ENVIRONMENTAL AND PLANNING LAW IN NEW SOUTH WALES

ENVIRONMENTAL AND PLANNING LAW IN NEW SOUTH WALES

Rosemary Lyster
BA, LLB, LLM (Natal)

Zada Lipman
BA (Hons) (Wits), LLB (UNISA), LLM (Qld)

Nicola Franklin
BA, LLB (Natal)

Graeme Wiffen
BA, LLB (Syd), LLM (York, Canada)

Linda Pearson
BA (Syd), LLB (UNSW), LLM, MPP (Syd)

THE FEDERATION PRESS
2007

Published in Sydney by:
The Federation Press
PO Box 45, Annandale, NSW, 2038
71 John St, Leichhardt, NSW, 2040
Ph (02) 9552 2200 Fax (02) 9552 1681
E-mail: info@federationpress.com.au
Website: http://www.federationpress.com.au

National Library of Australia
Cataloguing-in-Publication entry
Environmental and planning law in New South Wales

Includes index.
ISBN 978 186287 630 9

1. Environmental law – New South Wales. 2. Regional planning – Law and legislation – New South Wales. I. Lyster, Rosemary.

344.944046

Text printed on
100% recycled paper

Typeset by The Federation Press, Leichhardt, NSW.
Printed by Ligare Pty Ltd, Riverwood, NSW.

LIST OF CHAPTERS

For detailed Table of Contents, see over

CONTENTS

PREFACE

Writing a book entitled *Environmental and Planning Law in New South Wales* in the 21st century is, by anyone's account, a challenging project. This is so for a number of reasons. First, there has been a proliferation of environmental law statutes in the past three decades, which cover almost every aspect of the built and natural environment. So it is unusual for one author to be an expert on every single aspect of environmental law, although authors like Dr Gerry Bates and Professor Douglas Fisher still manage ably to produce solely authored texts in this area. This means that it is more common, as with this book, to find a number of co-authors contributing chapters in their special areas of expertise.

Secondly, since the mid-to-late 1990s, the New South Wales government has attempted to achieve greater integration between discrete pieces of legislation which regulate quite different environmental problems. This has been done for two different reasons. One of these is the realisation, following the 1992 United Nations Conference on the Environment (the Rio Conference), that the earth's natural systems are interconnected and cannot be managed separately. This is evidenced by the drafting, at that conference, of documents relating to global climate change, the conservation of biological diversity and the protection of the world's forests, which are of course all interrelated. Coupled with this were the exhortations contained in the Rio Declaration and Agenda 21 to world leaders to integrate decision-making on environmental, social and economic issues, so as to achieve sustainable development. Another, equally important, reason for the move towards integration in New South Wales was the review and reform of all laws which restrict competition and create unnecessary duplication, as required under National Competition Policy (discussed comprehensively in Chapter 1).

The consequence of legislative integration for the reader of this book is that information may appear in more than one chapter. For example, the Building Sustainability Index (BASIX), which sets a greenhouse gas emissions target for buildings in New South Wales, is mentioned in both Chapter 3 (Development Control) and Chapter 5 (Energy Law and global climate change). Similarly, the 2003 native vegetation reform package is relevant for Chapter 4 (Environmental Assessment), Chapter 7 (Integrated Natural Resource Management) and Chapter 8 (Conservation of Biodiversity). Bearing this in mind, the authors have attempted to provide ample cross-references between the chapters.

What do the authors see as the strengths of this book? First and foremost, this book is written by leading environmental law academics who have been teaching, and researching and writing, in their chosen areas of specialisation for many years. Not only is the law accurately presented, but in many instances the policy behind the law is also explained. This is because the authors have been following the developments in their specialist areas every step of the way over a significant period of time. They are able to provide insights into the legislative and policy changes, and the consequences of those changes, for the environment and for society. The authors have also traced the development of the case law in the Land and Environment Court of New South Wales, the New South Wales Court of Appeal, and the High Court, for years. Moreover, to ensure that the book is useful for a wide readership, the authors have had most chapters reviewed by practitioners. Their reviews have been most encouraging. In this regard, the authors would like to thank the following people for giving so generously of their time: Michelle Astridge, Michael Causer and Rebecca Dixon at Mallesons Stephen Jaques; Camilla Charlton and Edmund Lee at DLA Phillips Fox; and Robert Ghanem, Kirsty Ruddock, Jacquie Svenson and Rachel Walmsley at the New South Wales Environmental Defender's Office.

The second major strength of the book is its explicit acknowledgement that economic rationalism has played a significant role in shaping regulatory schemes for managing the environment, including the establishment of markets in water, metropolitan water infrastructure, carbon, biodiversity, native vegetation and salinity. While these markets may still be emerging, the authors question (in Chapter 1 and elsewhere) whether they will help or hinder attempts to achieve ecologically sustainable development – the other most significant influence on the development of environmental law in Australia. Also, the book includes a discussion of Corporate Social Responsibility which is regarded by many as a 'market' mechanism, in the sense that compliance by corporations with environmental and social standards is voluntary and directed at improving 'the bottom line'. For these reasons the authors are confident that this book will contribute to the broader regulatory debate and be useful to policy makers, and to those who make, and enforce, the law.

Thirdly, the book represents the most recently updated account of the state of environmental law in New South Wales. As far as is humanly possible, the authors have ensured that the law is updated to 1 February 2007, while accepting that it is likely to be outdated in some significant respect very shortly. Such is the nature of environmental lawmaking!

Now to some explanation of the chapters. Chapter 1 (co-authored by Zada Lipman and Rosemary Lyster) provides an Overview of Environmental Law in Australia, including a comprehensive discussion of the common law, ecologically sustainable development, market mechanisms and the resolution of disputes by the Land and Environment Court of New South Wales. Chapters 2 (Land Use Planning – authored by Linda Pearson), 3 (Development Control – authored by Linda Pearson) and 4 (Environmental Assessment – authored by Nicola Franklin) need to be read together. Chapters 2 and 3 discuss the framework for environmental planning, and the determination of development applications, in New South Wales under the *Environmental Planning and Assessment Act 1979* (NSW) (EPAA). Environmental assessment traverses issues at both the planning and development control stage. The issues are brought together in Chapter 4 which examines the procedural framework for environmental assessment under the EPAA. The discussion is extended to environmental assessment and approval at the Commonwealth level under the *Environment Protection and Biodiversity Conservation Act 1999* (Cth). Chapters 5 and 6 (authored by Rosemary Lyster) deal with Energy Law and Global Climate Change, and Water, two of the most pressing natural resource issues, respectively. Chapters 7 (Integrated Natural Resource Management – co-authored by Rosemary Lyster, Graeme Wiffen and Edmund Lee (Senior Associate, DLA Phillips Fox)), 8 (Conservation of Biodiversity – co-authored by Rosemary Lyster and Graeme Wiffen) and 9 (Protected Areas – authored by Graeme Wiffen) need also to be read together. This is because, as explained above, attempts to manage natural resources, in an integrated way, and the conservation of biodiversity have resulted in legislative schemes which overlap. Chapter 10 (authored by Graeme Wiffen) discusses Australia's complicated system of heritage laws at the national and State levels. Chapter 11 (authored by Zada Lipman) provides a comprehensive account of Pollution control while in Chapter 12 (authored by Zada Lipman) the management of Waste, Chemicals, Contaminated Land and Dangerous Goods is discussed together in a holistic and innovative way. The book concludes with Chapter 13 (Corporate Social Responsibility - authored by Rosemary Lyster). Rosemary Lyster is the overall editor of the book.

It is difficult in a co-authored work of this nature for each author to individually acknowledge and thank the many people who have supported their efforts. Nevertheless, the authors are sure that these people know who they are. The authors wish to thank Rosemary Lyster for her editorial work on the book, while all of the co-authors acknowledge each other's generous teamwork and contribution. The authors also wish to thank Andrew Petersen, PricewaterhouseCoopers Legal, for allowing them to access the Environmental News Network (*eNNA)* archive which was written by Rosemary Lyster during her time as a legal consultant to the firm. Finally, grateful thanks go to Chris Holt and Kathy Fitzhenry of The Federation Press for their forbearance, support and assistance in bringing this extensive piece of work to fruition.

Rosemary Lyster
Zada Lipman
Nicola Franklin
Graeme Wiffen
Linda Pearson

February 2007

ABOUT THE AUTHORS

Rosemary Lyster is an Associate Professor in the Faculty of Law, University of Sydney, where she teaches Administrative Law and Environmental Law. She is the Director of the Australian Centre for Environmental Law Sydney. Rosemary is co-editor of the *Asia Pacific Journal of Environmental Law* and is the Energy and Water Special Editor of the *Environmental and Planning Law Journal*. She is co-chair of the Special Working Group on Water and Wetlands within the IUCN Commission on Environmental Law, and is a member of the Commission's Special Working Group on Energy and Climate Change. Rosemary is a legal consultant to Mallesons Stephen Jaques.

Zada Lipman is a Professor in the Division of Law, Macquarie University. Over the past 25 years, she has been involved in teaching and researching in the area of environmental law. She is currently teaching pollution law and planning law. Zada is the Australian editor of the *Environmental Liability Journal* and is the New South Wales and Pollution Special Editor of the *Environmental and Planning Law Journal*. Zada is a member of the IUCN – the World Conservation Union Commission on Environmental Law. She is a member of the Commission's Special Working Group on Enforcement and Compliance and a member of the Special Working Group on Oceans, Coasts and Coral Reefs.

Nicola Franklin is a Senior Lecturer in the Faculty of Law, University of Sydney. She is Coordinator of the Faculty's Environmental Law Program, Deputy Director of the Australian Centre for Environmental Law Sydney and co-editor of the *Asia Pacific Journal of Environmental Law*.

Graeme Wiffen teaches law at Macquarie University, Sydney, and writes on legal aspects of the protection of natural and cultural heritage. He is a member of the Australian branch of the International Committee for Monuments and Sites (ICOMOS) and is the Australian representative and vice president of ICOMOS' international scientific committee on legal issues. Graeme is currently on the executive of the National Parks Association of New South Wales.

Linda Pearson teaches Administrative Law and Environmental Law at the Faculty of Law, University of New South Wales. She has been a member of a number of administrative tribunals and is currently a Judicial member of the Administrative Decisions Tribunal of NSW. She is the author of *Local Government Law in New South Wales* (Federation Press), and has written on such topics as jurisdictional fact in planning law, and implementing the precautionary principle in land use decision-making.

ABBREVIATIONS

AAU	Assigned Amount Unit
ABARE	Australian Bureau of Agricultural and Resource Economics
ACCC	Australian Competition and Consumer Commission
ACF	Australian Conservation Foundation
ACP	Abatement Certificate Provider
ADJR	*Administrative Decisions (Judicial Review) Act 1977* (Cth)
AFCP	Alternative Fuels Conversion Program
AGO	Australian Greenhouse Office
AGVET Code	*Agricultural and Veterinary Chemicals Code* (Cth)
ANZECC	Australian and New Zealand Environment and Conservation Council
AONM	Australian Obligated Nuclear Material
AP	Assessment Plan
ARA	Appropriate regulatory authority
ASEAN	Association of South East Asian Nations
ASIC	Australian Securities and Investment Commission
AVCAA	*Agricultural and Veterinary Chemicals (Administration) Act 1992* (Cth)
AWS	Australian Water Services (Pty) Ltd
BASIX	Building Sustainability Index
BCM	Bromochloromethane
BDAC	Biological Diversity Advisory Council
BPA	*Building Professionals Act 2005* (Cth)
CA	Clean Air
CAMAC	Australian Corporations and Markets Advisory Committee
CAMBA	Agreement between the Governments of Australian and the People's Republic of China for the protection of Migratory Birds and their Environment 1986
CBD	Convention on Biological Diversity 1992
CCO	Chemical control order
CCS	Carbon Capture and Storage
CDM	Clean Development Mechanism
CER	Certified Emission Reduction
CFC	Chloroflurocarbon
CGERG	Council of Australian Government's (COAG) Greenhouse and Energy Reporting Group
CHO	Chief Health Officer
CITES	Convention on the International Trade in Endangered Species 1973
CLERP 9 Act	*Corporate Law Economic Reform Program (Audit Reform and Corporate Disclosure) Act 2004* (Cth)
CLMA	*Contaminated Land Management Act 1997* (NSW)
CMA	Catchment Management Authority
CMAA	*Catchment Management Authorities Act 2003* (NSW)
CMS	*Convention on the Conservation of Migratory Species of Wild Animals 1979*
COAG	Council of Australian Governments
COP	Conference of the Parties
CPA	Competition Principles Agreement
CPA	*Coastal Protection Act 1979* (NSW)
CSO	Community Service Obligations
CSR	Corporate Social Responsibility
DA	Development Application

DCP	Development control plan
DEC	Department of Environment and Conservation
DEUS	Department of Energy Utilities and Sustainability
DJSI	Dow Jones Sustainability Indexes
DNSP	Distribution Network Service Provider
DSM	Demand side management
E2WG	Energy Efficiency Working Group
EA	Environmental assessment
EIS	Environmental Impact Statement
EMP	Environment Management Plan
EMS	Environmental Management System
EOAM	Environmental Outcomes Assessment Methodology
EPA	Environment Protection Authority
EPAA	*Environmental Planning and Assessment Act 1979* (NSW)
EPAR	*Environmental Planning and Assessment Regulation 2000* (NSW)
EPBCA	*Environment Protection and Biodiversity Conservation Act 1999* (Cth)
EPBCR	*Environment Protection and Biodiversity Conservation Regulation 2000* (Cth)
EPHC	Environment Protection and Heritage Council
EPI	Environmental Planning Instrument
ERA	Energy Resources of Australia
ERU	Emission Reduction Unit
ESA	*Electricity Supply Act 1995* (NSW)
ESD	Ecologically Sustainable Development
ESG	Environmental, societal and governance
ETA	*Environmental Trust Act 1998* (NSW)
FMA	*Fisheries Management Act 1994* (NSW)
GBE	Government Business Enterprise
GGAP	Greenhouse Gas Abatement Program
GMO	Genetically Modified Organisms
GRI	Global Reporting Initiative
GTA	*Gene Technology Act 2000* (Cth)
GTMC	Gene Technology Ministerial Council
GTR	Gene Technology Regulator
HBFC	Hydrobromofluorocarbon
HCFC	Hydrochlorofluorocarbon
HFC	Hydrofluorocarbon
ICMM	International Council on Mining and Metals
ICZM	Integrated Coastal Zone Management
IGAE	Intergovernmental Agreement on the Environment
IGAMDB	Intergovernmental Agreement on Addressing Water Overallocation and Achieving Environmental Objectives in the Murray-Darling Basin
IGANWI	Intergovernmental Agreement on a National Water Initiative
IP	Implementation Plan
IPART	Independent Pricing and Regulatory Tribunal
IHAP	Independent Hearing and Assessment Panel
ILO	International Labour Organisation
IPCC	Intergovernmental Panel on Climate Change
IRM	Integrated Resource Management
ISO	International Organisation for Standardisation
JAMBA	Agreement between the Governments of Japan and Australia for the Protection of Migratory Birds and Birds in Danger of Extinction and their Environment 1974
JI	Joint Implementation
LEC	Land and Environment Court
LECA	*Land and Environment Court Act 1979* (NSW)

LEP	Local Environmental Plan
LGA	*Local Government Act 1993* (NSW)
LGGR	*Local Government (General) Regulation 2005*
LUAC	Large User Abatement Certificates
MAB	Man and Biosphere Program
MARPOL	Convention for the Prevention of Pollution from Ships 1973 / 1978
MBI	Market-based instrument
MCE	Ministerial Council on Energy
MCMPR	Ministerial Council on Mineral and Petroleum Resources
MDBC	Murray-Darling Basin Commission
MDBMC	Murray-Darling Basin Ministerial Council
MNSP	Market Network Service Provider
MOU	Memoranda of Understanding
MPA	*Marine Parks Act 1997* (NSW)
MP Act	*Marine Pollution Act 1987* (NSW)
MPR	*Marine Parks Regulation 1999* (NSW)
MP Regulation	*Marine Pollution Regulation 2006* (NSW)
MRET	Mandatory Renewable Energy Target
MSW	Municipal Solid Waste
NAP	National Action Plan for Salinity and Water Quality
NCA	National Competition Agreements
NCC	National Competition Council
NCP	National Competition Policy
NEM	National Electricity Market
NEMMCO	National Electricity Market Management Commission
NEPA	*National Environmental Policy Act 1969* (United States)
NEPC	National Environment Protection Council
NEPCA	*National Environment Protection Council Act 1994* (Cth)
NEPM	National Environment Protection Measure
NFEE	National Framework for Energy Efficiency
NGAC	NSW Greenhouse Gas Abatement Certificate
NGL	National Gas Law
NGO	Non-government organisation
NHMRC	National Health and Medical Research Council
NHT	Natural Heritage Trust
NHTA	*National Heritage Trust Act 1997* (Cth)
NICNAS	National Industrial Chemicals Notification and Assessment Scheme
NLWRA	National Land and Water Resources Audit
NPWA	*National Parks and Wildlife Act 1974* (NSW)
NRC	Natural Resources Commission
NRCA	*Natural Resources Commission Act 2003* (NSW)
NRET	NSW Renewable Energy Target
NRMMC	Natural Resource Management Ministerial Council
NRMSC	Natural Resource Management Standing Committee
NVA	*Native Vegetation Act 2003* (NSW)
NVCA	*Native Vegetation Conservation Act 1997* (NSW)
NWI	National Water Initiative
OECD	Organization for Economic Co-operation and Development
OPA	*Ozone Protection Act 1989* (NSW)
OSCAR	Online System for Challenge Activity Reporting
PAS	Priorities Action Statement
PEOA	*Protection of the Environment Operations Act 1997* (NSW)
PEP	Protection of the environment policy
PER	Public environment report
POP	Persistent organic pollutant

PRI	Principles for Responsible Investing
PROTEA	*Protection of the Environment Administration Act* 1991
PVP	Property Vegetation Plan
PVRP	Photovoltaic Rebate Program
R & DG	Renewable and Distributed Generation
RAC	Refrigeration and Air Conditioning
RCA	*Radiation Control Act 1990* (NSW)
RDGWG	Renewable and Distributed Generation Working Group
RE(E)A	*Renewable Energy (Electricity) Act 2000* (NSW)
REC	Renewable Energy Certificate
RECP	Renewable Energy Commercialisation Program
REF	Review of environmental factors
REP	Regional Environmental Plan
RFA	Regional Forest Agreement
RGP	Regulatory guiding principle
RPP	Renewable Power Percentage
RPS	Renewable Portfolio Standard
RMU	Removal unit
RRG	Remote Renewable Generation
SCA	Sydney Water Catchment Authority
SEAC	Social and Economic Advisory Council
SEE	Statement of Environment Effects
SEPP	State Environmental Planning Policy
SFE	Sydney Futures Exchange
SIS	Species Impact Statement
SOC	State Owned Corporation
SOCA	*State Owned Corporations Act 1989* (NSW)
SRI	Socially Responsible Investing
SWA	*Sydney Water Act 1994* (NSW)
SWMOP	State Water Management Outcomes Plan
TBL	Triple Bottom Line
TNSP	Transmission Network Service Provider
TSCA	*Threatened Species Conservation Act 1995* (NSW)
TPA	*Trade Practices Act 1974* (Cth)
UNCED	United Nations Conference on Environment and Development 1992
UNEP	United Nations Environment Program
UNEP FI	United Nations Environment Programme Finance Initiative
UNESCO	United Nations Educational, Scientific and Cultural Organization
UNFCCC	United Nations Framework Convention on Climate Change
VRET	Victorian Renewable Energy Target
WA	*Wilderness Act 1987* (NSW)
WARRA	*Waste Avoidance and Resource Recovery* Act *2001* (NSW)
WBCSD	World Business Council for Sustainable Development
WELS	*Water Efficiency Labelling Scheme Act 2005* (Cth)
WEPWG	Wind Energy Policy Working Group
WETAG	Wind Energy Technical Advisory Group
WMA	*Water Management Act 2000* (NSW)
WRPCA	*Waste Recycling and Processing Corporation Act 2001* (NSW)
WSSD	World Summit on Sustainable Development
WMO	World Meteorological Organisation
WWF	World Wide Fund for Nature

TABLE OF CASES

TABLE OF STATUTES

New South Wales

Queensland

South Australia

Tasmania

Victoria

Australian Capital Territory

1

OVERVIEW OF ENVIRONMENTAL LAW IN AUSTRALIA

This chapter provides an overview of environmental law in Australia, while pointing out that, until the 1970s, environmental law was not recognised as a separate body of legal principle. Environmental controls were distributed over a number of statutes which dealt with land use planning, local government law and pollution control. In New South Wales, the planning scheme dated back to measures adopted in 1945[1] which in turn were modelled on the United Kingdom *Town and Country Planning Act 1932*. Planning schemes made under the legislation focused on infrastructure and technical issues. They did not incorporate environmental assessment and protection. Further, there was no transparency in planning matters and no community involvement in the process. There were also no comprehensive controls to regulate pollution. The most substantive tools available to litigants were the traditional common law remedies, such as nuisance, trespass and negligence.

Having provided a comprehensive analysis of common law remedies, and some of their inadequacies, the powers of the Commonwealth and NSW governments to enact environmental legislation are discussed. It is important to note that under the Constitution the Commonwealth has no head of power over the environment although it has used a number of other powers to legislate in this area. More recently, however, the Commonwealth and State governments have worked together in the context of 'cooperative federalism' to devise environmental policy in the areas of pollution control, environmental impact assessment, heritage conservation, natural resource management, salinity and water quality, water reform and the restructuring of energy markets. The policies devised at the intergovernmental level are then usually incorporated into environmental legislation enacted by State governments, and often supported by payments from the Commonwealth.

This chapter also discusses the most significant influences on the recent development of environmental law in Australia, namely the internationally recognised concept of sustainable development and the trend to create markets to deliver specific environmental outcomes. The move to establish markets is underpinned by an economic rationalist approach currently favoured by the Commonwealth and NSW governments.

Finally, attention is drawn to the institutions which resolve conflict in environmental disputes. In the NSW context, the Land and Environment Court plays a prominent role since it has both a judicial review and an appellate jurisdiction. The availability of alternative dispute resolution mechanisms to resolve environmental conflict is also mentioned.

---

1 The *Local Government (Town and Country Planning) Amendment Act 1945* (NSW) inserted a new Pt XIIA entitled 'Town and Country Planning Schemes' into the *Local Government Act 1919* (NSW).

The common law: an inadequate source of environmental law

Common law, or judge-made law, has been developed over centuries, first in the United Kingdom and then in Australia after colonisation. The main common law causes of action relevant to environmental protection are the torts of private nuisance, public nuisance, trespass and negligence. These causes of action have proved largely ineffective as a means of protecting the environment since their emphasis is on protection and enforcement of private rights and obligations and not on the protection of public rights and interests. This has made it difficult in most cases for third parties to obtain standing. Common law remedies are also reactive, rather than proactive. Instead of focusing on actions which can prevent pollution, the traditional common law causes of action generally involve seeking compensation for damage which has already occurred, although in appropriate cases an injunction may be granted to prevent an unlawful action. Common law actions also depend on problems being brought before the courts, which results in piecemeal law reform

There is little doubt today that common law causes of action are ineffective as a means of protecting the environment in a wide range of circumstances and that they are largely being superseded by legislation. As Lord Scarman, a judge of the English House of Lords and a former Chairman of the English Law Commission, commented:

> Tied to concepts of property, possession, and fault, the judges have been unable by their own strength to break out of the cabin of the common law and tackle the broad problems of land use in an industrial and urbanised society. The challenge appears, at this moment of time, to be likely to overwhelm the law. As in the area of the social challenge, so also the guarding of our environment has been found to require an activist, intrusive role to be played by the executive arm of government.[2]

Most statutes dealing with the environment provide criminal sanctions for breaches, rather than civil remedies. Civil remedies have two particular advantages over criminal prosecution. First, they seek to compensate for damage caused, which may often exact a greater financial penalty from the polluter than criminal prosecution. Further, the civil standard requires proof to be established on the balance of probabilities, which is less demanding than the criminal standard of proof.

It is interesting to note that there has been a resurgence of common law actions in Australia over the past 10 years, particularly in the area of negligence. Most of these actions have been brought against public authorities for compensation for an alleged breach of a statutory duty.

Some of the more frequently used common law actions are discussed below.

Nuisance

Private nuisance

Private nuisance was described in *Sedleigh-Denfield v O'Callaghan* by Lord Atkin as follows:

---

2 *English Law – The New Dimension* (Stevens, 1974) at 53.

> [A] wrongful interference with another's enjoyment of his land or premises by the use of land or premises either occupied or in some cases owned by oneself.[3]

Private nuisance has limitations as a remedy to pursue public interest litigation, since the litigant must establish and prove certain essential elements to succeed. In the first place, the litigant must have an interest in the land affected.[4] Knowledge or foresight of the risk of harm by the defendant must also be established. Furthermore, the plaintiff must prove that the nuisance constitutes a substantial interference with the enjoyment of the land.[5] That is, actual damage must be proved; nuisance per se is not actionable. The plaintiff must also establish that the interference is unreasonable, since the law of private nuisance is largely concerned with striking a balance between the competing uses of adjoining landowners.[6] The test of 'unreasonableness' is an objective one and the question to be considered is:

> [W]hether the neighbour is using his property reasonably, having regard to the fact that he has a neighbour. The neighbour who is complaining must remember, too, that the other man can use his property in a reasonable way and there must be a measure of give and take, live and let live.[7]

Factors relevant to the determination of whether the interference is unreasonable in the circumstances include the locality of the land, the time, the duration (whether temporary or permanent), the mode of commission, the nature of the nuisance, the potential for harm and the character and extent of harm, as well as any alternative action which may have been taken.[8] Thus, a barking dog in a noisy inner city suburb may well be tolerated whereas this may not be so in quiet garden suburbia. Similarly, the occupier in a suburb already polluted is unlikely to find a sympathetic hearing if a nearby factory discharges into the atmosphere as it has always done.[9]

If successful, the plaintiff may recover damages or claim an injunction to restrain the wrongful conduct. Situations in which the tort of private nuisance has had widespread use in controlling disturbances having environmental consequences include: air pollution from odours,[10] gases, smoke, fumes and dust,[11] water pollution,[12] and offensive noise and vibrations.[13] However, the common law does not recognise any right to the maintenance of a view.[14]

---

3 [1940] AC 880 at 896-897.

4 See *Oldham v Lawson (No 1)* [1976] VR 654; *Read v J Lyons & Co Ltd* [1947] AC 156 at 183.

5 *Munro v Southern Dairies Ltd* [1955] VLR 332.

6 *Sedleigh-Denfield v O'Callaghan* [1940] AC 880 at 903; *Elston v Dore* (1982) 149 CLR 480 at 488.

7 *Kennaway v Thompson* [1981] QB 88 at 94; [1980] 3 All ER 329 at 333.

8 See *Van Son v Forestry Commission of NSW* (1995) 86 LGERA 108.

9 See *Gillingham C v Medway Dock* [1993] QB 343.

10 *Aldred's Case* (1610) 9 Co Rep 57b; 77 ER 816; *Allen v Gulf Oil Refining Ltd* [1981] AC 1001.

11 *Halsey v Esso Petroleum Co Ltd* [1961] 1 WLR 683; *St Helen's Smelting Co v Tipping* (1865) 11 HL Cas 642; 11 ER 1483.

12 *Allen v Gulf Oil Refining Ltd* [1981] AC 1001; *Gartner v Kidman* (1962) 108 CLR 12; *Van Son v Forestry Commission of NSW* (1995) 86 LGERA 108; *Lawrence v Kempsey Shire Council* (1995) 87 LGERA 49.

13 *Munro v Southern Dairies Ltd* [1955] VLR 332; *Don Brass Foundry Pty Ltd v Stead* (1948) 48 SR (NSW) 482; *Halsey v Esso Petroleum Co Ltd* [1961] 1 WLR 683.

14 *Day v Pinglen* (1981) 34 ALR 545; *Kent v Johnson, Minister of State for Works* (1973) 21 FLR 177.

Public nuisance

Public nuisance is distinct from private nuisance although the grounds on which an action may be brought are very similar. At common law, public nuisance is also a crime. The advantage of public nuisance is that, unlike private nuisance which requires proof of an interference with an interest in land, public nuisance does not. The complainant need have no interest in land. Further, while a private nuisance generally requires repetition, an isolated action may amount to a public nuisance

Like private nuisance, public nuisance also provides for tortious liability. However, to complain of a public nuisance, the plaintiffs must be affected in some way over and above the rest of the public generally. As Sholl J stated in *Walsh v Ervin*:

> [A]n individual cannot sue alone for relief in respect of a nuisance ... unless he has sustained some particular damage, in the sense of some substantial injury, directly and not merely consequential, beyond that suffered by the public generally.[15]

Where a person suffers to the same extent as other members of the community, that person is left to seek the assistance of the Attorney-General, who must lend his or her name to allow an action to proceed. The disadvantage is obvious as it places the decision in the hands of a public officer amenable to political pressure.[16] This makes public nuisance difficult to prove in actions based on pollution, as invariably the damage from, for example, smog emanating from industrial premises, pervades a complete area with equal effect

In *Ball v Consolidated Rutile*,[17] the court held open the possibility that pollution of water which resulted in the death of fish, thus interfering with the public right to fish, could constitute a public nuisance. The plaintiffs were licensed fishermen. A mining company had created a sand dune abutting Moreton Bay. Part of the dune slipped into the water causing damage to the plaintiff's prawn nets. The value of the lost catches was substantial and fishing subsequently became uneconomical. The plaintiffs claimed they had suffered special loss over and above the public generally because of the damage to their nets and the economic loss resulting from an inability to continue fishing. The court held that a licence to fish did not confer any special rights other than those held in the public generally. Nor did it confer a right for the waters to be kept clear of pollution deposits, such as the dune slippage. Moreover, the deposit of material in fishing grounds which made it more difficult to catch fish did not constitute a public nuisance.

It should be noted that s 125 of the *Local Government Act 1993* (NSW) extends the common law remedy of 'public nuisance'. This section empowers a council to abate a public nuisance or to order a person responsible for a public nuisance to abate it. According to the explanatory note to s 125, a nuisance is 'public' if it materially affects the reasonable comfort and convenience of a sufficient class of people to constitute the public or a section of the public.

---

15 [1952] VLR 361 at 368.

16 See *Kent v Johnson, Minister of State for Works* (1973) 21 FLR 177; *Johnson v Kent* (1975) 132 CLR 164; *A-G v Board of Water Supply and Sewerage* (1916) 16 SR (NSW) 437; and the article by WK Hancock, 'The Battle of Black Mountain', Department of Economic History, ANU, Canberra, 1976, which illustrate the political nature of an Attorney-General's decision to lend his or her name to a suit. Although in the *Kent* case the Attorney-General was eventually persuaded to bring the action, the plaintiffs ended up conducting it. The plaintiffs were ultimately unsuccessful with the court refusing to accept that the construction of a tower on a mountain, which a sector of the public found visually and aesthetically displeasing, amounted to a public nuisance.

17 [1991] Qd R 524.

Defence of statutory authority

A statutory authority carrying out authorised works is given a measure of protection against liability for nuisance as a result of exercising its statutory powers. In relation to nuisance, it seems that the defence of statutory authority will only succeed where the activity is authorised by statute and which, despite the taking of reasonable precautions, constitutes a nuisance. The nuisance must be the 'inevitable consequence' of the performance of the statutory duty or exercise of power to be justified by the statute.[18] 'Inevitable consequences' means that there was, 'in the light of contemporary scientific knowledge then available, no reasonable way' the permitted function could be performed without causing the damage.[19] Furthermore:

> [The] criterion of inevitability is not what is theoretically possible but what is possible according to the state of scientific knowledge at the time, having also in view a certain common sense appreciation, which cannot be rigidly defined, of practical feasibility in view of situation and of expense.[20]

These authorities were applied by Young J in *Lawrence v Kempsey Shire Council*,[21] where a council was held liable for damages in relation to a nuisance arising from sewage effluent entering a creek and flowing onto the plaintiff's land. Young J rejected the defence of statutory authority after imposing the following test: 'Did the council act taking all reasonable regard and care for the interests of other persons?' A similar approach was adopted in *Van Son v Forestry Commission of NSW*,[22] where the Forestry Commission was held liable to a downstream landowner for siltation caused by logging operations which polluted water used for domestic purposes.[23]

Trespass

Trespass is rarely invoked to protect the environment. Trespass involves the unauthorised direct physical interference with the plaintiff's exclusive possession of his or her land. The advantage of an action in trespass is that is unnecessary to prove actual damage. However, like private nuisance, the only persons having title to sue are those in exclusive possession of land or who have some recognised proprietary interest constituting possession.[24] Further, it is only immediate or direct acts that can be the subject of an action for trespass. In *Southport Corporation v Esso Petroleum Co Ltd*,[25] an oil spill caused by the defendant had polluted the plaintiff's property. The plaintiff's action in trespass failed because the oil had been carried there by the tide, and consequently did not constitute an immediate or direct act.

---

18 *York Bros (Trading) Pty Ltd v Commissioner of Main Roads* [1983] 1 NSWLR 391 at 397 per Powell J.

19 Ibid.

20 *Manchester Corporation v Farnworth* [1930] AC 171 at 183.

21 (1995) 87 LGERA 49.

22 (1995) 86 LGERA 108.

23 See also *Allen v Gulf Oil Refining Ltd* [1981] AC 1001 and *Tate and Lyle Food and Distribution Ltd v Greater London Council* [1983] 2 AC 509.

24 *National Provincial Bank Ltd v Ainsworth* [1965] AC 1175.

25 [1954] 2 QB 182.

Negligence

Negligence is rapidly becoming a strong ground on which causes of action may be based to seek a remedy for injuries, damage to property or economic loss. The litigant must prove that the defendant owed the litigant a duty of care, that the duty of care was breached by the polluter and that the litigant suffered foreseeable damage or loss as a result of that breach.

The basis of the tort of negligence is that all persons owe a duty of care to avoid injury to others who might reasonably be foreseen as likely to be injured by their acts or omissions.[26] Once a duty of care is established, it is necessary to determine whether that duty has been breached. This turns on whether the appropriate standard of care has been met. The High Court test formulated in *Wyong Shire Council v Shirt*[27] is to ask whether a reasonable man in the defendant's position would have foreseen that his conduct involved a risk of injury to the plaintiff or to a class of persons including the plaintiff. If the answer is in the affirmative, the court must then determine what a reasonable man would do by way of response to the risk. The perception of the reasonable man's response requires an evaluation of the magnitude of the risk and the degree of the probability of its occurrence. It also requires an examination of the expense, difficulty and inconvenience of taking alleviating action and any other conflicting responsibilities which the defendant may have

The more hazardous the activity, the higher the standard of care required. Formerly, under the doctrine in *Rylands v Fletcher*,[28] a person who brought a hazard onto his or her land for their own purposes, was strictly liable for all ensuing damage that was a 'natural consequence' of its escape. However, in *Burnie Port Authority v General Jones Pty Ltd*,[29] the High Court effectively abolished this doctrine and absorbed it into the tort of negligence. In that case, the Port Authority had allowed an independent contractor to carry out unguarded welding operations on the Port Authority's premises in close vicinity of cartons of a highly flammable substance. The substance caught fire, causing substantial damage. The High Court found that the Port Authority had breached its duty of care and was liable to General Jones in negligence. The high standard of care imposed by the High Court effectively means that, if harm does occur during an ultra-hazardous activity, the standard of care has not been met. Thus, for practical purposes the abolition of the strict liability rule in *Rylands v Fletcher* may not have a significant impact.

Negligent exercise of a statutory duty

When a public authority, such as a local council, exercises its power in a manner which causes loss or damage to the plaintiff, the courts will generally have little difficulty in finding a duty of care. It becomes more difficult to decide whether a duty is owed in situations where the loss or damage results from failure to exercise a statutory power. This discussion will examine the tests applied by the High Court in establishing when public authorities will owe a duty of care to persons suffering damage as a result of their failure to exercise a statutory duty.

---

26 *Donoghue v Stevenson* [1932] AC 562.

27 (1980) 146 CLR 40.

28 (1866) LR 1 Ex 265.

29 (1994) 179 CLR 520.

In recent years, the High Court has propounded a number of different approaches for determining whether a public authority owes a duty of care to a plaintiff. In *Sutherland Shire Council v Heyman*,[30] the High Court applied the concept of 'general reliance' to establish the necessary proximity in which a duty of care would arise. In terms of this approach, a council owes a duty of care to those members of the public who would 'generally rely' on it to exercise its powers in circumstances where they are particularly vulnerable and where the council is empowered to protect them from the actual loss that occurred.

In *Alec Finlayson Pty Ltd v Armidale City Council*,[31] a council was held liable in negligence to a developer for losses arising as a result of land contamination. The land had previously been used as a timber treatment plant, and the council was aware of the substances used on the site and their potential danger, but nevertheless rezoned the land for residential development and subsequently granted subdivision approval and building consents. The council appealed to the Full Federal Court which upheld Burchett J's decision that the council owed the developer a duty of care when granting subdivision and building consents.[32]

In more recent judgments,[33] the High Court has departed from the tests of 'general reliance', 'foreseeability' and 'proximity' as concepts sufficient to establish a duty of care. The test currently favoured by a majority of the High Court is known as the 'salient factors' test. This approach has been applied by the High Court in a number of recent decisions. In *Pyrenees Shire Council v Day*,[34] the alleged negligence was the council's failure to direct and ensure that a defective fireplace be repaired. The result was a fire which caused extensive damage to a shop premise and adjoining premises. The salient factors which rendered the council liable, were its statutory exercise of control over the risk of fire, and special knowledge of the fire risk. Similarly, in *Brodie v Singleton Shire Council*,[35] the High Court referred to the 'significant and special measure of control' which highway authorities exercised over the safety of the person or property. This combination of direct control, power, and the undertaking of functions in accordance of power, gave rise to a duty of care. This led the court to abolish the longstanding highway immunity rule which provided that highway authorities were not liable for non-feasance (failure to act) as opposed to misfeasance (a positive act by the authority).

The most recent pronouncement on this issue is the decision of the High Court in *Graham Barclay Oysters Pty Ltd v Ryan*.[36] This case concerned the liability in negligence of growers and distributors of oysters and the relevant local and State government, for harm suffered by consumers of oysters. The consumers contracted the hepatitis A virus as a consequence of eating oysters which had been harvested from Wallis Lake which had been polluted by human faecal contamination. The case against the council was that it had not exercised its powers under the *Local Government Act 1993* (NSW) to monitor the water in the lake for contamination, warn oyster farmers of contamination and to take steps to bring about a cessation of harvesting

30 (1985) 157 CLR 424.

31 (1994) 51 FCR 378.

32 *Armidale City Council v Alex Finlayson Pty Ltd* (1999) 104 LGERA 9.

33 See *Pyrenees Shire Council v Day* (1998) 192 CLR 330 and *Perre v Apand Pty Ltd* (1999) 198 CLR 180.

34 (1998) 192 CLR 330.

35 (2001) 206 CLR 512 at 559.

36 (2002) 77 ALJR 183.

On appeal, the High Court unanimously rejected any finding of negligence against the council. The High Court held that the council did not owe the plaintiffs a duty of care. Nor had it been shown that the council was the cause of the plaintiff's damage for although council arguably could have done more to prevent the outbreak; it had not been established that the harm could have been prevented – 'short of prohibiting the cultivation of oysters in Wallis Lake altogether'.[37]

In *Ryan*, a majority of the High Court applied the 'salient factors' test to determine whether the council owed a duty of care to the plaintiff. An important factor in determining that no duty of care existed was the council's lack of control over the risk of harm that eventuated. Although the council had statutory power to monitor and intervene to protect the environment, it had no control over all risks of harm which could result from the conduct of independent commercial enterprises in its area. The council did not have direct responsibilities in relation to the cultivation, harvesting and supply of oysters. Nor did council's conduct directly affect the oyster consumers as there were many levels of decision-making between council's conduct and the consumers

The disadvantage of the 'salient factors' test in *Ryan* and other cases is that it provides no conceptual framework for determining when a duty of care will exist.[38] The result is that cases will continue to be decided on an ad hoc basis. Equally unfortunately, three of the High Court judges did not apply the 'salient factors' test and preferred to adopt their own tests for establishing the existence of a duty of care.

Although no hard and fast rule can be laid down, the above analysis indicates that the salient factors which the High Court will examine to determine the existence of a duty of care are as follows:

- *Statutory powers* – whether the imposition of a duty of care is consistent with the council's statutory powers;
- *Proximity* – whether the relationship between the parties is one of neighbourhood in Lord Atkin's sense in *Donoghue v Stevenson*;
- *Control* – whether the council is in a position of control and has the power to control the situation that brought about the harm;
- *Knowledge* – whether the council must know, or ought to have known, of an existing risk of harm to the plaintiff, or a specific class of persons who included the plaintiff (rather than the general public);
- *Vulnerability* – whether the claimant is vulnerable in the sense that he or she could not reasonably be expected adequately to safeguard her or himself;
- *Reasonableness* – whether it is reasonable in all the circumstances to impose a duty of care.

Policy matters and justiciability

In earlier cases there was an attempt by the courts to distinguish between policy and operational matters.[39] According to this approach, only operational decisions are

37 Ibid at 188 per Gleeson J.

38 See further J Swanton and B McDonald, 'Liability in Negligence for Pure Economic Loss' (2000) 74 *ALJ* 17.

39 *Sutherland Shire Council v Heyman* (1985) 157 CLR 424; *Alec Finlayson Pty Ltd v Armidale City Council* (1994) 51 FCR 378.

capable of being the subject of a duty of care. Policy matters are not justiciable. However, that distinction did not gain uniform acceptance and its value and utility have been questioned.[40] In the *Ryan* case, Gleeson CJ did find the idea behind the distinction relevant in some situations and considered that it could operate to limit negligence liability in certain circumstances. He observed as follows:

> Decisions as to raising revenue, and setting priorities in the allocation of public funds between competing claims on scarce resources, are essentially political. So are decisions about the extent of government regulation of private and commercial behaviour that is proper.[41]

Statutory exemption clauses

With the imposition of greater statutory responsibilities on the providers of public services and managers of public resources, for community good, parliaments have shown more willingness to exempt statutory authorities from the consequences of their own negligence as long as the activities complained of were done in good faith in the pursuit of their statutory responsibilities. The courts' attitude to such exemption clauses is to treat them strictly, because they affect common law rights; and as a general rule of statutory interpretation, the courts take the view that common law rights should not be affected unless by clear or necessary and unambiguous statutory intent. For example, in *Puntoriero v Water Administration Ministerial Corporation*,[42] the High Court held that a clause exempting the Corporation from any action for loss or damage 'suffered as consequence of the exercise of a function' did not excuse the negligence of the respondent for adding chemicals to water used for irrigation by the appellants, leading to the destruction of their potato crops.

The Local Government Act 1993 (NSW)

An important exemption clause for local councils is found in s 733 of the *Local Government Act 1993*. Section 733(1) exempts councils from liability in respect of advice furnished, action taken or anything done or omitted to be done which relates to flooding or its nature or extent, provided the decision was taken in good faith. Section 733(2) exempts councils from liability in respect of advice furnished, action taken or anything done or omitted to be done in relation to natural hazards in the coastal zone, provided that the decision was taken in good faith. Good faith will be assumed where council acts substantially in accordance with the Coastline Management Manual. Section 733(3) extends these immunities to the preparation or making of an environmental planning instrument; a development control plan; the granting or refusal of consent to a development application; the determination of an application for a complying development certificate; the imposition of conditions; advice furnished in a s 149 certificate under the *Environmental Planning and Assessment Act 1979* (NSW); the carrying out of coastal management works; and any other thing done or omitted to be done in the exercise of a council's functions

---

40 *Pyrenees Shire Council v Day* (1998) 192 CLR 330 at 393-394; *Romeo v Conservation Commission of the Northern Territory* (1998) 151 ALR 263; *Stovin v Wise* [1996] AC 923 at 951-953.

41 (2002) 77 ALJR 183 at 186.

42 (1999) 104 LGERA 419 at 451.

Section 733 was considered by the NSW Court of Appeal in *Kempsey Shire Council v Lawrence*.[43] In that case, Clarke JA held that a defence under s 733(1) involves two stages. The first is to identify for what conduct the appellant, in the absence of s 733, would be liable and the second is whether such conduct comes within paras (a) or (b) of s 733(1). His Honour identified the conduct for which the council would be liable as the release of effluent into the creek in such condition that it increased the nutrients in the water and damaged the respondent's land, and said that under s 733 that conduct would be exempt from liability if (a) it was done in good faith and (b) it related to the likelihood of the land being flooded or the nature or extent of any such flooding. His Honour was prepared to assume that the council in that case had acted in good faith but found against the council on the second point

The requirement for the council to have acted in good faith was considered in *Mid-Density Development Pty Ltd v Rockdale Municipal Council*,[44] where it was held that lack of good faith is not limited to dishonesty, but involves more than honest ineptitude. It involves acting honestly without any ulterior motive. In *Lamont v Wyong Shire Council*,[45] his Honour held that though negligence or gross negligence would not be sufficient to avoid the protection afforded by the section, a lack of honest endeavour to undertake the task for which the council has the responsibility would be sufficient. These cases suggest that before council can rely on a good faith defence, it must conscientiously apply itself in the exercise of its duties and disclose any information about possibility of flooding or natural hazards on a s 149(2) certificate or when providing other data.[46]

It is clear that the immunity from liability conferred in s 733 will not always protect councils who would otherwise be liable. However, no hard and fast rule can be laid down and each case has to be decided on its own facts.

The Civil Liability Act 2002 (NSW)

The *Civil Liability Act 2002* was amended in 2002 to restrict the potential liability of public authorities, such as councils. It is limited to actions for death or personal injury.

The Act changes the common law liability of public authorities in a number of respects:

- It requires a court to consider the financial and other resources that are reasonably available to the authority for the purpose of exercising their functions in deciding whether a duty of care is owed and whether it has been breached (s 42).
- It restores the non-feasance rule in relation to a roads authority as it was before the decision of the High Court in *Brodie v Singleton Shire Council*[47] (s 45).

---

43 [1996] A Torts R ¶63-141 at 81-375.

44 (1993) 81 LGERA 104 at 113-114.

45 Unreported, NSWSC, Palmer AJ, 13 December 1991.

46 See P Romano, P Grech and D Bewsher, 'Minimising Legal Liability Risks When Disseminating Flood Data, unpublished paper, 39th Annual Floodplain Management Conference, May 1999, <http://www.bewsher.com.au/PAPERS/CNF25-3.HTM>.

47 (2001) 206 CLR 512.

- It imposes a new test to determine whether a duty of care has been breached, namely whether it was 'in the circumstances so unreasonable that no authority having the functions of the authority in question could properly consider the act or omission to be a reasonable exercise of its functions' (s 43(2)).
- It introduces the element of 'factual causation' and 'scope of liability' causation as a prerequisite to a determination of negligence (s 5D).
- It excludes liability for obvious risks. A person who suffers harm from an obvious risk is presumed to have been aware of the risk (s 5G(1)). The defendant does not owe a duty of care to warn the plaintiff of that risk (s 5H).
- It excludes liability for harm suffered by another as a result of the materialisation of an inherent risk (s 51).

The Act will make it considerably more difficult for a litigant to bring proceedings against a council, particularly in relation to claims for personal injury or death. Whether the Act will be extended to other claims against public authorities remains to be seen.

Procedural obstacles to common law actions and statutory reform

Standing to sue

Standing to sue is an obstacle to actions by private citizens in public interest litigation. The leading case in Australia is *Australian Conservation Foundation v Commonwealth*.[48] In that case, the Australian Conservation Foundation (ACF) sought an injunction to challenge a proposal to build a resort and tourist area in Queensland. The High Court rejected the ACF's claim for standing, applying the rule in the English decision in *Boyce v Paddington Borough Council* as follows:

> A plaintiff can sue without joining the Attorney-General in two cases: first where the interference with the public right is such as that some private right of his is at the same time interfered with; and, secondly, where no private right is interfered with, but the plaintiff in respect of his public right, suffers special damage peculiar to himself from the interference with the public right.[49]

The High Court reformulated the second limb of the test by substituting the criterion of 'special interest' for 'special damage'. The High Court held that a special interest does not mean a mere intellectual or emotional concern and denied the ACF standing on the grounds of insufficient interest. This decision is still binding law in Australia although subsequent more liberal courts have often granted standing to public interest plaintiffs by distinguishing the case before them on the facts. Also, relying on the 'person aggrieved' standing test provided in the *Administrative Decisions (Judicial Review) Act 1977* (Cth), the Federal Court has granted standing to the ACF to challenge the decision of the Minister for Resources to grant a woodchip

48 (1980) 146 CLR 493.

49 [1903] 1 Ch 109 at 11.

licence.[50] This decision suggests that today any large environmental organisation will be granted standing to bring an action in its area of involvement; however, individual plaintiffs and small groups will still have difficulty.

Most Australian jurisdictions have reformed their laws on an ad hoc basis by including open standing provisions in environmental statutes.[51] A number of other statutes, both in New South Wales and in other States, have also introduced open standing provisions.[52] The standing provisions in the New South Wales *Protection of the Environment Operations Act 1997* (PEOA) are the most generous. Not only can any person bring an action to remedy or restrain a breach (or threatened or apprehended breach) of that Act (s 252), but any person may bring an action to restrain a breach (or a threatened or apprehended breach) of *any other Act* if the breach is likely to cause harm to the environment, regardless of whether any right of that person has been infringed (s 253). Accordingly, even if a statute does not contain 'open standing' provisions, as is the case with some of the older mining statutes, access to the court would still be available.

Traditionally, the federal government has been reluctant to grant standing to third parties. Most Commonwealth legislation, such as the *Environment Protection and Biodiversity Conservation Act 1999* (Cth) (EPBCA), does not have an open standing provision, but grants standing to any 'interested person' to apply to the Federal Court for an injunction to prevent or remedy a breach of the Act, or to review a decision taken under the Act. The definition of 'interested person' in the Act includes an organisation whose objects include the protection of the environment and which has engaged in environmental protection or conservation activities for the past two years or more. This test of standing seems relatively easy to satisfy but it would be preferable to have an open standing provision as in New South Wales and most of the other States.

Security for costs

The courts are empowered to order applicants to give security for the payment of costs that may be awarded against them. The courts are generally disinclined to require security for costs in public interest litigation but this is not always the case and is a matter of concern for the applicant.[53]

Undertaking for damages

A party applying for an injunction may be required to provide an undertaking for damages. The damage suffered by the defendants could potentially run into millions of dollars, if construction of a major development was halted by an injunction. Fortunately, this requirement has been relaxed in public interest actions. In deciding whether to grant an injunction, the courts regard such an undertaking as only one

---

50 *ACF v Minister for Resources and Harris-Daishowa (Australia) Pty Ltd* (1989) 76 LGRA 200. The court based its decision on a combination of ACF's involvement in the issue of the South East Forests, its funding and support from government, and public perception of the need for the protection of the environment and for bodies such as the ACF to act in the public interest to counter economic exploitation. See also *North Coast Environmental Council v Minister for Resources* (1994) 127 ALR 617.

51 See also discussion of LEC at p 41.

52 See, eg, *Environmentally Hazardous Chemicals Act 1985* (NSW) s 57; *National Parks and Wildlife Act 1987* (NSW) s 176A; *Threatened Species Conservation Act 1995* (NSW) s 147.

53 See *Razorback Environment Protection Society Inc v Wollondilly Council* [1999] NSWLEC 8.

factor to be taken into account. This trend has been continued by the EPBCA s 478, which expressly constrains the court from requiring an undertaking for damages when dealing with matters under the Act.

Costs

Lack of resources is one of the greatest obstacles facing public interest litigants in Australia. Legal costs are high and so are fees for expert evidence. Legal aid is not always available and public interest litigants are often thrown back on their own resources, although legal firms occasionally take on high profile public interest cases on a conditional basis or for no fee. Consequently, a prospective litigant not only faces the prospect of meeting their own costs, but may also have to contend with paying the other party's costs if unsuccessful.

It should be noted that some of the statutory courts and tribunals, such as the NSW Land and Environment Court, do not award costs to the successful applicants in certain cases.[54]

Legislation: the primary source of environmental law

Given the shortcomings of the common law, legislation has emerged as the primary source of environmental law. Legislation is created by State and Commonwealth Parliaments. Most environmental legislation is enacted by the States, but the Commonwealth is playing an increasingly important role. Acts of Parliament are binding on all courts and judges. Only if an Act is unconstitutional, that is, beyond the power of the Commonwealth or State Parliament, can the Act be declared invalid by the State court (in the case of a State Act) and the High Court (in the case of a federal Act).

A statute may delegate power to the Governor-General or Governor to make Regulations to deal with certain matters or empower a public authority, local council, minister or public servant to make some form of legal instrument. Delegated legislation does not have the same status as Acts of Parliament and can be declared invalid by the courts.

The division of legislative power between the Commonwealth and State Parliaments in the Australian Constitution has had a considerable influence on the development of environmental law in Australia.[55] Under the Constitution, the legislative powers of the federal government are limited to those matters specified in the Constitution while the residue of powers rests with the States. Environmental issues were not contemplated when the Constitution was enacted and consequently no reference is made to the environment. Thus, the States were traditionally considered to have primary responsibility for environmental matters.[56] State Parliaments have power under their Constitutions to make law 'for the peace, order and good government' of their respective territories.

54 See the discussion of LEC at pp 41-42.

55 See further Zada Lipman, 'Environmental Management in a Multi-Jurisdictional System: An Australian Perspective' (1996) 3 *SAJELP* 105 at 106-107.

56 M Crommelin, 'Resources Law and Public Policy' (1983) 15 *UWALR* 1.

In the environmental context, statutes have been enacted by State governments to cover a wide range of environmental issues including biodiversity, biotechnology, chemicals, energy, environmental planning and assessment, heritage, native vegetation, natural resource management, pollution, waste and water. In recent times, the New South Wales government has made deliberate attempts to integrate as far as possible the consent provisions of the environmental planning and assessment regime and also the management of natural resources.

Local government is not mentioned in the Australian Constitution despite the fact that, at the time of federation, each colony had some form of local government. It is accorded some recognition in State constitutions, but its powers and functions are subsidiary to, and derivative from, the States. Today there are about 673 local councils in Australia to whom State governments have devolved many of their everyday planning and decision-making powers.

Legislative powers of the Commonwealth

The Commonwealth Parliament has full plenary power to legislate in respect of federal Territories, including those that are self-governing or outside Australia (Constitution s 122). The Commonwealth Parliament has some exclusive powers (eg, Constitution ss 52, 90) but in most cases Commonwealth powers are exercised concurrently with the States. The Constitution confers legislative power on the Commonwealth Parliament primarily through s 51, which lists 39 heads of power held concurrently with the States. Where legislative powers are exercised concurrently, conflicts and inconsistencies may arise. Section 109 of the Constitution provides a mechanism for resolving inconsistencies in areas of concurrent legislative competence, whereby a Commonwealth law prevails over a State law, rendering the latter invalid to the extent of the inconsistency. There is no presumption that an Act of the Commonwealth Parliament will take precedence over a State law.

Although the Commonwealth has no direct powers to legislate on environmental matters it has used a number of other powers to pass environmental legislation. The main heads of power on which the Commonwealth has relied, and can rely, to legislate with respect to the environment are discussed below.[57]

The external affairs power

Section 51(xxix) of the Constitution confers power on the Commonwealth to legislate with respect to external affairs. The seminal decision on the ambit of this power in relation to the environment was *Commonwealth v Tasmania* (*Tasmanian Dam* case).[58] Before this decision, it was settled law that legislation could be valid under the external affairs power in two situations, namely:

- where a matter is of international concern, even though its primary operation is within Australia;
- where the matter is one which occurs outside Australia.

An issue which arose in the *Tasmanian Dam* case was whether legislation, not otherwise within Commonwealth power, would be valid under the external affairs

57 For a fuller discussion, see J Crawford, 'The Constitution and the Environment' (1991) 13 *Syd LR* 11.

58 (1983) 158 CLR 1.

power where it purports to implement an international treaty or convention which Australia has ratified.

Briefly, the facts of the case involved a proposal by the Hydro-Electric Corporation, a statutory authority in Tasmania, to construct a dam on the Gordon-below-Franklin river. The Tasmanian government had passed legislation authorising the proposal. Australia had ratified the *Convention for the Protection of the World Cultural and Natural Heritage 1975* (World Heritage Convention) and the Franklin river was on the World Heritage List. The campaign against the dam became a national issue in the federal elections in 1983 and featured prominently in the outcome. The new Labor government enacted the *World Heritage Properties Conservation Act 1983*[59] to prevent the construction of the dam. This action was justified by the federal government principally on the basis that it was meeting its international obligations under the World Heritage Convention. The Tasmanian government instituted an action in the High Court challenging the constitutional validity of the legislation.

The validity of the Act was upheld by the High Court (by a majority of four to three). The High Court construed the external affairs power very broadly to enable the Commonwealth to pass legislation, not otherwise within power, to implement an international convention. However, the court did place certain restrictions on the exercise of this power. First, the court can examine the bona fides of the legislation and; and, secondly, the legislation has to be in reasonable conformity with the Convention.

The intervention of the federal government in land-use issues within the States was extremely controversial and, while there was enormous support in many quarters, the Tasmanian and Queensland governments expressed concern that it challenged the very basis of federalism. However, undeterred by these criticisms, the federal government continued to use these powers to override State government projects in Tasmania and Queensland. These actions generated a great deal of political controversy and resulted in two further constitutional challenges in the High Court. In both cases the High Court confirmed the broad view of Commonwealth power enunciated in the *Tasmanian Dam* case.[60] These High Court decisions greatly extended the federal government's powers over domestic environmental policy and have been a prominent source of federal environmental legislation. This has paved the way for the Commonwealth to play a more active role in environment protection.

The corporations power

Section 51(xx) of the Constitution permits the federal government to make laws with respect to foreign corporations, and trading or financial corporations formed within the limits of the Commonwealth. This provision clearly confers full plenary power on the federal government to legislate in respect of foreign companies trading in

59 This Act was repealed in 2000. The Commonwealth's obligations under the World Heritage Convention are now implemented by the *Environment Protection and Biodiversity Conservation Act 1999* (EPBCA). The EPBCA requires the Commonwealth to consult with the affected State before nominating a site for World Heritage listing unless the site is under imminent threat.

60 See *Richardson v Forestry Commission (Tas)* (1988) 164 CLR 261 (this dispute concerned the constitutional validity of Commonwealth legislation establishing a Commission of Inquiry to determine whether the Lemonthyme Forests should be nominated for World Heritage Listing. In *Queensland v Commonwealth* (1989) 167 CLR 232, the High Court held that the Commonwealth nomination and listing of the Queensland Wet Tropics were not reviewable.

Australia, as well as power to regulate the trading and financial activities (and activities incidental thereto) of trading and financial corporations formed under Australian law.[61] However before the *Tasmanian Dam* case it was unclear whether the power extended to all actions of a trading or financial corporation, or only to their trading and financial activities. Three of the judges in the *Tasmanian Dam* case took a broad view, holding that the power should extend to the regulation of *any* acts undertaken by corporations for the purpose of engaging in trading activities.

A further issue which arose in the *Tasmanian Dam* case was whether the Hydro-Electric authority could properly be classified as a 'trading' corporation. The majority of the High Court decided that a corporation is a trading corporation if a substantial part of its activities are trading activities. Since a major function of the Hydro-Electric Corporation was the sale of electricity, it satisfied this test. The broad interpretation of this head of power has also been relied on by the Commonwealth as a mandate to pass a number of environmental statutes.

The High Court has continued to take a broad view of the corporations power. In *New South Wales v Commonwealth*,[62] the High Court by a 5-2 majority held that the *Workplace Relations Amendment (Work Choices) Act 2005* was a valid use of the corporations power. Moreover, the High Court held that the corporations power is not limited to laws with respect to the external relationships of corporations, but can include relationships between corporations and actual or prospective employees. This decision makes it possible for the Commonwealth to control the environmental operations of corporations and to include environment conditions in contracts of employment.

The trade and commerce power

Section 51(i) of the Constitution confers power to make laws with respect to 'trade and commerce with other countries and among the States'. Since most manufacturing or resource extraction is for foreign or interstate trade, this power is of particular importance in respect to environmental management. The federal government used this power to intervene in relation to sand mining proposals on Fraser Island, off the coast of Queensland. The federal government invoked its power under the now repealed *Environment Protection (Impact of Proposals) Act 1974* (Cth) to order an inquiry into the proposal. It subsequently refused to grant an export licence. Since there was no domestic market for rutile and zircon, this effectively blocked the mining proposal. The validity of the legislation was upheld by the High Court in *Murphyores Inc Pty Ltd v Commonwealth*.[63]

Section 51(i) was traditionally thought to be limited to foreign trade, since s 92 of the Constitution prohibits barriers on inter-state trade. The High Court decision in *Cole v Whitfield*[64] has overturned the view that s 92 of the Constitution precludes the Commonwealth from regulating interstate trading activities. In the *Whitfield* case, the High Court made it clear that s 92 only has application in relation to laws which are 'protectionist' or 'discriminatory'. This decision opened up the possibility of federal control of interstate exports on environmental grounds.

---

61 *Strickland v Rocla Concrete Pipes Ltd* (1971) 124 CLR 468.

62 [2006] HCA 52.

63 (1976) 136 CLR 1.

64 (1988) 165 CLR 360.

Financial powers

The federal government could also make use of its extensive financial powers to legislate on environmental matters: the Commonwealth has a general taxing power, limited only by s 114 (taxes on State property) and the prohibitions against discrimination against States or parts of a State in s 51(ii). The power may be exercised in such a way as to have an effect in areas where the federal government has no legislative power. The federal government could therefore use its fiscal powers to tax environmentally unsound products or grant deductions for money expended on developing new technologies to prevent pollution.

Section 96 of the Constitution empowers the federal government to make grants to States, either absolutely or subject to conditions. This section could be used to further environmental objectives, eg, to require the States to adopt new pollution technology or standards.

The federal government could also use moneys appropriated under s 81 of the Constitution to finance environmental projects within the States. Section 83 of the Constitution provides that such moneys can be expended for 'the purposes of the Commonwealth'. This raises the question whether 'purposes of the Commonwealth' are limited to powers conferred in the Constitution or whether it extends to any purposes which the Commonwealth may have in mind. In *Victoria v Commonwealth* (*AAP* case),[65] a majority of the High Court upheld the validity of expenditure for purposes which were not otherwise within constitutional power. The High Court again took a broad view of Commonwealth spending power in *Davis v Commonwealth*,[66] holding that the federal government is entitled to spend money for purposes which are incidental to its legislative powers. Arguably, the federal government could use s 81 to by-pass the States and appropriate funds for national programs to other bodies within the States. It would not be forced to depend on the States to carry out its wishes, as it is in the case of a grant under s 96 of the Constitution.

Consequently, it would seem that, given the range of existing Commonwealth powers in the Constitution and the broad interpretation of certain powers by the High Court, the lack of a specific head of power in relation to the environment is of little practical significance. Clearly, the Commonwealth has power to act to protect the environment in all significant areas. The real issue is whether it has the political will to do so.

The emergence of co-operative federalism

Notwithstanding the broad mandate that the High Court has conferred on the federal government to control land-use decisions in the States, in the late 1980s the federal government decided to adopt a policy of co-operation, favouring consensus based arrangements with the States. According to Fowler,[67] these arrangements fall into four categories:

- broad strategic agreements which attempt to delineate areas of jurisdiction and responsibility such as the Intergovernmental Agreement on the Environment 1992;

65 (1975) 134 CLR 338.

66 (1988) 63 ALJR 35.

67 'New National Directions in Environmental Protection and Conservation' in B Boer et al, *Environmental Outlook* (Federation Press, 1994) 113 at 115.

- national strategies which address specific areas, such as the National Strategy for Ecologically Sustainable Development 1992;
- agreements establishing jurisdictions for environmental management such as joint arrangements for the management of world heritage sites in Queensland and Tasmania; and
- agreements for the adoption of national standards and guidelines in specific areas, eg, the national guidelines formulated by the Australian and New Zealand Environment and Conservation Council (now subsumed into the Environment Protection and Heritage Council) in relation to areas such as air, noise, water, waste.

The agreements are all important for the development of environmental law and policy, but the most important initiative for delineating federal/State powers over the environment has been the Intergovernmental Agreement on the Environment.

The Intergovernmental Agreement on the Environment

The Intergovernmental Agreement on the Environment (IGAE) purports to facilitate a co-operative national approach to the environment. The Agreement was concluded by the Commonwealth, States and the Local Government Association in May 1992. The inclusion of the Local Government Association recognised the emerging role of local government in environmental management in Australia. It was strongly supported by the States who regarded it as a means of restricting Commonwealth intervention in land-use planning in the States.

The IGAE introduced three important initiatives. First, it attempts to delineate the respective roles and responsibilities of the Commonwealth, States and local government. The Agreement defines the roles of the respective governments in relation to environment protection in terms of a co-operative approach. It defines the Commonwealth's role as 'safeguarding and accommodating national environmental matters' and acknowledges the primary responsibility of the States for environmental matters within their own boundaries (paras 2.21, 2.2). However, it largely fails to resolve the demarcation issue, as it fails to define and clarify the ambit of 'national' environmental matters. The only environmental areas specified as falling under the exclusive jurisdiction of the Commonwealth are foreign policy, particularly in relation to the ratification and implementation of internal conventions; and the prevention of policies and practices by one State which could have significant adverse consequences in another (para 2.2). Commonwealth powers are further restricted by an undertaking to consult the States before ratifying an international convention (para 2.5.2).

The IGAE also provides some mechanisms for avoiding duplication of functions between different levels of government and reducing the number of disputes on environmental issues (para 2.5). It envisages an accommodation of Commonwealth and State interests through Commonwealth accreditation of State practices and procedures.

Second, the IGAE acknowledged the need for uniform environmental measures across Australia. It provided for the creation of the National Environment Protection Council with power to make National Environment Protection Measures (Sch 4).

Third, the agreement recognised the need to adopt sound environmental practices and procedures as a basis for ecologically sustainable development. This required the effective integration of economic and environmental considerations in decision-making processes. The IGAE elaborates that ecologically sustainable development (ESD) can be achieved by the implementation of the precautionary principle, intergenerational equity, conservation of biological diversity and ecological integrity, and improved valuation pricing and incentive mechanisms. The undertaking in the IGAE to adopt these principles has had a significant influence on environmental legislation. There has been a proliferation of legislation throughout Australia incorporating these principles.[68]

Ministerial Councils

The commitment to co-operative federalism has led to the Commonwealth government adopting a structure of Ministerial Councils and Advisory Councils to enable other jurisdictions, industry and NGOs to have a direct input into the formulation of environmental policy. It has been observed that the ability of these councils to make policy 'ranges from the deliberative to the merely consultative' but that even those councils whose role is merely consultative have some influence in setting the public policy agenda.[69]

The Council of Australian Governments

The Council of Australian Governments (COAG) is the principal ministerial council and was formed in 1992. It is constituted by the Prime Minister, the six State Premiers and two Territory Chief Ministers. COAG's role is to facilitate structural reform across Australian jurisdictions. It deals with a number of issues, including micro-economic reform, social and regulatory reform and environmental matters. It has radically reformed intergovernmental environmental responsibilities. In 1997, COAG undertook a review of Commonwealth and State involvement in environmental issues with a view to furthering the policy of co-operative federalism which had begun in the IGAE. The review concluded with a Heads of Agreement on Commonwealth/State Roles and Responsibilities for the Environment. The Agreement acknowledged that the Commonwealth had a valid role in environment protection and specified the matters of 'national environment significance' for which the Commonwealth was responsible. It also provided for formal accreditation of State environmental assessment and decision-making processes, a matter which had stagnated under the IGAE. The review was endorsed by the COAG meeting in 1997. The federal government did not let matters remain at policy level, as it had done in the case of the IGAE, but acted immediately to reform existing environmental legislation to give effect to the COAG agreement. The outcome was the *Environment Protection and Biodiversity Conservation Act 1999* (Cth).

As mentioned in Chapters 5, 6 and 7, COAG has also played a significant role in restructuring the electricity market, providing the impetus for major water reforms, and developing the National Action Plan on Salinity and Water Quality.

---

68 See p 25, n 72.

69 L Pearson, 'Intergovernmental Relations, Federalism and Environmental Policy', unpublished paper, Environmental Justice and The Legal Process Conference, Cape Town, 1998.

The National Environment Protection Council and Environment Protection and Heritage Council

The National Environment Protection Council (NEPC) was established under the *National Environment Protection Council Act 1994* (Cth) and complementary State legislation. The Council comprises an Environment Minister from each jurisdiction in Australia. The Council has the responsibility to develop National Environment Protection Measures (NEPMs). These measures are limited to pollution issues and waste disposal. The Council has already made a number of measures which include the National Ambient Air Quality Guidelines and National Guidelines for Contaminated Sites (see Chapter 11).

Following an agreement by COAG in 2001, the NEPC was subsumed into a new Environment Protection and Heritage Council (EPHC). In addition to the NEPC, the EPHC also comprises the environment protection components of the Australian and New Zealand Environment Conservation Council and Heritage Ministers' Meetings.

Ministerial Council on Energy

The Ministerial Council on Energy (MCE) was established by COAG in 2001 and plays a key role in implementing COAG's national energy policy framework. The MCE is the national policy and governance body for the Australian energy market, including electricity and gas. It has played a key role in recent initiatives to continue with energy market reform, as discussed in Chapter 5. In addition to energy market reform, the kinds of issues with which the MCE has recently been engaged are energy efficiency, energy security and renewable and distributed generation. The Council comprises ministers with responsibility for energy from the Australian Government and all States and Territories. The MCE is assisted in its work by the Standing Committee of Officials of the Ministerial Council on Energy.

The Natural Resources Management Ministerial Council

The Natural Resources Management Ministerial Council (NRMMC) consists of the Commonwealth, State and Territory government ministers, including the New Zealand government ministers, responsible for primary industries, natural resources, environment and water policy. The Council is essentially an intergovernmental forum for consulting, and co-ordinating action, on natural resource management issues. The terms of reference of the Council are discussed in Chapter 7. The Council meets twice a year and is supported by one permanent Standing Committee, the Natural Resource Management Standing Committee (NRMSC), comprising the departmental heads, or CEOs, of relevant Commonwealth, State, Territory and New Zealand government agencies.

The Gene Technology Ministerial Council

The Gene Technology Ministerial Council (GTMC) is an intergovernmental Council established by the intergovernmental Gene Technology Agreement 2001 (the Agreement). The functions of the GTMC include:

- issuing policy principles, policy guidelines and codes of practice to govern the activities of the Gene Technology Regulator (see Chapter 8);

- approving Regulations proposed under the *Gene Technology Act 2000* (Cth) (GTA);
- approving the appointment (and, if necessary, the dismissal) of the Regulator, and the chairpersons of the Gene Technology Advisory Committee, the Gene Technology Community Consultative Committee, and the Gene Technology Ethics Committee, and advising the responsible Commonwealth Minister on the appointment of the members of those bodies;
- ensuring co-ordination with other Ministerial Councils on gene technology matters particularly the harmonisation of regulatory processes relating to GM products; and
- generally overseeing the implementation of the GTA.

The Murray-Darling Basin Ministerial Council

The Murray-Darling Basin Ministerial Council (MDBMC) was established at an intergovernmental meeting of ministers in 1985. Its operation and functions are specified in the Murray-Darling Basin Agreement. The MDBMC considers the use and distribution of riparian resources from the nation's largest river system, the Murray Darling, and environmental issues related to the use of water resources from the basin, notably salinisation. The Ministerial Council comprises the ministers responsible for land, water and environmental resources within the contracting governments (ie, the governments of New South Wales, Victoria, South Australia, Queensland and the Commonwealth).

Major influences on the development of Australian environmental law

International environmental law

Australia is a party to over 100 international conventions and agreements which either deal exclusively with environmental issues or impacts on the environment. It also maintains an active participation in a number of international environmental bodies such as the United Nations Environment Program and the United Nations Commission on Sustainable Development. Given Australia's significant international involvement, it is hardly surprising that developments in international environmental law have played, and continue to play, a considerable role in domestic policy and legislation. However, implementation of international obligations is heavily dependent on political and economic considerations.

Ratification of international treaties is a function of the executive government under s 61 of the Australian Constitution, but international obligations accepted by Australia do not form part of Australia's legal system until they have been incorporated into national law by legislation. Australia's acceptance of its international obligations is complicated by the federal system and the policy of co-operative federalism. The Commonwealth has agreed to notify and consult with affected States in the 'negotiation, joining or implementation of international agreements', and to include them in negotiations if appropriate (IGAE para 2.3.2). This complicates and extends the process of ratifying a convention.

Key multilateral conventions for the environment, which Australia has ratified, fall into four broad areas: biodiversity and conservation; hazardous substances; marine protection; and atmospheric pollution. The Commonwealth government has enacted a number of statutes to give effect to its obligations under these conventions. In some cases these statutes apply in the States while in other instances the States have enacted complementary legislation.

Australia's international obligations on biodiversity and conservation have been consolidated in the *Environment Protection and Biodiversity Conservation Act 1999* (Cth). Domestic legislation regulating international transfers of hazardous wastes is dealt with in the *Hazardous Waste (Regulation of Exports and Imports) Act 1989*. Australia has met its obligations under the *Stockholm Convention on Persistent Organic Pollutants 2001* and the *Rotterdam Convention on the Prior Informed Consent Procedure for Certain Hazardous Chemicals and Pesticides in International Trade 1998* through 2004 amendments to existing legislation, such as the *Industrial Chemicals (Notification and Assessment) Act 1989* and the *Agricultural and Veterinary Chemicals Act 1994*. The federal government has also enacted a number of statutes to give effect to its international obligations relating to marine pollution.

However, Australia has been less successful in meeting its international obligations on atmospheric pollution. The *Ozone Protection and Synthetic Greenhouse Gas Management Act 1989* (Cth) deals comprehensively with ozone depletion, but does not fully address Australia's obligations on climate change. Australia is the only developed country, other than the United States, who has yet to ratify the Kyoto Protocol (see Chapter 5).

The influence of the above conventions and the principal domestic legislation giving effect to them will be discussed in more detail in later chapters. Environmental policy and legislation in Australia have also been heavily influenced by non-binding international agreements, in particular, the principle of ecologically sustainable development.

Ecologically sustainable development

The concept of ecologically sustainable development (ESD) has had a significant impact on environmental management in Australia at a national, State and local level. Sustainable development may be defined as 'development which meets the needs of present generations without compromising the ability of future generations to meet their needs'. This definition, which has been adopted by the international community, first appeared in *Our Common Future* (the Brundtland Report). The 1987 Report, produced by the World Commission on Environment and Development, was the culmination of international research and investigation into the state of the global environment. The 21-member Commission, chaired by Norwegian Prime Minister, Gro Harlem Brundtland, heard evidence from public meetings held on all five continents over three years. The Report included environmental strategies for achieving sustainable development by the year 2000 and beyond, and was hailed by the United Nations Environment Program as the most important document of the decade.

The 1992 United Nations Conference on Environment and Development (the Rio Conference) was a landmark in the development of sustainable development.

The purpose of the Conference was to formulate strategies to achieve 'sustainable development'[70] worldwide.

The Rio Declaration

The principal objectives of the Rio Declaration were to establish 'a new and equitable global partnership through the creation of new levels of co-operation among States, key sectors of societies and people', and developing international agreements which would 'respect the interests of all and protect the integrity of the global environmental and developmental system'. The Declaration proclaimed human beings, entitled to a healthy and productive life in harmony with nature, to be at the centre of concerns of sustainable development (Principle 1). It also reaffirmed the sovereign right of states to exploit their resources, while bearing in mind their obligation to not allow domestic activities to cause transboundary damage to the environment (Principle 2).

Perhaps the most influential principles of the Declaration have proved to be the principles of intergenerational equity, the precautionary principle and the polluter-pays principle. Intergenerational equity requires current rates of development to equitably meet the development and environmental needs of present and future generations (Principle 3). The precautionary approach is that 'where there are threats of serious or irreversible damage, lack of full scientific certainty shall not be used as a reason for postponing cost-effective measures to prevent environmental degradation' (Principle 15). Finally, the polluter-pays principle envisages the 'internalisation of environmental costs and the use of economic instruments, taking into account the approach that the polluter should, in principle, bear the cost of pollution (Principle 16).

Other enduring Rio principles are poverty alleviation (Principle 5), the common but differentiated responsibilities of countries to achieve sustainable development (Principle 7), capacity building and technology transfer (Principle 9), and public participation in decision-making (including women and indigenous people) (Principles 10, 20 and 22). States were also called on to enact effective environmental laws (Principle 11), including the provision of compensation for the effects of pollution and other forms of environmental degradation (Principle 13), environmental impact assessment (Principle 17), and effective legal remedies (Principle 10).

Agenda 21

Agenda 21 sets out a number of programs which establish the basis for action, objectives, activities and means of implementing the agreements reached at the Rio Conference. It sets out the challenges which the world needs to confront and deal with in the 21st century, and advocates strongly the development of global partnerships including the involvement of international, regional and sub-regional organisations. Agenda 21 states that considerable financial resources will need to be devoted to achieving sustainable development in developing countries, while economies in transition will need to be given special attention. The program

70 'Sustainable development' was defined in *Our Common Future* (1987 Report to the UN General Assembly by the World Commission on Environment and Development) as 'development which meets the needs of the present without compromising the ability of future generations to meet their own needs'.

areas of Agenda 21 include: social and economic dimensions, the conservation and management of resources, strengthening the role of major groups and means of implementation.

The World Summit on Sustainable Development

In 2002, the World Summit on Sustainable Development (WSSD) was held to assess the progress made in achieving the goals set out at the 1992 United Nations Conference on Environment and Development (the Rio Conference). The WSSD became known as the 'Rio +10' Conference. Leading up to the WSSD, the UN Secretary-General, Kofi Annan, proposed the development of the WEHAB initiative which focused on five key areas namely Water, Energy, Health, Agriculture and Biodiversity. These themes were regarded as integral to a coherent international approach to the implementation of sustainable development. These initiatives were specifically incorporated into the final outcome of the WSSD which was the Plan of Implementation of the World Summit on Sustainable Development.[71]

ESD in Australia

Australia participated in the United Nations Conference on Environment and Development 1992 (UNCED) and adopted the Rio Declaration on Environment and Development and Agenda 21. Much of Australia's domestic environmental policy on sustainable development reflects the influence of these documents.

The formulation of the precautionary principle in the Rio Declaration has been adopted in many national jurisdictions, including Australia. In Australia, the precautionary principle is generally expressed as a key component of ecologically sustainable development and has been incorporated as part of the national policy on the environment. In December 1992, six months after UNCED, each tier of government in Australia adopted the National Strategy for Ecologically Sustainable Development. The inclusion of the prefix 'ecologically' before the term 'sustainable development' was an important Australian innovation. The National Strategy committed all levels of Australian government to the promotion of 'development that improves the total quality of life, both now and in the future, in a way that maintains the ecological processes on which life depends'. The Strategy also established an Intergovernmental Committee to supervise the implementation of ESD within each jurisdiction.

The Intergovernmental Agreement on the Environment 1992 also includes a commitment to ESD principles. While there is no formal or compulsory implementation strategy for ESD principles, they have been incorporated in a large number of federal, State and Territory statutes.[72]

ESD principles are beginning to be applied by the Australia courts, particularly the precautionary principle. The seminal case on the precautionary principle is *Leatch v Director-General of National Parks and Wildlife Service*,[73] where Stein J applied

71 See <http://www.un.org/esa/sustdev/documents/WSSD_POI_PD/English/WSSD_PlanImpl.pdf#search=%22Plan%20of%20implementation%22> (accessed 1 September 2006).

72 Stein, 'Are Decision-makers too Cautious with the Precautionary Principle' (2000) 17 *EPLJ* 3, in an appendix lists 119 statutes which incorporate ESD principles.

73 (1993) 81 LGERA 270.

the principle to refuse a licence 'to take or kill' an endangered species (the Giant Burrowing Frog) in the context of a development proposal for a link road. The *National Parks and Wildlife Act 1974* (NSW), under which the Director-General of the National Parks and Wildlife Service granted the licence, had no express provision requiring consideration of the precautionary principle. His Honour nevertheless concluded that:

> While there is no express provision requiring consideration of the 'precautionary principle', consideration of the state of knowledge or uncertainty regarding a species, the potential for serious or irreversible harm to an endangered fauna and the adoption of a cautious approach in protection of endangered fauna is clearly consistent with the subject matter, scope and purpose of the Act.

And:

> [T]he precautionary principle is a statement of commonsense ... It is directed towards the prevention of serious or irreversible harm to the environment in situations of scientific uncertainty. Its premise is that where uncertainty or ignorance exists concerning the nature or scope of environmental harm (whether this follows from policies, decisions or activities), decision-makers should be cautious.[74]

Stein J held that, since the evidence left in doubt key questions as to the populations, habitat and behavioural characteristics of the frog, he was unable to conclude with any degree of certainty that a licence should be granted.

Although subsequent judgments in the Land and Environment Court have endorsed the precautionary principle as a relevant consideration in environmental decision-making, it has generally not been decisive in influencing the outcome of the case.[75] However, in a recent decision *Bentley v BGP Properties Pty Ltd*[76] (discussed extensively in Chapter 8), Preston CJ emphasised that the objects of the *National Parks and Wildlife Act 1974* (NSW) are to be achieved by applying the principles of ecologically sustainable development, as set out in s 2A(2) of the Act. His Honour stated that 'the conservation of biological diversity and ecological integrity is one of the pillars of ecologically sustainable development'.[77] His Honour also noted that the requirement for prior assessment and study of the impacts of a proposed action likely to damage threatened species, populations or ecological communities is an important component of the precautionary principle,[78] intergenerational equity,[79] and can facilitate the internalisation of external environmental costs.[80] In this case, the defendant had been charged with picking a threatened species contrary to s 118A(2) of the *National Parks and Wildlife Act*. Having addressed the objective seriousness of the offence, the seriousness of environmental harm and the defendant's actions, which were planned and deliberate, the defendant was convicted of the charge, fined the amount of $40,000 and ordered to pay the prosecutor's costs.

---

74 Ibid at 282-283.

75 See *Nicholls v Director-General of National Parks and Wildlife Service* (1994) 84 LGERA 397; *Greenpeace Australia Ltd v Redbank Power Co* (1995) 86 LGERA 143; and *North Compass v Hornsby Council* (unreported, NSWLEC, 26 August 1996); see also R Lyster, '*Friends of Hinchinbrook v Minister for the Environment*: The relevance of the precautionary principle' (1997) 14 *EPLJ* 390.

76 [2006] NSWLEC 34.

77 Ibid at [58].

78 Ibid at [68].

79 Ibid at [69].

80 Ibid at [70].

The significance of this case is that it is the first instance in which ESD principles have been referred to when convicting a person of a criminal offence under the *Threatened Species Conservation Act 1995* (NSW).

Economic rationalism

In addition to the influence exerted by the principles of ecologically sustainable development on Australian governments, the governments have shown an increasing interest in recent years to use the 'market' as a key aspect of environmental management. Before this, environmental management rested primarily on a form of regulation known as 'command-and-control' regulation. Essentially, 'command-and-control' regulation envisages the enactment of a statute, which prohibits the undertaking of an environmentally harmful activity without the granting of a permit, or licence, by a consent authority. Conditions may be attached to the permit which constrains the undertaking of the activity within the confines of the imposed conditions.

Traditionally, 'command-and control' statutes have governed the regulation of every type of environmental problem including planning, pollution, the conservation of biodiversity and natural resource management. Recently, while 'command-and-control' regulation still plays a vital role in environmental management, there is a tendency to introduce market mechanisms to achieve environmental outcomes.

The economic rationalist theory, which underpins the move towards the 'market', is based on neoclassical economics which claims that economic resources are better allocated through unfettered market forces than by government intervention. Coupled with this economic philosophy is a political philosophy that questions the nature and proper role of the state, favouring a minimal or residual state. There is a loss of faith in government both as a regulator and as a service provider. Neoclassical economics promises a smaller more efficient state in keeping with the fundamental tenets of liberal political philosophy. Liberalism promotes 'rationality, individuality, equality, liberty from interference from others or the State unless justified, the availability of legal rights, and the protection of the private sphere of life which is conventionally deemed to be "not the State's interest".'[81]

Under the neoclassical paradigm, it is expected that social needs will be met when the market is allowed to allocate public goods, without interference from the State, which is regarded as an impediment to the smooth allocation of resources. Within this paradigm, it is believed that market mechanisms have a number of advantages over traditional command-and-control strategies. With regard to allocation, market forces are likely to direct resources in a cost-effective manner at a lower overall cost while maintaining environmental quality. Market mechanisms relieve the state of much of its responsibility for decision-making. Rather, it is individual operators and investors who will regulate their activities to best position themselves in the market.

For environmental lawyers, the critical question is whether or not the 'market' is likely to result in the achievement of ecologically sustainable development. As the ensuing analysis demonstrates, there are numerous concerns about the move to the 'market'.

---

81 H Barnett, *Introduction to Feminist Jurisprudence* (Cavendish Publishing, 1998) at 121.

Creating markets to manage natural resources

One of the most interesting aspects of a new regulatory philosophy for managing natural resources is the move towards using 'markets' in the areas of water, carbon, renewable energy, salinity and biodiversity.[82]

The creation of such markets is evident in international instruments like the Kyoto Protocol which now provides for the establishment of an international emissions trading scheme for greenhouse gases. Closer to home, the Australian government has established a trading scheme in renewable energy certificates (RECs), as discussed in Chapter 5, while COAG is committed to a national water trading market, as discussed in Chapter 6. The New South Wales and ACT governments, meanwhile, have established a Greenhouse Benchmarks Scheme where the trading of greenhouse abatement certificates is an integral aspect of the Scheme, as discussed in Chapter 5.

A market in ecosystem services

In addition to these initiatives is an interest in using markets properly to value ecosystem services. Ecosystem services have been defined as 'the conditions and processes through which natural ecosystems, and species that make them up, sustain and fulfil human life'.[83] They include the provision of goods[84] as well as regenerating processes.[85] The services, which are regarded by economists as natural capital, supply 'for free' a stream of goods and other support services similar to those supplied by human and human-made capital. Heal et al[86] claim that there are two reasons that our ecosystem services are threatened. These include the unprecedented rate at which humanity is altering natural ecosystems and the processes that they control, and the failure of policy-makers to recognise the natural capital of these services. The result is that the ecosystem services underpinning the production of goods have no market value due to the fact that there is no market to capture and express their value. There are also no efficient price mechanisms to signal scarcity or degradation of the services. A further difficulty is that, as classic 'public goods', the ecosystem services cannot be exclusively controlled.

One of the keys to establishing markets in ecosystem services is to recognise the many different goods and services delivered by a single ecosystem and the interaction between them. A single system may deliver carbon storage and sequestration services, biodiversity, salinity and water purification services. According to Heal et al, policy-makers need to ask themselves three questions:

- what combinations of goods and services can be produced and what are the tradeoffs among services?

---

82 See R Lyster, '(De)regulating the rural environment' (2002) 19 *EPLJ* 34.

83 G Heal, G C Daily, PR Ehrlich, J Salzman, C Boggs, J Hellmann, J Hughes, C Kremen, T Ricketts, 'Protecting Natural Capital Through Ecosystem Service Districts' (2001) 30 *Stanford Environmental LJ* 333 at 336.

84 Such goods include food, pharmaceuticals, durable materials, energy, industrial products and biodiversity: ibid at 337.

85 These include cycling and filtration processes, translocation processes, stabilising processes, and life-fulfilling functions: ibid.

86 Ibid at 340-341.

- what are the policy variables that deliver different combinations of the outputs?
- which of these alternative product mixes is best for society?[87]

Before making any firm decisions, an explicit accounting of ecosystem services is required as well as the impacts on those services of alternative courses of action.[88]

Australian governments at the Commonwealth and State levels have already established schemes to recognise and create markets in ecosystem services in the areas of salinity management, native vegetation conservation and biodiversity protection. These are discussed in Chapters 7 and 8.

Criticisms of markets in natural resources and ecosystem services

Eckersely notes that a market in various natural resources

> enables environmental assets to be put to their highest valued combination of uses. We may not achieve an optimal environmental outcome, but this is not the point: rather, the concern is simply to achieve an *optimal allocation* of environmental resources.[89]

Efficiency is achieved in a competitive market where economic exchanges continue until it is impossible to make anyone better off without making somebody worse off. However, this approach only examines the allocation of resources, not property and income distribution. By taking the original distribution of property rights as a given, efficiency provides a limited performance principle for environmental and social policy-making.[90] Environmental organisations, Aboriginal people and others are unlikely to have the same bargaining power in the market as other well-resourced purchasers of environmental property rights.

In addition, markets do not exercise caution or intervene to redress imbalances in the public interest, neither do they do it to protect discrete interests. As neo-classical economic theory insists, the market will allocate resources to the highest value use, not necessarily to those most in need of it.

One of the mechanisms that corrects a potentially detrimental allocation of resources, like water, in a command-and-control framework is the opportunity for public participation. Very often, natural resource legislation allows for notice-and-comment procedures so that objections to applications for allocations, or development, may be made by those affected. However, in a market the only type of participation that is recognised is financial participation by those who can afford to enter the market. Clearly, the goal of efficiency, well served by the market, is often at odds with the principle of equity.

This seems to have been recognised by the New South Wales government with its establishment in August 2006 of the Aboriginal Water Trust (discussed in Chapter 6). The government has established this Trust to help Aboriginal people to enter the commercial water market and to encourage innovative methods of water use. This acknowledges the intimate cultural and economic relationship which

---

87 Ibid at 345.

88 Ibid at 360.

89 R Eckersley, 'Rationalising the Environment: How Much AM I Bid?' in S Rees, G Rodley and F Stilwell (eds), *Beyond the market: alternatives to economic rationalism* (Pluto Press, 1993) 237 at 242.

90 Ibid.

Aboriginal people have with water. Funding will be provided where water is a core component of plans to expand or establish an Aboriginal-owned business. In this case, applications must be made to the Aboriginal Water Trust. Funding will be made available either through specific purpose grants or interest payment subsidies or as 'in kind' contributions. The Trust will also be in a position to help Aboriginal enterprises secure additional funding and equity participation from the private sector.

Problems with measuring ecosystem services

In order for a market in ecosystem services to be established, each service needs to be identified, measured, endowed with property rights and priced in the marketplace. This acknowledges the existence and value of the service and allows buyers, willing and able to do so, to trade in the resource. This much is clear from all of the major policy documents that have been developed in recent years in Australia proposing recourse to the market as a natural resource management strategy.

Experience with wetland mitigation trades in the United States has shown that there are considerable difficulties associated with such assumptions. As Boyd et al[91] note:

> The exchange of complex environmental assets creates significant challenges for implementation, however. In particular, ecosystem exchanges, such as wetland mitigation trades, require more than good ecological analysis. They require the conscientious application of economic analysis in order to guarantee that trades preserve what is valuable about ecosystems. In most cases, regulators are not adequately equipped, financially or technically, to judge the relative value of environmental assets to be exchanged in such markets. Until these challenges are met, badly regulated ecosystem trades may undermine, rather than advance, the achievement of environmental and social welfare objectives.[92]

Most Australian policy documents which promote the use of markets to manage natural resources do so with reference to the success of air emissions trading programs under the *Clean Air Act 1990* in the United States. However, as Boyd et al note, '[a]ir emission trading differs significantly from trades involving more complex, heterogeneous, environmental assets such as habitat, water quality, and biodiversity'.[93] Ecosystem trading systems require complex bio-physical comparisons and trade-specific environmental valuation.

Consequently, there are significant legal, economic and practical implications for ecosystem trading. While the social costs of air pollution from different sources and the attendant environmental damage caused by them are relatively easy to compare, this is not the case with ecosystem services. Damage to land, a watershed or species is difficult to compare and rank since they are all highly idiosyncratic. This is because the social value of habitat or a species depends on location in the landscape, relationship to human activities and changes over time.[94] Boyd et al conclude that, '[w]ithout these environmental asset valuation methods, confidence

---

91 J Boyd, D King and LA Wainger, 'Compensation for Lost Ecosystem Services: The Need for Benefit-Based Transfer Ratios and Restoration Criteria' (2001) 20 *Stanford Environmental LJ* 393.

92 Ibid at 394.

93 Ibid.

94 Ibid at 395.

in ecosystem exchange is impossible. In short, a ton of sulphur dioxide (SO2) may be a ton of SO2 anywhere, but an acre here may not be worth an acre elsewhere'.[95]

The principal concern is that in practice regulators tend to value the strictly biophysical or functional site characteristics rather than valuing the ecosystem services. While biophysical characterisation is fundamental to any ecosystem evaluation they do not value the social value of an ecosystem. This is a major weakness of the wetland mitigation scheme in the United States as wetland mitigation projects, and particularly off-site mitigation projects, involve the exchange of one wetland for another, either explicitly or implicitly.

While an extensive review of the essential components of ecosystem service valuation is beyond the scope of the present discussion, the following basic principles of valuation are instructive. In addition to understanding the contribution of inputs to outputs, ecosystem services must be valued by paying attention to: scarcity and substitution; complementary goods and services; and marginal analysis. Greater scarcity and a relative lack of substitutes will increase the value of ecosystem services. Also the value of ecosystems increases when their complementary goods and services are accurately assessed and when the combination of these services is adequately appreciated. Marginal analysis, meanwhile, requires the realisation that 'the value of a wetland acre or individual in a biotic population is a decreasing function of the number already protected. In other words, the value of the only existing … wetland is greater than the value of the millionth'.[96]

In addition to understanding the basic principles of service valuation, it is necessary for regulators who are establishing markets to understand the temporal and spatial aspects of the analysis. Temporal analysis of ecosystems must demonstrate sensitivity to the fact that ecosystems provide benefits over lengthy periods of time, while spatial analysis requires an understanding that the services delivered by ecosystems depend on the landscape context in which those functions and services arise.[97]

Meanwhile, the environmental concerns about markets in ecosystem services are numerous. If trading commences in services that have not been appropriately valued by agencies there could be serious environmental damage. The risk of inappropriate valuation has been clearly enunciated by Boyd et al. There is the further risk that offsets will be allowed to occur where there is no clear appreciation of the value of services that will be lost. How then can agencies determine what type of ecosystem should be established to replace that which will be destroyed during the offset process?

It is not suggested that the search for alternative methods of regulation be abandoned. However, policy-makers in Australia need to ensure that, before rushing to the market, they are confident that the services that are traded are properly evaluated and accounted for. They need to consider whether natural resource markets need to be regulated so as to achieve ecologically sustainable outcomes.

Policy-makers need to make explicit the links between natural resources law, which is essentially command-and control in nature, and natural resource markets.

95 Ibid.

96 Ibid at 405-406.

97 Ibid at 406-407.

They need to consider also whether existing law needs to be amended, or new laws enacted to support the market.[98]

These considerations underpin a belief that the government should retain ultimate political responsibility for the ecologically sustainable management of Australia's natural resources, albeit while it establishes an appropriate mix of command-and-control and market instruments.

National Competition Policy in Australia (NCP)

In addition to adopting markets to manage natural resources, economic rationalism has also been responsible for a move in Australia towards deregulation, corporatisation or privatisation, and increased competition. These processes need to be assessed in relation to their consequences for ecologically sustainable development.

The origins of the processes may be found in 1992, when COAG commissioned an Independent Commission of Inquiry into National Competition Policy chaired by Professor Fred Hilmer (Hilmer Inquiry). The deregulation principle was enthusiastically endorsed by the Hilmer Inquiry which recommended specifically that legislation be reviewed to strategically surrender regulation in specific areas and to introduce innovative forms of regulation.

Acting on the recommendations of the Hilmer Inquiry, COAG signed three agreements: the Competition Principles Agreement (CPA); the Conduct Code Agreement; and the Agreement to Implement the National Competition Policy and Related Reforms in 1995. The agreements were designed to: improve efficiency of the economy through competition; remove regulatory impediments to productivity; and ensure that public sector businesses operate along the same market and profit oriented lines as the private sector.

The reforms can be outlined as: the review and reform of all laws which restrict competition by the year 2000; the restructuring of public sector monopoly businesses covering the electricity, gas, water and road transport industries; the introduction of competitive neutrality so that public businesses do not enjoy unfair advantages and to extend the operation of Pt IV of the *Trade Practices Act 1974* to government business enterprises; to facilitate access to nationally significant infrastructure services to promote competition in related markets;[99] and the extension of price surveillance to government business enterprises which retain a market monopoly.[100]

Following the signing of these agreements, regulation review units were set up at the Commonwealth and State levels to reduce regulatory barriers to competition. In New South Wales, for example, the government developed the NSW Government Policy Statement of Legislation Review. In 1997, guidelines entitled *Consulting on Reform: A Consultation Framework for Review of Anti-Competitive Legislation* were developed to ensure that the reviews were conducted in an open and transparent

---

98 See, eg, the *Carbon Rights Legislation Amendment Act 1998* (NSW), which amends the *Conveyancing Act 1919* (NSW) to recognise that a right associated with carbon sequestration from the atmosphere may be a species of forestry right; see also the *Protection of the Environment Operations Amendment (Tradeable Emission Schemes) Act 2000* (NSW).

99 See Pt IIIA of *Trade Practices Act 1974* (Cth) which gives a firm the right to require another firm to give it access to certain infrastructure it owns.

100 'National Competition Policy – Some Facts', <http://www.ncc.gov.au> at 1.

manner allowing for public participation. In addition, all proposals for new legislation, or for amendments to existing statutes, are required to take account of NCP and are reviewed by officials in the Cabinet Office.

The Commonwealth agreed at COAG to make special payments in the order of $16 billion over 1997-98 and 2005-08 to States and Territories on satisfactory progress in implementing NCP reforms. Eligibility for these payments was assessed by the National Competition Council (NCC) in June 1997, 1999 and 2001.[101] The legislation review deadline for all jurisdictions to complete legislation reviews was 30 June 2002.[102]

Review of laws that restrict competition

Under cl 5 in the Competition Policy Agreements (CPA), all governments agreed that legislation should not restrict competition unless it can be demonstrated that the benefits of the restriction to the community outweigh the costs and the objectives of legislation can only be achieved by restricting competition. The NCC has indicated the matters which can be taken into account in establishing interventions in public interest. Clause 1(3) of the CPA lists several issues that can be taken into account including: government legislation and policies that relate to ecologically sustainable development; social welfare and equity considerations including community service obligations imposed on government business enterprises; economic and regional development, including employment and investment growth; and the efficient allocation of resources.[103]

Despite the assurance in cl 1(3) of the CPA, land use and natural resource approvals systems have been prime targets for deregulation under the review process.[104] Environmental regulation is by its very nature a 'regulatory impediment to productivity' and may interfere with the 'efficient allocation of resources'. Although governments are permitted to take ecologically sustainable development into account during the process of regulation review, conventional environmental regulation is under the spotlight as never before. Competition principles have infiltrated the deliberations of intergovernmental policy-makers, like COAG, and have influenced the development of natural resource strategies adopted at both the Commonwealth and State levels of government.

Restructuring of public sector monopoly businesses

In line with national competition policy, the majority of public sector monopoly businesses in Australia have either been corporatised or privatised. The corporatisation of publicly owned entities, like airlines, banking, post, telecommunications and utilities (electricity, water and gas), is often a precursor to full privatisation. Corporatisation involves 'converting agencies from a statutory authority structure

---

101 Ibid at 4.

102 Council of Australian Government's Meeting, 3 November 2000, Canberra, Communiqué, Attachment B.

103 Ibid at 7.

104 See, eg, the 1997 amendments to the *Environmental Planning and Assessment Act 1979* (NSW) which introduced the concepts of 'integrated development' and 'accredited certifiers' as well as the overhaul of Commonwealth environmental impact assessment procedures under the EPBCA to avoid duplication of State and Commonwealth procedures.

(established by an Act of Parliament) or a departmental structure to a company structure (in conformity with Companies legislation applying to the private sector)'.[105] Such a corporation is known as a government business enterprise (GBE), or State Owned Corporation (SOC), and may be incorporated under the *Corporations Act 2001* (Cth). The government usually has a controlling or substantial interest.[106] Full privatisation occurs when the SOC is sold to private investors, involving a total divestment of government ownership and responsibility for the operations of the corporation.

Where public sector businesses, like Sydney Water (discussed in Chapter 6), have been corporatised, the corporatised entity has generally been expected to comply with community service objectives (CSOs). For example, the *State Owned Corporations Act 1989* (NSW) (SOCA) provides that the principal objectives of State Owned Corporations are:

> (a) to be a successful business and, to this end:
>   (i) to operate at least as efficiently as any comparable businesses, and
>   (ii) to maximise the net worth of the State's investment in the SOC, and
> (b) to exhibit a sense of social responsibility by having regard to the interests of the community in which it operates, and
> (c) where its activities affect the environment, to conduct its operations in compliance with the principles of ecologically sustainable development contained in section 6(2) of the *Protection of the Environment Administration Act 1991*, and
> (d) to exhibit a sense of responsibility towards regional development and decentralisation in the way in which it operates.
> (2) Each of the principal objectives of a SOC is of equal importance. (ss 8, 20E)

Social impacts of restructuring

In keeping with the tenets of sustainable development which seek to integrate economic, social and environmental considerations, it is important to consider the social implications of restructuring. Consumer concerns about privatised and corporatised utilities are numerous. Will the services so crucial to human health and well-being be provided to all, without discrimination? While this may be a goal of public service providers, the privatised or corporatised utilities have a profit motive and may neglect the needs of less lucrative 'clients'. Will the service itself, and the quality of the service, be maintained so as to not impact on human health and well-being? How will the services be provided – on the basis of a pre-paid meter, or by payment of an account at regular intervals? What are the consequences of not buying tokens to insert in the meter, or of mounting debt and an inability to service the debt? When can the service provider disconnect the 'consumer' from the service?

The question is whether or not CSOs of the type mentioned above are enforceable. The reality of this concern was illustrated in *Yarmirr v Australian Telecommunications Corporation*.[107] Here a representative of an Aboriginal community sought review of the corporatised Telecom's failure to provide the community with

---

105 H Michael, 'Statement before the Industrial Relations Commission of NSW (IRC No 789 of 1993)', cited by Wettenhall Roger, 'Corporations and Corporatisation: An Administrative History Perspective' (1995) 6 *PLR* 7 at 11.

106 Ibid at 19.

107 (1990) 96 ALR 739.

interim telephone services. A plan to extend standard telephone services to their remote area had been substantially delayed. They claimed that the provision of a satellite telephone service would alleviate difficulties which they experienced with a high frequency radio telephone, subject to provision of the standard service at a later date. Section 27(4) of the *Australian Telecommunications Corporation Act 1989* (Cth) provided that:

> Telecom shall ensure:
>
> (a) that, in view of the social importance of the standard telephone service, the service is reasonably accessible to all people in Australia on an equitable basis, wherever they reside or carry on business.

The Aboriginal community's attempt to enforce the community service obligation in s 27(4) of the Act did not meet with success in the Federal Court. Burchett J held that no error of law had been made and that the discharge of the obligations required Telecom to determine priorities in pursuing each ideal with respect to the services made available to communities around Australia.

Meanwhile, there have been numerous examples of corporatised or privatised utility failure. In Melbourne, the explosion of a temperature valve at the Longford gas station, operated by the private utility, Esso, left Melbournians without an energy source for weeks. The explosion also resulted in the death of, and horrific injuries to, workers.[108] In New Zealand, the corporatised Mercury Energy was responsible for a total power failure in the central business district of Auckland due to serious infrastructural collapse. The charge levelled at all of these utilities is that they allowed profit motives to override all other concerns including safety and consumer welfare.

Environmental impacts of restructuring

Concern about the environmental impacts of the restructured National Electricity Market is discussed in Chapter 5. However, it is also possible that utility failure can impact on the environment in a direct way. Gas explosions at facilities and failure of electricity supplies or sewage systems create obvious environmental hazards. It should also be remembered that the McClellan Inquiry which investigated the circumstances surrounding the Sydney Water 'boil water' alerts in 1998 (discussed in Chapter 6) found that Australian Water Services (Pty) Ltd (AWS) was selected as the preferred tenderer to operate the plant because it offered the lowest price – $40 million less than the nearest tender price. This was in spite of the fact that it had not proved its treatment process to the satisfaction of the technical assessment team. In addition, the Inquiry found that the Water Board undertook the design and tender stage of the project before publishing an environmental impact statement (EIS). This was despite the fact that the Water Board, before its corporatisation as Sydney Water, was required under provisions of the *Environmental Planning and Assessment*

---

108 Employees, and former employees, interviewed about the activities of Esso all pointed to the fact that the plant was inadequately maintained, that staff training to deal with accidents was deficient, that staff had been cut back and that incidents at the plant were not properly accounted for in accordance with risk management and accounting procedures. It was also alleged that both with respect to this incident, and another in Hong Kong, vital information regarding the accidents was withheld from Commissions and Coronial Inquiries: *The 7.30 Report*, Australian Broadcasting Corporation, 3 May 1999.

Act 1979 (NSW) to prepare an EIS before deciding whether to proceed with the development of improved facilities by the private sector. By the time the EIS process was finalised, the preliminary contractual arrangements had imposed considerable time cost pressures on the Board. At that stage, it was unlikely that the project would not proceed, irrespective of the outcome of the EIS.

Conclusion

It is clear that economic rationalism has had a considerable influence on the environmental policy and regulatory framework in Australia. As discussed, it has led to the establishment, and proposed creation, of markets in various areas of environmental law. The restructuring of the water and energy services sector is another consequence of this economic theory. Environmental lawyers will need to keep abreast of these developments and assess their implications for ecologically sustainable development in Australia.

Courts and tribunals

A unique feature of Australian environmental law is the establishment of a number of specialist statutory courts and tribunals to adjudicate environmental matters: in New South Wales, the Land and Environment Court; in Victoria, the Victorian Civil and Administrative Tribunal; in Queensland, the Planning and Environment Court; in South Australia, the Environment Resources and Development Court; in Tasmania, the Resource Management and Planning Appeal Tribunal; and in Western Australia, the Town Planning Appeal Tribunal. An appeal against a Commonwealth decision lies to the Federal Court.

Tribunals operate outside the court system and are intended to provide a speedier and less expensive way of resolving disputes. There is generally a right of appeal to a higher tribunal or a court. Even without such provision, however, a court may review the process by which a Tribunal made a decision. Tribunals are not vested with criminal jurisdiction and criminal proceedings have to be commenced in the appropriate court of criminal jurisdiction.

Merits appeals and judicial review

Depending on the jurisdiction of the court, it may hear challenges as to the merits of a decision or conduct judicial review proceedings.

Merits appeal

An appeal on the merits is only available where it is expressly provided by statute. A merits appeal involves the court standing in the shoes of the original decision-maker and deciding what the correct decision should be. If the court disagrees with the decision, it can overturn it and substitute its own. Merits appeals are widely available to applicants under environmental legislation. For example, s 97 of the *Environmental Planning and Assessment Act 1979* gives the applicant a right of merits appeal within 12 months of the determination of a development application, or deemed refusal. Third party merits appeals are seldom provided in environmental legislation. However, s 98 of the *Environmental Planning and Assessment Act 1979* gives objectors a right of merits appeal in relation to designated development. The appeal has to be brought within 28 days of the determination.

Judicial review

Judicial review proceedings involve the court inquiring into the *legality* of the decision. If the decision-maker followed the correct procedures and the decision was within power, the decision cannot be overturned by the court, notwithstanding that the court would not have come to the same conclusion. If the plaintiff is successful in alleging an illegality, the decision will be declared invalid by the court. However, the decision-maker can subsequently make the same decision, provided the correct procedures are followed, and it will not be susceptible to challenge in the courts. This should be borne in mind when contemplating judicial review. However, in some cases the ensuing publicity results in a decision-maker reconsidering its original decision. Given the limited availability of third party merits appeals, public interest challenges are generally by way of judicial review.

Most environmental statutes have open standing provisions permitting any person to bring an action to enforce a breach of the legislation, for example, s 123 of the *Environmental Planning and Assessment Act 1979*. However, even where a statute does not have such a provision, judicial review is always available under the more general provisions of administrative law to applicants who can show the necessary 'standing' to bring the action. The types of grounds for judicial review available to applicants under administrative law include:

- that the decision-make took account of an irrelevant consideration, or failed to consider a relevant consideration;[109]
- that the decision-maker acted ultra vires (beyond power);[110]
- that the decision-maker did not observe procedural fairness;[111]
- that the decision was so unreasonable, that no reasonable decision-maker properly applying his or her mind to the matter could have made it.[112]

These aspects will be more clearly illustrated in the context of the NSW Land and Environment Court.

The NSW Land and Environment Court

In 1979, the NSW government introduced a package of reforms designed to transform the planning system and rationalise the diversified jurisdictions of the numbers of courts and tribunals involved in land use and enforcement decisions. This package included the *Environmental Planning and Assessment Act 1979*, the *Heritage Act 1979* and the *Land and Environment Court Act 1979* (LECA). The *Environmental Planning and Assessment Act 1979* introduced a new planning system, while the LECA established a new specialist court.

---

109 *Parramatta City Council v Hale* (1982) 47 LGRA 319; *Carstens v Pittwater Council* (1999) 111 LGERA 1.

110 *Randwick City Council v Minister for the Environment* [1998] FCA 1376.

111 *Australian Broadcasting Tribunal v Bond* (1990) 170 CLR 321.

112 *Associated Provincial Picture Houses Ltd v Wednesbury Corporation* [1948] 1 KB 223; *Parramatta City Council v Hale* (1982) 47 LGRA 319.

The Land and Environment Court (LEC) commenced operations in September 1980. It is one of the oldest specialist environmental courts in the world. Since its establishment, it has created an impressive body of environmental jurisprudence and has been an important catalyst in the development of environmental law in Australia. Its two-tiered structure enables it to declare and enforce the law as well as to review the merits of the decisions of certain bodies.

The LEC is a superior court of record with rank equivalent to the Supreme Court in NSW (LECA s 5). It is constituted by six judges and nine Commissioners. The Commissioners are lay experts with specialist knowledge in specific areas, such as town planning or engineering.

The court has provided a model for the establishment of similar courts in Queensland, South Australia and Tasmania. It has also generated considerable international interest.[113]

The Jurisdiction of the Land and Environment Court

The LEC has a mixed jurisdiction, which requires it to deal not only with all merits appeals relating to land use and environmental issues, but also with all civil and criminal enforcement matters, and judicial review. The LEC has original jurisdiction in merits appeals, but in judicial review proceedings it is a court of first instance.

The LEC has jurisdiction to hear any matter falling within its jurisdiction and all matters ancillary thereto. As a superior court of record, it has also inherent jurisdiction.[114] Its jurisdiction is purely statutory – it has not been given jurisdiction over common law actions, such as negligence or nuisance or civil claims for environmental damage. It cannot award damages except where provided for by statute.

The jurisdiction of the LEC is divided into seven classes according to the nature of the subject-matter in question. The class of the litigation affects its scope and the remedy available. These classes are as follows:

Class 1 – environmental planning and protection appeals (LECA s 17)

Appeals in this class lie from a range of environment protection statutes, dealing with areas such as planning, pollution, heritage and threatened species. They are often appeals by applicants against decisions by local councils and constitute more than half of the court's workload. They also include a small number of third party merits appeals, which have made an important contribution to the development of environmental law.

Class 2 – local government and miscellaneous appeals and applications (LECA s 18)

These appeals are mainly confined to matters arising under the *Local Government Act 1993* but extend to a number of other statutes dealing with water supply, catchment management and noxious weeds.

---

113 The Environment Court Project: Final Report of the Department of Environment, Transport and the Regions (2000) (the Grant Report) conducted by Professor Grant of Cambridge University recommended the introduction of an environmental court in the United Kingdom. It strongly commended the NSW LEC. The British government rejected the proposal. See <http://www.odpm.gov.uk/>.

114 See *Longwon Pty Ltd v Warringah Shire Council* (1993) 33 NSWLR 13 (CA).

Class 3 – land tenure, valuation, rating and compensation matters (LECA s *19)*

This class includes appeals against land valuations and compensation for land which has been compulsorily acquired by the State. It also includes land claims under the *Aboriginal Land Rights Act 1983*.

Merits appeals – appeals in classes 1-3

Appeals in classes 1-3 are full merits appeals. Appeals in these 3 classes involve a *de novo* rehearing of the matter. Issues of fact and questions of law may be considered. The LEC has original jurisdiction over the merits of the decision and 'stands in the shoes' of the original decision-maker. This means that the court has all the powers and responsibilities of the original decision-maker and is not bound by the original decision.

Proceedings in class 1, 2 or 3 of the court are conducted with as little formality and technicality and as expeditiously as possible (LECA s 38(1)). The court is not bound by the rules of evidence and may inform itself on any matters as it thinks appropriate (LECA s 38(2)). Proceedings in class 1, 2 or 3 can be delegated to one or more Commissioners for hearing and disposal. In practice, the majority of appeals in class 1, 2 or 3 are heard by Commissioners. Commissioners do not decide legal questions and if a question of law arises during a hearing, it must be referred to a judge for determination. Judgments of the Commissioners are final, except that an appeal lies to a judge of the LEC on a question of law. Complex matters are heard before a judge who may be assisted by a Commissioner if scientific or technical matters are involved. In this situation, the Commissioner acts in a purely advisory role. An appeal lies from a decision of an LEC judge to the Court of Appeal in classes 1, 2 or 3 on a question of law. Until recently, costs in class 1, 2 or 3 could only be awarded in exceptional circumstances, but can now be awarded where it is 'fair and reasonable' to do so.

Class 4 – environmental planning and protection and development and development contract – civil enforcement (LECA s *20)*

This class deals with civil enforcement as well as judicial review of environmental decisions. These matters may only be heard by a judge of the LEC. The civil enforcement jurisdiction involves the hearing and disposing of proceedings arising under the specific enforcement provisions of a large number of environmental statutes.

Judicial review is concerned with procedural breaches of environmental legislation and occurs where the decision-making authority has misunderstood its legal obligations, for example, taking account of irrelevant considerations. In Class 4 matters, the LEC is the court of first instance and has exclusive jurisdiction (LECA s 71). The LEC has power to issue injunctions and other orders. An appeal lies from a decision of an LEC judge in class 4 to the Court of Appeal. This may be a full appeal on the law and the facts.

Decisions in class 4 are widely regarded as the most important area of the court's jurisdiction and have greatly contributed to the development of an environmental jurisprudence and increased public awareness and concern for the environment. This process has been facilitated by the enactment of environmental legislation with 'open standing' provisions.

Class 5 – environmental planning and protection – summary criminal enforcement (LECA s 21)

This class involves criminal enforcement and prosecution. The LEC exercises summary criminal jurisdiction over a number of environmental statutes. Foremost among these are prosecutions under the *Protection of the Environment Operations Act 1997*. Prosecutions under this legislation are brought by the Environment Protection Authority and local councils.

Jurisdiction in this class is exercised by a judge. An appeal lies from a decision of a judge of the LEC to the Court of Criminal Appeal. Although the role of the court in class 5 is primarily involved with construing legislation pertaining to environmental offences, its decisions have made an important contribution to the literature on environmental crime.

Class 6 – appeals by defendants from convictions relating to environmental offences (LECA s 21A)

This class deals with appeals from convictions or sentences by the Local Courts for environmental offences. Only appeals as of right are dealt with in this class.[115]

Class 7 – other appeals by defendants relating to environmental offences[116]

This class also deals with appeals from convictions by the Local Courts for environmental offences. Only appeals which require the leave of the LEC are dealt with in this class.

An appeal lies from a decision of a judge of the LEC in class 6 or 7 to the Court of Criminal Appeal.

Alternative dispute resolution

Alternative dispute resolution is well integrated into the procedures of the LEC and facilitates quicker and cost-effective resolution of disputes. Several forms are available.

Issues conferences

Issues conferences were introduced in 1991. They are mandatory in complex class 1 matters, class 3 compensation matters and class 4 matters. The purpose is to narrow the issues, explore matters for settlement and reduce time and costs.

Conciliation conferences

These conferences may be held in classes 1, 2 and certain class 3 matters. These conferences are conducted by commissioners at any early stage in the proceedings. Originally these proceedings were mandatory in every case. However, now they are

115 These are appeals under ss 31 or 42 of the *Crimes (Local Courts Appeal and Review) Act 2001*. Section 31 deals with appeals by the defendant against conviction or sentence, while s 42 deals with appeals by the Director of Public Prosecutions against the sentence imposed.

116 Ibid s 21B. These are appeals under ss 32 or 43 of the *Crimes (Local Courts Appeal and Review) Act 2001*. Section 32 deals with appeals by the defendant against a conviction in their absence or following a plea of guilty. Section 43 deals with appeals by the Director of Public Prosecutions.

only held at the request of both parties. If an agreement is reached, the matter will be disposed of without further hearing. If the conciliation does not succeed, the matter is heard by the court in the usual way. Conciliation conferences are reported to have a high settlement rate of approximately 85%.[117]

Mediation and neutral evaluation

Since 1991 the LEC has offered mediation as an alternative to litigation in classes 1, 2, 3 and 4 of its jurisdiction (LECA Pt 5A). Mediation is available at any stage of the proceedings at the option of the parties. The court can also refer matters to mediation, but participation is voluntary. Mediation is informal and confidential. It is defined as 'a structured negotiation process in which a mediator, as a neutral and independent party, assists the parties to a dispute to achieve their own resolution of the dispute' (s 61B(1)).

Anything said in mediation cannot be used in any proceedings before a court or tribunal. If the matter is not resolved, the matter will be heard by the LEC and the judge will not be told of anything which took place during the mediation conference. If parties reach agreement, they can either have an informal agreement or have it given the force of a court order so that it is binding.

According to Stein J, the success rate for mediated disputes is around 70%.[118] There is also considerable time and cost savings as mediation takes about a quarter of the time of contested hearings.

The LEC also offers neutral evaluation of disputes. Neutral evaluation is voluntary and confidential. It is defined as process in which 'the evaluator seeks to identify and reduce the issues of fact and law in dispute. The evaluator's role includes assessing the relative strengths and weakness of each party's case and offering an opinion as to the likely outcome of the proceedings' (s 61B(2)). Costs of mediation or neutral evaluation are borne equally by the parties. A court list of approved mediators is available, but parties are free to choose their own mediator.

Procedural achievements of the LEC

The LEC has demonstrated how a specialist court can contribute to the development of environmental law, both procedurally and substantively. Substantively, in a number of important decisions the LEC has used its unique combination of a merits appeals jurisdiction, judicial review and criminal jurisdiction to develop an impressive body of environmental jurisprudence. This has been elaborated by the Court of Appeal, the High Court and academic writers. Transparency and public awareness of decisions have been stimulated by publication in specialist law reports and on the internet.

The LEC has also introduced a number of procedural innovations that have facilitated access to justice. Some of its achievements are discussed below.

---

117 See Hon Justice Stein, 'Down Under Perspective of the Environmental Court Project', unpublished paper, the UK Environment Association Seminar on the Final Report of the Environmental Court Project, London, 27 June 2002, p 5.

118 Ibid.

Standing

The *Environmental Planning and Assessment Act 1979* (EPAA) contains an open standing provision which gives any person a right to bring proceedings in the court 'for an order to remedy to restrain a breach or threatened breach of the Act, whether or not any right of that person had been or may be infringed as a consequence of that breach' (s 123). This section paved the way for public interest matters to be brought in the LEC. Public interest matters generally involve important points of law and incorporate values which are important to the whole community.

The open standing provision was challenged shortly after the commencement of the Act. The LEC was quick to reject an argument that the section should be narrowly construed and that it did not relieve the appellant of establishing the common law requirement of a private right or a 'special interest' in the subject-matter of the action.[119] The broad interpretation of open standing by the LEC was affirmed by the Court of Appeal in *Sydney City Council v Building Owners' and Managers Association of Australia Ltd*.[120]

Concerns that open standing provisions would 'open the floodgates' and that the court would be deluged with appeals have been proved to be unfounded. According to Justice Stein, the reality of open standing is that the influx of litigants has been barely enough to 'wet the wellingtons'.[121] Court statistics show that the number of proceedings brought by third parties under the various open standing provisions in New South Wales have never exceeded 20% of registrations for civil enforcement and review in any year.[122]

Costs in public interest litigation

Lack of resources is one of the greatest obstacles facing prospective litigants. Legal costs are high and so are the fees for experts. In civil enforcement and judicial review (Class 4) proceedings, because the jurisdiction of the court is similar to a conventional court, the general rule is that costs follow the event – ie, the unsuccessful party pays the costs of the successful party. This can be a significant deterrent to public interest litigants as although they can often raise funds for their legal expenses, they also have to contend with paying the other party's costs if unsuccessful. This could largely negative the advantages of providing open standing provisions. Justice Toohey (a former justice of the High Court) observed in an address to the National Environmental Law Association in 1989 that 'there is little point in opening the doors of the courts if litigants cannot afford to enter'.

Already in 1988, the LEC had attempted to overcome this obstacle by adopting the view that the public interest nature of the proceedings is a significant factor to be considered in awarding costs.[123]

---

119 See *Rowley v NSW Leather Trading Co Pty* Ltd (1980) 46 LGRA 250; *National Trust (NSW) v Minister Administering Environmental Planning and Assessment Act* (1981) 53 LGRA 37.

120 (1985) 55 LGERA 444.

121 Hon Justice P Stein, 'New Directions in the Prevention and Resolution of Environmental Disputes – Specialist Environmental Courts', unpublished paper, The SE Asian Regional Symposium on the Judiciary and the Law of Sustainable Development, UNEP/UNDP, Manila, 6 March 1999, p 7.

122 Ibid.

123 See, eg, *Campbell v Lord Howe Islands* (unreported, NSWLEC, 24 June 1998).

This issue came before the LEC again in 1994 in *Oshlack v Richmond River Council*.[124] In that case, Stein J reviewed the earlier cases and stated some of the principles applicable to an award of costs in public interest litigation. Applying these principles, His Honour declined to award costs against the unsuccessful party who had brought the action in the public interest. That ruling was reversed by the Court of Appeal in *Richmond River Council v Oshlack*,[125] but reinstated in 1998 by a majority of the High Court in *Oshlack v Richmond River Council*.[126] However, a subsequent judgment of the High Court confined this ruling to the special features of the NSW legislation.[127]

Security for costs

Ordering an applicant to give security for payment of costs which may be awarded against them can be an impediment to public interest litigation. In practice these applications are rarely and seldom successful.[128] The LEC has taken the view that the public interest nature of litigation is a significant factor to be taken into account in considering the award of costs.[129]

Undertaking for damages

The traditional common law rule is that the giving of an undertaking as to damages is a condition precedent to the granting of an interim injunction. The damage suffered by the defendants could potentially run into millions of dollars if construction of a major development was halted by an injunction. The LEC has consistently held that where the laws are concerned with the protection of the environment such an undertaking is a factor to be taken into account in exercising its discretion.[130]

The review of the Land and Environment Court

From inception, the LEC was intended to be 'a novel concept bringing together in one body the best attributes of a traditional court system and of a lay tribunal system'.[131] While it enjoyed strong support from the government of the day, some members of the judiciary and legal profession were opposed to the creation of a specialist court outside the existing system which they saw as undermining traditional values.

The two-tiered structure of the LEC has also been particularly controversial. Since the creation of the LEC its opponents have argued that merits appeals would be better dealt with by an administrative tribunal and that the court should restrict itself to legal questions and judicial review. A public review of the LEC was undertaken by a Working Party under the Chairmanship of Justice Cripps QC in 2000. This review was restricted to development applications and dealt mainly with

124 (1994) 82 LGERA 236.
125 (1996) 39 NSWLR 622.
126 (1998) 193 CLR 72.
127 *South-West Forest Defence v Conservation Department* (1998) 72 ALJR 1008.
128 Stein, above n 121, at 10.
129 *Byron Shire Business for the Future Inc v Byron Shire Council* (1994) 83 LGERA 59.
130 *Ross v State Rail Authority* (1987) 70 LGRA 91.
131 *Hansard*, Second Reading Speech, Legislative Assembly, 14 November 1979, 3051.

perceived problems with the merits appeal system. A submission by 172 local councils expressed concern about the high cost of litigation, inconsistent decisions, inadequate regard for the environment and its alleged pro-development bias.[132]

Most of the criticism was directed at decisions of the Commissioners who some critics considered less able to determine planning appeals than judges. This view was rejected by the Cripps Report[133] which pointed out that Commissioners have often more extensive planning qualifications than judges and are better equipped to evaluate expert evidence. Commissioners are also more cost-effective than appointing additional judges. The Report also found that there was insufficient evidence to support allegations of inadequate regard for the environment or a pro-development bias.[134]

The Report expressed concern at the high costs of litigation which is estimated to be in the vicinity of $20,000 to $25,000 per day for each party. Factors contributing to the high costs are the duplication of expert evidence and unnecessary cross-examination.

The Cripps Report recommended that the current system of merits review should be retained. It accepted that merits review provided a safeguard for the rights of individuals as well as protecting the public interest. Further, it considered that a division of responsibilities for merit review between a court and a tribunal would detract from the 'one stop shop' approach, would involve additional expenditure in creating the new body, and could lead to confusion and duplication of responsibilities between the court and the tribunal.

The Cripps Report made 37 recommendations to improve the handling of merits appeals and minimise the cost of litigation. These recommendations have not all been adopted but in 2004 the Chief Judge of the LEC introduced a number of changes in classes 1, 2 and 3 of the court's jurisdiction in 2004 primarily directed at reducing costs.[135] Some of the principal reforms are:

- Compulsory issues conferences are to be conducted in complex class 1 proceedings to identify the real issues in dispute and lay out a blue-print for the hearing to resolve them as efficiently as possible.
- Class 1 matters are to commence with a view on site conducted by a Commissioner. Objectors are to be encouraged to present their view informally.
- Parties must advise the court at the first callover whether the matter is appropriate for case management and/or mediation.
- Court-appointed experts are to be encouraged in suitable matters. Although parties will be consulted on the choice of expert, they will have to give reasons why a court expert should not be appointed;
- A Code of Conduct has been introduced for expert witnesses, which emphasises the need to confer, and outlines their duty to the court.

---

132 Report of the Land and Environment Court Working Party, NSW Attorney General, 2001 (Cripps Report).

133 Ibid at 56.

134 Ibid at 13.

135 These changes effected additions and changes to the LEC Practice Directions as well as amendments to the LEC Rules 1996. They commenced operation in February and March 2004. Justice Peter McClellan, 'Land and Environment Court – Achieving the Best Outcome for the Community', EPLA Conference, Newcastle, 28-29 November 2003.

- Cross-examination in merits appeals is to be curtailed. Although in the past it has been only available by leave of the court, it was, nevertheless, often excessive.
- In the past the LEC's discretion to award costs was only exercised in merits appeals in exceptional cases.[136] Costs can now be awarded where it is 'fair and reasonable' to do so.
- To ensure more transparency of merit decisions by Commissioners, their decisions are being published on the internet.
- Consideration was to be given to holding 'paper' appeals in appropriate cases.

136 Practice Directions 10, 10A.

2

LAND USE PLANNING

Planning is a term which covers a broad range of meanings. In the context of land use, it can include strategic planning, the development of urban policy, for example in provision of infrastructure such as housing and transport, and more focused reference to urban and regional, or town and country, planning.[1]

Planning processes relevant to environmental issues include management of protected areas by all levels of government, including management of community land by local government; water catchment management; and controls on activities which may impact on native vegetation. Plans of management for protected areas, including under the *Local Government Act 1993*, are discussed in Chapter 9. Catchment management is discussed in Chapter 7. The primary focus of this chapter is on land use planning, or the regulation of land use, through the controls established under the *Environmental Planning and Assessment Act 1979* (EPAA).

The EPAA was passed in 1979, in a regulatory climate very different from that of today. The objects of the EPAA are set out in s 5, and as originally enacted were:

> The objects of this Act are:
>
> (a) to encourage:
>
> (i) the proper management, development and conservation of natural and artificial resources, including agricultural land, natural areas, forests, minerals, water, cities, towns and villages for the purpose of promoting the social and economic welfare of the community and a better environment;
>
> (ii) the promotion and co-ordination of the orderly and economic use and development of land;
>
> (iii) the protection, provision and co-ordination of communication and utility services;
>
> (iv) the provision of land for public purposes;
>
> (v) the provision and co-ordination of community services and facilities; and
>
> (vi) the protection of the environment;
>
> (b) to promote the sharing of the responsibility for environmental planning between the different levels of government in the State, and
>
> (c) to provide increased opportunity for public involvement and participation in environmental planning and assessment.

Subsequent amendments have added to s 5(a) '(vii) ecologically sustainable development' and '(viii) the provision and maintenance of affordable housing', and expanded s 5(a)(vi), which now reads:

---

1 B Gleeson and N Low, *Australian Urban Planning: New Challenges, New Agendas* (Allen & Unwin, 2000) at 12.

(vi) the protection of the environment, including the protection and conservation of native animals and plants, including threatened species, populations and ecological communities, and their habitats.

The EPAA does not in terms direct decision-makers to have regard to the objects of the Act when making decisions. However, these objects are relevant in consideration, in particular, of 'the public interest' in decision-making under the EPAA: *Carstens v Pittwater Council*;[2] *BGP Properties Pty Ltd v Lake Macquarie City Council*;[3] *Telstra Corporation Ltd v Hornsby Shire Council*.[4] The objects are also relevant in the making of environmental planning instruments, which must be made for the purpose of achieving any of the objects of the EPAA (s 24).

The objects of the EPAA reflect a number of themes that had emerged by the second half of the 20th century: a concern for the balancing of economic growth and environmental protection; a desire to achieve a greater degree of co-ordination in decision-making between State and local government; and the growing demand for increased opportunities for public participation in the decision-making process.

Issues in planning control

Who decides – State or local government?

As noted above, one of the objects of the EPAA is to 'promote the sharing of the responsibility for environmental planning between the different levels of government in the State'. The delineation of appropriate division of responsibilities between State and local government has been a significant issue since the introduction of comprehensive planning legislation in New South Wales in 1945, in Pt XIIA of the *Local Government Act 1919*.

The first comprehensive planning legislation was introduced following the Commonwealth-State Housing Agreement in 1945, under which the federal government agreed to provide funds to the States for public housing, on condition that the States ensured that there was adequate legislation to control town planning. Before this, planning controls were minimal, and essentially negative. Nineteenth century legislation allowing local government to control the subdivision of land, the erection of roads and building standards was supplemented by the *Local Government Act 1919*, which allowed local government to restrict undesirable development. This was primarily achieved through s 309 (in Pt XI), under which councils could proclaim residential districts from which offensive uses were excluded.

The focus was initially on local government. The Cumberland County Council was created with representatives of the Sydney City Council and from 5 to 12 other councils, to prepare the County of Cumberland Planning Scheme (covering the County of Cumberland, which was essentially then metropolitan Sydney). Local councils were given the power to prepare more detailed local planning schemes, either alone or as a joint scheme with other councils. The Minister and local councils had the power to regulate interim development, that is, development during the

2 (1999) 111 LGERA 1.
3 [2004] NSWLEC 399.
4 (2006) 146 LGERA 10.

preparation of a local planning scheme, or during suspension of its provisions or those of the County of Cumberland Planning Scheme. This position was not without difficulty, however, as the Cumberland County Council had to rely on the support of the relevant Minister to co-ordinate activities of other State government agencies. Further, the role of the local council was limited in the finalisation of a planning scheme, which was formally made by the Minister following a report by the Town and Country Planning Advisory Committee, with no more than three-quarters of its members coming from the council.

The County of Cumberland was disbanded in 1963 with the creation of the State Planning Authority. Central control of planning by the State government has since then been in the hands of either a statutory authority or a government department, currently the Department of Planning. Local councils continued to have primary responsibility for the preparation of local planning schemes, subject to ultimate approval by the Minister. While there were some legislative amendments under the *Local Government (Town and Country Planning) Amendment Act 1962* to speed up the process, preparation and approval of a planning scheme was still a lengthy process. Many councils relied on the interim development controls available in Pt XIIA, and either did not prepare a planning scheme or used the interim development control provisions to 'spot rezone' land without reference to the prescribed planning scheme.

By the early 1970s the complexity of both the planning process and the approvals system was apparent. An added impetus to reform came in the growing awareness of environmental issues, and in particular the need to ensure consideration of environmental factors in development control decision-making. The EPAA came into effect on 1 September 1980, and introduced three types of environmental planning instruments (EPIs): State environmental planning policies (SEPPs), regional environmental plans (REPs), and local environmental plans (LEPs). The State government has primary responsibility for the formulation and implementation of SEPPS and REPs, and local government has primary responsibility for the formulation of LEPs. When the EPAA was first enacted, there was no hierarchy in these three types of EPIs: s 36 of the EPAA provided that to the extent of any inconsistency the provisions of a later instrument were to prevail over any earlier instrument, unless a contrary intention appeared. Section 36 was amended in 1996 and again in 2005, and its current operation is discussed below.

Gleeson and Low characterise the legislative changes introduced in New South Wales (as well as in other States such as Victoria) in the 1970s and 1980s, including the reference in the EPAA to 'environmental planning', as reflecting green democratic aspirations.[5] They trace a shift during the 1980s and 1990s, driven by a larger political-economic reform agenda, leading to reductions in participation and accountability through such means as involvement of the private sector in development control.[6] It is arguable that such measures as the introduction of standard instruments (discussed below) can be seen in this context.

The balance of responsibilities for planning and development control between State and local government has shifted since the enactment of the EPAA. The amendment of s 36 in 2005 to introduce a formal hierarchy of planning instruments

5 B Gleeson and N Low, 'Unfinished Business: Neoliberal Planning Reform in Australia' (2000) 18 *Urban Policy and Research* 7 at 7.

6 Ibid at 12-18.

is one example of this. The Minister can make amendments to a draft LEP, including matters of substance, and under the 2005 amendments to the EPAA has power to transfer provisions of SEPPs or REPs (with or without modification) to the principal LEP for the local government areas to which the existing provisions apply (EPAA Sch 6 cl 91). In development control, the Minister has always had power under the EPAA (initially conferred by s 101) to 'call in' particular development applications for determination, qualified to situations 'where the Minister considers it expedient in the public interest to do so, having regard to matters of significance for State or regional environmental planning'. The 1985 amendments to the EPAA gave the Minister power to call in and make decisions for applications to consent to development which would otherwise be prohibited, thus bypassing the planning process. The 1997 amendments to the EPAA introduced the concept of 'State significant development' for which the Minister was the consent authority, and these provisions have been amended again, with the introduction of Pt 3A (Major Projects) (discussed below).

Binding or flexible planning controls?

Part XIIA (Town and Country Planning Schemes) in the *Local Government Act 1919* was modelled on the 1932 United Kingdom legislation, the *Town and Country Planning Act*. The planning schemes introduced under Pt XIIA shared the essential characteristics of the United Kingdom model, that is, they were binding as a matter of law on both members of the public and the council.

The environmental planning instruments made under the EPAA are also binding. They have varied, however, in the extent to which they impose specific controls, or allow flexibility. Local Environmental Plans primarily operate through specification of zones, in which certain types of development are permissible without needing development consent, or require consent, or are prohibited, and through specification of development standards for development. Flexibility in zoning has been achieved by specifying objectives for particular zones, and requiring councils to determine development applications by reference to consistency with zone objectives. In some LEPs there are no prohibited uses identified, and the council can approve any development that it regards as being consistent with the objectives of the zone: *Manly Council v Hortis*.[7] Flexibility in development consent decision-making has been achieved through SEPP 1 Development Standards (discussed below), under which a council can decide to waive compliance with a particular development standard.

The introduction of the Standard Instrument for LEPs (discussed below) will achieve uniformity in terms and definitions used in LEPs across the State. However, it will also reduce flexibility, both for zoning, and characterisation of particular uses, through prescription of zones and definitions. This may achieve some regulatory simplification, although it will also reduce the ability of localities to make regulatory choices that reflect social and ecological diversity.[8]

7 (2001) 113 LGERA 321.

8 Gleeson and Low, above n 5, at 23.

Separate systems, or integrated planning controls?

The current system is based on sector-specific approaches to regulation. The various chapters in this book dealing with such matters as pollution, natural resource management, heritage and water are a reflection of this. There are some attempts at integration, for example, in the provisions for assessment of development characterised as 'integrated development' under Div 5 of Pt 4 of the EPAA (see Chapter 3). However, it remains the case that a particular project may require consideration of a number of regulatory regimes. Recent amendments to the EPAA, in the introduction of Pt 3A (see Chapter 4), limit this requirement for projects which are assessed under Pt 3A.

Planning under the Environmental Planning and Assessment Act 1979

Types of planning instruments

The EPAA establishes three types of EPIs:

- State environmental planning policies (SEPPs)
- regional environmental plans (REPs)
- local environmental plans (LEPs)

The EPAA includes within the definition of EPI a 'deemed environmental planning instrument'. Deemed EPIs are those remaining planning scheme ordinances, or interim development orders, made under Pt XIIA of the *Local Government Act 1919*, and continued in force after the EPAA commenced. It is not clear how many such instruments are still in force. However, there are some deemed EPIs which are still the principal planning instrument in an area: *Direct Factory Outlets Homebush v Strathfield Municipal Council*.[9]

Other instruments and documents relevant in land use control include:

- development control plans (DCPs);
- directions under s 117(2) of the EPAA;
- circulars from the Department of Planning;
- strategies and policies, such as the Metropolitan Strategy.

SEPPs and REPs, and some LEPs, are available online at <www.legislation.nsw.gov.au>. An amendment to an existing EPI will require an amending EPI, which will require compliance with the same procedure as the initial EPI (set out below). However, under s 73A of the EPAA, inserted in 2005, some amendments can be made without complying with that procedure. These include corrections of obvious misdescriptions, spelling or numbering errors or grammatical mistakes, and which address matters in the principal instrument that are of a 'consequential, transitional, machinery or other minor nature' (s 73A(2)). A council that wishes to amend a LEP under s 73A is required to inform the Department, which refers the proposal to the LEP Review Panel (see below), which may decide that the proposed amendment is not within the scope of s 73A (Department of Planning, Planning Circular PS 06-014).

---

9 [2006] NSWLEC 318.

State Environmental Planning Policies

Types

SEPPs are intended to address matters of significance for environmental planning for the State (s 37(1)). Some SEPPs apply to specific sites or projects, for example, *SEPP 3 – Castlereagh Liquid Waste Disposal Depot, SEPP 7 – Port Kembla Coal Loader, SEPP – 29 Western Sydney Recreation Area, SEPP 31 – Sydney (Kingsford Smith) Airport, SEPP 39 – Spit Island Bird Habitat, SEPP 41 – Casino/Entertainment Complex, SEPP 43 – New Southern Railway, SEPP 47 – Moore Park Showground, SEPP 51 – Eastern Distributor, SEPP 54 – Northside Storage Tunnel, SEPP 67 – Macquarie Generation Industrial Development Strategy, SEPP 73 – Kosciuszko Ski Resorts*, and *SEPP – Development on Kurnell Peninsula 2005*.

Many SEPPs establish policy frameworks for matters of environmental significance. These include *SEPP 14 – Coastal Wetlands* (which restricts activities such as land clearing and drainage work on over 1300 identified wetlands); *SEPP 19 – Bushland in Urban Areas* (which is designed to protect bushland in public open space zones and reservations, and to ensure that bush preservation is given high priority when LEPs are prepared); *SEPP 26 – Littoral Rainforests* (which applies to 18 local government areas on the Pacific coast); and *SEPP 71 – Coastal Protection*. SEPP 71 is considered in detail in Chapter 7.

There are a number of SEPPs focusing on particular industries or activities of significance in land use decision-making. Some make permissible with consent development that would otherwise be prohibited under an EPI: for example, *SEPP 22 – Shops and Commercial Premises* which permits certain changes of use within business zones; and SEPP 63, which makes development associated with the Parramatta Rail Link, Liverpool-Parramatta Transitway, the Cross City Tunnel and the Bondi Beach Rail Link permissible without development consent. *SEPP (Seniors Living) 2004* replaced the former *SEPP 5 – Housing for Older People or People with Disability*, under which such housing was permissible in residential areas. *SEPP (Seniors Living) 2004* applies to land zoned for urban purposes, and permits development for the purpose of any form of seniors housing, and seniors housing in the form of a hostel or residential care unit on land adjoining land zoned for urban purposes. In certain specified local government areas, development applications under *SEPP (Seniors Living) 2004* can only be made by the Director-General of the Department of Housing, or by a local government or community housing provider (*SEPP (Seniors Living) 2004* Sch 3). The Department of Housing, and local government or community housing providers, need not comply with many of the development standards imposed by the *SEPP (Seniors Living) 2004*.

Some SEPPs have been made to overcome conflict between local and State government strategies, for example *SEPP 53 – Metropolitan Residential Development*, under which the Minister can alter local planning controls to facilitate medium density development of sites located close to transport, employment and services. This SEPP is not the only mechanism by which the State government has attempted to implement its residential strategies. Development for the purpose of multi unit housing on sites in the Ku-ring-gai area listed in Sch 4 to SEPP 53 is declared in cl 15 of Sch 2 to *SEPP (Major Projects) 2005* as development to which Pt 3A of the EPAA applies (discussed in Chapter 4).

Other SEPPs provide policy or other planning detail: *SEPP 6 – Number of Storeys in a Building, SEPP 10 – Retention of Low-cost Rental Accommodation, SEPP 11 – Traffic Generating Developments, SEPP 15 – Rural Land-sharing Communities, SEPP 21 – Caravan Parks, SEPP 30 – Intensive Agriculture, SEPP 33 – Hazardous and Offensive Development, SEPP 36 – Manufactured Home Estates, SEPP 45 – Permissibility of Mining, SEPP 62 – Sustainable Aquaculture, SEPP 65 – Design Quality of Residential Flat Development.*

Two significant SEPPs of this type are *SEPP 1 – Development Standards*, and *SEPP 4 – Development Without Consent and Miscellaneous Exempt and Complying Development.*

SEPP 1 – Development Standards

A 'development standard' is a provision of an EPI which specifies requirements or fixes standards in respect of any aspect of development, and includes numerical standards such as floor space of a building, area of land, and bulk, scale, size, height and density of a building; and other requirements such as character, location, density, provision of open space and facilities for vehicle movements, road patterns and drainage (EPAA s 4(1)). Under SEPP 1, a person intending to carry out development that would otherwise be restricted by a development standard can make a development application for that development, supported by a written objection (referred to as a 'SEPP 1 objection') that compliance with that development standard is unreasonable or unnecessary in the circumstances of the case. The consent authority can, with the concurrence of the Director-General of the Department of Planning ('Director'), grant development consent if satisfied that the objection is well grounded and that the granting of consent is consistent with the aims of SEPP 1. Those aims are stated in cl 3 to be to provide flexibility in the application of planning controls operating by virtue of development standards, in circumstances where strict compliance would be unreasonable or unnecessary or tend to hinder the objects specified in s 5(a)(i) and (ii) of the EPAA. The Land and Environment Court upheld the validity of SEPP 1 in *IDA Safe Constructions Pty Ltd v Woollahra Municipal Council*,[10] holding that even though the administration of SEPP 1 would operate at the local level, the principles embodied in it were of significance for State environmental planning.

The most significant issue in the application of SEPP 1 has been in identifying whether a particular provision is properly characterised as a 'development standard'. In *North Sydney Municipal Council v PD Mayoh Pty Ltd (No 2)*,[11] the Court of Appeal distinguished provisions which describe the characteristics of particular land on which particular development is prohibited, from those which specify how and to what extent permissible development can be carried out. A development standard regulates permissible development. The difficulty in determining whether a particular provision in an EPI is a development standard arises from the difficulty in distinguishing conditional prohibition from regulation. For some time the Land and Environment Court has applied the two-step analysis of Giles JA in *Strathfield Municipal Council v Poynting*.[12] The first step is to determine whether a provision

10 (1981) 48 LGRA 62.

11 (1990) 71 LGRA 222.

12 (2001) 116 LGERA 319.

prohibits the development under any circumstances, in which case it will be a provision controlling development and not a development standard. The second step is to determine whether the provision specifies a requirement or fixes a standard in relation to an aspect of the (non-prohibited) development. The Court of Appeal has noted the difficulties which this approach causes in some contexts, and has restated that the critical question will be to define the elements of the proposed development which are essential elements in the context of the LEP: *Blue Mountains City Council v Laurence Browning Pty Ltd.*[13]

A draft SEPP (Application of Development Standards) 2004 was exhibited in 2004 and, if gazetted, will replace SEPP 1. The draft SEPP continues the flexibility in application of development standards, but shifts the obligation to the applicant to demonstrate how a proposed departure from a development standard will result in a better environmental planning outcome than could have been achieved had the standard been complied with, and that the proposed development would be in the public interest by being consistent with the aims and objectives expressed in or implied from the relevant zone, or the development standard. Demonstration of a better environmental planning outcome will require the applicant to show that there are unusual site characteristics, or the proposed development comprises exceptional design quality, social or economic benefit to the community, above and beyond that which could have been achieved had the development standard been complied with. There are restrictions on the deviation from development standards relating to subdivision for development proposed in certain zones (including, for example, rural, non-urban, environmental protection and coastal protection), and for setbacks along the River Murray. The draft SEPP is intended to be in place for four years, during which councils will be required to incorporate appropriate flexibility into their LEPs. Clause 24 of the Standard Instrument – Principal Local Environmental Plan makes provision for a consent authority to grant consent for development that contravenes a development standard. The applicant must demonstrate that compliance is unreasonable or unnecessary and that there are sufficient environmental planning grounds to justify contravening the development standard.

SEPP 4 – Development Without Consent and Miscellaneous Exempt and Complying Development

SEPP 4 Development Without Consent and Miscellaneous Exempt and Complying Development allows development for a purpose 'which is of minor environmental significance', development for some public utility undertakings, and development on certain land reserved under the *National Parks and Wildlife Act 1974* to be carried out without development consent where the development is not prohibited and can be carried out in accordance with certain predetermined development standards. Under SEPP 4, changes in the type of shop or commercial premises, industry or light industry, places of public worship, or cable telecommunications connections, are permissible without consent. There are some restrictions, eg, use of shops as sex shops. Written notice must be given to the council. Many councils have included similar provisions in their LEPs, and so SEPP 4 will not apply.

13 [2006] NSWCA 331.

SEPP (Major Projects) 2005

SEPP (Major Projects) 2005, as discussed in Chapter 4, was gazetted on 1 August 2005, and identifies development to which the development assessment and approval processes under Pt 3A of the EPAA apply. Part 3A applies to the carrying out of major infrastructure or other development that is, in the opinion of the Minister, of significance for State or regional environmental planning, and is declared to be a Pt 3A project by order of the Minister, or by a SEPP. Schedule 1 to *SEPP (Major Projects) 2005* includes a range of classes of development, grouped into nine groups: Agriculture, Timber, Food and Related Industries; Mining, Petroleum, and Extractive Industries; Chemical and Manufacturing Industries; Other Manufacturing, Distribution and Storage Facilities; Residential, Commercial or Retail projects; Tourism and Recreational Projects; Health and Public Service Facilities; Transport, Energy and Water Infrastructure; Resource and Waste Related Industries. These specified classes of development are identified by reference both to their type and scale, including in some instances the amount of capital investment value. Schedule 2 includes specific sites, ranging from specified developments in the coastal zone to sites such as Kurnell, Rhodes Peninsula, certain Sydney Harbour Foreshore sites, and development with a capital investment value above $5 million at the Australian Museum, Redfern-Waterloo Authority sites and Sydney Olympic Park. *SEPP (Major Projects) 2005* also identifies as a 'critical infrastructure project' for the purposes of Pt 3A the proposed Kurnell Desalination Plant.

SEPP (Sydney Region Growth Centres) 2006 is the initial planning instrument for the implementation of the Metropolitan Strategy released on 4 December 2005, and provides for the release of land for residential, employment and other urban development in the North West and South West growth centres of the Sydney region. The Minister can declare any precinct to be released for urban development, and any application for development consent for specified large scale development must be accompanied by an assessment of the consistency of the proposed development with the relevant growth centre structure plan (*Environmental Planning and Assessment Regulation 2000* (EPAR) cll 275, 276).

Procedure for making SEPPs

The Director or Minister for Planning may decide to prepare a SEPP (s 37). The draft is prepared by the Director, and the Minister has a discretion whether or not to publicise the draft, and whether or not to seek submissions from the public (s 39(2)). Attempts to challenge decisions limiting consultation, or not to publicise, have been unsuccessful: *Minister for Urban Affairs and Planning v Rosemount Estates Pty Ltd*;[14] *Save the Showground for Sydney Inc v Minister for Urban Affairs and Planning*.[15] The Minister recommends to the Governor, who makes the SEPP (s 39(4)).

Regional Environmental Plans

Types

Regional environmental plans cover issues of regional significance, such as urban growth, and extractive industries, and are also made by the Minister for Planning.

---

14 (1996) 91 LGERA 31.

15 (1997) 95 LGERA 33.

Regional environmental plans apply in the Greater Metropolitan Region, the Hunter Illawarra, North Coast, Sydney and Western NSW regions. Two Greater Metropolitan Region REPs relate to water catchments: Drinking Water Catchments REP No 1, gazetted 9 June 2006, which applies to 16,000 square kilometres of the catchments supplying drinking water to Sydney, Blue Mountains and the Illawarra; and REP No 2 Georges River Catchment, intended to co-ordinate land use planning and development control in the Georges River and its tributaries. The Western New South Wales REPs include Kosciuszko REP 1998 Snowy River, which applies to the Snowy River local government area outside the Kosciuszko National Park; Western Division REP No 1 Extractive Industries, which provides controls for extractive industries in the Western Division; and Willandra Lakes REP No 1 World Heritage Property, which applies to the Willandra Lakes Region in the Shires of Wentworth and Balranald and is intended to manage the Willandra Lakes World Heritage Property.

Procedure for making REPs

The Director or Minister may decide to prepare a REP (s 40). The draft is prepared by the Director, taking into consideration whether any SEPP is affected by the subject-matter of the draft REP, and any environmental study (s 44). The Director must notify any council whose area (or part of the area) is situated in the relevant region, and any other relevant public authorities, of the reasons for deciding to prepare the draft REP, its general aims and objectives, a general description of the land to which it is intended to apply, and any other matters that the Director thinks fit (s 45). The Director may request information from any public authority (s 46). The draft REP must be publicly exhibited, and any person may make submissions (ss 47, 48). The Director may decide to hold a public inquiry (s 49(1)(a)). The Director may make changes to the draft REP, having regard to the findings and recommendations of any public inquiry, and any written submissions (s 49(1)(b)). Amendments need not relate to such findings or submissions, and may include changes of substance (s 49(1)(b)). The Director may decide to re-exhibit an amended draft REP (s 49(1)(c)). The Minister has the power to make changes, which may include changes of substance, to the draft submitted by the Director, before making the REP (s 51).

The notification and consultation requirements for REPs have been strictly applied by the courts. In *Leichhardt Municipal Council v Minister for Planning and Director of Planning*,[16] the Court of Appeal held that failure to consult as required by s 45 invalidated Greater Metropolitan Regional Environmental Plan 1. While s 45 has been amended since this decision to specify the particular matters which the Director is required to notify under s 45(2), it is likely that failure to comply would still invalidate any plan. The specific conferral in s 50 on the Minister of power to amend a draft REP presented by the Director would probably overcome the effect of the decision of the Court of Appeal in *Leichhardt Municipal Council v Minister for Planning (No 2)*.[17] In that decision the Court of Appeal held invalid a REP which was significantly different from the draft that had been exhibited, resulting in a REP that was not the product of the process set out in Div 3 of Pt 3 of the EPAA.

---

16 (1992) 78 LGERA 306.

17 (1995) 87 LGERA 78.

Local Environmental Plans

Procedure for making local environmental plans

An LEP may relate to the whole, or part of, a local government area (s 54(1)). Two or more councils may decide to prepare an LEP in respect of the whole, or any part of, the land within their areas (s 54(2)). One example of a joint LEP is the Waverley and Woollahra Joint Local Environmental Plan 1991—Bondi Junction Commercial Centre, which sets out the planning parameters for the redevelopment of Bondi Junction. The Minister may direct a council to prepare an LEP (s 55(1)).

An LEP may be made in order to consolidate existing LEPs, to replace older planning instruments or to rezone particular land in the area. Unless the LEP is simply amending previous LEPs, an environmental study must be prepared before the draft LEP is prepared. An environmental study is required in other circumstances only if the Director-General of the Department of Planning requires it (ss 57(1), 74(2)).

Councils routinely prepare LEPs to rezone particular parcels of land. Such 'spot rezoning' constitutes approximately half the proposals for draft LEPs notified to the Department (Department of Planning Circular PS06-015 15 June 2006). The Department encourages councils to prepare one amendment, or a limited number of amendments, each year, to reduce the administrative load and to ensure consistency and a strategic approach to planning issues.

If a council decides to prepare an LEP, it must notify the Department of Planning (s 54(4)). In 2006 the Department introduced a departmental LEP Review Panel. The Panel consists of the Director, senior executives from the Department of Planning, and a nominee from the Local Government and Shires Associations. The function of the Panel is to review notifications under s 54, and provide preliminary advice on each proposal by evaluating it against set criteria, advising the Director or the Minister, and councils on the proposal.

The council must consult with, and may request information from, relevant public authorities, in preparing an LEP (ss 62, 63). After preparing a draft LEP, the council must submit it to the Department of Planning for a certificate to allow the draft LEP to be publicly exhibited (ss 64, 65(1)). The draft LEP is exhibited for a period of at least 28 days, during which members of the public may make submissions (EPAA ss 66(1), 67; EPAR cl 13). There may be a public hearing arranged by the council if a person making a submission requests it and the council considers that the issues raised in the submission are of such significance that they should be the subject of a hearing before the council decides whether changes should be made to the draft LEP (s 68(1)). The report of any public hearing must be made public (s 68(2)). The council must consider this report, and any public submissions, in deciding whether to amend the draft LEP, and these must also be provided, together with the reasons for any amendments, to the Department of Planning when the council submits its final version of the draft LEP (s 68(3), (4)). The draft may be reviewed again by the departmental LEP Review Panel before being submitted to the Minister for approval. The final decision to approve the LEP is made by the Minister, following a report by the Director-General (ss 69, 70). The Minister can alter the draft as submitted, if there are matters which in the Minister's opinion are of significance for State or regional environmental planning, which can include changes of substance (s 70(1), (1A)).

The courts have insisted on compliance with the procedural requirements set out in the EPAA for LEPs. In particular, public notice under s 66 of the exhibition of a draft LEP must be accurate and complete, and if it is misleading the resulting LEP will be invalid: *Canterbury District Residents & Ratepayers Association Inc v Canterbury Municipal Council;*[18] *Litevale Pty Ltd v Lismore City Council;*[19] *El Cheikh v Hurstville City Council.*[20] A failure to include all specified matters (such as non-compliance with an applicable s 117 Direction) in a report to the Minister under s 69 has also been held to invalidate the resulting LEP: *Belongil Progress Association Inc v Byron Shire Council.*[21]

Planning administrator

The Minister may appoint a planning administrator, or a panel (or both), to exercise functions of a council if the council has failed to comply with or carry out any of its obligations under the planning legislation, or the Minister is of the opinion that the council's performance in dealing with planning and development matters, unsatisfactory because of the manner in which the council has dealt with those matters or the time taken, if the council agrees, or if the Independent Commission Against Corruption recommends this (s 118(1)). Section 118(12) defines failure to comply with obligations under the planning legislation to include a failure to comply with or carry out the provisions of the EPAA, an EPI, a direction under s 55 (to prepare a draft LEP), s 94A(provision of public amenities), or s 117, and a failure to comply with the requirements of a staged repeal program under s 33B (see below). The Minister must obtain the concurrence of the Minister for Local Government. The council would be entitled to the opportunity to present a case before the appointment is made: *Balmain Association Inc v Planning Administrator for Leichhardt Council.*[22]

Environmental studies

An environmental study may be required before a draft REP or LEP is prepared. An environmental study will be required if the proposed REP or LEP is the first such instrument applying to the relevant land, or if the Minister (in the case of a proposed REP) or the Director (in the case of a proposed LEP) so directs (s 74). A local environmental study will be required where a council proposes provisions in its LEP which are inconsistent with a s 117 Direction (for example, affecting existing industrial zonings, or zonings on flood-prone land). A local environment study may be required where the proposed amending LEP will allow major residential, tourist, commercial or industrial development, or allow a proposal that will have significant economic or employment generating potential.

An environmental study will generally provide detailed information about the environment of the land, including existing natural, social and economic issues, a review of potential land uses, and an analysis of environmental, economic and social implications arising from rezoning (Department of Planning Circular PS 06-013 2

---

18 (1991) 73 LGRA 317.

19 (1997) 96 LGERA 91.

20 [2006] NSWCA 173.

21 (1999) 106 LGERA 202.

22 (1991) 25 NSWLR 615.

May 2006). An environmental study may be independently prepared by the council, or rely on material provided by proponents, provided the council reviews this material before adopting it (Circular PS 06-013). If the draft LEP is proposed to rezone particular land, the council can recover the cost of an environmental study from the person who made the request for the rezoning amendment (EPAA s 57; EPAR cl 15).

Relationship between EPIs

Section 36 of the EPAA makes provision for dealing with inconsistencies between planning instruments:

> (1) In the event of an inconsistency between environmental planning instruments and unless otherwise provided:
>
> (a) there is a general presumption that a State environmental planning policy prevails over a regional environmental plan or local environmental plan made before or after the policy, and
>
> (b) there is a general presumption that a regional environmental plan prevails over a local environmental plan made before or after the regional environmental plan, and
>
> (c) the general presumptions of the law as to when an Act prevails over another Act apply to when one kind of environmental planning instrument prevails over another environmental planning instrument of the same kind.
>
> (4) Nothing in this section prevents an environmental planning instrument from being expressly amended by a later environmental planning instrument, of the same or a different kind, to provide for the way in which an inconsistency between them is to be resolved.

This version of s 36 was inserted in 2005. As initially enacted, there was no general presumption that an EPI of one type prevailed over an EPI of another type, and the provisions of a later instrument prevailed over the provisions of an earlier instrument unless the contrary intention appeared. The extent of this provision was considered by the Court of Appeal in *Coffs Harbour Environment Centre Inc v Minister for Planning and Coffs Harbour City Council* (1994) 84 LGERA 324. Kirby P noted that there would be inconsistency if there is 'want of consistency or congruity', 'lack of accordance or harmony' or 'incompatibility, contrariety or opposition'.[23] Mahoney JA commented that two planning instruments may be inconsistent 'if the general principles or general provisions provided by each are different', or if 'the later instrument enacts a provision which is a qualification or an exception to a general principle stated in the earlier instrument'.[24]

Under amendments made to the EPAA in 1996, a SEPP could prevail over a REP or LEP if it so provided, and a REP could prevail over an LEP if it so provided. The 2005 amendments to s 36 both entrench the hierarchy of planning instruments, and clarify that instruments higher in the hierarchy prevail over instruments made subsequently, an issue that was also discussed by the Court of Appeal in *Coffs Harbour Environment Centre Inc v Minister for Planning*.[25]

23 (1994) 84 LGERA 324 at 331.

24 Ibid at 345.

25 (1994) 84 LGERA 324.

Content of environmental planning instruments

An EPI may make provision for any of the following:

- protecting, improving or utilising, the environment;
- controlling development;
- reserving land for use for various public purposes;
- providing, maintaining and retaining affordable housing;
- protecting or preserving trees or vegetation;
- protecting and conserving native animals and plants, including threatened species, populations and ecological communities, and their habitats;
- controlling advertising;
- protecting and conserving vulnerable ecological communities. (s 26)

Legislation may also authorise the inclusion of other matters in an EPI.

Standard Instruments

Section 33A (inserted in the EPAA with effect from 30 September 2005) allows the Governor to prescribe the standard form and content of LEPs and other EPIs. An EPI may then declare that the applicable mandatory provisions of a standard instrument are adopted or set out the mandatory provisions, and any of the non-mandatory provisions, that are to apply (s 33A(2)). If the standard instrument is subsequently amended, the EPI is automatically amended to include any changes to the standard instrument (s 33A(4)).

A standard instrument for preparing LEPs was gazetted on 30 March 2006, the Standard Instrument (Local Environmental Plans) Order 2006. This Order sets out 34 standard zones, grouped in eight categories: rural, residential, business, industrial, special purpose, recreation, environment protection and waterways. The standard instrument sets out a Dictionary of standard definitions relating to land uses, and those definitions are mandatory. The land use terms are grouped into general categories (including advertising, building and works, home activities, industry, primary industry, residential accommodation, retail and business). Other terms are defined, including administrative terms, heritage terms and terms used in maps. Terms which are not defined in the Standard Instrument continue to be defined using the ordinary meaning of the word.

The intention behind the introduction of the LEP Standard Instrument was to achieve consistency and efficiency. In his Second Reading speech, the then Minister for Planning and Infrastructure commented that the standard LEP would reduce the existing zoning categories from 3100 to around 25, and the 1700 existing definitions to fewer than 300.[26]

With the introduction of the Standard Instrument for LEPs, the Model Provisions, and s 71 directions, have been repealed. The Model Provisions contain definitions and general provisions relating to such matters as foreshore building lines, tree preservation and certain types of development such as motor showrooms. Councils were free to adopt any or all of the Model Provisions in their LEPs. Despite the repeal, the Model Provisions continue in force for those LEPs which adopted

---

26 *Hansard*, NSW Legislative Assembly, 27 May 2005.

them (Sch 6 cl 93). The Directions under s 71 related to the format, structure and content of LEPs, and are replaced by the Standard Instrument provisions.

Staged review of environmental planning instruments

Section 33B was inserted in the EPAA with effect from 30 September 2005. Under s 33B, in order to facilitate the staged implementation of standard instruments and periodic review of existing instruments, the Minister may publish a staged repeal program for existing EPIs. The EPIs identified through this process will be automatically repealed at the time specified for repeal (s 33B(3)). The Minister may make a LEP, adopting the mandatory provisions of the standard instrument, to take effect after repeal while a replacement LEP is being prepared under the Act. While the Minister has not yet published a program for staged repeals of LEPs, he has directed councils to prepare their principal LEPs using the Standard Instrument within the next two, three or five years.

Special provisions for LEPs

Section 117 of the EPAA enables the Minister to direct any public authority or person having functions under the EPAA or an EPI to exercise those functions at or within such times as are specified in the direction. A consolidated and updated set of s 117 Directions was issued on 30 September 2005. There are transitional provisions in the *Environmental Planning and Assessment Amendment (Miscellaneous) Regulation 2006* which enable the former s 117 Directions to continue to apply to draft LEPs at advanced stages of preparation.

The new s 117 Directions cover 28 matters. Some apply to all councils when preparing a draft LEP, while others apply only to specified councils. Under some of these Directions, councils cannot include provisions in an LEP that require concurrence or consultation of a Minister or public authority, alter provisions relating to business or industrial zones, or identify development as designated development, without the approval of the Director. In some instances, an environmental study will be required to justify a proposed inconsistency with a s 117 Direction.

Development control plans

Development control plans (DCPs) can be prepared by a council in relation to LEPs, or by the Director in relation to REPs or SEPPs. A DCP can be prepared to make more detailed provision with respect to development, or to make provision for advertised development, or for publication or advertising of specified development, or to specify criteria to be taken into account by a council in making an order under Pt 6 of the EPAA (s 74C(1)). Under an amendment made to the EPAA in 2005, only one DCP made by the same relevant planning authority may apply in respect of the same land (s 74C(2)). This means that a council may prepare a DCP, and the Department of Planning may also prepare a DCP, relating to the same land. In many instances this new limitation will require councils to consolidate existing DCPs, several of which may apply in different ways to the same land. Unless directed otherwise by the Minister, a council could choose to make one DCP for its entire area, or localities within its area, or to have a site specific DCP. If the latter option is adopted, the council would have to exclude the application of other DCPs. The consequence of non-compliance with the limitation of one DCP to each site is that all DCPs applying to that site have no effect (s 74C(2)). Councils have until the earlier of 31 March 2011, or the time the principal LEP which applies to the same land as the DCP adopts the provisions of the Standard Instrument (Local Environmental Plans) Order 2006 (EPAR cl 289A).

A provision of a DCP will be of no effect to the extent that it is inconsistent with an EPI, or contains provisions which prevent compliance with an EPI (EPAA s 74C(5)). This reflects the position reached under the previous provisions relating to DCPs. In *Guideline Drafting and Design v Marrickville Municipal Council*[27] the Land and Environment Court held that a provision of a DCP that restricted the location of refreshment rooms to ground floors of buildings was inconsistent with the relevant planning instrument under which refreshment rooms were a permissible use and was invalid. However, some restrictions imposed by a DCP may be able to stand consistently with the provisions of an EPI. In *North Sydney Council v Ligon 302 Pty Ltd (No 2)*,[28] the Court of Appeal held that a provision in a DCP that was restrictive or prohibitive unless certain conditions were met would not necessarily be contrary to the relevant planning instrument.

Part 3 of the EPAR sets out the procedures for preparation of DCPs by councils. A draft DCP must be publicly exhibited for at least 28 days, and any person may make submissions (cll 18, 20). A council can approve the DCP, with amendments, or decide not to proceed, and must give notice of its decision in a local newspaper within 28 days (cl 21).

An EPI may require a DCP to be prepared for a site before development can be carried out (s 74D). These DCPs are prepared by the owner of the land and submitted to the relevant planning authority (s 74D(3)). If the planning authority refuses to make the DCP, or delays for more than 60 days, the owner of the land may make a development application despite the absence of the DCP (s 74D(5)). The planning authority may require further information before deciding whether to make the DCP (EPAR cl 25). Section 74D took effect on 30 September 2005, and replaces previous requirements for the preparation of a master plan for particular development sites. Schedule 6 to the EPAA contains transitional provisions, which include that provisions of an EPI requiring the preparation of a master plan are to be construed as requiring the preparation of a DCP, and that master plans prepared before 30 September 2005 are taken to be a DCP under s 74D of the EPAA (Sch 6 cl 95).

Zoning

One of the central provisions in a LEP is to establish zones for areas of land, and to specify for each zone development that is permissible without needing consent, or development that requires consent, and development that is prohibited. Under the Standard Instrument (LEP), there are 34 standard zones for councils to use when preparing LEPs. Each standard zone has one or more core objectives for development in the zone, and councils can prepare additional local objectives, provided they are not inconsistent with the core objectives and compulsory land uses.

27 (1988) 64 LGRA 275.

28 (1996) 93 LGERA 23.

Older planning instruments specify zoning provisions in the form of a table. More recent planning instruments list for each zone provisions which reflect the three-fold classification of development in ss 76, 76A and 76B of the EPAA: namely, development that is permissible without development consent, development that requires development consent and development that is prohibited. The planning instrument will be accompanied by a map which identifies the relevant zones.

The land use table in the Standard Instrument (Local Environmental Plans) Order 2006 specifies for each zone the objectives of the zone, and sets out the threefold classification of development permitted without consent, permitted with consent, and prohibited. For each zone there is a direction that certain development must be included as either 'permitted without consent' or 'permitted with consent'. For example, under Zone RU4 Rural Small Holdings, extensive agriculture, farm buildings, horticulture, roads and roadside stalls must be included as either 'permitted without consent' or 'permitted with consent'. The Standard Instrument contains other mandatory provisions, for example, for Zone R3 Medium Density Residential, boarding houses, child care centres, community facilities, group homes, multi dwelling housing, neighbourhood shops, places of public worship, seniors housing and shop top housing are permitted with consent. Councils can supplement the mandated permitted and prohibited land uses for each zone. The Department's LEP Practice Note PN 02-002 states that councils should maximise the range of uses that are permissible with or without consent.

Existing uses

Planners do not start the planning process with a clean slate, and they must accommodate the range of uses that will already be in place. If occupiers are required to discontinue uses which do not conform to the new planning instrument, there would be significant pressure for compensation. The alternative, to prepare a planning instrument that simply reflects the status quo, would largely destroy any benefits to be gained by planning.[29] The EPAA continues the approach of planning schemes under Pt XIIA, in allowing existing uses to continue 'as a transitional derogation designed, for a time only, to cushion the impact of new general planning laws upon private owners with established use of their land which has continued without abandonment'.[30]

Existing use rights arise when an EPI comes into force which has the effect of changing the status of a particular development or use. An EPI may specify that the particular use is now prohibited, or that it requires consent where consent was not previously required. Section 106 of the EPAA defines 'existing use' to mean the use of a building, work or land for a lawful purpose immediately before the coming into force of an EPI which would have the effect of prohibiting that use. Development for which consent was granted before the commencement of a provision of an EPI which would prohibit the use, and which has been carried out within one year after the date of commencement of that EPI to the extent so as to ensure that the consent would not lapse, is also an 'existing use'.

---

29 M Wilcox, *The Law of Land Development in New South Wales* (Law Book Co, 1967) at 260.

30 *North Sydney Municipal Council v Boyts Radio & Electrical Pty Ltd* (1989) 16 NSWLR 50 at 51 per Kirby P.

The reference to 'lawful purpose' in s 106 is a reference to planning considerations, and not the general law, so that only those uses commenced with consent (if consent was previously required), or permissible without requiring consent, are included in s 106: *Sydney City Council v Ke Su Investments Pty Ltd (No 2)*;[31] *Steedman v Baulkham Hills Shire Council*.[32]

Section 107(1) allows an existing use to continue. Existing use rights attach to the premises, and not the owner or occupier of those premises. Existing use rights are lost if the use is abandoned (s 107(2)(e)), and there is a presumption that a use is abandoned if the use ceases for a continuous period of 12 months (s 107(3)). Abandonment is a question of fact. An existing use can be continued even if there have been interruptions or breaks, so long as those interruptions are not of such a kind as to constitute a termination or abandonment of that use. Both objective and subjective factors are relevant, including the intention of the person relying on existing use rights. For example, if premises are vacant because of renovation work, or if the owner is having difficulty finding a tenant, such a break may not necessarily be evidence of abandonment: *Woollahra Municipal Council v Banool Developments Pty Ltd*;[33] *Woollahra Municipal Council v TAJJ Investments Pty Ltd*.[34]

Part 5 of the EPAR contains provisions which regulate existing uses. Under cl 41, an existing use can be enlarged, expanded or intensified, altered or extended, rebuilt, or changed to another use. An amendment made to the EPAR in 2006 qualifies this, by specifying that the other use must be a use that may be carried out with or without development consent. Before this, the EPAR permitted change of an existing use to another use which would itself be prohibited. Development consent is required for any of these changes (EPAR cll 42, 43, 44, 45).

The EPAA also covers the situation where an EPI comes into effect requiring development consent for a use where consent was not previously required. This is not an 'existing use' as defined in s 106. Section 109 allows such a use to be continued until abandoned, and makes similar provision for a presumption of abandonment after 12 months (s 109(3)). Any alteration, extension or rebuilding, enlargement or intensification of the use, or increase in the area of land actually physically and lawfully used, will require development consent (s 109(2)).

Characterisation

As noted above, the zoning provisions of EPIs will specify uses that are permissible without consent being required, or permissible with development consent, or prohibited. Characterisation of the purpose of a proposed, or existing, use, is required in order to determine its status under the relevant EPI.

The applicable EPI may contain a definition. For example, *SEPP 9 – Group Homes* defines 'dwelling' to mean 'a room or suite of rooms occupied or used, or so constructed or adapted as to be capable of being occupied or used as a separate domicile'. The Standard Instrument (Local Environmental Plans) Order 2006 defines 'entertainment facility' to mean 'a theatre, cinema, music hall, concert hall, dance

31 (1983) 51 LGRA 186.
32 (1991) 72 LGRA 265.
33 (1973) 129 CLR 138.
34 (1982) 49 LGRA 123.

hall, amusement centre and the like'. If a term is not defined in the EPI, its meaning will be how that word is understood in ordinary usage, which is usually found by consulting a dictionary. The definition in the EPI may itself refer to other terms (as is the case with 'entertainment facility' in the Standard Instrument), and those meanings will also need to be determined by reference to their ordinary meaning.

The general approach to characterisation for planning purposes was set out by Kitto J in *Shire of Perth v O'Keefe*:

> The application of the by-law in a particular case is therefore not to be approached through a meticulous examination of the details of processes or activities, or through a precise cataloguing of individual items of goods dealt in, but by asking what, according to ordinary terminology, is the appropriate designation of the purpose being served by the use of the premises at the material date.[35]

Difficulties can arise when characterising a use which has more than one purpose. The traditional view is that, if one purpose is dominant, any subordinate use can be disregarded in deciding the status of the development: *Warringah Shire Council v Raffles*.[36] If, however, there is no dominant purpose, but two or more independent purposes, the status of each must be considered: *Foodbarn Pty Ltd v Solicitor General*.[37] A use which can be said to be ancillary to another use is not automatically precluded from being an independent use, and it is a question of fact and degree: *Baulkham Hills Shire Council v O'Donnell*.[38]

Characterisation of development in the context of existing use rights raises additional issues, as a broad definition or characterisation of the existing use will enable its continuation, favouring private over social rights: *North Sydney Municipal Council v Boyts Radio & Electrical Pty Ltd*.[39] The approach is usually to define the purpose of the use, rather than to descend to the detail of the particular activities carried on: *Royal Agricultural Society of New South Wales v Sydney City Council*.[40] All uses of the land at the relevant time, which will generally be the date of the coming into effect of a planning instrument that required development consent, or prohibited, the claimed existing use, must be considered. So long as it is real, a minor use cannot be ignored, even if it is overshadowed by other uses of the land: *Steedman v Baulkham Hills Shire Council (No 2)*.[41]

Characterisation of proposed development may arise not only in deciding whether the development is permissible or prohibited, but in determining whether additional procedural requirements apply, for example, as designated development. Here, too, the attempt to characterise uses as 'dominant' or 'ancillary' may be misleading. As discussed at p 69, designated development is development declared to be so in an EPI or the EPAR. Part 1 of Sch 3 to the EPAR lists a number of categories as designated development. If a particular part of an overall development is designated development because it falls within one of those categories (for example, sewerage treatment plant for a large scale residential development), it does not

---

35 (1964) 110 CLR 529 at 535.
36 (1978) 38 LGRA 306.
37 (1975) 32 LGRA 157.
38 (1990) 69 LGRA 404.
39 (1989) 16 NSWLR 50.
40 (1987) 61 LGRA 305.
41 (1993) 31 NSWLR 562.

matter whether it is subsidiary or ancillary to some other form of development to which the application relates, or whether it constitutes an independent use of the land. The crucial question will be whether the application is 'in respect of' designated development: *Penrith City Council v Waste Management Authority;*[42] *Residents Against Improper Development Inc v Chase Property Investments Pty Ltd.*[43] If so, the additional environmental assessment and public participation requirements will apply (see Chapter 4).

While the characterisation of a use is a question of fact, it is a jurisdictional fact. The determination of the consent authority as to how a particular development is to be characterised is a matter which can be reviewed by the Land and Environment Court. The court will be able to have regard to additional evidence that was not before the consent authority, and will make its own determination of the appropriate characterisation, rather than assessing the reasonableness of the consent authority's determination: *Woolworths Ltd v Pallas Newco Pty Ltd.*[44]

Challenges to EPIs

The Land and Environment Court has jurisdiction to hear and determine challenges to the validity of an EPI, in Class 4 of its jurisdiction (*Land and Environment Court Act 1979* s 20).

Most such challenges are based on failure to comply with the procedures prescribed by the EPAA and the EPAR, in particular, the requirements for public notification. The Land and Environment Court has generally insisted on compliance with these procedural requirements, declaring invalid the resulting LEP where there has been a procedural defect: *Canterbury District Residents & Ratepayers Association Inc v Canterbury Municipal Council;*[45] *Smith v Wyong Shire Council.*[46] Challenges can be made on other grounds, for example, failure to have regard to all relevant material: *Gales Holdings Pty Ltd v Minister for Infrastructure and Planning.*[47]

Section 35 attempts to limit challenges, and provides:

> The validity of an environmental planning instrument shall not be questioned in any legal proceedings except those commenced in the Court by any person within three months of the date of its publication in the Gazette.

This provision is similar to s 101 of the EPAA, which applies to challenges to the validity of development consents. The construction of that provision is discussed in Chapter 3. It is likely that the courts will apply similar reasoning to the construction of s 35, and allow challenge on any ground before three months, and after three months where the instrument does not conform to the threefold principle in *R v Hickman; ex parte Fox & Clinton.*[48] Under this principle, decisions could be challenged where it is manifest that the decision is not a bona fide attempt to exercise the power; where it does not relate to the subject-matter of the legislation;

---

42 (1990) 71 LGRA 376.
43 [2006] NSWCA 323.
44 [2004] NSWCA 422.
45 (1991) 73 LGRA 317.
46 (2003) 132 LGERA 148.
47 [2006] NSWCA 388.
48 (1945) 70 CLR 598.

or where it is not reasonably capable of reference to the power given to the decision-maker. It is also likely that s 35 would not protect against breach of, or non-compliance with, a restriction or requirement which is construed as being of such significance in the legislative scheme that it constitutes a limitation or requirement that is variously expressed in the authorities as 'essential', 'indispensable', 'imperative' or 'inviolable'.[49] The precise application of these principles is a matter of debate, in particular the extent to which the alleged defect must be apparent on the face of the instrument.[50]

The validity of DCPs and other instruments, such as s 117 Directions, can also be challenged, on the basis of failure to comply with procedural requirements or consistency with the requirements of the EPAA.[51]

49 *Lesnewski v Mosman Municipal Council* [2005] NSWCA 99.

50 *Maitland City Council v Anambah Homes Pty Ltd* [2005] NSWCA 455.

51 *Westfield Developments Pty Ltd v Sutherland Shire Council* (1987) 28 APA 375; *Lainson v Sutherland Shire Council* (1998) 108 LGERA 1.

3

DEVELOPMENT CONTROL

Development can take many forms, including the use of land, and physical activity on land for a particular purpose such as the erection of a building. As originally enacted, the *Environmental Planning and Assessment Act 1979* (EPAA) drew a distinction between development which requires development consent, and activities which do not require development consent but which require approval under other legislation, for example, mining or forestry, or which are to be carried out by a government agency. Assessment of the environmental impacts of development which required development consent was to be carried out under Pt 4 of the Act. Part 5 of the Act provided the process for assessment of environmental impacts of activities that did not require development consent under Pt 4.

The environmental assessment of various types of activities has become more complex. Part 4 of the EPAA now sets out the processes for assessment of most forms of proposed development on land, including the erection of buildings, subdivision, and the use of land for a particular purpose. Additional requirements are specified in Pt 4 for development identified in advance as likely to have a significant environmental impact, which is characterised as designated development, and development which is likely to have an impact on threatened species or habitat. Proposals for such development may require the preparation and consideration of an environmental impact statement (EIS) or species impact statement (SIS). Some projects may be identified in advance in the provisions of an environmental planning instrument (EPI), or by the Minister for Planning, as major infrastructure, or other projects of State or regional environmental significance. Assessment of those projects is managed under Pt 3A of the EPAA. Other types of development may not require a formal consideration, and may be approved by the issue of a certificate, for example, a complying development certificate.

This chapter outlines the processes of application for development consent, and consideration and determination of those applications, under Pt 4 of the EPAA. The additional requirements for assessment of environmental impact of designated development, and development on land that is critical habitat or is likely significantly to affect threatened species, populations or ecological communities or their habitats, are discussed in Chapter 4 at p 120. The assessment of projects under Pt 3A of the EPAA, and the environmental assessment under Pt 5 of activities that do not require development consent is also discussed in Chapter 4.

Requirement for development consent

Sections 76, 76A and 76B of the EPAA set out the threefold classification that is central to the operation of Pts 4 and 5 of the EPAA.

If an EPI provides that specified development may be carried out without the need for development consent, a person may carry that development out in accordance with the EPI (s 76(1)). The applicable EPI may impose some requirements (for example, notification requirements) and environmental assessment of the development may be required under Pt 5 of the EPAA (see Chapter 4). An EPI may identify development of a specified class or description that is of minimal environmental impact as 'exempt' development (s 76(2)). Exempt development can be carried out without development consent, unless it is proposed for land that is critical habitat, or is (or is part of) a wilderness area. Exempt development does not require environmental assessment under Pt 5 of the EPAA (s 76(3)). Other activities which do not require development consent, but which are carried out by government agencies or which require approval under other legislation, will need to be assessed under Pt 5 of the EPAA.

If the applicable EPI provides that specified development can only be carried out with development consent, consent must be obtained, and the development must be carried out in accordance with that consent (s 76A(1)). Consent can be obtained by a consent authority making a determination to grant development consent (s 76A(2)(a)). The EPI may specify that development that can be addressed by predetermined development standards is 'complying' development (s 76A(5)). There are limitations imposed by s 76A(6). An EPI cannot specify as complying development, development that is designated development, development for which concurrence is required (other than concurrence of the consent authority or the Director-General of National Parks and Wildlife), development on land that is critical habitat, wilderness area, or on which there is an item of the environmental heritage, or which is identified in the EPI as an environmentally sensitive area. Consent for complying development can be obtained by the issue of a complying development certificate (s 76A(2)(b)).

The applicable EPI may state that specified development is prohibited on certain land, or that development cannot be carried out on land, with or without development consent. If it does, a person must not carry out the development (s 76B).

EPIs, particularly local environmental plans (LEPs), reflect this threefold classification by specifying for each of the zones development that is permissible without consent, development that requires consent and development that is prohibited. One of these categories will be a residual category: for example, the EPI may specify particular types of development as permissible without consent, and others as permissible with development consent, and state that all development other than the types specifically identified is prohibited.

An important exception to the prohibition in s 76B to carrying out development where the applicable EPI states that it is prohibited is in the right to continue an existing use and, with consent, to modify, expand or alter the use. A further exception to the requirement in s 76A to obtain development consent is provided for in s 109, which permits continuation of a use without consent where an EPI comes into effect that requires that consent be obtained. Existing use rights and the right to continue lawful uses are discussed in Chapter 2 at p 61.

Consent authority

If development consent is required, it must be obtained from the relevant 'consent authority'. The consent authority will be the local council or, if the Act, the regulations or the applicable EPI so specify, a Minister or other public authority (s 4). LEPs will specify the council as consent authority. Councils are also the consent authority under many SEPPs, for example *SEPP 19 – Bushland in Urban Areas*. If the council is not the consent authority, it will still receive a copy of the development application (s 77(4)).

Development

The term 'development' is critical to the operation of Pt 4 of the EPAA. It is defined in s 4 to mean:

- the use of land;
- subdivision of land;
- erection of a building;
- carrying out of a work;
- demolition of a building or work;
- any other act, matter or thing referred to in s 26 that is controlled by an EPI.

As discussed in Chapter 2, s 26 sets out the matters that may be included in an EPI. An EPI may make provision to control advertising (s 26(1)(g)), in which case advertising will be 'development' for the purposes of Pt 4.

Use

The 'use' of land will generally be for a particular purpose, and it is the purpose of that use that will be relevant in deciding whether the use is permissible or not. A 'use' need not be a continuing activity, and can include a one-off event such as a rock concert[1] or a weekend music and arts festival.[2]

As discussed in Chapter 2, the process of characterisation of a current or proposed use can be difficult. The consent authority must form a view as to the appropriate characterisation, in order to decide whether it has the power to grant consent or not. However, its conclusion on that issue is subject to review by the Land and Environment Court (LEC). The characterisation of a use is a jurisdictional fact, which means that the court has the power to decide for itself, on the evidence available to it at the time it is deciding the issue, how to characterise the use.[3]

Subdivision

Subdivision of land means the division of land into two or more parts that, after the division, are obviously adapted for separate occupation, use or disposition. Subdivision can be carried out by conveyance, transfer or partition, or by any agreement, dealing, plan or instrument, and includes registration of a plan of subdivision under the *Conveyancing Act 1919* and a strata plan under the strata legislation (s 4B(1)). However, there are some dealings in land that are not 'subdivision' for the purposes of the definition of 'development'. These include a lease of a building or

1 *South Sydney City Council v Paul Dainty Corp Pty Ltd* (1992) 75 LGRA 202.
2 *Gosford City Council v Popran Creek Pty Ltd* (1995) 89 LGERA 208.
3 *Woolworths Ltd v Pallas Newco Pty Ltd* [2004] NSWCA 422.

part of a building; opening of a public road; the acquisition of land (voluntary or compulsory) under legislation; and certain transactions under the *Conveyancing Act* (s 4B(3)).

Erection of a building

For the purposes of the definition of 'development', a building includes part of a building, and any structure or part of a structure, but does not include a manufactured home, a moveable dwelling or associated structure, or a temporary structure within the meaning of the *Local Government Act 1993* (s 4). The placing of a structure on land constitutes development – for example, *Aquatic Airways Pty Ltd v Warringah Shire Council*[4] where the placement of weights on the bed of Pittwater, and the securing of those weights to a pontoon by means of chains, was held to be the erection of a building.

Carrying out of a work

The carrying out of a work includes physical activity on land. In *Parramatta City Council v Brickworks Ltd*,[5] the High Court held that a 'work' is the 'physical product of labouring operations'. Not all physical activity on land will constitute a 'work', and it is a matter of degree. For example, in *Kiama Municipal Council v French*,[6] the placement of soil on agricultural land which raised the soil level by approximately 10 centimetres was held not to be a work. In *Kavanagh v Baulkham Hills Shire Council*,[7] the construction of a BMX track was held to be a 'work', having regard to its size and shape, the height of proposed earthworks, the material and the method of construction.

Types of development

The procedure set out in Pt 4 of the EPAA for application for development consent and the determination of applications may vary, depending on the type of development. Additional requirements are set out for designated development, advertised development and integrated development.

Designated development

Designated development is development that is declared to be designated development by an EPI, or by the regulations (s 77A). *SEPP 14 – Coastal Wetlands*, for example, declares that clearing, draining or filling, or construction of a levee, on land that is subject to the SEPP, is designated development. Section 117 Direction No 10 states that councils are not to identify development as designated development, and an LEP can only be inconsistent with this direction if the council can satisfy the Director-General that a particular provision should be varied having

4 (1990) 71 LGRA 10.
5 (1972) 128 CLR 1 at 24.
6 (1984) 54 LGRA 42.
7 (1983) 48 LGRA 370.

regard to the objects of the EPAA, and the class of development is likely to have a significant impact on the environment. Part 1 of Sch 3 to the *Environmental Planning and Assessment Regulation 2000* (EPAR) lists a range of development as designated development (cl 4). Developments are listed by type, scale and, in some instances, also by proximity to environmentally sensitive areas such as natural waterbodies or wetlands or drinking water catchments. For example, paper pulp or pulp industries with an intended production capacity of more than 30,000 tonnes a year (or 70,000 tonnes a year if at least 90% of the raw material is recycled and if no bleaching or de-inking is done), or that release effluent or sludge within 100 metres of a natural body or wetland or in an area of high watertable or in a drinking water catchment, are designated development. Alterations or additions to development may not be designated development if they do not significantly increase the environmental impacts of the total development (cl 35, Sch 3). In deciding whether an alteration or addition is designated development, the consent authority must consider the impact of the existing development, the likely impact of the proposed alterations or additions, any proposals to mitigate environmental impacts and manage any residual risk, or to facilitate compliance with relevant standards, codes of practice or guidelines published by the Department or other public authorities (cl 36, Sch 3).

Advertised development

Advertised development is development that is not designated development, and which is identified as advertised development by the regulations, an EPI or a development control plan (DCP) (s 4). Advertised development includes development for the purposes of a scheduled activity at any premises under the *Protection of the Environment Operations Act 1997* that is not designated development (s 4).

Examples of EPIs which specify certain development as advertised development include *SEPP 19 – Bushland in Urban Areas*, which states that disturbance of bushland zoned or reserved for public open space requires the consent of the council, and that this is advertised development (cl 6(1), (2)). *SEPP 33 – Hazardous and Offensive Development* provides that development for the purposes of potentially hazardous or potentially offensive industry is advertised development. An LEP may identify types of development as 'advertised development', for example development which comprises the demolition of a heritage item, or the use of a building which is a heritage item.[8]

The EPAR identifies as advertised development certain types of integrated development (referred to as 'nominated integrated development'); development on land that is or is part of critical habitat or is likely significantly to affect threatened species, populations or ecological communities or their habitats ('threatened species development'); and development that is, pursuant to *SEPP 62 – Sustainable Aquaculture*, Class 1 aquaculture ('Class 1 aquaculture development') (cl 5). Development which was formerly State-significant development under the now repealed s 76A(7) of the EPAA, and which falls within the transitional provisions, is also advertised development (cl 5(3)).

8 *Centro Properties Ltd v Hurstville City Council* [2006] NSWLEC 78.

Integrated development

Integrated development is development other than complying development that requires development consent, and one or more of approvals under the following legislation:

- *Fisheries Management Act 1994* ss 144, 201, 205, 219;
- *Heritage Act 1977* s 58;
- *Mine Subsidence Compensation Act 1961* s 15;
- *Mining Act 1992* ss 63, 64;
- *National Parks and Wildlife Act 1974* s 90;
- *Petroleum (Offshore) Act 1991* s 9;
- *Protection of the Environment Operations Act 1997* ss 43(a), 47 and 55, ss 43(b), 48 and 55, ss 43(d), 55 and 122;
- *Roads Act 1993* s 138;
- *Rural Fires Act 1997* s 100B;
- *Water Management Act 2000* ss 89, 90, 91. (s 91(1))

Section 91(1A), (2), (3) and (4) limit the provisions of s 91(1), for example, development which requires approval under s 138 of the *Roads Act* is not integrated development if it requires the development consent of a council and the approval of the same council (s 91(3)).

Development that requires approval under the above specified provisions of the *Heritage Act*, *Water Management Act* or *Protection of the Environment Operations Act* is referred to in the EPAR as 'nominated integrated development', and is advertised development (cl 5(1)(b)).

Complying development

Complying development is development which requires development consent and which, under an EPI, can be addressed by specified predetermined development standards (s 76A(5)). Development that cannot be identified as complying development includes designated development, and development which requires concurrence of a person other than the consent authority or the Director-General of National Parks and Wildlife, or which applies to land that is critical habitat, part of a wilderness area, comprises or has certain items of environmental heritage, or is identified in the EPI as an environmentally sensitive area. Complying development can be carried out if a complying development certificate has been issued, and the development is carried out in accordance with that certificate and any applicable provisions of an EPI, DCP or the regulations (s 84A(1)).

A 'complying development certificate' is a certificate that states that proposed development is complying development and will comply with relevant development standards and, if it involves the erection of a building, identifies the relevant classification of the building under the Building Code of Australia (s 85(1)).

An application for a complying development certificate can be made to the council, or to an accredited certifier (discussed below at p 91). There may be a requirement imposed by a DCP publicly to notify the application. The only matters to be considered are whether the proposed development is complying development; whether it complies with the relevant development standards; and, if the development is complying development because of the provisions of an LEP, or an LEP and DCP, which specifies standards and conditions for the complying development, whether the proposed development complies with those standards and conditions (s 85A). If the proposed development does comply with any applicable standards and the requirements of the regulations, the council or certifier must issue the complying development certificate, within seven days (s 85A(7), (8)). Building work must comply with the requirements of the Building Code of Australia, and meet fire safety requirements (EPAR cll 130, 131). The council or certifier can impose conditions if required by the regulations, an EPI or a DCP, and must impose a condition relating to contribution to public amenities and public services if required (s 85A(6), (9)). If the development involves any building, subdivision or demolition work, there must be a sign erected on the site advising details of the certifier and principal contractor, and prohibiting unauthorised entry to the site (EPAR cl 136B). If the building is, or is to become, a BASIX affected building (see p 73), the complying development certificate must include a condition that the commitments listed in the BASIX certificate must be fulfilled (EPAR cl 136D).

A complying development certificate lapses five years after the date endorsed on the certificate, unless the development is physically commenced on the land before that date (s 86A).

Development applications

Formal requirements

A 'development application' (DA) is an application for consent under Pt 4 of the EPAA to carry out development. An application for a complying development certificate is not a development application (s 4). A DA can be made by the owner of the land, or any other person with the written consent of the owner (EPAR cl 49). Failure to obtain the consent of the owner means that the DA is defective, and any development consent granted before obtaining the consent of the owner will be invalid.[9] However, a consent authority can consider a DA and grant development consent so long as the consent of the owner is obtained before the consent is granted.[10] If the owner withdraws consent before the DA is determined, the consent authority can still continue to deal with the application on its merits.[11]

A DA made by the lessee of Crown land requires the written consent of the Crown. If the DA is made by a public authority, the consent of the owner of the land to which it relates is not required, but the public authority must serve a copy of the application on the owner (cl 49(2)).

A single application may be made for one or more of the types of development specified in the definition of 'development' in s 4 (s 78A(2)). If approval is also required under the *Local Government Act 1993*, for example, to install a temporary structure on the land, and the consent authority is a council, the applicant can apply for development consent and the *Local Government Act* approval in the one application (s 78A(3)). If the council grants development consent, it is taken to have granted

9 *King v Great Lakes Shire Council* (1986) 58 LGRA 366.

10 *Woolworths Ltd v Bathurst City Council* (1987) 63 LGRA 55.

11 *Stafford Quarries Pty Ltd v Kempsey Shire Council* (1992) 72 LGRA 52.

the relevant approval under the *Local Government Act* (s 78A(5)). The council can impose a condition that the approval is granted only to the applicant, and does not run with the land to which it applies, and can impose a condition that approval is granted for a specified time (s 78A(6)).

The information required in a DA is specified in Pt 1 of Sch 1 to the EPAR. In addition to information describing the proposed development, the DA must indicate whether the land is, or is part of, critical habitat; whether the development is likely significantly to affect threatened species, populations or ecological communities or their habitats; list any approvals of the kind referred to in s 91(1); and provide the estimated cost of the development.

Clause 2 of Pt 1 of Sch 1 lists the documents that must accompany the DA. These include a site plan of the land; a sketch of the development; and a statement of environmental effects. If the development involves the erection of a building, the DA must include an A4 plan of the building indicating its height and external configuration. If the development involves building work to alter, expand or rebuild an existing building, the DA must include a scaled plan of the existing building. A DA involving change of use of a building must include details of existing and proposed fire safety provisions. If the DA involves subdivision work, it must include preliminary engineering drawings of the work to be carried out.

From 1 July 2005, a DA for any development that involves the erection of a BASIX affected building, or which involves a change of building use by which a building becomes a BASIX affected building, must be accompanied by a BASIX certificate for the development (EPAR cl 2A, Sch 1). From 1 October 2006 BASIX applies to renovation work valued at $100,000 or more, and to the installation of a swimming pool (or pool and spa) with a capacity greater than 40,000 litres.

The Building Sustainability Index (BASIX) was introduced from 1 July 2004 when the SEPP – Building Sustainability Index (BASIX) 2004 and *Environmental Planning and Assessment Amendment (Building Sustainability Index (BASIX)) Regulation 2004* came into effect. BASIX applies to residential development, and requires assessment of how the proposed development performs by reference to several sustainability indices, including savings in mains-supplied potable water consumption, greenhouse gas emissions and thermal performance. The BASIX assessment process is an online program, which assesses the house or unit design using information such as site location, house size, type of building materials and fittings for hot water, cooling and heating (see also p 230).

The statement of environmental effects required by cl 2(1)(c) of Sch 1 to the EPAR must indicate the environmental impacts of the development, how the environmental impacts of the development have been identified, the steps to be taken to protect the environment or to lessen the expected harm to the environment, and any matters required to be indicated by any guidelines issued by the Director-General (cl 2(4) Sch 1). There are additional requirements for a statement of environmental effects if the DA relates to residential flat development to which *SEPP 65 – Design Quality of Residential Flat Development* applies (cl 2(5)).

If the DA is in respect of designated development, it must be accompanied by an EIS, instead of the statement of environmental effects (s 78A(8)(a)). If the DA is in respect of land that is, or is a part of, critical habitat or is likely to affect threatened species, populations or ecological communities or their habitats, it must be accompanied by a SIS prepared in accordance with Div 2 of Pt 6 of the *Threatened Species*

Conservation Act 1995 (s 78A(8)(b)). The requirements for an EIS and a SIS are discussed in Chapter 4 at p 136.

Staged development

A 'staged development application' is a DA that sets out concept proposals for the development of a site, and for which detailed proposals for separate parts of the site are to be the subject of subsequent development applications (s 83B(1)). The applicant must request that the DA is to be treated as a staged development application. If consent is granted on determination of a staged development application, a further DA will be needed for development on any part of the site, unless the staged development application also provided the required details of the to carry out development, and consent is granted for that first stage of the development (s 83B(3)).

Public notification

The EPAA imposes obligations to notify applications for designated development and advertised development. Apart from these requirements (discussed below), if the DA relates to the erection of a building, the consent authority must make available to interested persons extracts of the DA which are sufficient to identify the applicant and the land to which the DA relates, and which contain a plan of the building indicating its height and external configuration (EPAR cl 56).

Designated development

The formal requirements for notification of an application for consent to carry out designated development are set out in s 79(1) of the EPAA. In summary, those requirements are:

- the DA, together with the accompanying information (which will include the EIS), must go on public exhibition for a period of not less than 30 days;
- the consent authority must give written notice of the DA to owners or occupiers of adjoining land, and (if practicable) to owners and occupiers of land the use and enjoyment of which may be detrimentally affected if the designated development is carried out;
- notice of the DA must be exhibited on the land; and
- notice of the DA must be published in newspapers.

During the period of public exhibition and submission, any person is entitled to inspect the DA and accompanying information, and to make submissions to the consent authority (s 79(4), (5)). Submissions by way of objections to the DA must set out the grounds of the objection (s 79(5)).

Public exhibition is not required if the DA is amended, substituted or withdrawn and later replaced before it has been determined by the consent authority, and the consent authority has complied with the public exhibition and notification requirements, and the consent authority determines that the amended, substituted or later application differs only in minor respects from the original application (s 79(6)).

Advertised development

The notification and publication requirements for advertised development are set out in the EPAR. The consent authority must give written notice of the DA to owners and occupiers of adjoining land and to public authorities which may have an interest in the determination of the application, and publish notice of the application in a local newspaper (cll 87, 88). The written notice must include a description of the land, the name of the applicant and the consent authority, a description of the proposed development, a statement that the application may be inspected, and a statement that any person may make submissions (cl 89(1)). The minimum period for exhibition is 14 days, or 30 if the application is for nominated integrated development or threatened species development (cl 89(3)). The notice of an application for integrated development must include that it is integrated development and state the approvals required (cl 89(2)(a)). Notice of an application for threatened species development must state that it is threatened species development (cl 89(2)(b)).

During the period of public exhibition and submission, any person is entitled to inspect the DA and accompanying information, and to make submissions to the consent authority. Submissions by way of objections to the DA must set out the grounds of the objection (cl 91).

The notification provisions do not apply to an amended or substituted DA where the consent authority has complied with the notification requirements for the original application, and the consent authority is of the opinion that the amended, substituted or later application differs only in minor respects from the original application (cl 90).

Assessment

Consultation and concurrence

The consent authority may be required by the applicable EPI to consult with, or obtain the concurrence of, a specified person or authority. The consent authority must consult, or obtain concurrence, unless the consent authority decides to refuse development consent (EPAA s 79B(1)). However, if the consent authority is the Minister, the Minister is required only to consult (s 79B(2)).

If the DA relates to development on land that is, or is part of, critical habitat, or is likely significantly to affect a threatened species, population or ecological community or habitat, the consent authority cannot grant consent without the concurrence of the Director-General of National Parks and Wildlife. If the Minister is the consent authority, consultation with the Minister administering the *Threatened Species Conservation Act 1995* is required (EPAA s 79B(3)).

The person whose concurrence is required may grant concurrence (which may be subject to conditions), or refuse concurrence. In doing so, that person is required to consider any matters specified in the EPI which imposes the concurrence requirement (s 79B(8)). If that person does not respond within the time allowed, the consent authority can go ahead and determine the DA without the concurrence of the specified person (s 79B(11)). Otherwise, if the consent authority determines the DA without obtaining concurrence, or not subject to any conditions of the concurrence, the development consent is voidable (s 79B(10)).

Integrated development

The consent authority must forward a DA for development which is 'integrated development' to the authority or authorities whose approval is required under the applicable legislation within two days after the DA is lodged (EPAR cl 66). The approval body may request additional information (cl 67). The approval body must notify the consent authority in writing, within 40 days, of its general terms of approval, including whether or not it will grant approval (cl 70). If the DA has to be publicly notified, this period is extended to 21 days after receiving the last of the submissions made during the applicable submission period, or after the consent authority notifies the approval body that no submissions were made (cl 70(1)(b)). If the approval body fails to advise the consent authority whether it will grant the approval, or of the general terms of its approval, the consent authority can determine the DA. If the consent authority grants development consent, the approval body cannot refuse to grant approval, and its approval must not be inconsistent with the development consent (s 91A(5)).

If the approval body advises that it will not grant an approval that is required for the development to be lawfully carried out, the consent authority must refuse development consent (s 91A(4)). If the approval body advises that it will grant approval, and the consent authority decides to grant development consent, the consent must be consistent with the general terms of approval proposed to be granted by the approval body, and the consent authority can impose any condition that the approval body could impose as a condition of its approval (s 91A(3)). If the consent authority decides to refuse development consent, it must advise the approval body (EPAR cl 70(2)).

If the approval body advises the consent authority of the general terms of its approval, and the consent authority grants development consent, the approval body must grant approval to any application for approval made within three years after the date on which development consent is granted, if the consent has not lapsed or been revoked (s 93(1)).

Evaluation

Section 79C sets out the matters which the consent authority is required to take into consideration in determining a DA:

> (1) In determining a development application, a consent authority is to take into consideration such of the following matters as are of relevance to the development the subject of the development application:
> (a) the provisions of:
> (i) any environmental planning instrument, and
> (ii) any draft environmental planning instrument that is or has been placed on public exhibition and details of which have been notified to the consent authority (unless the Director-General has notified the consent authority that the making of the draft instrument has been deferred indefinitely or has not been approved), and
> (iii) any development control plan, and
> (iiia) any planning agreement that has been entered into under section 93F, or any draft planning agreement that a developer has offered to enter into under section 93F, and

(iv) the regulations (to the extent that they prescribe matters for the purposes of this paragraph),

that apply to the land to which the development application relates,

(b) the likely impacts of that development, including environmental impacts on both the natural and built environments, and social and economic impacts in the locality,

(c) the suitability of the site for the development,

(d) any submissions made in accordance with this Act or the regulations,

(e) the public interest.

Section 79C does not refer to the principles of ecologically sustainable development. However, one of the objects of the EPAA, as stated in s 5(a)(vii), is to encourage ecologically sustainable development. The LEC has held that, in requiring a consent authority to take into account 'the public interest', s 79C(1)(e) obliges the consent authority to have regard to the principles of ecologically sustainable development in cases where issues relevant to those principles arise.[12] The Act defines ecologically sustainable development as having the same meaning as it has in s 6(2) of the *Protection of the Environment Administration Act 1991*, and so the applicable principles of ecologically sustainable development are the precautionary principle, the principle of inter-generational equity, the conservation of biological diversity and ecological integrity, and improved valuation, pricing and incentive mechanisms.

Section 79C(1)(a)(i) requires the consent authority to take into consideration the provisions of any relevant EPI. An EPI may provide specific criteria for assessment of particular types of development, for example, *SEPP 32 – Urban Consolidation (Redevelopment of Urban Land)*, which requires the Minister as consent authority to consider the effect of development on the streetscape; privacy of, and availability of sunlight to, adjoining owners; noise; and whether adequate provision has been made for car parking and access. *SEPP 55 – Remediation of Land* requires the consent authority to consider whether the land is contaminated and, if it is, whether it is satisfied that the land is suitable in its contaminated state, or will be after remediation, for the purpose for which the development is proposed to be carried out (SEPP 55 cl 7). An EPI may impose development standards. If those development standards are non-discretionary, and the development complies with those standards, the consent authority is not entitled to refuse consent on the basis of those standards.

The consent authority is required under s 79C(1)(a)(ii) to consider the provisions of any draft exhibited EPI, and is entitled to give weight to its perception of the likely, or unlikely, imminence of the relevant provisions of the draft EPI coming into force. If the draft EPI has in fact come into force, the consent authority is entitled to regard its provisions as certain and imminent. Even if the draft EPI contains transitional provisions stating that it is not to apply to the application before the consent authority, the consent authority is still entitled to have regard to its provisions as a matter relating to the 'public interest', referred to in s 79C(1)(e).[13]

The consent authority is required by s 79C(1)(a)(iii) to consider the provisions of any development control plan. While not determinative, provisions in a DCP setting

12 *Carstens v Pittwater Council* (1999) 111 LGERA 1; *BGP Properties Pty Ltd v Lake Macquarie City Council* (2004) 138 LGERA 237; *Port Stephens Pearls Pty Ltd v Minister for Infrastructure and Planning* [2005] NSWLEC 426; *Telstra Corporation Ltd v Hornsby Shire Council* (2006) 146 LGERA 10.

13 *Terrace Tower Holdings Pty Ltd v Sutherland Shire Council* [2003] NSWCA 289.

standards which are directly relevant to the application for consent (for example, minimum distances for the location of brothels from sensitive uses such as schools) are entitled to significant weight.[14] The principles relevant to the consideration of development control plans were summarised by McClellan CJ in *Stockland Development Pty Ltd v Manly Council*[15] in the following terms:

- A development control plan adopted after consultation with interested persons, including the affected community, will be given significantly more weight than one adopted with little or no community consultation.
- A development control plan which has been consistently applied by a council will be given significantly greater weight than one which has only been selectively applied.
- A development control plan which can be demonstrated, either inherently or perhaps by the passing of time, to bring about an inappropriate planning solution, especially an outcome which conflicts with other policy outcomes adopted at a State, regional or local level, will be given less weight than a development control plan which provides a sensible planning outcome consistent with other policies.
- Consistency of decision-making must be a fundamental objective of those who make administrative decisions. That objective is assisted by the adoption of development control plans and the making of decisions in individual cases which are consistent with them. If this is done, those with an interest in the site under consideration or who may be affected by any development of it have an opportunity to make decisions in relation to their own property which is informed by an appreciation of the likely future development of nearby property.

The consent authority may be faced with a range of policies relevant to the proposed development. Planning policies may be adopted by a council, or by other authorities, such as the State government's Metropolitan Strategy for Sydney. Policies do not have statutory force, but will still be relevant in consideration of the public interest, and the consent authority is entitled to have regard to them in making value judgments.[16] The matters relevant when determining the weight to be given to a planning policy adopted by a council were summarised by McClellan CJ in *Stockland Development Pty Ltd v Manly Council*[17] in the following terms:

- the extent, if any, of research and public consultation undertaken when creating the policy;
- the time during which the policy has been in force and the extent of any review of its effectiveness;
- the extent to which the policy has been departed from in prior decisions;
- the compatibility of the policy with the objectives and provisions of relevant environmental planning instruments and development control plans;
- the compatibility of the policy with other policies adopted by a council or by any other relevant government agency;

14 *Zhang v Canterbury City Council* (2001) 51 NSWLR 589; *Deancliff Developments Pty Ltd v Hornsby Shire Council* [2005] NSWCA 271.

15 [2004] NSWLEC 472 at [87].

16 *Terrace Tower Holdings Pty Ltd v Sutherland Shire Council* [2003] NSWCA 289; *Direct Factory Outlets Homebush Pty Ltd v Strathfield Municipal Council* [2006] NSWLEC 318.

17 [2004] NSWLEC 472 at [92].

- whether the policy contains any significant flaws when assessed against conventional planning outcomes accepted as appropriate for the site or area affected by it.

The EPAR sets out additional matters that must be considered for particular types of development, including development on land to which the Government Coastal Policy applies, and the requirement to have regard to fire safety considerations for change of building use that does not involve rebuilding, alteration or extension of the building (cll 92, 93).

Section 79C(1)(b) requires the consent authority to consider the likely impacts of the proposed development, including environmental impacts on both the natural and built environments. For development other than designated development, the DA must be accompanied by a statement of environmental effects, which must indicate the environmental impacts of the development, how those impacts have been identified, the steps to be taken to protect the environment or to lessen expected harm, and any matters required to be indicated in guidelines by the Director-General (EPAR cl 2(1)(c), (4), Sch 1). The relatively limited role of the statement of environmental effects has been acknowledged by the courts, reflecting as it does the applicant's perception of likely environmental impacts rather than an independent assessment.[18] A council may reject a DA which is not accompanied by a statement of environmental effects (cl 51(1)(b)). It is, however, open to a council to consider, and grant consent to, a DA which is not accompanied by a statement of environmental effects where the absence is not in a particular case of such significance as to prevent it from performing its statutory duty to consider the likely environmental impacts of the proposed development.[19] Assessment of environmental impacts for designated development, development on land that is critical habitat or is likely significantly to affect threatened species, major projects covered by Pt 3A of the Act, and for activities which do not require development consent, is discussed in Chapter 4.

In considering the likely impacts of a proposed development under s 79C(1)(b), the consent authority is also required to consider social and economic impacts in the locality. Economic impacts including likely employment generation, viability of existing and future businesses, and impact on property values, are relevant considerations.[20] Section 79C(1)(c) requires consideration of the suitability of the site for the development, which may include how the proposal fits in the locality and whether the site attributes are appropriate for the proposed development. A proposed development is expected to accommodate the impact of existing lawful development on adjoining or nearby land.[21]

While the weight to be given to each of the s 79C factors is a matter for the consent authority, the consent authority is obliged to consider those factors which are objectively of relevance for the application.[22] The consideration must be a

---

18 *MCC Energy Pty Ltd v Wyong Shire Council* [2006] NSWLEC 581.

19 *Cranky Rock Road Action Group Inc v Cowra Shire Council* [2006] NSWCA 339.

20 *Lakeside Plaza Pty Ltd v Legal & General Properties No 2 Ltd* (1992) 76 LGRA 60; *Patra Holdings Pty Ltd v Minister for Land and Water Conservation* (2001) 119 LGERA 231.

21 *Inghams Enterprises Pty Ltd v Kira Holdings Pty Ltd* (1996) 90 LGERA 68; *Concrite Pty Ltd v South Sydney City Council* (2001) 117 LGERA 87.

22 *Everall v Ku-ring-gai Municipal Council* (1991) 72 LGRA 369; *Parramatta City Council v Hale* (1982) 47 LGRA 319.

genuine consideration, and mere advertence to a matter required to be taken into account will not be sufficient.[23] Difficulties can arise in determining whether a council, as a collective decision-maker, has actually taken mandatory considerations into account. Where a majority of councillors deprive the minority of an opportunity to consider relevant material, the decision may be invalid.[24] A challenger must establish that a mandatory consideration was not taken into account, and that this error was material to the decision.[25]

Planning principles

Since September 2003 the LEC has published judgments of Commissioners which include planning principles. These are available on the court's website. At the time of writing there are 39 judgments identified as containing planning principles. These planning principles cover such matters as aesthetics, redevelopment, ESD principles, noise, privacy and views. The planning principles are described as being statements of a desirable outcome from; a chain of reasoning aimed at reaching; or a list of appropriate matters to be considered in making, a planning decision. The planning principles are not legally binding, and are intended to promote consistency within the court, and to assist consent authorities when making planning decisions, including where there is a void in policy; or where policies expressed in qualitative terms allow for more than one interpretation; or where policies lack clarity. For example, *Tenacity Consulting Ltd v Warringah Council*[26] sets out an approach in assessing whether proposed sharing of views is reasonable, as involving a four-stage assessment: the assessment of views to be affected, valuing water views, iconic views, and whole rather than partial views; consideration of from what part of the property the views are obtained; assessment of the extent of the impact; and assessment of the reasonableness of the proposal that is causing the impact. The planning principles are intended as guidelines to assist resolution of issues that commonly arise in merits review cases, and must not be applied if they result in the misapplication of the EPAA provisions.[27]

Determination

The consent authority determines a DA by granting consent, which may be subject to conditions, or by refusing consent (s 80(1)). If the consent authority does not determine the DA within 40 days (or 60 days in the case of designated development, integrated development or development requiring concurrence), it is deemed to have refused the application for the purposes of any appeal rights (s 82(1), EPAR cl 113).

When calculating the length of an assessment period for the purposes of the deemed refusal provisions, the day on which the DA is lodged and the following day are disregarded (EPAR cl 107). The time for determination is extended if the

23 *Zhang v Canterbury City Council* (2001) 51 NSWLR 589; *Centro Properties Ltd v Hurstville City Council* (2004) 135 LGERA 257.

24 *Parramatta City Council v Hale* (1982) 47 LGRA 319.

25 *Minister for Aboriginal Affairs v Peko Wallsend Ltd* (1986) 162 CLR 24.

26 [2004] NSWLEC 140.

27 *Stromness Pty Limited v Woollahra Municipal Council* [2006] NSWLEC 587.

concurrence of a person or authority is required, or if the consent authority requests further information from the applicant (cll 106-112). The assessment period 'clock' stops if a request for additional information is made by the consent authority within 25 days from the start of the deemed refusal period, or by a referral body within 25 days of receiving the DA from the consent authority (cll 109, 110, 111). The assessment period 'clock' restarts if the applicant gives the requested information to the consent authority, or notifies the consent authority that the information will not be provided. If a referral body makes the request for additional information, the 'clock' restarts two days after the consent authority refers the requested information, or notifies the referral agency that the information will not be provided. The 'clock' can be restarted by the consent authority if the applicant does not give the requested information within the time specified (which must be reasonable) or any further time allowed. The consent authority must notify the applicant of the effect of the stop the clock provisions on the assessment period (cl 112).

The consent authority may grant consent for the whole development; for the development, except for a specified excluded part or aspect; or for a specified part or aspect of the development (s 80(4)). The specific provisions for staged development in Div 2A of Pt 4 have been set out above.

The consent authority cannot determine a DA for designated development until after the period for submissions has ended or, if a submission has been made within the submission period, until 21 days after a copy of that submission has been sent to the Director-General (s 80(9)).

The consent authority must give notice of its determination to the applicant, to any objector (if the application is for designated development) and any other persons as required by the regulations (s 81(1)). If the consent authority is not the council, it must notify the council of the determination (s 81(2)). Notice must be sent within 14 days after the date of the determination and specify the date of the determination (EPAR cll 101(1), 100(1)(d)). Clause 100 of the EPAR sets out the requirements of the notice. If the application has been granted, the written notice must include:

- the terms of any conditions imposed, and the reasons for imposing those conditions;
- whether the applicant has the right to request review
- if the consent is for staged development, whether a subsequent development application is required for any part of the site;
- the date on which the determination was made;
- the date from which consent operates;
- the date on which the consent will lapse;
- whether the Act gives the applicant, or any objector, the right of appeal against the determination.

If the application has been refused, the notice must include the reasons for the refusal, and notification of whether there are any appeal rights.

A development consent can be granted for a period of up to five years. Consent may be granted for a shorter period, except for staged development. A development consent for the erection or demolition of a building or the subdivision of land must be granted for at least two years (s 95).

Development consent

Conditions

The consent authority may impose a condition on the development consent if:

- it relates to any matter referred to in s 79C of relevance to the development;
- it requires the modification or surrender of a consent granted under the EPAA or an existing use right;
- it requires the modification or cessation of development (including the removal of buildings and works used in connection with that development) carried out on land;
- it limits the period during which development may be carried out in accordance with the consent;
- it requires the removal of buildings and works (or any part of them) at the end of the period during which the development may be carried out;
- it requires the carrying out of works (whether or not being works on land to which the application relates) relating to any matter referred to in s 79C(1) relevant to the development;
- it modifies details of the development the subject of the development application;
- it is authorised under s 80(3), (5), 80A(5)-(9), 94, 94A, 94EF or 94F. (s 80A(1))

The general test for the validity of a condition is that it must be imposed for a planning purpose; it must relate fairly and reasonably to the development for which the consent is given; and it must be reasonable.[28] The test of 'reasonableness' is the *Wednesbury* test, namely, whether the condition is so unreasonable that no reasonable decision-maker could have imposed it.[29] A condition which does not meet these requirements, or which is not authorised under s 80A(1), will be invalid. Depending on how central the condition is to the development consent, the invalidity of the condition may invalidate the consent as a whole.[30]

A condition may be imposed which limits the period during which the development may be carried out (s 80A(1)(d)). This can be used to limit a proposed use, such as a brothel, to a probationary or trial period, for example a period of 12 months.[31]

Conditions requiring monetary contributions can only be imposed under s 94, and not under the general power to impose conditions under s 80A.[32] Section 94 does not prevent the council from imposing a condition requiring the carrying out of works, even works such as road works, which may benefit the public, where the condition satisfies the *Newbury* test.[33]

---

28 *Newbury District Council v Secretary of State for the Environment* [1981] AC 578; *Western Australia Planning Commission v Temwood Holdings Pty Ltd* [2004] HCA 63.

29 *Woolworths Ltd v Pallas Newco Pty Ltd* [2004] NSWCA 422; *Westfield Management Ltd v Perpetual Trustee Co Ltd* [2006] NSWCA 245.

30 *Greek Australian Finance Corporation v Sydney City Council* (1974) 29 LGRA 130; *Association for Berowra Creek Inc v Minister for Planning* [2003] NSWLEC 38.

31 *Zhang v Canterbury City Council* (2001) 51 NSWLR 589.

32 *Fitch v Shoalhaven City Council* (1987) 67 LGRA 165.

33 *Fairfield City Council v N & S Olivieri Pty Ltd* [2003] NSWCA 41.

A condition can be expressed in terms of express outcomes or objectives that are to be achieved, and clear criteria against which achievement of the outcome or objective can be assessed (s 80A(4)). The Court of Appeal has adopted a purposive approach to this provision, holding that the term 'outcomes' is not to be understood in its ordinary meaning of a result or visible effect, but rather in the sense of a broader objective, which will not be sufficient to identify a particular result. Objectives can be identified in a manner which includes the criteria, so long as the criteria are clear. Section 80A(4) is intended to allow a condition to require a variation of a proposal where the intended result is sufficiently identified, but the means of achieving it are left to the applicant.[34]

Finality

The consent authority must frame conditions which actually deal with the issues relating to the matters listed in s 79C, and it cannot postpone the resolution of difficult issues, or refer them to others for determination. Central matters such as floor space ratio, height and position of any building on the site, and measures to reduce environmental impact, must be decided at the time of granting consent.[35] The consent authority must deal with such matters by imposing conditions and cannot, for example, rely on a deed entered into with the developer dealing with that matter.[36] A development consent which leaves open the possibility that the development carried out will be significantly different from the development for which consent was sought, or which lacks finality or is uncertain, may be invalid.[37] These two categories may overlap in circumstances where a development consent is granted subject to a condition which allows for significant variation of the development proposed.[38]

Matters which are ancillary to the core purpose of the development can be made the subject of a condition which requires the applicant to carry out a specified aspect of the development to the satisfaction of the consent authority, or specified person (s 80A(2)).

A consent authority may grant consent subject to a condition that the consent is not to operate until the applicant satisfies that consent authority as to any matter specified in the condition (s 80(3)). A 'deferred commencement' consent must be identified as such (EPAR cl 95(1)). The consent authority may specify the period within which the applicant must provide evidence sufficient to enable it to be satisfied of the specified matters and, if so, the consent authority must notify the applicant whether it is satisfied (cl 95). A development consent subject to a deferred commencement condition will lapse if the applicant fails to satisfy the consent authority as to the specified matter within five years from the grant of the consent, or within any shorter period specified by the consent authority (s 95(6)). The consent authority cannot use a deferred commencement consent to leave unresolved, and for

---

34 *Kindimindi Investments Pty Ltd v Lane Cove Council* [2006] NSWCA 23.

35 *Lend Lease Management Pty Ltd v Sydney City Council* (1986) 68 LGRA 61; *Mison v Randwick Municipal Council* (1991) 73 LGRA 349; *Jungar Holdings Pty Ltd v Eurobodalla Shire Council* (1989) 70 LGRA 79.

36 *Kindimindi Investments Pty Ltd v Lane Cove Council* [2006] NSWCA 23.

37 *Hurstville City Council v Renaldo Plus 3 Pty Ltd* [2006] NSWCA 248.

38 *Kindimindi Investments Pty Ltd v Lane Cove Council* [2006] NSWCA 23.

future determination, issues relevant to the impact of the proposed development, or to avoid the obligation to consider all relevant matters as required by s 79C.[39]

Conditions requiring financial or other contributions

If the consent authority is satisfied that the development will or is likely to require the provision of or increase the demand for, public amenities and public services within the area, the consent authority may impose a condition requiring the dedication of land, or the payment of a monetary contribution, or both (s 94(1)). The dedication or contribution must be reasonable, and can be for provision, extension or augmentation of public amenities or public services (s 94(2)). The public amenities and services are those provided in the local government area.[40] However, if there is a joint contributions plan (discussed below), a condition can be imposed wholly or partly for the benefit of an adjoining area (s 94C). The term 'public amenities and public services' is not defined in the Act. The LEC has held that the phrase is to be interpreted broadly, to reflect the changes in services and amenities provided by local government over time. So long as a facility is operated or used for the benefit of the public, it will provide a public service or amenity.[41] This may include facilities such as council administrative offices, works depots and childcare centres.[42] The public amenities and public services which can be funded through s 94 contributions or s 94A levies do not include water supply and sewerage services (s 93C).

The consent authority can impose a condition requiring monetary contribution towards the recoupment of the costs of providing public amenities or public services if these have already been provided, and the development will benefit from those amenities or services (s 94(3)). The contribution towards recoupment must be reasonable (s 94(4)). Calculation of such costs was for some time based on the actual money paid by the council at the time for the capital costs of carrying out the work, rather than by discounting the current cost or indexing the historical cost.[43] Section 94(3) now allows the council to recover costs indexed in accordance with cl 25I of the EPAR, which is based on the CPI. The consent authority may accept dedication of land in part or full satisfaction of such a condition (s 94(5(a)). The consent authority may accept the provision of a material public benefit in part or full satisfaction of a condition either for provision of public amenities or services, or to recoup the cost of such amenities or services already provided (s 94(5)(b)). If the applicant has already provided land, money, or a material public benefit within the area or an adjoining area, the consent authority must take that into account (s 94(6)).

The consent authority must have evidence to justify its prediction about future need for provision, or increased demand, for public amenities or public services.[44]

As an alternative to the provision of a monetary contribution or the dedication of land under s 94, the consent authority may require the applicant to pay a levy of a percentage of the proposed cost of carrying out the development (s 94A(1), (2)). The

39 *Remath Investments No 6 Pty Ltd v Botany Bay Council (No 2)* (unreported, NSWLEC, Talbot J, No 10649 of 1996, 11 December 1996); *Weal v Bathurst City Council* (2000) 111 LGERA 181.

40 *Parramatta City Council v Peterson* (1987) 61 LGRA 286.

41 *Stockland (Constructors) Pty Ltd v Shellharbour Council* [1996] NSWLEC 123.

42 *Arkibuilt Pty Ltd v Ku-ring-gai Council* [2006] NSWLEC 502.

43 *Allsands Pty Ltd v Shoalhaven City Council* (1993) 78 LGERA 435.

44 *Lake Macquarie City Council v Hammersmith Management Pty Ltd* (2003) 132 LGERA 225.

money paid in the form of a levy must be used for the provision, extension or augmentation of public amenities or public services, or to recoup the cost of amenities or services already provided (s 94A(3)). The maximum levy is 1% of the cost of the development (EPAR cl 25K). The cost of the development is determined by adding up all the costs and expenses incurred in carrying out the development, and include costs incurred in:

- erecting any building, or carrying out any work, including costs of and incidental to demolition, excavation and site preparation, decontamination or remediation;
- doing anything necessary to enable the use of the land to be changed;
- preparing, executing and registering the plan of subdivision and any related covenants, easements or other rights.

The consent authority cannot take into account:

- the cost of the land on which the development is to be carried out;
- costs of any repairs to any building or works on the land that are to be retained in connection with the development;
- costs associated with marketing or financing the development (including interest on any loans);
- costs associated with legal work carried out or to be carried out in connection with the development;
- project management costs associated with the development;
- the cost of building insurance in respect of the development;
- the costs of fittings and furnishings, including any refitting or refurbishing, associated with the development (except where the development involves an enlargement, expansion or intensification of a current use of land);
- the costs of commercial stock inventory; or
- any taxes, levies or charges (other than GST) paid or payable in connection with the development by or under any law. (EPAR cl 25J)

The Minister has power under s 94E to direct a consent authority as to the public amenities or services in relation to which a condition may be imposed; the means of calculating a monetary contribution; the maximum amount of a monetary contribution; the things, or types of things, that may be accepted as a material public benefit; the type or area of development in respect of which a levy can be imposed under s 94A and the maximum percentage of the levy; and the use of monetary contributions or levies for purposes other than which they were paid (s 94E(1)). The consent authority must comply with such a direction, and cannot impose a condition that is not in accordance with the direction, even if that direction is contrary to the provisions of Pt 4 Div 6 or a contributions plan (s 94E(2), (3)).

On 10 November 2006 the Minister issued a direction under s 94E to consent authorities imposing restrictions on the imposition of levies under s 94A. The maximum 1% levy can only be imposed for development with a proposed cost above $200,000. The maximum rate of the levy for development where the proposed cost is between $100,001 and $200,000 is 0.5%, and a s 94A levy cannot be imposed for development where the proposed cost is less than $100,000. Irrespective of the proposed cost of carrying out the development, a s 94A levy cannot be imposed on development:

- for the purpose of disabled access;
- for the sole purpose of affordable housing;
- for the purpose of reducing the consumption of mains-supplied potable water, or reducing the energy consumption of a building;
- for the sole purpose of the adaptive reuse of an item of environmental heritage; or
- other than the subdivision of land, where a s 94 condition has been imposed under a previous development consent relating to the subdivision of land on which the development is proposed to be carried out.

If the consent authority is a council, any conditions imposed under s 94 or 94A must be authorised by a contributions plan (s 94B(1)).[45] Other consent authorities (for example, the Minister) can impose such a condition even if it is not authorised by a contributions plan, but they must have regard to any contributions plan before imposing the condition (s 94B(2)).

A contributions plan may be made by a council alone, or in conjunction with other councils (s 94EA(1)). The Minister can direct the preparation of a joint contributions plan by two or more councils (s 94E(1)(f)). The Minister can direct a council to approve, amend or repeal a contributions plan. If the council fails to act in accordance with such direction or, if the council consents, the Minister can make, amend or repeal a contributions plan (s 94EAA(2)). The council must forward a copy of its contributions plan to the Minister (s 94EA(4)).

The contributions plan must provide details of formulas to be used in calculating contributions, rates for different types of development, how the percentage of any s 94A levy is determined, council's policy on timing and deferral of payment, a map showing specific public amenities and services supported by a works schedule, and priorities for expenditure of contributions and levies (EPAR cl 27). The council must put a draft contributions plan on public exhibition, and consider any submissions received during the period of public exhibition when deciding whether to approve the plan, with or without amendments (cll 28, 29, 30, 31(1)). The council must give public notice of its decision in a local newspaper within 28 days, and the contributions plan comes into effect either on the date that notice is published, or on a later date if specified in the notice (cl 31(2), (4)). If the council decides not to proceed with the contributions plan, it must give reasons for that decision in the notice (cl 31(3)).

Contributions made in accordance with a s 94 condition must be held by the council and applied for a public purpose, within a reasonable time.[46] If the cost of providing the public amenities or services has increased by the time that the s 94 contributions are applied, the council is not required to construct all the public amenities and facilities identified in the contributions plan. Reduction or substitution of works for which contributions have been required must be authorised by amendment of the contributions plan.[47]

If the proposed development is in an area identified in a SEPP as having a need for affordable housing, the consent authority must consider whether the develop-

45 *Baulkham Hills Shire Council v Group Development Services Pty Ltd* [2005] NSWCA 315.

46 *Frevcourt Pty Ltd v Wingecarribee Shire Council* [2005] NSWCA 107; *Levadetes v Hawkesbury Shire Council* (1988) 67 LGRA 190; *Idameneo (No 9) Pty Ltd v Great Lakes Shire Council* (1990) 70 LGRA 27.

47 *Frevcourt Pty Ltd v Wingecarribee Shire Council* [2005] NSWCA 107.

ment will reduce the availability of affordable housing in the area, or will create a need for affordable housing in the area. If either applies, or the proposed development is allowed only because of the initial zoning of the site, the consent authority can impose a condition requiring the dedication of part of the land, or other land owned by the applicant, for the provision of affordable housing, or a condition requiring the payment of monetary contribution to be used for the purpose of providing affordable housing (s 94F(1), (2)). The condition must be authorised by an LEP or regional environment plan (REP), and be in accordance with a scheme for dedications or contributions set out or adopted by such a plan (s 94F(3(b)).

SEPP 70 – Affordable Housing (Revised Schemes) identifies that there is a need for affordable housing in the City of Sydney, Willoughby and Leichhardt areas within the Greater Metropolitan Region. Section 4 of the EPAA defines 'affordable housing' as meaning housing for very low income households, low income households or moderate income households. Clause 8 of SEPP 70 states that very low income households are those whose gross income is less than 50% of the median household income for the Sydney Statistical Division according to the Australian Bureau of Statistics. Low income households are those whose gross income falls within the range of 50 to 80%, and moderate income households are those whose gross income falls within the range of 80 to 120% of median household income.

The consent authority is required to consider the principles set out in Sch 2 to SEPP 70 before imposing such a condition (SEPP 70 cl 10). These principles reflect the need to create mixed and balanced communities. The dedication or contribution for affordable housing must be reasonable, having regard to the extent of the need in the area for affordable housing, the scale of the proposed development and any other dedication or contribution required under s 94 (s 94F(3)).

Planning agreements

As an alternative to the imposition of conditions under s 94 or s 94A, contributions can be made by the developer for public purposes through a planning agreement. A planning agreement is a voluntary agreement entered into by one or more planning authorities, and a developer who is seeking either a change in an EPI or who has made or is making a development application (s 93F(1)).

Under a planning agreement the developer may be required to dedicate land free of cost, pay a monetary contribution, or provide any other material public benefit, or any combination of them, to be used for or applied towards a public purpose. A public purpose includes the provision, or the recovery of the costs, of public amenities or public services, affordable housing, transport or other infrastructure relating to land, the funding of recurrent expenditure relating to the provision of public amenities or public services, affordable housing or transport or other infrastructure, the monitoring of the planning impacts of development, or the conservation or enhancement of the natural environment (s 93F(2)). There need be no connection between the development and the object of expenditure of any money required to be paid by a provision in a planning agreement (s 93F(4)).

A planning agreement may exclude the application of s 94 or 94A to the development, or may state whether the contribution under the planning agreement is to be taken into consideration under s 94(6) (s 93F(5), (6)). A planning agreement cannot exclude the application of s 94 or 94A unless the consent authority for the development or the Minister is a party to the agreement (s 93F(3A)). A planning agreement may be registered by agreement of any person with an interest in the land and, if it is registered, is binding and enforceable on subsequent owners of the land (s 93H).

Lapsing, modification and revocation

A development consent lapses five years after the date on which it operates, or earlier if granted for a shorter period (s 95(1), (2)). Development consent for the erection of a building, the subdivision of land or the carrying out of a work does not lapse if building, engineering or construction work is physically commenced on the land to which the consent applies (s 95(4)). The work must relate to the building, subdivision or work, and must be in accordance with the terms of the development consent.[48] For development which comprises the subdivision of land, the term 'engineering work' in the phrase 'building, engineering or construction work' is to be given a broad meaning to include all the activities associated with, and forming a necessary part of, the discipline of engineering applicable to the subdivision of land. That may include physical survey or geotechnical investigation work.[49] The relevant work must be commenced on the land in a physical sense, and off-site work such as design and planning work does not constitute physical commencement of the development for the purposes of s 95(4).[50] If the development is a use of land, the consent will lapse unless the use is actually commenced before the relevant date (s 95(5)). If the initial consent was granted for a period of less than five years, the applicant or any other person entitled to rely on the consent can apply to the consent authority for an extension on one year. The extension may be granted if the consent authority is satisfied that the applicant has shown good cause (s 95A).

The applicant can apply to the consent authority for modification of a development consent. The modification can include the amendment or disallowance of a condition requiring monetary contribution imposed under s 94.[51] If the application is for a change to the consent which is more than the correction of a minor error, misdescription or miscalculation, the consent authority must first consider whether the proposed modification is of minimal environmental impact. If it is so satisfied, and is also satisfied that the development to which the consent as modified is substantially the same as the original development, the consent authority can modify the consent, subject to complying with any requirement in the regulations or any development control plan to notify the application. The consent authority must consider any submissions made in response (s 96(1A)). In other circumstances, if the consent authority is satisfied that the development to which the consent as modified is substantially the same as the original development, it must consult with the relevant Minister or authority whose concurrence was required, or approval body if it is integrated development; notify the application if the regulations or a DCP plan requires; and consider any submissions received (s 96(2)). If the consent relates to land that is, or is part of, critical habitat, or the development is likely significantly to

48 *Iron Gates Development Pty Ltd v Richmond-Evans Environmental Society Inc* (1992) 81 LGERA 132; *Detala Pty Ltd v Byron Shire Council* [2002] NSWCA 404.

49 *Hunter Development Brokerage Pty Ltd v Cessnock City Council* [2005] NSWCA 169.

50 Ibid.

51 *Arkibuilt Pty Ltd v Ku-ring-gai Council* [2006] NSWLEC 502.

affect a threatened species, population, ecological community, or habitat, the consent authority must comply with the requirements of s 79B(3) to (7), which include the requirement to obtain concurrence of the Director-General of National Parks and Wildlife or (if the consent authority is a Minister) to consult (s 96(5)). The consent authority can impose conditions when determining an application for modification.[52]

The consent authority can modify a development consent granted by the LEC (s 96AA(1)). The consent authority must consider the matters referred to in s 79C and, if the development is on land that is critical habitat, or is likely significantly to affect threatened species, concurrence of the Director-General of National Parks and Wildlife will be required (s 96AA(1A), (1B)).

The Director-General, or a council, can revoke or modify a development consent, if satisfied that the development should not be carried out or completed, or should not be carried out or completed except with modifications. This consideration is made having regard to the provisions of a draft SEPP or REP, for the Director-General, or a draft LEP, in the case of the council (s 96A(1)). A consent granted by the LEC or the Minister cannot be revoked or modified (s 96A(9)). Any person who will be adversely affected is entitled to written notice and the opportunity to appear to show cause why the consent should not be revoked or modified (s 96A(3)). Compensation is payable for expenditure incurred between the date on which the consent becomes operative and the date of service of notice of the proposed revocation or modification which is rendered abortive by the revocation or modification (s 96A(7)).

Certification of development

Part 4A of the Act sets out the processes for certification of certain stages in development control. The following certificates can be issued:

- compliance certificate;
- construction certificate;
- occupation certificate;
- subdivision certificate. (s 109C(1))

A single certificate may deal with any number of matters (s 109C(1A)).

A *compliance certificate* may be issued to certify that specified building or subdivision work has been completed as specified and complies with plans and specifications; that a condition attached to a development consent or complying development certificate has been complied with; that a specified building has a specified classification in accordance with the Building Code of Australia; that any specified aspect of development complies with any other provisions prescribed by the regulations; or that any specified aspects (including design) complies with specified standards or requirements (s 109C(1)(a)). A compliance certificate relating to building work or subdivision work can only be issued where the certifying authority is satisfied that a development consent or complying development certificate is in force (s 109G).

A *construction certificate* is a certificate to the effect that work completed in accordance with specified plans and specifications will comply with the requirements of

52 *1643 Pittwater Road Pty Ltd v Pittwater Council* [2004] NSWLEC 685.

the regulations relating to the erection of buildings and subdivision of land (s 109C(1)(b)). The certifying authority must be satisfied that the requirements of any regulations relating to erection of buildings or subdivision of land are met, and that any required long service levy has been paid (s 109F(1)). A construction certificate cannot be issued after the building work or subdivision work to which it relates has been physically commenced on the land (s 109F(1A)).

An *occupation certificate* authorises the occupation and use of a new building or a change of building use for an existing building (s 109C(1)(c)). There are two types of occupation certificates: an interim occupation certificate or a final occupation certificate (s 109H), and occupation or use of a new building is not permitted unless an occupation certificate has been issued (s 109M). A change of building use also requires an occupation certificate (s 109N).

A *subdivision certificate* authorises the registration of a plan of subdivision (s 109C(1)(d)). The certifying authority must be satisfied of a range of matters listed in s 109J(1), which includes whether the applicant has complied with the conditions of any development consent. If subdivision work is required for the subdivision, the certifying authority must be satisfied that the work has been completed, or that agreement has been reached for payment for work to be completed by the consent authority, or for security for work to be carried out by the applicant (s 109J(2)).

Compliance certificates, construction certificates and occupation certificates can be issued by a consent authority, the council or an accredited certifier. A subdivision certificate can be issued by the consent authority or council, if the subdivision is the subject of development consent. If the subdivision is not the subject of development consent, the subdivision certificate can only be issued by the council. For subdivision carried out by or on behalf of the Crown or a prescribed person, the subdivision certificate can be issued by the Crown or prescribed person, or any person acting on their behalf. If an EPI identifies subdivision as being of a kind for which an accredited certifier can issue a subdivision certificate, the subdivision certificate can be issued by an accredited certifier (s 109D).

Part 8 of the EPAR deals with certification of development. In particular, cll 145 and 146 apply to the issue of a construction certificate. A certifying authority must not issue a construction certificate for building work unless satisfied:

- that the plans and specifications for the building include such matters as each relevant BASIX certificate requires;
- that the design and construction of the building are not inconsistent with the development consent;
- that the proposed building will comply with the relevant requirements of the Building Code of Australia. (cl 145(1))

A certifying authority must not issue a construction certificate for subdivision work unless satisfied that the design and construction of the work are not inconsistent with the development consent (cl 145(2)). A certifying authority must not issue a construction certificate for building work or subdivision work under a development consent unless satisfied that each condition or agreement requiring the provision of security, each condition requiring the payment of a monetary contribution or levy, and each other condition of the development consent that must be complied with before the issue of a construction certificate may be issued, has been complied with (cl 146).

The Land and Environment Court has held that the limitation imposed in Pt 4A of the EPAA and in EPAR cl 145 on the power of a certifying authority to issue a construction certificate by reference to the satisfaction of the certifying authority treats that satisfaction according to a subjective standard. That is, a certifier who in fact is satisfied that the design and construction of a building is not inconsistent with the relevant development consent does not commit an offence against s 109ZH of the EPAA, which makes it an offence to make any statement that is false or misleading in a material particular in connection with the issue of a Pt 4A certificate.[53] Further, the reference to the satisfaction of the certifying authority as to consistency or compliance means that judicial review challenges to the issue of a certificate are limited. The court must determine whether the certifying authority was in fact satisfied of the relevant matters, and the formation of that opinion may be challenged on the basis that it is manifestly unreasonable. However, if the certifying authority is in fact satisfied, the court has no role in determining whether or not there is consistency or compliance.[54]

Amendments to the EPAA made by the *Environmental Planning Legislation Amendment Act 2006* will significantly alter this position. Those amendments have removed the references to the satisfaction of the certifying authority in ss 109F, 109G, 109H and 109J, and specify that construction, compliance, occupation and subdivision certificates must not be issued unless the relevant requirements are met. At the time of writing the amendments are not in force, as amendments to the EPAR are required to remove equivalent references to the satisfaction of the certifying authority. Once these amendments come into effect, it is likely that the Land and Environment Court will need to reconsider whether consistency or compliance is a jurisdictional fact, that is, a matter which the court must decide, in determining challenges to the issue of Pt 4A certificates.

Accredited Certifiers

The framework for accrediting, auditing and investigating, private certifiers is, at the time of writing, provided in Pt 4A of the Act. The *Building Professionals Act 2005* (BPA) will replace those provisions when it comes into effect, expected to be in 2007. Under the BPA the Building Professionals Board will replace four accreditation bodies, the Department of Planning, Engineers Australia, Planning Institute of Australia, and the Professional Surveyors Occupational Association, in the role of accrediting private certifiers. The Building Professionals Board will also take on the role of processing complaints, auditing and investigating the conduct of private certifiers, and disciplinary proceedings.

Appeals and review

If the consent authority is a council, an applicant for development consent can request the council to review its determination of the application, other than an application for a complying development certificate, or an application in respect of designated development, integrated development or an application by the Crown

53 *Warringah Council v Moy* [2005] NSWLEC 416.

54 *Lesnewski v Mosman Municipal Council* [2004] NSWLEC 99, affirmed *Lesnewski v Mosman Municipal Council* [2005] NSWCA 99.

(EPAA s 82A). The determination cannot be reviewed after the time for appealing the determination to the LEC has expired, unless an appeal has been lodged, or after any appeal has been disposed of by the LEC (s 82A(2A)). The council can confirm or change its determination (s 82A(4A).

The LEC has jurisdiction to consider applications for review of development consent decisions on the merits, and challenges to the legality of the development decision-making process.

Merits appeals

As discussed in Chapter 1, appeals against decisions made under the EPAA are included in Class 1 of the LEC jurisdiction, and are heard by one or more Commissioners or by a Judge (*Land and Environment Court Act 1979* (LECA s 33). These appeals are appeals on the merits, which means that the court takes a fresh look at the issues, and exercises all the powers and discretions of the original decision-maker. The court has the power to substitute a decision for that of the original decision-maker, and can have regard to fresh or additional evidence that was not before the original decision-maker (LECA s 39).

Developer appeals

The applicant for, or holder of, development consent can appeal to the LEC against the following decisions:

- refusal of an application for extension of development consent granted for less than five years (EPAA s 95A(3));
- refusal of application to modify a development consent granted by the consent authority or the court (ss 96(6), 96AA(3));
- revocation or modification of the development consent (s 96A(5));
- determination of application for development consent (s 97(1));
- imposition, or refusal to release, security (s 98A(1));
- refusal to issue a construction certificate, a final occupation certificate or a subdivision certificate, or to issue a construction certificate subject to conditions (s 109K(1));
- refusal to issue a building certificate (s 149F(1)).

The right to appeal under s 97 against the consent authority's determination of an application for development consent can include an appeal against a decision to refuse consent, or conditions imposed, and can include an appeal against any decision made on internal review under s 82A. The time within which the appeal must be brought varies, in some instances being 40 days (modification applications under s 96), in others, three months (revocation or modification of development consent) and in others, 12 months (appeals against refusal of consent, or conditions, under s 97).

Objector appeals

A person who has made a submission in writing objecting to an application for designated development can appeal against a determination to grant consent (EPAA s 98). Such an appeal must be lodged within 28 days after notice of the decision is given. An objector can appeal, with leave, against a decision relating to an application for modification of a development consent for designated development, also within 28 days (s 96(4)).

Enforcement and judicial review

As discussed in Chapter 1, the LEC has jurisdiction (Class 4) to deal with applications for enforcement of the provisions of the EPAA and other environmental laws, and applications for review of the exercise of functions and the making of decisions under planning or environmental laws (LECA s 20(1), (2)). Planning and environmental laws include the EPAA, the *Coastal Protection Act 1979*, the *Contaminated Land Management Act 1997*, the *Environmentally Hazardous Chemicals Act 1985*, the *Heritage Act 1977*, certain Parts of the *Local Government Act 1993*, the *National Parks and Wildlife Act 1974*, the *Native Vegetation Act 2003*, the *Ozone Protection Act 1989*, the *Pesticides Act 1999*, the *Protection of the Environment Operations Act 1997* and the *Threatened Species Conservation Act 1995* (LECA s 20(3)).

Enforcement proceedings can be brought by any person to remedy or restrain a breach of the Act (EPAA s 123). A breach of the Act may include the carrying out of development without having the required consent, or failure to comply with the terms of a development consent. The court may also be asked to determine whether a development consent, or any conditions imposed by it, are valid. Judicial review of development control decision-making focuses on whether the decision-maker has exceeded the limits of the powers conferred under the legislation. The court has upheld several challenges based on a failure to comply with procedural obligations, for example, the notification provisions applicable to advertised development and designated development. Notification requirements are regarded as an important part of the process of promoting public participation referred to in the objects of the EPAA, and failure to comply with those requirements will invalidate any development consent granted.[55] Not all procedural defects will result in the invalidity of a development consent, and the test for determining the issue of validity is to ask whether it was the purpose of the legislation that an act done in breach of a legislative provision should be invalid.[56] For example, failure to provide a statement of environmental effects with a DA will not necessarily invalidate a development consent granted, so long as the consent authority has properly considered the matters required under s 79C of the EPAA (see p 76).[57] Decisions involving the formation of an opinion by the consent authority require that the consent authority has, in fact, formed the relevant state of satisfaction. Such decisions must also not be affected by any material misdirection in law, and must not be so unreasonable that no reasonable decision-maker could properly have arrived at the decision.[58]

If the court determines that one or more conditions imposed on development consent are invalid, it must determine whether those conditions can be severed, or whether the invalidity of the conditions invalidates the consent as a whole. This is

55 *Johnson v Lake Macquarie City Council* (1996) 91 LGERA 331.

56 *Project Blue Sky Inc v Australian Broadcasting Authority* (1998) 194 CLR 355.

57 *Cranky Rock Road Action Group Inc v Cowra Shire Council* [2006] NSWCA 339.

58 *King v Bathurst Regional Council* [2006] NSWLEC 505.

determined by asking whether severing the invalid condition would leave the consent operating differently from the manner in which the whole would have operated, or whether the condition under challenge relates to matters fundamental to the development or goes to the root of the planning permission itself.[59]

Section 102 applies to development consents granted by the Minister, and states that the only requirements of the Act that are mandatory in connection with the validity of a development consent are those listed in s 102(2):

- a requirement that a development application to carry out designated development and its accompanying information be publicly exhibited for the minimum period of time;
- a requirement that a development application to carry out development, being development, other than designated development, to which some or all of the public notification provisions apply, be publicly exhibited for the minimum period of time;
- a requirement that a development application to carry out advertised development and its accompanying information be publicly exhibited for the minimum period of time prescribed by the regulations.

The term 'mandatory' as used in s 102 (which was introduced in 1997) reflects previous case law which distinguished between 'mandatory' legislative requirements, which had to be complied with strictly, and 'directory' requirements, where substantial compliance would suffice. Since the decision of the High Court in *Project Blue Sky Inc v Australian Broadcasting Authority*,[60] the courts have posed the question as being whether there is a legislative purpose to invalidate any act that fails to comply with the requirements. In *Association for Berowra Creek Inc v Minister for Planning*,[61] Lloyd J held that s 102 does not apply where the defect in the development consent amounts to a jurisdictional error. In that case, which concerned a consent for extensions to a marina and car parking, the Minister had failed to classify the proposed development as designated development, which was a jurisdictional error, and so s 102 did not prevent the court from making a declaration that the consent was invalid.

Whether or not a defect in the decision-making process results in the LEC making a declaration or determination that a development consent is invalid may depend on the timing of the application for review, and the exercise by the court of its discretion, both general and in the exercise of the powers conferred by s 25B of the EPAA.

Time limitation

Section 101 provides:

> If public notice of the granting of a consent or a complying development certificate is given in accordance with the regulations by a consent authority or an accredited certifier, the validity of the consent or certificate cannot be questioned in any legal proceedings except those commenced in the Court by any person at any time before the expiration of 3 months from the date on which public notice was so given.

59 *Maitland City Council v Anambah Homes Pty Ltd* [2005] NSWCA 455.
60 (1998) 194 CLR 355.
61 [2003] NSWLEC 38.

The public notice referred to in s 101 is a notice published in a local newspaper describing the land and the development the subject of the application, which states that the development consent is available for public inspection at the consent authority's principal office (EPAR cl 124).

The courts generally construe provisions such as s 101 which attempt to limit or restrict judicial review strictly. There has been a divergence of views in the LEC, with some decisions supporting the view that challenges based on bad faith or manifest jurisdictional error could still be made after three months,[62] while others have held that no challenge could be made.[63] More recently, the Court of Appeal has considered s 101, and there is now authority to support the construction that s 101 allows challenge to the validity of a development consent – on any ground before three months, and after three months where the consent does not conform to the threefold principle in *R v Hickman; ex parte Fox & Clinton*.[64] Under this principle, decisions could be challenged where it is manifest that the decision is not a bona fide attempt to exercise the power; where it does not relate to the subject-matter of the legislation; or where it is not reasonably capable of reference to the power given to the decision-maker. It is also likely that s 101 would not protect against breach of, or non-compliance with, a restriction or requirement which is construed as being of such significance in the legislative scheme that it constitutes a limitation or requirement that is variously expressed in the authorities as 'essential', 'indispensable', 'imperative' or 'inviolable'.[65] The precise application of these principles is a matter of debate, in particular the extent to which the alleged defect must be apparent on the face of the document.[66]

Discretion

If the LEC decides that a development consent is invalid because of failure to comply with preliminary steps, whether or not those preliminary steps should have been taken by the consent authority or by any other person or body, it may, instead of declaring or determining that the consent is invalid, make an order suspending the operation of the consent in whole or in part, and specifying terms the compliance with which will validate the consent (LECA ss 25A, 25B(1)). Those terms can include a requirement to carry out again steps already carried out, or steps not yet carried out, or requiring other acts, matters or things to be done or omitted (LECA s 25B(2)). Section 25A does not apply to all causes of invalidity, and there is a divergence of views in the LEC on the ambit of the term 'steps preliminary to the granting of a development consent'. For example, lack of finality and certainty in a development consent were held not to result in invalidity as a consequence of a step preliminary to the granting of the development consent in *Glowpace Pty Ltd v South Sydney City Council*.[67] In *Centro Properties Pty Ltd v Warringah Council (No 2)*[68] and *Woolworths Ltd v Wyong Shire Council*,[69] Pain J held that failure to consider a

62 *Woolworths Ltd & Kenlida Pty Ltd v Bathurst City Council* (1987) 63 LGRA 55.

63 *Coles Supermarkets Australia Pty Ltd v Minister for Urban Affairs and Planning* (1996) 90 LGERA 341.

64 (1945) 70 CLR 598.

65 *Lesnewski v Mosman Municipal Council* [2005] NSWCA 99.

66 *Maitland City Council v Anambah Homes Pty Ltd* [2005] NSWCA 455.

67 (2000) 111 LGERA 84.

68 (2003) 132 LGERA 45.

69 [2005] NSWLEC 607.

mandatory matter under s 79C of the EPAA is not a preliminary step, but rather is part of the decision. A broader construction of the scope of ss 25A and 25B was adopted by Lloyd J in *Kindimindi Investments Pty Ltd v Lane Cove Council*.[70] In *GPT Ltd v Wollongong City Council (No 2)*,[71] Biscoe J suggested an approach which would limit the power in s 25B to curing procedural and not substantive defects. While the LEC is required to consider making an order under s 25B instead of declaring or determining that a consent is invalid (LECA s 25E), it still retains a discretion. The court has refused to exercise the discretion where the step (consideration of a draft SEPP) would have necessitated the re-opening of the whole of the consideration of the application.[72]

The LEC has a general discretion to refuse to make an order. Factors such as the public interest in enforcement of the law, and impact on the respondent and others, will be relevant.[73]

70 [2006] NSWLEC 399.

71 [2006] NSWLEC 401.

72 *Noble v Cowra Shire Council* (2001) 114 LGERA 440; *Centro Properties Ltd v Hurstville City Council* [2006] NSWLEC 78; *Belmore Residents' Action Group Inc v Canterbury City Council* [2006] NSWLEC 530.

73 *Warringah Shire Council v Sedevcic* (1987) 10 NSWLR 335; *ACR Trading Pty Ltd v Fat-Sel Pty Ltd* (1987) 11 NSWLR 67; *Liverpool City Council v Roads and Traffic Authority* (1991) 74 LGRA 265.

4

ENVIRONMENTAL ASSESSMENT

This chapter explains the framework for assessing development that requires consent or approval, or is to be undertaken by a public authority. In New South Wales, this involves examining the procedures in Pts 3A, 4 and 5 of the *Environmental Planning and Assessment Act 1979* (NSW) (EPAA). This is done in Section 1 of this chapter. We are only concerned in this Section with the procedures and documentation that may be required. Chapter 3 discussed the determination of a development application.

In addition to assessment under the EPAA, a proposal may also require assessment and approval by the Commonwealth under the *Environment Protection and Biodiversity Conservation Act 1999* (Cth) (EPBCA). Section 2 of this chapter examines the Commonwealth's role under this Act.

At Commonwealth level, assessment of environmental impact performs the function of identifying those actions that require Commonwealth environmental approval. The EPBCA carves out the Commonwealth's role in approving actions, whether taken in the Commonwealth, a State or Territory, by reference to matters of national environmental significance, as well as to Commonwealth actions and Commonwealth land. However, in order to trigger the assessment and approval requirements, an action must be likely to have a significant impact on a matter protected by the Act. Environmental assessment is thus pivotal.

At State level, environmental planning instruments (EPIs) identify, through zoning, locality planning or otherwise, those developments that require government approval. In deciding whether to approve the carrying out of development, assessment of environmental impact will frequently be central. Where the discretion is at large, it will provide the overarching considerations. An EPI may reduce or remove discretion by fixing standards or requirements, or imposing prohibitions, that resolve some or all of the issues in advance of particular applications. Through prior planning, jurisdictional constraints may be imposed on decision-makers at the development control stage. For example, zone objectives or environmental performance criteria may have to be satisfied before assessing a particular proposal on its merits. These can serve to both inform and confine the discretionary issues in assessing environmental impact. But in the absence of an absolute prohibition or an inflexible standard, the discretion to approve development will invariably involve, to varying degrees, an assessment of the environmental consequences of proposed development. The focus of assessment, depending on the nature of the proposal, will range from weighing up the acceptability of likely impacts to determining how, if at all, uncertain impacts, which threaten serious or irreversible environmental damage, can be prevented.

At the development control stage, the issue for lawmakers is how best to assist consent or approval authorities in making an informed decision in the light of likely or uncertain environmental consequences. The choices for the decision-maker at this stage are likely to be limited. A contest between the applicant, the consent authority and interested members of the public has been engaged. If prior policy-making or planning was not adequately informed by environmental considerations, the contest may well be intractable. Yet it is at this stage that the legislative tools for informing decision-makers are at their most developed. Development control legislation has long included requirements for environmental impact statements and other documentation of impacts, and opportunities for public participation and commissions of inquiry, at the time of approving physical actions or the use of land.

Decision-makers may also be assisted by the precautionary principle – not only in determining the application, but also in deciding whether documentation of environmental impacts is required and is adequate. The precautionary principle is a method of decision-making that guides assessment where there are threats of serious or irreversible environmental damage and scientific uncertainty. It shifts the focus of assessment from the acceptability of the likely impacts to preventing threatened impacts. The precautionary principle is of considerable utility in exposing for scrutiny the types of uncertainty that must be factored into assessment and in prompting decision-makers to examine technical and scientific information more critically. Application of the principle helps to ensure that uncertainties attending environmental concerns do not exclude them from due consideration along with other priorities.[1] In particular, as a decision-making tool the precautionary principle carries implications relating to evidentiary burdens, the presentation of scientific and technical material, the examination of experts, and the sourcing and weighing of evidence.[2]

Environmental impact assessment law has served important educative and democratic purposes. It has enhanced the internalisation of environmental considerations by proponents and public decision-makers, and it has underlined the need for full environmental disclosure and public discussion of development proposals. While the achievement of these objectives may be flawed, the purposes remain valid and crucial. Mechanisms are available to enhance the reliability and independence of environmental assessment and the accountability of public and private decision-makers. Poor science, token public participation and flabby political will can be addressed through a range of action-forcing and reporting measures and cultural changes. The fatal flaw in environmental impact assessment law is, however, its project focus. Both the *Environmental Planning and Assessment Act 1979* (NSW) and the *Environment Protection and Biodiversity Conservation Act 1999* (Cth) are predominantly concerned with mechanisms to assess the impacts of individual projects, development proposals, activities or actions. It is well understood that the environment is not impacted by a single project, but by the interaction and cumulative impact of decisions, actions and natural processes, spatially and temporally. Cumulative impacts and long-term affects cannot be effectively addressed at the stage of implementing a project. Further, project-by-project assessment pre-empts future decisions on the type and timing of development, and increases the cost burden of

---

1 See Jacqueline Peel, *The Precautionary Principle in Practice* (Federation Press, 2005).

2 See especially *Telstra Corporation Ltd v Hornsby Shire Council* (2006) 146 LGERA 10.

environmental mitigation.[3] Choosing the no-go option and evaluating alternative uses of land is highly constrained when assessing an individual project in the context of existing development and permissive environmental planning instruments.

Requirements to consider an environmental impact statement when approving single projects have deflected attention from the crucial need to subject choices made at the policy or planning level to assessment for their environmental impact. Sustainable policy and decision-making requires this. An integrated perspective, which transcends time and space, can only be achieved at this level. It is widely acknowledged that strategic environmental assessment is where attention should be focused.[4] This would certainly include land use planning.[5] It may also extend to the formal and open environmental assessment of proposed legislation[6] or international agreements, sectoral and cross-sectoral issues, and the adoption of new technologies.

As discussed in Chapter 2, provision is made under the EPAA for environmental studies as part of the regional and local environmental planning process (ss 41, 57). However, this is not mandatory where an existing EPI is being amended in whole or in part, unless the Minister (in the case of REPs) or the Director-General (in the case of LEPs) directs otherwise (s 74(2)). Where a study is undertaken, it must be a study 'of the land', which requires assessing alternative uses of the land rather than a particular proposal, even in the case of a spot-rezoning.[7] Further, unlike environmental impact statements, the study must be prepared by, or on behalf of, the planning authority, rather than a developer.[8]

Recent amendments to the *Threatened Species Conservation Act 1995* (NSW) (TSCA) encourage planning authorities, particularly local councils, to address biodiversity conservation at the planning stage. The incentive is that the Minister for the Environment can confer biodiversity certification on an EPI if satisfied that the EPI, in addition to any other relevant measures to be taken, will lead to the overall improvement or maintenance of biodiversity values (s 126G). Biodiversity values include threatened species, populations and ecological communities, and their habitats. The effect of certification is, subject to the conditions of certification, to dispense with the requirements for species impact statements and related concurrence requirements at the development control stage (s 126I). Biodiversity certification may be used in conjunction with 'the biobanking scheme' as a means to offset impacts of development on biodiversity (Pt 7A). Certification and the biobanking scheme are discussed in Chapter 8.

---

3 David James, 'Environmental Impact Assessment: Improving Processes and Techniques' (1995) 2 *Australian Journal of Environmental Management* 78 at 80-81.

4 See Ralf Buckley, 'Strategic Environmental Assessment' (1997) 14 *EPLJ* 174; S Marsden and S Dovers (eds), *Strategic Environmental Assessment in Australasia* (Federation Press, 2002); C Wood, 'Strategic Assessment in Australia and New Zealand' (1992) 7 *Project Appraisal* 143; John Court, Colin Wright and Alasdair Guthrie, 'Environmental Assessment and Sustainability: Are We Ready for the Challenge?' (1996) 3 *Australian Journal of Environmental Management* 42.

5 See AL Brown and GT McDonald, 'From Environmental Impact Assessment to Environmental Design and Planning' (1995) 2 *Australian Journal of Environmental Management* 65.

6 See Simon Marsden, 'Applying EIA to Legislative Proposals: Practical Solutions to Advance ESD in Commonwealth and State Policy-Making' (1997) 14 *EPLJ* 159. Regulatory impact assessment of statutory rules is required by the *Subordinate Legislation Act 1989* (NSW)

7 *Burns Philp Trustee Co Ltd v Wollongong City Council* (1983) 49 LGRA 420.

8 If the study is of particular land to enable the carrying out of development on that land, a council may recover from the proposed developer the costs and expenses incurred in preparing the study, provided the developer agrees: EPAA s 57(5); EPAR cl 15.

Section 1: Environmental Planning and Assessment Act 1979 (NSW)

Key terms

EPAA Parts 3A, 4 and 5

The structure of the EPAA reflects the acknowledgement at the time of its drafting that all development requiring government approval and public development should undergo some level of assessment. Parts 4 and 5 of the EPAA deal with project assessment. Development requiring consent is assessed under Pt 4. Part 5 of the Act catches development not requiring consent under the Act, but requiring some other approval, or being undertaken by or on behalf of a public authority. Both Pts 4 and 5 include requirements for environmental impact statements (EISs); but they are mutually exclusive. A development proposal is assessed under either Pt 4 or Pt 5.

This structure has become unsettled over the years with the introduction of exempt and complying development and in 2005 with the enactment of Pt 3A. Exempt and complying developments are not subject to environmental impact assessment. Part 3A provides a mechanism for the Planning Minister to remove from the framework of Pts 4 and 5, projects which in the opinion of the Minister are of state or regional environmental planning significance or public development which would otherwise be assessed under Pt 5. Under Pt 3A, the form of environmental assessment is a matter of discretion not prescription, but it must nonetheless be undertaken.

Different terminology

Parts 3A, 4 and 5 use different terminology to describe the proposal, the person proposing to carry out the proposal and the decision-maker. Under Pt 3A, the proposal is referred to as a *project,* the person proposing to carry out the project is referred to as the *proponent* and the approval authority is the Minister. Under Pt 4, the proposal is referred to as *development,* the person proposing to carry out the development is referred to as the *applicant* and the decision-maker is the *consent authority*. Under Pt 5, the proposal is referred to as an *activity,* the person proposing to carry out the activity is the *proponent* and the decision-maker is the referred to as the *determining authority*. A determining authority may also be the proponent.

The terms 'project', 'development' and 'activity' bear a similar meaning in terms of the actions to which they apply,[9] namely –

- the use of land;
- the subdivision of land;
- the erection of a building;
- the carrying out of a work;
- the demolition of a building or work;

9 EPAA ss 4 ('development'), 75A ('project'), 110 ('activity').

- any other act, matter or thing referred to in s 26 that is controlled by an environmental planning instrument (EPI) (for the purposes of Pt 4) or that is prescribed by the regulations (for the purposes of Pt 5).

Levels of environmental assessment

All development requiring consent or approval must be assessed for its environmental impact. A general duty to take into account environmental impact is imposed on consent authorities under Pt 4 s 79C(1) and on determining authorities under Pt 5 s 111. Although there is no such general duty imposed on the Minister under Pt 3A, environmental impact is an implied mandatory consideration in making decisions under that Part.[10] Further, environmental assessment must be informed by the objects of the EPAA which encourage ecologically sustainable development (ESD).[11]

To assist in the duty to consider environmental impact, the EPAA requires particular proposals under Pts 4 and 5 to be accompanied by a formal evaluation or assessment of environmental impact prepared by or on behalf of the applicant or proponent. The Act includes requirements for two types of document: an *environmental impact statement* (EIS) and a *species impact statement* (SIS).

Decision-makers may also be assisted by the report and recommendations of a public inquiry. Under the EPAA, the Minister has a discretion to appoint a commission of inquiry for a variety of purposes, including to inquire into the environmental aspects of a proposal under Pts 3A, 4 and 5 (s 119) the Minister may derive assistance from an Independent Hearing and Assessment Panel.

It should be noted that EISs and SISs are the only types of assessment documents provided for in the Act and that the majority of development applications will not be accompanied by documentation of this type. The binary nature of the decision as to whether a formal assessment process must and has been followed – yes or no – creates dilemmas,[12] including when assessing the adequacy of the assessment document.[13] As discussed below, failure to comply with the requirements relating to EISs and SISs leads to the invalidity of any consent or approval.

The application form prescribed in Sch 1 to the *Environmental Planning and Assessment Regulation 2000* (EPAR) for development that requires consent under Pt 4 requires the application to include a statement of environmental effects (SEE). Failure to do so, however, will not lead to invalidity.[14] Under Pt 5, guidelines issued for public authorities other than local councils, encourage the discipline of documenting consideration of environmental factors by determining authorities, which may extend to a preparing a review of environmental factors (REF) in order to determine the nature and extent of the authority's obligations.[15] A REF, however, has no legislative basis.

---

10 *Gray v Minister for Planning* [2006] NSWLEC 720 at [115] per Pain J.

11 See *Telstra Corporation Ltd v Hornsby Shire Council* (2006) 146 LGERA 10; *Gray v Minister for Planning* [2006] NSWLEC 720 esp at [114]-[115], [117] per Pain J.

12 Arthur Conacher and Jeanette Conacher, *Environmental Planning and Management in Australia* (Oxford University Press, 2000) at 227.

13 *Bell v Minister of Urban Affairs & Planning* (1997) 95 LGERA 86.

14 *Cranky Rock Road Action Group Inc v Cowra Shire Council* [2006] NSWCA 339.

15 NSW Department of Planning, *Is an EIS required? – Best Practice Guidelines for Part 5 of the EPAA 1979* (1995).

The types of development application that must be accompanied by an EIS or SIS are discussed in the following sections. The final part of this Section discusses some key issues relating to environmental impact assessment procedures. In that context, the matters that must addressed in an EIS or SIS are outlined.

Triggering the requirement for an EIS or SIS

There are two approaches to identifying which proposals should require formal documentation of their environmental impact. One approach is to identify particular types of development – to list them or categorise them. The other approach is to require an assessment of each proposal to determine whether it is likely to significantly impact on the environment. Both approaches are used in the EPAA.

Under Pt 4 of the EPAA, the requirement for an EIS is triggered using the listing or categorical approach. Classes of development which require an EIS are referred to as *designated development*. Characterisation of development as designated development in discussed under the heading, 'EPAA Part 4 – Development assessment', below. Under Pt 5, each proposed activity must be assessed to determine whether it is *likely to significantly affect the environment*.

The requirement for a SIS, which may be required under Pt 4 or Pt 5, is triggered if the proposal:

- is on land that is, or is a part of, critical habitat;
- is likely to significantly affect threatened species, populations or ecological communities, or their habitats.

In the final part of this Section, which discusses key issues relating to environmental impact procedures, the expression 'likely to significantly affect the environment' is discussed.

Threatened species, biodiversity certification of EPIs and biobanking

The terms *critical habitat* and *threatened species, populations or ecological communities* take their meaning from the TSCA and the *Fisheries Management Act 1994* (FMA) (EPAA s 4(1)). They are identified and listed under those Acts: see Chapter 8. For the purpose of the EPAA, a reference to 'threatened species, populations and ecological communities' does not include a reference to any vulnerable ecological community. This exclusion does not apply to any threatened species or endangered population that forms part of a vulnerable ecological community (EPAA s 5D).

In the introduction to this chapter it was pointed out that recent amendments to the TSCA empower the Minister for the Environment to confer biodiversity certification on an EPI if satisfied that the EPI will lead to the overall improvement or maintenance of biodiversity values (TSCA s 126G). Biodiversity values include threatened species, populations and ecological communities, and their habitats. The certification may be limited to specified threatened species, populations and communities or to specified parts of the land to which the EPI applies, and it may be limited to specified development or activities (TSCA s 126H). The effect of certification is, subject to the conditions of certification, to dispense with the requirements for SISs and related concurrence requirements under Pts 4 and 5 of the EPAA (TSCA s 126I).

Biodiversity certification may also be conferred on the native vegetation reform package, with the effect that development consent to clearing of native vegetation that has the benefit of biodiversity certification does not require the preparation of a SIS or consultation between Ministers.[16] An order conferring biodiversity certification on the native vegetation reform package, but excluding private native forestry, took effect on 1 December 2005.

The TSCA amendments also introduced a biodiversity banking and offsets scheme (TSCA Pt 7A). Under this scheme, biobank sites may be established by means of biobanking agreements entered into between the Minister and the owners of the land concerned (ss 127D–127L). Management actions carried out, or proposed to be carried out, on biobank sites that improve biodiversity values create tradeable biodiversity credits that can be used to offset the impact of proposed development on biodiversity values (ss 127V–127ZI).[17] A biobanking statement may be issued in respect of any development that is 'development for which biobanking is available' – that is to say, development that requires development consent under Pt 4, an activity to which Pt 5 applies, and Pt 3A projects (s 127ZJ). The Director-General may only issue a biobanking statement if the proposed development will 'improve or maintain biodiversity values' (s 127ZL(1), (2)). This is determined on the basis of an assessment of the development in accordance with the biobanking assessment methodology, including the number and class of biodiversity credits to be retired as an offset against the negative impact of the development on biodiversity values. The party proposing to carry out development must demonstrate that all cost effective on-site measures to minimise any negative impact of the development on biodiversity values will be carried out (s 127ZL(4)(d)). The statement may apply generally to the proposed development or may be limited to a specified aspect or a specified part of the land or by reference to its potential impact on specified biodiversity values. The effect of a biobanking statement is that the development described in the statement is taken to be development that is not likely to significantly affect any threatened species, population or ecological community or its habitat (ss 127ZO, 127ZP). Thus the requirements relating to SISs under Pts 4 and 5, and the related requirements for concurrence or consultation, do not apply to the proposal. Further, the consent authority under Pt 4, or the determining authority under Pt 5, is not required to take into consideration the likely impact of the development or activity on biodiversity values.[18] If consent or approval is granted, any conditions specified in the biobanking statement, including conditions relating to the retirement of credits, must be imposed as conditions of the consent or approval.

Biodiversity certification and the biobanking scheme, including the biobanking assessment methodology, are discussed in Chapter 8.

EPAA Part 3A – Projects determined by the Minister

Introduction

Part 3A authorises the Planning Minister to determine development proposals for infrastructure or other projects which, in the Minister's opinion, are of State or

16 *Native Vegetation Act 2003* s 14(4); TSCA s 126D.

17 Management actions under a biobanking agreement for which biodiversity credits may be created are taken to be exempt development for the purposes of the EPAA: TSCA s 127K.

18 TSCA s 127ZO(5), qualifying EPAA s 79C; and TSCA s 127ZP(7), qualifying EPAA s 111.

regional environmental planning significance.[19] The Minister declares the projects to which Pt 3A applies. Streamlined procedures are provided for approval of Pt 3A projects. In particular, the form of environmental assessment is not prescribed but rather tailored by the Director-General to the particular proposal. Concept plans may be approved following a procedure similar to that for projects, and subsequent assessment lies in the discretion of the Minister. A range of requirements and powers under other regulatory regimes are limited in their application to a Pt 3A project. Appeals and civil enforcement proceedings are restricted. An even more streamlined procedure is provided for determining 'critical infrastructure projects'. Any project to which Pt 3A applies may also be declared to be a critical infrastructure project if, in the Minister's opinion, the project is essential for the State for economic, environmental or social reasons (s 75C).

Part 3A was inserted in the Act in August 2005. It replaces the 'State significant development' provisions in Pt 4, which empowered the Minister to call-in a development application, or call-in prohibited development. Projects for which the Minister is the consent authority are now for the most part processed under Pt 3A. Pt 3A does not preclude the Minister from being identified as the consent authority for development assessed under Pt 4. For example, *SEPP (Major Projects) 2005* identifies in Sch 6 development requiring consent under Pt 4 for which the Minister is the consent authority. Further, the Minister is the consent authority under Pt 4 for proposed designated development in respect of which the Minister has directed that an inquiry be held by a commission of inquiry (s 80(7)).

Relationship of Part 3A to other Parts of the Act

Parts 4 and 5 of the EPAA do not apply to an approved project, including the declaration of the project as a Pt 3A project and any approval or other requirements under Pt 3A for the project (s 75R(1)). Further, regional environmental plans (REPs) and local environmental plans (LEPs) have no application to an approved Pt 3A project (s 75R(3)). With respect to critical infrastructure projects, even State environmental planning policies (SEPPs) do not apply to the project unless the SEPP expressly so provides (s 75R(2)).

When Pt 3A was initially inserted, it precluded approval being granted to a Pt 3A project or concept plan for a project (other than critical infrastructure) if the project would be 'wholly prohibited' under an EPI.[20] This raised uncertainty. Could the Minister grant consent to the whole of a project provided any one of its purposes was permissible or should the project be characterised by reference to its dominant purpose? The Act was amended in 2006 to give primacy to s 75J(3), which provides that EPIs (other than SEPPs) do not apply to or in respect of an approved project. In deciding whether or not to grant approval, the Minister may, but is not required to, take into account the provisions of any EPI that would otherwise apply.[21] Further,

---

19 The State Department publishes a NSW *State Development Monitor* which provides detailed statistical and case studies about decisions made by the Department and Minister for Planning on development proposals: *New South Wales State Development Monitor 2005-2006* (NSW Government, Department of Planning: September 2006) <http://www.planning.nsw.gov.au/corporate_publications/pdf/nsw_development_monitor_2005-06.pdf> (accessed 23 September 2006).

20 EPAA ss 75J(3) (projects), 75O(3) (concept plans). These subsections were replaced by *Environmental Planning Legislation Amendment Act 2006* (NSW).

21 EPAA ss 75J(3) (projects), 75O(3) (concept plans).

the Minister may directly amend an EPI to authorise the carrying out of development that is an approved project, or development that is a project for which a concept plan has been approved (s 75R(3A)). This includes removing or modifying any restrictions or prohibitions on the project in the planning instrument. The exemption of Pt 3A projects from prohibitions in REPs and LEPs can be modified by regulation. The regulations may keep alive prohibitions in a REP or LEP by precluding approval for a class of project, other than a critical infrastructure project.[22]

A Pt 3A declaration can be made even if consent or approval has been granted under Pt 4 or Pt 5 (s 75ZA). This has the unusual effect of revoking the existing consent or approval, thus requiring a fresh consent to be obtained from the Minister under Pt 3A. The consent or approval is revived if the declaration is subsequently revoked without any approval of the project under Pt 3A (s 75ZA(2)).

The declaration of a project as a Pt 3A project can be amended or revoked at any time, including after the project has been approved (s 75B(5)). If the declaration is revoked after approval has been given under Pt 3A, the approval is taken to be a development consent for the project granted under Pt 4 (s 75ZA(3)).

Part 3A projects

The Minister may declare development to be a Pt 3A project by way of a SEPP or by order published in the *Gazette* (including an order amending a SEPP) (s 75B(1)). The declaration can apply to the carrying out of a particular development or class of development, or to development for a program or plan of works or activities. The Minister must be of the opinion that the project is of State or regional environmental planning significance. This jurisdictional requirement is not one which the courts have closely supervised,[23] thus giving the Minister an extremely broad discretion as to the projects for which the Minister is the approval authority. A further type of project that may be identified as a Pt 3A project is an activity under Pt 5 for which the proponent is also the determining authority, and which in the opinion of the proponent would require an EIS under that Part.

If only part of a development is declared to be a Pt 3A project, the other parts ('related development') are also taken to be a Pt 3A project and the development must be dealt with as a single project (s 75B(3)). This does not apply if the declaration is specifically limited to an aspect of the development or a particular period of carrying it out (s 75B(4)).

The Minister may declare a Pt 3A project to be a 'critical infrastructure project' if the Minister is of the opinion that the project is of a category that is essential to the State for economic, environmental or social reasons (s 75C). The declaration may be made at the time of declaring the project to be a Pt 3A project or at a later time, and need not use the same method (s 75C(2)). Special procedures apply to Pt 3A projects which have also been declared to be critical infrastructure. The Act contains a definition of 'major infrastructure development' but the definition is not expressly given any work to do. This is because any development that is declared to be a project to which Pt 3A applies may also be declared to be a critical infrastructure

---

22 EPAA ss 75J(3) (projects), 75O(3) (concept plans).

23 *Leichhardt Municipal Council v Minister for Planning* (1992) 78 LGERA 306; *Medway v Minister for Planning* (1993) 80 LGERA 121.

project, provided that the Minister is of the opinion that it is essential for the State for economic, environmental or social reasons.[24]

SEPP (Major Projects) 2005 identifies a range of Pt 3A projects and critical infrastructure. The SEPP is an improvement on the practice before 2005 which saw some 85 EPIs being gazetted under which the Minister was made the consent authority.

SEPP (Major Projects) 2005 describes the development to which it applies in different ways:

- Schedule 1 lists classes of development together with thresholds – for example, development that employs 20 or more people for the purpose of feedlots, piggeries, poultry egg or meat production or dairies.
- Schedule 2 identifies development on specified sites – for example, development for specified purposes within the coastal zone.
- Schedule 3 identifies State significant sites – for example, the Sydney Opera House, Lunar Park and Redfern-Waterloo Authority sites.
- Schedule 5 lists critical infrastructure projects – currently the Kurnell Desalination Plant and development for the purposes of redeveloping the Royal North Shore Hospital site and the Liverpool Hospital site.

Characterisation of a proposal to ascertain whether it falls within a Schedule depends on the Planning Minister's opinion.[25] If the Minister decides that the proposed project falls within the SEPP, the Minister in respect of some projects has a further discretion as to whether to call in the proposed project for determination under Pt 3A. For example, development for the purpose of residential, commercial or retail projects with a capital investment value of more than $50 million is not *per se* a project that must be processed under Pt 3A. The Minister must also form the view that the proposal is important in achieving State or regional planning objectives.[26]

The SEPP provides a procedure for identifying new State-significant sites,[27] but it is not a precondition of doing so.[28] The Minister may require the Director-General to undertake a study, or to make arrangements for a study to be undertaken, for the purpose of determining whether any development on the site should be declared to be a project to which Pt 3A applies and the appropriate development controls for the site. Any such study must assess, amongst other things, the suitability of the site for any proposed land use, taking into consideration the ESD principles and any State or regional planning strategy. The Director-General must make arrangements for the study to be publicly exhibited with an invitation to the public to make written submissions.

Proposals to create a State-significant site can be considered concurrently with a specific development proposal for the site, usually in the form of a concept plan. The

---

24 The definition of 'major infrastructure development' is development, whether or not carried out by a public authority, for the purpose of roads, railways, pipelines, electricity generation, electricity or gas transmission or distribution, sewerage treatment facilities, dams or water reticulation works, desalination plants, trading ports or other public utility undertakings: EPAA s 75A.

25 *SEPP (Major Projects) 2005* cll 6, 6A. Projects identified in the SEPP are not Pt 3A projects if they already have consent or approval under Pts 4 or 5 of the Act.

26 *SEPP (Major Projects) 2005* cl 13(1).

27 *SEPP (Major Projects) 2005* cl 8.

28 *SEPP (Major Projects) 2005* cl 8(6).

Department claims that this allows it to process planning changes in less than 12 months in contrast with the years it may take to process a draft LEP.[29]

Obtaining approval for Part 3A projects

The Minister is the approval authority for Pt 3A projects, including for projects for which the Minister is the proponent (s 75D). The person proposing to carry out all or part of the project is the proponent (s 75A).[30] On application to the Minister for approval, the Director-General must prepare the 'environmental assessment requirements' and notify the proponent of these requirements (s 75F). This is done in consultation with relevant public authorities and having regard to any published guidelines. The Director-General has a discretion as to the form of the environmental assessment, but that does not make environmental assessment discretionary. There must be some form of environmental assessment.[31] Importantly, in scoping the environmental assessment, the Director-General must exercise his or her discretion in accordance with the objects of the Act, which include the encouragement of ESD principles.[32]

The Director-General may require the proponent to include in the environmental assessment a statement of the commitments the proponent is prepared to make for environmental management and mitigation measures on the site (s 75F(6)), and these can be made conditions of any approval (s 75J(5)).

The public has the right to view the environmental assessment and make submissions (s 75H(3), (4)). Before accepting the environmental assessment for public exhibition, the Director-General must form a view as to whether it complies with the environmental assessment requirements for the project.[33] Unlike the more structured regime for environmental assessment under Pts 4 and 5, Pt 3A contains no objective criteria in terms of which the Director-General can be held accountable.[34] However, the Director-General must have regard to relevant matters and these include ESD principles.[35] In *Gray v Minister for Planning*,[36] Pain J held that the Director-General had failed to take into account intergenerational equity and the precautionary principle when he decided that the environmental assessment for a proposed coal mine was adequate, and that this constituted a failure to comply with a legal requirement. The environmental assessment that had been placed on public exhibition did not include an analysis of the potential greenhouse gas emissions from the burning of coal by third parties. Her Honour held that there was a sufficiently proximate link between the proposed mining and the emission of greenhouse gases to require that this be addressed in the assessment.[37]

After the public exhibition, the proponent may be required to respond to issues raised in the submissions (s 75H(6)). The proponent may also be required to prepare

29 *New South Wales State Development Monitor 2005-2006*, above n 19, at 15.

30 The Minister may certify a person to be a 'proponent'.

31 *Gray v Minister for Planning* [2006] NSWLEC 720 at [70] per Pain J.

32 Ibid at [115].

33 Ibid at [72] per Pain J.

34 Ibid at [79]-[82].

35 Ibid.

36 Ibid at [135], [126].

37 Ibid at [83]-[100].

a preferred project report outlining any proposed changes to minimise environmental impact, or to prepare a revised statement of commitments (s 75H(6)). If that entails significant changes to the 'nature of the project', the proponent may be required to make the preferred project report 'available to the public' (s 75H(7)).[38]

An Independent Hearing and Assessment Panel (IHAP) may be appointed to assess any aspect of the project, and must be appointed if the Minister is the proponent of the project (s 75G). The IHAP's role is advisory. It is not subject to the direction of the Minister. Experts, officers of the Minister's Department or officers of other public authorities may be appointed to the IHAP, provided they do not have regulatory functions in connection with the project. The name given to this tribunal is disingenuous. There is no requirement for it to hold hearings. It may invite submissions from 'interested persons' (s 75G(4)).

The Director-General must prepare a report to the Minister, which must include:[39]

- a copy of the proponent's environmental assessment and any preferred project report;
- any advice provided by public authorities;
- a copy of any report of a IHAP;
- a copy of or reference to the provisions of any SEPP that substantially govern the carrying out of the project;
- a copy of or reference to the provisions of any EPI that would, but for Pt 3A, substantially govern the carrying out of the project and that have been taken into consideration in the environmental assessment of the project;
- any environmental assessment undertaken by the Director-General;
- a statement relating to compliance with the environmental assessment requirements. (s 75I)

The Minister must take into account the Director-General's report, any advice provided by the Minister having portfolio responsibility for the proponent if the proponent is a public authority, and the findings or recommendations of a commission of inquiry if the Minister has directed that an inquiry be held (s 75J(2)).[40]

On approving the project, the Minister may make modifications (s 75J(4)) and may impose conditions (s 75J(4)), including conditions requiring a special or local infrastructure contribution, or an affordable housing contribution (s 75R(4)). Obligations in a statement of commitments made by the proponent or in a planning agreement entered into under s 93F can be made conditions of approval (s 75J(5)).

The terms of the Minister's approval can be modified at a later stage, on the application of the proponent (s 75W). The modification power is not limited by any reference to the project remaining substantially the same. The Director-General can require prior assessment.

---

38 See *Leichhardt Municipal Council v Minister for Planning (No 2)* (1995) 87 LGERA 78 where the Court of Appeal held invalid a REP which was significantly different from the draft that had been exhibited and was thus not a product of the consultation procedures in EPAA Pt 3.

39 See further EPAR 2000 cl 8B; *Tugun Cobaki Alliance Inc v Minister for Planning and RTA* [2006] NSWLEC 396.

40 In *Tugun Cobaki Alliance Inc v Minister for Planning and RTA* [2006] NSWLEC 396, it was held that s 75I does not require the Minister to consider the proponent's response to issues raised in submissions or to read the proponent's environmental assessment.

Following recent amendments to the TSCA, the Minister may approve a project subject to a condition that the proponent acquire and retire, in accordance with Pt 7A of TSCA, biodiversity credits of a specified number and class (EPAA s 75JA). The retirement of some or all of the biodiversity credits may be deferred pending the completion of any rehabilitation or restoration action proposed to be taken on the site, after the project has been substantially completed, that will restore or improve the biodiversity values affected by the project.[41] The power to require the proponent to acquire and retire biodiversity credits exists whether or not a biobanking statement was obtained under Pt 7A in respect of the project. If a biobanking statement is obtained, the Minister may impose the conditions specified in the statement, and these conditions are not appealable (EPAA s 75JA(4), (5)).

Fast-tracking critical infrastructure projects

The procedure for obtaining consent to critical infrastructure projects is essentially the same as for other EPAA Pt 3A projects. There are, however, some special features which make it easier and faster to obtain approval for critical infrastructure projects. Most of these are discussed elsewhere, but it is convenient to summarise them here. First, EPIs, including SEPPs, do not apply to the carrying out of the project unless a SEPP expressly relates to the project (s 75R(2)) It is of no consequence that a REP or LEP prohibits or restricts the critical infrastructure project and the regulations cannot keep alive any such prohibition, as they can in relation to other Pt 3A projects.[42] Secondly, neither the proponent nor any objector has a right to appeal the Minister's determination on the merits (ss 75K, 75L and 75Q). Thirdly, only the Minister can institute civil enforcement proceedings (ss 75T, 75X(5)). Fourthly, there are limited requirements for the certification of construction and subdivision work (s 75S). Fifthly, administrative enforcement powers under natural resource legislation, protection of the environment legislation and local government legislation cannot be used so as to interfere with the carrying out of an approved project (s 75U(3)).

Concept plans

The Minister can authorise or require an applicant to apply for approval of a concept plan for a Pt 3A project, including a critical infrastructure project (s 75M). The application merely outlines the scope of the project, any development options, any proposals to conduct the development in stages, and any other matters required by the Director-General. A detailed description of the project is not required. The application may also include an application to carry out any part or aspect of the project (s 75M(3A)). A procedure similar to that for project approval must be followed, including environmental assessment and public consultation.[43]

41 Division 7 of Pt 7A of TSCA applies in respect of any such arrangement as if it were a deferred retirement arrangement approved by the Director-General of the Department of Environment and Conservation under that Division.

42 See EPAA ss 75J(3) (projects), 75O(3) (concept plans).

43 EPAA ss 75F (environmental assessment requirements for approval), 75G (independent hearing and assessment panels), 75H (environmental assessment and public consultation) and 75I (Director-General's environmental assessment report) apply with respect to a concept plan in the same way as they apply with respect to approval to carry out a project: s 75N.

Approval of the concept plan may be given subject to satisfactory arrangements being made to fulfil obligations in a statement of commitments made by the proponent (including by entering into a planning agreement) before the project or a stage of the project is finally approved (s 75O(5)).

When giving approval to a concept plan, the Minister determines subsequent environmental assessment requirements for the project or stages of the project (s 75P). The Minister may require further assessment or no assessment at all. If no further assessment is required for the project, or a stage of the project, the Minister may grant approval without further application or assessment or reporting. Another option is for the Minister to require that the project be assessed under Pts 4 or 5 of the Act, subject to any modifications of the procedures under those Parts as the Minister determines. For example, the Minister may declare that a stage of the development is not designated development (s 75P(2)(e)). Or the Minister may declare a stage of the project to be exempt or complying development (s 75P(2)(d)). In any event, the project would not be processed as integrated development (s 75P(2)(b)).

If the project or a stage of the project is to be approved under Pt 4, the Minister may direct that a provision of an EPI which prohibits or restricts the carrying out of the project does not have affect.[44] The determination of a development application for the project under Pt 4 must be generally consistent with the terms of approval of the concept plan (s 75P(2)). The Minister can direct that conditions be imposed for the purpose of fulfilling obligations in a statement of commitments made by the proponent (s 75P(2)(a1)). Those conditions cannot be modified except with the Minister's approval and cannot be appealed. Nor can the Minister's direction be appealed.

Part 3A Appeals

If the project is critical infrastructure there is no appeal. Neither the proponent nor an objector can appeal the determination (ss 75K, 75L and 75Q).

For other Pt 3A approvals, the proponent[45] and, if the project is designated development, objectors (s 75L)[46] have rights of appeal to the Land and Environment Court. There are limitations on these rights of appeal. First, a proponent who is a public authority cannot appeal the determination. Secondly, the project must be one to which Pt 4 would have applied but for Pt 3A. Thirdly, there are no rights of appeal if an IHAP or commission of inquiry was appointed.[47]

A fourth limitation on rights of appeal is that, even if the project is designated development, there is no objector right of appeal if a concept plan for the project has been approved (s 75L(1)(b)). The proponent has a right of appeal, but not objectors. Nor, if a concept plan has been approved, do objectors not have a right to be heard as a party to a proponent appeal. Objectors who want to be made a party to an appeal would have to apply under s 39A of the *Land and Environment Court Act 1979*.

---

44 EPAA s 75P(2)(c1) (other than a project of a class prescribed by the regulations).

45 EPAA ss 75K (projects), 75Q (concept plans).

46 On an appeal by a proponent against the determination of designated development, objectors to designated development have a right to be heard as if a party to the proponent appeal: s 75K(3).

47 Similarly, where the Minister under Pt 4 has directed that an inquiry be held by a commission of inquiry in relation to any proposed designated development, thus becoming the consent authority, neither the applicant nor an objector has a right of appeal: EPAA s 80(8).

If a proponent appeals the determination of a concept plan, and the court allows the appeal, it is the Minister and not the court who must approve the concept plan. The Minister must do so 'in the manner determined by the Court' (EPAA s 75Q(3)). Further, the court does not have jurisdiction to make any determination as to subsequent environmental assessment or to give directions to the Minister in that respect.

Observing the law

As discussed in Chapter 1, in New South Wales the legal right of any person to enforce the law through the civil jurisdiction of the Land and Environment Court, without having to show common law standing or obtain the fiat of the Attorney-General, is entrenched. Section 123 of the EPAA provides that any person may apply to the Land and Environment Court for an order to remedy or restrain a breach of the Act, an EPI, development consent, an administrative order under Pt 6 Div 2A or a planning agreement under s 93F. Proceedings under s 123 include judicial review of the legality of government decisions and proceedings to remedy or restrain breaches of the legislation by other persons. This is compendiously known as 'civil enforcement'. The *Protection of the Environment Operations Act 1997* (NSW) s 253 provides in even broader terms that any person may bring proceedings in the court for an order to restrain a breach, or a threatened or apprehended breach, of any Act, or any statutory rule, if the breach is likely to cause harm to the environment.

EPAA Part 3A seriously undermines these important rights. First, there is an attempt to narrow the scope of review. Section 75X(5) provides that the 'only requirement of this Part that is mandatory in connection with the validity of an approval of a project or of a concept plan for a project is a requirement that an environmental assessment with respect to the project is made publicly available'. The broadest interpretation of this provision would be that breach of any of the other procedures cannot result in invalidity and cannot be remedied or restrained by the court. However, it is to be expected that the court would read down this provision, as it does with other privative clauses, on the presumption that the legislature does not intend to limit a court's ability to supervise the legality of administrative decisions.[48] A narrower interpretation is readily available. The court's jurisdiction to make orders turns on whether there has been a breach of the legislation. A range of consequences, rather than simply invalidity, may attend a breach of legislation, and the mandatory/directory distinction is not helpful in discerning the consequence intended.[49] In *Tugun Cobaki Alliance Inc v Minister for Planning and RTA*,[50] Jagot J preferred a restrictive interpretation. While no breach of Pt 3A was made out in that case, her Honour indicated that the section must be construed as an expression of Parliament's intention that the only provision breach of which will *necessarily* lead to invalidity is the requirement to make the environ-

48 *Plaintiff S157/2002 v Commonwealth* (2003) 211 CLR 476 at [32], [35] and [65]. A restrictive interpretation has been given to a similar provision in s 102 of the EPAA. In *Association for Berowra Creek Inc v Minister for Planning* [2003] NSWLEC 38, the court held that the provision is directed to 'procedural requirements' and cannot apply where the relevant omission amounts to a jurisdictional error, such as the failure to classify development as designated development.

49 *Project Blue Sky Inc v Australian Broadcasting Authority* (1998) 194 CLR 355.

50 [2006] NSWLEC 396.

mental assessment publicly available.[51] The consequence of other breaches will need to be worked out on a case-by-case basis, and could also include invalidity. In *Gray v Minister for Planning*,[52] Pain J held that the failure of the Director-General to take into account ESD principles when deciding whether an environmental assessment under Pt 3A was adequate could give rise to invalidity. Her Honour was of the view that s 75X(5) could not prevent review in this case having regard to the objects of the EPAA and the significance of the Director-General's role in the Pt 3A environmental assessment process.

Secondly, with respect to critical infrastructure projects, 'open standing' has been removed. Only the Minister can bring or approve civil enforcement proceedings under the EPAA, *Protection of the Environment Operations Act 1997* (NSW) and s 20(2) of the *Land and Environment Court Act 1979* (NSW) in relation to critical infrastructure projects (EPAA s 75T). The restriction extends from the declaration of the project as a Pt 3A project through to the carrying out of the critical infrastructure project, and covers authorisations under other legislation. This, in effect, makes the Minister's decisions immune from judicial supervision on grounds of legality. It purports to put the Minister above the law. It also prevents any person other than the Minister from enforcing compliance with an approval for a critical infrastructure project and with the conditions imposed on the approval.

Thirdly, there is an attempt to place a time limit on applying for judicial review. Proceedings challenging the validity of an approval for a Pt 3A project must be commenced within three months after public notice of the decision was given (s 75X(4)). A similar provision applies to development consents under Pt 4 and has been interpreted restrictively (s 101).[53] This was discussed in Chapter 3.

Fast-tracking other approvals

A range of approvals and authorisations under other regulatory regimes are not required for an approved Pt 3A project, or for any investigative or other activities required for the purpose of complying with any environmental assessment requirements in connection with an application for approval of a project or concept plan (s 75U(1), (4)). Thus prohibitions on undertaking an activity without approval or authorisation do not apply.[54] The following approvals are not required:

- concurrence under Pt 3 of the *Coastal Protection Act 1979*;
- a permit under s 201, 205 or 219 of FMA;
- an approval under Pt 4, or an excavation permit under s 139, of the *Heritage Act 1977*;
- a permit under s 87, or a consent under s 90, of the *National Parks and Wildlife Act 1974*;

51 Ibid at [184].

52 [2006] NSWLEC 720 at [143].

53 See *Woolworths Ltd v Pallas Newco Pty Ltd* [2004] NSWCA 422; *Lesnewski v Mosman MC* [2005] NSWCA 99; *Maitland City Council v Anambah Homes Pty Ltd* [2005] NSWCA 455.

54 Note also that, under the *National Parks and Wildlife Act 1974*, actions that are essential for carrying out an approved Pt 3A project provide the same defence to a prosecution relating to harm to native fauna, threatened species, habitat and reserved land as a development consent under Pt 4, or environmental assessment under Pt 5, provide: *National Parks and Wildlife Act 1974* ss 98(5), 118A(3), 118C(5), 118D(2), 156A(2).

- an authorisation referred to in s 12 of the *Native Vegetation Act 2003* to clear native vegetation or State protected land;
- a permit under Pt 3A of the *Rivers and Foreshores Improvement Act 1948;*
- a bush fire safety authority under s 100B of the *Rural Fires Act 1997;*
- a water use approval under s 89, a water management work approval under s 90 or an activity approval under s 91 of the *Water Management Act 2000.* (EPAA s 75U(1))

Other approvals and authorisations must be sought, but in respect of some the regulator's discretion is fettered, at least until the first renewal or review of the approval. Section 75V(1) of the EPAA specifies a range of approvals that cannot be refused if the approval is necessary for carrying out an approved project. Further, the approval must be substantially consistent with the Pt 3A approval. It is only when an application is made for a renewal or further authorisation (whether or not following the expiry or lapsing of the initial approval) that the regulator's discretion is restored (s 75V(3)). In the case of an environment protection licence under the *Protection of the Environment Operations Act 1997,* the licence can be considered afresh after the first review of the licence under s 78 of that Act.

The specified approvals, which must be granted and cannot be inconsistent with the Pt 3A approval, are:

- an aquaculture permit under s 144 of FMA;
- an approval under s 15 of the *Mine Subsidence Compensation Act 1961;*
- a mining lease under the *Mining Act 1992;*
- a production lease under the *Petroleum (Onshore) Act 1991;*
- an environment protection licence under Chapter 3 of the *Protection of the Environment Operations Act 1997* (for any of the purposes referred to in s 43 of that Act);
- a consent under s 138 of the *Roads Act 1993;*
- a licence under the *Pipelines Act 1967.*

If a concept plan is approved, but approval to carry out the project requires consent under Pt 4 and that consent is granted, the above-mentioned approvals cannot be refused if the approval is necessary for carrying out the project (s 75V(2)). The approval must be substantially consistent with the development consent.

Restrictions on administrative enforcement

Where approvals and authorisations under other regulatory regimes are not required, or the regulator's discretion is fettered, the advantages of licensing as a tool to manage compliance and create incentives to go beyond compliance are diminished. In addition, Pt 3A removes altogether specified administrative enforcement powers with respect to the carrying out of critical infrastructure projects. The following orders or notices cannot be made or given so as to prevent or interfere with the carrying out of an approved critical infrastructure project:

- an interim protection order within the meaning of the *National Parks and Wildlife Act 1974* or the TSCA;
- a stop work order under Pt 6A of the *National Parks and Wildlife Act 1974,* Pt 7 of TSCA or Pt 7A of FMA;

- an environment protection notice under Chapter 4 of the *Protection of the Environment Operations Act 1997*;
- an order under s 124 of the *Local Government Act 1993*. (EPAA s 75U(3))

A further restriction relating to critical infrastructure projects is that only the Minister or the Director-General can issue enforcement orders under EPAA Pt 6 Div 2A.[55]

Finally, a restriction which applies to all Pt 3A projects is that heritage orders under Pt 6 Div 8 of the *Heritage Act 1977*, to prevent harm to buildings, works, relics or places, cannot be made so as to prevent or interfere with the carrying out of an approved project (EPAA s 75U(2)).

Post-approval monitoring and auditing

After approval of a Pt 3A project, the Planning Department retains a monitoring and compliance role (Pt 6 Divs 2B and 2C).[56] The Minister may require monitoring or environmental audits by imposing conditions on an approved project (s 122C). These conditions may be imposed at the time of approving the project or at any other time, and may be varied or revoked. The purpose of monitoring is to provide data on compliance with the approval or on the environmental impact of the project (s 122B(1)). An 'environmental audit' of a project is defined as a periodic or particular documented evaluation of an approved project to provide information to the proponent of the project and to the Department on compliance with the approval or on the project's environmental management or impact (s 122B(2)). Information must be provided in connection with a monitoring report or environmental audit even if the information might incriminate the person (s 122F). The information is admissible in evidence in any prosecution of the proponent for any offence under any legislation. And the Minister may publish the information in such manner as the Minister considers appropriate.

The Minister can make administrative enforcement orders under Pt 6 Div 2A of the EPAA in relation to Pt 3A projects (s 121B(1)(aa)), as well as initiate civil or criminal enforcement proceedings.

EPAA Part 4 – Development assessment

Development that requires consent

Part 4 of the EPAA establishes the framework for assessing development that requires consent under an EPI. As previously stated, we are only concerned in this chapter with the procedures and documentation that may be required. Chapter 3 discussed the types of development application and the determination of a development application. Characterisation of development to decide whether it requires consent was discussed in Chapter 2.

It should also be noted that an EPI will identify a range of exempt and complying development. Exempt development can be carried out in accordance with the EPI without being assessed under either Pts 4 or 5. It must by definition be 'of

55 EPAA s 75R(5); EPAR cl 8I.

56 See *New South Wales State Development Monitor 2005-2006*, above n 19.

minimal environmental impact' (s 76(2)). Complying development is development that can be addressed by specified predetermined development standards (s 76A(5), (6)). The proposal is assessed against those development standards and if it complies a complying development certificate, which enables the development to be carried out, must be issued (s 85A). Environmental assessment more generally is not relevant.

If the development requires consent, but is not complying development, an application must be made to the consent authority which, for Pt 4 applications, will usually be the local council. As discussed in the previous section, projects for which the Minister is the consent authority are now for the most part processed under Pt 3A. However, the Minister is not precluded from being identified as the consent authority for development assessed under Pt 4.[57]

All development requiring consent must be assessed for its environmental, social and economic impact. This is required by s 79C(1) of the EPAA, as discussed in Chapter 3. The consent authority will be assisted in this task by documentation prepared by the applicant and by public participation. The documentation required by the Act and regulations, and requirements for public participation, are discussed below. Before this, 'designated development' is explained. Development characterised as designated development has important consequences for both public participation and environmental assessment.

Designated development

Designated development is development identified as such in Sch 3 to the EPAR or in an EPI (EPAA s 77A). The declaration of development as designated development says nothing about whether the development is permissible. The purpose of the declaration is to attach special procedures for environmental assessment and public participation to an application for development that requires consent.

Three important consequences follow from the declaration. First, the development application must be accompanied by an EIS prepared by the applicant.[58] Secondly, neighbours and the public generally must be given notice and have the right to inspect the application and accompanying documentation, and to make submissions.[59] Thirdly, persons who have made a submission by way of objection ('objectors'[60]) have the right to appeal against the grant of development consent (s 98). It is a merits appeal; that is to say, a full rehearing of the application by the Land and Environment Court in its Class 1 jurisdiction. If the applicant appeals, objectors have the right to be made parties to the proceedings (s 97(4)).

These important consequences make it all the more critical to the characterise the development properly. Characterisation is probably a jurisdictional fact, with the consequence that the Land and Environment Court can review the consent authority's determination *de novo*.[61]

---

57 See *SEPP (Major Projects) 2005* Sch 6.

58 EPAA s 78A(8)(a); EPAR Pt 6 Div 4 and Sch 2.

59 EPAA s 79; EPAR Pt 6 Div 5.

60 EPAA s 4 'objector'.

61 See the reasoning in *Timbarra Protection Coalition Inc v Ross Mining NL* (1999) 46 NSWLR 55; *Woolworths Ltd v Pallas Newco Pty Ltd* [2004] NSWCA 422; *Corporation of the City of Enfield v Development Assessment Commission* (2000) 199 CLR 135.

Schedule 3 to the EPAR lists designated development by class. The classes of development are not described by reference to their purpose. The Schedule simply describes the type of development and sets out thresholds and qualifications in an effort to ensure that only those developments that are likely to have a significant impact are processed as designated development. The following is an example:

> Wood or timber milling or processing works (being works, other than joineries, builders supply yards or home improvement centres) that saw, machine, mill, chip, pulp or compress timber or wood:
> (a) that have an intended processing capacity of more than 6,000 cubic metres of timber per year and:
> (i) are located within 500 metres of a dwelling not associated with the milling works, or
> (ii) are located within 40 metres of a natural waterbody or wetland, or
> (iii) burn waste (other than as a source of fuel), or
> (b) that have an intended processing capacity of more than 50,000 cubic metres of timber per year.

That example is a reminder that the application and any consent that is granted should specify its intended capacity or output. If the application does not do so and is not processed as designated development, a consent granted that authorises production in excess of the threshold is invalid.[62]

Although the Schedule does not describe development by reference to its purpose, the Land and Environment Court has nevertheless used the 'dominant purpose test' to characterise a proposal which has more than one purpose.[63] If the dominant purpose is not designated development, the court has not required the application to comply with the requirements for designated development. Most of the Land and Environment Court cases concerned sewerage treatment plants, which inevitably serve the main purpose of the proposal. In the result, sewerage treatment plants for large residential or resort development have escaped the environmental assessment requirements for designated development, even though they fall within the Schedule. The Land and Environment Court's approach was held to be erroneous in the recent decision of the Court of Appeal in *Residents Against Improper Development Inc v Chase Property Investments Pty Ltd*.[64] The correct approach is to ask whether any part of the overall proposal is designated development and whether the application is 'in respect of' designated development. If it is, it matters not whether the designated development component is an independent use or a use that is subsidiary or ancillary to some other part, or the overall purpose, of the proposal.[65] It would be contrary to the environmental protection objectives of the Act if designated development were to lose that character because it forms part of a greater but non-designated development.[66] Further, the question whether the development application is 'in respect of' designated development should not be

62 *Levenstrath Community Association Inc v Tomies Timber* [2000] NSWLEC 95.

63 See *Hynes Urban Planners Pty Ltd v Hawkesbury CC* [2003] NSWLEC 1, overruling *Maxwell v Hornsby Council* (2002) 121 LGERA 186.

64 [2006] NSWCA 323.

65 Ibid esp at [121]-[172], [178]-[179] per Tobias JA, with whom Giles JA and McClellan CJ at CL agreed.

66 Ibid at [182].

narrowly framed. An application is 'in respect of' designated development where a not insignificant part of the development can be so categorised.[67]

Under EPAR Sch 3, if the development application is for alterations or additions to an approved or existing development, it must be asked whether the alterations or additions significantly increase the environmental impacts of the total development compared with the existing or approved development. The total development is the existing development together with the additions or alterations. The application would not be for designated development if, in the opinion of the consent authority, the alterations or additions do not significantly increase the environmental impacts of the total development (EPAR Sch 3 cl 35). In making this assessment, the Regulation requires a range of factors to be considered, including previous environmental management performance, the number and nature of all past changes and their cumulative effects, the degree to which the potential environmental impacts can be predicted with adequate certainty, any proposals to mitigate the environmental impacts and any proposals to facilitate compliance with relevant standards (EPAR Sch 3 cl 36).[68] The Land and Environment Court has held that the question 'Are alterations or additions designated development?' is only asked if the proposed development is designated development; but to determine this, the total development including alterations and additions must be characterised.[69] That is an appropriate approach where neither the alterations or additions nor the existing development constitute on their own designated development, but when taken as a whole come within a class of designated development. However, in light of the Court of Appeal's decision in *Residents Against Improper Development Inc v Chase Property Investments Pty Ltd*,[70] that approach should not be allowed to prevent the question from being asked simply because a component of the application or of the existing development, while being designated development, is overshadowed by non-designated development.

Public participation

Applications requiring public participation

Public participation is an essential ingredient of local and regional environmental planning under Pt 3 of the Act, as discussed in Chapter 2. At the development assessment stage, however, public participation rights are limited. The only statutory requirements for public participation relate to 'designated development' and 'advertised development'. Public participation may also be provided for in a development control plan. The limited rights to participate at the development assessment stage reflect a rule-based approach to planning, which has been steadily eroded. The rule-based approach assumes that the important discretionary decisions are made at the planning stage and that assessment of particular developments is merely implementation of the prohibitions, requirements and standards put in place

67 Ibid at [180]-[189].

68 See NSW Department of Urban Affairs and Planning, *Is an EIS required for Alterations and Additions? A Guide for Applicants and Consent Authorities* (2000-01), <http://www.planning.nsw.gov.au/assessingdev/pdf/gu_alteration.pdf> (accessed 23 September 2006).

69 *Mitchell v Vella* (1998) 101 LGERA 333.

70 [2006] NSWCA 323.

by the planning instrument. On this assumption, it is only necessary to single out the 'big, bad' developments, which are permitted in some zones, for further public participation in the decision as to whether they should go ahead. Planning, however, has become increasingly discretionary and understandably so in the context of rapid urban change. Static zonings, including categorical prohibitions, can only be amended through time consuming and cumbersome processes. Environmental planners have responded by increasing the range of developments that are permissible within a zone or locality, depending on an assessment of the likely performance of a particular proposal and its consistency with the objectives of the zone or the desired future character of the locality. Public input to inform discretionary decisions has thus become increasingly important at the development assessment stage.

In addition to designated development, public participation can be provided for by identifying development as 'advertised development' in the regulations or in an EPI (ss 29A, 79A(1)). Councils may also identify advertised development, or otherwise provide for public participation, in a development control plan (s 74C), or council policy.[71] Although development control plans are not binding documents, the Act requires development applications to be notified or advertised in accordance with the requirements of a development control plan (ss 29A, 79A(2)).[72]

The EPAR identifies the following development as advertised development:

- development on critical habitat or development that is likely to significantly affect threatened species, populations or ecological communities or their habitats, thus requiring a SIS ('threatened species development');
- integrated development that requires an approval under the *Heritage Act 1977*, the *Water Management Act 2000* or the *Protection of the Environment Operations Act 1997* ('nominated integrated development');
- Class 1 aquaculture development under *SEPP 62 – Sustainable Aquaculture* ('Class 1 aquaculture development'). (EPAR cl 5)

Failure to comply with the requirements

The Land and Environment Court and Court of Appeal have consistently recognised the importance of public participation.[73] Thus the consequence of not complying strictly with requirements for public participation will lead to the invalidity of any consent.[74] The court is very unlikely to refuse a remedy in its discretion.[75] However, the Land and Environment Court is under a statutory obligation to consider making an order suspending a declaration of invalidity and specifying the terms required to validate the consent.[76]

71 A policy or practice of consultation may generate a legitimate expectation attracting a duty to observe procedural fairness: *Nelson v Burwood MC* (1991) 75 LGRA 39.

72 See *Lesnewski v Mosman Municipal Council* [2005] NSWCA 99.

73 *Helman v Byron Shire Council* (1995) 88 LGERA 349; *Litevale Pty Limited v Lismore City Council* (1997) 96 LGERA 91; *Monaro Acclimatisation Society v Minister for Planning* (unreported, NSWLEC, Stein J, 2 March 1989).

74 *Curac v Shoalhaven CC* (1993) 81 LGERA 124 (notification); *Johnson v Lake Macquarie City Council* (1996) 91 LGERA 331 (exhibition period); *Maybury v Minister for Planning* (1995) 87 LGERA 154 (landowners but not occupiers notified of designated development); *Coffs Harbour City Council v Arrawarra Beach Pty Ltd* [2006] NSWLEC 365 (notice misleading).

75 *Curac v Shoalhaven CC* (1993) 81 LGERA 124.

76 *Land and Environment Court Act 1979* Pt 3 Div 3.

Public inquiries

Public participation under the EPAA is by and large of the notice-and-comment type. The application and accompanying documents are exhibited and the public is invited to make submissions. The procedures for advertised and designated development also seek to ensure that persons who are likely to be particularly affected receive personal notice. However, the statutory procedures do not address the conditions that affect the quality of public debate, or fair access to that debate.[77] Nor do they recognise the variety of ways in which public deliberation can be fostered.[78]

Public inquiries provide more substantial opportunities for public participation. Under the EPAA, the Minister has a discretion to appoint a commission of inquiry for a variety of purposes, including to inquire into the environmental aspects of a proposal (s 119). Commissioners are independent of the Minister and their findings and recommendations operate as advice to the Minister. The commission of inquiry must be conducted in accordance with procedural fairness.[79] This includes, as Brennan J has observed, the general principle, founded firmly on the requirements of procedural fairness, that *ex parte* communications must not be taken into account without giving the parties whose interests might be affected an opportunity to correct or contradict the information.[80] With respect to *ex parte* communications following completion of the public inquiry, a distinction has been drawn between information and arguments relating to the local situation and the merits of the proposal, which must be disclosed,[81] and policy advice which can be obtained without the need to reopen the public inquiry.[82] It is thus surprising, and worrying, that the Land and Environment Court has held that procedural fairness does not extend beyond the conclusion of the hearing, even if new information is subsequently provided by the applicant.[83]

Some local councils have set up Independent Hearing and Assessment Panels (IHAP).[84] More controversial development applications, including those in respect of which there are unresolved objections, are referred to the panel which conducts a public hearing and independently assesses the application.[85] The IHAP report to council is advisory only.

---

77 See, for example, Cass Sunstein, 'Beyond the Republican Revival' (1988) 97 *Yale LJ* 1539; Carol Pateman, *Participation and Democratic Theory* (Cambridge University Press, 1970); Carol Pateman, *The Disorder of Women: Democracy Feminism and Political Theory* (Polity Press, 1989).

78 See the report prepared for the NSW Department of Urban Affairs and Planning by Lyn Carson and Katharine Gelber, *Ideas for Community Consultation – A discussion on principles and procedures for making consultation work* (2001), <http://www.planning.nsw.gov.au/planfirst/pdf/principles_procedures_final.pdf#search=%22public%20participation%22> (accessed 23 September 2006).

79 *Lindemans Wines Pty Ltd v Woodward* (1981) 46 LGRA 14; EPAA s 120.

80 *Minister for Aboriginal Affairs v Peko-Wallsend Ltd* (1986) 162 CLR 24 at 58-60.

81 *Errington v Minister of Health* [1935] 1 KB 249.

82 *Bushell v Secretary of State for the Environment* [1981] AC 75.

83 *Valley Watch Inc v Minister for Planning* (1994) 82 LGERA 209.

84 For example, Fairfield, Liverpool, Sutherland and Warringah Councils. See also Warringah LEP 2000 cl 15(2).

85 See NSW Independent Commission Against Corruption risks in the NSW development approval process: discussion paper (22 December 2005), <http://www.icac.nsw.gov.au/files/pdf/ICAC_Discussion_Paper_DEC.pdf> (accessed 23 September 2006).

Documentation accompanying a development application

Statement of environmental effects

EPAR Sch 1 identifies a range of information that must accompany a development application, including a site plan, a sketch of the development and a statement of environmental effects. If the application is for designated development or development that is on critical habitat or likely to significantly affect threatened species, populations or ecological communities or their habitats, more substantial documentation evaluating environmental impact is required.

The site plan will indicate existing vegetation and trees on the land and the location and uses of buildings on sites adjoining the land. The statement of environmental effects must indicate the environmental impacts of the proposed development, how the environmental impacts have been identified, the steps to be taken to protect the environment or to lessen the expected harm to the environment, and any matters required to be indicated by any guidelines issued by the Director-General. These matters only have to be 'indicated'. An EPI may require more. For example, Warringah LEP 2000, in respect of a particular category of development, requires a statement of environmental effects that gives reasons justifying the proposal having regard to biophysical, economic and social considerations and the ESD principles.[86]

Further information must accompany applications for certain types of development. If the application relates to residential flat development to which *SEPP 65 – Design Quality of Residential Flat Development* applies, the statement of environmental effects must include an explanation of the design in terms of the design quality principles set out in Pt 2 of the SEPP (EPAR Sch 1 Pt 1 cl 2(5)). Applications relating to BASIX affected buildings must be accompanied by a BASIX certificate.[87]

Environmental impact statements (EIS)

An EIS must accompany a development application for designated development (EPAA s 78A(8)). Characterisation of development as designated development was discussed previously. EPAR Sch 2 prescribes the matters that must be addressed in an EIS. Schedule 2 applies also to EISs required under Pt 5 and is discussed in the final part of this Section.

Species impact statements (SIS)

A SIS must accompany an application for development on critical habitat, or development that is likely to significantly affect threatened species, populations or ecological communities or their habitats, excluding vulnerable ecological communities (EPAA s 78A(8)). In deciding whether a SIS is required, regard must be had to the factors listed in EPAA s 5A and an approach based on the precautionary principle is appropriate.[88] The s 5A considerations are discussed in the final part of this Section.

86 Warringah LEP 2000 cl 15 and Sch 15.

87 BASIX is discussed in Chapter 5.

88 *BT Goldsmith Planning Services v Blacktown City Council* [2005] NSWLEC 210; *Gales Holdings Pty Ltd v Tweed Shire Council* [2006] NSWLEC 85; *Gales Holdings Pty Ltd v Tweed Shire Council* [2006] NSWLEC 212. See also *Providence Projects Pty Ltd v Gosford City Council* [2006] NSWLEC 52.

A SIS may have to be prepared if after lodging the development application there is a new listing of an endangered species, population or ecological community. The list for vulnerable species, however, is frozen for a period of 12 months from the time a valid application is lodged (s 105A).

SISs must be prepared in accordance with Pt 6 Div 2 of TSCA. The requirements are discussed in the final part of this Section.

If a SIS is required, consent cannot be granted without the concurrence of the Director-General of National Parks or the Director of NSW Fisheries (EPAA s 79B(3)-(7)). If the Minister is the consent authority, there is only the requirement for consultation at the ministerial level. The Director-General and the Minister administering the TSCA or FMA must have regard to matters listed in the Act as relevant considerations, including the ESD principles (EPAA s 79B(5)). Concurrence may be granted on condition that the applicant undertake specified 'voluntary action' which the Director-General considers will significantly benefit threatened species conservation (TSCA s 126N). This could include a monetary contribution (TSCA s 126N(2)(d)).

As explained in the introduction to this Section, if biodiversity certification is conferred on an EPI under the TSCA, any development for which consent is required under the EPI is taken to be development that is not likely to significantly affect any threatened species, population or ecological community, or its habitat (TSCA s 126I). Thus neither a SIS nor concurrence would be required. The issue of a biobanking statement has the same effect of dispensing with these requirements (TSCA s 127ZO).

Failure to comply with the requirements

Failure to obtain a SIS or EIS, and to do so before the public participation process, will invalidate any consent granted.[89] In *Helman v Byron Shire Council,* the Court of Appeal held that public participation requirements are in the nature of a condition precedent to any consideration of a development application and reception of impact assessment documents cannot bypass the participation process.[90] Further, the Land and Environment Court has held that it is not appropriate to suspend a declaration of invalidity under s 25B of the *Land and Environment Court Act 1979* as the effect of a failure to lodge an impact statement is that a fundamental requirement is outstanding.[91] Until it is complied with there are crucial issues that cannot be resolved.

Helman's case was approved in *Timbarra Protection Coalition Inc v Ross Mining NL* where the Court of Appeal held that the question whether a SIS is required is a jurisdictional fact.[92] This means that the consent authority's decision as to whether a proposal is likely to significantly affect threatened species, populations or ecological communities or their habitats, is provisional in the sense that on an application for review in the Land and Environment Court's Class 4 jurisdiction, the Court must decide the question *de novo.* The court does not simply ask whether the consent authority's decision was reasonably open, but rather must decide for itself on fresh

89 *Helman v Byron Shire Council* (1995) 87 LGERA 349 (fauna impact statement). See also *Botany Bay City Council v Remath Investments No 6 Pty Ltd* (2000) 111 LGERA 446.

90 Ibid.

91 *Coffs Harbour City Council v Arrawarra Beach Pty Ltd* [2006] NSWLEC 365.

92 (1999) 46 NSWLR 55. See also *Plumb v Penrith City Council* [2002] NSWLEC 223.

evidence whether a SIS is required. This intense standard of review is derived from the significant role that a SIS plays in the legislative scheme, such that it is appropriate to describe it as an 'essential condition' or 'essential preliminary'. The same reasoning no doubt applies to characterisation of designated development, as well as to the requirements for EISs and SISs under Pt 5.

In contrast, the Court of Appeal has upheld the Land and Environment Court's rulings that a development application that is not accompanied by any of the documents specified in EPAR Sch 1, including a statement of environmental effects, is not invalid.[93] The legislative intention that this is so is derived from the marked differences between the requirements for an EIS and SIS, on the one hand, and those for a statement of environmental effects, on the other.[94] The differences lie in the legislative source of the obligations and the nature and degree of prescription, together with the consequence that a SEE is a less reliable document. More particularly, the remedy for a deficient development application lies with the consent authority. The consent authority has the power to reject an application that is unaccompanied by a SEE (EPAR cl 51(b)) or to request the applicant to provide additional information (EPAR cl 54(1)). Ultimately, the consent authority can refuse to grant consent having regard to s 79C matters, including any uncertainty as to environmental impact. The difficulty, of course, for those who oppose proposed development on environmental grounds is that challenging the consent authority's discretion is onerous and unpredictable: see Chapter 3. On the other hand, there is little doubt that a SEE is prone to being an advocacy document, requiring little, if any, expertise and not subject to effective external constraints. The problem must in part lie with the restricted range of designated developments requiring a more formal EIS under Pt 4. EPAR Sch 3 does not, for example, capture large residential or tourist development. To avoid the problem of over-inclusion in Sch 3, more use could be made of the power to identify designated development in an EPI.

EPAA Part 5 – Assessment of activities not requiring development consent

Part 5 applies to an activity that does not require consent under Pt 4 and is not a Pt 3A project. This could be either public or private development, provided that, in the case of private development, the activity requires a government approval, other than development consent.

Part 5 has two central requirements:

- a duty to take into account to the fullest extent possible all matters affecting or likely to affect the environment by reason of a proposed activity; and
- a duty to consider an EIS if the activity is likely to significantly affect the environment (including critical habitat) or threatened species, populations or ecological communities, or their habitats, and to engage in public participation informed by the EIS.

93 *Cranky Rock Road Action Group Inc v Cowra Shire Council* [2006] NSWCA 339, affirming *Cranky Rock Road Action Group Inc v Cowra Shire Council* [2005] NSWLEC 674.

94 See especially *MCC Energy Pty Ltd v Wyong Shire Council* [2006] NSWLEC 581 at [61]-[67] per Jagot J, approved by the Court of Appeal in *Cranky Rock Road Action Group Inc v Cowra Shire Council* [2006] NSWCA 339 at [87] per Tobias JA, Young CJ and Campbell J agreeing.

The original intention of Pt 5 was to catch development which escaped environmental assessment under Pt 4 and to ensure that all public authorities undertaking activities that do not require development consent internalise environmental considerations, regardless of the terms of their statutory mandate. Part 5 continues to serve this function but with exceptions brought about by amendments to the Act. The most notable of these is the power vested in the Minister to declare an activity to be a Pt 3A project, where the proponent of the activity is also the determining authority and is of the opinion that Pt 5 requires the preparation and consideration of an EIS. While the external scrutiny of the Planning Minister is highly desirable in such circumstances, it was already provided for in Pt 5.[95] The provisions were repealed on introduction of Pt 3A with the consequence that public development which is likely to significantly affect the environment is either processed under Pt 3A, where environmental assessment is not prescribed but is in the discretion of the Director-General, and where there is no equivalent of s 111 or under Pt 5, with no requirement for ministerial approval. Another retreat from the original intention of Pt 5 was the re-definition of 'activity' to mean essentially the same as 'development'. 'Activity' was initially defined much more broadly than 'development' so as to trigger environmental assessment from an early stage in project planning – when formulating the proposal, making financial outlays, resuming or leasing land and so forth.

The ambit of Part 5

To bring Pt 5 into play:

- there must be an *activity*;
- that is proposed to be undertaken by a *determining authority* or requires the *approval* of a determining authority.

Activity

'Activity' is defined in the same way as 'development', that is:

- the use of land;
- the subdivision of land;
- the erection of a building;
- the carrying out of a work;
- the demolition of a building or work; and
- any other act, matter or thing referred to in EPAA s 26 that is prescribed by the regulations. (s 110(1))

Interpretation of these terms was discussed in Chapter 3. A significant case under Pt 5 is the decision of the Land and Environment Court in *Sustainable Fishing and Tourism Inc v Minister for Fisheries*.[96] In that case it was held that commercial fishing constituted the 'use of land'. Thus in granting a commercial fishing licence under FMA, the Minister for Fisheries had to comply with Pt 5 of the EPAA. EPAA Pt 5 was subsequently amended to provide for strategic environmental assessment

95 EPAA Pt 5 Div 4 (now repealed).

96 (2000) 106 LGERA 322.

of commercial fisheries and to dispense with the need for environmental assessment of individual applications for licences (Pt 5 Div 5).

Excluded from the definition of 'activity' is development:

- that requires consent under Pt 4;
- that is prohibited development;
- that is development identified in an EPI as 'exempt development' – that is, development 'of minimal environmental impact' (s 76(2));
- that is development being carried out in compliance with an order under Pt 6 Div 2A;
- that is of a class or description that is prescribed by the regulations. (s 110(1))

Further, Pt 3A projects are not subject to Pt 5 (ss 75R(1), 110(2)).[97]

Although the existing use provisions fall within Pt 4, an existing use that needs approval other than development consent is caught by Pt 5.[98]

SEPP 4 – Development Without Consent and Miscellaneous Exempt and Complying Development exempts a range of development from the need to obtain development consent, thus bringing Pt 5 into play. The exemptions include:

- the construction of water storage dams, sewage treatment works and electricity transmission lines by or on behalf of a public authority;
- development on land dedicated or reserved under the *National Parks and Wildlife Act 1974*;
- classified roads within the meaning of the *Roads Act 1993*;
- bushfire hazard reduction that is consistent with a bush fire management plan under the *Rural Fires Act 1997*.

In addition, schedules to local environmental plans may exempt from the need to obtain development consent a range of public utility undertakings relating to the supply of gas, water, electricity, sewerage and transport.[99]

Characterisation of a proposal as an 'activity' is a jurisdictional fact, which means that on an application for judicial review the Land and Environment Court can review the decision of the determining authority *de novo*.[100] Where the activity has more than one purpose, a 'dominant purpose' approach to characterisation of the activity has been used:[101] see Chapter 2. This has the consequence that if the dominant purpose does not require government approval, Pt 5 is not brought into play. However, interdependent purposes may require independent characterisation having regard to their character, extent and other features.[102]

---

97 See also EPAA s 75P(2)(c).

98 *Vaughn-Taylor v David Mitchell-Melcann Pty Ltd* (1991) 73 LGRA 366 (CA).

99 See Environmental Planning and Assessment Model Provisions 1980.

100 *Coles Holdings v Tweed Shire Council* (1999) 110 LGERA 235.

101 *Brown v EPA (No 2)* (1992) 78 LGERA 119. However, see the recent decision of the Court of Appeal relating to characterisation of designated development: *Residents Against Improper Development Inc v Chase Property Investments Pty Ltd* [2006] NSWCA 323.

102 *Penrith City Council v Waste Management Authority* (1990) 71 LGRA 376 (characterisation of designated development under EPAA Pt 4).

Determining authority

'Determining authority' in relation to an activity means a Minister or public authority by or on whose behalf the activity is to be carried out, or whose approval is required in order to enable the activity to be carried out (EPAA s 110(1)). The term 'public authority' includes local government and statutory State-owned corporations within the meaning of the *State Owned Corporations Act 1989* (EPAA s 4(1)).[103] Commonwealth Ministers and public authorities cannot be determining authorities.[104] Further, the phrase 'on whose behalf' does not include an authority that merely consults with, or furthers the interests of, a public authority.[105] Thus, the Federal Airports Corporation, in carrying out dredging for the third runway at Sydney airport, could not be said to be acting on behalf of a NSW public authority, the Maritime Services Board, merely because the dredging served the long-term interest of the Board in constructing a new dock facility at the dredging site.[106] In particular, the Board had no legal power to direct or supervise or control the activities of the Federal Airports Corporation.

There are some statutory exemptions.[107] For example, authorities granting fire permits under the *Rural Fires Act 1997* are not determining authorities within the meaning of Pt 5.[108] The Director-General of the Department of Environment and Conservation is not a determining authority when granting a licence under the TSCA to harm or pick threatened species, populations or ecological communities or damage habitat (TSCA s 99).[109] Nor is the Director-General a determining authority when granting general and scientific licences under the *National Parks and Wildlife Act 1974* (ss 120, 132C), or approving a property management plan under the TSCA (s 113B).

Where there is more than one determining authority, the Minister may nominate one of them as the determining authority responsible for discharging the obligations relating to obtaining and considering an EIS where Pt 5 so requires (EPAA s 110A). This does not absolve the other determining authorities from the more general obligation to take into account all matters affecting or likely to affect the environment by reason of the activity (s 110A(2)), subject to the exemption for activities, or part thereof, that have been approved or are to be carried out by another determining authority after environmental assessment under Pt 5 (s 110E).

Approval

The definition of 'approval' is broad and inclusive. It includes a consent, licence or permission, or any form of authorisation. It also includes the 'provision of financial accommodation by a determining authority to another person' (s 110(1)). The term 'approval' has been held to include a renewal of an approval.[110]

---

103 For company State-owned corporations, see *State Owned Corporations Act 1989* s 37A.

104 *Botany Municipal Council v Federal Airports Corporation* (1992) 175 CLR 453.

105 *Citizens Airport Environment Assoc Inc v Maritime Services Board* (1993) 79 LGERA 254.

106 Ibid.

107 In addition to the examples given in this paragraph, see *Protection of the Environment Operations (General) Regulation 1998* cl 45.

108 *Rural Fires Act 1997* s 96.

109 See also FMA s 221B.

110 *Brown v EPA (No 2)* (1992) 78 LGERA 119.

Duties under Part 5

Part 5 imposes two important obligations: a general duty to take into account, to the fullest extent possible, all matters affecting or likely to affect the environment (s 111); and a duty to consider an EIS if the activity is likely to significantly affect the environment, including critical habitat, or threatened species, populations or ecological communities, or their habitats (s 112). As part of the duty to consider an EIS, there must be public exhibition of the statement and consideration of submissions from any member of the public.

Considerations relevant to assessing the impact on critical habitat, threatened species, populations or ecological communities, and their habitats are amplified in EPAA s 5A. Section 5A is discussed in the final part of this Section. It should be noted that, if the list of vulnerable species is amended after an EIS has been obtained and notified, the duties under Pt 5 do not arise in relation to that species (s 110D). This exemption ceases if the activity has not commenced, or an approval has not been granted, by a determining authority within 12 months from the date of notification of the EIS.

As explained in the introduction to this Section, if biodiversity certification is conferred on an EPI under the TSCA, an activity that does not require consent under the EPI is taken to be an activity that is not likely to significantly affect any threatened species, population or ecological community, or its habitat (TSCA s 126I). The issue of a biobanking statement for a proposed activity has the same effect (TSCA s 127ZP). Further, the s 111 duty is qualified by not requiring the determining authority to consider the effect of the activity on biodiversity values (TSCA s 127ZP(7)).

Section 111: The duty to have regard to environmental affects

Section 111 imposes a general duty on determining authorities, in their consideration of an activity, to examine and take into account to the fullest extent possible all matters affecting or likely to affect the environment by reason of that activity. This obligation applies *notwithstanding the provisions of any Act or any instrument made under an Act*.

The thinking behind this obligation, and its language, can be sourced to the *United States National Environmental Policy Act* of 1969 (NEPA) – the seminal environmental impact assessment legislation. The requirement is designed to make environmental protection a part of the mandate of all public bodies. It precludes a public body from arguing that it has no statutory authority to concern itself with the environmental impacts of its activities.[111] In the case which laid the foundation for subsequent interpretation of NEPA, the phrase 'to the fullest extent possible' was said to set a high standard for public decision-making, which must be rigorously enforced by the reviewing courts.[112] The phrase has elicited a more sceptical response from the NSW Court of Appeal, which has substituted 'reasonably practicable' for 'possible'.[113] Further, in supervising compliance with this obligation, the Land and Environment Court has shown considerable deference to the expertise of the determining authority.[114]

---

111 See *Calvert Cliffs' Coordinating Committee v United States ACE* 449 F 2d 1109 (DC Cir, 1971).

112 Ibid per Skelly Wright J.

113 *Guthega Development Pty Ltd v Minister* (1987) 7 NSWLR 353; *Transport Action Group Against Motorways Inc v Roads and Traffic Authority* (1999) 104 LGERA 133 at [68].

114 *Drummoyne Municipal Council v Roads and Traffic Authority* (1989) 67 LGRA 155.

The regulations set out an extensive list of factors that must be taken into account in considering environmental impact, including any long-term affects on the environment and any cumulative environmental affect with other existing or likely future activities (EPAR cl 228(1)). Alternatively, the Director-General may establish guidelines in relation to the consideration of activities generally or of a particular kind (EPAR cl 228(3)). General guidelines have been issued at State level, amplifying the relevant factors.[115] They provide a structured process by which the relevant factors can be interpreted and the level of assessment determined. A feature of these guidelines is that they envisage documentation of the duty to have regard to relevant considerations, thereby enhancing greater accountability.[116]

Without limiting the generality of the s 111 duty, a determining authority must consider the affect of an activity on:

- any biobanking agreement entered into under Pt 7A of TSCA that applies to the land;
- any relevant conservation agreement entered into under the *National Parks and Wildlife Act 1974*;
- any joint management agreement entered into under the TSCA;
- any wilderness area (within the meaning of the *Wilderness Act 1987*);
- the register of critical habitat;
- threatened species, populations and ecological communities, and their habitats;
- protected fauna or protected native plants within the meaning of the *National Parks and Wildlife Act 1974*. (s 111(2))

Section 112: The duty to obtain and consider an EIS

The second obligation under Pt 5 relates to formal documentation of environmental assessment. A determining authority must not carry out an activity, or grant an approval in relation to an activity that is likely to significantly affect the environment unless the determining authority has obtained and has examined and considered an EIS in respect of the activity (s 112(1)).[117] If the activity is likely to significantly affect critical habitat, or threatened species, populations or ecological communities, or their habitats, a SIS or an EIS that includes a SIS must be obtained and considered. These triggers are discussed in the final part of this Section.

The Court of Appeal has held that the decision as to whether a SIS is required under Pt 4 is a jurisdictional fact and thus reviewable *de novo* in the Land and Environment Court's Class 4 jurisdiction.[118] The same reasoning is undoubtedly applicable to EISs and SISs required under Pt 5, thus displacing the Land and Environment Court's more deferential standard of scrutiny. Historically, the Land

115 NSW Department of Urban Affairs and Planning, *Is an EIS Required? Best Practice Guidelines for Part 5 of the Environmental Planning and Assessment Act 1979*, <http://www.planning.nsw.gov.au/assessingdev/pdf/gu_isaneisrequired.pdf> (accessed 23 September 2006).

116 Amongst other things this avoids the surprising decision in *Rundle v Tweed Shire Council* (1989) 68 LGRA 308 at 326 that the determining authority had constructively complied with s 111, even though it was not aware of its responsibilities under Pt 5.

117 Activities in respect of which an EIS must be prepared may also be prescribed; see EPAR cll 244G, 244H in relation to rail infrastructure facilities.

118 *Timbarra Protection Coalition Inc v Ross Mining NL* (1999) 46 NSWLR 55.

and Environment Court has only inquired as to whether the consent or determining authority had acted reasonably, having regard to the material actually or constructively before it. Jurisdictional fact review requires the court to determine the existence of the fact afresh. To this end the court receives fresh evidence which, subject to the rules of evidence, may be more or different from the material considered by the consent or determining authority.[119] Further, the High Court has rejected a doctrine of deference to the administrator's finding.[120]

In its consideration of an EIS, the determining authority is under an express duty to consider:

- any representations made during the public consultation process;
- the report of any commission of inquiry or other examination; and
- for the purpose of assessing any affect on a threatened species, population or ecological community or its habitat, the terms of any recovery plan or threat abatement plan relating to the land. (ss 112(1), 112A)

The duty to invite and consider public submissions

If an EIS has been prepared for an activity, it must be publicly exhibited and any person may inspect it and make submissions (s 113(1), (2)).

The determining authority must respond to the environmental assessment process, including public submissions. As soon as practicable after a decision has been made to carry out the activity, or refrain from doing so, the determining authority must prepare and make public a report commenting on:

- the EIS;
- any representations made to it about the proposed activity;
- the affects of the proposed activity on the environment;
- the proponent's proposals to mitigate any adverse affects of the activity on the environment;
- the findings and recommendations of any report on the EIS and submissions prepared by the Director-General (s 113(5));
- the findings and recommendations of any commission of inquiry;
- any advice given to it by the Minister (under EPAA s 114) following a commission of inquiry. (EPAR cl 243)

The report must also give full particulars of the determining authority's decision on the proposed activity and, if the authority has granted approval to the carrying out of the activity, any conditions or modifications imposed or required by the authority.

Exemptions from the section 111 and section 112 duties

Exemptions to the s 111 and s 112 duties were created by amendments to the Act in 2005 and 2006. Sections 111 and 112 do not apply to:

- a modification of an activity, following environmental assessment, that will reduce its overall environmental impact;

---

119 See *Corporation of the City of Enfield v Development Assessment Commission* (2000) 199 CLR 135.
120 Ibid.

- a routine activity (such as the maintenance of infrastructure) that the Minister determines has a low environmental impact and that is carried out in accordance with a code approved by the Minister;
- an activity (or part of an activity) that has been approved, or is to be carried out, by another determining authority after environmental assessment under Pt 5. (s 110E)

Decision-making

Relevant considerations

An EIS, and related submissions, consultations and inquiry reports, are only relevant considerations for the decision-maker or concurrence authority. The function of the assessment process is to inform decision-makers, but not to determine the outcome. Having considered the relevant matters, the determining authority may approve the activity, subject to conditions or modifications designed to reduce or eliminate any detrimental environmental impacts, or determine that the activity should not go ahead (s 112(4)).

Concurrence where a SIS is required

In relation to critical habitat, or activities that are likely to significantly affect threatened species, populations or ecological communities or their habitats, there are requirements to obtain concurrence or to consult before determining that an activity can go ahead. If a Minister is a determining authority, the Minister must not carry out, or approve, an activity, unless that Minister has consulted with the Minister administering the TSCA (EPAA s 112B). Where the determining authority is not a Minister, the concurrence of the Director-General of National Parks and Wildlife must be obtained (s 112C). The Minister administering the TSCA may, if the Minister considers that it is appropriate, elect to act in the place of the Director-General. Both the Director-General and the Minister must have regard to considerations listed in the Act, including the ESD principles (ss 112D, 112E).

Modifications

The proposed activity may be modified having regard to its environmental impacts. EPAA s 112(4) provides that if a determining authority is satisfied that the activity will detrimentally affect the environment (including critical habitat) or threatened species, populations or ecological communities, or their habitats, it may:

- where it is granting approval to a proponent, impose such conditions or require such modifications as will in its opinion eliminate or reduce the detrimental effect of the activity on the environment, or refuse approval;
- where it is also the proponent of the activity, modify the proposed activity so as to eliminate or reduce the detrimental effect of the activity on the environment, or refrain from undertaking the activity.

If the modifications are such that the activity is likely to have significant new impacts on the environment, the question arises as to whether the Pt 5 assessment process must begin afresh. The question was answered by amendments to the Act in

2005 and 2006 which exempt a determining authority from the s 111 and s 112 duties when modifying an activity, that has already been assessed, so as to reduce its overall environmental impact (s 110E(a)). 'Modify' was given an expansive meaning in *Transport Action Group Against Motorways Inc v Roads and Traffic Authority*.[121] It covers changes falling short of a radical transformation of the original activity. Further, it was held in that case that a modification can have a new detrimental affect, which was not addressed in the environmental impact assessment, provided it eliminates or reduces the detrimental affect of the activity viewed as a whole.

No appeal under Part 5

Part 5 does not create any rights of appeal against the determining authority's decision. Unlike Pt 4, persons who have made a submission by way of objection do not have a right of appeal on the merits. They may seek judicial review of the decision under EPAA s 123, on grounds of non-compliance with the law. Judicial review is concerned only with issues of legality and not the merits of the decision.

The proponent does not have a right of appeal under Pt 5, but may have a right of appeal under the legislation requiring government approval of the activity.

Environmental impact statements: key issues

In designing a statutory scheme for environmental assessment, a number of key issues need to be resolved, including:[122]

- What levels of assessment should be required for which projects?
- What should trigger the requirement for an assessment document?
- Who decides whether an assessment document is triggered?
- At what stages should environmental assessment be required?
- Who should prepare the assessment document?
- What should the assessment document address?
- What mechanisms of external scrutiny, including public participation, should be put in place?
- What should be the function of the assessment document in decision-making?
- How should the requirements be enforced?
- Is provision made for post-approval monitoring and auditing?

The ways in which Pts 3A, 4 and 5 of the EPAA resolve these issues have for the most part been outlined above. The final part of this Section addresses the outstanding issues.

---

121 (1999) 104 LGERA 133. See also *Schaffer Corp Ltd v Hawkesbury CC* (1992) 77 LGRA 21.

122 See generally Ian Thomas and Mandy Elliot, *Environmental Impact Assessment in Australia – Theory and Practice* (4th ed, Federation Press, 2005); Christopher Wood, *Environmental Impact Assessment: A Comparative Review* (Longman, 1995); Nick Harvey, *Environmental Impact Assessment – Procedures Practice and Prospects in Australia* (Oxford University Press, 1998); Alan Gilpin, *Environmental Impact Assessment: Cutting Edge for the Twenty-first Century* (Cambridge University Press, 1995); Conacher and Conacher, above n 12.

Triggering the requirement for an assessment document

Likely to significantly effect the environment

As previously explained, the trigger for an EIS under Pt 4 of the EPAA uses the listing or categorical approach. Types of development requiring an EIS are listed and are referred to as 'designated development'. In contrast Pt 5 requires the preparation and consideration of an EIS if the proposed activity is 'likely to significantly affect the environment'.

In deciding whether an activity is likely to significantly affect the environment, the EPAR sets out an extensive list of factors that must be taken into account (cl 228(1)). Alternatively, the Director-General may establish guidelines relating to activities generally or activities of a particular kind (cl 228(3)). General guidelines have been issued at State level, providing a structured process for identifying and analysing the issues and evaluating the likely environmental significance of impacts.[123]

Litigation has also provided guidance in determining whether an activity is likely to significantly affect the environment. First, it has been held that 'likely' means a real chance or possibility, rather than 'more probable than not'.[124] In *Booth v Bosworth*, Branson J, in considering the similar expression in the EPBCA, inclined to the view that the expression 'likely' should be understood in the sense of 'prone', 'with a propensity' or 'liable'.[125] This would be consistent with the precautionary principle and would tend to avoid the risk to the environment which would flow from the need for scientific certainty or confidence. The expression 'likely' is typical of EIA legislation and a reflection of the era in which such legislation emerged.[126] The legal frameworks for environmental impact assessment were bedded down at a time when environmental decision-making focused on harm or danger - on responding to known hazards or remedying damage. The precautionary principle subsequently emerged as a legal tool to guide decision-makers and, in particular, to alert them to uncertainties relating to causation and effect, and our incomplete knowledge base. Use of the term 'likely' should not be an invitation to ignore uncertain impacts. Where there is a risk of serious or irreversible damage, lack of scientific certainty about the potential impacts will not itself justify a decision that the action is not likely to have a significant impact.

Secondly, 'significantly' means 'important' or 'more than ordinary'.[127] That is only a partial definition as significance can be statistical, ecological or social, or arise from the planning context.[128] The Department of Planning has observed that it depends on:[129]

---

123 NSW Department of Urban Affairs and Planning, above n 68.

124 *Jarasius v Forestry Commission of NSW* (1988) 71 LGRA 79 at 94; *Drummoyne Municipal Council v Roads and Traffic Authority of NSW* (1989) 67 LGRA 155 at 163; *Drummoyne Municipal Council v Maritime Services Board* (1991) 72 LGRA 186 at 193; *Oshlack v Richmond River Shire Council and Iron Gates Development Pty Ltd* (1993) 82 LGERA 222.

125 *Booth v Bosworth* (2001) 114 FCR 39 at [97]-[98].

126 The seminal legislation was the US *National Environmental Protection Act 1969* (NEPA).

127 *Jarasius v Forestry Commission of NSW* (1988) 71 LGRA 79; *Drummoyne Municipal Council v Maritime Services Board* (1991) 72 LGRA 186; *Oshlack v Richmond River Shire Council and Iron Gates Development Pty Ltd* (1993) 82 LGERA 222.

128 Thomas and Elliot, above n 122, at 143-144.

129 NSW Department of Planning, above n 21, at 48.

- fact or degree and is conditioned by the circumstances of the environment;
- the context and intensity;
- the existence of pre-established legal limits or precedents;
- the level of social or political acceptance.[130]

In *Bailey v Forestry Commission*,[131] Hemmings J accepted that in each case it is relevant to consider not only the absolute qualitative environmental affects of the activity, but also those in the context of existing adverse impacts arising from the subject environment. His Honour approved the approach in *Hanly v Kleindienst*[132] which requires the proposed activity to be viewed in the light of at least two relevant factors:

- the extent to which the action will cause adverse environmental effects in excess of those created by existing uses in the area affected; and
- the absolute quantitative adverse environmental effects of the action itself, including the cumulative harm that results from its contribution to existing adverse conditions or uses in the affected area.

The term 'environment' encompasses all aspects of the surroundings of humans, whether affecting any human as an individual or in his or her social groupings (s 4(1)). Social and economic affects must be factored in,[133] but if these are the only significant affects it is unlikely that an EIS would be required.[134] Questions of scale are important. In the first Pt 5 case, *Kivi v Forestry Commission of NSW*,[135] it was made clear that consideration should not be confined to the likely impacts on the immediate geographical area in which the proposed activity would occur. The court looked to the whole undertaking of which the activity formed a part in order to understand its cumulative and continuing affect. This approach, however, cannot be used to diminish the significance of likely impacts.[136] Nor is it relevant that the zoning of the area permits the activity without the need for development consent.[137]

A determining authority may select the activity it proposes to assess,[138] but the activity cannot be erroneously described so as to lessen its likely impacts.[139] The likelihood of significant environmental affects should be determined having regard to the 'raw' activity, not the activity as proposed to be conditioned or modified by the determining authority. In *Drummoyne Municipal Council v Maritime Services Board*,[140] the officer who assessed the proposal determined that the marina extension as proposed would be likely to significantly affect the environment. However,

---

130 But see *Jarasius v Forestry Commission of NSW* (1988) 71 LGRA 79 at 93.

131 (1989) 67 LGRA 200.

132 471 F 2d 823 (1972).

133 *Severn Shire Council v Water Resources Commission* (1982) 47 LGRA 257.

134 See Brian Preston, 'The EIS Threshold Test: When is an Activity Likely to Significantly Affect the Environment' (1990) 7 *EPLJ* 147 at 158.

135 (1982) 47 LGRA 35.

136 *Jarasius v Forestry Commission of NSW* (1988) 71 LGRA 79; *Bailey v Forestry Commission of NSW* (1989) 67 LGRA 200.

137 *Bailey v Forestry Commission of NSW* (1989) 67 LGRA 200.

138 *Prineas v Forestry Commission of NSW* (1984) 53 LGRA 160 (CA).

139 *Liverpool City Council v Roads and Traffic Authority and Interlink Roads Pty Ltd* (1991) 74 LGRA 265.

140 (1991) 72 LGRA 186.

the likely affects could be avoided by the imposition of conditions. Conditional approval was granted without obtaining and considering an EIS. The Land and Environment Court held that the approval was invalid.[141] Of course, and desirably, the proponent should consider environmental impacts from an early stage of concept development and option selection, thereby incorporating ameliorative measures into the proposal.[142]

Likely to significantly effect threatened species, populations or ecological communities

The requirement for a SIS, both under Pts 4 and 5, is triggered if the proposal is on land that is, or is a part of, critical habitat or is likely to significantly affect threatened species, populations or ecological communities, or their habitats. Judicial interpretation of the term 'likely to significantly affect the environment', discussed above, is also relevant to deciding whether a SIS is required. In particular, an approach based on the precautionary principle is appropriate.[143] In addition, EPAA s 5A sets out a list of mandatory considerations. The s 5A considerations are more generally relevant to decision-makers in their consideration and determination of development proposals, or in deciding whether concurrence should be granted.

EPAA s 5A requires the following to be taken into account:

- in the case of a threatened species, whether the action proposed is likely to have an adverse effect on the life cycle of the species such that a viable local population of the species is likely to be placed at risk of extinction;
- in the case of an endangered population, whether the action proposed is likely to have an adverse effect on the life cycle of the species that constitutes the endangered population such that a viable local population of the species is likely to be placed at risk of extinction;
- in the case of an endangered ecological community or critically endangered ecological community, whether the action proposed:
  - o is likely to have an adverse effect on the extent of the ecological community such that its local occurrence is likely to be placed at risk of extinction, or
  - o is likely to substantially and adversely modify the composition of the ecological community such that its local occurrence is likely to be placed at risk of extinction;
- in relation to the habitat of a threatened species, population or ecological community:

141 Ibid. See also *Enfield City v Development Assessment Commission* (1996) 91 LGERA 277 at 300. This approach was not followed by the Court of Appeal when deciding whether a modification under Pt 5 eliminates or reduces the detrimental affect of a proposal. In this context it is the conditional change that is to be tested: *Transport Action Group Against Motorways Inc v Roads and Traffic Authority* (1999) 104 LGERA 133 at [81] per Mason P, Sheller JA agreeing.

142 See *Smyth v Nambucca Shire Council* (1999) 105 LGERA 65 at [10]; *Eastlakes Golf Club v Botany Bay City Council* [2006] NSWLEC 343 at [62].

143 *BT Goldsmith Planning Services v Blacktown City Council* [2005] NSWLEC 210; *Gales Holdings Pty Ltd v Tweed Shire Council* [2006] NSWLEC 85; *Gales Holdings Pty Ltd v Tweed Shire Council* [2006] NSWLEC 212. See also *Providence Projects Pty Ltd v Gosford City Council* [2006] NSWLEC 52.

- o the extent to which habitat is likely to be removed or modified as a result of the action proposed,[144] and
- o whether an area of habitat is likely to become fragmented or isolated from other areas of habitat as a result of the proposed action, and
- o the importance of the habitat to be removed, modified, fragmented or isolated to the long-term survival of the species, population or ecological community in the locality;

- whether the action proposed is likely to have an adverse effect on critical habitat (either directly or indirectly);
- whether the action proposed is consistent with the objectives or actions of a recovery plan or threat abatement plan;
- whether the action proposed constitutes or is part of a key threatening process or is likely to result in the operation of, or increase the impact of, a key threatening process.[145]

Section 5A has colloquially, but misleadingly, been referred to as the 'eight-part test'. It now comprises seven, not eight, parts. The complexity of the original test led to its amendment, bringing the scale of assessment down to local level and providing more comprehensive tests for endangered ecological communities and the assessment of impact on habitat. It is not a test, but rather a set of factors that must be taken into account in arriving at a conclusion as to whether there is likely to be a significant affect on threatened species, populations or ecological communities or their habitat. The Land and Environment Court has recognised that the question is not answered by finding a positive answer to one or more of the factors; nor is a negative answer required if only one of the eight factors carries an affirmative answer.[146] Furthermore, s 5A does not exhaust the inquiry. There may be other relevant facts and circumstances which are not specifically referred to in s 5A.[147] Cumulative impact is a relevant matter.[148]

Stage at which assessment is required

The legal requirements for environmental assessment suffer two crippling shortcomings. First, they focus on the single project. Secondly, they focus unduly on a single document.

The project focus of environmental impact assessment law is arguably a fatal flaw in its design. It obscures the fact that decisions taken at the policy or strategic level pre-empt choices at the project stage. Environmental assessment of alternatives

---

144 A quantitative approach based on the size of the area is not appropriate: *BT Goldsmith Planning Services Pty Ltd v Blacktown City Council* [2005] NSWLEC 210 at [80]-[82].

145 'Key threatening process' has the same meaning as in TSCA and Pt 7A of FMA.

146 *Plumb v Penrith City Council* [2002] NSWLEC 223 at [36]-[37]; *Masterbuilt Pty Ltd v Hornsby Shire Council* [2002] NSWLEC 170; *Carstens v Pittwater Council* (1999) 111 LGERA 1 at [59]-[61]; *Gales Holdings Pty Limited v Tweed Shire Council* [2006] NSWLEC 85.

147 *Plumb v Penrith City Council* [2002] NSWLEC 223 at [37].

148 *BT Goldsmith Planning Services Pty Limited v Blacktown City Council* [2005] NSWLEC 210.

is a planning activity. At the project stage, its contribution is limited to design changes and mitigation measures.[149]

The focus on a stand-alone document encourages a perception that environmental assessment is a one-off hurdle to be overcome and undermines the justification for proponent-prepared documents, namely the internalisation of environmental considerations.[150] It has been suggested that if environmental impact assessment is to have continuing utility at the project stage it should be an iterative process, engaged in over the life of the project: '[I]t must transform from being directed at the production of a stand-alone report to a process able to contribute apposite environmental advice in good time for each of the decision-points in the planning process'.[151]

Even at the project stage, it may only become apparent at a late stage of option selection and design that an EIS is required. Under EPAA Pt 4, an EIS must accompany a development application and is considered by the consent authority when determining whether development should go ahead and, if so, under what conditions. Under Pt 5, if an EIS must be prepared, it must be considered before carrying out an activity or granting an approval in relation to an activity (s 112(1)). As previously explained, 'development' and 'activity' are confined to physical actions. When the EPAA was initially passed, 'activity' was a much broader concept encompassing the decision-making process leading up to the implementation of a proposal, including financial outlays, the entering into of a lease and the resumption of an easement. Thus, where the determining authority was also the proponent, an EIS could be required at an early stage of project planning. However, the definition was amended to bear the same meaning as 'development' under Pt 4. Thus there is a real danger that pre-emptive decisions will diminish the weight of an EIS prepared only at the point of deciding whether to carry out the activity. It is not open to argue the rule against bias where commercial considerations predominate because a public authority has earlier locked itself into agreements, or expended money.[152]

Where the determining authority is also the proponent, the duty under EPAA s 111 to consider environmental impacts to the fullest extent reasonably practicable arguably arises at an early stage and continues through implementation of the activity. Section 111 requires a determining authority to take account of environmental factors 'in its consideration of an activity'. As the Court of Appeal has recognised, the duty does not arise at any specific time and thus may be designed to entail a continuous monitoring of the development.[153] This is now qualified by an amendment to the EPAA in 2005, which provides that the s 111 duty does not apply to a modification of an activity already assessed where that will reduce its overall environmental impact (s 110E(a)).

It has been held that Pt 5 permits, in appropriate circumstances, an EIS which adequately assesses the overall activity without necessarily at that time also assessing the detail of the site specific impacts.[154] This would be especially appropriate for multi-stage projects, which are particularly prone to fragmentation and hence

---

149 See Brown and McDonald, above n 5.

150 Ibid.

151 Ibid at 71.

152 *Blue Mountains City Council v Prospect County Council* (1992) 74 LGRA 129

153 *Guthega Development Pty Ltd v Minister* (1987) 7 NSWLR 353 at 367.

154 *Bailey v Forestry Commission of NSW* (1989) 67 LGRA 200.

pre-emption of decisions at later stages. Further EISs may be required before carrying out site-specific proposals.

Under Pt 3A, the Minister may approve a concept plan and environmental assessment will occur at that earlier stage (s 75N). Subsequent environmental assessment of the project or stages of the project is in the Minister's discretion (s 75P).

What must the assessment document address?

Environmental impact statements

An EIS, whether required under Pt 4 or Pt 5, must be prepared in accordance with Sch 2 to the EPAR (cll 72, 230). It must include:

- a summary of the EIS;
- a statement of the objectives of the development or activity;
- an analysis of any feasible alternatives to the carrying out of the development or activity, having regard to its objectives, including the consequences of not carrying out the development or activity;
- an analysis of the development or activity, including:
  - a full description of the development or activity, and
  - a general description of the environment likely to be affected by the development or activity, together with a detailed description of those aspects of the environment that are likely to be significantly affected, and
  - the likely impact on the environment of the development or activity, and
  - a full description of the measures proposed to mitigate any adverse effects of the development or activity on the environment, and
  - a list of any approvals that must be obtained under any other Act or law before the development or activity may lawfully be carried out;
- a compilation of proposed mitigation measures;
- the reasons justifying the carrying out of the development or activity in the manner proposed, having regard to biophysical, economic and social considerations, including the following ESD principles:
  - the 'precautionary principle',
  - 'intergenerational equity',
  - 'conservation of biological diversity and ecological integrity',
  - 'improved valuation, pricing and incentive mechanisms'.

The Director-General of the Department of Planning may stipulate further matters that must be addressed in the EIS. This 'scoping' is an important step in tailoring the assessment to the particular project and the applicant or proponent is under an obligation to consult the Director (cll 73, 231).

Species impact statement

A SIS, whether required under Pt 4 or Pt 5, must be prepared in accordance with s 110 of TSCA (ss 78A(8)(b), 112(1A)). It must include a full description of the action proposed, including its nature, extent, location, timing and layout. Further, it must include, to the fullest extent reasonably practicable, the following information relating to threatened species or populations:

- a general description of the threatened species or populations known or likely to be present in the area that is the subject of the action and in any area that is likely to be affected by the action;
- an assessment of which threatened species or populations known or likely to be present in the area are likely to be affected by the action;
- for each species or population likely to be affected, details of its local, regional and State-wide conservation status, the key threatening processes generally affecting it, its habitat requirements and any recovery plan or threat abatement plan applying to it;
- an estimate of the local and regional abundance of those species or populations;
- an assessment of whether those species or populations are adequately represented in conservation reserves (or other similar protected areas) in the region;
- an assessment of whether any of those species or populations is at the limit of its known distribution;
- a full description of the type, location, size and condition of the habitat (including critical habitat) of those species and populations and details of the distribution and condition of similar habitats in the region;
- a full assessment of the likely effect of the action on those species and populations, including, if possible, the quantitative effect of local populations in the cumulative effect in the region;
- a description of any feasible alternatives to the action that are likely to be of lesser effect and the reasons justifying the carrying out of the action in the manner proposed, having regard to the biophysical, economic and social considerations and the ESD principles;
- a full description and justification of the measures proposed to mitigate any adverse effect of the action on the species and populations, including a compilation of those measures;
- a list of any approvals that must be obtained under any other Act or law before the action may be lawfully carried out, including details of the conditions of any existing approvals that are relevant to the species or population.

Similar information is required in relation to ecological communities.

As with EISs, the Director-General of National Parks and Wildlife may stipulate further matters that must be addressed in the SIS (TSCA s 111). Further, the Director-General may limit or modify the matters to be included in a particular SIS (TSCA s 111(3)).

Every SIS must include details of the qualifications and experience in threatened species conservation of the person preparing the statement and of any other person who has conducted research or investigations relied on in preparing the statement (TSCA s 110(4)).

Compliance with the statutory requirements

The Land and Environment Court in its Class 4 jurisdiction can supervise compliance with the statutory requirements relating to the contents of EISs and SISs. The court's supervisory jurisdiction was established in the decision of Cripps J in *Prineas v Forestry Commission of NSW*.[155] The case, however, laid down a less than rigorous standard of review, making it difficult to challenge successfully the adequacy of an EIS or SIS. The court eschewed a standard of perfection. However, its preferred test of 'substantial compliance'[156] has condoned EISs that are less than satisfactory.[157] For example, in *Prineas* the environmental assessment of proposed rainforest logging was held to be adequate even though it failed to assess a number of important issues, including the cumulative impact of future hardwood logging in the vicinity, feasible alternatives to rainforest logging, Aboriginal cultural heritage and endangered species.

Substantial compliance must be determined in light of the purpose of environmental assessment, which is to alert the decision-maker and the public to the inherent problems of the proposal, to encourage public participation and to ensure that the decision-maker takes a hard look at what is proposed.[158] In particular, the statement must not be superficial, subjective or non-informative. It must be sufficiently specific to direct a reasonably intelligent and informed mind to the possible environmental consequences of the proposed development.[159]

More than 30 years of testing the quality of EISs in the courts have produced what Raff describes as a 'common law of EIA'.[160] Raff distils 10 basic principles from the case law dealing with NEPA-style EISs. These are:

- An assessment cannot be restricted to site-specific environmental affects.[161] Provided there is a real and sufficient link, it should address direct and indirect impacts, including upstream and downstream impacts, and impacts that result from further activities that are made possible or facilitated by the proposal.[162]
- The assessment must contain a statement of alternative courses of action and their environmental significance even if it is beyond the power of the proponent to implement them.[163]
- Greater plans must be assessed in addition to single phases in their execution.[164]

---

155 (1983) 49 LGRA 402 (NSWLEC); affirmed on appeal (1984) 53 LGRA 160.

156 *Prineas v Forestry Commission of NSW* (1983) 49 LGRA 402. The same approach applies to SISs: *NSW Land and Housing Corporation v Campbelltown City Council* (2002) 126 LGERA 348, and to environmental assessments under Pt 3A: *Gray v Minister for Planning* [2006] NSWLEC 720 at [149]-150].

157 For example, *Prineas v Forestry Commission of NSW* (1983) 49 LGRA 402; *Bell v Minister of Urban Affairs & Planning* (1997) 95 LGERA 86.

158 *Prineas v Forestry Commission of NSW* (1983) 49 LGRA 402; *Schaffer Corp Ltd v Hawkesbury CC* (1992) 77 LGRA 21 (overruled on different grounds in *Egan v Hawkesbury CC* (1993) 79 LGERA 321); *Liverpool City Council v Roads and Traffic Authority and Interlink Roads Pty Ltd* (1991) 74 LGRA 265.

159 *Prineas v Forestry Commission of NSW* (1983) 49 LGRA 402; *Schaffer Corp Ltd v Hawkesbury CC* (1992) 77 LGRA 21.

160 Murray Raff, 'Ten Principles of Quality in Environmental Impact Assessment' (1997) 14 *EPLJ* 207.

161 See *Bell v Minister of Urban Affairs & Planning* (1997) 95 LGERA 86.

162 See *Gray v Minister for Planning* [2006] NSWLEC 720 at [83]-[100].

163 See *Jarasius v Forestry Commission of NSW* (1988) 71 LGRA 79 at 100.

164 See *Jarasius v Forestry Commission of NSW* (1988) 71 LGRA 79 at 96; *Bailey v Forestry Commission of NSW* (1989) 67 LGRA 200 at 210.

- A large project should not be segmented into smaller phases.[165]
- The range of alternatives that must be discussed is limited to realistic alternatives that will be reasonably available within the time intended for the activity.
- Alternative courses of action must include the option of doing nothing.
- The assessment must engage in a real inquiry and not merely dispose of alternatives in favour of a decision which has already been arrived at.
- Environmental affects are not to be disregarded merely because they are difficult to identify or quantify.[166]
- The EIA must take a 'hard look' at the environmental consequences of the project and what that entails.
- The findings of EIA must be presented in clear language and the methodologies employed to arrive at them must be explained.

To these principles should be added the emerging 'common law' of ESD. An approach to environmental assessment informed by ESD requires, amongst other things, sufficient information of impacts that are cumulative, ongoing and long term.[167] In *Gray v Minister for Planning*,[168] Pain J held that the Director-General had failed to take into account intergenerational equity and the precautionary principle when he decided that the environmental assessment under EPAA Pt 3A of a proposed coal mine was adequate, and that this constituted a failure to comply with a legal requirement. The environmental assessment that had been placed on public exhibition did not include an analysis of the potential greenhouse gas emissions from the burning of coal by third parties. Her Honour held that there was a sufficiently proximate link between the proposed mining, the purpose of which was for use as fuel in power stations, and the emission of greenhouse gases which contribute to global warming, to require assessment of the greenhouse gas impacts.

Despite these important principles, the court will look to the EIS as a whole to determine as a matter of fact and degree whether it passes muster. Viewed in this context, omissions or defects may not be so significant as to invalidate the whole statement.[169] A troubling aspect of the court's reasoning is the reliance placed on members of the public to remedy omissions by raising the issues themselves.[170]

Changes to the proposed development may be made between the exhibition of the EIS and the determination of the proposal, but not so as to result in a completely different proposal.[171]

---

165 However, it is for the proponent to select the activity: *Prineas v Forestry Commission of NSW* (1984) 53 LGRA 160 (CA) per Hutley JA.

166 See *Gray v Minister for Planning* [2006] NSWLEC 720 esp at [138] per Pain J.

167 Ibid.

168 Ibid at [135], [126].

169 *Bell v Minister of Urban Affairs & Planning* (1997) 95 LGERA 86. See also *Gray v Minister for Planning* [2006] NSWLEC 720 at [149]-[150] per Pain J.

170 See *Prineas v Forestry Commission of NSW* (1983) 49 LGRA 402; *Bell v Minister of Urban Affairs & Planning* (1997) 95 LGERA 86.

171 *Schaffer Corp Ltd v Hawkesbury CC* (1992) 77 LGRA 21. See also *Transport Action Group Against Motorways Inc v Roads and Traffic Authority* (1999) 104 LGERA 133 (CA).

External scrutiny and enforcement

It is crucial that there be external scrutiny of the important decisions made by consent and determining authorities. This is all the more so where the proponent is also the decision-maker. It is also vital that there be external scrutiny of the quality of environmental assessment documents. As the statement is prepared or commissioned by the proponent or applicant, the temptation to produce an advocacy document is great.

The public and the Land and Environment Court have an important role to play in external scrutiny. As previously discussed, the assessment documents must be publicly exhibited and submissions invited and considered. Any person has the right to apply to the Land and Environment Court to remedy or restrain non-compliance with the legislation (subject to the restrictions previously discussed in relation to Pt 3A). On judicial review, the court will closely supervise the decision as to whether an EIS is required.[172] The court can also ensure that the prescribed procedures have been followed and that the EIS substantially complies with the requirements. The determination as to whether the development should go ahead is also judicially reviewable on grounds of legality. Remedies, however, are in the discretion of the court.[173]

The Minister and Department of Planning can play a role. Under Pt 3A, the Director-General's role in determining the form and adequacy of the environmental assessment is pivotal.[174] Under Pt 5 external scrutiny by the Department is discretionary. The Department may examine a Pt 5 EIS, and any submissions made, and report its findings and recommendations to the determining authority (s 113(5)). The Department's report must be made public (s 113(6)). More generally, a Commission of Inquiry may be appointed by the Minister (s 119).

Before 2005, a determining authority who was also the proponent could not go ahead with an activity, in respect of which an EIS was required, without the approval of the Planning Minister. This requirement has been repealed. The Minister now has a discretion to call in, under Pt 3A, a Pt 5 activity for which the proponent is also the determining authority, and which in the opinion of the proponent would require an EIS under Pt 5 (s 75B(2)(b)).

As discussed previously, if a SIS is required, either under Pt 4 or Pt 5, consent cannot be granted without the concurrence of the Director-General of National Parks or the Director of NSW Fisheries. If the Minister is the consent authority, there is only the requirement for consultation at the ministerial level.

Post-approval auditing

Post-approval monitoring and auditing provide important feedback on, and accountability for, the predictions made in an EIS and the judgments made at the time of deciding that the project should go ahead. Accountability is enhanced if monitoring and auditing reports are made public. Monitoring and auditing are also important mechanisms in ensuring compliance with conditions of approval. Despite

---

172 *Timbarra Protection Coalition Inc v Ross Mining NL* (1999) 46 NSWLR 55.

173 See, for example, *Liverpool City Council v Roads and Traffic Authority and Interlink Roads Pty Ltd* (1991) 74 LGRA 265 where a remedy was refused on grounds of futility.

174 See *Gray v Minister for Planning* [2006] NSWLEC 720.

these advantages, monitoring and auditing is not systematically required and has been described as the weakest link in environmental assessment procedures.[175]

As previously outlined, EPAA Pt 3A makes provision for post-approval monitoring and auditing (Pt 6 Divs 2B and 2C). The Minister is expressly empowered to impose conditions requiring monitoring and reporting, and environmental audits, at the time of approving the project or at any other time, and these conditions may be varied or revoked (s 122C). Both compliance and impact monitoring and auditing can be required (s 122B(2)). There are no similar provisions in Pts 4 or 5, although monitoring requirements can be imposed as a condition of development consent or in determining the terms on which a Pt 5 activity can go ahead.

A significant difficulty in imposing effective monitoring conditions and in responding to feedback is that development consent under Pt 4 is final and conditions attached to the consent cannot leave open the possibility that the development carried out will be significantly different from the development for which consent was granted.[176] Subsequent modifications of the development can only be made on the application of the person entitled to act on the development consent. This clearly restricts the capacity of consent authorities to respond to scientific uncertainty and engage in adaptive management. The principle of finality does not apply to Pt 5 activities, at least where the determining authority is also the proponent.[177]

Section 2: *Environment Protection and Biodiversity Conservation Act 1999* (Cth)

Overview

Since 1974, the Commonwealth has had in place legislation to assess environmental impact. Before 2000, the legislation made a commitment to assessing the environmental impact of Commonwealth proposals, recommendations, agreements, expenditure and decisions if there would be a significant affect on the environment.[178] In practice, such wide-ranging strategic assessment was not undertaken. The legislation is most remembered for litigation it spawned relating to Commonwealth decisions in respect of export approval (following, for example, woodchipping or sandmining) and foreign exchange approval (for resort development, by way of example). In these respects, the legislation overlapped State assessment and approval processes. In 1992, the Commonwealth and States entered into an intergovernmental agreement – the Intergovernmental Agreement on the Environment (IGAE) – which sought to confine the role of the Commonwealth to matters of national environmental significance, avoid duplication of Commonwealth and State assessment processes and agree on overarching principles for environmental regulation and decision-making. The Commonwealth's commitments under the IGAE relating to environmental assessment and approval were embodied in the *Environ-*

175 Nicole Malone, 'Environmental Impact Monitoring' (1997) 14 *EPLJ* 222. See also Harvey, above n 122.

176 *Mison v Randwick Municipal Council* (1991) 73 LGRA 349.

177 *Transport Action Group Against Motorways Inc v Roads and Traffic Authority* (1999) 104 LGERA 133.

178 *Environment Protection (Impact of Proposals) Act 1974* (Cth).

ment Protection and Biodiversity Conservation Act 1999 (EPBCA), which came into force on 16 July 2000.

The objects of the EPBCA include:

- to provide for the protection of the environment, especially those aspects of the environment that are matters of national environmental significance;
- to promote ESD through the conservation and ecologically sustainable use of natural resources;
- to assist in the co-operative implementation of Australia's international environmental responsibilities. (s 3(1)(b))

ESD comprises the principle that decision-making processes should effectively integrate both long-term and short-term economic, environmental, social and equitable considerations (s 3A). It also comprises the precautionary principle, the principle of intergenerational equity, the principle that conservation of biological diversity and ecological integrity should be a fundamental consideration in decision-making, and principles relating to the valuation and pricing of environmental resources (s 3A).

The Federal Court has adopted a purposive interpretation of the EPBCA. The objects of the Act, particularly with regard to the precautionary principle,[179] biodiversity conservation[180] and Australia's international obligations,[181] have informed the court's understanding of its provisions.[182] In *Queensland Conservation Council Inc v Minister for the Environment and Heritage*,[183] Kiefel J recognised the 'high public policy' apparent in the objects of the Act, taking the view that no narrow approach should be taken to the interpretation of legislation having objects of this kind. In *Brown v Forestry Tasmania (No 4)*,[184] Marshall J expressly applied the approach of Mason CJ and Deane J in *Teoh's* case[185] in favouring a construction of the Act, as far as the language of the legislation permits, that is in conformity and not in conflict with Australia's international obligations.

The identification of 'matters of national environmental significance' that require Commonwealth assessment and approval is inevitably contentious. Ecological impacts elude political jurisdictions not only because of their transboundary affects but because they are uncertain, long-term and cumulative. The choices made in the EPBCA are necessarily governed by constitutional considerations. However, Australia's international commitments are not fully reflected in the Act despite the Commonwealth's constitutional capacity derived from the external affairs power. A conspicuous omission from the EPBCA is greenhouse impacts.

Part 3 of the EPBCA identifies as *matters of national environmental significance*, requiring Commonwealth assessment and approval, actions that are likely to have a significant impact on:

---

179 *Booth v Bosworth* (2001) 114 FCR 39 at [97]-[98].

180 Ibid at [105]; *Humane Society International Inc v Kyodo Senpaku Kaisha Ltd* [2006] FCAFC 116 at [22]; *Brown v Forestry Tasmania (No 4)* [2006] FCA 1729 at [294]-[301].

181 *Brown v Forestry Tasmania (No 4)* [2006] FCA 1729 at [294]-[301]; *Minister for Environment and Heritage v Queensland Conservation Council Inc* (2004) 139 FCR 24 at [2]; *Booth v Bosworth* (2001) 114 FCR 39 at [115] per Branson J.

182 See also *Minister for the Environment and Heritage v Queensland Conservation Council Inc* (2004) 139 FCR 24 at [52].

183 [2003] FCA 1463 at [40].

184 [2006] FCA 1729 at [301].

185 *Minister for Immigration and Ethnic Affairs v Teoh* (1995) 183 CLR 273 at 287.

- the World Heritage values of a World Heritage property;
- the National Heritage values of a National Heritage property;
- the ecological character of a declared Ramsar wetland;
- nationally listed threatened species and communities;
- listed migratory species;
- the environment, if it is a nuclear action;
- the Commonwealth marine environment, or the environment generally if the action is taken within a Commonwealth marine area.

Further matters of national significance may be added by regulation if they fall within the Commonwealth's constitutional powers.

Part 3 of the EPBCA also triggers environmental assessment and approval where an action is likely to have a significant impact on:

- the environment of Commonwealth land, even if taken outside Commonwealth land;
- the environment generally, if the action is undertaken by the Commonwealth.

When the EPBCA is triggered, the proposed action requires the approval of the Commonwealth Environment Minister, following an assessment procedure determined by the Minister within the framework of Pt 8 of the Act. The action is referred to as a *controlled action* (s 67) and the prohibitions in Pt 3 on undertaking controlled actions without approval are referred to as *controlling provisions* (s 67). The Act mandates consideration of the precautionary principle, to the extent that this can be done consistently with the other provisions of the Act, in deciding whether or not an action is a controlled action and whether or not to grant an environmental approval (s 391). There is a range of *exemptions* from the need for Commonwealth assessment and approval, including for classes of actions addressed in a *bilateral agreement* entered into between the Commonwealth and a State or Territory.

The taking of a controlled action without approval, or an exemption, carries criminal consequences or liability for civil penalties. Remediation may also be ordered by the Minister or by the Federal Court. The action may be enjoined by injunction, including a 'public interest injunction'. Public interest litigants are also given extended standing to seek judicial review of Commonwealth government decisions made under the Act.

Commonwealth and State responsibilities

The EPBCA states that in order to achieve its object of protecting the environment and promoting ESD, it is appropriate to strengthen intergovernmental co-operation and minimise duplication, and to focus the role of the Commonwealth on matters of national environmental significance (ss 3(2)(a) and (b), 44). At the same time, it is not the intention of the EPBCA to exclude or limit the concurrent operation of any law of a State or Territory (s 10). Thus an action impacting on a matter on national environmental significance may be subject to requirements for assessment and approval under both Commonwealth and State or Territory laws. Duplication can be avoided by agreement between the Commonwealth and State or Territory accrediting State or Territory practices, procedures, processes or environmental systems.

Bilateral agreements

The Commonwealth may enter into an agreement with a State or Territory for a broad range of purposes, extending at its broadest to 'protection of the environment' and 'promoting the conservation and ecologically sustainable use of natural resources' (s 45(2)). In practice bilateral agreements are directed at securing agreement on actions that will not need Commonwealth assessment, allowing the Commonwealth to rely on State or Territory assessment processes for the class of actions covered by the agreement (s 47). This is referred to as an assessment bilateral. An approvals bilateral may also be made; that is to say, an agreement declaring that a specified class of actions do not need the Commonwealth Minister's approval because they will be dealt with under a State or Territory management arrangement or authorisation process that has been accredited by the Minister (s 46). A bilateral agreement may also provide for State accreditation of Commonwealth processes and decisions (s 48(1)(a)).

Bilateral agreements do not have any effect in relation to an action in a Commonwealth area or an action by the Commonwealth or a Commonwealth agency, unless the agreement expressly provides otherwise (s 49).

Assessment bilaterals have been entered into with the Northern Territory,[186] Queensland,[187] Tasmania[188] and Western Australia.[189] Six years into the operation of the EPBCA, the only approvals bilateral that has been entered into is with New South Wales relating to actions approved and taken in accordance with the bilaterally accredited Management Plan for the Sydney Opera House.[190]

Criteria to be met before making a bilateral agreement

There are detailed substantive and procedural criteria in the Act and regulations that must be met before the Environment Minister may enter a bilateral agreement, including requirements that the agreement is consistent with Australia's international obligations.[191] The public must be given an opportunity to comment on a draft agreement (s 49A), and a notice of intention to enter into an agreement, the draft agreement and the final agreement, together with a statement of the

186 *An Agreement between the Commonwealth of Australia and the Northern Territory under section 45 of the Environment Protection and Biodiversity Conservation Act 1999 (Cth) relating to environmental impact assessment,* 31 May 2002 <http://www.deh.gov.au/epbc/assessmentsapprovals/bilaterial/nt/index.html> (accessed 1 November 2006).

187 *An Agreement between the Australian Government and the State of Queensland under section 45 of the Environment Protection and Biodiversity Conservation Act 1999 (Cth) relating to environmental impact assessment,* 13 August 2004 <http://www.deh.gov.au/epbc/assessmentsapprovals/ bilateral/qld/index.html> (accessed 1 November 2006).

188 *An agreement between the Commonwealth of Australia and the State of Tasmania under section 45 of the Environment Protection and Biodiversity Conservation Act 1999 (Cth) relating to environmental impact assessment,* 12 December 2005 <http://www.deh.gov.au/epbc/assessmentsapprovals/bilateral/tasmania/index.html> (accessed 1 November 2006).

189 *An agreement between the Commonwealth of Australia and Western Australia under section 45 of the Environment Protection and Biodiversity Conservation Act 1999 (Cth) relating to environmental impact assessment,* 16 August 2002 <http://www.deh.gov.au/epbc/assessmentsapprovals/bilateral/wa/index.html> (accessed 1 November 2006).

190 <http://www.deh.gov.au/epbc/assessmentsapprovals/bilateral/sydneyoperahouse/index.html>, 22 December 2005 (accessed 1 November 2006).

191 EPBCA ss 50-56. *Environment Protection and Biodiversity Conservation Regulations 2000* (EPBCR) Pt 2B (bilaterally accredited management plans); Pt 3 (relating to assessment bilaterals).

Environment Minister's reasons for entering into the agreement, must all be published (ss 45(3), (4), 49A).

Before entering into an assessment bilateral, the Environment Minister must be satisfied that assessment of an action in the manner specified in the agreement will include assessment of the likely impacts of the action on the matters protected by Pt 3 of the EPBCA (s 47(2)). The agreement must specify the manner of assessment, which need not be a procedure prescribed by a law of the State or Territory (s 47(1), (3)). If the action requires Commonwealth approval under Pt 9 of the EPBCA, the agreement must provide for the Environment Minister to receive a report including enough information about the relevant impacts of the action to enable the Minister to make an informed decision (s 47(4)).

An approvals bilateral depends on the Commonwealth Environment Minister accrediting a State or Territory 'management arrangement' or 'authorisation process' and then declaring that a class of actions does not require approval under the EPBCA 'wholly or partly' by reference to the fact that the taking of the action has been approved by the State or Territory in accordance with that management arrangement or authorisation process. Neither term is meaningfully defined in the Act, save that a management arrangement must be in force under a law of the State or Territory that is a party to the agreement, while an authorisation process need only be 'set out' in the State or Territory's law (ss 46(2), (2A), 528). However, the Minister can only accredit a management arrangement or authorisation process if satisfied that:

- the arrangement or process and the law of the State or Territory under which it is in force or 'set out' meet the criteria prescribed by the regulations; and
- there has been or will be adequate assessment of the likely impacts of the action on each matter protected by the provision of Pt 3 specified in the agreement; and
- actions approved in accordance with the management arrangement or process will not have unacceptable or unsustainable impacts on the matter protected. (s 46(3))

Before accrediting a management arrangement or authorisation process, it must be tabled in both Houses of the Commonwealth Parliament and is subject to disallowance by either House (s 46(4)-(8)).

Termination of a bilateral agreement

A bilateral agreement ceases to have effect at the time when the agreement so provides, but must be reviewed by the Minister at least once every five years (s 65).

The Commonwealth Environment Minister may unilaterally suspend or cancel an agreement - generally or in relation to a specified class of actions - if the Minister is not satisfied that the State or Territory has complied with, or will comply with, the agreement and has not given effect to the agreement in a way that accords with the objects of the Act and promotes the discharge of Australia's international obligations (s 59). There must be prior consultation with the appropriate Minister of the State or Territory (s 58). Provision is also made for the emergency suspension of an agreement where the State or Territory is not complying with it and as a result a significant impact on a protected matter is occurring or is imminent (s 60).

Assessment of non-controlled actions by agreement with a State

The Environment Minister and a Minister of a State or Territory may make an agreement for assessment of the environmental impact of an action that is not a controlled action and that is to be undertaken in the State or Territory (s 167). It must be an action that is to be taken by a constitutional corporation, or is to be taken for the purposes of international or interstate trade or commerce, or an action the assessment of which is an appropriate means of giving effect to Australia's international obligations (s 166(1)). An agreement can also be made for the strategic assessment of a policy, plan or program (s 166(2)).

The agreement may select a form of assessment provided for in Pt 8 of the EPBCA (ss 168, 169). The recommendation report or report of a commission of inquiry, and any recommendations made by the Environment Minister, as provided for in the agreement, is given to each State or Territory Minister who is party to the agreement (ss 169(4), 170).

'Action'

Requirements for Commonwealth environmental assessment and approval apply to controlled actions. 'Action' is defined as including:[192]

- a project;
- a development;
- an undertaking;
- an activity or series of activities;
- an alteration of any of the things mentioned above. (s 523)

The Act expressly excludes from the definition a decision by a government body (Commonwealth, State or Territory) to grant a governmental authorisation, however described, for another person to take an action (s 524). That exclusion relates to regulatory, not planning, functions.[193] However, the outer limits of what constitutes 'an activity or series of activities' remain unclear. In *Save the Ridge Inc v National Capital Authority*,[194] Wilcox J and Moore J were of the view that it is at least arguable that planning activities may fall within the term. In subsequent proceedings, however, the planning decision in question - amendments to the National Capital Plan to permit a freeway to be built - was held not to be an action.[195] But actions authorised by and taken under a plan are not excluded.[196]

Where an area is subdivided for the purpose of performing work on that land over a period of time - such as in forestry operations - the planned activities in total may be found to constitute a 'project' and/or an 'undertaking' and/or 'an activity or series of activities'.[197] The Act recognises the artificiality of fragmenting a larger

---

192 The definition of action is certainly wide enough to include the clearing and cultivation of land: *Minister for the Environment and Heritage v Greentree (No 2)* [2004] FCA 741.

193 *Save the Ridge Inc v National Capital Authority* [2004] FCAFC 209 at [23] per Wilcox J, Moore J agreeing; [2005] FCA 17 at [18].

194 [2004] FCAFC 209.

195 *Save the Ridge Inc v Commonwealth* [2005] FCA 17 per Whitlam J.

196 *Brown v Forestry Tasmania (No 4)* [2006] FCA 1729 at [51]-[53].

197 Ibid at [62]-[65].

proposal into a series of individual actions, thereby avoiding scrutiny under the EPBCA, by empowering the Minister to reject a referral if satisfied that the action is a component of a larger proposal (s 74A). This is discussed below in the context of referrals.

Provision of funding by way of a Commonwealth, State or Territory grant is expressly excluded from the definition (s 524A). Also excluded are actions that were specifically authorised before the commencement of the Act (s 43A) and actions occurring immediately before the commencement of the Act which have lawfully continued (s 43B). This is further elaborated under the heading, 'Exemptions', below.

Strategic assessment

The EPBCA provides for the strategic assessment of proposed policies, plans or programs, if the Environment Minister so agrees (Ch 4 Pt 10 Div 1). It also mandates strategic assessment of Commonwealth-managed fisheries before deciding whether to adopt a plan of management, and further assessment if the impact of fisheries actions turns out to be significantly greater than earlier assessed (Ch 4 Pt 10 Div 2).

The advantages of strategic environmental assessment are widely acknowledged.[198] Above all, it is at the policy or planning stage, rather than when implementing individual projects, that alternatives and cumulative impacts can more effectively be assessed and an integrated perspective brought to bear on the type and timing of development within a region. In particular, strategic assessment allows more effective analysis of the cumulative affects of both small and large projects. Further, it facilitates the co-ordination of government agencies and policies, including non-environmental agencies and policies, and the internalisation of environmental considerations at a policy- or plan-making level. It also provides opportunities for public participation at a strategic point in decision-making.

Strategic environmental assessment may make later project assessment simpler or unnecessary. It may avoid decisions that precipitate proposals with significant environmental impacts or proposals on inappropriate sites. It provides data for later environmental assessment. And it allows generic mitigation measures to be developed for later projects.

These advantages of strategic assessment depend for their realisation on the legislative model. A weakness in the EPBCA, as in the NSW legislation, is that it is project focused. As previously discussed, the controlling provisions apply to 'actions'. This does, however, extend to a 'series of activities'. More pertinently, the EPBCA sets up a framework for strategic environmental assessment of policies, plans or programs. The framework is fleshed out through agreement between the Environment Minister and the person responsible for the adoption or implementation of the policy, plan or program, including the terms of reference and the method of proceeding (s 146). The agreement must include a program for public participation before finalising the report on likely impacts, but public participation is not required in finalising the terms of reference.

It should be borne in mind that the strategic assessment would not be comprehensive, but rather directed at the impacts of actions under the policy, plan

198 See Buckley, above n 4; Marsden and Dovers, above n 4; Wood, above n 4; Court, Wright and Guthrie, above n 4; Brown and McDonald, above n 5; James, above n 3, at 80-81.

or program on a matter protected by a provision of Pt 3. However, the agreement may provide for the assessment of other likely impacts if the actions are to be taken in a State or Territory, and the appropriate State or Territory Minister so requests. The Environment Minister's role, after receiving the final assessment report, is to provide recommendations to the person responsible for the adoption or implementation of the policy, plan or program, including recommendations as to how it should be modified.

If the impacts of actions under a policy, plan or program have been assessed within this framework, the assessment report must be taken into consideration by the Minister when deciding the appropriate level of assessment of individual actions taken under the policy, plan or program (s 87(3)(b)). For example, if relevant impacts have been assessed at the strategic level, the Minister could decide that an individual action need only be assessed on preliminary documentation rather than by preparation and consideration of an EIS.

The Minister may go further and endorse the policy, plan or program, in accordance with the agreement, if satisfied that the assessment report adequately addresses the impacts and that recommended modifications have been incorporated (s 146(2)(f)). If the endorsed policy, plan or program is embodied in a management arrangement or authorisation process, the Minister may make a declaration under s 33 (discussed below), or make a bilateral agreement, declaring that specified actions approved in accordance with the management arrangement or authorisation process do not need approval under the EPBCA. Further, following amendments to the Act in 2006, the Minister may approve the taking of an action or a class of actions in accordance with an endorsed policy, plan or program without the need for further environmental assessment and approval (s 146B). The approval is deemed to have been granted under Pt 9 (s 146D). The provisions in Pt 9 relating to the imposition of conditions, compliance with conditions, variation of conditions and suspension and revocation of approvals apply to such approval. In deciding whether to give approval and the conditions to be attached, the Minister's discretion is constrained in a manner similar to that applying to the discretion to grant approval under Pt 9 (discussed below) (ss 146F-146M).

The amendments to the Act allowing actions to be approved following strategic assessment of a policy, plan or program provide an incentive to developers and State, Territory and local governments, through agreement with the Environment Minister, to subject broad-scale development plans to environmental assessment at an early stage of planning. However, the power needs to be exercised with caution as general concept assessments do not obviate the possibility that site-specific impact assessments may be needed as plans are implemented.

Controlling provisions

Part 3 contains the controlling provisions – that is to say, the circumstances in which an action requires an environmental approval. Non-compliance with the requirements carries both civil and criminal consequences for the person taking the action. There is a limitation on liability for actions taken by third parties (ss 25AA, 28AB). A person who takes the primary action cannot be prosecuted, or a civil penalty imposed, for impacts caused by a secondary action not taken at the direction or request of the person taking the primary action. The third party, however, will be liable for taking an action that has a significant impact on a matter protected by Pt 3. Whether an event or circumstance consequential upon a secondary action is an 'impact' turns on the statutory definition of that term (s 527E) and is discussed below.

World Heritage properties

A person must not, without approval, take an action that has or will have a significant impact on the *World Heritage values* of a declared World Heritage property, or is likely to do so.[199] A property not yet on the World Heritage list, but which is the subject of a current declaration under the EPBCA, is covered by the prohibition (s 13(2)). Declaration and listing of World Heritage properties, the meaning of cultural and natural heritage, and offences in relation to World Heritage properties, are discussed in Chapter 10.

National Heritage places

Approval is required for an action that has or will have, or is likely to have, a significant impact on the *National Heritage values* of a National Heritage place.[200] The prohibition on such action without approval applies to:

- a constitutional corporation;
- the Commonwealth or a Commonwealth agency;
- any person:
    - where the action is for the purposes of trade or commerce;
    - where the action is to be taken in a Commonwealth area or a Territory;
    - where the action impacts on indigenous heritage values;
    - where the action is to be taken in an area in respect of which Australia has obligations under Art 8 of the Biodiversity Convention, and prohibition of the action is appropriate and adapted to give effect to Australia's obligations under that Article.

The listing of National Heritage properties, the meaning of heritage values, and offences in relation to National Heritage places, are discussed in Chapter 10.

Ramsar wetlands

A person must not, without approval, take an action that has or will have a significant impact on the *ecological character* of a declared Ramsar wetland, or is likely to do so.[201] A declared Ramsar wetland is a wetland, or part of a wetland, designated by the Commonwealth under Art 2 of the Ramsar Convention for inclusion in the List of Wetlands of International Importance maintained under that Convention (s 17(1)). A designation is effective in creating a declared Ramsar wetland even if the Commonwealth, at the time of the designation, fails to describe the boundaries of

---

199 EPBCA ss 12 (civil penalty), 15A (offences).

200 EPBCA ss 15B (civil penalty), 15C (offences).

201 EPBCA ss 16 (civil penalty), 17B (offences).

the site precisely.[202] Also included in the meaning of a declared Ramsar wetland is a wetland, or part of a wetland, that is the subject of a current declaration by the Minister under the EPBCA (s 17(2)).

'Ecological character' has the same meaning as in the Ramsar Convention and is discussed in Chapter 9, together with the process for listing Ramsar wetlands and offences relating to Ramsar wetlands.

Listed threatened species and ecological communities

A person must not, without approval, take an action that has or will have, or is likely to have, a significant impact on:[203]

- a listed threatened species included in the extinct in the wild category;
- a listed threatened species included in the critically endangered category;
- a listed threatened species included in the endangered category;
- a listed threatened species included in the vulnerable category;
- a listed threatened ecological community included in the critically endangered category;
- a listed threatened ecological community included in the endangered category.

Species listed under the EPBCA as conservation dependent or extinct, and ecological communities listed in the vulnerable category, are not included in the prohibition. The listing of threatened species and ecological communities, and related offences, are discussed in Chapter 8.

Listed migratory species

A person must not, without approval, take an action that has or will have a significant impact on a listed migratory species, or is likely to do so.[204] The list of migratory species is maintained by the Environment Minister and must include, and only include:

- all species from time to time included in appendices to the Bonn Convention[205] and for which Australia is a Range State under the Convention; and
- all species from time to time included in lists established under JAMBA[206] and CAMBA;[207] and
- all native species from time to time identified in a list established under an international agreement approved by the Minister. (s 209)

The Minister may approve an international agreement if satisfied it is an agreement relevant to the conservation of migratory species (s 209(4)).

---

202 *Minister for the Environment and Heritage v Greentree (No 2)* [2004] FCA 741 at [117]-[137].

203 EPBCA ss 18 (civil penalty), 18A (offences).

204 EPBCA ss 20 (civil penalty), 20A (offences).

205 *Convention on the Conservation of Migratory Species of Wild Animals*, done at Bonn, 23 June 1979.

206 The Agreement between the Governments of Japan and Australia for the Protection of Migratory Birds and Birds in Danger of Extinction and their Environment, 6 February 1974.

207 Agreement between the Governments of Australia and the People's Republic of China for the protection of Migratory Birds and their Environment, 20 October 1986.

Issues relating to listed migratory species, including offences, are discussed in Chapter 8.

Nuclear actions

Approval is required for a nuclear action that has, will have or is likely to have a significant impact on the environment.[208] The prohibition on such action without approval applies to:

- a constitutional corporation;
- the Commonwealth or a Commonwealth agency;
- any person
    - o for the purposes of interstate or overseas trade or commerce, or
    - o where the nuclear action is to take place in a Territory.

A nuclear action means any of the following:[209]

- establishing or significantly modifying a nuclear installation;
- transporting spent nuclear fuel or radioactive waste products arising from reprocessing;
- establishing or significantly modifying a facility for storing radioactive waste products arising from reprocessing;
- mining or milling uranium ore;
- establishing or significantly modifying a large-scale disposal facility for radioactive waste;
- de-commissioning or rehabilitating any facility or area in which one of the above activities has been undertaken;
- any other action prescribed by the regulations. (s 22)

Commonwealth marine area

A person must not, without approval, take in a Commonwealth marine area an action that has, will or is likely to have a significant impact on the environment.[210] Further, a person must not take outside a Commonwealth marine area, but in the Australian jurisdiction, an action that has or will have a significant impact on the environment in a Commonwealth marine area, or is likely to do so.[211] The Commonwealth marine area includes the water, seabed and airspace within Australia's exclusive economic zone and over the continental shelf, with the exception of coastal waters within the jurisdiction of the States and the Northern Territory (s 24). It also includes any area of sea or seabed that is within a Commonwealth reserve.

There are exceptions for fishing in a fishery in Commonwealth waters that is managed by a State or the Northern Territory and for fishing outside Commonwealth marine areas that is permitted under a law of a State or Territory (s 23(5), (6)). With respect to fisheries in coastal waters managed by the Commonwealth,

208 EPBCA ss 21 (civil penalty), 22A (offences).

209 The terms used are further defined in this section and in the EPBCR Pt 2.

210 EPBCA ss 23(1) (civil penalty), 24A(1), (2) (offences).

211 EPBCA ss 23(2) (civil penalty), 24A(3), (4) (offences).

approval is required for fishing that has or will have a significant impact on the environment in those coastal waters, or is likely to do so.[212]

The prohibitions relating to the marine environment do not apply to the Commonwealth or a Commonwealth agency (s 23(4)(d)). As discussed below, actions by the Commonwealth or a Commonwealth agency having a significant impact on the environment are regulated under s 28.

Matters of national environmental significance can be added by regulation

Further matters of national environmental significance may be added by regulation, if they fall within the Commonwealth's constitutional powers – for example, they are appropriate and adapted to give effect to Australia's international obligations or relate to action taken by a constitutional corporation (s 23(5)). There must be consultation with the States and Territories (s 23(3)).[213] If so added, a person must not take an action without approval that is prescribed by the relevant regulation (ss 25(1), (2), 25A). An amendment to the Act in 2006 removed the requirement that the Minister review the scope of protected matters every five years.

Commonwealth land

A person (other than the Commonwealth or a Commonwealth agency) must not, without approval, take an action on Commonwealth land that has, will or is likely to have a significant impact on the environment.[214] Nor must a person (other than the Commonwealth or a Commonwealth agency) take, without approval, an action outside Commonwealth land that has or will have a significant impact on the environment on Commonwealth land, or is likely to do so.[215] For the purpose of this prohibition, Commonwealth land excludes the Commonwealth marine area (s 27).

The definition of 'environment' includes the heritage values of places (s 528). Thus this prohibition includes among its aims the protection of the Commonwealth Heritage values (defined in s 341D) of a Commonwealth Heritage place on Commonwealth land. With respect to Commonwealth Heritage places outside the Australian jurisdiction – that is to say, places owned or leased by the Commonwealth or a Commonwealth agency (s 341C(2)) – a person must not without approval take an action that has, will have or is likely to have a significant impact on the environment in a Commonwealth Heritage place.[216]

Commonwealth actions

The Commonwealth or a Commonwealth agency must not without approval take inside or outside the Australian jurisdiction an action that has, will or is likely to have a significant impact on the environment inside or outside the Australian jurisdiction.[217]

212 EPBCA ss 23(3) (civil penalty), 24A(5), (6) (offences).

213 Consultation does not mean that the Commonwealth must secure agreement: s 23(3A).

214 EPBCA ss 26(1) (civil penalty), 27A(1), (2) (offences).

215 EPBCA ss 26(2) (civil penalty), 27A(3), (4) (offences).

216 EPBCA ss 27B (civil penalty), 27C (offences).

217 EPBCA s 28 (civil penalty).

The Minister may exempt from this requirement all or a specified class of action taken by a Commonwealth agency if the Minister is satisfied that the agency's action must comply with the law of a State or Territory dealing with environmental protection (s 28(4), (5)). The Minister must be satisfied that an object of the State or Territory law is to protect the environment or promote the conservation and ecologically sustainable use of natural resources, and that the likely impacts are adequately addressed.

As previously explained, the definition of 'action' excludes the grant of a governmental authorisation (ss 524(2), 524A). However, before authorising certain actions that are likely to have a significant impact on the environment, Commonwealth agencies are required to obtain and consider advice from the Environment Minister following environmental assessment (s 162). This is explained below.

Exemptions

There is a range of exemptions, or mechanisms to create exemptions, from requirements for Commonwealth approval, namely:

- bilateral agreements between the Commonwealth and a State or Territory, accrediting the State or Territory environmental system;
- actions specifically authorised before the commencement of the Act and actions occurring immediately before the commencement of the Act which have lawfully continued (referred to below, for convenience, as 'existing uses');
- actions covered by ministerial declarations and accredited management arrangements or accredited authorisation processes;
- actions covered by ministerial declarations and bioregional plans;
- actions covered by conservation agreements;
- actions authorised following the Minister's advice;
- action taken 'in a specified manner';
- activities impacting on threatened or migratory species introduced for conservation purposes;
- forestry operations in certain regions;
- actions in the Great Barrier Reef Marine Park;
- exemptions in the national interest;
- national security or emergency exemptions;
- telecommunications facilities.

The rationale for most of the exemptions is that there is an alternative method of assessment and approval – in effect, an alternative means to achieve the objects of the EPBCA. It was in recognition of this that the Federal Court in *Brown v Forestry Tasmania (No 4)*[218] was prepared closely to scrutinise forestry practices under a Regional Forest Agreement (RFA) to ensure that protection of threatened species was actually delivered. In the event the court found that the forestry operations were not being carried out in accordance with the RFA, and were unlikely to do so

218 [2006] FCA 1729.

in the future, and thus s 38 of the EPBCA did not provide an exemption for Forestry Tasmania's operations. The same reasoning can be applied to other exemptions that provide an alternative method of delivering the objects of the EPBCA. For an exemption to apply, it is not sufficient that mere lip service is paid to the alternative process. More generally, the reasoning applies to the Minister's discretion to create exemptions by approving alternative processes. The touchstone is whether the objects of the Act will nevertheless be achieved, including biodiversity conservation and implementation of Australia's international obligations.[219]

Bilateral agreements

Bilateral agreements between the Commonwealth and a State or Territory, accrediting the State or Territory environmental system, were discussed previously. Approval is not required for actions covered by an approvals bilateral provided that the action is taken in accordance with the bilaterally accredited management arrangement or authorisation process (ss 29, 30).

Existing uses

The EPBCA exempts existing uses – that is to say, uses existing immediately before the commencement of the Act (16 July 2000) – from the requirement to obtain an environmental approval under the Act. It addresses two situations: first, actions that were specifically authorised before the commencement of the Act (s 43A) and, secondly, actions occurring immediately before the commencement of the Act which have lawfully continued (s 43B).

For the first exemption to apply, it is necessary to establish that:

- the action consists of a use of land, sea or seabed; and
- before the commencement of the Act, the action was authorised by a specific environmental authorisation; and
- immediately before the commencement of the Act, no further specific environmental authorisation was necessary to allow the action to be taken lawfully; and
- at the time the action is taken, the specific environmental authorisation continues to be in force. (s 43A)

'Environmental authorisation' means an authorisation under a law of the Commonwealth, a State or a Territory that has, as one of its objects, to protect the environment or to promote the conservation and ecologically sustainable use of natural resources (s 43A(2)). 'Specific environmental authorisation' means an environmental authorisation that either:

(a) identifies the particular action by reference to acts and matters uniquely associated with that action; or

(b) was issued or granted following a consideration of the particular action by reference to acts and matters uniquely associated with that action.

The definition of 'specific environmental authorisation' was introduced in 2006. Paragraph (a) of the definition is intended to overcome, in part, the broad interpre-

219 See *Brown v Forestry Tasmania (No 4)* [2006] FCA 1729 at [294]-[301].

tation given to the exemption in *Minister for the Environment and Heritage v Greentree (No 2)*.[220] In that case Sackville J held, first, that the exemption does not require the occupier actually to have acted in relation to the land in a particular way before the commencement of the EPBCA. It is noteworthy that the subsequent amendment to the Act does not put a limit on the period within which the action must actually commence following the grant of an authorisation in order to avoid the need for EPBCA approval. Secondly, Sackville J held that the requirement for the action to be 'specifically authorised' does not mean that the authorisation must only relate to a single site or to a single activity on land. It was enough in that case that a local environmental plan authorised within the zone development for the purpose of agriculture, including vegetation clearance and de-silting, without the need to obtain consent.[221] In the event, however, the clearing of the Ramsar wetland was found to require a further environmental authorisation – under the *Native Vegetation Conservation Act 1997* (NSW). Thus the exemption did not apply to the clearing.[222] It was otherwise with respect to the de-silting of the watercourse.[223] It is to be hoped that the definition inserted in 2006 will overcome the second part of this ruling.

If the environmental authorisation is renewed or extended, it is taken to be a new authorisation unless the renewal or extension authorises the same action that was authorised before the commencement of the Act and could properly be given without any further consideration of environmental impact (s 43A(1A)). If those provisos cannot be established, consideration would need to be given to whether the action needs assessment and approval under the EPBCA at the time of renewal or extension.

The second exemption addresses 'actions which are lawful continuations of use' but not authorised by a specific environmental authorisation. Approval is not required if:

- the action is a lawful continuation of a use of land, sea or seabed; and
- was occurring immediately before the commencement of the EPBCA. (s 43B)

A use does not 'continue' for the purpose of this exemption if it involves an enlargement, expansion or intensification of the use (s 43B(3)(a)).[224] Nor does it continue if there is either a change in location or a change in the nature of the activities, and the change results in a substantial increase in the impact of the use on the land, sea or seabed (s 43B(3)(b)).

The s 43B exemption does not apply, but the s 43A exemption may apply, if:

- before the commencement of the Act, the action was authorised by a specific environmental authorisation; and
- at the time the action is taken, the specific environmental authorisation continues to be in force.

---

220 [2004] FCA 741.

221 Ibid at [152]-[156].

222 Ibid at [178].

223 Ibid at [180].

224 For NSW cases on the meaning of the terms enlargement, expansion or intensification, see *South Sydney CC v Houlakis* (1996) 92 LGERA 401 (CA); *Nymboida Shire Council v Skar Industries Pty Ltd* (1998) 99 LGERA 178; *King v Lewis* (1995) 88 LGERA 183 (CA); *Archibald v Byron Shire Council* [2003] NSWCA 292.

NSW law on existing uses is discussed in Chapter 2, including case law on characterisation of the use at the relevant time and the inquiry into whether the use as characterised has continued.[225]

Actions covered by ministerial declarations and accredited management arrangements or accredited authorisation processes

The Environment Minister may accredit a Commonwealth 'management arrangement' or 'authorisation process' for the purpose of making a declaration that actions approved under, and taken in accordance with, the management arrangement or authorisation process do not require approval (ss 32, 33). Before amendments to the Act in 2006, the exemption was confined to accredited management plans in force under a law of the Commonwealth. In broadening the Minister's options, the amendment provides no meaningful definition of 'management arrangement' or 'authorisation process', except that the former must be 'in operation' under a law of the Commonwealth, and the latter must be 'set out' in a law of the Commonwealth (ss 32(c), 33(2), (2A)).[226] It would seem that a management arrangement could simply be 'a policy' (s 528 'management arrangement'). Provided the policy is consistent with the enabling Act, and has not been abandoned, it could be said to be 'in operation'. Policies, however, are flexible, and require decision-makers to entertain exceptions.

More meaningful (although committed to the subjective discretion of the Minister) are the jurisdictional constraints placed on the power to accredit an arrangement or process and to make a declaration. Before accrediting a management arrangement or authorisation process, the Minister must be satisfied that:

- the management arrangement or authorisation process and the law under which it is in operation, or in which it is set out, meet the criteria prescribed by the regulations; and
- there has been or will be adequate assessment of the likely impacts of the approved actions on the matters protected by Pt 3; and
- actions approved or taken in accordance with the arrangement or process will not have unacceptable or unsustainable impacts on the matter protected by Pt 3 to which the declaration relates. (s 33(3))

The management arrangement or authorisation process must be tabled in each House of the Commonwealth Parliament and, if opposed by resolution of either House, the Minister cannot accredit it (s 33(4)-(8)).

Before making a declaration, the Minister must be satisfied in relation to various matters designed to ensure, amongst other things, that the declaration accords with the objects of the Act and Australia's international obligations, and promotes the management of the place or the survival of the species or community (ss 34A-34F). Declarations may be revoked (s 35). Actions which have commenced but which have not been completed before the revocation continue to be covered by the declaration.

---

225 See *Shire of Perth v O'Keefe* (1964) 110 CLR 529; *Royal Agricultural Society of NSW v Sydney CC* (1987) 61 LGRA 305 (CA); *North Sydney MC v Boyts Radio & Electrical Pty Ltd* (1989) 16 NSWLR 50 (CA); *Steedman v Baulkham Hills Shire Council (No 2)* (1993) 31 NSWLR 562 (CA); *Hudak v Waverley MC* (1990) 70 LGRA 130.

226 See also EPBCA s 528.

Actions covered by ministerial declarations and bioregional plans

The Minister may by declaration exempt actions taken in accordance with a 'bioregional plan' applying to a Commonwealth area or part thereof (ss 37, 37A). Bioregional plans can be made by the Minister, after consultation, for a bioregion that is within a Commonwealth area (s 176(1)). With respect to bioregions that are not wholly within a Commonwealth area, the Minister may co-operate in the preparation of a bioregional plan, including by providing financial or other assistance (s 176(2), (3)). Plans may address priorities, strategies and actions to achieve objectives relating to biodiversity and heritage values, and important economic and social values (s 176(4)). Before an amendment to the Act in 2006, the existence of a bioregional plan was only a relevant consideration in decision-making. The 2006 amendment empowers the Minister to declare that an action or class of actions specified 'wholly or partly' by reference to the fact that it is in accordance with a bioregional plan does not require approval (s 37A). The intention is to create an incentive for interested persons to have their activities considered within the context of developing bioregional plans.

In making a declaration, the Minister must take into account ESD principles, and economic and social matters, and cannot make a declaration if it is considered that the action would have unacceptable or unsustainable impacts on a matter protected by Pt 3 (s 37B). There are further prescribed criteria in respect of which the Minister must be satisfied, including that the declaration is not inconsistent with Australia's obligations under specified international treaties (ss 37C-37H). A declaration relating to specified nuclear actions cannot be made (s 37J).

Actions covered by conservation agreements

Approval is not required for actions included in a class of actions declared in a conservation agreement not to require approval under Pt 9 (ss 37M, 306A). The action must be taken in accordance with any conditions specified in the declaration. Conservation agreements are discussed in Chapter 8.

Actions authorised following Minister's advice

As previously outlined, the definition of 'action' excludes the grant of a governmental authorisation for another person to take an action (s 524). However, before authorising certain actions, Commonwealth agencies are required to refer the proposed authorisation to the Environment Minister for assessment and advice (ss 160, 161, 162). If the Minister is satisfied, on the basis of the information in the referral, that the action is not likely to have a significant impact on the environment, assessment need not be undertaken or advice given (ss 160(1A), 161A). The action is deemed not to be a controlled action. If assessment is required, it is undertaken as if the referral were a controlled action (s 162). The Minister then gives non-binding advice as to whether the agency should give the authorisation and any conditions that should be imposed (s 163). If the advice is not followed, the agency must report its reasons to the Minister (s 164). The authorised action does not require separate approval under the EPBCA. Subsequent authorisations may be given without obtaining the Minister's advice if the agency is satisfied that the earlier advice covers the likely impacts or that the likely impacts are not significantly different in nature and do not significantly add to the impacts (s 160(3), (4)).

The actions which must be referred to the Minister are set out in the Act and regulations. They are (s 160(2)):

- the entry by the Commonwealth, under Australia's foreign aid program, into a contract, agreement or arrangement for the implementation of a project that has, will have or is likely to have a significant impact on the environment anywhere in the world;
- the adoption or implementation of a plan for aviation airspace management involving aircraft operations that have, will have or are likely to have a significant impact on the environment;
- the adoption or implementation of a major development plan, as defined in the *Airports Act 1996*;
- any other actions prescribed by the regulations; which currently are (EPBCR reg 6.01):
  - o an action authorised by a permit under the *Environment Protection (Sea Dumping) Act 1981*,
  - o an action authorised by a Basel permit, or by a variation of a Basel permit, under the *Hazardous Waste (Regulation of Exports and Imports) Act 1989*,
  - o an action authorised by a grant, renewal or variation of a permit or the grant of an exemption certificate under the *Sea Installations Act 1987*,
  - o an action authorised by a permit or authority under the *Wildlife Protection (Regulation of Exports and Imports) Act 1982*,
  - o an action authorised by a permit or authority (however described) under the *Great Barrier Reef Marine Park Act 1975* or the *Great Barrier Reef Marine Park Regulations 1983*.

Action taken 'in a particular manner'

In deciding whether an action is a controlled action, the Minister may take the view that, if the action is taken in a particular manner, it would not be likely to have a significant impact on a matter protected by Pt 3 and thus would not fall within a controlling provision. If so, the action may be undertaken without approval, provided it is carried out in a manner consistent with that specified by the Minister (s 77A). The initial referral of the proposed action to the Minister may include alternative proposals with respect to location, time frames and proposed activities (s 72(3)).

A question arises as to whether compensatory measures may be built into the proposed action so as to take advantage of this exemption. It would seem not as the Minister, when deciding whether an action is a controlled action, must have regard to all likely adverse impacts and must disregard any likely beneficial impacts (s 75(2)). The Department's 'Particular Manner' guidelines state that mitigating measures must be designed directly to avoid or lessen adverse impacts rather than compensate for them.[227]

227 See Department of the Environment and Heritage, Guideline on application of 'Particular Manner' in decision-making under the EPBCA <http://www.deh.gov.au/epbc/publications/pubs/particularmanner.pdf> (accessed 10 November 2006).

Activities impacting on threatened or migratory species introduced for conservation purposes

With respect to listed threatened species and communities, and listed migratory species, the Minister may exempt particular persons, or a class of person, from the need to obtain approval if satisfied that the species has been introduced into the area covered by the exemption for the purpose of contributing to its conservation (s 517A). The Minister must be satisfied that impacts on the species, or their habitat, would be incidental to, and not the purpose of, carrying out the activities. The exemption must specify the activities to which it applies. If the person primarily responsible for carrying out the activities is not the person responsible for introducing the species, he or she must have agreed to its introduction.

Forestry operations in certain regions

Approval is not required for forestry operations if they are in a region that is part of a RFA, within the meaning of the *Regional Forest Agreements Act 2002* (Cth), and are taken in accordance with that agreement (s 38). Forestry operations are not in accordance with the agreement, and the exemption will not apply, if mere lip service is paid to the RFA.[228]

The exemption does not apply to forestry operations that are in a World Heritage property, a Ramsar wetland, or incidental to another action the primary purpose of which does not relate to forestry (s 42).

Actions in the Great Barrier Reef Marine Park

Approval is not required for actions taken in the Great Barrier Reef Marine Park, provided the action is authorised under a zoning plan or a plan of management made under the *Great Barrier Reef Marine Park Act 1975*, or a permission granted under that Act (s 43).

Exemptions in the national interest

The Environment Minister may exempt a person from the requirements for assessment and/or approval if the Minister is satisfied that it is in the national interest to grant the particular exception (s 158). In determining the national interest, the Act states that the Minister may consider Australia's defence or security or a national emergency, but this does not limit the matters that the Minister may consider. The exemption cannot apply retrospectively (s 158(6)).

National security or emergency exemptions

The Environment Minister may exempt the Commonwealth or a Commonwealth agency from the need to get approval if the Minister is satisfied that this is necessary in the interests of Australia's defence or security or to deal with a national emergency (s 28(2)(c), (3)).

228 *Brown v Forestry Tasmania (No 4)* [2006] FCA 1729.

Telecommunications facilities

Approval is not required if an action is authorised by a facility installation permit granted under the *Telecommunications Act 1997* (Sch 3 cl 28). This exempts actions such as erecting a mobile tower. Before issuing a permit, the Australian Communications and Media Authority must consult the Environment Secretary (Sch 3 cl 28).

Is a proposal a controlled action?

Referring a proposal to the Minister

The Environment Minister decides whether an action is a controlled action and which provisions of Pt 3 are controlling provisions for the action (s 75(1)). Persons, including Commonwealth, State and Territory agencies, that propose to take an action that they think may be a controlled action must refer the proposal to the Minister (s 68). This includes a party to a contract, agreement, arrangement or understanding for whose benefit the action is proposed to be taken, but not a subcontractor (s 68A).[229]

Thus those proposing to take an action must make judgments about whether the proposed action is likely to have a significant impact on a protected matter. The Department of Environment and Heritage has prepared guidelines to assist in the decision as to whether a referral should be made.[230] It has also prepared associated industry guidelines, which provide specific guidance for industry sectors, and guidelines on specific threatened species and ecological communities.[231] The guidelines have had to be amended from time to time following litigation showing the Minister to have misunderstood his statutory functions. The *Nathan Dam*[232] case is discussed below. Another example is the case brought by the Humane Society International challenging the Minister's advice to persons holding State permits to kill a specified number of grey-headed flying foxes (a nationally listed vulnerable species) that they did not need approval under the EPBCA.[233] Effectively the advice purported to exempt them from their statutory obligation to refer proposed actions. The purported exemption was held not to be authorised by the Act.

Referrals may also be made to the Minister by a State or Territory, or by an agency of the Commonwealth, a State or Territory that is aware of a proposal by another person to take an action, if the State, Territory or agency has administrative responsibilities relating to the action. This includes local government. The Environment Minister may also request a referral (s 70). If the matter is not then referred, the Minister may make a determination as if it had been.

---

229 A reference to a contract, agreement, arrangement or understanding includes a reference to a proposed contract etc.

230 Department of the Environment and Heritage 'Significant Impact Guidelines' (May 2006) 1.1 Matters of National Environmental Significance, <http://www.deh.gov.au/epbc/publications/pubs/nes-guidelines.pdf> (accessed 1 November 2006); 1.2 Actions on, or impacting upon, Commonwealth land and Actions by Commonwealth Agencies, <http://www.deh.gov.au/epbc/publications/pubs/commonwealth-guidelines.pdf> (accessed 1 November 2006).

231 See <http://www.deh.gov.au/epbc/policy/#guidelines> (accessed 1 November 2006).

232 *Queensland Conservation Council Inc v Minister for Environment and Heritage* [2003] FCA 1463, affirmed on appeal (2004) 139 FCR 24.

233 *Humane Society International Inc v Minister for Environment and Heritage* [2003] FCA 65.

It is an offence to take an action that has been referred to the Minister while the Minister's decision is pending (s 74AA(1)). An offence is also committed if an action is taken after the Minister has requested referral of the action and the referral has not been made (s 74AA(3)).

In order to inform the Minister's decision as to whether an action is a controlled action, the Act requires:

- the referral to provide prescribed information (EPBCA s 72; EPBCR reg 4.03 and Sch 2) and the Minister may request further information from the person proposing to take the action (s 76);
- the Environment Minister to invite other Commonwealth, State or Territory Ministers having responsibilities relating to the proposal to provide information or comments (s 74(1), (2));[234]
- the referral to be published on the internet (subject to exemptions for commercially confidential information[235]) with an invitation to the public to comment (s 74(3)).

Information provided on referral

The *Environment Protection and Biodiversity Conservation Regulations 2000* (EPBCR) prescribe the information that must be provided with the referral, including a description of the proposal, the nature and extent of likely impacts, and a description of important features of the project area and the affected area, including the current state of the environment (EPBCR Sch 2). This last-mentioned description must state the source of the information, how recent it is, how its reliability was tested and what uncertainties there are. The consequence of non-compliance with the Regulations is yet to be tested in court. Nonetheless, it is an offence under the Act recklessly or negligently to provide information that is false or misleading in a material particular (s 489).

Importantly, the Minister may reject a referral if satisfied that the action is a component of a larger proposal and request referral of the larger action (s 74A). However, the Minister does not have a fact-finding role[236] and must rely on information provided in the referral or request further information in this respect from the person proposing to take the action (s 76(2)). In *Mees v Roads Corporation*,[237] the major issue was whether information provided to the Minister by the State of Victoria in relation to a proposed motorway was false or misleading. The State of Victoria had made two referrals to the Commonwealth Minister on the same day, each relating to sections of a proposed motorway. The Federal Court found that the information given was misleading in failing to inform the Minister of the strong chance that a link would be built at some time in the future between the two

---

234 The Minister may also invite the Heritage Council to comment where heritage values are relevant: EPBCA s 74(1A), (1B).

235 EPBCA s 74(3A). The onus lies on the person claiming commercial confidentiality to demonstrate to the Minister that release of the information would cause competitive detriment to the person; the information is not in the public domain; the information is not required to be disclosed under another law of the Commonwealth, a State or a Territory; and the information is not readily discoverable: s 74(3B).

236 *Mees v Roads Corporation* [2003] FCA 306 at [118].

237 [2003] FCA 306.

sections. It was not to the point that the Minister was capable of discerning the truth or that the applicant in the litigation had taken steps to enlighten the Minister. Because the Minister must make a decision on the information provided in the referral, it is important that the referral document contain information that is truthful and complete, so as not to mislead. Anything less would subvert the purpose of the EPBCA.[238] However, the architecture of the EPBCA[239] and the hazards of public interest litigation failed to provide an effective remedy against this fragmentation. The application for an injunction was not pressed and the court declined in its discretion to grant a declaration.[240] Subsequent proceedings against the Commonwealth Environment Minister failed. The challenge to the Minister's decision that a section of the motorway was not a 'controlled action' was out of time and the Minister's decision that he could not reconsider his earlier decision because there was no 'substantial new information', as required by s 78 of the Act, was not a reviewable decision.[241] The litigation imposed a heavy cost burden on the public interest applicant.[242]

The 2006 amendments to the Act introduced two changes relevant to the *Mees* litigation. First, the Minister may request the person proposing to take the action to provide information about whether or not the action is a component of a larger action that the person proposes to take (s 76(2)). Secondly, any person may request the Minister to reconsider the decision that an action is a controlled action and which provisions are the controlling provisions (ss 78A-78C). However, the grounds on which the Minister may revoke the decision and substitute a new decision remain limited (s 78). The grounds include that substantial new information about likely impacts has become available or that there has been a substantial and unforeseen change in circumstances relating to likely impacts. The timeframe is also limited as the Minister cannot revoke the decision once approval has been granted or the action has been taken.

Likely to have a significant impact

In deciding whether the proposed action is a controlled action and which provisions of Pt 3 are the controlling provisions, the Minister must consider *all likely adverse impacts*[243] on matters protected by Pt 3 and must disregard any beneficial impacts the action will or is likely to have (s 75(2)). The Minister must consider any public comments received in response to publication of the referral on the internet (ss 74(3),

238 Ibid at [118] per Gray J.

239 See *Mees v Roads Corporation* [2003] FCA 306 at [120]-[122] on the issues surrounding the granting of injunctions under EPBCA s 475 and the problems of Crown immunity. The issues were not resolved because the application for an injunction was not pressed: *Mees v Roads Corporation* [2003] FCA 410.

240 *Mees v Roads Corporation* [2003] FCA 410.

241 *Mees v Minister for the Environment and Heritage* [2005] FCAFC 5, affirming *Mees v Kemp* [2004] FCA 366.

242 *Mees v Roads Corporation* [2003] FCA 410; *Mees v Kemp (No 2)* [2004] FCA 549.

243 The Minister must not consider any adverse impacts of an exempt RFA forestry operation or a forestry operation in an RFA region (for example, when considering the impacts of an action that will use timber from an RFA region): EPBCA s 75(2B). With respect to actions proposed to be taken partly in and partly outside Commonwealth areas, where the controlling provision relates to National Heritage places, Commonwealth marine areas or Commonwealth land, the Minister must consider only those impacts of that part of the action that is taken in or on a Commonwealth area, a Territory, a Commonwealth marine area or Commonwealth land: s 75(2A).

75(1A)). The ultimate question is whether the action is *likely* to have a *significant impact* on a protected matter.

The extent of inquiry into impacts that the Environment Minister must undertake was addressed in the important *Nathan Dam* case, decided in 2004.[244] A proposal to construct a dam in Central Queensland had been referred to the Minister. The dam would be situated on a river which, 500 kilometres downstream, flowed into the Great Barrier Reef World Heritage Area. Once in operation the dam would make controlled discharges of water for agricultural, industrial, urban and environmental uses. The Minister took the view that the Act required him only to consider the impacts of the construction and operation of the dam by the entity proposing it and not potential downstream impacts consequent on other persons' decisions. The Minister therefore did not consider the potential cumulative impacts on the Great Barrier Reef of downstream irrigation of agricultural land and associated chemical use, including in cotton farming. It was held that the Minister had misunderstood his statutory function by giving too narrow an interpretation to 'impacts'. 'Impact' is not confined to the direct physical effects of the action. It includes indirect effects and it includes effects which are sufficiently close to the action to allow it to be said that they are, or would be, the consequences of the action.[245]

Further, an impact may be significant because the action contributes to the cumulative effects on the protected matter, notwithstanding that on its own the impact is insignificant relative to other impacts. In *Brown v Forestry Tasmania (No 4)*,[246] it was held that loss of habitat for endangered species caused by proposed forestry operations, while relatively insignificant in the context of other factors impacting on the species, can still be considered significant in the context of legislation which is designed to protect native species and, in particular, prevent the extinction, and promote the recovery, of threatened species.

Subsequent to the *Nathan Dam* case, an amendment to the Act in 2006 inserted a definition of 'impact' (s 527E). Although the statutory test of causation is different from, and narrower than, the way in which impact has been interpreted by the Federal Court, it does not exclude indirect, secondary or cumulative impacts. It is wide enough to include downstream or downwind impacts, upstream impacts and facilitated impacts. However, it must be established that the action is *a substantial cause* of the indirect consequence (s 527E(1)). Further, with respect to actions taken by another person as a consequence of the primary action, where the secondary action is not taken at the direction or request of the person undertaking the primary action, a consequential event or circumstance is only 'an impact' if:

- the primary action facilitates *to a major extent* the secondary action; and
- both the secondary action and the consequential event or circumstance are:
  - o within the contemplation of the primary person, or
  - o a reasonably foreseeable consequence of the secondary action. (s 527E(2))

In short, the definition of 'impact' inserted in 2006 compounds the questions of fact and degree that may have to be addressed in order to trigger the assessment

244 *Queensland Conservation Council Inc v Minister for Environment and Heritage* [2003] FCA 1463, affirmed on appeal (2004) 139 FCR 24.

245 *Minister for the Environment and Heritage v Queensland Conservation Council* (2004) 139 FCR 24 at [53].

246 [2006] FCA 1729 at [93]-[102].

and approval process. In the case of secondary impacts, it must be established not only that a likely impact is *significant,* but that the secondary impact was *substantially caused* by the primary action and was facilitated *to a major extent* by the primary action and was *reasonably foreseeable.* This clearly sits uneasily with the Act's object to promote ESD. It is to be hoped that a precautionary approach will be built into the interpretation of the statutory definition – in particular the expressions 'substantially caused' and 'to a major extent' – in a manner similar to the acknowledgement that 'likely to significantly affect' is not an invitation to ignore uncertainty.[247]

Prior to 'impact' being defined in the Act, Dowsett J in *Wildlife Preservation Society of Queensland Proserpine/Whitsunday Branch Inc v Minister for the Environment& Heritage,* doubted that greenhouse gas emissions consequent on the burning of coal sourced from a proposed mine could cause an impact on a protected matter, which could be said to be an impact of the proposed mine.[248] This stands in contrast to the decision of Pain J in *Gray v Minister for Planning*[249] concerning environmental assessment in NSW: see Section 1 of this chapter. Dowsett J did not need finally to resolve causation issues relating to the global warming impacts as the Minister's delegate had considered the possible impact of greenhouse gases generated in the extraction, transportation and burning of coal won from the proposed mine and concluded that there would not be a relevant impact for the purposes of Pt 3. Dowsett J found no legal error in the delegate's approach. The case contains a reminder of the need to focus attention on what is being protected by Pt 3 and to identify the actual effect on that protected matter. The likely significance of the impact of any action will vary, depending on which protected matter is being considered. Dowsett J warned that 'it will usually be erroneous to speak of a "significant impact" for the purposes of Pt 3 as if a particular action and its consequences might affect all protected matters in the same way and to the same extent'.[250]

The term 'significant' in the formula for triggering assessment is widely accepted as meaning 'important, notable or of consequence having regard to its context or intensity'.[251] In *Booth v Bosworth,* Branson J, without finally deciding, inclined to the view that the expression 'likely' should not be translated as 'more likely than not', but rather understood in the sense of 'prone', 'with a propensity' or 'liable'.[252] This would be consistent with the precautionary principle and would tend to avoid the risk to biological diversity and the environment generally which would flow from the need for scientific certainty or confidence. The term 'likely' is not a reason to ignore uncertain impacts. The Department's 'Significant Impact Guidelines' recognise that, where there is a risk of serious or irreversible damage, lack of scientific certainty about the potential impacts will not itself justify a decision that the action is not likely to have a significant impact.[253]

---

247 See *Booth v Bosworth* (2001) 114 FCR 39 at [97]-[98].

248 [2006] FCA 736 at [72].

249 [2006] NSWLEC 720.

250 Ibid at [40].

251 *Booth v Bosworth* (2001) 114 FCR 39 at [99] per Branson J; *Minister for the Environment and Heritage v Greentree (No 2)* [2004] FCA 741 at [191] per Sackville J.

252 *Booth v Bosworth* (2001) 114 FCR 39 at [97]-[98].

253 Department of the Environment and Heritage 'Significant Impact Guidelines' (May 2006) 1.1 Matters of National Environmental Significance, <http://www.deh.gov.au/epbc/publications/ pubs/nes-guidelines.pdf> (accessed 1 November 2006) at 4, 8.

In *Booth v Bosworth*,[254] it was held that the disappearance of the spectacled flying fox from the Wet Tropics World Heritage Area, or a dramatic reduction in its numbers, would significantly impact on the World Heritage values of the area by detracting from its biological diversity and from the significance of the habitats contained within it for *in situ* conservation. It would also detract from the record contained in that area of the mixing of the faunas of the Australian and Asian continental plates. Approximately 20% of the population of adult female spectacled flying foxes were being killed by an aerial electric grid erected to protect a lychee orchard in close proximity to the World Heritage Area.

The Minister's decision

On receiving a referral, the Minister may decide, on the basis of the information in the referral, that the proposed action would clearly have unacceptable impacts on a protected matter (ss 74B, 74C). If so, the person proposing to take the action may withdraw the referral, refer a new modified proposal or request reconsideration (s 74C(3)). The Act sets out a procedure for reconsideration, which must include an opportunity for public comment and a report by the Environment Secretary on the likely impacts of the proposed action (s 74D). If, after reconsideration, the Minister still considers that it is clear that the action would have unacceptable impacts, the Minister must refuse to approve the taking of the action (s 74D(4)).

If the Minister decides that an action is a controlled action, the Minister must determine which provisions of Pt 3 are the controlling provisions (s 75(1)), designate a person as proponent of the action (s 75(3), (4)), and decide on the approach to be used for assessing the relevant impacts.

Once the decision is made, the Minister has only limited power to revoke it and substitute a new decision. The power is limited because of the timeframe – the decision cannot be revoked once approval has been granted or the action has been taken – and in terms of the grounds for reconsideration. The Minister can only make a new decision (s 78):[255]

- if satisfied that this is warranted by the availability of substantial new information about likely impacts; or
- if satisfied that this is warranted by a substantial change in circumstances relating to likely impacts that was not foreseen at the time of the first decision; or
- an exemption no longer applies (including, with respect to the 'particular manner' exemption, because the Minister is satisfied that the action will not be taken in the manner identified (s 78(1)(b)); or
- any person (other than a Minister of a State or self-governing Territory) requests reconsideration on any of the above grounds (s 78A); or
- the proposed action is to be taken in a State or Territory and within 10 business days of being notified of the decision, the Minister of the State or Territory requests reconsideration (s 79).

254 [2001] FCA 1453.

255 See *Mees v Minister for the Environment and Heritage* [2005] FCAFC 5 esp at [68]-[75].

The ability of any person to request reconsideration was added by amendment to the Act in 2006. However, it does not broaden the grounds on which the Minister can substitute a new decision. In reconsidering the decision, the public must be invited to comment (s 78B(6)). So also must the designated proponent be invited to comment if the request was made by a person other than the designated proponent (s 78B(2)). However, the Minister need not reveal the identity of the person who made the request (s 78B(3)). Following reconsideration, the Minister must either confirm the decision, or revoke the decision and substitute a new decision (s 78C(1)).

Decision not affected by subsequent listing event

Once the Minister has decided whether or not an action is a controlled action, the decision and any other approval process decision is not affected by a subsequent 'listing event'[256] – that is to say, new listings of species, Ramsar wetlands, or heritage properties or places; up-listing of species; and changes to boundaries of Ramsar wetlands or heritage properties or places (s 158A). The listing event is to be disregarded in making any further approval process decision and in doing anything in relation to the relevant action pursuant to the making of an approval process decision (s 158A(4)). An approval process decision includes all the key steps in the assessment and approval process, including a reconsideration of whether the action is a controlled action, the appropriate form of assessment, whether to approve the action and the conditions to be attached (s 158A(1)). It is surprising and troubling that such disregard for a new or amended listing should set in at such an early stage. This is all the more so given that the focal point of assessment and approval is protection of matters of national environmental significance. The certainty sought for development proposals is clearly privileged over environmental protection.

The Act further provides that the validity of any approval process decision made before the listing event occurred is not affected by the listing event, nor can it be revoked, varied, suspended, challenged, reviewed, set aside or called in question because of, or for reasons relating to, the listing event (s 158A(3)).

Environmental assessment

The relevant impacts of a controlled action must be assessed at some level before the Minister decides whether or not to approve it. An assessment may be done:

- by a process laid down under a bilateral agreement; or
- by a process specified in a declaration by the Minister; or
- under Pt 8 which provides for assessment:
    - by an accredited assessment process, or
    - on the referral information, or
    - on preliminary documentation provided by the proponent, or
    - by a public environment report, or
    - by an EIS, or
    - by a public inquiry.

256 Subsequent also to commencement of this section, which was inserted by *Environment and Heritage Legislation Amendment Act (No 1) 2006* Item 322.

Bilateral agreement

Part 8 does not apply if the action is to be taken in a State or Territory and is covered by a bilateral agreement between that State or Territory and the Commonwealth (s 83). The exemption from Pt 8 only applies if the action has been assessed in the manner specified in the bilateral agreement. The assessment provided for in the agreement must meet the criteria specified in Sch 1 to the EPBCR (reg 3.06).

Declaration of the Minister

The Minister may make a declaration that a class of actions assessed by the Commonwealth or a Commonwealth agency in a specified manner does not need to be assessed under Pt 8 (s 84). The manner of assessment that may be specified is not limited to assessment provided for under a law of the Commonwealth (s 84(4)).

A declaration may only be made if the Minister is satisfied that the assessment as specified in the declaration:

- includes an assessment of the likely impacts on the matter protected by Pt 3; and
- meets the standards prescribed in the regulations; and
- if the action requires approval under Pt 9, the Minister will receive enough information about the relevant impacts to make an informed decision.

The Minister must also be satisfied in relation to various matters designed to ensure, amongst other things, that the declaration accords with the objects of the Act and Australia's international obligations, and promotes the management of the place or the survival of the species or community.[257] Declarations must be published (s 84(5)) and may be revoked (s 84(6)).

Part 8 – Choosing the appropriate form of assessment

For actions that must be assessed under Pt 8, the Environment Minister must select the appropriate form of assessment. Implicit in the range of assessment procedures provided for in the Act is that proposed actions will differ in the complexity of their likely impacts, the extent and types of uncertainty, and the spectrum of issues that need further investigation and analysis. It is important to bear in mind that the assessment is directed to the likely impacts on the matter protected by the provision of Pt 3 that the Minister has decided is a controlling provision (s 82).[258] The assessment may address other likely impacts if the action is to be taken in a State or Territory and the appropriate State or Territory Minister has so requested, but this is for the purpose of assisting the State or Territory in making decisions about the action.[259]

---

257 EPBCA s 84(3A) applies ss 34A-34F.

258 With respect to actions proposed to be taken partly in and partly outside Commonwealth areas, where the controlling provisions relate to National Heritage places, Commonwealth marine areas and Commonwealth land, the relevant impacts are those impacts of that part of the action that is taken in or on a Commonwealth area, a Territory, a Commonwealth marine area or Commonwealth land: s 82(4).

259 EPBCA ss 97(3) (public environment report), 102(3) (EIS), 107(4) (public inquiries).

The decision as to the appropriate form of assessment is based on the information in the referral documentation and must be made at the same time as deciding that the action is a controlled action (ss 87, 88). An amendment to the Act in 2006 removed the requirement that the proponent provide 'preliminary information' and the requirement that the Minister seek comments from relevant State and Territory Ministers. State and Territory Ministers are now asked for comments on the appropriate form of assessment at the referral stage (s 74(2)).

The Minister must also consider any strategic environmental assessment of a policy, plan or program of which the action is a part (s 87(3)(b)). This is consistent with the benefits of strategic assessment, which include that strategic assessment may make later project assessment simpler or unnecessary.

Assessment by an accredited assessment process

The Minister may decide on a case-by-case basis to accredit a Commonwealth, State or Territory assessment process provided the Minister is satisfied that:

- the process is to be carried out under a law of the Commonwealth, a State or a Territory; and
- the process and the law meet the standards prescribed by the regulations; and
- the process will ensure that the relevant impacts of the action are adequately assessed; and
- the Minister will receive a report of the outcome of the process that will provide enough information on the relevant impacts of the action to make an informed decision whether or not to approve the action. (s 87(4))

Assessment on referral information

Amendments to the Act in 2006 introduced a new level of 'assessment on referral information'. The Minister may decide on this form of assessment only if satisfied that the action meets the criteria prescribed in the regulations (s 87(4A)).

If the Minister decides that this is the appropriate form of assessment, the Environment Secretary must prepare a draft recommendation report (within 30 business days) relating to whether the taking of the action should be approved and, if approval is recommended, any conditions that should be attached (s 93(1), (2)). The draft recommendation report must be published on the internet[260] with an invitation to anyone to comment (within 10 business days) and the final recommendation report must take account of any comments received (s 93(3)-(5)).

Assessment on preliminary documentation

If the Minister decides that the relevant impacts can be assessed on preliminary documentation, the Minister may request further specified information, including information about strategies for mitigating any adverse impacts (s 95A). The designated proponent must publish for public comment so much of the information

260 Material may be omitted if the Secretary is satisfied that it is commercial-in-confidence, or if it would be exempt under the *Freedom of Information Act 1982* on grounds of security of the Commonwealth or providing advice to the Minister: EPBCA s 93(3A).

provided on the referral, and on request by the Minister, as the Minister specifies (s 95). If comments are received, the designated proponent must prepare for the Minister a document that sets out the information previously provided, with any changes or additions needed to take account of the comments, and a summary of the comments and how they have been addressed (s 95B). This document must be made public. The Environment Secretary must then prepare for the Minister a recommendation report relating to whether the taking of the action should be approved and, if approval is recommended, any conditions that should be attached (s 95C).

Assessment by public environment report or EIS

The procedure for assessment by public environment report or EIS is the same. The Minister plays a key role in scoping the assessment. The Minister must give the designated proponent of the action written guidelines for the preparation of the draft public environment report or EIS (PER or EIS guidelines).[261] These could be standard guidelines[262] or guidelines tailored to the particular assessment.[263] The Minister has a discretion as to whether to invite anyone to comment on draft tailored guidelines.[264] Standard guidelines can be prepared for an industry sector, for a particular controlling provision or for particular categories of actions.[265]

After the draft report or statement has been prepared, the designated proponent must invite public comment.[266] The draft can only be published for public comment if the Minister is satisfied that the draft report or statement is in accordance with the guidelines.[267] Following the period for public comment, the designated proponent must finalise the report, taking into account any comments received, and publish the final report, including a summary of any comments and how those comments have been addressed.[268]

The Environment Secretary must then prepare for the Minister a recommendation report relating to whether the taking of the action should be approved and, if approval is recommended, any conditions that should be attached.[269]

Public access to recommendation reports

Any person has a right of access, on request, to the Environment Secretary's recommendation report after the Minister has decided whether or not to approve the taking of the action concerned (s 135A). Information may be withheld if the Secretary is satisfied that it is commercial-in-confidence or if it is exempt under the *Freedom of Information Act 1982* for reasons of the security of the Commonwealth or that it provides advice to the Minister (s 135A(4)). The onus is on the person claiming commercial-in-confidence to demonstrate to the Secretary that:

---

261 EPBCA ss 96A (public environment report), 101A (EIS).
262 EPBCA ss 96A(2), 96B (public environment report); 101A(2), 101B (EIS).
263 EPBCA ss 96A(2), 97 (public environment report); 101A(2), 102 (EIS).
264 EPBCA ss 97(5) (public environment report), 102(5) (EIS).
265 EPBCA ss 96B(3) (public environment report), 101B(3) (EIS).
266 EPBCA ss 98 (public environment report), 103 (EIS).
267 EPBCA ss 98(2) (public environment report), 103(2) (EIS).
268 EPBCA ss 99 (public environment report), 104 (EIS).
269 EPBCA ss 100 (public environment report), 105 (EIS).

- release of the information would cause competitive detriment to the person; and
- that the information is not in the public domain; and
- that is not required to be disclosed under another law of the Commonwealth, a State or a Territory; and
- that is not readily discoverable. (s 135A(5))

Provision is also made for the Minister to permit the designated proponent to withhold from publication so much of the assessment documentation that is commercial-in-confidence (s 170BA).

Assessment by public inquiry

The Minister may appoint a commissioner or commissioners to carry out an inquiry into the impacts of a proposed action (s 107). An inquiry may be appointed initially or after a draft public environment report or draft EIS has been published (s 90). Commissioners are independent of government. They are not subject to any directions by an employee of the Commonwealth or by a Commonwealth agency (s 109(2)).[270]

The Minister must specify the terms of reference and may also specify the manner in which the commission is to carry out the inquiry (s 107). It is likely that a reviewing court would require any such specification to be consistent with the common law principles of procedural fairness and would be prepared to supplement them with common law notions of fair procedure.[271]

The presumption is that hearings will be held in public and that any submission or evidence given to the commission in writing will be made public (s 110). The commission can compel persons to give evidence and produce documents (s 111), and an individual is not excused on the ground of self-incrimination (s 112(4)). However, information provided is not admissible in evidence in criminal proceedings against the person.[272] Commissioners have powers of entry and inspection for the purposes of their inquiry (ss 114-117).

Commissioners must report to the Minister and publish their reports (ss 121, 122).

Decision whether to approve an action

After receiving the assessment documentation[273] or the report of a commission of inquiry, the Environment Minister must decide whether or not to approve the controlled action and, if so, on what conditions (s 133). The Minister may approve 'one or more' alternative proposals if the referral included alternative proposals (s 133(1A)).[274]

270 See also EPBCA s 127 (termination of appointment).

271 *Re Minister for Immigration and Multicultural Affairs; Ex p Miah* (2001) 206 CLR 57.

272 EPBCA s 112(5) (except in proceedings for providing false or misleading information).

273 'Assessment documentation' is defined in EPBCA s 133(8).

274 See EPBCA s 72(3) permitting a referral to include alternative proposals relating to location, time frames and activities.

The person proposing to take the action and the designated proponent must be afforded procedural fairness. In this respect, the Act contains an 'exhaustive statement of the requirements of the natural justice hearing rule' (s 131AA).

Before deciding, the Minister must invite comments, including on social and economic matters, from other Commonwealth Ministers who have administrative responsibilities relating to the action (s 131). The Minister may also request further information from any person the Minister considers appropriate, including State or Territory Ministers where relevant (s 132). The Minister has a discretion as to whether to publish the proposed decision for public comment (s 131A).

If the action is to be taken in a State or Territory, and is an action in respect of which the Commonwealth has constitutional powers, the Minister, before deciding whether or not to grant approval, may request the appropriate Minister of the State or Territory to advise the method that has been used to assess the certain and likely impacts of the action on things other than matters protected by the controlling provisions for the action (s 132A).[275] This discretion replaces what was previously a constraint on the Minister's power to grant approval. Before the 2006 amendments to the Act, the Minister could not grant an approval until the Minister had received notice from a State or Territory that the certain and likely impacts of the action on things other than matters protected by the controlling provisions had been assessed 'to the greatest extent practicable'. The Minister is no longer so constrained and can make a decision in the absence of a notice from the State or Territory, even if one has been requested.

Variation of proposed action

At any time before the Minister's decision granting or refusing approval, or identifying and notifying a particular manner for taking the proposed action,[276] the person who referred the action for assessment and approval may request the Minister to accept a variation to the action (s 156A). The Minister cannot accept a varied proposal unless the Minister is satisfied that the character of the varied proposal is substantially the same as the character of the original proposal (s 156B(2), (3)). If the Minister does not accept a variation, the person may withdraw the original proposal and refer the new proposal (s 170C). The Minister's decision must be published (s 156E(3)).

Constraints on the power to grant approval

The Act stipulates three sets of constraints on the power of the Minister to grant approval.

First, the Minister must not act inconsistently with Australia's international obligations under:

- the World Heritage Convention (s 137);
- the Ramsar Convention (s 138);

275 There are exceptions for nuclear actions, actions taken entirely in Commonwealth areas and actions taken by Commonwealth agencies, where the relevant impacts of the action have been assessed under Pt 8.

276 But not if the referral has been rejected under s 74A or withdrawn, or a decision has been made that the action is not a controlled action: EPBCA s 156A(2).

- the Biodiversity Convention, the Apia Convention or CITES (s 139);
- the Bonn Convention, the CAMBA, the JAMBA, or an international agreement approved under s 209(4) (s 140).

Secondly, the Minister must not act inconsistently with:

- the Australian World Heritage management principles and any plan that has been prepared for the management of a declared World Heritage property (s 137);[277]
- the National Heritage management principles, any agreement to which the Commonwealth is party in relation to a National Heritage place, and any plan that has been prepared for the management of a National Heritage place (s 137A);[278]
- a Commonwealth recovery plan or threat abatement plan in relation to threatened species and endangered communities (s 139).

Thirdly, the Minister must not approve an action consisting of or involving the construction or operation of any of the following nuclear installations:

- a nuclear fuel fabrication plant;
- a nuclear power plant;
- an enrichment plant;
- a reprocessing facility. (s 140A)

Relevant and irrelevant considerations

The Act stipulates mandatory considerations for the Minister in deciding whether or not to approve the taking of an action, and what conditions to attach. These are:

- matters relevant to any matter protected by a provision of Pt 3 that the Minister has decided is a controlling provision for the action;
- economic and social matters. (s 136)[279]

In considering these matters, the Minister must take into account:

- the ESD principles, which are defined in the Act to include the precautionary principle, the principle of intergenerational equity, conservation of biological diversity and ecological integrity and improved valuation, pricing and incentive mechanisms (s 3A);
- the recommendation report, finalised public environmental report or EIS, any report of a commission of inquiry and any assessment report;
- any other information the Minister has on the relevant impacts of the action (including, for example, a strategic assessment of a policy, plan or program under which the action is to be taken);
- any relevant comments given to the Minister;
- any notice from a State or Territory stating the method that has been used to assess the certain and likely impacts of the action on things other than matters protected by the controlling provisions;

---

277 With respect to plans of management, see ss 316 and 321.

278 With respect to plans of management, see ss 324S and 324X.

279 See also EPBCA s 134(4).

- in relation to listed threatened species or ecological communities, any approved conservation advice for the species or community.[280] (s 136)

The Minister may also consider the environmental history of the person to be granted an approval – that is to say, whether the person is a suitable person to be granted an approval, having regard to the person's history in relation to environmental matters, and if the person is a body corporate, the history of its executive officers in relation to environmental matters (s 136(4)). If the person is a body corporate – that is, a subsidiary of another body or company – the history of the parent body and its executive officers in relation to environmental matters is relevant.

The Act states that the matters stipulated in the Act, which the Minister must or may take into account, exhaust the range of relevant consideration (s 136(5)). This not only prevents a reviewing court from implying further considerations that must as a matter of law be taken into account, but confines the Minister to considering matters protected by Pt 3, rather than environmental impacts more broadly. If the assessment has addressed other impacts at the request of a State or Territory, this is for the purpose of assisting the State or Territory in making decisions about the action.[281]

Conditions

The Minister may attach a condition to the approval if satisfied that the condition is necessary or convenient for protecting the matter, or repairing or mitigating damage to the protected matter (s 134).[282] In deciding whether to attach a condition, the Minister must consider any relevant conditions that have been, or are likely to be, imposed on the action under a law of a State or Territory or another law of the Commonwealth (s 134(4)). The Minister must also consider the desirability of ensuring as far as practicable that the condition is a cost-effective means to achieve the object of the condition – for both the Commonwealth and the person taking the action.

The Act gives a non-exhaustive list of conditions that could be attached (s 134(3)). A condition could require the deposit of security to ensure compliance and meet any liability if the Commonwealth takes measures to repair and mitigate damage caused by a contravention.[283] Alternatively, the holder of the approval may be required to insure against any specified liability of the holder to the Commonwealth. Conditions may be imposed requiring environmental monitoring or testing and periodic environmental audits. Compliance with a specified industry standard or code of practice can be required. A condition may also be imposed requiring the preparation and implementation of a plan approved by the Minister for managing the impacts of the approved action, such as a plan for conserving habitat of a species or ecological community.

Conditions may be imposed which require compensatory activities, or a financial contribution, to support the protection or repair of the protected matter, or

---

280 EPBCA s 266B requires the Minister to ensure there is approved conservation advice for each threatened species and threatened ecological community.

281 EPBCA ss 97(3) (public environment report), 102(3) (EIS), 107(4) (public inquiries).

282 Non-compliance with conditions is an offence; civil penalties are also available: EPBCA s 142.

283 The Commonwealth has power to do so under EPBCA s 499.

mitigation of damage to it – whether or not the action itself gives rise to the need for protection and whether or not the damage may be caused by the action (s 134(1)(a), (3)(aa) and (ab)). However, if the compensatory activities are not reasonably related to the taking of the action, the holder of the approval must consent to the condition (s 134(3A)(a)). The holder must also agree to any condition requiring a financial contribution (s 134(3A)(b)). Once the holder has agreed, and the condition has been attached, the holder cannot resile (s 134(3B)). Any person to whom the approval is later transferred is taken to have consented to the condition, and cannot withdraw that consent.

Conditions may be imposed requiring a person taking the action to comply with conditions specified in an instrument – for example, a consent or approval, made or granted under a law of a State or Territory or another law of the Commonwealth (s 134(3)(c)). It is not necessary that the instrument exist at the time of approval (s 134(3C)). Further, any variations to the instrument are automatically incorporated into the approval granted under the EPBCA (s 134(3C)).

Approval is granted to a person

An approval attaches to persons, not to the land. It approves the taking of the action specified in the approval by:

- the holder of the approval (that is, the person named in the approval);
- a person who is authorised, permitted or requested by the holder of the approval to take the action; and
- a person who is authorised, permitted or requested by another person with the consent or agreement of the holder of the approval, to take the action. (s 133(2A))

In authorising, permitting or requesting another person to undertake any part of the action, reasonable steps must be taken to ensure that the other person is informed of any condition that restricts or regulates the action and that the other person complies with any such condition (s 134(1A)). This duty is a condition of all approvals.

Provision is made for the transfer of approvals to another person. The Minister must consent to any transfer (s 145B). In deciding whether consent should be granted, the Minister may consider whether the transferee would be a suitable person to be granted the approval, having regard to the transferee's history in relation to environmental matters, and whether the transferee can comply with the conditions attached to the approval. 'Environmental history' was explained above in the context of granting the initial approval.

Appeals

There is no appeal against the Minister's decision.

Post-approval monitoring and auditing

Authorised officers may enter premises under a warrant issued by a magistrate and exercise a range of monitoring powers for the purpose of ascertaining compliance with the Act and regulations (ss 407-412). It is an offence to fail to answer questions or provide information, records or documents in response to a requirement of the authorised officer (s 412A).

Environmental audits may be required by a condition attached to an approval (s 134(3)(d)) or on the direction of the Minister to the holder of an approval (*directed environmental audit*) (s 458). A directed environmental audit can be required if the Minister believes or suspects on reasonable grounds that the holder has contravened, or is likely to contravene, a condition of approval; or that the likely impacts of the approved action on the protected matter are significantly greater than was indicated in the information available to the Minister when approval was granted (s 458(1)). The audit may be directed to issues of compliance or risks to the environment (s 458(3)). An independent environmental auditor must be appointed and approved by the Minister (s 459). Auditors conducting directed environmental audits are subject to various offences, including for failure to take into account any relevant information or document, or making a statement that is false or misleading in a material particular (ss 460, 461). The Minister must be provided with the audit report (s 461).

Variation, suspension and revocation of approvals

The Minister may revoke, vary or add to conditions attached to an approval (s 143), or suspend an approval (s 144). The circumstances in which this may be done include where a condition has been contravened, or where the Minister believes that the action will have a significant impact that was not identified in the initial assessment. In order to suspend the approval in the case of unanticipated impacts, the Minister must reasonably believe that approval would not have been granted had the information been available at the time (s 144(1), (2)). A particular circumstance in which the Minister may suspend an approval is where there has been non-compliance with a condition relating to the timing of the action, which was of essence to the grant of approval – for example, to protect a threatened species at a certain time of year (s 144(2A)). During the period in which an approval is suspended, the relevant provision of Pt 3 applies as if the Minister had not granted approval (s 144(4)).

Conditions can also be revoked, varied or added to where the Minister is satisfied that an impact is substantially greater than the impact that was identified in assessing the action (s 143(1)(ba)). However, in this respect and with respect to unanticipated impacts, it must be recalled that the Minister cannot have regard to 'listing events' occurring after the decision that the action is a controlled action (s 158A(1)(g)). Listing events include new listings of species, Ramsar wetlands, or heritage properties or places; up-listing of species; and changes to boundaries of Ramsar wetlands or heritage properties or places (s 158A).

The holder of the approval can agree to a proposed revocation, variation or addition of conditions, but the Minister must be satisfied that this is necessary or convenient for protecting the matter or repairing or mitigating damage to a matter (s 143(1)(c)).

Approvals may be revoked in circumstances similar to suspensions (s 145). There is an additional circumstance in which approvals can be revoked; namely where the Minister believes that the person proposing to take the action, or the designated proponent, negligently, deliberately or by omission did not accurately identify the impacts in the information available to the Minister when the approval was given (s 145(2A)).

In deciding whether or not to revoke, vary or add to any conditions, or to suspend or revoke an approval, the Minister may have regard to the person's history in relation to environmental matters (ss 143(3), 144(3), 145(3)). 'Environmental history' was explained above in the context of granting the initial approval.

Approvals that have been suspended or revoked can be reinstated on request, which is considered in the same way as initial approvals (s 145A).

Compliance and enforcement

Judicial review of administrative decisions

Judicial review of government decisions to ensure compliance with the law is available in the Federal Court under the *Administrative Decisions (Judicial Review) Act 1977* (ADJR Act). The court can review decisions that have been made, conduct engaged in for the purpose of making a decision, and failure to make a decision (ADJR Act ss 5, 6, 7) (referred to below simply as the 'decision'). The grounds of review are confined to questions of legality and not the merits of the decision. If the decision is not one to which the ADJR Act applies,[284] proceedings can be brought under s 39B of the *Judiciary Act 1903* (Cth).[285] The advantages of using the ADJR Act include its simplified remedies and, in the absence of a specific duty to give reasons under the EPBCA, the general right to obtain reasons for a decision that is reviewable under the ADJR Act.[286] The further important advantage of applying under the ADJR Act is that a broader range of persons has standing to bring the proceedings. The EPBCA expressly extends standing to individuals, organisations or associations (whether incorporated or not) that have engaged in a series of activities in Australia or an external Territory for protection or conservation of, or research into, the environment, at any time in the two years immediately before the decision the subject of review (EPBCA s 487).[287] In the case of an organisation or association, this must be one of its objects or purposes at the time of the decision. This test for standing gives statutory blessing to, and removes uncertainty about, the 'Sackville factors', which had been evolving in the Federal Court in relation to environmental interest groups before enactment of the EPBCA.[288]

Minister's powers to obtain information or documents

As discussed below, there are administrative, civil and criminal enforcement options where requirements to obtain environmental approvals and comply with approvals are not observed. In order to investigate or prevent an offence, or a contravention of

284 See, for example, *Humane Society International Inc v Minister for Environment and Heritage* [2003] FCA 65.

285 Proceedings may also be brought in the original jurisdiction of the High Court: Australian Constitution s 75(iii), (v). On judicial review, including the jurisdiction of the courts, see M Aronson, B Dyer and M Groves, *Judicial Review of Administrative Action* (3rd ed, Lawbook Co, 2004).

286 ADJR Act s 13, subject to ss 13A, 14.

287 The applicant must be an Australian citizen or ordinarily resident in Australia, or be incorporated or otherwise established in Australia or an external Territory. A person acting on behalf of the unincorporated organisation may apply for review: EPBCA s 488.

288 *Australian Conservation Foundation v Minister for Resources* (1989) 76 LGRA 200; *North Coast Environment Council Inc v Minister for Resources (No 2)* (1994) 127 ALR 617 (Sackville J); *Tasmanian Conservation Trust Inc v Minister for Resources* (1995) 127 ALR 580 (Sackville J).

a civil penalty provision, the Minister is equipped with powers to obtain information or documents (EPBCA Pt 17 Div 15A). An individual is not excused from giving information (including by answering a question) or from producing documents on the ground of self-incrimination (s 486J(1)). However, there are use-immunity provisions – the information or document is not admissible in evidence against the person in any civil or criminal proceedings, except criminal proceedings relating to failure to comply with a requirement to give information or a document (s 486J(2)).

Civil enforcement: injunctions

Contraventions of the Act or regulations can be remedied by civil injunction, even if the contravention is a criminal offence (s 475).[289] Proceedings can be brought in the Federal Court by the Minister or an 'interested person' or person acting on behalf of an unincorporated organisation that is an 'interested person' (s 475(1)). The definition of 'interested person' extends standing in the same way as for applicants for judicial review, thus allowing persons to bring proceedings if they have been engaged in environmental conservation or research in Australia in the previous two years (s 475(6), (7)).[290] The ability of public interest litigants to enforce the Act has assumed importance in light of the Commonwealth's poor record on enforcement. The first injunction under the EPBCA was granted to a wildlife researcher and member of the Queensland Conservation Council to restrain use of an aerial electric grid to protect a lychee orchard from spectacled flying foxes.[291]

Both prohibitory injunctions – restraining conduct constituting a contravention – and mandatory injunctions – requiring positive action to avoid a contravention – may be sought (s 475(2), (3), (4)).[292] A prohibitory injunction may be coupled with an order requiring the person to do something, including repair or mitigate damage to the environment (s 475(3)). Either type of injunction may be granted without having to show past or likely future contraventions or that there is a significant risk of injury or damage to human beings or the environment (s 479). It is enough that a person has engaged, is engaging, or proposes to engage, in conduct consisting of an act or omission that constitutes a contravention of the Act or the regulations.

An interim injunction may be granted (s 475(5)). It must be shown that there is a serious issue to be tried and that the balance of convenience lies in favour of granting the application.[293] However, the court may require an undertaking as to

289 See *Mees v Roads Corporation* [2003] FCA 306 at [120]-[122] on the limitations of confining the injunction to contraventions of the Act and the problems of Crown immunity. The issues were not resolved because the application for an injunction was not pressed: *Mees v Roads Corporation* [2003] FCA 410.

290 The applicant must be an Australian citizen or ordinarily resident in Australia, or be incorporated or otherwise established in Australia or an external Territory. In the case of organisations or associations, its objects or purposes must at the time of the conduct or, if the application relates to proposed conduct, at any time of the application, have environmental conservation or research as one of its objects or purposes.

291 *Booth v Bosworth* (2001) 114 FCR 39.

292 The powers conferred on the Federal Court are in addition to and do not limit any other powers of the Court: EPBCA s 480.

293 For a discussion of relevant factors, including that, although considerable environmental damage had been done, there was a reasonable possibility of remediation of the site, see: *Minister for the Environment & Heritage v Greentree* [2003] FCA 857 at [14]-[20].

damages as a condition of granting an interim injunction. An amendment to the Act in 2006 repealed the provision precluding the court from doing so. Further, an order that the applicant provide security for costs may be made in the discretion of the court.[294]

The nature of public interest injunctions was recognised by the Full Court in *Humane Society International Inc v Kyodo Senpaku Kaisha Ltd*.[295] The Humane Society – a public interest organisation having as one of its objects the protection and conservation of the environment – sought a declaration and injunction against the respondent, a Japanese company, alleging that its fleet of whalers was in breach of the EPBCA by killing and injuring Antarctic minke whales in that part of the Australian Whale Sanctuary that is adjacent to the Australian Antarctic Territory. The issue for the court was whether to grant leave to serve the application on the respondent in Japan. At first instance, leave was refused for two reasons, both of which had been pressed by the Commonwealth Attorney-General.[296] First, it was held that prosecution of the action 'may upset the diplomatic status quo under the Antarctic Treaty and be contrary to Australia's long term national interests, including its interests connected with its claim to territorial sovereignty to the Antarctic'. Secondly, the action was held to be futile because of 'the difficulty, if not impossibility, of enforcement of any court order'.[297] The court at first instance further stated that:

> Futility will be compounded by placing the Court at the centre of an international dispute (indeed helping to promote such a dispute) between Australia and a friendly foreign power which course or eventuality the Australian Government believes not to be in Australia's long term national interests.[298]

The appeal by the Humane Society was upheld, the Full Court unanimously holding that there is no room for political considerations where Parliament has provided that the action is justiciable in an Australian court and the applicant has satisfied each of the required conditions for obtaining leave.[299] The Full Court was divided on the question of futility. The majority, Black CJ and Finkelstein J, disagreed with the primary judge for several reasons, including that it is no bar to the grant of an injunction that its purpose is entirely educative.[300] What was being sought in the proceedings was a statutory public interest injunction. A public interest injunction may be granted in the court's discretion even though there might be no prospect of the conduct being repeated by the respondent or even though it may prove difficult or even impossible to enforce it. The majority observed:[301]

> Parliament has determined that it is in the public interest that the enforcement provisions of the EPBC Act should be unusually comprehensive in scope. …
>
> Although 'deterrence' is more commonly used in the vocabulary of the law than 'education', the two ideas are closely connected and must surely overlap in areas

294 See *Save the Ridge Inc v Commonwealth* [2004] FCA 1167.

295 [2006] FCAFC 116.

296 *Humane Society International Inc v Kyodo Senpaku Kaisha Ltd* [2005] FCA 664.

297 [2005] FCA 664 at [27] and [28].

298 Ibid at [35].

299 [2006] FCAFC 116 at [10]-[13] per Black CJ and Finkelstein J, Moore J agreeing on this issue.

300 Ibid at [14]-[27].

301 Ibid at [19], [22].

> where a statute aims to regulate conduct. Thus, there being a 'matter' ..., the grant of a statutory public interest injunction to mark the disapproval of the Court of conduct which the Parliament has proscribed, or to discourage others from acting in a similar way, can be seen as also having an educative element. For that reason alone the grant of such an injunction may be seen, here, as potentially advancing the regulatory objects of the EPBC Act. Indeed, some of those objects are expressed directly in the language of 'promotion' ...

Court order to remediate

In addition to its other powers, and without the need to grant an injunction, the Federal Court is equipped with power to make a remediation order against a person who has or is contravening the Act or regulations, whether or not the conduct constitutes an offence (ss 480A, 480C). An application for a remediation order can only be made by the Minister (s 480A(5)). A remediation order requires the defendant to take action to repair or mitigate damage that may or will be, or that has been, caused to the environment by the contravention. The order may be in general terms (for example, requiring the person to take whatever action is necessary to repair or mitigate the damage), or it may require the person to take particular action to repair or mitigate the damage (s 480A(3)). The defendant may also be required to provide security for taking the action (s 480A(4)). The Act sets out a non-exhaustive list of relevant considerations in deciding whether to grant an order (s 480A(2)). A remediation order can be discharged or varied by the Federal Court on the application of the Minister (s 480B).

Minister's power to make remediation determinations

The 2006 amendments to the Act equipped the Minister with a new and relatively speedy administrative enforcement option. The Minister may make a remediation determination in respect of a person who the Minister considers has taken an action which contravenes a civil penalty provision of Pt 3 (s 480D). The determination requires the person to take action to repair or mitigate damage to the matter protected that has been, will be or is likely to be caused by the contravention. The remediation action that the person is required to take must be specified (s 480E(1)); but could be a requirement to prepare and implement a plan, approved by the Minister, for taking action. Other possible requirements include:

- compliance with a specified industry standard or code of practice in taking action;
- the taking of reasonable steps to obtain any Commonwealth, State or Territory approval or authority needed to carry out action;
- the spending of a specified amount of money on the taking of action;
- the payment to a specified person of a specified amount or money, for the purpose of activities directed towards the protection and conservation of the matter protected;
- the payment to the Commonwealth of a specified amount of money as security for the taking of the action;
- monitoring, auditing or reporting to the Minister in relation to the taking of action. (s 480E(2))

If action is required to be taken on land that is not owned or occupied by the person who is the subject of the determination, the Minister, before making the determination, must take all practicable steps to notify and seek comment from the owner or occupier of the land, and take any comments into account (s 480F).

The person who is the subject of the determination may apply for a reconsideration of the determination by the Minister, who may affirm or vary it or set it aside (s 480J). Alternatively, the person may apply to the Federal Court to have the remediation determination set aside (s 480K). The court must do so, and only do so, if satisfied that the person did not contravene the civil penalty provision or the remediation action is not a reasonable measure to repair or mitigate damage (s 480K(2), (4)). Whether this right to apply for reconsideration is an adequate substitute for the right to be afforded procedural fairness before the Minister makes a remediation determination may be doubted, unless the determination was made in circumstances of urgency.[302]

Compliance with the remediation determination is enforceable by order of the Federal Court on application of the Minister (s 480L). Non-compliance can also incur a civil penalty, equivalent to the penalty the court could order for contravention of the relevant provision of Pt 3 (s 480M).

The Minister may vary or revoke a remediation determination (s 480N).

Civil penalties

The EPBCA includes numerous civil penalty provisions – an enforcement strategy that is well used in other areas of law (such as trade practices), but has not hitherto been a feature of environmental law in either the Commonwealth or New South Wales. Civil penalty provisions include proscriptions against taking without approval an action that is likely to have a significant impact on matters of national environmental significance,[303] proscriptions relating to activities involving Commonwealth land or undertaken by the Commonwealth or a Commonwealth agency,[304] prescriptions that action be taken in a particular manner (s 77A), and the requirement to comply with conditions of approval (s 142).[305]

A contravention of a civil penalty provision is not a criminal offence (s 483).[306] The provision can be enforced by application to the Federal Court for an injunction (discussed above) or for an order that the wrongdoer pay to the Commonwealth a

---

302 See *Re Minister for Immigration and Multicultural Affairs; Ex p Miah* (2001) 206 CLR 57; *Marine Hull & Liability Co Ltd v Hurford* (1985) 67 ALR 77.

303 EPBCA ss 12(1) (World Heritage), 15B (National Heritage), 16 (Ramsar wetlands), 18 (listed threatened species and communities), 20 (listed migratory species), 21 (nuclear actions), 23 (activities involving the marine environment), 25 (additional matters of national environmental significance).

304 EPBCA ss 26 (activities involving Commonwealth land), 27B (Commonwealth Heritage places overseas), 28 (Commonwealth actions).

305 A person who is not the holder of the approval is not liable if he or she was not informed of the condition and could not reasonably have been expected to be aware of the condition: EPBCA s 142(1A). However, the holder of the approval may be liable; see s 134(1A).

306 Nevertheless the High Court has recognised that proceedings for a civil penalty have both civil and criminal characteristics: *Chief Executive Officer of Customs v Labrador Liquor Wholesale Pty Ltd* [2003] HCA 49. See also *Minister for the Environment and Heritage v Greentree (No 3)* [2004] FCA 1317 at [53]-[57]. A useful discussion can be found in Australian Law Reform Commission 95 *Principled Regulation: Federal Civil and Administrative Penalties in Australia* (2003), <http://www.austlii.edu.au/au/other/alrc/publications/reports/95/> (accessed 1 November 2006).

pecuniary penalty (ss 481, 485).[307] Only the Minister can bring an application for a pecuniary penalty order (s 481(1)).[308]

Wrongdoers include those who are in any way, directly or indirectly, knowingly concerned in, or party to, a contravention (s 484). In *Minister for the Environment and Heritage v Greentree (No 2)*, the Federal Court did not need to rely on this section in finding that proceedings may be brought not only against the person who physically 'takes an action', but also against a person who gives instructions from a position of authority to an employee requiring the employee to carry out the particular action.[309] Amendments to the Act in 2006 confirm the liability of principals and employers for actions taken on their behalf. This is discussed below, together with the liability of landholders, corporations and persons concerned in the management of a body corporate.

In fixing the quantum of a civil penalty, the court must have regard to the nature and extent of the contravention and any loss or damage suffered, the circumstances in which the contravention took place, and whether the person has previously been found by the court in proceedings under the EPBCA to have engaged in similar conduct (s 481(3)). These considerations are not exhaustive.[310] In *Minister for Environment and Heritage v Greentree (No 3)*,[311] the contravention incurring civil penalties was deliberate and sustained, and had caused serious environmental damage to a Ramsar wetland. On the other hand, the wetland was not pristine at the relevant time and there was some prospect of the site being rehabilitated albeit over a lengthy period and subject to climatic conditions. Further, the wrongdoers had not previously been found by the Court to have engaged in similar conduct. It was relevant that the action was taken in the course of commercial operations; however, the evidence did not establish that the wrongdoers obtained substantial financial benefits from their contraventions. The further considerations taken into account in setting a total penalty of $450,000 included:[312]

- that high maximum penalties reflect the public expression by Parliament of the seriousness of the offence;
- that substantial penalties should act as both a general and specific deterrent;
- that the respondents had not shown contrition for their conduct or unqualified acknowledgment that their conduct was wrong;
- that penalties should not ordinarily be increased because the contravener does not display a co-operative attitude, although depending on the circumstances co-operation might count in favour of the contravener;
- that there was no evidence that substantial pecuniary penalties would cause any financial hardship;

307 The double jeopardy rule applies: a person is not liable to more than one pecuniary penalty in respect of the same conduct: EPBCA s 481(4).

308 The application must be brought within six years of the contravention of the civil penalty provision.

309 [2004] FCA 741 at [207]-[208] per Sackville J.

310 *Minister for Environment and Heritage v Greentree (No 3)* [2004] FCA 1317 at [50], [68] ff per Sackville J.

311 Ibid.

312 Ibid at [68]-[79]. Greentree was ordered, as an individual, to pay $150,000 and the private company of which he was the sole director was ordered to pay $300,000. Greentree and the company were also ordered to pay the Minister's costs.

- that in the absence of evidence of financial hardship or other special considerations, the fact that a person who has deliberately contravened the EPBCA is the subject of an adverse costs order will not ordinarily warrant a reduction in the penalty;
- that it is important to consider the totality of the penalties imposed to ensure that they fairly reflect the statutory criteria and do not result in unfairness.

Conduct constituting a contravention of a civil penalty provision will usually also constitute a criminal offence. Criminal proceedings may be brought against a person for conduct that is substantially the same regardless of whether a pecuniary penalty order was made against the person (s 486C). Evidence given in the proceedings for a pecuniary penalty order is not admissible in the criminal proceedings (s 486D). However, if a person has already been convicted of an offence, the Federal Court cannot make a pecuniary penalty order in respect of substantially the same conduct (s 486A). Further, if criminal proceedings are started against the person, any pending proceedings for a pecuniary penalty order are stayed (s 486B). The proceedings for the order may be resumed if the person is not convicted of the offence.

Enforceable undertakings relating to contraventions of Part 3 civil penalty provisions

The Minister may accept an enforceable financial undertaking from a person whom the Minster considers has taken an action in contravention of a civil penalty provision of Pt 3. This alternative to pursuing litigation was introduced by amendment to the Act in 2006, modelled on enforceable undertaking provisions in other Commonwealth legislation, such as the *Trade Practices Act 1974*.[313] The undertaking is to pay a specified amount, within a specified period, to the Commonwealth or some other specified person, for the purpose of activities directed towards the protection and conservation of the protected matter (EPBCA s 486DA). The person may only withdraw or vary the undertaking with the consent of the Minister (s 486DA(3)). If the person fails to comply with the undertaking, the Minister may apply to the Federal Court for an order enforcing the terms of the undertaking (s 486DB).

Criminal enforcement

The Act creates a range of offences, including offences relating to requirements to obtain environmental approvals,[314] breaching conditions of approval (ss 142A, 142B) and providing false or misleading information (ss 489, 490, 491).[315] These offences expose individuals, corporations, persons concerned in the management of corporations, non-corporate principals, employers and landholders to liability carrying potentially substantial fines and, in the case of individuals, terms of imprisonment.

313 *Trade Practices Act 1974* (Cth) ss 87B, 87C.

314 EPBCA ss 15A (offences relating to declared World Heritage properties), 15C (offences relating to National Heritage places), 17B (offences relating to declared Ramsar wetlands), 18A (offences relating to threatened species etc), 20A (offences relating to listed migratory species), 22A (offences relating to nuclear actions), 24A (offences relating to marine areas), 27A (offences relating to Commonwealth land), 27C (offences relating to Commonwealth Heritage places overseas), 74AA (offence of taking action before decision made in relation to referral).

315 Further offences relate to the conduct of public inquiries: see ss 111, 112, 114, 119, 120.

Most of the offences relating to requirements to obtain environmental approvals are punishable on conviction by imprisonment for a maximum term of seven years and/or a maximum fine of 420 penalty units.[316] The offence arises where an action is taken without approval that results, will result or is likely to result in a significant impact on the protected matter. Chapter 2 of the *Criminal Code* (Cth), which sets out the general principles of criminal responsibility, applies to all offences against the Act (with the exception of corporate criminal responsibility, which is discussed below). Under the *Criminal Code*, intention must be proved except for the result element of the offence, in respect of which it is enough to prove recklessness.[317] With respect to one element of the offence, the EPBCA creates strict liability; namely, the circumstance (as the case may be) that the property is a declared World Heritage property (s 15A(1A), (2A)), the place is a National Heritage place and the heritage values are National Heritage values,[318] the wetland is a declared Ramsar wetland (s 17B(1A), (2A)), the species or community is a listed threatened species or ecological community (s 18A(1A), (2A)), or listed migratory species (s 20A(1A), (2A)), the area is a Commonwealth marine area[319] or the action is taken on Commonwealth land (s 27A(1A), (2A), (3A), (4A)). Thus the prosecution does not have to show that the defendant knew or was reckless as to this fact. The only defence to the strict liability element of the offence is reasonable mistake of fact.[320] This defence is discussed in the context of NSW law in Chapter 11.

Where approval has been granted, it is a strict liability offence to contravene, by act or omission, any condition attached to the approval (s 142B). However, a person who is not the holder of the approval is not liable if he or she was not informed of the condition and could not reasonably have been expected to be aware of the condition (s 142B(2)). In this situation, the holder of the approval would be liable if the holder authorised, permitted or requested the other person to undertake any part of the action, but failed to take reasonable steps to ensure that the other person was informed of conditions of approval and complied with conditions. This duty is itself a condition of approval with which the holder must comply (s 134(1A)).

It is also an offence, carrying double the penalty, to contravene a condition, by act or omission, where the person is reckless as to that fact, and the contravention either:

- results or will result in a significant impact on a matter protected by Pt 3 – in which case strict liability applies (s 142A(1), (2)); or
- is likely to have a significant impact on a matter protected by a provision of Pt 3 and the person is reckless as to that fact (s 142A(3)).

Liability of corporations, non-corporate principals and employers

The EPBCA contains its own code of corporate responsibility, modelled on corresponding provisions in the *Great Barrier Reef Marine Park Act 1975*[321] and the *Trade*

316 The *Crimes Act 1914* (Cth) s 4B(3) lets a court fine a body corporate up to five times the maximum amount the court could fine an individual.

317 *Criminal Code* s 5.6. Recklessness can be established by proving intention, knowledge or recklessness: s 5.4(4).

318 EPBCA s 15C(1A), (2A), (3A), (4A), (5A), (6A), (7A), (8A), (9A), (10A). See also s 27C(1A), (2A).

319 EPBCA s 24A(1A), (2A), (3A), (4A). See also s 24A(5A), (6A).

320 *Criminal Code* (Cth) ss 6.1, 9.2.

321 *Great Barrier Reef Marine Park Act 1975* s 64.

Practices Act 1974.[322] It makes corporations and non-corporate principals and employers vicariously liable for actions taken on their behalf by directors, agents and employees.

First, in relation to the physical elements of an offence or contravention, a corporation is attributed with any conduct engaged in on behalf of the corporation (including failing or refusing to engage in conduct):

- by a director,[323] employee or agent of the body corporate within the scope of his or her actual or apparent authority; or
- by any other person at the direction or with the consent or agreement (whether express or implied) of a director, employee or agent of the body corporate, where the giving of the direction, consent or agreement is within the scope of the actual or apparent authority of the director, employee or agent. (s 498B(1), (8))

Where it is necessary to establish the state of mind of the corporation in relation to particular conduct, it is sufficient to show that the person whose conduct is attributed to the corporation had the relevant state of mind (s 498B(2)). State of mind includes a reference to the knowledge, intention, opinion, belief or purpose of the person, and the person's reasons for the intention, opinion, belief or purpose (s 498B(6)).

Persons other than bodies corporate are liable in a similar way for the conduct and state of mind of their employees or agents (s 498B(3), (4)).

By requiring an individual to have the relevant state of mind, and by excluding Pt 2.5 of the *Criminal Code* (EPBCA s 498B(9)), the EPBCA misses the opportunity to hold corporations liable for organisational blameworthiness.[324] The *Criminal Code*, which applied before the amendment of the EPBCA in 2006, attributes intention, knowledge or recklessness to the corporation if it expressly, tacitly or impliedly authorised or permitted the commission of the offence, and this may be established by proving that a corporate culture existed within the body corporate that directed, encouraged, tolerated or led to non-compliance or that the body corporate failed to create and maintain a corporate culture that required compliance.[325] Importantly, the *Criminal Code* goes a considerable way towards forcing corporations not only to put in place effective compliance programs and due diligence systems, but also to foster a culture of compliance that cannot be masked by formal documents.

The EPBCA does, nevertheless, encourage the implementation of due diligence systems. Corporations, non-corporate principals and employers can avoid liability if they can establish that they took reasonable precautions and exercised due diligence to avoid the conduct of their director, agent or employee (s 498B(1), (3)). The EPBCA provides a non-exhaustive list of relevant factors; namely the steps (if any) that the body or person took directed towards ensuring:

---

322 *Trade Practices Act 1974* s 84.

323 A reference to a director of a body corporate includes a reference to a constituent member of a body corporate incorporated for a public purpose by a law of the Commonwealth, of a State or of a Territory: EPBCA s 498B(7).

324 Brent Fisse, 'The Attribution of Criminal Liability to Corporations; A Statutory Model' (1991) 13 *Syd LR* 277. See also Brent Fisse, *Howard's Criminal Law* (5th ed, Law Book Co, 1990); Brent Fisse and John Braithwaite, *Corporations, Crime and Accountability* (Cambridge University Press, 1993).

325 *Criminal Code* s 12.3.

- that it arranges regular professional assessments of its compliance with the Act and the regulations and implements any appropriate recommendations arising from the assessment;
- that it has an appropriate system established for managing the effects of its activities on the environment;
- that directors, employees and agents have a reasonable knowledge and understanding of relevant requirements in the Act and the regulations. (s 498B(5).

Liability of directors and persons concerned in the management of a body corporate

Contraventions of the Act by a body corporate expose 'executive officers' of the corporation to liability. An executive officer is a person who is concerned, or takes part, in the management of the body corporate, by whatever name called (s 493).

First, an executive officer may be ordered to pay a civil penalty if the corporation contravenes a civil penalty provision of Pt 3 or breaches a condition of approval and:

- the officer knew that, or was reckless or negligent as to whether, the contravention would occur; and
- the officer was in a position to influence the conduct of the body in relation to the contravention; and
- the officer failed to take all reasonable steps to prevent the contravention. (s 494)

Secondly, criminal liability arises in the same way where the corporation contravenes an offence relating to the provision of false or misleading information (s 495(1)).[326] The executive officer is guilty of an offence punishable on conviction by imprisonment for a term not exceeding two years (s 495(1)).[327]

Thirdly, in respect of a range of offences related to matters of national environmental significance and Commonwealth land, and the offence of breaching conditions of approval, an executive officer is deemed to have committed the same offence as the corporation if:[328]

- the officer was reckless as to whether the contravention would occur; and
- the officer was in a position to influence the conduct of the body in relation to the contravention; and
- the officer failed to take all reasonable steps to prevent the contravention. (s 495(2), (3))

---

326 The offences are EPBCA ss 489 (providing false or misleading information to obtain approval or permit), 490 (providing false or misleading information in response to a condition of an approval or permit), 491 (providing false or misleading information to authorised officer etc).

327 The *Crimes Act 1914* (Cth) s 4B(2) provides the alternative of a fine.

328 The offences are EPBCA ss 15A (offences relating to declared World Heritage properties), s 15C (offences relating to National Heritage places), 17B (offences relating to declared Ramsar wetlands), 18A (offences relating to threatened species etc), 20A (offences relating to listed migratory species), 22A (offences relating to nuclear actions), 24A (offences relating to marine areas), 27A (offences relating to Commonwealth land), 27C (offences relating to Commonwealth heritage places overseas), 142A (offence of breaching conditions on approval).

In determining whether an executive officer failed to take all reasonable steps to prevent the contravention, the EPBCA provides a non-exhaustive list of relevant factors, namely:

- what action (if any) the officer took directed towards ensuring:
  - that the corporation arranges regular professional assessments of its compliance with the Act and the regulations, and implements any appropriate recommendations arising from the assessment,
  - that the corporation has an appropriate system established for managing the effects of its activities on the environment,
  - that employees, agents and contractors have a reasonable knowledge and understanding of the relevant requirements in the Act and the regulations; and
- what action (if any) the officer took when he or she became aware that the corporation was contravening the Act, regulations or any environmental management plan imposed as a condition of approval. (s 496)

Liability of landholders for other people's actions

Owners, lessees or occupiers of land (*landholders*) (s 496A) can be held liable for the contraventions of others that take place on their land. Liability is both criminal and civil. Liability for civil penalties arises where another person has contravened a civil penalty provision of Pt 3 or breached conditions of approval and the landholder:

- knew that, or was reckless or negligent as to whether the contravention would occur; and
- was in a position to influence the conduct of the actor in relation to the contravention; and
- failed to take all reasonable steps to prevent the contravention. (s 496B)

Criminal liability arises where another person commits a Pt 3 offence or the offence of breaching approval conditions and the landholder:

- was reckless as to whether the contravention would occur; and
- was in a position to influence the conduct of the actor in relation to the contravention at the time when the contravention occurred; and
- failed to take all reasonable steps to prevent the contravention. (s 496C)

In determining whether a landholder failed to take all reasonable steps to prevent the contravention, it is relevant to consider:

- what action (if any) the landholder took directed towards ensuring that the person who contravened the Act had an appropriate system established for managing the effects of its activities on the environment; and
- what action (if any) the landholder took on becoming aware that there was a substantial risk of a contravention. (s 496D)

Liability for loss or damage caused by a contravention

A person who contravenes the Act or the regulations – whether or not the contravention is an offence or breach of a civil penalty provision – is liable to compensate an affected person who has suffered loss or damage arising from the contravention (s 500). Loss or damage includes expenses and liabilities reasonably incurred in mitigating or preventing any damage relating to the environment. Joint and several liability applies (s 500(4)).

Compensation may have to be paid to the Commonwealth where the Minister takes steps to mitigate or prevent damage relating to the environment in the circumstances authorised by s 499 of the EPBCA.

The EPBCA in practice

The EPBCA gained prominent news coverage in 2006 over the decision of the Minister not to approve the Bald Hills wind farm in Victoria on the basis of its threat to the endangered orange-bellied parrot. The wind farm had generated strong local opposition and there were suggestions that the Minister was motivated by political considerations.[329] What gained less prominence in the news were the statistics of referrals, assessments and approvals over the first six years of the Act's operation. Over these six years, approximately 60 wind farm referrals were made under the assessment and approval provisions of the EPBCA and only the Bald Hills proposal was refused approval.[330] The decision was subsequently reversed and approval granted.

The Department's statistics for the first six years reveal that there were only 1932 referrals, of which only 424 were determined to be controlled actions.[331] Of these, only four failed to obtain approval. Remarkably, also, 10 approvals were granted without any conditions attached. The exemption for actions carried out in a particular manner was used in 281 cases.

The low number of referrals is surprising overall, but especially in respect of some industry sectors. The agricultural and forestry sector, for example, only produced 55 referrals in six years. Research by the Australia Institute reveals that fewer than 10 of the agricultural referrals involved any significant land clearing, despite millions of hectares of native vegetation being cleared since July 2000.[332] The research also found that approximately 35 to 40 dam and weir developments were referred in the six years, but none was prevented from proceeding and enforceable conditions were imposed on fewer than 10% of these developments.[333]

The low number of referrals is of heightened concern when placed in the context of minimal enforcement. There have been only two enforcement actions brought by

329 See Andrew Macintosh, *Environment Protection and Biodiversity Conservation Act – An Ongoing Failure* (Australia Institute, October 2006), <http://www.tai.org.au/documents/downloads/WP91.pdf> (accessed 22 November 2006).

330 See Andrew Macintosh and Christian Downie, 'Wind Farms – The facts and fallacies', Discussion Paper No 91 (Australia Institute, October 2006), <http://www.tai.org.au/documents/dp_ fulltext/DP91.pdf> (accessed, 22 November 2006).

331 Australia, Department of the Environment and Heritage, *Environment Protection and Biodiversity Conservation Act 1999 Activity Report – 30 June 2006*, <http://www.deh.gov.au/epbc/statistics/pubs/epbc-activity-report.pdf> (accessed 22 November 2006).

332 Macintosh, above n 329, at 3. See further Andrew Macintosh and Debra Wilkinson, 'Environment Protection and Biodiversity Conservation Act – A Five Year Assessment' Discussion Paper No 81 (Australia Institute, July 2005), <http://www.tai.org.au/documents/dp_fulltext/DP81.pdf> (accessed 22 November 2006) esp at 6-8.

333 Ibid.

the Department. In the one successful case for taking action without approval,[334] it took the Commonwealth some 10 months before instituting legal proceedings. The proceedings were for a civil penalty, not a criminal prosecution. It is claimed that 80% of the clearing of a Ramsar wetland occurred while the Commonwealth was trying to negotiate a settlement with the defendants.[335]

With respect to assessment of controlled actions,[336] most are assessed on only preliminary documentation - 67%. Seventeen per cent were assessed by accredited process, 7% by EIS, 3% by public environment report and 6% were assessed under bilateral agreements. No public inquiry has been appointed.

334 *Minister for the Environment and Heritage v Greentree (No 2)* [2004] FCA 741.

335 Macintosh and Wilkinson, above n 332, at 14-16.

336 See Australia, Department of the Environment and Heritage, above n 331.

5

ENERGY LAW AND GLOBAL CLIMATE CHANGE

It is virtually impossible to discuss energy law without first explaining how our use of energy is directly correlated with the now well-recognised phenomenon of global climate change. The 2003 Australian Greenhouse Inventory,[1] which is the most recently available, shows that the combined energy sector (including stationary energy, transport and fugitive emissions from fossil fuel extraction and distribution) made up 68% of Australia's total greenhouse gas emissions. Electricity generation comprised 71% of these and 35% of Australia's net emissions. Therefore, from an environmental law perspective, it is crucial that the international framework for attempting to counteract global climate change is well understood. It is also important to situate the Australian and the NSW governments' stance on controlling emissions from the energy sector, particularly from electricity, within the international framework.

Global climate change

Global climate change formed an important part of the agenda at the 1992 United Nations Conference on Environment and Development (the Rio Conference) largely as a result of the research collated by the Intergovernmental Panel on Climate Change (IPCC). The IPCC was established in 1988 by the World Meteorological Organization (WMO) and the United Nations Environment Programme (UNEP) due to a concern about increased greenhouse gas emissions and the potential for global climate change. The role of the IPCC is to assess scientific, technical and socio-economic information relevant to understanding the scientific basis of risk of human-induced climate change, its potential impacts and options for adaptation and mitigation. The assessments are based mainly on peer-reviewed and published scientific/technical literature.

The IPCC has three Working Groups and a Task Force. Working Group I assesses the scientific aspects of the climate system and climate change; Working Group II assesses the vulnerability of socio-economic and natural systems to climate change, including the negative and positive consequences of climate change, and options for adapting to it; Working Group III assesses options for limiting greenhouse gas emissions and otherwise mitigating climate change; and the Task Force on National Greenhouse Gas Inventories is responsible for overseeing the IPCC's National Greenhouse Gas Inventories Program.[2] The First IPCC Assessment Report

1 See <http://www.greenhouse.gov.au/inventory/2003/index.html#summary> (accessed 16 January 2006).

2 See <www.ipcc.ch/about/about.htm> (accessed 26 July 2005).

was completed in 1990 and played a significant part in persuading the international community to adopt the United Nations Framework Convention on Climate Change (UNFCCC).

Almost 10 years after the adoption of the UNFCCC, the IPCC released its most recent scientific research on climate change in a report entitled IPCC Third Assessment Report – Climate Change 2001.[3] Importantly, climate change science and modelling has improved to such an extent since the Rio Conference that the IPCC is more confident of its predictions. It presented the following collective picture of warming and climate change. Surface temperatures have increased 0.6 degrees over the 20th century, which is the largest increase in the past 1000 years. The 1990s was the warmest decade with 1998 being the warmest year ever recorded. Sea-ice extent decreased 10-15%, thickness in Arctic sea-ice declined 40% in summer. The global average sea level has risen and ocean heat has increased. Other climate changes have occurred like precipitation, cloud cover, and high and low temperatures.

Emissions of GHGs and aerosols continue to alter the atmosphere to affect climate. The concentration of carbon dioxide has increased 31% since 1750. The current rate of increase is unprecedented in 20,000 years. Three-quarters of the increase in the past 20 years is due to fossil fuel burning. The concentration of methane has increased 151% since 1750, and more than half of these emissions are anthropogenic. The concentration of NO_2 increased 17% and one-third of these emissions are anthropogenic. Natural factors make a small contribution. Consequently, there is newer and stronger evidence that most of the global warming over the past 50 years is attributable to human activities.

Based on long-term studies of 20 years, the IPCC's Report also pointed to the impact of global climate change including recent regional climate changes, particularly temperature increases, which have already affected many physical and biological systems. These include: the shrinking of glaciers, thawing of permafrost, later freezing and earlier break-up of ice on rivers and lakes, longer growing seasons, shifts of plant and animal ranges, declines in plant and animal populations, earlier flowering of trees, and emergence of insects and egg-laying birds.[4]

Natural systems are vulnerable to climate change and some will be irreversibly damaged because of limited adaptive capacity. Many human systems are also sensitive to climate change and some are vulnerable like water, food security, forestry, coastal zones and marine systems (fisheries), human settlements (sea-level rise and flooding), disease, increased demand for energy, industry, insurance and other financial services.

The IPCC stated that adaptation is a necessary strategy at all scales to complement climate change mitigation efforts. However, those with least resources have least opportunity for adaptation and so are most vulnerable, while vulnerability varies across regions.

The IPCC's Fourth Assessment Report is scheduled for publication in 2007.

---

3 See <http://www.grida.no/climate/ipcc_tar/> (accessed 16 November 2004).

4 Note that anthropogenic climate change has been listed as a key threatening process under Sch 3 to the *Threatened Species Conservation Act 1995* (NSW).

The Stern Review Report

The Stern Review Report[5] entitled 'The Economics of Climate Change' leaves the global community in no doubt that climate change 'is the greatest and widest ranging market failure ever seen'. The Review, commissioned by the UK Chancellor of the Exchequer, provides an economic analysis of the impacts of climate change as well as the economics of stabilising greenhouse gases in the atmosphere. One of the fundamental policy recommendations of the Review is that the establishment of a carbon price, through tax, trading or regulation, is an essential foundation for climate change policy. The Review also emphasises the importance of technology policy and the removal of barriers to behavioural change. According to Stern, '[l]eaving out any one of these elements will significantly increase the costs of action' to reduce greenhouse gas emissions. Also, Stern makes it clear that the benefits of concerted early action outweigh the costs of mitigation and that 'it is already very clear that the economic risks of inaction in the face of climate change are very severe'.

The Review confirms the scientific consensus that greenhouse gas levels in the atmosphere are rising and are human induced. Current levels are at 430 parts per million (ppm) CO_2 compared with 280ppm before industrialisation, resulting already in a warming of global temperatures of 0.5 degrees, with at least another half degree over the next few decades already locked into the atmosphere. By 2050 this is likely to rise to 550ppm even if emissions do not continue to grow beyond current rates. However, given the likelihood of an acceleration in emissions this level could be reached as early as 2035. At this level there is a 77-99% chance that the global average temperature will rise by 2-3 degrees Celsius. Most worrying, under a business as usual scenario, emissions could treble by the end of the century resulting in a 50% chance that temperatures will rise by 5 degrees. As Stern reports, '[t]his would take humans into unknown territory'.

The Review concludes by calling for urgent co-ordinated action and international multilateral co-operation over the next 10-20 years to move towards a more sustainable path. Flows of carbon finance to developing countries must also be increased, while deforestation must be curbed at the same time as preserving remaining areas of natural forest.

International instruments on global climate change

Principal amongst the international instruments on global climate change are the UNFCCC,[6] and its associated Kyoto Protocol,[7] which together require the stabilisation of global greenhouse gas emissions to 1990 levels. However, in order to elucidate the essentials of a sustainable energy policy, it is also important to understand the basic underpinnings of the Rio Declaration[8] and Agenda 21,[9] which

5 See <http://www.hm-treasury.gov.uk/independent_reviews/stern_review_economics_climate_change/stern_review_report.cfm> (accessed 7 December 2006).

6 (1992) 31 ILM 849; 1771 UNTS 108 (in force 29 May 1992).

7 (1998) 37 ILM 22; UN Doc FCCC/CP/1997/L.7/Add.1 (in force 16 February 2005).

8 A/CONF.199/CRP/7. See <www.unep.org/Documents/Default.asp?DocumentID=78&ArticleID=1163> (accessed 16 March 2005).

9 A/CONF 151/26; discussed in NA Robinson (ed), *Agenda 21: Earth's Action Plan* (Oceana Press, 1993), <www.un.org/esa/sustdev/documents/agenda21/English> (accessed 31 January 2005).

established the parameters for nations to move towards sustainable development. The energy and climate change outcomes of the 2002 World Summit on Sustainable Development will also be mentioned, as they enunciate the global community's most recent commitments to a program of action towards developing a sustainable energy framework.

These international environmental law instruments contain a number of key messages for energy policy development, particularly in light of the growing imperative for the world to move towards a carbon constrained economy. They are that energy use should be ecologically sustainable; renewable energy technologies should be promoted and adequately represented in the energy fuel mix; national energy efficiency programs should be pursued; market distortions and perverse subsidies, which impede a sustainable energy market, should be removed; national energy markets should function in a way that promotes sustainable development; and grid extensions are not necessarily the preferred method of increasing access to electricity. As will become evident later in this chapter, the Australian government has not paid sufficient attention to a number of these messages, while the New South Wales government has taken some significant steps towards integrating them in its overall strategy to reduce the greenhouse gas emissions from the energy sector.

United Nations Conference on Environment and Development (UNCED)

As mentioned in Chapter 1, sustainable development was the focus of the 1992 UNCED held in Rio de Janeiro. At that Conference, five important international documents were developed: the Rio Declaration, Agenda 21, United Nations Framework Convention on Climate Change (UNFCC), the Convention on Biological Diversity (CBD) and the Statement of Principles for the Sustainable Management of Forests.[10] These documents have formed the basis for global initiatives to achieve sustainable development, and are all relevant to global climate change in one way or another. For example, the management of the world's forests has a significant bearing on global climate change, and climate change in turn will, and already does, have significant impact on the earth's biodiversity. Although in Chapter 1 we discuss the Rio Declaration, Agenda 21 and the Johannesburg Plan of Implementation extensively, it is instructive in this chapter to refer to those aspects of the instruments that relate to a sustainable energy law framework.

The Rio Declaration

As discussed in Chapter 1, perhaps the most influential principles of the Declaration have proved to be the principles of intergenerational equity, the precautionary principle and the polluter pays principle. The principle of intergenerational equity requires current rates of development equitably to meet the development and environmental needs of present and future generations (Principle 3). The precautionary

10 A/CONF.151/26 (Vol III).

principle is that, 'where there are threats of serious or irreversible damage, lack of full scientific certainty shall not be used as a reason for postponing cost-effective measures to prevent environmental degradation' (Principle 15). Finally, the polluter pays principle envisages the 'internalisation of environmental costs and the use of economic instruments, taking into account the approach that the polluter should, in principle, bear the cost of pollution' (Principle 16). All of these principles are highly relevant to the development of a sustainable energy law framework.

Agenda 21

Chapter 9 of Agenda 21 also makes specific reference to the protection of the atmosphere, referring to the 1985 Vienna Convention for the Protection of the Ozone Layer, the 1987 Montreal Protocol on Substances that Deplete the Ozone Layer as amended, and the 1992 United Nations Framework Convention on Climate Change. The first two instruments provide for the protection of the ozone layer, while, as already mentioned, the UNFCC is directed at global greenhouse gas emissions. However, the links between ozone protection and global climate change should not be missed as many of the gases developed to take the place of ozone depleting gases have now been found to be 'synthetic greenhouse gases'.[11]

Agenda 21 specifies that activities undertaken to protect the atmosphere should be integrated with social and economic development, taking into account the needs of developing countries to achieve sustained economic growth and eradicate poverty (Chapter 9.3). The two Agenda 21 program areas relevant to our purposes are: improving the scientific basis for decision-making; and promoting sustainable development though energy development, efficiency and consumption (Chapter 9.5). Various activities are recommended for improving the scientific basis for decision-making including: promoting and co-operating on research initiatives to better understand 'the levels of greenhouse gas concentrations, that would cause dangerous anthropogenic interference with the climate system and the environment as a whole, and the associated rates of change that would not allow ecosystems to adapt naturally'.

With respect to energy resources, Agenda 21 provides that governments should: develop economically and environmentally sound energy sources, including renewable energy systems (Chapter 9.12(a), (d)); review current energy supply mixes to determine how new and renewable energy systems could be increased (Chapter 9.12(f)); promote the use of improved energy-efficient technologies (Chapter 9.12(c)); and establish labelling programs for products to inform decision-makers and consumers about opportunities for energy efficiency (Chapter 9.12(l)).

The United Nations Framework Convention on Climate Change (UNFCCC)

The Preamble to the UNFCCC[12] contained the following principles relevant to energy and sustainable development: that the earth's climate and adverse effects are

11 See, eg, legislative activity by the Australian government in this regard enacting the *Ozone Protection and Synthetic Greenhouse Gas (Import Levy) Act 1995; Ozone Protection and Synthetic Greenhouse Gas (Manufacture Levy) Act 1995; Ozone Protection and Synthetic Greenhouse Gas Management Act 1989; Ozone Protection and Synthetic Greenhouse Gas Management Regulations 1995.*

12 See <http://unfccc.int/resource/docs/convkp/conveng.pdf>.

a common concern of humankind; that the greenhouse effect will increase warming of the earth's surface and atmosphere and adversely affect natural ecosystems and humankind, although uncertainties in predictions of climate change were noted;[13] that there is a need for an appropriate international response in accordance with common but differentiated responsibilities; that developed countries should take immediate action to develop comprehensive strategies; that the climate system should be protected for present and future generations (intergenerational equity); and that responses to climate change should be co-ordinated with social and economic development. The precautionary principle is also recognised as a guiding principle for all signatories to the UNFCCC. The ultimate objective of the UNFCCC is to achieve stabilisation of greenhouse gas concentrations in the atmosphere at a level that would prevent dangerous anthropogenic interference with the climate system.

The most relevant commitments for our purposes are: to develop, update, publish and make available national inventories of anthropogenic emissions and removals of sinks (Art 4.1(a)); to enact effective legislation to achieve the objectives of the UNFCCC; to formulate, implement publish and update national and regional programs to mitigate climate change (Art 4.1(b)); to manage sustainably sinks and reservoirs of greenhouse gases (Art 4.1(d)); and to take climate change into account when undertaking environmental impact assessment (Art 4.1(f)). Developed countries are required to take the lead in reducing emissions by adopting national policies. Parties should also undertake and share appropriate research on global climate change, while educating the public about global climate change and its effects (Art 6). The Parties are also required at Conferences of the Parties (CPOs) regularly to review progress made in implementing the UNFCCC.

The Kyoto Protocol

At the third Conference of the Parties in 1997, signatories to the UNFCCC met to develop a Protocol for advancing the goals of the Convention. The Protocol is now known as the Kyoto Protocol.[14] It has had a chequered history with negotiations over its implementation failing (at COP 6 at The Hague) and being reinvigorated (in Bonn), only to have the United States and Australia withdraw from the Protocol. This withdrawal has severely undermined international multilateral efforts to curb greenhouse gas emissions. The United States is the largest emitter of greenhouse gases. Australia emits about 1.5% of the world's greenhouse gases but Australians are among the highest per capita emitters in the world.

The most important feature of the Protocol is that the so-called Annex B parties agreed to specific individual targets for reducing greenhouse gas emissions, so that overall emissions in the first commitment period 2008-12 would be at 5% below 1990 levels. Parties must have achieved demonstrable progress is achieving these targets by 2005. Economies in transition are permitted to use a year other than 1990 as their baseline (Art 3).

Under Art 3.3, reductions in greenhouse gas emissions resulting from forestry activities, limited to afforestation, reforestation and deforestation since 1990, may be

13 Although the 2001 IPCC Third Assessment Report provides far greater certainty.

14 See <http://unfccc.int/resource/docs/convkp/kpeng.html> (accessed 16 November 2004).

used to meet the commitments of each Party. It was also agreed that, in addition to these, human-induced activities relating to revegetation, forest management, cropland management and grazing land management could be counted toward commitments in the second and subsequent commitment periods.[15] However, a Party may choose to have them counted for its first commitment period, provided that the activities have taken place since 1990. To comply with Art 3, Parties must keep an annual inventory of anthropogenic emissions and removals of sinks (Art 7). Information in the inventory must be reviewed by expert review teams, selected from those nominated by Parties and intergovernmental organisations. The inventory must provide a thorough and comprehensive technical assessment of all aspects of implementation, including a report on problems with fulfilling commitments. The inventories must be circulated to all Parties (Art 8).

Developing countries did not commit themselves to any binding targets under the Protocol, although those that ratified the UNFCCC remain obliged to comply with those commitments. At COP 8 in Marrakesh, new guidelines were adopted to be followed by developing countries, which are required to report on their emissions, and the steps they are taking to meet their commitments under the UNFCC. The Protocol also provides that developed countries should provide new financial resources to assist developing countries to meet their commitments (Art 11).

Quite obviously, Parties must have in place a national system for estimating anthropogenic emissions and removals of sinks, relying on methodologies that are acceptable to the IPCC. The Parties are required regularly to review and revise their methodologies (Art 5). Parties must also formulate cost-effective national and regional programs to mitigate climate change from the energy, transport, industry, agricultural and other sectors. Information on these programs must be submitted to the Conference of the Parties. Parties are also expected to promote strategies for technology transfers, to co-operate in scientific and technical research, and develop education and training programs (Art 10).

To actually achieve the Kyoto targets, each Party should implement the following policies and measures: the enhancement of energy efficiency; the enhancement of sinks and reservoirs; sustainable forms of agriculture; research on renewable energy and environmentally sound technologies; reduction of market imperfections; encourage reforms in relevant sectors to reduce greenhouse gases, for example, transport; reduce methane in waste management; and share and exchange information (Art 2).

Under the Protocol, Parties must regularly review implementation of the Protocol to assess the environmental, economic and social effects of measures taken as well as cumulative impacts. They must also exchange information on measures taken, and seek co-operation of international, intergovernmental and non-governmental bodies which can act as observers at Conferences of Parties (Art 13).

A very innovative aspect of the Protocol is that Parties are allowed to achieve their emission reduction targets by relying on the 'flexibility mechanisms' or 'least

15 See the Report of the Conference of the Parties on the Second Part of its Sixth Session, held at Bonn from 16 to 27 July 2001, <http://unfccc.int/resource/docs/cop6secpart/05a02.pdf> (accessed 16 November 2004) at 10. This provision is included in Art 3.4, also known as the 'Australia clause', as it was a concession proposed, and won, by the Australian government in Bonn. The Australian government successfully persuaded the international community to allow a more generous accounting of emissions reductions resulting from halting broadscale land clearing.

cost abatement measures'. These include joint implementation (JI) (Art 6), the clean development mechanism (CDM) (Art 12) and emissions trading (Art 17). Joint implementation means that developed countries can invest in projects in other developed countries to acquire credits to assist in meeting assigned amounts, if generated in the first commitment period 2008-12. Participation in JI projects must be voluntary and is open to public and private entities. A JI project must be one that would not normally be undertaken by the receiving Party and must, in this sense, be 'additional' (Art 6(b)). The acquisition of emission reduction units, derived from a JI project, by a Party must be 'supplemental' to domestic actions for the purposes of meeting its emission reduction target (Art 6(d)).

The CDM allows developed countries to invest in emission reducing projects in developing countries, and to obtain certified emission reductions towards meeting assigned amounts. This allows developed countries not only to meet their emission reduction targets outside of their own jurisdictions, but also to find a ready export market for their sustainable energy technologies. Emission reductions resulting from each project activity must be certified by operational entities on the basis of: voluntary participation approved by each Party involved; real, measurable, and long-term benefits related to the mitigation of climate change; and reductions in emissions that are additional to any that would occur in the absence of the certified project activity (Art 12(5)). Participation may involve public and private entitles (Art 12(9)). Certified emission reductions obtained between 2000 and 2008 may be used to achieve compliance in the first commitment period (Art 12(10)).

At COP 6, at The Hague, the use of sinks as CDM projects proved contentious. However, this was resolved in Bonn, where it was agreed that this would be allowed, but limited to afforestation and reforestation projects during the first commitment period that would be capped at 1% of base-year emissions. There was also considerable concern about the appropriate regulation of CDM projects being 'exported' to developing countries. It was agreed at COP 6.5 that an Executive Board of the Clean Development Mechanism (CDM) should be established. This Board is now established and has released the Modalities and Procedures of the CDM: Role of the Executive Board.[16]

With respect to emissions trading, now that the Kyoto Protocol has been ratified, the Parties will establish and participate in an international emissions trading regime. Under this scheme, developed countries can trade emissions to meet their assigned amounts. One of the issues that had to be resolved between the Parties was the concern that Annex I Parties could 'oversell' units and subsequently be unable to meet their own emissions targets. At the Bonn negotiations, it was agreed that each Party be required to hold a minimum level of emission reduction units (ERUs), certified emission reductions (CERs), assigned amount units (AAUs) and removal units (RMUs) in its national registry. This is known as the 'commitment period reserve'.[17] This reserve is calculated as the lower of the following: 90% of the Party's assigned amount, as defined in Articles 3.7 and 3.8 of the Protocol,[18] or the level of

16 Decision 15/CP.7, <http://cdm.unfccc.int/EB/rules/modproced.html#CEB>.

17 See <http://unfccc.int/kyoto_mechanisms/emissions_trading/items/2731txt.php> (accessed 16 November 2004).

18 This calculation is likely to be relevant to Annex I Parties which prove, at the end of the commitment period, to be 'net buyers' of units under the mechanisms.

national emissions indicated in the Party's most recent emissions inventory (multiplied by five, for the five years of the commitment period).[19]

To participate in the flexibility mechanisms, Annex I Parties must meet the following eligibility requirements: they must have ratified the Kyoto Protocol; they must have calculated their assigned amount in terms of tonnes of CO_2-equivalent emissions;[20] they must have in place a national system for estimating emissions and removals of greenhouse gases within their territory; they must have in place a national registry to record and track the creation and movement of ERUs, CERs, AAUs and RMUs, and must annually report such information to the secretariat; and they must annually report information on emissions and removals to the secretariat.[21]

To establish eligibility each Annex I Party must submit a report on the above information to the secretariat, at the latest by 1 January 2007 (or a year after becoming a Party to the Protocol, whichever is later). This report will be reviewed, and any questions arising will be dealt with by the Enforcement Branch of the Compliance Committee within 16 months of submission through a set of expedited procedures. A Party which is found not to meet the eligibility requirements may seek reinstatement of eligibility through a further expedited procedure.[22]

In spite of making these flexibility mechanisms available to Parties, the Marrakech Accords require that domestic actions (as opposed to use of the mechanisms) constitute a 'significant element' of the efforts made by each Annex I Parties to meet their target. While they do not set a quantified proportion that is to be met through domestic action, the Protocol requires that Annex I Parties provide information in their national communications under the Protocol to demonstrate that their use of the mechanisms is 'supplemental to domestic action' to achieve their targets.[23]

Compliance with the Protocol will be monitored by a Compliance Committee comprising two branches: a Facilitative Branch and an Enforcement Branch. The facilitative branch will provide advice and assistance to Parties to promote compliance, whereas the enforcement branch has the power to determine consequences for Parties not meeting their commitments. The branches each comprise 10 members, including one representative from each of the five official UN regions (Africa, Asia, Latin America and the Caribbean, Central and Eastern Europe, and _Western Europe and Others), one from the small island developing states, as well as two each from Annex I and non-Annex I Parties. Decisions of the Facilitative Branch may be taken by a three-quarters majority, but decisions of the Enforcement Branch require, in addition, a double majority of both Annex I and non-Annex I Parties. The Committee also meets in a Plenary composed of members of both branches.[24]

The Protocol entered into force on 16 February 2005, on the 90th day after the date on which not less than 55 Parties to the Convention, incorporating Annex I

19 This calculation is likely to be relevant to Annex I Parties which prove, at the end of the commitment period, to be 'net sellers' of units under the mechanisms.

20 As referred to in Arts 3.7 and 3.8 and Annex B of the Protocol.

21 FCCC/CP/2001/13/Add.2, <http://unfccc.int/resource/docs/cop7/13a02.pdf#page=2> (accessed 16 November 2004.)

22 Ibid.

23 Ibid.

24 See FCCC/CP/2001/13/Add.3, <http://unfccc.int/resource/docs/cop7/13a03.pdf#page=64> (accessed 16 November 2004).

Parties that accounted in total for at least 55% of the total carbon dioxide emissions for 1990 ratified the Protocol (Art 25). After the United States' and Australia's withdrawal from the Protocol there was considerable concern that it would never be ratified. However, on 4 November 2004, Russia ratified the Protocol in a move that is generally regarded as a quid pro quo for the admission of Russia to the World Trade Organisation. Russia's ratification was important as her emissions account for 17% of overall emissions from developed countries and, without Russia the Protocol could not have come into force.

Johannesburg Plan of Implementation

The Plan of Implementation, which represents the final text negotiated at the 2002 World Summit on Sustainable Development, builds on the achievements made since UNCED and seeks to expedite the realisation of the remaining goals. Under the Plan, all nations have committed themselves to undertaking concrete actions and measures at all levels. They have also committed to enhancing international co-operation, taking into account the Rio Principles, including the principle of common but differentiated responsibilities as set out in principle 7 of the Rio Declaration on Environment and Development. These efforts are intended to promote the integration of the three mutually reinforcing pillars of sustainable development - economic development, social development and environmental protection. Clause 19 of the Plan of Implementation deals specifically with energy while cl 36 deals with climate change and reiterates that change in the earth's climate and its adverse effects are a common concern of humankind.[25] The Plan reaffirms that the United Nations Framework Convention on Climate Change is the key instrument for addressing climate change and reaffirms countries' commitments to achieving the stabilisation of greenhouse gas concentrations in the atmosphere at a level that would prevent dangerous anthropogenic interference with the climate system.

Australia's climate change and energy profile

Vulnerability to climate change

The latest scientific data and predictions made by the IPCC,[26] regarding Australia, indicates that: water resources are already stressed in some areas and are therefore highly vulnerable, especially with respect to salinisation; a warming of 1 degree Celsius would threaten the survival of species that are currently growing near the upper limit of their temperature range, notably in marginal alpine regions;[27] food production is threatened because agricultural activities are particularly vulnerable to regional reductions in rainfall in southwest and inland Australia; with respect to industry and human settlement, the trend toward greater population and investment in exposed regions will increase its vulnerability to cyclones and storm surges;

25 For the full text of cll 19 and 36, see <http://www.johannesburgsummit.org/html/document/summit_docs/plan_final1009.doc>.

26 Intergovernmental Panel on Climate Change, Climate Change 2001: Impacts, Adaptation and Vulnerability 51-54 (2001), <http://www.ipcc.ch/index.html>.

27 Note that anthropogenic climate change has been listed as a key threatening process under Sch 3 to the *Threatened Species Conservation Act 1995* (NSW).

and many natural ecosystems in Australia have a limited capacity to adapt to global climate change.

In 2006, the CSIRO released a report on the climate change impacts on Australia.[28] The report indicates that Australia is already experiencing significant climate change as a result of human-induced global warming. Over the past century, the average surface air temperature has risen by .07 degrees Celsius accompanied by declining regional precipitation in the east and west of the country. By the year 2030, Australia's annual average temperatures are expected to increase to 0.4-2.0 degrees Celsius above 1990 levels and to 1-6 degrees Celsius by 2020. Average precipitation in southwest and southeast Australia will continue to decline while the northwest might experience increased precipitation. Sea levels may rise between 8-88 centimetres resulting in the erosion and inundation of Australia's coastline.

Australia's biodiversity will suffer particularly in sensitive areas like the Great Barrier Reef which has already been significantly damaged by bleaching over the past two decades. However, with an increase of 1 degree Celsius, coral communities are expected to contract and a considerable loss of species is anticipated. Although some agricultural areas will benefit from increased precipitation and longer growing periods, these will not be sustained over the long term and Australia will face increasing challenges with accessing sufficient water for agricultural, commercial and domestic purposes. Australia's public infrastructure and health systems are likely to be severely impacted by extreme weather events such as cyclones, heat waves and extreme precipitation events. Also, if the ocean's thermohaline circulation were to slow, or ice sheets in West Antarctica or Greenland were to collapse, this would have important impacts on Australia's climate and coastline.

How Australia uses energy

A recent analysis of Australia's energy use has been provided in the August 2004 report of the Australian Bureau of Agricultural and Resource Economics (ABARE) entitled *Australian energy: National and state projections to 2019-20*.[29] The report states that, since 1973-74, total primary energy use in Australia grew by some 2.6% per annum, compared with an economic growth rate of 3.2% per annum. In 2000-01 Australia's total primary energy consumption was 5037 petajoules (PJ). Primary energy consumption is projected to grow at an average of 2.1% over the period 2019-20, while gross domestic product is assumed by ABARE to grow by 3.4% per annum. This means that by 2019-20 total primary energy consumption would grow by 50% reaching 7515 PJ. The report affirms that fossil fuels are Australia's major energy sources. Australia's energy needs are provided by oil (35%), black coal (28%), natural gas (19%) and brown coal (13%). Uranium is not used currently as an energy source in Australia.

The largest users of stationary energy are the manufacturing and construction sectors. ABARE forecasts an industry demand growth of 50% to 2020, attributed to

28 BL Preston and RN Jones, *Climate Change Impacts on Australia and the Benefits of Early Action to Reduce Global Greenhouse Gas Emissions* (CSIRO, February 2006), <http://www.csiro.au/files/files/p6fy.pdf> (accessed 1 May 2006).

29 See M Akmal, S Thorpe, A Dickson, G Burg and N Klijn, *Australian energy: National and state projections to 2019-20* (ABARE: 2004), <http://abareonlineshop.com/product.asp?prodid=12776> (accessed 20 June 2005).

growth in the iron and steel sector as well as non-ferrous metals such as alumina refining and aluminium smelting. Our focus on greenhouse gas emissions in the energy sector in this book is justified by the fact that energy production and use contributed 68% of Australia's greenhouse gas emissions in 2002, and is expected to be 72% by 2020. Greenhouse gas emissions from the energy sector are expected to grow by more than 30% to 2020. The biggest single source of energy emissions is electricity, accounting for two-thirds of stationary energy emissions. Coal is the major source of base load electricity generation and its combustion accounts for 92% of electricity emissions. However, it seems that electricity emissions will grow somewhat slower than electricity use, as there is a relative shift from brown coal to natural gas in electricity generation.

Nevertheless, Australia's fuel mix will continue to be dominated by coal and oil with coal expected to account for more than 70% of the mix.

Growth in domestic use of natural gas is projected to remain strong with total consumption expected to be 1828 PJ by 2019-20. However, energy consumed per dollar of economic output is expected to decline so that by 2019-20 18% less energy will be required. Australia's reliance on imported liquid fuel is expected to increase by 29% by 2019-20.

Uptake of renewable energy in Australia[30]

As discussed below, a mix of renewable energy technologies is expected to be developed to meet the Mandatory Renewable Energy Target of sourcing 2% more electricity from renewable sources by 2010 (the Mandatory Renewable Energy Target (MRET)), as prescribed by the *Renewable Energy (Electricity) Act 2000* (Cth). Before the enactment of this legislation, Australia's renewable energy sector generated approximately 16,000 GWh of electricity representing 10.5% of Australia's electricity market. This was largely electricity generated from hydro-electric sources from Tasmania and the Snowy Mountains Scheme. In order to meet the MRET, renewable energy generation from minor sources of energy, other than hydro, will need to increase about 60% above 1997 levels to a point where 9500 GWh of renewable energy is generated.

The mix of renewable energy technologies, as at 18 August 2003, was the following: hydro – 36%; solar hot water heaters – 26%; wind – 11%; bagasse cogeneration – 10%; landfill gas – 8%; wood waste – 4%; black liquor – 4%; and sewage gas – 1%. These figures demonstrate that a wide range of renewable energy technologies have entered the electricity markets since the introduction of the MRET. For example, largely due to the MRET, the solar hot water system has grown by 30% per annum from 19,000 to 30,000 systems. The wind industry reported an annual growth rate of 118% between 1999 and 2002. Wind power is expected to grow 16% a year from a small base over the entire outlook period and to contribute around 36% to the additional renewable energy generated between 2001-02 – 2010-11. Electricity generated from biomass is expected to increase by 10% per year, accounting for 33% of the total growth over the same period.

---

30 Most of the information given in this section is sourced from *Renewable Opportunities – A Review of the Operation of the Renewable Energy (Electricity) Act 2000* especially the section entitled 'Progress Towards MRET Objectives', <http://www.mretreview.gov.au/report/index.html> (accessed 23 August 2005).

Sales of renewable electricity, equipment and services for 2002-03 were approximately $1.8 billion, of which 14.5% were expected to be exports, amounting to $226.5 million. These sales were less than half of the Renewable Energy Action Agenda (discussed below) target of $4 billion sales in 2010. Projected employment is 6189 people. Installed capacity for this period was 7616.4 MW which, when large hydro generation is removed, amounted to 680 MW.

A number of investors are concerned that investment in renewable energy projects will cease after 2007 because the capacity to deliver the 2010 MRET target will have already been installed. Also there is no commitment on the part of the Australian government to continue the target beyond 2020. This has reduced the payback period for investments which is typically 15 years.

Nuclear energy for Australia?

The possibility of establishing a nuclear fuel industry in Australia has long been dismissed on environmental grounds. However, in March 2005, the Minister for Industry, Tourism and Resources established an inquiry into Australia's uranium resources. As a result of global climate change, the global demand for uranium resources has escalated as nuclear energy is a non-fossil fuel source of energy. It is regarded as being a 'greenhouse friendly' type of fuel, although critics state that the greenhouse intensity of building and operating nuclear power stations is often not factored into the overall calculation of intensity. The federal Minister for Industry and Resources has indicated that he will be disappointed if uranium exports do not double or triple over the next 10 years, possibly creating a $2 billion export industry.

The Minister subsequently requested the Commonwealth House of Representatives Standing Committee on Industry and Resources to inquire into the strategic importance of Australia's uranium resources.

The Committee published its report, 'Australia's uranium – Greenhouse friendly fuel for an energy hungry world',[31] in November 2006. The Committee reached the following conclusions:

- Uranium: demand and supply – the demand for uranium worldwide is projected to increase by 22% by 2050 compared with 2004 as a result of new reactor capacity being built, combined with capacity upgrades and life extensions of existing reactors. Australia possesses 36% of the world's uranium but only supplies 23% of world production. There is great potential for Australia to become the world's premier supplier of uranium.
- Australia's uranium resources, production and exploration – the value of Australia's in situ uranium resources is A$270 billion. Exploration activity and expenditure have increased in Australia due to an increase in the uranium price and an expected decrease in secondary supplies. Additional funding should be given to explore deep uranium deposits.
- Greenhouse gas emissions and nuclear power – nuclear power plants currently save about 10% of greenhouse gas emissions world-wide which represents an immense saving of emissions. Renewable energy and energy efficiency alone will not meet growing demands for abatement.

31 See <http://www.aph.gov.au/house/committee/Isr/uranium/report/front.pdf> (accessed 11 December 2006).

- Radioactive waste – the nuclear power industry manages its waste more explicitly and transparently than many other sources of energy, while the levels of waste are small. The generation, management and transportation of radioactive waste does not present an unacceptable risk.
- The safety of the nuclear fuel cycle – while the nuclear energy industry can never be risk free, the safety record of nuclear power surpasses that of all other energy industries. Nevertheless, certain recommendations are made to protect uranium industry workers.
- The global non-proliferation regime – the proliferation of nuclear weapons has been successfully limited by the global safeguards regime. However, the regime now faces weakening political support for the non-proliferation regime. The Committee recommends that the Australian government takes steps to counter challenges to the regime.
- Australia's bilateral safeguards – this policy has been effective to date. There is no potential for Australian Obligated Nuclear Material (AONM) to be diverted for use by terrorists or for Australian radioactive materials to be used in 'dirty bombs'.
- Strategic importance of Australia's uranium – given the strategic importance of Australia's uranium resources, the development of new uranium deposits should be actively encouraged.
- Uranium industry regulation and impact on Aboriginal communities – the regulatory regime governing uranium mining has protected the environment from harmful impacts, although pollution problems occur on closure and rehabilitation. Care must be taken to ensure that uranium mining does not impact on local Aboriginal communities.
- Impediments to the uranium industry's development – the prohibition on uranium mining in some States as well as a lack of alignment between the Australian and State governments on the issue is the principal impediment. All legislative impediments to uranium mining and exploration should be repealed. Negative public perceptions are also a factor.
- Value adding – fuel cycle services industries in Australia – the Committee makes various recommendations regarding the skills base and research and development activity needed to support Australia's participation in the nuclear fuel cycle.

The Committee makes 14 recommendations with respect to issues discussed in the Report.

Meanwhile, in June 2006, the Prime Minister appointed a taskforce to undertake a Review of Uranium Mining, Processing and Nuclear Energy in Australia. In December 2006, the Taskforce, chaired by Ziggy Switkowski, released its report entitled, 'Uranium Mining, Processing and Nuclear Energy – Opportunities for Australia?'.[32] The key findings of the Review are that:

- Skills shortages and government policies, which are restricting the growth of the uranium industry, should be urgently addressed as there is support for the expansion of uranium mining and exportation.

---

32 See <http://www.dpmc.gov.au/umpner/docs/draft_report/full_report.pdf> (accessed 11 December 2006).

- Uranium mining regulations should be rationalised to establish a consistent approach to environmental and radiation protection while maintaining high industry standards.
- If uranium conversion, enrichment and fuel fabrication occurred domestically an additional $1.8 billion in value could be added to uranium processing. However, there are commercial, technological and legal barriers which make market entry difficult, and there is limited opportunity for Australian companies to compete in these areas.
- Nuclear power would be between 20-50% more expensive to produce than coal or gas-fired power, but nuclear and renewable would only be competitive in Australia's fuel mix if the costs of greenhouse gas emissions were explicitly recognised. Even then, private investment in building nuclear reactors would require government support.
- It will take at least 10-15 years for nuclear power to be delivered to the grid. The industry should be regulated by a single national regulator.
- If the first nuclear reactor is built in 2020, a third of Australia's electricity could be produced by 25 reactors by 2050.
- New reactor designs are now safer, more efficient and produce less radioactive waste than those involved in the Three Mile Island and Chernobyl accidents.
- Nuclear plants could reduce Australia's greenhouse gas emissions by between 8-18% by 2050.
- There is consensus that nuclear waste should be disposed of in deep repositories. Australia has areas which are suitable for such disposal although none will be needed before 2050.
- Australia will need to have a strong, transparent and national regulatory regime to manage a successful nuclear power generation program.
- Australian involvement in the nuclear fuel cycle will not change the risk of the proliferation of nuclear weapons and Australia's energy grid will not become more vulnerable to terrorist attack.

In spite of these findings, concerns have been raised with regard to the use of nuclear energy in Australia.[33] First, nuclear power itself generates greenhouse gases because of the significant use of energy required to mine, mill and enrich the uranium for the fuel rods. Even where high-grade uranium ores are used, it takes seven to 10 years to 'pay back' the energy used in the construction and fuelling of a typical reactor. Secondly, for a large-scale deployment of nuclear power to be sustainable in the long term, breeder reactors would have to be used, which create their own fuel in the form of plutonium. To date, these reactors have not generated sufficient new fuel. Ultimately, this would result in plutonium, a highly hazardous radioactive material, being transported around the world in increasing quantities, potentially with associated risks for nuclear terrorism. Thirdly, despite significant government support for the nuclear energy industry globally, it remains one of the most expensive ways to reduce greenhouse gas emissions. At no time has the same level of support been forthcoming to support the development and commercialisation of energy efficiency

33 See article by Professor Stuart White in *Sydney Morning Herald*, 13 June 2005.

and renewable energy technologies. Finally, with the well-known difficulties of disposing of the waste associated with nuclear energy, the technology may well exacerbate, rather than solve, environmental problems. Perhaps one of the greatest concerns is that a focus on a nuclear energy industry in Australia will detract support and funding for the nascent sustainable energy industry.

Profile of greenhouse gas emissions

In June 2005, the Australian Greenhouse Office released a paper entitled *State and Territory Greenhouse Gas Emissions – An Overview*.[34] It is the latest available estimate of emissions from the States and Territories. Total emissions in Australia amounted to 541.8 million tonnes. The breakdown is as follows:

- New South Wales: 151.5 million tonnes (Mt) = 28%
- Queensland: 145.1 Mt = 26.8%
- Victoria: 117.0 Mt = 21.6%
- Western Australia: 70.4 Mt = 13.0%
- South Australia: 30.9 Mt = 5.7%
- Northern Territory: 17.7 Mt = 3.3%
- Tasmania: 7.2 Mt = 1.3%, and
- Australian Capital Territory: 1.3 Mt = 0.2%.

Emissions from the Stationary Energy sector, including production of electricity and other direct combustion of fossil fuels (other than Transport), account for 48% of national greenhouse gas emissions. On a State and Territory basis this is broken down as follows:

- Victoria 29.5% (67% of all emissions)
- New South Wales 27.2% (48% of all emissions)
- Queensland 22.5% (40% of all emissions)
- Western Australia 13.2% (48% of all emissions)
- South Australia 5.3% (45% of all emissions)
- Northern Territory 1.5% (23% of all emissions), and
- Tasmania 0.9% (31% of all emissions).

The information indicates, not surprisingly, that the majority of emissions emanate from New South Wales and Victoria and that in those States emissions from the stationary energy sector are the most significant. As we demonstrate in this chapter, the Commonwealth and NSW governments have focused primarily on this sector in order to reduce greenhouse gas emissions.

The National Electricity Market

Since a high proportion of Australia's greenhouse gas emissions emanate from the stationary energy, especially the electricity, sector, it is important to understand the efforts of the Council of Australian Governments (COAG) to establish a National

34 See <http://www.greenhouse.gov.au/inventory/stateinv/index.html>.

Electricity Market (NEM). Also, research has shown that the restructuring of electricity sectors around the world has had profound environmental consequences, especially in relation to increased greenhouse gas emissions. Consequently, environmental lawyers are concerned to see what measures are taken by governments to offset the rise in emissions.

The NEM was formally launched in December 1998. It was established to operate consistently with four principles: freedom of choice for consumers to trade with retailers and traders; open access to interstate interconnected transmission and distribution networks; no legislative or regulatory barriers discriminating against new participants in generation and retail supply; and no legislative or regulatory barriers discriminating against interstate and intrastate trade.[35]

The NEM is a wholesale electricity market that operates across Queensland, New South Wales, Victoria, the Australian Capital Territory and South Australia. Inter-regional trade between these jurisdictions is facilitated by interconnectors which transmit power between regions to meet energy demands which local generators cannot meet, or when the price of electricity in another region is sufficiently low that it displaces local supply. Tasmania joined the NEM when the construction of the Basslink between Victoria and Tasmania was completed in 2005.

The NEM was established by co-operative legislation in all participating States to set up the NEM and to provide for access arrangements.[36] The operation of the NEM is now regulated under the *National Electricity Law* as set out in the Schedule to the *National Electricity (South Australia) Act 1996* of South Australia, as amended by the *National Electricity (South Australia) (New National Electricity Law) Amendment Act 2005*, and the *Australian Energy Market Regulations 2005* (Cth).

Participants in the NEM include generators;[37] market customers (electricity retailers and end-use customers);[38] network service providers who own, operate or control either a transmission (TNSPs) or distribution (DNSPs) system;[39] market net-

35 See R Coroneos, 'The regulatory framework of the NEM: its impact on NSW distributors and opportunities for further reform' (1999) 7 *AJAL* 5; see also A Rann, *Electricity Industry Restructuring – A Chronology* (Parliamentary Library Background Paper 21: 1997-8); and John Quiggan, 'Market-oriented reform in the Australian electricity industry' (2001) 12(1) *Economic & Labour Relations Review* 126 at 127.

36 *National Electricity (New South Wales) Act 1997* (NSW); *Electricity – National Scheme (Queensland) Act 1997* (Qld); *National Electricity (South Australia) Act 1996* (SA); *National Electricity (Victoria) Act 1997* (Vic); *Electricity (National Scheme) Act 1997* (ACT).

37 Generators produce and sell electricity. There are four categories of generators: market generators whose entire output is sold on the NEM spot market; non-market generators which sell their entire supply directly to a local retailer or customer; schedules generators which have a capacity over 30 MW and whose output is regulated by NEMMCO's dispatch instructions; and non-scheduled generators which have a generating capacity of less than 30 MW, but which are still required to register with NEMMCO.

38 Market customers comprise both electricity retailers and end-use customers. Retailers purchase wholesale electricity through the spot market, or from local generators who sell their entire output to them. The electricity is then sold to customers, increasingly within a contestable retail market. End-use customers purchase electricity directly from the spot market which they then consume.

39 TNSPs control the high voltage transmission assets that carry electricity between generators and distributors, while DNSPs operate the low voltage substations and wires that transport electricity from these substations to customers. Distributors hold a franchise over the regions in which their poles and wires are installed but must also be given access to customers outside their regions by using rival distribution networks; see Rann, above n 35, at 3.

work service providers (MNSPs);[40] and special participants who may be appointed by the National Electricity Market Management Commission (NEMMCO) to perform various functions such as taking responsibility for operations during power system emergencies.

The NEM is essentially a continuous-time auction market that allows generators and users of electricity to enter half-hourly bids, indicating willingness to supply or demand electricity. Together, the bids form aggregate demand and supply schedules. Market clearing occurs every five minutes in recognition of the fact that available capacity and consumption can fluctuate. The despatch price is determined at the intersection of the aggregate demand and supply schedules. Generator bids equal to or less than the dispatch price are accepted, as are user bids that are equal to or greater than the dispatch price. The spot price of electricity is determined when the dispatch prices are averaged over a half-hour period, and this is the price actually paid to generators by purchasers. Not all purchases occur in this way, however, as participants can enter into bilateral arrangements or trade electricity in a forward market. Based on the vagaries of supply and demand, the spot price for electricity can vary from $20 MWh one day to $10,000 MWh the next. However, $10,000 is the regulatory limit for the price of one MWh of electricity.

The National Electricity Market and greenhouse gas emissions

Hamilton and Denniss[41] argue convincingly that, although greenhouse gas emissions from the electricity sector have been increasing steadily since 1994, there was a 10.35% spike in emissions in 1998. This was the first year of the operation of the NEM. Their proposition has been supported by data released by the Australian Greenhouse Office.[42] Hamilton and Denniss point to the fact that the average prices charged to industrial and commercial users (which account for 70% of the market) fell by nearly 22% between 1991-92 and 1997-98.[43] The fall in price led in turn to a 6.3% increase in demand, which exceeded the long-term average increase of around 2.5%. Hamilton and Denniss ascribe the large fall in the price of electricity to attempts by Victoria's privatised brown coal generators to win market share at the expense of Victoria's gas generators and black coal generators in New South Wales. They show that in 1998 around 3500 GWh was exported from Victoria into New South Wales, while only 600 GWh flowed in the other direction (excluding flows from the Snowy Mountains Hydro-Electric Authority). This net energy transfer of 2900 GWh northward is in sharp contrast with the pattern in preceding years which saw nearly equal northward and southward energy transfers.

---

40 MNSPs are entrepreneurial interconnectors, with a minimum capacity of 30 MW, that offer their capacity to transport power into the market through a bidding process similar to that used by generators. Currently there is only one MNSP, called Directlink, which operates between New South Wales and Queensland. MNSPs are unregulated interconnectors whereas all other interconnectors are regulated, originally by State governments but increasingly by the Australian Competition and Consumer Commission (ACCC). They receive a fixed rate of return that takes into account the value of their asset base and is reviewed every five years by the ACCC.

41 Clive Hamilton and Richard Denniss, 'Generation Emissions?, The Impact of Microeconomic Reform on the Electricity Industry' (2001) 20(3) *Economic Papers* 15 at 18. See also *Greenhouse Gas Emissions and the Productivity Growth of Electricity Generators* (Productivity Commission, 2001) and *National Competition Policy: Some Impacts on Society and the Economy* (National Competition Council, 1999).

42 See *Analysis of Trends* (Australian Greenhouse Office, 2000) at 18.

43 Hamilton and Denniss, above n 41, at 19.

Hamilton and Denniss state that, although the fall in the price of electricity to contestable customers is seen as the 'jewel in the crown' of microeconomic reform in Australia, there is no doubt that this has been very damaging to the environment.[44] They conclude that:

> As long as the impacts of economic activity on the environment are excluded from the definition of 'economic efficiency' competition policy cannot guarantee improved welfare. Increased competition has the capacity to improve welfare in some situations, but only after significant market failures, particularly externalities, have been removed.[45]

If one looks at the increase in emissions that has already occurred since the establishment of the NEM, it is clear that the market cannot continue to exist in an environmental policy vacuum driven principally by competition principles. For this reason, it is interesting to note what the Australian and NSW governments have done to counteract global warming and to control emissions from the electricity sector.

Response of the Australian government to global climate change

It is clear, from the discussion below, that the Australian government is committed to investing significant amounts of money in finding a technological solution to global climate change. The government favours, in particular, the concept of geo-sequestration and the development of clean coal technologies. Since preparing to enter negotiations on the Kyoto Protocol, the government has been at pains to protect the fossil fuel base of the Australian economy. For this reason, it has assiduously refused to ratify the Protocol or to establish a domestic emissions trading scheme. However, this position may be modified with the announcement by the Prime Minister on 13 November 2006 that the government will establish a working group with business to examine a carbon trading scheme. The Prime Minister cautioned that such a scheme should not harm Australia's competitiveness in key industries.[46]

Refusal to ratify Kyoto Protocol

The Australian government has claimed that the Protocol will not be effective, and will damage Australia's economy. While it continues to insist that it will not ratify the Protocol, it will be difficult to construct an energy policy that is consistent with the principles of ESD. This is because the Protocol is regarded by the international community as an important instrument to begin combating one of the most significant barriers to ESD – global climate change.

To understand the government's stance on the Kyoto Protocol it is necessary to analyse the position which it adopted going into the Kyoto negotiations in December 1997. Before Kyoto, the government insisted that it wanted the outcome

44 Ibid at 20.

45 Ibid at 27.

46 Wendy Frew, 'PM thaws on carbon trading', *Sydney Morning Herald*, 14 November 2006.

of the negotiations to be fair and achievable, defining a fair outcome as one where the costs of reducing greenhouse emissions would be shared equitably by all countries.[47]

In developing its pre-Kyoto position, the government relied on economic modelling undertaken by ABARE.[48] ABARE concluded that the cost to the Australian economy of reducing greenhouse emissions would be 22 times higher than the loss estimated by the average European country, and six times higher than America's. This meant that Australia would be expected to sacrifice jobs even though it only contributes 1% of the world's emissions compared with 19% for United States, and 14% for the European Union. For Australia to meet the proposed target it would have to sacrifice highly efficient coal mining, mineral processing[49] and agricultural production.[50] Australia also argued that the target would result in the displacement of emissions to neighbours.[51] As a result, Australia argued strongly for the principle of *differentiation* to be accepted and adopted when setting national emissions reduction targets as this would also encourage developing countries to participate in reduction programs.[52]

There has been a great deal of criticism of the government's position at Kyoto particularly since it relied entirely on ABARE modelling to reach the conclusions that it did. ABARE modelling did not consider the potential losses to Australia like the social, environmental and economic costs of bushfires, floods and tropical cyclones, natural disasters resulting in loss of crops and production and widespread property damage. ABARE also did not account for benefits to the Australian economy of developing and selling renewable energy technologies like solar and wind, in which it has been recognised as a world leader.[53]

The most recent report which refutes the Australian government's position is the Allen Consulting Group's report, *Deep Cuts in Greenhouse Gas Emissions*,[54] which was commissioned by the Business Roundtable on Climate Change to assess the likely impact that taking significant policy action to bring about deep cuts in greenhouse gas emissions by 2050 would have on the Australian economy and community. The deep cuts referred to are a 60% reduction on 2000 levels by 2050. Given

---

47 In the federal government's view, uniform international emissions targets, of reducing emissions to 5% below that of 1990, would not be fair while the EU allowed some countries to reduce their emissions by 30% while others would increase emissions by 40%. Furthermore, based on anticipated economic growth, Australia's emissions would probably increase by 40% compared with 1990 levels.

48 ABARE is a public sector economic research agency located in Commonwealth Department of Primary Industry and Energy.

49 In particular, energy based commodities like the processing of aluminium which produces high emissions.

50 Australia's food and fibre production results in high methane emissions from cattle and sheep (second highest per capita in the world).

51 For example, if Australia were to be penalised for emissions produced in processing natural liquid gas for export to neighbours, neighbours would not get the benefit of a less polluting energy source.

52 Note that ABARE forecast that by 2004 emissions from developing countries will exceed those from developed countries.

53 See, eg, the Allen Consulting Group, *Sustainable Energy Jobs Report* (2003) and the *Sustainable Energy Jobs Report: Wind Manufacturing Case Study* (2003). The Reports conclude that, in a competitive energy market, the States that establish a strong and dynamic sustainable energy sector will build a significant first mover advantage.

54 See <http://www.allenconsult.com.au/resources/GHG2050%20FINAL.pdf> (accessed 24 April 2006).

that emissions from Australia's stationary energy sector have increased 40% above 1990 levels, and that the economy is expected to grow by 130% over the stipulated period, achieving such deep cuts is a daunting task. Clearly, major changes in technology will be required. The report draws on the estimates made by the CSIRO about feasible changes in existing technologies, as well as other sources. The key assumptions about the energy sector included in the report are that by 2050:

- electricity will be generated almost entirely by renewables and fossil fuels;
- emissions from the use of fossil fuels will be sequestered using carbon capture and storage (CCS) technologies;
- transport will be based on hydrogen fuel cells and hybrid vehicles;
- energy will be used more efficiently by all sectors;
- production of coal will be reduced while exports of uranium and LPG will be significantly increased.

Two emission reduction scenarios are presented: the 'early action' and the 'delayed action' scenarios. These scenarios are based on the adoption of greenhouse gas abatement measures that already exist in Australia and a business-as-usual projection for the Australian economy. Under the 'early action' scenario, emission reductions strategies would be implemented in 2013 whereas under the 'delayed action' scenario action would only begin in 2022, but reach the same overall reduction profile as under the 'early action' scenario.

Under the 'early action' scenario, GDP will grow at 2.1% a year to reach an estimated $2 trillion by 2050. Under the 'delayed action' scenario GDP will grow at 1.9% to reach $1.84 trillion by 2050. The important conclusion is that the negative impact on Australia's economy of deep cuts in greenhouse gas emissions is not as severe as might be anticipated. Significantly, costs to the economy are exacerbated where action is delayed. GDP would be 13% lower than a business-as-usual scenario, and 6% lower than under the 'early action' scenario.

Funding for climate change

As part of its commitment to developing responses to global climate change, without ratifying Kyoto, the Australian government established the Australian Greenhouse Office (AGO) to conduct research and to administer the Commonwealth government's climate change packages, Safeguarding the Future: Australia's Response to Climate Change[55] and the Measures for a Better Environment package announced as part of Australia's new tax system in 1999.[56]

It is interesting to note that in 2002 the activities of the AGO were reviewed and, although it maintains its status as an executive agency, its powers have been subordinated to some extent to the Department of Foreign Affairs and Tourism. Also the AGO is now required to report more formally to both the Ministers for the

55 Statement by John Howard, Prime Minister of Australia, *Safeguarding the Future: Australia's Response to Climate Change* (20 November 1997), <http://www.greenhouse.gov.au/ago/safeguarding.html>.

56 See AGO, <http://www.greenhouse.gov.au/measures> (accessed 15 April 2004). This package was announced in May 1999 as part of the introduction of the Goods and Services Tax (GST) in Australia. It was negotiated with the Australian Democrats who allowed the GST legislation to pass in the Senate based on the additional greenhouse initiatives contained in the package.

Environment and Heritage and the Minister for Industry and Resources. This is to cure the perception that the AGO has displayed a bias towards environment rather than industry interests.[57] Given the fact that some industry interests have militated against the ratification of the Kyoto Protocol, this consultation requirement is likely to constrain the activities of the AGO, at least to some extent.

Safeguarding the Future

The 1997 Safeguarding the Future package includes:

- the Greenhouse Challenge, which is a voluntary industry program to reduce greenhouse gas emissions, drive continuous improvement and enhance knowledge and understanding of the best ways of managing greenhouse gas emissions ($27.1 million);
- the Renewable Energy Equity Fund, which is an investment program to encourage the commercialisation of research and development in renewable energy technologies ($19.5 million); and
- the Renewable Energy Commercialisation Program (RECP), which is a grant program to support innovative renewable energy equipment and technologies ($29.6 million).[58]

Measures for a Better Environment

The 1999 revised tax system package, Measures for a Better Environment, includes the following programs:

- Greenhouse Gas Abatement Program (GGAP)[59] to support financially activities likely to result in substantial emissions reductions or substantial sink enhancement, particularly in the first Kyoto Protocol commitment period of 2008-12 ($400 million);
- Renewable Remote Power Generation Program to increase the uptake of renewable energy in remote areas, especially to meet the energy needs of Indigenous people ($179.9 million);
- Photovoltaic Rebate Program (PVRP) to encourage the long-term use of photovoltaic technology especially by granting subsidies for the use of solar hot water systems ($34.6 million);

---

57 Key recommendations include: revoking the AGO's status as an executive agency and incorporating it in Environment Australia while retaining its distinct identity; allowing the AGO to continue to lead domestic greenhouse policy but requiring it to take a subordinate position to the Department of Foreign Affairs and Trade on international greenhouse issues; and that a whole-of-government approach be adopted to greenhouse policy, rather than favouring environmental interests; see Hon Warwick L Smith, *Independent Review of the Australian Greenhouse Office* (June 2002, released 4 February 2003) at iii.

58 See also *Renewable Energy (Electricity) Act 2000* (Cth).

59 The aims of the Program are to: fund initiatives that will result in sustained reductions in emissions during the first commitment period (2008-12); be cost effective while having a least cost impact on the economy; be consistent with the principles of ecologically sustainable development; and generate the use of new technologies and provide opportunities particularly for rural and regional Australia. See *The Heat is On: Australia's Greenhouse Future,* Report of the Senate Environment, Communications, Information Technology and Arts Reference Committee (November 2000) at 120.

- Alternative Fuels Conversion Program (AFCP) to reduce emissions and improve urban air quality by encouraging heavier commercial road vehicles and public transport buses to operate on compressed natural gas, or liquefied petroleum gas ($71.4 million); and
- extension of the RECP program with additional funding for industry development component ($26 million).[60]

The total value of the programs is $873.70 million.

Another 'no-regrets' initiative of the AGO has been the Greenhouse Friendly/ Greenhouse Free program, which is an endorsement for products with greenhouse emissions offset by projects financed by companies and approved by the AGO. The AGO provides companies with approved methods for estimating greenhouse emission reductions from abatement projects and a list of Greenhouse Challenge accredited verifiers so proposed abatement projects can be independently verified.[61]

Various commentators, including the AGO, have serious doubts as to whether or not the federal government's 'no-regrets' policy will deliver any significant reductions in emissions.

Establishment of a renewable energy trading scheme

To date, the only enforceable piece of legislation passed by the Australian government in relation to energy and climate change is the *Renewable Energy (Electricity) Act 2000* (Cth) (RE(E)A).[62] The Act introduces a 2% Renewable Portfolio Standard (RPS) for Australia in addition to the 10% which already exists. This 10% is derived from historic investment in hydro-electric schemes in Tasmania and New South Wales, dating back to the 1950s. As is clear from the Act, an RPS scheme typically requires retailers to purchase a proportion of their electricity from renewable energy sources. Renewable energy credits (RECs) are created which may then be traded between those retailers which have difficulty in meeting their legal obligations, and

60 For example, the aim of the *National Average Fuel Consumption Target* is to impose new fuel efficiency standards to secure a 15% fuel efficiency improvement target by 2010 over business as usual. Note that the *Fuel Quality Standards Act 2000* (Cth) has been passed by the federal government to enable it to make mandatory national quality standards for fuel supplied in Australia. The standards will be based on international standard vehicle and emission control technologies. Standards will be set for petrol, diesel and liquefied petroleum gas. One of the main objectives of the Act is to reduce pollutants and emissions arising from the use of fuel that may cause environmental, greenhouse and health problems. The *Fuel Quality Standards Act* was amended in 2004, to insert Pt 2A relating to Renewable Fuel into the Act. Part 2A sets out a regulatory regime in relation to the inclusion of cellulosic biomass ethanol, and other renewable fuel, in fuel supplied for use in motor vehicles in Australia. A 2005 amendment to the *Fuel Quality Standards Act* inserted s 22A into the principal Act to establish the requirement for ethanol content in fuel which is at least 4% from 1 July 2009, at least 7% from 1 July 2012 and at least 10% from 1 July 2015. In addition, a new labelling system for passenger vehicles sold in Australia has been introduced. The label is required under a new Australian Design Rule (ADR) 81/00 Fuel Consumption Labelling for Light Vehicles and must state the fuel consumption in litres per 100 kilometres to enable consumers to make decisions based on fuel efficiency and environmental protection.

61 Greenhouse Friendly Certification Program, <http://www.greenhouse.gov.au/greenhousefriendly/index.html> (accessed 14 April 2004).

62 For a detailed discussion of this Act, see Adrian Bradbrook and Alexandra S Wawryk, 'Government Initiatives Promoting Renewable Energy for Electricity Generation in Australia' (2002) 25(1) *UNSWLJ* 124 at 146-153.

those which have the capacity to produce excess credits.[63] RPSs are a common measure for promoting the commercialisation of renewable energy. The Standard set in various countries is as follows: the Netherlands - 10% by 2020,[64] Denmark - 20% by 2010,[65] the United States - 10% by 2019,[66] and the United Kingdom - 10.4% by 2010.[67]

Despite the popularity of a RPS, the real question is whether or not an RPS scheme is consistent with a competitive electricity market. The reason that it is favoured by regulators is that by creating a tradeable market in RECs it seems to require a minimal amount of government interference, and this is consistent with the economic theory underlying a restructured market. However, it is arguable that a RPS is not administratively simple. One has only to consider the role of the Renewable Energy Regulator under the RE(E)A to realise that the Regulator's task in verifying RECs, ensuring compliance with the scheme and assessing penalties for breach of the Act is quite complex.[68]

Also there is a legitimate debate about whether or not a RPS is competitively neutral when existing renewables are considered. Those utilities with an existing high level of renewables will be less severely impacted by a RPS than others.[69] In fact suppliers with excess renewable energy credits may see rate reductions as they sell their excess credits to other suppliers, whose rates increase. If competitive neutrality is a concern, it may be possible to limit the RPS to new renewable energy generation.[70]

Others note that the system gives renewable energy technologies an unfair market advantage in that customers and the market should select the types of electricity that are used, rather than being forced to select one source over another.[71]

---

63 See, for example, Tim Woolf and Bruce Biewald, 'Efficiency, Renewables and Gas: Restructuring as if Climate Mattered' (1998) January/February *The Electricity Journal* 64; Karen Palmer, Dallas Burtraw, Ranjit Bharvirkar, Anthony Paul, *Restructuring and the Cost of Reducing Nox Emissions in Electricity Generation* (Resources for the Future, 2001); Sebastian Crawford and Jeff Angel, *Green or Black? Renewable Energy Policy in Australia* (Total Environment Centre, 2002); Steven L Clemmer, Alan Nogee, Michael C Brower, Paul Jefferiss, *A Powerful Opportunity: Making Renewable Electricity the Standard* (Union of Concerned Scientists Publications, 1999); David Mills, 'Reducing Greenhouse Gas Emission Through Electricity Industry Reform: A Market-Oriented Emissions Reduction Scheme' (2000) 12 *World Resources Review* 58; Annex I Expert Group on the United Nations Framework Convention on Climate Change *Penetration of Renewable Energy in the Electricity Sector: Working Paper No 15* (Organisation for Economic Co-operation and Development, 1998); Ryan Wise, Steven Pickle, Charles Goldman, 'Renewable energy policy and electricity restructuring: A California case study' (1998) 26 *Energy Policy* 465; Simone Espey, 'Renewable portfolio standard: a means for trade with electricity form renewable energy sources' (2001) 29 *Energy Policy* 55.

64 *Dutch Electricity Act 1998.*

65 *Energy 21*; see also Jens Hauch, 'The Danish Electricity reform (2001) 29 *Energy Policy* 509 at 510.

66 *Energy Policy Act 2002* (US).

67 The Renewables Obligation Order 2002 No 914 made under the *Utilities Act 2000* (UK); for a detailed discussion of the scheme, see also Bradbrook and Wawryk, above n 62, at 142-144.

68 RE(E)A ss 11-16, 41, 48-50, 52, 58-59, 69, 71-73, 102-105, 135-141; see also Wise et al, above n 63, at 471.

69 This has certainly been a concern in the Australian context where existing hydro-electricity generators were able to surrender the highest number of RECs in the first year of the operation of the RE(E)A; see Bradbrook and Wawryk, above n 62, at 150.

70 Wise et al, above n 63, at 472.

71 See Bradbrook and Wawryk, above n 62, at 133.

Creating renewable energy certificates

Under the Act accredited power stations are given a 1997 eligible renewable power baseline. Power stations create renewable energy certificates (RECs) when they generate power using eligible renewable energy sources[72] that exceed the 1997 baseline (RE(E)A s 18). Certificates can also be created by installations of solar hot water heaters that are installed after January 2001 and which replace non-renewable heaters (ss 18-30).

A person needs to be registered before they can create a certificate and needs to be accredited before a certificate can be issued in relation to power generated by it. Every certificate must be registered on creation as must every transfer of a certificate. Once a certificate is surrendered by a liable party it loses its validity. Any person can apply to the Regulator to be registered under the Act. Any registered person can apply to the Regulator for accreditation as an accredited power station. A power station is eligible for accreditation. If an application for accreditation is approved, the power station must be allocated a unique identification code of which is must be advised (Pt 2).

It is an offence of strict liability to create a certificate that one is not entitled to create. A penalty can be imposed in respect of the creation of each improperly created certificate. Certificates must be created electronically containing a unique identification code, the electronic signature of the person who created the certificate, the date on which the electricity was generated and the date on which the certificate was created. Certificates must be registered with the Regulator. Once registered the certificates can be transferred to any person, subject to the Regulator being notified. Any body accredited by the Australian Securities and Investments Commission or similar body can act as a broker in renewable energy certificates between renewable electricity generators, liable parties and third parties (Pt 2, Div 4).

Renewable energy sources

The following energy sources are 'eligible renewable energy sources':[73]

(a) hydro;
(b) wave;
(c) tide;
(d) ocean;
(e) wind;
(f) solar;
(g) geothermal-aquifer;
(h) hot dry rock;
(i) energy crops;
(j) wood waste;
(k) agricultural waste;
(l) waste from processing of agricultural products;
(m) food waste;

72 Eligible renewable energy sources are defined in RE(E)A s 17.

73 These definitions take account of the amendments contained in the *Renewable Energy (Electricity) Amendment Act 2006* (Cth).

(n) food processing waste;
(o) bagasse;
(p) black liquor;
(q) biomass-based components of municipal solid waste;
(r) landfill gas;
(s) sewage gas and biomass-based components of sewage;
(t) any other energy source prescribed by the regulations.

However, the following energy sources are not eligible renewable energy sources:

(a) fossil fuels;
(b) waste products derived from fossil fuels (s 17).

Under the 2006 amendments to the Act, the opportunities for generating bioenergy have been increased. The amendments remove the requirement that a bioenergy crop be produced for the 'primary purpose' of renewable energy generation. This means that plantations, agricultural crops and biomass that would normally go to landfill can be used to generate renewable energy. Types of bioenergy projects that may now become eligible include short-cycle plantations, such as energy crops, wood waste from existing plantations and 'supplementary fuel' plantations. Also, the definition of municipal solid waste (MSW) is amended to include all biomass material that would otherwise be landfill, including material that is directly sourced from a licensed landfill or licensed waste transfer station. This will increase the amount of green waste available as fuel for MSW generators.

'Liable entities' under the Act

The legislation is directed primarily at 'liable entities' (RE(E)A s 35), that is, entities that make a 'relevant acquisition' of electricity that is either a wholesale acquisition or a notional wholesale acquisition. A wholesale acquisition is essentially an acquisition from NEMMCO (s 32). A notional wholesale acquisition is where a person acquires electricity from a generator and that person is not registered under the National Electricity Code, or where there is less than 1 kilometre between the point at which the electricity is generated and the point at which the electricity is used. The electricity must be transmitted and distributed on a line that is used solely for this specific purpose (s 33). These exceptions give effect to the government's agreement not to regulate self-generators under the scheme.

Liable entities are required to achieve individual renewable energy targets based on their projected market share of consumption, which can be projected three years in advance (ss 36-43).[74] A liable entity calculates its target with reference to the renewable power percentage (RPP) that must be achieved in any given year. The RPP should be set by Regulation before 31 March each year and must relate to the required gigawatt hours (GWhs), or mandatory renewable energy target (MRET), as set out in the Act (s 40). The Act requires the following:

74 Note that Green Power sales will not be able to be used by energy suppliers to meet their MRET obligations.

Required GWh of renewable source electricity	
Year	**Required additional GWh**
2001	300
2002	1100
2003	1800
2004	2600
2005	3400
2006	4500
2007	5600
2008	6800
2009	8100
2010 and later years	9500

A liable entity must surrender RECs to the Renewable Energy Regulator in discharge of its renewable energy liabilities under the Act (s 41). So, if a liable entity makes a relevant acquisition of 100,000 MWh or electricity in a given year, it would multiply that by the RPP to work out the number of RECs it has to surrender. For example, the RPP for the year 2001 was 0.24%. Consequently, an acquisition of 100,000 MWh would require the entity to surrender 240 certificates to discharge its liability that year.

Calculating the RPP

Since the liability to acquire RECs is dependent on the RPP, it is important to be able to predict what the RPP will be. Determining the RPP is largely dependent on the annual target for additional renewable energy acquisitions for the market as a whole, as set out in the table reproduced above. However, there are two alternative methods for calculating the RPP for a given year. The most likely means is that the Governor-General will simply determine the RPP by making a regulation (s 39(1)). Alternatively, if this does not occur, the Act provides a formula under s 39(2) for calculating the RPP.

When making the RPP by regulation (s 39(1)), the following factors are to be considered (s 39(3)):

- *(a)* *the required GWh of renewable source electricity for the year* (see the targets set out in the table above)
- *(b)* *the amount estimated as the total amount of electricity that will be acquired under relevant acquisitions during the year; and*
- *(c)* *the amount by which the required GWhs of renewable source electricity for all previous years* (according to the table in s 40) *has exceeded, or has been exceeded by, the amount for renewable source electricity required under the scheme in those years.* (The amount required under the scheme is calculated by multiplying the total amount of electricity acquired during the year by the RPP for that year (s 39(4).)

In other words, the annual RPP is set after considering the annual target, the estimated total acquisition of electricity for the following year and the market's shortfalls or surpluses in previous years. Hence the RPP is determined by many factors which have a relatively high level of uncertainty, which will be discussed further below.

As mentioned above, it is anticipated that the RPP will be set by regulation each year. However in the event that it is not set, the Act provides for a default RPP, known as an *interim RPP* (s 39(2)). The interim power percentage for the year is:

(a) for the year commencing on 1 January 2001 – 0.24% and
(b) for any later year – the rate worked out using the formula:

$$\frac{\textit{Renewable power percentage for the previous year} \times \textit{Required GWh for the year} \text{ (s 40)}}{\textit{Required GWh for the previous Year}}$$

The Act specifically provides that where a regulation is made under s 39(1), the formula set out in s 39(2) should not be used to set the RPP. Only the factors referred to s 39(3) should be considered. In other words, the simple calculation provided in s 39(2) is superseded by the more complicated list of factors which must be considered when making a regulation.

Lodging energy acquisition statements

A liable entity which acquired electricity under a relevant acquisition during a year must lodge an energy acquisition statement for the year on or before 14 February in the following year setting out the name and postal address of the liable entity, the amount of electricity acquired under relevant acquisitions during the year, the value, in MWh, or renewable energy certificates being surrendered for that year, and any carried forward shortfall or surplus for the previous year, and any carried forward surplus for the current year (RE(E)A Pt 5).

The statement must be lodged with the Regulator accompanied by details of all renewable energy certificates being surrendered for that year. Only valid certificates can be surrendered and must have been created before the end of the year to which the acquisition statement relates. The liable person must be recorded in the register of certificates as the owner of the certificate.

Renewable energy shortfall statements must also be submitted. The Act provides for a self-assessment mechanism for reporting certificate shortfalls to the Regulator. If a liable entity lodges a renewable energy shortfall statement and has not previously lodged a shortfall statement for that year with the Regulator, the statement is regarded as the assessment of the entity's shortfall. If a liable party has lodged an energy acquisition statement without lodging a shortfall statement and the Regulator is of the opinion that the party has a shortfall, an assessment of liability may be made by the Regulator on the entity's behalf. The Regulator can also make necessary amendments and additions to assessments. Liable entities who are dissatisfied with an assessment can lodge written objections to the Regulator within 60 days of an assessment being made, setting out the grounds for the objection. A late objection can also be made but must be accompanied by a written request for an extension of time. The Regulator must make an objection decision either allowing or disallowing the objection. If the liable entity proceeds to appeal before the Administrative Appeals Tribunal or the Federal Court it can only rely on the matters covered by the objection. The Act provides that penalties may be charged for failing to provide statements and information and for making false and misleading statements.

Auditing of 'liable entities'

The affairs of registered persons and liable entities may be audited under the Act. Authorised officers who are offices or employees of the Office of Renewable Energy Regulator may be appointed by the Regulator. An authorised officer, for the purposes of substantiating information supplied under the Act, may enter any premises and exercise monitoring powers provided for under the Act. This includes, amongst others, searching premises, examining activities, taking photographs, videos or audio recordings and inspecting documents. The penalty for giving false and misleading evidence or documents to an authorised officer is imprisonment for one year (RE(E)A Pt 11).

Registers

The Regulator must maintain electronic registers of registered persons, accredited power stations and renewable energy certificates, which must be available for inspection on the internet.

Trading renewable energy certificates

The Act envisages that a market in RECs might develop where one liability entity is in possession of excess RECs and another has too few RECs to meet its obligations under the Act. To this end a REC which is registered may be transferred to any person (RE(E)A s 27). However, a liable entity will face a non tax-deductible penalty of $40 MWh if it has not acquired sufficient RECs (see s 6). An entity can carry forward a 10% shortfall to the following year thus reducing its liability to pay the penalty (s 36).

In the first year of the operation of the Act 659,000 RECs were surrendered to the Regulator representing an oversupply of RECs for 2001 to a factor of 2.2.[75] Early assessment of the legislation, however, indicates that the Act will not deliver the 2% increase in renewable energy. This is because energy consumption in Australia is likely to double by 2010. The legislation as it currently stands will only deliver a 0.9% increase in renewable energy.[76]

Securing Australia's energy future?

Following the release of the Parer Review into the National Electricity Market (NEM) (see below), the Prime Minister released the much-awaited energy policy for Australia entitled *Saving Our Energy Future*. The focus on technological solutions is disappointing given the clear need to develop a legally enforceable obligation to

75 See <http://www.orer.gov.au/pubs/bioenergy.pdf> (accessed 12 August 2002).

76 See Origin Energy report, produced by McLennan Magasanik Associates, which shows that the legislation will only produce a 0.9% increase in renewable energy in 2010.

reduce greenhouse gas emissions. The policy makes it clear that the Australian government is committed to adopting a range of technological measures to reduce greenhouse gas emission. Under the policy, a $500 million fund is established to demonstrate low-emission technologies to reduce greenhouse gas emissions including primarily geosequestration (ie, sequestration of carbon dioxide underground). Geosequestration is an important part of the Howard government's energy policy. It has also been adopted as a research priority by COAL21, the partnership between the coal mining industry, the coal-fired electricity generation industry, and Commonwealth and State research bodies such as the CSIRO.

In light of this, the Ministerial Council of Mineral and Petroleum Resources (MCMPR) released Carbon Dioxide Capture and Geological Storage: Australian Regulatory Guiding Principles (RGPs)[77] in December 2005 in order to achieve a nationally consistent approach to the implementation of this technology. The RGPs take into account principles of Ecologically Sustainable Development, the Intergovernmental Agreement on the Environment, Principles of Good Regulation and relevant COAG Occupational Health and Safety Principles.

Solar Cities

The government is committed to implementing a range of energy efficiency measures. These include: committing $75 million to Solar Cities trials requiring firms using more than 0.5 petajoules of energy a year to undertake every five years. The assessments will be conducted in accordance with strict standards and will be reported publicly.

In April 2005, the Australian government released the Programme Guidelines for Solar Cities.[78] It is anticipated that the first critical infrastructure components and market arrangements for Solar Cities will be in place in 2006-07. The impacts will be monitored, analysed and reported through to 2012-13. The Prime Minister has announced that the first Solar Cities are to be located in North Adelaide, Townsville and Blacktown.[79]

Energy efficiency opportunity assessments

As part of the Australian government's commitment in *Securing Our Energy Future* to increasing energy efficiency, the *Energy Efficiency Opportunities Act 2006* (Cth) was enacted. The object of the Act is to improve the identification and evaluation of energy efficiency opportunities by large energy-using businesses which use more than half a petajoule of energy per year. These corporations must register on the Register of Corporations for the Energy Efficiency Opportunities Scheme. The Act distinguishes between a holding company which is a body corporate, and a controlling corporation which is a constitutional corporation which does not have a holding company registered in Australia.

Under the Act, corporations must undertake an assessment of their energy efficiency opportunities to a minimum standard to improve the way in which

---

77 See <http://www.industry.gov.au/assets/documents/itrinternet/Regulatory_Guiding_Principles_for_CCS20051124145652.pdf> (accessed 1 May 2006).

78 See <http://www.greenhouse.gov.au/solarcities/guidelines.html>.

79 See <http://www.greenhouse.gov.au/solarcities/> (accessed 8 December 2006).

opportunities are identified and evaluated; and to report publicly on the outcomes of their assessment to demonstrate to the community that their energy use is being effectively managed. Registered corporations are required to submit assessment plans (AP) every five years. The AP must set out a proposal for assessing the opportunities for improving energy efficiency, and set a deadline for doing all of the actions set out for assessing energy efficiency opportunities.

A registered corporation must report publicly on the way in which the corporation has carried out the proposal in its AP for assessing the opportunities to improve energy efficiency. It must also report on the results of carrying out the proposal and how the corporation has responded to the results. Inspectors are given powers under the Act to inspect and monitor activities under the Act. Civil and criminal penalties apply to a breach of the Act.

A major weakness of the Act is that ultimately the obligation to take energy efficiency measures is discretionary. Corporations retain the right to decide whether or not to pursue the opportunities that have been identified, based on their commercial assessment of the options available.

The Act must be read together with the *Energy Efficiency Opportunities Regulations 2006* (Cth).

Small scale renewable energy

The government will provide an additional $100 million to target strategic research, development and commercialisation of smaller scale renewable energy technologies. It will also maintain support for the Mandatory Renewable Energy Target (see below) through to 2020 but with no increase in the target beyond the existing 2% by 2010. It will provide $230 million to continue projects like the Remote Renewable Generation (RRG) and Greenhouse Gas Abatement programs (GGAP), and provide $34 million to remove specific barriers to the deployment of renewable energy like wind forecasting, improved electricity storage options and better grid connection rules.

Asia-Pacific Partnership on Clean Development and Climate

Australia has joined the Asia-Pacific Partnership on Clean Development and Climate[80] established on 28 July 2005 at the Association of South East Asian Nations (ASEAN) Regional Forum meeting. Member nations include the United States, Australia, China, India, Japan and South Korea which together account for around 50% of the world's greenhouse gas emissions, energy consumption, GDP and population. The six countries will work together to: develop, deploy and transfer existing and emerging clean technology; meet increased energy needs and explore ways to reduce the greenhouse intensity of their economies; build human and institutional capacity; and seek ways to engage the private sector. The parties have included the following areas for collaboration in the agreement: energy efficiency; clean coal; integrated gasification combined cycle; liquefied natural gas; carbon capture and storage; combined heat and power; methane capture and use; the

80 Office of the Prime Minister, 28 July 2005 and the Australia Institute, 28 July 2005, <http://www.pm.gov.au/news/media_releases/media_Release1482.html> (accessed 16 October 2005).

development of next-generation nuclear power and the use of civilian nuclear power; fusion power; hydrogen energy distribution; geothermal energy; biotechnology; nanotechnology; rural/village energy systems; advanced transportation; building and home construction and operation; bioenergy; agriculture and forestry; hydropower; wind power; solar power; and other renewables.

The agreement states that the partnership is consistent with efforts under the United Nations Framework Convention on Climate Change and will complement, but not replace, the Kyoto Protocol. Unlike the Kyoto Protocol, which imposes mandatory limits on greenhouse gas emissions, this pact permits participating countries to set their own goals for reducing emissions individually, with no mandatory enforcement mechanism.

Given the membership of the partnership, and the wide-ranging commitments to develop technologies to address greenhouse gas emissions, it is to be hoped that significant reductions are delivered. However, there has been some scepticism about the announcement. The Australia Institute, for example, has labelled the pact as nothing but a charade which conceals Australia's burgeoning greenhouse gas emissions and the abject failure of the Australian government's policies. The Institute points to the fact that study after study shows that voluntary agreements do not produce any meaningful reductions in greenhouse gas emissions.[81] The authors are also critical of greenhouse gas emissions reduction schemes which rely solely on voluntary commitments.

COAG responses to global climate change

Given the greenhouse implications of the National Energy Market, it was with some optimism that environmental lawyers greeted the announcement of COAG that it would be reviewing Australia's energy policy. This seemed an opportune moment for a thorough overhaul of the policy and legal framework of the energy market, and to move towards a sustainable energy framework. At its meeting on 8 June 2001,[82] COAG accepted that it needed to provide effective policy leadership to meet the opportunities and challenges facing the energy sector in Australia. Consequently, COAG agreed to establish a new Ministerial Council on Energy (MCE) and to provide it with a series of priority tasks for its consideration and resolution.

Priority issues for consideration were: identifying any impediments to the full realisation of the benefits of energy market reform; identifying strategic directions for further energy market reform; examining regulatory approaches that effectively balance incentives for new supply investment, demand responses and benefits to consumers; assessing the potential for regions and small business to benefit from energy market development; *assessing the relative efficiency and cost effectiveness of options within the energy market to reduce greenhouse gas emissions from the electricity and gas sectors, including the feasibility of a phased introduction of a national system of greenhouse emission reduction benchmarks* (emphasis added); and identifying means of encouraging the wider penetration of natural gas including increased upstream gas competition, value-adding processes for natural gas and potential other uses such as

81 See <http://www.tai.org.au/> (accessed 16 October 2005).

82 See COAG Communiqué, 8 June 2001, <http://www.coag.gov.au/meetings/080601/index.htm#energy> (accessed 3 February 2005).

distributed generation, because it is an abundant, domestically available and clean energy resource. This marks the first occasion on which COAG identified greenhouse gas emissions as a challenge facing the energy sector in Australia.

The subsequent review of the NEM, entitled *Towards a Truly National and Efficient Energy Market* (Parer Review), contained eight principal chapters, covering governance and regulatory arrangements; electricity market mechanism and structure; electricity transmission; electricity financial market development; demand side participation and full retail contestability in electricity; increasing the wider penetration of gas; options to reduce greenhouse gas emissions; and rural and regional issues. It is not possible to reproduce the Parer Review in full.

For our purposes, the Parer Review made a number of recommendations to assist embedded (renewable energy) generators to access the NEM. The Review recommended that the newly formed NER introduce a mandatory code of practice governing arrangements between distribution companies and prospective embedded generators.

With respect to counteracting the greenhouse impact of the NEM, the review recommended the introduction of a national economy-wide greenhouse gas emissions trading scheme to replace the following existing government greenhouse gas abatement initiatives: the Commonwealth Mandatory Renewable Energy Target; the NSW Greenhouse Gas Reduction Scheme; the Queensland 13 percent Gas Scheme; Generator efficiency standards; and the Greenhouse Gas Abatement Program – Stationary Energy projects. The Review also recommended greater penetration of natural gas into the national energy framework.

In 2003, the COAG MCE accepted a number of these recommendations.[83] What is remarkable is that in spite of the substantial overhaul of the *National Electricity Law*, made in response to the recommendations, no provisions were inserted into the Law to ensure that the NEM achieves the reduction of greenhouse gas emissions. It seems almost inconceivable that such an opportunity could have been missed by the MCE. The recommendation to establish a domestic emissions trading scheme was ignored.

In spite of this oversight, COAG continues to develop policies and frameworks on climate change, renewable energy and the increasing penetration of gas.

COAG to develop Climate Change Plan of Action

In February 2006, the Council of Australia Governments (COAG) agreed to adopt a new Climate Change Plan of Action while establishing a high-level interjurisdictional Climate Change Group to implement the Plan. Key initiatives of the Plan include:

- developing a national framework to enhance the uptake of renewable and low emissions technologies as well as funding a study to identify gaps in technology development;
- developing a national climate change adaptation strategy to allow business and community decision-makers to manage the risks associated with climate change;

83 See Ministerial Council on Energy Communiqué, Perth 11 December 2003, <http://www. industry.gov.au/assets/documents/itrinternet/MCE-Dec03-Communique20031211171220.pdf?CFID=2495&CFTOKEN=81125836> (accessed 3 February 2005).

- funding a $100,000 study to establish a Centre for Climate Change Science and Knowledge to support scientifically Australia's decision-making on climate change;
- acceleration of work by Ministerial Councils investigating ways of strengthening emissions-reporting approaches; and
- requiring all Ministerial Councils to consider the climate change implications of their decisions and activities.

National Framework for Energy Efficiency

In November 2002, the Ministerial Council on Energy endorsed a proposal for the development of a National Framework for Energy Efficiency (NFEE), comprising an energy efficiency policy and efficiency programs for Australia. A new body, known as the Energy Efficiency Working Group (E2WG), was established to provide strategic advice on these issues through the Standing Committee of Officials to the Ministerial Council on Energy. The NFEE will enhance Australia's energy efficiency performance, reduce energy demand and lower greenhouse gas emissions right across the economy. In particular, the NFEE promotes demand-side energy efficiency in the residential, commercial and industrial sectors, and also seeks to overcome the barriers and challenges to energy efficiency measures. Development of the NFEE occurs with the involvement of the Commonwealth and State governments as well as key stakeholders.

The NFEE is divided into Stage One and Stage Two. Stage One has resulted in the development of integrated and inter-linked policy packages covering:

- residential and commercial buildings;
- commercial/industrial and government energy efficiency;
- appliance and equipment energy efficiency;
- trade and professional training and accreditation;
- commercial/industrial sector capacity building;
- consumer and finance sector awareness.

In December 2004, the MCE also approved eight high level implementation plans for the NFEE Stage One covering the years 2005-07. Implementation Committees and E2WG are responsible for delivering NFEE Stage One and for developing the NFEE Stage Two policy program. Stage Two is being developed now that the Productivity Commission has presented its report entitled *The Private Cost Effectiveness of Improving Energy Efficiency*[84] to the Australian government, which was favourably received.[85]

Impediments to the uptake of renewable energy

The Ministerial Council on Energy (MCE) has established a special working group known as the Renewable and Distributed Generation Working Group (RDGWG) to take responsibility for developing wind energy policy, as well as developing a

84 See <http://www.pc.gov.au/inquiry/energy/finalreport/index.html> (accessed 2 May 2006).

85 See <http://www.greenhouse.gov.au/energy/publications/pubs/government-response.pdf> (accessed 2 May 2006).

national Code of Practice for Embedded Generation and the Improving Grid Accessibility initiative. In 2006, the Ministerial Council on Energy Standing Committee of Officials released a Discussion Paper entitled *Impediments to the Uptake of Renewable and Distributed Energy*.[86] The paper notes that while the *National Electricity Law* and Rules govern the operation of the wholesale National Electricity Market and establish an access regime for electricity transmission and distribution, it is the State governments that are responsible for regulating distribution and retail pricing, and the licensing of distributors, retailers and generators. This will change when retail and distribution functions are transferred to a national regulator by the end of 2006, and economic regulation of distribution networks are transferred by January 2007. The transfer of economic regulation of distribution networks provides an opportunity to establish a nationally consistent approach to Renewable and Distributed Generation (R & DG).

Although there are different impediments to R & DG, depending on the size of the generator, there are a number of impediments commonly faced by all generators. These are:

- Approvals processes for R & DG projects can be complex and inconsistent across jurisdictions.
- Per-unit generation costs are generally higher than conventional technologies.
- There is no strategic regional focus on planning for R & DG technologies and current network planning tends to be incremental.
- It is often difficult for new technologies to obtain planning approval, financing and skilled labour while access to support infrastructure can be difficult.
- Economic signals for distributed and close-to-load generation is often muted or lost because of a lack of locational and cost reflective pricing (and associated metering).
- Incremental connection costs can be potentially prohibitive for new R & DG projects, particularly where projects require network augmentations or provision of major new line. Although the National Electricity Rules require connection agreements to be fair and reasonable it may be necessary to develop further guidance on what this amounts to. Network connection regulations can also be complex.
- Network Service Provider concerns about the reliability of R & DG may be a barrier to active uptake.

The paper states that these problems can only be overcome if emerging technology issues are adequately addressed, R & DG proponents and consumers are able to participate effectively in the market, and the network is capable of managing increased levels of R & DG in a cost-effective manner.

These problems are likely to be substantially ameliorated by the National Code of Practice for Embedded Generation[87] which was released in draft form in February

86 See <http://www.mce.gov.au/assets/documents/mceinternet/DiscussionPaperImpedimentstoUptakeRDG20060222140112.pdf> (accessed 1 May 2006).

87 See <http://www.mce.gov.au/assets/documents/mceinternet/DraftCoPEGforWeb20060221154032%2Epdf> (accessed 8 December 2006).

2006. The Draft Code deals with matters such as Arrangements for Connection; Technical Requirements and Commercial Arrangements.

Wind energy policy

Two other groups have been established under RDGWG – the Wind Energy Policy Working Group (WEPWG) and the Wind Energy Technical Advisory Group (WETAG). These groups are required to pay particular attention to the barriers which wind energy generators may face when seeking to connect new generating plant to the national electricity grid.

In March 2005, the WEPWG released a Discussion Paper entitled *Integrating Wind Farms into the National Electricity Market* for comment.[88] In addition, in May 2006, the Minister for the Environment and Heritage released a discussion paper entitled *A National Code for Wind Farms*.[89] The Discussion Paper points to the need for a Code that will ensure that a consistent approach is taken towards public participation, environmental, heritage, Indigenous and biodiversity issues. Given the release of these papers, it is likely that there will be further policy and regulatory activity in 2007 regarding the development of wind energy resources in Australia.

Wider penetration of gas

Although COAG initially focused on the reform of the NEM, the Ministerial Council on Energy has also agreed to establish a Gas Market Leaders group to develop a gas market development plan.[90] The Plan will meet the MCE's objectives of accelerating the development of a reliable, secure and competitive natural gas market. Key elements of the plan will include:

- the level of information that should be provided to the market in order to increase transparency with regard to system capabilities, and supply and demand information including secondary trades;
- the manner of communicating this information to the market, eg using market-based electronic facilities;
- the extent to which market arrangements, including the phasing in of spot market trading at major trading nodes, should be adopted to promote greater levels of liquidity and competition;
- considering whether the publication of an annual report would be beneficial to gas market development;
- an implementation timetable, including milestones; and
- the identification of State-based regulatory and rule-making requirements needed to facilitate the implementation of the plan.

---

88 See <http://www.mce.gov.au/assets/documents/mceinternet/WEPWGDiscussionPaperMar0520050510160534%2E.pdf> (accessed 16 January 2007).

89 See <http://www.greenhouse.gov.au/renewable/publications/pubs/wind-discussionpaper.pdf> (accessed 16 January 2007).

90 MCE, *Energy Market Reform Bulletin* No 52, 8 November 2005.

In addition, the MCE released for comment its *Statement of Approach – A New Legislative Framework for Gas.*[91] The following principles have been adopted with respect to developing this regulatory framework:

- Wherever feasible alignment with the new electricity regulatory regime should occur.
- The regulatory framework should be enshrined in the National Gas Law (NGL), while procedural and technical details will remain in the new Gas Rules.
- The Rule change process will be enshrined in the NGL and will be sufficiently flexible to allow the details of the Regulation to be responsive to the needs of market participants.
- General legislative principles which confer and determine the scope of functions, powers, rights and obligations should be included in the NGL.

Given the amount of work undertaken by the MCE with respect to a greater penetration of gas into Australia's energy mix, it seems that legislative reform of this energy sector is imminent.

State government co-operation on energy and climate change

Green Power

As Bradbrook[92] notes, '[g]reen power schemes are designed to enhance the use of renewable energy resources in the production of electricity in order to improve the environment and to reduce atmospheric carbon emissions'. Under Green Power schemes, consumers pay an additional premium to their electricity supply company because the cost of generating electricity from renewable energy resources is almost always higher than that produced from fossil fuels. The premium allows the electricity supply company to offset the increased cost of producing electricity from renewable energy and financially promotes the development energy resources. On payment of the premium, the electricity supply company purchases additional electricity generated from renewable energy, to match the agreed amount of electricity in respect of which the premium was paid.

Australia's Green Power program is a national accreditation program and is a collaborative arrangement between the State governments, administered by the NSW Department of Energy Utilities and Sustainability (DEUS). By choosing a Green Power product, energy suppliers agree to purchase the equivalent amount of energy produced from renewable sources so reducing reliance on electricity derived from fossil fuels. Stringent environmental and reporting standards have been set for renewable energy products offered by electricity suppliers to commercial and

---

91 See <http://www.mce.gov.au/assets/documents/mceinternet/MCESoA20050913164120%2Epdf> (accessed 1 May 2006).

92 See R Lyster and A Bradbrook, *Energy Law and the Environment* (Cambridge University Press, 2006) Chapter 6: see also A Bradbrook, 'Green Power Schemes: The Need for a Legislative Base' (2002) 26 *MULR* 15; AS Wawryk, 'Green Pricing and Green Power Marketing: Demand-side Mechanisms for Promoting "Green Power" in Deregulated Electricity Markets' in AJ Bradbrook and RL Ottinger (eds), *Energy Law and Sustainable Development* (IUCN, 2003).

domestic customers across Australia. All Green Power products are independently audited.

In the 1 July–30 September 2006 Quarterly Status Report, the following sales of Greenpower were reported: There are 324,442 residential customers consuming 130,309 MWh of renewable energy and 19,586 commercial customers consuming 134,045 MWh of renewable energy.[93]

A national emissions trading scheme

Until recently the Australian government indicated that it will not establish a domestic carbon emissions trading scheme in Australia. Nevertheless, in a March 2005 communiqué, the State and Territory Premiers and Chief Ministers announced that a multi-jurisdictional greenhouse gas emissions trading scheme will be developed. A key issue is whether or not the scheme will be able to link in with other international carbon markets. Currently, if a country has not ratified the Kyoto Protocol, domestic trading schemes cannot be linked either to an international or to the European Emissions Trading Schemes.

In September 2005, the Inter-jurisdictional Working Group on Emissions Trading released a consultation paper entitled 'A National Emissions Trading Scheme'.[94] The proposed Scheme is a national cap-and-trade scheme, which is based on achieving the national emissions abatement target of 108% of 1990 levels between 2008-12. It will apply initially to the stationary energy sector (including electricity, coal and gas) and will cover all six greenhouse gases mentioned in the Kyoto Protocol

Permits will be allocated both administratively and by way of auction. The tradeable permit to emit greenhouse gases will entitle the holder to emit 1 tonne of CO_2-e in a year. It is proposed that both annual and long term permits be allocated to provide investor certainty. Non-compliance to surrender permits will be a strict liability civil offence which will attract an automatic monetary penalty. Banking and borrowing provisions, such as those which exist under the *Renewable Energy (Electricity) Act 2000* (Cth), are being considered. Drawing on the experience of other Australian trading schemes, the penalty for non-compliance is likely to be set at a level to encourage compliance and set a price ceiling for the permit market.

To meet the emissions cap, liable parties can choose to either cut their emissions, invest in offset projects or acquire more permits. Offset credits can be generated by planting forests, reducing methane emissions from waste, energy efficient industrial processes and carbon capture and storage. In addition, projects that generate credits under the clean development mechanism (CDM) and joint implementation (JI) mechanisms of the Kyoto Protocol will be recognised for offset credits. The offsets will need to be rigorously verified using widely accepted accounting standards.

The adverse effects of the scheme, as well as any need for structural adjustments, will need to be addressed. Mechanisms should be included to recognise early abatement action by participants and to accommodate new entrants into the market.

---

93 See <http://www.greenpower.gov.au/downloads/reportsaudits/2006Q3Report.pdf> (accessed 14 December 2006).

94 See <http://www.emissionstrading.net.au/__data/assets/pdf_file/413/background.pdf> (accessed 14 December 2006).

New South Wales initiatives on energy and climate change

NSW Greenhouse Plan

In 2003, Premier Bob Carr established the NSW Greenhouse Office, a specialist policy office in the Cabinet Office reporting directly to the Premier. It co-ordinates and develops government policy to adapt to climate change and reduce emissions. It provides whole-of-government advice on climate change and participates in interstate greenhouse forums. It is guided by the NSW Greenhouse Advisory Panel and has responsibility for developing a Greenhouse Strategy for New South Wales.

In December 2005, the NSW government released its Greenhouse Plan.[95] The Plan indicates that New South Wales is responsible for over a quarter of Australia's greenhouse gas emissions. This represents per capita emissions of 23 tonnes per person per year compared with 10 tonnes per person in the UK, Germany and Japan and about 13 tonnes per person in other industrialised countries. Stationary emissions (including fossil fuel combustions in electricity and heat production, and manufacturing and construction industries) make up half of NSW emissions with transport accounting for 15% and agriculture accounting for 14%. The Plan makes it clear that a concerted effort is needed now to slow and reverse projected growth in emissions.

Consequently, the NSW government has committed itself to reducing the State's emissions by 60% by 2050, and to return emissions to 2000 levels by 2025. New South Wales is also advocating that the 60% reductions by 2050 goal be adopted as a national aspirational target. The essential features of the Plan are to:

- educate the community about climate change and build partnerships across the economy through awareness raising campaigns and holding a series of Best Practice Roundtables;
- improve understanding about climate change and begin to develop adaptation strategies to deal with its impacts through research programs, environmental monitoring and capacity building;
- limit the growth of greenhouse emissions while establishing carbon sinks;
- adopting a long-term strategy to avoid dangerous climate change;
- facilitate the uptake by business of new international market opportunities for low-emissions goods and services; and
- work with other national and international governments to work towards a co-ordinated global solution.

The government has also committed $24 million which will include $10 million for Climate Action grants to promote emission reduction technologies, $7.5 million for a new Climate Change Awareness Program, $2 million for a Climate Change Impact Research Program, $2 million for a Climate Change Adaptation Program, and $2.3 million for a new Greenhouse Gas Emissions Reduction Projects Program to fund carbon sequestration, emissions trading and rating heavy vehicle emissions.

---

95 See <http://www.greenhouseinfo.nsw.gov.au/__data/page/927/28-11_FINAL_NSW_GH_Plan_web.pdf> (accessed 24 April 2006).

Creating a carbon sequestration right

The NSW government was the first to recognise a carbon sequestration right as a separate legal right under the *Carbon Rights Legislation Amendment Act 1998* (NSW). It did this in 1998, as a joint initiative between the NSW government and State Forests of New South Wales, when both parties expected that the world's first futures exchange in carbon would be launched on the Sydney Futures Exchange. Although this did not eventuate, the legislation recognises that a carbon credit derived from the planting of forests needs to be identifiable as a legal entity separate from the tree itself. Consequently, the Act defines carbon sequestration and a carbon sequestration right as follows:

> [C]arbon sequestration by a tree or forest means the process by which the tree or forest absorbs carbon dioxide from the atmosphere, and a carbon sequestration right in relation to land means a right conferred on a person by agreement or otherwise to the legal, commercial or other benefit (whether present or future) of carbon sequestration by any existing or future tree or forest on the land after 1990.[96]

The Act amends the *Conveyancing Act 1919* (NSW) to recognise that rights associated with carbon sequestrated by trees and forests from the atmosphere may be a species of forestry right.

A baseline-and-credit greenhouse trading scheme

A baseline-and-credit, as opposed to a cap-and-trade, greenhouse emissions trading scheme is already operating in New South Wales. In 1995, the NSW government made it a licence condition for electricity retailers to adopt greenhouse gas emission benchmarks. A 2001 review of compliance[97] with the licence condition indicated that only two out of 22 retailers had complied with the condition. Consequently, in January 2003, the NSW government introduced an enforceable greenhouse benchmark scheme (the Scheme) for electricity retailers and large users of electricity by enacting the *Electricity Supply Amendment (Greenhouse Gas Emission Reduction) Act 2003* (NSW). The amending legislation inserted Pt 8A into the *Electricity Supply Act 1995* (NSW) (ESA). In addition, the government has made the *Electricity Supply (General) Amendment (Greenhouse Gas Abatement Certificate Scheme) Regulation 2003.*

The ESA requires participants to achieve a benchmark of 7.27 tonnes of carbon dioxide equivalent of greenhouse gas emissions per head of State population by the calendar year 2007, which remains as a benchmark until the calendar year 2012 (s 97B). This amounts to approximately 25% reduction in emissions compared with business as usual. It also makes a broad range of benchmark participants subject to the benchmark, including electricity retailers (as well as generators retailing

---

96 The first forest dedicated to the reduction of greenhouse gases was planted on 10 October 2002. The forest is being established with the cooperation of Integral Energy, Planning NSW and State Forests of NSW. The five-hectare site will slowly be transformed with the planting of 5000 native trees and shrubs. As the plants and shrubs grow they will soak in 50 tonnes of greenhouse gases each year during the forests' 40-year growth cycle. Each tonne can be converted into a carbon credit which could be traded and become of financial value to Integral Energy: see Media Release, NSW Minister for Forestry and Energy, 10 October 2002.

97 Independent Pricing and Regulatory Tribunal, *Electricity distribution and retail licences Compliance report for 2000/01 – Report to the Minister for Energy*, at 4.

electricity), large electricity users, and projects of State significance (s 97BB). In 2005, the definition of 'large customer' was amended to include customers which together with other 'related entities' use 110 GWh or more per year of electricity at a single site in New South Wales, or this amount at more than one site as long as one of the sites uses 50 GWh each year.[98] 'Related entity' of a customer has been defined as a related body corporate of the customer, a joint venture partner, or an entity with which the customer has various relationships under the law of trusts. The Act establishes the NSW Independent Pricing and Regulatory Tribunal (IPART) as the regulatory body that will determine the liability of benchmark participants, and assess their compliance with the Scheme (s 97H). Benchmark participants are also required to lodge an annual greenhouse gas benchmark statement each year with IPART (ESA s 97CB).

The following activities are recognised for the valid creation of a NSW Greenhouse Abatement Certificate (NGAC) equivalent to one tonne of CO_2eq abated: generation of electricity that results in reduced greenhouse gas emissions; reduction in electricity consumption; and carbon sequestration that results in reduced greenhouse gas emissions (s 97DA). Large retail electricity users may elect to be liable directly under the Scheme and create Large User Abatement Certificates (LUACs) from reductions in greenhouse gas emissions associated with reduced consumption (s 97EC(4)).

Participants will be liable for a civil penalty of $10.50 per tonne of CO_2eq target shortfall for the relevant calendar year (the penalty may be CPI indexed under the regulations) (s 97CA(2), (3)). Criminal penalties may also be imposed for failure to comply with the operation of the Scheme, including the failure to co-operate with IPART (ss 97CB(5), 97DD(5), 97EF(7)).

The Greenhouse Gas Benchmark Rules detail the methodology on how the Scheme will operate, for example, the calculations of the benchmark participants targets and possible shortfalls. The Rules are very detailed and cannot be reproduced here but it is essential that they be consulted and applied in practice. They include the following: Greenhouse Gas Benchmark Rule (Compliance) No 1 of 2003; Greenhouse Gas Benchmark Rule (Generation) No 2 of 2003 (3 October 2003); Greenhouse Gas Benchmark Rule (Generation) No 2 of 2003 (11 June 2004); Greenhouse Gas Benchmark Rule (Demand Side Abatement) No 3 of 2003 (3 October 2003); Greenhouse Gas Benchmark Rule (Demand Side Abatement) No 3 of 2003 (11 June 2004); Greenhouse Gas Benchmark Rule (Large User Abatement Certificates) No 4 of 2003; Greenhouse Gas Benchmark Rule (Carbon Sequestration) No 5 of 2003.

The *Electricity Supply (General) Amendment (Greenhouse Gas Abatement Certificate Scheme) Regulation 2003* sets up the abatement certificate scheme under Pt 8A of the Act. The Regulation sets the criteria for the following aspects of the abatement certificate regime. In order to be eligible to create a certificate, the participant must be accredited by the Scheme Administrator. Applications for the accreditation and the transfer of certificates must be made to the Scheme Administrator. A register of accredited abatement certificate providers (ACPs) must be kept. IPART or the Scheme Administrator may at any time conduct or require audits to be conducted of ACPs with respect to the creation of certificates, eligibility for accreditation and compliance with any condition of accreditation.

98 See *Energy Supply (Amendment) Act 2005* (NSW).

The Building Sustainability Index

The *SEPP (Building Sustainability Index: BASIX) 2004* requires all new housing in New South Wales to be designed and built to use 40% less mains supply water and produce 25% lower greenhouse gas emissions than average housing of the same type. The greenhouse gas target rose to 40% from July 2006. Developments will effectively meet the target for greenhouse gas reduction if they include: an efficient hot water system and well designed buildings that make the most of natural cooling, heating and lighting. Good design will reduce the number of days and hours air conditioners need to be used and the required size of air-conditioning systems. The SEPP prevails over any other environmental planning instrument to the extent of any inconsistency and ensures that the BASIX scheme is implemented in a consistent way throughout the State. The SEPP must be read in conjunction with the *Environmental Planning and Assessment Regulation 2000.*

The Regulation was amended by *Environmental Planning and Assessment Amendment (Building Sustainability Index: BASIX) Regulation 2004* to incorporate BASIX provisions into the development assessment process. The Regulations require that a development application must be accompanied by a BASIX certificate, issued no earlier than three months before the date on which the application is made. Together, these pieces of delegated legislation implement the NSW government's commitment to achieving energy and water efficiency outcomes.

The SEPP and Regulations apply across the State to a proposed 'BASIX affected building'. This was initially defined in the Regulation as: single dwelling houses built on a single allotment of land (whether attached or detached); dual occupancy: that is two dwelling houses (whether attached or detached) on a single allotment of land, including strata title dual occupancy; and a guest house, boarding house, lodging house or hostel (including a backpackers hostel), being a building with a gross floor area of less than 300 square metres. However, from 1 October 2005, BASIX applied to all multi-unit construction in New South Wales, and from 1 October 2006 it applied to alterations and additions to all homes. However, the Minister for Planning has agreed to lower the BASIX energy target for high rise residential buildings of six storeys or more. The target has been reduced from 25% to 20% for such buildings. The NSW government agreed to lower the target after extensive lobbying by the Property Council of NSW because of the continued high cost of compliance with BASIX for high rise buildings. Applicants will now need to generate separate BASIX certificates for buildings six storeys and over, and for those that are five storeys and under. Multiple BASIX certificates may be lodged with a single development application in this instance.

From 2007, all homes sold will have to prove that they are either BASIX compliant, or that they have been fitted with water efficiency measures under Sydney Water's Retrofit program.

However, in 2006, the Planning Minister, Frank Sartor, ordered a review of BASIX amidst lobbying by the building industry in the State on the grounds that compliance with BASIX is impacting on housing affordability.[99]

---

99 A Davies, 'Cheaper, not so green homes', *Sydney Morning Herald*, 2 May 2006.

Demand side management

Demand side management (DSM) is a crucial policy strategy that can be adopted along with a range of other measures to reduce greenhouse gas emissions from the stationary energy sector. Essentially, it comprises strategies which encourage all users of electricity to reduce their consumption thus reducing the demand for electricity services. The International Energy Agency[100] defines the goals of DSM as:

- Reduce peak demand especially when the utilisation of power comes close to its limits of availability
- Shift the loads between times of day or even seasons
- Fill the demand valleys to better utilise existing power resources
- Reduce overall demand (strategic savings) in the context of delivering the required energy services by use of less energy (not a reduction in services)
- Provide strategic growth especially to shift between one type of supply to another with more favourable characteristics, for example, in terms of environment.

The NSW government committed itself to achieving demand side management with the passage of the *Energy Administration Amendment (Water and Energy Savings) 2005* (NSW). This Act changes the name of the *Energy Administration Act 1987* to the *Energy and Utilities Administration Act 1987.* It prescribes energy and water savings measures but the focus here is only on the energy provisions.

Part 6A is inserted into the Act and establishes 'designated energy users'. A designated energy user is any State agency or any other person prescribed by a savings order that uses energy. An Energy Savings Fund is established to provide funding to:

- encourage energy savings;
- address peak demand for energy;
- stimulate investment in innovative energy savings measures;
- increase public awareness and acceptance of the importance of energy savings measures;
- develop cost effective energy savings measures that reduce greenhouse gas emissions arising from the use of energy; and
- pay for the contributions made by the State for the purposes of national energy regulation.

The Fund will include payments made by contributions received from designated energy users; money advanced by the Treasurer for the Fund, money appropriated by Parliament, the proceeds of the investment of money in the Fund, money directed or authorised to be paid into the Fund under the Act or any other law; and all money received from voluntary contributions. Money may be paid out of the Fund, on the approval of the Minister, to fund all or any part of the cost of any energy saving measures, the cost of administering the Fund, and the Minister's expenses associated with the Minister's functions under the Act. The Minister may also approve selection criteria to be applied to determine the kinds of energy savings measures that will be eligible for funding. A person applying for funding

100 International Energy Agency *Strategic Plan 2004-2009: IEA Demand Side Management Programme,* <http://dsm.iea.org/NewDSM/Work/plan/DSMStrategy.pdf> (accessed on 4 May 2005).

for an energy savings measure may be required to submit an energy savings action plan detailing the measures, and providing any other information requested by the Minister. In approving payments out of the Fund, the Minister may obtain advice from a committee established under the Act, or any other person the Minister thinks relevant.

The Minister may, by order published in the *Gazette*, require any one or more distribution network service provider to make an annual contribution for a specified financial year to the Energy Savings Fund. The same specifications apply to the Minister's powers to make this order as apply to the placing of an order on State water agencies. The Minister for Energy and Utilities has now placed orders on utilities to make annual contributions to the Savings Funds. Distribution network service providers must make an annual contribution to the Energy Savings Fund for the financial year 1 July 2005. The contributions are as follows: Energy Australia – $18,973,999.00; Integral Energy – $12,050,000.00; Country Energy – $8,977,000.00. These contributions were paid in quarterly instalments on the first day of August 2005, November 2005, February 2006 and May 2006.

Designated energy users are required to prepare draft energy savings action plans. A draft energy savings plan must include the following:

- a description of the designated energy user's current energy usage;
- a list of individual energy savings measures prioritised in terms of water saved, cost effectiveness and potential benefits;
- a statement concerning the energy savings measures included on that list that will be implemented in the four-year period following the approval of the plan.

The Minister may then approve the draft plans after consultation with the designated energy users, and may make such alterations as the Minister thinks fit. Notice of such approval must be given within 14 days. The plan comes into effect the day on which written notice is given and expires on the fourth anniversary of its commencement, unless revoked sooner by the Minister.

The Minister has already declared the State's 200 highest energy users to be 'designated energy users', and has ordered them to prepare draft energy savings action plans for his approval.[101]

The penalty for not submitting a draft savings action plan is $5000. Directors of the corporation are taken to have contravened the Act, and be personally liable, if they knowingly authorised or permitted the contravention. However, it is a defence to prosecution if the defendant can prove that it has a reasonable excuse for not preparing or submitting a plan. Also, the plans do not have to be implemented unless the designated energy users are directed to do so by the Minister by way of regulations. The Minister may establish standing or special committees for the purpose of advising the Minister.

The Minister may require an energy service provider (energy services corporations within the meaning of the *Energy Service Corporations Act 1995* (NSW)) to furnish the Minister with information on the identity of its consumers as well as the amount of energy or water that is being provided to a consumer.

---

101 For the names of the corporations, see *NSW Government Gazette No 132*, 28 October 2005.

NSW Renewable Energy Target

In 2006, the NSW government announced the establishment of a NSW Renewable Energy Target (NRET).[102] The target is 15% of end use consumption by 2020 with an interim target of 10% by 2010. The target will be imposed on all electricity retailers and will require them to purchase their share of renewable energy from accredited renewable generation sources. Retailers will be given individual targets based on their levels of supply to customers. The renewable energy can be sourced from generation occurring anywhere within the National Electricity Market. Retailers will not be allowed to offset GreenPower purchases against their liability under NRET, and there will be no double-dipping between NRET and renewable energy generated to satisfy benchmarks under the Greenhouse Benchmarks Scheme. There will be an enforceable penalty for non-compliance, which will include an automatic CPI escalator. Tradeable renewable energy certificates will be created by generators under certain circumstances. The NSW government is keen to have the NRET function as consistently as possible with the Victorian Renewable Energy Target (VRET)[103] to reduce the costs of compliance for business. To this end, the NSW government is investigating the possibility of NRET being administered by the Victorian Essential Services Commission. It is expected that legislation for the NRET will be enacted in 2007 with the first target level being set for 2008.

102 See <http://www.deus.nsw.gov.au/publications/nret%20explanatory%20paper%20final.pdf> (accessed 17 December 2006).

103 VRET requires 10% end use consumption to be renewable by 2016, <http://www.esc.vic.gov.au/public/Energy/Consultations/VRET/Victorian+Renewable+Energy+Target+Scheme+(VRET).htm> (accessed 17 December 2006).

6

WATER

The world water crisis

It is important to set any discussion about the current status of water law in Australia in a broader international context. This context highlights the fact that water resource management is a significant global problem that has demanded the attention of world leaders. It also emphasises that the earth's water resources are extremely precarious.

Only 2.53% of water on earth is freshwater. The rest is saltwater. Two thirds of all freshwater is locked up in glaciers and permanent snow cover. The available freshwater is reduced by pollution, estimated at 2 million tonnes of waste per day, while global climate change is expected to increase scarcity by 20%. The area of irrigated land is expected to increase 22% in the next 25 years and water withdrawals are expected to increase by 14%. Added to this is the fact that the global population is growing as is per capita use of water. Currently, 50% of people in developing countries are exposed to polluted water while many people live without adequate access to water. In Latin America and the Caribbean this amounts to 15% of the population, in Asia 20% and in Africa 40%. No wonder then that the international community has made water resource management a key sustainability issue.

International initiatives on water

There have been various international initiatives to focus attention on the precarious state of the world's water resources. Two important conferences were held in 1992. These were the Dublin Conference on Water and Development[1] and the United Nations Conference on the Environment and Development (the Rio Conference). The essential principles to emerge from the Dublin Conference were that:

- Water is a finite and valuable resource, essential to sustain life, development and environment.
- Water development and management should be based on a participatory approach involving users, planner and policy-makers at all levels.
- Water has an economic value in all its competing uses and should be recognised as an economic good.

Meanwhile, Chapter 18 of Agenda 21[2] (an outcome of the Rio Conference) focused on the following program areas for the freshwater sector:

---

1 See <http://www.gdrc.org/uem/water/dublin-statement.html> (accessed 26 February 2006).

2 See <http://www.un.org/esa/sustdev/documents/agenda21/> (accessed 26 February 2006).

- integrated water resources development and management;
- water resources assessment;
- protection of water resources, water quality and aquatic ecosystems;
- drinking-water supply and sanitation;
- water and sustainable urban development;
- water for sustainable food production and rural development; and
- the impact of climate change on water resources.

Since 1992, the most significant international initiatives on water have been the declaration by the United Nations in 2000 of the Millennium Development Goals,[3] and the 2002 World Summit on Sustainable Development. In terms of the Millennium Development Goals, all nations agreed to halve by 2015 the proportion of people who are unable to reach or to afford safe drinking water, and the proportion of people who do not have access to basic sanitation. Sections 23-28 of the Plan of Implementation,[4] the outcome of the World Summit on Sustainable Development, are devoted to principles underpinning the protection and management of water. These international principles provide a framework for discussing the management of water resources in Australia.

Australia's water resources

A recent audit of Australian water resources has shown a considerable state of degradation. Most of the river systems in Australia are currently overallocated. One third of rivers are in an extremely poor condition while 40% of rivers show clear signs of degradation. It is estimated that within 20 years the drinking water in Adelaide will fall below World Health Organization salinity standards in two days out of five.

The most recently available report on the state of water resources in New South Wale is the 2003 NSW State of Environment report. [5] The information contained in the report is based on information gathered under the National Land and Water Resources Audit (NLWRA). The Audit commenced in 1997 and reported in 2002 with a mission to 'provide data, information and nationwide assessments of Australia's land, water and biological resources to support sustainable development'. A special study of New South Wales was conducted under the Audit. The NLWRA's main findings were that the State has the poorest aquatic biota condition in the country, with macroinvertebrate communities impaired along 50% of the length of the rivers assessed. The environmental condition of 97% of the assessed river length in New South Wales has been modified as a result of: catchment disturbance from land-use changes and clearing; elevated levels of nutrients (especially total phosphorus) and suspended sediments; altered hydrologic regimes; and modified aquatic habitat.

---

3 See <http://www.un.org/millenniumgoals/> (accessed 26 February 2006).

4 See <http://www.johannesburgsummit.org/html/documents/summit_docs/2309_planfinal.htm> (accessed 26 February 2006).

5 See <http://www.epa.nsw.gov.au/soe/soe2003/chapter5/chp_5.1.htm#5.1.47> (accessed 10 March 2006.

It is no surprise then that over the past 12 years Australian governments have been working together significantly to reform the water sector and to place it on a more ecologically sustainable footing. This is in spite of the fact that the Commonwealth government has no express constitutional power to manage water resources. Such powers are vested in the States (see Chapter 1).

The beginning of water reform in Australia

In 1994, the Council of Australian Governments (COAG) adopted a strategic framework for the reform of the Australian water industry covering:

- natural resource management;
- pricing;
- a more rigorous approach to future investment;
- trading in water entitlements; and
- institutional reform.

A key component of the COAG agreement was that the principle of ecologically sustainable development[6] should underpin all water management in Australia, in recognition of the fact that past practices of over-allocation have impacted heavily on species, river health, ecosystems and wetlands.

As mentioned in Chapter 1, the Commonwealth agreed at COAG to make special payments in the order of $16 billion over 1997-98 and 2005-08 to States and Territories upon satisfactory progress in implementing National Competition Policy (NCP) reforms. Eligibility for these payments was to be assessed by the National Competition Council (NCC) in June 1997, 1999 and 2001.[7] In 1995 the COAG agreement on water reform was linked to National Competition Policy payments. The First Tranche of payments did not impose any obligations with respect to water. However, the Second Tranche payments in 1999-2000 depended on the implementation of a strategic framework for the efficient and sustainable reform of Australian water. A key feature of this process was that rights to water be separated from rights to land and that property rights in water be recognised. Third Tranche payments depended on States giving full effect to and continuing to observe all COAG agreements on water. The progress of the States in implementing the water reform agenda was closely monitored by the National Competition Council. This function has now been taken over by the National Water Commission.

The National Water Initiative

In August 2003, COAG met to give further impetus to the national water reform process, especially to the creation of a water trading market. At its meeting COAG agreed to:

6 This is defined as adherence to the precautionary principle, intergenerational equity, the conservation of biological diversity and the polluter pays principle; see the 1993 Intergovernmental Agreement on the Environment.

7 Ibid at 4.

- increase the productivity and efficiency of water use;
- sustain rural and urban communities; and
- ensure the health of rivers and groundwater systems.

COAG concluded that investment, in the context of fully functioning water markets, in new, more efficient production system is being hampered by uncertainty over the long-term access to water in some areas. COAG agreed to develop a National Water Initiative which was further articulated at its meeting on 24 June 2004.

The Commonwealth, State and Territory governments subsequently entered into two agreements namely, the Intergovernmental Agreement on a National Water Initiative (IGANWI)[8] and the Intergovernmental Agreement on Addressing Water Overallocation and Achieving Environmental Objectives in the Murray-Darling Basin (IGAMDB).[9] Together they represent the most significant policy statements on water resource management to date. The IGANWI was signed by, and will be implemented by the Commonwealth, NSW, Victorian, Queensland, South Australian, ACT and Northern Territory governments. The Tasmanian and Western Australian governments did not sign, not being part of the proposed eastern seaboard water market. The IGAMDB was signed by, and will be implemented by the Commonwealth, NSW, Victorian, South Australian and ACT governments.

Some of the key elements of the IGANWI are the following:

Water access entitlements and planning framework

Here, the main features are the security and commercial certainty of water access entitlements and the return of previously overallocated or overdrawn surface and groundwater systems to environmentally sustainable levels of extraction. The governments agreed that :

- security and commercial certainty of access entitlements need to be enhanced by:
    - o clearly specifying the statutory nature of the entitlements;
    - o clearly assigning the risks arising from future changes to the consumptive pool;
    - o having a compatible system of water access entitlements across jurisdictions to improve investment certainty;
    - o being competitively neutral and minimising transaction costs on water trades, and
    - o protecting the integrity of water access entitlements from unregulated growth in interception through land-use change (eg, farms dams and bores; interception and storing of overland flows; and large-scale plantation forestry).

With respect to environmental factors, the governments agreed that:

- water sources and their dependent ecosystems need to be statutorily protected;

8 See <http://www.coag.gov.au/meetings/250604/iga_national_water_initiative.pdf> (accessed 26 February 2006).

9 See <http://www.coag.gov.au/meetings/250604/iga_water_overallocation_murray_darling.pdf> (accessed 26 February 2006).

- a planning process must ensure that adequate productive, environmental and other public benefit considerations are taken into account;
- surface and groundwater systems must be managed in accordance with adaptive management principles;
- water systems must be returned to environmentally sustainable levels of extraction;
- water systems of high conservation value must be identified and managed; and
- Indigenous needs must be recognised.

It was also agreed that States must modify their existing legislation and administrative regimes where necessary to ensure that their water access entitlement and planning frameworks incorporate these features. More specifically, the consumptive use of water will require a water access entitlement, separate from the land, which must be a perpetual or open-ended share of the consumptive pool as determined by a water plan. The entitlements must be: exclusive, able to be traded, given, bequeathed or leased; be able to be subdivided or amalgamated; be mortgagable; be enforced and enforceable; and be recorded in publicly accessible water registers.

According to the agreement, entitlement holders must bear the risks of any reduction in their water allocation if the consumptive pool is reduced as a result of seasonal or long-term changes in climate and periodic natural events such as bushfires and drought. If their allocation is reduced as a result of better scientific understanding of sustainable water extraction levels:

- entitlement holders must bear the risk until 2014;
- after 2014, and for each subsequent 10-year period, risks must be borne by entitlement holders to the extent of the first 3% of the reduction;
- the State and Commonwealth governments will share one-third: two-thirds respectively of the risks in reduction between 3% and 6%;
- thereafter, the States and Commonwealth will then share any reduction greater than 6% equally.

Environmental water must be given statutory recognition and have the same degree of security as water access entitlements, and may be traded on the temporary water market when not required to meet environmental outcomes. Water plans must secure ecological outcomes and resource security outcomes by determining the share in the consumptive pool and the rules to allocate water during the life of the plan. Substantial progress must have been made by 2010 towards adjusting all overallocated and/or overused systems.

Water markets and trading

It is clear that the establishment of a water trading market has been a specific policy imperative of COAG since the early days of the water reform process in 1994. The NWI gave added impetus to this phenomenon. Under the NWI, the States and Territories agreed to facilitate the operation of efficient water markets between States and Territories, where water systems are shared or hydrologic connections will permit water trading. Institutional and regulatory arrangements must be in place by 2007 to facilitate interstate and intrastate trade, and manage differences in entitlement reliability, supply losses, supply source constraints, trading between systems and cap requirements. In particular, any barriers to the temporary trade of water *must be immediately removed*. Importantly, *barriers to permanent trade out of water irrigation areas must also be immediately removed up to an annual threshold limit of 4% of total water entitlement of that area*, subject to a review, by 2009 with a move to *full and open trade by 2014 at the latest*, except in the southern Murray-Darling Basin where action to remove barriers to trade are provided for separately. However, the trading aspects of the NWI will be accelerated as a result of the Summit on the Southern Murray-Darling Basin held in November 2006. Permanent interstate trade in the southern MDB States commenced on 1 January 2007.[10]

Best practice water pricing

The governments agreed to implement water pricing and institutional arrangements to promote the economically efficient and sustainable use of water resources, water infrastructure assets, and government resources devoted to the management of water. Pricing must also ensure sufficient revenue streams to:

- allow the efficient delivery of services;
- facilitate the efficient functioning of water markets;
- give effect to the user pays principle;
- avoid perverse or unintended pricing outcomes; and
- provide mechanisms for the release of unallocated water.

In particular, the governments have agreed to move continuously towards upper bound pricing by 2008 and by 2006 to develop appropriate pricing policies for recycled and stormwater and trade wastes, as well as the development of national guidelines for customers' water accounts that provide information of their water use compared with equivalent households in the community. States will also be required to report independently, publicly and on an annual basis to benchmark pricing and service quality for metropolitan, non-metropolitan and rural water delivery agencies.

Urban water reform

There were significant suggestions for reform of the urban water sector under the NWI which have resulted in a number of recent initiatives.

Water Efficiency Labelling Scheme

Under the NWI, COAG agreed to enact a Water Efficiency Labelling Scheme. This has resulted in the enactment of the *Water Efficiency Labelling Scheme Act 2005* (Cth) (WELS) and the gazetting of the *Water Efficiency Labelling and Standards Regulations 2005* (Cth). Complementary legislation and Regulations exist in the States and Territories. The *Water Efficiency Labelling Scheme Act 2005* (NSW) commenced on 27 April 2005. The scheme covers showerheads, washing machines, dishwashers and

10 See <http://www.pm.gov.au/docs/key_outcomes_MDB_summit.pdf> (accessed 17 December 2006).

toilets and is likely to cut water consumption by 5% per annum which amounts to 58 billion litres a year.

WELS essentially provides for water efficiency labelling and the making of water efficiency standards. The Scheme is a national co-operative scheme between the Commonwealth and the States. Under Pt 4 of the Act, the Minister may determine that water-use or water-saving products are WELS products, but the Minister can only do this if there is agreement amongst a majority of participating States and Territories. Such a determination must set out the WELS standard for the product. The standards must set out: criteria for rating the products in relation to either/both water efficiency and general performance, and also the requirements for communicating WELS ratings on product labels.

'Smart water mark'

Under the NWI, COAG also agreed to develop and implement a labelling system for household gardening equipment; review the effectiveness of current water restrictions; and manage leakage, excess pressure, overflows and other maintenance needs. A Smart Approved Water Mark scheme has now been established which proposes a voluntary labelling scheme.[11]

National Guidelines for Water Recycling

Consistently with the NWI, National Guidelines for Water Recycling were developed by the Natural Resource Management Ministerial Council and Environment Protection and Heritage Council in October 2005. The Guidelines were released under the auspices of the National Water Quality and Management Strategy and contain an Overview and Risk Management Approach.

The Guidelines reiterate that widespread drought and population movement to Australia's cities have increased pressure on fresh water supplies. National guidelines on water recycling are needed because State and Territory governments have been developing their own, resulting in inconsistencies and a lack of uniformity.

The Guidelines provide a generic risk-assessment and management framework that is applicable to all types of water recycling but it also provides specific guidelines for the uses of recycled water identified as priority uses. These include:

- Large-scale treated sewage and grey water to be used for:
    - residential garden watering, car washing, toilet flushing and clothes washing;
    - irrigation for urban recreational and open space, agricultural and horticulture;
    - fire protection and fire fighting systems; and
    - industrial uses, including cooling water.
- Grey water treated on-site to be used for residential garden watering, car washing, toilet flushing and clothes washing.

The risk-management framework comprises 12 elements, based on the Australian Drinking Water Guidelines, that need to be addressed and these are grouped into

11 See <http://www.wsaa.asn.au/smartwatermark/smartabout.htm> (accessed 17 December 2006).

the following four general areas: commitment to the responsible use and management of recycled water; system analysis and management; supporting requirements, including employee training, community involvement, R&D, and systems for documentation and reporting; and a review which includes an evaluation and audit process to ensure that the management system is functioning satisfactorily.

The National Water Commission

The Australian government has established a National Water Commission which has a number of general and specific functions. Its general functions are:

- to assist with the implementation of the National Water Initiative (NWI) and to promote the objectives and outcomes of the NWI;
- on the request of the Minister, to make recommendations to the Commonwealth, COAG or the Minister on matters of national significance relating to water; and
- to advise the Commonwealth or COAG whether or not State and Territory governments are implementing their commitments under the NWI or the COAG water reform agenda and, if not, to recommend an appropriate fine to be levied.

To assist with the implementation of the NWI, the Australian Government Water Fund (worth $2 billion) was established by the Australian government to invest in water infrastructure, improved water management, and better practices in the stewardship of Australia's scarce water resources. The Fund comprises three programs: Water Smart Australia; Raising National Water Standards; and the Community Water Grants programs. The most relevant fund for the urban water sector is the Water Smart Australia program. It will fund large-scale projects that will make a significant contribution to the sustainable and efficient management of Australia's water resources. In particular, funding will be given to projects that: desalinate water for use in cities and towns; recycle and reuse stormwater, 'grey' water and waste water from sewage; provide alternatives to ocean outfalls and the better management of sewage in our coastal cities, or develop water efficient housing design. As such, the Water Smart program provides a likely source of funding to private sector investment in the urban water services sector.

New Department for the Environment and Water Resources

On 25 January 2007, in an address to the National Press Club,[12] the Prime Minister announced that he will be writing to all State and Territory leaders to request them to transfer the power of water management over the Murray-Darling Basin to the Commonwealth government. This is likely to have a significant bearing on the way that water is managed in the Basin and will fundamentally alter the water law framework in New South Wales. Since this proposal is in its early stages it is too early to comment on these changes. Consequently, the law, as it currently exists, governing the management of water resources in the Murray-Darling Basin and New South Wales, is presented in this chapter.

---

12 See <http://www.pm.gov.au/news/speeches/speech2341.html> (accessed 27 January 2007).

The Prime Minister's announcement includes the establishment of a new Department to be known as the Department for the Environment and Water Resources. The Honourable Malcolm Turnbull has been appointed the Minister for the Environment and Water Resources. This development is not surprising given the establishment by the Prime Minister, on 26 September 2006, of a new Office of Water Resources in his office. The Office was established to provide and coordinate policy advice across Commonwealth agencies and report directly to the Prime Minister. More specifically, the Office was established to further implement the National Water Initiative and the Living Murray Initiative (mentioned below). The Prime Minister's then Parliamentary Secretary, Malcolm Turnbull, was appointed as head of the Office.

In addition to requesting State and Territory governments to transfer power over the Murray-Darling Basin to the Commonwealth, the Prime Minister has announced a 10 point plan, with $10 billion in associated funding, to address over-allocation and efficiency issues in the Basin. The details of the funding are as follows:

- $6 billion for irrigation infrastructure especially the lining or piping of major delivery channels, improved metering and the installation of drip systems. Under this package:
    - $3 billion will come from Commonwealth funding and $750 million from irrigation companies. 50% of the savings will be retained by irrigators while the other 50% will be held by the Commonwealth for water security and sustaining river systems and wetlands,
    - $1.5 billion will be spent on farm water efficiency,
    - $225 million will be spent on installing accurate water meters, and
    - $500 million will be devoted to improving the efficiency and effectiveness of river operations and storages;
- $3 billion will be used to correct the problem of over-allocation in the Murray-Darling Basin by adjusting water entitlements;
- $480 million will be allocated for a significant upgrade of the Bureau of Meteorology;
- a Taskforce will investigate the potential for further land and water development in the Northern Territory;
- further restrictions on extractions will be imposed to restore the Great Artesian Basin;
- applications by State and Territory governments to the Australian Water Fund (see above) to support urban water utilities will have to be accompanied by a commitment to building further infrastructure, such as dams.

The Murray-Darling Basin

The Murray-Darling Basin extends across four States including New South Wales, Victoria, South Australia, and Queensland, as well the entire Australian Capital Territory. The Basin is just over one million square kilometres in extent and comprises about 14% of the continental landmass. It includes the three largest rivers in Australia, including the Darling River at 2740 kilometres, the Murray at 2530 kilometres and the Murrumbidgee at 1690 kilometres. All of NSW's inland rivers drain into the Basin and, for this reason, the various initiatives that have been developed for the Basin have a bearing on law and policy in New South Wales.

The Basin is an extremely important area in terms of biodiversity and ecology, although human activities have seriously impacted on these aspects of the Basin. There are also approximately 30,000 wetlands in the Murray-Darling Basin of which 12 have been listed under the Ramsar *Convention on Wetlands*. The main environmental impacts in the Basin include the over-allocation of water, changed water flows, land clearing, increasing in-stream and dryland salinity, and weeds and feral pests.[13]

Murray-Darling Basin Act 1993 (Cth)

The *Murray-Darling Basin Act 1993*, which was preceded by the 1992 Murray-Darling Basin Agreement, provides the legal framework for the management of the Basin's natural and environmental resources. The Agreement is analogous to transboundary watercourse agreements between sovereign states. It established the Murray-Darling Basin Ministerial Council (MDBMC) comprising the Commonwealth, State and Territory governments. The Murray-Darling Basin Commission (MDBC) is the executive arm of the Commission and comprises representatives of the relevant State, Territory and Commonwealth government agencies with responsibility for land, water and the environment. A Community Advisory Committee has been established to advise the Council. The functions of the Commission are to set the policy and direction for natural resources management in the Basin, and to promote and co-ordinate effective planning and management for the equitable sustainable and efficient use of water, land and other resources.[14]

The 1997 Cap on extractions

One of the most important early interventions in over-allocation in the Murray-Darling Basin was the imposition in 1997 of 'the Cap' which limits extractions to those allowed in 1993-94 and requires water needs for future irrigation to be met within the Cap. The Cap marked the end of the expansionary phase of water industry in the Murray-Darling Basin, and highlighted the need for a reallocation of water. In 2000, the MDBMC commissioned a comprehensive review of the operation of the Cap on water diversions from the Basin's rivers. The key conclusions and recommendations were that:

- the Cap should be maintained as it is an essential first step towards achieving a balance between environmental needs and consumptive use;
- there is no certainty that the current level of the Cap represents a sustainable level of diversions;
- the Cap has ensured security of supply at a valley level and provided a framework within which water trading and related reforms could be developed;
- all forms of water use should be included in the Cap, such as diversions from floodplain and overland flows, farm dams and tree plantations, as they are recognised and can be quantified;

13 See generally <http://www.deh.gov.au/water/basins/murray-darling.html> (accessed 16 January 2007).

14 *Murray-Darling Basin Act 1993* (Cth) s 9.

- groundwater should be managed on an integrated basis with surface water within the spirit of the Cap;
- intrastate equity issues outside the jurisdiction of the Commission should be dealt with by the particular government concerned;
- a high priority should be given to the finalisation of the compliance tools (computer simulation models) to determine Cap compliance; and
- a Sustainable Rivers Audit should be developed and implemented.

It should be noted that all water sharing plans developed in New South Wales (see below) for water management areas in the Murray-Darling Basin refer to the 1997 Cap on extractions. Many of these plans refer to the Cap to set the maximum amount of water available for allocation[15] and yet, as the Review of the Cap shows, there is uncertainty about whether or not this level of extraction is sustainable.

1999 Murray-Darling Basin Salinity Audit and 2001-15 Salinity Strategy

Another significant initiative of the MDBC was the conducting of a salinity audit in 1999 which identified serious salinity risks for the Basin. Dryland salinity is one of the most serious environmental problems facing Australian natural resource managers. Although it might well be a natural phenomenon in Australia it has been exacerbated by a number of inappropriate land use practices. These include the clearing of native vegetation, urban development, river regulation, and the irrigation of crops and pastures. Consequently, the 2001-15 Salinity Strategy was developed. There are nine key elements to the Strategy including:

- developing capacity to implement the Strategy;
- identifying values and assets at risk;
- setting salinity targets;
- managing trade-offs with the available within-valley options;
- implementing salinity and catchment management plans;
- redesigning farming systems;
- targeting reforestation and vegetation management;
- constructing salt interception works; and
- ensuring Basin-wide accountability, monitoring, evaluating and reporting.

As part of the Strategy, the MDBC will receive audits every five years for each valley so as to assess impacts on river salinity and progress towards targets. The Strategy itself will be reviewed in 2007 and 2015.

2002 Murray-Darling Basin Integrated Catchment Management Framework

This policy was prepared by the MDBMC and its Community Advisory Committee and focuses on providing governments with a consistent, uniform decision-making process, and encouraging greater co-operation in the use of water. It sets out a way

15 See, eg, cl 30 of the Water Sharing Plan for the Gwydir Regulated River Water Source, <http://www.dipnr.nsw.gov.au/water/sharing/pdf/gwydirreg_gazetted.pdf> (accessed 14 March 2006).

forward for determining the targets for water sharing, water quality and biodiversity in the Murray-Darling Basin Valley. It also acknowledges some serious issues that need to be resolved which include the continuing decline in water quality and ecosystems, the competition and conflict between agricultural, urban and environmental sectors for water resources and the fact that the Murray-Darling Basin land, water and other environmental resources are often overused.

The Living Murray

The Living Murray is one of the most significant programs attempting to address the natural resource management crisis facing the River Murray. It comprises four key program areas: water recovery; statutory support; environmental delivery; and works and measures. The program is administered by the Murray-Darling Basin Commission, through The Living Murray Board.[16] The 2003 *Intergovernmental Agreement on Addressing Water Overallocation and Achieving Environmental Objectives in the Murray-Darling Basin* (IGAMDB), mentioned above, is a key element to the Living Murray program. It establishes the framework to implement the governments' commitment to:

- invest $500 million to address water allocation in the MDB;
- implement arrangements for cost-effective, permanent recovery of water;
- achieve the agreed environmental objectives of the Living Murray First Step decision;
- provide water on an ongoing basis to meet agreed environmental objectives in the MDB; and
- improve management of environmental water in the MDB.

Under the First Step decision, an average of 500 gigalitres of water per year (built up over five years), must be released into the river system, at six critical ecological sites.

These initiatives in the Murray-Darling Basin inevitably have a bearing on the management of water and other natural resources in New South Wales.

The New South Wales Water Management Act 2000

As mentioned above, the reform of water law in the States and Territories is required as part of the COAG agreement to reform the Australian water sector. Each of the States and Territories has passed legislation to give effect to the agreement, and the legislation is still being continually amended to incorporate crucial aspects of the 2003 National Water Initiative. In New South Wales, the Act is known as the *Water Management Act 2000* (NSW) (WMA) and came into effect on 1 July 2004. It must be read together with significant amendments to the Act in 2004 and 2005. The WMA must also be situated within the context of the natural resource reforms which occurred in New South Wales in 2003 (see Chapter 7). These reforms, represented by the *Native Vegetation Act 2003* (NSW), *Catchment Management Act 2003*

---

16 See also the 2004 The Living Murray Business Plan which deals with the following: Targets; Water Recovery; Water Application (establishing the process for developing watering plans for the assets and Living Murray Environmental Watering Plan – Interim Arrangements); Accounting for Environmental Water; Consultation and Communication, and Risk Management, Monitoring, Audit and Review.

(NSW) and the *Natural Resources Commission Act 2003* (NSW), have attempted to integrate water resource management within the overall framework for managing natural resources and native vegetation on a catchment basis.

It is also important to note that, where water sharing plans have not been made for a water management area in New South Wales, the *Water Act 1912* (NSW) continues to apply.

State's water rights and abolition of common law riparian rights

The WMA makes it quite clear that the State's water rights are vested in the Crown (s 392) and that any right that the owner of riparian land would have at common law with respect to the flow of any river, estuary or lake through or past the land, or to the taking or using of water from any such river, estuary or lake, is abolished (s 393). Consequently, the right to use water arises only as a result of the licensing process. There are a few exceptions. These include: basic landholder rights, which allow a landholder to take water for domestic consumption and stock watering without a licence (s 52); harvestable rights, which allow landholders to retain 10% of rainwater run off (s 53); and native title rights, whereby an Aboriginal community can take water without a licence but *only* if its native title rights have been determined under the *Native Title Act 1993* (Cth) (WMA s 54).

Under amendments made by the *Water Management Amendment Act 2004* (the 2004 amendments), owners or occupiers of land recently subdivided must abide by any restrictions placed on their rights to take water, for domestic purposes and stock watering purposes, by the Regulations. Also, the amendments make it clear that 'stock watering' relates to 'stock being raised on the land but does not include the use of water in connection with the raising of stock animals on an intensive commercial basis that are housed or kept in feedlots or buildings while they are being raised' (s 52(3)).

Objects

The objects of legislation are important as they may be used by administrators and the courts to interpret statutory obligations especially where provisions of the Act are ambiguous. The objects of the WMA reflect the essential goals of the COAG water reform agreement. They are to provide for the sustainable and integrated management of the water sources of the State for the benefit of both present and future generations and, in particular:

- (a) to apply the principles of ecologically sustainable development, and
- (b) to protect, enhance and restore water sources, their associated ecosystems, ecological processes and biological diversity and their water quality, and
- (c) to recognise and foster the significant social and economic benefits to the State that result from the sustainable and efficient use of water, including:
  - (i) benefits to the environment, and
  - (ii) benefits to urban communities, agriculture, fisheries, industry and recreation, and
  - (iii) benefits to culture and heritage, and
  - (iv) benefits to the Aboriginal people in relation to their spiritual, social, customary and economic use of land and water,

(d) to recognise the role of the community, as a partner with government, in resolving issues relating to the management of water sources,
(e) to provide for the orderly, efficient and equitable sharing of water from water sources,
(f) to integrate the management of water sources with the management of other aspects of the environment, including the land, its soil, its native vegetation and its native fauna,
(g) to encourage the sharing of responsibility for the sustainable and efficient use of water between the Government and water users,
(h) to encourage best practice in the management and use of water. (s 3)

The objects of the WMA reflect not only the ethos of the COAG water reform process. The objects and the water management principles (s 5) also reflect the principles of ecologically sustainable development as discussed in Chapter 1.

Strategic planning for water

Another significant feature of the WMA is that for the first time in New South Wales a legislative framework is in place to plan strategically for the use of water. This is provided for by requiring the Governor, by order published in the Gazette, to establish a State Water Management Outcomes Plan[17] (SWMOP) for the development, conservation, management and control of the State's water resources in furtherance of the objects of this Act. All water management plans made under the WMA must be consistent with the SWMOP.

The objects of a SWMOP are as follows:

(a) to set the over-arching policy context, targets and strategic outcomes for the management of the State's water sources, having regard to:
  (i) relevant environmental, social and economic considerations, and
  (ii) the results of any relevant monitoring programs,
(b) to promote the water management principles established by this Act,
(c) to give effect to any government policy statement in relation to salinity strategies. (s 6)

In addition, the Minister is required, by order published in the Gazette, to classify water sources for the purposes of this Act. Water sources are to be classified as follows:

(a) as to the extent to which they are at risk (that is, the extent to which harm to the water source or its dependent ecosystems is likely to occur),
(b) as to the extent to which they are subject to stress (that is, the extent to which harm to the water source or its dependent ecosystems has occurred or is occurring),
(c) as to the extent of their conservation value (that is, the extent to which their intrinsic value merits protection from risk and stress). (s 7)

Classes of environmental water

Classes of environmental water are recognised for the first time under the WMA. The classes include:

---

17 See <http://www.dlwc.nsw.gov.au/care/water/sharing/pdf/swmoppart1.pdf> (accessed 24 March 2006).

(i) water that is committed by management plans for fundamental ecosystem health or other specified environmental purposes, either generally or at specified times or in specified circumstances, and that cannot, to the extent committed, be taken or used for any other purpose ('planned environmental water'),

(ii) water that is committed by conditions of access licences for specified environmental purposes, either generally or at specified times or in specified circumstances ('adaptive environmental water') (s 8). Such water may be committed by a licence holder to the environment for altruistic purposes.

Rules for the identification, establishment and maintenance of each class of environmental water ('environmental water rules') must be established for all of the water sources in the State, by way of incorporation in a management plan, as soon as practicable. A management plan must contain provisions relating to adaptive environmental water. Note that the environmental water rules relating to a water source do not need to specify that a minimum quantity of water is required to be present in the water sources at all times (s 8(2)).

As a result of amendments to the WMA in 2005,[18] s 8(1A) was inserted into the Act to provide that a management plan must commit water as 'planned environmental water' in at least two of the following ways:

- by reference to the commitment of the physical presence of water in the water source;
- by reference to the long-term average annual commitment of water as planned environmental water;
- by reference to the water that is not committed after the commitments to basic landholder rights, and for sharing and extraction under any other rights, have been met.

Section 8A was also inserted into the Act as a result of the 2005 amendments. It provides that 'planned environmental water' may be provided for the water source when the Minister cancels a supplementary access licence, and any other category or subcategory of licence held by the Minister. Such water may only be used for the specific purpose identified in the management plan.

Sections 8B, 8C, 8D and 8E, relating to 'adaptive environmental water', are also inserted into the Act. Section 8B states that, if a management plan so provides, the holder of an access licence can request the Minister to impose an adaptive environmental water condition on the whole or part of the access licence (eg, for altruistic reasons so that the water can be used for environmental rather than consumptive purposes). But before imposing an adaptive environmental water condition on an access licence, the Minister must approve a special plan which sets out the way in which the condition will be implemented. The plan must form part of the adaptive environmental water condition. This condition may be amended or revoked by the Minister at the request of the licence holder.

Section 8C gives the Minister some flexibility with respect to managing 'adaptive environmental water' by dispensing with the need to follow the licensing provisions in Pt 2 of Chapter 3. This will be the case where an access licence is

---

18 See *Water Management Amendment Act 2005* (NSW).

granted to the Minister, a catchment management authority or other public body provided that:

- works result in water savings in the system (the water source to which the management plan applies excluding); and
- the share component of the licence is equivalent to the value of water savings being made in the system; and
- an adaptive environmental water condition is imposed on the licence.

Section 8D provides that, if the relevant management plan so provides, the Minister may keep an access licence surrendered by the holder of the licence or transfer it to a catchment management authority or other public body and even change the licence to a different category if:

- the licence has been surrendered as a result of water savings made from water recycling, works or other measures; and
- the share component of the licence is equivalent to the value of water savings being made in the system; and
- an adaptive environmental water condition is imposed on the licence.

Section 8E stipulates that an adaptive environmental water condition is a mandatory condition when it is attached to an access licence, and the terms of the condition must further the objectives of the relevant management plan. If a condition requires water to be left in the water source for environmental purposes, then the water allocation account must be debited when the water is available. However, if the condition requires that the water be taken from a water source, the water allocation account must be debited when it is taken. For the purposes of auditing compliance, a licence to which s 8C relates must not be accounted for as extraction whereas a licence to which ss 8B or 8D apply must be accounted for as extraction. An adaptive environmental water condition may be the subject of a dealing in accordance with the Act, if the special plan attached to the condition so provides.

Water management plans

From a strategic planning perspective, one of the most significant innovations is the requirement that water management plans be developed for all water management areas in New South Wales. These may be made with respect to water sharing,[19] water use, drainage management, floodplain management, aquifer interference activities and environmental protection provisions (Pt 3).

State Water Management Outcomes Plan

As mentioned above, all water management plans must be consistent with the SWMOP and will be supplemented by Implementation Plans (IPs) prepared by the Department of Land and Water Conservation. The IPs will set out detailed rules for river flows and water access as well as transfer principles and rules supporting the trade of water entitlements.[20]

19 For water sharing plans currently made, see <http://www.dlwc.nsw.gov.au/care/water/sharing/index.html> (accessed on 24 March 2006).

20 WMA Pt 5.

Core provisions

With respect to each of the water management plans, the Act stipulates the core provisions to be included in the plans. For example, all of the water management plans which have been made in NSW are water sharing plans and the core provisions of these plans must deal with the following matters:

(a) the establishment of environmental water rules and provisions relating to adaptive environmental water;
(b) the identification of water to satisfy basic landholder rights;
(c) the identification of water for extraction under access licences;
(d) the establishment of access licence dealing rules for the area or water source, although s 20(4)(b) stipulates that a water sharing plan must not deal with any matter that is already dealt with under the access licence dealing principles made under s 71Z(2) of the WMA (see below);
(e) the establishment of a bulk access regime for the extraction of water under access licences, having regard to the rules already mentioned in (a)-(e) above. (s 20)

Significantly, if water management plans include any environment protection provisions, controlling development in a water management area, these must be included in the relevant regional environmental planning policy (ss 34, 46). These provisions go some way towards ensuring integration between environmental planning instruments under the *Environmental Planning and Assessment Act 1979* (NSW) and the WMA.

Making the plan

There is provision in the WMA for water management plans to be made either by water management committees or by the Minister. Where a committee is constituted, the following interested and affected parties will be represented: water user groups, conservation groups, local government, catchment management boards, local Aboriginal communities, numerous government agencies and 'other interests as required'.[21] The management committee is required to take into account the socio-economic impact of a draft plan as well as any provisions of any relevant catchment actions plan under the *Catchment Management Authorities Act 2003* (NSW). Requiring consideration of catchment action plans, a provision inserted by the 2004 amendments, is another indication of an attempt by the NSW government to better integrate natural resource management across the State. The WMA spells out the procedures for making a management plan which include public exhibition of the plan (ss 36-41). A draft plan made by water management committees must be approved by the Minister.[22] The WMA also provides that, if a management committee fails to prepare a draft management plan, in accordance with its terms of reference, the Minister can make a Minister's plan (s 15(3)).

However, given the urgent need for water management plans to be developed for highly stressed rivers, all of the plans have been developed by the Minister in

21 WMA Pt 2.

22 For a critical appraisal of Water Management Committees, see R Lyster, '(De)regulating the rural environment' (2001) 18 *EPLJ* 447.

accordance with his powers under the Act (s 50) to make plans for a water management area for which there is currently no water management plan, and which extend to the making of a plan even if a draft management plan has been submitted by a committee (s 50(5)). The plans are all water sharing plans. As part of the 2004 amendments, before making a Minister's plan, the Minister must get the concurrence of the Minister for the Environment (s 50(3)).

The right to challenge the validity of management plans, and the exercise of any plan-making functions by the Minister, a management committee and the Director-General, is limited to three months from the date that a plan, or any amendments to a plan, are gazetted. Challenges may only be brought before the Land and Environment Court (s 47).

The making of a Minister's plan was challenged on appeal in the NSW Supreme Court in *Nature Conservation Council of NSW v The Minister*.[23] The subject of the appeal was the making by the Minister of the following environmental health water rule in the *Water Sharing Plan for the Gwydir Regulated River Water Source 2003*:

> (a) water volume in excess of the long-term limit established in clause 30 of this Plan may not be taken from this water source and used for any purpose.

Clause 30 (Volume of long-term extraction limit) provides:

> This Plan establishes a long-term extraction limit for this water source being the lesser of:
> (a) the long-term average annual extraction from this water source that would occur with the water storages and water use development that existed in 1999/2000, the share components existing at the commencement of this Plan and application of the water management rules defined in this Plan, or
> (b) the long-term average annual extraction from this water source that would occur under Cap baseline conditions.

The Nature Conservation Council asserted that s 8(2) of the WMA required that the Plan contain 'provisions for the identification, establishment and maintenance' of water that would be committed to fundamental ecosystem health at all times. Instead, the part of the Plan which purported to comply with this obligation was simply a volume of water *in excess* of a long-term extraction limit. On appeal, the Supreme Court upheld the NCC's submission. The court held that the Act requires that water is constantly provided for, and available, absent acute drought conditions, to protect fundamental ecosystem health. A rule expressed in terms of an amount in excess of an extraction limit was not a rule within the meaning of s 8(2) of the Act.

In spite of finding that the environmental health water rule did not comply with the WMA, the court did not declare the water sharing plan to be invalid. It relied on the decision of the High Court of Australia in *Project Blue Sky Inc v Australian Broadcasting Authority*.[24] In that case, the High Court held that failure to comply with a statutory requirement does not necessarily result in invalidity. In determining whether or not invalidity results, a court should ascertain whether or not it is Parliament's intention that the breach of the legislation result in invalidity. Where a declaration of invalidity may result in commercial inconvenience (such as having to amend or cancel access licences already granted on the basis of a water sharing plan) the court will find that Parliament does not intend to have the Plan declared invalid.

23 [2005] NSWCA 9.

24 (1998) 194 CLR 355.

The court also rejected a submission made by the NCC that pursuant to s 35(1) of the WMA a management plan must contain performance indicators to measure the success of strategies for reaching the objectives of the plan. As long as a plan specifies indicators in general terms, with a more detailed mode of assessment provided for in an appendix, this is sufficient.

As mentioned above, as a result of a 2005 amendment to the WMA, the environmental water rules relating to a water source do not need to specify that a minimum quantity of water is required to be present in the water sources at all times (s 8(2)). This statutory amendment seeks to overcome the type of argument raised by the NCC in this case.

Duration of, and changes to, plans

Generally, water management plans have a lifespan of 10 years. However, under provisions brought in under the 2004 amendments to further secure water entitlements, the Minister may extend the duration of a water sharing management plan for another 10 years, taking into account a report of the Natural Resources Commission (NRC). More than one such extension can be made. The report of the NRM must include a five-year review of the water sharing plan and indicate the extent to which the provisions have achieved the State-wide natural resource management standards and targets which are set out for the catchment management area. The NRC must then advise the Minister whether changes to the water sharing provisions are warranted. The NRC must call for, and consider, public submissions and also have regard to any other relevant State-wide and regional government policies or agreements that apply to the catchment management area. The NRC's report must be made available to the public after the Minister has decided to extend a plan, or within six months, whichever occurs first (s 43A).

A new s 43A(3A) was inserted into the Act under 2005 amendments to provide that if a report provided by the National Resources Commission recommends changes to a management plan which result in a reduction in water allocations, and compensation may be payable under s 87AA of the WMA, the Commission must state whether the purpose of the changes are to: restore water to the environment because of natural reduction in inflow (which under the National Water Initiative does not attract compensation); or whether better scientific knowledge indicates that allocations to the environment were not adequate (which does attract compensation).

The 2004 amendments to the WMA also give the Minister the power to amend a management plan at any time if satisfied that it is in the public interest to do so, or in order to give effect to an order of the Land and Environment Court relating to the validity of the plan (s 45(1)). One of the situations where the Minister may amend a plan is in order to allow a catchment management authority, the Minister or other public body to obtain an access licence (containing conditions for adaptive environment water use) as a result of the additional water, that has been conserved by public expenditure or works, becoming available (s 45(2)). Before amending a plan, the Minister must obtain the concurrence of the Minister for the Environment (s 45(3)). If, as a result of an amendment, the bulk access regime will be varied and a management committee for the area is constituted, then the Minister must consult with the committee (s 45(7)). The Minister can also repeal a management plan but may not repeal a plan that deals with water sharing (s 45(5)).

Under 2005 amendments, a new s 46 is inserted into the WMA to provide for the making or amendment of management plans. It states that if a Minister makes a replacement management plan or amends an existing management plan which may result in compensation, the Minister must issue a statement regarding whether the changes were necessary because of natural causes, or better scientific knowledge or a change in government policy. This affects the right to compensation (see the discussion on the compensation provisions below).

Access licences

Subject to a few exceptions, water may not be used except in accordance with an access licence issued by the Department of Natural Resources.

The *Water Management Act 2000* (NSW) facilitates the establishment of a water market by providing for access entitlements to water which comprise both a share entitlement as well as an extraction entitlement. There are a number of innovative features with respect to licences granted under the WMA. The share component of the entitlement allocates the holder a share in the total amount of water available for extraction. The share is separate from, and not linked to, the extraction entitlement which allows water to be extracted at a specified location and at a specified rate. Note that the extraction component of an access licence may authorise the taking of water from a water source other than that mentioned in the share component if the two water sources are vertically abutting (either wholly or partly) water sources (s 56(4A). Share entitlements can be traded freely whereas trade in extraction entitlements may vary according to environmental conditions.

Secondly, access entitlements are not linked to ownership of the land, as was previously the case before the enactment of the WMA. This is a crucial reform and is intended to facilitate the trade in water entitlements as required under the 1994 COAG water reform agreement. Thirdly, access licences may only be allocated in accordance with the bulk access regime stipulated in the water sharing plan prepared for the particular water management area. This links the allocation of water to the strategic planning process provided by the WMA. Access licences may also be granted to the Minister, a catchment management authority or other public body by the Minister, without the need for approval under Pt 2 of the Act, on condition that the licence is granted only for environmental purposes (s 65(3)).

Share or extraction components of access licences can be amended under s 68A of the Act. Such amendments can be made so as to alter the water management area or water source to which the share component of the licence relates, or the location from which water may be taken in accordance with the extraction component of the licence. However, these amendments can only be made because erroneous location data has resulted in the holder taking water from a different source, and at the time when the access licence was recorded in the register, the licence could just as easily have been granted authorising the taking of water from that source. There are also a number of provisions in the WMA with respect to the co-holding of access licences.

Water allocation accounts

Licence holders keep track of their right to extract water by way of water allocation accounts which are attached to each access licence.

Categories of access licences and priorities between them

The WMA introduces various categories of access licences and then creates priorities between them. The point of this is that in times of water scarcity, water will be allocated and priority will be given to the most important, and most secure, types of licences first. The categories of licences are as follows:

(a) regulated river (high security) access licences;[25]
(b) regulated river (general security) access licences;[26]
(c) regulated (conveyance) access licences;
(d) unregulated river access licences;[27]
(e) aquifer access licences;
(f) estuarine water access licences;
(g) coastal water access licences;
(h) supplementary water access licences;
(i) major utility access licences;
(j) local water utility access licences;
(k) domestic and stock access licences;
(l) such other categories of access licence as may be prescribed by the regulations. (s 57)

For the sake of clarity, a regulated river in New South Wales is one on which dams and weirs have been constructed in order to regularise the availability of water for irrigation, and also to provide flood mitigation. The regulated rivers in New South Wales are the Barwon-Darling, the Manoi, the Gwydir, the Lachlan, the Macquarie-Cudgegong, the Murray-Lower Darling, the Murrumbidgee, and the Hunter. All other rivers in New South Wales are unregulated.

Under the WMA, the following priorities for distributing water are to be observed in relation to access licences:

(a) local water utility access licences, major utility access licences and domestic and stock access licences have priority over all other access licences;
(b) regulated river (high security) access licences have priority over all other access licences (other than those referred to in para (a));
(c) access licences (other than those referred to in paras (a), (b) and (d)) have priority between themselves as prescribed by the regulations;
(d) supplementary water access licences have priority below all other licences. (s 58)

However, it is important to note that a management plan may provide for different rules of priority for categories of licences other than those established under s 58(1) of the Act (s 58(3)). Also, in times of severe water shortage, the Minister can determine that first priority is to be given to: the taking of water for domestic purposes by

25 A regulated river is one on which water containment works like weirs and dams have been constructed. A high security licence is one where the licence holder is guaranteed a regular allocation owing to the nature of the agricultural activity, eg vineyards, orchards.

26 A general security licence is one where no guarantees are made regarding an allocation and in any given year the holder of a general security licence may only receive 60% of the actually allocation specified in the licence.

27 An unregulated river is one that does not have a dam or weir constructed on it.

persons exercising basic landholder rights, and the taking of water for domestic purposes or essential town services authorised by an access licence. Second priority is to be given to the needs of the environment.

Third priority is to be given to:

- the taking of water for stock purposes by persons exercising basic landholder rights; and
- in the case of regulated rivers, the taking of water for purposes authorised by a regulated river (high security) access licence; and
- the taking of water for the purposes authorised by a major utility access licence or local water utility access licence; and
- the taking of water for the purposes of electricity generation authorised by a major utility access licence; and
- the taking of water for purposes authorised by a domestic and stock access licence or by persons exercising any other water rights in relation to stock; and
- the taking of water for purposes authorised by a conveyance access licence in connection with the supply of water for any other purpose or need referred to in this paragraph.

Fourth priority is to be given to the taking of water for purposes authorised by any other category or subcategory of access licence (s 60(3)).

This gives clear direction to the Minister regarding how to choose between various access licence holders during periods of severe drought.

Duration of access licences

Originally, the WMA provided that an access licence had effect for 15 years, except in the case of a local or major water utility access licence which had effect for 20 years. The holder of an access licence could, at any time within the 12 months before the access licence expired, apply to the Minister for renewal of the access licence. A major utility could apply to the Minister for the access licence to be extended for another five years (ss 69, 70). However, under the 2004 amendments, these provisions are deleted in favour of a section which simply says that 'an access licence ceases to be in force on the date that the cancellation of the licence is recorded in the Access Register' (s 69). This is a very significant amendment to the WMA and means that a licence can last in perpetuity. As mentioned above, security of access to entitlements, and the recognition of entitlements as property rights, are essential ingredients of COAG's decision to establish a water trading market in Australia.

Trading access licences

To provide a legal basis for the water market, the WMA contains various provisions relating to the trading of access entitlements. Entitlements may be transferred, assigned, subdivided, and traded interstate. The Minister may regulate or prohibit the kind of trading rules which may be adopted in a management plan by adopting access licence dealing principles.[28] One of the most important points to notice about

28 These principles have now been made. They can be found in the Access Licence Dealing Principles Order 2002, <http://www.legislation.nsw.gov.au/fullhtml/inforce/subordleg+1032+2002+FIRST+0+N+#pt.1> (accessed 17 December 2006).

trading is that each trade must be approved by the Minister before it can occur (s 71A). The Minister will only grant consent if the dealing complies with the water management principles, the access licence dealing principles, and the access licence dealing rules established by any relevant management plan. This provision is regarded by some as curious given the free market ethos underpinning the move toward water trading. However, important environmental considerations require ministerial oversight of such trades. Clearly, if the access licence is subject to a registered security interest then the security holder must consent to the dealing (ss 71A-71L).

Apart from these legal constraints to trading, other constraints on the transferability of access licences include technical and economic constraints (ss 71A-71L). Technical constraints include factors such as the transmission losses occurred through seepage and evaporation. For this reason, water should only be transferred between certain zones. Also there are capacity limits in storage works and water ways and, to meet minimum in-stream flow, transfers should be geographically bounded.

Economic constraints are also evident particularly as there is a risk that the large-scale movement of water may impact on local economies.

It is important to note that the 2005 amendments to the WMA make it clear that the access licence dealing rules, which are core provisions of the water sharing plan, referred to in s 20(d) of the WMA, can prohibit any dealing with respect to access licences. This amendment was made to prevent the type of challenge to such rules as occurred in *Murrumbidgee Horticulture Council Inc v Minister of Land and Water Conservation* (see below).

Challenging the lawfulness of access dealing rules

The lawfulness of such access dealing rules was challenged in *Murrumbidgee Horticulture Council Inc v Minister for Land and Water Conservation*.[29] This case was a challenge to the Murrumbidgee Regulated River Water Sharing Plan ('the Plan'), brought by 1000 high security access licence holders with properties along the Murrumbidgee River. The main ground of the Council's case was that cl 53(8) of the Plan (which imposes a deadline of 1 September each year for high security water trading) was invalid, because:

- By reducing the amount of water traded by high security access licence holders, the Plan was increasing the amount of water available to access licence holders with a lower priority. This was not consistent with s 58(1) of the *Water Management Act 2000* (the Act), which sets out the priorities between access licence holders.
- It did not comply with cl 10 of the Access Licence Dealing Principles Order (the Principles Order), which requires that access licence dealing rules should allow maximum flexibility in order to promote social and economic benefits.
- It was not consistent with Target 16a of the State Water Management Outcomes Plan (SWMOP), which provides that all share components of access licences should be tradeable. The Council argued that a constraint should

29 [2002] NSWLEC 213.

not be imposed on the water trading market, as cl 53(8) does, in order to increase the quantity of environmental water available.

Pain J rejected all of the Council's arguments. The main points of her judgment were:

- Clause 53(8) was not inconsistent with s 58 of the Act. The Act does not give access licence holders an unfettered right to deal in water. The fact that a plan did not meet, or did not completely meet, a target set by the SWMOP would not necessarily make that plan invalid. Even if the Plan was inconsistent with Target 16a of the SWMOP, the Plan met other targets in the SWMOP, relating to environmental objectives.
- Regardless of cl 10 of the Principles Order, cl 53(8) of the Plan was justified by cl 7(1) and (2) of the Principles Order, which require that dealings should not adversely affect environmental water and should enhance water quality. The overall aim of reducing water extraction from the Murrumbidgee River, in order to achieve compliance with the Murray-Darling Basin Cap, was to improve water quality and the condition of the aquatic environment in the river.
- The Plan, made under Pt 5 of Chapter 2 of the Act, was compliant in general terms with the Principles Order and was consistent in general terms with the SWMOP, as required by the Act. The fact that a plan did not meet, or did not completely meet, a target set by the SWMOP would not necessarily make that plan invalid. Even if the Plan was inconsistent with Target 16a of the SWMOP, the Plan met other targets in the SWMOP, relating to environmental objectives.

Environmental consequences of water trading

It is instructive to reflect at this point on a pilot water trading project that was recently established within the Murray-Darling Basin. In 2000, the CSIRO conducted a review of the trading trial and presented some interesting findings.[30] Fifty-one trades involving 9.5GL of water have been allowed to move between South Australia, Victoria and New South Wales. The trades are worth over $9.9 million with over 90% of the water moving to South Australia. The demand for water in South Australia has been driven primarily by investment in the wine and dairy industries as well as in horticulture. Access to water in South Australia is more restricted than in the other two States resulting in an escalation in the price of water. The economic impacts of the trades have been positive since 99% of the water traded was not being used at its origin. Consequently, it has moved to a high value use and resulted and increased the efficiency of water use.

However, there is some concern that, while the market may move resources to their highest value use, this use might not be the most ecologically sustainable use over the long term. The CSIRO's review of the pilot water trading project within the Murray-Darling Basin indicates that trading has resulted in an increase in salinity in river systems. This is despite the fact that participants in the pilot project have committed themselves to:

30 CSIRO Land and Water, Policy and Economic Research Unit, *Inter-State Water Trading: A Two Year Review*, December 2000.

> establish a procedural framework and set of standards so that the Scheme is accountable and does not result in increased levels of salinity, reduction in environmental flows or degradation of the natural environment.

These objectives are supposed to be met by a series of environmental clearance procedures in each State. The CSIRO noted, however, that analysis of the pilot project is made difficult as a result of the different licensing systems, including different environmental management and planning frameworks, in each State.

Nevertheless, the CSIRO reported on several environmental consequences of the pilot scheme. First, environmental flows in all areas upstream of the final destination of the water will be greater resulting in slightly altered seasonal flow patterns. Secondly, there is a distinctly negative impact on river salinity, particularly at Morgan in South Australia. The problem with salinity impacts is that each State has a different regime for controlling the impact.

It is interesting to note that the Australian Conservation Foundation (ACF) recommended that the National Competition Council (NCC) partly suspend payments to New South Wales for failing adequately to progress a whole-of-government process for determining and mitigating the ecological impacts of water trading.[31] The ACF found that the Department of Land and Water Conservation had failed to issue a consultation paper on the ecological effects of water trading despite serious concern amongst agency staff, conservationists and land holders. Rather, it seemed that regional staff of the agency were extolling the virtues of trading without discussing some of the environmental impacts.

The water availability risk market

An interesting development, and one which indicates the extent to which 'the market' has become a reality with respect to water entitlements, is that the Sydney Futures Exchange (SFE) has conceived of a market in water availability risk to provide affected parties with a tool to hedge against drought conditions. The SFE states that the risk of water availability is a reality for users of water in the Australian rural economy. However, unlike participants in the equity, money or commodity markets, these users have no market into which users and investors can effectively hedge the risk. The SFE regards the implications of this as 'profound' not only for farmers but also service providers and investors who seek large scale capital investment opportunities. Such investors will either avoid the sector or price the risk accordingly, which can result in inefficiencies. The key features of the market in water availability risk are:

- the development of a series of market benchmarks or indices of water availability based on the logical aggregation of key water storage dams (to be known as SFE State Water Indexes); and
- the listing of futures contracts on each regional index to provide a market mechanism for parties to hedge against the future value of the index.

The SFE has engaged in widespread key participant and stakeholder consultation in this regard. The NSW indexes, which provide a snapshot of water availability across

---

31 S Blanch, *Submission to the National Competition Council regarding its Third Tranche Assessment of Government's Progress with Implementing National Competition Policy* (Australian Conservation Foundation, May 2001.

the State, have been developed by State Water and the SFE through a Project Team and Steering Committee.[32]

The proposed SFE Water Futures Market will be a financial market with the contracts being settled in cash. There will be no physical delivery of water. Rather buyers and sellers will have price exposure to the respective SFE State Water Index that results in realised cash profits or losses.

New South Wales government enters the water market

In July 2006, the NSW Department of Environment and Conservation launched NSW Riverbank which is a $105 million environmental fund set up to buy water for the most stressed and valued rivers and wetlands in NSW, over the next five years. NSW Riverbank will be buying water from willing sellers within the existing water sharing and water management framework. It will participate in the water market on the same basis as other buyers and acquisitions will be managed in such a way as not to distort water prices. Initial areas of focus include Macquarie Marshes, the Gwydir and Lowbidgee wetlands and the Narran Lakes.

Riverbank will be managed by DEC and funded through the existing NSW Environmental Trust. The Trust will establish a special water subcommittee to advise it, including independent members with water market and ecological expertise.

Registering access licences

All access licences, and all transactions relating to access licences, must be registered in the Water Access Licence Register which must be kept by the Minister. The register must record: ministerial action in relation to the licence; any general dealing in the licence; any dealing on default in relation to the licence; any caveat lodged in relation to, or any security interest held over, the licence, as well as any devolution of the licence. Any alteration in a co-holder's tenancy arrangement in relation to the licence must also be registered (s 71). Information in the register must be made available to the public, subject to any conditions imposed by the Minister (s 71J).

Registration is very important to facilitate a market in water. As an access licence is no longer attached to the land, and can be traded, interests in an access licence need to be registered in the same way as land is registered. This is particularly important from the perspective of financial institutions which may want to treat an access licence as the subject of a security interest. Financial institutions have expressed concern about the fact that agricultural land, which is the subject of a security interest, may lose its value where water rights are not attached to ownership of the land.

Ministerial interference with access licences and compensation provisions

The powers of the Minister to manage water in the public interest are extensive under the WMA. In some instances, compensation is payable but not in others. The rules relating to ministerial interference with access licences are as follows:

32 See <http://www.statewater.com.au/indexes/index.asp> (accessed 20 March 2006).

Temporary water restrictions

The Minister may also impose temporary water restrictions if it is necessary to do so in the public interest (such as to cope with a water shortage or a threat to public health or safety). This may occur if the Minister directs that, for a specified period, the taking of water from a specified water source is totally prohibited or is restricted as specified in the order. The order must be broadcast on television and radio and published in the newspaper. No compensation is payable in this instance (s 323).

Embargoes on applying for licences

The Minister may, by order published in the Gazette, effectively declare an embargo on the making of applications for access licences in a specified water management area and declare that they may only be acquired by auction, tender or other means (s 65). These orders would obviously be made where there is an acute water shortage in a particular water management area, and would provide a mechanism for new entrants into the water market.

Cancellation and suspension of licences

The Minister may also cancel or suspend access licences if the licence holder does not comply with the conditions of the licence, is convicted of an offence, or has not paid any fees, charges or civil penalties relating to the licence (s 78). No compensation is payable for the suspension or cancellation of an access licence, or for any error in the Access Register, or for the registration of a security interest or caveat in the Access Register (s 81A).

Acquisition of licences

In the case of severe drought, the Minister may, by notice in writing served on their holders, compulsorily acquire access licences if it is in the public interest to acquire them. A person would then be entitled to compensation from the State for the market value of the licence as at the time it was compulsorily acquired. The amount of compensation payable will be determined by agreement between the Minister and the person entitled to compensation or, if agreement cannot be reached, by the Valuer-General (s 79).

Variation of the bulk access regime

A holder of an access licence (other than a supplementary water access licence) whose water allocations are reduced as a consequence of the variation of a bulk access regime may claim compensation for loss suffered as a consequence of that reduction. However, rights to compensation are contingent on a number of factors relating to the making and amending of management plans. Essentially, what s 87 makes clear is that:

- compensation is payable only in respect of a reduction in water allocations occurring during the period for which the first management plan that established the bulk access regime concerned is in force, excluding any period for which the plan has been extended under s 43A(1) (s 87(9));
- compensation may not be claimed if the variation of the bulk access regime results from the making of a new management plan where the original plan, establishing the bulk access regime, has expired (s 87(2)(a1));

- where a management committee makes a plan for an area, for which no plan previously existed, there will be no compensation if as a result the bulk access regime is altered (s 87(2)(b));
- if the Minister amends a management plan 'in the public interest' or as a result of a decision of the Land and Environment Court relating to the validity of the plan, no compensation is payable (s 87(2)(c)).

However, subject to the 2005 amendments, rendered necessary by the NWI, ss 87AA and 87AB of the WMA now stipulate that compensation is payable in certain circumstances for reductions in water allocations arising *after* the initial period that the management plan is in force. These compensation provisions apply to the following categories of access licences:

- regulated river (high and general security) access licences;
- Murrumbidgee and Coleambally Irrigation (conveyance) access licences;
- unregulated river access licences; aquifer access licences; and
- other categories of licences stipulated by regulation.

The holders of such licences are entitled to compensation if the reductions are as a result of a change in government policy or because of more accurate scientific knowledge. Compensation is not payable if the reduction occurred while the first management plan was in force; or because of changes to a plan required by the Land and Environment Court, or where reductions are needed in water allocations for the purpose of restoring water to environment because of natural reductions. Compensation under these new provisions is conditional on the Commonwealth providing funding for compensation. Compensation will not be payable where a person's conduct has been unconscionable, misleading, deceptive or where negligent, false or misleading representations are made.

The amount of compensation is determined on the advice of the Valuer-General who must have regard to the market value of the water to the claimant for compensation as a consequence of the variation of the bulk access regime (s 87(5), (6)). An appeal may be made to the Land and Environment Court where a person is dissatisfied with the amount of compensation offered, or with any delay in the payment of compensation (s 87(7)).

Keeping water allocation accounts

The Minister is required to keep an account of the water allocations that are assigned between one access licence holder and another, and the interstate transfer of water allocations.

Approvals

The granting of an access licence does not entitle the holder to actually use the water. Permission to use it must be granted under one of the following types of approvals: a water use approval; a water management works approval; and a water activity approval (ss 89, 90, 91). Approvals can also be granted to use water taken from a source outside of New South Wales which has been acquired as a result of a water trade (s 89(2)). Approvals may be granted subject to conditions (ss 100-103) and may be amended, surrendered, suspended, varied or cancelled by the Minister (ss 107-109).

Ministerial directions and guidelines concerning waste of water

The Minister may by notice in writing order a landholder to use water beneficially, and not waste it or use it improperly, where water is being used under the authority of a water use approval, a domestic and stock right, or a water supply work. The Minister can also order that domestic and stock water be used in accordance with any guidelines established by the Minister. The Minister's guidelines must be placed on public exhibition and the public is entitled to make submissions on them (s 325).

Penalties and offences

A person who breaches the WMA is guilty of an offence and is liable to pay a significant fine. In the case of a corporation the penalty is $250,000 and, in the case of a continuing offence, to a further penalty not exceeding $120,000 for each day the offence continues. In the case of an individual, the penalty is $120,000 and, in the case of a continuing offence, a further penalty of $60,000 for each day the offence continues.

The 2004 amendments also provide for administrative and civil penalties if the holder of an access licence takes water illegally, whether or not the person has been prosecuted. The Minister is empowered to debit up to five times the amount of the water taken from any water allocations credited to the account for the licence. Alternatively, or in addition, to this, the Minister can order the holder of the licence to pay a civil penalty amounting to five times the fee or charge in respect of the water taken. The Minister can take these actions after notifying the holder of the access licence in writing of the proposed action, and giving the person an opportunity to make submissions (s 85B).

Conclusions

Clearly, the WMA, and particularly the 2004 and 2005 amendments to the WMA, are intended to stimulate the creation of an open water trading market. Access entitlements are separate from the land and are divided into share and extraction entitlements; the 2004 amendments granted perpetual licences and, necessarily, extended the duration of water management plans; entitlements must be registered in the Water Access Licence Register; and access licences may be traded. The 2005 amendments especially go some way towards implementing the agreements reached by COAG under the NWI. Coupled with this move to the market is a regulatory framework that attempts to situate the market within an environmentally sustainable regulatory paradigm. The granting of access licences depends on the making of water sharing plans which must be developed after environmental considerations have been taken into account. The Natural Resources Commission is given a role in advising the Minister on any changes that are needed to the plans. The Minister is given extensive powers to amend water sharing plans, to place embargoes on new licences, and to acquire licences where it is in the public interest to do so. Trades must be approved by the Minister. It remains to be seen, with the benefit of hindsight, whether or not the WMA, and the NWI for that matter, have struck the right balance between market mechanisms and environmental sustainability.

National Water Commission penalises New South Wales for performance on water reform

In spite of the attempts of the NSW government to implement the NWI, it has recently been found wanting by the National Water Commission, which has taken over the function of assessing performance on water reform from the National Competition Council. In 2006, National Competition Policy payments totalling $820.4 million will be paid by the Commonwealth government to the States and Territories for implementing their water reform commitments. Their progress in meeting commitments has been assessed by the National Water Commission. Four jurisdictions have been assessed as meeting the majority of the obligations and so are receiving their full entitlement for 2005-06. They are Queensland, Victoria, Tasmania and the ACT. Western Australia's performance has yet to be fully assessed. New South Wales has been reimbursed 50% of the 2004-05 suspension of payment for unsatisfactory performance ($13 million of a $26 million suspension) but a further $13 million has been suspended for the 2005-06 period until further progress is made.

Also further specific suspensions of $26.2 million were agreed to by the Australian government where the obligations relating to interstate trading in the southern Murray-Darling Basin are outstanding. Trading in this area is integral to the NWI and has been a central part of the COAG water reform agenda since 1994. In this regard, the following suspensions apply: NSW – $13.3 million, Victoria – $9.9 million, and South Australia – $3 million. This means that $26.3 million worth of NCP payments have been suspended with respect to New South Wales.

The Supply of Water in New South Wales

As well as understanding the process for allocating water access licences in NSW, it is important to have an overview of the major water corporations which have the responsibility of delivering water to the agricultural and urban sectors. In the agricultural sector, this responsibility is vested in the State Water Corporation, Irrigation Corporations and private irrigation entities. In the urban context, the relevant bodies are the Sydney Water Corporation, the Sydney Catchment Authority, the Hunter Water Corporation, water supply authorities and local government authorities (also known as local water utilities).

The Supply of Rural Water

State Water Corporation

The State Water Corporation was corporatised in 2004 under the *State Water Corporation Act 2004* (NSW) and delivers bulk water in regional and rural New South Wales to all authorised users such as river pumpers, irrigation companies, towns, farms, mines and electricity generators. It also has the responsibility of delivering water for the environment from its storage facilities, as well as unlicensed stock and domestic users on regulated rivers.

The functions of the Corporation are to capture, store and release water and construct, maintain and operate dams and weirs on the regulated rivers of New South Wales (s 6). One of the important functions of State Water in this regard is providing information to the Minister about dam levels in NSW. Where levels rise, additional available water determinations may be announced which has the effect of giving licence holders increased water allocations for extraction. State Water also has the delegated power to collect various water charges and even to suspend access licences or works approval and to impose penalties where users exceed their water allocations. The Corporation exercises its functions under an operating licence granted by the Governor (s 11) and is regulated by the Independent Pricing and Regulatory Tribunal (s 17).

Irrigation corporations

Irrigation areas were set up historically in south and south-west New South Wales as an incentive to encourage returning servicemen to settle in the inland parts of the State. The principal agricultural activity in these areas are fruit and cotton cultivation. The irrigation schemes were corporatised under the *Irrigation Corporatisation Act 1994* (NSW) which has been repealed now that the corporations are regulated under Chapter 4 Pt 1 of the WMA. Irrigation corporations are incorporated under the *Corporations Act 2001* (Cth) and include Coleambally Irrigation Limited, Jemalong Irrigation Limited, Western Murray Irrigation Limited, Murray Irrigation Limited, and Murrumbidgee Irrigation Limited.

The activities of these corporations are governed by operating licences which authorise them to carry on the business of supplying water. Corporations are required (in accordance with a management plan and business plan) to provide, construct, maintain, manage and operate efficient, co-ordinated and commercially viable systems and services for supplying water (WMA s 123(2)). Irrigation corporations are issued with a single access licence, effectively a bulk water licence, in which the shareholders of the corporation are issued shares.

Irrigation corporations and the NWI

Irrigation corporations have historically prohibited the trade of water outside of their irrigation districts. This is because trade may compromise the value of the bulk access licence, which is the corporation's most significant asset. Essentially, permanent water trades might leave irrigation assets stranded; increase the financial burden on remaining water users; result in increased water prices; jeopardise the viability of remaining water users; and impact on communities' social and economic vitality. However, under the National Water Initiative, New South Wales is required, in the Southern Murray-Darling Basin, to make 'necessary legislative changes to give effect to the Heads of Agreement between Government and major irrigation corporations to permit increased trade including to remove barriers to trade up to the interim threshold limit'. As mentioned above under the discussion of the NWI trading agreement, the interim threshold limit amounts to permanent trade out of all water irrigation areas of 4% per annum of total water access entitlements.

It is important to note that WMA s 71ZA now allows the Minister to order an irrigation corporation to pay a civil penalty if the corporation prevents arrangements being made for the reduction in the share component of an access licence, held by it, for the purpose of permanently transferring a member's entitlement to water to another access licence that is not held by the corporation. This applies only to a regulated river (high security) access licence and a regulated river (general security) access licence held by the corporation. Consistently with the NWI, this does not apply to preventing a transfer that would result in the share component of an access licence held by the irrigation corporation being reduced, in any period commencing on 1 July in any year and ending on 30 June (inclusive) in the following year, by an amount of more than 4% of the share component that applied to the access licence at the beginning of that period. This percentage may be changed by Regulation. The amount of the initial civil penalty is up to $500,000 and a further civil penalty not exceeding $20,000 may be imposed for each day that the circumstances giving rise to the initial civil penalty continue to exist.

Murray Irrigation Limited, for example, has amended its constitution to take account of the NWI.[33] The new Constitution:

- allows the Murray Irrigation Board of Directors discretion over the enforcement of current restrictions on the trading of the company's water entitlements;
- allows shareholders, at the discretion of the Board, to sell their Murray Irrigation Water Entitlements to individuals or organisations which do not own land in the company's area of operations;
- provides amalgamated landholdings with their original voting rights.

Shareholders will be allowed to choose whether to sell their water entitlements and keep the accompanying shares, or sell the water entitlements and return the shares to Murray Irrigation. However, when entitlements are sold to people who do not own land in the area of operations, a 'retail tagging' regime will apply. Here, a buyer will buy a Murray Irrigation Water Access licence entitlement but will not own shares and will not have any voting rights in Murray Irrigation. The effect of this is that regardless of who owns the water, or where the water is used, the owners of the entitlement will continue to own a Murray Irrigation entitlement and this will not be converted to an entitlement in another jurisdiction. The buyer will be required to pay Murray Irrigation's fixed water charges each year. This is known as the 'retail tag'.

When shareholders sell entitlements to other Murray Irrigation shareholders they can choose to sell the entitlements and shares together, or sell the entitlements and keep the shares, or sell the entitlements and return the shares to the company.

An exit fee will be charged on all share components traded from Murray Irrigation's licence. This is a one-off contribution to the company's fixed operating and capital costs and recognises the increasing burden which the permanent trade of water places on the region's remaining water users. The exit fee will be paid by the buyer.

Private irrigation districts and private water trusts

Other water supply authorities regulated under the WMA are private irrigation districts and private irrigation trusts (Chapter 4 Pt 2). Private irrigation districts were originally set up under the *Private Irrigation Districts Act 1973* (NSW). They are now established under the provisions of the WMA.[34] A private water supply district

33 See <http://www.murrayirrigation.com.au/download/3263515.pdf> (accessed 24 March 2006).

34 A private water supply district or a private water supply and irrigation district may be constituted by the Governor upon the petition of three or more landholders to the Minister.

or a private water supply and irrigation district may be constituted by the Governor upon the petition of three or more landholders to the Minister (s 142). A private irrigation board of management must be established for each private irrigation district (s 148). Members of the private irrigation board are elected and may be removed from office by the Governor by proclamation in the Gazette (s 149). The private irrigation board must determine the quantity of water to be allocated for irrigation to each holding within the district (s 176). It must also supply water for domestic and stock purposes as well as for irrigation (s 182). The water must be supplied to the boundary of each holding as well as to other points agreed upon by the board and the landholder.

Private water trusts are established under WMA (Chapter 4 Pt 4). The members of a private irrigation trust (s 223) must maintain and administer the trust's water management works in a water supply district (s 227). In order to raise money for the performance of their functions, members of a private water trust can fix and levy rates on land within the water supply district (s 232(1)). The WMA also provides for rates in connection with the supply of water for stock and domestic purposes and in connection with the construction and maintenance of flood works and irrigation (s 232(1)). The Fish River Water Supply Scheme is also regulated subject to the WMA. The Fish River water supply works at Oberon are controlled and administered by the Minister for Natural Resources (s 241). To supply someone with water, the Minister may at all times use and repair the works even if a local council is charged with the care and management of the works (s 242).

Any person who wishes to accept a supply of water from the Fish River water supply works must enter into a contract with the Minister on such terms and conditions as the Minister thinks fit (s 243(1)). The Minister may publish in the Gazette the price to be paid per kilolitre for water supplied in any year and may also fix a minimum amount to be paid irrespective of the quantity of water supplied (s 243(3)). A local council that is supplied with water from the works must not supply water to any premises situated outside the council area (s 244).

The supply of metropolitan water

Sydney Water Corporation

Water is supplied to the Sydney Metropolitan Region by the Sydney Water Corporation (Sydney Water). Sydney Water is also responsible for sewage treatment and stormwater management in the Region. Consistently with National Competition Policy principles, the Sydney Water Board was corporatised, and converted to the Sydney Water Corporation (Sydney Water) under the *Sydney Water Act 1994* (NSW) (SWA). As such, Sydney Water became a State Owned Corporation for the purposes of the *State Owned Corporations Act 1989* (NSW). Sydney Water exercises its functions in accordance with the Sydney Water's Operating Licence 2005–2010.[35] Reference should also be made here to the Hunter Water Corporation which is the other major metropolitan water utility in NSW. It was corporatised in 1991, and is subsequently also a State Owned Corporation. The regulatory framework governing Hunter

35 See <http://www.sydneywater.com.au/Publications/_download.cfm?DownloadFile=Legislation Acts/OperatingLicence.pdf> (accessed 16 March 2006).

Water is very similar to that relating to Sydney Water and for this reason no further mention will be made of Hunter Water.

Objectives of Sydney Water

The principal objectives of Sydney Water are:

- to be a successful business;
- to exhibit a sense of social responsibility by having regard to the interests of the communities in which it operates;
- to conduct its operations in compliance with the principles of ecologically sustainable development;
- to protect public health by supplying safe drinking water to its customers and other members of the public in compliance with the requirements of any operating licence.

All of these objectives are of equal importance (SWA s 21).

In addition, Sydney Water has the following special objectives:

- to reduce risks to human health; and
- to prevent the degradation of the environment. (s 22(1))

In implementing these special objectives, Sydney Water may adopt the following means:

- reducing the environmental impact of its discharges into or onto the air, water or land of substances likely to cause harm to the environment;
- minimising its creation of waste by the use of appropriate technology, practices and procedures;
- reducing its use of energy, water and other materials and substances;
- re-using and recovering energy, water and other materials and substances, used or discharged by it, by the use of appropriate technology, practices and procedures. (s 22(3))

Sydney Water Corporation must include in its annual report a statement on its implementation of its special objectives. The Environment Protection Authority must review the statement as soon as possible after it is published and, within three months, make its evaluation of the statement available for public inspection. The evaluation must include an opinion as to whether the best environmental outcome has been achieved (s 22(7)).

Regulatory consequences of the 1998 'boil water' alert

In 1998, Sydney Water was forced to issue numerous 'boil water' alerts as a result of the detection of *cryptosporidium* and *giardia* in the water. All customers were required to boil water for one minute before using it. The NSW government subsequently established the Sydney Water Inquiry[36] to investigate the circumstances of the boil water alerts. The Inquiry found that there were two probable causes for the presence of *cryptosporidium* and *giardia* in Sydney water in June/July 1998. They were that heavy rains in the catchment, following a period of significant drought, carried the

36 *Sydney Water Inquiry* (New South Wales Premier's Department, 1998).

organisms into the stored catchment waters. In addition, operational difficulties at the principal treatment plant allowed a greater than usual number of pathogens to pass into the 'treated' water.

Based on the outcomes of the Inquiry, the NSW government enacted three statutes to protect human health and the environment. These include *Water Legislation Amendment (Drinking Water and Corporate Structure) Act 1998*, the *Sydney Water Catchment Management Act 1998* and the *State Environmental Planning Policy No 58 – Protecting Sydney's Water Supply. The Water Legislation Amendment (Drinking Water and Corporate Structure) Act 1998* fundamentally restructured Sydney Water and gives the Minister wide powers to intervene in its activities. The first amendment of note is that the term 'water provider' does not only include various corporatised utilities, like Sydney Water, but also 'any person who treats or supplies water' on behalf of a corporatised person. This definition lends itself to the interpretation that fully privatised utilities which treat or supply water on behalf of corporatised utilities are covered by the provisions of the amending legislation. The legislation also applies to 'any person supplying drinking water in the course of a commercial undertaking (other than that of supplying bottled or packaged drinking water)'.

The amending legislation also disestablished Sydney Water as a *company* State Owned Corporation (SOC) and re-established it as a *statutory* SOC. This means that it is no longer incorporated under the *Corporations Act*. Moreover, the Board of the reconstituted Sydney Water Corporation is now obliged to follow the directions of the Minister relating to the public interest and government policy. The Minister is not required to consult with the Board before making a direction in the public interest, and may do so in the case of urgency, public health and public safety. The Minister is required to give a statement of reasons for issuing the directions. Sydney Water has been placed under a statutory obligation to comply with the Minister's direction.

In addition, the amending legislation amends the *Public Health Act 1991* by inserting Pt 2A entitled 'Safety of drinking water'. This Part gives the Chief Health Officer (CHO) powers to prepare advice for the public on the safety of drinking water. The water supplier must publish the advice or face a penalty of 10,000 penalty units. The CHO may also direct the supplier to correct any misleading information. The Director General is vested with the following powers: to issue 'boil water' advice; to enter premises for the purpose of inspecting them; to require the testing of water; to require information and to give directions to the supplier.

Regulating compliance with operating licence

As mentioned above, Sydney Water exercises its functions in accordance with an operating licence. The Independent Pricing and Regulatory Tribunal (IPART) monitors compliance with the licence which sets quality and performance standards for:

- customer and consumer rights;
- drinking water (health and aesthetic), environmental and other water quality;
- infrastructure performance, water continuity and pressure and sewage overflow;
- pricing;
- water conservation and demand management;

- environment – ESD indicators and plans;
- dispute resolution.

Environmentally sustainable development (ESD) Indicators have been developed and gazetted (cl 9.2.1 Operating Licence) covering: Ecological integrity and/or Biodiversity Indicators; Social and Public Health Indicators; and Economic Indicators.[37] All of these indicators must be reported against.

Complaints with regard to the service provided by Sydney Water can be made to the Consumer, Trader and Tenancy Tribunal constituted under the *Consumer Claims Act 1998* (NSW). Complaints[38] about the service may be made to the Energy and Water Ombudsman.[39] In addition, any person may bring proceedings in the Supreme Court for an order to restrain a breach (or a threatened or apprehended breach) of a customer contract by Sydney Water (SWA s 103).

Memoranda of Understanding

Sydney Water interacts, and has some overlapping functions, with a number of other governments agencies. As a result, Sydney Water is required to enter into memoranda of understanding (MOUs) with these agencies (SWA s 34). Sydney Water has a Memorandum of Understanding with the Department of Environment and Conservation,[40] which regulates the environmental performance of Sydney Water's activities under the *Protection of the Environment Operations Act 1997* (NSW). Sydney Water also has MOUs with NSW Health[41] and the Department of Natural Resources.[42]

Conclusions

What is interesting about the Sydney Water case study is the NSW government's response to the 'boil water' alert and the Sydney Water Inquiry. The government by its subsequent regulatory interventions seemed to indicate a lack of confidence in the neoliberal philosophy that underpins National Competition Policy, and its insistence on the restructuring of public sector monopoly businesses. Of course, it is common for governments to corporatise utilities as a precursor to full privatisation. Yet, far from moving towards the privatisation of Sydney Water, the 'boil water' alerts resulted in the utility being subjected to greater regulation and far closer government scrutiny and control.

---

37 See <http://www.sydneywater.com.au/Publications/_download.cfm?DownloadFile=Plans Strategies/EcologicallySustainableDevelopmentIndicators.pdf> (accessed 23 March 2006).

38 These include disputed accounts, disconnection or restriction of supply, actions of a service provider which affect property, and the supply of water services such as delays in connection or quality of supply; see 'Making complaints', <http://www.ewon.com.au/making_complaint/index.html> (accessed 16 March 2005).

39 The NSW Energy and Water Ombudsman Scheme has been established by means of a company limited by guarantee, the Energy & Water Ombudsman (NSW) Limited.

40 See draft, <http://www.sydneywater.com.au/Publications/MemorandaOfUnderstanding/DraftMoUWithTheDEC.cfm> (accessed 23 March 2006).

41 See <http://www.sydneywater.com.au/Publications/_download.cfm?DownloadFile=MemorandaOfUnderstanding/SydneyWaterMoUwithNSWHealth.pdf> (accessed 23 March 2006).

42 See <http://www.sydneywater.com.au/Publications/_download.cfm?DownloadFile=MemorandaOfUnderstanding/SydneyWaterMoUwithDLWC.pdf> (accessed 23 March 2006).

Sydney Catchment Authority

One of the most important outcomes resulting from the Sydney Water Inquiry was the establishment of the Sydney Water Catchment Authority (SCA) under the *Sydney Water Catchment Management Act 1998*. The SCA has the following objectives:

- to ensure that the catchment areas and the catchment infrastructure works are managed and protected so as to promote water quality, the protection of public health and public safety, and the protection of the environment;
- to ensure that water supplied by it complies with appropriate standards of quality;
- to conduct operations in compliance with the principles of ecologically sustainable development;
- to manage the Authority's catchment infrastructure works efficiently, economically and in accordance with sound commercial principles. In implementing these objectives, the Authority has the special objectives of minimising risks to human health and preventing the degradation of the environment. (s 14)

The SCA's primary function is to protect the quality and quantity of water in catchment areas (s 15) and is responsible for bulk water in the Greater Sydney region. It also has a number of specific functions which include:

- supplying water to the Sydney Water Corporation;
- supplying water to water supply authorities, prescribed local councils or prescribed county councils;
- supplying water to other persons and bodies;
- managing and protecting the catchment areas and the catchment infrastructure works vested in or under the control of the Authority;
- undertaking research on catchments generally and particularly with regard to the health of catchment areas; and
- protecting and enhancing the quality of water controlled by the Authority. (s 15)

The SCA exercises its functions in accordance with an operating licence granted by the Governor for a period of five years (ss 25, 28). IPART is the licence regulator for the SCA (s 30A).

The preservation of water quality in the Sydney Catchment is further regulated under *SEPP 58 – Protecting Sydney's Water Supply*[43] which aims 'to ensure that development in the hydrological catchment from which Sydney draws it drinking water supply does not have a detrimental impact on water quality' (SEPP 58 s 3(a)). In addition, the SEPP provides for a notification and concurrence role for the Chief Executive of the Sydney Catchment Authority where development[44] in the catch-

43 State Environmental Planning Policies (SEPPs) are prepared in accordance with the *Environmental Planning and Assessment Act 1979* (NSW) and are strategic planning documents which either permit or constrain development in a particular area.

44 The type of development referred to under this provision is designated development under the *Environmental Planning and Assessment Act 1979* (NSW). Where development is designated the application for development must be accompanied by an environmental impact statement and objectors to the development have a right of third party appeal to the Land and Environment Court.

ment is likely to impact on water quality. It also ensures that development is assessed and controlled consistently within the catchment (SEPP 58 s 3(b), (c)).

Under s 10 of the SEPP, a consent authority under Pt 4 of the *Environmental Planning and Assessment Act 1979* (NSW) (EPAA), a proponent or determining authority under Pt 5 of the EPAA, and the Chief Executive of the SCA, when deciding whether or not to grant concurrence, must consider the following:

- whether the development or activity will have a neutral or beneficial effect on the water quality of rivers, streams or groundwater in the hydrological catchment, including during periods of wet weather;
- whether the water quality management practices proposed to be carried out as part of the development or activity are sustainable over the long term;
- whether the development or activity is compatible with relevant environmental objectives and water quality standards for the hydrological catchment when these objectives and standards are established by the government.

Water supply authorities and local councils

Water supply authorities whose activities are regulated under the *Water Management Act 2000* (NSW) (WMA) include: Benerembah Irrigation District Environment Protection Trust, Broken Hill Water Board, Cobar Water Board, Upper Parramatta River Catchment Trust, Australian Inland Energy Water Infrastructure, Gosford City Council and Wyong Council.

Where water supply authorities have not been designated, local councils can act as the local water utility to supply water to customers within their municipalities. Local councils are entitled to take water in accordance with access licences granted under the WMA. The share component of their licences must be expressed as a specified volume per year (s 56). Local water utility access licences have priority over all other access licences along with major utility access licences and domestic and stock access licences (s 58). Where there is a severe water shortage and the rules of distribution are suspended by the Minister, the needs of local water utilities will enjoy first priority in relation to domestic water supplies (s 60(3)(a)).

The 2006 Metropolitan Water Plan

Sydney consumes about 600GL of water per year and has done so for the past 20 years. However, consumption is projected to increase as the population moves to 4.5 million people in 2011 and to 4.9 million by 2021. Increased consumption patterns are likely to coincide with reduced availability of water because of global climate change. The 2006 Metropolitan Water Plan (the Plan),[45] developed by the NSW government, deals with the following major aspects of water supply management:

- increasing recycling;
- reducing demand;
- increasing supply;

45 See <http://www.waterforlife.nsw.gov.au/__data/assets/pdf_file/1446/wfl2006.pdf> (accessed 17 December 2006).

- improving catchment and river health; and
- creating a dynamic water industry.

With regard to supply, in addition to the current available supply from dams (which are at approximately 43% of capacity in 2006), the NSW government expects to secure further supplies from:

- water savings (145 billion litres per year);
- recycling (70 billion litres per year);
- additional sources – deep water extraction, groundwater extraction and desalination (77 billion litres per year).

Demand management

The NSW government has already undertaken a number of initiatives with respect to demand management.

Labelling of products for water efficiency

The government has enacted the *Water Efficiency Labelling and Standards (New South Wales) Act 2005* which gives effect in New South Wales to the labelling scheme introduced by the Commonwealth under the *Water Efficiency Labelling Scheme Act 2005* (Cth) (discussed above).

Building Sustainability Index (BASIX)

The Building Sustainability Index has been incorporated into the *Environmental Planning and Assessment Act 1979* (NSW), attendant Regulations and the *State Environment Planning Policy (Building Sustainability Index: BASIX) 2004*. It applied originally to local government areas in Sydney. Under BASIX, all new housing, multi-unit developments and additions and alterations in NSW are required to be designed and built to use 40% less mains supply water and produce 25% lower greenhouse gas emissions than was previously the case. For water, developments will be required to achieve a rating of 40 for water conservation. Achieving this rating will mean that the development can potentially reduce mains supply water use by 40%. From 2007, all homes sold will have to prove that they are either BASIX compliant, or that they have been fitted with water efficiency measures under Sydney Water's *Retrofit* program.

BASIX is discussed in more detail in Chapter 5.

Water savings

Demand management has been mandated in the utilities and large user sectors by the *Energy Administration Amendment (Water and Energy Savings) Act 2005* (NSW). The Act changed the name of the *Energy Administration Act 1987* (NSW) to the *Energy and Utilities Administration Act 1987* (NSW). The objects of the Act in relation to water are specifically 'to reduce the demand for water in water savings areas; and to stimulate investment in innovative water savings measures'. Part 6A is inserted into the *Energy and Utilities Administration Act* and establishes 'designated water users' which are defined as any local council that is located in a water savings area, or any other person prescribed by a savings order that uses water in a water savings area.

The Act also establishes a Water Savings Fund, worth $30 million per year over the next four years, to provide funding to: encourage water savings; the recycling of water (especially in Sydney Water's area of operations: Sydney, Blue Mountains and Illawarra); to reduce the demand for water; to stimulate investment in innovative water savings measures; and increase public awareness and acceptance of the importance of water savings measures. The Minister has already required Sydney Water to make the following annual contributions to the Water Savings Fund: $1,000,000.00 to be paid before 15 August 2005; $6,000,000.00 to be paid before 30 September 2005; $7,500,000.00 to be paid before 31 December 2005; $7,500,000.00 to be paid before 31 March 2006, and $7,500,000.00 to be paid by 30 June 2006. This Fund provides another vehicle, in addition to the Water Smart Programme funded by the Australian government, for private sector involvement in urban water projects.

In addition, under the Act, the top 200 water users in NSW are now required to prepare water savings action plans that must be approved by the Minister.

Applications may also be made to the NSW government for funding from the Water Savings Fund to undertake water savings measures.

Metropolitan water pricing

IPART is responsible for setting the maximum prices that can be charged by metropolitan water agencies for monopoly water and wastewater services. In 2005, IPART made a price determination with respect to prices charged by Sydney Water. The determination is for the period 1 October 2005 – 30 June 2009. In making the determination, IPART was influenced by the following factors: scarcity of water; the importance of maintaining and renewing water, wastewater and other services; population growth; and higher operating costs and increasing complexity.

In relation to Sydney Water:

- The decision sets prices which will generate revenue of $6,014 million between 1 October 2005 and 30 June 2009. This is adequate to meet Sydney Water's efficient costs of providing water, wastewater and stormwater services. On average, prices will increase by 5% above inflation in the first year, and by 1.1% above inflation in each of the remaining years.
- Step pricing has been introduced to provide a strong conservation signal with respect to discretionary water use. Consequently, water usage up to 400 kilolitres per year will be charged at $1.13/kL (increasing to $1.23/kL in 2008-09). Usage beyond this amount will be charged at $1.44/kL (increasing to $1.84/kL in 2008-09). The water service charge will be reduced by 42% over the determination period.
- Non-residential wastewater charges will be increased from $1.15/kL to $1.24/kL in 2008-09. Wastewater service charges for all customers will rise from the current $346.66 per annum to $384 per annum to reflect the increased costs of providing these services to a growing population.
- The residential stormwater service charge will increase by $20 (from the current $25.04) or 80% above inflation over the 2005 determination period. For non-residential customers this charge will increase by $44 (from $70.64) or 62% above inflation over the determination period.

For Sydney Water's residential customers, the determination is expected to increase the bill of a customer with average water consumption (250kL per year) by 7% in

2005-06, by a further 4% in 2006-07 and 5% in 2008-09. These increases include the effect of inflation. An average customer could avoid any real increase in their water bill by reducing consumption by 11.7%.

For low-income large family customers there are special measures which will moderate the impact of the price of the price changes. The Tribunal will be requiring Sydney Water to develop a rebate system where each member of a large low-income household will be able to use up to 80kL per annum at the lower tier price.

For commercial and industrial customers, the determination will increase their bills depending on the customer's level of consumption.

Investing in infrastructure

The 2006 Metropolitan Plan commits the NSW government to considerable spending on infrastructure including: investing $106 million in dam modifications to extract currently inaccessible water at the bottom of Sydney's dams; investing $4 million to undertake field trials for supplementing water supplies with groundwater; investing $4 million to develop plans for establishing a desalination plant if needed in times of drought; conducting consultations to ascertain the feasibility of constructing Shoalhaven transfer infrastructure at the cost of $250 million in the first stage and $430 million in the second stage; and commissioning additional research to better understand the effect of climate change on Sydney's water supplies.

Of course, major infrastructure projects will need to be assessed under the *Environmental Planning and Assessment Act 1979* (NSW). In order to avoid any lengthy delays, the NSW government has enacted the *SEPP (Sydney Metropolitan Water Supply) 2004* which has the following aims:

- to facilitate development for water supply infrastructure to enable deep water extraction from dams supplying water to the Sydney metropolitan area;
- to facilitate investigation into the availability of groundwater to augment water supply to the Sydney metropolitan area (including carrying out exploratory drilling);
- to suspend the operation of the EPAA to enable the deep water extraction to occur promptly. This means that it does not require development consent, or any other approval, permit or authorisation required by an environmental planning instrument. It extends to all development that is incidental to deep water access infrastructure including the clearing of native vegetation, environmental management works and the demolition, refurbishment or alteration of any existing pumping stations, pipelines and other water supply infrastructure. The same provisions apply to groundwater investigations.

Any development carried out by or on behalf of the Sydney Catchment Authority for the purposes mentioned above will not need development consent and can simply be assessed under Pt 5 of the *Environmental Planning and Assessment Act.*

Sydney's desalination plant

Under the Plan, the NSW government controversially committed itself to the construction of a desalination plant for Sydney. While it has resiled from this position agreeing to focus more on accessing underground sources of water, a pilot plant will still be built.

The building of a desalination plant has required substantial regulatory changes. As a result amendments have been made to *SEPP (Sydney Metropolitan Water Supply) 2004*, mentioned above. A new cl 7A is inserted into the SEPP stating that development for the purposes of the desalination plant (including a pilot plant) may be carried out by, or on behalf of, Sydney Water Corporation without development consent under Pt 4 of the *Environmental Planning and Assessment Act 1979*. However, it will still be assessed under the critical infrastructure provisions under Pt 3A of the Act.[46] This also applies to all other activities necessary to develop a desalination plant including: access, investigation, temporary structures, the clearing of native vegetation, tunnelling and other works associated with the construction of the plant; temporary laydown areas for construction use; environment management works; and pipelines (and tunnelling) to discharge seawater concentrate from a pilot plant to a sewer line or directly to the ocean. The declaration by the Minister for Planning has now declared the desalination plant to be critical infrastructure. As such, the plant is expected to be given approval 12 months earlier than would have occurred under normal planning provisions.

Environmental protection

Under the Plan, the government has also committed itself to: implement new environmental flow regimes in the Hawkesbury-Nepean, Woronora and Shoalhaven Rivers; build new outlet works at dams and weirs to allow environmental flow releases to be made; and monitor on an ongoing basis the environmental releases before building works at successive dams.

Urban Water Reform and New Investment Opportunities in NSW

Although, like all of Australia's urban water utilities, the urban utilities in NSW remain in government ownership, there can be no doubt that the provision of urban water services is currently undergoing significant change. These changes provide greater opportunities for private sector involvement. This is because State governments are becoming increasingly aware of the threat to their continuing ability to provide urban water services in the face of decreasing availability of supply. As a result, there is a major focus on assessing various ways of securing an urban water supply. The scenarios being canvassed are the building of recycled water facilities and desalination plants, the introduction of demand management practices and the establishment of funds to assist large users of water to engage in demand management. All of this requires a fundamental policy and regulatory shift and provides an opportunity for increased private sector involvement in the urban water sector.

Private sector water service providers

The NSW government included in its 2006 Metropolitan Water Plan a discrete section on 'Creating a dynamic and competitive metropolitan water industry'. The

---

46 See discussion of Pt 3A (critical infrastructure) in Chapter 4.

government has followed up on its commitment to encourage private sector participation in the water, recycled water and wastewater services market by enacting the *Water Industry Competition Act 2006* (NSW).

The objects of the Act are:

(a) to establish a licensing scheme to provide for private sector involvement in the supply of water and the provision of sewerage services, and
(b) to establish an access regime to ensure that certain monopoly infrastructure services involved in the supply of water and the provision of sewerage service are available to persons seeking access to them, and
(c) to facilitate the resolution of disputes between certain persons operating sewerage infrastructure and persons seeking access to the contents of that infrastructure, and
(d) to facilitate the resolution of disputes between private sector bodies and their customers in relation to the supply of water and the provision of sewerage services, and
(e) to enact provisions to facilitate the construction, maintenance and operation of infrastructure of the supply of water and the provision of sewerage services, and
(f) to protect private sector involvement in the supply of water and the provision of sewerage services by means of the creation of an offence for that purpose.[47]

The licence

Under Part 2 of the *Water Industry Competition Act 2006*, two types of licences may be applied for – a network operator's licence and a retail supplier's licence. IPART must consider all applications for a licence and, after considering any submissions received from the public, must furnish a report on the application to the Minister. The Minister may determination an application and must notify IPART of the decision after which relevant information about the licence must be posted on IPART's website. The licence must specify the activities that are authorised as well as the area of operations and may have conditions attached to it. Both the Minister and IPART may take action to enforce the conditions of the licence.

Access to infrastructure services

Part 3 of the *Water Industry Competition Act 2006* makes it clear that the Act is intended to promote the economically efficient use and operation of, and investment in, significant water industry infrastructure so as to promote effective competition in upstream and downstream markets. However, the operation of Pt 3 is restricted to the areas of operation of Sydney Water and Hunter Water. Infrastructure services will be made the subject of coverage declarations if they meet certain criteria. If the services do not meet the criteria they may be made the subject of a binding non-coverage declaration.

The criteria provided by s 23 are that:

---

47 See <http://143.119.255.90/isysquery/c73c6857-552a-4fe7-bcb8-e1171b4676f8/1/doc/> (accessed 16 January 2007).

- the infrastructure is State significant;
- it is not economically feasible to duplicate infrastructure;
- access by third parties is necessary to promote a material increase in competition;
- the safe use by third parties can be ensured; and
- access is not contrary to the public interest.

The Act sets out detailed provisions relating to: coverage declarations, revocation of coverage declarations, binding non-coverage declarations, access undertakings, access agreements and access determinations, and administration of the access regime. Disputes are to be dealt with generally under the *Commercial Arbitration Act 1984* (NSW).

Part 5 deals with sewer mining while Pt 6 provides for the operation of a retail water market. Part 6 relates to work (particularly on public roads and reserves) that needs to be carried out by a licensed network operator in order to construct water infrastructure. Part 7 sets out the offences under the Act while Pt 8 refers to IPART's licence auditing and regulatory powers under the Act.

Services Sydney: a case study

The *Water Industry Competition Act* is better understood in the context of the Services Sydney's tussle for private sector access to services traditionally offered by State-owned corporations.

Services Sydney Pty Ltd submitted a proposal to the NSW government in 2002 to allow it to provide various private sector sewage transmission and interconnection services. Services Sydney has claimed that the proposal will offer wider water conservation outcomes than those included in Sydney Water's WaterPlan21.

On 3 March 2004, the National Competition Council (NCC) received an application from Services Sydney declaring the following services currently provided by Sydney Water: a service for the transmission of sewage via Sydney Water's Sydney Sewage Reticulation Network from the customer collection points to the interconnection points (transmission services); and a service for the connection of new trunk main sewers owned and operated by Services Sydney to the existing Sydney Sewage Reticulation Network at the interconnection points (interconnection service).

Under the declaration provision of Pt IIIA of the *Trade Practices Act 1974* (Cth), a business wanting access to a particular service must apply to the NCC to have the service declared. The Council then makes a recommendation. Declaration of a service gives the applicant access to the service either through an agreement with the service provider or, if this is not forthcoming, then through arbitration by the Australian Consumer and Competition Commission (ACCC). The NCC can only recommend that a declaration be made if access would promote competition in at least one market other than the market for the service, it would be uneconomical for anyone to develop another facility to provide the service and the facility is of national significance.

In December 2005, the NCC handed down its recommendation that each of the following services should be declared for a period of 50 years under Pt IIIA of the TPA:

- a service for the transportation of sewage via the North Head Reticulation Network, the Bondi Reticulation Network, and the Malabar Reticulation Network from a customer's boundary trap to points of interconnection; and
- a service for the connection of new sewers to the North Head Reticulation Network, the Bondi Reticulation Network, and the Malabar Reticulation Network at points of interconnection.

Conclusions

A number of issues emerge from the latest developments in the urban water sector. First, it is clear that State governments in Australia no longer expect to be able to bear the financial burden of delivering water services to the growing populations in Australia's major cities. For this reason, there is a growing commitment, both at the Commonwealth and State government levels, to seek private sector investment in the water sector. At the same time, governments like the NSW government have made it clear that, where infrastructure projects are urgently needed, regulatory changes will be made to cut down on the barriers to development normally faced by the private sector. In particular, planning laws may be changed to facilitate the development. Secondly, the move towards relying more heavily on the private sector is directly related to the increasing threats to the supply of water in the urban environment. Evidence of the impact of climate change on water supplies, and ever-growing populations, have made the provision of enhanced water infrastructure imperative. The new infrastructure that will be needed is likely to be: to provide recycled water facilities; to allow greater extractions from existing dams; or to build desalination plants. Quite apart from infrastructural needs, there are also opportunities for the private sector to develop the technologies that will assist in delivering the demand management outcomes that will become increasingly important. Finally, there is a clear message coming from various agencies in Australia, including IPART and the NWC – it is that there is a valid role for the private sector in the provision of water and sanitation services, and that the private sector's participation should be allowed and protected.

All of these developments indicate that the private sector's participation in providing water services to Australia's urban communities will continue to grow in the years ahead.

7

INTEGRATED NATURAL RESOURCE MANAGEMENT

Key natural resource management challenges

There can be no doubt that some of the key natural resource management (NRM) challenges for Australia in the 21st century are the following: global climate change; water resource management; the broadscale clearing of native vegetation; soil conservation, including the reversal of dryland salinity; and the sustainable management of coastal areas and marine resources. Perhaps one of the greatest challenges for natural resource managers is to try to manage resources in an integrated way since the degradation of one resource inevitably impacts on the other. The new wave of natural resource management is therefore 'integrated resource management' (IRM). This is a planning and decision-making process that attempts to co-ordinate resource use to optimise its long-term sustainable benefits and to minimise conflicts among users of the resource. IRM attempts to balance the economic, environmental, and social requirements of society, consistently with the principles of ecologically sustainable development (ESD).

In this chapter we discuss developments in natural resource management at the Commonwealth and especially the NSW levels of government including integrated catchment management, native vegetation conservation, dryland salinity and coastal management. In particular, we focus on the new natural resource management regime in New South Wales encapsulated in the *Natural Resources Commission Act 2003* (NSW), the *Catchment Management Act 2003* (NSW), and the *Native Vegetation Act 2003* (NSW). Clearly, the way in which natural resources are managed and regulated has a significant bearing on the conservation of biological diversity which we discuss in the following chapter. Energy and water resource management are dealt with extensively in Chapters 5 and 6.

Commonwealth involvement in natural resource management

This chapter is devoted largely to assessing NRM under New South Wales State laws, as, historically, this has been an area that the States administer. However, as has happened in various other areas of environmental law and policy, the Commonwealth and State governments have attempted to find common approaches to some natural resource issues, particularly dryland salinity. They have done this in the context of co-operative federalism, discussed in Chapter 1. The Commonwealth government has also contributed considerable amounts of funding to resolving various natural resource management problems around Australia. It has done this by establishing the Natural Heritage Trust and by participating in and funding the

National Action Plan on Salinity and Water Quality. The result is that, even though the Commonwealth lacks express constitutional power to manage natural resources, it is able to influence considerably NRM policy by funding projects which deliver natural resource outcomes.

The Natural Heritage Trust

Perhaps the most significant initiative on the part of the Commonwealth government has been the establishment of the Natural Heritage Trust (NHT)[1] under the *National Heritage Trust Act 1997* (Cth) (NHTA). The main feature of the Act is the establishment of the National Heritage Trust Reserve with $1.35 billion from the sale of part of the Commonwealth's interest in Telstra. With further funding devoted to the Trust in subsequent budgets, the Trust now amounts to a $3 billion investment. The preamble to the NHTA 'recognises the need for urgent action to redress the current decline, and to prevent further decline, in the quality of Australia's natural environment'. The main objective of the reserve is to 'conserve and replenish Australia's natural capital infrastructure'. Money from the Reserve is spent on the 'environment, sustainable agriculture and natural resources management (s 3). There are four major programs under the NHT including:

- the Landcare Program which aims to reverse land degradation and promote sustainable agriculture;
- the Bushcare Program which contributes to conserving and restoring habitat for native flora and fauna;
- the Rivercare Program which aims to improve water quality and environmental condition in river systems and wetlands; and
- the Coastcare Program which invests in activities that contribute to protecting coastal catchments, ecosystems and the marine environment.

Delivery of these programs is integrated in some instances with delivery under the National Action Plan on Salinity and Water Quality (see below). Funds are allocated to projects at the local, regional and national level. Local projects are funded through the Envirofund which announces various rounds of funding for which applications are assessed to conserve biodiversity and promote sustainable resource use. National applications for funding are assessed under the National Competitive Program, while regional applications are assessed under the Regional Competitive Program.

Bilateral agreements have been negotiated between the Commonwealth and the States and Territories to implement the programs of the Natural Heritage Trust.

National Heritage Trust investigates use of market-based instruments in NRM

As mentioned in Chapter 1, there is an increasing interest in the use of market-based instruments (MBIs) to manage natural resources. In 2004, the NHT demonstrated its own interest in MBIs by publishing *Managing Our Natural Resources: Can Markets Help?*[2] The NHT claims that MBIs have the following benefits:

---

1 See <http://www.nht.gov.au/about-nht.html> (accessed 6 September 2006).

2 See <http://www.nrm.gov.au/publications/nrm-mbi/pubs/nrm-mbi.pdf> (accessed 6 September 2006); see also *Investigating new approaches – A Review of Natural Resource Management Pilots and Programs in Australia that Use Market-based Instruments*, <http://www.napswq.gov.au/mbi/pubs/review.pdf> (accessed 6 September 2006).

- they have the potential to deliver NRM outcomes at a lower cost than many traditional government instruments;
- they encourage change by those who can achieve the change most cheaply;
- they have the potential to deliver positive incentives to achieve better NRM compared with negative, or penalty, incentives;
- they seek to correct 'market failure'; and
- they can reduce compliance costs.

The NHT states that MBIs can be used to complement traditional policy tools and in fact often rely on a regulatory framework to operate effectively. The types of instruments discussed in the document include:

- price-based MBIs such as auctions of land management contracts, subsidies and grants, rebates and taxes;
- quantity based MBIs such as cap and trade schemes and offsets; and
- market friction (making markets work better) such as better risk management, leveraging private sector involvement and product differentiation.

The document provides a number of examples of each of these MBIs which are already operating in Australia, or are at the pilot stage of development.

Co-operative federalism and natural resource management

As mentioned in Chapter 1, the Commonwealth and State and Territory governments have formed Ministerial Councils to facilitate the national implementation of plans and programs that would not otherwise be possible because of the limitations imposed by the division of constitutional powers between the Commonwealth, State and Territory governments. One such council is the Natural Resource Management Ministerial Council (NRMMC) which consists of the Commonwealth, State and Territory government ministers, including the New Zealand government ministers, responsible for primary industries, natural resources, environment and water policy. The Council is essentially an intergovernmental forum for consultation and the coordination of action on natural resource management issues. The terms of reference of the Council are:

- to develop policies and strategies for national approaches to the conservation, sustainable use and management of Australia's land, water, vegetation and biological resources
- to oversee the development and implementation of national natural resource management programs including the National Action Plan for Salinity and Water Quality (NAP), the Natural Heritage Trust (NHT) and other agreed programs
- to monitor and evaluate the outcomes of these policies, strategies and programs and the health of the nation's natural resources
- to promote community understanding of and engagement with the key challenges associated with the sustainable use and management of Australia's land and water, vegetation and biological resources, and
- to liaise with other Ministerial Councils and other bodies on matters relevant to the activities of the Council.[3]

3 See <http://www.mincos.gov.au/about_nrmmc.htm> (accessed 6 September 2006).

The Council meets twice a year and is supported by one permanent Standing Committee, the Natural Resource Management Standing Committee (NRMSC), comprising the departmental heads, or CEOs, of relevant Commonwealth, State, Territory and New Zealand government agencies.

The National Action Plan on Salinity and Water Quality

Dryland salinity is one of the most serious environmental problems facing Australian natural resource managers. Although it might well be a natural phenomenon in Australia it has been exacerbated by a number of inappropriate land use practices. These include the clearing of native vegetation, urban development, river regulation, and the irrigation of crops and pastures. In October 1999, the Murray-Darling Basin Ministerial Council released a Salinity Audit of the Murray-Darling Basin entitled *Salt: Our Challenge for the 21st century*. The study estimated that the total economic impact of salinity in the Murray-Darling Basin is $46 million per year. Nationally, it is estimated that 2.5 million hectares of cultivated land is currently affected by salinity and that it is likely to rise to 12 million hectares at the current rate of increase. Its impact on land and water degradation costs Australia $3.5 billion per year with a resultant reduction in bird species of 50% in agricultural areas.

In 2000, the Council of Australian Governments (COAG) responded to the Salinity crisis by developing the National Action Plan for Salinity and Water Quality[4] (NAP) and the Intergovernment Agreement on a National Action Plan for Salinity and Water Quality. An integral aspect of the NAP is the signing of bilateral agreements between the Commonwealth and State or Territory Governments to develop action plans in 21 priority regions affected by salinity and water quality problems. At the regional level the NAP and the NHT are jointly delivered. The Commonwealth and State governments have devoted $1.4 billion in funding to support the NAP.

Integrated delivery of the NAP and NHT

Rather than deal separately with salinity and other natural resource issues, the Commonwealth and State governments have agreed to develop accredited integrated natural resource management plans for 56 regions in Australia. The national objectives and outcomes for regional natural resource management plans (NRM plans), which include biodiversity objectives, are the following:

- Promote sustainable resource use, particularly sustainable agriculture
- Protect and improve the condition of land, water (including groundwater) and vegetation resources that provide the ecosystem services that support sustainable resource use industries
- Improve water quality and environmental condition in surface and ground water systems including wetlands and estuaries while maintaining the economic and social values derived from water use
- Protect our coastal catchments, ecosystems and the marine environment
- Reverse the decline in the extent and quality of native vegetation and maintain and restore habitat for flora and fauna

---

4 See <http://www.napswq.gov.au/publications/vital-resources.html> (accessed 6 September 2006).

- Protect and manage places and values of national environmental significance, including threatened species and communities, listed migratory species, Ramsar wetlands of international importance, world heritage areas and national heritage places, and
- Promote Indigenous community participation in the planning and delivery of Regional NRM outcomes.[5]

Essentially, regional plans identify the region's natural resource management targets and strategies for implementation. They are developed as a partnership between government and the community and include investment strategies for implementing the plan.

In 2004, the Australian government announced special *Guidelines for Indigenous Participation in Natural Resource Management.*[6] The Guidelines emphasise that Indigenous people have a significant role to play in the management of natural resources in Australia. Regional NRM groups in Australia have been asked to consider the following principles in undertaking their management functions:

- appropriate processes should be established to facilitate Indigenous representation in NRM groups, however, Indigenous people may not have authority to speak about various matters;
- peak Indigenous groups such as Land councils should be consulted on land and water management issues;
- Indigenous historical and archaeological sites should be protected by NRM plans;
- all Indigenous owned or managed land should be identified in plans and managed with prescribed uses in mind;
- regional NRM groups should build on existing partnerships between Indigenous people and other landowners;
- regional plans should acknowledge Indigenous interests and relationships in land and water;
- where plans refer to legislative requirements and responsibilities, matters relating to Indigenous land and water management should be included;
- Indigenous views should be taken into account in all NRM issues not only those identified as 'Indigenous'; and
- the views of Indigenous people need to be incorporated in the planning process.

The principles have been integrated into various pieces of environmental legislation in New South Wales including the *National Parks and Wildlife Act 1974* (NSW) and the *Water Management Act 2000* (NSW).

National Market-based Instruments (MBI) Pilots Program

As one of the implementation strategies for the NAP, the Commonwealth, State and Territory governments agreed in 2003 jointly to fund $5 million to establish the National Market-based Instruments Programme. The funding covers the establish-

5 See <http://www.nrm.gov.au/national/index.html> (accessed 6 September 2006).

6 See <http://www.nrm.gov.au/indigenous/publications/participation-guidelines/index.html> (accessed 17 December 2006).

ment of 10 natural resource management projects using market-based instruments (MBIs) in some of the 21 priority NAP regions. In November 2006, the Natural Resource Management Ministerial Council announced that up to $5 million in extra funding will support nine new projects under Round Two of the MBI Pilot Programme. All projects are approved by the Natural Resource Management Ministerial Council on the recommendation of an advisory panel. Round One projects, approved in 2002, trialled a range of MBIs and operated through to 2006.

The new Integrated Natural Resource Management regime in New South Wales

Before the 2003 natural resource management reforms in New South Wales, there was little co-ordination between the management of native vegetation, threatened species, catchments and water. However, the reforms have brought about a far greater integration of natural resource management (NRM). The principal bodies vested with the responsibility of achieving NRM are the Natural Resources Commission (NRC) and the Catchment Management Authorities (CMAs). The functions of these bodies, described below, indicate the ways in which they are expected to implement integrated NRM.

Natural Resources Commission Act 2003 (NSW)

The *Natural Resources Commission Act 2003* (NSW) (NRCA) commenced on 23 January 2004. The Act defines natural resource management for the purpose of the Act as extending to matters relating to the management of water, native vegetation, salinity, soil, biodiversity, coastal protection and any other matters prescribed by regulations (s 5). It establishes an independent Commission and provides for the appointment of a Commissioner to advise the government on NRM. The functions of the Commission include:

- recommending State-wide standards and targets for natural resource management issues;
- recommending the approval (under the *Catchment Management Authorities Act 2003*) of catchment action plans consistent with the above standards that promote such targets;
- undertaking audits of those plans;
- co-ordinating or undertaking significant natural resource and conservation assessments;
- undertaking inquiries on natural resource management issues; and
- arranging for information to be gathered and disseminated on natural resource management issues. (NRCA s 13)

In the performance of its specific functions, the Commission must be guided by the principles of ecologically sustainable development, the social and economic implications of its recommendations and advice, an integrated approach to natural resource management issues, indigenous knowledge of natural resource management, and State and national legislation and policies that are relevant to natural resource management (NRCA s 14).

In September 2005, the NSW government adopted the *Standard for Quality Natural Resource Management*[7] recommended by the NRC. The Standard is intended to provide a quality assurance framework to CMAs (see below) with respect to the way in which they manage natural resources in different landscapes and communities. CMAs will be held accountable to the Standard but they will retain sufficient discretion to allow them to respond to diverse situations. The Standard promotes an adaptive management approach to NRM as is evidenced by the seven key aspects of NRM which are included in the Standard. They are: the 'collection and use of knowledge; determination of scale; opportunities for collaboration; community engagement; risk management; monitoring and evaluation; and information management.' Together these aspects relate to the four conventional stage of adaptive management – planning, implementation, audit and response. The Standard also specifies a Required Outcome for each component of the Standard which CMAs must achieve. Guidance is also given on how to achieve each Required Outcome. Finally, the Standard advises CMAs on the type of evidence that can be provided to demonstrate compliance with the Required Outcomes.

In February 2006, the NSW government adopted the NRC's recommended State-wide Targets.[8] These include targets on biodiversity, water, land and community. Each of these targets is broken down into macro-environmental and specific priority targets.

With respect to its advisory role, at the time of writing the NRC was:

- providing formal advice about any proposed changes to the Environmental Outcomes Assessment Methodology in accordance with the *Native Vegetation Regulation 2005*;
- conducting a review to provide advice on the potential for Landscape Vegetation Plans that may be submitted by multiple landholders under the *Native Vegetation Act 2003* (see below);
- supervising the environmental impact of the cloud seeding operations in the Snowy Mountains under the *Snowy Mountains Cloud Seeding Trial Act 2004*;
- advising the Department of Planning on coastal protection issues under the *SEPP 71 – Coastal Development*;
- preparing to audit Water Sharing Plans under the *Water Management Act 2000*;
- preparing to advise the NSW Department of Environment and Conservation and some specialist committees on threatened species under the *Threatened Species Legislation Amendment Act 2004*.[9]

As mentioned in Chapter 6, in deciding whether or not to extend the duration of a water sharing management plan for another 10 years, the Minister must take into account a report of the NRC. Furthermore, where the NRC recommends such changes which result in a reduction in water allocations, and compensation may be payable under s 87AA of the *Water Management Act 2000* (NSW), the Commission must state whether the purpose of the changes are to restore water to the environ-

7 See <http://www.nrc.nsw.gov.au/_documents/Standard%20for%20quality%20NRM.pdf> (accessed 17 December 2006).

8 See <http://www.nrc.nsw.gov.au/_documents/Fact%20sheet%20-%20State-wide%20targets%20for%20NRM.pdf> (accessed 17 December 2006).

9 See <http://www.nrc.nsw.gov.au/> (accessed 6 September 2006).

ment because of natural reduction in inflow (which under the National Water Initiative does not attract compensation); or whether better scientific knowledge indicates that allocations to the environment were not adequate (which does attract compensation).

The NRC also has various functions under the *Threatened Species Conservation Act 1995* (NSW) (TSCA) as discussed in Chapter 8. For example, the NRC may initiate the listing of a threatened species. Also, the Minister may not suspend or revoke biodiversity certification of the native vegetation reform package generally, or with respect to a particular Catchment Management Authority, unless the Minister has considered an audit undertaken by the NRC (TSCA s 126E).

Catchment Management Authorities Act 2003 (NSW)

The *Catchment Management Authorities Act 2003* (CMAA) establishes CMAs and devolves to them certain NRM functions. The following CMAs have been established in NSW:

- Border Rivers–Gwydir Catchment Management Authority;
- Central West Catchment Management Authority;
- Hawkesbury–Nepean Catchment Management Authority;
- Hunter–Central Rivers Catchment Management Authority;
- Lachlan Catchment Management Authority;
- Lower Murray–Darling Catchment Management Authority;
- Murray Catchment Management Authority;
- Murrumbidgee Catchment Management Authority;
- Namoi Catchment Management Authority;
- Northern Rivers Catchment Management Authority;
- Southern Rivers Catchment Management Authority;
- Sydney Metropolitan Catchment Management Authority; and
- Western Catchment Management Authority. (Sch 1)

CMAs have the general function of carrying out or funding catchment activities in accordance with the CMAA, or any other Act, or Environmental Planning Instruments (EPIs). For example, as discussed below, CMAs have functions under the *Native Vegetation Act 2003*. In addition, under the *Water Management Act 2000* (WMA) the Minister may authorise a CMA to exercise the following functions:

- assisting the Minister or a management committee in the development of, in consultations about or in the implementation of management plans;
- managing adaptive environmental water under access licences;
- monitoring water quality and other environmental health objectives of management plans (including in connection with a review or audit of any such plan). (s 389A(1))

A CMA may, with the approval of the Minister, acquire, hold and deal with access licences (s 389A(2)).

CMAs also have the capacity to be appointed as the consent authority for development under the *Environmental Planning and Assessment Act 1979* (CMAA s 14).

The specific functions of CMAs include developing catchment action plans; the provision of financial assistance for programs; entering contracts or doing any work with respect to catchment activities; assisting landholders to implement catchment action plans; and providing education and training in connection with NRM (s 15).

In developing a draft catchment action plan, a CMA must include the following:

- the results that are expected to be achieved by implementing the plan and the time by which the results will be achieved;
- for the purposes of annual implementation programs, the priorities for the funding or carrying out of the CMA's catchment activities in its area of operations; and
- any other matter that the Minister may direct to be included in the plan. (CMAA s 20(1))

A draft plan may also include provisions that relate to water quality or other non-regulatory water management issues, and must include any provisions relating to environmental water functions that are required by s 30A. In formulating a draft plan, the authority must have regard to the provisions of any environmental planning instrument under the *Environmental Planning and Assessment Act 1979* (NSW) (EPAA) that applies to land within its area of operations, and other existing NRM plans (including any such plans in the course of preparation) for its area of operations. The CMA must also have regard to the fact that the plan must comply with any State-wide NRM standards and promote the State-wide targets (CMAA s 20(1A)).

The CMA must consult widely on the draft plan by giving notice of the preparation of the plan and publicly exhibiting it as required in the Regulations. A draft catchment action plan must also be submitted to the Minister and the Natural Resources Commission after which the Minister must seek the advice of the NRC as to whether or not to approve the plan (CMAA s 22). The Minister can either approve the draft plan or refer it to the CMA for alteration. A plan must not be approved by the Minister unless the Minister is satisfied (having consulted with the NRC) that the plan complies with the State-wide NRM standards, and promotes the achievement of State-wide NRM targets (s 23). As soon as a plan has been approved it must be published in a way that makes it accessible to the persons within the catchment and the Minister must place a copy of it on the website of the Department of Natural Resources (s 24). A plan may be amended, replaced or revoked (s 25). A CMA must keep the plan under a regular and periodic review and the Minister must ensure that the plans are audited every five years by the NRC or an independent person appointed by the Minister (s 25).

The CMAs have been granted $550 million over four years ($436.5 million from the Natural Heritage Trust and National Action Plan on Salinity and Water Quality plus $115 million for operational costs).

As mentioned below, in relation to native vegetation, CMAs administer and manage applications for development consent and Property Vegetation Plans under the *Native Vegetation Act 2003*.

Conserving native vegetation

The conservation of native vegetation is important for many reasons. These include maintaining ecosystem, species and genetic diversity as well as the economic, technological and social health of human societies. The extent of native vegetation cover has been used in the State as a general indicator of the state of ecosystem diversity in the absence of other more detailed information. Currently, this indicator is regarded as providing the most comprehensive information available about terrestrial ecosystem diversity in New South Wales. The clearing of native vegetation has been identified as the most important pressure acting on vegetation communities and is consequently an important indicator of pressure on terrestrial ecosystems in the State.

The NSW State of Environment 2003 Report[10] affirms the fact that terrestrial habitats are severely impacted by the clearing of native vegetation constituting a major threat to biodiversity. Given the extent of clearing in NSW, even small amounts of additional clearing can impact heavily on biodiversity. Other environmental impacts associated with the clearing of native vegetation include soil degradation, such as erosion and salinity, a decline in aquatic ecosystem health and water quality, and climate change. The Report states that although the rate of native vegetation clearing has slowed in recent years, compared with the 1960s and 1970s, native woody vegetation is still being permanently removed at a considerable rate each year. It is difficult to ascertain the exact rate of clearing given the high differential in figures produced by different organisations. Figures given in the Report estimate that around 25,000–33,000 hectares of native woody vegetation were permanently removed each year in New South Wales in the early to mid-1990s. However, other estimates state that the clearing rate is 60,000–100,000 hectares per year. Some studies even suggest that, in some regions, clearing levels are 8–10 times higher than the figures based on satellite-data studies. The recent Auditor-General's report (see below) suggested that there were 30,000 hectares of illegal clearing in 2005.[11]

The clearing of native vegetation is highly bioregion specific. For example, results show that over 50% of native vegetation has been cleared in the NSW South-western Slopes, Nandewar, Brigalow Belt South, South-eastern Highlands and New England Tableland bioregions, while much of the native vegetation has been retained in the Australian Alps, Simpson Strzelecki Dunefields, Mulga Lands, Channel Country and Broken Hill Complex bioregions. In most areas more than 70% of the original grassy woodlands have been lost to clearing with significant consequences for threatened species.[12]

History of native vegetation legislation in New South Wales

The NSW government has sought to regulate native vegetation on private land through legislation requiring a landholder to obtain consent from the appropriate regulatory authority for permission to clear. Historically, statutes such as the *Western Lands Act 1901* (NSW), the *Soil Conservation Act 1938* (NSW), and the *Rivers and Foreshores Improvement Act 1948* (NSW) have indirectly preserved native vegetation as permission was required to clear any vegetation, native or exotic, dead or alive. As well, Tree Preservation Orders made under the EPAA apply to certain types and sizes of native and exotic vegetation primarily in metropolitan areas.

10 See <http://www.dec.nsw.gov.au/soe/soe2003/> (accessed 6 July 2006).
11 Ibid Chapter 6.
12 Ibid.

However, between August 1995 and December 1997, the government legislated directly to regulate the clearing of native vegetation on private lands through *SEPP 46 – Protection and Management of Native Vegetation*. This SEPP was repealed when the *Native Vegetation Conservation Act 1997* (NSW) came into effect on 1 January 1998. The *Native Vegetation Conservation Act* has since been repealed by the *Native Vegetation Act 2003*.

SEPP 46 and the National Vegetation Conservation Act 1997 (NSW)

SEPP 46 – Protection and Management of Native Vegetation

In August 1995, the NSW government gazetted *SEPP 46 – Protection and Management of Native Vegetation* (SEPP 46) as an environmental planning instrument under the EPAA. SEPP 46 applied to the majority of freehold land in the central and eastern divisions of New South Wales and prohibited the clearing of native vegetation without development consent by the Director-General of the Department of Land and Water Conservation, as it was then known. Not all clearing activities required development consent. Native vegetation could be cleared if the activity fell within the exemptions provided under Sch 3, eg clearing to construct rural structures, or the clearing of regrowth.

SEPP 46 was enforced by prosecuting alleged offenders for a breach of the EPAA, in which case the maximum penalty was $110,000. During the time that SEPP 46 was in force, the Department commenced 17 prosecutions for approximately 6500 hectares of clearing. The Department withdrew from four of these prosecutions. Of the remaining cases there were 11 penalty hearings and two contested hearings. The Department was unsuccessful in convicting the defendants in the two contested hearings.[13] Where the defendants pleaded guilty, the Land and Environment Court ordered that the charges proceed without conviction against three of the defendants. For the remaining eight proceedings, penalties totalled almost $100,000 with over 2000 hectares of land protected through consent orders.

Native Vegetation Conservation Act 1997

The *Native Vegetation Conservation Act 1997* (NVCA) sought to manage and conserve native vegetation in New South Wales through development consents, regional vegetation management plans, and property agreements. By consolidating the clearing provisions for 'protected lands' under the *Soil Conservation Act 1938* and on leased land under the *Western Lands Act 1901*, the NVCA became a 'one stop shop' for development consent applications, assessments and approvals for clearing native vegetation.

Native vegetation could be cleared if a person held a valid development consent, or if the activity was permissible under the regional vegetation management plan, or if the activity was exempt. The various exemptions which applied under SEPP 46 were saved into the NVCA.

13 *Windouran Pastoral Company Pty Ltd v Director-General of Department of Land and Water Conservation* [2000] NSWCCA 65 which overturned *Director-General of Department of Land and Water Conservation v Crawford* (unreported, NSWLEC, Talbot J, 3 April 1997) and *Director-General of Department of Land and Water Conservation v Pye* [1998] NSWLEC 292.

Difficulties with enforcement under the NVCA

The Department has experienced significant difficulties in attempting to enforce the NVCA. In *Director-General of the Department of Land and Water Conservation v Bailey*,[14] the defendant cleared approximately 84 hectares to construct a farm dam in 2000, with further clearing in 2002. The defendant claimed that the clearing was 'designated development' within the meaning of the EPAA. This meant that development consent under the NVCA was not required, and that the clearing was to construct a farm dam, which also did not require consent as the activity is listed in Sch 3 to SEPP 46. The prosecutor claimed that 'clearing to a minimum extent … necessary for the construction, operation and maintenance of farm structures', within the meaning of the exemption, meant that the landholder may only construct 'minor' farm structures resulting in minimum harm to the environment. Talbot J of the Land and Environment Court rejected the prosecutor's argument. On appeal, the Court of Criminal Appeal agreed with his Honour.

This case centred on the statutory interpretation of two exemptions. The NVCA provided a number of exemptions from the classification of land (eg, residential, State Forests and National Parks) to certain Local Government Areas (primarily metropolitan Sydney Councils), and types of clearing authorised under other statutes (eg, the *Rural Fires Act 1997*, the *Mining Act 1992*, and the *Roads Act 1993*). The NVCA was silent on whether a landholder was required to obtain consent under the EPAA, before clearing native vegetation, for the purpose of undertaking 'designated development'.[15] In relation to the rural structure exemption, Talbot J commented that clearing rural structures to the minimum extent necessary for the construction of farm structures is referable to the amount of clearing, not to the rural structure itself.

In *Holmes v Director-General of the Department of Infrastructure, Planning and Natural Resources*,[16] the Director-General served a direction for remedial work under s 47 of the NVCA (the Notice) on Mr Holmes for clearing over 1000 hectares of invasive native scrub which the Director-General was satisfied had caused soil erosion and/or land degradation. The Notice, which purported to be in effect for 10 years, prohibited the landholder from clearing any native vegetation, required a fence to be installed, stock to be removed, and prohibited any cleared vegetation from being moved, removed or burnt.

Mr Holmes challenged the validity of the Notice on the grounds that the Notice was *ultra vires* as the NVCA did not allow the Director-General to make the Notice which contained prohibitory conditions. Lloyd J of the Land and Environment Court agreed with Mr Holmes and held that any direction for remedial work must require the carrying out of specified work in positive terms. Accordingly, the Notice was invalid to such an extent that no part of the Notice could survive.

Push for reform of native vegetation regulatory framework

In 2002 and 2003, four documents were released which sparked a change in native vegetation laws. The first was a highly critical performance audit in 2002 by the

---

14 (2003) 128 LGERA 1; [2003] NSWLEC 160.

15 Note that under the *Native Vegetation Act 2003* consent to clear native vegetation to undertake 'designated development' is now required, thus reversing the decision in *Bailey*.

16 (2005) 139 LGERA 102.

Auditor-General. The second and third documents were released by the Wentworth Group of Concerned Scientists, *Blueprint for a Living Continent* and *A New Model for Landscape Conservation in New South Wales*. These documents suggested that there should be a refocusing of native vegetation laws from the regional level to individual property holders. The culmination was the Final Report of the Native Vegetation Reform Implementation Group which proposed 48 recommendations to reform natural resource management in New South Wales. It was this last report that was the catalyst for the cognate legislation – the *Natural Resources Commission Act* 2003, the *Catchment Management Act* 2003 and the *Native Vegetation Act* 2003.

Current legislative regime: the Native Vegetation Act 2003 (NSW)

The *Native Vegetation Act 2003* (NVA) outlines the framework for native vegetation management. The Act relies on the *Native Vegetation Regulation 2005* to implement key aspects of the NVA. The NVA does not incorporate the protected land provisions originally in the *Soil Conservation Act* 1938, which were subsequently incorporated into the NVCA. The NVA does make a savings provision for State-protected land by providing that the provisions of the NVCA continue to have effect with respect to exotic and dead trees until a State Environmental Planning Policy under the EPAA otherwise provides.

Key concepts

The operation of the NVA depends on six key concepts. These are 'native vegetation', 'remnant native vegetation', 'regrowth and protected regrowth', 'broadscale clearing', and 'routine agricultural management activities'. These concepts are all defined in Pt 2 of the NVA (ss 6-11).

In relation to native vegetation and its conservation, 'native vegetation' is vegetation that existed in New South Wales before European settlement and includes trees, understorey plants and groundcover. 'Remnant native vegetation' means any native vegetation other than regrowth, where 'regrowth' is any native vegetation that has regrown since 1 January 1983 for land in the Western Division and 1 January 1990 for land outside the Western Division. Alternatively, regrowth may be in accordance with a date specified in a property vegetation plan. 'Protected regrowth' may be identified in an environmental planning instrument or plan such as a property vegetation plan or natural resource management plan, or an interim protection order. Native vegetation is cleared if it is cut down, felled, thinned, logged or removed or if it is killed, destroyed, poisoned, ringbarked, uprooted or burnt.

'Broadscale clearing' means the clearing of any remnant native vegetation or protected regrowth. 'Routine agricultural activities' may be classified as any activity which a landholder regularly undertakes as part of a rural enterprise and includes the construction, operation and maintenance of rural infrastructure; the removal of noxious weeds under the *Noxious Weeds Act 1993*; the control of noxious animals under the *Rural Lands Protection Act 1998* (NSW); the lopping of native vegetation for stock fodder; and the maintenance of public utilities.

The Regulations provide that native vegetation cleared for the construction, operation and maintenance of rural infrastructure must be used for that purpose within 12 months or 18 months depending on where the land is situated. Native vegetation may only be cleared to obtain construction timber if it does not cause land degradation and is carried out in conjunction with a restoration program. As well, certain buffer distances for rural infrastructure have been prescribed for the Western Division and specified catchment management authorities' areas.

Native vegetation which comprises feral native plant species may only be cleared where the Minister has ordered that a species of native vegetation is a feral species for specified land where the species is outside the natural range, and the local CMA has recommended that the plant species is feral, and the Minister has consulted with the Natural Resources Commission and the Minister for the Environment.

Clearing native vegetation

Native vegetation may be cleared if the landowner has been given development consent to clear the land, or the clearing of native vegetation has been undertaken in accordance with an approved Property Vegetation Plan (PVP). Clearing is permissible only where the clearing 'improves or maintains' environmental outcomes. Development applications must be assessed in accordance with the Environmental Outcomes Assessment Methodology (EOAM), incorporated into the Act by Regulation, to determine whether proposed broadscale clearing will improve or maintain environmental outcomes. Under the EOAM, the clearing will be assessed in accordance with its impacts on the following environmental values: water quality; salinity; biodiversity; and land degradation. The methodology may not be amended unless the Minister has sought the advice of the Natural Resources Commission. The advice must be made public. Concurrence from the Minister for the Environment is required where the Minister for Natural Resources makes any amendments that relate to biodiversity. With respect to clearing to be undertaken under a PVP, the impacts of the proposed clearing and the benefits of offsets must also be assessed against each environmental value.

The Regulations specify that in determining a development application to clear land s 79C matters under the EPAA are not taken into account. Furthermore, a development application for clearing does not have to specify whether the vegetation comprises critical habitat and threatened species, populations or ecological communities. Where development consent has been granted to construct a single dwelling under the EPAA no further approval is required under the NVA.

There are exceptions to the requirement to obtain consent for clearing. For example, native vegetation that is classified as non-protected regrowth may be cleared without consent. As well, native vegetation that is required for 'routine agricultural management', to continue 'existing farming activities' or for sustainable grazing does not require consent. Clearing for 'routine agricultural management' is permissible after the grant of any statutory approval for a building, work or structure. 'Existing farming activities' do not include the clearing of 'remnant vegetation'.

Property Vegetation Plans

A landholder, or a group of landholders, may submit a Property Vegetation Plan (PVP) for approval by the Minister, the CMA or other government agency as an alternative to applying for development consent. A PVP runs with the land for the duration of the plan and is not affected by a change in ownership of the land. A PVP may also be registered on title.

The NVA provides that a group of landholders may submit a draft PVP. In 2006, the Natural Resources Commission conducted a public review on the potential for landscape or multi-farm vegetation management plans to produce better economic and environmental outcomes than small-scale or single-farm plans. Landscape vegetation plans cover multiple properties and are large enough to allow vegetation management actions and trade-offs to occur within the boundaries of the area. It is envisaged that such plans may produce better environmental and economic benefits. The plans will be developed by a group of landholders who are seeking private benefits over land which they own and over which they have stewardship responsibilities.

The *Native Vegetation Regulation 2005* sets out the detailed provisions relating to PVPs.

Requirements of PVPs

A PVP must:

- contain a description of the land to which the PVP applies as well as specify the address and particulars of title of the land to which the PVP applies;
- specify the period for which the PVP has effect and the nature of the clearing that is proposed by the PVP, and the period within which the clearing may occur;
- include a rectified satellite or aerial photograph or topographical map identifying any land which is the subject of proposed broadscale land clearing, land identified for regrowth, native vegetation that is protected regrowth or remnant vegetation, and land on which native vegetation management activities will be carried out under the PVP;
- specify the nature of the clearing that is proposed and the period within which it may occur (with 15 years being the maximum time that a PVP can have effect);
- specify the distance of a riparian buffer from the banks of the relevant water course;
- detail the financial incentives that have been offered to undertake any management actions under the PVP;
- include details of any offsets that are proposed by the PVP; and
- include details of the extent to which the PVP excludes clearing for routine agricultural management or other activities from being 'permitted clearing'.

PVPs that change 'regrowth' date

Under the NVA 'regrowth' means any native vegetation that has regrown since the earlier of the following dates: 1 January 1983 in the case of land in the Western Division and 1 January 1990 in the case of any other land. The Regulations provide that a PVP cannot be approved if it sets the regrowth date earlier than these dates unless the Minister is satisfied that the native vegetation has been cleared according to existing rotational farming practices, on at least two occasions, since 1950, in the case of land not in the Western Division, or 1943 for land in the Western Division.

The PVP can also only be approved if it requires that regrowth is cleared only if it occurs consistently with those existing rotational farm practices.

Termination of PVPs

Rights of procedural fairness are granted under the Regulations. A PVP cannot be terminated by the Minister unless he or she has given the landholder notice of the termination and given the landholder 14 days within which to make a written submission. The Minister must have regard to the submission before deciding whether or not to terminate the PVP.

Information about PVPs and development consents

The Minister must make publicly available on the internet:

- the GPS co-ordinates of land subject to a development consent or PVP that provides for broadscale clearing of native vegetation;
- the number of hectares authorised to be cleared; and
- the number of hectares to which offsets apply.

Each CMA, established under the *Catchment Management Act 2003*, must keep available for inspection detailed information about the clearing authorised by a development consent or PVP that provides for broadscale clearing of native vegetation as well as information about the agreed offsets.

A bona fide prospective purchaser of the land must be given details of financial incentives available under a PVP for the management of natural resources and details for the provision and expenditure of those financial incentives.

All information must be made available within 10 days after development consent is granted or a PVP is approved.

Variation of PVPs

Where a PVP proposes broadscale clearing of native vegetation, the Minister is not to approve a variation of the PVP unless the PVP could have been approved under s 29 of the Act, ie, that it will maintain or improve environmental outcomes.

Other provisions

The Regulations allow a landholder to include information on the social and economic impacts of activities such as clearing, natural resource management activities, or the continuation of existing farming practices in a PVP. The impacts may include on-farm impacts, impacts to the regional community and other impacts established by the Natural Resources Commission.

The Regulations also prescribe the content of a PVP and a 'continuing use PVP', the procedure to vary and terminate a PVP, and the publication of certain information on the internet and by inspection. More detailed information about a PVP may be obtained by a prospective purchaser of land where a PVP applies.

Enforcement

The NVA provides for criminal, civil and administrative enforcement similar to the provisions of the NVCA. Clearing of native vegetation in contravention of the Act constitutes an offence. The maximum penalty is found in s 126 of the EPAA which provides for a maximum pecuniary penalty of $1,100,000, the planting of vegetation and/or the giving of a security for performance.

The administrative mechanisms of stop work orders and directions for remedial work are almost identical in the 1997 and 2003 native vegetation legislation. The NVA allows authorised officers to issue a penalty notice for a contravention. A landholder who has cleared native vegetation in contravention of the Act may be fined $3300 (for an individual) or $5500 (for a company). Where a landholder fails to comply with a stop-work order or direction for remedial work, the penalty notice is $1650 (for an individual) or $3300 (for a company). If the Department prosecutes a landholder for a failure to comply with a direction for remedial work or stop work order, the maximum penalty is $110,000 (for an individual) or $220,000 (for a company).

Financial assistance package for farmers

In June 2006, the NSW government established a package to help farmers who have been affected by the NVA and the *Native Vegetation Regulation 2005*. The $37 million package funded by the Environmental Trust is available for three years from 1 July 2006 and includes:

- Farmer Exit Assistance ($12 million) – where farmers can demonstrate loss of commercial viability as a result of being refused permission to clear native vegetation and who have passed the Relative Hardship Test – that is, the landholder must show that the area of native vegetation being conserved on their farm is greater than the catchment average for each landscape type. The NSW government may offer to purchase the property to be on-sold under strict environmental management conditions. The money generated by the sale will be added to a revolving pool fund to be used to purchase further properties.
- Sustainable Farming Grants ($15 million) – where farmers have suffered real financial hardship as a result of the legislation a grant may be awarded to improve the economic and environmental viability of the property. Farmers must have been refused consent to clear, satisfy the Relative Hardship Test, exhausted all Property Vegetation Plan options, and have completed, or complete, a sustainable farm management course.
- Offset Pools – where farmers are not able to avail themselves of the 'offset' actions available under the *Native Vegetation Act*, because they are not able to establish the offsets either on-farm or on an adjoining property, they may access the CMA's Offset Pool. The CMAs will broker agreements with farmers to create this pool and some farmers will even be paid to provide the offsets. Again, the farmers must have been refused consent to clear, satisfy the Relative Hardship Test, exhausted all Property Vegetation Plan options, and have completed, or complete, a sustainable farm management course.

The Draft Code of Practice for Private Native Forestry

In July 2006, the Department of Natural Resources released a draft code of practice for Private Native Forestry for comment. The Code aims to regulate the clearing of native vegetation on private property for forestry purposes. The Department hopes to use the Code to require landholders to have either development consent or a PVP to harvest timber for private native forestry. The landholder must prove that the harvesting of timber will 'improve or maintain' the environment.

The Auditor-General's 2006 report

In July 2006, the Auditor-General released a report following up on his previous audit in 2002.[17] The report claimed that approximately 74,000 hectares of native vegetation was cleared in 2005, comprising 44,000 hectares of approved clearing and 30,000 hectares of illegal clearing. These figures omit exempt clearing, being clearing that is legally carried out without approval. No figure was provided on the size of exempt clearing.

The Report noted that the issues raised in the 2002 report in relation to accountability, targets and monitoring have been addressed and that there has been considerable progress towards achieving the government's objectives to end broadscale clearing of native vegetation and to maintain productive landscapes.

The Report also noted that the cognate legislation has more clearly defined the responsibilities for native vegetation within the government, with the establishment of the Natural Resources Commission providing advice and CMAs responsible for clearing approvals.

Market mechanisms to protect and enhance native vegetation

As mentioned in Chapter 1, in addition to the direct regulation, governments have been developing alternative mechanisms to manage natural resources, including native vegetation. The Victorian BushBroker program and the NSW Biobanking scheme are examples of market-based instruments that endeavour to commoditise a natural resource which may be bought and sold.

Under the BushBroker programme, BushBroker registers and trades native vegetation credits in Victoria. Native vegetation credits are created by entering into an agreement with a public agency, through a credit auction (such as BushTender), by direct contribution from the applicant to the landholder or through a public conservation reserve system. BushBroker registers, lists, extinguishes and controls the quality of native vegetation credits.

The NSW Biodiversity Banking and Offset Scheme (BioBanking)[18] is discussed extensively in Chapter 8.

Coastal zone protection

Australia's coastal zone is 36,000 kilometres long and includes a wide range of climatic, geological and oceanographic regimes including a mix of terrestrial, estuarine and marine ecosystems which all interact with each other, and support a wealth of biodiversity. The conservation of this biodiversity is crucial to the broad

---

17 See <http://www.audit.nsw.gov.au/publications/reports/performance/performance_reports.htm> (accessed 6 September 2006).

18 For further information on Biobanking, see P Curnow and L Fitz-Gerald, 'Biobanking in New South Wales: legal issues in the design and implementation of a biodiversity offsets and banking scheme' (2006) 23 *EPLJ* 298.

range of commercial and non commercial activities which it supports. Coastal zone protection is pursued, in Australia, through national and State policies and specialist State laws. Australia is also a signatory to a number of conventions which are relevant to coastal zone management. These include:

- The *Ramsar Convention*;
- The *World Heritage Convention*;
- The Japan-Australia Migratory Bird Agreement (JAMBA);
- The China-Australia Migratory Bird Agreement;
- Agreements under the *Convention for the Prevention of Pollution from Ships*;
- The *United Nations Convention on the Law of the Sea*; and
- The Global Programme of Action for protecting the marine environment from land-based sources of pollution 1995.

Co-operative federalism

A national Framework for a National Co-operative Approach to Integrated Coastal Zone Management was approved by the Natural Resource Management Ministerial Council in October 2003 to protect coastal and estuarine water quality, coastal biodiversity and the economic base of coastal areas around Australia.

Framework for a National Co-operative Approach to Integrated Coastal Zone Management (ICZM)

The Framework[19] states that:

> The fundamental goal of ICZM is to maintain, restore or improve the quality of coastal ecosystems and the societies they support. A defining feature of ICZM is that it seeks to address both development and conservation needs within a geographically specific place - a single community, estuary or nation - and within a specified timeframe.[20]

The key coastal zone pressures identified in the Framework are: population growth and demographic shifts; industry trends; protection of the coastal resource base; and climate change. The key themes for national action include:

- a catchment-coast-ocean continuum, which requires an integration of coastal zone management with: the National Heritage Trust and National Action Plan on Salinity and Water Quality initiatives; the Integrated Oceans Management Collaborative Approach; Australia's Oceans Policy; the regional marine planning process; Australian, State and local government initiatives; and Australia's obligations under the international conventions mentioned above;
- coastal issues for national collaboration which include: land and marine-based sources of pollution; managing climate change; introduced pest plants and animal; allocation and use of coastal resources; and capacity building.

An Implementation Plan for the Framework has also been developed.

---

19 See <http://www.deh.gov.au/coasts/publications/framework/index.html> (accessed 11 September 2006).

20 Ibid at 7.

New South Wales

The NSW Government's Coastal Protection Package in June 2001 subjected planning in the coastal zone to stronger government direction under the *Coastal Protection Act 1979,* and two State Environmental Protection Policies: *SEPP 71 – Coastal Protection,* and *SEPP (Major Projects) 2005.*

Coastal Policy

The New South Wales Coastal Policy 1997 promotes 'the ecologically sustainable development of the New South Wales coastline' by setting out goals, objectives and actions.

The policy applies development control to the 'coastal zone' discussed below. Councils are guided by the policy when making local environmental plans for, and deciding development applications in, the coastal zone, using the legislative instruments discussed below.[21]

Coastal Protection Act 1979

The *Coastal Protection Act 1979* (CPA) regulates the use and occupation of the coastal region of New South Wales and facilitates coastal protection works (s 1) to provide for the protection of the coastal environment for the benefit of both present and future generations (s 3). The Act binds the Crown, so far as the legislative power of Parliament permits, in all its capacities (s 5).

The specific objects of the legislation include:

- to protect the environment of the coastal region, its associated ecosystems, ecological processes and biological diversity, and its water quality;
- to promote the orderly and balanced utilisation and conservation of the coastal region and its natural and man-made resources;
- to recognise and foster the significant social and economic benefits to the State that result from a sustainable coastal environment;
- to promote public pedestrian access to the coastal region; and
- to acquire land in the coastal region for environmental protection in the coastal region. (s 3)

In exercising functions under the Act, the Minister must promote the 'principles of ecologically sustainable development' as described in s 6(2) of the *Protection of the Environment Administration Act 1991* (CPA ss 4, 37A).

Coastal zone

The legislation makes provision for maps of the coastal zone, which includes coastal waters of the State, land, the seabed, subsoil and airspace. The maps outlining the coastal zone are available for inspection at the offices of the Department of Planning and councils within the coastal zone (CPA ss 4A, 4B).

---

21 See Environmental Defender's Office New South Wales (Ltd), Fact Sheets, Topic 4 – Natural Resources <www.edo.org.au/edonsw/site/factsh/fs04_6.php> (access 17 December 2006).

Generally, the western boundary of the coastal zone is one kilometre landward of the western boundary of the coastal waters of the State, or around any bay, estuary, coastal lake or lagoon. It follows the length of any coastal river inland generally at a distance of one kilometre from each bank of the river, to one kilometre, beyond the limit of any mangroves on the river or, in the absence of mangroves, beyond the tidal limit of the river.

The coastal zone extends into the metropolitan area but the boundary excludes:

- the parts of the local government areas of Pittwater, Warringah, Manly, Woollahra, Waverley, Randwick and Sutherland that are unlikely to be affected by coastal processes, including coastal wave and wind action; and
- the waters of Sydney Harbour and Botany Bay.

Development in the coastal zone

Development regulated in the coastal zone includes:

- the erection or removal of buildings;
- the carrying out of a work;
- a change in the use of any building or work;
- the subdivision of land; and
- the clearing or propagation of marine and other vegetation.

This list may be added to in the Regulations (CPA s 37).

General supervision of coastal zone

The legislation limits the powers of public authorities that might be inconsistent with principles of ecologically sustainable development or adversely impact on the coastal zone. Without the concurrence of the Minister administering the CPA, an authority must not carry out, grant a right, or consent to development in, or the use or occupation of, any part of the coastal zone (ss 38, 40-45). This restriction applies generally to areas described by an order of the Governor, or to functions set out in the Coastal Protection Regulations (s 39). A regulation does not apply to an area that is subject to an environmental planning instrument under the EPAA other than a SEPP (s 39).

Entry, inspection, and testing

Persons authorised by the Minister may carry out inspections of the coastal zone and any development within it. The authorised person, after reasonable notice to the owner or occupier, may enter a development, carry out tests, investigations, surveys, experiments, boring, drilling and exploration, take samples and measurements, and record information (s 48).

It is an offence to obstruct, hinder or interfere with an authorised person (s 49), or to interfere with, damage, destroy a vehicle, vessel or equipment used by authorised persons in carrying out these functions (s 50).

Enforcement by notice

In addition to any other means of enforcement, a person who does anything without the concurrence of the Minister, required by the CPA or other legislation, may be served with a notice requiring that the person stop the action, or do whatever is specified in the notice as necessary to restore the coastal zone to its previous condition. If the person fails to comply with a notice, the Minister may do whatever is required by the notice and recover the expense from the person as a debt in any court of competent jurisdiction. The Act sets out procedures for serving a notice (s 51). The Minister may give directions to any public authority as to the exercise of its functions that affect the coastal zone, with which the public authority must comply (s 52).

Carrying out of works in the coastal zone by the Minister

The Minister may direct that works for the preservation, protection, maintenance, restoration or improvement of the coastal zone or any part of the coastal zone should be carried out under the *Public Works Act 1912*. Work worth more than $1,000,000 must be authorised by the Governor. The work is deemed to be an authorised work under the *Public Works Act 1912* (CPA s 55).

Coastal zone management plans

Councils whose areas are included in the coastal zone prepare draft coastal zone management plans under the Act (CPA s 55B), providing for:

- beach environment and amenity;
- emergency actions including under the *State Emergency and Rescue Management Act 1989*, during periods of beach erosion; and
- public access to beaches, headlands and waterways, particularly where public access is threatened or affected by accretion. (CPA s 55C)

The Minister may issue guidelines for draft coastal zone management plans (s 55D).

A draft coastal zone management plan must be publicly exhibited, and details must be given in a newspaper circulating in the locality (s 55E). The council must consider any submissions made as a result on the consultation process (s 55F). When approved by the Minister (s 55G), a plan must be published in the *Government Gazette* (s 55H). Copies must be made available for public inspection at the council's offices (s 55J).

Breach of coastal zone management plan

It is an offence to carry out work relating to beach erosion, except in accordance with the coastal zone management plan (s 55K). The Minister or a council may bring proceedings in the Land and Environment Court for an order to remedy or restrain a breach of a coastal zone management plan (s 55L). The Minister or a council may order:

- a person not to deposit material on a beach likely to affect beach erosion or public access to a beach or headland, or to remove the material; and
- a person who is the owner or occupier of land that has a frontage to a beach is not to erect any structure at the boundary of the land likely to affect beach erosion or public access to a beach or headland, or to remove the structure.

The Act applies relevant provisions of the *Local Government Act 1993* to the Minister's order (CPA s 55M and *Local Government Act* Chapter 7, Pt 2, Div 3 and s 678).

A person who carries out work in compliance with an order under the CPA is not subject to Pt 5 of the EPAA (CPA s 55M).

Modification of doctrine of erosion and accretion

The CPA modifies the doctrine of erosion and accretion for land with a water boundary, within the coastal zone, or which adjoins the tidal waters of Sydney Harbour or Botany Bay, or their tributaries. The area of the land may not be increased if a perceived trend by way of accretion is not likely to be indefinitely sustained by natural means, or if a consequence of the implementation of the doctrine would be to restrict or deny public access to a beach, headland or waterway. To this end, the CPA restricts the powers of the courts, the Registrar-General, and the Minister administering the *Crown Lands Act 1989* under Pt 7 of the *Surveyors (Practice) Regulation 2001* (CPA s 55N).

Restoration orders

The Land and Environment Court may order a person to take steps to:

- prevent, control, abate or mitigate any harm to the environment or any loss of amenity caused by the person;
- to make good any resulting environmental damage; or
- to prevent any continuance or recurrence.

'Environment' and 'harm' have the same meanings as in the *Protection of the Environment Operations Act 1997* (CPA s 56A).

Proceedings for offences

The Local Court hears proceedings for offences against the CPA (s 59). The maximum penalties are:

- for offences against the Act – $11,000; or
- for offences against the Regulations – $1100.

Coastal Protection Regulation 2004

This Regulation prohibits the carrying out of development on any part of the coastal zone, except with the concurrence of the Minister for Natural Resources. It also prohibits public authorities from granting any rights or consent to the use or occupation of the coastal zone, without the Minister's consent The Regulation extends to the coastal zone below the mean high water mark, excluding any estuary, lake or artificial harbour.

It is important to note also that the *Native Vegetation Conservation (Savings and Transitional) Amendment (Minimal Clearing Exemption) Regulation 2004* bans minimal clearing of native vegetation in the coastal zone.

State Environmental Planning Policy No 71 – Coastal Protection

SEPP 71 – Coastal Protection was made under the EPAA and commenced on 1 November 2002. SEPP 71 places considerable restrictions on developments along the NSW coast to ensure:

- that development in the NSW coastal zone is appropriate and suitably located;
- a consistent and strategic approach to coastal planning and management; and
- a clear development assessment framework for the coastal zone.

Aims of policy

The aims of the Policy are generally to encourage a strategic approach to coastal management and to protect and manage the natural, cultural, recreational and economic attributes of the NSW coast. Management must be in accordance with the principles of ecologically sustainable development. The Policy also has more specific aims, including to:

- maintain and increase public access to coastal foreshores;
- protect and preserve Aboriginal cultural heritage, and Aboriginal places, values, customs, beliefs and traditional knowledge; and
- to protect and preserve visual amenity, beach environments, native coastal vegetation, marine environment and rock platforms.

Finally, the Policy is to ensure that the type, bulk, scale and size of any development is appropriate for the location, and protects and improves the natural scenic quality of the surrounding area.

The Policy pursues these aims by:

- identifying State-significant development in the coastal zone; and
- requiring certain development applications to be referred to the Director-General for comment; and
- identifying master plan requirements for certain development in the coastal zone.

The Policy applies to all land and development in the coastal zone, with minor exceptions (cl 4), and prevails over other environmental planning instruments (cl 5).

Matters for consideration by local councils

The Policy sets out matters for consideration by a council when preparing a draft local environmental plan, and by a consent authority when determining a development application to carry out development on land to which the Policy applies. These include:

- the aims of the Policy set out above;
- protecting the environment – to conserve animals and fish and their habitats; marine vegetation, the water quality of coastal waterbodies, and existing wildlife corridors;
- reducing conflict between land-based and water-based coastal activities;
- encouraging compact towns and cities;
- the cumulative impacts of the proposed development on the environment; and
- efficient water and energy usage.

Clause 92 of the *Environmental Planning and Assessment Regulation 2000* requires Government Coastal Policy to be taken into consideration by consent authorities when determining development applications in local government areas to which it applies (cl 8).

The Policy identifies instances of significant coastal development (cl 9) and requires a council to send a copy of development applications to the Director-General for guidance.

Master plans

The Policy requires the preparation of a master plan for sensitive subdivisions by a land owner for approval by the Minister, after public consultation. A consent authority is required to take the master plan into consideration. Master plans are available for inspection at council offices (cll 18-26).

State Environmental Planning Policy (Major Projects) 2005

This SEPP, discussed more extensively in Chapter 2, identifies development to which assessment and approval provisions in Pt 3A of the EPAA apply. The Minister for Planning is the approval authority for development and sites nominated in the Policy. Schedule 2, cl 1, to the SEPP lists categories of development in coastal areas to which Pt 3A of the Act applies.

Coastal Lands Protection Scheme

The Government's Coastal Lands Protection Scheme aims to bring significant coastal lands into public ownership, with long-term management and care. The Scheme, which commenced in 1973, identifies lands for protection and acquisition. These usually include features like headlands, dunes, hinterland, coastal lagoons and lakes, particularly where the original vegetation is still dominant. Land is also acquired on an opportunistic basis. The main criteria for acquisition are:

- public access to the foreshore;
- scenic quality; and
- ecological values of regional, State and national significance.

As at June 2006, about 15,314 hectares have been acquired for new coastal national parks and reserves, administered by the Department of Environment and Conservation (national parks), the Department of Lands (Crown Reserves) and local councils (public reserves).

8

CONSERVING BIODIVERSITY

Introduction

This chapter discusses the policy and legislative initiatives adopted by the Commonwealth and NSW governments in their attempts to conserve Australia's unique biodiversity. It refers especially to efforts to conserve biodiversity outside protected areas, although it is also important to remember the role of protected areas, discussed in Chapter 9, in conserving biodiversity. In reading this chapter, it will also be necessary to refer to Chapter 7, in particular the native vegetation reform package.

The Convention on Biological Diversity

The objectives of the *Convention on Biological Diversity*[1] are the conservation of biological diversity, the sustainable use of its components and the fair and equitable sharing of the benefits arising out of the utilisation of genetic resources, including by appropriate access to genetic resources and by appropriate transfer of relevant technologies, taking into account all rights over those resources and to technologies, and by appropriate funding (Art 1). Article 6 of the Convention imposes an obligation on nations to adopt national strategies, plans or programs to conserve biological resources, and to integrate, as far as possible, the conservation and sustainable use of biological diversity into relevant sectoral or cross-sectoral plans, programs and policies. Components of biodiversity must be identified and monitored (Art 7).

The Convention also refers to the importance of conserving biodiversity *in situ*, that is both in and outside of protected areas (Art 8). As a last resort biodiversity should also be conserved *ex situ* in places like zoos or botanical gardens (Art 9.) Countries should integrate the conservation and sustainable use of biological resources into national decision-making, while adopting measures to avoid or minimise adverse impacts on biological diversity. The customary use of biological resources should be protected and encouraged (Art 10). The environmental impacts of proposed projects that are likely to have significant adverse effects on biological diversity should be assessed so as to avoid or minimise such effects and, where appropriate, allow for public participation in such procedures (Art 14). The Contracting Parties also recognise that technology includes biotechnology, and that both access to and transfer of technology among Contracting Parties are essential elements for the attainment of the objectives of the Convention (Art 16).

---

1 31 ILM 818 (1992).

The Parties to the Convention have adopted the Strategic Plan for the *Convention on Biological Diversity* in which they have agreed to achieve by 2010 a significant reduction of the current rate of biodiversity loss at the global, regional and national level as a contribution to poverty alleviation and to the benefit of all life on earth.

Cartagena Protocol on Biosafety 2000: recognising the potential impacts of biotechnology on biodiversity

There is considerable controversy about whether, and to what extent, genetically modified organisms (GMOs)[2] pose a threat to the biodiversity of the earth.[3] It is important, for the purposes of this chapter, to note that GMOs are organisms, plants or animals which are *not* derived from traditional breeding techniques. They are produced using biotechnological methods knows as recombinant DNA, which is the latest evolution of genetic engineering. It involves the transfer of an alien gene into the genetic code of an organism such that the organism bears certain 'desired' new characteristics. The potential risks presented by GM crops for biodiversity include:

- the impact on non-target organisms such as insects, birds and micro/fauna and flora;
- gene transfer from the GM crop into related species;
- persistence or invasiveness of GM crops;
- the potential adverse effects of altered farm management practices, required by GM crops, on biodiversity; and
- the potential adverse impact on the centre of the origin of species.[4]

Yet, there are many who extol the environmental benefits of GM crops which require fewer fertilisers, herbicides and pesticides. Others point to the fact that there will be nine billion people by 2050 concentrated in developing countries. Their food security is tenuous given the shrinkage of available farmland and decreasing productivity caused by housing, infrastructure and climate change.

Under the *Convention on Biological Diversity*, the handling of biotechnology and the distribution of its benefits is provided for by requiring the parties to consider the need for a 'protocol setting out appropriate procedures, including, in particular, advance informed agreement, in the field of the safe transfer, handling and use of any living modified organism resulting from biotechnology that may have adverse effect on the conservation and sustainable use of biological diversity' (Art 19(3)).

Article 19(3) in the Convention gave rise to the negotiation of the Cartagena Protocol[5] which acknowledges the growing public concern over the rapid expansion of modern biotechnology and its potential to impact adversely on biological diversity and human health.[6] It also recognises, however, that if modern biotechnology is

---

2 This term is preferred by the author but may be used interchangeably with the term 'living modified organisms' as adopted in the Cartagena Protocol.

3 See, eg, S Kolehmainen 'Precaution Before Profits: An Overview of Issues in Genetically Engineered Food and Crops' (2001) 20 *Vancouver Environmental LJ* 267.

4 See T Simpson, 'Environmental Risk Assessment of GMOs Under Directive 2001/18: An Effective Safety-Net or a "Collective Illusion"' (2003) 25(2) *EIPR* 79 at 81.

5 See <http://www.biodiv.org/doc/legal/cartagena-protocol-en.pdf> (accessed 27 July 2006).

6 H Baumuller, 'The Cartagena Protocol on Biosafety-Environmental Perspectives' (2001) 18 *EPLJ* 46; and B Eggers and R Mackenzie, 'The Cartagena Protocol on Biosafety' [2000] *Journal of International Economic Law* 525.

used with adequate safety measures for the environment and human health, it has great potential for human well-being. The Protocol specifically acknowledges that many countries, particularly developing countries, have little capacity to cope with the potential risks associated with living modified organisms.

Consequently, the objective of the Protocol is to ensure an adequate level of protection for the safe transfer, handling and use of living modified organisms (hereafter 'organisms') derived from modern biotechnology. Relying on the precautionary principle, the level of protection should take into account risks to biological diversity and human health, and should focus on transboundary movements (Art 1). The Protocol does not apply to the transboundary movement of organisms which are pharmaceuticals for humans as these are regulated under other relevant international agreements or organisations (Art 5).

The centrepiece of the Protocol is the 'advance informed agreement procedure' which requires the exporting Party to notify the Competent National Authority (Art 19) of the importing Party about its first intentional transboundary movement of an organism (Arts 8-10 and 12).[7] The importing Party must acknowledge receipt of the notification (Art 9) and then decide, within 90 days of notification, whether the importation can proceed with or without the written consent of the importing party (Art 10(2)). The importing Party is required to carry out an assessment of the risk posed to biodiversity and human health by the organisms, taking into account recognised risk assessment techniques and the precautionary principle (Arts 10(1), (6), 12). The exporting Party can be required by the importing Party to undertake a risk assessment and bear the cost (Arts 15, 16). If importation is only allowed upon written consent, the importing Party must notify the notifier and the Biosafety Clearing-House (Art 20)[8] of its decision to: approve the import, with or without conditions, including how the decision will apply to subsequent imports of the same organism; prohibit the import; or request additional relevant information (Art 10(3)).[9] The advance informed agreement procedure does not apply to organisms in transit or destined for contained use in the importing country (Art 6). Different provisions apply to organisms intended for direct use as food or feed, or for processing (Art 11).

Parties should also develop risk management strategies to deal with the risks associated with the transboundary movement of organisms (Art 16). They must also notify potentially affected States and the Biosafety Clearing-House (Art 20) if an unintentional transboundary movement occurs (Art 17). Parties must also ensure that organisms that are subject to intentional transboundary movement are handled, packaged and transported under conditions of safety, taking into consideration relevant international rules and standards (Art 18).

Appropriate domestic measures aimed at preventing and penalising illegal transboundary movements of organisms should be adopted by Parties. The affected Party may also request the Party of origin to dispose of the organisms by repatriation or destruction at its own expense. The Biosafety Clearing-House must be informed of all cases of illegal transboundary movements (Art 25).

---

7 Annex I of the *Protocol* sets out the information that must be included in such notification.

8 The Biosafety Clearing-House provides a mechanism to facilitate the exchange of scientific, technical, environmental and legal information on, and experience with, living modified organisms; and assists Parties to implement the Protocol, taking into account the special needs of developing countries and small island states.

9 This notification must take place within 270 days of notification by the exporting Party.

As discussed below, the *Gene Technology Act 2000* (Cth) represents the Australian government's response to obligations imposed under the *Convention on Biological Diversity*.

Status of Australia's biodiversity

Australia, along with Brazil, China and Mexico, is a mega-diverse country in respect of biodiversity. This means that these countries cover less than 10% of the global surface yet hold more than 70% of the world's biodiversity. Australia has over one million species of plants, animals and micro-organisms, which is an extremely large number compared with other continents. More than 80% of our plants and animals are unique and found only in Australia. Yet the release of the *2006 Red List of Threatened Species* by the World Conservation Union[10] showed that Australia is one of four countries with the highest number of threatened species. Australia has a total of 639 critically endangered, endangered and vulnerable species in each group of organisms, [11] a total of 2129 extinct, threatened and other species of animals,[12] and 171 extinct, threatened and other species of plants. [13]

One of the most recent Australian audits of our biodiversity is the Australian Terrestrial Biodiversity Assessment 2002,[14] which itself exposed a crisis in loss of biodiversity in Australia. State and Territory agencies worked closely with the independent National Land and Water Resources Audit to create an Australia-wide database on terrestrial biodiversity. The key findings were as follows:

Wetlands and riparian zones

The condition of nationally important wetlands is generally good particularly in northern Australia, however, many wetlands are declining. Information on a number of nationally important wetlands in subregions is unavailable but it is clear that the condition of riparian zones is degraded and declining across much of southern and eastern Australia which means that recovery is unlikely in the medium term.

Threatened ecosystems and species

The Assessment identified 2891 threatened ecosystems and other ecological communities across Australia. Ninety-four per cent of bioregions in Australia have one or more threatened ecosystems particularly in the highly cleared regions of southern and eastern Australia. Of these, 50% are eucalypt forest and woodlands with shrubby or grassy understorey threatened as a result of extensive clearing. The subregions of Victoria and New South Wales contain the highest number of threatened species.

10 See <http://www.iucn.org/themes/ssc/redlist2006/redlist2006.htm> (accessed 18 July 2006).

11 See <http://www.iucnredlist.org/info/tables/table5> (accessed 18 July 2006).

12 See <http://www.iucnredlist.org/info/tables/table6a> (accessed 18 July 2006).

13 See <http://www.iucnredlist.org/info/tables/table6b> (accessed 18 July 2006).

14 See <http://audit.ea.gov.au/anra/vegetation/docs/biodiversity/bio_assess_contents.cfm> (accessed 18 July 2006).

Mammals and birds

Mammal extinction has been substantial within the past 200 years. Twenty-two Australian mammals are now extinct and this represents a third of the world's most recent extinctions. A further eight species exist only on islands. The distribution of mammals in arid and semi-arid parts of Australia has contracted massively, particularly with respect to the small to medium critical weight range species. Populations of some species of birds have reduced markedly with 29 species showing significant decrease in agricultural areas over the past 20 years. Birds most affected are the grassland, woodland and ground nesting guilds.

Eucalypts and acacias

Critical areas for the protection of these species have been identified as the Murray-Darling Basin and south-west Western Australia.

Threatening processes

Vegetation clearing represents the most significant threat to species and ecosystems in eastern Australia, as are overgrazing, exotic weeds, feral animals and changed fire regimes, which also threaten wetlands and riparian zones. These threats are widespread and pervasive. Fragmentation of remnants as well as salinity and firewood collection also threaten biodiversity.

Conserving biodiversity outside protected areas under the Environment Protection and Biodiversity Conservation Act 1999 (Cth)

The major piece of Commonwealth legislation for the conservation of biodiversity is the *Environment Protection and Biodiversity Conservation Act 1999* (Cth) (EPBCA), which followed the development of a national biodiversity strategy.

The National Strategy for the Conservation of Australia's Biological Diversity was issued in 1996, by the Commonwealth government, and recognises the need to strengthen activities and improve policies, practices and attitudes to achieve conservation and sustainable use of biological diversity. It accepted that biological diversity is best conserved *in situ*, with the co-operation of indigenous peoples and the community in general.

Other significant policy documents relating to biodiversity conservation are the:

- Biodiversity Conservation Outcomes and Targets for Natural Resource Management of the Natural Resources Management Ministerial Council; and
- National Biodiversity and Climate Change Action Plan, 2004-2007.

The major constitutional basis for the EPBCA is the external affairs power, as the Act gives effect to major international treaties: the *World Heritage Convention* and the *Ramsar Convention*, discussed in Chapter 4, and the *Convention on Biological Diversity* (the Biodiversity Convention), discussed in this chapter.

According to the Biodiversity Convention 'biological diversity' means the variability among living organisms from all sources including, inter alia, terrestrial, marine and other aquatic ecosystems and the ecological complexes of which they are part; this includes diversity within species, between species, and of ecosystems' (Biodiversity Convention Art 2 and EPBCA s 528).

Components of biodiversity are defined in the EPBCA to include: species, habitats, ecological communities, genes, ecosystems and ecological processes (s 172(4)).

Biodiversity conservation focuses on genetic diversity, species diversity and ecosystem diversity.[15]

The EPBCA adopts two quite distinct approaches to the conservation of biodiversity by:

- assessing and deciding whether or not to approve 'actions' that are likely to impact significantly on 'matters of national environmental significance' (which include wetlands of international importance (Ramsar wetlands), listed threatened species and ecological communities, listed migratory species, and the marine environment (EPBCA Chapter 2); and
- the conservation of biodiversity (EPBCA Chapter 5).

The assessment and approval provisions of the EPBCA are discussed in Chapter 4 of this book. Here the focus is Chapter 5 of the Act. It is, of course, rather artificial to separate the environmental assessment provisions and the conservation of biodiversity provisions since the assessment and approvals processes inevitably impact on attempts to conserve biodiversity. Nevertheless, these parts of the EPBCA have been divided into separate chapters for the sake of comprehensively discussing the environmental assessment and approval provisions at the Commonwealth and NSW government levels in one chapter, and the conservation of biodiversity in this chapter. Therefore, to get a comprehensive view of biodiversity conservation *in situ* at the Commonwealth level it is important to cross-refer to Chapter 4.

Management schemes for conserving biodiversity

The focus of the conservation of biodiversity under Chapter 5 of the EPBCA is on setting up forward management schemes. Initial steps in this forward planning are the preparation of inventories, surveys and bioregional plans. The inventories and surveys are of species and communities on Commonwealth land and in Commonwealth marine areas such as cetaceans, listed threatened species, listed threatened ecological communities, listed migratory species and listed marine species (ss 172 and 173).

Bioregional plans

Bioregional plans are made by the Minister after consultation, and are taken into account in decision-making under the Act. Plans relate to bioregions in Commonwealth areas, and include:

15 Australian Museum Online, <http://www.austmust.gov.au/biodiversity/what/levels.htm> (accessed 2 August 2006).

- the components of biodiversity, their distribution and conservation status;
- important economic and social values;
- objectives and priorities, strategies and actions;
- mechanisms for community involvement;
- the monitoring and review of the plan. (s 176)

Listing species, communities and key threatening processes

The legislation requires the preparation of a list of threatened species, ecological communities and key threatening processes (Pt 13, s 178 *et seq*).

Threatened species

The list of threatened species is divided into the following categories of native species:

- extinct – the last member of the species has died;
- extinct in the wild – known only to survive in cultivation, in captivity, or as a naturalised population well outside its past range, or has not been recorded in its known or expected habitat, despite exhaustive surveys over a timeframe appropriate to its life cycle and form;
- critically endangered – facing an extremely high risk of extinction in the wild in the immediate future;
- endangered – not critically endangered, but facing a very high risk of extinction in the wild in the near future;
- vulnerable – not critically endangered or endangered, but facing a high risk of extinction in the wild in the medium-term future;
- conservation dependent – the species is the focus of a specific conservation program, the cessation of which would result in the species becoming vulnerable, endangered, or conservation dependent within a period of five years, or the species is a species of fish that is the focus of a plan of management, under Commonwealth, State or Territory law, to maximise its chances of long-term survival in nature the cessation of which would adversely affect the species' conservation status. (ss 179, 180, 186)

Threatened ecological communities

The categories in the list of threatened ecological communities are:

- critically endangered – an extremely high risk of extinction in the wild in the immediate future;
- endangered – not critically endangered, but facing a very high risk of extinction in the wild in the near future; and
- vulnerable – not critically endangered nor endangered, but facing a high risk of extinction in the wild in the medium-term future (ss 181, 182).

Key threatening processes

A threatening process threatens the survival, abundance, or evolutionary development of a native species or ecological community. It is listed as a key threatening process if it:

- could cause a native species or an ecological community to become eligible for listing in any category, other than a 'conservation dependent' category;
- could cause a listed threatened species or a listed threatened ecological community to become eligible to be listed in another category representing a higher degree of endangerment; or
- adversely affects two or more listed threatened species (other than conservation dependent species) or two or more listed threatened ecological communities. (ss 183, 188)

Scientific Committee

A Scientific Committee called the Threatened Species Scientific Committee advises the Minister on nominations and strategies for preventing a species or community becoming threatened (ss 189, 190).

Listing process

Subdivision AA of Part 1, Div 1 of the EPBCA sets out a listing process for the three lists, referred to above, threatened species (s 178), threatened ecological communities (s 181) and key threatening processes (s 183). The usual process is based on an annual cycle of 12-month assessment periods. The process is similar to the listing process for heritage lists described in Chapter 10.

First, the Minister may designate a conservation theme for an assessment cycle, for example, that priority should be given to a particular species or region of Australia (s 194D).

The public is then invited to nominate items for listing in one of the three lists (s 194E). The Minister gives the nominations to the Scientific Committee, but may reject nominations considered to be vexatious, frivolous or not made in good faith (s 194F). The Scientific Committee prepares a list for the Minister of items that it thinks should be assessed, and may include its own items. In deciding on the list, the Committee may have regard to any themes designated by the Minster, its own opinion as to priorities, its capacity to make assessments and any other matter it thinks relevant (s 194G). The Committee also includes its reasons (s 194J). The Minister finalises the list and may, for any appropriate reason, include further items or omit items (s 194K). The Committee makes the finalised list available to the public (s 194L), and invites public comment (s 194M).

The Committee makes a written assessment of the eligibility for listing of the items in the finalised list, which it gives to the Minister (s 194N). The Minister then decides whether to list the assessed items (s 194Q).

The Committee co-ordinates with the Australian Heritage Council on any matter that the Council is assessing that is relevant to the Committee's assessment work (s 194S).

Protecting habitats

Habitats are vital to the survival of a listed threatened species or threatened ecological community. The EPBCA establishes a Register of critical habitats, maintained with scientific advice and available for public inspection (s 207A).

It is an offence in a Commonwealth area, knowingly, to damage a critical habitat for a listed threatened species, other than a conservation dependent species, a cetacean, or a listed threatened ecological community (s 207B).

When the Commonwealth sells or leases property the site of a critical habitat for a listed threatened species or threatened ecological community, it takes steps to protect the habitat. Sale contracts will contain a covenant that binds all future owners (s 207C).

Offences

It is an offence, in a Commonwealth area, to:

- take an action resulting in the death or injury of; or
- to trade, take, keep, or move,

a member of a listed threatened species, other than a conservation dependent species, or listed threatened ecological community (ss 196, 197) Any person involved in such an activity must notify the Department (s 199).

It is an offence to take an action that might harm a member of a listed species or community. Defences include:

- authorisation – if the action is:
    - o authorised by a permit under the Act, or under the *Great Barrier Reef Marine Park Act 1975*;
    - o taken under a conservation agreement, recovery plan or an accredited plan or regime;
    - o covered by an approval;
    - o one of a class of actions, declared by the Minister not to require an approval, taken in accordance with an accredited management plan; (s 197)
- necessity – if the action was necessary to relieve suffering by a member of a listed threatened species or ecological community, to prevent a risk to human health, human life or property, or by a government agency as part of law enforcement (s 212);
- unavoidability – if the action is the result of an unavoidable accident, and is not caused by negligent or reckless behaviour (ss 196-196E and 197).

Permits

The Minister may issue a permit authorising a person to take an action without committing an offence (ss 200-207). It is an offence to contravene a condition of a permit. The Commonwealth Administrative Appeals Tribunal reviews the Minister's decision on permits.

Actions may be permitted that are:

- significant for the conservation of the listed threatened species or ecological community, where any impact is incidental to the action;
- not adverse to the survival in nature of the species or ecological community;
- consistent with a recovery plan;
- significant for Indigenous tradition; or
- necessary to control pathogens.

The permit holder is expected to take all reasonable steps to minimise impacts.

Migratory species

Each year 2 million migratory shore birds spend the summer months in Australia to and from their breeding grounds on the Russian tundra. Their 'flyways' consist of a chain of wetlands in Eastern and South-east Asia, Australia, New Zealand and the Arctic circle. The protection of migratory species in Australia is based on three international agreements:

- 1979 *Convention on the Conservation of Migratory Species of Wild Animals* (CMS or Bonn Convention);[16]
- Agreement between the Government of Australia and the Government of the People's Republic of China for the Protection of Migratory Birds in Danger of Extinction and their Environment 1986 (CAMBA);
- Agreement between the Government of Japan and the Government of Australia for the Protection of Migratory Birds and Birds in Danger of Extinction and their Environment 1974 (JAMBA).

Lists

As with the other categories, protection is based on a list, which includes migratory species, that are native species, or are included in the appendices of the Bonn Convention, or the annexes established under JAMBA or CAMBA.

The list is published in the Commonwealth *Gazette* (s 209).

Offences

The offences in relation to migratory species are similar to the offences for threatened species or communities discussed above, that is, to take an action that results in the death or injury of, or to trade, take, keep, or move, a member of a listed migratory species in a Commonwealth area, other than a member of a listed threatened species or a cetacean (ss 211-211E).

The defences, set out in s 212, are similar to those in s 197 for listed species and communities, discussed above.

Permits

As with other actions that would otherwise be prohibited under this part of the legislation, the Minister may issue a permit allowing an action in relation to a

16 See <http://www.cms.int/documents/convtxt/cms_convtxt.htm> (accessed 27 July 2006).

migratory species. The Minister may issue a permit if one of the criteria set out above for permits is generally satisfied (ss 210-223).

National Shorebird Conservation Taskforce

A National Shorebird Conservation Taskforce has been established with funding from the Natural Heritage Trust to accelerate on-ground conservation of the shorebird sites. The project is co-ordinated by the World Wide Fund for Nature (WWF). Project activities include: the development of site management plans to be included in catchment plans, on-ground rehabilitation works and bird counting programs, and community education programs.

The National Task Force comprises representatives from the WWF, Birds Australia, the Australasian Wader Study Group, Wetland Care Australia, Wetlands International - Oceania, the Conservation Council of Western Australia, the Tasmanian Conservation Trust, the Marine and Coastal Community Network, Environment Australia, and the ANZECC Wetlands and Migratory Shorebirds Taskforce.

The Taskforce will assist with implementing the 1993 National Plan for Shorebird Conservation in Australia.[17]

Whales

The Australian Whale Sanctuary was 'established to give formal recognition of the high level of protection and management afforded to cetaceans in Commonwealth marine areas and prescribed waters' (s 225). Relevant to New South Wales, the sanctuary comprises:

- the waters of Australia's exclusive economic zone; and
- so much of the coastal waters of a State as are set out in the *Environment Protection and Biodiversity Conservation Regulations 2000* (Cth) (EPBCR). (ss 224, 226, 227)

Whales property of the Commonwealth

A cetacean killed, injured or taken in the Australian Whale Sanctuary, or in the waters beyond its outer limits becomes the property of the Commonwealth (s 246).[18]

Offences

It is an offence for a person, in the sanctuary and in waters beyond its limits:

- to take any action that results in the death or injury of a cetacean;
- after an illegal killing, to deal with parts of a cetacean;

17 See <http://www.biodiversity.ea.gov/biodiversity/migratory/waterbirds/pubs/natplanshore.pdf> (accessed 15 December 2006).

18 With regard to efforts to enforce these provisions against a Japanese whaling company in the Australian Whales Sanctuary, which is adjacent to the Australian Antarctic Territory, see *Humane Society International Inc v Kyodo Senpaku Kaisha Ltd* [2005] FCA 678 and *Humane Society International Inc v Kyodo Senpaku Kaisha Ltd* [2006] FCAFC 116; see also Sam Blay and Karen Bubna-Litic, 'The interplay of international law and domestic law: The case of Australia's efforts to protect whales' (2006) 23 *EPLJ* 465.

- to take, keep, move or interfere with a cetacean;
- to have possession of a cetacean or of products made from a cetacean; or
- to treat a cetacean that has been unlawfully imported. (ss 229-236)

There is no offence if the cetacean was not a member of a listed threatened species, or if the action was covered in an accredited plan of management (s 245).

The master of a foreign whaling vessel who brings the vessel into an Australian port without permission is guilty of an offence (s 236). For the defences, see s 231.

Plans of management

The Commonwealth Minister accredits plans of management, regimes and policies in respect of whales, made under Commonwealth, State or Territory law, which meet two minimum conditions, that:

- persons engaged in fishing are to take all reasonable steps to ensure that cetaceans are not killed or injured; and
- any fishery is not likely adversely to affect the conservation status of a species or a population of cetacean. (s 245)

Permits

Permits may be issued for otherwise prohibited actions. The criteria are that the:

- action will contribute significantly to the conservation of cetaceans;
- interference from the action is incidental to, and not the purpose of, the action;
- action will not adversely affect the conservation status of a species or a population of cetacean;
- action is consistent with any recovery plan or wildlife conservation plan; and
- permit holders will take all reasonable steps to minimise any interference with cetaceans.

Whale watching is regulated under the EPBCR (ss 237-244).

Listed marine species

There is a list of marine species set out in s 248 of the EPBCA. The list is amended on advice from the Scientific Committee, to include further marine species that occur naturally in Commonwealth marine areas to ensure their long-term conservation (ss 250, 251).

Prohibited actions

It is an offence for a person to take an action that results in the death or injury of, or to take, trade, keep or move, a member of a listed marine species in a Commonwealth area (ss 253-254C). Offences must be notified to the Secretary of the Department of Environment and Heritage (s 256). For defences, see s 255.

Permits for otherwise prohibited action may be issued under the usual criteria (ss 257-264).

Plans of management

The Minister may accredit plans, regimes and policies under Commonwealth and State law, if the plan requires persons engaged in fishing under the plan to take all reasonable steps to ensure that members of a listed marine species are not killed or injured, and that a fishery is not likely to affect adversely the conservation status of a species or a population of listed marine species (s 265).

Matters of national environmental importance

Four of the categories of species and communities protected by the Act under the heading of conservation of biodiversity are also included as matters of national environmental significance under the EPBCA. This aspect is discussed in Chapter 4.

Planning for the conservation of biodiversity

The EPBCA provides for the preparation, administration and enforcement of various types of plans to conserve biodiversity:

- recovery plans;
- threat abatement plans; and
- wildlife conservation plans.

Copies of proposed plans are made available for public comment, and comments are taken into account (ss 275, 276, 278).

Recovery plans

After a threat to a listed threatened species or listed threatened ecological communities has been recognised, the Minister may decide to have a recovery plan for research and management actions necessary for their long-term survival in nature (ss 270, 269A). A plan of a State may be adopted for this purpose (ss 269A, 277).

Threat abatement plans

Threat abatement plans provide for research, management and other actions necessary to reduce a key threatening process, listed under the EPBCA (s 183) to an acceptable level for the long-term survival in nature of native species and ecological communities affected (s 271). Plans are prepared, if the Minister decides, or within 90 days of a listing of a key threatening process (s 270A) and are made jointly with the relevant State. Plans are subject to public comment and consultation (ss 270A, 275, 276). If a plan is revoked, reasons are given (s 283A).

Wildlife conservation plans

Wildlife conservation plans are for the protection, conservation, and management of:

- a listed migratory species and marine species that occur in Australia;
- a species of cetacean that occurs in the Australian Whale Sanctuary; and
- for a conservation dependent species, other than a listed threatened species. (s 286)

When a recovery plan is implemented for a species, the wildlife conservation plan is replaced by the recovery plan (s 299).

Effect of plans

The Commonwealth complies with recovery, threat abatement and wildlife conservation plans (ss 268, 286). The Department reports on the making and adoption of recovery plans and threat abatement plans in its Annual Report to the Commonwealth Parliament (s 284).

Marine environment

The EPBCA makes separate provision for environmental protection in the marine environment. This covers the sea, the seabed and airspace inside the seaward boundary of the 200 nautical mile exclusive economic zone, except State waters (s 24). This is a fairly clear area of Commonwealth constitutional authority. Management systems are discussed in Chapter 9.

Conservation agreements

Voluntary agreements, called 'conservation agreements' in the EPBCA, promote:

- biodiversity;
- the heritage values of World Heritage properties, and National and Commonwealth Heritage places;
- the ecological character of a declared Ramsar wetland; and
- the environment, in respect of the impact of a nuclear action, in a Commonwealth marine area, or on Commonwealth land

of world, national and Commonwealth heritage places (s 304) and, under the agreement, may provide financial, technical and other assistance (s 306).

Conservation agreements must, in the view of the Commonwealth, have a net benefit to the conservation of biodiversity or heritage values, and be consistent with at least one of the Australian World Heritage, National Heritage, or Commonwealth Heritage values (s 305). Agreements are legally binding on the parties, and their successors in title (Chapter 5, Pt 14).

A conservation agreement may provide, for example, for:

- activities to promote National or Commonwealth Heritage values, or for controlling or prohibiting actions or processes that might adversely affect them;
- access for persons authorised by the agreement for monitoring compliance; and
- requiring a person to give an authorised person requested information. (s 306)

A notice of a conservation agreement is published in the *Gazette*, unless notice would result in harm to components of biodiversity, or disclose matters that are commercial-in-confidence (s 309).

A public list of conservation agreements is publicly available (s 309).

Tax incentives for conservation agreements

In 2003 greater tax incentives were made available under the *Income Tax Assessment Act 1997* (Cth) to landowners who sign voluntary conservation agreements. The legislation aims to:

- provide a tax incentive to landowners who have taken the initiative to help conserve Australia's environment;
- encourage more people to enter into formal covenants that protect important environmental sites;
- include commitments to on-ground action such as fencing off rare plants, seed collecting and tree planting; and
- allow landowners to claim an income tax deduction for any decrease in land value that results from signing a conservation agreement, provided the landowner receives no payment for entering into it.

The legislation covers a conservation covenant between a landowner and an authorised body such as the State or a local government authority.

Conserving biodiversity outside protected areas in New South Wales

In New South Wales, legislation to protect aspects of biological diversity was enacted even before the Rio Conference. The major example is the *National Parks and Wildlife Act 1974* (NSW) (NPWA), which is discussed in Chapter 9. The traditional focus of these laws has been the conservation of nature in protected areas, but these laws also play a vital role in the conservation of aspects of biological diversity outside reserves. Under the NPWA this is especially so with respect to fauna, marine mammals and protected plants (see pp 372ff). In recent times, the NPWA has been supplemented by laws which more closely reflect the principles of the *Convention on Biological Diversity*. An important example of this is the *Threatened Species Conservation Act 1995* (NSW).

Threatened Species Conservation Act 1995 (NSW)

The *Threatened Species Conservation Act 1995* (TSCA) provides for the listing of endangered species, populations, and ecological communities, as well as species presumed extinct in Sch 1. Schedule 2 to the TSCA contains a list of vulnerable species, while Sch 3 to the Act contains a list of key threatening processes (TSCA s 8). The TSCA must be read together with the NPWA which makes it an offence to harm any animal that is a threatened species, population or ecological community without a licence (NPWA s 118A). Applicants for development consent under the *Environmental Planning and Assessment Act 1979* (NSW) (EPAA) may be required to submit a species impact statement if the activity is likely to significantly affect threatened species, populations or ecological communities, or their habitat (EPAA ss 77(3), 90(1)(c2), (c3)). In addition, as soon as possible after each endangered species, population and ecological community is listed, the Director-General must prepare a recovery plan to promote their recovery to a position of viability in nature, and a threat abatement plan to neutralise the effects of a key threatening process.

It is also important to note that the *Threatened Species Legislation Amendment Act 2004* (NSW) effected some significant changes to the original regime envisaged under the TSCA in its original form. These include: new categories for listing; amended criteria for listing; the involvement of the Natural Resources Commission in the listing process; amendments to the Scientific Committee's power to consider nominations and propose final determinations; the establishment of two new Committees; requiring the Director-General to develop a Priorities Action Statement for developing recovery and threat abatement plans; and introducing the concept of biodiversity certification.

Listing provisions

Listing threatened species

Relying on the opinion of the Scientific Committee, the following species may be listed in Sch 1 to the TSCA:

- endangered species;
- endangered populations;
- endangered ecological communities; and
- species presumed extinct

Under Sch 1A the following may be listed:

- critically endangered species; and
- critically endangered ecological communities

The category of 'critically endangered' was inserted into the TSCA as a result of the 2004 amendments.

Note that any endangered or critically endangered species, species presumed extinct and any endangered or critically endangered ecological community that is also listed as threatened under the EPBCA is marked with an asterisk to show that the species is considered to be a threatened species nationally (TSCA s 6).

Under Sch 2 the following may be listed:

- vulnerable species;
- vulnerable ecological communities .

Again, any vulnerable species or vulnerable ecological community that is listed as a threatened species or a threatened ecological community under the EPBCA is marked with an asterisk to show that it is considered to threatened nationally (TSCA s 7).

Key threatening processes are listed under Sch 3 to the TSCA (TSCA s 8).

The TSCA also requires that as soon as practicable after a species or ecological community that is or was indigenous to New South Wales becomes a listed threatened species or a listed threatened ecological community under the EPBCA, the Scientific Committee is to consider whether the species or ecological community should be listed under the TSCA. If a species or ecological community is so listed it must be marked with an asterisk to show its national status (TSCA s 9).

Criteria for listing

Before the 2004 amendment, species could be listed if they were *likely to become extinct.* Now, the following criteria apply to the listing of species:

- *Species presumed extinct* – if, despite targeted surveys, a species has not been recorded in its known/expected habitat in New South Wales over a time frame appropriate to its life cycle and form.
- *Critically endangered species* – if it is facing an *extremely high risk* of extinction in New South Wales in the immediate future. Criteria for determining this will be set out in the Regulations. This category of species was introduced in the 2004 amendments.
- *Endangered species* – if it is facing a *very high risk of extinction* in New South Wales in the near future and it is not eligible to be listed as a critically endangered species.
- *Vulnerable species* – if it is facing a *high risk* of extinction in New South Wales in the medium-term future and it not eligible to be listed as an endangered or critically endangered species.

Listing endangered populations and ecological communities

Originally, ecological communities could be listed if they were *likely to become extinct* or were *already extinct.* The 2004 amendments also proposed new 'triggers' for listing population, ecological communities. They are:

- Endangered populations – may be listed if there is a *very high risk of extinction* in New South Wales in the near future. Currently under the Act, a population can be listed if it is facing a high risk of extinction.
- Ecological communities may be listed as:
  - o *A critically endangered ecological community* if it is facing an *extremely high risk of extinction* in the near future. This is a new category of community and must be listed in Sch 1A to the Act;
  - o *An endangered ecological community* if it is facing a *very high risk of extinction* in New South Wales in the near future and it is not eligible to be listed as a critically endangered ecological community;
  - o *A vulnerable ecological community* if it is facing a *high risk* of extinction in New South Wales in the medium-term future and it not eligible to be listed as an endangered or critically endangered ecological community.

Matters to be taken into account before listing

The *Threatened Species Conservation Amendment (Listing Criteria) Regulation 2005* inserts Pt 3 into the Regulation. This Part prescribes the criteria for a determination by the Scientific Committee of the matters that must be taken into account before listing species, populations and ecological communities under the *Threatened Species Conservation Act 1995* (NSW). The Criteria for Listing of species include: reduction in the population size of the species; restricted geographic distribution of species and low numbers of mature individuals of the species. The Criteria for Listing of endangered populations include: large reduction in population size; highly restricted geographic distribution of the population; and low, or very low, numbers of mature individuals in the population. The Criteria for listing ecological communities are: reduction in the geographical distribution of the ecological community; restricted geographic distribution of the ecological community; and reduction in ecological function of the ecological community.

Listing key threatening processes

Key threatening processes may be listed if they adversely affect threatened species, populations or ecological communities or could cause those that are not threatened to become threatened. Originally, a process can only be listed if it affected two or more species, populations or communities.

Natural Resources Commission may initiate listing

A further innovation of the 2004 amendments is that the National Resources Commission (NRC) may initiate action for listing. The NRC and the Minister may also give directions to the Committee requiring it to undertake an investigation for the purpose of identifying species, population and communities that are potentially threatened. This provision reflects the attempts of the NSW government to better integrate natural resource management and the conservation of biodiversity.

Considering nominations and making final determinations

The Scientific Committee's powers to consider nominations was also substantially amended by the 2004 amendments requiring greater interaction between the Committee, the Minister and the NRC. The TSCA now requires the Scientific Committee to give notice of any nominations for listing to the Minister and the NRC within 14 days after nomination. Also instead of considering each application as it is submitted, the Scientific Committee must determine priorities for considering nominations according to the degree and immediacy of the threat, taxonomic distinctiveness and any advice or recommendations on the priorities received from the Minister or NRC. In making these recommendations, the Minister and NRC may consider State-wide issues of concern in biodiversity conservation. Also in rejecting a nomination, or making a final determination, the Committee will have to notify the NRC as well as the Minister.

The Act also proposes that, before making a final determination, the Scientific Committee should give the Minister notice in writing of its proposed final determination. Under the present Act, the Committee has six months within which to make a final determination on a listing without having to notify the Minister. The Minister then has two months to decide whether or not to refer the matter back to the Committee for reasons of a scientific nature. If the Minister does refer it back then the Committee must consider the matter further before making a final determination within three months. The Committee can also request the Minister to extend its period of determination from six months to two years.

In addition, the Act imposes an obligation on the Committee to review the lists at least every two years to assess whether any changes are necessary. The NRC and Minister are given the power to give advice and make recommendations to the Committee regarding priorities for undertaking such reviews.

Protecting critical habitat

Land comprising the habitat of an endangered species, population or ecological community or critically endangered species or ecological community that is critical to the survival of the species, population or ecological community may be declared to be the critical habitat of the species, population or ecological community (TSCA s 37). The Director-General is responsible for identifying the critical habitat of each endangered species, population and ecological community or critically endangered species or ecological community (TSCA s 38). However, The Director-General must consult with the Scientific Committee before preparing a recommendation for the identification of critical habitat and must have regard to its advice in preparing any recommendation with regard to identifying critical habitat (TSCA s 39). After considering the advice of the Scientific Committee, the Director-General must prepare a recommendation for identifying the critical habitat of that species, population or ecological community. In so doing, the Director-General must consider the likely social and economic consequences of the making of the recommendation in the manner proposed (TSCA s 40).

There are extensive publication and community consultation obligations placed on the Director-General once a recommendation for identification has been prepared (TSCA s 41). The submissions received from the public and any advice given by the Scientific Committee in respect of the recommendation must be taken into account by the Director-General (TSCA s 42). After considering these, and making any amendments, the Director-General must forward the recommendation to the Minister along with the submissions and advice already received (TSCA s 42). The Minister must consider the recommendation while taking into account, amongst other things, the social and economic consequences, as well as consequences for landholders, of the declaration of critical habitat (TSCA s 44). The Minister must then advise the Director-General as to whether or not the recommendation should be amended in any way and, if the Minister so recommends, the Director-General must amend the recommendation (TSCA s 46).

Following this, the Minister will approve the recommendation, with or without any amendments; refuse the recommendation; or refer it back to the Director-General for further consideration. If the Minister approves of a recommendation then the Minister will declare the land to be critical habitat, by notice in the *Gazette* (TSCA s 47). It is then up to the Director-General personally to give notice to all persons known to the Director-General who may be affected by the declaration, including landholders, public authorities, financial institutions who may have a mortgage over the property and others (TSCA s 48). A public authority is obliged to have regard to the existence of critical habitat in relation to the use of land that it owns or controls that is within or contains critical habitat, or in exercising its functions in relation to land that is within or contains critical habitat (TSCA s 50). Declarations may be amended or revoked by the Minister (TSCA s 49).

The Regulations may prohibit or regulate the carrying out of specified actions, or actions of a specified class or description, on specified critical habitat (TSCA s 51).

Preparing recovery plans, threat abatement plans and the Priorities Action Statement

Recovery plans

The TSCA provides that the Director-General may prepare a recovery plan for each endangered species (other than a species presumed extinct), population and ecological community and each critically endangered species and ecological community to promote the recovery of the species, population or ecological community to a position of viability in nature. Recovery plans for vulnerable species and vulnerable ecological communities may also be prepared. A recovery plan may contain provisions for more than one species, population or ecological community and may be made for part of a range of a species, population or ecological community. If the Director-General decides to prepare a recovery plan for a vulnerable ecological community, the recovery plan must be prepared within five years after that decision is made (TSCA s 56).

Threat abatement plans

The Director-General may prepare a threat abatement plan for each key threatening process which is essentially a management strategy to abate, ameliorate or eliminate the adverse effects of the key threatening process on threatened species, populations or ecological communities, or even to prevent species, populations or ecological communities from becoming threatened. A threat abatement plan may contain provisions relevant to more than one key threatening process (TSCA s 74). The Director-General may, with the approval of the Minister, make arrangements with the Director of NSW Fisheries for the joint preparation of a threat abatement plan under this Act and Pt 7A of the *Fisheries Management Act 1994* (TSCA s 74A).

In deciding which measures to include in threat abatement plans, the Director-General must have regard to the following:

- the objects of this Act;
- the likely social and economic consequences of the making of the plan, including the desirability of minimising any significant adverse social and economic consequences;
- the most efficient and effective use of available resources for the conservation of threatened species, populations and ecological communities.

The Director-General must also consider, when preparing a threat abatement plan, ways in which the public can co-operate in the abatement, amelioration or elimination of the adverse effects of key threatening processes on the prospects of survival of threatened species, populations or ecological communities and their recovery to a position of viability in nature. The special knowledge or interest that Indigenous people may have in the species, population or ecological community concerned, and in the measures to be contained in the plan, must also be considered (TSCA s 75).

A threat abatement plan must state the criteria for assessing the achievement of the objective, and identify the actions needed to abate, ameliorate or eliminate the effects of the key threatening process. It must also identify the persons or public authorities who are responsible for the implementation of the measures included in the plan and, where practicable, provide a proposed timetable for the implementation of the plan. The estimated cost of the measures included in the plan must be stated, and the date by which the plan should be subject to review by the Director-General must be given. The plan may also include any other matter relating to the impact of the plan that the Director-General considers appropriate (TSCA s 77).

Before completing the preparation of the draft threat abatement plan, the Director-General must consult with the chief executive officer of a public authority that will have responsibility for implementing the plan. The chief executive officer of the public authority must approve the inclusion of the measure in the plan (TSCA s 78).

There are extensive publication and consultation provisions in the TSCA. Notice must be given to the Scientific Committee, all affected public authorities and the public. The TSCA sets out what must be included in the notice (TSCA s 79). The Director-General must consider all written submissions received as a result of the notification and consultation provisions and may amend the draft threat abatement plan accordingly (TSCA s 80). The Director-General must then forward the draft threat abatement plan to the Minister, and provide the Minister with a summary of any advice and submissions received (TSCA s 81). The Director-General may be requested by the Minister to amend the plan and upon effecting the amendments the Director-General must return the plan to the Minister (TSCA s 82).

As soon as practicable after the Minister approves a threat abatement plan, the Director-General must give a copy of the threat abatement plan to the Scientific Committee, publish notice of the approval of the plan in a newspaper circulating generally throughout the State and, if the threat abatement plan is likely to affect a particular area or areas (other than the State as a whole), in a newspaper circulating generally in that area or areas. All public authorities that the Director-General knows is likely to be affected by the plan must be notified and the Director-General must publish notice of the approval of the plan in the Gazette. The Director-General must also make a copy of the threat abatement plan available for public inspection (TSCA s 84). The Director-General is required to keep each threat abatement plan under review and, if the Director-General considers that any change (other than a minor change) should be made, a new plan must be prepared in accordance with the procedures already described (TSCA s 85).

Ministers and public authorities (including the Director-General) must take appropriate actions to implement the measures included in a threat abatement plan for which they are responsible and must not make decisions that are inconsistent with the provisions of a plan (TSCA s 86). They must report to Parliament annually on the measures they have taken to implement the plans (TSCA s 87).

Developing a Priorities Action Statement

As a result of the 2004 amendments, Pt 5A of the TSCA now requires the Director-General to determine priorities for preparing recovery plans for species and ecological communities by developing a Priorities Action Statement (PAS). This represents a move away from the previous process of preparing plans for each threatened species and key threatening process. It attempts to integrate planning for the recovery of threatened species with urban and rural land use planning, decision-making and landscape restoration decisions.

The PAS must set out the strategies to be adopted for promoting the recovery of species, populations and communities to a position of viability and managing each key threatening process. Relative priorities between each of these must be established as well as key performance indicators to facilitate reporting on the success of all of these strategies. The Priorities Action Statement must be reviewed every three years and amended accordingly. Upon reviewing the Statement the Director-General must include a report on the achievements in implementing the strategies identified in the Statement. The Director-General in performing these functions must consult with the NRC, the Scientific Committee, the new Biodiversity Advisory Council (see below), the Social and Economic Advisory Council (see below) and other relevant government agencies. Before adopting the Statement, the Director-General must engage in public notice and comment procedures and consider all submissions

In July 2006, the Department of Environment and Conservation released a draft PAS. Under the draft PAS there are 25 recovery plans for threatened species and 12 threat abatement strategies for key threatening processes.

The objectives of the PAS are to:

- convert as many species as possible from threatened to non-threatened status;
- abate or eliminate the impacts of key threatening processes;
- provide a comprehensive and strategic approach to recovering threatened species;
- involve stakeholders in working together to implement the PAS actions.

Specific priority actions cover such things as:

- surveys to clarify the distribution of a species ;
- weed and pest management programs;
- guidelines for threatened species issues in development assessments;
- research into factors influencing the survival of threatened species;
- community education programs to raise awareness of a species or threat in a particular area.

The PAS is expected to benefit catchment management authorities, planning authorities, land managers, Aboriginal communities and researchers, scientists, students, and conservation and community groups.

Offences under Part 8A of the National Parks and Wildlife Act 1974 (NSW)

While the TSCA provides for the listing of threatened species, endangered population or endangered ecological community and the protection of critical habitat, Pt 8A of the NPWA creates various offences with respect to the matters listed under the TSCA. It is important to note that 'any person' may bring proceedings in the Land and Environment Court to enforce these provisions (NPWA s 176A).

Harming animals or picking plants

It is an offence to 'harm' any animal that is a threatened species, endangered population or endangered ecological community (NPWA s 118A). 'Harm' is defined in the NPWA as hunting, shooting, poisoning, netting, snaring, spearing, pursuing, capturing, injuring or killing, but changing the habitat of an animal is not included within this definition. It is also an offence to pick any plant that is a threatened species, population or ecological community. 'Pick' is defined as gathering, plucking, cutting, pulling up, destroying, poisoning, taking, digging up, removing or injuring.

The penalty for harming an animal or picking a plant in respect of any endangered species, population or ecological community is $220,000 or imprisonment for two years or both and, in a case where an animal of any endangered species, population or ecological community is harmed, an additional $100,000 in respect of each animal that is harmed, Where a vulnerable species has been harmed or picked the penalty is $500,000 or imprisonment for one year or both and, in a case where an animal of any vulnerable species is harmed, an additional $5000 penalty units in respect of each animal that is harmed.

It is a defence to a prosecution for an offence of harming an animal or picking a plant if the accused proves that the act constituting the alleged offence:

- was authorised by a general licence under s 120 (fauna), a licence under s 131, 132 or 132A (native plants), a scientific licence under s 132C, issued under the NPWA, or a licence granted under Pt 6 of the TSCA; or
- has already been determined by the Director-General, under s 95(2) of the TSCA, to be action not likely to significantly affect threatened species, populations or ecological communities, or their habitats; or
- was authorised by a property vegetation plan approved under the *Native Vegetation Act 2003,* on the ground that the act was covered by the biodiversity certification provisions of the native vegetation reform package (see below) when the plan was approved; or
- was essential for the carrying out of:
    - development in accordance with a development consent within the meaning of the EPAA, or
    - an activity by a determining authority within the meaning of Pt 5 of that Act, or
    - an activity in accordance with an approval of a determining authority within the meaning of Pt 5 of that Act, or
    - a project approved under Pt 3A of the EPAA, or
- was authorised by, and done in accordance with, a conservation agreement, or a joint management agreement entered into under Pt 7 of the TSCA; or
- was authorised to be done under the *State Emergency and Rescue Management Act 1989* or the *State Emergency Service Act 1989* and was reasonably necessary in order to avoid a threat to life or property; or
- was not done for commercial purposes and was done in relation to a plant that was cultivated by the person, or by another person, as a hobby; or
- was done in relation to a plant that was obtained from a person authorised to grow and sell it by a licence issued under s 132.

This section does not apply in relation to any emergency fire fighting act authorised to be done under the *Rural Fires Act 1997* (NPWA s 118A(3)).

In relying on a defence, the burden of proof rests on the accused.

In *Bentley v BGP Properties Pty Ltd,*[19] the defendant was prosecuted for the slashing, clearing and excavation of land at Redhead in the local government area of the

19 [2006] NSWLEC 34.

City of Lake Macquarie, between 1 August 2001 and 7 December 2001. In doing so, the defendant damaged thousands of plants of the vulnerable species Tetratheca juncea.

The common name of the species is Black-eyed Susan which has been listed as a vulnerable species under the TSCA. A key factor threatening the species is habitat clearance resulting in direct destruction of individual plants, fragmentation of populations of plants and reduction of the range and distribution of the species. The defendant was charged with picking a threatened species contrary to s 118A(2) of the NPWA. The defendant pleaded guilty to the charge and the court's task was to determine the appropriate sentence for the defendant's crime.

In imposing a sentence, Preston CJ emphasised that the objects of the NPWA are to be achieved by applying the principles of ecologically sustainable development, as set out in s 2A(2) of the Act. His Honour stated that 'the conservation of biological diversity and ecological integrity is one of the pillars of ecologically sustainable development',[20] and that 'maintaining ecological integrity involves maintaining ecosystem health'.[21] His Honour also noted that the requirement for prior assessment and study of the impacts of a proposed action likely to damage threatened species, populations or ecological communities (such as prescribed under Pt 6 of TSCA, and Pts 4 or 5 of EPAA) is a key means of achieving ecologically sustainable development.[22] The requirement is also an important component of the precautionary principle,[23] intergenerational equity,[24] and can facilitate the internalisation of external environmental costs.[25]

With respect to the fact that the sentence must serve the purpose of general or public deterrence, his Honour said that:

> It is the duty of the Court to see that the sentence which is imposed will operate as a powerful factor in preventing the commission of similar crimes by those who might otherwise be tempted by the prospect that only light punishment will be imposed … [t]his factor is particularly relevant to environmental offences. Persons will not be deterred from committing environmental offences by nominal fines.[26]

Furthermore:

> The offence provisions, including [section] 118A(2) of the NPW Act, are themselves designed to warn potential offenders of the seriousness with which the community views conduct which contravenes these requirements to protect threatened species, populations and ecological communities, to deter persons from such conduct and to punish those who nevertheless persist in engaging in such conduct. The Court must be alive to considerations of this kind and, by the sentence it passes, show its abhorrence of crimes against the environment and significant components of it such as threatened species, populations and ecological communities.[27]

Having addressed the objective seriousness of the offence, the seriousness of environmental harm and the defendant's actions, which were planned and deliberate,

20 Ibid at [58].
21 Ibid at [61].
22 Ibid at [67].
23 Ibid at [68].
24 Ibid at [69].
25 Ibid at [70].
26 Ibid at [139],[140].
27 Ibid at [148], [149].

the defendant was convicted of the charge, fined the amount of $40,000 and ordered to pay the prosecutor's costs. Preston CJ noted that the defendant expressed no contrition or remorse and made no attempt to rehabilitate the land or to prevent further damage to the land since the clearing.[28] In addition, other than co-operating with the prosecutor in the investigation of the offence and in the early, interlocutory stages of the proceedings, there had been little other co-operation.[29]

The significance of this case is that it is the first instance in which the principles of ecologically sustainable development have been referred to when convicting a person of a criminal offence under the TSCA.

Harming critical habitat

In addition, a person must not harm any critical habitat (NPWA s 118C). The burden of proof resting on the prosecution differs according to whether or not a map of critical habitat was published in the *Gazette* before the offence was committed. If it was, the prosecution does not have to prove that the person knew that the habitat was declared as critical habitat. However, if the map was not published, then it will be necessary for the prosecution to prove that the person knew, or ought to have known, that it was critical habitat. The maximum penalty for harming critical habitat is $20,0000 or imprisonment for two years or both.

The defence provisions relating to the harming of critical habitat are slightly different from those relating to harming or picking threatened species and endangered population or ecological communities. Here, it is a defence to a prosecution if the act constituting the alleged offence:

- was authorised by a licence granted either under the NPWA or under Pt 6 of the TSCA; or
- has already been determined by the Director-General, under s 95(2) of the TSCA, to be action not likely to significantly affect threatened species, populations or ecological communities, or their habitats; or
- was essential for the carrying out of:
    - development in accordance with a development consent within the meaning of the EPAA, or
    - an activity by a determining authority within the meaning of Pt 5 of that Act, or
    - an activity in accordance with an approval of a determining authority within the meaning of Pt 5 of that Act, or
    - a project approved under Pt 3A of the EPAA, or
- was authorised by, and done in accordance with, a conservation agreement, or a joint management agreement entered into under Pt 7 of the TSCA; or
- was authorised to be done under the *Rural Fires Act 1997, State Emergency and Rescue Management Act 1989* or the *State Emergency Service Act 1989* and was reasonably necessary in order to avoid a threat to life or property. (NPWA s 118C(5))

In relying on a defence, the burden of proof rests with the accused.

28 Ibid at [259].

29 Ibid at [266].

Damaging habitat of threatened species, endangered population or endangered ecological community

A person must also not damage any habitat of a threatened species, an endangered population or an endangered ecological community if the person is aware of its status as habitat (NPWA s 118D). The penalty is $100,000 or imprisonment for one year or both.

The defence provisions are the same as for harming or picking threatened species and endangered populations or communities (NPWA s 118D(2)). The burden of proof rests with the accused.

General defence under Part 8A of National Parks and Wildlife Act 1974

It is a general defence to prosecution under Pt 8A of the NPWA if the accused is able to prove that the act constituting the offence: amounted to the clearing of native vegetation that constitutes 'a routine agricultural management activity' (this is defined at length in s 118G(2)), or a routine farming practice activity (other than clearing of native vegetation). However, the clearing must not exceed the minimum extent reasonably necessary for carrying out the exempt activities, and the clearing will not be exempt from prosecution if it is done for a work, building or structure before the grant of any required statutory approval or other authority (NPWA s 118G(3)). It will also be a defence to prosecution if the activity amounts to the clearing of non-protected regrowth, the continuation of existing farming activities, or sustainable grazing, all permitted under the *Native Vegetation Act 2003*.

Licensing provisions

The licensing provisions under the TSCA appear in Pt 6 of the Act.

A person can apply to the Director-General for a licence to:

- harm any animal that is, or is part of, a threatened species, population or ecological community; or
- pick any plant that is, or is part of, a threatened species, population or ecological community; or
- damage critical habitat; or
- damage to habitat of a threatened species, population or ecological community.

For example, a licence may be issued under this section to authorise an Aboriginal person to harm animals or pick plants for cultural purposes. But note that a 'general licence' issued under s 120 of the NPWA, discussed above, may authorise one of these actions only for the welfare of an animal, or if there is a threat to life or property (TSCA s 91).

If the proposed action is not on land that is critical habitat and the application is not accompanied by a species impact statement, the Director-General must decide whether the action is likely to significantly affect threatened species, populations or ecological communities, or their habitats. The Director-General must take into account the following:

- any assessment guidelines issued and in force under s 94A;
- in the case of a threatened species, whether the action proposed is likely to have an adverse effect on the life cycle of the species such that a viable local population of the species is likely to be placed at risk of extinction;
- in the case of an endangered population, whether the action proposed is likely to have an adverse effect on the life cycle of the species that constitutes the endangered population such that a viable local population of the species is likely to be placed at risk of extinction
- in the case of an endangered ecological community or critically endangered ecological community, whether the action proposed
    - o is likely to have an adverse effect on the extent of the ecological community such that its local occurrence is likely to be placed at risk of extinction, or
    - o is likely to modify substantially and adversely the composition of the ecological community such that its local occurrence is likely to be placed at risk of extinction;
- in relation to the habitat of a threatened species, population or ecological community
    - o the extent to which habitat is likely to be removed or modified as a result of the action proposed, and
    - o whether an area of habitat is likely to become fragmented or isolated from other areas of habitat as a result of the proposed action, and
    - o the importance of the habitat to be removed, modified, fragmented or isolated to the long-term survival of the species, population or ecological community in the locality,
- whether the action proposed is likely to have an adverse effect on critical habitat (either directly or indirectly);
- whether the action proposed is consistent with the objectives or actions of a recovery plan or threat abatement plan; and
- whether the action proposed constitutes or is part of a key threatening process or is likely to result in the operation of, or increase the impact of, a key threatening process (TSCA s 94).

Within seven days of receiving an application for a licence, the Director-General must place a copy on the register of licence applications and notify the public of the application in a newspaper circulating throughout the State. The public must be given the opportunity to make comments within 28 days (TSCA s 96).

In considering whether to grant or to refuse to grant a licence application, the Director-General must take into account the following:

- any species impact statement;
- any written submissions received;
- the factors specified in the listings provisions in the TSCA (ss 10-15);
- any relevant recovery plan or threat abatement plan;
- the principles of ecologically sustainable development;
- whether the action proposed is likely irretrievably to reduce the long-term viability of the species, population or ecological community in the region;

- whether the action proposed is likely to accelerate the extinction of the species or ecological community or place it at risk of extinction; and
- the likely social and economic consequences of granting or refusing to grant a licence application. (TSCA s 97)

After considering an application for a licence and any accompanying material, the Director-General may grant the application, unconditionally or subject to conditions or restrictions, or refuse the application (TSCA s 99). The Director-General may attach a condition to the licence requiring the licensee to make a monetary contribution towards the cost of preparation of a recovery plan for any threatened species, population or ecological community, or any of their habitats, likely to be affected by the action (TSCA s 101(1)(b)). A licence may be cancelled by the Director-General (TSCA s 105). An applicant for a licence, or a person who has made written submissions about an application for a licence, or a person to whose licence conditions or restrictions have been attached, or whose licence has been varied or cancelled may, if dissatisfied with the Director-General's decision, appeal to the Land and Environment Court (TSCA s 106).

'Any person' may bring proceedings in the Land and Environment Court to enforce the provisions of the TSCA (TSCA s 147).

Administrative orders

In addition to the various offences which are set out in the TSCA, for which a person may be criminally prosecuted, the TSCA also provides for the making of administrative orders. The making of interim protection orders is mentioned in Chapter 9.

Stop work orders

Although this section is subject to various exceptions, if the Director-General is of the opinion that any action is being, or is about to be, carried out that is likely to result in one or more of the following:

- harm to a threatened species, population or ecological community (so far as animals are concerned); or
- picking of a threatened species, population or ecological community (so far as plants are concerned); or
- damage to critical habitat; or
- damage to habitats of threatened species, populations or ecological communities;

the Director-General may order that the action is to cease and that no action, other than those specified in the order, be carried out in or in the vicinity of the critical habitat or the habitat of the threatened species, population or ecological community within a period of 40 days after the date of the order (TSCA s 114).

Joint management and conservation agreements

The TSCA allows the Director-General to enter into a joint management agreement with public authorities for the management, control, regulation or restriction of an action that is jeopardising the survival of a threatened species, population or ecological community (TSCA s 121).

Also where a conservation agreement, discussed in Chapter 9, relating to land has been entered into under the NPWA for the conservation of critical habitat or the conservation of threatened species, populations or ecological communities, or their habitats, the agreement may also make provision for: assistance in connection with maintaining and promoting sustainable farming practices and achieving the objects of this Act; implementing the requirements of a recovery plan that relates to the land; and ensuring the continued and appropriate agricultural use of the land by the owner of the land (TSCA s 126).

New Biological Diversity Advisory Council (BDAC) and Social and Economic Advisory Council (SEAC)

The 2004 amendments also led to the establishment of two new Committees. The BDAC is comprised of members who have expertise in biological diversity, biological science and environmental science. The BDAC will advise the Minister, the Director-General and the NRC on the likely impacts on biodiversity of actions taken under the Act following the listing of threatened species, populations and ecological communities or key threatening processes and other related matters (TSCA s 141B). Another Committee, the SEAC, will comprise members who have expertise in natural resource management, economics, social impact assessment and the industry or agriculture sectors. The SEAC will have the same advisory functions as the BDAC (TSCA s 141C).

Understanding the interaction between TSCA and the Environmental Planning and Assessment Act 1979 (NSW)

The TSCA must be read together with other pieces of legislation such as the *Environmental Planning and Assessment Act 1979* (EPAA). The interactions between the TSCA and the EPAA, as they existed before the introduction of the native vegetation and natural resource management reforms, will be explained first before the reforms are set out.

The TSCA interacts with the EPAA in two primary ways – with respect to environmental planning instruments (EPIs) and applications for development consent. Where native plants and animals, including threatened species, populations and ecological communities, and their habitats, have been listed under the TSCA, EPIs may make provision for protecting them. Also, if land is declared to be critical habitat then it must be properly identified in the EPI applying to that land. EPIs may also include provisions protecting and conserving vulnerable ecological communities (EPAA s 26(1A)).

If a development application is made under Pt 4 of the EPAA in respect of land that is critical habitat, or if the activity is likely to significantly affect threatened species, populations or ecological communities, then a species impact statement must be supplied by the applicant and must be taken into account by the consent authority. The content of a species impact statement is discussed in Chapter 4. In addition, the consent authority must get the concurrence of the Director-General of the Department of Environment and Conservation unless a Minister is the consent authority in which case the concurrence of the Minister for the Environment must be obtained.

Similarly, under Pt 5 of the EPAA, a determining authority must not carry out an activity, or grant approval to an activity, that is likely to significantly affect the environment (including critical habitat) or threatened species, population or ecological communities, or their habitats. If development is taking place under Pt 5 of the Act, and the determining authority is not a Minister, the Director-General of the Department of Environment and Conservation must concur. Where the determining authority is a Minister, an activity must not be approved unless the Minister for the Environment has been consulted.

In deciding whether there is likely to be a significant effect on threatened species, populations or ecological communities or their habitats the following factors must be taken into account:

- in the case of a threatened species, whether the action proposed is likely to have an adverse effect on the life cycle of the species such that a viable local population of the species is likely to be placed at risk of extinction;
- in the case of an endangered population, whether the action proposed is likely to have an adverse effect on the life cycle of the species that constitutes the endangered population such that a viable local population of the species is likely to be placed at risk of extinction;
- in the case of an endangered ecological community or critically endangered ecological community, whether the action proposed:
    - o is likely to have an adverse effect on the extent of the ecological community such that its local occurrence is likely to be placed at risk of extinction, or
    - o is likely to modify substantially and adversely the composition of the ecological community such that its local occurrence is likely to be placed at risk of extinction;
- in relation to the habitat of a threatened species, population or ecological community:
    - o the extent to which habitat is likely to be removed or modified as a result of the action proposed, and
    - o whether an area of habitat is likely to become fragmented or isolated from other areas of habitat as a result of the proposed action, and
    - o the importance of the habitat to be removed, modified, fragmented or isolated to the long-term survival of the species, population or ecological community in the locality;
- whether the action proposed is likely to have an adverse effect on critical habitat (either directly or indirectly);
- whether the action proposed is consistent with the objectives or actions of a recovery plan or threat abatement plan;
- whether the action proposed constitutes or is part of a key threatening process or is likely to result in the operation of, or increase the impact of, a key threatening process. (EPAA Pt 5A)

The Minister for the Environment may, with the concurrence of the Minister for Planning, issue assessment guidelines by order in the *Gazette* for determining whether an action is likely to significantly affect threatened species, population or ecological communities or their habitats (TSCA s 94A).

The Director-General, meanwhile, is required to take the following factors into account before granting concurrence to any activities proposed under Pts 4 and 5 of the EPAA:

- any species impact statement prepared in relation to the activity;
- any assessment report prepared by or on behalf of the proponent;
- any representations made under s 113 concerning the species impact statement;
- any relevant recovery plan or threat abatement plan;
- whether the activity is likely to reduce the long-term viability of the species, population or ecological community in the region;
- whether the activity is likely to accelerate the extinction of the species, population or ecological community or place it at risk of extinction;
- the principles of ecologically sustainable development;
- the likely social and economic consequences of granting or of not granting concurrence. (EPAA s 79B(5))

The consent and concurrence provisions do not apply to development that may affect vulnerable ecological communities.

Another important aspect of the interactions between the TSCA and the EPAA is that 'any person' can enforce the provisions of the EPAA. This is relevant where there has been a failure to submit a species impact assessment, or environmental impact statement, or for any other relevant breach of the EPAA (EPAA s 123).[30]

Understanding the impact of the native vegetation reform package on the interaction between the TSCA and EPAA

In spite of what has been discussed above, regarding the interaction between the TSCA and the EPAA, the native vegetation reform package has had a significant impact on these interactions.

Biodiversity certification affecting the clearing of native vegetation

Under the biodiversity certification provisions of Pt 7 Div 4 of the TSCA, the Minister may confer biodiversity certification on the native vegetation reform package for the purposes of the Act. The reform package includes: the *Native Vegetation Act 2003;* State-wide standards and targets for natural resource management issues recommended under the *Natural Resources Commission Act 2003;* catchment action plans under the *Catchment Management Authorities Act 2003,* and protocols and guidelines adopted by regulation under the *Native Vegetation Act 2003,* the *Catchment Management Authorities Act* and the *Natural Resources Commission Act* (TSCA ss 126B, 126C). While the certification is in force, all land within the area of operations of each catchment management authority has the benefit of that biodiversity certification. Biodiversity certification has the effect that the clearing of native vegetation, authorised by a property vegetation plan developed under the *Native Vegetation Act,* will not need to be licensed under the NPWA. The obtaining of development consent for

30 See, for example, *Corkhill v Forestry Commission of New South Wales* [1990] NSWLEC 77 and *Oshlack v Iron Gates Pty Ltd and Richmond River Council* (1997) 130 LGERA 189.

the clearing of native vegetation on the land will also not require preparation of a species impact statement or consultation between Ministers (TSCA s 126D).

The Minister may suspend or revoke biodiversity certification of the native vegetation reform package generally, or with respect to a particular catchment management authority, if the Minister is of the opinion that the package will fail to conserve threatened species, populations and ecological communities. The Minister may only form this opinion based on the outcomes of any audit undertaken by the NRC, results of an investigation conducted by the Director-General or other circumstances prescribed by Regulation (TSCA s 126E).

Biodiversity certification of environmental planning instruments

Under Pt 7 Div 5 of the TCSA, the Minister may also confer biodiversity certification on an EPI if satisfied that the EPI seeks to promote the conservation of threatened species, populations and ecological communities. In deciding whether or not to confer certification, the Minister must consider, amongst other things, the likely social and economic consequences of implementing the EPI; the most effective and efficient use of resources for conserving threatened species, population and communities; the principles of ecologically sustainable development; and whether any land has been reserved for conservation purposes under the NPWA.

An EPI cannot be biodiversity certified unless the proposed certification when the EPI is publicly exhibited under s 66 of the EPAA and copies of all submissions received have been provided to the Minister. Certification may be subject to conditions. The effect of certification of an EPI is that any development requiring development consent under Pt 4 of the EPAA will be taken to be development that is not likely to significantly affect any threatened species, population or ecological community or its habitat. The same is true of development being undertaken under Pt 5 of the EPAA. Biodiversity certification for an EPI remains in force for as long as the Minister determines, or if no period is determined, then for 10 years. Certification may be renewed for a further 10 years if the Minister has reviewed the EPI to take account of any new listings under the Act. The certification may also be suspended or revoked if the EPI fails to conserve threatened species, populations and ecological communities, or if the consent authority has failed to comply with a direction from the Minister to review the EPI in response to any new listings. Notice of certification must be given to the Director-General of the Department of Infrastructure, Planning and Natural resources, must be placed on the website of the Department of Environment and Conservation and to each local council to which the EPI applies.

Certification also affects the Director-General's powers of concurrence with respect to developments, undertaken under Pts 4 and 5 of the EPAA. Under the Act, the Director-General may grant concurrence if the developer agrees to take voluntary action that the Director-General considers will significantly benefit threatened species conservation. The voluntary action includes reserving land under Pt 4 of the NPWA or entering into a conservation agreement relating to land under the Act, securing the land for conservation purposes by a method considered by the Director-General to be satisfactory, action to restore habitat or a monetary contribution.

Accreditation of person to prepare threatened species assessments and surveys

The Director-General must institute arrangements for the accreditation of suitably qualified and experienced persons to undertake and prepare surveys and assessments for use in connection with biodiversity certification of EPIs and for assessing under s 5A of the EPAA significant effects on threatened species, populations and ecological communities.

Creating a market in biodiversity credits under the TSCA

Clearly, one of the 'ecosystem services' which can be traded in the market is a biodiversity credit. As mentioned earlier, the key to markets in ecosystem services is to identify the many services that can be delivered by a single ecosystem. The planting of a stand of trees, for example, may deliver many different ecosystem services including carbon sinks, reduced salinity and biodiversity protection. In an ecosystem services trading system, each service would need to be identified and measured to determine the appropriate number of credits that should be allocated to the delivery of the service. The pool of credits would then need to be managed to match buyers' needs with ecosystem service supply.

To this end, the NSW Government has enacted the *Threatened Species Conservation Amendment (Biodiversity Banking) Act 2006*, also discussed in Chapter 4. This follows the release by the NSW Department of Environment and Conservation (DEC) of the *BioBanking: A Biodiversity Offsets and Banking Scheme – Working Paper*,[31] released in December 2005. The key elements of the Act, which inserts a new Pt 7A into the principal Act, are the following:

Biobanking agreements

In accordance with biobanking agreements entered into between the Minister for the Environment and owners of land, biobanking sites may be established on land in New South Wales. Key features include:

- The agreements will authorise or require a land owner to carry out certain management actions on the land in order to preserve biodiversity value.
- Biobanking agreements must be registered on title to land and will generally last in perpetuity and can be varied in limited circumstances.
- Entry into an agreement leads to automatic entitlement to registration of the biobank site, although this may be cancelled where the conditions of an agreement are breached.
- The management actions are exempt from the requirement for development consent or environmental assessment under the EPAA (unless otherwise provided for by Regulation).
- The agreements can be enforced by any person in the Land and Environment Court.

Development cannot be carried out on a biobanking site simply by suspending the biobanking agreement under the EPAA, except with the concurrence of the Minister for the Environment (Div 2).

---

31 See <http://www.environment.nsw.gov.au/resources/biobanking05661.pdf> (accessed 24 July 2006).

Creation of biodiversity credits

Biodiversity credits may be created by the Director-General in respect of management actions carried out on a biobanking site. The number and class of credits that can be created on a site will be determined in accordance with the biobanking assessment methodology which is to be published by the Minister in the Gazette. The methodology will contain rules with respect to:

- the management actions in respect of which credits can be created The circumstances in which development will be regarded as improving or maintaining biodiversity values, including where impacts are being offset against biodiversity credits;
- any impacts which cannot be offset by the retirement of biodiversity credits (Div 3).

Credits may be cancelled or suspended by the Director-General on account of wrongdoing by the person who created the credit, and credits may also be compulsorily retired because of wrongdoing. Failure to comply with an order to retire credits attracts a penalty of $550,000 (Div 5).

Trading in biodiversity credits

The Act sets up a biodiversity credit trading scheme subject to the Regulations (Div 4).

Essentially, a credit may be traded to any person. On the first transfer of a biodiversity credit, the regulations may require the payment of an amount into the Biobanking Trust Fund which will fund management actions carried out by land owners (Div 7).

Biobanking statements

The proponent of development and activities under Pts 4 and 5 of the EPAA, or a project under Pt 3A of the Act, may apply to the Director-General for a biobanking statement, unless the development requires approval under the *Native Vegetation Act 2003* or is excluded by Regulations.

The application must include an assessment of the likely impacts of the development on biodiversity values and a description of the biodiversity credits which will be retired in order to allow the development to proceed, and must show that all cost effective measures are being taken on the site to minimise any impacts on biodiversity values. Failure to comply with an order to retire credits attracts a penalty of $1,100,000.

The Director-General may issue a biobanking statement only if a development will improve or maintain biodiversity values. In relation to projects under Pt 3A, the Minister may direct the Director-General to issue a biobanking statement.

Where a biobanking statement is issued, the development is not required to be assessed in accordance with the threatened species provisions contained in Pts 4 and 5 of the EPAA. Also the requirement to obtain the concurrence of the Minister for the Environment falls away. Nevertheless, the development must be carried out in accordance with the conditions contained in the biobanking statement.

Biobanking statements will lapse after two years if no further action has been taken with regard to the development by that time (Div 6).

Registers

The Director-General must keep a register of biobank sites, biodiversity credits and biobanking statements (Div 8).

Conclusions

The 2004 amendments to the TSCA have streamlined to a considerable extent the granting of consent to activities that may nevertheless result in 'harm' to threatened species and the clearing of native vegetation. Intrinsic to the reforms is the idea that biodiversity can be adequately protected using all of the new processes, as well as providing for offsets and biodiversity banking.

The new regime for managing natural resources, threatened species and native vegetation is very new and is still in the process of being implemented. Time will tell whether or not the reforms in NSW manage to deliver better environmental outcomes, as well as better economic outcomes for landholders and developers.

Fisheries Management Act 1994 (NSW)

Part 7A of the *Fisheries Management Act 1994* (FMA) inserts provisions into the Act for protecting aquatic species such as fish and marine vegetation. They are very similar to those for listing and managing terrestrial threatened species, endangered populations and endangered ecological communities, for listing key threatening processes and protecting critical habitat. A Fisheries Scientific Committee is responsible for recommending listings to the Minister (FMA s 220G). Where the listing of a key threatening process is likely to have an impact on both terrestrial and aquatic environments, the Chairperson of the Committee may consult with the Chairperson of the Threatened Species Scientific Committee to determine whether the nomination should also be considered by that Committee under the TSCA (FMA s 200IA). Recovery and threat abatement plans may be made and a Threatened Species Priorities Action Statement must be prepared by the Director-General (FMA s 220ZVB). Licences may be issued to authorise harm to aquatic threatened species, populations or ecological communities or damage habitat (FMA s 220ZW) while stop work orders may be given (FMA s 221O) and joint management agreements entered into (FMA s 221V).

Assessing the risk of genetically modified organisms to Australia's biodiversity

The possible risks to biodiversity posed by genetically modified organisms have been set out above in the section on the Cartagena Protocol. We will now discuss provisions in Australian legislation to assess and mitigate these risks.

In Australia, GMOs are regulated under a number of different Acts. These include the *Gene Technology Act 2000* (Cth), the *Food Acts* in the States[32] which in the

32 See *Food Act 2003* (NSW), *Food Act 2006* (Qld), *Food Act 2001* (SA), *Food Act 2003* (Tas), *Food Act 1984* (Vic), *Food Act 2001* (ACT).

case of GM foods must be labelled consistently with Standard A18,[33] the *Quarantine Act 1908* (Cth) and the *Imported Food Control Act 1992* (Cth), administered by the Australian Quarantine and Inspection Service, and the *Customs Act 1901* (Cth) which vests various powers in the Australian Customs Service.

Gene Technology Act 2000 (Cth) (GTA)

For the purposes of releasing GMOs into the environment, the most relevant legislation is the *Gene Technology Act*. This Act regulates 'dealings' with GMOs (defined as live, viable organisms that have been modified by techniques of gene technology) and dealings with GM products not currently regulated by existing regulators (GTA Pt 4). A 'dealing' includes conducting experiments with, making, developing, producing, manufacturing, breeding, propagating, using in the course of manufacture of a thing, growing, raising, culturing or importing. The Act prohibits any 'dealing with' GMOs unless the dealing is exempt, a notifiable low risk dealing, is licensed, or is on the Register of GMOs. Before the Governor-General declares that a 'dealing' is a notifiable low risk dealing, the Regulator must be satisfied that the 'dealing' would not involve the intentional release of a GMO into the environment (GTA s 74). The Act is administered by the Gene Technology Regulator (GTR) who reports directly to Parliament and is the final decision-maker on applications relating to 'dealings'. These include GM agricultural crops, GM animals or fish, GM micro-organisms designed for bio-remediation and GM viruses and vaccines. The Act also requires the establishment of a publicly available database of all approvals of GMOs and GM products in Australia (GTA Pt 9 Div 6).

Three advisory committees are established under the Act: the Gene Technology Technical Advisory Committee to advise exclusively on licence applications; the Gene Technology Ethics Committee and the Gene Technology Community Consultative Group. The Consultative Group comprises 12 members appointed by the Minister who have skills and experience in environmental issues, consumer issues, the impact of gene technology on the community, issues relevant to the biotechnology industry, issues relevant to gene technology research, and public health issues (GTA Pt 8).

If the GTR is satisfied that a 'dealing' involving the intentional release of a GMO into the environment may pose significant risks to the health and safety of people, before approving the 'dealing', the GTRs must prepare a Risk Assessment and Risk Management Plan. Public participation is only called for if the GTR believes that the 'dealing' will pose a significant risk to health and safety of people and the environment. The Regulator must also seek advice on the risk assessment and the risk management plan from the States; the Gene Technology Technical Advisory Committee; each Commonwealth authority or agency prescribed by the Regulations for the purposes of this paragraph; the Environment Minister; and any local council that the Regulator considers appropriate (TSCA Pt 5 Div 4).

There are no third party appeals or statutory standing for judicial review (GTA Pt 12 Div 2). Also the GTR is not specifically required to take the precautionary

33 On 28 July 2000, ANZFSC agreed on a genetically modified food labelling regime and Standard A18 now requires the labelling of food and food ingredients: where novel DNA and/or protein is present in the final food or where the food has altered characteristics. However, the Standard allows an ingredient to contain up to 1% unintended presence of genetically modified product.

principle into account in making a decision whether or not to license a 'dealing', but the principle is included in the Act as a means of achieving the object of the Act (GTA s 4). The object is 'to protect the health and safety of people, and to protect the environment, by identifying risks posed by or as a result of gene technology, and by managing those risks through regulating certain dealings with GMOs' (GTA s 3).

NSW moratorium on planting of GM trial crops

The NSW government, like other State and Territory governments, enacted legislation giving effect to the *Gene Technology Act 2000* (Cth) in New South Wales. The Act is the *Gene Technology Act 2003* (NSW). However, given Australia's federal system of government even if an intentional release of a GMO crop into the environment is authorised by the GTR, there is no guarantee that it can be released into the environment. This is because a number of State governments have placed moratoria on the planting of GM crops in their jurisdictions. The NSW government, for example, enacted the *Gene Technology (GM Crop Moratorium) Act 2003* (NSW) which designates New South Wales as an area in which certain GM plants may not be cultivated for marketing purposes. The moratorium was initially intended to expire on 3 March 2006 but has been extended to 2008. The moratorium operates to the extent that the Minister can prohibit the cultivation in New South Wales of a specified GM food plant or class of GM food plants. A breach of the Act is an offence attracting a fine of $125,000 for a corporation, or $50,000 or imprisonment for two years, or both, for a person who cultivates the GM food plant, either intentionally or negligently. A person can be ordered to destroy a plant or the Minister can seize and dispose of an offending plant. Inspectorial powers are conferred on persons appointed by the Director-General. Exemption from the operation of the moratorium order may be conferred.

To indicate the effect of the NSW moratorium, in July 2003, the Federal Gene Technology Regulator made a decision, under the *Gene Technology Act*, to issue a licence in respect of application DIR 021/2002 from Bayer CropScience Pty Ltd. This was the first step in the phased commercial release of InVigor® canola in Australia. However, the NSW government released Moratorium Order Number 1 prohibiting cultivation of InVigor canola in the State.[34] In May 2004, the NSW Minister for Agriculture then granted an exemption from the moratorium with respect to three sites in NSW. The exemption was for GM canola to be planted as part of research trial by Bayer CropScience Pty Ltd (Bayer).[35]

The Minister attached the following extensive conditions of consent: Bayer must notify the Director-General in writing of the date of the planting, and forecasted date of flowering and harvesting of the canola and must notify neighbours of the date of planting and the location of the site. Bayer must also provide evidence to the Director-General that planting equipment has been cleaned after the planting, and a buffer zone of at least 50 metres must extend in all directions from the edge of the site, which must be inspected at least once every 35 days commencing 14 days before the forecasted flowering of the GM canola at the site and concluding when flowering of the GM canola ceases. If plants in the buffer zone are detected then the

34 *NSW Government Gazette*, Special Supplement No 119, 25 July 2003.

35 *NSW Government Gazette*, Special Supplement, Exemption Orders Number 4, 5, 6, No 89, 25 May 2004.

GM canola at the site must be destroyed; Bayer must also give the Director-General evidence of the measures taken to clean equipment after the harvesting of the GM canola.

After harvesting, the canola seeds must be stored in a locked, sealed container and marked 'GM canola seed', or rendered unviable by autoclaving or burning, or transported in an unbreakable and sealed container to a location outside New South Wales; Bayer must provide evidence to the Director-General of measures taken to clean equipment used to transport the GM canola from the site; Bayer must, within three months of the harvest, or after rain, lightly till the site when germination of any canola seed is likely.

Grazing is prohibited unless the tillage has taken place, and deep cultivation (ie to a depth of more than 50 millimetres) is prohibited in the 12 months following the harvest. After the harvest, GM must not be planted at the site before 3 March 2006 unless authorised by the Director-General.

The site must be inspected for volunteer plants until 3 March 2006 and records of the inspection must be kept. Bayer must make available to the Director-General any data relating to the trials conducted at the site, including but not limited to the trial design, results of experiments and any other results required by the Director-General within seven days of a written request. Bayer must hold and maintain, and must ensure that all subcontractors are beneficiaries under, a public liability insurance policy that provides coverage to the equivalent of 10 million Euros for any losses that it may incur in connection with the cultivation of GM canola in research trials conducted in accordance with the exemption.

The exhaustive conditions attached to the permit to release GMOs into the environment, as well as the moratorium, are an indication of the cautious approach which the NSW government has adopted with regard to their safety.

The *Gene Technology Act* was reviewed in 2006. One of the most significant recommendations contained in the Review, entitled *Statutory Review of the Gene Technology Act 2000 and the Gene Technology Agreement*,[36] was that the moratoria imposed by the State governments are causing detrimental impacts and are hampering the collection of information which would assist farmers in deciding whether or not to grow GM crops. In addition, the moratoria are impacting negatively on the agricultural and research sectors. For these reasons, the Review recommended that the Commonwealth and State governments reconfirm their commitment to a nationally consistent scheme for gene technology.[37]

36 See <http://www.health.gov.au/internet/wcms/publishing.nsf/Content/9F34C91EA9E219E2CA2571410009A47E/$File/Stat_Review_GeneTechAct.pdf> (accessed 18 January 2007).

37 Ibid at 92-97.

9
PROTECTED AREAS

New South Wales has a wide network of parks and reserves under Commonwealth and State legislation, collectively called protected areas.

Protected areas, the best known being national parks, have historically been reserved for a variety of reasons, both natural and cultural. Two reasons give a new urgency to creating new reserves. The first is the conservation of biodiversity, and the network is being evaluated in terms of its comprehensiveness and representativeness in relation to biodiversity. Another important influence on the creation of protected areas is the rate of development, particularly on the coast, where active measures are being taken to reserve land, not only for its biodiversity value but also to preserve views, landscapes, access and amenity.

This legislation may also restrict the use of private land, and government land not included in the system of parks and reserves, and supplements the major schemes dealing with vital concerns in the conservation of biodiversity, threatened species, native vegetation and the management of coastal areas, dealt with in Chapters 7 and 8.

This chapter also looks at an interesting new feature of privately owned reserves.

The Commonwealth legislation on protected areas is the *Environment Protection and Biodiversity Conservation Act 1999* (Cth) (EPBCA). While there are no Commonwealth reserves in New South Wales under the EPBCA, the legislation is important in facilitating links between the Commonwealth's international responsibilities, such as for world heritage places and Ramsar sites, and State reserves. World heritage places in New South Wales, for example, are also reserved lands under NSW legislation. The main NSW legislation to be discussed is the *National Parks and Wildlife Act 1974* (NSW) (NPWA).[1]

While the schemes of management for all categories of reserved lands show many similarities, similarities that are increasing as the legislation is amended, there are still many differences. Thus, at this stage, it is still useful to discuss the various categories of reserves and declared lands under their enabling legislation, rather than attempting an ambitious synthesis.

IUCN Categories

Increasingly, the diversity of parks, reserves and declared lands at the Commonwealth and State levels is being classified according to the IUCN Protected Areas Management Categories.[2] IUCN, the International Union for the Conservation of

1 The legislation in this chapter binds the Crown as well as individuals: see, eg, EPBCA s 4; NPWA s 3.

2 NPWS, *State of the Parks 2004* (2004) at 7; EPBCA s 347.

Nature, also known as the World Conservation Union, is a large international organisation that, for example, is named in the *World Heritage Convention* as an advisor to UNESCO on world heritage sites with natural heritage values.

Protected areas are defined by IUCN as:

> An area of land and/or sea especially dedicated to the protection and maintenance of biological diversity, and of natural and associated cultural values resource, and managed through legal or other effective legal means.[3]

The IUCN categories, particularly numbers 1a to 3, apply to parks and reserves. The IUCN categories, with some further explanation from the EPBCA, are:

- IUCN Category 1a – **strict nature reserve**: protected area managed mainly for science.

  EPBCA description: containing outstanding or representative ecosystems, geological or physiological feature or species;
- IUCN Category 1b – **wilderness area**; protected area managed mainly for wilderness protection.

  EPBCA description: a large area of land or sea that:
  - o is unmodified, or only slightly modified;
  - o retains its natural character; and
  - o does not contain permanent or significant habitation.
- IUCN Category 2 – **national park**; protected area managed mainly for ecosystem protection and recreation.

  EPBCA description: an area of land or sea in natural condition;
- IUCN Category 3 – **natural monument**; protected area managed mainly for conservation of specific natural features.

  EPBCA description: containing a specific natural feature, or natural and cultural feature, of outstanding value because of its rarity, representativeness, aesthetic quality or cultural significance;
- IUCN Category 4 – **habitat/species management area**; protected area managed mainly for conservation through management intervention.

  EPBCA description: containing species habitat;
- IUCN Category 5 – **protected landscape/seascape**; protected area managed mainly for landscape/seascape conservation and recreation.

  EPBCA description does not refer to seascape but of containing an area of land with a distinct character and significant aesthetic, cultural or ecological value from the interaction of people and nature;
- IUCN Category 6 – **managed resource protected area**; protected area managed mainly for the sustainable use of natural ecosystems.

  EPBCA description: containing natural systems, largely unmodified by technology.[4]

---

3 IUCN, *Guidelines for Protected Area Management Categories* (Gland, 1974); quoted in P Figgis, *Australia's National Parks and Protected Areas* (ACIUCN Occasional paper No 8, 1999) at 1.

4 For the IUCN categories, see <www.iucn.org>, and for the legislative amplification, EPBCA ss 346, 347.

This chapter in considering protected areas pursues the following issues:

- whether the land is in public or private ownership;
- formalities in the initiating action and revocation;
- whether the scheme allows for administration outside the relevant public service department through trusts and committees;
- the widespread requirements for plans of management; and
- enforcement measures.

Commonwealth protected areas

The EPBCA provides for the setting up and management of the following categories of protected areas:

- world heritage places, and national and Commonwealth heritage places, where the major concern is heritage conservation, discussed in Chapter 10;
- reserves and conservation zones;
- wetlands of international significance; and
- biosphere reserves.

Commonwealth reserves

Twenty-one Commonwealth reserves have been declared under the EPBCA, six Commonwealth national parks, 13 marine protected areas and two botanic gardens.[5] While none is located in New South Wales, there is a Commonwealth reserve at Jervis Bay, a Commonwealth territory on the NSW South Coast. Of the marine reserves in Australian waters, the Solitary Islands Marine Reserve is located off the NSW North Coast, near Coffs Harbour, with a proposed reserve near the Victoria/ NSW border.

Conservation zone

A conservation zone has interim protection, while being assessed for its suitability as a Commonwealth reserve (ss 390C-390E).

Declaration of a Commonwealth reserve

Reserves are formally created by a proclamation of the Governor-General, which also names the reserve and sets out its purpose. The proclamation is issued following a period of public consultation (ss 344-351). Commonwealth reserves comply with the IUCN protected areas management categories and criteria in the *Environment Protection and Biodiversity Conservation Regulations 2000* (Cth) (EPBCR).

Land in reserves

Commonwealth reserves comprise:

---

5 See <www.deh.gov.au/parks/index.html> (accessed 16 January 2007).

- in Australia – land owned or leased by the Commonwealth, and the sea in a Commonwealth marine area; or
- outside Australia – land or sea for which Australia has obligations relating to biodiversity or heritage under an international agreement (s 343).

Property and usage rights in a reserve, other than over minerals, are vested in the Director of National Parks (ss 345A, 350(7) – usage right defined).

The EPBC legislation and plans of management do not affect:

- prior property and usage rights (s 359); or
- traditional use for hunting, food gathering, ceremonial or religious purposes unless modified to preserve biodiversity (s 359A).

Administration

The Director of National Parks administers reserves and conservation zones (s 514B). The Director consults State agencies and relevant Aboriginal Land Councils (s 514D). The Minister administering the EPBCA may give instructions as to the Director's functions, and has to approve certain contracts and leases (s 514D). An Annual Report is submitted by the Secretary of the Department administering the legislation to the Commonwealth Parliament (s 516).

Boards may be appointed for reserves that include Indigenous people's land, leased to the Director. A Board prepares plans of management, takes management decisions and advises the Minister on development. The appointment is by agreement with the Land Council or the traditional owners, and the Board has a majority of Indigenous members (ss 377-383). Boonderee Reserve in the Jervis Bay Territory is managed jointly with the Indigenous population (s 390).

Wardens, rangers and inspectors may be appointed from the Commonwealth, State or Territory public service or police force (ss 392-399). Wardens and inspectors have extensive powers of entry and seizure (Pt 17).

Plans of management

A plan of management provides for the protection, conservation and management of a reserve. The Director of National Parks prepares plans of management in conjunction with the Board of the reserve, if there is one. Notice of a draft plan is given in the *Gazette* and in a national daily newspaper, inviting public comment (ss 366-370). Plans are approved by the Minister, and after approval are presented to both Houses of Parliament. Either House may disallow a plan.

The following actions may only be taken in a reserve in accordance with its management plan: kill, injure, take, trade, keep, or move a member of a native species; damage heritage; carry on an excavation; erect any structure; carry out works, or carry on commercial activities. There is a civil penalty of 550 penalty units for individuals, and 5000 for corporations (s 354).[6] Mining is prohibited unless approved by the Governor-General, and carried out in accordance with the management plan (s 355). There are further restrictions in the EPBCR.

---

6 A penalty unit is $110: *Crimes Act 1914* (Cth) s 4AA.

Offences

It is an offence to take any action that may result in a significant effect on the environment on Commonwealth land (s 27A).[7] Environment includes heritage values and social, economic and cultural aspects (s 528).

Commonwealth marine protected areas

Marine protected areas are a category of Commonwealth reserve, comprising water, with the seabed below, and the airspace above, inside the seaward boundary of Australia's exclusive economic zone, except:

- waters, where the rights are vested in the State; and
- waters within State limits or over the continental shelf. (s 24)

Offences

It is an offence to take an action that has, will have or is likely to have a significant impact on the environment in a marine protected area (ss 23, 24A). This prohibition also covers actions in the coastal waters of a State that may significantly impact on the environment in Commonwealth controlled coastal waters.

Protected areas outside Commonwealth reserves

The EPBCA protects sites for which the Commonwealth has responsibility under international conventions. In New South Wales these sites are not in Commonwealth reserves but may be State protected areas, or be covered by planning law.

Ramsar sites – wetlands of international importance

Ramsar wetlands are wetlands of international importance, recognised under the *Convention on Wetlands* (the Ramsar Convention) (Ramsar, Iran, 1971), which aims for the conservation and 'wise use' of wetlands. Wise use is defined as:

> the sustainable utilisation of wetlands for the benefit of mankind in a way compatible with the maintenance of the natural properties of the ecosystem. (Recommendation 3.3)

Sustainable utilisation is defined as:

> human use of a wetland so that it may yield the greatest continuous benefit to present generations while maintaining its potential to meet the needs and aspiration of future generations. (Recommendation 3.3)[8]

There are agreed criteria for assessing a site's uniqueness, rarity or representativeness, or the flora, fauna or ecological communities it supports.

---

7 This provision is discussed in Chapter 10.

8 See <www.deh.gov.au/water/wetlands/database/directory/convention.html#ramsar> (accessed 16 January 2007), Department of Environment and Heritage.

There are 11 Ramsar sites in New South Wales, covering an area of 270,000 hectares. Ramsar sites may be on public or private land, and 85% of the NSW sites are in the NSW park system.[9]

Declaration

The formal step for creating a Ramsar site is:

- designation by the Commonwealth for inclusion in the List of Wetlands of International Importance kept under Art 2 of the Ramsar Convention; or
- declaration by the Minister of a site that has not yet been designated and is under threat.

The Minister may declare a site if satisfied that:

- the wetland is of international significance, because of its ecology, botany, zoology, limnology or hydrology; and
- its ecological character is under threat. (s 17)

The declaration giving the site interim protection is by notice in the Commonwealth *Government Gazette.*

Public notice is given after a wetland is designated in, or deleted from, the Ramsar list, or if its boundaries are altered (s 327).

Sites in New South Wales may only be designated if the Minister is satisfied that the Commonwealth has used its best endeavours to reach an agreement with the State, and with any owner or occupier (s 326).

Managing wetlands

Wetlands are managed in accordance with the Ramsar Convention; Australian Ramsar management principles; and the plan of management (ss 330, 334). Australian Ramsar management principles are found in Sch 6 to the EPBCR (s 335).

Plans of Management

For a wetland within the land or coastal waters of a State, the Commonwealth uses its best endeavours to ensure a management plan for the wetland is prepared and implemented in co-operation with the State (ss 332, 333). The Commonwealth may provide the State and members of the public with financial and other assistance for the protection or conservation of a wetland (ss 336, 333). Management plans are binding on the Commonwealth and its agencies in carrying out work that may affect a wetland. Public notice is given of the making of a plan (s 329), which is reviewed at least every five years (s 331).

Offences

It is an offence to take an action likely to have a significant impact on the ecological character of a declared Ramsar wetland (s 16).

There is a range of defences under the EPBCA that, while very technical in their wording, have the effect of underpinning the extensive management provisions of the Act. Actions are prohibited, by provisions like s 16, unless covered by some broader management scheme, that is, unless:

---

9 State of the Parks 2004, above n 2, at 29.

- approved under Pt 9 of the EPBCA;
- Part 4 of the Act lets the person take the action without an approval;
- covered by a decision of the Minister (the Minister's decision is under Div 2 of Pt 7 of the Act and is to the effect that, in this case, s 16 is not a controlling provision for the action. If the decision was made because the Minister believed the action would be taken in a certain manner (see s 77), the action must be taken in that manner);
- taken by the Commonwealth or a Commonwealth agency;
- taken according to a special environmental assessment process under s 160(2); or
- the action is permitted under State law. (ss 23-24A)

Biosphere reserves

Australia has 12 biosphere reserves as part of the World Network of Biosphere Reserves of the International Co-ordinating Council of the Man and the Biosphere Program (MAB) of the United Nations Educational, Scientific and Cultural Organization (UNESCO). MAB was launched in 1971 to support sustainable relationships between people and their environment. Biosphere reserves provide a global network of sites for co-operative research and to demonstrate the sustainable use goals of the World Conservation Strategy. UNESCO acts on nominations submitted by participating countries.

There are two biosphere reserves in New South Wales – Kosciuszko and Yathong National Parks.[10]

Purposes of a biosphere reserve

A biosphere reserve includes protected areas and surrounding lands managed for both conservation and sustainable use of natural resources. A reserve:

- contains examples of characteristic ecosystems of one of the world's natural regions;
- is managed for objectives ranging from complete protection to intensive yet sustainable production where people are an integral component;.
- is a regional centre for monitoring, research, education and training on natural and managed ecosystems;
- operates as a model program for managing land and water to meet human needs while conserving natural processes and biological resources; and
- is an example of voluntary co-operation to conserve and use resources for the well-being of people everywhere.

Management of biosphere reserves

The Commonwealth co-operates with New South Wales over plans of management for biosphere reserves within the State that comply with Australian Biosphere Reserves Management Principles, set out in the EPBCR (EPBCA s 338). The

---

10 See <www.deh.gov.au/parks/biosphere/index.html> (accessed 16 January 2007), Department of Environment and Heritage.

Commonwealth may give financial and other assistance for the protection or conservation of a biosphere reserve (s 341). The Commonwealth and its agencies take all reasonable steps to ensure that they carry out any work that may affect a biosphere reserve consistently with the Australian biosphere reserves management principles, and the management plan (s 339).

New South Wales Protected Areas

Protected areas in New South Wales are regulated under a variety of statutes of the NSW Parliament, of which the *National Parks and Wildlife Act 1976* (the NPWA) is the most important. As at 2004, the National Parks and Wildlife Service (NPW Service) controlled 5,986,921 hectares of land or 7.4% of the land area of the State in 661 parks and reserves of different classification.[11] The NPW Service refers to its lands as the 'parks system',[12] which commentators characterise as areas locked away in parks or other form of 'sanctuary'.

NSW parks system

The popular image of protected areas in New South Wales is of parks, particularly national parks.

> Historically there has been a plethora of different reserve categories and varied terminology ... However, the prevailing public idea of a nature conservation reserve is embodied in a national park. The predominant model of national park in Australia has been the publicly owned, non-inhabited, minimal interference, park ... Human use, in the form of recreation, has always been a value of the reserves, but the conservation of nature and scenic beauty were seen as the primary objectives ... This model sometimes called the Yellowstone or sanctuary model, accords with the IUCN's classification categories I-III ... different streams in global thinking are converging to question whether this model will be the predominant protected area of the future.[13]

These streams of thinking include social considerations – for example, with 'severe population pressures and pressing social needs ... the strictly protected model of reserves, which excludes resource use and human activities other than recreation, is neither feasible or morally acceptable ... The way forward is seen to be the integration of economic and conservation goals'.[14]

Elsewhere this debate concentrates on the 'economic needs of indigenous and local communities around or in protected areas'.[15] In Australia, where these social pressures are less urgent, the debate centres on access to natural resources in national parks, particularly through mining and forestry.

Another concern about the NSW parks system is whether it is adequate in representing and conserving biodiversity? This is measured by the CAR (comprehensive and representative) principle;

11 State of the Parks, above n 2, at 8.
12 Ibid *passim*.
13 Figgis, above n 3, at 89.
14 Ibid at 10.
15 Ibid at 9.

> *comprehensive and representative*: to protect significant ecological features and landforms occurring across New South Wales and to protect samples of as many of the state's ecosystems and habitats as possible, which in turn will protect the natural processes, plant and animal communities and species that occur within these ecosystems.[16]

This is an application of a national strategy that provides targets for reservation.

> *Comprehensiveness* articulates the need to conserve each overall element of biodiversity.
>
> *Representativeness* is an extension of comprehensiveness and entails ensuring that the full variety of biodiversity is given protection and that sufficient samples are selected to withstand such events as fire and disease.

The *State of the Parks 2004 Report* examines the representativeness of the NSW park system 'in the context of bioregions within New South Wales and the relative percentage of each that is protected both in the NSW park system and by private land conservation programs across the state'.[17] This criterion is further refined, and the report measures progress and identifies priorities by reference to considerations like vegetation communities, wetlands, geological landscapes and wilderness.[18]

The reference in the Report to 'private land conservation programs across the state' suggests another criticism of the sanctuary model, its adequacy as a response to conservation. Figgis notes that:

> [I]nternational debates stress the need to incorporate protection of biodiversity into many tenures. There is broad consensus that strictly protected islands alone will not achieve the global need to conserve the earth's biodiversity and that existing islands need to be incorporated into interlinked networks of sustainably managed lands.[19]

This is not only because there will never be sufficient of these islands, but also because the islands will be threatened by activities on adjoining lands.

As was seen in Chapter 7, New South Wales has introduced important legislation to conserve biodiversity on private land, which, with the legislation described in this chapter, has the potential to replace 'archipelagos of isolated islands of nature' with 'networks of well protected areas connected by buffers, corridors and linkages of sympathetically managed adjacent lands. Biodiversity would in this way be integrated into many land uses and tenures'.[20]

National Parks and Wildlife Act

The main NSW legislation for protected areas is the NPWA. The Act contains a comprehensive and lengthy set of objects organised around:

- the conservation of nature;
- the conservation of objects, places and features for their cultural values; and

16 State of the Parks, above n 2, at 22.
17 Ibid at 26.
18 Ibid at 26 et seq.
19 Figgis, above n 3, at 2.
20 Ibid at 16.

- the fostering of public appreciation and management through the application of management principles. (s 2A)[21]

The conservation of nature includes the conservation of habitat, ecosystems and ecosystem processes; biological diversity; landforms and landscapes and natural features.

The reference in the objects to cultural values is to values within landscape, including in:

- places, objects and features of significance to Aboriginal people;
- places of social value to the people of New South Wales; and
- places of historic, architectural or scientific significance. (s 2A(b))

Thirdly, the administration of the Act is to foster public appreciation, understanding and enjoyment of nature and cultural heritage, in an overall management system for reserved lands.

Examination of a proposal for a reserve takes into account:

- the establishment of a comprehensive, adequate and representative reserve system;
- the desirability of protecting the full range of natural and cultural heritage, wilderness, and world heritage values; and
- the maintenance of natural processes. (s 7)

The objects of the legislation are to be achieved by applying the principles of ecologically sustainable development (s 2A(2)), as defined in the *Protection of the Environment Administration Act 1991* (s 5).

Types of reserves and declared areas

The NSW parks system consists of reserves and declared areas. Reserves are categorised as:

- national parks (s 30E);
- historic sites (s 30F);
- regional parks (s 30H);
- karst conservation reserves (s 30J);
- nature reserves (s 30J);
- State conservation areas (s 30G); and
- Aboriginal areas (s 30K).

Declared areas may be public land with other uses, or private land, and its values are protected by restricting use. Categories of declared land are:

- wild rivers (s 61);
- protected archaeological areas (s 65);
- wildlife refuges (s 68); and
- wildlife management areas (s 69).

---

21 The majority of references to legislation in this chapter are to the NPWA and will be given in this form. The text will make it clear when other legislation is being referred to.

Reserves

The categories of reserves under the NPWA are defined by the purposes for which an area is reserved. Purposes common to all reserves include research and monitoring.

National parks

The purposes of a national park are to identify, protect and conserve areas containing outstanding or representative ecosystems, natural or cultural features or landscapes or phenomena for public appreciation, inspiration and sustainable visitor use and enjoyment. Management principles include pursuing those principles and:

- the conservation of biodiversity and ecosystem functions and cultural values; and
- the protection of geological and geomorphological features, natural phenomena and ecological integrity. (s 30E)

Historic sites

The purposes of a historic site are to identify, protect and conserve areas associated with a person, event or historical theme, or containing a building, place, feature or landscape of cultural significance. Management principles include:

- the conservation of places, objects, features and landscapes of cultural value, and of natural values;
- provision for sustainable visitor use and enjoyment; and
- research and monitoring. (s 30G)

Regional parks

The purposes of regional parks are to identify, protect and conserve areas in a natural or modified landscape that are suitable for public recreation and enjoyment. Management principles include:

- the provision of opportunities, in an outdoor setting, for recreation and enjoyment in natural or modified landscapes;
- the identification, interpretation, management and conservation of the park so as to maintain and enhance significant landscape values;
- conservation of natural and cultural values; and
- sustainable visitor use and enjoyment and public appreciation and understanding. (s 30H)

Karst conservation reserve

A karst environment is an area of land, including subterranean land that has developed in soluble rock through the process of solution, abrasion or collapse, together with its associated bedrock, soil, water, gases and biodiversity (s 5(1)). The purposes of a karst conservation reserve are to identify, protect and conserve areas, including subterranean land, containing outstanding or representative examples of karst landforms and natural phenomena. Management principles include:

- the conservation of the karst environment including its catchment values, cultural values, and biodiversity and ecosystem functions;
- the protection of geological and geomorphological features and natural phenomena; and
- provision for sustainable visitor use. (s 30I)

Nature reserves

The purposes of nature reserves are to identify, protect and conserve areas of outstanding, unique or representative ecosystems, species, communities and natural phenomena. Management principles include:

- the conservation of biodiversity and ecosystem functions;
- the protection of geological and geomorphological features and natural phenomena; and
- promotion of public appreciation. (s 30J)

State conservation areas

The purposes of State conservation areas are to identify, protect and conserve areas with significant or representative ecosystems, landforms or natural phenomena or places of cultural significance. Management principles include:

- the conservation of biodiversity, ecosystem functions and of places, objects and features of cultural value;
- the protection of natural phenomena and the maintenance of natural landscapes; and
- sustainable visitor use and enjoyment of the area and buildings, including adaptive reuse; appropriate research and monitoring. (s 30G)

Aboriginal areas

The purposes of Aboriginal areas are to identify, protect and conserve areas associated with a person, event or historical theme, or containing a building, place, object, feature or landscape, of:

- natural or cultural significance to Aboriginal people; or
- importance in improving public understanding of Aboriginal culture and its development and transitions.

Management principles include:

- conserving natural values, buildings, places, objects, features and landscapes of cultural value to Aboriginal people in accordance with their cultural values;
- allowing the use of the area by Aboriginal people for cultural purposes; and
- promoting public understanding and appreciation of the Aboriginal area's natural and cultural values and significance. (ss 30K, 62)

Declaration of reserves

The formal step creating a reserve under the Act is a notice, signed by the Governor, in the NSW *Government Gazette* (s 30A). Notices reserving land as a national park or historic site (s 35) or a State conservation area (s 47D) are given to both Houses of Parliament and may be disallowed.

Generally the procedure for varying or revoking a reserve is the same as for creating it. National parks, historic sites (s 37), nature reserves (s 52) and karst conservation reserves (s 58M) may only be revoked by an Act of Parliament.

Interests in land

The land that may be reserved under the NPWA may be Crown lands, other government land and land for which the National Parks and Wildlife Reserve Trust is the trustee.[22] The Minister may acquire land in private ownership by agreement or compulsorily (s 30B), under the terms of the *Land Acquisition (Just Terms Compensation) Act 1991* (ss 145, 146). Private persons may also enter into conservation agreements with the government to maintain their land for conservation purposes.

When land is reserved, existing interests in the land are not affected, but possibly may not be renewed or extended (see national park or historic site (s 39); State conservation area (s 47H); regional park (s 47ZA); State recreation area (s 49(4), nature reserve (s 58); karst conservation reserves (s 58S)).

Reserved land may not be sold or leased, except as allowed in the NPWA (see national park or historic site (s 40); State conservation area (s 47I); regional park (s 47Z); State recreation area (s 49(4)); nature reserve (s 53); karst conservation reserves (s 58N)).

Restrictions of activity in reserves

The NPWA restricts many activities in reserves.

Mining

Mining and prospecting in a reserve under the *Mining Act 1992, Offshore Minerals Act 1999* and *Petroleum (Onshore) Act 1991* may only be carried out with the approval of the Minister (see national park or historic site (NPWA s 41); State conservation area (s 47J)). Under s 41 the Minister gives notice of an approval to both Houses of the NSW Parliament, and it may be disallowed. The NPWA applies this section to regional parks (s 47ZA), nature reserves (s 54), karst conservation reserves (s 58O) and Aboriginal areas (s 62).

Forestry

The *Forestry Act 1916* does not apply to lands within a national park or historic site (NPWA s 42), State conservation area (s 47J), regional park (s 47ZA), nature reserve (s 55) or karst conservation reserve (s 58P).

Soil Conservation

The *Soil Conservation Act 1938* applies to reserved land but experimental and research work carried out under the Act requires the concurrence of the Minister

---

22 This Trust relates to certain State forests dedicated as Crown Reserves. See *Forest and National Parks Estate Act 1998* (NSW) s 9; *National Park Estate (Southern Region Reservations) Act 2000* (NSW) s 8.

(see national park and historic sites (NPWA s 43); State conservation area (s 47K); regional parks (s 47ZA); nature reserve (s 58); karst conservation reserve (s 58S)).

Fisheries

The *Fisheries Act 1916* continues to apply to reserved land, except that leases under the Act affecting reserves require the concurrence of the Minister (see national park or historic site (NPWA s 44); State conservation areas (s 47K); regional parks (s 47ZA); nature reserve (s 58); karst conservation reserve (s 58S)).

Declared areas

Declared areas under the NPWA - namely, wild rivers, protected archaeological areas, wildlife refuges and wildlife management areas - are also defined by their purposes.

Wild rivers

The purpose of declaring a wild river is to identify, protect and conserve a water course of natural origin with substantially natural flow and containing examples of biological, hydrological and geomorphological processes substantially undisturbed since European occupation. Management principles include:

- restoration and maintenance of the natural biological, hydrological and geomorphological processes associated with wild rivers and their catchment; and
- the identification, conservation and appropriate management of Aboriginal objects and places. (s 61)

A statutory authority may not carry on any development in relation to a wild river without consulting the Minister administering the NPWA (s 61).

Protected archaeological area

The purpose of declaring a protected archaeological area is to protect an Aboriginal object or place (s 65). The Director-General, with the consent of the owner or occupier, may regulate entry and use of protected archaeological areas (s 65).

Wildlife refuge

The purposes of a wildlife refuge are:

- preserving, conserving, propagating and studying wildlife;
- conserving and studying the natural environment; and
- creating simulated natural environments. (s 68)

Wildlife management areas

The purposes of wildlife management areas are:

- propagating fauna for game;
- providing suitable land for hunting fauna as game;

- conserving and studying natural environments; and
- creating simulated natural environments. (s 69)

Who declares?

The Director-General may declare a wild river (s 61), the Minister a protected archaeological area (s 65), and the Governor a wildlife refuge (s 68) or a wildlife management area (s 69). Declared areas may be on State government or private land, and declaration requires the consent of the owner or occupier (see protected archaeological area, s 65; wildlife refuge, s 72; wildlife management areas, s 69).

Joint management of reserved lands – Aboriginal land

Part 4A of the NPWA provides for a system of joint management of reserved lands in New South Wales with Aborigines, to protect Aboriginal cultural values without extinguishing Aboriginal land rights or interests (s 71C). This Aboriginal land is described in the Act as:

- ALR Act land (*Aboriginal Land Rights Act 1983*); and
- land reserved under Sch 14 to the NPWA.

ALR Act lands are lands recognised under the Aboriginal land rights process. Under the scheme, the Aboriginal Land Council in which the lands are vested leases them to the Minister for reservation under Pt 4A of the NPWA.

Schedule 14 lands are lands already reserved under the NPWA that are subsequently identified as having cultural significance to Aborigines. The reservation is revoked so that the land can be vested in Local Aboriginal Land Councils or the New South Wales Aboriginal Land Council, on behalf of Aboriginal owners, and then leased back to the Minister. The land is then again reserved under the NPWA in accordance with Pt 4A. While at first sight this may seem rather circular, the effect is to set up the basis for the recognition of cultural significance to Aborigines and joint management. Land is currently reserved under Sch 14 of the NPWA as the Biamanga, Gulaga, Jervis Bay, Kinenega, Mungo and Mootwingee National Parks, the Mootwingee and Mount Grenfell Historic Sites and the Coturaundee and Mount Yarrowyck nature reserves.[23] Listing in Sch 14 is by Act of Parliament (s 71AW) as is a deletion (s 71BM).

Negotiations

Negotiations are required for two purposes under Pt 4A:

- for land that is already reserved – to determine whether the existing reservation should be revoked so that land may be reserved anew, subject to joint management under the Part; and
- for land subject to a land rights claim under the *Aboriginal Land Rights Act 1983* – to determine whether the claimants would be agreeable to having the land reserved under Pt 4A. (s 71F)

---

23 See <www.nationalparks.nsw.gov.au> follow link to Aboriginal heritage (accessed 16 January 2007).

This process may require the selection of representatives for negotiations both before and after Aboriginal owners are identified (71G). The Minister selects a negotiating panel, which will adequately represent the wishes of Aboriginals who have a cultural association with the lands (s 71I). The panel participates in the negotiations between the Minister and the Aboriginal Land Council, advises on the cultural significance to Aboriginals of the ALR Act lands and recommends a name for the proposed reserve (s 71I). Any disagreements are referred to mediation (s 71K).

When negotiations are completed in respect of ALR Act lands, reservation is by the Governor by notice published in the *Gazette*. ALR lands may be reserved as a national park, historic site, State conservation area, regional park, nature reserve, karst conservation reserve or Aboriginal area (s 71Y).

If negotiations result in a proposal to reclassify lands reserved under the NPWA and then entered in Sch 14, a notification is laid before each House of Parliament, and the proposal may be disapproved (s 71N).

Reclassification is by the Governor by proclamation in the *Gazette*, which revokes the existing reservation under the NPWA and vests the land in an Aboriginal Land Council, which leases the land to the Minister (s 71O). On publication of the proclamation, the lease takes effect and the lands are reserved, with the appropriate classification, under the NPWA.

No consideration is payable to the Crown by an Aboriginal Land Council on the vesting in the Council land, nor is any stamp duty owed (s 71V).

Leases

The requirements under the NPWA for a lease of Sch 14 lands and ALR Act lands are detailed, including requirements that the lease include:

- a term of at least 30 years, with renewals by agreement;
- an acknowledgement that Aboriginals may enter and use the lands for hunting or fishing or gathering of traditional foods for domestic, ceremonial and cultural purposes in accordance with the tradition of the Aboriginal owners, while complying with the provisions of the NPWA concerning the protection of animals, trees, timber, plants, flowers and vegetation;
- an acknowledgement that the public generally has access to the lands in accordance with the NPWA, and any plan of management; and
- continuing consultation between the Minister and the Aboriginal Land Council. (s 71AD)

Leases are reviewed at least every five years (ss 71AH, 71AI). The Minister pays rent under Pt 4A (s 71AE).

Boards of management

A board of management, with Aboriginal owners as a majority of members, is established when Aboriginal lands are reserved (ss 71AN, 71AM). A board has the care, control and management of the lands, including preparing plans of management and the supervision of money. It considers proposals from Aboriginals for carrying out cultural activities (such as hunting and gathering).

Proposals for additions to Schedule 14

Any person or body may propose to the Director-General that lands reserved under the NPWA have cultural significance to Aboriginals and should be listed in Sch 14. The proposal is widely circulated (s 71AS). The Director-General assesses the proposal and reports to the Minister on whether the lands contain places that are:

- of spiritual or mythological importance in Aboriginal custom or lore;
- used for the conduct of ceremonial activities; or
- significant for their association with Aboriginal life after occupation of the area by persons of European extraction. (s 71AT)

The Director-General's Report includes comments on:

- the presence of Aboriginal burials or remains;
- the rarity of the types of Aboriginal sites and objects on the lands, and their diversity, and antiquity;
- whether the lands have been listed on Commonwealth heritage lists for their Aboriginal cultural significance.

Native title rights

A board of management, and the NPW Service, are subject to the preservation of native title rights and interests (if any) that exist in relation to the lands (s 71BI). If a determination is made under s 253 of the *Native Title Act 1993* (Cth) that native title exists, the Minister, the Aboriginal Land Council and the board of management enter into arrangements with the native title holders to ensure native title is preserved (s 71BH). Any dispute is arbitrated (s 71BJ).

Administration of the NSW Parks system

The administrative structure for reserved and declared lands includes the Department of Environment and Conservation (Parks and Wildlife Division), the Director-General, and councils and committees under the NPWA. Some reserves have boards and trusts.[24]

Department of Environment and Conservation

The Department consists of the Director-General and persons appointed under the *Public Service Act 1979* for the administration of the NPWA, the *Wilderness Act 1987* and the *Threatened Species Conservation Act 1995* (s 6). The Department submits an Annual Report to Parliament (*Annual Reports (Departments) Act 1985*; NPWA s 144B).

Director-General

The Director-General of the Department of Environment and Conservation has a wide range of statutory functions (ss 7, 8).

24 The NPWA, and popular usage, continue to refer to the National Parks and Wildlife Service, and the Director-General of National Parks and Wildlife. The administration of the NSW parks system has, however, been reorganised and legally these references should now be read as references to the Department of Environment and Conservation and the Director-General of the Department of Environment and Conservation (Public Sector Employment and Management (Environment and Conservation) Order 2003 cl 6(3) and (5), Administrative Changes Orders).

Councils and committees

The NPWA provides for different councils and committees as part of its administrative structure:

- Audit and Compliance committee to oversee the Director-General's obligations (s 9);
- National Parks and Wildlife Advisory Council to provide advice to the Minister and the Director-General (s 23(1)); and
- special advisory committees (s 25).

Regional Advisory committees

New South Wales is divided into administrative regions and a regional advisory committee is constituted for each region (s 24), to advise the Director-General and the Council on activities, policies and management and other plans for the region (s 25).

Aboriginal Cultural Heritage Advisory Committee

The Aboriginal Cultural Heritage Advisory Committee advises on the identification, assessment and management of Aboriginal cultural heritage, including on plans of management and the heritage impact permit process (s 28).

Boards and trusts for reserves

The NPWA makes provision for trusts and boards for reserves. These include:

- trust boards for State conservation areas (see ss 47GB-47GG); and
- trusts for regional parks (ss 47S -47YT).

Enforcement officers

Persons are appointed as authorised officers for the national parks legislation, under the *Protection of the Environment Operations Act 1997* (Chapter 7), for the purposes of compliance and contravention, obtaining information and administering the legislation (s 156B). The national parks legislation is the NPWA, *Threatened Species Conservation Act 1995*, *Wilderness Act 1987* and the *Marine Parks Act 1997* (s 156B).

Police officers, and fisheries officers under the *Fisheries Management Act 1994* (FMA) are *ex officio* rangers under the NPWA (s 16). Ex officio and honorary rangers (s 17) have the powers of officers of the NPW Service (ss 19, 20).

It is an offence to impersonate or assault officers of the service, or to resist or obstruct them in the exercise of their duties (s 169). It is also an offence to attempt to corrupt them (s 170).

Functions and powers of enforcement officers.

Enforcement powers include to:

- require persons suspected of an offence to give their name and address (ss 157, 158);
- serve penalty notices (s 160);

- stop and search a vehicle, enter and search premises, and seize incriminating articles (s 164).

There are detailed provisions for the removal of unauthorised structures (ss 160A, 160B, forfeiture of property).

Financial provisions

National Parks and Wildlife Fund

The National Parks and Wildlife Fund (s 137) for the purposes of the NPWA (s 139) comprises government money and moneys received for leases, licences, royalties, rents and other fees, franchises, easements community service contributions and penalties (s 138).

Charges

The NPW Service imposes charges on users of the parks system. The holder of a lease or licence for lands in a reserve contributes to the costs of community service in the reserve (s 140); royalties are charged on fauna and skins (s 142); and there are more general fees and charges for services provided under the NPWA, the *Wilderness Act* and the *Threatened Species Act*. These services include entering and using a park or reserve, using other facilities, and using vehicles and vessels (s 143).

Plans of management

An important management tool for achieving objectives under the NPWA is the plan of management, which is

> [A] legal document that outlines how an area will be managed in the years ahead. It identifies the available knowledge of the park and sets out the values of the area, plus management objectives and strategies. The plan is closely linked to other generally more detailed plans such as conservation management plans, pest species management plans, fire management strategies and threatened species recovery plans, which may either contribute to or flow from the plan of management.[25]

The Director-General prepares of a plan of management for each reserve and declared area (s 72). Operations in the area must be in accordance with the relevant plan (s 81).

Plans of management cover:

natural values

- the conservation of biodiversity;
- the protection of geological and geomorphological features,
- the protection of wilderness values,
- the maintenance and reinstatement of natural processes,
- the rehabilitation of landscapes,

---

25 State of the Parks 2004, above n 2, at 35.

- the preservation of catchment values, and
- the protection and management of wild rivers;

cultural values

- the protection and appreciation of objects, places and structures of cultural significance, and tracts of land, landscape values and scenic features,
- the potential for used by Aboriginal people for cultural purposes, and
- the adaptive reuse of buildings and structures;

public use

- opportunities for public appreciation of natural and cultural heritage values,
- sustainable visitor use,
- the appropriate and ecologically sustainable use of the reserved land, and
- the encouragement of research;

reserve in its context

- the natural resource management and the land use management plans and practices of land affecting the reserved land,
- the regional, national and international context of the reserved land, maintaining national and international significance and compliance with national and international agreements,
- the social and economic context of the reserve, and
- fire management.

Plans of management within a conservation area relate to the objects of the conservation agreement, and for land within a State forest to those of the *Forestry Act 1916* (s 72AA).

A single plan of management may be prepared for contiguous reserves, and with the co-operation from the other State or Territory, a joint plan of management may relate to contiguous areas across borders (s 72A).

Public exhibition and consultation

Notice is given of the preparation of a plan of management to advisory committees, the water authority for any relevant catchment and to the public, and representations are invited (s 73A). The Minister adopts plans of management, after considering any representations made in the consultation process (s 73B).

Leases, licences and easements

Leases and licences may be granted under the NPWA over reserved land for purposes set out in the legislation, consistently with its conservation values and plan of management. Purposes include:

- for national parks and historic sites – accommodation and facilities for tourists, and to the preservation of the area;
- for nature reserve and karst conservation reserves – the erection of buildings consistent with the relevant management principles.

Further general provisions relate to:

- leases for the adaptive reuse of existing buildings (s 151B(2));
- short-term licences in modified natural areas for other uses (s 151B(3)).

Where land is acquired for conserving threatened species, populations or threatened communities or to protect Aboriginal objects and places, a lease or licence may be granted for those purposes (s 151(2)). Leases and licences are not granted in a wilderness area (s 153A).

The NPWA makes provision for:

- head leases (s 151A and Sch 15).
- Kosciuszko National Park (ski resort area under the *Environmental Planning and Assessment Act 1979* (EPAA Sch 6, Pt 8A).

These provisions allow limited use for permanent residential accommodation (s 151C).

The NPW Service keeps a register of leases and other interests available for public inspection (s 151D).

The legislation allows for licences to carry on trades, businesses or occupations (s 152(1)) and franchises for the sale of goods and services, the provision of public transportation, or the supply of other facilities and amenities, within a national park or historic site (s 152(3)).

Easements over land

The Minister may grant easements or rights of way in a reserve for access, the construction of pipelines, the transmission of electricity and for other necessary purposes (ss 153, 153B-153D).

Enforcement

The NPWA provides a variety of enforcement mechanisms, such as offence provisions and the making of orders to support its management.

Offences

The NPWA provides for a range of offences for activities that may imperil the values of reserved and declared lands. Examples are collected here to give the breadth of the concerns of the legislation.

Animals

It is an offence to harm an animal or discharge a prohibited weapon in a park or reserve (see national park or historic site (s 45); State conservation area (s 47J); regional park (s 47ZA); nature reserve (s 56); karst conservation reserve (s 58Q); nature reserve (s 56); wildlife refuge, wildlife management area, conservation area or area subject to a wilderness protection agreement (s 70)).

Firearms, weapons and trap

Possession of a firearm, explosive, net, trap, or hunting device; the use of a dog or other animal for the purpose of taking or killing animals, and being accompanied by a dog, is prohibited in a nature reserve (s 56), a karst conservation reserve (s 58Q), a wildlife refuge, wildlife management area, conservation area or area subject to a wilderness protection agreement (s 70).

Flora

Except as part of a permitted forestry operation or as the occupier of lands in a reserve, a person may not fell, cut, destroy, injure, pick, remove or set fire to any tree, timber, plant, flower, or vegetation, or be in possession of any native plant, in a nature reserve (s 57), a karst conservation reserve (s 58R), a wildlife refuge, a wildlife management area, conservation area, or area subject to a wilderness protection agreement (s 71).

Fauna

The harming of animals within a national park (s 45), nature reserve (s 56), wildlife refuge, wildlife management area, conservation area or area subject to a wilderness protection agreement (s 70) is an offence.

Vehicles

The NPWA provides for parking and mooring offences (s 159).

Orders

Allowing a public official to make an order requiring compliance with the legislation is often a speedy mechanism for achieving its objects.

Stop work orders

The Director-General may order that any action that is likely to affect significantly:

- protected fauna or native plants or their environment;
- an Aboriginal object or Aboriginal place; or
- any other item of cultural heritage on reserved land;

is to stop and may specify what actions may be carried out in the vicinity. An order takes effect when it is affixed in a conspicuous place, or the person about to perform the action is notified. It operates for 40 days and may be extended. The order does not affect development and project approval under the EPAA.

Persons who may be affected by the order are not entitled to prior notification (s 91BB) and must comply (s 91AA). The person may appeal to the Minister, who may confirm, modify or rescind the order, consistently with the principles of ecologically sustainable development (s 91CC, and see *Protection of the Environment Administration Act 1991* s 6).

A stop work order prevails over an inconsistent approval, notice or order under any other Act that requires or permits the environment to be affected significantly (s 91FF).

The Director-General consults with the person served with a stop work order, and, if satisfactory arrangements cannot be made for the environment, may proceed to an interim protection order.[26]

26 See below p 372.

Reserves under other legislation

Other categories of reserves and declared areas are administered under other NSW legislation:

- marine protected areas – marine parks and aquatic reserves;
- Crown reserves;
- flora reserves;
- State parks;
- State forests;
- local government reserves; and
- wilderness areas

Marine protected areas

> Marine protected areas are coastal, estuarine or oceanic areas managed to conserve biodiversity. They range from small, highly protected areas that focus on species or community protection, to large multiple use areas that include complex linkages of ecosystems and habitats. Marine protected areas may include reefs, seagrass beds, rocky platforms, mangroves, estuarine waters, mudflats, salt marshes, shipwrecks, archaeological sites, and coastal and offshore areas of airspace, seabed and water. ...
>
> Marine protected areas are one of the primary tools used, within a broader integrated coastal and marine management framework, for the conservation of biodiversity. Other tools used include fishery management strategies, fishing closure notifications, estuary and catchment management plans, conservation agreements, threatened species recovery plans, threat abatement plans and habitat protection plans.[27]

Some national parks and nature reserves have important marine components. Other marine protected areas are marine parks and aquatic reserves. These are complemented by inter-tidal protected areas, which are temporary fishing closures under the *Fisheries Management Act 1994* (FMA) (Pt 2, Div 1).

Development in marine protected areas

Development is restricted in marine protected areas.

Mining

It is unlawful to prospect or mine for minerals in an aquatic reserve (FMA s 197B) or a marine park (*Marine Parks Act 1997* (MPA) s 18) unless authorised by an Act of Parliament. The *Offshore Minerals Act 1999*, the *Mining Act 1992*, the *Petroleum (Onshore) Act 1991* and the *Petroleum (Submerged Lands) Act 1982* do not apply to an aquatic reserve (FMA s 197B).

Development

Before determining a development application in aquatic reserves and marine parks under the EPAA, a consent or determining authority must take the objects of,

27 Marine Parks Authority, <www.mpa.nsw.gov.au> (accessed 16 January 2007).

respectively, the FMA or the MPA, management and zoning plans and the permissible uses of the area, into consideration, and obtain the concurrence of the Ministers (FMA s 197C; MPA ss 19, 20).

The provisions of s 79B(8) to (11) of the EPAA apply to this requirement to obtain the concurrence of the relevant Ministers in the same way as they apply to a requirement on a consent authority to obtain concurrence under an environmental planning instrument. In applying s 79B reference is made to the objects of the FMA or MPA and to the permissible uses of the area (FMA s 197C; MPA s 20).

The Minister administering Pt 3 of the *Coastal Protection Act 1979* must notify the Authority of any intention to concur in the use or occupation of, or development within, a marine park (MPA s 21).

Marine parks

Marine parks are established under the MPA which in many ways is similar to the NPWA. Its objects are:

- to conserve marine biological diversity and marine habitats through a comprehensive system of marine parks;
- to maintain ecological processes in marine parks and, where consistent with these objects;
    - o to provide for ecologically sustainable use of fish and marine vegetation in marine parks; and
    - o to provide opportunities for public appreciation, understanding and enjoyment of marine parks. (s 3)

Land

A marine park may include an area of sea or tidal waters, land covered by water, and adjacent water and land (MPA s 6). This includes land reserved under the NPWA or any other Act for a public purpose. This land may continue to be used for its public purpose if that is consistent with the MPA (MPA s 11).

Declaration of an area as a marine park does not affect any aquaculture permit or aquaculture lease under the FMA but any renewal is subject to the MPA (MPA, s 14).

Declaration of marine parks

The Governor declares a marine park by proclamation in the *Gazette* (MPA s 5). Revocation is by Act of Parliament (MPA s 8). A declaration of a marine park revokes a declaration of an aquatic reserve under the FMA (MPA, s 10).

Administration of marine parks

The management structure for marine parks includes the following bodies.

Marine Parks Authority

The Marine Parks Authority, consisting of the Directors-General of the Premier's Department, NSW Fisheries, and National Parks and Wildlife, is subject to the direction of the relevant Ministers. It is a statutory body representing the Crown (MPA s 29).

The Authority:

- considers proposals for marine parks, and the appropriate classification of areas within them;
- prepares an operational plan for each marine park;
- manages and controls activities that may affect marine biological diversity, marine habitats and marine ecological processes in marine parks;
- provides for the ecologically sustainable use of marine parks;
- disseminates information; and
- encourages public appreciation and scientific research.

The NPW Service, NSW Fisheries and other government departments provide staff for the Authority (s 31).

Marine Parks Advisory Council

The Marine Parks Advisory Council consists of the Directors-General of NSW Fisheries and National Parks and Wildlife; representatives of the Commonwealth government, and of the interests of marine conservation, Aboriginal people, the tourism industry, commercial fishers, recreational fishers and scuba divers. There is also a member with expertise in marine science (s 32).

The Advisory Council, when requested by one of the relevant Ministers or the Authority, gives advice on marine parks, including on:

- proposals for marine parks and the appropriate classification of areas; and
- the conservation of marine biological diversity within, and the ecologically sustainable use, of marine parks. (s 33)

Marine Parks advisory committees

There is an advisory committee for each marine park of at least nine members representing similar interest to those on the Advisory Council. An advisory committee advises the relevant Ministers and the Authority on the marine park's management (s 35).

Marine Parks Fund

The Marine Parks Fund consists of fees and other money received from administrative functions and gifts and bequests. Expenses in the administration of this Act are paid out of the Fund, including the expenses of the Advisory Council and advisory committees (s 42).

Plans of Management

Plans of management are called operational plans under the MPA, and are prepared for marine parks by the Authority for submission to the relevant Ministers (ss 23, 24). The Ministers give public notice of the proposed plan and consider any comments before the plan is adopted (s 25). The Authority and marine park rangers follow operational plans (s 27). An operational plan for a marine park prevails over any plan of management under the NPWA over the same area (s 28). Operational plans are regularly reviewed by the advisory committee and the Authority (ss 26A-26C).

Marine park closures

A 'marine park closure' occurs when the relevant Ministers prohibit a specified activity (including the taking of fish) in a marine park (s 20A). Unless urgent (s 20C), a closure is notified in the *Gazette*, in the media, and in a prominent place adjacent to the marine park (MPA s 20B). Closure may take effect for up to five years (s 20C).

Enforcement

Marine park rangers

Marine park rangers are appointed from the staff of the NPW Service, fisheries officers, and the staff of other government departments and public or local authorities (s 35A).

Offences

The MPA provides for specific offences, and applies provisions from other legislation.

Contravention of a provision of the *Marine Parks Regulation 1999* (MPR) is an offence (s 17A). It is also an offence to carry out any activity in contravention of a marine park closure (s 20G).

In addition, Divs 1 to 4 of Pt 9 (Enforcement) of the FMA are applied to a marine park ranger in the same way as they apply to a fisheries officer. An offence against the provisions as applied is an offence against the MPA (MPA s 36).

Sections 157, 158 and 159 of the NPWA also apply to offences under the MPA, so that an offence against the provisions so applied is an offence against the MPA (MPA s 37).

Penalty notices

A marine park ranger may serve a penalty notice on a person for an offence prescribed by the MPR. If the amount of the penalty in the notice is paid no further proceedings are taken for any alleged offence (s 38).

Proceedings for offences

Proceedings for an offence against the MPA are dealt with summarily before a Local Court, or the Land and Environment Court. In a Local Court, the maximum monetary penalty is $20,000 (s 39). Proceedings must be brought within two years of the offence (s 40).

Directors and others concerned in the management of a corporation that has contravened the marine parks legislation are liable if they knowingly permitted the contravention.

Removal of property from marine parks

The Authority may direct a person responsible for any unused property in a marine park to remove it. It is an offence to fail to do so. Under the MPA, 'unused property' is:

- any sunken or wrecked vessel; or
- any abandoned property; or
- anything unlawfully erected or placed.

The Authority may itself remove any unused property and dispose of it or, if it is reasonable to do so, destroy it, and recover its reasonable expenses from the person responsible for the unused property (s 20H).

Other legislation including the FMA and the NPWA continue to apply to marine parks (MPA ss 5, 36, 37).

Aquatic reserves

The second of the three types of marine protected areas, introduced above, are aquatic reserves under the FMA.

The purpose of an aquatic reserve is to conserve the biodiversity of fish and marine vegetation and, in particular, in the reserve:

- the protection of fish habitat, threatened species, populations and ecological communities;
- species management; and
- educational activities and scientific research. (s 194)

An important activity is to regulate the taking of fish (ss 194-197).

Declaration

Aquatic reserves are declared by the Minister by notice published in the *Gazette* (s 194) with, for private land, the consent of the owner, or for public waters, the consent of the appropriate public authority (s 195). The revocation of an aquatic reserve is tabled in both Houses of Parliament and may be disallowed (s 196).

Land

The area of an aquatic reserve may be private land or public waters (s 195). A declaration is not affected by any existing interests in land in the area (s 195C), but any aquaculture lease or public purpose may continue (s 194).

Regulations

The *Fisheries Management (Aquatic Reserves) Regulation 2002*:

- prohibits or regulates the taking of fish or marine vegetation from aquatic reserves;
- provides for the management, protection and development of aquatic reserves, and
- classifies areas within an aquatic reserve for different uses (such as recreational uses or as a sanctuary). (s 197)

Plans of management

A management plan for an aquatic reserve is made by Regulation. The Minister first arranges for draft management plans for aquatic reserves providing for:

- the objectives of the aquatic reserve and the regulation of activities to achieve the objectives; and
- performance indicators for, and reviews of, the management plan.

The draft is made available for public submissions.

A plan of management may create offences with penalties of up to 1000 penalty units (s 197A).

Enforcement

Aquatic reserve notification

The Minister may prohibit specified activities (including the taking of fish) in an aquatic reserve by an 'aquatic reserve notification' (s 197E). Except in an emergency, an aquatic reserve notification is published in the *Gazette* and the media, and exhibited in a prominent place adjacent to the reserve (s 197F). A notification takes effect on the first publication and may remain in force for up to five years (s 197G).

Offences

It is an offence to contravene an aquatic reserve notification, or to be in possession of an animal, plant, rock, sand or other thing taken in contravention of an aquatic reserve notification (s 197K).

Other land-based protected areas

While most protected areas are protected under the NPWA, there are also important systems under other legislation. This chapter discusses:

- Crown reserves - State parks;
- flora reserves;
- local government reserves; and
- wilderness areas

Crown reserves – State parks

The NSW Department of Lands controls 12.7 million hectares of land, which includes areas managed for conservation purposes.[28] These areas include 10 State parks 'which are high-use Crown recreation reserves, located in accessible locations across the State ... on inland water sources and ... on the coast. ... The focus is on providing public recreation, as well as preserving the environment'.[29]

Flora reserves

Flora reserves are established under the *Forestry Act 1916* for the preservation of native flora (s 25A). Land set aside for a flora reserve may include Crown lands and State forests.

Dedication

The dedication of a flora reserve is by the Governor, by notice in the *Gazette*, and may only be revoked by an Act of Parliament (s 16A).

28 Department of Lands, Corporate Brochure, March 2006, <www.lands.nsw.gov.au> (accessed 24 July 2006).

29 Ibid, follow link to State Parks (accessed 17 January 2007).

Plan of management

The equivalent to the plan of management required for other protected areas is a detailed written scheme of the operations proposed to be undertaken in a flora reserve to preserve native flora. A written scheme is drawn up by the Forestry Commission and submitted to the Minister. Operations on a flora reserve comply with the working plan (s 25A).

Protected areas under the Local Government Act 1993

Local government councils control large areas of land, classified as community or operational land, under the *Local Government Act 1993* (NSW) (LGA). Community land includes land with environmental and cultural aspects protected through plans of management (s 35). Councils must prepare plans of management for community lands, which categorise the land, set out objectives and performance targets, how these are to be achieved and how performance is to be measured. Relevant categories include: natural areas, including bushlands, wetlands, escarpments, watercourses and foreshores; parks; and areas of cultural significance (s 36).

Special obligations apply to community land comprising the habitat of endangered species (ss 36A, 36B), significant natural features (s 36C) or areas of cultural significance. Cultural significance is Aboriginal, historical or cultural significance (s 36D).

Core objectives for the management of natural area community land include to:

- conserve biodiversity and maintain ecosystem function;
- maintain its natural state and setting;
- provide for its restoration and regeneration; and
- provide for sustainable community use and access. (ss 36E-40)

Plan of managements are available for public inspection at council offices.

A council cannot dispose of community land, but may grant a lease or licence (s 45) for limited purposes (s 46) set out in the plan of management (s 46).

Wilderness areas

Wilderness areas are reserved under the *Wilderness Act 1987* (WA). Wilderness is

- an area that, with its plant and animal communities, is in a state that has not been substantially modified by humans or is capable of being restored to such a state;
- of a sufficient size to make its maintenance in such a state feasible; and
- capable of providing opportunities for solitude and appropriate self-reliant recreation. (s 6)

Management principles for a wilderness area are to:

- restore and protect its unmodified state and its plant and animal communities;
- preserve its capacity to evolve in the absence of significant human interference; and
- permit opportunities for solitude and appropriate self-reliant recreation. (s 9)

Declaration of wilderness areas

The Minister declares an area of land to be a wilderness area by notification in the *Gazette*. The declaration does not affect any existing interest in the land, except as provided by an agreement (s 8).

Anyone may submit a proposal for a wilderness area to the Director of National Parks, who notifies the owner of the area proposed. The Director has up to two years to consider a proposal and advise the Minister (s 7).

Wilderness protection agreements and conservation agreements

Land may become a wilderness area through a wilderness protection agreement or a conservation agreement, or by being reserved or dedicated under the NPWA (NPWA, s 59; WA s 10).

Wilderness protection agreements are agreements between the Minister and another authority in the NSW government over land owned by the State. They require the consent of persons with an interest in the land.

An agreement may require the Minister or a statutory authority to carry out specified activities including providing financial or technical assistance and advice, and may cover any other matter relating to the protection of the area, including the implementation of a plan of management, restricting the use of the area, and restricting or requiring specified activities (WA s 12).

Draft wilderness protection agreements are made available to the public, by notice and exhibition, and forwarded to the National Parks and Wildlife Advisory Council (WA s 11). The Minister considers submissions from the public or the Council (s 10). The Director keeps a public register of wilderness protection agreements (s 14).

A statutory authority may not carry out any development, or approve a change of use, in a wilderness area until written notice is given to the Minister, parties to the agreement and the owner, and the Minister has consented. The Minister may only consent to a development that will not adversely affect the area (s 15).

A conservation agreement under the NPWA may relate to wilderness (WA s 16).

Administration

Director-General

The *Wilderness Act* is administered by the Director-General of the NPW Service whose functions include identifying wilderness areas; their protection, management and maintenance; and promoting educational activities and scientific research. The provisions of the NPWA relating to wilderness areas prevail over the *Wilderness Act* (WA s 5).

Dunphy Wilderness Fund

The Dunphy Wilderness Fund is a Special Deposits Account in the Treasury for money received in connection with the *Wilderness Act*, including from gifts (WA s 23; NPWA s 148).

The NPW Service includes wilderness areas in its Annual Report to the State Parliament (WA s 24).

Plans of management

Plans of management are prepared for wilderness areas. A draft plan is referred to the National Parks and Wildlife Advisory Council for comment. The Minister may adopt a plan of management with the consent of the other party to a wilderness or conservation agreement. A plan of management is given effect to by the Director and the other party to an agreement (WA ss 17-19).

Enforcement

Any person may bring proceedings in the Land and Environment Court for an order to remedy or restrain a breach of the *Wilderness Act*, whether or not affected by the breach. Proceedings for an offence against the regulations shall be dealt with summarily before a Local Court (s 30).

Conservation measures outside of protected areas under NPWA

In addition to the protective legislation for the conservation of biodiversity, discussed in Chapter 8, the NPWA also provides for conservation outside reserves and declared lands. Three major strategies are:

- interim protection orders;
- conservation agreements; and
- measures for the protection of fauna and flora in the State.

Interim protection orders

Interim protection orders are directed at private individuals for the preservation, protection and maintenance of:

- land and its fauna and plants;
- threatened species, populations and ecological communities and critical habitat of endangered species, populations and ecological communities; and
- any Aboriginal object or place. (NPWA s 91B)

Interim protection orders are made by the Minister on the recommendation of the Director-General:

- over land with natural, scientific or cultural significance;
- over land where it is intended to carry out any power, authority, duty or function of the Director-General relating to fauna, native plants, threatened species, populations or ecological communities, or critical habitat, of endangered species populations or ecological communities. (s 91A)

Failure to comply by a person given notice is an offence (s 91G).

Orders have effect for up to two years, and cease to have effect if the land is reserved or dedicated under the NPWA (ss 91D, 91E). There is a public register of interim protection orders (s 91I).

Prior notice to affected persons is not required (s 91C). When an order is made, notice is given in the *Gazette* and to affected persons (s 91F). An affected owner or occupier of land may appeal to the Land and Environment Court against the making of the order. The court may have regard to any hardship caused by the order and the purpose in making it (s 91H).

Conservation agreements

Conservation agreements are under the NPWA, and are made between the Minister administering the NPWA and owners of land. The Nature Conservation Trust of New South Wales established under the *Nature Conservation Trust Act 2001* may negotiate agreements. The consent of the owner and of any person with an interest in the land is required. Conservation agreements may also be over government owned or Crown land (NPWA s 69B). There is a public register of conservation agreements (s 69H).

Conservation agreements cover areas containing:

- scenery, natural environment or phenomena worthy of preservation or of special scientific interest;
- the sites of buildings, objects, monuments or events of national significance; or
- Aboriginal objects or places of special significance.

The purposes of conservation agreements include:

- the study, preservation, protection, care of fauna, native plants or other flora and of karst environments; and
- the conservation of critical habitats, threatened species, populations or ecological communities or other habitats. (s 69C)

A conservation agreement may regulate access to the area and the activities of the owner; set out financial arrangements and contain terms for the conservation or enhancement of the conservation area, including for plans of management (s 69C). The agreement may place requirements on the Minister and the Nature Conservation Trust, including to provide financial and other assistance (s 69C).

The Minister may terminate an agreement, without compensation, if the area is no longer needed, or able to be used, for the purposes of the agreement (s 69D(4)).

A conservation agreement runs with the land and is enforceable by and against subsequent owners (s 69E). Details are kept at the Land Titles Office (s 69F).

A conservation agreement is enforced in the Land and Environment Court. Damages may be only be awarded against an owner for a breach of an agreement arising out of an intentional or reckless act or omission by the owner, or a previous owner. In assessing damages for a breach of an agreement, the court has regard to any relevant matter, which may include any detriment to the public interest that arose from the breach and any financial or other benefit that the owner sought to gain from the breach (s 69G).

Statutory authorities may not carry out development in a conservation area without the consent of the Minister (s 69I) with disputes referred to the Premier (s 69J).

The Director-General may, after consulting with the owner, cause a plan of management to be prepared for a conservation area (s 72).

A conservation agreement is a regulatory instrument under s 28 of the EPAA and, therefore, may be suspended by an environmental planning instrument made under that Act (s 69KA).

Conservation of fauna

The NPWA nominates the Director-General as the 'authority' for the protection and care of fauna (Pt 7, s 92).

Fauna in the State is categorised under the NPWA as protected or unprotected. The legislation nominates what is unprotected, so that all fauna is protected unless listed in Sch 11 to the Act (s 93). Fauna may be declared to be unprotected within a specified locality in the State. The locality must be outside a national park, historic site or nature reserve, and the fauna may not be from a threatened species, population or ecological community (s 96). Schedule 12 lists threatened interstate fauna, but at present does not contain any items (s 94).

Protected fauna is the property of the Crown, until captured or killed in accordance with the NPWA. Exceptions are protected fauna that:

- at the time of its birth, is in the lawful possession of any person other than the Crown;
- is imported into New South Wales; or
- is of a class or description listed in the Regulations, until it is liberated. (s 97)

Harming protected fauna

It is an offence to:

- harm any protected fauna;
- harm game birds for sporting or recreational purposes, even if they are unprotected in that locality; or
- use any substance, animal, firearm, explosive, net, trap, hunting device or instrument or means whatever for the purpose of harming any protected fauna. (s 98)

It is a defence if the action was required by any law, or taken under a licence. The NPWA creates categories of licences:

- general licence (s 120);
- occupier's licence (s 121);
- trapper's licence (s 123);
- emu licence (s 125A); and
- scientific licence (s 132C).

Licences are also issued under Pt 6 of the *Threatened Species Conservation Act*.

It is also a defence if the action:

- was authorised by a conservation agreement, or by joint management agreement under Pt 7 of the *Threatened Species Conservation Act*;
- was essential for carrying out development under the EPAA. (NPWA s 98)

Finally, it is a defence if the animal concerned was in someone's lawful possession or had escaped and that the act was reasonably necessary for promoting the welfare of the animal or for securing its return (s 100).

A similar offence relates to harming threatened interstate fauna (s 99).

Feeding fauna

Officers of the NPW Service may give directions to stop feeding protected fauna, or to stop any activity that is causing the animal distress (s 99A).

Buying, selling or possessing protected fauna

A person may not buy, sell or have in their control any protected fauna, unless covered, for example, by an exemption set out in an order of the Governor, or unless a court is satisfied that there were reasonable grounds for the person to believe that the act was covered by a licence (Pt 9, Div 2). or by an aviary registration certificate (s 128).

If an animal was incapable of fending for itself in its natural habitat, the person must notify the Director-General that the animal has come into the person's possession (s 101).

The Director-General may give directions to a person who keeps protected fauna in confinement or in a domesticated state, respecting food, drink and shelter, and the welfare of the fauna (s 102).

Harming fauna for sale

A person must not harm fauna for the purpose of sale, unless the action is covered by a licence. Dingos, ferrets, foxes, hares, rabbits and any species of fauna named in an order are not included in this prohibition (s 103).

Use of certain substances for harming fauna

A person must not, without the Director-General's consent, use any substance set out in the Regulations for harming protected fauna (s 110).

Method of shooting fauna

A person may only use a firearm of a kind habitually raised at arm's length and fired from the shoulder without other support, for the purpose of harming protected fauna (s 111).

Harming snakes

A person shall not be convicted for harming a snake unless it is proved that the person could have no grounds for reasonably believing that the snake was likely to endanger a person or property (s 112).

Licences for dealing with fauna

The NPWA provides for licensing activities with respect to fauna.

There are two broad licences. A general licence (ss 120, 129) authorises a person to harm, obtain, hold, exhibit, dispose of or keep under control any protected fauna. It would usually not operate in reserves, nor authorise the harming of protected fauna solely for scientific, educational or conservation purposes (s 132C).

An occupier's licence authorises an owner or occupier of land to harm, or permits the holder of a general licence or a trapper's licence to harm and dispose of fauna found on the land. A condition may be imposed requiring labels, tags, slips or other objects to be attached to the skin or carcase of harmed fauna, which the NPW Service will supply. Occupier's licences are not issued for threatened species, populations or ecological communities, or for sporting or recreational purposes (ss 121, 129).

The NPWA also provides for business licences for carrying on the business of a:

- trapper (generally outside protected areas and not for threatened species, populations or ecological communities) (ss 123, 129);
- fauna dealer (except in respect of dingos, ferrets, foxes, hares, rabbits or any species named in an order of the Governor published in the *Gazette*) (s 104);
- skin dealer (s 105); or
- emu breeder (s 105A).

An aviary registration certificate is issued for specified premises authorising a person to deal in birds that are protected fauna. Buyers from the holder of the certificate must also have a licence (s 128).

Licences are also required to:

- import or export protected fauna (ss 126 and 106);
- exhibit protected fauna (ss 120 and 107); or
- liberate any animal (other than a homing pigeon or a captured animal which is native to New South Wales) (ss 108, 127).

Marine mammals

Part 7A of the NPWA sets out special provisions for marine mammals.

Administration

Marine Mammals Advisory Committee

The Marine Mammals Advisory Committee (s 112A, Sch 8A) advises the Minister on the conservation and protection of marine mammals, including strandings, and on the preparation of plans of management (s 112B).

Plans of management for marine mammals

The NPWA provides for plans of management for populations of marine mammals to deal with:

- their population distribution and abundance;
- threats to their survival;
- research and educational activities; and
- national and international agreements. (s 112C)

Public notice is given of the proposed plan of management inviting representations. The plan is then forwarded to the Marine Mammals Advisory Committee for consideration and advice, which the Minister considers for adoption (s 112D) and is given effect to by the Director-General (s 112E).

Licences – marine mammals

A licence, referred to above for a person to harm fauna or obtain fauna for exhibition or other purposes (see ss 120, 132C), will not be granted for a marine mammal unless the officer issuing the licence is satisfied that the marine mammal is required for genuine scientific or educational purposes or for the conservation or protection of marine mammals (s 112F).

Approaching marine mammal

It is an offence to approach a marine mammal any closer than is set out in the *National Parks and Wildlife Regulation 2002* or to interfere with a marine mammal, without a general licence (s 120), scientific licence (s 132C), or a licence under Pt 6 of the *Threatened Species Conservation Act*. Interfere includes to harass, chase, herd, tag, mark or brand the mammal. References in the NPWA to harming fauna includes approaching or interfering with marine mammals (s 112G).

Proceedings are heard by the Land and Environment Court. If the court is satisfied that the person committed the offence in the course of commercial operations relating to the killing of marine mammals, the maximum penalty is 2000 penalty units.

Conservation and native flora

The NPWA nominates the Director-General as the authority for the protection of native plants (s 114).

Plans of management

The Director-General may cause a flora plan of management to be prepared for any commercial activity that might adversely affect the conservation of a species or group of native plants, consulting the Scientific Committee, established under Pt 8 of the *Threatened Species Conservation Act*. The following matters are considered in the preparation of a flora plan of management:

- the ecology of the species;
- the sustainability of the proposed management regime;
- Aboriginal cultural practices;
- standards to be adhered to in the picking or growing of plants;
- whether limits need to be imposed on the number of licences that may be issued for a commercial activity if a licence is required to carry out the activity;
- protocols for the extraction of plant material from the wild;
- consistency with any threat abatement plan, or recovery plan, within the meaning of the *Threatened Species Conservation Act*;
- monitoring of the activity.

A draft flora plan of management is publicly exhibited before adoption and any representations are considered (s 115A).

The Forestry Commission must not issue a licence under the *Forestry Act 1916* for the removal of any protected native plant from a State forest, timber reserve or Crown land, unless the plant would be damaged or destroyed in the taking of timber, products or forest materials or other activity authorised by the *Forestry Act*, and subject to a condition that the removal will accord with any relevant flora plan of management (s 116).

Licensing and plants

The NPWA provides for the following licences relating to plants:

- licence to pick protected native plants – authorising a person to pick specified protected native plants, including a plant of a threatened species that has been grown in accordance with a licence under s 132;
- licence to grow native plants for sale – authorising an owner or occupier of private land to grow protected native plants for sale (s 132);
- import and export licences for protected native plants – authorising a person to import or export protected native plants (s 132A).

A licence issued authorising the picking of a protected native plant in the wild is subject to any relevant flora plan of management for the protected native plant adopted under s 115A (s 133).

Restriction on picking or possession of native plant

It is offence to pick a protected native plant or have it in one's possession. Exceptions to this blanket prohibition are where the action was:

- in a nature reserve or wildlife refuge or in Aboriginal lands (see s 57(7));
- in respect of a plant grown upon private land picked by or with the consent of the owner, lessee or occupier of that land;
- authorised under a conservation agreement, or a joint management agreement under Pt 7 of the *Threatened Species Conservation Act*;
- pursuant to a licence under s 131 or 132C of the NPWA, the *Forestry Act*, or the *Threatened Species Conservation Act* Pt 6;
- pursuant to a duty imposed on the person under any Act; or
- in respect of a protected native plant cultivated as a hobby and not for commercial purposes.

In a prosecution, proof that a protected native plant was found in the possession of the defendant is prima facie evidence of an offence and the defendant bears the onus of proof to disprove this (s 117).

Restriction on selling of native plant

It is an offence to sell a protected native plant. It is a defence that the protected native plant was picked or sold under a licence under the NPWA (s 131 commercial purposes, ss 132, 132A). It is also a defence if both the supplier of the plant, and the person who received it, cultivate plants as a hobby (s 118).

Conservation and threatened species

The NPWA supports the *Threatened Species Conservation Act* by setting out offence provisions for protecting threatened species, endangered populations, endangered ecological communities and their habitats. These are discussed in Chapter 8.

Private national parks

A relatively new development is the emergence of privately owned reserves, set up by community and other groups, usually incorporated under the *Corporations Act 2001* (Cth).

One group which maintains properties in New South Wales is the Australian Bush Heritage Fund:

> a national, independent, non-profit organisation. It is committed to protecting Australia's animals and plants and their habitats. It acquires – by purchase, gift or bequest – land and water of outstanding ecological significance to protect and enhance its natural values. Funds are raised by tax-deductible donations from the public and funding organisations.

The fund has over 660,000 hectares of Australia's conservation lands in 22 reserves in six States with examples of at least 154 vegetation communities (59 of conservation significance), at least 102 species of plants of conservation significance and at least 54 species of birds or animals at risk.[30]

Another major conservation group is the Australian Wildlife Conservancy, which has over 917,000 hectares of land in 14 reserves that it calls sanctuaries, protecting over 250 ecosystems, 100 threatened ecosystems and 135 threatened animal species.[31] 'Its aim is to own tracts of land that that contain every single native species … In short it wants to be Australia's Noah'.[32]

These organisations attract large donations and perform extremely important conservation work. They have a different relationship to the legislation discussed in this Chapter than do public reserves. While they would follow the provisions protecting flora and fauna that apply generally in the State, for legal structures and mechanisms relating to the ownership and administration of their land they would look to legislation that regulates corporations and charities. Their landholdings are growing at a very fast rate and the adequacy of these legal structures to support such important site-specific environmental work may need to be reviewed.

Conclusion

This chapter describes the legislative basis for parks and reserves in New South Wales. The largest category is land reserved under the NPWA, particularly as national parks. For historical reasons, land is also held under other legislation, for example, by the long standing administrations of Crown lands and forestry, and new policy needs have led to the creation of new administrations.

The chapter shows how the traditional reasons for reserving land based on broad environmental, cultural and recreational needs are being joined by the need to meet new pressures in biodiversity conservation, and from rapid development in desirable locations. It also shows how a modern social need for reconciliation has led to innovative schemes for joint management of reserved lands with Aboriginal groups.

The latest development is increasing ownership of large areas lands, important for biodiversity, by non-profit organisations relying on a combination of public and private funding. These developments augment provisions in protected areas legislation for controlling activities, deleterious to the conservation of biodiversity, outside reserves.

Protected areas in New South Wales are a dynamic and vital aspect of the environment and environmental law in the State.

---

30 Australian Bush Heritage Fund, *Annual Report 2004/2005*, <www.bushheritage.asn.au> (accessed 24 July 2006), unpaginated.

31 See <www,australianwildlife.org/about AWC.asp> (accessed 16 January 2007).

32 Bearup, G, 'To save a sunburnt country', *Sydney Morning Herald Good Weekend*, 13 January 2007, 17.

10

HERITAGE

This chapter reviews the laws that protect and conserve heritage in New South Wales at the three levels of government: Commonwealth, State and local. The major piece of Commonwealth legislation is the *Environment Protection and Biodiversity Conservation Act 1999* (Cth) (EPBCA). State legislation centres on the *Heritage Act 1974* (NSW). Finally, local government councils administer heritage laws as part of their land use planning functions, primarily through local environmental plans under the *Environmental Planning and Assessment Act 1979* (NSW) (EPAA). All categories of heritage can be covered by this legislation. There is, however, other specialist legislation dealing with heritage objects and Indigenous heritage, and the chapter discusses these. Before discussing heritage legislation that applies in New South Wales, this chapter first looks at meanings of heritage.

What is heritage?

When people think of heritage, they usually think of old buildings, even grand old buildings. Modern heritage practice and legislation goes far beyond this view:

> In contemporary Australia [the] material remnants of the past, including place, buildings, archaeological sites and objects are termed 'heritage' – 'the things we want to keep' – 'places in the heart'. Places and objects contribute to a sensory and emotional perception of belonging, of home and community. We measure our lives against them; they are things that keep us anchored, the fundamental values we take our bearings from, every day.[1]

Modern ideas of heritage even extend beyond the 'material remnants of the past' to natural heritage and intangible heritage, like traditional forms of knowledge and cultural practice and places with social significance. The law that relates to heritage protection reflects these wide and expanding views of heritage.

In the context of this book, it is useful, in considering what is covered by heritage laws, to note a modern trend, where the same laws apply to heritage and environmental issues. The major example is the EPBCA which consolidates the Commonwealth's national environment protection legislation and, by recent amendments, incorporates national heritage laws.

1 J Lydon and T Ireland (eds), *Object lessons: Archaeology & Heritage in Australia* (Australian Scholarly Publishing, 2005) at 1.

Many applaud this development and argue that environment is to a large extent part of heritage, in that there is little of Australia that is natural in the sense of not being impacted upon by humans:

> In Australia the whole landscape is a cultural place, in that it is an artifact of humanity; people have been modifying or giving human meaning to the landscape for at least 60,000 years, and most of Australia has been affected by this.[2]

While in this chapter an attempt will be made at times to divide heritage into different categories for discussion, this quote explains why these categories will often merge, so that it is as useful to talk just in terms of heritage.

Categories of heritage significance

There are two important initial questions in heritage conservation: what is to be conserved, and why. The first leads to the Australian use of the word 'place', discussed below. The second relates to types of heritage significance.

While the distinction is being challenged, it is useful, initially, to identify heritage items by reference to two main categories of significance, either cultural or natural.

This distinction is made in the *Convention for the Protection of the World Cultural and Natural Heritage* (World Heritage Convention),[3] which protects cultural heritage, in Art 1, and natural heritage, in Art 2, of outstanding universal value.

Natural heritage

Article 2 of the World Heritage Convention illustrates the range of items included in the term natural heritage:

> Article 2
>
> For the purposes of the Convention, the following shall be considered as 'natural heritage':
>
>> natural features consisting of physical and biological formations or groups of such formations, which are of outstanding universal value from the aesthetic or scientific point of view; geographical and physiographical formations and precisely delineated areas which constitute the habitat of threatened species of animals and plants of outstanding universal value from the point of view of science or conservation; natural sites or precisely delineated natural areas of outstanding universal value from the point of view of science, conservation or natural beauty.

The Australian Natural Heritage Charter includes a definition of natural heritage that recognises that natural heritage has significance for humans, as well as an intrinsic significance as nature.

> Natural significance means the importance of ecosystems, biological diversity and *geodiversity* for their existence value, or for present or future generations in terms of their scientific, social, aesthetic and life support value.[4]

2 M Pearson and S Sullivan, *Looking after Heritage Places* (Melbourne University Press, 1995) at 5.

3 UNESCO, 16 November 1972, 27 UST 37, 1037 UNTS 151.

4 Australian Heritage Charter Art 1.2; Australian Committee for IUCN (1996) at 6

Cultural heritage

There are many views of what constitutes cultural heritage. Some still reflect a focus on old and important buildings, as suggested by the title of an influential early document addressing the conservation of cultural heritage, the Athens Charter for the Restoration of Historic Monuments (1931). A tendency to equate cultural heritage with monuments, a monuments approach to heritage, favouring grand old buildings is identified as deriving from Europe. This view finds some support in the World Heritage Convention:

> Article 1
>
> For the For the purposes of this Convention, the following shall be considered as 'cultural heritage':
>
> **monuments:** architectural works, works of monumental sculpture and painting, elements or structures of an archaeological nature, inscriptions, cave dwellings and combinations of features, which are of outstanding universal value from the point of view of history, art or science;
>
> **groups of buildings:** groups of separate or connected buildings which, because of their architecture, their homogeneity or their place in the landscape, are of outstanding universal value from the point of view of history, art or science;
>
> **sites:** works of man or the combined works of nature and man, and areas including archaeological sites which are of outstanding universal value from the historical, aesthetic, ethnological or anthropological point of view.

Cultural landscapes

As one reaction to the monuments view of heritage, more importance has been given recently to the last category in this definition, 'sites', and in particular to the words 'the combined works of nature and man'. From this has developed the concept of the cultural landscape to reflect cultural values in natural places. This move also reflects that many of the peoples of the world do not have a history of built heritage, or have buildings that are less old and less grand than in Europe, but may have modified the landscape or invested natural features with spiritual and cultural values. In this sense elements of natural heritage are recognised as having cultural significance.

Other values

The definitions in legislation with effect in New South Wales show further development from a cultural, or cultural/natural, focus. Australia's first National Heritage legislation, the *Australian Heritage Commission Act 1975* (Cth), included natural, and had an expansive definition of cultural to include aesthetic, historic and scientific. Interestingly, it also included the value or category of significance, 'social', a word of potentially very wide import.[5] Its focus was Australia's National Estate and provided that:

> The national estate consists of those places, being components of the natural environment of Australia or the cultural environment of Australia, that have aesthetic,

5 See C Johnston, *What is Social Value?* (Australian Heritage Commission Technical Publications Series Number 3, AGPS, 1992).

> historic, scientific, or social significance or other special value for future generations as well as for the present community. (s 4(1))

These broad concepts of heritage are included in the current national legislation, the EPBCA, which provides that the:

> *heritage value* of a place includes the place's natural or cultural environment having aesthetic, historic, scientific or social significance, or other significance, for current and future generations of Australians. (s 528)

Note the addition of the catchall 'or other significance'. Notice also that this latest Australian definition continues the Australian use of the word 'place', a much broader and more inclusive word than building or monument.

The relevant definition in the State legislation in New South Wales is earlier but just as comprehensive. The *Heritage Act 1977* (NSW) protects what is referred to as the environmental heritage, the definition of which also reflects the move away from a strict cultural/natural distinction and a focus on buildings, by referring to 'those places, buildings, works, relics, movable objects, and precincts that are of State or local heritage significance'. 'State' and 'local' heritage significance are then defined to include significance in relation to 'the historical, scientific, cultural, social, archaeological, architectural, natural or aesthetic value of the item' (s 4).

Place

Place is an important concept in discussing heritage laws in New South Wales in moving on from a narrow focus on buildings. The important Burra Charter of Australia ICOMOS[6] provides a good explanation of 'place', and how it links up with significance. This quote shows how expansive this concept is:

> 1.1 *Place* means site, area, land, landscape, building or other work, group of buildings or other works, and may include components, contents, spaces and views.
>
> Place as used in this charter has a broad scope: it is geographically defined and includes its natural and cultural features. Place can be used to refer to small things, such as a milestone, and large areas, such as a cultural landscape. A memorial, tree, the site of an historical event, an urban area or town, an industrial plant, an archaeological site, a stone arrangement, a road or travel route, a site with spiritual and religious connotations – all of these can fit under the term.
>
> 1.2 *Cultural significance* means aesthetic, historic, scientific, social or spiritual value for past, present or future generations.
>
> Cultural significance is embodied in the place itself, its fabric, setting, use, associations, meanings, records, related places and related objects.
>
> Places have a range of values for different individuals or groups.
>
> Australian conservation practice and heritage legislation is based on the concept of cultural significance; ie that the values (significance) of a place can be described and that retaining significance is the primary objective of conservation of the place. Some acts use slightly different terms – such as 'heritage significance' or 'cultural heritage value' – but the concept is the same as cultural significance …

6 Australia ICOMOS, the Australia ICOMOS Charter for Places of Cultural Significance, see P Marquis-Kyle and M Walker, *The Illustrated Burra Charter: Good Practice for Heritage Places* (ICOMOS, 2004).

> The cultural significance of a place may change as the result of the continuing history of the place. Understanding of cultural significance may change as a result of new information.
>
> A place may have different meanings to different groups.[7]

With a sense, now, of how expansive the concept of heritage is, the question of how heritage is protected by legislation in New South Wales can be addressed.

Regulatory regimes in New South Wales

Under regulatory regimes, this chapter looks at international conventions and domestic legislation that applies in New South Wales.

International charters and conventions

International charters and conventions have been an important influence on heritage conservation law and practice in Australia.

Charters are drawn up regionally and nationally, often by heritage groups and professional bodies. They are not sets of rules, but are 'statements of general principles, reflecting particular philosophical positions about the past and the role the past plays in the present – as well as about our role as present custodians of the environment and our responsibilities towards the future'.[8] The Australian Burra Charter, just mentioned, fits into a tradition inspired by European Charters, particularly by the:

- Athens Charter for the Restoration of Historic Monuments, adopted at the First International Congress of Architects and Technicians of Historic Monuments in Athens in 1931; and
- Venice Charter, the International Charter for the Conservation and Restoration of Monuments and Sites, adopted at the Second International Congress of Architects and Technicians of Historic Monuments in Venice in 1964.

The Venice Charter is now the international instrument guiding the work of professionals involved in heritage conservation.[9]

There are functional connections between charters and conventions and charters can prepare the way for conventions.

Conventions are also common in international law and in heritage matters and 'emanate from intergovernmental organizations such as UNESCO. These norms are considered public international law, and before being adopted and applied, they are subject to meticulous preparation and consultations between states to ensure the widest possible consensus'.[10] The World Heritage Convention is only one of many that relate to heritage conservation.

---

7 Marquis-Kyle and Walker, ibid at 11.

8 W Logan, 'Introduction: Voices from the periphery: the Burra Charter in Context' (2004) 18(1) *historic environment* 6.

9 B Boer and G Wiffen, *Heritage Law in Australia* (Oxford University Press, 2006) at 36.

10 J-L Luxen, 'Reflections on the use of Heritage Charters and Conventions' (2004) 19(2) *Conservation* 6.

UNESCO, the United Nations Educational, Scientific and Cultural Organization, has been important in the preparation of Conventions. Important heritage conventions administered by UNESCO are:

- *Hague Convention on the Protection of Cultural Heritage in Times of Armed Conflict 1954* (the Hague Convention);
- *Convention on the Means of Prohibiting and Preventing the Illicit Import, Export and Transfer of Ownership of Cultural Property 1970* (UNESCO Convention).
- *Convention concerning the Protection of the World Cultural and Natural Heritage 1972* (World Heritage Convention);
- *Convention on the Protection of the Underwater Cultural Heritage 2001* (Underwater Cultural Heritage Convention);
- *Convention on the Safeguarding of the Intangible Cultural Heritage 2003* (Intangible Cultural Heritage Convention).[11]

World Heritage Convention

The World Heritage Convention is the most significant Convention for Australia. Australia was the fourth country to ratify the Convention, which provides the Commonwealth Parliament with its main constitutional power to legislate for heritage protection. The Convention was adopted by UNESCO in 1972 and is administered by UNESCO's World Heritage Centre in Paris.

> The Convention provides a permanent legal, administrative and financial framework for international co-operation in safeguarding the cultural and natural heritage of 'outstanding universal value' …
>
> The Convention establishes the World Heritage List, which is divided into natural and cultural properties, with provision for mixed natural and cultural nominations …[12]

There is a World Heritage Committee of 21 members chosen from the States Parties (Art 8).

> The Committee uses regularly updated *Operational Guidelines* developed under the Convention to spell out in detail how the Convention should be administered, what criteria should be adopted for assessing outstanding universal value and the manner in which States Parties are to implement the Convention.[13]

Article 11 of the Convention establishes a List of World Heritage in Danger.[14]

Australian heritage legislation

The heritage legislation that has effect in New South Wales deals with the wide range of places of heritage significance by creating inventories of heritage places. The inventories are a series of lists administered by national, State and local

---

11 List taken from Boer and Wiffen, above n 9, at 35. For an extensive database of Charters and Conventions, see <www.icomos.org>.

12 Boer and Wiffen, above n 9, at 65.

13 Ibid.

14 For a discussion of the World Heritage Convention, see Boer and Wiffen, above n 9, Chapter 3.

governments. This last stage in this system for New South Wales was put in place by the heritage amendments to the EPBCA in 2004.

The national listing system is based on two assumptions: that heritage concerns can to a large extent concentrate on individual places or items that can be listed, and that government responsibility for heritage can efficiently be allocated according to the divisions of responsibility between the tiers of government in the Australian federation: national; State and Territory; and local. Both of these assumptions can be questioned.

While heritage precincts and cultural landscapes may be listed, the use of lists may have the effect of obscuring the inter-connectedness of different heritage items. Secondly, the division of heritage responsibility according to an item's national, State or local significance between the different levels of government may diminish another sense of connectedness, of heritage places as part of broader stories. The repealed *Australian Heritage Commission Act 1975*, for example, used the concept of the National Estate to emphasise the national significance of all heritage items in Australia. Even this broader view may be challenged.

> In focusing on national character this narrative strongly downplayed both internal complexity, as well as the nation's broader entanglement within histories or prior indigenous occupation, colonialism, empire, migration and global capitalism.[15]

The division of responsibility for heritage between the tiers of government in Australia is the result of an agreement of the Council of Australian Governments (COAG) of which New South Wales along with the other Australian governments is a member. COAG issued the 1992 Intergovernmental Agreement on the Environment and in 1997 reached agreement on the responsibility for heritage, under which the parties:

> 6. ***Agree*** to the rationalisation of the existing Commonwealth/State arrangements for the identification, protection, and management of places of heritage significance through the development, within twelve months, of a co-operative national heritage strategy which will: (i) set out the roles and responsibilities of the Commonwealth and the States; (ii) identify criteria, standards and guidelines, as appropriate, for the protection of heritage by each level of government; (iii) provide for the establishment of a list of places of national heritage significance; and (iv) maximise Commonwealth compliance with State heritage and planning laws.[16]

Responsibility for heritage is divided between the Commonwealth on the one hand and the States and the two largely self-governing Territories, the Northern Territory and the Australian Capital Territory, on the other. In New South Wales and the other States responsibility is then allocated between the State and local government.

Despite the COAG agreement, the States have not formally transferred constitutional power to the Commonwealth. Therefore, what legislative and administrative steps the Commonwealth may actually take are still subject to the interpretation of the terms of the Constitution.

The Commonwealth is responsible for what is designated as world, national and Commonwealth heritage places. Under the Constitution, the Australian Parliament may protect items in Commonwealth areas, and this is the basis for its list of Com-

15 Lydon and Ireland, above n 1, at 2.

16 Heads of Agreement on Commonwealth/State Roles and responsibilities for the Environment, November 1997, Art 6, <http://www.deh.gov.au/epbc/about/agreement/preamble.html>.

monwealth Heritage Places. The Commonwealth's powers to give effect to other aspects of the COAG agreement are less straightforward. Therefore the provisions in the EPBCA protecting heritage items on its other lists are more complex as to which actions may be controlled.

Heritage lists in New South Wales

The legislative inventories or lists in New South Wales operate at the national, State and local government levels. Much of the remainder of this chapter discusses the details of these lists.

National

The main Commonwealth lists are created under the EPBCA. These are:

- declared World Heritage properties – places inscribed on or being considered for the World Heritage List under the World Heritage Convention;
- National Heritage List – a limited number of iconic places of national significance; and
- Commonwealth Heritage List – heritage places located in a Commonwealth area.

The Register of the National Estate created under the repealed *Australian Heritage Commission Act 1975* was retained under s 5 of the *Australian Heritage Council Act 2003*.

State

The main list under NSW legislation is the State Heritage Register under the *Heritage Act 1977* (NSW), which lists places, buildings, works, relics, movable objects or precincts of State heritage significance (s 32).

The *Heritage Act* is also the basis for the:

- Register of Shipwrecks (s 49); and
- Heritage and Conservation Register of State government agencies (s 170).

The EPAA regulates land use planning in New South Wales. Under this Act, heritage places are included as schedules to:

- State environmental planning policies (SEPPs);
- regional environmental plans (REPs); and
- local environmental planning policies (LEPS).

Local

Local government councils in New South Wales have a significant role in the legal protection of heritage primarily under local environmental plans (LEPS) under the EPAA, referred to above.

Community groups

Professional and community groups in New South Wales maintain lists of heritage places that do not have legal force but are influential. The best known is that of the

National Trust of Australia (NSW), which maintains the National Trust Register of, currently, 12,000 landscapes, townscapes, buildings, industrial sites, cemeteries and other items or places which the Trust determines have cultural significance and are worthy of conservation.[17]

Commonwealth heritage legislation

The Commonwealth Parliament has enacted two comprehensive pieces of legislation dealing with broad categories of heritage, the *Australian Heritage Commission Act 1975* and the EPBCA.

The *Australian Heritage Commission Act*, prompted by the emphasis on nationalism at the time, referred to Australia's heritage as its National Estate. The National Estate was given an expansive definition following the 1972 World Heritage Convention. As mentioned above, the Convention, as an innovation, had included both cultural and natural heritage.

The EPBCA, as amended in 2004, replaced the *Australian Heritage Commission Act* and covers all the major categories of heritage, including Indigenous and non-indigenous cultural heritage, and natural heritage. There are important categories of delegated legislation under the EPBCA (s 323). The *Environment Protection and Biodiversity Conservation Regulations 2000* (Cth) (EPBCR) and the various types of orders that the Minister and other officials may make have important legal effects and are referred to below.

The EPBCA is based on the interpretation of a number of Commonwealth powers in s 51 of the Australian Constitution by the High Court in cases beginning, for environmental matters, with the *Tasmanian Dams* case in 1983.[18]

These constitutional powers are concurrent powers with the States, whereby the Commonwealth Parliament could pass legislation to override the legislation of the States. The EPBCA, however, does not preclude New South Wales and the other States from also making heritage laws, as it provides that generally it 'is not intended to exclude or limit the concurrent operation of any law of a State or Territory' (s 10).

> [The Act] promotes a partnership approach to environmental protection and biodiversity conservation through:
> (i) bilateral agreements with States and Territories;
> (ii) conservation agreements with landholders;
> (iii) recognising and promoting indigenous peoples' role in, and knowledge of, the conservation and ecologically sustainable use of biodiversity; and
> (iv) the involvement of the community in management planning. (s 3(2)(g))

Principles of ecologically sustainable development (s 3A) and the precautionary principle are taken into account in decision-making under the Act (ss 3A(b), 391).

The Act deals with heritage places as matters of national environmental significance. There are also heritage protection provisions under the general category of the conservation of biodiversity and heritage.

There are seven matters of national environmental significance in the EPBCA and three clearly relate to heritage. These are the major heritage lists of places of World, National and Commonwealth Heritage significance.

---

17 See <http://www.nsw.nationaltrust.org.au/register/default.asp> (accessed 16 January 2007).
18 *Commonwealth v Tasmania* (1983) 158 CLR 157.

The EPBCA protects heritage places by identifying prohibited actions and providing for criminal consequences. Under the Act 'the Minister [may] decide whether an action that has, will have or is likely to have a significant impact' on a matter of national environmental significance, should proceed. A person is prohibited from taking an action 'without the Minister having given approval or decided that approval is not needed' (EPBCA Chapter 2, 'Protecting the Environment', s 11).

The Act also sets out strategies for the long-term management of heritage places. Prohibited actions are then permitted if carried out in an approved way under one of these schemes.

Chapter 5 of the Act sets out detailed provisions for the conservation of biodiversity and heritage, providing further protection for the protected places of World Heritage (Pt 15, Div 1), National Heritage (Pt 15, Div 1A) and Commonwealth Heritage (Pt 15, Div 3A).

EPBCA Partnership model

The partnership model under the EPBCA, described in the previous part, is illustrated by the case of the Sydney Opera House. Preparation is well under way to support the nomination of the Opera House if the Commonwealth and New South Wales governments so decide. A bilateral agreement under the EPBCA is ready, which supports the continued management of the property by the State government, and stipulates what actions by the State will not require approval by the Commonwealth under the EPBCA, assessment of potential impacts by the State, monitoring of the site and dispute resolution.[19]

Buffer zones

In recent years, the World Heritage Committee through amendments to the Operational Guidelines for the World Heritage Convention is paying more attention to the creation of buffer zones to protect World Heritage sites. It is likely that buffer zones in Australia will be provided under State legislation as part of partnership arrangements under the EPBCA.

> In the event that the Sydney Opera House is inscribed on the World Heritage List, a buffer zone will come into force by an amendment to the *Harbour REP* (Regional Environment Plan under the *Environment Planning and Assessment Act 1974 (NSW)*). The buffer zone will be subject to additional planning rules and provisions aimed at further protecting the World Heritage values of the property. The Minister for Planning will be required to ensure that any development within the buffer zone satisfies certain criteria for consideration before granting consent under the Harbour REP.
>
> To be approved any development will need to preserve the World Heritage values of the Sydney Opera House; to preserve views and vistas between the property and other public places within the buffer zone; and to avoid any diminution of the Sydney Opera House when viewed from other public places within the

19 Agreement between the Australian Government and the State of New South Wales under s 45 of the *Environment Protection and Biodiversity Conservation Act 1999* (Cth) relating to actions approved and taken in accordance with the bilaterally accredited management plan for the Sydney Opera House, <www.deh.gov.au/heritage/world heritage>.

zone. Any proposed development within the buffer zone would need to address these matters in its application.[20]

Commonwealth heritage lists

This chapter now discusses the details of the protection of heritage places under the EPBCA.

World Heritage properties

World Heritage properties are protected as a matter of national environment significance (Pt 3, Div 1, Subdiv A) and as protected areas requiring to be managed (Pt 15).

The Commonwealth Parliament's ratification of the World Heritage Convention provides the constitutional basis for these provisions in the Act.

The Act protects a 'declared World Heritage property' which is a property:

- included in the World Heritage List kept under Art 11 of the World Heritage Convention; or
- specified in a declaration by the Minister in the *Gazette*. (s 13)

Listed properties

Australia has 16 World Heritage places recognised as of outstanding universal significance, listed on the World Heritage List. The properties in New South Wales, and the category of values for which they were listed, are:

- Willandra Lakes Region (natural and cultural significance);
- Lord Howe Island group (natural);
- Central Eastern Rainforest reserves (natural); and
- Greater Blue Mountains Area (natural).[21]

The Sydney Opera House is a potential nomination for inclusion.

The World Heritage Committee of UNESCO enters properties on the World Heritage List established under the Convention, after the properties are nominated by a national government. Before nominating a property to the Committee, the Australian government uses its 'best endeavours to reach agreement' with any owner or occupier of the property and, in New South Wales, with the State government, on the proposed submission and management arrangements for the property (s 314).

Public notice

Public notice is given when:

- a property is submitted to the World Heritage Committee or a submission is withdrawn;

---

20 Australian Government Department of Environment and Heritage, Sydney Opera House Nomination by the Government of Australia for inscription on the World Heritage List, Part 5, Protection and Management of the Property, Canberra, 2006, <www.deh.gov.au/heritage> at 69.

21 See Boer and Wiffen, above n 9, at 20.

- the boundaries of a property are extended or restricted; or
- a property is included in, or removed from, the World Heritage List. (s 315)

Properties that may be specified in a declaration and thus attract protection under the EPBCA are:

- properties submitted to the World Heritage Committee for the World Heritage List; or
- properties with World Heritage values that are under threat. (s 14)

Unless the threat is imminent, the Commonwealth government will consult the NSW government on a proposal to include a specified property in the State in a declaration (s 14).

Offences

A person is guilty of an offence for taking an action, or recklessly taking an action, with a significant impact on the World Heritage values of a declared World Heritage property (s 15A). A note in s 15A refers to Chapter 2 of the *Criminal Code* (Cth) which sets out general principles of criminal responsibility.

The defences to these offences are linked to the Act's management provisions. An offence will not be committed if other procedures under the EPBCA have been taken. These are:

- that there is prior approval or exemption, or, in the words of the Act:
    - o an approval of the taking of the action is in operation under Pt 9 of the EPBCA;
    - o Part 4 of the Act lets the person take the action without an approval under Pt 9;
- that a management scheme is in force that covers the proposed action or, in the words of the Act:
    - o there is in force a decision of the Minister under Pt 7 Div 2 of the Act that s 15A is not a 'controlling provision' for the action, and if the decision was made because the Minister believed that the action would be taken in a manner specified in the notice of the decision under s 77, the action is taken in that manner;
    - o the action is an action described in s 160(2) (which describes actions whose authorisation is subject to a special environmental process). (s 15A)

Managing World Heritage properties

Part 15 of the EPBCA includes World Heritage properties amongst the protected areas regulated under the Act. Part 15 requires management plans for World Heritage properties, consistent with:

- Australia's obligations under the World Heritage Convention; and
- Australian World Heritage management principles.

Australian World Heritage management principles are set out in the EPBCR and contain principles for the management of natural and cultural heritage as defined in the World Heritage Convention (s 323).

The Commonwealth uses its best endeavours to ensure that a plan for World Heritage properties in New South Wales is prepared and implemented in co-operation with the NSW government (s 321).

Public notice is given of the making of a plan (s 317). Plans are reviewed every 5 years as to whether they remain consistent with Australian World Heritage management principles (s 319).

Commonwealth responsibilities

The Commonwealth and its agencies take all reasonable steps to act consistently with the World Heritage Convention, Australian World Heritage management principles and a property's management plan (s 322). The Commonwealth may give financial and other assistance to New South Wales and to any other person for the protection or conservation of a declared World Heritage property (s 324).

National and Commonwealth Heritage significance

The EPBCA creates two other heritage lists:

- National Heritage List of National Heritage places; and
- Commonwealth Heritage List of Commonwealth Heritage places (Chapter 5, Pt 15)

as a 'a written record of places and their heritage values' (ss 324C(1) and 341C(1)). Thus, the concepts of a place and its values, introduced above, are important as the bases of the lists.

National Heritage place

A National Heritage place is a place within the Australian jurisdiction with a National Heritage value (s 324C). The EPBCA protects heritage values. A place has a National Heritage value if it meets one of the National Heritage criteria set out in the EPBCR, and the 'National Heritage value of the place is the place's heritage value that causes the place to meet the criterion' (s 324D). The list of National Heritage places is thought likely to develop into a list of a relatively small number of iconic sites.

Commonwealth Heritage place

A Commonwealth Heritage place is a place with a Commonwealth heritage value. A place has a Commonwealth Heritage value if it meets one of the Commonwealth Heritage criteria set out in the EPBCR, and the Commonwealth Heritage value of the place is the place's heritage value that causes the place to meet the criterion (s 341D). Commonwealth Heritage places are places in a Commonwealth area or, if outside the Australian jurisdiction, owned or leased by the Commonwealth or one of its agencies (s 341C) – that is, areas where the Commonwealth has some administrative authority.

Criteria

The EPBCR contain criteria for the cultural, natural, Indigenous and historic and other heritage values (ss 324D and 341D; regs 10.01A and 10.03A).[22]

22 For a discussion of indigenous heritage in Australia, see Boer and Wiffen, above n 9, Chapter 9.

Place

When referring to National or Commonwealth Heritage places:

> 'place' includes:
> (a) a location, area or region; and
> (b) a building or other structure, or group of buildings or other structures (which may include equipment, furniture, fittings and articles associated or connected with the building or structure, or group of buildings or structures); and
> (c) in relation to the protection, maintenance, preservation or improvement of a place – the immediate surroundings of a thing in paragraph (a) or (b). (s 528)

The introduction to this chapter has stressed the breadth of what may be termed heritage in Australian legislation. Note how this is reflected in this definition, which includes things 'associated or connected with ' a 'building or site', and 'the immediate surroundings'.

Values

The EPBCA protects the values of heritage places. As indicated above, heritage value is tied in with the criteria set out in the EPBCR (ss 324D and 341D).

The two categories have different thresholds. National Heritage places have *outstanding* heritage value to the nation (s 324D and reg 10.01A(2)) and Commonwealth Heritage places have *significant* heritage values (s 341D and reg 10.03A). Therefore, a place has heritage value because of the place's outstanding or significant:

- importance in the course, or pattern, of Australia's natural or cultural history;
- possession of uncommon, rare or endangered aspects of Australia's natural or cultural history;
- potential to yield information that will contribute to an understanding of Australia's natural or cultural history;
- importance in demonstrating the principal characteristics of a class of Australia's natural or cultural places or environments;
- importance in exhibiting particular aesthetic characteristics valued by a community or cultural group;
- importance in demonstrating a high degree of creative or technical achievement at a particular period;
- strong or special association with a particular community or cultural group for social, cultural or spiritual reasons;
- special association with the life or works of a person, or group of persons, of importance in Australia's natural or cultural history; or
- importance as part of Indigenous tradition. (regs 10.01A and 10.03A)

Location of a place

The location of a heritage place may be important for what the Commonwealth may do to protect it.

The Commonwealth's constitutional powers are most extensive in Commonwealth areas. Relevant to New South Wales, a Commonwealth area consists of land, and the airspace over it:

- owned or leased by the Commonwealth or a Commonwealth agency;
- in Jervis Bay;
- the coastal sea of Australia;
- the continental shelf and the waters over it;
- the waters of the exclusive economic zone and sea bed under those waters; and
- any other area of land, sea or seabed included in a Commonwealth reserve. (s 525)

Commonwealth Heritage places are heritage places in Commonwealth areas, or places outside Australia owned or leased by the Commonwealth or an agency (341C).

Management principles

The introduction to this chapter stressed that the EPBCA is designed to focus as much on long-term management as on the use of prohibitions and criminal sanctions. The EPBCR set out National and Commonwealth Heritage management principles, which are similar for both types of place (ss 341Y and 324Y; and EPBCR Schs 5B and 7B).

- The objective in managing places is to identify, protect, conserve, present and transmit, to all generations, their National or Commonwealth Heritage values.
- The management of places should use the best available knowledge, skills and standards for those places, and include ongoing technical and community input to decisions and actions that may have a significant impact on their National or Commonwealth Heritage values.
- The management of places should respect all heritage values of the place and seek to integrate, where appropriate, any Commonwealth, State, Territory and local government responsibilities for those places.
- The management of places should ensure that their use and presentation is consistent with the conservation of their National or Commonwealth Heritage values.
- The management of places should make timely and appropriate provision for community involvement, especially by people who:
  - have a particular interest in, or association with, the place; and
  - may be affected by the management of the place.
- Indigenous people are the primary source of information on the value of their heritage and the active participation of Indigenous people in identification, assessment and management is integral to the effective protection of Indigenous heritage values.
- The management of places should provide for regular monitoring, review and reporting on the conservation of National or Commonwealth Heritage values. (EPBCR Schs 5B and 7B)

Listing process

Heritage places derive much of their protection from being entered on a heritage list. Therefore, it is important to understand the listing process, including who nominates a place for listing and who decides whether to list. The processes for listing on the National Heritage List and the Commonwealth Heritage List are very similar and will be discussed together. The questions of how open the process is, and whether there is scope for public involvement at its various stages, will be addressed.

As will be seen proposing a place for listing on the two lists is by the Minister, the Australian Heritage Council or the public. Proposals for listing considered vexatious, frivolous or not in good faith may be rejected. The Australian Heritage Council provides expert advice on the suitability of a place for listing.

Usual listing process

The EPBCA describes a 'usual process' for listing, based on annual cycles of 12-month assessment periods, that is similar for the consideration of items for listing on the National Heritage List (Pt 15, Div 1A, Subdiv BA) and Commonwealth Heritage List (Pt 15, Div 3A, Subdiv BA).

The Minister invites nominations from the public of places for listing on each list (National Heritage List s 324J, and the Commonwealth Heritage List s 341H). Before calling for nominations for the National Heritage List, the Minister may set out heritage themes to be given priority in that assessment period (s 324H). Nominations are referred to the Australian Heritage Council (ss 324JA, 341H and 341J).

The Council prepares a list called the priority assessment lists, of places that it thinks should be assessed. These may be places nominated by the public or added by the Council. In considering what to include in the priority assessment list the Council has regard to, for:

- the National heritage list – any heritage themes nominated by the Minister; and
- for both the National and Commonwealth Heritage lists – the Council's own views as to what should be given priority, its capacity to make assessments while still performing its other functions and any other matter it considers appropriate. (ss 324JB, 324JC, 341JA, 341JB)

In the past all nominations were considered unless rejected as vexatious, frivolous or not in good faith. These provisions, inserted in 2006, may have the result that not all nominations from the public are considered.

> These amendments have the potential to allow the delay or indefinite postponement of assessment and eventual entry of a place on (a heritage list). The new process constitutes a departure from the principle of having an independent listing process based on heritage significance and a separation of the listing decision from downstream management decisions.[23]

The priority assessment lists are then referred to the Minister with details of why places have been included (ss 324JC, 341JC). The Minister finalises this list and, at this stage, may add or remove places (ss 324JE, 341JD). The finalised list is made

23 Australian Network of Environmental Defender's Offices Submission on the Environment and Heritage Amendment Bill (No 1) 2006, <www.edu.org.au> (accessed 23 January 2007), at 15.

available to the public (ss 324JF, 341JE). The Council invites public comment on the places on the priority assessment list (ss 324JG, 341JF), and then provided the Minister with an assessment of these places (ss 324JH, 341JG). Unless an extension is given, the assessment takes place within the assessment period (ss 324JI, 341JH). The Minister then includes an assessed place in the National or Commonwealth Heritage List, by a notice in the *Gazette* that sets out the assessed place's National or Commonwealth Heritage values. The Minister may also decide, in writing, not to include the assessed place in a List. The Minister's decisions are notified to the public, and, if practicable, notice of a decision to list is given to owners and occupiers of the place (ss 324JJ, 341JI).

Emergency listing

The EPBCA describes a standard emergency process for including places in the National Heritage List (Pt 15, Div 1A, Subdiv BB) and Commonwealth Heritage List (Pt 15, Div 3A, Subdiv BB).

If the Minister believes that a place has a National or Commonwealth heritage value that is under a likely and imminent threat of significant impact, the Minister may, by notice in the *Gazette,* include the place on the National Heritage List (s 324JL) or the Commonwealth Heritage List (s 341JK). The Minister then asks the Australian Heritage Council to assess the place (ss 324JM, 341JL). The Council publishes a notice, inviting comments (ss 324JN, 341JM). The Council then provides the Minister with its assessment of the place (ss 324JM, 324JP, 341JN, 341JO). The Minister has 12 months from the listing of the place to decide whether it should continue to be listed (ss 324JQ, 341JP).

Co-ordination with the Threatened Species Scientific Committee

Heritage in Australian heritage legislation includes natural aspects and the EPBCA provides a formal process for the Australian Heritage Council to co-ordinate with the Threatened Species Scientific Committee in making its assessments of places for listing on the National or Commonwealth Heritage Lists (ss 324JR, 324JS, 341JQ, 341JR).

Removal of places

The Minister may remove a place from the National or Commonwealth Heritage lists that no longer has, or contributes to, a relevant heritage value, or for defence or security reasons. The removal is notified in the *Gazette* with a statement of reasons, and on the internet. If the removal is for the loss of National or Commonwealth Heritage values, the instrument of removal is tabled in both houses of the Commonwealth Parliament and may be disallowed (ss 341L and 324L). The Minister seeks the advice of the Australian Heritage Council and public comment before removing a place (ss 341M and 324M).

A place must be removed from the Commonwealth Heritage List if it is no longer in a Commonwealth area (s 341L).

List of Overseas Places of Historic Significance to Australia

The 2006 amendments to the EPBCA removed the process whereby places outside Australia with National Heritage values could be placed on the National Heritage list and created a new List of Overseas Places of Historic Significance to Australia (s 390K). This list is the responsibility of the Minister, who may include a place on this list by a notice in the *Gazette*. The notice includes a statement of the place's historic significance to Australia, which must be 'outstanding'. The regulations may set out any matters the Minister is to have regard to in coming to this decision (s 390L). A place may also be removed from the list, or varied, by notice in the *Gazette* (s 390M). Up-to-date copies of the List of Overseas Places of Historic Significance to Australia are made publicly available free on request and on the internet (s 390Q).

Before taking any action, the Minister, currently the Environment Minister, informs the Minister for Foreign Affairs, and any other Minister whom the Environment Minister believes should be informed, and invites their comment (s 3390N). The Minister may also ask the Australian Heritage Council for advice (s 390P).

Consequences under the Environment Protection and Biodiversity Conservation Act 1999

The EPBCA provides civil and criminal penalties for taking an action 'that has, will have or is likely to have a significant impact' on the values of a National Heritage place (s 15B).

Offences in relation to Commonwealth Heritage places are covered by the general provision in the EPBCA that a person must not take an action on Commonwealth land, likely to have a significant impact on the environment, within Australia (s 27A), or in a Commonwealth Heritage place outside the Australian jurisdiction (s 27B). 'Environment' is defined to include the heritage values of places (s 528).

As National Heritage places may be located outside Commonwealth areas, the legal position under the Constitution is more complex. The main provisions of the EPBCA, s 15B 'Requirement for approval' and s 15C 'Offences', create offences by persons whose activities the Commonwealth may regulate. These include the Commonwealth itself, corporations and, in some circumstances, individuals.

The Commonwealth may regulate its own activities and those of Commonwealth agencies. 'Commonwealth agency' is a wide ranging concept and includes:

- Ministers in the Commonwealth government;
- persons who hold an office under a Commonwealth law;
- persons appointed to a position by the Governor-General or a Minister;
- bodies corporate established for a public purpose by a law of the Commonwealth; and
- companies where the Commonwealth owns more than half of the voting stock. (s 528)

As for corporations, the Commonwealth may, under its corporations power, regulate the activities of 'foreign corporations, and trading and financial corporations formed within the limits of the Commonwealth' (Constitution s 51(xx)). The EPBCA describes these as constitutional corporations (ss 15B(1) and 15C(1)).

As for individuals, the Commonwealth may only regulate the actions of individuals under one of its other powers, for example, where:

- the person is an accessory to the actions of the Commonwealth, or a constitutional corporation;
- the person is engaged in trade or commerce across Australia's internal or international borders;
- the prohibited action takes place in a Commonwealth area, or a Territory;
- the threatened heritage values are Indigenous values;
- the action and the place are outside the Australian jurisdiction; or
- Australia has obligations under a treaty (ss 15B and 15C).

The Act provides for civil penalties of up to 5000 penalty units for an individual and 50,000 for a corporation (s 15B), and criminal penalties of imprisonment for up to seven years, a fine of up to 420 penalty units, or both (s 15C(13)). A penalty unit is $110.[24]

Responsibilities of Commonwealth agencies

The Commonwealth and its agencies have added responsibility for places they own that have or might have National or Commonwealth Heritage values.

They must assist the Minister and the Australian Heritage Council to identify, assess and monitor a place's National or Commonwealth Heritage values (ss 324Z and 341Z) and keep a register of places and any heritage values (s 341ZB). They also must not take any action that has, will have or is likely to have an adverse impact on the National or Commonwealth Heritage values of places unless:

- there is no feasible and prudent alternative to taking the action;
- all measures that can reasonably be taken to mitigate the impact of the action on those values are taken (s 341ZC); and
- the agency has asked the Minister for advice (s 341ZD).

Where a Commonwealth agency signs a contract to sell a National or Commonwealth Heritage place, it must:

- give the Minister 40 days notice; and
- unless it is unnecessary or impractical – include a covenant in the contract to protect the place's National or Commonwealth Heritage values.

If the agency has not included a covenant, or if the covenant is insufficient to ensure the protection of the place's values, the Minister is informed before a contract is entered into. The Minister then attempts to enter into a conservation agreement with the prospective buyer, or informs the agency of what other measures it might take (ss 341ZE and 324ZA).

Commonwealth agencies prepare a heritage strategy, consistent with Commonwealth Heritage management principles, for managing places they own or control to identify and conserve their heritage values (s 341ZA). The strategy includes a statement of the agency's objective for the management of its heritage places and how this operates within the agency's corporate planning framework. The strategy also outlines various processes, including, for example, for:

---

24 See *Crimes Act 1914* (Cth) s 4AA.

- consultation and liaison with other government agencies, and the community:
- resolution of conflict;
- monitoring, reviewing and reporting; and training and promoting community awareness. (EPBCR Sch 7C)

Commonwealth agencies produce management plans to protect and manage the values of Commonwealth Heritage places it owns or controls (s 341S). Public notice is given of a plan (s 341S).

EPBCA as developing legislation

There is surprisingly little case law on the use of the EPBCA, and on its application to heritage issues. Recent interesting cases raise the issue of the type of legislation it is, and of the significance of including national laws for the protection of heritage places, including World Heritage properties, within national environmental legislation. What is the significance for heritage protection of the following?

> The EPBC Act is a member of a global family of laws based upon the United States National Environment Policy Act of 1969, triggering environmental impact assessment for projects that 'are likely to have a significant impact on the environment'.[25]

In relation to World Heritage places the wording is 'significant impact on the World Heritage values of a declared World Heritage property' (s 15A), and two interesting cases examine the import of these words.

Flying Foxes case[26]

This case relates to the Wet Tropics World Heritage Area. The facts are that a farmer had erected 14 aerial electric fences, in a grid pattern to electrocute flying foxes attacking the farmer's lychee orchard. The orchard was 60 hectares in area and the grids were 6.4 kilometres in length. The orchard was adjacent to the Wet Tropics World Heritage Area in Queensland. Deaths of flying foxes in the 2000-01 season from electrocution from impact with the grid were estimated at 9900 to 10,880. The total Australian population of the Spectacled Flying Fox was estimated at less than 100,000. The farmer's actions could halve that population within five years and make the species endangered. The court was satisfied that the action of installing and operating the grid, taken outside the World Heritage area, was likely to have a significant impact on the world heritage values of the Wet Tropics World Heritage Area. The animal is 'part of the record of the mixing of faunas of the Australian and Asian continental plates following their connection'. Also, the species 'contributes to the character of the Wet Tropics World Heritage Area as "one of the most significant regional ecosystems in the world" and as an important and significant natural habitat for in-situ conservation'.[27] The court granted an injunction restraining the operation of the grid.

25 McGrath, C, 'Swirls in the stream of Australian environmental law: Debate on the EPBC Act' (2006) 23 *EPLJ* 165 at 182, citing Wood, C, *Environmental Impact Assessment: A Comparative Review* (Prentice Hall, 1995) Chapter 9.

26 *Booth v Bosworth* (2001) 114 FCR 39; [2001] FCA 1453, discussed in McGrath, above n 24.

27 *Booth v Bosworth*, taken from Summary at [2001] FCA 1453.

Subsequently, the farmer sought administrative approval for the grid, which was refused. The Queensland State Government announced that it would no longer approve the use of grids.

Note that the farmer's orchard was adjacent to, not in, the World Heritage area, and the values seen to be affected were the continued existence of the flying foxes.

The action was brought by a member of the public, also raising issues of public interest litigation and rules as to standing to approach the courts.

Nathan Dam case[28]

A second even more startling case considered the building of a dam, and whether actions of persons other than the dam builder could be seen in the words of s 15A, as 'likely to have a significant impact on the World Heritage values of a declared World Heritage property'. More striking for heritage, perhaps, is that those actions were 500 kilometres from the World Heritage area.

This case also arose in Queensland and related to the Great Barrier Reef World Heritage Area. A major dam was proposed in the centre of the State to supply water for an expansion of agriculture in the area. There was a likelihood that chemicals from the agricultural development, particularly cotton farming, that the dam would facilitate would have a significant impact on the Great Barrier Reef World Heritage Area. The Great Barrier Reef World Heritage Area was 500 kilometres downstream and the Commonwealth Minister for the Environment, who is responsible for the administration of the EPBCA, refused to consider the dam building as an activity to which he should have regard under the EPBCA. Justice Kiefel in the Federal Court decided that that decision was incorrect and that the potential impacts should be considered.

The court did not seem to be concerned at the distance of the dam from the World Heritage place, and in its summary concentrates on the question of whose actions the Minister must consider:

> The Environment Minister considered that the relevant statutory provisions requires him only to consider the effects of the operation of the dam by the entity proposing it and did not extend to consequences which might follow other persons' decisions to use chemicals. The Court has held that the enquiry is a wider one and the Environment Minister is therefore obliged to reconsider the matter.[29]

For heritage advocates, these cases are exciting examples of using the environmental impact assessment model of legislation in heritage legislation, and how this can lead to very broad inquiries as to the impact of actions on heritage places.

State heritage legislation

The *Heritage Act 1977* (NSW) is the most comprehensive piece of State legislation relating to heritage. The Act sets up the Heritage Council with a co-ordinating role for the State's heritage. It also sets up the State Heritage Register, which, before

---

28 *Queensland Conservation Council v Minister for Environment and Heritage* [2003] FCA 1463 (Kiefel J), affirmed on appeal, *Minister for Environment and Heritage v Queensland Conservation Council* (2004) 139 FCR 24, discussed in McGrath, above n 25.

29 Taken from Summary at [2003] FCA 1463.

1988, was a record of permanent conservation orders placed on properties to give them protection. Under the 1988 amendments to the *Heritage Act*,[30] New South Wales moved to a listing system. Protection is given to heritage items entered on the State Heritage Register.

Items are also protected under the *Heritage Act* when:

- covered by an Interim Heritage order;
- covered by a Heritage Agreement;
- declared to be an historic shipwreck; or
- listed on the Heritage and Conservation Register of a NSW government instrumentality.

Additionally, orders may be made under the Act for temporary protection.

Other agencies with an interest in heritage will be discussed below. The National Parks and Wildlife Service, part of the NSW Department of Environment and Conservation, holds sites with heritage values, and the Historic Houses Trust is a specialist body in the area of the built heritage.

The *Heritage Act* protects items of the 'environmental heritage', which it defines as 'places, buildings, works, relics, movable objects and precincts of State or local heritage significance' (s 4). State or local significance is determined through historic, scientific, cultural, social, archaeological, architectural, natural or aesthetic value (ss 4, 4A). The word 'cultural' includes Indigenous heritage.

Heritage administration

Heritage protection in the State government is administered by:

- the Minister with responsibility for the *Heritage Act*;
- the NSW Heritage Council established under the *Heritage Act*; and
- public servants in the NSW Heritage Office at Parramatta.

The Minister currently administering the *Heritage Act* is the Minister for Planning in the NSW government. As explained below, it is the Minister who decides whether a heritage item should be listed in the State Heritage Register, with the protection that entails.

The Heritage Council is created by the *Heritage Act* (s 7) to advise the Minister on the protection of heritage items. The Council consists of 15 members chosen for their expertise:

- the chairperson;
- four government members – the Government Architect, the Director-General of National Parks and Wildlife, the Director of the Heritage Office and an officer in the Minister's Department;
- four members nominated by relevant organisations – the National Trust of Australia (NSW), the Royal Australian Historical Society, the Labor Council of New South Wales, the New South Wales Chapter of the Royal Australian Institute of Architects, and the New South Wales Division of the Royal Australian Planning Institute; and

---

30 *Heritage Amendment Act 1988.*

- six members from persons with expertise in Aboriginal heritage; the building development and property industries; corporate promotion; the conservation of the environmental heritage; local government; movable heritage; natural heritage; the property rights of citizens, and rural interests. (ss 8, 9)

The main function of the Heritage Council is to advise the Minister, including on such topics as conservation, exhibition and display, and access and information. The Heritage Council makes recommendations to the Minister on listing items on the State Heritage Register (s 32), on grants and loans from the Heritage Conservation Fund and the Heritage Incentive Fund (s 106) and on heritage agreements (s 39).

The Heritage Council maintains the following databases:

- the State Heritage Register;
- the register of interim heritage orders, other orders and notices under the *Heritage Act*, and heritage agreements (s 22).
- the State Heritage Inventory listing items of State and local significance (s 21); and
- the Register of Shipwrecks (s 49).

The Heritage Council issues certificates as to whether an item is on the State Heritage Register or is affected by an interim heritage order or other orders (ss 120M, 167).

State Heritage Register

The State Heritage Register lists places, works, relics, movable objects or precincts that the Minister considers to be of State heritage significance. The Minister directs that an item be listed, but only on the recommendation of the Heritage Council (s 32).

The State Heritage Council's criteria are whether an item:

- is important in the course or pattern of NSW cultural or natural history;
- has strong or special association with the life or works of a person, or group of persons, of importance in NSW cultural or natural history;
- is important in demonstrating aesthetic characteristics and/or a high degree of creative or technical achievement in New South Wales;
- has strong or special association with a particular community or cultural group in New South Wales for social, cultural or spiritual reasons;
- has potential to yield information that will contribute to an understanding of NSW cultural or natural history;
- possesses uncommon, rare or endangered aspects of New South Wales' cultural or natural history; or
- is important in demonstrating the principal characteristics of a class of New South Wales' cultural or natural places, or environments.[31]

The first step in listing on the State Heritage Register is a recommendation to the Minister from the Heritage Council (ss 32, 33).

31 See <www.heritage.gov.au/docs/criteria.pdf> (accessed 13 July 2006).

Public notice is given that the Council is considering making a recommendation for listing an item. Submissions are invited by written notice to affected owners or occupiers, and by a notice published in a newspaper in the locality (s 33). Submissions may include issues relating to heritage significance that:

- the item is not of heritage significance; and
- the item's long-term conservation is not necessary.

The Act also makes it clear that submissions may address questions that go beyond heritage significance, that listing would;

- make the item incapable of reasonable or economic use, or
- cause undue financial hardship. (s 33)

The Minister has 14 days after receiving a recommendation from the Heritage Council to consider their advice and make a decision whether to direct listing, or to seek further advice. The Minister may refer the question to a Ministerial Review Panel, or to a Commission of Inquiry. A Ministerial Review Panel is appointed by the Minister and reports within 30 days (s 35). A Commission of Inquiry follows the procedures set out in s 120 of the EPAA. Owners, mortgagees lessees of relevant land, owners of other items, the local council, the Heritage Council and, if granted leave, any other person may appear before a Commission of Inquiry (s 36).

The Heritage Council gives affected owners and occupiers notice of the Minister's decision. If the decision is to list, it proceeds with the listing and gives notice in the *Gazette*. The listing takes effect from the date of publication in the *Gazette* (s 37). A similar procedure is followed for removal of a listing of an item (s 38).

Interim listing

Interim heritage orders may be made by the Minister (s 24) or, if authorised by the Minister, by local councils (s 25) over places, works, relics, movable objects or precincts that, on further study, may be of State or local heritage significance. An order takes effect when it is published in the *Gazette* and remains in force for up to 12 months. Orders may be revoked (s 29).

Notice is not given of an interim heritage order until it is made (s 26). Then the order is published in the *Gazette*, and notice is given to the Chairperson of the Heritage Council, affected owners or occupiers, and in a newspaper in the locality (s 28). An affected owner or occupier may appeal to the Land and Environment Court against the making of an interim heritage order (s 30).

Prior approval of work

The major device for protecting items under the *Heritage Act* is through the concept of controlled activities (Pt 4, Div 2). Prior approval from the Heritage Council is required before a controlled activity may be carried out that may affect heritage items listed on the State Heritage Register or covered by an interim heritage order. Controlled activities are:

- demolishing the building or work;
- damaging or despoiling the place, precinct or land;
- moving, damaging or despoiling the relic or movable object;

- excavating any land to expose or move a relic;
- carrying out any development of the site;
- altering the building, work, relic or movable object;
- displaying notices or advertisements; or
- damaging, destroying or removing trees or other vegetation on the place. (s 57)

A local council is the approval body for items covered by an interim heritage order made by the council (s 56). Councils have no control over actions that are part of State Significant Development or development by the Crown (s 57).

The Minister or local councils may exempt activities from the approval process (s 57), which relate to minor maintenance work on an item.[32] Heritage agreements under the Act may also specify permitted activities.

Approvals under other legislation that are inconsistent with approvals under the *Heritage Act* are void (s 68).

Approvals

For approval of a controlled activity, an owner makes application to the 'approval body', that is the Heritage Council or the local council. The approval body may approve an application, with or without conditions, or refuse it. An application that would result in the demolition of the item must be refused, unless the item is unsafe, will be relocated or is part of a precinct that will not have its significance detrimentally affected by the demolition (s 63).

The Heritage Council or local council gives public notice of applications for activities that it believes would materially affect the significance of a heritage item in a daily newspaper, and places any plans, specifications or similar documents, lodged with the application, on public exhibition. The public may make written representations (s 61). Notice is also given of the decision (s 76).

An applicant dissatisfied with the decision may appeal under Pt 4, Div 4, Subdivs 1 and 2 of the Act to:

- the Minister from a decision of the Heritage Council; or
- the NSW Land and Environment Court –
    - from a decision of the Heritage Council that was part of an integrated development application under the EPAA (s 3L); or
    - from the decision of a local council (s 70A).

The Minister may appoint a Commission of Inquiry to hold a hearing and prepare a report (ss 71, 78).

Heritage agreements

Heritage agreements provide another form of protection for listed items. Under general contract and property law, an owner may, of course, agree to do whatever is

32 See NSW Heritage Office, *Standard Exemptions for works requiring heritage Council Approval* (Heritage Information Series, 2006), <www.heritage.gov.au/docs/info_standard exemptios2006.pdf> (accessed 13 July 2006).

necessary to maintain the heritage significance of a property, which the *Heritage Act* facilitates (Pt 3B – Heritage Agreements). The Minister, after advice from the Heritage Council, may enter into a heritage agreement with the owner of an item listed on the State Heritage Register (s 39).

A heritage agreement may include provisions relating to:

- conservation of the item;
- financial, technical and professional advice or assistance;
- the review of the valuation of the item or land;
- restrictions on the use of the item or the land;
- requirements that work be carried out;
- standards for any works;
- restrictions on kinds of works that may be carried out;
- exemption from restrictions on controlled activities; and
- public appreciation and public inspection of the item. (s 40)

The Registrar-General notes the heritage agreement against the title of the affected land and the agreement binds subsequent owners.

Action may be taken against a breach or a threatened breach of a heritage agreement by injunction proceedings in the Land and Environment Court (s 44).

Other measures for the conservation of the environmental heritage

The *Heritage Act* provides other ways for conserving heritage items, and some apply to items that are not listed on the State Heritage Register or covered by an interim heritage order (Pt 6).

Curtailing other laws

Many heritage items are old and will not meet modern planning and building standards, for example, fire protection standards.[33] Therefore, the Act provides that the Minister may protect a heritage item and its heritage values by suspending any other Act, rule, regulation, by-law, ordinance, proclamation, agreement, covenant, or instrument that regulates, restricts or prohibits the conservation of a listed heritage item (s 129).

In a controversial move, a recent piece of legislation went the other way and excluded the operation of the *Heritage Act*. The *Redfern-Waterloo Authority Act 2004* provides that the *Heritage Act* does not apply in the area of the Act. The Minister responsible for this area must, however, consult the Heritage Council on development proposals that would otherwise come within the provisions of the *Heritage Act*. The development may proceed if the Minister is satisfied that it is necessary for the 'sustainable improvement of the operational area'.[34]

---

33 See, eg, *Royal Automobile Club of Australia v Council of City of Sydney* (1991) 74 LGRA 121.

34 *Redfern-Waterloo Authority Act 2004* (NSW) s 29.

Financial assistance

The Minister, on the recommendation of the Heritage Council, may give grants or loans for heritage items from two funds under the Act – the Heritage Conservation Fund (s 103) and the Heritage Incentive Fund (s 105A). The Minister may also execute a guarantee for the repayment of money used for conservation purposes (s 108).

Relief from rates and taxes

A heritage valuation is made for land affected by a listing on the State Heritage Register for the calculation of rates and taxes, including land tax, that takes into account the restricted uses that the listing involves (Pt 6, Div 6).

Acquisition or resumption

Acquisition of a heritage item may be achieved under the *Heritage Act* by a corporation established under the Act called the 'Minister administering the *Heritage Act 1977*' (s 102). Acquisition by agreement or compulsory process follows procedures under the *Land Acquisition (Just Terms Compensation) Act 1991* and the *Public Works Act 1912* (s 112). The corporation may also accept gifts for the purposes of the Act (s 115).

Maintenance and repair

The Heritage Council may give an owner an order to bring a heritage item up to standard (ss 120, 120A, 120B). The *Heritage Regulation 2005* sets out minimum standards of maintenance and repair for heritage items to provide protection from damage or deterioration due to weather; damage or destruction by fire; for security (including fencing and surveillance measures to prevent vandalism), and essential maintenance and repair necessary to prevent serious or irreparable damage or deterioration (ss 118, 119; *Heritage Regulation* Pt 3). The Land and Environment Court may hear appeals against the order (ss 120F, 120L). The order binds subsequent owners of the land (s 120H).

There are a number of steps that may be taken if an order is not complied with.

The Heritage Council make carry out the work, doing whatever is necessary or convenient to give effect to its order. The Council may recover its expenses from the person who should have complied with the order (s 120K).

The corporation may resume or appropriate the land (s 121).

The Minster may order that no development or use of the land take place for up to 10 years, other than for conservation reasons, or that any development may not exceed the building envelope occupied by the building at the time the maintenance and repair order was served (s 121).

Protective orders

The *Heritage Act* provides for a variety of orders that may be made by the Heritage Council to protect heritage items.

Stop work orders – unlisted items

The Minister or the Chairperson of the Heritage Council may order that work that may harm a building, work, relic, or place not on the State Heritage Register not be carried out, for a period of up to 40 days. The order takes effect without notice when affixed to the endangered item (s 136) and prevails over permission for the work given under other legislation (s 137A).

Orders of the court

Where a person has committed an offence under the *Heritage Act*, the Land and Environment Court may, in addition to any other order it may make (s 155):

- restrain use of a building;
- order demolition; or
- require restoration or reinstatement of land to its condition before the breach of the *Heritage Act*. (s 154)

State government owned heritage items

Australian governments and their agencies own a large amount of property, some of which will have heritage significance. Some agencies, like the Historic Houses Trust, are specifically set up for the purpose of holding heritage items and will be discussed in more detail below. Other agencies use heritage items in their ordinary work. New South Wales has, for example, many heritage schools, railway stations and hospitals still being used for their original purpose. The *Heritage Act*, like the EPBCA, makes particular provision for heritage items in government hands.

Recent legislation discussed in this chapter 'binds the Crown', so that the government and government agencies have the same duties under heritage legislation as natural and corporate individuals (EPBCA s 4; *Heritage Act* s 5).

Heritage and Conservation Register

New South Wales government agencies keep a Heritage and Conservation Register containing details of heritage items:

- listed on the State Heritage Register or subject to an interim heritage order;
- listed in an environmental planning instrument under the EPAA; or
- covered by guidelines issued by the Heritage Council as possibly suitable for these categories.

The Heritage and Conservation Register is available for public inspection and a copy is supplied to the Heritage Council.

Items on a Heritage and Conservation Register are to be maintained with due diligence according to the State Owned Heritage Management Principles. The agency must also comply with any heritage asset management guidelines issued by the Heritage Council. An agency reports on its compliance with these requirements, and on the condition of any items entered in its register, in its Annual Report to Parliament made under the *Annual Reports (Statutory Bodies) Act 1984* or the *Annual Reports (Departments) Act 1985*.

An agency notifies the Heritage Council removes any item from, or transfers ownership, ceases to occupy, or demolishes, an item in its Register (s 170).

National Parks and Wildlife Act 1974 (NSW)

The NSW government is the owner of a huge area of land in the State's parks system that is maintained for what might broadly be seen as heritage purposes. This land is generally seen as important for its natural values, and the *National Parks and Wildlife Act 1974* (NPWA) is comprehensively discussed in Chapter 9 largely from this perspective. The Act and the parks system managed under it are, however, also important for maintaining land for its cultural values, both Indigenous and non-indigenous, as is apparent in some of the titles to the major categories of parks and reserves:

- national parks (s 30E);
- historic sites (s 30F);
- regional parks (s 30H);
- karst conservation reserves (s 30J);
- State conservation areas (s 30G); and
- Aboriginal areas (s 30K).

When the Act refers to cultural values it generally refers to cultural values within landscape, including in:

- places, objects and features of significance to Aboriginal people;
- places of social value to the people of New South Wales; and
- places of historic, architectural or scientific significance. (s 2A(b))

Heritage objects

In the past, heritage law has to a large extent maintained a traditional distinction between land and objects or, in legal terminology, between real and personal property. This distinction is becoming less relevant in modern heritage legislation and much of the commentary above on heritage items applies both to land and objects. Nonetheless, because of its previous importance it is useful to discuss the distinction.

The Commonwealth EPBCA provides for the listing of a 'place', which is defined to include:

> (b) a building or other structure, or group of buildings or other structures (which may include equipment, furniture, fittings and articles associated or connected with the building or structure, or group of buildings or structures) ... (s 528, emphasis added)

Similarly the *Heritage Act* defines 'environmental heritage' as those 'places, buildings, works, *relics, moveable objects* and precincts that are of State or local heritage significance' (emphasis added). In the *Heritage Act*, a relic is any deposit, object or material evidence more than 50 years old relating to the non-Aboriginal settlement of New South Wales. Relics are part of the environmental heritage if of historic, scientific, cultural, social, archaeological, architectural, natural or aesthetic significance to the State, or to the local area (s 4(1)).

Objects under specialist legislation

Heritage law needs also to protect objects that have become separated from places to which they give significance. There are specialised laws dealing with the import and export of objects and with shipwrecks. These are of limited relevance to this book and are only mentioned for the sake of completeness.

Commonwealth and State museums

While they are outside the scope of a book concentrating on environmental law, major holders of heritage objects in New South Wales are museums located in the State, such as Commonwealth museums, like the National Maritime Museum, and State museums like the Australian Museum, the Art Gallery of New South Wales, the Powerhouse Museum and the State's extensive network of regional museums and galleries.

National Parks and Wildlife Act 1974

Special provision is made for Aboriginal objects under Pt 6 of the NPWA. This is discussed below under Indigenous Heritage.

Movable cultural heritage

The *Protection of Movable Cultural Heritage Act 1986* (Cth) was passed by the Australian Parliament to give effect in Australia to the *International Convention on the Means of Prohibiting and Preventing the Illicit Import, Export and Transfer of Ownership of Cultural Property*.[35] The Act regulates the import and export of objects important to Australia for ethnographical, archaeological, historical, literary, artistic, scientific or technological reasons. Categories of objects are set out in the legislation. The most relevant here are:

- objects recovered from the soil or inland waters;
- objects recovered from the coastal sea or waters above the continental shelf, or the seabed or subsoil beneath the sea or water;
- objects relating to Aborigines or Torres Strait Islanders.

Further categories in the *Protection of Movable Cultural Regulations 1987* (Cth) include:

- archaeological objects of non-Australian origin;
- natural science objects.

Schedule 1 to the Regulations sets out the National Heritage Control List of objects from these categories that are subject to export control. Class A objects may only be exported with a certificate and Class B objects may be exported in accordance with a certificate or a permit (s 8). The National Cultural Heritage Committee advises the Minister on applications for certificates.

---

35 Paris, 17 November 1970; Aust TS 1990 No 2; 823 UNTS 231.

Historic shipwrecks

Historic shipwrecks are a particular category of heritage item, and those in New South Wales are regulated under the:

- *Historic Shipwrecks Act 1976* (Cth);
- Part 3C of the *Heritage Act*; and
- *Marine Parks Regulation 1999* (NSW) reg 18.

Historic Shipwrecks Act 1976 (Cth)

The *Historic Shipwrecks Act* provides for a Register of Historic Shipwrecks as a list of historic shipwrecks setting out details of ships, associated articles and protected zones. The Register is available for public inspection (s 12). Items are entered in the Register by a declaration of the Commonwealth Minister in the government *Gazette* that:

- the remains of a ship situated in Australian waters or in waters above the continental shelf of Australia;
- Dutch shipwrecks; and
- Papua New Guinea shipwrecks;

are of historic significance (s 5). Articles associated with the ship may be registered even if removed from the site (s 5). A protected zone is an area of sea or land, containing a historic wreck or relic (s 7).

A person in possession of an article relating to a historic shipwreck must notify the Minister (s 9). The Minister may grant permits authorising exploration for or recovery of shipwrecks and relics. The permit may authorise actions that would otherwise be prohibited (s 15).

Heritage Act 1977 (NSW)

Part 3C of the *Heritage Act* protects historic shipwrecks in State waters. The NSW Minister, with the advice of the Heritage Council, may declare the remains of a ship to be an historic shipwreck, by order in the *Gazette* (s 48). The Heritage Council maintains a Register of Shipwrecks (s 49). It is an offence to move, damage or destroy an historic shipwreck without an excavation permit under s 139 of the Act, unless for safety reasons or in an environmental emergency (s 51).

Marine Parks Regulation 1999 (NSW)

Marine parks legislation in New South Wales provides for the creation of special purpose zones in marine parks. The objects for a special purpose zone may cater for special facilities and features in the zone, such as 'shipwrecks' (reg 18).

Alternatives to listing

This chapter has concentrated on the protection of heritage items through the device of listing in heritage inventories operating in New South Wales. Important heritage items, both natural and cultural, are protected under legislation that uses general concepts from property law, like ownership and covenants.

Protection through ownership

An owner of a heritage item may protect simply through the normal rights of ownership. The parks system under the NPWA, discussed above and in Chapter 9, is a very important example of this. The *Heritage Act*, as discussed above, also uses the concept of property rights by assisting owners to enter into conservation agreements with heritage bodies.

Commonwealth alternatives – Sydney Harbour Federation Trust Act 2001 (Cth)

At the Commonwealth level, an important statutory owner of heritage items in New South Wales is a Commonwealth agency, the Sydney Harbour Federation Trust. This Trust was established to take control of land with important cultural and natural heritage values on the shores of Sydney Harbour at Georges Heights, Middle Head, North Head and Watsons Bay, near the entrance to Sydney Harbour, and at Cockatoo Island and Woolwich, further into the Harbour (Trust land). This land was originally acquired in the 19th century for defence purposes, a use which is now redundant. The Commonwealth Parliament, under the *Sydney Harbour Federation Trust Act 2001*

> intends to conserve and preserve land in the Sydney Harbour region for the benefit of present and future generations of Australians. ... Suitable land with significant environmental and heritage values will be returned to the people of Australia.
>
> The Parliament intends to establish the Sydney Harbour Federation Trust as a transitional body to manage the land and facilitate its return in good order. The Trust will transfer suitable land to New South Wales for inclusion in the national parks and reserves system. (Preamble)

The Act established the Sydney Harbour Federation Trust whose objects include:

> (a) to ensure that management of Trust land contributes to enhancing the amenity of the Sydney Harbour region;
> (b) to protect, conserve and interpret the environmental and heritage values of Trust land; ...
> (d) to establish and manage suitable Trust land as a park on behalf of the Commonwealth as the national government ... (s 6)

A major function of the Trust is 'to rehabilitate, remediate, develop, enhance and manage Trust land, by itself or in cooperation with other institutions or persons, in accordance with the plans' (s 7).

The Trust is required to 'co-operate with New South Wales, affected councils and the community in furthering the above objects' (s 6). In a recent example, the New South Wales Government leased its interest in 72 hectares of land at the former School of Artillery site, North Head to the Trust to 'create a sanctuary on North Head which will focus on the fauna, flora and geology of this iconic location'.[36]

The Act requires plans to be prepared for the Trust land (Pt 5) and submitted to the Minister for approval (s 31). The Commonwealth and its agencies must act in accordance with the relevant plan in carrying out activities on the land (s 37). The Trust establishes community advisory committees for each plan area (s 57).

---

36 Hon Greg Hunt, Hon Tony Abbot, 'Wildlife Sanctuary planned for Sydney's North Head', Joint Media Release, 3 January 2007, <www.harbourtrust.gov.au/downloads/acrobat/media/mrnorth headhandover.pdf> (accessed 23 January 2007).

The Act was originally envisaged to have a 10-year life span and by the end of that time all Trust assets including Trust land were to be transferred to New South Wales (s 66), although the recent initiative at North Head may mean that this time-line is under review.

New South Wales alternatives

At the State level, other important legislation creates organisations to be the owner of significant heritage items.

Historic Houses Trust of New South Wales

The Historic Houses Trust is set up under the *Historic Houses Act 1980* (NSW). The Trust owns a number of significant heritage properties in State government ownership including the important colonial houses: Government House, Sydney; Elisabeth Farm, Parramatta; and Vaucluse House and Elisabeth Bay House on Sydney Harbour.

The Trust may accept property 'by gift inter vivos, devise or bequest' and may agree to accept the property subject 'to conditions' (s 8). The Trust has accepted the gift of more recent houses, including Rose Seidler House, Wahroonga, designed by a famous architect, Harry Seidler.

The Trust is to:

- manage and maintain, as house museums, buildings vested in or acquired by the Trust, having regard to their historic and architectural interest;
- conserve the buildings and manage and maintain their grounds; and
- provide such educational and cultural services in relation to the building as would increase public knowledge and enjoyment of the buildings and of their place in the heritage of the State. (s 7)

The Historic Houses Trust of New South Wales has the legal status of a corporation (s 5). It is managed by a Board of nine Trustees (s 6), subject to the direction and control of the Minister (s 5). The Minister approves the acquisition of buildings suitable as house museums, and alterations and improvements to the Trusts historic houses (s 10).

National Trust of Australia (New South Wales)

The National Trust of Australia (New South Wales), set up under the *National Trust of Australia (New South Wales) Act 1990* (NSW), has similarities with the Historic Houses Trust but is a community organisation. The National Trust began in 1945, and has its own legislation, passed in 1960, and replaced by the present Act.

The National Trust is a corporation, incorporated under this legislation. It does not have shareholders, but is constituted by members (s 4), who meet in general meeting (s 10), and do not receive dividends (s 26). The Board of directors consists of the Executive Director, and 12 elected members (Sch 1, cl 2). The Executive Director is in charge of day-to-day management (ss 11, 8).

The National Trust is mainly known for its collections of cultural heritage significance, particularly historic properties, but also artworks, furniture and objects. It also owns properties with natural heritage values.

The National Trust acquires items by purchase or gift. Gifts may have conditions attached by the donors (s 14). These conditions may be altered when just and equitable, taking into account the National Trust's ability to carry out its objects generally, and the intentions of the donor. Permission for alterations is given by the Attorney-General, for property worth less than $500,000, or the NSW Supreme Court in other cases (s 17).

The National Trust is subject to the general law of trusts and other general legislation, including the *Trustee Act 1925* (NSW) (s 22) and parts of the *Companies (New South Wales) Code*, particularly the provisions relating to auditing of accounts (ss 30, 34, 36).

The National Trust submits an Annual Report and Financial Statements to the NSW Parliament (s 35). The Minister may direct the Auditor-General to inspect, examine and audit and report on the books and accounts of the Trust, as if the Trust were an authority under the *Public Finance and Audit Act 1983* (NSW).

Covenants

The *Conveyancing Act 1919* (NSW) building on the traditional concept of the covenant has created a scheme that has proved useful in the protection of heritage items. Both the National Trust and the Historic Houses Trust, for example, have applied a protective covenant to properties they owned but did not wish to retain. A covenant enabled them to sell properties ensuring that their heritage significance could be maintained. The Trusts could enforce the covenants after they had given up ownership. This avenue, under the *Conveyancing Act*, is also available to other owners of heritage properties.

A public or local authority constituted by an Act of Parliament, or a corporation prescribed for the purposes of the legislation, may impose restrictions on the use of, or impose public positive covenants on, any land it owns (s 88D). For land it does not own, it needs the consent of those with an interest in the land. The body taking advantage of the covenant does not need to own other land in the area which takes the benefit of the restriction or public covenant (s 37). A covenant may set out requirements for maintenance and consequences for failure to meet the requirements (s 87A).

Local government heritage

Local councils regulate heritage items of local significance under the EPAA and the *Heritage Act 1977* (NSW). The *Heritage Act* was amended in 1999 to identify shared roles of the Heritage Council and local government councils in heritage matters.

In 2002, the State government delegated some approval functions for minor works on items of State significance to councils with appropriate skill and expertise. Council may in turn delegate their powers under s 377 of the *Local Government Act 1993* (NSW) to council officers.

Interim heritage orders

The Minister, on the advice of the Heritage Council, may make interim heritage orders under the *Heritage Act* on items of local significance. Local councils are authorised to make interim heritage orders when, in the opinion of the Heritage Office, the council:

- has undertaken a comprehensive heritage study; and
- the heritage schedule in the local council's local environmental plans is comprehensive.

Many councils, or groups of councils, employ heritage officers and advisors on a full-time or consultancy basis. The Heritage Council hosts a Local Government Heritage Incentive Scheme to support councils in their heritage functions, particularly for employing heritage advisors, which is a prerequisite to councils receiving a delegation from the Heritage Council of approval functions, and from the Minister to make Interim Heritage Orders.

Planning legislation

While local government councils' responsibilities are referred to in the *Heritage Act*, they carry out their responsibilities primarily through developing and interpreting environmental planning instruments, which comprise local environmental plans (LEPs) and development control plans, made under the EPAA. The link between the two Acts is a 1985 ministerial directive under s 317 of the EPAA for councils to include heritage provisions in the drafting local planning instruments.

Local environmental plans

Annexed to a council's local environmental plan is a list of heritage items in its area. Development consent is required from a council for work on heritage items listed in an LEP. The heritage provisions in LEPs include definitions and objectives, and standard clauses that cover:

- advertising development proposals;
- notice of demolition to the Heritage Council;
- development:
    - affecting sites of Aboriginal significance;
    - in the vicinity of heritage items; and
    - in heritage conservation areas; and
- conservation incentives.[37]

Local environmental plans are approved by the Minister, advised by the Heritage Council and Department of Planning.

Development control plans

Development control plans are prepared by councils to specify more detailed management policies for consideration of items listed in a LEP and of matters required under s 79C 'Matters for Consideration' of the EPAA.

Local government Heritage Committees

Many councils in New South Wales have established a Heritage Committee for their area, as a committee of the council under s 377 of the *Local Government Act 1993*,

---

37 NSW Heritage Office, *Local Government Heritage Guidelines* (2002) *passim*.

chaired by a councillor with council staff and community representatives as members. The NSW Heritage Office lists the following as committee functions:

- prepare and monitor a heritage policy;
- provide advice to council on local heritage management;
- raise community awareness of heritage conservation through publications, seminars, public displays, and annual heritage awards;
- make recommendations on the collection and recording of local heritage material or artefacts;
- compile a register of local heritage suppliers and heritage consultants;
- make recommendations on the nomination and deletion of items in the heritage schedule of councils' local environment plan;
- supervise funding submissions to other agencies, including heritage grants from the NSW Heritage Incentives Program;
- comment on specific development applications before council.[38]

Some councils may see their roles differently, particularly as to the last function, preferring the committee to advise on policy rather than on individual cases.

Indigenous heritage

The law and practice relating to Indigenous cultural heritage is changing quickly, and it is useful to discuss it under its own heading. The major pieces of Commonwealth and State heritage legislation, discussed in this chapter, cover Indigenous along with other aspects of cultural significance. There is also specialist legislation that should be noted.

Boer makes the general point that:

> The Federal, State, and Territory legislation can ... be classified into two basic types. The first approaches Indigenous cultural heritage as evidence of past occupations and customs, concentrating more on the archaeological aspects of the heritage of Aboriginal and Torres Straits Islanders; this type of legislation reflects outdated and old-fashioned approaches. The second type recognises the Aboriginal and Torres Strait Islander heritage as part of a living and still developing set of traditions, to which present day Aboriginal people and Torres Strait Islanders can directly relate.[39] Increasingly, it is the second approach that dominates the legislative drafting concerned with this heritage.[40]

Commonwealth Indigenous heritage legislation

Important Commonwealth legislation for the recognition and protection of Indigenous heritage applies in New South Wales.

---

38 Ibid at 4.2.4.

39 This concept is summed up by Janke, T, *Our Culture: Our Future*, Report on Indigenous Cultural and Intellectual Property, Michael Frankel & Co, prepared for the Australian Institute of Aboriginal and Torres Strait Islander Studies, Canberra, at xvii, cited in Boer and Wiffen, above n 9, at 261: 'For indigenous peoples, cultural heritage is a living and evolving tradition. Its continued practice is vital to the identity and cultural survival of Indigenous groups. So any definition of heritage must be a living one which recognises the continual transmission of Indigenous heritage'.

40 Boer and Wiffen, n 9, at 265.

Aboriginal and Torres Strait Islander Heritage Protection Act 1984 (Cth)

The purposes of the *Aboriginal and Torres Strait Islander Heritage Protection Act* are:

> [T]he preservation and protection from injury or desecration of areas and objects in Australia and in Australian waters, being areas and objects that are of particular significance to Aboriginals in accordance with Aboriginal tradition. (s 4)

This is amplified by the definitions:

> 'Aboriginal tradition' means the body of traditions, observances, customs and beliefs of Aboriginals generally or of a particular community or group of Aboriginals, and includes any such traditions, observances, customs or beliefs relating to particular persons, areas, objects or relationships. (s 3)

The Act does not exclude or limit State or Territory laws capable of operating concurrently with it (s 7). The Minister administering the legislation consults the State government before making a declaration to protect an area or object in a State or Territory (s 13(2)). The Minister will revoke a declaration if 'satisfied that the law of a State ... makes effective provision for the protection of an area (or) object' (s 13).

An area or object has suffered 'injury or desecration' if the use or significance of the area, in accordance with Aboriginal tradition, is adversely affected; if entry into the area, or passage through it, is inconsistent with Aboriginal tradition; or if the object is used or treated inconsistently with Aboriginal tradition (s 3(2)).

The Minister may make protective declarations over areas of land or water. Emergency declarations for up to 60 days may be made on behalf of an Aboriginal person or group, if a threat is seen to be serious and immediate (ss 9, 11, 18). The Minister may make a declarations on the basis of an expert report, and after any public submissions are considered (ss 10, 11).

Declarations may also be made to protect objects (s 12) including human remains (s 3). The discovery of Aboriginal must be reported. The Minister then consults with relevant Aboriginal people (ss 20, 21).

Protection of Movable Cultural Heritage Act 1986 (Cth)

Class A objects on the National Cultural Heritage Control List under the Act include sacred and secret Aboriginal ritual objects, bark and log coffins, human remains, rock art and dendroglyphs (carved trees) (*Protection of Movable Cultural Heritage Regulations 1987* Sch 1.3). The National Cultural Heritage Committee which advises the Minister on movable cultural heritage includes an Aborigine or Torres Strait Islander (s 17(1A)).

Environment Protection and Biodiversity Conservation Act 1999 (Cth)

The EPBCA includes significant provisions relating to the role of Australia's Indigenous peoples in heritage and environmental protection. Included in the objects of the Act are:

- 'to promote a cooperative approach to the protection and management of the environment involving governments, community, land-holders and indigenous peoples' (s 3(1)(d));

- 'to recognise the role of indigenous people in the conservation and ecologically sustainable use of Australia's biodiversity' (s 3(1)(f)); and
- 'to promote the use of indigenous peoples' knowledge of biodiversity with the involvement of, and cooperation with, the owners of that knowledge' (s 3(1)(g)).

The Act recognises that places may have Indigenous heritage value, being 'a heritage value of the place that is of significance to Indigenous persons in accordance with their practices, observances, customs, traditions, beliefs or history' (s 528). It is an offence to take an action likely to have a significant impact on the National Heritage values of a National Heritage place that are Indigenous heritage values (ss 15B(4), 15C(7), (8)).

The Act also provides formal consultation procedures with Aboriginal owners and organisations, for example, when the Minister is considering a proposal to take a controlled action that might affect the Indigenous heritage value of a National or Commonwealth Heritage place (s 74(1A)).

A conservation agreement may be made with Indigenous persons or organisations that have usage rights over land (s 305(5)(a)-(d)).

Australian Heritage Council Act 2003 (Cth)

The Australian Heritage Council includes a representative of Indigenous people (s 7(3)), and the Register of the National Estate contains places that are important in Indigenous tradition (s 22).

New South Wales legislation and Indigenous heritage

Heritage Act 1977 (NSW)

The *Heritage Act* deals with Aboriginal heritage items other than relics and places or areas not within national parks.

National Parks and Wildlife Act 1974 (NSW)

The NPWA has the most detailed provisions for Indigenous heritage in New South Wales legislation.

> Over the past few years the New South Wales National Parks and Wildlife Service (NPWS), has paid a great deal of attention to the identification, registration, and protection of Aboriginal heritage. There has been an increased involvement of Aboriginal experts, land councils, and communities.[41]

The NPWA adopts the definition of Aboriginal person in the *Aboriginal Land Rights Act 1983* (NSW) (s 4) as a person who:

(a) is a member of the Aboriginal race of Australia;
(b) identifies as an Aboriginal person;
(c) is accepted by the Aboriginal community as an Aboriginal person. (s 5)

---

41 Boer and Wiffen, above n 9, at 282. See discussion of Aboriginal land in the NSW parks system in Chapter 9.

Aboriginal places

A place of special significance for Aboriginal culture may be declared an Aboriginal place by the Minister administering the Act by order published in the *Gazette* (s 84).

Aboriginal objects

Certain Aboriginal objects including abandoned objects are deemed to be, and to always have been, the property of the Crown. No compensation is payable (s 83).

Director-General's responsibilities

The Director-General of National Parks and Wildlife is the authority for the protection of Aboriginal objects and Aboriginal places in New South Wales, particularly for their proper care, preservation, restoration and protection (s 85).[42]

The Director-General may dispose of Aboriginal objects that are the property of the Crown by returning them to an Aboriginal owner, entitled and willing to accept them in accordance with Aboriginal tradition. The *National Parks and Wildlife Regulation 2002* makes provision for safekeeping when there is no owner, and for settling disputes (s 85A, reg 88).

The Director-General may issue permits for dealing with Aboriginal objects (s 87). It is an offence, without a permit, to:

- disturb or excavate land to discover an Aboriginal object;
- disturb or move an Aboriginal object that is Crown property;
- take possession of, or remove, an Aboriginal object in land reserved under the Act. (s 86)

It is also an offence, without the consent of the Director-General or in accordance with Aboriginal tradition, knowingly to destroy, deface or damage an Aboriginal object or place. A person refused consent, or dissatisfied with its terms may appeal to the Minister (s 90).

Only the Australian Museum Trust may remove an Aboriginal object from a national park, historic site, nature reserve, karst conservation reserve, Aboriginal area, State conservation area or regional park (s 87).

Notification of Aboriginal sites of objects

A person aware of the location of an Aboriginal object must notify the Director-General (s 91).

Conclusion

Heritage legislation illustrates a rare degree of consensus in legislation in the Australia federation. With the passing of the *Heritage Act 2004* (ACT), the legislation of the Commonwealth, States and the two major self-governing Territories is very similar, and is consistent with the administrative arrangements between the jurisdictions agreed to by the Council of Australian Governments in 1994. That agreement has resulted in a series of heritage lists administered by the three levels of government with responsibility in New South Wales. This chapter discussed these laws.

---

42 But see Chapter 9, n 24.

The heritage amendments to the Commonwealth's EPBCA passed by the Australian Parliament towards the end of 2003 facilitated this division of responsibility. As discussed above, the amendments replaced the national view of heritage of the Register of the National Estate, compiled under the repealed *Australian Heritage Commission Act*. While the government, responding to widespread concern, retained the Register of the National Estate in the new *Australian Heritage Council Act* (s 21), its significance is reduced in favour of the new lists under the EPBCA. It is not clear what remains of the 30 years' experience in working out a systematic way of setting up criteria and guidelines for identifying items of Australia's National Estate, and the 14,000 items, represented by the Register of the National Estate. The options seem to be that the Register may remain static as an historical record or may be added to by the Australian Heritage Council as the only list over which it has control.

The new Commonwealth laws are very complex. The new scheme had to navigate the inadequate provision for Commonwealth activities in heritage in the Constitution. A second major factor was the federal government's wish to include heritage in the already complicated environmental protection provisions of the EPBCA. It will be seen whether the systems provided by the Act to deal with issues of environmental protection, while opening up exciting possibilities, may be more complex than is necessary for heritage protection.

Place or values of the place

The protective and enforcement provisions of the EPBCA are expressed to protect the *values* of a heritage place, and not the place itself, as under the former *Australian Heritage Commission Act*. The significance of this change is also not clear.

Who decides?

The Australian legislation is not consistent on who identifies a place as having heritage values. Many argue that this is a different question from who decides whether a place with heritage values should be protected. One response would then be that these two questions may be answered by different decision-makers.

One view is that the identification of heritage values and significance should be a question for experts, relying on the systems and methods of identification that have been developed in Australia over the past 25 years. Whether a place with identified heritage values should be protected may be a much more contentious question involving competing views as to the allocation of community resources.

> Heritage is in some sense a political issue but primarily it should be a technical issue: Does this have cultural aesthetic value to the community? Heritage can be very prone to political pressure and political mood swings, and there is a sense it needs to be raised above that.[43]

The distinction is also made in the Burra Charter, Australia's eminent document on the approach to be taken in heritage preservation. Referring to Art 6.1 of the

43 Senate Committee Inquiry into the Environment and Heritage Legislation Amendment Bill (No 2) 2000 and the Australian Heritage Council Bill 2000 Report, 3.6, quoting the submission of the Environmental Defender's Office.

Charter, Australia ICOMOS in its submission to the Senate Committee inquiring into the then proposed new Commonwealth laws argued:

> A major issue in heritage conservation is the need to clearly separate heritage places and values from their management. Past experience warns that where these matters are dealt with together, management issues can cloud or otherwise influence decisions about whether a place has certain heritage values, or any values at all.[44]

The laws applying in New South Wales disagree with the Australia ICOMOS position. Under both the Commonwealth legislation and the NSW *Heritage Act*, it is the Minister who decides whether an item should be entered on the Heritage Register or list. Under the Commonwealth legislation, the Minister also decides whether a proposed development that might affect the heritage significance of the listed item should be approved. Under the *Heritage Act*, this is formally the decision of the Heritage Council.

This question is important in relation to the final comment that might be made about the NSW heritage law system. In both jurisdictions, the heritage legislation is highly discretionary, concentrating on providing a process for what is otherwise a discretionary decision. There is little provision for judicial or other oversight of the Minister's decision other than public opinion and the ballot box. This may be the major flaw in what seems otherwise a well crafted, even elegantly worded, set of laws.

44 Ibid at 2.

11

POLLUTION

Introduction

The Commonwealth government has limited responsibility for pollution regulation and consequently most matters are dealt with by the States. Most Commonwealth legislation occurs as a result of international obligations incurred as a result of treaty ratification. Commonwealth legislation relating to hazardous waste, industrial chemicals, pesticides, dangerous goods and ozone protection is discussed in Chapter 12. This chapter discusses Commonwealth and NSW environment protection legislation and marine pollution.[1]

Commonwealth responsibilities for national environment protection measures

The Intergovernmental Agreement on the Environment (IGAE)[2] provides for a co-operative approach to environmental management. Two important initiatives resulting from the IGAE were the establishment of a Commonwealth Environment Protection Agency (Environment Australia) and a National Environment Protection Council. The Commonwealth Environment Protection Agency has no national role despite its renaming as 'Environment Australia'. It is not an independent body, but part of the Commonwealth Department of the Environment and Heritage which has responsibility for other matters. It has no regulatory functions and no authority over the State environment protection authorities. It is responsible for administering federal environmental legislation and for formulating guidelines for environmental protection.

Following recommendations in the IGAE on the need for uniform national environment protection measures, the federal government passed the *National Environment Protection Council Act 1994* (Cth) (NEPCA). This Act created a National Environment Protection Council (NEPC) with power to pass National Environment Protection Measures (NEPMs) (ss 8, 12). Complementary legislation has been passed by each of the States, for example, the *National Environment Protection Council (New South Wales) Act* 1995.

The NEPC comprises a ministerial representative from each of the States and Territories, as well as the Commonwealth (s 9). The NEPC is a statutory body but

1 The author wishes to acknowledge the editorial assistance of Elizabeth Lamaro BSc, LLB (Hons) (Macq).

2 May 1992.

since 2001 has operated under the umbrella of the Environment Protection and Heritage Council of Australia and New Zealand. This Council was created by amalgamating the NEPC, the environment protection components of the Australian and New Zealand Environment and Conservation Council (ANZECC) and Heritage Ministers Meetings.

NEPMs can only be made in relation to a very limited range of matters:

- ambient air quality;
- ambient water quality;
- noise, where uniformity is required because of the existence of a national market for goods or services;
- assessment of site contamination;
- environmental impacts associated with hazardous wastes;
- motor vehicle emissions;
- the reuse and recycling of used materials. (s 14(1))

NEPMs may take the form of standards, goals, guidelines or protocols (NEPCA s 6(1)). There is no commitment to legally binding standards. It is clear that NEPMs will be confined to ambient measures and will not extend to point-source pollution. Consequently, NEPMs will have no direct regulatory control over industry or individuals. Setting appropriate standards will be the responsibility of State governments.

The Council must give advance notice of its intention to make a draft NEPM and an impact statement must then be prepared and exhibited for public comment (NEPCA ss 16-19). Promulgation of a NEPM requires a two-thirds majority of the NEPC (s 28). The final NEPM must be tabled in the Commonwealth Parliament and can be disallowed by either House (s 21). Once a NEPM has been made, it is the responsibility of each of the States and the Commonwealth to implement and enforce it (s 7). The Act imposes no sanctions for non-compliance with a NEPM. The only mechanism for monitoring State compliance is a duty to report annually to the Council on the implementation and effectiveness of NEPMs (s 23). These reports, together with a report from the Council, are tabled in the Commonwealth Parliament (s 24).

At the time of writing, seven NEPMs have been made: National Pollutant Inventory 1998 (varied 2000), Ambient Air Quality 1998 (varied 2003), Movement of Controlled Waste Between States and Territories 1998 (varied 2004), Assessment of Site Contamination 1999, Diesel (Vehicles Emissions) Measure 2001, Air Toxics NEPM 2004, and Used Packaging Materials 2004. The National Pollutant Inventory requires industries who use certain toxic substances to report their annual emissions and transfers to air, land and water to a national database or inventory. This data is listed on a publicly available internet database. The NEPM on Ambient Air Quality sets uniform standards and monitoring and reporting protocols for certain air pollutants. It does not apply to indoor air pollution. The NEPM on Movement of Controlled Waste Between States and Territories aims to minimise the impact on the environment from the movement of hazardous and controlled wastes across State and Territory borders by establishing an agreed set of objectives and benchmarks for managing hazardous waste. The NEPM for Assessment of Site Contamination establishes a nationally consistent approach to the assessment of site contamination and ensures sound environmental management practices. The NEPM for Diesel

(Vehicles Emissions) provides a framework for the management of emissions from in-service diesel vehicles by ensuring they are properly maintained. This NEPM improves the information database available on ambient air toxics, for example, polycyclic aromatic hydrocarbons and heavy metals and aldehydes. The Used Packaging Materials NEPM aims to reduce degradation arising from the disposal of used packaging and conserve virgin materials through encouragement of reuse and recycling of used packaging materials by complementing the voluntary strategies in the National Packaging Covenant. The Covenant is an industry self-regulatory instrument which aims to ensure that all participants in the packaging chain play their part in waste reduction. The NEPM applies to non-participants in the Covenant to ensure that participants are not unfairly disadvantaged in the market place. The NEPM will also assist in achieving the waste reduction and recycling objectives of the Covenant.[3]

Protection of the Environment Operations Act 1997 (NSW)

Until the 1960s, in New South Wales the most substantive tools to control pollution were the traditional common law remedies. However, these were orientated towards the protection of private rather than public interests which inhibited the resolution of pollution problems. As community environmental consciousness developed, the political process responded positively by enacting a number of statutes designed directly to control pollution. The first generation of environmental statutes focused on basic discharges and emissions, such as air, waste and noise. The *Protection of the Environment Administration Act 1991* (PROTEA) was the first stage in the reform of NSW pollution legislation. It established the Environment Protection Authority (EPA) and provides guidelines for its general responsibilities and management structure. The EPA is currently part of the Department of Environment and Conservation.

The *Protection of the Environment Operations Act 1997* (PEOA) was the second-stage in the reform process and undertakes a major restructuring and streamlining of pollution legislation. The Act adopts a more integrated proactive approach to pollution control and recognises that pollution prevention is an essential component of an environment protection system. It is also typical of the neo-liberal approach in that it aims at cost-effective environment protection and inducements to industry through economic measures and incentives.

The PEOA operates in conjunction with other NSW statutes such as the *Contaminated Land Management Act 1997*, the *Marine Pollution Act 1987*, the *Local Government Act 1993*, the *Environmentally Hazardous Chemicals Act 1985*, the *Ozone Protection Act 1989*, the *Environmental Trust Act 1998* and the *Waste Avoidance and Resource Recovery Act 2001*.

The PEOA came into force on 1 July 1999. The PEOA repeals and consolidates all previous NSW legislation dealing with pollution regulation. It rationalises, simplifies and strengthens the regulatory regime dealing with air and water pollution, noise control and waste management. The PEOA was reviewed in 2003, and extensively amended by the *Protection of the Environment Operations Amendment Act 2005*.

3 See further 'NEPMs and their Administration', EPHC Secretariat, <www.ephc.gov.au>.

The following instruments and strategies are now available in New South Wales under the PEOA to prevent and/or control pollution:

- designation of the appropriate regulatory authority;
- protection of the environment policies;
- environment protection licensing;
- environment protection notices, and other notices directed to specific companies, individuals or public authorities;
- general criminal laws directed to individuals and companies at large;
- enforcement procedures;
- environmental audits; and
- economic measures.

Objects

The PEOA has three main objects:

- to 'protect, restore and enhance the quality of the environment in New South Wales having regard to the need to maintain ecologically sustainable development';
- to ensure increased opportunities for public involvement and access to information; and
- to reduce risks to human health and prevent degradation of the environment. (s 3)

The Dictionary to the PEOA provides that ecologically sustainable development has the same meaning as in s 6(2) of the PROTEA. The PROTEA states that ecologically sustainable development (ESD) can be achieved through the precautionary principle; intergenerational equity; conservation of biological diversity and ecological integrity; and improved valuation and pricing of environmental resources (PROTEA s 6(2)(a)-(d)). This definition has now been incorporated in a large number of statues in Australia (see discussion of ESD in Chapter 1 at pp 22-26).

The PEOA provides a number of mechanisms to facilitate public involvement and access to information on development proposals and licensing functions. This takes place through public registers of regulatory action, integrated development assessment, the licence review and variation process, and the notification provisions of the Act.

The mechanisms which are used to prevent environmental degradation include pollution prevention, cleaner production, reduction to harmless levels of discharge of substances likely to cause harm to the environment, recycling and progressive environmental improvements (PEOA s 3(d)). These approaches indicate a move away from a reliance on 'end-of-pipe' controls, such as licensing of point source emissions, to a new more holistic approach that encompasses pollution prevention and environmental improvement. This is a departure from the media-specific approach adopted in former pollution control legislation which focused separately on air, noise, water and land and which failed to take account of the complex cross-media effects of pollution.

However, while the general aim of the PEOA is to prevent pollution, the Act also recognises that pollution cannot be totally eliminated. It therefore provides a two-tiered system to regulate pollution on a daily basis. The EPA is responsible for regulating the higher environmental risk activities listed in Sch 1 by licensing, while local councils and other public authorities regulate the lower risk non-scheduled activities. The PEOA also introduces economic instruments such as load-based licensing, tradeable credits and financial assurances to complement the traditional licensing structure.

Appropriate regulatory authority

Under the PEOA, responsibility for initiating pollution control lies with the 'appropriate regulatory authority' (ARA). The PEOA differentiates clearly between premises regulated by the EPA and those that are the responsibility of other public authorities.

The EPA is the ARA for scheduled works or activities requiring a licence, and activities involving the State government or a public authority (PEOA s 6). Local councils are the ARA for non-scheduled or unlicensed works and activities, except where a licence is held to control unscheduled water pollution, or where a public authority, other than a local council is declared by regulation[4] to be an ARA (s 6).

An ARA may only exercise functions in, or in relation to, its area (s 6(4)). The marine authority – that is, the Minister administering the *Ports Corporatisation and Waterways Management Act 1995* or the Waterways Authority (PEOA Dictionary) – is the 'appropriate regulatory authority' in connection with noise control notices and noise abatement directions relating to boats (s 263). Police officers are also given powers in connection with noise and vehicle emissions (s 275(a)). There are special provisions in the PEOA dealing with noise control measures. For non-scheduled premises, the local council has the power to issue noise control notices (s 264).

Protection of the environment policies

The PEOA makes provision for protection of the environment policies (PEPs). These provide a statutory framework for NSW government decisions affecting the environment. The policies also provide a means of formalising guidelines or codes of practice developed by the EPA and for implementing NEPMs.

A PEP can be made for the purpose of protecting the NSW environment and, in particular, to further the objectives of the EPA and to manage the cumulative impact of existing and future human activities on the environment, having regard to ESD principles, as well as reducing the risks to human health and preventing environmental degradation (s 10). A PEP can specify environment protection goals, standards, guidelines or protocols (s 11).

---

4 The following authorities have been declared by regulation as ARAs: the Marine Parks Authority for non-scheduled activities in marine parks: *Protection of the Environment Operations (General) Regulation 1998* (PEO (Gen) Regulation) cl 64; the Waterways Authority for non-scheduled activities involving non-pilotage in navigable waters: s 64A; the Director-General of National Parks and Wildlife for non-scheduled activities in Kosciuszko National Park; the Sydney Organising Committee for the Olympic Games for premises occupied or carried on by SOCOG: POE (Gen) Regulation cl 65; EPA for non-scheduled activities on the route of the light rail system under s 104N(2) of the *Transport Administration Act 1988* (NSW), except for buildings or structures included in the route: PEO (Gen) Regulation cl 66; the EPA for outdoor entertainment activities relating to certain Trust lands, Homebush Bay and the Opera House: PEO (Gen) Regulation cl 67.

Chapter 2 of the PEOA outlines the contents and the procedures for developing and implementing PEPs. PEPs may be made with respect to:

- the whole or any part of the State;
- the environment generally or any part of it;
- any activity that may impact, or has impacted, on the environment;
- any form of pollution;
- any aspect of waste. (s 11(4))

In preparing a draft PEP, the EPA must have regard to a number of matters including the environmental, economic and social impact of the policy, relevant environmental planning instruments under the *Environmental Planning and Assessment Act 1979* (NSW) (EPAA) and NEPMs (s 13).

The EPA must prepare an impact statement when making a draft PEP. The impact statement must address a number of matters. These include the desired environmental outcomes, the reason for the PEP and the environmental impact of not making it, a statement of the alternative methods of achieving these outcomes and the reasons why those alternatives have not been adopted (s 16(2)).

During the preparation of the draft PEP, the EPA is required to consult with public authorities, organisations or persons as the Minister directs, or which it considers appropriate (s 18). The PEP and impact statement must be advertised for at least three months for public comment (s 17(3)). The EPA must submit the PEP to the Minister together with a report on submissions received and any consultation undertaken (s 20). Once a PEP has been made, it must be taken into account by the EPA and other regulatory authorities when making a decision under the pollution legislation. PEPs must also be considered by planners when granting a consent or approval under the EPAA, or in preparing an environmental planning instrument (s 29).

Failure to comply with a procedural requirement will not invalidate a PEP provided that there has been substantial compliance with the requirements (s 38). The validity of a PEP can only be challenged within three months after the date of publication in the *Gazette* (s 37). A PEP may not create an offence for contravention of its provisions (s 36).

At the time of writing, no PEPs have been made. The reasons are not clear, although it is possible that the lengthy consultation and public consultation process involved has been a deterrence. They have not even been used for implementing NEPMs as was originally contemplated. The Report on the Review of the PEOA 1997 (2003) by the Department of Environment and Conservation (DEC) (PEOA Review Report (2003)) attributes the lack of PEPs to the fact that the particular issues they may have addressed have been more readily dealt with through other instruments. According to the Report, the DEC is exploring potential subjects for PEPs. Initially, it was proposed to replace the *Clean Waters Regulations 1972*, which classified a number of waters, with a PEP. Instead the Regulations have been repealed and replaced with a general requirement that environmental values of water, as provided for in the Australian and New Zealand Guidelines for Fresh and Marine Water Quality 2000, be considered in licensing functions or when issuing prevention notices.

Licences

Licensing is a core strategy under the PEOA. The Act introduces one integrated licensing system that controls all forms of air, noise, water and waste pollution from licensed activities. Licences are issued exclusively by the EPA. The move from annual licences required under the previous legislation is intended to give industry sufficient time to implement effective environment protection measures such as pollution reduction programs.[5]

The public have only a limited right to participate in licensing decisions, namely in relation to licence reviews and variations (see pp 431-432). The rationale for this is greater efficiency and also the need to protect industrial and commercial secrets. The PEOA provides that, if a licence application is granted or refused, any person can request a written statement of reasons from the EPA (s 61). Each regulatory authority is required to keep a public register of licensing applications and other decisions (s 308 discussed at pp 472-473).

When is a licence required?

Licences may be issued for the following activities:

- scheduled development work at any premises (s 47);
- scheduled activities at any premises (s 48);
- scheduled activities not based on premises (s 49); and
- non-scheduled activities that may cause water pollution (s 122).

Licences are required for development work and activities listed in Sch 1 to the Act if they meet a specified threshold. Scheduled development work is construction work to enable scheduled activities to be carried on at any premises (s 47). A licence can be granted to cover both the work and the carrying on of the proposed activity. Alternatively, after the completion of the work, the licence can be amended to allow the carrying on of the scheduled activity as well (this is known as staged licensing). Scheduled activities comprise, for the most part, the heavy industrial polluters as well as certain quarrying and mining activities. These activities correspond very closely to the schedule of designated development under the EPAA (see pp 430-431). The activities listed are those undertaken at specific premises (Pt 1 of Sch 1) as well as non premises-based activities relating to the commercial transportation of specific types of waste (Pt 2 of Sch 1).

Once a licence has been issued, the EPA is responsible for the regulation of all mediums of pollution (air, noise, water and waste) generated from that work or activity. Only one licence is required for each site. The principle of 'one site, one regulator' applies which means that once premises are licensed by the EPA for one medium, the EPA is the ARA for all forms of pollution arising from that work or those activities (ss 6(1), 44). Pollution control may be initiated by the EPA through conditions on licences or through variations to existing licences. Non-scheduled premises will be regulated by means of clean-up or prevention notices (see pp 435-466).

Some activities that may cause water pollution are listed in Sch 1 to the PEOA and will require a licence, eg aquaculture. A licence may also be sought for an activity not listed in Sch 1 that may cause water pollution, but this is not mandatory. The advantage of obtaining a licence is that compliance with the conditions of the licence provides a defence to the offence of polluting waters (s 122). This is a curious provision, since if the EPA decides that a licence is unnecessary the person will be

---

5 NSW Government Green Paper, *Protection of the Environment Operations Bill 1996*, Public Discussion Paper (EPA, Sydney 1996) at 13.

deprived of a defence if prosecuted for water pollution. Presumably, in these cases an environment protection notice will be issued requiring specific action to be taken (see pp 435-436).

Relevant factors in granting a licence

The PEOA requires the EPA to take certain factors into consideration when deciding whether a licence should be granted, namely:

- any PEPs;
- ecologically sustainable development;
- the nature of the pollution being caused or likely to be caused, the impact of that pollution on the environment and any practical measures that could be taken to prevent or mitigate its effects;
- any green offset scheme or works, or tradeable emission scheme under Pt 9.3 of the Act;
- whether the applicant is a fit and proper person as elaborated in s 83;
- environmental values of water affected by the activity and the practical measures that could be taken to restore or maintain those values;
- environmental impact statements (EISs) or species impact statements;
- any 'practical measures' to prevent, control, abate or mitigate that pollution and to protect the environment from harm;
- public submissions under the PEOA or the EPAA;
- industry waste reduction plans or regional waste plans. (s 45)

The EPA may grant or refuse an application for the issue of a licence. When a licence is granted it is subject to a number of conditions. If the EPA intends to refuse a licence, it must first give notice to the applicant and provide an opportunity to make submissions (s 55). If the EPA does not issue a licence within 60 days of the application, it is taken to have been refused (s 287). An appeal may be made to the Land and Environment Court against the EPA's decision (s 287). The EPA must provide the applicant with reasons for refusal including any significant environmental or other issues involved and any relevant standards, outcomes or requirement. The EPA must also provide third parties with reasons if they so request.

Licence fees

An annual fee prescribed by the *Protection of the Environment Operations (General) Regulation 1998* (PEO (Gen) Regulation) is payable. Administrative fees are also charged for the issue of a licence. (The applicable fees are set out in cll 6(2), 12, 13 and Sch 1 of the PEO (Gen) Regulation.)

In general, the fees are linked to the type and scale of activity involved. In addition, the EPA has introduced a system of load-based licensing, which effectively implements a polluter pays system, based on the volume and toxicity of discharges (see p 547).

Licence conditions

A licence may be issued subject to conditions or unconditionally (s 63(1)). The Act provides a non-exhaustive list of examples of conditions that may be attached to a licence. These include a requirement for the licence holder to perform any of the following:

- monitoring and certification of compliance with licensing requirements including independent certification, if so required (s 66);
- conducting mandatory environmental audits (ss 67, 174-179);
- conducting and submitting pollution studies and pollution reduction programs to the EPA (s 68);
- providing financial assurances to guarantee funding of remediation or pollution reduction programs (ss 70, 296-307);
- requiring remediation work in connection with the activities authorised (s 71);
- providing information about waste, or regulating the management, storage, handling, transportation or disposal of waste (ss 75-76);
- requiring the licensee to have insurance cover (s 72);
- requiring the implementation of tradeable emission schemes, green offset schemes or works, or other economic measures (ss 69, 293-295).

The list of conditions outlined above are not exhaustive. The EPA has a wide discretion to attach other conditions to a licence, such as a requirement to introduce new pollution control equipment or update processes and industrial plants as new technology becomes available. To this extent, pollution licensing could potentially overlap with a prevention notice. Any conditions imposed should reasonably relate to the subject of the licence. This principle was developed by the House of Lords in *Newbury District Council v Secretary of State for the Environment*[6] and followed by the NSW Land and Environment Court by Bignold J in *EPA v Cleary Bros (BOMBO) Pty Ltd*.[7]

To increase operator accountability, the licence holder may be required to provide a statement certified by the holder or another person approved by the holder as correct, indicating compliance with licence conditions, particulars of, and reasons for any failure to comply with the conditions, action taken, or to be taken, to prevent the recurrence of that failure or to mitigate the effects of that failure and the fee payable in relation to the licence (s 66(3)).

Pollution reduction programs

The legality of bonding arrangements attached as conditions to licences was debatable under the law which existed before the PEOA. As a result, bonds were based on contractual principles dependent on the voluntary agreement of those involved. There is no longer any doubt as to the legal status of bonding arrangements, as the PEOA specifically provides that financial assurances to guarantee funding of remediation can be attached as a condition of a licence (ss 70, 296-307 – see p 476). Also, there is specific provision for requiring pollution studies and/or reduction programs to be undertaken and submitted for approval to the EPA, as a condition of a licence (s 68(1), (2)). A pollution reduction program may include requirements to carry out works or to install plant for the purpose of preventing, controlling, abating

6 [1981] AC 578.
7 (1996) 92 LGERA 101.

or mitigating pollution (s 68(3)). Since licences no longer expire after one year, pollution reduction programs can now be more effectively implemented. The increasing emphasis placed on fixing self-monitoring conditions and certification of compliance with licensing requirements also provides a firm basis for prosecution. The EPA now has access to information and records on the financial position of particular companies (s 191), but EPA licensing officers must have sufficient expertise to negotiate realistic and efficient pollution reduction targets in light of this information.

The EPA makes regular use of pollution reduction programs to require licensees to carry out remediation works and upgrade plant and equipment (PEOA Review Report (2003)). According to the Report, more than 150 pollution reduction programs are negotiated each year, with the annual value directed to reducing pollution ranging between $24 million and $417 million.

Practical measures

The PROTEA allocates general responsibility to the EPA for ensuring that the best practicable measures are taken for environmental protection (s 7(2)(a)). In effect, this requires the EPA to balance the environmentally damaging effect of pollution against the economic and social benefits the community would receive from the activity, while at the same time, recognising the significant economic implications for the polluter.[8] This requires the polluter to utilise the best technology already in use or available commercially.

Integration of licensing and development control

The PEOA also facilitates better integration between environment protection and the development consent process under the EPAA by integrating some aspects of the licensing system under the PEOA with the development control system under the EPAA. The PEOA provides that a licence that relates to a development requiring development consent under Pt 4 of the EPAA (controlled development) must not be granted or varied by the EPA until development consent has been granted (s 50). However, applications can be submitted for consideration simultaneously to the EPA and the relevant council or consent authority.

In almost all cases, development which requires a licence under the PEOA will be designated development under the EPAA. Works and activities listed in Sch 1 to the PEOA (scheduled activities) require a licence, while works listed in Sch 3 to the *Environmental Planning and Assessment Regulation 2000* require an EIS. The EPAA requires an EIS to be advertised for public submissions. Schedule 1 to the PEOA and Sch 3 to the EPAA are very similar with the result that an activity that constitutes designated development under the EPAA will almost always require a licence under the PEOA. Under s 91 of the EPAA, development which requires development consent under that Act and an approval under the PEOA and any of the Acts listed is known as integrated development (see Chapter 3). Where an application is made for consent to integrated development, the council must provide the EPA with a copy of the development application including the EIS. The EPA must inform the consent council whether it will grant a licence and, if so, the general terms of any

8 See *Brown v EPA (No 2)* (1992) 78 LGERA 119.

licence proposed to be granted. If the consent authority approves the application, the conditions of the development consent must be consistent with the terms proposed by the EPA (s 91A(3)). If the EPA indicates that it will not grant a licence, development consent must be refused (s 91A(4)). If the EPA does not respond, it cannot later refuse to grant a licence and any licence granted must not be inconsistent with the development consent (s 91A(5)). It should be noted that if the Planning Minister approves a major project under Pt 3A of the EPAA, and the activity also requires a PEOA licence, the licence must be issued (EPAA s 75V).

The integration of licensing and development control essentially means that the pollution aspects of a development may be scrutinised in the development consent determination process through the provisions for public participation under the EPAA. There is no provision for advertising or public participation in relation to new licence applications under the PEOA. This means that the only opportunity for public participation in the licensing process is at the determination of the development application stage. A major advantage with giving the EPA the discretion to grant or refuse an environmental protection licence is that the EPA has the expertise to make detailed assessment of issues of pollution which often a local council does not. Thus, where councils face the difficult task of assessing development proposals with significant pollution implications, there is a safeguard to the environment since the EPA must also issue a licence. Developers are also better placed to make a decision on whether to proceed with a development if they can ascertain the requirements of a licence at the development consent stage. According to the PEOA Review Report (2003), more than 80 new developments are referred to the EPA each year.

Variation of licence

The EPA may vary a licence or the conditions attached to it at any time, either upon the licence holder's application or on its own initiative, except that a licence granted in relation to integrated development may not be amended until after the first review date (PEOA s 78). Licence variation applications relating to works that require development consent may not be granted until that consent is obtained (s 50).

Variation may include the attachment, substitution, removal or amendment of a condition (s 58(2)). This provision enables the EPA to implement higher standards based on increased knowledge of the causes and effects of the pollution. The EPA must invite and consider public submissions before a licence is varied if the licence will permit a significant increase in the environmental impact of the activity and the variation did not undergo environmental assessment and public consultation under the EPAA (s 58(6)).

Licence review

Licences must be reviewed at least every five years (s 78(1)). Before a review of a licence takes place, public notice must be given. However, the EPA is not required to invite or consider submissions. It should be noted that principles of administrative law suggest the EPA should consider public submissions as a relevant consideration when making its decision. The EPA is required to report a failure to give public notice to the Board of the EPA and in their Annual Report with a statement of reasons for the failure (s 78(3)). The EPA must audit, on an industry-wide or regional basis, compliance with licence requirements and whether they reflect best practice in relation to the matters regulated (s 78(4A)). No proceeding may be brought in respect of any failure to comply with the notification procedures (s 78(5)).

Termination of licence

Once granted, a licence remains in force until it is suspended, revoked or surrendered (s 77). The EPA may revoke or suspend a licence at any time after taking into account the considerations listed in s 45 (ss 58, 79, 81).[9] In practice it will only do so where there are persistent breaches of the Act or licence conditions, and where the licence holder fails to improve their performance. When a civil action is brought, the court, if satisfied that a breach will be committed unless restrained, may suspend any environment protection licence (s 253). Apart from this instance, only the Minister has power to suspend or revoke a licence if the licence holder is convicted of a major pollution offence (s 82(1)). A major pollution offence is one which has caused or is likely to cause environmental harm, and is punishable by a penalty of $1 million or more in the case of a corporation, or $250,000 or more in the case of an individual (s 82(2)). A licence holder may also choose to surrender their licence. This requires the EPA's written approval (s 80(1)). The EPA may refuse an application if there will be an ongoing environmental impact, and it is appropriate to manage that impact though conditions of the licence (s 80(1B)).

Discharge of domestic and trade waste to sewers

Domestic and trade waste are discharged into sewers operated by the Sydney Water Corporation and the Hunter Water Corporation. Sydney Water operates water, sewerage and stormwater drainage systems in Sydney, Illawarra and the Blue Mountains under the *Sydney Water Act 1994.* The Hunter Water Corporation operates in the Newcastle, Cessnock, Maitland, Lake Macquarie and Port Stephens areas pursuant to the *Hunter Water Act 1991.* In some areas, such as Wyong and Gosford, access to sewers are regulated under the *Water Management Act 2000.* Outside these areas, discharges are regulated by local councils under the *Local Government Act 1993* and the *Local Government (Approvals) Regulation 1999.*

Because domestic discharges differ from industrial waste, different regulations apply in metropolitan areas, and households are usually connected automatically to the sewer system and pay a fixed fee per quarter. Householders are not required to obtain a licence, but Sydney Water, Hunter Water and other water supply authorities must obtain a licence from the EPA in accordance with the PEOA.

Trade waste schemes

Sydney Water and Hunter Water operate the main trade waste schemes in metropolitan areas but since the systems are similar, only Sydney Water's scheme is discussed. The *Sydney Water Act 1994* (SWA) requires Sydney Water to conduct its operations in compliance with the principles of ecologically sustainable development

---

9 Procedural fairness concepts apply and the licence holder must be given an opportunity to make submissions in relation to the proposed revocation or suspension: PEOA s 79(4).

(s 21(1)(b)). Sydney Water is also required to reduce its consumption of energy and water, and its discharges of pollution to the environment (s 23). It is an offence to discharge any substance into a work owned by Sydney Water, unless the written agreement of the Corporation has been obtained (s 49(1)). Discharges may be made in accordance with a contract or arrangement with Sydney Water (s 49(2)). A condition of Sydney Water's licence requires it to regulate discharges in trade waste contracts or agreements with customers.

The Trade Waste Policy and Management Plan 2004 sets out the conditions under which Sydney Water agrees to accept trade wastewater. Trade wastewater is defined to include any liquid and substances which may be produced at premises in an industrial or commercial activity, excluding domestic waste water. Fees are levied according to the quality, quantity and type of waste discharged. The Trade Waste Plan specifically emphasises that Sydney Water's relationship with business and industry is that of a service provider.

Industrial and commercial customers

A distinction is made between industrial and commercial customers. Certain commercial businesses may not require a permit to discharge trade waste provided that they install standard pre-treatment equipment as specified by Sydney Water. For example, businesses such as hairdressers and dry cleaners can obtain a deemed permit if they install approved pollution control equipment. Other commercial premises, such as hospitals, motels, butchers, service stations and so forth, require a formal permit from Sydney Water. Permits have no fixed term.

Industrial customers, such as abattoirs and oil refineries, must negotiate a formal agreement with Sydney Water and are subject to more stringent requirements under the Trade Waste Policy and Plan than commercial customers. An agreement is normally for a period of three years. Detailed conditions are set out in agreements and permits, including acceptance standards, rate and volume of discharge, arrangements for monitoring and auditing of the wastewater discharge, pre-treatment maintenance schedules and any improvement programs which industry agrees to undertake. Industrial customers are required to notify the existence of a current 'due diligence' program within six months of the granting of the permit. Where there is a breach of an agreement or permit, the default notice procedure outlined in individual agreement and permit documents applies. The Plan provides for suspension of trade wastewater discharges where Sydney Water reasonably believes it will present a potential threat to staff, treatment works or the environment. The Plan makes brief mention of criminal penalties. Offenders may be prosecuted under the *Sydney Water Act 1994*. Alternatively, a prosecution could be brought for pollution of waters under s 120 of the PEOA.

Individual industrial trade waste agreements can be inspected on the Sydney Water website (<www.sydneywater.nsw.gov.au>).

Local councils

Outside metropolitan areas, domestic and trade waste discharges are the responsibility of local councils. Councils may grant an approval to discharge waste into their sewers (*Local Government Act 1993* s 68). The *Local Government (General) Regulation 2005* (LGGR) provides that an application for approval to discharge trade waste into a sewer under the control of the council, or that which connects with such a sewer must be accompanied by the information required by Table 1 to the Liquid Trade Waste Management Guidelines (cl 25). Council may attach conditions to an approval having regard to Table 5 to the Guidelines (cl 32). The concurrence of the Director-General of the Department of Energy, Utilities and Sustainability is required for treated or untreated trade waste discharges (cl 28). An application for approval to install a sewage management facility must be accompanied by plans, specifications of the work to be done, a detailed site assessment and operational and maintenance information (cl 26). The LGGR provides detailed criteria which the council must consider in determining applications for approval to install, alter or operate sewage systems, including environment and health protection matters and performance standards (cll 39-30, 36-38). Sewage management facilities must be accredited (cl 41). An annual fee may be levied for these services (*Local Government Act 1993* s 501).

Notices

Notices are a major administrative tool for ensuring compliance with the provisions of the PEOA. There are many different kinds of notices, the most important of which are known as environment protection notices. These notices are designed to promote a proactive stance to environment protection in addition to remedying an existing problem. In other words, instead of waiting for pollution to occur, they can be used to prevent pollution occurring in the first place. There are three kinds of environment protection notices: clean-up notices, prevention notices and prohibition notices (s 90). Other notices which can be issued under the PEOA are, compliance cost notices (see p 437), notices relating to work on licensed premises (see pp 438-439), noise control notices (see p 438), and notices to repair motor vehicles (see p 439) (PEOA ss 104, 86, 264, 161). Notices are able to deal with all media and waste management. Notices can be issued to persons outside New South Wales if the matter affects the environment of the State (PEOA s 109). However, clean-up, prevention and prohibition notices cannot be issued so as to prevent or interfere with the carrying out of a 'critical infrastructure project' approved under Pt 3 of the EPAA (EPAA s 75U(3)(c)).

Except for prohibition notices which can only be issued by the Minister for the Environment, notices can be issued by the 'appropriate regulatory authority'. Regulatory authorities can recover an administrative fee of $320 for issuing a clean-up or prevention notice. They may extend the time for payment of the fee or waive payment in whole or in part. Reasonable costs and expenses incurred can also be recovered by issuing a compliance cost notice.

Failure to comply with an environment protection notice is an offence. The maximum penalty that may be imposed is $1 million for a corporation and $250,000 for an individual. In both cases, additional penalties apply for each day the offence continues (PEOA ss 91, 97, 102)). Similar penalties apply for persons who wilfully obstruct others in carrying out action in compliance with a notice (s 112).

Agents, employees or contractors of a council or the EPA are given wide powers to enter premises at any reasonable time for the purposes of exercising their functions in relation to environment protection notices (s 111(1)). Unlike the powers available to authorised officers (s 197), it seems that this power may be wide enough to permit entry to residential premises without the owner's consent.

As at 2003 the EPA had issued 157 clean-up notices and 31 prevention notices to both licensed and unlicensed facilities. Only three cost recovery notices were used (PEOA Review Report (2003)). An average of 13 clean-up notices and four prevention notices were issued per council, with 46% using compliance cost notices. Most notices were issued by councils in urban areas (PEOA Review Report (2003)).

Clean-up notices

Clean-up notices are intended to provide a quick response to 'pollution incidents' although in practice they are sometimes used to deal with pollution which has occurred over a period of time (eg, ground water contamination). They can be used to prevent or clean up pollution. They may be issued by the 'appropriate regulatory authority' to either the occupier of premises or the person reasonably suspected of causing a pollution incident, or both (s 91(1)). In an emergency, the notice can be given by the EPA even if it is not the appropriate regulatory authority (s 91(2)). The notice must generally be in writing but may be given orally. An oral notice must be acted on immediately but will lapse within 72 hours unless confirmed in writing (s 93(1)-(3)). Provision for oral clean-up directions ensures that immediate action can be taken, either to prevent a potential pollution incident or to mitigate any likely environmental impacts. A clean-up notice can be issued immediately after an event that may cause pollution, without waiting for the pollution to occur. This enables preventative measures to be taken.

A 'pollution incident' extends to actual or potential leaks, spills or escapes, and includes unlawful depositing of waste but does not cover incidents involving only the emission of noise (PEOA Dictionary). Before the 2005 amendments to the Act, odour incidents were excluded from the ambit of a clean-up notice but this has been changed so that immediate action can be required to clean up odorous materials.

'Clean-up action' is broadly defined in the PEOA Dictionary as to:

- include action to prevent, minimise, remove, disperse, destroy or mitigate pollution;
- ascertain the nature and extent of the incident and potential pollution; and
- prepare and carry out a remedial plan of action. It includes action to remove or store waste that has been disposed of on land unlawfully.

The clean-up notice must specify the clean-up action required and the time for compliance (s 91(1)). The clean-up notice may require periodic reports regarding progress on the carrying out of the clean-up action (s 91(3)).

Public authorities may be ordered to undertake clean-ups by the EPA or may do so at their own discretion (s 92(1)). This can occur whether or not a polluter or occupier has been served with a notice to undertake clean-up action.

It is an offence to fail to comply with a clean-up notice (s 91(5)). There is no right of merits appeal against a clean-up notice. This may explain why clean-up notices have sometimes been issued in preference to a remediation order under the *Contaminated Land Management Act 1997* where a merits appeal is available.

In keeping with the polluter pays principle, the person who has complied with the clean-up notice, despite not having caused the pollution, may recover the cost of complying with the notice from the polluter (s 91(4)).

Prevention notices

Prevention notices are intended to address ongoing pollution problems. They can be issued by the appropriate regulatory authority to either (or both) the occupier of premises or the person carrying on the activity, where there are reasonable grounds to believe that an activity is being conducted in an 'environmentally unsatisfactory manner' (s 96(1)). 'An environmentally unsatisfactory manner' is defined in s 95 of the PEOA as follows:

- it is carried on in contravention of, or in a manner that is likely to lead to a contravention of, the Act, the regulations or a condition attached to a licence including a condition of a surrender of a licence or an exemption issued;
- it causes, or is likely to cause, a pollution incident,
- it is not carried on by such practicable means as may be necessary to prevent, control or minimise pollution; or
- it is not carried on in accordance with good environmental practice.

'Good environmental practice' is not defined but presumably will be determined by the regulatory authority with regard to the circumstances and industry practice. Examples of actions which may be required by a prevention notice include:

- installing, repairing, altering, replacing, maintaining or operating control equipment or other plant;
- ceasing to carry on, or not commencing to carry on, an activity, or requiring the person to review the carrying out of an activity;
- preparing a plan of action to control prevent or minimise pollution or waste. (s 96(3))

The types of action listed in s 96(3) are not exhaustive and are similar to the usual conditions attached to a licence.

When determining the action to be specified in relation to an activity that has caused water pollution, the appropriate regulatory authority must consider the environmental values of water affected, and the practical measures that could be taken to restore or maintain them, and any guidelines issued by the EPA (s 96(3A)).

Thus, prevention notices could be used by a council to regulate unlicensed activities in much the same manner as the EPA regulates licensed activities by way of conditions on licences.

Prevention notices must be in writing and must specify the actions required. If no time limit is set, the notice is ongoing. Unlike licences there is no provision for a periodic review. If the occupier receives the notice and is not the person carrying on the activity, they must take all available steps to cause the activity to cease (s 96(4)). If the recipient does not comply with the prevention notice, the appropriate regulatory authority may effect the necessary improvements and recover the costs incurred (ss 98, 100, 104(4)).

An offence is committed if the requirements of a prevention notice are not complied with (s 97), but a merits appeal may be made to the Land and Environment Court within 21 days of issue (s 289). Prevention notices operate from the date the notice is issued, or from the date specified to the notice (s 99). If an appeal is made, the Land and Environment Court may stay the notice. The provision for an appeal means that it may be preferable to issue a clean-up notice where a quick response is required.

Prohibition notices

The Minister for the Environment has the power to issue a written prohibition notice directing either the occupier of the premises or the person carrying on an activity or both, to cease carrying on the activity where it is of the opinion that an emission or discharge of pollution from (or within) premises in which an activity is carried on, is:

- causing or likely to cause harm to the environment;
- likely to be injurious to public health;
- causing or likely to cause discomfort or inconvenience to any persons not associated with the management or operation of the activity. (s 101(1))

The notice may direct the occupier of the premises and/or the person carrying on the activity to cease the activity or any aspect of it, for the time specified in the notice (s 101(2)). Further notices may be issued on the expiry of the earlier notice. If the occupier receives the notice and is not the person carrying on the activity, they must take all available steps to cause the activity to cease (s 101(3)).

Failure to comply with a prohibition notice is an offence and no right of appeal is provided (s 102). If the notice is not complied with, the EPA may take action to achieve compliance and recover the costs incurred from the recipient of the notice (ss 103, 104(4)).

Compliance cost notice

The appropriate regulatory authority can issue a compliance cost notice to recover expenses that they have incurred in connection with the issue of notices. The types of expenses that can be recovered are:

- monitoring action under the notice;
- ensuring compliance with the notice;
- taking action because the recipient failed to comply; and
- any other associated matters. (s 104)

An exception is that the EPA is not permitted to recover costs incurred in monitoring action under a prevention notice (s 104(3)). This is presumably because the activities regulated by the EPA already incur a licensing fee.

A public authority which has undertaken a clean-up action, either voluntarily or at the direction of the EPA can also recover those costs by issuing a compliance cost notice (s 104(2)). The polluter is liable to compensate any person who complies with a notice and was not responsible for the pollution (s 105(2)).

Unpaid amounts specified in a compliance cost notice can be recovered as a debt in a court of competent jurisdiction (s 105(1)). Payment can be secured by registering it as a charge on land owned by the debtor (s 106(1)). The authority that lodges or registers the notice may require the recipient to pay costs and expenses incurred in respect of the lodgement or registration of the notice and the resulting charge (including the costs of discharging the charge (s 107(8)).

Other notices

The PEOA provides for various circumstances in which the appropriate regulatory authority can issue notices requiring the recipient to undertake or cease an activity.

Noise control notices

With regard to noise pollution, the appropriate regulatory authority[10] may by notice prohibit the occupier of premises or the person carrying on, or proposing to carrying on, any activity, from using or operating articles or carrying on the activity, during certain days or times that when measured at any specified point (whether within or outside the premises), emit noise in excess of a specified level (s 264). If no times are specified in the notice, it operates at all times. An offence is not automatically committed by those who breach the requirements of a noise control notice. It must also be established that noise was emitted which 'was able to be detected or perceived outside those premises without the aid of an instrument, machine or device' (s 265(2)). There is a right of merits appeal against a noise control notice (s 267). The notice operates from the day the notice is given, or the day specified in the notice. If an appeal is brought, the court may stay the notice.

The 2005 amendments to the PEOA bring the noise control notice into line with other environment protection notices by providing for a cost recovery system, namely:

- an administrative fee may be levied for issuing the notice;
- a compliance cost notice may be issued to recover all or any reasonable costs incurred by the authority in connection with monitoring action under the notice; ensuring the notice is complied with; and any other matters.

Unpaid amounts may be recovered as a debt in a court of competent jurisdiction. If the person who complies with the notice was not the person who caused the noise, the cost of complying may be recovered from the person responsible (s 267B).

Smoke abatement notices

These notices enable local councils to respond to smoke from domestic solid fuel heaters. Householders can cause unnecessary smoke even with an Australian Standard-compliant heater if they turn down the air circulation excessively, or burn wet or inappropriate fuel. To combat this problem, a local council officer can issue a smoke abatement notice if 'excessive smoke' is being emitted from a chimney on residential premises, or has been emitted within the past seven days (s 135B). 'Excessive smoke' is defined as a visible plume of smoke from a chimney which continues for at least 10 minutes and which, for at least 30 seconds, extends at least 10 metres from the point of emission (s 135A). Notices commence 21 days after issue and continue to operate for six months or until revoked. Failure to comply with a smoke abatement notice is an offence.

Breach of licensing requirements

If the occupier carries out scheduled development work or activities in contravention of the licensing requirements of the Act, the EPA may issue a notice requiring the occupier to remove the work that has been carried on, or to restore the premises to their previous state (s 86(1)). The notice operates from the date of issue, unless

10 Note that the Waterways Authority is the appropriate regulatory authority in relation to noise emanating from vessels in navigable waters, as well as premises used in connection with vessels and situated adjacent to, or partly or wholly over, navigable waters (s 263).

another date is specified. If an appeal is made, the Land and Environment Court may stay the notice. It is an offence to contravene the requirements of a notice (s 86(3)).

Notice to control motor vehicle emissions

An authorised officer of the EPA may direct the owner of a motor vehicle to service or repair the vehicle or to install or adjust an anti-pollution device, so that it no longer emits excessive air impurities. This is done by written notice when the officer reasonably suspects that the motor vehicle emits excessive air impurities (s 161). It is an offence to use a motor vehicle if the requirements of the notice have not been complied with (s 161(4)).

Noise abatement directions

An authorised officer or a police officer may issue a noise abatement direction if offensive noise is being, or has at any time within the past seven days been, emitted from premises (s 276). The Waterways Authority can issue notices in relation to vessels in navigable waters (s 275(b)). A direction may be given to the occupier of the premises or the person responsible for making the noise, or both. 'Offensive noise' is defined in broad terms. It is sufficient that the noise is likely to be harmful to a person outside the premises or to interfere unreasonably with their comfort or repose (PEOA Dictionary). Everything depends on the facts of each case, for example, the time at which the noise is made and the nature of the locality.

Once a noise abatement direction has been issued, the offensive noise must cease and not start up again during the next 28 days or an offence is committed, unless there is a reasonable excuse (s 277). A direction cannot be made to affect the activities of government or public authorities or any scheduled activity or work for which a licence is held (s 278), unless the direction is issued by an authorised officer appointed by the EPA.

The police have the power to enter premises to seize equipment that is being used to contravene a noise abatement direction provided they have a warrant (s 282). Unless they have obtained a warrant, they may not enter residential premises without the occupier's consent.

Criminal offences

Introduction

Classification of statutory offences

Most offences at common law consist of an *actus reus* (an act) and a *mens rea* (a state of mind). The *actus reus* refers to physical elements of the crime, that is, the act, the circumstances and the consequences, and the *mens rea* to all the mental elements. Generally a person does not incur liability for an offence unless they also have a guilty mind. However, there are many statutory exceptions to this. In some cases a statute may specify that *mens rea* is not a requirement for liability. In other cases, a statute may create an offence without specifying the relevant mental state. In *He*

Kaw Teh v R,[11] the High Court provided some assistance in determining when *mens rea* applies where this is not expressly stated in the statute. The court classified statutory offences into three categories:

(1) where *mens rea* or a guilty mind is an essential component of the offence;
(2) where the offence is one of strict liability so that the prosecution does not have to prove the *mens rea*. However, a defence of honest and reasonable mistake of fact is available;
(3) where the offence creates an absolute liability to which no defence is available.

The High Court pointed out that as a general rule, in the absence of a contrary statutory intent, *mens rea* applies to all statutory offences.[12] The presumption that *mens rea* is an essential ingredient in every offence can be displaced either by the words of the statute creating the offence or by a clear legislative intent to the contrary. To determine the legislative purpose, regard should be had to the language of the section, the subject-matter of the statute, the consequences of the offence for the community and the potential consequences for the accused if convicted.[13]

The common feature of offences of strict liability and absolute liability is that they dispense with proof of *mens rea*. However, strict liability offences allow a defence of honest and reasonable mistake of fact. Strict liability is therefore a middle ground between imposing absolute liability and requiring proof of negligence or intention.

Hierarchy of offences

The PEOA categorises environmental offences in three main groups or tiers. The first tier deals with serious offences. The second tier contains the mid-range offences which were previously dealt with in other pollution legislation, namely, the *Clean Air Act 1961* (NSW), the *Clean Waters Act 1970* (NSW), the *Noise Control Act 1975* (NSW), the *Pollution Control Act 1970* (NSW) and the (now repealed) *Waste Minimisation and Management Act 1995* (NSW). The third tier of the Act provides an 'on-the-spot' infringement notice system for dealing with minor environmental offences.

In the case of tier one (serious) offences, some form of mental element is required to establish criminal liability. These offences accordingly attract the most severe penalties, including imprisonment. Tier two offences fall into three broad categories:

- polluting, causing and permitting pollution or environmental harm
- offences pertaining to administrative breaches; and
- offences relating to enforcement.

Tier three offences are less serious. They generally fall into the same categories as the mid-range offences but, because of their lesser impact, do not warrant the imposition of high penalties.

---

11 (1985) 157 CLR 523.

12 See *Sherras v De Rutzen* [1985] 1 QB 918 at 921, adopted by Gibbs J in *He Kaw Teh* (1985) 157 CLR 523.

13 *He Kaw Teh* (1985) 157 CLR 523 at 529-530 per Gibbs CJ.

Tier one offences

Tier one offences are set out in ss 115-117 of the PEOA. Since these offences are serious, proof of *mens rea* in the form of intention or negligence is required. The 2005 amendments increased fines to provide a greater deterrent and to bring them into line with penalties for equivalent offences in other jurisdictions. The maximum penalty for a tier one offence for a corporation is $5 million for an offence that is committed wilfully and $2 million where it is committed negligently. An individual is liable to a maximum penalty of $1 million for wilful offences and/or seven years' imprisonment, and $500,000 and/or four years' imprisonment for an offence involving negligence (s 119).

It is interesting that the legislature saw fit to increase the maximum penalties available, since the Land and Environment Court has rarely imposed the maximum monetary penalty and a custodial sentence has only been imposed on one occasion. In *EPA v Gardner*,[14] Lloyd J convicted Gardner of an offence of 'wilfully disposing of waste in a manner which was likely to harm the environment'. The defendant Gardner, a caravan park operator, had discharged untreated sewerage into a river for 128 weeks. The results of this discharge was the growth of viruses near an oyster farm, representing a serious danger to human health. Gardner was sentenced to 12 months' imprisonment, with a minimum non-parole period of nine months. In addition, he was fined $250,000, the maximum penalty for an individual at that time, and ordered to pay the prosecution's costs of $170,000.[15]

In *EPA v Keogh*,[16] the defendant was fined $12,000 and sentenced to two months' imprisonment for failing to comply with an order of the court to remove illegally dumped waste. The period of imprisonment was suspended for 12 months to enable the defendant to remediate the site. The defendant failed to comply with this order and became the second person in New South Wales to be imprisoned for an environmental offence, although technically the sentence was for contempt of court.[17]

The tier one offences provided by the PEOA are:

- s 115(1) – 'wilfully or negligently dispos[ing] of waste in a manner that harms or is likely to harm the environment';
- s 116(1) – 'wilfully or negligently caus[ing] any substance to leak, spill or otherwise escape (whether or not from a container[18]) in a manner that harms or is likely to harm the environment';
- s 117(1) – 'wilfully or negligently caus[ing] any controlled substance (within the meaning of the *Ozone Protection Act 1989*) to be emitted into the atmosphere in contravention of the regulations under the Act and in a manner that harms or is likely to harm the environment'.[19]

---

14 [1997] NSWLEC 169.

15 *EPA v Gardner* [1997] NSWLEC 212.

16 [1999] NSWLEC 231.

17 *EPA v Keogh* [2000] NSWLEC 237.

18 Container is defined in s 116(5) to include 'anything for the purpose of storing, transporting or handling the substance concerned'. Thus it includes ships, trucks, aircraft and pipelines.

19 Section 117 is designed to complement the restrictions on ozone-depleting substances in the *Ozone Protection Act 1989* (NSW). There are eight controlled substances specified in Sch 1 to that *Ozone Protection Act*. These substances correspond with those in the Montreal Protocol 1988 and the *Ozone Protection and Synthetic Greenhouse Gas Management Act 1989* (Cth). This system is sufficiently flexible to accommodate any additions to the schedule of controlled substances in future revisions of the Montreal Protocol.

Where a contravention of s 116(1) (escape of substances) occurs, the net of liability also extends to a wide range of persons listed in s 116(2) provided they are shown to have 'wilfully or negligently, in a material respect, caused or contributed to the conditions which gave rise to the commission of the offence'. These persons are:

- the possessor of the substance;
- the owner of the container;
- the owner or occupier of the land on which the substance or container was located;

at the time of the leak, spill or escape.

Liability of owners

If the person who has committed an offence under s 115(1), 116(1) or 117(1) is not the owner of the waste or substance, the owner is also liable. 'Owner' includes the person who was the owner immediately before the disposal or escape (ss 115(3), 116(5), 117(2)).

These provisions are designed to prevent waste generators and other persons from off-loading waste and other substances to unlicensed or unscrupulous operators. The legislation has stopped short of imposing strict liability on owners as the defence in s 118 (no control and reasonable precautions and due diligence) is available (see pp 448-449).

The definition of owner of waste and other substances does not include a financial institution that is acting solely as a holder of a security interest. In that case, the person who has control of the waste or substance is taken to be the owner (PEOA Dictionary). Under former environment protection legislation there was no protection for lenders. Hence, a lender, despite not being in any way responsible for environmental damage, could become liable for an environmental offence, clean-up costs and damages to third parties by being categorised as an owner. The protection in the PEOA is, however, limited to situations where the lender is acting solely in that capacity. If a financial institution assumes possession and day-to-day control of the premises, it loses the protection.

Actus reus for tier one offences

Liability for a tier one offence is contingent on the disposal, emission or escape taking place in a manner which 'harms or is likely to harm the environment'.

What is 'waste'?

The ordinary dictionary meaning of 'waste' is extended by a wide definition in the PEOA Dictionary to include:

(a) any substance (whether solid, liquid or gaseous) that is discharged, emitted or deposited in the environment in such volume, constituency or manner as to cause an alteration in the environment, or

(b) any discarded, rejected, unwanted, surplus or abandoned substance, or

(c) any otherwise discarded, rejected, unwanted, surplus or abandoned substance intended for sale or for recycling, processing, recovery or purification by a separate operation from that which produced the substance, or

(d) any processed, recycled, re-used or recovered substance produced wholly or partly from waste that is applied to land, or used as fuel, but only in the circumstances prescribed by the regulations, or

(e) prescribed by the regulations to be waste.

What constitutes 'disposal of waste'?

An essential part of the *actus reus* for an offence under s 115(1) is the disposal of waste. In *EPA v Anning*,[20] Lloyd J considered whether the deposit of large quantities of tyres for reuse and sale constituted 'disposal of waste' for the purposes of s 5(1) of the *Environmental Offences and Penalties Act 1989* (NSW): now s 115(1) of the PEOA. Lloyd J interpreted the word 'dispose' broadly to include depositing tyres for future reuse as well as final deposits or disposals.[21] His Honour pointed out that if 'dispose' was to denote a final resting place only, the object of the Act would be defeated. This interpretation has been adopted in s 115(3) of the PEOA, which defines 'dispose' to include 'dump, abandon, deposit, discard, reject, discharge or emit anything that constitutes waste' as well as to 'cause or permit the disposal of waste'.

In considering whether there had been a disposal of waste, Lloyd J found that tyres intended for resale and reuse did not constitute 'waste' as then defined since they were not a 'substance'. Subsequent legislative amendments have overcome this problem. The Act now defines 'substance' to include 'matter or thing'. The definition of 'waste' has been broadened to 'include any unwanted or surplus substance (whether solid, liquid or gaseous). Further, a substance is not precluded from being waste merely because it may be reprocessed, recovered, reused or recycled': PEOA Dictionary. In effect, if the facts in *Anning* were to be decided today, the outcome would be different.

What is 'harm or likely harm to the environment'?

'Harm' is defined in the Dictionary to the PEOA as including 'any direct or indirect alteration of the environment that has the effect of degrading the environment and, without limiting the generality of the above, includes any act or omission that results in pollution'. 'Pollution' is widely defined to mean water, air, noise or land pollution within the broad meanings set out in the PEOA (PEOA Dictionary). 'Air pollution', for example, is defined as 'the emission into the air of any air impurities' which include smoke, dust, gases, fumes, mists, odours and so forth (PEOA Dictionary). The definition of 'water pollution' is equally wide and extends to almost any action that changes the physical, chemical or biological condition of air or water.

This comprehensive definition of 'harm' overcomes the evidentiary difficulties experienced by the State Pollution Control Commission in *State Pollution Control Commission v Caltex Refining Co Pty Ltd*.[22] The then Commission had initiated five prosecutions against Caltex for exceeding its licence limits of five milligrams per litre of phenols into Botany Bay by nearly six times the discharge limits. The charges

---

20 (1998) 100 LGERA 354.

21 Lloyd J found support for this interpretation in *R v Metropolitan Stipendiary Magistrate, Ex parte London Waste Regulation Authority* [1993] 3 All ER 113.

22 Unreported, NSWLEC, 50082-84/90, 50098/90 and 50102/90, 10 August 1990.

were, however, subsequently withdrawn because the Act (*Environmental Offences and Penalties Act 1989* (NSW)) did not define 'harm' and the Commission believed that the evidence was insufficient to prove harm to the environment.

In *Matthews v Goulburn Wool Processors Pty Ltd*,[23] Smart J held that in relation to the now repealed *Clean Waters Act 1970* (NSW), 'likely' means 'a real or not remote chance or possibility regardless of whether it is less or more than a 50% chance'. This definition of 'likely' has been consistently applied by the Land and Environment Court in relation to tier two offences. In *EPA v Anning*,[24] Lloyd J held that this definition of 'likely' applied also to 'likely harm to the environment' in tier one offences.

What is the environment?

The Dictionary to the PEOA also provides a comprehensive definition of 'environment', covering not only land, waters and the atmosphere, but also any organic or inorganic matter and any living organism, and interacting natural ecosystems, as well as human-made or modified structures. This definition is a departure from the human-centred approach which formerly characterised legislation of this kind. It is sufficiently broad to extend to greenhouse, ozone and atmospheric problems. At the same time it will cover substances which travel some distance from source and enter the food chain. Most pollution legislation in Australia has adopted a similar model.

Mens rea for tier one offences

The *mens rea* required to establish an offence under ss 115, 116 and 117 of the PEOA is wilfulness or negligence. 'Wilfully' suggests a deliberate or intentional act and requires a subjective test.

In considering whether a defendant has acted negligently, the courts apply an objective test. In *EPA v N*,[25] Hunt CJ at CL said:

> What must be considered is whether the risk of such harm was foreseeable to the reasonable person in the position of the defendant, not whether the defendant subjectively foresaw the risk himself.

Does mens rea apply to both components of an offence?

While it is clear from the wording of the legislation that *mens rea* must be shown in relation to the first component of the offence, namely the act of 'disposal' of waste or 'escape' of substances, it is unclear whether there is any such requirement in relation to the second component of 'harm or likely harm' to the environment under ss 115(1), 116(1) and 117(1) of the PEOA.

This matter was settled by the Court of Criminal Appeal in *EPA v N*,[26] where it was held by Hunt CJ at CL (with whom Enderby and Allen JJ agreed) that in a prosecution for an offence under s 5(1) of the *Environmental Offences and Penalties Act 1989* (NSW) (now s 115 of the PEOA), the prosecution must establish not only that the person charged with the offence wilfully or negligently disposed of the waste but also that the person 'either intended or was aware that the waste which he or

23 (1987) 10 NSWLR 419 at 420.
24 (1998) 100 LGERA 354.
25 (1992) 26 NSWLR 352 at 358-359.
26 (1992) 26 NSWLR 352.

she was disposing of would or was likely to harm the environment'.[27] Hunt CJ at CL also held that actual knowledge of harm to the environment was not essential and that it would be sufficient to show 'wilful blindness'.[28] According to this doctrine, someone who deliberately refrains from making inquiries, preferring not to know the result or avoiding the truth, may for some purposes be treated as having the equivalent of knowledge or reckless disregard for the facts.[29] The same reasoning would apply to ss 115, 116 and 117 of the PEOA since similar wording is used.

The standard of negligence

The PEOA is silent as to whether the relevant standard of negligence is the criminal standard, that is 'gross negligence' or 'recklessness', or a higher civil standard. This matter was considered in *State Pollution Control Commission v Kelly*,[30] where a company was charged under s 6(1) of the *Environmental Offences and Penalties Act 1989* (NSW) (now s 116 of the PEOA) for negligently causing a substance to leak, spill or escape from a container. Hemmings J rejected the argument by the defence that only gross departures from appropriate standards of conduct should lead to conviction, stating: '[I]n my opinion, s 6 compels the objective determination in each case of a standard of care, rather than nominate a degree of departure which is necessary to constitute negligence'.[31] Accordingly, the standard of care will vary according to the severity of the case. Hemmings J then stated that 'negligence in this context in my opinion is the failure to exercise such care, skill and foresight that would be expected of a reasonable person in the particular situation of the person charged'.[32] Hemmings J also held that 'negligence is an element of the offence which the prosecutor must prove beyond reasonable doubt'. The *Kelly* case left some uncertainty as to the appropriate standard of negligence for tier one offences.

The standard of negligence was clarified in the decision of the NSW Court of Criminal Appeal in *EPA v Ampol Ltd*.[33] Ampol was the owner and lessor of a fuel depot containing underground tanks which were used for storing petroleum products. While filling the tank, an employee of the lessee of the depot, Brir Pty Ltd, allowed the underground tank to overflow into the stormwater system, thereby polluting a nearby creek. It was alleged that Ampol was negligent in not providing for a draining, bunding and holding or shut-off system or tank alarm to ensure the containment of a spillage of this kind. The system used was the kind commonly found in the petroleum industry, and complied with all regulatory instruments and EPA requirements. Ampol had also provided a manual to the lessee to ensure that the correct operational procedures were followed.

Ampol was charged with a tier one offence in that, as owner of land on which the substance or container was located at the time of the escape, it 'negligently, in a material respect, caused or contributed to the conditions which gave rise to the commission of the offence' (s 116(2)(c)). Pearlman J referred the case to the Court of

27 Ibid at 356.

28 Ibid at 358.

29 *State Pollution Control Commission v Hunt* (1990) 72 LGRA 316 at 325; *He Kaw Teh v R* (1985) 157 CLR 523 at 531, 536.

30 Unreported, NSWLEC, Hemmings J, 50190/90, 50191/90 and 50226/90, 26 June 1991.

31 Ibid at 15.

32 Ibid at 15.

33 (1993) 81 LGERA 433.

Criminal Appeal for clarification of the standard of negligence. Mahoney JA (with whom Campbell and James JJ agreed) held that when concerned with the word 'negligence' appearing in a criminal statute, its meaning is to be determined by standard statutory construction, that is, what is meant by the term as it appears in the statute. Further, the question of whether the contribution to the relevant conditions was made negligently within the meaning of the statute must be assessed having regard to the contribution and the conditions in question and the circumstances of the case.

On the return of the matter to the Land and Environment Court, Pearlman J, in convicting Ampol, adopted a statutory measure based on the obligations imposed by the statute to avoid or minimise environmental harm.[34] She pointed out that the risk of harm to the environment was foreseeable, and relevant pollution prevention equipment such as bunding, a shut-off valve and a high level alarm were not used. Consequently, the fact that Ampol had carried out and complied with relevant industry codes, standards and practices, did not absolve it from liability; rather, the defendant had 'a general obligation to avoid or minimise environmental harm'.[35] Since Ampol's conduct did not amount to 'negligence' in the criminal sense, Pearlman J quite clearly applied a higher standard of care of a civil type. In fact, the standard seems even more demanding than the civil standard of care, which would be met by compliance with standard industry practice. Pearlman J imposed a penalty of $75,000 on Ampol. Interestingly, Pearlman J found the offence committed by Ampol – 'contributing to conditions that gave rise to the offence' (s 116(2)) – equivalent in seriousness to that of causing a spill (s 116(2)). Consequently, her Honour found that Ampol should not receive a lesser penalty than the $50,000 penalty that was imposed on Brir Pty Ltd, the lessee of Ampol's depot which had caused the diesel fuel to escape into a stormwater drain.[36]

Ampol's appeal to the Court of Criminal Appeal against the conviction was dismissed.[37] Special leave to appeal to the High Court was refused.[38]

The implications of the *Ampol* case are highly significant for all sectors of industry. It means that owners of property have to conduct an assessment of their sites, whether or not they are leased to others. Where environmental harm is a foreseeable risk of on-site activities, the owner will have to expend capital on control equipment or construction works so that any potential spill will be contained. To ensure that any loss is recoverable, the lessor should also ensure that an appropriate indemnity clause is included in the contract with the lessee.

The decision in *EPA v Warringah Golf Club*[39] and *EPA v Warringah Golf Club (No 2)*[40] also illustrates the high standard of care that is expected. The EPA prosecuted a golf superintendent and his employer, the Warringah Golf Club, for the negligent release of a highly toxic pesticide, Gusathion Turf Insecticide Liquid. The facts giving rising to this offence were as follows. An insect pest was discovered on one of the greens and it was decided to spray it with a pesticide, Gusathion, to

34 *EPA v Ampol Ltd* (1994) 82 LGERA 247.

35 Ibid at 255.

36 *EPA v Brir Pty Ltd* (1995) 85 LGERA 450.

37 *Ampol Ltd v EPA* (unreported, NSWCA, 60139/95, 26 October 1995).

38 *Ampol Ltd v EPA* (unreported, HCA, 15 June 1996).

39 [2003] NSWLEC 140.

40 (2003) 129 LGERA 211.

prevent it spreading. However, mechanical problems arose and the pesticide spray unit failed to operate. It was parked on a concrete slab in the workshop area to enable repairs to be carried out. The golf course superintendent disconnected one of the hose lines to drain the tanks to determine the location of the blockage. The chemical solution flowed across the concrete slab and was hosed off by the defendant. This resulted in the pesticide flowing into a stormwater drain which led directly into Brookvale Creek. It ultimately migrated into Manly Lagoon resulting in the death of more than 10,000 fish. In total over four tonnes of dead fish and eels were collected for disposal by Manly and Warringah Councils. At least 12 species of fish within the Lagoon perished. In addition, dead and dying ducks, cormorants and herons were observed by local residents.

The chemical Gusathion was found in the Lagoon and in samples of fish that died. The active ingredient of Gusathion is azinphos-ethyl which has a very high toxicity to fresh water invertebrates and fish. It has been estimated that one teaspoon of azinphos-ethyl in an Olympic size swimming pool would destroy aquatic life within a matter of hours. Approximately 10 litres of Gusathion containing 400 grams per litre of azinphos-ethyl was used by the defendant for spraying.

The golf course superintendent was convicted under s 116(1) of the PEOA for negligently causing a substance to escape in a manner that harmed or was likely to harm the environment.[41] The defendant pleaded guilty to the offence. At the time of the hearing the defendant was unemployed. Cowdroy J decided against imposing a fine but sentenced the defendant to 250 hours of community service work. In addition, the defendant was ordered to pay $1236 for tipping fees and disbursements for the disposal of dead fish by the council. He was also required to pay the prosecutor's costs.

The Warringah Golf Club was prosecuted separately for an offence under s 116(2) of the PEOA in that, being an occupier of land on which a substance was located at the time of escape, it negligently in a material respect contributed to the conditions that gave rise to the commission of an offence.

The Land and Environment Court found that the Warringah Golf Club had been criminally negligent. The case again illustrates the high standard of care which is imposed for statutory negligence under the PEOA. The court found that the club had contributed to the conditions giving rise to the offence by failing, 'to implement fundamental safeguards and procedures to protect the environment from harm in the event of an accident or the careless or negligent performance of duties by the defendant's employees'. In particular, the handling of chemicals in the area and servicing of equipment on the concrete slab and the regular hosing down of the slab near the stormwater pit and Brookvale Creek made it reasonably foreseeable that substances previously spilt could be washed into the waterway. There was no bunding or other protective device around the concrete slab or stormwater grate to contain a spill, and no washdown bay on the golf course to clean or repair machinery safely. In short, it was an accident waiting to happen. The club also had no written policies or guidelines for the safe handling of chemicals and no access to equipment to deal with a spill.

The court imposed a penalty of $250,000 on the golf club and ordered it to contribute $190,000 towards the prosecutor's costs. The club was also ordered to

---

41 *EPA v Coggins* (2003) 126 LGERA 219.

reimburse Warringah and Manly Councils for costs of $50,500 for clean-up expenses and the investigation. In addition, the court made ancillary orders requiring the club to carry out specific works and publish the offence.

Defences to tier one offences

Defence of lawful authority

Under ss 115(2) and 116(4) it is a defence for a person in proceedings for an offence under ss 115(1) and 116(1) respectively to show that the disposal or emission took place with 'lawful authority'. 'Lawful authority' is not defined in the Act. The possession of a licence under the PEOA would probably constitute lawful authority for the purposes of the section. It is also possible that the EPA or other public authority may give consent in certain situations to the disposal of waste, for example, under ss 145-146. It should be noted that the onus of proving lawful authority lies with the defendant.

Defence of lack of control and due diligence

It is a defence to a tier one offence where the person establishes:

(1) that the commission of the offence was due to causes over which the person had no control; and

(2) that the person took reasonable precautions and exercised due diligence to prevent the commission of the offence. (s 118)

Both parts of this defence must be proven by the defendant in order to succeed. The defendant bears the onus of proof for this defence (s 118). The scope of this defence is likely to be limited. In particular, it is unlikely to extend to the principal offences in tier one where the prosecution is required to prove negligence or wilfulness by the defendant, since an event which occurs because of forces over which the defendant had no control or where due diligence has been exercised is unlikely to have occurred as a result of negligence or wilfulness.

Parliamentary debates indicate that this defence was intended to protect employees who commit the offence of pollution under orders from their employer.[42] However it has not proven to be very successful in this aim. In *State Pollution Control Commission v Hunt*,[43] Bignold J held that the defendant's evidence that he committed the offence in pursuance of his supervisor's orders only served to diminish his penalty, not provide a defence to liability.

The defence can place a role in relation to constructive offences where the offence of another is sought to be imputed to the person in question. For example, it could be relied on by corporations to escape liability for acts of employees. It could also be used by owners of substances and waste. In *State Pollution Control Commission v Blue Mountains City Council*,[44] the previous version of this defence (*Environmental Offences and Penalties Act 1989* s 7) was successfully raised by the Blue Mountains City Council to escape liability for an offence committed at a waste dump which they owned. The offence was committed by an employee of a waste-

42 *Hansard*, Legislative Council, 21 September 1989, pp 10,394, 10,399.

43 (1990) 72 LGRA 316.

44 (1991) 72 LGRA 345.

disposal company retained by the council to oversee the management of a tip. Stein J held that the defence was made out since the council could not have been aware of, and had no control over, the employee's actions. At that time, the first part of the defence in *Environmental Offences and Penalties Act* s 7 (lack of control) was the same as that in s 118 of the PEOA, but the second part required proof that it was impracticable to make provision against the happening of the offence. The second part of s 118, on the other hand, requires the defendant to demonstrate reasonable precautions and due diligence. This means that the judgment is not entirely relevant, except for Stein J's evaluation in relation to the question of lack of control in the first part of the defence.

The common law defence of honest and reasonable mistake of fact does not apply to tier one offences.[45]

Tier two offences

Tier two offences are all other offences under the PEOA and regulations which are not tier one offences (s 114(2)). Where tier two offences are dealt with by way of penalty notice, they are classified as tier three offences (s 114(3) (see p 466).

Tier two offences can be divided into four broad categories:

- polluting, causing, or permitting pollution (ss 120 (waters), 124-135 (air), 136-141 (noise), 142A-142E (land) and 143-144A (waste));
- failure to comply with the regulatory scheme, for example, carrying out scheduled development work or scheduled activities without the appropriate environment protection licence (ss 47, 48, 49) and breaching the conditions of a licence (s 64);
- failure to comply with an environment protection notice, eg, a clean-up notice (ss 91(5), 97, 102); and
- failure to comply with directions issued by authorised officers.

The maximum penalties for offences relating to water, air and noise pollution when dealt with as tier two offences, are $1 million for corporations and $250,000 for individuals (ss 123, 132, 141). Daily penalties of $120,000 for corporations and $60,000 for individuals apply for continuing offences. Unless otherwise stated, these penalties apply in respect of all tier two offences.

Actus reus

What is pollution?

It is an offence to pollute or to cause or permit pollution. In New South Wales, 'pollution' is very broadly defined to include water, air, noise or land pollution (PEOA Dictionary). Land, air and noise pollution are also widely defined (PEOA Dictionary).

The definition of water pollution is particularly broad. 'Pollution of waters' is defined to include the introduction into waters of any solid, liquid or gas which changes the physical, chemical or biological condition of waters (PEOA Dictionary). It also includes the range of factors specified in the PEO (Gen) Regulation cl 52 read with Sch 3. These are very extensive and include animal and plant matter, ashes, oil,

45 *State Pollution Control Commission v Australian Iron & Steel Ltd* (1992) 74 LGRA 337.

radioactive substances and so forth. It is not essential to discharge directly into the waters. It is sufficient for it to be put in a position from which it ends up in waters or is likely to do so (PEOA Dictionary).

The definition of water pollution in the Act is meant to catch all modes of pollution, for example, the disposal of a small amount of heated water into a lake would effect a change in the physical and biological condition of the lake and would constitute pollution. In *Electricity Commission of New South Wales v EPA*,[46] the Court of Criminal Appeal held that the defendant was guilty of polluting waters even though the waters which had been polluted were entirely on its own land and had been specially constructed as a cooling pond for adjacent power stations. The court drew attention to the broad definition of 'waters' (PEOA Dictionary), which includes water stored in artificial works, mains, pipes and channels. It countered suggestions that, on this reasoning, an offence would be committed every time someone used chlorine in their swimming pool, by arguing that this would not involve a change in the condition of the water as contemplated by the definition of 'pollute'. It also pointed to the fact that the law does not concern itself with trifles.

Result offences

It has been held in New South Wales at least, that pollution offences are 'result' offences, that is, the *actus reus* consists of both the defendant's conduct and the harm resulting from that conduct.[47] In *Brownlie,* a case primarily involving the question of extra-territorial application of pollution legislation, Gleeson CJ pointed out that a necessary element of the offence is the consequential pollution which the conduct produces in New South Wales, irrespective of where it is committed. In result offences (eg, pollution), the prosecution also has to prove a link between the defendant's act and the prohibited consequences. In these cases a defendant only incurs liability where his or her conduct is a cause of the substantive criminal harm.

Causing pollution

The term 'cause' as used in pollution legislation has been given a wide interpretation by the courts. The most commonly prosecuted offence is that of causing or permitting pollution of waters. In the leading British case on pollution and causation, *Alphacell Ltd v Woodward*,[48] Lord Wilberforce held that it is necessary for the prosecution to prove 'some active operations or chain of operations involving as the result the pollution of the stream'. If pollution results, it is irrelevant that the defendant did not intend to cause it. This interpretation was followed in New South Wales in *Majury v Sunbeam Corp Ltd*.[49] McClemens CJ at CL found that the defendant had 'caused' the waters to be polluted since the entire process of storing potassium cupro cyanide, the control of the tanks, the method of working and the drainage system were all under the defendant's exclusive control. The drainage system was designed in such a way that any leakages would flow directly into the nearby river.

46 (1992) 28 NSWLR 494.

47 *Brownlie v State Pollution Control Commission* (1992) 27 NSWLR 78; *EPA v Bathurst* (1995) 89 LGERA 79.

48 [1972] AC 824 at 834.

49 [1974] 1 NSWLR 659.

In later NSW decisions on the point, the courts have continuously applied a wide interpretation of 'cause'.[50]

Causation – acts of third parties

An issue that requires clarification and that was not settled in the *Alphacell* or *Majury* cases is whether acts of third parties or natural forces remove the causal connection so that the defendant cannot be held liable for causing the pollution. According to the House of Lords, in *Empress Car Co (Abertillery) Ltd v National Rivers Authority*,[51] the test to be imposed, is whether the defendant did something which caused a situation where pollution could escape and the act of a third party or a natural event which causes the pollution, although not necessarily foreseeable in a particular case, is nonetheless 'in the generality a normal and familiar fact of life' as opposed to an act or event which is 'abnormal and extraordinary'.[52] For example, there is nothing extraordinary or abnormal about leaky pipes or lagoons, or about people putting unlawful substances in the sewage system or acts of ordinary vandalism. On the other hand, a terrorist attack would be something so unusual that one would not regard the defendant's conduct as having caused the pollution.[53] The test imposed by the House of Lords has been approved in a number of decisions of the Land and Environment Court.[54]

Mens rea

Polluting or causing pollution

The PEOA does not specify whether any guilty intent (*mens rea*) applies in relation to tier two offences. Traditionally, pollution offences have been described as offences of strict liability, meaning it is unnecessary to prove the *mens rea* element of the offence. This means that all that need be shown is that the defendant was responsible for the act or emission which resulted in pollution. This was held in England in *Alphacell Ltd v Woodward*,[55] and affirmed by the House of Lords in *Empress Car Co (Abertillery) Ltd v National Rivers Authority*,[56] as a matter of public policy and was followed in New South Wales in *Majury v Sunbeam Corp Ltd*.[57] In *State Pollution Control Commission v Tiger Nominees Pty Ltd*,[58] Hemmings J held that s 16(1) of the *Clean Waters Act 1970* (NSW) (now s 120 of the PEOA) 'creates an offence of strict liability in respect of which *mens rea*, knowledge or negligence are

---

50 See *Cooper v ICI Australia Operations Pty Ltd* (1987) 64 LGRA 58; *Tiger Nominees Pty Ltd v State Pollution Control Commission* (1992) 25 NSWLR 715; *Jones v John Lysaght (Aust) Ltd* (1983) 51 LGRA 90; *Environmental & Earth Sciences Pty Ltd v EPA* (1999) 103 LGERA 434; *EPA v Multiplex Constructions Pty Ltd* (2000) 112 LGERA 1).

51 [1998] 1 All ER 481.

52 Ibid at 491.

53 Ibid.

54 See *EPA v Multiplex Constructions Pty Ltd* (2000) 112 LGERA 1; *EPA v Shell Co of Australia Ltd* [2000] NSWLEC 132.

55 [1972] AC 824.

56 [1998] 1 All ER 481.

57 [1974] 1 NSWLR 659 at 664.

58 (1991) 72 LGRA 337 at 342.

not ingredients'.[59] It has also been held that the offences of causing air pollution are strict liability offences.[60] A similar finding has been made in relation to s 63 of the now repealed *Waste Minimisation and Management Act 1995* (NSW) (now s 143 of the PEOA).[61] Since the offences in tier two of this Act are similar to those in former legislation, they have continued to be regarded as offences of strict liability. Tier two offences are subject to a common law defence of honest and reasonable mistake of fact (see discussion at pp 464-466) and *He Kaw Teh v The Queen*[62]).

Permitting pollution

Where legislation uses the word 'permit', some knowledge is required. A measure of control over the emission must be shown. In *Rochford Rural District Council v Port of London Authority*,[63] Darling J briefly considered the meaning of the word 'permit'. His Honour held that 'if a man knowingly permits a thing to happen he certainly suffers it to happen'.[64] This approach was followed in New South Wales in *State Pollution Control Commission v Tiger Nominees Pty Ltd*,[65] where Hemmings J suggested that '"permit" probably must require knowledge and involves a failure to prevent the pollution'. It has also been applied in other New South Wales decisions.[66]

Water pollution

The PEOA prohibits absolutely the pollution of any waters. [67] Section 120 of the PEOA provides that a person must not

- pollute any waters;
- cause any waters to be polluted; or
- permit any waters to be polluted.

It is a defence to a charge of water pollution that the person held a licence and the pollution was in accordance with the conditions of the licence (s 122). In *EPA v ADI Ltd*,[68] Talbot J held that the onus of proof in establishing that the licence conditions had not been contravened rested with the defendant.

---

59 See also *Cooper v ICI Australia Operations Pty Ltd* (1987) 64 LGRA 58 at 65; *Tiger Nominees Pty Ltd v State Pollution Control Commission* (1992) 25 NSWLR 715; *State Rail Authority New South Wales v Hunter Water Board* (1992) 28 NSWLR 721 at 722; *EPA v Water Board* (1993) 79 LGERA 103 per Bignold J; *EPA v Australian Iron and Steel Pty Ltd (No 2)* (1993) 78 LGERA 373; *EPA v Multiplex Constructions Pty Ltd* (2000) 112 LGERA 1.

60 *EPA v Water Board* (1993) 79 LGERA 103; *EPA v Australian Iron and Steel Pty Ltd (No 2)* (1993) 78 LGERA 373.

61 *Owen v Willtara Construction Pty Limited* [1998] NSWLEC 216.

62 (1985) 157 CLR 523.

63 [1914] 2 KB 916 at 924.

64 See also *Alphacell Ltd v Woodward* [1972] AC 824.

65 (1991) 72 LGRA 337 at 342.

66 See *EPA v Multiplex Constructions Pty Ltd* (2000) 112 LGERA 1.

67 Note that a person who discharges pollutants into a sewer with the consent of the person in whom the sewer is vested is exempted from the provisions of s 120: PEO (Gen) Regulation cl 55. See other exemptions in Chapter 3 of the PEO (Gen) Regulation.

68 [1998] NSWLEC 279.

Air pollution

The PEOA attempts to prevent and control air pollution, although for practical purposes it recognises that, for the present, the minimisation of air pollution is more realistic. Air pollution is defined as the emission into the air of any air impurity. Air impurity includes smoke, dust, cinders, solid particles of any kind, gases, fumes, mists, odours and radioactive substances (PEOA Dictionary).

There are five offences relating to air pollution (ss 124-129). They do not apply to premises used only for residential purposes (s 131). Air pollution offences require proof of air pollution outside the premises. This can be established by proof that air pollution was caused on the premises, unless the defendant can prove that the air pollution did not cause air pollution outside the premises (s 127).

Operation and maintenance work on plant (other than domestic)

It is an offence for an occupier to operate a plant, carry out maintenance work on plant, or deal with materials in such a manner as to cause air pollution from the premises, if it results from a failure to maintain the plant in an efficient condition or to operate it in a 'proper and efficient manner' (ss 124, 125, 126(1)). The phrase 'proper and efficient manner' is not defined in the Act but some assistance can be derived from case law. Failing to start control equipment[69] has been held to be equivalent to failing to operate equipment in a 'proper and efficient manner'.[70] 'Proper and efficient' must also be considered in relation to harm to the environment, therefore, control equipment is not operating properly and efficiently if it is simultaneously causing pollution.[71] To establish an offence it is sufficient to prove an inefficient condition of control equipment sufficient to create the possibility of air pollution.[72]

Dealing with materials

An occupier commits an offence if he or she deals with materials in such a manner as to cause air pollution from premises, if the pollution is due to a failure to 'deal with those materials in a proper and efficient manner' (s 126(1)). 'Deal' is defined to mean process, handle, move, store or dispose of materials (s 126(2)). In *Jones v John Lysaght (Australia) Ltd*,[73] the Land and Environment Court found that the defendant had caused pollution, notwithstanding that the fire causing the damage had resulted from the actions of a third party who had been present with the consent of the defendant. The fire was directly linked to a failure to store materials in a proper and efficient manner. This case was followed by Stein J in *EPA v Australian Iron & Steel Pty Ltd (No 2)*.[74]

---

69 'Control equipment' refers to apparatus used or designed to prevent, limit or regulate pollution or to monitor or to give warning of pollution (PEOA Dictionary). See also discussion of the general offence of failing to maintain or operate control equipment efficiently (s 167) discussed at p 458.

70 *Smith v Cnizonom Pty Ltd* (unreported, NSWLEC, Cripps J, Nos 50011-2/81, 25 March 1982).

71 *State Pollution Control Commission v Shell Refining (Australia) Pty Ltd* (unreported, NSWLEC, Cripps J, Nos 50171-3/89, 1 July 1990, BC 9003120).

72 *Smith v Calsil Ltd* (1982) 47 LGRA 132 per McLelland CJ.

73 (1983) 51 LGRA 90.

74 (1992) 78 LGERA 373.

In *EPA v Yolarno Pty Ltd*,[75] a company was convicted of three air pollution offences arising from a failure to 'deal with materials in a proper and efficient manner'. The defendant had discharged effluent waste water from abattoirs into aneorobic ponds on the premises. The ponds were already overloaded with effluent and caused emission of unpleasant odours and gases into the atmosphere. The defendant company was ordered to spend $30,000 on rehabilitation works and to publish the details of the offence.

Emission standards

It would be unrealistic to attempt to prohibit all forms of air pollution. Instead, the PEOA allows for standards to be set in respect of the concentration and rate of emissions from any premises. Emissions of air impurities in excess of the prescribed standards is an offence (s 128).

Emission standards have been laid down for a variety of different types of air pollutants that relate to plant and equipment. The *Clean Air (Plant and Equipment) Regulation 1997* has been repealed. A number of its provisions have been transferred to the *Protection of the Environment Operations (Clean Air) Regulation 2002* (CA Regulation) and new provisions have been introduced. The new Pt 4 of the CA Regulation classifies both scheduled and non-scheduled activities and plant based on their age. Six emission limit groups are established for scheduled premises. Emission limits are set based on the classification and phase-out dates for the least stringent limits applicable to the older activities and plant. Older industry must review emission standards and progressively modify or replace existing plant. More stringent limits are set for future industry. Prescribed standards of concentration for air impurities for scheduled premises are set out in Schs 2, 3 and 4 of the CA Regulation. Maximum emission levels have also been specified for non-scheduled premises, with respect to solid particles, smoke and soot (Sch 6), the use of high sulphur liquid fuels and the transport and storage of volatile organic liquids (CA Regulation Pts 5 and 6). These have to be attained even at the expense of installing new equipment and plants, although in practice the standards are not set so high as to impose unduly onerous economic burdens on industry.

Odours

Occupiers of premises at which scheduled activities are carried on under the authority of a licence must not cause or permit the emission of an offensive odour (s 129(1)). This is defined as an odour that, by reason of its strength, nature, duration, character or quality, is harmful to, or unreasonably interferes with, the comfort of a person outside the premises from which it is emitted (PEOA Dictionary). It is a defence if the environmental protection licence pertaining to the premises contemplates the emission of the odour and the relevant conditions aimed at minimising the odour have been complied with, or the odour only affects those engaged in the management or operation of the premises (s 129(2)). In *EPA v Shoalhaven Starches Pty Ltd*,[76] an occupier of scheduled premises was convicted under s 129(1) for causing offensive odours from licensed premises arising from stored wastewater in effluent ponds. This was the third prosecution of the company in 10 years. The court

75 [2004] NSWLEC 764 and [2004] NSWLEC 765.

76 [2006] NSWLEC 496.

imposed a fine of $125,000 plus EPA costs of $235,000. The company was also ordered to publicise the offence and pay for an independent environmental audit at an estimated cost of $400,000.

There is no specific offence relating to the emission of odour from unlicensed premises. However, in an appropriate case this could be prosecuted as an offence causing air pollution.[77]

Open fires and incinerators

The EPA may prohibit the burning of open fires or specified classes of incinerators for a period of up to seven days, when it is of the opinion that meteorological conditions warrant it (s 133(1), (2)). This is achieved by an order published in a daily newspaper circulated in New South Wales or broadcast by radio or television (s 133(4)). An authorised officer is empowered to issue a notice requiring any fire to be extinguished immediately. Authorised officers also have a general power to order that fires be extinguished where they are health hazards or likely to cause 'serious discomfort or inconvenience' (s 134).

Land pollution and waste

Land pollution

A blanket prohibition on land pollution was introduced in 2005. A person who pollutes land, or causes or permits land to be polluted, commits an offence (s 142A).

A number of defences are provided, namely if the person establishes that:

- the activity that polluted the land was authorised by regulation, and that the regulation was not contravened;
- the pollution was regulated by a licence and the conditions of the licence were not contravened;
- the substance placed on the land was a pesticide, fertiliser, manure or like material which could be lawfully used;
- that the substance was placed into an unlicensed landfill site notified to the EPA in accordance with, and operated in accordance with, the regulations.

Waste

The PEOA provides for the following offences in relation to waste:

- transporting waste to a place that cannot lawfully be used as a waste facility, or causing or permitting waste to be so transported (s 143);
- for an owner or occupier to use land, or cause or permit land to be used as a waste facility when it cannot lawfully be used for that purpose (s 144).

In each case, the defendant bears the onus of establishing lawful authority (ss 143(2), 144(2)).

Specific defences are provided for unlawful transportation of waste, namely:

- if the owner did not transport the waste and established that the commission of the offence was due to causes over which he or she had no control,

77 See *EPA v Yolarno Pty Ltd* [2004] NSWLEC 764 and [2004] NSWLEC 765 discussed at p 454.

and the owner exercised reasonable precautions and due diligence (s 143(3));

- if a notice in a form approved by the EPA was given to the defendant by the owner or occupier of the place to which the waste was transported which stated that the place could lawfully be used as a waste facility, and was certified by the owner or occupier as being correct, and the defendant had no reason to believe that the place could not lawfully be so used (s 143(3A)).

For the purposes of s 143, 'owner' of waste includes the person who was the owner of the waste immediately before it was transported. 'Waste' includes any unwanted or surplus substance (whether solid, liquid or gaseous). A substance is not precluded from being waste merely because it may be reprocessed, re used or recycled.

The EPA has had little difficulty in obtaining convictions for waste offences. For example, in *EPA v Fernando*,[78] the defendant and his company were convicted of an offence under s 143(1)(a) of the Act (transporting waste to a place that could not lawfully be used as a waste facility). The defendant operated a cleaning service business. After removing several drums of chemicals from a printing company's premises, he disposed of the drums on a dirt road. Some of the drums contained hazardous waste and were flammable but no harm to the environment resulted because of prompt action by the fire brigade. Fernando was fined $60,000. The court took a number of factors into account in mitigation of penalty, including an undertaking to clean up the site. The company, a trust involved in charitable work, was fined $5000.[79]

It is also an offence for a person to supply (or cause or permit supply of) false or misleading information about waste to another in the course of dealing with waste unless the person can prove that he or she took all reasonable steps to verify the accuracy of the information (s 144AA). This offence is intended for situations where unscrupulous operators are claiming a waste is, for example, uncontaminated with asbestos or a lower risk waste, when it in fact contains hazardous contaminants and should be classified as a hazardous waste, with the result that it is accepted or disposed of inappropriately and at lower cost.[80]

Littering

It is an offence to litter in a public place or open private place (s 145). It is also an offence to deposit advertising material in a place other than a mail box or under the door of premises (s 146A(1)). A person is not excused from being convicted of an offence of depositing litter in a public place where the forces of nature cause the mobility of litter, for example, it blows into water. A more serious offence of aggravated littering is committed if the circumstances in which the litter was deposited, caused or contributed to appreciable danger to harm to persons, animals, or property, or was reasonably likely to do so (s 145A).

If litter is deposited from a motor vehicle, the driver or owner are both guilty of an offence, unless they provide a statutory declaration disclosing the name and

---

78 (2003) 129 LGERA 416.

79 See also *EPA v Pannowitz* [2006] NSWLEC 219 discussed at p 471.

80 EPA Issues Paper: Review of the PEOA 1997.

address of the person responsible, or satisfy the responsible officer that they do not know the name and address, and could not with reasonable diligence have ascertained it (s 146). Exceptions apply where litter is deposited from vehicles involved in public transportation or from stolen vehicles (s 146).

Noise pollution

It is impossible to ban all noise, as the activities of society would cease to function. The PEOA controls noise by setting standards or limits on noise production from specified sources. Alternatively, where a specified limit is impracticable due to the complex nature of the noise, the offence is to cause offensive noise (see noise abatement directions at p 439). The Act does not extend to noise produced in the work environment, such as factories. It is intended only to control noise as it affects the community, such as noise from industrial premises, transport, loud parties and dogs, to name a few of the many likely sources. The distinction between occupational noise and community noise is maintained by directing the application of the Act at noise which is heard outside the premises, or which is the subject of a prescribed level or standard. There is no provision in the Act for setting general noise emission standards, although standards are prescribed in relation to certain articles.

There are four main offences relating to noise pollution (ss 136-140). A person commits an offence if he or she:

- sells an article which emits noise that is in excess of the prescribed level, provided the article is of a class prescribed by the regulations (s 136);
- sells an article which is not fitted in the prescribed manner with noise control equipment of a prescribed class or, if fitted, is not maintained as required by the regulations (s 137(2));
- causes noise due to a failure to maintain the plant in an efficient condition, or to operate the plant in a proper and efficient manner (s 139); or
- causes noise due to a failure to deal with materials in a proper and efficient manner (s 140(1)).

It is a defence to a prosecution for failing to maintain control equipment if the defendant can prove that he or she took all reasonable steps to ensure the equipment was properly maintained (s 137(3)). A defence is also available to employees and sales staff who are charged with selling articles which emit excessive noise (s 138).

Hours of use are prescribed for certain articles such as lawnmowers, chainsaws, air conditioners, power tools and musical instruments. They cannot be used on residential premises during certain hours if they emit noise which can be heard in a 'habitable' room of a neighbouring house (*Protection of the Environment Operations (Noise Control) Regulation 2000* cll 50-52). Where building and vehicle intruder alarms do not cease sounding after the maximum time permitted in the Regulation, an authorised officer may turn off the alarm or otherwise disable it (PEOA s 198A).

Noise abatement orders

The occupier of any premises can complain to a justice of the peace (usually the magistrate at a Local Court) that their occupation is being affected by 'offensive noise' (s 268(1)). 'Offensive noise' is broadly defined to include noise that by reason of its level, nature, character or quality, or the time at which it is made, is harmful to a person outside the premises, or unreasonably interferes with their comfort or repose (PEOA Dictionary). The person alleged to be making or contributing to the noise, or the occupier of the premises from which it is alleged to be emitted, may then be summoned to appear before a Local Court (s 268(2)). The court can make a noise abatement order directing the defendant to abate the offensive noise, or prevent it re-occurring, or both (s 268(4)). An order cannot be issued against the State or a public authority, or if it affects an activity subject to a licence or an activity prescribed by the regulations (s 270). The only recourse is to complain to the EPA. Contravening a noise control order is an offence. An appeal lies to the Land and Environment Court (s 271).

Duty to notify pollution incidents

The PEOA requires various persons including the polluter, the occupier, an employee or an employer to notify the appropriate regulatory authority, usually the EPA or local council, of pollution incidents as soon as practicable, where 'material harm' to the environment is caused or threatened (s 148). Material harm includes actual or potential harm to the health or safety of humans beings or to ecosystems that is not trivial or results in actual or potential loss or property damage of an amount exceeding $10,000 (s 147(1)). Odour incidents need not be reported. Failure to notify the EPA is a tier two offence. However, any notification is not admissible in evidence against the person for an offence or for the imposition of a penalty.

A person is also excused from notification if there are reasonable grounds for believing that the incident has already come to the notice of the relevant authorities (s 151(1)).

Offences relating to licences and control equipment

It is an offence to carry out scheduled work or activities without obtaining a licence (ss 47-49). The onus of proof in establishing that a licence is held rests with the defendant.[81] If a licence is held, it is an offence to contravene the conditions of the licence. It is an offence for an occupier to fail to maintain any control equipment in an efficient condition, or to fail to operate it in a proper and efficient manner (s 167). In *EPA v Water Board*,[82] Bignold J held that the duty to maintain control equipment in an efficient condition includes a duty to put it in such condition if it is not already in it.

Offences relating to environment protection notices

Notices are an important administrative tool for ensuring compliance with environment protection legislation (see p 434). Failure to comply with an environmental protection notice is an offence (ss 91(5) (clean-up notices), 97 (prevention notices), 102 (prohibition notices)).

Powers of investigation and related offences

Effective enforcement of environmental protection measures is reliant on inspection and investigation to ensure compliance with such measures. In addition to regular

---

81 *EPA v Brown & Hatton Rural Pty Ltd* (1992) 77 LGRA 383.

82 (1993) 79 LGERA 103.

inspections, authorised officers also enjoy wide powers to enter and inspect premises and vehicles, without a search warrant in many instances, to monitor compliance with the legislative provisions (s 196).

The EPA, the appropriate regulatory authority or an authorised officer can issue a notice requiring a person to furnish information or records in connection with any matter relating to its functions or responsibilities under the Act (ss 191-193). Authorised officers can request proof of a suspect's name and address. Failure to provide this information is not an offence but the authorised officer can arrest the person and bring them before a magistrate (s 204).

There are a number of offences aimed at facilitating investigations and enforcement by authorised officers. For example, occupiers and other personnel are guilty of an offence if they obstruct an authorised officer (s 211(3)), furnish false or misleading information (ss 190-5, 211(2)), or refuse to answer questions (ss 203-204). The EPA or any other regulatory authority may require a corporation to nominate a director or officer to be the corporation's representative for the purpose of answering questions (s 203(2)). Answers given by a nominee bind the corporation (s 203(3)).

An individual or corporation, however, is not guilty of an offence of failing to furnish information or to answer a question unless they were warned that failure to comply is an offence. The individual or corporation cannot refuse to comply with these requirements on the ground of self-incrimination (s 212(2)). In the case of an individual, however, the answer given or information supplied cannot be used in criminal proceedings against such a person if the person objected at the time to answering on the ground that the answer might incriminate them, or if the person was not warned of their right to object to furnishing the information on the ground of self-incrimination (s 212(3)). This protection is consistent with the decision of the High Court in *EPA v Caltex Refining Co Pty Ltd*,[83] where the High Court held that the privilege against self-incrimination only applies for the benefit of natural persons and not for corporations.

Vicarious liability

Vicarious liability is the term applied to circumstances where a person is held legally liable for the actions of another. In this context, vicarious liability is seen as a form of strict liability, because the person found to be vicariously liable need not have had a guilty mind. In fact, the person held vicariously liable may not even have known about the commission of the offence.

In New South Wales, the question of whether Parliament intended to impose vicarious criminal liability for strict liability offences has been considered in a number of decisions. In *Tiger Nominees Pty Ltd v State Pollution Control Commission*,[84] Gleeson CJ (with whom Mahoney JA and Campbell J agreed) found that the imposition of vicarious liability was consistent with the long title of the *Clean Waters Act 1970* (NSW), the purpose of the Act and the definition of 'pollute' in s 5. Vicarious liability only arises where the employee is acting within the course of his or her employment.[85] An employee performing improper or unauthorised acts that relate to employment duties is still considered to be acting within the scope of employment.

83 (1993) 178 CLR 477.

84 (1992) 25 NSWLR 715.

85 Ibid at 721 per Gleeson CJ.

Independent contractors

After some conflict as to whether vicarious criminal liability could attach for the acts of employees of independent contractors under the repealed *Clean Waters Act 1970* (NSW),[86] the decision in *State Pollution Control Commission v Australian Iron & Steel Ltd*[87] made it clear for the first time that persons could be held vicariously liable for the acts of employees of independent contractors in circumstances where they exercised sufficient control over such workers. Again, in *EPA v Multiplex Constructions Pty Ltd*,[88] Lloyd J considered control to be a crucial factor in determining the existence of vicarious liability. The terms of the contract between the parties are important in determining whether such control is exercised. In that case, the EPA prosecuted a developer, Multiplex, for water pollution resulting from breach of a fuel line on a finger wharf in Woolloomooloo Bay. The pollution had been caused by an employee of a subcontractor retained by an independent contractor McConnell Dowell who had been retained by Multiplex. The court acquitted Multiplex because they had not exercised control over the employee who had caused the pollution. Although they had given directions as to what work was to be done, they had not given instructions as to how the work was to be carried out. The EPA subsequently prosecuted McConnell Dowell with the same result.[89] It should be noted that these prosecutions were instituted under s 16(1) of the now repealed *Clean Waters Act* 1970 as they occurred before the commencement of the PEOA. Had the PEOA been in force, the result may have been different, at least in respect of McConnell Dowell, depending on whether the test in s 257 of the PEOA had been satisfied.

The PEOA changes the control test by providing for occupiers' liability in certain circumstances. Section 257 provides that the occupier of premises from which pollution has occurred is taken to have caused the pollution, unless the occupier proves that someone other than an agent, licensee, employee, contractor or subcontractor was responsible, and that the occupier took reasonable steps to prevent the pollution. Presumably, 'reasonable steps' will correspond closely with 'due diligence'. 'Occupier' is defined as a person who has the management and control of premises or the current licence holder. Clearly, if an independent contractor falls into the range of persons covered by this section, the test will be based on 'occupation' rather than control.

Corporate liability

Since corporations are artificial persons, a difficulty arises in determining how they can be held liable for an offence which requires proof of a guilty mind or some form of intent. This dilemma was overcome in England in the early 20th century where the courts held that a company could be convicted of a criminal offence where the necessary fault could be found in a corporate officer who is in effect the 'directing mind and will' of the company.[90] The common law basis of corporate criminal

---

86 Compare *State Pollution Control Commission v Blue Mountains City Council (No 2)* (1991) 73 LGRA 337 at 348 and *State Pollution Control Commission v Tiger Nominees Pty Ltd* (1991) 72 LGRA 337 at 342-343.

87 (1992) 74 LGRA 387.

88 (2000) 112 LGERA 1.

89 *EPA v McConnell Dowell* [2003] NSWLEC 70.

90 *Lennards Carrying Co Ltd v Asiatic Petroleum Co Ltd* [1915] AC 705, as elaborated in *Tesco Supermarkets Ltd v Nattrass* [1972] AC 153.

liability, as laid down in *Tesco* and other case law, limited the responsibility of a corporation to the conduct and fault of the board of directors, the managing director or persons to whom a function of the board had been wholly delegated. This approach has been adopted in Australia and, unless abrogated by statute, continues to apply. It has many disadvantages, including opportunity for evasion, particularly on the part of large corporations, since decisions which cause pollution are seldom made at board level, but are often taken by middle management or diffused throughout the organisation.

The PEOA overcomes the problems of the *Tesco* principle by extending the range of persons whose state of mind can be attributed to the corporation to persons lower down the corporate ladder, such as employees or agents. Thus, where it is necessary to establish the state of mind of a corporation, it is sufficient to show that an officer, employee or agent (acting within their capacity as such) had that state of mind (s 169(4)). 'State of mind' is defined to include a person's knowledge, intention, opinion, belief or purpose and the reasons therefore. This provision operates in addition to any liability that the corporation may have incurred for an offence which it has committed (s 169(3)).

Offences by directors and managers

Corporate policy is determined by an organised collective of individuals. Thus any effective response to environmental problems must target the decision dynamics within the corporation. At common law, corporate officers are not liable for offences committed by their corporations. New South Wales, like most Australian jurisdictions, has introduced legislation imposing personal criminal liability on corporate officers to complement sanctions against the corporations themselves. Liability for corporate offences arises solely by virtue of the officer's position in the organisation.

The Act provides that where a corporation contravenes a provision of the Act, each person who is a director of the corporation, or who participates in the management of the corporation, is taken to have contravened the same provision irrespective of whether proceedings are taken against the company or whether it is convicted of the contravention (s 169(1)). The terms 'directors' or 'persons concerned in the management of the corporation' are not defined and will presumably be interpreted in accordance with the *Corporations Act 2001* (Cth) and case law.[91] In considering the meaning of the phrase 'concerned in management' in the context of s 556 of the *Companies (New South Wales) Code*, it is necessary to consider the precise role the person played in the corporation, rather than simply the title or the position the person occupies in the corporate structure.[92] In *Barac v Farnell*,[93] the court held that being concerned in the management of a corporation means to take an active part in running the corporation, and to be responsible for decision-making and the

91 See s 9 of the *Corporations Act* provides a detailed definition of 'director', which includes a person occupying or acting in a position of director of a body corporate (whether or not so named, validly appointed or duly authorised to act), or a person in accordance with whose directions or instructions the directors of the corporation are accustomed to act. In the case of a body corporate incorporated overseas, a director will include a member of its board, a person occupying or acting in a position of membership of the board, or a person in accordance with whose directions or instructions the directors of the corporation are accustomed to act. Presumably, this definition would include alternate and nominee directors.

92 *Holpitt Pty Ltd v Swaab* (1992) 105 ALR 421.

93 (1994) 125 ALR 241.

direction of the corporation to such an extent that the functions are suggestive of control, not merely the carrying out of routine duties. The larger the corporation, the more likely it is that senior management and even those lower down on the corporate ladder may exercise managerial functions.[94] In a case under the *Companies (Victoria) Code*, Ormiston J interpreted the phrase, 'those who are concerned in the management of [a] corporation' very widely. If applied in this way, it could refer to senior management, middle management or lesser employees who have been delegated full discretionary responsibilities. It could also extend to persons outside the corporation such as financiers, receivers and liquidators.[95]

Defences

Defences for directors

Directors and managers are provided with two statutory defences: first, that the officer was not in a position to influence the conduct of the corporation in relation to the contravention; and, second, that the officer exercised all due diligence (reasonable care) to prevent the contravention (s 169(1)(b), (c)). The defences are available in a prosecution for any offence, whether or not it is a tier one offence or an offence of strict liability. It has not been judicially determined what degree of influence is required or how far removed the director or manager should be to rely on the defence that the director could not have influenced the corporation in relation to the contravention. Given the assumption that corporate officer liability is intended to improve corporate environmental performance, prosecutors may have to demonstrate actual influence and even control of relevant aspects of the corporation. This may be difficult to establish, particularly in the case of larger companies.

Due diligence appears to be the most useful defence for corporations and corporate officers. (This defence is discussed below.) Formerly, directors had an additional defence of lack of 'knowledge', but this was removed by the 2005 amendments as it was considered out of touch with modern principles of corporate responsibility, which expect managers and directors to be aware of the environmental effects of their businesses (PEOA Review Report (2003)). The removal of the 'no knowledge' defence is intended to facilitate the prosecution of directors. Directors and senior management will now have to show that their companies have taken the appropriate precautions, such as risk management, to avoid prosecution.

The NSW EPA has indicated in its Prosecution Guidelines that it will not prosecute corporate officers unless there is some evidence directly linking that person with the corporation's unlawful activity (see discussion at pp 471-472). The prosecution record of the EPA is consistent with this undertaking. All of the directors prosecuted in New South Wales have been directly involved in the commission of the offence by the corporation.[96] Overall, the fines imposed have not been

---

94 See *AWA Ltd v Daniels* (1992) 7 ACSR 759 at 832-833 per Rogers J; on appeal *Daniels v Anderson* (1995) 16 ACSR 607.

95 *Commissioner for Corporate Affairs v Bracht* [1989] VR 821.

96 See, eg, *State Pollution Control Commission v Kelly* (1991) 5 ACSR 607; *EPA v Suciu* (1998) 98 LGERA 330; *EPA v Morgan* (unreported, NSWLEC, Bannon J, 1996); *McConnell Dowell Constructors (Aust) Pty Ltd v EPA* (1996) 93 LGERA 364; *Morgan v EPA* (unreported, NSWCCA, 25 October 1996 (stated case)). For details of other prosecutions, see T Howard, 'Liability of Directors for Environmental Crime: The Anything-but-Level Playing Field in Australia' (2000) 17 *EPLJ* 250 at 262.

significant. Most prosecutions have involved directors of small companies, an inevitable consequence of requiring 'hands-on' involvement. Consequently, most prosecutions have not relied on the 'status offence' provision, but have prosecuted the directors in their personal capacity. However, in a recent decision, *EPA v Perry*,[97] Perry, a sole director of KP Recycling Pty Ltd, was prosecuted for the company's offence of negligently disposing of waste in a manner that harmed, or was likely to harm, the environment under s 115 of the PEOA. The offence related to the abandonment of 3000 used tyres on a site where the company had operated a recycling plant. The company had gone into liquidation and abandoned the premises. Perry was initially fined $100,000 which was reduced to $30,000 having regard to mitigating factors and his capacity to pay. Although Perry's conviction was regarded as 'status liability' by virtue of his position as director, the court found that as sole director of KP Recycling at the relevant time, he was in any event personally responsible for the decision to cease the business operation which led to the offence.[98] Since this decision there have been further prosecutions of directors for offences committed by their corporations, for example, *EPA v Pannowitz; EPA v Steepleton Pty Ltd*[99] (discussed at p 471) and *EPA v Obaid*.[100]

Due diligence

Due diligence is an important defence and is particularly useful for corporations (for tier one offences) and corporate officers (all offences). Because it is a statutory defence, it is only available where the Act expressly provides for it. It is available to all defendants under tier one of the Act (s 118 discussed at pp 448-449). However, it is generally not available for tier two offences, with two exceptions: for an owner of unlawfully transported waste (s 143(3)), and for corporate officers (s 169(1)(c)).

'Due diligence' is not defined in the legislation but has been described by the House of Lords as being 'the converse of negligence' or 'lack of care for the consequences of his physical acts on the part of the person doing them'.[101] In Australia, the defence was first developed in areas such as the *Corporations Law* and trade practices legislation. In *Universal Telecasters (Qld) v Guthrie*,[102] the Full Federal Court outlined the requirements of the defence of due diligence under s 85(1)c) of the *Trade Practices Act 1974* (Cth) as follows:

- the defence requires not only the establishment of a proper system to guard against a contravention, but also adequate supervision to ensure it is properly carried out;
- the system must cover all material aspects and dimensions of the business; and
- the mere fact that a system proves inadequate to prevent a contravention does not necessarily establish that it is defective.

---

97 (2004) 135 LGRA 431.

98 See further R Mohr and R Fox, 'Status Liability Anxiety – director convicted for environmental crime of company' (2005) 2(7) *Contract Management* 104 at 104.

99 [2005] NSWLEC 175.

100 [2005] NSWLEC 171.

101 *Tesco Supermarkets v Nattrass* [1972] AC 153 at 199.

102 (1978) 32 FLR 360.

There is little judicial authority in Australia on the defence of due diligence in relation to environmental offences. In the seminal NSW case, *State Pollution Control Commission v Kelly*, Hemmings J stated:[103]

> Due diligence ... depends on the circumstances of the case, but *contemplates a mind concentrated on the likely risks.* The requirements are not satisfied by precautions merely as a general matter in the business of the corporation, unless also designed to prevent the contravention. Whether a defendant took the precautions that ought to have been taken must always be a question of fact and ... must be decided according to the standard of a reasonable man in the circumstances.

This statement highlights the importance of risk assessment in establishing the due diligence defence. This aspect was elaborated in a case on air pollution in Western Australia in *Payne v Tiwest Pty Ltd*.[104] In that case, the court applied the test adopted in *Romeo v Conservation Commission (NT)*[105] (a civil case), namely whether the risk was 'so remote that a reasonable man, careful of the safety of his neighbour, would think it right to neglect it'.

In the *Payne* case, the defence of due diligence succeeded because the extensive risk analysis undertaken by the company had failed to identify and quantify the risk that eventuated. The incident was the result of a complex set of circumstances that were unlikely to be repeated and the probability of it occurring was very low, approximately once every 4000 years. The consequences of the emission were also not life threatening. Arguably, the risk assessment approach to due diligence in the *Payne* case would apply equally in New South Wales. It seems that a preliminary risk assessment analysis is necessary to determine the risk and the contributing factors. This involves an analysis of the likelihood of occurrence and its severity. Strategies should then be developed to manage or reduce the risk (a due diligence program). These strategies must be directed to preventing the occurrence of the risk, and where this fails to mitigate any potential environmental impact which may occur. The extent of the risk depends on the particular industry, the nature of the activity and the sensitivity of the environment. The risk management strategy should also provide for continuous monitoring.

A risk assessment strategy can also be integrated into a broader based environmental management system. Such a system is an important voluntary measure in achieving due diligence and preventing pollution. It can be established informally within the company, or the company may seek certification to some external standard, such as the international standard ISO 14001.

'Honest and reasonable mistake'

The common law defence of 'honest and reasonable mistake' is only available where proof of guilty knowledge or intention is not required, that is, the offence is one of strict liability.[106]

The defence derives from the decision of the High Court in *Proudman v Dayman*,[107] where Dixon J stated:

---

103 (1991) 5 ACSR 607 at 608-609.

104 [2005] WASC 141.

105 (1998) 192 CLR 431.

106 *He Kaw Teh v The Queen* (1985) 157 CLR 523.

107 (1943) 67 CLR 536 at 540.

> As a general rule an honest and reasonable belief in a state of facts which, if they existed, would make the defendant's act innocent affords an excuse for doing what would otherwise be an offence.

In New South Wales, it has been established in a number of judicial decisions that the defence of 'honest and reasonable mistake of fact' applies to tier two offences under the environment protection legislation.[108]

The decision of the Court of Criminal Appeal in *State Rail Authority of New South Wales v Hunter Water Board*[109] provides guidance on the requirements of the defence. In that case, water pollution had resulted from the escape of diesel oil from a break in an underground PVC pipe. The defence of honest and reasonable mistake was based on the depot manager's belief that there had been no problems with the installation of the pipe, that he was absolutely certain that the system would work, and that the pipe was maintenance free. Gleeson CJ found that the defence did not apply since it would be inconsistent with the legislative purpose to conclude that a defendant would be excused on the basis simply that he or she had no particular reason to apprehend that the operation of the plant and equipment in question would, or might, result in pollution. Gleeson CJ identified the following requirements as necessary to establish the defence:

(1) The mistake must be one of fact, not law, and one which would render the actions of the defendant 'innocent'. So, for example, defendants cannot argue that they had breached discharge standards in the past without being prosecuted and this had led them to believe that the standards were only targets;[110]

(2) There must be a positive belief that the consequences will not ensue. The belief must be sufficiently specific to relate it to the elements of the particular offence. In *State Rail Authority of New South Wales v Hunter Water Board*,[111] the court held that the defendant was required to have a positive belief that the pipe did not leak, and that if it did the oil would not cause pollution.

(3) The mistake must be honest and reasonable. In *State Rail Authority of New South Wales v Hunter Water Board*, the court found that the depot manager's belief that the pipe would not leak was unreasonable. In *EPA v Milpharma Pty Ltd*,[112] the defence succeeded in relation to a charge of polluting waters under s 16(1) of the *Clean Waters Act 1970* (now PEOA s 120). Bignold J found that the belief by the managing director, that there would be no overflow from the waste water tank into Sydney Water's sewer, was honestly and reasonably held, and had not been displaced by the prosecution beyond reasonable doubt. This belief was corroborated by an expert, who concluded that the incident was purely accidental and unforeseeable.

---

108 See, eg, *Woodward v Cleary Bros (BOMBO) Pty Ltd* (1984) 54 LGRA 409 at 412-413; *Cooper v ICI Australia Operations Pty Ltd* (1987) 64 LGRA 58 at 65-66; *State Pollution Control Commission v Australian Iron and Steel Ltd* (1992) 74 LGRA 387 at 393; *Hunter Water Board v State Rail Authority of NSW (No 1)* (1992) 75 LGRA 15 at 19; *State Rail Authority of NSW v Hunter Water Board* (1992) 28 NSWLR 721; *EPA v Brazel* (2002) 119 LGERA 72; *EPA v Milpharma Pty Ltd* [1994] NSWLEC 189.

109 (1992) 28 NSWLR 721.

110 See *SPCC v Broken Hill Pty Co Ltd (No 1)* (1991) 74 LGRA 351.

111 (1992) 28 NSWLR 721.

112 [1994] NSWLEC 189.

It has been held that the defence of 'honest and reasonable mistake' does not include a requirement of 'due diligence'.[113]

If the evidence raises the possibility of an honest and reasonable mistake of fact, the burden of proof lies with the prosecution to prove beyond a reasonable doubt that the defendant had no such belief or that the belief was unreasonable.[114]

From the cases, it appears that the defence of honest and reasonable mistake is not easy to establish. This is often due to the defendant's failure to establish that the mistaken belief held was honest and reasonable.

Tier three offences

Tier three offences are tier two offences under the PEOA and the *Protection of the Environment Operations (Penalty Notices) Regulation 2004* (Penalty Notices Regulation) which can be dealt with by way of a penalty notice (ss 114, 222). Authorised officers are persons belonging to a class of officers or employees prescribed by Penalty Notices Regulation in relation to the offence. Depending on the offence, an authorised officer could be an employee of a local council, the EPA, Sydney Water Corporation and a range of other authorities. A penalty notice can be served by an authorised officer either personally or by post or, if authorised by the regulations, left on a vehicle or at other premises in respect of which the offence was committed (s 224). The notice contains a fine and must be paid within 28 days (ss 223, 227). Rather than paying the penalty, the offender can opt to go to court and fight the charge (s 223). In comparison with other offences under the PEOA, tier three offences are intended for relatively minor infringements. The EPA Prosecution Guidelines 1993 (revised 2003) provide guidance as to when a penalty notice is appropriate, namely, when the breach is minor; if the breach is a 'once-off'; and if a penalty notice will deter future breaches. Penalties for tier three offences vary according to the offence. The highest penalty that can be imposed is $5000 for certain waste offences (ss 144, 144A(1)) for corporate offenders and $1500 for an individual. Tier three water pollution offences attract a penalty of $750 for individuals and $1500 for corporations. The important qualification to penalty notices is that another enforcement officer or the EPA may withdraw a penalty notice regarded as inappropriate and take formal proceedings for a tier two offence (s 228).

Environmental audits

The PEOA provides for mandatory and voluntary environmental audits (Chapter 6). An environmental audit is defined as:

> a documented evaluation of an activity (including an evaluation of management practices, systems and plant) for either or both of the following purposes:
> (a) to provide information to the persons managing the activity on compliance with legal requirements, codes of practice and relevant policies relating to the protection of the environment,
> (b) to enable those persons to determine whether the way the activity is carried on can be improved in order to protect the environment and to minimise waste. (s 172)

113 *Australian Iron and Steel Pty Ltd v EPA (No 2)* (1992) 29 NSWLR 497 at 510-511.

114 *He Kaw Teh v The Queen* (1985) 157 CLR 523.

In certain circumstances, the EPA may require a mandatory environmental audit as a condition of a licence (s 174). This may only be imposed if the EPA reasonably suspects that the holder of the licence has contravened the Act on one or more occasions and this has resulted in harm or likely harm to the environment (s 175). The EPA may require the audit to be undertaken by an approved environmental auditor, and that an environmental audit report be prepared and submitted (s 174). Although the PEOA makes provision for regulations to deal with accreditation of auditors, unlike the requirements of the *Contaminated Land Management Act 1997*, the government does not currently propose to introduce an accreditation scheme for PEOA audits (s 173, discussions with EPA). The supply of false or misleading information to an auditor by a licensee is an offence. An environmental auditor who omits to supply information or provides false or misleading information in an audit report also commits an offence (s 177). Information supplied by a person in connection with a mandatory audit can be used as evidence in a prosecution and the privilege against self-incrimination does not apply (ss 178, 179).

The PEOA provides protection for voluntary audits to encourage industry to undertake regular compliance audits. A voluntary environmental audit can be undertaken in relation to licensed or unlicensed activities (s 180). Documents prepared for the sole purpose of a voluntary environmental audit are not admissible in evidence in proceedings against any person unless the person seeks to rely on them (ss 182(1), 183). The EPA cannot obtain a copy of a voluntary audit or request information in relation to it (s 182(2)).

Enforcement

Criminal proceedings

Public authorities

Criminal proceedings for an offence against the PEOA may be instituted by the EPA (s 217). However, provision is also made for proceedings to be instituted by other appropriate regulatory authorities, other than an excluded offence (s 218(1)). For example:

- a local authority may institute proceedings for an offence under the Act or regulations;
- a water supply authority may institute proceedings for a water pollution offence;
- the Waterways Authority may institute proceedings for a noise pollution offence in, on, or adjacent to boats (s 218(3));
- police officers may institute proceedings for a noise pollution offence, a littering offence or an offence against the regulations relating to the operation of a motor vehicle (s 218(4)).

Regulatory authorities other than the EPA may not institute proceedings for excluded offences, which are offences committed in relation to:

- scheduled activities;
- licensed activities or work (ie scheduled development work);
- premises occupied by, or activities carried on by, the State or a public authority;

- in the case of a noise pollution offence – a vessel in navigable waters or premises used in connection with vessels and situated adjacent to, or partly or wholly over, navigable waters. (s 218(6))

The amount of any fine imposed in a prosecution brought by a council is to be paid to the council.[115] This provides a strong incentive for councils to pursue a policy of vigorous prosecution in relation to pollution offences.

Private prosecutions

Any person may institute proceedings for an offence against the PEOA if the Land and Environment Court grants leave to bring the proceedings (s 219(1)). This makes initiating criminal proceedings much more onerous than civil proceedings, where leave of the court does not have to be granted. Before granting leave, the court must be satisfied:

- the EPA has decided not to take any relevant action or has not reached a decision within 90 days of being asked to do so;
- the proceedings are not an abuse of process of the court;
- the EPA has been notified of the proceedings; and
- the particulars of the offence disclose a *prima facie* case. (s 219(2))

Relevant action by the EPA is not limited to the institution of criminal proceedings, but includes action under the PEOA to prevent, control, abate or mitigate any harm to the environment caused by the offence, or to prevent its continuance or recurrence (s 219(3)).

The Local Court, where tier two offences can ordinarily be prosecuted as an alternative to the Land and Environment Court (s 215), is not empowered to grant leave to bring a private prosecution.

Civil proceedings

Any person may bring an action to restrain a breach or apprehended breach of the PEOA, or of any other Act, if the breach is likely to cause harm to the environment, regardless of whether any right of the person has been infringed (ss 252, 253). The court is empowered to make such orders as it thinks fit to *remedy or restrain* the breach of the PEOA (s 252(6)), but, in the case of another Act, the court may only *restrain* a breach which causes harm to the environment (s 253(4)).

Court enforceable undertakings

Following the 2005 amendments to the PEOA, the EPA can accept court enforceable undertakings in connection with any matter in relation to which the EPA has a function under the PEOA (s 253A). If the EPA considers that the person who gave the undertaking has breached any of its terms, the EPA may apply to the Land and Environment Court for appropriate orders, such as:

115 *Local Government Act 1993* s 694; *Sutherland Shire Council v Pedy Concrete Co Pty Ltd* (1992) 77 LGRA 333.

- an order directing compliance with the undertaking;
- an order to pay a sum up to the amount of any financial benefit obtained directly or indirectly as a result of the breach;
- any order that the court considers appropriate to compensate any person who has suffered loss or damage as a result of the breach;
- an order suspending or revoking any licence held by the person;
- an order requiring the person to prevent, control, abate, mitigate or make good any actual or likely harm to the environment caused by the breach
- any other order that the court considers appropriate. (s 253A(4)(a)-(g))

A person can withdraw or vary the undertaking at any time, but only with the consent in writing of the EPA.

Prosecutions in practice

Over the past decade, the EPA has averaged about 100 prosecutions per year for pollution offences relating to water pollution, waste, littering, motor vehicles, breaches of licences, pesticides and other offences, with a 95% success rate. In 2002-03, 156 prosecutions were commenced. The total value of fines for the 2002-03 financial year were $1.1 million (PEOA Review Report (2003)). However, most of these prosecutions were for minor offences, such as smoky vehicles. After motor vehicles, most prosecutions occurred for water pollution, followed by breach of licence conditions, waste and pesticides. In 2004-05, 127 prosecutions were commenced. Only 46 tier two convictions were recorded. There were numerous convictions for breaches of the regulations, but these were for more trivial offences and the penalties were small (DEC Annual Report 2004-05).

There have been relatively few prosecutions for tier one offences. In 2004 only one conviction was recorded.[116] To date, the courts have only imposed the maximum penalty on one occasion.[117]

Penalty notices have been issued for a variety of offences. In 2004 most penalty notices were issued for littering from motor vehicles (4924), followed by water pollution offences (1350), smoky vehicles (1184) and waste (524). Overall, over 10,000 penalty notices were issued, with the total fines imposed amounting to approximately $4,800,000 (DEC Annual Report 2004). The number of penalty notices issued by the EPA was roughly half of those issued by local government officers. The decline in prosecutions for more serious offences and the large increase in penalty notices suggest that regulatory authorities may be issuing penalty notices for offences instead of bringing a prosecution under tier two of the PEOA. This is reinforced by the fact that in 2004 only six convictions were recorded for the tier two offence of 'polluting waters'.

Powers of the court – sentencing

As an alternative to imposing a fine or a term of imprisonment, the court may dismiss a charge, discharge the offender conditionally, defer sentence or order a

116 *EPA v Perry* (2004) 135 LGRA 431.

117 *EPA v Gardner* [1997] NSWLEC 212: $250,000 plus 12 months' imprisonment, discussed at p 441.

defendant to pay a fine, without recording a conviction.[118] These options are applied having regard to the trivial nature of the offence, extenuating circumstances in which the offence was committed and any other matter that the court thinks proper to consider (*Crimes (Sentencing Procedure) Act 1999* (NSW) s 10).

Part 8.3 of the PEOA provides a range of innovative sentencing options. The courts now have broad powers to make a range of ancillary orders in addition to, or as an alternative to, a fine or gaol term. For example, a convicted defendant can also be ordered to:

- pay an additional penalty estimated as any monetary benefit acquired or accruing to the offender as a result of the commission of the offence (s 249);
- publicise the offence and its environmental or other consequences and any other orders made against the person (s 250(1)(a));
- notify any person who is aggrieved or affected by the offender's conduct of the facts relating to the conviction and the orders made (s 250(1)(b));
- carry out a specified project for the restoration or enhancement of the environment in a public place or for the public benefit (s 250(1)(c)); if the EPA is a party to the proceedings, a financial assurance may be required to be paid to the EPA to ensure compliance (s 250(1)(g));
- carry out an environmental audit (s 250(1)(d));
- order a person to take action to clean-up, make good any environmental damage or take action to prevent or investigate further harm (s 245);
- pay any costs or expenses incurred by a public authority or other person who has taken action to mitigate environmental harm or suffered loss or damage as a consequence thereof. This includes costs incurred at the time of the offence; costs incurred after conviction; and any costs incurred by the regulatory authority in investigating the offence (ss 246-248);
- order the offender to pay an amount to the Environmental Trust or a specified environmental organisation for the purposes of a specified project for the restoration or enhancement of the environment or for general environmental purposes (s 250(1)(e));
- order the offender to attend or establish a training course (s 250(1)(f), (g)).

These powers should operate as a deterrent for prospective polluters. The power to order details of an offence to be publicised may often be a greater deterrent for a large corporation than a monetary penalty. The introduction of projects for the public benefit is also important in that it enables the court to deal more effectively with defendants who have no financial means or assets.

Community service orders are being increasingly invoked for environmental offences. In *EPA v White*,[119] a company director was convicted of an offence of negligently disposing of waste in a manner that would be likely to harm the environment. White was fined $25,000 and sentenced to 400 hours community service. He was also required to pay $18,590.70 for remediation of the environment and to

118 Section 243 of the PEOA provides that the court may deal with the offence according to the *Crimes (Sentencing Procedure) Act 1999* (NSW) ss 10, 11 (dismiss offender; discharge conditionally), 12 (defer sentence).

119 (1996) 92 LGERA 263.

contribute $11,000 towards the prosecutor's costs. In *EPA v Coggins*,[120] the superintendent of a golf course was sentenced to 250 hours community service for negligently permitting a pesticide to pollute a nearby creek.

A number of sentencing alternatives were utilised in *EPA v Warringah Golf Club Ltd (No 2)*.[121] The golf club was convicted of an offence under s 116(2) in that it had negligently contributed to the conditions which gave rise to the offence by an employee (see *Coggins* case above). It was ordered to carry out specific works to prevent short-term spillages at an estimated cost of $73,789 (the club had already installed bunding at a cost of $6614), and to pay the expenses of public authorities in removing over four tonnes of dead fish. It was also ordered to publish a notice in its regular newsletter informing members of the offence.

EPA v Pannowitz[122] illustrates the potentially serious consequences for persons who do not comply with court orders. This case arose out of the decision in *EPA v Steepleton*,[123] where Steepleton, a corporation, and Pannowitz, the sole director, pleaded guilty to an offence under s 143(1) of the Act for transporting waste to a place that could not lawfully be used as a waste facility. Fines of $40,000 and $20,000 were imposed on Steepleton and Pannowitz respectively, and both parties were ordered to pay costs. In addition, Pannowitz was ordered to publicise both convictions in the *Newcastle Herald* and *Waste Management and Environment*. Pannowitz was subsequently convicted of contempt of court because the notice placed did not comply with the court order and also deliberately included words which were not part of the order and incorrect. He was sentenced to 300 hours of community service.

These innovative new penalty options overcome the drawbacks of the previous system which was confined to punishing past behaviour without providing for any positive environmental outcome. They also provide a means of dealing with impecunious defendants. The EPA has published guidelines as to when it will seek an environmental court order.[124]

Prosecution guidelines

The EPA issued prosecution guidelines in 1993 indicating how it will exercise its prosecutorial powers. These guidelines have been revised several times, most recently in 2003. They are not legally binding on the EPA or any other organisation. They provide criteria to determine:

- the basis on which the EPA will make a decision to prosecute;
- how the appropriate defendant will be determined;
- which charges to lay;
- the appropriate mode of trial;
- co-operative measures which may influence the EPA's decision to prosecute or which may operate as important mitigating factors on sentence; or
- indemnification of witnesses. (para 2.1 at 3)

---

120 (2003) 126 LGERA 219.

121 (2003) 129 LGERA 211.

122 [2006] NSWLEC 219.

123 [2005] NSWLEC 175.

124 See <http://www.environment.nsw.gov.au/legal>.

The guidelines point out that, in criminalising breaches of environmental law, a primary, though not the sole, aim of Parliament is deterrence. Prosecution, however, may not always be the appropriate response. Hence, sufficiency of evidence is not the sole criteria for prosecution. Rather, prosecution will be used as part of an overall strategy for achieving EPA objectives where it is in the public interest. Factors to be considered in determining whether the public interest requires a prosecution include: the seriousness of the offence; the harm or potential harm to the environment; the degree of culpability of the alleged offender in relation to the offence; whether the offender had been dealt with previously by non-prosecutorial means; the likely outcome of a prosecution; the prevalence of the alleged offence; and the need for deterrence (para 3.7 at 5-6).

Generally, the appropriate defendant will be the person primarily responsible for the offence, that is, the person who committed the act, formed the intention or created the material circumstances giving rise to the breach (para 5.2 at 10). Where an offence is committed by employees/agents/officers of a corporation in the course of their employment, proceedings will usually be instituted against the corporation (para 6.2 at 11). The employee and not the corporation will be prosecuted where the employee should have known that the activity was illegal or where a senior employee has not taken reasonable steps to inform the employer of the impropriety of the practice. In so far as corporations are concerned, the existence and effective implementation of compliance programs by the corporation are a relevant factor to be considered along with all the other material in deciding whether to prosecute. Compliance programs need not have a direct impact on the offence (para 19.1 at 26).

In deciding whether directors or corporate managers should be prosecuted, the crucial issue is the person's actual control or influence over the conduct of the corporation in relation to its criminal conduct. Proceedings will generally only be instituted where there is evidence linking a director or manager with the corporation's illegal activity. It is sufficient if the linkage is of a negligent nature (para 8.3 at 13). If, however, there is clear evidence of wrongdoing on the part of the director, charges will generally be brought against both the director and the corporation.

Public registers and other information

In a move to ensure greater access to information regarding the environment, each regulatory authority is required to keep a public register recording information including:

- details relating to each licence application, any conditions imposed on each licence and licensing decisions made by the authority including those to vary, suspend, revoke or approve the surrender of a licence and conditions of the licence;
- details of each certification supplied certifying compliance with the conditions of a licence;
- details of each environment protection notice or noise control notice;
- details of any exemption granted by the EPA;
- a summary of the conclusions of any audit report in connection with a mandatory environmental audit; and
- details of convictions in prosecutions and results in civil proceedings before the Land and Environment Court brought under the PEOA. (s 308)

Members of the public may obtain a copy of any part of the register from the appropriate authority (s 309(2)). There is also a formalised system to allow public access to self-monitoring data (s 320(3)). The EPA has established a public register which is available at DEC offices and on the internet.[125] As of 2003 only 61% of councils had established public registers (PEOA Review Report (2003)).

The National Pollutant Inventory, which has been released as a National Environment Protection Measure and given effect to in New South Wales through the PEO (Gen) Regulation cll 57D-57F, is also a valuable source of information to the community (<www.npi.gov.au>).

State of the Environment Reports are also important sources of information. They are required to be prepared by the EPA every four years (FROTEA s 10).

Economic measures

The EPA is provided with power under the Act to institute economic measures to protect the environment in a cost-effective way. Schemes involving economic measures are an extension of the 'polluter pays' principle. A market-based approach to pollution control can have advantages of cost-effectiveness, flexibility and efficiency. For corporations, these schemes can provide significant incentives to introduce innovation in pollution control technology.

Load-based licensing

Load-based licensing was introduced by the PEOA and has gradually been phased in (for details of the scheme, see POE (Gen) Regulation). Load-based licensing applies only to licensed activities or premises. In conformity with the polluter pays principle, licence fees are linked to the load of pollutants discharged into the environment. Fees are based on load, harmfulness and location. Annual pollutant load limits have been introduced and independently certified annual licence returns and reporting of loads is required. Previously, pollutant concentration limits in discharges sought to prevent acute local area problems, but failed to control the cumulative impact of emissions in broader waterways and airsheds. Load-based licensing creates an incentive for the largest polluters to reduce annual pollution loads below licensed levels and not merely avoid breaching daily limits. Load fees affect the largest licensed activities, such as sewage treatment plants, smelters, power stations, paper mills, mines, chemical industries and refineries. According to the PEOA Review Report (2003), about 270 activities fall within the load-based licensing scheme which accounts for the majority of point-source emissions in New South Wales. By 2002 the scheme had reportedly tracked over 460 million kilograms of air pollutants and 140 million kilograms of water pollutants.

Load Reduction Agreements allow licensees in the scheme immediately to reduce their licence fees if they commit to achieving specific environmental outcomes. The savings in licence fees can be committed to environmental improvement. The PEOA Review (2003) reported that, from the time of its introduction until 2003, licensees had agreed to prevent a total of nearly 4000 tonnes of pollution a year. This involved 23 licensees saving a combined total of over $9.7 million in licence fees.

---

125 See <www.epa.gov.nsw.au>.

Tradeable emission permits

The EPA is required to consider any tradeable emission scheme or other scheme involving economic measures when exercising its licensing functions (ss 45(e), 69, Part 9.3A). Tradeable emission schemes operate as important financial incentives for innovation in pollution control technology once the set standard is achieved. Under the tradeable emission scheme, for example, the polluter must pay a higher penalty in the form of tradeable emission permits which must be purchased in the market place for higher levels of pollution, but when pollution control technology reduces emissions below a certain level set by the EPA, the polluter receives a financial reward for lower levels of pollution in the form of tradeable emission credits which can be sold in the market place.

Since 1995, the EPA has operated a tradeable emissions scheme for the Hunter River. The scheme now operates under the *Protection of the Environment Operations (Hunter River Salinity Trading) Regulation 2002*. The scheme seeks to reduce salinity levels in the Hunter River which have increased due to irrigation and the discharge of saline water from 22 coal mines and two power stations. The scheme has been implemented through licences issued for the discharge of saline waste water to the Hunter River. Licence holders must also hold credits in the scheme. Licence conditions include restrictions on the amount and time of saline discharges so as to maintain ecological quality given variable river flow conditions. The scheme which is limited to industry participants allows internet-based trading 24 hours a day. Licensees may transfer discharge entitlements among themselves, although this is subject to EPA veto if the trade would impair the environment. According to the EPA this scheme has been highly successful, with an average in-river salinity halved and no exceedances of water quality goals occurring due to discharges under the scheme (PEOA Review Report (2003)).

Green offsets

Green offset schemes were introduced by the 2005 amendments to the PEOA. A green offset scheme is a form of emission trading involving small numbers of participants at any one time. Green offset is action taken outside, but near to a licensed premise, to reduce pollution. This creates green offset credits which may be traded with other licensed premises. These schemes are intended 'to carry out a specified program for the restoration or enhancement of the environment that is related to a licensed activity', 'to prevent, control, abate, mitigate or otherwise offset any harm to the environment arising (wholly or partly) from any licensed activity' or 'to make good any environmental damage arising (wholly or partly) from a licensed activity' (s 295O(1)(a)-(c)).

In diminishing the environmental impact of a licensed activity, a green offset scheme may include any of the following elements:

- 'contractual agreements or other arrangements between the person who arranges or implements or manages a green offset scheme and other participants in the scheme' (s 295O(2)(a));
- creation of a market for entitlements to participate in a green offset scheme (s 295O(2)(b));
- creation of green offset credits (s 295O(2)(c));

- initiation of, or further sale or allocation of green offset credits (s 295O(2)(d));
- provision for the holding of green offset credits by participants (s 295O(2)(e));
- the payment of contributions to the scheme for works under the scheme (s 295O(2)(f));
- implementation of works by participants into the scheme (s 295O(2)(g));
- payment of administrative costs relating to the scheme (s 295O(2)(h);
- rights and duties of participants in the scheme (s 295O(2)(i));
- trading of green offset credits or of any entitlements conferred by them (including restrictions on trading and any other dealings) (s 295O(2)(j));
- safeguards against anti-competitive behaviour by participants in the scheme (s 295O(2)(k));
- the alteration, suspension, cancellation or forfeiture of green offset credits, or other rights or entitlements under the scheme (s 295O(2)(l));
- provision for a register of green offset credits and participants and for the circumstances in which register information may be disclosed (s 295O(2)(m)).

Green offset works can include contractual or other arrangements between the licence holder and the person implementing the works, the implementation or arrangement of works, the payment of administration costs in relation to the works or the rights and duties of participants (s 295P(2)(a)-(c)). Green offset works may be part of a green offset scheme (s 295P(3)) and may, subject to licence conditions, be implemented by the holder of a licence or another person (s 295P(5)).

The detail concerning green offset schemes are to be dealt with by regulation (s 295Q(1)) and may include requirements or agreements relating to green offset schemes or works; criteria for activities that may be covered; inspection of premises; and the function of a manger of the scheme and accountability arrangements. The regulations must make provision for appropriate criteria and methodologies for determining whether specific licensing condition outcomes have been met; and evaluation on a periodic basis of the schemes or works and publication of such evaluations (s 295Q(2)(a)(b)). In 2006, cl 57T was inserted into the *Protection of the Environment Operations (General) Amendment Regulation* 2006 to provide for evaluation of a green offset scheme by the EPA at intervals of not more than five years, as well as at the end of the scheme. Where a green offset work is not part of a green offset scheme, the EPA must determine the appropriate intervals for evaluation. The evaluation must be reported on and the manager of the scheme or work must give the EPA information relating to their effectiveness (cl 57T).

The Minister has the power to review periodically a green offset regulation (s 295Q(4)) and a duty to ensure the public is given an opportunity to make submissions to the review (s 295Q(5)) by giving notice to invite the public to make submissions within a period of not less than 21 days (s 295Q(6)(a)-(c)).

The regulations may authorise the EPA to cancel, suspend or order the forfeiture of green offset credits or the right to participate in a green offset scheme (s 295R(1)(a)-(c)). The EPA may manage or appoint a manager (s 295R(2)) or participate in a green offset scheme and may order administration costs (s 295S) or contributions (s 295T) to be paid.

A Green Offsets Fund under the control of the EPA is to be established to collect contributions, proceeds from sale of credits, investment moneys and bequests, and other money appropriated by Parliament (s 295U(2), (3)). Moneys paid out of the fund will be used for the purpose of green offset scheme costs, management and administration of schemes and works and for compliance enforcement costs (s 295U(4)).

Financial assurances

Financial assurances may be attached as conditions to licences to secure funding towards the carrying out of remediation work or pollution reduction programs (s 296(1)). A financial assurance may be in the form of a bank guarantee, a bond or another form of security specified by the regulatory authority (s 298(2)). To require a financial assurance, the regulatory authority must be satisfied that it is justified by the degree of risk of environmental harm associated with the activities; the remediation work that may be required; the environmental record of the holder; and other prescribed matters (s 299). The regulatory authority can determine the amount of the assurance, which must not exceed the total likely costs and expenses that may be incurred in carrying out the work or program required (s 300(2)).

If the holder of the licence fails to carry out any work or program covered by a financial assurance, the appropriate regulatory authority can have the work carried out and recover the reasonable costs and expenses from the financial assurance (s 303). However, before doing so, the regulatory authority must give notice to, and consider any representations by, the licence holder (s 303). If the regulatory authority then decides to realise the financial assurance, the licence holder must be notified and reasons must be provided (s 303(6)). Disputes can be referred to the Land and Environment Court (s 307). After the work has been carried out, any excess amounts must be returned to the licence holder (s 303(7)). Any shortfall may be recovered from the licence holder as a debt (s 303(8)). A financial assurance lapses if the regulatory authority has given written notice to the licence holder that the work or program for which the financial assurance was required has been satisfactorily carried out (s 304). The fact that a financial assurance has been called upon does not preclude a prosecution of the licence holder (s 306).

According to the PEOA Review Report, as at 2003 40 financial assurances were attached to licences ranging from $8000 to $1.5 million, but the EPA had not needed to call upon them.

Marine pollution

There is a plethora of legislation on marine pollution in Australia. This chapter deals only with those sources of marine pollution which result from the use of ships or sea dumping. Land-based sources of marine pollution are dealt with under pollution control legislation, mainly the PEOA. Australian legislation on marine pollution is a direct response to its undertakings under international conventions. Two key international conventions are discussed in this chapter – the *International Convention for the Prevention of Pollution from Ships 1973/78* (MARPOL 73/78) and the *Convention on the Prevention of Marine Pollution by the Dumping of Wastes and Other Matter 1972* (the London Convention) and 1996 Protocol.

Commonwealth/State disputes concerning jurisdiction over the territorial sea were settled by the High Court in 1975 in favour of the Commonwealth.[126] However, the Commonwealth subsequently negotiated an agreement with the States to return jurisdiction of the territorial sea to the States extending to three nautical miles (5.5 kilometres) from the low water mark. This agreement was termed the Offshore Constitutional Settlement 1979. This agreement was given legislative force in the *Coastal Waters (State Title) Act 1980* (Cth), *Coastal Waters (State Powers) Act 1980* (Cth) whilst equivalent legislation was enacted by the States and Territories.

Accidental or operational discharges from ships

MARPOL 73/78

MARPOL 73/78 is the main international convention dealing with the prevention and minimisation of marine pollution by ships from operational or accidental causes. It is a combination of two treaties adopted in 1973 and 1978 respectively and updated by amendments through the years. It currently includes six technical Annexes:

Annex 1: Regulations for the Prevention of Pollution by Oil;
Annex II: Regulations for the Control of Pollution by Noxious Liquid Substances in Bulk;
Annex III: Prevention of Pollution by Harmful Substances Carried by Sea in Packaged Form;
Annex IV: Prevention of Pollution by Sewage from Ships;
Annex V: Prevention of Pollution by Garbage from Ships;
Annex VI: Prevention of Air Pollution from Ships (entered into force 19 May 2005 – not in force in Australia)

State parties must accept Annexes I and II, but the other Annexes are voluntary. All Annexes are in force for Australia, except Annex VI.

Protection of the Sea (Prevention of Pollution from Ships) Act 1983 (Cth)

The Commonwealth enacted the *Protection of the Sea (Prevention of Pollution from Ships) Act 1983* (Cth) to give effect to Australia's international obligations under the MARPOL Convention. The Act applies both within and outside Australia and extends to every external Territory and to the Exclusive Economic Zone (s 6). The legislation includes a rollback provision, which means that Commonwealth law ceases to apply in any State jurisdiction which has enacted equivalent legislation. New South Wales enacted the *Marine Pollution Act 1987* (NSW) (MP Act) and the *Marine Pollution Regulation 2006* to give effect to its obligations under MARPOL. However, the NSW legislation only covers obligations imposed by Annex I (oil) and Annex II (chemicals). Thus, apart from some provisions in the Regulation, it does not cover Annexes III (packaged goods), Annex IV (sewage) and Annex V (garbage), so the Commonwealth legislation applies to these areas. The provisions of the Commonwealth legislation are briefly discussed below.

126 *New South Wales v Commonwealth* (1975) 135 CLR 337.

Criminal offences

The Commonwealth legislation provides for the following main offences:

- discharging oil or oily mixtures into the sea (s 9);
- discharging noxious substances into the sea (s 21);
- discharging packaged harmful substances into the sea (s 26AB);
- discharging untreated sewage into the Antarctic sea (s 26BC) or other seas (s 26BD);
- disposing of garbage into the sea (s 26F).

In a prosecution of the polluter, it must be shown that the discharge or disposal was reckless or negligent. The owner and the master, on the other hand, are strictly liable. These are indictable offences with a maximum penalty of $220,000 (2000 penalty units). Offences can be prosecuted summarily in which case lesser penalties apply (ss 9, 21, 26D, 26F).

Defences

A defence is provided where the discharge was:

- for the safety of human beings or a ship at sea (ss 9(2)(c), 21(2)(c));
- released through unintentional damage to the ship or its equipment, providing reasonable precautions were taken in mitigation (ss 9(2)(d), 21(2)(d), s 26DF);
- accidental loss of specified synthetic materials, eg fishing nets, and reasonable preventive measures were taken (s 26F(10));
- for the purpose of combating specific pollution incidents (s 21(2)(e));
- in compliance with permissible conditions of discharge/disposal (s 21(4)).

Duty to notify

There is a duty to report incidents which have resulted in, or are likely to cause, unauthorised discharges of oil/oily mixtures (s 11), noxious substances (s 22) or packaged harmful substances (s 26B). The primary duty is on the master to notify either a prescribed Australian officer or the government of a foreign country, depending on where the incident took place, and to furnish a report if requested. If the master is unable to comply or the ship is abandoned due to the incident, the duty falls to the ship's owner, agent, charterer, manager or operator. It is a defence if the person proves they were not aware of the incident or that they did not know or suspect that the master was unable to comply with the notification procedures.

Record books

Oil tankers or ships over a specified tonnage are required to keep oil record books (s 12(5)). Similar provisions apply to certain ships carrying liquid substances in bulk (s 23(5)). Garbage record books must be kept by ships over 400 tonnes or carrying 15 or more persons on an overseas voyage (s 26FA).

Regulation of packaged goods, sewage and garbage

Regulation of packaged goods, sewage and garbage takes the form of a prohibition on discharge or disposal. Power is given to order discharge of sewage at a reception facility if the retention poses a risk of discharge (s 26DAA). There are extensive provisions in relation to disposal of garbage. Placards are required to be displayed in ships over 12 metres in length to inform passengers and crew that certain kinds of garbage cannot be disposed of into the sea, and the conditions of disposal (s 26FD). Conditions of disposal are based on the nature and degradability of garbage, the amount of the discharge; and the distance from land. A shipboard waste management plan is also required (s 26FC).

Enforcement

Inspectors have been given wide powers to ensure compliance with the legislation and the MARPOL convention generally. These powers include the power to require information; board ships; require the production of record books; require a person to answer questions; and seize items. Where pollution discharges are reasonably suspected, ships may be detained in certain cases (s 27A). It is an offence to fail to comply with a request of an inspector or to provide misleading information (s 27).

Prosecutions

Prosecutions are the responsibility of the Australian Maritime Safety Authority and can be brought at any time, except in the case of a foreign ship where a three-year limit applies (s 29). The Commonwealth legislation makes no provision for requiring the polluter to clean up any pollution caused, although this is a requirement in most State legislation, including the *Marine Pollution Act 1987* (NSW) (ss 46-47).

The Commonwealth Act lifts the corporate veil. Where it is necessary to show the state of mind of the corporation, the state of mind of a director, officers or agent is attributed to the corporation (s 28(5)). Similarly, conduct by a director, officer or agent or their delegate is regarded as the conduct of the corporation (s 28(6)).

Marine Pollution Act 1987 (NSW)

The *Marine Pollution Act 1987 (*MP Act) is designed to implement the MARPOL Convention in New South Wales. The Act is supported by the *Marine Pollution Regulation 2006* (MP Regulation).

The MP Act covers 'State waters', namely, the territorial sea up to 3 nautical miles from the coast (s 3(1)). It also covers major ports. The MP Act does not deal with land-based discharges, except those which occur during transfer operations. Land-based discharges are dealt with under the PEOA. In the event of an inconsistency between the PEOA and the MP Act, the MP Act prevails except in relation to pollution relating to transfer operations (PEOA s 7(3)).

The scheme of the MP Act is absolute prohibitions coupled with exceptions. Military ships and foreign government non-commercial ships are exempted from its provisions (MP Regulation cl 39).

Prevention of pollution by oil

This part of the NSW legislation covers Australia's international obligations under Annex I of MARPOL 73/78.

Criminal offences

There is a general prohibition on the discharge of oil or oily mixtures from a ship into the State waters. Where a discharge occurs, the master and the owner (s 8(1)), and each crew member and person involved in the operation or maintenance of the ships (s 8A(1)), and each person whose act causes the discharge are guilty of an offence (s 8A(3)). In each case, the maximum penalty is a fine of $10 million for a corporation and $500,000 for an individual. Generally, strict liability applies, but where a person whose act causes the discharge is prosecuted under s 8A(3), intention, recklessness or negligence must be established.

Oil residue, that is oil which remains after oily mixtures have been separated, must be retained on board the ship. It can be off-loaded into reception facilities at oil loading terminals which are required to be provided under the terms of the MARPOL Convention (Regulation 12 of Annex 1). Since discharges are difficult to prove, the Act provides for an offence of failing to retain residues while in coastal waters. In such circumstances, the master and the owner are each guilty of an offence with a maximum penalty of $10 million for a corporation and $500,000 for an individual offender (MP Act s 9(1)).

Defences

The Act provides for a number of defences, namely:

- where the discharge is necessary to ensure the ship's safety or to save life at sea;
- if the discharge resulted from damage to the ship or its equipment and all reasonable precautions were taken after the occurrence of the damage or the discovery of the discharge for the purpose of preventing or minimising the escape;
- in the case of an oily mixture, if the discharge was authorised to combat a specific pollution incident;
- if the discharge was authorised by the NSW Maritime Authority for training purposes. (s 8(2))

The defence bears the burden of establishing these defences.

Exemptions

Apart from the defences, there are also exceptions to the general prohibition on discharges in line with the MARPOL Convention. Ships are allowed to discharge oil provided they meet certain conditions in relation to, inter alia, the place, rate and ratio (to cargo) of discharge. Conditions of discharge are dependent on the type of ship, the nature of the discharge and its source. Discharges of oil or oily mixtures from oil tankers must be made more than 50 nautical miles from land and not within special areas; must be made en route; must be below a certain threshold of litres per nautical mile and not exceed a certain ratio of total cargo (MP Act s 8(4)).

Insurance

All ships carrying a cargo of more than 2000 tons of oil in bulk, except non-commercial government ships, must not enter State waters without adequate insurance against oil damage (MP Act s 13B(2)). An inspector may detain a ship if he or she believes on reasonable grounds that no insurance is held. Both the master and the owner are guilty of an offence if no insurance is held (s 13B(3)), or if a ship that has been detained leaves port before being released (s 13B(5)). The maximum penalty is $110,000 for a corporation and $55,000 for an individual.

Control of pollution by noxious liquid substances in bulk

This part of the NSW legislation covers Australia's international obligations under Annex II of MARPOL 73/78.

Criminal offences

Legislation governing the discharge of liquid noxious substances is generally the same as for the discharge of oil.

There is a general prohibition on the discharge of liquid substances, including a mixture containing such a substance being carried as cargo in bulk from a ship into the sea, with defences and exceptions. Where a discharge occurs, the master and the owner (s 18(1)), and each crew member and person involved in the operation or maintenance of the ships (s 18A(1)), and each person whose act caused the discharge are guilty of an offence (s 18A(3)). In each case, the maximum penalty is a fine of $10 million for a corporation and $500,000 for an individual.

Generally, strict liability applies, but where a person whose act causes the discharge is prosecuted under s 18A(3), intention, recklessness or negligence must be established.

Defences

Defences are identical to those provided in relation to oil pollution offences (s 18(2)).

Exemptions

Consistent with obligations under MARPOL, no offence is committed if there has been compliance with conditions of discharge in relation to, inter alia, the category of substance discharged; the state of the ship's tank; approval for the discharge; and the place, rate and ratio of discharge (s 18(4)-(12)).

As a rule there is a more stringent regime for substances posing a threat to the marine environment and human health. Tanks containing such substances must first be washed, residues discharged into reception facilities and remaining residues diluted before they can be discharged (s 18(4)(a)-(c)). Conditions include discharges outside of special areas, a certain distance from land, at a prescribed speed and below the water line of the ship, in waters of a specified depth. It is not an offence to discharge clean or segregated ballast or bilge water, a mixture caused by tank cleaning or de-ballasting operations, in certain circumstances (s 18(4)-(13)). Certain listed substances such as castor oil, glycerine, molasses, liquid sulphur and wine are also exempted (s 18(11)).

Record books

Oil tankers or ships over 400 tonnes are required to keep an oil record book in which they record occurrences and operations in relation to the ship (MP Act s 11(1)). They are to be carried on board at all times, be available for inspection at all reasonable times, contain true and proper details and be retained for a period of time after completion. Non-compliance constitutes an offence punishable with a maximum penalty of 1000 penalty units for a corporation and 200 for an individual offender (MP Act ss 11, 13).

Trading ships on an intrastate voyage carrying liquid substances in bulk are required to carry a cargo record book in which they record occurrences and operations relating to the ship (s 23(5)). Cargo record books must be carried on board at all times, be available for inspection at all reasonable times, contain true and proper details, and be retained for a period of time after completion (s 23(4)).

Transfer operations

This part of the NSW legislation pertains to both Annex I and Annex II of MARPOL 73/78.

Criminal offences

The Act makes it an offence to discharge oil, an oily mixture or any other liquid into State waters on the seaward side of the first isolating valve on land, from:

- a ship or place on land in or in connection with a transfer operation; or
- any apparatus or purpose-built pipeline used in or in connection with a transfer operation, whether or not it is being used. (s 26(1))

It is an offence to transfer oil at night unless consent has been obtained from the harbour master, the Maritime Authority or the Minister (s 32). Consent may be general and/or conditional, such as at a port where oil transfer operations are a regular occurrence.

Strict liability applies for offences relating to the discharge of oil and liquid substances (s 27(1)). Liability extends to a number of persons in addition to the polluter. Liability is determined according to where the apparatus is situated – on a ship or on land. In relation to a discharge from an apparatus on land, the occupier of the place, the owner of the apparatus and the person in charge of the operation could all be liable (see definition of 'appropriate person' in s 25(1)). The following cases indicates the wide range of persons who can be held liable.

In *Filipowski v Fratelli D'Amato*,[127] 294,000 litres of oil were spilt from the carrier *Laura D'Amato* into Sydney Harbour during a transfer operation. Prosecutions were brought against the ship owner, the chief officer and the master in relation to the illegal discharge. All defendants pleaded guilty to an offence under s 27(1) of the MP Act. Talbot J found that the defendants had not followed good marine practice because of their failure properly to test the cargo discharge system, and properly to manage the discharge of cargo. The ship owner was fined $510,000 and the chief officer $110,000. No conviction was recorded in respect of the master as he did not have personal control over the system which had failed. The defendant company was also ordered to pay the prosecutor's costs of $400,000. In imposing the penalty, Talbot J took into account that the defendants had pleaded guilty and that $4.5 million had been paid by their insurers towards clean-up costs.

127 (2000) 108 LGERA 108.

Defences

It is a defence if the discharge was authorised for the purpose of combating pollution or carried out in accordance with a PEOA licence (s 27(2)).

Duty to notify

In the event of an oil pollution incident which has resulted, or in all probability will result, in unauthorised discharges of oily mixtures or noxious substances, the master or certain other persons associated with the ship are required to notify the Maritime Authority without delay (ss 10, 20). The primary duty is on the master, but if the master is unable to comply or the ship is abandoned due to the incident, the duty falls to the owner, agent, charterer, manager or operator to notify the appropriate authorities and, if requested, prepare a report (ss 10(3), 20(3)). It is a defence if the person proves they were not aware of the incident or that they did know or suspect that the master was unable to comply with the notification procedures. Failure to notify or to provide a report when requested, or to make a false or misleading statement in a report, is an offence punishable by a maximum penalty of $2,750,000 for a corporation and $120,000 for an individual.

A similar reporting duty applies in relation to discharges during transfer operations. The duty falls on a range of 'appropriate' persons, basically the owner and master and those involved (ss 28, 25). It is a defence if the person proves an inability to comply (s 28(2)).

Notification under these proceedings cannot be used as evidence for a prosecution (ss 10(9), 20(9), 28(5)).

Enforcement

Inspectors have wide-ranging powers to ensure compliance with the Act and the MARPOL Convention generally (s 53(1)(a)(b)). It is an offence to obstruct an inspector or to make false or misleading statements (s 53(3)). Inspectors are generally immune from liability provided they acted in good faith. They have statutory responsibilities and must not unnecessarily delay a ship from going to sea (s 53(4)).

Powers of the Maritime Safety Authority

The Maritime Safety Authority is empowered to take all necessary measures to prevent or mitigate a serious pollution threat from oil or other noxious substances to Australia's coastline. Expenses and liabilities incurred by the Authority are recoverable from the owner or master of the ship, the polluter or an 'appropriate person' (ss 46, 47). A ship may be detained as security for payment of costs and expenses incurred (s 52A).

If a discharge occurs, or the Minister believes there is a probability of a discharge, he or she can issue a notice for:

- action to be taken, or prohibited, in relation to a ship, its cargo, a place on land, an apparatus, facility or pipeline;
- prohibiting the removal of a ship or its cargo. (s 48)

Prosecutions

A prosecution must be brought within two years of the commission of the offence (s 54). Proceedings are brought by the Maritime Safety Authority. Offences under the Act may be dealt with summarily by either the Land and Environment Court or a Local Court (s 55).

Recovery of damages

A person who suffers damage to property, or incurs cost or expenses in preventing or mitigating damage from an illegal discharge, may recover the costs as a debt from the person who caused the discharge, or the owner or master of the ship (s 51).

Liability of corporate officers

The Act provides for personal liability for directors or corporate officers. If a corporation commits an offence, directors or persons concerned in the management of the corporation are deemed to have contravened the same provision if they knowingly authorised or permitted the contravention (s 56(1)). It is not necessary for corporations to be prosecuted or convicted in order for this section to apply.

Sewage and waste

Although these aspects are not dealt with in the MP Act, Pt 7 of the MP Regulation contains some provisions regulating disposal of sewage and waste and requiring a licence to be held under the PEOA.

Intentional dumping at sea

London Convention 1972 and Protocol 1996

The London Convention 1972 limits the discharge of waste that is generated on land and disposed of at sea. It permits dumping of waste at sea, except for those materials on a banned list (Annex I). Materials which are not as harmful are listed in Annex II (the 'grey' list) and require a permit before dumping is permitted. Dumping of high-level radioactive waste is prohibited and a moratorium on the dumping of low-level radioactive waste has been in place since 1983. Incineration of wastes at sea is prohibited under amendments adopted in 1993.

The 1996 Protocol is a separate agreement that updated the Convention. The Protocol entered into force on 24 March 2006 and replaces the London Convention. It represents a major change of approach to the question of how to regulate the use of the sea as a depository for waste materials in that, in essence, dumping is prohibited, except for materials on an approved list (Annex I).

Article 3 of the Protocol affirms the 'precautionary approach' which requires that 'appropriate preventative measures are taken when there is reason to believe that wastes or other matter introduced into the marine environment are likely to cause harm even when there is no conclusive evidence to prove a causal relation between inputs and their effects'.

The Protocol requires parties to ensure that pollution is not transferred from one part of the environment to another.

Prohibitions and permits

Parties are required by the Protocol to prohibit the dumping of any waste or other matter with the exception of those listed in Annex I (Art 4). These are:

- dredged material;
- sewage sludge;
- fish waste, or material resulting from industrial fish processing operations;
- vessels and platforms or other man-made structures at sea;
- inert, inorganic geological material;
- organic material of natural origin; and
- bulky items primarily comprising iron, steel, concrete and similar unharmful materials for which the concern is physical impact. This is limited to circumstances, where such waste is generated at locations, such as small islands with isolated communities, having no practicable access to disposal options other than dumping.

The only exceptions to this are contained in Art 8 which permits dumping to be carried out in cases of *force majeure* caused by stress of weather, or in any case which constitutes a danger to human life or a real threat to vessels.

Incineration of wastes at sea is specifically prohibited (Art 5). Parties are required to prohibit export of waste or other matter to other countries for dumping or incineration at sea (Art 6).

Permits are required for dumping that is not prohibited and parties are required to designate an authority to issue permits in accordance with the Protocol.

Environment Protection (Sea Dumping) Act 1981 (Cth)

This Act was originally enacted to fulfil Australia's international responsibilities under the London Convention 1972. It has now been amended to meet the obligations imposed by the 1996 Protocol. The Act is administered by the Department of the Environment and Heritage, or the Great Barrier Reef Marine Park Authority if dumping is to take place within the Great Barrier Reef Marine Park. It applies to all Australian wasters from the low water mark out to the limits of the Exclusive Economic Zone. It applies to the coastal waters of each State, unless the States have enacted complementary legislation. In such a case, the Commonwealth legislation is 'rolled' back except where the dumping of 'seriously harmful' material is proposed (s 9). 'Seriously harmful' material is defined to include radioactive material and other prescribed substances (s 4).

New South Wales has not enacted complementary legislation and thus the Commonwealth legislation applies in its entirety.

The Act regulates the deliberate loading and dumping of wastes and other matters at sea from ships, aircraft and platforms. It also applies to incineration of waste and other matter on ships and platforms. It applies to all vessels, aircraft or platforms in Australian waters and to all Australian vessels or aircraft in any part of the ocean. Foreign military vessels and aircraft are exempted from the provisions of the legislation. However, Australian Defence Force vessels and aircraft are exempted only in situations of armed conflict and emergencies (s 7). The Act also exempts activities (other than a vessel, aircraft or platform) relating to the exploration, mining and processing of offshore seabed mineral resources (s 5).

Permits

Permits are required for a range of activities. These are:

- dumping of waste (controlled material) (s 10A);
- dumping by a vessel, aircraft or platform (s 10A);
- incineration of waste (controlled material) at sea (s 10B);
- loading of waste for dumping or incineration at sea (s 10C);
- export for the purpose of dumping or incineration (s 10D);
- placement of artificial reef (s 10E).

Permit applications are made to the Minister (s 18(1)). The Minister has wide powers to require the applicant to research and monitor the consequences of dumping wastes into the sea, as well as to investigate alternatives (ss 18(3), 19(9)). The applicant may be required to enter into an agreement with the Commonwealth to pay the expenses incurred for such research and monitoring. If the application falls within the purview of the *Environment Protection and Biodiversity Conservation Act 1997* (Cth), the Minister must obtain a report under that Act before granting a permit (s 19(3)). The decision whether to grant a permit is discretionary (s 19(1)). However, in exercising discretion the Minister is bound by a range of considerations:

- a permit for dumping or loading for dumping may only be granted for controlled material that is within Annex I to the Protocol, and may only be granted in accordance with Annex II to the Protocol;
- a permit cannot be granted for incineration at sea or loading for incineration at sea, except in an emergency where there is no other feasible solution; and
- a permit cannot be granted for an artificial reef placement of seriously harmful material. 'Seriously harmful material' includes radioactive material. (s 19(5)-(8A))

A permit may be suspended or revoked if a condition is breached or it is necessary to do so in order to regulate activities with which the Act is concerned (s 20). Conditions may be imposed, revoked, suspended or varied when granting a permit or at any time while a permit is in force (s 21).

Currently about 30 permits are issued in Australia each year, mainly for the dumping of uncontaminated dredge spoil, disposal of illegal vessels and burials at sea.[128]

Criminal offences

It is a strict liability offence to carry out an activity specified in ss 10A-10E otherwise than in accordance with a permit. Three categories of penalties are provided for. For dumping or incineration of seriously harmful material, the penalty is imprisonment for up to 10 years and/or a $220,000 fine. If the offending material is not within Annex 1 to the Protocol – imprisonment for up to two years and/or a $55,000 fine. In any other case, the penalty is imprisonment for up to one year and/or a fine up to $27,500. The defendant can also be tried summarily, in which case lesser penalties apply (s 37). In addition to the polluter, a range of other 'responsible' persons can be held liable, namely, the owner and person in charge of the offending craft, and the owner of the offending material. However, it must be proved that they *knew* that the offending craft or material would be used in committing the offence, or were *reckless*

128 For further reference, see Department of the Environment and Heritage, 'Dumping Wastes at Sea', July 2002, <http://www.deh.gov.au/coasts/pollution/dumping/dumping.html>.

as to whether it would be so used, and that they did not take reasonable steps to prevent it (s 10F). The same penalties apply as those for the primary offender.

It is also an offence to breach the conditions of a permit if the person knew of the condition at the time of the act, or was reckless as to its existence. This offence is punishable by imprisonment for up to one year or a fine up to $27,500, or both (s 36).

Defences

The Act provides for a number of exceptions or defences. The defendant bears the evidential burden of proving a defence. It is not an offence if the prohibited action:

- took place in waters that are not Australian under the imprimatur of a permit granted by another country in accordance with the Protocol;
- was necessary for the safety of human life or of a vessel, aircraft or platform in a case of *force majeure* by stress of weather;
- was the only way to avert threat to human life, or to the safety of the vessel, aircraft or platform, and there was every probability that the damage caused by the conduct would be less than would otherwise occur. The conduct must be carried out to minimise the likelihood of damage to human or marine life and be reported to the Minister as soon as practicable. (s 15(1)-(3))

Enforcement

Enforcement is the responsibility of inspectors. Members of the Australian Federal Police, the police forces of a State or Territory and Customs Officers are *ex officio* inspectors (s 27). The Minister also has the power to appoint inspectors (s 26). Inspectors have wide-ranging powers to investigate and prevent the commission of offences under the Act. These include the power to board vessels, aircraft or platforms (s 29(2)) and to enter premises with a warrant (s 30(2), (3)).

Remedies

The Attorney-General or an 'interested' person may seek an injunction to restrain a person from engaging in conduct that constitutes an offence relating to dumping, loading (for dumping), incineration, or placement of an artificial reef (s 33). An 'interested' person includes a person whose use or enjoyment of any part of the sea, or of the air space above, or of the seabed or subsoil beneath, any part of the sea is, or is likely to be, adversely affected by the conduct concerned.

The Minister has power to take all necessary steps to mitigate any damage or remedy any situation caused by dumping where he or she considers that such dumping may obstruct or endanger vessels or harm human life or the marine environment (s 16). The costs can be recovered from the defendant on conviction (s 17). The amount expended is recoverable as a debt and operates as a charge upon the vessel, aircraft or platform (s 17(1), (3)). The vessel may be detained as security for payment (s 17(3)).

There is no time limit for bringing a prosecution (s 37A).

12

WASTE, CHEMICALS, CONTAMINATED LAND AND DANGEROUS GOODS

Waste

Growing concern about the amounts and types of waste being consigned to landfill and the increasing shortage of land in urban areas has resulted in a change of focus from waste disposal to waste prevention and recycling. To reflect these changes, the *Waste Avoidance and Resource Recovery Act 2001* (NSW) (WARRA) replaces the *Waste Minimisation and Management Act 1995* (NSW). The Waste Recycling and Processing Corporation has been established by the *Waste Recycling and Processing Corporation Act 2001* (NSW) (WRPCA) as a State-owned corporation with responsibility for the operation of most waste facilities located in the Sydney area. Local councils and private operators have responsibility for managing waste facilities outside the metropolitan area. The WARRA and the WRPCA are the principal statutes governing the management of waste in New South Wales. The *Protection of the Environment Operations Act 1997* (NSW) (PEOA) also plays an important role in the licensing of waste facilities and activities and in the day-to-day regulation of waste.

The NSW government has two primary goals in relation to waste:

- to encourage resource recovery from wastes and waste avoidance; and
- to protect the environment from potential negative impacts. (*Issues Paper: Review of the Protection of the Environment Operations Act 1997*, NSW EPA (2003) (PEOA Issues Paper (2003))

Waste recovery and waste avoidance

The NSW government has addressed its goal of achieving resource recovery and waste avoidance through mechanisms provided under the WARRA and the adoption of the Waste Avoidance and Resource Recovery Strategy and Performance Report 2006 (Waste Strategy) for New South Wales. Policy and planning functions are the responsibility of the Director-General of the NSW Department of Environment and Conservation.

The WARRA focuses on waste avoidance and resource recovery. This is reflected in the objectives of the Act which include:

- encouraging the most efficient use of resources and reducing environmental harm in accordance with ecologically sustainable development (ESD) principles;

- ensuring that resource management options are considered against a hierarchy of the following order: avoidance of unnecessary resource consumption, resource recovery and disposal. (s 3)

To ensure consistency with the PEOA the same definition of waste applies under the WARRA (see discussion in Chapter 11 at pp 442-443).

Waste strategies

The WARRA provides for the development of a waste strategy for New South Wales. The strategy must be based on continuous improvement and benchmarked against international best practice. It must also include targets for waste reduction, resource recovery and the diversion of waste from landfill disposal (s 12(2)). Waste strategies must be replaced every two years. The adequacy of a waste strategy may be assessed by various means, including the technique of life cycle analysis (s 12(6)). A waste strategy must be advertised for public comment for at least 28 days and public comments must be taken into consideration in finalising the strategy (s 12(7)). In accordance with this mandate, the NSW Waste Strategy was adopted in 2003. This Strategy was superseded by the Waste Avoidance and Resource Recovery Strategy 2006. The Waste Strategy 2006 combines a performance report against the recycling and other targets set in 2003. It updates the 2003 Strategy but retains the current targets. It proposes priority areas and actions to guide the work of key groups in NSW to minimise environmental harm from waste disposal, and the conservation and efficient use of resources. Councils may be requested to give reasons for any non-compliance with the objectives of the current waste strategy (s 14(1)).

Extended producer responsibility schemes

The *Waste Minimisation and Management Act 1995* (NSW) provided for industry waste reduction plans. Plans were made in relation to the dairy industry, tyres, soft drinks, beer, and used packaging materials. These schemes were largely unsuccessful and all, except the plan for used packaging materials, were repealed by the WARRA at the same time as the repeal of the 1995 Act. The Used Packaging Materials Industry Waste Reduction Plan continued to operate until its replacement by regulations implementing the Used Packaging Materials National Environment Protection Measure by amendments to the *Protection of the Environment Operations (Waste) Regulation 2005* in 2006 (discussed at pp 490-491). The WARRA replaces industry waste reduction plans with extended producer responsibility schemes.

An extended producer responsibility scheme aims to ensure that producers take physical or financial responsibility for the environmental impacts of their products throughout the products' life cycle. It includes 'upstream' impacts from choice of materials and manufacturing processes and 'downstream' impacts associated with the use and disposal of products. Part 4 of the WARRA introduces an extended producer responsibility scheme which is defined as 'a scheme in which a producers' responsibility for their products (including physical or financial responsibility) is extended to the post-consumer stage of the product's life-cycle' (s 15(1)). The extended producer responsibility scheme includes product stewardship, defined as 'shared responsibility for the life-cycle of products including the environmental impact of the product from the extraction of virgin materials, to manufacturing, to consumption and through to and including ultimate disposal and post-disposal consequences' (s 15(2)).

The Director-General is required to publish an annual priority statement with respect to any extended producer responsibility scheme that it proposes to recommend for implementation. These schemes are to be advertised and public submissions invited. A report must be published on any submissions received (s 18(1)). The priority statement identifies only those wastes or products that would be suitable for management through an extended producer responsibility scheme. Other wastes are controlled under the PEOA. The first priority statement in 2004 listed 16 wastes of concern, with nine to receive priority focus namely: computers, televisions, nickel cadmium batteries, used tyres, plastic pages, agricultural/ veterinary chemicals, AGVET chemical containers, mobile phones/batteries and packaging waste. No regulatory action was proposed in the 2004 priority statement, but industries were placed on notice of the need to develop voluntary schemes to reduce waste created by their sector. The second priority statement, released in 2005-06, has not identified any new wastes of concern because of the need to focus on current priority wastes. The wastes identified for priority focus for 2005-06 are computers, mobile phones, office paper, paint, plastic bags, televisions and tyres. The priority statement states that if the industry does not develop adequate initiatives to address these types of waste, the Minister may decide to make regulations to implement an extended producer responsibility scheme. The computer industry, in particular, is targeted for regulation in the absence of satisfactory progress towards a voluntary scheme. Overall, the priority statement expresses a preference for the use of voluntary schemes.

Section 16 of the WARRA empowers the Minister to make regulations to implement extended producer responsibility schemes. Any regulation would apply to a product sector and could specify outcomes to be achieved, as well as the mechanism to achieve those outcomes. However, the Minister is not to recommend a regulation to implement an extended producer responsibility scheme unless satisfied that it is necessary having regard to the following factors:

- the volume of waste requiring ultimate disposal or the toxicity of the waste generated;
- the existence of a national or voluntary scheme that adequately addresses waste issues;
- economic analysis supporting the scheme; and
- constitutional or other impediments. (s 17(1))

Failure to observe these factors will not give rise to an action to challenge or invalidate the regulation (s 17(2)). Breaches will be dealt with in a Local Court (s 26). The maximum penalty for a breach is $22,000 for an individual and $44,000 for a corporation. The rationale for the Local Court to have jurisdiction instead of the Land and Environment Court is not clear. The penalties provided for are also much lower than penalties available under the PEOA. Proceedings for offences under the WARRA and Regulations are dealt with under Chapter 8 of the PEOA (PEOA s 213).

Used packaging materials

The *Protection of the Environment Operations (Waste) Amendment (Used Packaging Materials) Regulation 2006* inserted a new Pt 5B into the *Protection of the Environment*

Operations (Waste) Regulation 2005 (Waste Regulation) to implement the National Environment Protection (Used Packaging Materials) Measure in New South Wales. These regulations replace the Used Packaging Materials Industry Waste Reduction Plan which was introduced under the *Waste Minimisation and Management Act 1995*. The Used Packaging Materials NEPM is the regulatory underpinning for the voluntary strategies in the National Packaging Covenant. Part 5B of the Waste Regulation regulates the activities of NSW companies who are not signatories to, or fail to comply with, the National Packaging Covenant. It applies to all brand owners of products as well as retailers who provide plastic bags to consumers. It does not apply to persons who have signed, and are complying with, the National Packaging Covenant; have made an arrangement with the EPA which will produce equivalent outcomes; or have a turnover of less than $5 million per annum. The Waste Regulation makes provision for the EPA to set targets for the recovery of specified waste materials used in packaging produced, having regard to the targets set in the National Packaging Covenant (cl 46J). Persons to whom the Waste Regulation applies must recover waste material used in packaging in accordance with EPA targets. Recovered materials must be reused and recycled, preferably within Australia (cl 46K). Consumers must be given adequate information on where to take packaging for reuse or recycling (cl 46K). Brand owners must prepare a waste action plan (cl 46L). Full records must be kept.

National Packaging Covenant

The National Packaging Covenant is a voluntary industry self-regulatory agreement with specific targets and performance indicators. It is an agreement based on the principles of shared responsibility through product stewardship. It is designed to minimise environmental impacts arising from the disposal of used packaging. It also aims to conserve resources through better design and production processes and facilitate the reuse and recycling of used packaging materials. It establishes a framework for the effective life cycle management of consumer packaging and paper products through a collaborative approach between all sectors of the packaging supply chain, consumers, collectors, re-processors and all spheres of government. It also commits industry to a package to make kerbside recycling more economically sustainable.

The Covenant was extensively reviewed in 2005 to ensure improved performance. Key changes made were to require more consistent data-reporting and the inclusion of packaging waste occurring away from homes and workplaces. The following three overarching targets were set:

- recycle 65% of post-consumer packaging by 2010;
- recycle 25% of plastics and non-recyclable paper and cardboard packaging by 2010;
- to have no increase in packaging going to landfill compared to the 2003 level. (National Packaging Covenant 2005)

NEPM for Used Packaging Materials

The NEPM for Used Packaging Materials is intended to reduce environmental degradation arising from the disposal of used packaging, to improve kerbside recycling, and to conserve virgin materials through the encouragement of reuse and recycling of used consumer packaging materials. The NEPM focuses on:

- materials used for packaging retail products consumed in industrial, commercial and domestic premises and public places;
- materials used for packaging food and beverages intended for consumption in public places or in commercial provision of food services to individuals in hotels and restaurants;
- consumer paper; and
- distribution packaging that contains multiples of products intended for consumer use. (NEPM (Used Packaging Materials) cl 7)

In 2005 the NEPM was amended to ensure consistency with the strengthened National Packaging Covenant and to provide for continuation of the co-regulatory arrangement until 2010. New South Wales is collaborating with other States to develop a NEPM for Product Stewardship to enable the implementation of more national co-regulatory approaches for other product sectors.

Protecting the environment from waste

The PEOA provides the legislative framework to protect the environment from potential impacts from waste. It regulates waste primarily through licensing and tracking requirements and offence provisions, and also uses the economic mechanism of imposing a waste levy on the disposal of waste at licensed facilities.

Classification of waste

In order to determine how waste should be managed, all waste must be classified into one of eight categories. These categories are: inert, solid, industrial, hazardous, Group A, B or C, and non-controlled aqueous liquid waste. These categories are specified in Sch 1 Pt 3 of the PEOA and elaborated in the Environmental Guidelines: Assessment, Classification and Management of Liquid and Non-Liquid Wastes DEC NSW (1999). The highest risk categories are hazardous, industrial and Group A wastes. Generally, the origin of the wastes determines the classification. For example, domestic waste is automatically classified as solid waste, building and demolition waste not containing asbestos are inert wastes, asbestos wastes are industrial waste, dangerous goods are hazardous waste, non-aqueous liquids and controlled aqueous liquids are group A wastes, liquid grease trap wastes from food are Group B wastes and septic tank waste is Group C waste. If a waste cannot be automatically classified, it must be analysed in accordance with EPA guidelines (PEOA Issues Paper (2003)). The classification of the waste determines:

- the type of facility that may be used to dispose of the waste;
- whether a licence is required to dispose of, transport, process, or manage the waste;
- whether movement of the waste must be tracked.

Waste Recycling and Processing Corporation Act 2001 (NSW)

The *Waste Recycling and Processing Corporation Act 2001* (WRPCA) establishes the Waste Recycling and Processing Corporation as a statutory state owned corporation trading as the 'Waste Service' (s 4). The Corporation has a number of objectives including:

- operating as a successful business;
- protecting the environment by conducting its operations in accordance with ESD principles;
- minimising any adverse health and environmental impacts of its activities and services relating to waste management and secondary resource recovery. (s 5(1))

The Corporation is managed by a Board of Directors (s 7). The chief executive officer may, but need not be, appointed as a director. The chief executive officer is appointed by the board after consultation with the voting shareholders and the Minister (s 8).

The Corporation has a range of functions. It is required to establish, maintain and operate waste facilities and secondary resource facilities, although in practice this is limited to the Sydney metropolitan area. It is required to conduct businesses or provide services relating to waste and secondary resource recovery, including waste management and secondary resource management services. It is also empowered to trade in waste and secondary resources and to research, develop and implement alternative waste management technologies (s 6(1)). In exercising these functions, the Waste Recycling and Processing Corporation must strive to achieve international best practice in waste management and act in accordance with ESD principles (s 6(4), (5)). The Minister can adopt environmental reporting indicators, including ESD development indicators for use by the Corporation. These indicators must include a methodology for making comparisons to international best practice in waste management (s 15(2)). A proposed environmental reporting indicator must be published and any submissions must be taken into account (s 15(3)).

Waste levies

Waste levies are an important source of funding and also provide an incentive for waste avoidance and waste recovery. The Waste Regulation provides details relating to the calculation of contributions payable by occupiers of waste facilities licensed under the PEOA and exemptions and rebates in respect of such contributions.

Licensing requirements for waste facilities, transportation and management

Schedule 1 to the PEOA sets out criteria to determine when a licence will be required. This depends on the type and volume of waste handled and what is being done with it. In general, the following facilities or activities must be licensed:

- facilities that treat, reprocess, dispose of hazardous, industrial and Group A and B wastes, or that store or dispose of tyres, and landfill sites (waste facilities);
- generators or storers of hazardous, industrial or Group A wastes (waste activities);
- transporters of hazardous, industrial, Group A, B, and C waste (waste transporters);
- mobile plants that treat, process or reprocess industrial, hazardous, and Group A wastes (mobile waste processors).

Only one licence is required for scheduled activities under the PEOA - there is no separate waste licence.

Waste facilities

Waste facilities must conform to the requirements of the *Environmental Planning and Assessment Act 1979* (EPAA) and any relevant environmental planning instruments together with the licensing requirements of the PEOA (see below). Waste management facilities, or facilities or works that dispose of, sort, store or process solid or liquid waste, are designated development under Sch 3 to the *Environmental Planning and Assessment Regulation 2000. SEPP 3 – Castlereagh Liquid Waste Depot Sites* provides for the continuation and expansion of the Castlereagh Liquid Waste Depot.

Waste facilities are listed in Sch 1 to the PEOA and must be licensed. In the case of putrescible waste landfill sites, a licence may only be granted to a person who is not a public authority, if the public authority holds a supervisory licence in respect of the facility. Furthermore, a condition must be imposed on the licence requiring the occupier to charge for the disposal in accordance with the directions of the public authority holding the supervisory licence (PEOA s 87).

SEPP 48 – Major Putrescible Landfill provides for the assessment and determination of proposals for major putrescible landfill sites. It applies to applications for sites which have the capacity to receive more than 75 tonnes of putrescible waste per annum or 650 tonnes over the lifetime of the facility, as well as applications to extend existing sites to receive that capacity.

It should be noted that *SEPP 33 – Hazardous and Offensive Development* redefines the definitions of hazardous and offensive industries where that term is used in an environmental planning instrument (EPI). It overrides provisions in an EPI that prohibit development for the purposes of a storage facility on the ground that it is hazardous or offensive if it is not so defined in the SEPP. Further, in determining whether a development is hazardous or offensive the consent authority has to take account of measures proposed to reduce its impact. This SEPP facilitates a range of development with consent in industrial zones which would previously have been prohibited. It also means that councils have to make a merit assessment of any pollution control measures proposed.

Waste activities

A licence is required for generating or storing hazardous, industrial and Group A waste. Those transporting wastes into, out of, or within the region for payment must hold a licence under the PEOA if they transport in loads over 200 kilograms of:

- hazardous or industrial waste;
- group A waste: certain liquid waste (non-aqueous waste and controlled aqueous waste);
- group B waste: food waste; and
- group C waste: sewage waste.

A licence is also required to transport used, rejected or unwanted tyres in loads over 2 tonnes (PEOA Sch 1).

These licensing provisions also apply to local council garbage disposal services. The powers of council to arrange for the provision of garbage collection services falls within a council's general power to provide services and facilities, and carry out activities, appropriate to the current and future needs within its local community (*Local Government Act 1993* (LGA) s 24). A council is required to make and levy an annual charge for the provision of domestic waste management services (LGA s 496).

Waste tracking

Cradle-to-grave management systems are imposed for higher risk wastes. The Waste Regulation and the EPA's Environmental Guidelines: Assessment, Classification and Management of Liquid and Non-Liquid Wastes (Waste Guidelines) require these wastes to be tracked to ensure they are safely transported to lawful waste facilities and dealt with appropriately. The types of wastes to which waste-tracking requirements apply, are specified in Sch 1 to the Waste Regulation. The Regulation places obligations on producers, consignors, transporters and receivers of scheduled waste to obtain certain authorisations to transport and receive the waste and to carry, complete or keep certain documentation in relation to the transportation of the waste. The Waste Regulation deals only with waste transported within New South Wales. When wastes are transported interstate, they fall under the national requirements of the Controlled Waste NEPM.

Waste management

The Waste Regulation imposes a number of requirements to ensure safe management of higher risk wastes. These requirements include:

- specifying requirements to be met by persons transporting, collecting, storing or disposing of any type of asbestos waste;
- specifying requirements to be met by persons disposing of clinical waste at a facility that is not licensed under the Act;
- prohibiting the application of certain residue waste to land used for growing vegetation unless the waste was lawfully sold as a soil improving agent or trace element product within the meaning of the *Fertilisers Act 1985* (NSW) or was exempted from the provisions by the EPA;
- requiring the reporting of certain matters to the EPA by the occupiers of landfill sites that are not licensed under the Act;
- requiring persons to store waste in an environmentally safe manner and to take certain measures when transporting waste;
- permitting the EPA to grant approvals to enable waste to be assessed and classified in accordance with the procedures relating to the immobilisation of waste set out in Environmental Guidelines: Assessment, Classification and Management of Liquid and Non-Liquid Wastes issued by the EPA;
- revising the formula for calculating contributions payable;
- establishing a scheme to promote waste reduction by councils and allowing the EPA to pay councils for achieving waste reduction goals;
- revising the record-keeping requirements of the occupier of a scheduled waste facility;
- clarifying what the EPA can consider when determining the contribution to be paid by occupiers of a scheduled waste facility who has not kept adequate records; and
- allowing an authorised agent to act as a consignor of waste transported from a waste facility, on behalf of the occupier of the waste facility.

(See Explanatory Note to the Waste Regulation.)

The provisions in the Waste Regulation relating to contributions and waste reduction by councils resulted from a 2006 amendment to Sch 2 to the PEOA (cl 5A) entitled 'Local council waste reduction scheme' which provides for regulations to be made in respect of:

- the establishment and administration of a scheme for recycling, resource recovery and other reduction of waste by local councils;
- the making of payments to local councils from money appropriated by Parliament for that purpose; and
- requirements to be met by local councils to be eligible to receive payments under the scheme.

The amendment assists with the fulfilment of the NSW City and Country Environment Restoration Program which, inter alia, aims to achieve the targets of the NSW Waste Strategy.

Waste offences

The PEOA provides for a number of waste offences. The most serious offence is the tier one offence of 'wilfully or negligently disposing of waste in a manner which harms or is likely to harm the environment' (PEOA s 115(1) (see Chapter 11 at p 441). Once an offence under s 115(1) is established, the owner of the waste is also liable (s 115(2)) unless he or she can show that the illegal dumping was due to causes over which they had no control, and that they took reasonable precautions and exercised due diligence to prevent it (PEOA s 118). The maximum penalty for a corporation is $5 million for an offence that is committed wilfully, and $2 million where it is committed negligently. An individual is liable to a maximum penalty of $1 million for wilful offences and/or seven years' imprisonment and $500,000 and/or four years' imprisonment for an offence involving negligence (s 119) (see Chapter 11 at p 440). The PEOA also provides for a number of tier two and tier three waste offences (see Chapter 11 at pp 449-459, 466). The Waste Regulation provides additional offences, such as providing false information about waste (cl 40). For discussion of the definition of waste and when waste ceases to be waste (eg, by recycling), see Chapter 11 at pp 442-443. For discussion of ownership of waste at various stages of its generation, transport and disposal, see Chapter 11 at pp 455-456, 442.

Commonwealth regulation of waste

The Commonwealth focus is on hazardous waste. The Commonwealth has developed a number of strategies for safe management and disposal of different types of hazardous waste. It also controls the exports and imports of hazardous waste as required by the *Convention on the Control of Transboundary Movements of Hazardous Wastes and their Disposal 1989* (Basel Convention).

Exports of hazardous waste

The past 30 years have seen an unprecedented increase in production of new products that generate hazardous waste. In 1990 the United Nations Environment Program (UNEP) estimated the annual global generation of hazardous waste to be approximately 300 to 500 million tons. Most of this waste originates in developed countries. The introduction of stringent controls on disposal of this waste has resulted in an escalation in disposal costs. This increased cost has led, in some cases, to the export of hazardous wastes to developing countries for final disposal or recycling. Since most developing countries do not have the capacity to handle these wastes safely, these exports pose a risk of serious harm to human health and the environment. To address these concerns, the international community adopted the Basel Convention in 1989 which came into force in 1992.

Basel Convention

The Basel Convention seeks to control and limit the movement of waste, based on a process of prior informed consent. At first the Convention did not ban exports of hazardous waste. The result was that some Parties began to bypass their obligations under the Basel Convention by claiming they were exporting a commodity for recycling, and not waste for disposal. To address this problem, the Convention was amended to ban all exports of hazardous wastes from OECD to non-OECD (largely developing) countries. The ban applied immediately to waste exports for final disposal, while recycling was prohibited from December 1997. To ensure that the ban would be effective, it was adopted as an amendment to the Convention in 1995. The ban has not yet received the required number of ratifications to come into force. Key obligations imposed under the Convention are as follows:

- to minimise the quantity and severity of the hazardous wastes generated;
- to ensure the availability of adequate disposal facilities for environmentally sound management within their own territory;
- to dispose of wastes as close as possible to their source of generation;
- to reduce the transboundary movements of hazardous wastes to a minimum, consistent with their environmentally sound management;
- to impose high penalties for illegal transboundary movements of hazardous waste;
- not to export or import hazardous wastes to non-Parties unless an Art 11 agreement has been concluded between the Parties. Article 11 permits Parties or non-Parties to enter into an agreement with other Parties or with non-Parties, as long as the agreement does not derogate from the environmentally sound management of the waste.

Hazardous Waste (Regulation of Exports and Imports) Act 1989 (Cth)

Consistently with the Basel Convention, the Commonwealth government has enacted the *Hazardous Waste (Regulation of Exports and Imports) Act 1989* (Hazardous Waste Act) to regulate the import and export of hazardous wastes. The Act is administered by Environment Australia.

The object of the Act is to regulate the export, import and transit of hazardous waste to ensure that it is managed in an environmentally sound manner so that human beings and the environment, both within and outside Australia, are protected from the harmful effects of the waste (s 3).

The aims of the Act are:

- to give effect to the Basel Convention; and
- to give effect to agreements of the kind mentioned in Art 11 of that Convention. (s 3)

As Australia has not yet ratified the ban amendment to the Convention (discussed at p 497), it is not included in the Hazardous Waste Act. The Act does not apply to movements of hazardous waste within Australia, but all industries throughout Australia have to comply with its requirements, should they wish to export or import hazardous waste.

Definition of hazardous waste

Definitions in the Hazardous Waste Act correspond with those in the Basel Convention. The Hazardous Waste Act defines 'waste' as a substance or object that: is proposed to be disposed of (s 4). 'Disposal' is defined as 'an operation specified in Annex IV to the Basel Convention' (s 4). Annex IV of the Basel Convention defines 'disposal' so as to cover final disposal as well as some recycling operations. This means that the Hazardous Waste Act will apply to hazardous waste that is intended for final disposal as well as some wastes intended for recycling or reclamation.

Waste is designated as hazardous under the Hazardous Waste Act if it belongs to any category contained in Annex I to the Basel Convention unless it does not possess any of the characteristics contained in Annex III. Annex I of the Convention sets out two categories of wastes to be controlled. The first category deals with waste streams and includes hospital and pharmaceutical waste, wastes from organic solvents, polychlorinated biphenyls, adhesives and so forth. The second category classifies wastes according to their constituents. The onus is then on a person who claims that the wastes are not hazardous to show they do not have any of the characteristics of Annex III. Annex III includes explosives, flammable liquids and solids, substances liable to spontaneous combustion, toxic and ecotoxic wastes. Wastes listed in Annex II of the Convention (household waste or residues arising from the incineration of household waste) are also classified as hazardous under the Hazardous Waste Act. Waste will also be treated as hazardous if it has been classified as hazardous in the domestic legislation of another country (ss 4, 4A).

The very general definitions of hazardous waste in Annexes I and III of the Basel Convention have led to confusion over which wastes should be classified as hazardous. To clarify this, lists of wastes have been compiled. These lists have been incorporated as Annexes VIII and IX of the Convention. Annex VIII lists wastes that are hazardous and subject to the Convention while Annex IX lists wastes that are non-hazardous. The Australian lists of hazardous wastes adopt the same classification.

Permits

To implement Australia's international obligations under the Basel Convention, the Hazardous Waste Act establishes a permit scheme for exports and imports of hazardous waste. An applicant for a permit must have a written contract covering all movements of waste. Two types of permits are provided for under the Act, a 'Basel permit' and a 'special permit'. Basel permits refer to permits issued under the substantive provisions of the Act (and the Basel Convention) while 'special permits' refer to permits issued under Art 11 arrangements (s 4) (see below).

A transit permit is required for 'transit' operations (s 13A)(1)). A proposal to bring hazardous waste into Australia and to take it out within 30 days is a 'transit proposal' so long as it is not proposed to dispose of the waste in Australia (s 4B).

Basel permits

Basel permits may only be issued for waste shipments between countries which are Parties to the Basel Convention. Before granting a Basel permit, the Minister must be satisfied that the prior informed consent procedures in Art 6 of the Basel Convention have been complied with. Article 6 of the Convention requires the notification and written consent of all States involved in a proposed transboundary movement of hazardous waste (including transit States) to be sought and granted before any movement is commenced (s 17(1)(b), (ba)).

The Minister must also be satisfied that the facility to which the waste is shipped will be able to deal with the waste in an 'environmentally sound' manner. To ensure consistency with the Basel Convention, the Hazardous Waste Act adopts the definition of 'environmentally sound management' in Art 2.8 of the Convention, namely 'taking all practicable steps to ensure that hazardous wastes or other wastes are managed in a manner which will protect human health and the environment against the adverse effects which may result from such wastes' (s 4E). For a permit to be granted, the applicant must be a 'suitable' person and have sufficient insurance cover (s 17(1)(c), (d)).

Although the Act provides that the Minister must grant a permit if these requirements are satisfied, he or she has a wide discretion to refuse a permit. A permit can be refused where the Minister considers that to grant it would be contrary to the public interest (s 17(3)). It can also be refused where the Minister is of the opinion that the hazardous waste could be dealt with in another way which would not pose a significant risk of injury to human beings or the environment and that, having regard to Australia's international obligations, it would be preferable to deal with the waste in that way (s 17(4)). A permit can also be refused where the Minister believes that the waste could be disposed of safely in Australia and that this would be consistent with the environmentally sound management of the waste and that, having regard to the desirability of using disposal facilities in Australia, the waste should not be exported (s 17(5)).

Export permits for final disposal of hazardous waste may be granted only in exceptional circumstances and then only if particulars of the export are specified in the regulations and the proposal is consistent with the environmentally sound management of the waste (s 18A(1), (2), (3)). In deciding whether there are exceptional circumstances, the Minister must have regard to the following:

- whether there will be a significant risk of injury or damage to human beings or the environment if the permit is not granted;
- whether the waste is needed for research or testing for the purposes of improving the management of hazardous waste; and
- any prescribed matters. (s 18A(4))

This provision is in keeping with Australia's obligations under the Basel Convention. 'Exceptional circumstances' contemplates a situation, for example, where a highly dangerous waste produced in a life-threatening industrial accident in Australia can only be processed safely by the manufacturer in another country.[1]

Special permits

Under the Basel Convention, Parties must not trade with non-Parties unless an agreement has been negotiated under Art 11. The Hazardous Waste Act also prohibits the issue of a 'Basel permit' for trade with non-Parties (s 17(7), (8)). The Hazardous Waste Act provides for regulations to be made to give effect to Art 11 agreements (s 13C). The regulations may specify the kinds of import, export and transit proposals that may be granted and provide for the granting of 'special permits' by the Minister to authorise an import, export or transit proposal (s 13D).

Australia is presently a party to three Art 11 agreements which are given effect to by the following regulations: the *Hazardous Waste (Regulation of Exports and Imports) (Imports from East Timor) Regulations 2003*; the *Hazardous Waste (Regulation of Exports and Imports) (Waigani Convention*[2]*) Regulations 1999*; and the *Hazardous Waste (Regulation of Exports and Imports) (OECD Decision) Regulations 1996*. The *Hazardous Waste (Regulation of Exports and Imports) (Imports from East Timor) Regulations* are intended to facilitate the reimportation of Australian defence force waste from East Timor.

The *Hazardous Waste (Regulation of Exports and Imports) (OECD Decision) Regulations* provide for the granting of a special permit for movements of hazardous waste between parties to the OECD Decision (Art 11 agreement) and specify the requirements for the issue of the permit. Although less onerous in some respects, the conditions for obtaining such permits are similar to those imposed for Basel permits. The Regulation gives effect to the OECD Decision of the Council C (92) 39/FINAL concerning the control of transboundary movements of wastes destined for recovery operations. This Regulation facilitates trade with OECD members who are non-Parties to the Basel Convention, such as the United States.

The *Hazardous Waste (Regulation of Exports and Imports) (Waigani Convention) Regulations 1999* give effect to Australia's obligations under the Waigani Convention. The Regulations enable Australia to assist South Pacific states in disposing of hazardous waste which these countries do not have the capacity to handle in an environmentally safe manner. For example, AusAid recently conducted a program which identified persistent organic pollutants in Pacific Island states and exported them to Australia for safe disposal.

Ministerial orders

Part 3 of the Hazardous Waste Act provides for ministerial orders in relation to hazardous waste. If a person imports, exports or carries out a transit operation in relation to hazardous waste without a permit, or contrary to the conditions of the permit, the Minister can order the waste to be dealt with in a certain way (s 34). If the hazardous waste in question is causing or likely to cause significant harm to

1 Hazardous Waste (Regulation of Exports and Imports) Amendment Bill 1995, Explanatory Memorandum, p 33.

2 The *Waigani Convention to Ban the Importation into Forum Island Countries of Hazardous and Radioactive Wastes and to Control the Transboundary Movement and Management of Hazardous Wastes within the South Pacific Region* 1995.

human health or the environment, the Minister may order it to be exported (in the case of imported waste) or imported (in the case of exported waste) (ss 35, 35A). An order to remedy or mitigate any damage may be made where there has been significant damage to human health or the environment, but no compensation may be awarded (s 36). If the order is not complied with, the Minister may take the necessary action and recover the costs from the person on whom the order was served (s 37). The Minister can also make an order authorising lawfully exported hazardous waste to be re-imported where it cannot be dealt with as intended (s 38).

Offences and penalties

Imports, exports or transit dealings in hazardous waste must not be undertaken without a permit or ministerial order, or contrary to the conditions of a permit or order (ss 39, 40, 40A). There are three levels of offence. The offence can be prosecuted as an offence of strict liability in which case a lesser penalty applies. If the offence was committed intentionally, recklessly or negligently, the maximum penalty is $275,000 for a corporation and two years' imprisonment for an individual offender (however, this will be subject to the discretion of the court to impose a fine under s 4B(2) of the *Crimes Act 1914* (Cth)). The Act defines 'negligence' in such a way to make it clear that 'gross negligence' is required (s 39(5)). It is a more serious offence if the contravention was intentional or reckless and the contravention injures, damages or is likely to cause injury or damage to human health or the environment (ss 39(6), 40(5), 40A(5)). In this case, the maximum penalty that can be imposed is five years' imprisonment in the case of an individual and $1,100,000 for a corporation (however, this will also be subject to the discretion of the court to impose a fine under s 4B(2) of the *Crimes Act*).

Corporate executive officer liability

The Act provides for personal liability for corporate executive officers for offences by the corporation (s 40B). Liability is not automatic – knowledge or recklessness, the ability to influence the conduct of the body in relation to the contravention and a failure to take reasonable steps to prevent the contravention must all be established in order to found a conviction (s 40B(1)). If convicted, an executive officer is liable to a maximum term of imprisonment of two years, or five years where harm or likely harm to human beings or the environment is established (see offences and penalties above).

The Act provides guidance on what is required to constitute 'all reasonable steps to prevent a contravention'. Amongst other things, the court is to have regard to whether the officer took any action directed towards ensuring an effective due diligence program is in place. The Act specifies the type of action that this will require (s 40B(4)).

It is commendable that the Act provides guidelines for determining whether 'all reasonable steps' have been taken. This defence, and the similar defence of 'due diligence', is becoming increasingly commonplace in environmental legislation (PEOA ss 118, 169(1)(c)), yet statutory guidelines as to how these requirements can be satisfied are rare. This is unfortunate, given that executive officers and other persons may be liable to heavy fines or imprisonment.

Standing for third parties

Individuals and organisations can bring proceedings under the *Administrative Decisions (Judicial Review) Act 1977* (Cth) to review a decision made under the Act. The Act widens the meaning of 'aggrieved' to expand the categories of persons who may seek review. An individual will be taken to be 'aggrieved' by the decision if he or she has engaged in research into hazardous waste, or protection of human health and the environment from its harmful effects for at least two years before the decision. In the case of an organisation the same criteria apply and these criteria must be included in its objects or purposes. Individuals and organisations must be resident or established in Australia (Hazardous Waste Act s 58A).

Strategies for dealing with hazardous chemicals

One group of chemicals, known as persistent organic pollutants (POPs), has been identified as posing the greatest dangers to human health and the environment. They are very hard to destroy and are resistant to degradation by chemical, physical or biological means. They are also bio-accumulative in humans, animals and plants. The term used in Australia for these wastes is 'scheduled' wastes, although they are also known as persistent organic pollutants.

In 1991 the former Australia and New Zealand Environment Conservation Council considered the recommendations of a joint taskforce for the construction of a high temperature incinerating disposal facility to dispose of these wastes, but opted instead for alternative disposal technologies. The National Strategy for the Management of Scheduled Wastes was adopted in 1992. The strategy focuses on emerging, alternative, non-incineration waste destruction technologies. Three management plans were established under the strategy, which specify threshold concentrations, quantities of chemicals to be covered and phase-out dates for three groups of chemical wastes:

- Organochlorine pesticides waste management plan;
- Hexachlorbenzene waste management plan; and
- Polychlorinated biphenyls management plan.

The Commonwealth also established a National Dioxins Program in 2001 which continues to monitor the level of dioxins in the environment. These measures assist in giving effect to Australia's international obligations under the *Stockholm Convention on Persistent Organic Pollutants 2001* which requires the elimination, restriction and safe disposal of some of the most dangerous POPs such as polychlorinated biphenyls, and so forth. Australia has developed a National Implementation Plan which was submitted to the Stockholm Convention Secretariat in August 2006. The Plan sets out how Australia will implement its obligations under the Stockholm Convention and provides details of current actions already taken in Australia and those proposed.

Movement of controlled wastes between States and Territories NEPM

The NEPM ensures that 'controlled' wastes that are to be moved between States and Territories are properly identified, transported and handled in an environmentally safe manner.[3] It provides a national framework for the management of the movement of controlled waste between States and Territories. These management systems include:

- tracking systems to ensure waste reaches appropriate facilities and which provide information for emergency services;
- prior notification systems which provide all jurisdictions with information to assess the appropriateness of the proposed movements of controlled wastes in terms of transportation and facility selection; and
- the licensing and regulation of generators, transporters and facilities so that tracking and notification functions are compatible with the requirements of all jurisdictions (see <www.ephc.gov.au>).

Chemicals

The past 50 years have witnessed an unprecedented growth in the chemical industry. In 2004 it was estimated that approximately 70,000 chemicals were available globally, with about 1500 new chemicals being introduced each year.[4] Some chemicals offer considerable benefits in areas such as health care, agriculture and industry. However, in many cases, the generation, use and disposal of these chemicals pose a serious risk to human health and the environment.

The Commonwealth government has legislated to impose requirements for the notification and assessment of new industrial chemicals under the *Industrial Chemicals (Notification and Assessment) Act 1989*. Industrial chemicals include a wide range of chemicals such as dyes, solvents, cement, adhesives, plastics, printing and photographic chemicals, paints, cleaning agents and cosmetics While this scheme provides a mechanism for the assessment of chemicals before their use, the National Chemicals Taskforce Review (EPHC 2003) identified a need to improve environmental management of chemicals at all states of their life cycle. This will be addressed through the National Framework for Chemicals Management in Australia which is currently under development by the Environment Protection and Heritage Council. According to a discussion paper released in 2006 the key elements for action are:

- strengthening environmental risk assessment;
- streamlining environmental controls;
- informing decisions; and
- prioritising action.

The *Environmentally Hazardous Chemicals Act 1985* (NSW) is the only comprehensive State legislation that regulates chemicals and chemical wastes.

---

3 'Controlled' wastes refer to those wastes in List 1 of the NEPM, provided they have one or more of the characteristics in List 2 to the NEPM. The wastes controlled are similar to those regulated by the Basel Convention.

4 UNEP-FAO News Release, 'Rotterdam Convention on Trade in Hazardous Chemicals and Pesticides Enters into Force', Horizons Solutions Site, <http://www.solutions-site.org/artman/publish/article_126.shtml> (accessed 2 January 2006).

Industrial Chemicals (Notification and Assessment) Act 1989 (Cth)

The *Industrial Chemicals (Notification and Assessment) Act 1989* establishes a national system of notification and assessment of industrial chemicals. The main focus of the Act is on the assessment of new industrial chemicals before their introduction (import or manufacture) into Australia, although it also addresses some existing chemicals. New chemicals are assessed for their health and environmental effects before they are used or released to the environment. Any new industrial chemicals introduced into Australia must be notified and/or assessed under the Act before they can be used commercially. Those chemicals already in use (existing chemicals) are assessed on a priority basis in response to specific concerns about potential health or environmental effects. The Act does not apply to radioactive chemicals or chemicals of an agricultural, veterinary or therapeutic nature.

A new industrial chemical is a chemical which is not listed in the Australian Inventory of Chemical Substances. To date, approximately 38,000 chemicals have been listed (<www.nicnas.gov.au>). All chemicals on the Inventory are defined as existing chemicals. The Inventory is available to the public (s 15), except for a confidential section (s 16). A chemical is to be included in the confidential section if publication of its particulars 'could reasonably be expected to prejudice substantially the commercial interests of the applicant and the prejudice outweighs the public interest in the publication of those particulars' (s 20E(2)(c)). There are time limits on how long it can remain in this section (s 19).

The industrial chemical assessment scheme is known as the National Industrial Chemicals Notification and Assessment Scheme (NICNAS). It was established in 1990 and is administered by the Department of Health and Ageing.

Application of Act

The Act makes provision for the validation of State and Territory notification laws which satisfy Commonwealth notification requirements (s 41). These roll-back provisions do not extend to the actual assessment of new chemicals. No States, except for New South Wales (*Environmentally Hazardous Chemicals Act 1985*), have enacted comprehensive legislation dealing with hazardous chemicals and chemical wastes.

The detailed regulatory systems controlling the use of chemicals and the disposal of chemical wastes have been left to the States to implement.

Object

The object of the *Industrial Chemicals (Notification and Assessment) Act 1989* (Cth) is to provide a national system for the assessment of industrial chemicals to:

- protect the Australian people and the environment by finding out the risks to occupational health and safety, to public health and to the environment that could be associated with the importation, manufacture or use of the chemicals;
- provide information, and making recommendations, about the chemicals to the appropriate Commonwealth, State and Territory regulatory bodies;

- give effect to Australia's obligations under international agreements relating to the regulation of chemicals; and
- collect statistics in relation to the chemicals, being a system under which information about the properties and effects of the chemicals is obtained from importers and manufacturers. (s 3)

Constitutional validity

The Act claims constitutional validity for the Commonwealth on the grounds that it implements obligations under international conventions (s 3(c); Constitution s 51(xxix)). It also relies on the powers with respect to corporations, foreign and trading corporations formed within the limits of the Commonwealth (ss 4, 21M(1); Constitution s 51(xx)); trade and commerce with other countries and among the States (ss 4, 21M(2)(c); Constitution s 51(i)); and supply to an authority or instrumentality of the Commonwealth or a Territory (ss 4, 21M(1)(d); Constitution s 122).

Introduction of new chemicals

A manufacturer or importer must apply for an assessment certificate for a new industrial chemical before its manufacture or import. A technical information dossier about the chemical must accompany the application (s 21D).

It is an offence to manufacture or import a new industrial chemical without an assessment certificate (s 21(1)). The maximum penalty for an offender is $33,000. Any person can apply for an injunction to prevent the commission of an offence under the Act and to require positive action to be taken (s 83).

There are several permits that can be issued without the requirement for an assessment certificate, namely:

- A commercial evaluation permit lasting for a period of two years (unless renewed) can be granted to enable commercial evaluation of quantities of chemicals not exceeding 4000 kilograms (ss 21(2)(a), 21A-21P).
- Low volume permits, lasting for a period of three years (unless renewed), can be issued for manufacture or importation of up to a total quantity of 100 kilograms (or 1000 kilograms in certain circumstances) of a chemical, Australia-wide (s 21(2)(b)), if the Director of the Industrial Chemicals Notification and Assessment Scheme is satisfied that the intended use does not constitute an unreasonable risk to occupational health and safety, public health or the environment (s 21U). Conditions can be varied after the permit has been issued. A permit can be cancelled if a condition is breached or if the information given in the application was materially false or misleading (ss 21W(6), 21Q-21ZB).
- An controlled use permit lasting for up to three years (unless renewed) can be granted for a new industrial chemical if the Director is satisfied that is a low risk to occupational health and safety, public health and the environment because its use, handling and disposal are highly controlled (ss 21(2)(c), 22A, 22F). The permit may be granted subject to conditions. The permit may be cancelled if a condition is breached or if the information given in the application was materially false or misleading (s 22J).

- The Minister for Health and Ageing can issue an introduction permit while the chemical is being assessed, if satisfied that it is in the public interest to act without delay, and that to do so is consistent with the 'reasonable protection' of occupational health and safety, public health and the environment (ss 21(2)(d), 30). A permit will be revoked if the application for assessment is withdrawn.

The Director must maintain a list of commercial evaluation permits, low volume chemicals and introduction permits, and publish details in the Chemical Gazette (ss 21J, 21ZA, 22N, 30(2)).

It is an offence to breach a condition of a commercial evaluation permit, a low volume permit or a controlled use permit (ss 21L(4), 21W, 22I). In each case, the penalty is a maximum of $33,000. In the case of a commercial evaluation permit and a low volume permit, a defence of 'reasonable excuse' is provided (ss 21L(4A), 21W(5A).

Assessments of new chemicals

The object of the assessment is to determine the risk of any adverse health, safety and environmental effects arising not only from manufacture, but also use, storage, handling and disposal of the chemical. This includes the extent to which this risk can be reduced by compliance with procedures relating to manufacture, use and discharge into the environment of the chemical or waste products (s 32). Certain chemicals of low concern can be self-assessed (ss 23A, 40K-40N). These chemicals are polymers of low concern, non-hazardous chemicals and other chemicals specified in the regulations (s 23A(1)). For these chemicals, the assessment report could be the application form (s 31). For other chemicals the application must be accompanied by a written notification statement about the chemical and any other assessment information available to the applicant (s 23(3), (10)). The notification statement must also contain the information specified in the Schedule to the Act. There are four parts to the Schedule (A-D) but not all parts need be addressed in a notification statement. It depends on the type of chemical which is proposed for introduction (s 23(4)-(8)). Generally, the requirements of the Schedule are directed at obtaining information about the properties of the chemical and the potential dangers it could pose to human health and the environment. In assessing a chemical, qualities which characterise POPs, namely persistence, bio-accumulation, potential for long-range environmental transport, adverse effects on human health and the environment, are also taken into account.

The assessment report

An assessment report must include a Material Safety Data Sheet, a summary of health, safety and environmental matters considered in the assessment and recommendations as may reasonably be made in relation to each of the following matters:

- precautions and restrictions to be observed during the importation, manufacture, handling, storage, use or disposal of the chemical to protect persons exposed to it;
- controls to limit emissions of the chemical into the environment, including permissible emission levels;

- packaging, labelling, handling and storage requirements;
- emergency measures;
- appropriate uses;
- means of disposal; and
- circumstances in which secondary notification is required. (s 33)

On completion of an assessment report about a chemical, a summary report and a full public report of the assessment must be prepared. After the applicant has been given the opportunity to request variations to this report (s 37), copies must be given to appropriate State and Commonwealth authorities, unless the application is withdrawn (s 38). A summary report must then be published in the Chemical Gazette, indicating where members of the public can obtain copies of the 'full public report'.

The public report

The public report consists of the assessment report, minus material exempted on the grounds of its potential to prejudice substantially the applicant's commercial interests, to the extent that it outweighs the public interest in publication (ss 38(5)(c), 34-35, 75). The applicant, or any other person, can apply within 28 days of the publication of the summary report to have the public report varied. The Director must publish details of the application for variation in the Chemical Gazette, and the applicant may provide additional information in support of the application within 28 days. Any other person may provide a written statement to the Director why a variation to the assessment should not be made. This must also be done within 28 days of the publication of the notice of variation (s 40). Full public reports are available on the NICNAS website (<www.nicnas.gov.au>).

In certain cases an assessment report may require the Director to be notified if circumstances occur in relation to the introduction of the chemical, or if a person who introduces a chemical becomes aware of a change in circumstances which may result in an increased risk of an adverse effect of the chemical on occupational health and safety, public health or the environment (s 64). This may then necessitate a re-assessment of the chemical (ss 67, 68).

After five years have elapsed, the applicant must be given an assessment certificate, and the particulars of the chemical must be included in the Inventory (s 14(1)). There is no provision for the assessment to be followed by Commonwealth regulation of the chemical. The issue of whether regulatory measures should be taken in light of the findings of the assessment is left to the States. The purpose of the assessment certificate is simply to certify that the chemical has been assessed under the provisions of the legislation, not to indicate that manufacture and use are safe, or that this will only be so under certain conditions. Proceedings cannot be taken against the Commonwealth by those who suffer damage as the result of relying on an assessment (s 101).

NICNAS compiles the assessments of industrial chemicals into reports, which are sent to relevant Commonwealth, State and Territories authorities. The reports may make recommendations, including restrictions or precautions relating to, manufacture, import, handling, storage, use, disposal, packaging and labelling. These recommendations may then be adopted by authorities as part of their control of the use of industrial chemicals.

Assessment of listed chemicals

Since NICNAS only commenced in 1990, most of the chemicals on the Australian Inventory of Chemical Substances have never been formally assessed. Therefore, NICNAS provides for the declaration of existing chemicals that are of most concern, called priority existing chemicals, because of their potential for adverse effects on occupational health and safety, public health or the environment.

NICNAS assesses chemicals on its own initiative or in response to concerns raised by governments, industry or the community. Nominated chemicals are screened and ranked against predetermined selection criteria. Chemicals that do not have to be notified as new chemicals, either because they are listed on the inventory or because they are exempt from notification, may also be selected and assessed under the priority existing chemical program. To date approximately 30 assessment reports of priority existing chemicals have been prepared (<www.nicnas.gov.au>).

Declaration of priority existing chemicals

There is no commitment in the legislation to the eventual assessment of all listed (existing) chemicals. However, the Director may recommend to the Minister that one or more industrial chemicals be declared priority existing chemicals if he or she has reasonable grounds for believing their manufacture, handling, storage, use or disposal may have a risk of adverse health or environmental effects. A recommendation by the Director (and any subsequent declaration by the Minister) must specify whether the declaration should apply to the chemical generally or whether it is restricted to the use of the chemical for specific purposes, or its manufacture, handling, storage or use in a specific geographical area or in specific circumstances, and whether a preliminary or full assessment is required. The recommendation (and any subsequent declaration) should also identify the matters to be taken into account in preparing the assessment report on the chemical and the information required to accompany the application (ss 50B, 51). Before making a recommendation to the Minister, the Director may publish a notice in the Chemical Gazette requiring persons involved in the manufacture or importation of the chemical to provide relevant information (s 48). There is no provision for members of the public to participate in this process unless the director considers that they have such information. The Director must prepare a summary of information supplied within 90 days and give notice in the Chemical Gazette as to where a copy of the summary can be obtained (s 50A). On the Director's recommendation, the Minister may then declare the chemical a priority existing chemical (s 51(1)).

The assessment report

Where a chemical becomes a priority existing chemical, a person has 28 days to apply for an assessment (s 55). It is an offence to import or manufacture a priority existing chemical unless those involved have applied for an assessment (s 56). If no application is made, the director can order an assessment (s 57(2)). Information may be sought by notice in the Chemical Gazette, not only from those involved in importation and manufacture, but from anybody thought to have it (s 58). Failure to comply with a notice requesting information, without reasonable excuse, is an offence (s 58(8)).

Matters which can be required to be considered in preparing an assessment report include:

- the properties of the chemical;
- its intended use;
- any adverse effects on the environment or persons that may result from the use; and
- the extent to which the environment, persons in a particular occupation or the public will be exposed to the chemical. (s 51(3))

If a full assessment is intended, further matters may be required (s 51(3), (5)). Information may be sought by notice in the Chemical Gazette (s 56). Failure to comply with a notice, without reasonable excuse, is an offence (s 58(8)).

During the period between declaration and the finalisation of the assessment, the Minister can take regulatory measures, where he or she has reasonable grounds for believing that an activity involving such a chemical, including use and manufacture, gives rise to 'an unacceptable risk of adverse health effects or adverse environmental effects'. In this situation, a notice must be issued prohibiting the activity (s 61).

On completion of the assessment, a draft assessment report must be prepared, followed by a final report, incorporating any variations or corrections (ss 60C, 60E). A final assessment report must include a summary of health, safety and environmental matters considered in the assessment, and recommend precautions and restrictions to be observed to ensure the safe handling, storage and disposal of the chemical (s 60B). Once the final assessment report is published and the certificate issued, the chemical ceases to be a priority existing chemical (s 62). Regulatory measures are again left to the States.

Registration scheme for importers and manufacturers

The Act establishes a registration scheme for certain importers and manufacturers of industrial chemicals (ss 80A-80W). It is an offence to knowingly or recklessly introduce industrial chemicals valued at $500,000 or more, in any registration year, without being registered (s 80B). Applications for registration must be made to the Director and must include specified information and a registration fee (s 80). If an application is approved, a registration certificate is issued which is valid for one year (ss 80H, 80J). Details of the person registered and information about the chemical (other than confidential commercial information) are then recorded in a publicly available Register of Industrial Chemical Introducers (s 80C). Registrations must be renewed annually (s 80K).

Environmentally Hazardous Chemicals Act 1985 (NSW)

The *Environmentally Hazardous Chemicals Act 1985* is intended to control the effect on the environment of chemicals and chemical wastes. The Act defines 'chemical' to include any chemical element, compound or complex and a component of a mixture, but does not include a physical mixture or a radioactive substance (s 3(1)).

Provisions in the *Environmentally Hazardous Chemicals Act* (ss 9, 12) dealing with unlisted chemicals and their assessment were never proclaimed and have now been repealed because of the creation at the Commonwealth level of a scheme for notification and assessment of new industrial chemicals under the *Industrial Chemicals (Notification and Assessment) Act 1989* (Cth).

The Act is administered by the EPA, assisted by the Hazardous Chemicals Advisory Committee which is established by the Act (ss 6-7).

Declared chemical wastes

The EPA may declare any chemical substance (including a mixture) to be a chemical waste where it is satisfied that it is, or is likely to be, stored in accumulating deposits, dumped or abandoned (s 10). The Act does not oblige the EPA to carry out an assessment before declaring a substance to be a chemical waste, although it has been its practice to do so.

Assessment of existing chemicals and declared chemical waste

The EPA is empowered to carry out an assessment of a listed chemical or activities proposed to be carried on in relation to a chemical, or a declared chemical waste, at any time (s 15(2)). Before making an assessment of an existing chemical, the EPA must first advertise its intentions and invite submissions (s 19). When making an assessment in relation to a chemical or declared chemical waste, the EPA must consider the likely effect on the environment (s 17(1), (2)). 'Environment' is defined to include 'all aspects of the surroundings of human kind, whether natural or artificial and whether living or inanimate' (s 3(1)). In assessing environmental impact, s 17(2) sets out a range of factors which the EPA may consider, including any matters relevant to the public interest and the protection of the environment. Other factors for consideration include the propensity of the substance to produce harmful effects in organisms or biological systems; the adequacy of measures proposed for its safe treatment and disposal; and the practicality of the manufacture or use of an alternative substance (s 17(2)).

Chemical control orders

After making an assessment the EPA may, but is not obliged to, make a Chemical Control Order (CCO) in respect of the chemical or declared chemical waste (s 22). A CCO may:

- absolutely prohibit specified activities in relation to an assessed chemical or declared chemical waste;
- absolutely prohibit specified activities, otherwise in accordance with the control order or a licence;
- permit the carrying on of an activity unconditionally or subject to such conditions as may be imposed by the order. (ss 22-24)

The EPA can only make a CCO absolutely prohibiting an activity in relation to a chemical or declared chemical waste which it has assessed, if it is reasonably considered necessary to prevent or minimise any adverse effect on the environment. Chemical Control Orders imposing an outright prohibition also require a recommendation from the Hazardous Chemicals Advisory Committee or the consent of the Minister (s 22(2)). Once a chemical is subject to a CCO, the legislation classifies it an 'environmentally hazardous chemical' (s 3(1)).

So far, only a small number of assessments of existing chemicals have been carried out. Five CCOs are currently in place in New South Wales: dioxin contaminated wastes, aluminium smelter wastes containing fluoride and/or cyanide (1986); dioxin contaminated waste materials (1986); polychlorinated biphenyl (1997); scheduled chemical wastes (2004); and organotin waste materials (1989).

There are no provisions allowing members of the public to initiate the procedures leading to the declaration of a chemical waste or the making of a CCO.

Reassessments

If the EPA or, on appeal, the court (see below) does decide to make a CCO, that is still not the end of the matter. Anybody who wishes to carry out an activity which is either prohibited or subject to a licensing requirement under the order can then apply to the EPA for an assessment of that specific activity (s 13(1)). The EPA has no option but to comply and the whole process is reactivated (s 15(1)). Alternatively, the EPA can order a reassessment on its own initiative (s 15(2)).

Before making the assessment, the EPA must have regard to any submissions made by the applicant (s 18). The EPA has broad powers to require the applicant to submit relevant information, and it can also take into account any information supplied by anybody else if it considers it to be reliable and relevant (ss 16, 18). In addition the EPA is entitled to have regard to the qualifications, experience and expertise of persons concerned in carrying on the activity (s 17(5)).

After conducting the assessment, the EPA can make a CCO permitting an activity which has been prohibited by a previous CCO provided it has obtained the recommendation of the Committee (s 23). The EPA can of course prohibit the activity with the consent of the Hazardous Chemicals Advisory Committee or Minister or require a licence.

Appeals against decisions involving CCOs

Appeals against failure to notify decision or decide on a CCO

The EPA has only 60 days in which to complete its assessment of an existing chemical or declared chemical waste and to decide whether it will make a CCO. If it fails to make a decision within 60 days, the applicant can appeal to the Land and Environment Court (s 37(1)). The court may order the EPA to make, or not make, an order (s 37(2)).

Appeals against CCOs or outcome of assessment

Any person who objects to a CCO, or a determination not to make a CCO, may appeal on one of three grounds:

- that the order was erroneous;
- that the CCO ought not to have been made, or ought to have been different;
- that an order should have been made. (s 38(1))

The court has wide powers, including the power to make a CCO or to substitute a different one (s 38(2)). The order has no effect until the appeal is decided, unless it has been classified as an emergency order (ss 42, 25(2)).

Licences

A CCO may prohibit activities in relation to chemicals or declared chemical wastes except under authority of a licence (s 24(1)). Licences are issued at the discretion of the EPA, who may grant a licence conditionally, unconditionally or refuse to grant a licence. Before making a decision, the EPA can, if it chooses, advertise the application but it does not have to do so (s 28(2)). Licences can be issued on a long-term basis or for temporary purposes where the EPA believes this to be appropriate (ss 29-30). In appropriate cases, the EPA may grant an application for the transfer of a licence (s 29A).

Licences can be temporarily suspended or withdrawn altogether where an offence under the Act has been committed or a provision of the CCO has been breached (s 31).

Appeals against licensing decisions

Third parties do not have a right of appeal against a decision by the EPA to grant a licence or in relation to any conditions which the EPA may impose. The Act confers a right of appeal on a person 'aggrieved' (presumably the applicant) to appeal against the refusal of an application for a licence or renewal thereof; a condition on a licence granted to the person; a variation of a condition attached to a licence; or the revocation or suspension of the person's licence (s 39(1)). Appeals must be brought within 30 days. The decision has no effect until the appeal has been heard.

The court may order the EPA to grant or renew the licence or order the conditions to be varied or not varied. Alternatively, it may rescind the revocation of the licence or decide to make no order (s 39(2)).

Criminal offences and proceedings

The Act provides for a number of criminal offences, including:

- carrying on an activity in relation to a chemical or declared chemical waste in contravention of a CCO (s 26);
- contravention of a condition of a licence (s 32(2)).

The maximum fine for a corporation for an offence is $137,500 and $66,000 in the case of an individual. Proceedings for offences under the Act or Regulations are to be taken by the EPA under Chapter 8 of the PEOA (PEOA s 213). Penalty notices for breaches of the Act can also be issued under the PEOA (PEOA s 213).

Corporate officer liability

The Act provides for personal liability for corporate officers for acts of their corporations (s 53). The Act provides that where a corporation contravenes a provision of the Act, each person who is a director of the corporation, or who participates in the management of the corporation, is taken to have contravened the same provision irrespective of whether proceedings are taken against the company or whether it is convicted of the contravention (s 53(1)). Directors and managers are provided with four statutory defences. These provisions and the defences available are substantially the same as those in the PEOA except that the defence of lack of knowledge of the contravention is still available (see Chapter 11 at pp 462-464).

Ozone-depleting substances and synthetic greenhouse gases

Montreal Protocol

Ozone is a naturally occurring gas, found in a layer of the stratosphere 15-30 kilometres above the earth's surface. Ozone-depleting substances, used widely in many industries, such as refrigeration, fire extinguishers and dry-cleaning, break down the ozone layer, resulting in an increase in damaging ultraviolet radiation at the earth's surface (DEH (2006)). International concern for protection of the ozone layer resulted in the *Vienna Convention for the Protection of the Ozone Layer* (Vienna Convention) in 1985. The Convention set the stage for international control of ozone-depleting substances. This led to the adoption of the Montreal Protocol on Substances that Deplete the Ozone Layer (Montreal Protocol) in 1987. The Protocol and subsequent amendments: London (1990), Copenhagen (1992), Vienna (1995) and Montreal (1997), Beijing (1999) set mandatory targets for phasing out the production and consumption of major ozone-depleting substances. The amendments accelerate the phase-out dates in accordance with improved scientific understanding about ozone depletion and advances in ozone benign technology. Australia has ratified the Vienna Convention, the Montreal Protocol and the amendments.

A summary of the current Montreal Protocol control measures is set out in the table on the following page.

Ozone Protection and Synthetic Greenhouse Gas Management Act 1989 (Cth)

Australia ratified the Ozone Convention and Montreal Protocol in September 1987 and May 1989 respectively, and subsequently enacted the *Ozone Protection Act 1989* (Cth) to give effect to its treaty obligations. The Act was extended in 2003 to cover synthetic greenhouse gases to meet Australia's international obligations under the Framework Convention on Climate Change 1992, and renamed as the *Ozone Protection and Synthetic Greenhouse Gas Management Act 1989*. The amendments extended the scope of the Act in three significant areas so as to:

- incorporate synthetic greenhouse gases used as replacements for ozone-depleting substances into the import, export and manufacturing licence system, but without any quotas or phase-outs;
- empower the Australian government to develop national end-use controls on the purchase, sale, handling and disposal of these gases, replacing current State and Territory requirements;
- allow the Australian government to implement the Beijing Amendment to the Montreal Protocol, banning the import and manufacture of bromochloromethane, and banning trade in certain ozone-depleting substances with non-Protocol countries. (<www.deh.gov.au/atmosphere/ozone/index.html>)

The Act regulates the manufacture, import and export of ozone-depleting substances through licensing and quotas to meet the target reductions in consumption required by the Montreal Protocol. Responsibility for implementing this control is shared between the Commonwealth, State and Territory governments. For its constitutional validity the Commonwealth statute relies not only on the external affairs power, but also on powers with respect to trading, financial and foreign

Summary of Montreal Protocol Control Measures

Ozone Depleting Substances	Developed Countries	Developing Countries
Chlorofluorocarbons (CFCs)	Phased out end of 1995[a]	Total phase out by 2010
Halons	Phased out end of 1993	Total phase out by 2010
Carbon tetrachloride	Phased out end of 1995[a]	Total phase out by 2010
Methyl chloroform	Phased out end of 1995[a]	Total phase out by 2015
Hydrochlorofluorocarbons (HCFCs)	Freeze from beginning of 1996[b] 35% reduction by 2004 65% reduction by 2010 90% reduction by 2015 Total phase out by 2020[c]	Freeze in 2016 at 2015 base level Total phase out by 2040
Hydrobromofluorocarbons (HBFCs)	Phased out end of 1995	Phased out end of 1995
Methyl bromide (horticultural uses)	Freeze in 1995 at 1991 base level[d] 25% reduction by 1999 50% reduction by 2001 70% reduction by 2003 Total phase out by 2005	Freeze in 2002 at average 1995-1998 base level 20% reduction by 2005[e] Total phase out by 2015
Bromochloromethane (BCM)	Phase out by 2002	Phase out by 2002

a With the exception of a very small number of internationally agreed essential uses that are considered critical to human health and/or laboratory and analytical procedures.
b Based on 1989 HCFC consumption with an extra allowance (ODP weighted) equal to 2.8% of 1989 CFC consumption.
c Up to 0.5% of base level consumption can be used until 2030 for servicing existing equipment.
d All reductions include an exemption for pre-shipment and quarantine uses.
e Review in 2003 to decide on interim further reductions beyond 2005.

Note:

1 The timetable set by the Montreal Protocol applies to bulk consumption of ozone depleting substances. Consumption is defined as the quantities manufactured or imported, less those quantities exported in any given year. Percentage reductions relate to the designated 'base year' for the substance. The Protocol does not forbid the use of existing or recycled controlled substances beyond the phase out dates.

The table was extracted from the website of the Department of the Environment and Heritage (<www.deh.gov.au/atmosphere/ ozone/legislation/ montp.html>).

corporations and trade and commerce among the States. The Act overrides State or Territory legislation to the extent that it is not capable of operating concurrently (s 4). The Act is administered by Environment Australia.

The substances controlled by the Act are listed in Sch 1 and are referred to as 'scheduled' substances. These substances are CFC (chlorofluorocarbon); halon 1211, 1301 and 2402; carbon tetrachloride, methyl chloroform; HBFCs (hydrobromofluorocarbon); HCFC (hydrochlorofluorocarbons), methyl bromide; bromochloromethane; HFC (hydrofluorocarbon); and PFC (perfluorocarbon). HFC and PFC are synthetic greenhouse substances, while the remainder are ozone-depleting substances (s 7).

Licensing

The Act regulates the manufacture, import and export of ozone-depleting substances and synthetic greenhouse gases through a licensing system directed to different chemicals and activities (Pt 3). The Act provides for four types of licences:

- a controlled substances licence;
- an essential uses licence;
- a used substances licence;
- a pre-charged equipment licence. (s 13A)

A controlled substances licence is required for the manufacture, export and import of HCFCs, methyl bromide and synthetic greenhouse gases (s 13A(2)). The Act imposes tradeable quotas on licensees of HCFC (ss 23-25).

An essential uses licence is required for the manufacture, import or export of specified stage-1 or stage-2 scheduled substances for uses which meet a limited range of essential use criteria. An essential use licence can also be obtained to import specified recycled or used HBFCs. A stage-1 scheduled substance is defined as a stage-1 CFC or a halon. A stage-2 scheduled substance means a stage-2 CFC, carbon tetrachloride, methyl chloroform or bromochloromethane (s 7, 13A(3)). These substances were phased out in 1996 and thus, by way of exception, a licence can permit some activities in relation to these chemicals.

A used substances licence allows the licensee to import or export specific recycled or used stage-1 or stage-2 scheduled substances, HCFCs or methyl bromide (s 13A(4)).

A pre-charged equipment licence allows the licensee to import air-conditioning or refrigeration equipment that is pre-charged with a substance that is, or contains, a HFC or HCFC (s 7). Product stewardship is required as a condition of a licence.

Licences are granted subjected to conditions under the Act. Examples of standard conditions imposed are that the applicant is a fit and proper person (s 16(4)) and that, except for a synthetic greenhouse gas licence, a licensee must only import from a county that is a Party to the Montreal Protocol (s 18(2), (3)). Licences stay in force for two years (s 8A) and, except for synthetic greenhouse gas licences, can be terminated by the Minister if this is necessary to give effect to amendments to the Protocol (s 19A(2)).

Licence fees are deposited into the Ozone Protection and Synthetic Greenhouse Gas Account which is used to fund the administration of the Act, the National Halon Bank, ozone-depleting substances phase-out programs and emission minimisation programs for both ozone-depleting substances and synthetic greenhouse gases (Pt VIIIA).

To ensure transparency in relation to dealings in scheduled substances (including synthetic greenhouse gases) and certain pre-charged equipment, licensees are required to provide quarterly reports to the Minister on the quantity of substances imported, exported, manufactured, recycled or destroyed (ss 46, 48). At the end of each financial year the Minister must prepare an annual report and present it to Parliament (s 68).

Quotas

A quota is required in addition to a controlled substances licence to manufacture, import or export HCFCs. Quotas are dealt with in Pt IV of the Act. Quotas are allocated by the Minister for the Environment having regard to Australia's international obligations and policies of the Commonwealth government in relation to the manufacture, importation or consumption of scheduled substances (s 28). Quotas can be traded (s 35). Quota periods generally last for two years (s 8(1)), and towards the end of this period application must be made for renewal (ss 27-28).

Controls on products and equipment

The Act imposes controls on the manufacture, import, export and distribution of certain products, which contain or rely on scheduled substances. These substances include dry-cleaning machinery, automotive air conditioning maintenance kits, extruded polystyrene packaging and insulation, aerosol products, refrigeration and air-conditioning equipment, and so forth (s 38 and Sch 4). These controls are contained in the *Ozone Protection and Synthetic Greenhouse Gas Management Regulations 1995* (Cth).

Controls on disposal and use of scheduled substances

Until 2005, the Commonwealth Act only controlled the manufacture, import and export of scheduled substances, while end-use controls were dealt with in State legislation. Section 45A of the Act now provides for regulations to be made to regulate the sale, purchase, disposal and use of scheduled substances. In 2005 the *Ozone Protection and Synthetic Greenhouse Gas Management Regulations 1995* were amended to impose licensing requirements and other controls on certain scheduled substances. The Commonwealth provisions override any inconsistent State legislation. However, under transitional arrangements, licences granted under State legislation will continue in force until their date of expiry, or until January 2007, whichever is the earlier (cl 136).

Part 6A of the Regulations gives effect to s 45A of the Act by imposing controls on the sale, purchase, acquisition, disposal, storage, use and handling of scheduled substances for refrigeration, air conditioning, fire protection; and methyl bromide (cl 100). Persons involved in refrigeration and air-conditioning (RAC) activities may be required to hold one or more of the following RAC industry permits:

- refrigerant handling licence (cl 111);
- refrigerant trading authority (cl 112);
- refrigerant and air-conditioning equipment manufacturing authority (cl 112); or
- Halon special permit (cl 113).

Persons involved in fire protection may be required to hold a fire protection industry permit (cl 313), namely an:

- existing agent handling licence (cl 321);
- existing agent trading authority; or
- Halon special permit.

The Regulations also impose restrictions on the use and sale of methyl bromide imported after January 2005 (cll 200-245).

Offences

It is an offence of strict liability to manufacture, import or export scheduled substances, unless licensed and within quota. The maximum penalty is $55,000 (s 13). Prosecutions are rare. In *Director of Public Prosecutions v Semal Pty Ltd*,[5] the defendant was prosecuted for importing an air conditioning refrigerant into Australia without a licence. The defendant pleaded guilty to seven charges of illegally importing chlorofluorocarbons, and was discharged on entering into a good behaviour bond of $5000 for 12 months and ordered to pay $168,000 to the Co-operative Research Centre for Southern Hemisphere Meteorology for ozone research within 12 months.

A defendant who knowingly or recklessly provides misleading or false information to the Minister is liable to imprisonment for up to two years (s 62).

Any person can apply for an injunction to prevent a breach of the Act or regulations (s 56). The court may not require an undertaking as to damages when granting an interim injunction (s 56(7)).

Exemptions

The Act provides for exemptions from provisions regulating ozone-depleting products (s 40). Application can be made to the Minister for an exemption for the import or manufacture of a banned product if the product is essential for medical, veterinary, defence, industrial or public safety purposes, and there is no practical alternative (s 40(3)). Only a very limited range of products meet these criteria and each application is carefully reviewed with reference to Montreal Protocol Guidelines (<www.deh.gov.au>).

Ozone Protection Act 1989 (NSW)

The *Ozone Protection Act 1989* (NSW) (OPA) provides for end-use controls on ozone-depleting substances and is designed to complement the Commonwealth Act which, until 2005, focused on manufacture, import and export of ozone-depleting substances. As the Commonwealth has now introduced its own control system, the continuing relevance of the NSW OPA is uncertain. However, the OPA may play a role in filling any gaps in Commonwealth legislation and meeting any deficiencies which could arise due to a lack of constitutional power. Licences granted under the OPA will continue in force until their date of expiry, or January 2007, whichever is the earlier (*Ozone Protection and Synthetic Greenhouse Gas Management Regulations 1995* (Cth) cl 136). The NSW *Ozone Protection Regulation 1997* has been repealed.

The object of the Act

The object of the Act is contained in s 3 and is stated to:

> provide for a system of controls on substances which when released into and dispersed in the atmosphere act as atmospheric pollutants that contribute to depletion of ozone in the stratospheric ozone layer.

The substances controlled under Sch 1 to the Act correspond with those in the Montreal Protocol and the Commonwealth Act. It is sufficiently flexible to accommodate

5 Unreported, Melbourne Magistrates Court, Smith M, No H540840, 8 June 1995.

any additions to the schedule of controlled substances in future revisions of the Montreal Protocol.

Guidance as to how the system of controls is to be implemented is to be found in the long title to the Act which provides that it is designed:

> to empower the regulation and prohibition of the manufacture, sale, distribution, use, emission, re-cycling, storage and disposal of stratospheric ozone depleting substances and articles which contain those substances …

Part 2 of the Act provides the underlying framework for the control of 'controlled' substances and controlled articles. The actual daily control of these substances and articles is governed by the *Ozone Protection and Synthetic Greenhouse Gas Management Regulations 1995* (Cth) (discussed above).

Offences

Proceedings for offences are dealt with under Chapter 8 of the PEOA (PEOA s 213). Very few prosecutions have been brought for offences against the OPA or Regulations. No convictions were recorded in 2004 (DEC Annual Report 2004-2005). The maximum penalty for an offence against the Act is $5500 for a corporation or $2200 for an individual offender. Consequently, more serious breaches are likely to be dealt with under the PEOA. Under s 117 of the PEOA it is an offence wilfully or negligently to cause any controlled substance to be emitted into the atmosphere in a manner that harms or is likely to harm the environment (s 117). The maximum penalty, which can be imposed is $5 million for a corporation for wilful offences, and $1 million and/or seven years' imprisonment in the case of an individual. As yet, no prosecutions have been brought.

Pesticides

Environmental protection has not always been the underlying aim of pesticide regulation. The control of pesticides previously focused on the protection of health and food quality whilst environmental concerns remained incidental. This policy has changed in more recent times along with major overhauls in the system by which regulation is administered.

The National Registration Scheme

Pesticide regulation was significantly transformed in 1992 with the advent of the National Registration Scheme. The Scheme was the result of an agreement between the Commonwealth, State and Territory governments and is applied nationally.

The current National Registration Scheme is implemented through a portfolio of Commonwealth legislation including:

Agricultural and Veterinary Chemicals Act 1994
Agricultural and Veterinary Chemicals (Administration) Act 1992
Agricultural and Veterinary Chemicals Code Act 1994

This legislation establishes a national scheme for the assessment and registration of agricultural and veterinary products through the Australian Pesticides and

Veterinary Medicines Authority. The primary piece of legislation is the *Agricultural and Veterinary Chemicals Code Act 1994*. The *Agricultural and Veterinary Code*, commonly referred to as the AGVET Code is attached in the Schedule to the *Agricultural and Veterinary Chemicals Code Act*.

AGVET Code

Presently, pesticide use is regulated in the following way. Pesticides must initially be approved for use and registered under the national uniform code known as the AGVET Code. The AGVET Code regulates the manufacture and supply of pesticides. Pesticide use and activities fall under the operation of the relevant State legislation.

The AGVET Code serves as a national regulatory benchmark. It consolidates a number of different concerns against which registration of a potential pesticide is to be considered and evaluated. The criteria are comprehensive and far reaching and include the potential to affect:

- human health;
- the environment;
- ecologically sustainable development;
- primary industry;
- trade and commerce.

The Australian Pesticides and Veterinary Medicines Authority

The Australian Pesticides and Veterinary Medicine Authority enforces the rules and regulations required by the AGVET Code. The Authority is established under the *Agricultural and Veterinary Chemicals (Administration) Act 1992* (AVCAA) and is responsible for the proper exercise of the functions and purposes of the AGVET Code regarding registration of pesticides.

The Authority is an independent body that comprises representatives from a number of key interest areas covering regulation of chemicals under State law, the agricultural and veterinary chemicals industry, consumer interest, occupational health and safety, and experience in managing a statutory authority or in the administration of Commonwealth policy (AVCAA s 14). Although no provision is made for a representative with environmental expertise, AVCAA s 8(1)(d) allows the Authority to engage in consultation with external environmental groups when a decision might require that specific environmental concerns be accounted for.

Functions of Authority

The Authority executes its functions under the AGVET Code on a national level and on behalf of all jurisdictions. Specifically, the Code provides the Authority with detailed operational provisions relating to the registration of pesticides. This is achieved through the full range of powers bestowed on the authority by the Code and the AVCAA including:

- evaluating, registering and reviewing pesticides and active constituents (Code ss 6, 18);
- issuing permits for activities using pesticides in a manner prohibited by the Code (Code s 108);

- introducing uniform standards for controlling the manufacture of chemical products (AVCAA s 7(1A)(k));
- regulating the supply of chemical products (AVCAA s 7(1A)(e));
- assessing the suitability of pesticides for sale in Australia (AVCAA s 7(1A)(a));
- providing information to, and co-operating with, State and Commonwealth governments in relation to the management of pesticide products (AVCAA s 7(1A)(b));
- keeping records of all registrations, permits and licences granted or issued under the AGVET Code (AVCAA s 7(1A)(c));
- analysing the effects of the use of pesticides in the States and Territories (AVCAA s 7(1A)(d));
- developing codes of practice, standards and guidelines regarding production, movement and sale of pesticides (AVCAA s 7(1A)(f)).

Persistent organic pollutants

The Stockholm Convention on Persistent Organic Pollutants 2001 requires the elimination and safe disposal of certain intentionally produced POPs which have been widely used as pesticides. The *Agricultural and Veterinary Chemicals Code Regulations 1995* (Cth) and the *Customs (Prohibited Imports) Regulations 1956* (Cth) give effect to a number of Australia's obligations under the Stockholm Convention.

Regulation of pesticides in New South Wales

AGVET Code NSW

The cornerstone of regulation in NSW is the AGVET Code. The Code has been adopted into NSW law through the enactment of the *Agricultural and Veterinary Chemicals (New South Wales) Act 1994*. By virtue of the operation of s 5 of the NSW Act, the AGVET Code applies as a law of New South Wales and is relevantly referred to as the AGVET Code NSW. Therefore, any registration under the AGVET Code is taken to fulfil the obligations of a registration under the AGVET Code NSW.

Registration

When is registration required?

Application for registration is dealt with under Pt 2 of the AGVET Code. The process involves an approval that is granted by the Authority following review of the application. The application must be in writing and contain all information necessary to enable the Authority to make a decision.

An application may be lodged for the following:

- approval of an active constituent for a proposed or existing pesticide;
- registration of a pesticide;
- approval of labelling relating to a pesticide. (Code s 10)

Relevant factors in granting registration or approval

The AGVET Code features a list of conditions that, if fulfilled, oblige the Authority to grant the relevant approval for registration. The object of the criteria is to scrutinise closely the potential effects of the application of the pesticide. The relevant considerations state that the pesticide:

- would not be likely to have an effect that is harmful to human beings;
- would not be likely to have an unintended effect harmful to animals, plant and the natural environment;
- would not unreasonably prejudice trade or commerce between Australia and foreign countries. (Code s 14(3))

The Authority must also examine potential adverse affects that may arise due to the composition of the pesticide itself (Code s 14(4)). Such considerations include:

- the toxicity of the constituent and its residues in relation to relevant living beings, ecosystems;
- the proposed method of manufacture for the relevant pesticide;
- the extent to which the constituent will contain impurities;
- whether any analysis of the pesticide has been undertaken and, if so, what were the results.

The ultimate approval hinges on whether each individual active constituent that makes up the pesticide has been approved, and that each application has provided satisfactory labelling of the pesticide (Code s 15). Approvals are not necessarily absolute though and may be subject to conditions that the Authority deems to be appropriate.

Public participation and notification

The Authority is obliged to invite public comment before ultimately determining an application for approval or registration. Notice is given to the public through publication in the Gazette (Code ss 12(1), 13(1)). Written responses must be submitted within 28 days and must outline whether the application should be accepted and on what basis. Submissions must be relevant to the considerations of the Authority, which is obliged to take the submissions into account.

Once the Authority approves or registers a chemical product, it must publish a notice stating this in the Gazette and in any other manner deemed appropriate (Code s 52(1)). The notice must specify the individual conditions that regulate the use of the pesticide as well as provide the date of approval or registration.

The Authority can invite the public to suggest active constituents for proposed or existing chemical products, or to propose products whose approval or registration might be reconsidered (Code s 30(1)). Notice must be given in the Gazette and in any other manner deemed appropriate. The notice must state the criteria to be taken into account. Any submission of this nature must give reasons based on the criteria in the notice. The Authority may also take the initiative in proposing the reconsideration of an approval, registration or label (Code s 31). Again, notice must be given and public submissions invited. Notice must also be given to anyone likely to be affected by the decision (Code s 32).

Permits

In the event that a person is required to use a prohibited pesticide, or use a registered pesticide in a prohibited way, the AGVET Code allows a permit to be obtained. A permit allows the prohibited activity to be carried out for a certain period and in accordance with conditions. Permits are granted in situations such as where a person wants to conduct a trial using an unregistered pesticide in order to determine whether an application is worth pursuing (Code s 108(2)).

Offences

The AGVET Code prohibits the manufacture of prohibited chemical products. If a person is found to have played any role in the manufacture of such products, they are liable to be convicted of an offence if they fail to provide a reasonable excuse (Code s 121(3)).

Suspension or cancellation of approval or registration

The Authority may cancel a registration or approval. There are a number of grounds for cancellation that vary from the failure to adhere to administrative rules and procedures, to more substantive matters concerning potential harmful effects of the pesticide.

The 'administrative' reasons for suspending or cancelling a registration include:

- a breach of a condition of the approval or registration;
- failure to provide the Authority with relevant information on application for reconsideration of an approval;
- failure to inform the Authority of the results of trials or experiments;
- failure to give the Authority a report or sample. (Code ss 36, 38)

The Authority is also entitled to cancel a registration or approval if it has reason to believe that the application of the pesticide could cause harm to people handling the substance, or if it is likely to be harmful to humans, animals, plants or the environment generally (Code s 41).

Appeals

Applicants can seek review of decisions by filing an application with the Administrative Appeals Tribunal (Code s 167). Any person may bring an action in the Federal Court of Australia for an injunction restraining a person from engaging in conduct that was, or would be an offence against the AGVET Code, or requiring a person to take action to comply (Code s 130).

Pesticides Act 1999 (NSW)

Whilst the AGVET Code (NSW) regulates the manufacture, supply, registration and approval of pesticides, the actual use and application falls under the operation of the *Pesticides Act 1999*. The Act came into force following criticism of the previous legislation, the *Pesticides Act 1978*, that ultimately led to its repeal. The operation and enforcement of the Act are the responsibility of the EPA, which is part of the Department of Environment and Conservation (ss 73, 108).

Definition of pesticides and agricultural products

The *Pesticides Act 1999* defines 'pesticide' to mean:

(a) an agricultural chemical product within the meaning of the Agvet Code, or
(b) a veterinary chemical product (within the meaning of the Agvet Code) that is represented as being suitable for, or is manufactured, supplied or used for, the external control of ectoparasites of animals.

Note. The Agvet Code defines an "**agricultural chemical product**" to be a substance or a mixture of substances that is represented, imported, manufactured, supplied or used as a means of directly or indirectly:

(a) destroying, stupefying, repelling, inhibiting the feeding of, or preventing infestation by or attacks of, any pest in relation to a plant, a place or a thing, or
(b) destroying a plant, or
(c) modifying the physiology of a plant or pest so as to alter its natural development, productivity, quality or reproductive capacity, or
(d) modifying an effect of another agricultural chemical product, or
(e) attracting a pest for the purpose of destroying it.

The term also includes insect repellants for use on human beings. (s 5(1))

Object

The Act operates consistently with the national registration scheme. The object of the Act is to:

- promote the protection of human health, the environment, property and trade in relation to the use of pesticides having regard to ESD principles;
- minimise risks to human health, the environment, property and trade;
- promote collaborative and integrated policies in relation to the use of pesticides; and
- establish a legislative framework to regulate the use of pesticides. (s 3)

Offences

The Act creates a number of offences concerning the use and possession of pesticides.

Offences can generally be divided into two broad categories, on-site and off-site. With regard to on-site contamination, the Act preserves the common law position that no legal liability is incurred for polluting one's own property. That being the case, the Act only provides on-site offences in regard to contraventions of statutory control measures.

However, liability for off-site contamination, such as allowing run off to enter a neighbour's premises, can be an offence under both the Act and common law (ss 8-11).

Wilful or negligent misuse of pesticides

The wilful or negligent misuse of pesticides is an offence where such use results in:

- actual or potential harm to people or property (s 7);
- harm to animals and plants that are not the target of pesticide use (s 8);
- material harm to endangered, vulnerable or protected animals (s 9).

No offence is committed under ss 7 and 8 if the 'on-farm/residential premises exception' applies. This exception applies where the person can establish that the only damage which occurred was on agricultural farm land, or on residential premises occupied by the accused (ss 7(2), 8(2)). The maximum penalties for these offences are $250,000 for corporations and $120,000 for individuals.

Misuse of pesticides

This offence deals with the use of a pesticide in a manner that:

- causes or is likely to cause harm to persons or property (s 10(1));
- causes harm to any non-target animal or plant (s 11(1)).

'Use' includes 'apply' or 'disperse' or 'prepare for use' (s 4). These are strict liability offences. However, defendants do not commit an offence if they can demonstrate that:

- the harm or damage was limited to agricultural land; and
- that they are the occupant of the relevant land. (ss 10(2), 11(2))

It is also a defence for a defendant to show that the commission of the offence was due to causes over which they had no control, and that the person took all reasonable precautions and exercised all due diligence to prevent the commission of the offence (ss 10(3), 11(3)). This defence is discussed in Chapter 11.

Possession and use of unregistered or restricted pesticides

It is an offence to possess or use an unregistered pesticide unless a permit is held and the person complies with the condition of the permit (ss 11, 12). It is also an offence to possess or use a restricted pesticide unless authorised by a certificate of competency or a pesticide control order (ss 16-17).

Failure to comply with directions on labels

It is an offence to keep a registered pesticide in a container that does not have an approved label (s 16). Before using a pesticide, a person is obliged to read the label or ensure that the label is explained to the person intending to use it (s 14).

Pesticides must be used in accordance with the instructions set out on the labels attached. The information contained on the labels specify the applications that have been approved and it is an offence to use the pesticide in manner that contravenes this (s 15(1)). It is a defence if the accused can demonstrate that they complied with the relevant instructions on an approved label or used the pesticide at a lower concentration level than that allowed on the label (s 15(3)). In *EPA v Gosford City Council*,[6] the defendant was prosecuted for disregarding a label instruction under s 33(1) of the, now repealed, *Pesticides Act 1978*. One of the defendant's employees had applied a registered pesticide on a school oval at 10 times the approved level. The employee and supervisor had falsified records to hide the error. The incident resulted in the death of approximately 50 ducks, and one teacher was ill for several weeks. The defendant pleaded guilty and was sentenced to a penalty of $16,000 (the maximum possible penalty at that time was $44,000). Although the court found that this was in the worst range of cases, the court took into account the fact that the

---

6 [2000] NSWLEC 154.

defendant had pleaded guilty, expressed remorse, co-operated with the EPA and introduced new systems to prevent the recurrence of the offence. The defendant also paid the EPA's costs of $12,000. This is the highest penalty awarded under the *Pesticides Act 1978*.[7]

Occupational health and safety

Employers must guard against the potential risks of pesticides adversely affecting the health of employees. This duty is provided by the *Occupational Health and Safety Regulation 2001* (NSW) and includes pesticides used in agriculture.

Penalty notices

Penalty notices may be issued for minor breaches of the Act or regulations for types of offences specified in the Regulations. A 'penalty notice' is a notice to the effect that, if the person served with the notice does not wish to have the offence dealt with by a court, they may pay the penalty (s 75). The penalty payable is prescribed in the Regulations but may not exceed $1500 (s 78). In 2004, 17 penalty notices were issued by DEC authorised officers (DEC Annual Report 2004-2005).

Enforcement

Proceedings for an offence under the Act can be commenced in the Land and Environment Court or a Local Court. Proceedings for an offence under the Act or Regulations may be instituted only by the EPA (s 73). Proceedings must be brought within three years after the date of the commission of the offence (s 72).

Pesticide control notices

Clean-up, prevention and compliance cost notices

The EPA can issue clean-up (ss 19-22) and prevention notices (ss 23-26) in relation to pesticide pollution. Compliance cost notices are available to recover expenses (ss 28-31). These notices are the same as the clean-up, prevention and compliance cost notices issued under the PEOA (discussed in Chapter 11 at pp 435-436, 437).

Defective equipment

Another form of notice relates to defective equipment. Defect notices, as they are called, prevent further use of equipment used in the application of pesticides until relevant repairs have been undertaken. Where an officer believes that a certain defect may result in consequent harm or damage then a notice may be delivered to the person to cease using the equipment (s 42).

Prohibited residue notices and orders

If an authorised officer reasonably suspects that agricultural produce contains a prohibited residue, he or she may issue a notice requiring the person not to part

7 In practice, a number of serious offences involving pesticides are prosecuted under the PEOA (see *EPA v Warringah Golf Club* [2003] NSWLEC 140; *EPA v Warringah Golf Club (No 2)* (2003) 129 LGERA 211 discussed in Chapter 11 at pp 446-447).

with the produce; retain it at the premises; or deal with it in any way reasonably necessary for public health (s 64). Once a notice has been issued, it remains in force for 14 days. After that period the Minister may make a prohibited residue order and may even order the destruction of the produce (s 65).

Pesticide control orders

The EPA has the power to make pesticide control orders. The EPA requires approval from the Minister and the order must be published in the Gazette and in certain newspapers. A pesticide control order can be made in relation to the protection of public health, property, the environment or trade, or to give effect to a policy or decision of the National Registration Authority with regard to a pesticide (s 38).

In achieving any of the listed goals and objectives, the EPA may request a control order to:

- prohibit or control the use of a pesticide; or
- authorise the use or possession of a restricted pesticide. (s 39)

Pesticide control orders are primarily issued to implement outcomes of a pesticide review. The orders specify the authorised users and the appropriate manner of use. To date, 15 pesticide control orders have been made. Thirteen orders relate to restricted pesticides. One sets rules for aerial spraying operations near residential and public buildings and another relates to baiting of crops for mouse plagues (<www.environment.nsw.gov.au/pesticides/pco.htm>).

Restricted pesticide

A restricted pesticide is a pesticide that may have a harmful effect on humans, or an unintended effect that is harmful to any animal, plant or to the environment. It also may require special knowledge, skill or qualifications in preparation or handling and special equipment to use the product safely. The Authority decides which pesticides meet any of these criteria and what special controls should be placed on their supply and use. Restricted pesticides, upon their declaration, are listed in Sch 4 to the *Agricultural and Veterinary Chemicals Code Regulations 1995* (Cth).

Anyone using a restricted pesticide must be authorised by either a pesticide control order or a certification of competency. The EPA generally issues pesticide control orders to allow the possession and use of restricted pesticides in New South Wales (<www.environment.nsw.gov.au/pesticides/pco.htm>).

It is an offence to possess or use a restricted pesticide unless authorised to do so by a certificate of competency issued by the EPA, or a pesticide control order. It is also necessary to comply with a list of conditions (*Pesticides Act 1999* (NSW) ss 17, 56-62).

Directions

An authorised officer, with the written approval of the EPA may give directions for the destruction of, or rendering harmless of, any pesticide if of the opinion that:

- it is necessary in the interest of public health or of any person;
- it is necessary because of any harm or risk of harm to any person, property, the environment or trade. (s 41)

Licensing

A licence is required for aerial pesticide operations (ss 45-55). A pilot (pesticide rating) licence is required for any person applying pesticides from an aircraft. Additionally, either the pilot themselves or the person employing the pilot must hold an aircraft (pesticide applicator) licence (ss 43, 45, 54).

Pesticide Codes of Practice

The Minister may make a pesticide code of practice on the recommendation of the EPA. The Code must be published in the Gazette. Pesticide Codes of Practice are a set of guidelines on the use and management of pesticides in the hope of ensuring best practice and use. The Codes of Practice are voluntary and non-binding. They may cover any specified pesticide or class of pesticide, any specified industry or their use (eg aerial spraying operations) (ss 69, 70).

Contaminated sites

There is no Commonwealth legislation that deals directly with contaminated sites although a number of policy documents and guidelines have been formulated. In 1992 the Australian and New Zealand Environment and Conservation Council (ANZECC) and the National Health and Medical Research Council (NHMRC) developed guidelines for site assessment (ANZECC and NHMRC, Australian and New Zealand Guidelines for the Assessment and Management of Contaminated Sites 1992). These Guidelines were aimed at protecting human health and the environment from contamination, while at the same time providing flexibility in land use. The Guidelines were followed in 1994 by a position paper on financial liability. The key operational principle in the position paper is the 'polluter-pays principle', which in essence directs that 'those who generate pollution and waste should bear the cost of containment, avoidance or abatement' (ANZECC *Financial Liability for Contaminated Site Remediation – A Position Paper,* April 1994, cl 4.02).

In 1999 the National Environment Protection (Assessment of Site Contamination) Measure was gazetted. The NEPM is essentially a revised and updated version of the 1992 Guidelines for site assessment. The desired environmental outcome of the NEPM is 'to provide adequate protection of human health and the environment, where site contamination has occurred, through the development of an efficient and effective national approach to the assessment of site contamination' (cl 5(2)). These policy documents have strongly influenced the management of contaminated sites and the allocation of financial liability in New South Wales.

Contaminated Land Management Act 1997 (NSW)

The main provisions dealing with site contamination in New South Wales are contained in the *Contaminated Land Management Act 1997* (CLMA). The CLMA promotes the 'polluter pays principle' by placing the primary responsibility for the clean-up on those responsible for the contamination. This is in contrast to the now repealed Pt V of the *Environmentally Hazardous Chemicals Act 1985* (NSW), where financial liability was primarily attributed to the occupier of contaminated land. Section 5(1) of the CLMA defines contamination to mean the presence in, on or under the land of a substance at such concentrations as to 'present a risk of harm to human health or any other aspect of the environment'.

The threshold test: 'significant risk of harm'

The CLMA gives the EPA power to regulate sites where contamination presents a significant risk of harm. The Act sets out a lengthy list of criteria which the EPA must take into account when deciding whether or not a site is a significant risk site (CLMA s 9). These criteria are elaborated in the Guidelines on Significant Risk of Harm from Contaminated Land and the Duty to Report (1999). If the EPA has reasonable grounds to believe that a site is actually or possibly contaminated in such a way as to present a significant risk of harm, it has wide power to take action For example, it can make records, investigate, employ community-based strategies to minimise risk, or any other lawful action (s 7). If, on the other hand, there are no reasonable grounds to believe that the land is contaminated in such a way as to present a significant risk of harm, the EPA may respond as it sees fit, but has no power to order an investigation or remediation (s 8). Generally, sites not causing a significant risk in their current zoning or use will not require any attention, unless a change of zoning or use is proposed. If a change is proposed, the site is dealt with by councils under the EPAA, in accordance with *SEPP 55 – Remediation of Land and the Planning Guidelines for Contaminated Land* (see below).

Investigation and remediation orders

If the EPA has reasonable grounds to **believe** that a site is contaminated in such a way as to present a significant risk of harm, it may take declare the land an investigation area. The EPA must give seven days' advance notice of the proposed declaration to the owner, or notional owner of land (see below), the polluter and the occupier of the land (s 15(4)). The declaration must be published in the Gazette and public submissions must be invited as to whether the EPA should issue an investigation order in relation to the area. Once a declaration has been made, the EPA may order an appropriate person (see below) or a public authority to investigate land and report on the nature and extent of the contamination, the nature and extent of the harm caused by the contamination, the risk that the contamination will cause such harm and the most appropriate means of remediation (s 17). Voluntary investigation proposals may also be submitted for EPA approval (s 19).

If land is **found** to be contaminated, whether or not as a result of an investigation, so as to present a significant risk of harm, the EPA may declare land to be a remediation site (CLMA s 21). Thus where land is found, independently of an investigation, to be a significant risk site, the EPA can bypass the investigation requirements and move directly to a declaration of a remediation site. Notification and publication procedures for remediation declarations are similar to those for an investigation declaration (s 21). Voluntary proposals to remediate contaminated land can also be agreed with the EPA (s 26).

Where the EPA considers the risk of harm presented by the contamination extremely significant or serious, it may make a remediation order at the same time as the declaration without complying with the publication and notification procedures (s 21(7)). After the land has been declared a remediation site, the EPA may order an appropriate person or public authority to remediate the site. In addition to the requirement to remediate, the EPA can order a wide range of action to be taken under a remediation order (ss 23, 24).

Failure to comply with an investigation or remediation order, without reasonable excuse, is an offence. The maximum penalty for a corporation is $137,500 and $66,000 for an individual. Daily penalties of $66,000 also apply (ss 17(4), 23(6)). The period for compliance, which must be specified in the order, must usually exceed by a reasonable amount the 21-day period allowed for lodging an appeal against the order in the Land and Environment Court (ss 18(2), 24(2)).

Sites which have been declared as remediation sites under the CLMA now fall within the type of project for which consent under Pt 3A of the EPAA is required. Schedule 1 to *SEPP (Major Projects) 2005* lists the projects which fall within Pt 3A, and remediation sites are specifically listed at para 28. (See discussion of Pt 3A in Chapter 2 at p 53.)

Financially responsible persons

The CLMA provides a hierarchy of 'appropriate persons' who may be liable for remediation or investigation (s 12). In keeping with the 'polluter pays' principle, the polluter is regarded as the most appropriate person to receive an investigation or remediation order. If it is not practicable to hold the polluter liable, the next preferred person is the owner of the land regardless of whether he or she was responsible for the contamination. The next person in the hierarchy becomes liable, if it is not 'practicable' to hold the first mentioned person liable. The choice of a person is not 'practicable' if there is no such person, the person cannot be located, or the person lacks the financial means to pay their debts (s 12(6)). If it is not practicable to hold the owner financially liable, then the notional owner of land will be held liable. A notional owner includes a mortgagee in possession of land and any other persons likely to benefit from the sale of the land (s 14(1)). The Act provides that a person will not be regarded as a notional owner merely because they have a mortgage or charge over the land unless they are in some way involved in the management of the land (s 14(2)(a)). This ensures that lenders will not be held financially liable for the clean-up of contaminated land when simply enforcing their right to recover their security, in the event that the polluter or the owner is unable to pay the costs of the clean-up.

Under the CLMA, the EPA is compelled to specify either an appropriate person or a public authority if investigation or remediation is required (s 12(1)). This means that, if no appropriate person can be located, the liability to investigate or remediate land could fall back on to a public authority (s 30). If the work is undertaken by the public authority on the basis that the appropriate person failed to comply with an order, the authority may recover the costs expended in seeking compliance with the order from that person (s 35). In the event that the owner is insolvent and the public authority has carried out the requirements of the investigation or remediation order, the public authority may recover all related costs and expenses so incurred in priority to any holder of a security over land (s 37). Likewise, an owner or occupier who was not responsible for the contamination, but who has complied with an investigation or remediation order, can recover a portion of those costs from each person who was responsible for the contamination (ss 32(3), 36(1), (4)).

Duty to notify EPA of contamination

In order to facilitate the EPA's functions, a person who has conducted activities on land which they know are causing a significant risk of harm has a duty to inform the EPA (s 60). This duty also applies to an owner who becomes aware that land has been contaminated in such a way as to present a significant risk of harm (s 60). This duty applies to current contamination and contamination which occurred before the commencement of the Act. Failure to notify is an offence. Information provided cannot be used for prosecution purposes, but it can result in an investigation or remediation declaration or order (s 60(4)).

Duty of EPA and local authorities to provide information

The EPA also has a duty to inform the local authorities of contaminated sites in their area (s 59). Site auditors must furnish the EPA and local authorities with copies of site audit statements which have been undertaken in their area (s 53B). Local authorities must include this information, in addition to details of investigation and remediation declarations and orders, on a planning certificate under s 149 of the EPAA.

The EPA is required to maintain a publicly available contaminated land sites register which records declarations of land as investigation or remediation sites, any investigation or remediation orders, any site audit statements, and any voluntary investigation or remediation proposals pertaining to the land (s 58(1)).

Audits and auditors

A site audit conducted under the CLMA is an independent review of an investigation or remediation which has been carried out to report on the nature and extent of any contamination; the nature and extent of the investigation or remediation; and what investigation or remediation remains necessary before the land is suitable for any specified use or range of uses (s 47(1)). The CLMA creates a scheme of accredited site auditors and site audit statements (ss 47-57). Site auditors must apply for EPA accreditation (s 50). Once accredited, auditors are eligible to conduct site audits for the EPA, councils, and the wider community. It is mandatory to engage a site auditor to report on work carried out as a result of an investigation or remediation order issued by the EPA or a voluntary investigation or remediation proposal (s 47(2)(a) and (a1)). Audits are also mandatory where they are required by SEPP 55, by a development consent condition or environmental planning instrument under the EPAA (ss 24(1)(d), 47(2)(b)).

The importance of ensuring the accuracy of an audit is well illustrated in *Charben Haulage Pty Ltd v Environmental and Earth Sciences Pty Ltd*.[8] The case highlights the advisability of retaining an EPA accredited auditor to sign off on any remediation. It also illustrates the potentially wide range of liability of environmental consultants for inaccurate statements in reports. Caltex obtained development consent to decommission a service station and remediate it for residential use. The remediation was required to be signed off by an accredited site auditor. Caltex commissioned an environmental consultant, Environmental and Earth Sciences Pty Ltd, to report on the remediation of the site. The consultant was not an EPA-

8 [2004] FCA 403.

accredited auditor. The consultant concluded that, following some remedial works on the site, it would be suitable for residential use. Caltex sold the property for mixed commercial and residential development. The EPA rejected the report because the consultant was not an EPA-accredited auditor. The purchaser engaged an accredited site auditor and an investigation disclosed that groundwater on the site was contaminated, that significant remediation was required and that the site was not suitable for the proposed use. The purchaser instituted proceedings against Caltex for breach of contract, and against Caltex and the consultant (EES) for breaches of the *Trade Practices Act 1974* (Cth) (TPA), negligent misstatement and negligence. Caltex was found liable for breaching the contract of sale in failing to reduce the contamination to a level necessary to permit the proposed development but was not found to have breached the TPA since it did not know that the contents of the report were incorrect or misleading. Caltex recovered the amount of its liability from EES who was held to have breached its contract to remediate and validate the site for residential use. Interestingly, the court found that, although EES had breached s 52 of the TPA, it was not liable for negligent misstatement, as it did not owe a duty of care to the purchaser, as the report was not produced for the purpose of the sale. However, EES was found liable under s 82 of the TPA for misleading conduct on the basis of significant misrepresentations in the report. The court ordered EES and Caltex to pay costs and damages of over $2 million to the purchaser.

The judgment in favour of Charben was set aside on appeal.[9] The Full Federal Court held that Caltex had not breached the contract of sale because of the special wording of the contract which had the effect of transferring the risk of future liability for contamination to Charben. The judgment against EES was also set aside because the court was not persuaded that Charben had relied on any particular statement in the report so as to induce Charben to purchase the site to its detriment. Charben's directors had not read the report and although their lawyer had done so, he had no knowledge of the EPA Guidelines. The court also found that EES had not breached the EPA Guidelines for failing to dig a well to test for contamination in ground water, as the Guidelines only required a well to be dug in certain circumstances, such as where ground water had been identified at the site.

Charben's application for special leave to appeal to the High Court was refused.

Corporate and director's liability

Criminal liability

To ensure that a corporation can be convicted for an offence involving *mens rea*, the CLMA provides that, where it is necessary to show intention on the part of a corporation, evidence that an officer, employee, or agent of a corporation (while acting in his or her capacity as such) had, at any particular time, a particular intention is evidence that the corporation had that intention (s 98(4)). Directors can also be held personally liable for offences by their corporations. The Act provides that, where a corporation contravenes the Act or the Regulations, each person who is a director of the corporation or who is concerned in the management of the

9 *Caltex Australia Petroleum Pty Ltd v Charben Haulage Pty Ltd* [2005] FCAFC 271.

corporation is taken to have contravened the same provision. Three statutory defences are provided if the director can satisfy the court that:

- the corporation contravened the provision without his or her knowledge (actual, imputed or constructive);
- the person was not in a position to influence the conduct of the corporation in relation to the contravention; or
- the person, if in such a position, used all due diligence to prevent the contravention by the corporation. (s 98(1))

A director may be proceeded against and convicted whether or not the corporation has been proceeded against or convicted (s 98(2)).

Section 98 corresponds with the similar provision in s 169 of the PEOA (see discussion at Chapter 11 at pp 462-464). However, it should be noted that recent amendments to s 169 of the PEOA Act have not been adopted in relation to s 98, specifically the abolition of the defence of lack of knowledge for directors, and the imputation of the state of mind of a director to the corporation.

Remedial orders

Enforcement

The provisions relating to criminal prosecutions and civil proceedings in the CLMA are consistent with those provided in the PEOA. Prosecutions under the Act are normally brought by the EPA. Other persons may institute proceedings with the leave of the Land and Environment Court (s 95). Any person may bring civil proceedings in the court for an order to remedy or restrain a breach of the Act (s 96).

Orders against directors or corporations

The CLMA gives the Land and Environment Court broad-ranging powers to prevent asset stripping and evasion of investigation and remediation orders by corporations. The court may order a director or person concerned in the management of a corporation to comply with an investigation or remediation order at their own expense, if the person was a director, or a person concerned in the management, of a corporation:

- that has been wound up within two years before the court's order has been made, and has failed to comply with the investigation or remediation order (s 63(1)); or
- that transferred land within two years before the court's order was made, and has failed to comply with the investigation or remediation order (s 64(1)).

Before making the order, the court must be satisfied that the person was a director or manager at the relevant time and there is reason to believe that the body corporate was wound up, or the land was transferred, as part of a scheme to avoid compliance with the investigation or remediation order (ss 63(3), 64(3)). A director or manager has three statutory defences, namely, lack of knowledge, lack of influence or due diligence (ss 63(5), 64(5)). These defences are identical to those available to directors in s 98 of the Act. Similarly, a holding company may be ordered to comply with an investigation or remediation order at their own expense, if the subsidiary has been wound up within two years before the court's order and has failed to comply with an investigation or remediation order (s 65(1), (3)). The Act provides a number of criteria to assist the court in determining whether the winding up, or the transfer of land, was part of a scheme to avoid compliance (ss 63(4), 64(4), 65(4)). The fact that the investigation or remediation order was made after steps were taken to wind up the corporation does not preclude the court from finding that it was wound up to avoid compliance (ss 63(7), 65(7)).

The role of the PEOA

The PEOA plays an important role in relation to the regulation and management of contaminated land. Potentially contaminating industries will generally require a licence under the PEOA. The EPA can attach conditions to a licence to require remediation work to be carried out by the licensee (PEOA s 71). To ensure that the licensee has sufficient funds to pay for a clean-up, the licensee may be required to maintain an insurance policy for the payment of expenses associated with clean-up action, and any compensation or damages resulting from pollution, or to provide a financial assurance (PEOA ss 70, 72). Where pollution incidents occur, notices can be issued to polluters and/or occupiers, directing them to take clean-up action (PEOA s 91).

The role of local authorities

Local councils also play a role in relation to contaminated land that is not a significant risk site under the CLMA. The EPAA contains provisions for planning; development control and environmental impact assessment (see Chapters 2-4). Presently, some contaminated treatment works are listed in the *Environmental Planning and Assessment Regulation 2000* (Sch 3), which means that an environmental impact statement must accompany the development application.

Part 7A of the EPAA overcomes the potential liability of local councils when dealing with contaminated land. The amendment was triggered by the Federal Court decision in *Alec Finlayson Pty Ltd v Armidale City Council.*[10] In that case, the Council was held liable to a developer and others for losses arising as a result of land contamination. Section 145B of the EPAA now exonerates planning authorities from liability for any action done in good faith in so far as it relates to contaminated land. A council is taken to have acted in good faith, in exercising a planning function, if its actions were substantially in accordance with the Planning Guidelines for Contaminated Land.[11] The purpose of the Guidelines is to assist consent authorities, developers and other parties to address the issue of land contamination in the planning and development control process. The Guidelines deal with the need for early investigation of contamination, the rezoning of land, the assessment of development applications and the notification of information.

SEPP 55 – Remediation of Land facilitates control over the remediation of contaminated land and ensures that appropriate information is furnished to councils, either

---

10 (1994) 84 LGERA 225. The decision was confirmed on appeal: *Armidale City Council v Alex Finlayson Pty Ltd* (1999) 104 LGERA 9.

11 Department of Urban Affairs and Planning and the EPA, 1998.

at the rezoning stage or with development applications, as appropriate. The SEPP requires a consent authority to consider whether land is contaminated and whether remediation is necessary before granting rezoning or development consent. The SEPP also specifies situations where development consent is required for remediation. This is the case where the remediation works may have a significant impact on the environment or where it does not comply with council's policy for contaminated land. Remediation work must be carried out in accordance with the Planning Guidelines for Contaminated Land and any other standards and guidelines (see EPA website <www.environment.nsw.gov.au>).

Local councils are also given a role in controlling pollution under the LGA. Local councils may give orders to the owner or occupier of land 'to do or refrain from doing such things as are specified in the order to ensure that land is, or premises are, placed or kept in a safe and healthy condition' or 'to do or refrain from doing such things as are specified in the order to prevent environmental damage, to repair environmental damage or to prevent further environmental damage' (LGA s 124).

Statutory Environmental Trust Fund

The *Environmental Trust Act 1998* (NSW) (ETA) creates an Environmental Trust consisting of five members: the Minister, the Secretary of the Treasury, the Director-General of the EPA, a nominee of the Nature Conservation Council and a nominee of the Local Government and Shires Associations (s 6). The main source of funding for the Trust is an indexed annual appropriation of $13.5 million each financial year (s 19). This amount is to be applied to the objects of the trust which are to encourage restoration and rehabilitation projects that will reduce pollution in New South Wales; to promote research into environmental problems; to promote environmental education; and to fund land acquisitions for the national park estate (s 7). The Trust is required to ensure that, during a financial year, a minimum amount is granted in relation to each of its objects, namely $1 million for restoration, $0.5 million for research and $0.5 million for environmental education (s 12). The ETA is an important source of funding for clean-ups of serious pollution that require immediate action and unlawful disposal of orphan waste; however, its usefulness is limited by the restriction that it spends no more than $0.5 million on these measures in any one year (s 16).

Dangerous goods

Transportation of dangerous goods

The transportation of dangerous goods is regulated by the Australian Code for the Transport of Dangerous Goods by Road and Rail (6th ed). The Australian Code is aligned with international practice based on the 'United Nations Recommendations on the Transport of Dangerous Goods'. The Code lays down standards for the packaging of dangerous goods, marking of packaging and containers for dangerous goods, transport in bulk and procedures for handling dangerous goods. The standards imposed by the Code have been adopted throughout Australia (eg, the *Road and Rail Transport (Dangerous Goods) Act 1997* (NSW)).

In addition to applying the general provisions of the Code, specific legislation has been enacted by the Commonwealth to ensure the safe transportation of dangerous goods. The *Road Transport Reform (Dangerous Goods) Act 1995* (Cth) s 3(1) and the *Road Transport Reform (Dangerous Goods) Regulations 1997* (Cth) regulate the transport of dangerous goods (other than explosives) by road and rail as part of a national scheme to ensure consistency throughout Australia. The Commonwealth Act is expressed to override any inconsistent State legislation dealing with the transport of dangerous goods by road (s 10). This legislation has been mirrored by the States and provides a consistent national approach.

The Commonwealth Act applies the standards and classification laid down in the Australian Code for the Transport of Dangerous Goods. The Commonwealth *Road Transport Reform (Dangerous Goods) Regulations 1997* provide for a national system of licensing and the creation of mutually recognised authorised authorities in the states for administering the legislation (Pt 15).

Road Transport Reform (Dangerous Goods) Regulations 1997 (Cth)

The *Road Transport Reform (Dangerous Goods) Regulations 1997* control matters such as:

- licensing of drivers and vehicles (Pts 18-20);
- packaging of dangerous goods (Pt 3);
- transportation of dangerous goods in bulk (Pt 4);
- freight containers (Pt 5);
- unit loads (Pt 6);
- marking and placarding (Pt 7);
- safety standards and insurance for vehicles (Pt 8);
- segregation of incompatible goods and stowage (Pt 9);
- transfer of dangerous goods in bulk (Pt 10);
- documents and provision of information (Pt 11);
- duties relating to personal protective and safety equipment (Pt 12);
- transport procedures (Pt 13);
- emergencies (Pt 14).

Road and Rail Transport (Dangerous Goods) Act 1997 (NSW)

The *Road and Rail Transport (Dangerous Goods) Act 1997*, in most respects, mirrors the Commonwealth legislation. The main difference is that the NSW Act also applies to rail transport as well as road transport. The Act provides a framework for the making of regulations to regulate the transport of dangerous goods by road and rail. The *Road and Rail Transport (Dangerous Goods) (Road) Regulation 1998* (NSW) adopts the Commonwealth Regulations.

Criminal offences

The Act provides for a number of offences relating to transportation of dangerous goods, namely:

- using or driving an unlicensed vehicle (s 35(1), (3));
- driving without a licence or accreditation (s 35(5));
- transporting goods too dangerous to be transported (s 36); and
- failing to ensure that goods are transported in a safe manner (s 37).

Generally, the maximum penalty for offences is $250,000 for a corporation and $50,000 and/or imprisonment for two years for an individual. However, if failure to transport dangerous goods safely involves death or serious injury, and the person involved in the transport failed to comply with the Act in circumstances where he or she knew or ought reasonably to have known that this would endanger the safety of persons, property or the environment, the maximum penalty is increased to $100,000 and/or imprisonment for four years for an individual, or $500,000 for a body corporate. In the first prosecution under the Act,[12] a consignor of flammable liquid was fined $45,000 for breach of s 37 (failing to ensure safe transport of dangerous goods).

Penalty notices may be issued for certain offences (s 38). The maximum penalty may not exceed $3000.

Proceedings for offences are brought by authorised officers and commenced in the Local Court or the Industrial Relations Commission in Court Session (s 39(1)). Proceedings must be brought within three years of the commission of the offence.

A number of prosecutions are brought under the *Road and Rail Transport (Dangerous Goods) (Road) Regulation 1998*. In 2004-05 there were 30 convictions. All defendants were prosecuted in the Local Court. Most penalties were low – the highest penalty recorded was $5000 for transporting dangerous goods in a vehicle that did not comply with the Code.[13]

Dangerous Goods under the Occupational Health and Safety Regulation 2001 (NSW)

Most dangerous goods are environmental hazards because they are toxic or harmful to humans or the environment. For this reason, dangerous goods are regulated throughout Australia. The *Dangerous Goods Act 1975* (NSW) has been repealed and subsumed into the *Occupational Health and Safety Regulation 2001* (Chapter 6A and Sch 5). The Regulations extend the Occupational Health and Safety System to dangerous goods, including dangerous goods stored or managed outside work-places.

Classification of dangerous goods

Dangerous goods are generally divided into classes according to their hazardous properties. Dangerous goods are defined as dangerous goods of class 2, 3, 4, 5, 6.1, 8 or 9 under the Australian Code for the Transport of Dangerous Goods by Road and Rail, goods too dangerous to be transported, and combustible liquids (cl 174A).

12 *EPA v Moama Refinery Pty Ltd* [2002] NSWLEC 244.
13 Speed-E-Gas (NSW) Pty Ltd (DEC Annual Report 2004-2005).

Obligations on manufacturers, importers and suppliers

Manufacturers or importers are required to identify whether goods are dangerous in accordance with the Code and, if so, whether they fall within the category of goods in the Code that are too dangerous to be transported. Manufacturers must assign to the goods the appropriate UN Number, Class, Subsidiary risk and Packing Group under the Code, except for combustible liquids where a special classification AS 1940 applies (cl 174G). Manufacturers and suppliers of dangerous goods must also ensure that goods are packaged and labelled in accordance with the Code and the legislation (cll 174H, 174I).

Material Safety Data Sheet

A manufacturer or importer of a hazardous substance or dangerous good must prepare a Material Safety Data Sheet for the substance before supplying it and provide a copy to suppliers and others. A supplier must provide the safety data sheet to employers and others who could be involved in handling or storing it. Employers must ensure that the safety data sheet is readily accessible to employees. There is also an obligation on occupiers to ensure they obtain and provide access to the data sheet (cll 174J-174M).

Hazard identification and risk assessment

An occupier of premises where dangerous goods are stored or handled must take measures to ensure that all persons, including members of the public, are not exposed to risks to their health and safety. Occupiers are required to undertake periodic risk assessments (at least every five years) and keep records of induction and training of employees likely to store or handle dangerous goods (cl 174Q). In undertaking risk assessments, occupiers must have regard to the risk control measures in cl 5. Clause 5 provides that when considering how to control a risk, where the elimination of the risk is not reasonably practicable, the following control measures, prioritised as follows, should be taken:

- substituting the hazard giving rise to the risk with a lesser risk hazard;
- isolating the hazard from the person at risk;
- minimising the risk by engineering;
- minimising the risk by administrative means (eg, safe working practices);
- using personal protective equipment.

A combination of the above measures is required to be taken if no single measure is sufficient.

Obligation of occupiers

An occupier of premises where dangerous goods are stored or handled is obliged to take specific risk control measures, namely:

- ensuring goods do not inadvertently become unstable, decompose or change so as to create a hazard that is different from the hazard originally created by the dangerous goods, or increase the risk associated with the dangerous goods (cl 174R);

- ensuring the dangerous goods are separated (cl 174S);
- ensuring incompatible goods are prevented from interacting with other substances on the premises (cl 174T);
- ensuring ignition sources are eliminated or controlled (cl 174U);
- ensuring that risks of atmospheric emissions are eliminated or reduced (cl 174V);
- ensuring that there is no contamination of food and personal products (cl 174W);
- ensuring dangerous goods in bulk in a container have stable foundations and that pipe work is installed so as to prevent excessive stress and protected from deterioration (cl 174X);
- ensuring that provision is made for the containment of spills and leaks (cl 174Y);
- ensuring any risk associated with transfers within, to or from the occupier's premises is eliminated or controlled (cl 174Z);
- ensuring that any pipe work or equipment, containing or associated with dangerous goods are protected from physical damage and stress (cl 174ZA);
- ensuring that safety equipment is provided, maintained and accessible to persons authorised to be on the premises (cl 174ZD);
- ensuring safe means of access to and from and within the premises (cl 174ZE);
- ensuring premises are secure from unauthorised persons or activities (cl 174ZT);
- ensuring appropriate lighting is available (cl 174ZU);
- ensuring the safe decommissioning of receptacles used in connection with dangerous goods (cl 174ZF);
- ensuring packaged dangerous goods are labelled in accordance with the Code and that the identity of any dangerous goods contained in an enclosed system (such as a pipe) is notified to any person who may handle them (cl 174ZH);
- ensuring that warning placards are erected (cll 174ZJ-174ZH).

Emergency planning

An occupier is required to take preventive measures to prepare for any emergency that could arise. Premises must be provided with a fire protection system that has been designed in accordance with the risk assessment system and takes account of the quantities of dangerous goods and other substances, and the conditions under which they are stored or handled. The system must be properly installed, tested and maintained. It must be easily accessible. If the fire protection system is inoperative, alternative measures must be available. If this results in a significant reduction in the effectiveness of the system, the relevant emergency services must be notified (cl 174ZB).

If dangerous goods are stored or handled in quantities that in total are likely to exceed the quantities specified in the table to Sch 5 (Manifest Quantity), occupiers must develop, implement and maintain a written plan for dealing with an emergency. The plan must be communicated to persons working on the premises and those on adjacent premises who may be exposed to risk. In developing or reviewing the plan, the occupier must seek advice from the NSW Fire Brigade. The plan must be reviewed if there is a change in circumstances such as to raise the possibility of an emergency of a kind not dealt with by the plan. Plans must also be reviewed at least every five years (cl 174ZC).

Incident responses and investigations

An occupier must respond to serious incidents, and certain other incidents involving dangerous goods at their premises, by ensuring that immediate action is take to assess and control any associated risks. Only essential personnel should remain in the vicinity of the incident and the risks to these persons should be reduced as far as reasonably practicable. These provisions apply to premises where dangerous goods are handled or stored regardless of whether or not they are places of work. However, they do not apply to emergency personnel (cl 174ZO).

Incidents involving dangerous goods must be investigated to determine the cause. A record must be kept for at least five years and be readily available, on request, to WorkCover. A risk assessment must be carried out, taking into account the results of the investigation into the incident. Any deficiencies in the risk control measures must be addressed. If the incident does not take place at a workplace, WorkCover may request information about the incident and any action taken by the occupier (cll 174ZP-174ZR).

Notification and register

Occupiers

An occupier of premises where dangerous goods are stored and handled in quantities that in total are likely to exceed the relevant quantities specified in the column headed 'Manifest Quantity' in the Table to Sch 5 must ensure that WorkCover is notified of the presence of such goods (cl 174ZS). The occupier must also keep a manifest of dangerous goods that contains information and site plans readily available for use by an inspector or the emergency services. The manifest must be kept, and be readily accessible, at the main entrance to the premises (cl 174ZN).

Employers

Employers are required to keep records of induction and training provided to employees who are likely to store and handle dangerous goods for at least five years (cl 174ZV). Employers are required to keep and maintain a register of dangerous goods stored or handled in the workplace. The register must include the relevant material safety data sheet for each dangerous good. It must be readily accessible to all employees involved in storing or handling dangerous goods (cl 174ZW). Employers are also obliged to record the results of a risk assessment relating to the storage and handling of dangerous goods and to ensure that any risk assessment report is readily accessible (cl 174ZX).

Self-service fuel dispensing units

Special requirements are placed on persons who keep dangerous goods, being vehicle fuel for sale or supply by means of a self-service fuel dispensing unit. These requirements apply to all dangerous goods, regardless of whether or not they are at a workplace. Proper operating instructions for the unit must be provided. The area must be adequately illuminated during the operation of the unit. A competent, trained and reliable person over 18 years must operate the unit

Both persons keeping self-service fuel dispensing units, and drivers of vehicles, have an obligation to ensure that the engine is stopped before the fuel tank is opened, and remains stopped while the fuel is dispensed. They must also ensure that there is no smoking in the area, and that no spark or ignition source is within 3 metres of a self-service fuel dispensing unit (including the nozzle of the hose) (cll 174ZZ, 174ZZA).

Liquefied gas cylinders, valves and balloons

There is a prohibition on keeping, conveying or using a cylinder containing, liquefied flammable gas, unless the cylinder is positioned so that the safety relief device communicates directly with the vapour space in the cylinder (cl 174ZZB).

Any cylinder or container containing dangerous goods (class 2) must, unless it is connected by permanent piping to a consuming device, ensure that its valve is kept securely closed at all times, except when it is being used. If piping is equipped with excess flow valves, the goods must not be conveyed unless each valve is set for the minimum diameter (cl 174ZZC).

There is a prohibition on filling a balloon or other collapsible container with flammable, toxic or anaesthetic gas, or keeping, conveying, selling or using a balloon or other collapsible container that contains such gas. An exception exists for scientific research or for medical purposes (cl 174ZZD).

Decommissioning of LPG tanks

If an LPG tank has been used to contain dangerous goods and two years have elapsed since any dangerous goods were last put in or taken from it, the owner must:

- remove any remaining dangerous goods from, and abandon, the tank in compliance with AS/NZS 1596-2002 *The Storage and Handling of LP Gas*; and
- notify WorkCover within seven days of the abandonment. (cl 174ZZE)

Radiation control

Radiation Control Act 1990 (NSW)

The object of the *Radiation Control Act 1990* (RCA) is to protect persons and the environment from exposure to harmful ionising and non-ionising radiation to the maximum extent that is reasonably practicable, taking into account social and economic factors and recognising the need for the use of radiation for beneficial purposes (s 3). More detailed controls, including safety requirements, are detailed in the *Radiation Control Regulation 2003* (NSW).

The Act establishes a Radiation Advisory Council consisting of 16 members appointed by the Minister. The Council's role is to advise the Minister on legislative changes, and measures to prevent or minimise the dangers arising from radiation (ss 29, 30). The EPA can also seek advice from the Council in the exercise of its functions under the Act (s 9A).

Licensing

Licences are required to possess, use, sell or give away any radioactive substance, ionising radiation apparatus or prescribed non-ionising radiation apparatus (s 6).

The EPA may not grant a licence unless it is satisfied that the applicant:

- is a natural person, and a fit and proper person to hold a licence;
- has appropriate knowledge of the principles and practices of radiation safety and protection applicable to the proposed activities; and
- meets the relevant requirements for licensing for use of the substance or apparatus set out in the National Directory.[14] (s 6(5))

The EPA can impose conditions on the licence.

Licensing offences

It is an offence to:

- possess, use, sell or give away any radiation substance or apparatus without a licence, or in non-compliance with the conditions of a licence (s 6(2));
- sell or give away any such substance or apparatus except to a person who holds a licence (s 6(3)).

In each case, the maximum penalty is $165,000 in the case of a corporation and/or $27,500 and two years' imprisonment in the case of an individual.

Registration

The Act imposes registration requirements on owners of sealed source devices and prescribed radiation apparatus. The types of radiation apparatus that have been prescribed are ionising radiation apparatus used or intended to be used for any medical, veterinary or dental diagnostic purpose; or for radiotherapy or radiotherapy planning purposes; and any cyclotron (*Radiation Control Regulation* cl 10).

Before it registers any devices or premises, the EPA must be satisfied that they comply with the Regulations and any relevant requirements in the National Directory (s 7(4)). A registration fee applies. Registration is subject to any conditions that may be imposed.

Registration offences

The Act provides for the following offences in respect to registration:

---

14 'National Directory' means the national guidance document entitled 'National Directory for Radiation Protection' approved by the Health Ministers for the States, Territories and Commonwealth from time to time (s 4).

- failure by an owner of a sealed radioactive source device or apparatus to register it in his or her name and to comply with any conditions of registration (s 7(2));
- where an owner of a registered sealed radioactive source device or apparatus allows an unlicensed person to use it (s 7(3));
- failure by an occupier of any premises on which unsealed radioactive source is kept or used, to register the premises in his or her name and to comply with any conditions of registration (s 8(1));
- where an occupier of registered premises allows an unlicensed person to use an unsealed source device (s 8(2)).

In each case, the maximum penalty is $165,000 in the case of a corporation and/or $27,500 and two years' imprisonment in the case of an individual.

Accreditation

Accreditation is necessary in order to carry on certain activities as a consulting radiation expert. It is an offence to carry on these activities without accreditation, and not in compliance with any conditions of accreditation (s 9(1)). Activities that require accreditation include advising on the design of premises to be registered in relation to radiation safety requirements and measuring radiation doses from ionizing radiation apparatus used for medical therapy (*Radiation Control Regulation 2003* cl 12). Before it accredits any person, the EPA must be satisfied that they have the necessary expertise and that they meet any relevant requirements in the National Directory (s 9(3)). Accreditation is subject to any conditions that may be imposed. An accreditation fee applies.

Conditions of licences, registrations or accreditations

A condition of a licence, registration or accreditation may be imposed by the EPA by written notice to the holder. The EPA may also vary or revoke a condition, or impose a further condition (s 10(1), (2)).

Termination, cancellation and surrender of licences, registrations or accreditations

Once granted, a licence, registration or accreditation remains in force for the specified term, unless it is cancelled or surrendered. A licence or registration may be renewed for a minimum period of one year (s 11). A registration of premises may be transferred (s 12). The holder of a licence, registration or accreditation can surrender it (s 13(1)).

The EPA may revoke or suspend a licence, registration or accreditation if satisfied:

- that it was obtained improperly;
- that the holder has contravened a condition;
- that the holder has been convicted of an offence against the Act or Regulations;
- that the holder of a licence or accreditation has ceased to hold the relevant qualifications; or

- that the holder of an accreditation has ceased working as a consulting radiation expert. (s 13(2)(a)-(e))

A decision to suspend or cancel a licence, registration or accreditation has no effect until the expiration of a period in which the holder may appeal against the decision, or an appeal is made, until the decision is confirmed or the appeal is withdrawn (s 13(3)). A licence, registration or accreditation that is surrendered or cancelled ceases to be of any force or effect or, if suspended, is invalid for the period to the suspension (s 13(4)).

Appeals

An appeal lies to the District Court against a decision of the EPA:

- to refuse to grant the person a licence, registration or accreditation;
- to impose or vary conditions of a licence, registration or accreditation; or
- to refuse to vary a licence or accreditation; or
- to suspend or cancel a licence, registration or accreditation. (s 14)

The appeal is a new hearing and new evidence may be adduced. The decision of the District Court is final and must be given effect to by the EPA (s 14(2), (3)).

Exemptions

The Regulations make provision for the Minister to grant an exemption from compliance with some of the requirements of the Act. The Minister is required to seek the advice of the Radiation Advisory Council before granting an exemption (s 39(1)). Examples of exemptions granted include exemptions from licensing requirements for certain persons, such as postgraduate students in a university undertaking research, and so forth (*Radiation Control Regulation 2003* (cl 8)). The Minister can also exempt premises from registration for use of radioactive substances specified in Sch 3B to the Regulations. These include substances such as americium 241 in industrial smoke detectors.

Liability of employers

If an employee commits an offence, the employer is taken to have committed the same offence, notwithstanding that the employee had contravened orders (s 22(1)). It is a defence if the employer establishes that he or she had no knowledge of the contravention and could not, by the exercise of due diligence, have prevented it (s 22(2)). Proceedings may be taken against an employer whether or not the employee has been proceeded against or convicted (s 22(3)).

Corporate officer liability

If a corporation commits an offence, each person who is a director of the corporation or concerned in the management of the corporation is taken to have contravened the same provision, if the person knowingly authorised or permitted the contravention. A person may be convicted whether or not the corporation is prosecuted (s 23). Unlike employees, directors are not provided with any specific defences.

Safety requirements

A number of requirements are specified in the *Radiation Control Regulation* to ensure radiation safety in the workplace. Amongst other requirements, an employer must ensure that:

- employees are not exposed to excessive amounts of ionising radiation (dose limits are specified in Sch 2) (cl 14);
- employees are fully aware of the hazards of radioactive substances and apparatus, as well as safety procedures and reporting requirements (cl 15);
- a radiation safety manual is prepared or adopted, if required (cl 16);
- exposed employees are issued with personal monitoring devices and records are kept of their exposure (cll 17-18);
- a monitoring device is installed and maintained on the premises, if required (cll 19-20);
- no person is exposed to ionising radiation for scientific or research purposes except as provided in the document *Administration of Ionizing Radiation to Human Subjects in Medical Research* (cl 22);
- radioactive substances and apparatus are not disposed of without EPA consent (cl 23);
- radioactive substances and apparatus are rendered inoperable before disposal, and records of their discharge must be kept (cll 23-24);
- safety requirements are observed in transporting radioactive substances (see *Code of Practice for the Safe Transport of Radioactive Material*) (cl 25);
- particulars of radiation accidents are reported and investigated, and records maintained (cl 28);
- faults in radiation apparatus must be reported to persons who have been exposed, and the faulty apparatus removed or repaired (cl 29);
- warning signs are displayed at premises where radiation apparatus or radioactive substances are kept (cl 36).

The maximum penalty for an offence against the Regulations is $2750.

Notices

An authorised officer may serve a written notice on a person if he or she believes on reasonable grounds that a contravention of the Act, Regulations or conditions of a licence has occurred; or if a person is responsible for any unnecessary exposure to, or contamination by, radiation (s 18). The notice may direct the person on whom it is served to take specified steps to comply with the direction within a specified time; and must inform the person that they have seven days in which to make submissions to the EPA as to why they should not comply (s 18(2)). The Council must be advised of the notices as soon as practicable. If the person fails to make a submission to the EPA or is unsuccessful, they must comply with the notice (s 18(4)). Failure to comply is an offence subject to a maximum penalty of $22,000 on conviction.

An appeal lies to the District Count against a decision of the EPA. Compliance with the notice is suspended until the appeal is determined or withdrawn. The appeal is a new hearing and new evidence can be adduced. The decision of the court is final and must be given effect to by the EPA (s 18(5)).

Directions

If the EPA believes a dangerous or potentially dangerous situation exists, involving actual or threatened exposure of any person, animal or thing or the environment to an excessive level of radiation or contamination of any person or premises by a radioactive substance, the EPA may give directions to avoid, remove or alleviate the danger. Directions may involve requiring a person to cease activities or to take action or to remove the substance or anything contaminated by it for disposal or treatment (s 19). The EPA can give any other direction it considers appropriate or take any action necessary to alleviate the danger (s 19(1)(a)-(d)). These directions may be given or action taken by the EPA or, with its prior approval, by an authorised officer, police officer or other EPA appointee (s 19(2)).

A direction may by given by notice in the Gazette or by personal service. Oral directions may be given in emergency situations, but must be confirmed in writing within 24 hours (s 19(3)).

It is an offence to contravene a direction or hinder any person exercising any function or complying with a direction. The maximum penalty is $165,000 for a corporation and $27,500 for an individual offender (s 19(4)).

Decontamination and acquisition of premises

The EPA may require or facilitate the decontamination or removal and disposal of premises contaminated by radioactivity. The EPA is also authorised to acquire contaminated premises. Premises are regarded as contaminated if there is a level of radioactivity of or above a prescribed level (s 21).

Increased penalty for offence causing serious harm

If a person is convicted of an offence in relation to licensing, registration, accreditation or an EPA direction and it is proved beyond reasonable doubt that the person knew that its commission was likely to cause serious harm to a person, animal or thing or the environment by exposure to radiation, the maximum penalty in respect of the offence is increased to $1.1 million in the case of a corporation and $165,000 and or two years' imprisonment in the case of an individual offender (s 24).

Penalty notices

An authorised officer or police officer may serve a penalty notice on a person who has contravened the Act or Regulations (s 25A). The notice contains a fine and must be paid within 28 days. If the penalty is paid, the person is not liable for any further proceedings (s 25A(5)). Penalty notices are available for a number of offences in the Act and regulations where the breach is of a minor nature. Those offences which can be dealt with by way of penalty notice are specified in Sch 4 to the Regulations. The maximum penalty prescribed is $1500 for a corporation and $750 for an individual.

Proceedings for offences

Offences can be prosecuted in a Local Court or in the Supreme Court. Proceedings in the Local Court require the consent of the EPA, while proceedings in the Supreme Court require the consent of the Minister. The maximum penalty which the Local Court may impose is $11,000 (s 25).

On conviction, the court may order forfeiture to the Crown of any radioactive substance or radiation apparatus in respect of which the offence was committed if it is the property of the defendant. The court may also order forfeiture of property seized by an authorised officer on application by the EPA (s 27).

Recovery of costs

If costs or expenses are incurred by the EPA or a public body in taking action or causing action to be taken in respect of danger or potential danger resulting from a contravention of the Act, those costs can be recovered from the responsible person in a court of competent jurisdiction as a debt (s 28).

Protection from personal liability

The Act exempts members of the Radiation Advisory Council, persons acting under their direction, or authorised officers from any personal liability for acts or omissions taken in good faith for the purposes of executing the Act (s 39A).

13

CORPORATE SOCIAL RESPONSIBILITY

What is Corporate Social Responsibility?

As we have discussed elsewhere in this book, market mechanisms are being relied on to achieve environmental and social outcomes. One such market mechanism is the concept of corporate social responsibility (CSR) to which corporations voluntarily commit in order to demonstrate that they have integrated environmental and social considerations into their overall management systems. Corporations expect that by doing this they will gain various benefits in the market. This chapter discusses the growing trend among global and Australian corporations to demonstrate that they conduct their activities in accordance with the notion of CSR. The World Business Council on Sustainable Development has defined CSR as:

> 'business' commitment to contribute to sustainable economic development, working with employees, their families, the local community, and society at large to improve their quality of life.[1]

Essentially, CSR is a concept whereby companies integrate social and environmental concerns in their business operations and in their interactions with their stakeholders on a voluntary basis. The Australian Corporations and Markets Advisory Committee (CAMAC), in its December 2006 Report entitled *The Social Responsibility of Corporations*,[2] outlines the various approaches to CSR including the compliance, philanthropic, business, and the social primacy approaches. The compliance approach to CSR emphasises that while companies are obliged to comply with the letter of the law they may also benefit by complying with the 'spirit' of the law. This means that companies may be expected to go beyond compliance to help safeguard the company against various reputational and other risks to longer term shareholder value.

The philanthropic approach involves companies giving financial, or other types of contributions, to the community and may extend to charitable causes. The business approach emphasises that it is likely to be in the company's own interests to take its social and environmental responsibilities into account. This involves both assessing the corporate benefit of CSR and the need for appropriate risk-management strategies. The social primacy approach requires company directors to take

---

1 See <http://www.wbcsd.org/templates/TemplateWBCSD1/layout.asp?type=p&MenuId=MzI3&doOpen=1&ClickMenu=LeftMenu> (accessed 31 March 2006); see also the WBCSD's publication entitled *CSR: making good business sense*, <http://www.wbcsd.org/DocRoot/IunSPdIKvmYH5HjbN4XC/csr2000.pdf> (accessed 31 March 2006).

2 See <http://www.camac.gov.au/camac/camac.nsf/byHeadline/PDFFinal+Reports+2006/$file/CSR_Report.pdf> (accessed 17 December 2006).

various ethical values or standards into account when making corporate decisions. The altruistic approach sees corporations playing an important role in solving social problems and advancing public welfare, given the privileged status of corporations in society especially their establishment as entities with limited liability.

In a practical sense, CSR expects that corporations will put strategies in place to deal with their environmental impacts. These would include: energy and water use; greenhouse gas emissions; whether or not materials used and products and services are ecologically sustainable; minimisation of, and responsible management of, both solid and hazardous wastes; emissions and discharges of pollutants into the air, land and water; impacts on biodiversity; the use of ozone-depleting substances; ensuring an ecologically sustainable supply chain; and compliance with legally binding obligations.

A commitment to socially, as opposed to environmentally, responsible performance would generally be demonstrated by the extent to which a corporation is properly engaged with stakeholders who are allowed to participate in its decision-making processes; compliance with minimum labour protection; HIV/AIDS; fair competition; and corporate governance. The CSR agenda can also drive consideration of corporate behaviour within the context of World Trade Organization activities, for example, the potential negative market access impacts of labelling or certification schemes and their compatibility with WTO rules. Being transparent is one of the key requirements of good corporate behaviour and so effective communication with key stakeholders like consumers, employees, community members, non-government organisation (NGOs), governments and relevant international institutions is crucial.

Impetus for CSR

The literature on CSR points to three fundamental reasons for the emergence, and adoption by corporations, of CSR. They are various global changes which have forced corporations to take CSR seriously, stakeholder expectations and the threat of climate change litigation. The growth of socially responsible investing (SRI) may also be regarded as providing an impetus for CSR and is discussed in a case study on CSR and the finance sector.

Global changes

The global forces which have driven companies to internalise the principles of CSR include far reaching changes, or revolutions, in technology and communications; markets; demographics and development; and values.[3] The communications revolution means that people all over the world have access to information about companies, and more especially about any breaches of environmental, health and safety and labour standards and regulations. The internet can be, and has been, used to mobilise powerful campaigns against corporations.

The revolution in markets has come about as a result of the collapse of Communism at the end of the 1980s and the endless processes of liberalisation, privati-

3 See generally D Grayson and A Hodges, *Corporate Social Opportunity!* (Greenleaf Publishing, 2004) at 24-34.

sation and globalisation facilitated by international trade law.[4] In this climate, the activities of corporations can be more closely scrutinised by funders which are approached by corporations wanting to raise funds on international financial markets. Their decision to invest will be based on a range of factors including environmental and social issues. Changing demographics may also impact on corporations. In the developed world these changes are evident in lower birthrates, an ageing population and increased cultural diversity. Corporations need to factor these into their corporate responses as well as realising that global inequalities are highly visible via 24-hour satellite TV and the internet. Significant increases in wealth, choice and education have also allowed people across the globe to express their values freely. Research has shown that, since the well-publicised corporate scandals and collapses of recent times, public trust in governments and companies has been in steep decline.

Stakeholder expectations

In addition to global changes, stakeholder expectations have provided an important impetus for getting corporations to engage with CSR. Stakeholders actually drive changes in corporate behaviour and also play a vital consultation role when corporations decide to devise a CSR strategy. With respect to CSR, corporations need to consider various stakeholders including: employees; investors; consumers; business partners and suppliers; non-governmental organisations (NGOs) and media campaigns; governmental, intergovernmental organisation and regulatory pressures; and community and society.[5]

- employees:
    - o need to trust an employer which mirrors their own values,
    - o expect an employer to assist with establishing a work-life balance, to make adequate contributions to health, well-being and pension needs, to provide training opportunities towards future employability, and respect their rights to privacy at work and at home, and
    - o expect an employer to be socially and environmentally responsible and to share their own social interests;
- investors:
    - o exert considerable pressure on corporations through 'socially responsible investment' (SRI) programs, which assist investors to make decisions based on the combination of good financial returns and socially, environmentally and ethically responsible business practices,
    - o expect that due diligence procedures adopted by corporations will include CSR issues and an assessment of reputation and operational risks, and that there are adequate corporate governance frameworks in place, and
    - o expect compliance with the law;

---

4 Grayson and Hodges give the example of coffee farmers in Cote d'Ivoire who check cocoa prices directly on the Chicago commodities exchange through their village cell phones, and who are no longer dependent on the biased price indicators of local traders: ibid at 26.

5 Ibid at 36-50.

- consumers:
    - o are increasingly making purchasing decisions based on the social, ethical and environmental credentials of a product as well as the integrity of product manufacturing and quality, for example, the use of genetically modified organisms, workplace practices (sweatshops) and food health and safety,
    - o want money raised from product purchases to be linked to contributions to social causes, and
    - o expect products to be properly labelled, responsibly marketed and distribution and access to be adequately covered;
- business partner and supplier relationships relate to the fact that business partners do not want to have their reputations affected by an extended supply chain which may turn out not to be compliant with social, environmental and ethical standards, while suppliers expect to receive technical support to meet these standards;
- NGOs:
    - o act as self-appointed corporate watchdogs and expect companies to be transparent and to have any triple bottom line or sustainability reports independently verified,
    - o expect to be engaged in an ongoing dialogue with corporations in a partnership which addresses social, economic and environmental challenges,
    - o expect corporations to pay penalties for breaking the law, and
    - o engage in media campaigns which can be particularly damaging to a corporation's reputation and profile as a good corporate citizen;[6]
- government, intergovernmental organisation and regulatory pressures:
    - o with an increasing number of former government responsibilities being privatised and contracted out, the government has oversight obligations over an ever growing corporate sector,
    - o corporations are being expected to engage increasingly in public policy formulation, public-private partnerships for the provision of services, and
    - o pressure from lobbyists and stakeholders resulting in governments imposing environmental, social and ethical obligations on corporations, as well as requiring corporations to engage in CSR-type activities;

---

6 One of the most recent successful NGO campaigns is the Greenpeace and Sea Shepherd campaign against Japan's whaling activities in December 2005. Greenpeace conducted a concerted consumer campaign against fishing companies linked to the whaling company Nissui. For example, 40,000 emails were sent to the chief executive of Sealord, a New Zealand company half owned by Nissui. In Argentina, a seafood company cancelled contracts with Nissui after 21,000 emails were sent to the company. Nissui and five other fishing companies will now get rid of their whaling fleet and Nissui has undertaken to stop processing and distributing whale meat in Japan: see A Darby, 'Japanese companies back out of whaling', *Sydney Morning Herald*, 4 April 2006, p 3.

- community and society concerns:
  - local communities are often affected by the activities of corporations and expect to be consulted, and
  - corporations are expected to treat Indigenous people and ethnic minorities fairly.

The 'value' proposition

Another view which has been advocated by a leading global sustainability strategy consultancy, Ecos Corporation, is that CSR is 'good for business' and that for this reason it motivates corporations to adopt it.[7] What Ecos Corporation advocates is that a primary focus should be placed on CSR creating value for corporations, rather than emphasising the moral imperative or social responsibility. A focus on value is likely to drive change within corporations for three principal reasons:

- value is more likely to be created if value is the focus of all actions and initiatives undertaken in the name of sustainability;
- financial markets are more likely to recognise and reward companies that consistently measure and report on creating value from sustainability;
- corporate sustainability is more likely to succeed in the long term if investor recognition creates a self-perpetuating loop which encourages more business action on sustainability.[8]

Ecos points to the fact that a variety of different studies conducted by business school professors at the Universities of Michigan and Harvard[9] consistently find a statistically significant, positive relationship between crude measures of social and environmental performance and financial performance.

Threat of climate change litigation

The threat of climate change litigation has arisen in recent years as non-government organisations have made it clear that they are looking for opportunities to hold corporations liable for the damage which their greenhouse gas emissions may cause. In 2003, an alliance of 70 environmental organisations, lawyers, academics and individuals in 29 countries, known as the Climate Justice Program, announced a strategy for worldwide climate change litigation. Climate litigation to date has included both public law and private law actions, although the majority of them have been public law actions.[10] Public law actions are those that are brought against

---

7 See P Gilding, M Hogarth, D Reed and CFA, *Single bottom line sustainability* (Ecos Corporation, 2002).

8 Ibid at 10.

9 See JD Margolis and JP Walsh, *People and Profits: The Search for a Link between a Company's Social and Financial Performance* (Lawrence Erlbaum Associates, 2000) and <http://www.sristudies.org> and <http://web.mit.edu/doncram/www/environmental/envir-fin-literature.html>, all cited by Gilding et al, above n 7, at 24.

10 For example, an action brought by an alliance of non-government organisations and cities in the United States against the US export credit agencies for funding fossil fuel projects under the *National Environmental Policy Act* (US) (NEPA) (see <http://www.climatelawsuit.org> for further information); an action brought by 12 States, several US cities and a number of NGOs against the Environmental Protection Agency for failing to regulate greenhouse gas emissions under the *Clean Air Act* (see <http://www.climatelaw.org/media/states.challenge/bush> for further information);

a government agency alleging that the agency has breached its duty to perform its statutory functions. In the case of climate change, the allegation would be that the agency has failed to take into account the consequences of greenhouse gas emissions for global climate change, in performing functions such as making policy and issuing licences and permissions.

However, as far as CSR is concerned, it is the threat of a private, or civil law, action that is of most concern for corporations. Under the law of torts, a person, including a corporation, can be sued for infringing another person's legal rights as a result of being either negligent or creating a nuisance. To bring an action under the law of negligence, a plaintiff would have to show that the defendant owed the plaintiff a duty to take reasonable care, that the defendant breached that duty by failing to take care, that the breach caused the injury or damage, and that the damage suffered by the plaintiff was not too remote a consequence of the breach of the duty. Of course, it is difficult for a plaintiff to establish the duty of care with respect to damage caused by global climate change because it must be established that the harm was reasonably foreseeable by the defendant. Also, according to the causation element in a negligence action, the plaintiff must be able to show, on a balance of probabilities, that the defendant's negligence caused, or materially contributed to, the damage caused by climate change.

The law of nuisance discriminates between private and public nuisances, but since an action based on private nuisance must relate to interferences with a person's use of his or her land, an action in climate change is much more likely to be based on public nuisance. A public nuisance is an interference with a public or a common law right such as the public's right to a clean and healthy environment, safety, enjoyment or comfort. In 2004, the first civil climate change action, based on public nuisance of global warming, was brought by the States of Connecticut, New York, California, Iowa, New Jersey, Rhode Island, Vermont and Wisconsin, and the City of New York. It was brought against six US energy companies, American Electric Power Company, Inc, American Electric Power Service Corporation, the Southern Company, Tennessee Valley Authority, XCEL Energy Inc and Cinergy Corporation, seeking an abatement of the defendants' ongoing greenhouse gas emissions. Their annual carbon dioxide emissions are approximately 650 million tons of carbon dioxide which makes them among the largest emitters of greenhouse gases in the world.

The public injuries mentioned by the plaintiffs are intensified and prolonged heat waves leading to increased heat-related deaths; increased respiratory problems like asthma caused by smog; various coastal impacts such as beach erosion, the inundation of coastal land, and the salinisation of water supplies from accelerated sea level rise; threats to California's water supply as a result of a reduction of mountain snow pack in California; impaired commercial shipping, recreation and hydropower generation caused by lowered Great Lakes water level; threats to human safety caused by more droughts and floods; and a widespread loss of bio-

(*cont*)

two separate actions brought in the NSW Land and Environment Court challenging the granting of development consent to new fossil fuel power stations under the *Environmental Planning and Assessment Act 1979* (NSW); and an appeal against a planning decision in Victoria to allow the extension of a coal mine to fuel a fossil fuel power station (see <http://climatelaw.org.media/CANA> Australia for further information).

diversity, including the loss of hardwood forests from the northern United States. Such impacts will also result in economic loss.[11]

Although such lawsuits pose significant challenges and obstacles, the exponential growth in climate change litigation has led commentators to say that such litigation 'against companies in carbon-intensive industries such as oil and gas, electric utilities, and automobile manufacturing seems inevitable'. In fact, similarities are being drawn between the liability of tobacco companies and emitters of greenhouse gas emissions for the damage caused because of 'consistent patterns of denial and deception by various companies ... [although] ... [t]he big difference is that the financial liability is going to be much greater for climate change'.[12]

It is clear that corporations which are heavy greenhouse gas emitters need to factor into their CSR strategies the ways in which they are dealing with their emissions (see Ceres report below).

Leading organisations involved in CSR

There are a number of international initiatives on CSR, a few of which deserve special mention because of their contribution to this issue.

Organisations developing the concept of CSR

There are a number of private sector initiatives which have helped to develop the concept of CSR as well as advocate its adoption by corporations. As can be seen, currently there is no agreed single definition of CSR, and no single institution with the mandate to develop one. However, there are a number of key themes inherent in the concept of CSR. They are:

- a commitment to sustainable development;
- engagement with key stakeholders;
- integrating CSR into management practices;
- reporting on social and environmental performance; and
- independent verification of reporting.

World Business Council for Sustainable Development

The World Business Council for Sustainable Development (WBCSD) is an alliance of 180 international companies which are committed to sustainable development through economic growth, ecological balance and social progress. Its membership is drawn from more than 30 countries and 20 major industrial sectors. It also liaises with a global network of approximately 50 national and regional business councils and partner organisations.

---

11 United States District Court for the Southern District of New York, 21 July 2004.

12 See, eg, William Baue, 'Climate Change Litigation Could Affect Companies' Market Value' *Social Funds.com*, 23 July 2003, <http://www.socialfunds.com/news/article.cgi/article1180.html> (accessed 22 April 2006); see also 'California's Climate Change Litigation Heralded at International Conference', Pacific Research Institute, 17 December 2004.

The WBCSD has played a very significant role in articulating the philosophy behind, and parameters of, CSR. The WBCSD has always stressed that sustainable development requires the integration of economic growth, ecological balance and social progress, and that CSR may be used as an engine for social progress. CSR is seen as providing a vision that can help companies maintain their 'licence to operate' in an increasingly globalised world.

One of the most important publications developed by the WBCSD is *CSR: making good business sense.*[13] In this publication the WBCSD states that:

- there are clear business and societal benefits to be gained from developing a coherent CSR strategy based on integrity, sound values and a long-term approach;
- the human face of business can be demonstrated through the development of a CSR strategy;
- the development of the strategy requires an open dialogue with all interested and affected stakeholders;
- although global standards and practices must be adhered to, CSR strategies should be implemented in a way that respects local and cultural differences; and
- specific initiatives must be taken as part of the commitment to local differences.[14]

The publication contains the following sections: Headlines - which explains how and why a corporation should approach CSR; Soundings - which points out the different regional perspectives on CSR; Practical Steps - which provides hands-on tools to develop and implement CSR strategies; CSR Navigator - which provides 12 points for guiding a corporation through its CSR direction and performance; and The Way Forward - which deals with questions and queries about CSR.

The WBCSD, along with other organisations, has been responsible for turning CSR into a mainstream business issue, rather than a fringe issue.

Ceres

Ceres[15] is the leading coalition of environmental, investor and advocacy groups in the United States, comprising over 80 organisations which work together for a sustainable future. Ceres has played a significant role in clarifying and developing the concept of CSR. This is principally through the development of the Ceres Principles which is a 10-point code of corporate environmental conduct which requires corporations to report periodically on environmental management structures and results. Over 50 companies have endorsed the Ceres Principles, including 13 Fortune 500 firms. Companies that endorse the Principles go voluntarily beyond the requirements of the law to abide by an environmental ethic. The Principles also give investors and others a benchmark against which to assess the environmental performance of companies.

The Ceres Principles include the following commitments:

---

13 Above n 1.

14 Above n 1, at 3.

15 For more information on Ceres, see <http://www.ceres.org/ceres/> (accessed 5 April 2006).

- protection of the biosphere;
- sustainable use of natural resources;
- reduction and disposal of wastes;
- energy conservation;
- environmental, health and safety risk reduction;
- safe products and services;
- environmental restoration;
- informing the public where health, safety and environment might be endangered;
- management commitment to implementing the principles;
- conducting audits and reporting on progress.

Perhaps one of the most groundbreaking reports to be released in recent time by Ceres is the 2006 'Corporate Governance and Climate Change: Making the Connection' report. It includes findings on how 20 of the world's biggest corporate emitters of greenhouse gases are factoring climate change risks and opportunities into their governance practices. The report features 14 specific governance actions that companies can take to address climate change.

The report identifies several problems areas including:

- lack of disclosure in securities filings;
- inadequate board reviews;
- undeveloped strategies to address risks and opportunities, including insufficient actions to reduce emissions.

The report states that effective corporate responses to climate change will be built on a foundation of well functioning environmental management systems and focused governance practices.

The climate change governance checklist identifies the following 14 specific actions that companies are taking to implement governance actions. These include:

- board level
    - o give direct oversight responsibility for environmental affairs to a committee of directors,
    - o monitor company response strategies and conduct a formal board-level review of climate change;
- management level
    - o require the chief environmental officer to report directly to the CEO, or the CEO's executive committee,
    - o factor greenhouse gas targets into employee compensation,
    - o CEO to make clear statement supporting company's climate change response;
- reporting
    - o ensure that the company's securities filings include a statement on material risks and opportunities posed by climate change,
    - o ensure that climate change and greenhouse issues are reported in sustainability or triple bottom line reports;

- emissions data
  - o greenhouse gas emissions savings and offsets from company projects should be calculated and registered,
  - o report results of company's emissions inventory directly to shareholders,
  - o establish emissions baseline (dating back at least 10 years) to gauge company's emissions trends,
  - o make projections and set firm company-wide targets to control future emissions,
  - o have emissions data verified by external auditor;
- other actions
  - o participate in voluntary greenhouse gas emissions trading schemes,
  - o purchase and/or develop renewable energy sources.

It may be that companies that comply with all of the suggestions made in this Report will be less vulnerable to climate change litigation.

SustainAbility

SustainAbility, a strategy consultancy and independent think tank which was established in 1987, specialises in the business risks and market opportunities of corporate responsibility and sustainable development. SustainAbility has offices in Europe and the United States and liaises with leading global companies and NGOs. It has played a substantial role in defining the ambit of CSR.

In 2005, SustainAbility released a leading report *The Changing Landscape of Liability: A Director's Guide to Trends in Corporate Environmental, Social and Economic Liability.*[16]

The Report notes that the landscape of liability is changing for the following reasons:

- the existence of a new legal landscape whereby causes of action, standards of evidence and procedural rules in court are shifting;
- there are new forms of legal activism including a highly profitable class action 'industry' and lawyers who are committed to social and environmental justice rather than to pursuing high salaries and career development;
- there is an accelerating shift in societal values and expectations as well as a demand for greater corporate accountability;
- there is a progressive 'internalisation' of social and environmental costs which brings businesses into the firing line for past and future impacts;
- there is a sense that technical compliance with the law is not enough and that escaping legal liability through subtle interpretations of the law is not acceptable; and
- recognition of the moral liability of companies, which usually exists and precedes any legislative activity in the area.

---

16 See <http://www.sustainability.com/insight/liability.asp> (accessed 10 April 2006).

SustainAbility notes that there is an increasing convergence between legal and moral liability. Deepening legal liability has the following consequences:

- the protection of the 'corporate veil' is weakening;
- legacies and liabilities are stretching further back in time and retrospective standards are being imposed;
- global standards are being applied and companies have supply chain accountability;
- increasing responsibility for consumer protection and risk disclosure;
- higher risk-management standards and increased investor suits;
- a lowering thresholds for compensation actions and increasing awards for damages.

Moral liability is hardening in the following ways:

- licence to operate – there must be compliance with the spirit of this principle, voluntary agreements will need to be struck and stakeholder outrage will need to be avoided;
- shareholder activism – increasing investment screening and risk and ethical resolutions being made;
- economic equity – demands for fair trade/pricing and responsible tax planning;
- governance – higher risk-management expectations and responsible investment/divestment;
- disclosure – pressure on 'creative' accounting, transparency regarding political lobbying and the increasing role of the whistleblower;
- goodwill – is vulnerable to CSR failures which damage reputation and result from market campaigns.

The key recommendations of the Report are that there is a need to shift from passive to active CSR; pursue the highest standards of CSR; ensure the alignment of standards and behaviours; make stakeholder engagement an essential and integral part of risk management; recognise that legal activism is a growing force for greater accountability; review on and off balance sheet risks; and apply new diligence to due diligence in investment and divestment processes.

The Report also presents four case studies to illustrate the changing landscape of liability. These include climate change; corporate accountability for human rights abuses in developing countries; obesity; and legacy or demands for continuing reparations related to pre-acquisition legacies.

Organisations endorsing CSR

Endorsement to the principles of CSR has come from a number of quarters.

UN Global Compact

The UN Global Compact was an initiative of UN Secretary-General Kofi Annan who, in 1999, advocated the establishment of a Compact between governments, corporations, labour and civil society organisations. The purpose of the Compact is to support universal environmental and social principles. The Global Compact was officially launched at the UN Headquarters on 26 July 2000. Now, hundreds of corporations from all over the world, and international labour and civil society organisations, are engaged in the Global Compact. The Global Compact is a purely voluntary initiative with two objectives:

- to mainstream the 10 principles in business activities around the world;
- to catalyse actions in support of UN goals.

The 10 universal principles include principles on human rights, labour standards, the environment and anti-corruption.[17]

OECD's Guidelines for Multinational Enterprises

In 2001, the Organization for Economic Co-operation and Development (OECD) developed Guidelines for Multinational Enterprises (the Guidelines)[18] which provide voluntary principles and standards for responsible business conduct. The Guidelines are endorsed by the governments of the OECD members as well as Argentina, Brazil and Chile and are intended to both complement and reinforce private efforts to define and implement responsible business conduct. The aims of the Guidelines are 'to ensure that the operations of multinational corporations are in harmony with government policies, to strengthen the basis of mutual confidence between enterprises and the societies in which they operate, to help improve the foreign investment climate and to enhance the contribution to sustainable development made by multinational enterprises'.[19] The Guidelines are complemented by implementation procedures whereby adhering governments agree to promote observance of the Guidelines. The following issues are dealt with by the Guidelines: Disclosure; Employment and Industrial Relations; Environment; Combating Bribery; Consumer Interests; Science and Technology; Competition and Taxation.

European Commission

In 2001, the European Commission released a Green Paper on promoting a European framework for Corporate Social Responsibility (CSR).[20] This was followed by an extensive consultation procedure on the concept of CSR. Finally in December 2002, the Commission adopted the Resolution of the Employment and Social Policy Council on CSR.[21]

The Commission's view, as stated in the Resolution, is that

> [A] strategy to promote CSR should be based on:
> - recognition of the voluntary nature of CSR;
> - a need for credibility and transparency of CSR practices;

---

17 See <http://www.unglobalcompact.org/AboutTheGC/TheTenPrinciples/index.html> (accessed 21 April 2006).

18 See <http://www.olis.oecd.org/olis/2000doc.nsf/4f7adc214b91a685c12569fa005d0ee7/d1bada1e70ca5d90c1256af6005ddad5/$FILE/JT00115758.DOC> (accessed 21 April 2006).

19 Ibid, Preface.

20 See <http://europa.eu.int/comm/employment_social/soc-dial/csr/greenpaper_en.pdf> (accessed 12 April 2006).

21 See <http://europa.eu.int/comm/employment_social/soc-dial/csr/csr_resolution.html> (accessed 12 April 2006).

- a focus on activities where Community involvement adds value;
- a balanced and broad approach to CSR, including economic, social and environmental issues as well as consumer interests;
- attention to the specific needs and characteristics of SMEs; and
- support of, and compatibility with, existing internationally agreed instruments.[22]

The Resolution emphasises that when businesses adopt CSR strategies they are 'going beyond compliance' to behave in a way not necessarily required by law, but which is relevant to broader questions of corporate governance and accountability. Also, given the complexity of business in a globalised world, CSR strategies should apply to the subsidiaries and subcontractors of a corporation. CSR strategies should address internal aspects such as human resource management and health and safety issues, as well as establishing a framework for social and civil dialogue.

Various initiatives are set out in the Resolution to be pursued by the Commission to promote CSR and to work with a Multi-Stakeholder Forum on CSR at the EU level. Member states are called upon to pursue CSR strategies at the national level.

Organisations setting standards

As mentioned above, stakeholders expect that, at a minimum, corporations will comply with all legal and other industry standards as part and parcel of their commitment to CSR. While every country has its own legislative framework for managing economic, environmental and social issues, considerable work has been done at the international level to develop standards with which corporations ought to comply.

International Organisation for Standardisation (ISO)

The ISO is a non-government organisation which is essentially a federation of the national standards bodies from 149 countries from all regions of the world and representing developed, developing and transitional economies. As a global network, the ISO sets standards for a wide range of products, services and organisational matters, which distil an international consensus from the broad base of stakeholder groups. The central secretariat is based in Geneva.

To date, the ISO has developed 15,036 standards for almost every sector of business, industry and technology. ISO standards are voluntary but in spite of this a number of standards, especially those concerned with health, safety or the environment, have been adopted in some countries as part of their regulatory framework. Also, although ISO standards are voluntary, in the environmental area, compliance with ISO standards has become a common market requirement.

For our purposes, the most important ISO standards are those which fall within the umbrella of ISO 14000.[23] ISO 14000 standards represent 'generic management system standards' which means that they can be applied to any organisation, whatever its product. The management system has a number of essential features which

22 Ibid.

23 For detailed information, see <http://www.iso.org/iso/en/prods-services/otherpubs/iso14000/index.html> (accessed 4 April 2006).

are spelled out in the relevant standards. ISO 14000 requires organisations to minimise harmful effects on the environment caused by its activities, and to achieve continual improvement of its environmental performance. ISO 14000 standards include:

- ISO 14001 and 14004 – environmental management systems;
- ISO 14020 – environmental labels and declarations;
- ISO 14030 – environmental performance evaluation;
- ISO 14040 – life cycle assessment;
- ISO 14062 – design for the environment; and
- ISO 14063 – environmental communication (on performance).[24]

New standard for greenhouse gases

The new ISO 14064 Standard on Greenhouse Gases Accounting and Verification is the latest addition to the ISO 14000 suite of International Standards for environmental management. It provides governments and industry with an integrated set of tools for programs aimed at reducing greenhouse gas emissions, as well as emissions trading. The Standard is intended to provide clarity and consistency between those reporting GHG emissions and their stakeholders. The Standard is the result of three years of research and engagement with the international community of governmental and business organisations, including 175 experts from 45 different countries. The Standard is intended to achieve the following outcomes:

- improve the quantification, monitoring, reporting and verification of GHG by promoting consistency, transparency and credibility;
- enable organisations to identify and manage GHG-related liabilities, assets and risks;
- stimulate emissions trading by facilitating the trade of GHG allowances or credits; and
- allow for the design, development and implementation of comparable and consistent GHG schemes or programs.

There are three standards under the ISO 14064 banner which can be used independently, or in an integrated way, to meet the needs of GHG accounting and verification. The standards are:

- ISO 14064-1:2006 Greenhouse Gases – Part 1: Specification with guidance at the organisation level for the quantification and reporting of GHG emissions and removals;
- ISO 14064-2:2006 Greenhouse Gases – Part 2: Specification with guidance at the project level for the quantification, monitoring and reporting of GHG emission reductions and removal enhancements;
- ISO 14064-3:2006 Greenhouse Gases – Part 3: Specification with guidance for the validation and verification of greenhouse gas assertions.

---

24 See <http://www.iso.org/iso/en/prods-services/otherpubs/iso14000/model.pdf> (accessed on 4 April 2006).

In early 2007, ISO 14065 will be published. This Standard will set out the specific requirements for accrediting bodies that undertake GHG validation or verification using ISO 14064.

Announcement of new standard for social responsibility

The ISO has announced that it will develop international standards for social responsibility, to be known as ISO 26000 guidance standard on social responsibility.[25] The decision to develop the international standards for social responsibility was made in June 2004 and is based on current trends and initiatives in the global economy. The ISO Social Responsibility standards are not intended to be used as certification, rather the objective is to produce guidance documents that are written in plain language and can be used by non-specialists. The new standards propose to add value to current international legal frameworks relevant to social responsibility, such as the UN Universal Declaration of Human Rights, and those adopted by the International Labour Organization (ILO), and other UN Conventions.

The new ISO Social Responsibility standards are not expected to be in place until 2008.

Organisations promoting reporting on CSR

Triple Bottom Line (TBL), or Sustainability, reporting may be used by corporations to demonstrate to capital markets and the general public that they are aware of, responding to, and managing their impacts on the environment and society. TBL reporting may benefit stakeholders by assisting shareholders and the market to assess how well corporations are dealing with non-financial risk. It helps investors with ethical concerns to make decisions and informs other stakeholders about the societal and environmental impact of the company. Some of the perceived benefits of producing a TBL or Sustainability Report are the ability to benchmark performance; improve operations and management; enhance reputation and capacity to recruit and retain excellent staff; improved management of risks; creation of market opportunities; greater control of environmental disclosure; satisfying any mandatory reporting requirements; and gaining the confidence of investors, insurers and financial institutions.[26]

The Global Reporting Initiative

The Global Reporting Initiative (GRI)[27] is the most influential international organisation in the field of reporting on CSR. GRI describes itself as a multi-stakeholder process and independent institution which incorporates the active participation of representatives from business, accountancy, investment, environmental, human rights, and research and labour organisations from around the world. It is an official collaborating centre of the UN Environment Programme (UNEP) and works in co-operation with UN Secretary-General Kofi Annan's Global Compact.

25 See <http://www.iso.org/iso/en/commcentre/pressreleases/archives/2005/Ref972.html> (accessed 4 April 2006).

26 See *The State of Sustainability Reporting in Australia 2005* at 32, <http://www.deh.gov.au/settlements/industry/corporate/reporting/pubs/survey2005.pdf> (accessed 31 March 2006).

27 See <http://www.globalreporting.org/> (accessed 31 March 2006).

GRI made a substantial contribution to the field of CSR by developing the *2002 Sustainability Reporting Guidelines*.[28] The GRI Guidelines, which provide a global benchmark for voluntary sustainability and TBL reporting, define 'environmental indicators' as an organisation's impacts on living and non-living systems, including eco-systems, land, air and water. Included within environmental indicators are the environmental impacts of products and services. 'Social indicators' are an organisation's impacts on the social system within which it operates. This in turn is divided into three clusters: labour practices, human rights and broader social issues which affect consumers, communities and other stakeholders. The GRI Guidelines are now very influential worldwide.[29]

Ceres

In addition to the GRI Guidelines is another set of guidelines known as the Ceres Reporting Requirements for Small Enterprises and Non-profit Organisations: Year 2002 Reporting.[30] These guidelines are based on the GRI Guidelines but are tailored to small manufacturers and service-based enterprises.

Organisations measuring CSR performance

The Dow Jones Sustainability Indexes

As discussed in the section on Socially Responsible Investment (SRI) below, investors are increasingly trying to diversify their portfolios by investing in companies that set industry-wide best practices with regard to CSR. The reason for this is that the companies which are the leaders in the area of CSR are expected to show superior performance and favourable risk/return profiles. Indeed, a growing number of investors are convinced that sustainability has become a catalyst for enlightened and disciplined management, and thus a crucial success factor. In response to this, Dow Jones Indexes, STOXX Limited and SAM Group worked together to launch the Dow Jones Sustainability Indexes (DJSI).[31] The indexes reflect the combined expertise and resources of three highly qualified partners: the publisher of the world's best known stock indicator, Dow Jones Indexes; the leading European index provider, STOXX Limited; and the internationally renowned pioneer in sustainability investing, SAM Group.

The DJSI now provide private and institutional investors with a global, rational, consistent, flexible index to benchmark the performance of their sustainability investments. They also provide an independent reliable index as a basis for derivatives and funds focused on sustainability companies. The DJSI are also beneficial for corporations as the Indexes provide a financial quantification of their sustainability strategies and their management of sustainability opportunities, risks and costs. The

---

28 See <http://www.globalreporting.org> (accessed 31 March 2006).

29 See also Institute of Social and Ethical Accountability: AA1000 Standards, <www.accountability.org.uk> (accessed 31 March 2006); and The Social Reporting Report published by SustainAbility, <www.sustainability.co.uk> (accessed 31 March 2006).

30 See <http://www.ceres.org> (accessed 27 March 2006).

31 For more information on DJSI, see <http://www.sustainability-index.com/htmle/sustainability/sustinvestment.html> (accessed 6 April 2006).

DJSI is expected also to provide investors and companies with insight into the trends and events which drive the global supply and demand of sustainable products and services. This will bring a greater appreciation of the benefits of integrating sustainability principles in both corporate and investment strategies.

As a testament to the increasing importance of providing Sustainability Indexes, four new Indexes have been launched recently including:

- STOXX Limited and SAM Group European Blue Chip Sustainability Indexes (31 January 2006);
- Dow Jones STOXX Sustainability 40 Index and the Dow Jones EURO STOXX Sustainability 40 Index (31 January 2006);
- Dow Jones Islamic Market Sustainability Index (23 January 2006); and
- Dow Jones Sustainability North America Index (23 September 2005).

FTSE4Good Index

Another Index for measuring the performance of companies that meet globally recognised CSR standards is the FTSE4Good Index Series. The Index has been designed to measure the performance of companies that meet globally recognised corporate responsibility standards. FTSE4Good can be used for four different purposes: as a basis for making investment decisions about socially responsible financial instruments and fund products; as a research tool to identify socially responsible companies; as a reference tool to provide companies with a transparent and evolving global corporate responsibility standard to aspire to and surpass; and as a benchmark index to track the performance of socially responsible investment portfolios.

To be included in the FTSE4Good Index the following Inclusion Criteria[32] must be met. A corporation must be:

- working towards environmental sustainability;
- developing positive relationships with clients;
- upholding and supporting universal human rights;
- ensuring good supply chain labour standards; and
- countering bribery.

Environmental performance

With respect to environmental performance, industry sectors are graded according to whether or not they have high, medium or low impacts on the environment. Companies are then screened according to their policies, management systems and levels of reporting.

Regarding environmental policy, the criteria distinguish between core and desirable indicators. The core indicators are:

- the adoption of an environmental policy that relates to all key issues;
- that responsibility for policy is taken at the board or departmental level; and
- that commitments are made to targets, auditing and reporting.

---

32 See <http://www.ftse.com/Indices/FTSE4Good_Index_Series/Downloads/FTSE4Good_Inclusion_Criteria_Brochure_Feb_06.pdf> (accessed 6 April 2006).

The desirable indicators include:

- adherence to globally applicable corporate standards;
- engagement with stakeholders;
- addressing product or service impacts in policy;
- making strategic moves towards sustainability.

With regard to management systems, corporations must be able to show that they have developed an outline of processes and responsibilities, manuals, action plans and procedures. They must also have internal audits and internal reporting procedures in place, as well as management review of the reports.

The core indicators for reporting include:

- publication of the text of the company's environmental policy;
- description of main impacts including quantitative data; and
- performance measured against targets.

The desirable indicators include reporting on the company's Environmental Management System (EMS), and on prosecutions, fines and accidents. Independent verification of reports is another desirable indicator, as are stakeholder dialogue and coverage of sustainability issues.

Social and stakeholder criteria

Like the environmental criteria, the social and stakeholder criteria are divided into policy, management and reporting criteria. The policy criteria are that a corporation must have an equal opportunity policy and adopt a Code of Ethics or Business Principles. With respect to management criteria, it must be shown that a corporation can provide evidence of:

- equal opportunity systems;
- health and safety systems;
- training and employee development systems;
- systems to maintain good employee relations including union recognition.

With respect to reporting, corporations must be able to demonstrate one of the following:

- they are making charitable donations in excess of $150,000;
- operating payroll giving schemes;
- providing gifts in kind or staff secondments to community schemes; or
- assigning responsibility for managing charitable programs to a senior manager.

Case studies on CSR

It would be difficult to find an industry sector that does not claim to embrace the principles of sustainability, and even corporate social responsibility. Here, two case studies are presented on industry groups that have generally been acknowledged as taking a lead in the area of CSR. They are the finance and the mining sectors. The interesting aspect about these case studies is that the finance sector does not have any direct environmental impacts. However, as the discussion below indicates, the finance sector is beginning to realise the impact of its corporate operations, and its lending and investing policies, on environmental and social issues. It is quite intriguing to discover the extent to which the finance sector has developed various instruments to govern its corporate behaviour. On the other hand, the mining sector has a very direct impact on the environment, and the fact that it has taken a lead on CSR is not at all surprising.

CSR and the finance sector

There have been a number of recent developments which more than anything else have raised the profile of CSR in the finance sector. These are:

- the partnership forged between the UN Environment Program (UNEP) and the Finance Sector;
- the development of the Equator Principles by the financial services industry; and
- the emergence of Socially Responsible Investing (SRI) allied with the release in 2006 of the Principles for Responsible Investing.[33]

UNEP Finance Initiative

The UNEP Finance Initiative represents a combination of two programs developed by UNEP in conjunction with commercial banks and the insurance sector

UNEP engages commercial banks

In 1991 a small group of commercial banks, including Deutsche Bank, HSBC Holdings, Natwest, Royal Bank of Canada, and Westpac, joined forces with UNEP to develop the banking industry's environmental agenda. In May 1992, before the UN Conference on Environment and Development (the Rio Summit Conference), the UNEP Statement by Banks on the Environment and Sustainable Development was launched in New York, and the Banking Initiative was formed. The Initiative:

- promoted the integration of environmental considerations into all aspects of the financial sector's operations and services; and
- fostered private sector investment in environmentally sound technologies and services.

UNEP and the insurance sector join forces

In 1995, UNEP joined forces with the insurance sector to launch the UNEP Statement of Environmental Commitment by the Insurance Industry. UNEP now works closely with over 275 financial institutions including commercial banks, investment banks, insurance and re-insurance companies, fund managers, multilateral development banks and venture capital funds to develop and promote the linkages between the environment and financial performance.

33 See also Australian Conservation Foundation, *False Profits: How Australia's Finance Sector Undervalues the Environment and What We Can Do About It* (2006).

The UNEP Statement by Financial Institutions on the Environment and Sustainable Development and the UNEP Statement of Environmental Commitment by the Insurance Industry focuses the commitment of financial institutions on environmental sustainability in the three key areas of their activities. The first is internal operations, looking at issues such as energy usage, resource use and waste generation. Secondly, the Statements emphasise normal processes of risk assessment and management that should identify and quantify environmental risk and, thirdly, they promote the development of products and services which will actively promote environmental protection. This is particularly relevant to asset management tools. The Statements also demand that the financial sector take a lead role in promoting environmental responsibility. The Statements expect signatories to conduct internal reviews and measure their activities against their environmental goals, share information with customers and other stakeholders, support research, engage in dialogue with other financial institutions, share best practice with them, and work with UNEP to review their success in implementing the Statements.

The UNEP Finance Initiative currently has over 230 signatories institutions from over 45 countries.

UNEP FI's 'Show Me the Money'

A 2006 report, entitled 'Show Me the Money: Linking Environmental Social and Governance Issues to Company Value',[34] has been developed by the UNEP FI Asset Management Working Group. The report relies on the expertise of over 22 different international financial services firms, including sell side research houses, asset management firms and an investment consultancy, while the factors linking environmental, social and governance (ESG) issues to company value were extracted from more than 1000 pages of financial analysis.

The key findings and recommendations are as follows:

- there is robust evidence that Environmental, Social and Corporate Governance (ESG) issues are material and affect shareholder value in both the short and long term;
- the impact of ESG issues on share price can be valued and quantified;
- key ESG issues are becoming apparent and their importance can vary between sectors.

Based on these findings the Group calls on investors, asset managers and financial service providers to act as links between ESG issues and company profitability.

The report goes on to say that investors and asset managers can:

- manage risk better if they consider ESG issues;
- potentially increase profits if they incorporate ESG into their investment decisions;
- tap into a growing market by embracing ESG issues in core investment processes.

Meanwhile, financial sector service providers need to improve their research by:

- undertaking more historical analysis of the effects of ESG issues;
- comparisons need to be made across all companies in a sector or industry;

---

34 See <http://www.unepfi.org/fileadmin/documents/show_me_the_money.pdf> (accessed 14 July 2006).

- systematic ESG frameworks developed by brokerage houses need to be consistent and user-friendly in order to be useful for the investment management industry.

Equator Principles and project finance

The Equator Principles were drafted as a result of a meeting of banks convened by the International Finance Corporation in London in October 2002 to discuss environmental and social issues in project finance. At that meeting, the banks decided to try to develop a banking industry framework for addressing environmental and social risks in project financing. This led to the drafting of the Equator Principles, which provide an industry approach for financial institutions in determining, assessing and managing environmental and social risk in project financing. These principles apply to projects with a total capital cost of $50 million or more. Signatories agree that they will only provide loans directly to projects if an environmental assessment report has been completed by the borrower to assist with the environmental and social screening of the project. For example, the environmental assessment (EA) report must address:

- baseline environmental and social conditions;
- requirements under host country laws and regulations, applicable international treaties and agreements;
- sustainable development and use of renewable natural resources;
- protection of human health, cultural properties, and biodiversity, including endangered species and sensitive ecosystems;
- use of dangerous substances;
- occupational health and safety;
- socio-economic impacts;
- land acquisition and land use;
- involuntary resettlement;
- impacts on indigenous peoples and communities;
- cumulative impacts of existing projects, the proposed project, and anticipated future projects;
- consideration of feasible environmentally and socially preferable alternatives;
- efficient production, delivery and use of energy; and
- pollution prevention and waste minimisation, pollution controls (liquid effluents and air emissions) and solid and chemical waste management.

The borrower or third party expert must also prepare an Environmental Management Plan (EMP) which draws on the conclusions of the EA. The EMP must address mitigation, action plans, monitoring, management of risk and schedules. About 20 of the world's major financial institutions have already adopted the Principles.

Socially responsible investing (SRI)

Socially responsible investing (SRI) refers to investment decisions which are made based on an integration of personal values and societal concerns. In other words,

SRI combines both the investor's financial needs and the impact of an investment on society. The types of institutions which are interested in SRI include corporations, universities, hospitals, foundations, insurance companies, pension funds, non-profit organisations, churches and synagogues.[35]

The three key SRI strategies which have evolved over the years include screening, shareholder advocacy, and community investment.[36]

Screening

Screening describes the process of deciding which corporate securities to include in, or exclude from, investment portfolios based on social or environmental criteria. Socially concerned investors will generally be looking for evidence of respectable employee relations; a commitment to community involvement; strong environmental impact policies and practices; respect for human rights on a global scale; and the manufacture and use of safe and useful products. Where corporations are weak in these areas, SRI investors are likely to avoid them.

Shareholder advocacy

Shareholder advocacy describes the use by a growing number of investors of their status as part-owners of companies to influence corporate behaviour.[37] Shareholder advocacy has proved to be a powerful tool for encouraging corporations to improve their social and environmental performance. Typically shareholder activists might employ the following strategies:

Dialogues

In order to change corporate behaviour, a coalition of investors will often request a dialogue with management on issues of concern. Individual investors, on the other hand, may initiate a dialogue by writing letters to corporate management in support of shareholder campaigns.

Shareholder resolutions

If dialogues are unsuccessful in changing corporate practices, or if a company refuses to discuss issues with shareholders, shareholder resolutions may be introduced at an annual general meeting by concerned investors, or written requests may be made to company management. Resolutions may take various forms such as requesting reports from management or proposing that the company consider changes in practices or policies. Individual shareholders can play an important role when it comes to voting on resolutions. This can be done either in person at the company's annual meeting or via a proxy ballot that is mailed or e-mailed to all investors before the annual meeting. In fact, proxy voting is the primary forum where management seeks affirmation of its corporate agenda, and where shareholders can influence the outcome of important issues.

---

35 See <http://www.socialinvest.org/Areas/SRIGuide/> (accessed 10 April 2006).

36 Ibid.

37 See <http://www.coopamerica.org/socialinvesting/shareholderaction/whattoknow.cfm> (accessed 10 April 2006).

Divestment campaigns

Finally, if all else fails, shareholders may divest, or sell off, their stock in the company in protest. Clearly, corporations are likely to take threats of divestment campaigns very seriously since divestment represents a potential drop in share price and loss of revenue. However, divestment is used as a last resort of shareholders, since it signals an end to attempts to negotiate.

Community investing

Community investing represents the investment of capital in communities underserved by traditional financial services.[38] Access is provided to products such as credit, equity, capital, and basic banking products that these communities would otherwise not have. In the United States and around the world, community investing assists local organisations with providing financial services to low-income individuals, and supplying capital for small businesses and vital community services, such as child care, affordable housing and healthcare. Other important services, such as education, mentoring and technical support, can also be provided whereby investors are able to build relationships between families, nonprofits, small businesses, and conventional financial institutions and markets.

Principles for Responsible Investment

The concept of responsible investment has been picked up by the former UN Secretary-General, Kofi Annan, who in 2005 invited a group of the world's largest institutional investors to assist with the development of the Principles for Responsible Investment (PRI). The process was co-ordinated by the UN Environment Programme Finance Initiative (UNEP FI) and the UN Global Compact. The Principles may be subscribed to by all institutional investors, investment managers and professional service partners. Phase 2 of the process will encourage additional investors to adopt the Principles while providing extensive resources to assist them in implementing the Principles and actions, and facilitate collaboration among the signatories.

The Principles[39] are as follows:

1 We will Incorporate Economic, Social and Corporate Governance (ESG) issues into investment analysis and decision-making processes.
2 We will be active owners and incorporate ESG issues into our ownership policies and practices.
3 We will seek appropriate disclosure on ESG issues by the entities in which we invest.
4 We will promote acceptance and implementation of the Principles within the investment industry.
5 We will work together to enhance our effectiveness in implementing the Principles.
6 We will each report on our activities and make progress towards implementing the Principles.

---

38 See <http://www.communityinvest.org/overview/what.cfm> (accessed 10 April 2006).

39 See <http://www.unpri.org/principles/> (accessed 27 July 2006).

CSR in the mining sector

The International Council on Mining and Metals (ICMM) is an international organisation which provides strategic leadership to the mining, minerals and metals industry with regard to integrating the principles of sustainable development into its practices. In addition to this, the ICMM is moving the industry towards CSR by requiring public reporting against the 10 ICMM Principles for sustainable development.

The ICMM Principles[40] are as follows:

- implement and maintain ethical business practices and sound systems of corporate governance;
- integrate sustainable development considerations within the corporate decision-making process;
- uphold fundamental human rights and respect cultures, customs and values in dealings with employees and others affected by the industry's activities;
- implement risk-management strategies based on valid data and sound science;
- seek continual improvement of health and safety performance;
- seek continual improvement of environmental performance;
- contribute to conservation of biodiversity and integrated approaches to land use planning;
- facilitate and encourage responsible product design, use, reuse, recycling and disposal of products;
- contribute to the social, economic and institutional development of the communities in which the sector operates; and
- implement effective and transparent engagement, communication and independently verified reporting arrangements with interested and affected stakeholders.

The ICMM has also committed its corporate members to public reporting against the 10 Principles. To this end, the ICMM Council has approved the Global Reporting Initiative Mining and Metals Sector Supplement[41] and produced a Resource Guide[42] to assist members with the task. These provide the basis for ICMM members to report their economic, environmental, human rights and social performance against the 10 Principles. They include specific performance indicators as well as principles for good reporting, such as completeness and materiality.

CSR in Australia

There are a number of legal obligations in Australian law which promote various aspects of CSR. In addition, the Australian government has encouraged TBL reporting by corporations.

---

40 See <http://www.icmm.com/publications/ICMM_Principles_en.pdf> (accessed 11 April 2006).

41 See <http://www.icmm.com/news/775MiningPilot.pdf> (accessed 11 April 2006).

42 See <http://www.icmm.com/uploads/1045Membersresourceguide_FINAL.pdf> (accessed 11 April 2006).

Legally binding reporting obligations in Australia[43]

To date, the publication of TBL Reports and the development of EMSs are voluntary in Australia. Other jurisdictions have made the mandatory disclosure of social and environmental issues in companies' annual reports and accounts.[44] However, as the following discussion shows, over the past decade legislation has been passed which increasingly imposes a legally binding obligation on corporations to report against their environmental and social performance.

Corporations Act 2001 (Cth)

A number of duties to report on environmental and social performance arise under the *Corporations Act 2001*.

Reporting on breaches of environmental law

In 1998, a new obligation to report against environmental and social performance was introduced into corporations law in Australia. Section 299(1)(f) of the *Corporations Act*, referring to annual directors' reports, states:

> if the entity's operations are subject to any particular and significant environmental regulation under a law of the Commonwealth or of a State or Territory – give details of the entity's performance in relation to environmental regulation.

Essentially, s 299(1)(f) requires companies to include details of breaches of environmental laws and licences in their annual reports.

Reporting on future prospects of a corporation

The legal obligations of directors to report were enhanced by *Corporate Law Economic Reform Program (Audit Reform and Corporate Disclosure) Act 2004* (Cth) (CLERP 9 Act), which inserted a new s 299A(1)) into the *Corporations Act*. This section states that, with respect to publicly listed companies, a director's annual report must:

> contain information that members of the company would reasonably require to make an informed assessment of:
> (a) the operations of the entity reported on; and
> (b) the financial position of the entity; and
> (c) the entity's business strategies and its prospects for future financial years.

The significance of this wording is its reference to the future prospects of the entity. It is arguable that companies may now be required to provide information about their past, present and future environmental performance, to the extent that it is likely to affect their business strategy and future financial prospects. However, in the absence of any judicial interpretation of this section, it may be preferable to regard such disclosure as being mandated only where there is a prospect of material contingent liability, rather than requiring detailed reporting of environmental compliance as a general matter. Of course, where there is a prospect of criminal

---

43 Rosemary Lyster is indebted to Eric Coonan, Senior Associate, PricewaterhouseCoopers Legal, for his assistance with writing this section.

44 For example, in 2002 the Johannesburg Stock Exchange became the first Stock Exchange in the world to require publicly listed companies to report to the standards set by the Global Reporting Initiative.

prosecution, then questions of materiality in the traditional sense become difficult. However, unless there is a likelihood of this action (ie, without there being an investigation or some other identifiable step in that direction having been taken) it would be unlikely that this would be something that would affect the financial position of the company. Also, it is possible that such disclosure is unlikely to be a necessary element of reporting on operations or business strategies.

Alleged breach of reporting obligations

It is interesting to note that, in April 2005, the Australian Conservation Foundation (ACF) wrote to the Australian Securities and Investments Commission (ASIC) to complain about a series of breaches of the *Corporations Act* arising out of materially misleading and inaccurate disclosures by Energy Resources of Australia (ERA) and its directors in ERA's 2004 Annual Report. In particular, the ACF alleged that misleading statements were made with respect to ERA's compliance with environmental legislation, and its failure to report accurately on pending prosecutions and serious operational deficiencies, which constitute overt and serious breaches of ss 299A and 299(1)(f) of the Act. The ACF alleged further that these may constitute criminal offences under Pt 9.4 of the Act. At the time, ERA was facing two charges relating to a contaminated water event at Ranger Uranium Mine under ss 23(5) and 39 of the *Mining Management Act* (NT) and a further charge under s 39 of the Act relating to a separate event where contaminated vehicles left the mine site in breach of de-contamination and clearance procedures, causing preventable radiation exposure to a local mechanic and his children.

The ACF stated that ERA's reference in its Annual Report to 'improving the management of radiation at Ranger was a focus in 2004 following a number of highly publicised breaches of ERA procedures resulting in the company's prosecution under the Mining Management Act' was materially misleading. The ACF requested ASIC to pursue an injunction under the Act, to seek a declaration of contravention, as well as prosecution of the company and its directors. The ACF also reported that breaches of this kind are 'endemic'.

Product Disclosure Statements

In 2001, reporting obligations were further enhanced under ss 1013A to 1013F of the *Corporations Act* requiring providers of financial products with an investment component to disclose the extent to which labour standards or environmental, social or ethical considerations are taken into account in investment decision-making. These amendments to the corporations law were brought in under the *Financial Services Reform Act 2001* (Cth) which now requires super funds, life insurers and managed investment funds to issue Product Disclosure Statements. Section 1013D(1) states that a Product Disclosure Statement must include the information which a person would reasonably require for the purpose of making a decision, as a retail client, whether to acquire the financial product. Section 1013D(1)(l) requires the following to be disclosed:

> if the product has an investment component – the extent to which labour standards or environmental, social or ethical considerations are taken into account in the selection, retention or realisation of the investment.[45]

45 Section 1013D(l).

In addition, ASIC was given the power to develop guidelines that must be complied with where a Product Disclosure Statement makes any claims that labour standards or environmental social or ethical considerations are taken into account in the selection, retention or realisation of the investment.[46]

In September 2003, ASIC released PS 168 Disclosure: Product Disclosure Statements (and other disclosure obligations).[47] The guidelines apply to three categories of products: those with an investment component, those offering multiple investment options, and those made up of different asset classes. The guidelines relate to the following issues:

- disclosing the extent to which labour standards and environmental, social or ethical issues are taken into account, including the methodology for taking them into account and the weight given to the standards;
- disclosing retention and realisation policies, including monitoring and review of compliance with the methodology for taking such issues into account;
- disclosing secondary sources to which consumers may wish to refer for the purposes of making a decision, including on the external agency, ratings system of index used, the weightings system used or lists of investments actually made.

Penalties for breach of the Corporations Act

It is an offence under the *Corporations Act* for a person to make, or authorise the making of, a statement that to the person's knowledge is false or misleading in a material particular when preparing a document for the purposes of the Act, including a document lodged with or submitted to ASIC. It is also an offence to omit, or authorise the omission of, any matter which has the effect that a document is to the person's knowledge misleading in a material respect (s 1311). It is also an offence to make a statement that is based on information that to the person's knowledge is false or misleading in a material particular, or to omit from the statement a matter which renders the information misleading in a material respect. It is even an offence to prepare a document, or make a statement, without having taken reasonable steps to ensure that the statement was not false or misleading. Chapter 2 of the *Criminal Code* (Cth) applies to offences under the *Corporations Act* (s 1308A). These offences are all relevant to the director's duties to publish financial reports (s 299(1)(f)), Product Disclosure Statements (s 1013D(1)(l)) and the prospects of the corporation for future financial years (s 299A(1)).

Mandatory reporting on greenhouse gas emissions

Under the Greenhouse Challenge Plus Programme, members are required to report publicly on their greenhouse gas emissions profile. This obligation arises as a result of the *Fuel Tax Act 2006* (Cth) which provides fuel tax credits to business taxpayers who are registered, or required to be registered, for GST (and to some non-profit bodies). A person cannot include more that $3 million in fuel tax credits in net fuel

46 Section 1013DA.

47 See <http://www.asic.gov.au/asic/pdflib.nsf/LookupByFileName/PS168.pdf/$file/PS168.pdf> (accessed 6 April 2006).

amounts in a financial year unless the person is a member of the Greenhouse Challenge Plus Programme. However, if a person is denied a credit on the basis of not being a member of the Programme, and subsequently becomes a member, a decreasing fuel tax adjustment will be made of the amount of credit that was originally denied.

This obligation to report on greenhouse gas emissions is very likely to be extended to all industry groups. In October 2006, the Council of Australian Government's (COAG) Greenhouse and Energy Reporting Group (CGERG) released a draft Regulation Impact Statement entitled *A national system for streamlined greenhouse and energy reporting by business.*[48] It proposes 'national purpose-built legislation' to provide for cost-effective mandatory reporting and disclosure on energy consumption and greenhouse gas emissions at the company level. This follows recommendations made by the Environment Protection and Heritage Council (EPHC) and the Ministerial Council on Energy (MCE) in April 2006 on the development of a nationally consistent framework for greenhouse and energy reporting by industry. A detailed proposal for a reporting system is to be completed by December 2006. The framework will provide for streamlined reporting of greenhouse and energy data by including: data collection through a single online entry point based on the Greenhouse Challenge Plus Programme's Online System for Challenge Activity Reporting (OSCAR); standardised greenhouse and energy reporting data set; and a consistent methodological approach.

False or misleading representations

The *Trade Practices Act 1974* (TPA) prohibits corporations from making false or misleading representations about a product or service.[49] It is not inconceivable that corporations may fall foul of the TPA where their TBL or Sustainability Reports are false or misleading. As such, the operation of trade practices law requires corporations to take particular care in publicly communicating any corporate position on CSR. Significantly, obligations imposed on corporations under trade practices law can arise not just in response to regulatory obligations but in relation to any public representations made.[50] Under trade practices law there is no need to demonstrate that the corporation intentionally made a false representation, it is enough to show that the representation was wrong.[51]

Further legislative reform?

CAMAC's report *The Social Responsibility of Corporations*, referred to above, responds to the following questions asked of it by the Parliamentary Secretary to the Treasurer, in March 2005, as follows:

- Should the *Corporations Act* be revised *to clarify the extent to which* directors may take into account the interests of specific classes of stakeholders or the broader community when making corporate decisions?

---

48 See <www.greenhouse.gov.au/reporting/pubs/ris.pdf> (accessed 17 December 2006).

49 TPA s 53.

50 See *Gardam v George Wills & Co Ltd* (1988) 82 ALR 415.

51 See *Given v CV Holland (Holdings) Pty Ltd* (1977) 15 ALR 439.

- Should the Act be revised *to require* directors to take into accounts the interests of specific classes of stakeholders or the broader community when making corporate decisions?

CAMAC does not support the revision of the *Corporations Act* in the manner suggested in these questions. CAMAC is of the view that the established formulation of directors' duties gives them sufficient flexibility to take relevant interests and broader societal considerations into account. The proposed changes may risk obscuring directors' accountability while not providing any meaningful clarification of their duties. However, where there are concerns about the environmental or social behaviour of corporations, or in the case of market failure, specific legislation may need to be enacted. Such legislation should apply to private and public sector organisations. In CAMAC's view the *Corporations Act* lacks this range of coverage.

- Should the *Corporations Act* require certain types of companies to report on the social and environmental impact of their activities?

CAMAC has concluded that s 299A of the *Corporations Act* already provides for this type of reporting. However, CAMAC recommends that this obligation should be extended beyond publicly listed companies to all listed entities.

- Should Australian companies be encouraged to adopt socially and environmentally responsible business practices and if so, how?

CAMAC does not see a need for the government to provide across the board fiscal or other incentives for corporations to operate in a socially responsible manner, and nor should government compel corporations to adopt a particular managerial style. However, in CAMAC's view, there is scope for additional 'light touch' approaches to be adopted by government. It is desirable for government to adopt a consistent whole-of-government approach to the development and implementation of policies and administrative arrangements that have implications for corporate conduct and practices. Government should lead by example in this area. There is also scope for encouraging continuing Australian participation in the development of voluntary industry codes and other guidelines at the international level. Government can play a role in co-ordinating private sector initiatives. According to CAMAC, it is ultimately for the companies themselves, and those who run them, to decide what business practices to adopt in response to the demands of CSR.

Australian government initiatives to promote CSR

As well as imposing certain legal obligations on corporations, the Australian government has undertaken a number of initiatives to encourage corporations to comply with the spirit of CSR.

A Guide to Triple Bottom Line Reporting

There are a number of self-regulatory codes of conduct in Australia[52] including:

- the Australian Minerals Industry Framework for Sustainable Development;
- the Mining Certification Evaluation Project;

52 As discussed in the CAMAC report: above n 2.

- the ASX Corporate Governance Council Principles of Good Corporate Governance and Best Practice;
- Standards Australia's Standard 8003-2003 Corporate Social Responsibility; and
- the Australian's Corporate Sustainability Index.

In June 2003, Environment Australia released *Triple Bottom Line (TBL) Reporting in Australia: A Guide to Reporting Against Environmental Indicators* (TBL Guide). The Guide has been produced for managers in business, community and government who want to improve the environmental performance of their organisations. It applies across all industry sectors. Environment Australia's TBL Guide is consistent with international initiatives in this area.[53]

The TBL Guide identifies the following benefits from TBL reporting:

- embedding sound corporate governance and ethics systems throughout all levels of the organisation;
- improving risk-management systems;
- formalising and enhancing communication with key stakeholders such as the finance sector, suppliers, community and customers;
- attracting and retaining competent staff; and
- ability to benchmark performance within industries and across industries.

The two principal aspects of the Reporting Guide are Environmental Management Indicators and Environmental Performance Indicators. The Environmental Management Indicator section comprises five Indicators. These include:

- Indicator 1: EMS Conformance which essentially means reporting on compliance with Environmental Management System Standard 14001.
- Indicator 2: Environmental Performance Improvement Process which provides information on how an organisation can identify and assess initiatives it has in place to enhance, and continually improve, its environmental performance.
- Indicator 3: Integration of Environment with other Business Management Systems which requires the integration of EMS with core business systems.
- Indicator 4: Due Diligence Processes which should indicate an organisation's ability to deal with the risks associated with mergers, acquisitions, divestments and closures.
- Indicator 5: Environmental liabilities which allow stakeholders, particularly analysts and investors to determine the current and future obligations of a corporation, which may impact on its sustainability and profitability.

Environmental Performance Indicators on the other hand assist an organisation to calculate and report on the impact its operations have on the environment, including flora, fauna, land, air and water. The Environmental Performance Indicators in the Guide are consistent with the GRI Indicators and include:

- energy;
- greenhouse;
- water;

---

53 See Environment Australia Guide Appendix A at 62.

- materials;
- waste – solid and hazardous;
- emissions and discharges to air, land and water;
- biodiversity;
- ozone-depleting substances;
- suppliers;
- products and services; and
- compliance.

The Guide gives a very detailed methodology for reporting on each Indicator. For example, under the Energy Indicator organisations are encouraged to calculate the financial cost of its energy consumption and to identify ways of improving energy use and efficiency. Obviously energy use has environmental impacts, especially, if the energy is derived from fossil fuels, with respect to the emission of greenhouse gas emissions.

State of sustainability reporting in Australia

In March 2006, the Minister for Environment and Heritage released *The State of Sustainability Reporting in Australia 2005*.[54] The project was conducted between May and September 2005 and gathered information from:

- companies in the Standard & Poor's/Australian Stock Exchange (S&P/ASX) 300 index;
- the top 100 private companies; and
- the top 100 unlisted public companies.

The report assesses the rate of production of stand-alone sustainability reports as well as sustainability sections in annual reports and on corporate websites; independent verification of sustainability reports; the benefits and impediments of producing a sustainability report; key audiences for sustainability reporting; and the use of the Global Reporting Initiative (GRI) Guidelines.

Of the top 486 companies researched for the Report, 24% are producing a sustainability report. Of these, 70% were stand-alone reports, 22% were sections of Annual Reports and 8% were website sections. The rate of reporting has increased steadily but slowly over the years while the number of companies using the GRI Guidelines has increased from 30% to 51%. Only 40% of these companies have had their Reports independently verified. Australia's rate of reporting is lower compared with the top 100 publicly listed companies in 16 other countries where the average reporting rate is 41%.

The rate of reporting within industry groups is as follows:

- manufacturing (35.3%);
- mining (19.3%);
- wholesale trade (10.9%);
- electricity, gas and water supply (9.2%);

---

54 The Report was compiled by the Centre for Australian Ethical Research (CAER) in collaboration with KPMG and Deni Greene Consulting Services, <http://www.deh.gov.au/settlements/industry/corporate/reporting/pubs/survey2005.pdf> (accessed 4 April 2006).

- finance and insurance (9.2%);
- property and business services (6.7%);
- communication services (2.5%).

CSR and the finance sector in Australia

There are two initiatives that have emerged in the finance sector in Australia which are worth mentioning. They are a Memorandum of Understanding (MOU) between the UN Environment Programme and the Victorian Environment Protection Authority (EPA Victoria) to ensure the continued promotion of the UNEP Finance Initiatives in Australasia,[55] and the development of an SRI Symbol by the Ethical Investment Association.

UNEP Financial Initiatives

Under the MOU, EPA Victoria will distribute material, including the newsletter, on behalf of the UNEP Financial Initiatives; solicit and co-ordinate Australian-based articles on the finance sector for the newsletter and other publications; hold conferences, seminars and meetings on behalf of UNEP; chair advisory committees to investigate environmental issues pertaining to the finance sector in Australasia, while including all levels of government in the Initiatives; and encourage Australian financial institutions to become signatories to the Initiatives.

The SRI Symbol

The Ethical Investment Association reports that research conducted by Mercer Investment Consulting conducted in 2005 revealed that 85% of Asian and Australian investment managers believe that within 10 years SRI practices will have become mainstream. For this reason, the SRI industry has collaborated with the NSW Department of Environment and Conservation (DEC) and the Victorian government to develop the SRI Symbol.[56] The SRI Symbol gives various assurances including that a product or service provides an investment opportunity which addresses labour standards and ethical, social and environmental considerations. It is also a recognisable visual mark which can be used on Product Disclosure Statements (mentioned above), marketing and other materials to alert investors and the media to the SRI nature of the product. The Symbol also demonstrates that products have been independently reviewed for authenticity and is expected to boost SRI activity. The trademark is owned and managed by the Ethical Investment Association. Fund managers, superannuation funds, dealer groups and financial advisers must apply to become licensees to use the Symbol and must satisfy stipulated eligibility requirements.

Sustainability indices in Australia

A number of sustainability indices are emerging in Australia in response to the growing need to measure the CSR performance of Australian corporations.

---

55 For more information, see <http://www.epa.vic.gov.au/programs/unep/default.asp> (accessed 22 April 2006).

56 For more information, see <http://www.eia.org.au/files/JHGFHFJQA7/SRI%20Symbol%20 Brochure.pdf> (accessed 22 April 2006).

Corporate Social Responsibility Index

The Corporate Social Responsibility Index is a collaboration between the St James Ethics Centre, *The Sydney Morning Herald* and Ernst and Young. It allows companies accurately to be benchmarked according to their corporate social responsibility practices. The primary focus areas are strategy, integration, management practice, performance and impact, and assurance and disclosure.

The 2004 Index, released on 4 April 2005, shows that Westpac scored first place in the ranking. It outperformed 133 companies in the United Kingdom. Westpac was followed closely by BP, BHP Billiton, Rio Tinto and Toyota Australia.

Australian Sustainability Index

In February 2005, the Victorian government launched the Australian Sustainability Index meaning that Australia is one of a handful of countries to have its own Sustainability Index. The Index will track the financial and sustainability performance of 70 Australian companies. Known as AuSSI, the Index comprises 40% of the 184 companies listed on the Australian Stock Exchange. Index values will be published in *The Australian* on a daily basis. A full review of index members will be published on an annual basis. EPA Victoria will help to fund the Index.

Critiques of CSR

It is interesting to note that there are two major, but widely conflicting, critiques of CSR. They emanate from economists who have been highly critical of the way in which CSR disrupts the fundamental tenets of capitalism and the free market, and non-government organisations which now want CSR to become a legal, rather than a voluntary, obligation.

Reaction from economists

The literature on CSR[57] refers frequently to the perspectives of two leading economists who have been highly critical of CSR. They refer to a piece written by Milton Friedman in 1970[58] and a report written by David Henderson, former chief economist of the OECD, entitled 'Misguided Virtue: False Notions of Social Corporate Social Responsibility'.[59] Friedman's critique of CSR was that:

---

57 See, eg, Charlotte Denny, 'Profit Motive', *The Guardian Weekly*, 15 November 2001; 'Curse of the ethical executive', *The Economist*, 15 November 2001; Russell Sparkes, 'A Pragmatic Approach to Corporate Social Responsibility – address given to the School of Management, London School of Economics, 19 Mary 2003, <http://cep.lse.ac.uk/seminarpapers/19-05-03-SPA.pdf> (accessed 14 April 2006).

58 See Milton Friedman, 'The social responsibility of business is to increase its profits', *New York Times*, 1970.

59 Henderson's publication includes the following chapters: The challenge of CSR; The rise of CSR; defining and interpreting CSR; Capitalism made anew: the CSR blueprint; Global Salvationism: a shared vision; Reducing welfare: the costs and risks of CSR; Companies, commitment and collectivism; and New developments and final thoughts; <http://www.iea.org.uk/files/upld-publication126pdf?.pdf> (accessed 13 April 2006).

> The doctrine of social responsibility ... is fundamentally subversive ... there is one and only one social responsibility of business – to use its resources and engage in activities designed to increase its profits so long as it engages in open and free competition without deception and fraud.[60]

Henderson states, meanwhile, that:

> In formulating their radical programme of change, the CSR adherents have taken a position which they do not make explicit and of which they may not be fully aware. *Defending the market economy is identified with making businesses more popular and more respected* [sic]. This is to be achieved by meeting 'society's expectations', through making a manifestly genuine commitment to CSR. How this response may affect competition and economic freedom is not directly considered. But ... there are good reasons to expect that both will be impaired, while at the same time the performance of enterprises will suffer. The likelihood of such an outcome is the greater because the strongest and most effective pressures for change come from organisations that are anti-business and hostile to free markets, while their arguments find support from the enthusiasts and zealots within the business world.[61]

Henderson goes on to say that CSR can best be attributed to 'the new millennium collectivism' which, aligned with 'global salvationist' ideas, is highly suspicious of the market which it misunderstands, leading to a bias in favour of interventionism. Yet, according to Henderson, this view is flawed for three reasons: a lack of understanding about economic theory; a failure to understand that a competitive profit-driven economy regards profitability as a means to higher things rather than a primary objective; and that market economies are anarchic and amoral leaving many people deprived, condemned excluded or marginalised.[62] Henderson concludes that CSR is flawed in its prescription and its diagnosis and is likely to bring about far-reaching changes in the business world, 'for purposes that are open to question and with worrying implications for the efficient conduct of enterprises'.[63]

Meanwhile, after the 2004 meeting of the World Economic Forum in Davos, Switzerland, *The Economist* noted in 'Two-Faced Capitalism' that:

> From an ethical point of view, the problem with conscientious (as opposed to fake) CSR is obvious: it is philanthropy at other people's expense. As a rule, so far as public companies are concerned, managers do not own the firms they work for. They are entrusted with the care of assets belonging to others, the firm's shareholders. Supporting good causes out of their own generous salaries, bonuses, deferred compensation, options packages and incentive schemes would be admirable; doing it out of income that would otherwise be paid to shareholders is a more dubious proposition. Anyway, is it really for managers and NGOs to decide social-policy priorities among themselves? In a democracy, that is a job for voters and elected politicians.[64]

---

60 As cited by Sparkes, above n 57, at 2.

61 Above n 59, at 142.

62 Ibid.

63 Ibid at 148.

64 See <http://www.economist.com/business/displayStory.cfm?story_id=2369912> (accessed 21 April 2006).

NGO disquiet

One of the most scathing attacks on CSR has come from Christian Aid which produced a report for the 2004 World Economic Forum in Davos entitled 'Behind the mask: The real face of CSR'.[65] In this report, Christian Aid presents case studies on the activities of Shell, British American Tobacco and Coca-Cola to its claim that CSR has become nothing more than a 'branch of PR'.[66] In addition, CSR is being used by corporations to block attempts to establish the mandatory international regulation of their activities because they are already behaving responsibly. However, according to Christian Aid the lack of such regulation means that the actions of the worst corporate abusers are left unrestrained while victims in developing countries lack access to adequate remedies. As well as calling for international regulation, Christian Aid believes that national legislation should be passed in all countries to ensure that the international regulatory regime is properly enforced. At the national level, Christian Aid called on the UK government to:

- enact legislation to make corporate social and environmental reporting and disclosure mandatory for British companies;
- impose a 'duty of care' on directors making them liable for the actions of their overseas companies;
- allow people harmed by British companies overseas to bring actions in the UK courts and also provide them with resources to enable them to bring the actions.

A pragmatic approach

Addressing the School of Management at the London School of Economics, Russell Sparkes attempted to offer a pragmatic approach to CSR. After referring to Friedman's criticism of CSR, which he says must be contextualised within the climate of big business in the late 1960s, he raises a number of objections to Henderson's attack on CSR. Sparkes' main objection is that Henderson 'does not understand, or does not want to understand, what CSR actually means. The efforts by NGOs to impose social and environmental constraints on business cannot be identified with CSR'. According to Sparkes, CSR should not be confused with anti-globalisation and anti-business thought.[67] Also, CSR is not an invitation for companies to act as charities, a function best left to foundations and publicly elected bodies. It simply means that corporations are responsive to the concerns of society. Sparkes prefers to define CSR in the following way:

> CSR describes the practical reality that companies are increasingly being judged not just by the products and profits they make, but also by *how* these profits are made. It is important to stress however that this definition is limited to the societal and environmental constraints put upon a company's core function of profit maximization by the provision of goods and services. Companies respond to these

65 See <http://www.christianaid.org.uk/news/media/pressrel/040121p.htm> (accessed 21 April 2006).

66 It is interesting to note that in 'The good company', *The Economist*, 20 January 2005, the writer agrees that 'CSR does not go very deep ... and it is little more than cosmetic treatment', http://www.economist.com/PrinterFriendly.cfm?Story_ID=3555212> (accessed 21 April 2006).

67 Sparkes, above n 57, at 3.

> constraints and respond to the two classes of 'stakeholders' who really do matter to them: customers and shareholders.[68]

Sparkes gives a number of examples of corporations, like Gap and Nike, whose sales were heavily affected by their breach of environmental or human rights standards.

Meanwhile, from the perspective of investors, CSR is rooted in corporate governance but goes far beyond it. In fact, investors, especially through socially responsible investment (SRI) funds, have far greater power than consumers to assert CSR issues. Sparkes gives the following figures which indicate the global SRI investment assets in 2001:

	US $bn
United States	2332.0
United Kingdom	326.6
Canada	31.4
Europe	17.6
Japan	1.9
Australia	1.1
Total	2710.6 [69]

Sparkes claims that the growth in shareholder activism evidenced in SRI 'reflects a growing political consensus among the Anglo-Saxon political establishment that corporate social responsibility must be encouraged'.[70] In addition, far from being an interference with corporate efficiency, SRI resolutions can act as a 'feedback mechanism alerting senior management to potential problems lying ahead'.[71] In this way, SRI has something to offer corporations by improving their behaviour.

Essentially, corporations must choose whether they want societal concerns to be dealt with through the price mechanism of the goods and capital markets, or government reregulation of the economy.[72]

Conclusions about CSR

As this discussion has shown, although there are common themes running through the various definitions of CSR, each organisation describing CSR has a slightly different interpretation of what it means. Nevertheless, CSR has gained a life of its own during recent times and a growing number of large multinational and national corporations commit extensive resources to developing their CSR strategies. These must be developed in consultation with identified stakeholders, must be reported against, independently verified and, if the research is to be believed, will ultimately deliver financial benefits to the corporation. Despite the voluntary underpinnings of CSR, various reporting obligations have become mandatory in Australia and, as indicated, these may even become more onerous. Certainly, the case studies, particularly on the finance sector, indicate that a commitment to CSR is being taken

68 Ibid at 4.

69 This figure is taken from Sparkes' book, *Socially Responsible Investment – a Global Revolution* (Society of Investment Professions, 2001).

70 Above n 57, at 7.

71 Ibid.

72 Ibid at 8.

very seriously by some of the world's largest institutional investors. Yet, CSR has its detractors. Economists fear that CSR will create inefficiencies in the market, while NGOs, which have been at the forefront of advocating CSR, may ultimately be disappointed by what it can deliver. What is certain is that environmental lawyers cannot ignore what has become a very significant market mechanism in controlling the environmental impacts of corporations.

INDEX

MORNINGSTAR®

Funds500™

Annual Sourcebook
2005 Edition

Introduction by
Christine Benz
and Russel Kinnel,
Co-Editors

Published by John Wiley & Sons, Inc., Hoboken, New Jersey
Published simultaneously in Canada

ISBN: 0-471-71030-X
ISBN: 0-582-71031-8

Printed in the United States of America
10 9 8 7 6 5 4 3 2 1

Table of Contents

As investors, we love a great buying opportunity.

In the late 1990s, for example, technology, telecom, and media stocks ascended to dizzying heights while everything else languished; you didn't have to be a genius to notice that some of the market's most unloved sectors—small-value stocks and real estate investments, in particular—were cheap and due for an upswing. Similarly, amid a flight to quality in the bond market in 2002, skittish investors bid up long-term Treasury bonds at the expense of all other fixed-income instruments. That trend spelled opportunity for those investors who were willing to venture beyond gilt-edged Treasuries and in 2003, corporate bonds trumped government securities (the typical high-yield bond fund gained 24% that year!).

Stocks and bonds have posted convincing gains over the past two years, however, so it's safe to say that there are fewer "home-run" opportunities right now than there were even a few years ago. Instead, the most successful mutual fund investors are apt be those who keep diversified portfolios and home in on those fund managers with proven track records of making money in a variety of market environments.

That's where this book comes in. We've taken the fund universe—at nearly 17,000 funds and counting—and edited it down to a far more manageable list of the 500 best and most notable offerings. You'll find every fund type you need to build a diversified all-weather portfolio, ranging from ultra-safe money market alternatives to sturdy core stock offerings to high-risk technology and telecommunications sector funds.

For each of these funds, we provide a one-page report that gives you all of the data and analysis you need to put a potential holding through its paces, including 10 years' worth of performance history, an overview of each fund's risks, and details about its manager, investment style and portfolio. This edition of the Morningstar Funds 500 also marks the debut of Morningstar's Fiduciary Grade, which summarizes each fund's shareholder-friendliness and encompasses factors such as board quality, expenses, and management compensation. The centerpiece of each fund report is Morningstar's Take—our analyst's critical evaluation of whether a given fund is worth buying or not.

For those investors who'd rather cut right to the chase, the book also gives you our exclusive Analyst Picks—the funds that our analysts consider to be the best and brightest within every category. While many investors base their fund-purchase decisions strictly on past performance, our Analyst Picks are those offerings that our analysts believe have the best future prospects. If you're looking for a short list of funds to investigate further, our Analyst Picks list is the best place to start.

Whatever your investing-experience level, goal, or time horizon, and whatever market conditions prevail in the future, we're confident that the Funds 500 has the data and analysis you need to make profitable decisions in the years ahead.

Christine Benz,
Co-editor
Morningstar Funds 500

Russel Kinnel,
Co-editor
Morningstar Funds 500

Year in Review

2004 started out shaky, but funds pulled through in the end.

by Karen Wallace, Managing Editor

Uncertainty surrounding rising interest rates, inflation, and the upcoming presidential elections weighed on investors throughout the first three quarters of the year. But the market gathered strength during the fourth quarter: The S&P 500 Index rose over 10%—buoying every diversified domestic-stock fund category well into the black. And although the market didn't rocket to the dizzying heights of 2003's rebound, many funds managed to post low double-digit returns in 2004.

Among diversified domestic-stock funds, the small-value category performed best, rising more than 20% for the year to date through Dec. 31, 2004. This is a familiar story to investors: Small value has also been the best-performing category since 2000, returning more than 16% on an annualized basis for the trailing five-year period through Dec. 31, 2004. In fact, smaller stocks have generally performed better than large-cap stocks over the period. (Many of our former Fund Analyst Picks in the small-cap categories have closed as their asset bases have ballooned.) A confluence of factors has shored up the performance of smaller-cap stocks. For one, the economic slowdown of recent years has hit larger companies harder than smaller companies, and smaller companies' earnings have held up better than those of larger firms. Also, in general, small cap stocks are thought to be more sensitive than large to improving economic conditions, so as the market clawed out of recession, they've done better than large caps. This, in turn, has justified small caps' higher stock prices. In addition, coming into 2000, small cap stocks' valuations were low relative to large caps', so they had more room to rise.

Meanwhile, in the opposite corner of Morningstar's domestic-equity style box, the large-growth category was the laggard among diversified, domestic-stock categories in 2004, rising "only" 8% through Dec. 31. The category also brings up the rear over the three- and five-year periods, when it lost 0.02% and more than 8%, respectively.

Value stocks' relative success is probably due to many separate factors, but much of it can be attributed to investors reining in their expectations from the days of so-called "irrational exuberance." That's what Fed Chairman Alan Greenspan termed the extraordinary speculative rally of the late 1990s, which we saw repeated on a smaller scale in the heady gains of 2003. The prices of many stocks—particularly tech issues—had gotten ahead of themselves, and investors thought value stocks looked even cheaper than usual by comparison.

So what should investors expect going forward? Will small-value fare continue to outperform other areas of the stock market? Although we don't have a crystal ball, we can say that it seems unlikely. It's more logical to conclude that after five years of impressive returns, small-value stocks are due for a breather. The price tags of many of these stocks have already been bid up. On the other hand, after five years in the doldrums, many large- and mega-cap companies look attractively priced compared with their historical valuations. Although it's nearly impossible to predict what direction the stock market will take in the short term, we wouldn't bet against a reversion to the mean over the long haul.

The Big Winners

Natural Resources

2004's biggest winners among specialized fund categories included the natural resources category, which jumped more than 28% for the year to date through Dec. 31. Although most natural-resources stocks did well last year, energy stocks performed the strongest, so funds with higher energy weightings outperformed more diversified funds in 2004. Funds that invested in smaller companies that are highly leveraged to the price of oil performed best of all. The top-performing fund in the category, for example, **State Street Research Global Resources** SSGRX, invests primarily in small- and mid-cap energy shares and was up more than 47% year to date through Dec. 31, 2004.

The fundamental factors that drove the price of oil higher last year included strong demand from China, steady demand from the United States, and limited spare capacity. However a confluence of events, for example, geopolitical tensions in Iraq, Russia, Nigeria, and Venezuela, and supply interruptions caused by Hurricane Ivan, pushed oil to a $55 peak last fall. Those factors have either resolved themselves or eased somewhat, so the price of oil has come off its highs. Many pundits expect the price of oil could fall even further if demand from China slows down.

Real Estate
Real estate funds also topped the charts last year, gaining more than 31% for the year to date through Dec. 31, 2004. In fact, real estate funds have outperformed every other fund category Morningstar tracks—including small-value funds—over the trailing three- and five-year periods. The same factors that have buoyed the diversified small-value offerings have also helped real estate funds; many funds that invest primarily in real estate investment trusts (REITs) and other types of real estate securities fall into the small- and mid-value style boxes.

More specifically, however, some of 2004's outstanding rise in real estate securities can be chalked up to a common investor behavior—performance chasing. Because the category has been on a tear, gaining more than 21% on an annualized basis over the past five years, many investors have jumped on board. But the real estate market is small—there aren't that many real estate securities, and the sector doesn't have a large total market cap. That means that inflows and outflows into real estate funds have a significant impact on real estate securities' prices.

Latin America
For the second year in a row, Latin America was the best-performing fund category of all in 2004—it soared 38% for the year to date through Dec. 31. Sharp surges in Brazilian and Mexican stocks are the main reason. That market, which suffered earlier in 2004 on political worries, bounced back with a vengeance thanks to positive macroeconomic and other developments. But keep in mind that Latin America funds have suffered losses in six of the past 10 calendar years, and they fell more than 15% in five of those six down years.

Fixed-Income Funds
Despite rising short-term interest rates, every bond-fund category Morningstar tracks finished the year with positive total returns in 2004. The top-performing group, the emerging-markets bond category, was up nearly 12% for the year to date through Dec. 31. Fears of rising interest rates in the United States downed this volatile category earlier in the year, but since May it surged back. Bond-rating agencies remain upbeat on Russia, as that country has aggressively paid down debt. High oil and commodity prices have helped producers such as Russia, Brazil, and Venezuela. Meanwhile, Turkey's improving public finances have also encouraged investors, as that country has strengthened its bid for European Union membership.

Among domestic investment-grade bond categories, an interesting trend developed in 2004. Even though the Fed raised interest rates five times last year, bonds with longer durations (in other words, bonds that are more sensitive to interest-rate changes) outperformed shorter-term bonds. The long-term bond category was up 6% for the year to date through Dec. 31, and the intermediate-term group gained nearly 4%. Meanwhile, the average short-term bond fund gained only 1.6%, and the ultrashort category eked out only a 1.2% return.

A combination of unexpectedly modest economic results, combined with investors' confidence that the Fed's aggressiveness will keep inflation under control, have helped keep a lid on long-term interest rates. Investors entered 2004 expecting interest rates would rise and bond prices would fall. But it appears that their pessimism was overdone. When the Federal Reserve raised rates, the central bank sent the rate up only 0.25% each time, versus expectations of 0.50% hikes.

And Finally, the Big Losers
Among the laggards in 2004, the precious metals category fell more than 8% through Dec. 31. This category has been a veritable roller-coaster ride for investors of late: Last year the price of gold bounced around quite a bit, based largely on strength and weakness in the U.S. dollar. This is quite an about-face from 2003—the category was a big winner that year, gaining more than 50%. These recent sharp runups and equally quick declines show just how turbulent the precious-metals category is. Because of this, in addition to their unimpressive long-term results and high costs, the funds are for aggressive investors only. They should play a very small role, if any, in a portfolio.

The biggest loser in 2004, the bear-market fund category, dropped more than 14% during the period. These funds are designed to profit in market downturns by employing risky trading strategies such as short-selling to bet on sinking stock prices. Naturally, they didn't fare well during last year's rising market. M

The Morningstar Fiduciary Grade for Funds

An introduction to our newest investors' aid.

by Christopher Traulsen, Fund Analyst and Kunal Kapoor, Director of Fund Analysis

For many investors, the search for an investment idea begins with familiar signposts, such as past performance and risk level. While these factors are important when considering whether or not to buy a fund, they don't take into account crucial intangibles. For instance, a fund's historical risk/reward profile doesn't tell you whether the interests of a management company and fund manager are aligned with those of the fund's shareholders. Nor do basic risk measures tell you anything about a fund firm's corporate culture. For example, when looking at a particular fund company, it's important to ask whether the organization, as Jack Bogle has put it, values salesmanship over stewardship. Does the firm take its responsibility to fund shareholders seriously and actually put their interests first?

Morningstar analysts have pondered these very questions since we began evaluating mutual funds in 1984. Our assessment of a firm's commitment to fund shareholders has frequently informed the investment recommendations we've made over the years. For instance, we've criticized boards for not safeguarding the interests of investors with fund closures and liquidations, questioned the value of many fund mergers, railed against high expenses, and complained about management turnover. Now we're taking the next step and presenting this research in a uniform fashion that will make it easier for investors to compare the corporate-governance track records of funds they own or are considering buying.

In this edition of Morningstar Funds 500, we mark the debut of Morningstar's new Fiduciary Grade for funds. (The grades appear above the Management and Strategy sections on the Morningstar page. You'll find that a majority of funds in this book carry the new grades.) The Fiduciary Grade serves as a handy way to assess key intangibles—such as the quality of a fund's board of directors or a fund firm's corporate culture—that can make the difference between a great investment and one to avoid. The grades, which will range from A (best) to F (worst), are not meant to be used in isolation or as simplistic buy/sell signals. Rather, they represent yet another valuable addition to our suite of investing research and tools, alongside our written Fund Analyst Reports and Morningstar Rating for funds.

In fact, the methodology for the Fiduciary Grade for funds is completely different from the Morningstar Rating for funds (the "star rating"), and the new Fiduciary Grade has no impact on a fund's star rating. The Morningstar Rating is a quantitative assessment of a fund's past performance—both return and risk. The Fiduciary Grade is determined using some quantitative measures, but it is primarily based on qualitative information gathered by Morningstar analysts. The letter grade assigned to each fund is based on the fund's score in five key areas. Read on for a brief synopsis of those components, each of which is weighted equally.

Regulatory Issues

This one is fairly straightforward. We examine each firm's record to determine if it has run afoul of regulators in the past three years. We also look at the gravity of the allegations and the subsequent reforms the firm has undertaken. For example, while Strong and AllianceBernstein both get dinged for their role in the fund scandals, we think the latter has done a far better job of addressing its problems than Strong has. As such, AllianceBernstein scores higher than Strong on this factor.

Board Quality

Our analysts have spent a great deal of time pulling together information about funds' boards, because we think the quality of a fund's board of directors is of paramount importance. For far too long, fund boards have looked the other way as investment-management firms have launched lousy funds, hiked expenses, or left underperforming managers on the job.

Because boards are in place to represent fund shareholders' interests, we're taking a close look at factors such as the number of funds that directors oversee, the relationships between directors and fund firms, and the performance of trustees in looking after fund shareholders' interests. We also examine whether trustees are investing alongside fundholders. For example, we like that all ICAP board members are paid in fund shares.

Manager Incentives

Over the past few months, we've been asking fund companies to complete a survey detailing the structure of fund managers' pay as well as the level of their investment in fund shares. We have not asked for specific salary figures; in our opinion, the structure of a manager's compensation—and his or her bonus in particular—is more important than the dollar amount of his or her pay. We believe that performance incentives can have a strong influence on the way a fund is run. A fund manager who is paid to beat an aggressive benchmark over a one-year period, for example, might be inclined to take much bigger risks than he or she otherwise would.

We also believe managers should eat their own cooking by investing in either the funds they run or other offerings run by their firm. Why? Because fund share ownership is an important reflection of whether a portfolio manager has conviction in his or her own process. Managers who invest alongside fund shareholders are also more likely to pay much closer attention to issues such as expenses and taxes than ones who do not. We don't believe it's a coincidence that firms such as Longleaf Partners, which requires that all employees invest in Longleaf's funds, are protective of fund shareholders' best interests.

Fees

It's easy for investors to overlook fund fees, because most don't know how much they're paying in hard dollars. Depending on a fund's expense ratio and the amount invested, fund shareholders could be saving tens of thousands of dollars over their investment lifetime by going with lower-cost options.

As such, the amount that a management company charges fund shareholders often speaks volumes about the priority the firm accords the interests of fund shareholders versus those of company stakeholders. That's why we examine whether fund investors are getting a good deal or the short end of the stick. For example, we've recently been critical of fee hikes at Evergreen that we thought were egregious. We pay attention to not only how a fund's expenses stack up relative to its peers, but also to trends in expenses to gauge whether a firm is appropriately passing on economies of scale to a growing fund's shareholders. Importantly, the scoring for this factor is within category and within distribution channel because we want to compare apples to apples.

Corporate Culture

No, we're not talking about dress codes or broadly assessing how a firm operates. Rather, we're focusing on how shareholder-focused management is by looking for tangible evidence that a firm has a deep-rooted understanding of its role as a fiduciary. This is the most subjective component of the grade by virtue of the sheer number of factors that can influence the depth of a firm's commitment to its fundholders.

Our analysts have spent a considerable amount of time evaluating criteria such as the quality of shareholder reports, a firm's willingness to close funds at appropriate asset levels, and the pattern of new fund launches. We examine how fund companies deal with these issues to gauge whether the long-term interests of fund shareholders have consistently been placed front and center—where they belong. We've also taken a close look at firms' usage of redemption fees and the ability to retain key personnel. Firms that embody these principles, such as Davis Advisors, score highly, while firms that we think fall short, such as Van Kampen, score poorly. M

Managers Who Deliver the Goods

These investors have added lots of value over the past three years.

by William Samuel Rocco, Fund Analyst

The U.S. stock market has been exceptionally turbulent over the past three years. After surging in the fourth quarter of 2001, domestic equities plummeted to double-digit losses the next year. They reversed course again in 2003, with most stocks gaining between 25% and 45%, before posting up-and-down but generally so-so returns during the first nine months of this year. What's more, the types of stocks that led the way also shifted back and forth during the period.

Although such turbulence is painful for investors, it also provides an excellent context for assessing which domestic-equity managers boast real talent. After all, it's one thing for managers to come through when their corner of the U.S. market mounts a sustained rally or even when their favorite type of domestic equities suffers a prolonged sell-off, but it's quite another for managers to deliver the goods in erratic conditions, with marked peaks and valleys and rotating market leadership.

Therefore, we thought it would be worthwhile to identify first-rate managers in each of Morningstar's nine diversified domestic-stock categories who have added a lot of value over the past three years. To do so, we began with a statistic called alpha, which measures the returns and volatility of a fund versus a relevant index to determine how much value a manager has added or subtracted relative to that benchmark. After screening for the funds with the highest three-year alphas through Sept. 30, 2004, relative to the appropriate style-specific or other benchmarks, we tossed out those with poor longer-term records or other problems and selected those we like best.

These high-alpha funds have many distinctive characteristics, but they do share some common qualities—besides having very talented managers. Many of these funds are willing to concentrate on a limited number of names or to buy stocks in bunches; several of them are flexible about where they look for stocks that meet their investment criteria; and quite a few of them have low portfolio turnover. Here are the details.

Large-Cap Growth

T. Rowe Price New America Growth PRWAX stands out from its large-growth rivals thanks to Joe Milano's deft execution of his flexible but disciplined strategy. Milano, unlike many of his peers, readily ventures outside the traditional growth areas. Indeed, **Harley-Davidson** HDI and energy-services and -equipment provider **Smith International** SII played key roles in the fund's top-notch showing in 2004. Milano also pays more attention to mid-cap opportunities than many of his large-growth rivals, and that open-mindedness has paid off throughout the early 2000s. His emphasis on low-debt, high-quality names and his patience have served the fund well in the past, and they should continue to do the same going forward.

Large-Cap Blend

Chris Davis and Ken Feinberg have added a lot of value at **Davis NY Venture** NYVTX by having the courage of their convictions. They readily build big positions in individual issues and industries as they strive to buy good companies trading at temporarily depressed prices, and they stick with their picks for the long haul. (Annual turnover is normally just 10%-25% here, and the fund's weighting in the financial sector often exceeds 40% of assets.) Such a hard-core approach would be dangerous in the hands of the unskilled, of course, but Davis and Feinberg are two of the most talented large-cap managers around. This fund beat the vast majority of its large-blend rivals in 2002 and 2003, and it did so again in 2004. And its recent success is certainly no fluke. The fund's five- and 10-year returns also rank in its group's top decile.

Large-Cap Value

Torray TORYX proves that a concentrated and patient style can also work quite well in the large-value category. Bob Torray and Doug Eby buy 35-40 large firms while they're on sale and hold on to them for the long haul. Although this focused approach courts considerable issue-specific risk, Torray and Eby have demonstrated they have the stock-picking chops to handle it. Although it has struggled this year, the fund boasts top-quartile three-year returns. What's more, its 10-year gains are significantly better—in both absolute and relative terms—and Torray and Eby have been around for more than a decade.

Mid-Cap Growth
We've decided to suggest two options in the mid-growth category. **Meridian Growth** MERDX is more price-conscious than most offerings in this group. That has served to dampen volatility and makes the fund suitable for risk-conscious mid-growth fans. Rick Aster, who has been at the helm for more than 20 years, has delivered impressive returns here over the past three years and the long run. Conversely, **TransAmerica Premier Growth** TPSCX is appropriate only for aggressive investors, because Chris Bonavico and Ken Broad normally invest in just 20-30 issues. They've put that concentration to good use. Although that fund has certainly had its rough spots, it has posted superior results over time.

Mid-Cap Blend
Thomas Putnam and John Fox of **FAM Value** FAMVX have also demonstrated that they have what it takes to manage a focused portfolio well. Putnam and Fox, who normally own 40-50 stocks and favor financial and industrial-materials issues, have delivered strong returns in a variety of environments, including this year's choppy climate. Moreover, because they're more bargain-oriented than most mid-blend skippers and insist that their purchases have rock-solid fundamentals, the fund has been less volatile than the majority of its rivals. The duo's low-turnover style also enhances tax efficiency.

Mid-Cap Value
Artisan Mid Cap Value ARTQX has demonstrated its mettle in good times and bad. After posting superior results in both 2002's sell-off and 2003's surge, the fund earned top-percentile returns in 2004's gyrating market. Scott Satterwhite and Jim Kieffer have accomplished this feat with a straightforward but strict strategy that leads them to favor issues in traditional value sectors such as financials and energy. And while this fund is still relatively young, Satterwhite and Kieffer have successfully applied the same-stock selection discipline they use here at **Artisan Small Cap Value** ARTVX over the longer run.

Small-Cap Growth
The pickings are a bit slim in the small-growth and other small-cap categories because so many of the best offerings in these groups are closed to new investors, but **T. Rowe Price New Horizons** PRNHX is well worth a look. Jack Laporte, who has been at the helm for 17 years, steadfastly adheres to his moderate discipline in all kinds of conditions, and he consistently turns in solid or better results. The fund has beaten its average small-growth peer throughout the early 2000s and achieved a top-quartile showing in 2004. The fund's 10- and 15-year returns are also strong.

Small-Cap Blend
Chuck Royce and Whitney George have guided **Royce Premier** RYPRX to topnotch returns over the past three years. That's particularly impressive given that micro-caps have been the best-performing portion of the small-cap universe in the early 2000s and Royce and George favor larger and more-established small companies with long records of profitability. (The fund's average market cap is about 50% bigger than the small-blend norm.) The fund's long-term returns are also good; it has been less volatile than most of its peers over time, and George and Royce have had considerable success on other small-cap offerings.

Small-Cap Value
American AAdvantage Small Cap Value AVPAX employs three subadvisors, each of which has had significant success elsewhere, and follows distinct disciplines. Brandywine Asset Management uses a quantitatively driven strategy to locate attractive bargains, while Barrow, Hanley, Mewhinney & Strauss relies on a more fundamental style that focuses on out-of-favor stocks with low valuations, and Hotchkis and Wiley takes a contrarian approach. The end result is a diverse but dedicated small-value portfolio that has delivered attractive returns in a variety of market conditions. Morningstar recently added this fund to its 401(k) plan after **Fidelity Low-Priced Stock** FLPSX closed. M

15 Funds for the Future

Don't be fooled by past performance.

by Russel Kinnel, Director of Fund Research

Finding a fund that was great in the past is a piece of cake. Go online and screen for strong returns or a high star rating and you can come up with hundreds in just seconds. The catch is that past performance doesn't tell you much about a fund's prospects.

There are two main reasons: A fund's fundamentals can change. For example, its expense ratio can rise, or past success can leave it overloaded with more money than its manager can effectively manage. Second, market trends distort fund returns in a way that makes it easy to confuse luck with skill.

If you understand the effects of both and coolly examine the key drivers of a fund's past success, you stand a good chance of finding a fund that's likely to outperform in the future. You can figure out which new popular funds will face rough seas and which ones won't be greatly affected by a larger asset base. You can also find funds that have escaped investors' attention because they're relatively new or simply didn't make the cover of *Money* and have never been overwhelmed with dollars.

I've carved up the 15 funds on this list into two groups. First, there are those that are relatively undiscovered and probably have greater potential upside, but are perhaps riskier bets. And the second group is those reliable veterans that should keep on chugging along.

Small and Nimble

Fidelity Spartan Short-Int Muni Inc FSTFX
Fidelity has quietly built the premier municipal-bond operation in the country. The firm has built outstanding analytical abilities with a great analyst staff and strong quantitative researchers to back it. While Fidelity's stock side labors under serious capacity constraints, the bond side has room to grow. I chose this fund because its relatively short maturity makes it a comfortable spot to be in a rising interest-rate environment.

ICAP Select Equity ICSLX
This is a great concentrated fund that has somehow avoided detection. Lead manager Rob Lyon and his group look for budget-priced stocks that boast a catalyst, such as a new product, to drive a higher share price. A number of their top-weighted picks have hit the mark, leading to superb long-term returns without any more volatility than the typical large-value offering.

Wasatch Heritage Growth WAHGX
Many of our favorite mid-growth funds are closing, becoming bloated, or both. So, we're going to stick our necks out for something really fresh. This fund was launched in June 2004, yet we're recommending it because Wasatch has built an outstanding track record in small caps. We think Wasatch can do just fine in mid-cap land and, in fact, the shop's managers followed many of today's mid-growth names when they were small caps. This fund even offers one improvement over Wasatch's small-cap funds: price. Wasatch has capped expenses at just 1.00% for now.

Western Asset Core Bond WATFX
We think the world of PIMCO's giant **Total Return** PTTRX, but this lesser-known gem also serves as a superb core fixed-income holding. This fund has at times courted more interest-rate sensitivity than the typical intermediate-term bond offering, and management has also focused on corporate bonds at the expense of gilt-edged Treasuries. Management has a record of getting those calls right over time, including cutting back on the fund's corporate stake and reducing its rate responsiveness in late 2003. While most retail investors will have to pay a bit more in expenses for the financial intermediary share class (which trades under the ticker WAPIX), we still think it represents quite a deal for an offering that boasts such a deep research staff.

Selected Special Shares SLSSX
Davis/Selected Advisers has long earned our admiration for its great work at two large-cap value funds, **Selected American** SLASX and **Davis NY Venture** NYVTX. At this fund, the team turns its attention to faster-growing stocks in the small- and mid-cap realm. That universe of stocks is fraught with potential pitfalls, but these managers aren't likely to throw risk control out the window.

PIMCO CommodityRealReturn Strategy PCRAX
OK, so the name is longer than a lot of Oscar acceptance speeches. Even so, this is a great fund that fills a valuable role in portfolios. The fund can serve as a great inflation hedge because it tracks commodity prices. Inflation spikes can damage your bond portfolio, so investing a little money in this fund can serve as useful insurance. Commodities are volatile, but used in moderation this fund can be a great diversifier.

PIMCO RCM Tax-Managed Growth DRTNX
This fund isn't at all related to PIMCO's bond group. Instead it's run by RCM, a growth shop that has a clever "grass-roots research" department that creates scores of field research reports to ensure that the reality on the ground matches up with the story company management is telling investors. What really makes this little fund appealing, though, is the fact that it's about the only one in existence that combines growth momentum investing with a tax-managed strategy.

Vanguard Selected Value VASVX
This fund hasn't gotten much attention, but I like the fund's prospects in what could be a low-returning environment for both stocks and bonds. Jim Barrow and Mark Giambrone focus on stocks that are cheap on an absolute basis, giving the fund room to make money no matter how overvalued the broad market is. Moreover, the fund's dividend focus could be an important advantage if dividends become a bigger component of total return than they have been in the recent past. Finally, the fund's low expense ratio will give it a leg up on its rivals in an environment of low absolute returns.

Old Reliables

Janus Mid Cap Value JMCVX
Perkins, Wolf, McDonnell & Co. launched its first fund in small-cap value space. That one worked so well that the shop launched this fund in 1998. So far, this fund has lived up to the high expectations set by its predecessor, and the fund's asset base hasn't yet outstripped management's abilities to run it effectively.

Fidelity Capital Appreciation FDCAX
Manager Harry Lange isn't shy about making bold bets here, but he also has an exceptional track record of making those bets pay off. Year-over-year performance, admittedly, has been a bit choppy, owing to Lange's sector bets and willingness to pay up for the names he likes. Still, as the offering's fine risk/return profile indicates, investors here have been handsomely compensated.

Vanguard Wellesley Income VWINX
This income-oriented fund won't thrive in every market, but its focus on dividend-paying stocks and high-quality bonds means that it's a sensible diversification tool for a portfolio tilted toward growth stocks. And as with all Vanguard funds, ultralow costs are a gift that keeps on giving.

Fidelity Asset Manager FASMX
This is another great conservative fund that holds both stocks and bonds. It typically keeps 50% of assets in stocks and usually maintains a modest cash stake. From there, lead manager Dick Habermann makes minor tactical adjustments to the fund's asset mix to take advantage of market currents. All told, this is a steady, all-weather offering that should suit conservative investors.

Dreyfus Appreciation DGAGX
This fund's unwavering focus on high-quality mega-cap companies has helped it deliver consistently superb results. The fund's tendency to underweight the technology sector holds it back when that sector rallies, but it also has made for a very smooth ride here. An added bonus: A very low turnover rate has led to excellent tax efficiency.

T. Rowe Price Equity-Income PRFDX
This fund might look a little slow when growth stocks rally, but its old-fashioned, value-leaning portfolio will ensure that its investors sleep easy at night. Manager Brian Rogers focuses on dividend-paying securities here, and while lots of large-cap value funds use a similar strategy, this one's execution has been better than most.

Vanguard Total Stock Market Index VTSMX
This could be the only domestic-stock fund you'll ever need. It offers exposure to 5,000 publicly traded U.S. companies—large and small, fast-growing and slow-growing—in a single, ultracheap package. Over time its returns have been extremely competitive relative to the broad universe of domestic-stock funds, and its returns look equally attractive on an aftertax basis. For investors who want simplicity without sacrificing diversification, it doesn't get much better than this. **M**

Category Killers: Seven Sector Fund Standouts with Real Expertise

Where to look for potential success rather than a flash in the pan.

by Russel Kinnel, Director of Fund Research

There's a special allure to a sector fund. You're hiring a specialist who knows the industry inside and out, and the industry is poised for tremendous growth. At least that's the pitch that fund companies often make.

In reality, sector funds are often run by second-string managers at second-string firms. Think of past duds such as Merrill Lynch Technology, Kemper Technology (nee Kemper Television), Kinetics Middle East Peace Fund (no, I'm not making that up), and AIM Global Financial.

Some sector-fund managers are real experts in their fields, but others are not. Often, the best investors in a sector are managing diversified funds rather than sector funds.

Fidelity actually makes a point of assigning to its sector funds managers who don't have experience in the relevant field because the firm wants its analysts to become well-rounded before they tackle a diversified fund. For example, **Fidelity Select Brokerage & Investment** FSLBX manager Brian Kennedy previously ran **Fidelity Select Multimedia** FBMPX. Heather Lawrence moved from **Fidelity Select Transportation** FSRFX to **Fidelity Select Banking** FSRBX. Moreover, Fidelity's sector fund managers are compensated based on the performance of their recommendations to managers of big diversified funds—not the returns of the sector funds they run.

And of course the "hot sector" promise rarely works, either. Usually fund companies don't get around to pushing a sector fund until that sector has enjoyed a strong rally and is due to cool off. In addition, investors tend to time their own purchases and sales poorly. Thus, we've found there's a wide gap between sector funds' published returns and the actual returns experienced by sector-fund shareholders. Why? Because so many people buy after a rally and sell after a correction.

Finally, sector funds often charge higher expenses than diversified funds, even though they may have fewer investment professionals contributing to it than the diversified fund. In short, sector funds rarely live up to the hype.

The good news is that there are a handful of sector funds that really do live up to their promise. They have the expertise, sound strategies, and reasonable expenses that enable long-term investors to earn attractive returns. If you're looking for a solid long-term investment rather than a quick killing, you can probably do quite well with these funds. I've chosen a few standouts whose industry expertise sets them apart.

Security Capital U.S. Real Estate SUSIX
Security Capital is a small name in the mutual fund world but a big name in the real estate world. Given this team's expertise in real estate investing, I'm amazed that this fund has only attracted $300 million in assets while lesser real estate funds have raked in billions. Managers Ken Statz, Kevin Bedell, and Anthony Manno have been with the fund since its 1996 inception, but each had many years of experience investing in real estate before that. The fund also has the support of seven analysts—more than any other real estate fund.

They use discounted cash-flow estimates to build a concentrated portfolio of real estate holdings, and they've shown a knack for good issue picks as well as good industry bets. For example, a contrarian bet on residential REITS paid off nicely in 2004.

Davis Financial RPFGX
Talk about areas of expertise. Chris Davis' grandfather made a killing in insurance stocks coming out of the Depression. Likewise, his father cleaned up as manager of **Davis NY Venture** NYVTX, a nominally diversified fund that had about half its assets in financials. Now Chris Davis and Ken Feinberg run the family flagship, as well as this financials-focused fund, and have distinguished themselves as two of the best investors in financials stocks that you can find east of Omaha. In fact, Warren Buffett has bought out more than a couple of their stock picks over the years, including GEICO. (Davis and Feinberg wisely kept the shares of **Berkshire Hathaway** BRK.B they got in return.) This fund's annualized 10-year returns of 15.31% rank in the top 20% of financials funds.

Vanguard Health Care VGHCX
This fund has almost everything you could want in a sector fund. First, it has an experienced manager in Ed Owens, who has put up great

returns for 20 years at this fund. You also get great analytical resources, thanks to Wellington Management's deep bench. And you get all that for just 0.28% a year—less than the cheapest health-care index fund charges. I also like the portfolio's heavy bias toward big pharmaceutical names, because the stocks appear cheaper than biotech and medical-device stocks right now. The bad news is that the fund is so big that it has no choice but to invest most of its assets in big pharma. In the past it has had some big gains in mid-caps. In addition, its $25,000 investment minimum means you've got to have a pretty big portfolio to make this niche fund a good fit.

T. Rowe Price Health Sciences PRHSX
If you want a health-care option with more flexibility than the Vanguard fund has, this is your fund. Manager Kris Jenner has just $1 billion to manage, and he's put that flexibility to good use by investing in lots of smaller drug and biotech stocks. Thus, if you want a health-care fund that will attempt to get into the next **Amgen** AMGN early, it's a nice option. Jenner has been at the helm since 2000, but his experience before that is helpful, too. He served as T. Rowe's biotech analyst for two years and was trained as a physician. T. Rowe's four health-care analysts support Jenner here.

PIMCO RCM Global Technology DRGTX
The technology world changes so quickly that finding an experienced management team that's devoting all its time to tech investing is an appealing—and all too rare—thing. Managers Huachen Chen and Walter Price have been running this fund for 10 years, and their great returns over that stretch prove they know their stuff. (Although this fund has the PIMCO name, it has nothing to do with PIMCO's bond group. RCM and PIMCO are both owned by Allianz, which decided to brand a lot of its funds as PIMCO.) RCM is a solid, growth-oriented firm that employs an army of part-time field researchers to verify that what management is saying is actually borne out in the marketplace. The only catch here is that the institutional share class is the only one with a decent expense ratio. Some fund supermarkets allow investors to buy PIMCO's institutional shares for a set fee, but that's about the only way to get in without getting overcharged on costs.

PIMCO CommodityRealReturn Strategy PCRAX
This fund is a bit of an outlier on my list of great sector funds. Whereas my other picks boast managers with years of experience in a given sector, PIMCO is experienced in bond and derivative investing rather than natural resources. However, we think this fund brings a lot to the table. Manager John B. Brynjolfsson uses derivatives linked to commodities such as oil and natural gas, grains, livestock, coffee, and industrial and precious metals. At the same time, he holds a bond portfolio to make good on the derivatives. It's a complicated strategy, but the fund shouldn't be that hard to use. Although it will likely be extremely volatile, studies have shown that commodities exposure can actually lower your overall portfolio's volatility and enhance returns; the fund can also serve to limit any losses you might suffer in your bond funds if inflation spikes. We prefer it to its commodity-focused counterpart run by Oppenheimer because the Oppenheimer fund is almost a pure play on oil. PIMCO CommodityRealReturn is apt to be a better portfolio diversifier than equity-based natural-resources funds, and because it's run by PIMCO, you can expect the firm to add value with its bond holdings.

T. Rowe Price Media & Telecommunications PRMTX
Manager Rob Gensler looks for companies with strong cash flows whose stocks are trading at reasonable valuations. That approach has paved the way to solid relative results under Gensler's watch. In fact, the fund has handily outpaced its typical rival since Gensler took the helm in January 2000. All told, Gensler's deft maneuvering in the sector, coupled with strong analytical support, make this fund an attractive entrant in the group.

Using Sector Funds in Your Portfolio
I wouldn't recommend scooping up a bunch of sector funds. However, you can effectively use one or two. If your portfolio has a glaring hole when you look at it on a sector basis, the funds can come in handy. Or they can simply work as a bet on a manager's expertise. As in many things in life, moderation is key to enjoyment. M

How to Use This Book

Tips for getting the most out of your Morningstar Funds 500.

by Christine Benz, Associate Director of Fund Analysis

Just as most professional stock-pickers agree that it's impossible to pick securities based solely on their past performance patterns, we at Morningstar have long argued that successful fund investing begins with fundamental analysis—not checking last year's leaders' lists. True, looking at the best-performing funds for any given time period can provide important clues about market trends, and that's why this book includes plenty of fund rankings. (See Pages 538-540.) But to truly understand a fund and the role it might play in a portfolio, investors have to drill down into its holdings, understand the manager's strategy, assess the shareholder-friendliness of the fund company, and evaluate its risk level.

Toward that end, this year's Morningstar Funds 500 is chock-full of all the data and analysis you need to make informed decisions. Read on as we walk through some of the best tools for doing just that. (The User's Guide that begins on Page 561 provides you with specific definitions of all of the data points in the book.)

Analyst Picks

Analyst Picks, a complete listing of which appears on Page 26, are Morningstar fund analysts' "best ideas" within every fund category. The analysts responsible for the picks within each fund category are charged with finding those offerings with strong track records, reasonable volatility, compelling strategies, great managers, and low expenses. We also look for our Analyst Picks to hail from firms that have a strong record of putting shareholders' interests first.

Many of our choices are fairly obvious. From staid large-value funds such as **American Funds Washington Mutual** AWSHX to high-octane mid-growth offerings such as **Turner Midcap Growth** TMGFX, our list of picks is full of well-known, well-run "category killers." Of course, some categories may be inappropriate for some investors. For example, even though our precious-metals picks offer topnotch returns on relative and absolute bases, we're not recommending that everyone go out and buy a gold fund. But once you've determined that you're looking for a certain type of fund, the Analyst Picks list is a natural next step.

Morningstar's Take

The text box in the lower left-hand quadrant of each individual fund page is the analysis, or "Morningstar's Take." Reading the analysis is an essential first step as you attempt to determine whether a fund is appropriate for your goals and risk tolerance. In it, the analyst sums up all of a fund's salient points by assessing its historical risk/reward profile relative to its peer group, discussing the manager's strategy, and noting any recent changes to the portfolio or its management. And because Morningstar analysts generally speak with each fund manager and have Morningstar's extensive database at their fingertips, the analysis can provide glimpses into a fund that you won't find anywhere else.

Fiduciary Grade

In an effort to summarize all of the factors that determine whether a fund company is shareholder-friendly, we developed our new fiduciary grades. The letter grades, which appear on the individual-fund pages, right below the fund's name, range from A to F. The grades take into account whether the fund company has had prior run-ins with securities regulators, the quality of the fund's board, the structure of the fund's manager incentives, the fund's expenses relative to its peers', and its corporate culture. For a complete overview of the fiduciary grades and how to use them, please see Page 7.

Star Ratings

For years, the Morningstar Rating for funds—the "star rating"—has been our best-known tool. This risk-adjusted rating is designed to give you a quick look at a fund's historical risk/reward profile, with 5 stars being the best rating and 1 star being the worst. The star rating is derived from a fund's standing within its category rather than within a broad asset class. For example, we rate a fund such as **Fidelity Low-Priced Stock** FLPSX alongside its category peers—other small-cap blend funds. That helps show you how well a fund has executed its particular style.

The star rating isn't predictive, and there may well be situations when a fund's star rating doesn't reflect its worthiness. For example, a fund that just gained a topnotch manager may sport a relatively low star rating, even though its prospects have recently improved. Nonetheless, searching for 4- and 5-star funds can be an effective way to determine—quickly—which funds merit further investigation and which do not.

Style Boxes/Morningstar Categories

The Morningstar style box, the nine-square grid that appears toward the bottom right-hand corner of each individual fund page, is designed to give you a visual snapshot of the type of securities a fund is buying. For stock funds, the style box shows you the size of companies in which a fund invests, as well as whether the fund manager buys growth- or value-oriented securities. For bond funds, the style box depicts a fund's sensitivity to interest rates as well as the average credit quality of the bonds in the portfolio. Armed with three years' worth of style boxes, we determine a fund's Morningstar category placement, which reflects how the fund has invested its assets over the past three years. (The Morningstar category appears in the top right-hand corner of each fund page.)

As a general rule of thumb, large-cap blend or large-cap value funds make the best core stock holdings, because they invest in the well-established companies that tend to dominate the market. For those seeking a core bond-fund holding, the intermediate-term bond category will generally be the best hunting ground. Such funds are typically well-diversified across government and corporate bonds and have some (although not extreme) sensitivity to interest-rate changes.

Just as Morningstar's style boxes and categories can help you make smart fund selections, they can also help you determine how to put the funds together into a well-diversified package. While you need not buy a fund in every single Morningstar category, building a portfolio of funds with varying investment styles is a sensible diversification strategy.

Sector Weightings

Sector weightings, which appear in the bottom right-hand corner of each stock fund page, pick up where a fund's investment-style box leaves off. Eyeballing a fund's sector weightings is an essential step on the road to understanding how a fund will behave and how you might use it (or not use it) to build a diversified portfolio. After all, funds may land in different Morningstar categories, but if their sector compositions are similar, it's possible that their performances will be, too.

You'll notice that we also provide you with a fund's three-year high and low weightings within each sector. Those figures can help put the fund's current sector positioning in context. For example, a fund that has a low current weighting in the technology-hardware sector but a far heftier three-year high weighting shouldn't necessarily be considered tame. After all, its manager has tilted the portfolio toward a very volatile sector once and may well do so again.

Tax Analysis

After three years of bear-market losses, many funds posted solid returns in 2003 and 2004, meaning that sizable capital gains could be in the offing. In an effort to help you know whether a fund is best suited to a taxable or tax-deferred account, we've developed our tax-analysis section, which is located on the left-hand side of every fund page. The section gives you an estimate of how much of a fund's return an investor in the highest tax bracket would be able to pocket after taxes. Pay particularly close attention to a fund's tax-adjusted return ranking within its category. If a fund's tax-adjusted return ranking is higher than its raw-return ranking, that could indicate that management is using a tax-efficient strategy. If the opposite is true, you might want to consider holding that fund in a tax-sheltered account such as an IRA.

Tables and Charts

For those of you who love lists (and who doesn't?) Pages 532-550 include an impressive array of fund data and rankings. In general, selecting funds from a list of short-term leaders is a poor investment strategy. But eyeballing the lists of top-performing funds over longer time frames—over the past five and 10 years, for example—can provide you with great ideas for further research. The lists of leaders and laggards over various time frames can also be a good way to get up to speed on recent market trends. Small-value funds dominate the three- and five-year domestic-equity funds' leader list on Page 538, for example, whereas aggressive, tech-stock-laden funds bring up the rear over these time frames. M

The Morningstar Stock-Fund Page

In this six-page walk-through, we briefly describe how each section of the page is relevant to your fund research and offer some tips on using these features to better analyze funds. More-detailed discussions of the elements presented in this section appear in the user's guide.

A Historical Investment Style Boxes

B Morningstar Rating

C Portfolio Manager(s) Profile and Fiduciary Grade

D Manager Strategy

E Performance

F Tax Analysis

G Morningstar's Take

H Operations

Data through December 31, 2004

Fidelity Contrafund

Analyst Pick	Ticker	Load	NAV	Yield	Total Assets	Mstar Category
	FCNTX	None	$56.74	0.1%	$44,484 mil	Large Growth

Governance and Management

Fiduciary Grade: B

Portfolio Manager(s)

Will Danoff has been at the helm since 1990 and is backed by Fidelity's deep research staff. He has adapted his style to the fund's size by holding more large caps, and he has cut the fund's turnover in recent years. He's also now running a new fund, Fidelity Advisor New Insights.

Historical Profile

Return: High
Risk: Low
Rating: ★★★★★ Highest

Investment Style Equity Stock %: 88% 85% 90% 94% 91% 89% 90% 94% 88%

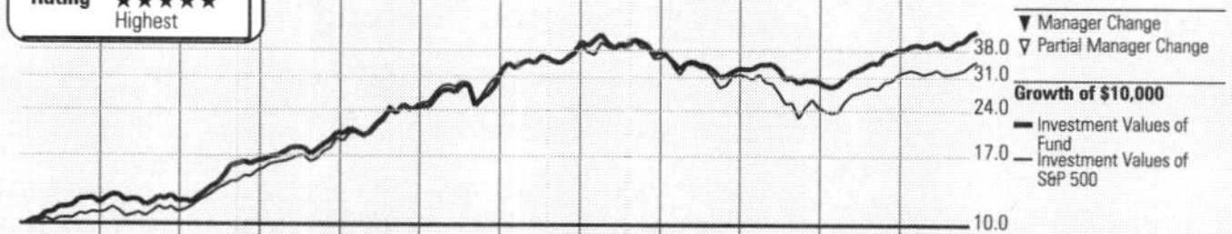

Performance Quartile (within Category)

Strategy

Call it forced evolution. As this fund's asset base grew in the 1990s, manager Will Danoff had to move away from mid-caps and small caps and adopt a growth-at-a-reasonable-price philosophy. He continues to keep a big part of the fund in mid-caps, but it is now dominated by larger fare. It has been more conservative than most of its large-blend rivals in recent years, with big underweightings in racy sectors such as technology, but Danoff is starting to ramp up its exposure to growth companies.

1993	1994	1995	1996	1997	1998	1999	2000	2001	2002	2003	12-04	History
30.84	30.28	38.02	42.15	46.63	56.81	60.02	49.18	42.77	38.60	49.35	56.74	NAV
21.43	-1.12	36.28	21.94	23.00	31.57	25.03	-6.80	-12.59	-9.63	27.95	15.07	Total Return %
11.37	-2.43	-1.25	-1.00	-10.35	3.00	3.99	2.30	-0.71	12.46	-0.72	4.20	+/-S&P 500
18.56	-3.74	-0.90	-1.18	-7.49	-7.14	-8.13	15.62	7.83	18.25	-1.80	8.77	+/-Russ 1000Gr
0.66	0.00	0.30	1.05	0.84	0.64	0.50	0.41	0.45	0.12	0.10	0.09	Income Return %
20.77	-1.12	35.98	20.89	22.16	30.93	24.53	-7.21	-13.04	-9.75	27.85	14.98	Capital Return %
13	46	22	30	70	50	73	24	12	1	46	5	Total Rtn % Rank Cat
0.18	0.00	0.09	0.38	0.35	0.30	0.28	0.24	0.22	0.05	0.04	0.05	Income $
2.25	0.22	3.13	3.45	4.56	4.22	10.22	6.62	0.00	0.00	0.00	0.00	Capital Gains $
1.06	1.00	0.96	0.79	0.67	0.61	0.62	0.84	0.91	0.99	0.98	—	Expense Ratio %
0.46	0.59	0.44	1.28	0.91	0.70	0.48	0.45	0.49	0.14	0.01	—	Income Ratio %
255	235	223	159	144	197	177	166	141	80	67	—	Turnover Rate %
6,193	8,682	14,832	23,798	30,809	38,821	46,927	40,220	32,321	27,695	36,051	44,484	Net Assets $mil

Performance 12-31-04

	1st Qtr	2nd Qtr	3rd Qtr	4th Qtr	Total
2000	5.56	-6.58	1.13	-6.54	-6.80
2001	-13.18	3.47	-8.80	6.70	-12.59
2002	2.88	-3.68	-9.86	1.18	-9.63
2003	-2.15	11.83	5.02	11.34	27.95
2004	3.75	2.36	-0.63	9.04	15.07

Trailing	Total Return%	+/- S&P 500	+/- Russ 1000Gr	%Rank Cat	Growth of $10,000
3 Mo	9.04	-0.19	-0.13	67	10,904
6 Mo	8.35	1.16	4.88	13	10,835
1 Yr	15.07	4.20	8.77	5	11,507
3 Yr Avg	9.99	6.41	10.17	1	13,306
5 Yr Avg	1.62	3.92	10.91	3	10,837
10 Yr Avg	13.81	1.74	4.22	4	36,459
15 Yr Avg	15.03	4.10	5.53	1	81,690

Tax Analysis	Tax-Adj Rtn%	%Rank Cat	Tax-Cost Rat	%Rank Cat
3 Yr (estimated)	9.95	1	0.04	7
5 Yr (estimated)	1.01	3	0.60	37
10 Yr (estimated)	11.77	5	1.79	63

Potential Capital Gain Exposure: 24% of assets

Rating and Risk

Time Period	Load-Adj Return %	Morningstar Rtn vs Cat	Morningstar Risk vs Cat	Morningstar Risk-Adj Rating
1 Yr	15.07			
3 Yr	9.99	High	Low	★★★★★
5 Yr	1.62	High	Low	★★★★★
10 Yr	13.81	High	Low	★★★★★
Incept	13.29			

Other Measures	Standard Index S&P 500	Best Fit Index S&P Mid 400
Alpha	7.2	2.7
Beta	0.54	0.31
R-Squared	63	33
Standard Deviation	11.05	
Mean	9.99	
Sharpe Ratio	0.79	

Portfolio Analysis 09-30-04

Share change since 06-04 Total Stocks:503	Sector	PE	YTD Ret%	% Assets
⊖ Avon Products	Goods	23.1	2.30	2.99
Berkshire Hathaway A	Financial	—	—	2.82
⊖ 3M Company	Ind Mtrls	22.8	0.28	2.81
⊖ EnCana	Energy	10.9	-6.47	2.02
⊕ Yahoo	Media	95.9	-4.56	1.74
⊖ Genentech	Health	84.1	-0.35	1.58
Samsung Electronics	Goods	—	—	1.22
⊕ American International G	Financial	16.3	2.91	1.19
⊕ Patterson Companies	Health	36.8	-1.34	1.18
⊕ Danaher	Ind Mtrls	25.8	-3.33	1.17
⊕ Newmont Mining	Ind Mtrls	44.6	-6.55	1.11
⊖ Nextel Communications	Telecom	11.0	0.43	1.08
⊖ Lockheed Martin	Ind Mtrls	19.8	-1.40	1.02
⊖ eBay	Consumer	82.9	-8.39	0.97
⊖ Golden West Financial	Financial	15.1	-2.20	0.94
⊕ Gillette	Goods	27.3	-1.74	0.93
⊕ Marvell Technology	Hardware	NMF	-2.73	0.92
⊖ Colgate-Palmolive	Goods	20.2	-2.11	0.89
⊕ Alcon	Health	41.2	-1.77	0.87
⊕ BP PLC ADR	Energy	20.8	-2.00	0.85

Current Investment Style

Value Blnd Growth — Large Mid Small

Market Cap	%
Giant	25.6
Large	36.6
Mid	32.2
Small	5.2
Micro	0.5

Avg $mil: 12,688

Value Measures		Rel Category
Price/Earnings	19.34	0.91
Price/Book	3.03	0.94
Price/Sales	1.68	0.79
Price/Cash Flow	8.12	0.74
Dividend Yield %	0.73	0.95

Growth Measures	%	Rel Category
Long-Term Erngs	14.20	1.01
Book Value	13.95	1.09
Sales	11.64	1.38
Cash Flow	20.71	1.24
Historical Erngs	32.22	2.22

Profitability	%	Rel Category
Return on Equity	21.05	1.17
Return on Assets	10.16	1.09
Net Margin	12.58	1.02

Sector Weightings	% of Stocks	Rel S&P 500	3 Year High	3 Year Low
Info	16.94	0.79		
Software	2.36	0.55	2	1
Hardware	6.40	0.63	7	1
Media	3.56	0.93	4	1
Telecom	4.62	1.47	5	0
Service	44.61	0.96		
Health	13.86	1.11	19	14
Consumer	10.09	1.11	14	10
Business	6.41	1.58	9	5
Financial	14.25	0.69	18	14
Mfg	38.45	1.20		
Goods	10.41	1.12	20	10
Ind Mtrls	16.19	1.28	16	14
Energy	11.01	1.54	11	5
Utilities	0.84	0.28	1	0

Composition

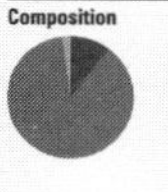

Cash	10.1
Stocks	87.9
Bonds	1.7
Other	0.3
Foreign (% of Stock)	19.9

Morningstar's Take by Christopher Traulsen 01-05-05

Fidelity Contrafund continues to impress.

This fund, which we recently moved to the large-growth category from large blend, has just posted another strong year. It finished 2004 up 15%, more than 7 percentage points ahead of the typical large-growth fund, and 4 percentage points ahead of the S&P 500 Index for the period.

Manager Will Danoff helped the fund's cause by a savvy move into Internet stocks such as Yahoo and eBay. He also correctly boosted the fund's energy stake, taking it from under 5% of the fund's equity portfolio up to nearly 11%, and overweighted industrials stocks. Both sectors benefited from the global economic recovery, and the resulting supply/demand imbalance that drove commodity prices up.

As always, the portfolio remains expansive. Despite lugging a $44 billion asset base, Danoff has shoehorned 32% of the fund into mid-cap stocks, and even has a smattering of small caps in the portfolio. He also has significant overseas exposure, with 18% of assets in foreign stocks. On the whole, relative to other large-growth funds, this offering is less aggressive than the norm. Danoff spreads its assets across more than 500 stocks, and while the fund's growth rates are well above category averages, its valuations are below those of its typical peer.

Danoff's eclecticism has paid off in spades: The fund owns top-flight three-, five-, and 10-year returns, while its diversification has helped make it less volatile than its average rival. We remain concerned with the fund's size, however. With an asset base of $44 billion, it's undeniably harder for Danoff to succeed than it was when the fund was much smaller. That said, Danoff has shown skill in handling the growth, and he has also reduced the fund's turnover in recent years, which should make the task more manageable. We continue to think this is a great core holding.

Address:	Fidelity Investments Company Boston MA 02109 800-343-3548	Minimum Purchase:	$2500	Add: $250	IRA: $2500
		Min Auto Inv Plan:	$2500	Add: $250	
		Sales Fees:	No-load		
Web Address:		Management Fee:	0.81%		
Inception:	05-17-67	Actual Fees:	Mgt:0.81%	Dist:6	
Advisor:	Fidelity Management & Research Co. (FMR)	Expense Projections:	3Yr:$502	5Yr:$651	10Yr:$1086
Subadvisor:	FMR Co., Inc. (FMRC)	Income Distrib:	Annually		
NTF Plans:	Fidelity Retail-NTF, CommonWealth NTF				

MORNINGSTAR® **Funds 500**

A Historical Investment Style Boxes

Does the manager stick with a consistent investment style year to year, or does he or she invest in different areas of the market as they become attractive? These are important questions to ask when building a portfolio. If you buy a fund to occupy a particular investment area, you will want it to maintain that position.

B Morningstar Rating

The star rating is a good way to identify funds that have provided the best balance of risk and return within their Morningstar Category. It sets out to separate the long-term winners from the losers. It's best used as a first screen, as a tool to narrow the field to a manageable group of funds to look at in-depth. Using it in other ways, such as a timing device, a predictive measure, or the sole reason to buy a fund, is not a good strategy.

C Management & Governance

The portfolio manager is the individual or individuals responsible for the overall fund strategy, as well as the buying and selling decisions for the securities in a fund's portfolio. To help investors know who is running a fund, we detail the fund's management with a brief biography. We note the manager's background, experience, analytical support, other funds managed, and whether the manager invests in his or her own fund. If a fund has a great record but new management, beware: The fund's best days may be behind it. This section also includes our analysts' Fiduciary Grades.

D Manager Strategy

While the Morningstar Category gives investors an idea of the kind of investments a manager makes, it does not fully capture the nuances of a manager's approach to picking stocks or bonds. In this section, Morningstar's analysts explain what criteria a manager uses in selecting securities, and how risky a given approach may be. On the equity side, the strategy description often focuses on what size and type of company a manager prefers, along with a discussion regarding how he or she balances growth and value factors. With bond funds, the strategy section explains whether the manager makes interest-rate and credit-quality bets, or whether management attempts to add value with individual security selection.

E Performance

The quarterly returns show the performance investors have seen over each calendar quarter in the past five years. This section is a good spot to quickly test your risk tolerance. Find the largest quarterly loss; if it makes you uneasy, you should probably look for less-volatile funds. The trailing returns section illustrates performance over short and long periods. We compare returns against appropriate benchmarks and peers: 1 is the best percentile; 100 is the worst.

F Tax Analysis

This section lists a fund's tax-adjusted returns and the percentage-point reduction in annualized returns that results from taxes, called the tax-cost ratio. For context, each figure is then given a percentile rank in the fund's category (1 is the best percentile; 100 is the worst). Examine the two returns figures together because high tax-adjusted returns do not necessarily mean the fund is tax-efficient. Also, a fund could be very tax-efficient, but if returns are poor to begin with, an investor will still pocket a low sum. This section is perhaps best used to determine whether a fund should be held in a tax-deferred or taxable account.

G Morningstar's Take

Our analysts interpret the data on the page and interview the fund's manager to uncover the strategies guiding investment decisions. They then succinctly detail how and why a fund has succeeded or failed, and what role—if any—it should play in your portfolio.

H Operations

Here we list where to write or call to obtain investment information from the fund. We also list the fund's minimum initial purchase and break down a fund's expenses into their components.

I Morningstar Category

The Morningstar Category is the first stage of digging into the fund's portfolio. We sort funds into peer groups based on the types of securities the funds hold. Each category is assigned using a fundamental analysis of a fund's portfolio over a three-year period. It is important to analyze the types of securities a fund holds. Portfolio analysis, and a fund's category, can tell you a lot about a fund's performance and future volatility. For example, investors can expect bumpier rides with funds in the small-cap growth category—those that focus on small, rapidly growing companies—than with large-cap value funds, which focus on well-established companies that are trading cheaply. In addition to portfolio analysis, the Morningstar categories also can help you diversify and evaluate the

The Morningstar Stock-Fund Page (continued)

I — Morningstar Category

J — Investment Value Graph

K — Performance Quartile Graph

L — History

M — Rating and Risk

N — Portfolio Analysis

Data through December 31, 2004

Fidelity Contrafund

Analyst	Ticker	Load	NAV	Yield	Total Assets	Mstar Category
Pick	FCNTX	None	$56.74	0.1%	$44,484 mil	Large Growth

Governance and Management

Fiduciary Grade: B

Portfolio Manager(s)

Will Danoff has been at the helm since 1990 and is backed by Fidelity's deep research staff. He has adapted his style to the fund's size by holding more large caps, and he has cut the fund's turnover in recent years. He's also now running a new fund, Fidelity Advisor New Insights.

Historical Profile
Return: High
Risk: Low
Rating: ★★★★★ Highest

Investment Style: Equity — Stock %: 88% | 85% | 90% | 94% | 91% | 89% | 90% | 94% | 88%

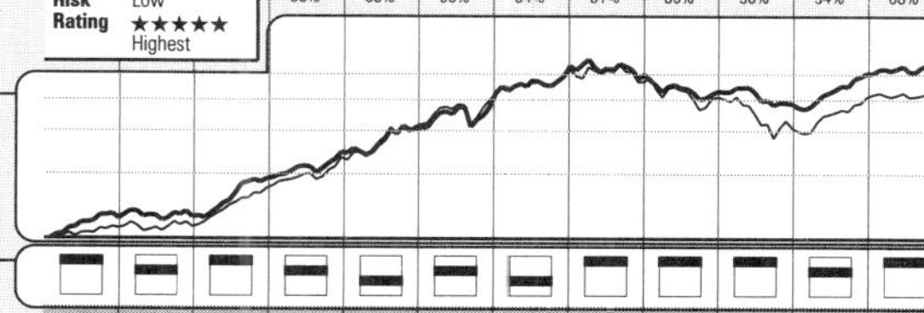

Performance Quartile (within Category)

Strategy

Call it forced evolution. As this fund's asset base grew in the 1990s, manager Will Danoff had to move away from mid-caps and small caps and adopt a growth-at-a-reasonable-price philosophy. He continues to keep a big part of the fund in mid-caps, but it is now dominated by larger fare. It has been more conservative than most of its large-blend rivals in recent years, with big underweightings in racy sectors such as technology, but Danoff is starting to ramp up its exposure to growth companies.

1993	1994	1995	1996	1997	1998	1999	2000	2001	2002	2003	12-04	History
30.84	30.28	38.02	42.15	46.63	56.81	60.02	49.18	42.77	38.60	49.35	56.74	NAV
21.43	-1.12	36.28	21.94	23.00	31.57	25.03	-6.80	-12.59	-9.63	27.95	15.07	Total Return %
11.37	-2.43	-1.25	-1.00	-10.35	3.00	3.99	2.30	-0.71	12.46	-0.72	4.20	+/-S&P 500
18.56	-3.74	-0.90	-1.18	-7.49	-7.14	-8.13	15.62	7.83	18.25	-1.80	8.77	+/-Russ 1000Gr
0.66	0.00	0.30	1.05	0.84	0.64	0.50	0.41	0.45	0.12	0.10	0.09	Income Return %
20.77	-1.12	35.98	20.89	22.16	30.93	24.53	-7.21	-13.04	-9.75	27.85	14.98	Capital Return %
13	46	22	30	70	50	73	24	12	1	46	5	Total Rtn % Rank Cat
0.18	0.00	0.09	0.38	0.35	0.30	0.23	0.24	0.22	0.05	0.04	0.05	Income $
2.25	0.22	3.13	3.45	4.56	4.22	10.22	6.62	0.00	0.00	0.00	0.00	Capital Gains $
1.06	1.00	0.96	0.79	0.67	0.61	0.62	0.84	0.91	0.99	0.98	—	Expense Ratio %
0.46	0.59	0.44	1.28	0.91	0.70	0.43	0.45	0.49	0.14	0.01	—	Income Ratio %
255	235	223	159	144	197	177	166	141	80	67	—	Turnover Rate %
6,193	8,682	14,832	23,798	30,809	38,821	46,527	40,220	32,321	27,695	36,051	44,484	Net Assets $mil

Performance 12-31-04

	1st Qtr	2nd Qtr	3rd Qtr	4th Qtr	Total
2000	5.56	-6.58	1.13	-6.54	-6.80
2001	-13.18	3.47	-8.80	6.70	-12.59
2002	2.88	-3.68	-9.86	1.18	-9.63
2003	-2.15	11.83	5.02	11.34	27.95
2004	3.75	2.36	-0.63	9.04	15.07

Trailing	Total Return%	+/- S&P 500	+/- Russ 1000Gr	%Rank Cat	Growth of $10,000
3 Mo	9.04	-0.19	-0.13	67	10,904
6 Mo	8.35	1.16	4.88	13	10,835
1 Yr	15.07	4.20	8.77	5	11,507
3 Yr Avg	9.99	6.41	10.17	1	13,306
5 Yr Avg	1.62	3.92	10.91	3	10,837
10 Yr Avg	13.81	1.74	4.22	4	36,459
15 Yr Avg	15.03	4.10	5.53	1	81,690

Tax Analysis	Tax-Adj Rtn%	%Rank Cat	Tax-Cost Rat	%Rank Cat
3 Yr (estimated)	9.95	1	0.04	7
5 Yr (estimated)	1.01	3	0.60	37
10 Yr (estimated)	11.77	5	1.79	63

Potential Capital Gain Exposure: 24% of assets

Rating and Risk

Time Period	Load-Adj Return %	Morningstar Rtn vs Cat	Morningstar Risk vs Cat	Morningstar Risk-Adj Rating
1 Yr	15.07			
3 Yr	9.99	High	Low	★★★★★
5 Yr	1.62	High	Low	★★★★★
10 Yr	13.81	High	Low	★★★★★
Incept	13.29			

Other Measures	Standard Index S&P 500	Best Fit Index S&P Mid 400
Alpha	7.2	2.7
Beta	0.54	0.61
R-Squared	63	83
Standard Deviation	11.05	
Mean	9.99	
Sharpe Ratio	0.79	

Portfolio Analysis 09-30-04

Share change since 06-04 Total Stocks:503	Sector	PE	YTD Ret%	% Assets
⊖ Avon Products	Goods	23.1	2.30	2.99
Berkshire Hathaway A	Financial	—	—	2.82
⊖ 3M Company	Ind Mtrls	22.8	0.28	2.81
⊖ EnCana	Energy	10.9	-6.47	2.02
⊕ Yahoo	Media	95.9	-4.56	1.74
⊖ Genentech	Health	84.1	-0.35	1.58
Samsung Electronics	Goods	—	—	1.22
⊕ American International G	Financial	16.3	2.91	1.19
⊕ Patterson Companies	Health	36.8	-1.34	1.18
⊕ Danaher	Ind Mtrls	25.8	-3.33	1.17
⊕ Newmont Mining	Ind Mtrls	44.6	-6.55	1.11
⊖ Nextel Communications	Telecom	11.0	0.43	1.08
⊖ Lockheed Martin	Ind Mtrls	19.8	-1.40	1.02
⊖ eBay	Consumer	82.9	-8.39	0.97
⊖ Golden West Financial	Financial	15.1	-2.20	0.94
⊕ Gillette	Goods	27.3	-1.74	0.93
⊕ Marvell Technology	Hardware	NMF	-2.73	0.92
⊖ Colgate-Palmolive	Goods	20.2	-2.11	0.89
⊕ Alcon	Health	41.2	-1.77	0.87
⊕ BP PLC ADR	Energy	20.8	-2.00	0.85

Current Investment Style (Value Blnd Growth / Large Mid Small)

Market Cap	%
Giant	25.6
Large	36.6
Mid	32.2
Small	5.2
Micro	0.5
Avg $mil: 12,688	

Value Measures		Rel Category
Price/Earnings	19.34	0.91
Price/Book	3.03	0.94
Price/Sales	1.68	0.79
Price/Cash Flow	8.12	0.74
Dividend Yield %	0.73	0.95

Growth Measures	%	Rel Category
Long-Term Erngs	14.20	1.01
Book Value	13.95	1.09
Sales	11.64	1.38
Cash Flow	20.71	1.24
Historical Erngs	32.22	2.22

Profitability	%	Rel Category
Return on Equity	21.05	1.17
Return on Assets	10.16	1.09
Net Margin	12.58	1.02

Sector Weightings	% of Stocks	Rel S&P 500	3 Year High	3 Year Low
Info	16.94	0.79		
Software	2.36	0.55	2	1
Hardware	6.40	0.63	7	1
Media	3.56	0.93	4	1
Telecom	4.62	1.47	5	0
Service	44.61	0.96		
Health	13.86	1.11	19	14
Consumer	10.09	1.11	14	10
Business	6.41	1.58	9	5
Financial	14.25	0.69	18	14
Mfg	38.45	1.20		
Goods	10.41	1.12	20	10
Ind Mtrls	16.19	1.28	16	14
Energy	11.01	1.54	11	5
Utilities	0.84	0.28	1	0

Composition

Cash	10.1
Stocks	87.9
Bonds	1.7
Other	0.3
Foreign (% of Stock)	19.9

Morningstar's Take by Christopher Traulsen 01-05-05

Fidelity Contrafund continues to impress.

This fund, which we recently moved to the large-growth category from large blend, has just posted another strong year. It finished 2004 up 15%, more than 7 percentage points ahead of the typical large-growth fund, and 4 percentage points ahead of the S&P 500 Index for the period.

Manager Will Danoff helped the fund's cause by a savvy move into Internet stocks such as Yahoo and eBay. He also correctly boosted the fund's energy stake, taking it from under 5% of the fund's equity portfolio up to nearly 11%, and overweighted industrials stocks. Both sectors benefited from the global economic recovery, and the resulting supply/demand imbalance that drove commodity prices up.

As always, the portfolio remains expansive. Despite lugging a $44 billion asset base, Danoff has shoehorned 32% of the fund into mid-cap stocks, and even has a smattering of small caps in the portfolio. He also has significant overseas exposure, with 18% of assets in foreign stocks. On the whole, relative to other large-growth funds, this offering is less aggressive than the norm. Danoff spreads its assets across more than 500 stocks, and while the fund's growth rates are well above category averages, its valuations are below those of its typical peer.

Danoff's eclecticism has paid off in spades: The fund owns top-flight three-, five-, and 10-year returns, while its diversification has helped make it less volatile than its average rival. We remain concerned with the fund's size, however. With an asset base of $44 billion, it's undeniably harder for Danoff to succeed than it was when the fund was much smaller. That said, Danoff has shown skill in handling the growth, and he has also reduced the fund's turnover in recent years, which should make the task more manageable. We continue to think this is a great core holding.

Address:	Fidelity Investments Company, Boston MA 02109, 800-343-3548	Minimum Purchase:	$2500	Add: $250	IRA: $2500
Web Address:		Min Auto Inv Plan:	$2500	Add: $250	
Inception:	05-17-67	Sales Fees:	No-load		
Advisor:	Fidelity Management & Research Co. (FMR)	Management Fee:	0.81%		
Subadvisor:	FMR Co., Inc. (FMRC)	Actual Fees:	Mgt:0.81%	Dist:ó	
		Expense Projections:	3Yr:$502	5Yr:$651	10Yr:$1036
		Income Distrib:	Annually		
NTF Plans:	Fidelity Retail-NTF, CommonWealth NTF				

MORNINGSTAR® **Funds 500**

role a fund might play in your portfolio. For example, you might head to the more-volatile categories (the small-cap groups or emerging markets) if you decided to spice up your large-cap-laden portfolio. Or you might want to tone down a growth-oriented portfolio with a value fund or two.

J Investment Value Graph

The Investment Value graph line shows a fund's performance trend, derived from the fund's historical growth of $10,000. It provides a visual depiction of how a fund has amassed its returns, including the performance swings its shareholders have endured along the way. The growth of $10,000 begins at the date of the fund's inception, or if the fund has been in existence for more than 12 years, then growth of $10,000 begins at the first year listed on the graph. Also, featured in the graph is the performance of an index (S&P 500 or MSCI EAFE), which allows investors to compare the performance of the fund with the performance of the benchmark index.

K Performance Quartile Graph

Here we show in which quartile a fund's calendar-year returns landed relative to its category. You can quickly gauge how consistent the fund's returns have been year to year.

L History

Use this table to spot trends over the past 12 years. Pay particular attention to the following statistics.

Expense Ratio

This percentage tells you how much it costs to own the fund each year. Generally, stick to funds with expense ratios lower than 1.25%. Many great domestic-stock funds keep expenses below 1%, and topnotch bond funds often change less than 0.75%. Raise the bar a little for international funds, because it costs more to do business overseas.

Turnover Rate

A low turnover figure (less than 30%) indicates a buy-and-hold strategy. A high rate (more than 100%) means the manager is doing a lot of buying and selling. (The average annual turnover for domestic-stock funds is about 85%.) If a fund has a high turnover rate, make sure the manager has a proven record as a good stock-picker; investors will end up the losers if a high-trading manager consistently buys and sells at the wrong time. Also, high turnover drives up a fund's costs because more brokerage commissions are being paid. High-turnover funds also tend to be less tax-efficient, although that is not always the case if the manager is offsetting gains with losses. Still, if a fund has a high turnover rate, check the fund's tax-efficiency. And watch for significant year-to-year changes in the turnover rate: It could indicate a new management style or a change in the fund's investment strategy.

Net Assets

A fund's asset size can also be an important consideration, especially for funds that focus on small-cap stocks or specialized areas of the market. In these cases, generally, the smaller the fund the better, because it can maneuver more nimbly in and out of market areas. Many small-cap funds close to new investors to keep a handle on asset size.

M Rating and Risk

This section breaks down the fund's risk, returns, and overall star rating over the three-, five-, and 10-year time periods. The Return versus Category section shows how the fund's returns compare with those of its peer group. The top 10% receive a high rating, the next 22.5% garner an "above-average" designation, and the middle 35% are rated "average." The next 22.5% of funds land in the "below-average" group, while the bottom 10% receive "low" ratings. Similarly, the Risk versus Category section ranks a fund's historical volatility versus that of its peer group, with those funds that have exhibited a lot of downside volatility faring worse than those that have not. The rationale here is that highly volatile funds are risky, but those offerings that tend to lose a lot of money are most worrisome to investors. The historical star ratings offer some clues regarding the consistency of a fund's historical risk-adjusted performance. Those with 5-star three-, five-, and 10-year results have often put up consistently strong risk-adjusted results, while those with universally poor marks have often languished year after year. Funds with markedly different short- and long-term results may have extreme strategies that produce feast-or-famine returns, or they may have experienced a manager change that has materially affected performance. The section also lists the fund's load-adjusted returns over the one-, three-, five-, and 10-year periods, as well as the annualized return since inception.

N Portfolio Analysis

Analyzing a fund's portfolio will give you an understanding of the fund's performance and potential volatility. First, note the fund's total holdings: The fund with fewer stocks will get more kick from its best performers, but if just a few holdings falter, the fund will lag. All things being equal, a fund with 50 or fewer stocks will be more volatile than a fund holding

O Other Measures

P Style Box

Q Sector Weightings

R Gowth and Value Measures

S Composition Information

Data through December 31, 2004

Fidelity Contrafund

Analyst Pick	Ticker	Load	NAV	Yield	Total Assets	Mstar Category
	FCNTX	None	$56.74	0.1%	$44,484 mil	Large Growth

Governance and Management

Fiduciary Grade: B

Portfolio Manager(s)

Will Danoff has been at the helm since 1990 and is backed by Fidelity's deep research staff. He has adapted his style to the fund's size by holding more large caps, and he has cut the fund's turnover in recent years. He's also now running a new fund, Fidelity Advisor New Insights.

Strategy

Call it forced evolution. As this fund's asset base grew in the 1990s, manager Will Danoff had to move away from mid-caps and small caps and adopt a growth-at-a-reasonable-price philosophy. He continues to keep a big part of the fund in mid-caps, but it is now dominated by larger fare. It has been more conservative than most of its large-blend rivals in recent years, with big underweightings in racy sectors such as technology, but Danoff is starting to ramp up its exposure to growth companies.

Historical Profile
Return: High
Risk: Low
Rating: ★★★★★ Highest

Investment Style: Equity Stock %: 88% 85% 90% 94% 91% 89% 90% 94% 88%

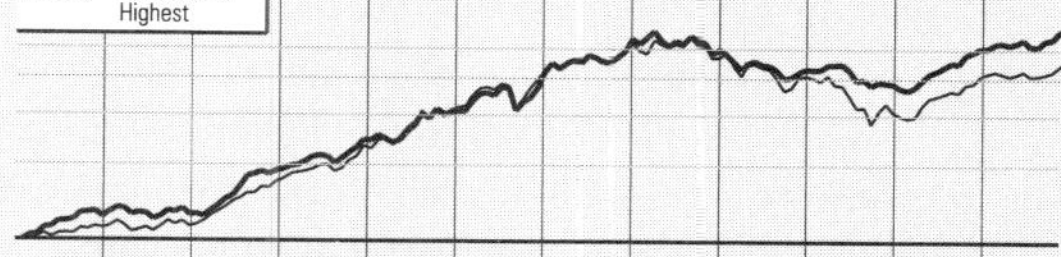

Performance Quartile (within Category)

1993	1994	1995	1996	1997	1998	1999	2000	2001	2002	2003	12-04	History
30.84	30.28	38.02	42.15	46.63	56.81	60.02	49.18	42.77	38.60	49.35	56.74	NAV
21.43	-1.12	36.28	21.94	23.00	31.57	25.03	-6.80	-12.59	-9.63	27.95	15.07	Total Return %
11.37	-2.43	-1.25	-1.00	-10.35	3.00	3.99	2.30	-0.71	12.46	-0.72	4.20	+/-S&P 500
18.56	-3.74	-0.90	-1.18	-7.49	-7.14	-8.13	15.62	7.83	18.25	-1.80	8.77	+/-Russ 1000Gr
0.66	0.00	0.30	1.05	0.84	0.64	0.50	0.41	0.45	0.12	0.10	0.09	Income Return %
20.77	-1.12	35.98	20.89	22.16	30.93	24.53	-7.21	-13.04	-9.75	27.85	14.98	Capital Return %
13	46	22	30	70	50	73	24	12	1	46	5	Total Rtn % Rank Cat
0.18	0.00	0.09	0.38	0.35	0.30	0.28	0.24	0.22	0.05	0.04	0.05	Income $
2.25	0.22	3.13	3.45	4.56	4.22	10.22	6.62	0.00	0.00	0.00	0.00	Capital Gains $
1.06	1.00	0.96	0.79	0.67	0.61	0.62	0.84	0.91	0.99	0.98	—	Expense Ratio %
0.46	0.59	0.44	1.28	0.91	0.70	0.48	0.45	0.49	0.14	0.01	—	Income Ratio %
255	235	223	159	144	197	177	166	141	80	67	—	Turnover Rate %
6,193	8,682	14,832	23,798	30,809	38,821	46,327	40,220	32,321	27,695	36,051	44,484	Net Assets $mil

Performance 12-31-04

	1st Qtr	2nd Qtr	3rd Qtr	4th Qtr	Total
2000	5.56	-6.58	1.13	-6.54	-6.80
2001	-13.18	3.47	-8.80	6.70	-12.59
2002	2.88	-3.68	-9.86	1.18	-9.63
2003	-2.15	11.83	5.02	11.34	27.95
2004	3.75	2.36	-0.63	9.04	15.07

Trailing	Total Return%	+/- S&P 500	+/- Russ 1000Gr	%Rank Cat	Growth of $10,000
3 Mo	9.04	-0.19	-0.13	67	10,904
6 Mo	8.35	1.16	4.88	13	10,835
1 Yr	15.07	4.20	8.77	5	11,507
3 Yr Avg	9.99	6.41	10.17	1	13,306
5 Yr Avg	1.62	3.92	10.91	3	10,837
10 Yr Avg	13.81	1.74	4.22	4	36,459
15 Yr Avg	15.03	4.10	5.53	1	81,690

Tax Analysis	Tax-Adj Rtn%	%Rank Cat	Tax-Cost Rat	%Rank Cat
3 Yr (estimated)	9.95	1	0.04	7
5 Yr (estimated)	1.01	3	0.60	37
10 Yr (estimated)	11.77	5	1.79	63

Potential Capital Gain Exposure: 24% of assets

Rating and Risk

Time Period	Load-Adj Return %	Morningstar Rtn vs Cat	Morningstar Risk vs Cat	Morningstar Risk-Adj Rating
1 Yr	15.07			
3 Yr	9.99	High	Low	★★★★★
5 Yr	1.62	High	Low	★★★★★
10 Yr	13.81	High	Low	★★★★★
Incept	13.29			

Other Measures	Standard Index S&P 500	Best Fit Index S&P Mid 400
Alpha	7.2	2.7
Beta	0.54	0.61
R-Squared	63	83
Standard Deviation	11.05	
Mean	9.99	
Sharpe Ratio	0.79	

Portfolio Analysis 09-30-04

Share change since 06-04 Total Stocks:503

	Sector	PE	YTD Ret%	% Assets
⊖ Avon Products	Goods	23.1	2.30	2.99
Berkshire Hathaway A	Financial	—	—	2.82
⊖ 3M Company	Ind Mtrls	22.8	0.28	2.81
⊖ EnCana	Energy	10.9	-6.47	2.02
⊕ Yahoo	Media	95.9	-4.56	1.74
⊖ Genentech	Health	84.1	-0.35	1.58
Samsung Electronics	Goods	—	—	1.22
⊕ American International G	Financial	16.3	2.91	1.19
⊕ Patterson Companies	Health	36.8	-1.34	1.18
⊕ Danaher	Ind Mtrls	25.8	-3.33	1.17
⊕ Newmont Mining	Ind Mtrls	44.6	-6.55	1.11
⊖ Nextel Communications	Telecom	11.0	0.43	1.08
⊖ Lockheed Martin	Ind Mtrls	19.8	-1.40	1.02
⊖ eBay	Consumer	82.9	-8.39	0.97
⊖ Golden West Financial	Financial	15.1	-2.20	0.94
⊕ Gillette	Goods	27.3	-1.74	0.93
⊕ Marvell Technology	Hardware	NMF	-2.73	0.92
⊖ Colgate-Palmolive	Goods	20.2	-2.11	0.89
⊕ Alcon	Health	41.2	-1.77	0.87
⊕ BP PLC ADR	Energy	20.8	-2.00	0.85

Current Investment Style

Value Blnd Growth / Large Mid Small

Market Cap	%
Giant	25.6
Large	36.6
Mid	32.2
Small	5.2
Micro	0.5

Avg $mil: 12,688

Value Measures		Rel Category
Price/Earnings	19.34	0.91
Price/Book	3.03	0.94
Price/Sales	1.68	0.79
Price/Cash Flow	8.12	0.74
Dividend Yield %	0.73	0.95

Growth Measures	%	Rel Category
Long-Term Erngs	14.20	1.01
Book Value	13.95	1.09
Sales	11.64	1.38
Cash Flow	20.71	1.24
Historical Erngs	32.22	2.22

Profitability	%	Rel Category
Return on Equity	21.05	1.17
Return on Assets	10.16	1.09
Net Margin	12.58	1.02

Sector Weightings	% of Stocks	Rel S&P 500	3 Year High	3 Year Low
Info	16.94	0.79		
Software	2.36	0.55	2	1
Hardware	6.40	0.63	7	1
Media	3.56	0.93	4	1
Telecom	4.62	1.47	5	0
Service	44.61	0.96		
Health	13.86	1.11	19	14
Consumer	10.09	1.11	14	10
Business	6.41	1.58	9	5
Financial	14.25	0.69	18	14
Mfg	38.45	1.20		
Goods	10.41	1.12	20	10
Ind Mtrls	16.19	1.28	16	14
Energy	11.01	1.54	11	5
Utilities	0.84	0.28	1	0

Composition

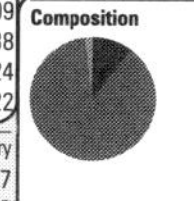

Cash	10.1
Stocks	87.9
Bonds	1.7
Other	0.3
Foreign (% of Stock)	19.9

Morningstar's Take by Christopher Traulsen 01-05-05

Fidelity Contrafund continues to impress.

This fund, which we recently moved to the large-growth category from large blend, has just posted another strong year. It finished 2004 up 15%, more than 7 percentage points ahead of the typical large-growth fund, and 4 percentage points ahead of the S&P 500 Index for the period.

Manager Will Danoff helped the fund's cause by a savvy move into Internet stocks such as Yahoo and eBay. He also correctly boosted the fund's energy stake, taking it from under 5% of the fund's equity portfolio up to nearly 11%, and overweighted industrials stocks. Both sectors benefited from the global economic recovery, and the resulting supply/demand imbalance that drove commodity prices up.

As always, the portfolio remains expansive. Despite lugging a $44 billion asset base, Danoff has shoehorned 32% of the fund into mid-cap stocks, and even has a smattering of small caps in the portfolio. He also has significant overseas exposure, with 18% of assets in foreign stocks. On the whole, relative to other large-growth funds, this offering is less aggressive than the norm. Danoff spreads its assets across more than 500 stocks, and while the fund's growth rates are well above category averages, its valuations are below those of its typical peer.

Danoff's eclecticism has paid off in spades: The fund owns top-flight three-, five-, and 10-year returns, while its diversification has helped make it less volatile than its average rival. We remain concerned with the fund's size, however. With an asset base of $44 billion, it's undeniably harder for Danoff to succeed than it was when the fund was much smaller. That said, Danoff has shown skill in handling the growth, and he has also reduced the fund's turnover in recent years, which should make the task more manageable. We continue to think this is a great core holding.

Address:	Fidelity Investments Company Boston MA 02109 800-343-3548	Minimum Purchase:	$2500	Add: $250	IRA: $2500
		Min Auto Inv Plan:	$2500	Add: $250	
		Sales Fees:	No-load		
Web Address:		Management Fee:	0.81%		
Inception:	05-17-67	Actual Fees:	Mgt:0.81%	Dist:0	
Advisor:	Fidelity Management & Research Co. (FMR)	Expense Projections:	3Yr:$502	5Yr:$651	10Yr:$1086
Subadvisor:	FMR Co., Inc. (FMRC)	Income Distrib:	Annually		
NTF Plans:	Fidelity Retail-NTF, CommonWealth NTF				

MORNINGSTAR® Funds 500

twice as many issues. Next, check the percentage of assets devoted to each security. A manager who follows a concentrated strategy will have large hunks of the fund's assets (more than 5% per stock) invested in its top holdings. Now identify each stock's sector to gain insight into where a fund's top holdings are concentrated and where its vulnerabilities lie. Then check the stocks' P/E ratios; high P/E's are another indication of possible future volatility. Each stock's year-to-date returns tell you which securities in which sectors are driving the performance of the fund up or down. Keep tabs on which positions the manager has increased or trimmed. A plus sign (+) means the fund has added shares to that holding; a minus sign (−) indicates a reduction. New additions are noted with a star burst (✱). If a position in a losing stock is new or expanded, the manager could be bargain-hunting.

O Other Measures

These numbers provide more views of risk. Alpha, Beta, and R-squared are three Modern Portfolio Theory statistics that measure how much you can expect a fund to follow a market index and whether the fund has added or subtracted value versus that benchmark. We compare all domestic- and international-equity funds with the S&P 500 and a Best Fit Index(the index with which the fund has the highest correlation).

R-squared

For beta and alpha to be reliable measures of risk and reward, a fund must have a high correlation with its index, as measured by R-squared. R-squared indicates how market-like a fund is. A high R-squared (between 85 and 100) indicates the fund's performance patterns have been in line with the index's. A fund with a low R-squared(70 or less) doesn't act much like the index.

Beta

Beta measures a fund's volatility relative to its benchmark. A beta of more than 1.0 means the fund is more volatile than the index and should outperform it when the index is rising and underperform it when the index is falling. A beta of less than 1.0 works the opposite way.

Alpha

Alpha measures excess returns per unit of risk. The higher the alpha the better. A positive alpha indicates the fund performed better in the past than its beta would predict. A negative alpha indicates the fund performed worse. Below these statistics, standard deviation measures risk as volatility by showing the range within which a fund's monthly returns have landed. The larger the number, the wider the range and more volatile the fund has been. To set a fund's standard deviation in context, compare it with others in the fund's category. The mean represents the annualized total return for a fund over the trailing three years.

Sharpe Ratio

The Sharpe ratio is a risk-adjusted measure similar to the star rating. The higher the Sharpe ratio (1.0 is pretty good), the better the fund's risk-adjusted performance has been.

P Style Box

For stock funds, Morningstar assigns style-box classifications based on portfolios' scores for Growth Measures, Value Measures, and average weighted market cap. For example, funds that invest predominantly in large-cap, fast-growing firms with high valuations typically land in large growth. By contrast, funds that specialize in smaller, slower-growing firms with modest valuations are assigned to the small-value style box.

Q Sector Weightings

Learn which sectors of the economy the fund invests in to gauge how diversified the fund is. A fund that has more than 25% of assets concentrated in one sector is almost certain to carry more risk than a more-diversified offering. Knowing the fund's weightings can help you maintain a well-diversified portfolio. Weightings are displayed relative to the S&P 500 for domestic-stock funds and to the category for international-stock funds. (We show relative subsector breakdowns for funds in our specialty categories.) The last two columns of the section give a fund's historical range of the percentage of assets held in each sector; here, you can see if a fund is bullish or bearish on particular sectors, based on its past weightings.

R Growth and Value Measures

This section lists a fund portfolio's current averages for various portfolio statistics, including price/earnings, price/cash flow, and historical earnings growth. To provide perspective, we compare these measures with the funds' category average.

S Composition Information

This section shows the percentage of assets devoted to cash, stocks, bonds, and other, along with what percentage of stock assets are invested in foreign securities. A large percentage of cash in Composition might indicate the fund is taking a defensive position.

The Morningstar Bond-Fund Page

In this two-page walk-through, we spotlight sections that are unique to the bond-fund page and offer some advice on using the page to select a bond fund. More-detailed discussions of the elements presented in this section appear in the user's guide.

A Yield

B Expense Ratio %

C Current Investment Style/ Duration Management

D Credit Analysis

PIMCO Total Ret Instl

Ticker	Load	NAV	Yield	SEC Yield	Total Assets	Mstar Category
PTTRX	None	$10.67	2.3%	2.14%	$77,547 mil	Intermediate-Term Bond

Governance and Management

Fiduciary Grade: B

Portfolio Manager(s)

Bill Gross and Pimco's extensive team of analysts and traders, who jointly received Morningstar's manager-of-the-year honors in 1998 and 2000, are widely acknowledged to be among the best in the business.

Strategy

Manager Bill Gross couples Pimco's long-term macroeconomic outlook with its take on short-term cyclical factors to determine this fund's sector weightings and duration. Although Gross will focus heavily on certain sectors, he doesn't make huge interest-rate bets against the Lehman Brothers Aggregate Index. (Such plays are typically plus or minus 20% of the index's duration.) However, he will occasionally invest in nonindex sectors of the market such as high-yield, developed-markets international, and emerging-markets debt.

Historical Profile
Return: High
Risk: Above Avg
Rating: ★★★★★ Highest

Investment Style Fixed Income — Income Rtn %Rank Cat: 16, 36, 23, 36, 22, 45, 60, 68, 90

▼ Manager Change
∇ Partial Manager Change

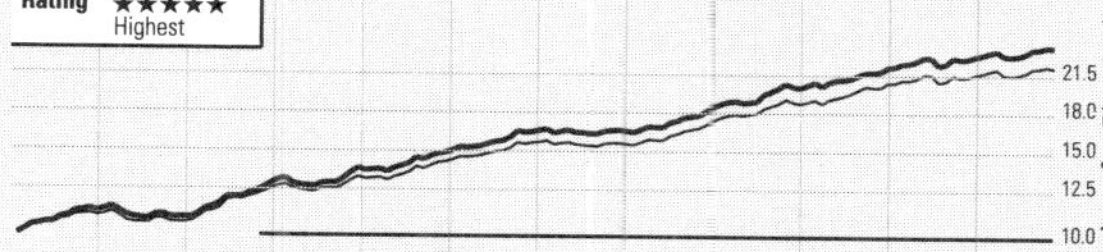

Growth of $10,000
— Investment Values of Fund
— Investment Values of LB Aggr

Performance Quartile (within Category)

1993	1994	1995	1996	1997	1998	1999	2000	2001	2002	2003	12-04	History
10.64	9.69	10.72	10.50	10.60	10.54	9.30	10.39	10.46	10.67	10.71	10.67	NAV
12.52	-3.58	19.79	4.69	10.17	9.77	-0.28	12.09	9.48	10.20	5.56	5.15	Total Return %
2.77	-0.66	1.32	1.06	0.52	1.08	0.54	0.46	1.04	-0.05	1.46	0.81	+/-LB Aggr
0.28	0.93	-1.64	2.00	0.74	-0.37	2.30	-0.35	0.66	-2.83	-0.41	-0.15	+/-LB 5-10YR
6.89	5.53	7.54	6.65	6.48	6.29	5.34	6.89	5.88	4.68	3.48	2.43	Income Return %
5.63	-9.11	12.25	-1.96	3.69	3.48	-6.22	5.20	3.60	5.52	2.08	2.72	Capital Return %
18	45	21	17	14	3	22	9	8	11	27	11	Total Rtn % Rank Cat
0.71	0.57	0.71	0.69	0.66	0.65	0.61	0.66	0.59	0.48	0.37	0.26	Income $
0.55	0.00	0.12	0.00	0.27	0.42	0.00	0.00	0.30	0.35	0.18	0.33	Capital Gains $
0.43	0.41	0.41	0.42	0.43	0.43	0.43	0.43	0.43	0.43	0.43	0.43	Expense Ratio %
7.07	6.27	6.72	6.85	6.60	6.06	5.91	6.25	6.57	5.16	4.17	2.73	Income Ratio %
90	177	98	221	173	206	154	223	448	445	234	273	Turnover Rate %
4,576	6,555	10,035	12,237	14,791	20,126	23,380	29,500	33,260	39,854	42,077	44,845	Net Assets $mil

Performance 12-31-04

	1st Qtr	2nd Qtr	3rd Qtr	4th Qtr	Total
2000	2.21	1.82	2.87	4.69	12.09
2001	2.86	-0.27	6.49	0.22	9.48
2002	0.65	3.33	3.43	2.45	10.20
2003	2.08	2.83	-0.18	0.75	5.56
2004	2.70	-2.18	3.25	1.38	5.15

Trailing	Total Return%	+/- LB Aggr	+/- LB 5-10YR	%Rank Cat	Growth of $10,000
3 Mo	1.38	0.43	0.40	18	10,138
6 Mo	4.67	0.49	-0.90	20	10,467
1 Yr	5.15	0.81	-0.15	11	10,515
3 Yr Avg	6.95	0.76	-1.10	9	12,233
5 Yr Avg	8.46	0.75	-0.61	4	15,009
10 Yr Avg	8.54	0.82	0.08	2	22,693
15 Yr Avg	8.69	0.99	0.37	2	34,901

Tax Analysis	Tax-Adj Rtn%	%Rank Cat	Tax-Cost Rat	%Rank Cat
3 Yr (estimated)	4.82	10	1.99	74
5 Yr (estimated)	5.95	6	2.31	80
10 Yr (estimated)	5.70	4	2.62	94

Potential Capital Gain Exposure: 0% of assets

Rating and Risk

Time Period	Load-Adj Return %	Morningstar Rtn vs Cat	Morningstar Risk vs Cat	Morningstar Risk-Adj Rating
1 Yr	5.15			
3 Yr	6.95	High	Avg	★★★★★
5 Yr	8.46	High	+Avg	★★★★★
10 Yr	8.54	High	+Avg	★★★★★
Incept	8.89			

Other Measures	Standard Index LB Aggr	Best Fit Index LB. U.S. Univ. Bd
Alpha	0.8	-0.1
Beta	0.98	1.03
R-Squared	95	97
Standard Deviation	4.61	
Mean	6.95	
Sharpe Ratio	1.22	

Morningstar's Take by Eric Jacobson 10-28-04

Bill Gross' successful 2004 decisions help explain how he attempts to pursue return while mitigating risk.

At first glance, his sector bets might appear to support the iconic image of Gross as a market gunslinger. By the end of this year's first quarter, for example, PIMCO Total Return had some 22% of its assets devoted to bonds outside of the United States. On the other hand, Gross has largely eschewed corporate bonds, maintaining a large underweighting relative to the fund's benchmark, the Lehman Brothers Aggregate Bond Index. So even though Gross missed out on some of corporates' gains--while they helped fuel many competitors--the fund has performed quite well thanks largely to its foreign bonds. Its 4.6% institutional share gains place in the intermediate-bond category's best decile--an extension of the fund's stellar record.

PIMCO makes a good argument, however, that investors shouldn't overestimate the impact of its foreign holdings. For one thing, thanks to hedging, this fund rarely takes on more than a few percentage points of nondollar exposure, which typically lends the bulk of volatility to such positions. In addition, the large early-2004 foreign stake was skewed to short maturities. As such, the portfolio's overall rate sensitivity was actually low relative to the benchmark. (Now that Gross has shifted to longer foreign bonds, they consume less of the fund.) Finally, PIMCO's analytics suggest that while its foreign-bond bets are important to the fund's success, they aren't likely to have nearly as much an impact as some of its other plays, such as interest-rate positioning, for example.

The bottom line is that while Bill Gross has the flexibility, and arguably the fortitude, to place more unusual bets than most, risk has always been part of the PIMCO calculus. That doesn't mean this fund can't underperform, but it does help explain how it has avoided many of the market's worst potholes. All in all, it remains one of our favorites.

Portfolio Analysis 09-30-04

Total Fixed-Income:5732	Date of Maturity	Amount $000	Value $000	% Net Assets
US Treasury Note (Fut)	12-20-04	—	—	10.17
EuroDollar (Fut)	06-13-05	—	—	8.47
FNMA 5%		7,258,400	7,279,043	6.04
EuroDollar (Fut)	09-19-05	6,112,001	5,928,029	4.92
US Treasury Note 2.5%	09-30-06	4,473,301	4,465,082	3.70
FNMA 5.5%		2,902,900	2,941,909	2.44
Euro Dollar (Fut)	12-13-04	2,804,250	2,739,612	2.27
US Treasury Note 3.875%	01-15-09	1,636,463	1,842,748	1.53
EuroDollar (Fut)	12-19-05	1,396,750	1,351,356	1.12
US Treasury Note 4.25%	01-15-10	1,046,239	1,214,577	1.01
US Treasury Note 3.625%	01-15-08	1,017,432	1,116,116	0.93
US Treasury Note 3.5%	01-15-11	984,551	1,114,658	0.92
FNMA 5%	03-01-34	605,405	600,772	0.50
US Treasury Note 3%	07-15-12	459,257	508,681	0.42
US Treasury Bond 5.375%	02-15-31	297,400	318,683	0.26
US Treasury Note 3.375%	01-15-07	269,824	288,364	0.24
United Mexican Sts Mtn B	08-15-31	246,890	281,455	0.23
US Treasury Bond 6.25%	05-15-30	175,600	208,470	0.17
Golden St Tob Securitiza	06-01-33	186,615	176,637	0.15
NJ Mtg Investors 2004-Wm	01-25-35	131,124	131,197	0.11

Current Investment Style
Duration: Short Int Long
Quality: High Med Low
[1] figure provided by fund

Avg Eff Duration[1]	4.3 Yrs
Avg Eff Maturity	6.0 Yrs
Avg Credit Quality	AAA
Avg Wtd Coupon	3.72%
Avg Wtd Price	106.05% of par

Coupon Range	% of Bonds	Rel Cat
0% PIK	1.9	0.5
0% to 6%	80.7	1.3
6% to 8%	14.6	0.5
8% to 10%	4.1	0.7
More than 10%	0.7	0.6

1.00=Category Average

Credit Analysis	% bonds 09-30-04		
US Govt	37	BB	1
AAA	52	B	0
AA	1	Below B	1
A	2	NR/NA	0
BBB	6		

Sector Breakdown	% of assets
US Treasuries	5
TIPS	6
US Agency	0
Mortgage Pass-Throughs	16
Mortgage CMO	4
Mortgage ARM	0
US Corporate	3
Asset-Backed	1
Convertible	0
Municipal	2
Corporate Inflation-Protected	0
Foreign Corporate	0
Foreign Govt	1

Composition			
Cash	55.7	Bonds	34.0
Stocks	0.0	Other	10.3

Special Securities	
Restricted/Illiquid Secs	Trace
Exotic Mortgage-Backed	0
Emerging-Markets Secs	Trace
Options/Futures/Warrants	Yes

Address:	PIMCO Funds Stamford, CT 06902 800-927-4648
Web Address:	www.pimcofunds.com
Inception:	05-11-87
Advisor:	PA Fund Management LLC
Subadvisor:	First Quadrant
NTF Plans:	N/A

Minimum Purchase:	$5000000	Add: $0	IRA: $0
Min Auto Inv Plan:	$0	Add: —	
Sales Fees:	No-load		
Management Fee:	0.25%, 0.18%A		
Actual Fees:	Mgt:0.25%	Dist:6	
Expense Projections:	3Yr:$138	5Yr:$241	10Yr:$542
Income Distrib:	Monthly		

MORNINGSTAR® **Funds 500**

A Yield

Yield provides instant gratification in the form of regular income payments, but basing your buy decision on a fund's high yield instead of total returns could cost you in the end. To pump up yields some funds use accounting tricks that can erode a fund's NAV over time. In other words, part of the "income" they are distributing to you is a return of your principal. Others invest in lower-quality debt and/or complex derivatives in an effort to enhance yield. Shrinking principal leads to smaller income checks, though, even if the yield percentage stays the same. Imagine a $10,000 investment in a fund carrying an NAV of $10 and yielding 7%. One year later, the fund still yields 7%, but its NAV has slipped to $9. Income would have dropped to $630 from $700.

Be wary if a fund has a high payout relative to its category and an NAV that is eroding, particularly in years when interest rates have declined. That fund may have to fight hard to keep writing big income checks.

B Expense Ratio %

It's critical to look for bond funds with low expenses. Expenses can eat into total returns, and typically, only a narrow difference separates the returns of the leaders and laggards of a bond category. Also, high-cost bond funds tend to be riskier than low-cost funds. Expenses are deducted from a fund's income payments. To keep yields at high-cost funds competitive, managers often make riskier investments, such as buying longer-duration issues, lower-quality debt, or complex derivatives. Managers with lower expense hurdles can offer the same returns without taking on the extra risk. How much is too much to pay? In general, broker-sold funds cost a bit more than no-load offerings, but that said, investors can find many government or corporate high-quality-bond funds with expense ratios of 0.75% or less. For specialty-bond funds, such as high yield or international bond, don't pay much more than 1%.

C Current Investment Style / Duration

The bond style box is based on a fund's credit quality and its duration. Check the fund's average credit quality and average effective duration in the column next to the style box. Credit quality is an important aspect of any bond fund, as it measures the creditworthiness of the fund's holdings. A fund with an average credit quality of AAA, for example, is less likely to get stung by defaults than a fund with an average credit quality of BBB. Duration is equally important, as it measures a fund's overall interest-rate risk. The longer a fund's duration, the more sensitive the fund is to shifts in interest rates. When rates fall, funds with longer durations benefit; when interest rates climb, shorter-duration funds are beneficial.

Most managers keep duration either pegged to a benchmark or within a prescribed range around a benchmark. For most investors, a fund with a disciplined duration strategy makes the most sense. First, such an approach confines managers' interest-rate bets. Few managers have proved they can consistently time the short-term direction of interest rates. Second, a fund with a consistent duration strategy may be easier to place in a portfolio. For example, a bond fund whose duration fluctuates dramatically poses asset-allocation problems for investors. Will the fund be a short-term fund or a long-term one? And how will it react to changes in interest rates?

First-time bond-fund buyers, especially those looking to cushion their stock-heavy portfolios, probably should stick with funds in the intermediate-term range (3.5 to six years). Intermediate-term bond funds have offered yields and returns similar to long-term bond funds but with less volatility.

D Credit Analysis

Average credit quality provides a snapshot of a portfolio's overall credit quality, while the Credit Analysis section shows the percentage of fixed-income securities that fall within each credit-quality rating, as assigned by Standard & Poor's or Moody's. The lower a bond's rating, the greater its default risk and the higher its yield. Bonds rated BBB and above are considered investment-grade issues; those rated BB and below are high-yield, commonly called junk bonds. Pay particularly close attention to a fund's weightings in below B and nonrated bonds. Often these issues are riskier bonds that are in danger of defaulting or that have already defaulted. They are also typically less liquid than higher-quality bonds.

Diversify with a good mix of high- and low-quality bonds (lean more toward the high-quality side), if not in one of the multisector bond funds (which tend to have relatively high expense ratios), then in a portfolio of two or three bond funds.

Fund Analyst Picks and Pans

Our analysts scrutinized more than 17,000 funds to come up with a handful of the best and worst funds for each category.

Analyst Picks

Morningstar Funds 500 Universe

Domestic Equity

Page	Fund Name	Category Name	Morningstar Rating
31	ABN AMRO/Montag & Caldwell Growth N	Large Growth	★★★★
35	American AAdvantage Small Cp Val Plan	Small Value	★★★★
64	American Funds Inc Fund of Amer A	Moderate Allocation	★★★★★
71	American Funds Washington Mutual A	Large Value	★★★★
74	Ariel Appreciation	Mid-Cap Blend	★★★★
92	Brandywine	Mid-Cap Growth	★★★★
99	Calamos Growth & Income A	Convertibles	★★★★★
103	Clipper	Large Value	★★★★★
112	Davis Appreciation & Income Class A	Convertibles	★★★★
113	Davis Financial A	Specialty-Financial	★★★
130	Eaton Vance Utilities A	Specialty-Utilities	★★★★★
208	FPA Paramount	Small Blend	★★
138	Fidelity Asset Manager	Moderate Allocation	★★★
143	Fidelity Capital Appreciation	Large Growth	★★★★
144	Fidelity Contrafund	Large Growth	★★★★★
145	Fidelity Convertible Securities	Convertibles	★★★★
150	Fidelity Dividend Growth	Large Blend	★★★★
183	Fidelity Select Technology	Specialty-Technology	★★★★
188	Fidelity Spartan 500 Index	Large Blend	★★★★
193	Fidelity Spartan Total Market Index	Large Blend	★★★
228	Harbor Capital Appreciation Instl	Large Growth	★★★★
234	ICAP Select Equity	Large Value	★★★★
246	Janus Mid Cap Value Investor	Mid-Cap Value	★★★★★
271	Marsico Focus	Large Growth	★★★★
276	Masters' Select Smaller Companies	Small Growth	—
292	Morgan Stanley Inst US Real Estate A	Specialty-Real Estate	★★★★
306	Oak Value	Large Blend	★★★★★
309	Oakmark I	Large Value	★★★★
312	Oakmark Select I	Large Value	★★★★★
326	PIMCO CommodityRealRet Strat A	Specialty-Natural Res	—
331	PIMCO RCM Global Technology Instl	Specialty-Technology	★★★★
321	Pax World Balanced	Moderate Allocation	★★★★★
341	Royce Premier Inv	Small Blend	★★★★
353	Security Capital U.S. Real Estate	Specialty-Real Estate	★★★★
354	Selected American Shares S	Large Blend	★★★★★

Domestic Equity

Page	Fund Name	Category Name	Morningstar Rating
355	Selected Special Shares S	Mid-Cap Blend	★★
360	Sound Shore	Large Value	★★★★
371	T. Rowe Price Equity-Income	Large Value	★★★★
372	T. Rowe Price Financial Services	Specialty-Financial	★★★
377	T. Rowe Price Health Sciences	Specialty-Health	★★★
383	T. Rowe Price Media & Telecom	Specialty-Communications	★★★★★
385	T. Rowe Price Mid-Cap Value	Mid-Cap Value	★★★★★
386	T. Rowe Price New America Growth	Large Growth	★★★★
390	T. Rowe Price Personal Strat Income	Conservative Allocation	★★★★★
406	TCW Galileo Value Opportunities I	Mid-Cap Blend	★★★★
413	Third Avenue Real Estate Value	Specialty-Real Estate	★★★★★
414	Third Avenue Small-Cap Value	Small Blend	★★★★
431	Turner Midcap Growth	Mid-Cap Growth	★★
433	Tweedy, Browne American Value	Mid-Cap Value	★★★
445	Vanguard 500 Index	Large Blend	★★★★
458	Vanguard Explorer	Small Growth	★★★★
463	Vanguard Growth Equity	Large Growth	★★
465	Vanguard Health Care	Specialty-Health	★★★★★
485	Vanguard Mid Capitalization Index	Mid-Cap Blend	★★★★
489	Vanguard Selected Value	Mid-Cap Value	★★★★
500	Vanguard Tax-Managed Balanced	Conservative Allocation	★★★
507	Vanguard Total Stock Mkt Idx	Large Blend	★★★★
509	Vanguard U.S. Value	Large Value	★★★★
511	Vanguard Wellesley Income	Conservative Allocation	★★★★★
512	Vanguard Wellington	Moderate Allocation	★★★★★
516	Wasatch Heritage Growth	Mid-Cap Growth	—
523	Weitz Value	Mid-Cap Value	★★★★

Analyst Picks

Morningstar Funds 500 Universe

International Equity

Page	Fund Name	Category Name	Morningstar Rating
40	American Century Global Gold Inv	Specialty-Precious Metals	★★★
58	American Funds Capital Inc Bldr A	World Allocation	★★★★
61	American Funds EuroPacific Gr A	Foreign Large Blend	★★★★
67	American Funds New Perspective A	World Stock	★★★★
68	American Funds New World A	Diversified Emerging Mkts	★★★
75	Artisan International Inv	Foreign Large Growth	★★★★
102	Causeway International Value Inv	Foreign Large Value	★★★★
120	Dodge & Cox International Stock	Foreign Large Value	★★★★
178	Fidelity Pacific Basin	Diversified Pacific/Asia	★★★★
190	Fidelity Spartan International Index	Foreign Large Blend	★★★
201	First Eagle Global A	World Allocation	★★★★★
229	Harbor International Instl	Foreign Large Value	★★★
233	ICAP Euro Select Equity	Europe Stock	★★★
256	Julius Baer International Equity A	Foreign Large Blend	★★★★★
279	Matthews Pacific Tiger	Pacific/Asia ex-Japan Stk	★★★★
284	Merrill Lynch Global Allocation A	World Allocation	★★★
296	Mutual European A	Europe Stock	★★★★
308	Oakmark Global I	World Stock	★★★★★
314	Oppenheimer Developing Markets A	Diversified Emerging Mkts	★★★★★
315	Oppenheimer Global A	World Stock	★★★★
370	T. Rowe Price Emerging Markets Stock	Diversified Emerging Mkts	★★★
382	T. Rowe Price Latin America	Latin America Stock	★★★★
387	T. Rowe Price New Asia	Pacific/Asia ex-Japan Stk	★★★
434	Tweedy, Browne Global Value	Foreign Small/Mid Value	★★★
457	Vanguard European Stock Index	Europe Stock	★★★
506	Vanguard Total Intl Stock Index	Foreign Large Blend	★★★★

Fixed Income

Page	Fund Name	Category Name	Morningstar Rating
119	Dodge & Cox Income	Intermediate-Term Bond	★★★★★
128	Eaton Vance Floating Rate A	Bank Loan	—
129	Eaton Vance Income Fund of Boston A	High Yield Bond	★★★★
207	FPA New Income	Intermediate-Term Bond	★★★
154	Fidelity Floating Rate High Income	Bank Loan	—
158	Fidelity Ginnie Mae	Intermediate Government	★★★★
174	Fidelity New Markets Income	Emerging Markets Bond	★★★★
184	Fidelity Short-Term Bond	Short-Term Bond	★★★★
189	Fidelity Spartan Interm Muni Income	Muni National Interm	★★★★★
191	Fidelity Spartan Municipal Income	Muni National Long	★★★★★
197	Fidelity Ultra-Short Bond	Ultrashort Bond	—
210	Franklin Federal Tax-Free Income A	Muni National Long	★★★★
227	Harbor Bond	Intermediate-Term Bond	★★★★★
265	Loomis Sayles Bond Ret	Multisector Bond	★★★★★
286	Metropolitan West Total Return Bond M	Intermediate-Term Bond	★★★★
304	Northeast Investors	High Yield Bond	★★★★
327	PIMCO Emerging Markets Bond A	Emerging Markets Bond	★★★
328	PIMCO Foreign Bond (US Dollar-Hedged) D	World Bond	★★★
329	PIMCO High Yield A	High Yield Bond	★★★
324	Payden Limited Maturity	Ultrashort Bond	★★
361	SSgA Yield Plus	Ultrashort Bond	★★
379	T. Rowe Price International Bond	World Bond	★★★
396	T. Rowe Price Spectrum Income	Multisector Bond	★★★★
397	T. Rowe Price Tax-Free High-Yield	High Yield Muni	★★★★
399	T. Rowe Price Tax-Free Short-Interm	Muni National Short	★★★★
400	T. Rowe Price U.S. Treasury Long-Term	Long Government	★★★
438	USAA Tax Exempt Intermediate-Term	Muni National Interm	★★★★★
440	USAA Tax Exempt Short-Term	Muni National Short	★★★★
461	Vanguard GNMA	Intermediate Government	★★★★★
466	Vanguard High-Yield Corporate	High Yield Bond	★★★★
467	Vanguard High-Yield Tax-Exempt	Muni National Long	★★★★★
468	Vanguard Inflation-Protected Secs	Intermediate Government	★★★★★
472	Vanguard Interm-Term Tax-Ex	Muni National Interm	★★★★
480	Vanguard Long-Term Investment-Grade Fund	Long-Term Bond	★★★★
481	Vanguard Long-Term Tax-Exempt	Muni National Long	★★★★★
482	Vanguard Long-Term U.S. Treasury	Long Government	★★★★
483	Vanguard Ltd-Term Tax-Ex	Muni National Short	★★★★
490	Vanguard Short-Term Bond Index	Short-Term Bond	★★★★
491	Vanguard Short-Term Federal	Short Government	★★★★
493	Vanguard Short-Term Tax-Ex	Muni National Short	★★★
505	Vanguard Total Bond Market Index	Intermediate-Term Bond	★★★★
525	Western Asset Core Bond Institutional	Intermediate-Term Bond	★★★★★

Analyst Pans

Morningstar Funds 500 Universe

Fund Name	Category Name	Morningstar Rating
AIM Income A	Intermediate-Term Bond	★
AIM Opportunities II A	Mid-Cap Growth	★★★
AXP Equity Value A	Large Value	★
AXP Selective A	Intermediate-Term Bond	★
AllianceBernstein Bond Corp Bd A	Long-Term Bond	★★
AllianceBernstein Bond U.S. Govt A	Long-Term Bond	★
AllianceBernstein Global Health Care A	Specialty-Health	★★★
AllianceBernstein Global Technology A	Specialty-Technology	★★★
AllianceBernstein New Europe A	Europe Stock	★★
AllianceBernstein Small Cap Growth A	Small Growth	★★★
American Heritage	World Stock	★
Ameristock Focused Value	Small Value	★
Berkshire Focus	Specialty-Technology	★
Columbia Asset Allocation T	Moderate Allocation	★★★
Columbia Federal Securities A	Intermediate Government	★★
Columbia Growth Stock A	Large Growth	—
Columbia Small Cap Growth Z	Small Growth	★★★
Columbia Young Investor A	Large Blend	—
Credit Suisse Emerging Markets Comm	Diversified Emerging Mkts	★
Credit Suisse International Focus Com	Foreign Large Blend	★★★
Delaware Balanced A	Moderate Allocation	★
Dreyfus A Bonds Plus	Intermediate-Term Bond	★★★
Dreyfus Founders Balanced F	Moderate Allocation	★
Dreyfus Founders Discovery F	Small Growth	★★★
Dreyfus Founders Passport F	Foreign Small/Mid Growth	★★
Dreyfus Premier Short Term Income D	Short-Term Bond	★★★
Eastern European Equity	Europe Stock	★★★★
Eaton Vance Balanced A	Moderate Allocation	★★
Evergreen Asset Allocation A	World Allocation	★★★★
Federated American Leaders A	Large Value	★★
Federated International Equity A	Foreign Large Growth	★★
Federated International Small Co A	Foreign Small/Mid Growth	★★
Fidelity Focused Stock	Large Growth	★★
First American Large Cap Value A	Large Value	★★
Frontier Equity	Small Blend	★
FundX Upgrader	Mid-Cap Blend	★★★
GAM International A	Foreign Large Blend	★★
Gabelli ABC	Conservative Allocation	★★★
GenomicsFund	Specialty-Health	★
Grand Prix A	Mid-Cap Growth	★
Granum Value	Mid-Cap Value	★★
Heartland Value	Small Value	★★★
Henlopen	Small Growth	★★★★
Ivy International A	Foreign Large Growth	★★
Jacob Internet	Specialty-Technology	★★★
John Hancock Large Cap Growth A	Large Growth	★
Kinetics Internet	Small Growth	★★★
Legg Mason Global Income	World Bond	★★
Legg Mason High-Yield Prim	High Yield Bond	★★
Loomis Sayles Core Plus Bond A	Intermediate-Term Bond	★★
MFS Emerging Growth A	Large Growth	★
MainStay Total Return B	Moderate Allocation	★★
Morgan Stanley Equally-Wtd S&P 500 A	Large Blend	★★★★★
Morgan Stanley Flexible Income B	Multisector Bond	★
Morgan Stanley Natural Resource Dev B	Specialty-Natural Res	★★
Morgan Stanley S&P 500 Index A	Large Blend	★★
Munder NetNet A	Specialty-Technology	★★
Nations Convertible Securities Inv A	Convertibles	★★★★
Nations Small Company Inv A	Small Growth	★★★
Nevis Fund	Small Growth	★

Fund Name	Category Name	Morningstar Rating
PBHG Emerging Growth	Small Growth	★
PBHG Growth	Mid-Cap Growth	★
Payden Growth & Income	Large Value	★★
Phoenix Market Neutral A	Conservative Allocation	★★
Phoenix-Engemann Balanced Return A	Moderate Allocation	★
Phoenix-Engemann Nifty Fifty A	Large Growth	★
ProFunds Ultra Biotechnology Inv	Specialty-Health	★
ProFunds UltraBull Inv	Large Blend	★
Putnam OTC Emerging Growth A	Mid-Cap Growth	★
Saratoga Health & Biotechnology A	Specialty-Health	★
Seligman Common Stock A	Large Blend	★
Seligman Global Growth A	World Stock	★★
Seligman High-Yield Bond A	High Yield Bond	★
Seligman Income and Growth A	Moderate Allocation	★★
Strong Balanced	Moderate Allocation	★★
Strong Growth 20 Inv	Large Growth	★★
Strong Short-Term Bond Inv	Short-Term Bond	★★
U.S. Global Investors Gold Shares	Specialty-Precious Metals	★★
Van Eck Global Hard Assets A	Specialty-Natural Res	★★★
Van Kampen Strategic Municipal Inc A	High Yield Muni	★★
Van Wagoner Emerging Growth	Small Growth	★
Waddell & Reed Adv Muni High-Inc A	High Yield Muni	★★★
Waddell & Reed Adv Municipal Bond A	Muni National Long	★★

Review Pages

This section offers a full-page report on each of the 500 funds.

ABN AMRO/Montag Gr N

Analyst Pick

Ticker	Load	NAV	Yield	Total Assets	Mstar Category
MCGFX	12b-1 only	$22.65	0.1%	$3,188 mil	Large Growth

Governance and Management

Fiduciary Grade: B

Portfolio Manager(s)

Ron Canakaris has been in charge of this fund since its 1994 inception and has a strong record in his 23 years with near-clone Enterprise Growth. Though Canakaris is the architect of the fund's strategy and leader of the research team, specific investment decisions are made by a committee of 14 portfolio managers with the help of five analysts.

Strategy

Manager Ron Canakaris and his 14-person investment team mix macroeconomic analysis with fundamental research. They stick to large-cap names, favoring those with earnings-growth rates of at least 10% but no more than 20%. They're not willing to pay through the nose, however, and will consider selling a stock when it reaches a 20% premium to their calculation of its intrinsic value.

Historical Profile
Return: Above Avg
Risk: Below Avg
Rating: ★★★★ Above Avg

Investment Style: Equity — Stock %: 96% 99% 99% 99% 96% 95% 98% 95%

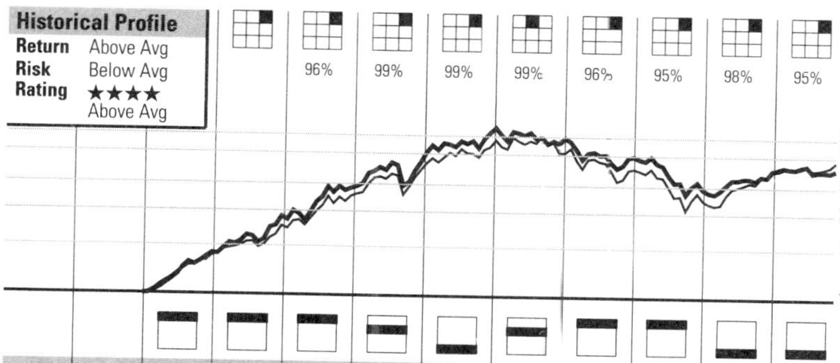

▼ Manager Change
▽ Partial Manager Change

Growth of $10,000 (37.0, 32.0, 25.0, 20.0, 15.0, 10.0)
— Investment Values of Fund
— Investment Values of S&P 500

Performance Quartile (within Category)

1993	1994	1995	1996	1997	1998	1999	2000	2001	2002	2003	12-04	History
—	9.77	13.52	17.80	23.25	29.65	34.64	27.83	24.12	18.60	21.79	22.65	NAV
—	-2.25*	38.68	32.72	31.85	31.85	22.51	-7.36	-13.33	-22.89	17.24	4.10	Total Return %
—	—	1.15	9.78	-1.50	3.28	1.47	1.74	-1.45	-0.80	-11.43	-6.77	+/-S&P 500
—	—	1.50	9.60	1.36	-6.86	-10.65	15.06	7.09	4.99	-12.51	-2.20	+/-Russ 1000Gr
—	0.00	0.27	0.04	0.00	0.00	0.00	0.00	0.00	0.00	0.09	0.15	Income Return %
—	—	38.41	32.68	31.85	31.85	22.51	-7.36	-13.33	-22.89	17.15	3.95	Capital Return %
—	—	16	3	20	50	78	27	15	19	97	82	Total Rtn % Rank Cat
—	0.01	0.03	0.00	0.00	0.00	0.00	0.00	0.00	0.00	0.02	0.03	Income $
—	0.00	0.00	0.14	0.21	0.94	1.65	4.08	0.00	0.00	0.00	0.00	Capital Gains $
—	—	1.30	1.28	1.23	1.12	1.05	1.03	1.06	1.06	1.06	—	Expense Ratio %
—	—	0.20	-0.06	-0.37	-0.22	-0.16	-0.14	0.10	0.23	0.29	—	Income Ratio %
—	—	—	26	19	30	32	67	60	38	39	—	Turnover Rate %
—	11	49	196	549	1,157	1,736	1,299	947	698	1,001	1,062	Net Assets $mil

Performance 12-31-04

	1st Qtr	2nd Qtr	3rd Qtr	4th Qtr	Total
2000	-2.86	-0.62	-8.52	4.90	-7.36
2001	-15.56	3.62	-9.98	10.04	-13.33
2002	-0.12	-13.62	-14.08	4.03	-22.89
2003	-0.59	8.92	-0.50	8.82	17.24
2004	1.70	2.26	-4.55	4.87	4.10

Trailing	Total Return%	+/- S&P 500	+/- Russ 1000Gr	%Rank Cat	Growth of $10,000
3 Mo	4.87	-4.36	-4.30	98	10,487
6 Mo	0.10	-7.09	-3.37	95	10,010
1 Yr	4.10	-6.77	-2.20	82	10,410
3 Yr Avg	-2.00	-5.58	-1.82	71	9,412
5 Yr Avg	-5.45	-3.15	3.84	29	7,556
10 Yr Avg	11.47	-0.60	1.88	16	29,620
15 Yr Avg	—	—	—	—	—

Tax Analysis	Tax-Adj Rtn%	%Rank Cat	Tax-Cost Rat	%Rank Cat
3 Yr (estimated)	-2.03	63	0.03	6
5 Yr (estimated)	-5.97	28	0.55	34
10 Yr (estimated)	10.93	9	0.48	7

Potential Capital Gain Exposure: 2% of assets

Rating and Risk

Time Period	Load-Adj Return %	Morningstar Rtn vs Cat	Morningstar Risk vs Cat	Morningstar Risk-Adj Rating
1 Yr	4.10			
3 Yr	-2.00	-Avg	Low	★★★
5 Yr	-5.45	+Avg	Low	★★★★
10 Yr	11.47	+Avg	-Avg	★★★★★
Incept	11.03			

Other Measures	Standard Index S&P 500	Best Fit Index S&P 500
Alpha	-5.1	-5.1
Beta	0.80	0.80
R-Squared	92	92
Standard Deviation	12.24	
Mean	-2.00	
Sharpe Ratio	-0.28	

Portfolio Analysis 11-30-04

Share change since 10-04 Total Stocks:36	Sector	PE	YTD Ret%	% Assets
Procter & Gamble	Goods	23.3	12.38	5.12
Gillette	Goods	27.6	23.94	5.10
Schlumberger	Energy	40.7	23.84	4.35
Johnson & Johnson	Health	20.6	25.17	4.32
⊕ ConocoPhillips	Energy	9.0	35.60	4.24
⊕ General Electric	Ind Mtrls	22.8	20.68	3.71
American International G	Financial	16.2	-0.53	3.69
⊖ United Parcel Service B	Business	28.5	16.40	3.64
⊕ Eli Lilly & Company	Health	24.3	-17.55	3.40
Genentech	Health	78.6	16.36	3.35
⊕ McDonald's	Consumer	19.7	31.48	3.26
Kohl's	Consumer	25.5	9.41	3.26
PepsiCo	Goods	22.5	13.82	3.24
Medtronic	Health	30.7	2.68	3.12
Boston Scientific	Health	32.3	-3.29	2.99
⊖ Caterpillar	Ind Mtrls	17.6	19.75	2.69
Bed Bath & Beyond	Consumer	27.6	-8.12	2.59
⊖ Qualcomm	Hardware	42.0	58.20	2.57
⊕ 3M Company	Ind Mtrls	23.5	-1.75	2.53
Pfizer	Health	22.0	-22.31	2.49

Current Investment Style

Value Blnd Growth — Large Mid Small

Market Cap	%
Giant	59.2
Large	40.8
Mid	0.0
Small	0.0
Micro	0.0
Avg $mil: 57,269	

Value Measures		Rel Category
Price/Earnings	20.23	0.95
Price/Book	4.25	1.32
Price/Sales	2.24	1.04
Price/Cash Flow	11.44	1.04
Dividend Yield %	1.28	1.66

Growth Measures	%	Rel Category
Long-Term Erngs	12.58	0.90
Book Value	13.39	1.05
Sales	12.81	1.50
Cash Flow	16.62	1.00
Historical Erngs	13.13	0.91

Profitability	%	Rel Category
Return on Equity	23.72	1.32
Return on Assets	10.94	1.17
Net Margin	13.77	1.12

Sector Weightings	% of Stocks	Rel S&P 500	3 Year High	3 Year Low
Info	8.76	0.41		
Software	2.19	0.51	8	1
Hardware	5.43	0.53	11	4
Media	1.14	0.30	7	1
Telecom	0.00	0.00	0	0
Service	53.05	1.14		
Health	23.97	1.92	26	20
Consumer	12.08	1.33	15	5
Business	8.49	2.10	9	2
Financial	8.51	0.41	16	7
Mfg	38.21	1.19		
Goods	17.33	1.86	27	17
Ind Mtrls	11.82	0.93	12	5
Energy	9.06	1.27	9	4
Utilities	0.00	0.00	0	0

Composition

Cash	5.2
Stocks	94.8
Bonds	0.0
Other	0.0
Foreign (% of Stock)	0.0

Morningstar's Take by David Kathman 10-12-04

ABN AMRO/Montag & Caldwell Growth remains a good large-growth option.

This fund's cautious growth strategy has served it well over the past decade. Manager Ron Canakaris and his team sift through the large-cap universe for companies with strong fundamentals and sustainable earnings growth of 10%-20% per year. From that group, they use a somewhat unusual combination of modest valuations and near-term earnings momentum to determine the portfolio. They prefer to buy stocks trading 10% to 25% below their estimated present value, and will start to trim a stock if it goes 20% over that value.

Though the process is mostly bottom up, macro considerations also come into play. For example, many technology stocks have started to look attractive on a valuation basis, but the managers have held off on buying them because high inventory levels make those companies' earnings outlooks doubtful. As a result, the fund holds very few tech names, and those are mainly consumer-oriented stocks such as Electronic Arts and Qualcomm.

Because the team uses a proprietary valuation method based on discounted cash flows, the portfolio can look expensive in terms of traditional measures such as P/E and price/sales, but it's a conservative portfolio in other ways. The fund is overweight relative to its peers in consumer and health care stocks, which the managers think will do well regardless of economic trends, and it's underweight in technology, as noted above. Lately they've been adding industrials such as Caterpillar and retailers such as Kohl's.

This moderately conservative strategy means that the fund tends to trail its large-growth peers in raging bull markets, as it did in both 1999 and 2003. However, it has otherwise been a solid performer, ranking in the top one-third of the large-growth category over the past five years with low volatility. It's a fine choice as a growth-leaning core fund.

Address:	680 E Swedesford Rd Wayne PA 19087 800-992-8151
Web Address:	www.abnamrofunds.com
Inception:	11-02-94*
Advisor:	Montag & Caldwell Inc.
Subadvisor:	None
NTF Plans:	Fidelity Retail-NTF, Schwab OneSource

Minimum Purchase:	$2500	Add: $50	IRA: $500
Min Auto Inv Plan:	$50	Add: $50	
Sales Fees:	0.25%B, 2.00%R		
Management Fee:	0.80% mx./0.60% mn., 0.06%A		
Actual Fees:	Mgt:0.66%	Dist:0.25%	
Expense Projections:	3Yr:$337	5Yr:$585	10Yr:$1294
Income Distrib:	Quarterly		

Aegis Value

Ticker	Load	NAV	Yield	Total Assets	Mstar Category
AVALX	Closed	$18.15	0.0%	$823 mil	Small Value

Governance and Management

Fiduciary Grade: C

Portfolio Manager(s)

Scott Barbee joined the fund's advisor, Aegis Financial Corp., in 1997. He's supported by two analysts, Tom Saberhagen and David Shapiro, who both joined Aegis in 2002.

Strategy

Manager Scott Barbee looks for stocks sporting very low P/E, price/cash-flow and price/book ratios. (That approach has typically led him to buy very small companies, but he's willing to look at larger names if they meet his strict criteria.) He then narrows the field to firms going through problems that he deems temporary, such as a weak division masking the power of a more productive one, and buys if they sell at a discount to his estimates of their intrinsic value. He'll sell when a stock hits that value. Barbee is willing to hoard cash when he can't find buying opportunities.

Historical Profile

Return Above Avg
Risk Low
Rating ★★★★★ Highest

Investment Style
Equity
Stock %

99% 58% 57% 65% 45%

▼ Manager Change
▽ Partial Manager Change

Growth of $10,000
— Investment Values of Fund
— Investment Values of S&P 500

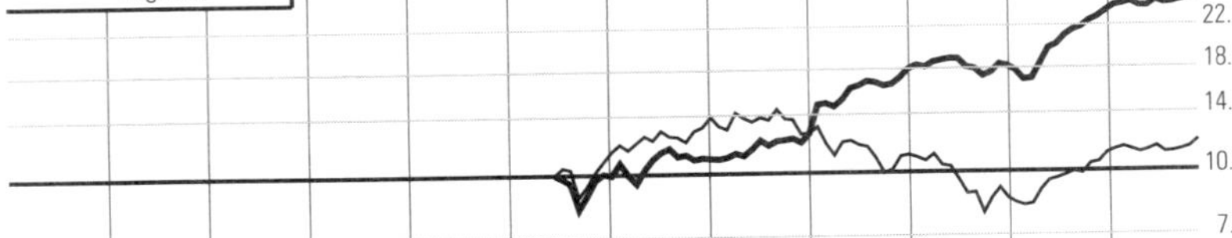

Performance Quartile (within Category)

1993	1994	1995	1996	1997	1998	1999	2000	2001	2002	2003	12-04	History
—	—	—	—	—	9.79	8.81	9.14	13.00	12.66	16.77	18.15	NAV
—	—	—	—	—	-0.85*	9.55	14.67	42.66	1.35	35.75	13.48	Total Return %
—	—	—	—	—	—	-11.49	23.77	54.54	23.44	7.08	2.61	+/-S&P 500
—	—	—	—	—	—	11.04	-8.16	28.64	12.78	-10.28	-8.77	+/-Russ 2000 VL
—	—	—	—	—	0.00	1.53	2.04	0.03	0.15	0.00	0.00	Income Return %
—	—	—	—	—	—	8.02	12.63	42.63	1.20	35.75	13.48	Capital Return %
—	—	—	—	—	—	27	66	3	5	81	95	Total Rtn % Rank Cat
—	—	—	—	—	0.08	0.15	0.18	0.00	0.02	0.00	0.00	Income $
—	—	—	—	—	0.04	1.70	0.76	0.04	0.49	0.41	0.87	Capital Gains $
—	—	—	—	—	—	1.50	1.50	1.50	1.50	1.50	1.50	Expense Ratio %
—	—	—	—	—	—	1.46	0.04	0.89	1.41	0.31	-0.34	Income Ratio %
—	—	—	—	—	—	33	50	10	29	15	27	Turnover Rate %
—	—	—	—	—	1	1	2	72	174	470	823	Net Assets $mil

Performance 12-31-04

	1st Qtr	2nd Qtr	3rd Qtr	4th Qtr	Total
2000	2.84	7.51	0.00	3.72	14.67
2001	16.08	12.25	-0.17	9.66	42.66
2002	3.92	1.70	-9.24	5.65	1.35
2003	-6.95	20.97	10.18	9.47	35.75
2004	5.25	0.68	0.06	7.03	13.48

Trailing	Total Return%	+/- S&P 500	+/- Russ 2000 VL	%Rank Cat	Growth of $10,000
3 Mo	7.03	-2.20	-6.17	99	10,703
6 Mo	7.09	-0.10	-6.28	93	10,709
1 Yr	13.48	2.61	-8.77	95	11,348
3 Yr Avg	16.01	12.43	-0.49	41	15,613
5 Yr Avg	20.63	22.93	3.40	11	25,543
10 Yr Avg	—	—	—	—	—
15 Yr Avg	—	—	—	—	—

Tax Analysis	Tax-Adj Rtn%	%Rank Cat	Tax-Cost Rat	%Rank Cat
3 Yr (estimated)	14.96	38	0.91	51
5 Yr (estimated)	19.33	10	1.08	56
10 Yr (estimated)	—	—	—	—

Potential Capital Gain Exposure: 14% of assets

Rating and Risk

Time Period	Load-Adj Return %	Morningstar Rtn vs Cat	Morningstar Risk vs Cat	Morningstar Risk-Adj Rating
1 Yr	13.48			
3 Yr	16.01	Avg	Low	★★★★
5 Yr	20.63	High	Low	★★★★★
10 Yr	—	—	—	—
Incept	16.63			

Other Measures	Standard Index S&P 500	Best Fit Index Mstar Small Value
Alpha	13.1	4.0
Beta	0.53	0.58
R-Squared	56	77
Standard Deviation	12.17	
Mean	16.01	
Sharpe Ratio	1.21	

Morningstar's Take by Greg Carlson 11-21-04

Aegis Value is closing its doors, but new investors shouldn't rush in.

On Nov. 30, 2004, this fund will close to new investors. Scott Barbee, the fund's manager since its inception, says heavy inflows and a lack of buying opportunities are driving that decision.

We're glad management has taken this step, but wish it had come much sooner. A distinctive investment style--Barbee insists on rock-bottom valuations, which he has typically found among the smallest companies--reaped superb early returns. That standout performance attracted investors in droves, swelling the fund's assets from $4 million in May 2001 to $750 million in October 2004. To cope, Barbee has had to alter the portfolio, nearly doubling the number of holdings since early-2001 while also making more frequent forays into the stocks of larger firms. Yet, Barbee still hasn't been able to put all of the fund's assets to work, as evidenced by its recent 54% cash stake.

By allowing the fund's growth to go unchecked until now, we think management has put itself in a bind. Try as he might to put the fund's cash to work, Barbee will have to do so without straying from the value discipline that has been pivotal to his past success--no simple feat. True, Barbee could further expand the portfolio to include more micro-cap names. But that option has been available all along and yet he hasn't exercised it, suggesting that such fare hasn't passed his valuation criteria or that Aegis lacks the resources to cover an even wider array of tiny firms.

All told, new investors weighing a purchase before the fund shuts its doors should think twice: Management amassed its stalwart record using a different style than it's likely to ply in the years ahead (since the portfolio will probably grow longer still, with a lesser emphasis on micro-caps). And while Barbee's approach should hold up even when extended beyond the micro-cap realm, we doubt he'll be able to reprise the terrific gains of years past.

Address:	1100 North Glebe Rd Arlington VA 22201 800-528-3780
Web Address:	www.aegisvaluefund.com
Inception:	05-15-98*
Advisor:	Berno Gambal & Barbee Inc
Subadvisor:	None
NTF Plans:	N/A

Minimum Purchase:	Closed	Add: —	IRA: —		
Min Auto Inv Plan:	Closed	Add: —			
Sales Fees:	No-load				
Management Fee:	1.20%, 0.30%A				
Actual Fees:	Mgt:1.20%	Dist:			
Expense Projections:	3Yr:$504	5Yr:$884	10Yr:$2011		
Income Distrib:	Annually				

Portfolio Analysis 08-31-04

Share change since 02-04 Total Stocks:73	Sector	PE	YTD Ret%	% Assets
⊕ Prime Hospitality	Consumer	—	—	3.29
⊕ Ryerson Tull A	Ind Mtrls	9.6	39.51	2.16
⊕ Standard Commercial	Goods	18.0	-1.08	2.04
⊕ PXRE Group	Financial	—	8.03	1.95
⊕ DiMon	Goods	7.7	4.38	1.95
Luby's	Consumer	86.1	103.25	1.88
⊕ Prime Group Realty Trust	Financial	—	2.55	1.76
⊕ Toys R Us	Goods	28.3	61.95	1.63
⊕ PMA Capital	Financial	—	102.15	1.62
Reliant Energy	Utilities	—	85.46	1.60
⊕ SCPIE Holdings	Financial	—	12.70	1.24
⊕ Sea Containers A	Ind Mtrls	20.3	8.53	1.14
☼ Imperial Sugar	Goods	10.9	34.82	1.12
⊕ Nash-Finch	Consumer	29.5	72.72	1.03
⊕ California First Nationa	Consumer	15.4	3.85	0.99
☼ Air France-KLM ADR	Business	—	—	0.95
Allmerica Financial	Financial	12.5	6.70	0.93
Atwood Oceanics	Energy	—	63.12	0.92
USEC	Ind Mtrls	—	22.88	0.90
Books-A-Million	Consumer	17.4	52.56	0.85

Current Investment Style

Value Blnd Growth; Large Mid Small

Market Cap	%
Giant	0.0
Large	0.0
Mid	10.6
Small	19.9
Micro	69.5
Avg $mil: 300	

Value Measures		Rel Category
Price/Earnings	5.52	0.35
Price/Book	0.77	0.46
Price/Sales	0.30	0.40
Price/Cash Flow	3.22	0.62
Dividend Yield %	1.37	1.14

Growth Measures	%	Rel Category
Long-Term Erngs	7.65	0.63
Book Value	-3.24	NMF
Sales	-2.82	NMF
Cash Flow	-13.21	NMF
Historical Erngs	4.37	0.91

Profitability	%	Rel Category
Return on Equity	-3.33	NMF
Return on Assets	-2.25	NMF
Net Margin	-3.15	NMF

Sector Weightings	% of Stocks	Rel S&P 500	3 Year High	3 Year Low
Info	0.46	0.02		
Software	0.00	0.00	2	0
Hardware	0.01	0.00	1	0
Media	0.00	0.00	0	0
Telecom	0.45	0.14	2	0
Service	45.07	0.97		
Health	0.00	0.00	1	0
Consumer	21.74	2.39	22	13
Business	4.05	1.00	14	4
Financial	19.28	0.93	19	7
Mfg	54.48	1.70		
Goods	23.39	2.51	23	6
Ind Mtrls	20.04	1.58	46	20
Energy	3.51	0.49	6	0
Utilities	7.54	2.55	10	0

Composition

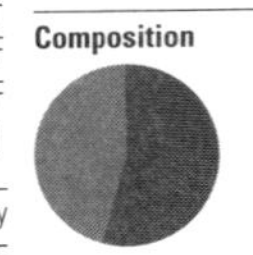

Cash	54.3
Stocks	45.3
Bonds	0.0
Other	0.4
Foreign (% of Stock)	3.7

AIM Constellation A

Ticker	Load	NAV	Yield	Total Assets	Mstar Category
CSTGX	5.50%	$22.84	0.0%	$6,742 mil	Large Growth

Governance and Management

Fiduciary Grade: C

Portfolio Manager(s)

Ken Zschappel is this fund's primary portfolio manager. He was recently added to the team that runs AIM Summit. Robert Lloyd, part of the Summit portfolio-management team since July 2001, was added here in May 2003. Christian Costanzo was also named a portfolio manager in May 2003, and Bryan Unterhalter was named as of mid-July 2003. Analysts here, including Costanzo and Unterhalter, have sector responsibilities.

Strategy

Depending on market environments, this mid- and large-cap fund invests between 10% and 50% of assets in core steady-growth companies and the rest in stocks with earnings-growth rates of 20% or more or accelerating earnings trends. The fund's approach typically leaves the bulk of its portfolio in high-growth areas, including consumer discretionary (retail, restaurants, and others), health care, technology, and financial services. However, without much of an eye toward a benchmark, the fund at times invests more heavily in more-staid areas.

Historical Profile

Return Average
Risk Above Avg
Rating ★★★ Neutral

Investment Style
Equity
Stock %

94%	98%	92%	95%	92%	99%	97%	99%	99%

▼ Manager Change
▽ Partial Manager Change

Growth of $10,000

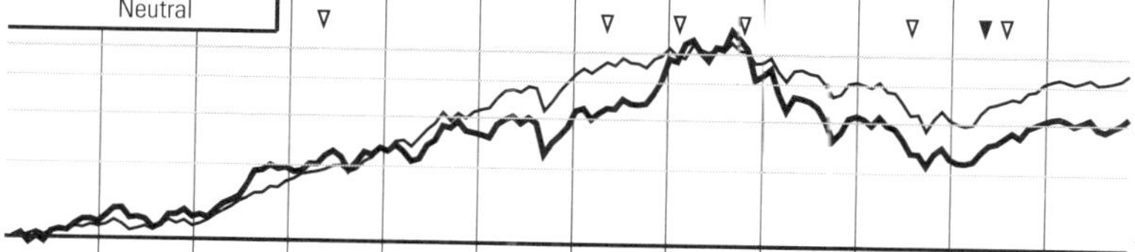

Performance Quartile (within Category)

1993	1994	1995	1996	1997	1998	1999	2000	2001	2002	2003	12-04	History
17.50	17.19	22.51	25.26	26.38	30.52	40.51	28.93	22.10	16.63	21.51	22.84	NAV
17.29	1.30	35.45	16.27	12.92	18.89	44.38	-10.37	-23.61	-24.75	29.34	6.18	Total Return %
7.23	-0.01	-2.08	-6.67	-20.43	-9.68	23.34	-1.27	-11.73	-2.66	0.67	-4.69	+/-S&P 500
14.42	-1.32	-1.73	-6.85	-17.57	-19.82	11.22	12.05	-3.19	3.13	-0.41	-0.12	+/-Russ 1000Gr
0.00	0.00	0.00	0.00	0.00	0.00	0.00	0.00	0.00	0.00	0.00	0.00	Income Return %
17.29	1.30	35.45	16.27	12.92	18.89	44.38	-10.37	-23.61	-24.75	29.34	6.18	Capital Return %
22	22	29	75	95	86	29	37	65	32	37	63	Total Rtn % Rank Cat
0.00	0.00	0.00	0.00	0.00	0.00	0.00	0.00	0.00	0.00	0.00	0.00	Income $
0.00	0.52	0.75	0.89	2.06	0.77	3.28	7.42	0.00	0.00	0.00	0.00	Capital Gains $
1.20	1.20	1.20	1.14	1.11	1.10	1.10	1.08	1.14	1.26	1.29	—	Expense Ratio %
-0.30	-0.20	-0.30	-0.27	-0.40	-0.47	-0.50	-0.61	-0.46	-0.74	-0.67	—	Income Ratio %
70	79	45	58	67	76	62	88	75	57	47	—	Turnover Rate %
2,925	3,704	7,377	11,915	13,991	14,304	17,920	15,905	10,635	6,376	6,862	5,788	Net Assets $mil

Performance 12-31-04

	1st Qtr	2nd Qtr	3rd Qtr	4th Qtr	Total
2000	14.32	-4.82	5.76	-22.11	-10.37
2001	-21.33	6.94	-23.34	18.44	-23.61
2002	-0.36	-14.12	-16.50	5.32	-24.75
2003	-1.86	13.42	4.00	11.74	29.34
2004	0.88	1.01	-5.29	10.02	6.18

Trailing	Total Return%	+/- S&P 500	+/- Russ 1000Gr	%Rank Cat	Growth of $10,000
3 Mo	10.02	0.79	0.85	47	11,002
6 Mo	4.20	-2.99	0.73	59	10,420
1 Yr	6.18	-4.69	-0.12	63	10,618
3 Yr Avg	1.10	-2.48	1.28	31	10,334
5 Yr Avg	-6.68	-4.38	2.61	41	7,077
10 Yr Avg	8.01	-4.06	-1.58	67	21,609
15 Yr Avg	11.06	0.13	1.56	24	48,235

Tax Analysis	Tax-Adj Rtn%	%Rank Cat	Tax-Cost Rat	%Rank Cat
3 Yr (estimated)	-0.78	49	0.00	1
5 Yr (estimated)	-8.50	53	0.83	50
10 Yr (estimated)	6.36	65	0.97	23

Potential Capital Gain Exposure: -4% of assets

Rating and Risk

Time Period	Load-Adj Return %	Morningstar Rtn vs Cat	Morningstar Risk vs Cat	Morningstar Risk-Adj Rating
1 Yr	0.34			
3 Yr	-0.78	Avg	Avg	★★★
5 Yr	-7.73	Avg	+Avg	★★★
10 Yr	7.40	-Avg	+Avg	★★
Incept	14.37			

Other Measures	Standard Index S&P 500	Best Fit Index Russ MG
Alpha	-2.3	-4.2
Beta	0.99	0.83
R-Squared	89	93
Standard Deviation	15.94	
Mean	1.10	
Sharpe Ratio	-0.02	

Morningstar's Take by Bridget Hughes 10-20-04

Is AIM Constellation's reliability here to stay?

For each of the past five calendar years, this large-growth fund has landed in the category's middle third, beating its typical rival in four of those years. This year, the fund is also close to the middle third: Its 4.4% loss through Oct. 19, 2004, lands at the group's 70th percentile.

We think, going forward, the offering's flexibility makes this kind of more-muted performance likely. While manager Ken Zschappel looks for strong earnings growth, he doesn't care where it comes from. In contrast, some growth funds stick only to certain areas of the market, including technology and health care, or limit how much their portfolios can deviate from growth benchmarks, such as the Russell 1000 Growth Index. Zschappel's only constraints are that a stock's market cap be at least $2 billion and its liquidity be sufficient enough for the $6.5 billion fund to trade it well.

Lately, Zschappel has been taking advantage of his flexibility. Although traditional growth stocks, including Cisco Systems, Dell, and Yahoo, remain top holdings as of Sept. 30, 2004, Zschappel has been adding to stocks from the basic materials, energy, and industrials areas. He's been moving away from consumer-discretionary stocks, particularly retailers, because he thinks that the little bit of inflation creeping into the economy will help curb U.S. consumers' long spending run.

Constellation's consistent record could signal good news ahead. Morningstar recently found that consistently above-average funds proved to be winners in the subsequent five-year period. That said, things could get harder for the fund if a narrow slice of the market pulls ahead or if large caps take off. (The fund regularly sports a hefty mid-cap stake.) All told, we continue to think there are better large-growth choices, but we're cautiously optimistic about this one.

Address:	Eleven Greenway Plz Houston TX 77046 800-347-4246
Web Address:	www.aiminvestments.com
Inception:	04-30-76
Advisor:	AIM Advisors, Inc.
Subadvisor:	AIM Capital Mgmt., Inc.
NTF Plans:	DATALynx NTF, Federated Tr NTF

Minimum Purchase:	$1000	Add: $50	IRA: $250
Min Auto Inv Plan:	$50	Add: $50	
Sales Fees:	5.50%L, 0.25%S		
Management Fee:	1.00% mx./0.63% mn.		
Actual Fees:	Mgt:0.63%	Dist:0.30%	
Expense Projections:	3Yr:$939	5Yr:$1224	10Yr:$2032
Income Distrib:	Annually		

Portfolio Analysis 06-30-04

Share change since 05-04 Total Stocks:128	Sector	PE	YTD Ret%	% Assets
Microsoft	Software	36.1	8.95	2.78
⊕ Cisco Systems	Hardware	24.5	-20.26	2.44
Microchip Technology	Hardware	26.7	-19.84	2.19
Biomet	Health	34.1	20.83	2.15
Teva Pharmaceutical Indu	Health	—	5.89	2.07
Pfizer	Health	22.0	-22.31	2.00
Caremark RX	Health	32.8	55.67	1.86
Dell	Hardware	34.0	24.01	1.84
Lamar Advertising A	Business	—	14.63	1.78
Analog Devices	Hardware	24.2	-18.69	1.78
CDW	Consumer	25.4	15.52	1.54
Clear Channel Communicat	Media	23.5	-27.57	1.52
Yahoo	Media	95.1	67.36	1.49
Lam Research	Hardware	21.5	-10.50	1.47
Fiserv	Business	21.3	1.64	1.47
Wal-Mart Stores	Consumer	23.4	0.51	1.27
MBNA	Financial	14.0	15.53	1.24
Robert Half Internationa	Business	51.7	26.95	1.23
⊖ Bed Bath & Beyond	Consumer	27.6	-8.12	1.18
Zimmer Holdings	Health	54.0	13.81	1.11

Current Investment Style

Value Blnd Growth — Large Mid Small

Market Cap	%
Giant	31.1
Large	46.5
Mid	22.4
Small	0.0
Micro	0.0
Avg $mil: 23,569	

Value Measures		Rel Category
Price/Earnings	22.92	1.08
Price/Book	3.10	0.96
Price/Sales	2.20	1.02
Price/Cash Flow	12.76	1.16
Dividend Yield %	0.56	0.73

Growth Measures	%	Rel Category
Long-Term Erngs	14.73	1.05
Book Value	10.10	0.79
Sales	7.08	0.83
Cash Flow	30.83	1.86
Historical Erngs	14.69	1.02

Profitability	%	Rel Category
Return on Equity	15.02	0.84
Return on Assets	7.45	0.80
Net Margin	11.44	0.93

Sector Weightings	% of Stocks	Rel S&P 500	3 Year High	3 Year Low
Info	32.93	1.53		
Software	5.40	1.26	8	4
Hardware	20.23	1.98	23	16
Media	5.91	1.54	6	1
Telecom	1.39	0.44	2	0
Service	52.72	1.14		
Health	19.68	1.57	23	16
Consumer	15.06	1.66	21	15
Business	7.82	1.93	11	7
Financial	10.16	0.49	17	9
Mfg	14.34	0.45		
Goods	3.92	0.42	7	2
Ind Mtrls	7.31	0.58	7	3
Energy	3.11	0.43	5	0
Utilities	0.00	0.00	0	0

Composition

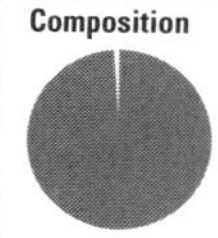

Cash	0.3
Stocks	98.3
Bonds	0.0
Other	0.6
Foreign (% of Stock)	4.1

AIM Energy Inv

Ticker	Load	NAV	Yield	Total Assets	Mstar Category
FSTEX	Closed	$27.83	0.0%	$448 mil	Specialty-Natural Res

Governance and Management

Fiduciary Grade: D

Portfolio Manager(s)

John Segner took over here in early 1997. Two research analysts support the fund.

Strategy

The fund holds 30-40 stocks and spreads assets among energy subsectors based on management's outlook for oil and natural gas. Management uses a bottom-up approach to select stocks in each area, emphasizing strong balance sheets and improving business prospects. Macroeconomic forecasts of supply and demand play a crucial role in the process.

Historical Profile

Return Above Avg
Risk Above Avg
Rating ★★★★ Above Avg

Investment Style: Equity Stock %

1993	1994	1995	1996	1997	1998	1999	2000	2001	2002	2003	12-04
	89%	95%	100%	97%	94%	83%	99%	93%	98%		

▼ Manager Change
▽ Partial Manager Change

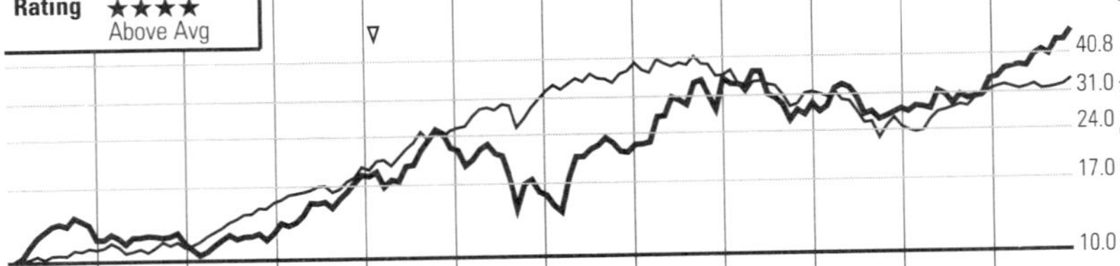

Performance Quartile (within Category)

History

1993	1994	1995	1996	1997	1998	1999	2000	2001	2002	2003	12-04	History
10.37	9.57	11.36	14.46	14.01	10.10	14.33	20.88	17.37	16.62	20.37	27.83	NAV
16.71	-7.25	19.80	38.84	19.09	-27.83	41.88	58.17	-16.81	-4.32	22.56	36.62	Total Return %
6.65	-8.56	-17.73	15.90	-14.26	-56.40	20.84	67.27	-4.93	17.77	-6.11	25.75	+/-S&P 500
—	—	—	—	2.15	-3.16	14.66	42.36	-1.22	8.94	-11.45	12.05	+/-GS NATR RES
1.22	0.52	0.97	0.33	0.42	0.08	0.00	0.00	0.00	0.00	0.00	0.00	Income Return %
15.49	-7.77	18.83	38.51	18.67	-27.91	41.88	58.17	-16.81	-4.32	22.56	36.62	Capital Return %
81	95	76	30	3	64	13	12	80	44	82	14	Total Rtn % Rank Cat
0.11	0.05	0.09	0.04	0.06	0.01	0.00	0.00	0.00	0.00	0.00	0.00	Income $
0.00	0.00	0.00	1.22	3.03	0.00	0.00	1.43	0.00	0.00	0.00	0.00	Capital Gains $
1.18	1.35	1.53	1.30	1.21	1.58	1.68	1.60	1.41	1.53	1.69	1.76	Expense Ratio %
0.86	0.65	0.72	0.54	0.39	0.01	-0.05	-0.26	-0.35	-0.34	-0.57	-0.35	Income Ratio %
190	123	300	392	249	192	279	109	166	144	144	123	Turnover Rate %
49	47	99	233	212	105	171	436	343	248	221	299	Net Assets $mil

Performance 12-31-04

	1st Qtr	2nd Qtr	3rd Qtr	4th Qtr	Total
2000	21.42	12.13	15.07	0.96	58.17
2001	-5.51	-5.83	-16.90	12.50	-16.81
2002	10.88	-6.39	-14.31	7.57	-4.32
2003	1.14	8.80	-2.79	14.57	22.56
2004	8.93	8.56	10.79	4.27	36.62

Trailing	Total Return%	+/- S&P 500	+/- GS NATR RES	%Rank Cat	Growth of $10,000
3 Mo	4.27	-4.96	-0.55	77	10,427
6 Mo	15.53	8.34	0.34	55	11,553
1 Yr	36.62	25.75	12.05	14	13,662
3 Yr Avg	17.01	13.43	3.88	46	16,020
5 Yr Avg	16.09	18.39	8.90	36	21,085
10 Yr Avg	15.64	3.57	—	24	42,764
15 Yr Avg	8.14	-2.79	—	69	32,344

Tax Analysis	Tax-Adj Rtn%	%Rank Cat	Tax-Cost Rat	%Rank Cat
3 Yr (estimated)	17.01	44	0.00	1
5 Yr (estimated)	15.71	37	0.33	42
10 Yr (estimated)	14.15	23	1.29	69

Potential Capital Gain Exposure: 27% of assets

Rating and Risk

Time Period	Load-Adj Return %	Morningstar Rtn vs Cat	Morningstar Risk vs Cat	Morningstar Risk-Adj Rating
1 Yr	36.62			
3 Yr	17.01	Avg	Avg	★★★
5 Yr	16.09	+Avg	+Avg	★★★
10 Yr	15.64	+Avg	+Avg	★★★★
Incept	9.32			

Other Measures	Standard Index S&P 500	Best Fit Index GS NATR RES
Alpha	15.3	3.8
Beta	0.60	1.00
R-Squared	21	81
Standard Deviation	22.87	
Mean	17.01	
Sharpe Ratio	0.69	

Portfolio Analysis 06-30-04

Share change since 05-04 Total Stocks:40	Sector	PE	YTD Ret%	% Assets
BP PLC ADR	Energy	20.7	22.07	4.85
Murphy Oil	Energy	16.5	24.71	4.80
ConocoPhillips	Energy	9.0	35.60	3.89
Nabors Industries	Energy	28.9	23.59	3.87
⊕ EOG Resources	Energy	16.5	55.21	3.72
Nexen	Energy	12.1	13.49	3.31
Valero Energy	Energy	7.0	97.64	3.30
Total SA ADR	Energy	17.0	23.39	3.26
Occidental Petroleum	Energy	10.1	41.27	3.18
Weatherford Internationa	Energy	27.8	42.50	2.99
Talisman Energy	Energy	15.2	44.37	2.95
Pioneer Natural Resource	Energy	15.3	10.60	2.93
Rowan Companies	Energy	—	11.78	2.93
☼ Kerr-McGee	Energy	20.9	28.52	2.92
⊕ Canadian Natural Resourc	Energy	11.4	71.21	2.88
⊖ Consol Energy	Energy	32.2	61.53	2.65
Maverick Tube	Ind Mtrls	7.2	57.40	2.60
Smith International	Energy	34.2	31.05	2.53
National Oilwell	Energy	36.9	57.83	2.45
⊖ FMC Technologies	Energy	23.4	38.20	2.45

Current Investment Style

Value Blnd Growth; Large Mid Small

Market Cap	%
Giant	14.6
Large	29.6
Mid	50.0
Small	5.8
Micro	0.0
Avg $mil: 8,670	

Value Measures		Rel Category
Price/Earnings	14.59	0.89
Price/Book	2.15	0.90
Price/Sales	0.95	0.79
Price/Cash Flow	5.27	0.66
Dividend Yield %	0.80	0.71

Growth Measures	%	Rel Category
Long-Term Erngs	7.88	0.73
Book Value	10.04	1.88
Sales	14.25	1.51
Cash Flow	16.27	2.42
Historical Erngs	37.81	1.82

Profitability	%	Rel Category
Return on Equity	13.55	1.08
Return on Assets	5.52	1.03
Net Margin	9.80	1.05

Industry Weightings	% of Stocks	Rel Cat
Oil & Gas	56.9	1.4
Oil/Gas Products	4.8	1.6
Oil & Gas Srv	29.2	1.1
Pipelines	1.5	1.1
Utilities	0.0	0.0
Hard Commd	3.1	0.3
Soft Commd	0.0	0.0
Misc. Indstrl	0.0	0.0
Other	4.5	0.6

Composition

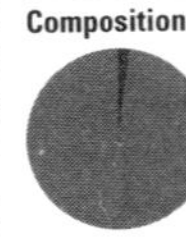

Cash	2.0
Stocks	98.0
Bonds	0.0
Other	0.0
Foreign (% of Stock)	18.6

Morningstar's Take by Dan McNeela 01-03-05

AIM Energy has its bright spots, but the overall picture is clouded.

This fund, which was named Invesco Energy until October 2004, is bound to come up on the radar screens of investors looking to bolster the energy stakes in their portfolios. It has an experienced and successful manager in John Segner, who has guided the fund for about eight years now. During that time, it has proved to be especially adept at finding the sweet spot of the energy market during rallies. Segner put the fund on the map with stellar campaigns in 1999 and 2000, with gains of better than 40% in each year. And relative to his energy-focused rivals, Segner's been more willing to hold oil service stocks and exploration and production firms, whose values are much more sensitive to changes in underlying commodity prices. That tendency also gives the fund a bias toward smaller-cap energy stocks.

In 2004, the fund was on target again. Segner largely stuck with the oil service stocks that lagged during the energy rally in 2003. As oil supplies remained tight, the prospects for services stocks such as National Oilwell and Weatherford International brightened considerably. Both holdings shook off disappointing returns in 2003 to post gains of better than 40% in 2004. All told, the fund gained 36.6% last year in one of the category's best performances.

Still, because of its somewhat aggressive positioning, the fund has not been great during downturns. That remains a concern given the run that energy stocks have had. Investors also have reason to be wary after AIM and Invesco ran afoul of industry regulators for allowing market-timers access to some of its funds. In October 2004, AIM agreed to a $375 million settlement and put forth reforms, but the firm has some work to do before it can win back investor confidence.

Overall, this does not look to be the most compelling option in the category.

Address:	11 Greenway Plaza Houston TX 77046 800-959-4246
Web Address:	www.aiminvestments.com
Inception:	01-19-84
Advisor:	AIM Advisors, Inc.
Subadvisor:	Invesco Institutional (n.a.), Inc.
NTF Plans:	Fidelity Retail-NTF, Schwab OneSource

Minimum Purchase:	Closed	Add: —	IRA: —
Min Auto Inv Plan:	Closed	Add: —	
Sales Fees:	0.25%B, 2.00%R		
Management Fee:	0.75% mx./0.35% mn.		
Actual Fees:	Mgt:0.75%	Dist:0.25%	
Expense Projections:	3Yr:$496	5Yr:$855	10Yr:$1867
Income Distrib:	Annually		

American AAdv SmCpVl Pln

Analyst Pick

Ticker	Load	NAV	Yield	Total Assets	Mstar Category
AVPAX	None	$19.91	0.3%	$1,896 mil	Small Value

Governance and Management

Fiduciary Grade:

Portfolio Manager(s)

Brandywine Asset Management runs 44% of the portfolio, while Hotchkis & Wiley; Barrow, Hanley, Mewhinney & Strauss, Inc.; and The Boston Company each manage between 15% and 18% of assets. The remaining 4% is held in cash. Each firm has a deep staff to support its work.

Strategy

The fund encompasses four distinct small-value strategies. It's unlikely the fund would deviate from that space because American AAdvantage monitors the subadvisors to ensure that they stick to small value. Brandywine Asset Management takes a more quantitative approach to value while The Boston Company, Hotchkis & Wiley, and Barrow, Hanley build their portfolios using more fundamental research.

Historical Profile

Return High
Risk Above Avg
Rating ★★★★ Above Avg

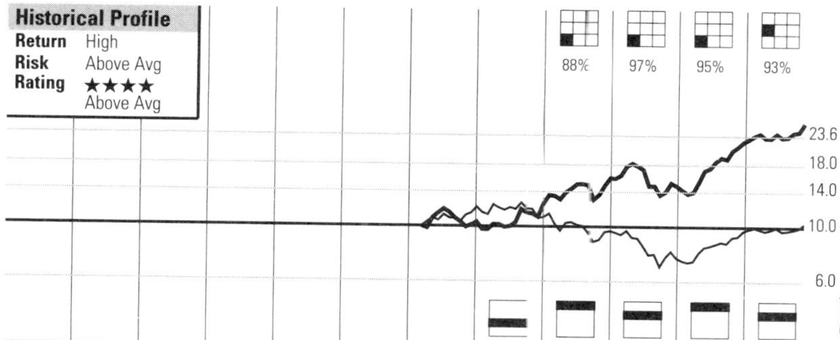

Investment Style: Equity, Stock %

▼ Manager Change
▽ Partial Manager Change

Growth of $10,000
— Investment Values of Fund
— Investment Values of S&P 500

Performance Quartile (within Category)

1993	1994	1995	1996	1997	1998	1999	2000	2001	2002	2003	12-04	History
—	—	—	—	—	—	9.30	10.69	12.73	11.45	16.84	19.91	NAV
—	—	—	—	—	—	4.04*	19.03	27.24	-6.92	51.28	23.19	Total Return %
—	—	—	—	—	—	—	28.13	39.12	15.17	22.61	12.32	+/-S&P 500
—	—	—	—	—	—	—	-3.80	13.22	4.51	5.25	0.94	+/-Russ 2000 VL
—	—	—	—	—	—	0.00	1.98	0.75	0.95	0.28	0.33	Income Return %
—	—	—	—	—	—	—	17.05	26.49	-7.87	51.00	22.86	Capital Return %
—	—	—	—	—	—	—	51	14	34	18	30	Total Rtn % Rank Cat
—	—	—	—	—	—	0.02	0.18	0.08	0.12	0.03	0.06	Income $
—	—	—	—	—	—	0.17	0.17	0.77	0.28	0.44	0.77	Capital Gains $
—	—	—	—	—	—	—	—	—	1.11	1.16	—	Expense Ratio %
—	—	—	—	—	—	—	—	—	0.52	0.39	—	Income Ratio %
—	—	—	—	—	—	—	—	—	81	75	—	Turnover Rate %
—	—	—	—	—	—	—	—	-	35	86	756	Net Assets $mil

Performance 12-31-04

	1st Qtr	2nd Qtr	3rd Qtr	4th Qtr	Total
2000	-2.04	-1.87	13.65	8.96	19.03
2001	4.21	15.17	-13.25	22.21	27.24
2002	11.55	-2.96	-20.90	8.71	-6.92
2003	-5.41	24.75	8.88	17.75	51.28
2004	8.08	-0.05	1.04	12.87	23.19

Trailing	Total Return%	+/- S&P 500	+/- Russ 2000 VL	%Rank Cat	Growth of $10,000
3 Mo	12.87	3.64	-0.33	47	11,287
6 Mo	14.05	6.86	0.68	18	11,405
1 Yr	23.19	12.32	0.94	30	12,319
3 Yr Avg	20.16	16.58	3.66	12	17,349
5 Yr Avg	21.31	23.61	4.08	9	26,271
10 Yr Avg	—	—	—	—	—
15 Yr Avg	—	—	—	—	—

Tax Analysis	Tax-Adj Rtn%	%Rank Cat	Tax-Cost Rat	%Rank Cat
3 Yr (estimated)	18.90	9	1.05	61
5 Yr (estimated)	19.71	8	1.32	65
10 Yr (estimated)	—	—	—	—

Potential Capital Gain Exposure: 12% of assets

Rating and Risk

Time Period	Load-Adj Return %	Morningstar Rtn vs Cat	Morningstar Risk vs Cat	Morningstar Risk-Adj Rating
1 Yr	23.19			
3 Yr	20.16	+Avg	+Avg	★★★★
5 Yr	21.31	High	+Avg	★★★★
10 Yr	—	—	—	—
Incept	18.79			

Other Measures	Standard Index S&P 500	Best Fit Index Russ 2000 VL
Alpha	16.7	3.3
Beta	0.96	1.00
R-Squared	65	97
Standard Deviation	21.44	
Mean	20.16	
Sharpe Ratio	0.89	

Portfolio Analysis 12-31-04

Share change since 11-04 Total Stocks:262	Sector	PE	YTD Ret%	% Assets
⊕ Del Monte Foods	Goods	15.3	5.96	1.43
⊕ Protective Life	Financial	11.1	28.45	1.32
⊕ NSTAR	Utilities	15.2	17.13	1.30
⊕ Lubrizol	Energy	22.0	17.03	1.09
⊕ MEMC Electronic Material	Hardware	13.7	37.73	1.08
WCI Communities	Financial	10.9	42.65	1.08
⊕ Allmerica Financial	Financial	12.5	6.70	1.07
Reinsurance Group of Ame	Financial	11.5	26.18	1.04
⊕ American Financial Group	Financial	4.4	20.38	1.04
⊕ Great Plains Energy	Utilities	—	0.40	1.03
⊕ Dana	Ind Mtrls	10.4	-3.11	1.02
⊕ National Fuel Gas	Utilities	10.3	20.95	1.01
⊕ Universal Health Service	Health	14.9	-16.59	1.00
⊖ Beazer Homes USA	Consumer	9.1	50.26	0.99
Furniture Brands Interna	Goods	14.4	-12.81	0.99
⊕ AGL Resources	Utilities	14.8	18.81	0.98
Health Net	Health	15.4	-11.71	0.94
Warnaco Group	Goods	—	35.42	0.93
⊕ OGE Energy Corp	Utilities	16.2	15.54	0.93
Alexander & Baldwin	Business	18.4	29.05	0.93

Current Investment Style

Value Blnd Growth / Large Mid Small

Market Cap	%
Giant	0.0
Large	0.0
Mid	61.7
Small	35.8
Micro	2.5
Avg $mil: 1,661	

Value Measures		Rel Category
Price/Earnings	4.57	0.91
Price/Book	1.63	0.98
Price/Sales	0.64	0.85
Price/Cash Flow	5.16	0.99
Dividend Yield %	1.39	1.16

Growth Measures	%	Rel Category
Long-Term Erngs	9.71	0.80
Book Value	7.35	1.70
Sales	5.50	1.76
Cash Flow	-4.91	NMF
Historical Erngs	8.53	1.77

Profitability	%	Rel Category
Return on Equity	13.98	1.53
Return on Assets	6.72	1.62
Net Margin	8.29	1.24

Sector Weightings	% of Stocks	Rel S&P 500	3 Year High	3 Year Low
Info	7.33	0.34		
Software	0.84	0.20	5	0
Hardware	4.41	0.43	7	0
Media	1.66	0.43	4	1
Telecom	0.42	0.13	1	0
Service	52.04	1.12		
Health	6.44	0.52	7	3
Consumer	10.78	1.19	22	11
Business	8.64	2.13	16	9
Financial	26.18	1.26	30	21
Mfg	40.62	1.26		
Goods	10.63	1.14	11	6
Ind Mtrls	11.16	0.88	13	9
Energy	4.52	0.63	7	2
Utilities	14.31	4.83	15	4

Composition

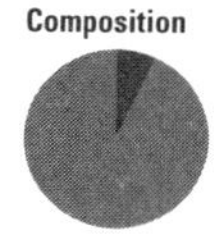

Cash	6.7
Stocks	93.3
Bonds	0.0
Other	0.0
Foreign (% of Stock)	2.2

Morningstar's Take by Terence Geenty 11-29-04

A recent subadvisor addition further strengthens this fund.

American AAdvantage Small Cap Value added a fourth subadvisor to its team in late September 2004. American AAdvantage hired The Boston Company to invest the cash that has streamed into this offering. Assets under management have climbed to about $1.5 billion, making this one of the larger open small-value funds. The Boston Company joins three other subadvisors assigned to this offering: Hotchkis & Wiley, Brandywine, and Barrow, Hanley, Mewhinney & Strauss.

Each of the fund's managers has achieved strong results using a consistent, value-based investment style. For example, Hotchkis & Wiley Small Cap Value, which is closed to new shareholders, boasts the best five-year return in the small-value category. More importantly, the fund attempts to combine subadvisors with distinct styles to identify a wide range of value opportunities. As the fund's assets grow, American AAdvantage will add more subadvisors to keep the fund nimble and its stock positions relatively liquid.

The combination of various value styles has generated solid results for this fund. Its year-to-date returns outpace the small-value category average by nearly 3.5 percentage points through Nov. 17, 2004, and its five-year return ranks in the group's top decile. However, the five-year record was built primarily by subadvisors Brandywine and Hotchkis & Wiley. (Barrow, Hanley was added in September 2003.) As more managers are added to this fund, performance may hew more closely to the small-value category average.

That caveat aside, this fund offers access to a number of well-regarded money managers that will stay true to small-value investing. Low expenses are another plus. Thus, this remains one of the top picks among open small-value options.

Address:	4151 Amon Carter Blvd Fort Worth TX 76155 800-388-3344
Web Address:	www.aafunds.com
Inception:	03-01-99*
Advisor:	AMR Investments
Subadvisor:	Multiple
NTF Plans:	Fidelity Retail-NTF, Schwab OneSource

Minimum Purchase:	$2500	Add: $50	IRA: $2500
Min Auto Inv Plan:	$2500	Add: $50	
Sales Fees:	No-load		
Management Fee:	0.54%		
Actual Fees:	Mgt:0.54%	Dist:	
Expense Projections:	3Yr:$368	5Yr:$638	10Yr:$1409
Income Distrib:	Annually		

AmCent Capital Val Inv

Ticker	Load	NAV	Yield	Total Assets	Mstar Category
ACTIX	None	$7.09	1.0%	$371 mil	Large Value

Governance and Management

Fiduciary Grade: B

Portfolio Manager(s)

Charles Ritter and Mark Mallon have been with this fund since its 1999 inception. During that time they've amassed an impressive record relative to the large-value category. Ritter and Mallon also manage American Century Large Company Value in a nearly identical manner. They're assisted by portfolio manager Brendan Healy and analyst Lon West, who came from USAA. The team may add a fifth member in the near future.

Strategy

The fund follows a fairly typical value strategy, screening for stocks that look cheap by various measures and then choosing those with decent growth prospects and solid balance sheets. True to the fund's tax-managed mandate, the managers will harvest losses when they can.

Historical Profile

Return Above Avg
Risk Average
Rating ★★★★ Above Avg

Investment Style
Equity
Stock %: 94% (1999), 89% (2000), 89% (2001), 90% (2002), 95% (2003), 95% (12-04)

▼ Manager Change
▽ Partial Manager Change

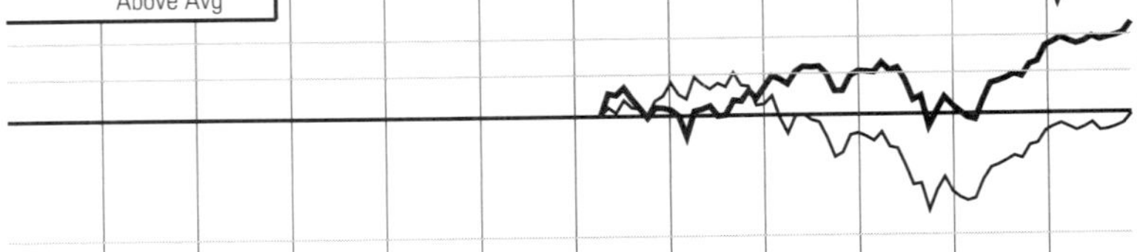

Performance Quartile (within Category)

History	1993	1994	1995	1996	1997	1998	1999	2000	2001	2002	2003	12-04
NAV	—	—	—	—	—	—	5.08	5.49	5.80	4.94	6.27	7.09
Total Return %	—	—	—	—	—	—	2.60*	9.75	6.78	-13.70	28.21	14.25
+/-S&P 500	—	—	—	—	—	—	—	18.85	18.66	8.39	-0.46	3.38
+/-Russ 1000 VI	—	—	—	—	—	—	—	2.74	12.37	1.82	-1.82	-2.24
Income Return %	—	—	—	—	—	—	0.00	1.60	1.10	1.12	1.25	1.16
Capital Return %	—	—	—	—	—	—	—	8.15	5.68	-14.82	26.96	13.09
Total Rtn % Rank Cat	—	—	—	—	—	—	—	49	9	17	47	31
Income $	—	—	—	—	—	—	0.05	0.08	0.06	0.07	0.06	0.07
Capital Gains $	—	—	—	—	—	—	0.00	0.00	0.00	0.00	0.00	0.00
Expense Ratio %	—	—	—	—	—	—	1.10	1.10	1.10	1.10	1.10	—
Income Ratio %	—	—	—	—	—	—	1.14	1.56	1.18	1.32	1.54	—
Turnover Rate %	—	—	—	—	—	—	—	73	56	42	22	—
Net Assets $mil	—	—	—	—	—	—	45	40	53	62	116	331

Performance 12-31-04

	1st Qtr	2nd Qtr	3rd Qtr	4th Qtr	Total
2000	-0.59	-2.18	6.48	6.00	9.75
2001	1.27	7.37	-9.72	8.77	6.78
2002	3.62	-7.32	-17.95	9.52	-13.70
2003	-6.07	17.67	2.01	13.71	28.21
2004	2.07	1.88	0.15	9.71	14.25

Trailing	Total Return%	+/- S&P 500	+/- Russ 1000 VI	%Rank Cat	Growth of $10,000
3 Mo	9.71	0.48	-0.67	36	10,971
6 Mo	9.87	2.68	-2.21	37	10,987
1 Yr	14.25	3.38	-2.24	31	11,425
3 Yr Avg	8.12	4.54	-0.45	18	12,639
5 Yr Avg	8.18	10.48	2.91	14	14,816
10 Yr Avg	—	—	—	—	—
15 Yr Avg	—	—	—	—	—

Tax Analysis	Tax-Adj Rtn%	%Rank Cat	Tax-Cost Rat	%Rank Cat
3 Yr (estimated)	7.69	13	0.40	27
5 Yr (estimated)	7.69	11	0.45	24
10 Yr (estimated)	—	—	—	—

Potential Capital Gain Exposure: 14% of assets

Rating and Risk

Time Period	Load-Adj Return %	Morningstar Rtn vs Cat	Morningstar Risk vs Cat	Morningstar Risk-Adj Rating
1 Yr	14.25			
3 Yr	8.12	+Avg	Avg	★★★★
5 Yr	8.18	+Avg	Avg	★★★★
10 Yr	—	—	—	—
Incept	7.55			

Other Measures	Standard Index S&P 500	Best Fit Index Schwab OneSource, Accutrade NTF
Alpha	4.5	-0.2
Beta	0.94	0.97
R-Squared	93	98
Standard Deviation	15.82	
Mean	8.12	
Sharpe Ratio	0.43	

Portfolio Analysis 09-30-04

Share change since 06-04 Total Stocks:91

	Sector	PE	YTD Ret%	% Assets
⊕ Citigroup	Financial	15.3	2.72	4.39
⊕ ExxonMobil	Energy	13.9	28.04	4.05
⊕ Freddie Mac	Financial	10.6	28.75	3.66
⊕ Bank of America	Financial	12.3	21.50	3.14
⊕ Royal Dutch Petroleum AD	Energy	—	14.31	2.61
SPDRs	—	—	—	2.38
⊕ Wells Fargo	Financial	15.5	8.97	2.11
⊕ Hewlett-Packard	Hardware	18.9	-7.28	1.87
⊕ ChevronTexaco	Energy	7.7	25.57	1.72
☼ J P Morgan Chase	Financial	19.4	9.97	1.52
⊕ McDonald's	Consumer	19.7	31.48	1.41
⊕ ConocoPhillips	Energy	9.0	35.60	1.40
⊕ Exelon	Utilities	16.1	37.55	1.36
⊕ US Bancorp	Financial	14.2	10.46	1.36
⊕ SBC Communications	Telecom	15.4	3.74	1.35
⊕ Wachovia	Financial	14.3	16.80	1.35
⊕ Allstate	Financial	12.8	23.12	1.32
⊕ Altria Group	Goods	13.3	18.38	1.31
⊕ Washington Mutual	Financial	13.9	10.05	1.29
⊕ Time Warner	Media	27.5	8.12	1.29

Current Investment Style

Value Blnd Growth — Large Mid Small

Market Cap	%
Giant	53.5
Large	31.9
Mid	14.4
Small	0.1
Micro	0.0
Avg $mil: 39,334	

Value Measures		Rel Category
Price/Earnings	13.40	0.89
Price/Book	2.06	0.91
Price/Sales	0.98	0.82
Price/Cash Flow	6.27	0.98
Dividend Yield %	2.30	1.13

Growth Measures	%	Rel Category
Long-Term Erngs	10.68	1.03
Book Value	5.94	1.05
Sales	5.11	1.22
Cash Flow	1.02	0.20
Historical Erngs	18.55	1.57

Profitability	%	Rel Category
Return on Equity	16.61	1.05
Return on Assets	9.07	1.16
Net Margin	10.36	1.01

Sector Weightings	% of Stocks	Rel S&P 500	3 Year High	3 Year Low
Info	14.50	0.67		
Software	1.94	0.45	2	1
Hardware	3.61	0.35	4	3
Media	2.76	0.72	3	1
Telecom	6.19	1.97	7	4
Service	50.88	1.10		
Health	7.57	0.61	9	8
Consumer	6.29	0.69	7	4
Business	3.65	0.90	5	3
Financial	33.37	1.61	35	31
Mfg	34.62	1.08		
Goods	9.84	1.05	10	7
Ind Mtrls	11.06	0.87	12	10
Energy	10.52	1.47	14	10
Utilities	3.20	1.08	7	3

Composition

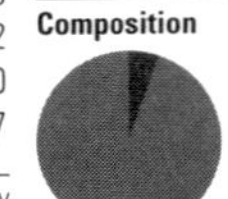

Cash	5.3
Stocks	94.6
Bonds	0.0
Other	0.0
Foreign (% of Stock)	4.8

Morningstar's Take by Dan Culloton 12-15-04

No fuss. No muss.

American Century Capital Value does no one thing spectacularly, but it does a lot of things well. It has an experienced management team that has amassed a fine record since this fund hit the market more than five years ago. From the offering's April 1999 inception through the end of November 2004 the portfolio has trounced the annualized 3.9% gain of the typical large-value fund with an annualized advance of nearly 7%.

The management team tries to keep things simple. It relies on a low-turnover brand of stock-picking that is heavily influenced by computer screens. The managers generally try to purchase stocks that have decent growth prospects, but have fallen out of favor because of transitory operational or industry-related factors. For example, earlier in the year the fund added to its stake in Royal Dutch Petroleum because the managers thought the stock's price underestimated its potential, despite doubts about the accuracy of the oil company's reserve accounting. Similarly, as concerns about rising interest rates weighed on Citigroup, this fund has maintained its large position because its managers think the financial conglomerate is large and diversified enough to weather rising rates.

This is a fairly standard, diversified value-investing strategy, but it has served this offering well. Furthermore, since American Century closed the no-load shares of near-twin American Century Large Company Value, this offering has represented the cheapest way to access this management team and strategy (although it's still more expensive than the average no-load large-value fund). In addition to having a lower expense ratio than the open share classes of American Century Large Value, a experienced management team, and steady approach, this fund has the added advantage of being tax-managed, making it a better idea than its load-bearing siblings for taxable accounts.

Address:	4500 Main St Kansas City MO 64141 800-345-2021
Web Address:	www.americancentury.com
Inception:	03-31-99*
Advisor:	American Century Investment Mgt Inc.
Subadvisor:	None
NTF Plans:	Schwab OneSource, Accutrade NTF

Minimum Purchase:	$2500	Add: $50	IRA: $2500
Min Auto Inv Plan:	$2500	Add: $50	
Sales Fees:	No-load		
Management Fee:	1.10% mx./0.90% mn.		
Actual Fees:	Mgt:1.10%	Dist:	
Expense Projections:	3Yr:$349	5Yr:$604	10Yr:$1334
Income Distrib:	Annually		

AmCent Equity Growth Inv

Ticker	Load	NAV	Yield	Total Assets	Mstar Category
BEQGX	None	$22.C8	1.1%	$1,818 mil	Large Blend

Governance and Management

Fiduciary Grade: B

Portfolio Manager(s)

Jeffrey Tyler, William Martin, and Thomas Vaiana make up the fund's portfolio-management team. A group of several quantitative analysts help them here.

Strategy

This fund keeps its sector weightings near the S&P 500 Index's, and computers try to pick better stocks in each sector. The fund's quantitative models look for low-valuation stocks that have growth potential as indicated by growth rates and other earnings and price-momentum factors.

Historical Profile

Return Above Avg
Risk Average
Rating ★★★★ Above Avg

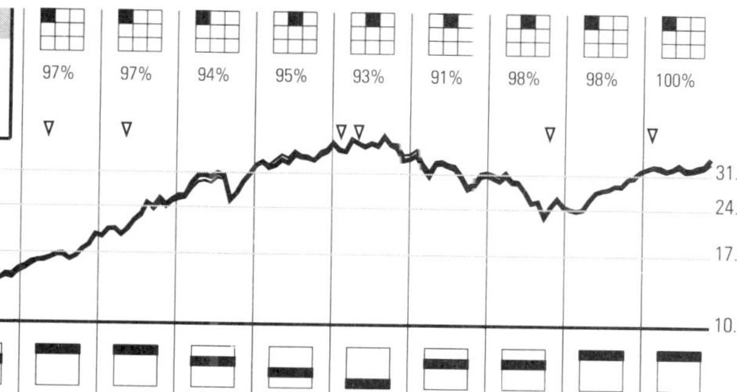

Investment Style
Equity
Stock %

▼ Manager Change
∇ Partial Manager Change

Growth of $10,000
— Investment Values of Fund
— Investment Values of S&P 500

Performance Quartile (within Category)

1993	1994	1995	1996	1997	1998	1999	2000	2001	2002	2003	12-04	History
12.12	11.53	14.24	15.96	19.04	22.71	26.23	21.77	19.24	15.19	19.60	22.08	NAV
11.42	-0.23	34.56	27.34	36.06	25.45	18.47	-10.95	-11.01	-20.32	30.27	13.98	Total Return %
1.36	-1.54	-2.97	4.40	2.71	-3.12	-2.57	-1.85	0.87	1.77	1.60	3.11	+/-S&P 500
1.24	-0.62	-3.21	4.89	3.21	-1.57	-2.44	-3.16	1.44	1.33	0.38	2.58	+/-Russ 1000
1.99	2.49	1.96	1.85	1.54	1.08	0.83	0.53	0.60	0.78	1.11	1.24	Income Return %
9.43	-2.72	32.60	25.49	34.52	24.37	17.64	-11.48	-11.61	-21.10	29.16	12.74	Capital Return %
42	52	44	9	5	40	61	85	35	30	17	10	Total Rtn % Rank Cat
0.23	0.30	0.22	0.26	0.24	0.20	0.19	0.14	0.13	0.15	0.17	0.24	Income $
0.66	0.26	1.01	1.85	2.31	0.88	0.43	1.47	0.00	0.00	0.00	0.00	Capital Gains $
0.75	0.75	0.71	0.63	0.69	0.69	0.68	0.67	0.68	0.69	0.69	—	Expense Ratio %
2.04	2.26	1.96	1.74	1.39	1.07	0.77	0.53	0.64	0.86	1.00	—	Income Ratio %
97	94	126	131	161	89	86	79	79	100	95	—	Turnover Rate %
96	98	159	274	771	2,019	2,317	1,912	1,477	988	1,194	1,548	Net Assets $mil

Performance 12-31-04

	1st Qtr	2nd Qtr	3rd Qtr	4th Qtr	Total
2000	2.74	-2.88	-0.88	-9.97	-10.95
2001	-11.84	7.61	-15.43	10.91	-11.01
2002	-0.42	-10.94	-16.80	7.99	-20.32
2003	-2.03	15.14	3.30	11.80	30.27
2004	3.08	1.81	-1.41	10.16	13.98

Trailing	Total Return%	+/- S&P 500	+/- Russ 1000	%Rank Cat	Growth of $10,000
3 Mo	10.16	0.93	0.36	26	11,016
6 Mo	8.60	1.41	0.79	20	10,860
1 Yr	13.98	3.11	2.58	10	11,398
3 Yr Avg	5.76	2.18	1.49	12	11,829
5 Yr Avg	-1.28	1.02	0.48	35	9,376
10 Yr Avg	12.50	0.43	0.34	10	32,473
15 Yr Avg	—	—	—	—	—

Tax Analysis	Tax-Adj Rtn%	%Rank Cat	Tax-Cost Rat	%Rank Cat
3 Yr (estimated)	5.38	11	0.36	30
5 Yr (estimated)	-1.85	32	0.58	31
10 Yr (estimated)	10.65	20	1.64	64

Potential Capital Gain Exposure: 9% of assets

Rating and Risk

Time Period	Load-Adj Return %	Morningstar Rtn vs Cat	Morningstar Risk vs Cat	Morningstar Risk-Adj Rating
1 Yr	13.98			
3 Yr	5.76	+Avg	Avg	★★★★
5 Yr	-1.28	Avg	Avg	★★★
10 Yr	12.50	+Avg	+Avg	★★★★
Incept	11.50			

Other Measures	Standard Index S&P 500	Best Fit Index Russ 1000
Alpha	2.2	1.5
Beta	0.95	0.96
R-Squared	97	97
Standard Deviation	15.21	
Mean	5.76	
Sharpe Ratio	0.29	

Portfolio Analysis 09-30-04

Share change since 06-04 Total Stocks:120	Sector	PE	YTD Ret%	% Assets
⊕ Johnson & Johnson	Health	20.6	25.17	3.15
⊕ IBM	Hardware	20.2	7.19	2.31
⊕ ChevronTexaco	Energy	7.7	25.57	2.31
⊕ Bank of America	Financial	12.3	21.50	2.36
⊕ Pfizer	Health	22.0	-22.31	2.53
⊕ ExxonMobil	Energy	13.9	28.04	2.07
⊕ Time Warner	Media	27.5	8.12	2.06
⊕ Countrywide Financial	Financial	9.0	48.15	2.06
⊖ TXU	Utilities	NMF	177.67	2.01
⊕ Wachovia	Financial	14.3	16.80	2.00
⊕ Walt Disney	Media	24.3	20.21	1.94
⊖ Eastman Kodak	Goods	—	27.90	1.94
⊖ J P Morgan Chase	Financial	19.4	9.97	1.91
⊕ McDonald's	Consumer	19.7	31.48	1.87
Motorola	Hardware	28.7	37.93	1.86
⊕ Gillette	Goods	27.6	23.94	1.86
⊕ Merck	Health	11.4	-27.76	1.82
⊕ Ford Motor	Goods	9.9	-6.00	1.79
⊕ Sunoco	Energy	12.9	62.69	1.71
⊕ Boeing	Ind Mtrls	14.7	24.86	1.71

Current Investment Style

Value Blnd Growth / Large Mid Small

Market Cap	%
Giant	39.8
Large	31.0
Mid	26.4
Small	2.9
Micro	0.0

Avg $mil: 23,527

Value Measures		Rel Category
Price/Earnings	13.77	0.81
Price/Book	2.37	0.90
Price/Sales	1.76	0.53
Price/Cash Flow	5.29	0.69
Dividend Yield %	1.55	1.05

Growth Measures	%	Rel Category
Long-Term Erngs	8.86	0.85
Book Value	5.47	0.70
Sales	5.58	0.97
Cash Flow	12.35	1.31
Historical Erngs	9.84	0.83

Profitability	%	Rel Category
Return on Equity	13.52	1.12
Return on Assets	8.56	0.99
Net Margin	9.67	0.85

Sector Weightings	% of Stocks	Rel S&P 500	3 Year High	3 Year Low
Info	19.06	0.89		
Software	1.70	0.40	6	2
Hardware	8.06	0.79	11	8
Media	4.48	1.17	6	2
Telecom	4.82	1.53	6	4
Service	46.38	1.00		
Health	13.33	1.07	17	13
Consumer	9.55	1.05	13	10
Business	4.65	1.15	5	3
Financial	18.85	0.91	24	13
Mfg	34.56	1.08		
Goods	11.86	1.27	16	3
Ind Mtrls	10.45	0.82	13	6
Energy	7.69	1.07	8	4
Utilities	4.56	1.54	5	2

Composition

Cash	0.2
Stocks	99.8
Bonds	0.0
Other	0.0
Foreign (% of Stock)	0.0

Morningstar's Take by Dan Culloton 12-15-04

American Century Equity Growth is a low-maintenance core holding.

This fund diligently adheres to quantitative models to pick a portfolio of large-cap stocks that it thinks can beat the S&P 500 without taking on significantly more risk. It stresses consistency over quick, short-lived bursts of performance and has amassed a credible record doing so. It has finished eight of the last 10 calendar years in the top half of the category and has beaten Vanguard 500 Index in 70% of the 43 rolling 10-year periods from the fund's 1991 inception through the end of November 2004.

The fund has built this record by paying close attention to its computer models. The offering uses the same system employed by American Century Income & Growth. Like its sibling, it attempts to craft a portfolio that resembles the S&P 500 at the sector and industry level. This fund, however, puts a heavier emphasis on its models' growth and momentum factors, which gives it more of a blend feel.

The management team can override the models if their own research exposes an opportunity. The squad also constantly examines and adjusts their tools (in recent years it has added an earnings quality component to the models). In general, however, the managers are content to follow the computer's lead. This year the models have been pointing the fund toward the shares of large, established companies still showing business and price momentum, such as McDonald's and CenterPoint Energy.

This fund will never set your heart aflutter with adrenaline-jolting returns, but it's not likely to do serious damage to your portfolio either. Furthermore, investors get access to an experienced management team, regimented process, and decent risk reward profile for a low expense ratio. Investors looking for a modest core holding could do worse.

Address:	4500 Main Street Kansas City MO 64111 800-345-2021
Web Address:	www.americancentury.com
Inception:	05-09-91
Advisor:	American Century Investment Mgt Inc.
Subadvisor:	None
NTF Plans:	Schwab OneSource, Accutrade NTF

Minimum Purchase:	$2500	Add: $50	IRA: $2500
Min Auto Inv Plan:	$2500	Add: $50	
Sales Fees:	No-load		
Management Fee:	0.70%		
Actual Fees:	Mgt:0.68%	Dist:	
Expense Projections:	3Yr:$217	5Yr:$378	10Yr:$844
Income Distrib:	Quarterly		

AmCent Equity Income Inv

Ticker	Load	NAV	Yield	Total Assets	Mstar Category
TWEIX	None	$8.11	2.3%	$3,928 mil	Large Value

Governance and Management

Fiduciary Grade: B

Portfolio Manager(s)

Phil Davidson has been at the helm since the fund's inception. Before that, Davidson spent 11 years as a manager for Boatmen's Trust Co. Scott Moore has roughly a decade of experience as an analyst and portfolio manager. Five analysts support them on this fund and on sibling American Century Value.

Strategy

Phil Davidson and Scott Moore employ an all-cap approach, focusing on stocks that are cheap relative to at least two valuation measures, such as price/earnings or price/cash flow and dividend yield. They also aim to create a portfolio with a yield that is two percentage points greater than the S&P 500 Index's by emphasizing higher-yielding stocks and holding a slew of convertibles. This income mandate means the fund has big stakes in dividend-rich utilities, energy, financials, and industrials stocks. The managers are quick to sell stocks they think have gotten too pricey; turnover is well above the mid-value norm.

Historical Profile

Return High
Risk Low
Rating ★★★★★ Highest

Investment Style: Equity Stock %: 81% 71% 77% 82% 64% 63% 65% 74% 69%

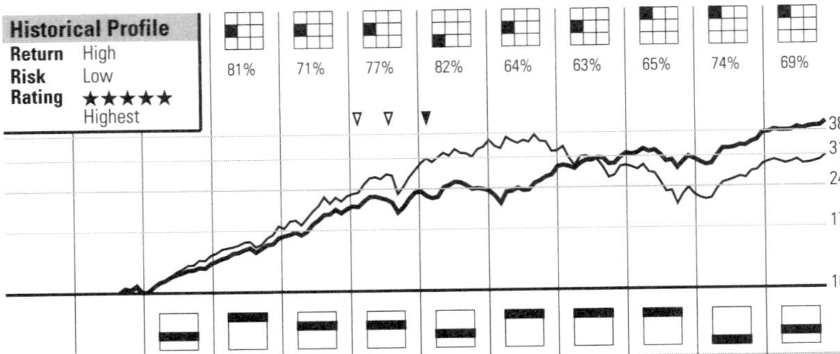

▼ Manager Change
▽ Partial Manager Change

Growth of $10,000
— Investment Values of Fund
— Investment Values of S&P 500

Performance Quartile (within Category)

1993	1994	1995	1996	1997	1998	1999	2000	2001	2002	2003	12-04	History
—	4.96	5.76	6.34	6.66	6.31	5.60	6.62	7.14	6.53	7.78	8.11	NAV
—	0.53*	29.62	23.31	28.26	12.97	-0.18	21.91	11.33	-5.00	24.25	12.53	Total Return %
—	—	-7.91	0.37	-5.09	-15.60	-21.22	31.01	23.21	17.09	-4.42	1.66	+/-S&P 500
—	—	-8.74	1.67	-6.92	-2.66	-7.53	14.90	16.92	10.52	-5.78	-3.96	+/-Russ 1000 VI
—	0.00	3.96	3.29	4.14	3.28	3.48	3.24	2.67	2.27	3.01	2.56	Income Return %
—	—	25.66	20.02	24.12	9.69	-3.66	18.67	8.66	-7.27	21.24	9.97	Capital Return %
—	—	74	19	39	47	75	8	4	1	83	54	Total Rtn % Rank Cat
—	0.05	0.19	0.19	0.26	0.22	0.22	0.18	0.18	0.16	0.19	0.20	Income $
—	0.02	0.45	0.55	1.16	0.96	0.48	0.00	0.04	0.10	0.12	0.42	Capital Gains $
—	—	1.00	0.98	1.00	1.00	1.00	1.00	1.00	1.00	1.00	1.00	Expense Ratio %
—	—	4.04	3.51	3.46	3.52	3.31	3.41	3.02	2.49	2.60	2.95	Income Ratio %
—	—	—	170	159	158	180	141	169	139	120	91	Turnover Rate %
—	24	97	187	297	326	328	385	832	1,241	2,105	2,919	Net Assets $mil

Performance 12-31-04

	1st Qtr	2nd Qtr	3rd Qtr	4th Qtr	Total
2000	-0.85	1.06	8.45	12.19	21.91
2001	-1.72	7.14	-3.25	9.28	11.33
2002	3.59	-4.71	-10.74	7.83	-5.00
2003	-4.14	13.63	2.31	11.49	24.25
2004	1.30	2.80	0.97	7.03	12.53

Trailing	Total Return%	+/- S&P 500	+/- Russ 1000 VI	%Rank Cat	Growth of $10,000
3 Mo	7.03	-2.20	-3.35	93	10,703
6 Mo	8.06	0.87	-4.02	65	10,806
1 Yr	12.53	1.66	-3.96	54	11,253
3 Yr Avg	9.93	6.35	1.36	7	13,285
5 Yr Avg	12.51	14.81	7.24	3	18,028
10 Yr Avg	15.34	3.27	1.51	4	41,668
15 Yr Avg	—	—	—	—	—

Tax Analysis	Tax-Adj Rtn%	%Rank Cat	Tax-Cost Rat	%Rank Cat
3 Yr (estimated)	8.11	10	1.66	88
5 Yr (estimated)	10.85	3	1.48	78
10 Yr (estimated)	11.52	7	3.31	97

Potential Capital Gain Exposure: 12% of assets

Rating and Risk

Time Period	Load-Adj Return %	Morningstar Rtn vs Cat	Morningstar Risk vs Cat	Morningstar Risk-Adj Rating
1 Yr	12.53			
3 Yr	9.93	High	Low	★★★★★
5 Yr	12.51	High	Low	★★★★★
10 Yr	15.34	High	Low	★★★★★
Incept	14.74			

Other Measures	Standard Index S&P 500	Best Fit Index Mstar Large Value
Alpha	6.7	4.4
Beta	0.66	0.67
R-Squared	88	93
Standard Deviation	11.57	
Mean	9.93	
Sharpe Ratio	0.75	

Morningstar's Take by Christopher Davis 11-01-04

American Century Equity Income won't always keep up with the Joneses, but we expect it to do just fine in the end.

This offering distinguishes itself from its mid-value rivals in several respects. Because managers Phil Davidson and Scott Moore employ an all-cap approach, their hunt for bargains isn't restricted solely to mid-caps. Davidson and Moore tend to flow freely to inexpensive, high-yielding stocks, wherever they reside. And with the managers finding large caps such as Microsoft, Bank of America, and Kraft Foods increasingly attractive in recent years, the fund's average market cap has risen steadily to $15.7 billion, more than double the category norm. Management augments these core holdings with a sizable chunk of income-generating preferred stocks and convertible bonds. Thus, it sports one of the largest yields in its group.

That mix can put the fund out of step with its peers. Its conservative, dividend-oriented strategy and sizable large-cap weighting led to a bottom decile finish in 2003's speculative, small-cap led market, for instance. Management has still been able to deliver respectable gains in up markets, though (the fund returned 24% in 2003) while preserving those gains through rough spots. The fund has lost money just twice--the worst loss was a relatively modest 5% drop in 2002--in the nine calendar years since its 1994 inception. Although the fund's lackluster 2003 campaign weighs on its three- and five-year returns, its 10-year marks are stellar. We'd note it handily topped its all-cap Russell 3000 Value bogy over all those stretches as well.

Management's all-cap strategy makes the fund a poor choice for those seeking pure mid-cap exposure. And its high-turnover approach and income-oriented strategy makes it a better choice for non-taxable accounts. However, given this offering's superb risk/reward profile, we find it easy to recommend.

Address:	P O Box 419200 Kansas City, MO 64141-6200 800-345-2021
Web Address:	www.americancentury.com
Inception:	08-01-94 *
Advisor:	American Century Investment Mgt Inc.
Subadvisor:	None
NTF Plans:	Schwab OneSource, Accutrade NTF

Minimum Purchase:	$2500	Add: $50	IRA: $2500
Min Auto Inv Plan:	$2500	Add: $50	
Sales Fees:	No-load		
Management Fee:	1.00%		
Actual Fees:	Mgt:1.00%	Dist:	
Expense Projections:	3Yr:$318	5Yr:$551	10Yr:$1219
Income Distrib:	Quarterly		

Portfolio Analysis 09-30-04

Share change since 06-04 Total Stocks:71	Sector	PE	YTD Ret%	% Assets
+ SPDRs	—	—	—	4.79
☆ S&P 500 Index (Fut)	—	—	—	4.56
− ExxonMobil	Energy	13.9	28.04	3.34
− Marsh & McLennan Compani	Financial	13.4	-29.80	3.18
+ SunTrust Banks	Financial	13.8	6.36	3.04
+ DuPont De Nemours E.I.	Ind Mtrls	22.3	10.42	2.44
+ Royal Dutch Petroleum AD	Energy	—	14.31	2.27
+ Kraft Foods	Goods	20.3	13.15	2.21
− BP PLC ADR	Energy	20.7	22.07	2.07
+ Ameren Pfd	—	—	—	2.07
+ Devon Engy 4.95%	—	—	—	2.05
+ Fpl Grp Pfd	—	—	—	1.98
+ Bank of America	Financial	12.3	21.50	1.86
☆ Altria Group	Goods	13.3	18.38	1.86
+ Commerce Bancshares	Financial	15.5	9.60	1.84
+ WGL Holdings	Utilities	14.8	16.08	1.69
+ Republic Services A	Business	21.8	32.45	1.48
+ Pitney Bowes	Ind Mtrls	19.6	17.24	1.45
− Emerson Electric	Ind Mtrls	22.8	11.09	1.43
− Bristol-Myers Squibb	Health	17.7	-7.27	1.41

Current Investment Style

Value Blnd Growth / Large Mid Small

Market Cap	%
Giant	37.8
Large	28.2
Mid	27.1
Small	6.4
Micro	0.5
Avg $mil: 18,517	

Value Measures		Rel Category
Price/Earnings	15.30	1.02
Price/Book	2.27	1.00
Price/Sales	1.16	0.97
Price/Cash Flow	8.33	1.31
Dividend Yield %	2.88	1.41

Growth Measures	%	Rel Category
Long-Term Erngs	8.71	0.84
Book Value	6.62	1.17
Sales	3.59	0.85
Cash Flow	4.05	0.78
Historical Erngs	7.69	0.65

Profitability	%	Rel Category
Return on Equity	18.47	1.16
Return on Assets	8.20	1.05
Net Margin	10.63	1.04

Sector Weightings	% of Stocks	Rel S&P 500	3 Year High	3 Year Low
Info	7.00	0.33		
Software	1.22	0.28	2	0
Hardware	2.00	0.20	2	0
Media	1.83	0.48	2	0
Telecom	1.95	0.62	7	2
Service	39.34	0.85		
Health	5.21	0.42	9	4
Consumer	1.60	0.18	4	2
Business	4.51	1.11	5	1
Financial	28.02	1.35	28	17
Mfg	53.66	1.67		
Goods	15.71	1.68	16	11
Ind Mtrls	14.69	1.16	30	15
Energy	11.59	1.62	14	8
Utilities	11.67	3.94	18	8

Composition

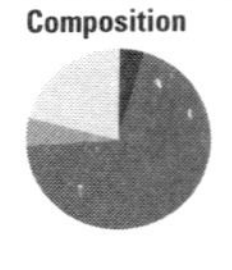

Cash	4.7
Stocks	69.2
Bonds	5.1
Other	21.1
Foreign (% of Stock)	9.1

AmCent Ginnie Mae Inv

Ticker	Load	NAV	Yield	SEC Yield	Total Assets	Mstar Category
BGNMX	None	$10.45	4.6%	3.84%	$1,595 mil	Intermediate Government

Governance and Management

Fiduciary Grade: B

Portfolio Manager(s)

Casey Colton had been the lead manager here since January 1994 but departed in September 2004. He was replaced by Alejandro H. Aguilar and Dan Shiffman. Both previously worked at the California pension system known as CalPERS and have several years of experience in the industry. Prior to joining CalPERS, Aguilar also managed portfolios for New York-based manager TIAA-CREF.

Strategy

Until recently, the fund held GNMAs and other issues with the full backing of Uncle Sam, and used a blended mortgage/Treasury index. But while supporting team members remain the same, two new arrivals took on day-to-day responsibility in early September 2004. The team may now hold up to 20% in mortgages and bonds from government-linked agencies such as FNMA and FHLMC. They may also use asset-backed and commercial mortgage securities. The fund's duration (a measure of interest-rate sensitivity) will typically stay within six months of the Salomon Brothers GNMA Index.

Historical Profile

Return Above Avg
Risk Low
Rating ★★★★ Above Avg

Investment Style: Fixed Income — Income Rtn %Rank Cat: 8, 17, 26, 12, 17, 10, 11, 11, 11

▼ Manager Change
∇ Partial Manager Change

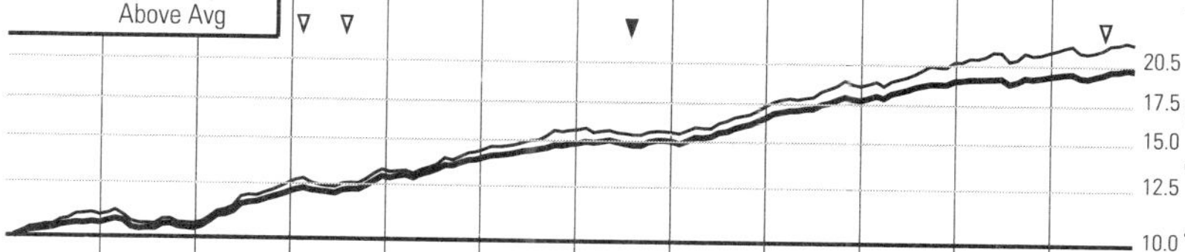

Growth of $10,000
— Investment Values of Fund
— Investment Values of LB Aggr

Performance Quartile (within Category)

History

1993	1994	1995	1996	1997	1998	1999	2000	2001	2002	2003	12-04	History
10.76	9.90	10.68	10.49	10.68	10.69	10.14	10.49	10.62	10.90	10.61	10.45	NAV
6.59	-1.67	15.85	5.21	8.79	6.32	0.99	10.35	7.43	8.30	2.02	3.12	Total Return %
-3.16	1.25	-2.62	1.58	-0.86	-2.37	1.81	-1.28	-1.01	-1.95	-2.08	-1.22	+/-LB Aggr
-4.07	1.71	-2.49	2.44	-0.80	-3.53	3.22	-2.89	0.20	-3.20	-0.34	-0.36	+/-LB Govt
6.69	6.51	7.78	6.94	6.88	6.23	6.28	6.72	6.21	5.60	4.72	4.64	Income Return %
-0.10	-8.18	8.07	-1.73	1.91	0.09	-5.29	3.63	1.22	2.70	-2.70	-1.52	Capital Return %
72	14	60	5	46	81	9	73	27	71	38	49	Total Rtn % Rank Cat
0.70	0.68	0.74	0.72	0.70	0.65	0.65	0.66	0.63	0.58	0.50	0.48	Income $
0.01	0.00	0.00	0.00	0.00	0.00	0.00	0.00	0.00	0.00	0.00	0.00	Capital Gains $
0.56	0.54	0.58	0.58	0.55	0.58	0.59	0.59	0.59	0.59	0.59	0.59	Expense Ratio %
7.31	6.12	7.08	6.98	6.84	6.49	5.98	6.57	6.57	5.75	5.19	2.77	Income Ratio %
71	49	120	64	105	133	119	133	143	218	356	356	Turnover Rate %
1,257	952	1,111	1,131	1,234	1,377	1,298	1,288	1,646	2,069	1,732	1,517	Net Assets $mil

Performance 12-31-04

	1st Qtr	2nd Qtr	3rd Qtr	4th Qtr	Total
2000	1.79	1.99	2.69	3.51	10.35
2001	2.94	0.83	3.61	-0.11	7.43
2002	0.99	3.37	2.45	1.27	8.30
2003	0.69	0.41	0.28	0.62	2.02
2004	1.06	-0.91	2.05	0.91	3.12

Trailing	Total Return%	+/- LB Aggr	+/- LB Govt	%Rank Cat	Growth of $10,000
3 Mo	0.91	-0.04	0.42	30	10,091
6 Mo	2.98	-1.20	-0.63	62	10,298
1 Yr	3.12	-1.22	-0.36	49	10,312
3 Yr Avg	4.44	-1.75	-1.26	57	11,392
5 Yr Avg	6.19	-1.52	-1.29	54	13,503
10 Yr Avg	6.76	-0.96	-0.70	34	19,235
15 Yr Avg	7.01	-0.69	-0.47	19	27,629

Tax Analysis	Tax-Adj Rtn%	%Rank Cat	Tax-Cost Rat	%Rank Cat
3 Yr (estimated)	2.61	49	1.75	78
5 Yr (estimated)	4.05	57	2.02	82
10 Yr (estimated)	4.31	34	2.29	84

Potential Capital Gain Exposure: -2% of assets

Rating and Risk

Time Period	Load-Adj Return %	Morningstar Rtn vs Cat	Morningstar Risk vs Cat	Morningstar Risk-Adj Rating
1 Yr	3.12			
3 Yr	4.44	Avg	-Avg	★★★
5 Yr	6.19	Avg	Low	★★★
10 Yr	6.76	+Avg	Low	★★★★
Incept	7.63			

Other Measures	Standard Index LB Aggr	Best Fit Index LB Mort
Alpha	0.4	-0.7
Beta	0.56	0.92
R-Squared	83	95
Standard Deviation	2.75	
Mean	4.44	
Sharpe Ratio	1.14	

Portfolio Analysis 09-30-04

Total Fixed-Income:24[illegible]3	Date of Maturity	Amount $000	Value $000	% Net Assets
GNMA 6%	09-20-34	200,000	207,300	11.39
GNMA 5.5%	07-15-33	173,548	131,583	7.23
GNMA 6.5%	10-15-34	110,000	115,981	6.37
GNMA 6%	07-20-34	101,532	104,517	5.74
FFCB FRN	03-29-07	94,750	94,808	5.21
GNMA 6.5%	09-15-32	365,702	92,647	5.09
GNMA 6%	10-15-34	80,000	82,925	4.56
GNMA 6.5%	01-15-33	249,698	66,482	3.65
GNMA 6.5%	05-15-31	319,302	57,381	3.15
GNMA 6.5%	04-15-32	233,823	51,446	2.83
GNMA 5.5%	03-15-34	50,175	47,947	2.63
GNMA 5.5%	06-15-33	55,302	43,744	2.40
GNMA 5.5%	06-15-33	50,753	40,246	2.21
GNMA 5.5%	04-15-33	55,652	38,359	2.11
GNMA 5.5%	11-15-33	40,000	36,390	2.00
GNMA 6.5%	10-15-31	129,164	32,188	1.77
GNMA 6.5%	06-15-33	44,940	25,807	1.42
GNMA 5%	03-15-34	21,856	21,382	1.17
GNMA 5%	02-15-34	20,000	18,405	1.01
GNMA 7%	05-15-32	109,484	17,031	0.94

Current Investment Style

Duration: Short Int Long — Quality: High Med Low

Avg Eff Duration[1]	2.6 Yrs
Avg Eff Maturity	4.3 Yrs
Avg Credit Quality	AAA
Avg Wtd Coupon	5.89%
Avg Wtd Price	63.76% of par

[1] figure provided by fund

Coupon Range	% of Bonds	Rel Cat
0% PIK	5.5	1.0
0% to 6%	51.6	0.7
6% to 8%	47.1	2.2
8% to 10%	1.3	0.6
More than 10%	0.1	0.1

1.00=Category Average

Credit Analysis	% bonds 09-30-04		
US Govt	0	BB	0
AAA	100	B	0
AA	0	Below B	0
A	0	NR/NA	0
BBB	0		

Sector Breakdown	% of assets
US Treasuries	0
TIPS	0
US Agency	0
Mortgage Pass-Throughs	90
Mortgage CMO	0
Mortgage ARM	0
US Corporate	5
Asset-Backed	0
Convertible	0
Municipal	0
Corporate Inflation-Protected	0
Foreign Corporate	0
Foreign Govt	0

Composition			
Cash	5.1	Bonds	94.9
Stocks	0.0	Other	0.0

Special Securities	
Restricted/Illiquid Secs	0
Exotic Mortgage-Backed	—
Emerging-Markets Secs	0
Options/Futures/Warrants	No

Morningstar's Take by Eric Jacobson 12-30-04

American Century Ginnie Mae is a fair bet to avoid trouble, with an option for better things to come.

One thing that we've always been able to say about this fund is that it's been fairly tame. Under its previous manager, the fund held a smattering of inflation-indexed and conventional Treasuries, and it sometimes bought mortgages in the forward market. The results have been decent, if not overly impressive. The fund has generated high income payouts, while doing a good job of preserving principal. But despite very nice 10- and 15-year returns relative to the intermediate government category, the fund's three- and five-year returns have been middling.

On the other hand, modest volatility has been the fund's hallmark. In part because of its benchmark-conscious ways, the fund's duration has been on the low side relative to other intermediate funds, including those focused almost exclusively on mortgages. As such, the fund's standard deviation of returns has been among the lowest of both groups over the long term.

We're enthusiastic, meanwhile, about a changing of the guard here. Hando Aguilar and Dan Shiffman took over day-to-day responsibility for this portfolio in the fall. Both have experience running mortgage money in the past at California's pension system (CalPERS), and Aguilar also worked at TIAA-CREF. In particular, we're hopeful that their specialty in securitized mortgages and asset-backed securities may help them apply research that can be used to pick undervalued bonds and thereby distinguish this portfolio--and its record--from its peers'.

Despite the fund's low-cost structure, though, its history of at- or below-benchmark rate sensitivity could continue to make that a challenge. Either way, we think this fund has a reasonable strategy and a promising management team. It's not begging to be bought, but there's no reason to leave it, either.

Address:	4500 Main Street Kansas City MO 64111 800-345-2021
Web Address:	www.americancentury.com
Inception:	09-23-85
Advisor:	American Century Investment Mgt Inc.
Subadvisor:	None
NTF Plans:	Schwab OneSource, Accutrade NTF

Minimum Purchase:	$2500	Add: $50	IRA: $2500
Min Auto Inv Plan:	$2500	Add: $50	
Sales Fees:	No-load		
Management Fee:	0.58%		
Actual Fees:	Mgt:0.58%	Dist:	
Expense Projections:	3Yr:$189	5Yr:$329	10Yr:$736
Income Distrib:	Monthly		

AmCent Global Gold Inv

Analyst Pick	Ticker	Load	NAV	Yield	Total Assets	Mstar Category
✔	BGEIX	None	$12.00	0.7%	$700 mil	Specialty-Precious Metals

Governance and Management

Fiduciary Grade: B

Portfolio Manager(s)

Bill Martin has run this fund since 1992, giving him one of the longest tenures in the precious-metals category. Two comanagers, John Schniedwind, American Century's CIO, and Joe Sterling, assist with stock selection.

Strategy

Manager Bill Martin runs this offering as a pure gold fund and stays away from other metals, such as palladium and platinum. Martin doesn't stick to any one geographic region, and the fund typically holds a mix of North American, Australian, and South African companies.

Historical Profile

Return Average
Risk Above Avg
Rating ★★★ Neutral

Investment Style
Equity
Stock %

99%	99%	96%	98%	93%	93%	91%	98%	99%

▼ Manager Change
∇ Partial Manager Change

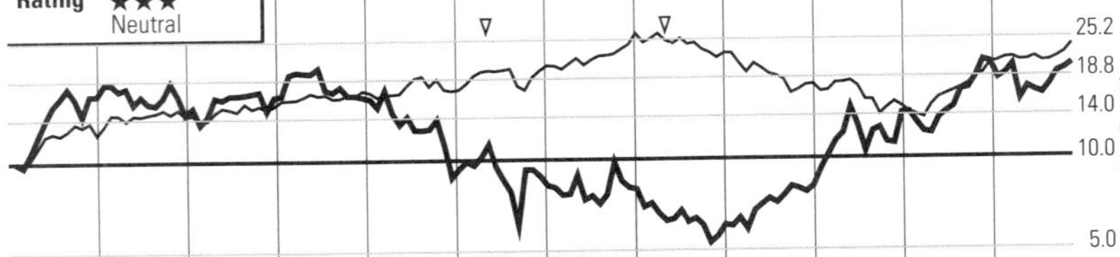

Growth of $10,000
— Investment Values of Fund
— Investment Values of MSCI EAFE

Performance Quartile (within Category)

1993	1994	1995	1996	1997	1998	1999	2000	2001	2002	2003	12-04	History
13.67	11.33	12.37	11.33	6.34	5.52	5.29	4.00	5.30	9.13	13.17	12.00	NAV
81.22	-16.75	9.25	-2.76	-41.47	-12.18	-3.18	-23.95	34.09	73.00	46.70	-8.17	Total Return %
48.66	-24.53	-1.96	-8.81	-43.25	-32.11	-30.21	-9.76	55.51	88.94	8.11	-28.42	+/-MSCI EAFE
—	—	—	—	—	—	-53.22	-0.39	32.99	77.28	-17.63	-22.05	+/-MSCI W Me&M
0.16	0.16	0.08	0.47	0.83	0.76	0.94	0.49	1.44	0.69	2.26	0.59	Income Return %
81.06	-16.91	9.17	-3.23	-42.30	-12.94	-4.12	-24.44	32.65	72.31	44.44	-8.76	Capital Return %
47	70	39	91	67	71	82	86	4	19	81	56	Total Rtn % Rank Cat
0.01	0.02	0.01	0.06	0.09	0.05	0.05	0.03	0.06	0.04	0.21	0.08	Income $
0.00	0.03	0.00	0.64	0.20	0.00	0.00	0.00	0.00	0.00	0.00	0.00	Capital Gains $
0.72	0.61	0.61	0.62	0.67	0.69	0.68	0.67	0.68	0.69	0.69	—	Expense Ratio %
0.23	0.20	0.17	0.46	0.93	0.75	1.04	1.19	0.99	0.57	0.22	—	Income Ratio %
28	42	28	45	28	68	53	17	17	34	22	—	Turnover Rate %
619	568	540	433	249	228	202	142	193	421	737	695	Net Assets $mil

Performance 12-31-04

	1st Qtr	2nd Qtr	3rd Qtr	4th Qtr	Total
2000	-17.01	2.18	-10.54	0.25	-23.95
2001	-3.50	26.11	9.56	0.57	34.09
2002	40.19	11.83	-1.33	11.84	73.00
2003	-13.47	16.50	19.65	21.63	46.70
2004	-2.05	-17.89	15.22	-0.91	-8.17

Trailing	Total Return%	+/- MSCI EAFE	+/- MSCI W Me&M	%Rank Cat	Growth of $10,000
3 Mo	-0.91	-16.23	-9.33	47	9,909
6 Mo	14.18	-0.82	-8.78	48	11,418
1 Yr	-8.17	-28.42	-22.05	56	9,183
3 Yr Avg	32.58	20.69	11.13	45	23,304
5 Yr Avg	18.90	20.03	12.18	38	23,763
10 Yr Avg	2.31	-3.31	—	72	12,566
15 Yr Avg	1.44	-2.79	—	67	12,392

Tax Analysis	Tax-Adj Rtn%	%Rank Cat	Tax-Cost Rat	%Rank Cat
3 Yr (estimated)	32.13	42	0.34	26
5 Yr (estimated)	18.49	35	0.34	36
10 Yr (estimated)	1.74	67	0.56	44

Potential Capital Gain Exposure: 11% of assets

Rating and Risk

Time Period	Load-Adj Return %	Morningstar Rtn vs Cat	Morningstar Risk vs Cat	Morningstar Risk-Adj Rating
1 Yr	-8.17			
3 Yr	32.58	Avg	+Avg	★★★
5 Yr	18.90	Avg	+Avg	★★★
10 Yr	2.31	-Avg	+Avg	★★
Incept	2.34			

Other Measures	Standard Index S&P 500	Best Fit Index JSE Gold ND
Alpha	34.0	14.5
Beta	0.38	0.73
R-Squared	3	67
Standard Deviation	51.67	
Mean	32.58	
Sharpe Ratio	0.61	

Portfolio Analysis 09-30-04

Share change since 06-04 Total Stocks:49	Sector	Country	% Assets
⊕ Newmont Mining	Ind Mtrls	United States	10.36
Barrick Gold	Ind Mtrls	United States	8.77
Placer Dome	Ind Mtrls	United States	8.45
⊕ Freeport-McMoRan Copper	Ind Mtrls	United States	5.20
Newcrest Mining Ltd	Ind Mtrls	Australia	4.71
Gold Fields Ltd	Ind Mtrls	South Africa	4.61
⊖ Harmony Gold Mining	Ind Mtrls	South Africa	4.55
Glamis Gold Ltd	Ind Mtrls	Canada	4.39
Meridian Gold	Ind Mtrls	United States	4.29
Anglogold Ashanti Ltd	Ind Mtrls	South Africa	3.49
Agnico-Eagle Mines Ltd	Ind Mtrls	Canada	3.38
Wheaton River Minerals L	Ind Mtrls	Canada	3.36
IAMGOLD	Ind Mtrls	Canada	3.19
⊕ Kinross Gold	Ind Mtrls	Canada	3.14
Goldcorp	Ind Mtrls	Canada	3.07
⊕ Bema Gold	Ind Mtrls	United States	2.99
Coeur d'Alene Mines	Ind Mtrls	United States	2.86
⊕ Anglogold Ashanti ADR	Ind Mtrls	South Africa	2.16
Crystallex Int'l	Ind Mtrls	Canada	1.76
Cambior	Ind Mtrls	Canada	1.75

Current Investment Style

Market Cap	%
Giant	0.0
Large	38.9
Mid	49.1
Small	10.8
Micro	1.2
Avg $mil: 3,267	

Value Measures		Rel Category
Price/Earnings	37.81	1.17
Price/Book	2.46	0.95
Price/Sales	3.82	1.19
Price/Cash Flow	16.93	1.03
Dividend Yield %	1.09	1.88

Growth Measures	%	Rel Category
Long-Term Erngs	20.27	0.96
Book Value	11.35	1.18
Sales	5.92	0.63
Cash Flow	-5.46	NMF
Historical Erngs	11.23	1.53

Composition

Cash	0.0	Bonds	0.0
Stocks	98.8	Other	1.3
Foreign (% of Stock)			53.6

Sector Weightings	% of Stocks	Rel MSCI EAFE	3 Year High	Low
Info	0.00	0.00		
Software	0.00	0.00	0	0
Hardware	0.00	0.00	0	0
Media	0.00	0.00	0	0
Telecom	0.00	0.00	0	0
Service	0.00	0.00		
Health	0.00	0.00	0	0
Consumer	0.00	0.00	0	0
Business	0.00	0.00	0	0
Financial	0.00	0.00	0	0
Mfg	100.00	2.59		
Goods	0.00	0.00	0	0
Ind Mtrls	100.00	8.13	100	100
Energy	0.00	0.00	0	0
Utilities	0.00	0.00	0	0

Regional Exposure	% Stock		
UK/W. Europe	0	N. America	76
Japan	0	Latn America	1
Asia X Japan	7	Other	16

Country Exposure	% Stock		
United States	46	Australia	7
Canada	29	Peru	1
South Africa	17		

Morningstar's Take by Lynn Russell 12-30-04

American Century Global Gold is a good choice for investors looking for exposure to gold, but it's still a very risky proposition.

Gold has been on a roller coaster in 2004, driven largely by the strength or weakness of the dollar. Most of the funds in the precious-metals funds group have posted losses, and this one is no exception. The fund's loss of 8% for the year to date through Dec. 28 lands right in the middle of the pack. Although it held winners such as Meridian Gold and Agnico-Eagle Mines, top 10 holdings such as Harmony Gold Mining Company and Anglogold Ashanti were among the industry's bigger losers.

But that's about what we would expect from this offering. This fund is essentially a vehicle for broad exposure to the gold-mining industry. Longtime manager Bill Martin starts with the companies in the Salomon Smith Barney Gold Mines Index, which includes around 65 gold producers that have publicly available shares. Rather than chasing the most speculative companies, he builds the fund's portfolio around an internal benchmark with the heaviest weightings to the largest companies such as Newmont Mining and Barrick Gold. The Index added 25 names to its list in 2004, so Martin has been adding a number of those companies to the fund's holdings, doubling the fund's stake in smaller companies to around 12% of the fund's portfolio. But that's still a lot less than the average for this group.

With the smaller producers and exploration companies typically getting the biggest boost from rising gold prices, the fund's relatively hefty stake in larger companies has meant that it can lag its more adventurous peers when gold rallies hard as it did in 2003. But the fund's longer-term record is competitive, and its expense ratio is among the lowest in the group. We also like this fund for its experienced management. All that said, we think this fund's potential volatility makes it appropriate for aggressive investors only.

Address:	4500 Main Street Kansas City MO 64111 800-345-2021
Web Address:	www.americancentury.com
Inception:	08-17-88
Advisor:	American Century Investment Mgt Inc.
Subadvisor:	None
NTF Plans:	Schwab OneSource, Accutrade NTF

Minimum Purchase:	$2500	Add: $50	IRA: $2500
Min Auto Inv Plan:	$2500	Add: $50	
Sales Fees:	No-load, 1.00%R		
Management Fee:	0.68%, 0.11%A		
Actual Fees:	Mgt:0.68%	Dist:	
Expense Projections:	3Yr:$217	5Yr:$378	10Yr:$844
Income Distrib:	Semi-Annually		

AmCent Global Gr Inv

Ticker	Load	NAV	Yield	Total Assets	Mstar Category
TWGGX	None	$7.79	0.2%	$322 mil	World Stock

Governance and Management

Fiduciary Grade: B

Portfolio Manager(s)

Henrik Strabo leads American Century's international effort, which consists of four other funds. Matthew Hudson started as an analyst here and was promoted to comanager in March 2002. Trevor Gurwich came aboard this fund in January 2004 after serving as a portfolio manager on two other American Century international offerings. Hudson and Gurwich run the portfolio here, while Strabo acts as an overseer.

Strategy

Companies with growing sales or profits are attractive to this fund's management, and the portfolio is full of fast growers, regardless of their countries, sectors, size, or price multiples. Management also favors firms with competent management and niche products, and earnings disappointments send a stock packing from the portfolio.

Historical Profile

Return Average
Risk Average
Rating ★★★ Neutral

Investment Style: Equity, Stock %: 90% 91% 85% 95% 94% 98% 95%

▼ Manager Change
∇ Partial Manager Change

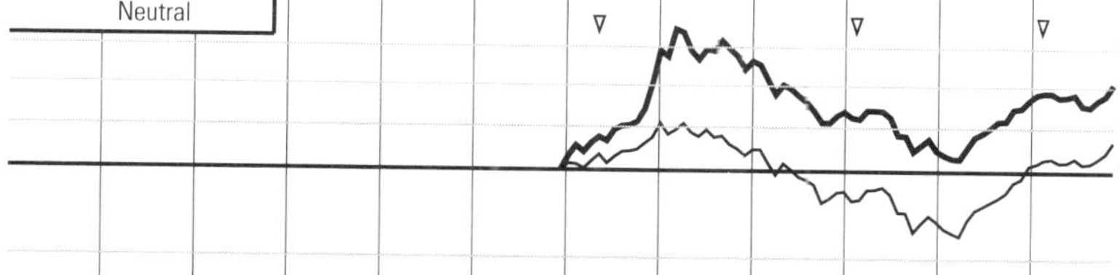

Growth of $10,000
— Investment Values of Fund
— Investment Values of MSCI EAFE

Performance Quartile (within Category)

1993	1994	1995	1996	1997	1998	1999	2000	2001	2002	2003	12-04	History
—	—	—	—	—	5.43	9.81	8.50	6.32	5.04	6.78	7.79	NAV
—	—	—	—	—	8.60*	86.09	-5.77	-25.65	-20.25	34.52	15.11	Total Return %
—	—	—	—	—	—	59.06	8.42	-4.23	-4.31	-4.07	-5.14	+/-MSCI EAFE
—	—	—	—	—	—	61.14	7.42	-8.85	-0.36	1.41	0.39	+/-MSCI World
—	—	—	—	—	0.00	0.00	0.00	0.00	0.00	0.00	0.20	Income Return %
—	—	—	—	—	—	86.09	-5.77	-25.65	-20.25	34.52	14.91	Capital Return %
—	—	—	—	—	—	6	34	87	54	47	47	Total Rtn % Rank Cat
—	—	—	—	—	0.00	0.00	0.00	0.00	0.00	0.00	0.01	Income $
—	—	—	—	—	0.00	0.26	0.75	0.00	0.00	0.00	0.00	Capital Gains $
—	—	—	—	—	—	1.30	1.30	1.30	1.32	1.31	—	Expense Ratio %
—	—	—	—	—	—	-0.60	-0.43	-0.06	0.13	0.00	—	Income Ratio %
—	—	—	—	—	—	133	123	232	278	152	—	Turnover Rate %
—	—	—	—	—	73	318	412	275	201	262	312	Net Assets $mil

Performance 12-31-04

	1st Qtr	2nd Qtr	3rd Qtr	4th Qtr	Total
2000	11.28	-9.42	0.31	-6.79	-5.77
2001	-17.76	-0.72	-14.55	6.58	-25.65
2002	0.95	-4.08	-17.97	0.40	-20.25
2003	-4.76	16.46	7.33	13.00	34.52
2004	4.57	-0.99	-2.99	14.60	15.11

Trailing	Total Return%	+/- MSCI EAFE	+/- MSCI World	%Rank Cat	Growth of $10,000
3 Mo	14.60	-0.72	2.66	15	11,460
6 Mo	11.17	-3.83	0.35	48	11,117
1 Yr	15.11	-5.14	0.39	47	11,511
3 Yr Avg	7.28	-4.61	0.33	49	12,347
5 Yr Avg	-2.85	-1.72	-0.40	59	8,654
10 Yr Avg	—	—	—	—	—
15 Yr Avg	—	—	—	—	—

Tax Analysis	Tax-Adj Rtn%	%Rank Cat	Tax-Cost Rat	%Rank Cat
3 Yr (estimated)	7.26	42	0.02	3
5 Yr (estimated)	-3.32	56	0.48	33
10 Yr (estimated)	—	—	—	—

Potential Capital Gain Exposure: 0% of assets

Rating and Risk

Time Period	Load-Adj Return %	Morningstar Rtn vs Cat	Morningstar Risk vs Cat	Morningstar Risk-Adj Rating
1 Yr	15.11			
3 Yr	7.28	Avg	Avg	★★★
5 Yr	-2.85	Avg	Avg	★★★
10 Yr	—	—	—	—
Incept	9.62			

Other Measures	Standard Index S&P 500	Best Fit Index Mstar Mid Core
Alpha	-3.0	-4.3
Beta	0.88	0.92
R-Squared	89	89
Standard Deviation	15.77	
Mean	7.28	
Sharpe Ratio	0.38	

Portfolio Analysis 09-30-04

Share change since 06-04 Total Stocks:100	Sector	Country	% Assets
⊕ ExxonMobil	Energy	United States	2.05
⊕ Gen Elec	Ind Mtrls	United States	2.04
⊕ BHP Billiton Ltd	Ind Mtrls	Australia	1.73
⊕ XTO Energy	Energy	United States	1.71
⊕ EnCana	Energy	Canada	1.55
Medtronic	Health	United States	1.55
⊕ Tyco International	Ind Mtrls	United States	1.52
⊕ Genentech	Health	United States	1.51
⊕ American Tower A	Telecom	United States	1.48
⊕ Danaher	Ind Mtrls	United States	1.45
⊕ Tesco	Consumer	U.K.	1.35
☼ TOTAL	Energy	France	1.35
☼ Rcs Mediagroup	Ind Mtrls	Italy	1.28
American Express	Financial	United States	1.27
⊕ ING Groep	Financial	Netherlands	1.26
⊖ Procter & Gamble	Goods	United States	1.24
⊕ Randstad Holding	Business	Netherlands	1.22
⊖ Citigroup	Financial	United States	1.22
Nextel Communications	Telecom	United States	1.22
⊕ Novartis	Health	Switzerland	1.21

Current Investment Style

Market Cap	%
Giant	41.0
Large	32.7
Mid	24.6
Small	1.7
Micro	0.0
Avg $mil: 19,560	

Value Measures		Rel Category
Price/Earnings	18.09	1.15
Price/Book	2.88	1.30
Price/Sales	1.64	1.40
Price/Cash Flow	5.96	0.94
Dividend Yield %	1.25	0.66

Growth Measures	%	Rel Category
Long-Term Erngs	13.64	1.13
Book Value	3.25	1.47
Sales	2.21	0.53
Cash Flow	9.61	1.64
Historical Erngs	9.41	1.10

Composition

Cash	4.3	Bonds	0.0
Stocks	95.0	Other	0.6
Foreign (% of Stock)			46.7

Sector Weightings	% of Stocks	Rel MSCI EAFE	3 Year High	3 Year Low
Info	14.51	0.87		
Software	2.43	2.25	5	0
Hardware	5.28	1.45	12	3
Media	1.62	0.71	5	1
Telecom	5.18	0.54	10	1
Service	48.96	1.09		
Health	15.74	2.17	20	9
Consumer	6.42	1.27	12	1
Business	7.37	1.35	14	3
Financial	19.43	0.72	24	13
Mfg	36.53	0.94		
Goods	11.20	0.82	24	10
Ind Mtrls	15.25	1.24	15	7
Energy	10.08	1.37	10	4
Utilities	0.00	0.00	1	0

Regional Exposure	% Stock		
UK/W. Europe	29	N. America	55
Japan	8	Latn America	0
Asia X Japan	4	Other	4

Country Exposure	% Stock		
United States	53	France	6
Japan	8	U.K.	4
Switzerland	7		

Morningstar's Take by Bridget Hughes 12-22-04

American Century Global Growth's advantages haven't translated into superior returns, but we're still optimistic.

There's a lot to like here. For starters, this world-stock fund is run as one portfolio. Whereas many rivals merely add separately run U.S. and foreign-stock portfolios together, this fund takes a truly global approach. That means ideas about foreign stocks and markets have implications for thoughts on U.S. issues and markets, and vice versa. We think this integrated approach is a better way to run a world-stock fund. In fact, we think there's little reason to buy funds that work otherwise. We also like the offering's multicap approach, especially considering American Century's success buying international small caps over the past decade. Furthermore, the fund's investment staff has grown over the past several years. That's led the fund to cut back on a number of small positions, giving it more conviction in well-researched names.

So far in the offering's six-year lifetime, however, these advantages haven't lent consistently strong returns. Sure, a tech-heavy portfolio helped it perform extremely well in 1999. But over the past five years, the offering's 1.6% annualized loss through Dec. 21, 2004, lands near the category's middle--not horrible, but certainly nothing to shout about.

We continue to think, however, that the fund has merit--particularly now. That's largely because large-growth stocks around the world have been among the markets' laggards for several years running. And this fund's current positioning--it's moved up the market-cap ladder over the past couple of years and continues to be aggressive in its sector allocations--means it stands to benefit if such stocks come back.

That doesn't mean there aren't risks, and the current energy overweight could backfire if oil prices come down. But we think there are enough pluses here to consider it for the long haul.

Address:	4500 Main St Kansas City MO 64111 800-345-3533
Web Address:	www.americancentury.com
Inception:	12-01-98*
Advisor:	American Century Investment Mgt Inc.
Subadvisor:	None
NTF Plans:	Schwab OneSource, Accutrade NTF

Minimum Purchase:	$2500	Add: $50	IRA: $2500
Min Auto Inv Plan:	$2500	Add: $50	
Sales Fees:	No-load, 2.00%R		
Management Fee:	1.30% mx./1.05% mn.		
Actual Fees:	Mgt:1.30%	Dist:	
Expense Projections:	3Yr:$413	5Yr:$715	10Yr:$1570
Income Distrib:	Annually		

AmCent Growth Inv

Ticker	Load	NAV	Yield	Total Assets	Mstar Category
TWCGX	None	$19.71	0.0%	$5,151 mil	Large Growth

Governance and Management

Fiduciary Grade: B

Portfolio Manager(s)

Greg Woodhams and Prescott LeGard were named comanagers here in mid-1998 and mid-2000, respectively. Tim Reynolds, who had comanaged sibling American Century Select since August 2001, came aboard in June 2003. All three managers served as analysts at other firms before joining American Century. The managers say they hold "material" positions in the fund, though they declined to specify any further.

Strategy

Management screens for companies with accelerating earnings-growth rates and favors those that can continue to deliver improving rates of growth. Although the fund has plenty of exposure to typical growth sectors, such as health care and technology, it will also pick up less-traditional industrial or consumer-staples names if their earnings are accelerating. Management's emphasis on sustainable growth means the fund is dominated by more-stable blue chips. With a median market cap that's among the highest in the group, management's giant-cap bias is evident.

Historical Profile

Return Average
Risk Average
Rating ★★★ Neutral

Investment Style: Equity Stock % — 100% | 95% | 91% | 93% | 92% | 87% | 91% | 98% | 99%

▼ Manager Change
▽ Partial Manager Change

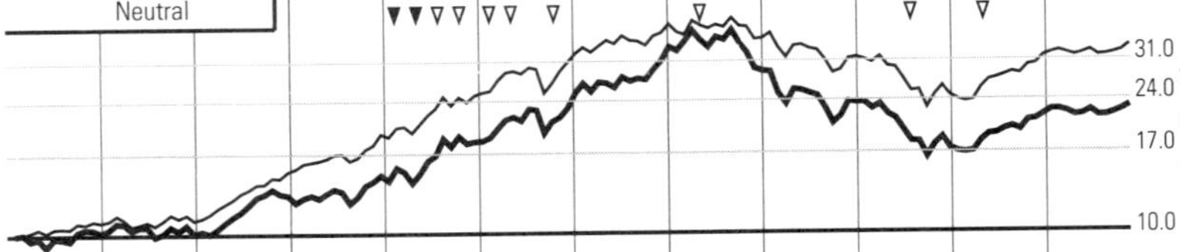

Growth of $10,000
▬ Investment Values of Fund
— Investment Values of S&P 500

Performance Quartile (within Category)

1993	1994	1995	1996	1997	1998	1999	2000	2001	2002	2003	12-04	History
22.40	18.74	19.39	21.88	24.01	27.16	32.28	24.00	19.52	14.42	17.94	19.71	NAV
3.76	-1.49	20.35	15.01	29.28	36.77	34.68	-14.71	-18.67	-26.13	24.41	9.91	Total Return %
-6.30	-2.80	-17.18	-7.93	-4.07	8.20	13.64	-5.61	-6.79	-4.04	-4.26	-0.96	+/-S&P 500
0.89	-4.11	-16.83	-8.11	-1.21	-1.94	1.52	7.71	1.75	1.75	-5.34	3.61	+/-Russ 1000Gr
0.23	0.23	0.37	0.94	0.00	0.00	0.00	0.00	0.00	0.00	0.00	0.04	Income Return %
3.53	-1.72	19.98	14.07	29.28	36.77	34.68	-14.71	-18.67	-26.13	24.41	9.87	Capital Return %
78	50	96	81	38	29	52	56	42	41	70	29	Total Rtn % Rank Cat
0.06	0.05	0.07	0.18	0.00	0.00	0.00	0.00	0.00	0.00	0.00	0.01	Income $
2.77	3.22	3.06	0.25	4.17	5.39	4.14	3.58	0.00	0.00	0.00	0.00	Capital Gains $
1.00	1.00	1.00	1.00	1.00	1.00	1.00	1.00	1.00	1.00	1.00	—	Expense Ratio %
0.20	0.30	0.40	-0.10	0.02	-0.02	-0.24	-0.30	-0.01	-0.04	0.05	—	Income Ratio %
94	100	141	122	75	126	92	102	114	135	159	—	Turnover Rate %
4,553	4,158	4,849	4,667	5,166	7,093	9,631	8,376	6,273	3,832	4,482	4,350	Net Assets $mil

Performance 12-31-04

	1st Qtr	2nd Qtr	3rd Qtr	4th Qtr	Total
2000	11.15	-4.07	-3.92	-16.75	-14.71
2001	-19.33	7.13	-17.89	14.62	-18.67
2002	-1.33	-15.42	-16.39	5.87	-26.13
2003	-2.15	12.47	2.14	10.67	24.41
2004	1.62	0.93	-1.90	9.24	9.91

Trailing	Total Return%	+/- S&P 500	+/- Russ 1000Gr	%Rank Cat	Growth of $10,000
3 Mo	9.24	0.01	0.07	63	10,924
6 Mo	7.16	-0.03	3.69	21	10,716
1 Yr	9.91	-0.96	3.61	29	10,991
3 Yr Avg	0.34	-3.24	0.52	40	10,102
5 Yr Avg	-6.87	-4.57	2.42	43	7,006
10 Yr Avg	8.73	-3.34	-0.86	54	23,094
15 Yr Avg	9.06	-1.87	-0.44	53	36,727

Tax Analysis	Tax-Adj Rtn%	%Rank Cat	Tax-Cost Rat	%Rank Cat
3 Yr (estimated)	0.33	35	0.01	2
5 Yr (estimated)	-7.39	40	0.56	34
10 Yr (estimated)	6.73	61	1.84	65

Potential Capital Gain Exposure: -12% of assets

Rating and Risk

Time Period	Load-Adj Return %	Morningstar Rtn vs Cat	Morningstar Risk vs Cat	Morningstar Risk-Adj Rating
1 Yr	9.91			
3 Yr	0.34	Avg	-Avg	★★★
5 Yr	-6.87	Avg	Avg	★★★
10 Yr	8.73	Avg	Avg	★★★
Incept	11.26			

Other Measures	Standard Index S&P 500	Best Fit Index Russ 1000Gr
Alpha	-3.0	0.3
Beta	0.95	0.92
R-Squared	95	95

Standard Deviation	14.76
Mean	0.34
Sharpe Ratio	-0.07

Morningstar's Take by Christopher Davis 10-15-04

American Century Growth Fund remains a worthwhile choice.

As is the case with its large-growth siblings, this offering employs an earnings-acceleration strategy. Management begins first by screening for firms with improving earnings--the approach first devised by American Century founder James Stowers III in the early 1970s. But rather than relying exlusively on backward-looking quantitative measures, it attempts to identify factors that predict growth will be sustained in the quarters to come. Management added PepsiCo in the second quarter of 2004, for instance, on the grounds that its snack food division is gaining market share overseas, which will enable the company to grow its earnings more quickly. They also like Pepsi's diversified product lineup, which they believe gives it an edge over chief rival Coca-Cola, which is much more reliant on its soft drink business.

To be sure, management's execution of that strategy hasn't been perfect. It was slow to recognize the technology sector's revival in 2003, for example, dampening the fund's returns in the year's buoyant market. On the whole, however, the fund's managers have generally gotten it right. After benefiting from a slew of tech and telecom names in the late 1990s, they turned to better-performing consumer staples and industrial holdings in the bear market. And in 2004, on-the-mark picks such as Carnival, Harley-Davidson, and Yahoo have pushed it into the large-growth category's top 20% for the year to date through Oct. 12.

Though the fund's long-term returns may not turn many heads, it has shown less volatility than either the large-growth average or the S&P 500. In addition to an appealing risk/reward profile, the fund boasts experienced management whose disciplined strategy has led to success at other American Century funds. While this offering isn't worthy of the large-growth elite, it's still a respectable core growth option.

Portfolio Analysis 09-30-04

Share change since 06-04 Total Stocks:75	Sector	PE	YTD Ret%	% Assets
⊖ Procter & Gamble	Goods	23.3	12.38	3.63
⊕ Microsoft	Software	36.1	8.95	3.57
⊖ Gen Elec	Ind Mtrls	22.8	20.68	3.34
⊖ Cisco Systems	Hardware	24.5	-20.26	3.30
Medtronic	Health	30.7	2.68	2.84
⊕ Johnson & Johnson	Health	20.6	25.17	2.67
⊕ Dell	Hardware	34.0	24.01	2.48
⊕ Intel	Hardware	19.8	-26.56	2.47
⊖ PepsiCo	Goods	22.5	13.82	2.41
⊖ Target	Consumer	22.3	36.14	2.21
⊕ Roche Holding	Health	—	—	2.16
⊖ Monsanto Company	Ind Mtrls	54.5	96.09	2.09
Pfizer	Health	22.0	-22.31	1.99
⊖ Yahoo	Media	95.1	67.36	1.93
CR Bard	Health	26.6	58.94	1.79
⊖ First Data	Business	18.8	3.72	1.76
Hospira	Health	—	—	1.76
⊖ Sprint	Telecom	—	55.24	1.74
⊖ American Express	Financial	20.3	17.60	1.73
⊖ Carnival	Goods	26.2	46.74	1.72

Current Investment Style

Value Blnd Growth; Large Mid Small

Market Cap	%
Giant	48.7
Large	35.4
Mid	16.0
Small	0.0
Micro	0.0

Avg $mil: 37,243

Value Measures		Rel Category
Price/Earnings	20.38	0.96
Price/Book	3.11	0.96
Price/Sales	2.28	1.06
Price/Cash Flow	10.77	0.98
Dividend Yield %	0.93	1.21

Growth Measures	%	Rel Category
Long-Term Erngs	12.99	0.92
Book Value	10.92	0.86
Sales	5.16	0.61
Cash Flow	17.58	1.06
Historical Erngs	10.04	0.69

Profitability	%	Rel Category
Return on Equity	18.49	1.03
Return on Assets	8.98	0.96
Net Margin	13.40	1.09

Sector Weightings	% of Stocks	Rel S&P 500	3 Year High	3 Year Low
Info	28.04	1.30		
Software	7.00	1.63	10	3
Hardware	14.97	1.47	18	12
Media	4.32	1.13	7	3
Telecom	1.75	0.56	2	0
Service	42.96	0.93		
Health	22.37	1.79	24	18
Consumer	8.45	0.93	13	3
Business	2.74	0.68	4	1
Financial	9.40	0.45	18	9
Mfg	28.99	0.90		
Goods	14.69	1.57	16	9
Ind Mtrls	11.11	0.88	12	6
Energy	3.19	0.45	6	1
Utilities	0.00	0.00	0	0

Composition

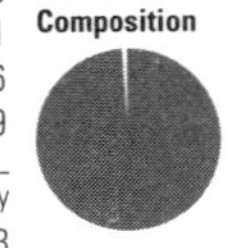

Cash	0.5
Stocks	98.7
Bonds	0.0
Other	0.8
Foreign (% of Stock)	5.0

Address:	4500 Main St Kansas City MO 64141 800-345-3533
Web Address:	www.americancentury.com
Inception:	10-31-58
Advisor:	American Century Investment Mgt Inc.
Subadvisor:	None
NTF Plans:	Schwab OneSource, Accutrade NTF

Minimum Purchase:	$2500	Add: $50	IRA: $2500
Min Auto Inv Plan:	$2500	Add: $50	
Sales Fees:	No-load		
Management Fee:	1.00% mx./0.88% mn.		
Actual Fees:	Mgt:1.00%	Dist:	
Expense Projections:	3Yr:$318	5Yr:$551	10Yr:$1219
Income Distrib:	Annually		

AmCent Inc & Growth Inv

Ticker	Load	NAV	Yield	Total Assets	Mstar Category
BIGRX	None	$30.67	1.9%	$5,275 mil	Large Value

Governance and Management

Fiduciary Grade: B

Portfolio Manager(s)

John Schniedwind, Kurt Borgwardt, and Zili Zhang are the day-to-day portfolio managers. Several quantitative analysts help with the fund's models.

Strategy

Like its sibling American Century Equity Growth, this fund keeps its sector and market-cap weights darn close to the S&P 500 index's and uses quantitative models to pick stocks based on valuations and a host of growth and momentum factors. In recent years the fund's managers have added an earnings quality factor to the models. This fund's models have more of a bias for cheap stocks than equity growth's, however, and they emphasize yield and risk control. To that end, the fund holds more than 250 names and keeps an eye on individual-position bets against the S&P 500 Index. Outperforming the benchmark is the goal.

Historical Profile

Return Average
Risk Above Avg
Rating ★★★ Neutral

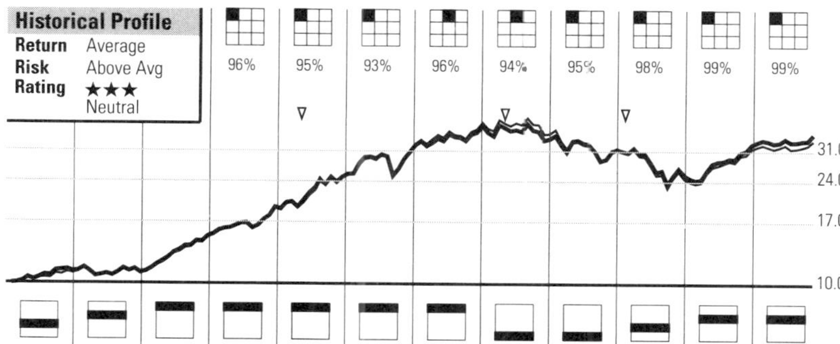

Investment Style: Equity Stock %

▼ Manager Change
▽ Partial Manager Change

Growth of $10,000
— Investment Values of Fund
— Investment Values of S&P 500

Performance Quartile (within Category)

History

1993	1994	1995	1996	1997	1998	1999	2000	2001	2002	2003	12-04	History
15.08	13.92	17.81	20.16	24.30	29.25	34.05	30.19	27.35	21.74	27.70	30.67	NAV
11.32	-0.55	36.87	24.15	34.44	27.67	17.95	-10.54	-8.37	-19.37	29.62	12.98	Total Return %
1.26	-1.86	-0.66	1.21	1.09	-0.90	-3.09	-1.44	3.51	2.72	0.95	2.11	+/-S&P 500
-6.75	1.43	-1.49	2.51	-0.74	12.04	10.60	-17.55	-2.78	-3.85	-0.41	-3.51	+/-Russ 1000 VI
3.03	2.83	3.07	2.52	1.94	1.46	1.15	0.85	1.01	1.20	1.98	2.13	Income Return %
8.29	-3.38	33.80	21.63	32.50	26.21	16.80	-11.39	-9.38	-20.57	27.64	10.85	Capital Return %
69	49	16	17	5	1	5	98	76	58	36	48	Total Rtn % Rank Cat
0.42	0.42	0.42	0.44	0.38	0.35	0.33	0.29	0.30	0.33	0.43	0.59	Income $
0.19	0.65	0.75	1.44	2.29	1.30	0.07	0.00	0.00	0.00	0.00	0.00	Capital Gains $
0.75	0.73	0.67	0.62	0.66	0.69	0.68	0.67	0.68	0.69	0.69	—	Expense Ratio %
2.90	2.96	2.61	2.32	1.81	1.31	1.08	0.89	1.07	1.34	1.80	—	Income Ratio %
31	68	70	92	102	86	58	64	61	67	67	—	Turnover Rate %
230	225	374	715	1,786	4,285	6,347	5,417	4,475	3,147	3,820	3,972	Net Assets $mil

Performance 12-31-04

	1st Qtr	2nd Qtr	3rd Qtr	4th Qtr	Total
2000	0.65	-4.17	-0.28	-6.98	-10.54
2001	-10.47	7.17	-13.43	10.30	-8.37
2002	1.14	-11.29	-17.05	8.34	-19.37
2003	-3.65	16.41	2.05	13.25	29.62
2004	2.73	2.05	-1.76	9.70	12.98

Trailing	Total Return%	+/- S&P 500	+/- Russ 1000 VI	%Rank Cat	Growth of $10,000
3 Mo	9.70	0.47	-0.68	35	10,970
6 Mo	7.77	0.58	-4.31	69	10,777
1 Yr	12.98	2.11	-3.51	48	11,298
3 Yr Avg	5.70	2.12	-2.87	51	11,809
5 Yr Avg	-0.65	1.65	-5.92	96	9,679
10 Yr Avg	12.78	0.71	-1.05	19	33,291
15 Yr Avg	—	—	—	—	—

Tax Analysis	Tax-Adj Rtn%	%Rank Cat	Tax-Cost Rat	%Rank Cat
3 Yr (estimated)	5.04	46	0.62	42
5 Yr (estimated)	-1.18	92	0.53	28
10 Yr (estimated)	11.23	10	1.37	26

Potential Capital Gain Exposure: 13% of assets

Rating and Risk

Time Period	Load-Adj Return %	Morningstar Rtn vs Cat	Morningstar Risk vs Cat	Morningstar Risk-Adj Rating
1 Yr	12.98			
3 Yr	5.70	Avg	Avg	★★★
5 Yr	-0.65	Low	Avg	★
10 Yr	12.78	+Avg	+Avg	★★★★
Incept	13.10			

Other Measures	Standard Index S&P 500	Best Fit Index S&P 500
Alpha	2.1	2.1
Beta	0.98	0.98
R-Squared	98	98
Standard Deviation	15.65	
Mean	5.70	
Sharpe Ratio	0.28	

Portfolio Analysis 09-30-04

Share change since 06-04 Total Stocks:116

	Sector	PE	YTD Ret%	% Assets
⊕ ChevronTexaco	Energy	7.7	25.57	5.31
⊕ Bank of America	Financial	12.3	21.50	4.78
J P Morgan Chase	Financial	19.4	9.97	3.35
Johnson & Johnson	Health	20.6	25.17	3.28
⊕ IBM	Hardware	20.2	7.19	2.87
⊖ Microsoft	Software	36.1	8.95	2.66
⊕ Merck	Health	11.4	-27.76	2.22
⊕ Countrywide Financial	Financial	9.0	48.15	2.19
⊕ AmerisourceBergen	Health	14.3	4.69	2.11
Ford Motor	Goods	9.9	-6.00	2.06
☼ Cigna	Health	8.4	42.87	2.04
⊕ Intel	Hardware	19.8	-26.56	2.03
⊖ Monsanto Company	Ind Mtrls	54.5	96.09	1.93
Pfizer	Health	22.0	-22.31	1.92
Time Warner	Media	27.5	8.12	1.71
⊕ May Department Stores	Consumer	13.7	4.58	1.66
⊖ Eastman Kodak	Goods	—	27.90	1.65
⊕ Walt Disney	Media	24.3	20.21	1.51
Bristol-Myers Squibb	Health	17.7	-7.27	1.42
⊕ SuperValu	Consumer	12.4	23.24	1.39

Current Investment Style

Value Blnd Growth / Large Mid Small

Market Cap	%
Giant	47.6
Large	25.8
Mid	25.0
Small	1.6
Micro	0.0
Avg $mil: 27,354	

Value Measures		Rel Category
Price/Earnings	13.17	0.88
Price/Book	2.10	0.93
Price/Sales	0.72	0.61
Price/Cash Flow	4.82	0.76
Dividend Yield %	2.17	1.06

Growth Measures	%	Rel Category
Long-Term Erngs	9.30	0.89
Book Value	4.67	0.83
Sales	5.51	1.31
Cash Flow	12.14	2.33
Historical Erngs	11.88	1.00

Profitability	%	Rel Category
Return on Equity	17.45	1.10
Return on Assets	7.61	0.97
Net Margin	9.70	0.95

Sector Weightings	% of Stocks	Rel S&P 500	3 Year High	3 Year Low
Info	20.75	0.97		
Software	2.93	0.68	4	3
Hardware	8.62	0.85	10	6
Media	3.63	0.95	4	3
Telecom	5.57	1.77	9	5
Service	46.00	0.99		
Health	14.57	1.17	15	10
Consumer	6.76	0.74	8	6
Business	3.82	0.94	4	3
Financial	20.85	1.00	24	17
Mfg	33.24	1.03		
Goods	12.23	1.31	14	7
Ind Mtrls	8.63	0.68	14	6
Energy	8.29	1.16	10	7
Utilities	4.09	1.38	5	4

Composition

Cash	0.2
Stocks	99.3
Bonds	0.0
Other	0.5
Foreign (% of Stock)	0.0

Morningstar's Take by Dan Culloton 12-15-04

American Century Income & Growth plays not to lose and wins.

This offering quietly goes about its business using a quantitatively influenced form of stock-picking to make small bets for or against large-cap stocks, usually members of the S&P 500. Its goal is to beat that benchmark not with quick, short-lived bursts of performance, but with consistent results. The fund has done a credible job, beating its typical large-value peer in seven of the last 10 calendar years and edging the biggest S&P 500 index fund available in all but one of the 48 rolling 10-year periods from 1990 through Nov. 30, 2004.

The fund has built this record by paying close attention to its computer models. The offering uses the same system employed by sibling American Century Equity Growth. Both management teams attempt to craft a portfolio that resembles the S&P 500 at the sector and industry level. However, American Century Income & Growth puts a heavier emphasis on its models' value-oriented elements, such as valuation and dividend yield.

The management team can override the models if its own research exposes an opportunity. The squad also constantly studies and adjusts its tools. (In recent years it has added an earnings-quality component to the models.) In general, however, the managers are content to follow their computers' leads. This year the models have been pointing the fund toward the shares of large established companies, such Motorola, Bank of America, and ChevronTexaco, that still look attractively priced.

This fund will never set your heart aflutter with adrenaline-jolting returns, but it's not likely to do serious damage to your portfolio either. Furthermore, investors get access to an experienced management team, regimented process, and decent risk/reward profile for a low expense ratio. Investors looking for a value-leaning core holding could do worse.

Address:	4500 Main Street Kansas City MO 64111 800-345-2021
Web Address:	www.americancentury.com
Inception:	12-17-90
Advisor:	American Century Investment Mgt Inc.
Subadvisor:	None
NTF Plans:	Schwab OneSource, Accutrade NTF

Minimum Purchase:	$2500	Add: $50	IRA: $2500
Min Auto Inv Plan:	$2500	Add: $50	
Sales Fees:	No-load		
Management Fee:	0.69%		
Actual Fees:	Mgt:0.69%	Dist:	
Expense Projections:	3Yr:$220	5Yr:$383	10Yr:$856
Income Distrib:	Quarterly		

AmCent Intl Disc Inv

Ticker	Load	NAV	Yield	Total Assets	Mstar Category
TWEGX	Closed	$13.47	0.0%	$1,271 mil	Foreign Small/Mid Growth

Governance and Management

Fiduciary Grade: B

Portfolio Manager(s)

Mark Kopinski has run this fund since January 1998, although he was also its manager for 10 months when American Century launched it in April 1994. Brian Brady joined the portfolio-management team in November 1998. Analyst Federico Laffan covers international small-caps. The fund also draws on the ideas of four emerging-markets analysts.

Strategy

Like most American Century funds, this offering bulks up on stocks with accelerating earnings. More so than its domestic counterparts, however, the managers also focus on other factors, emphasizing companies with good management, niche products, or rapidly growing revenues (even when profits are absent). The team buys small- and mid-cap stocks in the $1.5 billion to $5 billion range. American Century uses fair value pricing, when it determines such necessary.

Historical Profile

Return Above Avg
Risk Average
Rating ★★★★ Above Avg

Investment Style
Equity
Stock %: 99% 99% 92% 95% 82% 94% 95% 96% 92%

▼ Manager Change
▽ Partial Manager Change

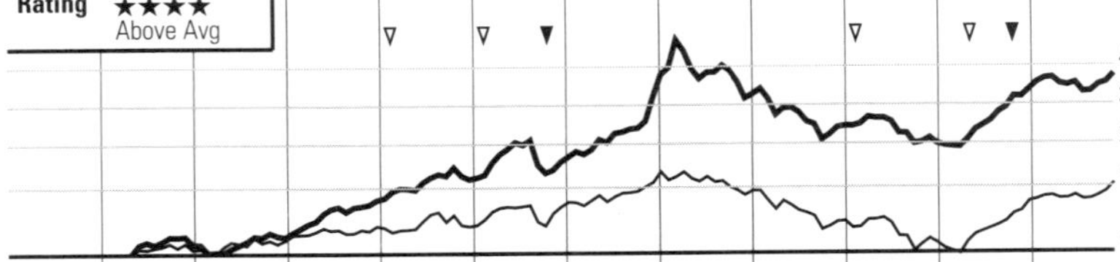

Growth of $10,000
▬ Investment Values of Fund
— Investment Values of MSCI EAFE

Performance Quartile (within Category)

1993	1994	1995	1996	1997	1998	1999	2000	2001	2002	2003	12-04	History
—	5.38	5.88	7.36	8.15	9.57	17.16	13.09	10.24	8.91	13.46	13.47	NAV
—	7.60*	9.89	31.18	17.48	17.86	88.54	-14.21	-21.77	-12.83	51.38	16.26	Total Return %
—	—	-1.32	25.13	15.70	-2.07	61.51	-0.02	-0.35	3.11	12.79	-3.99	+/-MSCI EAFE
—	—	-1.52	24.31	15.21	-0.83	60.56	-0.85	-0.38	2.97	11.96	-4.12	+/-MSCI Wd xUS
—	0.00	0.60	0.29	0.28	0.00	0.00	0.00	0.00	0.15	0.30	0.00	Income Return %
—	—	9.29	30.89	17.20	17.86	88.54	-14.21	-21.77	-12.98	51.08	16.26	Capital Return %
—	—	15	10	6	44	47	51	35	29	44	92	Total Rtn % Rank Cat
—	0.00	0.03	0.02	0.02	0.00	0.00	0.00	0.00	0.02	0.03	0.00	Income $
—	0.00	0.00	0.32	0.47	0.03	0.81	1.64	0.00	0.00	0.00	2.09	Capital Gains $
—	2.00	2.00	1.88	1.70	1.64	1.55	1.36	1.45	1.53	1.57	—	Expense Ratio %
—	-0.48	0.27	-0.31	-0.37	-0.36	-0.65	-0.64	0.10	0.35	0.27	—	Income Ratio %
—	—	168	130	146	178	110	113	180	224	215	—	Turnover Rate %
—	112	121	390	622	799	1,723	1,576	1,016	794	1,077	1,105	Net Assets $mil

Performance 12-31-04

	1st Qtr	2nd Qtr	3rd Qtr	4th Qtr	Total
2000	20.46	-15.62	1.15	-16.55	-14.21
2001	-14.67	1.88	-19.07	11.18	-21.77
2002	7.13	-3.37	-15.94	0.18	-12.83
2003	-2.81	18.36	14.63	14.79	51.38
2004	9.51	-4.14	-1.63	12.58	16.26

Trailing	Total Return%	+/- MSCI EAFE	+/- MSCI Wd xUS	%Rank Cat	Growth of $10,000
3 Mo	12.58	-2.74	-2.57	81	11,258
6 Mo	10.75	-4.25	-4.62	82	11,075
1 Yr	16.26	-3.99	-4.12	92	11,626
3 Yr Avg	15.33	3.44	3.11	65	15,340
5 Yr Avg	0.58	1.71	1.34	40	10,293
10 Yr Avg	14.50	8.88	8.56	15	38,731
15 Yr Avg	—	—	—	—	—

Tax Analysis	Tax-Adj Rtn%	%Rank Cat	Tax-Cost Rat	%Rank Cat
3 Yr (estimated)	14.37	64	0.83	93
5 Yr (estimated)	-0.37	40	0.94	75
10 Yr (estimated)	13.41	15	0.95	57

Potential Capital Gain Exposure: 25% of assets

Rating and Risk

Time Period	Load-Adj Return %	Morningstar Rtn vs Cat	Morningstar Risk vs Cat	Morningstar Risk-Adj Rating
1 Yr	16.26			
3 Yr	15.33	Avg	-Avg	★★★
5 Yr	0.58	Avg	Avg	★★★
10 Yr	14.50	+Avg	Avg	★★★★
Incept	14.20			

Other Measures	Standard Index S&P 500	Best Fit Index DJ 60%
Alpha	5.0	0.8
Beta	0.83	1.50
R-Squared	76	83
Standard Deviation	16.98	
Mean	15.33	
Sharpe Ratio	0.83	

Portfolio Analysis 09-30-04

Share change since 06-04 Total Stocks:122	Sector	Country	% Assets
⊖ Research In Motion Ltd	Hardware	Canada	2.97
☼ Petrokazakhstan Cl A	Energy	Canada	1.84
⊕ CSL Ltd	Health	Australia	1.77
☼ NOVA Chemicals	Ind Mtrls	Canada	1.74
Philippine Long Distance	Telecom	Philippines	1.72
Esprit Hldgs Ltd	Consumer	Hong Kong	1.69
⊖ Puma AG Rudolf Dassler S	Goods	Germany	1.68
Enagas	Energy	Spain	1.59
⊕ Geberit	Consumer	Switzerland	1.53
⊖ Anglo Irish Bank	Financial	Ireland	1.47
⊕ Wienerberger	Business	Austria	1.47
⊕ Hardman Resources Ltd	Energy	Australia	1.45
⊕ Gn Store Nord	Goods	Denmark	1.40
⊕ Storebrand	Financial	Norway	1.37
⊕ NHK Spring	Ind Mtrls	Japan	1.37
⊕ Phonak Holding Ltd	Health	Switzerland	1.34
⊕ Technip	Energy	France	1.31
☼ Lion Nathan Ltd	Goods	Australia	1.30
☼ NGK Insulators, Ltd	Ind Mtrls	Japan	1.27
⊖ Inchcape	Consumer	U.K.	1.24

Current Investment Style

Market Cap	%
Giant	0.0
Large	19.7
Mid	72.8
Small	7.5
Micro	0.0
Avg $mil: 2,333	

Value Measures		Rel Category
Price/Earnings	15.54	1.13
Price/Book	1.89	0.99
Price/Sales	0.86	1.05
Price/Cash Flow	4.72	0.95
Dividend Yield %	2.51	1.11

Growth Measures	%	Rel Category
Long-Term Erngs	278.40	6.02
Book Value	5.48	1.40
Sales	5.74	0.91
Cash Flow	13.05	2.81
Historical Erngs	13.31	1.43

Composition

Cash	5.4	Bonds	0.0
Stocks	91.7	Other	2.9
Foreign (% of Stock)			96.2

Sector Weightings	% of Stocks	Rel MSCI EAFE	3 Year High	3 Year Low
Info	11.00	0.66		
Software	0.00	0.00	4	0
Hardware	4.09	1.12	11	4
Media	1.42	0.62	6	0
Telecom	5.49	0.57	10	1
Service	36.07	0.81		
Health	7.48	1.03	13	1
Consumer	14.81	2.94	17	5
Business	6.14	1.13	15	4
Financial	7.64	0.28	16	8
Mfg	52.92	1.37		
Goods	11.86	0.87	28	12
Ind Mtrls	24.02	1.95	32	11
Energy	12.22	1.66	12	0
Utilities	4.82	0.90	5	0

Regional Exposure	% Stock		
UK/W. Europe	45	N. America	13
Japan	18	Latn America	0
Asia X Japan	22	Other	2

Country Exposure	% Stock		
Japan	18	Canada	9
U.K.	13	Germany	5
Australia	10		

Morningstar's Take by Bridget Hughes 11-22-04

Don't mistake American Century International Discovery's more grown-up portfolio for a safer investment.

Compared with its foreign small/mid-growth peers, this portfolio is a bit bigger. Its average market cap, for example, is greater than $2 billion. Upon purchase, its stocks must boast at least a $1.5-billion market cap (recently changed from $1 billion earlier this year). Many of its peers, in contrast, won't touch stocks that big. This portfolio also sports its share of large caps: Top holding Research in Motion has a market cap of $15 billion. As long as the fund's average market cap doesn't creep above $3.5 billion, the managers are comfortable holding some larger companies.

The fund, however, is in some respects as aggressive as its more-daring peers. Its bottom-up approach often puts it in just a few sectors at a time, and management is quite comfortable investing in emerging markets. High turnover also makes its portfolio less predictable. Consider recent changes. Whereas earlier this year, the fund was heavy in technology and Japan, it has roughly halved its stakes in those areas in the past six months. It has also taken down its emerging-markets exposure, but not by as big a margin.

The fund's aggressive nature makes it easier to understand its weak performance in 2004. For the year to date through Nov. 19, 2004, its 9.4% gain lands easily in the category's worst quartile. It's also one of the worst showings among funds that invest heavily in mid-caps. Tech and telecom burned earlier this year, as did Japan and some emerging-markets.

That doesn't mean we think the fund has lost its appeal; it's one of the few funds to focus on international mid-caps. Recent performance does, however, highlight the risks here and suggest the fund continue to serve in a more-specialized role.

Address:	4500 Main St, Kansas City MO 64111, 800-345-2021	Minimum Purchase:	Closed	Add: —	IRA: —
Web Address:	www.americancentury.com	Min Auto Inv Plan:	Closed	Add: —	
Inception:	04-01-94 *	Sales Fees:	No-load, 2.00%R		
Advisor:	American Century Investment Mgt Inc.	Management Fee:	1.75% mx./1.20% mn.		
Subadvisor:	None	Actual Fees:	Mgt:1.57%	Dist:	
		Expense Projections:	3Yr:$493	5Yr:$850	10Yr:$1854
		Income Distrib:	Annually		
NTF Plans:	Schwab OneSource, Accutrade NTF				

AmCent Intl Growth Inv

Ticker	Load	NAV	Yield	Total Assets	Mstar Category
TWIEX	None	$9.06	1.0%	$3,077 mil	Foreign Large Growth

Governance and Management

Fiduciary Grade: B

Portfolio Manager(s)

As a chief investment officer, Henrik Strabo leads American Century's international effort, which now consists of five funds. He has worked on this fund since August 1993. Keith Creveling was promoted from a large-cap Europe analyst to portfolio manager in 2002. The international team now totals about 20 investment professionals, up from fewer than 10 five years ago. Michael Perelstein joined the management team at the end of October 2004 with the idea that he'll eventually free Strabo to concentrate on his CIO duties. Perelstein is experienced but had only a so-so record at Schroder International.

Strategy

Henrik Strabo, Keith Creveling, and Michael Perelstein take American Century's signature growth approach overseas. They buy companies with accelerating earnings growth or other improvements in earnings trends, and they sell when growth slows. The fund can be more concentrated than its rivals when it comes to sectors and countries, as it uses a purely bottom-up approach with no regard to the weightings of its benchmark, the MSCI EAFE Index.

Historical Profile

Return Above Avg
Risk Average
Rating ★★★★ Above Avg

Investment Style: Equity, Stock %

100%	96%	97%	96%	81%	92%	95%	99%	98%

▼ Manager Change
▽ Partial Manager Change

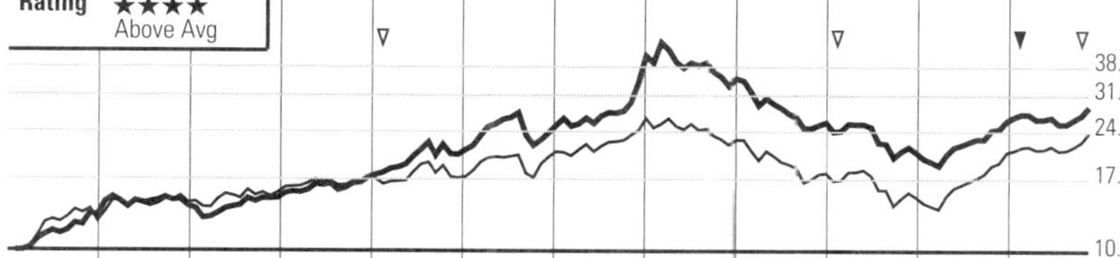

Performance Quartile (within Category)

1993	1994	1995	1996	1997	1998	1999	2000	2001	2002	2003	12-04	History
7.70	6.96	7.78	7.96	8.19	9.58	14.97	10.93	7.97	6.38	7.94	9.06	NAV
42.65	-4.76	11.89	14.43	19.72	19.01	64.44	-15.01	-26.79	-19.25	25.38	15.31	Total Return %
10.09	-12.54	0.68	8.38	17.94	-0.92	37.41	-0.82	-5.37	-3.31	-13.21	-4.94	+/-MSCI EAFE
10.44	-12.11	0.48	7.56	17.45	0.32	36.46	-1.65	-5.40	-3.45	-14.04	-5.07	+/-MSCI Wd xUS
0.00	0.00	0.10	0.00	0.35	0.20	0.06	0.00	0.28	0.70	0.90	1.16	Income Return %
42.65	-4.76	11.79	14.43	19.37	18.81	64.38	-15.01	-27.07	-19.95	24.48	14.15	Capital Return %
28	80	28	46	6	16	28	29	68	47	93	46	Total Rtn % Rank Cat
0.00	0.00	0.01	0.00	0.03	0.02	0.01	0.00	0.03	0.06	0.06	0.09	Income $
0.40	0.37	0.00	0.92	1.28	0.14	0.69	1.75	0.00	0.00	0.00	0.00	Capital Gains $
1.90	1.84	1.77	1.65	1.38	1.33	1.27	1.20	1.21	1.25	1.28	—	Expense Ratio %
-0.34	-0.53	0.25	-0.07	0.04	0.33	-0.06	-0.16	0.43	0.76	0.84	—	Income Ratio %
255	242	169	158	163	190	117	116	173	215	169	—	Turnover Rate %
944	1,272	1,258	1,361	1,784	2,640	4,521	4,755	3,311	2,318	2,617	2,471	Net Assets $mil

Performance 12-31-04

	1st Qtr	2nd Qtr	3rd Qtr	4th Qtr	Total
2000	4.49	-8.96	-6.40	-4.55	-15.01
2001	-17.38	-1.77	-13.42	4.19	-26.79
2002	-0.88	-2.28	-19.69	3.81	-19.25
2003	-9.09	16.03	4.31	13.95	25.38
2004	4.79	-2.16	-1.47	14.16	15.31

Trailing	Total Return%	+/- MSCI EAFE	+/- MSCI Wd xUS	%Rank Cat	Growth of $10,000
3 Mo	14.16	-1.16	-0.99	40	11,416
6 Mo	12.48	-2.52	-2.89	50	11,248
1 Yr	15.31	-4.94	-5.07	46	11,531
3 Yr Avg	5.30	-6.59	-6.92	74	11,676
5 Yr Avg	-6.19	-5.06	-5.43	52	7,265
10 Yr Avg	8.10	2.48	2.16	11	21,790
15 Yr Avg	—	—	—	—	—

Tax Analysis	Tax-Adj Rtn%	%Rank Cat	Tax-Cost Rat	%Rank Cat
3 Yr (estimated)	4.96	65	0.32	56
5 Yr (estimated)	-7.02	51	0.88	53
10 Yr (estimated)	6.55	13	1.43	77

Potential Capital Gain Exposure: -17% of assets

Rating and Risk

Time Period	Load-Adj Return %	Morningstar Rtn vs Cat	Morningstar Risk vs Cat	Morningstar Risk-Adj Rating
1 Yr	15.31			
3 Yr	5.30	Avg	-Avg	★★★
5 Yr	-6.19	Avg	Avg	★★★
10 Yr	8.10	+Avg	Avg	★★★★
Incept	9.42			

Other Measures	Standard Index S&P 500	Best Fit Index MSCI Wd xUS
Alpha	-5.4	-5.7
Beta	0.94	0.95
R-Squared	96	96

Standard Deviation	15.77
Mean	5.30
Sharpe Ratio	0.25

Portfolio Analysis 09-30-04

Share change since 06-04 Total Stocks:98	Sector	Country	% Assets
TOTAL	Energy	France	2.97
☼ BP	Energy	U.K.	2.90
⊖ Roche Holding	Health	Switzerland	2.56
⊕ Novartis	Health	Switzerland	2.43
⊕ BHP Billiton Ltd	Ind Mtrls	Australia	2.35
Smith & Nephew	Health	U.K.	2.03
Tesco	Consumer	U.K.	1.84
⊕ Erste Bank	Financial	Austria	1.74
Hoya	Goods	Japan	1.72
⊕ ING Groep	Financial	Netherlands	1.71
Telefonica	Telecom	Spain	1.64
Vivendi Universal	Media	France	1.60
⊕ Royal Bank Of Scotland G	Financial	U.K.	1.50
⊖ UBS	Financial	Switzerland	1.49
⊖ Reckitt Benckiser	Goods	U.K.	1.49
Credit Agricole	Financial	France	1.49
⊕ Toyota Motor	Goods	Japan	1.49
⊕ Mitsui & Co.	Ind Mtrls	Japan	1.47
SAP	Software	Germany	1.44
⊕ AXA	Financial	France	1.44

Current Investment Style

Value Blnd Growth — Large Mid Small

Market Cap	%
Giant	51.2
Large	38.0
Mid	10.2
Small	0.0
Micro	0.5
Avg $mil: 21,439	

Value Measures		Rel Category
Price/Earnings	14.72	0.99
Price/Book	2.17	1.04
Price/Sales	0.67	0.64
Price/Cash Flow	4.71	0.85
Dividend Yield %	2.16	1.06

Growth Measures	%	Rel Category
Long-Term Erngs	11.36	0.95
Book Value	0.90	0.52
Sales	6.79	1.47
Cash Flow	9.53	1.26
Historical Erngs	8.13	0.97

Composition

Cash	2.3	Bonds	0.0
Stocks	97.7	Other	0.0
Foreign (% of Stock)			99.0

Sector Weightings	% of Stocks	Rel MSCI EAFE	3 Year High	3 Year Low
Info	12.51	0.75		
Software	2.05	1.90	3	0
Hardware	1.46	0.40	9	1
Media	2.78	1.22	7	2
Telecom	6.22	0.65	12	1
Service	44.83	1.00		
Health	12.30	1.69	13	5
Consumer	5.53	1.10	9	2
Business	3.89	0.72	15	3
Financial	23.11	0.86	28	14
Mfg	42.67	1.10		
Goods	14.25	1.04	30	14
Ind Mtrls	15.02	1.22	15	3
Energy	10.89	1.48	11	5
Utilities	2.51	0.47	3	1

Regional Exposure	% Stock		
UK/W. Europe	70	N. America	3
Japan	16	Latn America	2
Asia X Japan	7	Other	2

Country Exposure	% Stock		
U.K.	18	Switzerland	9
Japan	16	Germany	8
France	15		

Morningstar's Take by Bridget Hughes 11-17-04

It's time for American Century International Growth to simply do better.

A success story during the bull market of the 1990s, this foreign large-growth fund's performance over the past three years has been nothing to write home about. Particularly troubling was its 2003 performance. While its 25.4% gain was certainly healthy in absolute terms, it ranked in the category's worst decile. Overall, its 3.6% annualized return for the trailing three-year period through Nov. 16, 2004, ranks near the category's worst quartile.

Recognizing performance problems, fund personnel have tried a multitude of tactics to improve results, and on paper, they seem helpful. The fund's analyst staff has been beefed up, it has hired a quantitative analyst to help the team sift through its sizeable stock universe, and it's made a couple of manager changes. Most recently, an experienced Michael Perelstein joined the management team at the end of October 2004, the idea being that he'll eventually take over for comanager Henrik Strabo, who will focus more on his duties as American Century's international CIO. Keith Creveling, comanager since March 2002, will remain on the fund.

Meanwhile, the fund's expense ratio is reasonable and, at under $3 billion, the high-turnover fund is still small enough to easily maneuver in its large-cap universe. Further, in order to better focus the analysts' efforts and as a sign of confidence in its analysts' ideas, the fund has reduced its number of holdings to around 100. Though still comparatively high, turnover has come down, as analysts believe they've found companies with more-sustainable growth trends.

The fund must now, however, demonstrate that these changes are leading to better performance. If there isn't improvement over the next year or so, we'd suggest shareholders start to explore other options in the fairly rich foreign large-growth field.

Address:	4500 Main St Kansas City MO 64111 800-345-2021
Web Address:	www.americancentury.com
Inception:	05-09-91
Advisor:	American Century Investment Mgt Inc.
Subadvisor:	None
NTF Plans:	Schwab OneSource, Accutrade NTF

Minimum Purchase:	$2500	Add: $250	IRA: $2500
Min Auto Inv Plan:	$2500	Add: $50	
Sales Fees:	No-load		
Management Fee:	1.50% mx./1.10% mn.		
Actual Fees:	Mgt:1.25%	Dist:	
Expense Projections:	3Yr:$395	5Yr:$683	10Yr:$1503
Income Distrib:	Annually		

AmCent Large Co Val Inv

Ticker	Load	NAV	Yield	Total Assets	Mstar Category
ALVIX	Closed	$6.49	1.5%	$1,245 mil	Large Value

Governance and Management

Fiduciary Grade: C

Portfolio Manager(s)

Charles Ritter and Mark Mallon have been with this fund since its 1999 inception. During that time they've amassed an impressive record relative to the large-value category. Ritter and Mallon also manage American Century Capital Value in a nearly identical manner. They're assisted by portfolio manager Brendan Healy and analyst Lon West, who came from USAA. The team may add a fifth member.

Strategy

The fund follows a fairly typical value strategy, screening for stocks that look cheap by a variety of measures and then choosing those with decent growth prospects and solid balance sheets. Management tries to avoid big sector bets.

Historical Profile

Return Above Avg
Risk Average
Rating ★★★★ Above Avg

Investment Style: Equity Stock %: 95% (1999), 89% (2000), 87% (2001), 90% (2002), 95% (2003), 96% (12-04)

▼ Manager Change
▽ Partial Manager Change

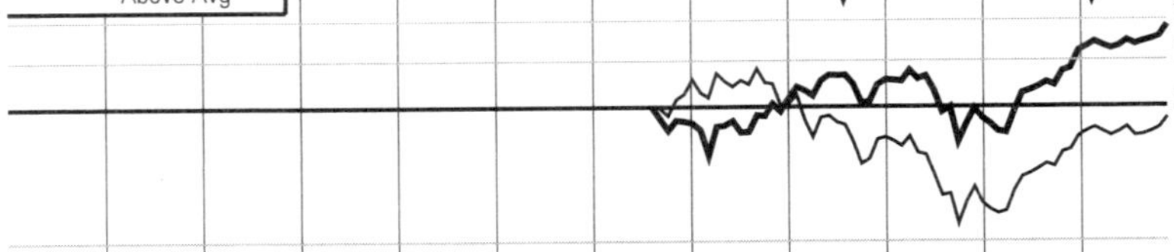

Growth of $10,000
— Investment Values of Fund
— Investment Values of S&P 500

Performance Quartile (within Category)

1993	1994	1995	1996	1997	1998	1999	2000	2001	2002	2003	12-04	History
—	—	—	—	—	—	4.67	5.04	5.35	4.56	5.79	6.49	NAV
—	—	—	—	—	—	-5.97*	9.68	7.47	-13.47	28.97	14.28	Total Return %
—	—	—	—	—	—	—	18.78	19.35	8.62	0.30	3.41	+/-S&P 500
—	—	—	—	—	—	—	2.67	13.06	2.05	-1.06	-2.21	+/-Russ 1000 VI
—	—	—	—	—	—	0.00	1.62	1.28	1.35	1.78	1.72	Income Return %
—	—	—	—	—	—	—	8.06	6.19	-14.82	27.19	12.56	Capital Return %
—	—	—	—	—	—	—	49	7	15	40	31	Total Rtn % Rank Cat
—	—	—	—	—	—	0.03	0.08	0.06	0.07	0.08	0.10	Income $
—	—	—	—	—	—	0.00	0.00	0.00	0.00	0.00	0.02	Capital Gains $
—	—	—	—	—	—	—	0.90	0.90	0.90	0.90	0.90	Expense Ratio %
—	—	—	—	—	—	—	1.72	1.62	1.34	1.75	1.58	Income Ratio %
—	—	—	—	—	—	—	51	55	34	30	61	Turnover Rate %
—	—	—	—	—	—	12	14	57	121	305	541	Net Assets $mil

Performance 12-31-04

	1st Qtr	2nd Qtr	3rd Qtr	4th Qtr	Total
2000	-1.33	-2.17	6.45	6.73	9.68
2001	1.10	8.06	-9.96	9.25	7.47
2002	3.66	-7.44	-17.67	9.53	-13.47
2003	-5.58	17.47	2.00	13.99	28.97
2004	2.01	1.91	0.29	9.62	14.28

Trailing	Total Return%	+/- S&P 500	+/- Russ 1000 VI	%Rank Cat	Growth of $10,000
3 Mo	9.62	0.39	-0.76	38	10,962
6 Mo	9.93	2.74	-2.15	35	10,993
1 Yr	14.28	3.41	-2.21	31	11,428
3 Yr Avg	8.44	4.86	-0.13	15	12,752
5 Yr Avg	8.49	10.79	3.22	12	15,030
10 Yr Avg	—	—	—	—	—
15 Yr Avg	—	—	—	—	—

Tax Analysis	Tax-Adj Rtn%	%Rank Cat	Tax-Cost Rat	%Rank Cat
3 Yr (estimated)	7.81	12	0.58	39
5 Yr (estimated)	7.91	10	0.53	28
10 Yr (estimated)	—	—	—	—

Potential Capital Gain Exposure: 15% of assets

Rating and Risk

Time Period	Load-Adj Return %	Morningstar Rtn vs Cat	Morningstar Risk vs Cat	Morningstar Risk-Adj Rating
1 Yr	14.28			
3 Yr	8.44	+Avg	Avg	★★★★
5 Yr	8.49	+Avg	Avg	★★★★
10 Yr	—	—	—	—
Incept	6.59			

Other Measures	Standard Index S&P 500	Best Fit Index Russ 1000 VI
Alpha	4.8	0.1
Beta	0.94	0.97
R-Squared	93	98
Standard Deviation	15.83	
Mean	8.44	
Sharpe Ratio	0.45	

Portfolio Analysis 09-30-04

Share change since 06-04 Total Stocks:91	Sector	PE	YTD Ret%	% Assets
⊕ Citigroup	Financial	15.3	2.72	4.43
⊕ ExxonMobil	Energy	13.9	28.04	4.10
⊕ Freddie Mac	Financial	10.6	28.75	3.68
⊕ Bank of America	Financial	12.3	21.50	3.16
⊕ Royal Dutch Petroleum AD	Energy	—	14.31	2.64
⊕ SPDRs	—	—	—	2.38
⊕ Wells Fargo	Financial	15.5	8.97	2.10
⊕ Hewlett-Packard	Hardware	18.9	-7.28	1.92
⊕ ChevronTexaco	Energy	7.7	25.57	1.71
☼ J P Morgan Chase	Financial	19.4	9.97	1.56
⊕ ConocoPhillips	Energy	9.0	35.60	1.43
⊕ McDonald's	Consumer	19.7	31.48	1.41
⊕ Exelon	Utilities	16.1	37.55	1.38
⊕ SBC Communications	Telecom	15.4	3.74	1.36
⊕ US Bancorp	Financial	14.2	10.46	1.35
⊕ Wachovia	Financial	14.3	16.80	1.34
⊕ Washington Mutual	Financial	13.9	10.05	1.33
⊕ Allstate	Financial	12.8	23.12	1.33
⊕ Altria Group	Goods	13.3	18.38	1.32
⊕ Time Warner	Media	27.5	8.12	1.30

Current Investment Style

Value Blnd Growth / Large Mid Small

Market Cap	%
Giant	53.5
Large	32.0
Mid	14.3
Small	0.2
Micro	0.0

Avg $mil: 39,300

Value Measures		Rel Category
Price/Earnings	13.41	0.89
Price/Book	2.06	0.91
Price/Sales	0.99	0.83
Price/Cash Flow	6.24	0.98
Dividend Yield %	2.30	1.13

Growth Measures	%	Rel Category
Long-Term Erngs	10.68	1.03
Book Value	5.15	0.91
Sales	4.96	1.18
Cash Flow	0.71	0.14
Historical Erngs	18.38	1.55

Profitability	%	Rel Category
Return on Equity	16.57	1.04
Return on Assets	9.05	1.16
Net Margin	10.35	1.01

Sector Weightings	% of Stocks	Rel S&P 500	3 Year High	3 Year Low
Info	14.69	0.68		
Software	2.00	0.47	2	1
Hardware	3.66	0.36	4	3
Media	2.76	0.72	3	1
Telecom	6.27	1.99	7	4
Service	50.77	1.09		
Health	7.62	0.61	9	8
Consumer	6.26	0.69	7	4
Business	3.63	0.90	5	3
Financial	33.26	1.60	34	31
Mfg	34.55	1.08		
Goods	9.75	1.05	10	7
Ind Mtrls	11.11	0.88	12	10
Energy	10.49	1.47	14	10
Utilities	3.20	1.08	7	3

Composition

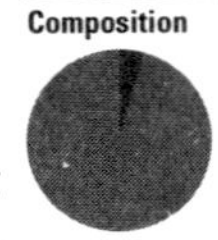

Cash	4.2
Stocks	95.8
Bonds	0.0
Other	0.0
Foreign (% of Stock)	4.8

Morningstar's Take by Dan Culloton 12-14-04

A lot of small things add up to big ones at American Century Large Company Value.

This fund has an experienced management team that has a fine record since its inception five years ago. From the offering's July 1999 launch through the end of November 2004 the portfolio has trounced the annualized 2.8% gain of the typical large-value fund with an annualized advance of nearly 6%.

The management team tries to keep things simple. It relies on a low-turnover brand of stock-picking that is heavily influenced by computer screens. The managers generally try to purchase stocks that have decent growth prospects, but have fallen out of favor because of transitory operational or industry-related factors. For example, earlier in the year the fund added to its stake in Royal Dutch Petroleum because the managers thought the stock's price underestimated its potential, despite doubts about the accuracy of the oil company's reserve accounting. Similarly, as concerns about rising interest rates weighed on Citigroup, this fund has maintained its large position because its managers think the financial conglomerate is large and diversified enough to weather rising rates.

This is a fairly standard, diversified value-investing strategy, but it has served this offering well. The only problem we have with this fund is that its cheapest shares are closed to new investors. The Investor share class is shut not due to capacity constraints (the fund's asset base remains reasonable for this category), but because a year ago, American Century introduced load-bearing shares of this fund. The expense ratios among most of this fund's shares with sales charges are below average for their peers with similar fee structures, but its cheapest share class remains off limits to new investors.

Despite this caveat, the fund's experienced management and sober approach make it worth keeping if you already own it, and keeping in mind if you don't.

Address:	P O Box 419200 Kansas City, MO 64141-6200 800-345-2021
Web Address:	www.americancentury.com
Inception:	07-30-99*
Advisor:	American Century Investment Mgt Inc.
Subadvisor:	None
NTF Plans:	Schwab OneSource, Accutrade NTF

Minimum Purchase:	Closed	Add: —	IRA: —
Min Auto Inv Plan:	Closed	Add: —	
Sales Fees:	No-load		
Management Fee:	0.90% mx./0.80% mn.		
Actual Fees:	Mgt:0.90%	Dist:	
Expense Projections:	3Yr:$286	5Yr:$497	10Yr:$1104
Income Distrib:	Quarterly		

AmCent Select Inv

Ticker	Load	NAV	Yield	Total Assets	Mstar Category
TWCIX	None	$38.08	0.2%	$4,110 mil	Large Growth

Governance and Management

Fiduciary Grade: B

Portfolio Manager(s)

John Sykora came aboard in September 2002 following a successful five-year stint at American Century Ultra. Keith Lee, who had been one of the fund's analysts for three years, was promoted to portfolio manager in June 2003. Lee was an analyst for American Century in the early 1990s, and before rejoining the firm in the late 1990s, he worked as an analyst for a hedge fund. The managers are assisted by three analysts.

Strategy

This offering is a tamer version of American Century Ultra and American Century Growth. Although its siblings employ similar earnings-acceleration strategies, managers John Sykora and Keith Lee better diversify the portfolio by sector and have a greater tolerance for companies whose earnings are improving at slower rates. Although the fund remains one of the large-growth group's more-temperate options, expect added volatility here; management has made larger bets against its S&P 500 benchmark. Further, the fund has become more reliant on nondividend-paying stocks.

Performance 12-31-04

	1st Qtr	2nd Qtr	3rd Qtr	4th Qtr	Total
2000	5.18	-3.05	-0.73	-9.83	-8.71
2001	-14.64	3.60	-13.91	7.49	-18.16
2002	-0.70	-12.90	-15.44	5.59	-22.77
2003	-2.39	15.92	1.43	8.68	24.74
2004	1.83	1.16	-4.48	9.10	7.35

Trailing	Total Return%	+/- S&P 500	+/- Russ 1000Gr	%Rank Cat	Growth of $10,000
3 Mo	9.10	-0.13	-0.07	66	10,910
6 Mo	4.21	-2.98	0.74	59	10,421
1 Yr	7.35	-3.52	1.05	50	10,735
3 Yr Avg	1.12	-2.46	1.30	31	10,340
5 Yr Avg	-5.03	-2.73	4.26	26	7,726
10 Yr Avg	9.50	-2.57	-0.09	42	24,782
15 Yr Avg	8.17	-2.76	-1.33	74	32,479

Tax Analysis	Tax-Adj Rtn%	%Rank Cat	Tax-Cost Rat	%Rank Cat
3 Yr (estimated)	1.06	27	0.06	11
5 Yr (estimated)	-5.30	23	0.28	17
10 Yr (estimated)	7.34	50	1.97	72

Potential Capital Gain Exposure: 10% of assets

Historical Profile

Return Above Avg
Risk Below Avg
Rating ★★★★ Above Avg

Investment Style: Equity Stock %	100%	96%	92%	93%	91%	90%	91%	98%	98%

▼ Manager Change
▽ Partial Manager Change

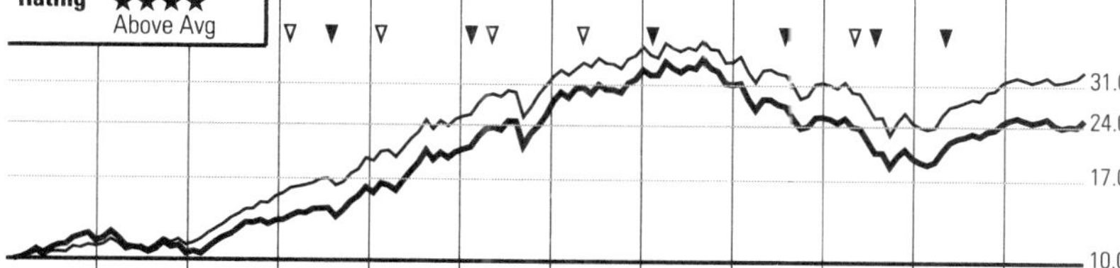

Performance Quartile (within Category)

1993	1994	1995	1996	1997	1998	1999	2000	2001	2002	2003	12-04	History
39.46	33.10	35.62	38.53	42.59	47.39	52.68	45.29	37.00	28.50	35.55	38.08	NAV
14.67	-8.04	22.67	19.22	32.19	35.72	22.23	-8.71	-18.16	-22.77	24.74	7.35	Total Return %
4.61	-9.35	-14.86	-3.72	-1.16	7.15	1.19	0.39	-6.28	-0.68	-3.93	-3.52	+/-S&P 500
11.80	-10.66	-14.51	-3.90	1.70	-2.99	-10.93	13.71	2.26	5.11	-5.01	1.05	+/-Russ 1000Gr
1.12	0.71	0.81	0.91	0.51	0.40	0.00	0.00	0.14	0.20	0.00	0.23	Income Return %
13.55	-8.75	21.86	18.31	31.68	35.32	22.23	-8.71	-18.30	-22.97	24.74	7.12	Capital Return %
32	94	94	53	18	34	79	32	38	19	68	50	Total Rtn % Rank Cat
0.43	0.28	0.27	0.32	0.20	0.17	0.00	0.00	0.06	0.07	0.00	0.08	Income $
4.47	2.87	4.66	3.68	7.93	9.79	5.10	2.73	0.00	0.00	0.00	0.00	Capital Gains $
1.00	1.00	1.00	1.00	1.00	1.00	1.00	1.00	1.00	1.00	1.00	—	Expense Ratio %
1.10	1.00	0.90	0.50	0.33	0.25	0.03	-0.11	0.15	0.21	0.03	—	Income Ratio %
82	126	106	105	94	165	130	67	98	168	84	—	Turnover Rate %
4,976	3,995	3,983	4,060	5,006	6,498	7,674	6,475	4,973	3,444	3,984	3,818	Net Assets $mil

Rating and Risk

Time Period	Load-Adj Return %	Morningstar Rtn vs Cat	Morningstar Risk vs Cat	Morningstar Risk-Adj Rating
1 Yr	7.35			
3 Yr	1.12	+Avg	-Avg	★★★★
5 Yr	-5.03	+Avg	Low	★★★★
10 Yr	9.50	Avg	-Avg	★★★★
Incept	9.26			

Other Measures	Standard Index S&P 500	Best Fit Index Russ 1000
Alpha	-2.2	-2.8
Beta	0.88	0.89
R-Squared	95	95
Standard Deviation	13.69	
Mean	1.12	
Sharpe Ratio	-0.02	

Portfolio Analysis 09-30-04

Share change since 06-04 Total Stocks:84	Sector	PE	YTD Ret%	% Assets
⊖ UnitedHealth Group	Health	23.8	51.38	5.49
⊖ Aramark	Consumer	18.9	-2.53	3.64
Gen Elec	Ind Mtrls	22.8	20.68	3.57
Four Seasons Hotel	Consumer	—	60.10	3.49
⊕ Microsoft	Software	36.1	8.95	3.48
⊕ Yankee Candle Company	Ind Mtrls	20.9	21.41	3.28
⊖ Carnival	Goods	26.2	46.74	3.15
Johnson & Johnson	Health	20.6	25.17	3.04
Dell	Hardware	34.0	24.01	2.77
⊖ Iac / Interactivecorp	Consumer	43.1	-18.60	2.57
American International G	Financial	16.2	-0.53	2.39
⊕ SLM	Financial	15.8	44.21	2.37
Weight Watchers Intl	Consumer	23.9	7.04	2.24
⊕ Citigroup	Financial	15.3	2.72	2.04
Altana Grp	Health	—	—	2.01
⊖ Eli Lilly & Company	Health	24.3	-17.55	2.01
⊖ PepsiCo	Goods	22.5	13.82	1.88
⊖ Nestle	Goods	—	—	1.73
Berkshire Hathaway A	Financial	—	—	1.55
⊕ eBay	Consumer	81.6	80.07	1.52

Current Investment Style

Value Blnd Growth — Large Mid Small

Market Cap	%
Giant	43.9
Large	33.0
Mid	19.1
Small	4.0
Micro	0.0
Avg $mil: 30,610	

Value Measures		Rel Category
Price/Earnings	19.12	0.90
Price/Book	3.36	1.04
Price/Sales	2.09	0.97
Price/Cash Flow	10.56	0.96
Dividend Yield %	0.92	1.19

Growth Measures	%	Rel Category
Long-Term Erngs	13.82	0.98
Book Value	16.10	1.27
Sales	10.19	1.20
Cash Flow	9.21	0.56
Historical Erngs	16.09	1.11

Profitability	%	Rel Category
Return on Equity	24.25	1.35
Return on Assets	12.44	1.33
Net Margin	14.58	1.18

Sector Weightings	% of Stocks	Rel S&P 500	3 Year High	3 Year Low
Info	13.13	0.61		
Software	5.31	1.23	5	2
Hardware	6.71	0.66	10	1
Media	0.06	0.02	8	0
Telecom	1.05	0.33	4	0
Service	60.60	1.31		
Health	21.11	1.69	23	14
Consumer	19.86	2.19	20	9
Business	4.87	1.20	7	4
Financial	14.76	0.71	21	13
Mfg	26.25	0.82		
Goods	13.61	1.46	17	8
Ind Mtrls	8.77	0.69	15	5
Energy	3.87	0.54	10	1
Utilities	0.00	0.00	1	0

Composition

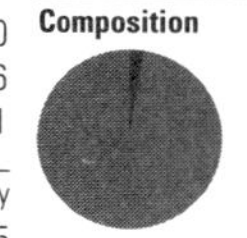

Cash	2.3
Stocks	97.7
Bonds	0.0
Other	0.0
Foreign (% of Stock)	7.9

Morningstar's Take by Christopher Davis 10-15-04

American Century Select Fund may have revved up its engine, but it's still no speed demon. And that's a good thing.

In constructing his portfolio, lead manager John Sykora has been willing to deviate substantially from his S&P 500 bogy. This approach contrasts markedly with that of his predecessors, whose benchmark-conscious style meant the fund straddled the large-blend and large-growth camps. Under Sykora, who came aboard in early 2003, the fund has marched deeper into large-growth territory.

Sykora, along with comanager Keith Lee, has hardly thrown caution to the wind, however. Pricier, faster-growing holdings such as Amgen, Cisco Systems, and eBay rub elbows here with less-expensive fare like Anheuser-Busch, Berkshire Hathaway, and Bank of New York, which still offer steady, if less-than-spectacular growth prospects. As such, the portfolio's price multiples align with those of its typical peer. The fund is also more diversified by sector than most rivals and features much less exposure to tech stocks than average.

Even so, Sykora's more growth-oriented tack means longtime shareholders should expect more volatility here than they might have grown accustomed to. In a fairly tough market for growth stocks in 2004, though, the fund has held its own. A light tech stake, coupled with winners like Carnival and Four Seasons, have pushed it a bit ahead of its large-growth rivals.

For those that can tolerate a bit bumpier ride, we think this offering is worth keeping. Sykora is experienced and helped build a strong record in his five years at American Century Ultra, which also shares this offering's earnings-acceleration ethos. Moreover, Lee was a longtime analyst for the fund prior to being named comanager in 2003, which means he's well versed in its strategy as well. With a sound strategy and seasoned management, we think this offering remains a respectable choice for large-growth exposure.

Address:	4500 Main St Kansas City MO 64141 800-345-2021
Web Address:	www.americancentury.com
Inception:	10-31-58
Advisor:	American Century Investment Mgt Inc.
Subadvisor:	None
NTF Plans:	Schwab OneSource, Accutrade NTF

Minimum Purchase:	$2500	Add: $50	IRA: $2500
Min Auto Inv Plan:	$2500	Add: $50	
Sales Fees:	No-load		
Management Fee:	1.00% mx./0.88% mn.		
Actual Fees:	Mgt:1.00%	Dist:	
Expense Projections:	3Yr:$318	5Yr:$551	10Yr:$1219
Income Distrib:	Annually		

AmCent Small Cap Val Inv

Ticker	Load	NAV	Yield	Total Assets	Mstar Category
ASVIX	Closed	$10.17	0.3%	$2,166 mil	Small Value

Governance and Management

Fiduciary Grade: B

Portfolio Manager(s)

Ben Giele and Kevin Laub have been here right from the start. Prior to February 1999, Giele was an analyst on the fund. Laub was named comanager in February 2003 but had joined the fund with Giele as an analyst. The pair is assisted by two analysts, James Pittman and Steve Roth. Both came aboard in 2002.

Strategy

Managers Ben Giele and Kevin Laub look for stocks that are cheap based on measures such as dividends, cash flow, earnings, and book value. They are quick to sell stocks that they think have appreciated beyond their fair value estimates, giving the fund a turnover rate considerably above the small-value norm. Sector weightings are kept within 10 percentage points of the S&P/Barra SmallCap Value Index's.

Historical Profile

Return Above Avg
Risk Average
Rating ★★★★ Above Avg

Investment Style
Equity
Stock %

96% 90% 85% 90% 91% 93% 94%

▼ Manager Change
∇ Partial Manager Change

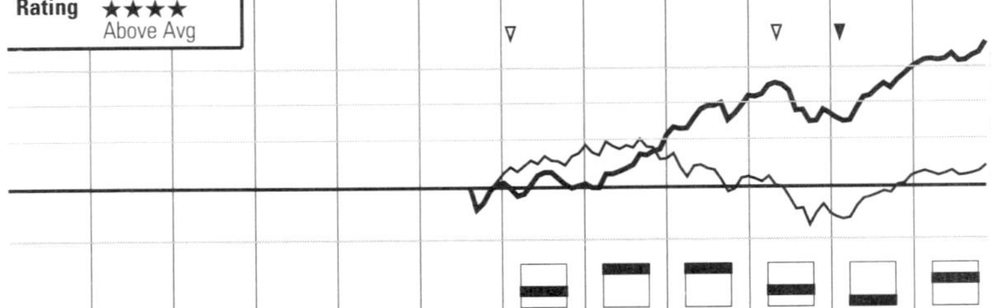

Growth of $10,000
— Investment Values of Fund
— Investment Values of S&P 500

Performance Quartile (within Category)

1993	1994	1995	1996	1997	1998	1999	2000	2001	2002	2003	12-04	History
—	—	—	—	—	5.12	4.73	6.32	8.02	6.79	9.18	10.17	NAV
—	—	—	—	—	3.31*	-0.86	39.41	30.52	-11.38	36.11	21.81	Total Return %
—	—	—	—	—	—	-21.90	48.51	42.40	10.71	7.44	10.94	+/-S&P 500
—	—	—	—	—	—	0.63	16.58	16.50	0.05	-9.92	-0.44	+/-Russ 2000 VL
—	—	—	—	—	0.00	1.06	1.08	0.59	0.00	0.75	0.31	Income Return %
—	—	—	—	—	—	-1.92	38.33	29.93	-11.38	35.36	21.50	Capital Return %
—	—	—	—	—	—	62	2	8	60	80	45	Total Rtn % Rank Cat
—	—	—	—	—	0.00	0.05	0.05	0.04	0.00	0.05	0.03	Income $
—	—	—	—	—	0.04	0.28	0.20	0.18	0.32	0.00	0.95	Capital Gains $
—	—	—	—	—	—	1.25	1.25	1.25	1.25	1.25	1.26	Expense Ratio %
—	—	—	—	—	—	1.02	1.04	1.10	0.27	0.37	0.59	Income Ratio %
—	—	—	—	—	—	153	178	144	73	104	110	Turnover Rate %
—	—	—	—	—	12	19	66	1,090	784	972	1,248	Net Assets $mil

Performance 12-31-04

	1st Qtr	2nd Qtr	3rd Qtr	4th Qtr	Total
2000	6.94	3.85	9.37	14.79	39.41
2001	4.71	16.48	-9.24	17.91	30.52
2002	7.48	-3.71	-19.04	5.76	-11.38
2003	-4.85	18.62	5.24	14.57	36.11
2004	5.94	3.67	-1.29	12.36	21.81

Trailing	Total Return%	+/- S&P 500	+/- Russ 2000 VL	%Rank Cat	Growth of $10,000
3 Mo	12.36	3.13	-0.84	59	11,236
6 Mo	10.90	3.71	-2.47	62	11,090
1 Yr	21.81	10.94	-0.44	45	12,181
3 Yr Avg	13.68	10.10	-2.82	68	14,691
5 Yr Avg	21.73	24.03	4.50	6	26,729
10 Yr Avg	—	—	—	—	—
15 Yr Avg	—	—	—	—	—

Tax Analysis	Tax-Adj Rtn%	%Rank Cat	Tax-Cost Rat	%Rank Cat
3 Yr (estimated)	11.99	69	1.49	75
5 Yr (estimated)	20.01	7	1.41	72
10 Yr (estimated)	—	—	—	—

Potential Capital Gain Exposure: 21% of assets

Rating and Risk

Time Period	Load-Adj Return %	Morningstar Rtn vs Cat	Morningstar Risk vs Cat	Morningstar Risk-Adj Rating
1 Yr	21.81			
3 Yr	13.68	Avg	-Avg	★★★
5 Yr	21.73	High	Avg	★★★★★
10 Yr	—	—	—	—
Incept	16.98			

Other Measures	Standard Index S&P 500	Best Fit Index Russ 2000 VL
Alpha	10.4	-0.4
Beta	0.84	0.84
R-Squared	67	93
Standard Deviation	17.39	
Mean	13.68	
Sharpe Ratio	0.72	

Portfolio Analysis 09-30-04

Share change since 06-04 Total Stocks:152	Sector	PE	YTD Ret%	% Assets
⊕ Sybase	Software	21.9	-3.06	2.54
⊖ iShares Russell 2000 Ind	—	—	—	1.85
⊕ Snap-on	Ind Mtrls	25.6	9.99	1.51
⊕ Platinum Underwriters Ho	Financial	16.1	4.76	1.37
⊕ Imation	Hardware	17.7	-8.48	1.33
⊖ Olin	Ind Mtrls	—	14.81	1.31
⊕ Bemis	Goods	18.5	19.23	1.30
⊖ Universal Health Service	Health	14.9	-16.59	1.27
⊖ Sensient Technologies	Goods	14.3	24.91	1.18
⊕ A.O. Smith	Ind Mtrls	18.3	-12.75	1.16
⊕ iShares Russell 2000 Val	—	—	—	1.16
⊕ iShares S&P SmallCap 600	—	—	—	1.15
⊕ United Defense Industrie	Ind Mtrls	14.2	48.21	1.10
⊕ HCC Insurance Holdings	Financial	17.0	5.19	1.09
⊖ Kaydon	Ind Mtrls	21.9	29.90	1.06
⊕ SkyWest	Business	13.1	11.79	1.04
⊕ Helmerich & Payne	Energy	70.9	23.36	1.01
⊖ Superior Industries Inte	Ind Mtrls	12.6	-32.12	1.00
⊕ THQ	Software	32.1	35.66	0.98
⊖ Idacorp	Utilities	18.2	6.37	0.96

Current Investment Style

Value Blnd Growth / Large Mid Small

Market Cap	%
Giant	0.0
Large	0.0
Mid	32.9
Small	63.9
Micro	3.2
Avg $mil: 1,198	

Value Measures		Rel Category
Price/Earnings	16.94	1.06
Price/Book	1.77	1.07
Price/Sales	0.89	1.19
Price/Cash Flow	6.83	1.32
Dividend Yield %	1.33	1.11

Growth Measures	%	Rel Category
Long-Term Erngs	11.23	0.93
Book Value	7.73	1.79
Sales	5.57	1.78
Cash Flow	-3.01	NMF
Historical Erngs	2.63	0.55

Profitability	%	Rel Category
Return on Equity	12.21	1.34
Return on Assets	5.73	1.38
Net Margin	8.48	1.27

Sector Weightings	% of Stocks	Rel S&P 500	3 Year High	Low
Info	14.96	0.70		
Software	7.11	1.65	9	4
Hardware	4.86	0.48	6	4
Media	2.94	0.77	3	1
Telecom	0.05	0.02	0	0
Service	47.64	1.03		
Health	8.37	0.67	12	7
Consumer	9.79	1.08	11	7
Business	10.81	2.67	11	6
Financial	18.67	0.90	20	13
Mfg	37.39	1.16		
Goods	9.12	0.98	13	8
Ind Mtrls	16.14	1.27	20	15
Energy	8.01	1.12	10	7
Utilities	4.12	1.39	7	4

Composition

Cash	4.6
Stocks	93.9
Bonds	0.0
Other	1.5
Foreign (% of Stock)	0.0

Morningstar's Take by Christopher Davis 12-01-04

There's good reason to stay the course with American Century Small-Cap Value, but shareholders should temper their expectations for its future.

Investors who flocked to this offering before it closed in 2001 may have wondered if they came aboard after its best days had come and gone. After trouncing its rivals as small-value stocks surged in 2000 and 2001, the fund lagged its rivals in the subsequent two years. It has gotten back in the saddle in 2004, however. Picks such as Bemis and Dade Behring Holdings have propelled the fund to an 18% gain for the year to date through Nov. 29, 2004, placing it well ahead of its typical rival.

Of course, whether the fund can produce strong returns in any given year isn't nearly as important as what it can deliver over the long haul. On that score, we think the fund should fare well. For one, it employs a consistent, disciplined strategy. Managers Ben Geile and Kevin Laub require their picks to trade in the cheapest third of the small-cap universe on at least two of five valuation measures and they move quickly to sell stocks that have gotten too pricey. We're heartened that strategy has not only been successful here, but it has also worked well in a similar incarnation at all-cap American Century Value. We also like the fact that Geile and Laub have been here from the fund's 1998 inception--first as analysts and then as managers--so they're partly responsible for its impressive record.

Nevertheless, investors may want to pare their stakes in this fund as they rebalance their portfolios. Small-value stocks--management's stomping grounds--have outpaced most areas of the market in recent years, leaving them with much higher valuations and less upside potential. As such, the group may be due for a cool down. While we think this offering's sound strategy and capable management continue to make it a worthy long-term holding, it's best held in smaller quantities.

Address:	P O Box 419200 Kansas City, MO 64141-6200 800-345-2021
Web Address:	www.americancentury.com
Inception:	07-30-98 *
Advisor:	American Century Investment Mgt Inc.
Subadvisor:	None
NTF Plans:	Schwab OneSource, Accutrade NTF

Minimum Purchase:	Closed	Add: —	IRA: —
Min Auto Inv Plan:	Closed	Add: —	
Sales Fees:	No-load		
Management Fee:	1.25%		
Actual Fees:	Mgt:1.25%	Dist:	
Expense Projections:	3Yr:$395	5Yr:$683	10Yr:$1503
Income Distrib:	Quarterly		

AmCent Tax-Free Bond Inv

Ticker	Load	NAV	Yield	SEC Yield	Total Assets	Mstar Category
TWTIX	None	$10.91	3.3%	2.77%	$597 mil	Muni National Interm

Governance and Management

Fiduciary Grade:

Portfolio Manager(s)

Ken Salinger took over in July 1999. He has been with the firm since 1992. Although he's the lead manager of this portfolio, he relies on a team of other American Century muni managers to help formulate strategy and high-level tactics.

Strategy

This fund employs a pretty conservative strategy. Its credit quality is generally high (with more than 80% of assets in AA or AAA rated bonds), and manager Ken Salinger keeps duration within a tight range of a self-selected peer group. He also looks for undervalued bonds and makes bets on the yield curve, adding or subtracting lower-rated securities as market yields dictate.

Historical Profile

Return Average
Risk Average
Rating ★★★★ Above Avg

Investment Style: Fixed Income — Income Rtn %Rank Cat: 54, 39, 27, 25, 32, 31, 50, 57, 53

▼ Manager Change
▽ Partial Manager Change

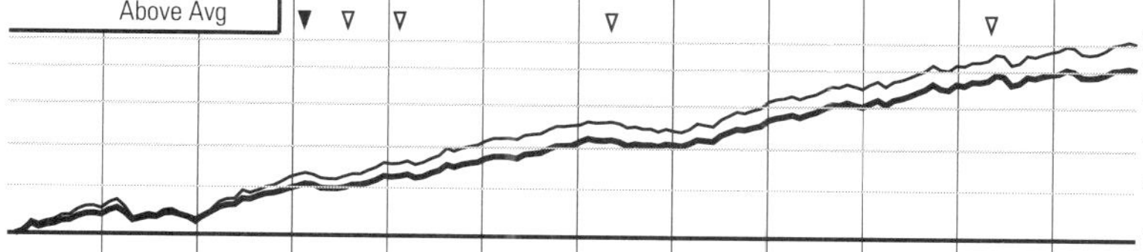

Growth of $10,000
— Investment Values of Fund
— Investment Values of LB Muni

Performance Quartile (within Category)

1993	1994	1995	1996	1997	1998	1999	2000	2001	2002	2003	12-04	History
10.66	9.88	10.48	10.37	10.54	10.58	9.99	10.46	10.45	10.96	10.99	10.91	NAV
9.10	-1.93	11.92	3.86	7.44	6.74	-0.93	9.77	5.25	9.12	3.99	2.65	Total Return %
-3.18	3.24	-5.54	-0.57	-1.75	0.26	1.13	-1.91	0.12	-0.48	-1.32	-1.83	+/-LB Muni
-3.67	2.84	-5.25	-0.68	-1.80	-0.02	0.31	-0.99	0.63	-1.05	-1.71	-1.50	+/-LB Muni 10YR
4.74	4.72	5.00	4.65	4.80	4.67	4.56	4.92	4.51	3.99	3.48	3.37	Income Return %
4.36	-6.65	6.92	-0.79	2.64	2.07	-5.49	4.85	0.74	5.13	0.51	-0.72	Capital Return %
78	18	85	43	53	3	19	39	11	33	57	57	Total Rtn % Rank Cat
0.48	0.49	0.48	0.48	0.49	0.48	0.47	0.43	0.46	0.41	0.38	0.36	Income $
0.13	0.08	0.07	0.02	0.09	0.17	0.02	0.00	0.09	0.02	0.02	0.00	Capital Gains $
0.72	0.60	0.60	0.60	0.58	0.51	0.51	0.51	0.51	0.51	0.51	0.51	Expense Ratio %
4.51	4.59	4.77	4.66	4.71	4.62	4.52	4.75	4.65	4.14	3.62	3.34	Income Ratio %
38	74	32	39	35	17	32	107	106	86	57	60	Turnover Rate %
97	77	82	79	133	147	161	163	316	556	605	590	Net Assets $mil

Performance 12-31-04

	1st Qtr	2nd Qtr	3rd Qtr	4th Qtr	Total
2000	1.98	1.70	2.08	3.63	9.77
2001	2.08	1.01	2.71	-0.63	5.25
2002	0.87	3.48	4.51	0.03	9.12
2003	0.79	2.25	-0.13	1.04	3.99
2004	1.07	-2.09	2.83	0.88	2.65

Trailing	Total Return%	+/- LB Muni	+/- LB Muni 10YR	%Rank Cat	Growth of $10,000
3 Mo	0.88	-0.37	0.05	27	10,088
6 Mo	3.73	-1.46	-1.27	55	10,373
1 Yr	2.65	-1.83	-1.50	57	10,265
3 Yr Avg	5.22	-1.22	-1.42	45	11,649
5 Yr Avg	6.12	-1.08	-0.92	29	13,458
10 Yr Avg	5.92	-1.14	-1.16	33	17,774
15 Yr Avg	6.42	-0.57	-0.66	24	25,430

Tax Analysis	Tax-Adj Rtn%	%Rank Cat	Tax-Cost Rat	%Rank Cat
3 Yr (estimated)	5.19	27	0.03	10
5 Yr (estimated)	6.04	18	0.08	32
10 Yr (estimated)	5.77	29	0.14	70

Potential Capital Gain Exposure: 1% of assets

Rating and Risk

Time Period	Load-Adj Return %	Morningstar Rtn vs Cat	Morningstar Risk vs Cat	Morningstar Risk-Adj Rating
1 Yr	2.65			
3 Yr	5.22	Avg	Avg	★★★
5 Yr	6.12	+Avg	Avg	★★★★
10 Yr	5.92	Avg	Avg	★★★★
Incept	6.12			

Other Measures	Standard Index LB Aggr	Best Fit Index LB Muni
Alpha	-0.8	-0.8
Beta	0.93	0.93
R-Squared	98	98

Standard Deviation	4.67
Mean	5.22
Sharpe Ratio	0.83

Portfolio Analysis 09-30-04

Total Fixed-Income:265	Date of Maturity	Amount $000	Value $000	% Net Assets
Chicago Ill Brd Ed 5.5%	12-01-31	13,355	15,215	2.52
Massachusetts St 5%	12-01-07	10,000	10,844	1.80
Maryland St 5%	08-01-07	10,000	10,819	1.79
Hawaii St 6.25%	03-01-06	10,000	10,617	1.76
Massachusetts St 5.25%	01-01-15	10,000	10,529	1.74
Engy Northwest Wash Elec	07-01-18	9,000	10,463	1.73
Birmingham Baptist Med C	11-15-16	10,000	10,000	1.66
Portland Ore Swr Sys 4%	06-01-08	8,200	8,654	1.43
King Cnty Wash 5.5%	12-01-12	7,145	8,192	1.36
Greenville Cnty S C Sch	12-01-24	7,110	7,382	1.22
New Jersey St Tran 5%	10-01-13	5,595	6,209	1.03
Long Island Pwr Auth 5%	12-01-06	5,790	6,155	1.02
Univ Colo Regts Partn In	10-01-22	5,000	5,734	0.95
New York N Y 5.75%	03-01-20	5,000	5,602	0.93
California St 5.625%	05-01-20	5,000	5,565	0.92

Current Investment Style

Duration: Short Int Long; Quality: High Med Low

[1]Avg Eff Duration	4.2 Yrs
Avg Eff Maturity	9.0 Yrs
Avg Credit Quality	AA
Avg Wtd Coupon	5.18%
Avg Wtd Price	108.92% of par

[1]figure provided by fund

Credit Analysis	% bonds 09-30-04		
US Govt	0	BB	0
AAA	73	B	0
AA	11	Below B	0
A	3	NR/NA	0
BBB	3		

Top 5 States	% bonds		
TX	9.2	CA	7.4
WA	7.9	IL	6.4
AZ	7.8		

Composition			
Cash	4.4	Bonds	95.6
Stocks	0.0	Other	0.0

Special Securities	
Restricted/Illiquid Secs	0
Options/Futures/Warrants	No

Sector Weightings	% of Bonds	Rel Cat
General Obligation	36.8	1.04
Utilities	14.9	1.35
Health	6.9	0.94
Water/Waste	11.9	1.20
Housing	0.3	0.05
Education	16.0	1.14
Transportation	4.4	0.80
COP/Lease	2.8	1.84
Industrial	5.7	0.64
Misc Revenue	0.0	0.00
Demand	0.2	0.48

Morningstar's Take by Eric Jacobson 01-06-05

American Century Tax-Free Bond has been paying a price, however modest, for its caution.

This fund has built its reputation on caution and simplicity. Chock full of AAA and AA rated issues, the fund takes on only minimal credit risk. The fund has historically kept its interest-rate sensitivity pretty close to that of a selected peer group, as well, in order to minimize the trouble that outsized bets can produce. And although manager Ken Salinger does have some freedom to use more eclectic tools, he hasn't generally loaded up on the futures, swaps, and derivatives that others have used both to hedge and to try to juice returns. Although not all such strategies are inherently risky, a misapplied hedge can easily cause a fund to lag under the wrong combination of circumstances.

But while a large degree of caution has become more fashionable among nearly all bond managers as interest rates have hovered near generational lows for the past two years, it hasn't been entirely beneficial here. Owing in part to its own benchmarking but also to a tactical decision to rein in the fund's interest-rate risk, its duration has been a bit short for some time. So even though some other managerial decisions have borne fruit, such as a short and long maturity spectrum placement, they haven't been sufficient to offset the fund's duration stance, as stable to falling market yields have benefited many rivals over the past two years. By contrast, this fund's returns in both 2003 and 2004 have been shy of the muni national intermediate category average.

That said, we don't view any of that as a major problem. The fund has still managed to generate solid long-term returns, it has been clear about its cautious mandate, and investors have indeed been well protected from bigger problems. Its modest cost structure also helps the fund's appeal, as it offsets a style that, by design, isn't meant to pump out fat returns. There are more exciting choices available, but this one is a nice, reasonable option.

Address:	4500 Main Street Kansas City MO 64111 800-345-2021
Web Address:	www.americancentury.com
Inception:	03-02-87
Advisor:	American Century Investment Mgt Inc.
Subadvisor:	None
NTF Plans:	Schwab OneSource, Accutrade NTF

Minimum Purchase:	$5000	Add: $50	IRA: $0
Min Auto Inv Plan:	$5000	Add: $50	
Sales Fees:	No-load		
Management Fee:	0.51%, 0.11%A		
Actual Fees:	Mgt:0.50%	Dist:	
Expense Projections:	3Yr:$163	5Yr:$285	10Yr:$640
Income Distrib:	Monthly		

AmCent Ultra Inv

Ticker	Load	NAV	Yield	Total Assets	Mstar Category
TWCUX	None	$29.50	0.0%	$24,050 mil	Large Growth

Governance and Management

Fiduciary Grade: B

Portfolio Manager(s)

Jim Stowers III has been part of this fund's management team since 1981. Bruce Wimberly, Jerry Sullivan, and Wade Slome handle day-to-day management. Wimberly has been at the helm since 1996. Sullivan came aboard in 2001. Slome joined in 2002 after serving as one of the fund's analysts. Four analysts are dedicated to the fund.

Strategy

Like all American Century growth offerings, management focuses on companies with accelerating earnings-growth rates and look for those whose growth is sustainable. Although the fund has exposure to traditional growth sectors, such as health care and technology, management will also pick up less-conventional industrial or consumer-staples stocks that meet its criteria. In a concession to the fund's size, management has recently cut turnover and now seeks companies that the fund can own for two to three years. Management is also far less likely to make the huge sector bets that were once the norm at this fund.

Historical Profile

Return Above Avg
Risk Average
Rating ★★★ Neutral

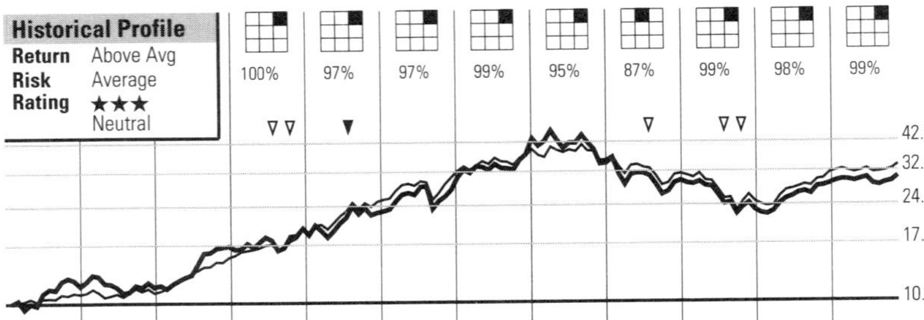

Investment Style
Equity
Stock %

▼ Manager Change
▽ Partial Manager Change

Growth of $10,000
— Investment Values of Fund
— Investment Values of S&P 500

Performance Quartile (within Category)

History

1993	1994	1995	1996	1997	1998	1999	2000	2001	2002	2003	12-04	History
21.39	19.95	26.11	28.09	27.30	33.41	45.78	32.37	27.64	21.18	26.65	29.50	NAV
21.81	-3.62	37.68	13.85	23.13	34.56	41.46	-19.91	-14.61	-23.15	25.83	10.69	Total Return %
11.75	-4.93	0.15	-9.09	-10.22	5.99	20.42	-10.81	-2.73	-1.06	-2.84	-0.18	+/-S&P 500
18.94	-6.24	0.50	-9.27	-7.36	-4.15	8.30	2.51	5.81	4.73	-3.92	4.39	+/-Russ 1000Gr
0.00	0.00	0.00	0.00	0.05	0.00	0.00	0.00	0.00	0.23	0.00	0.00	Income Return %
21.81	-3.62	37.68	13.85	23.08	34.56	41.46	-19.91	-14.61	-23.38	25.83	10.69	Capital Return %
12	69	19	86	69	39	34	76	21	21	58	24	Total Rtn % Rank Cat
0.00	0.00	0.00	0.00	0.01	0.00	0.00	0.00	0.00	0.06	0.00	0.00	Income $
0.00	0.65	1.30	1.69	7.07	3.12	1.38	4.41	0.00	0.00	0.00	0.00	Capital Gains $
1.00	1.00	1.00	1.00	1.00	1.00	1.00	0.99	0.98	0.99	1.00	—	Expense Ratio %
-0.60	-0.10	-0.30	-0.20	0.03	-0.08	-0.39	-0.64	-0.18	0.24	-0.09	—	Income Ratio %
53	78	87	87	107	128	42	62	86	92	82	—	Turnover Rate %
8,353	9,851	14,551	18,419	22,420	30,076	43,193	33,784	26,911	17,972	21,744	21,998	Net Assets $mil

Performance 12-31-04

	1st Qtr	2nd Qtr	3rd Qtr	4th Qtr	Total
2000	7.21	-10.31	0.23	-16.90	-19.91
2001	-17.49	10.45	-17.15	13.09	-14.61
2002	-1.05	-11.26	-15.41	3.47	-23.15
2003	-1.23	13.86	2.39	9.27	25.83
2004	3.41	1.74	-4.35	9.99	10.69

Trailing	Total Return%	+/- S&P 500	+/- Russ 1000Gr	%Rank Cat	Growth of $10,000
3 Mo	9.99	0.76	0.82	48	10,999
6 Mo	5.21	-1.98	1.74	43	10,521
1 Yr	10.69	-0.18	4.39	24	11,069
3 Yr Avg	2.29	-1.29	2.47	23	10,703
5 Yr Avg	-6.05	-3.75	3.24	35	7,320
10 Yr Avg	10.40	-1.67	0.81	30	26,896
15 Yr Avg	13.31	2.38	3.81	4	65,166

Tax Analysis	Tax-Adj Rtn%	%Rank Cat	Tax-Cost Rat	%Rank Cat
3 Yr (estimated)	2.26	20	0.03	6
5 Yr (estimated)	-6.55	32	0.53	32
10 Yr (estimated)	8.88	23	1.38	43

Potential Capital Gain Exposure: 22% of assets

Rating and Risk

Time Period	Load-Adj Return %	Morningstar Rtn vs Cat	Morningstar Risk vs Cat	Morningstar Risk-Adj Rating
1 Yr	10.69			
3 Yr	2.29	+Avg	-Avg	★★★★
5 Yr	-6.05	Avg	Avg	★★★
10 Yr	10.40	+Avg	Avg	★★★
Incept	13.73			

Other Measures	Standard Index S&P 500	Best Fit Index Russ 1000
Alpha	-1.0	-1.6
Beta	0.87	0.88
R-Squared	91	92
Standard Deviation	14.01	
Mean	2.29	
Sharpe Ratio	0.07	

Portfolio Analysis 09-30-04

Share change since 06-04 Total Stocks:149	Sector	PE	YTD Ret%	% Assets
Dell	Hardware	34.0	24.01	2.15
⊕ Medtronic	Health	30.7	2.68	2.13
Wal-Mart Stores	Consumer	23.4	0.51	1.95
UnitedHealth Group	Health	23.8	51.38	1.93
⊖ Citigroup	Financial	15.3	2.72	1.89
⊖ Microsoft	Software	36.1	8.95	1.84
⊖ Iac / Interactivecorp	Consumer	43.1	-18.60	1.68
⊕ SLM	Financial	15.8	44.21	1.64
⊖ Pfizer	Health	22.0	-22.31	1.62
⊖ American International G	Financial	16.2	-0.53	1.56
⊕ Teva Pharmaceutical Indu	Health	—	5.89	1.53
⊖ Gen Elec	Ind Mtrls	22.8	20.68	1.49
⊕ eBay	Consumer	81.6	80.07	1.49
⊖ Procter & Gamble	Goods	23.3	12.38	1.49
⊕ Apollo Group A	Consumer	NMF	19.02	1.48
First Data	Business	18.8	3.72	1.46
⊕ Yahoo	Media	95.1	67.36	1.32
Tyco International	Ind Mtrls	25.1	35.41	1.32
⊕ Amazon.com	Consumer	55.5	-15.83	1.32
⊖ Johnson & Johnson	Health	20.6	25.17	1.27

Current Investment Style

Value Blnd Growth (Large Mid Small)

Market Cap	%
Giant	40.1
Large	42.1
Mid	16.4
Small	1.4
Micro	0.0

Avg $mil: 29,245

Value Measures		Rel Category
Price/Earnings	20.36	0.96
Price/Book	3.39	1.05
Price/Sales	2.33	1.08
Price/Cash Flow	11.53	1.05
Dividend Yield %	0.79	1.03

Growth Measures	%	Rel Category
Long-Term Erngs	14.31	1.02
Book Value	14.37	1.13
Sales	11.81	1.39
Cash Flow	18.47	1.12
Historical Erngs	18.33	1.27

Profitability	%	Rel Category
Return on Equity	21.31	1.19
Return on Assets	12.04	1.29
Net Margin	14.54	1.18

Sector Weightings	% of Stocks	Rel S&P 500	3 Year High	3 Year Low
Info	19.03	0.89		
Software	7.68	1.79	8	1
Hardware	7.06	0.69	13	3
Media	3.45	0.90	6	3
Telecom	0.84	0.27	3	0
Service	62.21	1.34		
Health	18.72	1.50	27	17
Consumer	20.39	2.25	20	11
Business	7.51	1.85	8	4
Financial	15.59	0.75	20	11
Mfg	18.77	0.58		
Goods	8.44	0.90	10	7
Ind Mtrls	5.29	0.42	14	4
Energy	5.04	0.70	11	1
Utilities	0.00	0.00	0	0

Composition

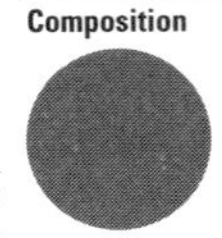

Cash	0.9
Stocks	99.1
Bonds	0.0
Other	0.0
Foreign (% of Stock)	2.2

Morningstar's Take by Christopher Davis 10-15-04

American Century Ultra can rise to the challenges posed by its strategy.

This offering faces some key tests in employing its earnings acceleration strategy. Screening for firms with improving earnings was novel when American Century founder James Stowers II first devised the approach in the early 1970s; its use is now commonplace among growth managers. That means the fund's edge flows not from its backward-looking quantitative screens, but from the ability to anticipate whose fundamentals will remain on the upswing in the quarters and years to come. Another hurdle, manager Wade Slome reports, is the current market environment. While companies continue to report strong results, the pace of earnings growth is slowing. The trick, he says, is to avoid richly priced names that are likely to come under pressure when earnings decelerate.

Management has generally executed its strategy well. When shares of Carnival slumped in the early 2003 run-up to the Iraq invasion, for example, management scooped up the cruise line on the grounds its earnings would improve once war worries subsided. After rebounding smartly last year, the stock has continued to buoy returns in 2004. In late 2003, management also began to slice the fund's exposure to tech holdings such as Cisco Systems and Intel, surmising the companies' earnings growth would slow faster than most investors expected. With both names faltering this year, that decision has been beneficial. The fund's 1% gain for the year to date through Oct. 11, 2004, lands in the large-growth group's top quartile.

To be sure, management's timing hasn't always been exactly right. It was too slow to pare the fund's tech weighting in 2000, for instance, and didn't ramp it quickly enough prior to the sector's 2003 revival. Management has acquitted itself over time, as the fund's fine long-term record attests. Given its size, this fund should be cheaper, but we regard this as a strong choice for large-growth exposure.

Address:	4500 Main St Kansas City MO 64141 800-345-2021
Web Address:	www.americancentury.com
Inception:	11-02-81
Advisor:	American Century Investment Mgt Inc.
Subadvisor:	None
NTF Plans:	Schwab OneSource, Accutrade NTF

Minimum Purchase:	$2500	Add: $50	IRA: $2500
Min Auto Inv Plan:	$2500	Add: $50	
Sales Fees:	No-load		
Management Fee:	1.00% mx./0.88% mn.		
Actual Fees:	Mgt:0.99%	Dist:	
Expense Projections:	3Yr:$314	5Yr:$545	10Yr:$1208
Income Distrib:	Annually		

AmCent Value Inv

Ticker	Load	NAV	Yield	Total Assets	Mstar Category
TWVLX	None	$7.39	1.0%	$2,857 mil	Large Value

Governance and Management

Fiduciary Grade: B

Portfolio Manager(s)

Prior to taking the helm upon this fund's 1993 inception in 1993, Phil Davidson spent 11 years as a manager for Boatmen's Trust Company. Comanager Scott Moore has roughly a decade of experience as an analyst and portfolio manager. Davidson and Moore also lead American Century Equity Income Fund, which has one of the mid-value category's better risk/reward profiles. After serving as one of the fund's analysts since 1998, Michael Liss was appointed comanager in early 2004. Five analysts support this offering and Equity Income.

Strategy

Managers Phil Davidson, Scott Moore, and Michael Liss employ an all-cap approach, looking for stocks that are cheap on measures such as dividends, cash flow, earnings, and book value. They apply these criteria rather strictly, so the fund has traditionally had scant exposure to growth sectors, including technology. The pair is quick to sell stocks that have gotten too pricey, which has given the fund high turnover in past years.

Historical Profile

Return Above Avg
Risk Average
Rating ★★★★ Above Avg

Investment Style: Equity Stock %

1994	1995	1996	1997	1998	1999	2000	2001	2002	2003	12-04
98%	95%	100%	98%	79%	81%	87%	97%	98%		

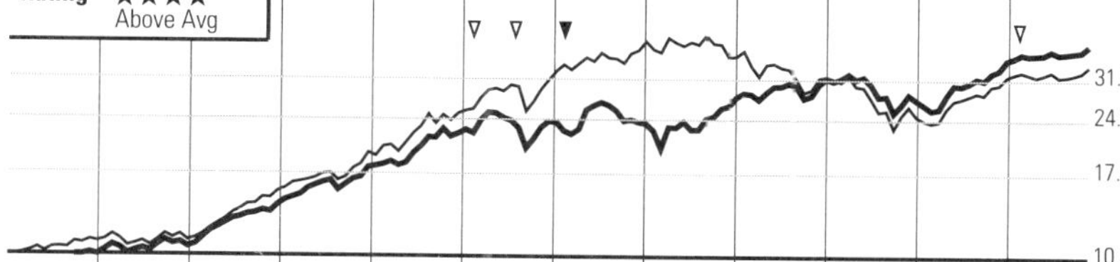

▼ Manager Change
∇ Partial Manager Change

Growth of $10,000
— Investment Values of Fund
— Investment Values of S&P 500

Performance Quartile (within Category)

History

1993	1994	1995	1996	1997	1998	1999	2000	2001	2002	2003	12-04	History
5.12	4.92	5.90	6.59	6.95	6.05	5.49	6.38	7.00	5.95	7.50	7.39	NAV
3.07*	3.99	32.80	24.25	26.01	4.99	-0.80	18.27	12.86	-12.69	29.06	14.36	Total Return %
—	2.68	-4.73	1.31	-7.34	-23.58	-21.84	27.37	24.74	9.40	0.39	3.49	+/-S&P 500
—	5.97	-5.56	2.61	-9.17	-10.64	-8.15	11.26	18.45	2.83	-0.97	-2.13	+/-Russ 1000 VI
0.00	2.49	2.72	1.89	1.80	1.23	1.49	1.81	1.30	0.93	1.43	1.16	Income Return %
—	1.50	30.08	22.36	24.21	3.76	-2.29	16.46	11.56	-13.62	27.63	13.20	Capital Return %
—	11	57	15	67	86	80	15	3	10	39	30	Total Rtn % Rank Cat
0.04	0.12	0.13	0.11	0.12	0.08	0.09	0.10	0.08	0.06	0.08	0.09	Income $
0.00	0.27	0.48	0.61	1.20	1.15	0.41	0.00	0.11	0.10	0.08	1.05	Capital Gains $
—	1.00	1.00	0.97	1.00	1.00	1.00	1.00	1.00	1.00	1.00	1.00	Expense Ratio %
—	3.37	2.65	2.17	1.86	1.38	1.19	1.48	1.71	1.19	1.19	1.26	Income Ratio %
—	—	145	145	111	130	130	115	150	151	102	122	Turnover Rate %
61	153	652	1,548	2,419	2,083	1,605	1,516	1,929	1,700	2,051	2,346	Net Assets $mil

Performance 12-31-04

	1st Qtr	2nd Qtr	3rd Qtr	4th Qtr	Total
2000	-2.20	-1.56	8.70	13.01	18.27
2001	-1.42	8.86	-7.34	13.51	12.86
2002	3.03	-6.60	-16.28	8.37	-12.69
2003	-5.41	15.72	3.72	13.68	29.06
2004	3.09	3.05	-1.00	8.74	14.36

Trailing	Total Return%	+/- S&P 500	+/- Russ 1000 VI	%Rank Cat	Growth of $10,000
3 Mo	8.74	-0.49	-1.64	63	10,874
6 Mo	7.66	0.47	-4.42	70	10,766
1 Yr	14.36	3.49	-2.13	30	11,436
3 Yr Avg	8.82	5.24	0.25	12	12,886
5 Yr Avg	11.46	13.76	6.19	4	17,203
10 Yr Avg	14.05	1.98	0.22	3	37,235
15 Yr Avg	—	—	—	—	—

Tax Analysis	Tax-Adj Rtn%	%Rank Cat	Tax-Cost Rat	%Rank Cat
3 Yr (estimated)	6.86	20	1.80	94
5 Yr (estimated)	9.86	5	1.44	75
10 Yr (estimated)	10.59	21	3.03	94

Potential Capital Gain Exposure: 9% of assets

Rating and Risk

Time Period	Load-Adj Return %	Morningstar Rtn vs Cat	Morningstar Risk vs Cat	Morningstar Risk-Adj Rating
1 Yr	14.36			
3 Yr	8.82	+Avg	-Avg	★★★★
5 Yr	11.46	High	Avg	★★★★★
10 Yr	14.05	+Avg	Avg	★★★★
Incept	12.99			

Other Measures	Standard Index S&P 500	Best Fit Index Russ 1000 VI
Alpha	5.3	1.0
Beta	0.86	0.89
R-Squared	90	94
Standard Deviation	14.72	
Mean	8.82	
Sharpe Ratio	0.51	

Portfolio Analysis 09-30-04

Share change since 06-04 Total Stocks:89	Sector	PE	YTD Ret%	% Assets
⊕ Union Pacific	Business	19.6	-1.28	3.57
⊕ Kraft Foods	Goods	20.3	13.15	2.87
⊖ SunTrust Banks	Financial	13.8	6.36	2.79
⊖ Martin Marietta Material	Ind Mtrls	20.6	16.14	2.78
⊕ Marsh & McLennan Compani	Financial	13.4	-29.80	2.57
⊕ New York Times A	Media	20.8	-13.42	2.55
⊕ Republic Services A	Business	21.8	32.45	2.37
⊕ AG Edwards	Financial	18.5	21.33	2.24
⊕ Unilever NV	Goods	21.2	6.49	2.20
⊖ Royal Dutch Petroleum AD	Energy	—	14.31	2.17
⊕ Bank of America	Financial	12.3	21.50	2.07
⊖ ExxonMobil	Energy	13.9	28.04	2.03
⊕ Synopsys	Software	19.8	-42.26	2.02
⊕ Brinker International	Consumer	26.9	5.76	1.79
⊖ Chubb	Financial	12.9	15.43	1.78
⊕ Bristol-Myers Squibb	Health	17.7	-7.27	1.76
⊕ Emerson Electric	Ind Mtrls	22.8	11.09	1.72
⊖ Freddie Mac	Financial	10.6	28.75	1.71
☼ AVX	Hardware	75.0	-23.37	1.62
⊕ Universal Health Service	Health	14.9	-16.59	1.60

Current Investment Style

Value Blnd Growth; Large Mid Small

Market Cap	%
Giant	30.4
Large	26.5
Mid	38.1
Small	5.0
Micro	0.0
Avg $mil: 13,653	

Value Measures		Rel Category
Price/Earnings	15.36	1.02
Price/Book	2.11	0.93
Price/Sales	1.15	0.97
Price/Cash Flow	6.73	1.05
Dividend Yield %	1.86	0.91

Growth Measures	%	Rel Category
Long-Term Erngs	10.70	1.03
Book Value	9.12	1.62
Sales	8.56	2.04
Cash Flow	5.18	0.99
Historical Erngs	15.14	1.28

Profitability	%	Rel Category
Return on Equity	18.94	1.19
Return on Assets	8.68	1.11
Net Margin	9.84	0.96

Sector Weightings	% of Stocks	Rel S&P 500	3 Year High	3 Year Low
Info	16.27	0.76		
Software	2.50	0.58	3	0
Hardware	5.49	0.54	6	2
Media	6.48	1.69	6	1
Telecom	1.80	0.57	6	2
Service	47.85	1.03		
Health	9.14	0.73	12	8
Consumer	4.35	0.48	4	2
Business	9.16	2.26	9	6
Financial	25.20	1.21	26	15
Mfg	35.87	1.12		
Goods	14.38	1.54	19	10
Ind Mtrls	10.65	0.84	21	11
Energy	6.30	0.88	12	6
Utilities	4.54	1.53	9	5

Composition

Cash	1.7
Stocks	98.3
Bonds	0.0
Other	0.0
Foreign (% of Stock)	6.5

Morningstar's Take by Christopher Davis 11-01-04

A disciplined strategy and veteran management burnish American Century Value's appeal.

Managers Phil Davidson, Scott Moore, and Michael Liss gravitate to market-leading firms with high profitability and solid balance sheets. They also require their picks to trade in the cheapest third of the market on at least two of five valuation measures, including the price-to-earnings ratio and dividend yield. Since higher-quality companies don't often trade at steep discounts, they look for those suffering temporary setbacks. The managers have been adding to its stake in consumer-products giant Unilever, for instance, which has been losing ground to rival Procter & Gamble. They point out, however, that P&G has discounted products aggressively in recent years thanks to cost-cutting measures, a well which it believes will soon run dry. They also like Unilever for its new management, strong balance sheet, and copious free cash flow.

The managers will add to struggling picks if they think the fundamentals remain strong and are also quick to trim their winners as they appreciate. As holdings like Freddie Mac and Toyota have posted handsome gains in 2004, they report slicing the fund's positions in the stocks throughout the year. The managers' strategy of adding on weakness and pruning on strength leads to relatively high turnover. The fund's turnover rate in 2003 weighed in at 122%, well above the mid-value norm.

That high-turnover approach hasn't made this fund a great choice for investors in taxable accounts. But for others seeking broad value exposure, we think it holds appeal. The fund's above-average market cap has hurt its relative standing in recent years versus its peers, but we'd point to the steadiness of its returns and the strength of its longer-term record. Management is also quite experienced and has executed its strategy consistently here. We still consider this offering a worthwhile choice.

Address:	P O Box 419200, Kansas City, MO 64141-6200, 800-345-2021
Web Address:	www.americancentury.com
Inception:	09-01-93*
Advisor:	American Century Investment Mgt Inc.
Subadvisor:	None
NTF Plans:	Schwab OneSource, Accutrade NTF

Minimum Purchase:	$2500	Add: $50	IRA: $2500
Min Auto Inv Plan:	$2500	Add: $50	
Sales Fees:	No-load		
Management Fee:	1.00% mx./0.85% mn.		
Actual Fees:	Mgt:1.00%	Dist:	
Expense Projections:	3Yr:$318	5Yr:$551	10Yr:$1219
Income Distrib:	Quarterly		

AmCent Veedot Inv

Ticker	Load	NAV	Yield	Total Assets	Mstar Category
AMVIX	None	$5.54	0.0%	$246 mil	Mid-Cap Growth

Governance and Management

Fiduciary Grade: C

Portfolio Manager(s)

Jim Stowers III has been at the helm since the fund's November 1999 inception. Stowers is one of the most experienced managers in the industry, though his other charge, American Century Ultra, is managed using more-traditional techniques. This fund's comanager, John Small, also worked on the team running Ultra. Stowers says he keeps a majority of his assets in this fund.

Strategy

Like all growth-oriented American Century offerings, this fund uses quantitative models to identify a universe of companies whose earnings-growth or revenue-growth rates are increasing. But management then employs technical analysis to home in on stocks with upward price momentum. Top holdings are typically kept to less than 2% of assets to minimize the risk of individual blowups, but the fund has no limits on sector concentration. It can invest in stocks in any market-cap and valuation range, although its emphasis on those with accelerating earnings and revenue keeps it in growth territory.

Historical Profile

Return Average
Risk Below Avg
Rating ★★★ Neutral

Investment Style
Equity
Stock %: 91% (1999), 95% (2000), 98% (2001), 99% (2002), 99% (2003), 99% (12-04)

▼ Manager Change
▽ Partial Manager Change

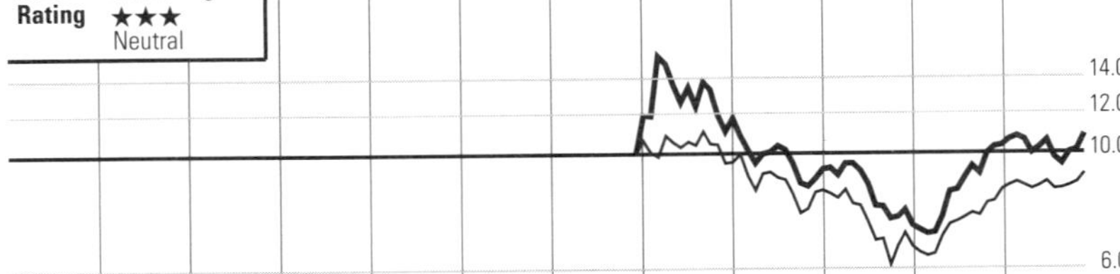

Growth of $10,000
— Investment Values of Fund
— Investment Values of S&P 500

Performance Quartile (within Category)

1993	1994	1995	1996	1997	1998	1999	2000	2001	2002	2003	12-04	History
—	—	—	—	—	—	5.92	5.84	4.66	3.63	5.17	5.54	NAV
—	—	—	—	—	—	18.40*	-1.35	-20.21	-22.10	42.42	7.16	Total Return %
—	—	—	—	—	—	—	7.75	-8.33	-0.01	13.75	-3.71	+/-S&P 500
—	—	—	—	—	—	—	10.40	-0.06	5.31	-0.29	-8.32	+/-Russ MG
—	—	—	—	—	—	0.00	0.00	0.00	0.00	0.00	0.00	Income Return %
—	—	—	—	—	—	—	-1.35	-20.21	-22.10	42.42	7.16	Capital Return %
—	—	—	—	—	—	—	46	50	28	20	88	Total Rtn % Rank Cat
—	—	—	—	—	—	0.00	0.00	0.00	0.00	0.00	0.00	Income $
—	—	—	—	—	—	0.00	0.00	0.00	0.00	0.00	0.00	Capital Gains $
—	—	—	—	—	—	—	1.50	1.50	1.50	1.50	—	Expense Ratio %
—	—	—	—	—	—	—	-0.92	-0.09	-0.31	-0.68	—	Income Ratio %
—	—	—	—	—	—	—	250	410	330	415	—	Turnover Rate %
—	—	—	—	—	—	73	343	245	175	236	232	Net Assets $mil

Performance 12-31-04

	1st Qtr	2nd Qtr	3rd Qtr	4th Qtr	Total
2000	25.17	-9.85	-0.90	-11.78	-1.35
2001	-17.98	7.93	-15.28	6.39	-20.21
2002	2.58	-8.58	-14.42	-2.94	-22.10
2003	-3.03	20.74	7.53	13.13	42.42
2004	2.51	-0.38	-5.11	10.58	7.16

Trailing	Total Return%	+/- S&P 500	+/- Russ MG	%Rank Cat	Growth of $10,000
3 Mo	10.58	1.35	-3.36	87	11,058
6 Mo	4.92	-2.27	-4.09	85	10,492
1 Yr	7.16	-3.71	-8.32	88	10,716
3 Yr Avg	5.94	2.36	-0.22	29	11,890
5 Yr Avg	-1.32	0.98	2.04	36	9,357
10 Yr Avg	—	—	—	—	—
15 Yr Avg	—	—	—	—	—

Tax Analysis	Tax-Adj Rtn%	%Rank Cat	Tax-Cost Rat	%Rank Cat
3 Yr (estimated)	5.22	29	0.00	1
5 Yr (estimated)	-1.32	28	0.00	1
10 Yr (estimated)	—	—	—	—

Potential Capital Gain Exposure: -31% of assets

Rating and Risk

Time Period	Load-Adj Return %	Morningstar Rtn vs Cat	Morningstar Risk vs Cat	Morningstar Risk-Adj Rating
1 Yr	5.01			
3 Yr	5.22	Avg	Avg	★★★
5 Yr	-1.32	Avg	-Avg	★★★
10 Yr	—	—	—	—
Incept	2.04			

Other Measures	Standard Index S&P 500	Best Fit Index Russ 2000
Alpha	3.0	-3.5
Beta	0.85	0.82
R-Squared	59	90
Standard Deviation	17.55	
Mean	5.94	
Sharpe Ratio	0.26	

Morningstar's Take by Christopher Davis 11-16-04

American Century Veedot Fund's attempt to build a better mousetrap hasn't succeeded lately, but it still holds some appeal.

This offering shares an earnings-acceleration strategy in common with its growth-oriented siblings. Managers Jim Stowers III and John Small begin first by screening for firms with improving earnings, but they don't stop there. The managers marry earnings-acceleration models with one that uses relative strength and other technical measures to help identify the right times to get in and out of stocks. Management's focus on price momentum, Stowers argues, enables it to avoid companies where fundamentals are on the upswing but share prices aren't rising.

By and large, that approach has been successful here. Since its December 1999 launch, the fund has handily outpaced both its typical mid-growth rival and its benchmark, the Wilshire 5000 Index. Management's models, however, aren't foolproof. In 2004, for example, they heavily favored semiconductor-related fare, which has been among the year's biggest losers. That has helped place the fund well behind the mid-growth average and its bogy for the year.

The fund's lackluster 2004 campaign underscores the most significant risk of investing here: There's no guarantee the managers' models will be able to replicate their past successes. The managers' focus on short-term technical indicators requires them to move rapidly into strong-performing stocks and ditch them quickly before they falter, a strategy that has often proven difficult to implement over long stretches of time.

Even so, there's still a case to be made for the fund. Management is highly experienced and employs a clear, consistent strategy. The fund's expense ratio is a bit of a hurdle, but its costs should decline as assets rise. This offering isn't core-holding material, but it could serve as a niche player in a diversified portfolio.

Portfolio Analysis 09-30-04

Share change since 06-04 Total Stocks:424	Sector	PE	YTD Ret%	% Assets
First Horizon	Health	25.2	103.47	0.94
⊖ Lone Star Technologies	Ind Mtrls	27.9	109.39	0.64
⊕ Airspan Networks	Hardware	—	55.14	0.57
☼ Tesoro Petroleum	Energy	6.4	118.67	0.57
⊕ Symmetricom	Telecom	—	33.38	0.54
ExxonMobil	Energy	13.9	28.04	0.52
Commercial Metals	Ind Mtrls	11.5	67.69	0.47
☼ Genzyme	Health	—	17.81	0.46
⊕ Symantec	Software	34.5	49.33	0.46
EGL	Business	30.2	70.02	0.45
☼ Sanmina-SCI	Hardware	—	-32.78	0.45
☼ Holly	Energy	11.6	105.62	0.45
MSC Industrial Direct Co	Business	28.4	32.26	0.44
☼ LifeCell	Health	12.7	64.84	0.43
☼ Aetna	Financial	16.9	84.67	0.43
☼ Covance	Health	26.6	44.59	0.43
☼ Allied Irish Banks ADR	Financial	7.6	35.89	0.43
⊕ Swift Energy	Energy	14.9	71.75	0.42
☼ AK Steel Holding	Ind Mtrls	—	183.73	0.42
⊕ Qualcomm	Hardware	42.0	58.20	0.42

Current Investment Style

Value Blnd Growth / Large Mid Small

Market Cap	%
Giant	2.4
Large	11.6
Mid	28.8
Small	40.0
Micro	17.2
Avg $mil: 1,525	

Value Measures		Rel Category
Price/Earnings	18.24	0.83
Price/Book	2.37	0.79
Price/Sales	1.18	0.67
Price/Cash Flow	7.14	0.74
Dividend Yield %	0.94	2.19

Growth Measures	%	Rel Category
Long-Term Erngs	13.69	0.87
Book Value	1.98	0.20
Sales	2.40	0.28
Cash Flow	0.71	0.06
Historical Erngs	-0.25	NMF

Profitability	%	Rel Category
Return on Equity	6.66	0.46
Return on Assets	3.21	0.45
Net Margin	5.28	0.55

Sector Weightings	% of Stocks	Rel S&P 500	3 Year High	3 Year Low
Info	20.03	0.93		
Software	3.46	0.80	11	2
Hardware	13.83	1.36	23	3
Media	0.54	0.14	7	1
Telecom	2.20	0.70	4	0
Service	40.82	0.88		
Health	10.14	0.81	24	8
Consumer	7.53	0.83	21	5
Business	11.57	2.86	13	7
Financial	11.58	0.56	26	9
Mfg	39.16	1.22		
Goods	4.62	0.50	11	4
Ind Mtrls	19.62	1.55	20	4
Energy	12.37	1.73	12	1
Utilities	2.55	0.86	3	0

Composition

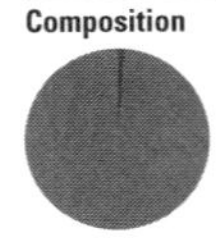

Cash	1.3
Stocks	98.7
Bonds	0.0
Other	0.0
Foreign (% of Stock)	2.8

Address:	4500 Main St Kansas City MO 64141 800-345-2021
Web Address:	www.americancentury.com
Inception:	11-30-99 *
Advisor:	American Century Investment Mgt Inc.
Subadvisor:	None
NTF Plans:	Schwab OneSource, Schwab Instl NTF

Minimum Purchase:	$2500	Add: $50	IRA: $2500
Min Auto Inv Plan:	$2500	Add: $50	
Sales Fees:	No-load, 2.00%R		
Management Fee:	1.50% mx./1.10% mn.		
Actual Fees:	Mgt:1.50%	Dist:	
Expense Projections:	3Yr:$693	5Yr:$814	10Yr:$1778
Income Distrib:	Annually		

AmCent Vista Inv

Ticker	Load	NAV	Yield	Total Assets	Mstar Category
TWCVX	None	$14.52	0.0%	$1,728 mil	Mid-Cap Growth

Governance and Management

Fiduciary Grade: B

Portfolio Manager(s)

Comanager Glenn Fogle has been a member of this fund's team since 1993. David Hollond joined the team as an analyst in 1998 and became comanager in March 2004 when David Rose, who had worked on the fund since February 2001, left. Analysts Brad Eixman and Chris Schaefer round out the team.

Strategy

This fund applies American Century's earnings-acceleration strategy to the mid-cap universe. Management uses models to screen for companies with improving prospects, looking primarily at earnings-growth rates. It researches companies to determine which can keep up earnings growth. The fund holds between 60 and 90 names, often stashing a good amount of assets in its top holdings. If management finds several companies with accelerating earnings in a particular area, it will often make rather large sector bets.

Historical Profile

Return Average
Risk Average
Rating ★★★ Neutral

Investment Style
Equity
Stock %

100% | 90% | 95% | 97% | 96% | 93% | 91% | 99% | 96%

▼ Manager Change
∇ Partial Manager Change

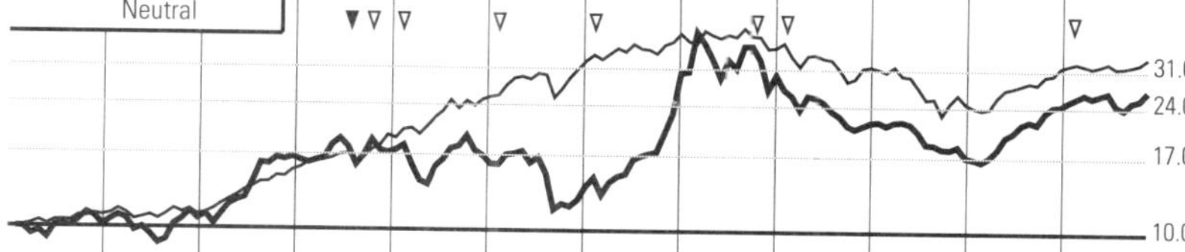

Growth of $10,000
— Investment Values of Fund
— Investment Values of S&P 500

Performance Quartile (within Category)

1993	1994	1995	1996	1997	1998	1999	2000	2001	2002	2003	12-04	History
10.27	10.72	14.60	14.51	12.42	10.65	22.21	15.33	11.10	8.78	12.54	14.52	NAV
5.45	4.68	46.13	7.56	-8.68	-14.25	119.11	-0.98	-27.59	-20.90	42.82	15.79	Total Return %
-4.61	3.37	8.60	-15.38	-42.03	-42.82	98.07	8.12	-15.71	1.19	14.15	4.92	+/-S&P 500
-5.74	6.84	12.15	-9.92	-31.22	-32.11	67.82	10.77	-7.44	6.51	0.11	0.31	+/-Russ MG
0.00	0.00	0.00	0.00	0.00	0.00	0.00	0.00	0.00	0.00	0.00	0.00	Income Return %
5.45	4.68	46.13	7.56	-8.68	-14.25	119.11	-0.98	-27.59	-20.90	42.82	15.79	Capital Return %
85	12	13	90	99	99	10	43	75	23	18	28	Total Rtn % Rank Cat
0.00	0.00	0.00	0.00	0.00	0.00	0.00	0.00	0.00	0.00	0.00	0.00	Income $
1.68	0.03	1.03	1.18	0.80	0.00	0.95	6.33	0.00	0.00	0.00	0.00	Capital Gains $
1.00	1.00	0.98	0.99	1.00	1.00	1.00	1.00	1.00	1.00	1.00	—	Expense Ratio %
-0.60	-0.80	-0.60	-0.70	-0.73	-0.42	-0.40	-0.65	0.31	-0.34	-0.57	—	Income Ratio %
133	111	89	91	96	229	187	135	290	293	280	—	Turnover Rate %
797	820	1,775	2,236	1,651	955	1,800	2,081	1,251	907	1,295	1,568	Net Assets $mil

Performance 12-31-04

	1st Qtr	2nd Qtr	3rd Qtr	4th Qtr	Total
2000	22.83	-10.70	10.18	-18.06	-0.98
2001	-21.00	5.12	-14.61	2.12	-27.59
2002	0.36	-6.37	-10.93	-5.49	-20.90
2003	0.11	18.32	6.54	13.18	42.82
2004	8.61	1.17	-6.10	12.21	15.79

Trailing	Total Return%	+/- S&P 500	+/- Russ MG	%Rank Cat	Growth of $10,000
3 Mo	12.21	2.98	-1.73	65	11,221
6 Mo	5.37	-1.82	-3.64	81	10,537
1 Yr	15.79	4.92	0.31	28	11,579
3 Yr Avg	9.37	5.79	3.21	9	13,083
5 Yr Avg	-1.27	1.03	2.09	35	9,381
10 Yr Avg	9.72	-2.35	-1.51	59	25,285
15 Yr Avg	9.68	-1.25	-1.32	60	39,986

Tax Analysis	Tax-Adj Rtn%	%Rank Cat	Tax-Cost Rat	%Rank Cat
3 Yr (estimated)	9.37	7	0.00	1
5 Yr (estimated)	-2.78	38	1.53	67
10 Yr (estimated)	8.12	46	1.46	32

Potential Capital Gain Exposure: 7% of assets

Rating and Risk

Time Period	Load-Adj Return %	Morningstar Rtn vs Cat	Morningstar Risk vs Cat	Morningstar Risk-Adj Rating
1 Yr	15.79			
3 Yr	9.37	High	-Avg	★★★★★
5 Yr	-1.27	Avg	Avg	★★★
10 Yr	9.72	Avg	+Avg	★★
Incept	10.73			

Other Measures	Standard Index S&P 500	Best Fit Index Wil 4500
Alpha	6.6	-0.4
Beta	0.66	0.80
R-Squared	49	81
Standard Deviation	15.48	
Mean	9.37	
Sharpe Ratio	0.52	

Portfolio Analysis 09-30-04

Share change since 06-04 Total Stocks:91	Sector	PE	YTD Ret%	% Assets
Boston Scientific	Health	32.3	-3.29	3.52
⊕ NII Holdings	Telecom	7.4	90.74	3.02
⊕ Qualcomm	Hardware	42.0	58.20	2.81
⊕ Aetna	Financial	16.9	84.67	2.33
☼ Nucor	Ind Mtrls	9.6	89.07	2.31
⊕ Symantec	Software	34.5	49.33	2.28
⊕ Chicago Mercantile Excha	Financial	37.9	218.54	2.25
⊕ Capital One Financial	Financial	12.5	37.61	2.18
⊕ Yellow Roadway	Business	21.5	54.02	2.08
☼ Textron	Ind Mtrls	30.4	32.17	2.02
☼ Cummins	Ind Mtrls	12.3	74.61	2.01
☼ North Fork Bancorporatio	Financial	15.4	10.24	1.99
☼ Zebra Technologies	Hardware	33.1	27.20	1.98
⊕ Station Casinos	Consumer	77.1	81.31	1.97
⊕ American Eagle Outfitter	Consumer	35.5	188.04	1.97
⊕ Expeditors International	Business	42.3	49.04	1.73
⊖ Copart	Business	24.9	58.55	1.63
⊕ Fisher Scientific Intern	Health	43.9	50.79	1.55
⊕ TCF Financial	Financial	13.3	28.60	1.50
⊖ CNF	Business	24.4	49.36	1.50

Current Investment Style

Value Blnc Growth; Large Mid Small

Market Cap	%
Giant	5.3
Large	27.0
Mid	58.2
Small	9.4
Micro	0.0
Avg $mil: 5,488	

Value Measures		Rel Category
Price/Earnings	19.35	0.88
Price/Book	3.09	1.03
Price/Sales	1.39	0.79
Price/Cash Flow	3.44	0.35
Dividend Yield %	0.69	1.60

Growth Measures	%	Rel Category
Long-Term Erngs	15.25	0.97
Book Value	10.20	1.02
Sales	4.50	0.52
Cash Flow	5.37	0.44
Historical Erngs	8.12	0.51

Profitability	%	Rel Category
Return on Equity	14.55	1.01
Return on Assets	8.11	1.13
Net Margin	11.34	1.18

Sector Weightings	% of Stocks	Rel S&P 500	3 Year High	3 Year Low
Info	21.54	1.00		
Software	3.42	0.80	7	1
Hardware	12.74	1.25	22	2
Media	1.55	0.40	10	0
Telecom	3.83	1.22	10	0
Service	48.86	1.05		
Health	12.16	0.97	33	12
Consumer	6.74	0.74	24	7
Business	15.52	3.83	19	2
Financial	14.44	0.70	20	8
Mfg	29.60	0.92		
Goods	2.55	0.27	12	1
Ind Mtrls	16.88	1.33	19	1
Energy	9.13	1.28	9	0
Utilities	1.04	0.35	2	0

Composition

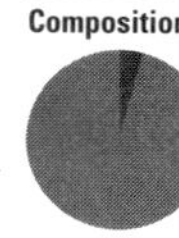

Cash	3.9
Stocks	96.0
Bonds	0.0
Other	0.0
Foreign (% of Stock)	3.4

Morningstar's Take by Dan Culloton 11-10-04

This fund hasn't found a magic bullet, but it has improved its aim.

Steps taken more than five years ago to smooth American Century Vista's performance have paid off. In late 1998 the fund honed the quantitative tools it uses to find stocks with accelerating earnings. Since then it has finished four of the past five years in its category's top half, including three top-quartile finishes, and is on pace for another above-average campaign in 2004.

At the same time the offering has reduced volatility by more quickly dumping stocks that show signs of deceleration or weakening price strength. Manager Glenn Fogle and his team also have paid closer attention to portfolio risk by meeting regularly to review the bear case for each stock in the fund. As a result the fund's three-year standard deviation through Oct. 31, 2004, is 55% of what it was at the end of 1998.

There are no guarantees the fund can keep it up. Its highly active approach (turnover is often more than 250%) isn't suited for every market environment. It has stumbled when the market abruptly shifted gears, such as in the fourth quarters of 2001 and 2002 and the third quarter of 2004. The fund's success also depends on its managers' ability to buy stocks that will do better than the shares they sell, over and over again, which is hard to sustain over the long term.

Nevertheless, the fund has some traits that correlate well with long-term success, including experienced management, low expenses, and a clearly articulated process. Fast trading usually increases tax and trading costs, but this fund still has a big tax loss to offset capital gains, and American Century does a good job squeezing transaction costs.

This offering isn't a cinch, but it gets credit for delivering what it promises: an aggressively managed growth fund. If you can live with frequent trading and the risk of occasionally being out of sync, the fund is worth consideration.

Address:	4500 Main St Kansas City MO 64141 800-345-2021
Web Address:	www.americancentury.com
Inception:	11-25-83
Advisor:	American Century Investment Mgt Inc.
Subadvisor:	None
NTF Plans:	Schwab OneSource, Accutrade NTF

Minimum Purchase:	$2500	Add: $50	IRA: $2500
Min Auto Inv Plan:	$2500	Add: $50	
Sales Fees:	No-load		
Management Fee:	1.00%		
Actual Fees:	Mgt:1.00%	Dist:	
Expense Projections:	3Yr:$318	5Yr:$551	10Yr:$1219
Income Distrib:	Annually		

Amer Funds Amcap A

Ticker	Load	NAV	Yield	Total Assets	Mstar Category
AMCPX	5.75%	$18.33	0.3%	$18,384 mil	Large Growth

Governance and Management

Fiduciary Grade: B

Portfolio Manager(s)

The fund is managed by a very seasoned four-person team of portfolio counselors. The average member boasts more than 24 years of experience with the firm. The team is backed by a large and talented legion of analysts. More than 140 investment professionals operate out of 11 offices around the globe.

Strategy

The fund favors established companies with proven records of steady, above-average growth. It owns its share of highfliers, such as Microsoft and Cisco Systems, but it's also willing to scoop up names that aren't very common in other growth portfolios, such as Altria Group. The resulting portfolio is well diversified across industries and individual names, and a usually large cash stake further keeps a lid on risk.

Historical Profile

Return High
Risk Low
Rating ★★★★★ Highest

Investment Style
Equity
Stock %: 87% 86% 78% 82% 73% 71% 69% 78% 81%

▼ Manager Change
▽ Partial Manager Change

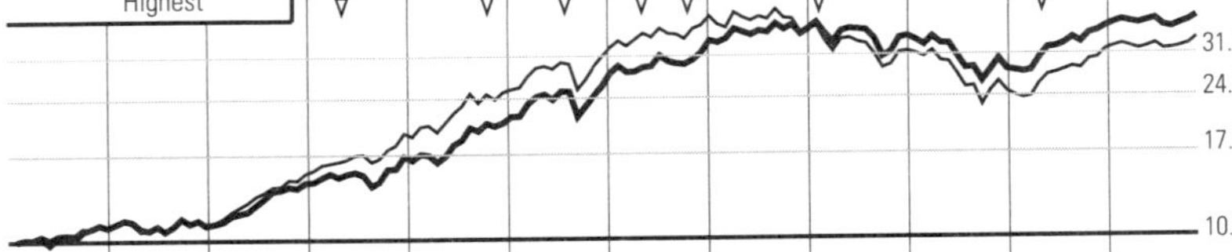

Growth of $10,000
— Investment Values of Fund
— Investment Values of S&P 500

Performance Quartile (within Category)

History

	1993	1994	1995	1996	1997	1998	1999	2000	2001	2002	2003	12-04
NAV	12.83	11.71	13.67	14.16	15.65	17.71	18.78	17.78	16.12	13.00	16.85	18.33
Total Return %	11.01	-0.24	28.71	14.16	30.55	30.02	21.78	7.50	-5.01	-18.66	29.64	9.81
+/-S&P 500	0.95	-1.55	-8.82	-8.78	-2.80	1.45	0.74	16.60	6.87	3.43	0.97	-1.06
+/-Russ 1000Gr	8.14	-2.86	-8.47	-8.96	0.06	-8.69	-11.38	29.92	15.41	9.22	-0.11	3.51
Income Return %	0.93	1.05	1.47	0.90	0.73	0.85	0.58	0.59	0.49	0.15	0.02	0.27
Capital Return %	10.08	-1.29	27.24	13.26	29.82	29.17	21.20	6.91	-5.50	-18.81	29.62	9.54
Total Rtn % Rank Cat	46	34	71	84	30	55	82	3	3	8	36	29
Income $	0.12	0.13	0.17	0.12	0.10	0.13	0.10	0.11	0.09	0.02	0.00	0.05
Capital Gains $	1.82	0.95	1.19	1.31	2.47	2.29	2.48	2.26	0.71	0.10	0.00	0.13
Expense Ratio %	0.73	0.72	0.71	0.71	0.69	0.68	0.67	0.68	0.67	0.71	0.77	0.73
Income Ratio %	1.02	0.89	1.16	1.16	0.81	0.62	0.70	0.72	1.18	0.58	0.25	0.11
Turnover Rate %	15	22	18	35	24	31	36	34	39	25	18	17
Net Assets $mil	3,079	2,877	3,533	3,784	4,537	5,830	7,188	7,655	7,596	6,683	10,322	13,319

Performance 12-31-04

	1st Qtr	2nd Qtr	3rd Qtr	4th Qtr	Total
2000	7.35	-1.24	0.85	0.54	7.50
2001	-8.38	8.37	-15.40	13.08	-5.01
2002	-0.31	-11.29	-14.34	7.37	-18.66
2003	-0.85	15.62	2.75	10.06	29.64
2004	2.61	1.85	-3.06	8.39	9.81

Trailing	Total Return%	+/- S&P 500	+/- Russ 1000Gr	%Rank Cat	Growth of $10,000
3 Mo	8.39	-0.84	-0.78	79	10,839
6 Mo	5.07	-2.12	1.60	46	10,507
1 Yr	9.81	-1.06	3.51	29	10,981
3 Yr Avg	5.01	1.43	5.19	9	11,580
5 Yr Avg	3.41	5.71	12.70	1	11,825
10 Yr Avg	13.64	1.57	4.05	5	35,918
15 Yr Avg	12.17	1.24	2.67	12	55,995

Tax Analysis	Tax-Adj Rtn%	%Rank Cat	Tax-Cost Rat	%Rank Cat
3 Yr (estimated)	2.82	16	0.14	24
5 Yr (estimated)	1.37	2	0.80	48
10 Yr (estimated)	10.89	9	1.84	65

Potential Capital Gain Exposure: 21% of assets

Rating and Risk

Time Period	Load-Adj Return %	Morningstar Rtn vs Cat	Morningstar Risk vs Cat	Morningstar Risk-Adj Rating
1 Yr	3.50			
3 Yr	2.96	+Avg	-Avg	★★★★
5 Yr	2.19	High	Low	★★★★★
10 Yr	12.97	High	Low	★★★★★
Incept	12.04			

Other Measures	Standard Index S&P 500	Best Fit Index Russ 1000
Alpha	1.5	0.9
Beta	0.91	0.93
R-Squared	93	94
Standard Deviation	14.88	
Mean	5.01	
Sharpe Ratio	0.25	

Portfolio Analysis 09-30-04

Share change since 06-04 Total Stocks:134	Sector	PE	YTD Ret%	% Assets
⊕ Fannie Mae	Financial	9.1	-2.33	2.21
First Data	Business	18.8	3.72	1.67
⊕ Lowe's Companies	Consumer	22.1	4.25	1.64
⊕ WellPoint Health Network	Health	—	—	1.61
Capital One Financial	Financial	12.5	37.61	1.61
⊕ Target	Consumer	22.3	36.14	1.57
⊖ HCA	Health	15.8	-6.00	1.42
Devon Energy	Energy	9.0	36.78	1.36
☼ Best Buy	Consumer	21.6	14.64	1.33
⊕ American International G	Financial	16.2	-0.53	1.32
⊖ eBay	Consumer	81.6	80.07	1.22
Express Scripts	Health	22.3	15.07	1.21
⊕ Applied Materials	Hardware	20.7	-23.80	1.21
⊕ Forest Laboratories	Health	18.0	-27.41	1.16
⊕ Microsoft	Software	36.1	8.95	1.14
Cisco Systems	Hardware	24.5	-20.26	1.14
⊖ Kohl's	Consumer	25.5	9.41	1.12
⊕ Carnival	Goods	26.2	46.74	1.11
Time Warner	Media	27.5	8.12	1.11
Avon Products	Goods	23.4	16.31	1.11

Current Investment Style

Value Blnd Growth / Large Mid Small

Market Cap	%
Giant	22.8
Large	47.1
Mid	27.9
Small	2.2
Micro	0.0

Avg $mil: 17,230

Value Measures		Rel Category
Price/Earnings	18.83	0.89
Price/Book	2.44	0.76
Price/Sales	1.32	0.61
Price/Cash Flow	8.21	0.75
Dividend Yield %	0.72	0.94

Growth Measures	%	Rel Category
Long-Term Erngs	13.84	0.99
Book Value	15.47	1.22
Sales	11.36	1.33
Cash Flow	10.08	0.61
Historical Erngs	18.29	1.26

Profitability	%	Rel Category
Return on Equity	16.09	0.90
Return on Assets	8.93	0.95
Net Margin	9.86	0.80

Sector Weightings	% of Stocks	Rel S&P 500	3 Year High	3 Year Low
Info	21.48	1.00		
Software	2.78	0.65	5	3
Hardware	11.50	1.13	15	12
Media	5.27	1.37	10	5
Telecom	1.93	0.61	6	1
Service	57.31	1.24		
Health	18.77	1.50	20	12
Consumer	19.65	2.16	20	16
Business	7.73	1.91	13	8
Financial	11.16	0.54	16	11
Mfg	21.20	0.66		
Goods	8.15	0.87	8	3
Ind Mtrls	7.31	0.58	7	4
Energy	5.29	0.74	5	1
Utilities	0.45	0.15	1	0

Composition

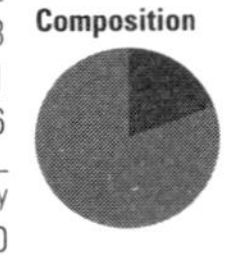

Cash	19.2
Stocks	80.7
Bonds	0.0
Other	0.1
Foreign (% of Stock)	0.0

Morningstar's Take by Paul Herbert 10-21-04

American Funds Amcap Fund remains a fetching option.

This fund and the typical large-growth fund don't have much in common. This one's managers focus on earnings growth, but also require holdings to possess ship-shape financial positions and reasonable valuations. Moreover, they build the portfolio from the bottom up, paying no mind to whether it bears any resemblance to a market benchmark. They also hold on to stocks for the long term and will devote a sizable portion of assets to cash.

Going its own way has been a boon for the fund over time. The fund's four managers and its team of analysts, who also run a portion of the fund, have consistently identified winners, including current favorites such as staffing firm Robert Half International and Yahoo. Over time, the fund has been an able performer, especially during times of stock market stress such as during the bear market that began at the turn of this century.

The fund's fine performance--which has extended into 2004 on the backs of strong runs from stocks such as those mentioned above--also owes to its institutional advantages. Its advisor can boast a massive analyst staff--140 (and growing) according to recent numbers--and also possesses the scale to keep costs very low. For all of these reasons, we have put the fund on a list of candidates for our domestic-stock Manager of the Year award.

That's not to say that our concerns regarding the firm's asset growth aren't an issue for this fund's shareholders. The shop's windfall means everyone's running a bit more money than she or he had previously. And while Amcap is significantly smaller than sibling Growth Fund of America, the two funds, and the firm's broader lineup, share many holdings in common.

In all, we continue to see a lot to like here, though we have some worries that the fund and its siblings could lose a step.

Address:	333 S Hope St - 52nd Floor Los Angeles CA 90071 800-421-0180
Web Address:	www.americanfunds.com
Inception:	05-01-67
Advisor:	Capital Research and Management Company
Subadvisor:	None
NTF Plans:	Federated Tr NTF

Minimum Purchase:	$250	Add: $50	IRA: $250
Min Auto Inv Plan:	$50	Add: $50	
Sales Fees:	5.75%L		
Management Fee:	0.49% mx./0.30% mn.		
Actual Fees:	Mgt:0.34%	Dist:0.25%	
Expense Projections:	3Yr:$795	5Yr:$958	10Yr:$1429
Income Distrib:	Semi-Annually		

Amer Funds Amer Bal A

Ticker	Load	NAV	Yield	Total Assets	Mstar Category
ABALX	5.75%	$18.00	2.0%	$44,974 mil	Moderate Allocation

Governance and Management

Fiduciary Grade: B

Portfolio Manager(s)

Like most American funds, this one is steered by a very experienced team. This fund's six portfolio counselors--Hilda L. Applbaum, J. Dale Harvey, Gregory D. Johnson, Mark R. MacDonald, Robert G. O'Donnell, and John H. Smet--boast an average of more than 15 years of investment experience with the firm. The managers are backed by a seasoned and deep team of research analysts, who are also responsible for managing a portion of the fund's assets.

Strategy

This fund keeps it simple. Its management tends to invest about 60% of the fund's assets in equities, with the remainder devoted to high-quality bonds and cash. The fund's stock portfolio is broadly diversified across sectors and individual names, with a bias toward value-priced securities. The managers typically buy mid- to large-cap stocks.

Historical Profile

Return: Above Avg
Risk: Average
Rating: ★★★★ Above Avg

Investment Style: Equity Stock %

1993	1994	1995	1996	1997	1998	1999	2000	2001	2002	2003	12-04
51%	55%	56%	55%	57%	58%	59%	64%	63%			

▼ Manager Change
▽ Partial Manager Change

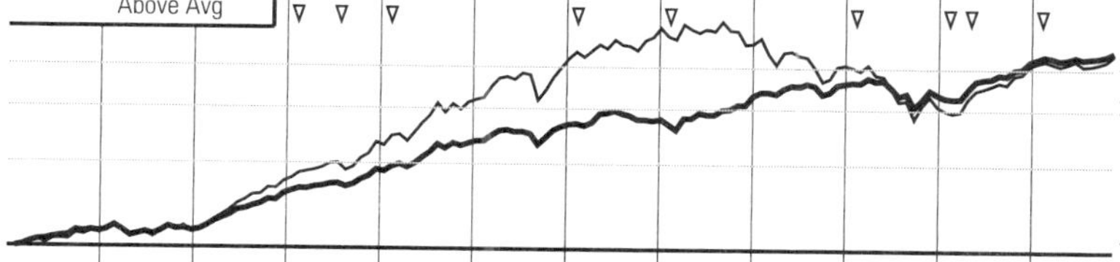

Growth of $10,000
— Investment Values of Fund
— Investment Values of S&P 500

Performance Quartile (within Category)

History

1993	1994	1995	1996	1997	1998	1999	2000	2001	2002	2003	12-04	History
12.57	12.00	14.15	14.55	15.68	15.76	14.42	15.47	15.85	14.42	17.29	18.00	NAV
11.27	0.34	27.13	13.17	21.03	11.13	3.47	15.85	8.19	-6.27	22.82	8.92	Total Return %
1.21	-0.97	-10.40	-9.77	-12.32	-17.44	-17.57	24.95	20.07	15.82	-5.85	-1.95	+/-S&P 500
-0.46	2.29	2.36	1.83	1.83	-1.26	-9.38	11.41	8.03	4.27	-1.24	-2.25	+/-DJ 60%
4.97	4.54	4.74	4.03	3.93	3.63	3.63	3.94	3.68	2.74	2.59	2.10	Income Return %
6.30	-4.20	22.39	9.14	17.10	7.50	-0.16	11.91	4.51	-9.01	20.23	6.82	Capital Return %
51	15	41	58	39	65	81	5	4	9	26	46	Total Rtn % Rank Cat
0.60	0.56	0.56	0.56	0.56	0.56	0.56	0.56	0.56	0.43	0.37	0.36	Income $
0.46	0.05	0.47	0.85	1.30	1.05	1.30	0.53	0.30	0.02	0.00	0.44	Capital Gains $
0.71	0.68	0.67	0.67	0.65	0.63	0.66	0.63	0.68	0.70	0.67	—	Expense Ratio %
4.74	4.76	4.38	4.01	3.74	3.57	3.59	3.93	3.26	2.79	2.38	—	Income Ratio %
28	32	39	44	44	54	48	16	50	41	32	—	Turnover Rate %
1,710	2,082	3,048	3,941	5,036	5,881	5,981	6,042	8,915	12,405	19,951	29,162	Net Assets $mil

Performance 12-31-04

	1st Qtr	2nd Qtr	3rd Qtr	4th Qtr	Total
2000	0.69	2.30	3.36	8.81	15.85
2001	1.23	4.77	-4.65	6.99	8.19
2002	3.47	-5.57	-11.53	8.44	-6.27
2003	-2.43	12.76	2.37	9.05	22.82
2004	2.48	0.58	-0.33	6.01	8.92

Trailing	Total Return%	+/- S&P 500	+/- DJ 60%	%Rank Cat	Growth of $10,000
3 Mo	6.01	-3.22	-1.47	72	10,601
6 Mo	5.67	-1.52	-1.86	69	10,567
1 Yr	8.92	-1.95	-2.25	46	10,892
3 Yr Avg	7.84	4.26	0.58	8	12,541
5 Yr Avg	9.47	11.77	4.23	3	15,721
10 Yr Avg	12.15	0.08	1.66	8	31,477
15 Yr Avg	10.90	-0.03	0.95	10	47,203

Tax Analysis	Tax-Adj Rtn%	%Rank Cat	Tax-Cost Rat	%Rank Cat
3 Yr (estimated)	4.65	31	1.02	71
5 Yr (estimated)	6.65	4	1.41	68
10 Yr (estimated)	9.07	14	2.17	76

Potential Capital Gain Exposure: 11% of assets

Rating and Risk

Time Period	Load-Adj Return %	Morningstar Rtn vs Cat	Morningstar Risk vs Cat	Morningstar Risk-Adj Rating
1 Yr	2.66			
3 Yr	5.73	+Avg	+Avg	★★★★
5 Yr	8.18	High	Avg	★★★★★
10 Yr	11.49	+Avg	-Avg	★★★★
Incept	6.53			

Other Measures	Standard Index S&P 500	Best Fit Index Russ 1000 VI
Alpha	4.6	1.3
Beta	0.67	0.68
R-Squared	93	95

Standard Deviation	11.08
Mean	7.84
Sharpe Ratio	0.59

Portfolio Analysis 09-30-04

Total Stocks:117 Share change since 06-30-04	Sectors	P/E Ratio	YTD Return %	% Net Assets
Gen Elec	Ind Mtrls	22.8	-3.01	1.88
⊕ Royal Dutch Petroleum ADR	Energy	—	-2.96	1.77
⊕ Altria Group	Goods	13.3	0.82	1.56
⊕ BellSouth	Telecom	12.7	-2.88	1.34
⊕ ExxonMobil	Energy	13.9	-2.75	1.28
Microsoft	Software	36.1	0.04	1.23
⊕ Freddie Mac	Financial	10.6	-3.68	1.19
⊕ Fannie Mae	Financial	9.1	-1.07	1.19
⊕ IBM	Hardware	20.2	-3.63	1.18

Total Fixed-Income:687	Date of Maturity	Amount $000	Value $000	% Net Assets
US Treasury Note 3.5%	11-15-06	500,000	508,830	1.29
US Treasury Note 6.25%	02-15-07	314,000	339,365	0.86
US Treasury Note 5.625%	05-15-08	275,000	299,192	0.76
US Treasury Bond 6.875%	08-15-25	234,000	293,815	0.75
FNMA	10-01-34	234,400	242,384	0.62
US Treasury Note 6.625%	05-15-07	190,000	208,377	0.53
US Treasury Note 6.875%	05-15-06	176,000	188,375	0.48
US Treasury Note 3%	11-15-07	181,000	181,565	0.46
US Treasury Note 5.75%	11-15-05	149,750	155,529	0.40

Equity Style
Style: Blend
Size: Large-Cap

Value Measures		Rel Category
Price/Earnings	15.92	0.96
Price/Book	2.41	0.99
Price/Sales	1.09	0.83
Price/Cash Flow	7.41	1.02
Dividend Yield %	2.03	1.29

Growth Measures	%	Rel Category
Long-Term Erngs	11.08	0.95
Book Value	6.34	1.10
Sales	6.58	1.08
Cash Flow	5.92	0.74
Historical Erngs	11.59	1.07

Market Cap %			
Giant	56.2	Small	0.0
Large	40.6	Micro	0.0
Mid	3.1	Avg $mil:	47,654

Composition

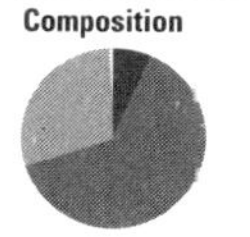

Cash	6.5
Stocks	63.3
Bonds	29.3
Other	0.9
Foreign (% of Stock)	7.9

Fixed-Income Style
Duration: Interm-Term
Quality: High

Avg Eff Duration[1]	4.1 Yrs
Avg Eff Maturity	5.5 Yrs
Avg Credit Quality	AA
Avg Wtd Coupon	5.35%

[1]figure provided by fund as of 09-30-04

Sector Weightings	% of Stocks	Rel S&P 500	3 Year High	3 Year Low
Info	22.88	1.06		
Software	2.98	0.69	3	2
Hardware	10.33	1.01	10	6
Media	2.83	0.74	3	1
Telecom	6.74	2.14	10	4
Service	42.18	0.91		
Health	11.83	0.95	13	11
Consumer	9.63	1.06	12	10
Business	3.18	0.79	4	1
Financial	17.54	0.84	22	14
Mfg	34.94	1.09		
Goods	11.12	1.19	11	6
Ind Mtrls	14.39	1.14	18	14
Energy	7.57	1.06	11	7
Utilities	1.86	0.63	5	2

Morningstar's Take by Paul Herbert 12-31-04

We like everything about American Funds American Balanced but its size.

No moderate-allocation fund has been more popular than this one during 2004, as it has raked in around $12 billion in inflows. As we have written before, asset growth can affect a fund manager's ability to trade in and out of stocks without affecting their prices. To minimize these types of trading costs, managers have often tweaked their strategies. Unfortunately, we have seen cases in which one move or the other has hurt fund performance.

As a result, we think the prudent step--and one that other popular balanced-fund advisors have taken lately--is to limit asset growth. Dodge & Cox announced that it is closing its Balanced fund in September, and Oakmark Equity & Income closed to fund supermarkets in May. American has never closed a fund and argues that its low-turnover approach and multiple-portfolio-counselor system allow it to run much more money than other shops.

We agree that these steps add capacity, but the firm now manages eight funds with asset bases greater than $30 billion, including this one, and there is significant overlap among the funds' holdings. Exiting these positions will become tougher.

In other regards, and like other American Funds, this offering stands out from the competition. It is constructed to serve as a long-term investor's entire portfolio, and over time it has trounced its category rivals without taking on excessive risks. Its managers look at risk in terms of losing money instead of in terms of staying close to a benchmark's performance--a viewpoint that helped the fund tremendously during the recent bear market. The fund also benefits from low costs and a world-class research effort.

All together, it's a nice package, but we remain concerned that asset bloat could cause the fund to lose some of its edge.

Address:	333 S Hope St - 52nd Floor Los Angeles, CA 90071 800-421-0180
Web Address:	
Inception:	01-03-33
Advisor:	Capital Research and Management Company
Subadvisor:	None
NTF Plans:	Federated Tr NTF

Minimum Purchase:	$250	Add: $50	IRA: $250
Min Auto Inv Plan:	$50	Add: $50	
Sales Fees:	5.75%L		
Management Fee:	0.42% mx./0.22% mn.		
Actual Fees:	Mgt:0.26%	Dist:0.25%	
Expense Projections:	3Yr:$777	5Yr:$927	10Yr:$1362
Income Distrib:	Quarterly		

Amer Funds Amer H/I A

Ticker	Load	NAV	Yield	SEC Yield	Total Assets	Mstar Category
AHITX	3.75%	$12.61	6.9%	—	$10,074 mil	High Yield Bond

Governance and Management

Fiduciary Grade: B

Portfolio Manager(s)

This fund is run by a team of managers (including David Barclay, Susan Tolson, and Abner Goldstine), each of whom is responsible for a segment of the portfolio. The managers communicate regularly and have access to vast research resources.

Strategy

The fund's management team targets issues with improving revenues and cash flows, much like stock-pickers do. The strategy has been capably executed over the long stretch, and it relies on a division of labor, with each of the fund's portfolio counselors getting a slice of the fund to manage individually. The group works together and shares resources, but each member has the final say on his or her portion of the portfolio. In general, the team has managed the fund more conservatively than its average high-yield fund peer.

Historical Profile

Return Above Avg
Risk Above Avg
Rating ★★★★ Above Avg

Investment Style: Fixed Income — Income Rtn %Rank Cat: 60, 70, 53, 42, 57, 51, 36, 44, 44

▼ Manager Change
▽ Partial Manager Change

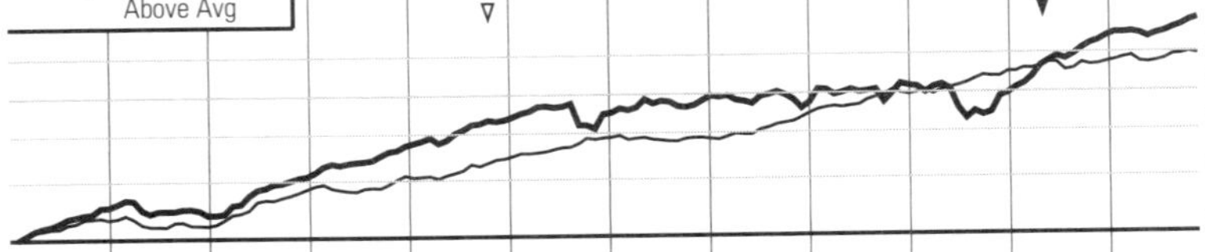

Growth of $10,000
— Investment Values of Fund
— Investment Values of LB Aggr

Performance Quartile (within Category)

1993	1994	1995	1996	1997	1998	1999	2000	2001	2002	2003	12-04	History
15.24	13.13	14.42	15.03	15.20	14.13	13.84	12.14	11.83	10.33	12.33	12.61	NAV
17.12	-5.11	20.68	13.75	12.20	1.64	7.54	-3.24	7.44	-3.59	28.87	9.78	Total Return %
7.37	-2.19	2.21	10.12	2.55	-7.05	8.36	-14.87	-1.00	-13.84	24.77	5.44	+/-LB Aggr
-1.79	-4.14	3.29	1.33	-0.43	1.06	4.26	1.97	1.66	-6.70	0.94	-2.18	+/-CSFB Glb HY
9.08	8.78	9.91	9.22	8.71	8.68	9.68	9.63	10.20	9.23	8.84	7.31	Income Return %
8.04	-13.89	10.77	4.53	3.49	-7.04	-2.14	-12.87	-2.76	-12.82	20.03	2.47	Capital Return %
78	81	5	33	69	35	21	20	13	73	18	49	Total Rtn % Rank Cat
1.26	1.28	1.25	1.28	1.26	1.27	1.31	1.27	1.19	1.04	0.88	0.87	Income $
0.30	0.08	0.08	0.02	0.34	0.05	0.00	0.00	0.00	0.00	0.00	0.00	Capital Gains $
0.87	0.86	0.89	0.87	0.82	0.81	0.82	0.82	0.83	0.88	0.75	0.67	Expense Ratio %
8.60	8.63	9.72	8.90	8.35	8.76	9.21	8.87	9.75	9.99	8.49	7.19	Income Ratio %
44	42	30	40	54	55	30	46	44	34	41	39	Turnover Rate %
789	798	1,211	1,671	2,194	2,573	2,871	2,620	3,290	3,892	6,831	7,408	Net Assets $mil

Performance 12-31-04

	1st Qtr	2nd Qtr	3rd Qtr	4th Qtr	Total
2000	-1.95	1.51	0.63	-3.40	-3.24
2001	3.50	1.03	-4.36	7.43	7.44
2002	-0.58	-9.06	-3.17	10.14	-3.59
2003	7.52	9.44	3.64	5.67	28.87
2004	1.70	-0.86	3.83	4.86	9.78

Trailing	Total Return%	+/- LB Aggr	+/- CSFB Glb HY	%Rank Cat	Growth of $10,000
3 Mo	4.86	3.91	0.30	29	10,486
6 Mo	8.88	4.70	-0.38	38	10,888
1 Yr	9.78	5.44	-2.18	49	10,978
3 Yr Avg	10.90	4.71	-2.98	39	13,639
5 Yr Avg	7.23	-0.48	-0.94	14	14,177
10 Yr Avg	9.09	1.37	0.47	4	23,870
15 Yr Avg	9.74	2.04	-0.35	7	40,316

Tax Analysis	Tax-Adj Rtn%	%Rank Cat	Tax-Cost Rat	%Rank Cat
3 Yr (estimated)	6.27	63	2.95	59
5 Yr (estimated)	2.93	28	3.28	48
10 Yr (estimated)	4.96	9	3.42	47

Potential Capital Gain Exposure: 3% of assets

Rating and Risk

Time Period	Load-Adj Return %	Morningstar Rtn vs Cat	Morningstar Risk vs Cat	Morningstar Risk-Adj Rating
1 Yr	5.66			
3 Yr	9.50	Avg	+Avg	★★★
5 Yr	6.42	+Avg	+Avg	★★★
10 Yr	8.68	+Avg	+Avg	★★★★
Incept	9.25			

Other Measures	Standard Index LB Aggr	Best Fit Index CSFB Glb HY
Alpha	9.4	-6.4
Beta	0.08	1.35
R-Squared	0	87
Standard Deviation	9.90	
Mean	10.90	
Sharpe Ratio	0.97	

Portfolio Analysis 09-30-04

Total Fixed-Income:626	Date of Maturity	Amount $000	Value $000	% Net Assets
Western Wireless 9.25%	07-15-13	79,675	81,667	0.87
Freeport-Mcmoran Copper	02-01-10	71,425	81,157	0.87
Nextel Partners 8.125%	07-01-11	72,075	76,760	0.82
Nextel Comms 7.375%	08-01-15	69,650	75,222	0.80
Amazon Com Cv 6.875%	02-16-10	59,550	74,922	0.80
Fuji Jgb Invt 144A FRN	12-31-49	61,565	72,315	0.77
Amer Tower 9.375%	02-01-09	66,322	70,633	0.75
Cinemark Usa 9%	02-01-13	58,218	65,350	0.70
Solectron 9.625%	02-15-09	54,425	60,548	0.65
Sanmina Sci 10.375%	01-15-10	51,750	59,448	0.63
Burns Philp Cap Pty 9.75	07-15-12	55,247	59,391	0.63
Ibj Pfd Cap 144A FRN	12-29-49	51,675	59,336	0.63
Cincinnati Bell 7.25%	07-15-13	56,925	55,075	0.59
Hollinger Partn Tr 144A	11-15-10	46,559	53,426	0.57
Young Broadcstg 10%	03-01-11	50,560	52,330	0.56
Pathmark Stores 8.75%	02-01-12	54,965	51,667	0.55
Qwest Svcs 144A 13.5%	12-15-10	43,215	50,670	0.54
Equistar Chemicals Lp /	05-01-11	43,875	50,237	0.54
Dynegy 144A 10.125%	07-15-13	43,390	50,115	0.54
Quintiles Transnational	10-01-13	46,900	49,949	0.53

Current Investment Style

Duration: Short Int Long — Quality: High Med Low

1 figure provided by fund

Avg Eff Duration[1]	3.6 Yrs
Avg Eff Maturity	5.1 Yrs
Avg Credit Quality	BB
Avg Wtd Coupon	8.39%
Avg Wtd Price	106.18% of par

Coupon Range	% of Bonds	Rel Cat
0% PIK	2.8	0.6
0% to 8%	37.2	1.0
8% to 11%	58.0	1.1
11% to 14%	4.5	0.7
More than 14%	0.3	1.5

1.00=Category Average

Credit Analysis		% bonds 09-30-04	
US Govt	1	BB	28
AAA	0	B	47
AA	0	Below B	10
A	3	NR/NA	0
BBB	10		

Sector Breakdown	% of assets
US Treasuries	1
TIPS	0
US Agency	0
Mortgage Pass-Throughs	0
Mortgage CMO	0
Mortgage ARM	0
US Corporate	83
Asset-Backed	1
Convertible	3
Municipal	0
Corporate Inflation-Protected	0
Foreign Corporate	5
Foreign Govt	1

Composition			
Cash	6.0	Bonds	88.3
Stocks	1.3	Other	4.4

Special Securities	
Restricted/Illiquid Secs	18
Exotic Mortgage-Backed	0
Emerging-Markets Secs	Trace
Options/Futures/Warrants	No

Morningstar's Take by Eric Jacobson 11-14-04

American High Income Trust's robust growth is worth watching over but not fretting over.

In a bit more than a year, this fund's assets have swelled by roughly $1.2 billion. In total it now boasts a $9.7 billion across all share classes. As such, the fund has surpassed its nearest rival, the $9.4 billion Vanguard corporate high yield to become the category's largest offering, and its recent growth alone would be enough to rank it in the top quartile according to size.

If nothing else that gives reason for pause. The average new high-yield issue in 2004 recently ran around $250 million, though some have been much larger. That suggests that for this fund, whose typical holding runs from $45 million to $110 million, getting big stakes in bonds its managers like must sometimes be a challenge. And to the degree that it hasn't been an issue in the past, it's logical to question whether it could become one in the future.

The fund's managers have been laboring to address that topic for a while. To begin with, the American Funds model is as well matched to running large portfolios as any. All together there are 27 people doing research for and managing this fund. That represents the addition of new help, as well as a broadening of research efforts. Comanager David Barclay explains, for example, that while the chemicals sector had been one of a few on the plate of one analyst, it's now the sole work of another. Importantly, Barclay also notes that it's typical for the fund to take as long as two years to build positions, making the need to buy big chunks at once less of an issue.

This fund has an excellent record, and advisor Capital Research has been a trustworthy steward. When its managers say they're not yet to the point at which its size constrains their investment discipline, we take them at their word. The optimal size of a fund is a target that moves with its market, though, so both of those and this fund's methods will be important to watch going forward.

Address:	333 S Hope St - 52nd Floor Los Angeles CA 90071 800-421-0180
Web Address:	www.americanfunds.com
Inception:	02-19-88
Advisor:	Capital Research and Management Company
Subadvisor:	None
NTF Plans:	Federated Tr NTF, Schwab Instl NTF

Minimum Purchase:	$250	Add: $50	IRA: $250
Min Auto Inv Plan:	$50	Add: $50	
Sales Fees:	3.75%L		
Management Fee:	0.45% mx./0.18% mn.		
Actual Fees:	Mgt:0.39%	Dist:0.24%	
Expense Projections:	3Yr:$606	5Yr:$776	10Yr:$1270
Income Distrib:	Monthly		

Amer Funds Amer Mut A

Ticker	Load	NAV	Yield	Total Assets	Mstar Category
AMRMX	5.75%	$25.48	1.7%	$14,966 mil	Large Value

Governance and Management

Fiduciary Grade: B

Portfolio Manager(s)

As with other American Funds, this fund's managers oversee several portfolios. The five portfolio counselors on this offering boast an average of 25 years of investment experience with the firm. Manager James Dunton has 40 years of experience. The firm's research staff, which plays a vital role, is equally seasoned. Many analysts at the firm follow a career analyst track and have covered their respective industries for decades.

Strategy

The fund aims to meet three goals: current income, capital growth, and conservation of principal. In pursuit of these objectives, management favors established, dividend-paying companies. And like most funds in the firm's roster, management likes to buy shares on the cheap. To smooth volatility, the fund typically has a sizable cash stake. Finally, the fund won't invest in companies that derive the majority of their revenues from tobacco or alcohol.

Historical Profile

Return Average
Risk Low
Rating ★★★★ Above Avg

Investment Style: Equity Stock %

72%	73%	72%	69%	73%	77%	76%	79%	84%

▼ Manager Change
∇ Partial Manager Change

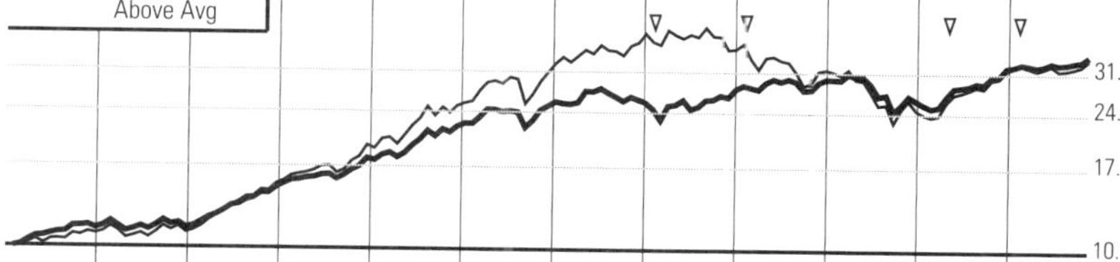

Growth of $10,000
— Investment Values of Fund
— Investment Values of S&P 500

Performance Quartile (within Category)

1993	1994	1995	1996	1997	1998	1999	2000	2001	2002	2003	12-04	History
21.77	20.11	24.33	25.76	29.21	29.65	23.83	23.87	24.05	20.32	24.38	26.48	NAV
14.28	0.33	31.38	16.22	26.39	14.76	-0.12	9.12	6.67	-12.18	23.32	10.74	Total Return %
4.22	-0.98	-6.15	-6.72	-6.96	-13.81	-21.16	18.22	18.55	9.91	-5.35	-0.13	+/-S&P 500
-3.79	2.31	-6.98	-5.42	-8.79	-0.87	-7.47	2.11	12.26	3.34	-6.71	-5.75	+/-Russ 1000 Vl
4.10	3.92	4.24	3.50	3.14	2.77	2.52	3.14	3.05	2.18	2.58	1.82	Income Return %
10.18	-3.59	27.14	12.72	23.25	11.99	-2.64	5.98	3.62	-14.36	20.74	8.92	Capital Return %
49	36	69	81	62	35	74	53	9	8	88	73	Total Rtn % Rank Cat
0.84	0.84	0.84	0.84	0.80	0.80	0.74	0.74	0.72	0.52	0.52	0.44	Income $
1.11	0.87	1.15	1.61	2.48	2.93	5.04	1.25	0.65	0.31	0.09	0.05	Capital Gains $
0.59	0.60	0.59	0.59	0.58	0.56	0.57	0.59	0.59	0.60	0.62	—	Expense Ratio %
3.83	4.07	3.92	3.36	2.95	2.75	2.67	3.29	2.67	2.15	2.32	—	Income Ratio %
22	18	23	24	19	29	42	29	45	31	24	—	Turnover Rate %
5,194	5,279	6,946	7,982	9,739	10,629	9,652	8,515	9,002	8,028	10,449	12,986	Net Assets $mil

Performance 12-31-04

	1st Qtr	2nd Qtr	3rd Qtr	4th Qtr	Total
2000	-1.94	-2.02	6.30	6.86	9.12
2001	-0.20	5.29	-5.30	7.20	6.67
2002	3.62	-6.29	-15.73	7.33	-12.18
2003	-3.70	13.05	2.14	10.90	23.32
2004	1.52	1.79	0.28	6.87	10.74

Trailing	Total Return%	+/- S&P 500	+/- Russ 1000 Vl	%Rank Cat	Growth of $10,000
3 Mo	6.87	-2.36	-3.51	94	10,687
6 Mo	7.17	-0.02	-4.91	76	10,717
1 Yr	10.74	-0.13	-5.75	73	11,074
3 Yr Avg	6.25	2.67	-2.32	42	11,995
5 Yr Avg	6.90	9.20	1.63	22	13,960
10 Yr Avg	11.94	-0.13	-1.89	37	30,892
15 Yr Avg	10.67	-0.26	-1.36	49	45,756

Tax Analysis	Tax-Adj Rtn%	%Rank Cat	Tax-Cost Rat	%Rank Cat
3 Yr (estimated)	3.23	68	0.90	60
5 Yr (estimated)	4.23	35	1.33	70
10 Yr (estimated)	8.80	59	2.23	77

Potential Capital Gain Exposure: 19% of assets

Rating and Risk

Time Period	Load-Adj Return %	Morningstar Rtn vs Cat	Morningstar Risk vs Cat	Morningstar Risk-Adj Rating
1 Yr	4.38			
3 Yr	4.17	Avg	Low	★★★
5 Yr	5.64	+Avg	Low	★★★★
10 Yr	11.28	Avg	Low	★★★★
Incept	11.96			

Other Measures	Standard Index S&P 500	Best Fit Index Russ 1000 Vl
Alpha	3.0	-0.8
Beta	0.76	0.78
R-Squared	92	97

Standard Deviation	12.52
Mean	6.25
Sharpe Ratio	0.39

Portfolio Analysis 09-30-04

Share change since 06-04 Total Stocks:127	Sector	PE	YTD Ret%	% Assets
⊕ IBM	Hardware	20.2	7.19	2.10
Gen Elec	Ind Mtrls	22.8	20.68	1.96
⊕ Fannie Mae	Financial	9.1	-2.33	1.95
⊕ BellSouth	Telecom	12.7	1.94	1.84
⊕ Bank of America	Financial	12.3	21.50	1.70
⊕ J P Morgan Chase	Financial	19.4	9.97	1.65
⊕ Abbott Laboratories	Health	22.1	2.61	1.65
Sprint	Telecom	—	55.24	1.62
⊕ General Motors	Goods	7.2	-21.48	1.56
⊕ Hewlett-Packard	Hardware	18.9	-7.28	1.48
Norfolk Southern	Business	—	55.12	1.46
⊕ Freddie Mac	Financial	10.6	28.75	1.45
⊕ Eli Lilly & Company	Health	24.3	-17.55	1.41
Marathon Oil	Energy	—	17.07	1.39
⊕ ChevronTexaco	Energy	7.7	25.57	1.37
⊕ Bristol-Myers Squibb	Health	17.7	-7.27	1.31
⊕ ExxonMobil	Energy	13.9	28.04	1.29
FNMA 6%	—	—	—	1.28
☼ St. Paul Travelers Compa	Financial	30.8	-3.15	1.25
⊖ ConocoPhillips	Energy	9.0	35.60	1.21

Current Investment Style

Value Blnd Growth — Large Mid Small

Market Cap	%
Giant	41.7
Large	44.7
Mid	13.6
Small	0.0
Micro	0.0
Avg $mil: 30,734	

Value Measures		Rel Category
Price/Earnings	14.35	0.95
Price/Book	2.08	0.92
Price/Sales	0.88	0.74
Price/Cash Flow	6.46	1.01
Dividend Yield %	2.42	1.19

Growth Measures	%	Rel Category
Long-Term Erngs	9.83	0.94
Book Value	5.79	1.03
Sales	3.61	0.86
Cash Flow	3.23	0.62
Historical Erngs	11.35	0.96

Profitability	%	Rel Category
Return on Equity	16.14	1.02
Return on Assets	7.78	0.99
Net Margin	9.51	0.93

Sector Weightings	% of Stocks	Rel S&P 500	3 Year High	Low
Info	14.40	0.67		
Software	0.72	0.17	1	0
Hardware	6.39	0.63	7	6
Media	0.57	0.15	1	0
Telecom	6.72	2.13	8	6
Service	42.93	0.93		
Health	10.63	0.85	11	8
Consumer	6.52	0.72	9	7
Business	4.06	1.00	5	4
Financial	21.72	1.05	25	20
Mfg	42.66	1.33		
Goods	8.99	0.96	10	7
Ind Mtrls	17.02	1.34	17	11
Energy	10.39	1.45	10	8
Utilities	6.26	2.11	11	6

Composition

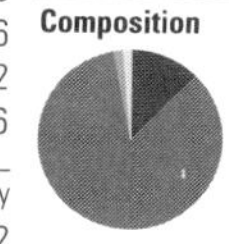

Cash	12.5
Stocks	84.3
Bonds	1.6
Other	1.6
Foreign (% of Stock)	1.1

Morningstar's Take by Paul Herbert 01-06-05

This mutual fund holds your hand and tells you everything will be okay, and it usually is.

American Funds American Mutual provides low-stress exposure to the equity market. In contrast to bolder peers who try only to grow capital, this fund's managers also try to produce current income and conserve principal. They target dividend-paying stocks and hold some bonds to boost the fund's yield--which at 1.9% recently was well above the large-value norm. They frequently stash more than 10% of assets in cash to keep the fund from giving up much ground in stock market downturns.

In recent years, the results of the fund's approach have been predictable performance and delightfully low volatility. As expected, it lagged its large-value peers during the 1990s but found its footing when such stocks skidded during the bear-market period, posting top-10% showings in 2001 and 2002. When low-quality stocks returned to favor in 2003, the fund again fell near the back of the pack. (Though its 23% return was nothing to sneeze at.) Its varying relative rankings shouldn't suggest it's a wildcat, though: The fund has offered one of its category's least-bumpy rides over time.

The fund's makeup allowed it to hang in there during 2004 as well. Again last year, the fund held a sizable cash stake--12.5% as of September--and favored the yield-rich telecom, utilities, and financials areas. It was left behind during rallies, especially the fourth quarter's, but when stocks skidded in March and July, its performance was first-rate. The fund lagged more than two thirds of its peers for the year, but given its cautious leanings, we're impressed by its 10.7% gain.

American Funds' recent popularity has made us concerned that the funds could lose a step if asset growth continues at its current clip, although that's less of a worry with this conservative, $14 billion offering.

In all, though, this fund is a keeper.

Address:	333 S Hope St - 52nd Floor Los Angeles, CA 90071 800-421-0180
Web Address:	
Inception:	02-21-50
Advisor:	Capital Research and Management Company
Subadvisor:	None
NTF Plans:	Federated Tr NTF

Minimum Purchase:	$250	Add: $50	IRA: $250
Min Auto Inv Plan:	$50	Add: $50	
Sales Fees:	5.75%L		
Management Fee:	0.38% mx./0.23% mn.		
Actual Fees:	Mgt:0.28%	Dist:0.23%	
Expense Projections:	3Yr:$762	5Yr:$901	10Yr:$1305
Income Distrib:	Quarterly		

Amer Funds CpIncBldr A

Analyst Pick	Ticker	Load	NAV	Yield	Total Assets	Mstar Category
✔	CAIBX	5.75%	$53.26	3.4%	$41,889 mil	World Allocation

Governance and Management

Fiduciary Grade: B

Portfolio Manager(s)

American Funds uses a multimanager system in which each of the fund's managers runs a portion of assets independently of the other managers. Many of the managers (also known as counselors) on this fund have been managing money for years, and many run other American Funds' portfolios as well.

Strategy

This fund has a razor-sharp focus on income. Its stock portfolio, for example, is filled with high-yielding names. Its bond portfolio consists mostly of U.S. Treasuries, investment-grade corporations, and mortgages. Although the fund's stock stake has hovered between 50% and 65%, its bond stake has varied widely: It has been as high as 40% and as low as 10% (with the remainder in cash).

Historical Profile

Return Above Avg
Risk Below Avg
Rating ★★★★ Above Avg

Investment Style Equity Stock %: 64% 65% 58% 63% 59% 59% 47% 62% 66%

▼ Manager Change
▽ Partial Manager Change

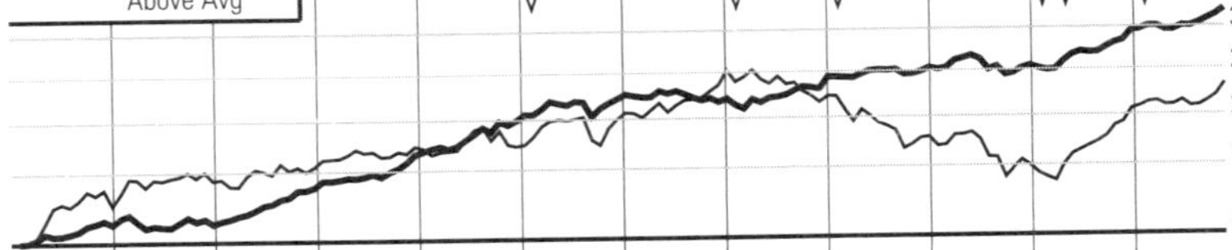

Growth of $10,000
— Investment Values of Fund
— Investment Values of MSCI EAFE

Performance Quartile (within Category)

History	1993	1994	1995	1996	1997	1998	1999	2000	2001	2002	2003	12-04
NAV	34.30	31.72	37.23	41.03	46.90	47.47	42.67	44.82	43.59	41.33	47.87	53.26
Total Return %	15.29	-2.26	25.05	17.64	23.33	11.75	-2.76	12.52	4.75	0.65	21.57	17.40
+/-MSCI EAFE	-17.27	-10.04	13.84	11.59	21.55	-8.18	-29.79	26.71	26.17	16.59	-17.02	-2.85
+/-DJ 60%	-1.97	-2.73	5.25	6.98	11.43	-0.57	-20.09	14.19	7.55	7.42	-5.81	4.43
Income Return %	5.17	4.97	5.63	5.01	4.68	4.22	4.18	4.80	4.73	4.76	4.84	3.85
Capital Return %	10.12	-7.23	19.42	12.63	18.65	7.53	-6.94	7.72	0.02	-4.11	16.73	13.55
Total Rtn % Rank Cat	83	34	1	1	1	42	100	1	13	20	63	15
Income $	1.59	1.67	1.75	1.83	1.89	1.95	1.96	2.01	2.08	2.04	1.97	1.82
Capital Gains $	0.12	0.10	0.50	0.73	1.61	2.81	1.54	0.94	1.17	0.52	0.17	0.90
Expense Ratio %	0.72	0.73	0.72	0.71	0.65	0.64	0.64	0.67	0.66	0.67	0.65	—
Income Ratio %	4.69	5.29	4.96	5.19	4.04	4.35	4.15	4.67	4.36	4.19	4.04	—
Turnover Rate %	11	36	18	28	28	24	21	41	37	36	27	—
Net Assets $mil	3,040	3,597	4,809	5,809	7,803	9,239	8,392	7,708	8,428	11,078	20,605	32,505

Performance 12-31-04

	1st Qtr	2nd Qtr	3rd Qtr	4th Qtr	Total
2000	-0.53	1.20	5.81	5.64	12.52
2001	-0.63	4.41	-2.66	3.73	4.75
2002	4.08	0.66	-8.60	5.10	0.65
2003	-2.12	10.49	2.36	9.82	21.57
2004	2.51	-0.08	4.03	10.18	17.40

Trailing	Total Return%	+/- MSCI EAFE	+/- DJ 60%	%Rank Cat	Growth of $10,000
3 Mo	10.18	-5.14	1.33	26	11,018
6 Mo	14.62	-0.38	4.84	6	11,462
1 Yr	17.40	-2.85	4.43	15	11,740
3 Yr Avg	12.83	0.94	2.54	24	14,364
5 Yr Avg	11.11	12.24	6.01	10	16,934
10 Yr Avg	12.81	7.19	3.18	9	33,379
15 Yr Avg	11.90	7.67	2.48	50	54,007

Tax Analysis	Tax-Adj Rtn%	%Rank Cat	Tax-Cost Rat	%Rank Cat
3 Yr (estimated)	8.73	70	1.72	100
5 Yr (estimated)	7.65	10	1.96	100
10 Yr (estimated)	9.70	9	2.18	55

Potential Capital Gain Exposure: 19% of assets

Rating and Risk

Time Period	Load-Adj Return %	Morningstar Rtn vs Cat	Morningstar Risk vs Cat	Morningstar Risk-Adj Rating
1 Yr	10.65			
3 Yr	10.63	Avg	-Avg	★★★
5 Yr	9.80	+Avg	-Avg	★★★★
10 Yr	12.14	+Avg	-Avg	★★★★
Incept	11.41			

Other Measures	Standard Index S&P 500	Best Fit Index MSCI Wd xUS
Alpha	5.9	5.7
Beta	0.48	0.49
R-Squared	81	81
Standard Deviation	9.27	
Mean	12.83	
Sharpe Ratio	1.25	

Portfolio Analysis 09-30-04

Total Stocks:184 Share change since 06-30-04	Sectors	P/E Ratio	YTD Return %	% Net Assets
⊕ SBC Communications	Telecom	15.4	-3.12	1.62
⊕ Altria Group	Goods	13.3	0.82	1.59
⊕ E.ON	Utilities	—	—	1.56
⊕ Verizon Communications	Telecom	32.4	-3.79	1.54
⊕ Bank of America	Financial	12.3	-3.85	1.43
⊕ Natl Grid Transco PLC	Utilities	—	—	1.42
⊕ HSBC Hldgs	Financial	—	—	1.26
⊕ Eni	Energy	—	—	1.10
⊕ Washington Mutual	Financial	13.9	-2.55	1.05

Total Fixed-Income:517	Date of Maturity	Amount $000	Value $000	% Net Assets
US Treasury Bond 9.375%	02-15-06	130,000	142,350	0.43
Deutsche Telekom Intl Fin	06-01-06	82,250	118,480	0.36
US Treasury Bond 12.75%	11-15-10	100,000	111,469	0.34
US Treasury Note 6.875%	05-15-06	100,000	107,031	0.33
Verizon Wireless Cap 5.37	12-15-06	91,600	95,932	0.29
FNMA	10-01-34	92,110	95,247	0.29
FHLMC 5.25%	01-15-06	80,000	82,761	0.25
FHLMC 5.75%	03-15-09	75,000	81,579	0.25

Current Investment Style

Value Blnd Growth / Large Mid Small

Market Cap	%
Giant	38.1
Large	36.6
Mid	23.8
Small	1.6
Micro	0.0
Avg $mil: 17,583	

Value Measures		Rel Category
Price/Earnings	13.21	0.95
Price/Book	1.99	1.04
Price/Sales	1.22	1.14
Price/Cash Flow	5.82	1.04
Dividend Yield %	4.32	1.51

Growth Measures	%	Rel Category
Long-Term Erngs	8.07	0.78
Book Value	3.92	1.48
Sales	2.91	0.73
Cash Flow	3.64	0.69
Historical Erngs	6.53	1.01

Sector Weightings	% of Stocks	Rel MSCI EAFE	3 Year High	3 Year Low
Info	15.57	0.94		
Software	1.22	1.13	1	0
Hardware	0.00	0.00	0	0
Media	0.32	0.14	1	0
Telecom	14.03	1.46	14	3
Service	39.86	0.89		
Health	2.06	0.28	3	0
Consumer	2.45	0.49	4	0
Business	3.39	0.62	4	1
Financial	31.96	1.18	46	30
Mfg	44.57	1.15		
Goods	13.18	0.96	15	13
Ind Mtrls	8.77	0.71	12	6
Energy	7.30	0.99	11	6
Utilities	15.32	2.86	21	15

Composition			
Cash	9.8	Bonds	22.5
Stocks	65.5	Other	2.2
Foreign (% of Stock)			53.1

Regional Exposure	% Stock		
UK/W. Europe	35	N. America	50
Japan	0	Latn America	0
Asia X Japan	14	Other	1

Country Exposure	% Stock		
United States	47	Netherlands	5
U.K.	13	Spain	3
Australia	6		

Morningstar's Take by Gareth Lyons 12-21-04

We like Capital Income Builder's feet-on-the-ground approach.

Thrill-seeking investors are likely to balk at this fund's mandate. The managers focus heavily on income and to a lesser extent on capital appreciation. The bond sleeve, which currently soaks up one quarter of assets, is comprised mostly of U.S. government and investment-grade debt. The equity portion, which accounts for 65% of the fund, has a conservative bias, too, as its large swath of dividend-paying stocks attests. In addition, portfolio turnover is less than one half of the category norm, meaning management isn't apt to shift the asset mix to latch on to the best-returning asset class in any given quarter.

The fund's behavior bears out that strategy. Its below-average performances in both 1999 and 2003 clearly show that this fund won't shine when speculative or growth-oriented issues are making hay. When markets are less exuberant, however, this fund typically wallops the competition. The team's disciplined approach and focus on capital conservation helped its shareholders emerge from the last bear market without any significant wounds. This year, the portfolio's ownership of income-generating stocks from the energy and utility sectors have helped the fund outpace most peers.

Such outperformance has attracted plenty of attention in recent years. With more than $31 billion under management, it is by far the biggest fund in its category. Advisor Capital Research and Management's multimanager setup and low-turnover approach help to allay our concerns somewhat. Nonetheless, we're not thrilled about the velocity in asset growth. Expecting this fund to keep expanding without impacting the investment style may be a leap of faith.

The fund is no doubt a compelling option, but to stay that way, we'd like to see its advisor set some limits on inflows.

Address:	333 S Hope St - 52 Floor Los Angeles CA 90071 800-421-0180
Web Address:	www.americanfunds.com
Inception:	07-30-87
Advisor:	Capital Research and Management Company
Subadvisor:	None
NTF Plans:	Federated Tr NTF

Minimum Purchase:	$250	Add: $50	IRA: $250
Min Auto Inv Plan:	$250	Add: $50	
Sales Fees:	5.75%L		
Management Fee:	0.31%		
Actual Fees:	Mgt:0.31%	Dist:0.22%	
Expense Projections:	3Yr:$774	5Yr:$922	10Yr:$1350
Income Distrib:	Quarterly		

Amer Funds CapWrldBd A

Ticker	Load	NAV	Yield	SEC Yield	Total Assets	Mstar Category
CWBFX	3.75%	$20.01	3.9%	3.22%	$2,049 mil	World Bond

Governance and Management

Fiduciary Grade: B

Portfolio Manager(s)

Five individual managers and a group of analysts each manages a slice of the fund. The managers have between five and 17 years on the fund. They also work on other American Funds bond funds, such as Intermediate Bond Fund of America and U.S. Government Securities. Their setup is slightly different than at other American Funds, with a couple of the managers acting more as specialists in their sectors.

Strategy

This fund primarily invests in investment-grade debt, but shareholders have voted to allow it to put up to 25% of assets in high-yield and emerging-markets bonds, although the managers generally stick to investment-grade debt in emerging markets. Management does make currency bets and country bets. It recently moved from a mostly foreign-currency benchmark, however, to one that's normally about 50% exposed to the U.S. dollar.

Historical Profile

Return Average
Risk Average
Rating ★★★ Neutral

Investment Style: Fixed Income — Income Rtn %Rank Cat: 76 64 55 56 79 85 81 57 57

▼ Manager Change
▽ Partial Manager Change

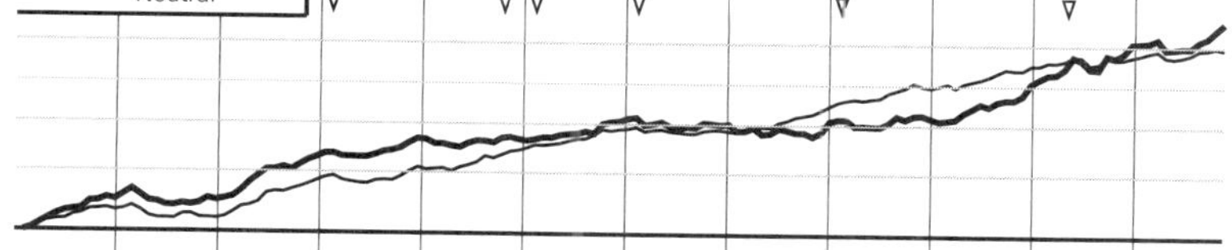

Growth of $10,000

— Investment Values of Fund
— Investment Values of LB Aggr

Performance Quartile (within Category)

1993	1994	1995	1996	1997	1998	1999	2000	2001	2002	2003	12-04	History
16.33	15.12	17.09	16.95	15.75	16.18	14.96	14.63	14.53	16.49	18.80	20.01	NAV
16.73	-1.43	21.41	6.34	-0.36	10.09	-2.16	1.46	1.53	16.45	18.86	11.38	Total Return %
6.98	1.49	2.94	2.71	-10.01	1.40	-1.34	-10.17	-6.91	6.20	14.76	7.04	+/-LB Aggr
1.61	-7.42	1.86	2.26	3.90	-7.70	2.91	4.09	5.07	-5.54	0.34	-0.76	+/-SB Wld Govt
6.71	6.02	8.14	5.67	5.17	5.18	5.05	3.59	2.21	2.78	4.68	4.23	Income Return %
10.02	-7.45	13.27	0.67	-5.53	4.91	-7.21	-2.13	-0.68	13.67	14.18	7.15	Capital Return %
41	20	21	80	74	44	45	59	51	35	21	20	Total Rtn % Rank Cat
0.98	0.96	1.20	0.95	0.86	0.80	0.80	0.53	0.32	0.40	0.76	0.78	Income $
0.08	0.00	0.00	0.23	0.28	0.32	0.07	0.00	0.00	0.00	0.00	0.10	Capital Gains $
1.19	1.11	1.12	1.09	1.07	1.06	1.08	1.12	1.12	1.08	1.04	1.02	Expense Ratio %
6.25	6.88	6.83	6.07	5.21	5.15	4.66	4.66	5.46	5.38	4.22	3.74	Income Ratio %
28	77	105	91	79	101	129	52	61	48	83	79	Turnover Rate %
526	563	698	815	710	626	515	417	383	544	935	1,427	Net Assets $mil

Performance 12-31-04

	1st Qtr	2nd Qtr	3rd Qtr	4th Qtr	Total
2000	-1.34	-0.20	-1.87	5.01	1.46
2001	-1.99	-0.15	3.32	0.41	1.53
2002	-0.21	6.80	1.83	7.31	16.45
2003	4.09	6.21	2.28	5.11	18.86
2004	2.03	-3.57	4.39	8.45	11.38

Trailing	Total Return%	+/- LB Aggr	+/- SB Wld Govt	%Rank Cat	Growth of $10,000
3 Mo	8.45	7.50	-2.19	37	10,845
6 Mo	13.21	9.03	-1.06	25	11,321
1 Yr	11.38	7.04	-0.76	20	11,138
3 Yr Avg	15.52	9.33	-1.96	29	15,416
5 Yr Avg	9.69	1.98	0.92	21	15,879
10 Yr Avg	8.21	0.49	0.88	27	22,013
15 Yr Avg	8.25	0.55	-0.41	25	32,841

Tax Analysis	Tax-Adj Rtn%	%Rank Cat	Tax-Cost Rat	%Rank Cat
3 Yr (estimated)	12.57	31	1.31	18
5 Yr (estimated)	7.50	18	1.25	14
10 Yr (estimated)	5.76	27	1.88	25

Potential Capital Gain Exposure: 11% of assets

Rating and Risk

Time Period	Load-Adj Return %	Morningstar Rtn vs Cat	Morningstar Risk vs Cat	Morningstar Risk-Adj Rating
1 Yr	7.21			
3 Yr	14.06	Avg	Avg	★★★
5 Yr	8.86	+Avg	Avg	★★★★
10 Yr	7.79	Avg	Avg	★★★
Incept	8.09			

Other Measures	Standard Index LB Aggr	Best Fit Index SB Wld Govt
Alpha	7.9	1.2
Beta	1.23	0.81
R-Squared	49	84
Standard Deviation	8.62	
Mean	15.52	
Sharpe Ratio	1.66	

Portfolio Analysis 09-30-04

Total Fixed-Income:485	Date of Maturity	Amount $000	Value $000	% Net Assets
Germany (Federal Republi	01-04-11	37,470	50,928	2.58
Japan (Government Cf) 0.	12-22-08	4,475,001	41,450	2.10
Japan (Government Cf) 0.	06-20-13	4,768,901	40,542	2.05
Poland (Republic Of) 8.5	05-12-07	131,500	38,686	1.96
Japan 10%	10-20-05	4,187,750	38,128	1.93
US Treasury Note 4.25%	08-15-13	33,250	33,754	1.71
US Treasury Bond 5.25%	02-15-29	29,750	30,968	1.57
France (Republic Of) 5%	10-25-11	22,220	29,866	1.51
France (Republic Of) 4%	04-25-09	22,550	28,905	1.46
US Treasury Note 5.75%	08-15-10	24,550	27,377	1.39
Sweden (Kingdom Of) 5%	01-28-09	180,750	26,160	1.32
Germany (Federal Republi	01-04-08	19,401	25,796	1.31
South Korea (Republic Of	09-09-08	—	25,311	1.28
Germany (Federal Republi	01-04-13	18,250	23,705	1.20
Eur Fwd Pur From Usd12/2		16,133	20,043	1.01
Jpy Fwd Pur From Usd12/1		2,184,039	19,946	1.01
Germany (Federal Republi	01-04-30	12,765	19,617	0.99
Germany (Federal Republi	01-04-24	12,750	19,387	0.98
Germany (Federal Republi	07-04-12	12,200	16,363	0.83
US Treasury Note 4.75%	11-15-08	14,500	15,377	0.78

Current Investment Style

Duration: Short Int Long — Quality: High Med Low

¹ figure provided by fund

Avg Eff Duration[1]	4.8 Yrs
Avg Eff Maturity	6.6 Yrs
Avg Credit Quality	AA
Avg Wtd Coupon	5.93%
Avg Wtd Price	94.07% of par

Coupon Range	% of Bonds	Rel Cat
0% PIK	0.9	0.6
0% to 6%	58.2	0.8
6% to 8%	22.1	1.2
8% to 10%	17.1	3.1
More than 10%	2.7	1.5

1.00=Category Average

Credit Analysis	% bonds 09-30-04		
US Govt	15	BB	4
AAA	34	B	7
AA	11	Below B	1
A	14	NR/NA	0
BBB	13		

Sector Breakdown	% of assets
US Treasuries	—
TIPS	—
US Agency	—
Mortgage Pass-Throughs	—
Mortgage CMO	—
Mortgage ARM	—
US Corporate	—
Asset-Backed	—
Convertible	—
Municipal	—
Corporate Inflation-Protected	—
Foreign Corporate	—
Foreign Govt	—

Composition			
Cash	24.6	Bonds	74.9
Stocks	0.1	Other	0.5

Special Securities	
Restricted/Illiquid Secs	6
Exotic Mortgage-Backed	0
Emerging-Markets Secs	—
Options/Futures/Warrants	Yes

Morningstar's Take by Lynn Russell 12-09-04

American Funds Capital World Bond is an attractive option for investors looking for global exposure.

It takes a more global--and more flexible--approach than many of its world-bond peers. The fund's managers invest in both U.S. and foreign government and corporate bonds, and, while the bulk of the portfolio is stashed in investment-grade securities, management also ventures into high-yield and emerging-markets securities. The fund's currency policy adds to its flexibility. Given its benchmark, the Lehman Brothers Global Aggregate, which contains roughly 40% U.S. bonds, the fund typically holds a substantial dollar stake. However, management has the flexibility to take on more or less currency exposure depending on its views of world markets.

Expecting a weaker dollar, the managers overweighted foreign currencies in 2004. That move has been a major contributor to near-term success, as the fund has gained 10.7% for the year to date through Dec. 7, and has outpaced 80% of its world-bond rivals. But currency isn't the only story here. Also helping were good country selection, including underweights in the U.S. and Japan, and stakes in corporate bonds.

The top-quartile performance in 2004 isn't typical for this fund, however; it doesn't often lead the category. But it seldom lags badly, either. That consistency has resulted in solid trailing returns: The fund's three-, five-, and 10-year trailing returns all land in the world-bond group's top third.

Like many global funds, this fund can be a hard fit in most portfolios. The fund's U.S. holdings limit its diversification potential for a domestic portfolio and its currency exposure brings some extra volatility to the table. That said, we think this fund is a good choice for investors looking to blanket the global fixed-income markets, given its experienced management, consistent track record, and reasonable costs.

Address:	333 S Hope St - 52 Floor Los Angeles CA 90071 800-421-0180
Web Address:	www.americanfunds.com
Inception:	08-04-87
Advisor:	Capital Research and Management Company
Subadvisor:	None
NTF Plans:	Federated Tr NTF

Minimum Purchase:	$250	Add: $50	IRA: $250
Min Auto Inv Plan:	$50	Add: $50	
Sales Fees:	3.75%L		
Management Fee:	0.57% mx./0.50% mn.		
Actual Fees:	Mgt:0.55%	Dist:0.27%	
Expense Projections:	3Yr:$688	5Yr:$917	10Yr:$1576
Income Distrib:	Quarterly		

Amer Funds CapWrldGI A

Ticker	Load	NAV	Yield	Total Assets	Mstar Category
CWGIX	5.75%	$33.89	2.5%	$33,223 mil	World Stock

Governance and Management

Fiduciary Grade: B

Portfolio Manager(s)

Like other American Funds, this offering uses a multimanager approach. Each manager--or counselor, as they are called here--runs his or her portion of assets independently. The newest manager on the team joined Capital Research in 1990. The managers also help run other American Funds offerings. As with all American Funds offerings, a portion of this fund's assets are managed by Capital Research & Management's analyst staff.

Strategy

This fund's managers are focused on yield. They buy a lot of blue-chip stocks with healthy dividends and hold them for the long term. They usually try to pick up stocks on the cheap, so the portfolio's price multiples are below the group norm. The managers use cash to moderate volatility, typically keeping the fund's stake in the double digits. The fund usually has a stake in emerging-markets companies and will sometimes hold preferred stock and convertibles debt.

Historical Profile

Return: High
Risk: Below Avg
Rating: ★★★★★ Highest

Investment Style: Equity Stock %: 83% 84% 75% 87% 70% 75% 75% 80% 84%

▼ Manager Change
▽ Partial Manager Change

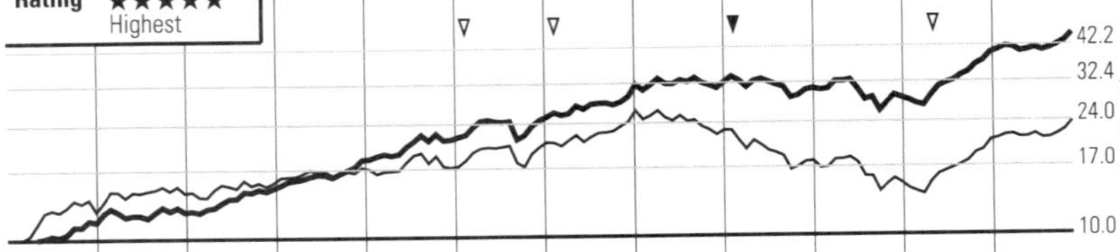

Performance Quartile (within Category)

1993	1994	1995	1996	1997	1998	1999	2000	2001	2002	2003	12-04	History
18.07	17.47	20.26	22.97	24.51	25.42	29.83	26.47	24.50	22.25	29.88	33.89	NAV
22.22*	1.22	21.39	21.54	17.99	16.20	27.30	1.38	-4.96	-7.15	39.07	19.42	Total Return %
—	-6.56	10.18	15.49	16.21	-3.73	0.27	15.57	16.46	8.79	0.48	-0.83	+/-MSCI EAFE
—	-3.86	0.67	8.06	2.23	-8.12	2.35	14.57	11.84	12.74	5.96	4.70	+/-MSCI World
0.00	2.91	3.59	3.50	2.83	2.31	2.00	1.78	1.91	2.14	2.86	2.91	Income Return %
—	-1.69	17.80	18.04	15.16	13.89	25.30	-0.40	-6.87	-9.29	36.21	16.51	Capital Return %
—	38	31	16	31	47	62	16	11	6	20	13	Total Rtn % Rank Cat
0.32	0.52	0.62	0.70	0.64	0.56	0.51	0.53	0.50	0.52	0.63	0.86	Income $
0.00	0.29	0.27	0.85	1.87	2.37	1.81	3.20	0.16	0.00	0.29	0.80	Capital Gains $
—	0.87	0.88	0.85	0.82	0.78	0.79	0.79	0.78	0.82	0.81	—	Expense Ratio %
—	3.11	3.24	3.28	2.53	2.25	1.93	2.08	2.05	2.22	2.70	—	Income Ratio %
—	19	26	30	32	39	34	41	45	32	27	—	Turnover Rate %
1,762	2,827	3,723	5,213	7,359	8,697	10,964	11,122	10,480	9,419	16,216	26,906	Net Assets $mil

Performance 12-31-04

	1st Qtr	2nd Qtr	3rd Qtr	4th Qtr	Total
2000	4.32	-1.09	-2.09	0.35	1.38
2001	-3.73	3.88	-11.20	7.02	-4.96
2002	5.43	-5.78	-15.18	10.21	-7.15
2003	-5.77	18.20	8.38	15.21	39.07
2004	4.09	-0.70	2.10	13.16	19.42

Trailing	Total Return%	+/- MSCI EAFE	+/- MSCI World	%Rank Cat	Growth of $10,000
3 Mo	13.16	-2.16	1.22	30	11,316
6 Mo	15.53	0.53	4.71	10	11,553
1 Yr	19.42	-0.83	4.70	13	11,942
3 Yr Avg	15.53	3.64	8.58	5	15,420
5 Yr Avg	8.24	9.37	10.69	8	14,857
10 Yr Avg	14.36	8.74	6.27	5	38,260
15 Yr Avg	—	—	—	—	—

Tax Analysis	Tax-Adj Rtn%	%Rank Cat	Tax-Cost Rat	%Rank Cat
3 Yr (estimated)	12.06	13	1.07	97
5 Yr (estimated)	5.47	11	1.40	86
10 Yr (estimated)	11.60	5	1.84	80

Potential Capital Gain Exposure: 23% of assets

Rating and Risk

Time Period	Load-Adj Return %	Morningstar Rtn vs Cat	Morningstar Risk vs Cat	Morningstar Risk-Adj Rating
1 Yr	12.55			
3 Yr	13.27	+Avg	-Avg	★★★★
5 Yr	6.97	+Avg	-Avg	★★★★
10 Yr	13.69	High	Low	★★★★★
Incept	13.55			

Other Measures	Standard Index S&P 500	Best Fit Index MSCI World
Alpha	4.7	9.6
Beta	0.86	0.91
R-Squared	92	94
Standard Deviation	16.03	
Mean	15.53	
Sharpe Ratio	0.89	

Portfolio Analysis 09-30-04

Share change since 06-04 Total Stocks:303	Sector	Country	% Assets
Altria Group	Goods	United States	1.85
⊕ Vodafone Grp	Telecom	U.K.	1.44
⊕ HSBC Hldgs	Financial	U.K.	1.22
⊖ Continental	Ind Mtrls	Germany	1.20
⊕ Diageo	Goods	U.K.	1.09
⊖ AstraZeneca	Health	U.K.	1.03
⊕ Shell Transport & Tradin	Energy	U.K.	1.03
Novo-Nordisk A S	Health	Denmark	0.98
⊕ Lloyds TSB Grp	Financial	U.K.	0.96
⊕ Sanofi-Synthelabo	Health	France	0.91
Soc Generale	Financial	France	0.88
E.ON	Utilities	Germany	0.85
Fortis	Financial	Netherlands	0.84
⊕ Nestle	Goods	Switzerland	0.83
⊕ J P Morgan Chase	Financial	United States	0.82
ING Groep	Financial	Netherlands	0.79
Scottish Power UK	Utilities	U.K.	0.77
☼ Cia Vale Rio Doce	—	Brazil	0.74
Daito Trust Construction	Business	Japan	0.73
Portugal Telecom, SGPS	Telecom	Portugal	0.72

Current Investment Style

Market Cap	%
Giant	41.5
Large	43.6
Mid	14.8
Small	0.1
Micro	0.0
Avg $mil: 18,023	

Value Measures		Rel Category
Price/Earnings	13.80	0.87
Price/Book	1.76	0.79
Price/Sales	1.02	0.87
Price/Cash Flow	5.10	0.80
Dividend Yield %	3.04	1.62

Growth Measures	%	Rel Category
Long-Term Erngs	10.19	0.85
Book Value	1.46	0.66
Sales	3.91	0.93
Cash Flow	6.49	1.11
Historical Erngs	6.77	0.79

Composition

Cash	10.6	Bonds	0.8
Stocks	84.2	Other	4.4
Foreign (% of Stock)			73.3

Sector Weightings	% of Stocks	Rel MSCI EAFE	3 Year High	3 Year Low
Info	18.00	1.08		
Software	0.43	0.40	1	0
Hardware	3.31	0.91	5	2
Media	2.25	0.99	2	1
Telecom	12.01	1.25	12	5
Service	38.76	0.87		
Health	8.39	1.16	9	6
Consumer	5.98	1.19	6	3
Business	2.61	0.48	3	1
Financial	21.78	0.81	28	21
Mfg	43.24	1.12		
Goods	15.27	1.12	18	15
Ind Mtrls	15.31	1.24	17	14
Energy	7.34	1.00	11	6
Utilities	5.32	0.99	7	5

Regional Exposure	% Stock		
UK/W. Europe	43	N. America	30
Japan	8	Latn America	3
Asia X Japan	14	Other	2

Country Exposure	% Stock		
United States	27	Netherlands	6
U.K.	15	Germany	6
Japan	8		

Morningstar's Take by Gareth Lyons 12-22-04

American Funds Capital World Growth & Income may be due for a cooling-off period, but its long-term appeal remains intact.

Many excellent funds become victims of their own success because they attract a flood of assets that can hamper a manager's flexibility and, in turn, hurt performance. This impressive fund hasn't suffered such a fate, however. While it assets have ballooned from $10 billion in 1999 to its current level of $28 billion, it has continued to beat more than 80% of peers in each of the past five years.

One might rightly argue that the past five years have favored this fund's style. It highlights high-yielding stocks and gravitates heavily toward value sectors like utilities and telecom services, which have been especially hot recently. The management team's appetite for undervalued stocks has also led them to overweight foreign and emerging markets relative to their world-stock peers; foreign markets have outperformed domestic bourses of late.

Even so, this fund's ability to handle its asset growth has played a vital role, as well. Like other offerings at American, assets here get divvied up among several different portfolio managers--each of whom oversees his or her portion independently. The managers use low-turnover approaches and typically buy up shares when others are selling. While such factors don't make this fund entirely immune to the harmful effects of asset growth, they help to allay our concerns considerably. If this fund's hot streak abates, investors shouldn't rush to conclude that it has grown too big. Instead, any underperformance would probably owe more to the fund's value-leaning, yield-focused style falling out of favor than asset bloat.

All the same, the strategy here has plenty of long-term appeal. The experienced management team also runs a diversified portfolio, which helps to keep a lid on volatility. Combined with the fund's low expense ratio, those traits make this an attractive core holding.

Address:	333 South Hope St-52nd Floor Los Angeles CA 90071 800-421-0180
Web Address:	www.americanfunds.com
Inception:	03-26-93 *
Advisor:	Capital Research and Management Company
Subadvisor:	None
NTF Plans:	Federated Tr NTF

Minimum Purchase:	$250	Add: $50	IRA: $250
Min Auto Inv Plan:	$50	Add: $50	
Sales Fees:	5.75%L, 0.25%S		
Management Fee:	0.60% mx./0.39% mn.		
Actual Fees:	Mgt:0.42%	Dist:0.25%	
Expense Projections:	3Yr:$822	5Yr:$1004	10Yr:$1530
Income Distrib:	Quarterly		

Amer Funds EuroPac A

Analyst Pick	Ticker	Load	NAV	Yield	Total Assets	Mstar Category
✔	AEPGX	5.75%	$35.63	1.4%	$51,644 mil	Foreign Large Blend

Governance and Management

Fiduciary Grade: B

Portfolio Manager(s)

Like all American Funds, this offering boasts many experienced managers, most of whom have been with the company for more than a decade. Each manager runs his or her portion of assets independently of the others. A portion of the portfolio (less than 25% of assets) is run by the firm's analyst staff.

Strategy

The fund divides assets among several portfolio counselors (managers), whose investment philosophies vary from growth-focused to value-oriented. In the aggregate, the fund's portfolio is well-diversified across countries and sectors, and its price multiples usually stay close to the category norms. Several of the managers like to pick up stocks on the cheap and then hold them for the long haul. The fund's turnover is quite low.

Historical Profile

Return Above Avg
Risk Below Avg
Rating ★★★★ Above Avg

Investment Style Equity Stock %: 84% 83% 82% 86% 79% 82% 85% 86% 87%

▼ Manager Change ▽ Partial Manager Change

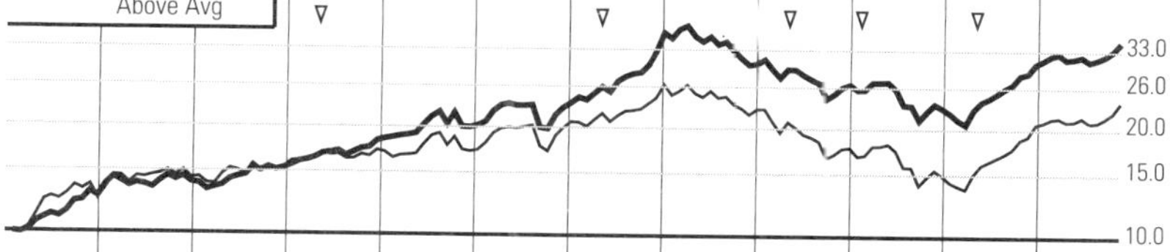

Performance Quartile (within Category)

1993	1994	1995	1996	1997	1998	1999	2000	2001	2002	2003	12-04	History
22.11	21.13	23.13	26.04	26.02	28.40	42.66	31.35	26.87	22.97	30.21	35.63	NAV
35.60	1.13	12.87	18.64	9.19	15.54	56.97	-17.84	-12.18	-13.61	32.91	19.69	Total Return %
3.04	-6.65	1.66	12.59	7.41	-4.39	29.94	-3.65	9.24	2.33	-5.68	-0.56	+/-MSCI EAFE
3.39	-6.22	1.46	11.77	6.92	-3.15	28.99	-4.48	9.21	2.19	-6.51	-0.69	+/-MSCI Wd xUS
1.45	1.49	2.33	1.90	1.78	1.40	1.03	0.50	2.09	0.90	1.35	1.68	Income Return %
34.15	-0.36	10.54	16.74	7.41	14.14	55.94	-18.34	-14.27	-14.51	31.56	18.01	Capital Return %
38	39	34	12	34	38	13	60	4	19	51	23	Total Rtn % Rank Cat
0.24	0.32	0.49	0.43	0.45	0.36	0.29	0.19	0.66	0.24	0.31	0.51	Income $
0.07	0.90	0.21	0.89	1.93	1.26	1.39	3.74	0.00	0.00	0.00	0.00	Capital Gains $
1.10	0.99	0.97	0.95	0.90	0.86	0.84	0.84	0.84	0.88	0.90	0.87	Expense Ratio %
1.40	1.13	1.80	2.09	1.77	1.64	1.45	0.93	1.89	1.21	1.06	1.08	Income Ratio %
10	21	16	22	26	31	32	29	37	27	29	25	Turnover Rate %
5,803	8,270	10,922	15,727	18,854	20,798	34,783	31,496	27,153	22,601	29,908	36,920	Net Assets $mil

Performance 12-31-04

	1st Qtr	2nd Qtr	3rd Qtr	4th Qtr	Total
2000	4.57	-6.70	-8.53	-7.93	-17.84
2001	-8.39	1.85	-14.02	9.48	-12.18
2002	1.56	-4.32	-17.58	7.87	-13.61
2003	-9.66	17.98	9.27	14.13	32.91
2004	6.79	-1.83	0.47	13.63	19.69

Trailing	Total Return%	+/- MSCI EAFE	+/- MSCI Wd xUS	%Rank Cat	Growth of $10,000
3 Mo	13.63	-1.69	-1.52	69	11,363
6 Mo	14.17	-0.83	-1.20	46	11,417
1 Yr	19.69	-0.56	-0.69	23	11,969
3 Yr Avg	11.18	-0.71	-1.04	22	13,743
5 Yr Avg	-0.17	0.96	0.59	17	9,915
10 Yr Avg	10.15	4.53	4.21	5	26,293
15 Yr Avg	10.33	6.10	5.92	1	43,692

Tax Analysis	Tax-Adj Rtn%	%Rank Cat	Tax-Cost Rat	%Rank Cat
3 Yr (estimated)	8.54	49	0.43	47
5 Yr (estimated)	-2.23	28	0.90	61
10 Yr (estimated)	8.20	8	1.19	53

Potential Capital Gain Exposure: 24% of assets

Rating and Risk

Time Period	Load-Adj Return %	Morningstar Rtn vs Cat	Morningstar Risk vs Cat	Morningstar Risk-Adj Rating
1 Yr	12.81			
3 Yr	9.01	Avg	-Avg	★★★
5 Yr	-1.34	+Avg	-Avg	★★★★
10 Yr	9.50	High	-Avg	★★★★★
Incept	13.09			

Other Measures	Standard Index S&P 500	Best Fit Index MSCI Wd xUS
Alpha	0.2	-0.1
Beta	0.91	0.92
R-Squared	96	96
Standard Deviation	15.99	
Mean	11.18	
Sharpe Ratio	0.62	

Portfolio Analysis 09-30-04

Share change since 06-04 Total Stocks:252	Sector	Country	% Assets
⊕ Sanofi-Synthelabo	Health	France	2.36
⊕ Vodafone Grp	Telecom	U.K.	1.59
⊖ AstraZeneca	Health	U.K.	1.59
⊕ France Telecom	Telecom	France	1.38
⊕ HSBC Hldgs	Financial	U.K.	1.31
⊖ Novo-Nordisk A S	Health	Denmark	1.23
⊖ Nestle	Goods	Switzerland	1.28
Telefonica	Telecom	Spain	1.24
⊕ Mitsui Sumitomo Insuranc	Financial	Japan	1.21
ING Groep	Financial	Netherlands	1.20
Kon Kpn Nv	Telecom	Netherlands	1.06
⊖ Canadian Natural Resourc	Energy	United States	1.02
⊕ Kookmin Bank	Financial	Korea	0.98
⊖ Honda Motor	Goods	Japan	0.92
⊕ Ahold(Kon)Nv	Consumer	Netherlands	0.91
Norsk Hydro	Energy	Norway	0.91
KDDI	Telecom	Japan	0.90
⊕ UCB Grp	Health	Belgium	0.90
Abn-Amro Hldgs Nv	Financial	Netherlands	0.88
Richemont(Cie Fin)	Goods	Switzerland	0.86

Current Investment Style

Value Blnd Growth / Large Mid Small

Market Cap	%
Giant	48.6
Large	43.0
Mid	8.4
Small	0.0
Micro	0.0

Avg $mil: 17,915

Value Measures		Rel Category
Price/Earnings	13.46	0.98
Price/Book	1.60	0.89
Price/Sales	0.93	1.02
Price/Cash Flow	3.23	0.66
Dividend Yield %	2.22	0.87

Growth Measures	%	Rel Category
Long-Term Erngs	11.1[illegible]	1.03
Book Value	-1.30	NMF
Sales	3.03	1.22
Cash Flow	5.35	0.95
Historical Erngs	12.73	2.28

Composition

Cash	9.8	Bonds	0.0
Stocks	86.9	Other	3.3

Foreign (% of Stock) 96.6

Sector Weightings	% of Stocks	Rel MSCI EAFE	3 Year High	3 Year Low
Info	22.61	1.36		
Software	0.31	0.29	2	0
Hardware	3.98	1.09	8	4
Media	2.83	1.24	6	3
Telecom	15.49	1.61	20	7
Service	39.86	0.89		
Health	11.02	1.52	14	10
Consumer	4.90	0.97	7	3
Business	2.74	0.50	6	2
Financial	21.20	0.79	21	12
Mfg	37.54	0.97		
Goods	17.18	1.26	24	17
Ind Mtrls	9.88	0.80	11	8
Energy	7.36	1.00	8	5
Utilities	3.12	0.58	3	1

Regional Exposure	% Stock		
UK/W. Europe	51	N. America	5
Japan	21	Latn America	5
Asia X Japan	17	Other	1

Country Exposure	% Stock		
Japan	21	Netherlands	7
U.K.	13	South Korea	6
France	8		

Morningstar's Take by Gareth Lyons 12-02-04

This impressive fund is steady, but never boring.

Among international offerings, American Funds EuroPacific Growth is one of the most moderately positioned funds. Like other American offerings, several managers pick stocks for the fund, with each person managing assets independently. They all share a distinctly long-term approach to stock picking, but their styles are different, ranging from growth to value. The end result is an extensive portfolio that is diversified across sectors and regions, which has made for consistent performance in all kinds of markets--a point neatly made by the fund's above-average showing in all but one of the past 11 years.

The steady returns also owe to this team's pioneering streak. Despite its sprawling portfolio, the fund is anything but benchmark-like. In fact, the managers invest heavily in emerging markets, and emphasize stocks and industries often shunned by their rivals. Their shared inclination to buy and hold picks for years allows them to add to holdings that are experiencing problems they believe to be short term in nature. For example, the team recently doubled its position in France Telecom on weakness, despite concerns about the French government's possible sale of its majority stake. And recent market jitters in India saw the team add to their favorite names from that country. Wild stock gyrations serve a practical purpose here, too. Because bouts of volatility often include surges in trading volumes, the team can more easily trade its preferred names.

Given how big this fund is getting, that contrarian tack is apt to play an even more vital role going forward. To be sure, the multi-manager setup and low-turnover approach limit our concerns about this offering's huge $46 billion asset base. But the rapid pace of flows here make us worry somewhat about how nimble this fund can remain--especially in often-illiquid emerging markets. That minor concern aside, this fund is a compelling option.

Address:	333 S Hope St - 52nd Floor Los Angeles CA 90071 800-421-0180
Web Address:	www.americanfunds.com
Inception:	04-16-84
Advisor:	Capital Research and Management Company
Subadvisor:	None
NTF Plans:	Federated Tr NTF

Minimum Purchase:	$250	Add: $25	IRA: $250
Min Auto Inv Plan:	$50	Add: $50	
Sales Fees:	5.75%L		
Management Fee:	0.69% mx./0.42% mn.		
Actual Fees:	Mgt:0.46%	Dist:0.25%	
Expense Projections:	3Yr:$828	5Yr:$1014	10Yr:$1553
Income Distrib:	Annually		

Amer Funds Fundamen A

Ticker	Load	NAV	Yield	Total Assets	Mstar Category
ANCFX	5.75%	$32.25	1.7%	$24,217 mil	Large Value

Governance and Management

Fiduciary Grade: B

Portfolio Manager(s)

The fund's four portfolio counselors boast an average of more than 20 years of investment experience. Investors would be hard-pressed to find managers and analysts who know their industries better. Gordon Crawford, for example, has covered media stocks for more than 30 years and is one of the most respected media investors in the business. The managers oversee other portfolios as well and are backed by a legion of analysts.

Strategy

This fund's investment team employs rigorous fundamental analysis to search for undervalued or overlooked companies that have solid long-term growth potential. Often, the managers let winners ride or pick up depressed growth stocks, occasionally pushing the fund into large-blend territory. The team doesn't limit its search to U.S. stocks, either, and generally devotes a sizable portion of assets to foreign stocks.

Historical Profile

Return Average
Risk Average
Rating ★★★ Neutral

Investment Style: Equity, Stock %: 92% 89% 89% 90% 85% 90% 89% 92% 92%

▼ Manager Change
▽ Partial Manager Change

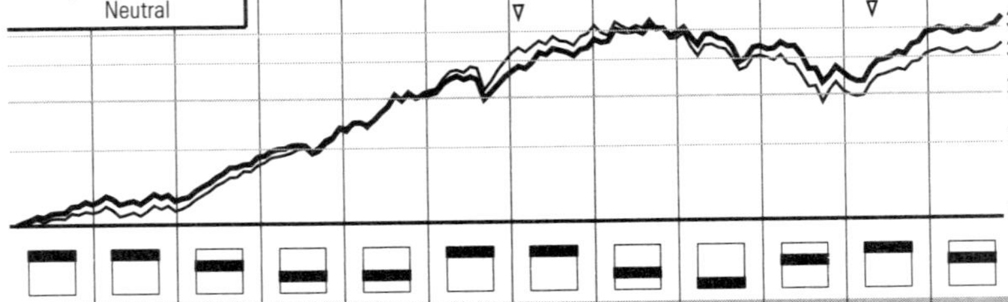

Growth of $10,000
— Investment Values of Fund
— Investment Values of S&P 500

Performance Quartile (within Category)

1993	1994	1995	1996	1997	1998	1999	2000	2001	2002	2003	12-04	History
18.15	17.50	22.29	24.54	27.40	28.92	32.59	31.16	27.45	22.23	23.85	32.25	NAV
18.16	1.33	34.21	19.99	26.67	16.72	24.58	4.27	-9.55	-17.34	31.96	13.91	Total Return %
8.10	0.02	-3.32	-2.95	-6.68	-11.85	3.54	13.37	2.33	4.75	3.29	3.04	+/-S&P 500
0.09	3.31	-4.15	-1.65	-8.51	1.09	17.23	-2.74	-3.96	-1.82	1.93	-2.58	+/-Russ 1000 VI
2.48	2.45	2.32	1.82	1.74	1.47	1.41	1.25	1.30	1.82	1.81	1.95	Income Return %
15.68	-1.12	31.89	18.17	24.93	15.25	23.17	3.02	-10.85	-19.16	30.15	11.96	Capital Return %
21	24	41	52	58	21	2	75	82	42	19	36	Total Rtn % Rank Cat
0.43	0.44	0.40	0.40	0.42	0.40	0.40	0.40	0.40	0.50	0.40	0.56	Income $
2.03	0.45	0.68	1.76	3.13	2.59	2.79	2.36	0.38	0.00	0.00	0.00	Capital Gains $
0.65	0.68	0.70	0.66	0.63	0.63	0.63	0.64	0.65	0.67	0.66	—	Expense Ratio %
2.43	2.45	2.08	1.78	1.54	1.47	1.33	1.28	1.41	1.68	2.08	—	Income Ratio %
29	23	25	39	45	53	46	43	29	38	31	—	Turnover Rate %
1,979	2,611	4,754	7,165	10,465	12,713	16,603	19,872	19,331	15,201	19,212	21,543	Net Assets $mil

Performance 12-31-04

	1st Qtr	2nd Qtr	3rd Qtr	4th Qtr	Total
2000	7.03	-1.08	0.88	-2.38	4.27
2001	-8.47	4.61	-15.48	11.77	-9.55
2002	2.43	-8.56	-17.59	7.10	-17.34
2003	-5.85	16.24	3.70	16.28	31.96
2004	1.69	1.08	0.94	9.79	13.91

Trailing	Total Return%	+/- S&P 500	+/- Russ 1000 VI	%Rank Cat	Growth of $10,000
3 Mo	9.79	0.56	-0.59	34	10,979
6 Mo	10.81	3.62	-1.27	22	11,081
1 Yr	13.91	3.04	-2.58	36	11,391
3 Yr Avg	7.50	3.92	-1.07	24	12,423
5 Yr Avg	3.22	5.52	-2.05	58	11,717
10 Yr Avg	13.27	1.20	-0.56	14	34,766
15 Yr Avg	12.13	1.20	0.10	12	55,696

Tax Analysis	Tax-Adj Rtn%	%Rank Cat	Tax-Cost Rat	%Rank Cat
3 Yr (estimated)	4.69	50	0.67	45
5 Yr (estimated)	1.04	70	0.95	51
10 Yr (estimated)	10.76	18	1.63	39

Potential Capital Gain Exposure: 18% of assets

Rating and Risk

Time Period	Load-Adj Return %	Morningstar Rtn vs Cat	Morningstar Risk vs Cat	Morningstar Risk-Adj Rating
1 Yr	7.36			
3 Yr	5.40	Avg	Avg	★★★
5 Yr	2.01	-Avg	Avg	★★
10 Yr	12.60	+Avg	Avg	★★★★
Incept	7.27			

Other Measures	Standard Index S&P 500	Best Fit Index Russ 1000 VI
Alpha	4.0	-0.7
Beta	0.93	0.96
R-Squared	90	95
Standard Deviation	15.72	
Mean	7.50	
Sharpe Ratio	0.39	

Portfolio Analysis 09-30-04

Share change since 06-04 Total Stocks:180	Sector	PE	YTD Ret%	% Assets
⊕ Suncor Energy	Energy	20.6	42.16	2.69
⊕ Microsoft	Software	36.1	8.95	2.47
⊖ Dow Chemical	Ind Mtrls	16.6	22.83	2.19
⊕ Royal Dutch Petroleum AD	Energy	—	14.31	1.98
Time Warner	Media	27.5	8.12	1.75
Altria Group	Goods	13.3	18.38	1.74
Boeing	Ind Mtrls	14.7	24.86	1.71
Deere & Company	Ind Mtrls	15.7	16.26	1.61
⊕ SBC Communications	Telecom	15.4	3.74	1.56
Gen Elec	Ind Mtrls	22.8	20.68	1.45
Lowe's Companies	Consumer	22.1	4.25	1.37
Limited Brands	Consumer	16.0	37.88	1.34
⊕ Caterpillar	Ind Mtrls	17.6	19.75	1.32
⊕ Fannie Mae	Financial	9.1	-2.33	1.26
News Corporation ADR A	Media	—	6.65	1.23
American International G	Financial	16.2	-0.53	1.17
⊕ Texas Instruments	Hardware	21.1	-15.90	1.16
⊕ Alcoa	Ind Mtrls	18.8	-15.75	1.13
Sanofi-Synthelabo	Health	—	—	1.11
⊕ ExxonMobil	Energy	13.9	28.04	1.10

Current Investment Style

Value Blnd Growth / Large Mid Small

Market Cap	%
Giant	41.9
Large	46.9
Mid	11.1
Small	0.1
Micro	0.0
Avg $mil: 29,429	

Value Measures		Rel Category
Price/Earnings	15.84	1.05
Price/Book	2.42	1.07
Price/Sales	1.19	1.00
Price/Cash Flow	6.59	1.03
Dividend Yield %	1.99	0.98

Growth Measures	%	Rel Category
Long-Term Erngs	10.27	0.99
Book Value	0.92	0.16
Sales	3.98	0.95
Cash Flow	5.74	1.10
Historical Erngs	7.74	0.65

Profitability	%	Rel Category
Return on Equity	15.66	0.99
Return on Assets	6.21	0.79
Net Margin	8.71	0.85

Sector Weightings	% of Stocks	Rel S&P 500	3 Year High	3 Year Low
Info	21.11	0.98		
Software	2.69	0.63	3	1
Hardware	7.02	0.69	12	6
Media	4.34	1.13	8	4
Telecom	7.06	2.24	7	4
Service	27.48	0.59		
Health	5.34	0.43	13	5
Consumer	5.83	0.64	6	5
Business	2.92	0.72	6	3
Financial	13.39	0.64	15	11
Mfg	51.40	1.60		
Goods	5.15	0.55	11	5
Ind Mtrls	26.44	2.09	31	14
Energy	16.21	2.26	16	10
Utilities	3.60	1.22	8	4

Composition

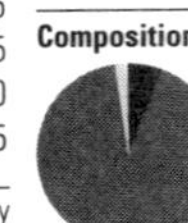

Cash	6.0
Stocks	91.7
Bonds	0.8
Other	1.5
Foreign (% of Stock)	26.5

Morningstar's Take by Paul Herbert 01-09-05

Recent results show part of the compelling American Funds Fundamental Investors' appeal.

This fund looked down early in 2004, but time has shown that it certainly wasn't out. After posting a striking 32% gain in 2003, thanks to some strong-performing industrials stocks, the fund looked a bit slow through this year's first eight months, amid mixed economic news. Its fortunes brightened down the year's home stretch, though, with holdings as diverse as Suncor Energy, Dow Chemical, and Altria Group delivering double-digit stock price gains from August to December. In all, the fund gained nearly 14% last year, making it the best performing among American's domestic-focused large-cap funds.

There's a lot more to get excited about here than just short-term performance, though. As the above examples may suggest, the fund's managers have the freedom to invest in large-cap stocks of all manner--making it more broadly diversified by style than most of its siblings. This wide reach puts it in good shape to benefit in growth rallies as well as value runups. It posted strong relative marks in both 2002 and 2003, for instance. And its volatility has been no greater than average, which owes to this broad scope, its managers' focus on higher-quality companies, and their attention to valuations. The fund has also shone over time. Its long-term returns have trounced its peers and the S&P 500 Index over a majority of rolling periods.

Such marks and American's fine reputation are well-known, however, and have led to significant inflows of late. This fund isn't as large as and hasn't been as popular recently as siblings such as Investment Company of America, but we think that asset growth is an issue because it holds many names in common with such funds. Other than that, it's tough not to like this fund.

Address:	333 S Hope St - 52nd Floor Los Angeles, CA 90071 800-421-0180
Web Address:	
Inception:	12-30-32
Advisor:	Capital Research and Management Company
Subadvisor:	None
NTF Plans:	Federated Tr NTF

Minimum Purchase:	$250	Add: $50	IRA: $25
Min Auto Inv Plan:	$50	Add: $50	
Sales Fees:	5.75%L		
Management Fee:	0.39% mx./0.24% mn.		
Actual Fees:	Mgt:0.27%	Dist:0.24%	
Expense Projections:	3Yr:$771	5Yr:$916	10Yr:$1339
Income Distrib:	Quarterly		

Amer Funds Grth Fund A

Ticker	Load	NAV	Yield	Total Assets	Mstar Category
AGTHX	5.75%	$27.38	0.3%	$95,266 mil	Large Growth

Governance and Management

Fiduciary Grade: B

Portfolio Manager(s)

First-rate. Six seasoned managers with an average of 28 years of experience call most of the shots here, and a huge staff of career analysts also runs a part of the fund. Each counselor manages money without the input of his five counterparts.

Strategy

The fund's six-member team of portfolio managers invests independently of each other but with a common flexible growth strategy. The team will invest in a mix of traditional growth stocks, turnaround situations, and cyclical names. The resulting portfolio is well diversified across industries and individual issues. Management also tends to park a good chunk of assets in cash at times, and the team is very sensitive to how much it pays for a stock. As a result, it may not be a chart-topper when speculative fare rules the roost, but the fund tends to be less volatile than most growth offerings.

Historical Profile

Return High
Risk Average
Rating ★★★★★ Highest

Investment Style: Equity Stock %

83%	83%	85%	85%	80%	79%	82%	88%	89%

▼ Manager Change
▽ Partial Manager Change

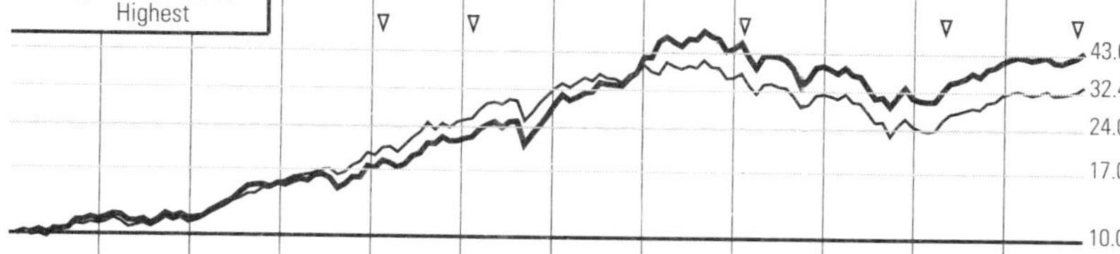

Growth of $10,000
— Investment Values of Fund
— Investment Values of S&P 500

Performance Quartile (within Category)

1993	1994	1995	1996	1997	1998	1999	2000	2001	2002	2003	12-04	History
13.38	12.77	15.27	16.57	18.78	22.40	29.14	27.08	23.71	18.47	24.54	27.38	NAV
14.54	0.02	29.75	14.84	26.86	31.78	45.70	7.49	-12.28	-22.02	32.90	11.95	Total Return %
4.48	-1.29	-7.78	-8.10	-6.49	3.21	24.66	16.59	-0.40	0.07	4.23	1.08	+/-S&P 500
11.67	-2.60	-7.43	-8.28	-3.63	-6.93	12.54	29.91	8.14	5.86	3.15	5.65	+/-Russ 1000Gr
0.49	0.64	1.14	0.72	0.78	0.48	0.20	0.50	0.17	0.08	0.03	0.37	Income Return %
14.05	-0.62	28.61	14.12	26.08	31.30	45.50	6.99	-12.45	-22.10	32.87	11.58	Capital Return %
34	31	66	81	49	50	27	4	11	15	19	15	Total Rtn % Rank Cat
0.06	0.09	0.14	0.11	0.13	0.09	0.05	0.14	0.05	0.02	0.01	0.09	Income $
0.49	0.52	1.14	0.86	2.06	2.21	3.19	4.09	0.00	0.00	0.00	0.00	Capital Gains $
0.77	0.78	0.75	0.75	0.72	0.70	0.70	0.70	0.71	0.75	0.76	0.70	Expense Ratio %
0.56	0.49	0.90	0.90	0.73	0.48	0.28	0.58	0.76	0.18	0.28	0.20	Income Ratio %
25	25	27	27	34	39	46	47	36	30	25	19	Turnover Rate %
5,062	5,274	7,891	9,675	12,248	16,247	27,407	37,006	36,347	31,104	48,074	60,323	Net Assets $mil

Performance 12-31-04

	1st Qtr	2nd Qtr	3rd Qtr	4th Qtr	Total
2000	17.64	-1.34	1.89	-9.11	7.49
2001	-14.11	9.54	-20.60	17.43	-12.28
2002	-1.27	-14.48	-13.64	6.93	-22.02
2003	-2.49	17.21	3.65	12.19	32.90
2004	3.46	1.06	-2.34	9.63	11.95

Trailing	Total Return%	+/- S&P 500	+/- Russ 1000Gr	%Rank Cat	Growth of $10,000
3 Mo	9.63	0.40	0.46	54	10,963
6 Mo	7.06	-0.13	3.59	21	10,706
1 Yr	11.95	1.08	5.65	15	11,195
3 Yr Avg	5.08	1.50	5.26	9	11,603
5 Yr Avg	1.81	4.11	11.10	3	10,938
10 Yr Avg	14.78	2.71	5.19	2	39,688
15 Yr Avg	13.12	2.19	3.62	6	63,546

Tax Analysis	Tax-Adj Rtn%	%Rank Cat	Tax-Cost Rat	%Rank Cat
3 Yr (estimated)	2.97	15	0.05	9
5 Yr (estimated)	0.00	4	0.61	37
10 Yr (estimated)	12.50	3	1.41	45

Potential Capital Gain Exposure: 18% of assets

Rating and Risk

Time Period	Load-Adj Return %	Morningstar Rtn vs Cat	Morningstar Risk vs Cat	Morningstar Risk-Adj Rating
1 Yr	5.51			
3 Yr	3.02	+Avg	Avg	★★★★
5 Yr	0.61	High	Avg	★★★★★
10 Yr	14.11	High	Avg	★★★★★
Incept	—			

Other Measures	Standard Index S&P 500	Best Fit Index Russ 1000
Alpha	1.5	0.8
Beta	1.00	1.01
R-Squared	93	94
Standard Deviation	16.28	
Mean	5.08	
Sharpe Ratio	0.23	

Portfolio Analysis 09-30-04

Share change since 06-04 Total Stocks:242	Sector	PE	YTD Ret%	% Assets
Time Warner	Media	27.5	8.12	2.50
⊕ American International G	Financial	16.2	-0.53	2.39
⊕ Microsoft	Software	36.1	8.95	2.36
⊕ Lowe's Companies	Consumer	22.1	4.25	1.94
⊕ Target	Consumer	22.3	36.14	1.87
⊕ Sanofi-Synthelabo	Health	—	—	1.73
Altria Group	Goods	13.3	18.38	1.58
⊕ Freddie Mac	Financial	10.6	28.75	1.40
⊕ Tyco International	Ind Mtrls	25.1	35.41	1.34
⊕ Biogen IDEC	Health	—	81.50	1.28
⊕ Schlumberger	Energy	40.7	23.84	1.20
⊕ Iac / Interactivecorp	Consumer	43.1	-18.60	1.18
⊕ Texas Instruments	Hardware	21.1	-15.90	1.15
⊕ Forest Laboratories	Health	18.0	-27.41	1.15
⊕ Fannie Mae	Financial	9.1	-2.33	1.13
⊕ Yahoo	Media	95.1	67.36	1.13
⊕ Vodafone Group PLC ADR	Telecom	—	11.74	1.10
⊕ Walgreen	Consumer	31.6	6.03	1.06
⊕ Comcast A	Media	81.0	1.49	1.03
⊕ Applied Materials	Hardware	20.7	-23.80	1.03

Current Investment Style

Value Blnd Growth; Large Mid Small

Market Cap	%
Giant	36.1
Large	48.3
Mid	15.3
Small	0.3
Micro	0.0
Avg $mil: 26,069	

Value Measures		Rel Category
Price/Earnings	19.37	0.91
Price/Book	2.27	0.70
Price/Sales	1.71	0.80
Price/Cash Flow	8.92	0.81
Dividend Yield %	0.79	1.03

Growth Measures	%	Rel Category
Long-Term Erngs	13.91	0.99
Book Value	8.26	0.65
Sales	7.68	0.90
Cash Flow	10.4	0.63
Historical Erngs	25.0	1.73

Profitability	%	Rel Category
Return on Equity	13.9	0.77
Return on Assets	6.95	0.74
Net Margin	9.29	0.75

Sector Weightings	% of Stocks	Rel S&P 500	3 Year High	3 Year Low
Info	30.31	1.41		
Software	4.07	0.95	5	3
Hardware	12.40	1.22	17	10
Media	9.98	2.60	13	10
Telecom	3.86	1.23	6	1
Service	42.32	0.91		
Health	13.71	1.10	16	13
Consumer	13.42	1.48	15	11
Business	5.79	1.43	9	6
Financial	9.40	0.45	15	9
Mfg	27.37	0.85		
Goods	6.27	0.67	7	3
Ind Mtrls	9.31	0.73	9	4
Energy	11.41	1.59	11	6
Utilities	0.38	0.13	1	0

Composition

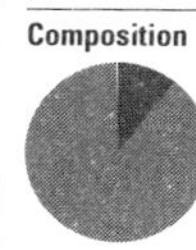

Cash	10.4
Stocks	88.9
Bonds	0.0
Other	0.7
Foreign (% of Stock)	15.0

Morningstar's Take by Paul Herbert 10-14-04

Growth Fund of America has plenty of appeal, but its burgeoning size remains the big question mark.

This fund's advisor deserves praise for constructing a research-intensive organization. Capital Research & Management has assembled a staff of more than 140 analysts and has a long-term goal of growing those ranks by 5%-7% a year. That's important to American Funds shareholders because the analysts manage a portion of each fund.

It's also important because this fund continues to gather new money at a very rapid pace. Its asset base stood at an estimated $79 billion at the end of August 2004, or about $25 billion more than a year earlier. Bringing in more analysts helps spread out buy and sell decisions among more folks, ideally reducing the chance of simultaneous increases or decreases to the fund's stakes in the same stocks. (Which would likely drive up the prices of stocks they're trying to buy, for instance.) The firm says that about 40 portfolio managers and analysts make such decisions for this fund. It may also increase the number of portfolio managers, and plans to disclose recent additions it has made to this fund soon.

While we admire the system in place--and believe that it's likely to do a better job handling growth that what many peers have in place--we are concerned about the pace of growth. American Funds' assets under management expanded by approximately 35% from August 2003 to August 2004--meaning everyone's running more money than she or he did just more than a year ago.

That being written, through Oct. 14, 2004, the fund continues to deliver lights-out performance. And it could continue doing well if large caps turn the tide on small caps. But our concern remains that, even with its tremendous resources, the pace of growth likely puts new pressures on investment personnel.

Address:	333 S Hope St - 52nd Floor Los Angeles, CA 90071 800-421-0180	Minimum Purchase:	$250	Add: $50	IRA: $250
Web Address:	www.americanfunds.com	Min Auto Inv Plan:	$50	Add: $50	
Inception:	01-01-59	Sales Fees:	5.75%L		
Advisor:	Capital Research and Management Company	Management Fee:	0.50% mx./0.26% mn.		
Subadvisor:	None	Actual Fees:	Mgt:0.31%	Dist:0.25%	
		Expense Projections:	3Yr:$804	5Yr:$973	10Yr:$1463
		Income Distrib:	Annually		
NTF Plans:	Federated Tr NTF				

Amer Funds Inc Fund A

Analyst Pick

Ticker	Load	NAV	Yield	Total Assets	Mstar Category
AMECX	5.75%	$18.56	3.5%	$53,576 mil	Moderate Allocation

Governance and Management

Fiduciary Grade: B

Portfolio Manager(s)

The fund's nine named portfolio "counselors" (managers) are a very seasoned bunch, with an average of more than 18 years with the fund's advisor, Capital Research and Management. Moreover, the firm boasts one of the deepest and most-skilled research benches in the fund business.

Strategy

The fund's managers favor stocks that pay high dividends, which typically leads the fund to large stakes in financials and utilities stocks and scant exposure to technology shares. On the bond side, the team keeps the fund's interest-rate risk fairly moderate and won't invest more than 20% of assets in issues rated below investment-grade--that sliver has been a tad below 10% in 2004.

Historical Profile

Return: High
Risk: Below Avg
Rating: ★★★★★ Highest

Investment Style
Equity Stock %: 53% 53% 47% 51% 51% 48% 44% 56% 61%

▼ Manager Change
▽ Partial Manager Change

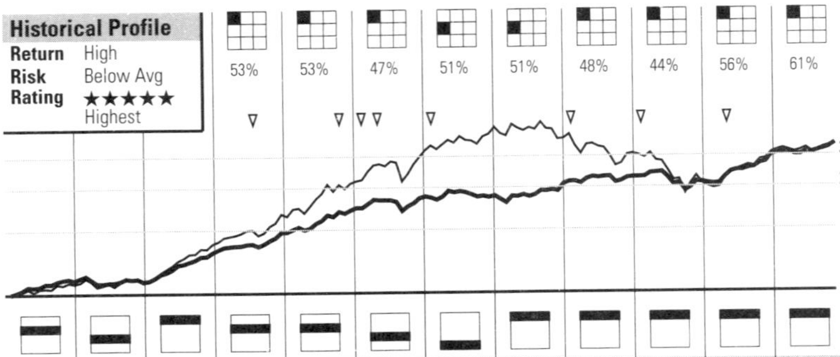

Growth of $10,000
— Investment Values of Fund
— Investment Values of S&P 500

Performance Quartile (within Category)

1993	1994	1995	1996	1997	1998	1999	2000	2001	2002	2003	12-04	History
14.39	13.14	15.87	16.52	17.77	17.34	15.74	15.94	15.82	14.35	17.18	18.56	NAV
14.01	-2.50	29.08	15.23	22.16	9.47	0.52	9.98	5.41	-4.37	25.27	12.92	Total Return %
3.95	-3.81	-8.45	-7.71	-11.19	-19.10	-20.52	19.08	17.29	17.72	-3.40	2.05	+/-S&P 500
2.28	-0.55	4.31	3.89	2.96	-2.92	-12.33	5.54	5.25	6.17	1.21	1.75	+/-DJ 60%
6.20	5.90	6.45	5.79	5.17	5.04	5.11	5.18	5.11	4.99	4.97	3.87	Income Return %
7.81	-8.40	22.63	9.44	16.99	4.43	-4.59	4.80	0.30	-9.36	20.30	9.05	Capital Return %
31	54	21	42	30	74	89	11	5	6	12	6	Total Rtn % Rank Cat
0.83	0.83	0.83	0.90	0.82	0.88	0.87	0.80	0.80	0.77	0.70	0.66	Income $
0.35	0.06	0.18	0.81	1.48	1.19	0.81	0.48	0.16	0.02	0.00	0.13	Capital Gains $
0.62	0.63	0.65	0.62	0.61	0.59	0.59	0.63	0.62	0.61	0.61	0.57	Expense Ratio %
6.05	5.92	6.12	5.56	5.09	4.75	4.99	5.52	5.18	4.66	4.98	4.15	Income Ratio %
29	26	26	38	41	35	44	35	44	36	28	27	Turnover Rate %
10,339	10,503	13,778	16,192	20,221	22,909	21,450	18,568	19,853	20,836	31,955	42,536	Net Assets $mil

Performance 12-31-04

	1st Qtr	2nd Qtr	3rd Qtr	4th Qtr	Total
2000	-0.44	-0.42	4.67	5.99	9.98
2001	0.44	4.62	-3.91	4.40	5.41
2002	3.22	-3.61	-10.29	7.13	-4.37
2003	-1.13	11.37	2.43	11.07	25.27
2004	1.96	0.15	2.71	7.67	12.92

Trailing	Total Return%	+/- S&P 500	+/- DJ 60%	%Rank Cat	Growth of $10,000
3 Mo	7.67	-1.56	0.19	30	10,767
6 Mo	10.58	3.39	3.05	2	11,058
1 Yr	12.92	2.05	1.75	6	11,292
3 Yr Avg	10.59	7.01	3.33	2	13,525
5 Yr Avg	9.42	11.72	4.18	3	15,685
10 Yr Avg	12.10	0.03	1.61	9	31,337
15 Yr Avg	10.85	-0.08	0.90	14	46,885

Tax Analysis	Tax-Adj Rtn%	%Rank Cat	Tax-Cost Rat	%Rank Cat
3 Yr (estimated)	6.65	9	1.64	95
5 Yr (estimated)	6.03	5	1.94	92
10 Yr (estimated)	8.66	19	2.49	92

Potential Capital Gain Exposure: 16% of assets

Rating and Risk

Time Period	Load-Adj Return %	Morningstar Rtn vs Cat	Morningstar Risk vs Cat	Morningstar Risk-Adj Rating
1 Yr	6.43			
3 Yr	8.43	High	Avg	★★★★★
5 Yr	8.13	High	-Avg	★★★★★
10 Yr	11.44	+Avg	Low	★★★★
Incept	10.98			

Other Measures	Standard Index S&P 500	Best Fit Index DJ 60%
Alpha	7.6	0.6
Beta	0.55	0.97
R-Squared	79	89
Standard Deviation	10.07	
Mean	10.59	
Sharpe Ratio	0.92	

Portfolio Analysis 09-30-04

Total Stocks:177 Share change since 06-30-04	Sectors	P/E Ratio	YTD Return %	% Net Assets
⊕ SBC Communications	Telecom	15.4	-3.12	1.82
⊕ Verizon Communications	Telecom	32.4	-3.79	1.71
⊕ Bank of America	Financial	12.3	-3.85	1.70
⊕ Dow Chemical	Ind Mtrls	16.6	-3.66	1.59
⊕ Bristol-Myers Squibb	Health	17.7	-2.90	1.36
⊕ General Motors	Goods	7.2	-4.02	1.16
⊕ Royal Dutch Petroleum ADR	Energy	—	-2.96	1.13
⊕ HSBC Hldgs	Financial	—	—	1.08
⊕ Weyerhaeuser	Ind Mtrls	—	-0.03	1.07

Total Fixed-Income:922	Date of Maturity	Amount $000	Value $000	% Net Assets
US Treasury Note 5.75%	11-15-05	239,500	248,742	0.54
FNMA	10-01-34	160,525	165,992	0.36
Sb Treas 144A FRN	12-29-49	122,070	144,261	0.31
Electnc Data Sys New 6%	08-01-13	123,000	124,267	0.27
US Treasury Note 3.625%	01-15-08	95,000	122,047	0.27
Ford Motor Cr 7.375%	10-28-09	105,000	115,132	0.25
Nextel Comms 7.375%	08-01-15	104,450	112,806	0.25
Celestica Cv	08-01-20	181,000	99,776	0.22
US Treasury Bond 6.875%	08-15-25	77,750	97,624	0.21

Equity Style
Style: Value
Size: Large-Cap

Value Measures		Rel Category
Price/Earnings	13.47	0.81
Price/Book	2.08	0.85
Price/Sales	1.00	0.76
Price/Cash Flow	6.05	0.83
Dividend Yield %	3.99	2.54

Growth Measures	%	Rel Category
Long-Term Erngs	7.56	0.65
Book Value	-2.27	NMF
Sales	0.01	0.00
Cash Flow	-0.97	NMF
Historical Erngs	3.16	0.29

Market Cap %			
Giant	42.1	Small	0.5
Large	39.9	Micro	0.1
Mid	17.5	Avg $mil:	25,399

Fixed-Income Style
Duration: Interm-Term
Quality: Medium

Avg Eff Duration [1]	4.1 Yrs
Avg Eff Maturity	5.8 Yrs
Avg Credit Quality	BBB
Avg Wtd Coupon	6.70%

[1]figure provided by fund as of 09-30-04

Sector Weightings	% of Stocks	Rel S&P 500	3 Year High	3 Year Low
Info	13.40	0.62		
Software	0.00	0.00	0	0
Hardware	0.44	0.04	1	0
Media	0.14	0.04	0	0
Telecom	12.82	4.07	13	4
Service	35.31	0.76		
Health	3.91	0.31	7	3
Consumer	3.53	0.39	6	3
Business	0.11	0.03	2	0
Financial	27.76	1.34	29	22
Mfg	51.30	1.60		
Goods	10.78	1.16	19	11
Ind Mtrls	16.46	1.30	23	16
Energy	11.37	1.59	11	9
Utilities	12.69	4.29	13	11

Composition

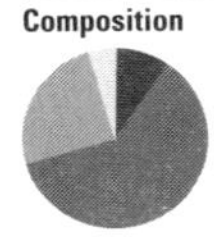

Cash	9.5
Stocks	60.9
Bonds	25.1
Other	4.6
Foreign (% of Stock)	27.5

Morningstar's Take by Paul Herbert 12-31-04

We find American Funds Income Fund of America appealing, though we have one worry.

We won't praise a fund if we aren't confident in its strategy and its advisor's ability to execute it. Neither matter has been an issue here. The fund's managers seek to offer current income and capital growth by investing in a mix of stocks, particularly blue-chip dividend-payers, and bonds, including high-yield issues. The strategy has been a recipe for success over time as the fund has consistently paid out more in income than most of its moderate allocation rivals and is a total-returns star.

But we can't get really excited unless we see that a manager is a strong fiduciary, and American Funds scores well on this measure, too. For instance, the firm has kept fees low, shown an unmatched ability to hire and retain topnotch talent, and steered clear of major regulatory issues.

Our major concern with American has been asset size. The company has enjoyed success in gathering assets in recent years, and that attention could make it more difficult for the funds to trade efficiently. Asset bloat is less of a problem at this $51.2 billion fund than it is at other stock-only funds, but it's an issue nonetheless given that the fund owns many of the same stocks as its siblings. Our bigger worry here is that asset growth could impact the fund's ability to invest in lower-rated bonds, which comprise more than 9% of its assets recently. This stake helps it to deliver a plump yield and has contributed to the fund's success in 2004 as low-grade paper is less sensitive to rising interest rates. But size could make it difficult for the fund to participate to a meaningful degree in smaller junk-bond offerings.

As a result, income-minded investors should keep an eye on the fund's yield. In all, though, we haven't noticed signs that the fund is experiencing trouble from its girth, and at this point, we continue to find it the class of its category.

Address:	333 S Hope St - 52nd Floor Los Angeles, CA 90071 800-421-0180
Web Address:	www.americanfunds.com
Inception:	12-31-70
Advisor:	Capital Research and Management Company
Subadvisor:	None
NTF Plans:	Federated Tr NTF

Minimum Purchase:	$250	Add: $50	IRA: $250
Min Auto Inv Plan:	$50	Add: $50	
Sales Fees:	5.75%L		
Management Fee:	0.24% mx./0.15% mn.		
Actual Fees:	Mgt:0.24%	Dist:0.23%	
Expense Projections:	3Yr:$762	5Yr:$901	10Yr:$1305
Income Distrib:	Quarterly		

Amer Funds Inv Co Am A

Ticker	Load	NAV	Yield	Total Assets	Mstar Category
AIVSX	5.75%	$30.75	1.7%	$75,867 mil	Large Value

Governance and Management

Fiduciary Grade: B

Portfolio Manager(s)

The fund is managed by a veteran nine-person team. The firm's research capabilities are hard to match as it employs more than 140 investment pros globally. Investors will also be hard-pressed to find analysts with greater industry expertise. Joyce Gordon, for example, has followed banks since 1987. Both managers and analysts are compensated in part based on how their picks perform versus a benchmark over a four-year moving average.

Strategy

The fund favors established blue-chip companies, many of which pay dividends. As a result, the fund has a decent stake of assets devoted to stocks in industries such as oil services, financials, and tobacco. But management is also willing to scoop up shares in depressed growth names. Thus, it isn't surprising to see stocks that are typically considered growth stocks in its portfolio. Management will also keep a decent chunk of assets parked in bonds and cash at times. This tack provides cushion when the market tumbles, but it may hold it back a bit during big rallies in the stock market.

Historical Profile

Return Average
Risk Low
Rating ★★★ Neutral

Investment Style
Equity
Stock %

88%	85%	81%	85%	78%	79%	72%	82%	82%

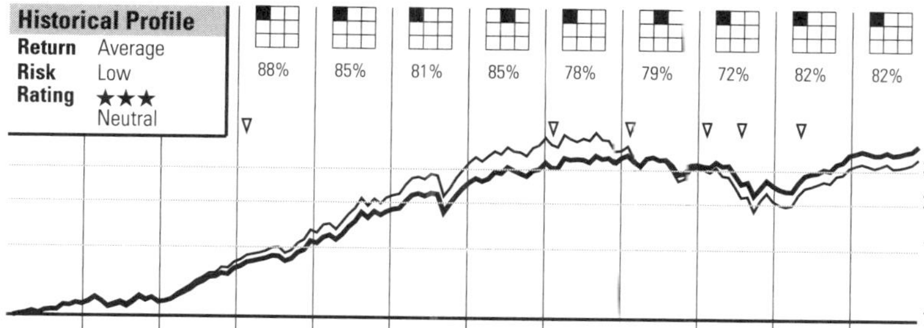

▼ Manager Change
▽ Partial Manager Change

Growth of $10,000
— Investment Values of Fund
— Investment Values of S&P 500

Performance Quartile (within Category)

1993	1994	1995	1996	1997	1998	1999	2000	2001	2002	2003	12-04	History
18.72	17.67	21.61	24.23	28.25	31.07	32.46	31.06	28.53	23.48	28.84	30.75	NAV
11.62	0.15	30.63	19.35	29.81	22.94	16.56	3.84	-4.59	-14.47	26.30	9.78	Total Return %
1.56	-1.16	-6.90	-3.59	-3.54	-5.63	-4.48	12.94	7.29	7.62	-2.37	-1.09	+/-S&P 500
-6.45	2.13	-7.73	-2.29	-5.37	7.31	9.21	-3.17	1.00	1.05	-3.73	-6.71	+/-Russ 1000 VI
2.66	2.59	2.86	2.33	2.08	1.83	1.66	1.63	1.70	1.84	2.23	1.82	Income Return %
8.96	-2.44	27.77	17.02	27.73	21.11	14.90	2.21	-6.29	-16.31	24.07	7.96	Capital Return %
66	41	71	57	26	4	9	76	52	21	64	83	Total Rtn % Rank Cat
0.47	0.48	0.50	0.50	0.50	0.51	0.51	0.52	0.52	0.52	0.52	0.52	Income $
0.75	0.60	0.91	1.03	2.60	2.94	3.04	2.08	0.59	0.46	0.21	0.36	Capital Gains $
0.59	0.60	0.60	0.59	0.56	0.55	0.55	0.56	0.57	0.59	0.59	—	Expense Ratio %
3.03	2.83	2.70	2.17	1.90	1.65	1.54	1.74	1.49	1.89	2.14	—	Income Ratio %
18	31	21	17	26	25	28	25	22	27	24	—	Turnover Rate %
19,005	19,280	25,678	30,875	39,718	48,498	56,095	56,212	54,315	46,129	58,353	64,880	Net Assets $mil

Performance 12-31-04

	1st Qtr	2nd Qtr	3rd Qtr	4th Qtr	Total
2000	3.63	-1.10	0.45	0.86	3.84
2001	-5.77	4.62	-10.24	7.82	-4.59
2002	2.02	-9.06	-14.51	7.84	-14.47
2003	-4.43	14.47	2.39	12.75	26.30
2004	1.48	0.59	-0.10	7.65	9.78

Trailing	Total Return%	+/- S&P 500	+/- Russ 1000 VI	%Rank Cat	Growth of $10,000
3 Mo	7.65	-1.58	-2.73	84	10,765
6 Mo	7.54	0.35	-4.54	72	10,754
1 Yr	9.78	-1.09	-6.71	83	10,978
3 Yr Avg	5.85	2.27	-2.72	49	11,860
5 Yr Avg	3.28	5.58	-1.99	58	11,751
10 Yr Avg	13.04	0.97	-0.79	16	34,066
15 Yr Avg	11.61	0.68	-0.42	19	51,945

Tax Analysis	Tax-Adj Rtn%	%Rank Cat	Tax-Cost Rat	%Rank Cat
3 Yr (estimated)	2.83	72	0.92	61
5 Yr (estimated)	0.89	72	1.15	61
10 Yr (estimated)	10.45	24	1.71	44

Potential Capital Gain Exposure: 27% of assets

Rating and Risk

Time Period	Load-Adj Return %	Morningstar Rtn vs Cat	Morningstar Risk vs Cat	Morningstar Risk-Adj Rating
1 Yr	3.47			
3 Yr	3.78	-Avg	Low	★★★
5 Yr	2.06	-Avg	Low	★★★
10 Yr	12.37	+Avg	-Avg	★★★★
Incept	12.56			

Other Measures	Standard Index S&P 500	Best Fit Index Russ 1000 VI
Alpha	2.4	-1.6
Beta	0.83	0.85
R-Squared	95	97
Standard Deviation	13.51	
Mean	5.85	
Sharpe Ratio	0.33	

Portfolio Analysis 09-30-04

Share change since 06-04 Total Stocks:187	Sector	PE	YTD Ret%	% Assets
Altria Group	Goods	13.3	18.38	3.75
⊕ SBC Communications	Telecom	15.4	3.74	2.27
⊕ Fannie Mae	Financial	9.1	-2.33	1.79
Dow Chemical	Ind Mtrls	16.6	22.83	1.78
⊕ Bank of America	Financial	12.3	21.50	1.75
Lowe's Companies	Consumer	22.1	4.25	1.58
⊕ Microsoft	Software	36.1	8.95	1.52
Caterpillar	Ind Mtrls	17.6	19.75	1.41
⊕ Gen Elec	Ind Mtrls	22.8	20.68	1.38
⊕ Target	Consumer	22.3	36.14	1.36
Time Warner	Media	27.5	8.12	1.33
⊕ J P Morgan Chase	Financial	19.4	9.97	1.32
⊖ Tyco International	Ind Mtrls	25.1	35.41	1.29
⊕ American International G	Financial	16.2	-0.53	1.27
⊕ Eli Lilly & Company	Health	24.3	-17.55	1.24
⊕ Royal Dutch Petroleum AD	Energy	—	14.31	1.23
⊕ Eni	Energy	—	—	1.21
⊕ ChevronTexaco	Energy	7.7	25.57	1.17
⊕ Verizon Communications	Telecom	32.4	20.25	1.11
Burlington Resources	Energy	10.9	58.50	1.05

Current Investment Style

Value Blnd Growth — Large Mid Small

Market Cap	%
Giant	49.6
Large	45.6
Mid	4.8
Small	0.0
Micro	0.0

Avg $mil: 42,544

Value Measures		Rel Category
Price/Earnings	15.29	1.02
Price/Book	2.35	1.04
Price/Sales	1.16	0.97
Price/Cash Flow	7.37	1.16
Dividend Yield %	2.23	1.09

Growth Measures	%	Rel Category
Long-Term Erngs	10.11	0.97
Book Value	5.57	0.99
Sales	2.78	0.66
Cash Flow	3.51	0.67
Historical Erngs	9.08	0.77

Profitability	%	Rel Category
Return on Equity	16.67	1.05
Return on Assets	7.24	0.92
Net Margin	9.25	0.91

Sector Weightings	% of Stocks	Rel S&P 500	3 Year High	3 Year Low
Info	22.44	1.04		
Software	1.86	0.43	2	1
Hardware	8.88	0.87	10	7
Media	3.33	0.87	7	3
Telecom	8.37	2.66	9	5
Service	30.76	0.66		
Health	6.30	0.50	12	6
Consumer	6.58	0.72	7	5
Business	2.86	0.71	4	3
Financial	15.02	0.72	19	13
Mfg	46.79	1.46		
Goods	12.19	1.31	15	10
Ind Mtrls	20.12	1.59	20	13
Energy	11.54	1.61	12	8
Utilities	2.94	0.99	5	3

Composition

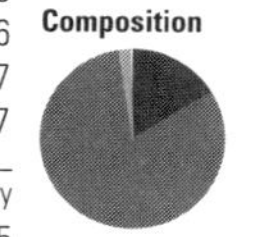

Cash	15.9
Stocks	81.6
Bonds	1.8
Other	0.6
Foreign (% of Stock)	10.8

Morningstar's Take by Paul Herbert 01-06-05

This research-driven fund's size is more of a concern than its recent sluggishness.

American Funds Investment Company of America has long been one of the biggest and best large-value funds. Its clearest advantage probably lies in its research resources. With nine experienced portfolio managers calling the shots and more than 140 analysts searching for blue-chip companies offering attractive price tags and the potential for future dividend growth, its depth is hard to match. Add the fund's low expenses--just 0.59% as of its most recent fiscal-year end--and it possesses a huge head start on the competition.

As we have expressed before, however, we're concerned that the fund could face some trials. Thanks to American Funds' great reputation and strong, consistent performance, the fund family has attracted plenty of attention lately. While the group may be equipped to handle growth better than almost any other active manager, we think it bears repeating that we have seen deleterious effects of asset growth many times. While it certainly isn't a cure-all, advisors that decide to close their funds help to head off these growing pains.

During 2004, we didn't see evidence that asset bloat had slowed this fund down, though it hasn't been a shining star. On balance, the fund's tendency toward cheaper mega-caps was a burden. While energy and industrials fare pitched in nice gains, telecom and health-care stocks weighed on performance. Favorites Microsoft and Time Warner also failed to keep pace with the market, and the fund lagged more than 80% of its peers last year. Finding opportunity in overlooked stocks is one of the fund's calling cards, though. And while some of its top choices may not have panned out in 2004, its strong long-term record suggests that shareholders have been compensated for the managers' pernicious ways.

We still find this an attractive fund, but we would be more comfortable if American Funds articulated a plan for managing asset growth.

Address:	333 S Hope St - 52nd Floor Los Angeles CA 90071 800-421-0180
Web Address:	
Inception:	01-01-34
Advisor:	Capital Research and Management Company
Subadvisor:	None
NTF Plans:	Federated Tr NTF

Minimum Purchase:	$250	Add: $50	IRA: $250
Min Auto Inv Plan:	$50	Add: $50	
Sales Fees:	5.75%L		
Management Fee:	0.39% mx./0.22% mn.		
Actual Fees:	Mgt:0.24%	Dist:0.23%	
Expense Projections:	3Yr:$744	5Yr:$870	10Yr:$1236
Income Distrib:	Quarterly		

Amer Funds New Econ A

Ticker	Load	NAV	Yield	Total Assets	Mstar Category
ANEFX	5.75%	$21.03	0.3%	$7,704 mil	Large Growth

Governance and Management

Fiduciary Grade: B

Portfolio Manager(s)

The team here is seasoned and influential. Its most senior member, Gordon Crawford, has been in the business for more than 30 years and wields significant influence with many of the media industry's top executives. The portfolio counselors are backed by an experienced and extensive team of research analysts who are based around the globe.

Strategy

This fund invests in companies whose prospects are tied to the information and services areas of the economy. The upshot of this approach is that the fund tends to have large stakes in technology and telecom, and it also boasts significant exposure to financial services and media. Management sometimes maintains a double-digit cash stake and will invest a good chunk of assets overseas. It generally prefers a growth-at-a-reasonable-price approach, but the fund owns everything from value names to hypergrowth stocks.

Historical Profile

Return Above Avg
Risk Above Avg
Rating ★★★ Neutral

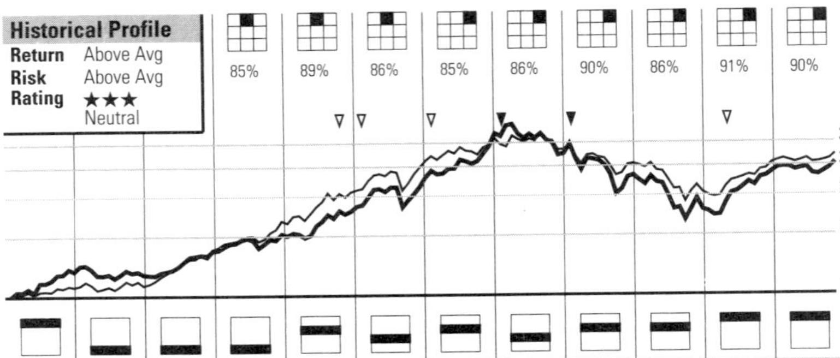

Investment Style
Equity
Stock %

▼ Manager Change
▽ Partial Manager Change

Growth of $10,000
— Investment Values of Fund
— Investment Values of S&P 500

Performance Quartile (within Category)

History

1993	1994	1995	1996	1997	1998	1999	2000	2001	2002	2003	12-04	History
15.89	13.74	16.18	16.98	19.97	22.95	29.82	22.14	18.30	13.54	18.77	21.03	NAV
30.99	-8.14	24.37	12.89	28.85	28.84	45.87	-16.20	-17.34	-26.01	38.71	12.45	Total Return %
20.93	-9.45	-13.16	-10.05	-4.50	0.27	24.83	-7.10	-5.46	-3.92	10.04	1.58	+/-S&P 500
28.12	-10.76	-12.81	-10.23	-1.64	-9.87	12.71	6.22	3.08	1.87	8.96	6.15	+/-Russ 1000Gr
0.83	1.07	1.39	0.87	0.77	0.70	0.79	0.00	0.00	0.00	0.08	0.40	Income Return %
30.16	-9.21	22.98	12.02	28.08	28.14	45.08	-16.20	-17.34	-26.01	38.63	12.05	Capital Return %
3	95	88	89	40	62	26	63	34	40	8	12	Total Rtn % Rank Cat
0.11	0.17	0.19	0.14	0.13	0.14	0.18	0.00	0.00	0.00	0.01	0.07	Income $
1.28	0.68	0.69	1.13	1.72	2.54	3.18	2.92	0.00	0.00	0.00	0.00	Capital Gains $
0.85	0.85	0.88	0.84	0.81	0.79	0.78	0.81	0.82	0.89	0.89	—	Expense Ratio %
0.76	1.25	1.33	0.85	0.66	0.60	0.42	0.42	0.02	-0.01	0.09	—	Income Ratio %
27	26	27	30	32	39	48	54	41	37	38	—	Turnover Rate %
2,117	2,594	3,546	4,132	4,985	6,531	10,865	10,438	8,159	5,262	6,885	7,151	Net Assets $mil

Performance 12-31-04

	1st Qtr	2nd Qtr	3rd Qtr	4th Qtr	Total
2000	8.18	-8.21	-5.17	-11.00	-16.20
2001	-13.10	8.16	-25.23	17.61	-17.34
2002	-1.20	-15.21	-19.24	9.37	-26.01
2003	-4.51	22.82	5.29	12.33	38.71
2004	3.84	-0.26	-3.50	12.51	12.45

Trailing	Total Return%	+/- S&P 500	+/- Russ 1000Gr	%Rank Cat	Growth of $10,000
3 Mo	12.51	3.28	3.34	12	11,251
6 Mo	8.57	1.38	5.10	12	10,857
1 Yr	12.45	1.58	6.15	12	11,245
3 Yr Avg	4.89	1.31	5.07	10	11,540
5 Yr Avg	-4.38	-2.08	4.91	22	7,994
10 Yr Avg	10.52	-1.55	0.93	29	27,190
15 Yr Avg	10.44	-0.49	0.94	32	44,350

Tax Analysis	Tax-Adj Rtn%	%Rank Cat	Tax-Cost Rat	%Rank Cat
3 Yr (estimated)	2.79	17	0.05	9
5 Yr (estimated)	-5.97	28	0.50	31
10 Yr (estimated)	8.45	29	1.28	38

Potential Capital Gain Exposure: 1% of assets

Rating and Risk

Time Period	Load-Adj Return %	Morningstar Rtn vs Cat	Morningstar Risk vs Cat	Morningstar Risk-Adj Rating
1 Yr	5.98			
3 Yr	2.84	+Avg	High	★★★★
5 Yr	-5.50	+Avg	+Avg	★★★
10 Yr	9.86	Avg	Avg	★★★
Incept	12.13			

Other Measures	Standard Index S&P 500	Best Fit Index Russ 1000
Alpha	1.2	0.3
Beta	1.25	1.27
R-Squared	92	93
Standard Deviation	20.83	
Mean	4.89	
Sharpe Ratio	0.17	

Morningstar's Take by Paul Herbert 10-21-04

You could do a lot worse than this fund, but it's not the best choice for broad large-growth exposure.

American Funds New Economy Fund has really shined in recent years. The media-, telecom-, and retail-focused fund prospered as those areas rallied in 2003. Its managers' emphasis on financially healthy companies selling at reasonable valuations was also a boon during 2001 and 2002, however, when rival funds that also rely heavily on this fund's favored sectors stumbled. As a result, the fund has amassed an enviable near-term record, even as conditions have varied during the past few years.

This has not always been the case, though. When its favored stomping grounds lagged in 2000, and areas such as health care and consumer staples kept some rivals afloat, it failed to keep up with the large-growth pack. And it also trailed its median peer in 1998, and from 1994 to 1996. To help measure a fund's staying power, we like to examine its performance over rolling periods versus its peers, and on this count, it has looked mediocre. Indeed, it has topped its peers in just 55 of the past 100 rolling periods.

The fund is showing strength during 2004, though. Rallying Internet stocks have certainly played a role in its relative success as Yahoo and eBay are among its top holdings. These have helped make up for stumbles from hardware picks such as Applied Materials, which have been hit as investors have fretted over news of slower-than-expected demand for their wares.

Institutional advantages lend this fund attractiveness. Still, unless you're in need of exposure to its chosen sectors, which include tech, media, retail, and financial services, you'll find superior--and more diversified--options.

Portfolio Analysis 09-30-04

Share change since 06-04 Total Stocks:154	Sector	PE	YTD Ret%	% Assets
Time Warner	Media	27.5	8.12	4.21
American International G	Financial	16.2	-0.53	3.20
Iac / Interactivecorp	Consumer	43.1	-18.60	2.88
Yahoo	Media	95.1	67.36	2.33
Carnival	Goods	26.2	46.74	2.24
⊕ Target	Consumer	22.3	36.14	2.11
⊕ First Data	Business	18.8	3.72	2.06
Freddie Mac	Financial	10.6	28.75	1.82
Schlumberger	Energy	40.7	23.84	1.77
⊕ Applied Materials	Hardware	20.7	-23.80	1.53
Wells Fargo	Financial	15.5	8.97	1.46
Kon Kpn Nv	Telecom	—	—	1.39
⊕ Texas Instruments	Hardware	21.1	-15.90	1.33
Lowe's Companies	Consumer	22.1	4.25	1.33
⊖ eBay	Consumer	81.6	80.07	1.29
Cisco Systems	Hardware	24.5	-20.26	1.28
☼ Telephone and Data Syste	Telecom	39.5	24.11	1.20
Soc Generale	Financial	—	—	1.19
⊕ Maxim Integrated Product	Hardware	27.9	-13.87	1.16
Capital One Financial	Financial	12.5	37.61	1.13

Current Investment Style

Value Blnd Growth; Large Mid Small

Market Cap	%
Giant	30.6
Large	42.3
Mid	24.7
Small	2.0
Micro	0.4
Avg $mil: 16,597	

Value Measures		Rel Category
Price/Earnings	18.27	0.86
Price/Book	2.06	0.64
Price/Sales	1.38	0.64
Price/Cash Flow	7.31	0.67
Dividend Yield %	0.99	1.29

Growth Measures	%	Rel Category
Long-Term Erngs	14.94	1.06
Book Value	4.94	0.39
Sales	6.48	0.76
Cash Flow	8.77	0.53
Historical Erngs	19.46	1.34

Profitability	%	Rel Category
Return on Equity	12.21	0.68
Return on Assets	6.17	0.66
Net Margin	9.76	0.79

Sector Weightings	% of Stocks	Rel S&P 500	3 Year High	3 Year Low
Info	36.50	1.70		
Software	1.99	0.46	5	2
Hardware	12.28	1.20	18	12
Media	12.98	3.38	20	13
Telecom	9.25	2.94	10	5
Service	53.97	1.16		
Health	2.23	0.18	4	0
Consumer	18.98	2.09	21	15
Business	12.91	3.19	14	10
Financial	19.85	0.96	27	17
Mfg	9.53	0.30		
Goods	4.13	0.44	4	2
Ind Mtrls	0.08	0.01	0	0
Energy	3.97	0.55	4	1
Utilities	1.35	0.46	1	0

Composition

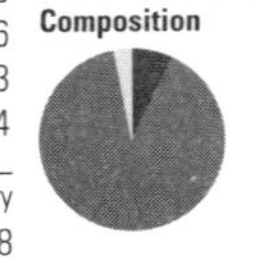

Cash	7.2
Stocks	89.7
Bonds	0.0
Other	3.1
Foreign (% of Stock)	26.4

Address:	333 S Hope St - 52nd Floor Los Angeles CA 90071 800-421-0180
Web Address:	www.americanfunds.com
Inception:	12-01-83
Advisor:	Capital Research and Management Company
Subadvisor:	None
NTF Plans:	Federated Tr NTF

Minimum Purchase:	$250	Add: $50	IRA: $250
Min Auto Inv Plan:	$50	Add: $50	
Sales Fees:	5.75%L		
Management Fee:	0.58% mx./0.35% mn.		
Actual Fees:	Mgt:0.40%	Dist:0.24%	
Expense Projections:	3Yr:$822	5Yr:$1004	10Yr:$1530
Income Distrib:	Annually		

Amer Funds New Persp A

Analyst Pick

Ticker	Load	NAV	Yield	Total Assets	Mstar Category
ANWPX	5.75%	$27.72	0.9%	$39,767 mil	World Stock

Governance and Management

Fiduciary Grade: B

Portfolio Manager(s)

American Funds uses a multimanager system at its offerings. Each portfolio manager runs a portion of assets, investing independently of the others. The managers' styles range from moderately aggressive to conservative. The average manager tenure here spans approximately two decades. All the managers also comanage other successful offerings, such as American Funds EuroPacific Growth and American Funds New Economy.

Strategy

This fund's managers typically buy out-of-favor companies and hold them for the long run. Although they tend to shop for bargains, they allow their winners to run, which pushes the fund into large-cap-growth territory. The managers never chase speculative stocks, though. The fund always has a sizable cash position. American Funds uses a fair-value pricing policy, although it only implemented such an approach within the past few years.

Historical Profile

Return: Above Avg
Risk: Average
Rating: ★★★★ Above Avg

Investment Style
Equity
Stock %: 87% 84% 83% 85% 81% 82% 85% 87% 92%

▼ Manager Change
▽ Partial Manager Change

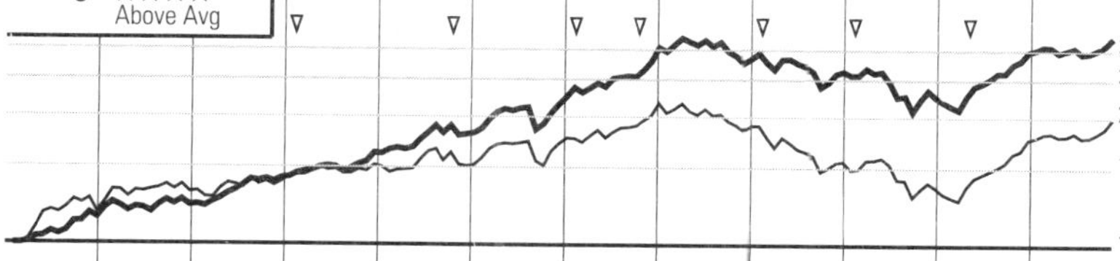

Growth of $10,000
— Investment Values of Fund
— Investment Values of MSCI EAFE

Performance Quartile (within Category)

1993	1994	1995	1996	1997	1998	1999	2000	2001	2002	2003	12-04	History
15.01	14.37	16.38	18.17	19.36	22.95	29.44	24.05	21.69	18.04	24.49	27.72	NAV
26.98	2.97	20.43	17.28	14.98	28.53	40.07	-7.24	-8.30	-16.05	36.76	14.27	Total Return %
-5.58	-4.81	9.22	11.23	13.20	8.60	13.04	6.95	13.12	-0.11	-1.83	-5.98	+/-MSCI EAFE
4.48	-2.11	-0.29	3.80	-0.78	4.21	15.12	5.95	8.50	3.84	3.65	-0.45	+/-MSCI World
1.71	1.54	2.17	1.98	1.60	1.35	0.74	0.66	1.54	0.77	0.98	1.05	Income Return %
25.27	1.43	18.26	15.30	13.38	27.18	39.33	-7.90	-9.84	-16.82	35.78	13.22	Capital Return %
72	11	37	42	46	11	46	39	16	23	35	56	Total Rtn % Rank Cat
0.21	0.23	0.31	0.32	0.29	0.26	0.17	0.20	0.37	0.17	0.18	0.26	Income $
0.37	0.84	0.60	0.69	1.21	1.57	2.34	3.10	0.00	0.00	0.00	0.00	Capital Gains $
0.87	0.84	0.83	0.82	0.79	0.77	0.77	0.79	0.78	0.82	0.82	0.78	Expense Ratio %
1.40	1.48	2.12	2.00	1.56	1.27	1.06	1.00	1.40	0.84	0.84	0.93	Income Ratio %
15	25	22	18	26	30	29	34	32	26	28	19	Turnover Rate %
5,086	6,540	9,292	12,895	16,203	21,257	32,173	31,304	27,787	22,166	29,053	33,735	Net Assets $mil

Performance 12-31-04

	1st Qtr	2nd Qtr	3rd Qtr	4th Qtr	Total
2000	6.69	-1.50	-7.34	-4.75	-7.24
2001	-7.11	4.37	-14.99	11.26	-8.30
2002	2.12	-8.85	-18.28	10.35	-16.05
2003	-8.20	19.99	7.35	15.67	36.76
2004	3.23	-0.28	-1.19	12.34	14.27

Trailing	Total Return%	+/- MSCI EAFE	+/- MSCI World	%Rank Cat	Growth of $10,000
3 Mo	12.34	-2.98	0.40	51	11,234
6 Mo	11.00	-4.00	0.18	51	11,100
1 Yr	14.27	-5.98	-0.45	56	11,427
3 Yr Avg	9.47	-2.42	2.52	32	13,119
5 Yr Avg	2.22	3.35	4.67	29	11,160
10 Yr Avg	12.55	6.93	4.46	9	32,618
15 Yr Avg	11.80	7.57	5.21	7	53,288

Tax Analysis	Tax-Adj Rtn%	%Rank Cat	Tax-Cost Rat	%Rank Cat
3 Yr (estimated)	6.99	44	0.32	43
5 Yr (estimated)	0.18	34	0.82	51
10 Yr (estimated)	10.41	16	1.32	52

Potential Capital Gain Exposure: 29% of assets

Rating and Risk

Time Period	Load-Adj Return %	Morningstar Rtn vs Cat	Morningstar Risk vs Cat	Morningstar Risk-Adj Rating
1 Yr	7.70			
3 Yr	7.33	Avg	Avg	★★★
5 Yr	1.01	Avg	Avg	★★★
10 Yr	11.89	+Avg	Avg	★★★★★
Incept	13.55			

Other Measures	Standard Index S&P 500	Best Fit Index MSCI World
Alpha	-2.0	3.2
Beta	0.99	1.07
R-Squared	91	97
Standard Deviation	17.78	
Mean	9.47	
Sharpe Ratio	0.46	

Morningstar's Take by Gareth Lyons 12-28-04

A so-so year for American Funds New Perspective doesn't dent its long-term appeal.

This fund's emphasis on large-cap growth names hasn't jibed with the market's recent penchant for smaller, value-priced stocks. Though its 14.4% year-to-date return through Dec. 28, 2004 isn't too bad on an absolute basis, it still trails its typical peer, not to mention the MSCI World Index.

While it may look a tad out of sync right now, the strategy here is consistent and well-proven. Each manager on this seven-member team picks stocks independently of the others, resulting in a broadly diversified portfolio. The fund typically has a moderate growth tilt, steering clear of both deep-value and speculative-growth fare. What's more, the managers are willing to hold on to picks that are experiencing near-term problems. (The fund currently has more than 12% of assets in the troubled tech hardware sector--nearly twice the category norm.)

The team here, which boasts decades of experience and is backed by a huge group of analysts, has shown repeated success plying its patient approach. And thanks to a broad portfolio and growth-at-a-reasonable-price bent, the fund has been a steady performer in both bull and bear markets.

For that reason, the fund has attracted plenty of attention lately, and asset flows here have been robust. The fund's wide global charter help to diminish our immediate worries that its $38 billion asset base has grown too unwieldy. Comforting, too, is word that advisor Capital Research & Management has added portfolio managers to the fund's multimanager setup to dilute the effects of asset growth. Even so, we're not sure that the structure in place here can allow the fund to keep on growing indefinitely without eventually sacrificing some flexibility. Make no mistake, this is a fine fund. But we'd like to see some specific dollar targets for closing the fund before asset bloat becomes a problem.

Address:	333 S Hope St - 52nd Floor Los Angeles CA 90071 800-421-0180
Web Address:	www.americanfunds.com
Inception:	03-13-73
Advisor:	Capital Research and Management Company
Subadvisor:	None
NTF Plans:	Federated Tr NTF

Minimum Purchase:	$250	Add: $50	IRA: $250
Min Auto Inv Plan:	$50	Add: $50	
Sales Fees:	5.75%L		
Management Fee:	0.60% mx./0.37% mn.		
Actual Fees:	Mgt:0.40%	Dist:0.24%	
Expense Projections:	3Yr:$810	5Yr:$983	10Yr:$1486
Income Distrib:	Annually		

Portfolio Analysis 09-30-04

Share change since 06-04 Total Stocks:217	Sector	Country	% Assets
Time Warner	Media	United States	2.68
⊕ Sanofi-Synthelabo	Health	France	2.18
⊖ Altria Group	Goods	United States	1.98
⊕ Vodafone Grp	Telecom	U.K.	1.98
⊖ AstraZeneca	Health	U.K.	1.71
Newmont Mining	Ind Mtrls	United States	1.41
⊖ Tyco International	Ind Mtrls	United States	1.29
⊕ Erste Bank	Financial	Austria	1.28
⊕ Deutsche Telekom	Telecom	Germany	1.28
Nestle	Goods	Switzerland	1.23
ING Groep	Financial	Netherlands	1.16
Telefonica	Telecom	Spain	1.16
Eni	Energy	Italy	1.12
⊕ Soc Generale	Financial	France	1.12
⊖ Motorola	Hardware	United States	1.09
⊕ American International G	Financial	United States	1.06
☼ France Telecom	Telecom	France	1.05
Microsoft	Software	United States	1.02
⊕ Honda Motor	Goods	Japan	1.01
Gen Elec	Ind Mtrls	United States	1.00

Current Investment Style

Value Blnd Growth / Large Mid Small

Market Cap	%
Giant	54.4
Large	38.3
Mid	7.3
Small	0.0
Micro	0.1

Avg $mil: 30,657

Value Measures		Rel Category
Price/Earnings	15.31	0.97
Price/Book	2.20	0.99
Price/Sales	1.18	1.01
Price/Cash Flow	5.97	0.94
Dividend Yield %	1.77	0.94

Growth Measures	%	Rel Category
Long-Term Erngs	10.39	0.91
Book Value	-1.14	NMF
Sales	0.25	0.06
Cash Flow	6.91	1.18
Historical Erngs	14.53	1.70

Composition

Cash	6.7	Bonds	0.0
Stocks	91.6	Other	1.8
Foreign (% of Stock)			58.4

Sector Weightings	% of Stocks	Rel MSCI EAFE	3 Year High	3 Year Low
Info	28.86	1.74		
Software	1.94	1.80	2	2
Hardware	12.34	3.38	15	9
Media	5.73	2.51	9	6
Telecom	8.85	0.92	10	3
Service	28.45	0.64		
Health	10.94	1.51	14	9
Consumer	3.19	0.63	5	3
Business	2.43	0.45	3	2
Financial	11.89	0.44	13	9
Mfg	42.69	1.10		
Goods	17.00	1.24	20	16
Ind Mtrls	16.18	1.32	20	16
Energy	7.76	1.06	9	4
Utilities	1.75	0.33	2	1

Regional Exposure	% Stock		
UK/W. Europe	40	N. America	42
Japan	8	Latn America	3
Asia X Japan	6	Other	1

Country Exposure	% Stock		
United States	41	France	7
U.K.	9	Netherlands	6
Japan	8		

Amer Funds New World A

Analyst Pick

Ticker	Load	NAV	Yield	Total Assets	Mstar Category
NEWFX	5.75%	$32.27	1.7%	$3,251 mil	Diversified Emerging Mkts

Governance and Management

Fiduciary Grade: B

Portfolio Manager(s)

The fund's managers, most of whom have been on the fund since its 1999 inception, all have long tenures at Capital Research & Management, the fund's parent, and several comanage other foreign offerings at the firm. In general, American Funds boasts an impressive lineup of international managers and research analysts. As with every American Fund, each manager here oversees his or her portion of assets independently.

Strategy

This fund splits its equity portfolio between emerging-markets stocks and developed-market names. However, stocks that come from developed economies must do considerable business in emerging markets. Typically, the fund's developed-market stake has hovered between one fourth and one third of assets. The portfolio holds a slug of multinationals, such as Samsung and Coca-Cola, and lacks many of the smaller-cap, speculative picks that are typical of emerging-markets funds. The fund can also put up to 25% of its assets in bonds.

Historical Profile

Return Below Avg
Risk Low
Rating ★★★ Neutral

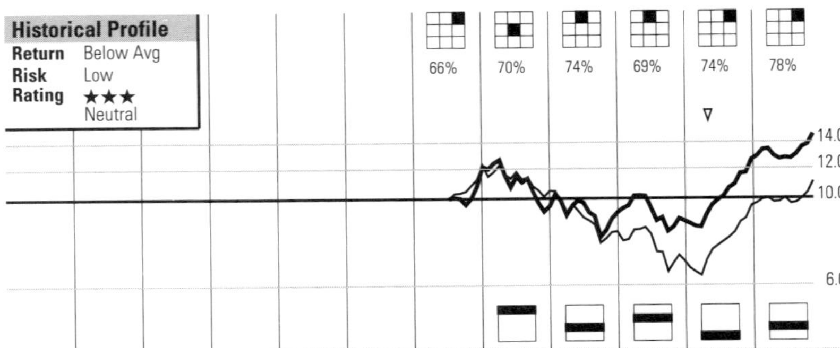

Investment Style: Equity, Stock % — 66% 70% 74% 69% 74% 78%

▼ Manager Change
▽ Partial Manager Change

14.0 / 12.0 / 10.0 / 6.0

Growth of $10,000
— Investment Values of Fund
— Investment Values of MSCI EAFE

Performance Quartile (within Category)

1993	1994	1995	1996	1997	1998	1999	2000	2001	2002	2003	12-04	History
—	—	—	—	—	—	28.29	22.01	20.58	19.38	27.18	32.27	NAV
—	—	—	—	—	—	20.97*	-20.90	-3.96	-4.62	43.36	20.79	Total Return %
—	—	—	—	—	—	—	-6.71	17.46	11.32	4.77	0.54	+/-MSCI EAFE
—	—	—	—	—	—	—	11.00	0.72	3.35	-8.23	-1.66	+/-MSCI EmrMkt
—	—	—	—	—	—	0.00	1.31	2.48	1.22	3.02	2.01	Income Return %
—	—	—	—	—	—	—	-22.21	-6.44	-5.84	40.34	18.78	Capital Return %
—	—	—	—	—	—	—	6	59	38	90	68	Total Rtn % Rank Cat
—	—	—	—	—	—	0.20	0.37	0.55	0.25	0.59	0.55	Income $
—	—	—	—	—	—	0.00	0.00	0.00	0.00	0.00	0.00	Capital Gains $
—	—	—	—	—	—	1.44	1.35	1.29	1.34	1.31	—	Expense Ratio %
—	—	—	—	—	—	1.83	1.61	2.15	1.65	1.86	—	Income Ratio %
—	—	—	—	—	—	—	30	40	32	30	—	Turnover Rate %
—	—	—	—	—	—	1,050	1,222	1,137	1,114	1,728	2,606	Net Assets $mil

Performance 12-31-04

	1st Qtr	2nd Qtr	3rd Qtr	4th Qtr	Total
2000	4.10	-9.44	-8.62	-8.18	-20.90
2001	-5.22	7.53	-18.32	15.38	-3.96
2002	10.54	-6.86	-12.98	6.45	-4.62
2003	-3.66	17.30	9.68	15.67	43.36
2004	6.37	-5.02	6.48	12.28	20.79

Trailing	Total Return%	+/- MSCI EAFE	+/- MSCI EmrMkt	%Rank Cat	Growth of $10,000
3 Mo	12.28	-3.04	-4.53	94	11,228
6 Mo	19.56	4.56	-5.89	93	11,956
1 Yr	20.79	0.54	-1.66	68	12,079
3 Yr Avg	18.21	6.32	-1.33	83	16,518
5 Yr Avg	4.64	5.77	2.55	40	12,546
10 Yr Avg	—	—	—	—	—
15 Yr Avg	—	—	—	—	—

Tax Analysis	Tax-Adj Rtn%	%Rank Cat	Tax-Cost Rat	%Rank Cat
3 Yr (estimated)	15.18	94	0.62	72
5 Yr (estimated)	2.68	56	0.71	76
10 Yr (estimated)	—	—	—	—

Potential Capital Gain Exposure: 19% of assets

Rating and Risk

Time Period	Load-Adj Return %	Morningstar Rtn vs Cat	Morningstar Risk vs Cat	Morningstar Risk-Adj Rating
1 Yr	13.85			
3 Yr	15.90	Low	Low	★★
5 Yr	3.41	Avg	Low	★★★
10 Yr	—	—	—	—
Incept	6.68			

Other Measures	Standard Index S&P 500	Best Fit Index MSCI EmrMkt
Alpha	8.1	3.2
Beta	0.76	0.73
R-Squared	79	91

Standard Deviation	15.78
Mean	18.21
Sharpe Ratio	1.08

Portfolio Analysis 09-30-04

Share change since 06-04 Total Stocks:157	Sector	Country	% Assets
⊕ Pt Telekomunikasi Indone	Telecom	Indonesia	2.82
Daelim Industrial	Business	Korea	2.67
Housing Development Fina	Financial	India	1.84
Kumgang Korea Chemical	Business	Korea	1.80
☼ Cia Vale Rio Doce	—	Brazil	1.71
⊕ OTP Bank	Financial	Hungary	1.65
Fomento Economico Mexica	Goods	Mexico	1.65
⊕ Erste Bank	Financial	Austria	1.56
Kingboard Chemical Hldgs	Ind Mtrls	Hong Kong	1.55
Votorantim Celulose e Pa	Ind Mtrls	Brazil	1.46
Philippine Long Distance	Telecom	Philippines	1.31
☼ Bses	Utilities	India	1.28
Russian Fedn 144A 2.25%	—	—	1.20
⊕ Cesky Telecom	Telecom	Czech Republic	1.20
⊕ Russian Federation 8.25%	—	Russia	1.16
Oriflame Cosmetics	—	Sweden	1.08
Portugal Telecom, SGPS	Telecom	Portugal	1.05
☼ Bk Rakyat	Financial	Indonesia	1.03
NHN	Business	Korea	1.00
Hindalco Industries Ltd	Ind Mtrls	India	1.00

Current Investment Style

Value Blnd Growth — Large / Mid / Small

Market Cap	%
Giant	26.3
Large	36.3
Mid	34.5
Small	2.8
Micro	0.1
Avg $mil: 5,880	

Value Measures		Rel Category
Price/Earnings	11.46	1.26
Price/Book	1.78	1.15
Price/Sales	0.98	1.18
Price/Cash Flow	4.63	1.06
Dividend Yield %	2.24	0.81

Growth Measures	%	Rel Category
Long-Term Erngs	15.32	0.79
Book Value	1.86	0.54
Sales	10.05	0.87
Cash Flow	7.69	1.03
Historical Erngs	6.91	1.00

Composition			
Cash	8.5	Bonds	11.2
Stocks	77.5	Other	2.8
Foreign (% of Stock)			89.0

Sector Weightings	% of Stocks	Rel MSCI EAFE	3 Year High	3 Year Low
Info	24.14	1.45		
Software	0.00	0.00	1	0
Hardware	3.73	1.02	4	3
Media	2.71	1.19	4	1
Telecom	17.70	1.84	21	7
Service	33.08	0.74		
Health	3.91	0.54	6	4
Consumer	3.07	0.61	5	3
Business	9.34	1.72	9	5
Financial	16.76	0.62	18	6
Mfg	42.77	1.11		
Goods	16.80	1.23	44	17
Ind Mtrls	19.12	1.55	19	13
Energy	3.51	0.48	6	2
Utilities	3.34	0.62	3	0

Regional Exposure	% Stock		
UK/W. Europe	15	N. America	12
Japan	3	Latn America	14
Asia X Japan	50	Other	6

Country Exposure	% Stock		
South Korea	14	Brazil	7
India	12	Mexico	6
United States	11		

Morningstar's Take by Gareth Lyons 12-21-04

American Funds New World's stability shouldn't be forgotten.

This fund's poor relative performance in 2003 demonstrated its difficulty in keeping up when emerging markets are on the tear. But, when those routinely volatile markets slip, like they did in June 2004 amid concerns about rising interest rates and higher oil prices, this fund held up remarkably well. What's more, as developing markets have rebounded sharply in recent months, this fund's 18.0% return for the year to date through Dec. 20 is just shy of the category norm.

Given the approach here, the fund is behaving just as we might expect. Unlike conventional funds in this category, the managers here invest only a portion of assets in developing-market stocks, combining them with emerging-market bonds and a collection of steadier multinational firms that accrue sizable revenues from emerging markets. The fund also distinguishes itself by holding sizable cash stakes. The idea is to give investors exposure to emerging markets without taking on all of the area's inherent risks, such as sky-high volatility, low trading volumes, high transaction costs, and a lack of publicly available financials.

We think the fund can fulfill that objective. Volatility here, as measured by the portfolio's three- and five-year standard-deviation readings, is the lowest in the category by far. True, the fund will be lead-footed during rallies. But what this fund lacks in sizzle, it makes up for in sensibleness. In this racy but important category, investors too often get wooed by an offering's eye-popping returns only to get jilted by its ensuing failure to preserve capital when markets slide. Of course, prudent risk management wouldn't matter much without strong stock-picking. On that front, the low-turnover approach of the experienced portfolio-management team and its deep research bench gets our enthusiastic nod. This fund won't satisfy the purest emerging-markets fans, but we think it's a solid choice.

Address:	333 South Hope St Los Angeles CA 90071 800-421-0180
Web Address:	www.americanfunds.com
Inception:	06-17-99 *
Advisor:	Capital Research and Management Company
Subadvisor:	None
NTF Plans:	Federated Tr NTF

Minimum Purchase:	$250	Add: $50	IRA: $250
Min Auto Inv Plan:	$50	Add: $50	
Sales Fees:	5.75%L, 0.05%S		
Management Fee:	0.85% mx./0.62% mn.		
Actual Fees:	Mgt:0.79%	Dist:0.24%	
Expense Projections:	3Yr:$960	5Yr:$1242	10Yr:$2042
Income Distrib:	Annually		

Amer Funds Sm World A

Ticker	Load	NAV	Yield	Total Assets	Mstar Category
SMCWX	5.75%	$31.20	1.0%	$12,669 mil	Small Growth

Governance and Management

Fiduciary Grade: B

Portfolio Manager(s)

Experienced and deep. The "novice" member of this fund's six-member roster of managers has nine years of investment experience with the firm, while senior portfolio counselor Gordon Crawford has 32 years under his belt. The managers also contribute to other funds in the firm's lineup. Value-oriented manager J. Dale Harvey, who is also a counselor on American Balanced, among other funds, recently joined the team.

Strategy

This fund's managers scour the globe for small-cap stocks with sound fundamentals. Normally, at least 80% of assets are invested in stocks that court market capitalizations between $50 million and $2 billion. In picking stocks, the team focuses on companies with experienced management, strong product lines, and solid balance sheets. The team also pays attention to how much it pays for a stock, which can cause the portfolio to swing between the growth and blend sections of the Morningstar style box.

Performance 12-31-04

	1st Qtr	2nd Qtr	3rd Qtr	4th Qtr	Total
2000	16.07	-9.91	-1.69	-17.86	-15.56
2001	-18.79	10.37	-25.22	23.31	-17.35
2002	2.27	-8.83	-17.97	1.65	-22.25
2003	-5.05	23.64	10.99	15.42	50.40
2004	7.28	-2.40	-0.75	13.32	17.76

Trailing	Total Return%	+/- S&P 500	+/- Russ 2000 Gr	%Rank Cat	Growth of $10,000
3 Mo	13.32	4.09	-1.76	62	11,332
6 Mo	12.47	5.28	4.31	9	11,247
1 Yr	17.76	6.89	3.45	19	11,776
3 Yr Avg	11.25	7.67	5.46	12	13,769
5 Yr Avg	-0.79	1.51	2.78	49	9,611
10 Yr Avg	9.87	-2.20	2.75	60	25,633
15 Yr Avg	—	—	—	—	—

Tax Analysis	Tax-Adj Rtn%	%Rank Cat	Tax-Cost Rat	%Rank Cat
3 Yr (estimated)	8.93	20	0.14	14
5 Yr (estimated)	-2.68	52	0.73	33
10 Yr (estimated)	7.70	61	1.39	40

Potential Capital Gain Exposure: 14% of assets

Historical Profile

Return Average
Risk Below Avg
Rating ★★★ Neutral

Investment Style: Equity Stock %

86%	90%	89%	89%	86%	88%	90%	90%	93%

▼ Manager Change
▽ Partial Manager Change

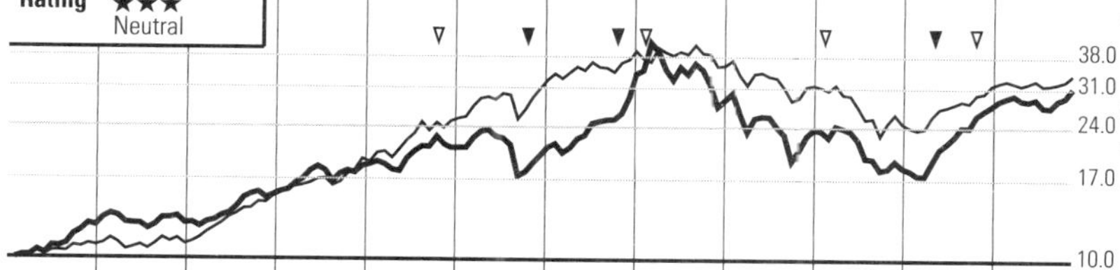

Growth of $10,000
▬ Investment Values of Fund
— Investment Values of S&P 500

Performance Quartile (within Category)

1993	1994	1995	1996	1997	1998	1999	2000	2001	2002	2003	12-04	History
23.58	21.41	23.50	25.61	25.98	24.63	39.14	27.78	22.92	17.82	26.77	31.20	NAV
30.04	-2.85	22.70	19.75	11.83	0.38	61.64	-15.56	-17.35	-22.25	50.40	17.76	Total Return %
19.98	-4.16	-14.83	-3.19	-21.52	-28.19	40.60	-6.46	-5.47	-0.16	21.73	6.89	+/-S&P 500
16.67	-0.42	-8.34	8.49	-1.12	-0.85	18.55	6.87	-8.12	8.01	1.86	3.45	+/-Russ 2000 Gr
0.32	0.47	1.08	0.51	0.39	0.35	0.06	0.00	0.14	0.00	0.17	1.16	Income Return %
29.72	-3.32	21.62	19.24	11.44	0.03	61.58	-15.56	-17.49	-22.25	50.23	16.60	Capital Return %
7	64	83	51	73	64	42	79	75	25	21	19	Total Rtn % Rank Cat
0.06	0.11	0.23	0.12	0.10	0.09	0.02	0.00	0.04	0.00	0.03	0.31	Income $
0.97	1.35	2.45	2.35	2.50	1.29	0.61	5.29	0.00	0.00	0.00	0.00	Capital Gains $
1.15	1.12	1.13	1.09	1.07	1.06	1.09	1.10	1.09	1.17	1.19	1.12	Expense Ratio %
0.33	0.38	0.97	0.68	0.40	0.27	0.12	—	-0.01	-0.32	-0.07	0.06	Income Ratio %
25	29	46	43	42	44	50	63	60	51	49	48	Turnover Rate %
2,713	3,483	4,766	7,073	8,667	8,109	12,374	11,329	8,723	6,180	9,200	11,117	Net Assets $mil

Rating and Risk

Time Period	Load-Adj Return %	Morningstar Rtn vs Cat	Morningstar Risk vs Cat	Morningstar Risk-Adj Rating
1 Yr	10.99			
3 Yr	9.08	+Avg	-Avg	★★★★
5 Yr	-1.96	Avg	-Avg	★★★
10 Yr	9.22	-Avg	-Avg	★★★
Incept	10.21			

Other Measures	Standard Index S&P 500	Best Fit Index Wil 4500
Alpha	7.9	-0.6
Beta	0.92	1.01
R-Squared	70	95
Standard Deviation	18.26	
Mean	11.25	
Sharpe Ratio	0.55	

Portfolio Analysis 09-30-04

Share change since 06-04 Total Stocks:413	Sector	PE	YTD Ret%	% Assets
Michaels Stores	Consumer	22.9	36.87	1.50
⊕ Ask Jeeves	Business	37.8	47.63	1.16
⊕ Daelim Industrial	Business	—	—	1.01
⊖ Aristocrat Leisure Ltd	Consumer	—	—	0.93
HDFC Bank Ltd	Financial	—	—	0.95
⊕ Eyetech Pharmaceuticals	Health	—	—	0.85
⊕ Integrated Circuit Syste	Hardware	20.5	-26.60	0.85
First Calgary Petroleums	Energy	—	—	0.83
Kingboard Chemical Hldgs	Ind Mtrls	—	—	0.78
⊕ Gemstar-TV Guide Interna	Goods	—	16.70	0.74
⊕ Spinnaker Exploration	Energy	23.9	8.68	0.74
CNET Networks	Media	NMF	64.66	0.70
⊖ Laureate Education	Consumer	32.0	53.14	0.68
⊕ Cathay General Bancorp	Financial	16.0	35.14	0.68
Helmerich & Payne	Energy	70.9	23.36	0.63
⊕ Quicksilver Resources	Energy	69.9	127.74	0.62
UnitedGlobalCom	Media	—	25.65	0.62
SBS Broadcasting	Media	32.3	23.47	0.60
Sirva	Business	—	-1.64	0.59
⊖ Millennium Chemicals	Ind Mtrls	—	—	0.59

Current Investment Style

Value Blnd Growth — Large Mid Small

Market Cap	%
Giant	0.0
Large	4.4
Mid	45.0
Small	44.6
Micro	6.0
Avg $mil: 1,377	

Value Measures		Rel Category
Price/Earnings	16.50	0.76
Price/Book	1.58	0.75
Price/Sales	0.83	0.55
Price/Cash Flow	5.60	0.70
Dividend Yield %	1.67	5.39

Growth Measures	%	Rel Category
Long-Term Erngs	15.34	0.89
Book Value	4.22	0.65
Sales	5.28	0.82
Cash Flow	4.62	0.34
Historical Erngs	7.99	0.59

Profitability	%	Rel Category
Return on Equity	10.70	1.08
Return on Assets	3.06	0.70
Net Margin	7.41	1.08

Sector Weightings	% of Stocks	Rel S&P 500	3 Year High	3 Year Low
Info	17.48	0.81		
Software	3.75	0.87	6	3
Hardware	7.13	0.70	15	5
Media	5.24	1.36	6	5
Telecom	1.36	0.43	2	1
Service	51.41	1.11		
Health	10.39	0.83	14	10
Consumer	14.98	1.65	29	15
Business	16.41	4.05	16	9
Financial	9.63	0.46	11	7
Mfg	31.11	0.97		
Goods	6.92	0.74	9	7
Ind Mtrls	15.53	1.23	16	8
Energy	8.24	1.15	8	4
Utilities	0.42	0.14	1	0

Composition

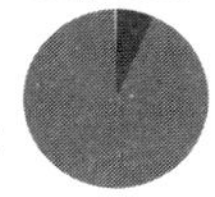

Cash	6.4
Stocks	92.8
Bonds	0.1
Other	0.7
Foreign (% of Stock)	48.3

Morningstar's Take by Paul Herbert 12-15-04

American Funds Smallcap World has some things going for it, but at the end of the day we expect moderate performance.

For this fund, small is beautiful. It sticks to stocks with market capitalizations below $2 billion at the time of purchase, making it one of the few mutual funds in existence to target both U.S. and foreign small- and mid-cap stocks. In typical American Funds fashion, several managers, drawing upon the research ideas of dozens of analysts, call the shots here. American Funds also has a 14-person team of small-cap generalists that contributes picks to this portfolio. The firm's size helps to keep costs down, as the fund's 1.19% expense ratio indicates.

These advantages, and a strong environment for small-cap investing, have clearly helped the fund to impressive absolute results lately. For the three-year period that ended Dec. 15, 2004, the fund had gained 10.75% per year. Part of the fund's success owes to some strong contrarian picks such as Australian gaming company Aristocrat Leisure, which has increased in price by more than 10 times in recent years, and U.S. software firm Novell.

We aren't confident that the fund will consistently beat the pack, though. While it hasn't been fund investors' favorite American Funds offering in recent years, the fund's asset base was north of $11 billion recently. At its size, it's hard for the fund's managers and analysts to establish meaningfully large positions in their favorite small-cap companies. It typically holds hundreds of stocks, and as of Nov. 30, 2004, only two of its picks took up more than 1% of assets. It's hard for any single pick to have a significant impact on performance, apart from less-common situations such as Aristocrat, with such a setup.

If you measure the fund's fine absolute showing versus the small group of funds with similar market-cap and regional mixes, it looks middling. We expect that kind of result, and not much more or less, from this fund going forward.

Address:	333 S Hope St - 52nd Floor Los Angeles CA 90071-1443 800-421-0180
Web Address:	www.americanfunds.com
Inception:	04-30-90
Advisor:	Capital Research and Management Company
Subadvisor:	None
NTF Plans:	Federated Tr NTF

Minimum Purchase:	$250	Add: $50	IRA: $250
Min Auto Inv Plan:	$50	Add: $50	
Sales Fees:	5.75%L, 0.25%S		
Management Fee:	0.80% mx./0.60% mn.		
Actual Fees:	Mgt:0.68%	Dist:0.25%	
Expense Projections:	3Yr:$931	5Yr:$1192	10Yr:$1935
Income Distrib:	Annually		

Amer Funds T/E Bd A

Ticker	Load	NAV	Yield	SEC Yield	Total Assets	Mstar Category
AFTEX	3.75%	$12.54	4.1%	3.19%	$3,664 mil	Muni National Interm

Governance and Management

Fiduciary Grade: B

Portfolio Manager(s)

The management team splits this fund's portfolio, with each manager responsible for a specific portion. The group includes Neil Langberg (who joined the fund in 1979), Brenda Ellerin (1998), David Hoag (1998), and Edward Nahmias (2000). The group is supported by at least two analysts.

Strategy

This fund's multiple managers have historically favored municipal issues with good structure, particularly noncallable bonds carrying predictable duration characteristics. The portfolio holds a larger stake in midgrade bonds rated A or BBB than most rivals in the muni national intermediate category, as well. Because the fund holds about 900 names, though, the effect of a possible default in one issue is diminished. The fund's duration, a measure of interest-rate sensitivity, will normally fall in a range of between 6.5 to eight years, with management considering seven to 7.5 years as roughly neutral.

Historical Profile

Return Above Avg
Risk Average
Rating ★★★★ Above Avg

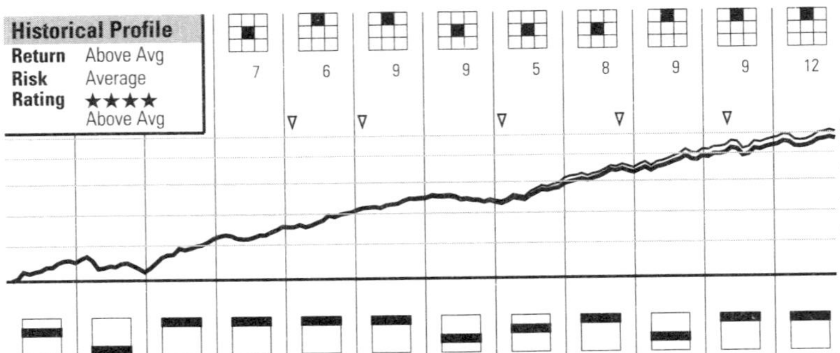

Investment Style
Fixed Income
Income Rtn %Rank Cat

▼ Manager Change
∇ Partial Manager Change

Growth of $10,000
▬ Investment Values of Fund
— Investment Values of LB Muni

Performance Quartile (within Category)

1993	1994	1995	1996	1997	1998	1999	2000	2001	2002	2003	12-04	History
12.37	11.11	12.23	12.09	12.47	12.41	11.50	11.97	12.01	12.42	12.52	12.54	NAV
11.71	-4.81	17.28	4.57	8.98	6.07	-2.32	9.67	5.57	8.44	5.18	4.37	Total Return %
-0.57	0.36	-0.18	0.14	-0.21	-0.41	-0.26	-2.01	0.44	-1.16	-0.13	-0.11	+/-LB Muni
-1.06	-0.04	0.11	0.03	-0.26	-0.69	-1.08	-1.09	0.95	-1.73	-0.52	0.22	+/-LB Muni 10YR
5.93	5.60	6.20	5.38	5.40	5.04	4.87	5.43	5.01	4.79	4.34	4.19	Income Return %
5.78	-10.41	11.08	-0.81	3.58	1.03	-7.19	4.24	0.56	3.65	0.84	0.18	Capital Return %
26	78	14	10	13	19	51	41	5	55	10	5	Total Rtn % Rank Cat
0.68	0.67	0.67	0.64	0.64	0.61	0.59	0.61	0.59	0.56	0.53	0.51	Income $
0.09	0.00	0.09	0.04	0.04	0.19	0.04	0.00	0.03	0.02	0.00	0.00	Capital Gains $
0.71	0.69	0.66	0.68	0.68	0.66	0.65	0.67	0.66	0.63	0.61	0.61	Expense Ratio %
5.62	5.53	5.87	5.35	5.27	4.98	4.78	5.22	4.98	4.73	4.33	4.23	Income Ratio %
16	22	49	27	14	23	15	29	21	8	8	8	Turnover Rate %
1,404	1,253	1,502	1,513	1,666	1,863	1,816	1,898	2,254	2,799	3,028	3,208	Net Assets $mil

Performance 12-31-04

	1st Qtr	2nd Qtr	3rd Qtr	4th Qtr	Total
2000	2.19	1.07	2.63	3.46	9.67
2001	2.35	1.16	2.94	-0.95	5.57
2002	0.88	3.45	4.09	-0.18	8.44
2003	0.99	2.45	0.20	1.46	5.18
2004	1.67	-1.83	3.43	1.11	4.37

Trailing	Total Return%	+/- LB Muni	+/- LB Muni 10YR	%Rank Cat	Growth of $10,000
3 Mo	1.11	-0.14	0.28	11	10,111
6 Mo	4.57	-0.62	-0.43	17	10,457
1 Yr	4.37	-0.11	0.22	5	10,437
3 Yr Avg	5.98	-0.46	-0.66	13	11,903
5 Yr Avg	6.63	-0.57	-0.41	12	13,785
10 Yr Avg	6.68	-0.38	-0.40	4	19,091
15 Yr Avg	6.61	-0.38	-0.47	11	26,120

Tax Analysis	Tax-Adj Rtn%	%Rank Cat	Tax-Cost Rat	%Rank Cat
3 Yr (estimated)	4.63	51	0.01	4
5 Yr (estimated)	5.80	32	0.02	8
10 Yr (estimated)	6.18	11	0.08	40

Potential Capital Gain Exposure: 5% of assets

Rating and Risk

Time Period	Load-Adj Return %	Morningstar Rtn vs Cat	Morningstar Risk vs Cat	Morningstar Risk-Adj Rating
1 Yr	0.46			
3 Yr	4.64	Avg	Avg	★★★
5 Yr	5.82	+Avg	Avg	★★★★
10 Yr	6.27	High	Avg	★★★★★
Incept	7.55			

Other Measures	Standard Index LB Aggr	Best Fit Index LB Muni
Alpha	-0.1	-0.1
Beta	0.93	0.93
R-Squared	99	99
Standard Deviation	4.69	
Mean	5.98	
Sharpe Ratio	0.99	

Portfolio Analysis 09-30-04

Total Fixed-Income:944	Date of Maturity	Amount $000	Value $000	% Net Assets
New York N Y City Transi	11-01-26	29,300	33,086	0.93
Tobacco Settlement Fing	05-15-30	29,920	26,599	0.75
Massachusetts Bay Transn	03-01-30	26,100	26,100	0.74
Shelby Cnty Tenn Health	09-01-20	21,400	22,970	0.65
Central Puget Sound Wash	02-01-28	21,940	21,945	0.62
Washington St Pub Pwr Sp	07-01-07	19,900	21,922	0.62
Arapahoe Cnty Colo Cap I	08-31-20	17,500	18,865	0.53
Badger Tob Asset Securit	06-01-27	18,555	17,829	0.50
Massachusetts St	09-01-16	17,500	17,500	0.49
Clark Cnty Nev Impt Dist	12-01-19	15,580	17,033	0.48
Fairfax Cnty Va Econ Dev	10-01-29	15,500	16,494	0.47
Montgomery Cnty Pa Indl	11-15-28	17,500	16,465	0.46
Harris Cnty Tex Health F	06-01-29	13,900	15,229	0.43
Sabine River Auth	05-01-22	14,000	14,980	0.42
Indiana Health Fac Fing	11-01-26	13,990	14,896	0.42

Current Investment Style

Duration: Short Int Long; Quality: High Med Low

[1]Avg Eff Duration	5.1 Yrs
Avg Eff Maturity	6.5 Yrs
Avg Credit Quality	AA
Avg Wtd Coupon	5.51%
Avg Wtd Price	107.20% of par

[1]figure provided by fund

Credit Analysis	% bonds 09-30-04		
US Govt	0	BB	10
AAA	43	B	2
AA	21	Below B	0
A	10	NR/NA	0
BBB	15		

Top 5 States	% bonds		
TX	12.6	WA	7.3
NY	10.0	CA	6.0
IL	9.7		

Composition			
Cash	3.7	Bonds	96.3
Stocks	0.0	Other	0.0

Special Securities	
Restricted/Illiquid Secs	0
Options/Futures/Warrants	No

Sector Weightings	% of Bonds	Rel Cat
General Obligation	25.5	0.72
Utilities	17.5	1.58
Health	15.8	2.13
Water/Waste	4.8	0.48
Housing	4.8	0.82
Education	9.5	0.67
Transportation	1.9	0.34
COP/Lease	1.6	1.01
Industrial	18.1	2.02
Misc Revenue	0.0	0.00
Demand	0.6	1.45

Morningstar's Take by Eric Jacobson 01-07-05

Tax-Exempt Bond Fund of America hits a very sweet spot in the bond world.

We generally think of bond funds as even better candidates for active management than stock funds. That largely owes to the fact that bonds continue to be traded in inefficient ways that were long ago discarded by the stock market. Except for a few highly liquid sectors, most bond trades involve human interaction, unpredictable pricing, and opaque and relatively high commissions. That's a good arena for active managers, as those who can exploit any or all of the aforementioned inefficiencies can get a leg up on the competition.

Indeed, the muni market is particularly ripe, given those traits, and the fact that it's even more fragmented than other bond sectors. There are thousands of issuers, many of whom have bonds with different structures and features. To that world the managers of this fund bring a style that focuses on ferreting out as much value as possible, particularly by uncovering midquality investment-grade bonds that look attractive.

Of course, other muni funds try to capitalize on inefficiencies and mispriced bond issues. Still, this fund's staff of managers and analysts have honed a very successful set of strategies. For one, they've focused on an intermediate level of rate sensitivity, thus taking on enough to get the income available from longer bonds, without gorging on the rate volatility that can put lots of capital at risk. By holding a lot of heavily researched midgrade bonds, meanwhile, they've captured lots of income, but mostly avoided the trouble of riskier junk and nonrated muni issues.

The proof here has been in the pudding. The fund has a terrific long-term record of top-quartile trailing returns and a moderate level of volatility, features that a very fair expense ratio has helped accentuate. Given its style, this is no proxy for a plain-vanilla index fund. For those who can tolerate a tad more risk, and who have a reasonable time horizon, however, it makes a terrific choice.

Address:	333 S Hope St - 52nd Floor Los Angeles CA 90071 800-421-0180
Web Address:	
Inception:	10-03-79
Advisor:	Capital Research and Management Company
Subadvisor:	None
NTF Plans:	Federated Tr NTF, Schwab Instl NTF

Minimum Purchase:	$250	Add: $50	IRA: $0
Min Auto Inv Plan:	$50	Add: $50	
Sales Fees:	3.75%L		
Management Fee:	0.35% mx./0.16% mn.		
Actual Fees:	Mgt:0.32%	Dist:0.25%	
Expense Projections:	3Yr:$578	5Yr:$729	10Yr:$1167
Income Distrib:	Monthly		

Amer Funds WashingtonA

Analyst Pick

Ticker	Load	NAV	Yield	Total Assets	Mstar Category
AWSHX	5.75%	$30.78	1.9%	$75,870 mil	Large Value

Governance and Management

Fiduciary Grade: B

Portfolio Manager(s)

This fund's team members all have long tenures. James Dunton, the longest-serving member, has been on board for more than 20 years and boasts 40 years of investment experience. In addition, the team is supported by a very deep bench of experienced investment analysts.

Strategy

This value fund invests by following this prudent investor rule: Buy the stocks of firms that have paid dividends in nine of the past 10 years. By mandate, the fund also can't own the stocks of tobacco and alcohol companies. The process has been tweaked over the years, but the overall spirit of its disciplined nature has been the same since 1952. The fund tends to be well diversified by stock and sector, although it's typically underweighted in tech, where dividends are more the exception than the rule.

Historical Profile

Return Average
Risk Below Avg
Rating ★★★★ Above Avg

Investment Style
Equity
Stock %

95%	96%	95%	96%	95%	95%	96%	96%	96%

▼ Manager Change
▽ Partial Manager Change

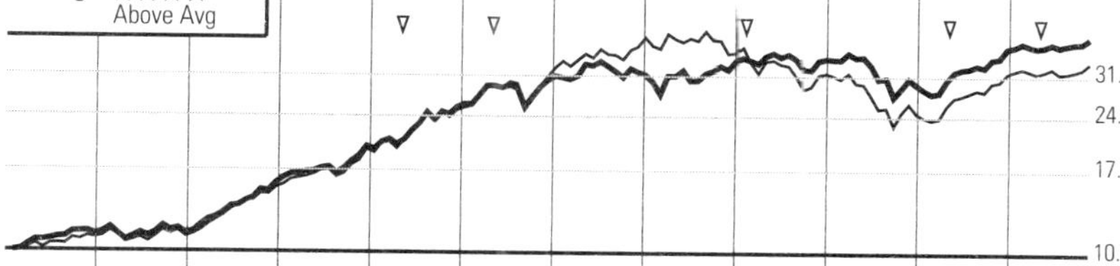

Growth of $10,000
— Investment Values of Fund
— Investment Values of S&P 500

Performance Quartile (within Category)

1993	1994	1995	1996	1997	1998	1999	2000	2001	2002	2003	12-04	History
17.78	16.84	21.97	24.54	30.35	32.91	29.56	29.03	28.25	23.51	28.78	30.78	NAV
13.05	0.49	41.22	20.18	33.29	19.37	1.16	9.06	1.51	-14.85	25.83	9.92	Total Return %
2.99	-0.82	3.69	-2.76	-0.06	-9.20	-19.88	18.16	13.39	7.24	-2.84	-0.95	+/-S&P 500
-5.02	2.47	2.86	-1.46	-1.89	3.74	-6.19	2.05	7.10	0.67	-4.20	-6.57	+/-Russ 1000 VI
3.42	3.53	3.73	2.85	2.55	2.02	1.77	1.98	1.91	1.93	2.32	2.07	Income Return %
9.63	-3.04	37.49	17.33	30.74	17.35	-0.61	7.08	-0.40	-16.78	23.51	7.85	Capital Return %
56	35	4	51	8	8	66	53	22	23	69	81	Total Rtn % Rank Cat
0.56	0.62	0.62	0.62	0.62	0.61	0.58	0.58	0.55	0.54	0.54	0.59	Income $
0.39	0.41	1.09	1.20	1.66	2.60	3.10	2.50	0.64	0.04	0.19	0.23	Capital Gains $
0.70	0.69	0.69	0.66	0.64	0.62	0.61	0.63	0.65	0.65	0.67	0.64	Expense Ratio %
3.33	3.29	3.57	2.98	2.56	2.08	1.84	1.91	1.95	1.72	2.28	2.14	Income Ratio %
19	24	26	23	20	18	28	26	25	22	21	12	Turnover Rate %
12,639	12,668	18,786	25,374	38,246	51,774	53,136	47,414	48,751	42,436	55,575	63,080	Net Assets $mil

Performance 12-31-04

	1st Qtr	2nd Qtr	3rd Qtr	4th Qtr	Total
2000	-0.82	-3.05	6.50	6.51	9.06
2001	-1.53	4.17	-7.41	6.89	1.51
2002	3.63	-7.36	-17.90	8.04	-14.85
2003	-4.92	15.94	1.25	12.73	25.83
2004	1.62	1.36	0.30	6.40	9.92

Trailing	Total Return%	+/- S&P 500	+/- Russ 1000 VI	%Rank Cat	Growth of $10,000
3 Mo	6.40	-2.83	-3.98	97	10,640
6 Mo	6.71	-0.48	-5.37	82	10,671
1 Yr	9.92	-0.95	-6.57	81	10,992
3 Yr Avg	5.60	2.02	-2.97	52	11,776
5 Yr Avg	5.45	7.75	0.18	34	13,039
10 Yr Avg	13.54	1.47	-0.29	12	35,603
15 Yr Avg	11.68	0.75	-0.35	18	52,436

Tax Analysis	Tax-Adj Rtn%	%Rank Cat	Tax-Cost Rat	%Rank Cat
3 Yr (estimated)	2.68	73	0.83	56
5 Yr (estimated)	2.94	49	1.22	64
10 Yr (estimated)	10.89	15	1.75	47

Potential Capital Gain Exposure: 21% of assets

Rating and Risk

Time Period	Load-Adj Return %	Morningstar Rtn vs Cat	Morningstar Risk vs Cat	Morningstar Risk-Adj Rating
1 Yr	3.60			
3 Yr	3.54	-Avg	-Avg	★★★
5 Yr	4.21	Avg	-Avg	★★★
10 Yr	12.87	+Avg	-Avg	★★★★
Incept	12.82			

Other Measures	Standard Index S&P 500	Best Fit Index Russ 1000 VI
Alpha	2.2	-2.2
Beta	0.87	0.90
R-Squared	93	98
Standard Deviation	14.31	
Mean	5.60	
Sharpe Ratio	0.30	

Portfolio Analysis 09-30-04

Share change since 06-04 Total Stocks:154	Sector	PE	YTD Ret%	% Assets
⊕ J P Morgan Chase	Financial	19.4	9.97	3.41
⊕ ChevronTexaco	Energy	7.7	25.57	2.90
⊕ ExxonMobil	Energy	13.9	28.04	2.85
⊕ Gen Elec	Ind Mtrls	22.8	20.68	2.71
⊕ Bank of America	Financial	12.3	21.50	2.39
Bristol-Myers Squibb	Health	17.7	-7.27	2.23
SBC Communications	Telecom	15.4	3.74	2.10
⊕ Fannie Mae	Financial	9.1	-2.33	2.05
Wells Fargo	Financial	15.5	8.97	2.00
⊖ Verizon Communications	Telecom	32.4	20.25	1.90
⊖ Eli Lilly & Company	Health	24.3	-17.55	1.73
General Motors	Goods	7.2	-21.48	1.63
Pfizer	Health	22.0	-22.31	1.58
⊕ BellSouth	Telecom	12.7	1.94	1.58
Lowe's Companies	Consumer	22.1	4.25	1.38
⊕ American International G	Financial	16.2	-0.53	1.32
Kimberly-Clark	Goods	17.8	16.12	1.22
International Paper	Ind Mtrls	—	-0.20	1.22
⊕ Sprint	Telecom	—	55.24	1.21
⊖ HSBC Holdings PLC ADR	Financial	19.8	12.54	1.19

Current Investment Style

Value Blnd Growth / Large Mid Small

Market Cap	%
Giant	48.3
Large	45.5
Mid	6.2
Small	0.0
Micro	0.0
Avg $mil: 41,681	

Value Measures		Rel Category
Price/Earnings	14.32	0.97
Price/Book	2.30	1.01
Price/Sales	1.06	0.89
Price/Cash Flow	6.85	1.07
Dividend Yield %	2.58	1.26

Growth Measures	%	Rel Category
Long-Term Erngs	9.59	0.92
Book Value	7.08	1.26
Sales	3.20	0.76
Cash Flow	-0.71	NMF
Historical Erngs	11.58	0.98

Profitability	%	Rel Category
Return on Equity	17.77	1.12
Return on Assets	8.56	1.09
Net Margin	10.38	1.02

Sector Weightings	% of Stocks	Rel S&P 500	3 Year High	3 Year Low
Info	12.66	0.59		
Software	1.25	0.29	1	1
Hardware	3.60	0.35	4	3
Media	0.29	0.08	1	0
Telecom	7.52	2.39	9	6
Service	43.51	0.94		
Health	10.05	0.80	12	10
Consumer	7.38	0.81	7	7
Business	2.42	0.60	3	2
Financial	23.66	1.14	25	22
Mfg	43.83	1.36		
Goods	10.25	1.10	12	9
Ind Mtrls	15.83	1.25	16	11
Energy	9.81	1.37	10	8
Utilities	7.94	2.68	10	8

Composition

Cash	2.9
Stocks	95.9
Bonds	0.0
Other	1.1
Foreign (% of Stock)	1.5

Morningstar's Take by Paul Herbert 01-06-05

This fund remains a favorite, though it's not worry-free.

We've paid a lot of well-deserved compliments to American Funds Washington Mutual Investors over the years. For instance, after a tough 1999 campaign, at least in relative terms, we offered "...patience and a long-term approach have always won out here." It may not have been obvious to fund investors at the time, but the fund has displayed a knack for recovering after tough spells over its history. As another sign of our enthusiasm, we made the fund an Analyst Pick in the large-value category a few years ago.

The fund's appeal comes back to its strategy and resource advantages. Its eight portfolio managers start with a variant of the prudent investor rule that leads them to buy blue-chip stocks with records of paying out dividends in at least nine of the past 10 years. This fund's universe, then, is made up mostly of financially sound firms run by disciplined executives, which makes them less susceptible to blowups. And, in addition to its large manager lineup, an army of analysts helps to uncover first-rate dividend payers.

This approach hasn't led to stellar near-term results, but in all it has been a hit. Yield-rich giant caps, such as the regional bells and drugmakers, have been out of style of late. The fund should be well-positioned when they return to favor, though. It has crushed rivals and bogys over time.

Our concern at this point relates to the fund's size. Due to fine performance and American's deserved strong reputation among fund investors, the fund has enjoyed significant inflows. While a value orientation and low-turnover demeanor in particular give the fund more room to grow than other funds, we have seen unfettered growth lead to performance erosion many times in the past. For this reason, we like to see firms articulate plans for dealing with asset growth. Otherwise, we have no quibbles here.

Address:	1101 Vermont Ave Nw Washington DC 20005 800-421-0180
Web Address:	www.americanfunds.com
Inception:	07-31-52
Advisor:	Capital Research and Management Company
Subadvisor:	None
NTF Plans:	Federated Tr NTF

Minimum Purchase:	$250	Add: $50	IRA: $250
Min Auto Inv Plan:	$50	Add: $50	
Sales Fees:	5.75%L, 0.25%S		
Management Fee:	0.40% mx./0.22% mn., 0.18%A		
Actual Fees:	Mgt:0.29%	Dist:0.24%	
Expense Projections:	3Yr:$771	5Yr:$916	10Yr:$1339
Income Distrib:	Quarterly		

Ameristock

Ticker	Load	NAV	Yield	Total Assets	Mstar Category
AMSTX	None	$40.54	2.6%	$1,935 mil	Large Value

Governance and Management

Fiduciary Grade: A

Portfolio Manager(s)

Nicholas Gerber has managed this offering since its August 1995 inception. He has been assisted by comanager Andrew Ngim since January 2000. Although Gerber has come a long way from the time when he ran the fund out of his basement, his research staff is still limited to Ngim and two other analysts.

Strategy

Nicholas Gerber sticks with stocks that have market caps of $15 billion or more, looking for cheaply priced companies with high dividend yields or fallen-growth stocks with bright long-term outlooks and reasonable valuations. He tends to hold on to stocks for the long haul, resulting in low turnover.

Historical Profile

Return Average
Risk Average
Rating ★★★ Neutral

Investment Style: Equity Stock %

1996	1997	1998	1999	2000	2001	2002	2003	2004
89%	100%	96%	98%	100%	91%	93%	94%	98%

▼ Manager Change
▽ Partial Manager Change

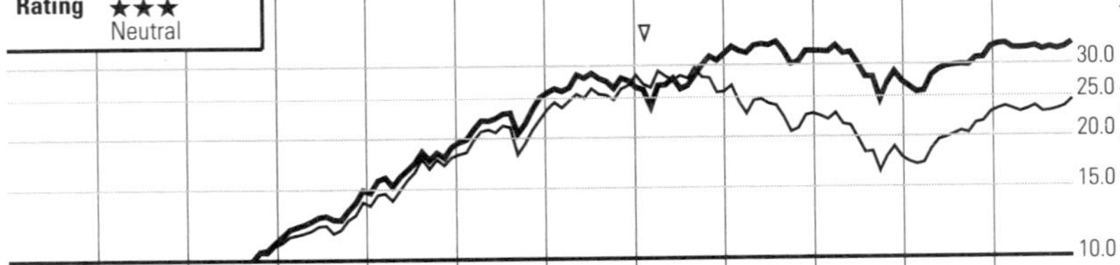

Growth of $10,000
▬ Investment Values of Fund
— Investment Values of S&P 500

Performance Quartile (within Category)

History

1993	1994	1995	1996	1997	1998	1999	2000	2001	2002	2003	12-04	History
—	—	16.96	21.18	26.81	34.91	35.11	40.22	40.40	33.04	39.41	40.54	NAV
—	—	14.29*	27.68	32.86	31.98	2.73	20.70	1.25	-16.00	21.27	5.52	Total Return %
—	—	—	4.74	-0.49	3.41	-18.31	29.80	13.13	6.09	-7.40	-5.35	+/-S&P 500
—	—	—	6.04	-2.32	16.35	-4.62	13.69	6.84	-0.48	-8.76	-10.97	+/-Russ 1000 VI
—	—	0.00	2.31	2.02	0.90	1.19	1.28	0.71	1.02	1.92	2.63	Income Return %
—	—	—	25.37	30.84	31.08	1.54	19.42	0.54	-17.02	19.35	2.89	Capital Return %
—	—	—	7	9	1	59	11	23	33	95	98	Total Rtn % Rank Cat
—	—	0.18	0.39	0.42	0.24	0.42	0.45	0.29	0.41	0.63	1.04	Income $
—	—	0.00	0.04	0.83	0.22	0.34	1.63	0.04	0.49	0.00	0.00	Capital Gains $
—	—	—	0.00	0.56	0.90	0.94	0.99	0.83	0.77	0.78	0.77	Expense Ratio %
—	—	—	2.40	2.40	1.48	1.22	1.51	1.50	1.31	1.97	1.96	Income Ratio %
—	—	—	—	22	12	9	31	6	14	3	6	Turnover Rate %
—	—	—	5	7	36	110	164	1,313	1,400	1,925	1,935	Net Assets $mil

Performance 12-31-04

	1st Qtr	2nd Qtr	3rd Qtr	4th Qtr	Total
2000	1.05	-2.03	14.41	6.55	20.70
2001	0.32	4.51	-10.10	7.42	1.25
2002	3.17	-9.86	-18.45	10.76	-16.00
2003	-5.24	14.76	0.72	10.72	21.27
2004	-0.74	1.07	-1.80	7.09	5.52

Trailing	Total Return%	+/- S&P 500	+/- Russ 1000 VI	%Rank Cat	Growth of $10,000
3 Mo	7.09	-2.14	-3.29	92	10,709
6 Mo	5.17	-2.02	-6.91	96	10,517
1 Yr	5.52	-5.35	-10.97	98	10,552
3 Yr Avg	2.44	-1.14	-6.13	88	10,750
5 Yr Avg	5.61	7.91	0.34	33	13,138
10 Yr Avg	—	—	—	—	—
15 Yr Avg	—	—	—	—	—

Tax Analysis	Tax-Adj Rtn%	%Rank Cat	Tax-Cost Rat	%Rank Cat
3 Yr (estimated)	1.67	83	0.75	50
5 Yr (estimated)	4.73	30	0.83	44
10 Yr (estimated)	—	—	—	—

Potential Capital Gain Exposure: 1% of assets

Rating and Risk

Time Period	Load-Adj Return %	Morningstar Rtn vs Cat	Morningstar Risk vs Cat	Morningstar Risk-Adj Rating
1 Yr	5.52			
3 Yr	2.44	-Avg	Avg	★★
5 Yr	5.61	Avg	Avg	★★★
10 Yr	—	—	—	—
Incept	14.19			

Other Measures	Standard Index S&P 500	Best Fit Index S&P 500
Alpha	-1.0	-1.0
Beta	0.95	0.95
R-Squared	93	93

Standard Deviation	15.18
Mean	2.44
Sharpe Ratio	0.07

Portfolio Analysis 11-30-04

Share change since 09-04 Total Stocks:51	Sector	PE	YTD Ret%	% Assets
Duke Energy	Utilities	—	30.21	4.24
Bank of America	Financial	12.3	21.50	4.14
Sara Lee	Goods	13.5	14.98	4.13
Merck	Health	11.4	-27.76	4.11
Fannie Mae	Financial	9.1	-2.33	3.96
Gen Elec	Ind Mtrls	22.8	20.68	3.85
Pfizer	Health	22.0	-22.31	3.80
Washington Mutual	Financial	13.9	10.05	3.58
Wyeth	Health	17.0	2.73	3.51
Bristol-Myers Squibb	Health	17.7	-7.27	3.45
Citigroup	Financial	15.3	2.72	3.27
Boeing	Ind Mtrls	14.7	24.86	3.23
DuPont De Nemours E.I.	Ind Mtrls	22.3	10.42	2.90
Albertson's	Consumer	20.2	8.87	2.55
Automatic Data Processin	Business	26.9	13.46	2.43
SBC Communications	Telecom	15.4	3.74	2.35
ExxonMobil	Energy	13.9	28.04	2.27
Dell	Hardware	34.0	24.01	2.24
Ford Motor	Goods	9.9	-6.00	2.20
General Motors	Goods	7.2	-21.48	2.17

Current Investment Style

Value Blnd Growth / Large Mid Small

Market Cap	%
Giant	61.8
Large	38.1
Mid	0.1
Small	0.0
Micro	0.0

Avg $mil: 66,899

Value Measures		Rel Category
Price/Earnings	14.45	0.96
Price/Book	2.64	1.16
Price/Sales	1.01	0.85
Price/Cash Flow	5.62	0.88
Dividend Yield %	2.76	1.35

Growth Measures	%	Rel Category
Long-Term Erngs	9.27	0.89
Book Value	7.92	1.40
Sales	1.63	0.39
Cash Flow	-3.25	NMF
Historical Erngs	1.15	0.10

Profitability	%	Rel Category
Return on Equity	19.64	1.24
Return on Assets	9.13	1.17
Net Margin	10.91	1.07

Sector Weightings	% of Stocks	Rel S&P 500	3 Year High	3 Year Low
Info	14.15	0.66		
Software	0.24	0.06	0	0
Hardware	6.76	0.66	15	7
Media	1.83	0.48	3	0
Telecom	5.32	1.69	10	5
Service	49.66	1.07		
Health	18.81	1.50	20	15
Consumer	5.74	0.63	6	3
Business	2.48	0.61	3	0
Financial	22.63	1.09	25	21
Mfg	36.20	1.13		
Goods	12.70	1.36	15	10
Ind Mtrls	13.71	1.08	14	12
Energy	5.46	0.76	6	4
Utilities	4.33	1.46	4	2

Composition

Cash	0.0
Stocks	98.0
Bonds	2.0
Other	0.0
Foreign (% of Stock)	1.7

Morningstar's Take by Kerry O'Boyle 12-20-04

Ameristock Fund is a solid offering mired in a bit of a slump.

It's been another tough year for this deep-value offering. Manager Nick Gerber looks for proven companies with solid balance sheets and good dividends that have a market cap of at least $15 billion and trade at discount to historical valuations. Unfortunately, high-quality names typically only trade at a discount when something has gone wrong. For example, a number of Ameristock's top 10 holdings--including Duke Energy, Fannie Mae, and Bristol-Myers Squibb--have had serious accounting and/or regulatory issues to address. Such troubled names can stay down for long periods of time until they fully resolve their problems.

That can weigh heavily on performance, as has been the case lately. The fund has struggled relative to its peers in the large-value category since the end of 2002. A heavy weighting--twice that of its typical rival--in drug stocks has been a drag on returns. The fund's bias toward mega-cap stocks hasn't helped either, as the market continues to favor smaller, more-nimble companies.

To be sure, the fund isn't without its charms. Once Gerber establishes a position in a name, he rarely lets it go. That takes the difficulty of timing out of the equation and ensures that the fund will eventually reap the benefit of any turnaround. In July, Gerber shed a name from the portfolio for the first time in 18 months when he sold AT&T after concluding that the firm's future prospects were no longer that bright. That kind of discipline means that the fund's volatility remains modest, despite the recent slide in performance.

To fully reap the rewards of this fund, investors must show equal discipline in riding out its rough stretches. The fund's low costs, tax-efficiency, and solid five-year track record make that easier to do. This offering remains a solid option.

Address:	1480 Moraga Rd 200 Moraga CA 94556 800-394-5064
Web Address:	www.ameristock.com
Inception:	08-31-95 *
Advisor:	Ameristock Corp
Subadvisor:	None
NTF Plans:	Fidelity Retail-NTF, Schwab OneSource

Minimum Purchase:	$1000	Add: $100	IRA: $1000
Min Auto Inv Plan:	$0	Add: —	
Sales Fees:	No-load		
Management Fee:	1.00% mx./0.75% mn.		
Actual Fees:	Mgt:0.77%	Dist: —	
Expense Projections:	3Yr:$265	5Yr:$460	10Yr:$1025
Income Distrib:	Semi-Annually		

Ariel

Ticker	Load	NAV	Yield	Total Assets	Mstar Category
ARGFX	12b-1 only	$53.17	0.0%	$4,197 mil	Small Value

Governance and Management

Fiduciary Grade: A

Portfolio Manager(s)

John Rogers, founder of Ariel Capital Management and architect of the firm's investment strategy, has managed this fund since its inception. He has more than 20 years of investment experience, specializing in small- and mid-cap stocks. Rogers works with about eight analysts. The analysts follow companies on their assignment lists closely, providing regular updates and recommendations.

Strategy

Manager John Rogers seeks out smaller-cap stocks that are selling at a discount of 40% or more to his estimate of their intrinsic values. He favors firms with strong brands or franchises that operate in consistent and stable industries, have sound balance sheets, generate lots of cash, and have strongly motivated management teams. The upshot of this approach is that the fund tends to have scant exposure to volatile sectors, such as technology and biotech, and big stakes in consumer goods, services, and industrial materials. The portfolio is typically concentrated in about 40 or fewer stocks.

Historical Profile

Return Average
Risk Below Avg
Rating ★★★★ Above Avg

Investment Style: Equity, Stock %: 99% 93% 93% 99% 90% 97% 95% 88% 82%

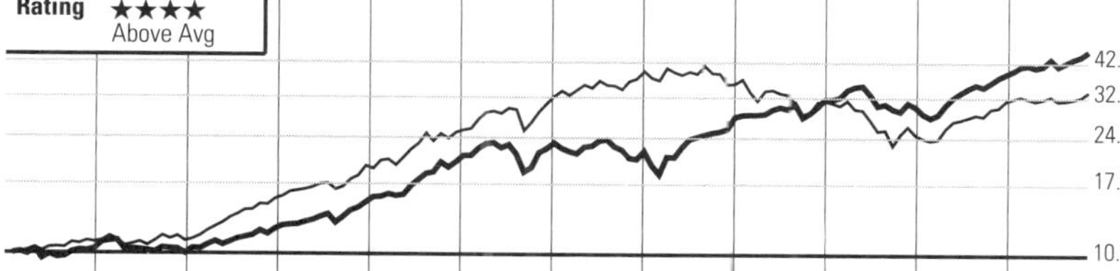

▼ Manager Change
▽ Partial Manager Change

Growth of $10,000
— Investment Values of Fund
— Investment Values of S&P 500

Performance Quartile (within Category)

History

1993	1994	1995	1996	1997	1998	1999	2000	2001	2002	2003	12-04	History
30.19	26.98	27.32	31.96	39.88	39.96	31.11	33.61	37.72	35.24	45.12	53.17	NAV
8.73	-4.22	18.52	23.51	36.44	9.89	-5.76	28.77	14.21	-5.18	28.04	21.97	Total Return %
-1.33	-5.53	-19.01	0.57	3.09	-18.68	-26.80	37.87	26.09	16.91	-0.63	11.10	+/-S&P 500
-15.04	-2.68	-7.23	2.14	4.66	16.34	-4.27	5.94	0.13	6.25	-17.99	-0.28	+/-Russ 2000 VL
1.02	0.77	1.62	0.00	0.45	0.20	0.19	0.79	0.33	0.00	0.00	0.05	Income Return %
7.71	-4.99	16.90	23.51	35.99	9.69	-5.95	27.98	13.83	-5.18	28.04	21.92	Capital Return %
87	81	79	46	13	2	84	14	62	23	97	43	Total Rtn % Rank Cat
0.30	0.23	0.44	0.00	0.14	0.08	0.08	0.25	0.1[illegible]	0.00	0.00	0.02	Income $
1.73	1.70	4.18	1.78	3.57	3.72	6.04	5.75	0.53	0.52	0.00	1.79	Capital Gains $
1.16	1.25	1.37	1.31	1.25	1.21	1.25	1.24	1.19	1.19	1.10	1.07	Expense Ratio %
0.72	0.56	1.18	0.57	0.23	0.30	0.27	0.65	0.59	-0.12	-0.05	0.06	Income Ratio %
13	9	16	17	20	22	38	48	24	6	4	16	Turnover Rate %
226	131	121	120	174	202	205	286	619	1,190	2,380	4,197	Net Assets $mil

Performance 12-31-04

	1st Qtr	2nd Qtr	3rd Qtr	4th Qtr	Total
2000	-4.21	14.03	4.94	12.34	28.77
2001	1.87	5.78	-7.29	14.32	14.21
2002	7.64	-3.55	-10.16	1.66	-5.18
2003	-5.51	17.63	4.26	10.48	28.04
2004	6.74	4.78	0.32	8.72	21.97

Trailing	Total Return%	+/- S&P 500	+/- Russ 2000 VL	%Rank Cat	Growth of $10,000
3 Mo	8.72	-0.51	-4.48	95	10,872
6 Mo	9.06	1.87	-4.31	88	10,906
1 Yr	21.97	11.10	-0.28	43	12,197
3 Yr Avg	13.98	10.40	-2.52	64	14,808
5 Yr Avg	16.84	19.14	-0.39	39	21,775
10 Yr Avg	16.24	4.17	1.07	21	45,036
15 Yr Avg	12.48	1.55	-1.54	69	58,362

Tax Analysis	Tax-Adj Rtn%	%Rank Cat	Tax-Cost Rat	%Rank Cat
3 Yr (estimated)	13.62	51	0.32	20
5 Yr (estimated)	15.58	41	1.08	56
10 Yr (estimated)	14.01	34	1.92	72

Potential Capital Gain Exposure: 23% of assets

Rating and Risk

Time Period	Load-Adj Return %	Morningstar Rtn vs Cat	Morningstar Risk vs Cat	Morningstar Risk-Adj Rating
1 Yr	21.97			
3 Yr	13.98	Avg	Low	★★★
5 Yr	16.84	Avg	-Avg	★★★★
10 Yr	16.24	+Avg	-Avg	★★★★
Incept	14.46			

Other Measures	Standard Index S&P 500	Best Fit Index Mstar Small Core
Alpha	11.1	3.3
Beta	0.62	0.67
R-Squared	53	80
Standard Deviation	14.39	
Mean	13.98	
Sharpe Ratio	0.88	

Portfolio Analysis 12-31-04

Share change since 11-04 Total Stocks:45	Sector	PE	YTD Ret%	% Assets
Caesars Entertainment	Consumer	62.6	85.97	4.06
Markel	Financial	21.8	43.58	3.59
Idex	Ind Mtrls	24.1	48.09	3.34
Janus Capital Group	Financial	3.8	2.71	2.95
Lee Enterprises	Media	23.5	7.20	2.78
Valassis Communications	Media	18.0	19.28	2.69
Neiman-Marcus A	Consumer	16.1	34.57	2.67
⊕ Invacare	Health	18.1	14.72	2.64
Energizer Holdings	Goods	17.4	32.30	2.45
Jones Lang LaSalle	Financial	23.1	80.46	2.37
ServiceMaster	Consumer	22.0	22.67	2.32
Hasbro	Goods	19.3	-7.90	2.30
Omnicare	Health	14.0	-14.07	2.28
Herman Miller	Goods	37.6	15.09	2.27
J.M. Smucker	Goods	21.0	6.11	2.25
⊕ Aramark	Consumer	18.9	-2.53	2.24
Waddell & Reed Financial	Financial	17.8	4.50	2.21
Brady A	Ind Mtrls	26.2	56.54	2.18
Anixter International	Ind Mtrls	21.0	46.40	2.16
American Greetings	Media	17.1	16.18	2.05

Current Investment Style

Value Blnd Growth; Large Mid Small

Market Cap	%
Giant	0.0
Large	0.0
Mid	73.0
Small	27.0
Micro	0.0

Avg $mil: 2,367

Value Measures		Rel Category
Price/Earnings	20.85	1.31
Price/Book	2.20	1.33
Price/Sales	1.31	1.75
Price/Cash Flow	8.70	1.68
Dividend Yield %	0.74	0.62

Growth Measures	%	Rel Category
Long-Term Erngs	11.59	0.96
Book Value	8.53	1.97
Sales	2.41	0.77
Cash Flow	4.46	2.06
Historical Erngs	14.98	3.11

Profitability	%	Rel Category
Return on Equity	18.68	2.05
Return on Assets	8.54	2.06
Net Margin	10.37	1.55

Sector Weightings	% of Stocks	Rel S&P 500	3 Year High	3 Year Low
Info	16.68	0.78		
Software	0.00	0.00	0	0
Hardware	3.15	0.31	4	2
Media	13.53	3.52	16	14
Telecom	0.00	0.00	0	0
Service	56.30	1.21		
Health	9.17	0.73	10	5
Consumer	19.24	2.12	21	15
Business	3.94	0.97	6	2
Financial	23.95	1.15	24	16
Mfg	27.01	0.84		
Goods	15.60	1.67	22	14
Ind Mtrls	11.41	0.90	17	11
Energy	0.00	0.00	0	0
Utilities	0.00	0.00	0	0

Composition

Cash	17.6
Stocks	82.4
Bonds	0.0
Other	0.0
Foreign (% of Stock)	0.0

Morningstar's Take by Kunal Kapoor 11-10-04

If there ever was a time to take a page out of Ariel Fund's manager's playbook, this is it.

John Rogers' has long distinguished himself as a talented stock-picker. But his slow and steady style is predicated on his ability to run a contrarian strategy, which means that he embraces stocks when they are out of favor and sells them when they catch the market's fancy.

It's a strategy that many of the fund's investors may want to pay attention to. With the small-cap rally continuing at an unabated pace, the relative attractiveness of small-cap funds, particularly those in the value space, has diminished--if not disappeared--relative to larger-cap offerings. That means investors who are only now beginning to invest in this fund--or ramp up their exposure to it, for that matter--must keep their expectations in check. Indeed, while we continue to think highly of this fund, it's important for investors to rebalance their portfolios periodically, so that recently strong performers, such as this fund, don't occupy a more-than-targeted allocation of a diversified portfolio's assets.

To be sure, we'll be the first ones to acknowledge that this advice hasn't paid off as yet. After all, this fund continues to rise strongly, already jumping a sizable 17% for the year to date through Nov. 9, 2004. But Rogers continues to stress that it's much tougher to find ideas for this portfolio--especially when compared with the mid-cap-oriented Ariel Appreciation, which he also manages--and we think it's wise for shareholders to take note of the fund's double-digit cash stake.

Still, we continue to like this fund despite our lingering concerns about its growing size. We just think that it's wise for shareholders to keep their expectations in check given the fund's fabulous 16.86% annual return over the trailing five years.

Address:	200 East Randolph Drive Chicago IL 60601 800-292-7435
Web Address:	www.arielmutualfunds.com
Inception:	11-06-86
Advisor:	Ariel Capital Management, LLC
Subadvisor:	None
NTF Plans:	Fidelity Retail-NTF, Schwab OneSource

Minimum Purchase:	$1000	Add: $50	IRA: $250
Min Auto Inv Plan:	$0	Add: $50	
Sales Fees:	0.25%B		
Management Fee:	0.65% mx./0.55% mn.		
Actual Fees:	Mgt:0.60%	Dist:0.25%	
Expense Projections:	3Yr:$350	5Yr:$606	10Yr:$1340
Income Distrib:	Annually		

Ariel Appreciation

Analyst Pick	Ticker	Load	NAV	Yield	Total Assets	Mstar Category
✔	CAAPX	12b-1 only	$47.67	0.1%	$3,265 mil	Mid-Cap Blend

Governance and Management

Fiduciary Grade: A

Portfolio Manager(s)

Eric McKissack left Ariel on Sept. 30, 2002. Firm founder John Rogers, who also manages Ariel, runs the show here. Rogers boasts more than 20 years of investment experience, specializing in small- and mid-cap stocks.

Strategy

Management hunts for stocks that are selling at discounts of 40% or more to its estimates of their intrinsic value. It favors firms with strong brands or franchises that operate in consistent and stable industries, have sound balance sheets, generate lots of cash, and have strongly motivated management teams. The portfolio is typically concentrated in 40 or fewer stocks, heavy in financials and consumer stocks, and light in technology fare.

Historical Profile

Return: Above Avg
Risk: Average
Rating: ★★★★ Above Avg

Investment Style: Equity Stock %: 97% 96% 94% 98% 94% 97% 97% 96% 96%

▼ Manager Change
▽ Partial Manager Change

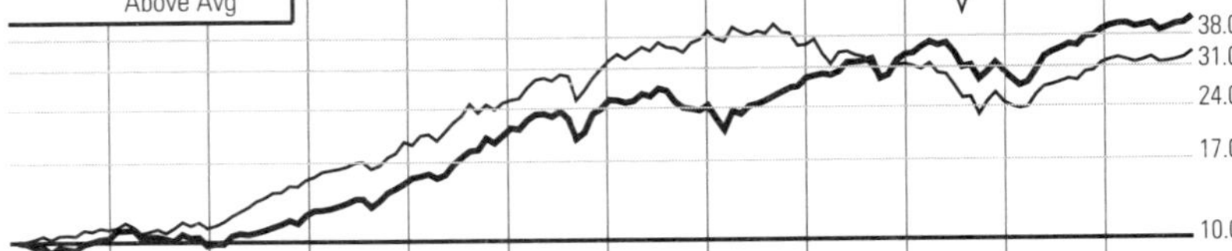

Growth of $10,000
— Investment Values of Fund
— Investment Values of S&P 500

Performance Quartile (within Category)

History

1993	1994	1995	1996	1997	1998	1999	2000	2001	2002	2003	12-04	History
22.89	19.51	22.24	26.07	32.82	35.69	30.97	32.53	37.02	33.06	43.30	47.67	NAV
7.95	-8.39	24.16	23.72	37.95	19.55	-3.79	18.82	16.23	-10.36	30.97	13.10	Total Return %
-2.11	-9.70	-13.37	0.78	4.60	-9.02	-24.83	27.92	28.11	11.73	2.30	2.23	+/-S&P 500
-5.98	-4.80	-6.76	4.54	5.71	0.44	-18.51	1.33	16.83	4.17	-4.62	-3.37	+/-S&P Mid 400
0.24	0.27	1.02	0.33	0.26	0.11	0.12	0.38	0.20	0.00	0.00	0.11	Income Return %
7.71	-8.66	23.14	23.39	37.69	19.44	-3.91	18.44	16.03	-10.36	30.97	12.99	Capital Return %
90	87	71	34	7	19	97	22	9	16	73	78	Total Rtn % Rank Cat
0.05	0.06	0.20	0.07	0.07	0.04	0.04	0.12	0.06	0.00	0.00	0.05	Income $
0.35	1.40	1.77	1.37	3.07	3.46	3.15	3.95	0.71	0.12	0.00	1.20	Capital Gains $
1.37	1.35	1.36	1.36	1.33	1.26	1.26	1.31	1.26	1.26	1.20	1.15	Expense Ratio %
0.33	0.17	0.61	0.50	0.07	0.25	0.13	0.25	0.35	-0.06	-0.06	0.01	Income Ratio %
56	12	18	26	19	20	24	31	28	13	32	19	Turnover Rate %
219	129	139	146	204	284	335	340	771	1,420	2,508	3,265	Net Assets $mil

Performance 12-31-04

	1st Qtr	2nd Qtr	3rd Qtr	4th Qtr	Total
2000	-3.71	4.56	8.02	9.26	18.82
2001	1.84	8.66	-10.00	16.70	16.23
2002	8.56	-6.77	-15.96	5.38	-10.36
2003	-7.05	21.84	4.14	11.05	30.97
2004	3.72	-0.04	-0.60	9.76	13.10

Trailing	Total Return%	+/- S&P 500	+/- S&P Mid 400	%Rank Cat	Growth of $10,000
3 Mo	9.76	0.53	-2.39	88	10,976
6 Mo	9.10	1.91	-0.69	59	10,910
1 Yr	13.10	2.23	-3.37	78	11,310
3 Yr Avg	9.91	6.33	-0.60	47	13,277
5 Yr Avg	12.90	15.20	3.37	9	18,343
10 Yr Avg	16.15	4.08	0.06	18	44,688
15 Yr Avg	13.37	2.44	-1.29	40	65,686

Tax Analysis	Tax-Adj Rtn%	%Rank Cat	Tax-Cost Rat	%Rank Cat
3 Yr (estimated)	9.72	37	0.17	20
5 Yr (estimated)	12.05	8	0.75	31
10 Yr (estimated)	14.57	13	1.36	24

Potential Capital Gain Exposure: 23% of assets

Rating and Risk

Time Period	Load-Adj Return %	Morningstar Rtn vs Cat	Morningstar Risk vs Cat	Morningstar Risk-Adj Rating
1 Yr	13.10			
3 Yr	9.91	Avg	Avg	★★★
5 Yr	12.90	+Avg	Avg	★★★★
10 Yr	16.15	+Avg	-Avg	★★★★
Incept	13.33			

Other Measures	Standard Index S&P 500	Best Fit Index Russ 1000 VI
Alpha	6.5	1.8
Beta	0.90	0.93
R-Squared	82	88
Standard Deviation	16.31	
Mean	9.91	
Sharpe Ratio	0.53	

Portfolio Analysis 12-31-04

Share change since 11-04 Total Stocks:35	Sector	PE	YTD Ret%	% Assets
⊕ Baxter International	Health	32.9	15.22	4.80
Northern Trust	Financial	20.4	6.77	4.80
MBIA	Financial	11.3	8.57	4.47
⊕ IMS Health	Business	19.3	-6.32	4.25
⊕ SunGard Data Systems	Business	17.5	2.24	4.17
Pitney Bowes	Ind Mtrls	19.6	17.24	3.77
Tribune	Media	20.6	-17.47	3.47
MBNA	Financial	14.0	15.53	3.39
Accenture	Business	21.7	2.58	3.37
⊕ Fisher Scientific Intern	Health	43.9	50.79	3.31
Yum Brands	Consumer	19.7	37.84	3.25
Franklin Resources	Financial	26.0	34.62	3.14
⊕ Banknorth Group	Financial	16.3	15.27	3.09
⊕ Black & Decker	Ind Mtrls	16.4	81.42	2.87
Cendant	Business	13.6	6.52	2.62
Omnicom Group	Business	21.6	-2.33	2.54
⊕ Clorox	Goods	23.2	23.93	2.47
Janus Capital Group	Financial	3.8	2.71	2.45
Interpublic Group of Com	Business	—	-14.10	2.40
Schering-Plough	Health	—	21.56	2.37

Current Investment Style

Value Blnd Growth / Large Mid Small

Market Cap	%
Giant	0.0
Large	48.8
Mid	51.2
Small	0.0
Micro	0.0

Avg $mil: 9,837

Value Measures		Rel Category
Price/Earnings	18.49	1.09
Price/Book	2.57	1.18
Price/Sales	1.84	1.74
Price/Cash Flow	8.48	1.36
Dividend Yield %	1.02	1.02

Growth Measures	%	Rel Category
Long-Term Erngs	11.57	0.92
Book Value	13.48	1.91
Sales	6.57	1.16
Cash Flow	9.22	1.23
Historical Erngs	17.35	1.54

Profitability	%	Rel Category
Return on Equity	21.09	1.53
Return on Assets	9.45	1.45
Net Margin	14.48	1.60

Sector Weightings	% of Stocks	Rel S&P 500	3 Year High	3 Year Low
Info	9.85	0.46		
Software	0.00	0.00	0	0
Hardware	0.00	0.00	0	0
Media	7.67	2.00	9	6
Telecom	2.18	0.69	4	2
Service	74.79	1.61		
Health	13.23	1.06	14	4
Consumer	6.65	0.73	15	4
Business	25.38	6.27	30	18
Financial	29.53	1.42	33	19
Mfg	15.36	0.48		
Goods	8.41	0.90	21	6
Ind Mtrls	6.95	0.55	10	6
Energy	0.00	0.00	0	0
Utilities	0.00	0.00	0	0

Composition

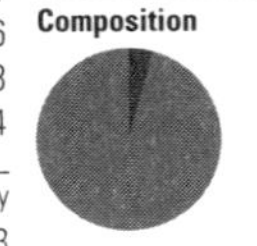

Cash	4.3
Stocks	95.7
Bonds	0.0
Other	0.0
Foreign (% of Stock)	0.0

Morningstar's Take by Kunal Kapoor 11-01-04

The rewards from Ariel Appreciation's strategy can take time to materialize, but they should be plentiful for shareholders.

This fund's manager, John Rogers, belongs to a fraternity of investors who value safety over sizzle. As a result, this portfolio tends to be among the most conservative in the value camp. It also means that Rogers doesn't feel constrained by a particular stylebox square or the need to stay fully invested. Lately, for instance, as the small- and mid-cap rally has gotten long in the tooth, Rogers has increasingly found new opportunities clustered among larger-cap stocks. In fact, while this fund remains near fully invested, Rogers' other charge, the small-cap leaning Ariel, has allowed cash to rise into the double digits.

Indeed, a byproduct of this approach is a portfolio that can significantly diverge from its peers, not only in terms of structure, but also performance. Consider, for instance, that as smaller stocks have continued to outperform over the trailing 12-month period through October 2004, this fund's large-cap bias has held it back. While it's up approximately 9%--a more-than-respectable absolute showing--it trails more than 75% of its peers during that stretch.

But patience is a must here. When Rogers invests in firms such as mutual fund company Janus, he's usually picking them off the bottom. That is, these firms tend to be out-of-favor with investors and often embroiled in controversy. As such, they can take time to turn around and regain investors' confidence, often holding the fund back. But Rogers has a knack for differentiating between businesses facing transitory versus permanent problems. The result is a passel of investments that can struggle in the short run but that have long-term potential. That's a fact borne out in Rogers' superlative long-term record and an important reason why investors must commit for the long run here.

Address:	200 East Randolph Drive Chicago IL 60601 800-292-7435
Web Address:	www.arielmutualfunds.com
Inception:	12-01-89
Advisor:	Ariel Capital Management, LLC
Subadvisor:	None
NTF Plans:	Fidelity Retail-NTF, Schwab OneSource

Minimum Purchase:	$1000	Add: $50	IRA: $250
Min Auto Inv Plan:	$0	Add: $50	
Sales Fees:	0.25%B		
Management Fee:	0.75% mx./0.65% mn.		
Actual Fees:	Mgt:0.70%	Dist:0.25%	
Expense Projections:	3Yr:$381	5Yr:$660	10Yr:$1455
Income Distrib:	Annually		

Artisan International Inv

Analyst Pick	Ticker	Load	NAV	Yield	Total Assets	Mstar Category
✔	ARTIX	None	$22.14	0.6%	$7,130 mil	Foreign Large Growth

Governance and Management

Fiduciary Grade: B

Portfolio Manager(s)

Mark Yockey, Morningstar's 1998 International Manager of the Year, has delivered exceptional results here and with his previous charge, United International Growth (now Waddell & Reed International Growth) where he got his start in 1990. He's supported by six analysts.

Strategy

The fund favors companies that are poised to enjoy superior earnings growth, but it is flexible in its pursuit of such issues. Thus, nontraditional growth stocks such as banks and insurers are often well-represented in the portfolio, and mid-cap names are also fairly common. This fund levies a 2% redemption fee on shares held less than 90 days and uses fair value pricing whenever necessary.

Historical Profile

Return Above Avg
Risk Above Avg
Rating ★★★★ Above Avg

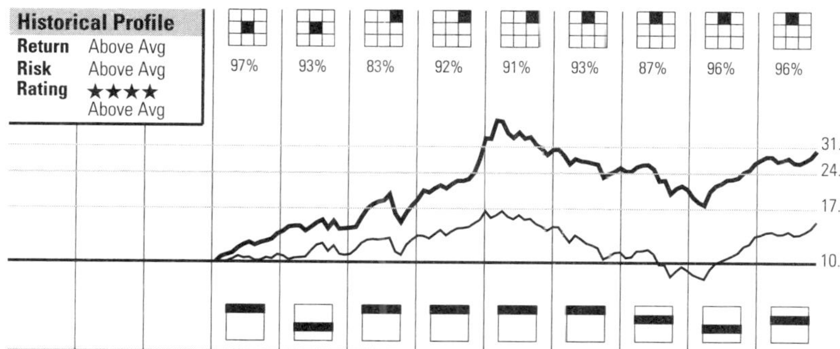

Investment Style
Equity
Stock %

▼ Manager Change
▽ Partial Manager Change

Growth of $10,000
— Investment Values of Fund
— Investment Values of MSCI EAFE

Performance Quartile (within Category)

1993	1994	1995	1996	1997	1998	1999	2000	2001	2002	2003	12-04	History
			97%	93%	83%	92%	91%	93%	87%	96%	96%	Stock %
—	—	10.00	13.32	12.46	16.12	28.50	21.90	18.36	14.79	18.91	22.14	NAV
—	—	0.00*	34.37	3.46	32.18	81.29	-10.59	-15.86	-18.90	29.14	17.76	Total Return %
—	—	—	28.32	1.68	12.25	54.26	3.60	5.56	-2.96	-9.45	-2.49	+/-MSCI EAFE
—	—	—	27.50	1.19	13.49	53.31	2.77	5.53	-3.10	-10.28	-2.62	+/-MSCI Wd xUS
—	—	—	0.00	1.48	0.28	0.15	0.00	0.30	0.55	1.19	0.65	Income Return %
—	—	—	34.37	1.98	31.90	81.14	-10.59	-16.16	-19.45	27.95	17.11	Capital Return %
—	—	—	2	69	2	14	15	14	42	75	27	Total Rtn % Rank Cat
—	—	0.00	0.00	0.20	0.04	0.02	0.00	0.07	0.10	0.18	0.12	Income $
—	—	0.00	0.11	1.13	0.24	0.54	3.55	0.00	0.00	0.00	0.00	Capital Gains $
—	—	—	2.50	1.61	1.45	1.38	1.27	1.22	1.21	1.20	1.22	Expense Ratio %
—	—	—	1.60	1.07	0.37	0.59	-0.10	0.45	0.82	1.35	0.64	Income Ratio %
—	—	—	57	104	109	79	99	72	51	15	55	Turnover Rate %
—	—	—	192	301	505	2,240	3,665	4,059	4,814	5,962	7,130	Net Assets $mil

Performance 12-31-04

	1st Qtr	2nd Qtr	3rd Qtr	4th Qtr	Total
2000	17.61	-10.02	-11.11	-4.95	-10.59
2001	-12.83	2.30	-14.08	9.82	-15.86
2002	0.87	-2.00	-21.38	4.35	-18.90
2003	-14.13	23.07	5.82	15.47	29.14
2004	6.08	-1.30	-2.37	15.21	17.76

Trailing	Total Return%	+/- MSCI EAFE	+/- MSCI Wd xUS	%Rank Cat	Growth of $10,000
3 Mo	15.21	-0.11	0.06	17	11,521
6 Mo	12.47	-2.53	-2.90	50	11,247
1 Yr	17.76	-2.49	-2.62	27	11,776
3 Yr Avg	7.24	-4.65	-4.98	49	12,333
5 Yr Avg	-1.48	-0.35	-0.72	14	9,282
10 Yr Avg	—	—	—	—	—
15 Yr Avg	—	—	—	—	—

Tax Analysis	Tax-Adj Rtn%	%Rank Cat	Tax-Cost Rat	%Rank Cat
3 Yr (estimated)	6.95	47	0.27	52
5 Yr (estimated)	-2.62	15	1.16	73
10 Yr (estimated)	—	—	—	—

Potential Capital Gain Exposure: 8% of assets

Rating and Risk

Time Period	Load-Adj Return %	Morningstar Rtn vs Cat	Morningstar Risk vs Cat	Morningstar Risk-Adj Rating
1 Yr	17.76			
3 Yr	7.24	Avg	+Avg	★★★
5 Yr	-1.48	+Avg	+Avg	★★★★
10 Yr	—	—	—	—
Incept	13.34			

Other Measures	Standard Index S&P 500	Best Fit Index MSCI EAFE
Alpha	-4.8	-4.8
Beta	1.09	1.09
R-Squared	93	93
Standard Deviation	19.03	
Mean	7.24	
Sharpe Ratio	0.31	

Portfolio Analysis 09-30-04

Share change since 06-04 Total Stocks:111	Sector	Country	% Assets
⊕ Fortis	Financial	Belgium	3.07
⊕ UBS	Financial	Switzerland	2.97
⊕ Kingfisher	Consumer	U.K.	2.83
Tesco	Consumer	U.K.	2.75
☆ ITV	Media	U.K.	2.63
Honda Motor	Goods	Japan	2.44
⊖ Nestle	Goods	Switzerland	2.18
Encana	Energy	Canada	2.12
⊖ Allianz	Financial	Germany	2.10
⊕ Ericsson AB (publ)	Hardware	Sweden	2.03
JC Decaux	Business	France	1.95
⊕ Grupo Televisa ADR	Media	Mexico	1.93
⊖ Muenchener Rueckversicher	Financial	Germany	1.86
⊕ British Sky Broadcasting	Media	U.K.	1.82
⊖ Credit Suisse Grp	Financial	Switzerland	1.78
Clariant Ltd	Ind Mtrls	Switzerland	1.68
Linde	Ind Mtrls	Germany	1.61
Promotora De Informacion	Media	Spain	1.60
⊖ Inbev	Goods	Belgium	1.57
⊕ Promise	Financial	Japan	1.45

Current Investment Style

Value Blnd Growth; Large Mid Small

Market Cap	%
Giant	41.4
Large	38.4
Mid	20.2
Small	0.0
Micro	0.0

Avg $mil: 15,819

Value Measures		Rel Category
Price/Earnings	14.91	1.01
Price/Book	2.09	1.00
Price/Sales	1.00	0.95
Price/Cash Flow	5.55	1.01
Dividend Yield %	1.93	0.95

Growth Measures	%	Rel Category
Long-Term Erngs	12.13	1.02
Book Value	0.03	0.03
Sales	1.62	0.35
Cash Flow	-4.50	NMF
Historical Erngs	7.12	0.85

Composition

Cash	0.8	Bonds	0.0
Stocks	95.9	Other	3.3

Foreign (% of Stock) 100.0

Sector Weightings	% of Stocks	Rel MSCI EAFE	3 Year High	Low
Info	23.30	1.40		
Software	0.00	0.00	0	0
Hardware	5.18	1.42	5	0
Media	10.90	4.78	11	4
Telecom	7.22	0.75	15	7
Service	47.84	1.07		
Health	3.97	0.55	8	3
Consumer	10.07	2.00	14	7
Business	6.20	1.14	6	0
Financial	27.60	1.02	40	22
Mfg	28.88	0.75		
Goods	13.48	0.99	31	12
Ind Mtrls	7.28	0.59	16	2
Energy	7.63	1.04	9	1
Utilities	0.49	0.09	1	0

Regional Exposure	% Stock		
UK/W. Europe	64	N. America	2
Japan	19	Latn America	5
Asia X Japan	7	Other	3

Country Exposure	% Stock		
Japan	19	Germany	8
U.K.	17	Spain	6
Switzerland	12		

Morningstar's Take by William Samuel Rocco 11-24-04

Artisan International remains wider-ranging and more appealing than most of its rivals.

Manager Mark Yockey is more price conscious than many of his counterparts, so he is less beholden to stocks in popular growth sectors and more open to opportunities in traditional value sectors. The fund, in fact, has had relatively light tech and health-care stakes for some time. And it continues to sport a relatively heavy financials weight. The fund has long held a sizable stake in that sector, and though Yockey recently profited on some European insurance names, he has added to his stakes in Spanish bank BBVA and the Japanese diversified financial-services firm Orix.

Moreover, Yockey is more open-minded about geography than many of his peers. For starters, he readily considers attractive stocks in Europe's smaller markets. Indeed, the fund has a hefty 7% of its assets in Spain, and it has 1% to 2% positions in Russia and the Czech Republic. Yockey also pays more attention to Latin America than most of his peers. And though the fund is one of the largest foreign large-growth offerings around, it still has 20% of its assets in mid-caps and an average market cap that's a bit less than the group norm.

Yockey, named Morningstar's International Manager of the Year in 1998, has executed his diversified and broad-based growth strategy deftly over the short and long term. The fund has gained 13% and outpaced nearly three fourths of its rivals this year, fueled by a diverse mix of picks, including the big Swiss bank UBS, the Canadian energy firm Encana, and the Mexican media giant Grupo Televisa. And though its flexible style has backfired at times, the fund earned top-quintile results in five of its first eight calendar years and thus boasts superior since-inception returns.

For all these reasons, we think this fund remains a terrific option for investors seeking broad growth-oriented exposure abroad.

Address:	875 East Wisconsin Avenue Suite 800 Milwaukee, WI 53202 800-344-1770
Web Address:	www.artisanfunds.com
Inception:	12-28-95 *
Advisor:	Artisan Partners Limited Partnership
Subadvisor:	None
NTF Plans:	Fidelity Retail-NTF, Schwab OneSource

Minimum Purchase:	$1000	Add: $50	IRA: $1000
Min Auto Inv Plan:	$50	Add: $50	
Sales Fees:	No-load, 2.00%R		
Management Fee:	1.00% mx./0.93% mn.		
Actual Fees:	Mgt:0.93%	Dist:	
Expense Projections:	3Yr:$387	5Yr:$670	10Yr:$1477
Income Distrib:	Annually		

Artisan Intl Sm Cap

Ticker	Load	NAV	Yield	Total Assets	Mstar Category
ARTJX	Closed	$17.56	0.6%	$621 mil	Foreign Small/Mid Growth

Governance and Management

Fiduciary Grade: B

Portfolio Manager(s)

Mark Yockey, who also runs Artisan International and was named Morningstar's International Manager of the year in 1998, is the lead manager here. He's supported by a team of six international analysts.

Strategy

Lead manager Mark Yockey focuses on firms with market caps of less than $3 billion that have good earnings prospects and reasonable valuations. Yockey, who considers opportunities from all over the globe and makes full use of the industry spectrum, readily builds country and sector weightings that are quite different from his bogy or peer group. This fund charges a 2% redemption fee on shares held fewer than 90 days, and it uses fair value pricing whenever necessary.

Historical Profile

Return Above Avg
Risk Average
Rating ★★★★★ Highest

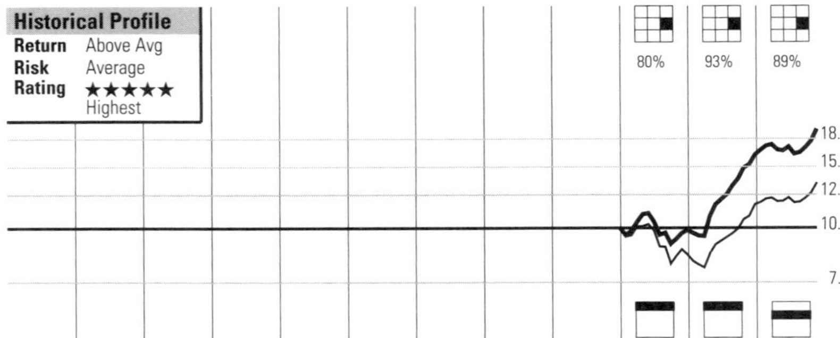

Investment Style
Equity
Stock %

▼ Manager Change
▽ Partial Manager Change

Growth of $10,000
— Investment Values of Fund
— Investment Values of MSCI EAFE

Performance Quartile (within Category)

1993	1994	1995	1996	1997	1998	1999	2000	2001	2002	2003	12-04	History
—	—	—	—	—	—	—	—	10.08	9.92	15.61	17.56	NAV
—	—	—	—	—	—	—	—	0.80*	-1.34	63.00	25.70	Total Return %
—	—	—	—	—	—	—	—	—	14.60	24.41	5.45	+/-MSCI EAFE
—	—	—	—	—	—	—	—	—	14.46	23.58	5.32	+/-MSCI Wd xUS
—	—	—	—	—	—	—	—	—	0.00	0.36	0.75	Income Return %
—	—	—	—	—	—	—	—	—	-1.34	62.64	24.95	Capital Return %
—	—	—	—	—	—	—	—	—	1	20	42	Total Rtn % Rank Cat
—	—	—	—	—	—	—	—	0.00	0.00	0.04	0.12	Income $
—	—	—	—	—	—	—	—	0.00	0.02	0.49	1.77	Capital Gains $
—	—	—	—	—	—	—	—	—	1.91	1.77	1.57	Expense Ratio %
—	—	—	—	—	—	—	—	—	-0.02	0.28	0.95	Income Ratio %
—	—	—	—	—	—	—	—	—	38	13	81	Turnover Rate %
—	—	—	—	—	—	—	—	—	108	164	621	Net Assets $mil

Performance 12-31-04

	1st Qtr	2nd Qtr	3rd Qtr	4th Qtr	Total
2000	—	—	—	—	—
2001	—	—	—	—	0.80 *
2002	4.07	0.10	-13.43	9.41	-1.34
2003	-3.83	26.83	14.46	16.75	63.00
2004	7.05	-1.50	-0.36	19.64	25.70

Trailing	Total Return%	+/- MSCI EAFE	+/- MSCI Wd xUS	%Rank Cat	Growth of $10,000
3 Mo	19.64	4.32	4.49	7	11,964
6 Mo	19.21	4.21	3.84	10	11,921
1 Yr	25.70	5.45	5.32	42	12,570
3 Yr Avg	26.44	14.55	14.22	12	20,214
5 Yr Avg	—	—	—	—	—
10 Yr Avg	—	—	—	—	—
15 Yr Avg	—	—	—	—	—

Tax Analysis	Tax-Adj Rtn%	%Rank Cat	Tax-Cost Rat	%Rank Cat
3 Yr (estimated)	24.70	12	1.38	100
5 Yr (estimated)	—	—	—	—
10 Yr (estimated)	—	—	—	—

Potential Capital Gain Exposure: 29% of assets

Rating and Risk

Time Period	Load-Adj Return %	Morningstar Rtn vs Cat	Morningstar Risk vs Cat	Morningstar Risk-Adj Rating
1 Yr	25.70			
3 Yr	26.44	+Avg	Avg	★★★★★
5 Yr	—	—	—	—
10 Yr	—	—	—	—
Incept	26.50			

Other Measures	Standard Index S&P 500	Best Fit Index MSCI Wd xUS
Alpha	13.9	13.5
Beta	0.94	0.95
R-Squared	86	86
Standard Deviation	19.76	
Mean	26.44	
Sharpe Ratio	1.28	

Portfolio Analysis 09-30-04

Share change since 06-04 Total Stocks:65	Sector	Country	% Assets
⊕ Banco Latinoamericano de	Financial	Panama	4.55
Vimpel-Communications AD	Telecom	Russia	3.35
Fraser & Neave Ltd	Ind Mtrls	Singapore	2.96
⊕ STADA Arzneimittel	Health	Germany	2.48
⊖ Clarins	Goods	France	2.45
⊖ Sulzer	Ind Mtrls	Switzerland	2.28
Gr Ed L'Espresso	Media	Italy	2.27
John Fairfax Hldgs	Media	Australia	2.17
⊕ Wienerberger	Business	Austria	2.15
Elekta	Health	Sweden	2.06
Precision Drilling Corp	—	—	2.02
⊖ Straumann Holding	Health	Switzerland	1.99
Colruyt	Consumer	Belgium	1.98
⊕ Intertek Grp	Business	U.K.	1.96
⊕ Schindler-Hldg Ag	Ind Mtrls	Switzerland	1.95
Creed	Financial	Japan	1.83
Komeri	Consumer	Japan	1.78
⊕ Bank Sarasin + Compagnie	—	—	1.71
☼ Natura Cosmeticos	—	Brazil	1.68
⊕ Kangwon Land	Consumer	Korea	1.67

Current Investment Style

Market Cap	%
Giant	0.0
Large	6.9
Mid	56.4
Small	27.2
Micro	9.5
Avg $mil: 1,381	

Value Measures		Rel Category
Price/Earnings	15.88	1.15
Price/Book	1.91	1.00
Price/Sales	1.06	1.29
Price/Cash Flow	4.47	0.90
Dividend Yield %	3.14	1.38

Growth Measures	%	Rel Category
Long-Term Erngs	13.67	0.30
Book Value	-16.00	NMF
Sales	1.57	0.25
Cash Flow	-6.01	NMF
Historical Erngs	-9.92	NMF

Composition

Cash	7.3	Bonds	0.0
Stocks	89.3	Other	3.3
Foreign (% of Stock)			100.0

Sector Weightings	% of Stocks	Rel MSCI EAFE	3 Year High	3 Year Low
Info	22.06	1.33		
Software	0.00	0.00	0	0
Hardware	1.56	0.43	2	0
Media	13.39	5.87	22	13
Telecom	7.11	0.74	11	0
Service	48.26	1.08		
Health	9.72	1.34	13	0
Consumer	13.65	2.71	25	11
Business	10.87	2.00	11	2
Financial	14.02	0.52	21	5
Mfg	29.70	0.77		
Goods	7.53	0.55	44	8
Ind Mtrls	16.09	1.31	16	0
Energy	5.43	0.74	7	0
Utilities	0.65	0.12	2	0

Regional Exposure	% Stock		
UK/W. Europe	56	N. America	0
Japan	7	Latn America	8
Asia X Japan	23	Other	6

Country Exposure	% Stock		
Switzerland	13	Japan	7
France	11	Russia	6
U.K.	7		

Morningstar's Take by William Samuel Rocco 11-29-04

Shareholders should take the so-so 2004 showing of the closed Artisan International Small Cap in stride.

The fund has earned undistinguished results in this year's choppy but generally favorable climate for smaller-cap-growth stocks abroad. Although No. 2 holding Vimpel Communications and several other names have thrived, some of manager Mark Yockey's picks have been sluggish or worse. Top holding Banco Latinoamericano de Exportaciones is essentially flat since Jan. 1 after zooming more than 300% in 2003. And German generic drugmaker STADA Arzneimittel has struggled, while Oriflame Cosmetics sank before Yockey sold it. Thus, the fund is in the middle of the foreign small/mid-growth pack for the year to date through Nov. 26.

But these results need to be put in perspective. The fund is up 18% since Jan. 1, which is quite heartening in absolute terms. What's more, it surged 63% and beat four fifths of its rivals in 2003's global rally, thanks to Banco Latinoamericano de Exportaciones, Australian newspaper chain John Fairfax, and several of Yockey's other picks. And it lost just 1% in 2002, while its average peer suffered a double-digit loss, as Yockey's stock selection in the consumer staples and other sectors was on the mark.

The fund, which opened in late 2001, has more than its superior since-inception returns and early success in a mix of conditions going for it. Yockey has earned strong long-term returns with his flexible growth strategy at Artisan International. This fund, which closed to new investors in the fall of 2003, still has a fairly modest asset base, and it continues to have a smaller average market cap and to be a better diversifier than most of its peers.

For all these reasons, we think this closed fund remains an excellent complement to most foreign large-value offerings and many other foreign large-cap funds.

Address:	875 East Wisconsin Avenue Suite 800, Milwaukee, WI 53202, 800-344-1770
Web Address:	www.artisanfunds.com
Inception:	12-21-01 *
Advisor:	Artisan Partners Limited Partnership
Subadvisor:	None
NTF Plans:	Fidelity Retail-NTF, Schwab OneSource

Minimum Purchase:	Closed	Add: —	IRA: —
Min Auto Inv Plan:	Closed	Add: —	
Sales Fees:	No-load, 2.00%R		
Management Fee:	1.25%		
Actual Fees:	Mgt:1.25%	Dist:	
Expense Projections:	3Yr:$496	5Yr:$855	10Yr:$1867
Income Distrib:	Annually		

Artisan Mid Cap Inv

Ticker	Load	NAV	Yield	Total Assets	Mstar Category
ARTMX	Closed	$23.56	0.0%	$4,763 mil	Mid-Cap Growth

Governance and Management

Fiduciary Grade: B

Portfolio Manager(s)

Andy Stephens has managed the fund since its inception in 1997. Before coming aboard here, he was a comanager at Strong Balanced. James Hamel, an analyst at the fund since 1997, was promoted to associate portfolio manager in October 2001. As of early 2004, six analysts support them.

Strategy

Manager Andy Stephens and his team look for dominant companies with accelerating profit cycles that are selling at attractive valuations. They seek a balance of stable and aggressive-growth stocks, and they pay more attention to valuations than many in the mid-growth set.

Historical Profile

Return Above Avg
Risk Average
Rating ★★★★ Above Avg

Investment Style
Equity
Stock %: 93% (1998), 96% (1999), 91% (2000), 95% (2001), 95% (2002), 96% (2003), 97% (12-04)

▼ Manager Change
▽ Partial Manager Change

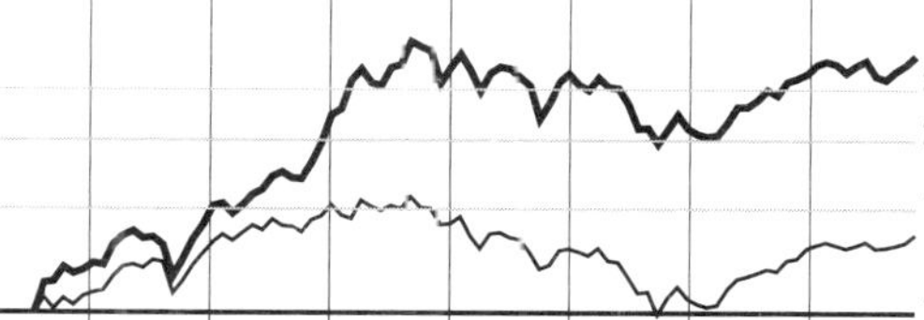

Growth of $10,000
— Investment Values of Fund
— Investment Values of S&P 500

Performance Quartile (within Category)

History

1993	1994	1995	1996	1997	1998	1999	2000	2001	2002	2003	12-04	History
—	—	—	—	12.01	14.36	21.69	26.60	25.79	19.56	25.78	29.56	NAV
—	—	—	—	28.14*	33.37	57.89	27.16	-3.04	-24.16	31.80	14.66	Total Return %
—	—	—	—	—	4.80	36.85	36.25	8.84	-2.07	3.13	3.79	+/-S&P 500
—	—	—	—	—	15.51	6.60	38.91	17.11	3.25	-10.91	-0.82	+/-Russ MG
—	—	—	—	0.00	0.00	0.00	0.00	0.00	0.00	0.00	0.00	Income Return %
—	—	—	—	—	33.37	57.89	27.16	-3.04	-24.16	31.80	14.66	Capital Return %
—	—	—	—	—	14	44	4	10	35	70	38	Total Rtn % Rank Cat
—	—	—	—	0.00	0.00	0.00	0.00	0.00	0.00	0.00	0.00	Income $
—	—	—	—	0.79	1.27	0.83	1.03	0.00	0.00	0.00	0.00	Capital Gains $
—	—	—	—	0.00	2.00	2.00	1.40	1.31	1.22	1.20	1.19	Expense Ratio %
—	—	—	—	0.00	-0.77	-1.13	-0.79	0.52	-0.77	-0.56	-0.77	Income Ratio %
—	—	—	—	—	236	203	246	154	121	27	101	Turnover Rate %
—	—	—	—	9	25	98	773	1,997	2,333	2,706	4,763	Net Assets $mil

Performance 12-31-04

	1st Qtr	2nd Qtr	3rd Qtr	4th Qtr	Total
2000	26.14	0.77	11.10	-9.96	27.16
2001	-11.43	12.18	-22.47	25.87	-3.04
2002	-2.06	-12.39	-18.07	7.89	-24.16
2003	-3.22	15.21	6.01	11.51	31.80
2004	5.04	1.77	-5.19	13.13	14.66

Trailing	Total Return%	+/- S&P 500	+/- Russ MG	%Rank Cat	Growth of $10,000
3 Mo	13.13	3.90	-0.81	47	11,313
6 Mo	7.26	0.07	-1.75	55	10,726
1 Yr	14.66	3.79	-0.82	38	11,466
3 Yr Avg	4.65	1.07	-1.51	42	11,461
5 Yr Avg	7.16	9.46	10.52	8	14,131
10 Yr Avg	—	—	—	—	—
15 Yr Avg	—	—	—	—	—

Tax Analysis	Tax-Adj Rtn%	%Rank Cat	Tax-Cost Rat	%Rank Cat
3 Yr (estimated)	4.65	35	0.00	1
5 Yr (estimated)	6.88	7	0.26	11
10 Yr (estimated)	—	—	—	—

Potential Capital Gain Exposure: 20% of assets

Rating and Risk

Time Period	Load-Adj Return %	Morningstar Rtn vs Cat	Morningstar Risk vs Cat	Morningstar Risk-Adj Rating
1 Yr	14.66			
3 Yr	4.65	Avg	Avg	★★★
5 Yr	7.16	High	Avg	★★★★
10 Yr	—	—	—	—
Incept	19.50			

Other Measures	Standard Index S&P 500	Best Fit Index Russ MG
Alpha	1.2	-1.2
Beta	1.08	0.94
R-Squared	83	94
Standard Deviation	18.71	
Mean	4.65	
Sharpe Ratio	0.18	

Morningstar's Take by William Samuel Rocco 11-11-04

Artisan Mid Cap, a closed fund, stands out in several ways.

Its distinctions begin with its strategy. Manager Andy Stephens pays more attention to valuations and diversification than many peers managers do. Thus, the fund often has moderate price multiples and sizable stakes in traditional value sectors.

Thanks to its price consciousness and breadth--and Stephens' stock-picking skill--the fund held up exceptionally well in the rough conditions of the early 2000s. While the typical mid-growth offering lost more than 50% of value between mid-March 2000 and the end of 2002, this fund lost less than 30% of its value during that period.

The fund has also distinguished itself in other climates. Though it lagged in 2003's rally, slowed by its high-quality bias as well as its diversification, it performed well in the late-1990s surges. And it has earned superior returns in this year's choppy conditions, as a mix of picks has thrived.

Alas, the fund's asset base also stands out. Though it closed to most new investors 2.5 years ago, the fund has grown to more than $5 billion in assets and is bigger than all but a handful of its mid-growth peers, due to inflows from existing shareholders and appreciation. Stephens has handled the fund's girth well so far. But it's worth noting that he can't be as agile as he once was and the portfolio's average market cap is higher than it used to be (though that's partly due to the fact that Stephens has been finding larger-cap opportunities). On a positive note, Artisan recently announced plans to shut the doors a little tighter. On January 24, 2005, the fund will stop accepting new accounts for employee benefit plans from all plan administrators (including those that already have relationships with Artisan).

We think the issues associated with the hefty asset base are less significant than fund's various strengths, and shareholders should certainly stay put. That said, shareholders need to understand this fund has evolved.

Address:	875 East Wisconsin Avenue Suite 800 Milwaukee, WI 53202 800-344-1770
Web Address:	www.artisanfunds.com
Inception:	06-27-97 *
Advisor:	Artisan Partners Limited Partnership
Subadvisor:	None
NTF Plans:	Fidelity Retail-NTF, Schwab OneSource

Minimum Purchase:	Closed	Add: —	IRA: —
Min Auto Inv Plan:	Closed	Add: —	
Sales Fees:	No-load		
Management Fee:	1.00% mx./0.93% mn.		
Actual Fees:	Mgt:0.96%	Dist:	
Expense Projections:	3Yr:$378	5Yr:$654	10Yr:$1443
Income Distrib:	Annually		

Portfolio Analysis 09-30-04

Share change since 06-04 Total Stocks:116	Sector	PE	YTD Ret%	% Assets
⊕ Aetna	Financial	16.9	84.67	1.55
⊕ Weatherford International	Energy	27.8	42.50	1.53
⊕ Caremark RX	Health	32.8	55.67	1.53
⊕ Smith International	Energy	34.2	31.05	1.49
⊕ EchoStar Communications	Media	NMF	0.85	1.44
⊕ Diebold	Hardware	22.2	5.00	1.43
⊕ MGIC Investment	Financial	12.7	21.42	1.39
⊖ CIT Group	Financial	13.2	29.28	1.37
⊕ Jabil Circuit	Hardware	28.2	-9.61	1.35
⊖ Precision Castparts	Ind Mtrls	26.0	44.97	1.34
⊕ Lamar Advertising A	Business	—	14.63	1.33
⊕ Kohl's	Consumer	25.5	9.41	1.33
⊕ Air Products and Chemica	Ind Mtrls	21.5	11.99	1.30
⊖ PACCAR	Ind Mtrls	15.6	47.28	1.30
⊖ Yahoo!	Media	95.1	67.36	1.26
⊕ Constellation Brands A	Goods	19.9	41.24	1.26
⊕ Boston Scientific	Health	32.3	-3.29	1.24
⊖ Danaher	Ind Mtrls	25.8	25.29	1.24
⊖ Thermo Electron	Health	27.2	19.80	1.23
⊕ Eaton	Ind Mtrls	18.5	36.07	1.23

Current Investment Style

Market Cap	%
Giant	1.3
Large	33.7
Mid	62.3
Small	2.8
Micro	0.0
Avg $mil: 6,366	

Value Measures		Rel Category
Price/Earnings	22.17	1.01
Price/Book	2.69	0.90
Price/Sales	1.80	1.02
Price/Cash Flow	11.31	1.17
Dividend Yield %	0.28	0.65

Growth Measures	%	Rel Category
Long-Term Erngs	14.59	0.93
Book Value	10.22	1.02
Sales	5.80	0.67
Cash Flow	11.05	0.91
Historical Erngs	10.34	0.65

Profitability	%	Rel Category
Return on Equity	14.66	1.02
Return on Assets	6.91	0.96
Net Margin	9.21	0.96

Sector Weightings	% of Stocks	Rel S&P 500	3 Year High	3 Year Low
Info	28.43	1.32		
Software	6.39	1.49	11	6
Hardware	16.41	1.61	22	9
Media	4.67	1.22	5	2
Telecom	0.96	0.30	3	0
Service	51.48	1.11		
Health	16.01	1.28	19	13
Consumer	12.42	1.37	13	2
Business	13.00	3.21	20	11
Financial	10.05	0.48	14	3
Mfg	20.09	0.63		
Goods	3.31	0.35	15	3
Ind Mtrls	11.65	0.92	12	5
Energy	5.13	0.72	8	3
Utilities	0.00	0.00	0	0

Composition

Cash	2.8
Stocks	97.2
Bonds	0.0
Other	0.0
Foreign (% of Stock)	3.5

Artisan Mid Cap Value

Ticker	Load	NAV	Yield	Total Assets	Mstar Category
ARTQX	None	$16.96	0.0%	$720 mil	Mid-Cap Value

Governance and Management

Fiduciary Grade: B

Portfolio Manager(s)

James Kieffer and Scott Satterwhite also manage Artisan Small Cap Value; they worked together at Wachovia before joining Artisan in 1997. They invest their own money in their funds and have equity stakes in Artisan Partners, the fund's advisor. One analyst, George Sertl, works with them.

Strategy

Managers James Kieffer and Scott Satterwhite look for 40 to 60 cash-producing companies with strong financial positions that sell at low valuations. They focus on companies with market caps between $1.5 billion and $10 billion while doing so. Because of their value discipline, investors can expect them to buy stocks in distressed industries and hold them until their prices appreciate close to their intrinsic values. Kieffer and Satterwhite trade infrequently and don't spend much time meeting with company management.

Historical Profile

Return High
Risk Average
Rating ★★★★★ Highest

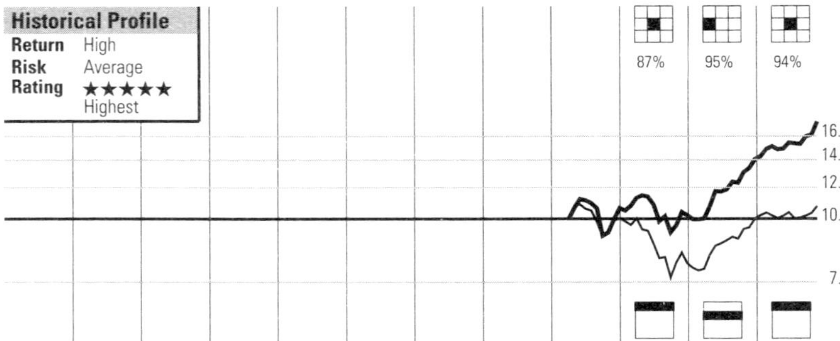

Investment Style
Equity
Stock %

▼ Manager Change
▽ Partial Manager Change

Growth of $10,000
— Investment Values of Fund
— Investment Values of S&P 500

Performance Quartile (within Category)

1993	1994	1995	1996	1997	1998	1999	2000	2001	2002	2003	12-04	History
—	—	—	—	—	—	—	—	10.60	10.19	13.69	16.96	NAV
—	—	—	—	—	—	—	—	6.93*	-3.87	36.83	26.20	Total Return %
—	—	—	—	—	—	—	—	—	18.22	8.16	15.33	+/-S&P 500
—	—	—	—	—	—	—	—	—	5.77	-1.24	2.49	+/-Russ MV
—	—	—	—	—	—	—	—	0.00	0.00	0.00	0.01	Income Return %
—	—	—	—	—	—	—	—	—	-3.87	36.83	26.19	Capital Return %
—	—	—	—	—	—	—	—	—	8	33	2	Total Rtn % Rank Cat
—	—	—	—	—	—	—	—	0.00	0.00	0.00	0.00	Income $
—	—	—	—	—	—	—	—	0.08	0.00	0.24	0.30	Capital Gains $
—	—	—	—	—	—	—	—	—	1.95	1.78	1.39	Expense Ratio %
—	—	—	—	—	—	—	—	—	-0.82	-0.34	0.73	Income Ratio %
—	—	—	—	—	—	—	—	—	168	12	54	Turnover Rate %
—	—	—	—	—	—	—	—	15	36	52	720	Net Assets $mil

Performance 12-31-04

	1st Qtr	2nd Qtr	3rd Qtr	4th Qtr	Total
2000	—	—	—	—	—
2001	—	11.02	-18.16	16.86	6.93 *
2002	5.94	-3.65	-14.51	10.16	-3.87
2003	-1.86	16.40	4.98	14.10	36.83
2004	7.45	2.11	3.53	11.11	26.20

Trailing	Total Return%	+/- S&P 500	+/- Russ MV	%Rank Cat	Growth of $10,000
3 Mo	11.11	1.88	-2.35	53	11,111
6 Mo	15.03	7.84	-0.40	6	11,503
1 Yr	26.20	15.33	2.49	2	12,620
3 Yr Avg	18.41	14.83	2.85	4	16,602
5 Yr Avg	—	—	—	—	—
10 Yr Avg	—	—	—	—	—
15 Yr Avg	—	—	—	—	—

Tax Analysis	Tax-Adj Rtn%	%Rank Cat	Tax-Cost Rat	%Rank Cat
3 Yr (estimated)	18.04	3	0.31	27
5 Yr (estimated)	—	—	—	—
10 Yr (estimated)	—	—	—	—

Potential Capital Gain Exposure: 12% of assets

Rating and Risk

Time Period	Load-Adj Return %	Morningstar Rtn vs Cat	Morningstar Risk vs Cat	Morningstar Risk-Adj Rating
1 Yr	26.20			
3 Yr	18.41	High	Avg	★★★★★
5 Yr	—	—	—	—
10 Yr	—	—	—	—
Incept	16.48			

Other Measures	Standard Index S&P 500	Best Fit Index Mstar Mid Value
Alpha	14.9	4.1
Beta	0.79	0.91
R-Squared	73	90

Standard Deviation	16.18
Mean	18.41
Sharpe Ratio	1.06

Portfolio Analysis 09-30-04

Share change since 06-04 Total Stocks:49	Sector	PE	YTD Ret%	% Assets
⊕ Student Loan	Financial	13.4	29.15	4.74
⊕ Apache	Energy	11.4	25.41	4.33
⊕ EOG Resources	Energy	16.5	55.21	4.15
⊕ Furniture Brands Interna	Goods	14.4	-12.81	3.63
⊕ White Mountains Insuranc	Financial	41.1	40.75	3.50
⊕ Countrywide Financial	Financial	9.0	48.15	3.46
⊕ XTO Energy	Energy	20.5	56.85	3.27
⊕ Alleghany	Financial	14.7	30.77	3.21
⊕ Old Republic Internation	Financial	10.3	1.89	3.17
⊕ Liz Claiborne	Goods	14.8	19.76	3.03
⊕ Nuveen Investment	Financial	22.6	51.57	2.78
⊕ Equitable Resources	Energy	13.0	45.53	2.34
⊕ Zale	Goods	13.1	12.29	2.24
⊕ Reebok International	Goods	15.3	12.83	2.19
⊕ Sherwin-Williams	Goods	16.3	30.70	2.11
⊕ AutoZone	Consumer	13.8	7.16	2.00
☼ Rent-A-Center	Consumer	13.7	-11.67	1.98
⊕ Washington Federal	Financial	15.1	7.15	1.86
⊕ Deluxe	Business	9.7	-6.35	1.79
⊕ BearingPoint	Business	95.1	-20.42	1.74

Current Investment Style

Value Blnd Growth — Large Mid Small

Market Cap	%
Giant	0.0
Large	9.6
Mid	79.8
Small	10.6
Micro	0.0
Avg $mil: 3,690	

Value Measures		Rel Category
Price/Earnings	13.84	0.90
Price/Book	1.91	0.99
Price/Sales	1.19	1.35
Price/Cash Flow	4.67	0.82
Dividend Yield %	0.74	0.52

Growth Measures	%	Rel Category
Long-Term Erngs	11.63	1.06
Book Value	9.87	1.75
Sales	4.64	0.97
Cash Flow	13.85	3.51
Historical Erngs	18.41	1.60

Profitability	%	Rel Category
Return on Equity	15.70	1.23
Return on Assets	8.06	1.33
Net Margin	13.60	1.55

Sector Weightings	% of Stocks	Rel S&P 500	3 Year High	Low
Info	4.47	0.21		
Software	3.67	0.85	4	0
Hardware	0.80	0.08	3	0
Media	0.00	0.00	1	0
Telecom	0.00	0.00	9	0
Service	52.80	1.14		
Health	6.05	0.48	6	0
Consumer	6.32	0.70	8	3
Business	10.62	2.62	11	6
Financial	29.81	1.44	40	27
Mfg	42.72	1.33		
Goods	17.38	1.86	19	6
Ind Mtrls	2.60	0.21	14	3
Energy	21.20	2.96	23	16
Utilities	1.54	0.52	12	1

Composition

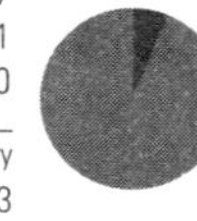

Cash	6.3
Stocks	93.7
Bonds	0.0
Other	0.0
Foreign (% of Stock)	1.2

Morningstar's Take by William Samuel Rocco 10-25-04

Artisan Mid Cap Value is beginning to get some of the attention it deserves.

This fund's asset base has grown from just over $50 million at the start of 2004 to a tad more than $309 million at the end of the third quarter. Performance has no doubt played a large role in this increased popularity. The fund has had more than twice the mid-value norm of 8% in the thriving energy sector all year, and some of Jim Kieffer and Scott Satterwhite's oil- and gas-related picks have earned exceptionally strong gains. Top-10 holdings EOG Resources and XTO Energy are both up about 50% since Jan. 1, 2004, for example. And several of the duo's selections in other sectors have surged. Thus, the fund leads all other mid-value offerings, with a 13.5% return for the year to date.

This year's success certainly isn't the only attraction here. This young fund posted relatively mild losses in rough 2002, buoyed by Kieffer and Satterwhite's selections in the mortgage, REIT, and other areas. It earned superior gains in the 2003 rally, thanks to the duo's picks in a variety of sectors. Overall, the fund has posted a 14% annualized return since opening in the spring of 2001, while the typical mid-value offering has earned an 8% annualized return during that period.

Kieffer and Satterwhite have much more than the past three and a half years here going for them. They've done a good job running Artisan Small Value the past seven years, and they had success running money for Wachovia in the mid-1990s. The facts that the fund can be nimble at its current size and that Artisan has a history of closing funds before they get too big are added plusses.

In short, this fund is well worth a look from mid-value fans. Remember, though, that the whole category has outperformed in recent years and can't keep that up forever.

Address:	875 East Wisconsin Avenue Suite 800 Milwaukee, WI 53202 800-344-1770
Web Address:	www.artisanfunds.com
Inception:	03-28-01 *
Advisor:	Artisan Partners Limited Partnership
Subadvisor:	None
NTF Plans:	Fidelity Retail-NTF, Schwab OneSource

Minimum Purchase:	$1000	Add: $50	IRA: $1000
Min Auto Inv Plan:	$50	Add: $50	
Sales Fees:	No-load		
Management Fee:	1.00% mx./0.93% mn.		
Actual Fees:	Mgt:1.00%	Dist:	
Expense Projections:	3Yr:$440	5Yr:$761	10Yr:$1669
Income Distrib:	Annually		

Artisan Small Cap

Ticker	Load	NAV	Yield	Total Assets	Mstar Category
ARTSX	Closed	$16.76	0.0%	$425 mil	Small Growth

Governance and Management

Fiduciary Grade: B

Portfolio Manager(s)

Carlene Murphy Ziegler has been on the job here since the fund's inception. She was joined by Marina Carlson in April 1999. Craigh Cepukenas recently became the third comanager after serving as an analyst on the fund for nine years. One analyst rounds out the team.

Strategy

The team here is price-conscious than the average small-growth manager. They search for stocks selling at discounts to their estimates of the private market values. Firms with improving returns on invested capital and positive free cash flow rank highly. Management tends to spread assets out widely across sectors and stocks.

Historical Profile

Return: Above Avg
Risk: Average
Rating: ★★★★ Above Avg

Investment Style: Equity, Stock %: 98% (1996), 97% (1997), 92% (1998), 98% (1999), 96% (2000), 95% (2001), 99% (2002), 96% (2003), 97% (12-04)

▼ Manager Change ▽ Partial Manager Change

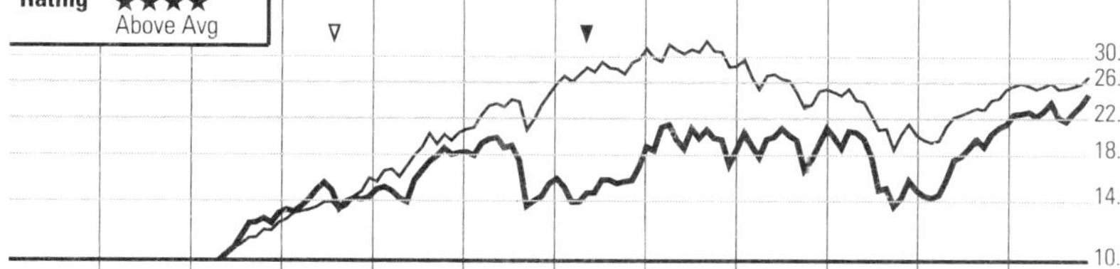

Performance Quartile (within Category)

1993	1994	1995	1996	1997	1998	1999	2000	2001	2002	2003	12-04	History
—	—	13.18	13.64	14.15	11.16	13.30	12.48	13.94	9.88	14.18	16.76	NAV
—	—	32.84*	11.86	22.67	-13.47	19.18	-1.40	12.21	-28.67	43.52	22.10	Total Return %
—	—	—	-11.08	-10.68	-42.04	-1.86	7.70	24.09	-6.58	14.85	11.23	+/-S&P 500
—	—	—	0.60	9.72	-14.70	-23.91	21.03	21.44	1.59	-5.02	7.79	+/-Russ 2000 Gr
—	—	0.00	0.00	0.00	0.00	0.00	0.00	0.00	0.00	0.00	0.00	Income Return %
—	—	—	11.86	22.67	-13.47	19.18	-1.40	12.21	-28.67	43.52	22.10	Capital Return %
—	—	—	79	33	98	81	37	10	58	53	9	Total Rtn % Rank Cat
—	—	0.00	0.00	0.00	0.00	0.00	0.00	0.00	0.00	0.00	0.00	Income $
—	—	0.10	1.07	2.58	0.96	0.00	0.66	0.06	0.06	0.00	0.53	Capital Gains $
—	—	2.00	1.52	1.41	1.33	1.37	1.35	1.34	1.31	1.39	1.27	Expense Ratio %
—	—	-0.59	-0.75	-0.73	-0.74	-0.67	-0.79	-0.68	-1.00	-0.98	-0.95	Income Ratio %
—	—	—	105	87	135	155	194	147	140	30	119	Turnover Rate %
—	—	270	296	39	67	59	139	154	102	100	425	Net Assets $mil

Performance 12-31-04

	1st Qtr	2nd Qtr	3rd Qtr	4th Qtr	Total
2000	12.86	-2.13	-5.17	-5.86	-1.40
2001	-4.25	17.07	-20.23	25.49	12.21
2002	-1.51	-12.67	-24.10	9.27	-28.67
2003	-2.73	23.83	5.29	13.17	43.52
2004	6.98	5.08	-5.14	14.51	22.10

Trailing	Total Return%	+/- S&P 500	+/- Russ 2000 Gr	%Rank Cat	Growth of $10,000
3 Mo	14.51	5.28	-0.57	38	11,451
6 Mo	8.62	1.43	0.46	45	10,862
1 Yr	22.10	11.23	7.79	9	12,210
3 Yr Avg	7.72	4.14	1.93	31	12,499
5 Yr Avg	6.70	9.00	10.27	19	13,830
10 Yr Avg	—	—	—	—	—
15 Yr Avg	—	—	—	—	—

Tax Analysis	Tax-Adj Rtn%	%Rank Cat	Tax-Cost Rat	%Rank Cat
3 Yr (estimated)	7.49	27	0.21	21
5 Yr (estimated)	6.24	16	0.43	20
10 Yr (estimated)	—	—	—	—

Potential Capital Gain Exposure: 15% of assets

Rating and Risk

Time Period	Load-Adj Return %	Morningstar Rtn vs Cat	Morningstar Risk vs Cat	Morningstar Risk-Adj Rating
1 Yr	22.10			
3 Yr	7.72	Avg	+Avg	★★★
5 Yr	6.70	+Avg	Avg	★★★★
10 Yr	—	—	—	—
Incept	10.28			

Other Measures	Standard Index S&P 500	Best Fit Index Russ 2000 Gr
Alpha	4.5	2.0
Beta	1.22	0.96
R-Squared	73	95
Standard Deviation	23.28	
Mean	7.72	
Sharpe Ratio	0.28	

Portfolio Analysis 09-30-04

Share change since 06-04 Total Stocks:78	Sector	PE	YTD Ret%	% Assets
⊕ MTC Technologies	Software	—	4.16	1.92
⊕ School Specialty	Ind Mtrls	18.3	13.38	1.85
⊕ Jackson Hewitt Tax Servi	Consumer	—	—	1.77
⊕ RC2	Goods	14.4	56.51	1.69
⊕ Pacer International	Business	19.9	5.14	1.68
⊕ Avocent	Hardware	NMF	11.20	1.63
⊕ Aeroflex	Hardware	30.3	3.50	1.62
⊕ TNS	Telecom	—	—	1.60
⊖ The First Marblehead	Financial	—	157.08	1.53
⊕ Texas Capital Bancshares	Financial	—	49.31	1.53
⊕ PSS World Medical	Health	26.6	3.77	1.57
⊕ W-H Energy Services	Energy	35.6	38.03	1.56
⊕ ElkCorp	Energy	22.4	29.15	1.51
⊕ LabOne	Health	23.9	-1.32	1.5[illegible]
⊕ Progress Software	Software	27.5	14.13	1.50
⊕ Too	Consumer	30.8	44.91	1.50
⊕ Findwhat.com	Business	25.7	-5.44	1.48
⊕ Inter-tel	Hardware	21.9	10.75	1.48
⊕ DSP Group	Software	12.5	-10.50	1.46
⊕ Autobytel	Consumer	24.0	-33.70	1.46

Current Investment Style

Value Blnd Growth; Large Mid Small

Market Cap	%
Giant	0.0
Large	0.0
Mid	7.0
Small	77.3
Micro	15.6

Avg $mil: 696

Value Measures		Rel Category
Price/Earnings	20.77	0.96
Price/Book	2.06	0.78
Price/Sales	1.36	0.91
Price/Cash Flow	6.13	0.77
Dividend Yield %	0.54	1.74

Growth Measures	%	Rel Category
Long-Term Erngs	17.74	1.03
Book Value	10.36	1.68
Sales	6.79	1.05
Cash Flow	9.[illegible]2	0.67
Historical Erngs	11.38	0.84

Profitability	%	Rel Category
Return on Equity	9.90	1.00
Return on Assets	6.62	1.51
Net Margin	8.[illegible]4	1.19

Sector Weightings	% of Stocks	Rel S&P 500	3 Year High	3 Year Low
Info	32.20	1.50		
Software	11.82	2.75	14	5
Hardware	16.67	1.63	18	10
Media	0.87	0.23	5	0
Telecom	2.84	0.90	8	2
Service	46.83	1.01		
Health	13.34	1.07	19	11
Consumer	9.03	0.99	19	9
Business	14.86	3.67	20	10
Financial	9.60	0.46	12	7
Mfg	20.96	0.65		
Goods	4.28	0.46	4	1
Ind Mtrls	9.91	0.78	10	5
Energy	6.77	0.95	9	4
Utilities	0.00	0.00	0	0

Composition

Cash	3.4
Stocks	96.6
Bonds	0.0
Other	0.0
Foreign (% of Stock)	1.1

Morningstar's Take by Dan McNeela 12-20-04

Shoppers for small-cap funds lost out on good opportunity, as Artisan Small Cap Fund has closed to new investors.

At the close of business on Dec. 17, 2004, this fund stopped accepting most new accounts. In doing so, Artisan fulfilled its promise to turn off the taps when assets in the fund reach the $400 million mark.

Limiting the fund's asset growth is a positive sign for investors. Staying small should help the managers continue to execute their strategy without worrying about impacting the market with their trading. Many rival small-cap funds have pushed their capacity limits by taking in more than $1 billion before closing.

The fund continues to deliver on the performance front as well. Its 19% year-to-date gain through December 13 ranks in the top decile of Morningstar's small-cap growth category. The fund's valuation discipline has served it well. Management sold some semiconductor stocks when they got expensive early in the year, avoiding a downturn that came in the late summer. Now with prices looking more attractive, management is wading back in.

The fund has also found interesting stock-specific stories. New comanager Craigh Cepukenas, who had been an analyst on the fund for nine years, led the effort on The First Marblehead Corporation. That firm has shown explosive growth as it becomes a bigger player in servicing student loans.

We also like the checks and balances that management has installed. Top positions rarely exceed 2% of assets and any of the three managers can veto an idea if he or she isn't comfortable with the investment thesis.

Investors who already own this fund should be pleased to hold it.

Address:	875 East Wisconsin Avenue Suite 800 Milwaukee, WI 53202 800-344-1770
Web Address:	www.artisanfunds.com
Inception:	03-28-95*
Advisor:	Artisan Partners Limited Partnership
Subadvisor:	None
NTF Plans:	Fidelity Retail-NTF, Schwab OneSource

Minimum Purchase:	Closed	Add: —	IRA: —
Min Auto Inv Plan:	Closed	Add: —	
Sales Fees:	No-load		
Management Fee:	1.00% mx./0.93% mn.		
Actual Fees:	Mgt:1.00%	Dist:	
Expense Projections:	3Yr:$403	5Yr:$697	10Yr:$1534
Income Distrib:	Annually		

Artisan Small Cap Value

Ticker	Load	NAV	Yield	Total Assets	Mstar Category
ARTVX	Closed	$17.61	0.0%	$1,400 mil	Small Value

Governance and Management

Fiduciary Grade: B

Portfolio Manager(s)

Scott Satterwhite has been on board since the fund's inception in late 1997. Before that, he amassed a strong record as manager of Wachovia Special Values. James Kieffer has been with the fund since its inception, starting as an analyst and moving up to comanager in mid-2000.

Strategy

Managers Scott Satterwhite and James Kieffer like small-cap stocks that are really cheap. They look for names that are selling at 30% to 50% discounts to their estimates of the companies' private-market values. They won't simply own a stock because it's on sale, however. They also want the safety that comes with owning cash-rich companies with limited debt loads. The managers also limit position sizes to 5% of assets.

Historical Profile

Return Above Avg
Risk Below Avg
Rating ★★★★ Above Avg

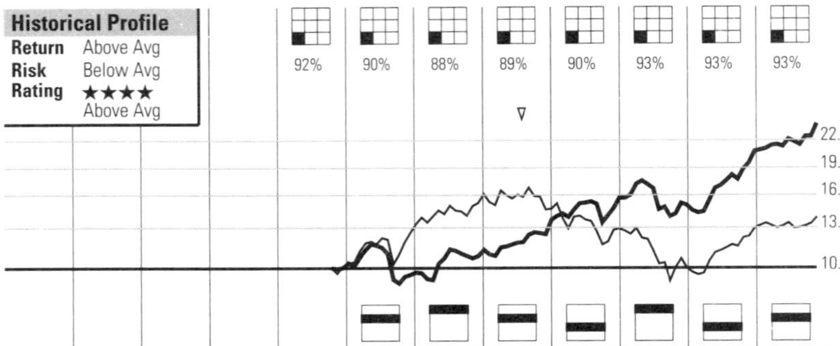

Investment Style
Equity
Stock %

▼ Manager Change
▽ Partial Manager Change

Growth of $10,000
— Investment Values of Fund
— Investment Values of S&P 500

Performance Quartile (within Category)

1993	1994	1995	1996	1997	1998	1999	2000	2001	2002	2003	12-04	History
—	—	—	—	10.31	9.14	10.16	11.70	12.68	11.60	16.08	17.61	NAV
—	—	—	—	3.10*	-5.76	15.42	20.83	15.04	-4.44	40.54	21.15	Total Return %
—	—	—	—	—	-34.33	-5.62	29.93	26.92	17.65	11.87	10.28	+/-S&P 500
—	—	—	—	—	0.69	16.91	-2.00	1.02	6.99	-5.49	-1.10	+/-Russ 2000 VL
—	—	—	—	0.00	0.00	0.30	0.52	0.14	0.00	0.00	0.00	Income Return %
—	—	—	—	—	-5.76	15.12	20.31	14.90	-4.44	40.54	21.15	Capital Return %
—	—	—	—	—	44	19	42	57	22	52	49	Total Rtn % Rank Cat
—	—	—	—	0.00	0.00	0.03	0.05	0.02	0.00	0.00	0.00	Income $
—	—	—	—	0.00	0.54	0.35	0.49	0.71	0.50	0.20	1.78	Capital Gains $
—	—	—	—	—	1.93	1.66	1.35	1.20	1.20	1.21	1.18	Expense Ratio %
—	—	—	—	—	-0.50	-0.45	0.60	0.45	-0.10	-0.21	-0.17	Income Ratio %
—	—	—	—	—	53	49	38	41	34	12	41	Turnover Rate %
—	—	—	—	24	54	143	335	523	566	616	1,400	Net Assets $mil

Performance 12-31-04

	1st Qtr	2nd Qtr	3rd Qtr	4th Qtr	Total
2000	1.57	3.00	6.68	8.26	20.83
2001	1.79	9.57	-11.80	16.94	15.04
2002	9.38	-2.81	-16.39	7.51	-4.44
2003	-3.97	18.04	3.95	19.26	40.54
2004	3.73	3.90	1.73	10.50	21.15

Trailing	Total Return%	+/- S&P 500	+/- Russ 2000 VL	%Rank Cat	Growth of $10,000
3 Mo	10.50	1.27	-2.70	83	11,050
6 Mo	12.41	5.22	-0.96	44	11,241
1 Yr	21.15	10.28	-1.10	49	12,115
3 Yr Avg	17.62	14.04	1.12	28	16,272
5 Yr Avg	17.73	20.03	0.50	30	22,617
10 Yr Avg	—	—	—	—	—
15 Yr Avg	—	—	—	—	—

Tax Analysis	Tax-Adj Rtn%	%Rank Cat	Tax-Cost Rat	%Rank Cat
3 Yr (estimated)	16.32	26	1.11	65
5 Yr (estimated)	16.11	34	1.38	71
10 Yr (estimated)	—	—	—	—

Potential Capital Gain Exposure: 26% of assets

Rating and Risk

Time Period	Load-Adj Return %	Morningstar Rtn vs Cat	Morningstar Risk vs Cat	Morningstar Risk-Adj Rating
1 Yr	21.15			
3 Yr	17.62	+Avg	-Avg	★★★★
5 Yr	17.73	+Avg	-Avg	★★★★
10 Yr	—	—	—	—
Incept	13.69			

Other Measures	Standard Index S&P 500	Best Fit Index Russ 2000 VL
Alpha	14.4	3.9
Beta	0.77	0.79
R-Squared	59	86
Standard Deviation	17.52	
Mean	17.62	
Sharpe Ratio	0.94	

Portfolio Analysis 09-30-04

Share change since 06-04 Total Stocks:106	Sector	PE	YTD Ret%	% Assets
⊕ Kellwood	Goods	10.9	-14.44	3.42
⊕ Stewart Information Serv	Financial	8.6	3.78	3.27
⊖ Plains Exploration & Pro	Energy	—	68.94	3.07
⊕ Hilb Rogal & Hobbs Compa	Financial	15.0	14.30	2.94
⊕ Stone Energy	Energy	9.1	6.22	2.67
⊕ Forest Oil	Energy	20.7	11.03	2.64
⊕ Zale	Goods	13.1	12.29	2.57
⊕ Simpson Manufacturing	Ind Mtrls	15.8	37.98	2.27
⊕ Advo	Business	21.1	13.82	2.06
⊕ PNM Resources	Utilities	17.8	39.12	1.99
⊕ St. Mary Land & Explorat	Energy	14.8	46.85	1.96
⊕ Kirby	Business	21.8	27.24	1.88
⊕ Superior Industries Inte	Ind Mtrls	12.6	-32.12	1.69
⊕ Payless ShoeSource	Consumer	—	-8.21	1.42
⊖ Cabot Oil & Gas A	Energy	18.1	51.42	1.40
⊖ USF	Business	27.3	12.18	1.33
Range Resources	Energy	35.8	117.27	1.32
⊕ Hollywood Entertainment	Consumer	10.7	-4.80	1.32
⊕ Watson Wyatt & Company H	Business	16.6	12.55	1.31
⊕ Movie Gallery	Consumer	12.0	2.75	1.30

Current Investment Style

Value Blnd Growth — Large / Mid / Small

Market Cap	%
Giant	0.0
Large	0.0
Mid	7.4
Small	82.3
Micro	10.3
Avg $mil:	860

Value Measures		Rel Category
Price/Earnings	14.80	0.93
Price/Book	1.63	0.98
Price/Sales	0.73	0.97
Price/Cash Flow	5.08	0.98
Dividend Yield %	0.59	0.49

Growth Measures	%	Rel Category
Long-Term Erngs	11.08	0.91
Book Value	7.04	1.63
Sales	0.44	0.14
Cash Flow	16.17	7.45
Historical Erngs	11.16	2.32

Profitability	%	Rel Category
Return on Equity	11.65	1.28
Return on Assets	5.92	1.43
Net Margin	8.25	1.23

Sector Weightings	% of Stocks	Rel S&P 500	3 Year High	3 Year Low
Info	4.98	0.23		
Software	0.95	0.22	3	0
Hardware	2.39	0.23	4	0
Media	0.55	0.14	2	0
Telecom	1.09	0.35	1	0
Service	44.61	0.96		
Health	2.11	0.17	3	1
Consumer	9.05	1.00	11	1
Business	18.70	4.62	19	10
Financial	14.75	0.71	17	14
Mfg	50.42	1.57		
Goods	8.01	0.86	11	7
Ind Mtrls	16.42	1.30	39	16
Energy	20.71	2.89	22	14
Utilities	5.28	1.78	9	2

Composition

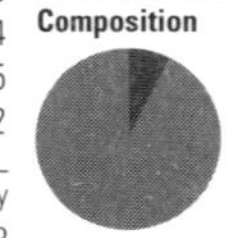

Cash	7.3
Stocks	92.7
Bonds	0.0
Other	0.0
Foreign (% of Stock)	1.1

Morningstar's Take by William Samuel Rocco 11-03-04

Long-closed Artisan Small Value remains stricter and stronger than most of its peers.

This fund remains more hard-core than most of its rivals. Scott Satterwhite and Jim Kieffer have historically paid even more attention to the traditional value sectors than most managers in their category do. Many of their peers have been finding bargains in the growth sectors, due to the persistent weakness in areas such as hardware and telecom and the ongoing strength in areas like industrials and commodities. But Satterwhite and Kieffer, low-turnover managers who prefer to keep cash limited, have largely stuck to their guns. The fund continues to sport one of the heftiest energy stakes in the group and heavy business-services and utilities stakes as well as light hardware and health-care positions.

The duo has executed its exacting strategy pretty well thus far in 2004 and in years past. The fund has gained about 1 percentage point more than the small-value norm for the year to date through November 2, buoyed by Plains Exploration & Production and other energy picks. It posted a mix of solid and good results during its first six calendar years. Overall, it has posted an 8.3% annualized return of since its late-1997 inception, whereas the typical small-value fund has earned a 4.0% annualized return over that period.

Investors in this closed offering have other reasons to be happy here. It has been less volatile than most of its small-value rivals over time, thanks to Satterwhite and Kieffer's uncompromising value style. The two managers have gotten off to a terrific start at Artisan Mid Cap Value--which is open to new investors--and they had a good bit of success at Wachovia before joining Artisan. And Artisan is a fairly fundholder-friendly shop.

In short, this fund is one of the strongest offerings in the small-value group.

Address:	875 East Wisconsin Avenue Suite 800 Milwaukee, WI 53202 800-344-1770
Web Address:	www.artisanfunds.com
Inception:	09-29-97 *
Advisor:	Artisan Partners Limited Partnership
Subadvisor:	None
NTF Plans:	Fidelity Retail-NTF, Schwab OneSource

Minimum Purchase:	Closed	Add: —	IRA: —
Min Auto Inv Plan:	Closed	Add: —	
Sales Fees:	No-load		
Management Fee:	1.00% mx./0.93% mn.		
Actual Fees:	Mgt:0.98%	Dist:	
Expense Projections:	3Yr:$375	5Yr:$649	10Yr:$1432
Income Distrib:	Annually		

Atlantic Whitehall Growth

Ticker	Load	NAV	Yield	Total Assets	Mstar Category
WHGFX	None	$14.54	0.0%	$ mil	Large Growth

Governance and Management

Fiduciary Grade: C

Portfolio Manager(s)

Fred Weiss and Jeff Thomas replaced Paul Blaustein as head stock-pickers in October 2003. Both have worked together at Atlantic Trust since 1989. They have no record running a public mutual fund, but they have an above-average record on institutional and separate accounts run in a similar style. They are supported by five full-time analysts.

Strategy

Despite a management change in 2003, don't expect a strategy change. This fund should continue to maintain a compact portfolio of about 35 to 40 stocks. It owns large, established companies that sport above-average growth in sales and earnings and sustainable competitive advantages. Valuation work takes a backseat to a focus on long-term growth, and sector bets are the norm here. This fund sports a very low turnover rate--once management finds a stock it likes, it tends to hold on for years.

Historical Profile

Return Above Avg
Risk Above Avg
Rating ★★★ Neutral

Investment Style: Equity, Stock %: 95% (1996), 96% (1997), 98% (1998), 92% (1999), 90% (2000), 85% (2001), 92% (2002), 100% (2003)

▼ Manager Change
▽ Partial Manager Change

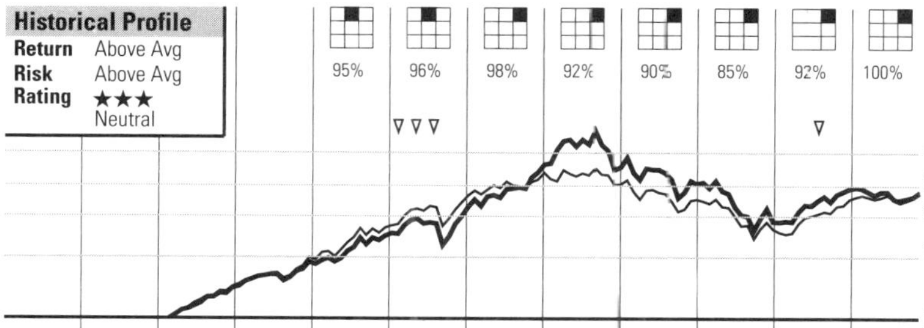

Performance Quartile (within Category)

1993	1994	1995	1996	1997	1998	1999	2000	2001	2002	2003	12-04	History
—	—	12.55	13.56	15.34	15.71	20.15	19.16	16.67	12.15	16.02	14.54	NAV
—	—	31.35*	20.64	29.91	24.89	42.54	-2.09	-13.00	-27.11	31.85	-0.46	Total Return %
—	—	—	-2.30	-3.44	-3.68	21.50	7.0[illegible]	-1.12	-5.02	3.18	-11.33	+/-S&P 500
—	—	—	-2.48	-0.58	-13.82	9.38	20.33	7.42	0.77	2.10	-6.76	+/-Russ 1000Gr
—	—	0.00	1.10	1.82	0.33	0.00	0.00	0.00	0.00	0.00	0.00	Income Return %
—	—	—	19.54	28.09	24.56	42.54	-2.09	-13.00	-27.11	31.85	-0.46	Capital Return %
—	—	—	41	35	75	32	12	14	48	23	96	Total Rtn % Rank Cat
—	—	0.13	0.14	0.24	0.05	0.00	0.00	0.00	0.00	0.00	0.00	Income $
—	—	0.45	1.45	1.96	2.85	2.23	0.58	0.00	0.00	0.00	1.41	Capital Gains $
—	—	0.89	0.89	0.89	0.94	0.93	1.24	1.33	1.33	1.39	—	Expense Ratio %
—	—	1.30	0.93	0.74	0.32	-0.23	-0.63	-0.55	-0.72	-0.70	—	Income Ratio %
—	—	37	27	44	92	6	7	1	9	[illegible]4	—	Turnover Rate %
—	—	89	89	110	135	143	132	148	135	161	—	Net Assets $mil

Performance 12-31-04

	1st Qtr	2nd Qtr	3rd Qtr	4th Qtr	Total
2000	21.64	1.18	-4.19	-16.97	-2.09
2001	-10.02	8.82	-21.06	12.56	-13.00
2002	2.46	-19.50	-17.89	7.62	-27.11
2003	-0.16	14.43	3.39	11.64	31.85
2004	-2.56	-0.06	-6.09	8.84	-0.47

Trailing	Total Return%	+/- S&P 500	+/- Russ 1000Gr	%Rank Cat	Growth of $10,000
3 Mo	8.84	-0.39	-0.33	71	10,884
6 Mo	2.21	-4.98	-1.26	85	10,221
1 Yr	-0.46	-11.33	-6.76	96	9,954
3 Yr Avg	-1.47	-5.05	-1.29	64	9,565
5 Yr Avg	-4.01	-1.71	5.28	20	8,149
10 Yr Avg	—	—	—	—	—
15 Yr Avg	—	—	—	—	—

Tax Analysis	Tax-Adj Rtn%	%Rank Cat	Tax-Cost Rat	%Rank Cat
3 Yr (estimated)	-1.91	62	0.45	70
5 Yr (estimated)	-4.38	17	0.39	24
10 Yr (estimated)	—	—	—	—

Potential Capital Gain Exposure: 0% of assets

Rating and Risk

Time Period	Load-Adj Return %	Morningstar Rtn vs Cat	Morningstar Risk vs Cat	Morningstar Risk-Adj Rating
1 Yr	-0.46			
3 Yr	-1.47	Avg	+Avg	★★
5 Yr	-4.01	+Avg	+Avg	★★★
10 Yr	—	—	—	—
Incept	11.66			

Other Measures	Standard Index S&P 500	Best Fit Index PSE Tech 100
Alpha	-4.8	-5.3
Beta	1.15	0.69
R-Squared	87	94
Standard Deviation	18.53	
Mean	-1.47	
Sharpe Ratio	-0.16	

Portfolio Analysis 11-30-04

Share change since 10-04 Total Stocks:44	Sector	PE	YTD Ret%	% Assets
⊖ Microsoft	Software	36.1	8.95	4.19
SLM	Financial	15.8	44.21	4.11
Vodafone Group PLC ADR	Telecom	—	11.74	3.87
UnitedHealth Group	Health	23.8	51.38	3.84
⊖ Comcast	Media	—	-13.77	3.53
⊖ Wells Fargo	Financial	15.5	8.97	3.48
⊕ Dell	Hardware	34.0	24.01	3.38
⊖ Medtronic	Health	30.7	2.68	3.26
Caremark RX	Health	32.8	55.67	3.18
⊖ Affiliated Computer Serv	Business	14.7	10.52	3.12
⊖ Costco Wholesale	Consumer	25.6	31.15	3.11
⊖ Cisco Systems	Hardware	24.5	-20.26	3.07
⊖ Amgen	Health	37.7	3.82	3.05
⊖ Maxim Integrated Product	Hardware	27.9	-13.87	2.73
⊖ Novartis AG ADR	Health	23.9	12.04	2.62
⊖ American International G	Financial	16.2	-0.53	2.56
⊖ Pfizer	Health	22.0	-22.31	2.50
ExxonMobil	Energy	13.9	28.04	2.50
Schlumberger	Energy	40.7	23.84	2.49
⊕ Analog Devices	Hardware	24.2	-18.69	2.47

Current Investment Style

Value Blnd Growth / Large Mid Small

Market Cap	%
Giant	57.8
Large	34.3
Mid	7.9
Small	0.0
Micro	0.0
Avg $mil: 53,899	

Value Measures		Rel Category
Price/Earnings	21.28	1.00
Price/Book	3.27	1.01
Price/Sales	2.16	1.00
Price/Cash Flow	12.91	1.17
Dividend Yield %	0.86	1.12

Growth Measures	%	Rel Category
Long-Term Erngs	14.62	1.04
Book Value	12.48	0.98
Sales	11.05	1.30
Cash Flow	18.88	1.14
Historical Erngs	18.63	1.29

Profitability	%	Rel Category
Return on Equity	19.40	1.08
Return on Assets	11.83	1.26
Net Margin	13.66	1.11

Sector Weightings	% of Stocks	Rel S&P 500	3 Year High	3 Year Low
Info	32.66	1.52		
Software	4.20	0.98	5	1
Hardware	17.93	1.76	37	18
Media	6.65	1.73	22	7
Telecom	3.88	1.23	4	0
Service	54.20	1.17		
Health	23.78	1.90	25	15
Consumer	9.52	1.05	11	5
Business	7.20	1.78	7	0
Financial	13.70	0.66	14	7
Mfg	13.15	0.41		
Goods	2.50	0.27	3	[illegible]
Ind Mtrls	3.33	0.26	4	2
Energy	7.32	1.02	7	3
Utilities	0.00	0.00	0	0

Composition

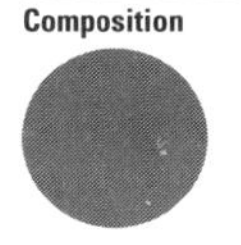

Cash	0.1
Stocks	99.9
Bonds	0.0
Other	0.0
Foreign (% of Stock)	8.1

Morningstar's Take by Gareth Lyons 10-20-04

Atlantic Whitehall Growth's new management team faces an uphill battle.

This fund's new managers, Fred Weiss and Jeff Thomas, took over about one year ago, and things look a little wobbly. Although the average large-growth fund has given up about 2% for the year to date through September 2004, this fund has lost 8.6%.

However, we don't think this short-term performance weakness is enough reason for shareholders to turn tail and run. True, Weiss and Thomas' predecessor, Paul Blaustein, was a talented and seasoned manager. But it's extremely early in this team's tenure, and given this fund's longtime bias toward the tech sector, it was bound to stumble when that very volatile sector did. (Top-10 holding Cisco alone has dipped 23% for the year to date through Oct. 18.)

More broadly, we're also heartened by the fact that both managers have run institutional assets in a similar growth-oriented style for several years, with above-average results. Like Blaustein, Weiss and Thomas will emphasize companies with above-average growth rates, with a focus on the tech and health-care sectors. In addition, the equity research team that supported the former manager remains intact. We think there's enough to build on here for current shareholders to take a wait-and-see approach.

All the same, new investors may want to hold off on putting money to work here. This team pursues an aggressive-growth investment approach and concentrates its bets on a compact list of about 40 names. Because individual stock positions wield considerable influence here, investors need to have the utmost confidence in management's stock-picking expertise. We'd like to see the dust settle a bit before we can properly assess this team's proficiency. A relatively high expense ratio also gives us pause.

Address:	50 Rockefeller Plaza New York NY 10020 800-994-2533
Web Address:	
Inception:	02-01-95*
Advisor:	Atlantic Trust Advisors, Inc.
Subadvisor:	None
NTF Plans:	Fidelity Retail-NTF, Schwab OneSource

Minimum Purchase:	$1000	Add: $50	IRA: $250
Min Auto Inv Plan:	$1000	Add: $500	
Sales Fees:	No-load, 0.25%S		
Management Fee:	0.85%, 0.15%A		
Actual Fees:	Mgt:0.80%	Dist:0.25%	
Expense Projections:	3Yr:$466	5Yr:$820	10Yr:$1817
Income Distrib:	Annually		

Atlas Global Growth A

Ticker	Load	NAV	Yield	Total Assets	Mstar Category
AGRAX	12b-1 only	$21.02	0.3%	$241 mil	World Stock

Governance and Management

Fiduciary Grade:

Portfolio Manager(s)

Bill Wilby, who has managed this fund since inception, has assumed managerial duties at subadvisor Oppenheimer Funds and is slowly transitioning off this fund. He is currently comanaging the fund with his chosen successor, Rajeev Bhaman, who has run Oppenheimer Developing Markets since late 1996 and has compiled a stellar record. Oppenheimer also recently hired a new senior Asia analyst, and the managers interact frequently with other portfolio managers on the strong Global Equity team, including George Evans, Frank Jennings, Mark Madden, and Dominic Freud.

Strategy

Manager Bill Wilby employs a theme-based strategy focusing on companies most likely to benefit from mass affluence, new technologies, restructuring, and aging. He is long-term oriented and keeps the portfolio well diversified. Rajeev Bhaman, who will eventually take over the portfolio, applies a similar investment discipline. This fund avoids stocks of tobacco companies as well as Indian names.

Historical Profile

Return Above Avg
Risk Above Avg
Rating ★★★★ Above Avg

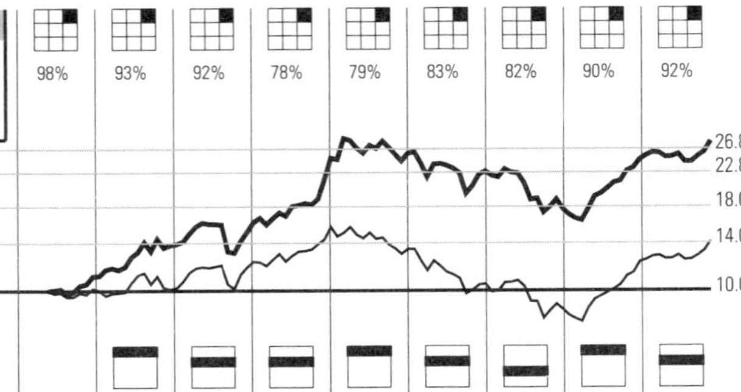

Investment Style
Equity
Stock %

▼ Manager Change
▽ Partial Manager Change

Growth of $10,000
— Investment Values of Fund
— Investment Values of MSCI EAFE

Performance Quartile (within Category)

1993	1994	1995	1996	1997	1998	1999	2000	2001	2002	2003	12-04	History
—	—	—	10.96	12.69	14.56	19.28	18.69	16.52	12.75	17.89	21.02	NAV
—	—	—	10.89*	24.35	16.19	55.85	3.24	-11.61	-22.82	40.31	17.79	Total Return %
—	—	—	—	22.57	-3.74	28.82	17.43	9.81	-6.88	1.72	-2.46	+/-MSCI EAFE
—	—	—	—	8.59	-8.13	30.90	16.43	5.19	-2.93	7.20	3.07	+/-MSCI World
—	—	—	0.00	0.00	0.00	0.00	0.01	0.00	0.00	0.00	0.30	Income Return %
—	—	—	—	24.35	16.19	55.85	3.23	-11.61	-22.82	40.31	17.49	Capital Return %
—	—	—	—	5	47	26	13	28	75	17	28	Total Rtn % Rank Cat
—	—	—	0.01	0.00	0.00	0.00	0.00	0.00	0.00	0.00	0.05	Income $
—	—	—	0.28	0.94	0.18	3.41	1.21	0.00	0.00	0.00	0.00	Capital Gains $
—	—	—	—	1.62	1.53	1.48	1.34	1.38	1.48	1.54	—	Expense Ratio %
—	—	—	—	0.14	0.04	0.49	0.15	-0.08	-0.03	0.06	—	Income Ratio %
—	—	—	—	64	75	103	54	44	39	38	—	Turnover Rate %
—	—	—	13	27	36	70	127	115	89	159	241	Net Assets $mil

Performance 12-31-04

	1st Qtr	2nd Qtr	3rd Qtr	4th Qtr	Total
2000	12.97	-3.31	-1.57	-3.98	3.24
2001	-14.98	8.18	-17.57	16.58	-11.61
2002	1.45	-8.95	-18.55	2.57	-22.82
2003	-7.76	20.66	8.88	15.79	40.31
2004	4.58	-0.86	-1.51	15.34	17.79

Trailing	Total Return%	+/- MSCI EAFE	+/- MSCI World	%Rank Cat	Growth of $10,000
3 Mo	15.34	0.02	3.40	11	11,534
6 Mo	13.60	-1.40	2.78	24	11,360
1 Yr	17.79	-2.46	3.07	28	11,779
3 Yr Avg	8.45	-3.44	1.50	39	12,755
5 Yr Avg	3.08	4.21	5.53	18	11,638
10 Yr Avg	—	—	—	—	—
15 Yr Avg	—	—	—	—	—

Tax Analysis	Tax-Adj Rtn%	%Rank Cat	Tax-Cost Rat	%Rank Cat
3 Yr (estimated)	8.42	34	0.03	5
5 Yr (estimated)	2.79	15	0.28	18
10 Yr (estimated)	—	—	—	—

Potential Capital Gain Exposure: 18% of assets

Rating and Risk

Time Period	Load-Adj Return %	Morningstar Rtn vs Cat	Morningstar Risk vs Cat	Morningstar Risk-Adj Rating
1 Yr	17.79			
3 Yr	8.45	Avg	+Avg	★★★
5 Yr	3.08	+Avg	+Avg	★★★★
10 Yr	—	—	—	—
Incept	13.09			

Other Measures	Standard Index S&P 500	Best Fit Index DJ 60%
Alpha	-3.0	-7.3
Beta	1.01	1.78
R-Squared	91	94
Standard Deviation	17.93	
Mean	8.45	
Sharpe Ratio	0.40	

Portfolio Analysis 12-31-04

Share change since 11-04 Total Stocks:148	Sector	Country	% Assets
⊕ Vodafone Grp	Telecom	U.K.	3.51
⊖ Sirius Satellite Radio	Media	United States	3.21
⊕ Ericsson AB (publ)	Hardware	Sweden	2.22
⊕ H&M Hennes & Mauritz	Consumer	Sweden	2.15
⊕ Royal Bank Of Scotland G	Financial	U.K.	1.94
⊕ Reckitt Benckiser	Goods	U.K.	1.92
⊕ Sanofi-Synthelabo	Health	France	1.75
⊕ J.P. Morgan Chase & Co.	Financial	United States	1.53
⊕ KDDI	Telecom	Japan	1.47
⊕ Advanced Micro Devices	Hardware	United States	1.34
⊕ Transocean	Energy	United States	1.22
⊕ Roche Holding	Health	Switzerland	1.12
⊕ HSBC Hldgs	Financial	U.K.	1.05
⊕ Technip	Energy	France	1.02
⊕ Wachovia	Financial	United States	1.00
⊕ Empresa Brasileira ADR	Ind Mtrls	Brazil	0.97
⊕ Cadbury Schweppes	Goods	U.K.	0.96
⊕ SAP	Software	Germany	0.95
⊕ France Telecom	Telecom	France	0.95
⊕ IBM	Hardware	United States	0.95

Current Investment Style

Value Blnd Growth — Large Mid Small

Market Cap	%
Giant	43.1
Large	40.0
Mid	16.8
Small	0.1
Micro	0.0
Avg $mil: 22,585	

Value Measures		Rel Category
Price/Earnings	17.73	1.12
Price/Book	2.62	1.18
Price/Sales	1.73	1.48
Price/Cash Flow	6.75	1.06
Dividend Yield %	1.61	0.86

Growth Measures	%	Rel Category
Long-Term Erngs	12.47	1.04
Book Value	-2.70	NMF
Sales	4.43	1.06
Cash Flow	13.63	2.33
Historical Erngs	12.87	1.50

Composition

Cash	7.9	Bonds	0.0
Stocks	92.0	Other	0.1
Foreign (% of Stock)			60.6

Sector Weightings	% of Stocks	Rel MSCI EAFE	3 Year High	3 Year Low
Info	33.17	2.00		
Software	4.45	4.12	15	4
Hardware	12.57	3.44	13	7
Media	7.81	3.43	10	3
Telecom	8.34	0.87	10	1
Service	42.66	0.95		
Health	12.90	1.78	22	13
Consumer	7.57	1.50	8	3
Business	2.52	0.46	3	1
Financial	19.67	0.73	21	12
Mfg	24.16	0.62		
Goods	11.50	0.84	20	10
Ind Mtrls	3.47	0.28	8	3
Energy	8.34	1.13	9	5
Utilities	0.85	0.16	1	0

Regional Exposure	% Stock		
UK/W. Europe	39	N. America	42
Japan	9	Latn America	4
Asia X Japan	6	Other	0

Country Exposure	% Stock		
United States	39	France	8
U.K.	16	Sweden	5
Japan	9		

Morningstar's Take by Dan Lefkovitz 12-23-04

Atlas Global Growth's manager transition is worth watching but not panicking over.

Bill Wilby, longtime manager of this long stellar fund, reports that he will be stepping down sometime in 2005 or early 2006. Since August, Wilby has been splitting his time between managing Atlas Global Growth and serving as the senior investment officer of subadvisor Oppenheimer Funds. He has been sharing portfolio management duties on this fund with Rajeev Bhaman, who formerly managed Oppenheimer Developing Markets and will become the sole manager of the Atlas Global Growth portfolio upon Wilby's departure.

One cause for concern is that Bhaman's previous experience was on an emerging-markets fund, whereas this portfolio is concentrated largely in developed markets. As of Nov. 30, this fund had roughly 80% of its portfolio in the United States, Europe, and Japan.

That said, we are heartened by the fact that Bhaman has an outstanding record. In his nearly eight years managing Developing Markets, the fund gained an average of 15% per year, trouncing the emerging-markets category average of 5%. We are encouraged that Wilby is grooming his successor over a substantial period of time and giving fundholders ample notice of his departure.

This transition is important because Atlas Global Growth and its near clone Oppenheimer Global have been so outstanding for so long. Wilby's long-term oriented, contrarian investing style has contributed to the fund's 12.7% average annual gain since its 1996 inception, a record that bests the fund's world-stock rivals by a wide margin. It's illustrative that several of the top contributors to the fund's above-average 2004 gains, such as Sirius Satellite Radio, have been in the portfolio for years. And it's encouraging that Bhaman also uses a patient, low-turnover style. So while no manager transition is completely seamless, this fine fund looks to be in good shape.

Address:	794 Davis Street First Floor, San Leandro CA 94577, 800-933-2852
Web Address:	www.atlasfunds.com
Inception:	04-30-96 *
Advisor:	Atlas Advisers Inc
Subadvisor:	OppenheimerFunds, Inc.
NTF Plans:	Fidelity Retail-NTF, Schwab OneSource

Minimum Purchase:	$2500	Add: $250	IRA: $250
Min Auto Inv Plan:	$250	Add: $250	
Sales Fees:	0.25%B, 2.00%R		
Management Fee:	0.80% mx./0.70% mn.		
Actual Fees:	Mgt:0.80%	Dist:0.25%	
Expense Projections:	3Yr:$486	5Yr:$839	10Yr:$1834
Income Distrib:	Annually		

Baron Asset

Ticker	Load	NAV	Yield	Total Assets	Mstar Category
BARAX	12b-1 only	$52.52	0.0%	$2,002 mil	Mid-Cap Growth

Governance and Management

Fiduciary Grade: B

Portfolio Manager(s)

Ron Baron has been at the helm since 1987, and given that he owns the advisor, he should be here for a long time. His firm employs more than 15 analysts and portfolio managers, but he's the driving force behind this fund's portfolio. Andrew Peck was named comanager on July 23, 2003. He worked as an analyst on the fund for five years before being named comanager and focuses on mid-cap stocks.

Strategy

Manager Ron Baron buys companies he thinks can double in price over the next four years, focusing on steady growers trading at prices that don't yet reflect their potential. He keeps turnover low and gets to know a company's management thoroughly before buying a full position. His attention to value and emphasis on steady growth keep the fund out of the technology sector, but it has frequently owned tech- and communications-related service companies.

Historical Profile

Return Above Avg
Risk Below Avg
Rating ★★★★ Above Avg

Investment Style: Equity Stock %

94%	94%	98%	99%	100%	99%	99%	96%	97%

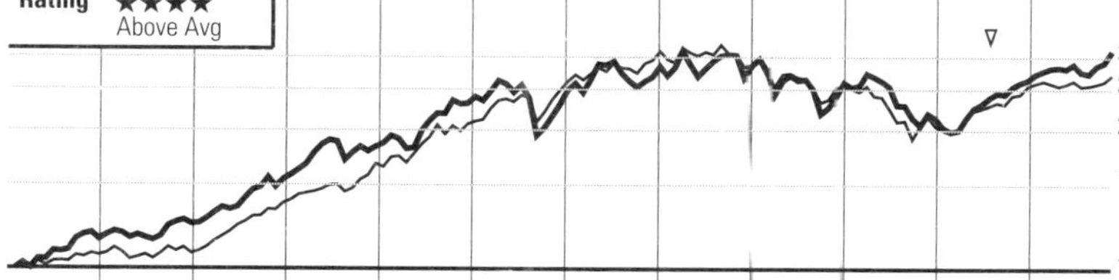

▼ Manager Change
▽ Partial Manager Change

Growth of $10,000
— Investment Values of Fund
— Investment Values of S&P 500

Performance Quartile (within Category)

1993	1994	1995	1996	1997	1998	1999	2000	2001	2002	2003	12-04	History
21.11	22.01	29.74	36.23	48.51	50.54	58.77	54.39	44.46	34.42	43.83	52.52	NAV
23.48	7.42	35.28	21.96	33.89	4.27	16.28	0.36	-10.12	-19.99	27.34	27.13	Total Return %
13.42	6.11	-2.25	-0.98	0.54	-24.30	-4.76	9.46	1.76	2.10	-1.33	16.26	+/-S&P 500
12.29	9.58	1.30	4.48	11.35	-13.59	-35.01	12.11	10.03	7.42	-15.37	11.65	+/-Russ MG
0.00	0.00	0.00	0.00	0.00	0.08	0.00	0.00	0.00	0.00	0.00	0.00	Income Return %
23.48	7.42	35.28	21.96	33.89	4.19	16.28	0.36	-10.12	-19.99	27.34	27.13	Capital Return %
14	9	36	23	6	85	88	40	23	18	89	1	Total Rtn % Rank Cat
0.00	0.00	0.00	0.00	0.00	0.04	0.00	0.00	0.00	0.00	0.00	0.00	Income $
0.77	0.66	0.03	0.04	0.00	0.00	0.00	4.61	4.07	1.18	0.00	2.99	Capital Gains $
1.80	1.60	1.40	1.40	1.30	1.32	1.31	1.33	1.37	1.33	1.34	1.34	Expense Ratio %
-0.70	-0.70	-0.50	-0.30	-0.50	0.11	-0.57	-1.09	-1.14	-1.16	-1.14	-0.90	Income Ratio %
108	56	35	19	13	23	16	3	4	6	28	20	Turnover Rate %
64	87	353	1,326	3,793	5,672	6,147	4,257	3 063	1,945	1,766	2,002	Net Assets $mil

Performance 12-31-04

	1st Qtr	2nd Qtr	3rd Qtr	4th Qtr	Total
2000	10.24	-10.46	9.21	-6.90	0.36
2001	-16.57	9.30	-18.91	21.55	-10.12
2002	6.03	-8.02	-17.78	-0.21	-19.99
2003	-7.09	17.73	6.37	9.44	27.34
2004	7.69	2.52	-1.03	16.35	27.13

Trailing	Total Return%	+/- S&P 500	+/- Russ MG	%Rank Cat	Growth of $10,000
3 Mo	16.35	7.12	2.41	8	11,635
6 Mo	15.15	7.96	6.14	2	11,515
1 Yr	27.13	16.26	11.65	1	12,713
3 Yr Avg	9.01	5.43	2.85	11	12,954
5 Yr Avg	3.16	5.46	6.52	21	11,683
10 Yr Avg	12.08	0.01	0.85	27	31,281
15 Yr Avg	11.57	0.64	0.57	29	51,667

Tax Analysis	Tax-Adj Rtn%	%Rank Cat	Tax-Cost Rat	%Rank Cat
3 Yr (estimated)	8.46	10	0.50	60
5 Yr (estimated)	2.15	19	0.98	43
10 Yr (estimated)	11.52	15	0.50	8

Potential Capital Gain Exposure: 61% of assets

Rating and Risk

Time Period	Load-Adj Return %	Morningstar Rtn vs Cat	Morningstar Risk vs Cat	Morningstar Risk-Adj Rating
1 Yr	27.13			
3 Yr	9.01	+Avg	-Avg	★★★★★
5 Yr	3.16	+Avg	-Avg	★★★★
10 Yr	12.08	+Avg	-Avg	★★★★
Incept	13.29			

Other Measures	Standard Index S&P 500	Best Fit Index Mstar Small Core
Alpha	6.2	-2.9
Beta	0.77	0.82
R-Squared	54	80
Standard Deviation	17.06	
Mean	9.01	
Sharpe Ratio	0.45	

Morningstar's Take by Christopher Traulsen 11-16-04

Changes at Baron Asset give it added appeal.

This mutual fund is having a great year. It's up 18.8% for the year to date through Nov. 15, 2004--among the very best showings in the mid-growth category. The fund has been fueled in part by casino concerns Wynn Resorts and Kerzner International. But across sectors, most of the fund's holdings have performed well (Charles Schwab and Krispy Kreme Doughnut are notable exceptions).

However, changes to the fund's portfolio construction are much more important to our thesis than recent performance. In the past, this fund was badly dented by large positions at the top of its portfolio. But, manager Ron Baron is now limiting top holdings to no more than 10% of assets at market (unless there are exceptional circumstances, and even then, all of the advisor's managers must sign off on the position), and has capped new positions at 2% of assets at cost during the first year of ownership. Both are key, as they would have helped the fund sidestep meltdowns at Schwab and Sotheby's in recent years (the fund still has a huge long-term profit in Schwab, despite its bear-market slide).

That's important. Baron is a great stock-picker, but his confidence in his own abilities has hurt this fund at times. The reduction in issue-specific risk should mesh nicely with the fund's identity as a lower-volatility way to invest in growth stocks: Baron rarely invests in tech and focuses mostly on relatively steady, service-oriented companies that are generating cash and trading at discounts to what Baron thinks they're worth. That's helped keep volatility here mild compared with the typical mid-growth fund, while Baron's stock-picking has delivered strong long-term returns.

For investors seeking small- and mid-cap growth exposure, this fund is well worth considering. It will make an estimated distribution of $3.05 per share to all shareholders of record as of Nov. 22, 2004, so investors may wish to wait until after that date to buy in.

Address:	767 Fifth Avenue, 49th Floor New York, NY 10153 800-992-2766
Web Address:	www.baronfunds.com
Inception:	06-12-37
Advisor:	Bamco Inc.
Subadvisor:	None
NTF Plans:	Fidelity Retail-NTF, Schwab OneSource

Minimum Purchase:	$2000	Add: $0	IRA: $2000
Min Auto Inv Plan:	$500	Add: $50	
Sales Fees:	0.25%B		
Management Fee:	1.00%		
Actual Fees:	Mgt:1.00%	Dist:0.25%	
Expense Projections:	3Yr:$415	5Yr:$718	10Yr:$1579
Income Distrib:	Annually		

Portfolio Analysis 09-30-04

Share change since 06-04 Total Stocks:58	Sector	PE	YTD Ret%	% Assets
⊖ ChoicePoint	Business	30.4	20.74	9.74
⊖ Apollo Group A	Consumer	NMF	19.02	5.28
Kerzner International	Consumer	24.5	54.13	5.24
⊖ Charles Schwab	Financial	32.9	1.77	4.29
XTO Energy	Energy	20.5	56.85	3.87
Wynn Resorts Ltd. Restri	—	—	—	3.56
⊖ Alexander's	Financial	—	72.47	3.10
Wynn Resorts	Consumer	—	138.92	3.02
Vail Resorts	Consumer	—	31.88	2.69
Anthem	Health	17.4	53.33	2.60
Chicago Mercantile Excha	Financial	37.9	218.54	2.56
Choice Hotels Internatio	Consumer	26.7	67.45	2.29
⊕ Commerce Bancorp NJ	Financial	19.8	23.89	2.19
⊕ Southern Union	Utilities	18.5	36.84	2.14
⊕ Manor Care	Health	19.1	4.21	2.12
Whole Foods Market	Consumer	45.4	43.11	2.04
Dollar Tree Stores	Consumer	17.3	-4.32	2.01
Arch Capital Group	Financial	9.1	-2.91	1.93
Polo Ralph Lauren	Goods	20.3	48.73	1.80
NVR	Consumer	12.2	65.11	1.75

Current Investment Style

Value Blnd Growth — Large Mid Small

Market Cap	%
Giant	0.0
Large	16.1
Mid	64.4
Small	18.6
Micro	0.9
Avg $mil: 3,494	

Value Measures		Rel Category
Price/Earnings	19.50	0.89
Price/Book	2.53	0.84
Price/Sales	1.63	0.92
Price/Cash Flow	8.0	0.83
Dividend Yield %	0.16	0.37

Growth Measures	%	Rel Category
Long-Term Erngs	15.13	0.96
Book Value	11.88	1.18
Sales	14.20	1.65
Cash Flow	2.89	0.24
Historical Erngs	19.97	1.26

Profitability	%	Rel Category
Return on Equity	15.75	1.10
Return on Assets	9.00	1.26
Net Margin	10.95	1.14

Sector Weightings	% of Stocks	Rel S&P 500	3 Year High	3 Year Low
Info	2.94	0.14		
Software	0.00	0.00	1	0
Hardware	0.00	0.00	0	0
Media	2.94	0.77	7	3
Telecom	0.00	0.00	0	0
Service	85.36	1.84		
Health	12.46	1.00	12	4
Consumer	34.36	3.78	49	34
Business	18.09	4.47	18	14
Financial	20.45	0.99	20	8
Mfg	11.71	0.36		
Goods	3.40	0.36	10	3
Ind Mtrls	0.00	0.00	9	0
Energy	6.03	0.84	6	3
Utilities	2.28	0.77	2	2

Composition

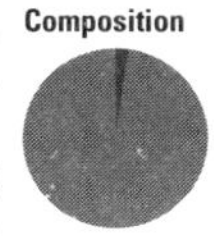

Cash	2.2
Stocks	97.3
Bonds	0.0
Other	0.6
Foreign (% of Stock)	0.0

Baron Growth

Ticker	Load	NAV	Yield	Total Assets	Mstar Category
BGRFX	Closed	$44.87	0.0%	$3,136 mil	Small Growth

Governance and Management

Fiduciary Grade: B

Portfolio Manager(s)

Ron Baron handles the stock-picking responsibilities here. He has run Baron Asset since 1987 and this fund since its inception. The advisory firm employs more than 15 analysts and portfolio managers.

Strategy

Manager and firm founder Ron Baron looks for businesses he thinks can double in price during the next four to five years, based on fundamentals such as rapidly growing earnings or cash flow, or improving margins. He also emphasizes quality of management and stays in close contact with the executives at the fund's holdings. Technology stocks rarely meet the fund's criteria, but the business-services, media, and communications sectors have been favorites.

Historical Profile

Return High
Risk Low
Rating ★★★★★ Highest

Investment Style: Equity Stock %: 94% 99% 96% 89% 98% 83% 99% 90% 91%

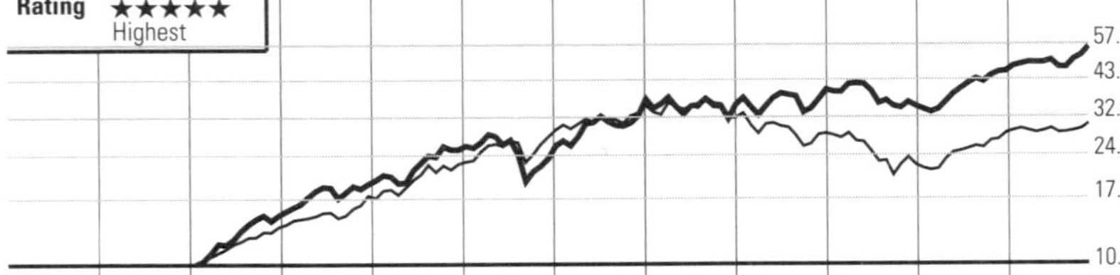

Performance Quartile (within Category)

	1993	1994	1995	1996	1997	1998	1999	2000	2001	2002	2003	12-04	History
	—	—	15.11	19.04	24.88	24.87	33.68	28.82	30.67	26.90	35.44	44.87	NAV
	—	—	52.69*	27.72	31.07	0.10	44.71	-4.59	12.67	-12.29	31.75	26.61	Total Return %
	—	—	—	4.78	-2.28	-28.47	23.67	4.51	24.55	9.80	3.08	15.74	+/-S&P 500
	—	—	21.50	16.46	18.12	-1.13	1.62	17.84	21.90	17.97	-16.79	12.30	+/-Russ 2000 Gr
	—	—	0.37	0.60	0.09	0.14	0.00	0.00	0.00	0.00	0.00	0.00	Income Return %
	—	—	52.17	27.12	30.98	-0.04	44.71	-4.59	12.67	-12.29	31.75	26.61	Capital Return %
	—	—	10	19	12	65	57	44	9	2	93	3	Total Rtn % Rank Cat
	—	—	0.04	0.09	0.02	0.04	0.00	0.00	0.00	0.00	0.00	0.00	Income $
	—	—	0.11	0.16	0.06	0.00	1.88	3.19	1.64	0.00	0.00	0.00	Capital Gains $
	—	—	2.00	1.50	1.40	1.37	1.37	1.36	1.36	1.35	1.36	1.33	Expense Ratio %
	—	—	1.10	1.20	0.40	0.20	-0.20	-0.78	-0.79	-1.16	-1.11	-0.89	Income Ratio %
	—	—	—	40	25	40	53	39	35	18	33	27	Turnover Rate %
	—	—	41	244	415	344	620	500	721	1,214	2,188	3,136	Net Assets $mil

Performance 12-31-04

	1st Qtr	2nd Qtr	3rd Qtr	4th Qtr	Total
2000	1.37	-6.80	1.38	-0.39	-4.59
2001	-7.77	18.66	-13.82	19.47	12.67
2002	4.53	-5.12	-11.37	-0.22	-12.29
2003	-2.49	17.96	5.53	8.55	31.75
2004	7.28	1.68	0.67	15.29	26.61

Trailing	Total Return%	+/- S&P 500	+/- Russ 2000 Gr	%Rank Cat	Growth of $10,000
3 Mo	15.29	6.06	0.21	22	11,529
6 Mo	16.06	8.87	7.90	2	11,606
1 Yr	26.61	15.74	12.30	3	12,661
3 Yr Avg	13.52	9.94	7.73	6	14,629
5 Yr Avg	9.48	11.78	13.05	10	15,728
10 Yr Avg	19.25	7.18	12.13	2	58,155
15 Yr Avg	—	—	—	—	—

Tax Analysis	Tax-Adj Rtn%	%Rank Cat	Tax-Cost Rat	%Rank Cat
3 Yr (estimated)	13.52	5	0.00	1
5 Yr (estimated)	8.74	10	0.68	30
10 Yr (estimated)	18.60	1	0.55	6

Potential Capital Gain Exposure: 42% of assets

Rating and Risk

Time Period	Load-Adj Return %	Morningstar Rtn vs Cat	Morningstar Risk vs Cat	Morningstar Risk-Adj Rating
1 Yr	26.61			
3 Yr	13.52	High	Low	★★★★★
5 Yr	9.48	+Avg	Low	★★★★★
10 Yr	19.25	High	Low	★★★★★
Incept	19.25			

Other Measures	Standard Index S&P 500	Best Fit Index Wil 4500
Alpha	10.6	3.6
Beta	0.66	0.78
R-Squared	55	86
Standard Deviation	15.02	
Mean	13.52	
Sharpe Ratio	0.82	

Morningstar's Take by Christopher Traulsen 12-15-04

Baron Growth is great in many respects, but the fund's board may need to act to keep it in fighting trim.

This fund, which closed to new investors in late 2003, is putting the finishing touches on a fine year. It's up 24.6% for the year to date through Dec. 14, 2004--among the very best performances in the small-growth category.

The reasons for the fund's strength are typical of what Baron does best--ferreting out interesting growth stories before others catch on. Wynn Resorts is one stock that has been a huge contributor in 2004. Baron bought it early in part because he knew Steve Wynn well and thought highly of him as a manager, and in part because he thought the company had great growth prospects in front of it, both in Las Vegas and in Macau.

It's also worth noting that the fund's lack of technology exposure has helped it in 2004. Baron typically stays clear of tech stocks, which he thinks are too unpredictable given his long-term investment approach. That has helped make the fund much less volatile than its typical small-growth peer, while Baron's stock-picking savvy has guided it to excellent long-term returns.

A cloud may be on the horizon, however. Despite closing to new investors in September 2003, the fund received about $1.1 billion in gross inflows in the fiscal year ended Sept. 30, 2004. That's almost as much as the $1.2 billion it pulled in in fiscal 2003 when it was open. (The firm's net inflows dropped to $501 million in 2004 from $815 million in 2003, due to increased redemptions.) Baron president Morty Schaja says the firm is analyzing the asset flows to determine the best course of action. It's the board who decides when to close a fund, however, and it's clear that the action it took in 2003 wasn't sufficient to stem the tide of new money. If the fund is to remain a strong offering, the board may well need to institute a harder close.

Address:	767 Fifth Avenue, 49th Floor New York, NY 10153 800-992-2766	Minimum Purchase:	Closed Add: — IRA: —
		Min Auto Inv Plan:	Closed Add: —
		Sales Fees:	0.25%B
Web Address:	www.baronfunds.com	Management Fee:	1.00%
Inception:	01-03-95*	Actual Fees:	Mgt:1.00% Dist:0.25%
Advisor:	Bamco Inc.	Expense Projections:	3Yr:$443 5Yr:$766 10Yr:$1680
Subadvisor:	None	Income Distrib:	Annually
NTF Plans:	Fidelity Retail-NTF, Schwab OneSource		

Portfolio Analysis 09-30-04

Share change since 06-04 Total Stocks:93	Sector	PE	YTD Ret%	% Assets
Amerigroup	Financial	24.7	77.40	3.45
Wynn Resorts	Consumer	—	138.92	3.14
Chicago Mercantile Excha	Financial	37.9	218.54	3.13
Station Casinos	Consumer	77.1	81.31	2.79
Four Seasons Hotel	Consumer	—	60.10	2.59
Kerzner International	Consumer	24.5	54.13	2.56
⊕ Encore Acquisition	Energy	14.4	41.62	2.45
Charles River Laboratori	Health	24.5	34.02	2.37
⊕ Strayer Education	Consumer	44.4	1.26	2.30
The First Marblehead	Financial	—	157.08	2.25
⊖ Cheesecake Factory	Consumer	39.7	10.59	2.24
ChoicePoint	Business	30.4	20.74	2.20
Centene	Financial	25.4	102.43	2.20
⊕ Edwards Lifesciences	Health	—	37.17	2.16
Arch Capital Group	Financial	9.1	-2.91	2.08
Wynn Resorts 144A Cv 6%	—	—	—	2.02
⊕ P.F. Chang's China Bistr	Consumer	62.4	10.75	1.96
⊕ Community Health Systems	Health	18.2	4.89	1.90
Manor Care	Health	19.1	4.21	1.74
Premcor	Energy	11.0	62.27	1.59

Current Investment Style

Value Blnd Growth; Large Mid Small

Market Cap	%
Giant	0.0
Large	0.4
Mid	54.8
Small	42.4
Micro	2.4
Avg $mil:	1,667

Value Measures		Rel Category
Price/Earnings	20.68	0.95
Price/Book	2.50	0.95
Price/Sales	1.45	0.97
Price/Cash Flow	8.05	1.00
Dividend Yield %	0.05	0.16

Growth Measures	%	Rel Category
Long-Term Erngs	16.35	0.95
Book Value	4.88	0.76
Sales	18.14	2.81
Cash Flow	4.50	0.33
Historical Erngs	19.23	1.42

Profitability	%	Rel Category
Return on Equity	11.75	1.19
Return on Assets	8.49	1.93
Net Margin	7.63	1.11

Sector Weightings	% of Stocks	Rel S&P 500	3 Year High	3 Year Low
Info	9.21	0.43		
Software	1.75	0.41	5	2
Hardware	0.13	0.01	0	0
Media	4.83	1.26	9	5
Telecom	2.50	0.79	3	0
Service	77.56	1.67		
Health	13.18	1.05	14	9
Consumer	33.76	3.72	39	32
Business	9.13	2.25	19	9
Financial	21.49	1.04	21	10
Mfg	13.22	0.41		
Goods	4.47	0.48	7	2
Ind Mtrls	1.33	0.10	6	1
Energy	6.30	0.88	6	2
Utilities	1.12	0.38	3	1

Composition

Cash	6.1
Stocks	90.8
Bonds	0.0
Other	3.1
Foreign (% of Stock)	2.9

Baron Small Cap

Ticker	Load	NAV	Yield	Total Assets	Mstar Category
BSCFX	12b-1 only	$22.08	0.0%	$1,782 mil	Small Growth

Governance and Management

Fiduciary Grade: B

Portfolio Manager(s)

Cliff Greenberg has managed the fund since its inception. He and firm founder Ron Baron share information. The advisory firm employs more than 15 analysts and portfolio managers.

Strategy

Manager Cliff Greenberg invests in firms that he thinks can double in price over the next three years, but he doesn't trade nearly as often as his rivals. He favors firms with strong competitive advantages and, above all, astute executive teams, but he will buy fallen angels, too. Greenberg's long-term bent keeps him clear of the volatile technology sector.

Historical Profile

Return Above Avg
Risk Low
Rating ★★★★ Above Avg

Investment Style — Equity Stock %: 96% | 95% | 83% | 97% | 88% | 96% | 91% | 90%

▼ Manager Change
▽ Partial Manager Change

Growth of $10,000
— Investment Values of Fund
— Investment Values of S&P 500

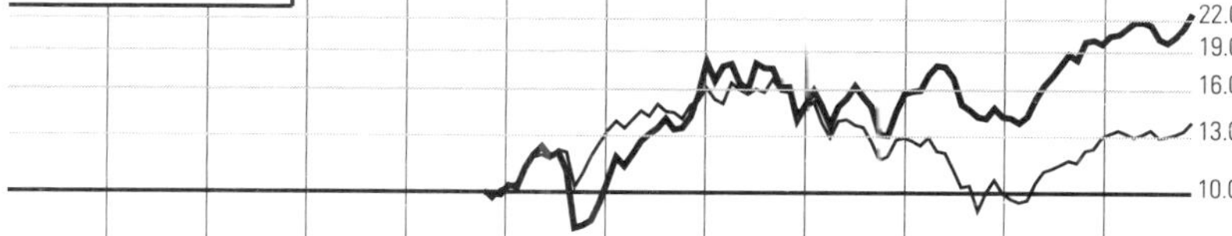

Performance Quartile (within Category)

1993	1994	1995	1996	1997	1998	1999	2000	2001	2002	2003	12-04	History
—	—	—	—	10.31	10.54	18.00	14.46	15.21	13.37	18.56	22.08	NAV
—	—	—	—	3.10*	2.23	70.78	-17.53	5.19	-9.66	38.82	22.16	Total Return %
—	—	—	—	—	-26.34	49.74	-8.43	17.07	12.43	10.15	11.29	+/-S&P 500
—	—	—	—	—	1.00	27.69	4.90	14.42	20.60	-9.72	7.85	+/-Russ 2000 Gr
—	—	—	—	0.00	0.00	0.00	0.00	0.00	0.00	0.00	0.00	Income Return %
—	—	—	—	—	2.23	70.78	-17.53	5.19	-9.66	38.82	22.16	Capital Return %
—	—	—	—	—	53	33	83	17	1	72	9	Total Rtn % Rank Cat
—	—	—	—	0.00	0.00	0.00	0.00	0.00	0.00	0.00	0.00	Income $
—	—	—	—	0.00	0.00	0.00	0.38	0.00	0.38	0.00	0.55	Capital Gains $
—	—	—	—	—	1.39	1.34	1.33	1.35	1.36	1.36	1.33	Expense Ratio %
—	—	—	—	—	-0.20	-0.99	-0.90	-0.68	-0.97	-0.87	-0.88	Income Ratio %
—	—	—	—	—	—	43	53	56	55	30	33	Turnover Rate %
—	—	—	—	285	470	1,089	746	704	748	1,051	1,782	Net Assets $mil

Performance 12-31-04

	1st Qtr	2nd Qtr	3rd Qtr	4th Qtr	Total
2000	-0.89	0.28	-10.29	-7.51	-17.53
2001	-8.78	19.41	-19.43	19.86	5.19
2002	9.01	-1.45	-15.97	0.08	-9.66
2003	0.22	19.55	7.74	7.53	38.82
2004	7.22	1.61	-5.14	18.21	22.16

Trailing	Total Return%	+/- S&P 500	+/- Russ 2000 Gr	%Rank Cat	Growth of $10,000
3 Mo	18.21	8.98	3.13	4	11,821
6 Mo	12.13	4.94	3.97	11	11,213
1 Yr	22.16	11.29	7.85	9	12,216
3 Yr Avg	15.28	11.70	9.49	5	15,320
5 Yr Avg	5.85	8.15	9.42	21	13,288
10 Yr Avg	—	—	—	—	—
15 Yr Avg	—	—	—	—	—

Tax Analysis	Tax-Adj Rtn%	%Rank Cat	Tax-Cost Rat	%Rank Cat
3 Yr (estimated)	14.92	4	0.31	29
5 Yr (estimated)	5.54	18	0.29	13
10 Yr (estimated)	—	—	—	—

Potential Capital Gain Exposure: 43% of assets

Rating and Risk

Time Period	Load-Adj Return %	Morningstar Rtn vs Cat	Morningstar Risk vs Cat	Morningstar Risk-Adj Rating
1 Yr	22.16			
3 Yr	15.28	High	Low	★★★★★
5 Yr	5.85	+Avg	Low	★★★★
10 Yr	—	—	—	—
Incept	12.78			

Other Measures	Standard Index S&P 500	Best Fit Index Russ 2000
Alpha	12.6	6.6
Beta	0.65	0.67
R-Squared	42	73
Standard Deviation	17.29	
Mean	15.28	
Sharpe Ratio	0.81	

Portfolio Analysis 09-30-04

Share change since 06-04 Total Stocks:80	Sector	PE	YTD Ret%	% Assets
Eagle Matls Cl E	Consumer	—	—	3.14
American Tower A	Telecom	—	70.06	2.92
⊖ Career Education	Consumer	20.6	-0.62	2.83
⊕ Immucor	Health	95.1	159.44	2.79
Anteon International	Business	27.9	16.12	2.50
Wynn Resorts	Consumer	—	138.92	2.50
⊕ Gaylord Entertainment	Consumer	—	39.13	2.47
⊕ Strayer Education	Consumer	44.4	1.26	2.45
United Surgical Partners	Health	34.1	24.55	2.44
Alamosa Holdings	Telecom	—	210.97	2.41
⊖ FLIR Systems	Ind Mtrls	27.4	74.77	2.18
⊕ Universal Technical Inst	Consumer	—	—	2.10
⊕ Apollo Group A	Consumer	NMF	19.02	2.03
Panera Bread	Consumer	41.3	2.02	1.92
⊕ Inamed	Health	36.4	31.63	1.90
⊕ Iron Mountain	Business	33.7	15.67	1.87
⊕ Quiksilver	Goods	23.0	68.02	1.8[illegible]
ChoicePoint	Business	30.4	20.74	1.76
WestJet Airlines Ltd	Business	—	—	1.66
Interactive Data	Business	25.8	31.28	1.60

Current Investment Style

Value Blnd Growth — Large / Mid / Small

Market Cap	%
Giant	0.0
Large	2.4
Mid	35.1
Small	50.1
Micro	12.3

Avg $mil: 1,203

Value Measures		Rel Category
Price/Earnings	23.47	1.08
Price/Book	2.64	1.00
Price/Sales	1.57	1.05
Price/Cash Flow	7.71	0.96
Dividend Yield %	0.11	0.35

Growth Measures	%	Rel Category
Long-Term Erngs	18.57	1.07
Book Value	5.30	0.82
Sales	11.[illegible]2	1.72
Cash Flow	29.65	2.19
Historical Erngs	16.91	1.25

Profitability	%	Rel Category
Return on Equity	12.50	1.27
Return on Assets	7.58	1.73
Net Margin	6.83	1.00

Sector Weightings	% of Stocks	Rel S&P 500	3 Year High	3 Year Low
Info	18.11	0.84		
Software	1.41	0.33	1	0
Hardware	0.00	0.00	1	0
Media	7.45	1.94	14	7
Telecom	9.25	2.94	9	0
Service	71.31	1.54		
Health	13.52	1.08	19	11
Consumer	35.89	3.95	37	31
Business	19.50	4.81	31	20
Financial	2.40	0.12	5	2
Mfg	10.56	0.33		
Goods	5.89	0.63	8	4
Ind Mtrls	4.30	0.34	4	1
Energy	0.00	0.00	1	0
Utilities	0.37	0.13	0	0

Composition

Cash	8.3
Stocks	90.3
Bonds	0.3
Other	1.1
Foreign (% of Stock)	2.6

Morningstar's Take by Christopher Traulsen 12-15-04

Baron Small Cap Fund continues to shine, but it may need to close to keep its healthy glow.

There's much to like about this fund. It's run by Cliff Greenberg, an experienced manager who uses a well defined style that meshes well with the research expertise at advisor Bamco. The firm prides itself on being a long-term investor in small-and mid-cap growth companies with superior management and finding those opportunities before others do--when they're still reasonably priced. Greenberg is very much cut from the same cloth, although he sticks mainly to small caps and is a bit more willing to bet on turnaround situations than the firm's other managers are.

The resulting portfolio looks much different than the typical small-growth fund's. Like other Baron managers, Greenberg rarely invests in technology, primarily because the prospects of firms in the sector tend to be so unpredictable that investing in them on a long-term basis is fraught with risk. Instead, Greenberg tends to favor service companies with more predictable earnings. The education area has long been a favorite, for example. Greenberg has recently reshuffled the fund's exposure there a bit, trimming struggling Career Education (the fund's former top holding) and adding to other holdings in the sector.

Greenberg has made his share of mistakes. For example, a big position in UnitedGlobalCom hurt the fund badly in 2000. However, his record on the whole is a very good one, with excellent returns and far less volatility than the category norm, and we think his style is fundamentally sound. Our one concern here is the fund's size--it has grown rapidly in recent years, and we'd hate to see Greenberg hamstrung by having to lug around a massive asset base. Greenberg says the fund's size isn't a problem yet, however, and the firm has indicated it will close the fund at about the same point it closed Baron Growth (roughly $2 billion). If the board makes sure that happens, it will help ensure this fund retains its appeal.

Address:	767 Fifth Avenue, 49th Floor New York, NY 10153 800-992-2766
Web Address:	www.baronfunds.com
Inception:	09-30-97*
Advisor:	Bamco Inc.
Subadvisor:	None
NTF Plans:	Fidelity Retail-NTF, Schwab OneSource

Minimum Purchase:	$2000	Add: $0	IRA: $2000
Min Auto Inv Plan:	$500	Add: $50	
Sales Fees:	0.25%B		
Management Fee:	1.00%		
Actual Fees:	Mgt:1.00%	Dist:0.25%	
Expense Projections:	3Yr:$425	5Yr:$734	10Yr:$1613
Income Distrib:	Annually		

Bernstein Intl Port

Ticker	Load	NAV	Yield	Total Assets	Mstar Category
SIMTX	None	$21.23	0.8%	$2,458 mil	Foreign Large Blend

Governance and Management

Fiduciary Grade: D

Portfolio Manager(s)

Like many of Bernstein's offerings, this fund is directed by a large team of analysts and portfolio managers. Since 1992, the team had been led by Andrew Adelson, who retired at the end of 2003. The group also runs a near-clone of this offering, Bernstein Tax-Managed International Portfolio, which has a solid record.

Strategy

Too soon to say. Team leader Andrew Adelson stepped down at the end of 2003, and the fund has recently been remade as a blend offering, with 50% of its assets managed by a growth team and the other half remaining with value managers. As international funds are especially susceptible to market-timing abuses, the team practices fair-value pricing on a case-by-case basis. If it perceives a need to reprice a security, a committee meets to determine the appropriate price; that new price is then reflected in the fund's NAV.

Performance 12-31-04

	1st Qtr	2nd Qtr	3rd Qtr	4th Qtr	Total
2000	-0.89	2.37	-5.19	0.59	-3.25
2001	-6.05	2.41	-14.44	5.77	-12.92
2002	4.61	0.72	-21.95	10.85	-8.84
2003	-7.18	24.94	5.80	13.58	39.35
2004	3.10	0.38	1.28	13.04	18.48

Trailing	Total Return%	+/- MSCI EAFE	+/- MSCI Wd xUS	%Rank Cat	Growth of $10,000
3 Mo	13.04	-2.28	-2.11	84	11,304
6 Mo	14.49	-0.51	-0.88	37	11,449
1 Yr	18.48	-1.77	-1.90	39	11,848
3 Yr Avg	14.60	2.71	2.38	4	15,051
5 Yr Avg	4.87	6.00	5.63	2	12,684
10 Yr Avg	—	—	—	—	—
15 Yr Avg	—	—	—	—	—

Tax Analysis	Tax-Adj Rtn%	%Rank Cat	Tax-Cost Rat	%Rank Cat
3 Yr (estimated)	14.19	4	0.36	39
5 Yr (estimated)	3.12	3	1.67	87
10 Yr (estimated)	—	—	—	—

Potential Capital Gain Exposure: 14% of assets

Historical Profile

Return High
Risk Average
Rating ★★★★★ Highest

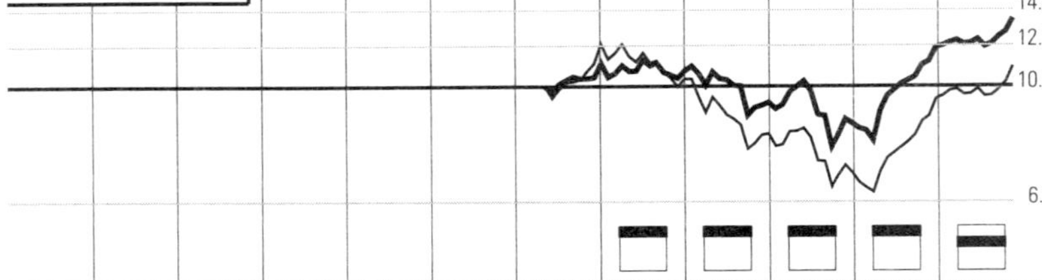

Investment Style
Equity
Stock %
98%

▼ Manager Change
▽ Partial Manager Change

Growth of $10,000
— Investment Values of Fund
— Investment Values of MSCI EAFE

Performance Quartile (within Category)

1993	1994	1995	1996	1997	1998	1999	2000	2001	2002	2003	12-04	History
—	—	—	—	—	—	21.25	17.20	14.53	13.09	18.07	21.23	NAV
—	—	—	—	—	—	10.43*	-3.25	-12.92	-8.84	39.35	18.48	Total Return %
—	—	—	—	—	—	—	10.94	8.50	7.10	0.76	-1.77	+/-MSCI EAFE
—	—	—	—	—	—	—	10.11	8.47	6.96	-0.07	-1.90	+/-MSCI Wd xUS
—	—	—	—	—	—	0.00	3.69	2.62	1.07	1.26	0.95	Income Return %
—	—	—	—	—	—	—	-6.94	-15.54	-9.91	38.09	17.53	Capital Return %
—	—	—	—	—	—	—	3	5	5	13	39	Total Rtn % Rank Cat
—	—	—	—	—	—	0.19	0.79	0.45	0.16	0.17	0.17	Income $
—	—	—	—	—	—	0.02	2.56	0.00	0.00	0.00	0.00	Capital Gains $
—	—	—	—	—	—	1.26	1.25	1.28	1.29	1.29	1.28	Expense Ratio %
—	—	—	—	—	—	2.23	1.09	1.06	0.97	1.63	0.76	Income Ratio %
—	—	—	—	—	—	—	24	45	67	28	92	Turnover Rate %
—	—	—	—	—	—	2,520	1,782	1,541	1,468	2,022	2,458	Net Assets $mil

Rating and Risk

Time Period	Load-Adj Return %	Morningstar Rtn vs Cat	Morningstar Risk vs Cat	Morningstar Risk-Adj Rating
1 Yr	18.48			
3 Yr	14.60	High	+Avg	★★★★★
5 Yr	4.87	High	Avg	★★★★★
10 Yr	—	—	—	—
Incept	6.14			

Other Measures	Standard Index S&P 500	Best Fit Index MSCI Wd xUS
Alpha	2.5	2.0
Beta	1.01	1.02
R-Squared	91	92
Standard Deviation	18.93	
Mean	14.60	
Sharpe Ratio	0.71	

Portfolio Analysis 10-31-04

Share change since 09-04 Total Stocks:100	Sector	Country	% Assets
Canon	Goods	Japan	3.20
⊕ Eni	Energy	Italy	2.64
TOTAL	Energy	France	2.32
⊕ Honda Motor	Goods	Japan	2.29
⊖ Vodafone Grp	Telecom	U.K.	2.17
HSBC Hldgs	Financial	U.K.	2.07
Sanofi-Synthelabo	Health	France	2.07
⊖ AGF	Financial	France	2.06
⊕ ING Groep	Financial	Netherlands	1.94
Tesco	Consumer	U.K.	1.94
BNP Paribas	Financial	France	1.87
Royal Bank Of Scotland G	Financial	U.K.	1.85
Arcelor Grp	Ind Mtrls	France	1.83
⊕ Novartis	Health	Switzerland	1.80
SAP	Software	Germany	1.70
Roche Holding	Health	Switzerland	1.57
Hoya	Goods	Japan	1.56
Carnival	Goods	U.K.	1.52
Continental	Ind Mtrls	Germany	1.50
Reckitt Benckiser	Goods	U.K.	1.49

Current Investment Style

Value Blnd Growth — Large / Mid / Small (Large Blend)

Market Cap	%
Giant	55.0
Large	33.7
Mid	11.3
Small	0.0
Micro	0.0
Avg $mil: 24,345	

Value Measures		Rel Category
Price/Earnings	12.68	0.93
Price/Book	1.97	1.09
Price/Sales	0.84	0.92
Price/Cash Flow	4.38	0.89
Dividend Yield %	2.40	0.94

Growth Measures	%	Rel Category
Long-Term Erngs	11.36	1.06
Book Value	-3.59	NMF
Sales	3.98	1.60
Cash Flow	3.08	0.55
Historical Erngs	5.23	0.94

Composition			
Cash	1.6	Bonds	0.0
Stocks	98.4	Other	0.0
Foreign (% of Stock)			99.4

Sector Weightings	% of Stocks	Rel MSCI EAFE	3 Year High	Low
Info	7.85	0.47		
Software	1.73	1.60	—	—
Hardware	2.72	0.75	—	—
Media	0.15	0.07	—	—
Telecom	3.25	0.34	—	—
Service	47.86	1.07		
Health	9.52	1.31	—	—
Consumer	8.20	1.63	—	—
Business	0.99	0.18	—	—
Financial	29.15	1.08	—	—
Mfg	44.27	1.15		
Goods	16.87	1.23	—	—
Ind Mtrls	19.17	1.56	—	—
Energy	8.23	1.12	—	—
Utilities	0.00	0.00	—	—

Regional Exposure	% Stock		
UK/W. Europe	69	N. America	5
Japan	22	Latn America	0
Asia X Japan	4	Other	0

Country Exposure	% Stock		
U.K.	27	Germany	7
Japan	22	Switzerland	6
France	14		

Morningstar's Take by Gareth Lyons 11-18-04

Despite Bernstein International Portfolio's efforts to diversify, we wouldn't jump in.

In late 2003, Alliance Bernstein decided it would better serve its client base of mostly high-net-worth individuals by transforming this traditionally value-driven fund into a blended one. The fund now targets a 50/50 split between growth and value stocks, with each category run by a separate team.

The move to broaden this fund's mandate seems logical. Because the fund will now own stocks from both the value and growth areas, shareholders who have long held this as their sole international large-cap fund should have a smoother ride going forward. And we can't help but notice that foreign value stocks have enjoyed a particularly good run over the past few years; it seems like opportune timing to increase exposure to growth issues, which could be overdue for improved relative performance. Shareholders should enjoy wider regional exposure, too. For example, the growth team is currently overweight U.K. stocks, while the value squad favors companies from Asia and continental Europe.

On the stock selection front, the growth and value teams are not exactly worlds apart, though. The growth camp--comprised of a dozen-plus investment professionals from Alliance who have earned reasonable success managing institutional accounts--plies a fairly moderate approach to growth investing. Recent additions, such as HSBC Holdings and Royal Bank of Scotland, appear to suggest a bias toward thriftiness rather than pure growth. That should serve the portfolio well when high-priced stocks hit trouble, but we don't expect the fund to shine during pure-growth spurts. A more important caveat, however, was the late-2003 retirement of the value team's talented longtime manager, Andrew Adelson. Granted, the same team that supported Adelson remains, but the departure of the key member who presided over this fund's impressive record is a notable loss. As a result, new investors should hold off.

Address:	1345 Avenue of the Americas Secaucus, NJ 07096 800-221-5672
Web Address:	www.bernstein.com
Inception:	05-03-99*
Advisor:	Alliance Capital Management L.P.
Subadvisor:	None
NTF Plans:	N/A

Minimum Purchase:	$25000	Add: $5000	IRA: $0
Min Auto Inv Plan:	$0	Add: —	
Sales Fees:	No-load		
Management Fee:	1.00% mx./0.85% mn., 0.25%A		
Actual Fees:	Mgt:0.96%	Dist:	
Expense Projections:	3Yr:$409	5Yr:$708	10Yr:$1556
Income Distrib:	Annually		

Bernstein Tx-Mgd Intl

Ticker	Load	NAV	Yield	Total Assets	Mstar Category
SNIVX	None	$22.58	0.7%	$5,281 mil	Foreign Large Blend

Governance and Management

Fiduciary Grade: D

Portfolio Manager(s)

Like many of Bernstein's offerings, this fund is directed by a large team of analysts and portfolio managers. Since 1992, the team had been led by Andy Adelson, who oversaw Bernstein's research process before taking the reins. Adelson retired at the end of 2003, though. Seth Masters manages the overall risk of the fund, which is now split between growth and value teams.

Strategy

Too soon to say. Team leader Andy Adelson stepped down at the end of 2003, and the fund has recently been remade as more of a blend offering, with 50% of the fund's assets managed by a growth team and the other half remaining with value managers. New manager Seth Masters, who manages the overall portfolio risk of the fund, will continue to execute tax-smart strategies. For example, he uses prudent trading strategies to offset capital-gains tax exposure by realizing capital losses.

Historical Profile

Return High
Risk Average
Rating ★★★★★ Highest

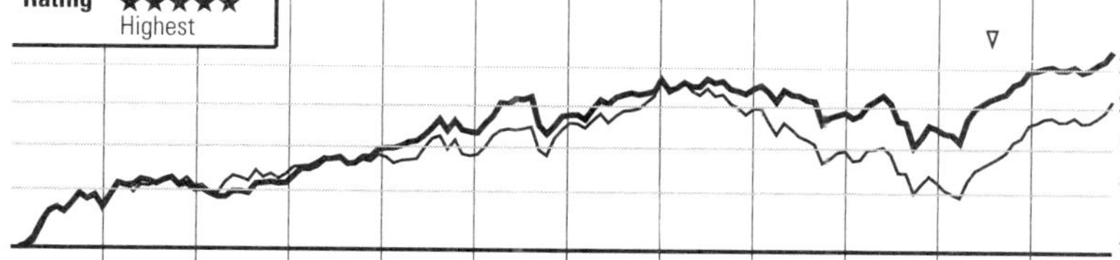

Investment Style: Equity Stock %

▼ Manager Change
▽ Partial Manager Change

Growth of $10,000
— Investment Values of Fund
— Investment Values of MSCI EAFE

Performance Quartile (within Category)

1993	1994	1995	1996	1997	1998	1999	2000	2001	2002	2003	12-04	History
			95%	95%	93%	93%		96%	84%	94%	99%	Equity Stock %
15.59	15.43	16.24	17.85	17.72	17.81	21.54	18.50	15.90	14.35	19.61	22.58	NAV
34.63	3.84	8.03	17.45	9.31	10.95	22.73	-5.05	-12.52	-8.51	38.83	17.58	Total Return %
2.07	-3.94	-3.18	11.40	7.53	-8.98	-4.30	9.14	8.90	7.43	0.24	-2.67	+/-MSCI EAFE
2.42	-3.51	-3.38	10.58	7.04	-7.74	-5.25	8.31	8.87	7.29	-0.59	-2.80	+/-MSCI Wd xUS
0.14	0.77	0.67	6.11	6.22	5.25	0.00	0.75	1.54	1.23	2.09	0.87	Income Return %
34.49	3.07	7.36	11.34	3.09	5.70	22.73	-5.80	-14.06	-9.74	36.74	16.71	Capital Return %
44	16	80	18	34	72	94	7	4	4	15	49	Total Rtn % Rank Cat
0.02	0.11	0.10	0.99	1.11	0.93	0.00	0.16	0.28	0.20	0.30	0.17	Income $
0.12	0.63	0.33	0.22	0.71	0.87	0.30	1.79	0.00	0.00	0.00	0.28	Capital Gains $
1.53	1.39	1.35	1.31	1.27	1.26	1.24	1.24	1.25	1.25	1.25	1.24	Expense Ratio %
1.27	1.13	1.17	1.37	1.37	0.98	0.80	40.62	1.14	1.04	1.59	0.79	Income Ratio %
21	24	30	22	26	30	32	41	46	64	28	71	Turnover Rate %
705	1,429	2,169	3,495	4,698	5,458	3,886	2,868	2,587	2,625	4,108	5,281	Net Assets $mil

Performance 12-31-04

	1st Qtr	2nd Qtr	3rd Qtr	4th Qtr	Total
2000	-1.62	2.03	-5.50	0.11	-5.05
2001	-6.97	3.49	-14.54	6.33	-12.52
2002	4.47	1.08	-21.98	11.04	-8.51
2003	-7.46	24.55	5.93	13.71	38.83
2004	2.75	-0.05	1.39	12.91	17.58

Trailing	Total Return%	+/- MSCI EAFE	+/- MSCI Wd xUS	%Rank Cat	Growth of $10,000
3 Mo	12.92	-2.40	-2.23	86	11,292
6 Mo	14.48	-0.52	-0.89	38	11,448
1 Yr	17.58	-2.67	-2.80	49	11,758
3 Yr Avg	14.30	2.41	2.08	6	14,933
5 Yr Avg	4.40	5.53	5.16	3	12,402
10 Yr Avg	8.88	3.26	2.94	16	23,414
15 Yr Avg	—	—	—	—	—

Tax Analysis	Tax-Adj Rtn%	%Rank Cat	Tax-Cost Rat	%Rank Cat
3 Yr (estimated)	13.72	5	0.51	55
5 Yr (estimated)	3.51	3	0.85	57
10 Yr (estimated)	7.38	14	1.38	72

Potential Capital Gain Exposure: 27% of assets

Rating and Risk

Time Period	Load-Adj Return %	Morningstar Rtn vs Cat	Morningstar Risk vs Cat	Morningstar Risk-Adj Rating
1 Yr	17.58			
3 Yr	14.30	High	+Avg	★★★★★
5 Yr	4.40	High	Avg	★★★★★
10 Yr	8.88	+Avg	-Avg	★★★★
Incept	9.47			

Other Measures	Standard Index S&P 500	Best Fit Index MSCI Wd xUS
Alpha	2.2	1.8
Beta	1.01	1.02
R-Squared	91	91
Standard Deviation	18.90	
Mean	14.30	
Sharpe Ratio	0.69	

Portfolio Analysis 10-31-04

Share change since 09-04 Total Stocks:99	Sector	Country	% Assets
⊖ Canon	Goods	Japan	3.21
Eni	Energy	Italy	3.04
Arcelor Grp	Ind Mtrls	France	2.36
⊕ Honda Motor	Goods	Japan	2.32
BNP Paribas	Financial	France	2.31
⊕ HSBC Hldgs	Financial	U.K.	2.01
AGF	Financial	France	2.00
⊖ Vodafone Grp	Telecom	U.K.	1.97
Nissan Motor	Goods	Japan	1.96
Tesco	Consumer	U.K.	1.91
⊕ TOTAL	Energy	France	1.80
⊕ ING Groep	Financial	Netherlands	1.80
⊕ Novartis	Health	Switzerland	1.76
⊕ Royal Bank Of Scotland G	Financial	U.K.	1.76
Sanofi-Synthelabo	Health	France	1.75
SAP	Software	Germany	1.66
Continental	Ind Mtrls	Germany	1.63
Hoya	Goods	Japan	1.58
Roche Holding	Health	Switzerland	1.56
UBS	Financial	Switzerland	1.52

Current Investment Style

Value Blnd Growth — Large Mid Small

Market Cap	%
Giant	55.5
Large	32.1
Mid	12.5
Small	0.0
Micro	0.0
Avg $mil: 24,458	

Value Measures		Rel Category
Price/Earnings	12.65	0.92
Price/Book	1.90	1.06
Price/Sales	0.82	0.90
Price/Cash Flow	4.37	0.89
Dividend Yield %	2.43	0.96

Growth Measures	%	Rel Category
Long-Term Erngs	11.17	1.04
Book Value	-2.45	NMF
Sales	4.05	1.63
Cash Flow	1.39	0.25
Historical Erngs	1.08	0.19

Sector Weightings	% of Stocks	Rel MSCI EAFE	3 Year High	3 Year Low
Info	8.31	0.50		
Software	1.69	1.56	2	0
Hardware	2.46	0.67	5	1
Media	0.15	0.07	1	0
Telecom	4.01	0.42	6	4
Service	45.90	1.03		
Health	8.90	1.23	10	0
Consumer	8.78	1.74	10	7
Business	0.75	0.14	5	0
Financial	27.47	1.02	30	23
Mfg	45.78	1.18		
Goods	17.79	1.30	34	18
Ind Mtrls	20.54	1.67	21	15
Energy	7.45	1.01	8	3
Utilities	0.00	0.00	3	0

Regional Exposure	% Stock		
UK/W. Europe	71	N. America	5
Japan	22	Latn America	0
Asia X Japan	3	Other	0

Composition			
Cash	1.3	Bonds	0.0
Stocks	98.7	Other	0.0
Foreign (% of Stock)			99.6

Country Exposure	% Stock		
U.K.	26	Germany	8
Japan	22	Switzerland	6
France	15		

Morningstar's Take by Gareth Lyons 11-18-04

Despite Bernstein Tax-Managed International Portfolio's efforts to diversify, we wouldn't jump in.

In late 2003, Alliance Bernstein decided it would better serve its client base of mostly high-net-worth individuals by transforming this traditionally value-driven fund into a blended one. The fund now targets a 50/50 split between growth and value stocks, with each category run by a separate team.

The move to broaden this fund's mandate seems logical. Because the fund will now own stocks from both the value and growth areas, shareholders who have long held this as their sole international large-cap fund should have a smoother ride going forward. And we can't help but notice that foreign value stocks have enjoyed a particularly good run over the past few years; it seems like opportune timing to increase exposure to growth issues, which could be overdue for improved relative performance. Shareholders should enjoy wider regional exposure, too. For example, the growth team is currently overweight U.K. stocks, while the value squad favors companies from Asia and continental Europe.

On the stock selection front, the growth and value teams are not exactly worlds apart, though. The growth camp--comprised of a dozen-plus investment professionals from Alliance who have earned reasonable success managing institutional accounts--plies a fairly moderate approach to growth investing. Recent additions, such as HSBC Holdings and Royal Bank of Scotland, appear to suggest a bias toward thriftiness rather than pure growth. That should serve the portfolio well when high-priced stocks hit trouble, but we don't expect the fund to shine during pure-growth spurts. A more important caveat, however, was the late-2003 retirement of the value team's talented longtime manager, Andrew Adelson. Granted, the same team that supported Adelson remains, but the departure of the key member who presided over this fund's impressive record is a notable loss. As a result, new investors should hold off.

Address:	1345 Avenue of the Americas Secaucus, NJ 07096 800-221-5672
Web Address:	www.bernstein.com
Inception:	06-22-92
Advisor:	Alliance Capital Management L.P.
Subadvisor:	None
NTF Plans:	N/A

Minimum Purchase:	$25000	Add: $5000	IRA: $0
Min Auto Inv Plan:	$0	Add: —	
Sales Fees:	No-load		
Management Fee:	1.00% mx./0.85% mn., 0.25%A		
Actual Fees:	Mgt:0.93%	Dist:	
Expense Projections:	3Yr:$397	5Yr:$686	10Yr:$1511
Income Distrib:	Annually		

Bjurman, Barry MicroCp Gr

Ticker	Load	NAV	Yield	Total Assets	Mstar Category
BMCFX	Closed	$30.75	0.0%	$650 mil	Small Growth

Governance and Management

Fiduciary Grade: B

Portfolio Manager(s)

Tom Barry has been managing this offering since its March 1997 inception. He relies on sell-side analysts, primarily from regional brokerages, for earnings projections, but he also works with a couple of in-house analysts. Barry also runs Bjurman, Barry's other funds, Bjurman, Barry Mid Cap Growth and Bjurman, Barry Small Cap Growth. Barry has worked for Bjurman, Barry as a portfolio manager since 1978.

Strategy

Manager Tom Barry screens the stock universe with market caps between $30 million and $300 million. Barry uses five models. Four look for fairly common growth criteria, including 12-month trailing earnings growth, 12-month forecasted earnings growth, P/E ratios relative to earnings-growth rates, and earnings revision. One, however, is less common and examines price/cash-flow ratios. Barry limits positions to 5% of assets and owns about 200 stocks.

Historical Profile

Return High
Risk Above Avg
Rating ★★★★★ Highest

Investment Style: Equity Stock %

1997	1998	1999	2000	2001	2002	2003	12-04
98%	100%	100%	96%	99%	95%	99%	99%

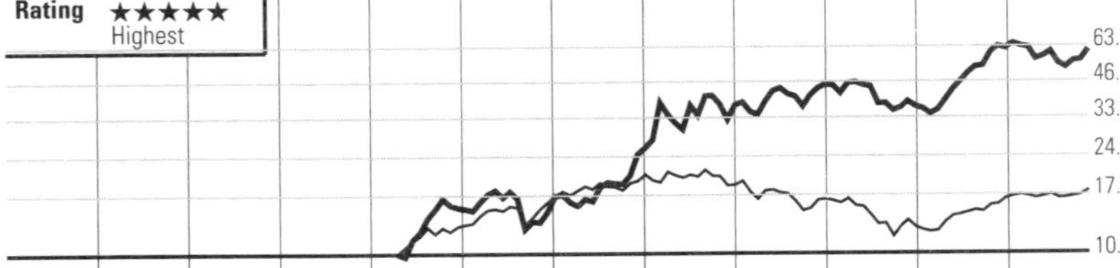

Performance Quartile (within Category)

1993	1994	1995	1996	1997	1998	1999	2000	2001	2002	2003	12-04	History
—	—	—	—	8.96	10.02	15.17	20.60	24.63	20.31	33.89	30.75	NAV
—	—	—	—	49.33*	11.83	53.31	45.57	19.56	-17.54	66.86	3.42	Total Return %
—	—	—	—	—	-16.74	32.27	54.67	31.44	4.55	38.19	-7.45	+/-S&P 500
—	—	—	—	—	10.60	10.22	68.00	28.79	12.72	18.32	-10.89	+/-Russ 2000 Gr
—	—	—	—	0.00	0.00	0.00	0.00	0.00	0.00	0.00	0.00	Income Return %
—	—	—	—	—	11.83	53.31	45.57	19.56	-17.54	66.86	3.42	Capital Return %
—	—	—	—	—	24	48	1	4	11	5	88	Total Rtn % Rank Cat
—	—	—	—	0.00	0.00	0.00	0.00	0.00	0.00	0.00	0.00	Income $
—	—	—	—	0.00	0.00	0.18	1.35	0.00	0.00	0.00	4.13	Capital Gains $
—	—	—	—	—	1.80	1.80	1.80	1.80	1.80	1.59	1.46	Expense Ratio %
—	—	—	—	—	-1.41	-1.58	-1.65	-1.05	-1.40	-1.16	-1.19	Income Ratio %
—	—	—	—	—	110	234	337	159	105	54	65	Turnover Rate %
—	—	—	—	4	10	16	91	275	400	898	650	Net Assets $mil

Performance 12-31-04

	1st Qtr	2nd Qtr	3rd Qtr	4th Qtr	Total
2000	34.28	8.20	8.98	-8.06	45.57
2001	-8.35	26.54	-14.94	21.21	19.56
2002	1.26	-2.93	-19.04	3.62	-17.54
2003	-3.10	28.35	14.81	16.86	66.86
2004	0.78	-3.84	-7.97	15.96	3.42

Trailing	Total Return%	+/- S&P 500	+/- Russ 2000 Gr	%Rank Cat	Growth of $10,000
3 Mo	15.96	6.73	0.88	16	11,596
6 Mo	6.72	-0.47	-1.44	61	10,672
1 Yr	3.42	-7.45	-10.89	88	10,342
3 Yr Avg	12.48	8.90	6.69	8	14,231
5 Yr Avg	19.89	22.19	23.46	2	24,769
10 Yr Avg	—	—	—	—	—
15 Yr Avg	—	—	—	—	—

Tax Analysis	Tax-Adj Rtn%	%Rank Cat	Tax-Cost Rat	%Rank Cat
3 Yr (estimated)	11.78	8	0.62	45
5 Yr (estimated)	18.84	2	0.88	37
10 Yr (estimated)	—	—	—	—

Potential Capital Gain Exposure: 47% of assets

Rating and Risk

Time Period	Load-Adj Return %	Morningstar Rtn vs Cat	Morningstar Risk vs Cat	Morningstar Risk-Adj Rating
1 Yr	3.42			
3 Yr	12.48	High	+Avg	★★★★
5 Yr	19.89	High	+Avg	★★★★★
10 Yr	—	—	—	—
Incept	26.90			

Other Measures	Standard Index S&P 500	Best Fit Index Russ 2000
Alpha	9.8	1.0
Beta	1.00	1.03
R-Squared	50	85
Standard Deviation	24.23	
Mean	12.48	
Sharpe Ratio	0.46	

Morningstar's Take by Kerry O'Boyle 12-13-04

Asset bloat may be taking its toll at Bjurman, Barry Micro-Cap Growth.

It hasn't been a good year for this offering. The fund has lost nearly 3% for the year to date through Dec. 10, 2004, compared with a 7.8% gain for the broader small-growth category. Manager Tom Barry cites a large stake in underperforming technology firms--currently 33% of assets--and surprising weakness among stocks with the highest expected earnings growth as reasons for the lackluster showing.

While these factors have certainly hurt, the fund's sizeable asset base hasn't helped. Although outflows have brought net assets down to $648 million recently, this is still by far the largest micro-cap fund in the category. And 70% of assets are in holdings that have a market cap greater than $300 million--outside of the range set for a stock to be eligible as a new purchase for the fund. That means that only 30% of assets are devoted to the 20 new ideas a week that Barry says his models generate--the kinds of stocks behind the fund's stellar performance prior to 2004.

Contrast that with Touchstone Micro-Cap Growth, the offering that Barry agreed to subadvise in June 2004 using the exact same style. More than 90% of the $30 million Touchstone fund is invested in stocks with market caps of less than $300 million. In the past three months alone, it has outperformed this fund by 3.5 percentage points. Granted, a comparison based on such a short time period needs to be taken with a grain of salt, but it is indicative of how a bloated asset base can lead to subtle strategy shifts that impact performance.

This offering's best days as a micro-cap vehicle could be behind it. While the fund may remain competitive within the broader small-cap group, it isn't the pure micro-cap play it once was. Plus, until Barry can overcome the asset issues and show that 2004's poor showing was an isolated case, shareholders should refrain from sending new money here.

Portfolio Analysis 09-30-04

Share change since 08-04 Total Stocks:157	Sector	PE	YTD Ret%	% Assets
Immucor	Health	95.1	159.44	2.45
Quality Systems	Software	28.7	34.11	2.08
Schnitzer Steel Industri	Ind Mtrls	10.5	-15.68	1.87
A.S.V.	Ind Mtrls	35.4	28.59	1.85
Comtech Telecomm	Hardware	21.7	30.64	1.83
Verint Systems	Software	62.6	61.04	1.76
eResearch Technology	Business	26.8	-6.47	1.72
SS&C Technologies	Software	25.3	11.52	1.61
Applied Signal Technolog	Hardware	28.9	54.66	1.58
Usana Health Sciences	Goods	24.1	11.77	1.53
Finish Line	Goods	17.6	22.50	1.53
Align Technology	Health	77.5	-34.89	1.49
Ceradyne	Ind Mtrls	37.3	151.95	1.48
Stratasys	Software	44.3	24.07	1.46
RC2	Goods	14.4	56.51	1.41
Palomar Medical Technolo	Health	66.6	147.81	1.41
TBC	Ind Mtrls	16.8	7.71	1.40
Rofin-Sinar Technologies	Ind Mtrls	21.1	22.83	1.39
Petroleum Development	Energy	17.7	62.74	1.37
Metal Management	Business	6.5	45.97	1.37

Current Investment Style

Market Cap	%
Giant	0.0
Large	0.0
Mid	0.0
Small	45.9
Micro	54.1
Avg $mil: 369	

Value Measures		Rel Category
Price/Earnings	19.34	0.89
Price/Book	2.69	1.02
Price/Sales	1.07	0.71
Price/Cash Flow	4.67	0.58
Dividend Yield %	0.19	0.61

Growth Measures	%	Rel Category
Long-Term Erngs	18.56	1.07
Book Value	13.61	2.11
Sales	13.76	2.13
Cash Flow	42.43	3.13
Historical Erngs	33.40	2.47

Profitability	%	Rel Category
Return on Equity	15.13	1.53
Return on Assets	9.35	2.13
Net Margin	9.56	1.40

Sector Weightings	% of Stocks	Rel S&P 500	3 Year High	3 Year Low
Info	26.84	1.25		
Software	10.54	2.45	17	4
Hardware	16.09	1.58	19	7
Media	0.21	0.05	0	0
Telecom	0.00	0.00	3	0
Service	40.62	0.88		
Health	20.32	1.63	24	12
Consumer	4.30	0.47	21	4
Business	10.90	2.69	18	10
Financial	5.10	0.25	9	3
Mfg	32.54	1.01		
Goods	7.70	0.83	12	6
Ind Mtrls	19.87	1.57	20	8
Energy	4.97	0.69	5	1
Utilities	0.00	0.00	0	0

Composition

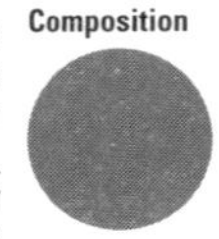

Cash	0.6
Stocks	99.4
Bonds	0.0
Other	0.0
Foreign (% of Stock)	3.4

Address:	10100 Santa Monica Blvd, Los Angeles CA 90067-4103, 800-227-7264	Minimum Purchase:	Closed	Add: —	IRA: —
Web Address:	www.bjurmanbarry.com	Min Auto Inv Plan:	Closed	Add: —	
Inception:	03-31-97 *	Sales Fees:	0.25%B		
Advisor:	Bjurman, Barry & Associates	Management Fee:	1.00%		
Subadvisor:	None	Actual Fees:	Mgt:1.00%	Dist:0.25%	
NTF Plans:	Fidelity Retail-NTF, Schwab OneSource	Expense Projections:	3Yr:$566	5Yr:$975	10Yr:$2116
		Income Distrib:	Annually		

BNY Hamilton SmCap Gr Is

Ticker	Load	NAV	Yield	Total Assets	Mstar Category
BNSIX	None	$15.54	0.0%	$775 mil	Small Growth

Governance and Management

Fiduciary Grade: C

Portfolio Manager(s)

John Lui has been managing this fund since its inception in April 1997. Before this, he spent time overseeing international equity and bond portfolios for both the Bank of New York and for Barclays Global Asset Management. This is his first stint as a retail-oriented fund manager. He's assisted by Nicole Kane, Jeffrey Thibault, and Jason Leinberger.

Strategy

Manager John Lui targets small-cap businesses that are growing earnings faster than the S&P 500 average. He particularly likes companies that have proprietary products or are industry leaders in niche markets. The fund keeps an eye on industry trends, which sometimes steers it toward a cluster of similarly positioned companies, though it generally avoids huge sector bets. Attention to valuation keeps Lui from buying companies with unjustified price multiples and also leads him to sell overvalued stocks. A low-turnover approach means that many of the fund's successful picks are allowed to grow into mid-caps.

Historical Profile

Return Average
Risk Average
Rating ★★★ Neutral

Investment Style: Equity Stock %

1997	1998	1999	2000	2001	2002	2003	12-04
93%	99%	91%	100%	100%	96%	96%	99%

▼ Manager Change
▽ Partial Manager Change

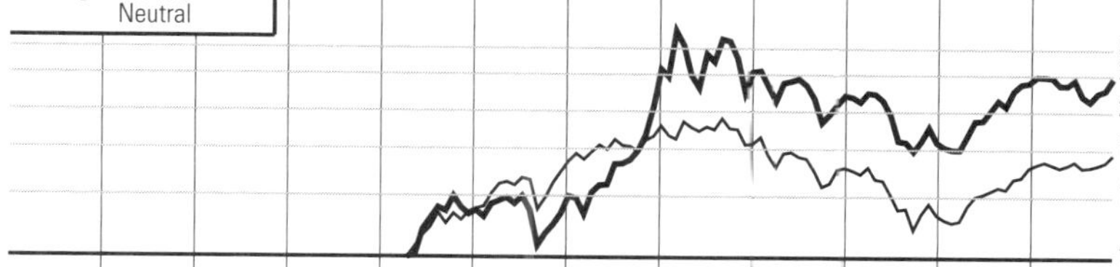

Growth of $10,000
— Investment Values of Fund
— Investment Values of S&P 500

Performance Quartile (within Category)

History

1993	1994	1995	1996	1997	1998	1999	2000	2001	2002	2003	12-04	History
—	—	—	—	11.93	12.46	22.78	17.83	15.53	11.89	15.63	15.54	NAV
—	—	—	—	28.57*	7.89	97.22	-1.41	-11.69	-22.12	37.73	5.59	Total Return %
—	—	—	—	—	-20.68	76.18	7.69	0.19	-0.03	9.06	-5.28	+/-S&P 500
—	—	—	—	—	6.66	54.13	21.02	-2.46	8.14	-10.81	-8.72	+/-Russ 2000 Gr
—	—	—	—	0.00	0.00	0.00	0.00	0.00	0.00	0.00	0.00	Income Return %
—	—	—	—	—	7.89	97.22	-1.41	-11.69	-22.12	37.73	5.59	Capital Return %
—	—	—	—	—	32	18	37	53	25	77	83	Total Rtn % Rank Cat
—	—	—	—	0.00	0.00	0.00	0.00	0.00	0.00	0.00	0.00	Income $
—	—	—	—	0.85	0.36	1.65	4.45	0.22	0.20	0.72	0.92	Capital Gains $
—	—	—	—	0.97	0.97	1.04	1.04	1.05	1.06	1.06	—	Expense Ratio %
—	—	—	—	-0.24	-0.19	-0.73	-0.51	-0.42	-0.58	-0.55	—	Income Ratio %
—	—	—	—	—	—	86	47	53	31	42	—	Turnover Rate %
—	—	—	—	134	188	389	404	349	284	377	681	Net Assets $mil

Performance 12-31-04

	1st Qtr	2nd Qtr	3rd Qtr	4th Qtr	Total
2000	13.70	-4.48	6.96	-15.13	-1.41
2001	-14.36	12.57	-20.79	15.64	-11.69
2002	1.42	-10.92	-17.74	4.80	-22.12
2003	-3.87	16.97	7.88	13.53	37.73
2004	3.01	-1.49	-6.57	11.38	5.59

Trailing	Total Return%	+/- S&P 500	+/- Russ 2000 Gr	%Rank Cat	Growth of $10,000
3 Mo	11.38	2.15	-3.70	89	11,138
6 Mo	4.06	-3.13	-4.10	83	10,406
1 Yr	5.59	-5.28	-8.72	83	10,559
3 Yr Avg	4.24	0.66	-1.55	56	11,327
5 Yr Avg	-0.28	2.02	3.29	46	9,861
10 Yr Avg	—	—	—	—	—
15 Yr Avg	—	—	—	—	—

Tax Analysis	Tax-Adj Rtn%	%Rank Cat	Tax-Cost Rat	%Rank Cat
3 Yr (estimated)	3.57	55	0.64	46
5 Yr (estimated)	-1.66	46	1.38	58
10 Yr (estimated)	—	—	—	—

Potential Capital Gain Exposure: 9% of assets

Rating and Risk

Time Period	Load-Adj Return %	Morningstar Rtn vs Cat	Morningstar Risk vs Cat	Morningstar Risk-Adj Rating
1 Yr	5.59			
3 Yr	4.24	Avg	-Avg	★★★
5 Yr	-0.28	Avg	Avg	★★★
10 Yr	—	—	—	—
Incept	13.65			

Other Measures	Standard Index S&P 500	Best Fit Index Russ 2000 Gr
Alpha	1.1	-0.9
Beta	0.98	0.79
R-Squared	70	95
Standard Deviation	18.51	
Mean	4.24	
Sharpe Ratio	0.16	

Portfolio Analysis 09-30-04

Share change since 06-04 Total Stocks:121	Sector	PE	YTD Ret%	% Assets
⊕ Dick's Sporting Goods	Consumer	29.3	44.47	2.79
⊕ UCBH Holdings	Financial	19.5	18.04	2.55
⊕ AC Moore Arts & Crafts	Consumer	31.2	49.59	2.19
⊕ Greater Bay Bancorp	Financial	17.4	-0.15	2.14
⊕ Columbia Sportswear	Goods	17.6	9.38	1.96
⊕ Semtech	Hardware	27.7	-4.04	1.84
⊕ Respironics	Health	27.6	20.24	1.83
⊕ Amsurg	Health	14.6	16.76	1.81
⊕ Performance Food Group	Consumer	20.8	-25.60	1.75
⊖ Electronics Boutique Hol	Consumer	17.5	87.59	1.74
⊕ Airgas	Ind Mtrls	21.8	24.36	1.71
⊕ Scholastic	Media	42.0	8.58	1.67
⊕ Hot Topic	Consumer	18.8	-41.63	1.64
⊕ Charles River Laboratori	Health	24.5	34.02	1.55
⊕ American Healthways	Health	41.8	38.42	1.52
⊕ FormFactor	Hardware	—	37.07	1.51
⊕ Fred's	Consumer	19.2	-43.61	1.50
⊕ Olin	Ind Mtrls	—	14.81	1.41
⊕ Proassurance	Financial	17.1	21.65	1.40
⊕ Bell Microproducts	Ind Mtrls	26.5	6.18	1.31

Current Investment Style

Market Cap	%
Giant	0.0
Large	0.0
Mid	27.2
Small	58.4
Micro	14.4
Avg $mil: 926	

Value Measures		Rel Category
Price/Earnings	22.62	1.04
Price/Book	2.14	0.81
Price/Sales	0.94	0.63
Price/Cash Flow	9.37	1.17
Dividend Yield %	0.27	0.87

Growth Measures	%	Rel Category
Long-Term Erngs	16.32	0.94
Book Value	8.45	1.31
Sales	5.94	0.92
Cash Flow	10.89	0.80
Historical Erngs	8.23	0.61

Profitability	%	Rel Category
Return on Equity	8.15	0.83
Return on Assets	2.54	0.58
Net Margin	5.46	0.80

Sector Weightings	% of Stocks	Rel S&P 500	3 Year High	3 Year Low
Info	22.39	1.04		
Software	4.13	0.96	5	3
Hardware	13.72	1.35	16	8
Media	4.54	1.18	8	5
Telecom	0.00	0.00	1	0
Service	60.34	1.30		
Health	21.23	1.70	21	18
Consumer	17.64	1.94	18	11
Business	8.95	2.21	10	7
Financial	12.52	0.60	16	11
Mfg	17.26	0.54		
Goods	5.01	0.54	8	5
Ind Mtrls	8.25	0.65	11	5
Energy	4.00	0.56	11	4
Utilities	0.00	0.00	0	0

Composition

Cash	1.2
Stocks	98.8
Bonds	0.0
Other	0.0
Foreign (% of Stock)	0.0

Morningstar's Take by Todd Trubey 11-15-04

BNY Hamilton Small Cap Growth has shifted its hunting ground lately, but its approach remains true.

This fund's impending shift to the small-growth category reflects some key recent changes. In the economic downturn lead manager John Lui moved the fund largely into mid-caps in order to avoid the severe risks that small firms have in bad times. While fund steadily held a 40% or lower stake in small-caps from 2000 to 2003, Lui started buying them heavily when he thought the economy had turned, and the fund now has a 75% stake in them.

From another angle, though, Lui's approach has always been consistent. He buys smaller firms that he believes will have much better long-term earnings growth than the average large firm and holds for a long time. That's why the fund's annual turnover is routinely below 50% while the average small-growth category member's is usually above 130%. Lui especially favors niche players or firms that cater to underserved customers. Oftentimes that means companies that pay close attention to defining and building strong brand identity.

Lui's belief in brands explains why many of his best picks have been retailers. The success of jeweler Tiffany in establishing its luxury-at-a-reasonable price brand, which the fund held from fall 1998 to fall 2002, sparked Lui's interest in Coach, which had huge gains from early 2001 to early 2004. Lui thinks that Columbia Sportswear (held here since early 2001) is similar. The firm has built a reputation for high-quality outdoor sportswear and leveraged it a bit--into shoes, for instance--but not willy-nilly.

The fund's risk/reward profile remains sound. True, the fund has lagged small-growth peers since its move back into those stocks. But the fund was more sturdy than average members of both the small-growth and mid-growth category during the bear market. So we still think it's an okay way to get moderate exposure to smaller growth stocks.

Address:	90 Park Ave. New York NY 10016 800-426-9363
Web Address:	www.bnyhamiltonfunds.com
Inception:	03-31-97*
Advisor:	The Bank of New York
Subadvisor:	None
NTF Plans:	Dreyfus LION-NTF

Minimum Purchase:	$1000000	Add: $0	IRA: $0
Min Auto Inv Plan:	$0	Add: —	
Sales Fees:	No-load		
Management Fee:	0.75%, 0.20%A		
Actual Fees:	Mgt:0.75%	Dist:	
Expense Projections:	3Yr:$331	5Yr:$574	10Yr:$1271
Income Distrib:	Annually		

Bogle Small Cap Gr Inv

Ticker	Load	NAV	Yield	Total Assets	Mstar Category
BOGLX	Closed	$26.33	0.0%	$335 mil	Small Blend

Governance and Management

Fiduciary Grade:

Portfolio Manager(s)

John Bogle Jr. built a strong record running N/I Numeric Investors Emerging Growth from June 1996 until February 1999. He then set up his own firm, Bogle Investment Management, in 1999. He has a small staff of analysts who assist with research.

Strategy

Manager John Bogle Jr. looks for stocks with market caps of $600 million or less. Beginning with this universe, he runs a series of quantitative screens that focus on various factors, including earnings improvement and cash flow. He then follows up with more fundamental work.

Historical Profile

Return Average
Risk Above Avg
Rating ★★★ Neutral

Investment Style
Equity
Stock %: 87% 97% 99% 99% 99% 100%

▼ Manager Change
▽ Partial Manager Change

Growth of $10,000
— Investment Values of Fund
— Investment Values of S&P 500

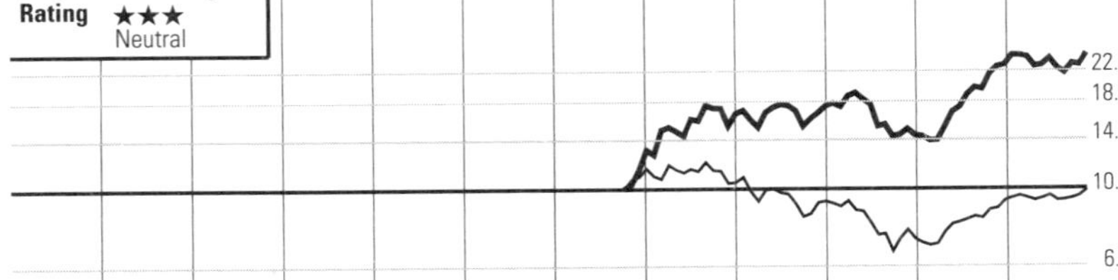

Performance Quartile (within Category)

	1993	1994	1995	1996	1997	1998	1999	2000	2001	2002	2003	12-04	History
	—	—	—	—	—	—	15.61	19.13	20.10	16.57	26.29	26.33	NAV
	—	—	—	—	—	—	30.08*	26.83	5.07	-17.56	58.66	10.78	Total Return %
	—	—	—	—	—	—	—	35.93	16.95	4.53	29.99	-0.09	+/-S&P 500
	—	—	—	—	—	—	—	29.85	2.58	2.92	11.41	-7.55	+/-Russ 2000
	—	—	—	—	—	—	0.00	0.00	0.00	0.00	0.00	0.00	Income Return %
	—	—	—	—	—	—	—	26.83	5.07	-17.56	58.66	10.78	Capital Return %
	—	—	—	—	—	—	—	12	65	65	8	96	Total Rtn % Rank Cat
	—	—	—	—	—	—	0.00	0.00	0.00	0.00	0.00	0.00	Income $
	—	—	—	—	—	—	0.00	0.66	0.00	0.00	0.00	2.48	Capital Gains $
	—	—	—	—	—	—	—	1.35	1.35	1.27	1.35	1.35	Expense Ratio %
	—	—	—	—	—	—	—	-0.68	-0.46	-0.20	-0.69	-0.70	Income Ratio %
	—	—	—	—	—	—	—	94	126	140	122	129	Turnover Rate %
	—	—	—	—	—	—	6	27	69	81	133	139	Net Assets $mil

Performance 12-31-04

	1st Qtr	2nd Qtr	3rd Qtr	4th Qtr	Total
2000	16.08	5.46	7.38	-3.52	26.83
2001	-8.73	16.38	-13.44	14.27	5.07
2002	6.72	-5.41	-18.93	0.73	-17.56
2003	-3.20	24.31	12.49	17.21	58.66
2004	5.52	-1.23	-3.36	9.98	10.78

Trailing	Total Return%	+/- S&P 500	+/- Russ 2000	%Rank Cat	Growth of $10,000
3 Mo	9.98	0.75	-4.11	92	10,998
6 Mo	6.29	-0.90	-4.54	94	10,629
1 Yr	10.78	-0.09	-7.55	96	11,078
3 Yr Avg	13.16	9.58	1.68	40	14,490
5 Yr Avg	14.06	16.36	7.45	37	19,305
10 Yr Avg	—	—	—	—	—
15 Yr Avg	—	—	—	—	—

Tax Analysis	Tax-Adj Rtn%	%Rank Cat	Tax-Cost Rat	%Rank Cat
3 Yr (estimated)	12.55	35	0.54	38
5 Yr (estimated)	13.39	31	0.59	22
10 Yr (estimated)	—	—	—	—

Potential Capital Gain Exposure: 23% of assets

Rating and Risk

Time Period	Load-Adj Return %	Morningstar Rtn vs Cat	Morningstar Risk vs Cat	Morningstar Risk-Adj Rating
1 Yr	10.78			
3 Yr	13.16	Avg	+Avg	★★★
5 Yr	14.06	Avg	+Avg	★★★
10 Yr	—	—	—	—
Incept	19.16			

Other Measures	Standard Index S&P 500	Best Fit Index Russ 2000
Alpha	10.2	2.3
Beta	0.91	0.92
R-Squared	55	91
Standard Deviation	20.95	
Mean	13.16	
Sharpe Ratio	0.57	

Morningstar's Take by Andrew Gogerty 12-07-04

Bogle Small Cap Growth's slump in 2004 doesn't tarnish its appeal.

This fund is in unfamiliar territory. Its 8.8% gain through Dec. 17, lands squarely in the bottom decile of the small-blend category. This is in stark contrast to the fund's competitive performance in the previous four years.

Its low energy stake has contributed to its underperformance, as that sector is up big in 2004. Manager John Bogle Jr. uses a quantitative modeling system to rank stocks on factors such as earnings quality, valuation, and cash flow, which show that earnings growth in the energy sector isn't attractive on a long-term basis. In addition, some of the fund's top picks have stumbled this year. Software maker Aspect Communication, a top five holding coming into 2004, has shed more than 33% this year.

Over time, however, this disciplined approach has served investors well. Unlike other quantitative funds that use static models, Bogle continuously looks for new ways to effectively measure earnings. For example, he added an R&D component to the model this year to measure how management reports research expenses in up and down markets. Bogle also adjusts his focus based on his outlook for the economy. In 2003, for instance, his focus on growth contributed to the fund's tremendous 59% gain. During the bear market, however, it was the model's earnings-quality screen that steered the fund clear of issues that used accounting tricks to boost earnings. We believe this combination of data enhancement and market focus will give the fund an edge over its peers.

We also find it encouraging that Bogle closed this fund in early 2002 when the fund's asset base was relatively small. This allows the fund to remain flexible, and Bogle has put shareholder interests above additional management fees. It remains a sound option.

Portfolio Analysis 12-31-04

Share change since 11-04 Total Stocks:164	Sector	PE	YTD Ret%	% Assets
⊖ Wesco International	Ind Mtrls	22.4	234.92	1.10
⊖ First Cash Financial Ser	Financial	21.5	56.25	1.08
⊖ Building Materials Holdi	Business	11.7	149.48	1.05
⊖ IPSCO	Ind Mtrls	—	159.34	1.04
⊖ Banco Itau Holding Finan	Financial	15.7	57.73	1.04
Dade Behring Holdings	Health	35.9	56.69	1.01
⊖ Tesoro	Energy	6.4	118.67	1.00
⊖ Carpenter Technology	Ind Mtrls	22.4	99.59	1.00
Witness Systems	Software	—	88.35	0.99
Rofin-Sinar Technologies	Ind Mtrls	21.1	22.83	0.98
⊖ Vintage Petroleum	Energy	—	90.70	0.97
⊖ Digi International	Hardware	39.0	79.06	0.97
⊖ Hub Group A	Business	33.8	142.66	0.97
Crown Holdings	Goods	—	51.66	0.96
⊖ Perkinelmer	Ind Mtrls	31.8	33.79	0.96
StanCorp Financial Group	Financial	12.0	32.88	0.94
⊖ Brink's Company	Business	27.7	75.38	0.93
Haemonetics	Health	23.4	51.57	0.91
7-Eleven	Consumer	24.7	49.22	0.90
⊖ Bright Horizons Family S	Consumer	33.1	54.19	0.90

Current Investment Style

Value Blnd Growth; Large Mid Small

Market Cap	%
Giant	1.0
Large	0.2
Mid	16.2
Small	62.7
Micro	19.9
Avg $mil: 877	

Value Measures		Rel Category
Price/Earnings	18.30	1.06
Price/Book	2.40	1.21
Price/Sales	0.73	0.77
Price/Cash Flow	4.37	0.75
Dividend Yield %	0.25	0.30

Growth Measures	%	Rel Category
Long-Term Erngs	14.13	1.04
Book Value	1.36	0.24
Sales	5.42	1.26
Cash Flow	31.20	6.32
Historical Erngs	14.93	2.00

Profitability	%	Rel Category
Return on Equity	8.66	0.83
Return on Assets	5.25	1.06
Net Margin	4.42	0.60

Sector Weightings	% of Stocks	Rel S&P 500	3 Year High	3 Year Low
Info	19.26	0.90		
Software	7.91	1.84	9	4
Hardware	10.00	0.98	16	8
Media	0.13	0.03	2	0
Telecom	1.22	0.39	5	0
Service	52.63	1.13		
Health	10.30	0.82	17	10
Consumer	10.67	1.18	14	9
Business	12.93	3.19	13	8
Financial	18.73	0.90	21	14
Mfg	28.10	0.87		
Goods	4.87	0.52	11	3
Ind Mtrls	18.77	1.48	21	11
Energy	4.46	0.62	6	0
Utilities	0.00	0.00	3	0

Composition

Cash	0.0
Stocks	100.0
Bonds	0.0
Other	0.0
Foreign (% of Stock)	6.9

Address:	57 River Street, Wellesley, MA 02481, 877-264-5346
Web Address:	
Inception:	09-30-99 *
Advisor:	Bogle Investment Management, LP
Subadvisor:	None
NTF Plans:	N/A

Minimum Purchase:	Closed	Add: —	IRA: —
Min Auto Inv Plan:	Closed	Add: —	
Sales Fees:	No-load		
Management Fee:	1.00%		
Actual Fees:	Mgt:1.00%	Dist:	
Expense Projections:	3Yr:$481	5Yr:$847	10Yr:$1879
Income Distrib:	Annually		

BostPtn SmCpII Inv

Ticker	Load	NAV	Yield	Total Assets	Mstar Category
BPSCX	Closed	$23.31	0.0%	$494 mil	Small Value

Governance and Management

Fiduciary Grade: C

Portfolio Manager(s)

David Dabora has run this fund since its mid-1998 inception. He has four small-cap analysts and more than a dozen other analysts working with him. Dabora has a six-figure investment in this fund and also invests in the portfolio's individual holdings Comanager Harry Rosenbluth is not involved in day-to-day management of the offering.

Strategy

Lead manager David Dabora focuses on fundamentally sound firms that are trading at discounts to their intrinsic values and that have catalysts for improvement, such as a new CEO or restructuring plan. He's quite risk-conscious, so he invests in more than 100 issues, keeps individual holdings small, and invests across the industry spectrum. The fund's cheapskate tendencies do sometimes result in sector concentration, though.

Historical Profile

Return Above Avg
Risk Above Avg
Rating ★★★★ Above Avg

Investment Style
Equity
Stock %

1999	2000	2001	2002	2003	12-04
95%	97%	98%	97%	100%	99%

▼ Manager Change
∇ Partial Manager Change

Growth of $10,000
— Investment Values of Fund
— Investment Values of S&P 500

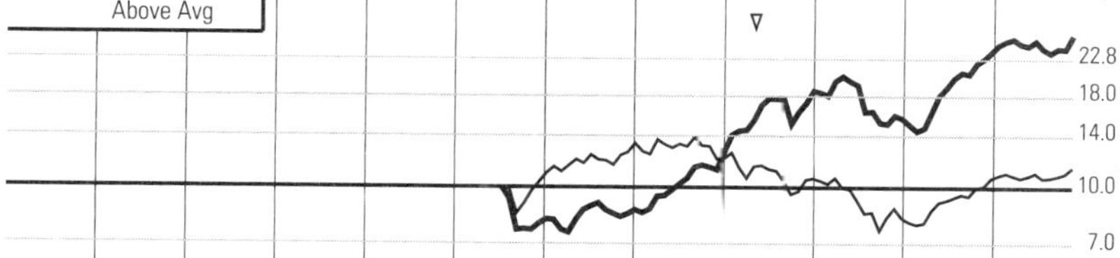

Performance Quartile (within Category)

1993	1994	1995	1996	1997	1998	1999	2000	2001	2002	2003	12-04	History
—	—	—	—	—	8.16	8.67	12.21	17.79	14.95	22.65	23.31	NAV
—	—	—	—	—	-18.40*	6.25	44.41	47.49	-15.94	52.90	16.47	Total Return %
—	—	—	—	—	—	-14.79	53.51	59.37	6.15	24.23	5.60	+/-S&P 500
—	—	—	—	—	—	7.74	21.58	33.47	-4.51	6.87	-5.78	+/-Russ 2000 VL
—	—	—	—	—	0.00	0.00	0.00	0.00	0.00	0.00	0.00	Income Return %
—	—	—	—	—	—	6.25	44.41	47.49	-15.94	52.90	16.47	Capital Return %
—	—	—	—	—	—	34	1	2	80	16	87	Total Rtn % Rank Cat
—	—	—	—	—	0.00	0.00	0.00	0.00	0.00	0.00	0.00	Income $
—	—	—	—	—	0.00	0.00	0.29	0.21	0.00	0.20	3.02	Capital Gains $
—	—	—	—	—	—	1.80	1.77	1.80	1.79	1.80	—	Expense Ratio %
—	—	—	—	—	—	-0.42	-0.40	-0.54	-1.00	-0.77	—	Income Ratio %
—	—	—	—	—	—	87	162	36	119	73	—	Turnover Rate %
—	—	—	—	—	—	—	1	382	205	316	346	Net Assets $mil

Performance 12-31-04

	1st Qtr	2nd Qtr	3rd Qtr	4th Qtr	Total
2000	8.88	8.26	12.72	8.69	44.41
2001	14.99	22.15	-14.87	23.35	47.49
2002	6.46	-2.59	-21.19	2.85	-15.94
2003	-5.82	29.19	8.91	15.39	52.90
2004	8.57	-1.22	-4.61	13.86	16.47

Trailing	Total Return%	+/- S&P 500	+/- Russ 2000 VL	%Rank Cat	Growth of $10,000
3 Mo	13.86	4.63	0.66	23	11,386
6 Mo	8.61	1.42	-4.76	89	10,861
1 Yr	16.47	5.60	-5.78	87	11,647
3 Yr Avg	14.40	10.82	-2.10	59	14,972
5 Yr Avg	26.10	28.40	8.87	2	31,884
10 Yr Avg	—	—	—	—	—
15 Yr Avg	—	—	—	—	—

Tax Analysis	Tax-Adj Rtn%	%Rank Cat	Tax-Cost Rat	%Rank Cat
3 Yr (estimated)	13.44	54	0.84	47
5 Yr (estimated)	25.10	2	0.79	38
10 Yr (estimated)	—	—	—	—

Potential Capital Gain Exposure: % of assets

Rating and Risk

Time Period	Load-Adj Return %	Morningstar Rtn vs Cat	Morningstar Risk vs Cat	Morningstar Risk-Adj Rating
1 Yr	16.47			
3 Yr	14.40	Avg	+Avg	★★★
5 Yr	26.10	High	+Avg	★★★★★
10 Yr	—	—	—	—
Incept	16.92			

Other Measures	Standard Index S&P 500	Best Fit Index Russ 2000 VL
Alpha	11.4	-1.7
Beta	0.92	1.00
R-Squared	54	91
Standard Deviation	21.35	
Mean	14.40	
Sharpe Ratio	0.62	

Portfolio Analysis 12-31-04

Share change since 11-04 Total Stocks:191	Sector	PE	YTD Ret%	% Assets
⊖ Apria HealthCare Group	Health	13.9	15.74	3.00
⊖ IPC Holdings	Financial	10.5	14.38	2.71
⊖ Platinum Underwriters Ho	Financial	16.1	4.76	1.93
⊖ Sola International	Health	—	46.49	1.70
⊖ Terex	Ind Mtrls	24.3	67.31	1.66
⊖ Assured Guaranty	Financial	—	—	1.60
⊖ United Online	Telecom	28.6	-31.33	1.59
⊖ Champion Enterprises	Consumer	—	68.86	1.52
⊖ Federal Agricultural Mor	Financial	11.8	-26.78	1.51
⊖ Scottish Re Group	Financial	11.1	25.78	1.49
⊖ Finish Line	Goods	17.6	22.50	1.22
⊖ Advanta	Financial	14.9	94.92	1.18
⊖ Earthlink	Telecom	19.3	15.20	1.15
⊖ Kindred Healthcare	Health	15.9	15.24	1.14
⊖ Conmed	Health	21.1	19.41	1.06
⊖ URS	Business	16.6	28.35	1.06
⊖ Service Corporation Inte	Consumer	17.7	38.22	1.05
⊖ Tetra Tech	Business	17.4	-32.66	1.04
⊖ Trammell Crow	Financial	27.3	36.68	1.04
⊖ Sierra Pacific Resources	Utilities	—	43.05	1.04

Current Investment Style

Value Blnd Growth — Large Mid Small

Market Cap	%
Giant	0.0
Large	0.0
Mid	11.4
Small	66.2
Micro	22.4
Avg $mil: 759	

Value Measures		Rel Category
Price/Earnings	15.88	0.99
Price/Book	1.60	0.96
Price/Sales	0.61	0.81
Price/Cash Flow	3.48	0.67
Dividend Yield %	0.50	0.50

Growth Measures	%	Rel Category
Long-Term Erngs	12.75	1.05
Book Value	3.29	0.76
Sales	4.27	1.36
Cash Flow	20.37	9.39
Historical Erngs	7.59	1.58

Profitability	%	Rel Category
Return on Equity	10.50	1.15
Return on Assets	5.49	1.32
Net Margin	6.76	1.01

Sector Weightings	% of Stocks	Rel S&P 500	3 Year High	3 Year Low
Info	5.55	0.26		
Software	0.25	0.06	5	0
Hardware	1.37	0.13	4	1
Media	1.15	0.30	3	1
Telecom	2.78	0.88	3	1
Service	73.80	1.59		
Health	11.48	0.92	17	11
Consumer	11.24	1.24	12	7
Business	19.71	4.87	21	14
Financial	31.37	1.51	33	23
Mfg	20.66	0.64		
Goods	8.12	0.87	9	6
Ind Mtrls	8.44	0.67	12	7
Energy	3.05	0.43	7	2
Utilities	1.05	0.35	3	1

Composition

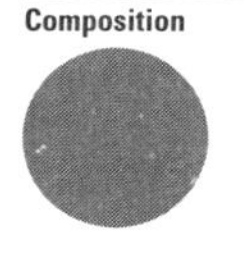

Cash	0.0
Stocks	99.3
Bonds	0.0
Other	0.7
Foreign (% of Stock)	1.6

Morningstar's Take by Laura Pavlenko Lutton 12-01-04

This closed offering has stumbled, but we would hold on.

After posting a stunning 52.9% gain in 2003 and beating more than three fourths of its small-value peers, Boston Partners Small Cap Value is having a rougher time this year. To be sure, it would be unfair to expect the fund to best its 2003 showing, but the fund's 11.26% gain for the year to date through Nov. 30, 2004, is one of the more anemic records in the category. The fund has been held back by its slim stake in soaring energy and industrial stocks, as well as losses among some top holdings, including United Online.

Short-term performance hiccups are to be expected at this offering given its strategy. Manager David Dabora invests in companies that are trading at discounts to his estimate of their fair values. His stock-picking criteria lead him more often to a few sectors, including financials, while keeping the fund light in other sectors, such as technology.

The fund's sector and industry bets do a lot to explain short-term performance problems here. In 2002, for example, the fund's 15.94% loss could be blamed in part on the fund's passel of financials stocks. And in 2004, several key insurance holdings have dragged on returns.

Over time, however, Dabora has shown he's a good stock-picker. In four of the last five calendar years, the fund has ended the year in the peer group's top third. Those strong performances have earned this offering one of the best five-year records in the category.

If we could change one thing, it would be this fund's rich expense ratio. At 1.80%, the offering is too pricey.

In the end, we think shareholders should stick with the offering. The small-value category is probably due to cool off after four years of relatively strong performance, but we're encouraged that this fund has held up well in a variety of market conditions.

Address:	400 Bellevue Pkwy Wilmington DE 19809 888-261-4073
Web Address:	
Inception:	06-30-98*
Advisor:	Boston Partners Asset Management LLC
Subadvisor:	None
NTF Plans:	Fidelity Retail-NTF, Schwab OneSource

Minimum Purchase:	Closed	Add: —	IRA: —
Min Auto Inv Plan:	Closed	Add: —	
Sales Fees:	0.25%B, 1.00%R		
Management Fee:	1.25%, 0.12%A		
Actual Fees:	Mgt:1.25%	Dist:0.25%	
Expense Projections:	3Yr:$566	5Yr:$1028	10Yr:$2308
Income Distrib:	Annually		

Brandywine

Analyst Pick

Ticker	Load	NAV	Yield	Total Assets	Mstar Category
BRWIX	None	$27.18	0.0%	$3,731 mil	Mid-Cap Growth

Governance and Management

Fiduciary Grade: A

Portfolio Manager(s)

Fund-family founder and chairman Foster Friess is still involved in the research process here, but Bill D'Alonzo, fund-family CEO and manager since inception, has the lead portfolio-manager role. D'Alonzo also steers the larger-cap Brandywine Blue, as well as Brandywine Advisors, another mid-cap offering. Friess is the fund's largest shareholder, while D'Alonzo has all of his investments in Brandywine Funds.

Strategy

The team looks for companies with rapidly increasing earnings (preferably in the 20% to 30% range annually), but it also requires a company to have three years of earnings history, $3 million in aftertax income, and a reasonable forward P/E ratio (compared with long-term norms for high-quality companies). Investing purely based on company-by-company considerations, the portfolio can become heavily skewed toward just a couple of sectors. Management also trades frequently, giving the fund a high turnover ratio.

Historical Profile

Return Average
Risk Below Avg
Rating ★★★★ Above Avg

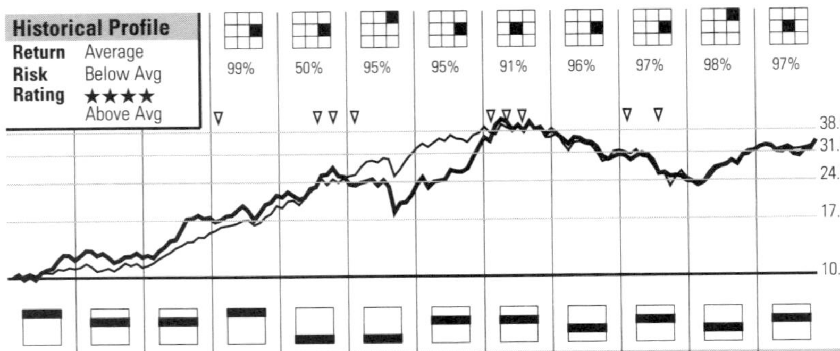

Investment Style
Equity
Stock %

▼ Manager Change
▽ Partial Manager Change

Growth of $10,000
— Investment Values of Fund
— Investment Values of S&P 500

Performance Quartile (within Category)

1993	1994	1995	1996	1997	1998	1999	2000	2001	2002	2003	12-04	History
24.97	23.50	28.08	33.69	30.89	30.28	42.88	29.39	23.35	18.28	24.03	27.18	NAV
22.58	0.02	35.75	24.92	12.02	-0.65	53.50	7.10	-20.55	-21.71	31.46	13.11	Total Return %
12.52	-1.29	-1.78	1.98	-21.33	-29.22	32.46	16.20	-8.67	0.38	2.79	2.24	+/-S&P 500
11.39	2.18	1.77	7.44	-10.52	-18.51	2.21	18.85	-0.40	5.70	-11.25	-2.37	+/-Russ MG
0.00	0.00	0.00	0.00	0.00	0.86	0.00	0.00	0.00	0.00	0.00	0.00	Income Return %
22.58	0.02	35.75	24.92	12.02	-1.51	53.50	7.10	-20.55	-21.71	31.46	13.11	Capital Return %
16	37	35	11	83	93	47	28	53	27	72	49	Total Rtn % Rank Cat
0.00	0.00	0.00	0.00	0.00	0.26	0.00	0.00	0.00	0.00	0.00	0.00	Income $
2.87	1.45	3.84	1.35	7.02	0.07	3.12	16.11	0.00	0.00	0.00	0.00	Capital Gains $
1.10	1.10	1.07	1.06	1.04	1.04	1.05	1.04	1.06	1.08	1.09	1.08	Expense Ratio %
-0.10	0.10	-0.40	-0.40	-0.30	0.60	-0.70	-0.60	-0.30	-0.50	-0.53	-0.55	Income Ratio %
150	190	194	203	192	264	209	244	284	273	279	247	Turnover Rate %
1,528	2,299	4,210	6,547	8,414	4,890	5,515	5,771	4,265	2,997	3,796	3,731	Net Assets $mil

Performance 12-31-04

	1st Qtr	2nd Qtr	3rd Qtr	4th Qtr	Total
2000	18.14	-5.21	-3.77	-0.62	7.10
2001	-12.39	1.98	-12.68	1.83	-20.55
2002	-1.93	-3.93	-13.27	-4.19	-21.71
2003	-1.48	15.82	2.11	12.82	31.46
2004	4.41	-2.15	-1.47	12.36	13.11

Trailing	Total Return%	+/- S&P 500	+/- Russ MG	%Rank Cat	Growth of $10,000
3 Mo	12.36	3.13	-1.58	62	11,236
6 Mo	10.71	3.52	1.70	14	11,071
1 Yr	13.11	2.24	-2.37	49	11,311
3 Yr Avg	5.19	1.61	-0.97	37	11,639
5 Yr Avg	-0.19	2.11	3.17	28	9,905
10 Yr Avg	11.12	-0.95	-0.11	42	28,703
15 Yr Avg	12.82	1.89	1.82	15	61,065

Tax Analysis	Tax-Adj Rtn%	%Rank Cat	Tax-Cost Rat	%Rank Cat
3 Yr (estimated)	5.19	30	0.00	1
5 Yr (estimated)	-2.28	34	2.09	82
10 Yr (estimated)	8.52	40	2.34	73

Potential Capital Gain Exposure: -7% of assets

Rating and Risk

Time Period	Load-Adj Return %	Morningstar Rtn vs Cat	Morningstar Risk vs Cat	Morningstar Risk-Adj Rating
1 Yr	13.11			
3 Yr	5.19	Avg	-Avg	★★★★
5 Yr	-0.19	Avg	Low	★★★★
10 Yr	11.12	Avg	-Avg	★★★★
Incept	13.63			

Other Measures	Standard Index S&P 500	Best Fit Index Mstar Small Core
Alpha	2.6	-5.8
Beta	0.67	0.77
R-Squared	48	82

Standard Deviation	15.29
Mean	5.19
Sharpe Ratio	0.25

Portfolio Analysis 09-30-04

Share change since 06-04 Total Stocks:106	Sector	PE	YTD Ret%	% Assets
⊕ Tyco International	Ind Mtrls	25.1	35.41	4.63
⊕ Phelps Dodge	Ind Mtrls	11.1	30.78	4.44
⊕ United States Steel	Ind Mtrls	—	47.19	3.92
⊕ MBNA	Financial	14.0	15.53	3.73
⊕ Motorola	Hardware	28.7	37.93	3.68
⊕ Aetna	Financial	16.9	84.67	3.54
Weatherford Internationa	Energy	27.8	42.50	3.45
⊕ Ingersoll-Rand A	Ind Mtrls	15.8	19.88	3.38
Allstate	Financial	12.8	23.12	3.26
⊕ Chesapeake Energy	Energy	13.1	22.90	2.75
⊕ Nextel Communications	Telecom	11.1	6.95	2.68
☼ Avaya	Hardware	24.5	32.92	2.56
⊕ Fisher Scientific Intern	Health	43.9	50.79	2.49
☼ J.C. Penney	Consumer	20.5	59.95	2.45
Nabors Industries	Energy	28.9	23.59	1.96
⊕ Consol Energy	Energy	32.2	61.53	1.81
Harman International Ind	Goods	48.4	71.77	1.78
⊕ Pentair	Business	24.0	93.44	1.64
⊕ Manpower	Business	18.2	3.24	1.61
☼ Danaher	Ind Mtrls	25.8	25.29	1.59

Current Investment Style

Value Blnd Growth — Large Mid Small

Market Cap	%
Giant	6.7
Large	35.2
Mid	50.5
Small	7.1
Micro	0.5

Avg $mil: 7,103

Value Measures		Rel Category
Price/Earnings	15.24	0.69
Price/Book	2.54	0.85
Price/Sales	1.13	0.64
Price/Cash Flow	4.61	0.48
Dividend Yield %	0.54	1.26

Growth Measures	%	Rel Category
Long-Term Erngs	14.26	0.91
Book Value	4.32	0.43
Sales	2.94	0.34
Cash Flow	-0.15	NMF
Historical Erngs	12.71	0.80

Profitability	%	Rel Category
Return on Equity	13.01	0.90
Return on Assets	6.16	0.86
Net Margin	7.70	0.80

Sector Weightings	% of Stocks	Rel S&P 500	3 Year High	3 Year Low
Info	12.60	0.59		
Software	0.54	0.13	5	1
Hardware	9.05	0.89	25	5
Media	0.00	0.00	9	0
Telecom	3.01	0.96	5	0
Service	42.78	0.92		
Health	5.64	0.45	32	5
Consumer	10.64	1.17	32	11
Business	14.45	3.57	14	2
Financial	12.05	0.58	20	3
Mfg	44.62	1.39		
Goods	3.66	0.39	16	4
Ind Mtrls	24.84	1.96	25	2
Energy	16.12	2.25	16	0
Utilities	0.00	0.00	0	0

Composition

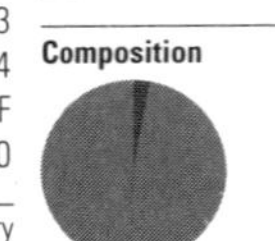

Cash	2.9
Stocks	97.1
Bonds	0.0
Other	0.0
Foreign (% of Stock)	3.2

Morningstar's Take by Karen Papalois 11-15-04

What's so great about Brandywine? Take a peek under the hood to find your answer.

At first glance, performance looks mediocre. Brandywine's 9.64% trailing 10-year return through Oct. 30, 2004, lands near the middle of the mid-growth pack. Moreover, it lags the S&P 500 by 1.36% annualized over the same time period.

Digging deeper, though, things don't look so bad. A look at the fund's 10-year returns on a rolling basis (where each month, one month drops off while one is added), shows that the fund has consistently beaten the mid-growth category, besting that group in 73% of 107 rolling 10-year periods. Morningstar recently found that funds that consistently outperform their peer groups turn out to be better investments in subsequent periods. Given the cyclical nature of the market, we wouldn't be surprised to see the fund back on top again. Further, despite double-digit losses during the bear market, it held up better than most mid-growth funds. This stability and resilience make it easier to own for the long haul.

Brandywine boasts other strengths that we think are key to its continued success. For one, the research effort is hearty. Along with lead manager Bill D'Alonzo, 27 people are dedicated to research. Each is charged with few companies (around nine stocks a piece). Under that framework, the team is able to dig deeper than many growth offerings', where analysts often track far more companies. As a result, researchers can delve into a firm's entire food chain by studying its customers, suppliers, and competitors. They also commission external researchers to focus on industry-wide factors and trends. Brandywine's deep research bench and contextual perspectives give it an advantage.

We also like Brandywine's attention to valuation. While that discipline can hold it back in strong rallies, it also helps it avoid big losses. Even though this fund hits its fair share of bumps and doesn't always stand at the top of the pack, it remains a favorite.

Address:	3908 Kennett Pike Greenville DE 19807 800-656-3017
Web Address:	www.brandywinefunds.com
Inception:	12-12-85
Advisor:	Friess Associates, LLC
Subadvisor:	Friess Associates of Delaware, LLC
NTF Plans:	N/A

Minimum Purchase:	$10000	Add: $1000	IRA: $10000
Min Auto Inv Plan:	$0	Add: —	
Sales Fees:	No-load		
Management Fee:	1.00%		
Actual Fees:	Mgt:1.00%	Dist:	
Expense Projections:	3Yr:$343	5Yr:$595	10Yr:$1317
Income Distrib:	Annually		

Bridgeway Balanced

Ticker	Load	NAV	Yield	Total Assets	Mstar Category
BRBPX	None	$11.57	0.7%	$28 mil	Conservative Allocation

Governance and Management

Fiduciary Grade: B

Portfolio Manager(s)

Richard Cancelmo, who is also Bridgeway's head of equity trading, has been at the helm since the fund's mid-2001 inception. His two decades in the investment industry include extensive options-trading experience and a stint from 1995 to 2000 managing the West University Fund (which trailed peers during the bull market because of its low-beta strategy).

Strategy

Manager Richard Cancelmo's chief goal is low volatility. He aims for a beta of no more than 0.40 relative to the S&P 500. At least 25% of assets are parked in high-quality bonds, mainly government issues; 30% are split between focused portfolios of growth and value stocks chosen by quantitative models; and the rest go into a basket of stocks meant to mimic the S&P 500. Cancelmo writes call or put options against most of the stocks in the growth and value portions and against a smaller percentage of stocks in the index portion.

Historical Profile

Return Above Avg
Risk Above Avg
Rating ★★★★ Above Avg

Investment Style
Equity
Stock %

▼ Manager Change
▽ Partial Manager Change

Growth of $10,000
— Investment Values of Fund
— Investment Values of S&P 500

Performance Quartile
(within Category)

History

1993	1994	1995	1996	1997	1998	1999	2000	2001	2002	2003	12-04	History
—	—	—	—	—	—	—	—	9.72	9.31	10.92	11.57	NAV
—	—	—	—	—	—	—	—	-2.29*	-3.51	17.82	7.61	Total Return %
—	—	—	—	—	—	—	—	—	18.58	-10.85	-3.26	+/-S&P 500
—	—	—	—	—	—	—	—	—	0.51	0.16	-1.40	+/-DJ 40%
—	—	—	—	—	—	—	—	0.00	0.64	0.52	0.71	Income Return %
—	—	—	—	—	—	—	—	—	-4.15	17.30	6.90	Capital Return %
—	—	—	—	—	—	—	—	—	54	13	22	Total Rtn % Rank Cat
—	—	—	—	—	—	—	—	0.05	0.06	0.05	0.08	Income $
—	—	—	—	—	—	—	—	0.00	0.01	0.00	0.10	Capital Gains $
—	—	—	—	—	—	—	—	—	0.94	0.94	0.94	Expense Ratio %
—	—	—	—	—	—	—	—	—	0.49	1.06	0.60	Income Ratio %
—	—	—	—	—	—	—	—	—	18	98	124	Turnover Rate %
—	—	—	—	—	—	—	—	2	6	14	28	Net Assets $mil

Performance 12-31-04

	1st Qtr	2nd Qtr	3rd Qtr	4th Qtr	Total
2000	—	—	—	—	—
2001	—	—	-7.70	5.86	-2.29*
2002	3.19	-1.60	-5.88	0.95	-3.51
2003	-0.32	8.30	2.59	6.39	17.82
2004	3.11	0.36	-0.80	4.83	7.61

Trailing	Total Return%	+/- S&P 500	+/- DJ 40%	%Rank Cat	Growth of $10,000
3 Mo	4.83	-4.40	-0.57	36	10,483
6 Mo	4.00	-3.19	-2.49	68	10,400
1 Yr	7.61	-3.26	-1.40	22	10,761
3 Yr Avg	6.95	3.37	-0.23	17	12,233
5 Yr Avg	—	—	—	—	—
10 Yr Avg	—	—	—	—	—
15 Yr Avg	—	—	—	—	—

Tax Analysis	Tax-Adj Rtn%	%Rank Cat	Tax-Cost Rat	%Rank Cat
3 Yr (estimated)	6.61	13	0.32	7
5 Yr (estimated)	—	—	—	—
10 Yr (estimated)	—	—	—	—

Potential Capital Gain Exposure: 8% of assets

Rating and Risk

Time Period	Load-Adj Return %	Morningstar Rtn vs Cat	Morningstar Risk vs Cat	Morningstar Risk-Adj Rating
1 Yr	7.61			
3 Yr	6.95	+Avg	+Avg	★★★★
5 Yr	—	—	—	—
10 Yr	—	—	—	—
Incept	5.22			

Other Measures	Standard Index S&P 500	Best Fit Index Mstar Small Core
Alpha	4.7	1.1
Beta	0.30	0.32
R-Squared	46	69
Standard Deviation	6.90	
Mean	6.95	
Sharpe Ratio	0.81	

Portfolio Analysis 09-30-04

Total Stocks:223 Share change since 06-30-04	Sectors	P/E Ratio	YTD Return %	% Net Assets
Nextel Communications	Telecom	11.1	0.53	1.78
⊕ Bristol-Myers Squibb	Health	17.7	-2.90	1.36
SBC Communications	Telecom	15.4	-3.12	1.31
⊕ General Motors	Goods	7.2	-4.02	1.04
E*Trade Financial	Financial	13.7	-11.17	1.03
⊕ Federated Department Stor	Consumer	15.2	-0.33	1.01
J.P. Morgan Chase & Co.	Financial	19.4	-1.99	0.96
⊕ Urban Outfitters	Consumer	42.4	-9.19	0.83
⊕ AT&T	Telecom	—	-2.73	0.75

Total Fixed-Income:15	Date of Maturity	Amount $000	Value $000	% Net Assets
Leucadia Natl 7.75%	08-15-13	700	725	3.11
US Treasury Note 2.25%	04-30-06	500	497	2.14
US Treasury Note 4%	06-15-09	300	304	1.31
US Treasury Note 2.5%	05-31-06	300	299	1.29
US Treasury Note 1.875%	12-31-05	300	298	1.28
US Treasury Note 1.875%	01-31-06	300	298	1.28
US Treasury Note 3.125%	04-15-09	300	293	1.26
US Treasury Note 3.5%	11-15-06	200	203	0.87
US Treasury Note 1.875%	11-30-05	200	199	0.85

Equity Style
Style: Blend
Size: Large-Cap

Value Measures		Rel Category
Price/Earnings	15.94	0.97
Price/Book	2.30	0.97
Price/Sales	0.96	0.74
Price/Cash Flow	7.08	1.02
Dividend Yield %	1.25	0.72

Growth Measures	%	Rel Category
Long-Term Erngs	11.25	1.01
Book Value	-0.51	NMF
Sales	1.14	0.25
Cash Flow	-5.38	NMF
Historical Erngs	10.66	1.13

Market Cap %			
Giant	16.4	Small	0.5
Large	52.1	Micro	0.0
Mid	31.0	Avg $mil:	14,205

Fixed-Income Style
Duration: —
Quality: —

Avg Eff Duration[1]	—
Avg Eff Maturity	—
Avg Credit Quality	—
Avg Wtd Coupon	3.57%

[1]figure provided by fund

Sector Weightings	% of Stocks	Rel S&P 500	3 Year High	3 Year Low
Info	24.76	1.15		
Software	4.03	0.94	7	2
Hardware	9.70	0.95	15	3
Media	2.73	0.71	5	3
Telecom	8.30	2.63	8	2
Service	48.21	1.04		
Health	11.85	0.95	15	11
Consumer	10.77	1.19	15	6
Business	5.21	1.29	11	3
Financial	20.38	0.98	26	18
Mfg	27.03	0.84		
Goods	9.46	1.01	15	8
Ind Mtrls	9.94	0.78	15	7
Energy	5.49	0.77	8	4
Utilities	2.14	0.72	4	2

Composition

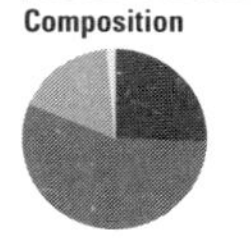

Cash	25.5
Stocks	55.7
Bonds	17.4
Other	1.4
Foreign (% of Stock)	0.2

Morningstar's Take by David Kathman 12-03-04

Bridgeway Balanced is a good way to moderate the volatility of a portfolio.

This fund is designed to provide a smooth ride for shareholders. Manager Richard Cancelmo strives to keep the fund's beta relative to the S&P 500 Index at 0.4--that means it will rise only 40% as much as the S&P when the market goes up, but will fall only 40% as much as the S&P when the market goes down. In fact, it has performed as advertised, losing much less than the S&P 500 in the 2002 bear market, but gaining much less in the 2003 bull market. Relative to other conservative-allocation funds, it ranks in the top 20% over the trailing three years, though that's largely due to its relatively high equity exposure.

Cancelmo achieves this result through an unusual mix of quantitative models and derivatives. About 45% of assets go into a basket of stocks designed to track the S&P 500. Another 30% is split between two smaller baskets representing growth and value stocks, determined by different quantitative screens. The rest of the fund, about 25% of assets, consists of bonds, mostly government issues.

Many of the fund's equity positions are represented not by the stocks themselves, but by cash-secured put options, which provide extra income but sometimes force Cancelmo to buy a falling stock. Cancelmo also writes covered calls on some of the stocks the fund does own; these also provide extra income, but sometimes force him to sell a rising stock.

Investors should think of this fund as a tool for diversifying a portfolio and lowering its overall volatility. In that respect, the fund's discipline and steadiness make it an excellent choice. We also like the fact that Bridgeway is an extremely shareholder-friendly shop which helps investors in lots of hidden ways, such as keeping trading costs to a minimum. Cancelmo is also the firm's head trader in addition to managing this fund, so he has lots of experience in that area.

Address:	5615 Kirby Drive Suite 518 Houston TX 77005-2448 800-661-3550
Web Address:	www.bridgewayfunds.com
Inception:	06-29-01 *
Advisor:	Bridgeway Capital Management Inc
Subadvisor:	None
NTF Plans:	ETrade No Load ETF

Minimum Purchase:	$2000	Add: $500	IRA: $2000
Min Auto Inv Plan:	$2000	Add: $200	
Sales Fees:	No-load		
Management Fee:	0.60%		
Actual Fees:	Mgt:0.60%	Dist:	
Expense Projections:	3Yr:$358	5Yr: —	10Yr: —
Income Distrib:	Annually		

Bridgeway Blue-Chip 35

Ticker	Load	NAV	Yield	Total Assets	Mstar Category
BRLIX	None	$7.18	1.7%	$39 mil	Large Blend

Governance and Management

Fiduciary Grade: A

Portfolio Manager(s)

Bridgeway Funds' founder John Montgomery runs all but one of Bridgeway's 11 funds. Two quantitative analysts assist him in testing new variables to potentially add to his models and in creating new models. Montgomery's background is unique: Prior to starting Bridgeway, he worked in mass-transit management, and with experience in statistics, he used quantitative models on his personal investment portfolio.

Strategy

Manager John Montgomery is attempting to track an index of his own creation. It is an equally weighted index that is composed of 35 of the market's largest names, meaning that Montgomery must rebalance the portfolio every quarter to ensure that the fund's assets are divided equally among the index's constituents. No industry is represented by more than four names. Montgomery also attempts to avoid paying capital-gains distributions.

Historical Profile

Return: Average
Risk: Average
Rating: ★★★ Neutral

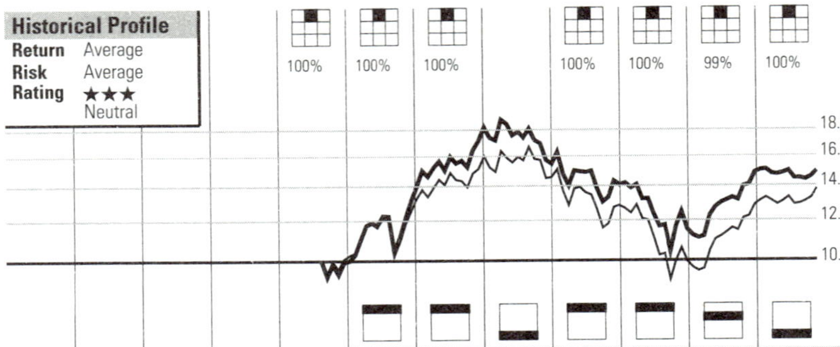

Investment Style
Equity
Stock %

▼ Manager Change
▽ Partial Manager Change

Growth of $10,000
— Investment Values of Fund
— Investment Values of S&P 500

Performance Quartile (within Category)

1993	1994	1995	1996	1997	1998	1999	2000	2001	2002	2003	12-04	History
—	—	—	—	5.00	6.92	8.95	7.51	6.75	5.45	6.97	7.18	NAV
—	—	—	—	0.00*	39.11	30.34	-15.12	-9.07	-18.02	28.87	4.79	Total Return %
—	—	—	—	—	10.54	9.30	-6.02	2.81	4.07	0.20	-6.08	+/-S&P 500
—	—	—	—	—	12.09	9.43	-7.33	3.38	3.63	-1.02	-6.61	+/-Russ 1000
—	—	—	—	0.00	0.61	0.96	0.98	1.08	1.29	0.97	1.78	Income Return %
—	—	—	—	—	38.50	29.38	-16.10	-10.15	-19.31	27.90	3.01	Capital Return %
—	—	—	—	—	2	14	94	22	18	27	93	Total Rtn % Rank Cat
—	—	—	—	0.00	0.03	0.07	0.09	0.08	0.09	0.05	0.12	Income $
—	—	—	—	0.00	0.00	0.00	0.00	0.00	0.00	0.00	0.00	Capital Gains $
—	—	—	—	—	0.15	0.15	0.15	0.15	0.15	0.15	0.15	Expense Ratio %
—	—	—	—	—	1.47	1.06	0.98	1.15	1.35	1.65	1.64	Income Ratio %
—	—	—	—	—	72	17	26	24	41	25	5	Turnover Rate %
—	—	—	—	—	2	6	7	6	6	23	39	Net Assets $mil

Performance 12-31-04

	1st Qtr	2nd Qtr	3rd Qtr	4th Qtr	Total
2000	3.46	-5.29	-3.76	-9.99	-15.12
2001	-9.32	6.17	-12.45	7.88	-9.07
2002	0.15	-12.28	-15.35	10.23	-18.02
2003	-2.94	16.07	1.30	12.91	28.87
2004	-0.57	1.30	-3.85	8.21	4.79

Trailing	Total Return%	+/- S&P 500	+/- Russ 1000	%Rank Cat	Growth of $10,000
3 Mo	8.21	-1.02	-1.59	79	10,821
6 Mo	4.04	-3.15	-3.77	90	10,404
1 Yr	4.79	-6.08	-6.61	93	10,479
3 Yr Avg	3.45	-0.13	-0.82	36	11,071
5 Yr Avg	-3.10	-0.80	-1.34	69	8,543
10 Yr Avg	—	—	—	—	—
15 Yr Avg	—	—	—	—	—

Tax Analysis	Tax-Adj Rtn%	%Rank Cat	Tax-Cost Rat	%Rank Cat
3 Yr (estimated)	2.95	33	0.48	40
5 Yr (estimated)	-3.55	62	0.46	24
10 Yr (estimated)	—	—	—	—

Potential Capital Gain Exposure: 4% of assets

Rating and Risk

Time Period	Load-Adj Return %	Morningstar Rtn vs Cat	Morningstar Risk vs Cat	Morningstar Risk-Adj Rating
1 Yr	4.79			
3 Yr	3.45	Avg	+Avg	★★★
5 Yr	-3.10	Avg	Avg	★★★
10 Yr	—	—	—	—
Incept	6.08			

Other Measures	Standard Index S&P 500	Best Fit Index S&P 500
Alpha	-0.1	-0.1
Beta	1.00	1.00
R-Squared	93	93
Standard Deviation	16.17	
Mean	3.45	
Sharpe Ratio	0.13	

Morningstar's Take by Bridget Hughes 12-22-04

Bridgeway Blue-Chip 35 Index Fund is in for a shake-up, though probably a very minor one. We still like the fund.

According to Bridgeway Funds' prospectus, manager John Montgomery rebalances the index that this fund mimics, the Bridgeway Blue-Chip 35 Index, every two or three years. (The last rebalancing was in December 2001, and the prospectus says the next will likely be in its fiscal year 2005, which runs from July 1, 2004, to June 30, 2005.) The benchmark is one of Montgomery's own creations, an equally weighted collection of 35 of the U.S. stock market's largest 150 companies by market cap. It's not a simple ranking, however: Montgomery won't own more than four companies in the same industry--choices are most likely needed from the banking and drugs areas, for example. And he won't own tobacco companies, which means Altria is out.

Assuming the rebalancing happens soon, investors should see the new index composition sometime in the next several months, as the portfolio is disclosed per SEC rules. But we don't expect many changes. In part, that's because Montgomery aims to limit capital-gains distributions here, and the last rebalancing resulted in few changes. Further, the biggest companies don't tend to change that much. Finally, given Montgomery's contrarian nature and the largest stocks' comparative weakness over the past few years, we think it's unlikely that he would opt for smaller (but still blue-chip) names that have outperformed.

While the fund's mega-cap profile has certainly hurt this year--its 4.2% year-to-date gain through Dec. 21, 2004, ranks in the large-blend category's worst decile--we continue to think this is an attractive option. We like the low expense ratio and attention to taxes. And we continue to believe that large companies will eventually return to favor after several years of lagging the overall market.

Address:	5615 Kirby Drive Suite 518 Houston TX 77005-2448 800-661-3550	Minimum Purchase:	$2000	Add: $500	IRA: $2000
		Min Auto Inv Plan:	$2000	Add: $100	
		Sales Fees:	No-load		
Web Address:	www.bridgewayfunds.com	Management Fee:	0.08%		
Inception:	07-31-97 *	Actual Fees:	Mgt:0.08%	Dist:	
Advisor:	Bridgeway Capital Management Inc	Expense Projections:	3Yr:$50	5Yr:$80	10Yr:$190
Subadvisor:	None	Income Distrib:	Annually		
NTF Plans:	ETrade No Load ETF				

Portfolio Analysis 09-30-04

Share change since 06-04 Total Stocks:36	Sector	PE	YTD Ret%	% Assets
⊕ SBC Communications	Telecom	15.4	3.74	3.29
General Electric	Ind Mtrls	22.8	20.68	3.07
ExxonMobil	Energy	13.9	28.04	3.03
Johnson & Johnson	Health	20.6	25.17	3.02
McDonald's	Consumer	19.7	31.48	3.01
⊕ Procter & Gamble	Goods	23.3	12.38	2.97
⊖ ChevronTexaco	Energy	7.7	25.57	2.95
Verizon Communications	Telecom	32.4	20.25	2.94
⊖ Bank of America	Financial	12.3	21.50	2.90
⊕ Berkshire Hathaway B	Financial	20.9	4.30	2.88
United Parcel Service B	Business	28.5	16.40	2.87
3M Company	Ind Mtrls	23.5	-1.75	2.87
Fannie Mae	Financial	9.1	-2.33	2.86
⊖ Microsoft	Software	36.1	8.95	2.84
⊖ Dell	Hardware	34.0	24.01	2.83
American International G	Financial	16.2	-0.53	2.81
IBM	Hardware	20.2	7.19	2.81
DuPont De Nemours E.I.	Ind Mtrls	22.3	10.42	2.79
Wells Fargo	Financial	15.5	8.97	2.78
⊕ Wal-Mart Stores	Consumer	23.4	0.51	2.76

Current Investment Style

Value Blnd Growth; Large Mid Small

Market Cap	%
Giant	89.0
Large	11.0
Mid	0.0
Small	0.0
Micro	0.0
Avg $mil: 101,249	

Value Measures		Rel Category
Price/Earnings	15.77	0.93
Price/Book	2.97	1.13
Price/Sales	1.52	1.06
Price/Cash Flow	7.73	1.01
Dividend Yield %	1.91	1.29

Growth Measures	%	Rel Category
Long-Term Erngs	10.30	0.89
Book Value	6.59	0.85
Sales	4.17	0.73
Cash Flow	9.24	0.98
Historical Erngs	7.98	0.68

Profitability	%	Rel Category
Return on Equity	21.01	1.20
Return on Assets	10.87	1.26
Net Margin	13.32	1.16

Sector Weightings	% of Stocks	Rel S&P 500	3 Year High	3 Year Low
Info	32.88	1.53		
Software	5.37	1.25	6	5
Hardware	15.87	1.56	18	14
Media	5.40	1.41	6	2
Telecom	6.24	1.98	8	4
Service	41.59	0.90		
Health	13.50	1.08	16	13
Consumer	8.32	0.92	9	7
Business	2.87	0.71	3	3
Financial	16.90	0.81	20	16
Mfg	25.54	0.80		
Goods	10.84	1.16	13	11
Ind Mtrls	8.73	0.69	9	6
Energy	5.97	0.83	6	5
Utilities	0.00	0.00	0	0

Composition

Cash	0.0
Stocks	100.0
Bonds	0.0
Other	0.0
Foreign (% of Stock)	0.0

Bridgeway Ul-Sm Co Mkt

Ticker	Load	NAV	Yield	Total Assets	Mstar Category
BRSIX	Closed	$17.77	0.1%	$806 mil	Small Blend

Governance and Management

Fiduciary Grade: A

Portfolio Manager(s)

Bridgeway Funds' founder John Montgomery runs all but one of Bridgeway's 11 funds. Two quantitative analysts assist him in testing new variables to potentially add to his models and in creating new models. Montgomery's background is unique: Prior to starting Bridgeway, he worked in mass-transit management, and with experience in statistics, he used quantitative models on his personal investment portfolio.

Strategy

This offering attempts to track the CRSP Cap-Based Portfolio 10 Index--a little-known benchmark comprising about 1,800 stocks that fall into the NYSE's bottom decile by market capitalization. Manager John Montgomery seeks to replicate the index's movements, currently by holding a representative sample of stocks. The fund's diversification, Montgomery argues, more than offsets the company-specific risk that comes with investing in these tiny firms, some of which ultimately go out of business. He also pays close attention to tax implications.

Historical Profile

Return High
Risk Average
Rating ★★★★★ Highest

Investment Style: Equity, Stock %: 100% (1998), 99% (1999), 99% (2001), 90% (2002), 90% (2003), 100% (12-04)

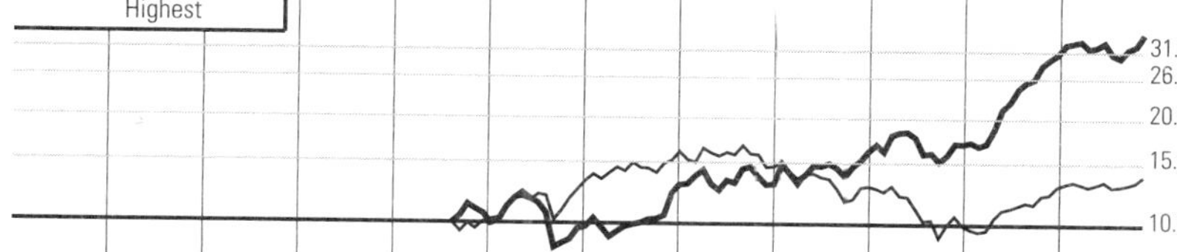

Performance Quartile (within Category)

1993	1994	1995	1996	1997	1998	1999	2000	2001	2002	2003	12-04	History
—	—	—	—	4.98	4.89	6.43	6.43	7.96	8.35	14.94	17.77	NAV
—	—	—	—	-0.40*	-1.81	31.49	0.67	23.98	4.90	79.43	19.13	Total Return %
—	—	—	—	—	-30.38	10.45	9.77	35.86	26.99	50.76	8.26	+/-S&P 500
—	—	—	—	—	0.74	10.23	3.69	21.49	25.38	32.18	0.80	+/-Russ 2000
—	—	—	—	0.00	0.00	0.00	0.66	0.18	0.00	0.00	0.18	Income Return %
—	—	—	—	—	-1.81	31.49	0.01	23.80	4.90	79.43	18.95	Capital Return %
—	—	—	—	—	28	15	90	8	1	2	48	Total Rtn % Rank Cat
—	—	—	—	0.00	0.00	0.00	0.04	0.01	0.00	0.00	0.03	Income $
—	—	—	—	0.00	0.00	0.00	0.00	0.00	0.00	0.04	0.00	Capital Gains $
—	—	—	—	—	0.75	0.75	0.75	0.75	0.75	0.75	0.67	Expense Ratio %
—	—	—	—	—	-0.38	-0.51	0.53	0.77	-0.05	-0.14	0.11	Income Ratio %
—	—	—	—	—	68	48	40	215	56	18	19	Turnover Rate %
—	—	—	—	40	58	69	64	59	100	752	806	Net Assets $mil

Performance 12-31-04

	1st Qtr	2nd Qtr	3rd Qtr	4th Qtr	Total
2000	9.95	-6.36	9.06	-10.34	0.67
2001	2.18	9.89	-6.37	17.93	23.98
2002	10.93	-1.47	-14.37	12.08	4.90
2003	0.48	30.87	15.94	17.69	79.43
2004	9.04	-0.92	-4.09	14.97	19.13

Trailing	Total Return%	+/- S&P 500	+/- Russ 2000	%Rank Cat	Growth of $10,000
3 Mo	14.97	5.74	0.88	12	11,497
6 Mo	10.27	3.08	-0.56	63	11,027
1 Yr	19.13	8.26	0.80	48	11,913
3 Yr Avg	30.89	27.31	19.41	1	22,424
5 Yr Avg	22.85	25.15	16.24	1	27,982
10 Yr Avg	—	—	—	—	—
15 Yr Avg	—	—	—	—	—

Tax Analysis	Tax-Adj Rtn%	%Rank Cat	Tax-Cost Rat	%Rank Cat
3 Yr (estimated)	30.84	1	0.04	3
5 Yr (estimated)	22.75	1	0.08	3
10 Yr (estimated)	—	—	—	—

Potential Capital Gain Exposure: 44% of assets

Rating and Risk

Time Period	Load-Adj Return %	Morningstar Rtn vs Cat	Morningstar Risk vs Cat	Morningstar Risk-Adj Rating
1 Yr	19.13			
3 Yr	30.89	High	+Avg	★★★★★
5 Yr	22.85	High	Avg	★★★★★
10 Yr	—	—	—	—
Incept	18.84			

Other Measures	Standard Index S&P 500	Best Fit Index Russ 2000
Alpha	27.4	18.8
Beta	0.92	0.89
R-Squared	58	88
Standard Deviation	23.55	
Mean	30.89	
Sharpe Ratio	1.27	

Portfolio Analysis 09-30-04

Share change since 06-04 Total Stocks:692	Sector	PE	YTD Ret%	% Assets
⊖ iShares Russell 2000 Ind	—	—	—	2.62
⊖ iShares Russell 2000 Val	—	—	—	2.52
Taser International	Ind Mtrls	NMF	361.03	1.54
Navarre	Consumer	31.2	189.47	1.14
Ask Jeeves	Business	37.8	47.63	0.90
First Horizon	Health	25.2	103.47	0.66
Amedisys	Health	19.3	113.65	0.61
Deckers Outdoor	Goods	25.3	129.22	0.53
LCA-Vision	Health	16.0	66.68	0.57
Ditech	Hardware	6.6	-21.73	0.54
Parlux Fragrances	Goods	25.6	336.51	0.5[illegible]
Metals USA	Ind Mtrls	4.1	84.21	0.49
Park-Ohio Holdings	Ind Mtrls	—	248.78	0.47
Edge Petroleum	Energy	18.4	44.07	0.46
Meridian Resource	Energy	20.8	1.85	0.46
Giant Industries	Energy	16.8	121.29	0.44
☼ Wilshire Bancorp	Financial	—	—	0.44
Ceradyne	Ind Mtrls	37.3	151.95	0.43
Boston Communications Gr	Hardware	9.7	-0.54	0.41
Ventiv Health	Business	25.3	122.08	0.41

Current Investment Style

Value Blnd Growth; Large / Mid / Small

Market Cap	%
Giant	0.7
Large	0.1
Mid	3.1
Small	11.1
Micro	85.0

Avg $mil: 205

Value Measures		Rel Category
Price/Earnings	16.?4	0.94
Price/Book	1.72	0.86
Price/Sales	0.63	0.66
Price/Cash Flow	3.66	0.63
Dividend Yield %	0.68	0.82

Growth Measures	%	Rel Category
Long-Term Erngs	15.45	1.14
Book Value	-0.22	NMF
Sales	1.39	0.32
Cash Flow	-5.0[illegible]	NMF
Historical Erngs	9.92	1.33

Profitability	%	Rel Category
Return on Equity	5.65	0.54
Return on Assets	1.55	0.31
Net Margin	6.22	0.85

Sector Weightings	% of Stocks	Rel S&P 500	3 Year High	3 Year Low
Info	16.38	0.76		
Software	5.18	1.20	8	5
Hardware	9.44	0.93	11	7
Media	0.60	0.16	1	0
Telecom	1.16	0.37	1	1
Service	58.90	1.27		
Health	16.59	1.33	19	13
Consumer	7.71	0.85	10	7
Business	10.37	2.56	15	10
Financial	24.23	1.17	27	19
Mfg	24.72	0.77		
Goods	6.33	0.68	10	6
Ind Mtrls	13.42	1.06	14	7
Energy	3.90	0.54	5	3
Utilities	1.07	0.36	1	1

Composition

Cash	0.0
Stocks	100.0
Bonds	0.0
Other	0.0
Foreign (% of Stock)	0.6

Morningstar's Take by Bridget Hughes 11-22-04

Is Bridgeway Ultra-Small Company Market Fund due for a stall?

Over time, the smallest of the smallest-cap stocks have proved superior investments. This passively managed small-blend fund, which buys the smallest 10% of stocks, is further testament to the superiority of the asset class: Its 23.2% annualized five-year return is among the best of all mutual funds'.

But while shareholders might safely assume there's ample opportunity to make money over the long haul here, they'd be wise to acknowledge the cyclicality of market leadership. Just consider this fund's 1998 performance: While the S&P 500 Index advanced more than 30%, this offering lost nearly 2%. And small caps have generally paced the market over the past four years--their legs could be tired soon. Further, investors know it would be silly to assume that a 23% annualized return is sustainable over the long term. All these factors suggest a dry spell could be coming.

In fact, a sluggish ultrasmall market may have already started. For the year to date through Nov. 19, 2004, this fund is up 11%. While that's certainly healthy in absolute terms, it lands the fund behind the typical small-blend fund, which invests in larger companies, mostly still small caps and some mid-caps. (The fund is still ahead of the S&P 500 Index, though.)

There is a silver lining to a weak ultrasmall market, however. One, it might give manager John Mongtomery more opportunity to harvest tax losses. While the fund paid a small distribution in 2003 and will again in 2004, Montgomery's goal is to minimize taxable distributions. Two, it could represent a buying opportunity for existing shareholders. (The fund is closed only to new investors.) Meanwhile, the fund serves as a good diversifier for S&P 500-like portfolios.

Address:	5615 Kirby Drive Suite 518 Houston TX 77005-2448 800-661-3550
Web Address:	www.bridgewayfunds.com
Inception:	07-31-97 *
Advisor:	Bridgeway Capital Management Inc
Subadvisor:	None
NTF Plans:	ETrade No Load ETF

Minimum Purchase:	Closed	Add: —	IRA: —
Min Auto Inv Plan:	Closed	Add: —	
Sales Fees:	No-load, 2.00%R		
Management Fee:	0.50%		
Actual Fees:	Mgt:0.50%	Dist:	
Expense Projections:	3Yr:$304	5Yr:$548	10Yr:$1245
Income Distrib:	Annually		

Brown Cap Small Co Instl

Ticker	Load	NAV	Yield	Total Assets	Mstar Category
BCSIX	Closed	$29.80	0.0%	$647 mil	Small Growth

Governance and Management

Fiduciary Grade: C

Portfolio Manager(s)

Keith Lee leads the management team of Robert Hall, Kempton Ingersol, and Amy Zhang. Lee has been with Brown Capital Management since 1991.

Strategy

This fund's managers search for promising growth businesses that they can invest in for the long haul. Because the managers look for companies with $250 million or less in operating revenue, the fund holds everything from micro- to mid-cap names. The fund sports huge weightings in volatile sectors such as technology and biotech.

Historical Profile

Return Average
Risk Average
Rating ★★★ Neutral

Investment Style — Equity Stock %: 85% 90% 93% 91% 100% 92% 92% 92% 99%

▼ Manager Change
▽ Partial Manager Change

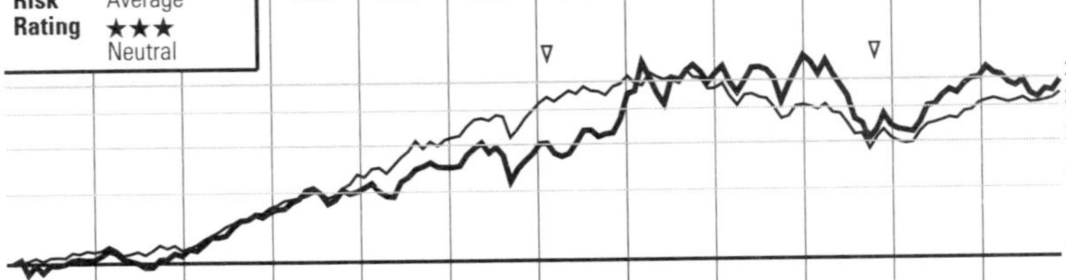

Growth of $10,000
— Investment Values of Fund
— Investment Values of S&P 500

Performance Quartile (within Category)

1993	1994	1995	1996	1997	1998	1999	2000	2001	2002	2003	12-04	History
10.97	11.24	13.99	16.00	18.29	21.42	28.70	31.23	35.17	20.98	29.73	29.80	NAV
5.83	4.81	33.91	17.08	15.78	18.39	44.02	15.30	13.33	-40.34	41.71	0.24	Total Return %
-4.23	3.50	-3.62	-5.86	-17.57	-10.18	22.98	24.40	25.21	-18.25	13.04	-10.63	+/-S&P 500
-7.54	7.24	2.87	5.82	2.83	17.16	0.93	37.73	22.56	-10.08	-6.83	-14.07	+/-Russ 2000 Gr
0.00	0.00	0.00	0.00	0.00	0.00	0.00	0.00	0.00	0.00	0.00	0.00	Income Return %
5.83	4.81	33.91	17.08	15.78	18.39	44.02	15.30	13.33	-40.34	41.71	0.24	Capital Return %
90	23	57	62	59	15	58	10	9	91	60	95	Total Rtn % Rank Cat
0.00	0.00	0.00	0.00	0.00	0.00	0.00	0.00	0.00	0.00	0.00	0.00	Income $
0.46	0.25	1.04	0.36	0.24	0.23	2.12	1.81	0.22	0.00	0.00	0.00	Capital Gains $
1.89	2.00	2.00	1.69	1.50	1.50	1.50	1.43	1.35	1.24	1.23	1.18	Expense Ratio %
-0.86	-1.34	-0.90	-0.50	-0.30	-0.68	-0.98	-0.94	-0.23	-0.83	-1.05	-1.03	Income Ratio %
—	23	33	23	13	12	28	28	8	7	1	1	Turnover Rate %
2	2	3	6	10	16	45	126	365	373	719	647	Net Assets $mil

Performance 12-31-04

	1st Qtr	2nd Qtr	3rd Qtr	4th Qtr	Total
2000	13.00	-1.25	10.04	-6.10	15.30
2001	-13.06	20.11	-22.32	39.72	13.33
2002	-3.55	-22.88	-26.95	9.79	-40.34
2003	-4.58	21.93	8.77	11.98	41.71
2004	1.61	-3.97	-6.55	9.92	0.24

Trailing	Total Return%	+/- S&P 500	+/- Russ 2000 Gr	%Rank Cat	Growth of $10,000
3 Mo	9.92	0.69	-5.16	96	10,992
6 Mo	2.72	-4.47	-5.44	91	10,272
1 Yr	0.24	-10.63	-14.07	95	10,024
3 Yr Avg	-5.37	-8.95	-11.16	96	8,474
5 Yr Avg	2.06	4.36	5.63	34	11,073
10 Yr Avg	13.11	1.04	5.99	21	34,278
15 Yr Avg	—	—	—	—	—

Tax Analysis	Tax-Adj Rtn%	%Rank Cat	Tax-Cost Rat	%Rank Cat
3 Yr (estimated)	-5.37	94	0.00	1
5 Yr (estimated)	1.77	30	0.28	13
10 Yr (estimated)	12.41	13	0.62	8

Potential Capital Gain Exposure: 9% of assets

Rating and Risk

Time Period	Load-Adj Return %	Morningstar Rtn vs Cat	Morningstar Risk vs Cat	Morningstar Risk-Adj Rating
1 Yr	0.24			
3 Yr	-5.37	Low	+Avg	★
5 Yr	2.06	Avg	Avg	★★★
10 Yr	13.11	+Avg	Avg	★★★★
Incept	12.02			

Other Measures	Standard Index S&P 500	Best Fit Index Mstar Small Growth
Alpha	-8.1	-8.1
Beta	1.36	0.94
R-Squared	71	93

Standard Deviation	23.75
Mean	-5.37
Sharpe Ratio	-0.29

Morningstar's Take by Kunal Kapoor 12-13-04

There's no way to sugarcoat it: Brown Capital Management Small Company has been lousy lately. But we think investors shouldn't give up on it.

This fund's performance for the trailing three-year period through Dec. 10, 2004, has been terrible. During that time, the fund has slipped 4.40% annually and lags more than 90% of its small-cap growth peers. Moreover, the fund's underperformance in 2004 owes partly to some mistakes. As such, it isn't unfair for shareholders to wonder if management has simply lost it.

They haven't. We like management's conviction and willingness to adhere to its strategy even in tough times. Unlike other small-cap managers, this team's goal is to identify small companies with less than $250 million in operating revenues that the fund can own for years. As such, turnover here is in the single digits--a fact that is almost unheard of in its category. That means the fund is inevitably going to go through some rough stretches as management chooses to ignore short-term hiccups in a firm's business with the singular goal of assessing its long-range potential. Moreover, the fund tends to be heavily concentrated in tech and health-care stocks, and the former have certainly hurt a bit in 2004.

This approach isn't an easy one to live with. The fund owns stakes in a multitude of firms whose stock prices are rich by traditional valuation metrics. That introduces a fair amount of short-term volatility to the portfolio. Moreover, because the fund is remarkably concentrated, the downside of a single bad call is severe.

Ultimately, however, these factors are less of an issue to long-term investors. As such, we're willing to wait out the lean periods with the expectation that management can deliver over lengthier frames, such as over five- and 10-years. We feel that the research they do is rigorous, thoughtful, and effective, even if it isn't infallible.

Portfolio Analysis 09-30-04

Share change since 03-04 Total Stocks:51

	Sector	PE	YTD Ret%	% Assets
Molecular Devices	Health	54.0	5.85	4.06
Affymetrix	Health	59.8	48.52	3.96
Symyx Technologies	Ind Mtrls	83.4	46.23	3.76
⊖ Transaction Systems Arch	Software	14.7	-10.87	3.68
Acxiom	Business	32.3	42.18	3.56
Cuno	Ind Mtrls	29.9	31.91	3.37
Ansys	Software	26.7	61.51	3.26
⊕ Cognex	Hardware	31.3	-0.43	3.12
⊖ PDI	Business	13.8	-16.90	3.04
⊖ Dionex	Health	28.0	23.14	3.00
Manhattan Associates	Software	30.1	-13.60	2.98
Dendrite International	Health	28.5	23.57	2.97
⊕ FEI	Hardware	59.0	-6.67	2.87
Techne	Health	28.3	2.80	2.87
Catalina Marketing	Business	—	48.90	2.79
Specialty Laboratories	Health	—	-34.25	2.78
FLIR Systems	Ind Mtrls	27.4	74.77	2.71
Diagnostic Products	Health	23.1	20.59	2.55
American Italian Pasta	Goods	14.2	-43.38	2.47
Albany Molecular Researc	Health	—	-25.78	2.43

Current Investment Style

Value Blnd Growth; Large Mid Small

Market Cap	%
Giant	0.0
Large	0.0
Mid	19.0
Small	51.9
Micro	29.1

Avg $mil: 682

Value Measures		Rel Category
Price/Earnings	27.95	1.29
Price/Book	2.44	0.93
Price/Sales	2.54	1.69
Price/Cash Flow	13.88	1.73
Dividend Yield %	0.02	0.06

Growth Measures	%	Rel Category
Long-Term Erngs	18.67	1.08
Book Value	6.73	1.04
Sales	4.39	0.68
Cash Flow	4.04	0.30
Historical Erngs	6.19	0.46

Profitability	%	Rel Category
Return on Equity	8.46	0.86
Return on Assets	4.87	1.11
Net Margin	7.78	1.14

Sector Weightings	% of Stocks	Rel S&P 500	3 Year High	3 Year Low
Info	32.57	1.52		
Software	21.67	5.04	31	22
Hardware	9.79	0.96	10	5
Media	0.00	0.00	2	0
Telecom	1.11	0.35	3	1
Service	51.33	1.11		
Health	37.69	3.02	43	35
Consumer	2.09	0.23	6	2
Business	11.55	2.85	14	12
Financial	0.00	0.00	0	0
Mfg	16.10	0.50		
Goods	6.13	0.66	6	1
Ind Mtrls	9.97	0.79	10	4
Energy	0.00	0.00	0	0
Utilities	0.00	0.00	0	0

Composition

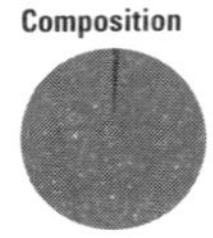

Cash	1.3
Stocks	98.7
Bonds	0.0
Other	0.0
Foreign (% of Stock)	0.0

Address:	116 South Franklin Street, Rocky Mount NC 27802, 877-892-4226
Web Address:	www.ncfunds.com
Inception:	07-23-92
Advisor:	Brown Capital Management Inc.
Subadvisor:	None
NTF Plans:	Schwab OneSource, Fidelity Instl-NTF

Minimum Purchase:	Closed	Add: —	IRA: —
Min Auto Inv Plan:	Closed	Add: —	
Sales Fees:	No-load		
Management Fee:	1.00%, 0.25%A		
Actual Fees:	Mgt:1.00%	Dist:	
Expense Projections:	3Yr:$375	5Yr:$649	10Yr:$1432
Income Distrib:	Quarterly		

Buffalo Small Cap

Ticker	Load	NAV	Yield	Total Assets	Mstar Category
BUFSX	Closed	$27.65	0.1%	$1,971 mil	Small Growth

Governance and Management

Fiduciary Grade: A

Portfolio Manager(s)

The team has recently changed. Kent Gasaway and Robert Male have both comanaged the fund since its April 1998 inception. However, in August 2003, long-tenured comanager Tom Laming and one stock analyst left the fund's advisor, Kornitzer Capital Management. In November 2003, Grant Sarris, a former small-cap manager with Waddell & Reed, was hired to replace Laming. Four analysts support Male, Gasaway, and Sarris.

Strategy

The managers employ numerous themes to direct stock selection, such as those related to demographic patterns and technological innovation. A growth-at-a-reasonable-price philosophy is used within these themes. Firms with strong earnings and cash flow, competitive products, and rock-solid balance sheets are fund favorites. Such stocks often sell for a premium, but management gets edgy when prices climb too high. The fund focuses on stocks with market caps of less than a $1 billion, but it occasionally buys some bigger companies. Its initial position in any one issue is small, but it holds on to winners. Turnover is very low.

Historical Profile

Return High
Risk Average
Rating ★★★★★ Highest

	1998	1999	2000	2001	2002	2003	12-04
Investment Style Equity Stock %	68%	98%	96%	91%	96%	93%	98%

▼ Manager Change
▽ Partial Manager Change

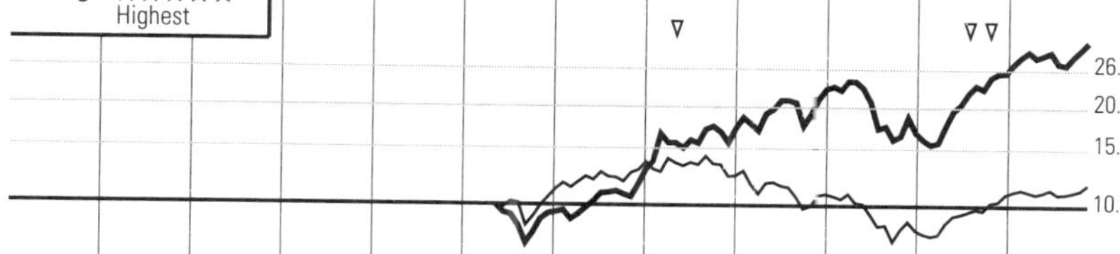

Growth of $10,000
— Investment Values of Fund
— Investment Values of S&P 500

Performance Quartile (within Category)

History

1993	1994	1995	1996	1997	1998	1999	2000	2001	2002	2003	12-04	History
—	—	—	—	—	9.63	12.76	15.24	19.96	14.80	22.18	27.65	NAV
—	—	—	—	—	-3.29*	34.79	33.69	31.18	-25.75	51.23	28.82	Total Return %
—	—	—	—	—	—	13.75	42.79	43.06	-3.66	22.56	17.95	+/-S&P 500
—	—	—	—	—	—	-8.30	56.12	40.41	4.51	2.69	14.51	+/-Russ 2000 Gr
—	—	—	—	—	0.00	0.00	0.00	0.00	0.00	0.00	0.08	Income Return %
—	—	—	—	—	—	34.79	33.69	31.18	-25.75	51.23	28.74	Capital Return %
—	—	—	—	—	—	67	2	1	42	19	1	Total Rtn % Rank Cat
—	—	—	—	—	0.04	0.00	0.00	0.00	0.00	0.00	0.02	Income $
—	—	—	—	—	0.00	0.21	1.67	0.03	0.03	0.20	0.88	Capital Gains $
—	—	—	—	—	—	—	1.12	1.04	1.01	1.02	1.01	Expense Ratio %
—	—	—	—	—	—	—	-0.27	-0.12	-0.44	-0.55	-0.53	Income Ratio %
—	—	—	—	—	—	—	42	31	6	23	22	Turnover Rate %
—	—	—	—	—	—	24	49	1,027	857	1,418	1,971	Net Assets $mil

Performance 12-31-04

	1st Qtr	2nd Qtr	3rd Qtr	4th Qtr	Total
2000	20.53	1.89	10.08	-1.11	33.69
2001	-1.77	23.45	-16.18	29.06	31.18
2002	5.61	-13.25	-23.00	5.26	-25.75
2003	-6.82	30.38	11.12	12.03	51.23
2004	15.87	-0.32	-3.01	15.00	28.82

Trailing	Total Return%	+/- S&P 500	+/- Russ 2000 Gr	%Rank Cat	Growth of $10,000
3 Mo	15.00	5.77	-0.08	28	11,500
6 Mo	11.54	4.35	3.38	16	11,154
1 Yr	28.82	17.95	14.51	1	12,882
3 Yr Avg	13.10	9.52	7.31	7	14,467
5 Yr Avg	20.47	22.77	24.04	2	25,374
10 Yr Avg	—	—	—	—	—
15 Yr Avg	—	—	—	—	—

Tax Analysis	Tax-Adj Rtn%	%Rank Cat	Tax-Cost Rat	%Rank Cat
3 Yr (estimated)	12.72	6	0.34	32
5 Yr (estimated)	19.63	2	0.70	31
10 Yr (estimated)	—	—	—	—

Potential Capital Gain Exposure: 29% of assets

Rating and Risk

Time Period	Load-Adj Return %	Morningstar Rtn vs Cat	Morningstar Risk vs Cat	Morningstar Risk-Adj Rating
1 Yr	28.82			
3 Yr	13.10	High	+Avg	★★★★
5 Yr	20.47	High	Avg	★★★★★
10 Yr	—	—	—	—
Incept	19.50			

Other Measures	Standard Index S&P 500	Best Fit Index Russ 2000
Alpha	9.9	0.7
Beta	1.26	1.14
R-Squared	68	90
Standard Deviation	26.25	
Mean	13.10	
Sharpe Ratio	0.45	

Portfolio Analysis 09-30-04

Share change since 06-04 Total Stocks:63	Sector	PE	YTD Ret%	% Assets
☼ Warner Chilcott plc (ADR	—	—	—	3.70
⊖ Pharmaceutical Product D	Health	41.7	53.10	3.2
⊖ Mentor	Health	25.0	44.90	2.98
⊖ Elan ADR	Health	—	295.50	2.95
Argosy Gaming	Consumer	24.0	79.68	2.88
Ameristar Casinos	Consumer	21.1	78.86	2.61
⊖ Covance	Health	26.6	44.59	2.60
⊖ Royal Caribbean Cruises	Goods	36.9	58.33	2.57
⊖ Penn National Gaming	Goods	34.8	161.89	2.45
WMS Industries	Consumer	—	28.02	2.43
⊖ Charles River Laboratori	Health	24.5	34.02	2.26
⊖ Cabot Microelectronics	Hardware	20.5	-18.22	2.18
⊖ American Medical Systems	Health	—	91.61	2.12
⊖ American Eagle Outfitter	Consumer	35.5	188.04	2.10
Borders Group	Consumer	14.1	17.47	2.09
Inamed	Health	36.4	31.63	2.06
⊖ Brunswick	Goods	18.1	57.47	1.87
⊕ FileNet	Software	53.4	-4.87	1.86
⊕ Rent-A-Center	Consumer	13.7	-11.67	1.80
Isle of Capri Casinos	Consumer	30.4	19.47	1.74

Current Investment Style

Value Blnd Growth — Large Mid Small

Market Cap	%
Giant	0.0
Large	5.6
Mid	40.8
Small	51.4
Micro	2.2

Avg $mil: 1,457

Value Measures		Rel Category
Price/Earnings	18.67	0.87
Price/Book	2.39	0.91
Price/Sales	1.13	0.79
Price/Cash Flow	4.63	0.58
Dividend Yield %	0.71	2.29

Growth Measures	%	Rel Category
Long-Term Erngs	15.1	0.87
Book Value	10.92	1.69
Sales	7.39	1.14
Cash Flow	18.24	1.35
Historical Erngs	1.81	0.13

Profitability	%	Rel Category
Return on Equity	11.64	1.18
Return on Assets	5.43	1.24
Net Margin	7.57	1.11

Sector Weightings	% of Stocks	Rel S&P 500	3 Year High	3 Year Low
Info	18.17	0.85		
Software	4.46	1.04	5	3
Hardware	13.71	1.34	19	9
Media	0.00	0.00	0	0
Telecom	0.00	0.00	0	0
Service	63.72	1.37		
Health	25.54	2.04	30	11
Consumer	29.28	3.22	40	25
Business	0.00	0.00	3	0
Financial	8.90	0.43	17	8
Mfg	18.12	0.56		
Goods	11.28	1.21	15	11
Ind Mtrls	6.84	0.54	8	4
Energy	0.00	0.00	2	0
Utilities	0.00	0.00	0	0

Composition

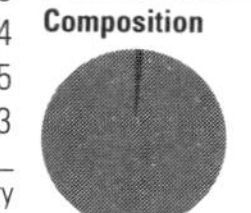

Cash	1.6
Stocks	98.3
Bonds	0.0
Other	0.1
Foreign (% of Stock)	9.8

Morningstar's Take by Gareth Lyons 12-13-04

It's time for Buffalo Small Cap to consider a hard close.

When this fund's asset base reached $1 billion in early 2002, Buffalo decided to close it to new investors looking to gain access through supermarkets, such as Schwab. Existing shareholders could add to their positions, but new investors were only allowed to access the fund by going directly to Buffalo. The move meant flows into the fund dissipated to a manageable trickle from a potentially harmful flood. But assets have ballooned anyway. Because the fund has notched a cumulative 75% over the past two years, it now hauls a worryingly large $2 billion, raising our concerns about this fund's future flexibility.

Admittedly, the strategy here allows for asset growth. Advisor Kornitzer Capital invests in its picks for the long haul, homing in on reasonably valued companies that stand to benefit from secular long-term trends, such as demographic shifts. That low-turnover approach isn't apt to encounter major liquidity problems, as the managers here buy and sell much less frequently than rivals who ply fast-trading strategies. Moreover, the team has always emphasized small- to mid-cap stocks with market-cap ranges of $500 million to $2.5 billion, only occasionally delving into risky, illiquid, micro-cap names.

But even though the managers have not strayed from their core strategy, we think the fund's rapid growth is a concern, especially given the portfolio here is spread across only 60 or so names. Indeed, some signs of stress have already appeared. For example, the fund's current position in J. Jill Group accounts for only 1.5% of assets, yet it represents almost 5 times the stock's average daily trading volume. Trading that name without affecting its stock price is likely to prove difficult. Of course, closing the fund to all channels won't deplete this fund's girth. But it would, at the very least, help to preserve some flexibility for this talented management going forward.

Address:	Kornitzer Capital Management Shawnee Mission KS 66205 800-492-8332
Web Address:	www.buffalofunds.com
Inception:	04-14-98 *
Advisor:	Kornitzer Capital Management, Inc.
Subadvisor:	None
NTF Plans:	Fidelity Retail-NTF, Schwab OneSource

Minimum Purchase:	Closed	Add: —	IRA: —
Min Auto Inv Plan:	Closed	Add: —	
Sales Fees:	No-load		
Management Fee:	1.00%		
Actual Fees:	Mgt:1.00%	Dist:	
Expense Projections:	3Yr:$322	5Yr:$558	10Yr:$1236
Income Distrib:	Semi-Annually		

Calamos Convertible A

Ticker	Load	NAV	Yield	Total Assets	Mstar Category
CCVIX	Closed	$21.20	2.5%	$1,225 mil	Convertibles

Governance and Management

Fiduciary Grade: B

Portfolio Manager(s)

John Calamos wrote the book on convertibles and has more than 20 years of experience investing in convertibles securities. Nick Calamos, who has comanaged the fund since 1988, developed the firm's quantitative models. New investors seeking access to their skills might consider Calamos Growth & Income, a slightly bolder convertible-based fund, given that this fund is closed.

Strategy

Comanagers John and Nick Calamos have traditionally focused on high-credit-quality issues that are trading at moderate conversion premiums, meaning the convertible is somewhat correlated with the underlying equity. Management uses a quantitative approach to identify attractively valued issues and backs that up with fundamental analysis and company visits. In February 2003, the fund dropped its investment-grade average credit-quality requirement and will likely carry more lower-rated credits.

Historical Profile

Return Above Avg
Risk Average
Rating ★★★★ Above Avg

Investment Style: Equity Stock %: 17% | 12% | 6% | 17% | 21% | 23% | 20% | 19%

▼ Manager Change
▽ Partial Manager Change

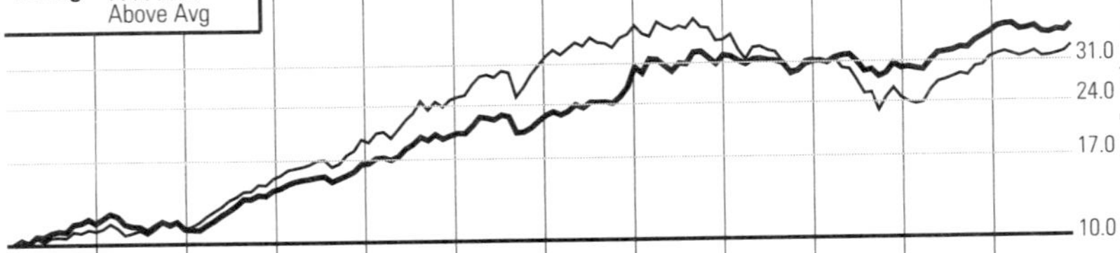

Performance Quartile (within Category)

1993	1994	1995	1996	1997	1998	1999	2000	2001	2002	2003	12-04	History
13.80	11.82	13.85	14.41	15.87	16.87	21.80	20.38	18.56	17.41	21.24	21.20	NAV
17.55	-7.04	29.25	16.70	20.81	11.64	35.11	7.25	-4.28	-4.56	25.01	7.54	Total Return %
7.49	-8.35	-8.28	-6.24	-12.54	-16.93	14.07	16.35	7.60	17.53	-3.66	-3.33	+/-S&P 500
1.14	-2.20	5.29	4.58	5.30	-0.57	-0.88	14.77	-1.37	-1.44	2.04	-0.77	+/-Merrill Lynch Convert
3.98	2.52	3.16	3.53	3.21	2.71	2.96	2.62	3.09	1.66	2.80	2.69	Income Return %
13.57	-9.56	26.09	13.17	17.60	8.93	32.15	4.63	-7.37	-6.22	22.21	4.85	Capital Return %
35	77	1	49	33	21	35	23	40	10	55	59	Total Rtn % Rank Cat
0.52	0.34	0.37	0.47	0.45	0.43	0.50	0.54	0.62	0.31	0.48	0.56	Income $
1.35	0.68	1.00	1.18	1.05	0.38	0.37	2.44	0.31	0.00	0.00	1.04	Capital Gains $
1.70	1.60	1.60	1.50	1.50	1.40	1.40	1.40	1.20	1.20	1.20	1.15	Expense Ratio %
3.20	2.80	3.30	3.00	2.80	3.30	2.60	2.30	2.50	2.70	3.80	2.36	Income Ratio %
73	73	42	65	52	76	78	91	93	37	36	67	Turnover Rate %
17	16	21	32	52	68	86	129	250	461	632	554	Net Assets $mil

Performance 12-31-04

	1st Qtr	2nd Qtr	3rd Qtr	4th Qtr	Total
2000	4.71	-2.35	7.52	-2.44	7.25
2001	-5.53	2.29	-7.37	6.93	-4.28
2002	2.21	-2.50	-9.13	5.39	-4.56
2003	-1.08	11.83	2.40	10.36	25.01
2004	5.37	-1.52	-2.48	6.27	7.54

Trailing	Total Return%	+/- S&P 500	+/- Merrill Lynch Convert	%Rank Cat	Growth of $10,000
3 Mo	6.27	-2.96	-0.09	82	10,627
6 Mo	3.64	-3.55	-1.17	94	10,364
1 Yr	7.54	-3.33	-0.77	59	10,754
3 Yr Avg	8.66	5.08	-0.21	42	12,829
5 Yr Avg	5.67	7.97	2.68	23	13,175
10 Yr Avg	13.73	1.66	2.73	4	36,203
15 Yr Avg	12.19	1.26	1.63	22	56,145

Tax Analysis	Tax-Adj Rtn%	%Rank Cat	Tax-Cost Rat	%Rank Cat
3 Yr (estimated)	4.99	57	1.14	45
5 Yr (estimated)	2.51	35	1.64	28
10 Yr (estimated)	10.52	8	2.15	38

Potential Capital Gain Exposure: 20% of assets

Rating and Risk

Time Period	Load-Adj Return %	Morningstar Rtn vs Cat	Morningstar Risk vs Cat	Morningstar Risk-Adj Rating
1 Yr	0.39			
3 Yr	6.20	Avg	Avg	★★★
5 Yr	4.22	Avg	-Avg	★★★
10 Yr	12.95	+Avg	Avg	★★★★★
Incept	10.99			

Other Measures	Standard Index S&P 500	Best Fit Index Mstar Mid Core
Alpha	5.8	0.0
Beta	0.56	0.62
R-Squared	70	88
Standard Deviation	10.77	
Mean	8.66	
Sharpe Ratio	0.68	

Portfolio Analysis 09-30-04

Total Fixed-Income:19	Date of Maturity	Amount $000	Value $000	% Net Assets
Ford Mtr Pfd	01-15-32	992	51,862	4.13
Tyco Intl Grp S A Cv 3.1	01-15-23	27,500	41,319	3.29
Intl Game Tech 144A Cv	01-29-33	37,000	29,415	2.34
Morgan Stanley 0.25%	04-01-09	28,600	26,562	2.12
Baxter Intl Pfd	02-16-06	485	26,069	2.08
Fluor 1.5%	02-15-24	24,000	25,170	2.01
Albertsons Pfd	05-16-07	960	24,864	1.98
Washington Mut		441	24,053	1.92
Washington Post		24	22,080	1.76
Royal Caribbean Cruises	02-02-21	41,000	21,833	1.74
Amerada Hess Pfd		270	21,551	1.72
Countrywide Financial		546	21,507	1.71
Anglo Amer Cv 3.375%	04-17-07	18,000	21,155	1.69
Givaudan Us Cv 1%	06-07-06	11,000	21,054	1.68
Cendant Cv 3.875%	11-27-11	20,000	20,225	1.61
Invitrogen 144A Cv 2%	08-01-23	18,300	20,222	1.61
Washington Mutual		514	20,087	1.60
Liberty Media 144A 0.75%	03-30-23	17,720	19,115	1.52
Travelers Ppty Cas Pfd	04-15-32	830	18,824	1.50
Neiman-Marcus A		318	18,285	1.46

Investment Style

Avg Eff Maturity	—
Avg Credit Quality	—
Avg Wtd Coupon	2.08%
Avg Wtd Price	104.69% of par

Coupon Range	% of Bonds	Rel Cat
0% PIK	0.0	0.0
0% to 8%	100.0	1.0
8% to 11%	0.0	0.0
11% to 14%	0.0	0.0
More than 14%	0.0	0.0

1.00=Category Average

Special Securities	
Restricted/Illiquid Secs	28
Emerging-Markets Secs	0
Options/Futures/Warrants	No

Composition	
Cash	0.3
Stocks	19.4
Bonds	18.5
Convertibles	44.8
Other	17.0

Credit Analysis		% bonds 09-30-04	
US Govt	—	BB	—
AAA	—	B	—
AA	—	Below B	—
A	—	NR/NA	—
BBB	—		

Morningstar's Take by Kerry O'Boyle 12-31-04

While not as adventurous as its sibling, Calamos Convertible is nevertheless a fine option.

This fund employs a relatively moderate approach to convertible investing. Whereas sister fund Calamos Growth & Income uses an aggressive style consisting of lower-quality convertibles and a hefty stake in equities, this fund plays it straight. Roughly 85% of its assets are held in convertible bonds or preferreds, and 65% of that total is devoted to investment-grade issues. That mix puts the fund roughly in line with its typical convertible-fund rivals, which seek to benefit from the downside protection offered by convert's fixed-income characteristics and most of the upside potential of a company's underlying stock.

Calamos' edge comes from an all-encompassing research approach that relies on both quantitative models and fundamental analysis. They look for firms with high revenue growth relative to industry peers and signs of sustainable growth in the form of superior cash flows and return on invested capital. In addition, they're willing to make top-down sector calls in an attempt to benefit from various market cycles.

Over the long run, results here have been impressive. In fact, while returns have been middling versus its convertible peers the past two years, the fund still boasts one of the best records over the trailing five-and 10-year periods through Dec. 30, 2004. A choppy stock market and a significant number of convertible issues being called has made for a difficult year for the fund. But it has surged in the second half of the 2004 relative to its peers, thanks to strong performances in the consumer arena--a heavy weighting for the fund--including holdings in cruise industry stalwarts Carnival and Royal Caribbean.

Overall, this offering has significantly outperformed the S&P 500 Index during the past decade with considerably less volatility and epitomizes the potential of a well-run convertible strategy.

Address:	Calamos Investment Trust Naperville, IL 60563 800-823-7386
Web Address:	www.calamos.com
Inception:	06-21-85
Advisor:	Calamos Advisors LLC
Subadvisor:	None
NTF Plans:	Federated Tr NTF, Fidelity Instl-NTF

Minimum Purchase:	Closed	Add: —	IRA: —
Min Auto Inv Plan:	Closed	Add: —	
Sales Fees:	4.75%L, 2.00%R		
Management Fee:	0.70%		
Actual Fees:	Mgt:0.70%	Dist:0.25%	
Expense Projections:	3Yr:$823	5Yr:$1078	10Yr:$1806
Income Distrib:	Quarterly		

Calamos Gr & Inc A

Analyst Pick	Ticker	Load	NAV	Yield	Total Assets	Mstar Category
✔	CVTRX	4.75%	$29.82	1.5%	$4,731 mil	Convertibles

Governance and Management

Fiduciary Grade: B

Portfolio Manager(s)

John Calamos wrote the book on convertibles. And he has more than 20 years of experience investing in convertible securities. Nick Calamos has comanaged the fund since 1988 and developed the firm's quantitative models. The pair also guide the highly successful Calamos Growth, which invests exclusively in stocks. The managers eat their own cooking: Most of their wealth is invested in the funds.

Strategy

Comanagers John and Nick Calamos couple convertible bonds and stocks in this fund. The convertibles are often low- and mid-quality issues from small- and mid-cap firms. Management uses a quantitative approach to identify attractively valued issues and backs that up with fundamental analysis and company visits.

Historical Profile

Return High
Risk Above Avg
Rating ★★★★★ Highest

Investment Style
Equity
Stock %

18%	20%	13%	14%	5%	24%	22%	37%	43%

▼ Manager Change
▽ Partial Manager Change

Growth of $10,000
▬ Investment Values of Fund
— Investment Values of S&P 500

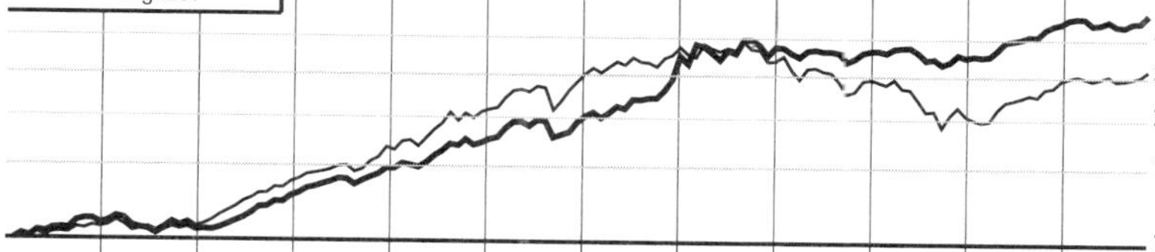

Performance Quartile (within Category)

1993	1994	1995	1996	1997	1998	1999	2000	2001	2002	2003	12-04	History
13.68	12.35	14.74	15.46	16.59	17.95	26.51	25.05	23.60	22.21	27.78	29.82	NAV
13.56	-5.31	29.13	19.22	23.34	17.62	52.94	6.86	-2.38	-4.10	27.57	9.67	Total Return %
3.50	-6.62	-8.40	-3.72	-10.01	-10.95	31.90	15.96	9.50	17.99	-1.10	-1.20	+/-S&P 500
-2.85	-0.47	5.17	7.10	7.83	5.41	16.95	14.38	0.53	-0.98	4.60	1.36	+/-Merrill Lynch Convert
2.76	2.23	3.52	2.09	2.53	1.96	2.64	2.30	2.49	1.80	2.28	1.65	Income Return %
10.80	-7.54	25.61	17.13	20.81	15.66	50.30	4.56	-4.87	-5.90	25.29	8.02	Capital Return %
70	41	4	31	8	12	2	32	19	7	37	37	Total Rtn % Rank Cat
0.36	0.30	0.43	0.29	0.38	0.32	0.47	0.59	0.61	0.42	0.50	0.46	Income $
1.08	0.30	0.71	1.68	2.00	1.17	0.28	2.73	0.21	0.00	0.00	0.16	Capital Gains $
2.00	2.00	2.00	2.00	2.00	2.00	2.00	1.70	1.40	1.30	1.30	1.14	Expense Ratio %
2.60	2.30	3.00	2.60	2.40	2.00	2.30	1.80	2.60	2.20	3.30	1.63	Income Ratio %
132	155	85	86	92	116	88	117	82	40	27	50	Turnover Rate %
5	4	4	8	10	16	24	65	173	474	1,634	2,507	Net Assets $mil

Performance 12-31-04

	1st Qtr	2nd Qtr	3rd Qtr	4th Qtr	Total
2000	7.06	-2.65	7.90	-4.98	6.86
2001	-6.65	4.13	-7.01	8.01	-2.38
2002	1.85	-2.65	-8.06	5.19	-4.10
2003	1.05	11.74	2.82	9.87	27.57
2004	3.56	-1.71	-1.21	9.06	9.66

Trailing	Total Return%	+/- S&P 500	+/- Merrill Lynch Convert	%Rank Cat	Growth of $10,000
3 Mo	9.06	-0.17	2.70	4	10,906
6 Mo	7.73	0.54	2.92	12	10,773
1 Yr	9.67	-1.20	1.36	37	10,967
3 Yr Avg	10.29	6.71	1.42	18	13,416
5 Yr Avg	6.95	9.25	3.96	13	13,993
10 Yr Avg	16.94	4.87	5.94	1	47,822
15 Yr Avg	14.68	3.75	4.12	1	78,040

Tax Analysis	Tax-Adj Rtn%	%Rank Cat	Tax-Cost Rat	%Rank Cat
3 Yr (estimated)	7.75	26	0.71	14
5 Yr (estimated)	4.53	15	1.31	13
10 Yr (estimated)	13.78	1	2.23	42

Potential Capital Gain Exposure: 14% of assets

Rating and Risk

Time Period	Load-Adj Return %	Morningstar Rtn vs Cat	Morningstar Risk vs Cat	Morningstar Risk-Adj Rating
1 Yr	4.46			
3 Yr	8.52	+Avg	Avg	★★★★
5 Yr	5.92	+Avg	Avg	★★★★
10 Yr	16.37	High	+Avg	★★★★★
Incept	14.24			

Other Measures	Standard Index S&P 500	Best Fit Index Wil 4500
Alpha	7.4	2.6
Beta	0.53	0.57
R-Squared	68	90

Standard Deviation	10.45
Mean	10.29
Sharpe Ratio	0.86

Portfolio Analysis 09-30-04

Total Fixed-Income:29	Date of Maturity	Amount $000	Value $000	% Net Assets
Ford Mtr Pfd	01-15-32	1,770	92,536	2.19
Washington Mutual		2,070	80,896	1.92
Starbucks		1,775	80,692	1.91
Home Depot		1,940	76,048	1.80
Valero Engy Cv		1,750	70,219	1.66
AES		7,000	69,930	1.66
Morgan Stanley 0.25%	04-01-09	75,000	69,656	1.65
International Game Tech		1,900	68,305	1.62
UnitedHealth Group		900	66,366	1.57
Microsoft		2,276	62,931	1.49
Archer Daniels Midland		3,500	59,430	1.41
Cendant		2,750	59,400	1.41
Liberty Media 0.75%	03-30-23	55,000	59,331	1.41
Harley-Davidson		990	58,846	1.39
Stanley Works		1,350	57,416	1.36
Penney J C Cv 5%	10-15-08	46,000	57,155	1.35
Electronic Arts		1,200	55,188	1.31
Health Mgmt Assoc Cv 1.5	08-01-23	53,000	54,855	1.30
Bausch & Lomb		775	51,499	1.22
Monsanto Company		1,400	50,988	1.21

Investment Style

Avg Eff Maturity	—
Avg Credit Quality	—
Avg Wtd Coupon	2.43%
Avg Wtd Price	108.68% of par

Coupon Range	% of Bonds	Rel Cat
0% PIK	1.5	0.1
0% to 8%	93.7	1.0
8% to 11%	6.3	2.0
11% to 14%	0.0	0.0
More than 14%	0.0	0.0

1.00=Category Average

Special Securities

Restricted/Illiquid Secs	17
Emerging-Markets Secs	1
Options/Futures/Warrants	No

Credit Analysis		% bonds 09-30-04	
US Govt	—	BB	—
AAA	—	B	—
AA	—	Below B	—
A	—	NR/NA	—
BBB	—		

Composition

Cash	2.8
Stocks	42.7
Bonds	15.1
Convertibles	32.3
Other	7.1

Morningstar's Take by Kerry O'Boyle 12-31-04

Calamos Growth & Income's mix of stocks and convertibles offers plenty of appeal for risk-conscious investors.

Unlike most of its convertible peers, this offering carries a hefty stake in straight equities--currently 40% of assets. That--plus a penchant for investing in lower-quality convertibles--makes it one of the more daring choices in the group. While this typically gives the fund an edge during strong stock market rallies, managers John and Nick Calamos have also been able to benefit from the defensive, fixed-income characteristics of their convertible holdings in minimizing losses during rough years.

The key here is the deft manner in which they manage risk in the portfolio. Calamos often uses stocks as a way to supplement the equity-sensitivity of their convertibles to the level of aggressiveness that they desire. For example, since 2002 the fund has owned the stock, and several convertibles, of Tyco International. As the stock appreciated toward what Calamos considered fair value--and the converts became more equity-sensitive-- they sold the stock to minimize their overall exposure but kept the convertibles. They believe that the company still has good upside potential, but that the converts give them an added measure of downside protection.

Calamos also uses top-down macroeconomic bets to drive their sector-allocation calls. This led them to trim back their technology holdings in the spring of 2004, after a good run. It has also kept them heavily invested in consumer discretionary stocks. Nick Calamos remains bullish on the economy and the average consumer--whom he doesn't think gets enough credit for managing personal debt.

All told, this offering is worthy of being one of our convertible Analyst Picks. While the fund's growing size--assets are now at $4.5 billion--is a concern and may be contributing to its large reliance on stocks, Calamos has handled that bloat well so far with another solid performance in 2004.

Address:	Calamos Investment Trust Naperville, IL 60563 800-823-7386
Web Address:	www.calamos.com
Inception:	09-22-88
Advisor:	Calamos Advisors LLC
Subadvisor:	None
NTF Plans:	Federated Tr NTF, Fidelity Instl-NTF

Minimum Purchase:	$1000	Add: $50	IRA: $500
Min Auto Inv Plan:	$1000	Add: $50	
Sales Fees:	4.75%L, 2.00%R		
Management Fee:	0.68%		
Actual Fees:	Mgt:0.68%	Dist:0.25%	
Expense Projections:	3Yr:$820	5Yr:$1073	10Yr:$1795
Income Distrib:	Quarterly		

Calamos Growth A

Ticker	Load	NAV	Yield	Total Assets	Mstar Category
CVGRX	4.75%	$52.98	0.0%	$13,684 mil	Mid-Cap Growth

Governance and Management

Fiduciary Grade: B

Portfolio Manager(s)

Calamos Asset Management, known for its convertible-bond expertise, employs techniques at this fund that are similar to those it uses in assessing underlying stocks in the convertibles market. John and Nick Calamos have managed the fund since its September 1990 inception, and John's son, John Jr., came on board in 1994.

Strategy

Management uses quantitative models to search for companies growing faster than their industry and sector peers as measured by earnings growth and returns on invested capital. It then digs deeply into company balance sheets to understand the business and looks for strong free cash flows and sustainable growth. Finally, in constructing the portfolio, management uses top-down macroeconomic analysis to identify promising sectors and themes to exploit with higher/lower weightings.

Historical Profile

Return High
Risk Average
Rating ★★★★★ Highest

Investment Style: Equity Stock %

100% | 100% | 97% | 98% | 100% | 98% | 85% | 98% | 99%

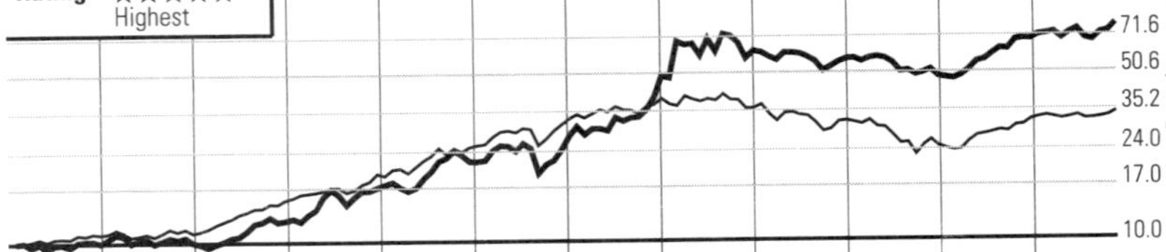

▼ Manager Change
▽ Partial Manager Change

Growth of $10,000
— Investment Values of Fund
— Investment Values of S&P 500

Performance Quartile (within Category)

1993	1994	1995	1996	1997	1998	1999	2000	2001	2002	2003	12-04	History
14.78	13.81	14.46	18.13	17.21	21.91	35.71	40.51	37.40	31.46	44.78	52.98	NAV
4.35	-5.70	27.50	37.91	24.22	27.31	77.70	26.59	-7.68	-15.88	42.34	18.65	Total Return %
-5.71	-7.01	-10.03	14.97	-9.13	-1.26	56.66	35.69	4.20	6.21	13.67	7.78	+/-S&P 500
-6.84	-3.54	-6.48	20.43	1.68	9.45	26.41	38.34	12.47	11.53	-0.37	3.17	+/-Russ MG
0.14	0.00	0.51	0.00	0.00	0.00	0.00	0.00	0.00	0.00	0.00	0.00	Income Return %
4.21	-5.70	26.99	37.91	24.22	27.31	77.70	26.59	-7.68	-15.88	42.34	18.65	Capital Return %
87	79	74	2	27	22	28	5	16	7	20	11	Total Rtn % Rank Cat
0.02	0.00	0.07	0.00	0.00	0.00	0.00	0.00	0.00	0.00	0.00	0.00	Income $
0.58	0.13	2.97	1.75	5.50	0.00	3.13	4.99	0.00	0.00	0.00	0.14	Capital Gains $
2.00	2.00	2.00	2.00	2.00	2.00	2.00	2.00	1.50	1.55	1.40	1.31	Expense Ratio %
-0.11	0.10	0.20	-0.80	-1.30	-1.50	-1.60	-1.70	-0.70	-1.10	-1.10	-0.96	Income Ratio %
57	87	104	252	174	206	184	175	91	79	60	54	Turnover Rate %
2	2	3	6	8	12	26	102	642	1,521	4,458	9,680	Net Assets $mil

Performance 12-31-04

	1st Qtr	2nd Qtr	3rd Qtr	4th Qtr	Total
2000	34.89	5.67	2.65	-13.48	26.59
2001	-8.57	6.24	-15.27	12.18	-7.68
2002	0.64	-4.44	-10.98	-1.75	-15.88
2003	0.70	16.16	10.60	10.02	42.34
2004	6.34	3.04	-3.85	12.61	18.65

Trailing	Total Return%	+/- S&P 500	+/- Russ MG	%Rank Cat	Growth of $10,000
3 Mo	12.61	3.38	-1.33	57	11,261
6 Mo	8.27	1.08	-0.74	43	10,827
1 Yr	18.65	7.78	3.17	11	11,865
3 Yr Avg	12.41	8.83	6.25	2	14,204
5 Yr Avg	10.67	12.97	14.03	2	16,602
10 Yr Avg	23.42	11.35	12.19	1	82,008
15 Yr Avg	—	—	—	—	—

Tax Analysis	Tax-Adj Rtn%	%Rank Cat	Tax-Cost Rat	%Rank Cat
3 Yr (estimated)	10.59	4	0.02	4
5 Yr (estimated)	9.13	2	0.43	19
10 Yr (estimated)	20.04	1	2.27	69

Potential Capital Gain Exposure: 20% of assets

Rating and Risk

Time Period	Load-Adj Return %	Morningstar Rtn vs Cat	Morningstar Risk vs Cat	Morningstar Risk-Adj Rating
1 Yr	13.01			
3 Yr	10.61	High	-Avg	★★★★★
5 Yr	9.60	High	Avg	★★★★★
10 Yr	22.83	High	Avg	★★★★★
Incept	18.72			

Other Measures	Standard Index S&P 500	Best Fit Index Russ 2000 Gr
Alpha	9.5	7.5
Beta	0.73	0.64
R-Squared	52	84

Standard Deviation	16.97
Mean	12.41
Sharpe Ratio	0.66

Morningstar's Take by Kerry O'Boyle 11-16-04

How long can this superb offering's hot streak last?

Calamos Growth has crushed the competition for most of the past decade. The all-cap offering's performance is simply topnotch, having landed in the top third of the mid-cap growth category year in and year out since 1995. Management's disciplined blend of macroeconomic sector calls along with strong, fundamentally driven bottom-up stock research has kept the fund in the right places at the right times. Lately, that approach has led them to favor larger, relatively stable companies like Qualcomm and Motorola based on their belief that the economic expansion is beginning to mature.

Still, much of the fund's performance in 2004 has come from aggressive-growth stories. Stocks such as Research in Motion--the maker of the Blackberry wireless platform--and antivirus software company Symantec have posted hefty returns, highlighting the stock-picking skills of John and Nick Calamos. Both stocks have been sizeable holdings in the portfolio since 2003, and the Calamoses have continued to add to their stakes as their prospects have continued to look promising.

But the fund is no longer as nimble as it was while it built its tremendous record. At more than $10 billion in assets, it's harder for the Calamoses to shift positions as quickly as they have done in the past to take advantage of their top-down calls. Moreover, with more than 200 holdings in the portfolio, they have to keep track of double the number of stocks they held just a few years ago. Finally, we're disappointed that the fund's fees haven't dropped as quickly as assets have risen, which means shareholders haven't fully benefited from the fund's economies of scale.

To be sure, this is still a highly capable offering. But investors should understand that given its increased size, it will be extremely difficult for the fund to duplicate its stunning past success, and it would be wise to keep expectations in check.

Portfolio Analysis 09-30-04

Share change since 06-04 Total Stocks:213	Sector	PE	YTD Ret%	% Assets
Yahoo	Media	95.1	67.36	2.99
⊕ Qualcomm	Hardware	42.0	58.20	2.90
⊕ Amazon.com	Consumer	55.5	-15.83	2.88
⊕ Research In Motion Ltd	Hardware	—	146.66	2.73
⊕ Motorola	Hardware	28.7	37.93	2.72
⊕ eBay	Consumer	81.6	80.07	2.49
⊕ Symantec	Software	34.5	49.33	2.16
⊕ Electronic Arts	Software	30.9	29.36	1.81
Zimmer Holdings	Health	54.0	13.81	1.74
⊕ Genentech	Health	78.6	16.36	1.54
⊕ Apple Computer	Hardware	NMF	201.36	1.49
⊕ Juniper Networks	Hardware	NMF	45.56	1.43
Coventry Health Care	Health	15.5	23.46	1.42
Autodesk	Software	46.6	209.62	1.34
XM Satellite Radio Holdi	Media	—	43.10	1.23
⊕ Boeing	Ind Mtrls	14.7	24.86	1.18
⊕ Quest Diagnostics	Health	19.8	31.66	1.13
International Game Tech	Consumer	28.1	-2.49	1.07
St. Jude Medical	Health	38.0	36.69	1.04
DR Horton	Consumer	10.7	41.36	1.03

Current Investment Style

Value Blnd Growth; Large Mid Small

Market Cap	%
Giant	11.4
Large	35.4
Mid	43.3
Small	9.4
Micro	0.4
Avg $mil: 7,671	

Value Measures		Rel Category
Price/Earnings	21.33	0.97
Price/Book	3.41	1.14
Price/Sales	1.90	1.07
Price/Cash Flow	9.09	0.94
Dividend Yield %	0.33	0.77

Growth Measures	%	Rel Category
Long-Term Erngs	15.31	0.97
Book Value	9.00	0.90
Sales	6.86	0.80
Cash Flow	20.45	1.68
Historical Erngs	14.87	0.94

Profitability	%	Rel Category
Return on Equity	17.27	1.20
Return on Assets	8.17	1.14
Net Margin	11.35	1.18

Sector Weightings	% of Stocks	Rel S&P 500	3 Year High	3 Year Low
Info	34.33	1.60		
Software	7.65	1.78	11	3
Hardware	19.67	1.93	25	2
Media	4.23	1.10	7	0
Telecom	2.78	0.88	3	0
Service	44.86	0.97		
Health	19.21	1.54	22	13
Consumer	14.99	1.65	48	15
Business	5.22	1.29	12	4
Financial	5.44	0.26	8	2
Mfg	20.80	0.65		
Goods	6.24	0.67	13	5
Ind Mtrls	8.18	0.65	8	1
Energy	6.38	0.89	6	0
Utilities	0.00	0.00	0	0

Composition

Cash	0.4
Stocks	99.5
Bonds	0.0
Other	0.1
Foreign (% of Stock)	4.4

Address:	Calamos Investment Trust Naperville, IL 60563 800-823-7386
Web Address:	www.calamos.com
Inception:	09-04-90
Advisor:	Calamos Advisors LLC
Subadvisor:	None
NTF Plans:	Federated Tr NTF, Fidelity Instl-NTF

Minimum Purchase:	$1000	Add: $50	IRA: $500
Min Auto Inv Plan:	$1000	Add: $50	
Sales Fees:	4.75%L, 2.00%R		
Management Fee:	0.83%		
Actual Fees:	Mgt:0.83%	Dist:0.25%	
Expense Projections:	3Yr:$870	5Yr:$1159	10Yr:$1979
Income Distrib:	Annually		

Calvert Tax-Fr Res Lim A

Ticker	Load	NAV	Yield	SEC Yield	Total Assets	Mstar Category
CTFLX	1.00%	$10.61	1.8%	2.10%	$1,219 mil	Muni National Short

Governance and Management

Fiduciary Grade: B

Portfolio Manager(s)

Tom Dailey runs the fund on a day-to-day basis. He also manages Calvert's taxable and tax-free money market portfolios. He was joined by Gary Miller in October 2003. They are backed by seven credit analysts who cover both taxable and tax-exempt securities.

Strategy

This fund buys munis with attractive yields and short maturities--generally less than three years--from various states. The fund's ultrashort duration limits its sensitivity to interest-rate changes, and although it invests in midquality bonds, it remains a relatively low-risk offering.

Historical Profile

Return Below Avg
Risk Low
Rating ★★ Below Avg

Investment Style
Fixed Income
Income Rtn %Rank Cat: 49 68 76 75 40 30 73 70 67

▼ Manager Change
▽ Partial Manager Change

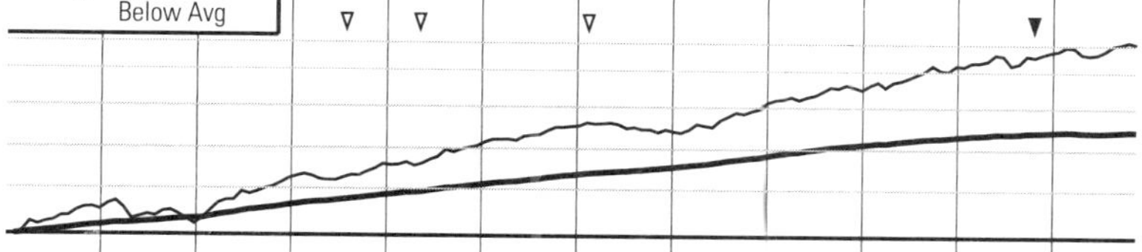

Growth of $10,000
— Investment Values of Fund
— Investment Values of LB Muni

Performance Quartile (within Category)

History

1993	1994	1995	1996	1997	1998	1999	2000	2001	2002	2003	12-04	History
10.72	10.59	10.72	10.69	10.70	10.71	10.64	10.66	10.69	10.74	10.74	10.61	NAV
4.02	2.42	5.55	3.94	4.07	3.87	2.86	4.52	4.46	3.10	1.91	0.62	Total Return %
-8.26	7.59	-11.91	-0.49	-5.12	-2.61	4.92	-7.16	-0.67	-6.50	-3.40	-3.86	+/-LB Muni
-2.20	1.74	-3.32	-0.50	-1.41	-1.34	0.90	-1.71	-2.13	-3.62	-0.77	-1.16	+/-LB Muni 3YR
3.64	3.66	4.30	4.22	3.98	3.76	3.52	4.33	4.18	2.62	1.88	1.84	Income Return %
0.38	-1.24	1.25	-0.28	0.09	0.11	-0.66	0.19	0.28	0.48	0.03	-1.22	Capital Return %
90	1	97	41	83	89	2	94	74	87	70	79	Total Rtn % Rank Cat
0.38	0.39	0.45	0.44	0.42	0.40	0.37	0.45	0.44	0.28	0.20	0.20	Income $
0.00	0.00	0.00	0.00	0.00	0.00	0.00	0.00	0.00	0.00	0.00	0.00	Capital Gains $
0.67	0.66	0.70	0.70	0.69	0.71	0.71	0.70	0.69	0.62	0.57	—	Expense Ratio %
3.59	3.60	4.21	4.17	3.91	3.70	3.47	4.22	4.09	2.57	1.88	—	Income Ratio %
14	27	33	45	52	45	77	82	63	47	31	—	Turnover Rate %
654	548	458	512	566	543	524	464	669	1,340	1,659	1,219	Net Assets $mil

Performance 12-31-04

	1st Qtr	2nd Qtr	3rd Qtr	4th Qtr	Total
2000	0.98	1.10	1.16	1.21	4.52
2001	1.39	1.11	1.10	0.78	4.46
2002	0.58	1.06	0.77	0.65	3.10
2003	0.61	0.57	0.43	0.28	1.91
2004	0.21	-0.31	0.39	0.33	0.62

Trailing	Total Return%	+/- LB Muni	+/- LB Muni 3YR	%Rank Cat	Growth of $10,000
3 Mo	0.33	-0.92	0.14	35	10,033
6 Mo	0.72	-4.47	-1.38	89	10,072
1 Yr	0.62	-3.86	-1.16	79	10,062
3 Yr Avg	1.87	-4.57	-1.84	86	10,572
5 Yr Avg	2.91	-4.29	-1.87	88	11,542
10 Yr Avg	3.48	-3.58	-1.49	95	14,079
15 Yr Avg	3.95	-3.04	—	100	17,880

Tax Analysis	Tax-Adj Rtn%	%Rank Cat	Tax-Cost Rat	%Rank Cat
3 Yr (estimated)	1.53	91	0.00	1
5 Yr (estimated)	2.70	92	0.01	20
10 Yr (estimated)	3.38	90	0.00	1

Potential Capital Gain Exposure: -1% of assets

Rating and Risk

Time Period	Load-Adj Return %	Morningstar Rtn vs Cat	Morningstar Risk vs Cat	Morningstar Risk-Adj Rating
1 Yr	-0.39			
3 Yr	1.53	-Avg	Low	★★
5 Yr	2.71	-Avg	Low	★★
10 Yr	3.38	-Avg	Low	★★
Incept	5.23			

Other Measures	Standard Index LB Aggr	Best Fit Index LB Muni 3YR
Alpha	0.1	0.1
Beta	0.08	0.17
R-Squared	55	68

Standard Deviation	0.53
Mean	1.87
Sharpe Ratio	0.98

Morningstar's Take by Lynn Russell 12-21-04

This fund may not look too appealing at first glance, but more cautious muni investors should take a second look.

As usual, Calvert Tax-Free Limited Reserves has trailed most of its muni-national short-term peers in 2004. The fund's year-to-date gain of 0.53% through Dec. 17, 2004, leaves it lagging more than 80% of its category rivals. The fund's ultrashort duration helped it hold up better than most of its rivals when interest rates jumped in April, but hindered performance when rates moved back down over the summer months. The fund's multifamily housing bonds also weighed on returns as that sector struggled to keep pace with other areas of the muni market.

By design, this fund seldom leads the pack. Managers Tom Dailey and Gary Miller keep a tight lid on the fund's interest-rate risk in order to keep its NAV stable. At just less than two thirds of a year, the fund's duration (a measure of sensitivity to interest-rate fluctuations) is one of the very shortest in this already-tame category. As a result, the fund has historically displayed less month-to-month volatility than any of its muni short competitors. The tradeoff for that relative stability, however, is a modest yield and an unimpressive long-term total return record compared with its muni national short-term rivals. The only time the fund really has a chance to shine is when rates jump sharply, as they did 1999.

But over the long term, this fund has provided a relatively calm place to ride out interest rate spikes while providing a better return than most muni money market offerings. That doesn't mean that the fund's NAV is as steady as that of a money market option--it's been hit this year--and, given the fund's 1% load, the fund is not practical for cash-management purposes. However, we think investors looking to balance the risks of a rate-sensitive municipal bond portfolio might find this fund to their liking.

Address:	4550 Montgomery Ave Ste 1000n Bethesda MD 20814 800-368-2748
Web Address:	www.calvertgroup.com
Inception:	03-04-81
Advisor:	Calvert Asset Management Co Inc.
Subadvisor:	None
NTF Plans:	Fidelity Instl-NTF, Schwab Instl NTF

Minimum Purchase:	$2000	Add: $250	IRA: $1000
Min Auto Inv Plan:	$2000	Add: $100	
Sales Fees:	1.00%L		
Management Fee:	0.50%		
Actual Fees:	Mgt:0.50%	Dist:	
Expense Projections:	3Yr:$281	5Yr:$415	10Yr:$806
Income Distrib:	Monthly		

Portfolio Analysis 12-31-04

Total Fixed-Income:192	Date of Maturity	Amount $000	Value $000	% Net Assets
West Va Econ Dev Auth	04-01-25	23,000	22,467	1.87
Indiana Transn Fin Auth	11-01-18	20,000	20,000	1.67
Birmingham Ala Pub Edl B	06-01-30	17,115	17,115	1.43
Michigan St Ctfs Partn	09-01-11	16,975	16,975	1.42
South Carolina St Hsg Fi		16,300	16,300	1.36
Louisiana Loc Govt Envir		16,000	16,000	1.33
Puerto Rico Comwlth 5%	07-01-18	14,625	15,683	1.31
Weslaco Tex Health Facs	06-01-23	15,475	15,475	1.29
Charter Mac Equity Issue	03-15-07	15,000	15,008	1.25
Massachusetts St Health	06-01-35	15,000	15,000	1.25
California St	05-01-33	15,000	14,999	1.25
Michigan Higher Ed Facs	06-01-34	13,500	13,500	1.13
Oxnard Calif Fing Auth	06-01-33	13,000	13,000	1.08
Yavapai Cnty Ariz Indl D	03-01-28	12,900	12,970	1.08
Maryland St Cmnty Dev Ad	03-01-20	13,000	12,967	1.08

Current Investment Style

Duration: Short Int Long — Quality: High Med Low

[1]Avg Eff Duration	0.7 Yrs
Avg Eff Maturity	0.8 Yrs
Avg Credit Quality	AA
Avg Wtd Coupon	3.34%
Avg Wtd Price	99.90% of par

[1]figure provided by fund

Credit Analysis	% bonds 12-31-04		
US Govt	0	BB	3
AAA	34	B	0
AA	25	Below B	0
A	15	NR/NA	13
BBB	9		

Top 5 States	% bonds		
CA	11.1	IN	5.3
TX	9.2	MA	5.0
PA	5.4		

Composition			
Cash	22.3	Bonds	77.7
Stocks	0.0	Other	0.0

Special Securities	
Restricted/Illiquid Secs	2
Options/Futures/Warrants	No

Sector Weightings	% of Bonds	Rel Cat
General Obligation	21.8	0.62
Utilities	0.7	0.08
Health	5.9	0.82
Water/Waste	8.4	0.80
Housing	20.5	2.75
Education	8.8	1.01
Transportation	5.9	1.39
COP/Lease	4.0	2.55
Industrial	22.0	1.45
Misc Revenue	0.0	—
Demand	1.9	3.02

Causeway Intl Value Inv

Analyst Pick

Ticker	Load	NAV	Yield	Total Assets	Mstar Category
CIVVX	12b-1 only	$16.17	1.4%	$2,345 mil	Foreign Large Value

Governance and Management

Fiduciary Grade: A

Portfolio Manager(s)

Sarah Ketterer and Harry Hartford managed Mercury HW International Value with success until June 2001. Ketterer directed the day-to-day operations at that fund from its inception in 1990; Hartford joined in 1994. Together with James Doyle, they started this fund in October 2001. They're supported by five sector analysts as well as two quantitative analysts.

Strategy

The managers rely on the same value style here as they did at their former charge. They pursue stocks that are cheap on many metrics, have superior return prospects, and pay dividends or repurchase their shares. They focus on large caps and mid-caps from developed markets and make full use of the industry spectrum, and they don't mind if their sector and country weights stand out. They normally keep the fund's currency exposure unhedged. And Causeway is aggressive about kicking out any market-timers who make it into the fund, and it uses a third-party fair valuation vendor.

Historical Profile

Return Above Avg
Risk High
Rating ★★★★ Above Avg

Investment Style: Equity Stock % — 93% (2001), 92% (2002), 94% (2003), 95% (12-04)

▼ Manager Change
∇ Partial Manager Change

Growth of $10,000
— Investment Values of Fund
— Investment Values of MSCI EAFE

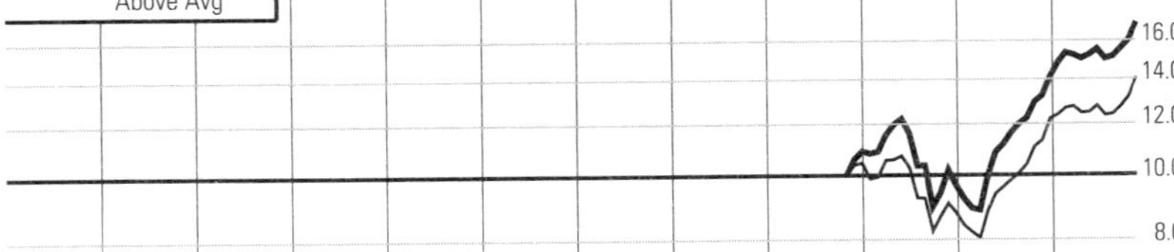

Performance Quartile (within Category)

	1993	1994	1995	1996	1997	1998	1999	2000	2001	2002	2003	12-04	History
	—	—	—	—	—	—	—	—	10.66	9.36	13.36	16.17	NAV
	—	—	—	—	—	—	—	—	6.66*	-11.18	45.53	26.31	Total Return %
	—	—	—	—	—	—	—	—	—	4.76	6.94	6.06	+/-MSCI EAFE
	—	—	—	—	—	—	—	—	—	4.62	6.11	5.93	+/-MSCI Wd xUS
	—	—	—	—	—	—	—	—	0.00	0.61	1.73	1.78	Income Return %
	—	—	—	—	—	—	—	—	—	-11.79	43.80	24.53	Capital Return %
	—	—	—	—	—	—	—	—	—	42	19	11	Total Rtn % Rank Cat
	—	—	—	—	—	—	—	—	0.01	0.07	0.16	0.24	Income $
	—	—	—	—	—	—	—	—	0.00	0.04	0.09	0.45	Capital Gains $
	—	—	—	—	—	—	—	—	—	1.27	1.27	1.23	Expense Ratio %
	—	—	—	—	—	—	—	—	—	1.69	1.55	1.31	Income Ratio %
	—	—	—	—	—	—	—	—	—	47	32	21	Turnover Rate %
	—	—	—	—	—	—	—	—	18	164	435	947	Net Assets $mil

Performance 12-31-04

	1st Qtr	2nd Qtr	3rd Qtr	4th Qtr	Total
2000	—	—	—	—	—
2001	—	—	—	—	6.66*
2002	5.72	0.62	-22.40	7.60	-11.18
2003	-8.12	25.47	9.45	15.34	45.53
2004	7.86	2.01	0.20	14.56	26.31

Trailing	Total Return%	+/- MSCI EAFE	+/- MSCI Wd xUS	%Rank Cat	Growth of $10,000
3 Mo	14.56	-0.76	-0.59	42	11,456
6 Mo	14.80	-0.20	-0.57	55	11,480
1 Yr	26.31	6.06	5.93	11	12,631
3 Yr Avg	17.75	5.86	5.53	18	16,326
5 Yr Avg	—	—	—	—	—
10 Yr Avg	—	—	—	—	—
15 Yr Avg	—	—	—	—	—

Tax Analysis	Tax-Adj Rtn%	%Rank Cat	Tax-Cost Rat	%Rank Cat
3 Yr (estimated)	16.95	18	0.68	67
5 Yr (estimated)	—	—	—	—
10 Yr (estimated)	—	—	—	—

Potential Capital Gain Exposure: 18% of assets

Rating and Risk

Time Period	Load-Adj Return %	Morningstar Rtn vs Cat	Morningstar Risk vs Cat	Morningstar Risk-Adj Rating
1 Yr	26.31			
3 Yr	17.75	+Avg	High	★★★★
5 Yr	—	—	—	—
10 Yr	—	—	—	—
Incept	19.05			

Other Measures	Standard Index S&P 500	Best Fit Index MSCI EAFE
Alpha	4.8	4.8
Beta	1.07	1.07
R-Squared	90	90
Standard Deviation	20.75	
Mean	17.75	
Sharpe Ratio	0.80	

Portfolio Analysis 12-31-04

Share change since 09-04 Total Stocks:71	Sector	Country	% Assets
⊕ Sanofi-Synthelabo	Health	France	2.61
⊕ Samsung Electronics	Goods	Korea	2.27
⊕ Takefuji	Financial	Japan	2.05
⊕ Promise	Financial	Japan	2.04
⊕ GlaxoSmithKline	Health	U.K.	2.00
⊕ Royal Bank Of Scotland G	Financial	U.K.	1.96
⊖ Amadeus Global Travel Di	Business	Spain	1.95
⊕ TPG	Business	Netherlands	1.95
⊕ Vinci	Business	France	1.93
⊕ ING Groep	Financial	Netherlands	1.87
⊕ Unilever	Goods	U.K.	1.84
⊕ Allied Irish Banks	Financial	Ireland	1.75
⊕ Enagas	Energy	Spain	1.73
⊕ Vodafone Grp	Telecom	U.K.	1.71
⊕ Koninklijke Philips Elec	Goods	Netherlands	1.71
⊕ British American Tobacco	Goods	U.K.	1.71
⊕ AXA	Financial	France	1.69
⊕ Aviva	Financial	U.K.	1.69
⊕ Henderson Land Developme	Financial	Hong Kong	1.68
⊕ Zurich Financial Service	Financial	Switzerland	1.68

Current Investment Style

Market Cap	%
Giant	43.5
Large	45.7
Mid	10.8
Small	0.0
Micro	0.0
Avg $mil:	22,968

Value Measures		Rel Category
Price/Earnings	12.69	0.94
Price/Book	2.19	1.33
Price/Sales	0.93	1.13
Price/Cash Flow	4.15	0.94
Dividend Yield %	2.75	0.99

Growth Measures	%	Rel Category
Long-Term Erngs	10.21	1.04
Book Value	-0.98	NMF
Sales	2.65	1.89
Cash Flow	7.96	2.58
Historical Erngs	1.92	0.69

Composition

Cash	4.8	Bonds	0.0
Stocks	95.2	Other	0.0
Foreign (% of Stock)			99.6

Sector Weightings	% of Stocks	Rel MSCI EAFE	3 Year High	3 Year Low
Info	18.02	1.08		
Software	0.00	0.00	0	0
Hardware	1.60	0.44	6	2
Media	2.65	1.16	4	0
Telecom	13.77	1.43	14	9
Service	50.69	1.13		
Health	7.02	0.97	7	3
Consumer	3.49	0.69	6	2
Business	11.81	2.17	12	7
Financial	28.37	1.05	30	25
Mfg	31.31	0.81		
Goods	15.83	1.16	24	16
Ind Mtrls	7.37	0.60	9	5
Energy	6.94	0.94	7	3
Utilities	1.17	0.22	5	0

Regional Exposure	% Stock		
UK/W. Europe	75	N. America	3
Japan	11	Latn America	0
Asia X Japan	12	Other	0

Country Exposure	% Stock		
U.K.	29	Netherlands	9
France	12	Spain	7
Japan	11		

Morningstar's Take by William Samuel Rocco 11-23-04

Causeway International Value won't be able to shine every year, of course, but we do expect it to be a long-term star.

This fund, which just had its three-year anniversary, has gotten off to a glowing start. After posting relatively limited losses in 2002's rough conditions, it produced a top-quintile 46% gain in 2003's rally. The fund benefited from a diverse mix of good picks last year, and it has done the same this year. Amadeus Global Travel Distribution of Spain, French construction and toll-road operator Vinci, and Telecom Corp. of New Zealand have all thrived. And several of the fund's financials picks, which make up a hefty 28% of assets, have prospered, including Canadian insurer Manulife Financial and Allied Irish Banks. The fund is up 18% and is in its group's top quintile for the year to date.

The fund will cool off at some point--no offering can dominate its rivals year in and year out--but we're quite bullish about its long-term prospects. And while its excellent three-year returns are one reason, they certainly aren't the only one.

The fund's managers rely on a risk-conscious style that favors larger firms from larger markets that appear cheap on a mix of measures, have good return potential, and repurchase their shares or pay dividends. They used the same approach while running Merrill Lynch International Value from 1990 through mid-2001, where they delivered good long-term risk-adjusted returns. That history makes us confident they will do the same here.

Due to its terrific start, sound and proven strategy, and seasoned and talented team of managers, we believe this fund is a superior option for those seeking a bargain-oriented foreign fund. The fund expects to make a small distribution in mid-December; interested investors might want to wait until after the fact to climb aboard.

Address:	1111 Santa Monica Blvd Los Angeles CA 90025 866-947-7000
Web Address:	www.causewayfunds.com
Inception:	10-26-01*
Advisor:	Causeway Capital Management LLC
Subadvisor:	None
NTF Plans:	Fidelity Retail-NTF, Schwab OneSource

Minimum Purchase:	$5000	Add: $100	IRA: $3000
Min Auto Inv Plan:	$5000	Add: $100	
Sales Fees:	0.25%B, 2.00%R		
Management Fee:	0.80%		
Actual Fees:	Mgt:0.80%	Dist:0.23%	
Expense Projections:	3Yr:$424	5Yr:$740	10Yr:$1638
Income Distrib:	Annually		

Clipper

Analyst Pick

Ticker	Load	NAV	Yield	Total Assets	Mstar Category
CFIMX	None	$89.68	0.6%	$7,057 mil	Large Value

Governance and Management

Fiduciary Grade: B

Portfolio Manager(s)

Not many funds can boast as much experience on their management teams. James Gipson and Michael Sandler have been at the helm since 1984. Bruce Veaco and Peter Quinn have also been with the fund's advisor since the late 1980s. Kelly Sueoka was named comanager in 2002, but has been with the firm since 1995. The team was named Morningstar's Domestic Equity Fund Manager of the Year in 2000.

Strategy

Management searches for established companies with dominant franchises but only buys those trading at discounts of at least 30% to its estimates of intrinsic value. Management uses discounted cash-flow analysis to estimate a company's worth but uses the sale price of comparable companies if the latter value is more conservative. The managers also look for factors such as insider buying and share-repurchase programs. The fund holds just 20 to 30 names. It eschews pricey sectors such as tech, and it will hold bonds or cash if the managers can't find stocks cheap enough and financially strong enough to meet their criteria.

Historical Profile

Return: High
Risk: Average
Rating: ★★★★★ Highest

Investment Style: Equity, Stock %: 76% 59% 61% 67% 60% 65% 92% 74% 75%

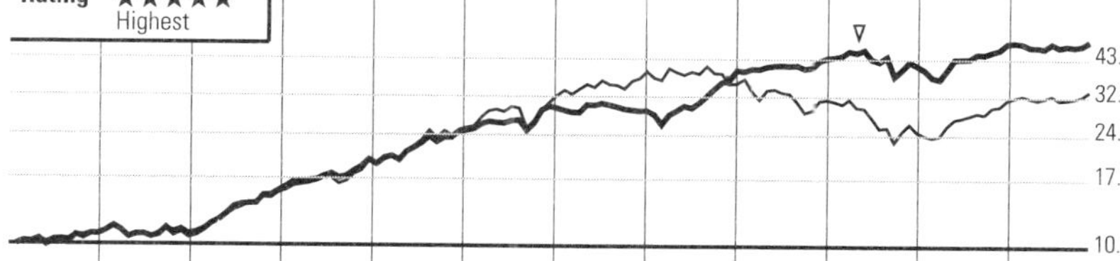

▼ Manager Change
▽ Partial Manager Change

Growth of $10,000
— Investment Values of Fund
— Investment Values of S&P 500

Performance Quartile (within Category)

History

	1993	1994	1995	1996	1997	1998	1999	2000	2001	2002	2003	12-04
NAV	50.05	46.09	60.74	67.57	76.86	75.37	65.28	79.25	83.53	75.73	87.97	89.68
Total Return %	11.26	-2.51	45.22	19.43	30.44	19.20	-2.02	37.40	10.26	-5.51	19.35	5.87
+/-S&P 500	1.20	-3.82	7.69	-3.51	-2.91	-9.37	-23.06	46.50	22.14	16.58	-9.32	-5.00
+/-Russ 1000 Vl	-6.81	-0.53	6.86	-2.21	-4.74	3.57	-9.37	30.39	15.85	10.01	-10.68	-10.62
Income Return %	1.46	1.41	1.64	1.37	2.01	2.26	2.98	2.86	1.36	1.29	0.96	0.65
Capital Return %	9.80	-3.92	43.58	18.06	28.43	16.94	-5.00	34.54	8.90	-6.80	18.39	5.22
Total Rtn % Rank Cat	70	72	1	56	22	8	84	2	5	1	97	98
Income $	0.75	0.71	0.76	0.83	1.36	1.63	2.25	1.87	1.08	1.08	0.73	0.57
Capital Gains $	6.73	2.00	5.42	4.27	9.83	12.86	6.16	8.38	2.75	2.11	1.62	2.81
Expense Ratio %	1.11	1.11	1.11	1.08	1.08	1.06	1.10	1.09	1.08	1.07	1.13	—
Income Ratio %	1.41	1.41	1.39	1.32	1.84	2.13	2.54	2.88	1.72	1.65	0.98	—
Turnover Rate %	64	45	31	24	31	65	63	46	23	48	25	—
Net Assets $mil	240	247	404	543	824	1,234	961	1,366	2,685	5,002	6,556	7,057

Performance 12-31-04

	1st Qtr	2nd Qtr	3rd Qtr	4th Qtr	Total
2000	-3.03	5.54	16.20	15.54	37.40
2001	1.03	3.02	-2.52	8.67	10.26
2002	5.71	-6.22	-12.34	8.73	-5.51
2003	-10.17	17.32	3.63	9.27	19.35
2004	-2.76	2.71	-2.31	8.51	5.87

Trailing	Total Return%	+/- S&P 500	+/- Russ 1000 Vl	%Rank Cat	Growth of $10,000
3 Mo	8.51	-0.72	-1.87	69	10,851
6 Mo	6.00	-1.19	-6.08	92	10,600
1 Yr	5.87	-5.00	-10.62	98	10,587
3 Yr Avg	6.08	2.50	-2.49	45	11,937
5 Yr Avg	12.58	14.88	7.31	3	18,084
10 Yr Avg	16.93	4.86	3.10	1	47,781
15 Yr Avg	14.23	3.30	2.20	4	73,570

Tax Analysis	Tax-Adj Rtn%	%Rank Cat	Tax-Cost Rat	%Rank Cat
3 Yr (estimated)	5.06	45	0.96	63
5 Yr (estimated)	10.94	3	1.46	76
10 Yr (estimated)	14.22	2	2.32	81

Potential Capital Gain Exposure: 13% of assets

Rating and Risk

Time Period	Load-Adj Return %	Morningstar Rtn vs Cat	Morningstar Risk vs Cat	Morningstar Risk-Adj Rating
1 Yr	5.87			
3 Yr	6.08	Avg	Avg	★★★
5 Yr	12.58	High	Avg	★★★★★
10 Yr	16.93	High	-Avg	★★★★★
Incept	15.48			

Other Measures	Standard Index S&P 500	Best Fit Index Mstar Large Value
Alpha	3.0	0.1
Beta	0.84	0.86
R-Squared	71	79
Standard Deviation	15.78	
Mean	6.08	
Sharpe Ratio	0.30	

Portfolio Analysis 09-30-04

Share change since 06-04 Total Stocks:27	Sector	PE	YTD Ret%	% Assets
Freddie Mac	Financial	10.6	28.75	9.36
American Express	Financial	20.3	17.60	5.28
Fannie Mae	Financial	9.1	-2.33	5.25
⊕ Altria Group	Goods	13.3	18.38	4.92
Tyco International	Ind Mtrls	25.1	35.41	4.55
Electronic Data Systems	Business	—	-3.82	4.43
El Paso	Energy	—	29.51	3.78
CVS	Consumer	21.1	25.61	3.43
⊕ Marsh & McLennan Compani	Financial	13.4	-29.80	3.10
Kraft Foods	Goods	20.3	13.15	3.05
Tenet Healthcare	Health	—	-31.59	3.00
⊕ Pfizer	Health	22.0	-22.31	2.85
⊖ UST, Inc.	Goods	22.4	42.18	2.68
HCA	Health	15.8	-6.00	2.08
⊕ Merrill Lynch & Company	Financial	12.6	3.12	2.01
Kroger	Consumer	66.5	-5.24	1.97
Wyeth	Health	17.0	2.73	1.83
Safeway	Consumer	—	-9.90	1.80
Johnson & Johnson	Health	20.6	25.17	1.45
Pitney Bowes	Ind Mtrls	19.6	17.24	1.36

Current Investment Style

Value Blnd Growth; Large Mid Small

Market Cap	%
Giant	57.1
Large	25.9
Mid	17.0
Small	0.0
Micro	0.0

Avg $mil: 28,949

Value Measures		Rel Category
Price/Earnings	14.35	0.95
Price/Book	1.83	0.81
Price/Sales	0.80	0.67
Price/Cash Flow	6.05	0.95
Dividend Yield %	2.57	1.26

Growth Measures	%	Rel Category
Long-Term Erngs	13.34	1.28
Book Value	6.46	1.15
Sales	5.52	1.31
Cash Flow	-16.20	NMF
Historical Erngs	20.42	1.72

Profitability	%	Rel Category
Return on Equity	14.12	0.89
Return on Assets	10.01	1.28
Net Margin	8.17	0.80

Sector Weightings	% of Stocks	Rel S&P 500	3 Year High	Low
Info	1.16	0.05		
Software	0.00	0.00	0	0
Hardware	0.00	0.00	0	0
Media	1.16	0.30	3	0
Telecom	0.00	0.00	0	0
Service	68.84	1.48		
Health	14.98	1.20	16	0
Consumer	9.62	1.06	20	9
Business	7.74	1.91	15	8
Financial	36.50	1.76	49	31
Mfg	29.99	0.93		
Goods	17.07	1.83	19	10
Ind Mtrls	7.88	0.62	19	8
Energy	5.04	0.70	5	0
Utilities	0.00	0.00	0	0

Composition

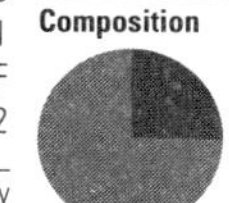

Cash	25.1
Stocks	74.8
Bonds	0.0
Other	0.0
Foreign (% of Stock)	0.0

Morningstar's Take by Christopher Traulsen 12-29-04

A subpar year doesn't shake our confidence in Clipper.

This fund's gain of 5.4% for the year to date through December 28, while fine in absolute terms, ranks in the 99th percentile of the large-value category. Picks including Tenet Healthcare, Electronic Data Systems (EDS), Fannie Mae, and Marsh & McLennan have slipped in the period.

Each of those names has been embroiled in some degree of controversy, and that isn't unusual here. The managers are disciplined value investors who pepper the portfolio with turnaround situations that are often experiencing significant business difficulties. They also take a long-term view and are rarely rattled by near-term price volatility.

The managers will also hold hefty cash or bond stakes when they can't find equities that meet their criteria. They haven't found much to buy lately, as is evident from the fund's 25% cash stake on September 30 (the most recent portfolio available). However, they did find some names to purchase in the third quarter. They continued to add to Marsh & McLennan even as the firm's shares fell sharply on word of Eliot Spitzer's insurance investigation in October and established a new position in Coca-Cola, which had fallen after repeatedly failing to hit its growth targets.

With a fund like this, short-term results are even less meaningful than usual. The managers' willingness to hold cash, their fondness for battered names, and the fund's concentration are all bound to cause its performance to deviate substantially from its average peer's at times. We don't know if picks like Coca-Cola and Marsh & McLennan will work out, but the managers typically have very conservative assumptions built into their valuations. They've also got history on their side. They've had much success with picks such as Tyco International and Altria over the years, and have guided the fund to top-flight long-term returns.

Address:	9601 Wilshire Blvd Ste 800 Beverly Hills CA 90210 800-776-5033
Web Address:	www.clipperfund.com
Inception:	02-29-84
Advisor:	Pacific Financial Research Inc.
Subadvisor:	None
NTF Plans:	Fidelity Retail-NTF, CommonWealth NTF

Minimum Purchase:	$25000	Add: $1000	IRA: $3000
Min Auto Inv Plan:	$25000	Add: $150	
Sales Fees:	No-load		
Management Fee:	1.00%		
Actual Fees:	Mgt:1.00%	Dist:	
Expense Projections:	3Yr:$356	5Yr:$617	10Yr:$1363
Income Distrib:	Annually		

Clipper Focus PBHG

Ticker	Load	NAV	Yield	Total Assets	Mstar Category
PBFOX	None	$17.33	0.3%	$1,189 mil	Large Value

Governance and Management

Fiduciary Grade: F

Portfolio Manager(s)

Despite this fund's youth, its managers boast a wealth of experience. James Gipson and Michael Sandler have been at the helm of sibling Clipper Fund since 1984. Bruce Veaco, Peter Quinn, and Douglas Grey have also been with the team since the 1980s. In 2000, the team won the Morningstar Domestic-Stock Manager of the Year Award for its work on Clipper Fund.

Strategy

This fund's managers search for established companies with dominant franchises but only buy those trading at discounts of at least 30% to their estimates of intrinsic value. They use discounted cash flow analysis to estimate a company's worth, but they will use the sale price of comparable companies if that value is more conservative. The managers also look for insiders who are buying company stock through share-repurchase programs. The fund is concentrated, typically holding between 20 and 30 names.

Historical Profile

Return Above Avg
Risk High
Rating ★★★★ Above Avg

Investment Style
Equity
Stock %

1998	1999	2000	2001	2002	2003	12-04
62%	85%	76%	92%	90%	96%	96%

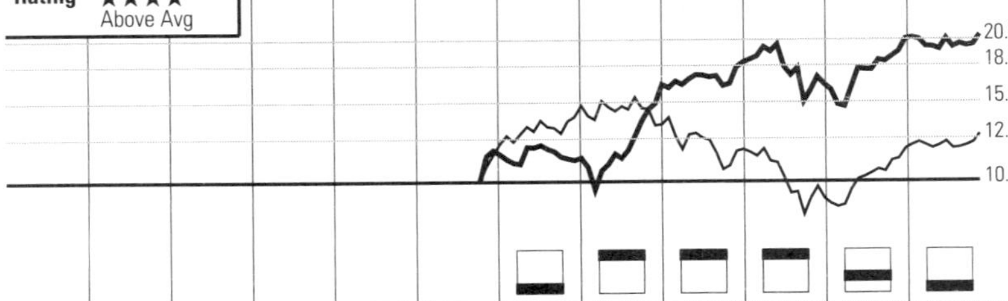

1993	1994	1995	1996	1997	1998	1999	2000	2001	2002	2003	12-04	History
—	—	—	—	—	11.77	11.28	15.53	15.19	13.22	16.50	17.33	NAV
—	—	—	—	—	17.91*	-1.89	44.29	11.82	-10.46	25.46	6.82	Total Return %
—	—	—	—	—	—	-22.93	53.39	23.70	11.63	-3.21	-4.05	+/-S&P 500
—	—	—	—	—	—	-9.24	37.28	17.41	5.06	-4.57	-9.67	+/-Russ 1000 VI
—	—	—	—	—	0.00	1.08	2.17	1.15	0.96	0.47	0.33	Income Return %
—	—	—	—	—	—	-2.97	42.12	10.67	-11.42	24.99	6.49	Capital Return %
—	—	—	—	—	—	84	1	4	5	73	97	Total Rtn % Rank Cat
—	—	—	—	—	0.02	0.13	0.24	0.18	0.15	0.06	0.05	Income $
—	—	—	—	—	0.00	0.14	0.41	1.92	0.24	0.02	0.23	Capital Gains $
—	—	—	—	—	—	1.40	1.40	1.40	1.40	1.45	1.48	Expense Ratio %
—	—	—	—	—	—	1.05	1.47	1.41	1.26	1.00	0.36	Income Ratio %
—	—	—	—	—	—	—	111	111	39	50	24	Turnover Rate %
—	—	—	—	—	2	92	312	341	641	1,104	1,173	Net Assets $mil

Performance 12-31-04

	1st Qtr	2nd Qtr	3rd Qtr	4th Qtr	Total
2000	-6.25	6.42	20.56	19.96	44.29
2001	0.02	4.76	-5.09	12.43	11.82
2002	7.97	-9.39	-15.95	8.89	-10.46
2003	-10.44	20.19	4.22	11.84	25.46
2004	-3.76	4.03	-3.63	10.71	6.82

Trailing	Total Return%	+/- S&P 500	+/- Russ 1000 VI	%Rank Cat	Growth of $10,000
3 Mo	10.71	1.48	0.33	16	11,071
6 Mo	6.69	-0.50	-5.39	82	10,669
1 Yr	6.82	-4.05	-9.67	97	10,682
3 Yr Avg	6.26	2.68	-2.31	42	11,998
5 Yr Avg	14.13	16.43	8.86	2	19,364
10 Yr Avg	—	—	—	—	—
15 Yr Avg	—	—	—	—	—

Tax Analysis	Tax-Adj Rtn%	%Rank Cat	Tax-Cost Rat	%Rank Cat
3 Yr (estimated)	5.80	35	0.43	29
5 Yr (estimated)	12.85	1	1.12	59
10 Yr (estimated)	—	—	—	—

Potential Capital Gain Exposure: 15% of assets

Rating and Risk

Time Period	Load-Adj Return %	Morningstar Rtn vs Cat	Morningstar Risk vs Cat	Morningstar Risk-Adj Rating
1 Yr	6.82			
3 Yr	6.26	Avg	High	★★★
5 Yr	14.13	High	High	★★★★★
10 Yr	—	—	—	—
Incept	13.64			

Other Measures	Standard Index S&P 500	Best Fit Index Mstar Large Value
Alpha	3.0	-0.5
Beta	1.02	1.04
R-Squared	74	80
Standard Deviation	19.17	
Mean	6.26	
Sharpe Ratio	0.26	

Portfolio Analysis 09-30-04

Share change since 06-04 Total Stocks:27	Sector	PE	YTD Ret%	% Assets
⊖ Freddie Mac	Financial	10.6	28.75	9.33
⊕ Altria Group	Goods	13.3	18.38	7.05
⊖ Tyco International	Ind Mtrls	25.1	35.41	6.67
⊖ Electronic Data Systems	Business	—	-3.82	6.06
⊕ Fannie Mae	Financial	9.1	-2.33	5.92
Kraft Foods	Goods	20.3	13.15	4.96
⊕ American Express	Financial	20.3	17.60	4.92
El Paso	Energy	—	29.51	4.84
⊕ Marsh & McLennan Compani	Financial	13.4	-29.80	4.08
Kroger	Consumer	66.5	-5.24	3.93
Wyeth	Health	17.0	2.73	3.74
Tenet Healthcare	Health	—	-31.59	3.66
Safeway	Consumer	—	-9.90	3.12
Pfizer	Health	22.0	-22.31	3.11
HCA	Health	15.8	-6.00	2.99
CVS	Consumer	21.1	25.61	2.93
⊕ Merrill Lynch & Company	Financial	12.6	3.12	2.89
⊖ UST, Inc.	Goods	22.4	42.18	2.67
Pitney Bowes	Ind Mtrls	19.6	17.24	2.58
Time Warner	Media	27.5	8.12	2.14

Current Investment Style

Value Blnd Growth — Large Mid Small

Market Cap	%
Giant	55.5
Large	28.1
Mid	16.5
Small	0.0
Micro	0.0
Avg $mil: 27,729	

Value Measures		Rel Category
Price/Earnings	14.58	0.97
Price/Book	1.86	0.82
Price/Sales	0.76	0.64
Price/Cash Flow	5.79	0.91
Dividend Yield %	2.60	1.27

Growth Measures	%	Rel Category
Long-Term Erngs	12.81	1.23
Book Value	5.20	0.92
Sales	5.43	1.29
Cash Flow	-16.20	NMF
Historical Erngs	14.34	1.21

Profitability	%	Rel Category
Return on Equity	13.53	0.85
Return on Assets	8.79	1.12
Net Margin	7.65	0.75

Sector Weightings	% of Stocks	Rel S&P 500	3 Year High	3 Year Low
Info	2.22	0.10		
Software	0.00	0.00	0	0
Hardware	0.00	0.00	0	0
Media	2.22	0.58	3	0
Telecom	0.00	0.00	0	0
Service	65.65	1.42		
Health	15.45	1.24	17	0
Consumer	10.35	1.14	20	10
Business	8.02	1.98	14	8
Financial	31.83	1.53	47	28
Mfg	32.12	1.00		
Goods	17.51	1.88	19	6
Ind Mtrls	9.59	0.76	14	10
Energy	5.02	0.70	7	0
Utilities	0.00	0.00	0	0

Composition

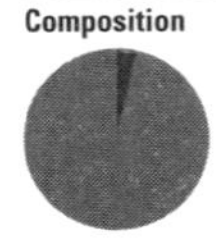

Cash	3.6
Stocks	96.4
Bonds	0.0
Other	0.0
Foreign (% of Stock)	0.0

Morningstar's Take by Christopher Traulsen 12-29-04

We wish this fund's board members were joking, but it appears they're serious.

This fund's board of directors recently reached an agreement with advisor Liberty Ridge Capital (formerly PBHG) to cap the expense ratio on the fund's no-load PBHG shares at 1.40% per year (it also capped A shares and Advisor Shares at 1.65% and B shares at 2.40%).

That's far too little, far too late. When this fund was merged in to the PBHG lineup in late 2001, one of the benefits of the merger for fund shareholders was supposed to be that PBHG's asset-gathering ability would help reduce expenses. This most decidedly hasn't happened. Assets under management have more than tripled, but the PBHG shares' expense ratio was 1.40% at the time of the merger, and it's still 1.40% (it actually rose to 1.49% before the board capped it). That's ridiculously high--the average no-load, large-value fund charges just 1.07%, and the management fee paid to the team from Clipper that actually runs this fund amounts to just 0.40% per year.

It's the board's job to negotiate fees, and we believe it has utterly failed in that regard. Here's a bright idea for the board: Instead of awarding the contract to Liberty Ridge at such a ridiculous fee, award the contract to Pacific Financial Research, the fund's renowned subadvisor, and cut Liberty out of the picture.

The fund has stumbled a bit this year as several big holdings have dropped sharply. We're not nearly as concerned about that, however, as we are with the fund's apparently lax governance. The fund's management team is highly experienced, and its value-oriented style has historically led it to invest in troubled companies from time to time. Over the long term, however, management has been right about enough of those names to deliver superior returns for shareholders.

But unless and until we see a substantial fee cut here, and preferably a new board, we can't recommend this offering.

Address:	PBHG Funds Kansas City, MO 64121-9534 800-433-0051
Web Address:	www.pbhgfunds.com
Inception:	09-10-98*
Advisor:	Liberty Ridge Capital, Inc.
Subadvisor:	Pacific Financial Research Inc.
NTF Plans:	Fidelity Retail-NTF, Schwab OneSource

Minimum Purchase:	$2500	Add: $0	IRA: $2000
Min Auto Inv Plan:	$500	Add: $25	
Sales Fees:	No-load		
Management Fee:	1.00%, 0.04%A		
Actual Fees:	Mgt:0.94%	Dist:	
Expense Projections:	3Yr:$443	5Yr:$766	10Yr:$1680
Income Distrib:	Annually		

Columbia Acorn A

Ticker	Load	NAV	Yield	Total Assets	Mstar Category
LACAX	5.75%	$25.93	0.0%	$13,859 mil	Small Growth

Governance and Management

Fiduciary Grade: D

Portfolio Manager(s)

In September 2003, legendary manager Ralph Wanger relinquished his position as head of the fund. His longtime comanager Chuck McQuaid is now at the helm, with Rob Mohn joining as his comanager. Mohn has served as a manager on Columbia Acorn USA for several years and has delivered fine results. John Park, the firm's longtime health-care analyst, had joined as a comanager but left in April 2004 to join another firm.

Strategy

Comanagers Chuck McQuaid, Rob Mohn, and their colleagues use a combination of top-down themes and fundamental research to put together this fund's sprawling portfolio of about 250 holdings. The managers are far more price-sensitive than their typical small-growth rival, and the portfolio usually has lower valuations and a much smaller technology weighting than the category norm. They have often favored business-services companies and financials.

Historical Profile

Return High
Risk Low
Rating ★★★★★ Highest

Investment Style
Equity
Stock %

2000	2001	2002	2003	12-04
92%	92%	83%	91%	93%

▼ Manager Change
∇ Partial Manager Change

Growth of $10,000
— Investment Values of Fund
— Investment Values of S&P 500

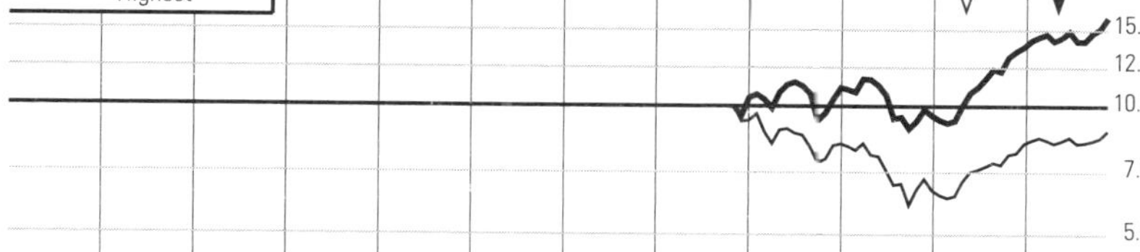

Performance Quartile (within Category)

1993	1994	1995	1996	1997	1998	1999	2000	2001	2002	2003	12-04	History
—	—	—	—	—	—	—	17.19	17.80	15.34	22.20	25.93	NAV
—	—	—	—	—	—	—	6.92*	5.56	-13.82	44.85	21.05	Total Return %
—	—	—	—	—	—	—	—	17.44	8.27	16.18	10.18	+/-S&P 500
—	—	—	—	—	—	—	—	14.79	16.44	-3.69	6.74	+/-Russ 2000 Gr
—	—	—	—	—	—	—	0.00	0.00	0.00	0.00	0.00	Income Return %
—	—	—	—	—	—	—	—	5.56	-13.82	44.85	21.05	Capital Return %
—	—	—	—	—	—	—	—	17	2	44	11	Total Rtn % Rank Cat
—	—	—	—	—	—	—	0.06	0.00	0.00	0.00	0.00	Income $
—	—	—	—	—	—	—	1.86	0.35	0.00	0.02	0.91	Capital Gains $
—	—	—	—	—	—	—	1.03	1.42	1.42	1.33	—	Expense Ratio %
—	—	—	—	—	—	—	0.39	-0.33	-0.45	-0.36	—	Income Ratio %
—	—	—	—	—	—	—	29	20	13	10	—	Turnover Rate %
—	—	—	—	—	—	—	17	304	713	2,000	2,668	Net Assets $mil

Performance 12-31-04

	1st Qtr	2nd Qtr	3rd Qtr	4th Qtr	Total
2000	—	—	—	—	6.92*
2001	-5.35	14.89	-18.69	19.38	5.56
2002	4.83	-8.25	-16.53	7.35	-13.82
2003	-2.80	19.85	8.79	14.30	44.85
2004	7.12	1.51	-0.91	12.35	21.05

Trailing	Total Return%	+/- S&P 500	+/- Russ 2000 Gr	%Rank Cat	Growth of $10,000
3 Mo	12.35	3.12	-2.73	79	11,235
6 Mo	11.33	4.14	3.17	17	11,133
1 Yr	21.05	10.18	6.74	11	12,105
3 Yr Avg	14.76	11.18	8.97	5	15,114
5 Yr Avg	—	—	—	—	—
10 Yr Avg	—	—	—	—	—
15 Yr Avg	—	—	—	—	—

Tax Analysis	Tax-Adj Rtn%	%Rank Cat	Tax-Cost Rat	%Rank Cat
3 Yr (estimated)	12.31	6	0.18	18
5 Yr (estimated)	—	—	—	—
10 Yr (estimated)	—	—	—	—

Potential Capital Gain Exposure: 39% of assets

Rating and Risk

Time Period	Load-Adj Return %	Morningstar Rtn vs Cat	Morningstar Risk vs Cat	Morningstar Risk-Adj Rating
1 Yr	14.09			
3 Yr	12.51	High	Low	★★★★★
5 Yr	—	—	—	—
10 Yr	—	—	—	—
Incept	11.94			

Other Measures	Standard Index S&P 500	Best Fit Index Russ 2000
Alpha	11.3	4.7
Beta	0.90	0.80
R-Squared	75	97
Standard Deviation	17.71	
Mean	14.76	
Sharpe Ratio	0.76	

Morningstar's Take by Todd Trubey 12-10-04

Problems surround Columbia Acorn, but they don't relate to performance or process.

This fund shouldn't be working so well. With $12.5 billion spread over 410 holdings, its returns should be sluggish. But its year-to-date gain of 17% through December 1 ranks in the top decile of its small-growth category. This isn't news, either: Since hitting $4 billion the fund has posted top quartile finishes in 2000, 2001, 2002 and was in the top half in 2003 when micro-caps leapt.

A few factors drove its success this year. Given the falling dollar, last year's move from 8% to 15% in foreign stocks has helped. Since 2003 the fund has had an above-average stake in energy stocks, the best small-cap sector in 2004. Finally, the fund's average market cap is $1.7 billion, and small-growth funds in that range generally topped those holding smaller firms. Lead manager Chuck McQuaid, though, says the key factor is his analysts' stock-picking.

Acorn is one of the most analyst-driven vehicles around, which is great when you have people like consumer discretionary specialist Susie Hultquist. She came to the firm in April 2000 with a distressed debt background, so she watches balance sheets as well as fashion. Given the shop's moderate, low-turnover approach, she only aims for five to 10 ideas per year and now has 24 stocks in the fund, two in the top ten. The fund started buying Coach at its IPO and it has risen 1000% since then. The fund added Chico's FAS in late 2001, and it has tripled.

We remain impressed with the investment process at advisor Wanger Asset Management, but we retain reservations. Happily, the board recently lowered the A-shares' once-high expenses to 1.18%, although given the fund's size we think it should drop more. But the larger problem here is the market-timing arrangements at Columbia and the lack of a final settlement with regulators. Current investors should hold on, but we don't now recommend the fund to new investors.

Address:	227 W Monroe Ste 3000 Chicago IL 60606 800-345-6611
Web Address:	
Inception:	10-16-00*
Advisor:	Columbia Wanger Asset Management, LP
Subadvisor:	None
NTF Plans:	DATALynx NTF, Federated Tr NTF

Minimum Purchase:	$50000	Add: $50	IRA: $50000
Min Auto Inv Plan:	$50	Add: $50	
Sales Fees:	5.75%L, 0.25%S		
Management Fee:	0.75% mx./0.65% mn., 0.05%A		
Actual Fees:	Mgt:0.69%	Dist:0.35%	
Expense Projections:	3Yr:$964	5Yr:$1282	10Yr:$2127
Income Distrib:	Semi-Annually		

Portfolio Analysis 08-31-04

Share change since 07-04 Total Stocks:410	Sector	PE	YTD Ret%	% Assets
XTO Energy	Energy	20.5	56.85	1.78
International Game Tech	Consumer	28.1	-2.49	1.39
Expeditors International	Business	42.3	49.04	1.17
⊕ Coach	Goods	37.4	49.40	1.10
AmeriCredit	Financial	14.3	53.48	1.07
TCF Financial	Financial	13.3	28.60	0.97
People's Bank	Financial	20.6	86.09	0.94
Harley-Davidson	Goods	20.5	28.70	0.93
Chico's FAS	Consumer	33.3	23.22	0.89
⊖ Ultra Petroleum	Energy	43.1	95.49	0.83
Michaels Stores	Consumer	22.9	36.87	0.80
First Health Group	Health	14.2	-4.15	0.74
Equitable Resources	Energy	13.0	45.53	0.73
Lincare Holdings	Health	16.1	41.79	0.70
Tellabs	Hardware	38.1	2.14	0.69
Western Gas Resources	Energy	21.1	24.56	0.63
SEI Investments	Business	24.6	38.82	0.63
ITT Educational Services	Consumer	32.8	1.24	0.68
Associated Banc-Corp	Financial	14.8	20.24	0.66
Western Wireless A	Telecom	—	59.59	0.66

Current Investment Style

Value Blnd Growth — Large Mid Small

Market Cap	%
Giant	0.0
Large	6.7
Mid	50.2
Small	35.4
Micro	7.6

Avg $mil: 1,669

Value Measures		Rel Category
Price/Earnings	17.81	0.82
Price/Book	2.37	0.90
Price/Sales	1.34	0.89
Price/Cash Flow	6.65	0.83
Dividend Yield %	0.90	2.90

Growth Measures	%	Rel Category
Long-Term Erngs	14.17	0.82
Book Value	5.47	0.85
Sales	4.32	0.75
Cash Flow	5.14	0.38
Historical Erngs	6.37	0.49

Profitability	%	Rel Category
Return on Equity	13.02	1.32
Return on Assets	6.29	1.43
Net Margin	8.39	1.31

Sector Weightings	% of Stocks	Rel S&P 500	3 Year High	3 Year Low
Info	16.08	0.75		
Software	5.69	1.32	8	6
Hardware	5.54	0.54	6	2
Media	2.26	0.59	3	2
Telecom	2.59	0.82	3	1
Service	53.55	1.15		
Health	9.97	0.80	11	9
Consumer	13.88	1.53	15	13
Business	12.82	3.17	16	12
Financial	16.88	0.81	23	15
Mfg	30.37	0.95		
Goods	9.22	0.99	12	9
Ind Mtrls	12.26	0.97	12	8
Energy	7.79	1.09	8	3
Utilities	1.10	0.37	2	1

Composition

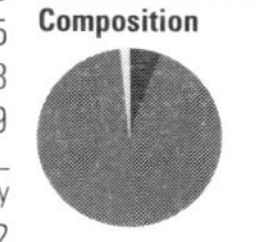

Cash	5.5
Stocks	92.8
Bonds	0.0
Other	1.7
Foreign (% of Stock)	15.8

Columbia Acorn Intl A

Ticker	Load	NAV	Yield	Total Assets	Mstar Category
LAIAX	5.75%	$28.75	0.5%	$2,075 mil	Foreign Small/Mid Growth

Governance and Management

Fiduciary Grade: D

Portfolio Manager(s)

After 11 years, Leah Zell stepped down as lead manager in September 2003. Zach Egan and Louis Mendes--who joined the fund as analysts in 1999 and 2001, respectively, and who were promoted to comanagers in May 2003--are now at the helm. Seven analysts work with them on the fund, and each member of the team is responsible for stock selection in his area of expertise.

Strategy

Management searches for smaller companies that are growing at above-average rates. The team also looks for good balance sheets, cash flow, and dividend yields and pays a lot of attention to valuations. Zach Egan and Louis Mendes monitor the aggregate portfolio to make sure its sector and other bets aren't too aggressive. The fund levies a 2% redemption fee on shares held less than 60 days.

Historical Profile

Return Below Avg
Risk Below Avg
Rating ★★ Below Avg

Investment Style Equity Stock %: 86% (2000), 91% (2001), 83% (2002), 93% (2003), 92% (12-04)

▼ Manager Change
▽ Partial Manager Change

Growth of $10,000
— Investment Values of Fund
— Investment Values of MSCI EAFE

Performance Quartile (within Category)

1993	1994	1995	1996	1997	1998	1999	2000	2001	2002	2003	12-04	History
—	—	—	—	—	—	—	23.85	18.35	15.32	22.45	28.75	NAV
—	—	—	—	—	—	—	-5.28*	-21.62	-16.46	46.94	28.91	Total Return %
—	—	—	—	—	—	—	—	-0.20	-0.52	8.35	8.66	+/-MSCI EAFE
—	—	—	—	—	—	—	—	-0.23	-0.66	7.52	8.53	+/-MSCI Wd xUS
—	—	—	—	—	—	—	0.00	0.00	0.05	0.30	0.69	Income Return %
—	—	—	—	—	—	—	—	-21.62	-16.51	46.64	28.22	Capital Return %
—	—	—	—	—	—	—	—	34	64	70	29	Total Rtn % Rank Cat
—	—	—	—	—	—	—	0.00	0.00	0.01	0.05	0.15	Income $
—	—	—	—	—	—	—	3.59	0.39	0.00	0.00	0.00	Capital Gains $
—	—	—	—	—	—	—	0.59	1.65	1.56	1.59	—	Expense Ratio %
—	—	—	—	—	—	—	0.40	0.03	0.30	0.57	—	Income Ratio %
—	—	—	—	—	—	—	63	45	52	40	—	Turnover Rate %
—	—	—	—	—	—	—	12	27	34	53	71	Net Assets $mil

Performance 12-31-04

	1st Qtr	2nd Qtr	3rd Qtr	4th Qtr	Total
2000	—	—	—	—	-5.28 *
2001	-12.45	-1.99	-18.87	12.58	-21.62
2002	2.23	-1.44	-19.96	3.58	-16.46
2003	-6.59	21.37	10.68	17.11	46.94
2004	6.77	1.63	1.86	16.63	28.91

Trailing	Total Return%	+/- MSCI EAFE	+/- MSCI Wd xUS	%Rank Cat	Growth of $10,000
3 Mo	16.63	1.31	1.48	46	11,663
6 Mo	18.80	3.80	3.43	12	11,880
1 Yr	28.91	8.66	8.53	29	12,891
3 Yr Avg	16.53	4.64	4.31	49	15,824
5 Yr Avg	—	—	—	—	—
10 Yr Avg	—	—	—	—	—
15 Yr Avg	—	—	—	—	—

Tax Analysis	Tax-Adj Rtn%	%Rank Cat	Tax-Cost Rat	%Rank Cat
3 Yr (estimated)	14.12	68	0.12	32
5 Yr (estimated)	—	—	—	—
10 Yr (estimated)	—	—	—	—

Potential Capital Gain Exposure: 30% of assets

Rating and Risk

Time Period	Load-Adj Return %	Morningstar Rtn vs Cat	Morningstar Risk vs Cat	Morningstar Risk-Adj Rating
1 Yr	21.50			
3 Yr	14.26	-Avg	-Avg	★★
5 Yr	—	—	—	—
10 Yr	—	—	—	—
Incept	2.45			

Other Measures	Standard Index S&P 500	Best Fit Index MSCI Wd xUS
Alpha	5.2	4.8
Beta	0.90	0.92
R-Squared	88	88
Standard Deviation	17.42	
Mean	16.53	
Sharpe Ratio	0.88	

Morningstar's Take by William Samuel Rocco 11-30-04

Columbia Acorn International has some real pluses, but it also has one big minus.

This fund has made positive moves. Due to reductions in certain administrative fees, the expense ratio will be 1.44% going forward, which is roughly 15 basis points lower than it had been and 55 basis points below the norm for a front-load offering in its group. The fund, which brought on a new Japan analyst in late 2003, hired a new basic-materials analyst this summer. That brings the total number of analysts to nine, including comanagers Zach Egan and Louis Mendes, and an energy analyst that covers both U.S. and foreign companies.

Meanwhile, the team's strategy draws on its firm's strengths and is more sensible than many of its peers'. Columbia Wanger Asset Management has long--and rightly--been respected for the quality of its smaller-cap research, and the team pursues overseas smaller caps with good growth prospects. The team also pays more attention to valuations and diversification than most of its peers, so the fund is less risky than most of its rivals.

Moreover, though the fund posted subpar results last year, it has thrived this year. It is up 24% and leads 89% of its peers, due to Talisman Energy, Billabong, and other picks. Thus, it has earned good overall results since Egan and Mendes took over in September 2003.

All that's encouraging,but the fund is part of the Columbia family, which had serious market-timing issues at its funds between 1998 and 2003. That firm, which reached an agreement in principle with regulators in March, has taken some good steps, but key details remain unclear and the market-timing was a major violation of the firm's fiduciary responsibilities. The merger of the Columbia and Nations funds exacerbates the situation.

All told, while current shareholders should stay, prospective investors should stay away until more progress is made.

Address:	227 W Monroe Ste 3000 Chicago IL 60606 800-345-6611	Minimum Purchase:	$1000 Add: $50 IRA: $25
Web Address:		Min Auto Inv Plan:	$50 Add: $50
Inception:	10-16-00 *	Sales Fees:	5.75%L, 0.25%S
Advisor:	Columbia Wanger Asset Management, LP	Management Fee:	1.20% mx./0.75% mn., 0.05%A
Subadvisor:	None	Actual Fees:	Mgt:0.81% Dist:0.35%
		Expense Projections:	3Yr:$337 5Yr:$585 10Yr:$1294
		Income Distrib:	Semi-Annually
NTF Plans:	DATALynx NTF, Federated Tr NTF		

Portfolio Analysis 08-31-04

Share change since 07-04 Total Stocks:148	Sector	Country	% Assets
Anglo Irish Bank	Financial	Ireland	2.44
☼ Grafton Group Uts(Compr	—	—	1.45
Kerry Grp	Goods	Ireland	1.42
Neopost	Ind Mtrls	France	1.41
Exel	Business	U.K.	1.37
Tullow Oil	Energy	U.K.	1.31
Talisman Energy	Energy	—	1.27
Billabong International	Goods	Australia	1.23
Fugro	Business	Netherlands	1.21
Aalberts Industries	Ind Mtrls	Netherlands	1.17
Daito Trust Construction	Business	Japan	1.13
Housing Development Fina	Financial	India	1.11
Geberit	Consumer	Switzerland	1.10
Abengoa	Business	Spain	1.09
Bank of Yokohama	Financial	Japan	1.07
OPG Groep	Health	Netherlands	1.06
Tenaris SA	Ind Mtrls	Luxembourg	1.05
⊕ DEPFA Bank	Financial	Germany	1.04
Global Bio-chem Technolo	Ind Mtrls	Hong Kong	1.04
Autogrill	Consumer	Italy	1.01

Current Investment Style

Market Cap	%
Giant	0.0
Large	20.1
Mid	46.5
Small	32.4
Micro	1.1
Avg $mil: 1,636	

Value Measures		Rel Category
Price/Earnings	14.37	1.04
Price/Book	2.18	1.14
Price/Sales	0.94	1.15
Price/Cash Flow	6.63	1.33
Dividend Yield %	2.40	1.06

Growth Measures	%	Rel Category
Long-Term Erngs	13.21	0.29
Book Value	2.44	0.62
Sales	6.49	1.03
Cash Flow	1.05	0.23
Historical Erngs	3.61	0.39

Composition

Cash	2.8	Bonds	0.0
Stocks	92.0	Other	5.2
Foreign (% of Stock)			99.7

Sector Weightings	% of Stocks	Rel MSCI EAFE	3 Year High	3 Year Low
Info	5.23	0.31		
Software	0.50	0.46	3	1
Hardware	2.56	0.70	4	1
Media	0.61	0.27	5	1
Telecom	1.56	0.16	2	0
Service	57.72	1.29		
Health	7.68	1.06	13	6
Consumer	13.78	2.73	14	7
Business	20.06	3.69	25	19
Financial	16.20	0.60	16	11
Mfg	37.06	0.96		
Goods	13.13	0.96	18	13
Ind Mtrls	19.24	1.56	21	11
Energy	3.85	0.52	6	4
Utilities	0.84	0.16	2	0

Regional Exposure	% Stock		
UK/W. Europe	61	N. America	1
Japan	17	Latn America	2
Asia X Japan	18	Other	1

Country Exposure	% Stock		
Japan	17	Netherlands	8
U.K.	13	France	6
Germany	9		

Columbia Acorn Select Z

Ticker	Load	NAV	Yield	Total Assets	Mstar Category
ACTWX	Closed	$2`.13	0.0%	$1,249 mil	Mid-Cap Growth

Governance and Management

Fiduciary Grade: D

Portfolio Manager(s)

This fund lost its longtime manager John Park in April 2004. He has been replaced by Ben Andrews, who cut his teeth as a software analyst at Acorn. Andrews receives considerable support from Acorn's large analyst staff.

Strategy

Historically, this fund's manager and the Acorn analyst team use a combination of investment themes and fundamental research to look for promising growth companies trading at discounts to the team's estimates of their worth. This fund is limited to fewer than three dozen holdings and will take large individual positions. It favors mid-caps to provide the needed liquidity to buy and sell such stakes. There is no indication that new manager Ben Andrews will be changing that strategy.

Historical Profile

Return High
Risk Low
Rating ★★★★★ Highest

Investment Style: Equity, Stock %: 100% 97% 95% 93% 95% 94% 90%

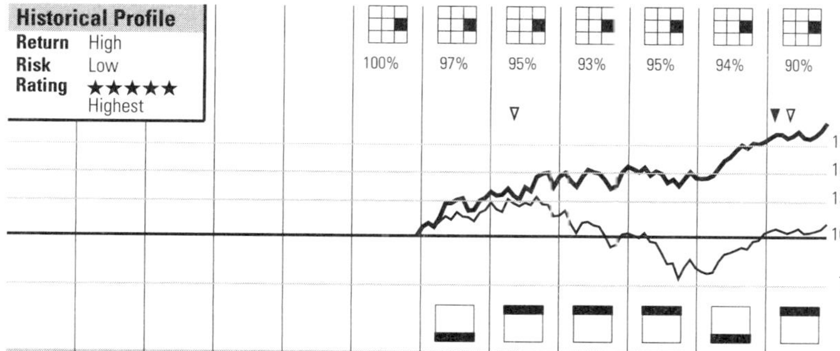

1993	1994	1995	1996	1997	1998	1999	2000	2001	2002	2003	12-04	History
—	—	—	—	—	10.71	13.70	14.13	15.23	14.04	18.20	21.13	NAV
—	—	—	—	—	7.10*	29.30	11.68	8.00	-7.81	30.61	18.58	Total Return %
—	—	—	—	—	—	8.26	20.78	19.88	14.28	1.94	7.71	+/-S&P 500
—	—	—	—	—	—	-21.99	23.43	28.15	19.60	-12.10	3.10	+/-Russ MG
—	—	—	—	—	0.00	0.00	0.00	0.00	0.00	0.00	0.00	Income Return %
—	—	—	—	—	—	29.30	11.68	8.00	-7.81	30.61	18.58	Capital Return %
—	—	—	—	—	—	77	20	2	1	76	11	Total Rtn % Rank Cat
—	—	—	—	—	0.00	0.00	0.00	0.00	0.00	0.00	0.00	Income $
—	—	—	—	—	0.00	0.14	1.09	0.03	0.00	0.13	0.44	Capital Gains $
—	—	—	—	—	1.35	1.37	1.34	1.35	1.26	1.12	—	Expense Ratio %
—	—	—	—	—	0.22	-0.62	-0.41	-0.44	-0.67	-0.63	—	Income Ratio %
—	—	—	—	—	173	101	116	82	40	16	—	Turnover Rate %
—	—	—	—	—	33	68	67	69	92	294	439	Net Assets $mil

Performance 12-31-04

	1st Qtr	2nd Qtr	3rd Qtr	4th Qtr	Total
2000	2.34	1.05	10.32	-2.11	11.68
2001	-6.86	11.25	-11.34	17.57	8.00
2002	-0.72	-4.30	-8.50	6.04	-7.81
2003	1.85	14.41	6.78	4.97	30.61
2004	5.38	1.93	-3.02	13.82	18.58

Trailing	Total Return%	+/- S&P 500	+/- Russ MG	%Rank Cat	Growth of $10,000
3 Mo	13.82	4.59	-0.12	32	11,382
6 Mo	10.39	3.20	1.38	17	11,039
1 Yr	18.58	7.71	3.10	11	11,858
3 Yr Avg	12.60	9.02	6.44	1	14,276
5 Yr Avg	11.48	13.78	14.84	1	17,218
10 Yr Avg	—	—	—	—	—
15 Yr Avg	—	—	—	—	—

Tax Analysis	Tax-Adj Rtn%	%Rank Cat	Tax-Cost Rat	%Rank Cat
3 Yr (estimated)	12.42	2	0.16	26
5 Yr (estimated)	10.94	1	0.48	22
10 Yr (estimated)	—	—	—	—

Potential Capital Gain Exposure: 22% of assets

Rating and Risk

Time Period	Load-Adj Return %	Morningstar Rtn vs Cat	Morningstar Risk vs Cat	Morningstar Risk-Adj Rating
1 Yr	18.58			
3 Yr	12.60	High	Low	★★★★★
5 Yr	11.48	High	Low	★★★★★
10 Yr	—	—	—	—
Incept	15.30			

Other Measures	Standard Index S&P 500	Best Fit Index Mstar Small Growth
Alpha	9.3	9.7
Beta	0.70	0.43
R-Squared	77	79
Standard Deviation	13.37	
Mean	12.60	
Sharpe Ratio	0.85	

Portfolio Analysis 08-31-04

Share change since 07-04 Total Stocks:28	Sector	PE	YTD Ret%	% Assets
TCF Financial	Financial	13.3	28.60	6.53
Harley-Davidson	Goods	20.5	28.70	6.36
First Health Group	Health	14.2	-4.15	5.76
McAfee	Software	18.2	92.35	5.37
ITT Educational Services	Consumer	32.8	1.24	4.37
Tellabs	Hardware	38.1	2.14	3.88
PeopleSoft	Software	NMF	16.24	3.87
Markel	Financial	21.8	43.58	3.68
Moody's	Business	32.5	44.06	3.36
Costco Wholesale	Consumer	25.6	31.15	3.22
Safeway	Consumer	—	-9.90	3.16
Expeditors International	Business	42.3	49.04	3.15
Herman Miller	Goods	37.6	15.09	3.05
Tektronix	Hardware	17.0	-3.86	2.98
Lincare Holdings	Health	16.1	41.79	2.97
Weight Watchers Intl	Consumer	23.9	7.04	2.96
⊕ Abercrombie & Fitch A	Consumer	23.6	92.74	2.85
Fair Isaac	Business	23.5	12.17	2.81
Coach	Goods	37.4	49.40	2.77
International Speedway A	Goods	29.0	18.96	2.54

Current Investment Style

Market Cap	%
Giant	0.0
Large	21.1
Mid	72.3
Small	6.5
Micro	0.0
Avg $mil: 4,231	

Value Measures		Rel Category
Price/Earnings	13.16	0.87
Price/Book	3.07	1.02
Price/Sales	1.62	0.92
Price/Cash Flow	3.49	0.98
Dividend Yield %	0.35	0.81

Growth Measures	%	Rel Category
Long-Term Erngs	14.42	0.92
Book Value	9.98	0.99
Sales	6.75	0.78
Cash Flow	1`.92	0.98
Historical Erngs	12.24	0.77

Profitability	%	Rel Category
Return on Equity	18.79	1.31
Return on Assets	1`.34	1.58
Net Margin	1`.29	1.17

Sector Weightings	% of Stocks	Rel S&P 500	3 Year High	3 Year Low
Info	24.07	1.12		
Software	16.39	3.81	18	7
Hardware	7.60	0.75	8	2
Media	0.00	0.00	9	0
Telecom	0.08	0.03	0	0
Service	59.63	1.29		
Health	9.67	0.77	26	3
Consumer	18.90	2.08	21	3
Business	17.04	4.21	21	13
Financial	14.02	0.68	19	3
Mfg	16.30	0.51		
Goods	16.30	1.75	22	9
Ind Mtrls	0.00	0.00	0	0
Energy	0.00	0.00	0	0
Utilities	0.00	0.00	4	0

Composition

Cash	9.7
Stocks	90.3
Bonds	0.0
Other	0.0
Foreign (% of Stock)	2.3

Morningstar's Take by Todd Trubey 11-08-04

Its mix of talent and uncertainty makes Columbia Acorn Select a tough nut to crack.

We've always been impressed with Columbia Wanger Asset Management's (CWAM) investment prowess, which is in sharp focus here. This fund showcases analysts' favorite stocks that have graduated from small-caps to mid-caps. So the fund typically holds less than 30 stocks, which is fewer than all but a handful of mid-growth category rivals. Since its late 1998 inception the fund has provided a smooth ride with stellar returns, although Wanger's keen attention to valuation causes it to lag peers in sharp rallies, as in 1999 and 2003.

Still, we remain concerned over the troubles the boutique shop's sale in 2000 have wrought. Founder Ralph Wanger sold his firm to Liberty (which merged with Columbia a year later) with an agreement CWAM would remains largely autonomous, and it has. But the fund's cheap no-load shares are now closed, and the load shares aren't cheap. Moreover, the rampant market-timing problems at Columbia, which affected three Acorn siblings but not this fund, showed that CWAM was hardly immune to troubles at its parent. Columbia's merger with similarly troubled Nations funds, and the fact that a March 2004 agreement in principle to settle with regulators is still not final, add to our concern.

Finally, new manager Ben Andrews must prove himself as John Park did over his five years. Focused portfolios, even when drawing on superior stock-picks, are tricky, but Park showed his skill in crafting one that had very low volatility. Andrews, a CWAM analyst for seven years, took the helm on May 1, 2004; especially given the fund's low turnover, it will take time for him to earn our full confidence.

All told, we advise investors to stand pat. There's no good reason now to buy its load shares. But current shareowners can be patient to see if Andrews develops and the shop's troubles subside.

Address:	227 W Monroe Ste 3000 Chicago IL 60606 800-345-6611
Web Address:	
Inception:	11-23-98 *
Advisor:	Columbia Wanger Asset Management, LP
Subadvisor:	None
NTF Plans:	Schwab OneSource

Minimum Purchase:	Closed	Add: —	IRA: —
Min Auto Inv Plan:	Closed	Add: —	
Sales Fees:	No-load		
Management Fee:	0.90%, 0.05%A		
Actual Fees:	Mgt:0.90%	Dist: —	
Expense Projections:	3Yr:$437	5Yr:$755	10Yr:$1657
Income Distrib:	Semi-Annually		

Columbia Acorn USA A

Ticker	Load	NAV	Yield	Total Assets	Mstar Category
LAUAX	5.75%	$24.77	0.0%	$869 mil	Small Growth

Governance and Management

Fiduciary Grade: D

Portfolio Manager(s)

Robert Mohn has been with Columbia Acorn USA's advisor, Columbia Wanger Asset Management, since 1992 and has managed this fund since its late-1996 inception. He became comanager on Columbia Acorn in mid-2003. Mohn draws heavily on the advisor's staff of domestic-equity analysts and portfolio managers. Like all Wanger portfolio managers, Mohn also has analyst duties. He covers financial-services stocks.

Strategy

Like its bigger sibling Columbia Acorn, Columbia Acorn USA hunts for fast-growing companies trading at discounts to its manager's estimates of their values. A proprietary valuation model, in-house research, and investment themes drive management's picks. This fund takes large positions in individual names.

Historical Profile

Return Above Avg
Risk Average
Rating ★★★★ Above Avg

Investment Style
Equity
Stock %: 97% (2000), 89% (2001), 90% (2002), 93% (2003), 94% (12-04)

▼ Manager Change
∇ Partial Manager Change

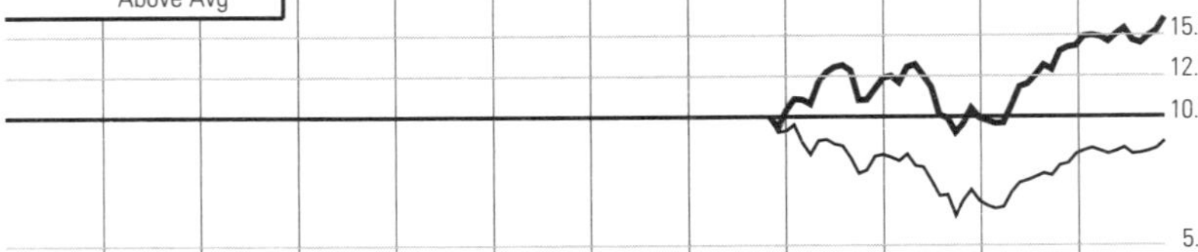

Growth of $10,000
▬ Investment Values of Fund
— Investment Values of S&P 500

Performance Quartile (within Category)

1993	1994	1995	1996	1997	1998	1999	2000	2001	2002	2003	12-04	History
—	—	—	—	—	—	—	14.88	17.50	14.18	20.74	24.77	NAV
—	—	—	—	—	—	—	6.90*	18.65	-18.97	46.26	20.12	Total Return %
—	—	—	—	—	—	—	—	30.53	3.12	17.59	9.25	+/-S&P 500
—	—	—	—	—	—	—	—	27.88	11.29	-2.28	5.81	+/-Russ 2000 Gr
—	—	—	—	—	—	—	0.00	0.00	0.00	0.00	0.00	Income Return %
—	—	—	—	—	—	—	—	18.65	-18.97	46.26	20.12	Capital Return %
—	—	—	—	—	—	—	—	5	15	37	13	Total Rtn % Rank Cat
—	—	—	—	—	—	—	0.00	0.00	0.00	0.00	0.00	Income $
—	—	—	—	—	—	—	0.00	0.15	0.00	0.00	0.14	Capital Gains $
—	—	—	—	—	—	—	—	1.84	1.74	1.65	—	Expense Ratio %
—	—	—	—	—	—	—	—	-1.13	-1.21	-1.26	—	Income Ratio %
—	—	—	—	—	—	—	39	24	31	7	—	Turnover Rate %
—	—	—	—	—	—	—	1	20	33	91	112	Net Assets $mil

Performance 12-31-04

	1st Qtr	2nd Qtr	3rd Qtr	4th Qtr	Total
2000	—	—	—	—	6.90 *
2001	3.49	21.56	-16.03	12.31	18.65
2002	5.94	-10.03	-21.40	8.16	-18.97
2003	-2.75	23.06	7.78	13.40	46.26
2004	4.87	4.55	-4.05	14.17	20.11

Trailing	Total Return%	+/- S&P 500	+/- Russ 2000 Gr	%Rank Cat	Growth of $10,000
3 Mo	14.17	4.94	-0.91	45	11,417
6 Mo	9.55	2.36	1.39	34	10,955
1 Yr	20.12	9.25	5.81	13	12,012
3 Yr Avg	12.49	8.91	6.70	8	14,234
5 Yr Avg	—	—	—	—	—
10 Yr Avg	—	—	—	—	—
15 Yr Avg	—	—	—	—	—

Tax Analysis	Tax-Adj Rtn%	%Rank Cat	Tax-Cost Rat	%Rank Cat
3 Yr (estimated)	10.26	13	0.03	4
5 Yr (estimated)	—	—	—	—
10 Yr (estimated)	—	—	—	—

Potential Capital Gain Exposure: 33% of assets

Rating and Risk

Time Period	Load-Adj Return %	Morningstar Rtn vs Cat	Morningstar Risk vs Cat	Morningstar Risk-Adj Rating
1 Yr	13.21			
3 Yr	10.29	+Avg	Avg	★★★★
5 Yr	—	—	—	—
10 Yr	—	—	—	—
Incept	13.47			

Other Measures	Standard Index S&P 500	Best Fit Index Russ 2000
Alpha	9.1	1.3
Beta	1.05	0.96
R-Squared	70	95
Standard Deviation	21.24	
Mean	12.49	
Sharpe Ratio	0.53	

Portfolio Analysis 08-31-04

Share change since 07-04 Total Stocks:131	Sector	PE	YTD Ret%	% Assets
Western Wireless A	Telecom	—	59.59	3.25
AmeriCredit	Financial	14.3	53.48	3.19
Edwards Lifesciences	Health	—	37.17	2.83
ESCO Technologies	Hardware	30.3	75.60	2.54
Quicksilver Resources	Energy	69.9	127.74	2.40
Commonwealth Telephone E	Telecom	17.5	31.55	2.03
Crown Castle Internation	Telecom	—	50.86	2.01
ITT Educational Services	Consumer	32.8	1.24	1.92
Aeropostale	Consumer	23.7	61.00	1.90
Micros Systems	Software	35.4	80.03	1.87
Kronos	Software	37.8	29.08	1.78
HCC Insurance Holdings	Financial	17.0	5.19	1.75
FMC Technologies	Energy	23.4	38.20	1.73
⊕ Zebra Technologies	Hardware	33.1	27.20	1.63
World Acceptance	Financial	16.4	38.31	1.63
First Health Group	Health	14.2	-4.15	1.59
Scotts	Ind Mtrls	22.7	24.27	1.45
⊕ Chicago Bridge & Iron	Business	27.1	39.16	1.39
JDA Software Group	Software	—	-17.51	1.35
Global Payments	Business	31.3	24.66	1.31

Current Investment Style

Market Cap	%
Giant	0.0
Large	0.0
Mid	45.0
Small	46.0
Micro	9.1
Avg $mil: 1,235	

Value Measures		Rel Category
Price/Earnings	19.18	0.88
Price/Book	2.26	0.86
Price/Sales	1.34	0.89
Price/Cash Flow	7.20	0.90
Dividend Yield %	0.31	1.00

Growth Measures	%	Rel Category
Long-Term Erngs	14.33	0.83
Book Value	5.44	0.84
Sales	4.09	0.63
Cash Flow	12.73	0.94
Historical Erngs	3.07	0.23

Profitability	%	Rel Category
Return on Equity	10.43	1.06
Return on Assets	5.40	1.23
Net Margin	5.92	0.86

Sector Weightings	% of Stocks	Rel S&P 500	3 Year High	3 Year Low
Info	29.88	1.39		
Software	9.15	2.13	16	9
Hardware	8.90	0.87	9	2
Media	3.53	0.92	5	3
Telecom	8.30	2.63	9	4
Service	48.96	1.06		
Health	13.77	1.10	22	14
Consumer	10.82	1.19	11	8
Business	12.01	2.97	16	12
Financial	12.36	0.60	15	11
Mfg	21.17	0.66		
Goods	4.43	0.47	6	3
Ind Mtrls	6.71	0.53	7	2
Energy	8.19	1.14	8	2
Utilities	1.84	0.62	6	1

Composition

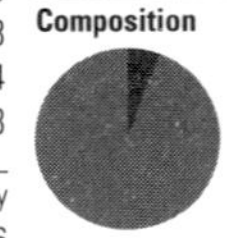

Cash	5.8
Stocks	94.0
Bonds	0.0
Other	0.2
Foreign (% of Stock)	1.7

Morningstar's Take by Todd Trubey 12-10-04

There's great talent at Columbia Acorn USA, but Columbia still has problems.

The small-growth funds run by Columbia Wanger Asset Management look different but have had similar success this year. While Columbia Acorn has a 16% foreign stake, this fund's is only 1.7%. This fund devotes nearly double the assets to tech and telecom that its sibling does (26% versus 14%). And while Acorn USA spreads $771 million across 131 stocks, Acorn invests $12.5 billion in 410 stocks. Yet through Nov. 30, 2004, both fund's year-to-date returns just miss the small growth category's top decile.

Manager Rob Mohn has long said that the funds use same ingredients for different recipes. This fund began as a domestic-only version of Acorn. It uses CWAM's growth-at-a-reasonable price approach, but more boldly than Acorn. While most analysts buy and sell stocks themselves in Acorn, Mohn uses their picks as a more traditional portfolio manager here.

This fund's results this year highlight good stock picks' ability to supercede apparently poor sector bets. Telecom has been wretched in 2004, with the average small-cap telecom stock down 10% through Nov. 30th. That would seem to hurt this fund--its 8% stake quadruples the small-growth category average. Yet the stocks that compose its apparent sector bet, Western Wireless, Crown Castle International, and Commonwealth Telephone Enterprises, have risen 49%, 57%, and 31% respectively through Nov. 30. CWAM found them during the bear market when trolling for firms that could escape the sector's wreckage.

We retain our long-held respect for the investment skill here but can't tout the fund to new investors. The fund's board has lowered the fund's once very high expenses to 1.52%, which is good news. But Columbia funds hasn't finalized its settlement in the market-timing scandal; to date we don't recommend sending new money to any Columbia fund.

Address:	227 W Monroe Ste 3000 Chicago IL 60606 800-345-6611
Web Address:	
Inception:	10-16-00*
Advisor:	Columbia Wanger Asset Management, LP
Subadvisor:	None
NTF Plans:	DATALynx NTF, Federated Tr NTF

Minimum Purchase:	$50000	Add: $50	IRA: $50000
Min Auto Inv Plan:	$50	Add: $50	
Sales Fees:	5.75%L, 0.25%S		
Management Fee:	0.95% mx./0.90% mn., 0.05%A		
Actual Fees:	Mgt:0.93%	Dist:0.35%	
Expense Projections:	3Yr:$1065	5Yr:$1420	10Yr:$2417
Income Distrib:	Semi-Annually		

Columbia Real Est Eq Z

Ticker	Load	NAV	Yield	Total Assets	Mstar Category
CREEX	None	$26.78	3.6%	$1,003 mil	Specialty-Real Estate

Governance and Management

Fiduciary Grade: F

Portfolio Manager(s)

David Jellison has run this fund since its 1994 inception and has been managing money for more than a decade. He conducts all of the fund's research.

Strategy

Management thinks supply-and-demand factors drive performance in mature, cyclical businesses--such as real estate--and uses such factors to emphasize and de-emphasize property subsectors. The fund invests primarily in REITs, which are required to pay out most of their income as dividends to shareholders, and it generally focuses on the largest securities it can find. A newer stake in forestry and paper stocks shows that it is willing to deviate from the category norm.

Historical Profile

Return Average
Risk Low
Rating ★★★ Neutral

Investment Style: Equity Stock %: 100% 100% 89% 86% 95% 97% 89% 97% 95%

▼ Manager Change
▽ Partial Manager Change

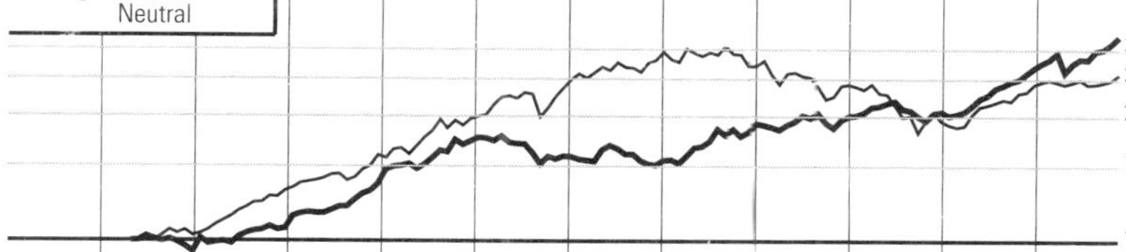

Growth of $10,000
- Investment Values of Fund
- Investment Values of S&P 500

Performance Quartile (within Category)

1993	1994	1995	1996	1997	1998	1999	2000	2001	2002	2003	12-04	History
—	11.72	12.71	16.16	18.80	15.76	14.57	17.89	18.04	17.81	23.16	26.78	NAV
—	1.76*	16.83	38.30	24.74	-12.34	-2.45	28.84	5.41	3.12	35.47	31.08	Total Return %
—	—	-20.70	15.36	-8.61	-40.91	-23.49	37.94	17.29	25.21	6.80	20.21	+/-S&P 500
—	—	4.59	1.26	5.07	4.66	0.12	-2.20	-6.95	-0.48	-0.59	-2.74	+/-Wil REIT
—	0.00	4.62	4.52	3.87	3.57	4.56	5.20	4.03	4.51	4.92	4.64	Income Return %
—	—	12.21	33.78	20.87	-15.91	-7.01	23.64	1.32	-1.39	30.55	26.44	Capital Return %
—	—	30	27	26	15	36	41	94	64	61	61	Total Rtn % Rank Cat
—	0.31	0.53	0.56	0.62	0.66	0.70	0.74	0.72	0.80	0.86	1.06	Income $
—	0.18	0.38	0.70	0.68	0.09	0.11	0.06	0.07	0.00	0.00	2.34	Capital Gains $
—	1.14	1.18	1.06	1.02	1.01	0.99	0.96	0.95	0.94	1.08	0.97	Expense Ratio %
—	6.28	6.71	6.23	4.87	4.60	5.66	5.16	4.65	5.30	3.09	3.78	Income Ratio %
—	8	54	46	34	6	29	25	41	53	—	28	Turnover Rate %
—	17	22	68	152	164	242	437	647	781	988	938	Net Assets $mil

Performance 12-31-04

	1st Qtr	2nd Qtr	3rd Qtr	4th Qtr	Total
2000	3.02	10.85	8.61	3.88	28.84
2001	-4.02	10.35	-5.05	4.82	5.41
2002	6.49	4.20	-9.86	3.10	3.12
2003	0.25	11.81	9.87	10.01	35.47
2004	10.60	-3.98	6.89	15.47	31.08

Trailing	Total Return%	+/- S&P 500	+/- Wil REIT	%Rank Cat	Growth of $10,000
3 Mo	15.47	6.24	-1.22	60	11,547
6 Mo	23.42	16.23	-2.84	73	12,342
1 Yr	31.08	20.21	-2.74	61	13,108
3 Yr Avg	22.34	18.76	-1.22	65	18,311
5 Yr Avg	19.98	22.28	-2.69	81	24,862
10 Yr Avg	15.67	3.60	0.42	15	42,875
15 Yr Avg	—	—	—	—	—

Tax Analysis	Tax-Adj Rtn%	%Rank Cat	Tax-Cost Rat	%Rank Cat
3 Yr (estimated)	20.03	63	1.89	61
5 Yr (estimated)	17.83	75	1.79	54
10 Yr (estimated)	13.46	15	1.91	56

Potential Capital Gain Exposure: 42% of assets

Rating and Risk

Time Period	Load-Adj Return %	Morningstar Rtn vs Cat	Morningstar Risk vs Cat	Morningstar Risk-Adj Rating
1 Yr	31.08			
3 Yr	22.34	Avg	Low	★★★
5 Yr	19.98	-Avg	-Avg	★★
10 Yr	15.67	+Avg	Low	★★★★
Incept	14.68			

Other Measures	Standard Index S&P 500	Best Fit Index Wil REIT
Alpha	20.2	2.3
Beta	0.38	0.83
R-Squared	20	95
Standard Deviation	15.33	
Mean	22.34	
Sharpe Ratio	1.38	

Morningstar's Take by Dan McNeela 12-06-04

Frustrations are growing with Columbia Real Estate Equity.

Despite looking good on an absolute basis, this fund's relative returns continue to lag. Its 26.5% year-to-date gain through Dec. 3, 2004, ranks behind nearly three fourths of its peers in Morningstar's specialty real estate category. Barring a late move, the fund is in danger of finishing below the category average for the fourth straight year.

At the heart of the fund's disappointing results is manager David Jellison's ongoing bet on paper stocks. The fund first acquired its stake in that industry in early 2002, when Jellison's top-down methodology pointed him toward those cyclical stocks. His thinking was that as the economy rebounded, pricing would firm up and profitability would improve. Jellison also believed that many REIT subsectors were fully valued, providing more motivation to invest in nontraditional areas.

The difficulty of consistently profiting from such calls has become readily apparent, however. The economy has indeed picked up since early 2002 and paper stocks have posted modest gains. But REIT stocks have continued to soar higher, leaving this fund in the dust.

Getting the fund turned around looks to be a challenge. Jellison questions how much longer the economy can support his paper stocks, and most REIT subsectors are even more expensive now. A correction among REITs could open the door, but investors will still be left to ask how well the fund will handle future shifts in the real estate market.

Two big-picture concerns remain. Columbia hasn't finalized its settlement with the SEC over market-timing allegations, and its future structure is uncertain given that Columbia's parent Fleet was acquired by Bank of America earlier in 2004.

All told, the current situation here is unappealing. We think investors have better opportunities to get real estate exposure at other firms.

Address:	1300 Sw Sixth Ave Portland OR 97207 800-345-6611
Web Address:	www.columbiafunds.com
Inception:	04-04-94 *
Advisor:	Columbia Management Advisors, Inc.
Subadvisor:	None
NTF Plans:	Fidelity Retail-NTF, Schwab OneSource

Minimum Purchase:	$100000	Add: $0	IRA: $0
Min Auto Inv Plan:	$25	Add: $25	
Sales Fees:	No-load		
Management Fee:	0.75%		
Actual Fees:	Mgt:0.75%	Dist:	
Expense Projections:	3Yr:$309	5Yr:$536	10Yr:$1190
Income Distrib:	Quarterly		

Portfolio Analysis 08-31-04

Share change since 07-04 Total Stocks:38	Sector	PE	YTD Ret%	% Assets
⊖ iStar Financial	Financial	29.3	24.56	4.81
Simon Property Group	Financial	37.3	46.10	4.70
Cousins Properties	Financial	6.2	27.28	4.68
⊕ Hilton Hotels	Consumer	36.1	33.34	4.44
⊖ Equity Residential	Financial	90.2	29.50	4.36
⊖ Alexandria Real Estate E	Financial	23.3	33.65	3.96
⊖ ProLogis Trust	Financial	25.1	41.03	3.72
⊖ General Growth Propertie	Financial	26.6	35.96	3.71
⊕ Host Marriott	Financial	—	40.88	3.60
Bowater Incorporated	Ind Mtrls	—	-3.19	3.25
⊖ Regency Centers	Financial	27.3	46.22	3.21
Public Storage	Financial	43.5	33.22	3.18
International Paper	Ind Mtrls	—	-0.20	3.02
⊕ Starwood Hotels & Resort	Consumer	33.9	64.71	2.96
Equity Office Properties	Financial	45.9	9.06	2.73
⊕ Kimco Realty	Financial	23.4	35.56	2.71
⊕ Marriott International A	Consumer	25.6	37.22	2.47
Duke Realty	Financial	33.1	16.66	2.46
St. Joe	Financial	57.6	74.18	2.37
AvalonBay Communities	Financial	58.1	65.02	2.10

Current Investment Style

Value Blnd Growth

Market Cap	%
Giant	0.0
Large	23.9
Mid	66.2
Small	8.9
Micro	1.1
Avg $mil: 4,484	

Value Measures		Rel Category
Price/Earnings	13.26	1.13
Price/Book	2.18	1.08
Price/Sales	2.26	0.61
Price/Cash Flow	12.76	1.06
Dividend Yield %	4.75	0.97

Growth Measures	%	Rel Category
Long-Term Erngs	7.36	1.04
Book Value	-0.38	NMF
Sales	3.40	2.05
Cash Flow	-5.62	NMF
Historical Erngs	4.46	5.79

Profitability	%	Rel Category
Return on Equity	10.09	0.98
Return on Assets	7.26	0.95
Net Margin	21.85	1.01

Sector Weightings	% of Stocks	Rel S&P 500	3 Year High	3 Year Low
Info	0.00	0.00		
Software	0.00	0.00	0	0
Hardware	0.00	0.00	0	0
Media	0.00	0.00	0	0
Telecom	0.00	0.00	0	0
Service	87.44	1.88		
Health	0.00	0.00	0	0
Consumer	11.43	1.26	11	1
Business	0.00	0.00	0	0
Financial	76.01	3.66	91	73
Mfg	12.56	0.39		
Goods	0.00	0.00	0	0
Ind Mtrls	12.56	0.99	14	6
Energy	0.00	0.00	0	0
Utilities	0.00	0.00	0	0

Composition

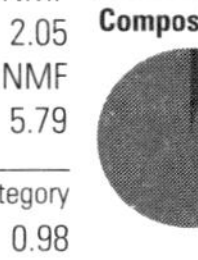

Cash	4.6
Stocks	95.4
Bonds	0.0
Other	0.0
Foreign (% of Stock)	1.5

Constel CIP Ultr Sh F/I I

Ticker	Load	NAV	Yield	SEC Yield	Total Assets	Mstar Category
TSDOX	None	$10.10	2.2%	2.89%	$381 mil	Ultrashort Bond

Governance and Management

Fiduciary Grade:

Portfolio Manager(s)

Roger Early took over as Turner Investment's fixed-income chief investment officer and portfolio manager of this fund at the beginning of 2002. He has roughly 20 years of experience, having run bond assets at Federated and Delaware. Paul Matlack and John McCarthy, with 17 and 15 years of experience, respectively, both worked with Early at Delaware.

Strategy

This fund typically holds half or more of its assets in collateralized mortgage-backed securities with good protection against excessive prepayments (also known as PAC CMOs). Management complements that stake with a small allocation to asset-backed securities and another large bucket of Treasury securities running from the shortest maturities to roughly two years, depending on management's evaluation of that part of the yield curve. Portfolio duration is generally kept at about 0.5 years.

Historical Profile

Return Average
Risk Below Avg
Rating ★★★ Neutral

Investment Style
Fixed Income
Income Rtn %Rank Cat

41	27	12	29	40	69	82	62	46

▼ Manager Change
∇ Partial Manager Change

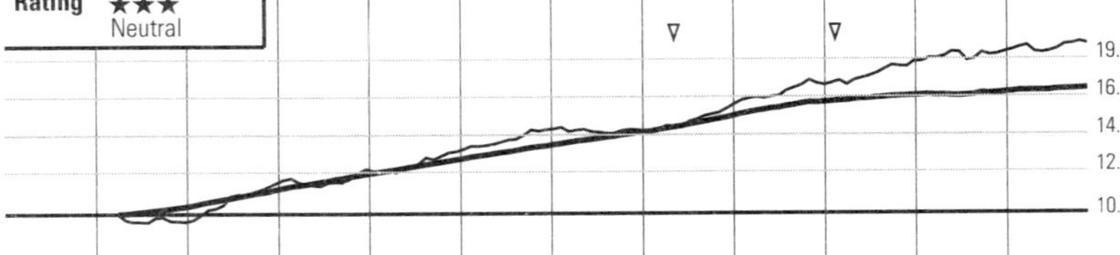

Growth of $10,000
— Investment Values of Fund
— Investment Values of LB Aggr

Performance Quartile (within Category)

1993	1994	1995	1996	1997	1998	1999	2000	2001	2002	2003	12-04	History
—	9.96	10.03	10.06	10.07	10.05	10.03	10.08	10.19	10.21	10.15	10.10	NAV
—	3.68*	7.61	6.41	6.30	5.84	5.41	6.99	5.81	2.66	1.35	1.74	Total Return %
—	—	-10.86	2.78	-3.35	-2.85	6.23	-4.64	-2.63	-7.59	-2.75	-2.60	+/-LB Aggr
—	—	1.63	1.32	0.73	0.47	0.26	0.66	2.32	0.86	0.17	-0.06	+/-6 Month CD
—	0.00	6.88	6.10	6.20	6.06	5.62	6.46	4.70	2.35	1.94	2.24	Income Return %
—	—	0.73	0.31	0.10	-0.22	-0.21	0.53	1.11	0.31	-0.59	-0.50	Capital Return %
—	—	52	31	52	12	6	38	49	48	59	20	Total Rtn % Rank Cat
—	0.40	0.66	0.60	0.61	0.59	0.55	0.63	0.46	0.24	0.20	0.23	Income $
—	0.00	0.00	0.00	0.00	0.00	0.00	0.00	0.00	0.01	0.00	0.00	Capital Gains $
—	—	0.00	0.00	0.00	0.00	0.00	0.36	0.36	0.36	0.41	—	Expense Ratio %
—	—	5.74	6.46	5.91	5.97	5.50	6.15	5.09	2.49	0.78	—	Income Ratio %
—	—	—	—	82	97	154	295	119	71	222	—	Turnover Rate %
—	—	—	1	1	1	5	22	117	565	418	374	Net Assets $mil

Performance 12-31-04

	1st Qtr	2nd Qtr	3rd Qtr	4th Qtr	Total
2000	1.51	1.71	1.72	1.88	6.99
2001	2.02	1.30	1.71	0.66	5.81
2002	0.63	0.86	0.76	0.38	2.66
2003	0.13	-0.23	1.12	0.33	1.35
2004	0.64	0.09	0.56	0.44	1.74

Trailing	Total Return%	+/- LB Aggr	+/- 6 Month CD	%Rank Cat	Growth of $10,000
3 Mo	0.44	-0.51	-0.19	34	10,044
6 Mo	1.01	-3.17	-0.12	28	10,101
1 Yr	1.74	-2.60	-0.06	20	10,174
3 Yr Avg	1.92	-4.27	0.33	42	10,587
5 Yr Avg	3.69	-4.02	0.79	48	11,986
10 Yr Avg	4.99	-2.73	0.83	44	16,273
15 Yr Avg	—	—	—	—	—

Tax Analysis	Tax-Adj Rtn%	%Rank Cat	Tax-Cost Rat	%Rank Cat
3 Yr (estimated)	1.12	26	0.78	30
5 Yr (estimated)	2.32	34	1.32	41
10 Yr (estimated)	3.07	28	1.83	58

Potential Capital Gain Exposure: -1% of assets

Rating and Risk

Time Period	Load-Adj Return %	Morningstar Rtn vs Cat	Morningstar Risk vs Cat	Morningstar Risk-Adj Rating
1 Yr	1.74			
3 Yr	1.92	Avg	Avg	★★★
5 Yr	3.69	Avg	-Avg	★★★
10 Yr	4.99	Avg	-Avg	★★★
Incept	4.95			

Other Measures	Standard Index LB Aggr	Best Fit Index LB Muni 3YR
Alpha	0.3	0.3
Beta	0.04	0.11
R-Squared	7	17
Standard Deviation	0.66	
Mean	1.92	
Sharpe Ratio	0.82	

Morningstar's Take by Eric Jacobson 10-31-04

It's so far so good at Constellation CIP Ultra Short Duration Fixed Income.

The changes at this fund require a scorecard thanks to numerous back and forth strategic shifts at former advisor, Turner. A few years ago that meant a management switch for this fund that brought in Roger Early. That left us with some concern given what a stalwart the fund was, but Early has largely proved himself capable of success. More recently, though, Turner decided to farm out the fund to subadvisor Chartwell, a firm that Early joined as part of the change. Not satisfied with that decision, Turner then elected to spin off a bunch of funds to a new firm called Constellation, run by Turner's former COO. The end result here is that Early now works for Chartwell, which subadvises the fund for Constellation. (There are now funds run by several different subadvisors but distributed by Constellation.)

Although Early has stayed with the fund, we have been a bit concerned that all of the tumult might make it difficult to perpetuate the fund's success. And there already has been one partial casualty: the fund's previously rock-bottom expense ratio.

The good news is that while the price tag has gone up some, it's not excessive, floating around 0.49%. And thus far Early has managed solid performance in 2004. With a duration (a measure of interest-rate sensitivity) of 0.6 years, he's kept the fund's rate sensitivity low--it proved stellar relative to other ultrashort funds when yields spiked in March and April 2004--yet good selection among CMOs (structured mortgages) has helped returns during the year's more bullish first and third quarters. The fund's 1.3% year-to-date gain places in the category's best quartile for the year to date through Oct. 29.

We never like to see this much of a musical chairs game, but thus far it doesn't seem to have badly bruised this fund. As such, we don't see any reason for investors to shy away.

Address:	1205 Westlakes Drive Berwyn, PA 19312 866-242-5742
Web Address:	www.constellationfundsgroup.com
Inception:	03-01-94*
Advisor:	Constellation Investment Mgmt Co., LP
Subadvisor:	Chartwell Investment Partners, LP
NTF Plans:	Schwab OneSource, ETrade No Load ETF

Minimum Purchase:	$2500	Add: $50	IRA: $2000
Min Auto Inv Plan:	$100	Add: $50	
Sales Fees:	No-load		
Management Fee:	0.25%, 0.10%A		
Actual Fees:	Mgt:0.25%	Dist:	
Expense Projections:	3Yr:$116	5Yr:$413	10Yr:$1259
Income Distrib:	Monthly		

Portfolio Analysis 12-31-04

Total Fixed-Income:94	Date of Maturity	Amount $000	Value $000	% Net Assets
FNMA CMO	04-25-32	15,000	15,154	3.97
FHLMC CMO	07-15-34	14,203	14,256	3.74
FNMA CMO	08-25-33	11,945	12,074	3.16
FHLMC CMO	08-15-32	11,754	11,910	3.12
FHLMC CMO	11-15-34	9,969	9,849	2.58
FHLBA 2.125%	01-27-06	9,750	9,741	2.55
GNMA CMO 4%	04-20-33	9,415	9,337	2.45
FHLMC CMO	12-15-32	9,124	9,152	2.40
FHLMC CMO	10-15-34	8,981	8,995	2.36
FHLMC CMO 4%	12-15-32	8,525	8,356	2.19
FHLMC CMO	11-15-34	7,956	7,982	2.09
FHLBA FRN	11-03-14	8,000	7,860	2.06
FHLMC CMO 6%	03-15-28	7,528	7,609	1.99
FNMA CMO	09-25-33	7,057	7,080	1.86
FHLMC CMO	05-15-34	6,250	6,276	1.64
FHLMC CMO	02-15-34	5,858	5,889	1.54
GNMA 7%	10-15-14	5,345	5,696	1.49
FNMA 7.5%	11-01-31	4,864	5,212	1.37
FHLMC CMO 3.79%	12-15-28	5,191	5,192	1.36
FNMA CMO	02-25-32	5,000	5,052	1.32

Current Investment Style

Duration: Short Int Long
Quality: High Med Low

¹ figure provided by fund

Avg Eff Duration¹	0.6 Yrs
Avg Eff Maturity	0.6 Yrs
Avg Credit Quality	AAA
Avg Wtd Coupon	3.15%
Avg Wtd Price	100.56% of par

Coupon Range	% of Bonds	Rel Cat
0% PIK	2.7	0.1
0% to 6%	90.7	1.1
6% to 8%	9.0	0.7
8% to 10%	0.3	0.1
More than 10%	0.0	0.0

1.00=Category Average

Credit Analysis		% bonds 12-31-04	
US Govt	97	BB	0
AAA	0	B	0
AA	0	Below B	0
A	0	NR/NA	3
BBB	0		

Sector Breakdown	% of assets
US Treasuries	0
TIPS	0
US Agency	3
Mortgage Pass-Throughs	6
Mortgage CMO	75
Mortgage ARM	0
US Corporate	4
Asset-Backed	0
Convertible	0
Municipal	0
Corporate Inflation-Protected	0
Foreign Corporate	0
Foreign Govt	0

Composition			
Cash	13.1	Bonds	86.9
Stocks	0.0	Other	0.0

Special Securities	
Restricted/Illiquid Secs	0
Exotic Mortgage-Backed	—
Emerging-Markets Secs	0
Options/Futures/Warrants	No

Constel Clover Sm Cap Val

Ticker	Load	NAV	Yield	Total Assets	Mstar Category
TCSVX	None	$26.96	0.0%	$592 mil	Small Value

Governance and Management

Fiduciary Grade:

Portfolio Manager(s)

Lawrence Creatura and Mike Jones have been at the helm since the fund's 1996 inception. Jones also comanages Constellation Clover Core Value, which has posted mixed results in recent years. They are assisted by seven industry analysts, most of whom have been with subadvisor Clover Capital Management for more than a decade. The managers report they are planning on hiring one more analyst.

Strategy

Managers Lawrence Creatura and Mike Jones favor a big-picture approach, evaluating economic conditions and industry trends before analyzing individual stocks. The pair focuses on small stocks because they think those are often the market's most undervalued issues. The fund's market cap tends to be below the category average, though it has risen as assets have grown. Creatura and Jones have also been willing to make large sector bets on occasion. The managers will venture into more-growth-oriented sectors such as health care and technology when they are cheap enough.

Historical Profile

Return Average
Risk Above Avg
Rating ★★ Below Avg

Investment Style: Equity Stock %

1996	1997	1998	1999	2000	2001	2002	2003	12-04
92%	97%	93%	100%	89%	99%	95%	99%	

▼ Manager Change
∇ Partial Manager Change

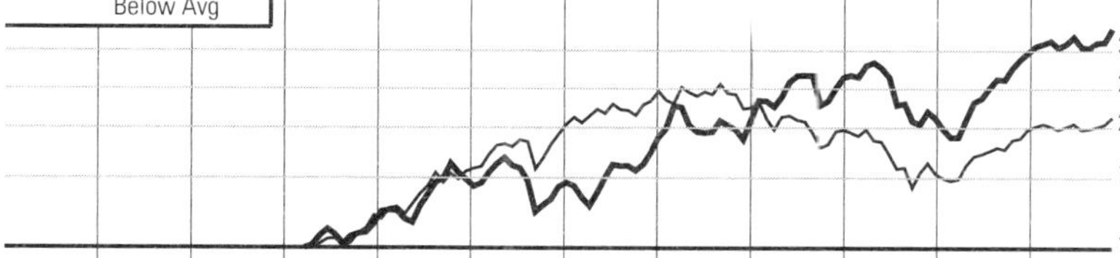

Growth of $10,000
— Investment Values of Fund
— Investment Values of S&P 500

Performance Quartile (within Category)

1993	1994	1995	1996	1997	1998	1999	2000	2001	2002	2003	12-04	History
—	—	—	12.11	12.80	12.79	15.26	15.39	19.55	15.45	22.44	26.96	NAV
—	—	—	22.72*	15.47	2.01	29.57	10.59	27.42	-20.75	45.32	20.14	Total Return %
—	—	—	—	-17.88	-26.56	8.53	19.69	39.30	1.34	16.65	9.27	+/-S&P 500
—	—	—	—	-16.31	8.46	31.06	-12.24	13.40	-9.32	-0.71	-2.11	+/-Russ 2000 VL
—	—	—	0.00	0.00	0.00	0.00	0.00	0.36	0.26	0.05	0.00	Income Return %
—	—	—	—	15.47	2.01	29.57	10.59	27.06	-21.01	45.27	20.14	Capital Return %
—	—	—	—	100	14	10	77	14	95	33	55	Total Rtn % Rank Cat
—	—	—	0.03	0.00	0.00	0.00	0.00	0.05	0.05	0.01	0.00	Income $
—	—	—	0.13	1.17	0.25	1.24	1.39	0.00	0.00	0.00	0.00	Capital Gains $
—	—	—	1.40	1.40	1.40	1.40	1.40	1.28	1.26	1.27	—	Expense Ratio %
—	—	—	-0.03	-0.64	-0.50	-0.10	-0.11	0.37	0.31	0.08	—	Income Ratio %
—	—	—	14	59	70	80	142	120	38	52	—	Turnover Rate %
—	—	—	6	15	17	20	37	412	503	480	592	Net Assets $mil

Performance 12-31-04

	1st Qtr	2nd Qtr	3rd Qtr	4th Qtr	Total
2000	18.81	-13.51	4.34	3.15	10.59
2001	7.80	19.40	-15.53	17.19	27.42
2002	6.99	-6.19	-22.37	1.70	-20.75
2003	-10.32	24.85	11.22	16.69	45.32
2004	6.95	2.38	-3.30	13.47	20.14

Trailing	Total Return%	+/- S&P 500	+/- Russ 2000 VL	%Rank Cat	Growth of $10,000
3 Mo	13.47	4.24	0.27	32	11,347
6 Mo	9.73	2.54	-3.64	79	10,973
1 Yr	20.14	9.27	-2.11	55	12,014
3 Yr Avg	11.43	7.85	-5.07	87	13,836
5 Yr Avg	14.28	16.58	-2.95	68	19,492
10 Yr Avg	—	—	—	—	—
15 Yr Avg	—	—	—	—	—

Tax Analysis	Tax-Adj Rtn%	%Rank Cat	Tax-Cost Rat	%Rank Cat
3 Yr (estimated)	11.38	75	0.04	3
5 Yr (estimated)	13.82	60	0.40	19
10 Yr (estimated)	—	—	—	—

Potential Capital Gain Exposure: % of assets

Rating and Risk

Time Period	Load-Adj Return %	Morningstar Rtn vs Cat	Morningstar Risk vs Cat	Morningstar Risk-Adj Rating
1 Yr	20.14			
3 Yr	11.43	-Avg	+Avg	★★
5 Yr	14.28	Avg	+Avg	★★
10 Yr	—	—	—	—
Incept	15.78			

Other Measures	Standard Index S&P 500	Best Fit Index Russ 2000 VL
Alpha	8.3	-4.8
Beta	0.99	1.04
R-Squared	62	94
Standard Deviation	21.19	
Mean	11.43	
Sharpe Ratio	0.48	

Portfolio Analysis 12-31-04

Share change since 11-04 Total Stocks:150	Sector	PE	YTD Ret%	% Assets
⊖ Felcor Lodging Trust	Financial	—	32.22	2.06
⊖ CMS Energy	Utilities	83.3	22.65	1.52
⊖ Stewart & Stevenson Serv	Ind Mtrls	—	47.10	1.40
⊖ Scottish Re Group	Financial	11.1	25.78	1.30
⊖ Reliant Energy	Utilities	—	85.46	1.30
⊖ AK Steel Holding	Ind Mtrls	—	183.73	1.27
⊖ Owens-Illinois	Ind Mtrls	—	90.50	1.24
⊖ AGCO	Ind Mtrls	12.1	8.69	1.24
⊖ South Financial Group	Financial	15.7	19.71	1.23
⊖ Providian Financial	Financial	14.3	41.50	1.19
⊖ Platinum Underwriters Ho	Financial	16.1	4.76	1.18
⊖ Men's Wearhouse	Consumer	20.2	27.79	1.09
⊖ Hooper Holmes	Health	32.4	-3.06	1.08
⊖ BankAtlantic Bancorp A	Financial	19.4	44.36	1.04
⊖ Scholastic	Media	42.0	8.58	1.00
⊖ Cumulus Media A	Media	40.9	-31.46	1.00
☼ Southern Union	Utilities	18.5	36.84	0.98
⊖ NICE-Systems ADR	Hardware	91.7	23.43	0.97
⊖ Webster Financial	Financial	13.3	12.57	0.95
⊖ BankUnited Financial A	Financial	20.0	23.89	0.95

Current Investment Style

Value Blnd Growth — Large Mid Small

Market Cap	%
Giant	0.0
Large	0.0
Mid	31.6
Small	53.8
Micro	14.6

Avg $mil: 1,043

Value Measures		Rel Category
Price/Earnings	18.18	1.14
Price/Book	1.67	1.01
Price/Sales	0.76	1.01
Price/Cash Flow	4.63	0.89
Dividend Yield %	0.67	0.56

Growth Measures	%	Rel Category
Long-Term Erngs	12.54	1.03
Book Value	2.02	0.47
Sales	3.11	0.99
Cash Flow	-0.53	NMF
Historical Erngs	-3.96	NMF

Profitability	%	Rel Category
Return on Equity	7.09	0.78
Return on Assets	3.98	0.96
Net Margin	6.31	0.90

Sector Weightings	% of Stocks	Rel S&P 500	3 Year High	3 Year Low
Info	10.22	0.48		
Software	1.83	0.43	4	0
Hardware	4.51	0.44	11	4
Media	3.17	0.83	3	[illegible]
Telecom	0.71	0.23	1	0
Service	59.24	1.28		
Health	7.86	0.63	9	2
Consumer	11.55	1.27	15	8
Business	11.20	2.77	13	8
Financial	28.63	1.38	30	23
Mfg	30.54	0.95		
Goods	6.39	0.68	10	5
Ind Mtrls	14.20	1.12	20	11
Energy	3.61	0.50	5	2
Utilities	6.34	2.14	8	5

Composition

Cash	0.7
Stocks	99.3
Bonds	0.0
Other	0.0
Foreign (% of Stock)	1.4

Morningstar's Take by Christopher Davis 12-01-04

Constellation Clover Small Cap Value holds appeal for long-term investors, but look before you leap.

Longtime managers Lawrence Creatura and Mike Jones blend top-down and bottom-up analysis at this offering. Emphasizing areas of they believe will benefit most from macroeconomic and industry wide trends, the managers look for stocks they believe are cheap. That strategy sounds simple enough, but to execute it well is no mean feat. Economic forecasting is notoriously difficult to get right consistently and even the most experienced value investors are often ensnared by "value traps"--seemingly cheap stocks that become even cheaper.

These days, Creatura and Jones have continued to give the portfolio a cyclical cast, with an eye toward consumer services names. That bet has had mixed results this year. Winners such as American Eagle Outfitters have helped but stinkers like Payless ShoeSource have hurt returns, contributing to the fund's bottom-third showing for the year to date through Nov. 30, 2004. This isn't the first time management has misfired. It prematurely bet economic recovery in 2002, a stance that backfired as the economy swooned, contributing to the fund's 21% loss for the year, one of the small-value group's worst showings. All told, 2004 is likely to mark the fund's fourth bottom-third showing in the past eight calendar years.

While returns here have been erratic in shorter time periods, the fund has fared well over the long haul. Indeed, it has nicely outpaced its small-value rivals since its March 1996 inception. To be sure, much of its record was earned with a smaller asset base and more exposure to micro-caps. But the fund has still delivered strong results even as assets have grown. while the same management team has been in place all along. Though the fund would have to be more predictable to join the ranks of the small-value elite, we think it's a respectable option in its category.

Address:	1205 Westlakes Drive Berwyn, PA 19312 866-242-5742
Web Address:	www.constellationfundsgroup.com
Inception:	02-28-96*
Advisor:	Turner Investment Partners, Inc.
Subadvisor:	Clover Capital Management Inc
NTF Plans:	Fidelity Retail-NTF, Schwab OneSource

Minimum Purchase:	$2500	Add: $500	IRA: $2000
Min Auto Inv Plan:	$100	Add: $100	
Sales Fees:	No-load		
Management Fee:	0.85%, 0.12%A		
Actual Fees:	Mgt:0.53%	Dist:	
Expense Projections:	3Yr:$512	5Yr:$908	10Yr:$2037
Income Distrib:	Quarterly		

Davis Appr & Income A

Analyst Pick

Ticker	Load	NAV	Yield	Total Assets	Mstar Category
RPFCX	4.75%	$27.50	2.4%	$295 mil	Convertibles

Governance and Management

Fiduciary Grade: A

Portfolio Manager(s)

Andrew Davis, has managed the fund since coming to the firm in 1993 from PaineWebber, where he managed convertible securities research. Jason Voss came to Davis Selected Advisers in 1998 and joined as comanager in fall 2000. The pair also manages Davis Real Estate, and at both funds they've shown a willingness to follow their mandates loosely, with mixed results.

Strategy

Managers Andrew Davis and Jason Voss prefer to own between 30 and 40 convertible securities from firms with strong management and reasonable valuations. They believe that a portfolio largely invested in convertibles can offer 80% of the S&P 500 index's upside return while avoiding 50% of its downside risk. When they can't find an ideal convertible they'll mix a convert with the firm's common stock or bundle stock and straight debt.

Historical Profile

Return: Average
Risk: Average
Rating: ★★★★ Above Avg

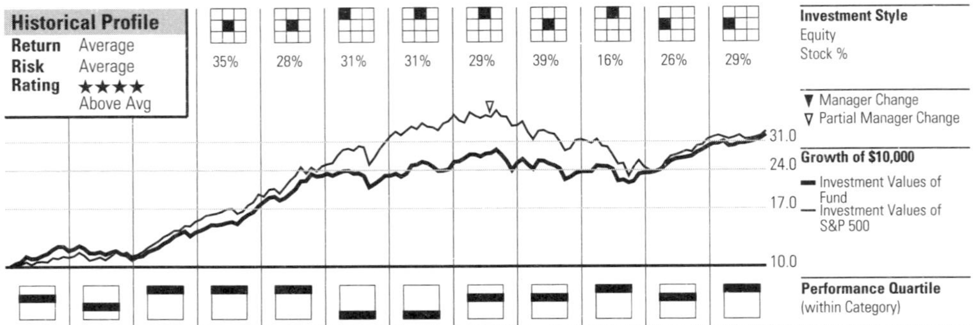

1993	1994	1995	1996	1997	1998	1999	2000	2001	2002	2003	12-04	History
17.45	15.57	18.22	21.22	25.26	23.76	25.21	23.96	21.36	20.30	24.95	27.50	NAV
17.30	-6.72	26.68	29.46	28.68	-1.80	12.97	-0.97	-7.56	-1.21	26.94	13.08	Total Return %
7.24	-8.03	-10.85	6.52	-4.67	-30.37	-8.07	8.13	4.32	20.88	-1.73	2.21	+/-S&P 500
0.89	-1.88	2.72	17.34	13.17	-14.01	-23.02	6.55	-4.65	1.91	3.97	4.77	+/-Merrill Lynch Convert
4.32	3.33	4.30	4.06	3.49	3.05	3.30	3.35	3.17	3.80	3.67	2.69	Income Return %
12.98	-10.05	22.38	25.40	25.19	-4.85	9.67	-4.32	-10.73	-5.01	23.27	10.39	Capital Return %
41	68	8	1	3	77	82	50	50	2	43	6	Total Rtn % Rank Cat
0.67	0.57	0.66	0.73	0.73	0.76	0.77	0.83	0.75	0.80	0.74	0.67	Income $
0.31	0.15	0.78	1.54	1.23	0.28	0.77	0.21	0.04	0.00	0.00	0.00	Capital Gains $
1.21	1.20	1.14	1.05	1.07	1.16	1.12	1.07	1.09	1.09	1.10	—	Expense Ratio %
3.89	4.06	3.87	3.34	3.00	3.27	2.99	3.02	3.31	3.69	3.38	—	Income Ratio %
62	45	54	43	24	14	33	25	20	34	33	—	Turnover Rate %
45	48	60	43	90	134	117	103	89	81	114	150	Net Assets $mil

Performance 12-31-04

	1st Qtr	2nd Qtr	3rd Qtr	4th Qtr	Total
2000	6.90	0.74	-0.90	-7.21	-0.97
2001	-5.38	4.77	-13.20	7.43	-7.56
2002	5.43	-3.14	-11.43	9.21	-1.21
2003	2.86	10.39	2.43	9.15	26.94
2004	4.69	-1.66	2.45	7.20	13.08

Trailing	Total Return%	+/- S&P 500	+/- Merrill Lynch Convert	%Rank Cat	Growth of $10,000
3 Mo	7.20	-2.03	0.84	40	10,720
6 Mo	9.83	2.64	5.02	2	10,983
1 Yr	13.08	2.21	4.77	6	11,308
3 Yr Avg	12.35	8.77	3.48	2	14,181
5 Yr Avg	5.36	7.66	2.37	28	12,983
10 Yr Avg	11.76	-0.31	0.76	27	30,399
15 Yr Avg	—	—	—	—	—

Tax Analysis	Tax-Adj Rtn%	%Rank Cat	Tax-Cost Rat	%Rank Cat
3 Yr (estimated)	9.35	8	1.08	41
5 Yr (estimated)	3.09	31	1.20	9
10 Yr (estimated)	9.18	23	1.83	9

Potential Capital Gain Exposure: 18% of assets

Rating and Risk

Time Period	Load-Adj Return %	Morningstar Rtn vs Cat	Morningstar Risk vs Cat	Morningstar Risk-Adj Rating
1 Yr	7.70			
3 Yr	10.54	High	+Avg	★★★★★
5 Yr	4.34	Avg	Avg	★★★
10 Yr	11.22	Avg	Avg	★★★★
Incept	10.59			

Other Measures	Standard Index S&P 500	Best Fit Index Merrill Lynch Convert
Alpha	9.7	2.7
Beta	0.47	1.09
R-Squared	54	74

Standard Deviation	10.67
Mean	12.35
Sharpe Ratio	1.04

Portfolio Analysis 09-30-04

Total Fixed-Income:6	Date of Maturity	Amount $000	Value $000	% Net Assets
Lehman Bros Hldgs 0.25%	08-23-11	12,400	12,877	4.97
SL Green Realty		245	12,702	4.90
Amer Express 144A Cv 1.8	12-01-33	11,100	11,766	4.54
Waste Connections FRN	05-01-22	8,260	9,320	3.59
Sealed Air 144A Cv 3%	06-30-33	9,000	9,034	3.48
Intl Rectifier Cv 4.25%	07-15-07	8,220	8,138	3.14
School Specialty Cv 3.75	08-01-23	6,500	7,889	3.04
Vornado Realty Trust		125	7,833	3.02
General Growth Propertie		246	7,616	2.94
Nco Grp Cv 4.75%	04-15-06	7,160	7,590	2.93
Aes Tr Iii Cv		169	7,485	2.89
Providian Finl Cv	02-15-21	14,200	7,313	2.82
Gtech Hldgs Cv 1.75%	12-15-21	3,900	7,264	2.80
CenterPoint Properties		163	7,108	2.74
Developers Diversified R		174	6,820	2.63
United Rentals Tr I Pfd		167	6,647	2.56
Amer Intl Grp 0.5%	05-15-07	6,895	6,619	2.55
Invision Tech Cv 3%	10-01-23	4,430	6,484	2.50
Masco Cv	07-20-31	10,600	5,221	2.01
Universal Hlth Svcs Cv 0	06-23-20	8,800	5,148	1.98

Morningstar's Take by Todd Trubey 12-01-04

Davis Appreciation & Income remains a stalwart convertible fund.

While this fund buys more than convertible bonds, they'll remain the fund's core. In mid-2003 the SEC required funds to invest 80% of assets as the fund's name suggests. Given few enticing converts, comanagers Andrew Davis and Jason Voss dropped "Convertible" from this fund's name but will keep at least a 65% convertible stake. For years they'd bought REITs and joined a firm's convertible to its stock, and in 2003 they opted to begin mixing a firm's straight debt and equity to create a "blended convertible."

In this way convertibles' nifty risk/reward profile became the fund's goal. Converts, compared with stocks, combine good upside potential with lower downside risk. Davis and Voss aim for 80% of the S&P 500 index's upside returns but half its downside risk. So far, they've done well. In 2003 the fund gained 27% versus the index's 29%. In 2004, through Nov. 30, the fund has gained 11% versus the index's 7% gain. Compared with its convertible peers, the fund has long had lower gains but better defense, which should continue.

The fund's moderation stems from a carefully constructed portfolio. The managers seek out 30 to 40 steady firms. They examine each firm's stock, debt, and convertibles, buying the latter if it's appealing enough. If it's not--or doesn't exist--they'll create a blended convert.

The fund does, though, have risks. Its REIT stake, now 20% of assets, has helped its relative returns and could hurt if the sector cools. And in any compact fund, a few poor picks can hurt badly. Finally, while the fund's few blended converts have done well, the practice isn't fully proven.

Still, we think this shop's fiduciary care will carry the day. In examining fund boards, management compensation, fees, corporate culture, and regulatory issues, no shop looks better than Davis. Investors seeking a safe convertible fund will like this Analyst Pick.

Investment Style	
Avg Eff Maturity	14.9 Yrs
Avg Credit Quality	BBB
Avg Wtd Coupon	2.31%
Avg Wtd Price	98.30% of par

Coupon Range	% of Bonds	Rel Cat
0% PIK	—	0.0
0% to 8%	0.0	0.0
8% to 11%	0.0	0.0
11% to 14%	0.0	0.0
More than 14%	0.0	0.0

1.00=Category Average

Special Securities	
Restricted/Illiquid Secs	12
Emerging-Markets Secs	0
Options/Futures/Warrants	No

Composition	
Cash	8.2
Stocks	28.6
Bonds	13.9
Convertibles	44.4
Other	4.8

Credit Analysis		% bonds 09-30-04	
US Govt	0	BB	10
AAA	6	B	25
AA	0	Below B	0
A	19	NR/NA	12
BBB	28		

Address:	2949 E. Elvira Road Tucson AZ 85706 800-279-0279
Web Address:	www.davisfunds.com
Inception:	05-01-92
Advisor:	Davis Selected Advisers LP
Subadvisor:	Davis Selected Advisers - NY, Inc.
NTF Plans:	DATALynx NTF, Federated Tr NTF

Minimum Purchase:	$1000	Add: $25	IRA: $1000
Min Auto Inv Plan:	$25	Add: $25	
Sales Fees:	4.75%L		
Management Fee:	0.75% mx./0.55% mn.		
Actual Fees:	Mgt:0.75%	Dist:0.14%	
Expense Projections:	3Yr:$808	5Yr:$1052	10Yr:$1752
Income Distrib:	Quarterly		

Davis Financial A

Analyst Pick

Ticker	Load	NAV	Yield	Total Assets	Mstar Category
RPFGX	4.75%	$41.00	0.0%	$975 mil	Specialty-Financial

Governance and Management

Fiduciary Grade: A

Portfolio Manager(s)

Chris Davis has managed this fund since 1991 and won't likely leave the family business soon. Ken Feinberg joined the firm in 1994 and became comanager of the fund in 1997. Feinberg has a considerable portion of his net worth invested in this and other Davis offerings. He also owns some of the portfolios' individual securities.

Strategy

Comanagers Chris Davis and Ken Feinberg focus on companies with sound financials and high-quality management that are trading at attractive valuations. They are opportunistic buyers and will often invest in companies that are under a cloud. The fund tends to hold each stock for several years, making for good tax efficiency. Its portfolio is quite compact, with only 30 names or so. Although management builds the portfolio stock by stock, the fund doesn't steer away from major industry bets when favorite names are found in the same line of business.

Historical Profile

Return: Average
Risk: Above Avg
Rating: ★★★ Neutral

Investment Style: Equity, Stock %

95%	93%	90%	99%	96%	87%	93%	100%	100%

▼ Manager Change
∇ Partial Manager Change

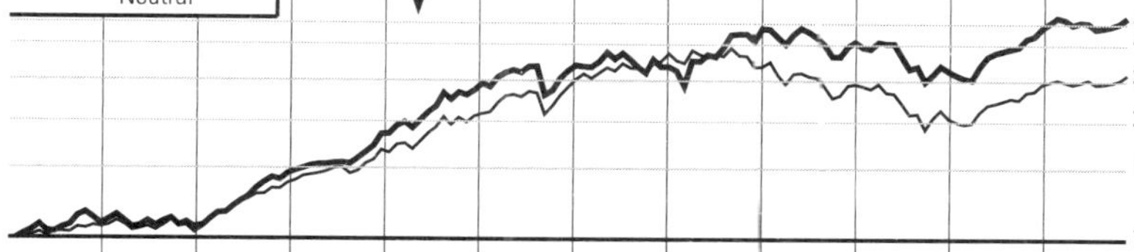

Growth of $10,000
▬ Investment Values of Fund
— Investment Values of S&P 500

Performance Quartile (within Category)

History

	1993	1994	1995	1996	1997	1998	1999	2000	2001	2002	2003	12-04
NAV	11.70	10.68	14.50	18.06	25.68	29.32	29.07	36.30	32.98	26.72	36.57	41.00
Total Return %	14.87	-4.55	50.51	31.50	44.53	14.17	-0.85	32.16	-9.13	-18.98	36.86	12.11
+/-S&P 500	4.81	-5.86	12.98	8.56	11.18	-14.40	-21.89	41.26	2.75	3.11	8.19	1.24
+/-DJ Finance	6.51	-0.27	-0.26	-2.34	-4.41	6.66	-2.37	5.22	-2.75	-6.63	4.63	-1.28
Income Return %	0.72	0.77	0.66	1.03	0.69	0.00	0.00	0.00	0.01	0.00	0.00	0.00
Capital Return %	14.15	-5.32	49.85	30.47	43.84	14.17	-0.85	32.16	-9.14	-18.98	36.86	12.11
Total Rtn % Rank Cat	60	80	10	46	58	17	39	21	84	91	27	60
Income $	0.08	0.09	0.07	0.15	0.13	0.00	0.00	0.00	0.00	0.00	0.00	0.00
Capital Gains $	1.08	0.40	1.50	0.87	0.30	0.00	0.00	1.93	0.00	0.00	0.00	0.00
Expense Ratio %	1.32	1.24	1.18	1.15	1.07	1.06	1.04	1.05	1.08	1.11	1.10	—
Income Ratio %	0.57	0.67	0.53	0.92	0.77	0.34	0.36	-0.21	-0.20	0.18	0.27	—
Turnover Rate %	70	44	42	26	6	11	18	35	18	15	9	—
Net Assets $mil	51	58	80	108	288	461	425	633	600	417	535	583

Performance 12-31-04

	1st Qtr	2nd Qtr	3rd Qtr	4th Qtr	Total
2000	4.30	2.97	18.16	4.14	32.16
2001	-10.66	9.31	-16.30	11.17	-9.13
2002	-0.15	-9.96	-16.66	8.13	-18.98
2003	-6.29	21.77	4.56	14.71	36.86
2004	6.51	-2.36	-2.18	10.22	12.11

Trailing	Total Return%	+/- S&P 500	+/- DJ Finance	%Rank Cat	Growth of $10,000
3 Mo	10.22	0.99	1.27	34	11,022
6 Mo	7.81	0.62	-2.46	85	10,781
1 Yr	12.11	1.24	-1.28	60	11,211
3 Yr Avg	7.53	3.95	-2.00	66	12,433
5 Yr Avg	8.34	10.64	-0.99	69	14,926
10 Yr Avg	17.07	5.00	-0.68	37	48,357
15 Yr Avg	—	—	—	—	—

Tax Analysis	Tax-Adj Rtn%	%Rank Cat	Tax-Cost Rat	%Rank Cat
3 Yr (estimated)	5.80	71	0.00	1
5 Yr (estimated)	7.06	74	0.21	10
10 Yr (estimated)	15.59	28	0.78	10

Potential Capital Gain Exposure: 43% of assets

Rating and Risk

Time Period	Load-Adj Return %	Morningstar Rtn vs Cat	Morningstar Risk vs Cat	Morningstar Risk-Adj Rating
1 Yr	6.79			
3 Yr	5.80	-Avg	+Avg	★★
5 Yr	7.29	-Avg	+Avg	★★
10 Yr	16.50	Avg	Avg	★★★
Incept	16.69			

Other Measures	Standard Index S&P 500	Best Fit Index MSCI World
Alpha	4.0	1.6
Beta	0.99	1.03
R-Squared	87	93
Standard Deviation	17.15	
Mean	7.53	
Sharpe Ratio	0.36	

Portfolio Analysis 09-30-04

Share change since 06-04 Total Stocks:24	Sector	PE	YTD Ret%	% Assets
American Express	Financial	20.3	17.60	10.99
⊕ Transatlantic Holdings	Financial	16.7	-3.74	8.50
⊖ Tyco International	Ind Mtrls	25.1	35.41	8.23
Golden West Financial	Financial	15.3	19.45	6.12
Citigroup	Financial	15.3	2.72	5.99
Dun & Bradstreet	Business	19.8	17.63	5.68
Berkshire Hathaway A	Financial	—	—	5.67
American International G	Financial	16.2	-0.53	5.41
⊖ Julius Baer Holding Ltd	Financial	—	—	4.32
Moody's	Business	32.5	44.06	4.46
Cincinnati Financial	Financial	14.5	14.24	4.37
Commerce Bancorp NJ	Financial	19.8	23.89	3.65
☼ J P Morgan Chase	Financial	19.4	9.97	3.49
⊖ Loews	Financial	—	43.59	3.21
Markel	Financial	21.8	43.58	2.98
⊖ Altria Group	Goods	13.3	18.38	2.94
Progressive	Financial	11.7	1.63	2.89
Sealed Air	Goods	20.4	-1.61	2.33
Providian Financial	Financial	14.3	41.50	2.20
H & R Block	Consumer	14.5	-9.99	2.14

Current Investment Style

Value Blnd Growth; Large Mid Small

Market Cap	%
Giant	39.9
Large	18.2
Mid	40.9
Small	0.0
Micro	1.0
Avg $mil: 17,720	

Value Measures		Rel Category
Price/Earnings	14.17	1.09
Price/Book	1.92	1.01
Price/Sales	1.64	0.88
Price/Cash Flow	4.12	1.11
Dividend Yield %	1.05	0.51

Growth Measures	%	Rel Category
Long-Term Erngs	12.45	1.07
Book Value	11.69	1.19
Sales	7.70	2.33
Cash Flow	23.34	1.66
Historical Erngs	16.40	0.82

Profitability	%	Rel Category
Return on Equity	15.04	0.94
Return on Assets	12.39	1.19
Net Margin	12.49	0.70

Industry Weightings	% of Stocks	Rel Cat
Intl Banks	10.7	0.8
Banks	4.7	0.2
Real Estate	0.0	0.0
Sec Mgmt	0.0	0.0
S & Ls	6.9	0.7
Prop & Reins	30.3	2.1
Life Ins	0.0	0.0
Misc. Ins	3.6	1.0
Other	43.9	2.8

Composition

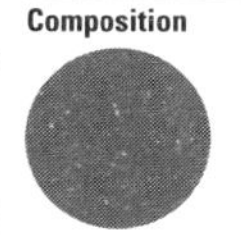

Cash	0.0
Stocks	100.0
Bonds	0.0
Other	0.0
Foreign (% of Stock)	5.4

Morningstar's Take by Laura Pavlenko Lutton 12-23-04

Recent insurance-industry investigations highlight Davis Financial's risks.

Most funds in the financials category can be sorted into two groups: those with very narrow industry focuses, such as brokerage- or bank-only funds, and those that take a more-diversified approach to stocks in the sector. This fund, however, doesn't fit neatly into either camp. Of the eight industries in the sector, it owns stocks in just five and keeps about 40% of the fund's assets completely outside the financials sector. The fund has an outsized stake in insurance stocks--about a third of the offering's assets. Managers Chris Davis and Ken Feinberg find insurance stocks often meet their investment criteria of steady growth, high-quality earnings, shareholder-friendly management teams, and cheap stock prices.

In addition to this quirky industry concentration, the fund holds just 24 stocks and makes big bets on its favorite names. Top holding American Express, for example, represents about 11% of assets.

As one might expect, this fund's strategy has yielded lumpy short-term returns. When the fund's favorite names or industries do well, this fund soars. But returns likewise suffer when a key pick stumbles. That was evident in 2004 when American International Group, a top holding, dropped on news that it was the subject of several regulatory and criminal investigations. That episode helped hold the offering to a below-average 11.70% gain for the year to date through Dec. 22.

Over the long term, however, shareholders have been rewarded for sticking around. To be sure, bottom-quartile finishes in 2001 and 2002 have hurt the fund's three- and five-year records, but Davis and Feinberg's deliberate stock-picking has led to impressive absolute and relative returns over the longer run.

Shareholders should be prepared for the occasional bump in the road here, but patient types have found a winner.

Address:	2949 E. Elvira Road, Tucson AZ 85706, 800-279-0279
Web Address:	www.davisfunds.com
Inception:	05-01-91
Advisor:	Davis Selected Advisers LP
Subadvisor:	Davis Selected Advisers - NY, Inc.
NTF Plans:	DATALynx NTF, Federated Tr NTF

Minimum Purchase:	$1000	Add: $25	IRA: $1000
Min Auto Inv Plan:	$25	Add: $25	
Sales Fees:	4.75%L		
Management Fee:	0.75% mx./0.55% mn.		
Actual Fees:	Mgt:0.64%	Dist:0.20%	
Expense Projections:	3Yr:$808	5Yr:$1052	10Yr:$1752
Income Distrib:	Semi-Annually		

Davis NY Venture A

Ticker	Load	NAV	Yield	Total Assets	Mstar Category
NYVTX	4.75%	$30.69	0.8%	$26,954 mil	Large Blend

Governance and Management

Fiduciary Grade: A

Portfolio Manager(s)

Comanager Chris Davis has been at the firm since 1991, and he plans to stick around at the family-run firm. Comanager Ken Feinberg began as a financial-stock analyst with the firm in 1994 and became comanager in 1998. Davis' family owns the firm and invests heavily in the funds. Other employees are also significant owners, and the bonus plan here is set up with an eye toward long-term outperformance.

Strategy

The managers try to buy great companies whose shares are temporarily depressed. They estimate a firm's intrinsic value based on their own earnings analysis in which they try to assess a firm's true cash earnings. They then look at those earnings relative to a return on adjusted invested capital. The idea is to figure out how well the company has historically allocated its capital.

Historical Profile

Return Above Avg
Risk Average
Rating ★★★★ Above Avg

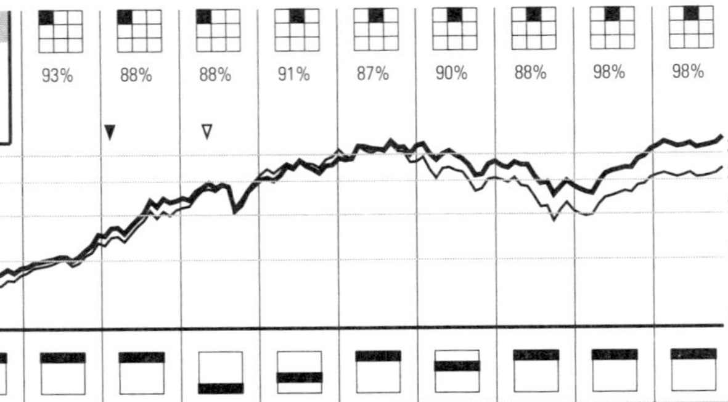

History

1993	1994	1995	1996	1997	1998	1999	2000	2001	2002	2003	12-04	History
11.97	11.16	14.52	17.50	22.33	25.01	28.76	28.74	25.43	20.94	27.52	30.69	NAV
16.09	-1.93	40.56	26.54	33.68	14.73	17.59	9.92	-11.41	-17.16	32.34	12.37	Total Return %
6.03	-3.24	3.03	3.60	0.33	-13.84	-3.45	19.02	0.47	4.93	3.67	1.50	+/-S&P 500
5.91	-2.32	2.79	4.09	0.83	-12.29	-3.32	17.71	1.04	4.49	2.45	0.97	+/-Russ 1000
2.36	1.00	1.34	1.24	1.31	0.47	0.01	0.19	0.10	0.51	0.88	0.84	Income Return %
13.73	-2.93	39.22	25.30	32.37	14.26	17.58	9.73	-11.51	-17.67	31.46	11.53	Capital Return %
21	76	4	11	11	77	65	8	39	14	10	19	Total Rtn % Rank Cat
0.26	0.12	0.15	0.18	0.23	0.11	0.00	0.05	0.03	0.13	0.19	0.23	Income $
0.58	0.45	1.01	0.70	0.83	0.48	0.62	2.64	0.00	0.00	0.00	0.00	Capital Gains $
0.89	0.87	0.90	0.87	0.89	0.91	0.90	0.88	0.89	0.92	0.95	0.92	Expense Ratio %
0.85	1.19	1.11	1.30	0.98	0.80	0.56	0.31	0.50	0.49	0.85	0.77	Income Ratio %
24	13	15	19	24	11	25	29	15	22	10	6	Turnover Rate %
938	1,091	1,798	2,659	4,655	6,820	8,139	10,600	10,463	8,258	11,563	15,108	Net Assets $mil

Performance 12-31-04

	1st Qtr	2nd Qtr	3rd Qtr	4th Qtr	Total
2000	9.84	-2.31	1.30	1.13	9.92
2001	-10.19	3.22	-14.19	11.38	-11.41
2002	-0.67	-9.94	-13.49	7.04	-17.16
2003	-5.59	18.66	2.43	15.33	32.34
2004	4.03	0.42	-1.18	8.85	12.37

Trailing	Total Return%	+/- S&P 500	+/- Russ 1000	%Rank Cat	Growth of $10,000
3 Mo	8.85	-0.38	-0.95	66	10,885
6 Mo	7.57	0.38	-0.24	35	10,757
1 Yr	12.37	1.50	0.97	19	11,237
3 Yr Avg	7.20	3.62	2.93	6	12,319
5 Yr Avg	3.71	6.01	5.47	7	11,998
10 Yr Avg	14.43	2.36	2.27	3	38,495
15 Yr Avg	13.53	2.60	2.45	4	67,090

Tax Analysis	Tax-Adj Rtn%	%Rank Cat	Tax-Cost Rat	%Rank Cat
3 Yr (estimated)	5.22	12	0.25	21
5 Yr (estimated)	2.13	10	0.56	30
10 Yr (estimated)	12.59	4	1.12	36

Potential Capital Gain Exposure: 22% of assets

Rating and Risk

Time Period	Load-Adj Return %	Morningstar Rtn vs Cat	Morningstar Risk vs Cat	Morningstar Risk-Adj Rating
1 Yr	7.04			
3 Yr	5.48	+Avg	Avg	★★★★
5 Yr	2.70	+Avg	-Avg	★★★★
10 Yr	13.87	High	Avg	★★★★★
Incept	13.32			

Other Measures	Standard Index S&P 500	Best Fit Index MSCI World
Alpha	3.7	1.6
Beta	0.90	0.92
R-Squared	91	95
Standard Deviation	15.05	
Mean	7.20	
Sharpe Ratio	0.39	

Morningstar's Take by Kunal Kapoor 12-29-04

Davis NY Venture embodies the best in a core mutual fund holding.

As numerous studies have demonstrated, mutual fund investors have done a lot worse than published returns may indicate. That's because investors are notorious for buying and selling funds at precisely the wrong time. There's a tendency among investors to buy funds after they've done well, and to sell them when they're underperforming. Unfortunately, this tendency also exists among professional money managers, who all too often invest with the rear-view mirror in plain sight.

On both those scores, we think this fund is different, and thus, compelling. First, it tends to be run on a fairly even keel, so extreme performances are rare. In general, the fund is more steady than flashy, so it's easier for investors to own, which hopefully translates into longer holding periods than is typical. At the management level, too, comanagers Chris Davis and Ken Feinberg have a long holding period and never adjust the portfolio to simply own issues that are driving the market at any one moment in time.

Viewed in that light, 2004's performance is all the more remarkable. With more than half its equity assets in financials, many may have expected this fund to give up some ground. After all, the financial media have been abuzz with stories about how financials are going to suffer in a rising-rate environment, and many professionals have been reducing their exposure to the sector. And while they may yet be proven right, the reality is that the fund owns a very diverse bunch of financials which have contributed nicely to its 12% gain for the year to date through Dec. 28, 2004. Moreover, the fund has done itself a favor by largely staying away from the drug stocks that have hurt many peers. However, the falling valuations in that sector have to be intriguing to this fund's managers, even if they haven't bitten yet.

Address:	2949 E. Elvira Road Tucson AZ 85706 800-279-0279	Minimum Purchase:	$1000 Add: $25 IRA: $1000
Web Address:		Min Auto Inv Plan:	$1000 Add: $25
Inception:	02-17-69	Sales Fees:	4.75%L, 0.25%S
Advisor:	Davis Selected Advisers LP	Management Fee:	0.75% mx./0.47% mn.
Subadvisor:	None	Actual Fees:	Mgt:0.51% Dist:0.25%
		Expense Projections:	3Yr:$754 5Yr:$960 10Yr:$1553
		Income Distrib:	Annually
NTF Plans:	DATALynx NTF, Federated Tr NTF		

Portfolio Analysis 10-31-04

Share change since 07-04 Total Stocks:65	Sector	PE	YTD Ret%	% Assets
American Express	Financial	20.3	17.60	7.46
Altria Group	Goods	13.3	18.38	4.84
Tyco International	Ind Mtrls	25.1	35.41	4.40
American International G	Financial	16.2	-0.53	4.33
Wells Fargo	Financial	15.5	8.97	3.84
⊕ HSBC Hldgs	Financial	—	—	3.76
Progressive	Financial	11.7	1.63	3.74
Berkshire Hathaway A	Financial	—	—	3.70
Costco Wholesale	Consumer	25.6	31.15	3.49
Golden West Financial	Financial	15.3	19.45	3.46
Citigroup	Financial	15.3	2.72	3.42
J.P. Morgan Chase & Co.	Financial	19.4	9.97	2.92
ConocoPhillips	Energy	9.0	35.60	2.73
Sealed Air	Goods	20.4	-1.61	2.51
Devon Energy	Energy	9.0	36.78	2.16
⊕ Comcast	Media	—	-13.77	2.16
Lexmark International	Hardware	20.0	8.09	1.87
Loews	Financial	—	43.59	1.81
⊕ Diageo	Goods	—	—	1.57
EOG Resources	Energy	16.5	55.21	1.55

Current Investment Style

Value Blnd Growth / Large Mid Small

Market Cap	%
Giant	50.4
Large	32.3
Mid	17.3
Small	0.0
Micro	0.0
Avg $mil: 31,973	

Value Measures		Rel Category
Price/Earnings	14.17	0.84
Price/Book	2.29	0.87
Price/Sales	1.43	0.99
Price/Cash Flow	5.60	0.73
Dividend Yield %	1.74	1.18

Growth Measures	%	Rel Category
Long-Term Erngs	10.57	0.91
Book Value	12.53	1.61
Sales	8.11	1.41
Cash Flow	12.30	1.30
Historical Erngs	17.55	1.49

Profitability	%	Rel Category
Return on Equity	18.51	1.06
Return on Assets	11.44	1.33
Net Margin	13.18	1.15

Sector Weightings	% of Stocks	Rel S&P 500	3 Year High	3 Year Low
Info	7.76	0.36		
Software	1.02	0.24	2	1
Hardware	2.27	0.22	8	2
Media	4.01	1.04	4	1
Telecom	0.46	0.15	0	0
Service	66.24	1.43		
Health	4.00	0.32	8	3
Consumer	5.97	0.66	9	5
Business	4.81	1.19	8	4
Financial	51.46	2.48	56	44
Mfg	26.00	0.81		
Goods	11.12	1.19	14	5
Ind Mtrls	6.13	0.48	13	6
Energy	8.75	1.22	9	4
Utilities	0.00	0.00	0	0

Composition

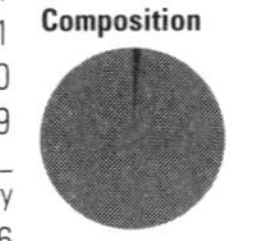

Cash	1.6
Stocks	98.4
Bonds	0.0
Other	0.0
Foreign (% of Stock)	13.1

Delafield

Ticker	Load	NAV	Yield	Total Assets	Mstar Category
DEFIX	12b-1 only	$25.21	0.0%	$345 mil	Small Value

Governance and Management

Fiduciary Grade:

Portfolio Manager(s)

Dennis Delafield and Vincent Sellechia have managed this fund since its 1993 inception. One analyst, who has been with the fund for seven years, rounds out the team. All three share research responsibilities.

Strategy

The fund combs the list of stocks hitting new lows in search of special situations--firms in the midst of a reorganization or management change--with lots of free cash flow. The pure bottom-up portfolio-construction process often leads to significant sector bets and a fairly concentrated portfolio. Management is willing to hold large cash stakes when compelling ideas are scarce, so the fund is rarely fully invested.

Historical Profile

Return Average
Risk Average
Rating ★★★ Neutral

Investment Style: Equity Stock % — 72% 73% 99% 99% 94% 75% 92% 75% 82%

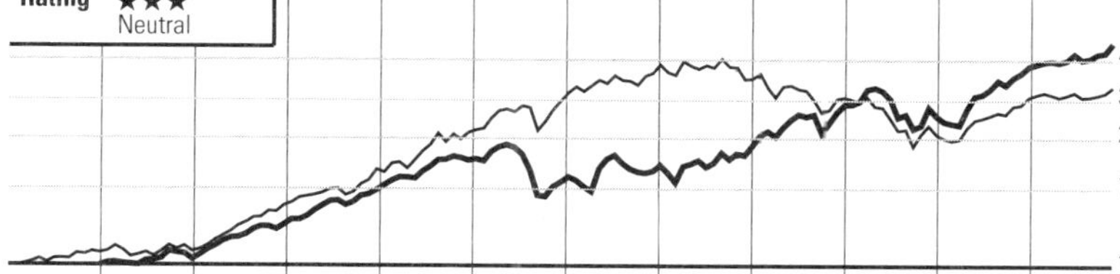

▼ Manager Change
∇ Partial Manager Change

Growth of $10,000
— Investment Values of Fund
— Investment Values of S&P 500

Performance Quartile (within Category)

History

1993	1994	1995	1996	1997	1998	1999	2000	2001	2002	2003	12-04	History
10.17	10.47	12.26	13.49	14.88	13.06	14.07	15.80	19.70	18.23	23.17	25.21	NAV
1.70*	5.59	27.41	26.35	19.66	-11.47	8.40	13.98	32.19	-7.46	40.13	20.85	Total Return %
—	4.28	-10.12	3.41	-13.69	-40.04	-12.64	23.08	44.07	14.63	11.46	9.98	+/-S&P 500
—	7.13	1.66	4.98	-12.12	-5.02	9.89	-8.85	18.17	3.97	-5.90	-1.40	+/-Russ 2000 VL
0.00	1.04	1.41	1.29	1.54	0.81	0.65	0.52	0.36	0.00	0.00	0.00	Income Return %
—	4.55	26.00	25.06	18.12	-12.28	7.75	13.46	31.83	-7.46	40.13	20.85	Capital Return %
—	13	26	27	94	76	28	69	6	37	54	51	Total Rtn % Rank Cat
0.00	0.11	0.14	0.16	0.21	0.12	0.09	0.07	0.06	0.00	0.00	0.00	Income $
0.00	0.16	0.89	1.84	1.03	0.00	0.00	0.16	1.13	0.00	2.38	2.78	Capital Gains $
—	1.78	1.65	1.29	1.29	1.24	1.25	1.25	1.25	1.20	1.32	—	Expense Ratio %
—	0.96	1.35	1.18	1.64	0.83	0.56	0.52	0.33	-0.09	-0.32	—	Income Ratio %
—	—	70	76	55	82	105	100	98	79	78	—	Turnover Rate %
—	10	45	61	146	104	86	99	199	144	247	345	Net Assets $mil

Performance 12-31-04

	1st Qtr	2nd Qtr	3rd Qtr	4th Qtr	Total
2000	-0.85	-0.57	5.41	9.69	13.98
2001	6.52	16.11	-11.90	21.31	32.19
2002	10.86	-6.14	-18.34	8.90	-7.46
2003	-5.76	22.88	6.63	13.49	40.13
2004	3.63	5.04	-0.04	11.07	20.85

Trailing	Total Return%	+/- S&P 500	+/- Russ 2000 VL	%Rank Cat	Growth of $10,000
3 Mo	11.07	1.84	-2.13	79	11,107
6 Mo	11.02	3.83	-2.35	60	11,102
1 Yr	20.85	9.98	-1.40	51	12,085
3 Yr Avg	16.15	12.57	-0.35	39	15,670
5 Yr Avg	18.75	21.05	1.52	23	23,614
10 Yr Avg	15.88	3.81	0.71	36	43,660
15 Yr Avg	—	—	—	—	—

Tax Analysis	Tax-Adj Rtn%	%Rank Cat	Tax-Cost Rat	%Rank Cat
3 Yr (estimated)	14.89	38	1.08	64
5 Yr (estimated)	17.51	21	1.04	55
10 Yr (estimated)	14.14	28	1.50	31

Potential Capital Gain Exposure: 25% of assets

Rating and Risk

Time Period	Load-Adj Return %	Morningstar Rtn vs Cat	Morningstar Risk vs Cat	Morningstar Risk-Adj Rating
1 Yr	20.85			
3 Yr	16.15	Avg	Avg	★★★
5 Yr	18.75	+Avg	+Avg	★★★★
10 Yr	15.88	Avg	Avg	★★★
Incept	14.91			

Other Measures	Standard Index S&P 500	Best Fit Index Mstar Mid Core
Alpha	12.6	2.0
Beta	1.00	1.09
R-Squared	73	88
Standard Deviation	20.45	
Mean	16.15	
Sharpe Ratio	0.73	

Morningstar's Take by Jeffrey Ptak 12-05-04

Delafield Fund is a hidden gem.

This fund's comanager, Vince Sellechia, recently observed that he and comanager Dennis Delafield run the fund as if they're entrusted not with a narrow slice of investors' portfolios but rather their entire net worth. It's a telling statement insofar as it explains the capital preservation-minded ethos that governs the process here. Management seeks firms whose stock prices have been felled by recent operational miscues, such as botched mergers, affording the chance to purchase at a steep discount to their estimate of intrinsic value.

A deep value strategy and loss aversion might seem like strange bedfellows. But there's merit to management's finicky approach. They seek firms boasting sturdy balance sheets and management teams that are proven cost-cutters or skilled capital allocators. Take recent purchase A.O. Smith, for instance, whose stock was pummeled when earnings sagged amid rising input costs and a slow transition to new Mexican production facilities. But Delafield and Sellechia liked the cash-generative nature of the company's small-motors and water heater businesses and thought the production hiccups would soon dissipate with cost-cutting moves eventually yielding fatter margins.

The fund stands out from its typical small-value peer in several respects. Management is market-cap agnostic and also not bashful about scooping up fallen growth stocks with loads of cash on their balance sheets. Moreover, they also run a concentrated portfolio, are willing to load up in given sectors, and don't hesitate to hoard cash.

This atypical look won't suit those seeking a cookie-cutter option. But we like the team's malleable definition of value, especially with small-caps looking rich. The fund's record is also impressive, as management has avoided prolonged losses while handily topping a benchmark that blends the S&P small-core and small-value indexes (appropriate given its wide wingspan) over the long haul. All told, it's a fine choice.

Address:	C/O Reich & Tang Asset Management LLC New York NY 10020-2302 800-221-3079	Minimum Purchase:	$5000	Add: $0 IRA: $250
Web Address:		Min Auto Inv Plan:	$5000	Add: —
Inception:	11-19-93 *	Sales Fees:	0.25%B, 2.00%R	
Advisor:	Reich & Tang Asset Management, LLC	Management Fee:	0.80% mx./0.70% mn., 0.21%A	
Subadvisor:	None	Actual Fees:	Mgt:0.80%	Dist:0.21%
NTF Plans:	Schwab OneSource, Schwab Instl NTF	Expense Projections:	3Yr:$462	5Yr:$797 10Yr:$1746
		Income Distrib:	Semi-Annually	

Portfolio Analysis 12-31-04

Share change since 09-04 Total Stocks:50	Sector	PE	YTD Ret%	% Assets
⊕ Foot Locker	Consumer	17.6	15.99	3.72
Thermo Electron	Health	27.2	19.80	3.29
ESCO Technologies	Hardware	30.3	75.60	2.79
⊕ Navistar International	Ind Mtrls	17.5	-8.17	2.75
⊕ Furniture Brands Interna	Goods	14.4	-12.81	2.70
⊕ Cytec Industries	Ind Mtrls	22.4	35.27	2.69
Ametek	Ind Mtrls	22.3	49.08	2.59
International Rectifier	Hardware	23.6	-9.80	2.53
⊖ Proquest	Business	15.7	0.85	2.59
⊕ Reynolds & Reynolds	Media	16.1	-7.18	2.51
⊕ Honeywell International	Ind Mtrls	20.5	8.21	2.30
Newell Rubbermaid	Goods	—	10.16	2.29
⊕ ElkCorp	Energy	22.4	29.15	2.24
⊕ Maytag	Goods	63.7	-21.85	2.06
⊕ Engelhard	Ind Mtrls	15.3	3.98	2.05
Hercules	Ind Mtrls	—	21.72	2.05
Ashland	Ind Mtrls	15.4	35.45	2.04
⊖ Unova	Ind Mtrls	—	10.20	2.02
⊕ Jones Apparel Group	Goods	14.8	4.84	1.97
Kennametal	Ind Mtrls	19.9	27.17	1.81

Current Investment Style

Value Blnd Growth — Large / Mid / Small

Market Cap	%
Giant	0.0
Large	3.1
Mid	65.3
Small	29.1
Micro	2.5
Avg $mil: 2,313	

Value Measures		Rel Category
Price/Earnings	18.50	1.16
Price/Book	2.40	1.45
Price/Sales	0.90	1.20
Price/Cash Flow	9.36	1.80
Dividend Yield %	1.05	0.88

Growth Measures	%	Rel Category
Long-Term Erngs	11.12	0.92
Book Value	4.86	1.12
Sales	0.95	0.30
Cash Flow	-1.47	NMF
Historical Erngs	6.01	1.25

Profitability	%	Rel Category
Return on Equity	11.39	1.25
Return on Assets	4.11	0.99
Net Margin	5.53	0.83

Sector Weightings	% of Stocks	Rel S&P 500	3 Year High	3 Year Low
Info	16.09	0.75		
Software	0.00	0.00	3	0
Hardware	12.35	1.21	41	3
Media	3.74	0.97	4	0
Telecom	0.00	0.00	2	0
Service	21.34	0.46		
Health	6.07	0.49	25	4
Consumer	4.62	0.51	5	0
Business	8.56	2.11	23	0
Financial	2.09	0.10	5	2
Mfg	62.57	1.95		
Goods	12.24	1.31	18	5
Ind Mtrls	42.09	3.32	42	7
Energy	8.24	1.15	19	6
Utilities	0.00	0.00	1	0

Composition

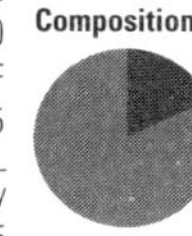

Cash	17.9
Stocks	82.1
Bonds	0.0
Other	0.0
Foreign (% of Stock)	0.0

Delphi Value Retail

Ticker	Load	NAV	Yield	Total Assets	Mstar Category
KDVRX	12b-1 only	$17.22	0.0%	$113 mil	Mid-Cap Value

Governance and Management

Fiduciary Grade: B

Portfolio Manager(s)

Scott Black has successfully run private accounts in the same way for decades. Four analysts help him evaluate the management teams and fundamentals of companies. Black is one of the largest shareholders of the fund. He is also part of the annual Barron's Roundtable, and a follower of Graham and Dodd investment philosophy.

Strategy

Stocks don't get into this fund just because they're cheap. Management doesn't distinguish stocks along "growth" or "value" lines; rather, it looks for great, growing businesses with low valuations and then holds them for a while. It looks for cheap names of any size in any industry, but insists on stocks with returns on equity of more than 15%, three- and five-year revenue- and earnings-growth rates that beat inflation, and clean balance sheets. Manager Scott Black also aims to keep capital-gains distributions low.

Historical Profile

Return Average
Risk Average
Rating ★★★ Neutral

Investment Style
Equity
Stock %

1998	1999	2000	2001	2002	2003	12-04
35%	95%	93%	95%	93%	94%	91%

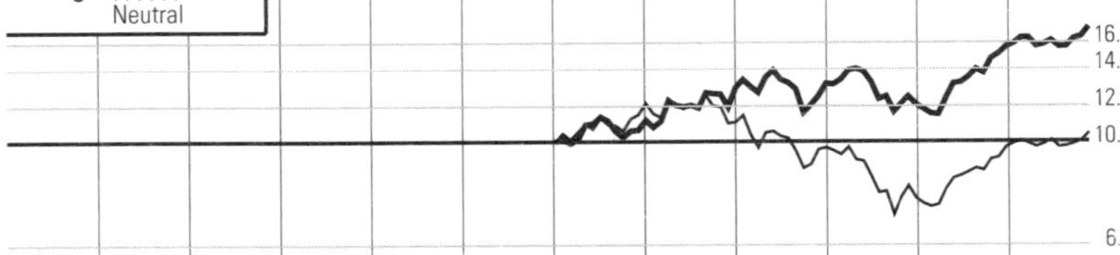

▼ Manager Change
▽ Partial Manager Change

Growth of $10,000
— Investment Values of Fund
— Investment Values of S&P 500

Performance Quartile (within Category)

1993	1994	1995	1996	1997	1998	1999	2000	2001	2002	2003	12-04	History
—	—	—	—	—	10.12	11.19	13.00	13.18	11.91	15.79	17.22	NAV
—	—	—	—	—	1.20*	11.30	17.30	1.90	-9.64	32.58	12.52	Total Return %
—	—	—	—	—	—	-9.74	26.40	13.78	12.45	3.91	1.65	+/-S&P 500
—	—	—	—	—	—	11.41	-1.88	-0.43	0.00	-5.49	-11.19	+/-Russ MV
—	—	—	—	—	—	0.02	0.00	0.00	0.00	0.00	0.00	Income Return %
—	—	—	—	—	—	11.28	17.30	1.90	-9.64	32.58	12.52	Capital Return %
—	—	—	—	—	—	42	56	70	29	60	89	Total Rtn % Rank Cat
—	—	—	—	—	0.00	0.00	0.00	0.00	0.00	0.00	0.00	Income $
—	—	—	—	—	0.00	0.07	0.12	0.07	0.00	0.00	0.55	Capital Gains $
—	—	—	—	—	1.75	1.75	1.71	1.64	1.63	1.64	—	Expense Ratio %
—	—	—	—	—	0.82	0.00	-0.12	-0.12	-0.13	-0.21	—	Income Ratio %
—	—	—	—	—	—	17	45	29	23	22	—	Turnover Rate %
—	—	—	—	—	5	31	45	45	44	53	62	Net Assets $mil

Performance 12-31-04

	1st Qtr	2nd Qtr	3rd Qtr	4th Qtr	Total
2000	10.01	-2.19	5.90	2.95	17.30
2001	-2.38	6.54	-15.01	15.29	1.90
2002	6.83	-5.47	-13.75	3.75	-9.64
2003	-4.87	17.03	4.83	13.60	32.58
2004	4.56	-1.39	0.92	8.13	12.52

Trailing	Total Return%	+/- S&P 500	+/- Russ MV	%Rank Cat	Growth of $10,000
3 Mo	8.13	-1.10	-5.33	92	10,813
6 Mo	9.13	1.94	-6.30	72	10,913
1 Yr	12.52	1.65	-11.19	89	11,252
3 Yr Avg	10.47	6.69	-5.09	56	13,481
5 Yr Avg	10.01	12.31	-3.47	65	16,112
10 Yr Avg	—	—	—	—	—
15 Yr Avg	—	—	—	—	—

Tax Analysis	Tax-Adj Rtn%	%Rank Cat	Tax-Cost Rat	%Rank Cat
3 Yr (estimated)	10.30	45	0.15	13
5 Yr (estimated)	9.78	57	0.21	12
10 Yr (estimated)	—	—	—	—

Potential Capital Gain Exposure: 38% of assets

Rating and Risk

Time Period	Load-Adj Return %	Morningstar Rtn vs Cat	Morningstar Risk vs Cat	Morningstar Risk-Adj Rating
1 Yr	12.52			
3 Yr	10.47	Avg	-Avg	★★★
5 Yr	10.01	Avg	Avg	★★★
10 Yr	—	—	—	—
Incept	10.37			

Other Measures	Standard Index S&P 500	Best Fit Index Russ MV
Alpha	7.2	-2.8
Beta	0.77	0.87
R-Squared	77	93
Standard Deviation	14.38	
Mean	10.47	
Sharpe Ratio	0.64	

Portfolio Analysis 11-30-04

Share change since 10-04 Total Stocks:76	Sector	PE	YTD Ret%	% Assets
⊕ Berkshire Hathaway B	Financial	20.9	4.30	2.67
XTO Energy	Energy	20.5	56.85	1.78
⊖ Denbury Resources	Energy	19.5	97.34	1.78
Southwest Bancorp	Financial	12.1	39.97	1.70
Pulitzer	Media	30.8	21.92	1.66
Washington Post	Media	27.8	25.21	1.66
Toll Brothers	Consumer	17.3	72.56	1.51
⊕ Gannett	Media	17.1	-7.23	1.48
Wells Fargo	Financial	15.5	8.97	1.46
DR Horton	Consumer	10.7	41.36	1.45
Cox Communications A	Media	—	—	1.39
Dow Chemical	Ind Mtrls	16.6	22.83	1.39
Teekay Shipping	Business	19.4	49.82	1.39
Bear Stearns Companies	Financial	10.9	29.25	1.38
IPC Holdings	Financial	10.5	14.38	1.38
Whiting Petroleum	Energy	—	64.40	1.37
OMI	Business	8.8	91.70	1.37
Liz Claiborne	Goods	14.8	19.76	1.35
Talisman Energy	Energy	15.2	44.37	1.34
⊕ News Corporation	Media	16.6	6.65	1.33

Current Investment Style

Value Blnd Growth — Large Mid Small

Market Cap	%
Giant	15.6
Large	24.3
Mid	43.7
Small	12.1
Micro	4.3
Avg $mil: 6,346	

Value Measures		Rel Category
Price/Earnings	13.50	0.88
Price/Book	2.02	1.05
Price/Sales	1.35	1.53
Price/Cash Flow	5.12	0.89
Dividend Yield %	1.06	0.74

Growth Measures	%	Rel Category
Long-Term Erngs	11.56	1.05
Book Value	10.61	1.88
Sales	4.46	0.93
Cash Flow	9.02	2.28
Historical Erngs	13.99	1.22

Profitability	%	Rel Category
Return on Equity	14.56	1.14
Return on Assets	7.98	1.31
Net Margin	13.99	1.59

Sector Weightings	% of Stocks	Rel S&P 500	3 Year High	3 Year Low
Info	17.96	0.84		
Software	0.00	0.00	0	0
Hardware	1.99	0.20	8	2
Media	15.97	4.16	19	16
Telecom	0.00	0.00	1	0
Service	50.39	1.09		
Health	0.94	0.08	2	0
Consumer	11.39	1.25	12	9
Business	3.02	0.75	6	2
Financial	35.04	1.69	38	30
Mfg	31.65	0.99		
Goods	8.03	0.86	9	5
Ind Mtrls	12.74	1.01	14	7
Energy	10.88	1.52	13	8
Utilities	0.00	0.00	0	0

Composition

Cash	8.6
Stocks	91.4
Bonds	0.0
Other	0.0
Foreign (% of Stock)	8.9

Morningstar's Take by Bridget Hughes 11-01-04

Delphi Value isn't making our bullish case for it any easier, but we continue to like the fund.

In some respects, this mid-value fund continues to look like an also-ran. Its performance since its late-1998 inception hasn't been much to write home about, at least compared with the rest of the mid-value group. Its 9.43% annualized return from Dec. 17, 1998, through Oct. 29, 2004, ekes past the category's 9.23%. On the risk side of the equation, the fund's volatility also has been middling, compared with the mid-value norm. Through the last week of October 2004, the fund's 5.2% gain lands in the category's worst third.

We still think more highly of the fund, however, than its 3-star Morningstar Rating for funds and category rankings suggest. Its all-cap approach means it's not a perfect representation of the mid-value universe of stocks. We think this fund's flexibility (it has no constraints on market cap or sector weightings) makes a comparison to the broader market, or more specifically the S&P 500 Index, appropriate. Judged on that basis, the fund has done well. It's also performed well compared with some highly regarded funds that use similar approaches, including Analyst Picks Tweedy, Browne American Value and Weitz Value.

We're also optimistic about its future. Despite the fund's youth, it's run by a very experienced value manager. Scott Black has been in the investment-management business for more than 20 years, and we like his sensible, time-tested approach. (Black's longer-term audited performance record on private accounts is very strong.) Although the fund could be due for a more-sluggish period--smaller, value-oriented stocks have outperformed the broader market over the past several years--we think its long-term prospects are bright.

This small fund does have a comparatively high expense ratio of 1.64%, but if the fund grows we would expect that to come down. All told, we think Delphi Value is an undiscovered gem.

Address:	Kobren Insight Funds Westborough, MA 01581 800-895-9936
Web Address:	www.kobren.com
Inception:	12-17-98*
Advisor:	Kobren Insight Management Inc
Subadvisor:	Delphi Management Inc
NTF Plans:	Fidelity Retail-NTF, Schwab OneSource

Minimum Purchase:	$2500	Add: $500	IRA: $2000
Min Auto Inv Plan:	$2500	Add: $500	
Sales Fees:	0.25%B		
Management Fee:	1.00%		
Actual Fees:	Mgt:1.00%	Dist:0.25%	
Expense Projections:	3Yr:$517	5Yr:$892	10Yr:$1944
Income Distrib:	Annually		

Dimensional US Micro Cp

Ticker	Load	NAV	Yield	Total Assets	Mstar Category
DFSCX	None	$15.12	1.8%	$3,380 mil	Small Blend

Governance and Management

Fiduciary Grade: B

Portfolio Manager(s)

A team of four portfolio managers, led by Robert Deere, runs this offering. Carl Snyder, Henry Gray, and Steve Clark round out the group. The fund's trading group, led by Jeanne Sinquefield, is critical to its operations.

Strategy

The fund invests in the smallest 4% of U.S. exchange-listed stocks to take advantage of the small-cap effect. The portfolio contains anywhere between 2,500 and 3,000 holdings, but it does not contain REITs, newly minted IPOs, or firms that management identifies as merger candidates or too highly leveraged. Though turnover is low, management is likely to sell a company when its market cap exceeds about $770 million.

Historical Profile

Return Above Avg
Risk High
Rating ★★★ Neutral

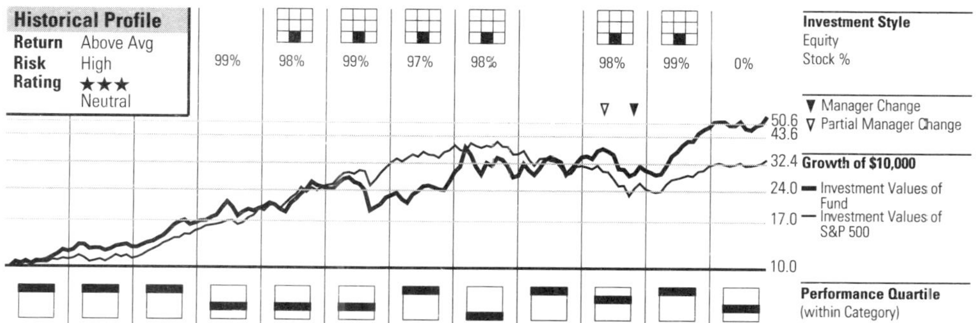

1993	1994	1995	1996	1997	1998	1999	2000	2001	2002	2003	12-04	History
8.25	8.49	10.53	11.20	11.78	10.76	12.61	9.64	10.01	8.53	13.32	15.12	NAV
20.97	3.09	34.48	17.65	22.78	-7.32	29.79	-3.60	22.77	-13.27	60.72	18.39	Total Return %
10.91	1.78	-3.05	-5.29	-10.57	-35.89	8.75	5.50	34.65	8.82	32.05	7.52	+/-S&P 500
2.09	4.91	6.03	1.16	0.42	-4.77	8.53	-0.58	20.28	7.21	13.47	0.06	+/-Russ 2000
0.25	0.18	0.51	0.26	0.23	1.28	3.49	3.89	0.51	0.16	2.42	2.04	Income Return %
20.72	2.91	33.97	17.39	22.55	-8.60	26.30	-7.49	22.26	-13.43	58.30	16.35	Capital Return %
24	16	14	75	71	69	18	93	9	34	6	53	Total Rtn % Rank Cat
0.02	0.02	0.04	0.03	0.03	0.15	0.38	0.43	0.05	0.02	0.21	0.27	Income $
0.62	0.00	0.84	1.16	1.89	0.00	0.89	1.93	1.71	0.14	0.18	0.36	Capital Gains $
0.70	0.65	0.62	0.61	0.60	0.59	0.61	0.56	0.56	0.56	0.56	—	Expense Ratio %
0.26	0.16	0.45	0.22	0.21	0.18	0.30	0.34	0.41	0.24	0.25	—	Income Ratio %
10	17	25	24	28	26	23	37	14	19	19	—	Turnover Rate %
643	663	946	1,187	1,437	1,360	1,452	1,378	1,663	1,533	—	3,380	Net Assets $mil

Performance 12-31-04

	1st Qtr	2nd Qtr	3rd Qtr	4th Qtr	Total
2000	21.09	-8.58	3.44	-15.82	-3.60
2001	0.73	21.83	-17.50	21.26	22.77
2002	6.99	-3.92	-20.70	6.39	-13.27
2003	-3.99	27.35	12.56	16.77	60.72
2004	6.46	0.14	-4.32	16.06	18.39

Trailing	Total Return%	+/- S&P 500	+/- Russ 2000	%Rank Cat	Growth of $10,000
3 Mo	16.06	6.83	1.97	8	11,606
6 Mo	11.05	3.86	0.22	46	11,105
1 Yr	18.39	7.52	0.06	53	11,839
3 Yr Avg	18.17	14.59	6.69	8	16,501
5 Yr Avg	14.32	16.62	7.71	35	19,526
10 Yr Avg	16.39	4.32	4.85	13	45,620
15 Yr Avg	14.82	3.89	3.73	8	79,481

Tax Analysis	Tax-Adj Rtn%	%Rank Cat	Tax-Cost Rat	%Rank Cat
3 Yr (estimated)	17.34	7	0.70	49
5 Yr (estimated)	11.97	40	2.06	90
10 Yr (estimated)	13.92	17	2.12	73

Potential Capital Gain Exposure: 36% of assets

Rating and Risk

Time Period	Load-Adj Return %	Morningstar Rtn vs Cat	Morningstar Risk vs Cat	Morningstar Risk-Adj Rating
1 Yr	18.39			
3 Yr	18.17	High	+Avg	★★★★
5 Yr	14.32	+Avg	High	★★★
10 Yr	16.39	+Avg	High	★★★
Incept	14.29			

Other Measures	Standard Index S&P 500	Best Fit Index Russ 2000
Alpha	14.9	6.3
Beta	1.01	0.98
R-Squared	63	97

Standard Deviation	22.56
Mean	18.17
Sharpe Ratio	0.75

Portfolio Analysis 08-31-04

Share change since 05-04 Total Stocks:0	Sector	PE	YTD Ret%	% Assets
⊕ U.S. Micro Cap Series	—	—	—	100.00

Morningstar's Take by Paul Herbert 12-01-04

Dimensional U.S. Micro Cap isn't as active as most offerings, but moves behind the scenes give it considerable appeal.

Don't look here if you're after a fund that changes positions based on forecasts about the directions of company earnings, interest rates, or the economy. This fund relies on a philosophy established years ago by academics who found that the stock market is highly efficient, and that you get paid by accepting the heightened risks associated with investing in cheap, small-cap stocks. Dimensional Fund Advisors (DFA), the fund's advisor, offers more than a dozen strategies that attempt to exploit this anomaly. This fund offers the best way to get exposure to the smallest stocks in the U.S. market: Its universe is the smallest 4% of stocks listed on American exchanges.

But while the fund is mostly passive, it differs from a traditional index fund in key respects. First, exclusion rules eliminate REITs, ADRs, and companies that are in bankruptcy or those with qualified financial statements. More importantly, DFA has taken steps to reduce the costs of trading, which can be high among the small-fry it targets. Sticking to a low-turnover strategy--its turnover rate checked in at less than 20% in 2003--helps. Another tool the firm has used is making block purchases of shares at below-market prices. Over time, Dimensional's trading practices have actually added 200 basis points to its returns. That margin accounts for more than 50% of its outperformance of the Russell 2000 Index for the 15-year period ended Oct. 31, 2004.

The fund may be set for a slowdown in performance if larger fare regains market leadership, but we think there's much to like here, including a low 0.56% expense ratio. You may have difficulty gaining access to its shares, as DFA targets institutional investors, but for those who can buy in, the fund has merit as a supporting piece of a well-diversified portfolio.

Address:	1299 Ocean Ave Santa Monica CA 90401 310-395-8005
Web Address:	www.dfafunds.com
Inception:	12-22-81
Advisor:	Dimensional Fund Advisors Ltd
Subadvisor:	None
NTF Plans:	N/A

Minimum Purchase:	$2000000	Add: $0	IRA: $0
Min Auto Inv Plan:	$0	Add: —	
Sales Fees:	No-load		
Management Fee:	0.50%		
Actual Fees:	Mgt:0.50%	Dist:	
Expense Projections:	3Yr:$195	5Yr:$340	10Yr:$762
Income Distrib:	Annually		

Current Investment Style

Value Blnd Growth / Large Mid Small

Market Cap	%
Giant	—
Large	—
Mid	—
Small	—
Micro	—
Avg $mil:	—

Value Measures		Rel Category
Price/Earnings	—	—
Price/Book	—	—
Price/Sales	—	—
Price/Cash Flow	—	—
Dividend Yield %	—	—

Growth Measures	%	Rel Category
Long-Term Erngs	—	—
Book Value	—	—
Sales	—	—
Cash Flow	—	—
Historical Erngs	—	—

Profitability	%	Rel Category
Return on Equity	—	—
Return on Assets	—	—
Net Margin	—	—

Sector Weightings	% of Stocks	Rel S&P 500	3 Year High	3 Year Low
Info	0.00	0.00		
Software	—	0.00	7	4
Hardware	—	0.00	12	7
Media	—	0.00	2	1
Telecom	—	0.00	2	1
Service	0.00	0.00		
Health	—	0.00	16	13
Consumer	—	0.00	14	11
Business	—	0.00	12	11
Financial	—	0.00	16	13
Mfg	0.00	0.00		
Goods	—	0.00	10	7
Ind Mtrls	—	0.00	16	15
Energy	—	0.00	5	4
Utilities	—	0.00	1	1

Composition

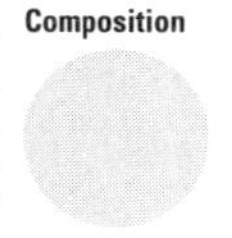

Cash	0.0
Stocks	0.0
Bonds	0.0
Other	100.0
Foreign (% of Stock)	0.0

Dodge & Cox Balanced

Ticker	Load	NAV	Yield	Total Assets	Mstar Category
DODBX	Closed	$79.35	2.0%	$20,091 mil	Moderate Allocation

Governance and Management

Fiduciary Grade: A

Portfolio Manager(s)

The fund's management team is deep, experienced, and talented. Stock selection and asset allocation are handled by the team from Dodge & Cox Stock. The bond portfolio is run by the squad from Dodge & Cox Income. The average tenure of the team members is nearly 15 years. They're supported by a bevy of industry and credit analysts.

Strategy

Management's typical mix of 60% to 65% stocks and 30% to 35% bonds is adjusted only moderately. The equity position mirrors the mid- to large-cap value Dodge & Cox Stock Fund, and management sticks to government and midquality corporate bonds on the fixed-income side of the portfolio.

Historical Profile

Return: High
Risk: Average
Rating: ★★★★★ Highest

Investment Style
Equity
Stock %: 58% 56% 59% 59% 61% 61% 63% 63% 59%

▼ Manager Change
▽ Partial Manager Change

Growth of $10,000
— Investment Values of Fund
— Investment Values of S&P 500

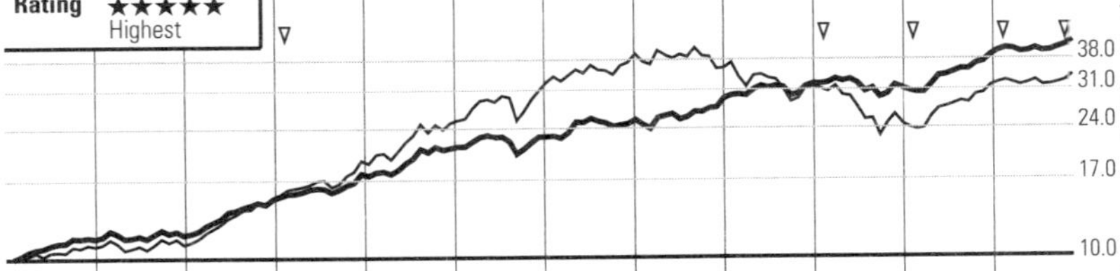

Performance Quartile (within Category)

History

	1993	1994	1995	1996	1997	1998	1999	2000	2001	2002	2003	12-04
NAV	46.40	45.21	54.60	59.82	66.78	65.22	65.71	63.42	65.42	60.75	73.04	79.35
Total Return %	15.95	1.99	28.02	14.76	21.19	6.69	12.06	15.14	10.05	-2.94	24.44	13.30
+/-S&P 500	5.89	0.68	-9.51	-8.18	-12.16	-21.88	-8.98	24.24	21.93	19.15	-4.23	2.43
+/-DJ 60%	4.22	3.94	3.25	3.42	1.99	-5.70	-0.79	10.70	9.89	7.60	0.38	2.13
Income Return %	3.97	3.85	4.90	3.70	3.77	3.41	3.47	3.91	3.44	2.91	2.76	2.21
Capital Return %	11.98	-1.86	23.12	11.06	17.42	3.28	8.59	11.23	6.61	-5.85	21.68	11.09
Total Rtn % Rank Cat	14	8	31	44	37	84	41	6	4	4	16	4
Income $	1.66	1.76	2.18	1.99	2.22	2.23	2.22	2.47	2.14	1.88	1.66	1.60
Capital Gains $	1.07	0.36	0.91	0.69	3.27	3.74	4.98	9.22	2.05	0.88	0.67	1.68
Expense Ratio %	0.60	0.58	0.57	0.56	0.55	0.54	0.53	0.53	0.53	0.53	0.54	—
Income Ratio %	3.67	3.94	3.85	3.60	3.39	3.29	3.18	3.70	3.28	3.12	2.57	—
Turnover Rate %	15	20	20	17	32	26	17	23	21	25	19	—
Net Assets $mil	487	725	1,800	3,630	5,077	5,693	5,138	4,909	6,040	7,885	13,196	20,031

Performance 12-31-04

	1st Qtr	2nd Qtr	3rd Qtr	4th Qtr	Total
2000	1.25	-1.09	5.16	9.33	15.14
2001	1.95	5.19	-5.22	8.27	10.05
2002	3.28	-2.93	-8.94	6.32	-2.94
2003	-2.86	12.32	3.78	9.88	24.44
2004	4.03	0.27	0.47	8.12	13.30

Trailing	Total Return%	+/- S&P 500	+/- DJ 60%	%Rank Cat	Growth of $10,000
3 Mo	8.12	-1.11	0.64	20	10,812
6 Mo	8.62	1.43	1.09	14	10,862
1 Yr	13.30	2.43	2.13	4	11,330
3 Yr Avg	11.02	7.44	3.76	1	13,684
5 Yr Avg	11.64	13.94	6.40	2	17,342
10 Yr Avg	13.95	1.88	3.46	2	36,910
15 Yr Avg	12.54	1.61	2.59	2	58,831

Tax Analysis	Tax-Adj Rtn%	%Rank Cat	Tax-Cost Rat	%Rank Cat
3 Yr (estimated)	9.81	2	1.09	75
5 Yr (estimated)	9.53	2	1.89	91
10 Yr (estimated)	11.58	1	2.08	70

Potential Capital Gain Exposure: 18% of assets

Rating and Risk

Time Period	Load-Adj Return %	Morningstar Rtn vs Cat	Morningstar Risk vs Cat	Morningstar Risk-Adj Rating
1 Yr	13.30			
3 Yr	11.02	High	Avg	★★★★★
5 Yr	11.64	High	Avg	★★★★★
10 Yr	13.95	High	Avg	★★★★★
Incept	—			

Other Measures	Standard Index S&P 500	Best Fit Index Russ MV
Alpha	8.0	0.8
Beta	0.57	0.62
R-Squared	84	92

Standard Deviation	10.30
Mean	11.02
Sharpe Ratio	0.95

Morningstar's Take by Dan Culloton 12-08-04

There's more to this fund than its performance.

Dodge & Cox Balanced has been on its game lately, with annualized returns ranking near the top of every trailing period. Investment styles ebb and flow, however, and there's a chance this fund's conservative style won't always look as good as it does now. (It trailed its peers, for example, in 1998.) In fact, the offering's managers have warned investors to temper their expectations for future equity and fixed-income returns.

This fund, however, has appeal beyond its relative ranking, whether it's leading or lagging. Its veteran managers, low expenses, rigorous research, long-term focus, and unblemished regulatory record are a hard combination to beat. The fund's huge size is a concern (its asset base has increased fourfold since 1999). The equity portion of the portfolio cannot hold as many significant positions in smaller-cap stocks as it once did. Still, the fact that this fund (and similar institutional accounts offered by the advisor) closed to new investors should mitigate the effects of asset growth.

There's also no sign the fund has abandoned the value-oriented, contrarian approach that has seen it through more than seven decades and numerous market cycles. True to form, as small-cap value stocks have soared in recent years the fund's stock managers have been picking up established large-cap growth stocks with attractive valuations, such as Liberty Media. On the fixed income side, the fund has kept its duration, a measure of interest-rate sensitivity, significantly shorter than Lehman Brothers Aggregate Bond Index and owned a lot of cash even though it has hurt so far this year. With inflation pressures building and interest rates at historic lows, the risks of rising rates over the long term is too great to take any other stance, the managers argue.

Such long-term thinking is a constant at this fund and a better reason to own it than its recent strong performance.

Portfolio Analysis 09-30-04

Total Stocks:89 Share change since 06-30-04	Sectors	P/E Ratio	YTD Return %	% Net Assets
⊕ Hewlett-Packard	Hardware	18.9	-4.39	1.80
⊕ Comcast A	Media	81.0	-0.18	1.72
AT&T Wireless Services	Telecom	—	—	1.69
⊕ HCA	Health	15.8	-0.70	1.54
⊕ News Corporation ADR A	Media	—	—	1.46
Schering-Plough	Health	—	2.06	1.38
⊖ Dow Chemical	Ind Mtrls	16.6	-3.66	1.35
⊕ Time Warner	Media	27.5	-3.91	1.33
McDonald's	Consumer	19.7	-2.99	1.31

Total Fixed-Income:238	Date of Maturity	Amount $000	Value $000	% Net Assets
FNMA 7.5%	08-01-17	111,012	118,188	0.64
At&T 8%	11-15-31	97,500	106,275	0.57
Ford Motor Cr 7.25%	10-25-11	97,920	105,963	0.57
FHLMC 6%	06-01-16	99,512	104,556	0.56
FNMA 6.5%	07-01-18	98,154	103,981	0.56
FNMA 6%	06-01-17	92,469	97,189	0.52
FNMA 6%	12-01-18	88,870	93,420	0.50
Comcast 5.3%	01-15-14	85,510	85,695	0.46
FNMA 5.5%	07-01-16	82,041	84,621	0.46

Equity Style
Style: Value
Size: Large-Cap

Value Measures		Rel Category
Price/Earnings	15.67	0.95
Price/Book	1.84	0.75
Price/Sales	0.91	0.69
Price/Cash Flow	5.94	0.82
Dividend Yield %	1.81	1.15

Growth Measures	%	Rel Category
Long-Term Erngs	10.04	0.86
Book Value	-5.77	NMF
Sales	1.93	0.37
Cash Flow	-31.41	NMF
Historical Erngs	6.88	0.63

Market Cap %			
Giant	28.2	Small	0.0
Large	55.4	Micro	0.0
Mid	16.4	Avg $mil:	19,827

Fixed-Income Style
Duration: Interm-Term
Quality: High

Avg Eff Duration [1]	3.7 Yrs
Avg Eff Maturity	6.4 Yrs
Avg Credit Quality	AA
Avg Wtd Coupon	6.54%

[1]figure provided by fund as of 09-30-04

Sector Weightings	% of Stocks	Rel S&P 500	3 Year High	3 Year Low
Info	20.00	0.93		
Software	0.88	0.20	1	1
Hardware	5.59	0.55	7	3
Media	8.21	2.14	8	0
Telecom	5.32	1.69	6	2
Service	45.63	0.98		
Health	12.25	0.98	12	8
Consumer	6.36	0.70	9	6
Business	8.18	2.02	9	8
Financial	18.84	0.91	22	19
Mfg	34.37	1.07		
Goods	6.93	0.74	9	6
Ind Mtrls	15.05	1.19	24	15
Energy	9.02	1.26	13	9
Utilities	3.37	1.14	4	2

Composition

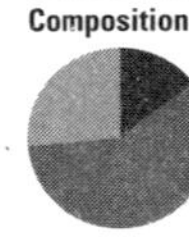

Cash	14.5
Stocks	59.1
Bonds	26.4
Other	0.0
Foreign (% of Stock)	16.0

Address:	Dodge & Cox Funds San Francisco, CA 94104 800-621-3979
Web Address:	www.dodgeandcox.com
Inception:	06-26-31
Advisor:	Dodge & Cox
Subadvisor:	None
NTF Plans:	N/A

Minimum Purchase:	Closed	Add: —	IRA: —
Min Auto Inv Plan:	Closed	Add: —	
Sales Fees:	No-load		
Management Fee:	0.50%		
Actual Fees:	Mgt:0.50%	Dist:	
Expense Projections:	3Yr:$173	5Yr:$302	10Yr:$677
Income Distrib:	Quarterly		

Dodge & Cox Income

Analyst Pick

Ticker	Load	NAV	Yield	SEC Yield	Total Assets	Mstar Category
DODIX	None	$12.84	4.2%	3.49%	$7,624 mil	Intermediate-Term Bond

Governance and Management

Fiduciary Grade: A

Portfolio Manager(s)

A deep, 11-member management team is responsible for the fund and all of the firm's institutional fixed-income accounts. Sector specialists on the team have both research and trading responsibilities. Dodge & Cox's 16-member analyst staff provides individual credit analysis and also supports the firm's equity products.

Strategy

Management strives to better its bogy, the Lehman Brothers Aggregate Bond Index, mainly through security selection. Thus, the fund is typically overweight in corporate bonds, especially midgrade issues. Management targets corporates and mortgage-backed securities with call-protection features so that it can hold on to its bonds for the long haul.

Historical Profile

Return High
Risk Below Avg
Rating ★★★★★ Highest

Investment Style: Fixed Income — Income Rtn %Rank Cat

1993	1994	1995	1996	1997	1998	1999	2000	2001	2002	2003	12-04
42	42	33	36	17	19	23	21	28			

▼ Manager Change
∇ Partial Manager Change

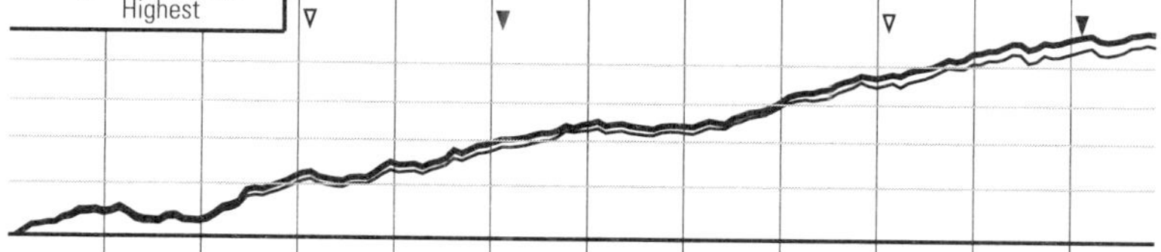

Growth of $10,000
— Investment Values of Fund
— Investment Values of LB Aggr

Performance Quartile (within Category)

1993	1994	1995	1996	1997	1998	1999	2000	2001	2002	2003	12-04	History
11.89	10.74	12.02	11.68	12.08	12.25	11.40	11.30	12.20	12.77	12.92	12.84	NAV
11.34	-2.89	20.21	3.61	10.00	8.08	-0.81	10.70	10.32	10.75	5.97	3.64	Total Return %
1.59	0.03	1.74	-0.02	0.35	-0.61	0.01	-0.33	1.88	0.50	1.87	-0.70	+/-LB Aggr
-0.90	1.62	-1.22	0.92	0.57	-2.06	2.07	-1.74	1.50	-2.28	0.00	-1.66	+/-LB 5-10YR
6.92	6.58	7.74	6.31	6.40	6.11	5.94	7.02	6.42	5.52	4.78	4.25	Income Return %
4.42	-9.47	12.47	-2.70	3.60	1.97	-6.75	3.68	3.90	5.23	1.19	-0.61	Capital Return %
33	25	17	34	17	36	37	37	4	6	23	58	Total Rtn % Rank Cat
0.78	0.76	0.81	0.74	0.73	0.72	0.71	0.78	0.74	0.66	0.60	0.54	Income $
0.17	0.05	0.03	0.00	0.00	0.06	0.04	0.00	0.06	0.05	0.00	0.00	Capital Gains $
0.60	0.54	0.54	0.50	0.49	0.47	0.46	0.46	0.45	0.45	0.45	—	Expense Ratio %
6.50	6.90	6.85	6.65	6.32	6.00	6.10	6.67	6.18	5.67	4.81	—	Income Ratio %
26	55	53	37	28	35	24	34	40	31	41	—	Turnover Rate %
180	195	303	533	705	952	974	1,021	1,512	3,405	5,697	7,624	Net Assets $mil

Performance 12-31-04

	1st Qtr	2nd Qtr	3rd Qtr	4th Qtr	Total
2000	2.11	1.32	2.72	4.17	10.70
2001	3.82	1.32	4.24	0.61	10.32
2002	0.98	3.12	3.81	2.45	10.75
2003	1.42	2.82	0.54	1.08	5.97
2004	1.86	-2.07	2.69	1.17	3.64

Trailing	Total Return%	+/- LB Aggr	+/- LB 5-10YR	%Rank Cat	Growth of $10,000
3 Mo	1.17	0.22	0.19	29	10,117
6 Mo	3.90	-0.28	-1.67	52	10,390
1 Yr	3.64	-0.70	-1.66	58	10,364
3 Yr Avg	6.75	0.56	-1.30	11	12,165
5 Yr Avg	8.24	0.53	-0.83	7	14,857
10 Yr Avg	8.12	0.40	-0.34	6	21,830
15 Yr Avg	8.11	0.41	-0.21	10	32,210

Tax Analysis	Tax-Adj Rtn%	%Rank Cat	Tax-Cost Rat	%Rank Cat
3 Yr (estimated)	5.20	5	1.45	34
5 Yr (estimated)	6.21	3	1.88	43
10 Yr (estimated)	5.75	3	2.19	51

Potential Capital Gain Exposure: 2% of assets

Rating and Risk

Time Period	Load-Adj Return %	Morningstar Rtn vs Cat	Morningstar Risk vs Cat	Morningstar Risk-Adj Rating
1 Yr	3.64			
3 Yr	6.75	High	Low	★★★★★
5 Yr	8.24	High	Low	★★★★★
10 Yr	8.12	High	-Avg	★★★★★
Incept	8.48			

Other Measures	Standard Index LB Aggr	Best Fit Index LB. U.S. Univ. Bd
Alpha	1.7	1.0
Beta	0.75	0.79
R-Squared	92	94
Standard Deviation	3.57	
Mean	6.75	
Sharpe Ratio	1.53	

Portfolio Analysis 09-30-04

Total Fixed-Income:269	Date of Maturity	Amount $000	Value $000	% Net Assets
US Treasury Note 6.625%	05-15-07	465,000	509,883	7.00
US Treasury Note 4.625%	05-15-06	450,000	465,557	6.39
At&T 8%	11-15-31	121,565	132,506	1.82
FNMA 5.5%	04-01-18	119,647	126,749	1.74
Ford Motor Cr 7.25%	10-25-11	109,900	118,927	1.63
FNMA CMO 7.5%	03-25-44	96,987	105,382	1.45
Wyeth 5.5%	02-01-14	99,875	101,321	1.39
Comcast 5.3%	01-15-14	99,100	99,315	1.36
General Mtrs Accep 6.875	09-15-11	87,520	91,810	1.26
At&T 7.3%	11-15-11	79,605	89,058	1.22
FNMA 6.5%	06-01-18	82,286	87,171	1.20
Xerox 7.125%	06-15-10	72,530	77,426	1.06
Aol Time Warner 7.625%	04-15-31	63,030	72,547	1.00
Hca 8.75%	09-01-10	54,550	63,943	0.88
FNMA 6%	02-01-19	57,886	60,739	0.83
FNMA 6.5%	07-01-17	55,697	59,003	0.81
FNMA 6%	01-01-19	56,230	59,002	0.81
FNMA 6%	07-01-17	54,251	56,925	0.78
FNMA 6%	03-01-16	54,099	56,858	0.78
FNMA 6%	03-01-14	53,767	56,511	0.78

Current Investment Style

Duration: Short Int Long — Quality: High Med Low

[1] figure provided by fund

Avg Eff Duration[1]	3.4 Yrs
Avg Eff Maturity	5.5 Yrs
Avg Credit Quality	AA
Avg Wtd Coupon	6.49%
Avg Wtd Price	107.46% of par

Coupon Range	% of Bonds	Rel Cat
0% PIK	0.5	0.1
0% to 6%	38.6	0.6
6% to 8%	55.3	1.9
8% to 10%	6.1	1.1
More than 10%	0.0	0.0

1.00=Category Average

Credit Analysis		% bonds 09-30-04	
US Govt	62	BB	8
AAA	0	B	3
AA	0	Below B	0
A	4	NR/NA	5
BBB	18		

Sector Breakdown	% of assets
US Treasuries	13
TIPS	0
US Agency	2
Mortgage Pass-Throughs	30
Mortgage CMO	8
Mortgage ARM	0
US Corporate	32
Asset-Backed	1
Convertible	0
Municipal	0
Corporate Inflation-Protected	0
Foreign Corporate	0
Foreign Govt	0

Composition			
Cash	14.2	Bonds	85.8
Stocks	0.0	Other	0.0

Special Securities	
Restricted/Illiquid Secs	Trace
Exotic Mortgage-Backed	0
Emerging-Markets Secs	0
Options/Futures/Warrants	No

Morningstar's Take by Dan Culloton 10-01-04

Dodge & Cox Income has looked wrong this year, but it's still the right choice.

This fund is on pace for its first year below the category average since 1990, but there's no need to fret. The fund trailed nearly 70% of its intermediate-term bond peers in the year to date through the end of September 2004 largely because it has committed itself to a conservative stance to guard against rising interest rates. At the start of this year, with bond yields at historic lows and the Federal Reserve poised to tighten monetary policy, that position seemed reasonable. Concerns about the vitality of the economy, however, have restrained interest rates in the second half of the year, even as the Fed has hiked its benchmark rate.

The fund's recent disappointment is not a sign of weakness, though. Rather, the management team's willingness to stick to its strategy, even though it has hurt short-term relative performance, is a sign of strength. This fund has built a long, successful record by keeping its eyes on the long term. With inflation pressure building and rates still at historic lows, the most prudent course remains a cautious one, the managers say. So they've kept the portfolio's duration (a measure of interest-rate sensitivity) shorter than the Lehman Brothers Aggregate Bond Index and the typical intermediate-term bond fund. The fund also continues to add value through opportunistic securities selection. It focuses on out-of-favor corporate bonds, such as those of AT&T. The offering is also emphasizing mortgage-backed securities whose underlying loans have low principal balances and delinquencies, and short amortization schedules because their cash flows are more predictable.

This fund's recent travails show that even long and consistent track records of success are no guarantee against occasional stumbles, but there is no cause for alarm and no signs this offering has abandoned its commitment to long-term investing and capital preservation. Stick with it.

Address:	Dodge & Cox Funds San Francisco, CA 94104 800-621-3979
Web Address:	www.dodgeandcox.com
Inception:	01-03-89
Advisor:	Dodge & Cox
Subadvisor:	None
NTF Plans:	N/A

Minimum Purchase:	$2500	Add: $100	IRA: $1000
Min Auto Inv Plan:	$2500	Add: $100	
Sales Fees:	No-load		
Management Fee:	0.50% mx./0.40% mn.		
Actual Fees:	Mgt:0.40%	Dist:	
Expense Projections:	3Yr:$144	5Yr:$252	10Yr:$567
Income Distrib:	Quarterly		

Dodge & Cox Intl Stock

Analyst Pick	Ticker	Load	NAV	Yield	Total Assets	Mstar Category
✔	DODFX	None	$30.64	0.8%	$3,376 mil	Foreign Large Value

Governance and Management

Fiduciary Grade: A

Portfolio Manager(s)

This fund is run by the Dodge & Cox International Policy Committee. The six-person committee is deep, talented, and experienced. The committee members have been at Dodge & Cox for an average of 16 years. Several members of the committee also serve on the committee that runs large-value Analyst Pick Dodge & Cox Stock.

Strategy

This fund's management team invests in stocks that it considers undervalued on a range of variables. It favors companies with good management, dominant competitive positions, and good growth potential. Because management takes such a long-term view, turnover is generally low here. Finally, management normally runs an unhedged portfolio and uses fair-value pricing whenever it thinks such an approach is warranted.

Historical Profile

Return Above Avg
Risk High
Rating ★★★★ Above Avg

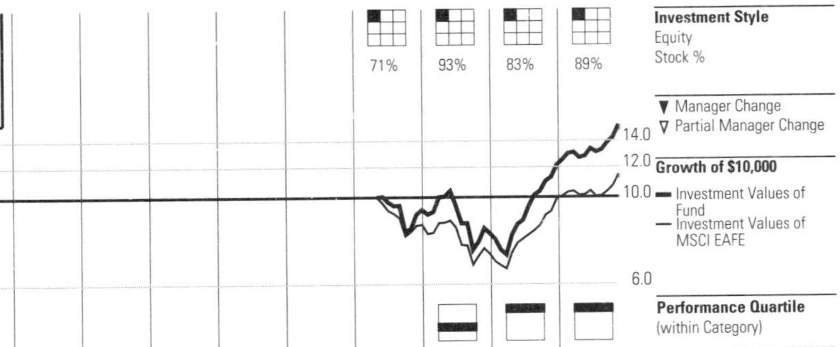

1993	1994	1995	1996	1997	1998	1999	2000	2001	2002	2003	12-04	History
—	—	—	—	—	—	—	—	18.42	15.81	23.48	30.64	NAV
—	—	—	—	—	—	—	—	-8.51*	-13.11	49.42	32.46	Total Return %
—	—	—	—	—	—	—	—	—	2.83	10.83	12.21	+/-MSCI EAFE
—	—	—	—	—	—	—	—	—	2.69	10.00	12.08	+/-MSCI Wd xUS
—	—	—	—	—	—	—	—	0.00	0.72	0.90	1.02	Income Return %
—	—	—	—	—	—	—	—	—	-13.83	48.52	31.44	Capital Return %
—	—	—	—	—	—	—	—	—	61	8	1	Total Rtn % Rank Cat
—	—	—	—	—	—	—	—	0.14	0.13	0.14	0.24	Income $
—	—	—	—	—	—	—	—	0.02	0.06	0.00	0.22	Capital Gains $
—	—	—	—	—	—	—	—	0.90	0.90	0.82	—	Expense Ratio %
—	—	—	—	—	—	—	—	1.74	1.30	1.54	—	Income Ratio %
—	—	—	—	—	—	—	—	23	12	11	—	Turnover Rate %
—	—	—	—	—	—	—	—	25	117	655	3,376	Net Assets $mil

Performance 12-31-04

	1st Qtr	2nd Qtr	3rd Qtr	4th Qtr	Total
2000	—	—	—	—	—
2001	—	—	-16.06	13.93	-8.51 *
2002	7.71	-5.04	-22.77	10.00	-13.11
2003	-11.70	22.64	18.46	16.49	49.42
2004	7.71	2.17	3.64	16.14	32.46

Trailing	Total Return%	+/- MSCI EAFE	+/- MSCI Wd xUS	%Rank Cat	Growth of $10,000
3 Mo	16.14	0.82	0.99	11	11,614
6 Mo	20.37	5.37	5.00	1	12,037
1 Yr	32.46	12.21	12.08	1	13,246
3 Yr Avg	19.81	7.92	7.59	11	17,198
5 Yr Avg	—	—	—	—	—
10 Yr Avg	—	—	—	—	—
15 Yr Avg	—	—	—	—	—

Tax Analysis	Tax-Adj Rtn%	%Rank Cat	Tax-Cost Rat	%Rank Cat
3 Yr (estimated)	19.42	10	0.33	29
5 Yr (estimated)	—	—	—	—
10 Yr (estimated)	—	—	—	—

Potential Capital Gain Exposure: 17% of assets

Rating and Risk

Time Period	Load-Adj Return %	Morningstar Rtn vs Cat	Morningstar Risk vs Cat	Morningstar Risk-Adj Rating
1 Yr	32.46			
3 Yr	19.81	+Avg	High	★★★★
5 Yr	—	—	—	—
10 Yr	—	—	—	—
Incept	13.61			

Other Measures	Standard Index S&P 500	Best Fit Index MSCI Wd xUS
Alpha	5.8	5.3
Beta	1.18	1.19
R-Squared	88	89
Standard Deviation	23.46	
Mean	19.81	
Sharpe Ratio	0.79	

Morningstar's Take by Kunal Kapoor 11-08-04

Dodge & Cox International Stock sets the bar high.

This fund distinguishes itself on many fronts but there are three that investors should really care about. The first two are easily explained and measured--namely, the fund has an experienced management team and rock-bottom expenses. Everyone on the team has been with Dodge & Cox since at least 1995, with one member having begun his tenure in 1972. And these folks get a head start on the competition with an expense ratio of just 0.82%, which is 74 basis points below the group norm. Thus, while the typical fund in this category costs investors $1,987 over 10 years (for a $10,000 investment), this fund charges $1,222.

The third factor working in this fund's favor is a measured approach. That is, this fund's managers distinguish themselves by closely examining what may go wrong with a potential investment. That may seem counterintuitive, but the reality is that nothing hampers the long-term compounding of capital more than capital losses. Thus, by focusing on an investment's downside, management gets comfortable with a range of possible outcomes, not just the positive ones.

Lately, this discipline has led the fund to the pharmaceutical sector and stock picks such as GlaxoSmithkline and Bayer. Comanager Diana Strandberg says that much of the bad news in the pharmaceutical sector is already priced into these firms' stocks, so their valuations are compelling. And the managers have added to numerous fund holdings, including those in the emerging markets. In fact, the 10 developing-market stocks in the portfolio account for 19% of assets. Meanwhile, the fund has sold off positions in Rolls Royce and Nortel Networks.

Management's willingness to go its own way can occasionally hobble the fund, and it's why investors should keep their expectations in check, even leaving aside the fund's strong recent run. But over the long haul, we think this fund will be tough to beat.

Portfolio Analysis 09-30-04

Share change since 06-04 Total Stocks:61	Sector	Country	% Assets
⊕ KT ADR	Telecom	Korea	3.04
⊕ Sony ADR	Goods	Japan	3.01
⊕ Unibanco Uniao de Bancos	Financial	Brazil	2.88
⊕ Vodafone Group PLC ADR	Telecom	U.K.	2.62
⊕ Royal Bank Of Scotland G	Financial	U.K.	2.58
⊕ Kookmin Bank ADR	Financial	Korea	2.58
⊕ Electrolux	Goods	Sweden	2.49
⊕ Akzo Nobel	Ind Mtrls	Netherlands	2.46
☼ News	—	Australia	2.44
Petroleo Brasileiro Sa P	Energy	Brazil	2.33
☼ Standard Bk Grp Limited	Financial	South Africa	2.33
⊕ Royal Dutch Petroleum AD	Energy	Netherlands	2.32
⊕ Nestle	Goods	Switzerland	2.17
⊕ Unilever NV	Goods	Netherlands	1.95
⊕ Bco Sant Cent Hisp	Financial	Spain	1.91
⊕ TOTAL	Energy	France	1.91
⊕ BHP Billiton Ltd	Ind Mtrls	Australia	1.90
⊕ Aderans	Goods	Japan	1.85
Stolt Offshore S.A. (ADR	Energy	Luxembourg	1.81
⊕ Norsk Hydro ASA ADR	Energy	Norway	1.78

Current Investment Style

Value Blnd Growth — Large Mid Small

Market Cap	%
Giant	37.3
Large	38.1
Mid	18.7
Small	5.1
Micro	0.8

Avg $mil: 11,921

Value Measures		Rel Category
Price/Earnings	13.65	1.01
Price/Book	1.53	0.93
Price/Sales	0.61	0.74
Price/Cash Flow	4.36	0.99
Dividend Yield %	2.92	1.05

Growth Measures	%	Rel Category
Long-Term Erngs	8.17	0.83
Book Value	2.86	6.22
Sales	1.26	0.90
Cash Flow	-3.39	NMF
Historical Erngs	2.20	0.79

Composition			
Cash	6.0	Bonds	0.0
Stocks	88.7	Other	5.3
Foreign (% of Stock)			100.0

Sector Weightings	% of Stocks	Rel MSCI EAFE	3 Year High	3 Year Low
Info	9.08	0.55		
Software	0.00	0.00	0	0
Hardware	2.78	0.76	5	0
Media	0.00	0.00	5	0
Telecom	6.30	0.66	6	2
Service	26.09	0.58		
Health	2.38	0.33	2	0
Consumer	2.70	0.54	12	3
Business	0.00	0.00	3	0
Financial	21.01	0.78	25	10
Mfg	64.85	1.68		
Goods	19.66	1.44	28	16
Ind Mtrls	30.41	2.47	43	30
Energy	12.13	1.65	12	2
Utilities	2.65	0.50	3	1

Regional Exposure	% Stock		% Stock
UK/W. Europe	55	N. America	1
Japan	17	Latn America	10
Asia X Japan	14	Other	3

Country Exposure	% Stock		% Stock
Japan	17	South Korea	8
U.K.	14	Brazil	6
Netherlands	9		

Address:	Dodge & Cox Funds San Francisco, CA 94104 800-621-3979	Minimum Purchase:	$2500 Add: $100 IRA: $1000
Web Address:	www.dodgeandcox.com	Min Auto Inv Plan:	$2500 Add: $100
Inception:	05-01-01 *	Sales Fees:	No-load
Advisor:	Dodge & Cox	Management Fee:	0.60%
Subadvisor:	None	Actual Fees:	Mgt:0.60% Dist:
NTF Plans:	N/A	Expense Projections:	3Yr:$268 5Yr:$466 10Yr:$1037
		Income Distrib:	Annually

Dodge & Cox Stock

Ticker	Load	NAV	Yield	Total Assets	Mstar Category
DODGX	Closed	$130.22	1.1%	$41,436 mil	Large Value

Governance and Management

Fiduciary Grade: A

Portfolio Manager(s)

This fund has an experienced and deep management team. The Dodge & Cox equity investment policy committee, which runs this fund, has nine members. The team is supported by nearly 20 analysts and five research assistants.

Strategy

This fund's management team invests in mid- and large-cap stocks that look cheap on a range of valuation measures. It favors companies with good management, dominant competitive positions, and good growth potential. Because management takes such a long-term view, the fund's turnover is just a fraction of the large-value category average.

Historical Profile

Return High
Risk Average
Rating ★★★★★ Highest

Investment Style: Equity Stock %

1993	1994	1995	1996	1997	1998	1999	2000	2001	2002	2003	12-04
	93%	89%	95%	92%	91%	89%	93%	90%	96%		

▼ Manager Change
▽ Partial Manager Change

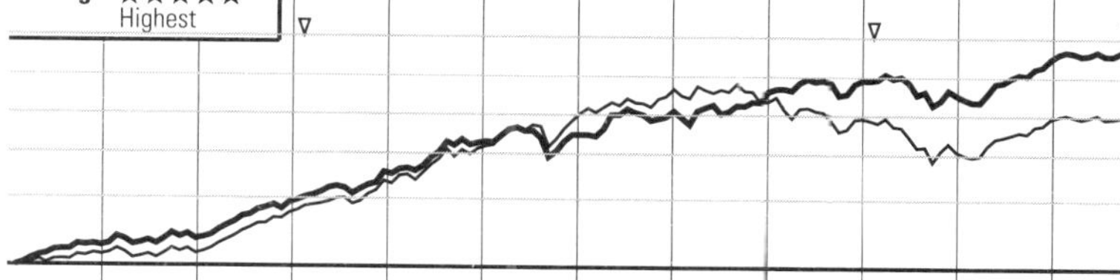

Growth of $10,000
— Investment Values of Fund
— Investment Values of S&P 500

Performance Quartile (within Category)

1993	1994	1995	1996	1997	1998	1999	2000	2001	2002	2003	12-04	History
53.23	53.94	67.83	79.81	94.57	90.70	100.52	96.67	100.51	88.05	113.78	130.22	NAV
18.31	5.17	33.38	22.27	28.40	5.40	20.21	16.31	9.33	-10.54	32.34	19.17	Total Return %
8.25	3.86	-4.15	-0.67	-4.95	-23.17	-0.83	25.41	21.21	11.55	3.67	8.30	+/-S&P 500
0.24	7.15	-4.98	0.63	-6.78	-10.23	12.86	9.30	14.92	4.98	2.31	2.68	+/-Russ 1000 VI
2.18	2.19	2.62	1.92	1.89	1.68	1.66	2.13	1.82	1.51	1.85	1.35	Income Return %
16.13	2.98	30.76	20.35	26.51	3.72	18.55	14.13	7.51	-12.05	30.49	17.82	Capital Return %
19	5	49	24	39	85	3	19	6	5	18	4	Total Rtn % Rank Cat
1.04	1.15	1.40	1.29	1.49	1.56	1.48	2.09	1.73	1.51	1.62	1.53	Income $
2.84	0.89	2.52	1.68	6.09	7.42	6.70	17.10	3.20	0.42	0.84	3.65	Capital Gains $
0.62	0.61	0.60	0.59	0.57	0.57	0.55	0.54	0.54	0.54	0.54	—	Expense Ratio %
1.95	2.16	2.07	1.79	1.67	1.63	1.46	2.13	1.80	1.74	1.72	—	Income Ratio %
15	7	13	10	19	19	18	32	10	13	8	—	Turnover Rate %
436	543	1,228	2,252	4,087	4,355	4,625	5,728	9,395	14,036	29,437	41,436	Net Assets $mil

Performance 12-31-04

	1st Qtr	2nd Qtr	3rd Qtr	4th Qtr	Total
2000	0.27	-2.22	6.24	11.66	16.31
2001	0.95	7.30	-10.23	12.44	9.33
2002	4.89	-6.22	-15.84	8.06	-10.54
2003	-5.29	16.59	5.24	13.88	32.34
2004	4.96	1.06	-0.26	12.64	19.17

Trailing	Total Return%	+/- S&P 500	+/- Russ 1000 VI	%Rank Cat	Growth of $10,000
3 Mo	12.64	3.41	2.26	4	11,264
6 Mo	12.35	5.16	0.27	8	11,235
1 Yr	19.17	8.30	2.68	4	11,917
3 Yr Avg	12.16	8.58	3.59	1	14,110
5 Yr Avg	12.40	14.70	7.13	3	17,940
10 Yr Avg	16.89	4.82	3.06	1	47,618
15 Yr Avg	14.44	3.51	2.41	2	75,625

Tax Analysis	Tax-Adj Rtn%	%Rank Cat	Tax-Cost Rat	%Rank Cat
3 Yr (estimated)	11.32	1	0.75	50
5 Yr (estimated)	10.64	4	1.57	82
10 Yr (estimated)	14.88	1	1.72	45

Potential Capital Gain Exposure: 24% of assets

Rating and Risk

Time Period	Load-Adj Return %	Morningstar Rtn vs Cat	Morningstar Risk vs Cat	Morningstar Risk-Adj Rating
1 Yr	19.17			
3 Yr	12.16	High	Avg	★★★★★
5 Yr	12.40	High	Avg	★★★★★
10 Yr	16.89	High	Avg	★★★★★
Incept	12.25			

Other Measures	Standard Index S&P 500	Best Fit Index Mstar Mid Core
Alpha	8.6	0.1
Beta	0.89	0.91
R-Squared	87	93
Standard Deviation	16.04	
Mean	12.16	
Sharpe Ratio	0.68	

Morningstar's Take by Dan Culloton 12-07-04

You don't need to ask Dodge & Cox Stock, "What have you done for me lately?" But one day you might be tempted to.

When you do the fund should still measure up. Its appeal goes beyond its recent streak of strong returns. Its veteran managers, low expenses, long-term focus, and unblemished regulatory record are a hard combination to beat. Nevertheless, investment styles ebb and flow, and someday value will fall out of favor just as growth did after 1999. Furthermore, the fund's large asset base could make it more difficult for it to repeat its past success. The fund now is more than eight times the size it was when it started its recent string of finishing six calendar years in its category's top fourth.

Despite those challenges, the fund has taken steps to ensure the continuity of the value-investing philosophy that has seen it through four decades of market cycles. The firm began preparing for the impending retirements of veteran team members A. Horton Shapiro and Harry Hagey three years ago by adding portfolio managers to the squad. The firm also has shut this fund, as well as Dodge & Cox Balanced and other equity accounts that work off the same list of approved stocks, to new investors.

That should help keep the fund from deviating from its strategy: Buying stocks that look cheap compared with their long-term growth rates or assets and holding them for years. The fund does own fewer mid-cap stocks than it has in the past, but its value discipline has as much to do with the shift as asset bloat. At the start of this year the fund found more attractive opportunities among large-cap growth stocks such as Liberty Media.

Fund performance is variable, but this fund's most endearing traits--seasoned management, low costs, long-term focus, and stubborn devotion to style--have been beneficial and constant. Remember that when you're tempted to ask it what it has done for you lately.

Portfolio Analysis 09-30-04

Share change since 06-04 Total Stocks:89	Sector	PE	YTD Ret%	% Assets
⊕ Hewlett-Packard	Hardware	18.9	-7.28	2.95
⊕ AT&T Wireless Services	Telecom	—	—	2.82
⊕ Comcast A	Media	81.0	1.49	2.80
⊕ HCA	Health	15.8	-6.00	2.43
⊕ News Corporation ADR A	Media	—	6.65	2.28
⊕ Time Warner	Media	27.5	8.12	2.23
⊕ Schering-Plough	Health	—	21.56	2.21
⊕ McDonald's	Consumer	19.7	31.48	2.19
⊕ Dow Chemical	Ind Mtrls	16.6	22.83	2.15
⊕ Union Pacific	Business	19.6	-1.28	2.12
⊕ Capital One Financial	Financial	12.5	37.61	2.11
⊕ AT&T	Telecom	—	-0.63	2.01
☼ J P Morgan Chase	Financial	19.4	9.97	1.98
⊕ ChevronTexaco	Energy	7.7	25.57	1.95
⊕ Sony ADR	Goods	47.7	13.04	1.94
⊕ Cardinal Health	Health	16.9	-4.73	1.92
⊕ Wachovia	Financial	14.3	16.80	1.88
⊕ Akzo Nobel NV ADR	Ind Mtrls	17.7	15.64	1.74
⊕ Electronic Data Systems	Business	—	-3.82	1.74
⊕ Xerox	Ind Mtrls	20.2	23.26	1.73

Current Investment Style

Value Blnd Growth / Large Mid Small

Market Cap	%
Giant	28.9
Large	56.0
Mid	15.1
Small	0.0
Micro	0.0
Avg $mil: 20,344	

Value Measures		Rel Category
Price/Earnings	15.73	1.05
Price/Book	1.84	0.81
Price/Sales	0.92	0.77
Price/Cash Flow	5.95	0.93
Dividend Yield %	1.85	0.91

Growth Measures	%	Rel Category
Long-Term Erngs	10.01	0.96
Book Value	-6.36	NMF
Sales	1.89	0.45
Cash Flow	-31.69	NMF
Historical Erngs	7.00	0.59

Profitability	%	Rel Category
Return on Equity	11.87	0.75
Return on Assets	5.34	0.68
Net Margin	6.86	0.67

Sector Weightings	% of Stocks	Rel S&P 500	3 Year High	3 Year Low
Info	20.22	0.94		
Software	0.78	0.18	1	1
Hardware	5.68	0.56	7	3
Media	8.21	2.14	8	0
Telecom	5.55	1.76	6	3
Service	45.00	0.97		
Health	12.24	0.98	12	9
Consumer	6.08	0.67	9	6
Business	8.08	2.00	9	7
Financial	18.60	0.90	22	19
Mfg	34.78	1.08		
Goods	6.93	0.74	8	6
Ind Mtrls	15.09	1.19	24	15
Energy	9.44	1.32	13	9
Utilities	3.32	1.12	4	2

Composition

Cash	3.5
Stocks	96.5
Bonds	0.0
Other	0.0
Foreign (% of Stock)	15.9

Address:	Dodge & Cox Funds San Francisco, CA 94104 800-621-3979
Web Address:	www.dodgeandcox.com
Inception:	01-04-65
Advisor:	Dodge & Cox
Subadvisor:	None
NTF Plans:	N/A

Minimum Purchase:	Closed	Add: —	IRA: —
Min Auto Inv Plan:	Closed	Add: —	
Sales Fees:	No-load		
Management Fee:	0.50%		
Actual Fees:	Mgt:0.50%	Dist:	
Expense Projections:	3Yr:$173	5Yr:$302	10Yr:$677
Income Distrib:	Quarterly		

Domini Social Equity

Ticker	Load	NAV	Yield	Total Assets	Mstar Category
DSEFX	12b-1 only	$29.54	1.0%	$1,500 mil	Large Blend

Governance and Management

Fiduciary Grade: B

Portfolio Manager(s)

A six-person committee at Kinder, Lydenberg, Domini, a Boston-based social-research firm, maintains the Domini 400 Social Index, which it licenses to this fund's manager, Domini Social Investments, LLC. State Street Global Advisors oversees the day-to-day management of the fund, including ensuring that assets are allocated in accordance with the index.

Strategy

This passively managed fund tracks the Domini 400 Social Index, which is made up of about 400 stocks that pass varied social screens. The screens eliminate companies that manufacture alcohol, tobacco, or firearms, provide services to gambling operations, own or operate nuclear power plants, or earn significant revenue from weapons contracting. The fund includes firms with strong records in environmental issues, workplace diversity, employee relations, community involvement, and product safety and usefulness.

Historical Profile

Return Average
Risk Above Avg
Rating ★★★ Neutral

Investment Style: Equity Stock %

1996	1997	1998	1999	2000	2001	2002	2003	2004
100%	100%	100%	100%	100%	100%	99%	100%	100%

▼ Manager Change
∇ Partial Manager Change

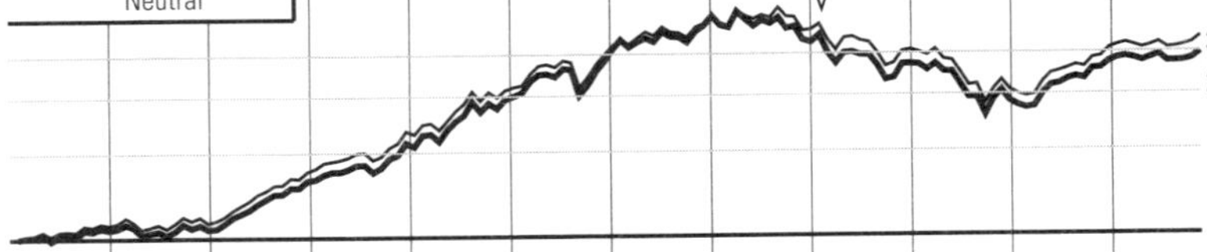

Growth of $10,000
— Investment Values of Fund
— Investment Values of S&P 500

Performance Quartile (within Category)

1993	1994	1995	1996	1997	1998	1999	2000	2001	2002	2003	12-04	History
12.43	12.10	16.11	19.35	26.22	34.40	41.89	34.57	27.37	21.60	27.31	29.54	NAV
6.53	-0.36	35.17	21.84	36.02	32.99	22.63	-15.05	-12.76	-20.69	27.13	9.26	Total Return %
-3.53	-1.67	-2.36	-1.10	2.67	4.42	1.59	-5.95	-0.88	1.40	-1.54	-1.61	+/-S&P 500
-3.65	-0.75	-2.60	-0.61	3.17	5.97	1.72	-7.26	-0.31	0.96	-2.76	-2.14	+/-Russ 1000
1.18	1.62	1.25	0.95	0.31	0.06	0.04	0.00	0.14	0.40	0.64	1.08	Income Return %
5.35	-1.98	33.92	20.89	35.71	32.93	22.59	-15.05	-12.90	-21.09	26.49	8.18	Capital Return %
83	55	41	46	5	4	32	94	62	33	50	64	Total Rtn % Rank Cat
0.14	0.20	0.15	0.15	0.06	0.02	0.01	0.00	0.05	0.11	0.14	0.29	Income $
0.07	0.08	0.08	0.12	0.03	0.45	0.27	0.98	2.75	0.00	0.00	0.00	Capital Gains $
0.75	0.75	0.90	0.98	0.98	1.17	0.98	0.96	0.93	0.92	0.92	0.95	Expense Ratio %
1.41	1.67	1.38	1.01	0.62	0.07	0.06	-0.05	0.06	0.32	0.63	0.55	Income Ratio %
4	8	6	5	1	5	8	—	—	13	8	8	Turnover Rate %
27	34	69	115	301	716	1,344	1,329	1,197	1,011	1,258	1,266	Net Assets $mil

Performance 12-31-04

	1st Qtr	2nd Qtr	3rd Qtr	4th Qtr	Total
2000	2.72	-5.28	-4.96	-8.15	-15.05
2001	-12.24	5.17	-14.26	10.24	-12.76
2002	-0.04	-12.14	-17.16	9.00	-20.69
2003	-3.56	15.06	3.14	11.08	27.13
2004	1.83	2.04	-3.74	9.24	9.26

Trailing	Total Return%	+/- S&P 500	+/- Russ 1000	%Rank Cat	Growth of $10,000
3 Mo	9.24	0.01	-0.56	46	10,924
6 Mo	5.15	-2.04	-2.66	84	10,515
1 Yr	9.26	-1.61	-2.14	64	10,926
3 Yr Avg	3.28	-0.30	-0.99	41	11,017
5 Yr Avg	-3.98	-1.68	-2.22	79	8,162
10 Yr Avg	11.55	-0.52	-0.61	29	29,833
15 Yr Avg	—	—	—	—	—

Tax Analysis	Tax-Adj Rtn%	%Rank Cat	Tax-Cost Rat	%Rank Cat
3 Yr (estimated)	3.03	32	0.24	20
5 Yr (estimated)	-4.59	77	0.64	34
10 Yr (estimated)	11.00	12	0.49	7

Potential Capital Gain Exposure: -7% of assets

Rating and Risk

Time Period	Load-Adj Return %	Morningstar Rtn vs Cat	Morningstar Risk vs Cat	Morningstar Risk-Adj Rating
1 Yr	9.26			
3 Yr	3.28	Avg	+Avg	★★★
5 Yr	-3.98	-Avg	+Avg	★★
10 Yr	11.55	+Avg	+Avg	★★★
Incept	10.42			

Other Measures	Standard Index S&P 500	Best Fit Index Russ 1000
Alpha	-0.3	-1.0
Beta	1.01	1.02
R-Squared	98	98
Standard Deviation	15.82	
Mean	3.28	
Sharpe Ratio	0.12	

Morningstar's Take by David Kathman 12-03-04

Domini Social Equity remains a good core fund for socially conscious investors, but it should cost less.

This fund offers broad large-cap stock exposure to investors who want to avoid certain types of companies for ethical reasons. It tracks the Domini 400 Social Index, which excludes businesses in the alcohol, tobacco, gambling, military weapons, and nuclear power industries. The index also excludes companies that fail a set of screening criteria designed to identify firms with good relationships to employees, shareholders, and the environment.

The Domini index includes 250 stocks from the S&P 500, 100 similarly sized stocks that also pass the screens (included to bring the sector weightings more in line with the S&P 500), and 50 smaller stocks that score especially well on the screens, such as Interface and Radio One. The presence of these smaller stocks, plus the absence of big names such as General Electric and ExxonMobil, means that this fund's average market cap is somewhat lower than the S&P 500's.

The Domini index also has more of a growth tilt than the S&P 500, because firms that fail the screening criteria tend to be industrial, energy, and utility names. Those sectors are underweighted in this fund relative to the S&P 500, and tech, telecom, and media stocks are correspondingly overweighted. That means the fund has tended to outperform the S&P 500 in growth markets and to underperform in bear markets. It has also lagged the index in the past two years, when cyclical and energy stocks have led the market.

Domini is a very shareholder-friendly shop in most respects, but our main issue with this fund is its 0.95% expense ratio. That's very high for a large-cap index fund, and it would be higher except for a fee waiver that's in place until November 30, 2005. Vanguard Calvert Social Index is cheaper, but also more volatile and less like the S&P 500. For investors seeking a milder socially responsible index fund, this one is a good choice, but its costs need to come down.

Address:	536 Broadway New York NY 10012-3915 800-762-6814
Web Address:	www.domini.com
Inception:	06-03-91
Advisor:	Domini Social Investments, LLC
Subadvisor:	State Street Global Advisors
NTF Plans:	Fidelity Retail-NTF, Schwab OneSource

Minimum Purchase:	$2500	Add: $100	IRA: $1500
Min Auto Inv Plan:	$1500	Add: $50	
Sales Fees:	0.25%B, 2.00%R		
Management Fee:	0.20%, 0.50%A		
Actual Fees:	Mgt:0.20%	Dist:0.25%	
Expense Projections:	3Yr:$348	5Yr:$618	10Yr:$1390
Income Distrib:	Semi-Annually		

Portfolio Analysis 09-30-04

Share change since 08-04 Total Stocks:400	Sector	PE	YTD Ret%	% Assets
⊕ Microsoft	Software	36.1	8.95	5.43
⊕ American International G	Financial	16.2	-0.53	3.20
⊕ Johnson & Johnson	Health	20.6	25.17	3.02
⊕ J P Morgan Chase	Financial	19.4	9.97	2.56
⊕ Procter & Gamble	Goods	23.3	12.38	2.52
⊖ Intel	Hardware	19.8	-26.56	2.33
⊕ Cisco Systems	Hardware	24.5	-20.26	2.21
⊕ Verizon Communications	Telecom	32.4	20.25	1.97
⊕ Wells Fargo	Financial	15.5	8.97	1.82
⊕ Coca-Cola	Goods	21.9	-16.12	1.77
⊕ Dell	Hardware	34.0	24.01	1.62
⊕ Home Depot	Consumer	19.0	21.47	1.58
⊕ SBC Communications	Telecom	15.4	3.74	1.55
⊕ PepsiCo	Goods	22.5	13.82	1.49
⊕ Merck	Health	11.4	-27.76	1.32
⊖ Amgen	Health	37.7	3.82	1.30
⊕ Time Warner	Media	27.5	8.12	1.29
⊕ American Express	Financial	20.3	17.60	1.18
⊕ Qualcomm	Hardware	42.0	58.20	1.15
⊕ 3M Company	Ind Mtrls	23.5	-1.75	1.13

Current Investment Style

Value Blnd Growth — Large Mid Small

Market Cap	%
Giant	52.6
Large	34.3
Mid	11.8
Small	1.1
Micro	0.1
Avg $mil: 37,872	

Value Measures		Rel Category
Price/Earnings	17.94	1.06
Price/Book	2.70	1.03
Price/Sales	1.68	1.17
Price/Cash Flow	7.52	0.98
Dividend Yield %	1.44	0.97

Growth Measures	%	Rel Category
Long-Term Erngs	11.97	1.04
Book Value	6.88	0.89
Sales	5.02	0.87
Cash Flow	8.83	0.93
Historical Erngs	16.66	1.41

Profitability	%	Rel Category
Return on Equity	19.15	1.09
Return on Assets	10.83	1.25
Net Margin	13.51	1.18

Sector Weightings	% of Stocks	Rel S&P 500	3 Year High	3 Year Low
Info	29.90	1.39		
Software	6.43	1.50	7	6
Hardware	12.47	1.22	15	10
Media	4.98	1.30	5	4
Telecom	6.02	1.91	8	5
Service	50.50	1.09		
Health	12.74	1.02	14	11
Consumer	10.71	1.18	11	9
Business	3.84	0.95	4	4
Financial	23.21	1.12	26	23
Mfg	19.59	0.61		
Goods	11.28	1.21	13	10
Ind Mtrls	5.87	0.46	6	4
Energy	1.90	0.27	2	1
Utilities	0.54	0.18	1	1

Composition

Cash	0.0
Stocks	100.0
Bonds	0.0
Other	0.0
Foreign (% of Stock)	0.0

Dreyfus Appreciation

Ticker	Load	NAV	Yield	Total Assets	Mstar Category
DGAGX	None	$38.69	1.3%	$4,436 mil	Large Blend

Governance and Management

Fiduciary Grade: C

Portfolio Manager(s)

Houston-based Fayez Sarofim & Co. has subadvised this fund for Dreyfus since 1990, but its eponymous leader has been managing money since 1958. An investment committee comprising Fayez Sarofim, Charles Sheedy, and several others with decades of experience makes portfolio decisions. The committee is supported by more than a dozen analysts.

Strategy

This fund is one of many plays on blue-chip names, but management's preference for companies with proven and well-known brands separates it from the pack. It holds more consumer-goods companies and fewer technology names than the typical large-blend fund. Management likes firms with high-quality earnings, clean balance sheets, and lots of free cash flow. The portfolio is more concentrated in individual stocks than many rivals. Management takes a buy-and-hold approach, which, in turn, translates into strong tax efficiency.

Historical Profile

Return Above Avg
Risk Below Avg
Rating ★★★★ Above Avg

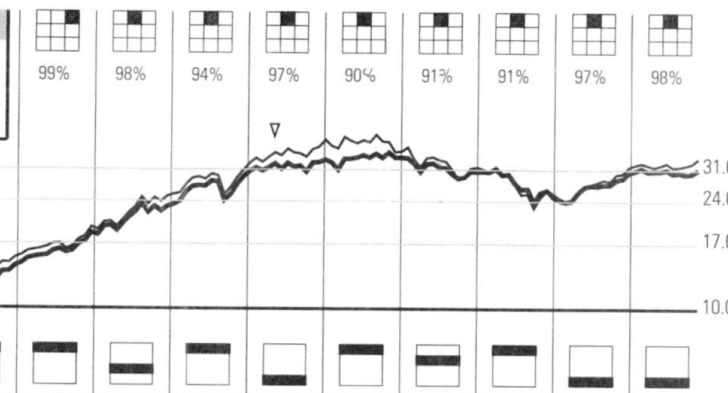

Investment Style
Equity
Stock %

▼ Manager Change
▽ Partial Manager Change

Growth of $10,000
— Investment Values of Fund
— Investment Values of S&P 500

Performance Quartile (within Category)

1993	1994	1995	1996	1997	1998	1999	2000	2001	2002	2003	12-04	History
14.92	15.17	20.55	25.58	32.38	42.07	45.73	42.94	38.02	31.20	37.14	38.69	NAV
0.71	3.62	37.88	25.67	27.85	30.85	9.97	1.30	-10.75	-17.14	20.39	5.57	Total Return %
-9.35	2.31	0.35	2.73	-5.50	2.28	-11.07	10.30	1.13	4.95	-8.28	-5.30	+/-S&P 500
-9.47	3.23	0.11	3.22	-5.00	3.83	-10.94	9.59	1.70	4.51	-9.50	-5.83	+/-Russ 1000
1.77	1.86	2.21	1.22	1.02	0.70	0.55	0.53	0.71	0.78	1.32	1.40	Income Return %
-1.06	1.76	35.67	24.45	26.83	30.15	9.42	1.17	-11.46	-17.92	19.07	4.17	Capital Return %
98	8	10	14	55	8	86	19	32	14	94	91	Total Rtn % Rank Cat
0.27	0.28	0.34	0.25	0.26	0.23	0.23	0.29	0.31	0.30	0.41	0.52	Income $
0.06	0.01	0.03	0.00	0.06	0.07	0.31	3.22	0.00	0.02	0.00	0.00	Capital Gains $
1.07	0.96	0.92	0.91	0.87	0.89	0.87	0.88	0.91	0.97	0.96	—	Expense Ratio %
1.66	1.86	2.28	1.34	0.99	0.75	0.51	0.64	0.72	0.90	1.28	—	Income Ratio %
10	7	5	5	1	1	12	4	5	2	5	—	Turnover Rate %
237	234	461	877	130	227	232	220	230	338	3,994	4,436	Net Assets $mil

Performance 12-31-04

	1st Qtr	2nd Qtr	3rd Qtr	4th Qtr	Total
2000	0.65	2.94	-1.98	0.24	1.80
2001	-10.83	3.79	-8.74	5.67	-10.75
2002	2.60	-11.28	-14.34	6.27	-17.14
2003	-4.28	12.96	0.71	10.55	20.39
2004	0.69	1.39	-3.59	7.26	5.57

Trailing	Total Return%	+/- S&P 500	+/- Russ 1000	%Rank Cat	Growth of $10,000
3 Mo	7.26	-1.97	-2.54	91	10,726
6 Mo	3.41	-3.78	-4.40	93	10,341
1 Yr	5.57	-5.30	-5.83	91	10,557
3 Yr Avg	1.74	-1.84	-2.53	71	10,531
5 Yr Avg	-0.88	1.42	0.88	32	9,568
10 Yr Avg	11.80	-0.27	-0.36	22	30,508
15 Yr Avg	10.59	-0.34	-0.49	31	45,262

Tax Analysis	Tax-Adj Rtn%	%Rank Cat	Tax-Cost Rat	%Rank Cat
3 Yr (estimated)	1.40	63	0.33	28
5 Yr (estimated)	-1.52	28	0.65	34
10 Yr (estimated)	11.21	10	0.53	9

Potential Capital Gain Exposure: 27% of assets

Rating and Risk

Time Period	Load-Adj Return %	Morningstar Rtn vs Cat	Morningstar Risk vs Cat	Morningstar Risk-Adj Rating
1 Yr	5.57			
3 Yr	1.74	Avg	-Avg	★★★
5 Yr	-0.88	+Avg	Low	★★★★
10 Yr	11.80	+Avg	-Avg	★★★★
Incept	12.78			

Other Measures	Standard Index S&P 500	Best Fit Index S&P 500
Alpha	-1.5	-1.5
Beta	0.81	0.81
R-Squared	91	91
Standard Deviation	12.94	
Mean	1.74	
Sharpe Ratio	0.03	

Portfolio Analysis 11-30-04

Share change since 10-04 Total Stocks:50	Sector	PE	YTD Ret%	% Assets
ExxonMobil	Energy	13.9	28.04	6.38
Altria Group	Goods	13.3	18.38	5.50
General Electric	Ind Mtrls	22.8	20.68	4.62
Intel	Hardware	19.8	-26.56	3.99
Citigroup	Financial	15.3	2.72	3.76
Pfizer	Health	22.0	-22.31	3.74
Procter & Gamble	Goods	23.3	12.38	3.49
ChevronTexaco	Energy	7.7	25.57	3.31
BP PLC ADR	Energy	20.7	22.07	3.29
⊖ Johnson & Johnson	Health	20.6	25.17	3.03
Coca-Cola	Goods	21.9	-16.12	2.88
Fannie Mae	Financial	9.1	-2.33	2.85
Walgreen	Consumer	31.6	6.03	2.74
PepsiCo	Goods	22.5	13.82	2.45
Microsoft	Software	36.1	8.95	2.35
Wal-Mart Stores	Consumer	23.4	0.51	2.31
McGraw-Hill Companies	Media	22.7	32.94	2.25
Bank of America	Financial	12.3	21.50	2.10
American Express	Financial	20.3	17.60	2.08
Nestle SA ADR	Goods	21.6	7.65	1.87

Current Investment Style

Value Blnd Growth — Large Mid Small

Market Cap	%
Giant	82.0
Large	18.1
Mid	0.0
Small	0.0
Micro	0.0
Avg $mil: 104,459	

Value Measures		Rel Category
Price/Earnings	15.43	0.91
Price/Book	3.21	1.23
Price/Sales	1.70	1.18
Price/Cash Flow	9.24	1.20
Dividend Yield %	2.17	1.47

Growth Measures	%	Rel Category
Long-Term Erngs	10.65	0.92
Book Value	13.51	1.74
Sales	8.27	1.44
Cash Flow	19.32	2.04
Historical Erngs	15.64	1.33

Profitability	%	Rel Category
Return on Equity	23.18	1.32
Return on Assets	11.67	1.35
Net Margin	12.81	1.12

Sector Weightings	% of Stocks	Rel S&P 500	3 Year High	3 Year Low
Info	11.65	0.54		
Software	2.40	0.56	3	2
Hardware	4.09	0.40	7	3
Media	5.16	1.34	5	4
Telecom	0.00	0.00	5	0
Service	43.82	0.94		
Health	11.34	0.91	21	11
Consumer	9.26	1.02	9	8
Business	1.21	0.30	1	1
Financial	22.01	1.06	23	19
Mfg	44.53	1.39		
Goods	22.05	2.36	25	13
Ind Mtrls	6.25	0.49	7	5
Energy	16.23	2.27	16	10
Utilities	0.00	0.00	0	0

Composition

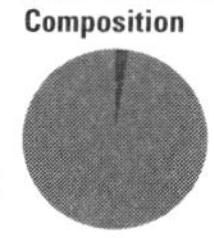

Cash	2.4
Stocks	97.6
Bonds	0.0
Other	0.0
Foreign (% of Stock)	8.9

Morningstar's Take by Gareth Lyons 10-01-04

While its recent underperformance is noteworthy, this fund remains a solid option.

This fund has been in a funk lately. Its perennial emphasis on blue chips was very much out of sync with 2003's proclivity for smaller, lower-quality companies. This year, however, that trend has subsided somewhat. True, smaller companies continue to prosper, but, amid fears of rising interest rates, investors have had less of an appetite for low-quality stocks. However, this fund has failed to benefit from that trend reversal. The portfolio, which is concentrated in about 50 names, has suffered at the hands of troubled stock picks such as Coke, Fannie Mae, and Merck. The fund's loss of 1.6% for the year to date through September lands in large blend's bottom quartile.

While this slipup can't be ignored, investors shouldn't count this management team out. Advisor Fayez Sarofim takes a distinctly long-term view of its investments. Given that turnover has averaged an annual rate of 5% over the past decade--a mere fraction of the category average--bouts of short-term performance weakness are inevitable. Granted, it's hard to know whether the fund's current batch of troubled picks will eventually turn around. But this management team's discipline of sticking with high-quality, cash-flow-rich companies usually pays off handsomely.

That patience shouldn't be mistaken for complacency, either. The managers here are continuously on the prowl for firms that meet their strict criteria, as recent addition Home Depot shows. Lead manager Charles Sheedy cites the home-improvement firm's large market-share, disciplined management team, and steady cash flow as key reasons for the purchase. (Interestingly, Sheedy had been evaluating the firm for over a year before pulling the trigger.)

We think discipline and patience gives this fund more than a fighting chance over the long haul. Those in search of benchmark-like performance should, though, consider other options.

Address:	The Dreyfus Corporation New York NY 10166 800-373-9387
Web Address:	www.dreyfus.com
Inception:	01-18-84
Advisor:	Dreyfus Corporation
Subadvisor:	Fayez Sarofim & Company
NTF Plans:	Fidelity Retail-NTF, Schwab OneSource

Minimum Purchase:	$2500	Add: $100	IRA: $750
Min Auto Inv Plan:	$100	Add: $100	
Sales Fees:	No-load		
Management Fee:	0.55% mx./0.28% mn.		
Actual Fees:	Mgt:0.55%	Dist:	
Expense Projections:	3Yr:$309	5Yr:$536	10Yr:$1190
Income Distrib:	Annually		

Dreyfus Emerging Leaders

Ticker	Load	NAV	Yield	Total Assets	Mstar Category
DRELX	Closed	$44.23	0.0%	$1,054 mil	Small Blend

Governance and Management

Fiduciary Grade: D

Portfolio Manager(s)

Hilary Woods and Paul Kandel have led the fund since late 1996. Their performance at mid-cap sibling Dreyfus New Leaders has been just average.

Strategy

Managers Hilary Woods and Paul Kandel invest in a mix of small- and mid-cap stocks, featuring both growth and value plays. Reflecting its Russell 2000 benchmark, the fund is typically diversified across sectors, with Woods focused on value-oriented sectors such as industrials and financials and Kandel focused on growth areas such as telecom and health care. The fund manages volatility by avoiding big sector and stock bets. A large asset base is the reason behind its move into mid-caps.

Historical Profile

Return Low
Risk Average
Rating ★ Lowest

Investment Style: Equity Stock %

1995	1996	1997	1998	1999	2000	2001	2002	2003	12-04
91%	98%	94%	95%	93%	95%	97%	95%	96%	

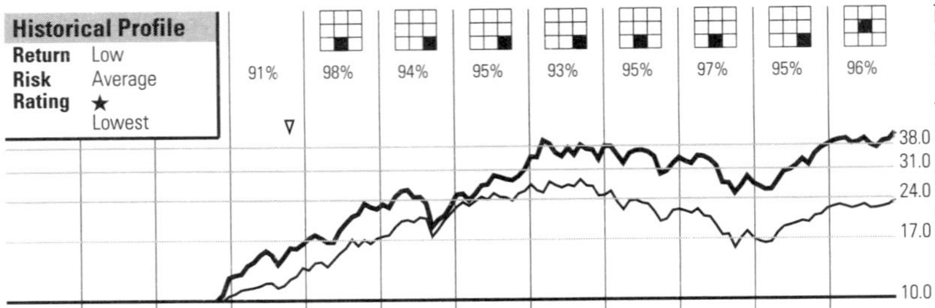

Performance Quartile (within Category)

1993	1994	1995	1996	1997	1998	1999	2000	2001	2002	2003	12-04	History
—	—	15.90	20.39	24.57	26.62	36.73	39.59	34.77	27.76	38.72	44.23	NAV
—	—	24.42*	37.40	33.91	8.56	38.25	9.49	-9.91	-20.16	39.48	14.23	Total Return %
—	—	—	14.46	0.56	-20.01	17.21	18.59	1.97	1.93	10.81	3.36	+/-S&P 500
—	—	—	20.91	11.55	11.11	16.99	12.51	-12.40	0.32	-7.77	-4.10	+/-Russ 2000
—	—	0.00	0.00	0.00	0.00	0.00	0.00	0.00	0.00	0.00	0.00	Income Return %
—	—	—	37.40	33.91	8.56	38.25	9.49	-9.91	-20.16	39.48	14.23	Capital Return %
—	—	—	8	18	5	6	67	98	77	60	85	Total Rtn % Rank Cat
—	—	0.03	0.00	0.00	0.00	0.00	0.00	0.00	0.00	0.00	0.00	Income $
—	—	0.00	1.41	2.67	0.05	0.07	0.59	0.84	0.00	0.00	0.00	Capital Gains $
—	—	—	1.16	1.39	1.39	1.38	1.26	1.29	1.34	1.38	1.31	Expense Ratio %
—	—	—	0.09	-0.62	-0.63	-0.49	-0.37	-0.39	-0.49	-0.56	-0.50	Income Ratio %
—	—	—	204	198	199	100	76	78	36	50	43	Turnover Rate %
—	—	17	61	129	156	612	1,417	1,362	1,004	1,269	1,054	Net Assets $mil

Performance 12-31-04

	1st Qtr	2nd Qtr	3rd Qtr	4th Qtr	Total
2000	11.92	-3.72	-1.09	2.72	9.49
2001	-13.92	11.77	-18.64	15.09	-9.91
2002	1.55	-8.33	-21.04	8.61	-20.16
2003	-4.97	18.35	4.68	18.48	39.48
2004	5.29	-0.10	-2.28	11.13	14.23

Trailing	Total Return%	+/- S&P 500	+/- Russ 2000	%Rank Cat	Growth of $10,000
3 Mo	11.13	1.90	-2.96	81	11,113
6 Mo	8.59	1.40	-2.24	80	10,859
1 Yr	14.23	3.36	-4.10	85	11,423
3 Yr Avg	8.35	4.77	-3.13	88	12,720
5 Yr Avg	4.64	6.94	-1.97	96	12,546
10 Yr Avg	—	—	—	—	—
15 Yr Avg	—	—	—	—	—

Tax Analysis	Tax-Adj Rtn%	%Rank Cat	Tax-Cost Rat	%Rank Cat
3 Yr (estimated)	8.35	82	0.00	1
5 Yr (estimated)	4.47	93	0.16	5
10 Yr (estimated)	—	—	—	—

Potential Capital Gain Exposure: 29% of assets

Rating and Risk

Time Period	Load-Adj Return %	Morningstar Rtn vs Cat	Morningstar Risk vs Cat	Morningstar Risk-Adj Rating
1 Yr	14.23			
3 Yr	8.35	-Avg	Avg	★★
5 Yr	4.64	Low	Avg	★
10 Yr	—	—	—	—
Incept	17.10			

Other Measures	Standard Index S&P 500	Best Fit Index Russ 2000
Alpha	5.0	-2.1
Beta	1.06	0.92
R-Squared	77	94
Standard Deviation	19.75	
Mean	8.35	
Sharpe Ratio	0.36	

Morningstar's Take by Gareth Lyons 11-22-04

Shareholders should consider selling this bloated fund.

Dreyfus Emerging Leaders, which is on track to end its fifth consecutive year in the small-blend category's bottom half, wasn't always bringing up the rear. From its launch in late 1995 through 1999, this fund consistently walloped the competition as managers Paul Kandel and Hilary Woods rooted out small- and micro-cap opportunities from a wide variety of industries. Not surprisingly, the successful run drew a flood of new investors. But the board of trustees and Dreyfus senior management, which has since changed, allowed assets to grow to well over $1 billion before closing the fund in mid-2000. Woods and Kandel have since been forced to buy bigger stocks to avoid owning too much of any one name. As the smallest of companies have enjoyed the best returns over the past few years, the managers' hands were tied.

The portfolio's recent migration to the mid-blend portion of the style box underlines our concerns. Top holdings Station Casinosand Davita, both of which sport market caps close to $3 billion, sit squarely in mid-cap land. Granted, the fund does hold smaller names, but those tend to be on the fringes. A recent purchase of small-cap tech firm Genesis Microchip represents less than 1% of assets here, for example. But the position accounts for a hefty 2.4% of the company's total shares outstanding and is nearly twice the stock's average daily trading volume. The risks of holding too much in such names are apt to keep this fund routinely skewed toward the upper reaches of small-cap territory.

Of course, that tilt should provide ballast when the smallest stocks hit the skids. However, investors presumably bought this fund to gain exposure to small stocks. Given that this offering has drifted from its original course, we'd explore other options.

Address:	The Dreyfus Corporation New York NY 10166 800-373-9387
Web Address:	www.dreyfus.com
Inception:	09-29-95 *
Advisor:	Dreyfus Corporation
Subadvisor:	None
NTF Plans:	Fidelity Retail-NTF, Schwab OneSource

Minimum Purchase:	Closed	Add: —	IRA: —
Min Auto Inv Plan:	Closed	Add: —	
Sales Fees:	No-load, 1.00%R		
Management Fee:	0.75%		
Actual Fees:	—	Dist:	
Expense Projections:	3Yr:$400	5Yr:$692	10Yr:$1523
Income Distrib:	Annually		

Portfolio Analysis 11-30-04

Share change since 10-04 Total Stocks:72

	Sector	PE	YTD Ret%	% Assets
Davita	Health	19.0	52.04	2.12
Affiliated Managers Grou	Financial	28.2	46.01	1.93
Petco Animal Supplies	Consumer	29.5	29.66	1.84
Harte-Hanks	Media	24.0	20.25	1.79
New Century Financial	Financial	5.7	63.77	1.75
⊖ Crown Holdings	Goods	—	51.66	1.74
Church & Dwight Company	Goods	18.5	28.24	1.73
⊖ Station Casinos	Consumer	77.1	81.31	1.71
Greater Bay Bancorp	Financial	17.4	-0.15	1.68
Wausau-Mosinee Paper	Ind Mtrls	40.3	35.24	1.66
United Defense Industrie	Ind Mtrls	14.2	48.21	1.65
First Midwest Bancorp	Financial	16.7	14.81	1.65
⊖ Trinity Industries	Ind Mtrls	—	11.40	1.63
Apria HealthCare Group	Health	13.9	15.74	1.61
Agrium	Ind Mtrls	—	3.13	1.61
Idex	Ind Mtrls	24.1	48.09	1.60
⊖ Olin	Ind Mtrls	—	14.81	1.59
⊖ Agnico-Eagle Mines Ltd	Ind Mtrls	—	14.17	1.58
Webster Financial	Financial	13.3	12.57	1.57
American Capital Strateg	Financial	9.0	23.48	1.56

Current Investment Style

Value Blnd Growth / Large Mid Small

Market Cap	%
Giant	0.1
Large	0.1
Mid	56.1
Small	43.7
Micro	0.1
Avg $mil: 1,582	

Value Measures		Rel Category
Price/Earnings	19.28	1.11
Price/Book	2.43	1.22
Price/Sales	1.25	1.32
Price/Cash Flow	5.70	0.97
Dividend Yield %	0.69	0.83

Growth Measures	%	Rel Category
Long-Term Erngs	13.43	0.99
Book Value	4.71	0.84
Sales	4.11	0.95
Cash Flow	9.95	2.01
Historical Erngs	7.86	1.05

Profitability	%	Rel Category
Return on Equity	12.52	1.20
Return on Assets	4.49	0.91
Net Margin	7.46	1.02

Sector Weightings	% of Stocks	Rel S&P 500	3 Year High	3 Year Low
Info	17.04	0.79		
Software	4.78	1.11	7	2
Hardware	7.72	0.76	12	5
Media	4.54	1.18	8	4
Telecom	0.00	0.00	2	0
Service	46.32	1.00		
Health	12.75	1.02	14	9
Consumer	7.97	0.88	11	4
Business	7.26	1.79	11	7
Financial	18.34	0.88	22	14
Mfg	36.64	1.14		
Goods	5.62	0.60	9	2
Ind Mtrls	18.97	1.50	21	15
Energy	9.82	1.37	13	5
Utilities	2.23	0.75	4	2

Composition

Cash	4.5
Stocks	95.5
Bonds	0.0
Other	0.0
Foreign (% of Stock)	5.0

Dreyfus Midcap Value

Ticker	Load	NAV	Yield	Total Assets	Mstar Category
DMCVX	Closed	$32.45	0.0%	$1,344 mil	Mid-Cap Blend

Governance and Management

Fiduciary Grade: D

Portfolio Manager(s)

Peter Higgins has been managing this fund since its inception in 1995. He also runs Dreyfus Small Company Value. David Daglio joined the fund as comanager in September 2003. Daglio is also a equity research analyst for Dreyfus' small- and mid-cap investment team.

Strategy

Lead manager Peter Higgins keeps a close eye on valuations, looking for cheap companies based on conventional measures such as P/E and price/book. He looks for a catalyst, such as corporate restructuring or industrywide events, that will boost earnings and trigger a stock-price increase. Unlike many other value investors, Higgins is willing to load up on technology stocks when he thinks they're cheap. As a result, the fund is much more volatile than average.

Historical Profile

Return Average
Risk High
Rating ★★★ Neutral

Investment Style: Equity Stock %: 96% (1995), 100% (1996), 99% (1997), 97% (1998), 97% (1999), 99% (2000), 100% (2001), 98% (2002), 100% (2003)

▼ Manager Change
∇ Partial Manager Change

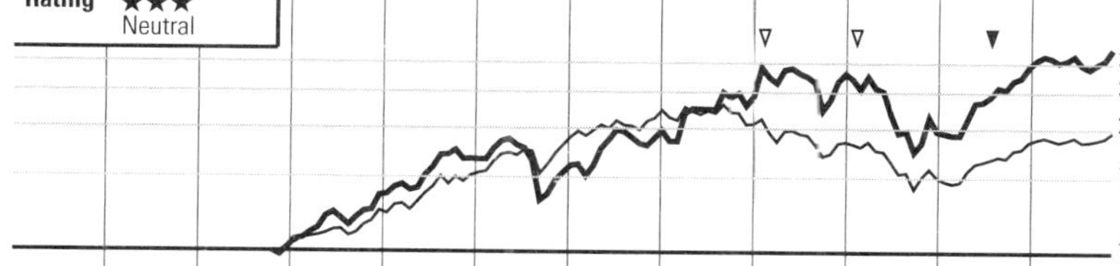

Growth of $10,000
- Investment Values of Fund
- Investment Values of S&P 500

Performance Quartile (within Category)

History

1993	1994	1995	1996	1997	1998	1999	2000	2001	2002	2003	12-04	History
—	—	13.54	16.83	20.52	17.80	21.46	23.94	26.23	17.53	27.61	32.45	NAV
—	—	8.73*	37.33	28.00	-4.21	28.06	27.46	17.10	-33.32	57.50	17.53	Total Return %
—	—	—	14.39	-5.35	-32.78	7.02	36.56	28.93	-11.23	28.83	6.66	+/-S&P 500
—	—	—	18.15	-4.24	-23.32	13.34	9.97	17.70	-18.79	21.91	1.06	+/-S&P Mid 400
—	—	0.00	0.30	0.00	0.00	0.00	0.00	0.00	0.00	0.00	0.00	Income Return %
—	—	—	37.03	28.00	-4.21	28.06	27.46	17.10	-33.32	57.50	17.53	Capital Return %
—	—	—	2	36	89	32	9	8	98	4	31	Total Rtn % Rank Cat
—	—	0.04	0.04	0.00	0.00	0.00	0.00	0.00	0.00	0.00	0.00	Income $
—	—	0.02	1.75	1.04	1.78	1.24	3.28	1.71	0.00	0.00	0.00	Capital Gains $
—	—	—	—	1.25	1.29	1.34	1.27	1.15	1.20	1.35	1.18	Expense Ratio %
—	—	—	—	-0.14	-0.25	-0.89	-0.38	-0.20	-0.51	-0.43	-0.37	Income Ratio %
—	—	—	—	155	169	257	242	192	177	158	145	Turnover Rate %
—	—	2	8	124	95	86	288	1,346	722	1,223	1,344	Net Assets $mil

Performance 12-31-04

	1st Qtr	2nd Qtr	3rd Qtr	4th Qtr	Total
2000	12.95	2.93	8.66	0.89	27.46
2001	9.57	6.98	-22.84	29.48	17.10
2002	-2.09	-23.23	-23.23	15.56	-33.32
2003	-2.57	26.41	9.12	17.19	57.50
2004	6.41	1.46	-5.37	15.03	17.53

Trailing	Total Return%	+/- S&P 500	+/- S&P Mid 400	%Rank Cat	Growth of $10,000
3 Mo	15.03	5.80	2.88	10	11,503
6 Mo	8.86	1.67	-0.93	64	10,886
1 Yr	17.53	6.66	1.06	31	11,753
3 Yr Avg	7.27	3.69	-3.24	75	12,343
5 Yr Avg	13.00	15.30	3.47	9	18,424
10 Yr Avg	—	—	—	—	—
15 Yr Avg	—	—	—	—	—

Tax Analysis	Tax-Adj Rtn%	%Rank Cat	Tax-Cost Rat	%Rank Cat
3 Yr (estimated)	7.27	66	0.00	1
5 Yr (estimated)	11.37	9	1.44	72
10 Yr (estimated)	—	—	—	—

Potential Capital Gain Exposure: 10% of assets

Rating and Risk

Time Period	Load-Adj Return %	Morningstar Rtn vs Cat	Morningstar Risk vs Cat	Morningstar Risk-Adj Rating
1 Yr	17.53			
3 Yr	7.27	-Avg	High	★★
5 Yr	13.00	+Avg	High	★★★
10 Yr	—	—	—	—
Incept	17.12			

Other Measures	Standard Index S&P 500	Best Fit Index Russ MG
Alpha	3.8	0.6
Beta	1.57	1.32
R-Squared	85	89
Standard Deviation	28.12	
Mean	7.27	
Sharpe Ratio	0.21	

Portfolio Analysis 11-30-04

Share change since 10-04 Total Stocks:135	Sector	PE	YTD Ret%	% Assets
⊕ Career Education	Consumer	20.6	-0.62	2.55
⊕ Cephalon	Health	—	5.10	2.40
⊖ Clear Channel Communicat	Media	23.5	-27.57	2.06
⊕ Navistar International	Ind Mtrls	17.5	-8.17	2.03
⊖ Unumprovident	Financial	—	16.09	2.02
⊕ E*Trade Financial	Financial	13.7	18.18	1.93
Nextel Communications	Telecom	11.1	6.95	1.77
Calpine	Utilities	—	-18.09	1.66
⊖ Omnicare	Health	14.0	-14.07	1.52
⊕ United Microelectronics	Hardware	27.1	-22.98	1.45
Genworth Financial	Financial	—	—	1.44
GlobalSantaFe	Energy	NMF	34.38	1.44
⊖ CIT Group	Financial	13.2	29.28	1.40
⊕ Boston Scientific	Health	32.3	-3.29	1.39
⊖ Knight Trading Group	Financial	—	-25.31	1.31
Patterson-UTI Energy	Energy	33.3	18.55	1.30
⊕ Marathon Oil	Energy	—	17.07	1.30
Office Depot	Consumer	16.4	3.89	1.30
⊖ Abercrombie & Fitch A	Consumer	23.6	92.74	1.27
⊕ Ivax	Health	20.8	-17.19	1.25

Current Investment Style

Value Blnd Growth; Large / Mid / Small

Market Cap	%
Giant	1.5
Large	25.1
Mid	66.6
Small	6.8
Micro	0.0

Avg $mil: 4,706

Value Measures		Rel Category
Price/Earnings	17.42	1.03
Price/Book	1.74	0.80
Price/Sales	0.81	0.76
Price/Cash Flow	6.59	1.05
Dividend Yield %	0.55	0.55

Growth Measures	%	Rel Category
Long-Term Erngs	13.26	1.06
Book Value	2.53	0.36
Sales	4.23	0.75
Cash Flow	-11.10	NMF
Historical Erngs	-0.32	NMF

Profitability	%	Rel Category
Return on Equity	10.09	0.73
Return on Assets	4.37	0.67
Net Margin	7.02	0.77

Sector Weightings	% of Stocks	Rel S&P 500	3 Year High	3 Year Low
Info	22.97	1.07		
Software	2.10	0.49	6	2
Hardware	13.95	1.37	18	13
Media	4.62	1.20	5	1
Telecom	2.30	0.73	7	2
Service	49.65	1.07		
Health	13.77	1.10	16	5
Consumer	16.14	1.78	16	5
Business	5.99	1.48	10	6
Financial	13.75	0.66	19	13
Mfg	27.38	0.85		
Goods	3.02	0.32	6	1
Ind Mtrls	7.19	0.57	13	7
Energy	13.17	1.84	15	10
Utilities	4.00	1.35	5	2

Composition

Cash	0.1
Stocks	99.9
Bonds	0.0
Other	0.0
Foreign (% of Stock)	6.5

Morningstar's Take by Todd Trubey 10-29-04

Dreyfus Midcap Value provides a thrilling ride.

Figuring out what this closed, somewhat unusual mid-blend fund does for an overall portfolio is key. For most shareowners, it should support a core large-cap holding by zigging when large-caps zag; on that score, it has done well. From 1996 to 1999 when large caps led the equity markets, the fund's 21% annualized returned lagged the S&P 500 Index's 26% mark. But when the S&P dove an average of 5% annually from 2000 to 2003, this fund gained 12% annually. And on a fundamental basis, this fund will slide into a portfolio nicely, not holding too many large or small caps.

Because comanagers Peter Higgins and Dave Daglio have an unusual approach, the fund's behavior can be quirky, especially over the short term. On the one hand, they're value managers who look for decent firms with positive catalysts trading at cheap prices. So the fund can do well versus its mid-blend category peers when value stocks do better--as it did in 2000. On the other hand, the managers are more contrarian than most and like to buy battered tech stocks. A dive into semiconductors made the fund look awful in 2002 but tremendous in 2003. Ultimately, shareholders here must be able to handle erratic returns.

After all, these comanagers see themselves primarily as bottom-up stock-pickers working the mid-cap universe. They opportunistically loaded up on Kmart in late 2003 and early 2004 when it traded below $30 per share and sold in June 2004 after it more than doubled. They're fearless, too: In July they bought Boston Scientific and Cardinal Health after those stocks plummeted on bad news. While the comanagers don't intentionally overload sectors compared to an index or peers, de facto sector bets are common and heavy.

Although certainly not for everyone, this quirky fund works well for its patient owners.

Address:	The Dreyfus Corporation New York NY 10166 800-373-9387
Web Address:	www.dreyfus.com
Inception:	09-29-95*
Advisor:	Dreyfus Corporation
Subadvisor:	None
NTF Plans:	Fidelity Retail-NTF, Schwab OneSource

Minimum Purchase:	Closed	Add: —	IRA: —
Min Auto Inv Plan:	Closed	Add: —	
Sales Fees:	No-load, 1.00%R		
Management Fee:	0.75%		
Actual Fees:	Mgt:0.75%	Dist:	
Expense Projections:	3Yr:$381	5Yr:$660	10Yr:$1455
Income Distrib:	Annually		

Dreyfus Prem Bal Opp J

Ticker	Load	NAV	Yield	Total Assets	Mstar Category
THPBX	Closed	$19.59	1.1%	$772 mil	Moderate Allocation

Governance and Management

Fiduciary Grade: D

Portfolio Manager(s)

Seasoned. Tom Plumb, principal of the fund's subadvisor, has been part of the management team of this fund since its 1987 inception and became lead manager in 1992. In 2002, David Duchow and Tim O'Brien, comanagers of Thompson Plumb Blue Chip, were appointed comanagers on this fund. Plumb has about $300,000 of his own money invested in the fund.

Strategy

Unlike many of his peers, manager Tom Plumb will look very broadly across the financial markets in search of value. He uses bonds to temper stock-price volatility, but his asset allocation is generally quite aggressive. Plumb buys growth companies that have fallen out of favor. On the bond front, he prefers intermediate-term, investment-grade issues. He'll adjust duration (a measure of interest-rate sensitivity) according to his view of the direction of interest rates and will opportunistically scoop up beaten-down bonds.

Historical Profile

Return: High
Risk: Above Avg
Rating: ★★★★ Above Avg

Investment Style: Equity Stock %

73% 70% 68% 64% 65% 67% 67% 67%

▼ Manager Change
∇ Partial Manager Change

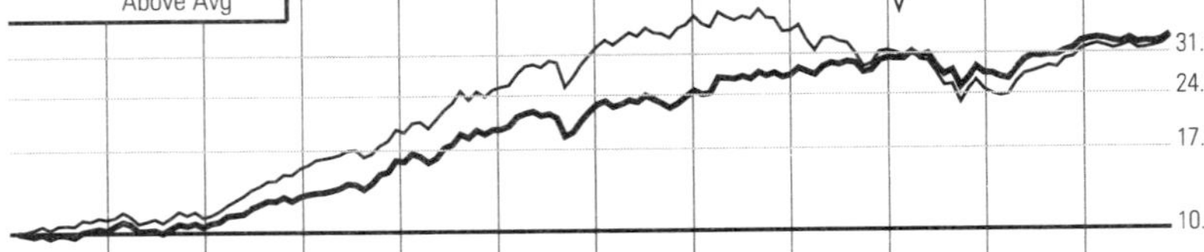

Growth of $10,000
— Investment Values of Fund
— Investment Values of S&P 500

Performance Quartile (within Category)

History

1993	1994	1995	1996	1997	1998	1999	2000	2001	2002	2003	12-04	History
13.65	12.02	13.33	14.84	16.29	17.70	17.67	17.08	17.35	15.47	18.61	19.59	NAV
4.45	1.47	20.03	23.09	22.54	16.87	8.87	10.21	11.07	-9.39	21.96	7.01	Total Return %
-5.61	0.16	-17.50	0.15	-10.81	-11.70	-12.17	19.31	22.95	12.70	-6.71	-3.86	+/-S&P 500
-7.28	3.42	-4.74	11.75	3.34	4.48	-3.98	5.77	10.91	1.15	-2.10	-4.16	+/-DJ 60%
1.91	2.06	1.91	1.71	0.87	1.16	1.20	1.51	1.51	1.47	1.62	1.11	Income Return %
2.54	-0.59	18.12	21.38	21.67	15.71	7.67	8.70	9.56	-10.86	20.34	5.90	Capital Return %
92	10	93	4	26	30	62	11	3	27	32	75	Total Rtn % Rank Cat
0.27	0.28	0.23	0.23	0.13	0.19	0.21	0.27	0.26	0.26	0.25	0.01	Income $
0.66	1.54	0.86	1.34	1.71	1.08	1.34	2.08	1.31	0.00	0.00	0.12	Capital Gains $
1.40	1.42	1.49	1.45	1.40	1.30	1.25	1.22	1.15	1.10	1.07	—	Expense Ratio %
1.89	1.84	1.71	1.32	1.04	1.16	1.24	1.42	1.73	1.91	1.90	—	Income Ratio %
92	110	111	135	77	83	67	78	58	79	42	—	Turnover Rate %
—	—	18	21	37	50	57	60	87	133	234	250	Net Assets $mil

Performance 12-31-04

	1st Qtr	2nd Qtr	3rd Qtr	4th Qtr	Total
2000	8.49	0.78	0.21	0.59	10.21
2001	0.12	6.55	-4.72	9.28	11.07
2002	3.69	-8.45	-12.39	8.95	-9.39
2003	-3.56	15.55	0.41	9.00	21.96
2004	1.40	0.27	-2.33	7.76	7.01

Trailing	Total Return%	+/- S&P 500	+/- DJ 60%	%Rank Cat	Growth of $10,000
3 Mo	7.76	-1.47	0.28	27	10,776
6 Mo	5.25	-1.94	-2.28	77	10,525
1 Yr	7.01	-3.86	-4.16	75	10,701
3 Yr Avg	5.75	2.17	-1.51	31	11,826
5 Yr Avg	7.68	9.98	2.44	5	14,477
10 Yr Avg	12.80	0.73	2.31	5	33,350
15 Yr Avg	10.92	-0.01	0.97	9	47,331

Tax Analysis	Tax-Adj Rtn%	%Rank Cat	Tax-Cost Rat	%Rank Cat
3 Yr (estimated)	5.27	22	0.45	31
5 Yr (estimated)	6.31	5	1.27	60
10 Yr (estimated)	10.71	5	1.85	54

Potential Capital Gain Exposure: 14% of assets

Rating and Risk

Time Period	Load-Adj Return %	Morningstar Rtn vs Cat	Morningstar Risk vs Cat	Morningstar Risk-Adj Rating
1 Yr	7.01			
3 Yr	5.75	+Avg	High	★★★
5 Yr	7.68	High	+Avg	★★★★★
10 Yr	12.80	High	+Avg	★★★★★
Incept	10.42			

Other Measures	Standard Index S&P 500	Best Fit Index Russ 1000 Vl
Alpha	2.5	-1.4
Beta	0.79	0.80
R-Squared	88	89
Standard Deviation	13.31	
Mean	5.75	
Sharpe Ratio	0.33	

Portfolio Analysis 11-30-04

Total Stocks:44 Share change since 10-31-04	Sectors	P/E Ratio	YTD Return %	% Net Assets
Cardinal Health	Health	16.9	-5.42	2.45
⊕ Corinthian Colleges	Consumer	21.3	-2.79	2.44
⊕ Career Education	Consumer	20.6	5.13	2.37
⊕ First Health Group	Health	14.2	0.91	2.37
Bisys Group	Business	23.1	-7.11	2.30
⊕ Electronic Data Systems	Business	—	-5.24	2.20
⊕ Pfizer	Health	22.0	-2.75	2.14
⊕ Microsoft	Software	36.1	0.04	2.10
General Electric	Ind Mtrls	22.8	-3.01	1.98

Total Fixed-Income:46	Date of Maturity	Amount $000	Value $000	% Net Assets
Philip Morris Cos 6.375%	02-01-06	10,315	10,578	1.48
Intl Lease Fin 4.75%	07-01-09	10,015	10,190	1.43
Marsh & Mclennan Cos 5.37	03-15-07	10,000	10,159	1.42
FNMA 5%	11-28-14	10,000	10,034	1.41
Morgan Stanley 4%	01-15-10	10,000	9,834	1.38
At&T Wireless Svcs 7.875%	03-01-11	8,000	9,368	1.31
Bristol Myers Squibb 4.75	10-01-06	7,750	7,940	1.11
FHLMC 2.375%	02-15-07	8,000	7,853	1.10
Goldman Sachs Grp 7.35%	10-01-09	6,000	6,805	0.95

Equity Style
Style: Blend
Size: Large-Cap

Value Measures		Rel Category
Price/Earnings	16.74	1.01
Price/Book	2.39	0.98
Price/Sales	0.98	0.74
Price/Cash Flow	6.22	0.86
Dividend Yield %	1.56	0.99

Growth Measures	%	Rel Category
Long-Term Erngs	12.02	1.03
Book Value	9.88	1.72
Sales	10.91	2.11
Cash Flow	12.47	1.56
Historical Erngs	9.70	0.89

Market Cap %			
Giant	45.2	Small	6.5
Large	26.5	Micro	0.0
Mid	21.8	Avg $mil:	26,131

Fixed-Income Style
Duration: Short-Term
Quality: High

Avg Eff Duration [1]	0.0 Yrs
Avg Eff Maturity	—
Avg Credit Quality	AA
Avg Wtd Coupon	5.43%

[1]figure provided by fund as of 11-30-04

Sector Weightings	% of Stocks	Rel S&P 500	3 Year High	3 Year Low
Info	15.04	0.70		
Software	3.16	0.73	7	3
Hardware	2.30	0.23	8	2
Media	5.98	1.56	8	4
Telecom	3.60	1.14	7	2
Service	68.71	1.48		
Health	20.68	1.65	24	20
Consumer	14.32	1.58	15	4
Business	19.54	4.82	20	12
Financial	14.17	0.68	22	9
Mfg	16.24	0.51		
Goods	7.07	0.76	7	2
Ind Mtrls	5.27	0.42	14	5
Energy	3.90	0.54	5	0
Utilities	0.00	0.00	0	0

Composition

Cash	3.9
Stocks	66.6
Bonds	27.5
Other	2.0
Foreign (% of Stock)	2.5

Morningstar's Take by Andrew Gogerty 12-29-04

Dreyfus Premier Balanced Opportunity has stumbled, but it remains a solid option.

This fund is on pace for an unfamiliar finish in 2004. Its 6.9% year-to-date gain through December 28 trails 74% of its moderate-allocation rivals and is in direct contrast to its otherwise consistent history. After all, this is only the second time in the past eight years that the fund has landed outside the category's top third.

Manager Tom Plumb's focus on health-care stocks (currently 21% of assets) has weighed heavily on returns this year as pharmaceutical stocks have fallen on negative news surrounding some of the industry's most visible drugs including Vioxx and Celebrex. But Plumb has stuck with his picks such as Pfizer, believing that the bad news is already reflected in its valuation. He also thinks the economy will grow at a slower pace in the near term, and that stable, high-quality companies such as Pfizer will thrive.

Plumb has also increased the fund's stake in business service firms such as Bisys Group and Fiserv. He believes that these firms will benefit from an increase in demand for compliance and accounting software in the financial industry. These picks have only posted moderate gains thus far, also limiting the fund. Still, we remain confident in Plumb, as he has posted a strong record by making prudent asset-allocation calls and investing across the market-cap spectrum.

We are also comfortable with Plumb's ability to handle asset growth. A fund merger and access to Dreyfus' distribution channel has increased fund assets to more than $700 million, and a potential merger with sibling Premier Balanced (pending shareholder approval) would add another $240 million. Plumb's strategy hasn't been impacted thus far, as his primary focus is on highly liquid issues such as large-cap stocks and Treasuries. But investors should remain watchful of this fund's expense ratio, as fund mergers have rarely resulted in lower fees over the long haul.

Address:	Dreyfus Premier Uniondale, NY 11556-0144 800-554-4611
Web Address:	www.dreyfus.com
Inception:	03-16-87
Advisor:	Dreyfus Corporation
Subadvisor:	Wisconsin Capital Management
NTF Plans:	Fidelity Retail-NTF, CommonWealth NTF

Minimum Purchase:	Closed	Add: —	IRA: —
Min Auto Inv Plan:	Closed	Add: —	
Sales Fees:	No-load		
Management Fee:	0.80%		
Actual Fees:	—	Dist:	
Expense Projections:	3Yr:$372	5Yr:$644	10Yr:$1420
Income Distrib:	Annually		

Dreyfus Prem Emerg A

Ticker	Load	NAV	Yield	Total Assets	Mstar Category
DRFMX	Closed	$13.61	0.4%	$1,049 mil	Diversified Emerging Mkts

Governance and Management

Fiduciary Grade: D

Portfolio Manager(s)

Kirk Henry has run this fund since its mid-1996 inception. He has more than a decade of experience as an international-value manager, and he has 10 analysts who work with him on this offering. He also runs no-load USAA Emerging Markets.

Strategy

Manager Kirk Henry won't buy a stock unless it is in the cheapest 40% of its market and is less expensive than the majority of its global competitors. Henry also insists on good earnings prospects and catalysts for improvement, and he sells holdings as soon as they appreciate out of the bottom 40% of their markets. It has a 1% redemption fee on shares held fewer than six months.

Historical Profile

Return Above Avg
Risk Below Avg
Rating ★★★★ Above Avg

Investment Style: Equity Stock %

1996	1997	1998	1999	2000	2001	2002	2003	2004
76%	91%	88%	87%	93%	92%	93%	94%	95%

▼ Manager Change
▽ Partial Manager Change

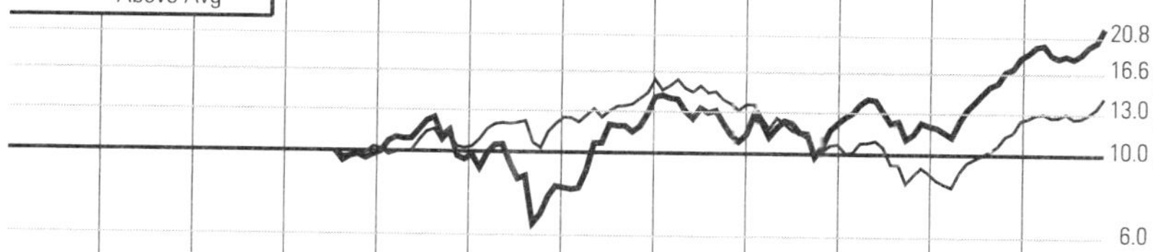

Performance Quartile (within Category)

1993	1994	1995	1996	1997	1998	1999	2000	2001	2002	2003	12-04	History
—	—	—	12.42	11.76	9.53	15.50	10.68	11.34	11.09	16.81	19.61	NAV
—	—	—	-0.30*	-1.53	-18.01	74.92	-20.30	7.70	-1.36	52.54	26.88	Total Return %
—	—	—	—	-3.31	-37.94	47.89	-6.11	29.12	14.58	13.95	6.63	+/-MSCI EAFE
—	—	—	—	11.92	9.66	10.83	11.60	12.38	6.61	0.95	4.43	+/-MSCI EmrMkt
—	—	—	0.00	0.14	0.77	1.15	0.86	1.50	0.84	0.96	0.45	Income Return %
—	—	—	—	-1.67	-18.78	73.77	-21.16	6.20	-2.20	51.58	26.43	Capital Return %
—	—	—	—	47	8	39	5	4	19	60	21	Total Rtn % Rank Cat
—	—	—	0.02	0.02	0.09	0.11	0.13	0.16	0.10	0.11	0.01	Income $
—	—	—	0.02	0.44	0.02	1.01	1.59	0.00	0.00	0.00	1.64	Capital Gains $
—	—	—	—	0.85	1.94	1.88	1.85	1.79	1.82	1.96	1.86	Expense Ratio %
—	—	—	—	0.07	0.54	1.42	1.48	1.02	2.18	0.90	0.97	Income Ratio %
—	—	—	—	20	87	88	106	78	62	49	47	Turnover Rate %
—	—	—	16	63	58	191	218	287	470	877	1,014	Net Assets $mil

Performance 12-31-04

	1st Qtr	2nd Qtr	3rd Qtr	4th Qtr	Total
2000	-1.23	-5.23	-8.82	-6.63	-20.30
2001	-1.31	9.01	-18.54	22.89	7.70
2002	12.26	-4.48	-15.38	8.70	-1.36
2003	-6.58	23.94	12.46	17.15	52.54
2004	8.15	-6.27	6.10	17.97	26.88

Trailing	Total Return%	+/- MSCI EAFE	+/- MSCI EmrMkt	%Rank Cat	Growth of $10,000
3 Mo	17.97	2.65	1.16	32	11,797
6 Mo	25.17	10.17	-0.28	55	12,517
1 Yr	26.88	6.63	4.43	21	12,688
3 Yr Avg	24.05	12.16	4.51	22	19,089
5 Yr Avg	10.38	11.51	8.29	11	16,385
10 Yr Avg	—	—	—	—	—
15 Yr Avg	—	—	—	—	—

Tax Analysis	Tax-Adj Rtn%	%Rank Cat	Tax-Cost Rat	%Rank Cat
3 Yr (estimated)	20.77	49	0.71	79
5 Yr (estimated)	7.37	17	1.57	98
10 Yr (estimated)	—	—	—	—

Potential Capital Gain Exposure: 32% of assets

Rating and Risk

Time Period	Load-Adj Return %	Morningstar Rtn vs Cat	Morningstar Risk vs Cat	Morningstar Risk-Adj Rating
1 Yr	19.58			
3 Yr	21.63	Avg	-Avg	★★★
5 Yr	9.08	+Avg	-Avg	★★★★
10 Yr	—	—	—	—
Incept	9.56			

Other Measures	Standard Index S&P 500	Best Fit Index MSCI EmrMkt
Alpha	12.1	5.6
Beta	0.91	0.89
R-Squared	77	95

Standard Deviation	20.03
Mean	24.05
Sharpe Ratio	1.15

Portfolio Analysis 11-30-04

Share change since 10-04 Total Stocks:153	Sector	Country	% Assets
⊖ Korea Electric Power	Utilities	Korea	2.78
⊖ Nedcor Ltd	Financial	South Africa	2.58
⊕ China Mobile	Telecom	Hong Kong	2.38
Telefonos de Mexico SA A	Telecom	Mexico	2.34
Petroleo Brasileiro ADR	Energy	Brazil	2.02
⊕ Samsung Electronics	Goods	Korea	1.70
Lukoil ADR	Energy	Russia	1.59
Reliance Industries Ltd	Ind Mtrls	India	1.58
⊖ KT ADR	Telecom	Korea	1.58
Coca-Cola Femsa SA ADR	Goods	Mexico	1.48
Anglo American	Ind Mtrls	U.K.	1.45
⊖ Old Mutual	Financial	U.K.	1.40
⊖ United Microelectronics	Hardware	Taiwan	1.34
☼ United Microelect	Hardware	Taiwan	1.31
Sasol Ltd	Ind Mtrls	South Africa	1.30
⊕ Sappi Ltd	Ind Mtrls	South Africa	1.29
Mahanagar Telephone Niga	Telecom	India	1.25
Kimberly-Clark de Mexico	Ind Mtrls	Mexico	1.25
⊖ Compal Electncs GDR 144A	Hardware	Taiwan	1.23
⊖ Nampak Ltd	Goods	South Africa	1.19

Current Investment Style

Value Blnd Growth

Market Cap	%
Giant	31.2
Large	31.3
Mid	31.6
Small	4.6
Micro	1.3
Avg $mil: 4,905	

Value Measures		Rel Category
Price/Earnings	10.28	1.13
Price/Book	1.31	0.85
Price/Sales	0.69	0.83
Price/Cash Flow	4.80	1.10
Dividend Yield %	3.40	1.24

Growth Measures	%	Rel Category
Long-Term Erngs	12.83	0.66
Book Value	7.59	2.19
Sales	11.58	1.00
Cash Flow	3.18	0.43
Historical Erngs	4.30	0.62

Composition

Cash	2.7	Bonds	0.0
Stocks	94.8	Other	2.5
Foreign (% of Stock)			99.5

Sector Weightings	% of Stocks	Rel MSCI EAFE	3 Year High	Low
Info	23.21	1.40		
Software	0.00	0.00	2	[illegible]
Hardware	7.71	2.11	8	[illegible]
Media	0.00	0.00	0	[illegible]
Telecom	15.50	1.61	16	13
Service	28.20	0.63		
Health	2.43	0.33	3	1
Consumer	4.51	0.89	6	4
Business	3.21	0.59	7	2
Financial	18.05	0.67	19	13
Mfg	48.58	1.26		
Goods	18.63	1.36	19	16
Ind Mtrls	17.06	1.39	23	16
Energy	7.07	0.96	11	7
Utilities	5.82	1.09	10	6

Regional Exposure	% Stock		
UK/W. Europe	3	N. America	1
Japan	0	Latn America	15
Asia X Japan	60	Other	21

Country Exposure	% Stock		
South Korea	19	India	12
Taiwan	12	Brazil	8
South Africa	12		

Morningstar's Take by William Samuel Rocco 11-21-04

The closed Dreyfus Premier Emerging Markets remains one of the best emerging-markets funds around.

This offering boasts an impressive management team. Kirk Henry has been running the fund since it opened in June 1996, which makes him one of the longer-serving managers in the category. Moreover, while Henry lost one of his analysts earlier this year, he plans to replace the departing analyst soon and he intends to hire an additional analyst in 2005. Thus, he has more analytical support than many of his counterparts.

Henry and his team follow a sound bargain-oriented discipline that moderates the considerable risk that comes with concentrating on emerging-markets stocks. Indeed, thanks to Henry's dedication to cheap stocks and issue diversification, the fund has been less volatile than most members of its wild category over time, and it has tended to hold up well in the developing world's many sell-offs. It lost 3 percentage points less than the group norm of 9.5% this spring, for example, thanks to its aversion to high-flying materials names--which tanked on fears of a slowdown in China--as well as its bias toward consumer staples and other defensive issues.

Furthermore, although its conservative style can be a liability in strong emerging-markets surges, the fund generally performs well in more moderate rallies and in mixed climates, thanks to Henry's stock selection. The fund posted top-decile returns in 2001's up-and-down conditions, for instance, as Henry made good picks in several countries and sectors. As a result, the fund boasts superior long-term returns.

The fund certainly isn't perfect--and it's quite volatile in absolute terms--but it remains a top-notch emerging-markets play.

Address:	200 Park Avenue, New York NY 10166, 718-895-1206
Web Address:	www.dreyfus.com
Inception:	06-28-96*
Advisor:	Dreyfus Corporation
Subadvisor:	None
NTF Plans:	Schwab OneSource

Minimum Purchase:	Closed	Add: —	IRA: —
Min Auto Inv Plan:	Closed	Add: —	
Sales Fees:	5.75%L, 1.00%R		
Management Fee:	1.25%		
Actual Fees:	Mgt:1.25%	Dist:	
Expense Projections:	3Yr:$582	5Yr:$1001	10Yr:$2169
Income Distrib:	Annually		

Eaton Vance Fltg Rt A

Analyst Pick

Ticker	Load	NAV	Yield	SEC Yield	Total Assets	Mstar Category
EVBLX	2.25%	$10.23	2.9%	3.37%	$3,817 mil	Bank Loan

Governance and Management

Fiduciary Grade: C

Portfolio Manager(s)

Scott Page and Payson Swaffield have comanaged this fund since its inception in early 2001 (The A shares opened in mid-2003). Page and Swaffield are quite experienced, having managed Eaton Vance Prime Rate Reserves (a continuously offered closed-end bank-loan fund) since 1996. They have amassed a solid long-term track record.

Strategy

Managers Payson Swaffield and Scott Page invest in senior-secured floating-rate bank loans, the majority of which earn junklike ratings. They favor companies with strong cash flows and positive earnings, and stay away from those that rely heavily on outside capital to finance their businesses. They also place a big emphasis on diversification by spreading assets widely across issues and industries. Overall, the fund has a slightly more defensive profile than the category norm.

Historical Profile

Return
Risk
Rating Not Rated

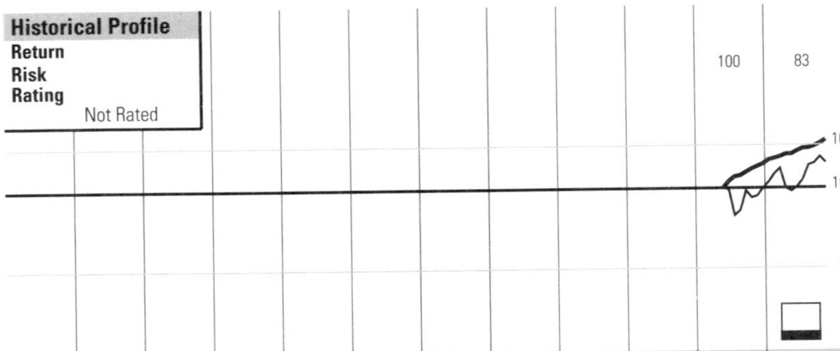

Investment Style
Fixed Income
Income Rtn %Rank Cat

▼ Manager Change
▽ Partial Manager Change

Growth of $10,000
— Investment Values of Fund
— Investment Values of LB Aggr

Performance Quartile (within Category)

1993	1994	1995	1996	1997	1998	1999	2000	2001	2002	2003	12-04	History
—	—	—	—	—	—	—	—	—	—	10.17	10.23	NAV
—	—	—	—	—	—	—	—	—	—	—	3.51	Total Return %
—	—	—	—	—	—	—	—	—	—	—	-0.83	+/-LB Aggr
—	—	—	—	—	—	—	—	—	—	—	1.66	+/-LB 1-5 YR
—	—	—	—	—	—	—	—	—	—	0.00	2.91	Income Return %
—	—	—	—	—	—	—	—	—	—	—	0.60	Capital Return %
—	—	—	—	—	—	—	—	—	—	—	87	Total Rtn % Rank Cat
—	—	—	—	—	—	—	—	—	—	0.18	0.29	Income $
—	—	—	—	—	—	—	—	—	—	0.00	0.00	Capital Gains $
—	—	—	—	—	—	—	—	—	—	1.09	—	Expense Ratio %
—	—	—	—	—	—	—	—	—	—	2.81	—	Income Ratio %
—	—	—	—	—	—	—	—	—	—	64	—	Turnover Rate %
—	—	—	—	—	—	—	—	—	—	387	1,179	Net Assets $mil

Performance 12-31-04

	1st Qtr	2nd Qtr	3rd Qtr	4th Qtr	Total
2000	—	—	—	—	—
2001	—	—	—	—	—
2002	—	—	—	—	—
2003	—	—	1.19	1.11	—*
2004	0.95	0.75	0.63	1.14	3.51

Trailing	Total Return%	+/- LB Aggr	+/- LB 1-5 YR	%Rank Cat	Growth of $10,000
3 Mo	1.14	0.19	0.99	67	10,114
6 Mo	1.77	-2.41	-0.11	76	10,177
1 Yr	3.51	-0.83	1.66	87	10,351
3 Yr Avg	—	—	—	—	—
5 Yr Avg	—	—	—	—	—
10 Yr Avg	—	—	—	—	—
15 Yr Avg	—	—	—	—	—

Tax Analysis	Tax-Adj Rtn%	%Rank Cat	Tax-Cost Rat	%Rank Cat
3 Yr (estimated)	—	—	—	—
5 Yr (estimated)	—	—	—	—
10 Yr (estimated)	—	—	—	—

Potential Capital Gain Exposure: 0% of assets

Rating and Risk

Time Period	Load-Adj Return %	Morningstar Rtn vs Cat	Morningstar Risk vs Cat	Morningstar Risk-Adj Rating
1 Yr	1.18			
3 Yr	—	—	—	—
5 Yr	—	—	—	—
10 Yr	—	—	—	—
Incept	2.85			

Other Measures	Standard Index LB Aggr	Best Fit Index
Alpha	—	—
Beta	—	—
R-Squared	—	—
Standard Deviation	—	
Mean	—	
Sharpe Ratio	—	

Portfolio Analysis 11-30-04

Total Fixed-Income:434	Date of Maturity	Amount $000	Value $000	% Net Assets
General Growth Propertie	11-12-08	54,175	54,437	1.01
Charter Communications O	04-27-11	53,865	53,802	0.99
Metro-Goldwyn-Mayer Stud	04-26-11	50,500	50,734	0.94
Regal Cinemas FRN	11-10-10	44,524	45,036	0.83
Community Health Systems	07-05-10	43,237	43,667	0.81
R.H. Donnelley Corporati	06-30-11	39,358	39,799	0.74
Qwest FRN	06-04-07	36,890	38,512	0.71
NextelCommunications FRN	12-15-10	37,853	37,943	0.70
Smurfit-Stone Container	11-01-11	37,190	37,835	0.70
Journal Register FRN	08-12-12	32,850	33,065	0.61
Centerpoint Engy FRN	10-07-06	32,759	32,912	0.61
Davita FRN	03-31-09	32,252	32,708	0.60
Boise Cascade Holdings L	09-29-10	32,091	32,670	0.60
Graphic Packaging Intl F	08-08-09	31,779	32,402	0.60
Dominos FRN	06-25-10	31,940	32,210	0.60
Emmis Oper FRN	11-10-11	31,100	31,463	0.58
Six Flags Theme Pks FRN	06-30-09	31,040	31,389	0.58
Nalco FRN	11-04-10	30,815	31,167	0.58
Directv Holdings Llc	03-06-10	29,841	30,315	0.56
Church & Dwight Co. Inc.	05-30-11	29,077	29,450	0.54

Current Investment Style

Duration: Short Int Long
Quality: High Med Low

[1] figure provided by fund

Avg Eff Duration[1]	—
Avg Eff Maturity	—
Avg Credit Quality	—
Avg Wtd Coupon	0.03%
Avg Wtd Price	101.20% of par

Coupon Range	% of Bonds	Rel Cat
0% PIK	99.5	2.0
0% to 6%	99.6	1.1
6% to 8%	0.2	0.0
8% to 10%	0.1	0.2
More than 10%	0.0	0.0

1.00=Category Average

Credit Analysis		% bonds 11-30-04	
US Govt	—	BB	—
AAA	—	B	—
AA	—	Below B	—
A	—	NR/NA	—
BBB	—		

Sector Breakdown	% of assets
US Treasuries	0
TIPS	0
US Agency	0
Mortgage Pass-Throughs	0
Mortgage CMO	0
Mortgage ARM	0
US Corporate	88
Asset-Backed	0
Convertible	0
Municipal	0
Corporate Inflation-Protected	0
Foreign Corporate	1
Foreign Govt	0

Composition			
Cash	11.3	Bonds	88.2
Stocks	0.1	Other	0.4

Special Securities	
Restricted/Illiquid Secs	Trace
Exotic Mortgage-Backed	0
Emerging-Markets Secs	0
Options/Futures/Warrants	No

Morningstar's Take by Scott Berry 11-22-04

We like Eaton Vance Floating Rate for its low volatility and proven management team.

This fund's managers keep a close eye on risk. Its bank loans are backed by assets that can be sold to repay loanholders should a borrower default. However, the assets aren't always enough to make loanholders whole, as we saw in 2001 and 2002 when a number of defaults socked investors with losses. To protect against such losses, managers Payson Swaffield and Scott Page place premiums on asset coverage and diversification (the fund's average loan size is just 0.21% of assets). Both methods have helped keep volatility to a minimum, while limiting losses. In fact, the fund's overall volatility is the lowest in the bank-loan category.

Swaffield and Page have led Eaton Vance's bank-loan effort since 1996 and have delivered good results during their tenure. Their funds failed to keep pace during a strong bank-loan rally in 2003, but they held up better than most during leaner periods in 2001 and 2002. And though the Eaton Vance bank loan funds don't rank at the top of the performance charts, they boast a category-best Sharpe Ratio (a measure of risk-adjusted performance).

We don't typically recommend new funds, but this fund, which opened in early 2001 and offered A shares in mid-2003, is basically a spin-off of Eaton Vance's older, more established bank-loan products. For years, Eaton Vance's bank-loan funds were structured as continuously offered closed-end funds, which allowed just quarterly redemptions. As liquidity and pricing have improved, Eaton Vance and others have launched true open-end bank-loan funds, such as this one, that allow daily redemptions. We think this structure will appeal to bank-loan newcomers.

This fund may not pack as big a punch as more-aggressive rivals, but we think its low volatility and seasoned management make it a good pick for investors willing to trade added return potential for added stability.

Address:	The Eaton Vance Building Boston MA 02109 800-225-6265
Web Address:	www.eatonvance.com
Inception:	05-05-03
Advisor:	Boston Management and Research
Subadvisor:	None
NTF Plans:	Federated Tr NTF, Fidelity Instl-NTF

Minimum Purchase:	$1000	Add: $50	IRA: $50
Min Auto Inv Plan:	$50	Add: $50	
Sales Fees:	2.25%L, 1.00%R		
Management Fee:	0.56%		
Actual Fees:	Mgt:0.56%	Dist:	
Expense Projections:	3Yr:$564	5Yr:$812	10Yr:$1524
Income Distrib:	Monthly		

Eaton Vance Inc Boston A

Analyst Pick

Ticker	Load	NAV	Yield	SEC Yield	Total Assets	Mstar Category
EVIBX	4.75%	$6.58	8.0%	5.57%	$1,814 mil	High Yield Bond

Governance and Management

Fiduciary Grade: C

Portfolio Manager(s)

Michael Weilheimer has run the fund since 1996. He was joined in January 2000 by Tom Huggins, who was a trader before becoming a portfolio manager. The pair is backed by six analysts who cover several sectors each.

Strategy

Management prefers bonds from issuers that have predictable cash flows. That means the fund has historically been light on cyclical issuers such as steel and paper companies and heavy on media, telecommunications, and cable companies. Management has also historically overweighted B rated bonds. The team has shown a willingness in the past few years, however, to make notable sector and credit-quality shifts to protect the portfolio from volatility and to jump on opportunities with gusto.

Historical Profile

Return Above Avg
Risk Average
Rating ★★★★ Above Avg

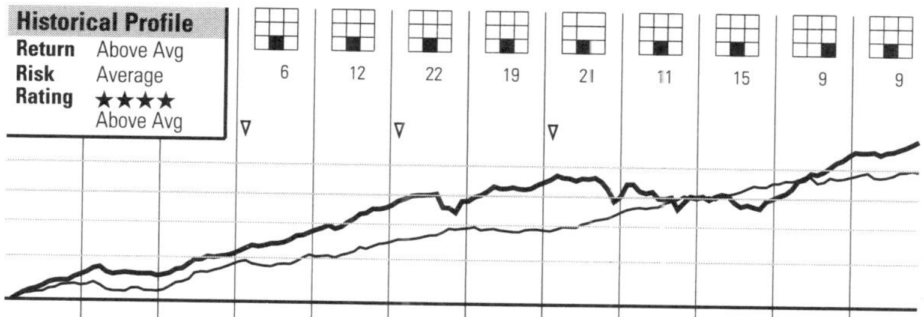

Investment Style: Fixed Income — Income Rtn %Rank Cat

▼ Manager Change
▽ Partial Manager Change

Growth of $10,000
— Investment Values of Fund
— Investment Values of LB Aggr

Performance Quartile (within Category)

1993	1994	1995	1996	1997	1998	1999	2000	2001	2002	2003	12-04	History
8.60	7.66	7.96	8.20	8.70	8.16	8.31	6.87	6.08	5.46	6.45	6.58	NAV
17.97	-1.29	15.29	13.74	16.27	2.90	12.19	-7.62	-0.14	-0.41	29.38	10.71	Total Return %
8.22	1.63	-3.18	10.11	6.62	-5.79	13.01	-19.25	-8.58	-10.66	25.28	6.37	+/-LB Aggr
-0.94	-0.32	-2.10	1.32	3.64	2.32	8.91	-2.41	-5.32	-3.52	1.45	-1.25	+/-CSFB Glb HY
11.84	10.21	11.28	10.52	9.86	9.50	10.39	10.95	12.11	10.11	10.42	8.47	Income Return %
6.13	-11.50	4.01	3.22	6.41	-6.60	1.80	-18.57	-12.25	-10.52	18.96	2.24	Capital Return %
61	22	77	34	4	25	5	58	73	45	15	29	Total Rtn % Rank Cat
0.91	0.84	0.82	0.80	0.77	0.79	0.81	0.87	0.79	0.59	0.55	0.53	Income $
0.00	0.00	0.00	0.00	0.00	0.00	0.00	0.00	0.00	0.00	0.00	0.00	Capital Gains $
1.03	1.04	1.09	1.07	1.05	1.04	1.01	1.04	1.06	1.07	1.02	1.06	Expense Ratio %
11.01	9.75	10.50	9.96	9.32	9.22	9.97	10.18	11.28	9.57	9.21	7.93	Income Ratio %
102	70	84	81	105	141	132	98	70	—	116	79	Turnover Rate %
103	98	113	154	209	248	385	638	819	832	1,212	1,326	Net Assets $mil

Performance 12-31-04

	1st Qtr	2nd Qtr	3rd Qtr	4th Qtr	Total
2000	2.69	-0.18	-1.87	-8.16	-7.62
2001	3.21	-4.08	-5.89	7.17	-0.14
2002	0.76	-3.46	-2.46	4.96	-0.41
2003	6.00	9.72	3.64	7.34	29.38
2004	1.77	0.23	3.05	5.32	10.71

Trailing	Total Return%	+/- LB Aggr	+/- CSFB Glb HY	%Rank Cat	Growth of $10,000
3 Mo	5.32	4.37	0.76	18	10,532
6 Mo	8.53	4.35	-0.73	53	10,853
1 Yr	10.71	6.37	-1.25	29	11,071
3 Yr Avg	12.57	6.38	-1.31	18	14,265
5 Yr Avg	5.64	-2.07	-2.53	47	13,157
10 Yr Avg	8.76	1.04	0.14	9	23,158
15 Yr Avg	9.41	1.71	-0.68	10	38,535

Tax Analysis	Tax-Adj Rtn%	%Rank Cat	Tax-Cost Rat	%Rank Cat
3 Yr (estimated)	7.12	43	3.29	84
5 Yr (estimated)	0.70	68	3.75	81
10 Yr (estimated)	4.18	14	3.74	82

Potential Capital Gain Exposure: -4% of assets

Rating and Risk

Time Period	Load-Adj Return %	Morningstar Rtn vs Cat	Morningstar Risk vs Cat	Morningstar Risk-Adj Rating
1 Yr	5.45			
3 Yr	10.76	Avg	Avg	★★★
5 Yr	4.62	Avg	+Avg	★★★
10 Yr	8.23	+Avg	Avg	★★★★
Incept	9.32			

Other Measures	Standard Index LB Aggr	Best Fit Index CSFB Glb HY
Alpha	11.3	-1.2
Beta	-0.01	1.01
R-Squared	0	93
Standard Deviation	7.19	
Mean	12.57	
Sharpe Ratio	1.57	

Portfolio Analysis 11-30-04

Total Fixed-Income:335	Date of Maturity	Amount $000	Value $000	% Net Assets
Nortel Networks Cv 4.25%	09-01-08	22,195	21,390	1.24
3815668 Cda 144A 8%	09-15-12	19,247	20,690	1.20
Universal City Dev Partn	04-01-10	16,080	18,733	1.09
Orion Pwr Hldgs 12%	05-01-10	14,185	17,944	1.04
Ugs 144A 10%	06-01-12	15,280	17,496	1.02
Crown European Hldgs Sa	03-01-13	13,895	16,500	0.96
Centennial Comms 10.125%	06-15-13	14,900	16,316	0.95
Insight Comms	02-15-11	16,320	15,749	0.91
Amkor Tech 7.75%	05-15-13	17,575	15,598	0.91
Dynegy 144A 10.125%	07-15-13	12,560	14,727	0.86
Rhodia 10.25%	06-01-10	13,065	14,567	0.85
Equistar Chemicals Lp /	05-01-11	12,550	14,558	0.85
Om Grp 9.25%	12-15-11	13,060	13,909	0.81
Western Wireless 9.25%	07-15-13	12,535	13,600	0.79
Waterford Gaming 144A 8.	09-15-12	12,258	13,177	0.77
Advcd Micro Devices 144A	11-01-12	12,855	13,176	0.77
NTL		187	13,001	0.76
Rainbow Natl Svcs 144A 1	09-01-14	11,690	12,450	0.72
Kabel Deutschland Gmbh 1	07-01-14	10,160	11,735	0.68
Venetian Casino Resort 1	06-15-10	10,205	11,685	0.68

Current Investment Style

Duration: Short Int Long — Quality: High Med Low

¹ figure provided by fund

Avg Eff Duration¹	3.5 Yrs
Avg Eff Maturity	6.8 Yrs
Avg Credit Quality	B
Avg Wtd Coupon	8.88%
Avg Wtd Price	106.10% of par

Coupon Range	% of Bonds	Rel Cat
0% PIK	7.0	1.5
0% to 8%	23.9	0.6
8% to 11%	62.0	1.1
11% to 14%	13.5	2.0
More than 14%	0.6	2.8

1.00=Category Average

Credit Analysis		% bonds 11-30-04	
US Govt	0	BB	7
AAA	9	B	57
AA	0	Below B	19
A	0	NR/NA	8
BBB	0		

Sector Breakdown	% of assets
US Treasuries	0
TIPS	0
US Agency	0
Mortgage Pass-Throughs	0
Mortgage CMO	0
Mortgage ARM	0
US Corporate	86
Asset-Backed	1
Convertible	2
Municipal	0
Corporate Inflation-Protected	0
Foreign Corporate	4
Foreign Govt	0

Composition			
Cash	7.9	Bonds	87.9
Stocks	1.6	Other	2.6

Special Securities	
Restricted/Illiquid Secs.	27
Exotic Mortgage-Backed	0
Emerging-Markets Secs	0
Options/Futures/Warrants	No

Morningstar's Take by Eric Jacobson 11-15-04

If history is any guide, Eaton Vance Income Fund of Boston's recent caution could prove to be a canary in a coal mine.

This fund's managers have tempered its aggressive tilt in 2004. We don't want to overstate the case, as its credit ratings haven't changed that much. Still, comanagers Michael Weilheimer and Thomas Huggins have taken steps to cut risk. They have trimmed bonds with zero-coupon structures, for example. They also sold some CCC bonds they felt were no longer paying enough to justify their risks. The pair have grown concerned that valuations are high, both on a relative basis among different high-yield strata and versus the Treasury market. So even though they don't view themselves as interest-rate bettors, the team has also shifted its focus to shorter-maturity bonds that are typically better protected in the event of a hiccup in the credit markets.

As we've alluded, that doesn't mean the fund has hidden in a cave. Weilheimer and Huggins continue to make individual picks they believe offer value. They own several smaller wireless names, for example, that carry low third-party ratings, but that are nothing like their old selves. Previously pouring cash into network buildouts, they now favor firms with lots of free cash flow and are taking steps to delever their balance sheets.

Why do we attach significance to this team's moves? The answer lies in their response to the market run up in telecom, in particular, prior to 2001. Unlike most typically aggressive managers, they slashed their riskiest holdings in time to avoid the market's worst 2001 and 2002 carnage.

This team doesn't predict that a bear high-yield market is around the corner. They simply don't want to be thick in the market's priciest bonds. If yields on such issues continue to grind lower, the fund may fall further behind. That seems a small price to pay to avoid bigger problems, though, and this team's record of success suggests their instincts are worth considering.

Address:	The Eaton Vance Building, Boston MA 02109, 800-225-6265
Web Address:	www.eatonvance.com
Inception:	06-15-72
Advisor:	Eaton Vance Management
Subadvisor:	None
NTF Plans:	DATALynx NTF, Federated Tr NTF

Minimum Purchase:	$1000	Add: $50	IRA: $50
Min Auto Inv Plan:	$1000	Add: $50	
Sales Fees:	4.75%L		
Management Fee:	0.62%		
Actual Fees:	Mgt:0.62%	Dist: —	
Expense Projections:	3Yr:$805	5Yr:$1047	10Yr:$1741
Income Distrib:	Monthly		

Eaton Vance Utilities A

Analyst Pick

Ticker	Load	NAV	Yield	Total Assets	Mstar Category
EVTMX	5.75%	$9.79	2.4%	$626 mil	Specialty-Utilities

Governance and Management

Fiduciary Grade: C

Portfolio Manager(s)

Judy Saryan took over management of the fund in March 1999. One development here: Eaton Vance named Saryan as a comanager of two recently launched funds, Eaton Vance Tax-Managed Dividend Income, and closed-end fund Eaton Vance Tax-Advantaged Dividend Income. These new responsibilities will require much of her time, but there is a great amount of overlap among the different funds' investable universes.

Strategy

Manager Judy Saryan has paid attention to earnings growth at times, but lately she has concentrated on companies with clean balance sheets, strong cash flow, and dividend growth. She has been more willing to devote a great percentage of the fund to foreign stocks than most rivals. Energy stocks, integrated oil concerns in particular, also play a role here.

Historical Profile

Return: High
Risk: Average
Rating: ★★★★★ Highest

Investment Style: Equity Stock %

1993	1994	1995	1996	1997	1998	1999	2000	2001	2002	2003	2004
	90%	83%	86%	86%	89%	96%	85%	91%	94%		

▼ Manager Change
▽ Partial Manager Change

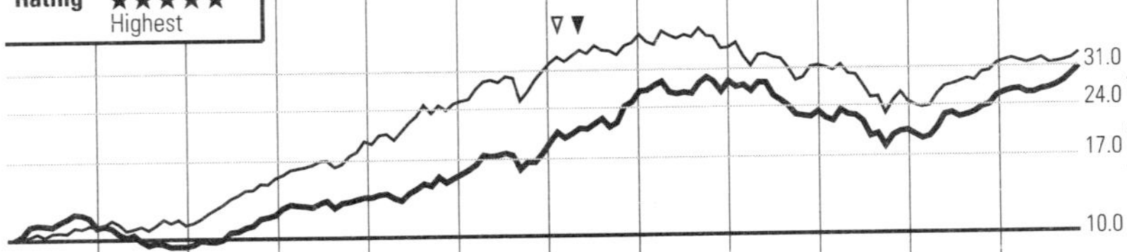

Growth of $10,000
— Investment Values of Fund
— Investment Values of S&P 500

Performance Quartile (within Category)

1993	1994	1995	1996	1997	1998	1999	2000	2001	2002	2003	12-04	History
9.13	7.63	9.13	8.77	8.45	10.15	11.65	10.06	7.74	6.58	8.04	9.79	NAV
9.57	-12.28	27.52	7.00	16.23	23.79	40.76	6.48	-18.94	-12.50	25.92	25.11	Total Return %
-0.49	-13.59	-10.01	-15.94	-17.12	-4.78	19.72	15.58	-7.06	9.59	-2.75	14.24	+/-S&P 500
-0.06	3.01	-4.46	-2.10	-6.77	4.91	46.78	-44.28	7.33	10.88	-3.47	-5.13	+/-DOWJNS UTIL
5.05	4.34	5.40	5.85	4.01	2.82	1.62	1.03	1.60	2.52	3.24	2.91	Income Return %
4.52	-16.62	22.12	1.15	12.22	20.97	39.14	5.45	-20.54	-15.02	22.68	22.20	Capital Return %
86	92	52	67	95	37	12	65	34	8	30	25	Total Rtn % Rank Cat
0.47	0.39	0.40	0.52	0.33	0.24	0.16	0.11	0.16	0.19	0.21	0.23	Income $
0.67	0.00	0.14	0.45	1.29	0.04	2.26	2.20	0.31	0.00	0.00	0.00	Capital Gains $
1.31	1.18	1.19	1.23	1.13	1.11	1.08	1.08	1.10	1.14	1.15	—	Expense Ratio %
4.64	4.90	4.49	5.59	4.06	2.75	1.33	1.18	1.62	2.99	2.81	—	Income Ratio %
63	107	103	166	169	78	93	149	169	146	106	—	Turnover Rate %
629	446	457	399	366	409	510	492	361	296	358	489	Net Assets $mil

Performance 12-31-04

	1st Qtr	2nd Qtr	3rd Qtr	4th Qtr	Total
2000	6.54	-7.10	10.62	-2.75	6.48
2001	-6.56	-3.33	-12.17	2.18	-18.94
2002	0.76	-7.52	-15.71	11.40	-12.50
2003	-4.27	17.26	0.21	11.94	25.92
2004	4.30	-0.34	5.96	13.60	25.11

Trailing	Total Return%	+/- S&P 500	+/- DOWJNS UTIL	%Rank Cat	Growth of $10,000
3 Mo	13.60	4.37	-0.87	15	11,360
6 Mo	20.37	13.18	-2.38	23	12,037
1 Yr	25.11	14.24	-5.13	25	12,511
3 Yr Avg	11.29	7.71	2.40	1	13,784
5 Yr Avg	3.54	5.84	-3.95	16	11,900
10 Yr Avg	12.64	0.57	1.64	3	32,880
15 Yr Avg	9.98	-0.95	2.34	1	41,659

Tax Analysis	Tax-Adj Rtn%	%Rank Cat	Tax-Cost Rat	%Rank Cat
3 Yr (estimated)	7.99	11	1.04	72
5 Yr (estimated)	0.40	23	1.88	79
10 Yr (estimated)	9.09	27	2.57	96

Potential Capital Gain Exposure: 21% of assets

Rating and Risk

Time Period	Load-Adj Return %	Morningstar Rtn vs Cat	Morningstar Risk vs Cat	Morningstar Risk-Adj Rating
1 Yr	17.91			
3 Yr	9.12	High	-Avg	★★★★★
5 Yr	2.32	+Avg	-Avg	★★★★
10 Yr	11.97	High	Avg	★★★★★
Incept	12.54			

Other Measures	Standard Index S&P 500	Best Fit Index Mstar Large Value
Alpha	8.0	5.0
Beta	0.81	0.83
R-Squared	72	80
Standard Deviation	15.85	
Mean	11.29	
Sharpe Ratio	0.63	

Portfolio Analysis 11-30-04

Share change since 10-04 Total Stocks:73	Sector	PE	YTD Ret%	% Assets
Entergy	Utilities	21.1	22.14	3.32
Verizon Communications	Telecom	32.4	20.25	3.26
Exelon	Utilities	16.1	37.55	3.23
Edison International	Utilities	45.8	52.08	3.22
PG & E	Utilities	3.7	19.84	3.21
TXU	Utilities	NMF	177.67	2.90
ADESA	Consumer	—	—	2.77
BellSouth	Telecom	12.7	1.94	2.59
SBC Communications	Telecom	15.4	3.74	2.43
⊕ E.ON	Utilities	—	—	2.40
Energy East	Utilities	18.3	24.39	2.37
TDC	Telecom	—	—	2.31
BCE	Telecom	18.1	12.67	2.14
Equitable Resources	Energy	13.0	45.53	2.10
ALLETE	Utilities	12.1	9.10	1.94
CMS Energy	Utilities	83.3	22.65	1.88
Enel	Utilities	—	—	1.88
Total SA ADR	Energy	17.0	23.39	1.84
BP PLC ADR	Energy	20.7	22.07	1.80
FirstEnergy	Utilities	15.2	16.62	1.77

Current Investment Style

Value Blnd Growth / Large Mid Small

Market Cap	%
Giant	26.8
Large	42.2
Mid	27.3
Small	3.7
Micro	0.0

Avg $mil: 13,447

Value Measures		Rel Category
Price/Earnings	14.92	0.98
Price/Book	1.83	1.04
Price/Sales	1.03	1.00
Price/Cash Flow	5.40	0.98
Dividend Yield %	2.75	0.92

Growth Measures	%	Rel Category
Long-Term Erngs	6.81	1.12
Book Value	4.06	2.67
Sales	2.31	0.57
Cash Flow	7.75	3.22
Historical Erngs	-2.26	NMF

Profitability	%	Rel Category
Return on Equity	14.94	1.32
Return on Assets	4.54	1.42
Net Margin	10.31	1.31

Industry Weightings	% of Stocks	Rel Cat
Telecom Srv	18.1	1.6
Electric Utls	47.5	0.8
Nat Gas Utls	8.7	0.9
Wireless Srv	2.4	0.5
Energy	17.1	2.0
Media	0.0	0.0
Network Eq	0.0	0.0
Water	2.0	2.9
Other	4.3	2.1

Composition

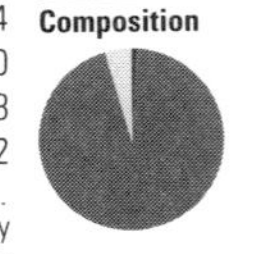

Cash	1.0
Stocks	94.3
Bonds	0.0
Other	4.7
Foreign (% of Stock)	34.5

Morningstar's Take by Paul Herbert 01-05-05

Eaton Vance Utilities remains our top utilities choice.

This fund stands apart from its rivals. While many utilities managers seek to balance safety and volatility by holding a mix of utilities and telecom stocks, this fund's manager doesn't stop there. For instance, finding regulatory climates friendlier in many foreign markets, Judy Saryan has placed about one third of the portfolio in overseas equities. The typical utilities offering stashes only 12% of assets abroad. In addition, the fund's 16% position in energy stocks--which is about two times the group norm--reflects Saryan's belief that integrated oil stocks are financially stronger and cheaper than utilities names.

This mix has worked well for the fund. When the category notched its worst showings in 2001 and 2002, due in large part to sliding telecom and unregulated utilities stocks in the United States, the fund's stake in issues like Canadian energy exploration firm Talisman Energy helped it to avoid disaster. In all, since Saryan's tenure began in early 1999, the fund hasn't finished a calendar year in the category's bottom third.

The fund held steady in 2004--managing to finish the year in the category's top quartile. Some of its foreign telecom picks slumped earlier in the year, as did Minnesota electric utility ALLETE, but most issues have rebounded nicely. (ALLETE stock gained more than 9% in 2004). The fund has also gotten a boost lately from its surging energy holdings: Top-10 holding TXU soared more than 160% in 2004. Saryan has not reduced the fund's energy stake, even with oil prices consistently above $40 per barrel. She said in summer 2004 that she finds these stocks attractive as long as the commodity price stays above $30 per barrel.

In all, an experienced manager, low fees, and the ability to keep its head above water in various market climates make this fund an appealing option.

Address:	The Eaton Vance Building Boston MA 02109 800-225-6265
Web Address:	www.eatonvance.com
Inception:	12-18-81
Advisor:	Boston Management and Research
Subadvisor:	None
NTF Plans:	DATALynx NTF, Federated Tr NTF

Minimum Purchase:	$1000	Add: $50	IRA: $1000
Min Auto Inv Plan:	$1000	Add: $50	
Sales Fees:	5.75%L, 0.25%S		
Management Fee:	0.75% mx./0.44% mn.		
Actual Fees:	Mgt:0.75%	Dist: —	
Expense Projections:	3Yr:$905	5Yr:$1146	10Yr:$1838
Income Distrib:	Monthly		

Eaton Vance Wld Health A

Ticker	Load	NAV	Yield	Total Assets	Mstar Category
ETHSX	5.75%	$10.66	0.0%	$2,619 mil	Specialty-Health

Governance and Management

Fiduciary Grade: C

Portfolio Manager(s)

Sam Isaly, founder of advisor OrbiMed Advisors, has been at the helm since 1989. Isaly is assisted by Sven Borho, Richard Klemm, Geoffery Hsu, and Trevor Polischuk, who have assisted him for at least several years but were named comanagers on Jan. 1, 2005. The firm specializes solely in health-care investing, with an unusually strong emphasis on the pharmaceutical and biotech industries. Isaly has a big investment in the fund and says he keeps 80% to 90% of his liquid assets in this and other accounts he manages.

Strategy

Management invests in pharmaceutical and biotechnology companies from both the United States and overseas. The fund has numerous quirks: an outsized biotech bet, one of the largest foreign stakes among offerings in its category, and a greater propensity for investing in small companies. Unlike many of its peers, the fund has scant exposure to health-care service providers and medical-equipment makers. Manager Sam Isaly tends to hang on to his picks for years, giving the fund a turnover far below the group norm.

Historical Profile

Return: Above Avg
Risk: Average
Rating: ★★★★ Above Avg

Investment Style: Equity — Stock %

1993	1994	1995	1996	1997	1998	1999	2000	2001	2002	2003	12-04
	93%	100%	83%	78%	90%	90%	86%	93%	96%		

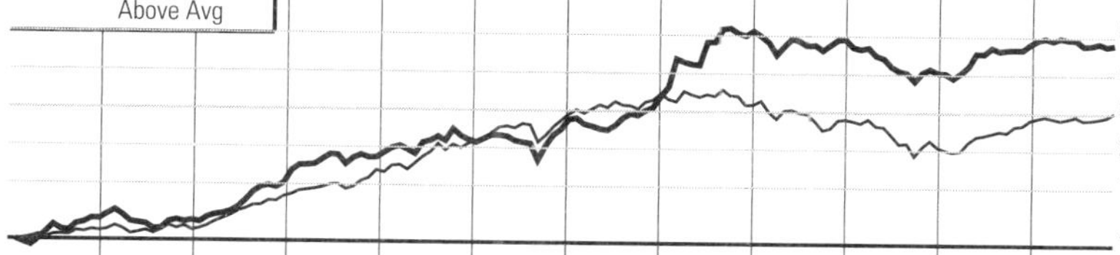

▼ Manager Change
▽ Partial Manager Change

Growth of $10,000
- Investment Values of Fund
- Investment Values of S&P 500

Performance Quartile (within Category)

1993	1994	1995	1996	1997	1998	1999	2000	2001	2002	2003	12-04	History
3.25	2.82	4.01	4.53	4.91	5.83	6.68	11.63	10.33	7.65	9.98	10.66	NAV
26.40	-6.32	61.11	18.25	10.50	23.53	23.98	81.56	-6.63	-25.94	30.46	6.81	Total Return %
16.34	-7.63	23.58	-4.69	-22.85	-5.04	2.94	90.66	5.25	-3.85	1.79	-4.06	+/-S&P 500
31.20	-17.10	6.25	-0.30	-26.38	-15.56	28.01	44.03	5.98	-5.13	11.03	2.26	+/-DJ Hlthcare
0.00	0.00	0.00	0.00	0.00	0.00	0.00	0.00	0.00	0.00	0.00	0.00	Income Return %
26.40	-6.32	61.11	18.25	10.50	23.53	23.98	81.56	-6.63	-25.94	30.46	6.81	Capital Return %
1	86	12	20	81	47	25	17	28	55	47	66	Total Rtn % Rank Cat
0.00	0.00	0.00	0.00	0.00	0.00	0.00	0.00	0.00	0.00	0.00	0.00	Income $
0.25	0.23	0.47	0.20	0.10	0.22	0.47	0.51	0.45	0.00	0.00	0.00	Capital Gains $
2.50	2.50	2.44	2.21	2.22	1.83	1.69	1.79	1.71	1.67	1.99	1.80	Expense Ratio %
-1.53	-1.65	-1.82	-1.81	-1.82	-1.21	-1.11	-1.29	-0.89	-0.90	-1.18	-1.08	Income Ratio %
77	49	45	66	14	34	41	31	24	38	27	13	Turnover Rate %
12	12	35	57	92	97	105	592	943	757	1,119	1,298	Net Assets $mil

Performance 12-31-04

	1st Qtr	2nd Qtr	3rd Qtr	4th Qtr	Total
2000	36.53	19.96	13.74	-2.53	81.56
2001	-19.26	13.42	-8.10	10.96	-6.63
2002	-7.36	-15.67	-12.14	7.90	-25.94
2003	0.13	18.93	3.73	5.61	30.46
2004	3.41	0.68	-3.18	5.96	6.81

Trailing	Total Return%	+/- S&P 500	+/- DJ Hlthcare	%Rank Cat	Growth of $10,000
3 Mo	5.96	-3.27	0.06	77	10,596
6 Mo	2.60	-4.59	1.60	56	10,260
1 Yr	6.81	-4.06	2.26	66	10,681
3 Yr Avg	1.05	-2.53	1.42	46	10,318
5 Yr Avg	11.84	14.14	8.33	20	17,498
10 Yr Avg	18.89	6.82	4.06	6	56,423
15 Yr Avg	16.76	5.83	—	12	102,191

Tax Analysis	Tax-Adj Rtn%	%Rank Cat	Tax-Cost Rat	%Rank Cat
3 Yr (estimated)	-0.92	63	0.00	1
5 Yr (estimated)	10.10	24	0.38	21
10 Yr (estimated)	17.07	6	0.94	27

Potential Capital Gain Exposure: 13% of assets

Rating and Risk

Time Period	Load-Adj Return %	Morningstar Rtn vs Cat	Morningstar Risk vs Cat	Morningstar Risk-Adj Rating
1 Yr	0.67			
3 Yr	-0.92	Avg	Avg	★★★
5 Yr	10.52	+Avg	Avg	★★★★
10 Yr	18.18	+Avg	Avg	★★★★
Incept	15.80			

Other Measures	Standard Index S&P 500	Best Fit Index DJ Hlthcare
Alpha	-1.8	2.0
Beta	0.82	1.11
R-Squared	60	72
Standard Deviation	16.15	
Mean	1.05	
Sharpe Ratio	-0.02	

Portfolio Analysis 11-30-04

Share change since 10-04 Total Stocks:34	Sector	PE	YTD Ret%	% Assets
Novartis	Health	—	—	7.75
Genzyme	Health	—	17.81	6.78
Amgen	Health	37.7	3.82	5.83
Pfizer	Health	22.0	-22.31	5.76
Takeda Chemical Industri	Health	—	—	4.68
Biogen IDEC	Health	—	81.50	4.51
⊖ MedImmune	Health	—	6.82	4.46
Schering-Plough	Health	—	21.56	4.07
Fujisawa Pharmaceutical	Health	—	—	4.07
Eli Lilly & Company	Health	24.3	-17.55	4.01
Altana Grp	Health	—	—	3.97
Genentech	Health	78.6	16.36	3.80
Affymetrix	Health	59.8	48.52	3.80
Serono	Health	—	—	3.73
Wyeth	Health	17.0	2.73	3.54
Gen-Probe	Health	44.3	23.97	3.48
Chugai Pharmaceutical	Health	—	—	2.77
OSI Pharmaceuticals	Health	—	132.09	2.42
Human Genome Sciences	Health	—	-9.28	2.37
NPS Pharmaceuticals	Health	—	-40.42	2.34

Current Investment Style

Value Blnd Growth — Large Mid Small

Market Cap	%
Giant	36.4
Large	26.6
Mid	21.1
Small	15.6
Micro	0.3

Avg $mil: 12,357

Value Measures		Rel Category
Price/Earnings	24.34	1.03
Price/Book	2.38	0.86
Price/Sales	4.45	1.57
Price/Cash Flow	10.20	0.94
Dividend Yield %	0.92	1.30

Growth Measures	%	Rel Category
Long-Term Erngs	4.89	0.92
Book Value	2.39	0.80
Sales	9.35	0.76
Cash Flow	6.14	0.33
Historical Erngs	-1.09	NMF

Profitability	%	Rel Category
Return on Equity	6.05	0.62
Return on Assets	0.96	0.31
Net Margin	7.11	0.93

Industry Weightings	% of Stocks	Rel Cat
Biotech	66.5	1.9
Drugs	28.4	1.0
Mgd Care	0.0	0.0
Hospitals	0.0	0.0
Other HC Srv	0.0	0.0
Diagnostics	0.0	0.0
Equipment	0.0	0.0
Good/Srv	5.1	1.1
Other	0.0	0.0

Composition

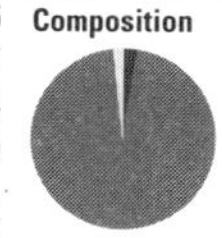

Cash	2.5
Stocks	95.7
Bonds	0.0
Other	1.8
Foreign (% of Stock)	29.6

Morningstar's Take by Christopher Davis 01-04-05

A unique approach and skilled management set Eaton Vance Worldwide Health Sciences apart from the crowd.

Most health-care offerings devote at least a small slice of their portfolios to medical-device makers, HMOs, and other health-care service providers. This offering, however, owns nothing but drug and biotechnology stocks. That reflects advisor OrbiMed Advisor's exclusive focus to both areas.

Few money managers are as specialized as OrbiMed. The firm has developed a wealth of analytical resources. Foremost among them is lead manager Sam Isaly, who has been at the helm here since 1989 and has three decades of experience in investing in health-care stocks. Isaly is assisted by four comanagers, including Sven Borho, who has followed European drug and global biotech stocks for the fund since 1991. Another, Richard Klemm, has a doctorate in molecular biology and has used his expertise to assess the prospects of emerging biotech firms for four years.

Isaly and his team unearthed a number of big winners in 2004, including Biogen Idec, OSI Pharmaceuticals, and Transkaryotic Therapies. However, large stakes in wayward pharmaceutical giants Pfizer and Eli Lilly, along with smaller holdings like NPS Pharmaceuticals, have weighed on returns. As a result, the fund's 7% gain in 2004 lagged nearly two-third of its peers.

Although the fund hasn't looked impressive lately, we're not terribly concerned. Isaly has compiled one of the health-care category's best long-term records. Importantly, we think the ingredients that led to his past success remain in place. Moreover, costs here are on he decline and Isaly expects the fund's expense ratio, which now stands at a pricey 1.81%, to fall to a more reasonable 1.60% this year. Though a flood of new assets in recent years means there's still a lot more room to cut costs here, we regard this fund as one of its category's better choices.

Address:	The Eaton Vance Building Boston MA 02109 800-262-1122
Web Address:	www.eatonvance.com
Inception:	07-26-85
Advisor:	Eaton Vance Management
Subadvisor:	Orbimed Advisers, Inc.
NTF Plans:	DATALynx NTF, Federated Tr NTF

Minimum Purchase:	$1000	Add: $50	IRA: $50
Min Auto Inv Plan:	$50	Add: $50	
Sales Fees:	5.75%L		
Management Fee:	0.25% mx./0.17% mn., 0.50%A		
Actual Fees:	Mgt:0.25%	Dist:0.25%	
Expense Projections:	3Yr:$1080	5Yr:$1445	10Yr:$2468
Income Distrib:	Annually		

Excelsior Val & Restruct

Ticker	Load	NAV	Yield	Total Assets	Mstar Category
UMBIX	None	$42.43	0.8%	$4,176 mil	Large Value

Governance and Management

Fiduciary Grade:

Portfolio Manager(s)

Seasoned and proved. Stock-pickers don't come much more talented than David Williams, who has managed the fund since its 1992 inception. Although he is supported by a pair of portfolio managers (Timothy Evnin and John McDermott, who also manage Excelsior Mid Cap Value) and is backed by U.S. Trust's analyst bench, Williams is the source of most of the fund's investment ideas.

Strategy

Manager David Williams looks for companies that he thinks can improve their bottom lines through reorganizations, consolidations, management turnover, or acquisitions. He isn't afraid to make significant sector bets, and the fund tends to hold some out-of-favor growth companies. He also buys smaller companies than many of his rivals, so the fund's median market cap is a fraction of the category average. Still, the portfolio is fairly well diversified, with large stakes in financials, cyclicals, and industrial firms, so its valuations look a lot like group norms.

Historical Profile

Return: High
Risk: High
Rating: ★★★★ Above Avg

Investment Style: Equity Stock %: 94% 95% 95% 95% 97% 99% 97% 95% 95%

▼ Manager Change ▽ Partial Manager Change

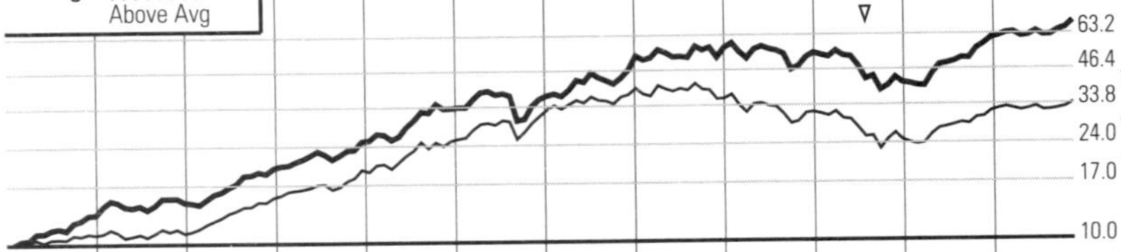

Performance Quartile (within Category)

History

1993	1994	1995	1996	1997	1998	1999	2000	2001	2002	2003	12-04	History
9.69	9.76	13.20	15.87	20.82	22.71	32.14	33.82	32.06	24.46	35.86	42.43	NAV
39.95	2.59	38.81	25.05	33.58	10.32	41.98	7.21	-4.96	-23.32	47.78	19.36	Total Return %
29.89	1.28	1.28	2.11	0.23	-18.25	20.94	16.31	6.92	-1.23	19.11	8.49	+/-S&P 500
21.88	4.57	0.45	3.41	-1.60	-5.31	34.63	0.20	0.63	-7.80	17.75	2.87	+/-Russ 1000 Vl
1.08	0.64	0.98	0.96	0.59	0.55	0.38	1.85	0.24	0.42	0.94	0.94	Income Return %
38.87	1.95	37.83	24.09	32.99	9.77	41.60	5.36	-5.20	-23.74	46.84	18.42	Capital Return %
1	18	7	14	7	62	1	62	55	82	1	4	Total Rtn % Rank Cat
0.08	0.06	0.09	0.12	0.09	0.11	0.09	0.59	0.08	0.13	0.23	0.34	Income $
0.02	0.12	0.24	0.47	0.27	0.14	0.00	0.00	0.00	0.00	0.00	0.00	Capital Gains $
0.99	0.99	0.98	0.91	0.91	0.89	0.93	0.90	1.05	0.94	0.99	0.99	Expense Ratio %
2.48	0.77	0.83	0.88	0.90	0.54	0.59	0.25	-0.54	0.27	0.65	0.78	Income Ratio %
9	75	82	56	62	30	43	13	15	3	16	4	Turnover Rate %
7	26	58	113	230	597	943	1,731	2,221	1,592	2,150	4,115	Net Assets $mil

Performance 12-31-04

	1st Qtr	2nd Qtr	3rd Qtr	4th Qtr	Total
2000	5.48	-5.81	5.74	2.06	7.21
2001	-9.25	8.63	-16.82	15.91	-4.96
2002	1.78	-12.65	-19.41	7.03	-23.32
2003	-3.27	22.18	4.45	19.71	47.78
2004	4.77	0.77	0.85	12.10	19.36

Trailing	Total Return%	+/- S&P 500	+/- Russ 1000 Vl	%Rank Cat	Growth of $10,000
3 Mo	12.10	2.87	1.72	5	11,210
6 Mo	13.06	5.87	0.98	4	11,306
1 Yr	19.36	8.49	2.87	4	11,936
3 Yr Avg	10.59	7.01	2.02	4	13,525
5 Yr Avg	6.63	8.93	1.36	24	13,785
10 Yr Avg	17.47	5.40	3.64	1	50,035
15 Yr Avg	—	—	—	—	—

Tax Analysis	Tax-Adj Rtn%	%Rank Cat	Tax-Cost Rat	%Rank Cat
3 Yr (estimated)	10.30	2	0.26	18
5 Yr (estimated)	6.28	18	0.33	17
10 Yr (estimated)	16.91	1	0.48	3

Potential Capital Gain Exposure: 27% of assets

Rating and Risk

Time Period	Load-Adj Return %	Morningstar Rtn vs Cat	Morningstar Risk vs Cat	Morningstar Risk-Adj Rating
1 Yr	19.36			
3 Yr	10.59	High	High	★★★★★
5 Yr	6.63	+Avg	High	★★★
10 Yr	17.47	High	High	★★★★★
Incept	17.86			

Other Measures	Standard Index S&P 500	Best Fit Index DJ 60%
Alpha	6.9	-6.2
Beta	1.10	1.88
R-Squared	88	93
Standard Deviation	19.45	
Mean	10.59	
Sharpe Ratio	0.48	

Portfolio Analysis 09-30-04

Share change since 06-04 Total Stocks:82	Sector	PE	YTD Ret%	% Assets
XM Satellite Radio Holdi	Media	—	43.10	4.75
Harman International Ind	Goods	48.4	71.77	4.00
Black & Decker	Ind Mtrls	16.4	81.42	3.73
⊕ Centex	Consumer	8.9	23.40	3.16
Harris	Hardware	27.4	64.22	2.42
Burlington Resources	Energy	10.9	58.50	2.24
Devon Energy	Energy	9.0	36.78	2.05
Avon Products	Goods	23.4	16.31	1.92
⊕ Dean Foods	Goods	19.5	0.24	1.73
America Movil SA ADR	Telecom	23.2	92.36	1.72
J P Morgan Chase	Financial	19.4	9.97	1.69
⊕ Union Pacific	Business	19.6	-1.28	1.69
⊕ Citigroup	Financial	15.3	2.72	1.67
ConocoPhillips	Energy	9.0	35.60	1.60
⊕ Zale	Goods	13.1	12.29	1.57
Freddie Mac	Financial	10.6	28.75	1.48
Lehman Brothers Holdings	Financial	11.7	14.22	1.48
⊕ Lafarge	Ind Mtrls	14.7	29.09	1.47
⊕ Consol Energy	Energy	32.2	61.53	1.44
⊕ PPG Industries	Ind Mtrls	18.1	9.67	1.43

Current Investment Style

Value Blnd Growth / Large Mid Small

Market Cap	%
Giant	18.6
Large	31.6
Mid	38.7
Small	10.1
Micro	0.9
Avg $mil: 9,176	

Value Measures		Rel Category
Price/Earnings	13.43	0.89
Price/Book	1.70	0.75
Price/Sales	0.90	0.76
Price/Cash Flow	4.46	0.70
Dividend Yield %	1.40	0.69

Growth Measures	%	Rel Category
Long-Term Erngs	11.40	1.10
Book Value	10.79	1.91
Sales	7.25	1.73
Cash Flow	7.10	1.36
Historical Erngs	21.00	1.77

Profitability	%	Rel Category
Return on Equity	16.80	1.06
Return on Assets	4.91	0.63
Net Margin	9.28	0.91

Sector Weightings	% of Stocks	Rel S&P 500	3 Year High	3 Year Low
Info	17.59	0.82		
Software	0.00	0.00	0	0
Hardware	7.22	0.71	13	7
Media	7.33	1.91	8	4
Telecom	3.04	0.97	3	0
Service	42.31	0.91		
Health	3.97	0.32	6	4
Consumer	6.69	0.74	9	7
Business	7.60	1.88	8	6
Financial	24.05	1.16	25	21
Mfg	40.10	1.25		
Goods	13.54	1.45	18	13
Ind Mtrls	12.86	1.01	18	11
Energy	9.67	1.35	10	4
Utilities	4.03	1.36	4	2

Composition

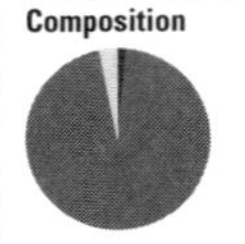

Cash	1.4
Stocks	95.3
Bonds	0.0
Other	3.3
Foreign (% of Stock)	6.3

Morningstar's Take by Jeffrey Ptak 12-23-04

Is Excelsior Value & Restructuring's manager most deserving of Morningstar Manager of the Year honors?

First things first: Fund manager David Williams' modus operandi is not for the faint of heart. Williams plies a malleable deep-value strategy that typically finds him at home amongst the market's unwanted, from fallen growth heroes to more mundane stories of firms struggling to right themselves from operational miscues. For instance, he scooped up XM Satellite Radio Holdings in 2002's fourth-quarter when the stock was plunging seemingly headlong toward bankruptcy. But Williams saw great promise in the firm's technology and thought the business would accelerate dramatically as the service took root amid a raft of impending product launches. His conviction was handsomely rewarded when the stock subsequently soared thanks to stronger-than-expected subscriber growth.

Standout picks such as these have been remarkably commonplace here. In fact, Williams has strung together one of the most impressive records of any diversified U.S. stock manager. The fund's 17.8% annualized return since its December 2002 inception tops the S&P 500 Index by a nearly unheard-of 7-percentage-point margin.

Given the fund's past and recent success--it has surged to a peer- and index-busting 18.7% return thus far in 2004--Williams should have contended strongly for Morningstar's Manager of the Year honors. But a cloud continues to hover over this fund's advisor (and Williams' employer), U.S. Trust, which disclosed some months ago that market-timers had targeted various Excelsior funds. U.S. Trust has not been publicly forthcoming about the nature or scope of what took place, declining even to identify the funds that were timed. For that reason and despite this fund's unquestionable merits, we're recommending that investors hold off on sending new monies to any Excelsior fund.

Address:	73 Tremont Street Boston MA 02108 800-446-1012
Web Address:	www.excelsiorfunds.com
Inception:	12-31-92
Advisor:	US Trust Company, NA Asset Mgt Division
Subadvisor:	None
NTF Plans:	Fidelity Retail-NTF, Schwab OneSource

Minimum Purchase:	$500	Add: $50	IRA: $250
Min Auto Inv Plan:	$500	Add: $50	
Sales Fees:	No-load		
Management Fee:	0.60%		
Actual Fees:	Mgt:0.60%	Dist:	
Expense Projections:	3Yr:$362	5Yr:$628	10Yr:$1386
Income Distrib:	Quarterly		

FAM Value

Ticker	Load	NAV	Yield	Total Assets	Mstar Category
FAMVX	None	$46.65	0.1%	$686 mil	Mid-Cap Blend

Governance and Management

Fiduciary Grade: A

Portfolio Manager(s)

Thomas Putnam has managed this fund since its inception in January 1987. John Fox joined him in May 2000. In addition to this fund, Putnam also manages FAM Equity-Income. Both have ownership stakes in this offering and its parent, Fenimore Asset Management.

Strategy

The managers look for fundamentally strong companies that are trading at a discount. Good growth records, high margins, and strong balance sheets are important fundamental factors. The fund prefers to invest in industry-leading firms with strong management teams.

Historical Profile
Return Above Avg
Risk Low
Rating ★★★★ Above Avg

Investment Style
Equity
Stock %

100% | 97% | 86% | 88% | 88% | 91% | 92% | 91% | 81%

▼ Manager Change
∇ Partial Manager Change

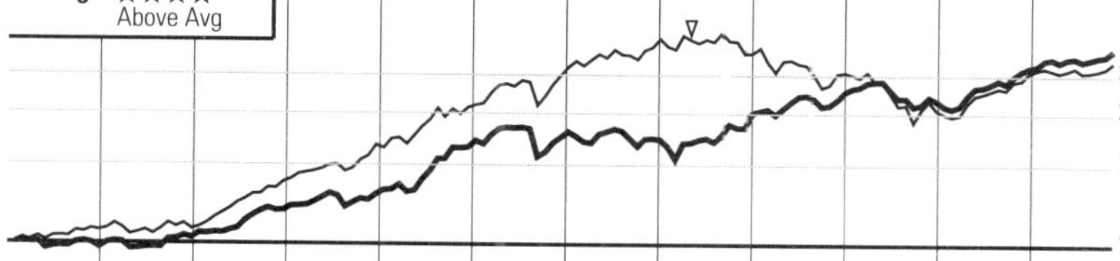

Growth of $10,000
— Investment Values of Fund
— Investment Values of S&P 500

Performance Quartile (within Category)

1993	1994	1995	1996	1997	1998	1999	2000	2001	2002	2003	12-04	History
20.40	21.04	24.58	26.53	35.76	34.44	31.35	32.70	36.17	33.69	41.15	46.65	NAV
0.21	6.83	19.73	11.22	39.06	6.19	-4.84	19.21	15.09	-5.33	24.98	16.86	Total Return %
-9.85	5.52	-17.80	-11.72	5.71	-22.38	-25.88	28.31	26.97	16.76	-3.69	5.99	+/-S&P 500
-13.72	10.42	-11.19	-7.96	6.82	-12.92	-19.56	1.72	15.69	9.20	-10.61	0.39	+/-S&P Mid 400
0.44	0.60	0.99	0.72	0.28	0.57	0.85	1.15	0.53	0.31	0.28	0.18	Income Return %
-0.23	6.23	18.74	10.50	38.78	5.62	-5.69	18.05	14.56	-5.64	24.70	16.68	Capital Return %
100	5	91	89	5	67	98	13	12	5	95	39	Total Rtn % Rank Cat
0.09	0.12	0.21	0.18	0.08	0.20	0.29	0.33	0.17	0.11	0.09	0.07	Income $
0.05	0.63	0.40	0.63	1.06	3.26	1.09	4.03	1.30	0.44	0.87	1.36	Capital Gains $
1.39	1.39	1.25	1.27	1.24	1.19	1.23	1.26	1.21	1.21	1.24	—	Expense Ratio %
0.57	0.58	0.92	0.64	0.25	0.57	0.86	1.08	0.56	0.30	0.26	—	Income Ratio %
5	2	10	12	9	17	16	9	10	18	9	—	Turnover Rate %
220	210	266	254	332	376	373	367	501	421	580	686	Net Assets $mil

Performance 12-31-04

	1st Qtr	2nd Qtr	3rd Qtr	4th Qtr	Total
2000	-2.49	3.40	9.59	7.88	19.21
2001	-1.04	13.04	-6.45	9.97	15.09
2002	6.75	-5.00	-10.14	3.89	-5.33
2003	-3.15	13.18	2.49	11.25	24.98
2004	6.05	0.55	0.59	8.95	16.86

Trailing	Total Return%	+/- S&P 500	+/- S&P Mid 400	%Rank Cat	Growth of $10,000
3 Mo	8.95	-0.28	-3.20	93	10,895
6 Mo	9.59	2.40	-0.20	48	10,959
1 Yr	16.86	5.99	0.39	39	11,686
3 Yr Avg	11.41	7.83	0.90	25	13,828
5 Yr Avg	13.66	15.96	4.13	7	18,969
10 Yr Avg	13.50	1.43	-2.59	50	35,478
15 Yr Avg	13.45	2.52	-1.21	28	66,385

Tax Analysis	Tax-Adj Rtn%	%Rank Cat	Tax-Cost Rat	%Rank Cat
3 Yr (estimated)	10.94	24	0.42	48
5 Yr (estimated)	12.56	7	0.97	43
10 Yr (estimated)	12.35	34	1.01	8

Potential Capital Gain Exposure: 43% of assets

Rating and Risk

Time Period	Load-Adj Return %	Morningstar Rtn vs Cat	Morningstar Risk vs Cat	Morningstar Risk-Adj Rating
1 Yr	16.86			
3 Yr	11.41	+Avg	Low	★★★★
5 Yr	13.66	High	Low	★★★★★
10 Yr	13.50	Avg	Low	★★★
Incept	12.95			

Other Measures	Standard Index S&P 500	Best Fit Index S&P Mid 400
Alpha	8.4	3.7
Beta	0.59	0.65
R-Squared	70	87
Standard Deviation	11.65	
Mean	11.41	
Sharpe Ratio	0.87	

Portfolio Analysis 06-30-04

Share change since 12-03 Total Stocks:45	Sector	PE	YTD Ret%	% Assets
White Mountains Insuranc	Financial	41.1	40.75	7.35
Brown & Brown	Financial	24.9	34.53	5.82
Kaydon	Ind Mtrls	21.9	29.90	3.47
Berkshire Hathaway A	Financial	—	—	2.75
Vulcan Materials	Ind Mtrls	20.8	17.34	2.65
Protective Life	Financial	11.1	28.45	2.62
⊕ Allied Capital	Financial	11.6	0.82	2.59
⊕ Idex	Ind Mtrls	24.1	48.09	2.54
Markel	Financial	21.8	43.58	2.42
Martin Marietta Material	Ind Mtrls	20.6	16.14	2.37
Reynolds & Reynolds	Media	16.1	-7.18	2.25
⊖ Yum Brands	Consumer	19.7	37.84	2.23
International Speedway A	Goods	29.0	18.96	2.21
Littelfuse	Hardware	20.4	18.53	2.20
Zebra Technologies	Hardware	33.1	27.20	2.16
Commonwealth Telephone E	Telecom	17.5	31.55	2.06
⊕ Liz Claiborne	Goods	14.8	19.76	1.97
⊕ Federated Investors B	Financial	17.0	5.00	1.88
☼ M & T Bank	Financial	18.1	11.55	1.79
Jones Apparel Group	Goods	14.8	4.84	1.74

Current Investment Style

Value Blnd Growth — Large Mid Small

Market Cap	%
Giant	0.0
Large	6.0
Mid	74.3
Small	16.0
Micro	3.8

Avg $mil: 2,637

Value Measures		Rel Category
Price/Earnings	17.30	1.02
Price/Book	2.44	1.12
Price/Sales	1.64	1.55
Price/Cash Flow	8.31	1.33
Dividend Yield %	1.30	1.30

Growth Measures	%	Rel Category
Long-Term Erngs	12.08	0.96
Book Value	9.45	1.34
Sales	5.45	0.96
Cash Flow	8.94	1.19
Historical Erngs	11.00	0.98

Profitability	%	Rel Category
Return on Equity	16.50	1.20
Return on Assets	8.31	1.28
Net Margin	12.88	1.42

Sector Weightings	% of Stocks	Rel S&P 500	3 Year High	3 Year Low
Info	15.23	0.71		
Software	0.00	0.00	1	0
Hardware	5.34	0.52	6	4
Media	6.90	1.80	8	6
Telecom	2.99	0.95	4	1
Service	55.67	1.20		
Health	4.14	0.33	8	4
Consumer	12.23	1.35	12	8
Business	0.00	0.00	6	0
Financial	39.30	1.89	43	38
Mfg	29.10	0.91		
Goods	12.15	1.30	12	6
Ind Mtrls	16.95	1.34	19	16
Energy	0.00	0.00	0	0
Utilities	0.00	0.00	0	0

Composition

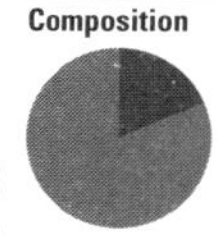

Cash	18.5
Stocks	81.4
Bonds	0.0
Other	0.2
Foreign (% of Stock)	0.0

Morningstar's Take by Karen Papalois 10-28-04

FAM Value sticks to its guns.

Portfolio managers Thomas Putnam and John Fox think of themselves as business owners when buying company stock. They favor firms with healthy financial statements, strong growth records and bargain valuations. Also, management holds on far longer than the typical value manager--as indicated by the fund's low turnover. So, what looks like style drift here--the fund has shifted from small value to mid-blend over the years-- is actually the result of the growth of the companies it owns.

This year, the fund added CarMax to its portfolio. Even though the used-car dealer is facing stiff competition from new cars, manager John Fox likes its business model. He highlights that the company offers consumers competitive financing and no-hassle ways to buy and sell cars. Moreover, Fox is optimistic about the dealer's prospects for expansion.

For the most part, such stock picks have led the fund to solid performance over the years. Its returns land in the top half of the mid-blend category for the trailing one-, three-, five- and 10-year periods through Oct. 19, 2004.

The strategy has resulted in good performance, but not without taking on a few risks. With 45 stocks in the portfolio and position sizes that can top 5% of assets, big declines in its top holdings can hurt the fund. Moreover, the portfolio keeps heavy stakes in some sectors. It has historically planted a hefty amount of assets in financial stocks, especially insurance firms. While none of its holdings have been directly implicated by the current scandal, controversy in the industry could affect them nonetheless. Fox remains optimistic about the fund's insurance stocks, though, especially top holding, White Mountains Insurance, which continues to grow through acquisitions.

Overall, this fund boasts a proven strategy and solid management and is a good option for investors seeking a mid-cap fund that tilts toward value.

Address:	118 N Grand St Cobleskill NY 12043 800-932-3271
Web Address:	www.famfunds.com
Inception:	01-02-87
Advisor:	Fenimore Asset Management, Inc.
Subadvisor:	None
NTF Plans:	Fidelity Retail-NTF, Schwab OneSource

Minimum Purchase:	$500	Add: $50	IRA: $100
Min Auto Inv Plan:	$500	Add: $50	
Sales Fees:	No-load		
Management Fee:	1.00%		
Actual Fees:	Mgt:1.00%	Dist:	
Expense Projections:	3Yr:$393	5Yr:$681	10Yr:$1500
Income Distrib:	Annually		

FBR Small Cap

Ticker	Load	NAV	Yield	Total Assets	Mstar Category
FBRVX	Closed	$41.81	0.0%	$1.012 mil	Small Growth

Governance and Management

Fiduciary Grade: B

Portfolio Manager(s)

Charles T. Akre has managed this fund since its year-end 1996 inception. Once an employee of the FBR Funds, Akre now subadvises this fund through his private asset-management firm, Akre Capital Management. In addition to this fund, Akre also runs some separate accounts and a hedge fund. He has a sizable portion of his and his family members' net worth invested in this offering.

Strategy

Manager Charles Akre seeks small-cap companies with sustainable returns on equity of 20% and higher. Company executives must manage their businesses with the shareholder in mind by reinvesting capital and avoiding dilutive options packages. Akre also keeps an eye on valuation, but he'll pay up for companies with higher-quality earnings and healthier balance sheets. He holds about 30 stocks, makes big bets on just a few sectors and has allowed cash to build to about one third of assets. This has led to volatile returns.

Historical Profile

Return High
Risk Low
Rating ★★★★★ Highest

Investment Style
Equity
Stock %

96% 93% 100% 100% 61% 62% 64% 76%

▼ Manager Change
▽ Partial Manager Change

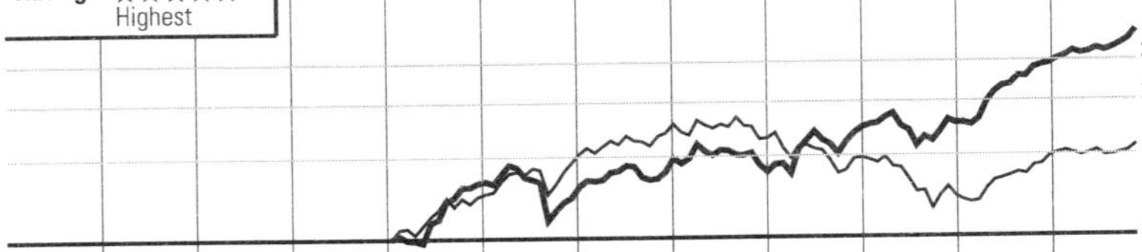

31.0
24.0 **Growth of $10,000**
17.0
10.0

— Investment Values of Fund
— Investment Values of S&P 500

Performance Quartile (within Category)

1993	1994	1995	1996	1997	1998	1999	2000	2001	2002	2003	12-04	**History**
—	—	—	12.00	16.82	15.75	18.84	16.50	21.71	22.28	32.45	41.81	NAV
—	—	—	0.00*	44.30	-3.52	19.62	-8.79	32.63	2.63	45.77	30.67	Total Return %
—	—	—	—	10.95	-32.09	-1.42	0.31	44.51	24.72	17.10	19.80	+/-S&P 500
—	—	—	—	31.35	-4.75	-23.47	13.64	41.86	32.89	-2.77	16.36	+/-Russ 2000 Gr
—	—	—	—	0.00	0.00	0.00	0.00	0.00	0.00	0.00	0.00	Income Return %
—	—	—	—	44.30	-3.52	19.62	-8.79	32.63	2.63	45.77	30.67	Capital Return %
—	—	—	—	4	75	80	57	1	1	40	1	Total Rtn % Rank Cat
—	—	—	0.00	0.00	0.00	0.00	0.00	0.00	0.00	0.00	0.00	Income $
—	—	—	0.00	0.49	0.43	0.00	0.65	0.17	0.00	0.03	0.57	Capital Gains $
—	—	—	—	1.65	1.65	1.92	1.95	1.95	1.94	1.60	—	Expense Ratio %
—	—	—	—	-0.79	-0.81	-1.46	-1.71	-1.34	-1.39	-0.75	—	Income Ratio %
—	—	—	—	—	78	24	3	26	13	16	—	Turnover Rate %
—	—	—	—	10	16	15	9	27	51	348	1,012	Net Assets $mil

Performance 12-31-04

	1st Qtr	2nd Qtr	3rd Qtr	4th Qtr	Total
2000	9.34	-3.64	-3.48	-10.31	-8.79
2001	-1.09	30.94	-13.38	18.23	32.63
2002	6.68	-8.03	-6.62	12.02	2.63
2003	2.56	23.15	6.16	8.72	45.77
2004	8.01	1.61	2.61	16.04	30.67

Trailing	Total Return%	+/- S&P 500	+/- Russ 2000 Gr	%Rank Cat	Growth of $10,000
3 Mo	16.04	6.81	0.96	15	11,604
6 Mo	19.07	11.88	10.91	1	11,907
1 Yr	30.67	19.80	16.36	1	13,067
3 Yr Avg	25.04	21.46	19.25	1	19,550
5 Yr Avg	18.78	21.08	22.35	2	23,644
10 Yr Avg	—	—	—	—	—
15 Yr Avg	—	—	—	—	—

Tax Analysis	Tax-Adj Rtn%	%Rank Cat	Tax-Cost Rat	%Rank Cat
3 Yr (estimated)	24.87	1	0.14	14
5 Yr (estimated)	18.46	2	0.27	12
10 Yr (estimated)	—	—	—	—

Potential Capital Gain Exposure: 25% of assets

Rating and Risk

Time Period	Load-Adj Return %	Morningstar Rtn vs Cat	Morningstar Risk vs Cat	Morningstar Risk-Adj Rating
1 Yr	30.67			
3 Yr	25.04	High	Low	★★★★★
5 Yr	18.78	High	Low	★★★★★
10 Yr	—	—	—	—
Incept	18.69			

Other Measures	Standard Index S&P 500	Best Fit Index Mstar Small Core
Alpha	21.7	12.8
Beta	0.72	0.72
R-Squared	58	76
Standard Deviation	17.38	
Mean	25.04	
Sharpe Ratio	1.38	

Portfolio Analysis 01-31-04

Share change since 06-03 Total Stocks:45	Sector	PE	YTD Ret%	% Assets
⊕ Markel	Financial	21.6	43.58	8.13
⊕ American Tower A	Telecom	—	70.06	7.83
Penn National Gaming	Goods	34.8	161.89	6.04
⊕ Multimedia Games	Consumer	12.8	-23.29	4.44
⊕ Americredit	Financial	14.3	53.48	3.44
⊕ Platinum Underwriters Ho	Financial	16.1	4.76	3.37
⊕ Unumprovident	Financial	—	16.09	3.08
CarMax	Consumer	29.6	0.39	3.07
⊕ PartnerRe	Financial	—	9.36	3.03
☼ Global Imaging Systems	Ind Mtrls	17.0	24.41	2.96
⊕ AES	Utilities	30.9	44.81	2.82
⊕ DR Horton	Consumer	10.7	41.36	2.73
☼ Liberty Media FRN	—	—	—	2.62
⊕ Allmerica Financial	Financial	12.5	6.70	2.42
⊕ Toll Brothers	Consumer	17.3	72.56	2.03
⊕ Alliance Gaming	Consumer	17.4	-43.98	1.98
☼ Kaneb Services LLC	Energy	20.3	44.32	1.92
☼ Hilb Rogal & Hamilton	Financial	15.0	14.30	1.91
Ryland Group	Consumer	7.8	30.51	1.58
⊕ Monarch Casino & Resort	Consumer	21.8	263.68	1.52

Current Investment Style

Value Blnd Growth; Large Mid Small

Market Cap	%
Giant	0.1
Large	0.6
Mid	56.8
Small	35.4
Micro	7.1
Avg $mil:	1,618

Value Measures		Rel Category
Price/Earnings	14.73	0.68
Price/Book	1.76	0.67
Price/Sales	0.86	0.57
Price/Cash Flow	3.06	0.38
Dividend Yield %	0.99	3.19

Growth Measures	%	Rel Category
Long-Term Erngs	14.73	0.85
Book Value	2.01	0.31
Sales	11.82	1.83
Cash Flow	25.18	1.86
Historical Erngs	-0.06	NMF

Profitability	%	Rel Category
Return on Equity	10.95	1.11
Return on Assets	4.47	1.02
Net Margin	-0.39	NMF

Sector Weightings	% of Stocks	Rel S&P 500	3 Year High	Low
Info	13.66	0.64		
Software	0.24	0.06	2	0
Hardware	0.00	0.00	4	0
Media	1.16	0.30	4	0
Telecom	12.26	3.89	13	2
Service	59.52	1.28		
Health	0.00	0.00	1	0
Consumer	24.59	2.71	27	14
Business	0.13	0.03	4	0
Financial	34.80	1.68	35	18
Mfg	26.82	0.83		
Goods	12.83	1.38	31	13
Ind Mtrls	4.71	0.37	15	2
Energy	5.57	0.78	6	0
Utilities	3.71	1.25	4	0

Composition

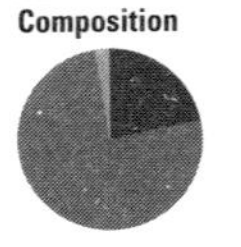

Cash	21.4
Stocks	76.0
Bonds	2.6
Other	0.0
Foreign (% of Stock)	0.0

Morningstar's Take by Laura Pavlenko Lutton 12-15-04

This closed fund is worth keeping, but we'd be mindful of its risks.

After more than doubling in size in nine months, FBR Small Cap closed its doors to new investors on Oct. 1, 2004. We think the fund's shareholders should benefit from FBR's decision to limit this offering's bulk. With assets nearing $1 billion, we think it's becoming more difficult to effectively execute this fund's unusual strategy.

To be sure, manager Chuck Akre has not changed this fund at its core. He continues to look for firms with high returns on equity and dependable growth, and he still especially likes gambling and insurance stocks. But he has made some changes to accommodate a larger asset base. First, he has expanded the portfolio to include about 60 stocks, up from 30 names in September 2002. Second, he hired a third full-time research analyst to help vet new stock ideas. Even with these efforts, Akre has had trouble putting this fund's new cash to work. The offering's cash position has remained at or above 25% of assets for months, and the fund could be left in the dust should the market take off suddenly. What's more, Akre and his researchers may be stretching to find enough stock ideas to soak up this offering's cash.

While we have these concerns about the fund, we don't think they're serious enough to warrant selling this offering. Thus far, Akre has continued to deliver strong performance. Some of the offering's long-time core holdings, including racetrack operator Penn National Gaming, have turned in sky-high gains, while newer themes, including housing, also have been strong. The fund is up 25.15% for the year to date through December 13--one of the best returns in the category for the period.

Given this fund's quirky, concentrated strategy, investors should be prepared for periods of severe underperformance. We'd also limit the offering to a tiny role in a portfolio.

Address:	FBR Family of Funds Arlington, VA 22209 888-888-0025
Web Address:	
Inception:	12-31-96*
Advisor:	FBR Fund Advisers Inc.
Subadvisor:	Akre Capital Management, LLC
NTF Plans:	Fidelity Retail-NTF, Schwab OneSource

Minimum Purchase:	Closed	Add: —	IRA: —
Min Auto Inv Plan:	Closed	Add: —	
Sales Fees:	0.25%B, 1.00%R		
Management Fee:	0.90%, 0.80%A		
Actual Fees:	Mgt:0.90%	Dist:0.25%	
Expense Projections:	3Yr:$505	5Yr:$871	10Yr:$1900
Income Distrib:	Annually		

Fidelity

Ticker	Load	NAV	Yield	Total Assets	Mstar Category
FFIDX	None	$29.88	1.3%	$10,812 mil	Large Blend

Governance and Management

Fiduciary Grade: B

Portfolio Manager(s)

John Avery managed Fidelity Advisor Balanced between early 1998 and early 2002, producing middling to subpar results. He did a good job in a shorter stint at Fidelity Advisor Growth & Income, however.

Strategy

Manager John Avery looks for stocks trading in the bottom quartile of their 10-year valuation range. He uses a mix of stable growers and economically sensitive stocks. Avery has recently positioned the fund to benefit from an economic upturn.

Historical Profile

Return Average
Risk Above Avg
Rating ★★★ Neutral

Investment Style Equity Stock %: 94% 92% 90% 93% 94% 89% 93% 99% 99%

▼ Manager Change
▽ Partial Manager Change

Growth of $10,000
— Investment Values of Fund
— Investment Values of S&P 500

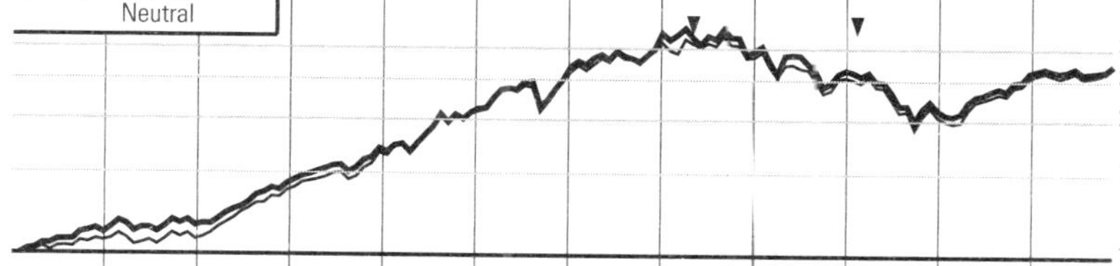

Performance Quartile (within Category)

1993	1994	1995	1996	1997	1998	1999	2000	2001	2002	2003	12-04	History
19.27	18.48	22.61	24.70	29.81	36.69	42.61	32.77	28.88	22.26	28.08	29.88	NAV
18.36	2.58	32.85	19.82	32.06	31.00	24.21	-10.97	-11.22	-22.25	27.26	7.84	Total Return %
8.30	1.27	-4.68	-3.12	-1.29	2.43	3.17	-1.87	0.66	-0.16	-1.41	-3.03	+/-S&P 500
8.18	2.19	-4.92	-2.63	-0.79	3.98	3.30	-3.18	1.23	-0.60	-2.63	-3.56	+/-Russ 1000
2.44	1.77	2.32	1.70	1.32	1.03	0.82	0.57	0.64	0.73	0.99	1.39	Income Return %
15.92	0.81	30.53	18.12	30.74	29.97	23.39	-11.54	-11.86	-22.98	26.27	6.45	Capital Return %
13	13	55	64	30	8	26	85	37	47	49	77	Total Rtn % Rank Cat
0.44	0.33	0.42	0.37	0.32	0.30	0.29	0.23	0.2[illegible]	0.21	0.22	0.39	Income $
2.55	0.94	1.40	1.82	2.35	1.81	2.21	5.20	0.00	0.00	0.00	0.00	Capital Gains $
0.66	0.65	0.64	0.60	0.59	0.56	0.55	0.56	0.5[illegible]	0.53	0.61	0.59	Expense Ratio %
2.94	1.85	2.18	1.71	1.34	1.01	0.87	0.57	0.55	0.82	0.93	0.89	Income Ratio %
261	207	157	150	107	65	71	113	16[illegible]	155	32	53	Turnover Rate %
1,546	1,886	3,214	4,451	6,530	10,563	16,114	15,070	12,45[illegible]	8,696	10,388	10,812	Net Assets $mil

Performance 12-31-04

	1st Qtr	2nd Qtr	3rd Qtr	4th Qtr	Total
2000	3.29	-4.84	-0.81	-8.68	-10.97
2001	-14.08	13.37	-18.30	11.55	-11.22
2002	-1.42	-11.83	-17.00	7.76	-22.25
2003	-2.11	12.65	2.49	12.60	27.26
2004	1.03	1.91	-2.50	7.43	7.84

Trailing	Total Return%	+/- S&P 500	+/- Russ 1000	%Rank Cat	Growth of $10,000
3 Mo	7.43	-1.80	-2.37	89	10,743
6 Mo	4.75	-2.44	-3.06	87	10,475
1 Yr	7.84	-3.03	-3.56	77	10,784
3 Yr Avg	2.19	-1.39	-2.08	65	10,671
5 Yr Avg	-3.35	-1.05	-1.59	71	8,434
10 Yr Avg	11.18	-0.89	-0.98	39	28,858
15 Yr Avg	10.51	-0.42	-0.57	32	44,774

Tax Analysis	Tax-Adj Rtn%	%Rank Cat	Tax-Cost Rat	%Rank Cat
3 Yr (estimated)	1.81	57	0.37	31
5 Yr (estimated)	-4.19	73	0.87	46
10 Yr (estimated)	9.33	41	1.66	65

Potential Capital Gain Exposure: -5% of assets

Rating and Risk

Time Period	Load-Adj Return %	Morningstar Rtn vs Cat	Morningstar Risk vs Cat	Morningstar Risk-Adj Rating
1 Yr	7.84			
3 Yr	2.19	Avg	-Avg	★★★
5 Yr	-3.35	-Avg	+Avg	★★
10 Yr	11.18	Avg	+Avg	★★★
Incept	10.45			

Other Measures	Standard Index S&P 500	Best Fit Index S&P 500
Alpha	-1.3	-1.3
Beta	0.92	0.92
R-Squared	98	98
Standard Deviation	14.33	
Mean	2.19	
Sharpe Ratio	0.06	

Portfolio Analysis 09-30-04

Share change since 06-04 Total Stocks:117	Sector	PE	YTD Ret%	% Assets
⊕ Gen Elec	Ind Mtrls	22.8	20.68	4.04
Microsoft	Software	36.1	8.95	4.03
⊕ American International G	Financial	16.2	-0.53	2.87
⊖ Pfizer	Health	22.0	-22.31	2.34
⊕ ExxonMobil	Energy	13.9	28.04	2.32
⊕ Bank of America	Financial	12.3	21.50	2.17
⊕ American Express	Financial	20.3	17.60	2.11
⊕ SBC Communications	Telecom	15.4	3.74	2.11
⊖ Citigroup	Financial	15.3	2.72	2.10
⊕ Boeing	Ind Mtrls	14.7	24.86	1.97
⊕ Verizon Communications	Telecom	32.4	20.25	1.96
Wells Fargo	Financial	15.5	8.97	1.87
⊕ Wal-Mart Stores	Consumer	23.4	0.51	1.80
⊖ Gillette	Goods	27.6	23.94	1.77
⊕ Johnson & Johnson	Health	20.6	25.17	1.75
⊖ Tyco International	Ind Mtrls	25.1	35.41	1.63
⊕ Home Depot	Consumer	19.0	21.47	1.56
⊕ Praxair	Ind Mtrls	21.0	17.32	1.50
⊖ 3M Company	Ind Mtrls	23.5	-1.75	1.48
⊕ Morgan Stanley	Financial	14.2	-2.25	1.45

Current Investment Style

Value Blnd Growth — Large / Mid / Small

Market Cap	%
Giant	62.9
Large	30.8
Mid	6.3
Small	0.0
Micro	0.0
Avg $mil: 57,544	

Value Measures		Rel Category
Price/Earnings	17.68	1.04
Price/Book	3.01	1.15
Price/Sales	1.76	1.22
Price/Cash Flow	8.97	1.17
Dividend Yield %	1.62	1.09

Growth Measures	%	Rel Category
Long-Term Erngs	11.11	0.96
Book Value	10.51	1.35
Sales	5.70	0.99
Cash Flow	20.03	2.12
Historical Erngs	8.71	0.74

Profitability	%	Rel Category
Return on Equity	19.57	1.12
Return on Assets	9.67	1.12
Net Margin	12.23	1.07

Sector Weightings	% of Stocks	Rel S&P 500	3 Year High	3 Year Low
Info	24.25	1.13		
Software	4.27	0.99	5	4
Hardware	8.32	0.82	10	5
Media	6.23	1.62	8	4
Telecom	5.43	1.72	5	3
Service	41.24	0.89		
Health	14.11	1.13	20	13
Consumer	6.04	0.67	9	4
Business	1.49	0.37	3	1
Financial	19.60	0.94	21	17
Mfg	34.50	1.07		
Goods	9.10	0.98	13	7
Ind Mtrls	18.01	1.42	22	12
Energy	7.00	0.98	8	6
Utilities	0.39	0.13	1	0

Composition

Cash	1.2
Stocks	98.8
Bonds	0.0
Other	0.0
Foreign (% of Stock)	3.7

Morningstar's Take by Greg Carlson 12-23-04

We don't see much reason to buy Fidelity Fund.

Fidelity's August 2004 announcement that it was cutting the expense ratio on four large- or all-cap index funds to a rock-bottom 0.10% casts a shadow over this fund. The move--seen widely as a shot across the bow of Vanguard and ETFs--also puts the onus on the firm's 20 actively managed large-blend funds, including this one, to make cases for themselves.

Within that group of Fidelity funds, this looks more like the S&P 500 index than most. Only three such siblings have tracked the bogy more closely than this fund over the past three years through Nov. 30, 2004. And as of Sept. 30, the fund's portfolio looks much like the index. While the fund has a modestly higher market cap, leans more toward growth stocks than the index, and has slightly different sector weightings, these differences are undramatic. Maybe most strikingly, the fund's six top holdings come from the index's top 10 names.

True, lead manger John Avery doesn't completely hug the index. In early 2004, because of his expectations of a continued recovery, he emphasized economically sensitive stocks. In late spring he bought more "late cycle" stocks, such as aerospace firms such as Honeywell International and Boeing, and media such as News Corp. and Time Warner. But while aerospace holdings held up OK this summer, media plummeted. All told, while the fund hasn't completely mirrored the bogy, it hasn't beaten it this year, either. Through Dec. 22, the fund lags the S&P 500 by more than 2 percentage points.

Certainly this fund isn't bad in and of itself. It does, after all, sport low fees, low turnover, and fairly stable management. On the other hand, its manager has a mediocre record here and elsewhere (including Fidelity Advisor Balanced and Fidelity Advisor Growth & Income). But the key issue is that, even within its family, it hardly seems to be the best bet.

Address:	82 Devonshire St Boston MA 02109 800-343-3548
Web Address:	www.fidelity.com
Inception:	04-30-30
Advisor:	Fidelity Management & Research Co. (FMR)
Subadvisor:	FMR Co., Inc. (FMRC)
NTF Plans:	Fidelity Retail-NTF, CommonWealth NTF

Minimum Purchase:	$2500	Add: $250	IRA: $500
Min Auto Inv Plan:	$2500	Add: $100	
Sales Fees:	No-load		
Management Fee:	0.38%		
Actual Fees:	Mgt:0.38%	Dist:	
Expense Projections:	3Yr:$183	5Yr:$318	10Yr:$714
Income Distrib:	Quarterly		

Fidelity Adv Eq Gr T

Ticker	Load	NAV	Yield	Total Assets	Mstar Category
FAEGX	3.50%	$45.71	0.0%	$10,091 mil	Large Growth

Governance and Management

Fiduciary Grade: B

Portfolio Manager(s)

Jennifer Uhrig has more than 15 years of investment experience, including her stint here, which began in January 1997. She receives the support of dozens of Fidelity industry analysts.

Strategy

Manager Jennifer Uhrig focuses on growth stocks, but she's more attentive to valuations than some of her category rivals. At times she can be mildly contrarian, loading up on growth stocks that are temporarily out of favor. She'll also add the occasional value play to the portfolio if she thinks it's cheap enough. In short, this is a stock-picker's fund with a growth bent.

Historical Profile

Return Average
Risk Average
Rating ★★★ Neutral

Investment Style: Equity Stock %

90%	98%	88%	96%	96%	98%	95%	99%	98%

▼ Manager Change
▽ Partial Manager Change

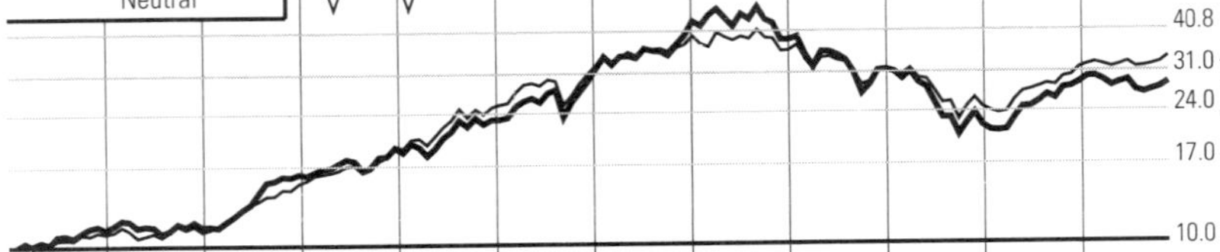

Growth of $10,000
- Investment Values of Fund
- Investment Values of S&P 500

Performance Quartile (within Category)

1993	1994	1995	1996	1997	1998	1999	2000	2001	2002	2003	12-04	History
29.02	28.36	37.51	42.01	46.24	57.09	71.61	59.57	48.69	33.77	44.52	45.71	NAV
14.85	-0.89	39.14	16.24	23.93	38.72	36.27	-11.48	-18.19	-30.64	31.83	2.67	Total Return %
4.79	-2.20	1.61	-6.70	-9.42	10.15	15.23	-2.38	-6.31	-8.55	3.16	-8.20	+/-S&P 500
11.98	-3.51	1.96	-6.88	-6.56	0.01	3.11	10.94	2.23	-2.76	2.08	-3.63	+/-Russ 1000Gr
0.00	0.28	0.21	0.46	0.00	0.00	0.00	0.00	0.00	0.00	0.00	0.00	Income Return %
14.85	-1.17	38.93	15.78	23.93	38.72	36.27	-11.48	-18.19	-30.64	31.83	2.67	Capital Return %
32	41	14	76	64	24	45	41	39	76	23	89	Total Rtn % Rank Cat
0.00	0.08	0.06	0.17	0.00	0.00	0.00	0.00	0.00	0.00	0.00	0.00	Income $
1.44	0.32	1.88	1.40	5.65	6.61	5.70	3.84	0.05	0.00	0.00	0.00	Capital Gains $
1.84	1.70	1.54	1.34	1.29	1.27	1.28	1.26	1.26	1.28	1.32	—	Expense Ratio %
-0.24	0.15	0.21	0.54	-0.08	-0.41	-0.43	-0.57	-0.37	-0.45	-0.35	—	Income Ratio %
160	137	97	76	108	122	82	99	106	93	62	—	Turnover Rate %
427	908	2,100	3,440	4,160	5,622	9,060	9,126	7,153	4,381	5,577	5,092	Net Assets $mil

Performance 12-31-04

	1st Qtr	2nd Qtr	3rd Qtr	4th Qtr	Total
2000	8.46	-3.41	-3.55	-12.39	-11.48
2001	-16.75	8.19	-22.07	16.54	-18.19
2002	-1.25	-18.43	-19.07	6.40	-30.64
2003	-2.99	16.54	5.13	10.91	31.83
2004	1.17	-0.02	-6.24	8.27	2.67

Trailing	Total Return%	+/- S&P 500	+/- Russ 1000Gr	%Rank Cat	Growth of $10,000
3 Mo	8.27	-0.96	-0.90	81	10,827
6 Mo	1.51	-5.68	-1.96	90	10,151
1 Yr	2.67	-8.20	-3.63	89	10,267
3 Yr Avg	-2.08	-5.66	-1.90	72	9,389
5 Yr Avg	-7.43	-5.13	1.86	50	6,798
10 Yr Avg	9.92	-2.15	0.33	35	25,749
15 Yr Avg	—	—	—	—	—

Tax Analysis	Tax-Adj Rtn%	%Rank Cat	Tax-Cost Rat	%Rank Cat
3 Yr (estimated)	-3.24	77	0.00	1
5 Yr (estimated)	-8.32	51	0.26	16
10 Yr (estimated)	8.14	35	1.27	38

Potential Capital Gain Exposure: -22% of assets

Rating and Risk

Time Period	Load-Adj Return %	Morningstar Rtn vs Cat	Morningstar Risk vs Cat	Morningstar Risk-Adj Rating
1 Yr	-0.92			
3 Yr	-3.24	-Avg	+Avg	★★
5 Yr	-8.08	Avg	Avg	★★★
10 Yr	9.53	Avg	Avg	★★★
Incept	9.96			

Other Measures	Standard Index S&P 500	Best Fit Index Russ 1000Gr
Alpha	-5.5	-1.6
Beta	1.13	1.10
R-Squared	94	95
Standard Deviation	17.43	
Mean	-2.08	
Sharpe Ratio	-0.20	

Portfolio Analysis 08-31-04

Share change since 05-04 Total Stocks:209	Sector	PE	YTD Ret%	% Assets
⊕ Pfizer	Health	22.0	-22.31	4.98
⊕ Cisco Systems	Hardware	24.5	-20.26	2.68
⊖ Microsoft	Software	36.1	8.95	2.52
⊕ Wal-Mart Stores	Consumer	23.4	0.51	2.34
⊕ Dell	Hardware	34.0	24.01	2.18
⊕ Johnson & Johnson	Health	20.6	25.17	2.02
⊕ American International G	Financial	16.2	-0.53	1.91
⊕ IBM	Hardware	20.2	7.19	1.89
⊕ Gen Elec	Ind Mtrls	22.8	20.68	1.79
⊕ Qualcomm	Hardware	42.0	58.20	1.77
⊕ Home Depot	Consumer	19.0	21.47	1.71
⊕ American Express	Financial	20.3	17.60	1.56
⊕ PepsiCo	Goods	22.5	13.82	1.52
⊕ Medtronic	Health	30.7	2.68	1.25
Schering-Plough	Health	—	21.56	1.20
⊕ 3M Company	Ind Mtrls	23.5	-1.75	1.16
⊕ Schlumberger	Energy	40.7	23.84	1.02
⊕ Wyeth	Health	17.0	2.73	1.02
⊖ Intel	Hardware	19.8	-26.56	0.99
First Data	Business	18.8	3.72	0.94

Current Investment Style

Market Cap	%
Giant	46.8
Large	29.0
Mid	20.8
Small	3.4
Micro	0.0
Avg $mil:	28,832

Value Measures		Rel Category
Price/Earnings	20.08	0.94
Price/Book	2.99	0.93
Price/Sales	1.98	0.92
Price/Cash Flow	10.20	0.93
Dividend Yield %	0.87	1.13

Growth Measures	%	Rel Category
Long-Term Erngs	13.83	0.98
Book Value	10.61	0.83
Sales	5.18	0.61
Cash Flow	11.08	0.67
Historical Erngs	7.58	0.52

Profitability	%	Rel Category
Return on Equity	16.92	0.94
Return on Assets	9.45	1.01
Net Margin	10.99	0.89

Sector Weightings	% of Stocks	Rel S&P 500	3 Year High	3 Year Low
Info	35.96	1.67		
Software	6.54	1.52	8	7
Hardware	25.17	2.47	31	19
Media	3.82	0.99	6	4
Telecom	0.43	0.14	2	0
Service	45.92	0.99		
Health	23.41	1.87	27	17
Consumer	9.20	1.01	11	7
Business	2.30	0.57	7	2
Financial	11.01	0.53	15	10
Mfg	18.12	0.56		
Goods	4.69	0.50	8	3
Ind Mtrls	7.58	0.60	8	4
Energy	5.85	0.82	6	4
Utilities	0.00	0.00	0	0

Composition

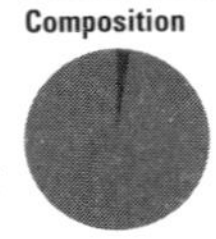

Cash	2.4
Stocks	97.6
Bonds	0.0
Other	0.0
Foreign (% of Stock)	6.8

Morningstar's Take by Greg Carlson 12-23-04

Despite Fidelity Advisor Equity Growth's disappointing recent performance, its manager makes it a viable option.

Jennifer Uhrig, who has run this fund since 1997, takes heed of her benchmark, the Russell 3000 Growth Index, but isn't held captive by it. For example, if opportunities cluster in a particular area, she's willing to give chase. And, far more often than not, Uhrig flouts consensus. For example, she owned a relatively light tech stake as the frenzy over that sector's prospects reached a fever pitch in the late 1990s. That stance paid off as the fund better withstood the downturn's early stages than its typical large-growth peer and its bogy.

Uhrig's mild contrarian ways shouldn't be confused for timidity. After tech firms were punished further after the September 11 terrorist attacks, she loaded up on the sector. Uhrig has, for the most part, kept the pedal to the metal ever since, with tech recently soaking up 32% of assets, one fourth higher than the Russell index's tally.

The fund's recent struggles highlight one of Uhrig's most attractive attributes: her resolve. Far from retreating in the face of tech's 2004 doldrums, Uhrig is standing fast, insisting that investors will eventually reward the exceptional growth prospects such firms offer. (The recent blowup of top-holding Pfizer, due to concerns over the side effects of its arthritis drug, Celebrex, has also dented returns.)

True, her patient, against-the-grain style can lead to prolonged dry spells. What's more, the fund's record during Uhrig's tenure--it has topped 55% of its rivals--isn't jawdropping. But Uhrig's focus on fast-growing but reasonably valued fare has kept excessive price risk at bay, as evidenced by the fund's below-average volatility. We'd need to see her string together a more consistent record of deft stock-picking to strongly endorse the fund. However, the fund's appealing risk/reward profile makes it worth a look all the same.

Address:	82 Devonshire St Boston MA 02109 800-522-7297
Web Address:	www.fidelity.com
Inception:	09-10-92
Advisor:	Fidelity Management & Research Co. (FMR)
Subadvisor:	FMR Co., Inc. (FMRC)
NTF Plans:	DATALynx NTF, Federated Tr NTF

Minimum Purchase:	$2500	Add: $100	IRA: $500
Min Auto Inv Plan:	$100	Add: $100	
Sales Fees:	3.50%L, 0.25%S		
Management Fee:	0.58%		
Actual Fees:	Mgt:0.58%	Dist:0.50%	
Expense Projections:	3Yr:$760	5Yr:$1058	10Yr:$1906
Income Distrib:	Semi-Annually		

Fidelity Adv Small Cap T

Ticker	Load	NAV	Yield	Total Assets	Mstar Category
FSCTX	3.50%	$24.63	0.0%	$2,684 mil	Small Growth

Governance and Management

Fiduciary Grade: B

Portfolio Manager(s)

Harry Lange has ample investing experience under his belt. He has managed and led the research effort at Fidelity Capital Appreciation since early 1996, generating above-average returns. Here, Lange relies more heavily on a team of dedicated analysts who chip in with research and investment ideas, meet with management teams, and work to assess the quality of a company's earnings and its potential for market-share growth.

Strategy

Manager Harry Lange is a classic stock-picker. He has generally focused on growth stocks, but he is not averse to make plays on out-of-favor areas and has put a sizable portion of the fund's assets in value fare. He prefers market leaders with additional opportunity for market-share growth. He's also been more attentive to valuations than many of his small-cap growth rivals.

Historical Profile

Return Average
Risk Below Avg
Rating ★★★ Neutral

Investment Style
Equity
Stock %

1998	1999	2000	2001	2002	2003	12-04
87%	92%	90%	92%	92%	92%	93%

▼ Manager Change
▽ Partial Manager Change

Growth of $10,000
— Investment Values of Fund
— Investment Values of S&P 500

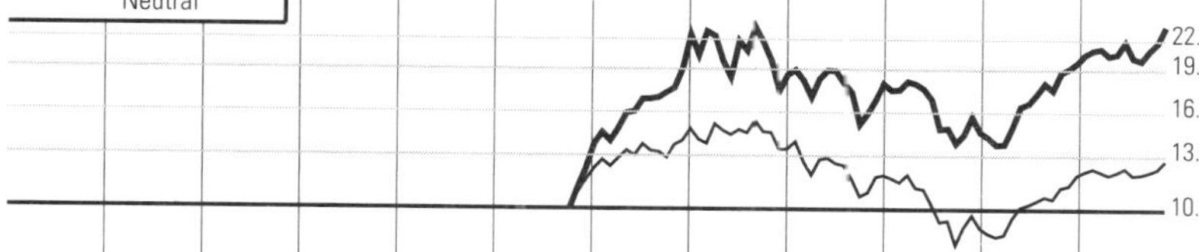

Performance Quartile (within Category)

History

	1993	1994	1995	1996	1997	1998	1999	2000	2001	2002	2003	12-04
NAV	—	—	—	—	—	13.88	22.80	18.73	18.00	14.33	19.94	24.63
Total Return %	—	—	—	—	—	38.80*	68.46	-17.55	-3.90	-20.39	39.15	23.52
+/-S&P 500	—	—	—	—	—	—	47.42	-8.45	7.98	1.70	10.48	12.65
+/-Russ 2000 Gr	—	—	—	—	—	—	25.37	4.88	5.33	9.87	-9.39	9.21
Income Return %	—	—	—	—	—	0.00	0.00	0.00	0.00	0.00	0.00	0.00
Capital Return %	—	—	—	—	—	—	68.46	-17.55	-3.90	-20.39	39.15	23.52
Total Rtn % Rank Cat	—	—	—	—	—	—	37	83	33	20	70	5
Income $	—	—	—	—	—	0.00	0.00	0.00	0.00	0.00	0.00	0.00
Capital Gains $	—	—	—	—	—	0.00	0.51	0.08	0.00	0.00	0.00	0.00
Expense Ratio %	—	—	—	—	—	1.93	1.56	1.53	1.57	1.61	1.59	—
Income Ratio %	—	—	—	—	—	-0.63	-0.77	-0.80	-0.89	-1.04	-1.23	—
Turnover Rate %	—	—	—	—	—	204	62	64	84	40	47	—
Net Assets $mil	—	—	—	—	—	100	603	668	669	577	890	1,312

Performance 12-31-04

	1st Qtr	2nd Qtr	3rd Qtr	4th Qtr	Total
2000	-0.64	-2.39	-0.73	-14.36	-17.55
2001	-9.88	13.21	-22.29	21.21	-3.90
2002	1.11	-8.19	-18.79	5.60	-20.39
2003	-5.72	21.47	6.52	14.07	39.15
2004	6.87	3.24	-3.95	16.56	23.52

Trailing	Total Return%	+/- S&P 500	+/- Russ 2000 Gr	%Rank Cat	Growth of $10,000
3 Mo	16.56	7.33	1.48	10	11,656
6 Mo	11.95	4.76	3.79	13	11,195
1 Yr	23.52	12.65	9.21	5	12,352
3 Yr Avg	11.02	7.44	5.23	13	13,684
5 Yr Avg	1.63	3.93	5.20	37	10,842
10 Yr Avg	—	—	—	—	—
15 Yr Avg	—	—	—	—	—

Tax Analysis	Tax-Adj Rtn%	%Rank Cat	Tax-Cost Rat	%Rank Cat
3 Yr (estimated)	9.71	15	0.00	1
5 Yr (estimated)	0.88	35	0.03	2
10 Yr (estimated)	—	—	—	—

Potential Capital Gain Exposure: 27% of assets

Rating and Risk

Time Period	Load-Adj Return %	Morningstar Rtn vs Cat	Morningstar Risk vs Cat	Morningstar Risk-Adj Rating
1 Yr	19.20			
3 Yr	9.71	+Avg	Avg	★★★★
5 Yr	0.91	Avg	-Avg	★★★
10 Yr	—	—	—	—
Incept	15.23			

Other Measures	Standard Index S&P 500	Best Fit Index Russ 2000
Alpha	7.6	0.3
Beta	1.04	0.92
R-Squared	74	94

Standard Deviation	20.25
Mean	11.02
Sharpe Ratio	0.48

Portfolio Analysis 08-31-04

Share change since 05-04 Total Stocks:209	Sector	PE	YTD Ret%	% Assets
Florida Rock Industries	Ind Mtrls	21.2	68.98	4.32
⊕ Mettler-Toledo Internati	Health	21.6	21.56	4.08
United Natural Foods	Consumer	37.4	73.21	3.48
⊕ Waste Connections	Business	20.4	36.02	3.20
MPS Group	Business	39.8	31.12	2.67
American Tower A	Telecom	—	70.06	2.12
Polycom	Hardware	45.9	19.47	2.02
⊕ Ctrip.com International	Business	—	—	1.71
⊕ Alamosa Holdings	Telecom	—	210.97	1.62
⊕ Wright Medical Group	Health	39.3	-6.25	1.59
Silicon Valley Bancshare	Financial	50.6	24.26	1.55
Molina Healthcare	Health	—	83.83	1.48
ResMed	Health	30.4	23.01	1.42
⊖ Whole Foods Market	Consumer	45.4	43.11	1.34
Actuant A	Ind Mtrls	50.7	44.06	1.30
Cooper Companies	Health	28.4	49.92	1.28
Teekay Shipping	Business	19.4	49.82	1.27
Brunswick	Goods	18.1	57.47	1.26
⊕ United Online	Telecom	28.6	-31.33	1.18
Liz Claiborne	Goods	14.8	19.76	1.16

Current Investment Style

Value Blnd Growth / Large Mid Small

Market Cap	%
Giant	0.0
Large	0.9
Mid	40.6
Small	42.8
Micro	15.7

Avg $mil: 1,075

Value Measures		Rel Category
Price/Earnings	19.01	0.88
Price/Book	2.28	0.87
Price/Sales	1.25	0.83
Price/Cash Flow	8.72	1.09
Dividend Yield %	0.25	0.81

Growth Measures	%	Rel Category
Long-Term Erngs	15.98	0.92
Book Value	-3.25	NMF
Sales	2.19	0.34
Cash Flow	2.74	0.20
Historical Erngs	9.15	0.68

Profitability	%	Rel Category
Return on Equity	10.21	1.03
Return on Assets	4.88	1.11
Net Margin	5.19	0.76

Sector Weightings	% of Stocks	Rel S&P 500	3 Year High	3 Year Low
Info	22.08	1.03		
Software	3.68	0.86	6	0
Hardware	9.05	0.89	14	9
Media	3.02	0.79	4	3
Telecom	6.33	2.01	6	0
Service	54.83	1.18		
Health	18.55	1.48	19	9
Consumer	12.22	1.35	16	12
Business	17.24	4.26	17	13
Financial	6.82	0.33	8	6
Mfg	23.08	0.72		
Goods	5.38	0.58	18	5
Ind Mtrls	15.02	1.19	17	12
Energy	2.54	0.35	3	2
Utilities	0.14	0.05	0	0

Composition

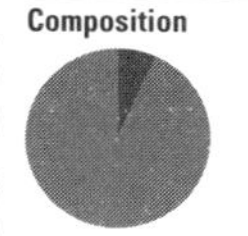

Cash	6.6
Stocks	93.4
Bonds	0.0
Other	0.0
Foreign (% of Stock)	7.9

Morningstar's Take by Christine Benz 12-14-04

We're fans of Fidelity Advisor Small Cap's manager, but potential investors should keep their expectations in check.

Within the small-growth group, it can be tough to find offerings with seasoned managers who have generated strong long-run returns without throwing risk control out the window. This one fits the bill, though. Both on this offering and on Fidelity Capital Appreciation, manager Harry Lange has demonstrated a deft touch that many growth managers seem to lack. As a former technology-fund manager, he has done a good job surfing the sector's cycles, upping his weighting in technology stocks when other managers are pessimistic and cutting back when rivals are euphoric (as many of his peers were earlier this year). Nor is he dogmatic about where he turns up growth stocks; trash haulers, natural food purveyors, and gravel companies have delivered solid gains here over the past year.

Investors buying in now should keep a few caveats in mind, though. First, smaller stocks have outperformed large for several years running; that trend will eventually reverse itself. And this fund's eclectic style means it will occasionally try its shareholders' patience. True, Lange's valuation-consciousness has generally helped the fund to above-average downside performance. In 2000, however, some weak stock picks led to greater losses than the typical small-growth fund endured. Finally, the fund's growing asset base is a concern. At $2.5 billion, it's one of the five largest small-growth funds. The fund's girth has yet to result in a perversion of Lange's style, but unabated asset growth will, at some point, affect how he runs the fund.

Would-be investors should also take care to choose the share class that best fits their estimated holding period. The T shares boast a lower sales charge than the A shares, but they also carry higher ongoing distribution fees than do the A shares.

Address:	82 Devonshire St Boston MA 02109 800-522-7297
Web Address:	www.fidelity.com
Inception:	09-09-98 *
Advisor:	Fidelity Management & Research Co. (FMR)
Subadvisor:	FMR Co., Inc. (FMRC)
NTF Plans:	DATALynx NTF, Federated Tr NTF

Minimum Purchase:	$2500	Add: $100	IRA: $500
Min Auto Inv Plan:	$100	Add: $100	
Sales Fees:	3.50%L, 0.25%S		
Management Fee:	0.45%		
Actual Fees:	Mgt:0.45%	Dist:0.50%	
Expense Projections:	3Yr:$834	5Yr:$1185	10Yr:$2173
Income Distrib:	Annually		

Fidelity Asset Mgr

Analyst Pick

Ticker	Load	NAV	Yield	Total Assets	Mstar Category
FASMX	None	$16.21	2.4%	$10,955 mil	Moderate Allocation

Governance and Management

Fiduciary Grade: B

Portfolio Manager(s)

There's a lot of experience here. Lead manager Dick Habermann has managed money for decades. Equity manager Charles Mangum has been successful Fidelity Dividend Growth Fund, a Fund Analyst Pick in the large-blend category. Mangum joined Fidelity in 1992 and, earlier in his career, managed multiple sector funds. Matt Conti and Jeff Moore handle the fund's high-yield and investment-grade bond portfolios, respectively.

Strategy

The fund has a neutral allocation mix of 50% stocks, 40% bonds, and 10% cash and lead manager Dick Habermann only slightly adjusts those weightings based on his economic outlook. Charles Mangum looks for stocks with reasonable valuations and decent growth prospects. Matt Conti and Jeff Moore use security selection, and not interest-rate bets, to drive returns in the fixed income portfolio.

Historical Profile

Return: Average
Risk: Average
Rating: ★★★ Neutral

Investment Style: Equity — Stock %: 44% 55% 45% 56% 49% 44% 40% 46% 46%

▼ Manager Change
▽ Partial Manager Change

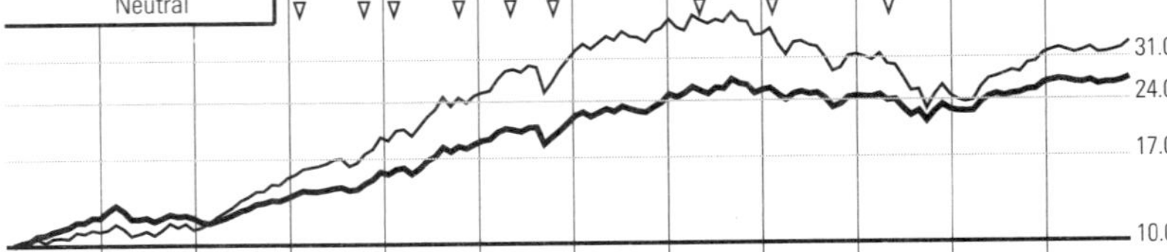

Growth of $10,000
— Investment Values of Fund
— Investment Values of S&P 500

Performance Quartile (within Category)

History

1993	1994	1995	1996	1997	1998	1999	2000	2001	2002	2003	12-04	History
15.40	13.83	15.85	16.47	18.35	17.39	18.38	16.82	15.50	13.80	15.76	16.21	NAV
23.29	-6.60	18.16	12.73	22.27	16.09	13.59	2.38	-3.93	-8.05	17.18	5.40	Total Return %
13.23	-7.91	-19.37	-10.21	-11.08	-12.48	-7.45	11.48	7.95	14.04	-11.49	-5.47	+/-S&P 500
11.56	-4.65	-6.61	1.39	3.07	3.70	0.74	-2.06	-4.09	2.49	-6.88	-5.77	+/-DJ 60%
4.48	2.62	3.36	3.97	3.75	3.31	3.26	3.58	3.92	3.07	2.78	2.50	Income Return %
18.81	-9.22	14.80	8.76	18.52	12.78	10.33	-1.20	-7.85	-11.12	14.40	2.90	Capital Return %
1	92	97	63	28	35	30	38	39	18	75	88	Total Rtn % Rank Cat
0.59	0.40	0.46	0.62	0.61	0.60	0.56	0.65	0.65	0.47	0.38	0.39	Income $
0.43	0.17	0.00	0.75	1.11	3.15	0.74	1.34	0.00	0.00	0.00	0.00	Capital Gains $
1.09	1.04	0.97	0.93	0.78	0.74	0.73	0.71	0.71	0.73	0.74	0.73	Expense Ratio %
4.28	3.63	4.27	3.64	3.39	3.19	3.01	3.32	3.51	3.31	2.82	2.12	Income Ratio %
98	109	137	131	79	136	104	109	133	129	120	78	Turnover Rate %
9,094	11,076	11,165	10,972	12,099	12,879	13,254	12,961	11,924	10,118	11,371	10,955	Net Assets $mil

Performance 12-31-04

	1st Qtr	2nd Qtr	3rd Qtr	4th Qtr	Total
2000	4.43	-0.51	2.44	-3.80	2.38
2001	-5.86	3.42	-7.79	7.00	-3.93
2002	0.77	-8.04	-7.39	7.14	-8.05
2003	-1.01	10.91	0.53	6.16	17.18
2004	1.58	-0.25	-1.45	5.55	5.40

Trailing	Total Return%	+/- S&P 500	+/- DJ 60%	%Rank Cat	Growth of $10,000
3 Mo	5.55	-3.68	-1.93	80	10,555
6 Mo	4.02	-3.17	-3.51	90	10,402
1 Yr	5.40	-5.47	-5.77	88	10,540
3 Yr Avg	4.33	0.75	-2.93	57	11,356
5 Yr Avg	2.24	4.54	-3.00	43	11,171
10 Yr Avg	9.14	-2.93	-1.35	45	23,979
15 Yr Avg	9.79	-1.14	-0.16	38	40,592

Tax Analysis	Tax-Adj Rtn%	%Rank Cat	Tax-Cost Rat	%Rank Cat
3 Yr (estimated)	3.36	51	0.93	65
5 Yr (estimated)	0.70	46	1.51	74
10 Yr (estimated)	6.87	49	2.08	70

Potential Capital Gain Exposure: 6% of assets

Rating and Risk

Time Period	Load-Adj Return %	Morningstar Rtn vs Cat	Morningstar Risk vs Cat	Morningstar Risk-Adj Rating
1 Yr	5.40			
3 Yr	4.33	Avg	Avg	★★★
5 Yr	2.24	Avg	Avg	★★★
10 Yr	9.14	Avg	Avg	★★★
Incept	10.14			

Other Measures	Standard Index S&P 500	Best Fit Index S&P 500
Alpha	1.4	1.4
Beta	0.58	0.58
R-Squared	90	90
Standard Deviation	9.55	
Mean	4.33	
Sharpe Ratio	0.31	

Portfolio Analysis 09-30-04

Total Stocks:365 Share change since 06-30-04	Sectors	P/E Ratio	YTD Return %	% Net Assets
American International Gr	Financial	16.2	2.25	2.73
Microsoft	Software	36.1	0.04	2.49
⊕ Home Depot	Consumer	19.0	-2.41	2.35
⊕ Pfizer	Health	22.0	-2.75	2.01
⊕ SBC Communications	Telecom	15.4	-3.12	1.95
⊖ Fannie Mae	Financial	9.1	-1.07	1.82
⊖ Cardinal Health	Health	16.9	-5.42	1.70
Clear Channel Communicati	Media	23.5	-6.03	1.67
⊕ Wyeth	Health	17.0	-0.85	1.62

Total Fixed-Income:1093	Date of Maturity	Amount $000	Value $000	% Net Assets
FNMA 5.5%	01-01-34	141,767	143,866	1.25
US Treasury Bond 7.875%	02-15-21	98,000	132,610	1.15
FNMA 2.5%	06-15-06	128,100	127,651	1.11
FNMA 0.06%	08-01-25	85,144	89,428	0.78
FNMA 0.05%	02-01-34	85,991	85,205	0.74
FNMA 0.04%	05-01-19	83,796	81,798	0.71
FNMA 4.5%	10-01-33	75,248	72,653	0.63
FNMA 3.125%	07-15-06	64,580	65,047	0.57
FNMA 0.05%	02-01-18	58,694	59,757	0.52

Equity Style
Style: Blend
Size: Large-Cap

Value Measures		Rel Category
Price/Earnings	15.33	0.93
Price/Book	2.35	0.96
Price/Sales	1.32	1.00
Price/Cash Flow	5.60	0.77
Dividend Yield %	1.73	1.10

Growth Measures	%	Rel Category
Long-Term Erngs	11.61	1.00
Book Value	6.30	1.10
Sales	5.70	1.10
Cash Flow	5.94	0.74
Historical Erngs	9.68	0.89

Market Cap %			
Giant	65.8	Small	0.6
Large	23.6	Micro	0.1
Mid	10.0	Avg $mil:	52,348

Fixed-Income Style
Duration: —
Quality: —

Avg Eff Duration[1]	—
Avg Eff Maturity	—
Avg Credit Quality	—
Avg Wtd Coupon	4.99%

[1]figure provided by fund

Sector Weightings	% of Stocks	Rel S&P 500	3 Year High	3 Year Low
Info	25.32	1.18		
Software	5.82	1.35	6	3
Hardware	7.21	0.71	7	6
Media	4.78	1.24	9	5
Telecom	7.51	2.38	8	4
Service	56.41	1.22		
Health	16.24	1.30	23	16
Consumer	10.63	1.17	11	6
Business	1.84	0.45	2	1
Financial	27.70	1.33	28	23
Mfg	18.27	0.57		
Goods	4.42	0.47	8	3
Ind Mtrls	7.90	0.62	9	7
Energy	4.66	0.65	8	5
Utilities	1.29	0.44	3	1

Composition

Cash	19.4
Stocks	46.4
Bonds	28.7
Other	5.5
Foreign (% of Stock)	8.3

Morningstar's Take by Andrew Gogerty 01-03-05

Fidelity Asset Manager remains a solid option for investors wanting consistency in a fund's asset allocation.

Investors won't find many surprises here. Lead manager Dick Habermann keeps a tight leash on the fund's makeup, only modestly adjusting its weightings among stocks, bonds, and cash based on his outlook on the economy. For instance, Habermann remains bullish on equities, but has only allowed that allocation to rise to 55% of assets (from a neutral weight of 50%) in 2004. Charles Mangum runs the equity portfolio, and he employs the same price-conscious, contrarian growth style here as at large-blend Analyst Pick Fidelity Dividend Growth. Habermann divides the fund's bond sleeve between high-yield and investment-grade issues and managers Matt Conti and Jeff Moore focus on security selection, not interest-rate bets, to drive returns.

Even with this strong pedigree, some investors may find appeal among its siblings. Fidelity's Freedom lineup targets certain retirement years from 2005 to 2040 by using a fund-of-funds structure to prepare investors for retirement. Those funds shift towards a higher fixed-income stake as their target years approach. This also provides investors diversified exposure to multiple mangers and investment styles.

Investors looking for more flexibility or a higher equity stake also have options. Sibling Fidelity Balanced Fund currently has approximately 70% devoted to equities, and it has a history of sizeable allocation shifts. Within the Asset Manager lineup, the Growth and Aggressive offerings have a higher equity allocation than this fund's current 55%.

In the end, though, investors must decide which combination of characteristics they prefer. Those wanting a static, core portfolio have a strong choice here. While the fund hasn't raced to the front of the pack, it has seldom fallen far behind. That steadiness combined with modest expenses and a seasoned management team are appealing.

Address:	82 Devonshire St Boston MA 02109 800-343-3548
Web Address:	www.fidelity.com
Inception:	12-28-88
Advisor:	Fidelity Management & Research Co. (FMR)
Subadvisor:	FMR Co., Inc. (FMRC)
NTF Plans:	Fidelity Retail-NTF, CommonWealth NTF

Minimum Purchase:	$2500	Add: $250	IRA: $2500
Min Auto Inv Plan:	$2500	Add: $100	
Sales Fees:	No-load		
Management Fee:	0.53%		
Actual Fees:	Mgt:0.53%	Dist:	
Expense Projections:	3Yr:$240	5Yr:$417	10Yr:$930
Income Distrib:	Quarterly		

Fidelity Asset Mgr: Aggr

Ticker	Load	NAV	Yield	Total Assets	Mstar Category
FAMRX	None	$11.31	0.5%	$399 mil	Large Growth

Governance and Management

Fiduciary Grade: B

Portfolio Manager(s)

In November 2002, Harry Lange replaced Bahaa Fam as the fund's equity portfolio manager. Lange has produced impressive results at Fidelity Capital Appreciation since assuming its reins in March 1996. Team leader Dick Habermann has been managing money at Fidelity since the early 1970s and has been on board here since the offering's September 1999 inception. Matt Conti handles the portfolio's fixed-income allocation.

Strategy

Lead manager Dick Habermann sets the fund's asset allocation. The fund's neutral stock weighting is 85%, but Habermann can raise that weight to 100% or lower it to 60%, depending on his assessment of the relative attractiveness of stocks, bonds, and cash. Within the stock portion, manager Harry Lange looks for reasonably priced growth stocks. The bond portfolio is focused on high-yield credits.

Historical Profile

Return High
Risk Above Avg
Rating ★★★★★ Highest

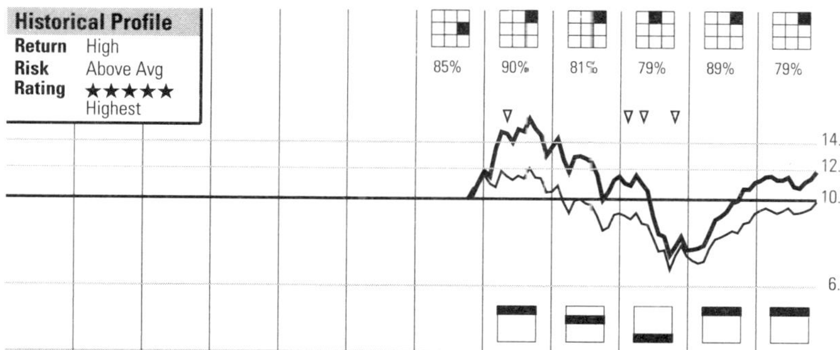

Investment Style
Equity
Stock %

▼ Manager Change
▽ Partial Manager Change

Growth of $10,000
— Investment Values of Fund
— Investment Values of S&P 500

Performance Quartile (within Category)

1993	1994	1995	1996	1997	1998	1999	2000	2001	2002	2003	12-04	History
—	—	—	—	—	—	11.93	13.03	10.76	6.93	10.24	11.31	NAV
—	—	—	—	—	—	20.05*	15.44	-15.72	-34.95	48.65	11.05	Total Return %
—	—	—	—	—	—	—	24.54	-3.84	-12.86	19.98	0.18	+/-S&P 500
—	—	—	—	—	—	—	37.86	4.70	-7.07	18.90	4.75	+/-Russ 1000Gr
—	—	—	—	—	—	0.00	1.09	1.69	0.65	0.87	0.59	Income Return %
—	—	—	—	—	—	—	14.35	-17.41	-35.60	47.78	10.46	Capital Return %
—	—	—	—	—	—	—	2	26	90	3	21	Total Rtn % Rank Cat
—	—	—	—	—	—	0.02	0.13	0.22	0.07	0.06	0.06	Income $
—	—	—	—	—	—	0.05	0.60	0.00	0.00	0.00	0.00	Capital Gains $
—	—	—	—	—	—	1.20	0.90	0.85	0.88	1.00	0.91	Expense Ratio %
—	—	—	—	—	—	4.06	1.32	1.55	0.87	0.63	0.52	Income Ratio %
—	—	—	—	—	—	—	338	255	240	131	86	Turnover Rate %
—	—	—	—	—	—	43	443	288	148	318	399	Net Assets $mil

Performance 12-31-04

	1st Qtr	2nd Qtr	3rd Qtr	4th Qtr	Total
2000	25.90	1.60	0.39	-10.10	15.44
2001	-13.66	8.27	-21.43	14.76	-15.72
2002	0.56	-21.16	-20.40	3.08	-34.95
2003	2.60	18.71	9.72	11.25	48.65
2004	3.81	-0.47	-2.74	10.51	11.05

Trailing	Total Return%	+/- S&P 500	+/- Russ 1000Gr	%Rank Cat	Growth of $10,000
3 Mo	10.51	1.28	1.34	38	11,051
6 Mo	7.48	0.29	4.01	18	10,748
1 Yr	11.05	0.18	4.75	21	11,105
3 Yr Avg	2.40	-1.18	2.58	22	10,737
5 Yr Avg	0.88	3.18	10.17	4	10,448
10 Yr Avg	—	—	—	—	—
15 Yr Avg	—	—	—	—	—

Tax Analysis	Tax-Adj Rtn%	%Rank Cat	Tax-Cost Rat	%Rank Cat
3 Yr (estimated)	2.16	20	0.23	40
5 Yr (estimated)	0.15	4	0.72	44
10 Yr (estimated)	—	—	—	—

Potential Capital Gain Exposure: -28% of assets

Rating and Risk

Time Period	Load-Adj Return %	Morningstar Rtn vs Cat	Morningstar Risk vs Cat	Morningstar Risk-Adj Rating
1 Yr	11.05			
3 Yr	2.40	+Avg	+Avg	★★★★
5 Yr	0.88	High	+Avg	★★★★★
10 Yr	—	—	—	—
Incept	4.39			

Other Measures	Standard Index S&P 500	Best Fit Index Russ MG
Alpha	-0.9	-3.1
Beta	1.08	0.93
R-Squared	83	90
Standard Deviation	18.42	
Mean	2.40	
Sharpe Ratio	0.06	

Portfolio Analysis 09-30-04

Share change since 06-04 Total Stocks:201	Sector	PE	YTD Ret%	% Assets
S&P 500 Index (Fut)	—	—	—	3.80
⊕ Genentech	Health	78.6	16.36	3.47
⊕ Univision Communications	Media	39.5	-26.25	2.37
⊕ Seagate Technology	Hardware	22.3	-5.50	2.28
☼ Research In Motion Ltd	Hardware	—	146.66	2.00
⊖ SBC Communications	Telecom	15.4	3.74	1.93
⊕ KLA-Tencor	Hardware	26.4	-20.43	1.67
KDDI	Telecom	—	—	1.66
⊕ Teradyne	Hardware	19.5	-32.93	1.60
FedEx	Business	27.9	46.40	1.56
⊕ Dell	Hardware	34.0	24.01	1.48
Zimmer Holdings	Health	54.0	13.81	1.48
⊕ Biogen IDEC	Health	—	81.50	1.45
☼ Altera	Hardware	26.2	-8.61	1.41
⊕ Samsung Electronics	Goods	—	—	1.35
⊕ EMC	Hardware	41.5	15.09	1.31
⊖ Whole Foods Market	Consumer	45.4	43.11	1.15
⊖ Microsoft	Software	36.1	8.95	1.07
⊖ Noble	Energy	51.7	39.02	1.02
⊕ Analog Devices	Hardware	24.2	-18.69	1.00

Current Investment Style

Market Cap	%
Giant	30.5
Large	35.3
Mid	30.6
Small	2.5
Micro	1.1
Avg $mil: 15,152	

Value Measures		Rel Category
Price/Earnings	20.31	0.95
Price/Book	1.70	0.53
Price/Sales	1.82	0.85
Price/Cash Flow	6.76	0.62
Dividend Yield %	0.71	0.92

Growth Measures	%	Rel Category
Long-Term Erngs	13.64	0.97
Book Value	12.53	0.99
Sales	5.30	0.62
Cash Flow	5.51	0.33
Historical Erngs	10.23	0.71

Profitability	%	Rel Category
Return on Equity	13.66	0.76
Return on Assets	6.88	0.74
Net Margin	8.96	0.73

Sector Weightings	% of Stocks	Rel S&P 500	3 Year High	3 Year Low
Info	43.77	2.04		
Software	4.50	1.05	7	1
Hardware	24.64	2.42	28	13
Media	8.87	2.31	20	0
Telecom	5.76	1.83	7	1
Service	40.64	0.88		
Health	17.13	1.37	20	10
Consumer	6.47	0.71	23	6
Business	6.56	1.62	7	0
Financial	10.48	0.50	20	8
Mfg	15.57	0.48		
Goods	5.12	0.55	6	1
Ind Mtrls	5.24	0.41	8	2
Energy	5.21	0.73	13	3
Utilities	0.00	0.00	2	0

Composition

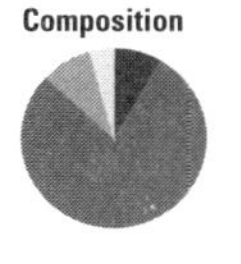

Cash	8.1
Stocks	78.8
Bonds	8.8
Other	4.3
Foreign (% of Stock)	19.1

Morningstar's Take by Andrew Gogerty 10-06-04

This fund's flexibility works well.

Fidelity Asset Manager: Aggressive isn't afraid to run with the crowd. Lead manager Dick Habermann let the fund's asset allocation loose in 2003, stashing 95% of assets into stocks. This is well above the fund's neutral target of 85% stocks and 15% bonds and allowed it to fully participate in the equity market's rally. The fund's 48% gain last year beat 97% of its large-growth peers.

Habermann still remains bullish on stocks this year, but in a muted way. The uncertainty in energy prices and the lull in the economy this summer have given him pause, and he cut back the fund's equity exposure to 86% of assets earlier this year. He has also trimmed the fund's bond exposure--which is made up entirely of high-yield credits--to 9%. Habermann thinks rising interest rates are a danger and that higher-yielding bonds will perform better in this environment.

Nevertheless, equity manager Harry Lange continues to display his stock-picking prowess. He has been betting on the health-care and consumer discretionary sectors this year, citing their strong growth potential. This has paid off, as shares of health-care equipment maker Zimmer Holdings and grocer Whole Foods have delivered strong double-digit gains thus far in 2004. Also, bond manager Matt Conti's stake in high-yield credits has continued to do well.

Investors should note the fund's biases, however. Performance has benefited from a slug of mid-cap names that could hold the fund back should the market turn back to mega-cap names. Also, Lange likes to see his winners run, resulting in pricey names in the portfolio at times.

Overall, though, the fund's flexibility is appealing. It remains a strong growth option.

Address:	82 Devonshire St Boston MA 02109 800-343-3548
Web Address:	www.fidelity.com
Inception:	09-24-99*
Advisor:	Fidelity Management & Research Co. (FMR)
Subadvisor:	FMR Co., Inc. (FMRC)
NTF Plans:	Fidelity Retail-NTF, CommonWealth NTF

Minimum Purchase:	$2500	Add: $250	IRA: $2500
Min Auto Inv Plan:	$2500	Add: $100	
Sales Fees:	No-load		
Management Fee:	0.58%		
Actual Fees:	Mgt:0.58%	Dist:	
Expense Projections:	3Yr:$309	5Yr:$536	10Yr:$1190
Income Distrib:	Annually		

Fidelity Asset Mgr: Grth

Ticker	Load	NAV	Yield	Total Assets	Mstar Category
FASGX	None	$14.82	2.2%	$3,733 mil	Moderate Allocation

Governance and Management

Fiduciary Grade: B

Portfolio Manager(s)

Experienced. Lead manager Dick Habermann has managed money for decades. Equity manager Charles Mangum has been successful Fidelity Dividend Growth, a Fund Analyst Pick in the large-blend category. Mangum joined Fidelity in 1992 and, earlier in his career, managed multiple sector funds. Matt Conti and Jeff Moore handle the fund's high-yield and investment-grade bond portfolios, respectively.

Strategy

Dick Habermann sets the fund's overall asset allocation but generally makes only limited bets: The fund tends to stick close to its neutral weighting of 70% stocks, 25% bonds, and 5% cash. Charles Mangum runs the equity portfolio; he is a growth-at-a-reasonable-price investor with a terrific record elsewhere. He has historically favored pharmaceuticals and financials over high-priced technology shares, but overall, he is a bit of a contrarian-growth investor. Matt Conti and Jeff Moore use security selection, and not interest-rate bets, to drive returns in the fixed-income portfolio.

Historical Profile

Return: Average
Risk: High
Rating: ★★ Below Avg

Investment Style
Equity
Stock %: 68% 72% 68% 71% 68% 64% 60% 65% 66%

▼ Manager Change
▽ Partial Manager Change

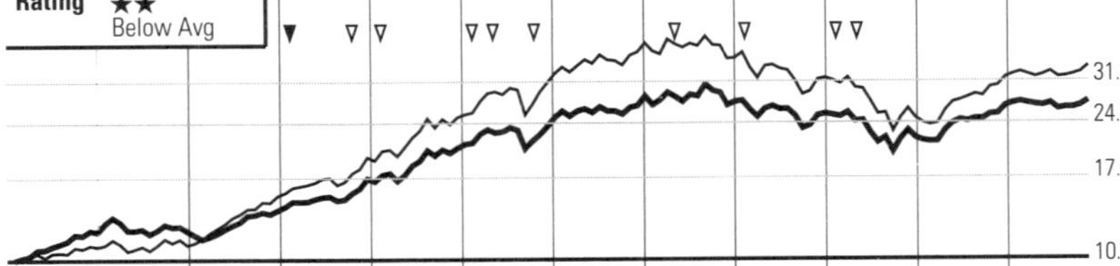

Growth of $10,000
- Investment Values of Fund
- Investment Values of S&P 500

Performance Quartile (within Category)

1993	1994	1995	1996	1997	1998	1999	2000	2001	2002	2003	12-04	History
14.25	12.84	15.17	16.35	18.48	18.68	19.67	15.91	14.34	11.97	14.28	14.82	NAV
26.32	-7.39	19.95	17.59	26.46	18.08	13.97	-3.55	-7.22	-14.05	21.93	6.05	Total Return %
16.26	-8.70	-17.58	-5.35	-6.89	-10.49	-7.07	5.55	4.66	8.04	-6.74	-4.82	+/-S&P 500
14.59	-5.44	-4.82	6.25	7.26	5.69	1.12	-7.99	-7.38	-3.51	-2.13	-5.12	+/-DJ 60%
0.76	1.33	1.79	2.83	2.45	1.89	2.41	2.34	2.64	2.51	2.59	2.24	Income Return %
25.56	-8.72	18.16	14.76	24.01	16.19	11.56	-5.89	-9.86	-16.56	19.34	3.81	Capital Return %
1	94	94	18	6	24	28	80	73	71	32	83	Total Rtn % Rank Cat
0.09	0.19	0.23	0.43	0.40	0.35	0.45	0.46	0.42	0.36	0.31	0.32	Income $
0.51	0.17	0.00	1.07	1.75	2.68	1.10	2.56	0.00	0.00	0.00	0.00	Capital Gains $
1.19	1.15	1.02	1.01	0.86	0.80	0.80	0.77	0.78	0.81	0.83	0.82	Expense Ratio %
3.02	2.64	3.16	2.51	2.36	2.49	2.38	2.46	2.62	2.73	2.53	1.77	Income Ratio %
97	104	119	138	70	150	101	197	143	101	72	67	Turnover Rate %
1,795	2,853	2,895	3,378	4,663	5,120	5,490	4,827	4,234	3,341	3,774	3,733	Net Assets $mil

Performance 12-31-04

	1st Qtr	2nd Qtr	3rd Qtr	4th Qtr	Total
2000	2.24	-1.34	2.47	-6.68	-3.55
2001	-8.99	4.77	-11.14	9.51	-7.22
2002	0.84	-11.83	-11.37	9.07	-14.05
2003	-2.17	14.35	0.60	8.35	21.93
2004	1.54	-0.07	-2.69	7.41	6.05

Trailing	Total Return%	+/- S&P 500	+/- DJ 60%	%Rank Cat	Growth of $10,000
3 Mo	7.41	-1.82	-0.07	38	10,741
6 Mo	4.51	-2.68	-3.02	87	10,451
1 Yr	6.05	-4.82	-5.12	83	10,605
3 Yr Avg	3.58	0.00	-3.68	71	11,113
5 Yr Avg	-0.11	2.19	-5.35	78	9,945
10 Yr Avg	9.09	-2.98	-1.40	47	23,870
15 Yr Avg	—	—	—	—	—

Tax Analysis	Tax-Adj Rtn%	%Rank Cat	Tax-Cost Rat	%Rank Cat
3 Yr (estimated)	2.76	61	0.79	55
5 Yr (estimated)	-1.56	79	1.45	70
10 Yr (estimated)	6.98	47	1.93	59

Potential Capital Gain Exposure: -11% of assets

Rating and Risk

Time Period	Load-Adj Return %	Morningstar Rtn vs Cat	Morningstar Risk vs Cat	Morningstar Risk-Adj Rating
1 Yr	6.05			
3 Yr	3.58	Avg	High	★★
5 Yr	-0.11	-Avg	+Avg	★★
10 Yr	9.09	Avg	High	★★★
Incept	9.75			

Other Measures	Standard Index S&P 500	Best Fit Index S&P 500
Alpha	0.3	0.3
Beta	0.82	0.82
R-Squared	94	94
Standard Deviation	13.19	
Mean	3.58	
Sharpe Ratio	0.17	

Portfolio Analysis 09-30-04

Total Stocks:187 Share change since 06-30-04	Sectors	P/E Ratio	YTD Return %	% Net Assets
American International Gr	Financial	16.2	2.25	3.81
Microsoft	Software	36.1	0.04	3.50
⊕ Home Depot	Consumer	19.0	-2.41	3.28
⊕ Pfizer	Health	22.0	-2.75	2.81
⊕ SBC Communications	Telecom	15.4	-3.12	2.73
⊖ Fannie Mae	Financial	9.1	-1.07	2.54
⊖ Cardinal Health	Health	16.9	-5.42	2.38
Clear Channel Communicati	Media	23.5	-6.03	2.34
⊕ Wyeth	Health	17.0	-0.85	2.27

Total Fixed-Income:1071	Date of Maturity	Amount $000	Value $000	% Net Assets
FNMA 5.5%	03-01-34	19,706	19,994	0.53
FNMA 2.5%	06-15-06	12,100	12,058	0.32
Tyco Intl Grp S A Cv 3.12	01-15-23	7,880	11,780	0.31
US Treasury Bond 7.875%	02-15-21	8,560	11,583	0.31
FNMA 0.04%	06-01-19	10,798	10,647	0.28
FNMA 5%	06-01-34	9,000	8,919	0.24
FNMA 4.5%	10-01-33	7,358	7,104	0.19
GNMA 0.06%	12-15-31	6,500	6,871	0.18
FNMA 3.125%	07-15-06	4,095	4,125	0.11

Equity Style
Style: Blend
Size: Large-Cap

Value Measures		Rel Category
Price/Earnings	15.38	0.93
Price/Book	2.39	0.98
Price/Sales	1.36	1.03
Price/Cash Flow	5.60	0.77
Dividend Yield %	1.69	1.08

Growth Measures	%	Rel Category
Long-Term Erngs	11.55	0.99
Book Value	6.71	1.17
Sales	5.94	1.15
Cash Flow	8.37	1.04
Historical Erngs	9.76	0.90

Market Cap %			
Giant	65.2	Small	0.2
Large	23.4	Micro	0.0
Mid	11.2	Avg $mil:	51,188

Fixed-Income Style
Duration: —
Quality: —

Avg Eff Duration[1]	—
Avg Eff Maturity	—
Avg Credit Quality	—
Avg Wtd Coupon	6.36%

[1]figure provided by fund

Sector Weightings	% of Stocks	Rel S&P 500	3 Year High	3 Year Low
Info	25.43	1.18		
Software	5.84	1.36	6	2
Hardware	7.41	0.73	7	5
Media	4.70	1.22	9	5
Telecom	7.48	2.37	8	4
Service	55.69	1.20		
Health	16.50	1.32	23	17
Consumer	10.25	1.13	10	6
Business	1.92	0.47	2	1
Financial	27.02	1.30	27	24
Mfg	18.88	0.59		
Goods	4.72	0.51	7	3
Ind Mtrls	8.12	0.64	9	7
Energy	4.92	0.69	8	4
Utilities	1.12	0.38	3	1

Composition

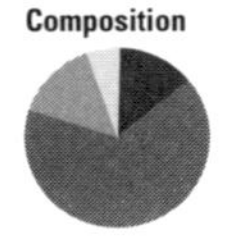

Cash	13.9
Stocks	66.1
Bonds	14.6
Other	5.5
Foreign (% of Stock)	9.2

Morningstar's Take by Andrew Gogerty 01-03-05

Fidelity Asset Manager: Growth's consistent asset allocation is appealing.

Investors won't find many surprises here. Lead manager Dick Habermann keeps a tight leash on the fund's makeup, only modestly adjusting its weightings among stocks, bonds, and cash based on his outlook on the economy. For instance, Habermann remains bullish on equities but has only allowed that allocation to rise to 76% of assets (from a neutral weight of 70%) in 2004. Charles Mangum runs the equity portfolio, and he employs the same price-conscious, contrarian growth style here as at large-blend Analyst Pick Fidelity Dividend Growth. Habermann divides the fund's bond sleeve between high-yield and investment-grade issues and managers Matt Conti and Jeff Moore focus on security selection, not interest-rate bets, to drive returns.

Even with this strong pedigree, some investors may find appeal among its siblings. Fidelity's Freedom lineup targets certain retirement years from 2005 to 2040 by using a fund-of-funds structure to prepare investors for retirement. Those funds shift toward a higher fixed-income stake as their target years approach. This also provides investors diversified exposure to multiple mangers and investment styles.

Investors looking for more flexibility or a different equity stake also have options. Sibling Fidelity Balanced currently has a similar 70% equity stake but will make sizable allocation shifts. Within the Asset Manager lineup, investors have a broad range of equity-exposure choices. The fund's Income sibling has a modest 20% neutral stake in equities, moving up to family sibling Aggressive, which hold's 85% in equities and falls into Morningstar's large-growth category.

In the end, though, investors must decide which combination of characteristics they prefer. Those wanting a static, more aggressive, core portfolio have a strong choice here. The fund is seasoned at the top, and its modest price tag adds to its appeal.

Address:	82 Devonshire St Boston MA 02109 800-343-3548
Web Address:	www.fidelity.com
Inception:	12-30-91
Advisor:	Fidelity Management & Research Co. (FMR)
Subadvisor:	FMR Co., Inc. (FMRC)
NTF Plans:	Fidelity Retail-NTF, CommonWealth NTF

Minimum Purchase:	$2500	Add: $250	IRA: $2500
Min Auto Inv Plan:	$2500	Add: $100	
Sales Fees:	No-load		
Management Fee:	0.58%		
Actual Fees:	Mgt:0.58%	Dist:	
Expense Projections:	3Yr:$265	5Yr:$460	10Yr:$1025
Income Distrib:	Annually		

Fidelity Balanced

Ticker	Load	NAV	Yield	Total Assets	Mstar Category
FBALX	None	$17.82	1.4%	$12,577 mil	Moderate Allocation

Governance and Management

Fiduciary Grade: B

Portfolio Manager(s)

Larry Rakers took over the stock portion of the fund in February 2002. He previously managed Fidelity Convertible Securities, as well as seven Fidelity sector funds. Fixed-income manager George Fischer came on board in March 2004. Fischer began managing government and mortgage bond offerings for the firm in June 2002 and previously spent six years running various Fidelity municipal-bond funds.

Strategy

On the equity side, manager Larry Rakers emphasizes moderate valuations and keeps sector weightings in between those of the Russell 3000 Index and the Russell 3000 Value Index. Rakers has shown more of a willingness to hold mid- and small-cap names than his predecessor, and the fund's median market cap falls well below the group average. George Fischer, who recently took over the fixed-income portion, sticks chiefly to high-quality bonds and doesn't make interest-rate bets.

Historical Profile

Return Above Avg
Risk Average
Rating ★★★★ Above Avg

Investment Style: Equity — Stock %: 56% 57% 57% 60% 55% 53% 55% 61% 66%

▼ Manager Change
▽ Partial Manager Change

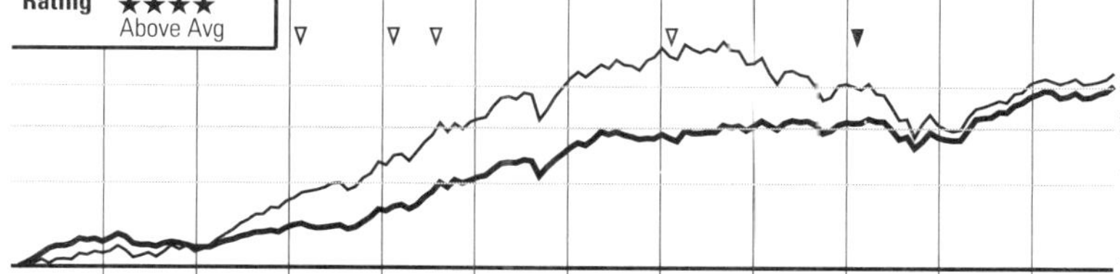

Growth of $10,000
— Investment Values of Fund
— Investment Values of S&P 500

Performance Quartile (within Category)

1993	1994	1995	1996	1997	1998	1999	2000	2001	2002	2003	12-04	History
13.39	12.29	13.52	14.08	15.27	16.36	15.36	15.19	14.90	13.29	16.75	17.82	NAV
19.28	-5.31	14.90	9.34	23.45	20.22	8.86	5.32	2.25	-8.49	28.24	10.94	Total Return %
9.22	-6.62	-22.63	-13.60	-9.90	-8.35	-12.18	14.42	14.13	13.60	-0.43	0.07	+/-S&P 500
7.55	-3.36	-9.87	-2.00	4.25	7.83	-3.99	0.88	2.09	2.05	4.18	-0.23	+/-DJ 60%
5.01	3.02	4.72	4.90	4.07	3.10	2.94	3.18	3.00	2.44	1.97	1.58	Income Return %
14.27	-8.33	10.18	4.44	19.38	17.12	5.92	2.14	-0.75	-10.93	26.27	9.36	Capital Return %
8	83	99	88	20	18	62	28	10	21	6	18	Total Rtn % Rank Cat
0.60	0.40	0.57	0.65	0.56	0.46	0.46	0.48	0.45	0.36	0.26	0.26	Income $
0.64	0.00	0.00	0.00	1.46	1.27	1.98	0.49	0.17	0.00	0.00	0.44	Capital Gains $
0.93	1.01	0.90	0.79	0.74	0.67	0.65	0.67	0.64	0.66	0.67	0.66	Expense Ratio %
5.07	4.09	5.33	4.12	3.58	2.97	2.67	2.98	3.05	2.79	2.17	1.63	Income Ratio %
162	157	269	247	70	135	157	139	115	150	137	99	Turnover Rate %
4,685	4,999	4,880	3,919	4,284	5,316	6,123	6,096	7,005	6,550	9,808	12,577	Net Assets $mil

Performance 12-31-04

	1st Qtr	2nd Qtr	3rd Qtr	4th Qtr	Total
2000	2.25	-0.97	2.96	1.01	5.32
2001	-2.13	4.87	-6.83	6.92	2.25
2002	2.42	-6.41	-10.89	7.13	-8.49
2003	-1.88	14.94	3.43	9.94	28.24
2004	3.34	-0.52	-0.54	8.50	10.94

Trailing	Total Return%	+/- S&P 500	+/- DJ 60%	%Rank Cat	Growth of $10,000
3 Mo	8.50	-0.73	1.02	16	10,850
6 Mo	7.91	0.72	0.38	23	10,791
1 Yr	10.94	0.07	-0.23	18	11,094
3 Yr Avg	9.19	5.61	1.93	4	13,018
5 Yr Avg	6.99	9.29	1.75	7	14,019
10 Yr Avg	11.02	-1.05	0.53	17	28,445
15 Yr Avg	10.34	-0.59	0.39	22	43,752

Tax Analysis	Tax-Adj Rtn%	%Rank Cat	Tax-Cost Rat	%Rank Cat
3 Yr (estimated)	8.31	3	0.81	56
5 Yr (estimated)	5.76	6	1.15	53
10 Yr (estimated)	8.73	17	2.06	69

Potential Capital Gain Exposure: 16% of assets

Rating and Risk

Time Period	Load-Adj Return %	Morningstar Rtn vs Cat	Morningstar Risk vs Cat	Morningstar Risk-Adj Rating
1 Yr	10.94			
3 Yr	9.19	High	+Avg	★★★★★
5 Yr	6.99	+Avg	Avg	★★★★
10 Yr	11.02	+Avg	Avg	★★★★
Incept	10.66			

Other Measures	Standard Index S&P 500	Best Fit Index DJ 60%
Alpha	5.9	-2.6
Beta	0.70	1.20
R-Squared	88	95
Standard Deviation	12.03	
Mean	9.19	
Sharpe Ratio	0.66	

Portfolio Analysis 10-31-04

Total Stocks:447 Share change since 07-31-04	Sectors	P/E Ratio	YTD Return %	% Net Assets
⊕ Citigroup	Financial	15.3	0.08	1.72
⊕ Bank of America	Financial	12.3	-3.85	1.44
⊖ Weatherford International	Energy	27.8	-3.70	1.11
⊕ General Electric	Ind Mtrls	22.8	-3.01	1.09
⊕ American International Gr	Financial	16.2	2.25	1.08
⊕ J.P. Morgan Chase & Co.	Financial	19.4	-1.99	1.07
⊕ National Oilwell	Energy	36.9	-3.83	0.75
⊖ Pride International	Energy	—	-0.24	0.74
⊕ SBC Communications	Telecom	15.4	-3.12	0.72

Total Fixed-Income:584	Date of Maturity	Amount $000	Value $000	% Net Assets
FNMA 5%	04-01-33	251,125	250,353	2.12
US Treasury Note 2.75%	07-31-06	192,600	193,495	1.64
US Treasury Note 2%	01-15-14	156,000	165,837	1.41
US Treasury Note 2.5%	05-31-06	143,503	143,677	1.22
FNMA 4.5%	11-01-33	139,925	136,082	1.15
US Treasury Note 3.25%	01-15-09	125,250	125,793	1.07
FNMA 5.5%	11-01-08	118,256	122,668	1.04
FNMA 0.04%	06-01-19	120,996	118,820	1.01
FNMA 5%	04-01-18	111,116	113,554	0.96

Equity Style
Style: Blend
Size: Large-Cap

Value Measures		Rel Category
Price/Earnings	17.11	1.03
Price/Book	2.12	0.87
Price/Sales	1.01	0.77
Price/Cash Flow	3.05	0.42
Dividend Yield %	1.13	0.72

Growth Measures	%	Rel Category
Long-Term Erngs	12.96	1.11
Book Value	5.21	0.91
Sales	4.09	0.79
Cash Flow	4.99	0.62
Historical Erngs	13.91	1.28

Market Cap %			
Giant	25.0	Small	11.0
Large	22.1	Micro	2.1
Mid	39.8	Avg $mil:	9,642

Fixed-Income Style
Duration: —
Quality: —

Avg Eff Duration [1]	—
Avg Eff Maturity	—
Avg Credit Quality	—
Avg Wtd Coupon	4.56%

[1]figure provided by fund

Sector Weightings	% of Stocks	Rel S&P 500	3 Year High	3 Year Low
Info	22.59	1.05		
Software	1.38	0.32	4	1
Hardware	10.92	1.07	12	5
Media	4.27	1.11	5	4
Telecom	6.02	1.91	7	2
Service	43.40	0.94		
Health	12.09	0.97	12	9
Consumer	5.74	0.63	11	6
Business	5.15	1.27	8	5
Financial	20.42	0.98	25	20
Mfg	34.00	1.06		
Goods	5.47	0.59	12	5
Ind Mtrls	15.12	1.19	15	13
Energy	10.75	1.50	11	7
Utilities	2.66	0.90	3	1

Composition

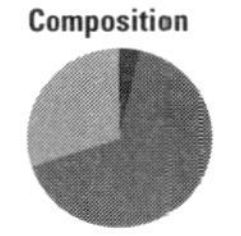

Cash	3.5
Stocks	66.3
Bonds	29.8
Other	0.5
Foreign (% of Stock)	8.3

Morningstar's Take by Andrew Gogerty 12-30-04

Fidelity Balanced continues to outpace its peers, but it requires patience.

A strong equity rally in 2004's second half has played right into manager Larry Rakers' hands. His bullish stance on stocks coming into the year was reflected in the fund's hefty equity stake of approximately 70%, its highest weighting in recent years. This move has paid off nicely, as stocks have surged in recent months.

While the fund is on pace to beat 75% of its moderate-allocation peers for the fourth consecutive year, investors should note that it lagged its rivals for most of the year. In fact, the fund's performance in 2004 highlights the risks of Rakers' style. Because he is willing to position the portfolio based on his macroeconomic views, its appearance, and hence, relative performance, can swing. Additionally, Rakers' willingness to roam the market-cap spectrum means that at just $8.6 billion, the fund's average market cap is well below the group norm of $27 billion. As such, the fund may lag if large caps return to dominance.

Still, the equity portfolio is diversified across sectors, which should keep volatility in check and also soften the impact of any miscues. In addition, bond manager George Fischer doesn't make interest rate bets and focuses only on issue selection. Recently, he has favored higher-quality issues such as governments and mortgages, believing low-quality debt is not worth the risk. To be sure, this does have the affect of increasing the fund's sensitivity to rate changes.

Overall, while the fund's strategy may result in short-term volatility, management's disciplined security selection and the fund's diversified approach should serve long-term investors well.

Address:	82 Devonshire Street Boston MA 02109 800-343-3548
Web Address:	
Inception:	11-06-86
Advisor:	Fidelity Management & Research Co. (FMR)
Subadvisor:	FMR Co., Inc. (FMRC)
NTF Plans:	Fidelity Retail-NTF, CommonWealth NTF

Minimum Purchase:	$2500	Add: $250	IRA: $2500
Min Auto Inv Plan:	$100	Add: $100	
Sales Fees:	No-load		
Management Fee:	0.44%		
Actual Fees:	Mgt:0.43%	Dist:	
Expense Projections:	3Yr:$224	5Yr:$390	10Yr:$871
Income Distrib:	Quarterly		

Fidelity Blue Chip Grth

Ticker	Load	NAV	Yield	Total Assets	Mstar Category
FBGRX	None	$41.71	0.9%	$23,578 mil	Large Growth

Governance and Management

Fiduciary Grade: B

Portfolio Manager(s)

John McDowell has run this fund since early 1996. He has managed diversified mutual funds for Fidelity since 1995 and has been running institutional money since the 1980s. He is supported by Fidelity's large and talented analyst staff.

Strategy

This fund scores points for truth in labeling, as manager John McDowell focuses it squarely on the market segment suggested by its moniker. McDowell, who has a background as an institutional money manager, doesn't take big chances. He likes giant-cap companies with good short- and long-term earnings-growth prospects, but he normally won't pay up for them unless their growth rates are very high. The fund's valuations are typically below the large-growth norm.

Historical Profile

Return Average
Risk Below Avg
Rating ★★★ Neutral

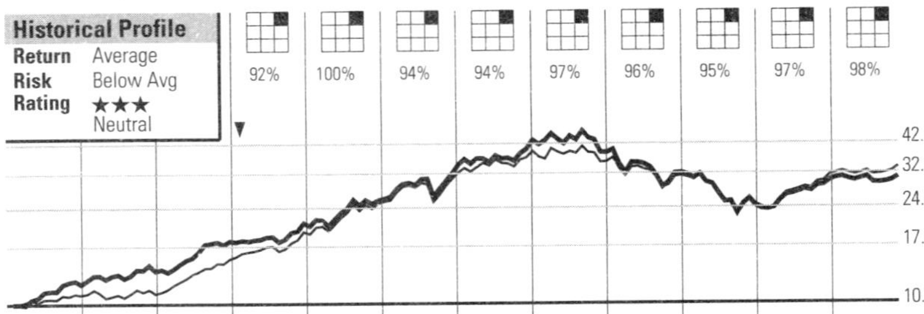

Investment Style
Equity
Stock %

▼ Manager Change
▽ Partial Manager Change

Growth of $10,000
— Investment Values of Fund
— Investment Values of S&P 500

Performance Quartile (within Category)

1993	1994	1995	1996	1997	1998	1999	2000	2001	2002	2003	12-04	History
24.17	25.95	30.77	32.69	39.46	50.39	60.11	51.53	42.94	31.94	39.63	41.71	NAV
24.50	9.85	28.38	15.38	27.02	34.76	24.26	-10.54	-16.55	-25.32	24.80	6.26	Total Return %
14.44	8.54	-9.15	-7.56	-6.33	6.19	3.22	-1.44	-4.67	-3.23	-3.87	-4.61	+/-S&P 500
21.63	7.23	-8.80	-7.74	-3.47	-3.95	-8.90	11.88	3.87	2.56	-4.95	-0.04	+/-Russ 1000Gr
0.04	0.00	0.48	0.93	0.81	0.25	0.28	0.00	0.12	0.30	0.69	0.99	Income Return %
24.46	9.85	27.90	14.45	26.21	34.51	23.98	-10.54	-16.67	-25.62	24.11	5.27	Capital Return %
8	2	75	78	48	38	75	38	31	36	67	62	Total Rtn % Rank Cat
0.01	0.00	0.12	0.28	0.26	0.10	0.14	0.00	0.06	0.13	0.22	0.39	Income $
4.12	0.58	2.47	2.25	1.75	2.06	2.07	2.52	0.00	0.00	0.00	0.00	Capital Gains $
1.25	1.22	1.02	0.95	0.78	0.70	0.70	0.86	0.87	0.74	0.69	0.67	Expense Ratio %
0.46	0.21	0.25	1.10	0.81	0.52	0.32	-0.02	0.01	0.25	0.64	0.48	Income Ratio %
319	271	182	206	51	49	38	40	46	33	24	23	Turnover Rate %
1,095	3,287	7,802	9,570	13,428	19,904	27,876	26,647	21,959	16,682	22,384	23,578	Net Assets $mil

Performance 12-31-04

	1st Qtr	2nd Qtr	3rd Qtr	4th Qtr	Total
2000	5.82	-2.09	-1.51	-12.33	-10.54
2001	-16.67	8.29	-18.41	13.34	-16.55
2002	-1.23	-15.70	-16.04	6.84	-25.32
2003	-1.82	13.20	2.44	9.61	24.80
2004	0.98	1.75	-4.52	8.31	6.26

Trailing	Total Return%	+/- S&P 500	+/- Russ 1000Gr	%Rank Cat	Growth of $10,000
3 Mo	8.31	-0.92	-0.86	80	10,831
6 Mo	3.42	-3.77	-0.05	72	10,342
1 Yr	6.26	-4.61	-0.04	62	10,626
3 Yr Avg	-0.32	-3.90	-0.14	50	9,904
5 Yr Avg	-5.86	-3.56	3.43	32	7,394
10 Yr Avg	8.82	-3.25	-0.77	52	23,286
15 Yr Avg	11.93	1.00	2.43	13	54,225

Tax Analysis	Tax-Adj Rtn%	%Rank Cat	Tax-Cost Rat	%Rank Cat
3 Yr (estimated)	-0.55	45	0.23	40
5 Yr (estimated)	-6.18	30	0.34	21
10 Yr (estimated)	7.62	44	1.10	29

Potential Capital Gain Exposure: 9% of assets

Rating and Risk

Time Period	Load-Adj Return %	Morningstar Rtn vs Cat	Morningstar Risk vs Cat	Morningstar Risk-Adj Rating
1 Yr	6.26			
3 Yr	-0.32	Avg	-Avg	★★★
5 Yr	-5.86	Avg	-Avg	★★★
10 Yr	8.82	Avg	-Avg	★★★
Incept	12.86			

Other Measures	Standard Index S&P 500	Best Fit Index Russ 1000Gr
Alpha	-3.7	-0.3
Beta	0.96	0.93
R-Squared	98	99
Standard Deviation	14.56	
Mean	-0.32	
Sharpe Ratio	-0.12	

Portfolio Analysis 10-31-04

Share change since 07-04 Total Stocks:173	Sector	PE	YTD Ret%	% Assets
Microsoft	Software	36.1	8.95	4.65
⊖ General Electric	Ind Mtrls	22.8	20.68	3.89
Pfizer	Health	22.0	-22.31	3.31
Johnson & Johnson	Health	20.6	25.17	2.42
⊕ Intel	Hardware	19.8	-26.56	2.21
⊖ Cisco Systems	Hardware	24.5	-20.26	2.09
⊕ Wal-Mart Stores	Consumer	23.4	0.51	2.04
American International G	Financial	16.2	-0.53	2.02
⊖ Citigroup	Financial	15.3	2.72	1.90
⊕ Procter & Gamble	Goods	23.3	12.38	1.87
Home Depot	Consumer	19.0	21.47	1.79
Dell	Hardware	34.0	24.01	1.67
⊖ Gillette	Goods	27.6	23.94	1.47
⊕ PepsiCo	Goods	22.5	13.82	1.45
Fannie Mae	Financial	9.1	-2.33	1.45
⊕ IBM	Hardware	20.2	7.19	1.41
⊕ Medtronic	Health	30.7	2.68	1.29
⊕ American Express	Financial	20.3	17.60	1.24
3M Company	Ind Mtrls	23.5	-1.75	1.20
⊕ UnitedHealth Group	Health	23.8	51.38	1.19

Current Investment Style

Value Blnd Growth — Large Mid Small

Market Cap	%
Giant	58.0
Large	31.5
Mid	10.4
Small	0.0
Micro	0.0
Avg $mil: 51,389	

Value Measures		Rel Category
Price/Earnings	19.30	0.91
Price/Book	3.08	0.95
Price/Sales	2.13	0.99
Price/Cash Flow	10.16	0.92
Dividend Yield %	1.16	1.51

Growth Measures	%	Rel Category
Long-Term Erngs	12.76	0.91
Book Value	14.12	1.11
Sales	7.95	0.93
Cash Flow	13.95	0.84
Historical Erngs	10.15	0.70

Profitability	%	Rel Category
Return on Equity	20.12	1.12
Return on Assets	10.24	1.09
Net Margin	13.00	1.06

Sector Weightings	% of Stocks	Rel S&P 500	3 Year High	3 Year Low
Info	25.99	1.21		
Software	6.47	1.50	7	4
Hardware	14.01	1.37	18	11
Media	4.59	1.20	5	4
Telecom	0.92	0.29	2	1
Service	47.87	1.03		
Health	20.29	1.62	23	20
Consumer	8.88	0.98	10	8
Business	4.84	1.20	6	4
Financial	13.86	0.67	17	13
Mfg	26.14	0.81		
Goods	9.91	1.06	11	9
Ind Mtrls	11.03	0.87	11	9
Energy	5.20	0.73	5	4
Utilities	0.00	0.00	0	0

Composition

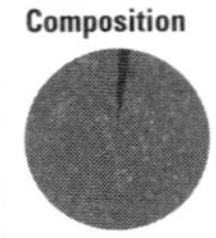

Cash	2.3
Stocks	97.7
Bonds	0.0
Other	0.0
Foreign (% of Stock)	2.4

Morningstar's Take by Christine Benz 10-19-04

Fidelity Blue Chip Growth has earned its keep.

This fund's official benchmark is the S&P 500, but manager John McDowell also keeps close watch on the Russell 1000 Growth Index when constructing this portfolio. As of the end of September 2004, in fact, eight of this fund's top 10 holdings also appeared in the Russell index's top 10. The fund's R-squared with the Russell 1000 Growth--a 99 out of 100--also indicates that its performance has been highly correlated with the benchmark's.

Any time you see a fund with such a high correlation to an index, it pays to check whether there are cheaper index alternatives available. And indeed, there is an iShares Russell 1000 Growth exchange-traded fund, which charges just 0.20% a year. This fund charges 0.68%.

We don't think investors need necessarily flee to the cheaper ETF, however, because this fund has charms of its own, albeit subtle ones. For starters, the fund has edged past the benchmark since McDowell took over here in 1996. (The ETF hasn't been around for the whole of McDowell's tenure, but its return will be lower than that of the index, which has no costs.) Moreover, the fund's volatility, as measured by its three-year standard deviation, is comfortably below that of the ETF, as McDowell has made a habit of downplaying the index's more-speculative names while giving greater play to higher-quality mega-caps. The portfolio's average market cap is more than $15 billion higher than the ETF's, and McDowell has top-weighted positions in stocks like Citigroup and General Electric, which do not appear in the index. As a result of that bias, the fund could reasonably be used as a core holding.

In addition to reducing volatility, the fund's mega-cap bias could hold it in good stead if such names, which have been badly out of favor for nearly five years, take market leadership. We continue to recommend this fund as a way to play a rebound in an unloved part of the market.

Address:	82 Devonshire St Boston MA 02109 800-343-3548
Web Address:	www.fidelity.com
Inception:	12-31-87
Advisor:	Fidelity Management & Research Co. (FMR)
Subadvisor:	FMR Co., Inc. (FMRC)
NTF Plans:	Fidelity Retail-NTF, CommonWealth NTF

Minimum Purchase:	$2500	Add: $250	IRA: $2500
Min Auto Inv Plan:	$2500	Add: $100	
Sales Fees:	No-load		
Management Fee:	0.47%		
Actual Fees:	Mgt:0.41%	Dist:	
Expense Projections:	3Yr:$218	5Yr:$379	10Yr:$847
Income Distrib:	Semi-Annually		

Fidelity Capital Apprec

Analyst Pick	Ticker	Load	NAV	Yield	Total Assets	Mstar Category
	FDCAX	None	$26.03	0.0%	$6,452 mil	Large Growth

Governance and Management

Fiduciary Grade: B

Portfolio Manager(s)

Harry Lange, manager here since March 1996, is a highly experienced stock-picker who has posted strong numbers at this fund and others, including a previous stint at Fidelity Select Computers. A former analyst, Lange performs much of the fund's research himself, but Fidelity's deep and talented staff of analysts also provides support.

Strategy

Manager Harry Lange's go-anywhere strategy and willingness to pay up for growth names make this a fairly unusual Fidelity offering. The fund's official benchmark is the S&P 500 Index, but Lange isn't afraid to make big bets on individual names and sectors. He will also make the occasional play on down-and-out parts of the market, and he sometimes looks overseas for his picks. The fund is also wide-ranging in terms of market capitalization and occasionally sports a decent slug of smaller-cap names.

Historical Profile

Return: High
Risk: Above Avg
Rating: ★★★★ Above Avg

Investment Style: Equity Stock %: 92% 95% 92% 94% 96% 95% 97% 96% 93%

▼ Manager Change
▽ Partial Manager Change

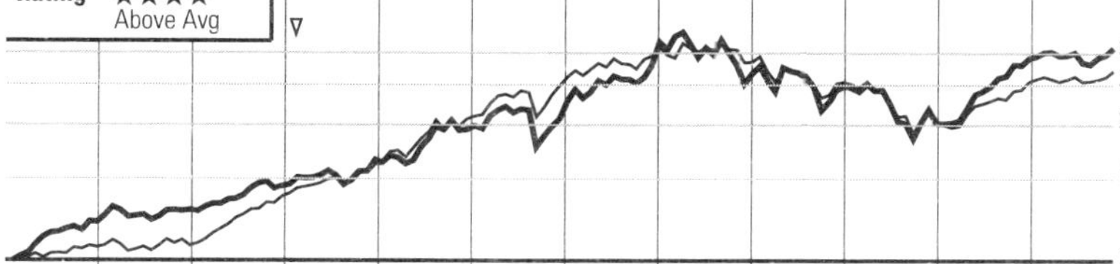

Performance Quartile (within Category)

History

	1993	1994	1995	1996	1997	1998	1999	2000	2001	2002	2003	12-04
NAV	16.92	15.31	16.78	17.64	19.38	22.07	29.87	22.23	20.35	16.18	24.51	26.03
Total Return %	33.41	2.52	18.77	15.12	26.52	16.95	45.84	-18.10	-7.56	-21.27	51.68	11.26
+/-S&P 500	23.35	1.21	-18.76	-7.82	-6.83	-11.62	24.80	-9.00	4.32	0.82	23.01	0.39
+/-Russ 1000Gr	30.54	-0.10	-18.41	-8.00	-3.97	-21.76	12.68	4.32	12.36	6.61	21.93	4.96
Income Return %	0.74	1.03	2.61	0.72	0.45	0.52	2.58	0.50	0.00	0.00	0.06	0.04
Capital Return %	32.67	1.49	16.16	14.40	26.07	16.43	43.26	-18.60	-7.56	-21.27	51.62	11.22
Total Rtn % Rank Cat	2	16	98	80	51	88	26	70	4	12	2	20
Income $	0.10	0.17	0.40	0.12	0.08	0.10	0.57	0.15	0.00	0.00	0.01	0.01
Capital Gains $	1.06	1.85	1.00	1.54	2.85	0.45	1.49	2.13	0.00	0.00	0.02	1.21
Expense Ratio %	0.86	1.17	1.06	0.80	0.66	0.67	0.65	0.63	0.91	1.03	0.88	0.91
Income Ratio %	0.93	1.22	2.31	1.24	0.43	0.46	0.56	0.15	0.17	-0.35	-0.31	-0.12
Turnover Rate %	120	124	87	205	176	121	78	85	120	80	54	72
Net Assets $mil	1,428	1,623	1,669	1,642	2,110	2,602	3,686	2,707	2,311	1,796	4,466	6,452

Performance 12-31-04

	1st Qtr	2nd Qtr	3rd Qtr	4th Qtr	Total
2000	6.43	-9.34	-3.47	-12.07	-18.10
2001	-10.71	12.64	-21.38	16.89	-7.56
2002	1.36	-12.29	-19.65	10.22	-21.27
2003	1.85	20.69	10.11	12.06	51.68
2004	4.20	-0.51	-3.15	10.81	11.26

Trailing	Total Return%	+/- S&P 500	+/- Russ 1000Gr	%Rank Cat	Growth of $10,000
3 Mo	10.81	1.58	1.64	32	11,081
6 Mo	7.32	0.13	3.85	19	10,732
1 Yr	11.26	0.39	4.96	20	11,126
3 Yr Avg	9.94	6.36	10.12	1	13,288
5 Yr Avg	0.12	2.42	9.41	5	10,060
10 Yr Avg	11.49	-0.58	1.90	15	29,673
15 Yr Avg	10.35	-0.58	0.85	34	43,811

Tax Analysis	Tax-Adj Rtn%	%Rank Cat	Tax-Cost Rat	%Rank Cat
3 Yr (estimated)	9.67	1	0.25	43
5 Yr (estimated)	-0.42	5	0.54	33
10 Yr (estimated)	9.73	16	1.58	54

Potential Capital Gain Exposure: 18% of assets

Rating and Risk

Time Period	Load-Adj Return %	Morningstar Rtn vs Cat	Morningstar Risk vs Cat	Morningstar Risk-Adj Rating
1 Yr	11.26			
3 Yr	9.94	High	+Avg	★★★★★
5 Yr	0.12	High	+Avg	★★★★
10 Yr	11.49	+Avg	+Avg	★★★★
Incept	12.69			

Other Measures	Standard Index S&P 500	Best Fit Index Russ 1000
Alpha	6.2	5.4
Beta	1.13	1.14
R-Squared	89	90
Standard Deviation	19.73	
Mean	9.94	
Sharpe Ratio	0.44	

Portfolio Analysis 10-31-04

Share change since 07-04 Total Stocks:198	Sector	PE	YTD Ret%	% Assets
⊕ Seagate Technology	Hardware	22.3	-5.50	3.57
⊕ Research In Motion Ltd	Hardware	—	146.66	3.05
⊖ Genentech	Health	78.6	16.36	2.90
⊕ Univision Communications	Media	39.5	-26.25	2.84
⊕ Altera	Hardware	26.2	-8.61	2.49
⊕ KLA-Tencor	Hardware	26.4	-20.43	2.37
⊕ Teradyne	Hardware	19.5	-32.93	2.37
⊕ FedEx	Business	27.9	46.40	2.06
⊖ SBC Communications	Telecom	15.4	3.74	1.93
⊕ EMC	Hardware	41.5	15.09	1.90
⊕ Dell	Hardware	34.0	24.01	1.89
⊕ Biogen IDEC	Health	—	81.50	1.84
⊕ Zimmer Holdings	Health	54.0	13.81	1.71
⊖ Microsoft	Software	36.1	8.95	1.42
⊕ Analog Devices	Hardware	24.2	-18.69	1.34
⊕ Royal Caribbean Cruises	Goods	36.9	58.33	1.33
⊖ Noble	Energy	51.7	39.02	1.33
⊕ St. Jude Medical	Health	38.0	36.69	1.22
⊕ Molex	Hardware	26.5	-13.65	1.19
⊖ KDDI	Telecom	—	—	1.18

Current Investment Style

Value Blnd Growth / Large Mid Small

Market Cap	%
Giant	30.8
Large	34.3
Mid	31.6
Small	2.3
Micro	1.1

Avg $mil: 14,834

Value Measures		Rel Category
Price/Earnings	21.80	1.02
Price/Book	1.87	0.58
Price/Sales	2.00	0.93
Price/Cash Flow	7.97	0.73
Dividend Yield %	0.63	0.82

Growth Measures	%	Rel Category
Long-Term Erngs	15.05	1.07
Book Value	12.68	1.00
Sales	5.32	0.62
Cash Flow	5.16	0.31
Historical Erngs	7.29	0.50

Profitability	%	Rel Category
Return on Equity	14.01	0.78
Return on Assets	7.24	0.77
Net Margin	8.73	0.71

Sector Weightings	% of Stocks	Rel S&P 500	3 Year High	3 Year Low
Info	47.85	2.23		
Software	5.61	1.30	7	3
Hardware	29.08	2.85	29	13
Media	8.44	2.20	22	8
Telecom	4.72	1.50	7	1
Service	36.32	0.78		
Health	15.11	1.21	19	11
Consumer	6.09	0.67	14	6
Business	7.29	1.80	9	5
Financial	7.83	0.38	14	3
Mfg	15.83	0.49		
Goods	5.63	0.60	10	5
Ind Mtrls	5.11	0.40	10	3
Energy	5.09	0.71	9	2
Utilities	0.00	0.00	0	0

Composition

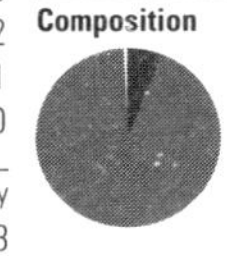

Cash	5.9
Stocks	93.2
Bonds	0.0
Other	0.9
Foreign (% of Stock)	15.9

Morningstar's Take by Christine Benz 10-16-04

Fidelity Capital Appreciation's manager is demonstrating the deft touch that makes this fund one of our favorites.

Given that this fund rode technology-hardware names to a gain of more than 50% in 2003, one might have expected to see it getting clobbered so far in 2004, as most of those very same names have sold off sharply amid rising inventories. Yet the fund has managed to stay roughly flat for the year to date through mid-October 2004, landing in the group's top quartile.

Manager Harry Lange's successful application of his contrarian-growth style is responsible for the relatively strong showing. Lange reduced the fund's exposure to the technology sector from close to 30% in late 2003 to 20% by the end of March 2004, a move that helped shelter the fund from the sector's recent weakness. Lange notes that he began increasing the fund's stake in the sector as it sold off sharply in the summer, however, and hard-hit names such as Teradyne, Seagate Technology, and KLA-Tencor numbered among the fund's top 10 holdings at the end of September. Lange acknowledges that corporations will still be judicious about spending on tech gear, but he also thinks the stocks are exceedingly cheap even given a backdrop of more-modest economic growth.

The timing of such maneuvers hasn't always worked out. Lange was early into tech stocks in 2002, for example. We'd also point out that the fund has enjoyed the tailwind of a relatively small average market cap amid a five-year rally in smaller-cap names. (True to form, however, Lange says he's adding to large caps these days.)

Lange's counter-punching strategy has intuitive appeal, and it's certainly hard to argue with his execution of it. This remains one of our favorite large-growth funds.

Address:	82 Devonshire St Boston MA 02109 800-343-3548
Web Address:	www.fidelity.com
Inception:	11-26-86
Advisor:	Fidelity Management & Research Co. (FMR)
Subadvisor:	FMR Co., Inc. (FMRC)
NTF Plans:	Fidelity Retail-NTF, CommonWealth NTF

Minimum Purchase:	$2500	Add: $250	IRA: $2500
Min Auto Inv Plan:	$100	Add: $100	
Sales Fees:	No-load		
Management Fee:	0.65%		
Actual Fees:	Mgt:0.65%	Dist:	
Expense Projections:	3Yr:$290	5Yr:$504	10Yr:$1120
Income Distrib:	Annually		

Fidelity Contrafund

Analyst Pick	Ticker	Load	NAV	Yield	Total Assets	Mstar Category
✔	FCNTX	None	$56.74	0.1%	$44,484 mil	Large Growth

Governance and Management

Fiduciary Grade: B

Portfolio Manager(s)

Will Danoff has been at the helm since 1990 and is backed by Fidelity's deep research staff. He has adapted his style to the fund's size by holding more large caps, and he has cut the fund's turnover in recent years. He's also now running a new fund, Fidelity Advisor New Insights.

Strategy

Call it forced evolution. As this fund's asset base grew in the 1990s, manager Will Danoff had to move away from mid-caps and small caps and adopt a growth-at-a-reasonable-price philosophy. He continues to keep a big part of the fund in mid-caps, but it is now dominated by larger fare. It has been more conservative than most of its large-blend rivals in recent years, with big underweightings in racy sectors such as technology, but Danoff is starting to ramp up its exposure to growth companies.

Historical Profile

Return: High
Risk: Low
Rating: ★★★★★ Highest

Investment Style — Equity Stock %: 88% 85% 90% 94% 91% 89% 90% 94% 88%

▼ Manager Change
▽ Partial Manager Change

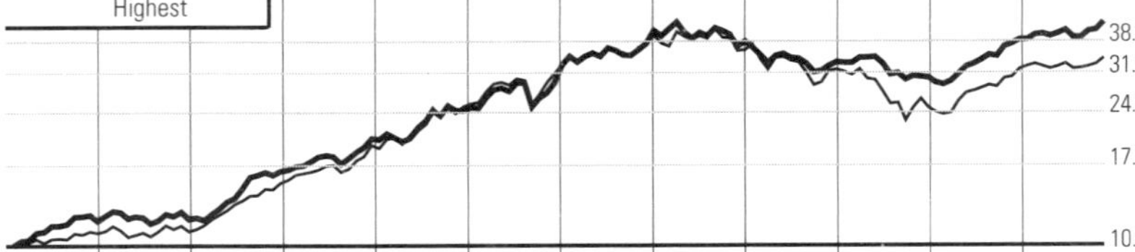

Performance Quartile (within Category)

History

	1993	1994	1995	1996	1997	1998	1999	2000	2001	2002	2003	12-04
NAV	30.84	30.28	38.02	42.15	46.63	56.81	60.02	49.18	42.77	38.60	49.35	56.74
Total Return %	21.43	-1.12	36.28	21.94	23.00	31.57	25.03	-6.80	-12.59	-9.63	27.95	15.07
+/-S&P 500	11.37	-2.43	-1.25	-1.00	-10.35	3.00	3.99	2.30	-0.71	12.46	-0.72	4.20
+/-Russ 1000Gr	18.56	-3.74	-0.90	-1.18	-7.49	-7.14	-8.13	15.62	7.83	18.25	-1.80	8.77
Income Return %	0.66	0.00	0.30	1.05	0.84	0.64	0.50	0.41	0.45	0.12	0.10	0.09
Capital Return %	20.77	-1.12	35.98	20.89	22.16	30.93	24.53	-7.21	-13.04	-9.75	27.85	14.98
Total Rtn % Rank Cat	13	46	22	30	70	50	73	24	12	1	46	5
Income $	0.18	0.00	0.09	0.38	0.35	0.30	0.28	0.24	0.22	0.05	0.04	0.05
Capital Gains $	2.25	0.22	3.13	3.45	4.56	4.22	10.22	6.62	0.00	0.00	0.00	0.00
Expense Ratio %	1.06	1.00	0.96	0.79	0.67	0.61	0.62	0.84	0.91	0.99	0.98	—
Income Ratio %	0.46	0.59	0.44	1.28	0.91	0.70	0.48	0.45	0.49	0.14	0.01	—
Turnover Rate %	255	235	223	159	144	197	177	166	141	80	67	—
Net Assets $mil	6,193	8,682	14,832	23,798	30,809	38,821	46,927	40,220	32,321	27,695	36,051	44,484

Performance 12-31-04

	1st Qtr	2nd Qtr	3rd Qtr	4th Qtr	Total
2000	5.56	-6.58	1.13	-6.54	-6.80
2001	-13.18	3.47	-8.80	6.70	-12.59
2002	2.88	-3.68	-9.86	1.18	-9.63
2003	-2.15	11.83	5.02	11.34	27.95
2004	3.75	2.36	-0.63	9.04	15.07

Trailing	Total Return%	+/- S&P 500	+/- Russ 1000Gr	%Rank Cat	Growth of $10,000
3 Mo	9.04	-0.19	-0.13	67	10,904
6 Mo	8.35	1.16	4.88	13	10,835
1 Yr	15.07	4.20	8.77	5	11,507
3 Yr Avg	9.99	6.41	10.17	1	13,306
5 Yr Avg	1.62	3.92	10.91	3	10,837
10 Yr Avg	13.81	1.74	4.22	4	36,459
15 Yr Avg	15.03	4.10	5.53	1	81,690

Tax Analysis	Tax-Adj Rtn%	%Rank Cat	Tax-Cost Rat	%Rank Cat
3 Yr (estimated)	9.95	1	0.04	7
5 Yr (estimated)	1.01	3	0.60	37
10 Yr (estimated)	11.77	5	1.79	63

Potential Capital Gain Exposure: 24% of assets

Rating and Risk

Time Period	Load-Adj Return %	Morningstar Rtn vs Cat	Morningstar Risk vs Cat	Morningstar Risk-Adj Rating
1 Yr	15.07			
3 Yr	9.99	High	Low	★★★★★
5 Yr	1.62	High	Low	★★★★★
10 Yr	13.81	High	Low	★★★★★
Incept	13.29			

Other Measures	Standard Index S&P 500	Best Fit Index S&P Mid 400
Alpha	7.2	2.7
Beta	0.54	0.61
R-Squared	63	83

Standard Deviation	11.05
Mean	9.99
Sharpe Ratio	0.79

Portfolio Analysis 09-30-04

Share change since 06-04 Total Stocks:503	Sector	PE	YTD Ret%	% Assets
⊖ Avon Products	Goods	23.4	16.31	2.99
Berkshire Hathaway A	Financial	—	—	2.82
⊖ 3M Company	Ind Mtrls	23.5	-1.75	2.81
⊖ EnCana	Energy	11.3	46.00	2.02
⊕ Yahoo	Media	95.1	67.36	1.74
⊖ Genentech	Health	78.6	16.36	1.58
Samsung Electronics	Goods	—	—	1.22
⊕ American International G	Financial	16.2	-0.53	1.19
⊕ Patterson Companies	Health	37.8	35.62	1.18
⊕ Danaher	Ind Mtrls	25.8	25.29	1.17
⊕ Newmont Mining	Ind Mtrls	45.6	-8.02	1.11
⊖ Nextel Communications	Telecom	11.1	6.95	1.08
⊖ Lockheed Martin	Ind Mtrls	19.9	9.97	1.02
⊖ eBay	Consumer	81.6	80.07	0.97
⊖ Golden West Financial	Financial	15.3	19.45	0.94
⊕ Gillette	Goods	27.6	23.94	0.93
⊕ Marvell Technology	Hardware	NMF	87.03	0.92
⊖ Colgate-Palmolive	Goods	20.3	4.14	0.89
⊕ Alcon	Health	41.6	33.78	0.87
⊕ BP PLC ADR	Energy	20.7	22.07	0.85

Current Investment Style

Value Blnd Growth — Large Mid Small

Market Cap	%
Giant	25.6
Large	36.6
Mid	32.2
Small	5.2
Micro	0.5

Avg $mil: 12,688

Value Measures		Rel Category
Price/Earnings	19.34	0.91
Price/Book	3.03	0.94
Price/Sales	1.68	0.78
Price/Cash Flow	8.12	0.74
Dividend Yield %	0.73	0.95

Growth Measures	%	Rel Category
Long-Term Erngs	14.20	1.01
Book Value	13.95	1.10
Sales	11.64	1.37
Cash Flow	20.71	1.25
Historical Erngs	32.22	2.23

Profitability	%	Rel Category
Return on Equity	21.05	1.17
Return on Assets	10.16	1.09
Net Margin	12.58	1.02

Sector Weightings	% of Stocks	Rel S&P 500	3 Year High	3 Year Low
Info	16.94	0.79		
Software	2.36	0.55	2	1
Hardware	6.40	0.63	7	1
Media	3.56	0.93	4	1
Telecom	4.62	1.47	5	0
Service	44.61	0.96		
Health	13.86	1.11	19	14
Consumer	10.09	1.11	14	10
Business	6.41	1.58	9	5
Financial	14.25	0.69	18	14
Mfg	38.45	1.20		
Goods	10.41	1.12	20	10
Ind Mtrls	16.19	1.28	16	14
Energy	11.01	1.54	11	5
Utilities	0.84	0.28	1	0

Composition

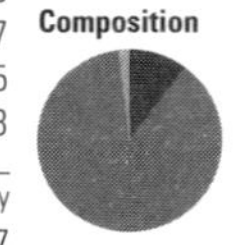

Cash	10.1
Stocks	87.9
Bonds	1.7
Other	0.3
Foreign (% of Stock)	19.9

Morningstar's Take by Christopher Traulsen 01-05-05

Fidelity Contrafund continues to impress.

This fund, which we recently moved to the large-growth category from large blend, has just posted another strong year. It finished 2004 up 15%, more than 7 percentage points ahead of the typical large-growth fund, and 4 percentage points ahead of the S&P 500 Index for the period.

Manager Will Danoff helped the fund's cause by a savvy move into Internet stocks such as Yahoo and eBay. He also correctly boosted the fund's energy stake, taking it from under 5% of the fund's equity portfolio up to nearly 11%, and overweighted industrials stocks. Both sectors benefited from the global economic recovery, and the resulting supply/demand imbalance that drove commodity prices up.

As always, the portfolio remains expansive. Despite lugging a $44 billion asset base, Danoff has shoehorned 32% of the fund into mid-cap stocks, and even has a smattering of small caps in the portfolio. He also has significant overseas exposure, with 18% of assets in foreign stocks. On the whole, relative to other large-growth funds, this offering is less aggressive than the norm. Danoff spreads its assets across more than 500 stocks, and while the fund's growth rates are well above category averages, its valuations are below those of its typical peer.

Danoff's eclecticism has paid off in spades: The fund owns top-flight three-, five-, and 10-year returns, while its diversification has helped make it less volatile than its average rival. We remain concerned with the fund's size, however. With an asset base of $44 billion, it's undeniably harder for Danoff to succeed than it was when the fund was much smaller. That said, Danoff has shown skill in handling the growth, and he has also reduced the fund's turnover in recent years, which should make the task more manageable. We continue to think this is a great core holding.

Address:	Fidelity Investments Company Boston MA 02109 800-343-3548
Web Address:	
Inception:	05-17-67
Advisor:	Fidelity Management & Research Co. (FMR)
Subadvisor:	FMR Co., Inc. (FMRC)
NTF Plans:	Fidelity Retail-NTF, CommonWealth NTF

Minimum Purchase:	$2500	Add: $250	IRA: $2500
Min Auto Inv Plan:	$2500	Add: $250	
Sales Fees:	No-load		
Management Fee:	0.81%		
Actual Fees:	Mgt:0.81%	Dist:	
Expense Projections:	3Yr:$502	5Yr:$651	10Yr:$1086
Income Distrib:	Annually		

Fidelity Convertible Sec

Analyst Pick

Ticker	Load	NAV	Yield	Total Assets	Mstar Category
FCVSX	None	$21.60	2.6%	$1,885 mil	Convertibles

Governance and Management

Fiduciary Grade: B

Portfolio Manager(s)

Management changes have been frequent at this fund. Most recently, in February 2002, Victor Thay took over the fund from Larry Rakers. Thay had a history of delivering solid returns with moderate volatility while in charge of various Fidelity Select funds from 1998 to 2002, but this is his first stint as a manager of a large, diversified offering.

Strategy

Manager Victor Thay takes a more moderate approach than many of his predecessors at this historically aggressive fund. Thay has lessened his reliance on straight equities and uses high-yield bonds to help boost income, making the fund more balanced than a number of its rivals. As before, the fund continues to draw from Fidelity's deep bench of analysts on both the bond and the stock side for research support.

Historical Profile

Return Above Avg
Risk Above Avg
Rating ★★★★ Above Avg

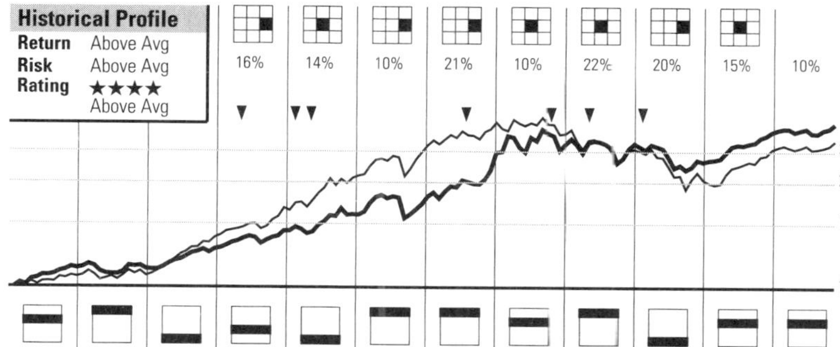

Investment Style
Equity
Stock %

▼ Manager Change
▽ Partial Manager Change

Growth of $10,000
— Investment Values of Fund
— Investment Values of S&P 500

Performance Quartile (within Category)

1993	1994	1995	1996	1997	1998	1999	2000	2001	2002	2003	12-04	History
16.45	15.36	16.77	17.56	17.51	18.49	24.28	20.78	19.93	16.34	20.17	21.60	NAV
17.79	-1.76	19.38	15.05	14.46	16.28	44.08	7.21	0.50	-13.89	28.32	10.21	Total Return %
7.73	-3.07	-18.15	-7.89	-18.89	-12.29	23.04	16.31	12.33	8.20	-0.35	-0.66	+/-S&P 500
1.38	3.08	-4.58	2.93	-1.05	4.07	8.09	14.73	3.41	-10.77	5.35	1.90	+/-Merrill Lynch Convert
4.77	4.96	5.03	4.70	4.04	3.60	3.18	2.90	4.55	4.24	4.41	2.85	Income Return %
13.02	-6.72	14.35	10.35	10.42	12.68	40.90	4.31	-4.05	-18.13	23.91	7.36	Capital Return %
30	19	84	61	90	16	23	28	1[illegible]	93	29	32	Total Rtn % Rank Cat
0.73	0.80	0.76	0.77	0.70	0.62	0.58	0.69	0.93	0.83	0.71	0.57	Income $
1.09	0.00	0.76	0.89	1.77	1.16	1.50	4.57	0.02	0.00	0.00	0.02	Capital Gains $
0.92	0.85	0.70	0.83	0.73	0.77	0.82	0.77	0.76	0.85	0.82	—	Expense Ratio %
4.62	4.61	4.59	4.48	3.46	3.21	2.85	2.96	3.40	4.76	4.46	—	Income Ratio %
312	318	203	175	212	223	246	262	282	138	136	—	Turnover Rate %
1,064	891	1,046	1,120	1,003	1,036	1,423	1,902	1,829	1,381	1,822	1,885	Net Assets $mil

Performance 12-31-04

	1st Qtr	2nd Qtr	3rd Qtr	4th Qtr	Total
2000	13.40	-0.01	3.37	-8.53	7.21
2001	-6.93	9.64	-15.95	17.19	0.50
2002	-0.70	-9.90	-9.89	6.80	-13.89
2003	2.83	12.15	1.84	9.25	28.32
2004	2.72	0.07	-1.03	8.34	10.21

Trailing	Total Return%	+/- S&P 500	+/- Merrill Lynch Convert	%Rank Cat	Growth of $10,000
3 Mo	8.34	-0.89	1.98	12	10,834
6 Mo	7.22	0.03	2.41	23	10,722
1 Yr	10.21	-0.66	1.90	32	11,021
3 Yr Avg	6.79	3.21	-2.08	80	12,178
5 Yr Avg	5.58	7.88	2.59	24	13,119
10 Yr Avg	13.20	1.13	2.20	8	34,551
15 Yr Avg	13.38	2.45	2.82	8	65,773

Tax Analysis	Tax-Adj Rtn%	%Rank Cat	Tax-Cost Rat	%Rank Cat
3 Yr (estimated)	5.33	63	1.37	61
5 Yr (estimated)	2.82	40	2.61	93
10 Yr (estimated)	9.68	16	3.11	95

Potential Capital Gain Exposure: 2% of assets

Rating and Risk

Time Period	Load-Adj Return %	Morningstar Rtn vs Cat	Morningstar Risk vs Cat	Morningstar Risk-Adj Rating
1 Yr	10.21			
3 Yr	6.79	Avg	+Avg	★★★
5 Yr	5.58	+Avg	+Avg	★★★
10 Yr	13.20	High	+Avg	★★★★
Incept	13.10			

Other Measures	Standard Index S&P 500	Best Fit Index Merrill Lynch Convert
Alpha	3.8	-4.5
Beta	0.63	1.40
R-Squared	74	93
Standard Deviation	11.70	
Mean	6.79	
Sharpe Ratio	0.47	

Portfolio Analysis 08-31-04

Total Fixed-Income:2	Date of Maturity	Amount $000	Value $000	% Net Assets
Yahoo Cv	04-01-08	40,500	62,142	3.62
Tyco Intl Grp S A Cv 3.1	01-15-23	39,900	61,199	3.56
Merrill Lynch Cv FRN	03-13-32	54,000	54,065	3.15
Comverse Tech Cv	05-15-23	40,400	47,369	2.76
Enzon Pharmaceuticals Cv	07-01-08	50,660	47,114	2.74
Cytyc 144A Cv 2.25%	03-15-24	35,000	39,200	2.28
Amer Express 144A Cv 1.8	12-01-33	36,500	38,918	2.27
Alza Cv	07-28-20	46,500	37,229	2.17
Freeport-Mcmoran Copper		35	33,701	1.96
EchoStar Communications		1,099	33,686	1.96
Nextel Partners Cv 1.5%	11-15-08	13,400	26,816	1.56
Crown Castle Intl 144A C	07-15-10	16,860	26,597	1.55
Chesapeake Engy Ffd Cv 1		284	26,499	1.54
Baxter Intl Pfd	02-16-06	492	25,589	1.49
Invitrogen Cv 2.25%	12-15-06	26,003	25,093	1.46
Idec Pharmaceuticals Cv	02-16-19	10,200	24,451	1.42
Mgi Pharma 144A 1.682%	03-02-24	32,400	24,319	1.42
Bausch & Lomb Cv FRN	08-01-23	17,700	23,823	1.39
Amer Tower 144A Cv 3.25%	08-01-10	15,400	22,094	1.29
Fisher Scientific Int 1	10-01-23	15,600	22,054	1.28

Investment Style	
Avg Eff Maturity	—
Avg Credit Quality	—
Avg Wtd Coupon	2.46%
Avg Wtd Price	107.34% of par

Coupon Range	% of Bonds	Rel Cat
0% PIK	—	0.0
0% to 8%	0.0	0.0
8% to 11%	0.0	0.0
11% to 14%	0.0	0.0
More than 14%	0.0	0.0

1.00=Category Average

Special Securities	
Restricted/Illiquid Secs	30
Emerging-Markets Secs	Trace
Options/Futures/Warrants	No

Composition	
Cash	1.4
Stocks	9.9
Bonds	9.2
Convertibles	69.3
Other	9.3

Credit Analysis	% bonds 08-31-04		
US Govt	—	BB	—
AAA	—	B	—
AA	—	Below B	—
A	—	NR/NA	—
BBB	—		

Morningstar's Take by Kerry O'Boyle 12-22-04

After a difficult run, Fidelity Convertible Securities appears to be regaining its stride.

Manager Victor Thay has faced a steep learning curve since taking charge of this offering in February 2002. Poor security selection that year and in the first half of 2004--as a tricky convertible market alternately rewarded solid credits and then equity-sensitive issues--has led to some terrible performance. The fund's 13.9% loss in 2002 landed it in the bottom decile of the category. And as recently as August 2004, it trailed more than 70% of its rivals for the year-to-date period.

But Thay seems to be finding his groove, and not just because the fund has surged during the second half of 2004 on the strength of health-care picks such as Cyctyc and Alza (now a wholly owned subsidiary of Johnson & Johnson). Thay is beginning to adjust better to the ebbs and flows of the convertible market. He has reduced the number of holdings in the portfolio from 221 at the end of 2003 to 129. He says that smaller position sizes are a lot more work for minimal payoff and recognizes the need to minimize trading and turnover to let his bets play out. The fund's pure equity stake has also diminished under Thay to 11% of assets, as he forsakes some potential upside for the greater downside protection offered by convertibles.

That has been a concern here in the past. The fund has historically held close to 20% of assets in straight equities--one of the more aggressive profiles in the category. That has helped to boost its long-term record, but at the cost of increased volatility relative to its peers.

This offering is an Analyst Pick on the strength of that performance, its low costs, and its solid analyst staff. While Thay has grown into the manager role nicely, his rocky start makes us leery of Fidelity's penchant for high manager turnover at this offering. And we'd be leery of any further upheaval given the complex variables involved with investing in convertibles. Still, this remains a solid option.

Address:	82 Devonshire St Boston MA 02109 800-343-3548
Web Address:	www.fidelity.com
Inception:	01-05-87
Advisor:	Fidelity Management & Research Co. (FMR)
Subadvisor:	FMR Co., Inc. (FMRC)
NTF Plans:	Fidelity Retail-NTF, CommonWealth NTF

Minimum Purchase:	$2500	Add: $250	IRA: $2500
Min Auto Inv Plan:	$2500	Add: $100	
Sales Fees:	No-load		
Management Fee:	0.64%		
Actual Fees:	Mgt:0.64%	Dist:	
Expense Projections:	3Yr:$271	5Yr:$471	10Yr:$1049
Income Distrib:	Annually		

Fidelity Destiny I

Ticker	Load	NAV	Yield	Total Assets	Mstar Category
FDESX	8.24%	$12.83	1.3%	$3,341 mil	Large Growth

Governance and Management

Fiduciary Grade: C

Portfolio Manager(s)

Karen Firestone, manager here since February 2000, has built a respectable long-term record at Fidelity Large Cap Stock, where she has consistently used the same growth-biased approach she uses here. She is also a longtime Fidelity analyst and has managed several sector funds. Moreover, she is backed by scores of talented analysts.

Strategy

Manager Karen Firestone spreads her bets across sectors, but she has a definite growth bent, too. Therefore, the portfolio typically has more in technology and health care than, for example, the S&P 500 Index. That contrasts with the style of previous manager George Vanderheiden, who tilted the portfolio toward value issues in areas such as financials. Still, Firestone is more valuation-conscious than many of her growth rivals, and when traditional growth sectors have weak fundamentals, she's willing to look at industrials and other slower-growing fare.

Historical Profile

Return Below Avg
Risk Below Avg
Rating ★★★ Neutral

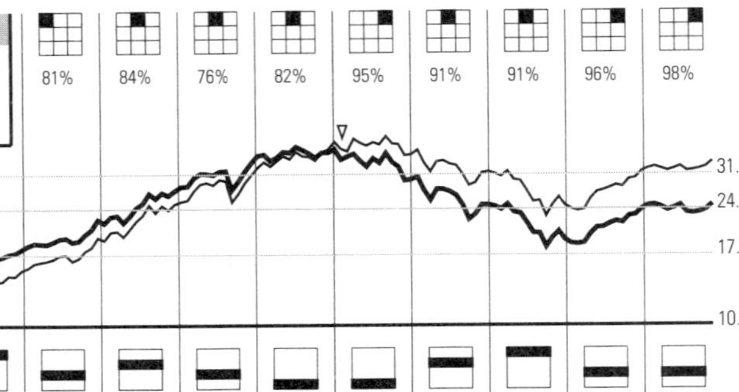

Investment Style
Equity
Stock %

▼ Manager Change
▽ Partial Manager Change

Growth of $10,000
— Investment Values of Fund
— Investment Values of S&P 500

Performance Quartile (within Category)

1993	1994	1995	1996	1997	1998	1999	2000	2001	2002	2003	12-04	History
16.81	14.61	18.74	20.03	23.64	26.95	24.33	15.55	12.74	9.75	12.16	12.83	NAV
26.42	4.43	36.95	18.55	30.92	25.63	4.96	-20.07	-17.29	-22.77	25.67	6.86	Total Return %
16.36	3.12	-0.58	-4.39	-2.43	-2.94	-16.08	-10.97	-5.41	-0.68	-3.00	-4.01	+/-S&P 500
23.55	1.81	-0.23	-4.57	0.43	-13.08	-28.20	2.35	3.13	5.11	-4.08	0.56	+/-Russ 1000Gr
1.69	2.02	2.94	2.40	2.35	1.78	1.63	0.53	0.77	0.71	0.92	1.32	Income Return %
24.73	2.41	34.01	16.15	28.57	23.85	3.33	-20.60	-18.06	-23.48	24.75	5.54	Capital Return %
6	7	21	57	28	73	99	77	34	18	60	55	Total Rtn % Rank Cat
0.25	0.34	0.43	0.45	0.47	0.42	0.44	0.13	0.12	0.09	0.09	0.16	Income $
2.05	2.53	0.81	1.73	2.03	2.17	3.44	3.78	0.00	0.00	0.00	0.00	Capital Gains $
0.66	0.70	0.68	0.65	0.38	0.33	0.31	0.25	0.37	0.44	0.46	0.47	Expense Ratio %
1.83	1.69	2.35	2.40	2.20	1.71	1.55	0.85	0.75	0.80	0.85	0.79	Income Ratio %
75	77	55	42	32	27	36	145	119	93	71	52	Turnover Rate %
3,154	3,208	4,279	4,903	6,140	7,365	7,223	5,126	3,969	2,879	3,420	3,278	Net Assets $mil

Performance 12-31-04

	1st Qtr	2nd Qtr	3rd Qtr	4th Qtr	Total
2000	-3.41	-3.23	-2.86	-11.96	-20.07
2001	-14.15	6.52	-18.71	11.26	-17.29
2002	0.55	-12.72	-16.73	5.68	-22.77
2003	-2.56	12.63	3.36	10.79	25.67
2004	1.32	1.30	-5.05	9.65	6.86

Trailing	Total Return%	+/- S&P 500	+/- Russ 1000Gr	%Rank Cat	Growth of $10,000
3 Mo	9.65	0.42	0.48	54	10,965
6 Mo	4.12	-3.07	0.65	61	10,412
1 Yr	6.86	-4.01	0.56	55	10,686
3 Yr Avg	1.22	-2.36	1.40	30	10,370
5 Yr Avg	-7.27	-4.97	2.02	48	6,856
10 Yr Avg	6.75	-5.32	-2.84	83	19,217
15 Yr Avg	9.55	-1.38	0.05	47	39,281

Tax Analysis	Tax-Adj Rtn%	%Rank Cat	Tax-Cost Rat	%Rank Cat
3 Yr (estimated)	-1.99	63	0.36	62
5 Yr (estimated)	-9.88	66	1.13	66
10 Yr (estimated)	3.79	89	1.94	71

Potential Capital Gain Exposure: -28% of assets

Rating and Risk

Time Period	Load-Adj Return %	Morningstar Rtn vs Cat	Morningstar Risk vs Cat	Morningstar Risk-Adj Rating
1 Yr	-1.95			
3 Yr	-1.64	Avg	-Avg	★★★
5 Yr	-8.85	Avg	-Avg	★★★
10 Yr	5.84	Low	Low	★★
Incept	14.23			

Other Measures	Standard Index S&P 500	Best Fit Index Russ 1000
Alpha	-2.2	-2.8
Beta	0.93	0.94
R-Squared	98	98
Standard Deviation	14.31	
Mean	1.22	
Sharpe Ratio	-0.01	

Portfolio Analysis 09-30-04

Share change since 06-04 Total Stocks:128	Sector	PE	YTD Ret%	% Assets
Microsoft	Software	36.1	8.95	4.03
Gen Elec	Ind Mtrls	22.8	20.68	3.18
⊕ Pfizer	Health	22.0	-22.31	2.75
⊖ American International G	Financial	16.2	-0.53	2.38
Cisco Systems	Hardware	24.5	-20.26	2.21
Dell	Hardware	34.0	24.01	2.11
⊖ Time Warner	Media	27.5	8.12	2.09
Wal-Mart Stores	Consumer	23.4	0.51	2.07
⊕ ExxonMobil	Energy	13.9	28.04	1.84
⊕ Citigroup	Financial	15.3	2.72	1.77
⊖ Tyco International	Ind Mtrls	25.1	35.41	1.72
Morgan Stanley	Financial	14.2	-2.25	1.66
⊕ Schlumberger	Energy	40.7	23.84	1.65
American Express	Financial	20.3	17.60	1.59
☼ J P Morgan Chase	Financial	19.4	9.97	1.59
⊕ Walt Disney	Media	24.3	20.21	1.53
⊖ Caterpillar	Ind Mtrls	17.6	19.75	1.48
⊖ Yahoo	Media	95.1	67.36	1.48
Home Depot	Consumer	19.0	21.47	1.46
⊕ Honeywell International	Ind Mtrls	20.5	8.21	1.43

Current Investment Style

Value Blnd Growth — Large Mid Small

Market Cap	%
Giant	57.1
Large	29.4
Mid	12.5
Small	0.9
Micro	0.0
Avg $mil: 43,985	

Value Measures		Rel Category
Price/Earnings	18.58	0.87
Price/Book	2.93	0.91
Price/Sales	1.83	0.85
Price/Cash Flow	9.49	0.86
Dividend Yield %	1.23	1.60

Growth Measures	%	Rel Category
Long-Term Erngs	12.17	0.87
Book Value	8.43	0.66
Sales	6.33	0.74
Cash Flow	11.50	0.69
Historical Erngs	7.15	0.49

Profitability	%	Rel Category
Return on Equity	17.13	0.95
Return on Assets	8.76	0.94
Net Margin	11.14	0.90

Sector Weightings	% of Stocks	Rel S&P 500	3 Year High	3 Year Low
Info	32.45	1.51		
Software	5.12	1.19	8	4
Hardware	14.57	1.43	18	11
Media	9.06	2.36	11	6
Telecom	3.70	1.17	4	2
Service	40.47	0.87		
Health	16.13	1.29	18	14
Consumer	6.51	0.72	10	6
Business	2.35	0.58	5	2
Financial	15.48	0.75	15	11
Mfg	27.08	0.84		
Goods	7.45	0.80	13	7
Ind Mtrls	12.96	1.02	13	9
Energy	6.40	0.89	8	5
Utilities	0.27	0.09	0	0

Composition

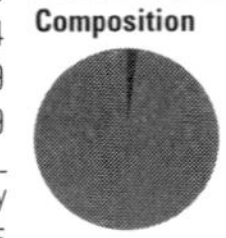

Cash	2.0
Stocks	97.9
Bonds	0.0
Other	0.0
Foreign (% of Stock)	5.7

Morningstar's Take by Greg Carlson 12-23-04

Fidelity Destiny boasts a competent skipper, but new investors should avoid it.

We've long been wary of the contractual plans through which this fund is sold, which require investors to commit to at least 10 years of systematic investments. The price of entry is quite high; investors pay commissions of up to 50% in the first year. Those who stick with the plan pay a more reasonable price over time, but investors who withdraw early may pay hefty penalties.

Recent developments underscore our concerns. In December 2004, First Command Financial Planning, one of the primary sellers of contractual plan funds, was censured and fined $12 million by the NASD for deceptive sales practices. What's more, First Command's data shows that only 43% of investors who started a 15-year plan completed their terms. The fine will be used to pay restitution to investors who have started a plan since Jan. 1, 1999, have since terminated it, and paid an effective sales charge of greater than 5%.

As a result, contractual plan funds face a murky future. A bill banning the sale of these funds was approved by the U.S. House of Representatives in October. (The Senate has yet to vote on it.) Just prior to the NASD's actions, First Command announced it would stop selling contractual plan funds. Also, Templeton Investment Counsel plans to merge its contractual plan offering, Templeton Capital Accumulator, into Templeton Growth, pending shareholder approval.

Fidelity, for its part, says it has no plans to shutter this fund. That's unfortunate, because First Command's own data suggest that many investors redeem their shares early in the life of their contracts, thereby incurring stiff penalties.

That said, current shareholders, who have already paid the load, should stick around. Since taking over in February 2000, manager Karen Firestone has amassed a respectable record compared with her large-growth rivals, and the fund's expense ratio is low.

Address:	82 Devonshire St Boston MA 02109 800-343-3548
Web Address:	www.fidelity.com
Inception:	07-10-70
Advisor:	Fidelity Management & Research Co. (FMR)
Subadvisor:	FMR Co., Inc. (FMRC)
NTF Plans:	N/A

Minimum Purchase:	$100	Add: $100	IRA: $100
Min Auto Inv Plan:	$100	Add: $100	
Sales Fees:	8.24%L		
Management Fee:	0.45%		
Actual Fees:	Mgt:0.45%	Dist:	
Expense Projections:	3Yr:$157	5Yr:$274	10Yr:$616
Income Distrib:	Annually		

Fidelity Destiny II

Ticker	Load	NAV	Yield	Total Assets	Mstar Category
FDETX	8.24%	$11.32	1.4%	$5,658 mil	Large Blend

Governance and Management

Fiduciary Grade: C

Portfolio Manager(s)

Adam Hetnarski, manager here since June 2000, is less experienced than this fund's former managers. He is, however, building a solid record as a diversified-fund manager, and he also was a seasoned analyst at Fidelity--at one time, specializing in tech firms--before taking over Fidelity Export & Multinational, which he guided to strong returns during a short stint.

Strategy

Adam Hetnarski looks for mid- and large-cap companies with rapid, sustainable, growth rates, but he's also willing to bet on turnarounds. Although Hetnarski's picks are eclectic, there's one constant: He trades them a lot. In the past, turnover rates at Hetnarski's funds have soared well into the triple digits. Hetnarski is willing to take on plenty of sector and issue-specific risk, so the fund could hit rough patches from time to time.

Historical Profile

Return: Below Avg
Risk: Average
Rating: ★★★ Neutral

Investment Style: Equity — Stock %: 77% | 83% | 91% | 93% | 93% | 88% | 84% | 90% | 90%

▼ Manager Change
▽ Partial Manager Change

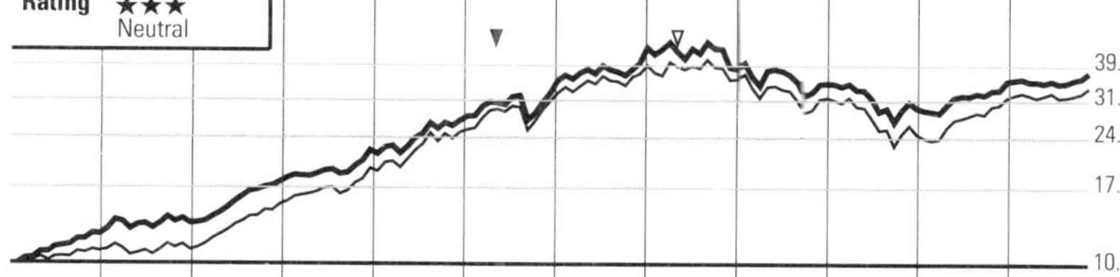

Performance Quartile (within Category)

History

1993	1994	1995	1996	1997	1998	1999	2000	2001	2002	2003	12-04	History
9.05	8.27	10.70	11.61	13.79	14.25	16.24	12.17	10.93	9.16	10.93	11.92	NAV
26.80	4.48	35.96	17.86	29.64	28.11	25.40	-13.75	-9.35	-15.37	20.23	10.60	Total Return %
16.74	3.17	-1.57	-5.08	-3.71	-0.46	4.36	-4.65	2.53	6.72	-8.44	-0.27	+/-S&P 500
16.62	4.09	-1.81	-4.59	-3.21	1.09	4.49	-5.96	3.10	6.28	-9.66	-0.80	+/-Russ 1000
1.13	1.84	2.70	2.34	2.15	0.87	0.77	0.49	0.82	0.82	0.87	1.51	Income Return %
25.67	2.64	33.26	15.52	27.49	27.24	24.63	-14.24	-10.17	-16.19	19.36	9.09	Capital Return %
2	5	34	77	45	23	22	92	23	7	94	40	Total Rtn % Rank Cat
0.09	0.17	0.22	0.25	0.25	0.12	0.11	0.08	0.10	0.09	0.08	0.17	Income $
0.73	0.99	0.31	0.75	0.97	3.34	1.43	1.80	0.00	0.00	0.00	0.00	Capital Gains $
0.84	0.80	0.80	0.78	0.53	0.48	0.47	0.56	0.55	0.43	0.50	0.55	Expense Ratio %
1.41	1.56	2.33	2.38	2.11	1.23	0.79	0.37	0.67	0.86	0.88	1.13	Income Ratio %
81	72	52	37	35	106	77	113	196	326	349	212	Turnover Rate %
1,260	1,468	2,208	2,797	3,808	4,997	6,329	5,495	4,938	4,080	5,079	5,405	Net Assets $mil

Performance 12-31-04

	1st Qtr	2nd Qtr	3rd Qtr	4th Qtr	Total
2000	3.51	-4.10	0.06	-13.16	-13.75
2001	-10.76	10.68	-15.64	8.79	-9.35
2002	-0.18	-9.53	-14.89	10.11	-15.37
2003	-3.38	12.54	0.60	9.91	20.23
2004	-0.37	0.55	0.73	9.60	10.60

Trailing	Total Return%	+/- S&P 500	+/- Russ 1000	%Rank Cat	Growth of $10,000
3 Mo	9.60	0.37	-0.20	37	10,960
6 Mo	10.40	3.21	2.59	5	11,040
1 Yr	10.60	-0.27	-0.80	40	11,060
3 Yr Avg	4.01	0.43	-0.26	28	11,252
5 Yr Avg	-2.53	-0.23	-0.77	55	8,797
10 Yr Avg	11.37	-0.70	-0.79	34	29,355
15 Yr Avg	12.93	2.00	1.85	5	61,964

Tax Analysis	Tax-Adj Rtn%	%Rank Cat	Tax-Cost Rat	%Rank Cat
3 Yr (estimated)	0.70	72	0.37	31
5 Yr (estimated)	-5.00	81	0.85	45
10 Yr (estimated)	8.53	53	1.71	68

Potential Capital Gain Exposure: 8% of assets

Rating and Risk

Time Period	Load-Adj Return %	Morningstar Rtn vs Cat	Morningstar Risk vs Cat	Morningstar Risk-Adj Rating
1 Yr	1.49			
3 Yr	1.07	-Avg	-Avg	★★★
5 Yr	-4.19	-Avg	Avg	★★
10 Yr	10.42	Avg	Avg	★★★
Incept	15.46			

Other Measures	Standard Index S&P 500	Best Fit Index S&P 500
Alpha	0.7	0.7
Beta	0.82	0.82
R-Squared	92	92
Standard Deviation	13.41	
Mean	4.01	
Sharpe Ratio	0.20	

Portfolio Analysis 09-30-04

Share change since 06-04 Total Stocks:111	Sector	PE	YTD Ret%	% Assets
⊕ Verizon Communications	Telecom	32.4	20.25	6.01
⊖ SBC Communications	Telecom	15.4	3.74	4.90
⊖ SLM	Financial	15.8	44.21	3.87
⊕ Pfizer	Health	22.0	-22.31	3.55
⊕ UnitedHealth Group	Health	23.8	51.38	3.29
⊖ Microsoft	Software	36.1	8.95	3.00
⊕ BellSouth	Telecom	12.7	1.94	2.95
⊕ Lockheed Martin	Ind Mtrls	19.9	9.97	2.94
⊖ Roche Holding	Health	—	—	2.65
⊕ Northrop Grumman	Ind Mtrls	18.3	15.68	2.62
⊕ Biomet	Health	34.1	20.83	2.08
⊖ Caremark RX	Health	32.8	55.67	1.95
⊖ Procter & Gamble	Goods	23.3	12.38	1.85
⊕ United Defense Industrie	Ind Mtrls	14.2	48.21	1.66
⊕ Honeywell International	Ind Mtrls	20.5	8.21	1.66
⊕ PepsiCo	Goods	22.5	13.82	1.61
⊖ Pixar	Media	29.3	23.55	1.59
☼ Lukoil ADR	Energy	—	—	1.53
⊕ Wal-Mart Stores	Consumer	23.4	0.51	1.43
⊖ Barr Pharmaceuticals	Health	37.4	-11.23	1.40

Current Investment Style

Value Blnd Growth — Large / Mid / Small

Market Cap	%
Giant	44.5
Large	31.3
Mid	21.2
Small	2.4
Micro	0.7
Avg $mil: 27,457	

Value Measures		Rel Category
Price/Earnings	19.57	1.16
Price/Book	2.58	0.98
Price/Sales	1.29	0.90
Price/Cash Flow	9.15	1.19
Dividend Yield %	1.54	1.04

Growth Measures	%	Rel Category
Long-Term Erngs	11.08	0.96
Book Value	9.47	1.22
Sales	7.52	1.31
Cash Flow	19.62	2.07
Historical Erngs	6.50	0.55

Profitability	%	Rel Category
Return on Equity	18.93	1.08
Return on Assets	9.26	1.07
Net Margin	11.70	1.02

Sector Weightings	% of Stocks	Rel S&P 500	3 Year High	3 Year Low
Info	29.13	1.36		
Software	3.79	0.88	12	4
Hardware	3.92	0.38	12	2
Media	4.56	1.19	16	1
Telecom	16.86	5.35	17	5
Service	39.02	0.84		
Health	27.11	2.17	27	15
Consumer	3.71	0.41	4	1
Business	1.80	0.44	8	2
Financial	6.40	0.31	13	6
Mfg	31.86	0.99		
Goods	10.01	1.07	18	1
Ind Mtrls	14.18	1.12	25	14
Energy	7.67	1.07	20	1
Utilities	0.00	0.00	2	0

Composition

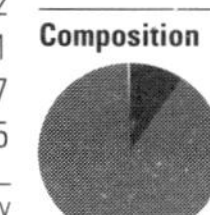

Cash	9.4
Stocks	90.0
Bonds	0.0
Other	0.6
Foreign (% of Stock)	10.8

Morningstar's Take by Greg Carlson 12-23-04

New investors should avoid Fidelity Destiny II.

We've long been wary of the contractual plans through which this fund is sold, which require investors to commit to at least 10 years of systematic investments. The price of entry is quite high; investors pay commissions of up to 50% in the first year. Those who stick with the plan pay a more reasonable price over time, but investors who withdraw early may pay hefty penalties.

Recent developments underscore our concerns. In December 2004, First Command Financial Planning, one of the primary sellers of contractual plan funds, was censured and fined $12 million by the NASD for deceptive sales practices. What's more, First Command's data shows that only 43% of investors who started a 15-year plan completed their terms. The fine will be used to pay restitution to investors who have started a plan since Jan. 1, 1999, have since terminated it, and paid an effective sales charge of greater than 5%.

As a result, contractual plan funds face a murky future. A bill banning the sale of these funds was approved by the U.S. House of Representatives in October. (The Senate has yet to vote on it.) Just prior to the NASD's actions, First Command announced it would stop selling contractual plan funds. Also, Templeton Investment Counsel plans to merge its contractual plan offering, Templeton Capital Accumulator, into Templeton Growth, pending shareholder approval.

Fidelity, for its part, says it has no plans to shutter this fund. That's unfortunate, because First Command's own data show that many investors redeem their shares early in the life of their contracts, thereby incurring stiff penalties.

That said, current shareholders, who have already paid the load, should stick around. Manager Adam Hetnarski's record is only so-so since taking over in June 2000, but a better record at previous stops is reason for optimism.

Address:	82 Devonshire St Boston MA 02109 800-343-3548
Web Address:	www.fidelity.com
Inception:	12-30-85
Advisor:	Fidelity Management & Research Co. (FMR)
Subadvisor:	FMR Co., Inc. (FMRC)
NTF Plans:	N/A

Minimum Purchase:	$50	Add: $50	IRA: $50
Min Auto Inv Plan:	$50	Add: $50	
Sales Fees:	8.24%L		
Management Fee:	0.59%		
Actual Fees:	Mgt:0.58%	Dist: —	
Expense Projections:	3Yr:$199	5Yr:$346	10Yr:$774
Income Distrib:	Annually		

Fidelity Discovery Fund

Ticker	Load	NAV	Yield	Total Assets	Mstar Category
FDSVX	None	$11.30	1.1%	$552 mil	Large Blend

Governance and Management

Fiduciary Grade: B

Portfolio Manager(s)

Adam Hetnarski took the reins here in February 2000, and he has had successful stints at other Fidelity offerings. He put up particularly big numbers during his short stint at Fidelity Export & Multinational. Hetnarski is also a former tech analyst for Fidelity.

Strategy

Adam Hetnarski tries to buy fast-growing companies. He considers most mid-caps and large caps fair game, and he said the fund could have a more pronounced mid-cap tilt over time. Although the fund has a definite growth bias, Hetnarski keeps an eye on valuations and has sometimes bought nontraditional growth fare such as Altria Group (formerly Philip Morris) and basic-materials stocks.

Historical Profile

Return Average
Risk Average
Rating ★★★ Neutral

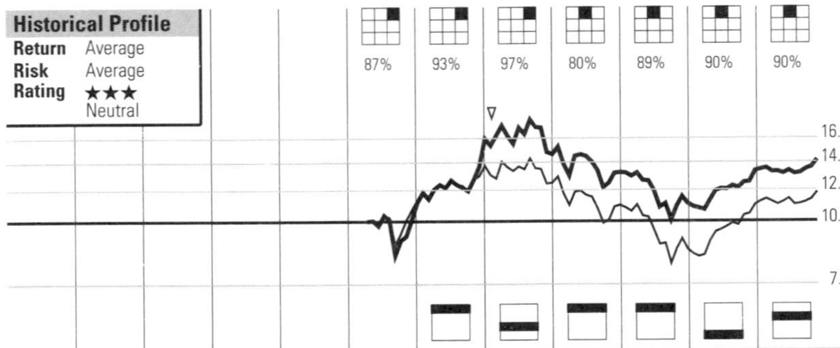

Investment Style
Equity
Stock %

▼ Manager Change
▽ Partial Manager Change

Growth of $10,000
— Investment Values of Fund
— Investment Values of S&P 500

Performance Quartile (within Category)

1993	1994	1995	1996	1997	1998	1999	2000	2001	2002	2003	12-04	History
—	—	—	—	—	11.14	14.91	11.49	10.35	8.67	10.34	11.30	NAV
—	—	—	—	—	—	42.52	-8.35	-9.59	-15.94	19.87	10.62	Total Return %
—	—	—	—	—	—	21.48	0.75	2.29	6.15	-8.80	-0.25	+/-S&P 500
—	—	—	—	—	—	21.61	-0.56	2.86	5.71	-10.02	-0.78	+/-Russ 1000
—	—	—	—	—	0.00	0.00	0.00	0.35	0.29	0.58	1.26	Income Return %
—	—	—	—	—	—	42.52	-8.35	-9.94	-16.23	19.29	9.36	Capital Return %
—	—	—	—	—	—	4	59	25	10	95	40	Total Rtn % Rank Cat
—	—	—	—	—	0.00	0.00	0.00	0.04	0.03	0.05	0.13	Income $
—	—	—	—	—	0.00	0.72	2.45	0.00	0.00	0.00	0.00	Capital Gains $
—	—	—	—	—	1.23	0.87	0.86	0.91	0.99	0.97	0.84	Expense Ratio %
—	—	—	—	—	-0.28	-0.01	-0.08	0.19	0.32	0.43	0.73	Income Ratio %
—	—	—	—	—	141	293	291	258	259	367	249	Turnover Rate %
—	—	—	—	—	538	1,374	1,451	1,032	672	655	552	Net Assets $mil

Performance 12-31-04

	1st Qtr	2nd Qtr	3rd Qtr	4th Qtr	Total
2000	7.58	-1.25	0.35	-14.03	-8.35
2001	-11.23	11.37	-15.96	8.81	-9.59
2002	-0.29	-9.59	-15.11	9.86	-15.94
2003	-3.58	12.44	0.64	9.86	19.87
2004	-0.48	0.58	0.79	9.64	10.62

Trailing	Total Return%	+/- S&P 500	+/- Russ 1000	%Rank Cat	Growth of $10,000
3 Mo	9.64	0.41	-0.16	36	10,964
6 Mo	10.51	3.32	2.70	4	11,051
1 Yr	10.62	-0.25	-0.78	40	11,062
3 Yr Avg	3.69	0.11	-0.58	32	11,148
5 Yr Avg	-1.57	0.73	0.19	39	9,239
10 Yr Avg	—	—	—	—	—
15 Yr Avg	—	—	—	—	—

Tax Analysis	Tax-Adj Rtn%	%Rank Cat	Tax-Cost Rat	%Rank Cat
3 Yr (estimated)	3.43	26	0.25	21
5 Yr (estimated)	-2.84	45	1.29	67
10 Yr (estimated)	—	—	—	—

Potential Capital Gain Exposure: -38% of assets

Rating and Risk

Time Period	Load-Adj Return %	Morningstar Rtn vs Cat	Morningstar Risk vs Cat	Morningstar Risk-Adj Rating
1 Yr	10.62			
3 Yr	3.69	+Avg	-Avg	★★★★
5 Yr	-1.57	Avg	+Avg	★★★
10 Yr	—	—	—	—
Incept	5.83			

Other Measures	Standard Index S&P 500	Best Fit Index S&P 500
Alpha	0.4	0.4
Beta	0.82	0.82
R-Squared	91	91
Standard Deviation	13.39	
Mean	3.69	
Sharpe Ratio	0.17	

Morningstar's Take by Greg Carlson 12-23-04

We expected better from Fidelity Discovery's manager, but we're still optimistic about the fund's prospects.

Adam Hetnarski, this fund's manager since February 2000, has struggled of late. Because he's consistently maintained a defensive stance, the fund held up well in the bear market but fared poorly in last year's rally. Given that high-priced fare has lagged more-steady names this year, one might have assumed the fund would once again be shining. However, it has posted just a middling showing through December 22.

That's due to Hetnarski's bold approach. He makes sector bets based on his macroeconomic view, and he seeks out firms that he believes have solid earnings growth potential. When he spies new opportunities, he doesn't hesitate to make rapid, sizable shifts. (Portfolio turnover has often been 250% or higher.) For example, the fund's energy weighting in 2004 fell from 10% in January to just 1% three months later, then rebounded to 9% by the end of July. The latter move was a result of Hetnarski's bet that oil prices, which had briefly pulled back, would rise again due to the uncertainty that has preceded the presidential election. That worked well, but he had a light energy stake going into February, when the sector also rallied. Also, a big wager on health care, which Hetnarski thought would thrive in a slowing economy, has produced mixed results.

All told, Hetnarski's record here is mediocre. However, he notched fine results in previous stints at Fidelity Select Technology and Fidelity Export & Multinational. What's more, although he runs another charge, Fidelity Destiny II, in an identical style, the two funds' combined asset base of $5.6 billion affords Hetnarski a good deal of flexibility.

As such, we think this offering is worth a look. However, Hetnarski's fast-moving approach, which he says he will moderate a bit in the future, means this fund is best taken in medium-sized doses, and should be stashed in a tax-deferred account.

Address:	82 Devonshire St Boston MA 02109 800-343-3548	Minimum Purchase: Min Auto Inv Plan: Sales Fees:	$2500 $2500 No-load	Add: $250 Add: $100	IRA: $2500
Web Address:	www.fidelity.com	Management Fee:	0.59%		
Inception:	04-01-98	Actual Fees:	Mgt:0.59%	Dist:	
Advisor:	Fidelity Management & Research Co. (FMR)	Expense Projections:	3Yr:$588	5Yr:$799	10Yr:$1409
Subadvisor:	FMR Co., Inc. (FMRC)	Income Distrib:	Semi-Annually		
NTF Plans:	Fidelity Retail-NTF, CommonWealth NTF				

Portfolio Analysis 09-30-04

Share change since 06-04 Total Stocks:111	Sector	PE	YTD Ret%	% Assets
⊖ Verizon Communications	Telecom	32.4	20.25	6.11
⊖ SBC Communications	Telecom	15.4	3.74	4.98
⊖ SLM	Financial	15.8	44.21	3.90
⊕ Pfizer	Health	22.0	-22.31	3.57
⊕ UnitedHealth Group	Health	23.8	51.38	3.30
⊖ Microsoft	Software	36.1	8.95	3.01
⊖ Lockheed Martin	Ind Mtrls	19.9	9.97	2.98
⊖ BellSouth	Telecom	12.7	1.94	2.96
⊖ Roche Holding	Health	—	—	2.66
⊖ Northrop Grumman	Ind Mtrls	18.3	15.68	2.63
⊖ Biomet	Health	34.1	20.83	2.09
⊖ Caremark RX	Health	32.8	55.67	1.97
⊖ Procter & Gamble	Goods	23.3	12.38	1.86
⊕ United Defense Industrie	Ind Mtrls	14.2	48.21	1.67
⊕ Honeywell International	Ind Mtrls	20.5	8.21	1.67
⊕ PepsiCo	Goods	22.5	13.82	1.62
⊖ Pixar	Media	29.3	23.55	1.60
☼ Lukoil ADR	Energy	—	—	1.53
⊕ Wal-Mart Stores	Consumer	23.4	0.51	1.44
⊖ Barr Pharmaceuticals	Health	37.4	-11.23	1.41

Current Investment Style

Value Blnd Growth / Large Mid Small

Market Cap	%
Giant	43.8
Large	31.6
Mid	21.5
Small	2.4
Micro	0.7
Avg $mil: 26,856	

Value Measures		Rel Category
Price/Earnings	19.83	1.17
Price/Book	2.60	0.99
Price/Sales	1.29	0.90
Price/Cash Flow	9.12	1.19
Dividend Yield %	1.55	1.05

Growth Measures	%	Rel Category
Long-Term Erngs	11.08	0.96
Book Value	9.39	1.21
Sales	7.41	1.29
Cash Flow	19.64	2.08
Historical Erngs	6.06	0.51

Profitability	%	Rel Category
Return on Equity	19.01	1.09
Return on Assets	9.28	1.08
Net Margin	11.65	1.02

Sector Weightings	% of Stocks	Rel S&P 500	3 Year High	3 Year Low
Info	29.42	1.37		
Software	3.84	0.89	13	4
Hardware	3.93	0.39	12	2
Media	4.58	1.19	16	2
Telecom	17.07	5.42	17	2
Service	38.58	0.83		
Health	27.65	2.21	28	15
Consumer	3.73	0.41	4	0
Business	1.86	0.46	8	1
Financial	5.34	0.26	9	5
Mfg	32.00	1.00		
Goods	10.05	1.08	12	5
Ind Mtrls	14.25	1.12	22	14
Energy	7.70	1.08	12	1
Utilities	0.00	0.00	6	0

Composition

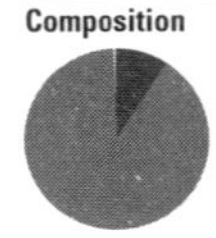

Cash	9.0
Stocks	90.2
Bonds	0.0
Other	0.7
Foreign (% of Stock)	11.1

Fidelity Diversified Int

Ticker	Load	NAV	Yield	Total Assets	Mstar Category
FDIVX	Closed	$28.64	0.5%	$23,420 mil	Foreign Large Growth

Governance and Management

Fiduciary Grade: B

Portfolio Manager(s)

In 2001, the fund lost its longtime manager Greg Fraser, who quit after a decade on the job. His replacement, Bill Bower, had a solid stint at Fidelity International Growth & Income (now Fidelity International Discovery). Thus far, Bower has done a fine job at this fund. Bower draws from Fidelity's rich regional research staff as well as a group of global sector analysts based in Boston.

Strategy

In the past, this fund's portfolio was filled with stocks picked by quantitative models that rely on earnings-momentum measures. Manager Bill Bower runs the fund with more of a fundamental approach, using a growth-at-a-reasonable-price strategy. It mainly focuses on larger-cap stocks, but it can also fish in small- and mid-cap waters. Bower runs a sprawling portfolio of more than 300 names, which makes this fund widely diversified. He isn't afraid to deviate somewhat from his benchmark, so the fund sometimes sports small but noticeable stakes in emerging markets stocks. Fidelity uses fair value pricing when necessary.

Historical Profile

Return High
Risk Below Avg
Rating ★★★★★ Highest

Investment Style
Equity
Stock %: 89% 80% 81% 88% 88% 90% 88% 93% 92%

▼ Manager Change
▽ Partial Manager Change

Growth of $10,000
— Investment Values of Fund
— Investment Values of MSCI EAFE

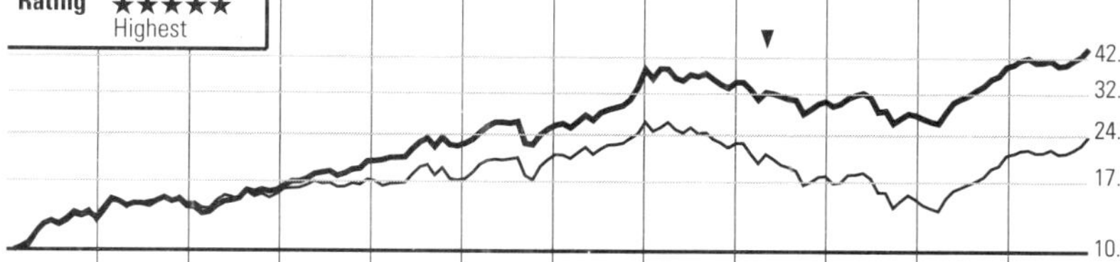

Performance Quartile (within Category)

History

	1993	1994	1995	1996	1997	1998	1999	2000	2001	2002	2003	12-04	History
	11.60	11.30	12.69	14.71	16.13	17.72	25.62	21.94	19.08	17.16	24.12	28.64	NAV
	36.67	1.09	17.97	20.02	13.72	14.39	50.65	-8.96	-12.99	-9.37	42.38	19.66	Total Return %
	4.11	-6.69	6.76	13.97	11.94	-5.54	23.62	5.23	8.43	6.57	3.79	-0.59	+/-MSCI EAFE
	4.46	-6.26	6.56	13.15	11.45	-4.30	22.67	4.40	8.40	6.43	2.96	-0.72	+/-MSCI Wd xUS
	0.12	0.26	1.95	1.18	1.29	1.43	1.41	2.15	0.05	0.68	1.75	0.62	Income Return %
	36.55	0.83	16.02	18.84	12.43	12.96	49.24	-11.11	-13.04	-10.05	40.63	19.04	Capital Return %
	61	20	11	15	21	51	56	7	4	5	14	17	Total Rtn % Rank Cat
	0.01	0.03	0.22	0.15	0.19	0.23	0.25	0.55	0.01	0.13	0.30	0.15	Income $
	0.10	0.39	0.41	0.36	0.41	0.47	0.70	0.81	0.00	0.00	0.00	0.06	Capital Gains $
	1.47	1.25	1.12	1.27	1.23	1.19	1.18	1.12	1.16	1.19	1.22	1.12	Expense Ratio %
	0.84	0.96	1.55	1.53	1.49	1.46	0.94	1.62	1.08	0.77	0.96	0.66	Income Ratio %
	56	89	101	94	81	95	73	94	86	55	51	55	Turnover Rate %
	239	306	341	754	1,536	2,157	4,908	6,580	6,379	7,135	13,559	23,420	Net Assets $mil

Performance 12-31-04

	1st Qtr	2nd Qtr	3rd Qtr	4th Qtr	Total
2000	0.27	-4.05	-3.16	-2.28	-8.96
2001	-11.76	2.53	-12.04	9.34	-12.99
2002	2.46	0.67	-17.17	6.08	-9.37
2003	-5.77	19.73	9.56	15.19	42.38
2004	6.72	-1.83	0.24	13.94	19.66

Trailing	Total Return%	+/- MSCI EAFE	+/- MSCI Wd xUS	%Rank Cat	Growth of $10,000
3 Mo	13.94	-1.38	-1.21	49	11,394
6 Mo	14.21	-0.79	-1.16	22	11,421
1 Yr	19.66	-0.59	-0.72	17	11,966
3 Yr Avg	15.58	3.69	3.36	2	15,440
5 Yr Avg	4.11	5.24	4.87	1	12,231
10 Yr Avg	13.00	7.38	7.06	1	33,946
15 Yr Avg	—	—	—	—	—

Tax Analysis	Tax-Adj Rtn%	%Rank Cat	Tax-Cost Rat	%Rank Cat
3 Yr (estimated)	15.30	1	0.24	48
5 Yr (estimated)	3.61	1	0.48	28
10 Yr (estimated)	12.00	1	0.88	43

Potential Capital Gain Exposure: 24% of assets

Rating and Risk

Time Period	Load-Adj Return %	Morningstar Rtn vs Cat	Morningstar Risk vs Cat	Morningstar Risk-Adj Rating
1 Yr	19.66			
3 Yr	15.58	High	-Avg	★★★★★
5 Yr	4.11	High	Low	★★★★★
10 Yr	13.00	High	-Avg	★★★★★
Incept	11.38			

Other Measures	Standard Index S&P 500	Best Fit Index MSCI Wd xUS
Alpha	4.6	4.2
Beta	0.87	0.88
R-Squared	95	95
Standard Deviation	15.97	
Mean	15.58	
Sharpe Ratio	0.90	

Portfolio Analysis 10-31-04

Share change since 07-04 Total Stocks:328	Sector	Country	% Assets
⊕ Vodafone Group PLC ADR	Telecom	U.K.	2.48
⊕ Novartis AG ADR	Health	Switzerland	2.12
⊕ BP PLC ADR	Energy	U.K.	1.98
⊕ HSBC Holdings PLC ADR	Financial	U.K.	1.58
⊖ Total SA ADR	Energy	France	1.54
⊕ Roche Holding	Health	Switzerland	1.47
⊖ Sanofi-Aventis ADR	Health	France	1.03
Toyota Motor ADR	Goods	Japan	1.02
⊕ UBS	Financial	Switzerland	1.00
⊕ Tesco	Consumer	U.K.	0.99
⊕ Samsung Electronics	Goods	Korea	0.91
⊕ Nestle	Goods	Switzerland	0.91
⊕ CSL Ltd	Health	Australia	0.87
⊕ ENI SpA ADR	Energy	Italy	0.85
⊕ Telefonica SA ADR	Telecom	Spain	0.84
⊕ BNP Paribas	Financial	France	0.84
⊕ Royal Bank Of Scotland G	Financial	U.K.	0.81
⊖ Sumitomo Mitsui Financia	Financial	Japan	0.80
⊖ EnCana	Energy	Canada	0.74
Reckitt Benckiser	Goods	U.K.	0.74

Current Investment Style

Value Blnd Growth — Large Mid Small

Market Cap	%
Giant	39.7
Large	35.5
Mid	21.8
Small	2.9
Micro	0.2

Avg $mil: 15,197

Value Measures		Rel Category
Price/Earnings	14.64	0.99
Price/Book	1.88	0.90
Price/Sales	1.10	1.05
Price/Cash Flow	5.31	0.96
Dividend Yield %	1.93	0.95

Growth Measures	%	Rel Category
Long-Term Erngs	13.48	1.13
Book Value	0.95	0.55
Sales	6.20	1.34
Cash Flow	-1.28	NMF
Historical Erngs	5.49	0.66

Composition

Cash	6.3	Bonds	0.9
Stocks	91.6	Other	1.1

Foreign (% of Stock) 95.6

Sector Weightings	% of Stocks	Rel MSCI EAFE	3 Year High	3 Year Low
Info	16.05	0.97		
Software	1.60	1.48	2	0
Hardware	3.43	0.94	6	3
Media	4.16	1.82	5	3
Telecom	6.86	0.71	8	3
Service	46.66	1.04		
Health	12.70	1.75	16	13
Consumer	5.75	1.14	6	2
Business	4.76	0.87	5	3
Financial	23.45	0.87	29	23
Mfg	37.29	0.96		
Goods	16.22	1.19	20	15
Ind Mtrls	10.75	0.87	12	9
Energy	8.70	1.18	10	8
Utilities	1.62	0.30	2	1

Regional Exposure % Stock

UK/W. Europe	64	N. America	11
Japan	13	Latn America	1
Asia X Japan	11	Other	0

Country Exposure % Stock

U.K.	22	France	9
Japan	13	Canada	7
Switzerland	11		

Morningstar's Take by Christopher Traulsen 12-01-04

The closing of Fidelity Diversified International makes sense.

Fidelity closed this fund to new investors on October 25. The move makes sense--the fund has grown tremendously in recent years, with its asset base swelling from $6.4 billion in 2001 to $18.7 billion as of Sept. 30, 2004. Manager Bill Bower had also been running another $4.3 billion in the same style at the Fidelity Advisor version of this offering, but that fund has now been handed off to Penelope Dobkin, which should help alleviate the burden on Bower.

This fund's popularity is understandable. Bower has put up excellent results since taking the helm in April 2001, and that performance came on the heels of a successful three-year stint at Fidelity International Discovery (formerly Fidelity International Growth and Income). From April 1, 2001, through Nov. 29, 2004 (a period roughly equal to Bower's tenure), Diversified International posted an annualized return of 11.02% per year. That compares favorably with the 2.42% per year the average foreign large-growth fund eked out over the period and also trounces the return of the broadly followed MSCI EAFE Index.

Bower has also kept risk reasonable here. Although he will venture into emerging markets (the fund had a 10% emerging-markets stake earlier this year), he keeps the portfolio well diversified across individual names and fairly broadly diversified across sectors of the market. Bower also has the advantage of being able to draw on Fidelity's staff of analysts with regional specialties and the firm's global sector analyst group, resources which few other investment advisors can match.

Investors in this fund have every reason to be satisfied with this choice.

Address:	82 Devonshire St Boston MA 02109 800-343-3548
Web Address:	www.fidelity.com
Inception:	12-27-91
Advisor:	Fidelity Management & Research Co. (FMR)
Subadvisor:	FMR Co., Inc. (FMRC)
NTF Plans:	Fidelity Retail-NTF, CommonWealth NTF

Minimum Purchase:	Closed	Add: —		IRA: —	
Min Auto Inv Plan:	Closed	Add: —			
Sales Fees:	No-load, 1.00%R				
Management Fee:	0.90%				
Actual Fees:	Mgt:0.90%	Dist:			
Expense Projections:	3Yr:$384	5Yr:$665		10Yr:$1466	
Income Distrib:	Annually				

Fidelity Dividend Growth

Analyst Pick

Ticker	Load	NAV	Yield	Total Assets	Mstar Category
FDGFX	None	$28.49	1.4%	$19,422 mil	Large Blend

Governance and Management

Fiduciary Grade: B

Portfolio Manager(s)

Charles Mangum is an experienced Fidelity manager and analyst. He has been on the job here since January 1997 and has built a fine record. He also runs the stock portion of Fidelity Asset Manager and Fidelity Asset Manager: Growth. Previously, Mangum, like most Fidelity skippers, ran several sector funds for the firm. His health-care bias dates back to his days as a health-care analyst. Mangum says that all of his 401(k) assets are in his funds, as are a sizable portion of his liquid assets.

Strategy

Charles Mangum is a counterpuncher, and if an area, including technology, has good-enough growth prospects and cheap-enough valuations, he'll give it a look. He has proved patient with his favorite stocks as the top holdings don't vary much from month to month. Most of the fund's turnover is generated by adjustments to position sizes rather than changes in names.

Historical Profile

Return Above Avg
Risk Above Avg
Rating ★★★★ Above Avg

Investment Style: Equity Stock %

94% 94% 95% 94% 95% 91% 89% 95% 95%

▼ Manager Change
∇ Partial Manager Change

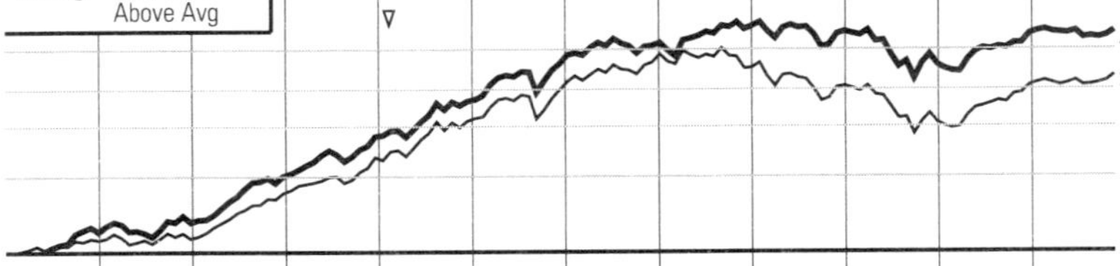

Growth of $10,000
— Investment Values of Fund
— Investment Values of S&P 500

Performance Quartile (within Category)

1993	1994	1995	1996	1997	1998	1999	2000	2001	2002	2003	12-04	History
12.11	12.37	15.84	20.09	23.27	28.73	28.99	29.96	28.33	22.32	27.30	28.49	NAV
21.72*	4.27	37.53	30.14	27.90	35.85	8.81	12.25	-3.74	-20.44	23.36	5.84	Total Return %
—	2.96	0.00	7.20	-5.45	7.28	-12.23	21.35	8.14	1.65	-5.31	-5.03	+/-S&P 500
—	3.88	-0.24	7.69	-4.95	8.83	-12.10	20.04	8.71	1.21	-6.53	-5.56	+/-Russ 1000
0.00	0.08	0.74	0.58	0.76	0.58	0.50	0.63	0.50	0.78	0.99	1.43	Income Return %
—	4.19	36.79	29.56	27.14	35.27	8.31	11.62	-4.24	-21.22	22.37	4.41	Capital Return %
—	6	12	5	55	2	87	5	9	31	82	89	Total Rtn % Rank Cat
0.01	0.01	0.09	0.09	0.15	0.13	0.14	0.18	0.15	0.22	0.22	0.39	Income $
0.05	0.24	1.07	0.37	2.19	2.19	2.14	2.40	0.33	0.00	0.00	0.00	Capital Gains $
2.50	1.40	1.19	0.99	0.92	0.86	0.84	0.74	0.94	0.95	1.02	0.89	Expense Ratio %
-0.73	0.13	0.78	0.86	0.99	0.64	0.58	0.52	0.54	0.90	0.94	0.75	Income Ratio %
90	291	162	129	141	109	104	86	88	81	51	37	Turnover Rate %
89	102	529	2,345	4,480	10,369	12,624	11,781	15,210	13,479	18,171	19,422	Net Assets $mil

Performance 12-31-04

	1st Qtr	2nd Qtr	3rd Qtr	4th Qtr	Total
2000	1.79	5.96	3.36	0.68	12.25
2001	-8.28	7.68	-12.70	11.64	-3.74
2002	0.81	-15.48	-15.42	10.39	-20.44
2003	-4.84	17.42	0.19	10.19	23.36
2004	1.39	0.61	-4.57	8.71	5.84

Trailing	Total Return%	+/- S&P 500	+/- Russ 1000	%Rank Cat	Growth of $10,000
3 Mo	8.71	-0.52	-1.09	69	10,871
6 Mo	3.75	-3.44	-4.06	91	10,375
1 Yr	5.84	-5.03	-5.56	89	10,584
3 Yr Avg	1.27	-2.31	-3.00	77	10,386
5 Yr Avg	2.33	4.63	4.09	11	11,221
10 Yr Avg	14.28	2.21	2.12	4	37,993
15 Yr Avg	—	—	—	—	—

Tax Analysis	Tax-Adj Rtn%	%Rank Cat	Tax-Cost Rat	%Rank Cat
3 Yr (estimated)	0.88	70	0.39	33
5 Yr (estimated)	1.64	11	0.67	35
10 Yr (estimated)	12.47	4	1.58	60

Potential Capital Gain Exposure: 8% of assets

Rating and Risk

Time Period	Load-Adj Return %	Morningstar Rtn vs Cat	Morningstar Risk vs Cat	Morningstar Risk-Adj Rating
1 Yr	5.84			
3 Yr	1.27	-Avg	+Avg	★★
5 Yr	2.33	+Avg	+Avg	★★★★
10 Yr	14.28	High	Avg	★★★★★
Incept	14.41			

Other Measures	Standard Index S&P 500	Best Fit Index S&P 500
Alpha	-2.2	-2.2
Beta	1.07	1.07
R-Squared	94	94
Standard Deviation	16.92	
Mean	1.27	
Sharpe Ratio	-0.01	

Portfolio Analysis 10-31-04

Share change since 07-04 Total Stocks:118	Sector	PE	YTD Ret%	% Assets
⊕ American International G	Financial	16.2	-0.53	5.37
Microsoft	Software	36.1	8.95	5.25
⊕ Home Depot	Consumer	19.0	21.47	5.19
⊖ Fannie Mae	Financial	9.1	-2.33	4.36
⊕ Pfizer	Health	22.0	-22.31	4.34
⊕ SBC Communications	Telecom	15.4	3.74	4.14
⊕ Cardinal Health	Health	16.9	-4.73	4.14
⊕ Wyeth	Health	17.0	2.73	3.83
Clear Channel Communicat	Media	23.5	-27.57	3.73
⊖ General Electric	Ind Mtrls	22.8	20.68	3.52
⊕ Bank of America	Financial	12.3	21.50	2.69
⊖ Citigroup	Financial	15.3	2.72	2.51
CVS	Consumer	21.1	25.61	2.20
Morgan Stanley	Financial	14.2	-2.25	2.20
⊖ Johnson & Johnson	Health	20.6	25.17	1.91
⊕ Cisco Systems	Hardware	24.5	-20.26	1.76
Tyco International	Ind Mtrls	25.1	35.41	1.45
⊕ J.P. Morgan Chase & Co.	Financial	19.4	9.97	1.42
⊖ S&P 500 Index (Fut)	—	—	—	1.40
⊕ Dell	Hardware	34.0	24.01	1.33

Current Investment Style

Value Blnd Growth; Large Mid Small

Market Cap	%
Giant	66.8
Large	22.9
Mid	10.3
Small	0.1
Micro	0.0
Avg $mil: 57,923	

Value Measures		Rel Category
Price/Earnings	15.84	0.94
Price/Book	2.45	0.94
Price/Sales	1.41	0.98
Price/Cash Flow	5.69	0.74
Dividend Yield %	1.66	1.12

Growth Measures	%	Rel Category
Long-Term Erngs	11.50	0.99
Book Value	8.46	1.09
Sales	6.39	1.11
Cash Flow	8.95	0.95
Historical Erngs	10.22	0.87

Profitability	%	Rel Category
Return on Equity	16.38	0.94
Return on Assets	9.83	1.14
Net Margin	12.23	1.07

Sector Weightings	% of Stocks	Rel S&P 500	3 Year High	3 Year Low
Info	26.24	1.22		
Software	6.08	1.41	6	2
Hardware	7.97	0.78	8	5
Media	4.89	1.27	9	5
Telecom	7.30	2.32	8	5
Service	57.16	1.23		
Health	17.25	1.38	23	17
Consumer	10.81	1.19	11	6
Business	1.59	0.39	3	1
Financial	27.51	1.33	28	22
Mfg	16.60	0.52		
Goods	3.81	0.41	7	4
Ind Mtrls	7.44	0.59	10	6
Energy	4.13	0.58	9	4
Utilities	1.22	0.41	2	0

Composition

Cash	3.1
Stocks	94.8
Bonds	0.0
Other	2.0
Foreign (% of Stock)	0.8

Morningstar's Take by Greg Carlson 12-23-04

Is Fidelity Dividend Growth due for a rebound?

This fund's manager, Charles Mangum, employs a price-conscious, contrarian growth strategy, which has led to sharp swings in annual relative performance since he took over in 1997. However, the fund has been quite consistent over longer spans: On Mangum's watch, it has beaten its benchmark, the S&P 500 Index, in 49 of 59 rolling three-year periods.

Most of the periods when the fund fell short ran from early in his tenure to early 2000, as Mangum's taste for steady-eddie firms resulted in a poor showing in latter stages of the bull market of the1990s. However, the fund far outpaced its bogy in the bear market. Because its management fee rises when the fund has beaten the index over the trailing three years (and vice versa), its expense ratio climbed from 2000 to 2003, despite significant asset growth. More recently, the fund has struggled again, and its expenses, which are calculated each July, have dropped accordingly (from 1.02% to 0.89%). Given the fund's turnaround after Mangum's style was last out of fashion, another reversal of fortune may be in the offing.

However, the fund may face another type of headwind. Mangum's avoidance of high-flyers certainly hurt last year, when speculative fare rallied sharply. But a recent focus on mega-cap stocks has also weighed on returns. Because Mangum now runs nearly $32 billion in the same style and tends to load up on his favorite picks, it's fair to question whether asset constraints have pushed Mangum--who has juiced returns in the past with forays into mid-caps--up the market-cap ladder. He says that's not the case and argues that larger firms boast more-attractive valuations. While that stance may soon pay off, we think Fidelity should consider closing the fund to preserve Mangum's distinctive investment style.

Over all, our confidence in Mangum trumps such concerns. This remains a fine choice.

Address:	82 Devonshire St Boston MA 02109 800-343-3548
Web Address:	www.fidelity.com
Inception:	04-27-93 *
Advisor:	Fidelity Management & Research Co. (FMR)
Subadvisor:	FMR Co., Inc. (FMRC)
NTF Plans:	Fidelity Retail-NTF, CommonWealth NTF

Minimum Purchase:	$2500	Add: $250	IRA: $2500
Min Auto Inv Plan:	$2500	Add: $100	
Sales Fees:	No-load		
Management Fee:	0.77%		
Actual Fees:	Mgt:0.77%	Dist:	
Expense Projections:	3Yr:$246	5Yr:$428	10Yr:$954
Income Distrib:	Annually		

Fidelity Equity-Inc

Ticker	Load	NAV	Yield	Total Assets	Mstar Category
FEQIX	None	$52.78	1.5%	$26,372 mil	Large Value

Governance and Management

Fiduciary Grade: B

Portfolio Manager(s)

Stephen Petersen has managed the fund since 1993, and he is supported by Fidelity's considerable research staff. He took on the added responsibility of running Fidelity Puritan's equity portfolio in early 2000.

Strategy

Manager Stephen Petersen generally invests in companies with dividend yields greater than the S&P 500 Index's. He spreads the portfolio across more than 200 stocks--mostly giant caps--and dabbles in bonds and convertibles for added income. The portfolio typically emphasizes financials and owns little in the technology arena.

Historical Profile

Return Average
Risk Average
Rating ★★★ Neutral

Investment Style
Equity
Stock %

1993	1994	1995	1996	1997	1998	1999	2000	2001	2002	2003	12-04
83%	89%	91%	91%	91%	92%	94%	95%	98%			

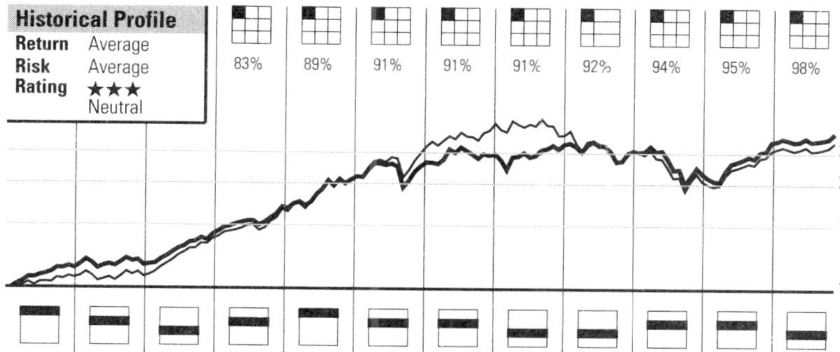

▼ Manager Change
▽ Partial Manager Change

Growth of $10,000
— Investment Values of Fund
— Investment Values of S&P 500

Performance Quartile (within Category)

1993	1994	1995	1996	1997	1998	1999	2000	2001	2002	2003	12-04	History
33.84	30.70	37.93	42.83	52.41	55.55	53.48	53.43	48.77	39.67	49.75	52.78	NAV
21.31	0.24	31.81	21.02	29.98	12.52	7.15	8.54	-5.02	-17.16	29.96	11.29	Total Return %
11.25	-1.07	-5.72	-1.92	-3.37	-16.05	-13.89	17.64	6.86	4.93	1.29	0.42	+/-S&P 500
3.24	2.22	-6.55	-0.62	-5.20	-3.11	-0.20	1.53	0.57	-1.64	-0.07	-5.20	+/-Russ 1000 VI
4.02	3.00	3.18	2.74	2.28	1.64	1.48	1.67	1.44	1.40	1.80	1.65	Income Return %
17.29	-2.76	28.63	18.28	27.70	10.88	5.67	6.87	-6.46	-18.56	28.16	9.64	Capital Return %
5	38	66	39	25	49	42	53	56	41	34	68	Total Rtn % Rank Cat
1.15	0.98	0.96	1.02	0.96	0.85	0.81	0.87	0.76	0.68	0.71	0.81	Income $
0.12	2.22	1.36	1.84	2.04	2.39	5.14	3.32	1.18	0.14	0.93	1.66	Capital Gains $
0.67	0.66	0.69	0.67	0.66	0.65	0.66	0.67	0.67	0.67	0.71	0.70	Expense Ratio %
4.02	3.55	3.37	2.86	2.46	1.90	1.54	1.42	1.63	1.41	1.57	1.63	Income Ratio %
84	70	50	39	30	23	30	26	20	23	23	25	Turnover Rate %
6,642	7,413	10,492	14,259	21,178	23,707	22,829	22,353	21,832	17,734	23,520	26,372	Net Assets $mil

Performance 12-31-04

	1st Qtr	2nd Qtr	3rd Qtr	4th Qtr	Total
2000	-2.36	-0.07	7.09	3.88	8.54
2001	-5.99	5.25	-12.22	9.35	-5.02
2002	3.73	-9.80	-19.09	9.42	-17.16
2003	-6.30	17.91	2.85	14.38	29.96
2004	1.75	1.63	-1.42	9.18	11.29

Trailing	Total Return%	+/- S&P 500	+/- Russ 1000 VI	%Rank Cat	Growth of $10,000
3 Mo	9.18	-0.05	-1.20	49	10,918
6 Mo	7.62	0.43	-4.46	71	10,762
1 Yr	11.29	0.42	-5.20	68	11,129
3 Yr Avg	6.21	2.63	-2.36	43	11,981
5 Yr Avg	4.31	6.61	-0.96	46	12,349
10 Yr Avg	11.94	-0.13	-1.89	37	30,892
15 Yr Avg	11.01	0.08	-1.02	35	47,911

Tax Analysis	Tax-Adj Rtn%	%Rank Cat	Tax-Cost Rat	%Rank Cat
3 Yr (estimated)	5.29	42	0.87	58
5 Yr (estimated)	3.14	46	1.12	59
10 Yr (estimated)	10.16	31	1.59	37

Potential Capital Gain Exposure: 26% of assets

Rating and Risk

Time Period	Load-Adj Return %	Morningstar Rtn vs Cat	Morningstar Risk vs Cat	Morningstar Risk-Adj Rating
1 Yr	11.29			
3 Yr	6.21	Avg	Avg	★★★
5 Yr	4.31	Avg	Avg	★★★
10 Yr	11.94	Avg	Avg	★★★
Incept	13.21			

Other Measures	Standard Index S&P 500	Best Fit Index Russ 1000 VI
Alpha	2.6	-2.3
Beta	1.01	1.03
R-Squared	95	98

Standard Deviation	16.51
Mean	6.21
Sharpe Ratio	0.30

Portfolio Analysis 10-31-04

Share change since 07-04 Total Stocks:206	Sector	PE	YTD Ret%	% Assets
⊕ Bank of America	Financial	12.3	21.50	3.30
ExxonMobil	Energy	13.9	28.04	3.27
⊕ Citigroup	Financial	15.3	2.72	2.79
⊖ J.P. Morgan Chase & Co.	Financial	19.4	9.97	2.54
⊕ American International G	Financial	16.2	-0.53	2.46
Fannie Mae	Financial	9.1	-2.33	1.92
⊕ SBC Communications	Telecom	15.4	3.74	1.72
Total SA ADR	Energy	17.0	23.39	1.64
Verizon Communications	Telecom	32.4	20.25	1.63
⊕ Wachovia	Financial	14.3	16.80	1.40
⊕ General Electric	Ind Mtrls	22.8	20.68	1.39
BP PLC ADR	Energy	20.7	22.07	1.37
BellSouth	Telecom	12.7	1.94	1.35
⊕ Viacom B	Media	36.1	-17.44	1.34
⊕ ChevronTexaco	Energy	7.7	25.57	1.28
Wells Fargo	Financial	15.5	8.97	1.26
Tyco International	Ind Mtrls	25.1	35.41	1.25
⊖ Johnson & Johnson	Health	20.6	25.17	1.15
Time Warner	Media	27.5	8.12	1.12
⊖ Schlumberger	Energy	40.7	23.84	1.06

Current Investment Style

Value Blnd Growth — Large Mid Small

Market Cap	%
Giant	52.6
Large	35.0
Mid	10.9
Small	1.4
Micro	0.0
Avg $mil: 40,533	

Value Measures		Rel Category
Price/Earnings	15.49	1.03
Price/Book	2.19	0.96
Price/Sales	1.23	1.03
Price/Cash Flow	5.43	0.85
Dividend Yield %	2.01	0.99

Growth Measures	%	Rel Category
Long-Term Erngs	10.51	1.01
Book Value	5.48	0.97
Sales	3.97	0.95
Cash Flow	6.78	1.30
Historical Erngs	13.77	1.16

Profitability	%	Rel Category
Return on Equity	15.52	0.98
Return on Assets	8.28	1.06
Net Margin	10.18	1.00

Sector Weightings	% of Stocks	Rel S&P 500	3 Year High	3 Year Low
Info	17.25	0.80		
Software	1.02	0.24	1	1
Hardware	4.70	0.46	5	3
Media	5.96	1.55	6	4
Telecom	5.57	1.77	7	4
Service	43.97	0.95		
Health	7.73	0.62	8	5
Consumer	3.27	0.36	7	3
Business	2.32	0.57	4	2
Financial	30.65	1.48	31	27
Mfg	38.78	1.21		
Goods	6.78	0.73	8	6
Ind Mtrls	16.87	1.33	19	15
Energy	12.12	1.69	15	11
Utilities	3.01	1.02	3	1

Composition

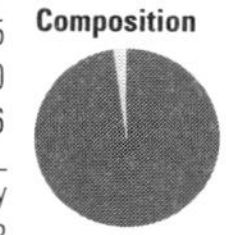

Cash	0.5
Stocks	97.7
Bonds	0.2
Other	1.6
Foreign (% of Stock)	9.4

Morningstar's Take by Christopher Traulsen 01-02-05

Fidelity Equity-Income is a solid core holding.

This fund isn't terribly exciting. Manager Stephen Petersen sticks mainly to large- and giant-cap, dividend-paying stocks, and rarely trades much. The fund's turnover rate clocked in at just 25% in fiscal 2004--well below the norm for the large-value category. Its portfolio is typically heavily tilted toward yield-rich financials and has also recently featured small overweights relative to its average peer in media stocks, telecom-service companies, and the soaring energy sector.

The latter was a boon for the fund in 2004, as oil prices soared in the face of supply constraints and booming demand. However, due to the fund's equity-income mandate and the constraints imposed by its massive asset base, Petersen focused mainly on giant integrated oil companies, which don't fare as well as oil-services and exploration and production companies when energy prices rise. The fund was also nicked by its media holdings, which stumbled in the face of a weaker than anticipated advertising environment, and by its focus on the largest companies. Small caps led the way in 2004, and funds that dipped down the market-cap ladder a bit generally fared better than those that did not.

The net result is that although the fund posted a strong absolute return of 11.3% in 2004, it lagged its average peer by just over 150 basis points. That doesn't concern us. Petersen has proved himself a fine manager over time, and with any fund (especially one as big as this), we'd rather see the manager focus on positioning it for the long term than on chasing near-term performance. Further, the fund's large-cap bias will eventually work in its favor, and that time may be coming soon--small caps have outperformed for six years now and could be due for a slowdown.

This fund won't suit investors looking for a fund that offers a chance of extreme outperformance, but for those seeking a core holding that won't offer too many surprises, it's a sound choice.

Address:	82 Devonshire Street Boston MA 02109 800-343-3548
Web Address:	www.fidelity.com
Inception:	05-16-66
Advisor:	Fidelity Management & Research Co. (FMR)
Subadvisor:	FMR Co., Inc. (FMRC)
NTF Plans:	Fidelity Retail-NTF, CommonWealth NTF

Minimum Purchase:	$2500	Add: $250	IRA: $2500
Min Auto Inv Plan:	$2500	Add: $100	
Sales Fees:	No-load		
Management Fee:	0.48%		
Actual Fees:	Mgt:0.48%	Dist:	
Expense Projections:	3Yr:$221	5Yr:$384	10Yr:$859
Income Distrib:	Quarterly		

Fidelity Equity-Inc II

Ticker	Load	NAV	Yield	Total Assets	Mstar Category
FEQTX	None	$24.01	1.5%	$12,915 mil	Large Value

Governance and Management

Fiduciary Grade: B

Portfolio Manager(s)

Stephen DuFour took the helm Feb. 1, 2000. At his former charge, Fidelity Balanced, he followed a contrarian strategy and delivered solid performance.

Strategy

This fund must invest at least 65% of its assets in dividend-paying securities and aims to meet or exceed the yield of the S&P 500 Index before fees. Manager Stephen DuFour seeks companies trading cheaply on the basis of P/E, price/cash flow, price/book, or price/sales. Most companies that are cheap enough to look at have some problems, so DuFour emphasizes figuring out whether management is aware of the problems, has viable plans to fix them, and is making progress in doing so.

Historical Profile

Return Average
Risk Average
Rating ★★★ Neutral

Investment Style: Equity Stock %: 86% 91% 90% 91% 81% 85% 94% 98% 99%

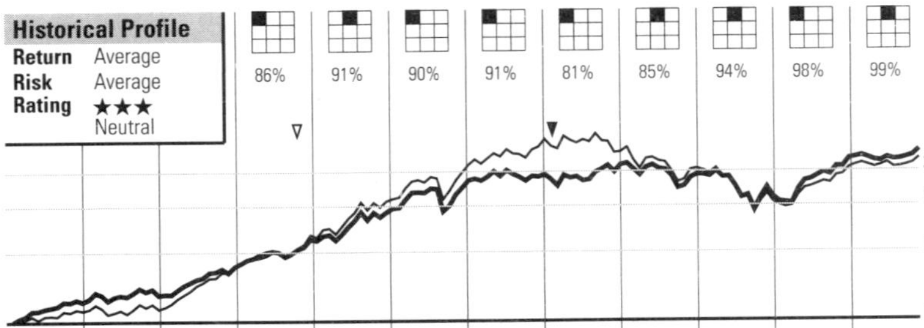

▼ Manager Change
▽ Partial Manager Change

Growth of $10,000
— Investment Values of Fund
— Investment Values of S&P 500

Performance Quartile (within Category)

1993	1994	1995	1996	1997	1998	1999	2000	2001	2002	2003	12-04	History
18.41	17.72	21.43	23.75	27.01	30.01	27.37	23.86	21.03	17.39	22.78	24.01	NAV
18.89	3.16	26.39	18.71	27.17	22.98	4.37	7.46	-7.16	-15.43	32.60	9.88	Total Return %
8.83	1.85	-11.14	-4.23	-6.18	-5.59	-16.67	16.56	4.72	6.66	3.93	-0.99	+/-S&P 500
0.82	5.14	-11.97	-2.93	-8.01	7.35	-2.98	0.45	-1.57	0.09	2.57	-6.61	+/-Russ 1000 VI
2.76	2.14	2.10	2.41	1.83	1.25	1.21	1.55	1.40	1.16	1.39	1.65	Income Return %
16.13	1.02	24.29	16.30	25.34	21.73	3.16	5.91	-8.56	-16.59	31.21	8.23	Capital Return %
14	16	89	64	53	3	51	60	70	27	16	82	Total Rtn % Rank Cat
0.45	0.39	0.37	0.51	0.43	0.33	0.36	0.42	0.33	0.24	0.24	0.37	Income $
0.73	0.88	0.55	1.14	2.63	2.65	3.50	4.98	0.79	0.21	0.00	0.61	Capital Gains $
0.88	0.81	0.75	0.72	0.68	0.66	0.64	0.63	0.62	0.63	0.64	—	Expense Ratio %
2.69	2.36	2.37	2.13	1.58	1.20	1.19	1.47	1.49	1.26	1.31	—	Income Ratio %
55	75	45	46	77	62	71	151	136	135	131	—	Turnover Rate %
5,022	7,698	11,977	15,238	16,977	19,454	17,580	13,915	12,212	9,401	12,256	12,915	Net Assets $mil

Performance 12-31-04

	1st Qtr	2nd Qtr	3rd Qtr	4th Qtr	Total
2000	-0.63	-3.97	9.05	3.27	7.46
2001	-7.48	4.75	-13.40	10.61	-7.16
2002	2.65	-10.75	-16.41	10.43	-15.43
2003	-4.94	19.60	3.56	12.62	32.60
2004	0.47	0.00	0.18	9.17	9.88

Trailing	Total Return%	+/- S&P 500	+/- Russ 1000 VI	%Rank Cat	Growth of $10,000
3 Mo	9.17	-0.06	-1.21	49	10,917
6 Mo	9.36	2.17	-2.72	46	10,936
1 Yr	9.88	-0.99	-6.61	82	10,988
3 Yr Avg	7.21	3.63	-1.36	28	12,323
5 Yr Avg	4.21	6.51	-1.06	47	12,290
10 Yr Avg	11.65	-0.42	-2.18	43	30,101
15 Yr Avg	—	—	—	—	—

Tax Analysis	Tax-Adj Rtn%	%Rank Cat	Tax-Cost Rat	%Rank Cat
3 Yr (estimated)	6.42	26	0.74	50
5 Yr (estimated)	2.62	53	1.53	80
10 Yr (estimated)	9.46	45	1.96	62

Potential Capital Gain Exposure: 17% of assets

Rating and Risk

Time Period	Load-Adj Return %	Morningstar Rtn vs Cat	Morningstar Risk vs Cat	Morningstar Risk-Adj Rating
1 Yr	9.88			
3 Yr	7.21	+Avg	+Avg	★★★★
5 Yr	4.21	Avg	Avg	★★★
10 Yr	11.65	Avg	Avg	★★★
Incept	14.20			

Other Measures	Standard Index S&P 500	Best Fit Index S&P 500
Alpha	3.5	3.5
Beta	1.06	1.06
R-Squared	96	96
Standard Deviation	17.42	
Mean	7.21	
Sharpe Ratio	0.34	

Morningstar's Take by Christopher Traulsen 01-02-05

Fidelity Equity-Income II's poor 2004 isn't cause for too much worry.

This fund just ended a year its manager would probably rather forget. It finished 2004 up 9.9%. That's good in absolute terms, but poor relative to the 12.8% showing of its average large-value peer. It's also somewhat surprising, given the fund's large overweight in the relatively strong-performing energy and telecom services sectors. However, picks in a variety of other sectors, including Charles Schwab, Morgan Stanley, IAC/InterActiveCorp, Viacom, and IBM have nicked the fund. Moreover, the fund's larger-cap bent held it back in a year when smaller stocks led the way.

The fund's mini-slump is a reflection of the types of situations favored by manager Stephen DuFour. He's attracted to companies that have been punished by the market, usually because something has gone wrong with their businesses. For example, he bought into brokers Charles Schwab and Morgan Stanley during the bear market on the theory that when stocks rallied again, trading volume would pick up and the brokers would benefit. Thus far, that theory has not been borne out.

Given that penchant, it's clear that investors will have to exercise patience here from time to time. That doesn't worry us so much, though. Many contrarian managers suffer through rough patches; the question is whether they make the wait pay off for investors down the line. In that regard DuFour has held his own: The fund's return is nearly even with its average large-value peer's over the course of his tenure here, and that measurement comes on the heels of one of the fund's worst periods of relative performance under DuFour.

This fund lacks the broad appeal of sibling Equity-Income, but its solid record under DuFour and reasonable costs make it worth a look. Given its high turnover, however, it's not well suited for taxable accounts.

Portfolio Analysis 08-31-04

Share change since 05-04 Total Stocks:95

	Sector	PE	YTD Ret%	% Assets
⊕ Verizon Communications	Telecom	32.4	20.25	5.39
⊖ ExxonMobil	Energy	13.9	28.04	5.20
⊕ Burlington Resources	Energy	10.9	58.50	5.03
⊖ American International G	Financial	16.2	-0.53	4.35
⊕ Gen Elec	Ind Mtrls	22.8	20.68	4.04
⊕ Fannie Mae	Financial	9.1	-2.33	3.59
⊕ Citigroup	Financial	15.3	2.72	3.40
⊕ Bank of America	Financial	12.3	21.50	3.39
⊖ Charles Schwab	Financial	32.9	1.77	3.19
⊕ Pfizer	Health	22.0	-22.31	3.14
⊕ Norfolk Southern	Business	—	55.12	2.59
⊕ J P Morgan Chase	Financial	19.4	9.97	2.51
⊕ Microsoft	Software	36.1	8.95	2.41
⊖ Dover	Ind Mtrls	20.3	7.18	2.36
⊕ SBC Communications	Telecom	15.4	3.74	2.29
⊕ Wells Fargo	Financial	15.5	8.97	2.19
⊕ News Corporation ADR	Media	16.6	6.65	2.00
⊕ Sprint	Telecom	—	55.24	1.94
⊖ Goodrich	Ind Mtrls	25.3	12.87	1.87
⊕ Iac / Interactivecorp	Consumer	43.1	-18.60	1.69

Current Investment Style

Value Blnd Growth; Large Mid Small

Market Cap	%
Giant	56.5
Large	28.9
Mid	14.2
Small	0.3
Micro	0.0

Avg $mil: 45,529

Value Measures		Rel Category
Price/Earnings	15.63	1.04
Price/Book	2.38	1.05
Price/Sales	1.52	1.28
Price/Cash Flow	6.97	1.09
Dividend Yield %	1.91	0.94

Growth Measures	%	Rel Category
Long-Term Erngs	10.52	1.01
Book Value	9.15	1.62
Sales	3.84	0.91
Cash Flow	11.74	2.25
Historical Erngs	12.77	1.08

Profitability	%	Rel Category
Return on Equity	17.30	1.09
Return on Assets	10.98	1.40
Net Margin	11.56	1.13

Sector Weightings	% of Stocks	Rel S&P 500	3 Year High	3 Year Low
Info	19.88	0.93		
Software	2.54	0.59	3	0
Hardware	2.90	0.28	11	3
Media	4.68	1.22	7	5
Telecom	9.76	3.10	10	5
Service	45.25	0.98		
Health	5.83	0.47	7	2
Consumer	5.59	0.62	7	0
Business	4.95	1.22	7	2
Financial	28.88	1.39	34	29
Mfg	34.86	1.09		
Goods	3.12	0.33	11	3
Ind Mtrls	15.53	1.23	17	12
Energy	14.44	2.02	14	9
Utilities	1.77	0.60	4	0

Composition

Cash	1.4
Stocks	98.6
Bonds	0.0
Other	0.0
Foreign (% of Stock)	3.7

Address:	82 Devonshire St Boston MA 02109 800-343-3548	Minimum Purchase:	$2500	Add: $250 IRA: $2500
Web Address:	www.fidelity.com	Min Auto Inv Plan:	$2500	Add: $100
Inception:	08-21-90	Sales Fees:	No-load	
Advisor:	Fidelity Management & Research Co. (FMR)	Management Fee:	0.48%	
Subadvisor:	FMR Co., Inc. (FMRC)	Actual Fees:	Mgt:0.48%	Dist:
		Expense Projections:	3Yr:$211	5Yr:$368 10Yr:$822
		Income Distrib:	Quarterly	
NTF Plans:	Fidelity Retail-NTF, CommonWealth NTF			

Fidelity Exp & Multinatl

Ticker	Load	NAV	Yield	Total Assets	Mstar Category
FEXPX	None	$19.64	0.5%	$1,643 mil	Large Blend

Governance and Management

Fiduciary Grade: B

Portfolio Manager(s)

Tim Cohen replaced Doug Chase at the fund's helm in February 2002. Cohen has managed a few of Fidelity's sector funds, including Fidelity Select Telecommunications and Fidelity Utilities. This is his first stint running a diversified fund, however.

Strategy

This fund is allowed to invest in export-oriented companies of any size, as well as multinationals. However, different managers have interpreted that mandate differently, resulting in numerous strategy changes. The fund's former manager, Doug Chase, invested in anything from deep-value to aggressive-growth stocks. Current skipper Tim Cohen favors companies with attractive earnings-growth prospects that are trading at reasonable valuations, leading to a decent exposure to the financials, health-care, and service sectors.

Historical Profile

Return High
Risk High
Rating ★★★★★ Highest

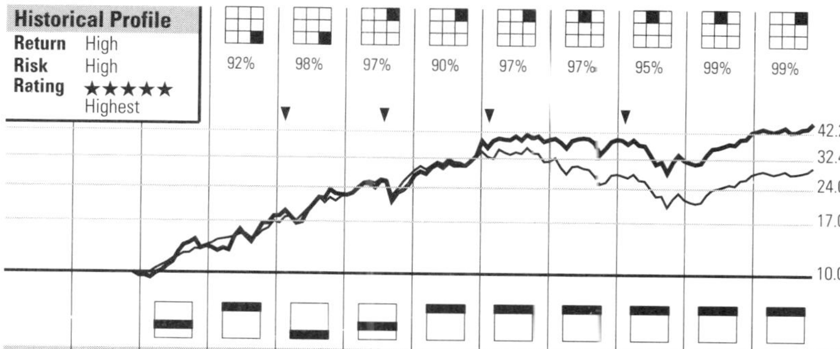

Investment Style
Equity
Stock %

▼ Manager Change
▽ Partial Manager Change

Growth of $10,000
— Investment Values of Fund
— Investment Values of S&P 500

Performance Quartile (within Category)

1993	1994	1995	1996	1997	1998	1999	2000	2001	2002	2003	12-04	History
—	10.24	12.72	16.75	17.02	19.88	21.97	16.88	16.97	13.75	18.16	19.64	NAV
—	2.50*	32.22	38.64	23.69	22.41	41.80	1.48	0.72	-18.66	32.62	13.59	Total Return %
—	—	-5.31	15.70	-9.66	-6.16	20.76	10.58	12.60	3.43	3.95	2.72	+/-S&P 500
—	—	-5.55	16.19	-9.16	-4.61	20.89	9.27	13.17	2.99	2.73	2.19	+/-Russ 1000
—	0.00	0.00	0.00	0.00	0.00	0.25	0.48	0.18	0.29	0.51	0.62	Income Return %
—	—	32.22	38.64	23.69	22.41	41.55	1.00	0.54	-18.95	32.11	12.97	Capital Return %
—	—	59	2	77	52	4	20	4	21	9	11	Total Rtn % Rank Cat
—	0.01	0.00	0.00	0.00	0.00	0.05	0.10	0.03	0.05	0.07	0.11	Income $
—	0.00	0.84	0.86	3.79	0.77	4.80	5.21	0.00	0.00	0.00	0.82	Capital Gains $
—	—	1.22	1.00	0.91	0.88	0.86	0.77	0.81	0.78	0.84	0.83	Expense Ratio %
—	—	-0.27	-0.39	-0.13	-0.25	0.23	0.38	0.21	0.19	0.60	0.15	Income Ratio %
—	—	245	313	429	281	265	380	170	228	139	96	Turnover Rate %
—	79	382	397	465	412	514	495	673	675	1,042	1,643	Net Assets $mil

Performance 12-31-04

	1st Qtr	2nd Qtr	3rd Qtr	4th Qtr	Total
2000	2.59	2.22	-1.91	-1.35	1.48
2001	-7.76	10.40	-14.78	16.06	0.72
2002	-0.35	-13.72	-16.79	13.70	-18.66
2003	-2.76	16.68	3.27	13.19	32.62
2004	1.82	3.03	-1.42	9.84	13.59

Trailing	Total Return%	+/- S&P 500	+/- Russ 1000	%Rank Cat	Growth of $10,000
3 Mo	9.84	0.61	0.04	32	10,984
6 Mo	8.28	1.09	0.47	25	10,828
1 Yr	13.59	2.72	2.19	11	11,359
3 Yr Avg	7.00	3.42	2.73	7	12,250
5 Yr Avg	4.60	6.90	6.36	6	12,522
10 Yr Avg	17.29	5.22	5.13	1	49,273
15 Yr Avg	—	—	—	—	—

Tax Analysis	Tax-Adj Rtn%	%Rank Cat	Tax-Cost Rat	%Rank Cat
3 Yr (estimated)	6.52	7	0.45	38
5 Yr (estimated)	2.43	9	2.07	91
10 Yr (estimated)	13.78	3	2.99	94

Potential Capital Gain Exposure: 14% of assets

Rating and Risk

Time Period	Load-Adj Return %	Morningstar Rtn vs Cat	Morningstar Risk vs Cat	Morningstar Risk-Adj Rating
1 Yr	13.59			
3 Yr	7.00	High	High	★★★★★
5 Yr	4.60	High	+Avg	★★★★★
10 Yr	17.29	High	High	★★★★★
Incept	17.13			

Other Measures	Standard Index S&P 500	Best Fit Index S&P 500
Alpha	3.3	3.3
Beta	1.11	1.11
R-Squared	97	97
Standard Deviation	18.17	
Mean	7.00	
Sharpe Ratio	0.31	

Portfolio Analysis 08-31-04

Share change since 05-04 Total Stocks:112	Sector	PE	YTD Ret%	% Assets
⊕ American International G	Financial	16.2	-0.53	5.61
⊕ Microsoft	Software	36.1	8.95	4.75
⊕ UnitedHealth Group	Health	23.8	51.38	3.49
⊖ Pfizer	Health	22.0	-22.31	2.95
⊕ Home Depot	Consumer	19.0	21.47	2.81
Ambac Financial Group	Financial	12.7	19.13	2.66
⊕ Morgan Stanley	Financial	14.2	-2.25	2.53
⊕ Procter & Gamble	Goods	23.3	12.38	2.36
⊕ ACE	Financial	9.6	5.26	2.09
⊕ Fannie Mae	Financial	9.1	-2.33	2.08
⊕ Intel	Hardware	19.8	-26.56	2.04
⊖ Tyco International	Ind Mtrls	25.1	35.41	2.01
⊕ Goldman Sachs Group	Financial	12.3	6.49	1.94
⊕ Cisco Systems	Hardware	24.5	-20.26	1.91
⊕ Dell	Hardware	34.0	24.01	1.85
⊕ Robert Half Internationa	Business	51.7	26.95	1.80
⊕ Honeywell International	Ind Mtrls	20.5	8.21	1.79
⊕ XL Capital	Financial	20.1	2.80	1.36
⊕ Univision Communications	Media	39.5	-26.25	1.33
⊕ Berkley WR	Financial	9.9	35.85	1.36

Current Investment Style

Value Blnd Growth — Large Mid Small

Market Cap	%
Giant	40.3
Large	27.2
Mid	28.6
Small	3.3
Micro	0.6
Avg $mil: 22,904	

Value Measures		Rel Category
Price/Earnings	15.70	0.93
Price/Book	2.50	0.95
Price/Sales	1.62	1.13
Price/Cash Flow	6.05	0.79
Dividend Yield %	0.85	0.57

Growth Measures	%	Rel Category
Long-Term Erngs	13.74	1.19
Book Value	13.80	1.78
Sales	9.18	1.60
Cash Flow	65.54	6.93
Historical Erngs	18.30	1.55

Profitability	%	Rel Category
Return on Equity	20.10	1.15
Return on Assets	13.11	1.52
Net Margin	12.54	1.10

Sector Weightings	% of Stocks	Rel S&P 500	3 Year High	3 Year Low
Info	20.65	0.96		
Software	6.47	1.50	7	3
Hardware	11.34	1.11	13	5
Media	2.84	0.74	9	3
Telecom	0.00	0.00	8	0
Service	56.16	1.21		
Health	14.57	1.17	22	12
Consumer	8.32	0.92	10	5
Business	6.56	1.62	7	3
Financial	26.71	1.29	27	14
Mfg	23.19	0.72		
Goods	3.81	0.41	8	3
Ind Mtrls	12.06	0.95	15	9
Energy	7.32	1.02	10	4
Utilities	0.00	0.00	0	0

Composition

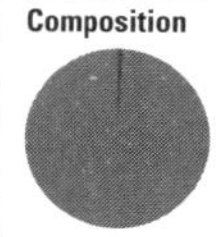

Cash	1.0
Stocks	99.0
Bonds	0.0
Other	0.0
Foreign (% of Stock)	4.2

Morningstar's Take by Andrew Gogerty 11-22-04

Fidelity Export & Multinational continues its winning ways.

Manager Tim Cohen follows a sensible tack here. Believing that stock prices do not always reflect a company's true growth potential, he looks for names with reasonable price multiples relative to their earnings-growth prospects. He will also play the contrarian card and go after shares of beaten-down names if he sees value. The fund's small asset base also affords Cohen greater flexibility than his colleagues at other, larger Fidelity funds. He can delve into smaller names when he spies opportunities and can also bulk up on his higher-conviction picks.

Even if the strategy isn't sexy, Cohen's results have been compelling. Since he took over here in February 2002, the fund has turned in a 6.4% annualized gain, which bests more than 90% of the large-blend category. (This is consistent with the fund's long-term results under other managers, which crush its rivals). The fund has benefited from an increased stake in Home Depot, which rebounded nicely after a poor 2002 campaign. Home Depot posted a strong 49% gain in 2003 and is up more than 19% again this year.

On the other hand, the fund isn't perfect. Cohen raised the fund's tech exposure because he thinks the area has long-term growth potential. Unfortunately, the fund's sizable stake in Cisco Systems has disappointed in 2004, posting a 20% loss. The fund's history of churning through managers has also spiked turnover at times, which can lead to higher tax bills for investors.

Still, Cohen's successful execution has continued the fund's dominance over its peers. Concern about stability at the helm remains, however, as Fidelity has shown a knack for tapping this fund's managers for greater duties. Nonetheless, the fund has done well, and its low costs make it an appealing choice. Those looking for an anchor for their portfolios should give this fund a look.

Address:	82 Devonshire St Boston MA 02109 800-343-3548
Web Address:	
Inception:	10-04-94 *
Advisor:	Fidelity Management & Research Co. (FMR)
Subadvisor:	FMR Co., Inc. (FMRC)
NTF Plans:	Fidelity Retail-NTF, CommonWealth NTF

Minimum Purchase:	$2500	Add: $250	IRA: $2500
Min Auto Inv Plan:	$2500	Add: $100	
Sales Fees:	No-load, 0.75%R		
Management Fee:	0.58%		
Actual Fees:	Mgt:0.58%	Dist:	
Expense Projections:	3Yr:$290	5Yr:$504	10Yr:$1120
Income Distrib:	Annually		

Fidelity Float Rt Hi Inc

Analyst Pick

Ticker	Load	NAV	Yield	SEC Yield	Total Assets	Mstar Category
FFRHX	None	$9.98	3.1%	3.39%	$2,162 mil	Bank Loan

Governance and Management

Fiduciary Grade: B

Portfolio Manager(s)

Christine McConnell leads the effort here and at Fidelity Advisor Floating Rate High Income. She has been with Fidelity since 1987, and she has worked as a high-yield bond analyst prior to taking the helm. She is backed by Fidelity's extensive research capabilities and a team of analysts. Fidelity's bank-loan group is part of its larger high-yield investment team.

Strategy

Manager Christine McConnell forms an economic outlook and tries to pick floating-rate bank loans that will perform well in that environment. She focuses on security, collateral, and covenants in an effort to find attractively priced loans. She will also look to take advantage of sector-related opportunities. In early 2004, for example, she has shifted assets into service-oriented sectors of the market, arguing their free cash flow makes them more attractive than others. The fund isn't a pure bank-loan play, as it owns a slew of plain-vanilla junk bonds.

Historical Profile

Return
Risk
Rating Not Rated

Investment Style
Fixed Income
Income Rtn %Rank Cat

2002	2003	12-04
100	74	49

▼ Manager Change
▽ Partial Manager Change

Growth of $10,000
— Investment Values of Fund
— Investment Values of LB Aggr

Performance Quartile (within Category)

1993	1994	1995	1996	1997	1998	1999	2000	2001	2002	2003	12-04	History
—	—	—	—	—	—	—	—	—	9.58	9.87	9.98	NAV
—	—	—	—	—	—	—	—	—	1.87*	6.46	4.47	Total Return %
—	—	—	—	—	—	—	—	—	—	2.36	0.13	+/-LB Aggr
—	—	—	—	—	—	—	—	—	—	3.11	2.62	+/-LB 1-5 YR
—	—	—	—	—	—	—	—	—	1.21	3.40	3.23	Income Return %
—	—	—	—	—	—	—	—	—	—	3.06	1.24	Capital Return %
—	—	—	—	—	—	—	—	—	—	75	60	Total Rtn % Rank Cat
—	—	—	—	—	—	—	—	—	0.12	0.32	0.31	Income $
—	—	—	—	—	—	—	—	—	0.00	0.00	0.01	Capital Gains $
—	—	—	—	—	—	—	—	—	0.94	0.86	0.84	Expense Ratio %
—	—	—	—	—	—	—	—	—	3.99	3.27	3.14	Income Ratio %
—	—	—	—	—	—	—	—	—	—	55	61	Turnover Rate %
—	—	—	—	—	—	—	—	—	65	956	2,162	Net Assets $mil

Performance 12-31-04

	1st Qtr	2nd Qtr	3rd Qtr	4th Qtr	Total
2000	—	—	—	—	—
2001	—	—	—	—	—
2002	—	—	—	1.86	1.87 *
2003	1.58	2.39	1.10	1.24	6.46
2004	1.06	0.82	0.99	1.52	4.47

Trailing	Total Return%	+/- LB Aggr	+/- LB 1-5 YR	%Rank Cat	Growth of $10,000
3 Mo	1.52	0.57	1.37	28	10,152
6 Mo	2.52	-1.66	0.64	29	10,252
1 Yr	4.47	0.13	2.62	60	10,447
3 Yr Avg	—	—	—	—	—
5 Yr Avg	—	—	—	—	—
10 Yr Avg	—	—	—	—	—
15 Yr Avg	—	—	—	—	—

Tax Analysis	Tax-Adj Rtn%	%Rank Cat	Tax-Cost Rat	%Rank Cat
3 Yr (estimated)	—	—	—	—
5 Yr (estimated)	—	—	—	—
10 Yr (estimated)	—	—	—	—

Potential Capital Gain Exposure: 1% of assets

Rating and Risk

Time Period	Load-Adj Return %	Morningstar Rtn vs Cat	Morningstar Risk vs Cat	Morningstar Risk-Adj Rating
1 Yr	4.47			
3 Yr	—	—	—	—
5 Yr	—	—	—	—
10 Yr	—	—	—	—
Incept	5.62			

Other Measures	Standard Index LB Aggr	Best Fit Index
Alpha	—	—
Beta	—	—
R-Squared	—	—

Standard Deviation	—
Mean	—
Sharpe Ratio	—

Morningstar's Take by Scott Berry 11-29-04

Investors nervous about rising interest rates may like what they find at Fidelity Floating Rate High Income.

This fund invests primarily in floating-rate bank loans. The borrowers on these loans typically earn junk-like credit ratings, but the loans themselves are backed by assets that can be sold off to pay loanholders if the borrower runs into financial difficulties. Further, the loans offer a floating stream of income that adjusts higher or lower based on interest-rate (typically the London Interbank Offered Rate or LIBOR) changes. If interest rates move higher over the next year, as many market pundits expect they will, the added income provided by the loans should allow it to weather the storm better than most bond fund types. Meanwhile, the improving economy should help limit defaults.

The fund hasn't yet been tested by an extended period of rising interest rates, but it has held its own during brief rate spikes. In both July 2003 and April 2004, for example, the fund's net asset value barely moved. It actually ended both months at the same level it started. Further, the fund's three-year standard deviation of returns (a measure of volatility) has been among the lowest in the bank-loan category. (The fund's no-load share class has only been open since September 2002, but its lettered share classes have been open since mid-2000.)

We like this fund for its low volatility, but it also earns credit for its reasonable costs. With the category's long-term returns in the midsingle digits, expenses can be a bitter pill to swallow. But at 0.84%, this fund's expense ratio ranks among the lowest in the group. The fund is the category's only true no-load offering, but its costs are in line with institutional share classes offered by both Franklin and Eaton Vance.

Portfolio Analysis 10-31-04

Total Fixed-Income:411	Date of Maturity	Amount $000	Value $000	% Net Assets
Charter Comm Op Term B 4	04-07-11	92,284	91,707	2.47
Qwest FRN	06-30-07	71,000	73,751	1.99
Echostar Dbs FRN	10-01-08	69,625	72,326	1.95
Nextel Comm Term E 12/15	12-15-10	63,342	63,500	1.71
Panamsat Corp Term B 8/2	08-20-11	51,000	51,510	1.39
Graham Pkg Trm B 1 Lien	10-04-11	37,200	37,665	1.02
Boise Cascade Term B 10/	10-26-11	36,920	37,566	1.01
Centerpoint Engy Houston	11-11-05	31,950	34,826	0.94
Boise Cascade Term C 10/	10-26-10	34,080	34,336	0.93
Ntl Investment Term B 6/	06-13-12	33,647	33,983	0.92
Jean Coutu Grp Pjc FRN	07-30-11	30,500	31,034	0.84
Donnelley(Rh) Term B2 6/	06-30-11	29,965	30,452	0.82
Community Health Term 8/	08-19-11	29,700	29,849	0.81
Allegheny Enrgy Term B 3	03-08-11	28,633	29,134	0.79
American Tower Term B 8/	08-31-11	27,431	27,843	0.75
Pemex Proj Fdg Master Tr	06-15-10	25,000	25,400	0.69
Rite Aid Term 9/21/09	09-21-09	25,000	25,250	0.68
Regal Cinemas Term 11/10	11-10-10	23,882	24,180	0.65
Loews Cin Ent Term 6/30/	06-30-11	23,400	23,722	0.64
Foundation Pa Term B 7/3	07-30-11	22,700	22,955	0.62

Current Investment Style

Duration: Short Int Long
Quality: High Med Low

¹ figure provided by fund

Avg Eff Duration[1]	—
Avg Eff Maturity	—
Avg Credit Quality	—
Avg Wtd Coupon	1.73%
Avg Wtd Price	101.66% of par

Coupon Range	% of Bonds	Rel Cat
0% PIK	30.0	0.6
0% to 6%	92.7	1.0
6% to 8%	2.9	0.3
8% to 10%	3.3	4.7
More than 10%	1.2	4.0

1.00=Category Average

Credit Analysis		% bonds 10-31-04	
US Govt	0	BB	27
AAA	0	B	29
AA	0	Below B	2
A	0	NR/NA	40
BBB	3		

Sector Breakdown	% of assets
US Treasuries	0
TIPS	0
US Agency	0
Mortgage Pass-Throughs	0
Mortgage CMO	0
Mortgage ARM	0
US Corporate	80
Asset-Backed	0
Convertible	0
Municipal	0
Corporate Inflation-Protected	0
Foreign Corporate	2
Foreign Govt	0

Composition			
Cash	18.2	Bonds	80.8
Stocks	0.0	Other	1.0

Special Securities	
Restricted/Illiquid Secs	4
Exotic Mortgage-Backed	0
Emerging-Markets Secs	0
Options/Futures/Warrants	No

Address:	Fidelity Group Boston, MA 02109 800-343-3548
Web Address:	www.fidelity.com
Inception:	09-19-02 *
Advisor:	FMR Co., Inc. (FMRC)
Subadvisor:	None
NTF Plans:	Fidelity Retail-NTF, Fidelity Instl-NTF

Minimum Purchase:	$2500	Add: $250	IRA: $2500
Min Auto Inv Plan:	$100	Add: $100	
Sales Fees:	No-load, 1.00%R		
Management Fee:	0.68%		
Actual Fees:	Mgt:0.68%	Dist:	
Expense Projections:	3Yr: —	5Yr: —	10Yr: —
Income Distrib:	Monthly		

Fidelity Four-in-One Idx

Ticker	Load	NAV	Yield	Total Assets	Mstar Category
FFNOX	None	$25.17	1.7%	$795 mil	Large Blend

Governance and Management

Fiduciary Grade: B

Portfolio Manager(s)

William Eigen, who has been with Fidelity since 1994 and also manages Fidelity Strategic Income, took over as manager here in October 2002.

Strategy

This fund of funds invests in four underlying Fidelity index funds. It tends to maintain constant weightings of about 55% of assets in Spartan 500 Index; 15% in Spartan Extended Market Index, which invests in mid- and small-cap stocks; 15% in Spartan International Index, which tracks the MSCI EAFE Index; and 15% in U.S. Bond Index, which invests in the high-quality, broadly diversified Lehman Brothers Aggregate Index.

Historical Profile

Return Above Avg
Risk Below Avg
Rating ★★★★ Above Avg

Investment Style: Equity Stock % — 81% 80% 81% 80% 81%

▼ Manager Change
▽ Partial Manager Change

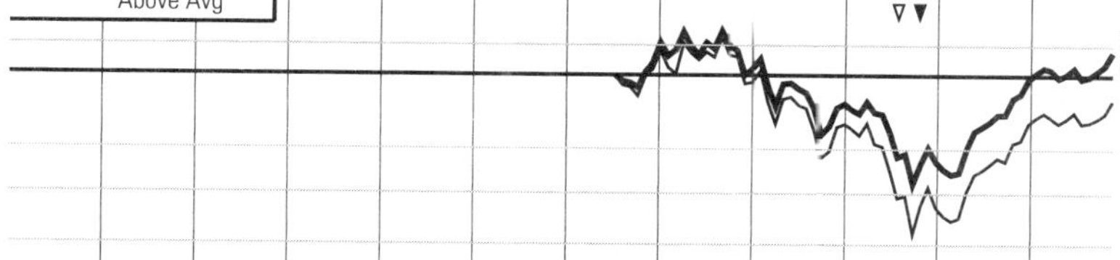

Growth of $10,000
— Investment Values of Fund
— Investment Values of S&P 500

Performance Quartile (within Category)

1993	1994	1995	1996	1997	1998	1999	2000	2001	2002	2003	12-04	History
—	—	—	—	—	—	27.69	24.91	21.93	18.05	22.80	25.17	NAV
—	—	—	—	—	—	11.74*	-7.65	-10.04	-15.97	28.25	12.34	Total Return %
—	—	—	—	—	—	—	1.45	1.84	6.12	-0.42	1.47	+/-S&P 500
—	—	—	—	—	—	—	0.14	2.4[illegible]	5.68	-1.64	0.94	+/-Russ 1000
—	—	—	—	—	—	0.00	2.06	1.8[illegible]	1.73	1.89	1.85	Income Return %
—	—	—	—	—	—	—	-9.71	-11.85	-17.70	26.36	10.49	Capital Return %
—	—	—	—	—	—	—	55	27	10	34	19	Total Rtn % Rank Cat
—	—	—	—	—	—	0.24	0.57	0.45	0.38	0.34	0.42	Income $
—	—	—	—	—	—	0.00	0.10	0.03	0.00	0.00	0.02	Capital Gains $
—	—	—	—	—	—	—	0.08	0.08	0.08	0.08	0.08	Expense Ratio %
—	—	—	—	—	—	—	2.20	1.77	1.77	1.87	1.76	Income Ratio %
—	—	—	—	—	—	—	2	19	21	18	7	Turnover Rate %
—	—	—	—	—	—	231	325	289	267	477	795	Net Assets $mil

Performance 12-31-04

	1st Qtr	2nd Qtr	3rd Qtr	4th Qtr	Total
2000	3.25	-3.19	-0.80	-6.87	-7.65
2001	-10.68	5.37	-12.89	9.72	-10.04
2002	0.59	-8.80	-14.24	6.80	-15.97
2003	-3.21	14.78	3.74	11.28	28.25
2004	2.89	0.60	-0.93	9.56	12.34

Trailing	Total Return%	+/- S&P 500	+/- Russ 1000	%Rank Cat	Growth of $10,000
3 Mo	9.56	0.33	-0.24	38	10,956
6 Mo	8.53	1.34	0.72	21	10,853
1 Yr	12.34	1.47	0.94	19	11,234
3 Yr Avg	6.58	3.00	2.31	9	12,107
5 Yr Avg	0.12	2.42	1.88	23	10,060
10 Yr Avg	—	—	—	—	—
15 Yr Avg	—	—	—	—	—

Tax Analysis	Tax-Adj Rtn%	%Rank Cat	Tax-Cost Rat	%Rank Cat
3 Yr (estimated)	5.90	8	0.64	53
5 Yr (estimated)	-0.62	22	0.74	39
10 Yr (estimated)	—	—	—	—

Potential Capital Gain Exposure: 4% of assets

Rating and Risk

Time Period	Load-Adj Return %	Morningstar Rtn vs Cat	Morningstar Risk vs Cat	Morningstar Risk-Adj Rating
1 Yr	12.34			
3 Yr	6.58	High	-Avg	★★★★★
5 Yr	0.12	+Avg	-Avg	★★★★
10 Yr	—	—	—	—
Incept	2.14			

Other Measures	Standard Index S&P 500	Best Fit Index MSCI World
Alpha	3.1	0.4
Beta	0.82	0.83
R-Squared	97	99
Standard Deviation	13.17	
Mean	6.58	
Sharpe Ratio	0.40	

Portfolio Analysis 08-31-04

Share change since 02-04 Total Stocks:0	Sector	PE	YTD Ret%	% Assets
⊕ Fidelity Spartan 500 Ind	—	—	—	55.34
⊕ Fidelity Spartan Extende	—	—	—	15.06
⊕ Fidelity Spartan Interna	—	—	—	15.01
⊕ Fidelity U.S. Bond Index	—	—	—	14.59

Current Investment Style

Value Blnd Growth — Large Mid Small

Market Cap	%
Giant	42.8
Large	31.0
Mid	18.3
Small	5.7
Micro	2.2
Avg $mil: 22,835	

Value Measures		Rel Category
Price/Earnings	16.37	0.97
Price/Book	2.31	0.88
Price/Sales	1.25	0.87
Price/Cash Flow	6.77	0.88
Dividend Yield %	1.68	1.14

Growth Measures	%	Rel Category
Long-Term Erngs	10.91	0.94
Book Value	4.52	0.58
Sales	3.35	0.58
Cash Flow	3.95	0.42
Historical Erngs	7.54	0.64

Profitability	%	Rel Category
Return on Equity	14.61	0.83
Return on Assets	5.34	0.62
Net Margin	9.89	0.86

Sector Weightings	% of Stocks	Rel S&P 500	3 Year High	3 Year Low
Info	20.64	0.96		
Software	3.74	0.87	4	3
Hardware	9.14	0.90	10	8
Media	3.92	1.02	4	4
Telecom	3.84	1.22	6	4
Service	48.45	1.04		
Health	12.35	0.99	15	12
Consumer	8.69	0.96	9	8
Business	4.75	1.17	5	5
Financial	22.66	1.09	23	19
Mfg	30.91	0.96		
Goods	9.58	1.03	11	10
Ind Mtrls	11.60	0.92	12	10
Energy	6.63	0.93	7	6
Utilities	3.10	1.05	4	3

Composition

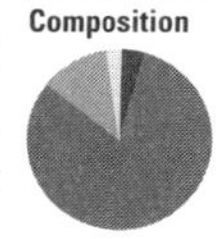

Cash	4.2
Stocks	81.2
Bonds	12.2
Other	2.4
Foreign (% of Stock)	15.0

Morningstar's Take by Gregg Wolper 11-30-04

Its siblings' cost cuts will help Fidelity Four-In-One Index, too.

In August 2004, Fidelity cut the expense ratios of five of its index funds to 0.10%. That cut nearly in half the cost of Fidelity's Spartan 500 Index, which had been charging 0.19%. It's even more significant for Fidelity Spartan International Index, which had been charging 0.47%, and Fidelity Spartan Extended Market Index, which had cost 0.40%.

Those cuts affect this offering, as well. Fidelity Four-In-One Index is a fund of funds whose portfolio consists of the three funds named above, plus Fidelity U.S. Bond Index (whose expense ratio remains at 0.32%). Thus, even with this offering's own fee of 0.08% added in, its overall expense ratio is bound to drop from its current level of 0.36%.

It's worth noting that the underlying funds' fee cuts are waivers rather than permanent reductions, so those expense ratios could revert to their old levels at some point down the line. And of course, a low cost alone isn't enough reason to own a fund. But this portfolio has other merits. It provides broad diversification, for one thing. And though the question of whether indexing is preferable to active management has no easy answer, this fund's shareholders at least don't have to worry that manager changes at the underlying offerings will hurt performance. And these index funds generally track their benchmarks well.

Fidelity Four-In-One's diversification has helped out this year, as its international and extended-market funds each has outperformed its S&P 500 fund through Nov. 29, 2004, putting its overall return in the category's top quartile. Its five-year return is in the same territory. That won't always happen, of course; when U.S. large caps lead the way, this fund will lag rivals that focus almost exclusively on those. But long-term investors who crave simplicity (and low costs) should keep it in mind.

Address:	1201 N Market St Wilmington DE 19899 800-343-3548
Web Address:	www.fidelity.com
Inception:	06-29-99*
Advisor:	Strategic Advisers, Inc.
Subadvisor:	None
NTF Plans:	Fidelity Retail-NTF, CommonWealth NTF

Minimum Purchase:	$10000	Add: $1000	IRA: $2500
Min Auto Inv Plan:	$10000	Add: $500	
Sales Fees:	No-load, 0.50%R		
Management Fee:	0.10%, 0.08%A		
Actual Fees:	Mgt:0.10%	Dist:	
Expense Projections:	3Yr:$211	5Yr: —	10Yr: —
Income Distrib:	Semi-Annually		

Fidelity Freedom 2010

Ticker	Load	NAV	Yield	Total Assets	Mstar Category
FFFCX	None	$13.62	2.1%	$8,419 mil	Conservative Allocation

Governance and Management

Fiduciary Grade: B

Portfolio Manager(s)

Ren Cheng of Fidelity oversees this and the other Fidelity Freedom funds. He has been managing it since October 1996. Because this is a fund of Fidelity funds, shareholders are also tapping into the managers of the underlying funds, most of whom are quite skilled, as well as Fidelity's strong research capabilities. At times, manager departures and shifts at underlying funds can raise concerns about individual funds.

Strategy

Aimed at investors planning to retire around 2010, this fund tries to match the performance of a customized benchmark of five indexes, using about 19 actively managed Fidelity funds. Although its assets include small caps and mid-caps, international stocks, and high-yield bonds, the bulk of assets is invested in large-cap domestic-stock funds and high-quality bond funds. The fund gradually changes its asset allocation to become more conservative. It is less aggressive than its Fidelity Freedom siblings with maturity dates further in the future.

Historical Profile

Return Average
Risk Above Avg
Rating ★★★ Neutral

Investment Style: Equity Stock %: 50% (1997), 56% (1998), 52% (1999), 45% (2000), 39% (2001), 45% (2002), 46% (2003)

▼ Manager Change
▽ Partial Manager Change

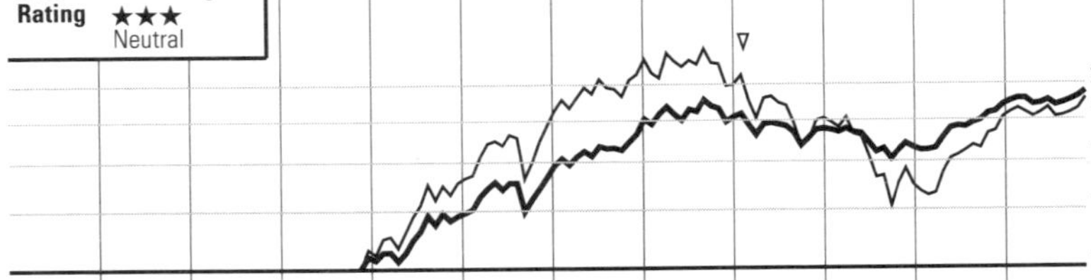

Growth of $10,000
— Investment Values of Fund
— Investment Values of S&P 500

Performance Quartile (within Category)

1993	1994	1995	1996	1997	1998	1999	2000	2001	2002	2003	12-04	History
—	—	—	10.19	11.69	13.30	14.87	13.84	12.61	11.44	13.02	13.62	NAV
—	—	—	2.99*	19.27	19.29	19.04	0.67	-4.34	-6.85	17.13	7.24	Total Return %
—	—	—	—	-14.08	-9.28	-2.00	9.77	7.54	15.24	-11.54	-3.63	+/-S&P 500
—	—	—	—	5.17	7.56	11.18	-6.12	-7.56	-2.83	-0.53	-1.77	+/-DJ 40%
—	—	—	0.00	3.65	3.04	3.75	3.20	2.73	2.47	2.46	2.24	Income Return %
—	—	—	—	15.62	16.25	15.29	-2.53	-7.07	-9.32	14.67	5.00	Capital Return %
—	—	—	—	19	7	6	76	81	81	16	27	Total Rtn % Rank Cat
—	—	—	0.11	0.37	0.35	0.49	0.46	0.37	0.31	0.28	0.29	Income $
—	—	—	0.00	0.09	0.28	0.42	0.67	0.27	0.00	0.09	0.05	Capital Gains $
—	—	—	—	0.08	0.08	0.08	0.07	0.08	0.07	0.08	0.08	Expense Ratio %
—	—	—	—	2.56	2.54	2.82	2.98	3.43	2.84	2.44	2.07	Income Ratio %
—	—	—	—	3	20	27	33	16	10	8	4	Turnover Rate %
—	—	—	—	123	914	1,644	2,313	3,491	4,330	6,787	8,419	Net Assets $mil

Performance 12-31-04

	1st Qtr	2nd Qtr	3rd Qtr	4th Qtr	Total
2000	4.57	-0.99	1.22	-3.94	0.67
2001	-6.50	3.91	-7.50	6.44	-4.34
2002	0.00	-5.02	-6.05	4.38	-6.85
2003	-0.35	8.62	2.11	5.98	17.13
2004	2.23	-0.62	0.00	5.56	7.24

Trailing	Total Return%	+/- S&P 500	+/- DJ 40%	%Rank Cat	Growth of $10,000
3 Mo	5.56	-3.67	0.16	17	10,556
6 Mo	5.56	-1.63	-0.93	36	10,556
1 Yr	7.24	-3.63	-1.77	27	10,724
3 Yr Avg	5.37	1.79	-1.81	39	11,699
5 Yr Avg	2.41	4.71	-3.89	72	11,264
10 Yr Avg	—	—	—	—	—
15 Yr Avg	—	—	—	—	—

Tax Analysis	Tax-Adj Rtn%	%Rank Cat	Tax-Cost Rat	%Rank Cat
3 Yr (estimated)	4.43	30	0.89	44
5 Yr (estimated)	1.09	72	1.29	49
10 Yr (estimated)	—	—	—	—

Potential Capital Gain Exposure: 4% of assets

Rating and Risk

Time Period	Load-Adj Return %	Morningstar Rtn vs Cat	Morningstar Risk vs Cat	Morningstar Risk-Adj Rating
1 Yr	7.24			
3 Yr	5.37	+Avg	+Avg	★★★★
5 Yr	2.41	-Avg	+Avg	★★
10 Yr	—	—	—	—
Incept	8.58			

Other Measures	Standard Index S&P 500	Best Fit Index DJ 60%
Alpha	2.7	-2.3
Beta	0.42	0.72
R-Squared	90	95
Standard Deviation	6.92	
Mean	5.37	
Sharpe Ratio	0.58	

Portfolio Analysis 09-30-04

Total Stocks:0 Share change since 03-31-04	Sectors	P/E Ratio	YTD Return %	% Net Assets
⊕ Fidelity Equity-Income	—	—	—	6.55
⊕ Fidelity Disciplined Equi	—	—	—	6.32
⊕ Fidelity	—	—	—	6.25
⊕ Fidelity Growth & Income	—	—	—	6.22
⊕ Fidelity Blue Chip Growth	—	—	—	5.94
⊕ Fidelity Mid-Cap Stock	—	—	—	3.61
⊕ Fidelity Growth Company	—	—	—	3.60
⊕ Fidelity OTC	—	—	—	2.72
⊕ Fidelity Europe	—	—	—	2.07

Total Fixed-Income:0	Date of Maturity	Amount $000	Value $000	% Net Assets
Fidelity Investment Grade		148,242	1,122,196	14.62
Fidelity Government Incom		108,029	1,110,534	14.46
Fidelity Intermediate Bon		68,762	726,816	9.47
Fidelity Capital & Income		35,362	285,729	3.72
Fidelity High Income		18,667	165,760	2.16

Equity Style
Style: Blend
Size: Large-Cap

Value Measures		Rel Category
Price/Earnings	16.97	1.03
Price/Book	2.61	1.10
Price/Sales	1.34	1.03
Price/Cash Flow	7.00	1.01
Dividend Yield %	1.35	0.78

Growth Measures	%	Rel Category
Long-Term Erngs	12.18	1.09
Book Value	7.53	1.37
Sales	5.32	1.16
Cash Flow	4.84	0.72
Historical Erngs	13.23	1.40

Market Cap %			
Giant	47.0	Small	3.1
Large	30.6	Micro	0.3
Mid	18.9	Avg $mil:	28,589

Fixed-Income Style
Duration: Interm-Term
Quality: High

Avg Eff Duration [1]	4.4 Yrs
Avg Eff Maturity	5.4 Yrs
Avg Credit Quality	AAA
Avg Wtd Coupon	5.16%

[1]figure provided by fund as of 09-30-04

Sector Weightings	% of Stocks	Rel S&P 500	3 Year High	3 Year Low
Info	26.00	1.21		
Software	5.44	1.27	8	5
Hardware	11.12	1.09	12	9
Media	4.73	1.23	5	3
Telecom	4.71	1.50	5	3
Service	45.70	0.99		
Health	14.86	1.19	18	14
Consumer	7.77	0.86	10	8
Business	4.07	1.00	5	4
Financial	19.00	0.92	20	16
Mfg	28.31	0.88		
Goods	8.49	0.91	9	8
Ind Mtrls	11.78	0.93	12	9
Energy	7.18	1.00	7	6
Utilities	0.86	0.29	1	1

Composition

Cash	16.2
Stocks	45.8
Bonds	37.5
Other	0.5
Foreign (% of Stock)	15.8

Morningstar's Take by Gregg Wolper 12-18-04

Fidelity Freedom 2010 provides quick help for investors who might otherwise leave their money in inappropriate alternatives.

This is a fund of funds that invests in a wide variety of other Fidelity funds. The idea is that people planning to retire in or around 2010 would own only this fund, thus getting strong management and diversification without having to choose a broad array of offerings themselves. This fund's underlying menu and the allocations therein are altered slowly by the Fidelity manager over time.

The result is a portfolio that contains 13 stock funds, five bond funds and a money-market offering. The equity side (currently about 47% of assets) focuses mostly, but not exclusively, on large U.S. companies, while the bond stake (roughly 44% of assets) primarily targets high-quality securities, though it includes some junk bonds. That's a reasonable mixture given the fund's purpose, and the underlying funds generally are sound.

But neither the mixture nor the particular funds included will necessarily suit everyone. For example, longer-term shareholders who now think it's possible they may retire several years earlier than 2010 might want to have a lower stock stake. This fund has a much higher equity allocation than the typical conservative-allocation fund, so while it has outperformed when stocks have been stronger than bonds, it risks suffering deeper losses when stocks slide. Meanwhile, those who feel comfortable picking and monitoring their own fund lineup can find funds from other firms preferable to some of this offering's choices.

However, many folks would rather not take the time that would require, or feel they lack the knowledge to do so. If that describes you, or if you simply lack better alternatives in your retirement plan, this or another Fidelity Freedom fund can serve you quite well as long as you understand its purpose.

Address:	1201 N Market St P O Box 1347 Wilmington DE 19899 800-343-3548
Web Address:	www.fidelity.com
Inception:	10-17-96 *
Advisor:	Strategic Advisers, Inc.
Subadvisor:	None
NTF Plans:	Fidelity Retail-NTF, CommonWealth NTF

Minimum Purchase:	$2500	Add: $250	IRA: $2500
Min Auto Inv Plan:	$2500	Add: $100	
Sales Fees:	No-load		
Management Fee:	0.10%, 0.08%A		
Actual Fees:	Mgt:0.08%	Dist:	
Expense Projections:	3Yr:$258	5Yr:$449	10Yr:$1000
Income Distrib:	Semi-Annually		

Fidelity Freedom 2020

Ticker	Load	NAV	Yield	Total Assets	Mstar Category
FFFDX	None	$13.96	1.9%	$9,338 mil	Moderate Allocation

Governance and Management

Fiduciary Grade: B

Portfolio Manager(s)

Ren Cheng of Fidelity oversees this and the other Fidelity Freedom funds. He has been managing it since its October 1996 inception. Because this is a fund of Fidelity funds, shareholders are also tapping into the managers of the underlying funds, most of whom are quite skilled, as well as Fidelity's strong research capabilities. At times, manager departures and shifts at the underlying funds can raise concerns about individual funds.

Strategy

The fund aims to match the performance of a customized benchmark of five indexes, using 17-20 actively managed Fidelity funds. It changes its asset allocation over time to become more conservative, with the expectation that shareholders plan to retire around 2020.

Historical Profile
Return Average
Risk Above Avg
Rating ★★★ Neutral

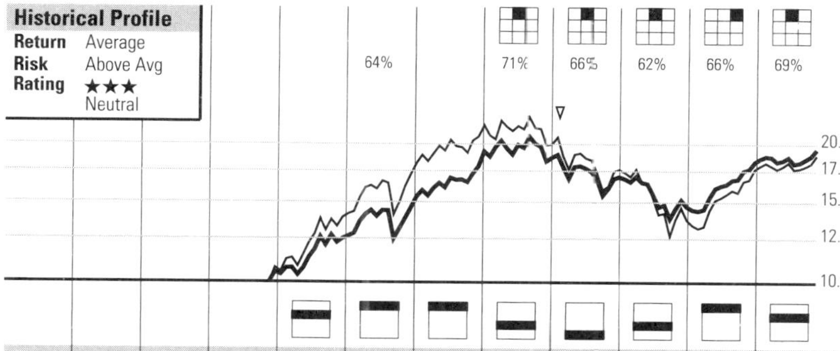

1993	1994	1995	1996	1997	1998	1999	2000	2001	2002	2003	12-04	History
—	—	—	10.24	11.93	13.95	16.38	14.56	12.58	10.64	13.02	13.96	NAV
—	—	—	3.29*	21.15	21.66	25.31	-3.03	-9.07	-13.71	24.90	9.55	Total Return %
—	—	—	—	-12.20	-6.91	4.27	6.07	2.81	8.38	-3.77	-1.32	+/-S&P 500
—	—	—	—	1.95	9.27	12.46	-7.47	-9.23	-3.17	0.84	-1.62	+/-DJ 60%
—	—	—	0.00	3.33	2.37	3.30	2.47	1.83	1.75	2.07	2.01	Income Return %
—	—	—	—	17.82	19.29	22.01	-5.50	-10.90	-15.46	22.83	7.54	Capital Return %
—	—	—	—	37	12	6	75	83	68	14	36	Total Rtn % Rank Cat
—	—	—	0.09	0.34	0.28	0.45	0.39	0.25	0.22	0.22	0.26	Income $
—	—	—	0.00	0.13	0.27	0.57	0.96	0.43	0.00	0.04	0.04	Capital Gains $
—	—	—	—	0.08	0.08	0.08	0.07	0.03	0.07	0.08	0.08	Expense Ratio %
—	—	—	—	1.75	1.76	2.03	2.07	2.23	2.03	1.96	1.85	Income Ratio %
—	—	—	—	21	15	18	28	15	10	6	3	Turnover Rate %
—	—	—	1	84	860	1,560	1,893	2,796	3,735	6,736	9,338	Net Assets $mil

Performance 12-31-04

	1st Qtr	2nd Qtr	3rd Qtr	4th Qtr	Total
2000	5.49	-2.03	0.62	-6.75	-3.03
2001	-9.96	5.27	-12.55	9.70	-9.07
2002	0.16	-8.59	-11.16	6.09	-13.71
2003	-1.32	12.40	3.32	8.99	24.90
2004	2.46	-0.09	-1.06	8.16	9.55

Trailing	Total Return%	+/- S&P 500	+/- DJ 60%	%Rank Cat	Growth of $10,000
3 Mo	8.16	-1.07	0.68	19	10,816
6 Mo	7.02	-0.17	-0.51	39	10,702
1 Yr	9.55	-1.32	-1.62	36	10,955
3 Yr Avg	5.69	2.11	-1.57	33	11,806
5 Yr Avg	0.81	3.11	-4.43	65	10,412
10 Yr Avg	—	—	—	—	—
15 Yr Avg	—	—	—	—	—

Tax Analysis	Tax-Adj Rtn%	%Rank Cat	Tax-Cost Rat	%Rank Cat
3 Yr (estimated)	4.95	26	0.70	49
5 Yr (estimated)	-0.37	65	1.17	54
10 Yr (estimated)	—	—	—	—

Potential Capital Gain Exposure: 8% of assets

Rating and Risk

Time Period	Load-Adj Return %	Morningstar Rtn vs Cat	Morningstar Risk vs Cat	Morningstar Risk-Adj Rating
1 Yr	9.55			
3 Yr	5.69	+Avg	+Avg	★★★★
5 Yr	0.81	Avg	+Avg	★★
10 Yr	—	—	—	—
Incept	8.72			

Other Measures	Standard Index S&P 500	Best Fit Index Russ 1000
Alpha	2.5	2.0
Beta	0.68	0.69
R-Squared	96	97
Standard Deviation	10.92	
Mean	5.69	
Sharpe Ratio	0.40	

Portfolio Analysis 09-30-04

Total Stocks:0 Share change since 03-31-04	Sectors	P/E Ratio	YTD Return %	% Net Assets
⊕ Fidelity Equity-Income	—	—	—	9.46
⊕ Fidelity Disciplined Equi	—	—	—	9.15
⊕ Fidelity	—	—	—	9.07
⊕ Fidelity Growth & Income	—	—	—	9.03
⊕ Fidelity Blue Chip Growth	—	—	—	8.65
⊕ Fidelity Mid-Cap Stock	—	—	—	5.26
⊕ Fidelity Growth Company	—	—	—	5.24
⊕ Fidelity OTC	—	—	—	3.94
⊕ Fidelity Europe	—	—	—	3.92

Total Fixed-Income:0	Date of Maturity	Amount $000	Value $000	% Net Assets
Fidelity Investment Grade		86,337	653,567	8.07
Fidelity Government Incom		62,959	647,214	7.99
Fidelity Intermediate Bon		40,067	423,504	5.23
Fidelity Capital & Income		44,475	359,361	4.44
Fidelity High Income		34,733	308,425	3.81

Equity Style
Style: Blend
Size: Large-Cap

Value Measures		Rel Category
Price/Earnings	16.88	1.02
Price/Book	2.58	1.06
Price/Sales	1.29	0.98
Price/Cash Flow	6.88	0.95
Dividend Yield %	1.36	0.87

Growth Measures	%	Rel Category
Long-Term Erngs	12.24	1.05
Book Value	7.09	1.24
Sales	5.30	1.02
Cash Flow	4.71	0.59
Historical Erngs	3.02	1.20

Market Cap %			
Giant	46.5	Small	3.0
Large	30.8	Micro	0.3
Mid	19.3	Avg $mil:	27,702

Composition

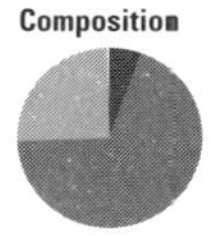

Cash	5.5
Stocks	68.7
Bonds	25.1
Other	0.8
Foreign (% of Stock)	18.5

Fixed-Income Style
Duration: Interm-Term
Quality: High

Avg Eff Duration [1]	4.4 Yrs
Avg Eff Maturity	5.4 Yrs
Avg Credit Quality	AAA
Avg Wtd Coupon	5.61%

[1]figure provided by fund as of 09-30-04

Sector Weightings	% of Stocks	Rel S&P 500	3 Year High	3 Year Low
Info	25.88	1.20		
Software	5.36	1.25	7	5
Hardware	10.86	1.06	12	9
Media	4.80	1.25	5	3
Telecom	4.86	1.54	5	3
Service	45.71	0.99		
Health	14.72	1.18	18	14
Consumer	7.66	0.84	10	8
Business	4.10	1.01	5	4
Financial	19.23	0.93	21	16
Mfg	28.43	0.89		
Goods	8.69	0.93	10	9
Ind Mtrls	11.68	0.92	12	9
Energy	7.22	1.01	7	3
Utilities	0.84	0.28	1	1

Morningstar's Take by Gregg Wolper 12-18-04

Fidelity Freedom 2020 has much in its favor, but it's appropriate only for a specific crowd.

This is a fund of funds that invests in a wide variety of other Fidelity funds. The idea is that people planning to retire in or around 2020 would own only this fund, thus getting strong management and diversification without having to choose a broad array of offerings themselves. This fund's underlying menu and the allocations therein are altered slowly by the Fidelity manager over time.

The result is a portfolio that contains 13 stock funds and five bond funds. The equity side (currently about 70% of assets) focuses mostly, but not exclusively, on large U.S. companies, while the bond stake (roughly 30% of assets) primarily targets high-quality securities, though it includes a significant amount in junk bonds. That's a reasonable mixture given the fund's purpose, and the underlying funds generally are sound.

But neither the mixture nor the particular funds included will necessarily suit everyone. For example, of the five international funds in this offering's portfolio, only one--Diversified International--is a real standout. Also, this fund has a higher equity allocation than the typical moderate-allocation fund, so while it has outperformed when stocks have been stronger than bonds, it has lagged when the reverse has been true, and risks suffering deeper losses than its typical category peer when stocks slide in the future.

Those who feel comfortable picking and monitoring their own funds likely could assemble a more-appealing collection than this one's group. However, many folks would rather not take the time that would require, or feel they lack the knowledge to do so. If that describes you, or if you simply lack better alternatives in your retirement plan, this or a Freedom sibling can serve you quite well as long as you understand its purpose.

Address:	1201 N Market St P O Box 1347 Wilmington DE 19899 800-343-3548
Web Address:	www.fidelity.com
Inception:	10-17-96*
Advisor:	Strategic Advisers, Inc.
Subadvisor:	None
NTF Plans:	Fidelity Retail-NTF, CommonWealth NTF

Minimum Purchase:	$2500	Add: $250	IRA: $2500
Min Auto Inv Plan:	$2500	Add: $100	
Sales Fees:	No-load		
Management Fee:	0.10%, 0.08%A		
Actual Fees:	Mgt:0.08%	Dist:	
Expense Projections:	3Yr:$269	5Yr:$468	10Yr:$1041
Income Distrib:	Semi-Annually		

Fidelity Ginnie Mae

Analyst Pick

Ticker	Load	NAV	Yield	SEC Yield	Total Assets	Mstar Category
FGMNX	None	$11.08	4.1%	4.01%	$4,036 mil	Intermediate Government

Governance and Management

Fiduciary Grade: B

Portfolio Manager(s)

William Irving worked as a quantitative fixed-income analyst before taking over this portfolio from Thomas Silvia, who became the head of Fidelity's bond-fund effort, in late 2004. He is backed by Fidelity's considerable research capabilities. Irving also took over Fidelity Inflation Protected Bond in late 2004.

Strategy

This fund plays it relatively safe. Fidelity bond funds don't bet on the direction of interest rates, and this fund is no exception. William Irving tries to add value through coupon selection and by occasionally dipping into adjustable-rate mortgages and CMOs. He also looks for issues likely to prepay at a slower rate than the market expects. The bulk of the fund is made up of plain-vanilla Ginnie Maes, though.

Historical Profile

Return Above Avg
Risk Low
Rating ★★★★ Above Avg

Investment Style
Fixed Income
Income Rtn %Rank Cat

24	19	17	13	6	17	26	76	24

▼ Manager Change
∇ Partial Manager Change

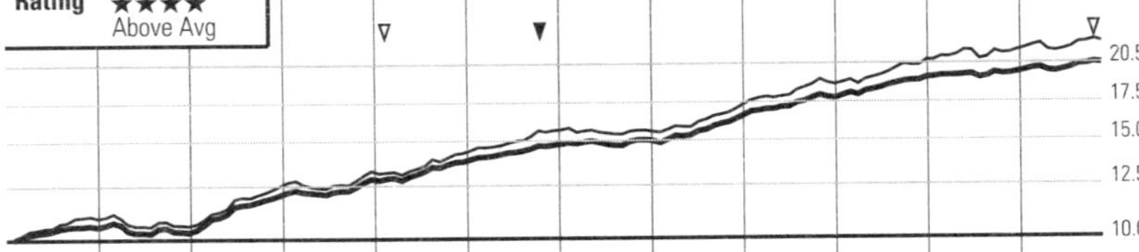

Growth of $10,000
— Investment Values of Fund
— Investment Values of LB Aggr

Performance Quartile (within Category)

1993	1994	1995	1996	1997	1998	1999	2000	2001	2002	2003	12-04	History
10.86	9.99	10.89	10.70	10.89	10.89	10.36	10.73	10.86	11.24	11.08	11.08	NAV
6.11	-2.00	16.61	4.86	8.70	6.38	1.25	10.74	7.24	8.66	2.20	4.20	Total Return %
-3.64	0.92	-1.86	1.23	-0.95	-2.31	2.07	-0.89	-1.20	-1.59	-1.90	-0.14	+/-LB Aggr
-4.55	1.38	-1.73	2.09	-0.89	-3.47	3.48	-2.50	0.01	-2.84	-0.16	0.72	+/-LB Govt
5.81	6.00	7.38	6.57	6.84	6.39	6.25	6.99	6.05	5.09	2.83	4.19	Income Return %
0.30	-8.00	9.23	-1.71	1.86	-0.01	-5.00	3.75	1.19	3.57	-0.63	0.01	Capital Return %
84	19	47	7	51	79	6	58	34	62	31	16	Total Rtn % Rank Cat
0.62	0.63	0.71	0.69	0.71	0.68	0.66	0.70	0.63	0.54	0.31	0.46	Income $
0.25	0.02	0.00	0.00	0.00	0.00	0.00	0.00	0.00	0.00	0.09	0.00	Capital Gains $
0.80	0.82	0.75	0.75	0.75	0.72	0.64	0.63	0.62	0.60	0.57	0.60	Expense Ratio %
7.26	7.03	7.24	6.69	6.75	6.58	6.43	6.67	6.40	5.15	3.25	3.64	Income Ratio %
259	303	210	107	98	172	73	75	120	327	262	155	Turnover Rate %
887	705	806	793	862	1,093	1,758	1,890	3,901	6,808	4,505	4,036	Net Assets $mil

Performance 12-31-04

	1st Qtr	2nd Qtr	3rd Qtr	4th Qtr	Total
2000	2.03	1.94	2.91	3.45	10.74
2001	2.49	0.99	3.76	-0.14	7.24
2002	1.29	2.99	2.61	1.51	8.66
2003	0.81	0.53	0.69	0.16	2.20
2004	1.79	-0.91	2.34	0.95	4.20

Trailing	Total Return%	+/- LB Aggr	+/- LB Govt	%Rank Cat	Growth of $10,000
3 Mo	0.95	0.00	0.46	26	10,095
6 Mo	3.31	-0.87	-0.30	39	10,331
1 Yr	4.20	-0.14	0.72	16	10,420
3 Yr Avg	4.99	-1.20	-0.71	32	11,573
5 Yr Avg	6.56	-1.15	-0.92	35	13,740
10 Yr Avg	7.00	-0.72	-0.46	18	19,672
15 Yr Avg	6.95	-0.75	-0.53	26	27,398

Tax Analysis	Tax-Adj Rtn%	%Rank Cat	Tax-Cost Rat	%Rank Cat
3 Yr (estimated)	3.41	21	1.50	54
5 Yr (estimated)	4.57	29	1.87	65
10 Yr (estimated)	4.65	13	2.20	72

Potential Capital Gain Exposure: 1% of assets

Rating and Risk

Time Period	Load-Adj Return %	Morningstar Rtn vs Cat	Morningstar Risk vs Cat	Morningstar Risk-Adj Rating
1 Yr	4.20			
3 Yr	4.99	+Avg	Low	★★★★
5 Yr	6.56	+Avg	Low	★★★★
10 Yr	7.00	+Avg	Low	★★★★
Incept	7.55			

Other Measures	Standard Index LB Aggr	Best Fit Index LB Mort
Alpha	1.1	0.2
Beta	0.50	0.83
R-Squared	85	96
Standard Deviation	2.47	
Mean	4.99	
Sharpe Ratio	1.49	

Portfolio Analysis 10-31-04

Total Fixed-Income:111	Date of Maturity	Amount $000	Value $000	% Net Assets
GNMA 0.05%	08-15-33	1,182,301	1,187,015	27.91
GNMA 0.06%	03-15-34	643,193	668,940	15.73
GNMA 0.06%	12-15-32	394,931	417,722	9.82
GNMA 0.06%	02-15-33	362,762	371,301	8.73
GNMA 0.04%	11-20-33	251,420	245,738	5.78
GNMA 0.07%	01-15-33	214,856	229,429	5.39
FNMA 4.5%	10-01-33	140,473	136,607	3.21
GNMA 7.5%	05-15-32	74,007	79,859	1.88
FHLMC 0.04%	11-01-19	64,378	63,231	1.49
GNMA CMO 6.5%	06-20-28	51,990	54,140	1.27
GNMA CMO 6.5%	05-16-31	33,139	34,079	0.80
GNMA CMO 6.5%	02-20-31	29,188	29,944	0.70
GNMA 8%	07-15-24	27,204	29,764	0.70
FNMA 5%	11-01-17	27,704	28,311	0.67
GNMA CMO 6%	10-20-30	20,573	20,771	0.49
GNMA CMO	03-16-43	318,942	20,519	0.48
GNMA CMO 5.5%	04-20-34	18,652	19,355	0.46
GNMA CMO	02-16-43	284,742	18,375	0.43
GNMA CMO 6%	10-20-31	15,041	15,453	0.36
FNMA CMO 5%	09-25-16	14,400	14,745	0.35

Current Investment Style

Duration: Short Int Long — Quality: High Med Low

¹ figure provided by fund

Avg Eff Duration¹	3.3 Yrs
Avg Eff Maturity	5.0 Yrs
Avg Credit Quality	AAA
Avg Wtd Coupon	1.12%
Avg Wtd Price	99.32% of par

Coupon Range	% of Bonds	Rel Cat
0% PIK	0.1	0.0
0% to 6%	91.1	1.2
6% to 8%	8.8	0.4
8% to 10%	0.1	0.0
More than 10%	0.0	0.0

1.00=Category Average

Credit Analysis	% bonds 10-31-04		
US Govt	99	BB	0
AAA	0	B	0
AA	0	Below B	0
A	0	NR/NA	1
BBB	0		

Sector Breakdown	% of assets
US Treasuries	0
TIPS	0
US Agency	0
Mortgage Pass-Throughs	82
Mortgage CMO	12
Mortgage ARM	0
US Corporate	0
Asset-Backed	0
Convertible	0
Municipal	0
Corporate Inflation-Protected	0
Foreign Corporate	0
Foreign Govt	0

Composition			
Cash	6.1	Bonds	93.9
Stocks	0.0	Other	0.0

Special Securities	
Restricted/Illiquid Secs	0
Exotic Mortgage-Backed	3
Emerging-Markets Secs	0
Options/Futures/Warrants	No

Morningstar's Take by Scott Berry 12-21-04

We don't think investors should be too concerned by this fund's recent management change.

On Nov. 1, 2004, manager Tom Silvia was replaced by William Irving. Irving has worked as a quantitative fixed-income analyst for Fidelity since 1999, helping build and maintain the prepayment models that Fidelity uses to value mortgage securities. Meanwhile, Silvia was promoted to head Fidelity's bond-fund effort. We think Irving's hands-on mortgage experience and Silvia's continued employment with Fidelity bode well for this fund's continued success.

Of course, the fund's reasonable expense ratio and steady approach provide a solid foundation for Irving to build on. At 0.60%, the fund's expense ratio provides it a small advantage over its average no-load intermediate government peer (0.68%), while the fund's duration-neutral approach helps limit wild performance swings. Rather than making adjustments to duration (a measure of interest-rate sensitivity), which has proved a difficult way for most manager to add value, Irving will try to find pockets of opportunity in issues with higher or lower coupons. He will also look for issues that are likely to prepay at faster or slower rates than the market expects.

Irving has a tough act to follow, but if he can simply duplicate Silvia's efforts, he'll be a success. Silvia took over the fund in late 1998 and helped it deliver solid results without much volatility during his tenure. In fact, the fund's three- and five-year trailing returns rank firmly in the category's best half, while its volatility (as measured by standard deviation of returns) ranks among the lowest in the group.

We hate to see good managers hand off funds to less-proven skippers, but we think investors have every reason to expect continued success here, given the quality of personnel and processes that are employed by Fidelity's bond group.

Address:	82 Devonshire St Boston MA 02109 800-343-3548
Web Address:	www.fidelity.com
Inception:	11-08-85
Advisor:	Fidelity Management & Research Co. (FMR)
Subadvisor:	Fidelity Intl Invest Advisors (U.K.) Ltd
NTF Plans:	Fidelity Retail-NTF, CommonWealth NTF

Minimum Purchase:	$2500	Add: $250	IRA: $2500
Min Auto Inv Plan:	$2500	Add: $100	
Sales Fees:	No-load		
Management Fee:	0.43%		
Actual Fees:	Mgt:0.43%	Dist:	
Expense Projections:	3Yr:$227	5Yr:$395	10Yr:$883
Income Distrib:	Monthly		

Fidelity Government Inc

Ticker	Load	NAV	Yield	SEC Yield	Total Assets	Mstar Category
FGOVX	None	$10.24	3.0%	2.94%	$4,478 mil	Intermediate Gove-nment

Governance and Management

Fiduciary Grade: B

Portfolio Manager(s)

George Fischer replaced former manager Tom Silvia in January 2003. Fischer has been a member of Fidelity's bond group for nearly 10 years, most recently as a manager of several municipal portfolios. Silvia continues to manage money, but now he also leads the firm's taxable-bond fund-management team.

Strategy

This fund's strategy involves rotating the fund's assets among U.S. Treasury bonds, U.S. agency securities, and mortgage bonds. Management also looks to add value through issue selection and yield-curve allocation. The fund's duration (a measure of interest-rate sensitivity) is tied to a benchmark index. As of Jan. 31, 2004, the fund's benchmark index was changed to a blend of the Lehman Brothers Government Bond Index (75%) and the Lehman Brothers Mortgage-Backed Securities Index (25%). The fund's duration is now closer to the category norm, but still a bit longer than average.

Historical Profile

Return Above Avg
Risk Above Avg
Rating ★★★★ Above Avg

Investment Style
Fixed Income
Income Rtn %Rank Cat

12	34	27	41	11	33	59	65	64

▼ Manager Change
▽ Partial Manager Change

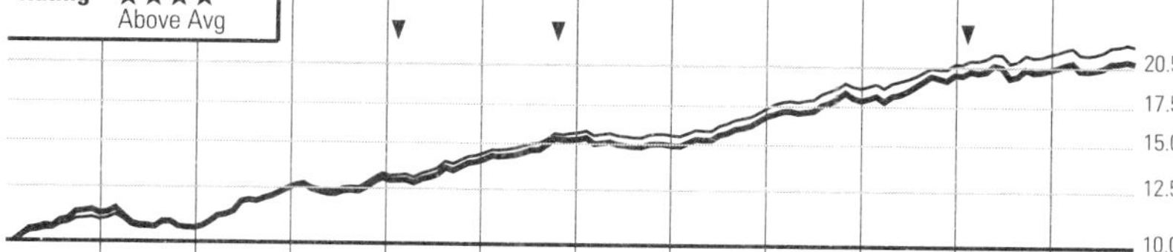

Growth of $10,000
▬ Investment Values of Fund
— Investment Values of LB Aggr

Performance Quartile (within Category)

1993	1994	1995	1996	1997	1998	1999	2000	2001	2002	2003	12-04	History
10.34	9.17	10.17	9.69	9.91	10.14	9.35	9.87	9.97	10.48	10.22	10.24	NAV
12.32	-5.21	18.07	2.08	8.93	8.59	-2.25	12.63	6.72	10.94	2.22	3.60	Total Return %
2.57	-2.29	-0.40	-1.55	-0.72	-0.10	-1.43	1.00	-1.72	0.69	-1.88	-0.74	+/-LB Aggr
1.66	-1.83	-0.27	-0.69	-0.66	-1.26	-0.02	-0.61	-0.5[illegible]	-0.56	-0.14	0.12	+/-LB Govt
6.86	6.17	6.88	6.82	6.51	6.23	5.72	6.83	5.72	4.36	3.18	3.05	Income Return %
5.46	-11.38	11.19	-4.74	2.42	2.36	-7.97	5.80	1.00	6.58	-0.96	0.55	Capital Return %
6	83	19	73	41	16	63	7	56	13	30	32	Total Rtn % Rank Cat
0.67	0.62	0.61	0.67	0.61	0.60	0.56	0.62	0.55	0.43	0.33	0.31	Income $
0.31	0.02	0.00	0.00	0.00	0.00	0.00	0.00	0.00	0.13	0.16	0.04	Capital Gains $
0.69	0.69	0.71	0.71	0.72	0.68	0.67	0.65	0.60	0.68	0.65	0.63	Expense Ratio %
6.40	6.26	6.36	6.52	6.48	5.82	5.91	6.27	5.91	4.50	3.56	3.01	Income Ratio %
323	402	391	124	199	289	168	131	214	284	253	224	Turnover Rate %
753	611	994	973	1,165	1,583	1,589	1,699	2,402	3,381	3,886	4,478	Net Assets $mil

Performance 12-31-04

	1st Qtr	2nd Qtr	3rd Qtr	4th Qtr	Total
2000	2.65	1.79	2.84	4.82	12.63
2001	2.17	0.05	5.17	-0.74	6.72
2002	-0.35	4.27	6.23	0.50	10.94
2003	0.81	2.29	-0.71	-0.16	2.22
2004	2.80	-2.76	2.86	0.76	3.60

Trailing	Total Return%	+/- LB Aggr	+/- LB Govt	%Rank Cat	Growth of $10,000
3 Mo	0.76	-0.19	0.27	47	10,076
6 Mo	3.64	-0.54	0.03	22	10,364
1 Yr	3.60	-0.74	0.12	32	10,360
3 Yr Avg	5.52	-0.67	-0.18	13	11,749
5 Yr Avg	7.15	-0.56	-0.33	12	14,124
10 Yr Avg	7.00	-0.72	-0.46	17	19,672
15 Yr Avg	7.29	-0.41	-0.19	7	28,734

Tax Analysis	Tax-Adj Rtn%	%Rank Cat	Tax-Cost Rat	%Rank Cat
3 Yr (estimated)	3.86	10	1.57	60
5 Yr (estimated)	5.14	9	1.88	66
10 Yr (estimated)	4.70	12	2.15	65

Potential Capital Gain Exposure: 1% of assets

Rating and Risk

Time Period	Load-Adj Return %	Morningstar Rtn vs Cat	Morningstar Risk vs Cat	Morningstar Risk-Adj Rating
1 Yr	3.60			
3 Yr	5.52	+Avg	+Avg	★★★★
5 Yr	7.15	+Avg	+Avg	★★★★
10 Yr	7.00	+Avg	+Avg	★★★★
Incept	8.74			

Other Measures	Standard Index LB Aggr	Best Fit Index LB Govt
Alpha	-1.6	-0.1
Beta	1.21	0.98
R-Squared	97	99

Standard Deviation	5.51
Mean	5.52
Sharpe Ratio	0.76

Portfolio Analysis 10-31-04

Total Fixed-Income:128	Date of Maturity	Amount $000	Value $000	% Net Assets
US Treasury Note 2.75%	07-31-06	461,550	463,695	9.02
US Treasury Note 3.25%	01-15-09	433,200	435,078	8.46
US Treasury Bond 3.625%	04-15-28	172,000	256,406	4.99
FNMA 3.25%	02-15-09	248,550	246,384	4.79
FNMA 0.05%	11-01-34	205,000	204,167	3.97
US Treasury Bond 8%	11-15-21	142,000	197,053	3.83
FHLMC 2.375%	04-15-06	133,000	132,566	2.58
US Treasury Note 4.75%	05-15-14	112,755	119,221	2.32
Israel St 5.5%	09-18-23	110,500	115,331	2.24
FNMA 0.04%	12-01-18	116,995	114,818	2.23
FNMA 0.06%	12-01-23	86,077	87,813	1.71
FNMA 3.25%	01-15-08	82,700	82,889	1.61
FNMA 2.375%	12-15-05	80,000	79,916	1.55
US Treasury Note 1.875%	07-15-13	75,000	79,640	1.55
US Treasury Note 2.625%	03-15-09	80,000	78,219	1.52
FNMA 0.06%	02-01-18	72,025	74,707	1.45
FHLMC 4.5%	01-15-14	73,400	73,805	1.44
Cssw Swap Irs 2/15/07 3m	02-15-07	68,735	68,775	1.34
FNMA 5.125%	01-02-14	65,000	66,784	1.30
US Treasury Note 4.25%	08-15-13	60,000	61,324	1.19

Current Investment Style

Duration: Short Int Long
Quality: High Med Low

¹figure provided by fund

Avg Eff Duration¹	4.5 Yrs
Avg Eff Maturity	6.1 Yrs
Avg Credit Quality	AAA
Avg Wtd Coupon	3.52%
Avg Wtd Price	106.98% of par

Coupon Range	% of Bonds	Rel Cat
0% PIK	1.7	0.3
0% to 6%	86.2	1.1
6% to 8%	13.2	0.6
8% to 10%	0.1	0.1
More than 10%	0.5	0.4

1.00=Category Average

Credit Analysis		% bonds 10-31-04	
US Govt	88	BB	0
AAA	0	B	0
AA	0	Below B	0
A	0	NR/NA	12
BBB	0		

Sector Breakdown	% of assets
US Treasuries	30
TIPS	7
US Agency	22
Mortgage Pass-Throughs	12
Mortgage CMO	6
Mortgage ARM	0
US Corporate	4
Asset-Backed	0
Convertible	0
Municipal	0
Corporate Inflation-Protected	0
Foreign Corporate	0
Foreign Govt	0

Composition			
Cash	20.4	Bonds	79.6
Stocks	0.0	Other	0.0

Special Securities	
Restricted/Illiquid Secs	0
Exotic Mortgage-Backed	—
Emerging-Markets Secs	0
Options/Futures/Warrants	No

Morningstar's Take by Scott Berry 12-10-04

Fidelity Government Income could face rough sledding if interest rates move higher, but it remains an appealing choice.

This fund is typically more sensitive to interest-rate changes than its average intermediate-government peer. That added risk isn't the result of a bet by manager George Fischer that interest rates will go lower, but rather reflects the added risk of the fund's benchmark index relative to the category norm. Unlike many of his peers, which make bets on the direction of interest-rates, Fischer keeps the fund's overall interest-rate sensitivity closely tied to the Lehman Brothers Government Bond Index.

The fund's added rate sensitivity worked in its favor in the early part of the decade, as rates moved lower and bond prices moved higher. However, two recent rate spikes have shown the fund's potential weakness. It lost 4.2% when rates moved higher in July 2003, for example, and lost 3.0% when rates jumped in April 2004. With the economy improving and the Federal Reserve ratcheting rates higher, further losses are certainly possible.

The fund's volatility should not be ignored, but we think long-term investors have a lot to like about it, including its management and expense ratio. Fischer has only been with the fund since January 2003, but he is a skilled and seasoned manager who had much success managing Fidelity municipal bond funds before shifting his attention to taxable government funds. Further, the fund is reasonably priced at 0.65%. That doesn't make it the group's cheapest, but it does provide a small advantage over the average no-load peer.

Overall, we like what this fund brings to the table. It may struggle to keep pace with its average peer if interest rates rise, but we think its skilled management and below-average expense ratio provide sustainable advantages that will allow it to continue to shine over the long term.

Address:	82 Devonshire St Boston MA 02109 800-343-3548
Web Address:	www.fidelity.com
Inception:	04-04-79
Advisor:	Fidelity Management & Research Co. (FMR)
Subadvisor:	Fidelity Intl Invest Advisors (U.K.) Ltd
NTF Plans:	Fidelity Retail-NTF, CommonWealth NTF

Minimum Purchase:	$2500	Add: $250	IRA: $2500
Min Auto Inv Plan:	$100	Add: $100	
Sales Fees:	No-load		
Management Fee:	0.43%		
Actual Fees:	Mgt:0.43%	Dist:	
Expense Projections:	3Yr:$208	5Yr:$362	10Yr:$810
Income Distrib:	Monthly		

Fidelity Growth & Income

Ticker	Load	NAV	Yield	Total Assets	Mstar Category
FGRIX	None	$38.21	1.4%	$32,106 mil	Large Blend

Governance and Management

Fiduciary Grade: B

Portfolio Manager(s)

Steve Kaye has been an analyst or portfolio manager for the firm since 1985. He has been at the helm of this fund since January 1993. Like Fidelity's other domestic-stock fund managers, he receives the support of dozens of talented industry analysts, though the final call is his to make.

Strategy

Steve Kaye's focus on valuations has consistently led him to underweight technology relative to the S&P 500 Index. He also favors steady growers over companies operating in more volatile industries. Kaye now favors middle-of-the-road financials and telecom-services names over shaky technology stocks.

Historical Profile

Return Average
Risk Low
Rating ★★★★ Above Avg

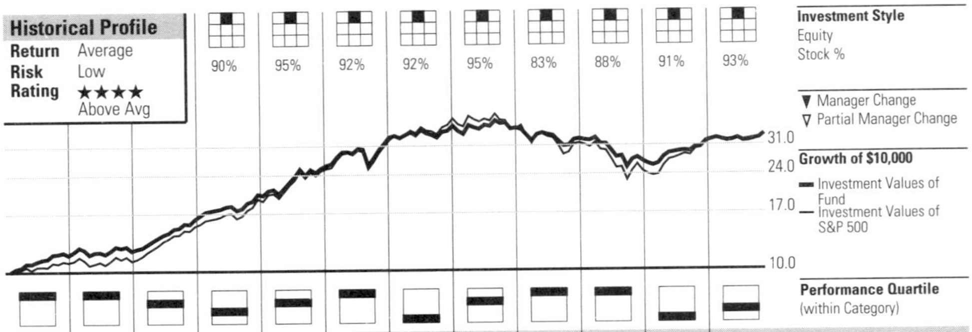

1993	1994	1995	1996	1997	1998	1999	2000	2001	2002	2003	12-04	History
22.22	21.09	27.05	30.73	38.10	45.84	47.16	42.10	37.38	30.31	35.63	38.21	NAV
19.53	2.27	35.38	20.02	30.17	28.31	10.42	-1.98	-9.35	-18.08	19.01	9.84	Total Return %
9.47	0.96	-2.15	-2.92	-3.18	-0.26	-10.62	7.12	2.53	4.01	-9.66	-1.03	+/-S&P 500
9.35	1.88	-2.39	-2.43	-2.68	1.29	-10.49	5.81	3.10	3.57	-10.88	-1.56	+/-Russ 1000
2.68	1.83	2.31	1.73	1.42	1.04	0.87	0.80	0.93	0.91	1.33	1.56	Income Return %
16.85	0.44	33.07	18.29	28.75	27.27	9.55	-2.78	-10.28	-18.99	17.68	8.28	Capital Return %
10	16	40	62	42	20	86	32	23	18	96	56	Total Rtn % Rank Cat
0.52	0.40	0.48	0.46	0.43	0.39	0.39	0.37	0.39	0.34	0.40	0.55	Income $
0.77	1.24	0.90	1.12	1.36	2.16	2.90	3.91	0.38	0.00	0.00	0.34	Capital Gains $
0.83	0.82	0.77	0.74	0.71	0.68	0.66	0.66	0.66	0.68	0.71	0.69	Expense Ratio %
2.67	2.09	2.21	1.82	1.43	1.02	0.88	0.82	0.94	0.94	1.29	1.13	Income Ratio %
87	92	67	41	38	32	35	41	46	36	33	30	Turnover Rate %
7,684	9,345	14,819	23,896	36,657	48,640	48,528	39,963	34,255	26,269	30,572	32,106	Net Assets $mil

Performance 12-31-04

	1st Qtr	2nd Qtr	3rd Qtr	4th Qtr	Total
2000	0.52	0.21	1.31	-3.96	-1.98
2001	-10.91	5.80	-9.64	6.45	-9.35
2002	0.83	-10.48	-14.03	5.58	-18.08
2003	-2.27	10.43	0.85	9.33	19.01
2004	1.34	1.11	-0.77	8.03	9.84

Trailing	Total Return%	+/- S&P 500	+/- Russ 1000	%Rank Cat	Growth of $10,000
3 Mo	8.03	-1.20	-1.77	82	10,803
6 Mo	7.20	0.01	-0.61	41	10,720
1 Yr	9.84	-1.03	-1.56	56	10,984
3 Yr Avg	2.31	-1.27	-1.96	62	10,709
5 Yr Avg	-0.99	1.31	0.77	32	9,515
10 Yr Avg	11.05	-1.02	-1.11	41	28,522
15 Yr Avg	11.53	0.60	0.45	16	51,390

Tax Analysis	Tax-Adj Rtn%	%Rank Cat	Tax-Cost Rat	%Rank Cat
3 Yr (estimated)	1.81	57	0.49	41
5 Yr (estimated)	-1.79	31	0.81	43
10 Yr (estimated)	9.68	36	1.23	42

Potential Capital Gain Exposure: 37% of assets

Rating and Risk

Time Period	Load-Adj Return %	Morningstar Rtn vs Cat	Morningstar Risk vs Cat	Morningstar Risk-Adj Rating
1 Yr	9.84			
3 Yr	2.31	Avg	Low	★★★
5 Yr	-0.99	Avg	Low	★★★★
10 Yr	11.05	Avg	Low	★★★★
Incept	13.81			

Other Measures	Standard Index S&P 500	Best Fit Index S&P 500
Alpha	-0.9	-0.9
Beta	0.75	0.75
R-Squared	95	95
Standard Deviation	11.80	
Mean	2.31	
Sharpe Ratio	0.08	

Portfolio Analysis 10-31-04

Share change since 07-04 Total Stocks:167	Sector	PE	YTD Ret%	% Assets
General Electric	Ind Mtrls	22.8	20.68	3.92
⊖ SLM	Financial	15.8	44.21	3.87
⊖ ExxonMobil	Energy	13.9	28.04	3.59
⊖ Microsoft	Software	36.1	8.95	3.40
⊕ Verizon Communications	Telecom	32.4	20.25	2.91
⊕ SBC Communications	Telecom	15.4	3.74	2.80
⊖ Pfizer	Health	22.0	-22.31	2.75
⊕ Wal-Mart Stores	Consumer	23.4	0.51	2.37
⊖ Fannie Mae	Financial	9.1	-2.33	2.08
⊖ UnitedHealth Group	Health	23.8	51.38	1.99
⊕ American International G	Financial	16.2	-0.53	1.92
⊖ Citigroup	Financial	15.3	2.72	1.88
⊕ Bank of America	Financial	12.3	21.50	1.77
Wells Fargo	Financial	15.5	8.97	1.55
BellSouth	Telecom	12.7	1.94	1.51
⊕ Home Depot	Consumer	19.0	21.47	1.49
Procter & Gamble	Goods	23.3	12.38	1.36
⊕ Omnicom Group	Business	21.6	-2.33	1.32
Johnson & Johnson	Health	20.6	25.17	1.18
⊖ Altria Group	Goods	13.3	18.38	1.12

Current Investment Style (Value Blnd Growth; Large Mid Small)

Market Cap	%
Giant	62.7
Large	32.6
Mid	4.4
Small	0.4
Micro	0.0
Avg $mil: 61,573	

Value Measures		Rel Category
Price/Earnings	17.24	1.02
Price/Book	2.93	1.12
Price/Sales	1.86	1.29
Price/Cash Flow	8.91	1.16
Dividend Yield %	1.81	1.22

Growth Measures	%	Rel Category
Long-Term Erngs	11.27	0.97
Book Value	12.20	1.57
Sales	6.77	1.18
Cash Flow	21.67	2.29
Historical Erngs	12.65	1.07

Profitability	%	Rel Category
Return on Equity	21.60	1.23
Return on Assets	11.56	1.34
Net Margin	12.66	1.11

Sector Weightings	% of Stocks	Rel S&P 500	3 Year High	3 Year Low
Info	21.62	1.01		
Software	4.00	0.93	6	4
Hardware	4.90	0.4[illegible]	6	1
Media	4.25	1.11	5	3
Telecom	8.47	2.69	8	4
Service	50.34	1.09		
Health	13.68	1.09	22	14
Consumer	9.92	1.09	10	7
Business	4.81	1.19	5	4
Financial	21.93	1.06	26	21
Mfg	28.04	0.87		
Goods	8.38	0.90	10	8
Ind Mtrls	11.93	0.94	12	9
Energy	6.55	0.91	7	5
Utilities	1.18	0.40	1	0

Composition

Cash	6.0
Stocks	93.2
Bonds	0.0
Other	0.8
Foreign (% of Stock)	4.4

Morningstar's Take by Christine Benz 10-02-04

Fidelity Growth & Income's appeal is more of a whisper than a shout, but that's what makes it such a fine core holding.

Don't look for this fund to top the charts in big equity-market rallies. In 1999 and again in 2003, as stocks were posting huge gains, the fund's return relative to its large-blend rivals landed in the group's bottom quartile. And while the fund's long-term returns under manager Steve Kaye are solid--besting those of the S&P 500 Index and the typical large-blend fund--they pale alongside those of flashier funds in the category, such as Legg Mason Value or Vanguard Primecap.

We think the fund holds significant appeal, however, particularly when you factor in its very low volatility relative to the typical large-blend fund. Kaye employs a valuation-sensitive approach and favors steady growers over companies operating in more volatile industries. That explains the fund's longtime underweighting of the tech sector relative to the S&P 500 Index. Kaye argues that most tech stocks remain quite overvalued even after their pullback this year, noting that the market isn't adequately factoring into their valuations the sector's extreme cyclicality.

Kaye's valuation-conscious discipline has the added benefit of keeping the fund in the game in sideways-moving markets such as this year's. With many of its rivals in the red for the year to date, this fund ekes into the black. In addition to correctly underweighting the tech sector, Kaye also made a profitable bet on regional Bells earlier this year, predicting that investor pessimism over the companies' prospects had reached an extreme. Top holding Sallie Mae has also been a big winner for the fund.

We also like this fund's prospects in a market that's favorable to the mega-cap stocks that Kaye tends to favor here. That bias has been a headwind for the fund for nearly five years running, but could work to its favor in the future.

This remains a solid core holding.

Address:	82 Devonshire St Boston MA 02109 800-343-3548
Web Address:	www.fidelity.com
Inception:	12-30-85
Advisor:	Fidelity Management & Research Co. (FMR)
Subadvisor:	FMR Co., Inc. (FMRC)
NTF Plans:	Fidelity Retail-NTF, CommonWealth NTF

Minimum Purchase:	$2500	Add: $250	IRA: $2500
Min Auto Inv Plan:	$2500	Add: $100	
Sales Fees:	No-load		
Management Fee:	0.48%		
Actual Fees:	Mgt:0.48%	Dist:	
Expense Projections:	3Yr:$218	5Yr:$379	10Yr:$847
Income Distrib:	Quarterly		

Fidelity Growth Company

Ticker	Load	NAV	Yield	Total Assets	Mstar Category
FDGRX	None	$56.07	0.1%	$25,180 mil	Large Growth

Governance and Management

Fiduciary Grade: B

Portfolio Manager(s)

Steve Wymer has a decade of managerial experience and has put up good overall numbers. Like all Fidelity managers, he receives the support of Fidelity's sizable analyst corps

Strategy

Manager Steve Wymer looks for firms with good growth prospects relative to their valuations. For example, Wymer currently has a number of tech stocks that are growing at a good clip and aren't very dependent on the corporate-IT spending cycle. In addition, the fund is underweighted in financials because he doesn't see much growth potential.

Historical Profile

Return Above Avg
Risk High
Rating ★★★ Neutral

Investment Style
Equity
Stock %

91%	95%	94%	97%	98%	98%	99%	99%	100%

▼ Manager Change
∇ Partial Manager Change

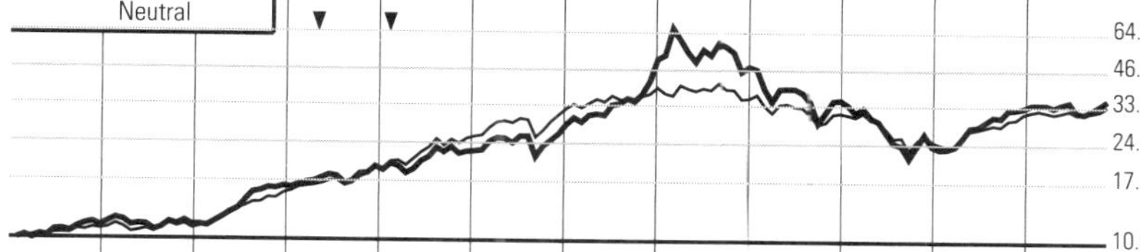

Growth of $10,000
— Investment Values of Fund
— Investment Values of S&P 500

Performance Quartile (within Category)

History

1993	1994	1995	1996	1997	1998	1999	2000	2001	2002	2003	12-04	History
29.06	27.26	36.29	40.46	43.32	51.02	84.30	71.43	53.22	35.42	50.07	56.07	NAV
16.19	-2.22	39.61	16.81	18.91	27.23	79.48	-6.32	-25.31	-33.45	41.36	12.12	Total Return %
6.13	-3.53	2.08	-6.13	-14.44	-1.34	58.44	2.78	-13.43	-11.36	12.69	1.25	+/-S&P 500
13.32	-4.84	2.43	-6.31	-11.58	-11.48	46.32	16.10	-4.89	-5.57	11.61	5.82	+/-Russ 1000Gr
0.25	0.76	0.59	0.78	0.54	0.21	0.00	0.00	0.00	0.00	0.00	0.14	Income Return %
15.94	-2.98	39.02	16.03	18.37	27.02	79.48	-6.32	-25.31	-33.45	41.36	11.98	Capital Return %
25	57	13	71	84	70	5	22	74	87	6	14	Total Rtn % Rank Cat
0.07	0.22	0.16	0.28	0.22	0.09	0.00	0.00	0.00	0.00	0.00	0.07	Income $
2.92	0.92	1.57	1.60	4.35	3.73	6.29	7.50	0.16	0.00	0.00	0.00	Capital Gains $
1.07	1.05	0.95	0.85	0.68	0.63	0.72	0.85	0.95	1.08	0.83	—	Expense Ratio %
0.43	0.64	0.76	0.96	0.54	0.24	-0.11	-0.31	-0.29	-0.38	-0.03	—	Income Ratio %
159	135	97	78	93	76	86	69	93	63	47	—	Turnover Rate %
2,543	2,993	6,279	9,273	10,509	11,440	24,337	30,397	22,742	14,798	22,609	25,180	Net Assets $mil

Performance 12-31-04

	1st Qtr	2nd Qtr	3rd Qtr	4th Qtr	Total
2000	18.78	-8.18	2.71	-16.37	-6.32
2001	-26.49	12.01	-26.04	22.66	-25.31
2002	-6.76	-19.65	-20.54	11.81	-33.45
2003	-0.31	19.31	8.50	9.54	41.36
2004	3.06	2.36	-6.40	13.55	12.12

Trailing	Total Return%	+/- S&P 500	+/- Russ 1000Gr	%Rank Cat	Growth of $10,000
3 Mo	13.55	4.32	4.38	7	11,355
6 Mo	6.29	-0.90	2.82	31	10,629
1 Yr	12.12	1.25	5.82	14	11,212
3 Yr Avg	1.80	-1.78	1.98	26	10,550
5 Yr Avg	-5.89	-3.59	3.40	33	7,382
10 Yr Avg	12.57	0.50	2.98	8	32,676
15 Yr Avg	12.88	1.95	3.38	7	61,554

Tax Analysis	Tax-Adj Rtn%	%Rank Cat	Tax-Cost Rat	%Rank Cat
3 Yr (estimated)	1.78	22	0.02	4
5 Yr (estimated)	-6.29	30	0.43	26
10 Yr (estimated)	11.25	8	1.17	32

Potential Capital Gain Exposure: -5% of assets

Rating and Risk

Time Period	Load-Adj Return %	Morningstar Rtn vs Cat	Morningstar Risk vs Cat	Morningstar Risk-Adj Rating
1 Yr	12.12			
3 Yr	1.80	+Avg	High	★★★
5 Yr	-5.89	Avg	High	★★★
10 Yr	12.57	High	High	★★★
Incept	14.49			

Other Measures	Standard Index S&P 500	Best Fit Index PSE Tech 100
Alpha	-1.7	-2.2
Beta	1.28	0.78
R-Squared	86	95
Standard Deviation	21.43	
Mean	1.80	
Sharpe Ratio	0.02	

Portfolio Analysis 08-31-04

Share change since 05-04 Total Stocks:249	Sector	PE	YTD Ret%	% Assets
⊕ Microsoft	Software	36.1	8.95	3.63
⊖ Pfizer	Health	22.0	-22.31	3.13
⊕ Network Appliance	Hardware	67.5	62.52	2.73
⊕ Qualcomm	Hardware	42.0	58.20	2.38
⊖ UnitedHealth Group	Health	23.8	51.38	2.23
⊕ Celgene	Health	95.6	18.18	2.14
⊕ Sepracor	Health	—	148.10	2.00
Boeing	Ind Mtrls	14.7	24.86	1.92
⊕ Research In Motion Ltd	Hardware	—	146.66	1.50
⊕ Johnson & Johnson	Health	20.6	25.17	1.38
⊖ Coach	Goods	37.4	49.40	1.38
⊖ Gen Elec	Ind Mtrls	22.8	20.68	1.35
Wal-Mart Stores	Consumer	23.4	0.51	1.33
Elan ADR	Health	—	295.50	1.29
Dell	Hardware	34.0	24.01	1.22
⊕ Southwest Airlines	Business	38.5	0.99	1.20
⊖ Yahoo	Media	95.1	67.36	1.09
⊕ Cognizant Technology Sol	Business	62.5	85.50	1.08
⊖ Xilinx	Hardware	25.2	-22.82	1.07
⊕ OSI Pharmaceuticals	Health	—	132.09	1.06

Current Investment Style

Value Blnd Growth / Large Mid Small

Market Cap	%
Giant	30.4
Large	31.1
Mid	28.0
Small	9.0
Micro	1.6
Avg $mil: 15,063	

Value Measures		Rel Category
Price/Earnings	22.18	1.04
Price/Book	3.54	1.10
Price/Sales	1.86	0.87
Price/Cash Flow	10.84	0.99
Dividend Yield %	0.57	0.74

Growth Measures	%	Rel Category
Long-Term Erngs	14.37	1.02
Book Value	7.14	0.56
Sales	5.38	0.63
Cash Flow	22.11	1.34
Historical Erngs	28.68	1.98

Profitability	%	Rel Category
Return on Equity	16.05	0.89
Return on Assets	6.22	0.66
Net Margin	10.54	0.86

Sector Weightings	% of Stocks	Rel S&P 500	3 Year High	3 Year Low
Info	32.92	1.53		
Software	8.84	2.06	11	9
Hardware	21.57	2.11	25	19
Media	1.91	0.50	4	2
Telecom	0.60	0.19	2	1
Service	49.40	1.06		
Health	28.37	2.27	28	22
Consumer	8.90	0.98	12	8
Business	7.70	1.90	8	3
Financial	4.43	0.21	6	4
Mfg	17.68	0.55		
Goods	8.34	0.89	10	8
Ind Mtrls	5.85	0.46	8	5
Energy	3.49	0.49	4	2
Utilities	0.00	0.00	0	0

Composition

Cash	0.3
Stocks	99.5
Bonds	0.0
Other	0.2
Foreign (% of Stock)	4.6

Morningstar's Take by Christine Benz 10-16-04

Fidelity Growth Company has more in its arsenal than many of its similarly aggressive rivals, and that's why we like it.

Unlike many of its siblings, which practice valuation-conscious growth strategies, this fund pushes the pedal to the metal. The portfolio's average price multiples and earnings-growth rates are typically higher than the category norm. Given that profile, the fund shone brightly in 1999's mega-bull tech market, stumbled badly in the bear market, then regained its footing in time to notch a tremendous 41% gain last year.

But unlike rivals that have exhibited a similar performance pattern, this fund isn't strictly reliant on the fortunes of the tech sector. The fund's showing in 2004--it lands around the category's top third for the year to date despite a bruising sell-off in tech-hardware stocks--demonstrates this fact. Although the fund has had roughly 35% of its assets in tech for much of this year, some of manager Steve Wymer's picks within the biotech arena--a longtime area of interest for him--have delivered strong gains. Additionally, steady-growth names such as Wal-Mart and Johnson & Johnson typically ballast Wymer's more-aggressive picks. Finally, it's worth noting that Wymer's stock picks within tech have actually been pretty good this year, with Internet-related names such as Yahoo and Google scoring big gains.

Make no mistake: The fund is still too aggressive to serve as a core holding. In addition, Wymer has long held a sizable percentage of mid-caps and smaller large caps alongside mega-cap names. That smaller-cap bias has been a distinct advantage over the past five years, but could work against it at some point in the future.

Those caveats aside, we still think the fund is a good, aggressive pick for investors who know what they're getting into.

Address:	82 Devonshire St Boston MA 02109 800-343-3548
Web Address:	www.fidelity.com
Inception:	01-17-83
Advisor:	Fidelity Management & Research Co. (FMR)
Subadvisor:	FMR Co., Inc. (FMRC)
NTF Plans:	Fidelity Retail-NTF, CommonWealth NTF

Minimum Purchase:	$2500	Add: $250	IRA: $2500
Min Auto Inv Plan:	$2500	Add: $100	
Sales Fees:	No-load		
Management Fee:	0.58%		
Actual Fees:	Mgt:0.58%	Dist:	
Expense Projections:	3Yr:$237	5Yr:$411	10Yr:$918
Income Distrib:	Annually		

Fidelity High Income

Ticker	Load	NAV	Yield	SEC Yield	Total Assets	Mstar Category
SPHIX	None	$9.09	7.5%	6.02%	$3,114 mil	High Yield Bond

Governance and Management

Fiduciary Grade: B

Portfolio Manager(s)

Fred Hoff took over this portfolio in June 2000 and works with Fidelity's extensive team of research analysts. He started with Fidelity as a high-yield analyst and has managed the high-yield portions of several asset-allocation funds.

Strategy

Manager Fred Hoff invests the bulk of the fund's assets in junk bonds, which offer handsome yields to compensate for their considerable credit risk. Hoff favors companies with strong management that show signs of improving financial situations. He has reined in the fund's risk over the last few years, cutting bonds rated below B and diversifying the portfolio across more issues.

Historical Profile

Return Average
Risk Above Avg
Rating ★★★ Neutral

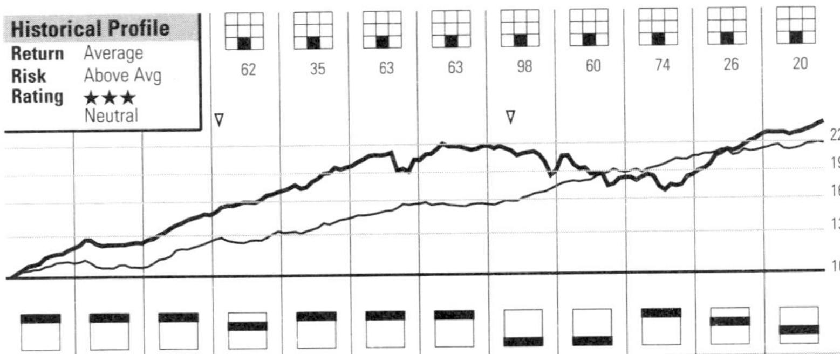

Investment Style: Fixed Income — Income Rtn %Rank Cat: 62, 35, 63, 63, 98, 60, 74, 26, 20

▼ Manager Change
▽ Partial Manager Change

Growth of $10,000 (22.6, 19.0, 16.0, 13.0, 10.0)
▬ Investment Values of Fund
— Investment Values of LB Aggr

Performance Quartile (within Category)

1993	1994	1995	1996	1997	1998	1999	2000	2001	2002	2003	12-04	History
12.17	11.46	12.21	12.54	13.03	12.11	12.00	9.45	8.13	7.60	8.94	9.09	NAV
21.86	3.21	18.53	14.16	15.92	3.30	8.92	-14.20	-4.84	1.48	27.48	9.69	Total Return %
12.11	6.13	0.06	10.53	6.27	-5.39	9.74	-25.83	-13.28	-8.77	23.38	5.35	+/-LB Aggr
2.95	4.18	1.14	1.74	3.29	2.72	5.64	-8.99	-10.62	-1.63	-0.45	-2.27	+/-CSFB Glb HY
10.30	8.56	10.73	9.21	9.33	8.58	8.97	7.27	9.88	8.03	9.38	7.87	Income Return %
11.56	-5.35	7.80	4.95	6.59	-5.28	-0.05	-21.47	-14.72	-6.55	18.10	1.82	Capital Return %
12	1	24	29	7	20	13	89	92	25	28	52	Total Rtn % Rank Cat
1.13	1.00	1.17	1.07	1.11	1.06	1.04	0.84	0.89	0.63	0.69	0.68	Income $
0.79	0.08	0.12	0.25	0.31	0.30	0.14	0.09	0.00	0.00	0.00	0.00	Capital Gains $
0.70	0.75	0.80	0.79	0.80	0.80	0.80	0.74	0.74	0.76	0.79	0.77	Expense Ratio %
9.57	8.07	8.41	8.85	8.51	8.57	9.20	9.85	10.68	10.44	8.82	7.67	Income Ratio %
136	213	172	170	102	85	68	50	55	69	81	84	Turnover Rate %
665	618	1,081	1,717	2,447	2,862	3,262	2,131	1,551	1,741	2,902	3,114	Net Assets $mil

Performance 12-31-04

	1st Qtr	2nd Qtr	3rd Qtr	4th Qtr	Total
2000	-1.88	-3.06	-0.86	-9.02	-14.20
2001	3.30	-5.81	-6.96	5.11	-4.84
2002	0.34	-5.89	0.37	7.08	1.48
2003	6.60	9.68	2.73	6.13	27.48
2004	1.29	-0.27	3.23	5.18	9.69

Trailing	Total Return%	+/- LB Aggr	+/- CSFB Glb HY	%Rank Cat	Growth of $10,000
3 Mo	5.18	4.23	0.62	21	10,518
6 Mo	8.58	4.40	-0.68	51	10,858
1 Yr	9.69	5.35	-2.27	52	10,969
3 Yr Avg	12.37	6.18	-1.51	20	14,189
5 Yr Avg	2.99	-4.72	-5.18	81	11,587
10 Yr Avg	7.42	-0.30	-1.20	27	20,457
15 Yr Avg	—	—	—	—	—

Tax Analysis	Tax-Adj Rtn%	%Rank Cat	Tax-Cost Rat	%Rank Cat
3 Yr (estimated)	9.19	12	2.83	50
5 Yr (estimated)	-0.18	76	3.08	36
10 Yr (estimated)	3.66	20	3.50	60

Potential Capital Gain Exposure: -25% of assets

Rating and Risk

Time Period	Load-Adj Return %	Morningstar Rtn vs Cat	Morningstar Risk vs Cat	Morningstar Risk-Adj Rating
1 Yr	9.69			
3 Yr	12.37	+Avg	Avg	★★★★
5 Yr	2.99	-Avg	+Avg	★★
10 Yr	7.42	+Avg	+Avg	★★★
Incept	10.48			

Other Measures	Standard Index LB Aggr	Best Fit Index CSFB Glb HY
Alpha	10.8	-2.3
Beta	0.07	1.09
R-Squared	0	88
Standard Deviation	8.05	
Mean	12.37	
Sharpe Ratio	1.38	

Portfolio Analysis 10-31-04

Total Fixed-Income:404	Date of Maturity	Amount $000	Value $000	% Net Assets
Ship Fin Intl 8.5%	12-15-13	40,195	40,798	1.35
Ntl Investment Term B 6/	06-13-12	40,000	40,400	1.33
Qwest FRN	06-30-07	37,390	38,839	1.28
Georgia Pac 9.5%	12-01-11	26,433	32,777	1.08
Aes 144A 8.75%	05-15-13	26,680	30,715	1.01
Primedia 7.625%	04-01-08	29,012	29,157	0.96
Csc Hldgs 7.625%	04-01-11	26,375	28,419	0.94
Ahold Fin U S A 8.25%	07-15-10	21,980	25,057	0.83
Cms Engy 7.75%	08-01-10	22,460	24,622	0.81
Celestica 7.875%	07-01-11	22,760	24,126	0.80
Sanmina Sci 10.375%	01-15-10	19,775	23,186	0.77
Invensys 144A 9.875%	03-15-11	22,030	23,021	0.76
Roller Bearing Hldg 144A	06-15-09	22,220	22,664	0.75
Iasis Cap 144A 8.75%	06-15-14	21,020	22,439	0.74
Cms Engy 8.9%	07-15-08	19,995	22,269	0.74
Us Oncology 144A 9%	08-15-12	19,610	21,179	0.70
Semicon Nt Partn Tr 144A	08-04-11	14,535	20,058	0.66
Aes 9.5%	06-01-09	17,342	19,922	0.66
Nextel Comms 7.375%	08-01-15	17,650	19,636	0.65
Allied Waste North Amer	01-01-06	18,965	19,629	0.65

Current Investment Style

Duration: Short Int Long — Quality: High Med Low

¹ figure provided by fund

Avg Eff Duration¹	—
Avg Eff Maturity	—
Avg Credit Quality	—
Avg Wtd Coupon	7.68%
Avg Wtd Price	103.58% of par

Coupon Range	% of Bonds	Rel Cat
0% PIK	7.5	1.6
0% to 8%	51.1	1.3
8% to 11%	46.0	0.8
11% to 14%	2.8	0.4
More than 14%	0.0	0.0

1.00=Category Average

Credit Analysis		% bonds 10-31-04	
US Govt	—	BB	—
AAA	—	B	—
AA	—	Below B	—
A	—	NR/NA	—
BBB	—		

Sector Breakdown	% of assets
US Treasuries	0
TIPS	0
US Agency	0
Mortgage Pass-Throughs	0
Mortgage CMO	0
Mortgage ARM	0
US Corporate	79
Asset-Backed	4
Convertible	0
Municipal	0
Corporate Inflation-Protected	0
Foreign Corporate	4
Foreign Govt	0

Composition			
Cash	12.1	Bonds	84.6
Stocks	1.4	Other	2.0

Special Securities	
Restricted/Illiquid Secs	20
Exotic Mortgage-Backed	0
Emerging-Markets Secs	0
Options/Futures/Warrants	No

Morningstar's Take by Scott Berry 11-12-04

We like what Fidelity High Income brings to the table.

This fund boasts a number of sustainable advantages. For starters, few firms dedicate more resources to their high-yield bond effort than Fidelity. Manager Fred Hoff is backed by 14 high-yield analysts and traders who comb the junk-bond market for opportunities while monitoring current holdings for signs of trouble. The group hasn't prevented the fund from hitting a few bumps in the road, but we see its depth as a long-term advantage. The fund also benefits from its built-in expense advantage. The fund isn't the cheapest in the high-yield category, but its 0.77% expense ratio provides the fund an edge over its average no-load category peer, which charges 0.94%.

The fund's advantages have helped Hoff, who took over the portfolio in mid-2000, to get this fund back on track. Hoff inherited a risky portfolio that was saddled with a number of troubled issues. It took him time to rework the fund into a more mainstream high-yield offering, but his efforts have largely paid off. The fund started showing signs of improvement in late 2001 and early 2002, and its three-year trailing return now ranks in the category's best quartile.

The fund's performance has been a bit sluggish in 2004 but not enough to cause concern. Hoff has positioned the fund rather defensively in recent months by holding floating-rate bank debt and some added cash. Both have held the fund back, but both should offer some protection for the fund if the interest rates move higher or if the high-yield bond market slumps. And although the fund lands in the category's bottom half for the year to date through Nov. 11, it has underperformed its average peer by just a narrow margin.

This fund hasn't stood out recently, but it has definite sustainable advantages. We think those advantages, along with Hoff's attention to risk, will pay off for long-term high-yield bond investors.

Address:	82 Devonshire St Boston MA 02109 800-343-3548
Web Address:	www.fidelity.com
Inception:	08-29-90
Advisor:	Fidelity Management & Research Co. (FMR)
Subadvisor:	FMR Co., Inc. (FMRC)
NTF Plans:	Fidelity Retail-NTF, CommonWealth NTF

Minimum Purchase:	$2500	Add: $250	IRA: $2500
Min Auto Inv Plan:	$2500	Add: $100	
Sales Fees:	No-load, 1.00%R		
Management Fee:	0.58%		
Actual Fees:	Mgt:0.58%	Dist:	
Expense Projections:	3Yr:$240	5Yr:$417	10Yr:$930
Income Distrib:	Monthly		

Fidelity Independence

Ticker	Load	NAV	Yield	Total Assets	Mstar Category
FDFFX	None	$17.83	0.6%	$4,705 mil	Large Growth

Governance and Management

Fiduciary Grade: B

Portfolio Manager(s)

Jason Weiner took over for Fergus Shiel in April 2003 following relatively successful stints at Fidelity OTC and Fidelity Discovery. Before leading those offerings, Weiner managed Fidelity Export & Multinational as well as sector funds such as Fidelity Select Air Transportation and Fidelity Select Computers. Weiner also manages the more concentrated Fidelity Fifty.

Strategy

Manager Jason Weiner, who took over for the departed Fergus Shiel in April 2003, pursues a bottom-up, stock-picking strategy, generally homing in on reasonably priced shares of companies with improving fundamentals and the potential for peer-besting rates of earnings growth. Turnaround stories will sometimes get his attention, too.

Historical Profile

Return Above Avg
Risk Above Avg
Rating ★★★ Neutral

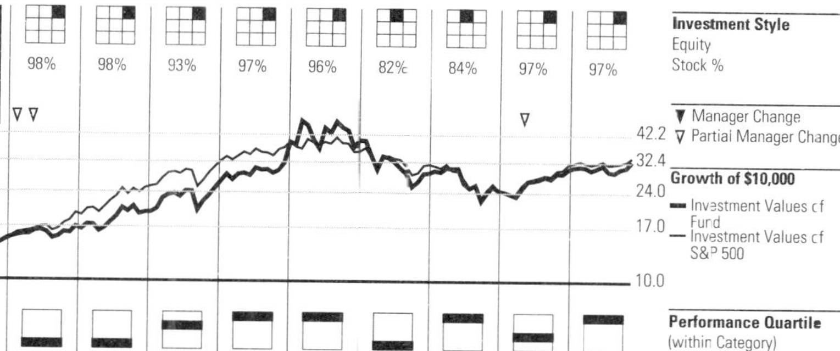

1993	1994	1995	1996	1997	1998	1999	2000	2001	2002	2003	12-04	History
18.14	16.24	18.19	17.29	16.85	20.51	25.85	22.01	15.77	13.07	16.06	17.83	NAV
22.13	0.06	24.28	8.33	18.54	35.89	47.03	1.70	-27.22	-15.82	23.66	11.65	Total Return %
12.07	-1.25	-13.25	-14.61	-14.81	7.32	25.99	10.80	-15.34	6.27	-5.01	0.78	+/-S&P 500
19.26	-2.56	-12.90	-14.79	-11.95	-2.82	13.87	24.12	-6.80	12.06	-6.09	5.35	+/-Russ 1000Gr
0.85	1.22	2.18	1.44	0.75	0.83	0.25	0.31	0.91	1.33	0.77	0.62	Income Return %
21.28	-1.16	22.10	6.89	17.79	35.06	46.78	1.39	-28.13	-17.15	22.89	11.03	Capital Return %
11	31	88	98	85	33	24	6	73	4	75	17	Total Rtn % Rank Cat
0.14	0.22	0.35	0.26	0.13	0.14	0.05	0.08	0.20	0.21	0.10	0.10	Income $
1.75	1.68	1.58	2.15	3.41	2.13	3.66	4.19	0.03	0.00	0.00	0.00	Capital Gains $
1.05	1.07	0.99	0.70	0.59	0.57	0.58	0.85	0.92	0.97	0.55	—	Expense Ratio %
0.80	1.13	1.92	1.26	0.66	0.68	0.25	0.19	0.95	1.41	1.00	—	Income Ratio %
101	72	108	230	205	266	310	249	187	191	166	—	Turnover Rate %
2,848	3,185	4,072	4,046	3,932	4,946	7,268	8,474	5,486	4,240	4,726	4,705	Net Assets $mil

Performance 12-31-04

	1st Qtr	2nd Qtr	3rd Qtr	4th Qtr	Total
2000	17.53	-2.52	0.54	-11.71	1.70
2001	-24.86	7.46	-21.28	14.49	-27.22
2002	5.14	-13.99	-15.78	10.53	-15.82
2003	-5.51	16.92	1.87	9.88	23.66
2004	1.93	2.02	-3.47	11.24	11.65

Trailing	Total Return%	+/- S&P 500	+/- Russ 1000Gr	%Rank Cat	Growth of $10,000
3 Mo	11.24	2.01	2.07	26	11,124
6 Mo	7.38	0.19	3.91	19	10,738
1 Yr	11.65	0.78	5.35	17	11,165
3 Yr Avg	5.14	1.56	5.32	9	11,623
5 Yr Avg	-2.96	-0.66	6.33	14	8,605
10 Yr Avg	10.62	-1.45	1.03	27	27,437
15 Yr Avg	11.10	0.17	1.60	23	48,497

Tax Analysis	Tax-Adj Rtn%	%Rank Cat	Tax-Cost Rat	%Rank Cat
3 Yr (estimated)	4.78	8	0.34	59
5 Yr (estimated)	-4.22	17	1.30	72
10 Yr (estimated)	7.62	43	2.71	95

Potential Capital Gain Exposure: -21% of assets

Rating and Risk

Time Period	Load-Adj Return %	Morningstar Rtn vs Cat	Morningstar Risk vs Cat	Morningstar Risk-Adj Rating
1 Yr	11.65			
3 Yr	5.14	High	+Avg	★★★★
5 Yr	-2.96	+Avg	High	★★★
10 Yr	10.62	+Avg	+Avg	★★★
Incept	13.33			

Other Measures	Standard Index S&P 500	Best Fit Index Russ 1000
Alpha	1.8	1.0
Beta	1.04	1.06
R-Squared	81	83
Standard Deviation	18.31	
Mean	5.14	
Sharpe Ratio	0.21	

Portfolio Analysis 08-31-04

Share change since 05-04 Total Stocks:149	Sector	PE	YTD Ret%	% Assets
⊕ Microsoft	Software	36.1	8.95	4.23
⊖ Pfizer	Health	22.0	-22.31	3.47
⊖ Clear Channel Communicat	Media	23.5	-27.57	2.39
Vodafone Group PLC ADR	Telecom	—	11.74	2.35
⊕ Carniva	Goods	26.2	46.74	2.29
⊕ Seagate Technology	Hardware	22.3	-5.50	2.13
First Data	Business	13.8	3.72	2.10
⊖ Crown Castle Internation	Telecom	—	50.86	1.97
⊕ Siebel Systems	Software	43.4	-24.64	1.97
⊖ BJ Services	Energy	21.8	30.07	1.87
⊕ American Express	Financial	20.3	17.60	1.74
⊖ Yahoo	Media	95.1	67.36	1.63
⊕ Ceridian	Business	22.1	-12.70	1.53
⊖ Tyco International	Ind Mtrls	25.1	35.41	1.52
⊕ Infosys Technologies Ltd	Software	—	—	1.51
⊖ Cisco Systems	Hardware	24.5	-20.26	1.46
⊖ Biogen IDEC	Health	—	81.50	1.36
⊖ American International G	Financial	16.2	-0.53	1.27
⊕ Kerzner International	Consumer	24.5	54.13	1.23
⊖ Viacom B	Media	36.1	-17.44	1.23

Current Investment Style

Value Blnd Growth / Large Mid Small

Market Cap	%
Giant	28.4
Large	26.0
Mid	35.7
Small	9.4
Micro	0.5
Avg $mil: 13,065	

Value Measures		Rel Category
Price/Earnings	21.51	1.01
Price/Book	2.35	0.73
Price/Sales	1.87	0.87
Price/Cash Flow	10.55	0.96
Dividend Yield %	0.56	0.73

Growth Measures	%	Rel Category
Long-Term Erngs	14.10	1.00
Book Value	9.46	0.74
Sales	6.84	0.80
Cash Flow	22.83	1.38
Historical Erngs	28.48	1.97

Profitability	%	Rel Category
Return on Equity	13.41	0.75
Return on Assets	7.52	0.80
Net Margin	7.91	0.64

Sector Weightings	% of Stocks	Rel S&P 500	3 Year High	3 Year Low
Info	29.63	1.38		
Software	9.53	2.22	10	0
Hardware	7.11	0.70	17	1
Media	7.51	1.96	18	8
Telecom	5.48	1.74	11	0
Service	47.19	1.02		
Health	19.91	1.59	20	2
Consumer	7.34	0.81	9	6
Business	12.18	3.01	12	7
Financial	7.76	0.37	24	7
Mfg	23.19	0.72		
Goods	5.17	0.55	33	3
Ind Mtrls	14.06	1.11	15	6
Energy	3.96	0.55	9	1
Utilities	0.00	0.00	2	0

Composition

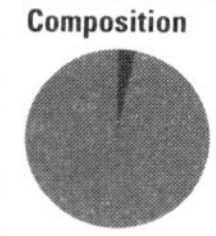

Cash	3.3
Stocks	96.5
Bonds	0.0
Other	0.2
Foreign (% of Stock)	12.0

Morningstar's Take by Andrew Gogerty 10-14-04

Fidelity Independence is showing signs of life, but investors should be aware of its risks.

After a poor showing relative to its large-growth peers in 2003, this fund is back on track in 2004. Its slight 0.1% loss through Oct. 13, 2004, tops 80% of its category rivals. The fund has benefited from an increased stake in natural resources, as iron-ore miners BHP Billiton and Companhia Vale Do Rio Doce have helped to buoy returns this year.

Manager Jason Weiner, who took over in April 2003, looks for companies with strong earnings potential that are trading at reasonable valuations. He also takes full advantage of the fund's flexibility to make sector- and stock-specific bets. Weiner has increased the fund's media stake to 10% of assets this year, double that of its typical rival, believing that the sector has strong growth potential. Still, top-holding Clear Channel has posted a stinging double-digit loss, even as Yahoo has jumped 52% thus far in 2004.

In fact, the fund has a potential boom-or-bust style under Weiner. While his sector and stock bets may not pay off immediately, the fund's turnover (currently 166%) indicates he might not wait for them to bear fruit anyway. As such, this approach could lead to heightened volatility should Weiner's picks be out of step with the market. This was the case in 2003, when biases toward technology and health-care stocks held the fund back.

Moreover, although Weiner has done relatively well at his former charges, he hasn't been great. So we're not ready to give our full endorsement here until Weiner can distinguish himself from other, more proven options. Analyst Pick and sibling Fidelity Capital Appreciation, for example, boasts a tested manager and stronger long-term returns.

Address:	82 Devonshire St Boston MA 02109 800-343-3548
Web Address:	www.fidelity.com
Inception:	03-25-83
Advisor:	Fidelity Management & Research Co. (FMR)
Subadvisor:	FMR Co., Inc. (FMRC)
NTF Plans:	Fidelity Retail-NTF, CommonWealth NTF

Minimum Purchase:	$2500	Add: $250	IRA: $2500
Min Auto Inv Plan:	$2500	Add: $100	
Sales Fees:	No-load		
Management Fee:	0.41%		
Actual Fees:	Mgt:0.41%	Dist:	
Expense Projections:	3Yr:$202	5Yr:$351	10Yr:$786
Income Distrib:	Annually		

Fidelity Inflation-Protec

Ticker	Load	NAV	Yield	SEC Yield	Total Assets	Mstar Category
FINPX	None	$11.41	1.3%	1.01%	$1,317 mil	Intermediate Government

Governance and Management

Fiduciary Grade: B

Portfolio Manager(s)

William Irving worked as a quantitative fixed-income analyst before taking over this portfolio from Thomas Silvia, who became the head of Fidelity's bond-fund effort, in late 2004. He is backed by Fidelity's considerable research capabilities. Irving also took over Fidelity Ginnie Mae effective Nov. 1, 2004.

Strategy

This fund sticks exclusively with U.S. Government Treasury Inflation-Protected Securities (commonly referred to as TIPS). Although management will fix the fund's overall risk characteristics--including interest-rate sensitivity--to that of an index, it will shift among different maturities depending on which of those appear cheap or expensive at a given time. The fund will also buy TIPS through forward contracts and invest the cash needed to back those purchases in ultra-short-term bonds.

Historical Profile

Return
Risk
Rating Not Rated

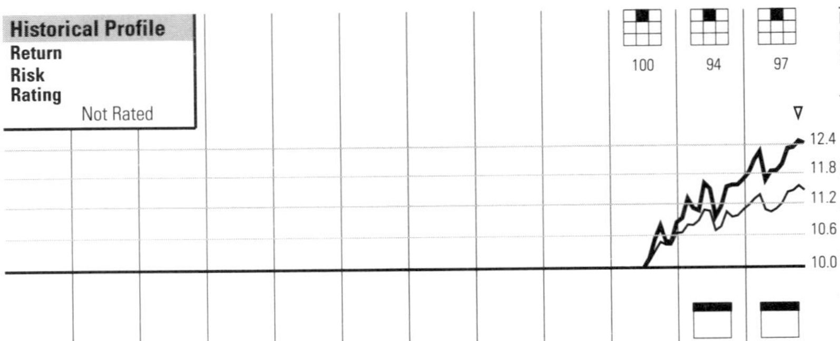

Investment Style
Fixed Income
Income Rtn %Rank Cat

▼ Manager Change
▽ Partial Manager Change

Growth of $10,000
— Investment Values of Fund
— Investment Values of LB Aggr

Performance Quartile (within Category)

History

1993	1994	1995	1996	1997	1998	1999	2000	2001	2002	2003	12-04	History
—	—	—	—	—	—	—	—	—	10.63	11.01	11.41	NAV
—	—	—	—	—	—	—	—	—	7.93*	7.75	8.24	Total Return %
—	—	—	—	—	—	—	—	—	—	3.65	3.90	+/-LB Aggr
—	—	—	—	—	—	—	—	—	—	5.39	4.76	+/-LB Govt
—	—	—	—	—	—	—	—	—	0.00	1.69	1.43	Income Return %
—	—	—	—	—	—	—	—	—	—	6.06	6.81	Capital Return %
—	—	—	—	—	—	—	—	—	—	3	3	Total Rtn % Rank Cat
—	—	—	—	—	—	—	—	—	0.11	0.18	0.16	Income $
—	—	—	—	—	—	—	—	—	0.05	0.26	0.34	Capital Gains $
—	—	—	—	—	—	—	—	—	0.50	0.50	0.50	Expense Ratio %
—	—	—	—	—	—	—	—	—	4.04	4.04	3.09	Income Ratio %
—	—	—	—	—	—	—	—	—	211	211	117	Turnover Rate %
—	—	—	—	—	—	—	—	—	398	724	1,317	Net Assets $mil

Performance 12-31-04

	1st Qtr	2nd Qtr	3rd Qtr	4th Qtr	Total
2000	—	—	—	—	—
2001	—	—	—	—	—
2002	—	—	7.68	0.52	7.93 *
2003	2.51	3.45	0.31	1.29	7.75
2004	4.90	-3.26	4.09	2.47	8.24

Trailing	Total Return%	+/- LB Aggr	+/- LB Govt	%Rank Cat	Growth of $10,000
3 Mo	2.47	1.52	1.98	3	10,247
6 Mo	6.66	2.48	3.05	1	10,666
1 Yr	8.24	3.90	4.76	3	10,824
3 Yr Avg	—	—	—	—	—
5 Yr Avg	—	—	—	—	—
10 Yr Avg	—	—	—	—	—
15 Yr Avg	—	—	—	—	—

Tax Analysis	Tax-Adj Rtn%	%Rank Cat	Tax-Cost Rat	%Rank Cat
3 Yr (estimated)	—	—	—	—
5 Yr (estimated)	—	—	—	—
10 Yr (estimated)	—	—	—	—

Potential Capital Gain Exposure: 4% of assets

Rating and Risk

Time Period	Load-Adj Return %	Morningstar Rtn vs Cat	Morningstar Risk vs Cat	Morningstar Risk-Adj Rating
1 Yr	8.24			
3 Yr	—	—	—	—
5 Yr	—	—	—	—
10 Yr	—	—	—	—
Incept	9.58			

Other Measures	Standard Index LB Aggr	Best Fit Index
Alpha	—	—
Beta	—	—
R-Squared	—	—
Standard Deviation	—	
Mean	—	
Sharpe Ratio	—	

Morningstar's Take by Eric Jacobson 01-07-05

For most TIPS investors, Fidelity Inflation Protected Securities is all that's needed.

If bells and whistles are your thing, this isn't your fund. There are other offerings that focus mostly on inflation-protected Treasuries but also employ additional tools to try and juice up their returns. And to be sure, there are successes among them. No matter how good those funds may be, however, there's no getting around the fact that by going beyond the TIPS universe, they run the risk of, if nothing else, not keeping pace with the broad TIPS market if others of their bets go awry.

By contrast, this is one of many plain-vanilla TIPS offerings. With the exception of some short-term bonds used mostly to sop up cash, this fund sticks exclusively with U.S. government-issued inflation-indexed bonds. In fact, one might say this fund takes things a step further. Although manager Bill Irving (who took over for the recently promoted Tom Silvia) does look to help bolster returns by over- or underweighting different bonds along the maturity spectrum, he does so sparingly. Following Fidelity protocol, meanwhile, he attempts to generally match the rate sensitivity of the Lehman Brothers TIPS index.

Clearly, the goal here is to try to at least match the returns of the index, with some attempt to outpace the bogy, using fairly targeted, low-risk bets. And though in some situations we might take issue with such a low-impact approach, it makes sense here. One reason is that despite lingering supply and demand imbalances that are quickly disappearing, there are only a handful of TIPS issues in the market, making bold moves difficult and potentially record wrecking. On the other hand, bolder players generally are so because they have no choice. That's because many rivals are priced so richly that the only way to compete is to take on more risk in the hope of jacking up returns. That's just not necessary for this fairly priced offering.

Portfolio Analysis 10-31-04

Total Fixed-Income:548	Date of Maturity	Amount $000	Value $000	% Net Assets
US Treasury Note 3%	07-15-12	214,400	252,963	15.60
US Treasury Bond 3.625%	04-15-28	140,300	209,150	12.90
US Treasury Note 1.875%	07-15-13	164,000	174,146	10.74
US Treasury Note 2%	01-15-14	162,000	172,215	10.62
US Treasury Note 3.875%	01-15-09	125,000	163,865	10.11
US Treasury Note 4.25%	01-15-10	107,000	141,253	8.71
US Treasury Note 3.5%	01-15-11	102,065	127,126	7.84
US Treasury Bond 2.375%	01-15-25	118,900	125,036	7.71
US Treasury Note 2%	07-15-14	89,600	93,182	5.75
US Treasury Note 3.625%	01-15-08	27,100	35,062	2.16
Bk One Oneseries 2002-2c	05-15-08	773	777	0.05
Sears Cr Acct Mstr Tr 20	08-15-09	719	721	0.04
Mbna Master Cc Tr Ii 200	01-15-09	656	658	0.04
Mbna Master Cc Tr Ii 200	10-15-08	648	650	0.04
Sears Cr Acct Mstr Tr 20	11-15-09	648	650	0.04
FNMA 6.25%	03-22-12	583	592	0.04
Sears Cr Acct Mstr Tr 20	08-15-09	583	584	0.04
Abs FRN	09-25-34	557	557	0.03
Americredit Auto Rec Tr	06-06-09	540	546	0.03
Long Beach Mtg Ln Tr 200	03-25-32	540	545	0.03

Current Investment Style

Duration: Short Int Long
Quality: High Med Low

¹ figure provided by fund

Avg Eff Duration¹	5.7 Yrs
Avg Eff Maturity	9.9 Yrs
Avg Credit Quality	AAA
Avg Wtd Coupon	2.98%
Avg Wtd Price	120.25% of par

Coupon Range	% of Bonds	Rel Cat
0% PIK	0.2	0.0
0% to 6%	99.6	1.3
6% to 8%	0.4	0.0
8% to 10%	0.0	0.0
More than 10%	0.0	0.0

1.00=Category Average

Credit Analysis	% bonds 10-31-04		
US Govt	95	BB	0
AAA	2	B	0
AA	1	Below B	0
A	1	NR/NA	0
BBB	1		

Sector Breakdown	% of assets
US Treasuries	13
TIPS	79
US Agency	0
Mortgage Pass-Throughs	0
Mortgage CMO	2
Mortgage ARM	0
US Corporate	0
Asset-Backed	3
Convertible	0
Municipal	0
Corporate Inflation-Protected	0
Foreign Corporate	0
Foreign Govt	0

Composition			
Cash	3.1	Bonds	96.9
Stocks	0.0	Other	0.0

Special Securities	
Restricted/Illiquid Secs	Trace
Exotic Mortgage-Backed	0
Emerging-Markets Secs	0
Options/Futures/Warrants	No

Address:	82 Devonshire St Boston MA 02109 800-343-3548
Web Address:	www.fidelity.com
Inception:	06-26-02 *
Advisor:	Fidelity Management & Research Co. (FMR)
Subadvisor:	Fidelity Intl Invest Advisors (U.K.) Ltd
NTF Plans:	Fidelity Retail-NTF, Fidelity Instl-NTF

Minimum Purchase:	$2500	Add: $500	IRA: $2500
Min Auto Inv Plan:	$100	Add: $100	
Sales Fees:	No-load		
Management Fee:	0.43%		
Actual Fees:	Mgt:0.43%	Dist: —	
Expense Projections:	3Yr: —	5Yr: —	10Yr: —
Income Distrib:	Monthly		

Fidelity Interm Bond

Ticker	Load	NAV	Yield	SEC Yield	Total Assets	Mstar Category
FTHRX	None	$10.52	3.5%	3.10%	$7,184 mil	Intermediate-Term Bond

Governance and Management

Fiduciary Grade: B

Portfolio Manager(s)

Manager Ford O'Neil has managed this fund since spring 1998. He works on Fidelity's intermediate-term/aggregate-bond team with a credit analyst, a quantitative analyst, a trader, and one other portfolio manager. O'Neil has also had success managing Fidelity U.S. Bond Index and will soon succeed Kevin Grant as manager of Fidelity Total Bond.

Strategy

Like all Fidelity bond funds, this offering eschews interest-rate bets. Manager Ford O'Neil ties the fund's duration that of the Lehman Brothers Intermediate Government/Credit Index. He tries to beat the index with a combination of sector plays, yield-curve positioning, and individual security selection. The fund's neutral mix is roughly 40% corporate bonds, 40% Treasury bonds, and 20% agency issues.

Historical Profile

Return Average
Risk Below Avg
Rating ★★★ Neutral

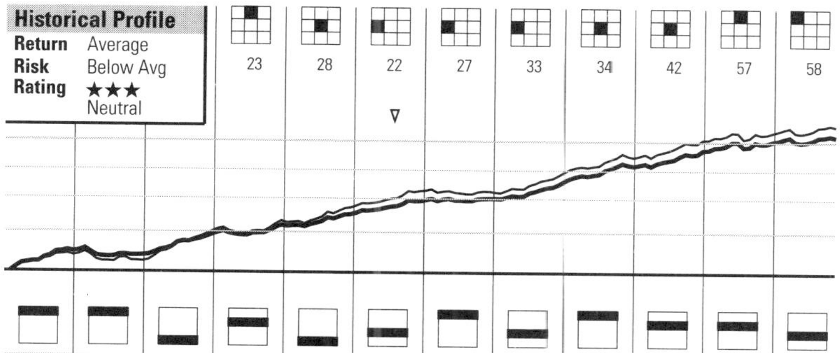

Investment Style
Fixed Income
Income Rtn %Rank Cat

History

1993	1994	1995	1996	1997	1998	1999	2000	2001	2002	2003	12-04	History
10.78	9.83	10.41	10.08	10.17	10.27	9.76	10.04	10.32	10.73	10.66	10.52	NAV
11.96	-2.01	12.81	3.65	7.57	7.32	0.96	9.75	8.83	9.16	4.96	3.20	Total Return %
2.21	0.91	-5.66	0.02	-2.08	-1.37	1.78	-1.88	0.39	-1.09	0.86	-1.14	+/-LB Aggr
-0.28	2.50	-8.62	0.96	-1.86	-2.82	3.84	-2.69	0.01	-3.87	-1.01	-2.10	+/-LB 5-10YR
7.50	6.16	6.57	6.53	6.61	6.32	6.06	6.71	6.01	5.05	3.76	3.51	Income Return %
4.46	-8.17	6.24	-2.88	0.96	1.00	-5.10	3.04	2.82	4.11	1.20	-0.31	Capital Return %
24	9	96	34	85	60	7	59	15	32	36	71	Total Rtn % Rank Cat
0.75	0.64	0.63	0.66	0.65	0.62	0.61	0.64	0.59	0.51	0.39	0.37	Income $
0.09	0.09	0.02	0.03	0.00	0.00	0.00	0.00	0.00	0.00	0.20	0.11	Capital Gains $
0.61	0.64	0.68	0.71	0.69	0.65	0.65	0.65	0.63	0.63	0.64	0.61	Expense Ratio %
7.44	6.88	6.31	6.48	6.46	6.37	6.00	4.93	6.45	5.44	4.47	3.48	Income Ratio %
51	81	75	169	116	90	108	102	73	78	117	120	Turnover Rate %
1,840	2,127	2,821	3,080	3,193	3,444	3,254	3,469	4,808	6,248	6,901	7,184	Net Assets $mil

Performance 12-31-04

	1st Qtr	2nd Qtr	3rd Qtr	4th Qtr	Total
2000	1.52	1.64	2.79	3.48	9.75
2001	3.38	0.69	4.48	0.06	8.83
2002	-0.01	3.15	3.86	1.91	9.16
2003	1.73	2.88	-0.13	0.41	4.96
2004	2.39	-2.43	2.72	0.57	3.20

Trailing	Total Return%	+/- LB Aggr	+/- LB 5-10YR	%Rank Cat	Growth of $10,000
3 Mo	0.57	-0.38	-0.41	80	10,057
6 Mo	3.30	-0.88	-2.27	78	10,330
1 Yr	3.20	-1.14	-2.10	71	10,320
3 Yr Avg	5.75	-0.44	-2.30	39	11,826
5 Yr Avg	7.15	-0.56	-1.92	38	14,124
10 Yr Avg	6.77	-0.95	-1.69	58	19,253
15 Yr Avg	7.00	-0.70	-1.32	63	27,590

Tax Analysis	Tax-Adj Rtn%	%Rank Cat	Tax-Cost Rat	%Rank Cat
3 Yr (estimated)	4.00	29	1.65	49
5 Yr (estimated)	5.07	28	1.94	48
10 Yr (estimated)	4.42	50	2.20	52

Potential Capital Gain Exposure: 1% of assets

Rating and Risk

Time Period	Load-Adj Return %	Morningstar Rtn vs Cat	Morningstar Risk vs Cat	Morningstar Risk-Adj Rating
1 Yr	3.20			
3 Yr	5.75	Avg	-Avg	★★★★
5 Yr	7.15	Avg	-Avg	★★★
10 Yr	6.77	Avg	Low	★★★
Incept	8.75			

Other Measures	Standard Index LB Aggr	Best Fit Index LB 5-10YR
Alpha	0.1	0.4
Beta	0.88	0.59
R-Squared	97	98
Standard Deviation	4.03	
Mean	5.75	
Sharpe Ratio	1.10	

Morningstar's Take by Scott Berry 10-28-04

Fidelity Intermediate Bond is Fidelity's most popular bond fund for good reason.

With roughly $7 billion in assets, this fund is the big toe in Fidelity's bond fund lineup. Large asset bases can at times hamper stock funds, as we've seen with Fidelity Magellan, but the same can't be said for most bond funds. In fact, in recent years, this fund has delivered some of its best relative returns since the early 1980s. Unlike Magellan and other stock funds that can be forced to become more indexlike with their purchases of larger and more-liquid stocks, bond funds can differentiate themselves through more-macro tools, such as sector allocation and yield-curve positioning (the fund's mix of short- and long-term bonds).

Those methods have helped this fund more than keep pace with its average peer over the long term, while its muted interest-rate risk has kept volatility to a minimum. In early 2004, for example, the fund's asset-backed and mortgage-backed securities performed well, while its relatively short duration (a measure of interest-rate sensitivity) provided some cushion against rising rates. With rates dipping lower more recently, the fund's year-to-date ranking has slipped a bit, but its three- and five-year trailing returns continue to rank in the category's best third.

The fund's solid returns and below-average volatility make it an appealing choice, but its skilled management and reasonable expense ratio provide the sustainable advantages that we look for in recommending a fund. Fidelity's bond group has proven itself over the years and continues to devote resources to improving its research capabilities and its overall investment process. Meanwhile, the fund's large size allows it to charge an expense ratio of just 0.61%, which provides the fund a built-in head start each year over its average no-load category peer.

We think this fund has all the tools to remain successful and think bond investors should consider it one of their better options.

Address:	82 Devonshire St Boston MA 02109 800-343-3548
Web Address:	www.fidelity.com
Inception:	05-23-75
Advisor:	Fidelity Management & Research Co. (FMR)
Subadvisor:	Fidelity Intl Invest Advisors (U.K.) Ltd
NTF Plans:	Fidelity Retail-NTF, CommonWealth NTF

Minimum Purchase:	$2500	Add: $250	IRA: $2500
Min Auto Inv Plan:	$2500	Add: $100	
Sales Fees:	No-load		
Management Fee:	0.43%		
Actual Fees:	Mgt:0.43%	Dist:	
Expense Projections:	3Yr:$214	5Yr:$373	10Yr:$835
Income Distrib:	Monthly		

Portfolio Analysis 10-31-04

Total Fixed-Income:928	Date of Maturity	Amount $000	Value $000	% Net Assets
US Treasury Note 3.125%	04-15-09	542,170	540,709	6.61
US Treasury Note 3.125%	05-15-07	482,615	487,516	5.96
Cssw Swap Irs 10/22/06 3	10-22-06	355,000	354,737	4.33
FNMA 0.06%	04-01-18	174,915	181,425	2.22
US Treasury Bond 12%	08-15-13	115,350	151,843	1.85
FNMA 6.25%	02-01-11	127,730	141,822	1.73
US Treasury Note 2%	01-15-14	120,000	127,567	1.56
FNMA 0.06%	02-01-32	107,681	113,453	1.39
FNMA 3 125%	03-16-09	110,800	108,328	1.32
FHLMC 0.04%	11-18-19	100,000	98,219	1.20
FNMA 0 05%	06-01-18	91,864	93,880	1.15
FNMA 2 5%	06-15-06	73,500	73,322	0.90
FNMA 0 06%	04-01-12	56,032	59,454	0.73
FNMA 6%	05-15-11	47,960	53,377	0.65
General Elec Cap 6%	06-15-12	44,700	49,078	0.60
FNMA 5 5%	03-15-11	44,645	48,417	0.59
GNMA 0.07%	05-15-32	41,115	43,906	0.54
Ford Motor Cr 7%	10-01-13	35,000	36,962	0.45
Petronas Cap 144A 7%	05-22-12	29,400	33,901	0.41
Bellsouth 5.2%	09-15-14	32,925	33,588	0.41

Current Investment Style

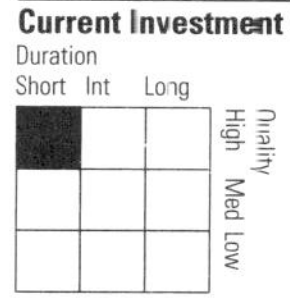

[1] figure provided by fund

Avg Eff Duration[1]	3.4 Yrs
Avg Eff Maturity	4.0 Yrs
Avg Credit Quality	AA
Avg Wtd Coupon	4.00%
Avg Wtd Price	103.30% of par

Coupon Range	% of Bonds	Rel Cat
0% PIK	6.7	1.7
0% to 6%	71.7	1.1
6% to 8%	24.2	0.8
8% to 10%	1.9	0.3
More than 10%	2.2	1.9

1.00=Category Average

Credit Analysis	% bonds 10-31-04		
US Govt	36	BB	1
AAA	13	B	0
AA	7	Below B	0
A	17	NR/NA	7
BBB	19		

Sector Breakdown	% of assets
US Treasuries	15
TIPS	2
US Agency	7
Mortgage Pass-Throughs	8
Mortgage CMO	12
Mortgage ARM	0
US Corporate	29
Asset-Backed	11
Convertible	0
Municipal	0
Corporate Inflation-Protected	0
Foreign Corporate	1
Foreign Govt	0

Composition			
Cash	14.1	Bonds	85.9
Stocks	0.0	Other	0.0

Special Securities	
Restricted/Illiquid Secs	4
Exotic Mortgage-Backed	1
Emerging-Markets Secs	0
Options/Futures/Warrants	No

Fidelity Interm Govt

Ticker	Load	NAV	Yield	SEC Yield	Total Assets	Mstar Category
FSTGX	None	$10.24	2.9%	3.04%	$941 mil	Intermediate Government

Governance and Management

Fiduciary Grade: B

Portfolio Manager(s)

George Fischer replaced Andrew Dudley in June 2002. Fischer is a Fidelity veteran and works closely here with Dudley, who is still with Fidelity as manager of Fidelity Short-Term Bond, and William Irving, manager of Fidelity Ginnie Mae and Fidelity Inflation-Protected Bond. Fischer also manages Fidelity Government Income and Fidelity Spartan Government Income.

Strategy

This fund follows the standard Fidelity formula. George Fischer abstains from interest-rate bets and keeps the fund's duration (a measure of interest-rate sensitivity) tied to that of the Lehman Brothers Intermediate Government Index. Within this framework, he makes moderate sector bets, moving among mortgage-backed securities, agency bonds, and Treasuries.

Historical Profile

Return: Average
Risk: Average
Rating: ★★★ Neutral

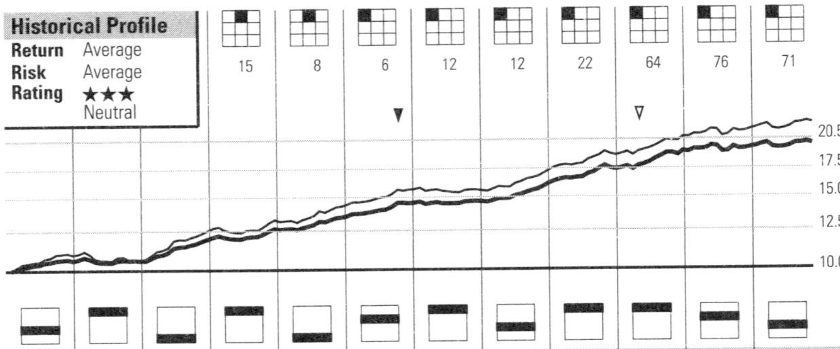

Investment Style: Fixed Income, Income Rtn %Rank Cat

▼ Manager Change
▽ Partial Manager Change

Growth of $10,000
— Investment Values of Fund
— Investment Values of LB Aggr

Performance Quartile (within Category)

1993	1994	1995	1996	1997	1998	1999	2000	2001	2002	2003	12-04	History
10.00	9.35	10.00	9.74	9.78	9.85	9.31	9.62	9.81	10.38	10.29	10.24	NAV
6.42	-0.95	13.93	4.14	7.69	7.45	0.64	10.33	7.93	10.23	1.92	2.40	Total Return %
-3.33	1.97	-4.54	0.51	-1.96	-1.24	1.46	-1.30	-0.51	-0.02	-2.18	-1.94	+/-LB Aggr
-4.24	2.43	-4.41	1.37	-1.90	-2.40	2.87	-2.91	0.70	-1.27	-0.44	-1.08	+/-LB Govt
5.88	5.70	6.79	6.74	7.24	6.74	6.27	6.81	5.94	4.27	2.81	2.89	Income Return %
0.54	-6.65	7.14	-2.60	0.45	0.71	-5.63	3.52	1.99	5.96	-0.89	-0.49	Capital Return %
75	5	87	17	86	49	15	73	13	25	42	75	Total Rtn % Rank Cat
0.58	0.56	0.62	0.65	0.68	0.64	0.60	0.62	0.56	0.41	0.29	0.29	Income $
0.23	0.00	0.00	0.00	0.00	0.00	0.00	0.00	0.00	0.00	0.00	0.00	Capital Gains $
0.65	0.65	0.65	0.62	0.54	0.38	0.53	0.63	0.60	0.59	0.60	0.60	Expense Ratio %
8.05	7.37	7.18	6.89	6.96	6.65	6.58	6.67	6.34	4.63	3.18	2.67	Income Ratio %
324	391	210	105	105	188	117	66	114	145	229	152	Turnover Rate %
1,357	831	830	713	758	760	820	766	918	1,367	1,116	941	Net Assets $mil

Performance 12-31-04

	1st Qtr	2nd Qtr	3rd Qtr	4th Qtr	Total
2000	1.52	1.74	2.74	3.97	10.33
2001	2.81	0.50	4.81	-0.34	7.93
2002	-0.10	3.96	5.04	1.05	10.23
2003	0.97	1.65	-0.40	-0.30	1.92
2004	2.25	-2.41	2.32	0.29	2.40

Trailing	Total Return%	+/- LB Aggr	+/- LB Govt	%Rank Cat	Growth of $10,000
3 Mo	0.29	-0.66	-0.20	85	10,029
6 Mo	2.62	-1.56	-0.99	80	10,262
1 Yr	2.40	-1.94	-1.08	75	10,240
3 Yr Avg	4.78	-1.41	-0.92	39	11,504
5 Yr Avg	6.50	-1.21	-0.98	38	13,701
10 Yr Avg	6.59	-1.13	-0.87	45	18,931
15 Yr Avg	6.52	-1.18	-0.96	64	25,791

Tax Analysis	Tax-Adj Rtn%	%Rank Cat	Tax-Cost Rat	%Rank Cat
3 Yr (estimated)	3.55	16	1.17	22
5 Yr (estimated)	4.73	20	1.66	42
10 Yr (estimated)	4.34	31	2.11	59

Potential Capital Gain Exposure: -3% of assets

Rating and Risk

Time Period	Load-Adj Return %	Morningstar Rtn vs Cat	Morningstar Risk vs Cat	Morningstar Risk-Adj Rating
1 Yr	2.40			
3 Yr	4.78	Avg	Avg	★★★
5 Yr	6.50	Avg	Avg	★★★
10 Yr	6.59	Avg	-Avg	★★★
Incept	6.69			

Other Measures	Standard Index LB Aggr	Best Fit Index LB Interm Tr
Alpha	-1.0	0.1
Beta	0.92	1.08
R-Squared	94	98
Standard Deviation	4.24	
Mean	4.78	
Sharpe Ratio	0.81	

Morningstar's Take by Scott Berry 12-22-04

Investors shouldn't dismiss this fund based on its middling recent results.

Fidelity Intermediate Government typically carries less interest-rate risk than its average intermediate-term government peer. That muted rate sensitivity can provide some protection for the portfolio when interest rates move higher, as they did in July 2003 and April 2004. But it can hamper returns when rates move lower or even when they stay flat, given that longer-term, more-rate-sensitive bonds tend to offer more yield than shorter-term issues. When rates plunged in 2000, for example, this fund underperformed more than 70% of its category peers. And though rates aren't far off their early-year levels, the fund has struggled to keep pace in 2004 as well.

The fund's short duration (a measure of interest-rate sensitivity) isn't a bet by manager George Fischer that rates will move lower but simply reflects the fund's chosen benchmark index, the Lehman Brothers Intermediate Government Bond Index. Fischer keeps duration closely tied to the index, while looking to add value through issue selection and sector allocation.

The fund's measured approach helps keep wild performance swings to a minimum, while its below-average expense ratio and skilled management give it an edge over many of its category peers. The fund's 0.60% expense ratio provides it a slight advantage over its average no-load competitor (0.68%), while Fidelity's deep research capabilities aid Fischer in his effort to uncover opportunities overlooked by others.

This fund may not pack as big a punch as its average category peer, but we think it's an appealing choice. Its muted interest-rate risk should offer some protection if rates rise in the near term. Meanwhile, its steady approach and built-in expense advantage should help it remain more than competitive with its average peer over the long run.

Portfolio Analysis 10-31-04

Total Fixed-Income:111	Date of Maturity	Amount $000	Value $000	% Net Assets
US Treasury Note 5.625%	05-15-08	125,116	136,240	13.36
US Treasury Note 3.625%	07-15-09	88,985	90,407	8.86
FHLMC 2.375%	04-15-06	67,125	66,906	6.56
FNMA 6%	05-15-11	55,860	62,170	6.10
FHLMC 2.875%	12-15-06	40,070	40,106	3.93
FNMA 5.5%	03-15-11	33,295	36,108	3.54
FHLMC 2.75%	10-15-06	28,780	28,760	2.82
FHLMC 4.375%	02-04-10	27,660	27,744	2.72
US Treasury Note 4.75%	05-15-14	23,950	25,323	2.48
US Treasury Note 2.75%	07-31-06	21,650	21,751	2.13
US Treasury Note 2%	01-15-14	20,000	21,261	2.08
FNMA 4.625%	10-15-14	20,000	20,158	1.98
FNMA 2.375%	12-15-05	20,000	19,979	1.96
FNMA 0.04%	11-01-19	20,000	19,625	1.92
Israel St U S Govt Gtd N	02-15-08	18,370	19,384	1.90
US Treasury Note 3.875%	05-15-09	18,000	18,506	1.81
Cssw Swap Irs 2/15/07 3m	02-15-07	18,045	18,055	1.77
FHLBA 5.8%	09-02-08	16,625	18,050	1.77
FHLMC 3.625%	09-15-08	17,391	17,579	1.72
FNMA 5.125%	01-02-14	16,000	16,439	1.61

Current Investment Style

Duration: Short Int Long; Quality: High Med Low

[1] figure provided by fund

Avg Eff Duration[1]	3.4 Yrs
Avg Eff Maturity	3.9 Yrs
Avg Credit Quality	AAA
Avg Wtd Coupon	4.15%
Avg Wtd Price	104.27% of par

Coupon Range	% of Bonds	Rel Cat
0% PIK	1.9	0.4
0% to 6%	91.5	1.2
6% to 8%	7.9	0.4
8% to 10%	0.6	0.3
More than 10%	0.1	0.1

1.00=Category Average

Credit Analysis		% bonds 10-31-04	
US Govt	96	BB	0
AAA	0	B	0
AA	0	Below B	0
A	0	NR/NA	4
BBB	0		

Sector Breakdown	% of assets
US Treasuries	31
TIPS	2
US Agency	43
Mortgage Pass-Throughs	7
Mortgage CMO	5
Mortgage ARM	0
US Corporate	3
Asset-Backed	1
Convertible	0
Municipal	0
Corporate Inflation-Protected	0
Foreign Corporate	0
Foreign Govt	0

Composition			
Cash	8.4	Bonds	91.6
Stocks	0.0	Other	0.0

Special Securities	
Restricted/Illiquid Secs	0
Exotic Mortgage-Backed	—
Emerging-Markets Secs	0
Options/Futures/Warrants	No

Address:	82 Devonshire St Boston MA 02109 800-343-3548
Web Address:	www.fidelity.com
Inception:	05-02-88
Advisor:	Fidelity Management & Research Co. (FMR)
Subadvisor:	Fidelity Intl Invest Advisors (U.K.) Ltd
NTF Plans:	Fidelity Retail-NTF, CommonWealth NTF

Minimum Purchase:	$2500	Add: $250	IRA: $2500
Min Auto Inv Plan:	$100	Add: $100	
Sales Fees:	No-load		
Management Fee:	0.65%		
Actual Fees:	Mgt:0.43%	Dist:	
Expense Projections:	3Yr:$192	5Yr:$335	10Yr:$750
Income Distrib:	Monthly		

Fidelity Intl Disc

Ticker	Load	NAV	Yield	Total Assets	Mstar Category
FIGRX	None	$28.20	0.5%	$2,504 mil	Foreign Large Blend

Governance and Management

Fiduciary Grade: B

Portfolio Manager(s)

In October 2004, William Kennedy replaced Penelope Dobkin, who had run the fund since April 2001, as its new manager. Kennedy had done a good job running Fidelity Pacific Basin for many years. He also managed Fidelity Advisor Japan for two years beginning in 2000 and served as director of equity research in Fidelity's Hong Kong office prior to that. He can call on the research of a large stable of Fidelity analysts

Strategy

This fund used to put a sizable chunk of its assets in bonds, but it's now a pure equity offering. Previous manager Penelope Dobkin, who was replaced in October 2004 by William Kennedy, looked around the globe for companies with decent growth prospects and reasonable prices. Most of the portfolio was in large companies, but it had a healthy amount of mid-caps, too. Kennedy is likely to use a similar style.

Historical Profile

Return: High
Risk: Above Avg
Rating: ★★★★★ Highest

Investment Style: Equity Stock %

66% 66% 88% 90% 92% 86% 87% 93% 95%

▼ Manager Change
▽ Partial Manager Change

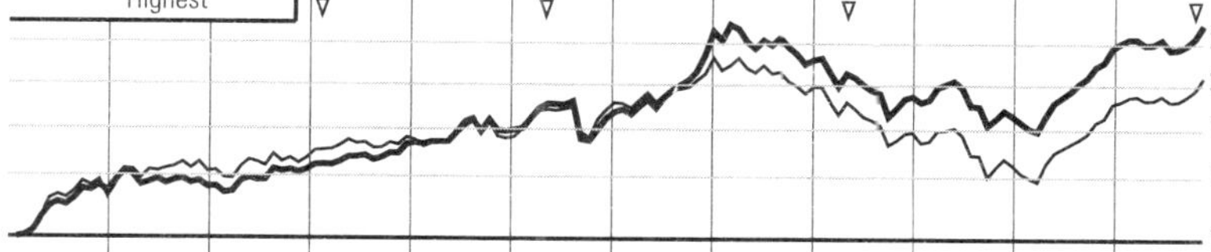

Growth of $10,000
- Investment Values of Fund
- Investment Values of MSCI EAFE

Performance Quartile (within Category)

History

1993	1994	1995	1996	1997	1998	1999	2000	2001	2002	2003	12-04	History
17.57	16.53	17.95	19.55	19.70	20.91	30.10	22.72	18.76	16.82	23.92	28.20	NAV
35.08	-2.87	12.23	12.69	7.12	9.98	53.71	-14.06	-17.43	-9.87	43.34	19.05	Total Return %
2.52	-10.65	1.02	6.64	5.34	-9.95	26.68	0.13	3.99	6.07	4.75	-1.20	+/-MSCI EAFE
2.87	-10.22	0.82	5.82	4.85	-8.71	25.73	-0.70	3.96	5.93	3.92	-1.33	+/-MSCI Wd xUS
0.46	0.00	3.63	1.62	1.89	0.46	1.58	1.69	0.00	0.48	1.07	0.63	Income Return %
34.62	-2.87	8.60	11.07	5.23	9.52	52.13	-15.75	-17.43	-10.35	42.27	18.42	Capital Return %
42	74	40	46	45	77	16	31	12	5	3	32	Total Rtn % Rank Cat
0.06	0.00	0.60	0.29	0.37	0.09	0.33	0.51	0.00	0.09	0.18	0.15	Income $
0.05	0.53	0.00	0.37	0.88	0.63	1.50	2.66	0.00	0.00	0.00	0.12	Capital Gains $
1.52	1.21	1.18	1.14	1.15	1.13	1.10	1.05	1.09	1.12	1.11	1.06	Expense Ratio %
0.87	2.16	2.98	2.76	2.33	1.62	0.69	0.63	0.91	0.59	1.08	0.92	Income Ratio %
24	173	141	95	70	143	94	104	81	63	81	87	Turnover Rate %
1,068	1,273	942	1,080	1,030	871	1,395	1,183	941	907	1,498	2,504	Net Assets $mil

Performance 12-31-04

	1st Qtr	2nd Qtr	3rd Qtr	4th Qtr	Total
2000	1.30	-5.81	-3.55	-6.61	-14.06
2001	-13.03	1.01	-15.58	11.34	-17.43
2002	4.74	-0.20	-18.00	5.16	-9.87
2003	-7.85	20.06	10.80	16.92	43.34
2004	5.10	-0.36	-2.71	16.85	19.05

Trailing	Total Return%	+/- MSCI EAFE	+/- MSCI Wd xUS	%Rank Cat	Growth of $10,000
3 Mo	16.85	1.53	1.70	3	11,685
6 Mo	13.68	-1.32	-1.69	59	11,368
1 Yr	19.05	-1.20	-1.33	32	11,905
3 Yr Avg	15.43	3.54	3.21	3	15,380
5 Yr Avg	1.77	2.90	2.53	5	10,917
10 Yr Avg	9.59	3.97	3.65	9	24,987
15 Yr Avg	8.32	4.09	3.91	14	33,161

Tax Analysis	Tax-Adj Rtn%	%Rank Cat	Tax-Cost Rat	%Rank Cat
3 Yr (estimated)	15.18	3	0.22	24
5 Yr (estimated)	1.05	5	0.71	47
10 Yr (estimated)	8.47	7	1.02	40

Potential Capital Gain Exposure: 21% of assets

Rating and Risk

Time Period	Load-Adj Return %	Morningstar Rtn vs Cat	Morningstar Risk vs Cat	Morningstar Risk-Adj Rating
1 Yr	19.05			
3 Yr	15.43	High	Avg	★★★★★
5 Yr	1.77	High	+Avg	★★★★★
10 Yr	9.59	High	+Avg	★★★★★
Incept	9.07			

Other Measures	Standard Index S&P 500	Best Fit Index MSCI Wd xUS
Alpha	3.7	3.3
Beta	0.95	0.96
R-Squared	96	96

Standard Deviation	17.44
Mean	15.43
Sharpe Ratio	0.81

Morningstar's Take by Gregg Wolper 11-27-04

Fidelity International Discovery's name change makes sense, but its manager change raises some questions.

This offering had been called Fidelity International Growth & Income, but its new moniker is more appropriate. Years ago, the fund had an income bent, but in recent years it has put little emphasis on providing income. Instead, under former manager Penelope Dobkin, who took the reins in April 2001, it has used a broad-ranging, growth-at-a-reasonable-price approach. Thus, the new name--which had been proposed for shareholder approval in the summer, along with the removal of income as an objective--is not intended to signal a new direction.

A more significant change, though, has also taken place. On Oct. 4, 2004, Fidelity took Dobkin off of this fund and reassigned her to Fidelity Advisor Diversified International, where she replaced Bill Bower. The new manager here at Fidelity International Discovery is William Kennedy, who had been manager of Fidelity Pacific Basin.

Kennedy has solid credentials in his area. He joined Fidelity as an analyst in 1994, had run Pacific Basin since 1998 (save for a one-year hiatus that ended in September 2003), and made that fund one of the better choices in its category. His GARP approach fits this fund's style. However, except for his work organizing a global sector-research group during his hiatus, his focus has been on Asia. This fund has roughly two thirds of its assets in Europe.

Kennedy may well prove a fine leader here. But given that his specialty is Asia and that this fund had flourished under Dobkin's direction--it landed in the foreign large-blend category's top quartile in 2001, 2002, and 2003--it's tough to argue that the fund is as appealing now as it was before the manager change.

Portfolio Analysis 10-31-04

Share change since 07-04 Total Stocks:229	Sector	Country	% Assets
⊖ BP PLC ADR	Energy	U.K.	2.97
⊕ TOTAL	Energy	France	2.33
Vodafone Grp	Telecom	U.K.	2.17
⊕ HSBC Hldgs	Financial	U.K.	1.90
⊕ Allianz	Financial	Germany	1.68
⊕ Deutsche Telekom AG ADR	Telecom	Germany	1.53
⊖ Shell Transport & Tradin	Energy	U.K.	1.44
⊕ Roche Holding	Health	Switzerland	1.36
Novartis	Health	Switzerland	1.32
⊕ ENI SpA ADR	Energy	Italy	1.13
☼ Nikkei 225 Fut	—	—	1.11
BNP Paribas	Financial	France	1.05
Danske Bank Grp	Financial	Denmark	1.04
⊕ Toyota Motor	Goods	Japan	1.02
⊕ UBS	Financial	Switzerland	0.95
France Telecom SA ADR	Telecom	France	0.92
⊖ Nestle	Goods	Switzerland	0.91
Vivendi Universal ADR	Media	France	0.83
Hypo Real Estate Holding	Financial	Germany	0.82
☼ BHP Billiton Ltd	Ind Mtrls	Australia	0.82

Current Investment Style (Value Blnd Growth; Large Mid Small)

Market Cap	%
Giant	45.4
Large	25.1
Mid	24.5
Small	4.9
Micro	0.0
Avg $mil: 14,960	

Value Measures		Rel Category
Price/Earnings	14.10	1.03
Price/Book	1.65	0.92
Price/Sales	0.88	0.97
Price/Cash Flow	4.64	0.94
Dividend Yield %	2.72	1.07

Growth Measures	%	Rel Category
Long-Term Erngs	12.40	1.15
Book Value	-0.72	NMF
Sales	3.74	1.50
Cash Flow	-1.83	NMF
Historical Erngs	2.47	0.44

Composition			
Cash	3.2	Bonds	0.0
Stocks	94.5	Other	2.3
Foreign (% of Stock)			99.0

Sector Weightings	% of Stocks	Rel MSCI EAFE	3 Year High	3 Year Low
Info	19.95	1.20		
Software	1.13	1.05	2	1
Hardware	3.42	0.94	11	3
Media	4.96	2.18	5	4
Telecom	10.44	1.09	11	4
Service	47.40	1.06		
Health	8.58	1.18	12	9
Consumer	7.59	1.51	8	3
Business	5.05	0.93	6	4
Financial	26.18	0.97	28	22
Mfg	32.65	0.84		
Goods	13.38	0.98	16	10
Ind Mtrls	7.30	0.59	11	5
Energy	9.26	1.26	14	6
Utilities	2.71	0.51	3	2

Regional Exposure	% Stock		
UK/W. Europe	70	N. America	1
Japan	14	Latn America	1
Asia X Japan	13	Other	1

Country Exposure	% Stock		
U.K.	18	Germany	11
Japan	14	Switzerland	8
France	12		

Address:	82 Devonshire St Boston MA 02109 800-343-3548
Web Address:	www.fidelity.com
Inception:	12-31-86
Advisor:	Fidelity Management & Research Co. (FMR)
Subadvisor:	FMR Co., Inc. (FMRC)
NTF Plans:	Fidelity Retail-NTF, CommonWealth NTF

Minimum Purchase:	$2500	Add: $250	IRA: $2500
Min Auto Inv Plan:	$2500	Add: $100	
Sales Fees:	No-load		
Management Fee:	0.73%		
Actual Fees:	Mgt:0.73%	Dist:	
Expense Projections:	3Yr:$359	5Yr:$622	10Yr:$1375
Income Distrib:	Annually		

Fidelity Intl Sm Cp

Ticker	Load	NAV	Yield	Total Assets	Mstar Category
FISMX	None	$23.28	0.3%	$1,412 mil	Foreign Small/Mid Growth

Governance and Management

Fiduciary Grade: B

Portfolio Manager(s)

Ben Paton has been at Fidelity since 1995 and Tokuya Sano since 1993, and both have worked as analysts. Sano has been on board since this fund's 2002 inception, but Paton joined the fund in early 2004 after European-based skipper L.C. Kvaal left Fidelity. This is the first time that either manager has run a public, U.S.-based fund.

Strategy

Managers Ben Paton and Tokuya Sano run a portion of assets independently. Paton focuses on European names while Sano invests in Asian stocks. Previous Europe manager L.C. Kvaal's strategy was best described as growth-at-a-reasonable-price, although it isn't clear whether Paton will alter that approach. Sector and regional bets are possible.

Historical Profile

Return
Risk
Rating Not Rated

Investment Style: Equity Stock % — 90% (2002), 85% (2003), 92% (12-04)

▼ Manager Change
▽ Partial Manager Change

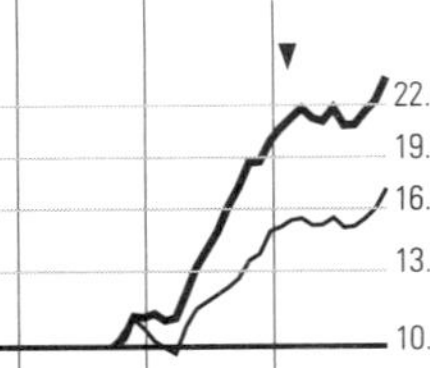

Growth of $10,000
▬ Investment Values of Fund
— Investment Values of MSCI EAFE

Performance Quartile (within Category)

1993	1994	1995	1996	1997	1998	1999	2000	2001	2002	2003	12-04	History
—	—	—	—	—	—	—	—	—	10.55	18.67	23.28	NAV
—	—	—	—	—	—	—	—	—	5.70*	80.25	29.43	Total Return %
—	—	—	—	—	—	—	—	—	—	41.66	9.18	+/-MSCI EAFE
—	—	—	—	—	—	—	—	—	—	40.83	9.05	+/-MSCI Wd xUS
—	—	—	—	—	—	—	—	—	0.00	0.19	0.32	Income Return %
—	—	—	—	—	—	—	—	—	—	80.06	29.11	Capital Return %
—	—	—	—	—	—	—	—	—	—	5	25	Total Rtn % Rank Cat
—	—	—	—	—	—	—	—	—	0.00	0.02	0.06	Income $
—	—	—	—	—	—	—	—	—	0.02	0.31	0.77	Capital Gains $
—	—	—	—	—	—	—	—	—	1.80	1.51	1.28	Expense Ratio %
—	—	—	—	—	—	—	—	—	-0.56	0.46	0.50	Income Ratio %
—	—	—	—	—	—	—	—	—	85	84	77	Turnover Rate %
—	—	—	—	—	—	—	—	—	16	748	1,412	Net Assets $mil

Performance 12-31-04

	1st Qtr	2nd Qtr	3rd Qtr	4th Qtr	Total
2000	—	—	—	—	—
2001	—	—	—	—	—
2002	—	—	—	10.45	5.70 *
2003	-0.19	26.02	23.06	16.45	80.25
2004	11.62	0.10	-1.34	17.42	29.43

Trailing	Total Return%	+/- MSCI EAFE	+/- MSCI Wd xUS	%Rank Cat	Growth of $10,000
3 Mo	17.42	2.10	2.27	25	11,742
6 Mo	15.84	0.84	0.47	41	11,584
1 Yr	29.43	9.18	9.05	25	12,943
3 Yr Avg	—	—	—	—	—
5 Yr Avg	—	—	—	—	—
10 Yr Avg	—	—	—	—	—
15 Yr Avg	—	—	—	—	—

Tax Analysis	Tax-Adj Rtn%	%Rank Cat	Tax-Cost Rat	%Rank Cat
3 Yr (estimated)	—	—	—	—
5 Yr (estimated)	—	—	—	—
10 Yr (estimated)	—	—	—	—

Potential Capital Gain Exposure: 24% of assets

Rating and Risk

Time Period	Load-Adj Return %	Morningstar Rtn vs Cat	Morningstar Risk vs Cat	Morningstar Risk-Adj Rating
1 Yr	29.43			
3 Yr	—	—	—	—
5 Yr	—	—	—	—
10 Yr	—	—	—	—
Incept	48.41			

Other Measures	Standard Index S&P 500	Best Fit Index
Alpha	—	—
Beta	—	—
R-Squared	—	—
Standard Deviation	—	
Mean	—	
Sharpe Ratio	—	

Portfolio Analysis 10-31-04

Share change since 04-04 Total Stocks:413	Sector	Country	% Assets
⊖ Steinhoff International	Goods	South Africa	1.85
☼ K+S Grp	Ind Mtrls	Germany	1.58
United Grp Ltd	Business	Australia	1.55
☼ Hikari Tsushin	Telecom	Japan	1.49
⊕ Orascom Tel Hldg	—	Egypt	1.43
⊕ Freenet.de	Business	Germany	1.40
⊕ Pfleiderer	Ind Mtrls	Germany	1.31
⊖ Bluescope Steel Ltd	Ind Mtrls	Australia	1.31
⊖ Stolt-Nielsen Sa	Business	Norway	1.24
Centennial Coal	Ind Mtrls	Australia	1.18
⊖ QBE Insurance Grp Ltd	Financial	Australia	1.14
☼ Lottomatica	Consumer	Italy	1.04
⊕ NOK	Goods	Japan	1.02
Nissin Kogyo	Ind Mtrls	Japan	1.00
⊖ Boral Ltd	Ind Mtrls	Australia	0.98
Nihon Dempa Kogyo	Hardware	Japan	0.97
☼ Kobe Steel, Ltd	Ind Mtrls	Japan	0.89
☼ Pkn Orlen	Energy	Poland	0.88
Toyo Ink Mfg.	Ind Mtrls	Japan	0.85
⊕ FAITH, INC.	Software	Japan	0.83

Current Investment Style

Market Cap	%
Giant	0.8
Large	16.3
Mid	36.3
Small	28.8
Micro	17.8
Avg $mil: 942	

Value Measures		Rel Category
Price/Earnings	14.11	1.02
Price/Book	2.08	1.09
Price/Sales	0.78	0.95
Price/Cash Flow	5.25	1.05
Dividend Yield %	2.72	1.20

Growth Measures	%	Rel Category
Long-Term Erngs	164.16	3.55
Book Value	-3.95	NMF
Sales	4.56	0.73
Cash Flow	5.70	1.23
Historical Erngs	11.88	1.28

Composition

Cash	2.6	Bonds	0.0
Stocks	91.7	Other	5.7
Foreign (% of Stock)			97.7

Sector Weightings	% of Stocks	Rel MSCI EAFE	3 Year High	Low
Info	16.22	0.98		
Software	3.94	3.65	5	3
Hardware	4.57	1.25	9	5
Media	3.53	1.55	5	3
Telecom	4.18	0.44	8	0
Service	38.90	0.87		
Health	7.13	0.98	14	6
Consumer	8.45	1.68	13	7
Business	11.34	2.08	14	11
Financial	11.98	0.44	14	12
Mfg	44.88	1.16		
Goods	11.76	0.86	17	12
Ind Mtrls	27.57	2.24	28	18
Energy	4.70	0.64	5	0
Utilities	0.85	0.16	1	0

Regional Exposure (% Stock)

UK/W. Europe	44	N. America	3
Japan	30	Latn America	1
Asia X Japan	15	Other	7

Country Exposure (% Stock)

Japan	30	Germany	9
U.K.	15	Norway	3
Australia	10		

Morningstar's Take by Bridget Hughes 12-02-04

Fidelity International Small Cap isn't in fighting shape.

For a fund family that's as research-intensive as Fidelity, you want its stock-picking on display. That's particularly true for inefficient slices of the market where research can really pay off. With this fund, it's tough to see that happening any time soon, and that's a shame, considering the international small-cap markets it fishes are about as inefficient as they come.

The problem is that the fund grew too big too quickly. Just over two years old, the offering is currently home to $1.2 billion. As a result, the portfolio now owns more than 400 stocks, up from fewer than 150 when the fund was launched. Top holdings thus generally consume no more than 1% of assets, while nearly 300 names get no more than one fourth of a percentage point (0.25%). That means a lot of stocks have to be going right to outperform. And each one of those many names requires continual research and monitoring.

So far the fund's bulk hasn't affected returns. In 2003, its 80.3% gain landed well in the foreign small/mid-growth category's best decile; through Dec. 1, 2004, its 24.4% advance also ranks in the group's top decile. But things could get more difficult because international small caps have been performing well as a group, particularly compared with large caps, for at least four years running. While the diffuse portfolio means it could prove a defensive option in a small-cap downturn, it could also make it harder for the fund to shine in a soberer environment.

It's possible that once investor inflows taper off, the managers could tighten up the portfolio, as they'll have more time to move slowly into and out of small caps, which can be very illiquid. (The managers weren't available for comment.) We think a smaller portfolio would better show off Fidelity's research talent. Meantime, Fidelity should close the fund, particularly if inflows continue at a rapid pace.

Address:	82 Devonshire St Boston MA 02109 800-343-3548
Web Address:	www.fidelity.com
Inception:	09-18-02 *
Advisor:	Fidelity Management & Research Co. (FMR)
Subadvisor:	FMR Co., Inc. (FMRC)
NTF Plans:	Fidelity Retail-NTF, CommonWealth NTF

Minimum Purchase:	$2500	Add: $250	IRA: $2500
Min Auto Inv Plan:	$100	Add: $100	
Sales Fees:	No-load, 2.00%R		
Management Fee:	0.88%		
Actual Fees:	Mgt:0.88%	Dist:	
Expense Projections:	3Yr:$486	5Yr:$839	10Yr:$1834
Income Distrib:	Annually		

Fidelity Invt Grade Bond

Ticker	Load	NAV	Yield	SEC Yield	Total Assets	Mstar Category
FBNDX	None	$7.53	3.3%	3.18%	$6,283 mil	Intermediate-Term Bond

Governance and Management

Fiduciary Grade: B

Portfolio Manager(s)

Kevin Grant has done a fine job with this charge since taking over in early 1997, but his tenure is near its end. Jeffrey Moore will take over here when Grant retires at the end of 2004. Moore manages the investment-grade bond portions of Fidelity's Asset Manager portfolios. He has managed bond portfolios at Fidelity since 2000.

Strategy

This fund is a plain-vanilla intermediate-term bond offering. Management avoids interest-rate bets by keeping the interest-rate sensitivity in line with its benchmark, while trying to add value with sector rotation and yield-curve plays. The fund holds a diversified mix of corporate bonds, Treasuries, and agency issues. Its benchmark is the Lehman Brothers Aggregate Bond Index, the bond market equivalent of the Standard & Poors 500.

Historical Profile

Return Above Avg
Risk Average
Rating ★★★★ Above Avg

Investment Style: Fixed Income — Income Rtn %Rank Cat

22	32	44	38	32	46	70	76	61

▼ Manager Change
▽ Partial Manager Change

Growth of $10,000
— Investment Values of Fund
— Investment Values of LB Aggr

Performance Quartile (within Category)

1993	1994	1995	1996	1997	1998	1999	2000	2001	2002	2003	12-04	History
7.89	6.85	7.38	7.12	7.28	7.39	6.89	7.16	7.34	7.57	7.55	7.53	NAV
16.23	-5.35	15.51	3.02	8.91	7.94	-1.01	10.84	8.54	9.37	4.67	4.53	Total Return %
6.48	-2.43	-2.96	-0.61	-0.74	-0.75	-0.19	-0.79	0.10	-0.88	0.57	0.19	+/-LB Aggr
3.99	-0.84	-5.92	0.33	-0.52	-2.20	1.87	-1.60	-0.28	-3.66	-1.30	-0.77	+/-LB 5-10YR
7.97	6.67	7.08	6.53	6.53	5.97	5.92	6.72	5.86	4.43	3.23	3.43	Income Return %
8.26	-12.02	8.43	-3.51	2.38	1.97	-6.93	4.12	2.68	4.94	1.44	1.10	Capital Return %
1	83	80	56	53	39	42	33	19	27	40	24	Total Rtn % Rank Cat
0.56	0.50	0.47	0.47	0.45	0.42	0.43	0.45	0.41	0.32	0.24	0.25	Income $
0.00	0.12	0.03	0.00	0.00	0.03	0.00	0.00	0.01	0.12	0.13	0.10	Capital Gains $
0.68	0.74	0.75	0.76	0.75	0.71	0.70	0.69	0.64	0.66	0.66	0.63	Expense Ratio %
7.74	6.94	7.00	6.58	6.53	6.12	5.77	6.21	6.31	5.18	3.86	3.16	Income Ratio %
74	61	90	134	120	207	167	115	225	230	276	238	Turnover Rate %
1,042	995	1,246	1,455	1,650	2,191	2,079	2,497	3,702	4,767	5,523	6,283	Net Assets $mil

Performance 12-31-04

	1st Qtr	2nd Qtr	3rd Qtr	4th Qtr	Total
2000	2.20	1.48	2.96	3.80	10.84
2001	2.96	0.47	4.60	0.32	8.54
2002	-0.20	2.83	4.07	2.41	9.37
2003	1.74	2.58	0.01	0.28	4.67
2004	2.59	-2.36	3.25	1.07	4.53

Trailing	Total Return%	+/- LB Aggr	+/- LB 5-10YR	%Rank Cat	Growth of $10,000
3 Mo	1.07	0.12	0.09	37	10,107
6 Mo	4.36	0.18	-1.21	28	10,436
1 Yr	4.53	0.19	-0.77	24	10,453
3 Yr Avg	6.17	-0.02	-1.88	23	11,968
5 Yr Avg	7.56	-0.15	-1.51	19	14,396
10 Yr Avg	7.14	-0.58	-1.32	39	19,930
15 Yr Avg	7.59	-0.11	-0.73	28	29,963

Tax Analysis	Tax-Adj Rtn%	%Rank Cat	Tax-Cost Rat	%Rank Cat
3 Yr (estimated)	4.32	18	1.74	56
5 Yr (estimated)	5.42	13	1.99	53
10 Yr (estimated)	4.75	31	2.23	55

Potential Capital Gain Exposure: 2% of assets

Rating and Risk

Time Period	Load-Adj Return %	Morningstar Rtn vs Cat	Morningstar Risk vs Cat	Morningstar Risk-Adj Rating
1 Yr	4.53			
3 Yr	6.17	+Avg	Avg	★★★★
5 Yr	7.56	+Avg	Avg	★★★★
10 Yr	7.14	Avg	-Avg	★★★
Incept	7.99			

Other Measures	Standard Index LB Aggr	Best Fit Index LB. U.S. Univ. Bd
Alpha	0.1	-0.7
Beta	0.97	1.01
R-Squared	97	99
Standard Deviation	4.46	
Mean	6.17	
Sharpe Ratio	1.09	

Portfolio Analysis 10-31-04

Total Fixed-Income:868	Date of Maturity	Amount $000	Value $000	% Net Assets
FNMA 0.06%	10-01-33	661,157	673,716	9.15
FNMA 0.05%	11-01-34	303,321	302,089	4.10
FNMA 0.04%	11-01-19	242,753	242,493	3.29
FNMA 0.07%	11-01-23	209,394	222,699	3.02
FNMA 0.06%	02-01-32	189,390	199,419	2.71
US Treasury Bond 6.125%	08-15-29	138,951	164,071	2.23
US Treasury Note 4%	11-15-12	138,820	140,360	1.91
US Treasury Note 2.75%	07-31-06	134,927	135,554	1.84
Boam Swap Irs 10/2/06 3m	10-02-06	96,000	96,164	1.31
US Treasury Note 2%	01-15-14	79,600	84,619	1.15
US Treasury Bond 6.375%	08-15-27	53,245	64,379	0.87
FNMA 0.04%	08-01-33	61,706	60,010	0.81
FNMA 0.06%	05-01-09	54,639	57,963	0.79
Pemex Prcj Fdg Master Tr	12-15-14	47,060	52,142	0.71
FNMA 4.625%	10-15-13	50,000	50,845	0.69
US Treasury Note 3.125%	05-15-07	50,000	50,508	0.69
Lbsp Swap Irs 9/14/06 3m	09-14-06	50,000	50,229	0.68
Mlcs Swap Irs 12/05/05 3	12-05-05	50,000	49,971	0.68
US Treasury Bond 8%	11-15-21	31,000	43,019	0.58
GNMA 0.07%	05-15-32	39,906	42,612	0.58

Current Investment Style

Duration: Short Int Long — Quality: High Med Low

¹figure provided by fund

Avg Eff Duration[1]	4.4 Yrs
Avg Eff Maturity	5.3 Yrs
Avg Credit Quality	AA
Avg Wtd Coupon	3.21%
Avg Wtd Price	104.58% of par

Coupon Range	% of Bonds	Rel Cat
0% PIK	5.4	1.3
0% to 6%	73.4	1.1
6% to 8%	23.9	0.8
8% to 10%	2.2	0.4
More than 10%	0.6	0.5

1.00=Category Average

Credit Analysis		% bonds 10-31-04	
US Govt	52	BB	1
AAA	8	B	0
AA	3	Below B	0
A	15	NR/NA	4
BBB	18		

Sector Breakdown	% of assets
US Treasuries	11
TIPS	1
US Agency	4
Mortgage Pass-Throughs	27
Mortgage CMO	9
Mortgage ARM	0
US Corporate	21
Asset-Backed	8
Convertible	0
Municipal	0
Corporate Inflation-Protected	0
Foreign Corporate	1
Foreign Govt	0

Composition

Cash	16.4	Bonds	82.9
Stocks	0.0	Other	0.7

Special Securities	
Restricted/Illiquid Secs	3
Exotic Mortgage-Backed	0
Emerging-Markets Secs	0
Options/Futures/Warrants	No

Morningstar's Take by Scott Berry 10-29-04

A management change at Fidelity Investment Grade Bond shouldn't have investors overly concerned.

Kevin Grant, who is retiring at the end of 2004, helped this fund deliver strong results during his seven-year tenure. In fact, the fund has ranked in the intermediate bond category's top half each of the past six years and is on pace to do so again in 2004. Prior to his arrival in 1997, the fund had struggled to keep pace with its average peer. Grant will be replaced by Jeffrey Moore, who currently manages the investment-grade bond portions of Fidelity's Asset Manager Funds.

We are confident that this fund's success will continue with Moore at the helm. Grant, along with entire Fidelity bond group, has put processes in place at this fund and others that allow them to squeeze value out of the bond market without introducing a lot of unwanted volatility. For starters, the fund's interest-rate sensitivity is tied to a benchmark index. That approach limits the damage that can be caused by ill-timed interest-rate bets, while still providing management an opportunity to add value through more-consistent methods, such as issue selection and sector allocation. We think this is where Fidelity has a sustainable advantage, given the resources and technology that it dedicates to its research capabilities.

Those capabilities have helped the fund cruise past its average peer in 2004. Early in the year, Grant scooped up high-coupon mortgage issues, which performed relatively well when the bond market tanked in the spring. A stash of mid-quality bonds has also worked in its favor, as their added yield has boosted returns. The fund gained 4.1% for the year to date through Oct. 28 and outperformed roughly 80% of its category peers.

Moore, who has managed bond portfolios for Fidelity since 2000, has a tough act to follow, but we expect he will continue to build on this fund's already-strong record.

Address:	82 Devonshire St, Boston MA 02109, 800-343-3548
Web Address:	www.fidelity.com
Inception:	08-06-71
Advisor:	Fidelity Management & Research Co. (FMR)
Subadvisor:	Fidelity Intl Invest Advisors (U.K.) Ltd
NTF Plans:	Fidelity Retail-NTF, CommonWealth NTF

Minimum Purchase:	$2500	Add: $250	IRA: $2500
Min Auto Inv Plan:	$2500	Add: $100	
Sales Fees:	No-load		
Management Fee:	0.43%		
Actual Fees:	Mgt:0.43%	Dist:	
Expense Projections:	3Yr:$227	5Yr:$395	10Yr:$883
Income Distrib:	Monthly		

Fidelity Leverage Co Stk

Ticker	Load	NAV	Yield	Total Assets	Mstar Category
FLVCX	None	$22.68	0.2%	$2,142 mil	Mid-Cap Blend

Governance and Management

Fiduciary Grade: B

Portfolio Manager(s)

Fidelity veteran Tom Soviero took charge of this fund in mid-July 2003. He has put in successful stints at Fidelity High-Income and Fidelity Advisor High Income Advantage, which he continues to manage. Soviero is backed by an experienced team of Fidelity analysts and looks to leverage Fidelity's high-yield and equity research.

Strategy

Manager Tom Soviero's strategy revolves around buying what he considers attractively valued stocks that issue high-yield debt or otherwise have leveraged capital structures. The fund itself is not leveraged. Soviero looks for companies that have a catalyst for improvement, such as a management change, a new product, or a pricing change. Soviero keeps the fund fairly concentrated in his favorites names. In fact, the fund's top-20 holdings recently accounted for more than half of the fund's net assets.

Historical Profile
Return High
Risk High
Rating ★★★★★ Highest

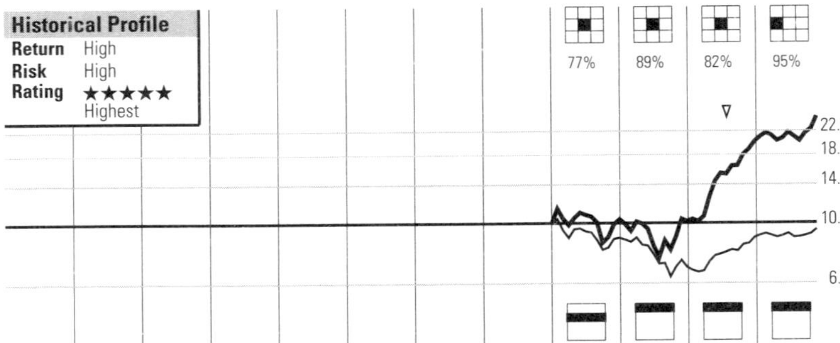

Investment Style
Equity
Stock %

▼ Manager Change
▽ Partial Manager Change

Growth of $10,000
— Investment Values of Fund
— Investment Values of S&P 500

Performance Quartile (within Category)

1993	1994	1995	1996	1997	1998	1999	2000	2001	2002	2003	12-04	History
—	—	—	—	—	—	—	10.07	10.18	10.00	19.33	22.68	NAV
—	—	—	—	—	—	—	0.70*	3.23	-1.77	96.31	24.46	Total Return %
—	—	—	—	—	—	—	—	15.11	20.32	67.64	13.59	+/-S&P 500
—	—	—	—	—	—	—	—	3.83	12.76	60.72	7.99	+/-S&P Mid 400
—	—	—	—	—	—	—	—	2.00	0.00	0.00	0.21	Income Return %
—	—	—	—	—	—	—	—	1.23	-1.77	96.31	24.25	Capital Return %
—	—	—	—	—	—	—	—	33	3	1	5	Total Rtn % Rank Cat
—	—	—	—	—	—	—	0.00	0.20	0.00	0.00	0.04	Income $
—	—	—	—	—	—	—	0.00	0.00	0.00	0.27	1.12	Capital Gains $
—	—	—	—	—	—	—	—	0.83	0.93	0.83	0.85	Expense Ratio %
—	—	—	—	—	—	—	—	1.12	1.16	0.07	0.23	Income Ratio %
—	—	—	—	—	—	—	—	230	203	79	35	Turnover Rate %
—	—	—	—	—	—	—	—	60	79	1,206	2,142	Net Assets $mil

Performance 12-31-04

	1st Qtr	2nd Qtr	3rd Qtr	4th Qtr	Total
2000	—	—	—	—	0.70 *
2001	-1.59	9.08	-21.18	22.00	3.23
2002	-1.96	-18.54	-3.44	27.39	-1.77
2003	4.40	44.06	6.63	22.41	96.31
2004	5.48	2.50	-0.57	15.76	24.46

Trailing	Total Return%	+/- S&P 500	+/- S&P Mid 400	%Rank Cat	Growth of $10,000
3 Mo	15.76	6.53	3.61	5	11,576
6 Mo	15.11	7.92	5.32	6	11,511
1 Yr	24.46	13.59	7.99	5	12,446
3 Yr Avg	33.89	30.31	23.38	1	24,002
5 Yr Avg	—	—	—	—	—
10 Yr Avg	—	—	—	—	—
15 Yr Avg	—	—	—	—	—

Tax Analysis	Tax-Adj Rtn%	%Rank Cat	Tax-Cost Rat	%Rank Cat
3 Yr (estimated)	33.00	1	0.66	73
5 Yr (estimated)	—	—	—	—
10 Yr (estimated)	—	—	—	—

Potential Capital Gain Exposure: 26% of assets

Rating and Risk

Time Period	Load-Adj Return %	Morningstar Rtn vs Cat	Morningstar Risk vs Cat	Morningstar Risk-Adj Rating
1 Yr	24.46			
3 Yr	33.89	High	High	★★★★★
5 Yr	—	—	—	—
10 Yr	—	—	—	—
Incept	25.45			

Other Measures	Standard Index S&P 500	Best Fit Index Merrill Lynch Convert
Alpha	30.2	9.9
Beta	1.42	2.93
R-Squared	69	76

Standard Deviation	34.66
Mean	33.89
Sharpe Ratio	0.95

Portfolio Analysis 10-31-04

Share change since 07-04 Total Stocks:97	Sector	PE	YTD Ret%	% Assets
⊖ Teekay Shipping	Business	19.4	49.82	6.84
⊖ AES	Utilities	30.9	44.81	6.70
⊖ General Maritime	Business	7.8	126.99	6.44
⊕ Forest Oil	Energy	20.7	11.03	4.30
⊕ Nextel Communications	Telecom	11.1	6.95	4.11
⊖ Tyco International	Ind Mtrls	25.1	35.41	3.90
⊕ CMS Energy	Utilities	83.3	22.65	3.22
⊖ NTL	Telecom	—	4.60	3.19
Qwest Communications Int	Telecom	—	2.78	3.05
⊖ Range Resources	Energy	35.8	117.27	2.94
⊕ OMI	Business	8.8	91.70	2.67
⊕ Davita	Health	19.0	52.04	2.19
ON Semiconductor	Hardware	—	-29.94	2.03
American Financial Group	Financial	4.4	20.38	1.91
⊖ Burlington Resources	Energy	10.9	58.50	1.89
⊖ Chesapeake Energy	Energy	13.1	22.90	1.81
☼ Crompton	Ind Mtrls	—	69.46	1.78
Owens-Illinois	Ind Mtrls	—	90.50	1.71
⊖ American Standard Compan	Business	18.2	23.10	1.68
⊖ Elan ADR	Health	—	295.50	1.64

Current Investment Style

Value Blnd Growth / Large Mid Small

Market Cap	%
Giant	4.4
Large	13.2
Mid	49.2
Small	29.8
Micro	3.5
Avg $mil: 3,361	

Value Measures		Rel Category
Price/Earnings	13.06	0.77
Price/Book	1.92	0.88
Price/Sales	0.51	0.48
Price/Cash Flow	3.93	0.63
Dividend Yield %	1.91	1.91

Growth Measures	%	Rel Category
Long-Term Erngs	11.82	0.94
Book Value	-5.41	NMF
Sales	-1.56	NMF
Cash Flow	30.35	4.05
Historical Erngs	18.79	1.67

Profitability	%	Rel Category
Return on Equity	8.42	0.61
Return on Assets	1.76	0.27
Net Margin	5.57	0.61

Sector Weightings	% of Stocks	Rel S&P 500	3 Year High	3 Year Low
Info	20.01	0.93		
Software	0.00	0.00	1	0
Hardware	4.19	0.41	8	1
Media	1.98	0.52	42	2
Telecom	13.84	4.39	18	8
Service	34.87	0.75		
Health	4.34	0.35	6	1
Consumer	3.06	0.34	11	3
Business	23.80	5.88	24	1
Financial	3.67	0.18	16	4
Mfg	45.12	1.40		
Goods	3.03	0.32	5	2
Ind Mtrls	13.95	1.10	14	8
Energy	17.69	2.47	18	2
Utilities	10.45	3.53	12	2

Composition

Cash	2.4
Stocks	95.4
Bonds	0.0
Other	2.1
Foreign (% of Stock)	10.5

Morningstar's Take by Scott Berry 10-29-04

Fidelity Leveraged Company Stock is best taken in small doses.

There's no denying this fund's success. Since its inception in late 2000, it has returned a jaw dropping 124%, besting all other diversified mid-cap stock funds by more than 25 percentage points. That success owes much to the stock picking ability of Tom Soviero and his predecessor, but favorable market conditions have also played a big role. The stocks of many high-yield bond issuers have rallied over the past two years as default rates have dropped and bankruptcy concerns have faded. Nextel, for example, has jumped from less than $5 per share to more than $25, while AES has climbed from less than $2 to more than $10. Both are top-10 holdings.

The fund carries a lot of risk though. High-yield bond issuers run the risk of not being able to refinance or pay back their debt when it comes due. When that happens, an issuer can be forced into bankruptcy and its stock can become worthless. Further, the fund is quite concentrated, with roughly 60% of its assets invested in its top-20 holdings. That concentration provides a lot of firepower but also creates a lot of volatility. The fund plunged 25% in mid-2002, for example, and its standard deviation of returns (a measure of volatility) lands near the very top of the charts.

The fund's added risk is a concern, but Soviero has managed it well thus far. His experience managing high-yield bond funds has made him quite familiar with the risks of investing in leveraged companies and has helped him sidestep a number of troubled issuers. He also benefits from Fidelity's high-yield and equity research capabilities.

Soviero's skilled management and the fund's early success shouldn't be ignored. However, given the fund's concentrated portfolio of leveraged companies, we don't think the fund is suitable for much more than a small slice of a diversified portfolio.

Address:	82 Devonshire St Boston MA 02109 800-343-3548
Web Address:	www.fidelity.com
Inception:	12-19-00*
Advisor:	Fidelity Management & Research Co. (FMR)
Subadvisor:	FMR Co., Inc. (FMRC)
NTF Plans:	Fidelity Retail-NTF, CommonWealth NTF

Minimum Purchase:	$10000	Add: $500	IRA: $2500
Min Auto Inv Plan:	$500	Add: $500	
Sales Fees:	No-load, 1.50%R		
Management Fee:	0.63%		
Actual Fees:	Mgt:0.63%	Dist:	
Expense Projections:	3Yr:$362	5Yr: —	10Yr: —
Income Distrib:	Semi-Annually		

Fidelity Low-Priced Stk

Ticker	Load	NAV	Yield	Total Assets	Mstar Category
FLPSX	Closed	$40.25	0.3%	$35,976 mil	Small Blend

Governance and Management

Fiduciary Grade: B

Portfolio Manager(s)

Joel Tillinghast has managed this fund since its inception. Not only is he one of the most experienced managers in the group, he also is one of the best. Tillinghast receives research support from a team of small-cap analysts and from Fidelity's industry analysts, but he does much of the research on his own. He was named Morningstar's Domestic Equity Fund Manager of the Year for 2002.

Strategy

This fund focuses on companies with share prices of $35 or less, but that is a marketing gimmick. The real story is that manager Joel Tillinghast buys mostly smaller-cap fare that offers a combination of reasonable valuations and solid growth prospects. He spreads the portfolio across hundreds of holdings. If he's finding the best opportunities overseas, Tillinghast is willing to devote a substantial chunk of the portfolio to foreign issues and larger-cap stocks. Tillinghast will let cash build if he can't find enough good investment opportunities. The fund closed to new investors on Dec. 31, 2003.

Historical Profile

Return High
Risk Low
Rating ★★★★★ Highest

Investment Style: Equity Stock %

1993	1994	1995	1996	1997	1998	1999	2000	2001	2002	2003	12-04
	80%	81%	89%	98%	94%	80%	85%	91%	86%		

▼ Manager Change
▽ Partial Manager Change

Growth of $10,000
— Investment Values of Fund
— Investment Values of S&P 500

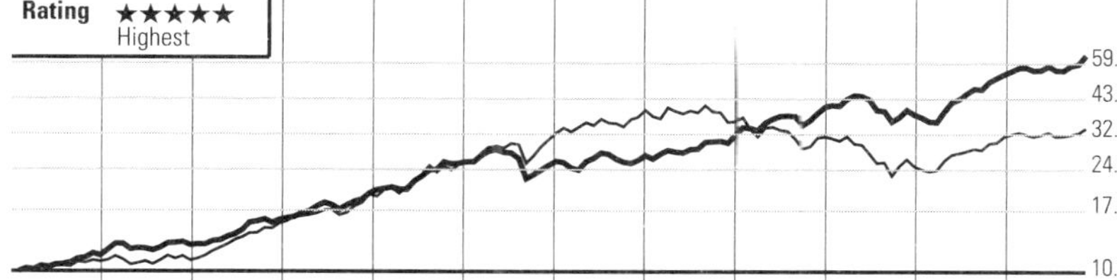

Performance Quartile (within Category)

1993	1994	1995	1996	1997	1998	1999	2000	2001	2002	2003	12-04	History
17.30	16.00	18.50	21.35	25.13	22.85	22.64	23.12	27.42	25.17	34.98	40.25	NAV
20.21	4.81	24.89	26.89	26.73	0.53	5.08	18.83	26.71	-6.18	40.85	22.24	Total Return %
10.15	3.50	-12.64	3.95	-6.62	-28.04	-15.96	27.93	38.59	15.91	12.18	11.37	+/-S&P 500
1.33	6.63	-3.56	10.40	4.37	3.08	-16.18	21.85	24.22	14.30	-6.40	3.91	+/-Russ 2000
1.02	0.55	1.46	1.33	1.34	0.81	0.67	0.75	0.70	0.11	0.08	0.35	Income Return %
19.19	4.26	23.43	25.56	25.39	-0.28	4.41	18.08	26.01	-6.29	40.77	21.89	Capital Return %
34	7	55	24	41	20	73	29	5	8	54	20	Total Rtn % Rank Cat
0.16	0.09	0.23	0.24	0.28	0.20	0.15	0.16	0.16	0.03	0.02	0.12	Income $
1.62	2.05	1.24	1.66	1.58	1.94	1.19	3.43	1.54	0.54	0.44	2.09	Capital Gains $
1.12	1.13	1.11	1.04	1.01	0.95	1.08	0.80	1.00	0.97	1.01	0.97	Expense Ratio %
1.00	0.51	1.31	1.46	1.36	1.10	0.52	0.58	0.92	0.34	0.05	0.15	Income Ratio %
47	54	65	79	45	47	24	15	44	26	23	28	Turnover Rate %
2,060	2,355	3,350	5,664	10,691	9,195	6,646	6,834	12,429	15,104	26,725	35,976	Net Assets $mil

Performance 12-31-04

	1st Qtr	2nd Qtr	3rd Qtr	4th Qtr	Total
2000	4.46	0.89	6.64	5.73	18.83
2001	3.94	12.90	-7.30	16.48	26.71
2002	6.97	-0.27	-16.98	5.93	-6.18
2003	-6.04	21.31	8.50	13.88	40.85
2004	5.86	1.24	0.20	13.83	22.18

Trailing	Total Return%	+/- S&P 500	+/- Russ 2000	%Rank Cat	Growth of $10,000
3 Mo	13.83	4.60	-0.26	29	11,383
6 Mo	14.06	6.87	3.23	12	11,406
1 Yr	22.24	11.37	3.91	20	12,224
3 Yr Avg	17.33	13.75	5.85	12	16,152
5 Yr Avg	19.45	21.75	12.84	4	24,318
10 Yr Avg	17.83	5.76	6.29	2	51,589
15 Yr Avg	18.18	7.25	7.09	1	122,507

Tax Analysis	Tax-Adj Rtn%	%Rank Cat	Tax-Cost Rat	%Rank Cat
3 Yr (estimated)	16.58	9	0.64	46
5 Yr (estimated)	17.86	5	1.33	66
10 Yr (estimated)	15.66	7	1.84	61

Potential Capital Gain Exposure: 33% of assets

Rating and Risk

Time Period	Load-Adj Return %	Morningstar Rtn vs Cat	Morningstar Risk vs Cat	Morningstar Risk-Adj Rating
1 Yr	22.24			
3 Yr	17.33	+Avg	Low	★★★★★
5 Yr	19.45	High	Low	★★★★★
10 Yr	17.83	High	Low	★★★★★
Incept	18.08			

Other Measures	Standard Index S&P 500	Best Fit Index Russ 2000 VL
Alpha	13.9	3.5
Beta	0.82	0.79
R-Squared	72	92

Standard Deviation	16.95
Mean	17.33
Sharpe Ratio	0.95

Portfolio Analysis 10-31-04

Share change since 07-04 Total Stocks:1036	Sector	PE	YTD Ret%	% Assets
⊕ DR Horton	Consumer	10.7	41.36	1.84
⊕ MBNA	Financial	14.0	15.53	1.78
Health Management Associ	Health	16.6	-4.89	1.56
Russell Index (Fut)	—	—	—	1.47
⊖ Next	Financial	—	—	1.35
⊖ Computer Sciences	Business	18.1	27.45	1.13
⊕ Safeway	Consumer	—	-9.90	1.12
⊖ Petroleo Brasileiro ADR	Energy	—	42.37	1.11
⊖ Lafarge	Ind Mtrls	14.7	29.09	1.08
⊕ Lincare Holdings	Health	16.1	41.79	1.08
⊖ PMI Group	Financial	11.4	12.61	1.08
⊖ CVS	Consumer	21.1	25.61	0.96
Doral Financial	Financial	13.3	55.06	0.86
Constellation Brands A	Goods	19.9	41.24	0.85
PacifiCare Health System	Health	21.5	67.22	0.79
⊖ Ford Motor	Goods	9.9	-6.00	0.77
Renal Care Group	Health	22.6	31.03	0.72
Tech Data	Ind Mtrls	17.5	14.39	0.71
⊕ Barratt Developments	Business	—	—	0.69
First Bancorp	Financial	17.2	62.27	0.67

Current Investment Style

Value Blnd Growth — Large Mid Small

Market Cap	%
Giant	3.3
Large	10.4
Mid	46.4
Small	29.1
Micro	10.9
Avg $mil: 1,877	

Value Measures		Rel Category
Price/Earnings	12.89	0.75
Price/Book	1.69	0.85
Price/Sales	0.57	0.60
Price/Cash Flow	5.52	0.94
Dividend Yield %	1.06	1.28

Growth Measures	%	Rel Category
Long-Term Erngs	12.92	0.95
Book Value	8.84	1.57
Sales	5.91	1.37
Cash Flow	2.42	0.49
Historical Erngs	9.84	1.32

Profitability	%	Rel Category
Return on Equity	15.84	1.52
Return on Assets	7.77	1.57
Net Margin	9.51	1.30

Sector Weightings	% of Stocks	Rel S&P 500	3 Year High	Low
Info	8.78	0.41		
Software	1.68	0.39	4	2
Hardware	5.13	0.50	7	5
Media	1.18	0.31	2	1
Telecom	0.79	0.25	1	1
Service	59.00	1.27		
Health	10.56	0.84	11	9
Consumer	18.67	2.06	26	18
Business	10.59	2.61	12	10
Financial	19.18	0.92	19	16
Mfg	32.22	1.00		
Goods	3.23	0.99	11	9
Ind Mtrls	13.09	1.43	18	13
Energy	4.26	0.59	4	2
Utilities	0.64	0.22	1	0

Composition

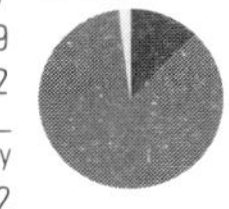

Cash	12.1
Stocks	85.8
Bonds	0.0
Other	2.1
Foreign (% of Stock)	26.0

Morningstar's Take by Laura Pavlenko Lutton 11-29-04

This fund's best days may be behind it.

It's easy to see why investors have flocked to Fidelity Low-Priced Stock. The closed small-blend offering has one of the best 10-year records in the category, and it has achieved those results with less volatility than its typical peer. Manager Joel Tillinghast has proven he's one of the best stock-pickers in the mutual fund world.

Thanks to this success, the fund grew to more than $25 billion before Fidelity closed it to new investors on Dec. 31, 2003. Assets are now approaching $32 billion, making this one of the largest offerings around.

The fund's girth poses significant challenges. Although Tillinghast invests in value-leaning stocks throughout the market-cap spectrum, he prefers smaller caps, and it's difficult for a fund this big to move in and out of these issues easily. Tillinghast has addressed this by expanding the fund's portfolio to more than 1,000 names and buying more mid-cap stocks.

Even so, Tillinghast has had trouble finding enough stocks that meet his strict valuation and financial-health criteria. Thus, cash has at times swelled to the midteens and has held back returns. Tillinghast also has faced turnover among the fund's analysts in 2004 since two small-cap researchers were promoted to run new funds.

These challenges don't appear insurmountable: The fund's 17.38% gain for the year to date through Nov. 26, 2004, puts the offering in the category's top third. Still, we wish Fidelity had limited this fund's size much earlier. Asking Tillinghast to run this enormous sum is like making a star basketball player shoot with one hand tied behind his back. The athlete probably remains a better shot than the average guy, but think of what he'd be capable of if his talent wasn't compromised.

In the end, we see little reason to sell one's stake in this fund, but we think it's not likely that the offering will remain a standout.

Address:	82 Devonshire Street Boston MA 02109 800-343-3548
Web Address:	
Inception:	12-27-89
Advisor:	Fidelity Management & Research Co. (FMR)
Subadvisor:	FMR Co., Inc. (FMRC)
NTF Plans:	Fidelity Retail-NTF, CommonWealth NTF

Minimum Purchase:	Closed	Add: —	IRA: —
Min Auto Inv Plan:	Closed	Add: —	
Sales Fees:	No-load, 1.50%R		
Management Fee:	0.77%		
Actual Fees:	Mgt:0.77%	Dist:	
Expense Projections:	3Yr:$328	5Yr:$569	10Yr:$1259
Income Distrib:	Semi-Annually		

Fidelity Magellan

Ticker	Load	NAV	Yield	Total Assets	Mstar Category
FMAGX	Closed	$103.79	1.2%	$63,296 mil	Large Blend

Governance and Management

Fiduciary Grade: B

Portfolio Manager(s)

Robert Stansky is an experienced manager who is backed by Fidelity's scores of analysts. Before taking over here, he ran Fidelity Growth Company from April 1987 to June 1996. Over that time Stansky produced an annualized return of 13.16%, compared with 10.00% for the average large-growth fund and 11.47% for the S&P 500. Stansky joined Fidelity in 1983 after earning an MBA from New York University.

Strategy

Robert Stansky likes to move into growth areas when they are temporarily depressed. Because the fund is so large, he cannot trade in and out of positions easily. He looks for stocks he can hold for several years. He favors stocks with above-average growth rates but marketlike prices. Stansky focuses on understanding the assumptions and expectations embedded in an analyst's estimates for a company to be certain that a company's growth engines will really work as expected. Because of the fund's size, it owns stocks across varied industries.

Historical Profile

Return Below Avg
Risk Average
Rating ★★ Below Avg

Investment Style
Equity
Stock %

89%	96%	92%	91%	95%	93%	93%	95%	98%

▼ Manager Change
▽ Partial Manager Change

Growth of $10,000

▬ Investment Values of Fund
— Investment Values of S&P 500

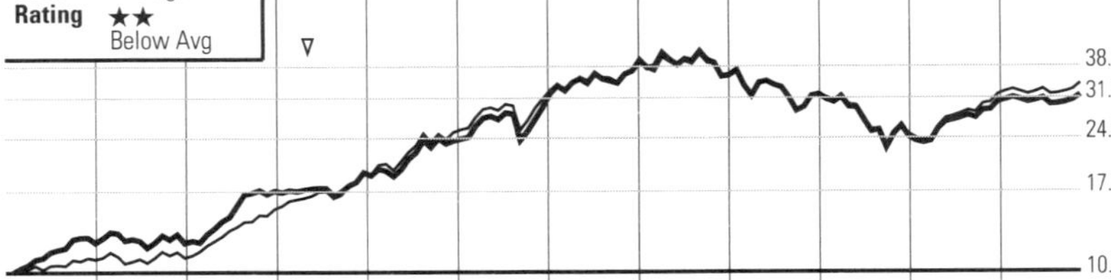

Performance Quartile (within Category)

1993	1994	1995	1996	1997	1998	1999	2000	2001	2002	2003	12-04	History
70.85	66.80	85.98	80.65	95.27	120.82	136.63	119.30	104.22	78.96	97.74	103.79	NAV
24.66	-1.81	36.82	11.69	26.59	33.63	24.05	-9.29	-11.65	-23.66	24.82	7.49	Total Return %
14.60	-3.12	-0.71	-11.25	-6.76	5.06	3.01	-0.19	0.23	-1.57	-3.85	-3.38	+/-S&P 500
14.48	-2.20	-0.95	-10.76	-6.26	6.61	3.14	-1.50	0.80	-2.01	-5.07	-3.91	+/-Russ 1000
1.22	0.18	0.88	1.41	1.57	0.72	0.63	0.20	0.39	0.61	0.96	1.27	Income Return %
23.44	-1.99	35.94	10.28	25.02	32.91	23.42	-9.49	-12.04	-24.27	23.86	6.22	Capital Return %
3	72	23	97	60	4	26	68	41	72	71	79	Total Rtn % Rank Cat
0.75	0.13	0.59	1.10	1.25	0.67	0.73	0.27	0.46	0.64	0.76	1.24	Income $
6.50	2.64	4.69	12.85	5.21	5.15	11.39	4.69	0.80	0.00	0.00	0.00	Capital Gains $
1.00	0.99	0.96	0.92	0.64	0.61	0.60	0.74	0.88	0.88	0.76	0.70	Expense Ratio %
2.11	1.07	0.39	0.95	1.75	0.77	0.66	0.46	0.29	0.43	0.82	0.83	Income Ratio %
155	132	120	155	67	34	37	28	17	5	21	13	Turnover Rate %
31,705	36,442	53,702	53,989	63,766	83,552	105,939	93,067	79,515	56,751	67,995	63,296	Net Assets $mil

Performance 12-31-04

	1st Qtr	2nd Qtr	3rd Qtr	4th Qtr	Total
2000	4.85	-3.96	-0.58	-9.40	-9.29
2001	-12.41	7.18	-15.36	11.18	-11.65
2002	-1.60	-13.72	-16.36	7.51	-23.66
2003	-2.88	14.25	1.48	10.85	24.82
2004	1.42	0.77	-2.77	8.17	7.49

Trailing	Total Return%	+/- S&P 500	+/- Russ 1000	%Rank Cat	Growth of $10,000
3 Mo	8.17	-1.06	-1.63	79	10,817
6 Mo	5.17	-2.02	-2.64	84	10,517
1 Yr	7.49	-3.38	-3.91	79	10,749
3 Yr Avg	0.80	-2.78	-3.47	81	10,242
5 Yr Avg	-3.87	-1.57	-2.11	78	8,209
10 Yr Avg	10.16	-1.91	-2.00	57	26,317
15 Yr Avg	10.78	-0.15	-0.30	25	46,443

Tax Analysis	Tax-Adj Rtn%	%Rank Cat	Tax-Cost Rat	%Rank Cat
3 Yr (estimated)	0.46	76	0.34	29
5 Yr (estimated)	-4.30	74	0.45	24
10 Yr (estimated)	8.54	52	1.47	55

Potential Capital Gain Exposure: 31% of assets

Rating and Risk

Time Period	Load-Adj Return %	Morningstar Rtn vs Cat	Morningstar Risk vs Cat	Morningstar Risk-Adj Rating
1 Yr	7.49			
3 Yr	0.80	-Avg	Avg	★★
5 Yr	-3.87	-Avg	Avg	★★
10 Yr	10.16	Avg	+Avg	★★★
Incept	18.91			

Other Measures	Standard Index S&P 500	Best Fit Index S&P 500
Alpha	-2.7	-2.7
Beta	0.99	0.99
R-Squared	99	99
Standard Deviation	15.10	
Mean	0.80	
Sharpe Ratio	-0.04	

Portfolio Analysis 09-30-04

Share change since 06-04 Total Stocks:211	Sector	PE	YTD Ret%	% Assets
⊖ American International G	Financial	16.2	-0.53	3.69
⊖ Citigroup	Financial	15.3	2.72	3.67
Gen Elec	Ind Mtrls	22.8	20.68	3.66
Microsoft	Software	36.1	8.95	3.28
Viacom B	Media	36.1	-17.44	2.67
⊖ Pfizer	Health	22.0	-22.31	2.57
⊖ ExxonMobil	Energy	13.9	28.04	2.41
Home Depot	Consumer	19.0	21.47	2.13
⊕ Bank of America	Financial	12.3	21.50	1.97
⊖ Johnson & Johnson	Health	20.6	25.17	1.80
⊕ ChevronTexaco	Energy	7.7	25.57	1.77
Wal-Mart Stores	Consumer	23.4	0.51	1.71
⊕ J P Morgan Chase	Financial	19.4	9.97	1.70
Tyco International	Ind Mtrls	25.1	35.41	1.68
Wells Fargo	Financial	15.5	8.97	1.60
Lowe's Companies	Consumer	22.1	4.25	1.57
⊖ Procter & Gamble	Goods	23.3	12.38	1.48
⊖ Cisco Systems	Hardware	24.5	-20.26	1.40
⊖ Fannie Mae	Financial	9.1	-2.33	1.37
American Express	Financial	20.3	17.60	1.34

Current Investment Style

Value Blnd Growth / Large Mid Small

Market Cap	%
Giant	67.3
Large	28.4
Mid	4.2
Small	0.1
Micro	0.0

Avg $mil: 64,807

Value Measures		Rel Category
Price/Earnings	16.71	0.99
Price/Book	2.58	0.98
Price/Sales	1.72	1.19
Price/Cash Flow	7.98	1.04
Dividend Yield %	1.48	1.00

Growth Measures	%	Rel Category
Long-Term Erngs	11.73	1.01
Book Value	9.26	1.19
Sales	7.32	1.28
Cash Flow	17.98	1.90
Historical Erngs	14.75	1.25

Profitability	%	Rel Category
Return on Equity	17.41	0.99
Return on Assets	9.62	1.11
Net Margin	11.77	1.03

Sector Weightings	% of Stocks	Rel S&P 500	3 Year High	3 Year Low
Info	25.83	1.20		
Software	4.56	1.06	5	4
Hardware	9.53	0.93	11	6
Media	8.62	2.24	9	8
Telecom	3.12	0.99	5	3
Service	48.17	1.04		
Health	12.44	1.00	16	12
Consumer	10.48	1.15	11	10
Business	1.85	0.46	2	2
Financial	23.40	1.13	26	21
Mfg	25.99	0.81		
Goods	5.71	0.61	8	6
Ind Mtrls	10.38	0.82	11	8
Energy	9.90	1.38	10	8
Utilities	0.00	0.00	0	0

Composition

Cash	2.0
Stocks	98.0
Bonds	0.0
Other	0.0
Foreign (% of Stock)	2.2

Morningstar's Take by Christine Benz 01-05-05

Fidelity Magellan isn't exactly an index-hugger, but its shareholders are probably beginning to wish it were.

For the past several years, the knock against this fund has been that it's nothing more than a closet index fund, making only tiny bets against the S&P 500 because it's too large to venture beyond the benchmark's biggest names. We've begged to differ, arguing that we've seen manager Bob Stansky bet against the index in a significant way on more than one occasion. In 2003, for example, he underweighted the tech sector versus the index, while in 2004 Stansky overweighted media stocks. (Viacom, which numbered among Magellan's top 10 holdings at the end of September, doesn't even crack the S&P's top 25.)

Trouble is, Stansky hasn't been getting enough of these bets right to merit our continued confidence in his abilities. The fund has now lagged the S&P 500 in four of the past five years. True enough, the mega-cap stocks that form the core of this portfolio have put the fund at a distinct disadvantage during the small-cap-led market of the past five years. That positioning isn't entirely under Stansky's control, as the fund's massive size limits him to the market's biggest stocks. But the bet against tech in 2003 and the fund's outsized stake in media stocks in 2004 were of Stansky's own doing, and they didn't work out. (The fund also had a larger Pfizer stake than the index coming into 2004's fourth quarter, and that stock's blowup may help explain the fund's poor fourth-quarter showing.)

We often urge investors to take a contrarian approach to managing their portfolios, adding to high-quality funds when they're down. And indeed, Stansky amassed a solid record at Fidelity Growth Company and at this fund early in his tenure. But this fund is far from topping our list, particularly given that Fidelity is now offering index funds for 0.10% per year.

Address:	82 Devonshire St Boston MA 02109 800-343-3548
Web Address:	www.fidelity.com
Inception:	05-02-63
Advisor:	Fidelity Management & Research Co. (FMR)
Subadvisor:	FMR Co., Inc. (FMRC)
NTF Plans:	Fidelity Retail-NTF, CommonWealth NTF

Minimum Purchase:	Closed	Add: —		IRA: —	
Min Auto Inv Plan:	Closed	Add: —			
Sales Fees:	No-load				
Management Fee:	0.57%				
Actual Fees:	Mgt:0.57%	Dist:			
Expense Projections:	3Yr:$532	5Yr:$704		10Yr:$1202	
Income Distrib:	Semi-Annually				

Fidelity Mid-Cap Stock

Ticker	Load	NAV	Yield	Total Assets	Mstar Category
FMCSX	None	$23.45	0.3%	$9,093 mil	Mid-Cap Growth

Governance and Management

Fiduciary Grade: B

Portfolio Manager(s)

Beso Sikharulidze, who took over for David Felman in June 2001, posted good returns during prior stints as manager of Fidelity Advisor Aggressive Growth, Fidelity Convertible Securities, and Fidelity Select Health Care.

Strategy

Beso Sikharulidze's approach differs from his predecessor's. While he continues to look for growing companies trading at reasonable valuations, the fund's sector weightings are a result of his stock selection, not conscious top-down bets. Thus, the fund's profile is more stable than it has been in the past. In addition, drawing on his previous experience, Sikharulidze will hold a modest stake in convertible securities at times to try to improve the fund's risk/return profile.

Historical Profile

Return Above Avg
Risk Average
Rating ★★★★ Above Avg

Investment Style: Equity Stock %

94%	95%	91%	93%	83%	73%	81%	92%	93%

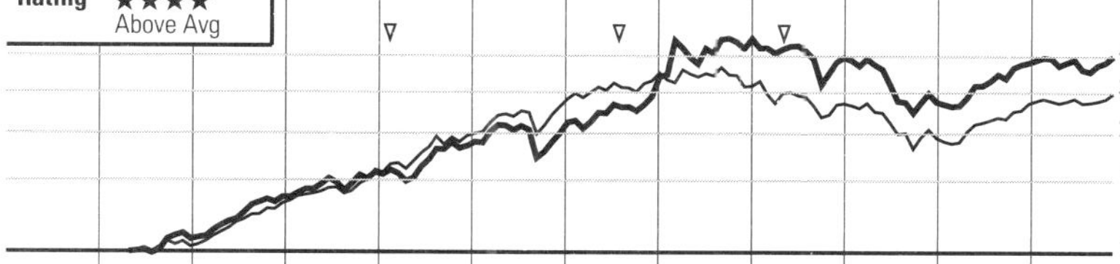

▼ Manager Change
∇ Partial Manager Change

Growth of $10,000
— Investment Values of Fund
— Investment Values of S&P 500

Performance Quartile (within Category)

1993	1994	1995	1996	1997	1998	1999	2000	2001	2002	2003	12-04	History
—	10.70	13.50	14.64	16.69	17.88	21.87	26.36	22.57	16.26	21.57	23.45	NAV
—	8.46*	33.92	18.12	27.08	15.18	39.83	32.37	-12.80	-27.59	33.26	9.05	Total Return %
—	—	-3.61	-4.82	-6.27	-13.39	18.79	41.17	-0.92	-5.50	4.59	-1.82	+/-S&P 500
—	—	-0.06	0.64	4.54	-2.68	-11.46	43.32	7.35	-0.18	-9.45	-6.43	+/-Russ MG
—	0.00	0.57	0.23	0.07	0.00	0.06	0.49	0.61	0.40	0.55	0.32	Income Return %
—	—	33.35	17.89	27.01	15.18	39.77	31.88	-13.41	-27.99	32.71	8.73	Capital Return %
—	—	44	41	19	56	67	1	30	51	62	78	Total Rtn % Rank Cat
—	0.00	0.06	0.03	0.01	0.00	0.01	0.10	0.16	0.09	0.09	0.07	Income $
—	0.14	0.74	1.26	1.77	1.28	2.59	2.50	0.00	0.00	0.00	0.00	Capital Gains $
—	—	1.22	1.00	0.96	0.86	0.74	0.86	0.87	0.87	0.66	0.65	Expense Ratio %
—	—	0.95	1.01	0.17	-0.10	0.08	-0.20	0.79	0.79	0.75	0.34	Income Ratio %
—	—	163	179	155	132	121	205	303	200	120	137	Turnover Rate %
—	126	1,160	1,695	1,763	1,784	2,286	7,011	6,547	5,132	8,049	9,093	Net Assets $mil

Performance 12-31-04

	1st Qtr	2nd Qtr	3rd Qtr	4th Qtr	Total
2000	23.27	-0.37	7.71	-0.16	32.07
2001	-10.05	5.54	-24.66	21.91	-12.80
2002	-0.89	-17.27	-18.40	8.21	-27.59
2003	-2.71	15.74	5.42	12.26	33.26
2004	3.15	-1.03	-3.95	11.22	9.05

Trailing	Total Return%	+/- S&P 500	+/- Russ MG	%Rank Cat	Growth of $10,000
3 Mo	11.22	1.99	-2.72	80	11,122
6 Mo	6.82	-0.37	-2.19	62	10,682
1 Yr	9.05	-1.82	-6.43	78	10,905
3 Yr Avg	1.71	-1.87	-4.45	72	10,522
5 Yr Avg	3.92	6.22	7.28	19	12,120
10 Yr Avg	14.65	2.58	3.42	7	39,241
15 Yr Avg	—	—	—	—	—

Tax Analysis	Tax-Adj Rtn%	%Rank Cat	Tax-Cost Rat	%Rank Cat
3 Yr (estimated)	1.57	67	0.14	23
5 Yr (estimated)	3.16	15	0.73	32
10 Yr (estimated)	12.55	9	1.83	46

Potential Capital Gain Exposure: 7% of assets

Rating and Risk

Time Period	Load-Adj Return %	Morningstar Rtn vs Cat	Morningstar Risk vs Cat	Morningstar Risk-Adj Rating
1 Yr	9.05			
3 Yr	1.71	-Avg	Avg	★★
5 Yr	3.92	+Avg	Avg	★★★★
10 Yr	14.65	High	-Avg	★★★★★
Incept	14.41			

Other Measures	Standard Index S&P 500	Best Fit Index Russ MG
Alpha	-1.6	-4.0
Beta	1.07	0.95
R-Squared	82	97
Standard Deviation	18.13	
Mean	1.71	
Sharpe Ratio	0.02	

Morningstar's Take by Andrew Gogerty 11-12-04

We remain concerned by Fidelity Mid-Cap Stock's expanding waistline.

At $8.4 billion, this fund is a beast. It's currently the third-largest offering in the mid-growth category, and second only to Calamos Growth among options still open to new investors. This fund is also not the pure mid-growth offering it once was. It devoted more than 81% of assets to mid-cap names in 2001, but this stake has steadily declined and now the fund has only 66% of assets in these names. Its weight in large-cap names has also increased over this time frame, from 8% to 14%. Trading costs are also a potential concern here, as the fund could have a difficult time moving in and out of positions in a timely manner without affecting their share prices.

In picking stocks, manager Beso Sikharulidze uses bottom-up analysis to look for companies that demonstrate sustainable growth and have strong balance sheets. He is more focused on valuation than many of his peers, and his focus on individual issues results in a more diversified portfolio across sectors. This will help to keep a lid on volatility, but the fund's sprawling portfolio will take the edge off even his best picks, as the fund's top 10 holdings barely soak up 10% of assets.

Further, the results during Sikharulidze's tenure have been lukewarm. The fund's 33% gain in 2003 was strong on an absolute basis, but his focus on valuation kept the portfolio light on tech issues, resulting in a poor showing compared with its peers. The fund also posted middling results during the end of the bear market, when we would've expected its value-conscious approach to shine.

In short, we'd like to see this fund close. Its size may begin to impinge on its strategy, and its vast number of holdings will dampen the impact of its winning picks. Sikharulidze's tempered style should avoid large blowups, but the fund's girth overshadows that positive. Investors would do well to shop for more-nimble offerings.

Address:	82 Devonshire St Boston MA 02109 800-343-3548
Web Address:	www.fidelity.com
Inception:	03-29-94 *
Advisor:	Fidelity Management & Research Co. (FMR)
Subadvisor:	FMR Co., Inc. (FMRC)
NTF Plans:	Fidelity Retail-NTF, CommonWealth NTF

Minimum Purchase:	$2500	Add: $250	IRA: $2500
Min Auto Inv Plan:	$2500	Add: $100	
Sales Fees:	No-load, 0.75%R		
Management Fee:	0.41%		
Actual Fees:	Mgt:0.41%	Dist:	
Expense Projections:	3Yr:$246	5Yr:$428	10Yr:$954
Income Distrib:	Semi-Annually		

Portfolio Analysis 10-31-04

Share change since 07-04 Total Stocks:370	Sector	PE	YTD Ret%	% Assets
⊕ Genentech	Health	78.6	16.36	3.44
☆ North Fork Bancorporatio	Financial	15.4	10.24	1.49
⊕ Lincare Holdings	Health	16.1	41.79	1.35
⊕ Fisher Scientific Intern	Health	43.9	50.79	1.07
Precision Castparts	Ind Mtrls	26.0	44.97	1.01
⊕ L-3 Communications Holdi	Hardware	20.6	43.54	0.93
⊖ Amphenol	Hardware	20.4	14.94	0.87
⊕ Toll Brothers	Consumer	17.3	72.56	0.85
⊕ Varian Semiconductor Equ	Hardware	28.4	-15.87	0.85
⊕ FileNet	Software	53.4	-4.87	0.81
⊕ Qiagen NV	Health	37.0	-8.45	0.81
⊖ Lam Research	Hardware	21.5	-10.50	0.77
⊕ Elan ADR	Health	—	295.50	0.77
Infosys Technologies ADR	Software	62.4	47.71	0.74
⊕ JC Decaux	Business	—	—	0.71
☆ Lastminute.com	Consumer	—	—	0.70
⊖ Symantec 144A Cv 3%	—	—	—	0.70
⊕ Harman International Ind	Goods	48.4	71.77	0.70
⊕ UnitedHealth Group	Health	23.8	51.38	0.69
⊕ Pharmion	Health	—	176.79	0.67

Current Investment Style

Value Blnd Growth; Large Mid Small

Market Cap	%
Giant	8.3
Large	14.1
Mid	63.3
Small	13.7
Micro	0.7
Avg $mil: 4,409	

Value Measures		Rel Category
Price/Earnings	20.31	0.92
Price/Book	2.58	0.86
Price/Sales	1.48	0.84
Price/Cash Flow	5.79	0.60
Dividend Yield %	0.55	1.28

Growth Measures	%	Rel Category
Long-Term Erngs	15.14	0.96
Book Value	11.41	1.14
Sales	9.16	1.07
Cash Flow	13.88	1.14
Historical Erngs	14.64	0.92

Profitability	%	Rel Category
Return on Equity	12.34	0.86
Return on Assets	6.03	0.84
Net Margin	8.92	0.93

Sector Weightings	% of Stocks	Rel S&P 500	3 Year High	3 Year Low
Info	26.15	1.22		
Software	6.24	1.45	12	5
Hardware	13.41	1.31	20	13
Media	2.51	0.65	7	3
Telecom	3.99	1.27	4	0
Service	56.29	1.21		
Health	25.76	2.06	26	12
Consumer	10.40	1.15	16	8
Business	9.77	2.41	13	7
Financial	10.36	0.50	16	10
Mfg	17.57	0.55		
Goods	4.51	0.48	7	4
Ind Mtrls	6.06	0.48	7	3
Energy	6.89	0.96	9	6
Utilities	0.11	0.04	1	0

Composition

Cash	3.8
Stocks	93.2
Bonds	0.5
Other	2.5
Foreign (% of Stock)	10.9

Fidelity New Markets Inc

Analyst Pick

Ticker	Load	NAV	Yield	SEC Yield	Total Assets	Mstar Category
FNMIX	None	$14.33	6.0%	5.59%	$1,089 mil	Emerging Markets Bond

Governance and Management

Fiduciary Grade: B

Portfolio Manager(s)

John Carlson has overseen this fund since 1995. Before that, he served as executive director of emerging markets for Lehman Brothers International. Carlson is supported by several experienced analysts. Some have worked on the fund for 10 years.

Strategy

John Carlson believes in a good defense. He usually chooses to invest heavily in countries that attract foreign direct investment. He treads lightly on corporate bonds, and he won't invest more than 10% of assets in local currencies. In the past, he has been quick to exit volatile markets, but lately the fund hasn't made too many drastic moves.

Historical Profile

Return Above Avg
Risk Average
Rating ★★★★ Above Avg

Investment Style
Fixed Income
Income Rtn %Rank Cat

1996	1997	1998	1999	2000	2001	2002	2003	12-04
73	13	59	54	32	47	55	64	37

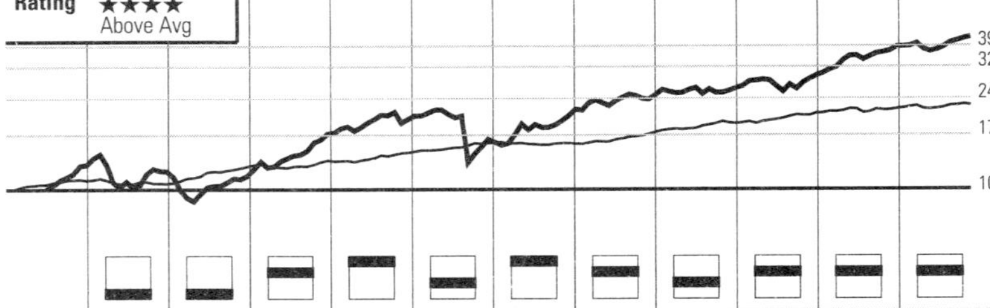

▼ Manager Change
▽ Partial Manager Change

Growth of $10,000
— Investment Values of Fund
— Investment Values of LB Aggr

Performance Quartile (within Category)

1993	1994	1995	1996	1997	1998	1999	2000	2001	2002	2003	12-04	History
13.07	10.19	9.95	12.96	12.97	8.99	11.13	11.39	10.91	11.32	13.90	14.33	NAV
38.84*	-16.55	7.97	41.39	17.52	-22.38	36.69	14.38	6.64	12.63	31.11	12.50	Total Return %
—	-13.63	-10.50	37.76	7.87	-31.07	37.51	2.75	-1.80	2.38	27.01	8.16	+/-LB Aggr
—	—	—	5.88	0.90	-17.08	19.88	1.56	-0.96	3.84	6.79	1.24	+/-
0.00	4.50	9.43	9.75	10.81	8.25	11.76	12.20	11.12	8.65	7.23	6.60	Income Return %
—	-21.05	-1.46	31.64	6.71	-30.63	24.93	2.18	-4.48	3.98	23.88	5.90	Capital Return %
—	100	83	30	15	57	8	26	61	36	30	47	Total Rtn % Rank Cat
0.55	0.57	0.92	0.93	1.32	1.02	1.01	1.30	1.21	0.91	0.79	0.88	Income $
0.17	0.20	0.00	0.00	0.87	0.20	0.00	0.00	0.00	0.00	0.05	0.33	Capital Gains $
1.24	1.28	1.17	1.09	1.08	1.13	1.07	0.99	0.99	1.00	1.00	—	Expense Ratio %
6.29	5.87	9.51	7.68	7.56	10.50	9.88	9.41	11.61	8.48	8.48	—	Income Ratio %
324	409	306	405	656	488	273	278	259	219	219	—	Turnover Rate %
284	180	174	306	371	207	214	258	293	425	866	1,089	Net Assets $mil

Performance 12-31-04

	1st Qtr	2nd Qtr	3rd Qtr	4th Qtr	Total
2000	9.15	-0.56	4.53	0.82	14.38
2001	1.82	5.13	-4.63	4.47	6.64
2002	7.35	-5.17	-2.42	13.38	12.63
2003	8.03	11.65	2.10	6.47	31.11
2004	3.16	-5.92	9.12	6.24	12.50

Trailing	Total Return%	+/- LB Aggr	+/-	%Rank Cat	Growth of $10,000
3 Mo	6.24	5.29	2.99	37	10,624
6 Mo	15.93	11.75	4.09	49	11,593
1 Yr	12.50	8.16	1.24	47	11,250
3 Yr Avg	18.44	12.25	3.85	34	16,615
5 Yr Avg	15.17	7.46	2.36	49	20,263
10 Yr Avg	14.45	6.73	—	25	38,562
15 Yr Avg	—	—	—	—	—

Tax Analysis	Tax-Adj Rtn%	%Rank Cat	Tax-Cost Rat	%Rank Cat
3 Yr (estimated)	15.29	24	2.66	25
5 Yr (estimated)	11.40	40	3.27	15
10 Yr (estimated)	10.21	9	3.70	10

Potential Capital Gain Exposure 9% of assets

Rating and Risk

Time Period	Load-Adj Return %	Morningstar Rtn vs Cat	Morningstar Risk vs Cat	Morningstar Risk-Adj Rating
1 Yr	12.50			
3 Yr	18.44	+Avg	+Avg	★★★★
5 Yr	15.17	Avg	Avg	★★★
10 Yr	14.45	+Avg	Avg	★★★★
Incept	13.70			

Other Measures	Standard Index LB Aggr	Best Fit Index
Alpha	12.1	0.6
Beta	1.00	1.24
R-Squared	16	89
Standard Deviation	12.57	
Mean	18.44	
Sharpe Ratio	1.37	

Portfolio Analysis 09-30-04

Total Fixed-Income:121	Date of Maturity	Amount $000	Value $000	% Net Assets
Russian Federation FRN	03-31-30	64,570	62,149	6.57
Brazil (Federative Repub	04-15-14	52,669	52,111	5.51
Brazil Federative Rep 11	08-17-40	31,125	34,922	3.69
FHLMC		34,866	34,497	3.65
United Mexican Sts Mtn B	04-08-33	32,745	34,431	3.64
Venezuela (Republic Of)	08-07-10	24,170	21,777	2.30
Venezuela Rep 9.25%	09-15-27	18,055	17,802	1.88
Russian Fedn 144A 2.25%	03-31-30	17,593	16,933	1.79
Russian Federation 11%	07-24-18	12,687	16,557	1.75
United Mexican Sts Mtn B	01-16-13	15,535	16,358	1.73
Peru Rep 9.125%	02-21-12	13,305	14,868	1.57
Russian Federation 12.75	06-24-28	9,092	13,820	1.46
Brazil Federative Rep 8.	04-15-24	14,345	13,771	1.46
Mobile Telesystems Fin S	01-30-08	12,710	13,473	1.42
Philippines Rep 8.375%	02-15-11	13,159	13,356	1.41
Petroliam Nasional Berha	10-15-26	11,310	13,275	1.40
Mexico-United Mexican St	12-30-19	11,355	13,013	1.38
Pemex Proj Fdg Master Tr	10-15-09	11,175	11,622	1.23
Brazil (Federative Repub	04-15-12	12,489	11,584	1.22
Brazil Federative Rep 14	10-15-09	8,605	11,100	1.17

Current Investment Style

Duration: Short Int Long
Quality: High Med Low

1 figure provided by fund

Avg Eff Duration[1]	—
Avg Eff Maturity	—
Avg Credit Quality	—
Avg Wtd Coupon	7.88%
Avg Wtd Price	102.83% of par

Coupon Range	% of Bonds	Rel Cat
0% PIK	7.9	2.0
0% to 6%	26.5	1.0
6% to 8%	20.2	1.1
8% to 10%	24.4	0.9
More than 10%	28.8	1.1

1.00=Category Average

Credit Analysis		% bonds 09-30-04	
US Govt	—	BB	—
AAA	—	B	—
AA	—	Below B	—
A	—	NR/NA	—
BBB	—		

Sector Breakdown	% of assets
US Treasuries	—
TIPS	—
US Agency	—
Mortgage Pass-Throughs	—
Mortgage CMO	—
Mortgage ARM	—
US Corporate	—
Asset-Backed	—
Convertible	—
Municipal	—
Corporate Inflation-Protected	—
Foreign Corporate	—
Foreign Govt	—

Composition			
Cash	8.9	Bonds	90.8
Stocks	0.0	Other	0.3

Special Securities	
Restricted/Illiquid Secs	10
Exotic Mortgage-Backed	0
Emerging-Markets Secs	—
Options/Futures/Warrants	No

Morningstar's Take by Dan Lefkovitz 12-10-04

In a roller-coaster year for emerging-markets bonds, Fidelity New Markets Income proves its mettle.

Manager John Carlson admits to being surprised by the stellar year emerging-markets bonds have posted in 2004. The asset class was coming off a frothy multiyear rally that saw this fund gain an average of nearly 20% per year between 1999 and 2003. Fearing that the good times might be over, Carlson positioned the portfolio defensively at the start 2004. He peeled back the fund's country overweightings and its interest-rate sensitivity. Those moves paid off this spring when emerging-markets bonds plummeted and the fund's losses were milder than its peers'.

But the asset class took off again in the summer, prompting Carlson to shift to a more aggressive stance. He upped the fund's exposure to countries such as Venezuela and steered the fund to an 11% overall gain for the year to date through Dec. 13, 2004, which trails the category average by less than 40 basis points. Carlson has now gone defensive again, in terms of both country weights and interest-rate exposure. This is not the first year that Carlson has successfully navigated ups and downs, either. In nearly 10 years at the helm, he has guided the fund to a 13.5% average annual gain, one of the category's best records.

Overall, Carlson has achieved his record through caution. The fund tends to hold a large number of bonds and its country allocation is usually close to that of its benchmark, the J.P. Morgan EMBI Global Index. When he overweights a country, it is because he likes its fundamentals. He favored Venezuela this year because the high price of oil has improved its debt position and he now has an overweighting on Brazil because he believes demand from China will continue to benefit Brazilian exports. In a still-volatile asset class (witness the sharp downturn in spring 2004) this fund's tempered approach, experienced management, and lower-than-average fees, give it an edge.

Address:	82 Devonshire Street Boston MA 02109 800-343-3548
Web Address:	www.fidelity.com
Inception:	05-04-93 *
Advisor:	Fidelity Management & Research Co. (FMR)
Subadvisor:	FMR Co., Inc. (FMRC)
NTF Plans:	Fidelity Retail-NTF, CommonWealth NTF

Minimum Purchase:	$2500	Add: $250	IRA: $2500
Min Auto Inv Plan:	$2500	Add: $100	
Sales Fees:	No-load, 1.00%R		
Management Fee:	0.69%		
Actual Fees:	Mgt:0.68%	Dist:	
Expense Projections:	3Yr:$359	5Yr:$622	10Yr:$1375
Income Distrib:	Monthly		

Fidelity New Millennium

Ticker	Load	NAV	Yield	Total Assets	Mstar Category
FMILX	Closed	$31.69	0.0%	$3,618 mil	Mid-Cap Growth

Governance and Management

Fiduciary Grade: B

Portfolio Manager(s)

Experienced. Fidelity has had lots of manager changes lately, but Neal Miller has been on board here since the fund's inception in 1992. He draws on Fidelity's deep bench of analysts.

Strategy

Manager Neal Miller combines top-down themes with Fidelity's crack stock-picking. Although high-growth names in rapidly growing industries form the core of the portfolio, Miller isn't afraid to delve into nontraditional growth areas like cyclicals or energy if he sees a catalyst. Although he will make large sector bets, Miller also spreads the fund's assets across more than 300 names, limiting issue-specific risk.

Historical Profile

Return Above Avg
Risk Above Avg
Rating ★★★★ Above Avg

Investment Style
Equity
Stock %: 94% 92% 95% 98% 93% 96% 97% 98% 96%

▼ Manager Change
▽ Partial Manager Change

Growth of $10,000
— Investment Values of Fund
— Investment Values of S&P 500

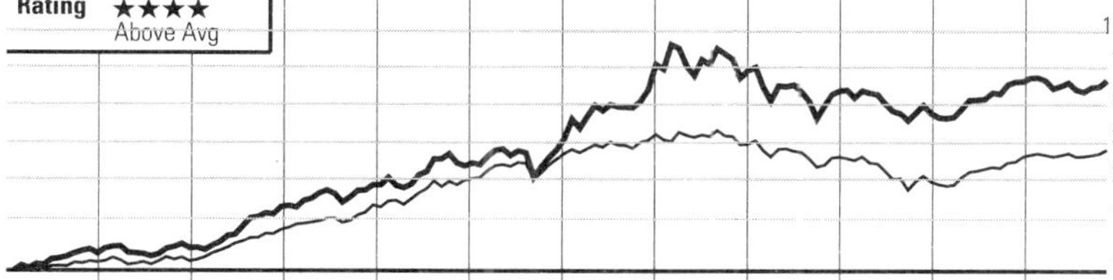

Performance Quartile (within Category)

1993	1994	1995	1996	1997	1998	1999	2000	2001	2002	2003	12-04	History
12.30	12.11	16.96	20.25	22.19	26.27	47.46	34.33	27.63	22.14	30.39	31.69	NAV
24.67	0.83	52.14	23.15	24.63	27.70	108.78	-6.03	-18.15	-19.87	37.31	4.28	Total Return %
14.61	-0.48	14.61	0.21	-8.72	-0.87	87.74	3.07	-6.27	2.22	8.64	-6.59	+/-S&P 500
13.48	2.99	18.16	5.67	2.09	9.84	57.49	5.72	2.00	7.54	-5.40	-11.20	+/-Russ MG
0.10	0.00	0.00	0.00	0.00	0.00	0.00	0.00	0.00	0.00	0.05	0.00	Income Return %
24.57	0.83	52.14	23.15	24.63	27.70	108.78	-6.03	-18.15	-19.87	37.26	4.28	Capital Return %
12	28	4	19	26	21	12	52	45	17	38	96	Total Rtn % Rank Cat
0.01	0.00	0.00	0.00	0.00	0.00	0.00	0.00	0.00	0.00	0.01	0.00	Income $
0.25	0.28	1.40	0.60	2.89	1.94	6.37	10.11	0.53	0.00	0.00	0.00	Capital Gains $
1.32	1.29	1.18	1.03	0.94	0.83	0.93	0.89	0.98	1.02	0.76	—	Expense Ratio %
-0.10	-0.05	-0.15	-0.17	-0.13	-0.13	-0.36	-0.36	-0.30	-0.38	0.02	—	Income Ratio %
204	199	176	158	142	121	116	97	85	91	97	—	Turnover Rate %
276	320	594	1,253	1,564	1,684	3,772	3,572	2,939	2,616	3,656	3,618	Net Assets $mil

Performance 12-31-04

	1st Qtr	2nd Qtr	3rd Qtr	4th Qtr	Total
2000	17.54	-10.82	5.97	-15.40	-6.03
2001	-26.06	17.35	-28.30	31.57	-18.15
2002	0.11	-11.89	-15.35	7.32	-19.87
2003	-3.57	18.55	5.97	13.35	37.31
2004	0.86	-2.06	-4.56	10.61	4.28

Trailing	Total Return%	+/- S&P 500	+/- Russ MG	%Rank Cat	Growth of $10,000
3 Mo	10.61	1.38	-3.33	86	11,061
6 Mo	5.56	-1.63	-3.45	78	10,556
1 Yr	4.28	-6.59	-11.20	96	10,428
3 Yr Avg	4.69	1.11	-1.47	41	11,474
5 Yr Avg	-2.47	-0.17	0.89	44	8,825
10 Yr Avg	18.57	6.50	7.34	2	54,922
15 Yr Avg	—	—	—	—	—

Tax Analysis	Tax-Adj Rtn%	%Rank Cat	Tax-Cost Rat	%Rank Cat
3 Yr (estimated)	4.68	34	0.01	2
5 Yr (estimated)	-3.64	44	1.20	54
10 Yr (estimated)	16.34	2	1.88	49

Potential Capital Gain Exposure: 16% of assets

Rating and Risk

Time Period	Load-Adj Return %	Morningstar Rtn vs Cat	Morningstar Risk vs Cat	Morningstar Risk-Adj Rating
1 Yr	4.28			
3 Yr	4.69	Avg	Avg	★★★
5 Yr	-2.47	Avg	+Avg	★★★
10 Yr	18.57	High	+Avg	★★★★
Incept	17.54			

Other Measures	Standard Index S&P 500	Best Fit Index Mstar Mid Growth TR
Alpha	1.5	1.8
Beta	1.05	0.86
R-Squared	74	89

Standard Deviation	19.49
Mean	4.69
Sharpe Ratio	0.17

Portfolio Analysis 08-31-04

Share change since 05-04 Total Stocks:240	Sector	PE	YTD Ret%	% Assets
Smith International	Energy	34.2	31.05	3.61
⊖ Boston Scientific	Health	32.3	-3.29	2.79
Puma AG Rudolf Dassler S	Goods	—	—	2.33
⊕ Genentech	Health	78.6	16.36	2.29
⊖ QLogic	Hardware	25.3	-28.78	2.26
☆ Gen Elec	Ind Mtrls	22.8	20.68	2.25
⊕ Adtran	Hardware	17.1	-37.70	2.19
⊖ Phelps Dodge	Ind Mtrls	11.1	30.78	2.17
⊕ McKesson	Health	15.8	-1.41	2.11
Cheesecake Factory	Consumer	39.7	10.59	2.09
⊖ Schlumberger	Energy	40.7	23.84	2.02
⊖ Thor Industries	Ind Mtrls	18.6	32.34	1.95
⊕ Zebra Technologies	Hardware	33.1	27.20	1.85
⊖ Garmin	Hardware	25.3	12.63	1.60
⊖ Winnebago Industries	Ind Mtrls	17.6	14.48	1.48
☆ Microsoft	Software	36.1	8.95	1.46
⊕ Cisco Systems	Hardware	24.5	-20.26	1.27
⊕ Harman International Ind	Goods	48.4	71.77	1.26
Roche Holding	Health	—	—	1.26
⊕ Waters	Health	27.6	41.10	1.14

Current Investment Style

Market Cap	%
Giant	13.4
Large	25.7
Mid	44.4
Small	15.7
Micro	0.8
Avg $mil: 6,834	

Value Measures		Rel Category
Price/Earnings	20.18	0.92
Price/Book	2.83	0.94
Price/Sales	1.31	0.74
Price/Cash Flow	12.18	1.26
Dividend Yield %	0.50	1.16

Growth Measures	%	Rel Category
Long-Term Erngs	14.42	0.92
Book Value	5.88	0.59
Sales	3.94	0.46
Cash Flow	10.71	0.88
Historical Erngs	12.09	0.76

Profitability	%	Rel Category
Return on Equity	13.86	0.96
Return on Assets	7.08	0.99
Net Margin	8.97	0.93

Sector Weightings	% of Stocks	Rel S&P 500	3 Year High	3 Year Low
Info	26.70	1.24		
Software	4.78	1.11	5	3
Hardware	16.81	1.65	38	17
Media	4.10	1.07	7	1
Telecom	1.01	0.32	3	1
Service	35.23	0.76		
Health	17.57	1.41	18	10
Consumer	9.09	1.00	18	9
Business	6.76	1.67	7	4
Financial	1.81	0.09	6	2
Mfg	38.08	1.19		
Goods	9.75	1.05	11	6
Ind Mtrls	18.62	1.47	19	8
Energy	9.05	1.26	9	5
Utilities	0.66	0.22	2	0

Composition

Cash	3.8
Stocks	96.2
Bonds	0.0
Other	0.1
Foreign (% of Stock)	11.0

Morningstar's Take by Christopher Traulsen 11-15-04

Fidelity New Millennium Fund still has the pieces in place to be a winner.

This fund--which remains closed to new investors--has struggled mightily in 2004. It's up just 0.7% for the year to date through Nov. 12, putting it in the category's worst decile for the period. The primary detractors from the fund's performance have been technology hardware stocks, as positions in Qlogic, Emulex, Foundry Networks, Adtran, and others have tanked thus far in 2004.

In hindsight, manager Neal Miller made a mistake in putting so many of his fund's eggs in that basket, but he appears to have learned from that. The fund's technology stake had fallen to 22.8% of assets by the end of September, down from 34% at the end of February. Miller isn't beholden to a benchmark, but he says he wants to rein in the fund's risk a bit.

That shouldn't prevent Miller from doing what he's always done here, however--spotting social and economic trends and the companies that are poised to benefit from them. Recently, for example, Miller has concluded that companies are going to need to improve their ability to close their annual books efficiently while meeting all the new Sarbanes-Oxley requirements. He's also keen on freight logistics given the expanding trade between China and the U.S.

Miller also can continue to draw on Fidelity's enormous resources to support him here. And--unlike most Fidelity funds--this one actually closed at a reasonable level of assets, and has remained closed. With an asset base of $3.3 billion, the fund remains nimble enough for Miller to invest as he sees fit.

Over time, the combination of Miller's trend-spotting, Fidelity's resources, and a relatively svelte asset base has produced excellent results here: The fund boasts top-flight long-term returns. It is more volatile than its average peer, but we continue to think highly of this offering.

Address:	82 Devonshire St Boston MA 02109 800-343-3548
Web Address:	www.fidelity.com
Inception:	12-28-92
Advisor:	Fidelity Management & Research Co. (FMR)
Subadvisor:	FMR Co., Inc. (FMRC)
NTF Plans:	Fidelity Retail-NTF, CommonWealth NTF

Minimum Purchase:	Closed	Add: —	IRA: —
Min Auto Inv Plan:	Closed	Add: —	
Sales Fees:	No-load		
Management Fee:	0.87%		
Actual Fees:	Mgt:0.87%	Dist:	
Expense Projections:	3Yr:$594	5Yr:$810	10Yr:$1431
Income Distrib:	Annually		

Fidelity OTC

Ticker	Load	NAV	Yield	Total Assets	Mstar Category
FOCPX	None	$34.69	1.2%	$8,143 mil	Large Growth

Governance and Management

Fiduciary Grade: B

Portfolio Manager(s)

Shep Perkins has run a number of communications-related sector funds for Fidelity. He also ran Select Medical Delivery for six months. Perkins received his B.A. from Amherst in 1993.

Strategy

The fund is tethered to the Nasdaq Composite Index. Management will adjust individual stock and industry weights, but the fund generally doesn't stray too far from its index. Because that's a pretty volatile index, high risk is baked into this fund. Manager Shep Perkins looks for fast growth and positive earnings surprises.

Historical Profile

Return Above Avg
Risk High
Rating ★★ Below Avg

Investment Style: Equity, Stock %: 92% 96% 97% 95% 97% 93% 88% 99% 100%

▼ Manager Change
▽ Partial Manager Change

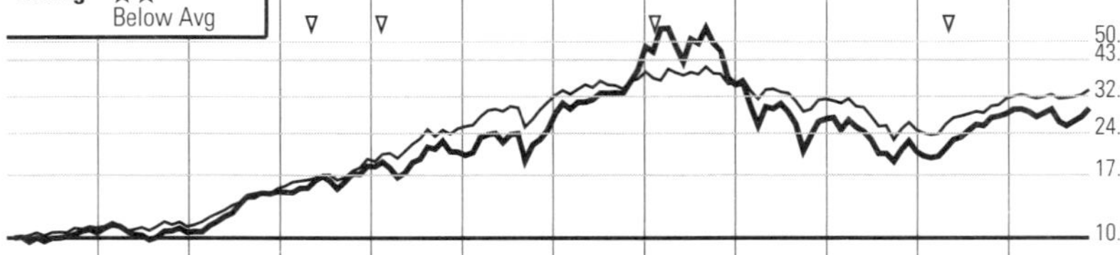

Growth of $10,000
— Investment Values of Fund
— Investment Values of S&P 500

Performance Quartile (within Category)

1993	1994	1995	1996	1997	1998	1999	2000	2001	2002	2003	12-04	History
24.14	23.27	30.33	32.71	33.45	43.63	67.97	41.05	31.17	23.91	32.47	34.69	NAV
8.33	-2.70	38.23	23.73	9.91	40.38	72.53	-26.81	-24.07	-23.29	35.80	8.12	Total Return %
-1.73	-4.01	0.70	0.79	-23.44	11.81	51.49	-17.71	-12.19	-1.20	7.13	-2.75	+/-S&P 500
5.46	-5.32	1.05	0.61	-20.58	1.67	39.37	-4.39	-3.65	4.59	6.05	1.82	+/-Russ 1000Gr
0.42	0.87	0.09	0.26	0.00	0.00	0.00	0.00	0.00	0.00	0.00	1.26	Income Return %
7.91	-3.57	38.14	23.47	9.91	40.38	72.53	-26.81	-24.07	-23.29	35.80	6.86	Capital Return %
61	61	17	17	97	20	6	92	67	22	13	44	Total Rtn % Rank Cat
0.10	0.21	0.02	0.08	0.00	0.00	0.00	0.00	0.00	0.00	0.00	0.41	Income $
3.42	0.00	1.80	4.32	2.52	2.38	5.51	12.66	0.00	0.00	0.00	0.00	Capital Gains $
1.08	0.88	0.81	0.82	0.84	0.75	0.74	0.75	0.94	1.09	1.12	0.89	Expense Ratio %
0.53	0.48	0.35	0.42	-0.15	-0.32	-0.16	-0.43	-0.40	-0.81	-0.71	-0.53	Income Ratio %
213	222	62	133	147	125	117	196	219	120	116	61	Turnover Rate %
1,343	1,381	2,350	3,387	3,858	5,476	11,705	10,979	8,070	5,974	7,940	8,143	Net Assets $mil

Performance 12-31-04

	1st Qtr	2nd Qtr	3rd Qtr	4th Qtr	Total
2000	16.20	-8.39	-3.45	-28.78	-26.81
2001	-28.06	19.40	-31.96	29.93	-24.07
2002	-0.96	-14.77	-16.50	8.83	-23.29
2003	-4.10	17.14	9.72	10.18	35.80
2004	1.66	1.94	-9.12	14.81	8.12

Trailing	Total Return%	+/- S&P 500	+/- Russ 1000Gr	%Rank Cat	Growth of $10,000
3 Mo	14.81	5.58	5.64	2	11,481
6 Mo	4.33	-2.86	0.86	58	10,433
1 Yr	8.12	-2.75	1.82	44	10,812
3 Yr Avg	4.05	0.47	4.23	13	11,265
5 Yr Avg	-8.94	-6.64	0.35	65	6,261
10 Yr Avg	11.04	-1.03	1.45	20	28,497
15 Yr Avg	11.19	0.26	1.69	18	49,089

Tax Analysis	Tax-Adj Rtn%	%Rank Cat	Tax-Cost Rat	%Rank Cat
3 Yr (estimated)	3.90	11	0.14	24
5 Yr (estimated)	-9.97	67	1.13	66
10 Yr (estimated)	9.00	21	1.84	65

Potential Capital Gain Exposure: -49% of assets

Rating and Risk

Time Period	Load-Adj Return %	Morningstar Rtn vs Cat	Morningstar Risk vs Cat	Morningstar Risk-Adj Rating
1 Yr	8.12			
3 Yr	4.05	+Avg	High	★★★★
5 Yr	-8.94	Avg	High	★★
10 Yr	11.04	+Avg	High	★★
Incept	14.50			

Other Measures	Standard Index S&P 500	Best Fit Index Mstar Small Growth
Alpha	0.8	1.0
Beta	1.13	0.75
R-Squared	77	92
Standard Deviation	20.33	
Mean	4.05	
Sharpe Ratio	0.13	

Portfolio Analysis 10-31-04

Share change since 07-04 Total Stocks:240	Sector	PE	YTD Ret%	% Assets
⊕ Microsoft	Software	36.1	8.95	13.38
Dell	Hardware	34.0	24.01	5.39
⊕ Intel	Hardware	19.8	-26.56	3.86
Yahoo	Media	95.1	67.36	2.61
Nextel Communications	Telecom	11.1	6.95	2.35
Ericsson Telephone ADR B	Hardware	—	77.91	2.23
Samsung Electronics	Goods	—	—	1.85
⊕ Flextronics Internationa	Hardware	—	-6.62	1.70
⊕ Alcatel SA ADR A	Hardware	—	21.63	1.41
⊕ Patterson-UTI Energy	Energy	33.3	18.55	1.37
Cognizant Technology Sol	Business	62.5	85.50	1.33
⊖ Ameritrade Holding	Financial	20.3	0.79	1.27
⊕ Comverse Technology	Hardware	—	39.00	1.24
⊖ Fifth Third Bancorp	Financial	14.1	-17.89	1.23
Motorola	Hardware	28.7	37.93	1.08
⊕ Qwest Communications Int	Telecom	—	2.78	1.00
NTL	Telecom	—	4.60	0.95
Applied Materials	Hardware	20.7	-23.80	0.94
Marvell Technology	Hardware	NMF	87.03	0.90
⊕ Lamar Advertising A	Business	—	14.63	0.90

Current Investment Style

Value Blnd Growth; Large Mid Small

Market Cap	%
Giant	32.5
Large	14.9
Mid	36.2
Small	13.3
Micro	3.0

Avg $mil: 11,340

Value Measures		Rel Category
Price/Earnings	22.44	1.06
Price/Book	2.81	0.87
Price/Sales	1.56	0.73
Price/Cash Flow	8.76	0.80
Dividend Yield %	0.34	0.44

Growth Measures	%	Rel Category
Long-Term Erngs	16.72	1.19
Book Value	4.74	0.37
Sales	0.95	0.11
Cash Flow	3.79	0.23
Historical Erngs	16.84	1.16

Profitability	%	Rel Category
Return on Equity	11.45	0.64
Return on Assets	6.01	0.64
Net Margin	8.32	0.68

Sector Weightings	% of Stocks	Rel S&P 500	3 Year High	3 Year Low
Info	64.21	2.99		
Software	20.30	4.72	27	19
Hardware	32.48	3.18	35	14
Media	5.00	1.30	6	0
Telecom	6.43	2.04	6	0
Service	28.10	0.61		
Health	10.46	0.84	20	10
Consumer	5.26	0.58	20	5
Business	7.86	1.94	14	7
Financial	4.52	0.22	7	4
Mfg	7.70	0.24		
Goods	3.53	0.38	4	1
Ind Mtrls	2.58	0.20	4	1
Energy	1.59	0.22	2	0
Utilities	0.00	0.00	0	0

Composition

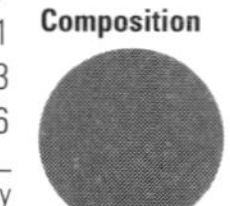

Cash	0.0
Stocks	100.0
Bonds	0.0
Other	0.0
Foreign (% of Stock)	11.8

Morningstar's Take by Christine Benz 10-16-04

Fidelity OTC faces competition on a few different fronts, and the comparisons don't favor it.

On the surface, this might look like a compelling pick. While it has been exceedingly volatile, its longer-term trailing returns are strong. Moreover, the fund managed to fare well in the disparate years of 2002 (the depths of the bear market) and 2003 (a euphoric rally). Finally, the fund's expenses are comfortably below the no-load category average.

Upon closer inspection, however, the fund looks less compelling. By charter, it must keep at least 80% of assets in stocks listed on the Nasdaq exchange, and the fund's official benchmark is the Nasdaq Composite Index. True, that restriction keeps it squarely focused on the fastest-growing companies, which usually list on Nasdaq. At the same time, however, the fund lacks the flexibility that some of its large-growth rivals have. So far in 2004, for example, some rivals have sought solace in energy-services names amid a bruising sell-off in tech shares. But this fund, because it's tied to the tech-heavy Nasdaq, has much less latitude to execute such maneuvers. The fund has lost more than 5% for the year to date through mid-October, landing in the large-growth group's bottom quartile.

And even for those investors who are looking for a fund that's tethered to the Nasdaq exchange, there are cheaper options. Fidelity now offers a Nasdaq Composite-tracking exchanged-traded fund for 0.30% per year, while Nasdaq 100 Trust Shares (Qubes), which offer purer exposure to the exchange's tech and biotech highfliers, can be had for just 0.18% per year. While this fund's expense ratio has dropped to 0.91% for the most recent fiscal year, its extra expense drag could prove difficult to make up over the long haul.

The fund has had several managers who have executed capably over the years, but we can't help but wonder whether investors really need a fund like this in the first place.

Address:	82 Devonshire St Boston MA 02109 800-343-3548
Web Address:	www.fidelity.com
Inception:	12-31-84
Advisor:	Fidelity Management & Research Co. (FMR)
Subadvisor:	FMR Co., Inc. (FMRC)
NTF Plans:	Fidelity Retail-NTF, CommonWealth NTF

Minimum Purchase:	$2500	Add: $250	IRA: $2500
Min Auto Inv Plan:	$2500	Add: $100	
Sales Fees:	No-load		
Management Fee:	0.86%		
Actual Fees:	Mgt:0.86%	Dist:	
Expense Projections:	3Yr:$240	5Yr:$417	10Yr:$930
Income Distrib:	Semi-Annually		

Fidelity Overseas

Ticker	Load	NAV	Yield	Total Assets	Mstar Category
FOSFX	None	$35.38	0.5%	$4,687 mil	Foreign Large Blend

Governance and Management

Fiduciary Grade: B

Portfolio Manager(s)

Rick Mace has worked at Fidelity since 1987 and has managed this fund for several years. He also oversees the foreign-stock portion of Fidelity Worldwide and helms world-allocation offering Fidelity Global Balanced. Mace is in charge of the firm's international-research team in Boston.

Strategy

This fund's sector and country weightings tend to move with those of the MSCI EAFE Index. Manager Rick Mace tries to get ahead of the index through stock-picking, although he will occasionally load up on a cluster of names when he finds a number of appealing picks. Mace's strategy is best described as growth at a reasonable price. Fidelity uses fair-value pricing on an as-needed basis.

Historical Profile

Return Average
Risk Above Avg
Rating ★★★ Neutral

Investment Style: Equity Stock %

86%	90%	81%	88%	93%	87%	98%	87%	93%

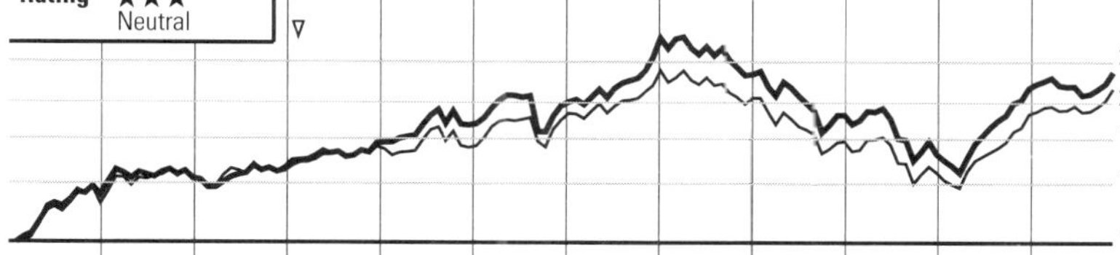

▼ Manager Change
∇ Partial Manager Change

Growth of $10,000
— Investment Values of Fund
— Investment Values of MSCI EAFE

Performance Quartile (within Category)

1993	1994	1995	1996	1997	1998	1999	2000	2001	2002	2003	12-04	History
27.43	27.30	29.07	30.84	32.54	35.98	48.01	34.37	27.42	22.00	31.43	35.38	NAV
40.05	1.27	9.06	13.10	10.92	12.84	42.89	-18.33	-20.22	-19.45	44.30	13.54	Total Return %
7.49	-6.51	-2.15	7.05	9.14	-7.09	15.86	-4.14	1.20	-3.51	5.71	-6.71	+/-MSCI EAFE
7.84	-6.08	-2.35	6.23	8.65	-5.85	14.91	-4.97	1.17	-3.65	4.88	-6.84	+/-MSCI Wd xUS
2.16	0.00	1.25	1.27	1.10	0.61	1.22	1.79	0.00	0.33	1.36	0.60	Income Return %
37.89	1.27	7.81	11.83	9.82	12.23	41.67	-20.12	-20.22	-19.78	42.94	12.94	Capital Return %
19	37	70	43	25	61	31	64	41	80	2	90	Total Rtn % Rank Cat
0.43	0.00	0.34	0.37	0.34	0.20	0.44	0.83	0.00	0.09	0.30	0.19	Income $
0.00	0.47	0.35	1.63	1.34	0.51	2.64	4.12	0.00	0.00	0.00	0.11	Capital Gains $
1.27	1.24	1.05	1.12	1.20	1.24	1.23	1.13	1.12	1.16	1.00	1.01	Expense Ratio %
1.00	0.90	1.78	1.74	1.28	0.82	0.85	0.55	0.63	0.42	0.75	0.55	Income Ratio %
64	49	49	82	68	69	85	132	95	72	104	79	Turnover Rate %
1,520	2,194	2,410	3,247	3,705	3,847	5,404	4,653	3,481	2,843	3,961	4,687	Net Assets $mil

Performance 12-31-04

	1st Qtr	2nd Qtr	3rd Qtr	4th Qtr	Total
2000	0.54	-5.26	-7.24	-7.57	-18.33
2001	-11.26	0.00	-18.39	10.16	-20.22
2002	2.19	-4.14	-20.74	3.74	-19.45
2003	-10.00	23.13	11.90	16.37	44.30
2004	5.82	-4.57	-1.58	14.23	13.54

Trailing	Total Return%	+/- MSCI EAFE	+/- MSCI Wd xUS	%Rank Cat	Growth of $10,000
3 Mo	14.23	-1.09	-0.92	48	11,423
6 Mo	12.43	-2.57	-2.94	84	11,243
1 Yr	13.54	-6.71	-6.84	90	11,354
3 Yr Avg	9.69	-2.20	-2.53	45	13,198
5 Yr Avg	-2.97	-1.84	-2.21	55	8,601
10 Yr Avg	6.61	0.99	0.67	37	18,966
15 Yr Avg	6.06	1.83	1.65	50	24,170

Tax Analysis	Tax-Adj Rtn%	%Rank Cat	Tax-Cost Rat	%Rank Cat
3 Yr (estimated)	9.48	37	0.19	21
5 Yr (estimated)	-3.65	51	0.70	46
10 Yr (estimated)	5.53	31	1.01	39

Potential Capital Gain Exposure: 6% of assets

Rating and Risk

Time Period	Load-Adj Return %	Morningstar Rtn vs Cat	Morningstar Risk vs Cat	Morningstar Risk-Adj Rating
1 Yr	13.54			
3 Yr	9.69	Avg	High	★★★
5 Yr	-2.97	Avg	+Avg	★★★
10 Yr	6.61	Avg	+Avg	★★★
Incept	12.82			

Other Measures	Standard Index S&P 500	Best Fit Index MSCI Wd xUS
Alpha	-2.4	-2.9
Beta	1.06	1.08
R-Squared	94	94
Standard Deviation	18.93	
Mean	9.69	
Sharpe Ratio	0.44	

Portfolio Analysis 10-31-04

Share change since 07-04 Total Stocks:167	Sector	Country	% Assets
⊖ Vodafone Grp	Telecom	U.K.	4.07
⊕ Deutsche Telekom AG ADR	Telecom	Germany	3.69
⊖ TOTAL	Energy	France	2.24
⊕ ASML Holding	Hardware	Netherlands	2.09
⊖ HSBC Hldgs	Financial	U.K.	1.98
Allianz	Financial	Germany	1.72
⊕ Sumitomo Mitsui Financia	Financial	Japan	1.70
⊖ Novartis	Health	Switzerland	1.57
⊕ UBS	Financial	Switzerland	1.50
⊖ BP	Energy	U.K.	1.37
⊕ Nomura Hldgs	Financial	Japan	1.21
BNP Paribas	Financial	France	1.18
⊖ Talisman Energy	Energy	Canada	1.16
⊕ ING Groep	Financial	Netherlands	1.15
⊕ Alcatel SA ADR A	Hardware	France	1.13
Toyota Motor	Goods	Japan	1.13
Telefonica S A	Telecom	Spain	1.11
⊖ Roche Holding	Health	Switzerland	1.09
The News Corporation Lim	Media	United States	1.07
⊕ Credit Suisse Grp	Financial	Switzerland	0.99

Current Investment Style

Market Cap	%
Giant	58.4
Large	25.6
Mid	15.4
Small	0.6
Micro	0.0
Avg $mil: 22,136	

Value Measures		Rel Category
Price/Earnings	13.85	1.01
Price/Book	1.93	1.07
Price/Sales	1.13	1.24
Price/Cash Flow	4.38	0.89
Dividend Yield %	1.86	0.73

Growth Measures	%	Rel Category
Long-Term Erngs	13.85	1.29
Book Value	-2.42	NMF
Sales	4.77	1.92
Cash Flow	5.09	0.91
Historical Erngs	5.38	0.96

Composition

Cash	6.6	Bonds	0.0
Stocks	92.8	Other	0.5
Foreign (% of Stock)			97.4

Sector Weightings	% of Stocks	Rel MSCI EAFE	3 Year High	3 Year Low
Info	33.73	2.03		
Software	2.39	2.21	2	0
Hardware	12.44	3.41	19	8
Media	4.30	1.89	5	1
Telecom	14.60	1.52	15	7
Service	40.94	0.92		
Health	8.68	1.20	12	9
Consumer	4.44	0.88	5	2
Business	1.06	0.19	1	0
Financial	26.76	0.99	34	24
Mfg	25.33	0.66		
Goods	9.44	0.69	14	9
Ind Mtrls	7.57	0.62	10	5
Energy	7.57	1.03	14	8
Utilities	0.75	0.14	1	0

Regional Exposure	% Stock		% Stock
UK/W. Europe	60	N. America	6
Japan	18	Latn America	3
Asia X Japan	12	Other	1

Country Exposure	% Stock		% Stock
U.K.	18	France	9
Japan	18	Switzerland	7
Germany	13		

Morningstar's Take by Dan Lefkovitz 11-29-04

Strategy changes have yet to pay off for this decent but unspectacular fund.

Fidelity Overseas is having a rough year. Its 9.4% return for the year through Nov. 18, 2004, is good in absolute terms, but lags the foreign large-blend category average by 4 percentage points. That puts the fund in the category's bottom quartile.

The underperformance can be blamed partially on sector allocation. Manager Rick Mace has overweighted technology-related shares such as hardware, which has recorded the worst year-to-date performance of the twelve sectors tracked by Morningstar. For example, ASM Holding, a Dutch maker of chip equipment and 1.4% of this fund's portfolio as of July 31, has lost 20% for the year to date. Meanwhile, the fund's underweighting in the utilities and industrial-materials sectors--among the year's top performers--has hurt.

This year's lagging performance means that the jury is still out on changes Mace made to his strategy earlier this year. He still employs a growth-at-a-reasonable price approach and keeps his sector and country allocations reasonably in line with those of his benchmark, the MSCI EAFE index. But he has decided to concentrate more of his portfolio in his top 50 picks. So far the change has yet to improve performance.

This fund has always been respectable, but far from stellar. Since Mace began running the portfolio in the spring of 1996, it has outpaced the category by an average of roughly 1 percentage point per year. But it has also been more volatile than its peers, and the fund has underperformed during difficult years like 2000 and 2002. This isn't a bad fund, but investors can get similar foreign-stock exposure at index fund Fidelity Spartan International Index. And if you are going to buy this fund, wait until after it makes a capital gains distribution on Dec. 3, 2004.

Address:	82 Devonshire St Boston MA 02109 800-343-3548
Web Address:	www.fidelity.com
Inception:	12-04-84
Advisor:	Fidelity Management & Research Co. (FMR)
Subadvisor:	FMR Co., Inc. (FMRC)
NTF Plans:	Fidelity Retail-NTF, CommonWealth NTF

Minimum Purchase:	$2500	Add: $250	IRA: $2500
Min Auto Inv Plan:	$100	Add: $100	
Sales Fees:	No-load, 1.00%R		
Management Fee:	0.92%		
Actual Fees:	Mgt:0.62%	Dist:	
Expense Projections:	3Yr:$331	5Yr:$574	10Yr:$1271
Income Distrib:	Annually		

Fidelity Pacific Basin

Analyst Pick	Ticker	Load	NAV	Yield	Total Assets	Mstar Category
	FPBFX	None	$19.77	0.4%	$497 mil	Diversified Pacific/Asia

Governance and Management

Fiduciary Grade: B

Portfolio Manager(s)

Dale Nicholls has managed Fidelity Advisor Japan since September 2003 and continues to run that fund in addition to this one. Nicholls began working as analyst in Fidelity's Tokyo office in 1996 and has managed sector funds available only in Japan. This fund was previously run by William Kennedy, who started in 1998 but took a one-year hiatus, from September 2002 to September 2003, to work in Fidelity's Boston headquarters.

Strategy

Fidelity hasn't provided specific details regarding the approach new manager Dale Nicholls will take with this fund. But he's likely to adhere to predecessor William Kennedy's growth-at-a-reasonable-price, benchmark-conscious, Japancentric approach.

Historical Profile

Return Average
Risk Average
Rating ★★★★ Above Avg

Investment Style: Equity Stock %: 97% 93% 94% 96% 94% 97% 97% 94% 97%

▼ Manager Change ▽ Partial Manager Change

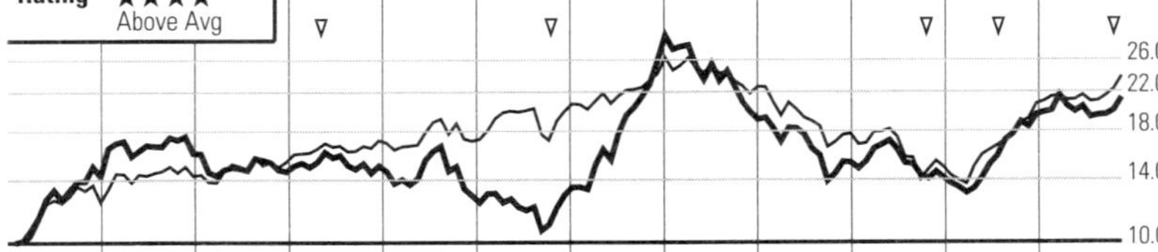

Performance Quartile (within Category)

1993	1994	1995	1996	1997	1998	1999	2000	2001	2002	2003	12-04	History
18.80	16.19	15.20	14.70	12.23	13.22	28.74	17.29	13.85	12.76	17.53	19.77	NAV
63.91	-2.81	-6.12	-2.76	-15.10	8.26	119.61	-35.32	-19.90	-7.87	38.69	14.08	Total Return %
31.35	-10.59	-17.33	-8.81	-16.88	-11.67	92.58	-21.13	1.52	8.07	0.10	-6.17	+/-MSCI EAFE
28.22	-15.64	-8.90	5.82	10.39	5.85	61.98	-9.55	5.49	1.42	0.21	-4.90	+/-MSCI Pac
1.11	0.11	0.00	0.53	1.70	0.16	1.97	3.90	0.00	0.00	1.25	0.46	Income Return %
62.80	-2.92	-6.12	-3.29	-16.80	8.10	117.64	-39.22	-19.90	-7.87	37.44	13.62	Capital Return %
40	50	100	100	34	6	6	68	47	11	52	84	Total Rtn % Rank Cat
0.13	0.02	0.00	0.08	0.25	0.02	0.26	1.12	0.00	0.00	0.16	0.08	Income $
0.27	2.02	0.00	0.00	0.00	0.00	0.00	0.23	0.00	0.00	0.00	0.13	Capital Gains $
1.59	1.54	1.32	1.24	1.31	1.72	1.36	1.22	1.45	1.50	1.17	1.19	Expense Ratio %
0.15	0.04	0.44	0.30	-0.04	-0.16	-0.24	-0.42	-0.11	-0.15	0.41	0.42	Income Ratio %
77	88	65	85	42	57	101	144	123	98	97	145	Turnover Rate %
527	476	469	447	214	227	989	447	331	297	430	497	Net Assets $mil

Performance 12-31-04

	1st Qtr	2nd Qtr	3rd Qtr	4th Qtr	Total
2000	-4.91	-9.44	-11.16	-15.45	-35.32
2001	-10.64	3.62	-21.42	10.10	-19.90
2002	7.44	-0.47	-12.42	-1.62	-7.87
2003	-7.45	16.17	16.84	10.40	38.69
2004	10.50	-5.73	-4.05	14.14	14.07

Trailing	Total Return%	+/- MSCI EAFE	+/- MSCI Pac	%Rank Cat	Growth of $10,000
3 Mo	14.14	-1.18	0.18	27	11,414
6 Mo	9.51	-5.49	-0.46	80	10,951
1 Yr	14.08	-6.17	-4.90	84	11,408
3 Yr Avg	13.38	1.49	-0.95	37	14,575
5 Yr Avg	-5.46	-4.33	-1.75	73	7,552
10 Yr Avg	3.36	-2.26	4.02	46	13,916
15 Yr Avg	3.51	-0.72	4.56	100	16,778

Tax Analysis	Tax-Adj Rtn%	%Rank Cat	Tax-Cost Rat	%Rank Cat
3 Yr (estimated)	13.16	32	0.19	42
5 Yr (estimated)	-6.06	53	0.63	44
10 Yr (estimated)	2.88	37	0.46	30

Potential Capital Gain Exposure: 8% of assets

Rating and Risk

Time Period	Load-Adj Return %	Morningstar Rtn vs Cat	Morningstar Risk vs Cat	Morningstar Risk-Adj Rating
1 Yr	14.08			
3 Yr	13.38	Avg	Avg	★★★
5 Yr	-5.46	-Avg	Avg	★★★
10 Yr	3.36	Avg	Avg	★★★★
Incept	5.85			

Other Measures	Standard Index S&P 500	Best Fit Index MSCI Pac
Alpha	4.3	0.0
Beta	0.73	0.93
R-Squared	57	93
Standard Deviation	16.99	
Mean	13.38	
Sharpe Ratio	0.71	

Portfolio Analysis 10-31-04

Share change since 07-04 Total Stocks:194	Sector	Country	% Assets
⊖ Toyota Motor	Goods	Japan	3.90
BHP Billiton Ltd	Ind Mtrls	Australia	1.69
East Japan Railway	Business	Japan	1.57
⊕ Fuji Photo Film	Goods	Japan	1.54
⊕ Techtronic Industries	Consumer	Hong Kong	1.49
⊖ Honda Mtr	Goods	Japan	1.47
Esprit Hldgs Ltd	Consumer	Hong Kong	1.32
⊖ Canon	Goods	Japan	1.28
Yamanouchi Pharmaceutica	Health	Japan	1.27
⊕ Konica Minolta Hldgs	Goods	Japan	1.17
Millea Hldgs	Financial	Japan	1.15
☼ Hikari Tsushin	Telecom	Japan	1.15
☼ Hyundai Motor	Goods	Korea	1.11
SFCG	Financial	Japan	1.08
Bridgestone	Ind Mtrls	Japan	1.07
USS	Consumer	Japan	1.05
Hoya	Goods	Japan	1.03
Aisin Seiki	Ind Mtrls	Japan	1.03
⊕ UFJ Hldgs	Financial	Japan	1.02
Ricoh	Ind Mtrls	Japan	1.02

Current Investment Style

Value Blnd Growth / Large Mid Small

Market Cap	%
Giant	30.2
Large	38.0
Mid	26.8
Small	5.0
Micro	0.0
Avg $mil: 5,205	

Value Measures		Rel Category
Price/Earnings	14.50	0.94
Price/Book	1.27	0.98
Price/Sales	0.63	0.67
Price/Cash Flow	4.31	0.89
Dividend Yield %	2.63	1.15

Growth Measures	%	Rel Category
Long-Term Erngs	26.87	1.93
Book Value	4.61	1.38
Sales	8.61	2.60
Cash Flow	0.63	0.21
Historical Erngs	18.40	1.16

Composition

Cash	1.3	Bonds	0.0
Stocks	97.4	Other	1.3
Foreign (% of Stock)			99.0

Sector Weightings	% of Stocks	Rel MSCI EAFE	3 Year High	3 Year Low
Info	10.93	0.66		
Software	1.15	1.06	1	0
Hardware	1.29	0.35	14	1
Media	0.93	0.41	4	1
Telecom	7.56	0.79	8	5
Service	49.01	1.10		
Health	6.20	0.85	7	3
Consumer	12.08	2.40	13	6
Business	8.64	1.59	9	2
Financial	22.09	0.82	30	22
Mfg	40.05	1.04		
Goods	22.14	1.62	28	19
Ind Mtrls	15.90	1.29	16	8
Energy	2.01	0.27	2	0
Utilities	0.00	0.00	3	0

Regional Exposure	% Stock		
UK/W. Europe	1	N. America	1
Japan	51	Latn America	0
Asia X Japan	47	Other	0

Country Exposure	% Stock		
Japan	51	South Korea	8
Australia	14	India	3
Hong Kong	9		

Morningstar's Take by Dan Lefkovitz 10-14-04

While not a plus, the manager change at Fidelity Pacific Basin is not a cause for serious concern.

In October 2004, Dale Nicholls replaced William Kennedy as manager of this fund. Nicholls has managed Fidelity Advisor Japan since September 2003 and will continue to run that fund in addition to this one.

Under Kennedy, this was a blue-chip-heavy fund that didn't deviate much from its benchmark, the MSCI All Country Pacific Index. This meant an especially hefty Japan stake. Kennedy also put more in Australia and less in emerging markets than his peers in the Diversified Pacific/Asia category, except for a foray into China in 2003. By July 31, 2004, Kennedy had grown the fund's Japan stake to 61%--well above the category average.

Fidelity declined to provide specific details about the approach Nicholls plans to take with this fund. However, given the way past manager changes have gone on Fidelity's specialized funds, Nicholls is unlikely to substantially alter Kennedy's growth-at-a-reasonable price, benchmark conscious style.

Considering that Nicholls' other fund has an all-Japan mandate, it also wouldn't be surprising if he preserved this fund's large-cap, Japancentric focus. That said, Nicholls' current portfolio at Fidelity Advisor Japan contains some names among its top holdings that aren't found in most large-cap-oriented Japan funds. Thus, it's possible that Nicholls will add spice to the Pacific Basin portfolio by dabbling in smaller fare.

We've noted before that Fidelity's specialized funds usually weather manager changes smoothly. Nicholls will be supported by Fidelity's formidable research team and will be aided by the fund's 1.17% expense ratio--the category's lowest. But given Nicholls' limited record running retail mutual funds available to U.S. investors, not to mention this fund's narrow regional mandate, it's wise to approach it with caution.

Address:	82 Devonshire St Boston MA 02109 800-343-3548
Web Address:	www.fidelity.com
Inception:	10-01-86
Advisor:	Fidelity Management & Research Co. (FMR)
Subadvisor:	FMR Co., Inc. (FMRC)
NTF Plans:	Fidelity Retail-NTF, CommonWealth NTF

Minimum Purchase:	$2500	Add: $250	IRA: $2500
Min Auto Inv Plan:	$2500	Add: $100	
Sales Fees:	No-load, 1.50%R		
Management Fee:	0.99%		
Actual Fees:	Mgt:0.99%	Dist:	
Expense Projections:	3Yr:$721	5Yr:$1027	10Yr:$1897
Income Distrib:	Annually		

Fidelity Puritan

Ticker	Load	NAV	Yield	Total Assets	Mstar Category
FPURX	None	$18.95	2.3%	$23,935 mil	Moderate Allocation

Governance and Management

Fiduciary Grade: B

Portfolio Manager(s)

Equity manager Stephen Petersen took the helm here in February 2000. He has built a strong record at Fidelity Equity-Income, which he has run since 1993. He also has experience managing gargantuan sums of money--a plus given Puritan's huge asset base. The bond portfolio was overseen by Kevin Grant until he retired in late 2004. Grant is succeeded by George Fischer, an experienced bond manager. As did Grant, Fischer will rely heavily on the rest of Fidelity's bond team in putting together this portfolio.

Strategy

Manager Stephen Petersen tries to ferret out blue chips with above-average dividend yields. That keeps him out of pricey, high-growth plays, but he picks up growth on the cheap where he can. Although Petersen holds some mid-caps, the fund's huge asset base leads him to emphasize the market's giants. Bond manager George Fischer eschews interest-rate bets. He keeps the bulk of the portfolio in high-quality credits, but he does dabble in high-yield debt. The fund typically has 60%-65% of its assets in stocks, although that figure has ranged higher or lower on occasion.

Performance 12-31-04

	1st Qtr	2nd Qtr	3rd Qtr	4th Qtr	Total
2000	-0.07	0.58	4.39	2.72	7.77
2001	-3.32	3.64	-6.80	5.96	-1.06
2002	2.21	-5.59	-10.74	6.92	-7.91
2003	-3.16	12.31	1.99	10.17	22.20
2004	2.10	0.38	0.11	6.51	9.27

Trailing	Total Return%	+/- S&P 500	+/- DJ 60%	%Rank Cat	Growth of $10,000
3 Mo	6.51	-2.72	-0.97	60	10,651
6 Mo	6.62	-0.57	-0.91	47	10,662
1 Yr	9.28	-1.59	-1.89	40	10,928
3 Yr Avg	7.14	3.56	-0.12	13	12,299
5 Yr Avg	5.57	7.87	0.33	12	13,113
10 Yr Avg	10.41	-1.66	-0.08	28	26,921
15 Yr Avg	10.51	-0.42	0.56	17	44,774

Tax Analysis	Tax-Adj Rtn%	%Rank Cat	Tax-Cost Rat	%Rank Cat
3 Yr (estimated)	5.81	17	1.24	83
5 Yr (estimated)	3.93	11	1.55	76
10 Yr (estimated)	7.99	30	2.19	78

Potential Capital Gain Exposure: 15% of assets

Historical Profile

Return Above Avg
Risk Below Avg
Rating ★★★★ Above Avg

Investment Style: Equity Stock % — 61% 62% 59% 62% 61% 60% 56% 61% 60%

▼ Manager Change
▽ Partial Manager Change

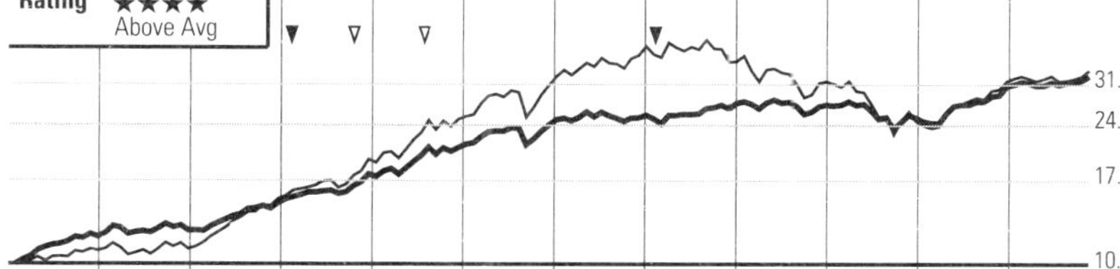

Growth of $10,000
— Investment Values of Fund
— Investment Values of S&P 500

Performance Quartile (within Category)

History

	1993	1994	1995	1996	1997	1998	1999	2000	2001	2002	2003	12-04
NAV	15.75	14.81	17.01	17.24	19.38	20.07	19.03	18.83	17.67	15.79	18.47	18.95
Total Return %	21.45	1.78	21.46	15.15	22.35	16.59	2.86	7.77	-1.06	-7.91	22.20	9.28
+/-S&P 500	11.39	0.47	-16.07	-7.79	-11.00	-11.98	-18.18	16.87	10.82	14.18	-6.47	-1.59
+/-DJ 60%	9.72	3.73	-3.31	3.81	3.15	4.20	-9.99	3.33	-1.22	2.63	-1.86	-1.89
Income Return %	5.05	3.50	3.36	3.80	4.03	3.57	3.26	3.28	3.24	2.86	2.89	2.50
Capital Return %	16.40	-1.72	18.10	11.35	18.32	13.02	-0.40	4.49	-4.30	-10.77	19.31	6.78
Total Rtn % Rank Cat	5	9	89	43	27	31	82	17	20	17	30	40
Income $	0.72	0.54	0.49	0.62	0.68	0.67	0.64	0.61	0.60	0.50	0.45	0.45
Capital Gains $	1.36	0.71	0.44	1.54	0.96	1.56	0.97	1.01	0.35	0.00	0.30	0.72
Expense Ratio %	0.74	0.79	0.77	0.72	0.66	0.63	0.63	0.64	0.63	0.64	0.66	0.64
Income Ratio %	4.89	4.00	3.50	3.44	3.69	3.40	3.23	3.24	3.23	3.03	3.03	2.46
Turnover Rate %	76	74	76	139	80	84	80	62	67	79	86	67
Net Assets $mil	8,988	11,769	15,628	18,502	22,822	25,682	24,371	21,369	20,315	18,031	21,964	23,935

Rating and Risk

Time Period	Load-Adj Return %	Morningstar Rtn vs Cat	Morningstar Risk vs Cat	Morningstar Risk-Adj Rating
1 Yr	9.27			
3 Yr	7.14	+Avg	Avg	★★★★
5 Yr	5.57	+Avg	-Avg	★★★★
10 Yr	10.41	+Avg	-Avg	★★★★
Incept	11.83			

Other Measures	Standard Index S&P 500	Best Fit Index Russ 1000 VI
Alpha	4.0	0.9
Beta	0.63	0.64
R-Squared	92	96

Standard Deviation	10.39
Mean	7.14
Sharpe Ratio	0.56

Portfolio Analysis 10-31-04

Total Stocks:212 Share change since 07-31-04	Sectors	P/E Ratio	YTD Return %	% Net Assets
ExxonMobil	Energy	13.9	-2.75	2.09
⊕ Bank of America	Financial	12.3	-3.85	2.00
⊕ Citigroup	Financial	15.3	0.08	1.68
⊖ J.P. Morgan Chase & Co.	Financial	19.4	-1.99	1.53
⊕ American International Gr	Financial	16.2	2.25	1.47
Fannie Mae	Financial	9.1	-1.07	1.23
Total SA ADF	Energy	17.0	-4.33	1.05
Verizon Communications	Telecom	32.4	-3.79	1.04
⊕ SBC Communications	Telecom	15.4	-3.12	1.04

Total Fixed-Income:706	Date of Maturity	Amount $000	Value $000	% Net Assets
FNMA 0.05%	11-01-34	766,000	762,888	3.21
FNMA 0.07%	09-01-23	185,802	197,566	0.83
US Treasury Note 2.75%	07-31-06	192,875	193,771	0.82
FNMA 0.06%	02-01-32	158,384	166,834	0.70
US Treasury Note 3.375%	12-15-08	152,200	153,722	0.65
FNMA 5%	09-01-17	148,230	151,479	0.64
FNMA 0.04%	11-01-19	128,000	128,240	0.54
FNMA 0.04%	08-01-33	116,928	113,714	0.48
US Treasury Note 5%	08-15-11	91,530	98,849	0.42

Equity Style
Style: Value
Size: Large-Cap

Value Measures		Rel Category
Price/Earnings	15.49	0.93
Price/Book	2.19	0.90
Price/Sales	1.22	0.92
Price/Cash Flow	5.46	0.75
Dividend Yield %	2.01	1.28

Growth Measures	%	Rel Category
Long-Term Erngs	10.50	0.90
Book Value	5.42	0.94
Sales	3.99	0.77
Cash Flow	6.69	0.84
Historical Erngs	13.86	1.28

Market Cap %			
Giant	52.6	Small	1.5
Large	34.9	Micro	0.0
Mid	11.1	Avg $mil:	40,407

Fixed-Income Style
Duration: —
Quality: —

Avg Eff Duration[1]	—
Avg Eff Maturity	—
Avg Credit Quality	—
Avg Wtd Coupon	4.34%

[1]figure provided by fund

Sector Weightings	% of Stocks	Rel S&P 500	3 Year High	3 Year Low
Info	17.47	0.81		
Software	1.02	0.24	1	0
Hardware	4.68	0.46	5	4
Media	5.98	1.56	6	4
Telecom	5.79	1.84	7	4
Service	43.46	0.94		
Health	7.70	0.62	8	5
Consumer	3.21	0.35	6	3
Business	2.32	0.57	4	2
Financial	30.23	1.46	32	29
Mfg	39.07	1.22		
Goods	6.85	0.73	8	6
Ind Mtrls	16.79	1.33	19	14
Energy	12.42	1.73	16	12
Utilities	3.01	1.02	3	1

Composition

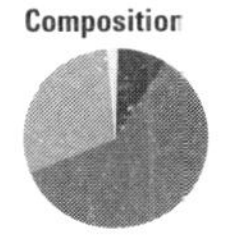

Cash	9.1
Stocks	59.7
Bonds	29.8
Other	1.5
Foreign (% of Stock)	9.7

Morningstar's Take by Christopher Traulsen 01-02-05

Fidelity Puritan gets the job done.

This fund has just put the finishing touches on another solid year. It ended 2004 up 9.3%, putting it squarely in the moderate-allocation category's top half for the period. It was helped by its healthy allocation to energy and industrials, both of which fared well in the face of strong global demand. Manager Stephen Petersen's focus on cheap, dividend-paying securities also kept the fund out of the technology sector--an area that struggled.

The fund won't always have it so good. Its value style comes in and out of favor, and the fund can lag when growth equities lead the market. Its 1999 return, for example, badly lagged the category average. However, Petersen's style also helps protect investors from the risks inherent in pricey growth stocks, as is evident from the fund's stalwart bear-market performance.

The fund's bond portfolio is also fairly tame. It focuses on high-quality, intermediate securities, though it will make small credit bets. In recent years, for example, the fund was helped by a foray into high-yield bonds. Petersen and his colleagues took that weighting down earlier this year, however, as the yield spread relative to higher-quality credits had narrowed.

Petersen has only been at the helm here since 2000, but he has built a fine long-term record at Fidelity Equity-Income, an all-equity offering run in the same fashion as this fund's equity portfolio. He has the advantage of being backed by Fidelity's deep research bench. Bond manager Kevin Grant recently retired and was replaced by George Fischer, but we don't expect any material changes to the fund's fixed-income style, as Fidelity's bond team has long used a team-oriented, uniform approach to managing bond portfolios.

We continue to think this fund is an excellent choice for relatively cautious investors. But those seeking broad equity exposure may wish to pair it with a small-cap fund and a growth offering, as Petersen sticks mainly to large-cap value stocks.

Address:	82 Devonshire Street Boston MA 02109 800-343-3548
Web Address:	
Inception:	04-16-47
Advisor:	Fidelity Management & Research Co. (FMR)
Subadvisor:	FMR Co., Inc. (FMRC)
NTF Plans:	Fidelity Retail-NTF, CommonWealth NTF

Minimum Purchase:	$2500	Add: $250	IRA: $2500
Min Auto Inv Plan:	$2500	Add: $100	
Sales Fees:	No-load		
Management Fee:	0.43%		
Actual Fees:	Mgt:0.43%	Dist:	
Expense Projections:	3Yr:$205	5Yr:$357	10Yr:$798
Income Distrib:	Quarterly		

Fidelity Real Estate Inv

Ticker	Load	NAV	Yield	Total Assets	Mstar Category
FRESX	None	$29.54	2.2%	$4,557 mil	Specialty-Real Estate

Governance and Management

Fiduciary Grade: B

Portfolio Manager(s)

The fund enjoys an experienced and deep management team. Manager Steve Buller has been in charge since October 1998 and served as an analyst on the fund before that. He is supported by one half-time and four full-time REIT analysts.

Strategy

This fund tends to favor real estate investment trusts (REITs) over real estate operating companies (REOCs). While doing so, it focuses on large, high-quality REITs with strong earnings and cash flow, and it moves at a relatively moderate pace.

Historical Profile

Return Average
Risk Average
Rating ★★★ Neutral

Investment Style: Equity Stock %

91%	94%	92%	88%	88%	86%	92%	95%	96%

▼ Manager Change
▽ Partial Manager Change

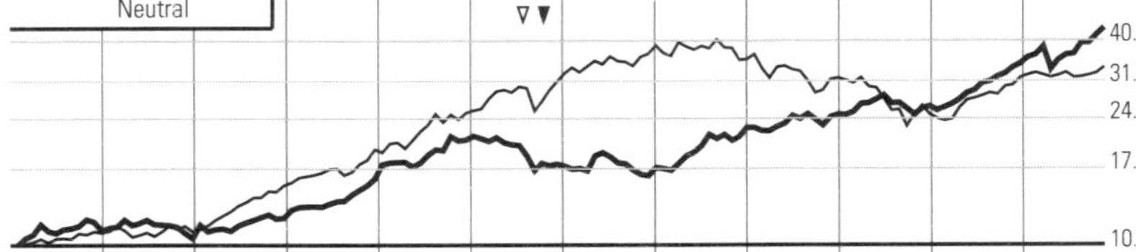

Growth of $10,000
— Investment Values of Fund
— Investment Values of S&P 500

Performance Quartile (within Category)

1993	1994	1995	1996	1997	1998	1999	2000	2001	2002	2003	12-04	History
13.57	13.20	13.88	18.03	20.45	15.54	14.70	18.50	18.52	18.39	23.71	29.54	NAV
12.51	2.04	10.92	36.22	21.39	-18.60	-0.97	31.38	9.50	5.77	33.78	34.15	Total Return %
2.45	0.73	-26.61	13.28	-11.96	-47.17	-22.01	40.48	21.38	27.86	5.11	23.28	+/-S&P 500
-2.95	-0.62	-1.32	-0.82	1.72	-1.60	1.60	0.34	-2.86	2.17	-2.28	0.33	+/-Wil REIT
4.84	4.72	5.49	5.29	4.45	3.86	4.51	5.05	4.31	4.26	2.97	2.90	Income Return %
7.67	-2.68	5.43	30.93	16.94	-22.46	-5.48	26.33	5.19	1.51	30.81	31.25	Capital Return %
80	50	80	50	45	73	22	15	40	29	76	30	Total Rtn % Rank Cat
0.60	0.63	0.71	0.72	0.79	0.77	0.69	0.73	0.78	0.77	0.54	0.67	Income $
0.00	0.00	0.00	0.00	0.56	0.41	0.00	0.00	0.89	0.43	0.26	1.34	Capital Gains $
1.16	1.13	1.03	0.95	0.90	0.84	0.86	0.88	0.82	0.79	0.84	0.83	Expense Ratio %
5.81	4.34	5.67	6.28	5.63	4.06	4.23	4.06	4.58	4.54	3.21	3.38	Income Ratio %
82	110	75	85	55	76	28	32	65	71	32	48	Turnover Rate %
424	556	709	1,722	2,480	1,239	724	1,037	1,245	1,720	2,712	4,557	Net Assets $mil

Performance 12-31-04

	1st Qtr	2nd Qtr	3rd Qtr	4th Qtr	Total
2000	2.90	12.77	7.88	4.94	31.38
2001	-2.24	11.02	-2.47	3.44	9.50
2002	7.54	6.08	-8.80	1.66	5.77
2003	1.49	9.94	9.85	9.15	33.78
2004	12.15	-5.38	8.47	16.56	34.15

Trailing	Total Return%	+/- S&P 500	+/- Wil REIT	%Rank Cat	Growth of $10,000
3 Mo	16.56	7.33	-0.13	45	11,656
6 Mo	26.43	19.24	0.17	30	12,643
1 Yr	34.15	23.28	0.33	30	13,415
3 Yr Avg	23.82	20.24	0.26	41	18,983
5 Yr Avg	22.25	24.55	-0.42	22	27,305
10 Yr Avg	14.98	2.91	-0.27	40	40,385
15 Yr Avg	13.89	2.96	2.05	1	70,353

Tax Analysis	Tax-Adj Rtn%	%Rank Cat	Tax-Cost Rat	%Rank Cat
3 Yr (estimated)	21.88	34	1.57	43
5 Yr (estimated)	20.07	18	1.78	53
10 Yr (estimated)	12.76	35	1.93	61

Potential Capital Gain Exposure: 32% of assets

Rating and Risk

Time Period	Load-Adj Return %	Morningstar Rtn vs Cat	Morningstar Risk vs Cat	Morningstar Risk-Adj Rating
1 Yr	34.15			
3 Yr	23.82	Avg	Avg	★★★
5 Yr	22.25	+Avg	Avg	★★★★
10 Yr	14.98	Avg	Avg	★★★
Incept	12.25			

Other Measures	Standard Index S&P 500	Best Fit Index Wil REIT
Alpha	22.1	1.5
Beta	0.33	0.93
R-Squared	12	99
Standard Deviation	17.16	
Mean	23.82	
Sharpe Ratio	1.32	

Morningstar's Take by William Samuel Rocco 12-21-04

Mainstream REIT fans are unlikely to be disappointed here--unless they're counting on big gains every year.

Fidelity Real Estate starts with some key advantages. Manager Steve Buller has been at the helm for more than six years and he served as an associate manager and analyst on the fund for years before that, so he's more experienced than many of his peers. He's supported by one of the bigger teams of real estate analysts around. And since its costs have declined nicely as its asset base has risen to more than $4 billion in assets, it boasts the lowest expense ratio of any actively run offering in its group and is about 50 basis points cheaper than its typical no-load rival.

Buller uses a straightforward strategy, so investors will find plenty of mainstream REIT exposure here. Buller, in fact, focuses on high-quality REITs with good earnings and cash flows and moves at a moderate pace, while many of his peers trade a fair amount and pay significant attention to less-established REITs or non-REIT real estate plays.

Buller has executed this no-frills strategy deftly over the short and longer term. For a number of reasons, he has made the fund more concentrated over the past 12 months or so. (The top 10 names now consume more than 50% of assets.) Most of his top picks have zoomed in 2004, so the fund has earned a near-top-quartile 32% gain. It has also posted superior overall results under Buller.

Due to that success and the fund's other strengths, we believe investors seeking no-frills REIT exposure are likely to be happy here over the long run. But it's crucial to note that real estate funds are on an extended hot streak--they've posted a 22% annualized gain and outpaced all other types of funds over the past five years--and that they can't sustain this torrid pace forever. Thus, interested investors should be prepared for a cool-to-cold spell and would be wise to slowly dollar-cost average into the fund.

Address:	82 Devonshire Street Boston MA 02109 800-544-8888
Web Address:	www.fidelity.com
Inception:	11-17-86
Advisor:	Fidelity Management & Research Co. (FMR)
Subadvisor:	FMR Co., Inc. (FMRC)
NTF Plans:	Fidelity Retail-NTF, CommonWealth NTF

Minimum Purchase:	$2500	Add: $250	IRA: $500
Min Auto Inv Plan:	$2500	Add: $100	
Sales Fees:	No-load, 0.75%R		
Management Fee:	0.58%		
Actual Fees:	Mgt:0.58%	Dist:	
Expense Projections:	3Yr:$287	5Yr:$498	10Yr:$1105
Income Distrib:	Quarterly		

Portfolio Analysis 10-31-04

Share change since 07-04 Total Stocks:51	Sector	PE	YTD Ret%	% Assets
⊕ Starwood Hotels & Resort	Consumer	33.9	64.71	7.33
⊕ Vornado Realty Trust	Financial	30.8	46.53	7.26
⊕ ProLogis Trust	Financial	25.1	41.03	6.44
⊕ Simon Property Group	Financial	37.3	46.10	5.76
⊕ Equity Office Properties	Financial	45.9	9.06	5.29
⊕ CBL & Associates Propert	Financial	16.8	41.69	5.26
⊕ General Growth Propertie	Financial	26.6	35.96	4.80
⊕ Reckson Associates Realt	Financial	11.5	43.02	4.76
⊕ Duke Realty	Financial	33.1	16.66	4.63
⊖ CenterPoint Properties	Financial	65.7	32.93	4.39
⊕ Public Storage	Financial	43.5	33.22	3.69
⊕ Boston Properties	Financial	23.9	40.60	3.54
⊕ Catellus Development	Financial	—	34.01	3.14
⊖ Apartment Investment & M	Financial	—	20.31	3.03
⊖ Rouse	Financial	—	—	2.56
⊖ Equity Residential	Financial	90.2	29.50	2.45
⊕ Kimco Realty	Financial	23.4	35.56	2.23
⊕ Federal Realty Investmen	Financial	37.8	40.53	1.86
⊕ Boardwalk Reit	Financial	—	—	1.67
⊕ Newcastle Investment	Financial	12.4	26.67	1.48

Current Investment Style

Value Blnd Growth; Large Mid Small

Market Cap	%
Giant	0.0
Large	22.2
Mid	69.6
Small	5.5
Micro	2.7
Avg $mil: 4,355	

Value Measures		Rel Category
Price/Earnings	15.54	1.08
Price/Book	2.24	1.11
Price/Sales	3.78	1.02
Price/Cash Flow	12.02	1.00
Dividend Yield %	4.50	0.92

Growth Measures	%	Rel Category
Long-Term Erngs	7.14	1.01
Book Value	1.02	6.80
Sales	4.02	2.42
Cash Flow	5.39	0.80
Historical Erngs	5.27	6.84

Profitability	%	Rel Category
Return on Equity	12.42	1.20
Return on Assets	9.27	1.21
Net Margin	23.46	1.08

Sector Weightings	% of Stocks	Rel S&P 500	3 Year High	3 Year Low
Info	0.00	0.00		
Software	0.00	0.00	0	0
Hardware	0.00	0.00	0	0
Media	0.00	0.00	0	0
Telecom	0.00	0.00	0	0
Service	99.29	2.14		
Health	0.00	0.00	0	0
Consumer	7.93	0.87	8	0
Business	0.30	0.07	0	0
Financial	91.06	4.39	99	91
Mfg	0.71	0.02		
Goods	0.00	0.00	0	0
Ind Mtrls	0.71	0.06	1	0
Energy	0.00	0.00	0	0
Utilities	0.00	0.00	0	0

Composition

Cash	4.2
Stocks	95.8
Bonds	0.0
Other	0.0
Foreign (% of Stock)	1.7

Fidelity Sel Electronics

Ticker	Load	NAV	Yield	Total Assets	Mstar Category
FSELX	None	$37.78	0.0%	$2,921 mil	Specialty-Technology

Governance and Management

Fiduciary Grade: B

Portfolio Manager(s)

This fund changes managers frequently. Former manager Samuel Peters took the helm here on Feb. 1, 2002, and left in early February 2004. He was replaced by James Morrow. Morrow has served as an analyst at Fidelity since 1998. He also ran Fidelity Select Business Services Outsourcing from July 2001 through October 2003. He's assisted by Fidelity's deep and talented staff of technology analysts.

Strategy

This offering focuses on electronics manufacturers and distributors. Companies that make semiconductors and semiconductor capital equipment generally figure prominently in its portfolio. Manager James Morrow tries to ascertain the state of the semiconductor cycle we're in. He then allocates assets to subindustries within the sector based on their attractiveness at the current part of the chip cycle, and he tries to buy companies within those subindustries that he thinks offer the best risk-reward prospects.

Historical Profile

Return Above Avg
Risk Above Avg
Rating ★★★ Neutral

Investment Style
Equity
Stock %: 91% 90% 92% 90% 92% 92% 93% 96% 99%

▼ Manager Change
▽ Partial Manager Change

Growth of $10,000
— Investment Values of Fund
— Investment Values of S&P 500

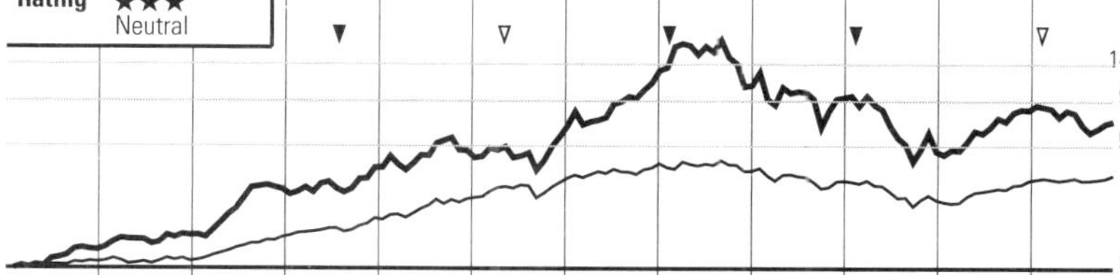

Performance Quartile (within Category)

1993	1994	1995	1996	1997	1998	1999	2000	2001	2002	2003	12-04	History
15.78	18.49	25.74	36.48	30.81	46.56	88.88	57.78	49.27	24.37	41.89	37.78	NAV
32.08	17.17	68.97	41.72	13.72	51.12	106.68	-17.54	-14.73	-50.54	71.89	-9.81	Total Return %
22.02	15.86	31.44	18.78	-19.63	22.55	85.64	-8.44	-2.85	-28.45	43.22	-20.68	+/-S&P 500
13.03	-3.70	21.26	21.69	-6.25	-3.48	-9.72	-1.32	0.86	-17.21	19.75	-21.54	+/-PSE Tech 100
0.00	0.00	0.00	0.00	0.00	0.00	0.00	0.00	0.00	0.00	0.00	0.00	Income Return %
32.08	17.17	68.97	41.72	13.72	51.12	106.68	-17.54	-14.73	-50.54	71.89	-9.81	Capital Return %
30	46	1	7	24	52	64	13	3	88	15	95	Total Rtn % Rank Cat
0.00	0.00	0.00	0.00	0.00	0.00	0.00	0.00	0.00	0.00	0.00	0.00	Income $
2.75	0.00	5.25	0.00	10.20	0.00	6.62	18.68	0.00	0.00	0.00	0.00	Capital Gains $
1.69	1.67	1.71	1.22	1.29	1.12	1.15	0.98	0.87	0.97	1.06	1.06	Expense Ratio %
-0.50	-0.52	-0.98	-0.28	-0.54	-0.42	-0.62	-0.46	-0.31	-0.59	-0.78	-0.70	Income Ratio %
293	163	205	366	341	435	160	125	63	57	70	50	Turnover Rate %
46	157	892	1,565	2,302	2,723	6,781	6,350	5,106	2,214	3,932	2,921	Net Assets $mil

Performance 12-31-04

	1st Qtr	2nd Qtr	3rd Qtr	4th Qtr	Total
2000	42.11	-3.51	-13.26	-30.67	-17.54
2001	-22.48	19.36	-37.41	47.25	-14.73
2002	1.99	-32.12	-37.41	14.15	-50.54
2003	1.11	25.16	16.99	16.10	71.89
2004	1.77	-5.58	-18.31	14.90	-9.81

Trailing	Total Return%	+/- S&P 500	+/- PSE Tech 100	%Rank Cat	Growth of $10,000
3 Mo	14.90	5.67	0.38	54	11,490
6 Mo	-6.14	-13.33	-12.07	96	9,386
1 Yr	-9.81	-20.68	-21.54	95	9,019
3 Yr Avg	-8.47	-12.05	-12.73	84	7,668
5 Yr Avg	-11.62	-9.32	-7.29	20	5,392
10 Yr Avg	16.45	4.38	-2.57	9	45,856
15 Yr Avg	18.62	7.69	0.15	1	129,530

Tax Analysis	Tax-Adj Rtn%	%Rank Cat	Tax-Cost Rat	%Rank Cat
3 Yr (estimated)	-8.47	81	0.00	1
5 Yr (estimated)	-12.49	20	0.98	62
10 Yr (estimated)	13.55	9	2.49	91

Potential Capital Gain Exposure: -103% of assets

Rating and Risk

Time Period	Load-Adj Return %	Morningstar Rtn vs Cat	Morningstar Risk vs Cat	Morningstar Risk-Adj Rating
1 Yr	-9.81			
3 Yr	-8.47	-Avg	+Avg	★★
5 Yr	-11.62	+Avg	+Avg	★★★
10 Yr	16.45	+Avg	+Avg	★★★
Incept	12.60			

Other Measures	Standard Index S&P 500	Best Fit Index PSE Tech 100
Alpha	-9.5	-10.9
Beta	2.16	1.42
R-Squared	71	91
Standard Deviation	38.80	
Mean	-8.47	
Sharpe Ratio	-0.26	

Portfolio Analysis 08-31-04

Share change since 05-04 Total Stocks:64	Sector	PE	YTD Ret%	% Assets
⊕ Analog Devices	Hardware	24.2	-18.69	10.04
⊕ Intel	Hardware	19.8	-26.56	9.97
⊕ National Semiconductor	Hardware	17.1	-8.80	9.43
⊕ Micron Technology	Hardware	46.2	-8.32	6.25
⊕ KLA-Tencor	Hardware	26.4	-20.43	6.18
⊕ Lam Research	Hardware	21.5	-10.50	4.41
⊕ Hon Hai Precision Indust	Business	—	—	3.19
⊖ Texas Instruments	Hardware	21.1	-15.90	3.07
⊖ Applied Materials	Hardware	20.7	-23.80	3.03
⊖ Motorola	Hardware	28.7	37.93	2.98
⊕ Altera	Hardware	26.2	-8.61	2.87
⊖ Xilinx	Hardware	25.2	-22.82	2.50
⊕ Flextronics Internationa	Hardware	—	-6.62	2.38
⊕ Teradyne	Hardware	19.5	-32.93	2.34
⊖ Samsung Electronics	Goods	—	—	1.91
⊕ Semiconductor Manufactur	Hardware	—	—	1.31
⊕ Marvell Technology	Hardware	NMF	87.03	1.29
⊖ Canon ADR	Goods	20.0	15.12	1.27
☼ LG Electronics	Goods	—	—	1.26
⊕ Taiwan Semiconductor Man	Hardware	26.4	-4.52	1.15

Current Investment Style

Value Blnd Growth — Large Mid Small

Market Cap	%
Giant	19.7
Large	26.8
Mid	44.2
Small	8.3
Micro	1.0

Avg $mil: 8,912

Value Measures		Rel Category
Price/Earnings	15.66	0.57
Price/Book	2.63	0.79
Price/Sales	1.63	0.55
Price/Cash Flow	12.49	1.00
Dividend Yield %	0.26	1.37

Growth Measures	%	Rel Category
Long-Term Erngs	18.93	1.12
Book Value	-0.48	NMF
Sales	0.41	0.13
Cash Flow	7.20	0.45
Historical Erngs	8.41	0.69

Profitability	%	Rel Category
Return on Equity	9.01	0.79
Return on Assets	6.33	0.99
Net Margin	9.02	0.86

Industry Weightings	% of Stocks	Rel Cat
Software	0.6	0.0
Hardware	3.9	0.3
Networking Eq	0.5	0.1
Semis	62.1	3.8
Semi Equip	22.3	5.1
Comp/Data Sv	0.1	0.0
Telecom	0.3	0.1
Health Care	0.4	0.1
Other	9.8	0.4

Composition

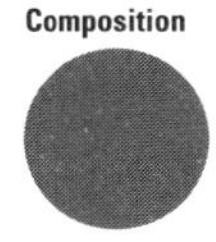

Cash	0.9
Stocks	99.1
Bonds	0.0
Other	0.0
Foreign (% of Stock)	17.1

Morningstar's Take by Christopher Traulsen 12-21-04

Fidelity Select Electronics is a taste that most investors probably don't need to acquire.

This fund isn't without appeal. It's advised by Fidelity, and as such, it has the backing of the small army of technology analysts the firm maintains in the U.S and in Asia. It also boasts reasonable expenses for a technology fund.

Still, we have serious reservations. The fund usually focuses roughly two thirds of its assets on semiconductor-related companies. The semiconductor industry has experienced tremendous long-term growth, and there's little to suggest it can't do so in the future. However, it's also extremely cyclical, and competition can be brutal. As a result this offering is very volatile.

The fund's performance thus far in 2004 is a case in point. The fund dropped 28% from the start of the year through Aug 12. It suffered a particularly steep decline in the summer as chip inventories began to build--a signal that demand was weakening. The fund has bounced back in recent months, but it's still down 11.8% for the year to date through Dec. 17.

James Morrow, who took the helm in early 2004, has made a few changes. He's cut the number of names, notably upping the fund's concentration. He has also increased the fund's exposure to chip companies that sell to the PC industry, while reducing the fund's exposure to communications-related firms. It's too early to say much about how those moves will play out--though the increased concentration could well make the fund even more volatile--but it's worth noting that the fund has built a great long-term record despite its many manager changes.

If you invest here, you need to be prepared to ride out significant losses in order to benefit from the fund's potential long-term strength. We don't think most investors need a tech fund, but if you do, we think a broader tech fund that has the freedom to benefit from multiple tech industries is the way to go.

Address:	82 Devonshire St Boston MA 02109 800-343-3548
Web Address:	www.fidelity.com
Inception:	07-29-85
Advisor:	Fidelity Management & Research Co. (FMR)
Subadvisor:	FMR Co., Inc. (FMRC)
NTF Plans:	Fidelity Retail-NTF, CommonWealth NTF

Minimum Purchase:	$2500	Add: $250	IRA: $2500
Min Auto Inv Plan:	$2500	Add: $100	
Sales Fees:	No-load, 0.75%R		
Management Fee:	0.58%		
Actual Fees:	Mgt:0.58%	Dist:	
Expense Projections:	3Yr:$613	5Yr:$838	10Yr:$1484
Income Distrib:	Semi-Annually		

Fidelity Sel Health Care

Ticker	Load	NAV	Yield	Total Assets	Mstar Category
FSPHX	None	$128.09	0.1%	$1,970 mil	Specialty-Health

Governance and Management

Fiduciary Grade: B

Portfolio Manager(s)

Sam Peters took the helm of this offering in early February 2004. Before taking charge, he ran Fidelity Select Banking and Fidelity Select Electronics, spending two years at each. He is backed by Fidelity's large team of analysts.

Strategy

Large-cap pharmaceutical companies have traditionally played starring roles here, though the fund's prior manager, Steve Calhoun, broadened the portfolio to include more exposure to other health-care subsectors, especially health-care services and medical devices. New manager Sam Peters hasn't altered that strategy significantly, though he says he plans to add to the fund's mid-cap stake and lighten its big-cap drug exposure.

Historical Profile

Return Average
Risk Below Avg
Rating ★★★★ Above Avg

Investment Style
Equity
Stock %: 87% 93% 92% 92% 94% 92% 92% 99% 99%

▼ Manager Change
▽ Partial Manager Change

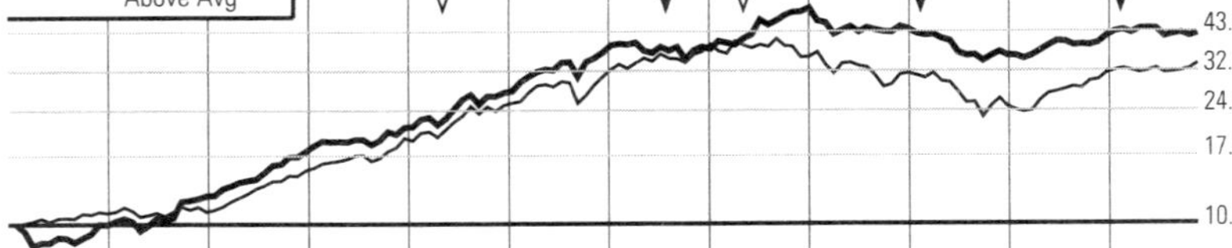

Growth of $10,000
▬ Investment Values of Fund
— Investment Values of S&P 500

Performance Quartile (within Category)

1993	1994	1995	1996	1997	1998	1999	2000	2001	2002	2003	12-04	History
63.62	70.80	97.57	95.40	101.87	136.77	124.82	150.13	127.26	101.98	118.01	128.09	NAV
2.42	21.46	45.86	15.46	31.15	41.28	-2.88	36.65	-15.01	-18.05	15.91	8.66	Total Return %
-7.64	20.15	8.33	-7.48	-2.20	12.71	-23.92	45.75	-3.13	4.04	-12.76	-2.21	+/-S&P 500
7.22	10.68	-9.00	-3.09	-5.73	2.19	1.15	-0.82	-2.40	2.76	-3.52	4.11	+/-DJ Hlthcare
0.11	0.98	0.84	0.68	0.27	0.19	0.06	0.20	0.09	0.16	0.18	0.11	Income Return %
2.31	20.48	45.02	14.78	30.88	41.09	-2.94	36.45	-15.10	-18.21	15.73	8.55	Capital Return %
46	1	67	30	15	3	87	74	62	11	95	49	Total Rtn % Rank Cat
0.07	0.62	0.59	0.65	0.25	0.19	0.08	0.24	0.13	0.20	0.18	0.13	Income $
0.00	5.74	4.92	15.95	20.73	6.17	7.85	18.63	0.19	2.42	0.00	0.00	Capital Gains $
1.46	1.55	1.36	1.30	1.32	1.18	1.05	1.05	0.97	0.96	0.99	0.99	Expense Ratio %
0.24	0.26	1.08	1.06	0.52	0.31	0.14	0.12	0.21	0.13	0.22	0.12	Income Ratio %
112	213	151	54	59	79	66	70	85	90	139	104	Turnover Rate %
573	796	1,449	1,242	1,632	3,032	2,427	3,124	2,511	1,825	1,957	1,970	Net Assets $mil

Performance 12-31-04

	1st Qtr	2nd Qtr	3rd Qtr	4th Qtr	Total
2000	3.29	20.83	3.48	5.81	36.65
2001	-18.22	1.64	0.28	1.96	-15.01
2002	-4.00	-12.76	-6.06	4.16	-18.05
2003	-0.08	11.43	-2.55	6.82	15.91
2004	2.17	3.16	-2.99	6.27	8.66

Trailing	Total Return%	+/- S&P 500	+/- DJ Hlthcare	%Rank Cat	Growth of $10,000
3 Mo	6.27	-2.96	0.37	73	10,627
6 Mo	3.09	-4.10	2.09	47	10,309
1 Yr	8.66	-2.21	4.11	49	10,866
3 Yr Avg	1.06	-2.52	1.43	46	10,321
5 Yr Avg	3.69	5.99	0.18	68	11,986
10 Yr Avg	13.77	1.70	-1.06	45	36,331
15 Yr Avg	15.35	4.42	—	23	85,166

Tax Analysis	Tax-Adj Rtn%	%Rank Cat	Tax-Cost Rat	%Rank Cat
3 Yr (estimated)	0.87	37	0.19	16
5 Yr (estimated)	3.00	70	0.67	44
10 Yr (estimated)	11.70	39	1.82	67

Potential Capital Gain Exposure: 28% of assets

Rating and Risk

Time Period	Load-Adj Return %	Morningstar Rtn vs Cat	Morningstar Risk vs Cat	Morningstar Risk-Adj Rating
1 Yr	8.66			
3 Yr	1.06	Avg	Low	★★★
5 Yr	3.69	Avg	-Avg	★★★
10 Yr	13.77	Avg	-Avg	★★★★
Incept	17.51			

Other Measures	Standard Index S&P 500	Best Fit Index DJ Hlthcare
Alpha	-1.5	1.2
Beta	0.54	0.88
R-Squared	53	93

Standard Deviation	11.23
Mean	1.06
Sharpe Ratio	-0.03

Portfolio Analysis 08-31-04

Share change since 05-04 Total Stocks:69	Sector	PE	YTD Ret%	% Assets
⊖ Johnson & Johnson	Health	20.6	25.17	10.61
⊕ Pfizer	Health	22.0	-22.31	7.60
Medtronic	Health	30.7	2.68	7.15
⊕ Abbott Laboratories	Health	22.1	2.61	5.75
⊕ UnitedHealth Group	Health	23.8	51.38	5.33
Genentech	Health	78.6	16.36	5.26
⊕ Baxter International	Health	32.9	15.22	5.01
⊕ Merck	Health	11.4	-27.76	4.90
Amgen	Health	37.7	3.82	4.29
Eli Lilly & Company	Health	24.3	-17.55	4.07
⊕ St. Jude Medical	Health	38.0	36.69	2.59
Biomet	Health	34.1	20.83	2.57
⊖ Schering-Plough	Health	—	21.56	2.41
Caremark RX	Health	32.8	55.67	2.01
Wyeth	Health	17.0	2.73	1.80
⊖ Boston Scientific	Health	32.3	-3.29	1.72
⊕ Alcon	Health	41.6	33.78	1.69
PacifiCare Health System	Health	21.5	67.22	1.54
☼ Guidant	Health	35.0	20.55	1.38
Biogen IDEC	Health	—	81.50	1.27

Current Investment Style

Value Blnd Growth; Large Mid Small

Market Cap	%
Giant	52.0
Large	30.6
Mid	15.6
Small	1.1
Micro	0.7
Avg $mil: 32,271	

Value Measures		Rel Category
Price/Earnings	20.36	0.86
Price/Book	3.39	1.23
Price/Sales	2.06	0.73
Price/Cash Flow	11.05	1.02
Dividend Yield %	1.06	1.49

Growth Measures	%	Rel Category
Long-Term Erngs	13.86	0.86
Book Value	17.39	1.13
Sales	9.62	0.78
Cash Flow	16.46	0.89
Historical Erngs	7.10	0.75

Profitability	%	Rel Category
Return on Equity	18.31	1.88
Return on Assets	8.76	2.83
Net Margin	12.20	1.60

Industry Weightings	% of Stocks	Rel Cat
Biotech	16.4	0.5
Drugs	42.2	1.5
Mgd Care	10.5	1.8
Hospitals	0.5	0.3
Other HC Srv	0.3	0.3
Diagnostics	2.1	2.1
Equipment	25.5	1.7
Good/Srv	1.8	0.4
Other	0.8	0.1

Composition

Cash	1.0
Stocks	99.0
Bonds	0.0
Other	0.0
Foreign (% of Stock)	0.1

Morningstar's Take by Christopher Davis 12-27-04

Fidelity Select Health Care has appealing attributes, but it's not the best of its breed.

We added this offering to our roster of Fund Analyst Picks in 2000 for several reasons. For one, we liked its sensible, moderate strategy. Focused on larger health-care names, the fund provided relatively mild-mannered exposure to a growth-oriented area of the market. And while management stability was hardly a strong suit, we had confidence in Fidelity's impressive research capabilities and analyst prowess. We also found it reassuring that the firm had cycled some of its most promising talent, including Fidelity Dividend Growth's Charles Mangum and Fidelity Growth & Income's Steven Kaye, through the fund over the years. Finally, in a pricey category, the fund's expense ratio was reasonable.

The fund has, however, lost some of its luster since we added it to our picks list. While its strategy remains intact and its costs are well below average, the fund has played host to a number of managers who have largely delivered underwhelming results in recent years. A reliance on out-of-favor big-cap drugmakers hasn't helped matters, but it hasn't distinguished itself greatly from rivals that employ similar approaches. In particular, our growing confidence in T. Rowe Price Health Sciences, weakens this fund's appeal.

You certainly can do much worse than this offering, though, and we'd expect it to look better in a market more hospitable to large-cap health-care stocks. The fund's low volatility is also a selling point. However, it falls short of the mark when compared with our other health-care favorites, Vanguard Health Care and the T. Rowe fund. Both of those offerings boast more experienced managers and superior records, making it difficult to include this fund in the ranks of the health-care category's elite.

Address:	82 Devonshire St Boston MA 02109 800-343-3548
Web Address:	www.fidelity.com
Inception:	07-14-81
Advisor:	Fidelity Management & Research Co. (FMR)
Subadvisor:	FMR Co., Inc. (FMRC)
NTF Plans:	Fidelity Retail-NTF, CommonWealth NTF

Minimum Purchase:	$2500	Add: $250	IRA: $2500
Min Auto Inv Plan:	$2500	Add: $100	
Sales Fees:	No-load, 0.75%R		
Management Fee:	0.58%		
Actual Fees:	Mgt:0.58%	Dist: —	
Expense Projections:	3Yr:$624	5Yr:$862	10Yr:$1544
Income Distrib:	Semi-Annually		

Fidelity Sel Technology

Analyst Pick	Ticker	Load	NAV	Yield	Total Assets	Mstar Category
✔ Analyst Pick	FSPTX	None	$60.19	0.3%	$2,205 mil	Specialty-Technology

Governance and Management

Fiduciary Grade: B

Portfolio Manager(s)

Like most Fidelity Select funds, this offering changes managers often. Sonu Kalra replaced Telis Bertsekas on Feb. 15, 2002. Before taking the helm here, Kalra had worked at Fidelity as an analyst covering various industries since 1998. His areas of coverage included media, Internet, and technology stocks. The potential ill effects of frequent manager changes are abated by Fidelity's vast tech research staff.

Strategy

This fund can invest in nearly any type of technology company, giving it broad latitude to emphasize different subsectors. However, its girth prevents it from making rapid, large-scale shifts. Current manager Sonu Kalra is a bottom-up stock-picker who favors companies that are market leaders, that are gaining market share, or that boast improving margins. Valuation is a secondary consideration, though Kalra gives it greater weight when IT spending is constrained.

Historical Profile

Return Above Avg
Risk Average
Rating ★★★★ Above Avg

Investment Style: Equity Stock %

1993	1994	1995	1996	1997	1998	1999	2000	2001	2002	2003	12-04
92%	87%	87%	88%	94%	92%	89%	99%	97%			

▼ Manager Change
∇ Partial Manager Change

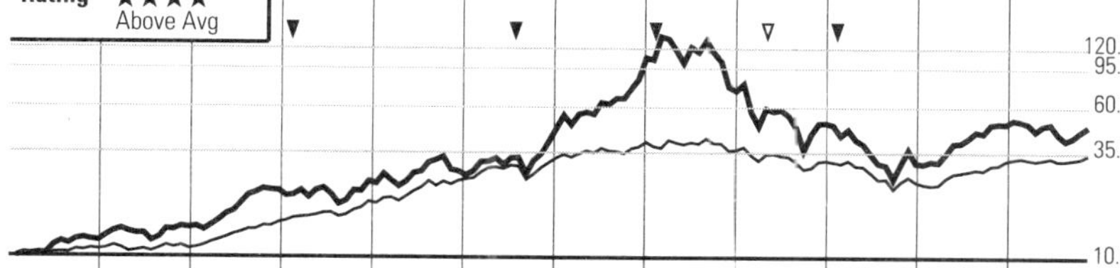

Growth of $10,000
— Investment Values of Fund
— Investment Values of S&P 500

Performance Quartile (within Category)

1993	1994	1995	1996	1997	1998	1999	2000	2001	2002	2003	12-04	History
38.73	41.36	51.31	55.68	45.28	78.86	152.39	88.72	60.60	37.70	60.09	60.19	NAV
28.65	11.13	43.81	15.82	10.33	74.16	131.75	-32.30	-31.70	-37.79	59.39	0.43	Total Return %
18.59	9.82	6.28	-7.12	-23.02	45.59	110.71	-23.20	-19.82	-15.70	30.72	-10.44	+/-S&P 500
9.60	-9.74	-3.90	-4.21	-9.64	19.56	15.35	-16.08	-16.11	-4.46	7.25	-11.30	+/-PSE Tech 100
0.38	0.00	0.00	0.00	0.00	0.00	0.00	0.00	0.00	0.00	0.00	0.27	Income Return %
28.27	11.13	43.81	15.82	10.33	74.16	131.75	-32.30	-31.70	-37.79	59.39	0.16	Capital Return %
50	69	67	69	38	18	46	52	38	19	35	67	Total Rtn % Rank Cat
0.13	0.00	0.00	0.00	0.00	0.00	0.00	0.00	0.00	0.00	0.00	0.16	Income $
3.70	1.50	8.05	3.68	15.69	0.00	19.80	20.73	0.00	0.00	0.00	0.00	Capital Gains $
1.64	1.54	1.56	1.39	1.44	1.30	1.20	1.04	0.94	1.13	1.22	1.14	Expense Ratio %
0.52	-0.65	-0.98	-0.52	-0.72	-0.45	-0.54	-0.34	-0.43	-0.73	-0.86	-0.80	Income Ratio %
259	213	102	112	549	556	339	210	133	184	153	127	Turnover Rate %
230	227	401	491	526	1,061	5,209	4,287	2,715	1,459	2,523	2,205	Net Assets $mil

Performance 12-31-04

	1st Qtr	2nd Qtr	3rd Qtr	4th Qtr	Total
2000	25.29	-9.44	-6.16	-36.42	-32.30
2001	-34.06	21.01	-38.25	38.64	-31.70
2002	-7.38	-25.39	-25.48	20.79	-37.79
2003	0.95	25.91	12.17	11.80	59.39
2004	0.28	-0.58	-14.37	17.64	0.43

Trailing	Total Return%	+/- S&P 500	+/- PSE Tech 100	%Rank Cat	Growth of $10,000
3 Mo	17.64	8.41	3.12	26	11,764
6 Mo	0.73	-6.46	-5.20	76	10,073
1 Yr	0.43	-10.44	-11.30	67	10,043
3 Yr Avg	-0.14	-3.72	-4.40	27	9,958
5 Yr Avg	-14.37	-12.07	-10.04	33	4,604
10 Yr Avg	13.07	1.00	-5.95	17	34,157
15 Yr Avg	16.05	5.12	-2.42	30	93,256

Tax Analysis	Tax-Adj Rtn%	%Rank Cat	Tax-Cost Rat	%Rank Cat
3 Yr (estimated)	-0.17	26	0.03	15
5 Yr (estimated)	-15.05	34	0.79	53
10 Yr (estimated)	9.90	17	2.80	95

Potential Capital Gain Exposure: -122% of assets

Rating and Risk

Time Period	Load-Adj Return %	Morningstar Rtn vs Cat	Morningstar Risk vs Cat	Morningstar Risk-Adj Rating
1 Yr	0.43			
3 Yr	-0.14	+Avg	Avg	★★★★
5 Yr	-14.37	Avg	Avg	★★★
10 Yr	13.07	+Avg	Avg	★★★★
Incept	13.58			

Other Measures	Standard Index S&P 500	Best Fit Index PSE Tech 100
Alpha	-2.8	-3.9
Beta	1.77	1.15
R-Squared	77	96
Standard Deviation	31.89	
Mean	-0.14	
Sharpe Ratio	-0.05	

Morningstar's Take by Christopher Traulsen 12-28-04

Fidelity Select Technology is a solid fund, but few investors need it.

Given its chosen vocation, this fund holds more appeal than many of its peers. Unlike most technology funds, it boasts a reasonably low expense ratio. It's also supported by the enormous resources of advisor Fidelity Management & Research. The firm maintains a technology analyst staff of more than 20 researchers, including several posted in key Asian countries. Finally, unlike some overly focused rivals, this fund has a broad mandate that allows its manager to invest in whichever technology subsectors he believes offer the best prospects.

In 2004, manager Sonu Kalra hasn't used that flexibility to great advantage. The fund is down 0.89% for the year to date through Dec. 27, 2004, compared with a 2.51% rise for the average tech fund. A bet on semiconductors has hurt the fund relative to its peers--the sector bounced back a bit in the fall, but it slumped sharply in the summer after inventories began to weaken. A large position in Cisco has also hurt the fund, as has a scant weighting in soaring Internet firms such as eBay.

Still, we aren't terribly concerned. Such short-term performance just isn't very meaningful. Over the long haul, the picture is considerably brighter. The fund has been a bit more volatile than the category norm, in part because it features rather large positions at the top of the portfolio. It's also worth noting that Fidelity runs so much money in this style that extensive forays into small caps or nimble sector rotations are not this fund's strong suit. Still, the fund's advantages have helped it handily best its average peer over the trailing three-, five-, and 10-year periods, despite enduring many manager changes.

That said, we don't think many investors need a tech fund. One can get plenty of technology exposure via diversified growth funds, and often pay much less for the privilege.

Portfolio Analysis 08-31-04

Share change since 05-04 Total Stocks:118	Sector	PE	YTD Ret%	% Assets
⊖ Microsoft	Software	36.1	8.95	9.61
⊕ Cisco Systems	Hardware	24.5	-20.26	8.70
⊕ Intel	Hardware	19.8	-26.56	7.80
Dell	Hardware	34.0	24.01	7.32
⊕ EMC	Hardware	41.5	15.09	5.73
⊕ National Semiconductor	Hardware	17.1	-8.80	2.71
⊕ Motorola	Hardware	28.7	37.93	2.56
⊕ Analog Devices	Hardware	24.2	-18.69	2.55
⊕ Oracle	Software	25.4	3.70	2.52
⊕ Qualcomm	Hardware	42.0	58.20	2.22
⊕ KLA-Tencor	Hardware	26.4	-20.43	1.90
Integrated Circuit Syste	Hardware	20.5	-26.60	1.72
⊕ Applied Materials	Hardware	20.7	-23.80	1.72
⊖ Yahoo	Media	95.1	67.36	1.61
⊕ eBay	Consumer	81.6	80.07	1.39
⊖ Apple Computer	Hardware	NMF	201.36	1.36
⊕ IBM	Hardware	20.2	7.19	1.20
⊖ Micron Technology	Hardware	46.2	-8.32	1.18
⊖ Veritas Software	Software	23.7	-22.88	1.11
☼ Marvell Technology	Hardware	NMF	87.03	1.03

Current Investment Style

Value Blnd Growth — Large Mid Small

Market Cap	%
Giant	45.3
Large	23.9
Mid	20.6
Small	8.6
Micro	1.6

Avg $mil: 23,181

Value Measures		Rel Category
Price/Earnings	21.62	0.78
Price/Book	3.17	0.95
Price/Sales	2.85	0.96
Price/Cash Flow	13.85	1.11
Dividend Yield %	0.10	0.53

Growth Measures	%	Rel Category
Long-Term Erngs	15.70	0.93
Book Value	4.53	0.91
Sales	-0.05	NMF
Cash Flow	4.76	0.30
Historical Erngs	14.15	1.16

Profitability	%	Rel Category
Return on Equity	13.39	1.17
Return on Assets	8.20	1.29
Net Margin	12.95	1.24

Industry Weightings	% of Stocks	Rel Cat
Software	18.7	0.9
Hardware	23.5	1.8
Networking Eq	11.3	1.6
Semis	24.9	1.5
Semi Equip	6.0	1.4
Comp/Data Sv	0.3	0.1
Telecom	0.1	0.1
Health Care	0.0	0.0
Other	15.1	0.6

Composition

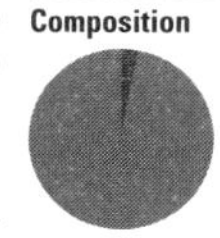

Cash	2.8
Stocks	97.2
Bonds	0.0
Other	0.0
Foreign (% of Stock)	6.7

Address:	82 Devonshire St Boston MA 02109 800-343-3548
Web Address:	www.fidelity.com
Inception:	07-14-81
Advisor:	Fidelity Management & Research Co. (FMR)
Subadvisor:	FMR Co., Inc. (FMRC)
NTF Plans:	Fidelity Retail-NTF, CommonWealth NTF

Minimum Purchase:	$2500	Add: $250	IRA: $2500
Min Auto Inv Plan:	$2500	Add: $100	
Sales Fees:	No-load, 0.75%R		
Management Fee:	0.58%		
Actual Fees:	Mgt:0.58%	Dist:	
Expense Projections:	3Yr:$632	5Yr:$869	10Yr:$1552
Income Distrib:	Semi-Annually		

Fidelity Sh-Term Bond

Analyst Pick

Ticker	Load	NAV	Yield	SEC Yield	Total Assets	Mstar Category
FSHBX	None	$8.98	2.5%	2.73%	$5,050 mil	Short-Term Bond

Governance and Management

Fiduciary Grade: B

Portfolio Manager(s)

Andrew Dudley has managed this fund since early 1997. As part of Fidelity's short- to intermediate-term bond team, he works with a credit analyst, a quantitative analyst, a trader, and one other portfolio manager. He has delivered impressive results during his tenure.

Strategy

Like all Fidelity bond funds, this offering doesn't make interest-rate bets. Manager Andrew Dudley ties the portfolio's duration (a measure of interest-rate sensitivity) to that of the Lehman Brothers 1-3 Year Government/Credit Index. He concentrates his efforts on moving among the corporate, Treasury, and mortgage sectors of the bond market, while looking to add value through individual issue selection. Dudley dips into the derivatives market here, but the derivatives don't alter its low-risk profile.

Historical Profile

Return Above Avg
Risk Average
Rating ★★★★ Above Avg

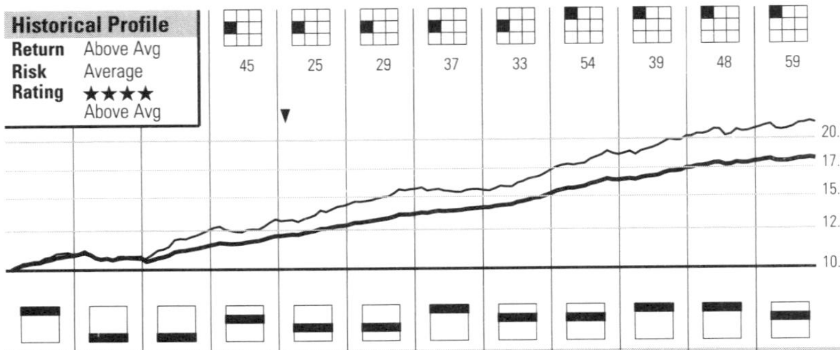

Investment Style
Fixed Income
Income Rtn %Rank Cat

▼ Manager Change
▽ Partial Manager Change

Growth of $10,000
— Investment Values of Fund
— Investment Values of LB Aggr

Performance Quartile (within Category)

1993	1994	1995	1996	1997	1998	1999	2000	2001	2002	2003	12-04	History
9.55	8.60	8.88	8.72	8.70	8.71	8.50	8.62	8.80	8.99	9.04	8.98	NAV
9.13	-4.09	9.82	4.77	6.21	6.14	3.29	7.85	7.63	6.70	3.57	1.86	Total Return %
-0.62	-1.17	-8.65	1.14	-3.44	-2.55	4.11	-3.78	-0.81	-3.55	-0.53	-2.48	+/-LB Aggr
2.03	-3.38	-3.06	0.10	-0.92	-1.49	1.20	-1.06	-1.40	-1.42	0.22	0.01	+/-LB 1-5 YR
7.30	6.15	4.96	5.93	6.37	6.04	5.77	6.35	5.52	4.47	3.00	2.53	Income Return %
1.83	-10.24	4.86	-1.16	-0.16	0.10	-2.48	1.50	2.11	2.23	0.57	-0.67	Capital Return %
8	98	80	34	61	58	20	40	38	22	19	33	Total Rtn % Rank Cat
0.66	0.57	0.41	0.51	0.54	0.51	0.49	0.53	0.46	0.39	0.27	0.23	Income $
0.00	0.00	0.13	0.06	0.00	0.00	0.00	0.00	0.00	0.00	0.00	0.00	Capital Gains $
0.77	0.80	0.69	0.68	0.70	0.70	0.65	0.62	0.58	0.58	0.57	0.57	Expense Ratio %
7.68	6.70	6.37	6.37	6.41	6.26	5.83	5.96	6.23	4.86	3.88	2.61	Income Ratio %
63	73	113	151	104	117	133	126	99	145	80	100	Turnover Rate %
2,470	1,515	1,197	996	875	842	1,333	1,773	3,339	5,195	5,406	5,050	Net Assets $mil

Performance 12-31-04

	1st Qtr	2nd Qtr	3rd Qtr	4th Qtr	Total
2000	1.16	1.78	2.29	2.40	7.85
2001	2.93	1.17	3.10	0.26	7.63
2002	0.33	1.84	2.57	1.83	6.70
2003	1.26	1.55	0.24	0.47	3.57
2004	1.39	-1.21	1.40	0.29	1.86

Trailing	Total Return%	+/- LB Aggr	+/- LB 1-5 YR	%Rank Cat	Growth of $10,000
3 Mo	0.29	-0.66	0.14	40	10,029
6 Mo	1.69	-2.49	-0.19	35	10,169
1 Yr	1.86	-2.48	0.01	33	10,186
3 Yr Avg	4.02	-2.17	-0.39	18	11,255
5 Yr Avg	5.49	-2.22	-0.72	21	13,063
10 Yr Avg	5.76	-1.96	-0.75	27	17,507
15 Yr Avg	5.93	-1.77	-0.79	44	23,729

Tax Analysis	Tax-Adj Rtn%	%Rank Cat	Tax-Cost Rat	%Rank Cat
3 Yr (estimated)	2.79	12	1.18	38
5 Yr (estimated)	3.80	14	1.60	43
10 Yr (estimated)	3.75	21	1.90	34

Potential Capital Gain Exposure: 0% of assets

Rating and Risk

Time Period	Load-Adj Return %	Morningstar Rtn vs Cat	Morningstar Risk vs Cat	Morningstar Risk-Adj Rating
1 Yr	1.86			
3 Yr	4.02	+Avg	Avg	★★★★
5 Yr	5.49	+Avg	Avg	★★★★
10 Yr	5.76	+Avg	-Avg	★★★★
Incept	6.06			

Other Measures	Standard Index LB Aggr	Best Fit Index LB. U.S. Univ. Bd
Alpha	0.6	0.2
Beta	0.42	0.44
R-Squared	89	91

Standard Deviation	1.97
Mean	4.02
Sharpe Ratio	1.36

Portfolio Analysis 10-31-04

Total Fixed-Income:873	Date of Maturity	Amount $000	Value $000	% Net Assets
EuroDollar (Fut)		5	1,233,859	18.30
FHLMC 2.75%	10-15-06	230,000	229,843	3.41
FNMA 6%	05-15-08	167,868	183,051	2.71
US Treasury Note 2.375%	08-31-06	111,000	110,735	1.64
FNMA 0.06%	04-01-18	97,180	100,815	1.49
FNMA 0.04%	11-01-19	93,500	93,675	1.39
FHLMC 2.85%	02-23-07	85,000	84,572	1.25
FHLMC 2.7%	03-16-07	84,000	83,612	1.24
US Treasury Note 4.375%	05-15-07	79,430	82,672	1.23
US Treasury Bond 12%	08-15-13	61,275	80,660	1.20
US Treasury Note 1.625%	02-28-06	74,920	74,226	1.10
FNMA 0.06%	10-01-10	57,554	61,113	0.91
FHLMC 0.04%	11-01-19	60,000	58,931	0.87
FNMA 3.125%	12-15-07	50,000	49,997	0.74
Bk One Oneseries 2002-2c	05-15-08	38,807	39,006	0.58
Ford Motor Cr 6.5%	01-25-07	30,780	32,339	0.48
US Treasury Bond 10%	05-15-10	30,740	32,012	0.47
US Treasury Bond 11.75%	02-15-10	30,180	31,001	0.46
Liberty Media FRN	09-17-06	29,637	29,973	0.44
Ford Motor Cr 6.875%	02-01-06	28,000	29,111	0.43

Current Investment Style

Duration: Short Int Long; Quality: High Med Low

[1] figure provided by fund

Avg Eff Duration[1]	1.9 Yrs
Avg Eff Maturity	2.7 Yrs
Avg Credit Quality	AA
Avg Wtd Coupon	3.49%
Avg Wtd Price	99.80% of par

Coupon Range	% of Bonds	Rel Cat
0% PIK	5.8	1.2
0% to 6%	81.7	1.1
6% to 8%	14.3	0.6
8% to 10%	1.7	0.6
More than 10%	2.3	2.7

1.00=Category Average

Credit Analysis		% bonds 10-31-04	
US Govt	28	BB	1
AAA	25	B	0
AA	6	Below B	0
A	17	NR/NA	6
BBB	18		

Sector Breakdown	% of assets
US Treasuries	6
TIPS	0
US Agency	10
Mortgage Pass-Throughs	6
Mortgage CMO	16
Mortgage ARM	0
US Corporate	16
Asset-Backed	18
Convertible	0
Municipal	0
Corporate Inflation-Protected	0
Foreign Corporate	0
Foreign Govt	0

Composition			
Cash	26.9	Bonds	73.1
Stocks	0.0	Other	0.0

Special Securities	
Restricted/Illiquid Secs	2
Exotic Mortgage-Backed	2
Emerging-Markets Secs	0
Options/Futures/Warrants	Yes

Morningstar's Take by Scott Berry 10-26-04

Fidelity Short-Term Bond is a good anchor for a broadly diversified portfolio.

This fund doesn't pack a big punch, but its steady returns can help balance the risks of longer-term bond funds and more-volatile stock funds. When the average long-term government bond fund dropped 6.75% in 1999, for example, this one returned 3.29%. And when the average large-cap stock fund plunged 22.7% in 2002, this fund jumped 6.7%. The fund has delivered positive returns each of the last nine years and even within the already conservative short-term bond category, its returns have been less volatile than most.

That's not to say this fund gets by on low volatility alone. Its three- and five-year trailing returns actually rank in the short-term bond category's top quartile, thanks to Andrew Dudley's skilled management and the fund's low price tag. In 2002, for example, Dudley shifted assets into mortgage-backed securities, which helped cushion the fund against a downturn in the corporate bond market. Meanwhile, the fund's 0.57% expense ratio provides a sustainable advantage that proves difficult for its higher-cost competitors to consistently overcome.

The fund's success has continued in 2004. Despite what has been a choppy market environment, the fund's net asset value recently checked in at the same level that it started the year. The fund's relatively short duration helped limit losses when interest rates spiked in the spring, while its asset-backed and mortgage-backed holdings fueled third-quarter gains. Overall, the fund has gained 1.94% for the year to date through Oct. 21, while its average category peer has gained 1.47%.

Rising interest rates could pressure this fund's absolute returns, but we think it will remain one of the category's more resilient offerings, given its proven approach and low costs. Investors who are looking for a conservative investment choice should like what they find here.

Address:	82 Devonshire St Boston MA 02109 800-343-3548
Web Address:	www.fidelity.com
Inception:	09-15-86
Advisor:	Fidelity Management & Research Co. (FMR)
Subadvisor:	Fidelity Intl Invest Advisors (U.K.) Ltd
NTF Plans:	Fidelity Retail-NTF, CommonWealth NTF

Minimum Purchase:	$2500	Add: $250	IRA: $2500
Min Auto Inv Plan:	$2500	Add: $100	
Sales Fees:	No-load		
Management Fee:	0.43%		
Actual Fees:	Mgt:0.43%	Dist:	
Expense Projections:	3Yr:$218	5Yr:$379	10Yr:$847
Income Distrib:	Monthly		

Fidelity Small Cap Indep

Ticker	Load	NAV	Yield	Total Assets	Mstar Category
FDSCX	None	$19.72	0.0%	$1,093 mil	Small Growth

Governance and Management

Fiduciary Grade: B

Portfolio Manager(s)

Before he began managing diversified funds in 2000, James Harmon was a member of Fidelity's small-cap analyst team. He also had a brief stint as manager of Fidelity's biotech fund. In short, his record as a diversified-fund manager is thin but promising.

Strategy

James Harmon buys a little of every kind of small-cap stock, using a style that he calls aggressive value. That may mean betting on turnarounds, making plays on cheap assets, or buying companies that are trading at discounts to his estimate of their discounted future free cash flows. He also looks for opportunities to trade in and out of a sector to make a quick profit. Because he's only required to invest 80% of the fund in small caps, Harmon exercises his right to buy a handful of larger-cap names.

Historical Profile

Return Average
Risk Low
Rating ★★★★ Above Avg

Investment Style
Equity Stock %: 84% 89% 91% 93% 90% 95% 93% 99% 92%

▼ Manager Change
▽ Partial Manager Change

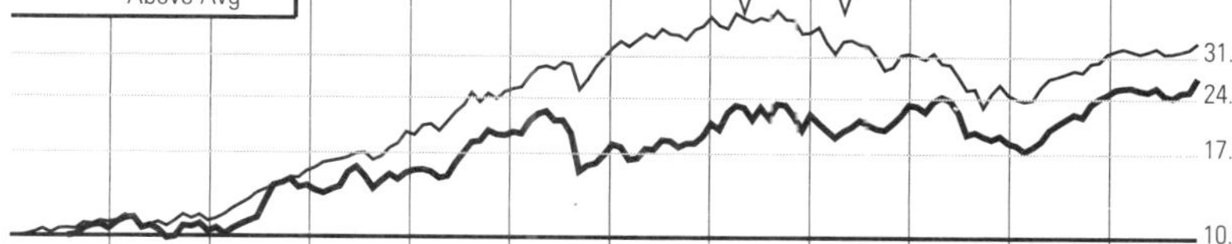

Growth of $10,000
— Investment Values of Fund
— Investment Values of S&P 500

Performance Quartile (within Category)

1993	1994	1995	1996	1997	1998	1999	2000	2001	2002	2003	12-04	History
10.82	10.45	12.39	13.56	15.93	14.19	16.09	16.23	16.30	13.30	17.94	19.72	NAV
8.82*	-3.32	26.63	13.63	27.25	-7.39	14.10	5.75	6.29	-20.83	34.89	15.02	Total Return %
—	-4.63	-10.90	-9.31	-6.10	-35.96	-6.94	14.85	18.17	1.26	6.22	4.15	+/-S&P 500
—	-0.89	-4.41	2.37	14.30	-8.62	-28.99	28.18	15.52	9.43	-13.65	0.71	+/-Russ 2000 Gr
0.00	0.09	0.77	0.08	0.97	0.19	0.63	0.19	0.00	0.00	0.00	0.00	Income Return %
—	-3.41	25.86	13.55	26.28	-7.58	13.47	5.56	6.29	-20.83	34.89	15.02	Capital Return %
—	67	71	74	22	89	87	25	16	21	86	34	Total Rtn % Rank Cat
0.02	0.01	0.08	0.01	0.13	0.03	0.09	0.03	0.00	0.00	0.00	0.00	Income $
0.04	0.00	0.77	0.51	1.14	0.62	0.00	0.74	0.44	0.00	0.00	0.89	Capital Gains $
—	1.18	0.90	0.99	0.90	0.97	0.82	0.84	0.74	0.91	0.93	0.91	Expense Ratio %
—	0.03	0.40	0.39	0.41	0.63	0.15	0.20	0.66	-0.52	-0.59	-0.49	Income Ratio %
—	210	182	192	176	88	173	159	450	290	220	95	Turnover Rate %
666	665	488	538	825	748	612	689	958	841	949	1,093	Net Assets $mil

Performance 12-31-04

	1st Qtr	2nd Qtr	3rd Qtr	4th Qtr	Total
2000	11.87	-1.22	1.57	-5.78	5.75
2001	-13.25	11.29	-5.87	16.96	6.29
2002	2.20	-6.58	-13.78	-3.83	-20.83
2003	-2.71	15.30	4.56	15.00	34.89
2004	4.52	-0.11	-2.78	13.31	15.02

Trailing	Total Return%	+/- S&P 500	+/- Russ 2000 Gr	%Rank Cat	Growth of $10,000
3 Mo	13.31	4.08	-1.77	63	11,331
6 Mo	10.17	2.98	2.01	25	11,017
1 Yr	15.02	4.15	0.71	34	11,502
3 Yr Avg	7.09	3.51	1.30	35	12,281
5 Yr Avg	6.66	8.96	10.23	19	13,804
10 Yr Avg	10.33	-1.74	3.21	55	26,726
15 Yr Avg	—	—	—	—	—

Tax Analysis	Tax-Adj Rtn%	%Rank Cat	Tax-Cost Rat	%Rank Cat
3 Yr (estimated)	6.85	32	0.22	22
5 Yr (estimated)	6.20	16	0.43	20
10 Yr (estimated)	9.31	37	0.92	22

Potential Capital Gain Exposure: 24% of assets

Rating and Risk

Time Period	Load-Adj Return %	Morningstar Rtn vs Cat	Morningstar Risk vs Cat	Morningstar Risk-Adj Rating
1 Yr	15.02			
3 Yr	7.09	Avg	Low	★★★★
5 Yr	6.66	+Avg	Low	★★★★
10 Yr	10.33	Avg	Low	★★★★
Incept	9.39			

Other Measures	Standard Index S&P 500	Best Fit Index Mstar Small Core
Alpha	4.5	-4.6
Beta	0.68	0.81
R-Squared	46	84
Standard Deviation	16.20	
Mean	7.09	
Sharpe Ratio	0.36	

Portfolio Analysis 10-31-04

Share change since 07-04 Total Stocks:133	Sector	PE	YTD Ret%	% Assets
⊖ Fisher Scientific Intern	Health	43.9	50.79	2.66
⊕ Affiliated Computer Serv	Business	14.7	10.52	2.49
⊕ Fidelity National Financ	Financial	10.2	32.24	2.14
⊕ Alliant Techsystems	Ind Mtrls	16.7	13.19	2.09
⊖ Corrections Corp of Amer	Business	13.2	40.31	2.09
⊕ BJ's Wholesale Club	Consumer	16.6	26.87	2.04
⊕ Philadelphia Consolidate	Financial	22.4	35.45	1.93
⊖ Renal Care Group	Health	22.6	31.03	1.78
⊕ NII Holdings	Telecom	7.4	90.74	1.68
⊕ Computer Sciences	Business	18.1	27.45	1.45
⊕ Jarden	Goods	27.5	58.89	1.41
⊖ Measurement Specialties	Ind Mtrls	14.8	24.62	1.27
⊕ Big 5 Sporting Goods	Consumer	19.1	39.45	1.25
⊕ The Geo Group	Business	13.8	16.58	1.21
Molina Healthcare	Health	—	83.83	1.19
⊕ W Holding Company	Financial	17.6	27.21	1.17
⊕ Mariner Health Care	Health	—	—	1.16
⊕ J2 Global Communications	Telecom	19.8	39.17	1.13
⊕ Bisys Group	Business	23.1	10.55	1.13
Montpelier Re Holdings	Financial	6.2	8.68	1.11

Current Investment Style

Value Blnd Growth / Large Mid Small

Market Cap	%
Giant	0.0
Large	1.6
Mid	38.1
Small	41.9
Micro	18.4
Avg $mil: 1,077	

Value Measures		Rel Category
Price/Earnings	16.21	0.75
Price/Book	1.88	0.71
Price/Sales	0.79	0.53
Price/Cash Flow	6.00	0.75
Dividend Yield %	0.30	0.97

Growth Measures	%	Rel Category
Long-Term Erngs	16.60	0.96
Book Value	13.46	2.09
Sales	11.06	1.71
Cash Flow	17.32	1.28
Historical Erngs	24.97	1.85

Profitability	%	Rel Category
Return on Equity	17.05	1.73
Return on Assets	8.10	1.85
Net Margin	10.96	1.60

Sector Weightings	% of Stocks	Rel S&P 500	3 Year High	3 Year Low
Info	7.54	0.35		
Software	2.20	0.51	6	0
Hardware	1.47	0.14	13	1
Media	0.34	0.09	3	0
Telecom	3.53	1.12	4	0
Service	69.60	1.50		
Health	11.89	0.95	43	12
Consumer	10.54	1.16	18	7
Business	17.47	4.31	26	11
Financial	29.70	1.43	30	6
Mfg	22.85	0.71		
Goods	6.21	0.67	6	3
Ind Mtrls	10.77	0.85	15	5
Energy	5.87	0.82	7	3
Utilities	0.00	0.00	0	0

Composition

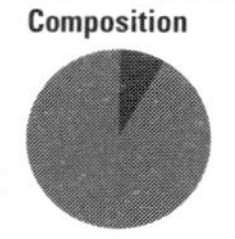

Cash	8.3
Stocks	91.8
Bonds	0.0
Other	0.0
Foreign (% of Stock)	2.0

Morningstar's Take by Laura Pavlenko Lutton 12-16-04

Fidelity Small Cap Independence has appeal.

This offering takes a sensible approach to small-growth investing. Manager James Harmon, who also runs this offering's near-twin Fidelity Small Cap Retirement, looks for companies with strong growth prospects and operations, but he's more mindful of valuation than the typical manager in this category. For example, Harmon has made Fidelity National Financial a top holding in the fund because he thinks the market isn't recognizing the earnings potential of the title insurer's information-services business. Harmon's fondness for cheaper stocks such as this one means the fund usually walks the line between the small-blend and the small-growth categories.

Because of this fund's more-moderate approach to small-growth investing, investors could consider it a worthy replacement for Fidelity Low-Priced Stock, the enormous small-blend offering that closed to new and many existing shareholders in 2004. While Low-Priced Stock leans more to value than growth, this offering's risk profile is comparable. To be sure, this fund makes some sector bets, but its individual stock weights are relatively tame. What's more, Harmon is supported by the same team of researchers that are feeding stock ideas into Low-Priced Stock, and he has demonstrated promise as a skilled stock-picker during his first few years at this fund. (The fund's three-year record is one of the better showings in the small-growth category.)

This fund also appears relatively nimble--certainly by Fidelity standards--at about $1 billion of assets. We think this fund is still small enough that Harmon can buy and sell stocks in this portfolio rather easily. It's worth noting, however, that this offering's trades are filled after those of Low-Priced Stock and the mega-huge Fidelity Contrafund when the funds have holdings in common. That trading rule could pose occasional liquidity issues here, but we don't think that's reason enough to rule out this offering.

Address:	82 Devonshire St Boston MA 02109 800-343-3548
Web Address:	www.fidelity.com
Inception:	06-28-93 *
Advisor:	Fidelity Management & Research Co. (FMR)
Subadvisor:	FMR Co., Inc. (FMRC)
NTF Plans:	Fidelity Retail-NTF, CommonWealth NTF

Minimum Purchase:	$2500	Add: $250	IRA: $2500
Min Auto Inv Plan:	$100	Add: $100	
Sales Fees:	No-load, 1.50%R		
Management Fee:	0.68%		
Actual Fees:	Mgt:0.68%	Dist:	
Expense Projections:	3Yr:$337	5Yr:$585	10Yr:$1294
Income Distrib:	Semi-Annually		

Fidelity SmCp Retirement

Ticker	Load	NAV	Yield	Total Assets	Mstar Category
FSCRX	None	$15.88	0.0%	$121 mil	Small Growth

Governance and Management

Fiduciary Grade: B

Portfolio Manager(s)

Before he began managing diversified funds in 2000, James Harmon was a member of Fidelity's small-cap analyst team. He also had a brief stint as manager of Fidelity's biotech fund. In short, his record as a diversified-fund manager is thin but promising.

Strategy

James Harmon buys a little of every kind of small-cap stock, using a style that he calls aggressive value. That may mean betting on turnarounds, making plays on cheap assets, or buying companies that are trading at discounts to his estimate of their discounted future free cash flows. He also looks for opportunities to trade in and out of a sector to make a quick profit. Because he's only required to invest 80% of the fund in small caps, Harmon exercises his right to buy a handful of larger-cap names.

Historical Profile

Return Average
Risk Low
Rating ★★★★ Above Avg

Investment Style
Equity
Stock %

2000	2001	2002	2003	12-04
83%	93%	94%	98%	92%

▼ Manager Change
∇ Partial Manager Change

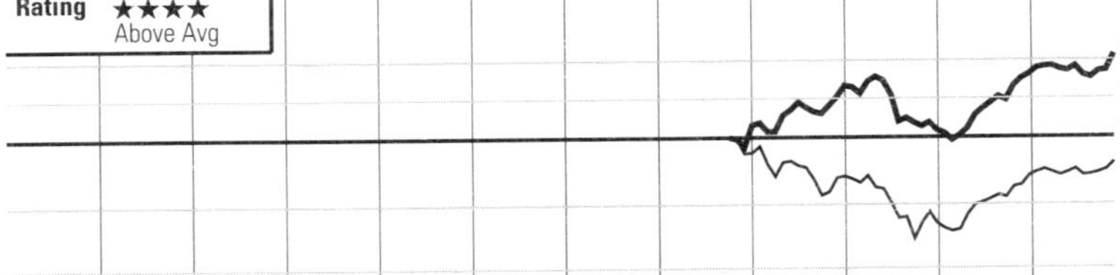

Growth of $10,000
— Investment Values of Fund
— Investment Values of S&P 500

Performance Quartile (within Category)

1993	1994	1995	1996	1997	1998	1999	2000	2001	2002	2003	12-04	History
—	—	—	—	—	—	—	10.84	13.30	10.27	13.81	15.88	NAV
—	—	—	—	—	—	—	8.40*	23.30	-21.04	34.47	14.99	Total Return %
—	—	—	—	—	—	—	—	35.18	1.05	5.80	4.12	+/-S&P 500
—	—	—	—	—	—	—	—	32.53	9.22	-14.07	0.68	+/-Russ 2000 Gr
—	—	—	—	—	—	—	0.00	0.00	0.00	0.00	0.00	Income Return %
—	—	—	—	—	—	—	—	23.30	-21.04	34.47	14.99	Capital Return %
—	—	—	—	—	—	—	—	3	21	86	34	Total Rtn % Rank Cat
—	—	—	—	—	—	—	0.00	0.00	0.00	0.00	0.00	Income $
—	—	—	—	—	—	—	0.00	0.06	0.29	0.00	0.00	Capital Gains $
—	—	—	—	—	—	—	—	0.93	0.92	0.86	0.99	Expense Ratio %
—	—	—	—	—	—	—	—	-0.15	-0.48	-0.49	-0.63	Income Ratio %
—	—	—	—	—	—	—	—	543	338	242	151	Turnover Rate %
—	—	—	—	—	—	—	2	25	48	79	121	Net Assets $mil

Performance 12-31-04

	1st Qtr	2nd Qtr	3rd Qtr	4th Qtr	Total
2000	—	—	—	6.80	8.40*
2001	-3.32	16.80	-5.83	15.95	23.30
2002	2.18	-6.63	-14.02	-3.75	-21.04
2003	-2.82	15.33	4.52	14.80	34.47
2004	4.49	-0.21	-2.71	13.35	14.99

Trailing	Total Return%	+/- S&P 500	+/- Russ 2000 Gr	%Rank Cat	Growth of $10,000
3 Mo	13.35	4.12	-1.73	61	11,335
6 Mo	10.28	3.09	2.12	24	11,028
1 Yr	14.99	4.12	0.68	34	11,499
3 Yr Avg	6.88	3.30	1.09	36	12,209
5 Yr Avg	—	—	—	—	—
10 Yr Avg	—	—	—	—	—
15 Yr Avg	—	—	—	—	—

Tax Analysis	Tax-Adj Rtn%	%Rank Cat	Tax-Cost Rat	%Rank Cat
3 Yr (estimated)	6.57	35	0.29	28
5 Yr (estimated)	—	—	—	—
10 Yr (estimated)	—	—	—	—

Potential Capital Gain Exposure: 18% of assets

Rating and Risk

Time Period	Load-Adj Return %	Morningstar Rtn vs Cat	Morningstar Risk vs Cat	Morningstar Risk-Adj Rating
1 Yr	14.99			
3 Yr	6.88	Avg	Low	★★★★
5 Yr	—	—	—	—
10 Yr	—	—	—	—
Incept	12.17			

Other Measures	Standard Index S&P 500	Best Fit Index Mstar Small Core
Alpha	4.3	-4.8
Beta	0.69	0.81
R-Squared	46	84
Standard Deviation	16.21	
Mean	6.88	
Sharpe Ratio	0.34	

Portfolio Analysis 10-31-04

Share change since 07-04 Total Stocks:133	Sector	PE	YTD Ret%	% Assets
⊕ Fisher Scientific Intern	Health	43.9	50.79	2.64
⊕ Affiliated Computer Serv	Business	14.7	10.52	2.54
⊕ Fidelity National Financ	Financial	10.2	32.24	2.19
⊕ Alliant Techsystems	Ind Mtrls	16.7	13.19	2.14
⊕ BJ's Wholesale Club	Consumer	16.6	26.87	2.09
⊖ Corrections Corp of Amer	Business	13.2	40.31	2.07
⊕ Philadelphia Consolidate	Financial	22.4	35.45	1.98
⊕ NII Holdings	Telecom	7.4	90.74	1.73
⊕ Renal Care Group	Health	22.6	31.03	1.71
⊕ Computer Sciences	Business	18.1	27.45	1.50
⊕ Jarden	Goods	27.5	58.89	1.46
⊖ Measurement Specialties	Ind Mtrls	14.8	24.62	1.32
⊕ Big 5 Sporting Goods	Consumer	19.1	39.45	1.24
⊕ The Geo Group	Business	13.8	16.58	1.23
⊕ Mariner Health Care	Health	—	—	1.21
⊕ W Holding Company	Financial	17.6	27.21	1.16
☼ Wellchoice	Financial	18.2	54.78	1.14
⊕ Bisys Group	Business	23.1	10.55	1.13
⊕ J2 Global Communications	Telecom	19.8	39.17	1.13
Molina Healthcare	Health	—	83.83	1.12

Current Investment Style

Value Blnd Growth — Large Mid Small

Market Cap	%
Giant	0.0
Large	1.7
Mid	38.2
Small	42.0
Micro	18.1
Avg $mil: 1,087	

Value Measures		Rel Category
Price/Earnings	16.19	0.75
Price/Book	1.88	0.71
Price/Sales	0.79	0.53
Price/Cash Flow	5.96	0.74
Dividend Yield %	0.30	0.97

Growth Measures	%	Rel Category
Long-Term Erngs	16.58	0.96
Book Value	13.49	2.09
Sales	11.12	1.72
Cash Flow	17.30	1.28
Historical Erngs	25.07	1.85

Profitability	%	Rel Category
Return on Equity	17.11	1.73
Return on Assets	8.08	1.84
Net Margin	10.88	1.59

Sector Weightings	% of Stocks	Rel S&P 500	3 Year High	3 Year Low
Info	7.58	0.35		
Software	2.22	0.52	6	0
Hardware	1.45	0.14	13	1
Media	0.33	0.09	3	0
Telecom	3.58	1.14	4	0
Service	69.28	1.49		
Health	11.78	0.94	43	12
Consumer	10.63	1.17	18	7
Business	17.56	4.34	26	11
Financial	29.31	1.41	29	6
Mfg	23.13	0.72		
Goods	6.22	0.67	6	3
Ind Mtrls	10.91	0.86	15	4
Energy	6.00	0.84	7	3
Utilities	0.00	0.00	0	0

Composition

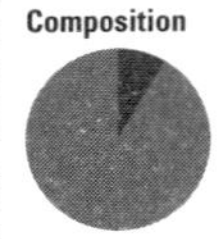

Cash	8.5
Stocks	91.5
Bonds	0.0
Other	0.0
Foreign (% of Stock)	2.0

Morningstar's Take by Laura Pavlenko Lutton 12-16-04

This is a decent small-cap option.

Fidelity Small Cap Retirement, the near clone of Fidelity Small Cap Independence, takes a sensible approach to small-growth investing. Manager James Harmon looks for companies with strong growth prospects and operations, but he's more mindful of valuation than the typical manager in this category. For example, Harmon has made Fidelity National Financial a top holding in the fund because he thinks the market isn't recognizing the earnings potential of the title insurer's information-services business. Harmon's fondness for cheaper stocks such as this one means the fund usually walks the line between the small-blend and the small-growth categories.

This fund's more-moderate approach to small-growth investing means investors could consider it a worthy replacement for Fidelity Low-Priced Stock, the enormous small-blend offering that closed to new and many existing shareholders in 2004. While Low-Priced Stock leans more to value than growth, this offering's risk profile is comparable. To be sure, this fund makes some sector bets, but its individual stock weights are relatively tame. What's more, Harmon is supported by the same team of researchers that are feeding stock ideas into Low-Priced Stock, and he has demonstrated promise as a skilled stock-picker during his first few years at this fund. (The fund's three-year record is one of the better showings in the small-growth category.)

This fund also appears relatively nimble--certainly by Fidelity standards. All told, Harmon runs about $2 billion in this style, and we think that sum is still small enough that Harmon can effectively buy and sell stocks. It's worth noting, however, that this offering's trades are filled after those of Low-Priced Stock and the mega-huge Fidelity Contrafund when the funds have holdings in common. That trading rule could pose occasional liquidity issues here, but we don't think that's reason enough to rule out this offering.

Address:	82 Devonshire St Boston MA 02109 800-343-3548
Web Address:	www.fidelity.com
Inception:	09-26-00*
Advisor:	Fidelity Management & Research Co. (FMR)
Subadvisor:	FMR Co., Inc. (FMRC)
NTF Plans:	Fidelity Retail-NTF, CommonWealth NTF

Minimum Purchase:	$2500	Add: $500	IRA: $2500
Min Auto Inv Plan:	$2500	Add: $100	
Sales Fees:	No-load, 1.50%R		
Management Fee:	0.72%		
Actual Fees:	Mgt:0.72%	Dist:	
Expense Projections:	3Yr:$353	5Yr: —	10Yr: —
Income Distrib:	Annually		

Fidelity Small Cap Stock

Ticker	Load	NAV	Yield	Total Assets	Mstar Category
FSLCX	None	$18.16	0.0%	$4,159 mil	Small Blend

Governance and Management

Fiduciary Grade: B

Portfolio Manager(s)

Paul Antico has been at the helm since the fund's March 1998 inception. He's supported by Fidelity's staff of four small-cap analysts and draws on the company's army of industry analysts for additional research. Small-cap research isn't generally a priority at Fidelity, however.

Strategy

Paul Antico is a pure bottom-up stock-picker who seeks companies with strong growth prospects, but he isn't willing to pay the extreme prices that pure growth managers do. He will buy turnaround plays and tends to avoid areas where valuations have run up. Antico spreads his picks across roughly 200 to 235 names and keeps individual stock positions fairly small, limiting the fund's exposure to company-specific risk. Turnover consistently runs over 100% per year.

Historical Profile

Return Average
Risk Average
Rating ★★★ Neutral

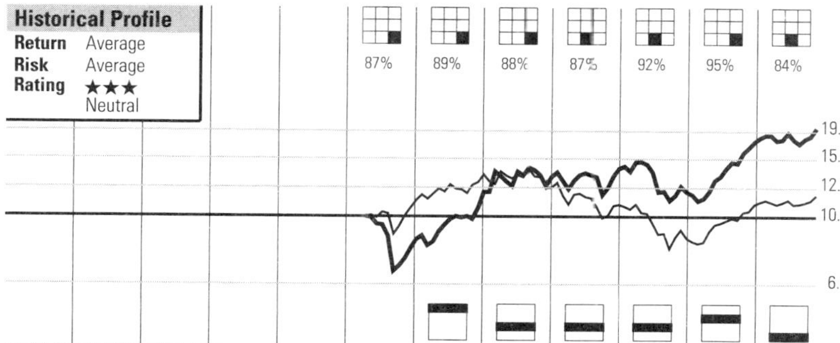

1993	1994	1995	1996	1997	1998	1999	2000	2001	2002	2003	12-04	History
—	—	—	—	—	8.91	12.71	13.51	14.36	11.84	17.10	18.16	NAV
—	—	—	—	—	-10.69*	42.65	11.84	6.44	-15.73	45.04	14.57	Total Return %
—	—	—	—	—	—	21.61	20.94	18.32	6.36	16.37	3.70	+/-S&P 500
—	—	—	—	—	—	21.39	14.83	3.95	4.75	-2.21	-3.76	+/-Russ 2000
—	—	—	—	—	0.00	0.00	0.32	0.15	0.00	0.00	0.00	Income Return %
—	—	—	—	—	—	42.65	11.52	6.29	-15.73	45.04	14.57	Capital Return %
—	—	—	—	—	—	4	54	55	56	40	82	Total Rtn % Rank Cat
—	—	—	—	—	0.02	0.00	0.04	0.02	0.00	0.00	0.00	Income $
—	—	—	—	—	0.00	0.00	0.65	0.00	0.31	0.07	1.33	Capital Gains $
—	—	—	—	—	1.48	0.99	1.13	1.07	1.07	1.10	1.08	Expense Ratio %
—	—	—	—	—	0.67	0.01	-0.0[illegible]	0.24	0.24	0.05	-0.34	Income Ratio %
—	—	—	—	—	75	170	120	151	132	116	96	Turnover Rate %
—	—	—	—	—	552	688	1,142	1,354	1,419	2,505	4,159	Net Assets $mil

Performance 12-31-04

	1st Qtr	2nd Qtr	3rd Qtr	4th Qtr	Total
2000	12.59	3.28	1.11	-4.86	11.84
2001	-8.51	12.54	-14.88	21.46	6.44
2002	5.08	-7.41	-18.73	6.57	-15.73
2003	-4.81	17.83	10.24	17.30	45.04
2004	4.91	1.86	-4.29	12.01	14.57

Trailing	Total Return%	+/- S&P 500	+/- Russ 2000	%Rank Cat	Growth of $10,000
3 Mo	12.01	2.78	-2.08	68	11,201
6 Mo	7.21	0.02	-3.62	92	10,721
1 Yr	14.57	3.70	-3.76	82	11,457
3 Yr Avg	11.88	8.30	0.40	60	14,004
5 Yr Avg	10.76	13.06	4.15	60	16,669
10 Yr Avg	—	—	—	—	—
15 Yr Avg	—	—	—	—	—

Tax Analysis	Tax-Adj Rtn%	%Rank Cat	Tax-Cost Rat	%Rank Cat
3 Yr (estimated)	11.05	56	0.74	51
5 Yr (estimated)	9.97	55	0.71	29
10 Yr (estimated)	—	—	—	—

Potential Capital Gain Exposure: 16% of assets

Rating and Risk

Time Period	Load-Adj Return %	Morningstar Rtn vs Cat	Morningstar Risk vs Cat	Morningstar Risk-Adj Rating
1 Yr	14.57			
3 Yr	11.88	Avg	Avg	★★★
5 Yr	10.76	Avg	Avg	★★★
10 Yr	—	—	—	—
Incept	11.70			

Other Measures	Standard Index S&P 500	Best Fit Index Russ 2000
Alpha	8.6	1.7
Beta	0.93	0.84
R-Squared	70	93
Standard Deviation	18.73	
Mean	11.88	
Sharpe Ratio	0.57	

Portfolio Analysis 10-31-04

Share change since 07-04 Total Stocks:230	Sector	PE	YTD Ret%	% Assets
⊖ Ingram Micro	Hardware	15.8	30.82	3.27
American Healthways	Health	41.8	38.42	2.68
⊕ Foot Locker	Consumer	17.6	15.99	2.29
⊕ Priority Healthcare	Health	18.2	-9.44	2.15
Tech Data	Ind Mtrls	17.5	14.39	1.57
⊕ Navistar International	Ind Mtrls	17.5	-8.17	1.44
⊕ EGL	Business	30.2	70.02	1.36
Timken	Ind Mtrls	22.3	32.68	1.25
⊕ Pep Boys	Consumer	23.9	-24.39	1.23
⊕ Wabash National	Ind Mtrls	19.0	-8.09	1.20
⊕ Arrow Electronics	Hardware	14.5	5.01	1.14
⊕ Labor Ready	Business	23.5	29.16	1.12
⊕ Cerner	Software	30.4	40.48	1.11
⊕ Mariner Health Care	Health	—	—	1.05
⊖ Amerigroup	Financial	24.7	77.40	1.02
⊕ Manitowoc	Business	22.2	21.59	1.01
⊕ Per-Se Technologies	Software	28.6	3.46	0.98
⊕ A.O. Smith	Ind Mtrls	18.3	-12.75	0.89
RONA	Consumer	—	—	0.87
⊖ Emmis Communications A	Media	—	-29.06	0.86

Current Investment Style

Value Blnd Growth — Large Mid Small

Market Cap	%
Giant	0.0
Large	0.4
Mid	34.1
Small	46.6
Micro	18.9
Avg $mil: 902	

Value Measures		Rel Category
Price/Earnings	18.67	1.08
Price/Book	1.93	0.97
Price/Sales	0.52	0.55
Price/Cash Flow	3.23	0.55
Dividend Yield %	0.50	0.60

Growth Measures	%	Rel Category
Long-Term Erngs	15.88	1.17
Book Value	3.02	0.54
Sales	0.49	0.11
Cash Flow	-2.19	NMF
Historical Erngs	8.92	1.19

Profitability	%	Rel Category
Return on Equity	8.61	0.82
Return on Assets	3.72	0.75
Net Margin	3.92	0.54

Sector Weightings	% of Stocks	Rel S&P 500	3 Year High	3 Year Low
Info	20.18	0.94		
Software	4.30	1.00	5	3
Hardware	10.43	1.02	10	7
Media	4.67	1.22	5	0
Telecom	0.78	0.25	3	1
Service	55.75	1.20		
Health	18.82	1.51	25	16
Consumer	12.21	1.34	18	9
Business	17.09	4.22	17	13
Financial	7.63	0.37	10	6
Mfg	24.06	0.75		
Goods	7.43	0.80	7	3
Ind Mtrls	16.19	1.28	25	16
Energy	0.44	0.06	1	0
Utilities	0.00	0.00	0	0

Composition

Cash	15.6
Stocks	84.0
Bonds	0.0
Other	0.4
Foreign (% of Stock)	14.3

Morningstar's Take by Christopher Traulsen 11-30-04

Fidelity Small Cap Stock is a solid offering. We hope it stays that way.

This fund fills a nice role in the Fidelity lineup of small-cap funds. Unlike Low Priced Stock, it's still small enough to emphasize small-cap stocks, and it's not nearly as volatile as Fidelity Value Strategies, another small-cap oriented offering. Its total returns haven't been as strong as Low Priced Stock's, but they've been much better than Value Strategies. In short, if you're looking for a small-cap offering at Fidelity, this fund, along with sibling Fidelity Small Cap Independence, are probably your best bets.

This fund's recent returns relative to its category might not look that impressive, but the fund rides the line between blend and growth and landed in the small-growth category until relatively recently. Compared with the small-growth category, it has excellent returns with below-average volatility. Compared with its new category, it still has peer-beating since-inception returns, but its volatility is a bit higher than the norm.

That profile stems from manager Paul Antico's style. He tries to find small-cap companies with strong growth prospects, but he also wants to keep risk in check. He pays more attention to valuations than a typical growth manager would, and also spreads the funds assets across more than 200 names, which helps limit issue-specific risk.

The fund is lagging a bit in 2004, due in large part to sizable underweights in energy and banks: two areas that have propelled many of the fund's peers. Two health-services picks--Accredo Health and Priority Healthcare, have also dented the fund. Still, Antico's long-term record suggests the fund should be just fine. We're more concerned about its size. At $3.7 billion in assets, the fund is getting bloated. We think the board should step up to the plate soon and close it.

For now, the fund is a sound choice for core small-cap exposure. If it's allowed to grow much larger, it may not be.

Address:	82 Devonshire St Boston MA 02109 800-343-3548
Web Address:	www.fidelity.com
Inception:	03-12-98*
Advisor:	Fidelity Management & Research Co. (FMR)
Subadvisor:	FMR Co., Inc. (FMRC)
NTF Plans:	Fidelity Retail-NTF, CommonWealth NTF

Minimum Purchase:	$2500	Add: $250	IRA: $2500
Min Auto Inv Plan:	$2500	Add: $100	
Sales Fees:	No-load, 2.00%R		
Management Fee:	0.90%		
Actual Fees:	Mgt:0.90%	Dist:	
Expense Projections:	3Yr:$331	5Yr:$574	10Yr:$1271
Income Distrib:	Semi-Annually		

Fidelity Spar 500 Idx

Analyst Pick	Ticker	Load	NAV	Yield	Total Assets	Mstar Category
✔	FSMKX	None	$83.36	1.7%	$12,113 mil	Large Blend

Governance and Management

Fiduciary Grade: B

Portfolio Manager(s)

This fund had been subadvised by Deutsche Asset Management for many years, but in mid-January 2003 Fidelity began managing it in-house. In August 2003, the unit of Fidelity that was running this and other Fidelity index portfolios, Geode Capital Management, was spun off and is now an independent entity. But Geode is still running this fund as a subadvisor, with the same individuals involved.

Strategy

This fund buys the stocks that make up the S&P 500 Index, as well as index futures, in an attempt to mimic the index's returns.

Historical Profile

Return: Above Avg
Risk: Average
Rating: ★★★★ Above Avg

Investment Style: Equity Stock %

92%	90%	96%	96%	98%	97%	97%	97%	97%

▼ Manager Change
▽ Partial Manager Change

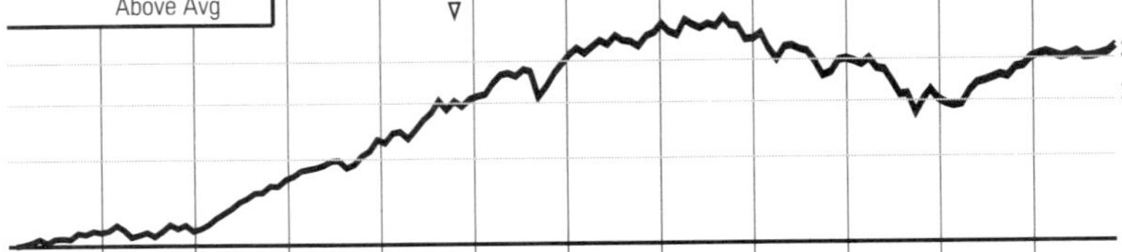

Growth of $10,000
- Investment Values of Fund
- Investment Values of S&P 500

Performance Quartile (within Category)

1993	1994	1995	1996	1997	1998	1999	2000	2001	2002	2003	12-04	History
34.60	34.15	45.32	53.42	68.50	85.29	100.89	90.76	78.89	60.47	76.60	83.36	NAV
9.62	1.02	37.00	22.59	33.03	28.48	20.65	-9.13	-12.05	-22.17	28.49	10.73	Total Return %
-0.44	-0.29	-0.53	-0.35	-0.32	-0.09	-0.39	-0.03	-0.17	-0.08	-0.18	-0.14	+/-S&P 500
-0.56	0.63	-0.77	0.14	0.18	1.46	-0.26	-1.34	0.40	-0.52	-1.40	-0.67	+/-Russ 1000
2.49	2.33	2.84	2.04	1.84	1.17	1.40	0.96	1.06	1.26	1.69	1.85	Income Return %
7.13	-1.31	34.16	20.55	31.19	27.31	19.25	-10.09	-13.11	-23.43	26.80	8.88	Capital Return %
59	27	20	35	17	18	41	65	46	45	30	37	Total Rtn % Rank Cat
0.80	0.80	0.96	0.91	0.97	0.79	1.19	0.97	0.96	0.99	1.02	1.41	Income $
0.18	0.00	0.37	1.05	1.38	1.68	0.70	0.00	0.00	0.00	0.00	0.00	Capital Gains $
0.44	0.45	0.45	0.45	0.44	0.19	0.19	0.19	0.19	0.19	0.19	0.19	Expense Ratio %
2.54	2.38	2.49	2.11	1.82	1.61	1.30	1.21	1.02	1.21	1.62	1.51	Income Ratio %
—	3	2	5	6	6	4	8	6	4	9	4	Turnover Rate %
300	307	689	1,598	3,870	7,150	10,438	9,572	8,602	6,788	9,825	12,113	Net Assets $mil

Performance 12-31-04

	1st Qtr	2nd Qtr	3rd Qtr	4th Qtr	Total
2000	2.26	-2.67	-0.99	-7.79	-9.13
2001	-11.90	6.07	-14.94	10.64	-12.05
2002	0.24	-13.44	-17.26	8.41	-22.17
2003	-3.19	15.38	2.59	12.12	28.49
2004	1.66	1.68	-1.90	9.21	10.73

Trailing	Total Return%	+/- S&P 500	+/- Russ 1000	%Rank Cat	Growth of $10,000
3 Mo	9.21	-0.02	-0.59	48	10,921
6 Mo	7.13	-0.06	-0.68	44	10,713
1 Yr	10.73	-0.14	-0.67	37	11,073
3 Yr Avg	3.46	-0.12	-0.81	36	11,074
5 Yr Avg	-2.42	-0.12	-0.66	52	8,847
10 Yr Avg	11.85	-0.22	-0.31	19	30,645
15 Yr Avg	—	—	—	—	—

Tax Analysis	Tax-Adj Rtn%	%Rank Cat	Tax-Cost Rat	%Rank Cat
3 Yr (estimated)	2.88	34	0.56	47
5 Yr (estimated)	-2.91	47	0.50	26
10 Yr (estimated)	10.99	13	0.77	17

Potential Capital Gain Exposure: 17% of assets

Rating and Risk

Time Period	Load-Adj Return %	Morningstar Rtn vs Cat	Morningstar Risk vs Cat	Morningstar Risk-Adj Rating
1 Yr	10.73			
3 Yr	3.46	Avg	+Avg	★★★
5 Yr	-2.42	Avg	Avg	★★★
10 Yr	11.85	+Avg	Avg	★★★★
Incept	11.16			

Other Measures	Standard Index S&P 500	Best Fit Index S&P 500
Alpha	-0.1	-0.1
Beta	1.00	1.00
R-Squared	100	100
Standard Deviation	15.56	
Mean	3.46	
Sharpe Ratio	0.13	

Portfolio Analysis 10-31-04

Share change since 07-04 Total Stocks:500	Sector	PE	YTD Ret%	% Assets
⊕ General Electric	Ind Mtrls	22.8	20.68	3.31
⊕ ExxonMobil	Energy	13.9	28.04	2.94
⊕ Microsoft	Software	36.1	8.95	2.80
⊕ Citigroup	Financial	15.3	2.72	2.11
⊕ Wal-Mart Stores	Consumer	23.4	0.51	2.10
⊕ Pfizer	Health	22.0	-22.31	2.01
⊕ S&P 500 Index (Fut)	—	—	—	1.71
⊕ Bank of America	Financial	12.3	21.50	1.67
⊕ Johnson & Johnson	Health	20.6	25.17	1.59
⊕ American International G	Financial	16.2	-0.53	1.45
⊕ IBM	Hardware	20.2	7.19	1.38
⊕ Intel	Hardware	19.8	-26.56	1.31
⊕ J.P. Morgan Chase & Co.	Financial	19.4	9.97	1.26
⊕ Procter & Gamble	Goods	23.3	12.38	1.20
⊕ Cisco Systems	Hardware	24.5	-20.26	1.19
⊕ ChevronTexaco	Energy	7.7	25.57	1.04
⊕ Verizon Communications	Telecom	32.4	20.25	0.99
⊕ Wells Fargo	Financial	15.5	8.97	0.93
⊕ Altria Group	Goods	13.3	18.38	0.91
⊕ Coca-Cola	Goods	21.9	-16.12	0.91

Current Investment Style

Value Blnd Growth — Large Mid Small

Market Cap	%
Giant	51.8
Large	37.8
Mid	10.2
Small	0.2
Micro	0.0
Avg $mil: 45,347	

Value Measures		Rel Category
Price/Earnings	16.82	0.99
Price/Book	2.66	1.02
Price/Sales	1.45	1.01
Price/Cash Flow	7.63	0.99
Dividend Yield %	1.66	1.12

Growth Measures	%	Rel Category
Long-Term Erngs	11.07	0.96
Book Value	7.13	0.92
Sales	4.72	0.82
Cash Flow	6.89	0.73
Historical Erngs	11.51	0.98

Profitability	%	Rel Category
Return on Equity	18.30	1.05
Return on Assets	9.37	1.09
Net Margin	12.06	1.05

Sector Weightings	% of Stocks	Rel S&P 500	3 Year High	3 Year Low
Info	21.78	1.01		
Software	4.62	1.07	5	4
Hardware	10.02	0.98	12	9
Media	3.85	1.00	4	4
Telecom	3.29	1.04	4	3
Service	46.25	1.00		
Health	12.52	1.00	15	13
Consumer	9.12	1.00	9	9
Business	4.04	1.00	4	3
Financial	20.57	0.99	21	20
Mfg	31.97	1.00		
Goods	9.18	0.98	10	9
Ind Mtrls	12.48	0.99	12	11
Energy	7.32	1.02	7	6
Utilities	2.99	1.01	3	3

Composition

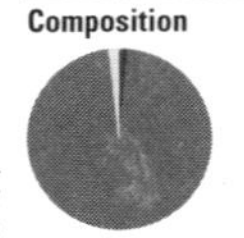

Cash	1.6
Stocks	96.7
Bonds	0.0
Other	1.7
Foreign (% of Stock)	0.0

Morningstar's Take by Gregg Wolper 12-13-04

Fidelity Spartan 500 Index is so cheap now it deserves a look.

On Aug. 31, 2004, Fidelity instituted a fee waiver in order to bring the expense ratio of this fund down to 0.10% from 0.19%. Even at the former price, the fund was much less costly than the typical actively managed large-blend fund and also one of the least-expensive choices of the subgroup of funds that passively track the S&P 500. Now that it costs just 0.10%, this fund stands as one of the very cheapest S&P 500 offerings available to ordinary investors.

That's significant. Index funds--particularly those that own large, easily traded stocks-- have few means of distinguishing themselves through performance. Costs can thus play a large role in differentiating returns. Although this fund isn't the absolute cheapest, it now has an advantage over the biggest and most well-known S&P 500 player--Vanguard 500 Index, which has an expense ratio of 0.18%--and an even more-pronounced advantage over some others. For the five-year period through Aug. 31, 2004, the Vanguard fund's return had beaten this one's by just 6 basis points (0.06 of a percentage point) annually. And for the three months through Dec. 10, 2004--with the new fee structure in place--the Fidelity fund has beaten its Vanguard rival by 1 basis point.

Still, don't go overboard in reacting to this change. For example, owners of the Vanguard fund need not switch, particularly if they would have to pay capital-gains taxes. After all, Vanguard funds are at least as adept at tracking their benchmarks as Fidelity's are; the difference in fees is slight; and there's no telling if that gap will exist permanently, because Fidelity's fee waiver can be lifted.

The move is, however, welcome. Fidelity Spartan 500 Index's lower cost makes it an even more-appealing alternative--both for indexing fans in particular and those who don't have access to high-quality, actively managed large-cap offerings.

Address:	82 Devonshire St Boston MA 02109 800-343-3548
Web Address:	www.fidelity.com
Inception:	03-06-90
Advisor:	Fidelity Management & Research Co. (FMR)
Subadvisor:	FMR Co., Inc. (FMRC)
NTF Plans:	Fidelity Retail-NTF, CommonWealth NTF

Minimum Purchase:	$10000	Add: $1000	IRA: $2500
Min Auto Inv Plan:	$10000	Add: $500	
Sales Fees:	No-load, 0.50%R		
Management Fee:	0.24%		
Actual Fees:	Mgt:0.05%	Dist:	
Expense Projections:	3Yr:$122	5Yr:$213	10Yr:$480
Income Distrib:	Semi-Annually		

Fidelity Spar IntermMuni

Analyst Pick

Ticker	Load	NAV	Yield	SEC Yield	Total Assets	Mstar Category
FLTMX	None	$10.15	3.9%	3.08%	$1,809 mil	Muni National Interm

Governance and Management

Fiduciary Grade: B

Portfolio Manager(s)

Douglas T. McGinley took over here in January 2003. He has also managed funds focusing on California, Florida, Michigan, and Ohio since June 2002. McGinley joined Fidelity in 1994 as a municipal fixed-income analyst and covered numerous sectors within the municipal-bond market over the subsequent eight years. Previously, he served as an assistant vice president in the corporate lending group at Bank One from 1988 to 1992.

Strategy

Manager Doug McGinley makes adjustments to the portfolio based on his outlook for the shape of the yield curve and for various sectors of the market. He also tries to find bargains based on a bond's credit quality and structure. No interest-rate bets are made, though, as the fund seeks to generally match the risk and interest-rate sensitivity characteristics of the Lehman Brothers 1-17 Year Muni Index.

Historical Profile

Return High
Risk Average
Rating ★★★★★ Highest

Investment Style: Fixed Income — Income Rtn %Rank Cat: 21, 23, 15, 13, 16, 16, 23, 20, 23

▼ Manager Change
∇ Partial Manager Change

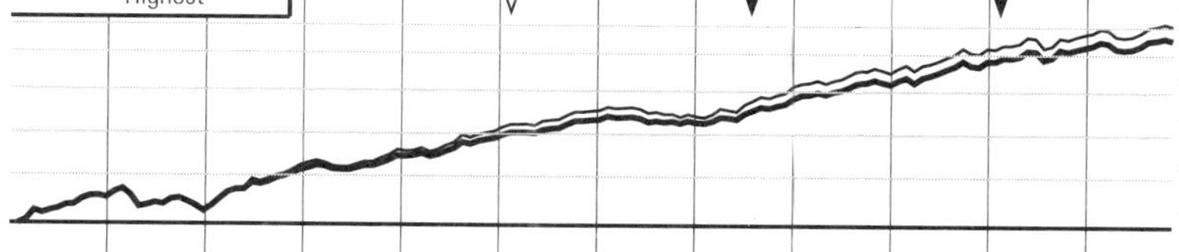

Growth of $10,000
- Investment Values of Fund
- Investment Values of LB Muni

Performance Quartile (within Category)

1993	1994	1995	1996	1997	1998	1999	2000	2001	2002	2003	12-04	History
9.99	8.99	9.80	9.70	9.94	9.98	9.41	9.78	9.85	10.23	10.21	10.15	NAV
12.24	-4.76	14.84	4.43	8.23	5.89	-1.06	9.25	5.43	9.02	5.30	3.74	Total Return %
-0.04	0.41	-2.62	0.00	-0.96	-0.59	1.00	-2.43	0.35	-0.58	-0.01	-0.74	+/-LB Muni
-0.53	0.01	-2.33	-0.11	-1.01	-0.87	0.18	-1.51	0.86	-1.15	-0.40	-0.41	+/-LB Muni 10YR
5.53	5.26	5.67	5.10	5.13	4.88	4.77	5.18	4.79	4.46	4.09	3.94	Income Return %
6.71	-10.02	9.17	-0.67	3.10	1.01	-5.83	4.07	0.69	4.56	1.21	-0.20	Capital Return %
18	75	34	17	35	28	21	49	8	38	8	15	Total Rtn % Rank Cat
0.52	0.51	0.50	0.49	0.49	0.47	0.47	0.48	0.46	0.43	0.41	0.39	Income $
0.24	0.02	0.00	0.03	0.05	0.06	0.00	0.00	0.00	0.06	0.14	0.04	Capital Gains $
0.57	0.56	0.57	0.56	0.55	0.50	0.48	0.49	0.39	0.43	0.43	—	Expense Ratio %
5.19	5.42	5.25	5.06	4.97	4.58	4.72	5.03	4.60	4.35	4.00	—	Income Ratio %
111	30	31	27	22	18	21	19	32	31	31	—	Turnover Rate %
1,195	881	941	901	912	1,146	1,061	1,210	1,487	1,752	1,797	1,809	Net Assets $mil

Performance 12-31-04

	1st Qtr	2nd Qtr	3rd Qtr	4th Qtr	Total
2000	2.00	1.37	2.00	3.58	9.25
2001	2.33	0.90	2.78	-0.61	5.48
2002	0.58	3.88	4.37	-0.02	9.02
2003	1.20	2.47	0.63	0.91	5.30
2004	1.62	-2.15	3.41	0.89	3.74

Trailing	Total Return%	+/- LB Muni	+/- LB Muni 10YR	%Rank Cat	Growth of $10,000
3 Mo	0.89	-0.36	0.06	25	10,089
6 Mo	4.33	-0.86	-0.67	26	10,433
1 Yr	3.74	-0.74	-0.41	15	10,374
3 Yr Avg	6.00	-0.44	-0.64	12	11,910
5 Yr Avg	6.54	-0.66	-0.50	17	13,727
10 Yr Avg	6.44	-0.62	-0.64	9	18,666
15 Yr Avg	6.49	-0.50	-0.59	18	25,682

Tax Analysis	Tax-Adj Rtn%	%Rank Cat	Tax-Cost Rat	%Rank Cat
3 Yr (estimated)	5.85	7	0.14	45
5 Yr (estimated)	6.45	11	0.08	32
10 Yr (estimated)	6.36	5	0.08	40

Potential Capital Gain Exposure: 5% of assets

Rating and Risk

Time Period	Load-Adj Return %	Morningstar Rtn vs Cat	Morningstar Risk vs Cat	Morningstar Risk-Adj Rating
1 Yr	3.74			
3 Yr	6.00	+Avg	Avg	★★★★★
5 Yr	6.54	High	Avg	★★★★★
10 Yr	6.44	High	Avg	★★★★★
Incept	6.40			

Other Measures	Standard Index LB Aggr	Best Fit Index LB Muni
Alpha	-0.1	-0.1
Beta	0.93	0.93
R-Squared	99	99

Standard Deviation	4.68
Mean	6.00
Sharpe Ratio	1.00

Portfolio Analysis 09-30-04

Total Fixed-Income:593	Date of Maturity	Amount $000	Value $000	% Net Assets
Hillsborough Cnty Fla In	09-01-25	18,000	18,400	1.03
San Antonio Tex Elec & G	02-01-06	17,500	17,059	0.96
Highlands Cnty Fla Healt	11-15-32	14,200	14,379	0.81
Washington St Pub Pwr Sp	07-01-07	15,130	14,066	0.79
Tobacco Settlement Fing	06-01-11	12,750	13,357	0.75
Washington St Pub Pwr Sp	07-01-10	16,000	12,966	0.73
Harris Cnty Tex	08-01-06	13,000	12,512	0.70
District Columbia	08-15-31	11,000	12,243	0.69
Texas St Tpk Auth 5.75%	08-15-38	10,110	11,123	0.62
Detroit Mich Sew Disp 5.	07-01-32	10,000	11,012	0.62
New Jersey St Transn Tr	06-15-23	10,000	10,964	0.61
Chicago Ill O Hare Intl	01-01-11	10,000	10,950	0.61
Chicago Ill O Hare Intl	01-01-08	9,820	10,721	0.60
Houston Tex Indpt Sch Di	08-15-11	13,740	10,653	0.60
Massachusetts St 5%	02-01-06	10,000	10,409	0.58

Current Investment Style

Duration: Short Int Long — Quality: High Med Low

¹Avg Eff Duration	5.4 Yrs
Avg Eff Maturity	8.6 Yrs
Avg Credit Quality	AA
Avg Wtd Coupon	4.40%
Avg Wtd Price	104.54% of par

¹figure provided by fund

Credit Analysis	% bonds 09-30-04		
US Govt	0	BB	0
AAA	68	B	0
AA	11	Below B	0
A	12	NR/NA	0
BBB	9		

Top 5 States	% bonds		
TX	19.5	WA	8.5
CA	11.9	NY	5.7
IL	11.4		

Composition			
Cash	2.0	Bonds	98.0
Stocks	0.0	Other	0.0

Special Securities	
Restricted/Illiquid Secs	0
Options/Futures/Warrants	No

Sector Weightings	% of Bonds	Rel Cat
General Obligation	31.9	0.90
Utilities	19.3	1.74
Health	6.7	0.90
Water/Waste	9.1	0.92
Housing	1.1	0.19
Education	12.2	0.87
Transportation	10.8	1.94
COP/Lease	0.7	0.47
Industrial	7.9	0.88
Misc Revenue	0.0	0.00
Demand	0.5	1.05

Morningstar's Take by Scott Berry 12-29-04

Moderate volatility, a proven approach, and low costs make Fidelity Spartan Intermediate Municipal Income easy for us to recommend.

This fund boasts an impressive record. Not only has it delivered peer-busting long-term returns--its three-, five-, and 10-year trailing returns all rank in the muni national intermediate bond category's best quartile, but it has done so with remarkable consistency. In fact, the fund's calendar-year returns have ranked in the category's top half each the last 10 years, while its standard deviation of returns (a measure of volatility) checks in lower than the category norm.

That success owes to three main factors. For starters, the fund's expense ratio provides it a sustainable and meaningful advantage over its average category peer. Meanwhile, the fund's approach helps ensure that management doesn't squander that advantage. Rather than making risky interest-rate bets, manager Doug McGinley looks to add value through more reliable methods, such as issue selection and sector allocation. Finally, the fund's success owes to McGinley and Fidelity's deep and talented municipal bond group, which has done an impressive job over the years of identifying market opportunities and aggressively taking advantage of them.

The fund's success continued in 2004. The added yield provided by the fund's A and BBB rated bonds juiced returns, while its overweight utility stake performed relatively well. Overall, the fund gained 3.5% for the year to date through Dec. 28 and outperformed nearly 90% of its category peers.

This fund could face some pressure if interest rates move higher, as its duration (a measure of interest-rate sensitivity) recently checked in a bit longer than the category norm. However, we remain big fans of this fund and think Fidelity's research capabilities and the fund's low costs will continue to make it tough to beat over the long term.

Address:	82 Devonshire Street Boston MA 02109 800-343-3548
Web Address:	www.fidelity.com
Inception:	04-15-77
Advisor:	Fidelity Management & Research Co. (FMR)
Subadvisor:	Fidelity Intl Invest Advisors (U.K.) Ltd
NTF Plans:	Fidelity Retail-NTF, CommonWealth NTF

Minimum Purchase:	$10000	Add: $1000	IRA: $0
Min Auto Inv Plan:	$500	Add: $500	
Sales Fees:	No-load, 0.50%R		
Management Fee:	0.34%		
Actual Fees:	Mgt:0.34%	Dist: —	
Expense Projections:	3Yr:$154	5Yr:$269	10Yr:$604
Income Distrib:	Monthly		

Fidelity Spar Intl Index

Analyst Pick

Ticker	Load	NAV	Yield	Total Assets	Mstar Category
FSIIX	None	$32.02	1.7%	$955 mil	Foreign Large Blend

Governance and Management

Fiduciary Grade: B

Portfolio Manager(s)

The fund had been subadvised by Deutsche Asset Management, one of the biggest indexers. But as of mid-January 2003, Fidelity took management duties in-house giving them to a group known as Geode. In August 2003, Geode Capital Management was spun off and is now a stand-alone firm, but it continues to manage this fund under a subadvisory agreement.

Strategy

The fund is designed to track the performance of the MSCI EAFE Index, a popular foreign-stock benchmark. Its portfolio consists primarily of large-cap stocks from developed markets. The fund imposes a 1% redemption fee on shares held fewer than 90 days. Fidelity uses fair value pricing when it deems the situation appropriate.

Historical Profile

Return Average
Risk Average
Rating ★★★ Neutral

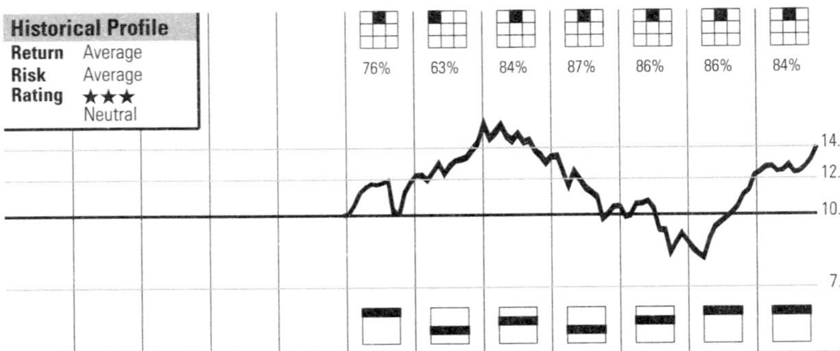

Investment Style
Equity
Stock %

▼ Manager Change
▽ Partial Manager Change

Growth of $10,000
— Investment Values of Fund
— Investment Values of MSCI EAFE

Performance Quartile (within Category)

1993	1994	1995	1996	1997	1998	1999	2000	2001	2002	2003	12-04	History
—	—	—	—	24.87	29.50	37.67	31.69	24.44	20.14	27.26	32.02	NAV
—	—	—	—	-0.08*	21.16	29.06	-14.90	-21.85	-15.99	38.34	19.86	Total Return %
—	—	—	—	—	1.23	2.03	-0.71	-0.43	-0.05	-0.25	-0.39	+/-MSCI EAFE
—	—	—	—	—	2.47	1.08	-1.54	-0.46	-0.19	-1.08	-0.52	+/-MSCI Wd xUS
—	—	—	—	0.00	1.94	1.29	0.77	1.01	1.60	2.74	2.02	Income Return %
—	—	—	—	—	19.22	27.77	-15.67	-22.86	-17.59	35.60	17.84	Capital Return %
—	—	—	—	—	10	75	35	51	39	18	21	Total Rtn % Rank Cat
—	—	—	—	0.06	0.48	0.38	0.29	0.32	0.39	0.55	0.55	Income $
—	—	—	—	0.00	0.13	0.00	0.08	0.00	0.00	0.00	0.07	Capital Gains $
—	—	—	—	—	0.35	0.36	0.35	0.35	0.35	0.39	0.47	Expense Ratio %
—	—	—	—	—	1.43	1.62	1.48	1.53	1.60	1.87	1.99	Income Ratio %
—	—	—	—	—	2	2	3	2	12	19	31	Turnover Rate %
—	—	—	—	21	40	186	349	319	346	455	955	Net Assets $mil

Performance 12-31-04

	1st Qtr	2nd Qtr	3rd Qtr	4th Qtr	Total
2000	-0.35	-4.38	-8.04	-2.89	-14.90
2001	-14.07	-0.15	-14.46	6.48	-21.85
2002	1.06	-2.15	-20.03	6.23	-15.99
2003	-7.75	19.23	7.93	16.53	38.34
2004	4.44	0.63	-0.77	14.93	19.86

Trailing	Total Return%	+/- MSCI EAFE	+/- MSCI Wd xUS	%Rank Cat	Growth of $10,000
3 Mo	14.93	-0.39	-0.22	26	11,493
6 Mo	14.05	-0.95	-1.32	50	11,405
1 Yr	19.86	-0.39	-0.52	21	11,986
3 Yr Avg	11.68	-0.21	-0.54	18	13,929
5 Yr Avg	-1.52	-0.39	-0.76	32	9,263
10 Yr Avg	—	—	—	—	—
15 Yr Avg	—	—	—	—	—

Tax Analysis	Tax-Adj Rtn%	%Rank Cat	Tax-Cost Rat	%Rank Cat
3 Yr (estimated)	10.89	18	0.71	76
5 Yr (estimated)	-2.12	27	0.61	39
10 Yr (estimated)	—	—	—	—

Potential Capital Gain Exposure: 4% of assets

Rating and Risk

Time Period	Load-Adj Return %	Morningstar Rtn vs Cat	Morningstar Risk vs Cat	Morningstar Risk-Adj Rating
1 Yr	19.86			
3 Yr	11.68	+Avg	Avg	★★★★
5 Yr	-1.52	Avg	Avg	★★★
10 Yr	—	—	—	—
Incept	5.31			

Other Measures	Standard Index S&P 500	Best Fit Index MSCI Wd xUS
Alpha	-0.1	-0.5
Beta	0.99	1.01
R-Squared	99	99

Standard Deviation	17.38
Mean	11.68
Sharpe Ratio	0.60

Morningstar's Take by Gregg Wolper 11-16-04

Fidelity Spartan International Index has made itself more appealing.

On Aug. 31, 2004, Fidelity instituted a fee waiver that drastically reduced the expense ratio of this fund, from 47 basis points (0.47%) to just 10 basis points. Even at the former price, the fund was a bargain compared to the actively managed offerings in the foreign large-blend category. After this cut, it's truly bare-bones cheap. By comparison, a prominent rival, Vanguard Developed Markets Index, which like this fund tracks the MSCI EAFE Index, currently has an expense ratio of 34 basis points. Thus, this offering has turned the cost advantage in its favor. (Meanwhile, a much smaller rival, E*Trade International Index, has cut its fee to 9 basis points.)

For index funds, such cost gaps are crucial, for they can't make up ground with stock selection. Over the trailing three-year period through Nov. 15, 2004, this fund's annualized return lags the Vanguard offering's by 33 basis points. The divergence can be explained by the cost advantage that fund had enjoyed, as well as the ability of its manager, Gus Sauter, to pick up a basis point here and there with his well-developed index-tracking techniques. Now this fund will be harder to beat.

That doesn't mean this fund is a clear choice, though. For one thing, Fidelity's fee waiver, though unlikely to be removed anytime soon, could be eliminated at some point. Second, as the three-year figures show, there's no guarantee this fund will beat its rival even with a lower cost. What's more, a different Vanguard index-tracker, Vanguard Total International Stock Index, might be preferable to either of these because it includes an emerging-markets weighting much closer to that of the typical foreign-stock fund. Still, there's no question this fund's cost cut is welcome news and makes it an even better deal than it was before.

Address:	82 Devonshire St Boston MA 02109 800-343-3548	Minimum Purchase:	$10000	Add: $1000 IRA: $10000
Web Address:	www.fidelity.com	Min Auto Inv Plan:	$500	Add: $500
Inception:	11-06-97 *	Sales Fees:	No-load	
Advisor:	Fidelity Management & Research Co. (FMR)	Management Fee:	0.34%	
Subadvisor:	FMR Co., Inc. (FMRC)	Actual Fees:	Mgt:0.34%	Dist:
		Expense Projections:	3Yr:$214	5Yr:$373 10Yr:$835
		Income Distrib:	Semi-Annually	
NTF Plans:	Fidelity Retail-NTF, CommonWealth NTF			

Portfolio Analysis 08-31-04

Share change since 02-04 Total Stocks:1037	Sector	Country	% Assets
⊕ BP	Energy	U.K.	2.28
⊕ HSBC Hldgs	Financial	U.K.	1.99
⊕ Vodafone Grp	Telecom	U.K.	1.79
⊕ FTSE 100 Index (Fut)	—	—	1.55
⊕ GlaxoSmithKline	Health	U.K.	1.40
⊖ TOTAL	Energy	France	1.34
⊕ Novartis	Health	Switzerland	1.32
⊕ Toyota Motor	Goods	Japan	1.32
☼ Royal Dutch Petroleum	Energy	Netherlands	1.24
☼ Dj Eurostoxx 50 Fut Sep0	—	—	1.23
⊕ Nestle	Goods	Switzerland	1.15
⊕ Royal Bank Of Scotland G	Financial	U.K.	0.97
⊕ UBS	Financial	Switzerland	0.91
⊕ TOPIX Index (Fut)	—	—	0.90
⊕ AstraZeneca	Health	U.K.	0.90
⊕ Roche Holding	Health	Switzerland	0.82
⊕ Shell Transport & Tradin	Energy	U.K.	0.82
⊕ Telefonica S A	Telecom	Spain	0.79
⊕ Sanofi-Synthelabo	Health	France	0.75
⊕ Barclays	Financial	U.K.	0.69

Current Investment Style

Value Blnd Growth / Large Mid Small

Market Cap	%
Giant	53.6
Large	33.0
Mid	13.0
Small	0.5
Micro	0.0
Avg $mil: 22,156	

Value Measures		Rel Category
Price/Earnings	13.92	1.02
Price/Book	1.75	0.97
Price/Sales	0.84	0.92
Price/Cash Flow	4.56	0.93
Dividend Yield %	2.75	1.08

Growth Measures	%	Rel Category
Long-Term Erngs	9.95	0.92
Book Value	-1.18	NMF
Sales	1.47	0.59
Cash Flow	3.43	0.61
Historical Erngs	4.90	0.88

Composition

Cash	7.6	Bonds	0.0
Stocks	84.5	Other	7.9
Foreign (% of Stock)			98.8

Sector Weightings	% of Stocks	Rel MSCI EAFE	3 Year High	Low
Info	15.14	0.91		
Software	0.70	0.65	1	1
Hardware	4.43	1.21	7	4
Media	2.36	1.04	3	1
Telecom	7.65	0.80	9	7
Service	45.24	1.01		
Health	8.65	1.19	10	9
Consumer	5.09	1.01	5	4
Business	4.76	0.87	5	4
Financial	26.74	0.99	28	21
Mfg	39.62	1.02		
Goods	14.20	1.04	17	14
Ind Mtrls	12.52	1.02	13	12
Energy	8.02	1.09	11	6
Utilities	4.88	0.91	5	5

Regional Exposure		% Stock	
UK/W. Europe	69	N. America	1
Japan	23	Latn America	0
Asia X Japan	7	Other	0

Country Exposure		% Stock	
U.K.	25	Switzerland	7
Japan	23	Germany	7
France	9		

Fidelity Spar Muni Inc

Analyst Pick	Ticker	Load	NAV	Yield	SEC Yield	Total Assets	Mstar Category
✔	FHIGX	None	$13.09	4.3%	3.39%	$4,619 mil	Muni National Long

Governance and Management

Fiduciary Grade: B

Portfolio Manager(s)

Christine Thompson took over this fund in 2002, but she has extensive experience as a Fidelity muni-fund manager. She's backed by numerous analysts and traders.

Strategy

This fund doesn't make big sweeping bets--it ties its interest-rate sensitivity to that of the Lehman Brothers Municipal Bond Index--and maintains minimal credit risk. Management focuses on yield-curve plays and the structure of the portfolio, such as a bias toward callable or noncallable bonds. The team also uses sophisticated analytics to measure market risk across the portfolio and to keep a close watch on how bonds will respond to different scenarios given their particular tax status or structure.

Historical Profile
Return: Above Avg
Risk: Average
Rating: ★★★★★ Highest

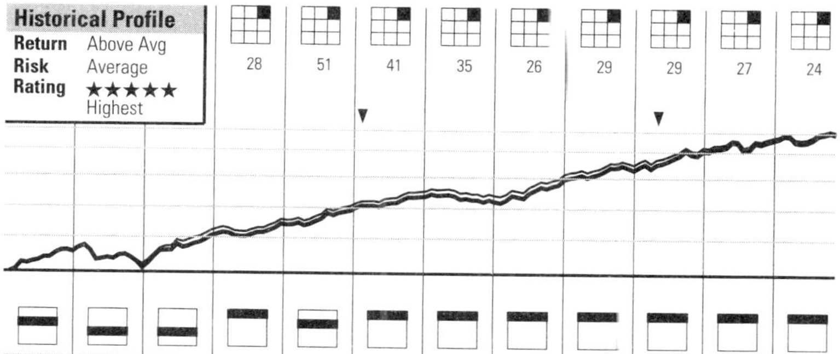

Investment Style
Fixed Income
Income Rtn %Rank Cat

▼ Manager Change
▽ Partial Manager Change

Growth of $10,000
— Investment Values of Fund
— Investment Values of LB Muni

Performance Quartile (within Category)

1993	1994	1995	1996	1997	1998	1999	2000	2001	2002	2003	12-04	History
12.95	11.25	12.36	12.27	12.68	12.82	11.91	12.70	12.68	13.22	13.18	13.09	NAV
13.11	-7.45	16.18	4.95	9.22	6.04	-2.48	12.30	5.00	10.48	5.80	4.73	Total Return %
0.83	-2.28	-1.28	0.52	0.03	-0.44	-0.42	0.62	-0.13	0.88	0.49	0.25	+/-LB Muni
-1.27	-0.11	-4.79	0.49	-1.62	-0.78	2.20	-2.94	0.13	0.45	-0.53	-1.83	+/-LB Muni 20YR
6.22	6.00	6.07	5.38	5.09	4.85	4.75	5.41	4.94	4.84	4.53	4.43	Income Return %
6.89	-13.45	10.11	-0.43	4.13	1.19	-7.23	6.89	0.06	5.64	1.27	0.30	Capital Return %
31	71	71	8	46	18	4	21	10	4	17	18	Total Rtn % Rank Cat
0.76	0.76	0.67	0.65	0.61	0.60	0.60	0.63	0.61	0.60	0.59	0.57	Income $
0.50	0.00	0.00	0.03	0.08	0.01	0.01	0.00	0.04	0.16	0.20	0.13	Capital Gains $
0.56	0.56	0.57	0.56	0.55	0.53	0.49	0.42	0.43	0.46	0.47	—	Expense Ratio %
5.85	6.21	5.69	5.32	4.92	4.75	4.77	4.98	4.80	4.62	4.42	—	Income Ratio %
53	48	50	53	31	25	28	4	27	23	23	—	Turnover Rate %
2,109	1,671	1,794	1,796	2,347	4,639	4,063	4,452	4,514	4,801	4,775	4,619	Net Assets $mil

Performance 12-31-04

	1st Qtr	2nd Qtr	3rd Qtr	4th Qtr	Total
2000	3.18	1.39	2.38	4.85	12.30
2001	2.17	0.75	3.01	-0.97	5.00
2002	0.92	3.96	5.41	-0.11	10.48
2003	1.32	3.08	-0.07	1.37	5.80
2004	2.10	-2.92	4.20	1.40	4.73

Trailing	Total Return%	+/- LB Muni	+/- LB Muni 20YR	%Rank Cat	Growth of $10,000
3 Mo	1.40	0.15	-0.58	28	10,140
6 Mo	5.66	0.47	-1.09	14	10,566
1 Yr	4.73	0.25	-1.83	18	10,473
3 Yr Avg	6.97	0.53	-0.66	6	12,240
5 Yr Avg	7.62	0.42	-0.92	5	14,437
10 Yr Avg	7.11	0.05	-0.84	5	19,875
15 Yr Avg	6.83	-0.16	-0.82	13	26,940

Tax Analysis	Tax-Adj Rtn%	%Rank Cat	Tax-Cost Rat	%Rank Cat
3 Yr (estimated)	6.75	5	0.21	56
5 Yr (estimated)	7.47	4	0.14	46
10 Yr (estimated)	7.01	6	0.09	38

Potential Capital Gain Exposure: 7% of assets

Rating and Risk

Time Period	Load-Adj Return %	Morningstar Rtn vs Cat	Morningstar Risk vs Cat	Morningstar Risk-Adj Rating
1 Yr	4.73			
3 Yr	6.97	High	+Avg	★★★★★
5 Yr	7.62	High	Avg	★★★★★
10 Yr	7.11	+Avg	Avg	★★★★★
Incept	7.22			

Other Measures	Standard Index LB Aggr	Best Fit Index LB Muni
Alpha	-0.1	-0.1
Beta	1.13	1.13
R-Squared	100	100

Standard Deviation	5.74
Mean	6.97
Sharpe Ratio	0.99

Portfolio Analysis 09-30-04

Total Fixed-Income:795	Date of Maturity	Amount $000	Value $000	% Net Assets
Louisville & Jefferson C	05-15-33	65,000	71,640	1.55
Washington St Pub Pwr Sp	07-01-12	56,550	63,460	1.37
New York N Y City Mun Wt	06-15-29	56,120	61,289	1.33
Texas St Tpk Auth 5.5%	08-15-39	37,550	39,913	0.86
Massachusetts St Wtr Res	08-01-39	33,000	36,591	0.79
Indianapolis Ind Loc Pub	07-01-33	35,240	36,578	0.79
Tobacco Settlement Fing	06-01-15	33,500	36,562	0.79
Intermountain Pwr Agy Ut	07-01-16	30,260	33,471	0.72
North Carolina Cap Facs	07-01-42	32,200	32,998	0.71
Engy Northwest Wash Elec	07-01-16	28,000	32,590	0.71
Intermountain Pwr Agy Ut	07-01-16	29,500	32,033	0.69
Mercer Cnty N D Pollutn	06-30-13	26,000	31,949	0.69
Texas St Tpk Auth 5.75%	08-15-38	27,550	30,309	0.66
Massachusetts St Indl Fi	08-01-06	30,800	29,495	0.64
Metropolitan Pier & Expo	06-15-41	26,420	29,136	0.63

Current Investment Style

Duration: Short Int Long; Quality: High Med Low

[1]Avg Eff Duration	7.3 Yrs
Avg Eff Maturity	16.1 Yrs
Avg Credit Quality	AA
Avg Wtd Coupon	4.87%
Avg Wtd Price	104.99% of par

[1]figure provided by fund

Credit Analysis	% bonds 09-30-04		
US Govt	0	BB	0
AAA	69	B	0
AA	14	Below B	0
A	10	NR/NA	1
BBB	7		

Top 5 States	% bonds		
IL	15.1	CA	8.9
TX	12.5	MA	7.1
NY	10.7		

Composition			
Cash	0.2	Bonds	99.8
Stocks	0.0	Other	0.0

Special Securities	
Restricted/Illiquid Secs	0
Options/Futures/Warrants	No

Sector Weightings	% of Bonds	Rel Cat
General Obligation	28.9	1.11
Utilities	20.5	1.55
Health	7.3	0.92
Water/Waste	14.4	1.30
Housing	1.1	0.15
Education	8.9	0.77
Transportation	10.4	1.37
COP/Lease	0.8	0.39
Industrial	6.9	0.53
Misc Revenue	0.0	0.00
Demand	0.8	2.81

Morningstar's Take by Eric Jacobson 12-13-04

Fidelity Spartan Municipal Income's leader was our Manager of the Year in 2003, but it really could have been any year.

When making those selections we clearly try to recognize managers who have enjoyed a good 12-month stretch. Every so often, though, particularly in the bond world (we select one each for international stocks, domestic stocks, and fixed-income) there are managers whose success is so consistent that they could easily be candidates in every year.

Fidelity's Christine Thompson (along with her team) is one such person. This fund--as well as others she runs--has earned a remarkably solid record, both over the long term, and year by year. We don't use the word remarkable lightly, either. Others who work for her, and some who preceded her, also deserve credit, but the bottom line is that of the 15 distinct, no-load Fidelity muni funds in our database with a 10-year record, all 15 place in the best quartiles of their respective categories.

The 2004 period for this fund is emblematic of Thompson's success. A benchmark-linked level of interest-rate sensitivity meant that she couldn't win thanks to a big rate bet. A high-quality portfolio, meanwhile, meant that she missed some of the year's fat credit rally. Yet, this fund has still managed a 4.5% gain for the year to date through Dec. 10 that places in the long-term muni category's upper echelon.

Much credit goes to picks among several revenue sectors such as hospitals, electric utilities, higher education, and water and sewer bonds. A focus on premium bonds--and away from those vulnerable to arcane market-discount tax laws--has also been helpful. Overall, these more moderate, tactical victories have carried the fund far.

We've also noted before that Fidelity always seems one step ahead of most rivals when it comes to using information wisely and recognizing pitfalls in the market. All in all, this fund and its manager inspire tremendous confidence.

Address:	82 Devonshire Street Boston MA 02109 800-343-3548
Web Address:	www.fidelity.com
Inception:	12-01-77
Advisor:	Fidelity Management & Research Co. (FMR)
Subadvisor:	Fidelity Intl Invest Advisors (U.K.) Ltd
NTF Plans:	Fidelity Retail-NTF, CommonWealth NTF

Minimum Purchase:	$10000	Add: $1000	IRA: $0
Min Auto Inv Plan:	$500	Add: $500	
Sales Fees:	No-load, 0.50%R		
Management Fee:	0.38%		
Actual Fees:	Mgt:0.38%	Dist:	
Expense Projections:	3Yr:$157	5Yr:$274	10Yr:$616
Income Distrib:	Monthly		

Fidelity Spar Sh-IntMuni

Ticker	Load	NAV	Yield	SEC Yield	Total Assets	Mstar Category
FSTFX	None	$10.38	2.6%	2.33%	$1,840 mil	Muni National Short

Governance and Management

Fiduciary Grade: B

Portfolio Manager(s)

In addition to this fund, Mark Sommer has, since June 2002, managed Fidelity funds focusing on New York, New Jersey, Connecticut, Maryland, and Pennsylvania. Sommer joined Fidelity's fixed-income quantitative research group in 1992 and began managing $4 billion in stable-value assets in 1997. Previously, Sommer was a scientist at Eolt, Beranek & Newman.

Strategy

Manager Mark Sommer does not place bets on the direction of interest rates. Instead, he keeps the fund's duration tied closely to that of the Lehman Brothers' 1-6 year Muni Index. In trying to add to returns, Sommer tries to find bonds selling at attractive valuations based on state, sector, maturity-spectrum, structure, or individual credit profiles.

Historical Profile

Return Above Avg
Risk Average
Rating ★★★★ Above Avg

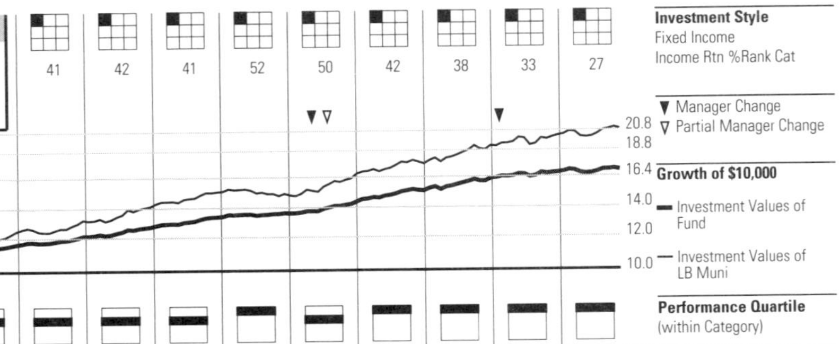

1993	1994	1995	1996	1997	1998	1999	2000	2001	2002	2003	12-04	History
10.11	9.66	10.04	10.00	10.11	10.16	9.93	10.12	10.27	10.52	10.48	10.38	NAV
7.12	-0.08	8.47	3.88	5.45	4.69	1.61	6.20	5.69	6.47	3.01	1.82	Total Return %
-5.16	5.09	-8.99	-0.55	-3.74	-1.79	3.67	-5.48	0.56	-3.13	-2.30	-2.66	+/-LB Muni
0.90	-0.76	-0.40	-0.56	-0.03	-0.52	-0.35	-0.03	-0.90	-0.25	0.33	0.04	+/-LB Muni 3YR
4.66	4.44	4.48	4.27	4.32	4.18	3.90	4.21	3.98	3.36	2.72	2.60	Income Return %
2.46	-4.52	3.99	-0.39	1.13	0.51	-2.29	1.99	1.71	3.11	0.29	-0.78	Capital Return %
34	45	29	44	33	43	21	35	3	25	22	14	Total Rtn % Rank Cat
0.45	0.44	0.42	0.42	0.42	0.41	0.39	0.41	0.40	0.34	0.28	0.27	Income $
0.01	0.00	0.00	0.00	0.00	0.00	0.00	0.00	0.02	0.06	0.07	0.02	Capital Gains $
0.55	0.47	0.55	0.54	0.55	0.55	0.55	0.54	0.41	0.45	0.47	—	Expense Ratio %
4.55	4.45	4.38	4.17	4.25	4.15	3.89	4.02	3.85	3.23	2.69	—	Income Ratio %
56	44	51	78	32	33	66	106	43	38	34	—	Turnover Rate %
1,188	913	905	737	699	639	765	958	1,189	1,683	1,839	1,840	Net Assets $mil

Performance 12-31-04

	1st Qtr	2nd Qtr	3rd Qtr	4th Qtr	Total
2000	1.02	1.22	1.55	2.28	6.20
2001	2.22	1.11	2.32	-0.05	5.69
2002	0.55	2.73	2.43	0.63	6.47
2003	0.85	1.16	0.86	0.12	3.01
2004	0.91	-1.36	1.92	0.36	1.82

Trailing	Total Return%	+/- LB Muni	-/- LB Muni 3YR	%Rank Cat	Growth of $10,000
3 Mo	0.36	-0.89	0.17	25	10,036
6 Mo	2.29	-2.90	0.19	15	10,229
1 Yr	1.82	-2.66	0.04	14	10,182
3 Yr Avg	3.75	-2.69	0.04	23	11,168
5 Yr Avg	4.62	-2.58	-0.16	21	12,534
10 Yr Avg	4.71	-2.35	-0.26	13	15,845
15 Yr Avg	5.02	-1.97	—	25	20,849

Tax Analysis	Tax-Adj Rtn%	%Rank Cat	Tax-Cost Rat	%Rank Cat
3 Yr (estimated)	3.66	17	0.09	100
5 Yr (estimated)	4.56	18	0.06	100
10 Yr (estimated)	4.68	8	0.03	34

Potential Capital Gain Exposure: 1% of assets

Rating and Risk

Time Period	Load-Adj Return %	Morningstar Rtn vs Cat	Morningstar Risk vs Cat	Morningstar Risk-Adj Rating
1 Yr	1.82			
3 Yr	3.75	+Avg	Avg	★★★★
5 Yr	4.62	+Avg	Avg	★★★★
10 Yr	4.71	+Avg	Avg	★★★★
Incept	4.77			

Other Measures	Standard Index LB Aggr	Best Fit Index LB Muni 3YR
Alpha	-0.3	-0.1
Beta	0.52	1.07
R-Squared	92	98

Standard Deviation	2.69
Mean	3.75
Sharpe Ratio	0.89

Portfolio Analysis 09-30-04

Total Fixed-Income:448	Date of Maturity	Amount $000	Value $000	% Net Assets
Massachusetts St 5%	02-01-06	40,000	41,637	2.28
Washington St 4%	01-01-08	33,175	34,903	1.91
Honolulu Hawaii City & C	10-01-09	26,940	33,302	1.82
California St Dept Wtr R	05-01-07	27,455	29,652	1.62
Nebraska Pub Pwr Dist	01-01-06	24,465	23,863	1.31
Highlands Cnty Fla Healt	11-15-32	20,300	20,555	1.13
Florida St Dept Environm	07-01-07	19,020	20,470	1.12
Tobacco Settlement Fing	06-01-13	17,500	18,753	1.03
Tobacco Settlement Fing	06-01-06	17,815	18,612	1.02
New Jersey St Transn Tr	12-15-08	15,000	16,237	0.89
Detroit Mich 5%	04-01-08	14,545	15,809	0.87
Wisconsin St Health & Ed	12-01-22	15,000	15,517	0.85
California Pollutn Ctl F	12-01-23	15,000	15,348	0.84
Clark Cnty Nev Sch Dist	06-15-09	13,890	15,298	0.84
Univ Tex Univ Revs 5%	08-15-09	13,555	14,904	0.82

Current Investment Style

Duration: Short Int Long; Quality: High Med Low

Avg Eff Duration[1]	2.9 Yrs
Avg Eff Maturity	3.4 Yrs
Avg Credit Quality	AA
Avg Wtd Coupon	4.37%
Avg Wtd Price	105.90% of par

[1]figure provided by fund

Credit Analysis	% bonds 09-30-04		
US Govt	0	BB	0
AAA	60	B	0
AA	18	Below B	0
A	13	NR/NA	3
BBB	6		

Top 5 States	% bonds		
TX	13.1	NY	7.3
IL	9.2	WA	7.0
CA	8.2		

Composition			
Cash	2.2	Bonds	97.8
Stocks	0.0	Other	0.0

Special Securities	
Restricted/Illiquid Secs	0
Options/Futures/Warrants	No

Sector Weightings	% of Bonds	Rel Cat
General Obligation	43.8	1.24
Utilities	14.5	1.56
Health	4.6	0.64
Water/Waste	10.6	1.01
Housing	0.1	0.02
Education	12.1	1.39
Transportation	4.5	1.05
COP/Lease	0.9	0.59
Industrial	5.0	0.33
Misc Revenue	0.0	—
Demand	3.8	5.97

Morningstar's Take by Eric Jacobson 12-24-04

All is well at Fidelity Spartan Short-Intermediate Municipal, but the fund has one feature worth watching.

There are many ways to measure performance, and the short end of the bond market has as many index options as any. Funds often try to pick benchmark indexes that will show them in the best light. That's one reason Morningstar segments fund categories as we do. Judging funds against indexes of their own choice would render a picture like that of Garrison Keillor's Lake Wobegon--one in which all funds are above average.

We bring that up because reconciling this fund's record with the way it's viewed by Fidelity is tricky. The firm uses the Lehman Brothers 1-6 Year Muni Bond Index because it simulates a group of funds this one sees as its rivals. Interestingly, though, the fund has lagged that benchmark somewhat over recent periods.

That doesn't concern us because it doesn't fully reflect peer-group realities. Against our muni-national short-term category, for example, the fund's history is impressive. Fidelity also reports high rankings versus its own select peer group. There are numerous index traits that could explain this anomaly. Because the fund has performed well versus its truest competitors, though, we think that real-world experience is more valuable than dwelling on the fund's showing versus a benchmark.

Of course, performance alone isn't enough to recommend a fund. This one's manager, Mark Sommer, who is part of a wildly successful Fidelity group, is also critical. The team avoids interest-rate bets, and has done a terrific job picking bonds.

That said, we will be keeping an eye on this fund's cost structure. Its expenses halfway through the fiscal year were an annualized 0.49%. That's low, but it represents a 19% increase from 2000. Given Fidelity's history, we don't expect it to rise much more, but if it does it could tarnish this fund's considerable appeal.

Address:	82 Devonshire Street Boston MA 02109 800-544-8888
Web Address:	www.fidelity.com
Inception:	12-24-86
Advisor:	Fidelity Management & Research Co. (FMR)
Subadvisor:	Fidelity Intl Invest Advisors (U.K.) Ltd
NTF Plans:	Fidelity Retail-NTF, CommonWealth NTF

Minimum Purchase:	$10000	Add: $1000	IRA: $0
Min Auto Inv Plan:	$10000	Add: $500	
Sales Fees:	No-load, 0.50%R		
Management Fee:	0.55%		
Actual Fees:	Mgt:0.55%	Dist:	
Expense Projections:	3Yr:$176	5Yr:$307	10Yr:$689
Income Distrib:	Monthly		

Fidelity Spar Tot Mkt Ix

Analyst Pick

Ticker	Load	NAV	Yield	Total Assets	Mstar Category
FSTMX	None	$33.05	1.4%	$2,774 mil	Large Blend

Governance and Management

Fiduciary Grade: B

Portfolio Manager(s)

Geode Capital Management took over as subadvisor to this fund and many of Fidelity's other index funds on Aug. 4, 2003. Fidelity founded Geode in 2001 but has since spun the firm off.

Strategy

This fund attempts to deliver returns close to those of the Wilshire 5000 Index. The fund will own all the large- and mid-cap stocks in that benchmark, but it holds a representative sample of the thousands of small-cap stocks in that index to keep trading costs within reason. The index's market-cap-based methodology tilts the portfolio decidedly toward large-cap stocks, but its broad exposure covers all sectors of the market.

Historical Profile

Return Average
Risk Above Avg
Rating ★★★ Neutral

Investment Style
Equity
Stock %

1998	1999	2000	2001	2002	2003	12-04
85%	91%	97%	97%	95%	92%	95%

▼ Manager Change
▽ Partial Manager Change

Growth of $10,000
— Investment Values of Fund
— Investment Values of S&P 500

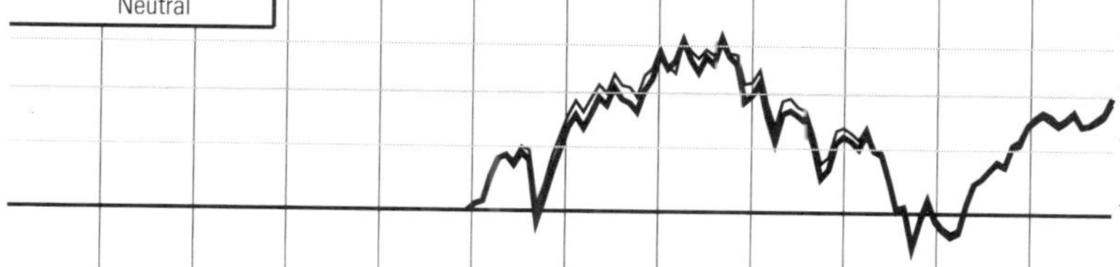

Performance Quartile (within Category)

1993	1994	1995	1996	1997	1998	1999	2000	2001	2002	2003	12-04	History
—	—	—	—	25.72	31.36	38.13	33.50	29.56	23.05	29.91	33.05	NAV
—	—	—	—	3.17*	24.03	23.23	-10.96	-10.79	-20.99	31.24	12.11	Total Return %
—	—	—	—	—	-4.54	2.19	-1.86	1.09	1.10	2.57	1.24	+/-S&P 500
—	—	—	—	—	-2.99	2.32	-3.17	1.66	0.66	1.35	0.71	+/-Russ 1000
—	—	—	—	0.00	0.90	0.93	0.79	0.96	1.08	1.39	1.57	Income Return %
—	—	—	—	—	23.13	22.30	-11.75	-11.75	-22.07	29.85	10.54	Capital Return %
—	—	—	—	—	46	29	85	33	35	13	21	Total Rtn % Rank Cat
—	—	—	—	0.08	0.23	0.29	0.30	0.32	0.32	0.32	0.47	Income $
—	—	—	—	0.00	0.28	0.19	0.18	0.00	0.00	0.00	0.00	Capital Gains $
—	—	—	—	—	0.25	0.27	0.26	0.25	0.25	0.25	0.25	Expense Ratio %
—	—	—	—	—	1.91	1.40	1.17	0.97	1.15	1.39	1.36	Income Ratio %
—	—	—	—	—	7	4	11	3	7	3	3	Turnover Rate %
—	—	—	—	20	166	756	1,028	1,103	1,033	1,970	2,774	Net Assets $mil

Performance 12-31-04

	1st Qtr	2nd Qtr	3rd Qtr	4th Qtr	Total
2000	3.86	-4.50	0.08	-10.30	-10.96
2001	-12.30	7.65	-16.00	12.49	-10.79
2002	0.91	-12.59	-16.87	7.74	-20.99
2003	-3.21	16.48	3.63	12.34	31.24
2004	2.54	1.21	-1.90	10.12	12.11

Trailing	Total Return%	+/- S&P 500	+/- Russ 1000	%Rank Cat	Growth of $10,000
3 Mo	10.12	0.89	0.32	27	11,012
6 Mo	8.03	0.84	0.22	28	10,803
1 Yr	12.11	1.24	0.71	21	11,211
3 Yr Avg	5.15	1.57	0.88	17	11,626
5 Yr Avg	-1.58	0.72	0.18	39	9,235
10 Yr Avg	—	—	—	—	—
15 Yr Avg	—	—	—	—	—

Tax Analysis	Tax-Adj Rtn%	%Rank Cat	Tax-Cost Rat	%Rank Cat
3 Yr (estimated)	4.66	16	0.47	39
5 Yr (estimated)	-2.04	34	0.47	25
10 Yr (estimated)	—	—	—	—

Potential Capital Gain Exposure: 7% of assets

Rating and Risk

Time Period	Load-Adj Return %	Morningstar Rtn vs Cat	Morningstar Risk vs Cat	Morningstar Risk-Adj Rating
1 Yr	12.11			
3 Yr	5.15	+Avg	Avg	★★★★
5 Yr	-1.58	Avg	+Avg	★★★
10 Yr	—	—	—	—
Incept	5.39			

Other Measures	Standard Index S&P 500	Best Fit Index Russ 1000
Alpha	1.6	0.9
Beta	0.98	0.99
R-Squared	99	99
Standard Deviation	15.58	
Mean	5.15	
Sharpe Ratio	0.24	

Portfolio Analysis 08-31-04

Share change since 02-04 Total Stocks:3675	Sector	PE	YTD Ret%	% Assets
⊕ Gen Elec	Ind Mtrls	22.8	20.68	2.46
⊕ ExxonMobil	Energy	13.9	28.04	2.17
⊕ S&P 500 Index (Fut)	—	—	—	2.15
⊕ Microsoft	Software	36.1	8.95	2.13
⊕ Pfizer	Health	22.0	-22.31	1.80
⊕ Citigroup	Financial	15.3	2.72	1.73
⊕ Wal-Mart Stores	Consumer	23.4	0.51	1.63
⊕ American International G	Financial	16.2	-0.53	1.34
⊕ Bank of America	Financial	12.3	21.50	1.32
⊕ Johnson & Johnson	Health	20.6	25.17	1.25
⊕ Procter & Gamble	Goods	23.3	12.38	1.04
⊕ IBM	Hardware	20.2	7.19	1.03
⊕ J P Morgan Chase	Financial	19.4	9.97	1.01
⊕ Intel	Hardware	19.8	-26.56	0.99
⊕ Cisco Systems	Hardware	24.5	-20.26	0.92
⊕ Verizon Communications	Telecom	32.4	20.25	0.79
⊕ Coca-Cola	Goods	21.9	-16.12	0.79
⊕ ChevronTexaco	Energy	7.7	25.57	0.76
⊕ Merck	Health	11.4	-27.76	0.72
⊕ Altria Group	Goods	13.3	18.38	0.72

Current Investment Style

Value Blnd Growth / Large Mid Small

Market Cap	%
Giant	40.8
Large	30.2
Mid	19.7
Small	7.1
Micro	2.2
Avg $mil: 22,491	

Value Measures		Rel Category
Price/Earnings	16.58	0.98
Price/Book	2.46	0.94
Price/Sales	1.33	0.92
Price/Cash Flow	6.95	0.90
Dividend Yield %	1.56	1.05

Growth Measures	%	Rel Category
Long-Term Erngs	11.37	0.98
Book Value	5.45	0.70
Sales	4.32	0.75
Cash Flow	5.51	0.58
Historical Erngs	11.23	0.95

Profitability	%	Rel Category
Return on Equity	17.55	1.00
Return on Assets	9.31	1.08
Net Margin	11.54	1.01

Sector Weightings	% of Stocks	Rel S&P 500	3 Year High	3 Year Low
Info	20.55	0.96		
Software	4.04	0.94	5	4
Hardware	8.98	0.88	11	8
Media	4.26	1.11	5	4
Telecom	3.27	1.04	4	3
Service	49.70	1.07		
Health	12.90	1.03	15	13
Consumer	9.27	1.02	10	9
Business	4.89	1.21	5	5
Financial	22.64	1.09	23	20
Mfg	29.74	0.93		
Goods	8.85	0.95	9	8
Ind Mtrls	11.14	0.88	11	10
Energy	6.81	0.95	7	6
Utilities	2.94	0.99	3	2

Composition

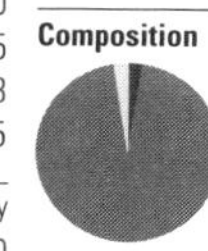

Cash	2.5
Stocks	94.8
Bonds	0.0
Other	2.7
Foreign (% of Stock)	0.[illegible]

Morningstar's Take by Dan McNeela 12-27-04

The new lower costs at Fidelity Spartan Total Market Index are a wonderful development.

On Aug. 31, 2004, Fidelity announced that it would cap the expense ratios of this offering and four other index funds at a miniscule 0.10% (or just 10 basis points). The expense cut, which was effective immediately, represents a 60% cut from the fund's former 0.25% price tag. Costs are especially important to index fund investors because these passively managed vehicles have few other methods for distinguishing themselves.

With that move, Fidelity served notice to Vanguard and other index fund providers that it was taking this part of its business very seriously. Vanguard Total Stock Market Index, which checks in at 0.20%, now costs twice as much as Fidelity's option. If the Fidelity fund's recent performance is any guide, it may have enough of an advantage to narrowly outperform its peers. In the three-year period ending Dec. 23, 2004, the fund was in a virtual tie with its Vanguard rival.

That said, costs shouldn't be investors' only consideration. Index funds such as this one that seek to match the Wilshire 5000 Index don't own all the stocks in the benchmark. Good index managers will effectively track their benchmarks while keeping transaction costs down. Subadvisor Geode Capital Management has done well here, but it has only run Fidelity's index funds since 2001.

Investors must also weigh two other factors. Fidelity is voluntarily waiving fees, indicating that it is willing to take a loss on this fund. If the cost reduction doesn't attract new assets, however, Fidelity may choose to start charging more. Investors with taxable accounts must also consider if switching to this fund would trigger any negative tax consequences.

At this point, however, it's hard to see Fidelity's bold move to cut costs as anything but a strong positive for index investors everywhere.

Address:	82 Devonshire St Boston MA 02109 800-343-3548
Web Address:	www.fidelity.com
Inception:	11-06-97 *
Advisor:	Fidelity Management & Research Co. (FMR)
Subadvisor:	FMR Co., Inc. (FMRC)
NTF Plans:	Fidelity Retail-NTF, CommonWealth NTF

Minimum Purchase:	$15000	Add: $1000	IRA: $15000
Min Auto Inv Plan:	$500	Add: $500	
Sales Fees:	No-load, 0.50%R		
Management Fee:	0.24%		
Actual Fees:	Mgt:0.24%	Dist:	
Expense Projections:	3Yr:$148	5Yr:$258	10Yr:$579
Income Distrib:	Semi-Annually		

Fidelity Strategic Inc

Ticker	Load	NAV	Yield	SEC Yield	Total Assets	Mstar Category
FSICX	None	$10.77	5.1%	4.71%	$3,166 mil	Multisector Bond

Governance and Management

Fiduciary Grade: B

Portfolio Manager(s)

Bill Eigen took over as lead manager in June 2001. He is responsible for the fund's sector-allocation decisions while a group of experienced sector specialists handle much of the fund's issue-selection duties. Mark Notkin handles high yield. Jonathan Kelly covers emerging markets. Andy Weir is responsible for developed-country debt. And George Fischer covers the fund's government exposure.

Strategy

Lead manager Bill Eigen uses a neutral asset-allocation mix as a baseline, then makes slight adjustments to that mix based on relative valuation and market outlook. The neutral mix is: 30% U.S. government issues, 40% U.S. high-yield obligations, 15% developed-nation sovereign debt, and 15% emerging-markets bonds. Fidelity sector specialists assist Eigen by handling much of the fund's issue-selection responsibilities.

Historical Profile

Return Above Avg
Risk Average
Rating ★★★★★ Highest

Investment Style
Fixed Income
Income Rtn %Rank Cat

1998	1999	2000	2001	2002	2003	12-04
100	68	76	80	63	52	49

▼ Manager Change
▽ Partial Manager Change

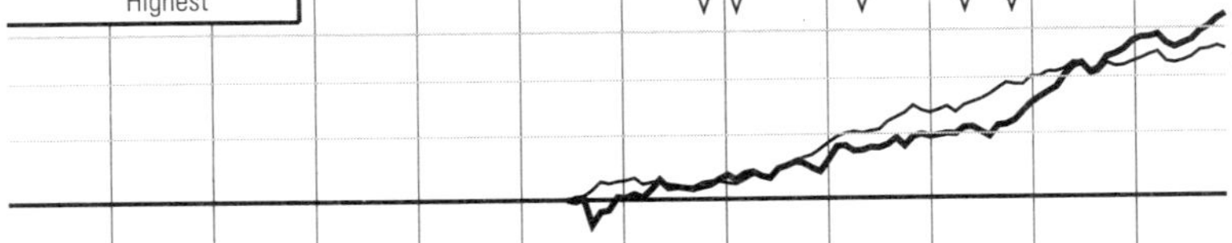

Growth of $10,000
— Investment Values of Fund
— Investment Values of LB Aggr

Performance Quartile (within Category)

History

1993	1994	1995	1996	1997	1998	1999	2000	2001	2002	2003	12-04	History
—	—	—	—	—	9.52	9.44	9.13	9.15	9.40	10.50	10.77	NAV
—	—	—	—	—	-0.65*	6.35	4.07	6.52	9.38	18.62	9.44	Total Return %
—	—	—	—	—	—	7.17	-7.56	-1.92	-0.87	14.52	5.10	+/-LB Aggr
—	—	—	—	—	—	6.18	-6.75	-1.57	-0.46	12.80	4.47	+/-LB. U.S. Univ. Bd
—	—	—	—	—	0.00	7.20	7.40	6.36	6.47	6.32	5.41	Income Return %
—	—	—	—	—	—	-0.85	-3.33	0.16	2.91	12.30	4.03	Capital Return %
—	—	—	—	—	—	19	16	15	20	37	26	Total Rtn % Rank Cat
—	—	—	—	—	0.39	0.66	0.68	0.56	0.57	0.58	0.55	Income $
—	—	—	—	—	0.00	0.00	0.00	0.00	0.00	0.03	0.13	Capital Gains $
—	—	—	—	—	1.09	1.10	0.99	0.94	0.84	0.80	—	Expense Ratio %
—	—	—	—	—	7.40	7.55	7.94	6.83	6.42	5.64	—	Income Ratio %
—	—	—	—	—	97	134	100	178	117	148	—	Turnover Rate %
—	—	—	—	—	24	41	63	163	771	2,320	3,166	Net Assets $mil

Performance 12-31-04

	1st Qtr	2nd Qtr	3rd Qtr	4th Qtr	Total
2000	0.84	0.86	1.45	0.86	4.07
2001	2.39	0.90	0.45	2.65	6.52
2002	0.66	0.57	1.98	5.95	9.38
2003	4.51	6.94	1.67	4.39	18.62
2004	1.80	-2.52	4.79	5.23	9.44

Trailing	Total Return%	+/- LB Aggr	+/- LB. U.S. Univ. Bd	%Rank Cat	Growth of $10,000
3 Mo	5.23	4.28	3.95	22	10,523
6 Mo	10.27	6.09	5.48	18	11,027
1 Yr	9.44	5.10	4.47	26	10,944
3 Yr Avg	12.40	6.21	5.55	18	14,200
5 Yr Avg	9.50	1.79	1.62	15	15,742
10 Yr Avg	—	—	—	—	—
15 Yr Avg	—	—	—	—	—

Tax Analysis	Tax-Adj Rtn%	%Rank Cat	Tax-Cost Rat	%Rank Cat
3 Yr (estimated)	9.95	12	2.18	44
5 Yr (estimated)	6.93	9	2.35	33
10 Yr (estimated)	—	—	—	—

Potential Capital Gain Exposure: 7% of assets

Rating and Risk

Time Period	Load-Adj Return %	Morningstar Rtn vs Cat	Morningstar Risk vs Cat	Morningstar Risk-Adj Rating
1 Yr	9.44			
3 Yr	12.40	+Avg	Avg	★★★★
5 Yr	9.50	+Avg	Avg	★★★★★
10 Yr	—	—	—	—
Incept	7.94			

Other Measures	Standard Index LB Aggr	Best Fit Index LB Credit
Alpha	7.3	6.4
Beta	0.72	0.67
R-Squared	39	57
Standard Deviation	5.47	
Mean	12.40	
Sharpe Ratio	2.04	

Portfolio Analysis 09-30-04

Total Fixed-Income:600	Date of Maturity	Amount $000	Value $000	% Net Assets
US Treasury Note 1.875%	07-15-13	77,950	81,754	3.11
Germany (Federal Republi	07-04-09	49,300	64,610	2.46
US Treasury Note 3.25%	01-15-09	50,700	50,724	1.93
Brazil (Federative Repub	04-15-14	37,312	36,916	1.40
US Treasury Bond 3.625%	04-15-28	22,350	33,210	1.26
US Treasury Note 2.5%	05-31-06	31,500	31,514	1.20
Russian Federation FRN	03-31-30	32,258	31,048	1.18
US Treasury Note 2.375%	08-31-06	30,000	29,889	1.14
US Treasury Note 4.25%	11-15-13	27,000	27,348	1.04
Japan	03-20-14	2,925,000	26,842	1.02
Federal Republic Of Germ	01-04-12	19,500	26,208	1.00
FNMA 3.25%	01-15-08	26,250	26,203	1.00
US Treasury Note 1.625%	02-28-06	25,500	25,240	0.96
FHLMC 3.625%	09-15-08	25,005	25,133	0.96
Nextel Comms 7.375%	08-01-15	23,405	25,102	0.96
Canada Govt 4.5%	09-01-07	30,000	24,409	0.93
Qwest Corp 8.875% 3/15/1	03-15-12	21,135	23,249	0.88
US Treasury Note 5.75%	08-15-10	18,000	20,066	0.76
Xerox 7.625%	06-15-13	17,830	19,256	0.73
US Treasury Bond 6.125%	08-15-29	16,500	19,230	0.73

Current Investment Style

Duration: Short Int Long — Quality: High Med Low

[1] figure provided by fund

Avg Eff Duration[1]	—
Avg Eff Maturity	—
Avg Credit Quality	—
Avg Wtd Coupon	6.13%
Avg Wtd Price	102.37% of par

Coupon Range	% of Bonds	Rel Cat
0% PIK	4.4	1.3
0% to 6%	44.5	1.0
6% to 8%	25.4	1.0
8% to 10%	20.1	1.0
More than 10%	10.0	1.0

1.00=Category Average

Credit Analysis	% bonds 09-30-04		
US Govt	—	BB	—
AAA	—	B	—
AA	—	Below B	—
A	—	NR/NA	—
BBB	—		

Sector Breakdown	% of assets
US Treasuries	10
TIPS	5
US Agency	4
Mortgage Pass-Throughs	2
Mortgage CMO	0
Mortgage ARM	0
US Corporate	49
Asset-Backed	1
Convertible	0
Municipal	0
Corporate Inflation-Protected	0
Foreign Corporate	7
Foreign Govt	15

Composition			
Cash	7.3	Bonds	91.2
Stocks	1.1	Other	0.4

Special Securities	
Restricted/Illiquid Secs	11
Exotic Mortgage-Backed	0
Emerging-Markets Secs	6
Options/Futures/Warrants	No

Morningstar's Take by Scott Berry 11-16-04

Fidelity Strategic Income is the complete package.

This fund's appeal starts with its price tag. At 0.77%, the fund's expense ratio provides it a definite sustainable advantage over its average multisector category peer. A lower expense burden allows the fund to pay out a competitive yield without lead manager Bill Eigen having to gorge on the riskiest bond issues. Over the long term, the fund's expense advantage creates a total-return hurdle that proves difficult for its higher-cost peers to overcome.

We also like this fund for its steady approach and deep management team. The fund invests heavily in the bond market's riskier segments, but Eigen keeps the portfolio well diversified and doesn't typically make large bets on any one issue or sector. He also relies heavily on a team of sector specialists in making individual issue selections. That allows him to take full advantage of Fidelity's research capabilities, which are difficult to match. Eigen's efforts and those of his team have helped keep the fund's standard deviation of returns (a common measure of volatility) slightly lower than the category norm.

Finally, we like this fund for its results. Eigen has made a number of timely adjustments to the fund's portfolio mix, while good issue selection and below-average costs have continued to work in its favor. For example, Eigen bulked up on high-yield bonds in mid-2004, and the fund profited as prices moved higher. Meanwhile, Eigen has maintained a sizable stake in emerging-markets debt, which has rallied sharply in recent years. Overall, the fund's one-, three-, and five-year trailing returns all rank in the category's best quartile.

Multisector-bond funds can be hard to fit into a investment plan given their added credit risk. However, we think this fund is good option for investors who are looking to add some diversification to an investment-grade portfolio.

Address:	82 Devonshire Street Boston MA 02109 800-343-3548
Web Address:	www.fidelity.com
Inception:	05-05-98*
Advisor:	Fidelity Management & Research Co. (FMR)
Subadvisor:	FMR Co., Inc. (FMRC)
NTF Plans:	Fidelity Retail-NTF, CommonWealth NTF

Minimum Purchase:	$2500	Add: $250	IRA: $2500
Min Auto Inv Plan:	$2500	Add: $100	
Sales Fees:	No-load		
Management Fee:	0.59%		
Actual Fees:	Mgt:0.58%	Dist:	
Expense Projections:	3Yr:$301	5Yr:$660	10Yr:$1455
Income Distrib:	Monthly		

Fidelity Struc Mid Cap VI

Ticker	Load	NAV	Yield	Total Assets	Mstar Category
FSMVX	None	$14.35	0.3%	$143 mil	Mid-Cap Value

Governance and Management

Fiduciary Grade: B

Portfolio Manager(s)

Ciaran O'Neill became manager here on Feb. 1, 2004. This is his first time running a public mutual fund. He replaced Robert Macdonald, who had run this offering since its November 2001 inception. O'Neill also manages Fidelity Structured Large Cap Value.

Strategy

Manager Ciaran O'Neill keeps this fund's sector weights within a few percentage points of those in the Russell MidCap Value Index. This move aligns the fund's risk profile with the index's, and emphasizes O'Neill's stock-picking ability. He takes his cues directly from Fidelity's analysts and several quantitative models.

Historical Profile

Return Average
Risk Average
Rating ★★★★ Above Avg

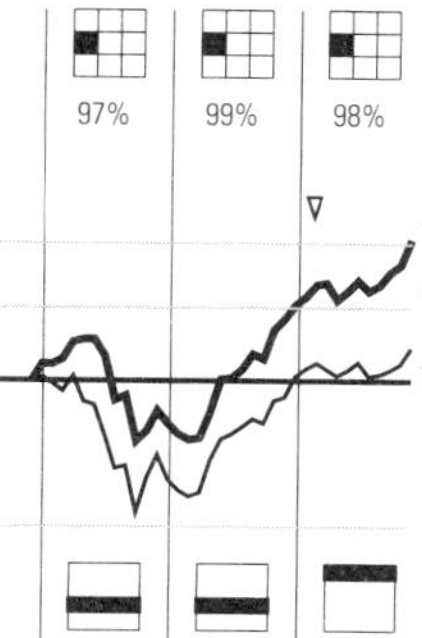

Investment Style: Equity, Stock %

▼ Manager Change
▽ Partial Manager Change

Growth of $10,000
— Investment Values of Fund
— Investment Values of S&P 500

Performance Quartile (within Category)

1993	1994	1995	1996	1997	1998	1999	2000	2001	2002	2003	12-04	History
—	—	—	—	—	—	—	—	10.59	9.08	12.08	14.35	NAV
—	—	—	—	—	—	—	—	6.00*	-13.52	33.49	21.87	Total Return %
—	—	—	—	—	—	—	—	—	8.57	4.82	11.00	+/-S&P 500
—	—	—	—	—	—	—	—	—	-3.88	-4.58	-1.84	+/-Russ MV
—	—	—	—	—	—	—	—	0.00	0.76	0.44	0.33	Income Return %
—	—	—	—	—	—	—	—	—	-14.28	33.05	21.54	Capital Return %
—	—	—	—	—	—	—	—	—	58	55	24	Total Rtn % Rank Cat
—	—	—	—	—	—	—	—	0.01	0.08	0.04	0.04	Income $
—	—	—	—	—	—	—	—	0.00	0.00	0.00	0.32	Capital Gains $
—	—	—	—	—	—	—	—	—	1.20	1.18	1.05	Expense Ratio %
—	—	—	—	—	—	—	—	—	0.59	0.79	0.55	Income Ratio %
—	—	—	—	—	—	—	—	—	68	113	97	Turnover Rate %
—	—	—	—	—	—	—	—	15	42	89	143	Net Assets $mil

Performance 12-31-04

	1st Qtr	2nd Qtr	3rd Qtr	4th Qtr	Total
2000	—	—	—	—	—
2001	—	—	—	—	6.00 *
2002	5.57	-3.40	-18.72	4.33	-13.52
2003	-3.41	15.74	4.73	14.03	33.49
2004	5.38	0.63	1.95	12.73	21.87

Trailing	Total Return%	+/- S&P 500	+/- Russ MV	%Rank Cat	Growth of $10,000
3 Mo	12.73	3.50	-0.73	20	11,273
6 Mo	14.93	7.74	-0.50	7	11,493
1 Yr	21.87	11.00	-1.84	24	12,187
3 Yr Avg	12.05	8.47	-3.51	38	14,068
5 Yr Avg	—	—	—	—	—
10 Yr Avg	—	—	—	—	—
15 Yr Avg	—	—	—	—	—

Tax Analysis	Tax-Adj Rtn%	%Rank Cat	Tax-Cost Rat	%Rank Cat
3 Yr (estimated)	11.72	31	0.29	25
5 Yr (estimated)	—	—	—	—
10 Yr (estimated)	—	—	—	—

Potential Capital Gain Exposure: 17% of assets

Rating and Risk

Time Period	Load-Adj Return %	Morningstar Rtn vs Cat	Morningstar Risk vs Cat	Morningstar Risk-Adj Rating
1 Yr	21.87			
3 Yr	12.05	Avg	Avg	★★★★
5 Yr	—	—	—	—
10 Yr	—	—	—	—
Incept	13.64			

Other Measures	Standard Index S&P 500	Best Fit Index Russ MV
Alpha	8.7	-2.6
Beta	0.82	0.96
R-Squared	77	99
Standard Deviation	15.73	
Mean	12.05	
Sharpe Ratio	0.69	

Portfolio Analysis 10-31-04

Share change since 07-04 Total Stocks:177	Sector	PE	YTD Ret%	% Assets
⊖ iShares Russell Midcap V	—	—	—	2.15
⊕ TXU	Utilities	NMF	177.67	1.24
⊕ PG & E	Utilities	3.7	19.84	1.23
⊕ Computer Sciences	Business	18.1	27.45	1.07
⊕ MBIA	Financial	11.3	8.57	1.06
⊕ Limited Brands	Consumer	16.0	37.88	1.06
⊕ Ambac Financial Group	Financial	12.7	19.13	1.00
⊕ Valero Energy	Energy	7.0	97.64	0.92
⊕ Equity Residential	Financial	90.2	29.50	0.91
⊕ Fidelity National Financ	Financial	10.2	32.24	0.89
☼ PPL	Utilities	12.0	26.14	0.85
⊕ Keyspan	Utilities	14.3	12.46	0.84
⊕ Bear Stearns Companies	Financial	10.9	29.25	0.83
☼ Public Service Enterpris	Utilities	14.8	24.38	0.83
⊕ Countrywide Financial	Financial	9.0	48.15	0.82
⊕ Occidental Petroleum	Energy	10.1	41.27	0.31
⊕ MGIC Investment	Financial	12.7	21.42	0.31
⊕ Torchmark	Financial	13.2	26.55	0.31
⊕ Constellation Energy Gro	Utilities	10.2	14.80	0.30
⊕ Sovereign Bancorp	Financial	16.4	-4.54	0.79

Current Investment Style

Value Blnd Growth; Large Mid Small

Market Cap	%
Giant	1.2
Large	25.1
Mid	65.0
Small	8.7
Micro	0.0
Avg $mil: 4,724	

Value Measures		Rel Category
Price/Earnings	13.35	0.87
Price/Book	1.85	0.96
Price/Sales	0.95	1.08
Price/Cash Flow	3.93	0.69
Dividend Yield %	1.45	1.01

Growth Measures	%	Rel Category
Long-Term Erngs	11.15	1.01
Book Value	13.58	2.41
Sales	3.25	1.73
Cash Flow	11.50	2.91
Historical Erngs	17.66	1.54

Profitability	%	Rel Category
Return on Equity	17.42	1.37
Return on Assets	3.99	1.48
Net Margin	13.11	1.49

Sector Weightings	% of Stocks	Rel S&P 500	3 Year High	3 Year Low
Info	4.64	0.22		
Software	0.47	0.11	2	0
Hardware	2.49	0.24	8	2
Media	0.03	0.01	3	0
Telecom	1.65	0.52	2	0
Service	54.77	1.18		
Health	4.99	0.40	7	5
Consumer	12.95	1.43	13	8
Business	6.15	1.52	10	6
Financial	30.68	1.48	34	25
Mfg	40.59	1.26		
Goods	9.98	1.07	10	5
Ind Mtrls	11.29	0.89	20	11
Energy	6.61	0.92	9	5
Utilities	12.71	4.29	13	9

Composition

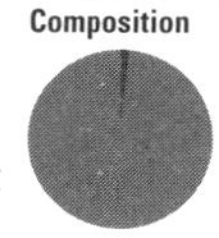

Cash	1.6
Stocks	98.4
Bonds	0.0
Other	0.0
Foreign (% of Stock)	1.4

Morningstar's Take by Dan Culloton 10-29-04

This fund has promise, but it still has to prove it can fulfill it.

Fidelity Structured Mid Cap Value uses a very disciplined process to provide exposure to the shares of undervalued midsized companies. The offering uses a variety of quantitative models as well as the insights of Fidelity's vaunted staff of fundamental analysts to locate stocks that look undervalued relative to the prospects of their underlying businesses.

The fund also employs strict controls in an effort to keep its overall risk profile in line with its benchmark, the Russell MidCap Value Index. The result is a portfolio that keeps sector allocations and average market cap close to its bogy and tries to differentiate itself with stock-picking.

That clear process and some other traits give this fund some appeal. It has a reasonable expense ratio. It's broadly diversified. Furthermore, Fidelity, which is well-known as a breeding ground for good stock-pickers, should have the resources to make this offering a success over the long run.

A couple factors temper our enthusiasm for this offering, though. First, manager Ciaran O'Neill has been at the helm for less than a year. He had experience as a Fidelity analyst before taking over this fund in February 2004, but this is his first stint as a retail mutual fund manager, so he doesn't have much of a record.

It's too early to definitively judge O'Neill's tenure, but it's not a forgone conclusion that he will succeed. The fund's record since its November 2001 inception is better than average for the mid-cap value category, but it has lagged its benchmark, the Russell MidCap Value Index, in each of the last two full years. So far in 2004, the fund is still beating its average peer, but it's also still trailing its bogy.

This fund deserves patience, but also circumspection until O'Neill proves he's capable of consistently beating the fund's category and benchmark index.

Address:	82 Devonshire Street Boston MA 02109 800-343-3548
Web Address:	www.fidelity.com
Inception:	11-15-01 *
Advisor:	Fidelity Management & Research Co. (FMR)
Subadvisor:	FMR Co., Inc. (FMRC)
NTF Plans:	Fidelity Retail-NTF, CommonWealth NTF

Minimum Purchase:	$2500	Add: $250	IRA: $2500
Min Auto Inv Plan:	$2500	Add: $100	
Sales Fees:	No-load, 0.75%R		
Management Fee:	0.58%		
Actual Fees:	Mgt:0.58%	Dist: —	
Expense Projections:	3Yr:$296	5Yr: —	10Yr: —
Income Distrib:	Annually		

Fidelity Total Bond

Ticker	Load	NAV	Yield	SEC Yield	Total Assets	Mstar Category
FTBFX	None	$10.63	3.4%	3.38%	$366 mil	Intermediate-Term Bond

Governance and Management

Fiduciary Grade: B

Portfolio Manager(s)

Kevin Grant has managed this fund since its inception in 2002, but he will be retiring at the end of 2004. Ford O'Neil, who will continue managing Fidelity Intermediate Bond and Fidelity U.S. Bond Index, takes over. He has had much success managing other funds, so we don't expect performance will slip here. Like Grant, O'Neil will be backed by Fidelity's large research staff.

Strategy

Management follows Fidelity's standard approach here. It looks to add value primarily through issue selection, sector allocation, and yield-curve positioning. Big interest-rate bets are strictly off-limits. The fund is broadly diversified across issues and sectors, but, unlike Fidelity Intermediate Bond and Fidelity Investment Grade Bond, it holds stakes in high yield and emerging-markets bonds. Its benchmark index is the Lehman Brothers US Universal Index.

Historical Profile

Return
Risk
Rating Not Rated

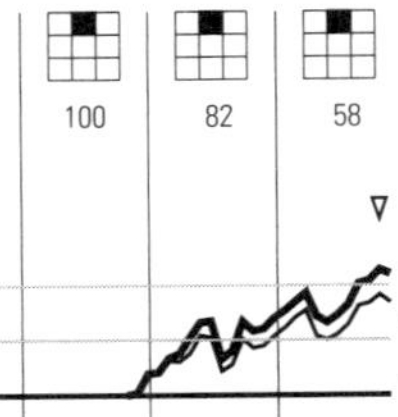

Investment Style
Fixed Income
Income Rtn %Rank Cat

▼ Manager Change
▽ Partial Manager Change

Growth of $10,000
— Investment Values of Fund
— Investment Values of LB Aggr

Performance Quartile (within Category)

1993	1994	1995	1996	1997	1998	1999	2000	2001	2002	2003	12-04	History
—	—	—	—	—	—	—	—	—	10.29	10.52	10.63	NAV
—	—	—	—	—	—	—	—	—	3.42*	5.87	5.47	Total Return %
—	—	—	—	—	—	—	—	—	—	1.77	1.13	+/-LB Aggr
—	—	—	—	—	—	—	—	—	—	-0.10	0.17	+/-LB 5-10YR
—	—	—	—	—	—	—	—	—	0.00	3.02	3.52	Income Return %
—	—	—	—	—	—	—	—	—	—	2.85	1.95	Capital Return %
—	—	—	—	—	—	—	—	—	—	24	6	Total Rtn % Rank Cat
—	—	—	—	—	—	—	—	—	0.05	0.31	0.36	Income $
—	—	—	—	—	—	—	—	—	0.00	0.06	0.09	Capital Gains $
—	—	—	—	—	—	—	—	—	—	0.65	0.65	Expense Ratio %
—	—	—	—	—	—	—	—	—	—	2.77	3.25	Income Ratio %
—	—	—	—	—	—	—	—	—	—	336	251	Turnover Rate %
—	—	—	—	—	—	—	—	—	45	300	366	Net Assets $mil

Performance 12-31-04

	1st Qtr	2nd Qtr	3rd Qtr	4th Qtr	Total
2000	—	—	—	—	—
2001	—	—	—	—	—
2002	—	—	—	—	3.42 *
2003	2.09	3.37	-0.04	0.37	5.87
2004	2.53	-2.19	3.52	1.60	5.47

Trailing	Total Return%	+/- LB Aggr	+/- LB 5-10YR	%Rank Cat	Growth of $10,000
3 Mo	1.60	0.65	0.62	12	10,160
6 Mo	5.17	0.99	-0.40	12	10,517
1 Yr	5.47	1.13	0.17	6	10,547
3 Yr Avg	—	—	—	—	—
5 Yr Avg	—	—	—	—	—
10 Yr Avg	—	—	—	—	—
15 Yr Avg	—	—	—	—	—

Tax Analysis	Tax-Adj Rtn%	%Rank Cat	Tax-Cost Rat	%Rank Cat
3 Yr (estimated)	—	—	—	—
5 Yr (estimated)	—	—	—	—
10 Yr (estimated)	—	—	—	—

Potential Capital Gain Exposure: 2% of assets

Rating and Risk

Time Period	Load-Adj Return %	Morningstar Rtn vs Cat	Morningstar Risk vs Cat	Morningstar Risk-Adj Rating
1 Yr	5.47			
3 Yr	—	—	—	—
5 Yr	—	—	—	—
10 Yr	—	—	—	—
Incept	6.72			

Other Measures	Standard Index LB Aggr	Best Fit Index
Alpha	—	—
Beta	—	—
R-Squared	—	—
Standard Deviation	—	
Mean	—	
Sharpe Ratio	—	

Morningstar's Take by Scott Berry 10-29-04

Fidelity Total Bond loses one skilled manager but gains another.

Kevin Grant has skippered this fund since its inception two years ago but will be retiring at the end of 2004. Fidelity veteran Ford O'Neil will take over the portfolio effective Dec. 1. O'Neil will continue to manage Fidelity Intermediate Bond and Fidelity U.S. Bond Index, both of which have been quite successful with him at the helm.

We think O'Neil was a logical choice to replace Grant and expect the transition will be seamless, given that Intermediate Bond and U.S. Bond Index hold many of the same sectors and issues as Total Bond. Unlike those funds, Total Bond holds a sizable high-yield bond stake (recently 8% of net assets). However, like Grant, O'Neil will lean on Fidelity's deep and talented high-yield bond team for help in that area.

Grant will be missed, but we think this fund still makes a good case for itself. In addition to O'Neil's skill and experience, the fund boasts a prudent approach and below-average costs. Its style, which is geared toward taking advantage of Fidelity research capabilities, is centered on issue selection and sector allocation. Interest-rate bets, which can result in wild performance swings, are off-limits. Meanwhile, the fund continually benefits from its built-in expense advantage. The fund currently charges 0.65%, while its average no-load intermediate bond category peer levies a 0.72% charge.

We think investors looking to hold a splash of higher-yielding junk bonds will like what they find here, but the fund's added risk should not be overlooked. It takes on more credit risk than the category norm, and its duration (a measure of interest-rate sensitivity) has at times run a bit longer than its average peer's. The fund held up reasonably well when rates spiked in early 2004, but investors shouldn't be surprised by a few performance hiccups now and then.

Portfolio Analysis 07-31-04

Total Fixed-Income:1199	Date of Maturity	Amount $000	Value $000	% Net Assets
FNMA 5%	08-01-34	42,610	41,558	9.20
FNMA 7%	05-01-18	32,623	34,537	7.65
FNMA 4.5%	09-01-18	17,988	17,718	3.92
FNMA 6.5%	05-01-08	11,798	12,475	2.76
US Treasury Note 4%	11-15-12	9,840	9,628	2.13
US Treasury Note 2.375%	08-15-06	9,591	9,530	2.11
Mlcs Fwsp Irs 6/21/06 3m	06-21-06	8,000	8,037	1.78
US Treasury Bond 8%	11-15-21	6,000	7,956	1.76
FHLMC 3.625%	09-15-08	8,000	7,921	1.75
FNMA 4.5%	09-01-33	6,646	6,285	1.39
FNMA 5.5%	08-01-34	5,998	6,017	1.33
US Treasury Note 1.625%	02-28-06	6,000	5,924	1.31
FNMA 4%	08-01-19	5,896	5,656	1.25
US Treasury Note 6.5%	02-15-10	4,500	5,094	1.13
US Treasury Note 5%	08-15-11	4,482	4,718	1.05
US Treasury Bond 9.875%	11-15-15	3,000	4,361	0.97
Jpsw Fswp Irs 4/07/08 3m	04-07-08	3,000	2,975	0.66
FNMA 4.625%	10-15-13	3,000	2,930	0.65
FHLMC 5.125%	08-20-12	2,418	2,421	0.54
FHLMC 5.875%	03-21-11	2,095	2,226	0.49

Current Investment Style
Duration: Short Int Long
Quality: High Med Low
[1] figure provided by fund

Avg Eff Duration[1]	4.8 Yrs
Avg Eff Maturity	5.5 Yrs
Avg Credit Quality	AA
Avg Wtd Coupon	5.43%
Avg Wtd Price	102.87% of par

Coupon Range	% of Bonds	Rel Cat
0% PIK	1.2	0.3
0% to 6%	55.3	0.9
6% to 8%	35.1	1.2
8% to 10%	7.3	1.3
More than 10%	2.3	2.0

1.00=Category Average

Credit Analysis		% bonds 07-31-04	
US Govt	55	BB	2
AAA	5	B	7
AA	3	Below B	2
A	9	NR/NA	2
BBB	15		

Sector Breakdown	% of assets
US Treasuries	11
TIPS	0
US Agency	4
Mortgage Pass-Throughs	29
Mortgage CMO	6
Mortgage ARM	0
US Corporate	25
Asset-Backed	5
Convertible	0
Municipal	0
Corporate Inflation-Protected	0
Foreign Corporate	1
Foreign Govt	1

Composition			
Cash	16.6	Bonds	80.7
Stocks	0.0	Other	2.6

Special Securities	
Restricted/Illiquid Secs	4
Exotic Mortgage-Backed	0
Emerging-Markets Secs	1
Options/Futures/Warrants	Yes

Address:	82 Devonshire St Boston MA 02109 800-343-3548
Web Address:	www.fidelity.com
Inception:	10-15-02 *
Advisor:	Fidelity Management & Research Co. (FMR)
Subadvisor:	FMR Co., Inc. (FMRC)
NTF Plans:	Fidelity Retail-NTF, CommonWealth NTF

Minimum Purchase:	$2500	Add: $250	IRA: $2500
Min Auto Inv Plan:	$100	Add: —	
Sales Fees:	No-load		
Management Fee:	0.43%		
Actual Fees:	Mgt:0.43%	Dist: —	
Expense Projections:	3Yr: —	5Yr: —	10Yr: —
Income Distrib:	Monthly		

Fidelity Ultra-Short Bd

Analyst Pick

Ticker	Load	NAV	Yield	SEC Yield	Total Assets	Mstar Category
FUSFX	None	$10.04	1.5%	2.13%	$763 mil	Ultrashort Bond

Governance and Management

Fiduciary Grade: B

Portfolio Manager(s)

Manager Andrew Dudley has run this fund since its inception. He has had much success at Fidelity Short-Term Bond, which he still manages, and we expect that success to continue here. Dudley is supported by a team of analysts and Fidelity's extensive research capabilities.

Strategy

Manager Andrew Dudley keeps the fund's overall interest-rate risk tied to the Lehman Brothers 6-Month Swap Index, which is typically a bit less sensitive to interest-rate changes than the ultrashort category as a whole. The bulk of the fund's assets are invested in asset-backed securities and mortgage-backed securities, but the fund does hold a small corporate bond stake. The fund also invests in floating-rate securities.

Historical Profile

Return
Risk
Rating
Not Rated

Investment Style
Fixed Income
Income Rtn %Rank Cat: 100 (2002), 85 (2003), 79 (12-04)

▼ Manager Change
∇ Partial Manager Change

Growth of $10,000 (11.2 / 10.6 / 10.0)
— Investment Values of Fund
— Investment Values of LB Aggr

Performance Quartile (within Category)

1993	1994	1995	1996	1997	1998	1999	2000	2001	2002	2003	12-04	History
—	—	—	—	—	—	—	—	—	10.02	10.06	10.04	NAV
—	—	—	—	—	—	—	—	—	0.94*	1.87	1.32	Total Return %
—	—	—	—	—	—	—	—	—	—	-2.23	-3.02	+/-LB Aggr
—	—	—	—	—	—	—	—	—	—	0.69	-0.48	+/-6 Month CD
—	—	—	—	—	—	—	—	—	0.00	1.47	1.49	Income Return %
—	—	—	—	—	—	—	—	—	—	0.40	-0.17	Capital Return %
—	—	—	—	—	—	—	—	—	—	24	43	Total Rtn % Rank Cat
—	—	—	—	—	—	—	—	—	0.07	0.15	0.15	Income $
—	—	—	—	—	—	—	—	—	0.00	0.00	0.00	Capital Gains $
—	—	—	—	—	—	—	—	—	—	0.55	0.55	Expense Ratio %
—	—	—	—	—	—	—	—	—	—	1.77	1.21	Income Ratio %
—	—	—	—	—	—	—	—	—	—	36	53	Turnover Rate %
—	—	—	—	—	—	—	—	—	80	354	763	Net Assets $mil

Performance 12-31-04

	1st Qtr	2nd Qtr	3rd Qtr	4th Qtr	Total
2000	—	—	—	—	—
2001	—	—	—	—	—
2002	—	—	—	0.68	0.94 *
2003	0.48	0.53	0.37	0.48	1.87
2004	0.54	-0.11	0.46	0.42	1.32

Trailing	Total Return%	+/- LB Aggr	+/- 6 Month CD	%Rank Cat	Growth of $10,000
3 Mo	0.42	-0.53	-0.21	42	10,042
6 Mo	0.88	-3.30	-0.25	47	10,088
1 Yr	1.32	-3.02	-0.48	43	10,132
3 Yr Avg	—	—	—	—	—
5 Yr Avg	—	—	—	—	—
10 Yr Avg	—	—	—	—	—
15 Yr Avg	—	—	—	—	—

Tax Analysis	Tax-Adj Rtn%	%Rank Cat	Tax-Cost Rat	%Rank Cat
3 Yr (estimated)	—	—	—	—
5 Yr (estimated)	—	—	—	—
10 Yr (estimated)	—	—	—	—

Potential Capital Gain Exposure: 0% of assets

Rating and Risk

Time Period	Load-Adj Return %	Morningstar Rtn vs Cat	Morningstar Risk vs Cat	Morningstar Risk-Adj Rating
1 Yr	1.32			
3 Yr	—	—	—	—
5 Yr	—	—	—	—
10 Yr	—	—	—	—
Incept	1.77			

Other Measures	Standard Index LB Aggr	Best Fit Index
Alpha	—	—
Beta	—	—
R-Squared	—	—
Standard Deviation	—	
Mean	—	
Sharpe Ratio	—	

Portfolio Analysis 10-31-04

Total Fixed-Income:668	Date of Maturity	Amount $000	Value $000	% Net Assets
Cwabs CMO	08-25-34	9,353	9,294	1.32
FNMA 0.06%	11-01-17	6,216	6,448	0.92
Bk One Oneseries 2002-2c	05-15-08	4,188	4,210	0.60
FNMA 6.25%	03-22-12	4,005	4,063	0.58
Dow Jones Cdx Indices Cd	03-20-10	4,000	3,996	0.57
Abs FRN	09-25-34	3,556	3,556	0.51
Gsamp Tr 2004-Ahl FRN	08-25-34	3,360	3,360	0.48
Liberty Media FRN	09-17-06	2,986	3,020	0.43
FNMA CMO 4.5%	05-25-20	2,943	2,953	0.42
Holmes Financing 8 Plc 2	07-15-40	2,927	2,929	0.42
Fieldstone Mtg Inv 2004-	01-25-35	2,912	2,911	0.41
British Telecom 7.625%	12-15-05	2,629	2,777	0.39
Adjustable Rate Mtg 2004	02-25-35	2,486	2,486	0.35
Sequoia Mtg Tr 2004-8 CM	09-20-34	2,445	2,447	0.35
Citibank Ccmt 2003-C1 FR	04-07-10	2,350	2,403	0.34
Mbna Master Cc Tr Ii 200	10-15-08	2,372	2,378	0.34
Morgan Stanley Cap 2004-	08-25-34	2,360	2,360	0.34
FNMA CMO 4.5%	05-25-34	2,344	2,345	0.33
Holmes Financing 8 Plc 2	04-15-11	2,335	2,335	0.33
Sears Cr Acct Mstr Tr 20	08-15-09	2,325	2,330	0.33

Current Investment Style

Duration: Short Int Long
Quality: High Med Low

¹ figure provided by fund

Avg Eff Duration¹	0.5 Yrs
Avg Eff Maturity	1.6 Yrs
Avg Credit Quality	A
Avg Wtd Coupon	2.67%
Avg Wtd Price	100.51% of par

Coupon Range	% of Bonds	Rel Cat
0% PIK	5.4	0.3
0% to 6%	90.4	1.1
6% to 8%	9.4	0.7
8% to 10%	0.2	0.1
More than 10%	0.0	0.0

1.00=Category Average

Credit Analysis		% bonds 10-31-04	
US Govt	19	BB	0
AAA	27	B	0
AA	8	Below B	0
A	14	NR/NA	28
BBB	10		

Sector Breakdown	% of assets
US Treasuries	0
TIPS	0
US Agency	1
Mortgage Pass-Throughs	2
Mortgage CMO	24
Mortgage ARM	0
US Corporate	5
Asset-Backed	28
Convertible	0
Municipal	0
Corporate Inflation-Protected	0
Foreign Corporate	0
Foreign Govt	0

Composition			
Cash	39.9	Bonds	60.1
Stocks	0.0	Other	0.0

Special Securities	
Restricted/Illiquid Secs	2
Exotic Mortgage-Backed	0
Emerging-Markets Secs	0
Options/Futures/Warrants	Yes

Morningstar's Take by Scott Berry 10-27-04

Fidelity Ultra-Short Bond has quickly become one of our favorite ultrashort bond funds.

Thus far, this fund has accomplished just what it set out to do. Its returns have easily bested those of an average taxable money market fund, while its volatility has been kept in check. For example, after gaining 1.87% in 2003, the fund gained 0.90% for the year to date through Sep. 30, 2004. In contrast, the average taxable money market gained just 0.61% and 0.47% during those periods. Meanwhile, the fund's net asset value has fluctuated just pennies per share since the fund's inception in mid-2002.

The fund's low volatility stems from its conservative approach. Manager Andrew Dudley keeps the fund's interest-rate sensitivity tied to the Lehman Brothers 6-Month Swap Index, which tends to be less rate-sensitive than the category norm. Dudley also shies away from credit risk. The fund holds corporate bonds, which carry some credit risk, but Dudley avoids below-investment-grade issues and recently held just 10% of the fund's assets in bonds rated BBB, the lowest investment-grade bond rating.

The fund's reasonable expense ratio seals the deal here. With an annual expense ratio of 0.55%, the fund isn't the cheapest ultrashort fund, but it is cheaper than its average no-load category peer. And in a category that often sees its winners and losers separated by a very narrow margin, small advantages add up in a hurry.

This fund's conservative strategy will likely prevent it from keeping pace with its more rate-sensitive peers during bond market rallies, but we think Dudley's safety-first approach makes the fund a good option for investors looking for a money-market alternative. Unlike a money market fund, this fund can lose money over short periods. However, its added return potential should appeal to investors that are comfortable with some limited principal fluctuations.

Address:	82 Devonshire St Boston MA 02109 800-343-3548
Web Address:	www.fidelity.com
Inception:	08-29-02 *
Advisor:	Fidelity Management & Research Co. (FMR)
Subadvisor:	Fidelity Intl Invest Advisors (U.K.) Ltd
NTF Plans:	Fidelity Retail-NTF, Fidelity Instl-NTF

Minimum Purchase:	$2500	Add: $250	IRA: $2500
Min Auto Inv Plan:	$100	Add: $100	
Sales Fees:	No-load, 0.25%R		
Management Fee:	0.43%		
Actual Fees:	Mgt:0.43%	Dist:	
Expense Projections:	3Yr: —	5Yr: —	10Yr: —
Income Distrib:	Monthly		

Fidelity Value

Ticker	Load	NAV	Yield	Total Assets	Mstar Category
FDVLX	None	$71.29	0.2%	$10,279 mil	Mid-Cap Value

Governance and Management

Fiduciary Grade: B

Portfolio Manager(s)

Richard Fentin has been at the helm since 1996 and is backed by Fidelity's deep research staff. A 23-year veteran of the firm, Fentin had a solid record at his previous charge, Fidelity Puritan, which he managed for almost a decade. He says he has owned shares of this fund since taking over but wouldn't disclose what percentage of his holdings it comprises.

Strategy

Manager Richard Fentin looks for stocks with low absolute valuations, typically on a price/sales or price/book basis. That approach has often led to an atypical portfolio. During Fentin's tenure, the fund has often been light on financial stocks relative to its peers. For a number of years, he loaded up on industrial stocks, but he's recently found more value in other corners of the market, such as tech and energy. Assets are spread among nearly 300 names, but Fentin's penchant for sector bets has resulted in slightly above-average volatility.

Historical Profile

Return Average
Risk Average
Rating ★★★ Neutral

Investment Style — Equity Stock %: 95% | 97% | 93% | 90% | 95% | 91% | 94% | 92% | 92%

▼ Manager Change
▽ Partial Manager Change

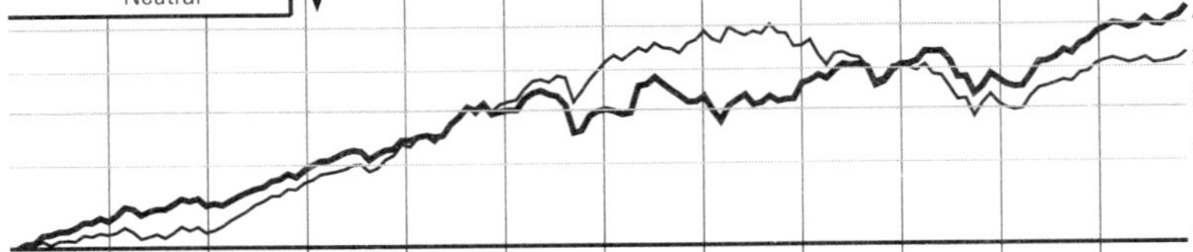

Growth of $10,000
— Investment Values of Fund
— Investment Values of S&P 500

Performance Quartile (within Category)

1993	1994	1995	1996	1997	1998	1999	2000	2001	2002	2003	12-04	History
40.23	40.81	49.64	51.54	54.04	46.35	43.81	46.35	51.51	46.39	62.07	71.29	NAV
22.94	7.63	27.13	16.85	21.08	0.18	8.55	8.10	12.25	-9.25	34.43	21.21	Total Return %
12.88	6.32	-10.40	-6.09	-12.27	-28.39	-12.49	17.20	24.13	12.84	5.76	10.34	+/-S&P 500
7.32	9.76	-7.81	-3.41	-13.29	-4.90	8.66	-11.08	9.92	0.39	-3.64	-2.50	+/-Russ MV
0.96	0.42	1.18	1.07	0.93	1.02	1.57	2.17	1.10	0.70	0.50	0.26	Income Return %
21.98	7.21	25.95	15.78	20.15	-0.84	6.98	5.93	11.15	-9.95	33.93	20.95	Capital Return %
31	10	50	63	78	59	51	87	27	24	51	27	Total Rtn % Rank Cat
0.34	0.17	0.48	0.53	0.48	0.55	0.73	0.95	0.51	0.36	0.23	0.16	Income $
2.80	2.28	1.73	5.92	7.95	7.15	5.62	0.00	0.00	0.00	0.05	3.71	Capital Gains $
1.11	1.08	0.96	0.88	0.66	0.61	0.54	0.48	0.77	0.95	0.98	0.93	Expense Ratio %
1.43	1.29	1.58	1.34	1.01	1.06	1.50	1.87	1.29	1.02	0.66	0.37	Income Ratio %
117	112	125	112	56	36	50	48	49	42	40	40	Turnover Rate %
1,716	3,720	5,746	7,080	7,914	5,523	4,383	3,522	5,238	5,092	6,984	10,279	Net Assets $mil

Performance 12-31-04

	1st Qtr	2nd Qtr	3rd Qtr	4th Qtr	Total
2000	-6.05	0.66	1.98	12.10	8.10
2001	2.91	8.70	-12.02	14.04	12.25
2002	8.76	-5.62	-19.27	9.53	-9.25
2003	-4.35	17.22	4.94	14.26	34.43
2004	4.96	3.67	0.00	11.39	21.21

Trailing	Total Return%	+/- S&P 500	+/- Russ MV	%Rank Cat	Growth of $10,000
3 Mo	11.39	2.16	-2.07	50	11,139
6 Mo	11.39	4.20	-4.04	43	11,139
1 Yr	21.21	10.34	-2.50	27	12,121
3 Yr Avg	13.93	10.35	-1.63	20	14,788
5 Yr Avg	12.40	14.70	-1.08	42	17,940
10 Yr Avg	13.38	1.31	-2.34	52	35,105
15 Yr Avg	12.92	1.99	-0.78	31	61,882

Tax Analysis	Tax-Adj Rtn%	%Rank Cat	Tax-Cost Rat	%Rank Cat
3 Yr (estimated)	13.39	17	0.47	38
5 Yr (estimated)	11.81	32	0.52	27
10 Yr (estimated)	11.24	50	1.89	50

Potential Capital Gain Exposure: 21% of assets

Rating and Risk

Time Period	Load-Adj Return %	Morningstar Rtn vs Cat	Morningstar Risk vs Cat	Morningstar Risk-Adj Rating
1 Yr	21.21			
3 Yr	13.93	+Avg	Avg	★★★★
5 Yr	12.40	Avg	Avg	★★★
10 Yr	13.38	Avg	Avg	★★★
Incept	14.44			

Other Measures	Standard Index S&P 500	Best Fit Index Russ MV
Alpha	10.3	-1.8
Beta	0.94	1.04
R-Squared	83	95
Standard Deviation	17.62	
Mean	13.93	
Sharpe Ratio	0.72	

Portfolio Analysis 10-31-04

Share change since 07-04 Total Stocks:259

Share change since 07-04	Sector	PE	YTD Ret%	% Assets
Fluor	Business	21.9	39.55	1.55
⊕ Xerox	Ind Mtrls	20.2	23.26	1.25
Precision Castparts	Ind Mtrls	26.0	44.97	1.19
⊕ Baxter International	Health	32.9	15.22	1.19
⊖ TXU	Utilities	NMF	177.67	1.10
⊕ Flextronics Internationa	Hardware	—	-6.62	1.10
⊕ Alcan	Ind Mtrls	53.1	5.87	1.02
Dade Behring Holdings	Health	35.9	56.69	0.98
⊕ Royal Caribbean Cruises	Goods	36.9	58.33	0.95
⊕ Ceridian	Business	22.1	-12.70	0.93
⊕ Celestica	Hardware	—	-6.37	0.91
⊕ Kennametal	Ind Mtrls	19.9	27.17	0.90
⊕ Alcoa	Ind Mtrls	18.8	-15.75	0.88
⊖ NCR	Hardware	26.7	78.43	0.85
⊕ Western Digital	Hardware	12.1	-8.06	0.85
Owens-Illinois	Ind Mtrls	—	90.50	0.85
Masco	Ind Mtrls	17.2	36.23	0.85
National Oilwell	Energy	36.9	57.83	0.81
⊕ Storage Technology	Hardware	20.8	22.76	0.80
⊕ Nucor	Ind Mtrls	9.6	89.07	0.78

Current Investment Style

Value Blnd Growth / Large Mid Small

Market Cap	%
Giant	6.4
Large	27.3
Mid	57.2
Small	8.5
Micro	0.5
Avg $mil: 5,672	

Value Measures		Rel Category
Price/Earnings	17.67	1.15
Price/Book	2.02	1.05
Price/Sales	0.86	0.98
Price/Cash Flow	7.78	1.36
Dividend Yield %	1.02	0.71

Growth Measures	%	Rel Category
Long-Term Erngs	12.85	1.17
Book Value	5.17	0.92
Sales	2.63	0.55
Cash Flow	0.95	0.24
Historical Erngs	17.37	1.51

Profitability	%	Rel Category
Return on Equity	10.86	0.85
Return on Assets	5.24	0.86
Net Margin	7.45	0.85

Sector Weightings	% of Stocks	Rel S&P 500	3 Year High	3 Year Low
Info	18.05	0.84		
Software	2.33	0.54	2	1
Hardware	9.74	0.95	10	4
Media	2.47	0.64	4	2
Telecom	3.51	1.11	4	3
Service	39.57	0.85		
Health	10.60	0.85	11	2
Consumer	7.45	0.82	10	7
Business	7.95	1.96	13	7
Financial	13.57	0.65	20	14
Mfg	42.37	1.32		
Goods	5.90	0.63	8	5
Ind Mtrls	21.04	1.66	21	19
Energy	10.00	1.40	13	10
Utilities	5.43	1.83	7	4

Composition

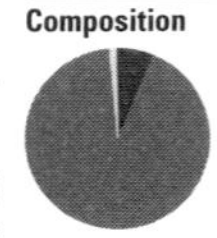

Cash	6.2
Stocks	92.2
Bonds	0.4
Other	1.2
Foreign (% of Stock)	6.9

Morningstar's Take by Greg Carlson 12-23-04

Fidelity Value has become more attractive, but a spotty history gives us pause.

Rich Fentin, this fund's manager since 1996, has hit his stride lately. Fentin, who seeks out stocks that are cheap on an absolute basis, is quite willing to load up on sectors where such names cluster. During much of his tenure, Fentin has held a bigger stake in industrial stocks than most mid-value rivals, a wager that juiced the fund's returns from 2001 through 2003. More recently, he has cut back on that sector and identified winners in areas such as tech, energy, and health care. As such, Fentin has beaten 75% of his rivals over the past three years through Dec. 22, 2004.

That said, Fentin has often misfired: Industrial names foundered during his first few years here. Meanwhile, he held only a minimal stake in financial stocks--which he found too pricey--during that stretch, thus missing out on that sector's rallies in 1996, 1997, and 2000. All told, this fund's returns, relative to its mid-value peers, are just middling on Fentin's watch. What's more, despite his price-conscious ethos and a portfolio spread across more than 250 stocks, the fund has been a bit more volatile than its typical rival.

Fentin met with more success while running Fidelity Puritan from 1987 to 1996, while also demonstrating an ability to spot bargains in other sectors: During the 1990 banking crisis, he scooped up a passel of financial names and subsequently rode the sector's resurgence to fat gains in the next two years before trimming his stake.

We're encouraged that Fentin has recently done well here without relying on big wagers. Nevertheless, given his checkered history, it's too soon to proclaim the fund a reliable option. It's also worth noting that the fund's solid returns of late have led to substantial inflows: At $9.8 billion, it's now the largest mid-value offering. While the fund's sprawling portfolio and Fentin's low-turnover style mitigate liquidity concerns, its asset growth bears watching.

Address:	82 Devonshire St Boston MA 02109 800-343-3548
Web Address:	www.fidelity.com
Inception:	12-01-78
Advisor:	Fidelity Management & Research Co. (FMR)
Subadvisor:	FMR Co., Inc. (FMRC)
NTF Plans:	Fidelity Retail-NTF, CommonWealth NTF

Minimum Purchase:	$2500	Add: $250	IRA: $2500
Min Auto Inv Plan:	$2500	Add: $100	
Sales Fees:	No-load		
Management Fee:	0.74%		
Actual Fees:	Mgt:0.74%	Dist:	
Expense Projections:	3Yr:$318	5Yr:$550	10Yr:$1225
Income Distrib:	Annually		

Fidelity Worldwide

Ticker	Load	NAV	Yield	Total Assets	Mstar Category
FWWFX	None	$13.25	0.6%	$1,169 mil	World Stock

Governance and Management

Fiduciary Grade: B

Portfolio Manager(s)

Rick Mace joined the fund in April 2001. Mace is also head of Fidelity's international funds group and manager of the flagship Fidelity Overseas Fund. Brian Hogan came on board in February 2002. He has experience both as a bond manager and as a manager of specialized equity funds. Both managers are served by a large analyst staff, including six global sector analysts who look around the world for the best picks regardless of geography.

Strategy

Managers Rick Mace and Brian Hogan don't make sizable country bets, preferring to focus on stock-picking. Mace, who sets the fund's regional allocations and invests overseas, is perhaps best characterized as a growth-at-a-reasonable-price investor. Brian Hogan manages the U.S. portion of the portfolio, which he runs independently from Mace. Fidelity has used a fair-value pricing policy on its international funds for several years.

Historical Profile

Return Average
Risk Average
Rating ★★★ Neutral

Investment Style: Equity — Stock %: 89% (1993), 91% (1994), 82% (1995), 92% (1996), 90% (1997), 88% (1998), 96% (1999), 95% (2000), 96% (2001)

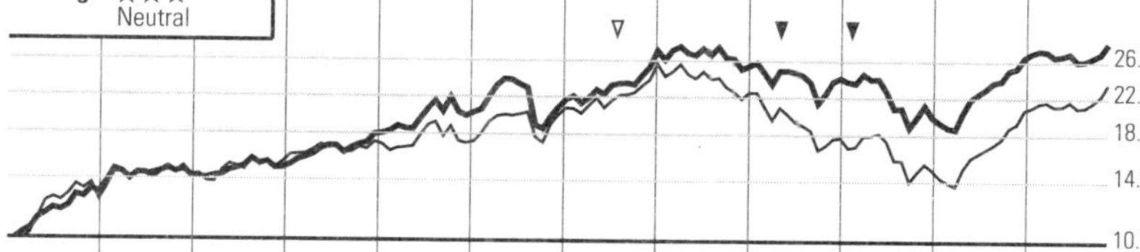

Performance Quartile (within Category)

History

	1993	1994	1995	1996	1997	1998	1999	2000	2001	2002	2003	12-04
NAV	13.03	12.68	13.44	15.39	15.95	16.53	19.90	15.63	14.66	11.88	16.37	18.25
Total Return %	36.55	2.96	7.19	18.72	12.08	7.18	30.80	-8.01	-6.21	-18.83	38.41	12.24
+/-MSCI EAFE	3.99	-4.82	-4.02	12.67	10.30	-12.75	3.77	6.[illegible]8	15.21	-2.89	-0.18	-8.01
+/-MSCI World	14.05	-2.12	-13.53	5.24	-3.68	-17.14	5.85	5.[illegible]8	10.59	1.06	5.30	-2.48
Income Return %	1.03	0.54	1.18	1.26	0.71	0.63	0.60	2.01	0.00	0.14	0.59	0.61
Capital Return %	35.52	2.42	6.01	17.46	11.37	6.55	30.20	-10.02	-6.21	-18.97	37.82	11.63
Total Rtn % Rank Cat	41	13	91	34	61	71	53	45	13	44	25	75
Income $	0.10	0.07	0.15	0.17	0.11	0.10	0.10	0.40	0.00	0.02	0.07	0.10
Capital Gains $	0.15	0.66	0.00	0.38	1.16	0.44	1.52	2.25	0.00	0.00	0.00	0.02
Expense Ratio %	1.40	1.32	1.16	1.18	1.16	1.12	1.07	1.04	1.05	1.20	1.28	1.19
Income Ratio %	1.99	1.40	2.05	1.71	1.24	0.91	0.47	0.48	0.29	0.19	0.28	0.29
Turnover Rate %	57	69	70	49	85	100	164	235	152	120	106	95
Net Assets $mil	340	704	654	926	1,145	1,014	1,125	928	807	642	957	1,169

Performance 12-31-04

	1st Qtr	2nd Qtr	3rd Qtr	4th Qtr	Total
2000	2.31	-1.08	-4.82	-4.51	-8.01
2001	-9.28	6.56	-15.16	14.35	-6.21
2002	2.32	-8.80	-17.69	5.68	-18.83
2003	-6.23	20.92	7.35	13.71	38.41
2004	3.36	-1.06	-2.15	12.18	12.24

Trailing	Total Return%	+/- MSCI EAFE	+/- MSCI World	%Rank Cat	Growth of $10,000
3 Mo	12.18	-3.14	0.24	57	11,218
6 Mo	9.76	-5.24	-1.06	62	10,976
1 Yr	12.24	-8.01	-2.48	75	11,224
3 Yr Avg	8.04	-3.85	1.09	42	12,611
5 Yr Avg	1.70	2.83	4.15	32	10,879
10 Yr Avg	8.08	2.46	-0.01	64	21,750
15 Yr Avg	—	—	—	—	—

Tax Analysis	Tax-Adj Rtn%	%Rank Cat	Tax-Cost Rat	%Rank Cat
3 Yr (estimated)	7.87	36	0.16	22
5 Yr (estimated)	0.80	28	0.88	57
10 Yr (estimated)	6.89	53	1.10	37

Potential Capital Gain Exposure: 15% of assets

Rating and Risk

Time Period	Load-Adj Return %	Morningstar Rtn vs Cat	Morningstar Risk vs Cat	Morningstar Risk-Adj Rating
1 Yr	12.24			
3 Yr	8.04	Avg	Avg	★★★
5 Yr	1.70	+Avg	Avg	★★★★
10 Yr	8.08	Avg	Avg	★★★
Incept	8.11			

Other Measures	Standard Index S&P 500	Best Fit Index MSCI World
Alpha	-2.9	2.0
Beta	0.94	1.02
R-Squared	91	97
Standard Deviation	16.68	
Mean	8.04	
Sharpe Ratio	0.40	

Morningstar's Take by Dan Lefkovitz 12-29-04

Its rough year aside, Fidelity Worldwide remains a decent if uninspiring choice.

Over the past few years, this portfolio has been heavy on technology stocks and tilted toward the U.S. market. Midway though 2004, for example, managers Rick Mace and Brian Hogan had more than one fourth of their portfolio in information-technology stocks and more than 55% of assets in U.S. stocks, both higher than the fund's peers in the world-stock category.

While the fund's tech exposure was a boost in 2003 when it landed in the category's top quartile, the stake has hurt this year. In 2004, technology hardware has been the second-worst performing of the 12 sectors tracked by Morningstar. Holdings such as Dutch chipmaker ASM Lithography and semiconductor manufacturer Analog Devices have dragged down performance. And the fund's large U.S. stake has hurt on a relative basis because stronger foreign currencies amplify gains in foreign stocks. (Mace and Hogan don't hedge the fund's currency exposure.) For the year to date, the fund lands in the category's bottom third.

This year's woes aside, Worldwide is a decent conservative fund. Mace and Hogan favor blue-chip multinationals such as General Electric and Vodafone. They spread assets across a far larger number of stocks than average: The fund currently holds more than 400 stocks, compared with the category average of 120. This has helped to make the fund less volatile than its typical peer and the S&P 500. Meanwhile, the fund's 26% total return since April 2001, when Mace took over the foreign portion of the portfolio, bests the world-stock category average by nine percentage points.

True, better options exist in the world-stock category, and for investors who already own a core U.S. stock fund, this offering's domestic-heavy portfolio will overlap considerably. Nevertheless, experienced management, low volatility, and low expenses make this fund a serviceable equity option.

Address:	82 Devonshire St Boston MA 02109 800-343-3548
Web Address:	www.fidelity.com
Inception:	05-30-90
Advisor:	Fidelity Management & Research Co. (FMR)
Subadvisor:	FMR Co., Inc. (FMRC)
NTF Plans:	Fidelity Retail-NTF, CommonWealth NTF

Minimum Purchase:	$2500	Add: $250	IRA: $2500
Min Auto Inv Plan:	$2500	Add: $100	
Sales Fees:	No-load, 1.00%R		
Management Fee:	0.86%		
Actual Fees:	Mgt:0.86%	Dist:	
Expense Projections:	3Yr:$356	5Yr:$617	10Yr:$1363
Income Distrib:	Annually		

Portfolio Analysis 10-31-04

Share change since 07-04 Total Stocks:383	Sector	Country	% Assets
⊕ General Electric	Ind Mtrls	United States	2.31
Microsoft	Software	United States	2.22
⊕ American International G	Financial	United States	1.84
⊖ Vodafone Group PLC ADR	Telecom	U.K.	1.76
⊕ Deutsche Telekom AG ADR	Telecom	Germany	1.75
⊖ Tyco International	Ind Mtrls	United States	1.45
⊕ ASML Holding NV	Hardware	Netherlands	1.09
⊕ Honeywell International	Ind Mtrls	United States	1.07
⊕ Bank of America	Financial	United States	1.06
⊖ Pfizer	Health	United States	1.05
⊕ Baxter International	Health	United States	1.03
⊖ Johnson & Johnson	Health	United States	0.90
⊕ SBC Communications	Telecom	United States	0.89
Allianz	Financial	Germany	0.87
⊕ ExxonMobil	Energy	United States	0.87
⊕ Home Depot	Consumer	United States	0.80
⊖ HSBC Holdings PLC ADR	Financial	U.K.	0.76
⊕ UnitedHealth Group	Health	United States	0.71
⊖ Wal-Mart Stores	Consumer	United States	0.63
⊕ Alcatel SA ADR A	Hardware	France	0.62

Current Investment Style

Market Cap	%
Giant	48.7
Large	28.4
Mid	19.9
Small	2.5
Micro	0.4
Avg $mil: 23,628	

Value Measures		Rel Category
Price/Earnings	15.97	1.01
Price/Book	2.25	1.01
Price/Sales	1.19	1.02
Price/Cash Flow	5.28	0.83
Dividend Yield %	1.50	0.80

Growth Measures	%	Rel Category
Long-Term Erngs	12.70	1.05
Book Value	3.69	1.67
Sales	4.20	1.00
Cash Flow	4.34	0.74
Historical Erngs	7.41	0.87

Composition

Cash	3.6	Bonds	0.0
Stocks	95.7	Other	0.8
Foreign (% of Stock)			45.2

Sector Weightings	% of Stocks	Rel MSCI EAFE	3 Year High	3 Year Low
Info	28.87	1.74		
Software	3.93	3.64	4	3
Hardware	11.12	3.05	12	7
Media	4.48	1.96	7	4
Telecom	9.34	0.97	9	3
Service	41.41	0.93		
Health	11.18	1.54	14	11
Consumer	5.70	1.13	9	5
Business	3.85	0.71	7	3
Financial	20.68	0.77	24	21
Mfg	29.71	0.77		
Goods	7.29	0.53	14	7
Ind Mtrls	13.62	1.11	14	9
Energy	7.49	1.02	9	6
Utilities	1.31	0.24	2	1

Regional Exposure	% Stock		
UK/W. Europe	27	N. America	56
Japan	8	Latn America	2
Asia X Japan	7	Other	0

Country Exposure	% Stock		
United States	55	Germany	7
Japan	8	France	4
U.K.	8		

First Eagle Fund of Am Y

Ticker	Load	NAV	Yield	Total Assets	Mstar Category
FEAFX	12b-1 only	$26.06	0.0%	$690 mil	Mid-Cap Blend

Governance and Management

Fiduciary Grade:

Portfolio Manager(s)

Harold Levy and David Cohen deserve full credit for this fund's sparkling record, as they've managed it since its 1987 inception. The analyst team has been bulked up from six analysts to eight.

Strategy

Comanagers Harold Levy and David Cohen look for companies in the midst of significant changes that are selling for less than the managers' estimates of the value of the companies' future cash flows. Often the changes affecting these companies are new management teams, major share repurchases, or elimination of a business segment.

Historical Profile

Return Average
Risk Low
Rating ★★★★ Above Avg

Investment Style: Equity Stock %

94%	97%	85%	94%	98%	100%	81%	96%	99%

▼ Manager Change
▽ Partial Manager Change

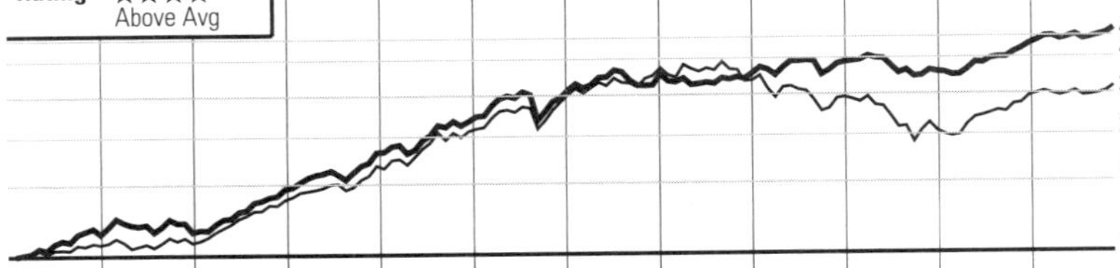

Growth of $10,000
▬ Investment Values of Fund
— Investment Values of S&P 500

Performance Quartile (within Category)

1993	1994	1995	1996	1997	1998	1999	2000	2001	2002	2003	12-04	History
15.04	12.70	16.96	18.30	19.33	21.43	20.56	20.47	21.58	20.02	23.99	26.06	NAV
23.85	-2.60	36.40	29.34	29.46	20.99	12.09	0.32	8.25	-7.23	22.21	15.91	Total Return %
13.79	-3.91	-1.13	6.40	-3.89	-7.58	-8.95	9.42	20.13	14.86	-6.46	5.04	+/-S&P 500
9.92	0.99	5.48	10.16	-2.78	1.88	-2.63	-17.17	8.85	7.30	-13.38	-0.56	+/-S&P Mid 400
0.00	0.00	0.00	0.00	0.00	0.00	0.00	0.00	0.00	0.00	0.00	0.00	Income Return %
23.85	-2.60	36.40	29.34	29.46	20.99	12.09	0.32	8.25	-7.23	22.21	15.91	Capital Return %
20	61	13	8	30	16	67	75	21	7	96	50	Total Rtn % Rank Cat
0.00	0.00	0.00	0.00	0.00	0.00	0.00	0.00	0.00	0.00	0.00	0.00	Income $
1.62	2.00	0.35	3.13	4.10	1.84	3.29	0.15	0.57	0.00	0.47	1.70	Capital Gains $
2.90	1.90	1.90	1.80	1.70	1.50	1.40	1.40	1.40	1.51	1.50	1.46	Expense Ratio %
-1.50	-0.70	-0.30	-0.20	-0.30	-0.40	-0.20	-0.20	-0.30	-0.82	-0.79	-0.63	Income Ratio %
141	110	81	93	98	83	55	55	83	51	44	45	Turnover Rate %
108	105	136	171	269	457	528	375	422	473	480	654	Net Assets $mil

Performance 12-31-04

	1st Qtr	2nd Qtr	3rd Qtr	4th Qtr	Total
2000	-3.11	-3.06	2.23	4.49	0.32
2001	-1.51	10.57	-9.29	9.59	8.25
2002	4.36	-7.10	-7.46	3.41	-7.23
2003	-2.20	8.99	4.08	10.16	22.21
2004	5.71	1.10	-0.66	9.18	15.91

Trailing	Total Return%	+/- S&P 500	+/- S&P Mid 400	%Rank Cat	Growth of $10,000
3 Mo	9.18	-0.05	-2.97	92	10,918
6 Mo	8.45	1.26	-1.34	70	10,845
1 Yr	15.91	5.04	-0.56	50	11,591
3 Yr Avg	9.53	5.95	-0.98	52	13,140
5 Yr Avg	7.37	9.67	-2.16	55	14,270
10 Yr Avg	16.02	3.95	-0.07	22	44,190
15 Yr Avg	13.41	2.48	-1.25	32	66,034

Tax Analysis	Tax-Adj Rtn%	%Rank Cat	Tax-Cost Rat	%Rank Cat
3 Yr (estimated)	9.04	47	0.45	50
5 Yr (estimated)	6.94	44	0.40	12
10 Yr (estimated)	14.04	20	1.71	50

Potential Capital Gain Exposure: 27% of assets

Rating and Risk

Time Period	Load-Adj Return %	Morningstar Rtn vs Cat	Morningstar Risk vs Cat	Morningstar Risk-Adj Rating
1 Yr	15.91			
3 Yr	9.53	Avg	Low	★★★★
5 Yr	7.37	Avg	Low	★★★
10 Yr	16.02	+Avg	Low	★★★★★
Incept	13.81			

Other Measures	Standard Index S&P 500	Best Fit Index Mstar Mid Core
Alpha	6.7	1.2
Beta	0.52	0.58
R-Squared	73	90
Standard Deviation	9.95	
Mean	9.53	
Sharpe Ratio	0.83	

Portfolio Analysis 10-31-04

Share change since 09-04 Total Stocks:51	Sector	PE	YTD Ret%	% Assets
⊖ Ball	Goods	20.9	49.08	6.53
Tyco International	Ind Mtrls	25.1	35.41	6.41
L-3 Communications Holdi	Hardware	20.6	43.54	5.31
Valeant Pharmaceuticals	Health	—	6.22	4.86
Storage Technology	Hardware	20.8	22.76	4.40
Manor Care	Health	19.1	4.21	4.15
Packaging Corporation of	Goods	74.7	10.60	3.62
Dean Foods	Goods	19.5	0.24	3.53
Shire Pharmaceuticals Gr	Health	21.3	10.17	3.02
NII Holdings	Telecom	7.4	90.74	2.90
Alliant Techsystems	Ind Mtrls	16.7	13.19	2.86
Hasbro	Goods	19.3	-7.90	2.52
Del Monte Foods	Goods	15.3	5.96	2.28
⊕ MedImmune	Health	—	6.82	2.24
Western Wireless A	Telecom	—	59.59	2.24
Celera Genomics Group	Health	—	-1.15	2.13
Guidant	Health	35.0	20.55	2.07
American Standard Compan	Business	18.2	23.10	1.87
Autoliv	Ind Mtrls	16.9	30.63	1.85
Pentair	Business	24.0	93.44	1.82

Current Investment Style

Value Blnd Growth / Large Mid Small

Market Cap	%
Giant	6.4
Large	8.2
Mid	78.8
Small	5.6
Micro	1.0
Avg $mil: 4,501	

Value Measures		Rel Category
Price/Earnings	18.20	1.08
Price/Book	2.44	1.12
Price/Sales	1.06	1.00
Price/Cash Flow	4.55	0.73
Dividend Yield %	0.43	0.43

Growth Measures	%	Rel Category
Long-Term Erngs	12.70	1.01
Book Value	8.89	1.26
Sales	5.54	0.98
Cash Flow	15.69	2.09
Historical Erngs	10.94	0.97

Profitability	%	Rel Category
Return on Equity	15.89	1.15
Return on Assets	6.14	0.94
Net Margin	6.02	0.66

Sector Weightings	% of Stocks	Rel S&P 500	3 Year High	3 Year Low
Info	16.12	0.75		
Software	0.00	0.00	2	0
Hardware	9.74	0.95	11	8
Media	0.00	0.00	1	0
Telecom	6.38	2.03	6	0
Service	43.71	0.94		
Health	32.29	2.58	42	28
Consumer	6.26	0.69	12	5
Business	5.16	1.27	16	3
Financial	0.00	0.00	7	0
Mfg	40.17	1.25		
Goods	22.82	2.45	26	8
Ind Mtrls	16.12	1.27	19	12
Energy	0.19	0.03	6	0
Utilities	1.04	0.35	1	0

Composition

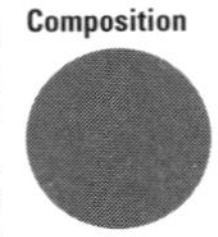

Cash	0.3
Stocks	99.3
Bonds	0.0
Other	0.4
Foreign (% of Stock)	4.5

Morningstar's Take by Dan McNeela 11-01-04

First Eagle Fund of America has a refreshing and profitable ability to take a contrarian view.

This fund doesn't fit easily into any particular style. Its dynamic approach to making money in the stock market involves using a variety of methods to determine a company's intrinsic value. Often an analysis of future cash flows reveals hidden gems, but comanagers Harold Levy and David Cohen also look at a firm's assets--including cash, patents, and licenses--to put a price tag on a company.

The fund often makes its best purchases when it reaches a different conclusion than most investors. At times, that means investing in troubled stocks such as Tyco, which the fund bought in mid-2002 after its well-publicized downfall. But buying when investors underreact to good news has been equally important. The fund's history with can maker Ball dates back to at least 1998. Since that time, the firm has built a dominant position through acquisitions, and the stock has more than tripled.

As a package, the portfolio exhibits a mild-mannered risk profile. As measured by the standard deviation of its returns, the fund has been about half as volatile the mid-blend category average. That's been true despite the fact that Levy and Cohen have owned a slug of risky biotech stocks. Management isn't prone to making big bets on the direction of the economy, so the fund hasn't had big performance swings based on GDP growth or employment statistics.

In 2004, the fund is delivering another solid year. Its 7.6% year-to-date gain through Oct. 29, 2004 ranks in the category's top third. A couple of big gains among beaten-down wireless stocks have given the fund a boost.

In all, there is a lot to like here. Levy and Cohen have proven themselves capable stock-pickers in their more than 15-year stint as comanagers. Given the fund's uniqueness, it makes a fine supporting player for those in search of mid-cap exposure.

Address:	1345 Avenue of the Americas New York NY 10105 800-334-2143
Web Address:	www.firsteaglefunds.com
Inception:	04-10-87
Advisor:	Arnhold and Bleichroeder Advisers, LLC
Subadvisor:	Iridian Asset Management LLC
NTF Plans:	Fidelity Retail-NTF, Schwab OneSource

Minimum Purchase:	$2500	Add: $100	IRA: $1000
Min Auto Inv Plan:	$100	Add: $100	
Sales Fees:	0.25%B, 2.00%R		
Management Fee:	1.00%		
Actual Fees:	Mgt:1.00%	Dist:0.25%	
Expense Projections:	3Yr:$474	5Yr:$818	10Yr:$1791
Income Distrib:	Annually		

First Eagle Glbl A

Analyst Pick	Ticker	Load	NAV	Yield	Total Assets	Mstar Category
✔	SGENX	5.00%	$38.81	1.1%	$10,686 mil	World Allocation

Governance and Management

Fiduciary Grade: A

Portfolio Manager(s)

Jean-Marie Eveillard, who plans to retire in January 2005, has managed the fund since 1979, and Charles de Vaulx, who has worked on it since 1987, became a full comanager in 1999. They rely on seven in-house analysts. Five of these analysts have been on board here for between three and eight years. This management group also makes the calls for siblings First Eagle Overseas, First Eagle Gold, and First Eagle U.S. Value.

Strategy

This fund was one of the first to apply value standards to markets worldwide, and it is still run according to those precepts. Management errs on the side of caution, favoring securities whose assets and cash flows appear undervalued by the market. Broad diversification also helps reduce risk. The fund invests more in stocks and less in bonds than most category rivals. The managers engage in currency hedging; they consider a 50% hedged position against a particular currency to be neutral but often veer far away from that level.

Historical Profile

Return: High
Risk: Average
Rating: ★★★★★ Highest

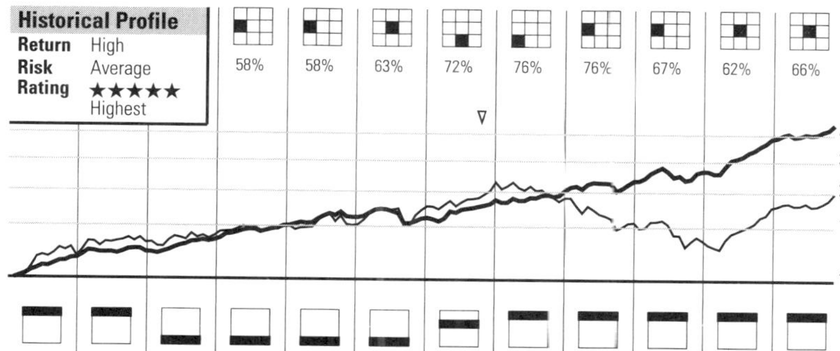

Investment Style: Equity, Stock %

▼ Manager Change
▽ Partial Manager Change

Growth of $10,000
— Investment Values of Fund
— Investment Values of MSCI EAFE

Performance Quartile (within Category)

1993	1994	1995	1996	1997	1998	1999	2000	2001	2002	2003	12-04	History
22.82	22.68	24.58	26.09	25.45	23.03	24.65	22.29	23.82	25.35	33.32	38.81	NAV
26.17	2.53	15.24	13.64	8.54	-0.26	19.56	9.72	10.21	10.23	37.64	18.37	Total Return %
-6.39	-5.25	4.03	7.59	6.76	-20.19	-7.47	23.91	31.63	26.17	-0.95	-1.88	+/-MSCI EAFE
8.91	2.06	-4.56	2.98	-3.36	-12.58	2.23	11.39	13.01	17.00	10.26	5.40	+/-DJ 60%
2.54	0.66	3.58	4.43	5.21	4.20	4.65	5.64	2.83	2.06	2.66	1.29	Income Return %
23.63	1.87	11.66	9.21	3.33	-4.46	14.91	4.08	7.38	8.17	34.98	17.08	Capital Return %
1	1	83	91	94	89	40	10	5	7	5	6	Total Rtn % Rank Cat
0.47	0.15	0.81	1.09	1.36	1.07	1.07	1.39	0.63	0.49	0.68	0.43	Income $
0.23	0.56	0.73	0.74	1.47	1.35	1.73	3.19	0.09	0.40	0.85	0.18	Capital Gains $
1.31	1.28	1.26	1.25	1.21	1.19	1.23	1.32	1.40	1.34	1.32	1.24	Expense Ratio %
3.69	2.34	2.70	3.71	3.08	2.80	2.75	2.68	2.20	2.14	1.91	1.46	Income Ratio %
18	24	13	10	13	21	10	12	29	20	7	5	Turnover Rate %
1,427	1,823	2,613	3,777	3,998	2,634	1,905	1,651	1,611	1,976	3,738	7,171	Net Assets $mil

Performance 12-31-04

	1st Qtr	2nd Qtr	3rd Qtr	4th Qtr	Total
2000	1.62	0.72	2.93	4.15	9.72
2001	1.79	6.13	-7.64	10.45	10.21
2002	8.02	1.79	-8.17	9.18	10.23
2003	-2.13	15.72	8.46	12.05	37.64
2004	5.46	-0.43	2.57	9.89	18.37

Trailing	Total Return%	+/- MSCI EAFE	+/- DJ 60%	%Rank Cat	Growth of $10,000
3 Mo	9.89	-5.43	1.04	55	10,989
6 Mo	12.72	-2.28	2.94	46	11,272
1 Yr	18.37	-1.88	5.40	6	11,837
3 Yr Avg	21.55	9.66	11.26	4	17,958
5 Yr Avg	16.78	17.91	11.68	5	21,719
10 Yr Avg	13.92	8.30	4.29	1	36,813
15 Yr Avg	12.70	8.47	3.28	1	60,098

Tax Analysis	Tax-Adj Rtn%	%Rank Cat	Tax-Cost Rat	%Rank Cat
3 Yr (estimated)	18.41	7	0.90	46
5 Yr (estimated)	13.55	5	1.76	79
10 Yr (estimated)	10.84	1	2.21	64

Potential Capital Gain Exposure: 22% of assets

Rating and Risk

Time Period	Load-Adj Return %	Morningstar Rtn vs Cat	Morningstar Risk vs Cat	Morningstar Risk-Adj Rating
1 Yr	12.45			
3 Yr	19.49	High	+Avg	★★★★★
5 Yr	15.59	High	Avg	★★★★★
10 Yr	13.34	High	Avg	★★★★★
Incept	12.76			

Other Measures	Standard Index S&P 500	Best Fit Index Mstar Mid Value
Alpha	13.3	10.4
Beta	0.56	0.64
R-Squared	78	86

Standard Deviation	11.89
Mean	21.55
Sharpe Ratio	1.72

Portfolio Analysis 10-31-04

Total Stocks:171 Share change since 09-30-04	Sectors	P/E Ratio	YTD Return %	% Net Assets
Rayonier	Ind Mtrls	15.2	-5.75	2.07
⊕ Shimano	Ind Mtrls	—	—	1.65
⊕ Costco Wholesale	Consumer	25.6	-2.25	1.53
Wendel Investissement	Ind Mtrls	—	—	1.39
⊕ Kuehne & Nagel Int'l	Business	—	—	1.38
Corporacion Financiera Al	Financial	—	—	1.31
Liberty Media	Media	—	-4.10	1.25
Nestle	Goods	—	—	1.23
Pargesa Holding	Financial	—	—	1.16

Total Fixed-Income:52	Date of Maturity	Amount $000	Value $000	% Net Assets
US Treasury Note 3%	07-15-12	93,800	105,041	1.28
Singapore (Republic Of) 2	10-01-07	75,000	46,181	0.56
US Treasury Note 4.25%	01-15-10	36,042	42,256	0.51
Emi Grp FRN	05-20-08	15,000	29,790	0.36
Malaysia	02-27-09	105,000	28,074	0.34
Hong Kong Monetary Author	12-17-07	175,000	23,659	0.29
Tyco Intl Grp S A 6.75%	02-15-11	20,500	23,216	0.28
Lucent Tech 7.25%	07-15-06	20,000	21,300	0.26

Current Investment Style

Value Blnd Growth / Large Mid Small

Market Cap	%
Giant	11.4
Large	24.6
Mid	49.8
Small	11.1
Micro	3.0

Avg $mil: 4,244

Value Measures		Rel Category
Price/Earnings	17.82	1.28
Price/Book	1.58	0.83
Price/Sales	1.04	0.97
Price/Cash Flow	3.79	1.57
Dividend Yield %	1.61	0.56

Growth Measures	%	Rel Category
Long-Term Erngs	12.02	1.17
Book Value	3.62	1.37
Sales	0.60	0.15
Cash Flow	2.23	0.43
Historical Erngs	0.08	0.01

Sector Weightings	% of Stocks	Rel MSCI EAFE	3 Year High	3 Year Low
Info	8.96	0.54		
Software	1.12	1.04	3	0
Hardware	0.27	0.07	3	0
Media	7.57	3.32	8	2
Telecom	0.00	0.00	3	0
Service	34.79	0.78		
Health	4.78	0.66	7	3
Consumer	10.71	2.13	15	9
Business	8.96	1.65	12	7
Financial	10.34	0.38	13	6
Mfg	56.25	1.45		
Goods	17.96	1.31	18	12
Ind Mtrls	32.10	2.61	45	31
Energy	6.19	0.84	8	2
Utilities	0.00	0.00	1	0

Regional Exposure	% Stock		
UK/W. Europe	37	N. America	38
Japan	16	Latn America	1
Asia X Japan	6	Other	2

Composition			
Cash	18.1	Bonds	7.9
Stocks	66.1	Other	7.9
Foreign (% of Stock)			64.8

Country Exposure	% Stock		
United States	35	Switzerland	8
Japan	16	U.K.	5
France	12		

Morningstar's Take by Gregg Wolper 12-23-04

First Eagle Global's superb 2004 ranking may be a bit misleading, but its great long-term record is not.

For the year to date though Dec. 22, 2004, this fund has a 16.9% gain that's near the world-allocation category's top. Comanager Charles de Vaulx says a variety of factors explain the nice result. Several holdings have benefited from takeover bids, including eyeglass-lens maker Sola. Energy stocks such as EnCana and Burlington Resources have soared as a result of rising oil and gas prices. And though Japan's market has lagged, De Vaulx says small-value stocks there--which is what this fund owns--have been strong.

But the fund's lofty ranking must be put into context. Small-value stocks have outperformed almost everywhere in 2004, and few other world-allocation funds specialize in that area. Note that sibling First Eagle Overseas, run by the same managers and featuring essentially the foreign slice of this portfolio, is lagging two thirds of its rivals this year even though it has a higher absolute return (19.5%) than this fund. That's because Morningstar divides foreign-only funds by style and First Eagle Overseas is in the small/mid-value group, where its large cash stake and partial currency hedge held it back. Global has the same traits, so if its category included many more similar rivals, it likely wouldn't be near the top this year.

However, the fund's long history proves it can ably and consistently capture solid returns without excessive volatility--and the long-term success of First Eagle Overseas shows that this is no quirk of category placement. The managers' strict value approach and willingness to wait years for results typically pay off. And it's likely to continue doing so even after longtime lead manager Jean-Marie Eveillard retires at the end of this year. Though Eveillard will be missed, De Vaulx and the analyst team have ample experience in their own right, and a firm commitment to the fund's unusual style.

Address:	1345 Avenue of the Americas New York NY 10105 800-334-2143
Web Address:	www.firsteaglefunds.com
Inception:	04-28-70
Advisor:	Arnhold and Bleichroeder Advisers, LLC
Subadvisor:	None
NTF Plans:	DATALynx NTF, Federated Tr NTF

Minimum Purchase:	$2500	Add: $100	IRA: $1000
Min Auto Inv Plan:	$100	Add: $100	
Sales Fees:	5.00%L, 2.00%R		
Management Fee:	0.75%		
Actual Fees:	Mgt:0.75%	Dist:0.25%	
Expense Projections:	3Yr:$897	5Yr:$1187	10Yr:$2011
Income Distrib:	Annually		

First Eagle Overseas A

Ticker	Load	NAV	Yield	Total Assets	Mstar Category
SGOVX	Closed	$21.77	1.1%	$7,631 mil	Foreign Small/Mid Value

Governance and Management

Fiduciary Grade: A

Portfolio Manager(s)

Jean-Marie Eveillard and Charles de Vaulx rely on six or seven experienced in-house analysts. Eveillard has been lead manager since its 1993 inception while de Vaulx has also been working on it since then and was named comanager in 1999. That group also makes the calls for siblings First Eagle Global, First Eagle Gold, and First Eagle U.S. Value. Eveillard plans to retire in January 2005.

Strategy

This fund seeks small- and mid-cap firms that management thinks are cheap relative to the value of their underlying assets or cash flows and have strong positions in their industry. Management also typically owns some bonds and gold-related assets and isn't afraid to have rather high cash stakes. To combat market-timers, there is a 2% redemption fee on investments held fewer than 90 days and investments from those identified as short-term market-timers are rejected. It typically hedges some of its currency exposure; a 50% hedged stance is considered neutral, but it often goes above or below that.

Historical Profile

Return High
Risk Low
Rating ★★★★★ Highest

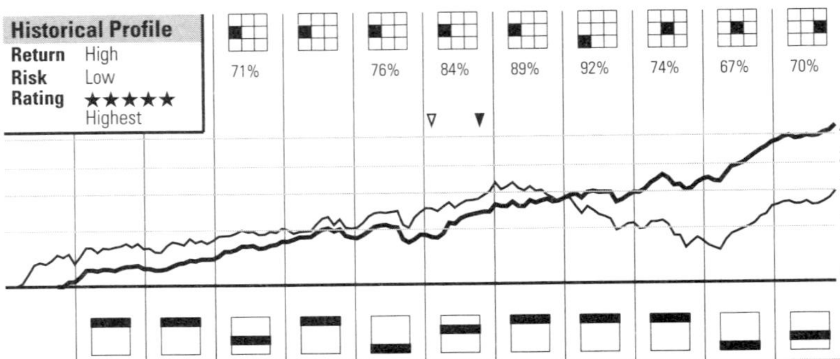

Investment Style
Equity
Stock %

▼ Manager Change
▽ Partial Manager Change

Growth of $10,000
▬ Investment Values of Fund
— Investment Values of MSCI EAFE

Performance Quartile (within Category)

1993	1994	1995	1996	1997	1998	1999	2000	2001	2002	2003	12-04	History
10.92	11.70	12.46	13.28	12.15	11.19	14.06	11.41	12.02	13.30	18.17	21.77	NAV
9.20*	7.79	11.79	14.53	3.02	2.53	33.19	5.68	5.35	12.53	41.41	21.83	Total Return %
—	0.01	0.58	8.48	1.24	-17.40	6.16	19.87	26.77	28.47	2.82	1.58	+/-MSCI EAFE
—	0.44	0.38	7.66	0.75	-16.16	5.21	19.04	26.74	28.33	1.99	1.45	+/-MSCI Wd xUS
0.00	0.48	3.74	4.82	6.21	4.67	1.56	5.41	0.00	1.75	3.57	1.32	Income Return %
—	7.31	8.05	9.71	-3.19	-2.14	31.63	0.27	5.35	10.78	37.84	20.51	Capital Return %
—	1	1	70	15	89	35	8	7	3	95	57	Total Rtn % Rank Cat
0.00	0.05	0.44	0.60	0.83	0.57	0.18	0.76	0.00	0.21	0.48	0.24	Income $
0.00	0.02	0.17	0.38	0.69	0.77	0.64	2.64	0.00	0.01	0.14	0.11	Capital Gains $
—	1.72	1.40	1.37	1.27	1.22	1.29	1.34	1.50	1.39	1.31	1.25	Expense Ratio %
—	-0.23	2.29	3.31	2.28	2.20	2.22	2.10	0.90	0.96	1.23	0.90	Income Ratio %
—	—	3	9	15	22	9	17	17	11	3	6	Turnover Rate %
36	438	543	850	964	593	484	388	450	912	2,944	4,267	Net Assets $mil

Performance 12-31-04

	1st Qtr	2nd Qtr	3rd Qtr	4th Qtr	Total
2000	2.49	1.11	1.24	0.73	5.68
2001	0.09	5.43	-8.89	9.57	5.35
2002	9.32	4.26	-10.51	10.33	12.53
2003	-1.95	16.64	10.72	11.68	41.41
2004	6.60	-0.15	2.95	11.18	21.83

Trailing	Total Return%	+/- MSCI EAFE	+/- MSCI Wd xUS	%Rank Cat	Growth of $10,000
3 Mo	11.18	-4.14	-3.97	90	11,118
6 Mo	14.46	-0.54	-0.91	54	11,446
1 Yr	21.83	1.58	1.45	57	12,183
3 Yr Avg	24.69	12.80	12.47	24	19,386
5 Yr Avg	16.63	17.76	17.39	8	21,580
10 Yr Avg	14.54	8.92	8.60	1	38,866
15 Yr Avg	—	—	—	—	—

Tax Analysis	Tax-Adj Rtn%	%Rank Cat	Tax-Cost Rat	%Rank Cat
3 Yr (estimated)	21.69	40	0.73	55
5 Yr (estimated)	13.48	8	1.70	91
10 Yr (estimated)	11.59	1	2.08	100

Potential Capital Gain Exposure: 28% of assets

Rating and Risk

Time Period	Load-Adj Return %	Morningstar Rtn vs Cat	Morningstar Risk vs Cat	Morningstar Risk-Adj Rating
1 Yr	15.74			
3 Yr	22.58	Avg	Low	★★★
5 Yr	15.44	High	Low	★★★★★
10 Yr	13.96	High	Low	★★★★★
Incept	13.84			

Other Measures	Standard Index S&P 500	Best Fit Index Mstar Mid Value
Alpha	15.9	13.1
Beta	0.59	0.67
R-Squared	74	79
Standard Deviation	13.18	
Mean	24.69	
Sharpe Ratio	1.79	

Portfolio Analysis 10-31-04

Share change since 09-04 Total Stocks:180	Sector	Country	% Assets
Wendel Investissement	Ind Mtrls	France	1.99
Shimano	Ind Mtrls	Japan	1.93
Corporacion Financiera A	Financial	Spain	1.68
Lindt & Sprungli	Goods	Switzerland	1.67
⊕ Kuehne & Nagel Int'l	Business	Switzerland	1.58
Samsung Electnc	—	Korea	1.58
EnCana	Energy	Canada	1.55
⊕ Pargesa Holding	Financial	Switzerland	1.50
⊕ Ono Pharmaceutical	Health	Japan	1.38
Nestle	Goods	Switzerland	1.36
Essilor Int'l	Goods	France	1.35
⊕ Vivendi Universal	Media	France	1.17
Altadis	Goods	Spain	1.15
Secom	Business	Japan	1.14
Freeport-McMoRan Copper	Ind Mtrls	United States	1.14
Newmont Mining	Ind Mtrls	United States	1.12
Heineken Hldg Nv	Goods	Netherlands	1.10
⊖ Eurazeo	Ind Mtrls	France	1.09
Aggregate Industries	Ind Mtrls	U.K.	1.07
⊕ France (Republic Of) 3.2	—	France	1.04

Current Investment Style

Value Blnd Growth — Large / Mid / Small

Market Cap	%
Giant	9.6
Large	18.1
Mid	48.9
Small	17.8
Micro	5.5
Avg $mil: 2,429	

Value Measures		Rel Category
Price/Earnings	17.35	1.28
Price/Book	1.41	0.87
Price/Sales	1.00	1.49
Price/Cash Flow	8.33	1.62
Dividend Yield %	2.06	0.76

Growth Measures	%	Rel Category
Long-Term Erngs	13.72	1.12
Book Value	2.64	24.00
Sales	-4.35	NMF
Cash Flow	0.48	1.30
Historical Erngs	0.45	0.45

Sector Weightings	% of Stocks	Rel MSCI EAFE	3 Year High	3 Year Low
Info	7.48	0.45		
Software	0.64	0.59	4	0
Hardware	0.78	0.21	2	0
Media	5.83	2.56	6	3
Telecom	0.23	0.02	0	0
Service	31.35	0.70		
Health	3.49	0.48	8	3
Consumer	6.98	1.38	10	6
Business	9.23	1.70	17	9
Financial	11.65	0.43	13	7
Mfg	61.17	1.58		
Goods	22.96	1.68	23	12
Ind Mtrls	34.36	2.79	40	33
Energy	3.67	0.50	5	0
Utilities	0.18	0.03	1	0

Composition			
Cash	15.7	Bonds	4.5
Stocks	70.5	Other	9.3
Foreign (% of Stock)			95.5

Regional Exposure	% Stock		
UK/W. Europe	54	N. America	8
Japan	23	Latn America	1
Asia X Japan	12	Other	2

Country Exposure	% Stock		
Japan	23	U.K.	7
France	17	United States	4
Switzerland	13		

Morningstar's Take by Gregg Wolper 11-27-04

It's understandable if First Eagle Overseas shareholders have concerns, but those concerns are largely uncalled for.

First off, shareholders of this closed fund might raise an eyebrow at its recent rankings. In 2003, the fund landed in the bottom decile of Morningstar's foreign small/mid value category, and for the year to date through Nov. 26, 2004, it lags about two thirds of that group. This year, a large cash stake, weakness in mining shares (despite the rise in gold prices), and a partial currency hedge on the euro and yen (which meant this fund got less of a boost than unhedged rivals from recent foreign-currency strength) have contributed to the below-average showing.

Another concern might be that cash stake, which reached 26% in January 2004 as managers Jean-Marie Eveillard and comanager Charles de Vaulx had trouble finding cheap, compelling opportunities. Finally, there's the fact that Eveillard, who has led sibling First Eagle Global for 25 years and this fund since its 1993 inception, will retire in January 2005.

These issues should not be overstated, though. First, the fine long-term records of this and the Global fund help put a year (or two or three) of subpar rankings into perspective. And look at what this fund did even in these years: A 41% return in 2003 and a 17.4% gain so far this year. Both figures top the MSCI EAFE Index and come after the fund uncannily posted gains throughout the bear market. Meanwhile, its cash stake has fallen sharply and was down to 14.4% in October.

Most crucially, Eveillard's departure should not cause alarm. Though Eveillard's talent and experience will be missed, De Vaulx is a quite capable manager in his own right. He began working on the Global fund in 1987, has taken much responsibility for this portfolio in more recent years, and can rely on an experienced analyst corps. This fund thus should continue to provide a pleasing home.

Address:	1345 Avenue of the Americas New York NY 10105 800-334-2143
Web Address:	www.firsteaglefunds.com
Inception:	08-31-93*
Advisor:	Arnhold and Bleichroeder Advisers, LLC
Subadvisor:	None
NTF Plans:	DATALynx NTF, Federated Tr NTF

Minimum Purchase:	Closed	Add: —	IRA: —
Min Auto Inv Plan:	Closed	Add: —	
Sales Fees:	5.00%L, 2.00%R		
Management Fee:	0.75%		
Actual Fees:	Mgt:0.75%	Dist:0.25%	
Expense Projections:	3Yr:$894	5Yr:$1182	10Yr:$2000
Income Distrib:	Annually		

FMI Focus

Ticker	Load	NAV	Yield	Total Assets	Mstar Category
FMIOX	None	$34.75	0.0%	$1,156 mil	Small Blend

Governance and Management

Fiduciary Grade: B

Portfolio Manager(s)

Lead manager Richard Lane has been with the fund since its inception in December 1996 and was named a portfolio manager in October 1997. He covers the media, financial-services, and manufacturing sectors. Comanager Glenn Primack joined in May 2001 and looks for values among technology and telecom stocks. In addition, the managers are supported by a staff of four analysts.

Strategy

The fund's managers have broad leeway in their stock selection. They look for small- and mid-cap names that trade for less than their calculations of private market value and that have strong market positions in their industries. The stocks must also have imminent catalysts for improved earnings growth. The managers will load up on individual positions and sectors.

Historical Profile

Return Below Avg
Risk High
Rating ★★ Below Avg

Investment Style Equity Stock %

1997	1998	1999	2000	2001	2002	2003	12-04
100%	100%	100%	80%	87%	89%	91%	84%

▼ Manager Change
∇ Partial Manager Change

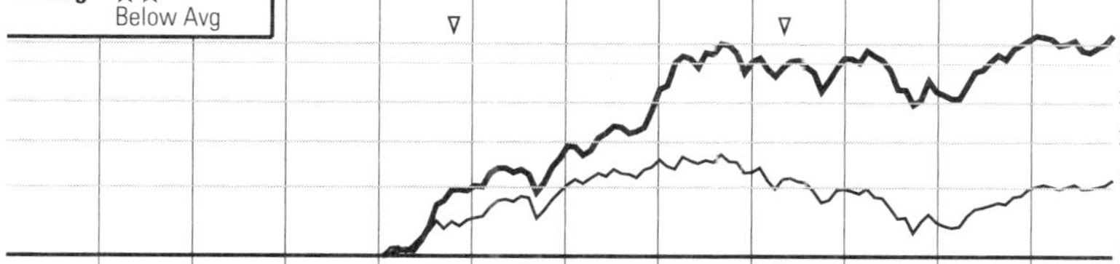

Growth of $10,000
— Investment Values of Fund
— Investment Values of S&P 500

Performance Quartile (within Category)

1993	1994	1995	1996	1997	1998	1999	2000	2001	2002	2003	12-04	History
—	—	—	10.23	14.77	19.26	26.12	28.81	29.54	22.97	34.02	34.75	NAV
—	—	—	2.45*	69.74	35.46	54.11	23.41	2.53	-22.24	48.11	7.05	Total Return %
—	—	—	—	36.39	6.89	33.07	32.51	14.41	-0.15	19.44	-3.82	+/-S&P 500
—	—	—	—	47.38	38.01	32.85	26.43	0.04	-1.76	0.86	-11.28	+/-Russ 2000
—	—	—	—	0.00	0.00	0.00	0.11	0.00	0.00	0.00	0.00	Income Return %
—	—	—	—	69.74	35.46	54.11	23.30	2.53	-22.24	48.11	7.05	Capital Return %
—	—	—	—	1	1	1	18	76	85	24	99	Total Rtn % Rank Cat
—	—	—	0.02	0.00	0.00	0.00	0.03	0.00	0.00	0.00	0.00	Income $
—	—	—	0.00	2.38	0.62	2.53	3.50	0.00	0.00	0.00	1.55	Capital Gains $
—	—	—	—	2.75	2.34	1.81	1.59	1.46	1.46	1.47	1.43	Expense Ratio %
—	—	—	—	-1.85	-1.94	-1.28	0.20	-0.60	-0.60	-0.71	-0.87	Income Ratio %
—	—	—	—	—	402	239	199	165	93	53	64	Turnover Rate %
—	—	—	—	9	29	53	268	295	599	1,229	1,156	Net Assets $mil

Performance 12-31-04

	1st Qtr	2nd Qtr	3rd Qtr	4th Qtr	Total
2000	28.60	2.65	5.66	-11.52	23.41
2001	-10.48	12.91	-20.91	28.27	2.53
2002	6.03	-13.70	-23.01	10.38	-22.24
2003	-5.01	24.24	8.26	15.91	48.11
2004	1.06	-1.37	-5.22	13.31	7.05

Trailing	Total Return%	+/- S&P 500	+/- Russ 2000	%Rank Cat	Growth of $10,000
3 Mo	13.31	4.08	-0.78	38	11,331
6 Mo	7.40	0.21	-3.43	90	10,740
1 Yr	7.05	-3.82	-11.28	99	10,705
3 Yr Avg	7.23	3.65	-4.25	90	12,330
5 Yr Avg	9.30	11.60	2.69	68	15,599
10 Yr Avg	—	—	—	—	—
15 Yr Avg	—	—	—	—	—

Tax Analysis	Tax-Adj Rtn%	%Rank Cat	Tax-Cost Rat	%Rank Cat
3 Yr (estimated)	6.96	89	0.25	18
5 Yr (estimated)	8.38	67	0.84	38
10 Yr (estimated)	—	—	—	—

Potential Capital Gain Exposure: 20% of assets

Rating and Risk

Time Period	Load-Adj Return %	Morningstar Rtn vs Cat	Morningstar Risk vs Cat	Morningstar Risk-Adj Rating
1 Yr	7.05			
3 Yr	7.23	-Avg	High	★
5 Yr	9.30	-Avg	High	★★
10 Yr	—	—	—	—
Incept	24.07			

Other Measures	Standard Index S&P 500	Best Fit Index Wil 4500
Alpha	3.8	-6.5
Beta	1.27	1.31
R-Squared	78	92
Standard Deviation	23.49	
Mean	7.23	
Sharpe Ratio	0.25	

Portfolio Analysis 09-30-04

Share change since 06-04 Total Stocks:101	Sector	PE	YTD Ret%	% Assets
iShares S&P SmallCap 600	—	—	—	4.09
Noble Energy	Energy	14.7	39.34	2.39
⊕ Manpower	Business	18.2	3.24	2.24
⊕ Pride International	Energy	—	10.19	2.20
⊖ Reinsurance Group of Ame	Financial	11.5	26.18	2.20
⊖ Ingram Micro	Hardware	15.8	30.82	2.10
⊕ Unova	Ind Mtrls	—	10.20	1.84
Airgas	Ind Mtrls	21.8	24.36	1.81
⊖ Polo Ralph Lauren	Goods	20.3	48.73	1.63
⊕ Kennametal	Ind Mtrls	19.9	27.17	1.59
⊖ Casella Waste Systems	Business	—	6.94	1.56
⊕ Proquest	Business	15.7	0.85	1.55
Republic Services A	Business	21.8	32.45	1.54
Kadant	Ind Mtrls	36.1	-5.31	1.50
⊕ Aspen Technology	Software	—	-39.47	1.38
⊕ W.W. Grainger	Business	22.0	42.69	1.36
⊕ Keane	Business	30.3	0.41	1.34
☼ Packaging Corporation of	Goods	74.7	10.60	1.32
⊖ PartnerRe	Financial	—	9.36	1.32
Smurfit-Stone Container	Ind Mtrls	—	0.59	1.26

Current Investment Style

Value Blnd Growth — Large Mid Small

Market Cap	%
Giant	0.0
Large	2.0
Mid	48.1
Small	36.2
Micro	13.6
Avg $mil:	1,387

Value Measures		Rel Category
Price/Earnings	20.03	1.16
Price/Book	1.81	0.91
Price/Sales	0.78	0.82
Price/Cash Flow	7.37	1.26
Dividend Yield %	0.44	0.53

Growth Measures	%	Rel Category
Long-Term Erngs	3.68	1.01
Book Value	2.79	0.49
Sales	1.41	0.33
Cash Flow	-4.54	NMF
Historical Erngs	9.37	1.25

Profitability	%	Rel Category
Return on Equity	5.67	0.54
Return on Assets	3.10	0.63
Net Margin	3.84	0.53

Sector Weightings	% of Stocks	Rel S&P 500	3 Year High	3 Year Low
Info	26.49	1.23		
Software	5.34	1.24	17	5
Hardware	14.34	1.41	23	9
Media	4.44	1.16	11	4
Telecom	2.37	0.75	2	0
Service	36.42	0.79		
Health	6.65	0.53	7	3
Consumer	5.39	0.59	11	4
Business	17.72	4.38	18	9
Financial	6.66	0.32	15	7
Mfg	37.09	1.15		
Goods	4.55	0.49	12	3
Ind Mtrls	22.20	1.75	25	16
Energy	10.17	1.42	10	2
Utilities	0.17	0.06	0	0

Composition

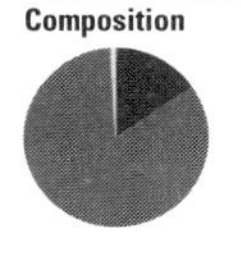

Cash	15.1
Stocks	83.9
Bonds	0.0
Other	1.0
Foreign (% of Stock)	2.8

Morningstar's Take by Kerry O'Boyle 12-01-04

This fund has lost a bit of its luster.

FMI Focus has taken investors on a roller-coaster ride the past few years. Despite posting a stunning 48% return in 2003, the fund lands in the bottom decile of the small-blend category for the trailing three-year period through Nov. 29, 2004.

The fund is again disappointing in 2004. Its 4% return for the year to date trails its typical peer by more than 10 percentage points. The fund has suffered from its large stakes in media and technology stocks. Manager Rick Lane added heavily to both groups in 2002--which boosted returns in 2003--but held on too long. Software-maker Aspen Technology and storage provider Emulex have been among the hardest-hit holdings, with both falling more than 40% so far this year.

While the fund's value-oriented, catalyst-driven, stock-picking approach has garnered success in the past, the recent rough spell is troubling. Lane's decision not to trim media and tech holdings that had reached his price targets in January 2004 was based on rosy political and economic themes--and a fear of building up too much cash. The fund has carried a double-digit cash stake all year (and roughly 4% of assets in a small-cap exchange-traded fund) because Lane has had a tough time finding new opportunities. But such top-down calls don't play to his stock-picking strengths, and the cash worries suggest that the fund might be suffering from growing pains. Assets have quadrupled since 2000, which corresponds with the fund's dry spell, and Lane says that more holdings and less turnover (not traits of the fund during its early years) are natural consequences of those increased assets.

Given Lane's proven stock-picking ability, current shareholders have reason to hang on, but new investors should steer clear until there's evidence that the fund has a handle on its asset bloat. We'd also like to see the fund's management fee come down given the surge in assets.

Address:	225 East Mason Street Milwaukee WI 53202 800-811-5311
Web Address:	www.fiduciarymgt.com
Inception:	12-16-96*
Advisor:	Fiduciary Management, Inc.
Subadvisor:	Broadview Advisors, LLC
NTF Plans:	N/A

Minimum Purchase:	$1000	Add: $100	IRA: $1000
Min Auto Inv Plan:	$1000	Add: $50	
Sales Fees:	No-load		
Management Fee:	1.25%, 0.20%A		
Actual Fees:	Mgt:1.25%	Dist:	
Expense Projections:	3Yr:$465	5Yr:$803	10Yr:$1757
Income Distrib:	Annually		

Forward Hoover Sm-Cp Eq

Ticker	Load	NAV	Yield	Total Assets	Mstar Category
FFSCX	12b-1 only	$18.45	0.0%	$192 mil	Small Growth

Governance and Management

Fiduciary Grade: C

Portfolio Manager(s)

Manager Irene Hoover has headed this offering since its 1998 inception, and shown resilience in down markets. She had a stunning three-year run at her previous charge, Jurika & Voyles Small-Cap Fund.

Strategy

Irene Hoover looks for growth companies trading at realistic price multiples. She looks at various valuation metrics, preferring a stock's P/E ratio to be less than two thirds of her estimate of the firm's earnings-growth rate. She also looks for catalysts, such as societal themes, management changes, or spinoffs, that are likely to produce higher growth rates.

Historical Profile

Return Above Avg
Risk Below Avg
Rating ★★★★★ Highest

Investment Style Equity Stock %: 100% 100% 100% 100% 100% 100%

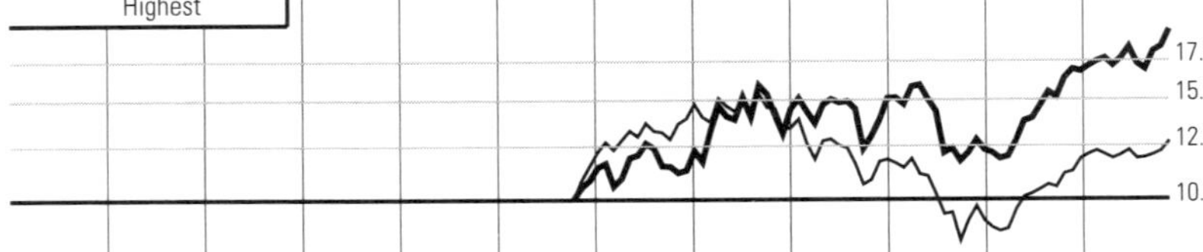

▼ Manager Change
▽ Partial Manager Change

Growth of $10,000
— Investment Values of Fund
— Investment Values of S&P 500

Performance Quartile (within Category)

1993	1994	1995	1996	1997	1998	1999	2000	2001	2002	2003	12-04	History
—	—	—	—	—	11.39	12.19	14.26	14.78	12.05	16.17	18.45	NAV
—	—	—	—	—	13.99*	7.03	17.88	4.27	-18.47	36.49	22.77	Total Return %
—	—	—	—	—	—	-14.01	26.98	16.15	3.62	7.82	11.90	+/-S&P 500
—	—	—	—	—	—	-36.06	40.31	13.50	11.79	-12.05	8.46	+/-Russ 2000 Gr
—	—	—	—	—	0.00	0.01	0.00	0.00	0.00	0.00	0.00	Income Return %
—	—	—	—	—	—	7.02	17.88	4.27	-18.47	36.49	22.77	Capital Return %
—	—	—	—	—	—	92	8	19	12	82	7	Total Rtn % Rank Cat
—	—	—	—	—	0.01	0.00	0.00	0.00	0.00	0.00	0.00	Income $
—	—	—	—	—	0.00	0.00	0.11	0.09	0.00	0.28	1.41	Capital Gains $
—	—	—	—	—	1.45	1.45	1.64	1.65	1.85	1.83	—	Expense Ratio %
—	—	—	—	—	0.21	-0.54	-1.06	-1.04	-1.34	-1.28	—	Income Ratio %
—	—	—	—	—	23	134	183	140	147	190	—	Turnover Rate %
—	—	—	—	—	30	47	97	116	92	128	187	Net Assets $mil

Performance 12-31-04

	1st Qtr	2nd Qtr	3rd Qtr	4th Qtr	Total
2000	19.36	3.57	1.26	-5.84	17.88
2001	-5.47	8.53	-16.75	22.07	4.27
2002	4.74	-9.30	-17.88	4.51	-18.47
2003	-2.57	16.35	8.71	10.75	36.49
2004	5.32	4.52	-1.69	13.44	22.77

Trailing	Total Return%	+/- S&P 500	+/- Russ 2000 Gr	%Rank Cat	Growth of $10,000
3 Mo	13.44	4.21	-1.64	59	11,344
6 Mo	11.53	4.34	3.37	16	11,153
1 Yr	22.77	11.90	8.46	7	12,277
3 Yr Avg	10.96	7.38	5.17	14	13,662
5 Yr Avg	10.92	13.22	14.49	8	16,790
10 Yr Avg	—	—	—	—	—
15 Yr Avg	—	—	—	—	—

Tax Analysis	Tax-Adj Rtn%	%Rank Cat	Tax-Cost Rat	%Rank Cat
3 Yr (estimated)	10.47	11	0.44	36
5 Yr (estimated)	10.57	6	0.32	15
10 Yr (estimated)	—	—	—	—

Potential Capital Gain Exposure: 26% of assets

Rating and Risk

Time Period	Load-Adj Return %	Morningstar Rtn vs Cat	Morningstar Risk vs Cat	Morningstar Risk-Adj Rating
1 Yr	22.77			
3 Yr	10.96	+Avg	-Avg	★★★★
5 Yr	10.92	+Avg	-Avg	★★★★★
10 Yr	—	—	—	—
Incept	12.15			

Other Measures	Standard Index S&P 500	Best Fit Index Russ 2000
Alpha	8.0	0.8
Beta	0.87	0.86
R-Squared	58	93
Standard Deviation	18.94	
Mean	10.96	
Sharpe Ratio	0.51	

Portfolio Analysis 11-30-04

Share change since 10-04 Total Stocks:104	Sector	PE	YTD Ret%	% Assets
⊖ Southwestern Energy	Energy	19.7	112.09	1.80
⊕ eFunds	Business	27.0	38.39	1.75
⊕ Foundry Networks	Hardware	27.8	-51.85	1.52
⊕ Tetra Technologies	Energy	36.7	16.75	1.45
Cree	Hardware	33.7	126.57	1.42
⊕ Micros Systems	Software	35.4	80.03	1.39
Peabody Energy	Energy	35.4	96.04	1.38
⊕ Montpelier Re Holdings	Financial	6.2	8.68	1.34
⊕ IMAX	Goods	—	4.29	1.31
⊕ Avocent	Hardware	NMF	11.20	1.29
☼ AGCO	Ind Mtrls	12.1	8.69	1.26
Lifepoint Hospitals	Health	16.1	18.23	1.17
Molina Healthcare	Health	—	83.83	1.15
☼ Digital Insight	Business	12.3	-26.08	1.14
Stratasys	Software	44.3	24.07	1.14
P.F. Chang's China Bistr	Consumer	62.4	10.75	1.12
☼ Titan International	Ind Mtrls	69.0	394.60	1.11
⊖ Steel Dynamics	Ind Mtrls	8.2	65.85	1.10
Scientific Games	Hardware	27.8	40.48	1.10
Bucyrus International A	Ind Mtrls	—	—	1.09

Current Investment Style

Value Blnd Growth / Large Mid Small

Market Cap	%
Giant	0.0
Large	0.0
Mid	33.5
Small	55.1
Micro	11.4
Avg $mil: 1,063	

Value Measures		Rel Category
Price/Earnings	22.64	1.04
Price/Book	2.62	1.00
Price/Sales	1.38	0.92
Price/Cash Flow	11.71	1.46
Dividend Yield %	0.15	0.48

Growth Measures	%	Rel Category
Long-Term Erngs	16.10	0.93
Book Value	6.29	0.98
Sales	3.70	0.57
Cash Flow	2.42	0.18
Historical Erngs	4.17	0.31

Profitability	%	Rel Category
Return on Equity	10.75	1.09
Return on Assets	6.49	1.48
Net Margin	8.43	1.23

Sector Weightings	% of Stocks	Rel S&P 500	3 Year High	3 Year Low
Info	22.62	1.05		
Software	9.13	2.12	9	0
Hardware	12.76	1.25	16	3
Media	0.73	0.19	2	1
Telecom	0.00	0.00	3	0
Service	50.85	1.10		
Health	5.73	0.46	16	6
Consumer	19.09	2.10	28	15
Business	10.33	2.55	14	5
Financial	15.70	0.76	18	8
Mfg	26.53	0.83		
Goods	3.24	0.35	8	2
Ind Mtrls	10.98	0.87	18	6
Energy	11.28	1.58	16	5
Utilities	1.03	0.35	1	0

Composition

Cash	0.0
Stocks	100.0
Bonds	0.0
Other	0.0
Foreign (% of Stock)	1.3

Morningstar's Take by Andrew Gogerty 12-16-04

If only Forward Hoover Small Cap Equity wasn't so pricey.

Its 19.6% gain through Dec. 13, 2004, places it ahead of 93% of its small-growth rivals. A historical overweight in the energy sector relative to its peers has paid off as rising commodity prices have fueled the sector's strong run. Currently, almost 15% of the fund is invested in energy stocks, compared with the category average of 6%. Manager Irene Hoover still likes natural-gas stocks, believing that an increase in future demand will continue to spur growth here. To be sure, this tack has hurt in years such as 2003, when the biggest gains were posted by speculative issues.

While the energy sector isn't the typical shopping ground for most growth managers, it fits Hoover's style. She prefers reasonably-priced firms with strong cash flows, low debt, and sustainable revenues. This leaves the portfolio underweight in areas such as tech and telecom, as Hoover believes many firms in these industries have less-proven business models, heavy debt, and a short or nonexistent history of positive cash flows. In fact, the fund has just 16% of its assets in these sectors, compared with the group norm of 23%. Although this focus may limit the fund's upside potential during big rallies, it also typically leads to less overall volatility. Still, we like that Hoover doesn't deviate from her strengths by chasing returns in hot sectors of the market, a common trait among the fund's more-aggressive peers.

What concerns us, however, are the fund's high fees. Its expense ratio of 1.83% is more than the 1.65% levy of its typical no-load peer and also higher than fees of fund's with similar assets. Until Forward steps up with a fee reduction, we can't give this fund our full endorsement.

Address:	433 California St. San Francisco CA 94104 800-999-6809
Web Address:	www.forwardfunds.com
Inception:	09-30-98*
Advisor:	Forward Management, LLC
Subadvisor:	Hoover Investment Management Co., LLC
NTF Plans:	Fidelity Retail-NTF, Schwab OneSource

Minimum Purchase:	$2500	Add: $100	IRA: $1000
Min Auto Inv Plan:	$500	Add: $50	
Sales Fees:	0.09%B, 2.00%R		
Management Fee:	1.05%, 0.35%A		
Actual Fees:	Mgt:1.05%	Dist:0.09%	
Expense Projections:	3Yr:$583	5Yr:$1011	10Yr:$2203
Income Distrib:	Annually		

FPA Capital

Ticker	Load	NAV	Yield	Total Assets	Mstar Category
FPPTX	Closed	$39.98	0.0%	$1,700 mil	Small Value

Governance and Management

Fiduciary Grade: B

Portfolio Manager(s)

Bob Rodriguez has been at the helm since the fund's 1984 inception. He is assisted by three analysts. Rodriguez also runs fixed-income offering FPA New Income in the same contrarian style he employs here. He was named Morningstar's Fixed-Income Manager of the Year in 2001 for his efforts at that fund.

Strategy

Manager Bob Rodriguez is a dyed-in-the-wool value investor. He looks for companies that are extremely cheap but that also have clean balance sheets, strong cash flows, and dominant market shares in their industries. When Rodriguez can't find stocks inexpensive enough to clear his strict valuation hurdles, he turns to cash or bonds. He invests without regard to where his picks land in the style box, but most tend to cluster in small- and mid-cap territory. This is a compact portfolio--it typically holds 35 to 40 stocks--and can concentrate picks in a handful of sectors. Rodriguez trades little, but the fund's tax efficiency is poor.

Historical Profile

Return Average
Risk High
Rating ★★ Below Avg

Investment Style: Equity Stock %

1993	1994	1995	1996	1997	1998	1999	2000	2001	2002	2003	12-04
		72%	82%	85%	99%	95%	94%	81%	73%	67%	

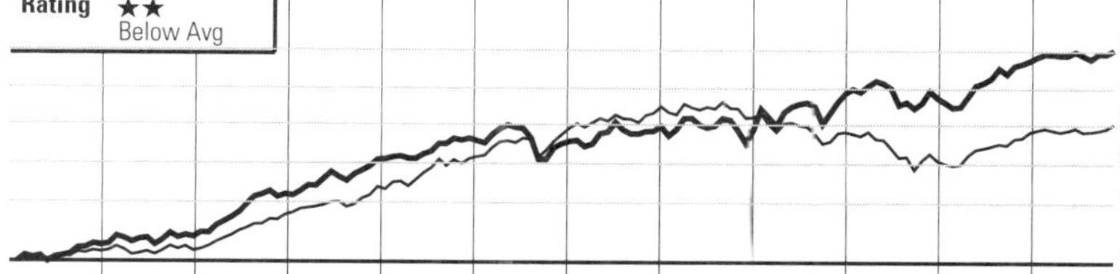

Performance Quartile (within Category)

1993	1994	1995	1996	1997	1998	1999	2000	2001	2002	2003	12-04	History
20.06	20.61	27.50	34.01	36.28	31.04	31.02	22.29	28.26	26.86	36.85	39.98	NAV
16.74	10.37	38.39	37.76	17.70	-0.42	14.24	-3.08	38.13	-3.86	38.54	12.62	Total Return %
6.68	9.06	0.86	14.82	-15.65	-28.99	-6.80	6.02	50.01	18.23	9.87	1.75	+/-S&P 500
-7.03	11.91	12.64	16.39	-14.08	6.03	15.73	-25.91	24.11	7.57	-7.49	-9.63	+/-Russ 2000 VL
0.27	0.21	0.68	1.29	1.27	1.89	0.71	0.49	0.13	0.00	0.07	0.00	Income Return %
16.47	10.16	37.71	36.47	16.43	-2.31	13.53	-3.57	38.00	-3.86	38.47	12.62	Capital Return %
62	1	3	1	98	23	23	95	4	21	63	97	Total Rtn % Rank Cat
0.05	0.04	0.14	0.34	0.42	0.65	0.22	0.14	0.03	0.00	0.02	0.00	Income $
1.70	1.34	0.73	2.60	2.84	4.79	4.03	7.76	2.39	0.33	0.33	1.48	Capital Gains $
1.06	1.03	0.95	0.87	0.84	0.83	0.86	0.86	0.89	0.84	0.87	0.83	Expense Ratio %
0.29	0.20	0.48	1.28	1.27	1.38	1.20	0.35	0.39	0.04	0.00	0.06	Income Ratio %
19	16	11	21	21	24	19	18	5	23	17	20	Turnover Rate %
154	192	353	568	731	674	539	384	552	616	1,128	1,700	Net Assets $mil

Performance 12-31-04

	1st Qtr	2nd Qtr	3rd Qtr	4th Qtr	Total
2000	7.29	-7.87	6.97	-8.34	-3.08
2001	3.23	21.77	-15.96	30.75	38.13
2002	6.72	-2.39	-15.86	9.68	-3.86
2003	-7.45	23.37	7.83	12.52	38.54
2004	5.75	2.39	-1.85	5.97	12.62

Trailing	Total Return%	+/- S&P 500	+/- Russ 2000 VL	%Rank Cat	Growth of $10,000
3 Mo	5.97	-3.26	-7.23	99	10,597
6 Mo	4.01	-3.18	-9.36	98	10,401
1 Yr	12.62	1.75	-9.63	97	11,262
3 Yr Avg	14.47	10.89	-2.03	59	14,999
5 Yr Avg	14.96	17.26	-2.27	63	20,079
10 Yr Avg	17.76	5.69	2.59	6	51,284
15 Yr Avg	17.61	6.68	3.59	1	113,937

Tax Analysis	Tax-Adj Rtn%	%Rank Cat	Tax-Cost Rat	%Rank Cat
3 Yr (estimated)	12.08	68	0.31	19
5 Yr (estimated)	11.58	79	1.89	87
10 Yr (estimated)	14.41	18	2.31	86

Potential Capital Gain Exposure: 26% of assets

Rating and Risk

Time Period	Load-Adj Return %	Morningstar Rtn vs Cat	Morningstar Risk vs Cat	Morningstar Risk-Adj Rating
1 Yr	6.71			
3 Yr	12.43	-Avg	Avg	★★
5 Yr	13.73	-Avg	High	★★
10 Yr	17.12	+Avg	High	★★★
Incept	—			

Other Measures	Standard Index S&P 500	Best Fit Index Russ 2000
Alpha	11.3	4.2
Beta	0.92	0.85
R-Squared	60	83
Standard Deviation	20.49	
Mean	14.47	
Sharpe Ratio	0.65	

Portfolio Analysis 12-31-04

Share change since 09-04 Total Stocks:30	Sector	PE	YTD Ret%	% Assets
⊕ Michaels Stores	Consumer	22.9	36.87	5.02
National Oilwell	Energy	36.9	57.83	4.77
⊕ Ensco International	Energy	51.8	17.23	4.09
Avnet	Business	16.9	-15.79	4.04
⊕ Patterson-UTI Energy	Energy	33.3	18.55	3.89
Reebok International	Goods	15.3	12.83	3.49
Trinity Industries	Ind Mtrls	—	11.40	3.35
⊕ Rowan Companies	Energy	—	11.78	3.14
Big Lots	Consumer	14.9	-14.64	3.07
Ross Stores	Consumer	22.6	9.82	3.03
Charming Shoppes	Consumer	15.1	70.99	2.98
☼ Fifth Third Bancorp 144A	—	—	—	2.94
Foot Locker	Consumer	17.6	15.99	2.55
Arrow Electronics	Hardware	14.5	5.01	2.45
⊖ Hutchinson Technology	Hardware	12.2	12.42	2.10
Zale	Goods	13.1	12.29	2.06
American Greetings	Media	17.1	16.18	2.00
Thor Industries	Ind Mtrls	18.6	32.34	1.83
⊕ Rent-A-Center	Consumer	13.7	-11.67	1.51
Westcorp	Financial	12.4	27.32	1.45

Current Investment Style

Value Blnd Growth / Large Mid Small

Market Cap	%
Giant	0.0
Large	0.0
Mid	72.3
Small	25.5
Micro	2.1

Avg $mil: 2,209

Value Measures		Rel Category
Price/Earnings	13.77	1.18
Price/Book	2.02	1.22
Price/Sales	0.67	0.89
Price/Cash Flow	4.70	0.91
Dividend Yield %	0.27	0.23

Growth Measures	%	Rel Category
Long-Term Erngs	14.41	1.19
Book Value	3.93	0.91
Sales	1.22	0.39
Cash Flow	-21.35	NMF
Historical Erngs	10.06	2.09

Profitability	%	Rel Category
Return on Equity	10.26	1.12
Return on Assets	5.64	1.36
Net Margin	4.96	0.74

Sector Weightings	% of Stocks	Rel S&P 500	3 Year High	3 Year Low
Info	13.94	0.65		
Software	0.00	0.00	0	0
Hardware	8.98	0.88	16	8
Media	3.01	0.78	4	0
Telecom	1.95	0.62	5	1
Service	41.07	0.89		
Health	1.22	0.10	1	0
Consumer	30.21	3.33	33	27
Business	6.07	1.50	8	4
Financial	3.57	0.17	13	4
Mfg	45.00	1.40		
Goods	8.35	0.89	8	3
Ind Mtrls	12.77	1.01	22	12
Energy	23.88	3.34	24	1
Utilities	0.00	0.00	0	0

Composition

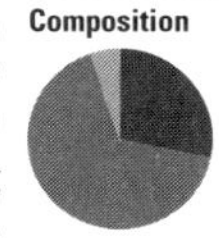

Cash	28.1
Stocks	66.6
Bonds	5.3
Other	0.0
Foreign (% of Stock)	0.0

Morningstar's Take by Christopher Davis 12-01-04

FPA Capital's manager has dimmed his view for the future. Shareholders might want to do the same.

California governor Arnold Schwarzenegger might call FPA Capital Fund manager Bob Rodriguez an economic girly man. While Rodriguez isn't forecasting doom and gloom for the economy, he expects muted returns--around 5% annually--for the equity market in the years ahead. And he points to a litany of risks investors don't fully appreciate, including the specter of rising interest rates, the widening trade deficit, high oil prices, and the potential for a federal cash crunch as baby boomers enter retirement. Given those potential troubles, Rodriguez argues valuations are excessive.

Rather than investing in overpriced stocks, Rodriguez has been content to sit on the sidelines. In fact, the fund's cash and bond holdings currently account for 36% of assets, nearly an all-time high. Rodriguez has broadened beyond small caps in his research efforts to include more mid-caps, including recent addition Rent-A-Center, but that has barely dented the fund's cash hoard.

To be sure, Rodriguez's willingness to load up on cash can subdue returns in rising markets, but it has also helped protect shareholders from suffering excessive losses. The fund has suffered losses in just four of Rodriguez's 19 calendar years at the helm, the largest being a 14% slide in 1990. And, fortunately, he has done just as good a job in creating capital as he has in preserving it. Indeed, the fund's 10-year return is among the mutual fund world's best.

While we don't doubt Rodriguez's ability to deliver superior results over the long haul, the fund's hefty cash stake may portend leaner times in the near term. The difficulty he has had in unearthing new ideas--in tandem with small caps' long-running supremacy over larger names--may suggest that small-cap rally has mostly run its course. It's certainly worth sticking with this closed fund, but keep your expectations in check.

Address:	11400 W Olympic Blvd Ste 1200 Los Angeles CA 90064 800-982-4372
Web Address:	www.FPAFunds.com
Inception:	02-01-68
Advisor:	First Pacific Advisors, Inc.
Subadvisor:	None
NTF Plans:	TD Waterhouse Ins NT

Minimum Purchase:	Closed	Add: —	IRA: —
Min Auto Inv Plan:	Closed	Add: —	
Sales Fees:	5.25%L, 2.00%R		
Management Fee:	0.75% mx./0.65% mn.		
Actual Fees:	Mgt:0.65%	Dist:	
Expense Projections:	3Yr:$776	5Yr:$961	10Yr:$1497
Income Distrib:	Semi-Annually		

FPA Crescent

Ticker	Load	NAV	Yield	Total Assets	Mstar Category
FPACX	None	$23.55	0.3%	$915 mil	Moderate Allocation

Governance and Management

Fiduciary Grade:

Portfolio Manager(s)

Steven Romick has been the lead manager for this fund since its inception in 1993 Prior to working for First Pacific Advisors, Romick was chairman of Crescent Management and a consulting security analyst for Kaplan, Nathan & Co. Since 2000, Romick has been supported by two savvy investment professionals, Dennis Bryan and Rikard Ekstrand.

Strategy

Unlike the majority of its moderate-allocation peers, this fund's equity portfolio is mostly focused on small companies with dirt-cheap valuations. Manager Steven Romick rarely keeps much more than 20% invested on the bond side, and he buys bonds and convertibles issued primarily by deeply undervalued companies. He'll also take short positions in stocks, but does so conservatively and to lower overall portfolio volatility.

Historical Profile

Return: High
Risk: Above Avg
Rating: ★★★★★ Highest

Investment Style
Equity
Stock %

65% | 66% | 66% | 61% | 44% | 46% | 41% | 44%

▼ Manager Change
▽ Partial Manager Change

Growth of $10,000
— Investment Values of Fund
— Investment Values of S&P 500

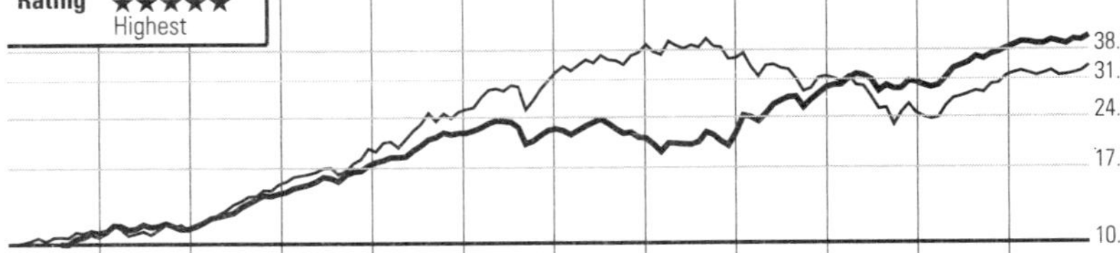

Performance Quartile (within Category)

1993	1994	1995	1996	1997	1998	1999	2000	2001	2002	2003	12-04	History
10.80	10.55	12.03	13.02	15.20	14.82	12.95	12.82	17.19	17.40	21.79	23.55	NAV
9.65*	4.22	26.04	22.88	21.95	2.79	-6.28	3.59	36.14	3.71	26.15	10.21	Total Return %
—	2.91	-11.49	-0.06	-11.40	-25.78	-27.32	12.69	48.02	25.80	-2.52	-0.66	+/-S&P 500
—	6.17	1.27	11.54	2.75	-9.60	-19.13	-0.85	35.98	14.25	2.09	-0.96	+/-DJ 60%
0.00	1.68	3.47	2.93	3.08	3.41	2.49	4.38	1.94	2.52	0.86	0.37	Income Return %
—	2.54	22.57	19.95	18.87	-0.62	-8.77	-0.79	34.20	1.19	25.29	9.84	Capital Return %
—	1	52	4	31	94	96	35	1	2	10	27	Total Rtn % Rank Cat
0.10	0.18	0.37	0.34	0.40	0.51	0.35	0.56	0.25	0.43	0.15	0.08	Income $
0.06	0.52	0.88	1.34	0.26	0.29	0.64	0.00	0.00	0.00	0.00	0.37	Capital Gains $
—	1.85	1.65	1.59	1.57	1.45	1.42	1.49	1.87	1.50	1.54	1.41	Expense Ratio %
—	1.61	2.16	3.35	2.80	3.62	3.67	2.26	2.79	1.73	2.06	0.67	Income Ratio %
—	—	101	100	45	18	36	10	37	34	39	20	Turnover Rate %
10	14	20	37	173	227	84	33	204	209	381	915	Net Assets $mil

Performance 12-31-04

	1st Qtr	2nd Qtr	3rd Qtr	4th Qtr	Total
2000	-3.40	-0.99	6.79	1.42	3.59
2001	8.19	15.04	-4.49	14.52	36.14
2002	6.52	-0.92	-6.07	4.62	3.71
2003	-2.24	14.64	4.73	7.48	26.15
2004	4.36	1.32	0.44	3.77	10.21

Trailing	Total Return%	+/- S&P 500	+/- DJ 60%	%Rank Cat	Growth of $10,000
3 Mo	3.77	-5.46	-3.71	96	10,377
6 Mo	4.23	-2.96	-3.30	89	10,423
1 Yr	10.21	-0.66	-0.96	27	11,021
3 Yr Avg	12.97	9.39	5.71	1	14,417
5 Yr Avg	15.25	17.55	10.01	1	20,333
10 Yr Avg	13.98	1.91	3.49	1	37,007
15 Yr Avg	—	—	—	—	—

Tax Analysis	Tax-Adj Rtn%	%Rank Cat	Tax-Cost Rat	%Rank Cat
3 Yr (estimated)	12.39	1	0.51	35
5 Yr (estimated)	14.35	1	0.78	33
10 Yr (estimated)	12.04	1	1.70	45

Potential Capital Gain Exposure: 11% of assets

Rating and Risk

Time Period	Load-Adj Return %	Morningstar Rtn vs Cat	Morningstar Risk vs Cat	Morningstar Risk-Adj Rating
1 Yr	10.21			
3 Yr	12.97	High	+Avg	★★★★★
5 Yr	15.25	High	+Avg	★★★★★
10 Yr	13.98	High	+Avg	★★★★★
Incept	13.26			

Other Measures	Standard Index S&P 500	Best Fit Index Mstar Small Core
Alpha	10.3	4.1
Beta	0.46	0.52
R-Squared	49	84

Standard Deviation	10.85
Mean	12.97
Sharpe Ratio	1.08

Morningstar's Take by Christopher Davis 01-07-05

FPA Crescent continues to go its own way, and we think it's for the best.

This moderate-allocation offering doesn't fit neatly in its category. While most funds in the group emphasize blue chips, longtime manger Steve Romick favors mid- and small caps. Also, although the fund's average market cap has risen in recent years, it remains far below the category norm. Moreover, most managed-allocation funds tend to maintain consistent equity and fixed-income exposure, but this one has no preset asset mix. The fund's asset allocation can fluctuate widely based on where Romick is finding bargains. Like his FPA counterparts, Romick will let his cash stake climb in the absence of compelling values.

With stocks up sharply from their bear-market lows in 2003, Romick says he found slim pickings in the equity market in 2004. Thus, he has been content to sit on the sidelines, as the fund's giant 50% cash stake attests. Growing exposure to energy-service stocks, which Romick believes will benefit from rising oil and natural-gas prices, and overseas holdings like U.K.-based Countrywide Assured have done little to decrease the fund's cash hoard.

To be sure, Romick's willingness to load up on cash can limit returns in rising markets--witness its bottom-decile showings in 1998 and 1999. But it has also helped protect shareholders from suffering excessive losses. In his 11 plus years at the helm, the fund has suffered just suffered one calendar year loss: a relatively mild 6% drop in 1999. Moreover, Romick has delivered stellar results over time. Indeed, the fund's trailing three-, five-, and 10-year returns rank among the category's best.

This offering won't suit those seeking a typical managed-allocation offering. But we think cautious investors craving small- and mid-cap exposure will find it appealing.

Portfolio Analysis 09-30-04

Total Stocks:35 Share change since 06-30-04	Sectors	P/E Ratio	YTD Return %	% Net Assets
Ensco International	Energy	51.8	-3.81	3.42
Michaels Stores	Consumer	22.9	3.00	2.81
⊕ Tate & Lyle Plc	—	—	—	2.62
⊕ Patterson-UTI Energy	Energy	33.3	-7.66	2.58
National Oilwell	Energy	36.9	-3.83	2.56
⊕ Assurant	Financial	—	—	2.35
Big Lots	Consumer	14.9	-8.16	2.03
⊕ SanDisk	Hardware	15.7	-3.92	2.01
Rowan Companies	Energy	—	-2.05	1.87

Total Fixed-Income:14	Date of Maturity	Amount $000	Value $000	% Net Assets
US Treasury Note 3.375%	01-15-07	10,162	10,860	1.35
Northland Cable Tv 10.25%	11-15-07	5,575	5,631	0.70
US Treasury Note 3.375%	01-15-12	4,800	5,436	0.68
Oregon Stl Mls 10%	07-15-09	4,900	5,341	0.67
Tenet Healthcare 144A 9.8	07-01-14	4,500	4,646	0.58
France Oatei Euro 3% 7/25	07-25-12	3,161	4,354	0.54
Western Finl Bk Irvine Ca	05-15-12	2,950	3,334	0.42
Kmart Fdg 8.8%	07-01-10	1,768	1,211	0.15
Frontiervision Oper Partn	10-15-06	980	1,166	0.15

Equity Style
Style: Blend
Size: Mid-Cap

Value Measures		Rel Category
Price/Earnings	19.64	1.19
Price/Book	2.00	0.82
Price/Sales	0.90	0.68
Price/Cash Flow	7.68	1.06
Dividend Yield %	0.49	0.31

Growth Measures	%	Rel Category
Long-Term Erngs	14.87	1.28
Book Value	5.80	1.01
Sales	3.58	0.69
Cash Flow	6.69	0.84
Historical Erngs	7.81	0.72

Market Cap %			
Giant	0.0	Small	22.9
Large	1.6	Micro	1.2
Mid	74.2	Avg $mil:	2,699

Fixed-Income Style
Duration: —
Quality: —

Avg Eff Duration [1]	—
Avg Eff Maturity	—
Avg Credit Quality	—
Avg Wtd Coupon	—

[1] figure provided by fund

Sector Weightings	% of Stocks	Rel S&P 500	3 Year High	3 Year Low
Info	13.19	0.61		
Software	0.63	0.15	1	0
Hardware	10.59	1.04	11	1
Media	0.00	0.00	0	0
Telecom	1.97	0.63	6	2
Service	41.89	0.90		
Health	0.97	0.08	2	0
Consumer	22.92	2.52	33	23
Business	3.66	0.90	10	4
Financial	14.34	0.69	16	10
Mfg	44.91	1.40		
Goods	4.69	0.50	7	2
Ind Mtrls	5.70	0.45	21	6
Energy	32.91	4.60	34	17
Utilities	1.61	0.54	2	0

Composition

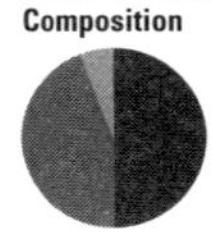

Cash	49.9
Stocks	44.1
Bonds	5.6
Other	0.4
Foreign (% of Stock)	0.0

Address:	11400 W. Olympic Blvd. Los Angeles CA 90064 800-982-4372
Web Address:	
Inception:	06-02-93 *
Advisor:	First Pacific Advisors, Inc.
Subadvisor:	None
NTF Plans:	Fidelity Retail-NTF, Schwab OneSource

Minimum Purchase:	$1500	Add: $100	IRA: $100
Min Auto Inv Plan:	$100	Add: $100	
Sales Fees:	No-load, 2.00%R		
Management Fee:	1.00%, 0.25%A		
Actual Fees:	Mgt:1.00%	Dist:	
Expense Projections:	3Yr:$446	5Yr:$771	10Yr:$1691
Income Distrib:	Semi-Annually		

FPA New Income

Analyst Pick

Ticker	Load	NAV	Yield	SEC Yield	Total Assets	Mstar Category
FPNIX	3.50%	$11.18	3.5%	—	$2,043 mil	Intermediate-Term Bond

Governance and Management

Fiduciary Grade: B

Portfolio Manager(s)

Seasoned and highly decorated. Manager Bob Rodriguez was named Morningstar Fixed-Income Manager of the Year for 2001. He has been at the fund's helm since 1984 and is supported primarily by Tom Atteberry, with whom he shares trading responsibilities. They're assisted by Steven Romick, Steven Geist, and Julian Mann.

Strategy

Unlike many of its intermediate-term bond peers, this fund doesn't pay attention to a broad market index. Instead, management seeks the best values, regardless of sector. That leaves the fund looking less like the norm and more like a contrarian. For example, the fund typically invests more in high yield than most peers, and it has gotten all of its Treasury exposure from inflation-indexed Treasuries since 1998. Management is less willing than many of its peers to take on interest-rate risk, however, especially when yields are low.

Performance 12-31-04

	1st Qtr	2nd Qtr	3rd Qtr	4th Qtr	Total
2000	3.01	-0.67	4.42	2.31	9.32
2001	5.68	1.76	3.23	1.19	12.33
2002	2.93	2.78	-3.00	1.85	4.52
2003	1.10	2.48	2.36	2.14	8.32
2004	0.80	0.80	0.36	0.63	2.60

Trailing	Total Return%	+/- LB Aggr	+/- LB 5-10YR	%Rank Cat	Growth of $10,000
3 Mo	0.63	-0.32	-0.35	77	10,063
6 Mo	0.98	-3.20	-4.59	99	10,098
1 Yr	2.60	-1.74	-2.70	86	10,260
3 Yr Avg	5.12	-1.07	-2.93	65	11,616
5 Yr Avg	7.36	-0.35	-1.71	27	14,263
10 Yr Avg	7.35	-0.37	-1.11	28	20,325
15 Yr Avg	8.17	0.47	-0.15	7	32,479

Tax Analysis	Tax-Adj Rtn%	%Rank Cat	Tax-Cost Rat	%Rank Cat
3 Yr (estimated)	2.29	82	1.53	40
5 Yr (estimated)	4.44	55	2.03	56
10 Yr (estimated)	4.42	50	2.38	72

Potential Capital Gain Exposure: -1% of assets

Historical Profile

Return Average
Risk Low
Rating ★★★ Neutral

Investment Style: Fixed Income — Income Rtn %Rank Cat: 47, 49, 1, 6, 4, 22, 43, 26, 59

▼ Manager Change
▽ Partial Manager Change

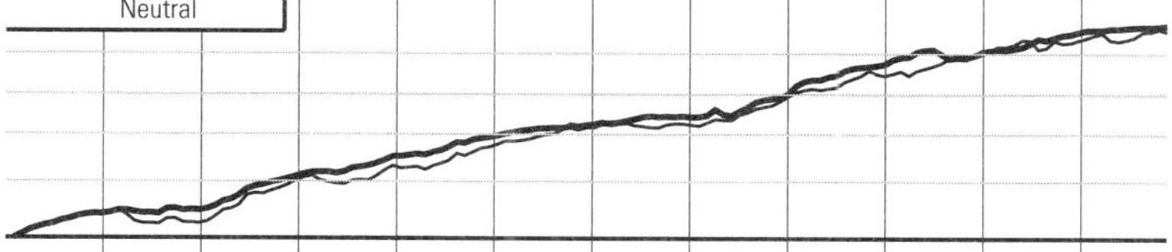

Growth of $10,000
— Investment Values of Fund
— Investment Values of LB Aggr

Performance Quartile (within Category)

1993	1994	1995	1996	1997	1998	1999	2000	2001	2002	2003	12-04	History
11.23	10.40	11.17	11.09	11.24	10.74	10.30	10.38	10.93	10.88	11.28	11.18	NAV
10.17	1.46	14.36	7.12	8.31	3.86	3.39	9.32	12.33	4.52	8.32	2.60	Total Return %
0.42	4.38	-4.11	3.49	-1.34	-4.83	4.21	-2.31	3.89	-5.73	4.22	-1.74	+/-LB Aggr
-2.07	5.97	-7.07	4.43	-1.12	-6.28	6.27	-3.12	3.51	-8.51	2.35	-2.70	+/-LB 5-10YR
6.50	6.60	6.60	6.21	6.30	7.71	6.78	7.69	6.30	5.03	4.56	3.50	Income Return %
3.67	-5.14	7.76	0.91	2.01	-3.85	-3.39	1.63	6.03	-0.51	3.76	-0.90	Capital Return %
56	1	89	2	71	98	2	67	2	94	11	86	Total Rtn % Rank Cat
0.69	0.71	0.67	0.67	0.68	0.84	0.71	0.77	0.64	0.54	0.49	0.39	Income $
0.07	0.27	0.00	0.16	0.05	0.08	0.09	0.08	0.07	0.00	0.00	0.00	Capital Gains $
0.73	0.74	0.68	0.63	0.59	0.59	0.60	0.61	0.58	0.58	0.61	0.62	Expense Ratio %
6.48	6.41	6.50	6.44	6.37	6.06	6.43	7.31	6.39	5.06	4.69	3.77	Income Ratio %
41	39	31	16	69	47	24	21	22	28	52	62	Turnover Rate %
115	130	234	375	563	582	515	486	705	1,088	1,202	2,043	Net Assets $mil

Rating and Risk

Time Period	Load-Adj Return %	Morningstar Rtn vs Cat	Morningstar Risk vs Cat	Morningstar Risk-Adj Rating
1 Yr	-0.99			
3 Yr	3.88	-Avg	Low	★★
5 Yr	6.60	Avg	Low	★★★
10 Yr	6.97	Avg	Low	★★★
Incept	—			

Other Measures	Standard Index LB Aggr	Best Fit Index CSFB Glb HY
Alpha	4.3	2.1
Beta	-0.11	0.13
R-Squared	3	9
Standard Deviation	2.72	
Mean	5.12	
Sharpe Ratio	1.38	

Morningstar's Take by Jeffrey Ptak 11-03-04

Still one of the best.

FPA New Income is in a rut. The fund's 2.2% return for the year through Nov. 2, 2004, trails virtually the entire intermediate-term bond category. The cause of this recent rut is hardly shrouded in mystery. Comanagers Bob Rodriguez and Tom Atteberry declared a "Buyer's Strike" on long-term Treasuries in June 2003, arguing that the yields on such bonds failed to compensate for the interest-rate risk they posed. As such, management has horded cash, explaining the fund's recent 0.7-year duration, which is a fraction of the group norm. But with long-term rates holding their ground this year, the fund has found itself out of step.

Rodriguez and Atteberry aren't budging, however. They observe that brisk demand for inflation-indexed Treasuries strongly suggests that inflation remains a concern amongst investors. That trend hasn't translated to rising long-term rates, they contend, because the market is assuming that companies would absorb, rather than pass along, the increased input prices they face (thereby compressing profit margins). However, they argue that the credit sector's generally stable condition contradicts this logic. Further, Rodriguez and Atteberry note that inflation has hovered near 2.9% since 1926. That's roughly double the rate implied by the current 10-year Treasury yield, a disconnect they think looks even more glaring given the looming twin budget and trade deficits and accelerating health-care costs.

Whether management is right or not is secondary to the consistency of process here. Management is sticking to the same contrarian guns that it has used to amass a tremendous record over the long haul. Most notably, they continue to take very seriously their responsibility to preserve shareholder capital. Fallow stretches like this most recent episode go with that territory. But their consensus-flouting instincts have been rewarded time and time again. We wouldn't bet against them.

Address:	11400 W Olympic Blvd Ste 1200 Los Angeles CA 90064 800-982-4372	Minimum Purchase:	$1500	Add: $100	IRA: $100
		Min Auto Inv Plan:	$100	Add: $100	
		Sales Fees:	3.50%L, 2.00%R		
Web Address:	www.FPAFunds.com	Management Fee:	0.50%		
Inception:	04-01-69	Actual Fees:	Mgt:0.50%	Dist:	
Advisor:	First Pacific Advisors, Inc.	Expense Projections:	3Yr:$539	5Yr:$678	10Yr:$1085
Subadvisor:	None	Income Distrib:	Quarterly		
NTF Plans:	TD Waterhouse Ins NT				

Portfolio Analysis 09-30-04

Total Fixed-Income:110	Date of Maturity	Amount $000	Value $000	% Net Assets
US Treasury Note 3.375%	01-15-07	416,812	437,040	22.54
FHLBA FRN	10-10-07	24,650	24,650	1.27
Landesbank Baden-Wurttem	08-06-07	23,500	23,218	1.20
Qwest Comms Intl 144A FR	02-15-09	24,045	22,903	1.18
FNMA 2%	05-18-07	22,800	22,800	1.18
FHLMC CMO 5.25%	10-15-26	22,341	22,788	1.18
FHLBA 2%	04-29-09	22,500	22,472	1.16
FHLBA 2%	05-11-07	21,900	21,907	1.13
FHLBA 2%	04-15-09	21,250	21,077	1.09
Bayerische Landesbank Gr	04-30-09	21,000	20,580	1.06
FHLMC CMO 5%	07-15-16	19,304	19,799	1.02
France O.A.T. Euro Cpi 3	07-25-12	13,961	19,232	0.99
Chase Mortgage Fin CMO 7	01-25-34	17,475	18,743	0.97
FHLBA 2%	10-08-09	18,750	18,574	0.96
Metaldyne 144A 11%	06-15-12	22,230	18,229	0.94
FNMA 6%	08-01-12	17,206	18,055	0.93
Bea Sys Cv 4%	12-15-06	18,000	18,000	0.93
Michaels Stores 9.25%	07-01-09	16,505	17,990	0.93
I2 Tech Cv 5.25%	12-15-06	18,900	17,577	0.91
Wells Fargo Mbs 2004-1 C	01-25-34	16,763	16,915	0.87

Current Investment Style

Duration: Short Int Long — Quality: High Med Low

1 figure provided by fund

Avg Eff Duration[1]	0.7 Yrs
Avg Eff Maturity	1.3 Yrs
Avg Credit Quality	AAA
Avg Wtd Coupon	4.41%
Avg Wtd Price	100.33% of par

Coupon Range	% of Bonds	Rel Cat
0% PIK	4.2	1.0
0% to 6%	81.4	1.3
6% to 8%	10.6	0.4
8% to 10%	2.3	0.4
More than 10%	5.7	5.0

1.00=Category Average

Credit Analysis	% bonds 09-30-04		
US Govt	64	BB	2
AAA	13	B	8
AA	0	Below B	6
A	0	NR/NA	1
BBB	1		

Sector Breakdown	% of assets
US Treasuries	0
TIPS	23
US Agency	7
Mortgage Pass-Throughs	4
Mortgage CMO	13
Mortgage ARM	0
US Corporate	11
Asset-Backed	2
Convertible	2
Municipal	0
Corporate Inflation-Protected	0
Foreign Corporate	0
Foreign Govt	0

Composition			
Cash	38.9	Bonds	58.5
Stocks	0.0	Other	2.6

Special Securities	
Restricted/Illiquid Secs	2
Exotic Mortgage-Backed	1
Emerging-Markets Secs	0
Options/Futures/Warrants	No

FPA Paramount

Analyst Pick

Ticker	Load	NAV	Yield	Total Assets	Mstar Category
FPRAX	5.25%	$13.93	0.0%	$257 mil	Small Blend

Governance and Management

Fiduciary Grade: B

Portfolio Manager(s)

Eric Ende and Steve Geist have been at the helm since March 2000. They have built a fine record at FPA Perennial, which Ende has led since 1995 and Geist has comanaged since 2000.

Strategy

Managers Eric Ende and Steve Geist look for small and midsize companies with strong returns on capital and clean balance sheets trading at a discount to the market's or their own historical price multiples. They hold a compact portfolio consisting of about 30 to 40 names, will concentrate their holdings in a limited number of sectors, and aren't afraid to let the fund's cash stake build if they can't find attractive investment ideas. With big stakes in both fast-growing hardware names and stodgier industrials, the managers' picks span the style box. The pair usually hangs on to their holdings for years.

Historical Profile

Return: Below Avg
Risk: Average
Rating: ★★ Below Avg

Investment Style: Equity, Stock %

65% | 67% | 83% | 77% | 68% | 82% | 95% | 84% | 71%

▼ Manager Change
▽ Partial Manager Change

Growth of $10,000
— Investment Values of Fund
— Investment Values of S&P 500

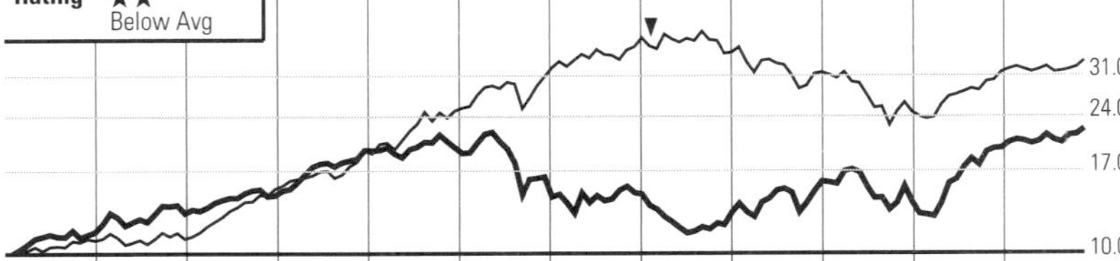

Performance Quartile (within Category)

History	1993	1994	1995	1996	1997	1998	1999	2000	2001	2002	2003	12-04
NAV	14.93	14.41	14.78	17.63	14.19	9.11	9.19	8.00	9.70	8.50	12.02	13.93
Total Return %	20.53	9.40	12.66	29.40	-1.76	-24.41	1.65	-10.96	21.67	-12.37	41.41	15.89
+/-S&P 500	10.47	8.09	-24.87	6.46	-35.11	-52.98	-19.39	-1.86	33.55	9.72	12.74	5.02
+/-Russ 2000	1.65	11.22	-15.79	12.91	-24.12	-21.86	-19.61	-7.94	19.18	8.11	-5.84	-2.44
Income Return %	1.92	1.78	2.12	1.90	1.91	1.81	0.77	1.86	0.40	0.00	0.00	0.00
Capital Return %	18.61	7.62	10.54	27.50	-3.67	-26.22	0.88	-12.82	21.27	-12.37	41.41	15.89
Total Rtn % Rank Cat	29	2	93	18	99	97	77	97	10	28	53	72
Income $	0.25	0.25	0.29	0.27	0.31	0.24	0.07	0.17	0.03	0.00	0.00	0.00
Capital Gains $	0.98	1.52	1.01	0.91	2.87	1.90	0.00	0.00	0.00	0.00	0.00	0.00
Expense Ratio %	0.89	0.90	0.89	0.87	0.86	0.92	1.03	1.17	1.20	1.17	1.15	0.99
Income Ratio %	1.83	1.69	2.25	1.94	1.84	1.14	0.57	1.22	0.92	-0.34	-0.47	-0.[illegible]6
Turnover Rate %	98	76	95	131	110	68	21	76	16	14	17	[illegible]6
Net Assets $mil	335	490	575	692	699	279	148	72	90	80	123	257

Performance 12-31-04

	1st Qtr	2nd Qtr	3rd Qtr	4th Qtr	Total
2000	-13.28	-9.66	2.51	10.87	-10.96
2001	-2.62	18.10	-12.85	21.40	21.67
2002	6.91	-9.35	-13.62	4.68	-12.37
2003	-8.47	26.48	9.65	11.40	41.41
2004	4.58	3.90	-0.38	7.07	15.89

Trailing	Total Return%	+/- S&P 500	+/- Russ 2000	%Rank Cat	Growth of $10,000
3 Mo	7.07	-2.16	-7.02	99	10,707
6 Mo	6.66	-0.53	-4.17	93	10,666
1 Yr	15.89	5.02	-2.44	72	11,589
3 Yr Avg	12.82	9.24	1.34	45	14,360
5 Yr Avg	9.24	11.54	2.63	69	15,556
10 Yr Avg	5.52	-6.55	-6.02	98	17,114
15 Yr Avg	7.91	-3.02	-3.18	96	31,327

Tax Analysis	Tax-Adj Rtn%	%Rank Cat	Tax-Cost Rat	%Rank Cat
3 Yr (estimated)	10.81	59	0.00	1
5 Yr (estimated)	7.85	70	0.20	7
10 Yr (estimated)	3.22	98	1.66	44

Potential Capital Gain Exposure: -45% of assets

Rating and Risk

Time Period	Load-Adj Return %	Morningstar Rtn vs Cat	Morningstar Risk vs Cat	Morningstar Risk-Adj Rating
1 Yr	9.81			
3 Yr	10.81	Avg	Avg	★★★
5 Yr	8.07	-Avg	Avg	★★
10 Yr	4.96	Low	Avg	★
Incept	—			

Other Measures	Standard Index S&P 500	Best Fit Index S&P Mid 400
Alpha	9.5	1.3
Beta	1.02	1.14
R-Squared	66	84

Standard Deviation	21.31
Mean	12.82
Sharpe Ratio	0.54

Portfolio Analysis 12-31-04

Share change since 09-04 Total Stocks:33

	Sector	PE	YTD Ret%	% Assets
⊕ Noble	Energy	51.7	39.02	3.77
⊕ Cal Dive International	Energy	23.4	68.95	3.68
CarMax	Consumer	29.6	0.39	3.35
⊕ North Fork Bancorporatio	Financial	15.4	10.24	3.31
⊕ SanDisk	Hardware	15.7	-18.40	3.20
⊕ Lincare Holdings	Health	16.1	41.79	3.19
⊕ O'Reilly Automotive	Consumer	21.6	16.83	3.15
⊕ Cognex	Hardware	31.3	-0.43	3.04
⊕ Engelhard	Ind Mtrls	15.3	3.98	3.01
⊕ Renal Care Group	Health	22.6	31.03	3.01
⊕ ScanSource	Ind Mtrls	25.8	36.26	2.84
⊕ Plantronics	Hardware	23.7	27.33	2.56
⊕ Arthur J. Gallagher & Co	Financial	15.7	3.18	2.53
⊕ Charles River Laboratori	Health	24.5	34.02	2.46
⊕ Health Management Associ	Health	16.6	-4.89	2.23
⊕ Crane	Ind Mtrls	—	-4.91	2.16
⊕ Bio-Rad Laboratories	Health	22.1	-0.52	2.13
Carnival	Goods	26.2	46.74	2.02
⊕ Oshkosh Truck	Ind Mtrls	20.5	34.70	1.99
Tidewater	Energy	48.3	21.49	1.97

Current Investment Style

Value Blnd Growth; Large Mid Small

Market Cap	%
Giant	0.0
Large	7.5
Mid	74.0
Small	18.5
Micro	0.1
Avg $mil: 3,063	

Value Measures		Rel Category
Price/Earnings	20.95	1.21
Price/Book	2.97	1.49
Price/Sales	1.57	1.65
Price/Cash Flow	11.70	2.00
Dividend Yield %	0.52	0.63

Growth Measures	%	Rel Category
Long-Term Erngs	15.07	1.11
Book Value	15.44	2.74
Sales	9.74	2.26
Cash Flow	14.85	3.01
Historical Erngs	13.88	1.86

Profitability	%	Rel Category
Return on Equity	15.01	1.44
Return on Assets	9.26	1.87
Net Margin	11.94	1.63

Sector Weightings	% of Stocks	Rel S&P 500	3 Year High	3 Year Low
Info	15.50	0.72		
Software	0.00	0.00	0	0
Hardware	15.50	1.52	27	16
Media	0.00	0.00	0	0
Telecom	0.00	0.00	0	0
Service	47.43	1.02		
Health	20.74	1.66	21	8
Consumer	13.25	1.46	17	12
Business	3.11	0.77	13	3
Financial	10.33	0.50	10	0
Mfg	37.08	1.15		
Goods	5.00	0.54	7	5
Ind Mtrls	18.85	1.49	26	17
Energy	13.23	1.85	13	7
Utilities	0.00	0.00	0	0

Composition

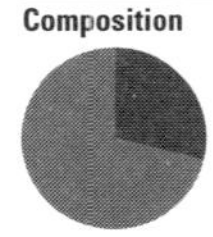

Cash	28.7
Stocks	71.3
Bonds	0.0
Other	0.0
Foreign (% of Stock)	0.0

Morningstar's Take by Christopher Davis 12-01-04

Star-struck investors make a mistake by overlooking FPA Paramount.

As a backward-looking performance measure, the Morningstar star rating isn't always a reliable gauge of future returns. That's especially the case with this offering, whose 2-star rating stems from the disastrous tenure of a former manager. But managers Eric Ende and Steve Geist have staged quite a turnaround, posting category-topping results since completing their portfolio overhaul in 2000.

The managers' success here stems from the same winning strategy they have employed at their longtime charge, FPA Perennial. The managers favor companies with high returns on equity, solid balance sheets, and strong growth prospects. They also pay close attention to valuation, running the portfolio with a contrarian bent. In early 2004, for instance, the managers added to oxygen-provider Lincare Holdings, which faltered on concerns that it would be hurt by proposed Medicare cutbacks. Ende believed worst-case fears of drastic reimbursement reductions were unlikely to materialize and thought the firm's industry-leading position and healthy profit margins would allow it to gain market share even if they did. Medicare cuts have been smaller than expected, though, and Lincare shares have since rallied sharply.

With a better long-term record, the fund's Perennial sibling has been more popular. But this fund is catching up: Assets have nearly doubled in the past year, rising to more than $200 million. Management hasn't been able to put all the new money to work, and the fund's cash stake now soaks up 26% of assets. And it could climb higher if inflows remain strong, suggesting the fund's board should consider closing the fund to new investors, if only temporarily. That swelling cash hoard, coupled with the sharp gains the fund's holdings have enjoyed in recent years, could dampen returns, at least in the short term. Even so, we think management's stock-picking prowess bodes well for the long haul.

Address:	11400 W Olympic Blvd Ste 1200 Los Angeles CA 90064 800-982-4372
Web Address:	www.FPAFunds.com
Inception:	09-08-58
Advisor:	First Pacific Advisors, Inc.
Subadvisor:	None
NTF Plans:	TD Waterhouse Ins NT

Minimum Purchase:	$1500	Add: $100	IRA: $100
Min Auto Inv Plan:	$100	Add: $100	
Sales Fees:	5.25%L, 2.00%R		
Management Fee:	0.75% mx./0.65% mn.		
Actual Fees:	Mgt:0.69%	Dist:	
Expense Projections:	3Yr:$871	5Yr:$1125	10Yr:$1849
Income Distrib:	Semi-Annually		

Franklin Bal Sh Invmt A

Ticker	Load	NAV	Yield	Total Assets	Mstar Category
FRBSX	Closed	$58.26	0.7%	$4,536 mil	Small Value

Governance and Management

Fiduciary Grade: C

Portfolio Manager(s)

Value-hound Bruce Baughman has managed this fund since April 1990. He's had ups and downs, but he generally has produced competitive returns with less volatility. Baughman is an accountant by training and pays close attention to company balance sheets. He's deliberate and prefers to be fully invested, but he won't compromise his investment style to do so.

Strategy

This fund employs a stricter-value discipline than many of its competitors. It requires price/book multiples in the bottom 20% of the universe it tracks. That stringent criterion has occasionally forced the fund to hold rather large cash positions, which at times have hindered performance.

Historical Profile

Return Average
Risk Low
Rating ★★★ Neutral

Investment Style: Equity Stock %

79%	93%	78%	91%	94%	99%	70%	75%	84%

▼ Manager Change
▽ Partial Manager Change

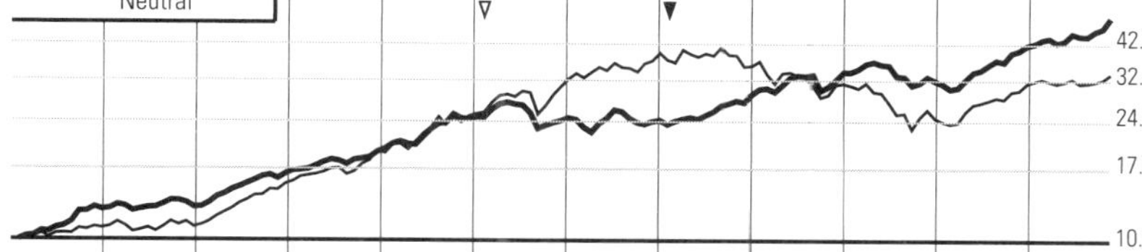

Growth of $10,000
▬ Investment Values of Fund
— Investment Values of S&P 500

Performance Quartile (within Category)

1993	1994	1995	1996	1997	1998	1999	2000	2001	2002	2003	12-04	History
21.85	21.62	26.68	28.49	33.54	31.60	30.47	35.67	40.02	37.09	47.57	58.26	NAV
25.57	1.50	30.04	17.50	25.97	-0.61	-1.53	20.47	17.70	-5.96	29.58	25.30	Total Return %
15.51	0.19	-7.49	-5.44	-7.38	-29.18	-22.57	29.57	29.58	16.13	0.91	14.43	+/-S&P 500
1.80	3.04	4.29	-3.87	-5.81	5.84	-0.04	-2.33	3.68	5.47	-16.45	3.05	+/-Russ 2000 VL
1.90	0.96	1.59	1.65	1.67	1.60	1.14	1.19	1.94	0.75	0.45	0.90	Income Return %
23.67	0.54	28.45	15.85	24.30	-2.21	-2.67	19.28	15.76	-6.71	29.13	24.40	Capital Return %
5	38	13	84	77	25	65	42	47	26	93	12	Total Rtn % Rank Cat
0.35	0.21	0.34	0.44	0.47	0.53	0.36	0.36	0.69	0.30	0.17	0.43	Income $
0.77	0.35	1.06	2.36	1.80	1.16	0.28	0.61	1.17	0.25	0.31	0.91	Capital Gains $
0.00	1.19	1.17	1.08	1.08	0.93	0.93	1.06	0.96	0.92	1.00	0.91	Expense Ratio %
1.89	0.99	1.30	1.69	1.59	1.47	1.19	1.00	2.14	0.63	0.35	0.67	Income Ratio %
31	25	29	35	25	12	18	9	27	11	13	7	Turnover Rate %
32	144	450	711	1,286	1,517	1,136	1,113	1,773	2,415	3,229	4,219	Net Assets $mil

Performance 12-31-04

	1st Qtr	2nd Qtr	3rd Qtr	4th Qtr	Total
2000	0.83	2.81	8.81	6.81	20.47
2001	1.96	12.61	-10.35	14.34	17.70
2002	6.35	-1.15	-13.45	3.35	-5.96
2003	-4.88	13.61	6.06	13.06	29.58
2004	5.36	3.43	1.87	12.87	25.30

Trailing	Total Return%	+/- S&P 500	+/- Russ 2000 VL	%Rank Cat	Growth of $10,000
3 Mo	12.87	3.64	-0.33	47	11,287
6 Mo	14.98	7.79	1.61	11	11,498
1 Yr	25.30	14.43	3.05	12	12,530
3 Yr Avg	15.15	11.57	-1.35	50	15,268
5 Yr Avg	16.71	19.01	-0.52	40	21,654
10 Yr Avg	15.09	3.02	-0.08	54	40,773
15 Yr Avg	—	—	—	—	—

Tax Analysis	Tax-Adj Rtn%	%Rank Cat	Tax-Cost Rat	%Rank Cat
3 Yr (estimated)	12.45	66	0.40	24
5 Yr (estimated)	14.55	51	0.68	33
10 Yr (estimated)	12.99	54	1.24	14

Potential Capital Gain Exposure: 36% of assets

Rating and Risk

Time Period	Load-Adj Return %	Morningstar Rtn vs Cat	Morningstar Risk vs Cat	Morningstar Risk-Adj Rating
1 Yr	18.10			
3 Yr	12.90	-Avg	Low	★★★
5 Yr	15.33	Avg	Low	★★★
10 Yr	14.41	Avg	Low	★★★
Incept	13.90			

Other Measures	Standard Index S&P 500	Best Fit Index Russ 2000 VL
Alpha	12.1	3.6
Beta	0.63	0.64
R-Squared	62	90
Standard Deviation	13.55	
Mean	15.15	
Sharpe Ratio	1.03	

Portfolio Analysis 09-30-04

Share change since 06-04 Total Stocks:112	Sector	PE	YTD Ret%	% Assets
Peabody Energy	Energy	35.4	96.04	2.30
Freddie Mac	Financial	10.6	28.75	2.26
CIT Group	Financial	13.2	29.28	2.12
Pulte Homes	Consumer	9.8	36.77	2.04
⊖ Aztar	Consumer	32.1	55.20	1.99
Old Republic Internation	Financial	10.3	1.89	1.99
United States Steel	Ind Mtrls	—	47.19	1.93
Teekay Shipping	Business	19.4	49.82	1.88
Bunge	Goods	13.3	75.28	1.85
Prudential Financial	Financial	14.5	33.31	1.75
American National Insura	Financial	15.2	27.12	1.60
Nucor	Ind Mtrls	9.6	89.07	1.47
⊖ Overseas Shipholding Gro	Business	9.6	64.92	1.47
Trinity Industries	Ind Mtrls	—	11.40	1.44
DR Horton	Consumer	10.7	41.36	1.40
Corn Products Internatio	Goods	19.2	57.18	1.32
Entergy	Utilities	21.1	22.14	1.24
PMI Group	Financial	11.4	12.61	1.19
⊖ Reliance Steel and Alumi	Ind Mtrls	33.9	18.18	1.18
IPC Holdings	Financial	10.5	14.38	1.15

Current Investment Style

Value Blnd Growth — Large Mid Small

Market Cap	%
Giant	3.8
Large	9.9
Mid	46.9
Small	36.9
Micro	2.6
Avg $mil: 2,578	

Value Measures		Rel Category
Price/Earnings	12.12	0.76
Price/Book	1.32	0.80
Price/Sales	0.60	0.80
Price/Cash Flow	4.75	0.92
Dividend Yield %	1.18	0.98

Growth Measures	%	Rel Category
Long-Term Erngs	12.38	1.02
Book Value	3.07	0.71
Sales	6.46	2.06
Cash Flow	7.90	3.64
Historical Erngs	7.61	1.58

Profitability	%	Rel Category
Return on Equity	8.03	0.88
Return on Assets	4.44	1.07
Net Margin	7.53	1.13

Sector Weightings	% of Stocks	Rel S&P 500	3 Year High	3 Year Low
Info	1.88	0.09		
Software	0.00	0.00	0	0
Hardware	1.70	0.17	5	2
Media	0.02	0.01	0	0
Telecom	0.16	0.05	0	0
Service	59.12	1.27		
Health	0.05	0.00	0	0
Consumer	18.20	2.00	30	18
Business	12.60	3.11	14	11
Financial	28.27	1.36	30	24
Mfg	39.00	1.21		
Goods	10.10	1.08	11	9
Ind Mtrls	17.55	1.39	18	10
Energy	5.88	0.82	6	1
Utilities	5.47	1.85	8	5

Composition

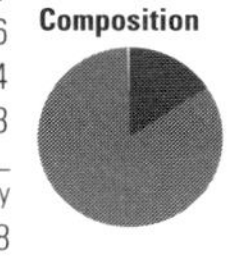

Cash	15.5
Stocks	83.9
Bonds	0.0
Other	0.6
Foreign (% of Stock)	5.3

Morningstar's Take by Dan Culloton 11-22-04

If the race really doesn't go to the swiftest, this fund is a good bet.

Franklin Balance Sheet Investment looks pokey compared with the average value fund. The fund doesn't rush anywhere. It follows a stringent, bottom-up stock-picking philosophy, buying stocks with low price/book ratios and underlying businesses strong enough to steadily increase those book values over time. It's willing to hang on to shares that meet its criteria for years (the fund's turnover rate implies a seven-year holding period). And given the choice between buying substandard stocks just to get fully invested or doing nothing, lead manager Bruce Baughman will do nothing, which often leads the fund to hold big cash stakes.

The fund has reduced its cash cushion since it closed to new investors a couple of years ago. Sidelined money still makes up about 17% of the fund, however, as it has trimmed strong performing stocks in the basic materials and sea transportation industries even as it found new opportunities in among capital intensive firms such as railroads Norfolk Southern and Kansas City Southern.

Over time, the fund's deliberate process has produced a strong risk/reward profile. Its cash pillow and tendency to avoid stocks in the more variable technology sectors has muted volatility, as measured by standard deviation. The fund's conservatism can look out of step when aggressive growth stocks rally, but it has put up strong long-term absolute returns. Its annualized gain of nearly 14% from the fund's April 1990 inception through the end of October 2004 is superior to the average small- or mid-cap value fund.

Although closed, size will continue to be a challenge for this $4 billion fund. For example, it required more than 11 days of Kansas City Southern's average trading volume to make the stock a less than 1% position. So far, the fund has compensated with patience and strong stock selection and there's no sign it's losing its touch. A slow and steady pace should keep it in the race.

Address:	One Franklin Parkway San Mateo CA 94403-1906 800-342-5236
Web Address:	www.franklintempleton.com
Inception:	04-02-90
Advisor:	Franklin Advisory Services, LLC
Subadvisor:	None
NTF Plans:	DATALynx NTF, Federated Tr NTF

Minimum Purchase:	Closed	Add: —	IRA: —
Min Auto Inv Plan:	Closed	Add: —	
Sales Fees:	5.75%L, 0.23%S, 2.00%R		
Management Fee:	0.63% mx./0.40% mn., 0.15%A		
Actual Fees:	Mgt:0.44%	Dist:0.23%	
Expense Projections:	3Yr:$869	5Yr:$1086	10Yr:$1707
Income Distrib:	Annually		

Franklin Fed T/F Inc A

Analyst Pick

Ticker	Load	NAV	Yield	SEC Yield	Total Assets	Mstar Category
FKTIX	4.25%	$12.16	4.6%	3.76%	$7,063 mil	Muni National Long

Governance and Management

Fiduciary Grade: C

Portfolio Manager(s)

Sheila Amoroso is a Franklin veteran and a proven municipal-bond manager. She has been a member of the fund's management since 1987 and has delivered solid results here and at other Franklin muni offerings. Francisco Rivera, Carrie Higgins, and John Wiley also contribute here.

Strategy

This income-oriented fund follows Franklin's plain-vanilla approach. Its management team, led by Sheila Amoroso, uses a buy-and-hold strategy in an effort to provide a steady stream of income, from which the bulk of the fund's total return is derived. Management doesn't make interest-rate bets and avoids potentially volatile derivative securities. And though the fund's duration floats with the market, it typically runs shorter than that of the category as a whole.

Historical Profile

Return Above Avg
Risk Low
Rating ★★★★ Above Avg

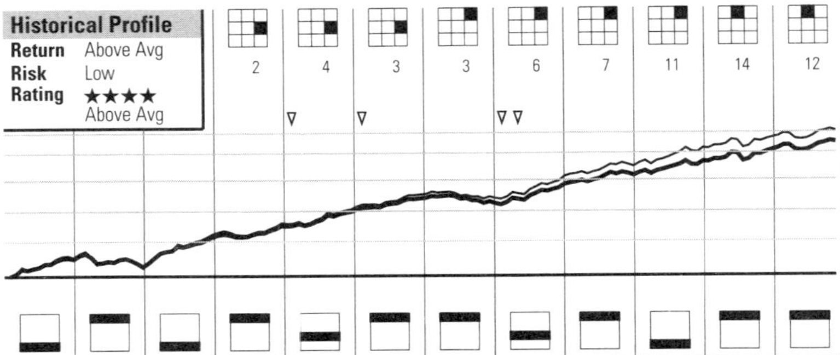

Investment Style
Fixed Income
Income Rtn %Rank Cat

▼ Manager Change
▽ Partial Manager Change

Growth of $10,000
▬ Investment Values of Fund
— Investment Values of LB Muni

Performance Quartile (within Category)

1993	1994	1995	1996	1997	1998	1999	2000	2001	2002	2003	12-04	History
12.53	11.29	12.19	12.01	12.35	12.39	11.39	11.85	11.76	11.98	12.09	12.16	NAV
11.25	-3.74	15.10	4.70	8.97	5.93	-2.79	10.14	4.63	7.19	5.84	5.39	Total Return %
-1.03	1.43	-2.36	0.27	-0.22	-0.55	-0.73	-1.54	-0.50	-2.41	0.53	0.91	+/-LB Muni
-3.13	3.60	-5.87	0.24	-1.87	-0.89	1.89	-5.10	-0.24	-2.84	-0.49	-1.17	+/-LB Muni 20YR
6.77	6.41	6.87	6.12	5.98	5.58	5.49	5.90	5.45	5.25	4.85	4.75	Income Return %
4.48	-10.15	8.23	-1.42	2.99	0.35	-8.28	4.24	-0.82	1.94	0.99	0.64	Capital Return %
78	6	84	12	52	24	8	72	20	81	16	6	Total Rtn % Rank Cat
0.79	0.78	0.75	0.73	0.70	0.67	0.66	0.65	0.63	0.60	0.57	0.56	Income $
0.00	0.00	0.00	0.00	0.00	0.00	0.01	0.00	0.00	0.00	0.00	0.00	Capital Gains $
0.51	0.52	0.59	0.57	0.58	0.59	0.60	0.60	0.60	0.60	0.61	0.61	Expense Ratio %
6.68	6.27	6.47	6.20	6.00	5.70	5.41	5.64	5.54	5.54	4.98	4.79	Income Ratio %
13	25	20	25	16	15	10	17	10	13	13	7	Turnover Rate %
7,060	6,561	7,211	7,032	7,096	7,189	6,570	6,430	6,576	6,737	6,577	6,303	Net Assets $mil

Performance 12-31-04

	1st Qtr	2nd Qtr	3rd Qtr	4th Qtr	Total
2000	2.62	1.27	2.39	3.51	10.14
2001	1.97	0.82	2.34	-0.55	4.63
2002	0.70	3.03	3.41	-0.09	7.19
2003	0.97	3.06	-0.31	2.02	5.84
2004	2.33	-2.38	3.59	1.85	5.39

Trailing	Total Return%	+/- LB Muni	+/- LB Muni 20YR	%Rank Cat	Growth of $10,000
3 Mo	1.85	0.60	-0.13	7	10,185
6 Mo	5.51	0.32	-1.24	19	10,551
1 Yr	5.39	0.91	-1.17	6	10,539
3 Yr Avg	6.14	-0.30	-1.49	23	11,957
5 Yr Avg	6.62	-0.58	-1.92	34	13,778
10 Yr Avg	6.42	-0.64	-1.53	33	18,631
15 Yr Avg	6.61	-0.38	-1.04	29	26,120

Tax Analysis	Tax-Adj Rtn%	%Rank Cat	Tax-Cost Rat	%Rank Cat
3 Yr (estimated)	4.61	55	0.00	1
5 Yr (estimated)	5.70	62	0.00	1
10 Yr (estimated)	5.96	35	0.00	1

Potential Capital Gain Exposure: 5% of assets

Rating and Risk

Time Period	Load-Adj Return %	Morningstar Rtn vs Cat	Morningstar Risk vs Cat	Morningstar Risk-Adj Rating
1 Yr	0.91			
3 Yr	4.61	Avg	Low	★★★
5 Yr	5.70	Avg	Low	★★★
10 Yr	5.96	+Avg	Low	★★★★
Incept	7.67			

Other Measures	Standard Index LB Aggr	Best Fit Index LB Muni 20YR
Alpha	0.2	-0.5
Beta	0.90	0.84
R-Squared	97	98
Standard Deviation	4.62	
Mean	6.14	
Sharpe Ratio	1.04	

Portfolio Analysis 09-30-04

Total Fixed-Income:861	Date of Maturity	Amount $000	Value $000	% Net Assets
Dallas Fort Worth Tex In	11-01-26	85,000	90,681	1.29
New York N Y 6.125%	08-01-25	63,965	69,684	0.99
North Carolina Eastn Mun	01-01-26	65,350	68,157	0.97
Puerto Rico Comwlth Hwy	07-01-36	62,000	62,544	0.89
Pope Cnty Ark Pollutn Ct	11-01-20	60,500	60,539	0.86
New York N Y City Mun Wt	06-15-33	55,000	58,759	0.84
Massachusetts St Tpk Aut	01-01-37	52,130	52,581	0.75
Golden St Tob Securitiza	06-01-28	50,000	51,101	0.73
California St 5%	02-01-32	49,000	49,355	0.70
Denver Colo City & Cnty	11-15-23	43,000	45,428	0.65
North Carolina Eastn Mun	01-01-23	39,030	45,075	0.64
Foothill / Eastern Trans	01-01-32	39,240	43,213	0.62
San Joaquin Hills Calif	01-15-21	50,000	42,378	0.60
Metropolitan Pier & Expo	12-15-28	39,580	40,731	0.58
Mississippi Busn Fin 5.8	04-01-22	40,000	40,249	0.57

Current Investment Style

Duration: Short Int Long; Quality: High Med Low

[1]Avg Eff Duration	5.0 Yrs
Avg Eff Maturity	18.8 Yrs
Avg Credit Quality	AA
Avg Wtd Coupon	5.33%
Avg Wtd Price	102.84% of par

[1]figure provided by fund

Credit Analysis	% bonds 09-30-04		
US Govt	0	BB	3
AAA	60	B	1
AA	11	Below B	1
A	11	NR/NA	1
BBB	13		

Top 5 States	% bonds		
NY	14.9	TX	6.1
CA	8.2	PA	4.7
IL	7.0		

Composition			
Cash	1.6	Bonds	98.4
Stocks	0.0	Other	0.0

Special Securities	
Restricted/Illiquid Secs	0
Options/Futures/Warrants	No

Sector Weightings	% of Bonds	Rel Cat
General Obligation	24.2	0.92
Utilities	14.8	1.11
Health	9.8	1.24
Water/Waste	13.6	1.23
Housing	5.1	0.72
Education	6.6	0.57
Transportation	12.8	1.69
COP/Lease	2.3	1.08
Industrial	10.7	0.83
Misc Revenue	0.0	0.00
Demand	0.2	0.81

Morningstar's Take by Scott Berry 12-10-04

Franklin Federal Tax-Free Income continues to impress.

This fund has lit up the charts over the last year. Its California holdings have performed extremely well thanks to that state's growing economy and improving budget situation. Meanwhile, management has kept the fund stocked with bonds that mature in 20 to 25 years. Those issues pump out a lot of yield, but don't carry quite as much interest-rate risk as 30-year issues. That added yield has fueled the fund's gains, as capital appreciation has been hard to come by recently. Overall, the fund gained 4.6% for the year to date through December 8 and outperformed roughly 95% of its muni-national long-term category peers.

The fund's added yield has also contributed to its long-term success. Management simply buys what it considers to be attractively valued bonds and holds them for their income. That often results in the fund owning a larger stash of older higher-coupon issues than its average peer. Not only do these bonds throw off a lot of tax-free income, but they tend to be less sensitive to interest-rate changes than newer, lower-coupon issues. When rates spiked in 1994 and 1999, for example, the fund bested more than 90% of its rivals. Overall, its three-, five-, and 10-year trailing returns rank firmly in the category's best half, while its standard deviation of returns (a measure of volatility) ranks among the lowest in the group.

One possible concern is that the fund could get reeled in by peers as its higher-coupon bonds mature or get called away. We've seen that to some extent in recent years, as the fund's income-return ranking has dipped a bit.

However, we think the fund's low cost and proven approach will keep it among the category's elite. In fact, the fund's 0.61% expense ratio provides a nearly insurmountable advantage over its higher-cost front-load category peers, a number of which charge more than 1.10%.

Address:	One Franklin Parkway San Mateo CA 94403-1906 800-342-5236
Web Address:	www.franklintempleton.com
Inception:	10-07-83
Advisor:	Franklin Advisers, Inc.
Subadvisor:	None
NTF Plans:	Fidelity Instl-NTF, Schwab Instl NTF

Minimum Purchase:	$1000	Add: $50	IRA: $0
Min Auto Inv Plan:	$50	Add: $50	
Sales Fees:	4.25%L, 2.00%R		
Management Fee:	0.63% mx./0.35% mn.		
Actual Fees:	Mgt:0.45%	Dist:0.09%	
Expense Projections:	3Yr:$612	5Yr:$751	10Yr:$1155
Income Distrib:	Monthly		

Franklin Growth A

Ticker	Load	NAV	Yield	Total Assets	Mstar Category
FKGRX	5.75%	$33.80	0.2%	$2,267 mil	Large Blend

Governance and Management

Fiduciary Grade: C

Portfolio Manager(s)

Jerry Palmieri has run this fund for nearly 40 years, making him one of the longest-tenured fund managers. His stock-picking has been good, but his asset allocation has been mixed. When stocks crashed in 1987, the fund gained more than 19%, and Palmieri was Morningstar's first Manager of the Year. But he kept a third of his money in cash in the late 1990s, missing the bull market's final run, and jumped back into stocks too early in 2002.

Strategy

This fund can own stocks of any size. In practice, though, manager Jerry Palmieri tries to buy industry leaders, skewing the fund toward large-cap stocks. He also has an eye for value, preferring to hold large cash stakes rather than pay inflated prices.

Historical Profile

Return Average
Risk Average
Rating ★★★ Neutral

Investment Style: Equity — Stock %: 81% | 100% | 74% | 67% | 88% | 100% | 99% | 98% | 100%

▼ Manager Change
▽ Partial Manager Change

Growth of $10,000
— Investment Values of Fund
— Investment Values of S&P 500

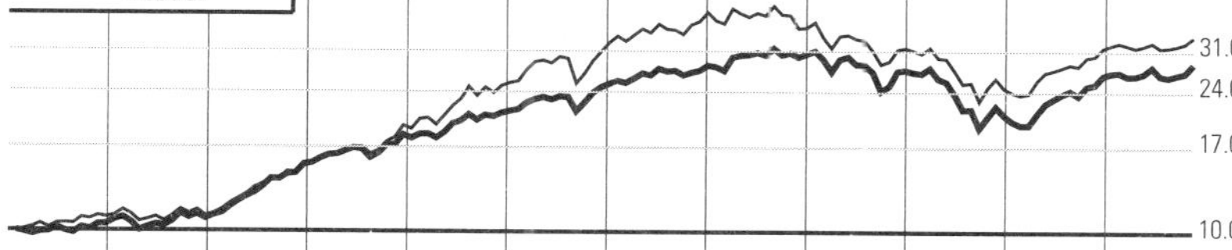

Performance Quartile (within Category)

1993	1994	1995	1996	1997	1998	1999	2000	2001	2002	2003	12-04	History
14.75	15.00	20.44	23.43	27.09	31.45	34.54	35.03	31.51	23.80	30.44	33.80	NAV
7.10	2.92	38.40	16.68	18.60	18.52	12.19	7.53	-9.47	-24.35	28.03	11.30	Total Return %
-2.96	1.61	0.87	-6.26	-14.75	-10.05	-8.85	16.63	2.41	-2.26	-0.64	0.43	+/-S&P 500
-3.08	2.53	0.63	-5.77	-14.25	-8.50	-8.72	15.32	2.98	-2.70	-1.86	-0.10	+/-Russ 1000
2.10	0.92	1.09	1.11	1.99	1.62	1.44	1.16	0.44	0.12	0.12	0.26	Income Return %
5.00	2.00	37.31	15.57	16.61	16.90	10.75	6.37	-9.91	-24.47	27.91	11.04	Capital Return %
80	10	8	86	89	66	82	1	24	77	38	30	Total Rtn % Rank Cat
0.30	0.14	0.16	0.23	0.47	0.44	0.45	0.40	0.16	0.04	0.03	0.08	Income $
0.08	0.04	0.15	0.20	0.24	0.21	0.26	1.67	0.05	0.00	0.00	0.00	Capital Gains $
0.64	0.77	0.90	0.87	0.89	0.88	0.89	0.93	0.91	0.96	1.06	0.98	Expense Ratio %
1.64	1.23	1.08	1.16	1.60	1.78	1.19	1.27	0.39	0.24	0.31	0.20	Income Ratio %
2	7	1	2	2	1	4	8	—	2	5	2	Turnover Rate %
567	538	803	1,110	1,509	1,899	2,194	2,139	1,884	1,320	1,608	1,659	Net Assets $mil

Performance 12-31-04

	1st Qtr	2nd Qtr	3rd Qtr	4th Qtr	Total
2000	5.27	3.03	-1.47	0.62	7.53
2001	-10.39	4.68	-15.37	14.03	-9.47
2002	1.27	-15.11	-18.75	8.30	-24.35
2003	-6.01	17.70	2.05	13.40	28.03
2004	-0.39	5.84	-4.71	10.79	11.30

Trailing	Total Return%	+/- S&P 500	+/- Russ 1000	%Rank Cat	Growth of $10,000
3 Mo	10.79	1.56	0.99	17	11,079
6 Mo	5.58	-1.61	-2.23	80	10,558
1 Yr	11.30	0.43	-0.10	30	11,130
3 Yr Avg	2.53	-1.05	-1.74	59	10,778
5 Yr Avg	0.97	3.27	2.73	18	10,495
10 Yr Avg	10.33	-1.74	-1.83	54	26,726
15 Yr Avg	9.81	-1.12	-1.27	55	40,703

Tax Analysis	Tax-Adj Rtn%	%Rank Cat	Tax-Cost Rat	%Rank Cat
3 Yr (estimated)	0.47	75	0.06	5
5 Yr (estimated)	-0.58	22	0.36	19
10 Yr (estimated)	9.11	44	0.52	8

Potential Capital Gain Exposure: 68% of assets

Rating and Risk

Time Period	Load-Adj Return %	Morningstar Rtn vs Cat	Morningstar Risk vs Cat	Morningstar Risk-Adj Rating
1 Yr	4.90			
3 Yr	0.53	-Avg	+Avg	★★
5 Yr	-0.22	+Avg	Avg	★★★★
10 Yr	9.68	Avg	-Avg	★★★
Incept	10.44			

Other Measures	Standard Index S&P 500	Best Fit Index Russ 1000
Alpha	-1.0	-1.7
Beta	1.04	1.05
R-Squared	95	95
Standard Deviation	16.53	
Mean	2.53	
Sharpe Ratio	0.07	

Portfolio Analysis 09-30-04

Share change since 06-04 Total Stocks:111	Sector	PE	YTD Ret%	% Assets
3M Company	Ind Mtrls	23.5	-1.75	3.07
Pfizer	Health	22.0	-22.31	2.94
Johnson & Johnson	Health	20.6	25.17	2.69
Yahoo	Media	95.1	67.36	2.60
Northrop Grumman	Ind Mtrls	18.3	15.68	2.56
Amgen	Health	37.7	3.82	2.53
Genentech	Health	78.6	16.36	2.52
Boeing	Ind Mtrls	14.7	24.86	2.48
General Dynamics	Ind Mtrls	17.5	17.40	2.45
IBM	Hardware	20.2	7.19	2.30
Tyco International	Ind Mtrls	25.1	35.41	2.28
Computer Sciences	Business	18.1	27.45	2.26
Illinois Tool Works	Ind Mtrls	22.1	11.75	2.24
United Technologies	Ind Mtrls	18.6	10.72	1.79
Schering-Plough	Health	—	21.56	1.65
Ingersoll-Rand A	Ind Mtrls	15.8	19.88	1.63
Textron	Ind Mtrls	30.4	32.17	1.62
Automatic Data Processin	Business	26.9	13.46	1.59
Emerson Electric	Ind Mtrls	22.8	11.09	1.48
Avery Dennison	Ind Mtrls	24.5	9.70	1.46

Current Investment Style (Value Blnd Growth; Large Mid Small)

Market Cap	%
Giant	37.7
Large	40.6
Mid	18.3
Small	3.1
Micro	0.3
Avg $mil: 22,132	

Value Measures		Rel Category
Price/Earnings	19.99	1.18
Price/Book	2.70	1.03
Price/Sales	1.21	0.84
Price/Cash Flow	9.83	1.28
Dividend Yield %	1.15	0.78

Growth Measures	%	Rel Category
Long-Term Erngs	12.00	1.04
Book Value	8.21	1.06
Sales	4.06	0.71
Cash Flow	7.58	0.80
Historical Erngs	0.14	0.01

Profitability	%	Rel Category
Return on Equity	15.78	0.90
Return on Assets	7.24	0.84
Net Margin	9.56	0.84

Sector Weightings	% of Stocks	Rel S&P 500	3 Year High	3 Year Low
Info	17.87	0.83		
Software	1.61	0.37	2	2
Hardware	10.25	1.00	12	8
Media	6.01	1.57	6	4
Telecom	0.00	0.00	0	0
Service	39.37	0.85		
Health	23.82	1.91	27	23
Consumer	2.61	0.29	4	3
Business	12.94	3.20	17	13
Financial	0.00	0.00	0	0
Mfg	42.76	1.33		
Goods	6.87	0.74	8	6
Ind Mtrls	32.17	2.54	32	27
Energy	3.72	0.52	4	3
Utilities	0.00	0.00	0	0

Composition

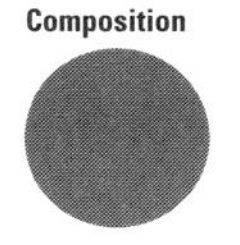

Cash	0.4
Stocks	99.6
Bonds	0.0
Other	0.0
Foreign (% of Stock)	4.1

Morningstar's Take by Dan Culloton 12-14-04

Franklin Growth has its moments, but others have more.

This fund has a consistent strategy, but an inconsistent record. Veteran manager Jerry Palmieri tries to buy large, established companies at favorable prices, and to hang onto them for years. Palmieri won't pay up for his stocks. The portfolio's average valuations are typically in line with those of the large-blend category, and he lets cash build if he thinks equities are too pricey. Palmieri, who is one of the most-tenured managers in the mutual fund industry, will hold stocks for decades if he remains pleased with their operating results. The fund's average turnover over the last decade implies a holding period of nearly 30 years.

There are virtues in this cautious, long-term approach. In the past, the strategy has muted the fund's volatility, helping it fall less than its peers when the market has retreated. Low turnover also has kept the fund's taxes and transaction costs low.

Some quirks, however, seem to stifle the fund's advantages. It has often lagged its competitors in rising markets. Its volatility, as measured by standard deviation, also has increased as it has shed the large cash stake that tempered the portfolio's behavior in the 1990s, but long-term returns have remained about average. Palmieri also avoids all financial-services stocks, not because he doesn't like the fundamentals of their businesses, but because he thinks it's a conflict of interest for a mutual fund to own them. Whether or not this odd stance is valid, it leaves the fund with no exposure to a sector that makes up about a fifth of the average large-blend portfolio and most core stock benchmarks.

Furthermore, the fund's expense ratio, which is about average for similarly sized peers with front-end loads, has increased in recent years. While the fund's long-term focus is admirable, there are other core stock funds with better risk/reward profiles.

Address:	One Franklin Parkway San Mateo CA 94403-1906 800-342-5236
Web Address:	www.Franklintempleton.com
Inception:	03-30-48
Advisor:	Franklin Investment Advisory Svs Inc.
Subadvisor:	None
NTF Plans:	DATALynx NTF, Federated Tr NTF

Minimum Purchase:	$1000	Add: $50	IRA: $250
Min Auto Inv Plan:	$50	Add: $50	
Sales Fees:	5.75%L		
Management Fee:	0.63% mx./0.36% mn.		
Actual Fees:	Mgt:0.46%	Dist:0.25%	
Expense Projections:	3Yr:$893	5Yr:$1126	10Yr:$1795
Income Distrib:	Annually		

Franklin Hi Yld T/F A

Ticker	Load	NAV	Yield	SEC Yield	Total Assets	Mstar Category
FRHIX	4.25%	$10.75	5.5%	4.58%	$5,429 mil	High Yield Muni

Governance and Management

Fiduciary Grade: C

Portfolio Manager(s)

John Wiley has been manager of this fund since 2000. He is a Franklin veteran with extensive experience managing tax-free money. Sheila Amoroso, John Hopp, Francisco Rivera, and a group of 15 analysts round out the team.

Strategy

This fund follows Franklin's basic buy-and-hold strategy. It avoids interest-rate bets and focuses on income more than on total return. Management looks to add value primarily through issue selection and sector allocation. The fund is more diversified than most high-yield muni funds, but credit risk is a concern as the fund typically holds 25%-30% of its assets in nonrated bonds. The fund also holds a few sizable individual positions, which could add to its volatility.

Historical Profile

Return Above Avg
Risk Average
Rating ★★★★ Above Avg

Investment Style: Fixed Income — Income Rtn %Rank Cat: 9, 10, 13, 10, 15, 40, 31, 25, 22

▼ Manager Change
▽ Partial Manager Change

Growth of $10,000
— Investment Values of Fund
— Investment Values of LB Muni

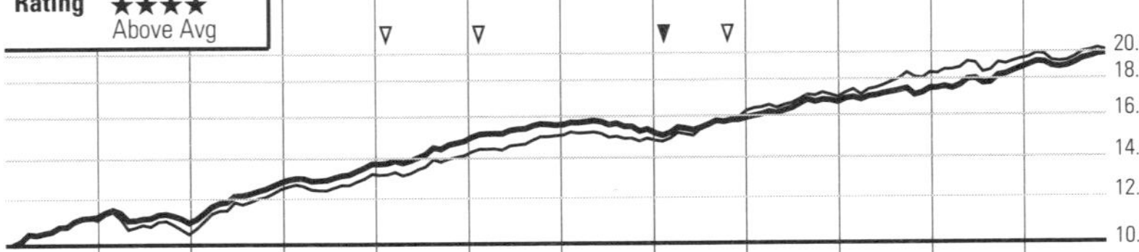

Performance Quartile (within Category)

History

	1993	1994	1995	1996	1997	1998	1999	2000	2001	2002	2003	12-04
NAV	11.38	10.35	11.26	11.19	11.64	11.51	10.51	10.47	10.49	10.42	10.63	10.75
Total Return %	13.27	-2.56	16.31	6.15	10.65	4.80	-3.24	5.86	5.89	5.19	7.99	6.88
+/-LB Muni	0.99	2.61	-1.15	1.72	1.46	-1.68	-1.18	-5.82	0.76	-4.41	2.68	2.40
+/-LB Muni 10YR	0.50	2.21	-0.86	1.61	1.41	-1.96	-2.00	-4.90	1.27	-4.98	2.29	2.73
Income Return %	7.44	6.76	7.30	6.70	6.44	5.85	5.78	6.23	5.74	5.89	5.85	5.68
Capital Return %	5.83	-9.32	9.01	-0.55	4.21	-1.05	-9.02	-0.37	0.15	-0.70	2.14	1.20
Total Rtn % Rank Cat	12	12	39	12	15	79	26	37	22	68	19	21
Income $	0.78	0.75	0.73	0.73	0.70	0.66	0.65	0.64	0.59	0.60	0.59	0.59
Capital Gains $	0.00	0.00	0.00	0.00	0.00	0.02	0.00	0.00	0.00	0.00	0.00	0.00
Expense Ratio %	0.54	0.53	0.60	0.61	0.62	0.61	0.62	0.61	0.62	0.62	0.62	0.62
Income Ratio %	7.45	6.79	6.92	6.68	6.41	5.98	5.64	5.92	5.90	5.78	5.69	5.62
Turnover Rate %	33	16	16	9	7	16	19	25	11	10	12	9
Net Assets $mil	3,327	3,124	3,694	4,310	5,226	5,897	5,154	4,733	4,605	4,432	4,455	4,597

Performance 12-31-04

	1st Qtr	2nd Qtr	3rd Qtr	4th Qtr	Total
2000	2.14	-0.16	2.22	1.56	5.86
2001	2.16	1.39	2.34	-0.11	5.89
2002	0.94	2.31	1.76	0.10	5.19
2003	-0.02	3.80	1.15	2.87	7.99
2004	2.15	-1.42	3.44	2.61	6.88

Trailing	Total Return%	+/- LB Muni	+/- LB Muni 10YR	%Rank Cat	Growth of $10,000
3 Mo	2.61	1.36	1.78	28	10,261
6 Mo	6.14	0.95	1.14	25	10,614
1 Yr	6.88	2.40	2.73	21	10,688
3 Yr Avg	6.68	0.24	0.04	38	12,141
5 Yr Avg	6.36	-0.84	-0.68	24	13,611
10 Yr Avg	6.55	-0.51	-0.53	16	18,860
15 Yr Avg	6.80	-0.19	-0.28	14	26,827

Tax Analysis	Tax-Adj Rtn%	%Rank Cat	Tax-Cost Rat	%Rank Cat
3 Yr (estimated)	5.15	65	0.00	1
5 Yr (estimated)	5.44	47	0.00	1
10 Yr (estimated)	6.08	20	0.01	15

Potential Capital Gain Exposure: -2% of assets

Rating and Risk

Time Period	Load-Adj Return %	Morningstar Rtn vs Cat	Morningstar Risk vs Cat	Morningstar Risk-Adj Rating
1 Yr	2.34			
3 Yr	5.15	Avg	Avg	★★★
5 Yr	5.44	Avg	Avg	★★★
10 Yr	6.09	+Avg	-Avg	★★★★
Incept	6.99			

Other Measures	Standard Index LB Aggr	Best Fit Index LB Muni CA
Alpha	1.9	2.2
Beta	0.66	0.62
R-Squared	76	78
Standard Deviation	3.80	
Mean	6.68	
Sharpe Ratio	1.41	

Portfolio Analysis 09-30-04

Total Fixed-Income:621	Date of Maturity	Amount $000	Value $000	% Net Assets
Pima Cnty Ariz Indl Dev	09-01-29	94,690	94,718	1.78
Farmington N Mex Pollutn	04-01-22	66,125	70,976	1.34
Klamath Falls Ore Elec 6	01-01-25	66,060	65,670	1.24
New York N Y City Indl D	08-01-12	74,000	59,876	1.13
Connecticut St Dev Auth	09-01-28	53,825	56,685	1.07
New Jersey Econ Dev Auth	09-15-23	73,030	56,452	1.06
Pima Cnty Ariz Indl Dev	09-01-29	53,500	53,516	1.01
Apache Cnty Ariz Indl De	03-01-28	53,150	53,164	1.00
Indiana Health Fac Fing	08-01-31	48,500	49,739	0.94
Director St Nev Dept Bus	01-01-40	48,000	48,611	0.91
San Joaquin Hills Calif	01-01-26	131,900	45,449	0.86
Henderson Nev Loc Impt D	08-01-18	42,065	45,199	0.85
San Joaquin Hills Calif	01-01-27	139,100	45,093	0.85
Eagle Cnty Colo Sports &	08-01-19	41,200	42,907	0.81
New Jersey Econ Dev Auth	09-15-19	54,420	42,623	0.80

Current Investment Style

Duration: Short Int Long — Quality: High Med Low

[1]Avg Eff Duration	5.5 Yrs
Avg Eff Maturity	18.1 Yrs
Avg Credit Quality	BBB
Avg Wtd Coupon	5.82%
Avg Wtd Price	99.26% of par

[1]figure provided by fund

Credit Analysis	% bonds 09-30-04		
US Govt	0	BB	16
AAA	22	B	5
AA	2	Below B	3
A	12	NR/NA	23
BBB	17		

Special Securities	
Restricted/Illiquid Secs	0
Options/Futures/Warrants	No

Top 5 States	% bonds		
CA	18.5	AZ	7.5
NY	9.2	PA	4.6
FL	8.7		

Composition			
Cash	1.0	Bonds	99.0
Stocks	0.0	Other	0.0

Sector Weightings	% of Bonds	Rel Cat
General Obligation	15.7	1.05
Utilities	13.7	1.60
Health	13.6	1.03
Water/Waste	7.5	1.08
Housing	4.9	0.62
Education	2.2	0.71
Transportation	4.3	0.56
COP/Lease	2.8	1.93
Industrial	35.0	0.97
Misc Revenue	0.0	—
Demand	0.2	2.67

Morningstar's Take by Scott Berry 12-21-04

Franklin High Yield Tax-Free Income is a good option for investors looking to diversify an otherwise high-quality municipal-bond portfolio.

This fund is no wallflower. It doesn't take on as much risk as some of the high-yield municipal-bond category's riskiest entrants, but with roughly two thirds of its assets invested in bonds rated BBB and below, it is a true high-yield muni fund. Those mid- and lower-rated holdings can add to the fund's volatility and can hamper returns when their finances weaken. In 2002, for example, the fund's airline holdings struggled due to bankruptcy concerns. The fund's small tobacco stake has also seen ups and downs in recent years, as litigation concerns have waxed and waned.

On the plus side, these holdings pump out lots of income, which can dampen the fund's overall interest-rate sensitivity. In fact, this fund lost less than most long-term general municipal-bond funds when interest rates spiked in 1994 and 1999. It has also proved itself versus its high-yield competitors, with three-year trailing returns that rank in the high-yield municipal-bond category's top half, and five- and 10-year returns that land in the group's best third.

The fund's long-term success owes much to its low costs, broad diversification, and good research capabilities. With an expense ratio of just 0.62%, the fund boasts a huge sustainable advantage over its higher-cost rivals. Meanwhile, the fund's added diversification--a result of its large asset base--helps limit the damage that can be caused by issue-specific credit problems. Finally, the fund benefits from its 15-member analyst staff, which can look far and wide for opportunities.

The fund's added credit risk makes it less suitable for conservative bond investors, but we think its solid long-term record, low costs, and broad diversification make it an appealing option for those looking to add a little spice to a muni portfolio.

Address:	One Franklin Parkway San Mateo CA 94403-1906 800-342-5236
Web Address:	www.franklintempleton.com
Inception:	03-18-86
Advisor:	Franklin Advisers, Inc.
Subadvisor:	None
NTF Plans:	DATALynx NTF, Schwab Instl NTF

Minimum Purchase:	$1000	Add: $50	IRA: $0
Min Auto Inv Plan:	$50	Add: $50	
Sales Fees:	4.25%L, 2.00%R		
Management Fee:	0.63% mx./0.45% mn.		
Actual Fees:	Mgt:0.46%	Dist:0.09%	
Expense Projections:	3Yr:$615	5Yr:$756	10Yr:$1166
Income Distrib:	Monthly		

Franklin Income A

Ticker	Load	NAV	Yield	Total Assets	Mstar Category
FKINX	4.25%	$2.52	6.2%	$30,576 mil	Conservative Allocation

Governance and Management

Fiduciary Grade: C

Portfolio Manager(s)

The fund is team-managed. Charles Johnson and Ed Perks run this fund. The former is the chairman of Franklin, while the latter is a 10-year veteran of the firm and has run Franklin Convertible Securities since early 1999.

Strategy

This fund's management takes a value-oriented, contrarian approach to investing. It buys beaten-down blue chips, utilities stocks, and high-yield bonds in an effort to provide shareholders a fat yield and an attractive total return. It will also venture into emerging-markets debt as opportunities present themselves.

Historical Profile

Return High
Risk High
Rating ★★★★★ Highest

Investment Style: Equity, Stock %: 29% 34% 32% 29% 31% 28% 32% 38% 38%

▼ Manager Change
∇ Partial Manager Change

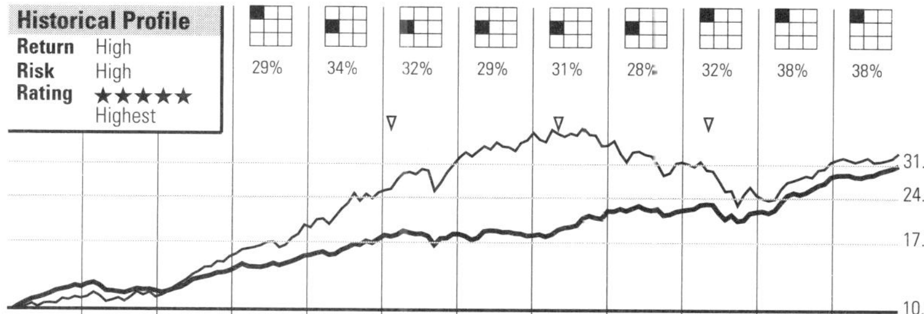

Performance Quartile (within Category)

History

1993	1994	1995	1996	1997	1998	1999	2000	2001	2002	2003	12-04	History
2.46	2.10	2.32	2.36	2.53	2.36	2.15	2.36	2.18	1.99	2.41	2.52	NAV
21.53	-6.38	21.29	10.45	16.85	0.95	-0.74	20.59	0.65	-1.06	30.96	12.17	Total Return %
11.47	-7.69	-16.24	-12.49	-16.50	-27.62	-21.78	29.69	12.53	21.03	2.29	1.30	+/-S&P 500
10.77	-5.15	3.13	1.56	2.75	-10.78	-8.60	13.80	-2.57	2.96	13.30	3.16	+/-DJ 40%
8.43	7.58	8.91	8.04	7.90	7.36	7.91	8.70	7.91	7.69	8.12	6.67	Income Return %
13.10	-13.96	12.38	2.41	8.95	-6.41	-8.65	11.89	-7.26	-8.75	22.84	5.50	Capital Return %
1	73	46	53	25	97	92	3	41	29	1	4	Total Rtn % Rank Cat
0.18	0.18	0.18	0.18	0.18	0.18	0.18	0.18	0.18	0.16	0.16	0.16	Income $
0.03	0.03	0.03	0.01	0.03	0.01	0.01	0.03	0.02	0.01	0.01	0.01	Capital Gains $
0.54	0.64	0.71	0.70	0.72	0.72	0.73	0.76	0.73	0.72	0.73	0.68	Expense Ratio %
7.84	7.37	8.26	8.27	7.45	6.83	7.46	8.01	7.54	6.67	6.63	5.11	Income Ratio %
25	23	59	25	16	22	17	24	28	51	48	32	Turnover Rate %
4,328	4,789	6,217	7,082	8,044	7,784	6,285	6,136	6,243	6,521	11,466	17,016	Net Assets $mil

Performance 12-31-04

	1st Qtr	2nd Qtr	3rd Qtr	4th Qtr	Total
2000	0.72	5.95	8.98	3.69	20.59
2001	0.21	1.50	-4.63	3.76	0.65
2002	4.42	-5.98	-5.94	7.14	-1.06
2003	1.47	14.24	3.16	9.51	30.96
2004	1.62	-0.45	4.24	6.36	12.17

Trailing	Total Return%	+/- S&P 500	+/- DJ 40%	%Rank Cat	Growth of $10,000
3 Mo	6.36	-2.87	0.96	9	10,636
6 Mo	10.88	3.69	4.39	3	11,088
1 Yr	12.17	1.30	3.16	4	11,217
3 Yr Avg	13.28	9.70	6.10	2	14,536
5 Yr Avg	12.02	14.32	5.72	1	17,639
10 Yr Avg	10.71	-1.36	1.56	2	27,661
15 Yr Avg	10.82	-0.11	2.02	1	46,695

Tax Analysis	Tax-Adj Rtn%	%Rank Cat	Tax-Cost Rat	%Rank Cat
3 Yr (estimated)	8.70	5	2.64	97
5 Yr (estimated)	7.83	5	2.90	98
10 Yr (estimated)	6.88	25	3.04	100

Potential Capital Gain Exposure: 10% of assets

Rating and Risk

Time Period	Load-Adj Return %	Morningstar Rtn vs Cat	Morningstar Risk vs Cat	Morningstar Risk-Adj Rating
1 Yr	7.41			
3 Yr	11.65	High	High	★★★★★
5 Yr	11.05	High	High	★★★★★
10 Yr	10.23	High	+Avg	★★★★★
Incept	11.07			

Other Measures	Standard Index S&P 500	Best Fit Index Mstar Mid Value
Alpha	10.5	4.2
Beta	0.47	0.54
R-Squared	59	73
Standard Deviation	10.19	
Mean	13.28	
Sharpe Ratio	1.18	

Portfolio Analysis 09-30-04

Total Stocks:72 Share change since 06-30-04	Sectors	P/E Ratio	YTD Return %	% Net Assets
⊕ Ameren	Utilities	15.6	-2.11	1.69
⊕ Dominion Resources	Utilities	22.2	-0.18	1.43
⊕ Pfizer	Health	22.0	-2.75	1.35
FirstEnergy	Utilities	15.2	-3.16	1.26
⊕ Royal Dutch Petroleum ADR	Energy	—	-2.96	1.19
⊕ Merck	Health	11.4	-3.02	1.07
⊕ Fifth Third Bancorp	Financial	14.1	-3.45	1.04
Canadian Oil Sands Tr	Energy	—	—	1.00
⊕ Public Service Enterprise	Utilities	14.8	-4.02	0.95

Total Fixed-Income:403	Date of Maturity	Amount $000	Value $000	% Net Assets
Nalco Fin Hldgs 144A	02-01-14	515,000	368,225	1.41
Pacific Gas & Elec 6.05%	03-01-34	300,000	306,397	1.17
Dynegy 6.875%	04-01-11	240,000	229,800	0.88
Charter Comms Hldgs	01-15-11	316,000	227,520	0.87
Qwest Cap Fdg 7.25%	02-15-11	245,000	219,888	0.84
Calpine 8.5%	02-15-11	325,000	209,625	0.80
Tenet Healthcare 7.375%	02-01-13	220,000	207,900	0.80
El Paso Engy 6.75%	05-15-09	205,000	205,000	0.78
Cablevision Sys 144A 8%	04-15-12	192,000	201,600	0.77

Equity Style
Style: Value
Size: Large-Cap

Value Measures		Rel Category
Price/Earnings	13.91	0.85
Price/Book	1.82	0.77
Price/Sales	0.98	0.75
Price/Cash Flow	5.42	0.78
Dividend Yield %	3.82	2.20

Growth Measures	%	Rel Category
Long-Term Erngs	6.12	0.55
Book Value	0.10	0.02
Sales	0.47	0.10
Cash Flow	-10.37	NMF
Historical Erngs	1.95	0.21

Market Cap %			
Giant	29.8	Small	0.7
Large	46.0	Micro	0.2
Mid	23.3	Avg $mil:	19,571

Composition

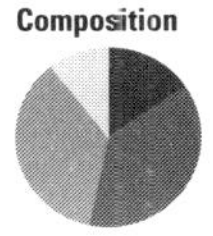

Cash	15.3
Stocks	37.8
Bonds	36.2
Other	10.7
Foreign (% of Stock)	10.5

Fixed-Income Style
Duration: —
Quality: —

Avg Eff Duration[1]	—
Avg Eff Maturity	—
Avg Credit Quality	—
Avg Wtd Coupon	6.31%

[1]figure provided by fund

Sector Weightings	% of Stocks	Rel S&P 500	3 Year High	3 Year Low
Info	6.32	0.29		
Software	0.00	0.00	0	0
Hardware	0.45	0.04	1	0
Media	0.00	0.00	0	0
Telecom	5.87	1.86	3	3
Service	25.28	0.54		
Health	10.67	0.85	11	0
Consumer	0.00	0.00	0	0
Business	0.33	0.08	0	0
Financial	14.28	0.69	14	5
Mfg	68.40	2.13		
Goods	3.68	0.39	5	2
Ind Mtrls	5.10	0.40	3	4
Energy	13.04	1.82	15	0
Utilities	46.58	15.74	81	47

Morningstar's Take by Andrew Gogerty 12-30-04

Franklin Income boasts a compelling record and healthy yield, but it isn't without risks.

Like many of its siblings, this fund's primary focus is delivering strong income and not just total return. Thus, its portfolio is loaded with stodgy, dividend-paying stocks and a hefty stake in low-quality debt. This tack can lead to significant sector bets, including the fund's current 49% stake in utilities. It also means added volatility and the likelihood that the fund won't always be in sync with the market.

This strategy has paid off, however. In 2004, for instance, the fund's 11.7% gain through December 28 tops 95% of its conservative-allocation peers. Its stake in utility companies has worked particularly well, as many of these firms refocus on their core businesses. The fund's high-yield issues have also done well amid improving corporate fundamentals and low interest rates. Moreover, this showing mirrors its long-term dominance over its peers.

While investors should expect this offering's biases to remain, comanagers Ed Perks and Charles Johnson continue to make changes at the margins. They have trimmed the fund's high-yield and utility stakes, believing that their strong runs have led to less opportunity for long-term price appreciation. Meanwhile, Perks and Johnson have increased the fund's health-care exposure by adding to picks such as Merck and Bristol-Myers Squibb. They believe these firms are trading below their true value, and that their stock prices don't reflect the future value of their drug pipelines.

In the end, this is a solid offering. Granted, the fund's potential volatility from its sector and high-yield concentration may turn off investors seeking a more tame, diversified option. But we think that Perks' and Johnson's experience in managing the fund's risks trumps these concerns.

Address:	One Franklin Parkway San Mateo CA 94403-1906 800-342-5236
Web Address:	www.Franklintempleton.com
Inception:	08-31-48
Advisor:	Franklin Advisers, Inc.
Subadvisor:	None
NTF Plans:	Schwab Instl NTF, TD Waterhouse Ins NT

Minimum Purchase:	$1000	Add: $50	IRA: $250
Min Auto Inv Plan:	$50	Add: $50	
Sales Fees:	4.25%L, 2.00%R		
Management Fee:	0.63% mx./0.36% mn.		
Actual Fees:	Mgt:0.46%	Dist:0.15%	
Expense Projections:	3Yr:$648	5Yr:$814	10Yr:$1293
Income Distrib:	Monthly		

Franklin Ins T/F Inc A

Ticker	Load	NAV	Yield	SEC Yield	Total Assets	Mstar Category
FTFIX	4.25%	$12.38	4.4%	3.52%	$1,838 mil	Muni National Long

Governance and Management

Fiduciary Grade: C

Portfolio Manager(s)

John Pomeroy is a Franklin veteran. He has been with this fund since 1989 and oversees many other Franklin muni funds. Jim Conn teams up with Pomeroy here. The fund also benefits from Franklin's extensive research capabilities.

Strategy

Lead manager John Pomeroy follows Franklin's standard buy-and-hold strategy. The fund's main focus is providing a steady stream of tax-free income, while steering clear of deliberate interest-rate bets. Pomeroy also avoids potentially volatile derivative securities. Finally, he invests almost exclusively in insured municipal bonds, so credit quality is not a concern.

Historical Profile

Return Average
Risk Below Avg
Rating ★★★ Neutral

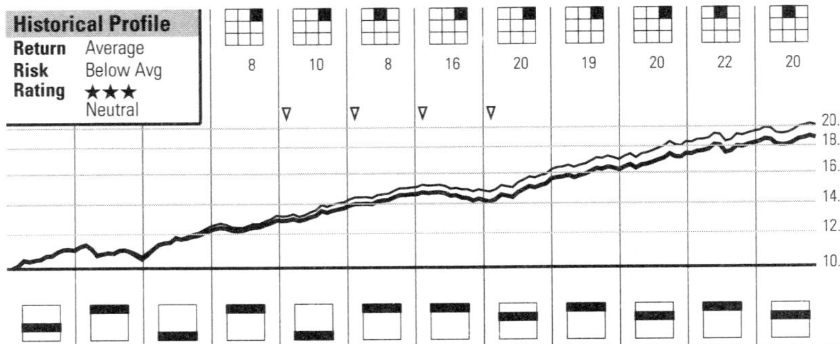

Investment Style
Fixed Income
Income Rtn %Rank Cat

▼ Manager Change
▽ Partial Manager Change

Growth of $10,000
▬ Investment Values of Fund
— Investment Values of LB Muni

Performance Quartile (within Category)

1993	1994	1995	1996	1997	1998	1999	2000	2001	2002	2003	12-04	History
12.70	11.54	12.37	12.16	12.32	12.30	11.26	11.97	11.91	12.34	12.44	12.38	NAV
11.84	-3.58	13.63	4.11	8.15	6.05	-3.46	12.08	4.57	8.70	5.46	4.13	Total Return %
-0.44	1.59	-3.83	-0.32	-1.04	-0.43	-1.40	0.40	-0.56	-0.90	0.15	-0.35	+/-LB Muni
-2.54	3.76	-7.34	-0.35	-2.69	-0.77	1.22	-3.16	-0.30	-1.33	-0.87	-2.43	+/-LB Muni 20YR
6.23	5.76	6.29	5.79	5.70	5.37	5.08	5.53	5.12	5.00	4.62	4.51	Income Return %
5.61	-9.34	7.34	-1.68	2.45	0.68	-8.54	6.55	-0.55	3.70	0.84	-0.38	Capital Return %
68	5	97	25	83	17	19	28	21	48	24	34	Total Rtn % Rank Cat
0.73	0.71	0.71	0.70	0.68	0.65	0.61	0.61	0.60	0.58	0.56	0.55	Income $
0.00	0.00	0.00	0.00	0.12	0.10	0.02	0.00	0.00	0.00	0.00	0.01	Capital Gains $
0.53	0.52	0.59	0.60	0.60	0.61	0.62	0.62	0.62	0.63	0.62	0.63	Expense Ratio %
6.22	5.79	6.00	5.81	5.68	5.44	5.11	5.23	5.23	4.90	4.73	4.45	Income Ratio %
8	7	14	14	19	28	13	13	10	8	12	9	Turnover Rate %
1,807	1,621	1,723	1,667	1,683	1,731	1,505	1,470	1,519	1,623	1,677	1,599	Net Assets $mil

Performance 12-31-04

	1st Qtr	2nd Qtr	3rd Qtr	4th Qtr	Total
2000	3.15	1.26	2.38	4.81	12.08
2001	1.68	0.68	2.51	-0.35	4.57
2002	0.88	3.00	4.40	0.21	8.70
2003	1.33	3.01	-0.48	1.52	5.46
2004	1.82	-2.66	3.56	1.44	4.13

Trailing	Total Return%	+/- LB Muni	+/- LB Muni 20YR	%Rank Cat	Growth of $10,000
3 Mo	1.44	0.19	-0.54	24	10,144
6 Mo	5.05	-0.14	-1.70	40	10,505
1 Yr	4.13	-0.35	-2.43	34	10,413
3 Yr Avg	6.08	-0.36	-1.55	27	11,937
5 Yr Avg	6.95	-0.25	-1.59	20	13,993
10 Yr Avg	6.24	-0.82	-1.71	40	18,318
15 Yr Avg	6.47	-0.52	-1.18	39	25,610

Tax Analysis	Tax-Adj Rtn%	%Rank Cat	Tax-Cost Rat	%Rank Cat
3 Yr (estimated)	4.55	59	0.00	1
5 Yr (estimated)	6.02	38	0.00	1
10 Yr (estimated)	5.74	50	0.04	17

Potential Capital Gain Exposure: 6% of assets

Rating and Risk

Time Period	Load-Adj Return %	Morningstar Rtn vs Cat	Morningstar Risk vs Cat	Morningstar Risk-Adj Rating
1 Yr	-0.30			
3 Yr	4.55	Avg	-Avg	★★★
5 Yr	6.02	Avg	-Avg	★★★
10 Yr	5.78	Avg	Low	★★★
Incept	7.13			

Other Measures	Standard Index LB Aggr	Best Fit Index LB Muni 20YR
Alpha	-0.2	-0.8
Beta	0.96	0.89
R-Squared	99	99

Standard Deviation	4.87
Mean	6.08
Sharpe Ratio	0.98

Portfolio Analysis 09-30-04

Total Fixed-Income:378	Date of Maturity	Amount $000	Value $000	% Net Assets
California St 5%	02-01-31	25,000	25,493	1.39
Jefferson Cnty Ala Swr 5	02-01-29	22,050	24,480	1.33
Harris Cnty Tex Health F	07-01-29	22,000	22,760	1.24
Harris Cnty-Houston Tex	11-15-30	21,325	22,091	1.20
Michigan St Trunk Line 5	11-01-30	20,000	20,777	1.13
Metropolitan Transn Auth	11-15-28	20,000	20,529	1.12
Orlando & Orange Cnty Ex	07-01-35	20,000	20,410	1.11
Corona Calif Ctfs Partn	09-01-20	15,000	20,008	1.09
Mesa Ariz Indl Dev Auth	01-01-25	18,000	19,488	1.06
Los Angeles Cnty Calif M	07-01-21	17,000	17,072	0.93
Jefferson Cnty Ala Swr 5	02-01-32	14,690	16,506	0.90
Medical Ctr Hosp Auth 5.	08-01-19	15,000	16,496	0.90
New York St Dorm Auth	07-01-26	15,000	16,212	0.88
Atlanta Ga Arpt 5.5%	01-01-26	13,750	15,637	0.85
Cleveland Ohio Arpt Sys	01-01-31	15,405	15,560	0.85

Current Investment Style

Duration: Short Int Long; Quality: High Med Low

[1]Avg Eff Duration	5.0 Yrs
Avg Eff Maturity	19.8 Yrs
Avg Credit Quality	AAA
Avg Wtd Coupon	5.33%
Avg Wtd Price	105.97% of par

[1]figure provided by fund

Credit Analysis	% bonds 09-30-04		
US Govt	0	BB	0
AAA	100	B	0
AA	0	Below B	0
A	0	NR/NA	0
BBB	0		

Top 5 States	% bonds		
TX	10.7	GA	7.4
MI	9.8	NY	7.2
FL	8.7		

Composition			
Cash	0.4	Bonds	99.3
Stocks	0.0	Other	0.3

Special Securities	
Restricted/Illiquid Secs	0
Options/Futures/Warrants	No

Sector Weightings	% of Bonds	Rel Cat
General Obligation	18.2	0.70
Utilities	3.7	0.28
Health	13.4	1.70
Water/Waste	24.7	2.23
Housing	1.9	0.27
Education	13.4	1.17
Transportation	9.1	1.20
COP/Lease	1.4	0.67
Industrial	13.6	1.05
Misc Revenue	0.0	0.00
Demand	0.5	1.85

Morningstar's Take by Scott Berry 12-13-04

We think Franklin Insured Tax-Free has a lot to offer conservative municipal bond investors.

For starters, management follows a restrained approach here. It avoids derivative securities, which can add to a fund's volatility, steers clear of interest-rate bets, which have proved to be a difficult way for most bond managers to add value, and invests almost exclusively in insured municipal bonds, which carry little if any credit risk. Rather, management simply buys what it considers to be attractively valued insured municipal bonds and holds them for their income.

The fund's approach is far from flashy, but it has produced solid long-term results. In fact, the fund's three- and five-year trailing returns rank in the muni national long-term category's top third and compare favorably with those of its average muni-insured peer. More impressive, though, has been the fund's below-average volatility, which owes much to the added yield provided by its stash of older less-rate-sensitive high-coupon bonds. Many of these issues have been called away in recent years, but the fund still holds a number of bonds with coupon rates of 6% and higher. These issues help dampen volatility and contribute to the fund's above-average yield.

Of course, the fund's conservative approach wouldn't be nearly as successful if not paired with a low-cost structure. At 0.63%, this fund's expense ratio ranks among the lowest in the broker-sold muni-bond universe. And with yields still low and fund returns tightly bunched, the fund's expense ratio provides it a nearly insurmountable advantage over its insured-muni subgroup peers.

We'll be keeping an eye on this fund to see if bond calls erode its yield advantage, but we think its expense advantage and proven approach are likely to keep it among the elite. As insured municipal-bond funds go, this one is easy to recommend.

Address:	One Franklin Parkway San Mateo CA 94403-1906 800-342-5236
Web Address:	www.franklintempleton.com
Inception:	04-03-85
Advisor:	Franklin Advisers, Inc.
Subadvisor:	None
NTF Plans:	Federated Tr NTF, Schwab Instl NTF

Minimum Purchase:	$1000	Add: $50	IRA: $0
Min Auto Inv Plan:	$50	Add: $50	
Sales Fees:	4.25%L, 2.00%R		
Management Fee:	0.63% mx./0.45% mn.		
Actual Fees:	Mgt:0.46%	Dist:0.10%	
Expense Projections:	3Yr:$618	5Yr:$761	10Yr:$1178
Income Distrib:	Monthly		

Franklin SmMid Cap Gr A

Ticker	Load	NAV	Yield	Total Assets	Mstar Category
FRSGX	5.75%	$34.16	0.0%	$8,938 mil	Mid-Cap Growth

Governance and Management

Fiduciary Grade: C

Portfolio Manager(s)

Ed Jamieson leads the management team here. He has managed the fund since 1992 and has put together a fine record. He's assisted by Michael McCarthy, a Franklin veteran who has worked on the offering for about a decade.

Strategy

This former small-cap fund now favors mid-cap stocks. It relies on a variety of quantitative screens and fundamental research from Franklin's pool of analysts to ferret out companies with growth rates of more than 15%, reasonable valuations, and some sort of sustainable competitive advantage.

Historical Profile

Return Average
Risk Above Avg
Rating ★★ Below Avg

Investment Style
Equity
Stock %

1993	1994	1995	1996	1997	1998	1999	2000	2001	2002	2003	12-04
92%	100%	90%	90%	100%	87%	89%	97%	95%			

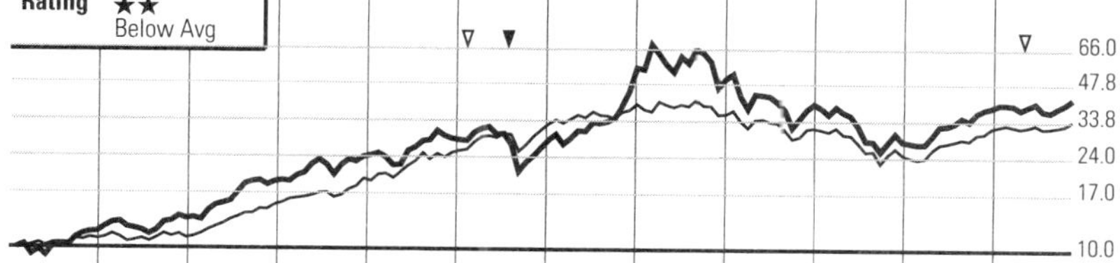

▼ Manager Change
▽ Partial Manager Change

Growth of $10,000
— Investment Values of Fund
— Investment Values of S&P 500

Performance Quartile (within Category)

1993	1994	1995	1996	1997	1998	1999	2000	2001	2002	2003	12-04	History
12.94	13.00	17.01	20.72	22.93	22.57	44.13	39.33	31.17	21.95	30.22	34.16	NAV
21.77	9.22	42.20	27.07	15.79	-0.02	97.08	-9.80	-20.53	-29.58	37.68	13.04	Total Return %
11.71	7.91	4.67	4.13	-17.56	-28.59	76.04	-0.70	-8.65	-7.49	9.01	2.17	+/-S&P 500
10.58	11.38	8.22	9.59	-6.75	-17.88	45.79	1.95	-0.38	-2.17	-5.03	-2.44	+/-Russ MG
0.39	0.17	0.11	0.40	0.44	0.63	0.19	0.55	0.21	0.00	0.00	0.00	Income Return %
21.38	9.05	42.09	26.67	15.35	-0.65	96.89	-10.35	-20.74	-29.58	37.68	13.04	Capital Return %
20	6	18	8	65	92	18	62	52	64	36	49	Total Rtn % Rank Cat
0.04	0.02	0.01	0.07	0.09	0.14	0.04	0.24	0.08	0.00	0.00	0.00	Income $
0.40	1.00	1.38	0.80	0.93	0.18	0.26	0.23	0.00	0.00	0.00	0.00	Capital Gains $
0.00	0.30	0.69	0.97	0.92	0.89	0.94	0.85	0.86	0.89	1.02	0.98	Expense Ratio %
0.84	0.24	0.25	0.09	0.10	0.32	0.30	0.24	0.23	-0.18	-0.41	-0.51	Income Ratio %
63	90	105	88	55	43	47	25	27	47	36	53	Turnover Rate %
15	40	246	800	2,756	3,961	8,820	10,956	8,523	5,540	7,860	7,729	Net Assets $mil

Performance 12-31-04

	1st Qtr	2nd Qtr	3rd Qtr	4th Qtr	Total
2000	13.71	-2.21	3.28	-21.46	-9.80
2001	-24.10	12.19	-25.14	24.68	-20.53
2002	-2.76	-16.63	-20.82	9.70	-29.58
2003	-2.41	18.81	4.40	13.74	37.68
2004	2.25	2.07	-4.22	13.08	13.04

Trailing	Total Return%	+/- S&P 500	+/- Russ MG	%Rank Cat	Growth of $10,000
3 Mo	13.08	3.85	-0.86	47	11,308
6 Mo	8.31	1.12	-0.70	43	10,831
1 Yr	13.04	2.17	-2.44	49	11,304
3 Yr Avg	3.10	-0.48	-3.06	58	10,959
5 Yr Avg	-4.71	-2.41	-1.35	60	7,857
10 Yr Avg	12.47	0.40	1.24	22	32,387
15 Yr Avg	—	—	—	—	—

Tax Analysis	Tax-Adj Rtn%	%Rank Cat	Tax-Cost Rat	%Rank Cat
3 Yr (estimated)	1.09	72	0.00	1
5 Yr (estimated)	-5.93	60	0.11	5
10 Yr (estimated)	11.14	19	0.60	11

Potential Capital Gain Exposure: 11% of assets

Rating and Risk

Time Period	Load-Adj Return %	Morningstar Rtn vs Cat	Morningstar Risk vs Cat	Morningstar Risk-Adj Rating
1 Yr	6.54			
3 Yr	1.09	-Avg	+Avg	★★
5 Yr	-5.83	Avg	+Avg	★★
10 Yr	11.81	+Avg	+Avg	★★★
Incept	12.41			

Other Measures	Standard Index S&P 500	Best Fit Index Russ MG
Alpha	-0.3	-3.0
Beta	1.19	1.04
R-Squared	85	97
Standard Deviation	20.14	
Mean	3.10	
Sharpe Ratio	0.09	

Portfolio Analysis 09-30-04

Share change since 06-04 Total Stocks:172	Sector	PE	YTD Ret%	% Assets
Tektronix	Hardware	17.0	-3.86	2.10
Thermo Electron	Health	27.2	19.80	1.92
⊖ Bunge	Goods	13.3	75.28	1.68
⊖ Coventry Health Care	Health	15.5	23.46	1.68
Pall	Health	23.0	9.51	1.58
Cabot	Ind Mtrls	18.3	23.54	1.53
Cognizant Technology Sol	Business	62.5	85.50	1.50
⊖ L-3 Communications Holdi	Hardware	20.6	43.54	1.41
Waters	Health	27.6	41.10	1.36
⊖ Mettler-Toledo Internati	Health	21.6	21.56	1.35
Fisher Scientific Intern	Health	43.9	50.79	1.33
CH Robinson Worldwide	Business	35.9	48.14	1.32
Lam Research	Hardware	21.5	-10.50	1.27
⊕ Newfield Exploration	Energy	12.5	32.58	1.25
⊕ Varian Medical Systems	Health	36.0	25.15	1.23
Avaya	Hardware	24.5	32.92	1.22
Moody's	Business	32.5	44.06	1.22
⊖ BorgWarner	Ind Mtrls	14.4	28.76	1.22
Federated Investors B	Financial	17.0	5.00	1.18
⊖ Providian Financial	Financial	14.3	41.50	1.17

Current Investment Style

Value Blnd Growth / Large Mid Small

Market Cap	%
Giant	0.0
Large	6.4
Mid	80.1
Small	12.8
Micro	0.7
Avg $mil:	3,213

Value Measures		Rel Category
Price/Earnings	20.39	0.93
Price/Book	2.69	0.90
Price/Sales	1.43	0.81
Price/Cash Flow	11.77	1.21
Dividend Yield %	0.33	0.77

Growth Measures	%	Rel Category
Long-Term Erngs	15.37	0.98
Book Value	11.00	1.10
Sales	9.78	1.14
Cash Flow	-0.38	NMF
Historical Erngs	16.44	1.03

Profitability	%	Rel Category
Return on Equity	15.74	1.09
Return on Assets	7.83	1.09
Net Margin	11.44	1.19

Sector Weightings	% of Stocks	Rel S&P 500	3 Year High	3 Year Low
Info	24.20	1.13		
Software	5.55	1.29	9	6
Hardware	15.51	1.52	23	15
Media	2.78	0.72	5	2
Telecom	0.36	0.11	2	0
Service	57.22	1.23		
Health	25.55	2.04	26	16
Consumer	6.79	0.75	9	6
Business	13.19	3.26	18	10
Financial	11.69	0.56	13	10
Mfg	18.59	0.58		
Goods	4.05	0.43	6	4
Ind Mtrls	8.95	0.71	9	4
Energy	5.59	0.78	8	3
Utilities	0.00	0.00	0	0

Composition

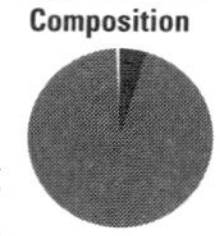

Cash	4.5
Stocks	94.6
Bonds	0.0
Other	0.9
Foreign (% of Stock)	3.3

Morningstar's Take by Dan Culloton 11-08-04

Size works against Franklin Small-Mid Cap Growth, but it has some things working for it, too.

This fund's assets have slipped some in recent years, but it remains one of the largest small-or-mid-cap funds. That has made it less nimble. For example, its 2% position in Thermo Electron gobbles up more than eight days of the medical equipment maker's average trading volume. Meanwhile, smaller funds, such as Needham Growth and Delafield, devote more of their portfolios to the stock but own less than a day's worth of trading volume each.

Carrying that much weight around could prevent this fund from leading the race in any one year; still, it has the resources at least stay in the contest. The fund's expense ratio is reasonable. It's among the cheapest mid-cap growth funds that charge a front-end load. More than 95% of mid-growth funds with similar fee structures are more expensive.

Veteran manager Ed Jamieson also practices a patient style of growth investing that relies on fundamental research. Jamieson is more of a maestro, orchestrating the ideas of Franklin's analysts, than a master stock selector. However, at his disposal he has a capable staff of more than 30 analysts who have served other Franklin growth funds well.

This year Jamieson and his squad have favored the shares of companies that could benefit from improved corporate spending and outsourcing trends. The fund added Rockwell Automation and Cognizant Technology Solutions this year because Jamieson thinks companies may be more likely to invest their money in cost-saving equipment and services than in labor as their profits improve. Those stocks have helped the fund post above-average results so far this year.

This fund wouldn't be our first choice among its peers because of its lack of flexibility and middling risk-adjusted returns. Still, decent costs, experienced management, and long-term focus make it an acceptable selection.

Address:	One Franklin Parkway San Mateo CA 94403-1906 800-342-5236
Web Address:	www.franklintempleton.com
Inception:	02-14-92
Advisor:	Franklin Advisers, Inc.
Subadvisor:	None
NTF Plans:	DATALynx NTF, Federated Tr NTF

Minimum Purchase:	$1000	Add: $50	IRA: $250
Min Auto Inv Plan:	$50	Add: $50	
Sales Fees:	5.75%L, 2.00%R		
Management Fee:	0.63% mx./0.40% mn.		
Actual Fees:	Mgt:0.46%	Dist:0.25%	
Expense Projections:	3Yr:$869	5Yr:$1086	10Yr:$1707
Income Distrib:	Semi-Annually		

Fremont Bond

Ticker	Load	NAV	Yield	SEC Yield	Total Assets	Mstar Category
FBDFX	None	$10.46	2.1%	2.81%	$879 mil	Intermediate-Term Bond

Governance and Management

Fiduciary Grade: D

Portfolio Manager(s)

Bill Gross and his extensive team of analysts and traders at Pimco are considered some of the best in the business. Gross has led this fund since its 1993 inception.

Strategy

This fund typically makes a series of bets against its benchmark, the Lehman Brothers Aggregate Index. Bill Gross relies on macroeconomic analysis to determine the fund's interest-rate sensitivity (duration usually stays within 20% of the index) and sector weightings, which can include high-yield, foreign bonds, and currency exposure.

Historical Profile

Return: High
Risk: Above Avg
Rating: ★★★★★ Highest

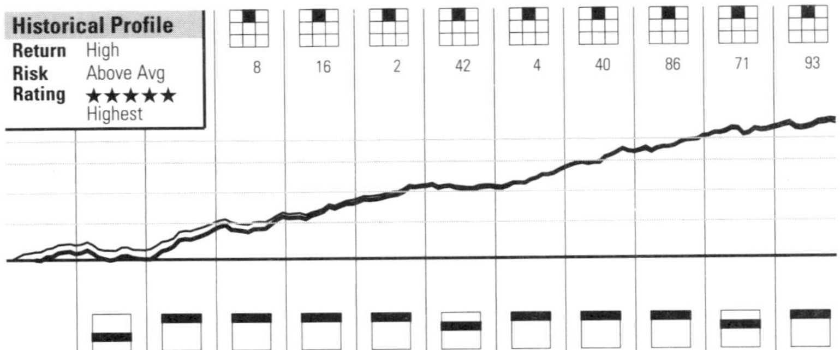

Investment Style
Fixed Income
Income Rtn %Rank Cat

▼ Manager Change
▽ Partial Manager Change

Growth of $10,000
— Investment Values of Fund
— Investment Values of LB Aggr

Performance Quartile (within Category)

History

1993	1994	1995	1996	1997	1998	1999	2000	2001	2002	2003	12-04	History
10.10	9.15	10.14	9.95	10.13	10.22	9.51	9.97	10.10	10.41	10.48	10.46	NAV
4.37*	-4.02	21.24	5.22	9.71	10.00	-1.24	12.77	9.77	9.78	5.32	5.10	Total Return %
—	-1.10	2.77	1.59	0.06	1.31	-0.42	1.14	1.33	-0.47	1.22	0.76	+/-LB Aggr
—	0.49	-0.19	2.53	0.28	-0.14	1.64	0.33	0.95	-3.25	-0.65	-0.20	+/-LB 5-10YR
0.00	5.60	7.66	6.99	6.86	7.23	5.87	7.72	5.95	3.90	3.42	2.23	Income Return %
—	-9.62	13.58	-1.77	2.85	2.77	-7.11	5.05	3.82	5.88	1.90	2.87	Capital Return %
—	54	10	11	23	2	50	5	6	19	30	11	Total Rtn % Rank Cat
0.37	0.55	0.68	0.69	0.66	0.71	0.58	0.71	0.57	0.39	0.35	0.23	Income $
0.01	0.00	0.22	0.00	0.09	0.18	0.00	0.00	0.25	0.27	0.13	0.32	Capital Gains $
0.50	0.66	0.60	0.68	0.61	0.60	0.60	0.62	0.57	0.59	0.61	—	Expense Ratio %
5.35	5.76	6.69	6.82	6.40	5.92	6.01	6.44	4.90	3.75	2.81	—	Income Ratio %
13	205	21	154	191	256	298	195	160	81	85	—	Turnover Rate %
12	60	93	73	109	216	175	298	783	1,228	851	879	Net Assets $mil

Performance 12-31-04

	1st Qtr	2nd Qtr	3rd Qtr	4th Qtr	Total
2000	2.92	1.94	2.91	4.44	12.77
2001	3.05	-0.07	6.37	0.23	9.77
2002	0.42	2.47	4.00	2.59	9.78
2003	2.05	2.82	-0.32	0.71	5.32
2004	2.94	-2.48	3.66	1.01	5.10

Trailing	Total Return%	+/- LB Aggr	+/- LB 5-10YR	%Rank Cat	Growth of $10,000
3 Mo	1.01	0.06	0.03	43	10,101
6 Mo	4.70	0.52	-0.87	19	10,470
1 Yr	5.10	0.76	-0.20	11	10,510
3 Yr Avg	6.71	0.52	-1.34	12	12,151
5 Yr Avg	8.51	0.80	-0.56	4	15,043
10 Yr Avg	8.63	0.91	0.17	1	22,882
15 Yr Avg	—	—	—	—	—

Tax Analysis	Tax-Adj Rtn%	%Rank Cat	Tax-Cost Rat	%Rank Cat
3 Yr (estimated)	4.90	8	1.70	53
5 Yr (estimated)	6.16	4	2.17	68
10 Yr (estimated)	5.91	2	2.50	84

Potential Capital Gain Exposure: 2% of assets

Rating and Risk

Time Period	Load-Adj Return %	Morningstar Rtn vs Cat	Morningstar Risk vs Cat	Morningstar Risk-Adj Rating
1 Yr	5.10			
3 Yr	6.71	High	+Avg	★★★★★
5 Yr	8.51	High	+Avg	★★★★★
10 Yr	8.63	High	+Avg	★★★★★
Incept	7.36			

Other Measures	Standard Index LB Aggr	Best Fit Index LB. U.S. Univ. Bd
Alpha	0.5	-0.4
Beta	1.01	1.06
R-Squared	95	97
Standard Deviation	4.72	
Mean	6.71	
Sharpe Ratio	1.15	

Morningstar's Take by Eric Jacobson 10-28-04

Fremont Bond is like a good dream that you're afraid you might wake up from.

We don't want to be overdramatic, but when it comes to bond funds, it's not much of a stretch to call this one dreamy. Through a quirk of business history, the fund is managed for Fremont by Pimco's Bill Gross, one of the biggest, and best, names in the bond-fund biz.

The significance is difficult to overstate. Gross has been fabulously successful at delivering strong, consistent returns to shareholders, and 2004 has been no exception. Despite a decision to shy away from corporate bond exposure in a year during which falling yields and rising prices have fueled the sector, the fund has earned a solid 4.6% gain through Oct. 28, 2004. Modest contributions from inflation-indexed Treasuries and emerging-market bond issues have helped. Gross hedges out most of the currency risk, but a focus on short European bonds early in the year and longer maturities more recently have also been a big help to the fund's bottom line.

A glance at the fund's longer record, including individual years and trailing returns, shows how successful Gross has been at making such deft plays and keeping the fund out of trouble. It's little wonder Morningstar has twice chosen him as our fixed-income Manager of the Year.

But while we stand by the 'dreamy' statement, our concern about 'waking up' relates to Fremont's involvement in the fund industry's market-timing scandal. There has been a flurry of suits and regulatory investigations, and Fremont has stated that its own investigation has uncovered some now-terminated timing arrangements. And though Fremont is being sold to a reputable firm, the dearth of information about the timing arrangements and steps taken to improve corporate governance remains a concern. As such, we don't think there's any reason to leave this fund, but we can't recommend sending new money until more questions are answered.

Address:	333 Market Street, Suite 2600 San Francisco CA 94105 800-548-4539
Web Address:	www.fremontfunds.com
Inception:	04-30-93*
Advisor:	Fremont Investment Advisors Inc
Subadvisor:	PA Fund Management LLC
NTF Plans:	ETrade No Load ETF

Minimum Purchase:	$2000	Add: $100	IRA: $1000
Min Auto Inv Plan:	$0	Add: $50	
Sales Fees:	No-load		
Management Fee:	0.40%, 0.10%A		
Actual Fees:	Mgt:0.40%	Dist:	
Expense Projections:	3Yr:$195	5Yr:$340	10Yr:$762
Income Distrib:	Monthly		

Portfolio Analysis 11-30-04

Total Fixed-Income:204	Date of Maturity	Amount $000	Value $000	% Net Assets
FNMA 5%		79,500	80,300	8.30
US Treasury Note 0.875%	04-15-10	49,816	49,395	5.11
US Treasury Note 3.875%	01-15-09	39,425	44,364	4.59
FNMA 5.5%		30,200	30,549	3.16
FHLMC CMO 6.5%	08-15-31	14,732	15,321	1.58
FNMA CMO 5%	04-25-33	9,114	9,204	0.95
Sears Cr Acct Mstr Tr 20	08-15-09	8,400	8,411	0.87
US Treasury Note 3.625%	01-15-08	7,640	8,369	0.87
Sears Cr Acct Mstr Tr 20	11-15-09	7,700	7,709	0.80
Peru Rep 9.125%	02-21-12	6,800	7,687	0.80
GNMA CMO	10-16-40	6,803	7,405	0.77
US Treasury Note 3%	07-15-12	5,809	6,459	0.67
Dg Fdg Tr Pfd 144A		1	6,131	0.63
Tennessee Gas Pipe 7%	10-15-28	6,145	6,053	0.63
Brazil Federative Rep 11	01-11-12	5,090	5,943	0.61
Daimler-Benz North Amerc	11-17-06	5,800	5,801	0.60
Tobacco Settlement Fing	06-01-39	5,350	5,329	0.55
FNMA 5.5%	03-01-18	4,739	4,895	0.51
US Treasury Note 2.5%	09-30-06	4,700	4,662	0.48
Small Busn Admin Gtd Ptn	08-10-11	4,407	4,632	0.48

Current Investment Style

Duration: Short Int Long
Quality: High Med Low

¹ figure provided by fund

Avg Eff Duration¹	4.5 Yrs
Avg Eff Maturity	6.4 Yrs
Avg Credit Quality	AA
Avg Wtd Coupon	4.54%
Avg Wtd Price	103.73% of par

Coupon Range	% of Bonds	Rel Cat
0% PIK	3.9	1.0
0% to 6%	79.2	1.2
6% to 8%	15.9	0.5
8% to 10%	3.4	0.6
More than 10%	1.4	1.2

1.00=Category Average

Credit Analysis		% bonds 11-30-04	
US Govt	0	BB	1
AAA	34	B	2
AA	1	Below B	0
A	59	NR/NA	0
BBB	2		

Sector Breakdown	% of assets
US Treasuries	6
TIPS	7
US Agency	1
Mortgage Pass-Throughs	18
Mortgage CMO	7
Mortgage ARM	0
US Corporate	4
Asset-Backed	2
Convertible	0
Municipal	1
Corporate Inflation-Protected	0
Foreign Corporate	0
Foreign Govt	1

Composition			
Cash	52.0	Bonds	47.0
Stocks	0.0	Other	1.0

Special Securities	
Restricted/Illiquid Secs	Trace
Exotic Mortgage-Backed	0
Emerging-Markets Secs	Trace
Options/Futures/Warrants	No

Fremont U.S. Micro-Cap

Ticker	Load	NAV	Yield	Total Assets	Mstar Category
FUSMX	Closed	$32.64	0.0%	$544 mil	Small Growth

Governance and Management

Fiduciary Grade: D

Portfolio Manager(s)

This management team has four senior members. Bob Kern handles semiconductor and services stocks. David Kern covers health care and software. Greg Weaver, who joined in 1997, handles communications and networking stocks. Stephen Roseman, who joined in 2003, oversees consumer-oriented stocks. Two analysts round out the team.

Strategy

Lead manager Bob Kern and his team look to invest in companies with innovative products that can grab market share or dominate an underserved niche. He is willing to invest before companies have a proven track record of success as long as the potential payoff is high enough. With that framework, he projects a firm's enterprise value as a guide to valuation. The team of four senior investment managers takes responsibility for certain sectors, with an emphasis on tech and health-care stocks.

Historical Profile

Return Above Avg
Risk Above Avg
Rating ★★★★ Above Avg

Investment Style: Equity Stock %

1995	1996	1997	1998	1999	2000	2001	2002	2003
74%	81%	85%	71%	80%	78%	86%	89%	

▼ Manager Change
▽ Partial Manager Change

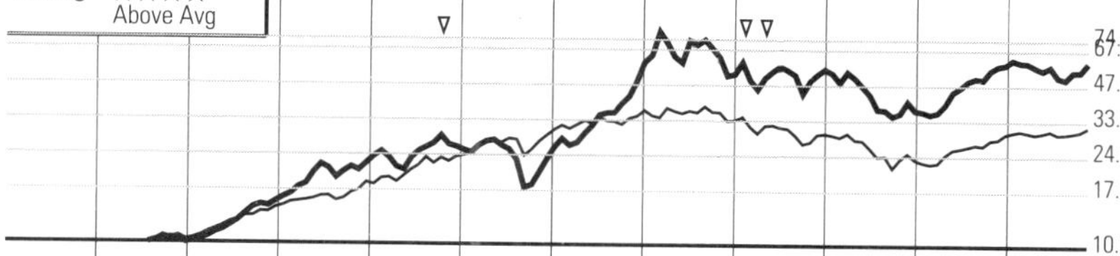

Growth of $10,000
— Investment Values of Fund
— Investment Values of S&P 500

Performance Quartile (within Category)

1993	1994	1995	1996	1997	1998	1999	2000	2001	2002	2003	12-04	History
—	10.13	15.10	21.50	20.28	20.86	39.35	26.87	28.29	18.98	29.73	32.64	NAV
—	1.50*	54.04	48.70	6.99	2.86	129.50	-10.62	5.28	-32.91	56.64	9.79	Total Return %
—	—	16.51	25.76	-26.36	-25.71	108.46	-1.52	17.16	-10.82	27.97	-1.08	+/-S&P 500
—	—	23.00	37.44	-5.96	1.63	86.41	11.31	14.51	-2.65	8.10	-4.52	+/-Russ 2000 Gr
—	0.00	0.00	0.00	0.00	0.00	0.00	0.06	0.00	0.00	0.00	0.00	Income Return %
—	—	54.04	48.70	6.99	2.86	129.50	-10.68	5.28	-32.91	56.64	9.79	Capital Return %
—	—	8	3	88	51	12	62	17	74	11	68	Total Rtn % Rank Cat
—	0.02	0.00	0.00	0.00	0.00	0.00	0.02	0.00	0.00	0.00	0.00	Income $
—	0.00	0.50	0.92	2.76	0.00	5.86	9.23	0.00	0.00	0.00	0.00	Capital Gains $
—	2.50	2.04	1.96	1.88	1.94	1.82	1.57	1.60	1.61	1.64	—	Expense Ratio %
—	0.68	-0.67	-0.51	-0.67	-1.22	-0.97	0.06	-0.47	-1.33	-1.47	—	Income Ratio %
—	129	144	81	125	170	164	117	93	68	105	—	Turnover Rate %
—	2	10	143	167	165	574	628	712	406	603	544	Net Assets $mil

Performance 12-31-04

	1st Qtr	2nd Qtr	3rd Qtr	4th Qtr	Total
2000	20.99	2.29	-7.25	-22.14	-10.62
2001	-13.66	25.17	-23.21	26.86	5.28
2002	-2.69	-19.91	-18.64	5.80	-32.91
2003	-1.90	27.71	8.12	15.64	56.64
2004	1.68	-3.31	-4.89	17.41	9.79

Trailing	Total Return%	+/- S&P 500	+/- Russ 2000 Gr	%Rank Cat	Growth of $10,000
3 Mo	17.41	8.18	2.33	7	11,741
6 Mo	11.67	4.48	3.51	15	11,167
1 Yr	9.79	-1.08	-4.52	68	10,979
3 Yr Avg	4.88	1.30	-0.91	51	11,537
5 Yr Avg	1.66	3.96	5.23	37	10,858
10 Yr Avg	20.17	8.10	13.05	1	62,800
15 Yr Avg	—	—	—	—	—

Tax Analysis	Tax-Adj Rtn%	%Rank Cat	Tax-Cost Rat	%Rank Cat
3 Yr (estimated)	4.88	45	0.00	1
5 Yr (estimated)	0.00	40	1.63	65
10 Yr (estimated)	17.53	3	2.20	81

Potential Capital Gain Exposure: -1% of assets

Rating and Risk

Time Period	Load-Adj Return %	Morningstar Rtn vs Cat	Morningstar Risk vs Cat	Morningstar Risk-Adj Rating
1 Yr	9.79			
3 Yr	4.88	Avg	+Avg	★★★
5 Yr	1.66	Avg	+Avg	★★★
10 Yr	20.17	High	+Avg	★★★★★
Incept	19.28			

Other Measures	Standard Index S&P 500	Best Fit Index Russ 2000 Gr
Alpha	2.0	-0.7
Beta	1.22	1.02
R-Squared	63	92
Standard Deviation	24.74	
Mean	4.88	
Sharpe Ratio	0.14	

Portfolio Analysis 09-30-03

Share change since 03-03 Total Stocks:87	Sector	PE	YTD Ret%	% Assets
⊕ NeoPharm	Health	—	-31.34	4.20
⊕ PDF Solutions	Hardware	—	8.12	3.33
⊕ Vixel	Software	—	—	2.99
Anaren	Hardware	30.5	-8.22	2.77
☼ Trident Microsystems	Hardware	64.2	-4.02	2.72
⊕ ATMI	Hardware	31.4	-2.93	2.69
⊖ Arthrocare	Health	58.4	30.86	2.36
⊕ Eclipsys	Software	—	75.52	2.35
⊕ Too	Consumer	30.8	44.91	2.20
⊕ Kroll	Business	—	—	2.01
⊕ BHA Group Holdings	Business	—	—	1.95
⊖ Harvard Bioscience	Health	44.5	-47.98	1.86
ICON PLC ADR	Health	18.8	-11.95	1.85
☼ Remec	Hardware	—	-15.67	1.84
☼ OPNET Technologies	Software	25.7	-48.82	1.83
⊕ Alloy	Consumer	—	54.89	1.73
⊖ Costar Group	Business	NMF	10.74	1.64
☼ California Pizza Kitchen	Consumer	28.6	14.26	1.61
⊕ Identix	Hardware	—	65.84	1.53
⊕ Advanced Neuromodulation	Health	41.9	-14.18	1.49

Current Investment Style

Value Blnc Growth / Large Mid Small

Market Cap	%
Giant	0.0
Large	0.0
Mid	0.0
Small	30.5
Micro	69.5
Avg $mil: 271	

Value Measures		Rel Category
Price/Earnings	28.10	1.29
Price/Book	1.69	0.64
Price/Sales	1.44	0.96
Price/Cash Flow	6.77	0.85
Dividend Yield %	0.04	0.13

Growth Measures	%	Rel Category
Long-Term Erngs	15.44	0.89
Book Value	9.77	1.51
Sales	5.33	0.83
Cash Flow	-22.45	NMF
Historical Erngs	4.92	0.36

Profitability	%	Rel Category
Return on Equity	-4.63	NMF
Return on Assets	-5.31	NMF
Net Margin	-4.26	NMF

Sector Weightings	% of Stocks	Rel S&P 500	3 Year High	3 Year Low
Info	42.31	1.97		
Software	11.29	2.63	14	6
Hardware	31.02	3.04	37	23
Media	0.00	0.00	2	0
Telecom	0.00	0.00	2	0
Service	46.95	1.01		
Health	20.35	1.63	24	14
Consumer	12.62	1.39	13	4
Business	13.03	3.22	18	13
Financial	0.95	0.05	6	0
Mfg	10.73	0.33		
Goods	4.76	0.51	13	2
Ind Mtrls	5.04	0.40	13	5
Energy	0.93	0.13	1	0
Utilities	0.00	0.00	0	0

Composition

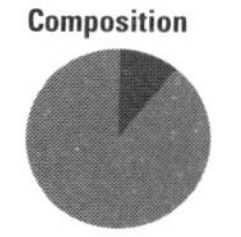

Cash	10.7
Stocks	89.4
Bonds	0.0
Other	0.0
Foreign (% of Stock)	4.1

Morningstar's Take by Dan McNeela 12-20-04

Deals with industry regulators and Affiliated Managers Group have helped clean up the mess at Fremont U.S. Micro-Cap.

On Nov. 4, 2004, Fremont agreed to a settlement with New York Attorney General Eliot Spitzer and the SEC to resolve allegations that it had permitted market-timing and late trading in its mutual funds. Fremont will pay $2.1 million in restitution and disgorgement and $2 million in civil penalties.

According to regulators, this fund had been a target of the improper trading in 2001 and 2002, as one of the market-timers made 20 exchanges in a year in amounts ranging from $13 million to $17 million. Fremont apparently allowed this activity, which clearly violated its prospectus, because the market-timer agreed to invest $10 million in another Fremont fund.

With Fremont's governance in question, it is encouraging that AMG has agreed to acquire the Fremont funds and act as the advisor. Many former Fremont employees are expected to join AMG, though Fremont previously stated that those involved in the improper trading are no longer with the firm.

Pending proxy approval, the fund's name will change to Managers Fremont Micro-Cap Fund. Its longtime subadvisor, Kern Capital Management, will continue to make the investment decisions. Lead manager Bob Kern is satisfied with the new affiliation because he has already been serving as a subadvisor for AMG on the Managers Special Equity.

Keeping Kern on board is crucial here, as he's proved himself very capable over long time periods. The fund's return in 2004 hasn't been great. It largely ignores energy stocks, which have led the market, because Kern thinks the area lacks the type of innovative company he seeks.

Investors have reason to be upset with past transgressions here, but we think there's enough reason to stick with it.

Address:	333 Market Street, Suite 2600 San Francisco CA 94105 800-548-4539
Web Address:	www.fremontfunds.com
Inception:	06-30-94 *
Advisor:	Fremont Investment Advisors Inc
Subadvisor:	Kern Capital Management LLC
NTF Plans:	Fidelity Retail-NTF, Schwab OneSource

Minimum Purchase:	Closed	Add: —	IRA: —
Min Auto Inv Plan:	Closed	Add: —	
Sales Fees:	No-load		
Management Fee:	2.50% mx./1.50% mn.		
Actual Fees:	Mgt:1.64%	Dist:	
Expense Projections:	3Yr:$517	5Yr:$892	10Yr:$1944
Income Distrib:	Annually		

Gabelli Asset

Ticker	Load	NAV	Yield	Total Assets	Mstar Category
GABAX	12b-1 only	$41.45	0.1%	$2,218 mil	Mid-Cap Blend

Governance and Management

Fiduciary Grade: D

Portfolio Manager(s)

Mario Gabelli has managed this fund since its March 1986 inception. He has clearly demonstrated management acumen, but his total compensation package is excessive ($37.5 million in 2002), and it's based on assets under management at his firm, rather than fund performance.

Strategy

Mario Gabelli first looks for firms trading at less than his estimates of the price a private buyer would pay for them. He buys those with improving fundamentals and clear catalysts that can drive their share prices higher. His style has led him to favor media and communications firms for some time, but industrials and consumer staples are also featured in the portfolio.

Historical Profile

Return Average
Risk Below Avg
Rating ★★★★ Above Avg

Investment Style: Equity, Stock %

▼ Manager Change
∇ Partial Manager Change

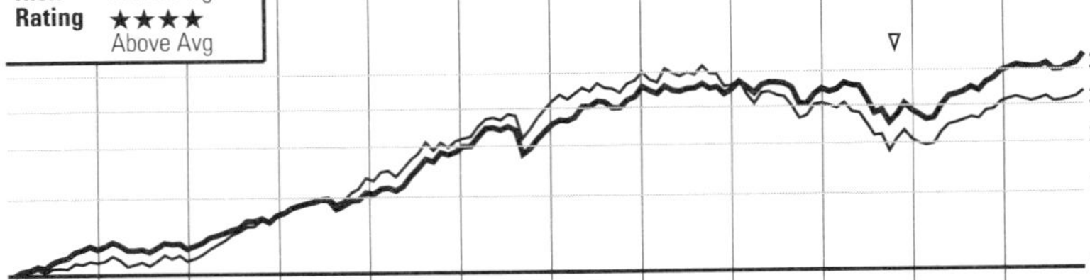

Performance Quartile (within Category)

	1993	1994	1995	1996	1997	1998	1999	2000	2001	2002	2003	12-04	History
				97%	99%	96%	93%	92%	87%	95%	99%	98%	Stock %
	23.30	22.21	25.75	26.42	31.85	35.47	40.84	33.90	32.97	28.25	36.26	41.45	NAV
	21.84	-0.15	24.94	13.36	38.07	15.93	28.49	-2.37	0.16	-14.27	30.57	16.49	Total Return %
	11.78	-1.46	-12.59	-9.58	4.72	-12.64	7.45	6.73	12.04	7.82	1.90	5.62	+/-S&P 500
	7.91	3.44	-5.98	-5.82	5.83	-3.18	13.77	-19.86	0.76	0.26	-5.02	0.02	+/-S&P Mid 400
	0.83	1.12	1.14	0.59	0.26	0.06	0.00	0.75	0.00	0.04	0.11	0.07	Income Return %
	21.01	-1.27	23.80	12.77	37.81	15.87	28.49	-3.12	0.16	-14.31	30.46	16.42	Capital Return %
	26	39	67	86	6	32	31	80	43	38	77	42	Total Rtn % Rank Cat
	0.17	0.26	0.25	0.15	0.07	0.02	0.00	0.31	0.00	0.01	0.03	0.03	Income $
	0.76	0.79	1.75	2.62	4.54	1.40	4.63	5.57	0.98	0.00	0.59	0.76	Capital Gains $
	1.31	1.28	1.33	1.34	1.38	1.36	1.37	1.36	1.36	1.38	1.38	—	Expense Ratio %
	0.82	1.10	0.95	0.52	0.22	0.06	-0.10	0.77	0.00	0.04	0.11	—	Income Ratio %
	16	19	26	15	22	21	32	48	15	8	7	—	Turnover Rate %
	948	982	1,090	1,082	1,334	1,594	1,994	1,909	1,911	1,683	1,733	2,218	Net Assets $mil

Performance 12-31-04

	1st Qtr	2nd Qtr	3rd Qtr	4th Qtr	Total
2000	0.22	-1.83	-0.10	-0.66	-2.37
2001	-2.57	7.33	-13.40	10.60	0.16
2002	3.76	-10.06	-15.37	8.55	-14.27
2003	-5.06	17.41	2.41	14.37	30.57
2004	3.06	1.85	-1.68	12.88	16.49

Trailing	Total Return%	+/- S&P 500	+/- S&P Mid 400	%Rank Cat	Growth of $10,000
3 Mo	12.88	3.65	0.73	26	11,288
6 Mo	10.99	3.80	1.20	29	11,099
1 Yr	16.49	5.62	0.02	42	11,649
3 Yr Avg	9.25	5.67	-1.26	55	13,040
5 Yr Avg	4.98	7.28	-4.55	72	12,751
10 Yr Avg	14.02	1.95	-2.07	43	37,137
15 Yr Avg	12.41	1.48	-2.25	64	57,819

Tax Analysis	Tax-Adj Rtn%	%Rank Cat	Tax-Cost Rat	%Rank Cat
3 Yr (estimated)	9.03	48	0.20	23
5 Yr (estimated)	3.99	68	0.94	41
10 Yr (estimated)	12.26	36	1.54	38

Potential Capital Gain Exposure: 47% of assets

Rating and Risk

Time Period	Load-Adj Return %	Morningstar Rtn vs Cat	Morningstar Risk vs Cat	Morningstar Risk-Adj Rating
1 Yr	16.49			
3 Yr	9.25	Avg	Avg	★★★
5 Yr	4.98	-Avg	-Avg	★★★
10 Yr	14.02	Avg	-Avg	★★★★
Incept	14.16			

Other Measures	Standard Index S&P 500	Best Fit Index Russ 1000 VI
Alpha	5.7	0.8
Beta	0.96	0.98
R-Squared	88	92
Standard Deviation	16.68	
Mean	9.25	
Sharpe Ratio	0.48	

Morningstar's Take by Kerry O'Boyle 10-26-04

The flagship Gabelli Asset is the best way for investors to benefit from the expertise of Mario Gabelli, but it requires patience.

This offering focuses on the core competencies of manager and firm founder Mario Gabelli--media, telecom, and industrial stocks. More than half of the fund's assets are devoted to those three sectors. Normally, such concentration in just a few areas would be cause for concern, but Gabelli has kept the fund's volatility low versus its mid-blend peers for more than a decade by spreading his bets across more than 400 holdings and hanging on to those stocks for the long haul.

Performance can be spotty, though, as the fund's heavy sector weightings drift in and out of favor. Its trailing three- and five-year returns through Oct. 22, 2004, for example, land it in the bottom third of the mid-blend category. Telecom stocks were battered severely when the stock market bubble burst in 2000, and media stocks have been slow to recover from a fall off in advertising spending. To be fair, the fund is likely to thrive should those sectors, and activity in another Gabelli specialty area--company mergers and acquisitions--pick up.

Still, investors should be wary of the glow of the fund's star manager. Mario Gabelli may be stretched a bit thin as the listed manager on 11 different offerings, the CEO of Gabelli Asset Management, and a frequent TV guest commentator. While Gabelli maintains that the number of funds he oversees is irrelevant and that it's the low-turnover, value-driven process he has created that's most important, investors need to understand that going in. Plus, the fund isn't cheap. Its 1.38% expense ratio is more expensive than it was a decade ago when the fund was less than half its current size.

Overall, fans of Gabelli will find this to be a capable offering. Its style has been distinctly out of favor the last few years and requires a long investment time horizon to reap its full benefits, but Gabelli's reputation is well-earned.

Address:	One Corporate Center Rye NY 10580 800-422-3554
Web Address:	www.gabelli.com
Inception:	03-03-86
Advisor:	Gabelli Funds, LLC
Subadvisor:	None
NTF Plans:	Fidelity Retail-NTF, Schwab OneSource

Minimum Purchase:	$1000	Add: $0	IRA: $250
Min Auto Inv Plan:	$0	Add: $100	
Sales Fees:	0.25%B, 2.00%R		
Management Fee:	1.00%, 0.10%A		
Actual Fees:	Mgt:1.00%	Dist:0.25%	
Expense Projections:	3Yr:$437	5Yr:$755	10Yr:$1657
Income Distrib:	Annually		

Portfolio Analysis 09-30-04

Share change since 06-04 Total Stocks:399	Sector	PE	YTD Ret%	% Assets
News Corporation ADR A	Media	—	6.65	3.49
⊖ Telephone and Data Syste	Telecom	39.5	24.11	2.50
Cablevision Systems A	Media	—	6.46	2.06
Liberty Media	Media	—	11.56	2.03
Neiman-Marcus	Consumer	—	—	1.76
Viacom A	Media	—	—	1.42
Deere & Company	Ind Mtrls	15.7	16.26	1.29
Time Warner	Media	27.5	8.12	1.21
ITT Industries	Ind Mtrls	18.4	14.79	1.20
Newmont Mining	Ind Mtrls	45.6	-8.02	1.17
AT&T Wireless Services	Telecom	—	—	1.11
Media General A	Media	—	0.81	1.03
Procter & Gamble	Goods	23.3	12.38	1.00
American Express	Financial	20.3	17.60	0.98
⊖ Navistar International	Ind Mtrls	17.5	-8.17	0.98
Genuine Parts	Consumer	19.3	36.90	0.96
Berkshire Hathaway A	Financial	—	—	0.95
⊖ Idex	Ind Mtrls	24.1	48.09	0.95
⊖ PepsiAmericas	Goods	16.1	25.93	0.95
⊖ Sprint	Telecom	—	55.24	0.95

Current Investment Style

Value Blnd Growth; Large Mid Small

Market Cap	%
Giant	15.8
Large	31.2
Mid	32.6
Small	17.1
Micro	3.3
Avg $mil: 7,075	

Value Measures		Rel Category
Price/Earnings	18.66	1.10
Price/Book	1.90	0.88
Price/Sales	0.96	0.91
Price/Cash Flow	7.45	1.19
Dividend Yield %	1.23	1.23

Growth Measures	%	Rel Category
Long-Term Erngs	11.33	0.90
Book Value	3.28	0.47
Sales	3.93	0.69
Cash Flow	-0.82	NMF
Historical Erngs	5.02	0.45

Profitability	%	Rel Category
Return on Equity	13.49	0.98
Return on Assets	4.56	0.70
Net Margin	5.75	0.63

Sector Weightings	% of Stocks	Rel S&P 500	3 Year High	3 Year Low
Info	33.13	1.54		
Software	0.12	0.03	1	0
Hardware	1.93	0.19	3	1
Media	20.34	5.30	21	15
Telecom	10.74	3.41	13	10
Service	21.58	0.47		
Health	3.05	0.24	3	2
Consumer	8.54	0.94	10	7
Business	3.68	0.91	4	4
Financial	6.31	0.30	7	6
Mfg	45.30	1.41		
Goods	16.42	1.76	19	15
Ind Mtrls	22.19	1.75	25	21
Energy	4.21	0.59	4	3
Utilities	2.48	0.84	3	2

Composition

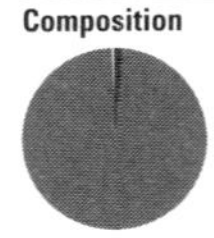

Cash	1.6
Stocks	97.8
Bonds	0.0
Other	0.6
Foreign (% of Stock)	14.0

Gabelli Glob Telecomm

Ticker	Load	NAV	Yield	Total Assets	Mstar Category
GABTX	12b-1 only	$17.23	0.5%	$211 mil	Specialty-Communications

Governance and Management

Fiduciary Grade: C

Portfolio Manager(s)

Mario Gabelli has been the lead manager here since 1995 and has managed mutual funds since 1986. He is supported on this fund by comanagers Ivan Arteaga and London-based Evan Miller, as well as Gabelli's New-York based telecom and media analysts. Gabelli has clearly demonstrated management acumen, but his total compensation package is excessive ($37.7 million in 2002), and it's based on assets under management at his firm rather than fund performance.

Strategy

Mario Gabelli brings his brand of value investing to the communications sector here, seeking companies that trade at discounts to the present value of their cash flows or breakup values. The fund is often broadly diversified across countries and individual names; it tends to avoid technology firms and has lower valuations than its rivals. The fund has a lower turnover rate than most in the category.

Historical Profile

Return Average
Risk Below Avg
Rating ★★★ Neutral

Investment Style: Equity Stock %

1994	1995	1996	1997	1998	1999	2000	2001	2002	2003	12-04
95%	91%	88%	70%	93%	93%	95%	100%	100%		

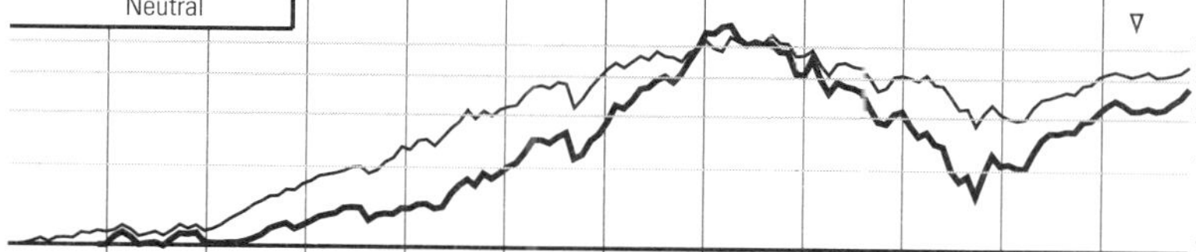

▼ Manager Change
▽ Partial Manager Change

Growth of $10,000
— Investment Values of Fund
— Investment Values of S&P 500

Performance Quartile (within Category)

1993	1994	1995	1996	1997	1998	1999	2000	2001	2002	2003	12-04	History
10.20	9.73	11.12	11.28	13.32	16.62	26.95	17.63	13.96	9.83	14.03	17.23	NAV
5.45*	-3.68	16.16	8.99	31.87	34.75	80.27	-24.08	-20.73	-29.58	42.73	23.37	Total Return %
—	-4.99	-21.37	-13.95	-1.48	6.18	59.23	-14.98	-8.85	-7.49	14.06	12.50	+/-S&P 500
—	1.47	-24.36	8.88	-8.77	-17.07	61.86	16.19	-7.96	4.97	35.40	4.67	+/-DJ Telecom
0.00	0.64	0.66	0.41	0.00	0.08	0.27	2.34	0.00	0.00	0.00	0.56	Income Return %
—	-4.32	15.50	8.58	31.87	34.67	80.00	-26.42	-20.73	-29.58	42.73	22.81	Capital Return %
—	67	100	62	25	67	15	15	3	30	46	27	Total Rtn % Rank Cat
0.10	0.07	0.06	0.05	0.00	0.01	0.05	0.63	0.00	0.00	0.00	0.08	Income $
0.00	0.03	0.12	0.79	1.55	1.30	2.90	2.15	0.02	0.00	0.00	0.00	Capital Gains $
2.54	1.80	1.75	1.72	1.74	1.60	1.48	1.45	1.52	1.66	1.62	—	Expense Ratio %
1.28	0.74	0.53	0.34	0.01	0.08	0.28	2.33	-0.45	-0.05	-0.38	—	Income Ratio %
—	14	24	7	9	20	60	49	5	8	11	—	Turnover Rate %
44	138	123	109	118	170	459	332	234	139	172	209	Net Assets $mil

Performance 12-31-04

	1st Qtr	2nd Qtr	3rd Qtr	4th Qtr	Total
2000	4.94	-10.15	-6.18	-14.18	-24.08
2001	-10.89	3.50	-19.86	7.25	-20.73
2002	-12.82	-21.94	-15.37	22.26	-29.58
2003	-1.93	26.24	0.99	14.16	42.73
2004	5.06	-2.10	3.46	15.94	23.37

Trailing	Total Return%	+/- S&P 500	+/- DJ Telecom	%Rank Cat	Growth of $10,000
3 Mo	15.94	6.71	7.72	58	11,594
6 Mo	19.95	12.76	5.06	34	11,995
1 Yr	23.37	12.50	4.67	27	12,337
3 Yr Avg	7.43	3.85	13.31	24	12,399
5 Yr Avg	-5.69	-3.39	9.67	22	7,461
10 Yr Avg	11.71	-0.36	7.26	29	30,264
15 Yr Avg	—	—	—	—	—

Tax Analysis	Tax-Adj Rtn%	%Rank Cat	Tax-Cost Rat	%Rank Cat
3 Yr (estimated)	7.37	21	0.06	20
5 Yr (estimated)	-6.44	22	0.80	73
10 Yr (estimated)	10.26	29	1.30	17

Potential Capital Gain Exposure: -3% of assets

Rating and Risk

Time Period	Load-Adj Return %	Morningstar Rtn vs Cat	Morningstar Risk vs Cat	Morningstar Risk-Adj Rating
1 Yr	23.37			
3 Yr	7.43	+Avg	-Avg	★★★★
5 Yr	-5.69	Avg	-Avg	★★★
10 Yr	11.71	Avg	Low	★★★
Incept	10.58			

Other Measures	Standard Index S&P 500	Best Fit Index Russ 1000
Alpha	3.9	2.9
Beta	1.39	1.40
R-Squared	84	84
Standard Deviation	24.79	
Mean	7.43	
Sharpe Ratio	0.25	

Morningstar's Take by Dan Lefkovitz 12-29-04

Geographic scope and attention to value give Gabelli Global Telecommunications an edge, but company-level issues dampen our enthusiasm for it.

This fund's foreign stake--over half of assets on Sept. 30--has boosted returns in recent years. One reason is that foreign-stock gains have been amplified as foreign currencies appreciated versus the dollar. Another is that foreign telecom, as in the U.S., is consolidating, and the fund is positioned to benefit. Canadian firm Rogers Communications, for example, is expanding through acquisition and gained 60% in 2004. Finally, comanager Ivan Arteaga says the team is finding foreign stock prices relatively low.

This attention to value has served investors well over time. Over the past 10 years, the fund has posted an impressive average annual return of nearly 12%. And during the bear market of the early 2000s, the fund lost less than its typical rival.

But the fund comes with a few notable caveats. For one thing, like any telecom fund, it is risky. Even though its bear market losses were relatively mild, it still lost 60%, a clear indication of the telecom sector's inherent volatility. What's more, investors who own a diversified fund probably already have plenty of telecom exposure.

We also have several concerns about Gabelli Asset Management's commitment to serving its fundholders well. Mario Gabelli is named manager on seven of the shop's funds, raising questions about whether he can adequately supervise so many offerings. In addition, fees on many funds are too high (this fund charges 1.62% versus 1.55% for its typical peer). Furthermore, the company could have been more forthcoming with fundholders regarding improper trading in the Global Growth fund and Marc Gabelli's diminished involvement in managing funds. Although we think Mario Gabelli is a topnotch investor, those concerns make it tough to give this fund an unqualified endorsement.

Portfolio Analysis 09-30-04

Share change since 06-04 Total Stocks:195	Sector	PE	YTD Ret%	% Assets
⊖ Sprint	Telecom	—	55.24	4.37
⊖ AT&T Wireless Services	Telecom	—	—	3.50
⊖ Telephone and Data Syste	Telecom	39.5	24.11	3.47
Deutsche Telekom AG ADR	Telecom	63.3	25.10	3.08
T.I.M.Spa	Telecom	—	—	2.88
⊖ Telefonica SA ADR	Telecom	36.4	31.63	2.67
Rogers Communications	Media	76.3	59.07	2.45
⊖ Verizon Communications	Telecom	32.4	20.25	2.38
Liberty Media	Media	—	11.56	2.30
⊖ Centurytel	Telecom	14.2	9.54	2.26
⊖ Swisscom AG ADR	Telecom	21.8	23.65	2.23
⊖ BCE	Telecom	18.1	12.67	2.20
⊖ Nextel Communications	Telecom	11.1	6.95	1.84
⊖ America Movil SA ADR	Telecom	23.2	92.36	1.80
⊖ Citizens Communications	Telecom	60.2	34.09	1.79
TeliaSonera	Telecom	—	—	1.78
⊖ United States Cellular	Telecom	38.5	26.09	1.67
KDDI	Telecom	—	—	1.60
⊖ Commonwealth Telephone E	Telecom	17.5	31.55	1.56
⊖ Alltel	Telecom	16.9	29.71	1.45

Current Investment Style

Value Blnd Growth; Large Mid Small

Market Cap	%
Giant	28.3
Large	40.1
Mid	25.0
Small	5.0
Micro	1.6
Avg $mil: 11,956	

Value Measures		Rel Category
Price/Earnings	20.64	0.98
Price/Book	1.66	0.82
Price/Sales	1.20	0.79
Price/Cash Flow	4.31	0.79
Dividend Yield %	1.30	1.19

Growth Measures	%	Rel Category
Long-Term Erngs	11.04	0.83
Book Value	-4.39	NMF
Sales	1.51	2.44
Cash Flow	11.26	1.18
Historical Erngs	0.85	0.31

Profitability	%	Rel Category
Return on Equity	9.39	0.88
Return on Assets	2.64	0.66
Net Margin	5.90	0.98

Industry Weightings	% of Stocks	Rel Cat
Telecom Srv	39.3	1.6
Wireless Srv	34.8	1.1
Network Eq	3.1	0.2
Semis	0.0	0.0
Big Media	2.3	0.7
Cable TV	13.6	4.9
Other Media	1.9	0.9
Soft/Hardwr	0.0	0.0
Other	5.0	0.4

Composition

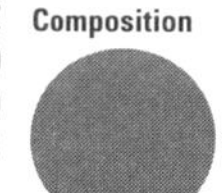

Cash	0.0
Stocks	99.9
Bonds	0.0
Other	0.1
Foreign (% of Stock)	52.9

Address:	One Corporate Center Rye NY 10580 800-422-3554
Web Address:	www.gabelli.com
Inception:	11-01-93 *
Advisor:	Gabelli Funds, LLC
Subadvisor:	None
NTF Plans:	Fidelity Retail-NTF, Schwab OneSource

Minimum Purchase:	$1000	Add: $0	IRA: $250
Min Auto Inv Plan:	$0	Add: $100	
Sales Fees:	0.25%B, 2.00%R		
Management Fee:	1.00%, 0.06%A		
Actual Fees:	Mgt:1.00%	Dist:0.25%	
Expense Projections:	3Yr:$511	5Yr:$881	10Yr:$1922
Income Distrib:	Annually		

Gabelli Growth

Ticker	Load	NAV	Yield	Total Assets	Mstar Category
GABGX	12b-1 only	$26.12	0.0%	$1,666 mil	Large Growth

Governance and Management

Fiduciary Grade: D

Portfolio Manager(s)

Howard Ward has been on the job here since January 1995. He is backed by two analysts dedicated exclusively to this fund, as well as Gabelli Asset Management's staff of analysts and portfolio managers. He previously managed Scudder Large Company Growth.

Strategy

Manager Howard Ward seeks big, well-known companies trading for less than what he thinks they're worth, based on his estimates of their growth during the next five years. He has recently boosted the number of holdings in the portfolio to more than 90 and tempered some of his sector bets in order to keep a lid on volatility. He hangs on to his stocks for the long haul, so the fund's turnover rate is fairly low.

Historical Profile

Return Average
Risk Above Avg
Rating ★★★ Neutral

Investment Style
Equity
Stock %

97% | 100% | 99% | 99% | 99% | 100% | 100% | 100% | 99%

▼ Manager Change
▽ Partial Manager Change

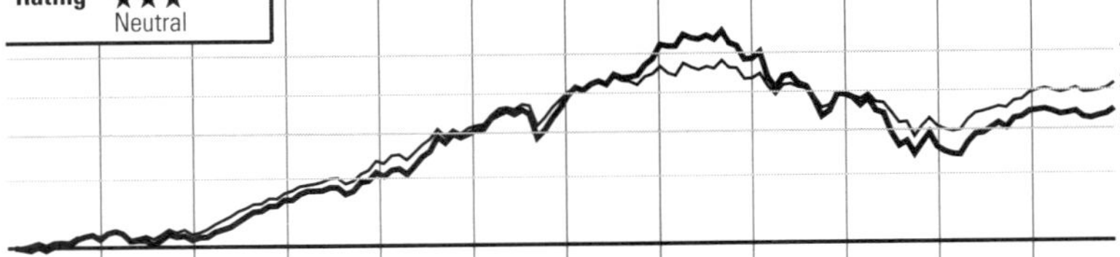

Growth of $10,000
— Investment Values of Fund
— Investment Values of S&P 500

Performance Quartile (within Category)

1993	1994	1995	1996	1997	1998	1999	2000	2001	2002	2003	12-04	History
23.26	19.68	22.16	24.14	28.63	35.40	46.51	37.79	28.68	18.99	24.95	26.12	NAV
11.26	-3.40	32.72	19.42	42.63	29.78	46.25	-10.57	-24.10	-33.79	31.38	4.69	Total Return %
1.20	-4.71	-4.81	-3.52	9.28	1.21	25.21	-1.47	-12.22	-11.70	2.71	-6.18	+/-S&P 500
8.39	-6.02	-4.46	-3.70	12.14	-8.93	13.09	11.85	-3.68	-5.91	1.63	-1.61	+/-Russ 1000Gr
0.42	0.37	0.28	0.11	0.01	0.00	0.00	0.00	0.00	0.00	0.00	0.00	Income Return %
10.84	-3.77	32.44	19.31	42.62	29.78	46.25	-10.57	-24.10	-33.79	31.38	4.69	Capital Return %
45	68	46	52	3	56	25	38	67	88	26	76	Total Rtn % Rank Cat
0.09	0.09	0.06	0.02	0.00	0.00	0.00	0.00	0.00	0.00	0.00	0.00	Income $
0.67	2.70	3.90	2.30	5.79	1.75	5.16	3.85	0.00	0.00	0.00	0.00	Capital Gains $
1.41	1.36	1.44	1.43	1.43	1.41	1.37	1.38	1.40	1.43	1.47	—	Expense Ratio %
0.22	0.31	0.22	0.12	-0.23	-0.33	-0.68	-0.63	-0.71	-0.68	-0.60	—	Income Ratio %
81	40	140	88	83	40	52	55	26	30	42	—	Turnover Rate %
696	484	526	623	952	1,864	3,155	3,835	2,958	1,905	1,751	1,666	Net Assets $mil

Performance 12-31-04

	1st Qtr	2nd Qtr	3rd Qtr	4th Qtr	Total
2000	7.72	-0.74	-5.73	-11.27	-10.57
2001	-20.19	3.38	-22.26	18.33	-24.10
2002	-3.00	-23.69	-15.31	5.62	-33.79
2003	-5.95	18.37	4.16	13.31	31.38
2004	-0.08	-0.08	-3.57	8.74	4.69

Trailing	Total Return%	+/- S&P 500	+/- Russ 1000Gr	%Rank Cat	Growth of $10,000
3 Mo	8.74	-0.49	-0.43	73	10,874
6 Mo	4.86	-2.33	1.39	49	10,486
1 Yr	4.69	-6.18	-1.61	76	10,469
3 Yr Avg	-3.07	-6.65	-2.89	84	9,107
5 Yr Avg	-9.17	-6.87	0.12	67	6,182
10 Yr Avg	10.25	-1.82	0.66	32	26,533
15 Yr Avg	9.54	-1.39	0.04	48	39,228

Tax Analysis	Tax-Adj Rtn%	%Rank Cat	Tax-Cost Rat	%Rank Cat
3 Yr (estimated)	-3.07	74	0.00	1
5 Yr (estimated)	-9.51	62	0.37	23
10 Yr (estimated)	8.43	30	1.65	57

Potential Capital Gain Exposure: -60% of assets

Rating and Risk

Time Period	Load-Adj Return %	Morningstar Rtn vs Cat	Morningstar Risk vs Cat	Morningstar Risk-Adj Rating
1 Yr	4.69			
3 Yr	-3.07	-Avg	High	★★
5 Yr	-9.17	Avg	+Avg	★★
10 Yr	10.25	Avg	+Avg	★★★
Incept	11.80			

Other Measures	Standard Index S&P 500	Best Fit Index Russ 1000Gr
Alpha	-6.5	-2.0
Beta	1.27	1.23
R-Squared	91	93

Standard Deviation	19.73
Mean	-3.07
Sharpe Ratio	-0.23

Portfolio Analysis 09-30-04

Share change since 06-04 Total Stocks:103	Sector	PE	YTD Ret%	% Assets
⊖ Time Warner	Media	27.5	8.12	3.17
⊖ Microsoft	Software	36.1	8.95	3.00
Walgreen	Consumer	31.6	6.03	2.67
⊖ Medtronic	Health	30.7	2.68	2.66
⊖ Amgen	Health	37.7	3.82	2.65
⊖ UnitedHealth Group	Health	23.8	51.38	2.52
⊖ Citigroup	Financial	15.3	2.72	2.35
⊖ Pfizer	Health	22.0	-22.31	2.17
⊕ Wal-Mart Stores	Consumer	23.4	0.51	2.07
Tiffany	Goods	22.6	-28.79	2.00
⊖ American International G	Financial	16.2	-0.53	2.00
⊖ State Street	Financial	15.3	-4.41	2.00
United Technologies	Ind Mtrls	18.6	10.72	1.79
⊖ Murphy Oil	Energy	16.5	24.71	1.72
⊖ Occidental Petroleum	Energy	10.1	41.27	1.70
⊖ Johnson & Johnson	Health	20.6	25.17	1.67
⊖ Symantec	Software	34.5	49.33	1.67
⊖ Schlumberger	Energy	40.7	23.84	1.66
⊖ L-3 Communications Holdi	Hardware	20.6	43.54	1.65
PepsiCo	Goods	22.5	13.82	1.60

Current Investment Style

Value Blnd Growth — Large Mid Small

Market Cap	%
Giant	44.0
Large	41.2
Mid	14.6
Small	0.3
Micro	0.0
Avg $mil: 33,825	

Value Measures		Rel Category
Price/Earnings	20.14	0.95
Price/Book	3.06	0.95
Price/Sales	2.10	0.98
Price/Cash Flow	11.68	1.06
Dividend Yield %	0.74	0.96

Growth Measures	%	Rel Category
Long-Term Erngs	13.82	0.98
Book Value	12.82	1.01
Sales	9.97	1.17
Cash Flow	18.80	1.14
Historical Erngs	15.74	1.09

Profitability	%	Rel Category
Return on Equity	18.00	1.00
Return on Assets	10.22	1.09
Net Margin	13.32	1.08

Sector Weightings	% of Stocks	Rel S&P 500	3 Year High	3 Year Low
Info	29.88	1.39		
Software	7.41	1.72	8	1
Hardware	13.11	1.29	24	13
Media	7.48	1.95	20	7
Telecom	1.88	0.60	3	1
Service	48.35	1.04		
Health	19.49	1.56	19	11
Consumer	14.10	1.55	14	5
Business	3.51	0.87	8	0
Financial	11.25	0.54	24	11
Mfg	21.77	0.68		
Goods	6.68	0.72	8	4
Ind Mtrls	5.71	0.45	6	0
Energy	9.38	1.31	9	0
Utilities	0.00	0.00	0	0

Composition

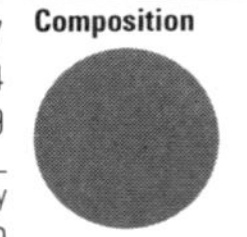

Cash	0.7
Stocks	99.3
Bonds	0.0
Other	0.0
Foreign (% of Stock)	3.3

Morningstar's Take by Kerry O'Boyle 10-13-04

A subtle strategy shift at Gabelli Growth addresses some concerns, but it's still too pricey.

Who says that veteran managers can't learn new tricks? Long-time skipper Howard Ward has taken some lessons from the recent bear market to heart. In 1999, Ward held only 40 stocks in the portfolio and nearly 50% of assets were devoted to hardware and media issues. While he managed to navigate the initial bursting of the tech bubble with relatively mild losses in 2000, that didn't last for long. A disappointing performance in 2001 and a disastrous 2002 highlighted the dangers of a fund concentrated in just a few names and sectors.

Fast forward to 2004, and shareholders now own a more diversified portfolio. It now holds more than 90 names and has milder sector biases. The fund's 8% media stake--while still more than its typical large-growth peer's--is less than half of what it was at the end of 2002. And hardware is a relatively moderate 18% of assets. Ward is also more conscious of the types of stocks he owns, leaning more toward steady growers, with fewer cyclicals and only a handful of emerging growth stories.

Unfortunately, the modified approach hasn't helped much thus far in 2004. Although a bet on oil stocks at the end of 2002 has paid off, Ward's favored semiconductor stocks have held the fund back. Overall, its performance trails more than two thirds of its peers through Oct. 13, 2004.

And we continue to dislike the fund's rich price tag. At 1.47%, its expense ratio is well above the 1.21% of its typical no-load rival. Moreover, its fees are 41 basis points (0.41) greater than the average of other actively managed funds with more than $1 billion in assets.

Those costs can put a serious dent in performance over time. While we consider the fund's strategy changes to be an improvement, the fund's fees still make it a less-than-compelling option.

Address:	One Corporate Center Rye NY 10580-1434 800-422-3554
Web Address:	www.gabelli.com
Inception:	04-10-87
Advisor:	Gabelli Funds, LLC
Subadvisor:	None
NTF Plans:	Fidelity Retail-NTF, Schwab OneSource

Minimum Purchase:	$1000	Add: $0	IRA: $250
Min Auto Inv Plan:	$0	Add: $100	
Sales Fees:	0.25%B, 2.00%R		
Management Fee:	1.00%, 0.10%A		
Actual Fees:	Mgt:1.00%	Dist:0.25%	
Expense Projections:	3Yr:$465	5Yr:$803	10Yr:$1757
Income Distrib:	Annually		

Gabelli Sm Cp Growth AAA

Ticker	Load	NAV	Yield	Total Assets	Mstar Category
GABSX	12b-1 only	$28.62	0.0%	$703 mil	Small Value

Governance and Management

Fiduciary Grade: D

Portfolio Manager(s)

Mario Gabelli has managed this fund since its 1991 inception. He's supported at this fund by a staff of nearly 20 analysts and portfolio managers. Gabelli has amassed some strong long-term records at funds such as Gabelli Value, but his total-compensation package is excessive ($37.5 million in 2002), and it's based on assets under management at his firm rather than on fund performance.

Strategy

Mario Gabelli values companies based on his estimates of their future cash flows or on what they might be worth to a potential buyer. He buys companies that trade at discounts to his estimates of their value, show improving fundamentals, and have some catalyst, such as industry consolidation, that will lead the market to recognize their value.

Historical Profile

Return Average
Risk Below Avg
Rating ★★★ Neutral

Investment Style: Equity Stock %

99%	90%	98%	96%	93%	93%	91%	99%	99%

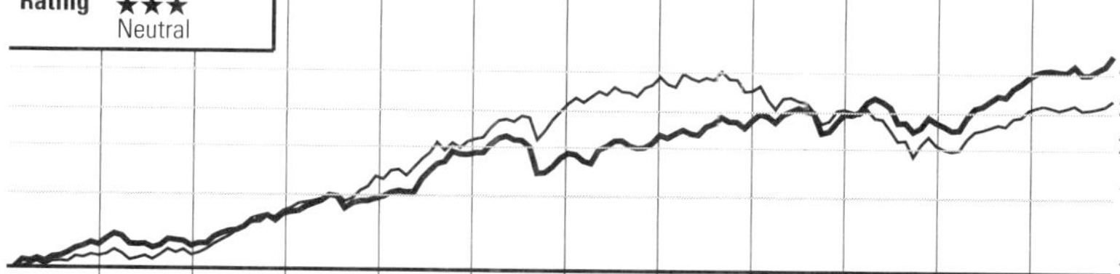

▼ Manager Change
∇ Partial Manager Change

Growth of $10,000
— Investment Values of Fund
— Investment Values of S&P 500

Performance Quartile (within Category)

1993	1994	1995	1996	1997	1998	1999	2000	2001	2002	2003	12-04	History
17.38	15.84	18.50	18.53	21.58	21.01	21.43	18.71	19.21	17.93	24.49	28.62	NAV
22.76	-2.93	25.25	11.88	36.47	-0.02	14.21	11.30	4.65	-5.34	37.56	21.68	Total Return %
12.70	-4.24	-12.28	-11.06	3.12	-28.59	-6.83	20.40	16.53	16.75	8.89	10.81	+/-S&P 500
-1.01	-1.39	-0.50	-9.49	4.69	6.43	15.70	-11.53	-9.37	6.09	-8.47	-0.57	+/-Russ 2000 VL
0.00	0.00	0.00	0.00	0.00	0.00	0.00	0.26	0.07	0.02	0.00	0.00	Income Return %
22.76	-2.93	25.25	11.88	36.47	-0.02	14.21	11.04	4.58	-5.36	37.56	21.68	Capital Return %
21	72	39	94	11	22	24	77	91	24	71	46	Total Rtn % Rank Cat
0.00	0.00	0.00	0.00	0.00	0.00	0.00	0.05	0.01	0.00	0.00	0.00	Income $
0.42	1.03	1.34	2.16	3.66	0.53	2.46	4.73	0.35	0.25	0.17	1.15	Capital Gains $
1.64	1.54	1.54	1.58	1.62	1.44	1.56	1.43	1.45	1.45	1.45	1.42	Expense Ratio %
0.03	-0.28	-0.24	-0.42	-0.36	-0.14	-0.34	0.26	0.30	-0.22	-0.22	-0.15	Income Ratio %
14	19	17	11	14	20	24	47	17	10	4	10	Turnover Rate %
215	196	229	217	293	321	338	374	440	453	521	703	Net Assets $mil

Performance 12-31-04

	1st Qtr	2nd Qtr	3rd Qtr	4th Qtr	Total
2000	3.78	2.38	3.65	1.07	11.30
2001	-1.39	10.73	-16.15	14.31	4.65
2002	8.90	-3.25	-15.81	6.71	-5.34
2003	-5.08	18.27	6.66	14.88	37.56
2004	5.19	2.99	-2.45	15.15	21.68

Trailing	Total Return%	+/- S&P 500	+/- Russ 2000 VL	%Rank Cat	Growth of $10,000
3 Mo	15.15	5.92	1.95	5	11,515
6 Mo	12.33	5.14	-1.04	45	11,233
1 Yr	21.68	10.81	-0.57	46	12,168
3 Yr Avg	16.58	13.00	0.08	35	15,844
5 Yr Avg	13.04	15.34	-4.19	82	18,457
10 Yr Avg	14.96	2.89	-0.21	56	40,315
15 Yr Avg	—	—	—	—	—

Tax Analysis	Tax-Adj Rtn%	%Rank Cat	Tax-Cost Rat	%Rank Cat
3 Yr (estimated)	16.17	28	0.35	22
5 Yr (estimated)	11.61	79	1.27	62
10 Yr (estimated)	13.01	49	1.70	45

Potential Capital Gain Exposure: 9% of assets

Rating and Risk

Time Period	Load-Adj Return %	Morningstar Rtn vs Cat	Morningstar Risk vs Cat	Morningstar Risk-Adj Rating
1 Yr	21.68			
3 Yr	16.58	Avg	-Avg	★★★★
5 Yr	13.04	-Avg	-Avg	★★
10 Yr	14.96	Avg	Avg	★★★
Incept	16.01			

Other Measures	Standard Index S&P 500	Best Fit Index Russ 2000 VL
Alpha	13.2	2.6
Beta	0.82	0.81
R-Squared	69	93
Standard Deviation	17.21	
Mean	16.58	
Sharpe Ratio	0.89	

Portfolio Analysis 09-30-04

Share change since 06-04 Total Stocks:472	Sector	PE	YTD Ret%	% Assets
Cablevision Systems A	Media	—	6.46	1.88
⊖ Clarcor	Ind Mtrls	21.5	25.62	1.64
Thomas Industries	Ind Mtrls	5.5	16.49	1.50
Thomas & Betts	Hardware	19.1	34.34	1.30
Liberty	Financial	28.1	7.83	1.18
⊖ Franklin Electric	Ind Mtrls	24.7	41.00	1.14
Vimpel-Communications AD	Telecom	75.2	47.51	1.12
Neiman-Marcus	Consumer	—	—	1.12
Greif A	Ind Mtrls	—	60.07	1.09
Chemed	Business	—	46.84	1.08
Modine Manufacturing	Ind Mtrls	20.5	27.68	1.07
⊖ Ametek	Ind Mtrls	22.3	49.08	1.06
CH Energy Group	Utilities	16.7	7.30	1.05
Pulitzer	Media	30.8	21.92	1.04
Hercules	Ind Mtrls	—	21.72	1.00
Sensient Technologies	Goods	14.3	24.91	0.98
⊖ Inamed	Health	36.4	31.63	0.98
Skyline	Consumer	65.5	22.05	0.91
⊖ Watts Water Technologies	Ind Mtrls	19.4	46.82	0.89
⊖ Sorin	Health	—	—	0.87

Current Investment Style

Value Blnd Growth — Large / Mid / Small

Market Cap	%
Giant	0.1
Large	1.3
Mid	24.7
Small	50.8
Micro	23.1
Avg $mil: 789	

Value Measures		Rel Category
Price/Earnings	18.88	1.18
Price/Book	1.58	0.95
Price/Sales	0.77	1.03
Price/Cash Flow	6.56	1.26
Dividend Yield %	1.20	1.00

Growth Measures	%	Rel Category
Long-Term Erngs	12.05	0.99
Book Value	1.54	0.36
Sales	1.11	0.35
Cash Flow	-3.20	NMF
Historical Erngs	-2.02	NMF

Profitability	%	Rel Category
Return on Equity	8.99	0.98
Return on Assets	2.95	0.71
Net Margin	3.86	0.58

Sector Weightings	% of Stocks	Rel S&P 500	3 Year High	3 Year Low
Info	18.50	0.86		
Software	0.66	0.15	1	0
Hardware	3.68	0.36	5	3
Media	11.16	2.91	14	10
Telecom	3.00	0.95	3	2
Service	30.35	0.65		
Health	6.68	0.53	7	3
Consumer	10.74	1.18	11	8
Business	6.87	1.70	8	6
Financial	6.06	0.29	8	6
Mfg	51.15	1.59		
Goods	10.70	1.15	14	10
Ind Mtrls	34.45	2.72	40	34
Energy	1.77	0.25	2	1
Utilities	4.23	1.43	5	4

Composition

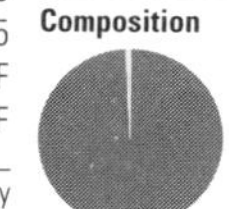

Cash	0.0
Stocks	99.0
Bonds	0.0
Other	1.0
Foreign (% of Stock)	6.4

Morningstar's Take by Kerry O'Boyle 12-02-04

Gabelli Small Cap Growth is a capable offering, but it's not among the elites of the small-cap world.

Don't let the name throw you. This is a sprawling, core small-cap option with a value bias. Noted manager Mario Gabelli looks for firms with solid fundamentals and catalysts for future growth that are trading at less than his estimate of their private-market value. This typically leads him to favor media firms that generate big cash flows, although Gabelli also specializes in finding values among industrial stocks.

Normally, such concentration in just a few sectors--the fund's nearly 35% stake in industrials, for example, is among the highest in the small-value category--would be cause for concern. But Gabelli has kept volatility low by spreading assets across more than 450 holdings and by patiently waiting for his picks to pay off. Turnover here tends to be miniscule.

Performance can be spotty, though, as those sectors drift in and out of favor. Thus far in 2004, for instance, the fund's returns have been mediocre, as its stake in surging industrials has been offset by continued weakness in media stocks. The lack of meaningful exposure to the financial and energy sectors hasn't helped, either.

We're also concerned that Mario Gabelli may be stretched a bit thin in his roles as manager of 11 different funds and CEO of Gabelli Asset Management. While Gabelli maintains that the number of funds he oversees is irrelevant and that it's the low-turnover, value-driven process he has created that's most important, investors need to understand this going in. Plus, the fund isn't cheap. Its 1.45% expense ratio is a bit rich for a no-load, small-cap blend or value offering.

In the end, Gabelli's reputation as a stock-picker is well-earned and over time the fund has been a decent performer. And it's likely the fund will thrive should media stocks rebound from their long slump. While not a standout, this is an adequate option for long-term investors.

Address:	One Corporate Center Rye NY 10580 800-422-3554
Web Address:	www.gabelli.com
Inception:	10-22-91
Advisor:	Gabelli Funds, LLC
Subadvisor:	None
NTF Plans:	Fidelity Retail-NTF, Schwab OneSource

Minimum Purchase:	$1000	Add: $0	IRA: $250
Min Auto Inv Plan:	$0	Add: $100	
Sales Fees:	0.25%B, 2.00%R		
Management Fee:	1.00%, 0.06%A		
Actual Fees:	Mgt:1.00%	Dist:0.25%	
Expense Projections:	3Yr:$459	5Yr:$792	10Yr:$1735
Income Distrib:	Annually		

Gabelli Value A

Ticker	Load	NAV	Yield	Total Assets	Mstar Category
GABVX	5.50%	$19.49	0.0%	$1,299 mil	Mid-Cap Blend

Governance and Management

Fiduciary Grade: D

Portfolio Manager(s)

Mario Gabelli has been managing mutual funds since the mid-1980s and has run this offering since its 1989 inception. He has clearly demonstrated management acumen, but his total compensation package is excessive ($37.5 million in 2002), and it's based on assets under management at his firm, rather than fund performance.

Strategy

As with his other funds, manager Mario Gabelli seeks companies that he estimates are trading at discounts to the present value of their future cash flow and that have a catalyst that will close those discounts. This offering is more concentrated in individual names than his flagship fund, Gabelli Asset, and is also much more concentrated in the media and communications sectors.

Historical Profile

Return Average
Risk Average
Rating ★★★ Neutral

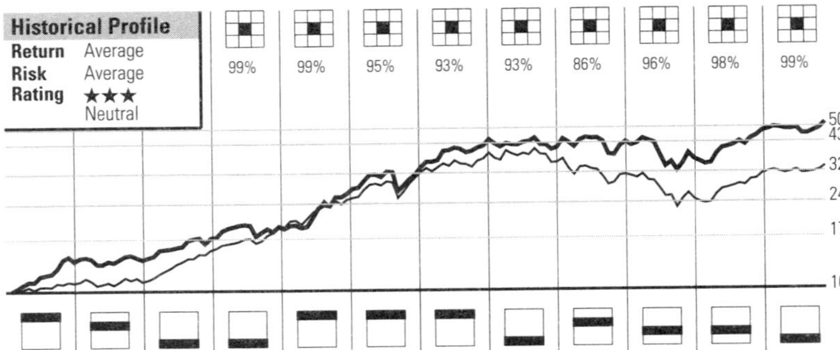

Investment Style
Equity
Stock %

▼ Manager Change
▽ Partial Manager Change

Growth of $10,000
▬ Investment Values of Fund
— Investment Values of S&P 500

Performance Quartile (within Category)

1993	1994	1995	1996	1997	1998	1999	2000	2001	2002	2003	12-04	History
12.09	10.49	11.62	11.52	14.30	16.08	19.45	16.13	16.43	13.81	17.97	19.49	NAV
39.45	0.00	22.56	8.65	48.23	23.23	31.92	-7.85	5.36	-15.95	31.87	12.78	Total Return %
29.39	-1.31	-14.97	-14.29	14.88	-5.34	10.88	1.25	17.24	6.14	3.20	1.91	+/-S&P 500
25.52	3.59	-8.36	-10.53	15.99	4.12	17.20	-25.34	5.96	-1.42	-3.72	-3.69	+/-S&P Mid 400
0.49	0.75	0.48	0.00	0.00	0.00	0.00	0.00	0.32	0.00	0.00	0.00	Income Return %
38.96	-0.75	22.08	8.65	48.23	23.23	31.92	-7.85	5.04	-15.95	31.87	12.78	Capital Return %
1	37	82	92	1	11	24	88	29	57	67	81	Total Rtn % Rank Cat
0.05	0.09	0.05	0.00	0.00	0.00	0.00	0.00	0.05	0.00	0.00	0.00	Income $
1.99	1.51	1.18	1.11	2.72	1.49	1.72	1.75	0.52	0.00	0.24	0.77	Capital Gains $
1.53	1.50	1.50	1.40	1.42	1.40	1.38	1.37	1.39	1.40	1.44	—	Expense Ratio %
0.38	0.73	0.42	-0.12	-0.45	-0.41	-0.40	-0.14	-0.30	-0.28	-0.35	—	Income Ratio %
21	67	65	37	44	46	59	66	29	16	8	—	Turnover Rate %
496	438	486	461	597	798	1,204	1,158	1,270	1,028	1,120	1,262	Net Assets $mil

Performance 12-31-04

	1st Qtr	2nd Qtr	3rd Qtr	4th Qtr	Total
2000	-3.86	1.02	-2.38	-2.80	-7.85
2001	0.68	8.56	-14.58	12.84	5.36
2002	3.29	-14.97	-14.62	12.09	-15.95
2003	-4.27	17.70	2.19	14.54	31.87
2004	2.89	-0.43	-2.93	13.41	12.78

Trailing	Total Return%	+/- S&P 500	+/- S&P Mid 400	%Rank Cat	Growth of $10,000
3 Mo	13.41	4.18	1.26	21	11,341
6 Mo	10.08	2.89	0.29	41	11,008
1 Yr	12.78	1.91	-3.69	81	11,278
3 Yr Avg	7.72	4.14	-2.79	71	12,499
5 Yr Avg	3.95	6.25	-5.58	78	12,137
10 Yr Avg	14.56	2.49	-1.53	34	38,934
15 Yr Avg	13.48	2.55	-1.18	24	66,648

Tax Analysis	Tax-Adj Rtn%	%Rank Cat	Tax-Cost Rat	%Rank Cat
3 Yr (estimated)	5.43	82	0.26	30
5 Yr (estimated)	1.91	80	0.85	38
10 Yr (estimated)	11.90	39	1.77	52

Potential Capital Gain Exposure: 35% of assets

Rating and Risk

Time Period	Load-Adj Return %	Morningstar Rtn vs Cat	Morningstar Risk vs Cat	Morningstar Risk-Adj Rating
1 Yr	6.57			
3 Yr	5.71	-Avg	+Avg	★★
5 Yr	2.78	-Avg	Avg	★★
10 Yr	13.92	Avg	Avg	★★★
Incept	12.97			

Other Measures	Standard Index S&P 500	Best Fit Index Russ 1000
Alpha	4.2	3.4
Beta	1.08	1.10
R-Squared	85	86
Standard Deviation	19.01	
Mean	7.72	
Sharpe Ratio	0.34	

Portfolio Analysis 09-30-04

Share change since 06-04 Total Stocks:149	Sector	PE	YTD Ret%	% Assets
⊕ Viacom A	Media	—	—	7.69
Media General A	Media	—	0.81	6.28
Cablevision Systems A	Media	—	6.46	4.59
⊖ Telephone and Data Syste	Telecom	39.5	24.11	3.24
Liberty Media	Media	—	11.56	3.15
Sprint	Telecom	—	55.24	2.70
Liberty	Financial	28.1	7.83	2.35
American Express	Financial	20.3	17.60	2.15
⊖ PepsiAmericas	Goods	16.1	25.93	1.92
Time Warner	Media	27.5	8.12	1.89
⊖ Newmont Mining	Ind Mtrls	45.6	-8.02	1.77
Vivendi Universal ADR	Media	—	32.08	1.72
⊖ Hilton Grp	Consumer	—	—	1.68
Dana	Ind Mtrls	10.4	-3.11	1.63
⊕ Honeywell International	Ind Mtrls	20.5	8.21	1.61
⊖ Navistar International	Ind Mtrls	17.5	-8.17	1.57
Thomas & Betts	Hardware	19.1	34.34	1.46
Archer Daniels Midland	Ind Mtrls	23.1	49.11	1.42
⊖ Hilton Hotels	Consumer	36.1	33.34	1.34
News Corporation ADR A	Media	—	6.65	1.30

Current Investment Style

Value Blnd Growth / Large Mid Small

Market Cap	%
Giant	8.5
Large	32.1
Mid	35.1
Small	22.5
Micro	1.9
Avg $mil: 5,573	

Value Measures		Rel Category
Price/Earnings	19.43	1.15
Price/Book	1.71	0.79
Price/Sales	0.91	0.86
Price/Cash Flow	7.22	1.16
Dividend Yield %	1.01	1.01

Growth Measures	%	Rel Category
Long-Term Erngs	10.77	0.86
Book Value	-1.31	NMF
Sales	2.75	0.49
Cash Flow	3.08	0.41
Historical Erngs	6.35	0.56

Profitability	%	Rel Category
Return on Equity	10.28	0.75
Return on Assets	2.77	0.43
Net Margin	3.30	0.36

Sector Weightings	% of Stocks	Rel S&P 500	3 Year High	3 Year Low
Info	49.64	2.31		
Software	0.06	0.01	0	0
Hardware	4.10	0.40	4	2
Media	34.81	9.07	39	30
Telecom	10.67	3.39	16	11
Service	19.56	0.42		
Health	0.78	0.06	1	1
Consumer	10.05	1.11	10	6
Business	3.79	0.94	4	4
Financial	4.94	0.24	6	5
Mfg	30.79	0.96		
Goods	10.15	1.09	11	10
Ind Mtrls	18.53	1.46	19	14
Energy	1.01	0.14	3	1
Utilities	1.10	0.37	3	1

Composition

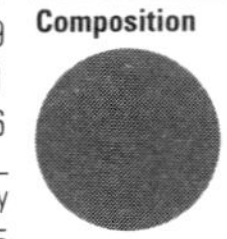

Cash	0.6
Stocks	99.4
Bonds	0.0
Other	0.0
Foreign (% of Stock)	11.3

Morningstar's Take by Kerry O'Boyle 10-27-04

Gabelli Value has less to show for its more compact portfolio.

This offering is the most concentrated option to which noted manager Mario Gabelli attaches his name. Currently, the portfolio contains 156 stocks, with 35% of assets in its top-10 holdings. Historically, however, that concentration has been significantly higher. Up until 2000, it wasn't unusual for Gabelli to stash more than 50% of the fund's assets in its top-10 stocks. In addition, more than half of its assets are typically invested in just three sectors of the market--media, telecom, and industrials--which Gabelli considers to be his firm's areas of core competency.

Unfortunately, Gabelli's bets on those top picks haven't paid off in recent years. After a strong run in the late 1990s, the fund has fallen on hard times, and its trailing five-year returns through Oct. 26, 2004, now land it in the bottom quartile of the mid-blend category. Media and telecom stocks have struggled mightily since the bursting of the stock market bubble in 2000. The concentrated approach hasn't stood out noticeably from its more diversified sibling, Gabelli Asset.

Investors attracted by the star power of Mario Gabelli should also understand just how much he has on his plate. He is the listed manager on 11 different funds, the CEO of Gabelli Asset Management, and a frequent TV guest commentator. Gabelli maintains that the number of funds he oversees is irrelevant and that it's the low-turnover, value-driven process he has created that's most important. Still, those looking for a more hands-on style may be disappointed.

Granted, Gabelli has hit such rough patches before and managed to bounce back. And the fund is likely to shine again should media and telecom stocks rebound strongly. But the combination of sector and individual security bets here has made it more volatile than the typical Gabelli-run offering. Fans of Gabelli are likely to be better off in one of his other, more diversified options.

Address:	One Corporate Center Rye NY 10580 800-422-3554
Web Address:	www.gabelli.com
Inception:	09-29-89
Advisor:	Gabelli Funds, LLC
Subadvisor:	None
NTF Plans:	DATALynx NTF, Federated Tr NTF

Minimum Purchase:	$1000	Add: $0	IRA: $250
Min Auto Inv Plan:	$0	Add: $100	
Sales Fees:	5.50%L, 2.00%R		
Management Fee:	1.00%, 0.10%A		
Actual Fees:	Mgt:1.00%	Dist:0.25%	
Expense Projections:	3Yr:$980	5Yr:$1294	10Yr:$2179
Income Distrib:	Annually		

Gabelli Westwood Bal AAA

Ticker	Load	NAV	Yield	Total Assets	Mstar Category
WEBAX	12b-1 only	$11.35	1.8%	$146 mil	Moderate Allocation

Governance and Management

Fiduciary Grade: C

Portfolio Manager(s)

Equity manager Susan Byrne is the founder and CEO of Westwood Holding Group and has a terrific long-term record as a stock-picker here and at Gabelli Westwood Equity. Mark Freeman has managed the bond portfolio since February 2001. He has been an analyst on the fund since 1998. Eight industry analysts assist the managers.

Strategy

Equity manager Susan Byrne scours the domestic-equity universe for companies that have posted positive earnings surprises but have yet to see upward estimate revisions from analysts. If the fundamentals check out, she's interested. The fund generally stakes about 60% of assets in stocks. Its bond stake is a conservative, intermediate-term portfolio.

Historical Profile

Return: Above Avg
Risk: Below Avg
Rating: ★★★★ Above Avg

Investment Style: Equity Stock %

60%	59%	63%	61%	61%	60%	61%	58%	58%

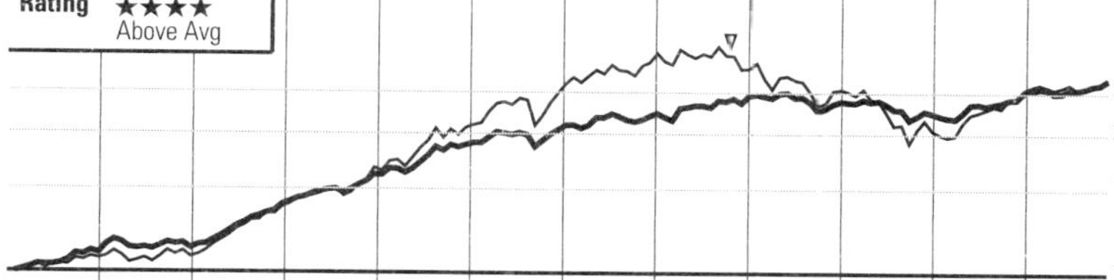

▼ Manager Change
▽ Partial Manager Change

Growth of $10,000
— Investment Values of Fund
— Investment Values of S&P 500

Performance Quartile (within Category)

1993	1994	1995	1996	1997	1998	1999	2000	2001	2002	2003	12-04	History
7.23	7.05	8.89	9.68	11.00	11.88	11.71	11.62	10.99	9.99	11.19	11.95	NAV
18.60	0.05	31.16	18.11	22.45	11.51	7.75	11.49	-3.26	-6.99	14.38	8.84	Total Return %
8.54	-1.26	-6.37	-4.83	-10.90	-17.06	-13.29	20.59	8.62	15.10	-14.29	-2.03	+/-S&P 500
6.87	2.00	6.39	6.77	3.25	-0.88	-5.10	7.05	-3.42	3.55	-9.68	-2.33	+/-DJ 60%
2.87	2.53	2.88	2.57	2.77	2.27	2.13	2.45	2.13	2.19	2.22	1.96	Income Return %
15.73	-2.48	28.28	15.54	19.68	9.24	5.62	9.04	-5.39	-9.18	12.16	6.88	Capital Return %
9	17	11	14	26	62	67	9	33	12	90	47	Total Rtn % Rank Cat
0.28	0.18	0.20	0.23	0.27	0.25	0.25	0.28	0.25	0.24	0.22	0.22	Income $
4.27	0.00	0.13	0.58	0.56	0.12	0.81	1.10	0.00	0.00	0.00	0.00	Capital Gains $
1.82	1.68	1.25	1.32	1.25	1.17	1.20	1.19	1.17	1.22	1.23	1.22	Expense Ratio %
1.90	1.55	2.47	2.62	2.60	2.37	2.06	2.21	2.23	2.25	2.10	1.92	Income Ratio %
192	168	133	111	110	77	86	65	37	78	56	41	Turnover Rate %
1	4	9	31	81	142	160	148	163	150	160	140	Net Assets $mil

Performance 12-31-04

	1st Qtr	2nd Qtr	3rd Qtr	4th Qtr	Total
2000	3.18	1.64	2.70	3.51	11.49
2001	-1.34	0.33	-8.03	6.27	-3.26
2002	1.13	-2.75	-9.19	4.13	-6.99
2003	-3.27	9.64	0.72	7.07	14.38
2004	1.45	-0.01	2.45	4.73	8.84

Trailing	Total Return%	+/- S&P 500	+/- DJ 60%	%Rank Cat	Growth of $10,000
3 Mo	4.73	-4.50	-2.75	91	10,473
6 Mo	7.30	0.11	-0.23	34	10,730
1 Yr	8.84	-2.03	-2.33	47	10,884
3 Yr Avg	5.01	1.43	-2.25	43	11,580
5 Yr Avg	4.54	6.84	-0.70	20	12,486
10 Yr Avg	11.03	-1.04	0.54	17	28,471
15 Yr Avg	—	—	—	—	—

Tax Analysis	Tax-Adj Rtn%	%Rank Cat	Tax-Cost Rat	%Rank Cat
3 Yr (estimated)	4.21	36	0.76	53
5 Yr (estimated)	3.26	16	1.22	57
10 Yr (estimated)	9.27	13	1.59	36

Potential Capital Gain Exposure: 13% of assets

Rating and Risk

Time Period	Load-Adj Return %	Morningstar Rtn vs Cat	Morningstar Risk vs Cat	Morningstar Risk-Adj Rating
1 Yr	8.84			
3 Yr	5.01	Avg	-Avg	★★★
5 Yr	4.54	+Avg	-Avg	★★★★
10 Yr	11.03	+Avg	Low	★★★★
Incept	10.68			

Other Measures	Standard Index S&P 500	Best Fit Index Mstar Large Value
Alpha	2.4	0.8
Beta	0.44	0.46
R-Squared	77	88
Standard Deviation	7.88	
Mean	5.01	
Sharpe Ratio	0.46	

Portfolio Analysis 09-30-04

Total Stocks:52 Share change since 06-30-04	Sectors	P/E Ratio	YTD Return %	% Net Assets
⊕ Lehman Brothers Holdings	Financial	11.7	2.19	1.61
⊖ ExxonMobil	Energy	13.9	-2.75	1.59
⊕ ChevronTexaco	Energy	7.7	-2.11	1.55
⊕ Starwood Hotels & Resorts	Consumer	33.9	-4.86	1.51
⊕ Kinder Morgan Energy Part	Energy	—	1.42	1.51
⊕ J P Morgan Chase	Financial	19.4	-1.99	1.50
⊖ Alcoa	Ind Mtrls	18.8	-5.63	1.49
⊖ Apache	Energy	11.4	-3.20	1.48
⊖ Burlington Resources	Energy	10.9	-4.28	1.48

Total Fixed-Income:30	Date of Maturity	Amount $000	Value $000	% Net Assets
US Treasury Note 3.5%	11-15-06	2,725	2,774	1.99
US Treasury Note 1.625%	10-31-05	2,750	2,734	1.96
US Treasury Note 6.125%	08-15-07	2,500	2,725	1.96
US Treasury Note 4.75%	05-15-14	2,000	2,100	1.51
US Treasury Note 5.75%	11-15-05	2,000	2,078	1.49
FHLMC 3.5%	09-15-07	2,000	2,022	1.45
FNMA 2%	01-15-06	2,000	1,988	1.43
Sec Cap Pac Tr 7.2%	03-01-13	1,600	1,802	1.29
Gte 6.46%	04-15-08	1,460	1,601	1.15

Equity Style
Style: Value
Size: Large-Cap

Value Measures		Rel Category
Price/Earnings	15.11	0.91
Price/Book	2.41	0.99
Price/Sales	1.41	1.07
Price/Cash Flow	8.54	1.18
Dividend Yield %	2.12	1.35

Growth Measures	%	Rel Category
Long-Term Erngs	9.59	0.82
Book Value	5.39	0.94
Sales	1.54	0.30
Cash Flow	3.02	0.38
Historical Erngs	13.97	1.29

Market Cap %			
Giant	36.2	Small	0.0
Large	46.6	Micro	2.5
Mid	14.7	Avg $mil:	26,983

Fixed-Income Style
Duration: Short-Term
Quality: High

Avg Eff Duration[1]	2.8 Yrs
Avg Eff Maturity	—
Avg Credit Quality	AAA
Avg Wtd Coupon	5.08%

[1]figure provided by fund as of 09-30-04

Sector Weightings	% of Stocks	Rel S&P 500	3 Year High	3 Year Low
Info	13.60	0.63		
Software	2.32	0.54	2	0
Hardware	5.03	0.49	11	5
Media	2.44	0.64	5	1
Telecom	3.81	1.21	7	2
Service	32.19	0.69		
Health	2.43	0.19	11	2
Consumer	3.80	0.42	4	1
Business	3.83	0.95	4	1
Financial	22.13	1.07	33	22
Mfg	54.21	1.69		
Goods	7.58	0.81	13	8
Ind Mtrls	23.18	1.83	23	13
Energy	19.92	2.78	20	14
Utilities	3.53	1.19	8	2

Composition

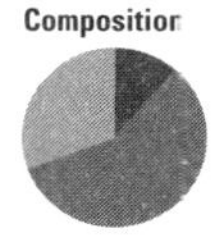

Cash	11.3
Stocks	58.0
Bonds	30.7
Other	0.0
Foreign (% of Stock)	2.5

Morningstar's Take by Kerry O'Boyle 12-20-04

Gabelli Westwood Balanced is a reliable moderate-allocation vehicle.

This offering is known for its mild approach. Management avoids radical asset-allocation calls, typically targeting a moderate 60% stake in equities with the remainder mostly in bonds and a bit of cash. The fund's mix of relatively tame dividend-paying stocks and investment-grade bonds has provided investors with strong performance, while courting only modest risk.

Equity manager Susan Byrne employs a value-oriented style in picking stocks. She often seeks companies with improved prospects not yet recognized by Wall Street. She also favors firms that offer hefty yields, which has helped to buoy returns during market downturns and kept volatility low compared with other moderate-allocation offerings.

On the bond side, manager Mark Freeman focuses on high-quality credits. He shuns high-yield--so-called "junk"--bonds in favor of a mix of Treasuries, government agency-backed issues, and solid corporate credits. In fact, the average credit quality for the bond portfolio is AAA. In addition, Freeman remains leery of interest-rate risk--the fund's duration (a measure of a portfolio's sensitivity to rate swings) is lower than normal and below average versus its benchmark.

The fund does run some risks, however. Large stakes in industrial and energy names--nearly double those of its typical peer--court sector risk. While those areas, especially energy, have boosted the fund's returns in 2004, the fund is vulnerable to a setback in those sectors should it occur. Also, Byrne's value bent can cause the fund to lag during big growth rallies, as evident in 1999.

Still, the fund has shown a knack for delivering strong performance while keeping volatility in check. Its overall modest approach makes it a solid option for most investors.

Address:	One Corporate Center Rye NY 10580 800-422-3554
Web Address:	www.gabelli.com
Inception:	10-01-91
Advisor:	Gabelli Advisers, Inc.
Subadvisor:	Westwood Management Corp
NTF Plans:	Fidelity Retail-NTF, Schwab OneSource

Minimum Purchase:	$1000	Add: $0	IRA: $250
Min Auto Inv Plan:	$0	Add: $100	
Sales Fees:	0.25%B, 2.00%R		
Management Fee:	0.75%		
Actual Fees:	Mgt:0.75%	Dist:0.25%	
Expense Projections:	3Yr:$390	5Yr:$676	10Yr:$1489
Income Distrib:	Quarterly		

Gateway Fund

Ticker	Load	NAV	Yield	Total Assets	Mstar Category
GATEX	12b-1 only	$24.31	1.2%	$2,104 mil	Conservative Allocation

Governance and Management

Fiduciary Grade:

Portfolio Manager(s)

Patrick Rogers has run the fund since 1994. Gateway has one trader as well as three other portfolio managers who work with Rogers to set its option strategy.

Strategy

The fund makes money by selling index call options. To cover the call options, the fund owns a broadly diversified portfolio of stocks. When stock prices go up, the fund's ownership of stocks compensates for losses on call options. To protect the fund from large losses in a declining market, management buys index put options.

Historical Profile

Return Average
Risk Above Avg
Rating ★★★ Neutral

Investment Style: Equity Stock %

95% | 95% | 92% | 99% | 99% | 94% | 98% | 100% | 100%

▼ Manager Change
▽ Partial Manager Change

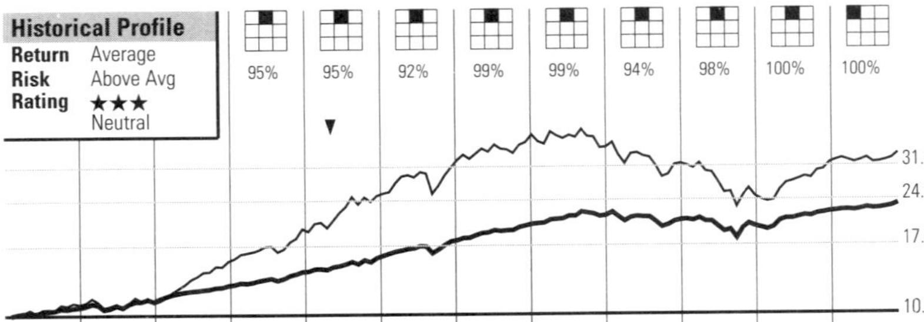

Growth of $10,000
— Investment Values of Fund
— Investment Values of S&P 500

Performance Quartile (within Category)

History

1993	1994	1995	1996	1997	1998	1999	2000	2001	2002	2003	12-04	History
15.85	15.48	16.91	18.48	18.85	21.02	23.67	22.92	21.98	20.76	23.00	24.31	NAV
7.40	5.57	11.04	10.53	12.35	12.26	12.97	6.61	-3.53	-4.86	11.61	6.95	Total Return %
-2.66	4.26	-26.49	-12.41	-21.00	-16.31	-8.07	15.71	8.35	17.23	-17.06	-3.92	+/-S&P 500
-3.36	6.80	-7.12	1.64	-1.75	0.53	5.11	-0.18	-6.75	-0.84	-6.05	-2.06	+/-DJ 40%
1.88	1.71	1.70	1.20	0.96	0.65	0.35	0.33	0.47	0.69	0.82	1.26	Income Return %
5.52	3.86	9.34	9.33	11.39	11.61	12.62	6.28	-4.00	-5.55	10.79	5.69	Capital Return %
94	4	98	50	64	31	11	23	74	68	57	31	Total Rtn % Rank Cat
0.29	0.27	0.26	0.20	0.18	0.12	0.07	0.08	0.11	0.15	0.17	0.29	Income $
0.51	0.97	0.01	0.00	1.73	0.01	0.00	2.24	0.02	0.00	0.00	0.00	Capital Gains $
1.11	1.21	1.19	1.14	1.07	0.99	0.98	0.98	0.97	0.97	0.97	—	Expense Ratio %
1.58	1.54	1.51	1.18	0.90	0.66	0.37	0.33	0.43	0.66	0.86	—	Income Ratio %
17	4	5	17	82	12	11	22	18	13	5	—	Turnover Rate %
207	165	176	194	255	464	922	1,492	1,285	1,285	1,406	2,104	Net Assets $mil

Performance 12-31-04

	1st Qtr	2nd Qtr	3rd Qtr	4th Qtr	Total
2000	3.34	2.86	2.31	-1.96	6.61
2001	-4.32	3.15	-7.34	5.50	-3.53
2002	1.36	-6.37	-8.49	9.55	-4.86
2003	-0.82	6.70	1.96	3.44	11.61
2004	1.22	1.59	0.30	3.71	6.95

Trailing	Total Return%	+/- S&P 500	+/- DJ 40%	%Rank Cat	Growth of $10,000
3 Mo	3.71	-5.52	-1.69	64	10,371
6 Mo	4.02	-3.17	-2.47	67	10,402
1 Yr	6.95	-3.92	-2.06	31	10,695
3 Yr Avg	4.33	0.75	-2.85	62	11,356
5 Yr Avg	3.16	5.46	-3.14	60	11,683
10 Yr Avg	7.40	-4.67	-1.75	67	20,419
15 Yr Avg	7.98	-2.95	-0.82	45	31,634

Tax Analysis	Tax-Adj Rtn%	%Rank Cat	Tax-Cost Rat	%Rank Cat
3 Yr (estimated)	4.00	37	0.32	7
5 Yr (estimated)	2.52	41	0.62	10
10 Yr (estimated)	6.70	29	0.65	3

Potential Capital Gain Exposure: 8% of assets

Rating and Risk

Time Period	Load-Adj Return %	Morningstar Rtn vs Cat	Morningstar Risk vs Cat	Morningstar Risk-Adj Rating
1 Yr	6.95			
3 Yr	4.33	Avg	High	★★★
5 Yr	3.16	Avg	+Avg	★★★
10 Yr	7.40	-Avg	Avg	★★
Incept	9.21			

Other Measures	Standard Index S&P 500	Best Fit Index S&P 500
Alpha	1.5	1.5
Beta	0.52	0.52
R-Squared	87	87
Standard Deviation	8.60	
Mean	4.33	
Sharpe Ratio	0.35	

Portfolio Analysis 12-31-04

Total Stocks:323 Share change since 11-30-04	Sectors	P/E Ratio	YTD Return %	% Net Assets
⊕ General Electric	Ind Mtrls	22.8	-3.01	4.18
⊕ ExxonMobil	Energy	13.9	-2.75	3.24
⊕ Citigroup	Financial	15.3	0.08	3.13
⊕ Microsoft	Software	36.1	0.04	2.82
⊕ Bank of America	Financial	12.3	-3.85	2.61
⊖ Altria Group	Goods	13.3	0.82	2.36
⊕ Pfizer	Health	22.0	-2.75	2.11
⊕ J.P. Morgan Chase & Co.	Financial	19.4	-1.99	1.86
⊕ Johnson & Johnson	Health	20.6	-0.85	1.85

Total Fixed-Income:0	Date of Maturity	Amount $000	Value $000	% Net Assets

Morningstar's Take by Dan McNeela 12-23-04

Gateway Fund accomplishes its mission.

This fund's management's number-one goal is to limit the volatility that can keep stock investors from getting a good night's sleep. It invests the fund's assets in a diversified basket of stocks, but it then locks in a certain income stream and buys protection against steep drops in the stock market.

Management generates income by selling call options on the S&P 500 index. In doing so, it trades away the fund's potential to appreciate in a rising market in exchange for premiums paid by other investors who buy those options. The fund uses about one third of the income it receives to buy put options, which act as a type of portfolio insurance. Owning put options, which gain in value when the market dips, helps cancel out the losses the fund would show if the stock market sinks.

The fund came out of the recent bear market bloodied but not broken. Its put options don't kick in until the market drops by anywhere from 6% to 10% and they typically last for three months. So when the S&P 500 lost 28% in the six-month period ending Sept. 30 2002, the fund took a 14% hit. That's a pretty steep short-term loss, but the fund showed some durability overall. From the beginning of the bear market in March 2000 through Sept. 2002, the fund lost a cumulative 11% while the S&P 500 lost a crushing 38%.

In 2004, the fund's unique strategy is putting it out in front of its conservative-allocation peers. Its 6.9% year-to-date gain through December 22 ranks near the category's top quartile. This may be the fund's time to shine. The Fed has started to hike interest rates, putting a damper on the bond market, and stock investors seem jittery about growth prospects and valuations.

This fund has proven that it can generate decent upside potential over time, while protecting investors from severe losses. That's not a bad combination.

Equity Style
Style: Value
Size: Large-Cap

Value Measures		Rel Category
Price/Earnings	16.96	1.03
Price/Book	2.80	1.18
Price/Sales	1.43	1.10
Price/Cash Flow	8.10	1.16
Dividend Yield %	2.41	1.39

Growth Measures	%	Rel Category
Long-Term Erngs	10.06	0.90
Book Value	7.91	1.44
Sales	3.61	0.79
Cash Flow	3.84	0.57
Historical Erngs	9.27	0.98

Market Cap %			
Giant	59.1	Small	4.4
Large	16.9	Micro	0.1
Mid	19.5	Avg $mil:	39,625

Composition

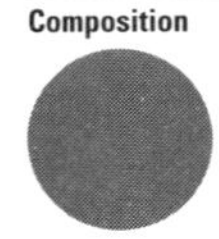

Cash	0.0
Stocks	99.8
Bonds	0.0
Other	0.2
Foreign (% of Stock)	4.0

Fixed-Income Style
Duration: —
Quality: —

Avg Eff Duration [1]	—
Avg Eff Maturity	—
Avg Credit Quality	—
Avg Wtd Coupon	—

[1]figure provided by fund

Sector Weightings	% of Stocks	Rel S&P 500	3 Year High	3 Year Low
Info	17.72	0.82		
Software	4.25	0.99	5	4
Hardware	7.53	0.74	12	7
Media	1.15	0.30	4	1
Telecom	4.79	1.52	6	3
Service	44.55	0.96		
Health	10.64	0.85	16	10
Consumer	7.99	0.88	10	8
Business	3.20	0.79	4	2
Financial	22.72	1.09	23	19
Mfg	37.74	1.17		
Goods	11.99	1.29	12	9
Ind Mtrls	13.50	1.07	15	11
Energy	8.07	1.13	8	5
Utilities	4.18	1.41	4	3

Address:	Rookwood Tower Cincinnati OH 45209 800-354-6339
Web Address:	www.gatewayfund.com
Inception:	12-07-77
Advisor:	Gateway Investment Advisers LP
Subadvisor:	None
NTF Plans:	Fidelity Retail-NTF

Minimum Purchase:	$1000	Add: $100	IRA: $500
Min Auto Inv Plan:	$1000	Add: $100	
Sales Fees:	0.35%B		
Management Fee:	0.92% mx./0.60% mn.		
Actual Fees:	Mgt:0.58%	Dist:0.35%	
Expense Projections:	3Yr:$309	5Yr:$536	10Yr:$1190
Income Distrib:	Annually		

George Putnam of BostonA

Ticker	Load	NAV	Yield	Total Assets	Mstar Category
PGEOX	5.25%	$18.06	1.7%	$5,621 mil	Moderate Allocation

Governance and Management

Fiduciary Grade: C

Portfolio Manager(s)

Jeanne Mockard handles the equity portion. Mockard has run several Putnam funds, including Putnam Utilities Growth & Income. Jeffrey Knight sets the asset-allocation mix. Raman Srivastava, named manager here in October 2004, oversees the bond portfolio on a daily basis, while Kevin Cronin, CIO for Putnam's core fixed-income group, more generally oversees the fixed-income sleeve. The previous bond manager, James Prusko, was dismissed from Putnam in October 2003 after allegedly quick-trading some of the firm's offerings.

Strategy

Jeanne Mockard and her team altered this fund's strategy when they took over in April 2000. The fund's equity portion is still filled with large-cap value stocks, but the fund leans more toward the S&P 500 than it did under previous management. The bond side consists mostly of corporate bonds and mortgages.

Historical Profile

Return Average
Risk Below Avg
Rating ★★★ Neutral

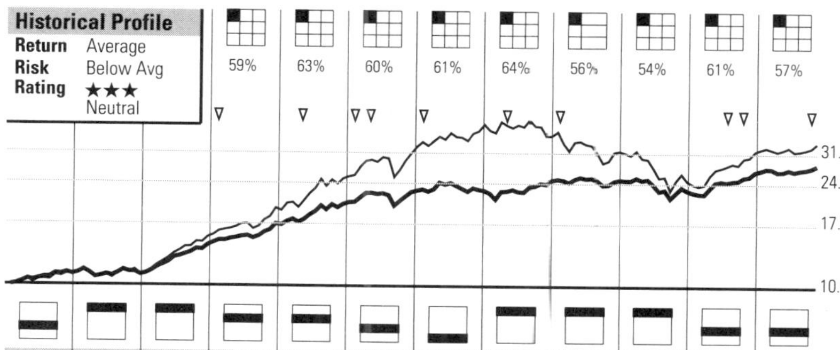

Investment Style
Equity
Stock %

▼ Manager Change
▽ Partial Manager Change

Growth of $10,000
— Investment Values of Fund
— Investment Values of S&P 500

Performance Quartile (within Category)

History

1993	1994	1995	1996	1997	1998	1999	2000	2001	2002	2003	12-04	History
13.86	12.91	15.50	16.40	17.98	18.04	16.28	17.17	16.74	14.80	16.98	18.06	NAV
10.90	-0.38	30.12	16.26	21.02	10.60	0.12	9.28	0.51	-8.42	17.39	8.32	Total Return %
0.84	-1.69	-7.41	-6.68	-12.33	-17.97	-20.92	18.38	12.39	13.67	-11.28	-2.55	+/-S&P 500
-0.83	1.57	5.35	4.92	1.82	-1.79	-12.73	4.84	0.35	2.12	-6.67	-2.85	+/-DJ 60%
4.70	4.18	4.54	4.30	3.64	3.38	3.37	3.55	3.07	3.35	2.40	1.85	Income Return %
6.20	-4.56	25.58	11.96	17.38	7.22	-3.25	5.73	-2.56	-11.77	14.99	6.47	Capital Return %
57	24	15	29	39	69	90	13	15	20	71	57	Total Rtn % Rank Cat
0.63	0.57	0.58	0.66	0.59	0.60	0.60	0.57	0.52	0.55	0.35	0.31	Income $
0.60	0.32	0.63	0.91	1.21	1.20	1.23	0.00	0.00	0.00	0.00	0.00	Capital Gains $
0.90	0.95	0.91	0.95	1.06	1.00	0.93	0.96	0.92	0.96	0.99	1.00	Expense Ratio %
4.34	4.15	4.58	4.07	3.51	3.11	3.10	3.32	3.11	2.75	2.50	1.90	Income Ratio %
89	101	103	119	135	126	128	141	333	132	121	166	Turnover Rate %
833	912	1,183	1,831	2,872	3,706	3,615	3,222	3,267	3,576	3,852	3,461	Net Assets $mil

Performance 12-31-04

	1st Qtr	2nd Qtr	3rd Qtr	4th Qtr	Total
2000	-0.75	-0.07	4.97	4.97	9.28
2001	-1.85	3.54	-5.42	4.57	0.51
2002	1.80	-5.44	-10.81	6.67	-8.42
2003	-2.99	11.65	0.56	7.78	17.39
2004	2.52	-0.57	0.29	5.96	8.31

Trailing	Total Return%	+/- S&P 500	+/- DJ 60%	%Rank Cat	Growth of $10,000
3 Mo	5.96	-3.27	-1.52	73	10,596
6 Mo	6.26	-0.93	-1.27	55	10,626
1 Yr	8.32	-2.55	-2.85	57	10,832
3 Yr Avg	5.21	1.63	-2.05	39	11,646
5 Yr Avg	5.05	7.35	-0.19	16	12,793
10 Yr Avg	10.00	-2.07	-0.49	34	25,937
15 Yr Avg	9.24	-1.69	-0.71	47	37,647

Tax Analysis	Tax-Adj Rtn%	%Rank Cat	Tax-Cost Rat	%Rank Cat
3 Yr (estimated)	2.37	68	0.93	65
5 Yr (estimated)	2.81	20	1.07	49
10 Yr (estimated)	7.17	42	2.05	68

Potential Capital Gain Exposure: 9% of assets

Rating and Risk

Time Period	Load-Adj Return %	Morningstar Rtn vs Cat	Morningstar Risk vs Cat	Morningstar Risk-Adj Rating
1 Yr	2.63			
3 Yr	3.33	Avg	Avg	★★★
5 Yr	3.92	+Avg	-Avg	★★★★
10 Yr	9.41	Avg	-Avg	★★★
Incept	5.93			

Other Measures	Standard Index S&P 500	Best Fit Index Russ 1000 VI
Alpha	2.2	-0.8
Beta	0.60	0.61
R-Squared	92	96
Standard Deviation	9.75	
Mean	5.21	
Sharpe Ratio	0.40	

Morningstar's Take by Laura Pavlenko Lutton 12-23-04

There's a new comanager at George Putnam Fund of Boston, but that doesn't change much.

Raman Srivastava was added as a manager on this offering in October 2004 and now handles day-to-day operations of this moderate-allocation fund's bond portfolio. Srivastava joins lead manager Jeanne Mockard, who invests the equity portion of this fund, Jeffrey Knight, an asset-allocation specialist, and Kevin Cronin, chief investment officer for Putnam's fixed-income group.

We view Srivastava's arrival as a nonevent. This fund's bond portfolio hews very closely to the Lehman Brothers Aggregate Bond Index. What's more, Srivastava doesn't select individual securities for the bond portfolio. He leaves that to teams of fixed-income investors at Putnam and instead works to keep a balance between types of bonds in the index. (Cronin, meanwhile, also supervises the bond portfolio, but not on a daily basis.)

Srivastava has joined a management team that is otherwise very experienced, and under Mockard's leadership, they've done a good job executing this offering's staid strategy. The fund's allocation between stocks and bonds doesn't stray much from the 60%/40% split, and Mockard invests the equity portion of the fund mainly in value-leaning large-caps. Mockard prefers to hold blue-chip names, but she occasionally picks up a turnaround name, such as Office Depot. She thinks earnings at the office-supplies retailer should benefit from an expected pick-up in corporate spending.

The fund's strategy understandably has led to stronger relative returns when value stocks are running, which was the case in the early 2000s. On the flip side, it hasn't looked as good during growth-led years such as 1999 and 2003. Over the long haul, however, the offering has produced competitive returns versus its typical category peer and funds with very similar strategies. In the end, we think this remains a solid core holding.

Address:	One Post Office Sq Boston MA 02109 800-225-1581	Minimum Purchase:	$500 Add: $50 IRA: $500
Web Address:	www.putnaminvestments.com	Min Auto Inv Plan:	$500 Add: $25
Inception:	11-05-37	Sales Fees:	5.25%L, 2.00%R
Advisor:	Putnam Investment Management Co.	Management Fee:	0.65% mx./0.38% mn.
Subadvisor:	None	Actual Fees:	Mgt:0.48% Dist:0.25%
NTF Plans:	Federated Tr NTF, Fidelity Instl-NTF	Expense Projections:	3Yr:$872 5Yr:$1091 10Yr:$1718
		Income Distrib:	Quarterly

Portfolio Analysis 09-30-04

Total Stocks:156 Share change since 06-30-04	Sectors	P/E Ratio	YTD Return %	% Net Assets
⊖ ExxonMobil	Energy	13.9	-2.75	3.04
⊖ Citigroup	Financial	15.3	0.08	2.42
⊕ Bank of America	Financial	12.3	-3.85	1.90
⊕ ChevronTexaco	Energy	7.7	-2.11	1.47
⊖ J P Morgan Chase	Financial	19.4	-1.99	1.43
⊖ Altria Group	Goods	13.3	0.82	1.41
⊖ Hewlett-Packard	Hardware	18.9	-4.39	1.39
⊖ Pfizer	Health	22.0	-2.75	1.27
⊕ Gen Elec	Ind Mtrls	22.8	-3.01	1.26

Total Fixed-Income:1300	Date of Maturity	Amount $000	Value $000	% Net Assets
FNMA 5.5%	10-01-34	169,745	171,946	2.93
FNMA 6.5%	11-01-34	128,300	134,254	2.29
FNMA 6%	11-01-34	115,300	118,795	2.02
FNMA 5%	10-01-19	75,200	76,375	1.30
FNMA 7.25%	01-15-10	38,135	44,265	0.75
FNMA 6.5%	03-01-34	33,422	35,107	0.60
FNMA 6.5%	06-01-33	29,070	30,536	0.52
Ffca Secured Fran 2000-1	09-18-27	15,802	18,082	0.31
FNMA 7%	01-01-34	14,358	15,246	0.26

Equity Style
Style: Value
Size: Large-Cap

Value Measures		Rel Category
Price/Earnings	13.83	0.83
Price/Book	2.17	0.89
Price/Sales	1.16	0.88
Price/Cash Flow	6.11	0.84
Dividend Yield %	2.05	1.31

Growth Measures	%	Rel Category
Long-Term Erngs	10.83	0.93
Book Value	10.75	1.87
Sales	4.75	0.92
Cash Flow	10.50	1.31
Historical Erngs	16.62	1.53

Market Cap %			
Giant	56.7	Small	0.0
Large	30.3	Micro	0.0
Mid	12.9	Avg $mil:	43,358

Fixed-Income Style
Duration: Interm-Term
Quality: High

Avg Eff Duration [1]	4.0 Yrs
Avg Eff Maturity	4.9 Yrs
Avg Credit Quality	AA
Avg Wtd Coupon	6.17%

[1] figure provided by fund as of 09-30-04

Sector Weightings	% of Stocks	Rel S&P 500	3 Year High	3 Year Low
Info	13.41	0.62		
Software	2.00	0.47	3	1
Hardware	5.92	0.58	7	5
Media	2.61	0.68	4	2
Telecom	2.88	0.91	7	3
Service	48.93	1.05		
Health	8.22	0.66	12	8
Consumer	5.98	0.66	7	4
Business	3.66	0.90	5	3
Financial	31.07	1.50	32	29
Mfg	37.66	1.17		
Goods	8.65	0.93	9	6
Ind Mtrls	14.96	1.18	15	8
Energy	10.80	1.51	11	9
Utilities	3.25	1.10	7	3

Composition

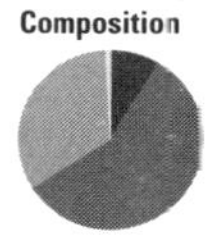

Cash	8.6
Stocks	57.3
Bonds	33.1
Other	1.0
Foreign (% of Stock)	1.3

Greenspring

Ticker	Load	NAV	Yield	Total Assets	Mstar Category
GRSPX	None	$20.91	3.1%	$130 mil	Moderate Allocation

Governance and Management

Fiduciary Grade:

Portfolio Manager(s)

Seasoned. Chip Carlson has managed this offering since 1987 and also manages separate accounts in the same style. Carlson is backed by three senior research analysts, all of whom he has worked with for more than a decade.

Strategy

This is a unique moderate-allocation fund. It favors deep-value sectors such as financials and energy, and it prefers small caps over the blue chips that populate the portfolios of most of its peers. What's more, big stakes in convertibles have given this fund one of the highest yields in the group. Cash stakes tend to run high.

Historical Profile

Return High
Risk Above Avg
Rating ★★★★ Above Avg

Investment Style
Equity
Stock %

64% 68% 63% 59% 66% 51% 36% 35% 45%

▼ Manager Change
▽ Partial Manager Change

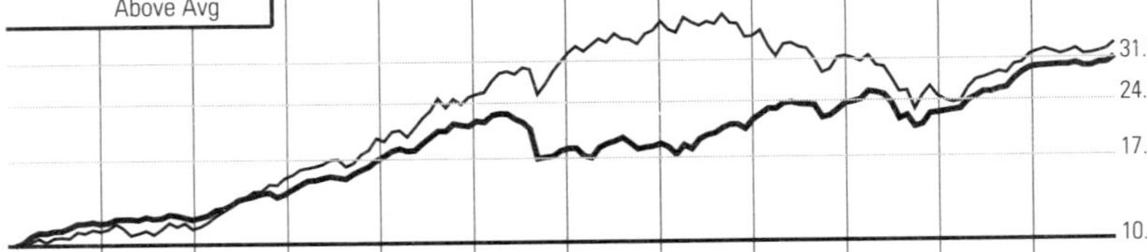

Growth of $10,000
— Investment Values of Fund
— Investment Values of S&P 500

Performance Quartile (within Category)

1993	1994	1995	1996	1997	1998	1999	2000	2001	2002	2003	12-04	History
13.96	13.39	15.05	17.24	20.04	16.10	15.41	16.98	17.74	15.70	19.96	20.91	NAV
14.69	2.88	18.74	22.65	23.95	-15.98	2.64	15.64	10.23	-5.99	31.34	8.69	Total Return %
4.63	1.57	-18.79	-0.29	-9.40	-44.55	-18.40	24.74	22.11	16.10	2.67	-2.18	+/-S&P 500
2.96	4.83	-6.03	11.31	4.75	-28.37	-10.21	11.20	10.07	4.55	7.28	-2.48	+/-DJ 60%
2.95	3.70	5.14	3.96	4.00	3.78	7.07	5.19	5.73	5.38	3.92	3.29	Income Return %
11.74	-0.82	13.60	18.69	19.95	-19.76	-4.43	10.45	4.50	-11.37	27.42	5.40	Capital Return %
24	6	96	4	16	100	84	6	3	8	3	51	Total Rtn % Rank Cat
0.40	0.51	0.68	0.59	0.68	0.75	1.12	0.79	0.96	0.94	0.61	0.65	Income $
1.41	0.45	0.14	0.56	0.60	0.04	0.00	0.00	0.00	0.00	0.00	0.10	Capital Gains $
1.31	1.27	1.06	1.04	1.00	1.01	1.08	1.24	1.19	1.19	1.14	—	Expense Ratio %
2.78	4.03	4.97	3.74	3.10	3.77	6.10	4.83	5.04	5.33	3.44	—	Income Ratio %
122	77	65	61	46	72	91	101	89	79	102	—	Turnover Rate %
30	50	72	91	181	114	61	47	51	51	109	130	Net Assets $mil

Performance 12-31-04

	1st Qtr	2nd Qtr	3rd Qtr	4th Qtr	Total
2000	-0.91	6.16	6.62	3.11	15.64
2001	6.77	2.76	-7.92	9.11	10.23
2002	7.50	-7.18	-13.46	8.88	-5.99
2003	2.29	11.02	2.56	12.76	31.34
2004	1.45	1.23	0.14	5.68	8.69

Trailing	Total Return%	+/- S&P 500	+/- DJ 60%	%Rank Cat	Growth of $10,000
3 Mo	5.68	-3.55	-1.80	77	10,568
6 Mo	5.83	-1.36	-1.70	65	10,583
1 Yr	8.69	-2.18	-2.48	51	10,869
3 Yr Avg	10.31	6.73	3.05	2	13,423
5 Yr Avg	11.34	13.64	6.10	2	17,110
10 Yr Avg	10.29	-1.78	-0.20	30	26,629
15 Yr Avg	9.84	-1.09	-0.11	36	40,870

Tax Analysis	Tax-Adj Rtn%	%Rank Cat	Tax-Cost Rat	%Rank Cat
3 Yr (estimated)	8.62	3	1.53	92
5 Yr (estimated)	9.44	2	1.71	85
10 Yr (estimated)	8.18	25	1.91	58

Potential Capital Gain Exposure: 15% of assets

Rating and Risk

Time Period	Load-Adj Return %	Morningstar Rtn vs Cat	Morningstar Risk vs Cat	Morningstar Risk-Adj Rating
1 Yr	8.69			
3 Yr	10.31	High	+Avg	★★★★★
5 Yr	11.34	High	+Avg	★★★★★
10 Yr	10.29	+Avg	+Avg	★★★
Incept	11.14			

Other Measures	Standard Index S&P 500	Best Fit Index Mstar Mid Core
Alpha	7.4	1.6
Beta	0.58	0.61
R-Squared	65	74
Standard Deviation	11.73	
Mean	10.31	
Sharpe Ratio	0.77	

Portfolio Analysis 11-30-04

Total Stocks:37 Share change since 10-31-04	Sectors	P/E Ratio	YTD Return %	% Net Assets
⊕ USI Holdings	Financial	15.7	-2.42	3.45
Wabash National	Ind Mtrls	19.0	-4.90	3.14
United National Group A	Financial	—	—	2.86
FTI Consulting	Business	13.0	-5.17	2.57
Suncor Energy	Energy	20.6	-7.15	2.57
Energen	Energy	17.3	-5.65	2.42
Michael Baker	Business	15.4	1.28	2.25
Allied Waste Industries	Business	—	-2.37	2.19
PPL	Utilities	12.0	-3.06	1.98

Total Fixed-Income:1	Date of Maturity	Amount $000	Value $000	% Net Assets
Bisys Grp Cv 4%	03-15-06	6,186	6,124	4.72
Akamai Tech Cv 5.5%	07-01-07	5,485	5,590	4.31
Brooks Automation Cv 4.75	06-01-08	5,488	5,334	4.11
Quanta Svcs Cv 4%	07-01-07	4,867	4,639	3.58
Amkor Tech Cv 5.75%	06-01-06	4,470	4,325	3.34
Sanmina Sci Cv	09-12-20	7,628	4,088	3.15
Mercury Interactive Cv 4.	07-01-07	3,933	3,975	3.07
Curagen Cv 6%	02-02-07	4,058	3,874	2.99
Ciena Cv 3.75%	02-01-08	3,817	3,287	2.54

Equity Style
Style: Value
Size: Small-Cap

Value Measures		Rel Category
Price/Earnings	15.13	0.91
Price/Book	1.83	0.75
Price/Sales	0.83	0.63
Price/Cash Flow	3.08	0.42
Dividend Yield %	0.68	0.43

Growth Measures	%	Rel Category
Long-Term Erngs	10.72	0.92
Book Value	13.41	2.34
Sales	2.43	0.47
Cash Flow	19.85	2.48
Historical Erngs	7.32	0.68

Market Cap %			
Giant	5.9	Small	34.8
Large	13.2	Micro	24.1
Mid	21.9	Avg $mil:	1,247

Fixed-Income Style
Duration: Short-Term
Quality: Low

Avg Eff Duration [1]	2.2 Yrs
Avg Eff Maturity	2.3 Yrs
Avg Credit Quality	B
Avg Wtd Coupon	4.03%

[1] figure provided by fund as of 11-30-04

Sector Weightings	% of Stocks	Rel S&P 500	3 Year High	3 Year Low
Info	7.25	0.34		
Software	0.00	0.00	0	0
Hardware	7.25	0.71	9	0
Media	0.00	0.00	6	0
Telecom	0.00	0.00	0	0
Service	61.32	1.32		
Health	4.07	0.33	9	4
Consumer	1.80	0.20	2	0
Business	24.82	6.13	30	10
Financial	30.63	1.48	41	26
Mfg	31.43	0.98		
Goods	0.00	0.00	5	0
Ind Mtrls	10.02	0.79	26	10
Energy	15.45	2.16	15	2
Utilities	5.96	2.01	20	6

Composition

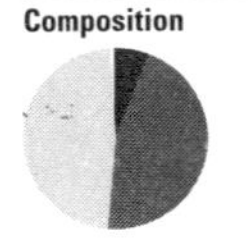

Cash	6.1
Stocks	45.1
Bonds	0.9
Other	47.9
Foreign (% of Stock)	5.7

Morningstar's Take by William Samuel Rocco 11-14-04

Greenspring has a lot more to offer than an offbeat portfolio, but it does require patience.

This fund stands out from its hybrid peers. Chip Carlson has little interest in the blue chips that dominate the stock portfolios of most moderate-allocation funds. Rather, he focuses on dirt-cheap mid- and small caps, such as top stock names Wabash National and USI Holdings. Thus, the fund typically sports one of the smallest average market caps in the category, along with below-average price multiples and hefty stakes in traditional value sectors such as financials and energy.

Carlson also takes an atypical approach with the fixed-income side of the portfolio. While most moderate-allocation managers concentrate on plain-vanilla government and high-quality corporate bonds, Carlson focuses on "busted" convertibles, which are lower-quality converts that trade like straight bonds because their underlying stocks are beaten up and which pay out substantial yields to maturity.

There's no arguing with the returns that Carlson has earned with his unusual approach. The fund has posted competitive results in 2004's topsy-turvy climate, buoyed by several of its busted converts and some of its energy and other stocks. And it boasts terrific five- and 10-year returns, after posting top-decile results during the first four calendar years of this decade.

Nevertheless, it's crucial to understand that the fund's bias toward cheap smaller caps gave it a big edge in the early 2000s and that it can really suffer when its style is out of favor, as its worst-quartile results in 1998 and 1999 attest. Thus, while we continue to believe this fund is a terrific long-term option for those who are comfortable with its atypical portfolio, such investors must understand that its early-2000s success can't be sustained indefinitely and that the rough spells can be quite painful here.

Address:	2330 West Joppa Road Suite 110 Lutherville MD 21093 800-366-3863
Web Address:	www.greenspringfund.com
Inception:	07-01-83
Advisor:	Corbyn Investment Management
Subadvisor:	None
NTF Plans:	Fidelity Retail-NTF, Schwab OneSource

Minimum Purchase:	$2000	Add: $100	IRA: $1000
Min Auto Inv Plan:	$1000	Add: $100	
Sales Fees:	No-load, 2.00%R		
Management Fee:	0.75% mx./0.65% mn., 0.04%A		
Actual Fees:	Mgt:0.75%	Dist:	
Expense Projections:	3Yr:$378	5Yr:$654	10Yr:$1443
Income Distrib:	Semi-Annually		

Harbor Bond

Analyst Pick	Ticker	Load	NAV	Yield	SEC Yield	Total Assets	Mstar Category
	HABDX	None	$11.83	2.8%	2.26%	$1,632 mil	Intermediate-Term Bond

Governance and Management

Fiduciary Grade: B

Portfolio Manager(s)

Bill Gross and his extensive team of analysts and traders at Pimco are considered some of the best in the business. Gross has led this fund since its 1987 inception.

Strategy

This fund makes a series of bets against its benchmark, the Lehman Brothers Aggregate Index. Manager Bill Gross relies on macroeconomic analysis to determine the fund's interest-rate sensitivity (duration is usually kept plus or minus 20% of the benchmark) and sector weightings. He also looks out for inefficiencies in the bond market. The fund may also carry exposure to junk debt, emerging-markets issues, foreign bonds, and currencies.

Historical Profile

Return High
Risk Average
Rating ★★★★★ Highest

Investment Style: Fixed Income — Income Rtn %Rank Cat: 42, 70, 64, 83, 92, 89, 14, 91, 79

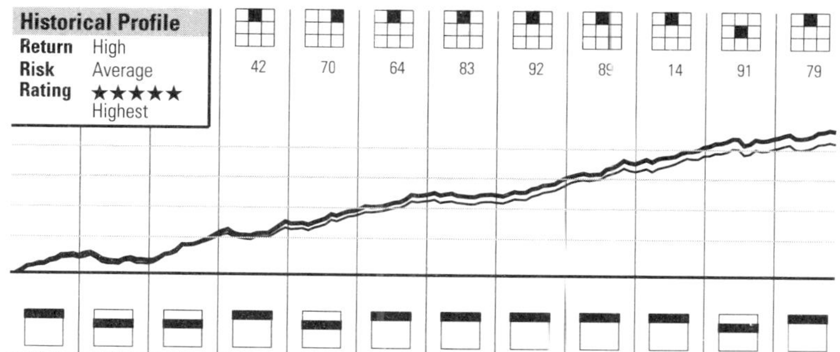

▼ Manager Change
∇ Partial Manager Change

Growth of $10,000 (21.5, 18.0, 15.0, 12.5, 10.0)
— Investment Values of Fund
— Investment Values of LB Aggr

Performance Quartile (within Category)

1993	1994	1995	1996	1997	1998	1999	2000	2001	2002	2003	12-04	History
11.31	10.28	11.41	11.24	11.37	11.28	10.68	11.23	11.42	11.70	11.83	11.83	NAV
12.41	-3.76	19.15	4.94	9.39	9.56	-0.33	11.34	9.03	10.63	5.30	5.47	Total Return %
2.66	-0.84	0.68	1.31	-0.26	0.87	0.49	-0.29	0.59	0.38	1.20	1.13	+/-LB Aggr
0.17	0.75	-2.28	2.25	-0.04	-0.58	2.55	-1.10	0.21	-2.40	-0.67	0.17	+/-LB 5-10YR
5.96	5.49	7.84	6.29	6.04	5.74	5.07	5.34	4.83	5.80	2.59	2.94	Income Return %
6.45	-9.25	11.31	-1.35	3.35	3.82	-5.40	6.00	4.15	4.83	2.71	2.53	Capital Return %
20	48	28	14	35	5	23	20	14	7	31	6	Total Rtn % Rank Cat
0.65	0.61	0.78	0.70	0.66	0.64	0.56	0.56	0.54	0.65	0.30	0.34	Income $
0.50	0.00	0.00	0.00	0.23	0.51	0.00	0.07	0.27	0.26	0.19	0.30	Capital Gains $
0.72	0.77	0.70	0.70	0.67	0.65	0.61	0.60	0.56	0.58	0.58	0.57	Expense Ratio %
6.19	6.29	7.11	6.40	6.04	5.41	5.35	6.16	1.64	4.37	3.43	2.21	Income Ratio %
120	151	89	193	252	278	271	494	53[illegible]	293	221	311	Turnover Rate %
172	167	233	288	385	494	618	787	1,006	1,369	1,527	1,613	Net Assets $mil

Performance 12-31-04

	1st Qtr	2nd Qtr	3rd Qtr	4th Qtr	Total
2000	2.17	1.74	2.54	4.46	11.34
2001	2.69	-0.30	5.84	0.62	9.03
2002	1.11	2.97	3.47	2.70	10.63
2003	2.37	2.62	-0.31	0.55	5.30
2004	2.65	-2.04	3.60	1.24	5.47

Trailing	Total Return%	+/- LB Aggr	+/- LB 5-10YR	%Rank Cat	Growth of $10,000
3 Mo	1.24	0.29	0.26	24	10,124
6 Mo	4.88	0.70	-0.69	16	10,488
1 Yr	5.47	1.13	0.17	6	10,547
3 Yr Avg	7.11	0.92	-0.94	8	12,288
5 Yr Avg	8.33	0.62	-0.74	6	14,919
10 Yr Avg	8.34	0.62	-0.12	3	22,279
15 Yr Avg	8.49	0.79	0.17	3	33,950

Tax Analysis	Tax-Adj Rtn%	%Rank Cat	Tax-Cost Rat	%Rank Cat
3 Yr (estimated)	5.15	5	1.83	63
5 Yr (estimated)	6.10	4	2.06	59
10 Yr (estimated)	5.78	2	2.36	69

Potential Capital Gain Exposure: 1% of assets

Rating and Risk

Time Period	Load-Adj Return %	Morningstar Rtn vs Cat	Morningstar Risk vs Cat	Morningstar Risk-Adj Rating
1 Yr	5.47			
3 Yr	7.11	High	Avg	★★★★★
5 Yr	8.33	High	Avg	★★★★★
10 Yr	8.34	High	Avg	★★★★★
Incept	8.71			

Other Measures	Standard Index LB Aggr	Best Fit Index LB. U.S. Univ. Bd
Alpha	1.1	0.3
Beta	0.95	1.00
R-Squared	94	96
Standard Deviation	4.49	
Mean	7.11	
Sharpe Ratio	1.29	

Portfolio Analysis 06-30-04

Total Fixed-Income:318	Date of Maturity	Amount $000	Value $000	% Net Assets
US Treasury Note (Fut)	12-20-04	258,300	289,478	9.92
EuroDollar (Fut)	09-19-05	178,750	173,370	5.94
Germany Fed Rep Bonds 10	12-08-04	116,100	166,729	5.72
Irs Usd Swp039712 R4.0lo	12-15-09	158,600	159,166	5.46
Interest Rate Swap Swp 0	12-15-09	139,900	140,399	4.81
FNMA 5%		131,000	131,145	4.50
US Treasury Note 2.5%	09-30-06	69,100	68,973	2.36
Interest Rate Swap Swp03	12-15-09	63,500	63,726	2.18
US Treasury Note 3.875%	01-15-09	54,398	61,255	2.10
EuroDollar (Fut)	12-13-04	55,500	54,221	1.86
EuroDollar (Fut)	12-19-05	36,500	35,314	1.21
FNMA 5.5%		21,800	22,093	0.76
Interest Rate Swap Swp04	06-18-34	15,600	20,400	0.70
US Treasury Bond (Fut)	12-20-04	17,600	19,751	0.68
FHLMC CMO 7%	10-15-30	15,472	16,244	0.56
Sears Cr Acct Mstr Tr 20	08-15-09	15,400	15,425	0.53
FNMA CMO 5%	04-25-33	15,157	14,961	0.51
Residential Asset Sec 20	05-25-26	14,783	14,761	0.51
FNMA 5%	03-01-34	14,486	14,375	0.49
Sears Cr Acct Mstr Tr 20	02-15-09	13,900	13,905	0.48

Current Investment Style

Duration: Short Int Long — Quality: High Med Low

¹figure provided by fund

Avg Eff Duration¹	4.7 Yrs
Avg Eff Maturity	6.2 Yrs
Avg Credit Quality	AA
Avg Wtd Coupon	1.90%
Avg Wtd Price	110.71% of par

Coupon Range	% of Bonds	Rel Cat
0% PIK	15.6	3.9
0% to 6%	87.4	1.4
6% to 8%	9.1	0.3
8% to 10%	2.9	0.5
More than 10%	0.7	0.6

1.00=Category Average

Credit Analysis	% bonds 06-30-04		
US Govt	0	BB	4
AAA	27	B	0
AA	63	Below B	0
A	0	NR/NA	0
BBB	6		

Sector Breakdown	% of assets
US Treasuries	0
TIPS	4
US Agency	0
Mortgage Pass-Throughs	6
Mortgage CMO	4
Mortgage ARM	0
US Corporate	5
Asset-Backed	0
Convertible	0
Municipal	3
Corporate Inflation-Protected	0
Foreign Corporate	0
Foreign Govt	1

Composition			
Cash	35.0	Bonds	29.0
Stocks	0.0	Other	36.1

Special Securities	
Restricted/Illiquid Secs	Trace
Exotic Mortgage-Backed	0
Emerging-Markets Secs	Trace
Options/Futures/Warrants	Yes

Morningstar's Take by Eric Jacobson 10-28-04

There are a scant few bond funds that can stack up against Harbor Bond.

There are, of course, other excellent bond funds. Many take themselves out of the running for us, however, whether because of limited access to individual investors or unattractive pricing structures.

One rival, meanwhile, has always been close on the heels of this offering. Fremont Bond is also run by Pimco's Bill Gross, and its expenses, as well as its record, have historically been within a hair of this fund's. That fund is currently off of our radar, though, as Fremont has yet to provide a full accounting of the market-timing arrangements the firm admits were executed by some of its employees in the past. Therefore, for individuals interested in hiring Bill Gross to run their money, we see no better choice than this offering.

The reasons for our enthusiasm are many. As we've alluded, the fund's 0.58% expense ratio, while not the lowest around, is sufficiently modest to allow plenty of performance to drop through to investors' bottom lines. That's simply an appetizer, though, for this capable offering. Subadvisor Pimco brings a stunning level of resources to this fund's table, not least of which is manager Bill Gross. Backed by scores of managers and analysts, Gross has a proven history of deftly picking among sectors and making astute interest-rate calls, while keeping risk firmly in check. Most recently, he's focused attention on (mostly hedged) foreign bonds, in particular, which have helped bolster returns, despite a misguided decision to underweight corporate bonds.

So while that has produced a category-slaying 5% gain for the year to date through Oct. 28, 2004, it's just another in a long string of victories. The fund has been remarkably consistent and has a terrific long-term record. No fund is perfect, and this one isn't a risk-free option. But for investors in search of a solid core bond fund choice, this one's a keeper.

Address:	One Seagate Toledo OH 43666 800-422-1050
Web Address:	www.harborfunds.com
Inception:	12-29-87
Advisor:	Harbor Capital Advisors
Subadvisor:	PA Fund Management LLC
NTF Plans:	N/A

Minimum Purchase:	$1000	Add: $100	IRA: $1000
Min Auto Inv Plan:	$1000	Add: $100	
Sales Fees:	No-load		
Management Fee:	0.50%		
Actual Fees:	Mgt:0.50%	Dist:	
Expense Projections:	3Yr:$205	5Yr:$357	10Yr:$798
Income Distrib:	Quarterly		

Harbor Capital App Instl

Analyst Pick	Ticker	Load	NAV	Yield	Total Assets	Mstar Category
✔	HACAX	None	$28.67	0.4%	$6,952 mil	Large Growth

Governance and Management

Fiduciary Grade: B

Portfolio Manager(s)

Sig Segalas and his staff at Jennison Associates have run this fund since 1990. The firm, which Segalas cofounded in 1969, focuses on large-growth investing. Unlike many shops, Jennison treats the analyst position as a career-track position, not a stepping-stone to a portfolio-management job. The result is a deep, talented analyst staff.

Strategy

This fund buys large-cap companies that are growing revenues faster than the S&P 500 average and that boast traits such as strong research and development and defensible franchises. Manager Sig Segalas also prefers to see strong unit-sales growth, which he thinks is key to the sustainability of a firm's growth rate. Although this is primarily a large-growth offering, it will hold smaller-cap names to get exposure to emerging areas, financials, and energy to help offset the risk in other holdings. The fund holds about 60 names, and it generally doesn't buy a new holding without selling an existing one.

Historical Profile

Return Above Avg
Risk Above Avg
Rating ★★★★ Above Avg

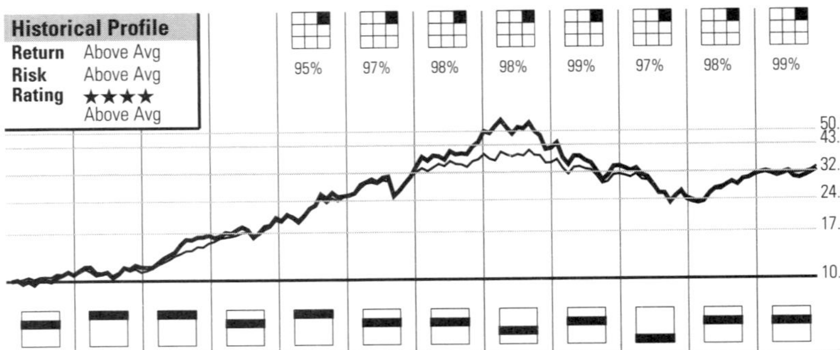

Investment Style
Equity
Stock %

▼ Manager Change
▽ Partial Manager Change

Growth of $10,000
▬ Investment Values of Fund
— Investment Values of S&P 500

Performance Quartile (within Category)

1993	1994	1995	1996	1997	1998	1999	2000	2001	2002	2003	12-04	History
16.37	16.71	22.69	26.33	29.47	37.99	50.65	35.58	29.23	20.21	26.32	28.67	NAV
12.12	3.37	37.82	19.85	31.46	36.80	45.81	-17.00	-17.74	-30.73	30.47	9.34	Total Return %
2.06	2.06	0.29	-3.09	-1.89	8.23	24.77	-7.90	-5.86	-8.64	1.80	-1.53	+/-S&P 500
9.25	0.75	0.64	-3.27	0.97	-1.91	12.65	5.42	2.68	-2.85	0.72	3.04	+/-Russ 1000Gr
0.22	0.23	0.15	0.09	0.25	0.22	0.00	0.00	0.11	0.13	0.24	0.42	Income Return %
11.90	3.14	37.67	19.76	31.21	36.58	45.81	-17.00	-17.85	-30.86	30.23	8.92	Capital Return %
43	9	19	48	24	29	26	67	36	76	31	33	Total Rtn % Rank Cat
0.03	0.04	0.03	0.02	0.07	0.07	0.00	0.00	0.04	0.04	0.05	0.11	Income $
1.13	0.17	0.31	0.86	4.85	2.28	4.60	6.17	0.00	0.00	0.00	0.00	Capital Gains $
0.86	0.81	0.75	0.75	0.70	0.68	0.66	0.64	0.66	0.69	0.71	0.67	Expense Ratio %
0.24	0.24	0.23	0.11	0.23	0.24	-0.05	-0.07	15.59	0.16	0.24	0.09	Income Ratio %
93	73	52	74	73	70	68	86	89	76	64	67	Turnover Rate %
150	239	989	1,682	2,906	4,697	7,947	7,786	6,792	4,912	6,607	6,825	Net Assets $mil

Performance 12-31-04

	1st Qtr	2nd Qtr	3rd Qtr	4th Qtr	Total
2000	12.81	-7.68	-4.28	-16.74	-17.00
2001	-16.33	4.40	-19.53	17.03	-17.74
2002	-2.63	-16.48	-17.50	3.25	-30.73
2003	-2.28	14.63	4.73	11.21	30.47
2004	1.25	1.80	-4.17	10.69	9.34

Trailing	Total Return%	+/- S&P 500	+/- Russ 1000Gr	%Rank Cat	Growth of $10,000
3 Mo	10.69	1.46	1.52	34	11,069
6 Mo	6.08	-1.11	2.61	34	10,608
1 Yr	9.34	-1.53	3.04	33	10,934
3 Yr Avg	-0.39	-3.97	-0.21	50	9,883
5 Yr Avg	-7.57	-5.27	1.72	52	6,746
10 Yr Avg	11.32	-0.75	1.73	17	29,223
15 Yr Avg	12.25	1.32	2.75	11	56,597

Tax Analysis	Tax-Adj Rtn%	%Rank Cat	Tax-Cost Rat	%Rank Cat
3 Yr (estimated)	-0.48	44	0.09	16
5 Yr (estimated)	-8.20	50	0.68	42
10 Yr (estimated)	10.13	14	1.07	27

Potential Capital Gain Exposure: -22% of assets

Rating and Risk

Time Period	Load-Adj Return %	Morningstar Rtn vs Cat	Morningstar Risk vs Cat	Morningstar Risk-Adj Rating
1 Yr	9.34			
3 Yr	-0.39	Avg	Avg	★★★
5 Yr	-7.57	Avg	Avg	★★★
10 Yr	11.32	+Avg	+Avg	★★★★
Incept	13.15			

Other Measures	Standard Index S&P 500	Best Fit Index Russ 1000
Alpha	-3.8	-4.5
Beta	1.05	1.06
R-Squared	94	94
Standard Deviation	16.27	
Mean	-0.39	
Sharpe Ratio	-0.11	

Portfolio Analysis 06-30-04

Share change since 05-04 Total Stocks:66	Sector	PE	YTD Ret%	% Assets
⊕ Gen Elec	Ind Mtrls	22.8	20.68	3.59
Microsoft	Software	36.1	8.95	3.57
⊕ Yahoo!	Media	95.1	67.36	3.44
eBay	Consumer	81.6	80.07	3.35
⊕ Schlumberger	Energy	40.7	23.84	2.87
⊕ J P Morgan Chase	Financial	19.4	9.97	2.76
Dell	Hardware	34.0	24.01	2.56
American Express	Financial	20.3	17.60	2.46
American International G	Financial	16.2	-0.53	2.23
Starbucks	Consumer	60.4	88.06	2.12
⊕ Electronic Arts	Software	30.9	29.36	2.09
⊖ Cisco Systems	Hardware	24.5	-20.26	2.08
Apple Computer	Hardware	NMF	201.36	1.95
⊕ Gilead Sciences	Health	36.9	20.08	1.90
⊕ Roche Holding AG ADR	Health	41.8	16.45	1.83
⊕ Target	Consumer	22.3	36.14	1.81
Whole Foods Market	Consumer	45.4	43.11	1.80
⊕ Genentech	Health	78.6	16.36	1.77
Caremark RX	Health	32.8	55.67	1.72
SAP AG ADR	Software	42.7	6.80	1.71

Current Investment Style

Value Blnd Growth — Large Mid Small

Market Cap	%
Giant	49.4
Large	38.0
Mid	12.7
Small	0.0
Micro	0.0
Avg $mil: 39,687	

Value Measures		Rel Category
Price/Earnings	24.57	1.16
Price/Book	3.65	1.13
Price/Sales	2.50	1.16
Price/Cash Flow	15.37	1.40
Dividend Yield %	0.55	0.71

Growth Measures	%	Rel Category
Long-Term Erngs	15.19	1.08
Book Value	14.96	1.18
Sales	8.01	0.94
Cash Flow	8.21	0.50
Historical Erngs	10.03	0.69

Profitability	%	Rel Category
Return on Equity	15.28	0.85
Return on Assets	7.72	0.82
Net Margin	12.52	1.02

Sector Weightings	% of Stocks	Rel S&P 500	3 Year High	3 Year Low
Info	37.08	1.73		
Software	9.54	2.22	10	4
Hardware	21.39	2.10	25	11
Media	6.03	1.57	8	6
Telecom	0.12	0.04	2	0
Service	47.90	1.03		
Health	18.20	1.46	21	16
Consumer	17.69	1.95	18	13
Business	0.00	0.00	3	0
Financial	12.01	0.58	19	12
Mfg	15.04	0.47		
Goods	5.62	0.60	12	4
Ind Mtrls	3.13	0.25	9	2
Energy	6.29	0.88	8	3
Utilities	0.00	0.00	0	0

Composition

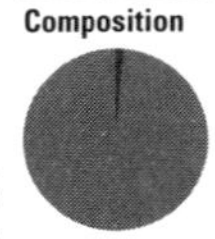

Cash	1.6
Stocks	98.4
Bonds	0.0
Other	0.0
Foreign (% of Stock)	7.3

Morningstar's Take by Christopher Traulsen 10-09-04

Harbor Capital Appreciation's latest moves help illustrate its strengths.

This fund typically has a lower annual turnover rate than its average large-growth peer. That's largely because manager Sig Segalas focuses on finding dominant companies that offer the prospect of strong earnings and revenue growth over the long haul, underpinned by qualities such as strong research and development programs and healthy growth in unit sales.

But that strategy doesn't mean Segalas is reluctant to trade when needed. He holds just 60 or so names here, so he has little patience with companies that aren't delivering operationally. That discipline can help the fund sidestep bad situations. In 2004's third quarter, for example, Segalas sharply cut back the fund's semiconductor exposure, saving the fund some pain.

Given his criteria, Segalas is rarely interested in IPOs, but he's participated in a couple this year. The fund now has an approximately 1% position in Google, most of which Segalas bought in the IPO. He also owns a big position in Yahoo and believed that Google's IPO price was simply too low relative to Yahoo's valuation for the gap to be sustainable. At least in the near-term, he has been proven right: Google has quickly jumped in price. Segalas also bought a position in Navteq, the dominant supplier of digital maps used in GPS devices. Both moves allowed him to get into younger, rapidly growing companies that dominate their niches.

In 2004, these moves and strong picks from a variety of sectors, including Yahoo, Whole Foods, and Schlumberger, have helped the fund lose considerably less money than its typical peer in a difficult environment for growth investing. The fund has also delivered extremely strong long-term returns under Segalas, and is backed by an experienced team of analysts at Jennison Associates. We think its investor share class should be cheaper, but otherwise, we continue to think highly of this large-growth offering.

Address:	One Seagate Toledo OH 43666 800-422-1050
Web Address:	www.harborfunds.com
Inception:	12-29-87
Advisor:	Harbor Capital Advisors
Subadvisor:	Jennison Associates, LLC
NTF Plans:	N/A

Minimum Purchase:	$50000	Add: $100	IRA: $50000
Min Auto Inv Plan:	$50000	Add: $100	
Sales Fees:	No-load		
Management Fee:	0.60%		
Actual Fees:	Mgt:0.60%	Dist:	
Expense Projections:	3Yr:$230	5Yr:$401	10Yr:$894
Income Distrib:	Annually		

Harbor Intl Instl

Analyst Pick	Ticker	Load	NAV	Yield	Total Assets	Mstar Category
✔	HAINX	None	$42.70	1.3%	$8,805 mil	Foreign Large Value

Governance and Management

Fiduciary Grade: B

Portfolio Manager(s)

Hakan Castegren, who has run this fund since its late-1987 inception, is the longest-serving manager in the foreign large-value group and was named Morningstar Manager of the Year in 1996. He's supported by four very experienced analysts: Jim LaTorre, Howard Appleby, Jean-Francois Ducrest, and Ted Wendell.

Strategy

Manager Hakan Castegren looks for undervalued large caps that have strong franchises, good restructuring plans, or other reasons to be optimistic about their earnings prospects. In addition, he considers macroeconomic factors and industry themes. He also has a long investment horizon and rarely hedges the fund's currency exposure. The fund has a 2% redemption fee on shares held fewer than 60 days, and it uses an outside service to set fair- value prices in certain situations.

Historical Profile

Return: Average
Risk: Above Avg
Rating: ★★★ Neutral

Investment Style: Equity — Stock %

90%		92%	91%	92%	92%	88%	93%	94%

▼ Manager Change
▽ Partial Manager Change

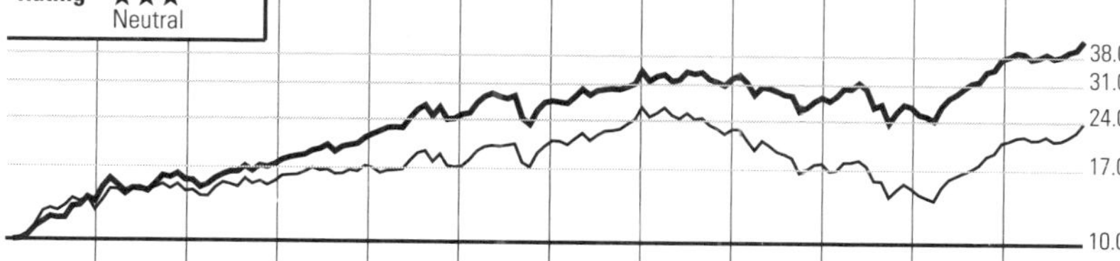

Growth of $10,000
— Investment Values of Fund
— Investment Values of MSCI EAFE

Performance Quartile (within Category)

1993	1994	1995	1996	1997	1998	1999	2000	2001	2002	2003	12-04	History
24.32	24.45	27.84	32.20	35.86	36.72	41.86	35.09	29.63	26.86	36.79	42.70	NAV
45.42	5.43	16.06	20.12	15.49	10.36	23.89	-4.97	-12.25	-6.38	40.95	17.97	Total Return %
12.86	-2.35	4.85	14.07	13.71	-9.57	-3.14	9.22	9.17	9.56	2.36	-2.28	+/-MSCI EAFE
13.21	-1.92	4.65	13.25	13.22	-8.33	-4.09	8.39	9.14	9.42	1.53	-2.41	+/-MSCI Wd xUS
1.26	1.01	1.66	1.50	1.25	1.61	1.77	1.69	0.76	1.13	1.88	1.51	Income Return %
44.16	4.42	14.40	18.62	14.24	8.75	22.12	-6.66	-13.01	-7.51	39.07	16.46	Capital Return %
19	29	15	17	16	56	55	76	34	18	35	87	Total Rtn % Rank Cat
0.21	0.25	0.41	0.42	0.40	0.58	0.65	0.71	0.27	0.34	0.51	0.56	Income $
0.00	0.94	0.13	0.80	0.90	2.30	2.86	3.79	0.88	0.54	0.56	0.15	Capital Gains $
1.20	1.10	1.04	0.99	0.97	0.94	0.92	0.92	0.91	0.87	0.89	0.86	Expense Ratio %
1.28	1.09	1.53	1.42	1.20	1.27	0.78	1.40	-5.70	1.45	1.83	1.25	Income Ratio %
16	29	14	10	6	14	48	10	7	16	21	12	Turnover Rate %
2,538	2,953	3,460	4,319	5,277	5,374	5,843	4,829	3,655	3,742	6,191	8,542	Net Assets $mil

Performance 12-31-04

	1st Qtr	2nd Qtr	3rd Qtr	4th Qtr	Total
2000	-2.22	1.93	-5.13	0.51	-4.97
2001	-10.74	2.59	-13.17	10.36	-12.25
2002	6.72	-0.60	-21.25	12.08	-6.38
2003	-9.16	20.74	9.37	17.50	40.95
2004	3.86	-0.31	1.81	11.91	17.97

Trailing	Total Return%	+/- MSCI EAFE	+/- MSCI Wd xUS	%Rank Cat	Growth of $10,000
3 Mo	11.91	-3.41	-3.24	91	11,191
6 Mo	13.94	-1.06	-1.43	72	11,394
1 Yr	17.97	-2.28	-2.41	87	11,797
3 Yr Avg	15.90	4.01	3.68	31	15,569
5 Yr Avg	5.36	6.49	6.12	38	12,983
10 Yr Avg	11.07	5.45	5.13	8	28,574
15 Yr Avg	11.01	6.78	6.60	17	47,911

Tax Analysis	Tax-Adj Rtn%	%Rank Cat	Tax-Cost Rat	%Rank Cat
3 Yr (estimated)	15.08	29	0.71	71
5 Yr (estimated)	4.14	39	1.16	66
10 Yr (estimated)	9.66	4	1.27	41

Potential Capital Gain Exposure: 38% of assets

Rating and Risk

Time Period	Load-Adj Return %	Morningstar Rtn vs Cat	Morningstar Risk vs Cat	Morningstar Risk-Adj Rating
1 Yr	17.97			
3 Yr	15.90	Avg	+Avg	★★★
5 Yr	5.36	Avg	+Avg	★★★
10 Yr	11.07	+Avg	+Avg	★★★★
Incept	13.81			

Other Measures	Standard Index S&P 500	Best Fit Index MSCI Wd xUS
Alpha	3.2	2.7
Beta	1.07	1.08
R-Squared	92	93
Standard Deviation	20.07	
Mean	15.90	
Sharpe Ratio	0.73	

Portfolio Analysis 06-30-04

Share change since 05-04 Total Stocks:72	Sector	Country	% Assets
BHP Billiton	Ind Mtrls	U.K.	3.21
Ericsson AB (publ)	Hardware	Sweden	3.08
Continental	Ind Mtrls	Germany	2.75
⊕ Bp	Energy	U.K.	2.45
ABB Ltd	Ind Mtrls	Switzerland	2.34
⊕ Petroleo Brasileiro Sa -	Energy	Brazil	2.15
Richemont(Cie Fin)	Goods	Switzerland	2.14
Canon	Goods	Japan	2.13
Credit Agricole	Financial	France	2.03
⊕ TOTAL	Energy	France	2.01
DBS Grp Hldgs Ltd	Financial	Singapore	1.94
⊕ Standard Chartered	Financial	U.K.	1.9-
⊕ Toyota Motor	Goods	Japan	1.90
Asahi Glass	Ind Mtrls	Japan	1.87
Novo Nordisk	Health	Denmark	1.83
Michelin Grp	Ind Mtrls	France	1.80
Sinopec	Energy	China	1.77
Nestle	Goods	Switzerland	1.72
⊕ Malayan Banking	Financial	Malaysia	1.71
Abn-Amro Hldgs Nv	Financial	Netherlands	1.69

Current Investment Style

Value Blnd Growth — Large / Mid / Small (Large Blend)

Market Cap	%
Giant	53.4
Large	39.4
Mid	7.3
Small	0.0
Micro	0.0
Avg $mil: 22,272	

Value Measures		Rel Category
Price/Earnings	14.34	1.10
Price/Book	1.37	1.19
Price/Sales	1.04	1.27
Price/Cash Flow	5.67	1.28
Dividend Yield %	2.12	0.76

Growth Measures	%	Rel Category
Long-Term Erngs	10.83	1.10
Book Value	0.98	2.13
Sales	1.63	1.16
Cash Flow	3.35	1.09
Historical Erngs	3.30	1.19

Composition

Cash	3.6	Bonds	0.0
Stocks	92.5	Other	3.9
Foreign (% of Stock)			100.0

Sector Weightings	% of Stocks	Rel MSCI EAFE	3 Year High	3 Year Low
Info	14.66	0.88		
Software	0.00	0.00	0	0
Hardware	5.85	1.60	6	0
Media	2.78	1.22	4	2
Telecom	6.03	0.63	6	0
Service	34.36	0.77		
Health	3.72	0.51	8	1
Consumer	1.87	0.37	3	2
Business	2.46	0.45	4	1
Financial	26.31	0.97	30	16
Mfg	50.98	1.32		
Goods	19.54	1.43	34	17
Ind Mtrls	19.40	1.58	31	19
Energy	10.97	1.49	12	8
Utilities	1.07	0.20	2	0

Regional Exposure	% Stock		
UK/W. Europe	63	N. America	0
Japan	20	Latn America	2
Asia X Japan	12	Other	3

Country Exposure	% Stock		
Japan	20	Switzerland	9
U.K.	16	Sweden	7
France	15		

Morningstar's Take by Gareth Lyons 11-28-04

A ho-hum year for Harbor International doesn't taint our enthusiasm.

Like most foreign large-value offerings, this fund has benefited from the continued strength in commodity-related stocks. For example, UK-based industrial-materials giant BHP Billiton, which is a top holding here, is up more than 35% this year so far. Due to some underperforming picks in the consumer-goods sector, however, this fund's 14.9% return for the year to date through Nov. 26 trails the category norm. Cutthroat pricing in the highly competitive digital-camera market have weighed heavily on positions in Olympus and Nikon. Jim LaTorre, one of four senior analysts that supports veteran skipper Hakan Castegran, readily admits that the team had underestimated the competitive landscape of the low end of the digital-camera market. As a result, the team has sold its stake in troubled Olympus.

To be sure, this value-oriented team is usually snapping up shares when others investors are selling. But knowing when to trim back has been an important part of manager Castegran's success, as well. And when his team's study of industry dynamics or company fundamentals raises red flags, the manager won't stick around. To hold on to a pick, which he typically does for years, the firm must maintain a sustainable franchise and operate in industry where barriers to entry are high. Generally, he finds such candidates among the largest names in the financial, telecom and consumer-goods industries. But the manager has a pioneering streak, too, as evidenced by the portfolio's overweighting in Malaysian stocks.

Of course, the occasional bet is sure to run into trouble. And the fund's emphasis of certain sectors is sure to produce the odd dry spell. But, as its stellar 10-year record suggests, this team's unwavering commitment to its disciplined strategy has a habit of paying off over the long haul. This dependable fund remains a fine option.

Address:	One Seagate, Toledo OH 43666, 800-422-1050
Web Address:	www.harborfunds.com
Inception:	12-29-87
Advisor:	Harbor Capital Advisors
Subadvisor:	Northern Cross Investments Ltd
NTF Plans:	N/A

Minimum Purchase:	$50000	Add: $100	IRA: $50000
Min Auto Inv Plan:	$50000	Add: $100	
Sales Fees:	No-load, 2.00%R		
Management Fee:	0.75%		
Actual Fees:	Mgt:0.75%	Dist:	
Expense Projections:	3Yr:$287	5Yr:$498	10Yr:$1108
Income Distrib:	Annually		

Harbor Large Cap Value

Ticker	Load	NAV	Yield	Total Assets	Mstar Category
HAVLX	None	$16.33	0.9%	$423 mil	Large Value

Governance and Management

Fiduciary Grade: B

Portfolio Manager(s)

Armstrong Shaw Associates became the subadvisor on this fund in 2001. The firm has run private accounts since 1984 in the same style that it uses here. The firm tends to hire individuals who have hands-on experience in industries outside of finance. It employs six analysts. Jeff Shaw is the only named manager here, but he chairs a committee of six managers who work on the fund.

Strategy

Management seeks out large-cap stocks trading at discounts of 30% or more to the team's estimates of their intrinsic values. To estimate intrinsic value, the team uses discounted cash-flow analysis and analyzes comparable transactions and historic valuations. The less agreement there is between the three methods' values, the greater the discount the managers demand. The managers keep sector weightings within twice those of the Russell 1000 Value Index's or within 15 percentage points of that index's, whichever is greater.

Historical Profile

Return Average
Risk Above Avg
Rating ★★★ Neutral

Investment Style: Equity Stock %

96% 96% 96% 98% 98% 95% 98% 93% 96%

▼ Manager Change
▽ Partial Manager Change

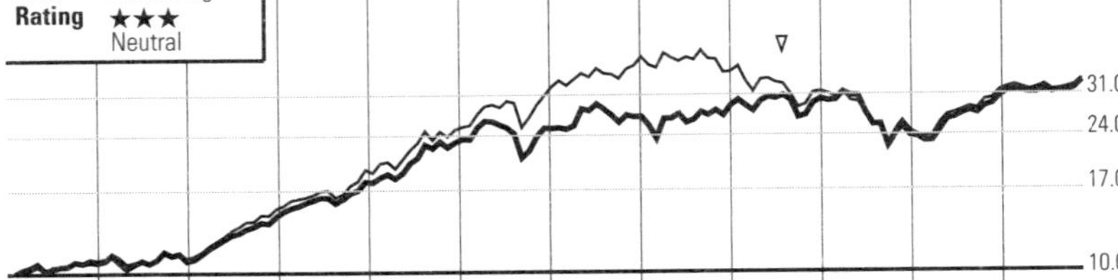

Growth of $10,000
— Investment Values of Fund
— Investment Values of S&P 500

Performance Quartile (within Category)

1993	1994	1995	1996	1997	1998	1999	2000	2001	2002	2003	12-04	History
13.21	11.88	14.34	14.79	15.20	14.34	13.55	14.03	14.39	11.31	14.36	16.33	NAV
8.38	0.70	35.37	20.02	31.20	6.92	7.59	7.16	4.10	-20.70	27.87	14.77	Total Return %
-1.68	-0.61	-2.16	-2.92	-2.15	-21.65	-13.45	16.26	15.98	1.39	-0.80	3.90	+/-S&P 500
-9.69	2.68	-2.99	-1.62	-3.98	-8.71	0.24	0.15	9.69	-5.18	-2.16	-1.72	+/-Russ 1000 VI
2.43	2.74	3.47	2.83	2.23	1.80	1.81	2.02	1.44	0.72	0.84	1.00	Income Return %
5.95	-2.04	31.90	17.19	28.97	5.12	5.78	5.14	2.66	-21.42	27.03	13.77	Capital Return %
87	32	29	52	17	81	40	63	13	69	49	26	Total Rtn % Rank Cat
0.33	0.36	0.41	0.40	0.33	0.27	0.26	0.27	0.20	0.10	0.10	0.14	Income $
1.10	1.07	1.27	2.00	3.74	1.63	1.57	0.19	0.00	0.00	0.00	0.00	Capital Gains $
0.88	1.04	0.90	0.83	0.83	0.79	0.76	0.80	0.77	0.77	0.77	0.68	Expense Ratio %
2.48	2.66	3.00	2.65	1.98	1.67	1.65	2.05	1.64	0.75	0.94	1.10	Income Ratio %
50	151	136	132	146	114	110	106	194	35	25	19	Turnover Rate %
60	57	92	117	175	177	155	142	160	143	235	400	Net Assets $mil

Performance 12-31-04

	1st Qtr	2nd Qtr	3rd Qtr	4th Qtr	Total
2000	-1.33	-2.43	4.87	6.15	7.16
2001	-3.31	8.15	-11.39	12.34	4.10
2002	4.31	-12.09	-19.06	6.83	-20.70
2003	-3.36	15.81	2.78	11.17	27.87
2004	2.79	1.59	-1.21	11.25	14.77

Trailing	Total Return%	+/- S&P 500	+/- Russ 1000 VI	%Rank Cat	Growth of $10,000
3 Mo	11.25	2.02	0.87	9	11,125
6 Mo	9.91	2.72	-2.17	36	10,991
1 Yr	14.77	3.90	-1.72	26	11,477
3 Yr Avg	5.18	1.60	-3.39	58	11,636
5 Yr Avg	5.36	7.66	0.09	35	12,983
10 Yr Avg	12.28	0.21	-1.55	31	31,844
15 Yr Avg	10.17	-0.76	-1.86	58	42,751

Tax Analysis	Tax-Adj Rtn%	%Rank Cat	Tax-Cost Rat	%Rank Cat
3 Yr (estimated)	4.86	48	0.30	20
5 Yr (estimated)	4.76	30	0.57	30
10 Yr (estimated)	9.07	54	2.86	92

Potential Capital Gain Exposure: 14% of assets

Rating and Risk

Time Period	Load-Adj Return %	Morningstar Rtn vs Cat	Morningstar Risk vs Cat	Morningstar Risk-Adj Rating
1 Yr	14.77			
3 Yr	5.18	Avg	Avg	★★★
5 Yr	5.36	Avg	+Avg	★★★
10 Yr	12.28	+Avg	+Avg	★★★
Incept	11.78			

Other Measures	Standard Index S&P 500	Best Fit Index Russ 1000 VI
Alpha	1.7	-3.0
Beta	0.98	0.99
R-Squared	91	92
Standard Deviation	16.17	
Mean	5.18	
Sharpe Ratio	0.24	

Portfolio Analysis 06-30-04

Share change since 05-04 Total Stocks:35	Sector	PE	YTD Ret%	% Assets
⊕ Comcast	Media	—	-13.77	3.62
⊕ Fannie Mae	Financial	9.1	-2.33	3.39
⊕ Citigroup	Financial	15.3	2.72	3.37
⊕ Anthem	Health	17.4	53.33	3.26
⊕ CVS	Consumer	21.1	25.61	3.22
⊕ Chubb	Financial	12.9	15.43	3.18
⊕ Allstate	Financial	12.8	23.12	3.14
Exelon	Utilities	16.1	37.55	3.13
⊕ DuPont De Nemours E.I.	Ind Mtrls	22.3	10.42	3.08
Abbott Laboratories	Health	22.1	2.61	3.08
American Express	Financial	20.3	17.60	3.07
⊕ Pitney Bowes	Ind Mtrls	19.6	17.24	3.06
Gen Elec	Ind Mtrls	22.8	20.68	3.06
Yum Brands	Consumer	19.7	37.84	3.06
⊕ Office Depot	Consumer	16.4	3.89	3.04
⊕ Emerson Electric	Ind Mtrls	22.8	11.09	3.04
⊕ Bank of America	Financial	12.3	21.50	3.02
Cendant	Business	13.6	6.52	3.00
⊕ Time Warner	Media	27.5	8.12	2.98
Devon Energy	Energy	9.0	36.78	2.73

Current Investment Style

Value Blnd Growth — Large Mid Small

Market Cap	%
Giant	34.6
Large	56.7
Mid	8.7
Small	0.0
Micro	0.0

Avg $mil: 32,509

Value Measures		Rel Category
Price/Earnings	14.47	0.96
Price/Book	2.16	0.95
Price/Sales	1.24	1.04
Price/Cash Flow	5.32	0.83
Dividend Yield %	1.72	0.84

Growth Measures	%	Rel Category
Long-Term Erngs	10.68	1.03
Book Value	9.74	1.73
Sales	7.63	1.82
Cash Flow	13.77	2.64
Historical Erngs	13.81	1.17

Profitability	%	Rel Category
Return on Equity	18.45	1.16
Return on Assets	4.93	0.63
Net Margin	9.75	0.95

Sector Weightings	% of Stocks	Rel S&P 500	3 Year High	3 Year Low
Info	13.39	0.62		
Software	0.00	0.00	1	0
Hardware	0.00	0.00	2	0
Media	11.85	3.09	12	6
Telecom	1.54	0.49	2	0
Service	54.07	1.17		
Health	10.95	0.88	14	9
Consumer	9.39	1.03	15	9
Business	3.10	0.77	10	3
Financial	30.63	1.48	31	26
Mfg	32.55	1.01		
Goods	1.02	0.11	3	0
Ind Mtrls	19.21	1.52	20	14
Energy	6.73	0.94	10	5
Utilities	5.59	1.89	6	3

Composition

Cash	7.3
Stocks	92.7
Bonds	0.0
Other	0.0
Foreign (% of Stock)	0.0

Morningstar's Take by Christopher Traulsen 12-29-04

Harbor Large Cap Value has the ingredients for success.

This fund has many of the ingredients we want to see in a sound investment. It features experienced managers: Jeff Shaw heads a team of six that runs this strategy for subadvisor Armstrong Shaw. The firm only invests in a single style and has been refining it since the firm's inception in 1984. The process is a disciplined one: The managers look for securities selling at less than 70% of their intrinsic values and don't veer from their criteria to chase performance. They also invest for the long term--turnover here has been in the 20%-35% range during the team's tenure. That should help keep trading costs down and help the fund's tax efficiency.

The team's style has been tested in a variety of markets since it took the helm at the end of September 2001. From what we've seen thus far, it's clear that investors here will need to share their managers' patience. The fund was nicked in 2002 by Electronic Data Systems and Amdocs, for example, and ended up losing slightly more than the category average that year. However, it has since bounced back, and the fund's return since Armstrong Shaw took the helm now bests that of its average peer. In 2004, despite an overweight in lagging media stocks, the fund has ridden a bevy of strong financials picks to a top-third return.

We have one beef here. After it was bought by Dutch firm Robeco, Harbor turned the original, low-expense share class of this offering into a high-minimum-investment "institutional" share class, limiting the ability of individuals to access it. It then rolled out a more expensive "investor" share class with lower minimums. That share class is more expensive than the average no-load, noninstitutional large-value fund's, which is disappointing. The fund's institutional shares are a good deal if you can get them, but its investor shares ought to be cheaper.

Address:	One Seagate Toledo OH 43666 800-422-1050
Web Address:	www.harborfunds.com
Inception:	12-29-87
Advisor:	Harbor Capital Advisors
Subadvisor:	Armstrong Shaw Associates
NTF Plans:	N/A

Minimum Purchase:	$50000	Add: $100	IRA: $50000
Min Auto Inv Plan:	$50000	Add: $100	
Sales Fees:	No-load		
Management Fee:	0.60%		
Actual Fees:	Mgt:0.60%	Dist:	
Expense Projections:	3Yr:$249	5Yr:$433	10Yr:$966
Income Distrib:	Semi-Annually		

Henlopen

Ticker	Load	NAV	Yield	Total Assets	Mstar Category
HENLX	None	$30.47	0.0%	$330 mil	Small Growth

Governance and Management

Fiduciary Grade:

Portfolio Manager(s)

This fund's advisor, Landis Associates, boasts more than 20 years of experience. Manager Michael Hershey has managed this fund since its late-1992 inception, while comanager Bruce Vogenitz began in July 1998. Hershey's son, Michael, also assists.

Strategy

Management searches for fast-growing firms of all sizes, although it favors small caps. The team isn't afraid to bulk up on individual names, nor does it limit its investable universe to the market's fastest-growing sectors, either. Instead, the squad tends to scour a swath of industries in search of cheap fare with catalysts for growth.

Historical Profile

Return: High
Risk: Above Avg
Rating: ★★★★ Above Avg

Investment Style
Equity
Stock %

1993	1994	1995	1996	1997	1998	1999	2000	2001	2002	2003	12-04
	96%	73%	97%	97%	99%	99%	98%	96%	100%		

▼ Manager Change
▽ Partial Manager Change

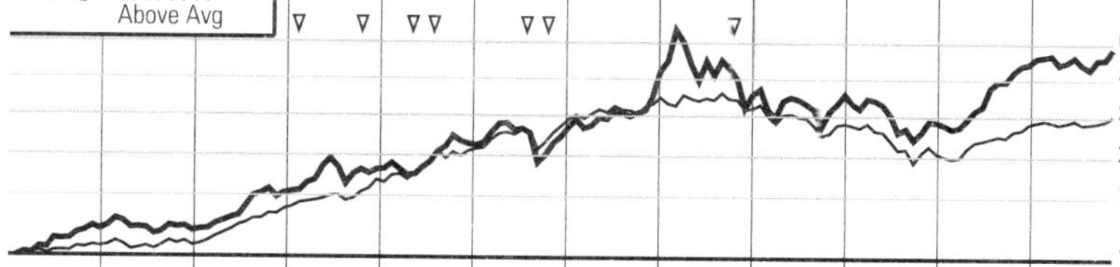

Growth of $10,000
— Investment Values of Fund
— Investment Values of S&P 500

Performance Quartile (within Category)

1993	1994	1995	1996	1997	1998	1999	2000	2001	2002	2003	12-04	History
12.51	11.98	14.22	14.89	14.80	17.28	26.08	19.89	19.93	15.82	26.10	30.47	NAV
29.86	-2.73	38.03	21.37	22.61	16.76	62.12	-18.55	0.75	-20.86	64.98	16.78	Total Return %
19.80	-4.04	0.50	-1.57	-10.74	-11.81	41.08	-9.45	12.63	1.23	36.31	5.91	+/-S&P 500
16.49	-0.30	6.99	10.11	9.66	15.53	19.03	3.88	9.93	9.40	16.44	2.47	+/-Russ 2000 Gr
0.00	0.00	0.00	0.00	0.00	0.00	0.00	0.00	0.00	0.00	0.00	0.04	Income Return %
29.86	-2.73	38.03	21.37	22.61	16.76	62.12	-18.55	0.75	-20.86	64.98	16.74	Capital Return %
8	61	38	43	33	16	41	87	23	21	5	23	Total Rtn % Rank Cat
0.00	0.00	0.00	0.00	0.00	0.00	0.00	0.00	0.00	0.00	0.00	0.01	Income $
0.44	0.19	2.26	2.14	3.31	0.00	1.38	1.23	0.04	0.00	0.00	0.00	Capital Gains $
2.00	2.00	2.00	1.80	1.60	1.50	1.50	1.40	1.30	1.40	1.58	1.38	Expense Ratio %
-0.70	-1.30	-1.20	-1.30	-0.70	-0.70	-0.60	-1.00	-0.70	-1.00	-1.04	-0.90	Income Ratio %
54	63	148	178	141	116	162	157	288	132	90	113	Turnover Rate %
5	9	17	31	33	44	113	222	151	76	161	330	Net Assets $mil

Performance 12-31-04

	1st Qtr	2nd Qtr	3rd Qtr	4th Qtr	Total
2000	28.30	-15.15	-6.01	-20.39	-18.55
2001	-17.50	16.70	-20.17	31.08	0.75
2002	-3.60	-12.87	-19.12	16.49	-20.86
2003	-4.17	19.46	23.80	16.41	64.98
2004	7.66	-1.46	-2.06	12.39	16.78

Trailing	Total Return%	+/- S&P 500	+/- Russ 2000 Gr	%Rank Cat	Growth of $10,000
3 Mo	12.39	3.16	-2.69	79	11,239
6 Mo	10.08	2.89	1.92	26	11,008
1 Yr	16.78	5.91	2.47	23	11,678
3 Yr Avg	15.10	11.52	9.31	5	15,248
5 Yr Avg	4.58	6.88	8.15	25	12,510
10 Yr Avg	17.14	5.07	10.02	4	48,647
15 Yr Avg	—	—	—	—	—

Tax Analysis	Tax-Adj Rtn%	%Rank Cat	Tax-Cost Rat	%Rank Cat
3 Yr (estimated)	15.09	4	0.01	2
5 Yr (estimated)	4.26	22	0.31	14
10 Yr (estimated)	14.38	5	2.10	77

Potential Capital Gain Exposure: 24% of assets

Rating and Risk

Time Period	Load-Adj Return %	Morningstar Rtn vs Cat	Morningstar Risk vs Cat	Morningstar Risk-Adj Rating
1 Yr	16.78			
3 Yr	15.10	High	+Avg	★★★★★
5 Yr	4.58	+Avg	+Avg	★★★
10 Yr	17.14	High	+Avg	★★★★
Incept	16.23			

Other Measures	Standard Index S&P 500	Best Fit Index Russ 2000 Gr
Alpha	12.2	9.3
Beta	1.14	0.96
R-Squared	57	84
Standard Deviation	26.40	
Mean	15.10	
Sharpe Ratio	0.53	

Morningstar's Take by Andrew Gogerty 12-13-04

Henlopen is under a dark cloud, and there are better options.

On June 22, 2004, the SEC filed a civil lawsuit against the fund's advisor, Landis Associates, and its manager, Michael L. Hershey. The complaint alleges that Hershey breached his fiduciary duty to a private client's managed account by investing its assets in a medical startup company in which Hershey was a shareholder and director and that he continued to invest the private account's assets there after it was clear that these investments were the medical company's only source of capital. In addition, the SEC is seeking an injunction against Hershey and the advisor. If granted, it would force both parties to terminate their relationship with the fund, which clouds the fund's future. Hershey and Landis, however, have denied these charges and are contesting them.

Despite these distractions, Hershey continues to search for fast-growing companies that he believes are undervalued. This year, he has increased the fund's stake in energy stocks. With more than 24% of assets in this sector, Hershey is betting that a decline in natural gas and other energy reserves will increase the need for drilling and exploration. Should the price of energy fall or demand for exploration decline, the fund could suffer. This move is typical of Hershey, though, as the fund has a history of making concentrated bets in sectors and individual picks. This has led to higher volatility than the typical small-growth offering, but investors have been rewarded for their patience. The fund's five-year trailing return through Dec. 10, 2004, tops 74% of its small-growth peers.

Unfortunately, despite the fund's strong performance, we recommend no new money be invested here. We think that uncertainty over the SEC's lawsuit and Hershey's future with the fund is a bad combination. Until more information is available, investors should look elsewhere.

Address:	Henlopen Fund Kennett Square, PA 19348 866-880-0032
Web Address:	www.henlopenfund.com
Inception:	12-02-92
Advisor:	Landis Associates LLC
Subadvisor:	None
NTF Plans:	Fidelity Retail-NTF, Schwab OneSource

Minimum Purchase:	$2000	Add: $500	IRA: $2000
Min Auto Inv Plan:	$2000	Add: $100	
Sales Fees:	No-load		
Management Fee:	1.00%, 0.20%A		
Actual Fees:	Mgt:1.00%	Dist:	
Expense Projections:	3Yr:$406	5Yr:$702	10Yr:$1545
Income Distrib:	Annually		

Portfolio Analysis 09-30-04

Share change since 06-04 Total Stocks:130	Sector	PE	YTD Ret%	% Assets
⊕ Southwestern Energy	Energy	19.7	112.09	1.53
⊕ Quicksilver Resources	Energy	69.9	127.74	1.41
☼ Building Materials Holdi	Business	11.7	149.48	1.37
Commercial Capital Banco	Financial	22.4	44.94	1.35
⊕ Burlington Resources	Energy	10.9	58.50	1.35
⊕ Aztar	Consumer	32.1	55.20	1.32
Cameco	Ind Mtrls	27.9	83.32	1.31
Offshore Logistics	Energy	10.6	32.42	1.31
EOG Resources	Energy	16.5	55.21	1.31
Ultra Petroleum	Energy	43.1	95.49	1.30
⊖ Lone Star Technologies	Ind Mtrls	27.9	109.39	1.25
☼ Markel	Financial	21.8	43.58	1.23
⊕ Questar	Energy	18.7	48.06	1.21
☼ Mohawk Industries	Goods	16.1	29.36	1.18
☼ Meridian Resource	Energy	20.8	1.85	1.17
Range Resources	Energy	35.8	117.27	1.16
Consol Energy	Energy	32.2	61.53	1.16
Masco	Ind Mtrls	17.2	36.23	1.14
Teekay Shipping	Business	19.4	49.82	1.14
☼ KB Home	Consumer	10.1	46.05	1.12

Current Investment Style

Value Blnd Growth — Large Mid Small

Market Cap	%
Giant	4.4
Large	7.3
Mid	28.1
Small	24.9
Micro	35.3
Avg $mil:	972

Value Measures		Rel Category
Price/Earnings	14.67	0.68
Price/Book	2.10	0.80
Price/Sales	0.91	0.61
Price/Cash Flow	5.72	0.71
Dividend Yield %	0.31	1.00

Growth Measures	%	Rel Category
Long-Term Erngs	16.86	0.97
Book Value	9.61	1.49
Sales	10.47	1.62
Cash Flow	18.58	1.37
Historical Erngs	10.45	0.77

Profitability	%	Rel Category
Return on Equity	12.05	1.22
Return on Assets	2.91	0.66
Net Margin	10.22	1.49

Sector Weightings	% of Stocks	Rel S&P 500	3 Year High	3 Year Low
Info	11.88	0.55		
Software	3.23	0.75	15	3
Hardware	5.50	0.54	18	6
Media	1.91	0.50	3	0
Telecom	1.24	0.39	3	0
Service	48.55	1.05		
Health	5.41	0.43	29	5
Consumer	17.92	1.97	18	6
Business	11.09	2.74	11	1
Financial	14.13	0.68	15	5
Mfg	39.56	1.23		
Goods	5.08	0.54	8	4
Ind Mtrls	10.28	0.81	11	3
Energy	24.14	3.37	24	8
Utilities	0.06	0.02	1	0

Composition

Cash	0.4
Stocks	99.5
Bonds	0.0
Other	0.0
Foreign (% of Stock)	12.4

ICAP Equity

Ticker	Load	NAV	Yield	Total Assets	Mstar Category
ICAEX	None	$44.01	1.6%	$948 mil	Large Value

Governance and Management

Fiduciary Grade: A

Portfolio Manager(s)

A team of managers led by Rob Lyon has run the fund since its inception. Prior to joining ICAP in 1988, Lyon served as director of research at Fred Alger Management.

Strategy

The fund's managers begin with a universe of 400 large-cap stocks and 50 mostly European ADRs. They then buy the 40 to 50 stocks with the best mix of attractive valuations, consistent or improving earnings, and catalysts for growth, such as product launches or management changes. The fund's sector weightings have shifted quite dramatically at times. Management will sell a stock if it reaches a predetermined price target.

Historical Profile

Return Average
Risk Average
Rating ★★★ Neutral

Investment Style: Equity Stock %: 97% 95% 89% 92% 94% 95% 94% 99% 99%

▼ Manager Change
∇ Partial Manager Change

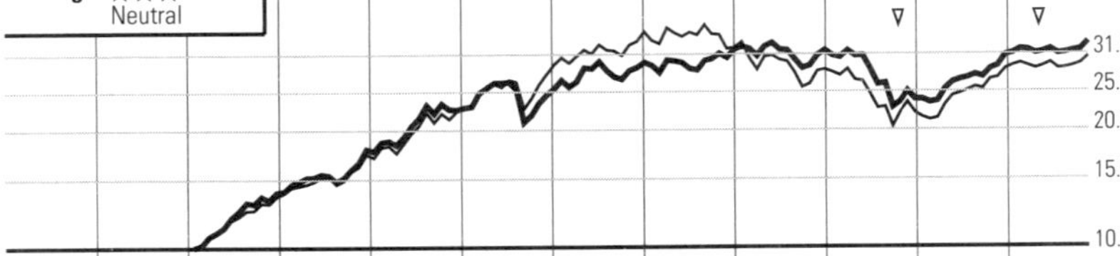

Growth of $10,000
— Investment Values of Fund
— Investment Values of S&P 500

Performance Quartile (within Category)

1993	1994	1995	1996	1997	1998	1999	2000	2001	2002	2003	12-04	History
—	20.00	26.03	31.16	35.12	38.63	43.14	43.66	43.01	32.07	40.89	44.01	NAV
—	0.00*	38.85	26.26	29.08	11.42	16.28	7.86	-0.61	-24.66	28.83	11.33	Total Return %
—	—	1.32	3.32	-4.27	-17.15	-4.76	16.96	11.27	-2.57	0.16	0.46	+/-S&P 500
—	—	0.49	4.62	-6.10	-4.21	8.93	0.85	4.98	-9.14	-1.20	-5.16	+/-Russ 1000 VI
—	—	1.40	1.15	1.22	1.43	1.33	1.13	0.85	0.85	1.16	1.76	Income Return %
—	—	37.45	25.11	27.86	9.99	14.95	6.73	-1.46	-25.51	27.67	9.57	Capital Return %
—	—	7	9	32	56	10	59	31	88	41	68	Total Rtn % Rank Cat
—	0.00	0.28	0.30	0.38	0.50	0.51	0.48	0.37	0.36	0.37	0.72	Income $
—	0.00	1.42	1.37	4.60	0.00	1.24	2.35	0.00	0.00	0.00	0.76	Capital Gains $
—	—	0.80	0.80	0.80	0.80	0.80	0.80	0.80	0.80	0.80	—	Expense Ratio %
—	—	1.49	1.15	1.06	1.39	1.22	1.13	0.87	0.96	1.03	—	Income Ratio %
—	—	105	125	121	133	118	116	87	85	97	—	Turnover Rate %
—	—	47	149	371	717	960	1,050	1,189	877	1,079	948	Net Assets $mil

Performance 12-31-04

	1st Qtr	2nd Qtr	3rd Qtr	4th Qtr	Total
2000	1.34	-4.85	5.79	5.74	7.86
2001	-3.77	3.73	-10.18	10.85	-0.61
2002	-0.26	-10.15	-19.67	4.65	-24.66
2003	-1.05	13.16	1.47	13.38	28.83
2004	3.08	0.32	-1.05	8.80	11.33

Trailing	Total Return%	+/- S&P 500	+/- Russ 1000 VI	%Rank Cat	Growth of $10,000
3 Mo	8.80	-0.43	-1.58	61	10,880
6 Mo	7.66	0.47	-4.42	70	10,766
1 Yr	11.33	0.46	-5.16	68	11,133
3 Yr Avg	2.61	-0.97	-5.96	86	10,804
5 Yr Avg	2.98	5.28	-2.29	61	11,581
10 Yr Avg	13.01	0.94	-0.82	16	33,976
15 Yr Avg	—	—	—	—	—

Tax Analysis	Tax-Adj Rtn%	%Rank Cat	Tax-Cost Rat	%Rank Cat
3 Yr (estimated)	2.14	78	0.46	31
5 Yr (estimated)	2.32	56	0.64	34
10 Yr (estimated)	11.69	6	1.17	17

Potential Capital Gain Exposure: 20% of assets

Rating and Risk

Time Period	Load-Adj Return %	Morningstar Rtn vs Cat	Morningstar Risk vs Cat	Morningstar Risk-Adj Rating
1 Yr	11.33			
3 Yr	2.61	-Avg	Avg	★★
5 Yr	2.98	Avg	-Avg	★★★
10 Yr	13.01	+Avg	Avg	★★★★
Incept	13.00			

Other Measures	Standard Index S&P 500	Best Fit Index Russ 1000 VI
Alpha	-0.7	-5.0
Beta	0.90	0.92
R-Squared	90	93
Standard Deviation	14.65	
Mean	2.61	
Sharpe Ratio	0.08	

Portfolio Analysis 11-30-04

Share change since 10-04 Total Stocks:48	Sector	PE	YTD Ret%	% Assets
⊕ Citigroup	Financial	15.3	2.72	4.71
Bank of America	Financial	12.3	21.50	4.60
J.P. Morgan Chase & Co.	Financial	19.4	9.97	3.38
⊖ ExxonMobil	Energy	13.9	28.04	3.31
⊕ Cendant	Business	13.6	6.52	3.30
⊖ ConocoPhillips	Energy	9.0	35.60	3.01
Wells Fargo	Financial	15.5	8.97	2.86
Comcast A	Media	81.0	1.49	2.86
Altria Group	Goods	13.3	18.38	2.83
⊖ General Electric	Ind Mtrls	22.8	20.68	2.81
Tyco International	Ind Mtrls	25.1	35.41	2.80
IBM	Hardware	20.2	7.19	2.76
⊖ Deere & Company	Ind Mtrls	15.7	16.26	2.75
⊕ Marathon Oil	Energy	—	17.07	2.64
Microsoft	Software	36.1	8.95	2.64
⊖ Sanofi-Aventis ADR	Health	23.0	9.75	2.56
St. Paul Travelers Compa	Financial	30.8	-3.15	2.55
Goldman Sachs Group	Financial	12.3	6.49	2.52
American International G	Financial	16.2	-0.53	2.35
Clear Channel Communicat	Media	23.5	-27.57	2.29

Current Investment Style

Value Blnd Growth; Large Mid Small

Market Cap	%
Giant	56.9
Large	39.1
Mid	4.0
Small	0.0
Micro	0.0

Avg $mil: 54,885

Value Measures		Rel Category
Price/Earnings	15.00	1.00
Price/Book	2.41	1.06
Price/Sales	1.28	1.08
Price/Cash Flow	6.30	0.99
Dividend Yield %	1.88	0.92

Growth Measures	%	Rel Category
Long-Term Erngs	9.99	0.96
Book Value	4.35	0.77
Sales	6.63	1.58
Cash Flow	7.16	1.37
Historical Erngs	14.11	1.19

Profitability	%	Rel Category
Return on Equity	16.07	1.01
Return on Assets	7.53	0.96
Net Margin	11.08	1.09

Sector Weightings	% of Stocks	Rel S&P 500	3 Year High	3 Year Low
Info	16.47	0.77		
Software	2.67	0.62	3	0
Hardware	4.13	0.40	5	2
Media	7.41	1.93	12	5
Telecom	2.26	0.72	6	2
Service	47.07	1.01		
Health	9.87	0.79	14	7
Consumer	5.27	0.58	10	3
Business	7.00	1.73	7	3
Financial	24.93	1.20	30	23
Mfg	36.46	1.14		
Goods	6.99	0.75	13	6
Ind Mtrls	12.87	1.02	15	10
Energy	12.38	1.73	12	5
Utilities	4.22	1.43	7	2

Composition

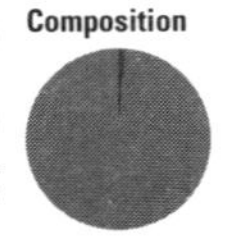

Cash	1.3
Stocks	98.7
Bonds	0.0
Other	0.0
Foreign (% of Stock)	7.0

Morningstar's Take by Kunal Kapoor 12-30-04

ICAP Equity isn't looking too hot right now, but we still like it.

Manager Rob Lyon and his team sprinkle some top-down analysis on what is otherwise a bottom-up driven process here. For instance, the fund has been playing growth in Asia throughout 2004 by investing in a bounty of energy, agricultural, and materials firms such as ConocoPhillips and Deere & Co. These moves have boosted the fund, but not by enough: The fund will likely close out the year in the large-value category's bottom half, a place it also resides in for the trailing five-year period through December 30. It has, however, outpaced the S&P 500 index during those stretches.

The index is an appropriate benchmark to compare the fund with because at its core is a stable of blue chips that Lyon invests in for relatively long periods. The fund owns shares in a number of well-known firms such as Citigroup and Altria, which provide a foil for picks such as R.R. Donnelly, a cost-cutting story that's not owned by a majority of rivals. What differentiates this fund, though, is Lyon's willingness to trade around individual positions to add incremental value. For instance, while the fund has maintained a core position in top-holding Bank of America, the size of the position has ebbed and flowed. Lyon boosted it after the stock initially dropped when it announced its acquisition of FleetBoston. He has since trimmed it a bit after it rallied nicely.

This approach, combined with low expenses and experienced management, make the fund appropriate for most equity investors. Nevertheless, we remain bigger fans of this fund's more-concentrated sibling, ICAP Select Equity. While that fund's focused nature has the potential to add some volatility, the risk/reward tradeoff up to this point has been superior. We think there's a good chance it'll stay that way and hence prefer that offering over this one.

Address:	225 West Wacker Chicago IL 60606 888-221-4227
Web Address:	www.icapfunds.com
Inception:	12-30-94*
Advisor:	Institutional Capital Corp
Subadvisor:	None
NTF Plans:	Schwab OneSource, Schwab Instl NTF

Minimum Purchase:	$1000	Add: $1000	IRA: $1000
Min Auto Inv Plan:	$1000	Add: $250	
Sales Fees:	No-load		
Management Fee:	0.80%, 0.18%A		
Actual Fees:	Mgt:0.80%	Dist:	
Expense Projections:	3Yr:$268	5Yr:$471	10Yr:$1055
Income Distrib:	Quarterly		

ICAP Euro Select Eqty

Analyst Pick

Ticker	Load	NAV	Yield	Total Assets	Mstar Category
ICEUX	None	$30.18	1.0%	$93 mil	Europe Stock

Governance and Management

Fiduciary Grade: A

Portfolio Manager(s)

Lead manager Rob Lyon, who has a strong record with ICAP's domestic funds and institutional accounts, has run the portfolio since its 1997 inception. He is supported by comanagers Matt Pickering and Jerry Senser.

Strategy

Like its domestically focused siblings, this fund features undervalued stocks. Management favors large European multinationals with catalysts for growth. Only a few make the cut, and the portfolio is the most concentrated among pan-Europe funds. The fund also sports a high turnover rate.

Historical Profile

Return Average
Risk Average
Rating ★★★ Neutral

Investment Style Equity Stock %

1998	1999	2000	2001	2002	2003	12-04
100%	97%	98%	90%	97%	93%	98%

▼ Manager Change
∇ Partial Manager Change

Growth of $10,000
— Investment Values of Fund
— Investment Values of MSCI EAFE

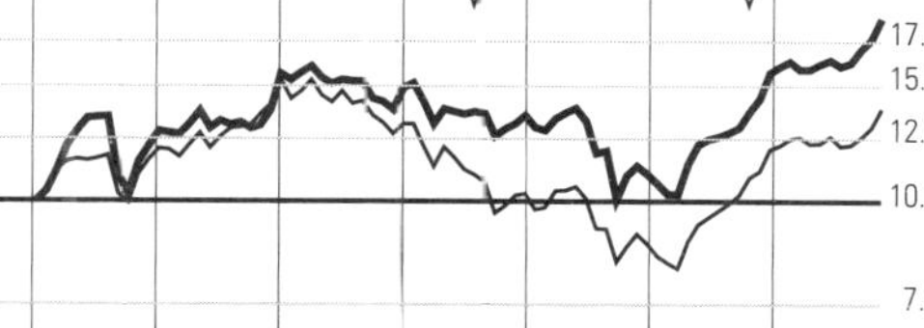

Performance Quartile (within Category)

1993	1994	1995	1996	1997	1998	1999	2000	2001	2002	2003	12-04	History
—	—	—	—	20.00	24.32	27.91	24.19	21.69	17.45	24.20	30.18	NAV
—	—	—	—	0.00*	27.40	22.03	-4.81	-8.95	-18.37	41.85	26.87	Total Return %
—	—	—	—	—	7.47	-5.00	9.38	12.47	-2.43	3.26	6.62	+/-MSCI EAFE
—	—	—	—	—	-1.10	6.10	3.59	10.95	0.01	3.31	5.99	+/-MSCI Eur
—	—	—	—	—	1.88	1.83	1.40	0.84	1.35	2.39	1.24	Income Return %
—	—	—	—	—	25.52	20.20	-6.21	-9.79	-19.72	39.46	25.63	Capital Return %
—	—	—	—	—	18	67	36	13	62	30	22	Total Rtn % Rank Cat
—	—	—	—	0.00	0.37	0.44	0.37	0.20	0.29	0.41	0.30	Income $
—	—	—	—	0.00	0.73	1.22	2.04	0.13	0.00	0.00	0.18	Capital Gains $
—	—	—	—	—	1.00	1.00	0.80	0.95	0.80	0.80	—	Expense Ratio %
—	—	—	—	—	1.69	1.71	1.53	0.72	1.48	1.89	—	Income Ratio %
—	—	—	—	—	272	245	370	267	276	218	—	Turnover Rate %
—	—	—	—	—	28	32	33	21	18	45	93	Net Assets $mil

Performance 12-31-04

	1st Qtr	2nd Qtr	3rd Qtr	4th Qtr	Total
2000	2.62	-4.56	-6.32	3.75	-4.81
2001	-11.70	3.46	-7.32	7.54	-8.95
2002	-1.21	-0.82	-23.77	9.29	-18.37
2003	-6.87	21.04	4.10	20.88	41.85
2004	1.24	3.30	3.71	16.98	26.87

Trailing	Total Return%	+/- MSCI EAFE	+/- MSCI Eur	%Rank Cat	Growth of $10,000
3 Mo	16.98	1.66	1.06	16	11,698
6 Mo	21.31	6.31	3.99	8	12,131
1 Yr	26.87	6.62	5.99	22	12,687
3 Yr Avg	13.68	1.79	2.70	34	14,691
5 Yr Avg	4.95	6.08	4.89	25	12,732
10 Yr Avg	—	—	—	—	—
15 Yr Avg	—	—	—	—	—

Tax Analysis	Tax-Adj Rtn%	%Rank Cat	Tax-Cost Rat	%Rank Cat
3 Yr (estimated)	12.99	31	0.61	63
5 Yr (estimated)	3.84	25	1.06	79
10 Yr (estimated)	—	—	—	—

Potential Capital Gain Exposure: 22% of assets

Rating and Risk

Time Period	Load-Adj Return %	Morningstar Rtn vs Cat	Morningstar Risk vs Cat	Morningstar Risk-Adj Rating
1 Yr	26.87			
3 Yr	13.68	Avg	+Avg	★★★
5 Yr	4.95	Avg	-Avg	★★★
10 Yr	—	—	—	—
Incept	10.24			

Other Measures	Standard Index S&P 500	Best Fit Index MSCI EASExJ
Alpha	1.0	1.8
Beta	1.09	0.99
R-Squared	90	96
Standard Deviation	20.39	
Mean	13.68	
Sharpe Ratio	0.61	

Portfolio Analysis 11-30-04

Share change since 10-04 Total Stocks:25	Sector	Country	% Assets
☼ GBL Groupe Bruxelles Lam	Ind Mtrls	Belgium	4.82
⊕ Telecom Italia S.p.A. (A	Telecom	United States	4.78
☼ Allianz	Financial	Germany	4.67
⊕ Total SA ADR	Energy	France	4.65
⊕ ING Group ADR	Financial	Netherlands	4.62
⊕ Siemens AG ADR	Hardware	Germany	4.61
⊕ E.ON AG ADR	Utilities	Germany	4.60
☼ Royal Bank Of Scotland G	Financial	U.K.	4.45
⊕ UBS	Financial	Switzerland	4.43
⊕ Vivendi Universal ADR	Media	France	4.42
⊕ Sanofi-Aventis ADR	Health	France	4.30
☼ Allied Domecq	Goods	U.K.	4.24
⊕ BASF AG ADR	Ind Mtrls	Germany	4.17
☼ Tesco	Consumer	U.K.	4.13
⊕ ENI SpA ADR	Energy	Italy	3.98
⊕ BP PLC ADR	Energy	U.K.	3.92
☼ Investor	Financial	Sweden	3.87
⊖ Nestle SA ADR	Goods	Switzerland	3.83
⊕ Barclays	Financial	U.K.	3.60
☼ GUS	Consumer	U.K.	2.98

Current Investment Style

Value Blnd Growth; Large Mid Small

Market Cap	%
Giant	68.9
Large	28.7
Mid	2.4
Small	0.0
Micro	0.0

Avg $mil: 43,815

Value Measures		Rel Category
Price/Earnings	13.35	0.99
Price/Book	1.80	0.89
Price/Sales	1.25	1.37
Price/Cash Flow	6.57	1.23
Dividend Yield %	2.90	1.11

Growth Measures	%	Rel Category
Long-Term Erngs	9.81	0.88
Book Value	-0.50	NMF
Sales	5.27	1.81
Cash Flow	10.74	2.21
Historical Erngs	1.48	0.35

Composition

Cash	2.3	Bonds	0.0
Stocks	97.7	Other	0.0

Foreign (% of Stock) 95.1

Sector Weightings	% of Stocks	Rel MSCI EAFE	3 Year High	Low
Info	14.14	0.85		
Software	0.00	0.00	0	0
Hardware	4.72	1.29	7	0
Media	4.53	1.99	11	0
Telecom	4.89	0.51	16	3
Service	45.61	1.02		
Health	7.02	0.97	16	6
Consumer	7.27	1.44	12	0
Business	2.68	0.49	5	0
Financial	28.64	1.06	34	7
Mfg	40.23	1.04		
Goods	10.64	0.78	32	8
Ind Mtrls	9.20	0.75	25	0
Energy	15.68	2.13	23	3
Utilities	4.71	0.88	8	0

Regional Exposure		% Stock	
UK/W. Europe	95	N. America	5
Japan	0	Latn America	0
Asia X Japan	0	Other	0

Country Exposure		% Stock	
U.K.	29	Switzerland	8
Germany	18	Netherlands	7
France	14		

Morningstar's Take by William Samuel Rocco 11-21-04

ICAP Euro Select Equity offers distinguished results as well as a distinctive portfolio.

This fund certainly isn't just another bland pan-Europe offering that looks a lot like the MSCI Europe Index. Rob Lyon, Matt Pickering, and Jerry Senser hold just 20 to 25 names in ICAP Euro Select Equity, so the fund is far more focused than both the typical pan-Europe offering and the index. And since the trio favors giant caps, the fund's average market cap is more than twice twice those of its typical peer and the index.

The three managers, unlike most of their peers, are comfortable when their stock selection leads to distinctive sector weights. Thanks to its hefty stakes in Total, Eni, and BP, the fund's energy stake is far bigger than that of typical pan-Europe funds and the index. And the trio trade rapidly; annual turnover normally exceeds 200%.

Lyon and his comanagers have executed their focused and fast-moving strategy well thus far in 2004. Barclays, which they bought in early summer after it and other British banks declined due to interest-rate concerns, has surged in recent months. The managers' energy stocks have also been winners. Thus, the fund is up 19% and well ahead of the average pan-Europe offering and the index for the year to date.

The fund has also earned superior returns over the long run, and it has suffered only moderate volatility along the way, as its value bias and stock selection have offset the risks of its concentration. And it has a fetching 0.80% expense ratio. Thus, we believe this fund is a terrific option for Europe fans. Such investors should note that it looks like the fund will make a small distribution later this year. They also might want to consider this fund for a tax-deferred account first. While the fund's high portfolio turnover hasn't been a problem in recent years, it could undermine tax efficiency over time.

Address:	225 West Wacker Chicago IL 60606 888-221-4227
Web Address:	www.icapfunds.com
Inception:	12-31-97*
Advisor:	Institutional Capital Corp
Subadvisor:	None
NTF Plans:	Schwab OneSource, Federated Tr NTF

Minimum Purchase:	$1000	Add: $1000	IRA: $1000
Min Auto Inv Plan:	$1000	Add: $250	
Sales Fees:	No-load, 2.00%R		
Management Fee:	0.80%, 0.18%A		
Actual Fees:	Mgt:0.80%	Dist:	
Expense Projections:	3Yr:$439	5Yr:$821	10Yr:$1893
Income Distrib:	Annually		

ICAP Select Equity

Analyst Pick	Ticker	Load	NAV	Yield	Total Assets	Mstar Category
✔	ICSLX	None	$34.35	1.6%	$281 mil	Large Value

Governance and Management

Fiduciary Grade: A

Portfolio Manager(s)

Rob Lyon is ICAP's chief investment officer and manager of each of the firm's retail mutual funds. Prior to joining ICAP in 1988, he served as director of research at Fred Alger Management. He is joined here by Jerry Senser, who took on comanager responsibilities in 2004.

Strategy

ICAP narrows a group of 450 large-cap U.S. and European names down to 50 by screening for stocks with attractive valuations, consistent to improving earnings, and catalysts for growth such as new product launches. Manager Rob Lyon further narrows this group by picking the 20 stocks with the most upside potential.

Historical Profile

Return Above Avg
Risk Average
Rating ★★★★ Above Avg

Investment Style
Equity
Stock %: 82% (1998), 94% (1999), 96% (2000), 91% (2001), 97% (2002), 94% (2003), 96% (12-04)

▼ Manager Change
▽ Partial Manager Change

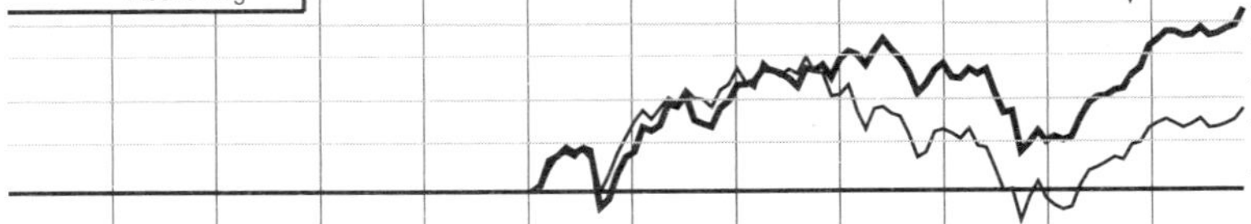

Growth of $10,000
— Investment Values of Fund
— Investment Values of S&P 500

Performance Quartile (within Category)

History

	1993	1994	1995	1996	1997	1998	1999	2000	2001	2002	2003	12-04
NAV	—	—	—	—	20.00	22.77	27.91	29.50	28.50	21.36	29.79	34.35
Total Return %	—	—	—	—	0.00*	15.33	27.17	9.49	-1.59	-24.53	40.68	17.98
+/-S&P 500	—	—	—	—	—	-13.24	6.13	18.59	10.29	-2.44	12.01	7.11
+/-Russ 1000 VI	—	—	—	—	—	-0.30	19.82	2.48	4.00	-9.01	10.65	1.49
Income Return %	—	—	—	—	—	1.45	1.70	1.15	0.53	0.56	0.99	1.90
Capital Return %	—	—	—	—	—	13.88	25.47	8.34	-2.12	-25.09	39.69	16.08
Total Rtn % Rank Cat	—	—	—	—	—	32	2	50	36	87	4	7
Income $	—	—	—	—	0.00	0.29	0.39	0.32	0.15	0.16	0.21	0.56
Capital Gains $	—	—	—	—	0.00	0.00	0.63	0.72	0.37	0.00	0.00	0.20
Expense Ratio %	—	—	—	—	—	0.80	0.80	0.80	0.80	0.80	0.80	—
Income Ratio %	—	—	—	—	—	1.82	1.63	1.24	0.54	0.64	0.88	—
Turnover Rate %	—	—	—	—	—	250	375	400	309	358	317	—
Net Assets $mil	—	—	—	—	—	10	24	38	54	38	80	281

Performance 12-31-04

	1st Qtr	2nd Qtr	3rd Qtr	4th Qtr	Total
2000	5.78	-3.27	2.85	4.04	9.49
2001	-2.08	5.73	-14.49	11.16	-1.59
2002	-1.87	-8.39	-19.06	3.71	-24.53
2003	1.67	15.53	3.00	16.27	40.68
2004	5.46	1.39	-0.42	10.80	17.98

Trailing	Total Return%	+/- S&P 500	+/- Russ 1000 VI	%Rank Cat	Growth of $10,000
3 Mo	10.80	1.57	0.42	14	11,080
6 Mo	10.34	3.15	-1.74	29	11,034
1 Yr	17.98	7.11	1.49	7	11,798
3 Yr Avg	7.79	4.21	-0.78	21	12,524
5 Yr Avg	6.18	8.48	0.91	27	13,496
10 Yr Avg	—	—	—	—	—
15 Yr Avg	—	—	—	—	—

Tax Analysis	Tax-Adj Rtn%	%Rank Cat	Tax-Cost Rat	%Rank Cat
3 Yr (estimated)	7.33	16	0.43	29
5 Yr (estimated)	5.56	23	0.58	31
10 Yr (estimated)	—	—	—	—

Potential Capital Gain Exposure: 10% of assets

Rating and Risk

Time Period	Load-Adj Return %	Morningstar Rtn vs Cat	Morningstar Risk vs Cat	Morningstar Risk-Adj Rating
1 Yr	17.98			
3 Yr	7.79	+Avg	Avg	★★★★
5 Yr	6.18	+Avg	Avg	★★★★
10 Yr	—	—	—	—
Incept	10.24			

Other Measures	Standard Index S&P 500	Best Fit Index MSCI World
Alpha	4.4	1.3
Beta	0.89	0.93
R-Squared	81	87

Standard Deviation	16.01
Mean	7.79
Sharpe Ratio	0.40

Portfolio Analysis 11-30-04

Share change since 10-04 Total Stocks:27	Sector	PE	YTD Ret%	% Assets
⊕ Microsoft	Software	36.1	8.95	6.33
⊕ Bank of America	Financial	12.3	21.50	6.27
⊕ Cendant	Business	13.6	6.52	5.91
⊕ Archer Daniels Midland	Ind Mtrls	23.1	49.11	5.02
⊖ Deere & Company	Ind Mtrls	15.7	16.26	4.60
⊕ Marathon Oil	Energy	—	17.07	4.58
⊕ J.P. Morgan Chase & Co.	Financial	19.4	9.97	4.50
⊕ Comcast A	Media	81.0	1.49	4.49
⊕ Altria Group	Goods	13.3	18.38	4.48
⊕ ConocoPhillips	Energy	9.0	35.60	4.46
⊕ Citigroup	Financial	15.3	2.72	4.30
⊕ St. Paul Travelers Compa	Financial	30.8	-3.15	4.27
⊖ Sanofi-Aventis ADR	Health	23.0	9.75	3.85
⊖ Tyco International	Ind Mtrls	25.1	35.41	3.76
⊕ Lowe's Companies	Consumer	22.1	4.25	3.62
⊖ Waste Management	Business	18.9	3.81	3.38
⊖ Goldman Sachs Group	Financial	12.3	6.49	2.83
RR Donnelley & Sons	Business	24.2	21.03	2.83
⊕ American International G	Financial	16.2	-0.53	2.72
Entergy	Utilities	21.1	22.14	2.62

Current Investment Style

Value Blnd Growth (Large / Mid / Small)

Market Cap	%
Giant	52.7
Large	41.4
Mid	5.9
Small	0.0
Micro	0.0
Avg $mil: 47,608	

Value Measures		Rel Category
Price/Earnings	14.62	0.97
Price/Book	2.25	0.99
Price/Sales	0.99	0.83
Price/Cash Flow	5.03	0.79
Dividend Yield %	1.79	0.88

Growth Measures	%	Rel Category
Long-Term Erngs	10.04	0.96
Book Value	3.85	0.68
Sales	7.54	1.80
Cash Flow	6.73	1.29
Historical Erngs	18.00	1.52

Profitability	%	Rel Category
Return on Equity	14.74	0.93
Return on Assets	7.21	0.92
Net Margin	10.73	1.05

Sector Weightings	% of Stocks	Rel S&P 500	3 Year High	3 Year Low
Info	13.03	0.61		
Software	6.60	1.53	7	0
Hardware	1.75	0.17	7	0
Media	4.68	1.22	19	0
Telecom	0.00	0.00	2	0
Service	49.88	1.08		
Health	6.72	0.54	14	5
Consumer	4.31	0.47	11	0
Business	12.93	3.19	14	4
Financial	25.92	1.25	32	21
Mfg	37.10	1.16		
Goods	6.86	0.74	18	3
Ind Mtrls	16.01	1.26	18	0
Energy	11.50	1.61	17	0
Utilities	2.73	0.92	11	0

Composition

Cash	4.0
Stocks	96.0
Bonds	0.0
Other	0.0
Foreign (% of Stock)	8.9

Morningstar's Take by Kunal Kapoor 12-29-04

Asia may be getting a lot of attention right now, but ICAP Select Equity found its way there sooner than rivals.

Banking on the massive amounts of financial stimuli pumped into the U.S. economy during the last downturn, this fund was well positioned for 2003's market rally. And it delivered, jumping more than 40% last year. And the fund has continued to hum along in 2004: Its 17.87% return for the year to date through Dec. 28, 2004, bests approximately 92% of its large-cap value rivals.

The reasons behind the fund's continued success are easy to identify. Late in 2003, manager Rob Lyon began to focus on growth in Asia--particularly China and India--and what opportunities that might present for the blue chips he favors. As such, the portfolio's exposure to energy, materials, and agricultural firms (which Lyon reckons will benefit most from those countries' development) rose. That move has already paid dividends, with picks such as ConocoPhillips and Archer Daniels Midland providing a boost.

Such moves also reflect other unique aspects of this fund. It remains among the few (that at least admit) to employing top-down analysis. In fact, the themes that resonate through the portfolio are a direct result of broad macroeconomic analysis. Moreover, Lyon and his team don't restrict their analysis to domestic issues or firms. The current portfolio, for instance, includes several foreign holdings, including European pharmaceuticals firm Sanofi-Aventis and GlaxoSmithkline.

We think this additional expertise is extremely important as industries become more global in nature. (Firms such as Sanofi and Glaxo, for instance, are among the three largest in their sectors, and can't even be ignored by U.S. managers.) Couple that with this offering's low expenses and experienced management, and it's clear to see why we consider it good enough to be an Analyst Pick.

Address:	225 West Wacker Chicago IL 60606 888-221-4227
Web Address:	www.icapfunds.com
Inception:	12-31-97 *
Advisor:	Institutional Capital Corp
Subadvisor:	None
NTF Plans:	Schwab OneSource, Schwab Instl NTF

Minimum Purchase:	$1000	Add: $1000	IRA: $1000
Min Auto Inv Plan:	$1000	Add: $250	
Sales Fees:	No-load		
Management Fee:	0.80%, 0.18%A		
Actual Fees:	Mgt:0.80%	Dist:	
Expense Projections:	3Yr:$339	5Yr:$617	10Yr:$1409
Income Distrib:	Quarterly		

ICM/Isabelle Sm Cap Invt

Ticker	Load	NAV	Yield	Total Assets	Mstar Category
IZZYX	12b-1 only	$16.30	0.0%	$86 mil	Small Value

Governance and Management

Fiduciary Grade: C

Portfolio Manager(s)

Warren Isabelle is the fund's founder and has been at the helm since March 1998. Prior to that, he posted great numbers at Pioneer Mid-Cap Value. Isabelle recently added two experienced analysts to his staff to assist him in stock-picking. He says that he has more than one third of his investable assets devoted to this fund.

Strategy

Manager Warren Isabelle favors beaten-down stocks that aren't on most investors' radar screens. Though the fund's sector concentration isn't as severe as in the past, it still sports huge industrial-materials and health-care stakes. Throughout 2003, Isabelle broadened the portfolio to include more than 80 names, but he's since reversed course. The fund now holds around 50 stocks.

Historical Profile

Return Low
Risk High
Rating ★ Lowest

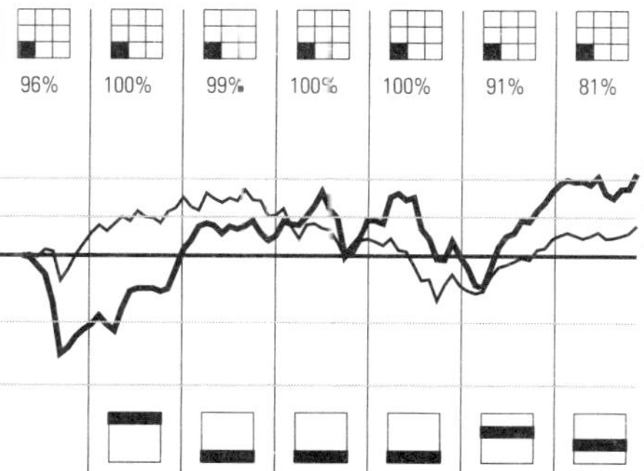

1993	1994	1995	1996	1997	1998	1999	2000	2001	2002	2003	12-04	History
—	—	—	—	—	6.91	10.33	10.87	11.83	9.76	13.80	16.30	NAV
—	—	—	—	—	-30.62*	49.49	7.73	8.83	-17.50	41.39	18.12	Total Return %
—	—	—	—	—	—	28.45	16.83	20.71	4.59	12.72	7.25	+/-S&P 500
—	—	—	—	—	—	50.98	-15.10	-5.19	-6.07	-4.64	-4.13	+/-Russ 2000 VL
—	—	—	—	—	0.00	0.00	0.00	0.00	0.00	0.00	0.00	Income Return %
—	—	—	—	—	—	49.49	7.73	8.83	-17.50	41.39	18.12	Capital Return %
—	—	—	—	—	—	4	82	78	86	50	73	Total Rtn % Rank Cat
—	—	—	—	—	0.00	0.00	0.00	0.00	0.00	0.00	0.00	Income $
—	—	—	—	—	0.00	0.00	0.25	0.00	0.00	0.00	0.00	Capital Gains $
—	—	—	—	—	1.95	1.95	1.82	1.74	1.71	1.88	—	Expense Ratio %
—	—	—	—	—	-1.31	-1.39	-0.43	-0.61	-1.08	-1.26	—	Income Ratio %
—	—	—	—	—	—	84	54	43	50	52	—	Turnover Rate %
—	—	—	—	—	1	10	75	87	67	67	71	Net Assets $mil

Performance 12-31-04

	1st Qtr	2nd Qtr	3rd Qtr	4th Qtr	Total
2000	15.00	-1.60	3.08	-7.64	7.73
2001	5.98	19.27	-29.11	21.46	8.83
2002	13.10	-0.30	-28.04	1.67	-17.50
2003	-15.68	31.83	8.02	17.75	41.39
2004	5.22	2.62	-6.24	16.68	18.12

Trailing	Total Return%	+/- S&P 500	+/- Russ 2000 VL	%Rank Cat	Growth of $10,000
3 Mo	16.68	7.45	3.48	4	11,668
6 Mo	9.40	2.21	-3.97	86	10,940
1 Yr	18.12	7.25	-4.13	73	11,812
3 Yr Avg	11.28	7.70	-5.22	88	13,780
5 Yr Avg	10.07	12.37	-7.16	93	16,156
10 Yr Avg	—	—	—	—	—
15 Yr Avg	—	—	—	—	—

Tax Analysis	Tax-Adj Rtn%	%Rank Cat	Tax-Cost Rat	%Rank Cat
3 Yr (estimated)	11.28	76	0.00	1
5 Yr (estimated)	9.90	89	0.15	7
10 Yr (estimated)	—	—	—	—

Potential Capital Gain Exposure: 30% of assets

Rating and Risk

Time Period	Load-Adj Return %	Morningstar Rtn vs Cat	Morningstar Risk vs Cat	Morningstar Risk-Adj Rating
1 Yr	18.12			
3 Yr	11.28	-Avg	High	★
5 Yr	10.07	Low	High	★
10 Yr	—	—	—	—
Incept	7.88			

Other Measures	Standard Index S&P 500	Best Fit Index Russ 2000 VL
Alpha	8.7	-6.2
Beta	1.13	1.18
R-Squared	53	81
Standard Deviation	26.33	
Mean	11.28	
Sharpe Ratio	0.38	

Portfolio Analysis 09-30-04

Share change since 06-04 Total Stocks:58	Sector	PE	YTD Ret%	% Assets
⊖ Crompton	Ind Mtrls	—	69.46	2.91
⊖ Ariad Pharmaceuticals	Health	—	-0.27	2.71
⊖ Willbros Group	Business	—	91.76	2.65
⊖ Denbury Resources	Energy	19.5	97.34	2.64
Magnum Hunter Resources	Energy	13.3	35.65	2.40
⊕ Olin	Ind Mtrls	—	14.81	2.39
Material Sciences	Ind Mtrls	—	77.94	2.36
Analogic	Health	63.5	9.95	2.24
⊖ Agilysys	Ind Mtrls	40.1	55.14	2.10
⊕ Newpark Resources	Business	—	7.52	2.05
⊕ Whiting Petroleum	Energy	—	64.40	1.96
AM Castle	Ind Mtrls	—	63.56	1.94
⊕ PMA Capital	Financial	—	102.15	1.92
⊖ PolyOne	Ind Mtrls	—	41.78	1.82
US Physical Therapy	Health	29.1	-1.97	1.77
⊕ Imation	Hardware	17.7	-8.48	1.75
Chiquita Brands Internat	Goods	21.9	-1.65	1.68
⊖ Cmnwlth Inds	Ind Mtrls	—	—	1.65
⊕ Lightbridge	Telecom	—	-33.63	1.64
⊕ Global Power Equipment	Ind Mtrls	65.0	47.31	1.64

Current Investment Style

Value Blnd Growth — Large Mid Small

Market Cap	%
Giant	0.0
Large	0.0
Mid	0.0
Small	52.5
Micro	47.5
Avg $mil:	406

Value Measures		Rel Category
Price/Earnings	18.80	1.18
Price/Book	1.50	0.90
Price/Sales	0.54	0.72
Price/Cash Flow	8.49	1.64
Dividend Yield %	0.61	0.51

Growth Measures	%	Rel Category
Long-Term Erngs	15.59	1.29
Book Value	-4.33	NMF
Sales	1.07	0.34
Cash Flow	-20.12	NMF
Historical Erngs	-5.56	NMF

Profitability	%	Rel Category
Return on Equity	-0.99	NMF
Return on Assets	-0.73	NMF
Net Margin	3.45	0.52

Sector Weightings	% of Stocks	Rel S&P 500	3 Year High	3 Year Low
Info	10.81	0.50		
Software	2.53	0.59	8	0
Hardware	6.28	0.62	12	5
Media	0.00	0.00	1	0
Telecom	2.00	0.63	2	0
Service	41.82	0.90		
Health	14.07	1.13	22	8
Consumer	1.74	0.19	5	2
Business	13.80	3.41	14	1
Financial	12.21	0.59	13	0
Mfg	47.39	1.48		
Goods	7.16	0.77	10	7
Ind Mtrls	31.69	2.50	51	30
Energy	8.54	1.19	9	1
Utilities	0.00	0.00	2	0

Composition

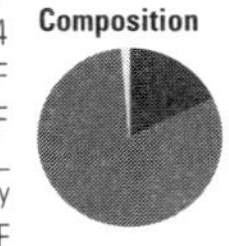

Cash	17.7
Stocks	80.8
Bonds	0.0
Other	1.5
Foreign (% of Stock)	3.5

Morningstar's Take by Christopher Davis 12-01-04

ICM/Isabelle Small Cap Value is easy to dismiss.

In 2003, manager Warren Isabelle took steps to moderate this fund's tough-to-stomach volatility. He strengthened its research capabilities, bringing aboard two new analysts to help broaden the portfolio beyond Isabelle's favorite stomping grounds, industrials and health care, to include more financials and energy stocks. Relying on increased analytical support, he expanded the portfolio to include 80 stocks, up from around 50, and lightened the fund's stake in its top holdings.

Unfortunately, those changes didn't have a beneficial effect. In fact, a number of the analysts' recommendations, including Hanger Orthopedic, Visteon, and Imation, have been liabilities this year. So despite the enormous gains enjoyed by longtime industrials holdings such as PolyOne and Crompton, the fund is up just 11% for the year to date through Nov. 30, 2004, placing it in the small-value category's worst 5%.

In 2004's third quarter, Isabelle jettisoned his efforts to limit volatility through added diversification. In a flurry of selling, he ditched losers such as Hanger and financial pick Brookline Bancorp, whittling the number of fund holdings to 56--the same level as in early 2003. Isabelle also says he expects to devote larger chunks of the portfolio to its largest holdings. The fund also remains heavily concentrated by sector--witness its outsized health-care and industrials stakes--and focused on beaten-down micro caps. As such, investors should continue to expect considerable volatility here.

Isabelle hasn't shown he can make the bumpy ride worthwhile, as the fund's lousy relative returns attest. That's particularly troubling given the dominance of smaller, cheaper names--Isabelle's bread and butter--in recent years. We're also dismayed by Isabelle's abrupt shift in strategy. Moreover, we think the fund's 1.88% expense ratio is excessive. Put simply, we think investors should look elsewhere.

Address:	ICM Series Trust Portland, ME 04101 800-472-6114
Web Address:	www.icmfunds.com
Inception:	03-12-98*
Advisor:	Ironwood Capital Management LLC
Subadvisor:	None
NTF Plans:	Fidelity Retail-NTF, Schwab OneSource

Minimum Purchase:	$1000	Add: $100	IRA: $1000
Min Auto Inv Plan:	$1000	Add: $100	
Sales Fees:	0.25%B		
Management Fee:	1.00%, 0.15%A		
Actual Fees:	Mgt:1.00%	Dist:0.25%	
Expense Projections:	3Yr:$567	5Yr:$976	10Yr:$2118
Income Distrib:	Annually		

Janus

Ticker	Load	NAV	Yield	Total Assets	Mstar Category
JANSX	None	$24.57	0.0%	$13,519 mil	Large Growth

Governance and Management

Fiduciary Grade: C

Portfolio Manager(s)

Blaine Rollins has managed this fund since January 2000, after longtime manager Jim Craig stepped down. Prior to his stint here, Rollins had successful runs at Janus Balanced and Janus Core Equity.

Strategy

The fund mixes pricey, high-growth stocks with more-stable growth names. Like most Janus managers, Blaine Rollins prizes companies that have significant free cash-flow yields and can deliver strong returns on invested capital. Rollins also likes firms that are able to steal market share from their competitors. For a fund of its size, it parks a lot of assets in its top holdings, and not all of its stocks are the biggest blue chips.

Historical Profile

Return Average
Risk Average
Rating ★★★ Neutral

Investment Style: Equity, Stock %: 83% 96% 96% 96% 95% 99% 99% 99% 98%

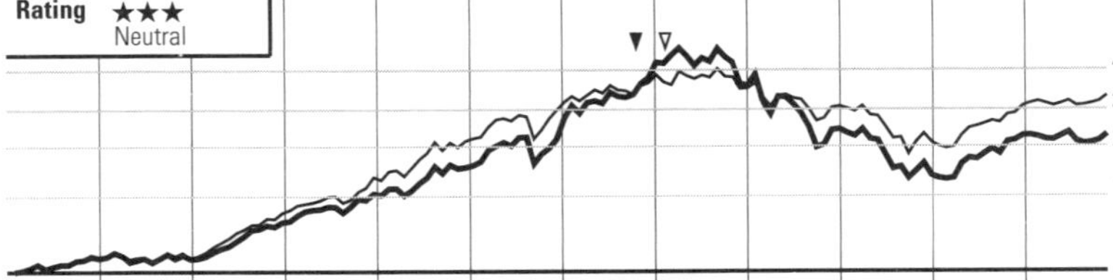

▼ Manager Change
▽ Partial Manager Change

Growth of $10,000
— Investment Values of Fund
— Investment Values of S&P 500

Performance Quartile (within Category)

1993	1994	1995	1996	1997	1998	1999	2000	2001	2002	2003	12-04	History
19.39	18.78	23.04	24.45	24.90	33.65	44.05	33.29	24.60	17.82	23.47	24.57	NAV
10.92	-1.10	29.43	19.61	22.72	38.89	47.13	-14.91	-26.10	-27.56	31.71	4.69	Total Return %
0.86	-2.41	-8.10	-3.33	-10.63	10.32	26.09	-5.81	-14.22	-5.47	3.04	-6.18	+/-S&P 500
8.05	-3.72	-7.75	-3.51	-7.77	0.18	13.97	7.51	-5.68	0.32	1.96	-1.61	+/-Russ 1000Gr
2.08	0.04	4.13	0.91	0.95	0.34	0.00	1.26	0.00	0.00	0.00	0.00	Income Return %
8.84	-1.14	25.30	18.70	21.77	38.55	47.13	-16.17	-26.10	-27.56	31.71	4.69	Capital Return %
48	45	68	49	73	23	24	57	77	51	24	76	Total Rtn % Rank Cat
0.39	0.01	0.78	0.21	0.23	0.08	0.00	0.55	0.00	0.00	0.00	0.00	Income $
0.94	0.39	0.49	2.92	4.75	0.82	5.22	3.84	0.00	0.00	0.00	0.00	Capital Gains $
0.92	0.91	0.86	0.85	0.86	0.87	0.84	0.84	0.83	0.84	0.89	0.90	Expense Ratio %
1.55	1.12	1.25	0.91	0.85	0.00	-0.14	-0.19	-0.16	-0.24	-0.17	-0.17	Income Ratio %
127	139	118	104	132	70	63	65	51	27	22	21	Turnover Rate %
9,200	9,401	12,466	15,890	19,200	25,491	42,330	39,174	25,622	15,426	17,123	13,519	Net Assets $mil

Performance 12-31-04

	1st Qtr	2nd Qtr	3rd Qtr	4th Qtr	Total
2000	10.44	-6.70	0.73	-18.02	-14.91
2001	-18.02	7.00	-25.82	13.57	-26.10
2002	-0.08	-16.23	-15.06	1.89	-27.56
2003	-1.85	14.12	3.96	13.11	31.71
2004	-2.51	4.98	-7.08	10.08	4.69

Trailing	Total Return%	+/- S&P 500	+/- Russ 1000Gr	%Rank Cat	Growth of $10,000
3 Mo	10.08	0.85	0.91	46	11,008
6 Mo	2.29	-4.90	-1.18	84	10,229
1 Yr	4.69	-6.18	-1.61	76	10,469
3 Yr Avg	-0.04	-3.62	0.14	46	9,988
5 Yr Avg	-8.88	-6.58	0.41	65	6,282
10 Yr Avg	9.32	-2.75	-0.27	43	24,378
15 Yr Avg	9.78	-1.15	0.28	45	40,537

Tax Analysis	Tax-Adj Rtn%	%Rank Cat	Tax-Cost Rat	%Rank Cat
3 Yr (estimated)	-0.04	39	0.00	1
5 Yr (estimated)	-9.35	61	0.52	32
10 Yr (estimated)	7.61	44	1.56	53

Potential Capital Gain Exposure: -34% of assets

Rating and Risk

Time Period	Load-Adj Return %	Morningstar Rtn vs Cat	Morningstar Risk vs Cat	Morningstar Risk-Adj Rating
1 Yr	4.69			
3 Yr	-0.04	Avg	Avg	★★★
5 Yr	-8.88	Avg	+Avg	★★★
10 Yr	9.32	Avg	Avg	★★★
Incept	14.14			

Other Measures	Standard Index S&P 500	Best Fit Index Russ 1000
Alpha	-3.4	-4.1
Beta	1.02	1.03
R-Squared	88	88
Standard Deviation	16.44	
Mean	-0.04	
Sharpe Ratio	-0.09	

Portfolio Analysis 11-30-04

Share change since 10-04 Total Stocks:107	Sector	PE	YTD Ret%	% Assets
⊖ Comcast	Media	—	-13.77	6.74
⊖ Time Warner	Media	27.5	8.12	6.43
⊖ Maxim Integrated Product	Hardware	27.9	-13.87	5.41
Cisco Systems	Hardware	24.5	-20.26	4.63
⊖ Linear Technology	Hardware	32.4	-7.10	4.10
⊖ United Parcel Service B	Business	28.5	16.40	3.02
Walgreen	Consumer	31.6	6.03	2.94
⊖ Univision Communications	Media	39.5	-26.25	2.69
Tyco International	Ind Mtrls	25.1	35.41	2.61
McDonald's	Consumer	19.7	31.48	2.37
⊖ 3M Company	Ind Mtrls	23.5	-1.75	1.99
⊖ Bank of New York	Financial	18.5	3.52	1.73
Lockheed Martin	Ind Mtrls	19.9	9.97	1.71
Amazon.com	Consumer	55.5	-15.83	1.68
Sysco	Consumer	26.0	3.69	1.55
⊕ Nokia ADR	Hardware	18.1	-6.14	1.43
Paychex	Business	38.9	-7.06	1.35
Boeing	Ind Mtrls	14.7	24.86	1.32
⊖ Illinois Tool Works	Ind Mtrls	22.1	11.75	1.30
⊖ Alcon	Health	41.6	33.78	1.30

Current Investment Style

Value Blnd Growth; Large Mid Small

Market Cap	%
Giant	32.2
Large	51.7
Mid	15.6
Small	0.4
Micro	0.0
Avg $mil: 23,932	

Value Measures		Rel Category
Price/Earnings	21.64	1.02
Price/Book	2.76	0.85
Price/Sales	1.96	0.91
Price/Cash Flow	11.81	1.07
Dividend Yield %	0.91	1.18

Growth Measures	%	Rel Category
Long-Term Erngs	14.24	1.01
Book Value	11.30	0.89
Sales	9.49	1.11
Cash Flow	9.50	0.57
Historical Erngs	14.16	0.98

Profitability	%	Rel Category
Return on Equity	17.80	0.99
Return on Assets	10.15	1.08
Net Margin	14.11	1.15

Sector Weightings	% of Stocks	Rel S&P 500	3 Year High	3 Year Low
Info	35.30	1.64		
Software	0.18	0.04	1	0
Hardware	17.77	1.74	23	10
Media	17.35	4.52	22	17
Telecom	0.00	0.00	0	0
Service	43.62	0.94		
Health	8.19	0.66	11	6
Consumer	17.22	1.90	17	9
Business	7.77	1.92	11	8
Financial	10.44	0.50	18	10
Mfg	21.07	0.66		
Goods	4.48	0.48	10	4
Ind Mtrls	15.13	1.19	15	8
Energy	1.20	0.17	1	0
Utilities	0.26	0.09	0	0

Composition

Cash	1.4
Stocks	98.2
Bonds	0.0
Other	0.4
Foreign (% of Stock)	6.4

Morningstar's Take by Dan McNeela 10-15-04

Investing in the Janus Fund is becoming a test of patience.

One need not look far down this fund's roster of stocks to see why it's having a rough 2004. Manager Blaine Rollins has sunk one third of its assets into the top five stocks, and all five had fallen by double digits for the year to date through Sept. 30. These five picks each hail from the media and hardware sectors, which have been among the least fertile areas in this year's market. And adding the lackluster performance of the top picks to the fund's combined 40% stake in media and hardware stocks only further shows why it's no surprise the fund has slipped 5.8% through Oct. 14.

That said, there are some encouraging signs below the surface. The fund's two big plays in the semiconductor area, Linear Technology and Maxim Integrated Products, have been among the least damaged in an industrywide pullback. Those two stocks also fueled much of the fund's success in 2003.

Rollins has shown the determination to ride through trying times. The fund's turnover averaged 25% in the past couple of years, which is less than one fourth of the category average. So when he sticks with stocks such as cable operators Time Warner and Comcast, whose businesses Rollins believe have performed fine fundamentally, there's some fundamental grounding to the decision.

And where Rollins has made moves, the fund has benefited. He dumped Viacom after becoming frustrated with the company's direction, and it has fallen steadily this year. He also pared back Texas Instruments to cut the fund's semiexposure, and that stock is off more than 25% this year. Rollins credits Janus' analyst staff with bringing in good new ideas and being the reason why the fund has remained competitive despite its challenges in 2004.

While it's understandable that some investors may have cold feet, we think there are enough optimistic signs to stay the course.

Address:	100 Fillmore St Denver CO 80206 800-525-3713
Web Address:	www.janus.com
Inception:	02-05-70
Advisor:	Janus
Subadvisor:	None

Minimum Purchase:	$2500	Add: $100	IRA: $500
Min Auto Inv Plan:	$500	Add: $100	
Sales Fees:	No-load		
Management Fee:	0.64%		
Actual Fees:	Mgt:0.64%	Dist:	
Expense Projections:	3Yr:$281	5Yr:$488	10Yr:$1084
Income Distrib:	Annually		

NTF Plans: Fidelity Retail-NTF, Schwab OneSource

Janus Balanced

Ticker	Load	NAV	Yield	Total Assets	Mstar Category
JABAX	None	$21.25	1.9%	$2,871 mil	Moderate Allocation

Governance and Management

Fiduciary Grade: C

Portfolio Manager(s)

Karen Reidy took the reins here Jan. 1, 2000. She trained as an assistant portfolio manager under Jim Craig at Janus Fund, and she's backed by Janus' deep bench of analysts. She also manages Janus Core Equity.

Strategy

Manager Karen Reidy has a fairly wide range in terms of asset allocation. The fund's stock and bond stakes can be as small as 40% or as large as 60%. On the equity side, she generally buys healthy growers, though she has tempered the stock portfolio's historical aggressiveness. As for bonds, she is not likely to make big interest-rate bets, preferring to actively manage the fund's credit risk as a primary method of adding value. Its internal benchmark is made up of 50% of the S&P 500, 40% Lehman Bros. Gov/Credit Index, and 10% three-month T-bills.

Historical Profile

Return Above Avg
Risk Below Avg
Rating ★★★★ Above Avg

Investment Style: Equity Stock %: 58% 54% 38% 41% 45% 45% 41% 58% 59%

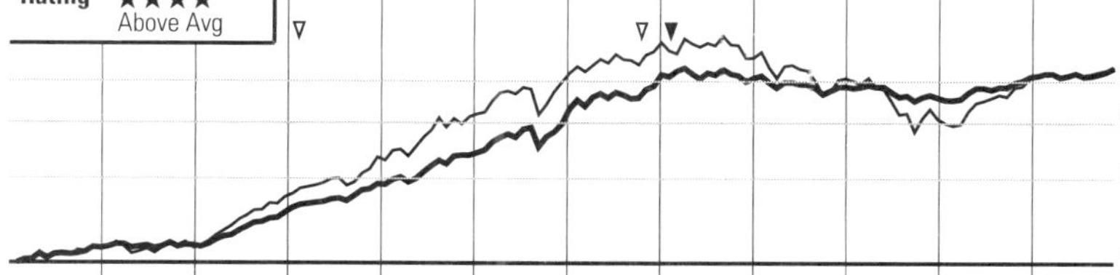

▼ Manager Change
▽ Partial Manager Change

Growth of $10,000
— Investment Values of Fund
— Investment Values of S&P 500

Performance Quartile (within Category)

1993	1994	1995	1996	1997	1998	1999	2000	2001	2002	2003	12-04	History
12.19	11.63	13.72	14.14	15.33	19.61	23.39	21.24	19.63	17.88	19.94	21.25	NAV
10.56	0.02	27.31	15.30	21.80	31.20	23.50	-2.16	-5.04	-6.56	13.74	8.71	Total Return %
0.50	-1.29	-10.22	-7.64	-11.55	2.63	2.46	6.94	6.84	15.53	-14.93	-2.16	+/-S&P 500
-1.17	1.97	2.54	3.96	2.60	18.81	10.65	-6.63	-5.20	3.98	-10.32	-2.46	+/-DJ 60%
1.98	4.66	9.26	1.91	2.54	2.32	2.35	4.17	2.52	2.42	2.09	2.06	Income Return %
8.58	-4.64	18.05	13.39	19.26	28.88	21.15	-6.33	-7.56	-8.98	11.65	6.65	Capital Return %
62	18	38	39	32	2	7	68	51	10	92	50	Total Rtn % Rank Cat
0.22	0.56	1.06	0.26	0.36	0.35	0.46	0.96	0.53	0.47	0.37	0.41	Income $
0.00	0.00	0.00	1.41	1.49	0.11	0.32	0.69	0.00	0.00	0.00	0.00	Capital Gains $
1.70	1.42	1.32	1.21	1.10	1.03	0.91	0.85	0.83	0.84	0.88	—	Expense Ratio %
2.15	2.28	2.52	2.35	2.63	2.34	2.37	2.92	2.73	2.44	2.00	—	Income Ratio %
131	167	185	151	139	73	64	87	117	88	73	—	Turnover Rate %
77	93	139	220	389	1,137	3,420	4,739	4,472	3,902	3,750	2,871	Net Assets $mil

Performance 12-31-04

	1st Qtr	2nd Qtr	3rd Qtr	4th Qtr	Total
2000	4.10	-2.97	-0.60	-2.56	-2.16
2001	-5.74	2.16	-5.94	4.84	-5.04
2002	0.92	-4.16	-5.32	2.04	-6.56
2003	-0.84	7.08	0.37	6.72	13.74
2004	2.01	0.20	0.07	6.28	8.71

Trailing	Total Return%	+/- S&P 500	+/- DJ 60%	%Rank Cat	Growth of $10,000
3 Mo	6.28	-2.95	-1.20	66	10,628
6 Mo	6.36	-0.83	-1.17	53	10,636
1 Yr	8.71	-2.16	-2.46	50	10,871
3 Yr Avg	4.93	1.35	-2.33	44	11,553
5 Yr Avg	1.43	3.73	-3.81	56	10,736
10 Yr Avg	12.01	-0.06	1.52	9	31,086
15 Yr Avg	—	—	—	—	—

Tax Analysis	Tax-Adj Rtn%	%Rank Cat	Tax-Cost Rat	%Rank Cat
3 Yr (estimated)	4.11	39	0.78	54
5 Yr (estimated)	0.27	53	1.14	53
10 Yr (estimated)	9.98	8	1.81	51

Potential Capital Gain Exposure: 0% of assets

Rating and Risk

Time Period	Load-Adj Return %	Morningstar Rtn vs Cat	Morningstar Risk vs Cat	Morningstar Risk-Adj Rating
1 Yr	8.71			
3 Yr	4.93	Avg	Low	★★★
5 Yr	1.43	Avg	Low	★★★
10 Yr	12.01	High	Avg	★★★★★
Incept	11.60			

Other Measures	Standard Index S&P 500	Best Fit Index DJ 60%
Alpha	2.4	-2.1
Beta	0.37	0.65
R-Squared	82	88
Standard Deviation	6.42	
Mean	4.93	
Sharpe Ratio	0.56	

Morningstar's Take by Dan McNeela 12-27-04

Janus Balanced Fund has passed some key tests.

One reason for investors to consider this fund is the even-keeled manner in which manager Karen Reidy has crafted its equity portfolio. Having directed the fund since the beginning of 2000, Reidy was first tested by an extended bear market and then grappled with a strong rally as the market pulled out of its funk. In focusing on free cash flow, the fund played better defense in 2002 by relying on turnaround stories and firms with dominant brands.

The fund wasn't in prime position to thrive during 2003's rebound, but its reluctance to chase those gains has given it an edge in 2004, as those rebounding tech stocks have lagged. Reidy remains convinced that the economic recovery is on track, but that hasn't overly influenced the fund's bottom-up strategy. Her general enthusiasm for stocks over bonds has the fund at its minimum allocation of 40% in fixed-income securities, however. Because the fund has held more in stocks, it has changed from Morningstar's conservative-allocation category to the moderate-allocation peer group. The fund's parameters haven't changed at all.

We are less optimistic about the the fixed-income portion of the fund. Reidy runs this part of the portfolio with some support from Janus' bond folks. But other premier funds of this type have a specialized fixed-income team in charge.

On the regulatory front, investors can take solace in the fact that Janus settled with the SEC after having allowed 12 large clients market-timing privileges in several of its funds. Importantly, top executives left the firm, giving new CEO Steve Scheid and new chief investment officer Gary Black a chance to put the scandal in the past.

With Reidy building a successful record as a stock-picker and making measured asset allocation decisions, this fund should remain competitive.

Address:	100 Fillmore St Denver CO 80206 800-525-3713
Web Address:	www.janus.com
Inception:	09-01-92
Advisor:	Janus
Subadvisor:	None
NTF Plans:	Fidelity Retail-NTF, Schwab OneSource

Minimum Purchase:	$2500	Add: $100	IRA: $500
Min Auto Inv Plan:	$500	Add: $100	
Sales Fees:	No-load		
Management Fee:	0.55%		
Actual Fees:	Mgt:0.55%	Dist:	
Expense Projections:	3Yr:$252	5Yr:$439	10Yr:$978
Income Distrib:	Quarterly		

Portfolio Analysis 11-30-04

Total Stocks:61 Share change since 10-31-04	Sectors	P/E Ratio	YTD Return %	% Net Assets
⊖ Roche Holding	Health	—	—	2.36
Marriott International A	Consumer	25.6	-3.14	2.28
⊕ Aetna	Financial	16.9	-0.14	2.20
⊕ Tyco International	Ind Mtrls	25.1	-0.92	2.07
⊕ ExxonMobil	Energy	13.9	-2.75	2.07
⊕ Time Warner	Media	27.5	-3.91	2.04
General Electric	Ind Mtrls	22.8	-3.01	2.03
⊕ Texas Instruments	Hardware	21.1	-9.14	2.00
J.P. Morgan Chase & Co.	Financial	19.4	-1.99	1.94

Total Fixed-Income:127	Date of Maturity	Amount $000	Value $000	% Net Assets
FHLMC 2.375%	04-15-06	31,470	31,203	1.10
FNMA 2.125%	04-15-06	26,718	26,400	0.93
FNMA 5%	01-15-07	25,235	26,126	0.92
FHLMC 1.875%	02-15-06	26,460	26,123	0.92
FNMA 2%	01-15-06	21,800	21,563	0.76
US Treasury Note 3.5%	11-15-06	21,045	21,242	0.75
US Treasury Note 5%	08-15-09	18,802	20,688	0.73
FNMA 5.5%	05-02-06	19,560	20,181	0.71
US Treasury Bond 5.25%	08-15-23	17,447	20,019	0.71

Equity Style
Style: Blend
Size: Large-Cap

Value Measures		Rel Category
Price/Earnings	17.57	1.06
Price/Book	2.75	1.13
Price/Sales	1.59	1.20
Price/Cash Flow	11.27	1.55
Dividend Yield %	1.18	0.75

Growth Measures	%	Rel Category
Long-Term Erngs	13.09	1.13
Book Value	7.97	1.39
Sales	4.17	0.81
Cash Flow	9.67	1.21
Historical Erngs	22.10	2.04

Market Cap %			
Giant	58.5	Small	0.0
Large	37.1	Micro	0.0
Mid	4.4	Avg $mil:	48,268

Fixed-Income Style
Duration: Interm-Term
Quality: High

Avg Eff Duration [1]	4.3 Yrs
Avg Eff Maturity	6.2 Yrs
Avg Credit Quality	AA
Avg Wtd Coupon	5.54%

[1]figure provided by fund as of 11-30-04

Sector Weightings	% of Stocks	Rel S&P 500	3 Year High	3 Year Low
Info	20.01	0.93		
Software	2.07	0.48	4	2
Hardware	11.60	1.14	15	5
Media	6.34	1.65	13	6
Telecom	0.00	0.00	1	0
Service	48.21	1.04		
Health	8.20	0.66	13	7
Consumer	13.22	1.46	14	4
Business	6.15	1.52	8	4
Financial	20.64	0.99	24	13
Mfg	31.78	0.99		
Goods	8.06	0.86	17	8
Ind Mtrls	16.12	1.27	18	8
Energy	7.60	1.06	9	4
Utilities	0.00	0.00	0	0

Composition

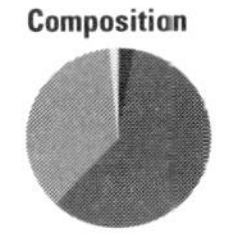

Cash	2.7
Stocks	59.0
Bonds	36.7
Other	1.6
Foreign (% of Stock)	17.4

Janus Contrarian Fund

Ticker	Load	NAV	Yield	Total Assets	Mstar Category
JSVAX	None	$13.24	0.2%	$2,602 mil	Mid-Cap Blend

Governance and Management

Fiduciary Grade: C

Portfolio Manager(s)

David Decker has been on-board since the fund's inception in February 2000. He also managed Janus Special Situations, which merged into this fund, from 1997 through February 2003. Special Situations' performance proved extremely volatile, compared with other mid-blend funds', but looked better compared with the S&P 500 Index's. He started his career at Janus in 1992 as a research analyst.

Strategy

David Decker looks for stocks with what he considers to be asymmetrical risk profiles, or a higher probability of upside and a smaller probability of limited downside. He likes companies with strong free cash flow and savvy management, and he isn't restrained by benchmark sector weightings or market-cap guidelines. He'll even buy stocks outside the U.S. and in emerging markets. Decker often buys these companies when controversy takes a swipe at their stock prices, making them temporarily cheap in his eyes. He'll typically hold them for the long haul, and the fund is quite concentrated.

Historical Profile

Return Above Avg
Risk Above Avg
Rating ★★★★ Above Avg

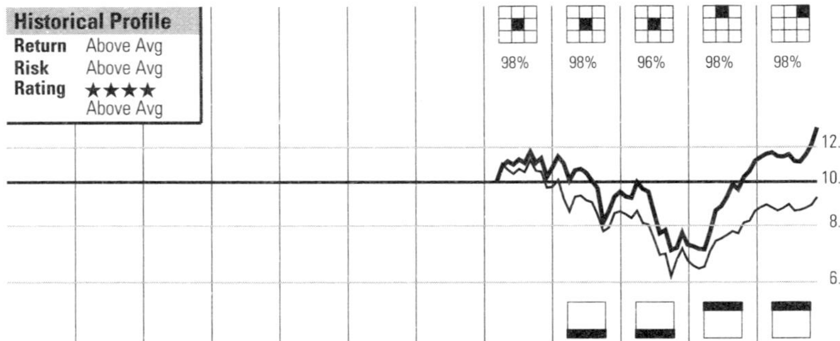

Investment Style
Equity
Stock %

▼ Manager Change
▽ Partial Manager Change

Growth of $10,000
▬ Investment Values of Fund
— Investment Values of S&P 500

Performance Quartile (within Category)

1993	1994	1995	1996	1997	1998	1999	2000	2001	2002	2003	12-04	History
—	—	—	—	—	—	—	10.52	9.26	7.06	10.82	13.24	NAV
—	—	—	—	—	—	—	7.75*	-11.74	-23.70	53.26	22.61	Total Return %
—	—	—	—	—	—	—	—	0.14	-1.61	24.59	11.74	+/-S&P 500
—	—	—	—	—	—	—	—	-11.14	-9.17	17.67	6.14	+/-S&P Mid 400
—	—	—	—	—	—	—	0.00	0.23	0.06	0.00	0.24	Income Return %
—	—	—	—	—	—	—	—	-11.97	-23.76	53.26	22.37	Capital Return %
—	—	—	—	—	—	—	—	88	84	6	7	Total Rtn % Rank Cat
—	—	—	—	—	—	—	0.25	0.02	0.01	0.00	0.03	Income $
—	—	—	—	—	—	—	0.00	0.00	0.00	0.00	0.00	Capital Gains $
—	—	—	—	—	—	—	0.99	0.91	0.98	1.01	—	Expense Ratio %
—	—	—	—	—	—	—	0.14	0.29	0.03	-0.17	—	Income Ratio %
—	—	—	—	—	—	—	72	77	60	44	—	Turnover Rate %
—	—	—	—	—	—	—	2,940	2,079	1,267	2,618	2,602	Net Assets $mil

Performance 12-31-04

	1st Qtr	2nd Qtr	3rd Qtr	4th Qtr	Total
2000	—	3.70	-1.78	-2.22	7.75 *
2001	-6.46	3.86	-22.31	16.94	-11.74
2002	4.97	-14.51	-17.33	2.85	-23.70
2003	-2.41	24.67	8.96	15.60	53.26
2004	4.34	-0.97	-0.18	18.87	22.61

Trailing	Total Return%	+/- S&P 500	+/- S&P Mid 400	%Rank Cat	Growth of $10,000
3 Mo	18.87	9.64	6.72	1	11,887
6 Mo	18.66	11.47	8.87	1	11,866
1 Yr	22.61	11.74	6.14	7	12,261
3 Yr Avg	12.76	9.18	2.25	15	14,337
5 Yr Avg	—	—	—	—	—
10 Yr Avg	—	—	—	—	—
15 Yr Avg	—	—	—	—	—

Tax Analysis	Tax-Adj Rtn%	%Rank Cat	Tax-Cost Rat	%Rank Cat
3 Yr (estimated)	12.72	12	0.04	5
5 Yr (estimated)	—	—	—	—
10 Yr (estimated)	—	—	—	—

Potential Capital Gain Exposure: 17% of assets

Rating and Risk

Time Period	Load-Adj Return %	Morningstar Rtn vs Cat	Morningstar Risk vs Cat	Morningstar Risk-Adj Rating
1 Yr	22.61			
3 Yr	12.76	+Avg	+Avg	★★★★
5 Yr	—	—	—	—
10 Yr	—	—	—	—
Incept	6.62			

Other Measures	Standard Index S&P 500	Best Fit Index Wil 4500
Alpha	9.2	0.2
Beta	1.07	1.09
R-Squared	77	90

Standard Deviation	20.71
Mean	12.76
Sharpe Ratio	0.56

Morningstar's Take by Bridget Hughes 11-01-04

It takes a special investor to own Janus Contrarian.

This isn't the most lovable mid-blend portfolio. A compact portfolio of often-controversial names is bound to make some uncomfortable. Take top holding Computer Associates, for example, which has been entangled in questions about its accounting and leadership for several years. Then there's EchoStar Communications, another top pick, which has suffered as investors evaluate its competitive landscape. The portfolio's 14% stake in Indian stocks, including a 5% position in Reliance Industries, could produce further agitation. After all, factors exogenous to firms in emerging markets can take a higher toll on returns. Consider 1997's Asian currency crisis, 1998's Russian debt default, and even India's most-recent election earlier in 2004. All three events sent their respective markets reeling--at least temporarily.

It's clear investors here need to think about the portfolio differently. Despite its appropriate placement in the mid-blend category, it's hardly a replica of the Russell Mid Cap Index, a fairly common benchmark among the group. Its most-recent portfolio lands in the large-growth section of the Morningstar style box. Manager David Decker's flexible approach simply has him searching for what he thinks are stocks with asymmetrical risk profiles--or a higher probability of upside and a lower probability of meaningful downside. Performance at this and Decker's previous charge, Janus Special Situations (which was merged into this fund in early 2003), has certainly been more volatile than the mid-blend group. Results look better when compared with the S&P 500 Index, a broader representation of the market and the fund's stated benchmark.

Perhaps the biggest challenge for investors is how to use the fund. Theoretically, its flexibility argues that it serves as an investor's only holding--it's Decker's only fund--but we think that's unrealistic and, frankly, too risky. We're more comfortable with the fund in a supporting role.

Address:	100 Fillmore St Denver CO 80206 800-525-3713
Web Address:	www.janus.com
Inception:	02-29-00 *
Advisor:	Janus
Subadvisor:	None
NTF Plans:	Fidelity Retail-NTF, Schwab OneSource

Minimum Purchase:	$2500	Add: $100	IRA: $500
Min Auto Inv Plan:	$500	Add: $100	
Sales Fees:	No-load		
Management Fee:	0.64%		
Actual Fees:	Mgt:0.64%	Dist:	
Expense Projections:	3Yr:$322	5Yr:$558	10Yr:$1236
Income Distrib:	Annually		

Portfolio Analysis 11-30-04

Share change since 10-04 Total Stocks:46	Sector	PE	YTD Ret%	% Assets
SK	Energy	—	—	6.45
⊕ EchoStar Communications	Media	NMF	0.85	5.18
⊖ Computer Associates Inte	Software	—	13.92	4.94
⊖ Reliance Industries Ltd	Ind Mtrls	—	—	4.21
Liberty Media	Media	—	11.56	4.05
⊕ Ceridian	Business	22.1	-12.70	4.00
Lear	Ind Mtrls	9.3	0.85	3.87
⊖ Tyco International	Ind Mtrls	25.1	35.41	3.79
⊖ Apple Computer	Hardware	NMF	201.36	3.67
Advanced Micro Devices	Hardware	33.0	47.79	3.63
J.P. Morgan Chase & Co.	Financial	19.4	9.97	3.12
Berkshire Hathaway B	Financial	20.9	4.30	2.99
⊖ Station Casinos	Consumer	77.1	81.31	2.79
Liberty Media Internatio	Media	—	—	2.74
SBS Broadcasting	Media	32.3	23.47	2.53
E*Trade Financial	Financial	13.7	18.18	2.33
Reckitt Benckiser	Goods	—	—	2.22
Tata Motors Ltd	Goods	—	—	2.20
Kinder Morgan Management	Energy	30.7	-5.26	2.17
ICICI Bank	Financial	—	—	2.07

Current Investment Style

Value Blnd Growth — Large Mid Small

Market Cap	%
Giant	24.4
Large	37.1
Mid	32.3
Small	5.5
Micro	0.7
Avg $mil: 10,492	

Value Measures		Rel Category
Price/Earnings	15.94	0.94
Price/Book	1.78	0.82
Price/Sales	0.91	0.86
Price/Cash Flow	6.44	1.03
Dividend Yield %	0.68	0.68

Growth Measures	%	Rel Category
Long-Term Erngs	101.98	8.13
Book Value	5.16	0.73
Sales	6.63	1.17
Cash Flow	3.49	0.47
Historical Erngs	37.97	3.38

Profitability	%	Rel Category
Return on Equity	13.16	0.96
Return on Assets	5.07	0.78
Net Margin	5.91	0.65

Sector Weightings	% of Stocks	Rel S&P 500	3 Year High	3 Year Low
Info	32.41	1.51		
Software	5.93	1.38	8	5
Hardware	7.41	0.73	8	5
Media	19.07	4.97	19	13
Telecom	0.00	0.00	0	0
Service	25.87	0.56		
Health	0.00	0.00	1	0
Consumer	4.15	0.46	11	4
Business	5.87	1.45	13	6
Financial	15.85	0.76	18	9
Mfg	41.71	1.30		
Goods	6.70	0.72	16	6
Ind Mtrls	19.59	1.55	23	15
Energy	13.25	1.85	15	7
Utilities	2.17	0.73	2	0

Composition

Cash	1.1
Stocks	97.7
Bonds	0.0
Other	1.2
Foreign (% of Stock)	35.8

Janus Core Equity

Ticker	Load	NAV	Yield	Total Assets	Mstar Category
JAEIX	None	$20.36	0.4%	$639 mil	Large Blend

Governance and Management

Fiduciary Grade: C

Portfolio Manager(s)

Karen Reidy has been lead manager since January 2000. She cut her teeth at Janus, serving as an assistant portfolio manager on Janus Fund. She's backed by the firm's large staff of analysts.

Strategy

Karen Reidy looks for companies with sustainable earnings growth, rising returns on capital, and strong free cash flows. Although in the past the fund was required to invest 65% of assets in income-producing securities, it no longer operates with any such restriction.

Historical Profile

Return Average
Risk Below Avg
Rating ★★★★ Above Avg

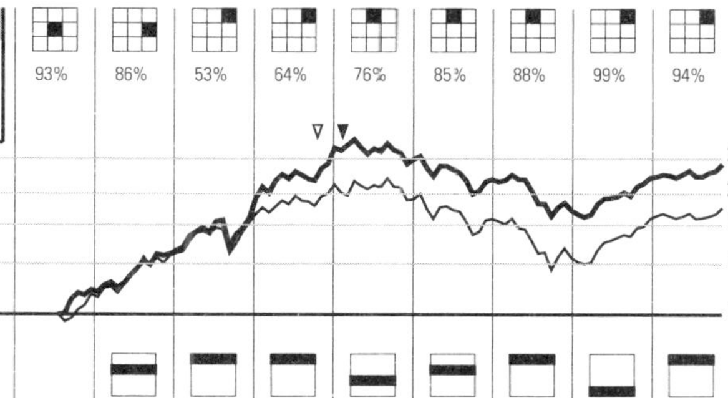

Investment Style
Equity
Stock %

▼ Manager Change
∇ Partial Manager Change

Growth of $10,000
▬ Investment Values of Fund
— Investment Values of S&P 500

Performance Quartile (within Category)

1993	1994	1995	1996	1997	1998	1999	2000	2001	2002	2003	12-04	History
—	—	—	11.08	13.54	18.72	25.14	20.53	17.98	14.63	17.97	20.36	NAV
—	—	—	15.59*	31.08	40.05	38.50	-7.16	-12.11	-18.02	23.27	13.77	Total Return %
—	—	—	—	-2.27	11.48	17.46	1.34	-0.23	4.07	-5.40	2.90	+/-S&P 500
—	—	—	—	-1.77	13.03	17.59	0.63	0.34	3.63	-6.62	2.37	+/-Russ 1000
—	—	—	0.00	0.61	0.41	0.83	3.35	0.73	0.62	0.43	0.46	Income Return %
—	—	—	—	30.47	39.64	37.67	-10.51	-12.84	-18.64	22.84	13.31	Capital Return %
—	—	—	—	37	1	6	53	48	18	82	11	Total Rtn % Rank Cat
—	—	—	0.06	0.07	0.06	0.15	0.84	0.15	0.11	0.06	0.08	Income $
—	—	—	0.42	0.88	0.18	0.58	1.85	0.00	0.00	0.00	0.00	Capital Gains $
—	—	—	1.71	1.45	1.21	1.01	0.93	0.93	0.89	0.96	—	Expense Ratio %
—	—	—	3.09	0.62	0.41	0.81	0.65	0.35	0.66	0.40	—	Income Ratio %
—	—	—	325	180	101	81	116	115	115	77	—	Turnover Rate %
—	—	—	29	89	349	948	964	817	698	706	639	Net Assets $mil

Performance 12-31-04

	1st Qtr	2nd Qtr	3rd Qtr	4th Qtr	Total
2000	5.61	-5.81	-1.04	-5.69	-7.16
2001	-10.42	4.45	-14.50	9.87	-12.11
2002	2.89	-9.62	-15.25	4.03	-18.02
2003	-2.87	11.19	1.46	12.50	23.27
2004	1.56	3.18	-1.38	10.10	13.77

Trailing	Total Return%	+/- S&P 500	+/- Russ 1000	%Rank Cat	Growth of $10,000
3 Mo	10.10	0.87	0.30	27	11,010
6 Mo	8.58	1.39	0.77	21	10,858
1 Yr	13.77	2.90	2.37	11	11,377
3 Yr Avg	4.76	1.18	0.49	20	11,497
5 Yr Avg	-1.27	1.03	0.49	35	9,381
10 Yr Avg	—	—	—	—	—
15 Yr Avg	—	—	—	—	—

Tax Analysis	Tax-Adj Rtn%	%Rank Cat	Tax-Cost Rat	%Rank Cat
3 Yr (estimated)	4.57	17	0.18	15
5 Yr (estimated)	-2.05	34	0.79	42
10 Yr (estimated)	—	—	—	—

Potential Capital Gain Exposure: -2% of assets

Rating and Risk

Time Period	Load-Adj Return %	Morningstar Rtn vs Cat	Morningstar Risk vs Cat	Morningstar Risk-Adj Rating
1 Yr	13.77			
3 Yr	4.76	+Avg	-Avg	★★★★
5 Yr	-1.27	Avg	-Avg	★★★★
10 Yr	—	—	—	—
Incept	12.66			

Other Measures	Standard Index S&P 500	Best Fit Index MSCI World
Alpha	1.5	-1.1
Beta	0.80	0.81
R-Squared	91	92

Standard Deviation	13.20
Mean	4.76
Sharpe Ratio	0.26

Portfolio Analysis 11-30-04

Share change since 10-04 Total Stocks:68	Sector	PE	YTD Ret%	% Assets
Marriott International A	Consumer	25.6	37.22	3.88
⊕ Tyco International	Ind Mtrls	25.1	35.41	3.64
J.P. Morgan Chase & Co.	Financial	19.4	9.97	3.46
⊖ Roche Holding	Health	—	—	3.45
General Electric	Ind Mtrls	22.8	20.68	3.38
⊕ ExxonMobil	Energy	13.9	28.04	3.31
Motorola	Hardware	28.7	37.93	3.18
⊕ Texas Instruments	Hardware	21.1	-15.90	3.17
⊕ Aetna	Financial	16.9	84.67	3.16
⊕ Time Warner	Media	27.5	8.12	2.88
Canadian National Railwa	Business	23.9	47.10	2.87
Freddie Mac	Financial	10.6	28.75	2.87
Starwood Hotels & Resort	Consumer	33.9	64.71	2.24
Honeywell International	Ind Mtrls	20.5	8.21	2.17
Berkshire Hathaway B	Financial	20.9	4.30	2.11
IBM	Hardware	20.2	7.19	2.08
Yahoo	Media	95.1	67.36	2.05
Citigroup	Financial	15.3	2.72	2.01
⊕ Lockheed Martin	Ind Mtrls	19.9	9.97	1.94
Reckitt Benckiser	Goods	—	—	1.84

Current Investment Style

Value Blnd Growth — Large Mid Small

Market Cap	%
Giant	53.8
Large	40.2
Mid	6.0
Small	0.0
Micro	0.0
Avg $mil: 42,205	

Value Measures		Rel Category
Price/Earnings	17.39	1.03
Price/Book	2.69	1.03
Price/Sales	1.58	1.10
Price/Cash Flow	10.73	1.40
Dividend Yield %	1.19	0.80

Growth Measures	%	Rel Category
Long-Term Erngs	13.31	1.15
Book Value	8.07	1.04
Sales	4.47	0.78
Cash Flow	10.30	1.09
Historical Erngs	23.71	2.01

Profitability	%	Rel Category
Return on Equity	16.32	0.93
Return on Assets	7.57	0.88
Net Margin	9.68	0.85

Sector Weightings	% of Stocks	Rel S&P 500	3 Year High	3 Year Low
Info	18.86	0.88		
Software	2.01	0.47	3	2
Hardware	11.16	1.09	13	4
Media	5.69	1.48	13	5
Telecom	0.00	0.00	[illegible]	0
Service	46.07	0.99		
Health	8.05	0.64	12	6
Consumer	12.50	1.38	14	6
Business	5.27	1.30	12	5
Financial	20.25	0.98	22	10
Mfg	35.06	1.09		
Goods	8.35	0.89	17	8
Ind Mtrls	20.22	1.60	20	10
Energy	6.49	0.91	10	4
Utilities	0.00	0.00	0	0

Composition

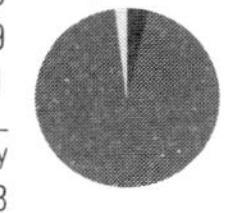

Cash	3.8
Stocks	94.0
Bonds	0.0
Other	2.2
Foreign (% of Stock)	19.8

Morningstar's Take by Dan McNeela 12-27-04

Janus Core Equity looks to be on the right road.

Having directed the fund since the beginning of 2000, manager Karen Reidy has been tested by a long and brutal bear market and then by a spirited rally in 2003. While the fund hasn't always come out on top, Reidy has displayed a welcome balance between recognizing changes in the investing environment and refraining from drastic tactical moves. Her focus on free cash flow put the fund in good position to play defense in 2002. Uncovering turnaround stories such as 3M Company and banking on steady firms with dominant brands such as Anheuser-Busch spared the fund from larger losses.

The fund wasn't in prime position to thrive during last year's rebound, but its reluctance to chase past gains has given it an edge in 2004, as once-rebounding tech stocks fizzled for much of the year. The fund has been pushed ahead in an uneven market. Its 13.3% year-to-date gain through Dec. 23 ranks near the top decile of the large-blend category.

Reidy remains convinced that the economic recovery is on track, but that hasn't meant a big bet on the most volatile names. Instead, she has stuck with hotel stocks that are benefiting from increased business travel, and FedEx, where improving economic growth boosts revenue. It is reassuring that the fund has gotten ahead with its growth-leaning portfolio because value stocks have generally had the upper hand in 2004.

On the regulatory front, investors can take solace in the fact that Janus settled with the SEC after granting 12 large clients market-timing privileges in several funds. Importantly, top executives left the firm, giving new CEO Steve Scheid and new chief investment officer Gary Black a chance to put the scandal in the past.

For those investors who are ready to give Janus another look, this offering has promise.

Address:	100 Fillmore St Denver CO 80206 800-525-3713
Web Address:	www.janus.com
Inception:	06-28-96*
Advisor:	Janus
Subadvisor:	None

Minimum Purchase:	$2500	Add: $100	IRA: $500
Min Auto Inv Plan:	$500	Add: $100	
Sales Fees:	No-load		
Management Fee:	0.60%		
Actual Fees:	Mgt:0.60%	Dist:	
Expense Projections:	3Yr:$293	5Yr:$509	10Yr:$1131
Income Distrib:	Annually		

NTF Plans: Fidelity Retail-NTF, Schwab OneSource

Janus Enterprise

Ticker	Load	NAV	Yield	Total Assets	Mstar Category
JAENX	None	$37.62	0.0%	$1,767 mil	Mid-Cap Growth

Governance and Management

Fiduciary Grade: C

Portfolio Manager(s)

Manager Jonathan Coleman became the manager of this fund at the end of January 2002. Coleman comanaged Janus Venture from 1997 to 2000. He then moved over to Janus Fund, where he served as assistant portfolio manager.

Strategy

Jonathan Coleman toned down the fund's aggressiveness after taking over in January 2002. He searches for fast-growing companies with management teams he likes that also have dominant market share in their industries. Unlike former manager Jim Goff, Coleman says he will spread the fund's assets into some decidedly stodgy sectors, such as industrials. He will also limit the fund's largest position sizes to about 3% of assets.

Historical Profile

Return Below Avg
Risk Above Avg
Rating ★★ Below Avg

Investment Style
Equity
Stock %: 97% 98% 98% 97% 96% 97% 86% 99% 99%

▼ Manager Change
▽ Partial Manager Change

Growth of $10,000
— Investment Values of Fund
— Investment Values of S&P 500

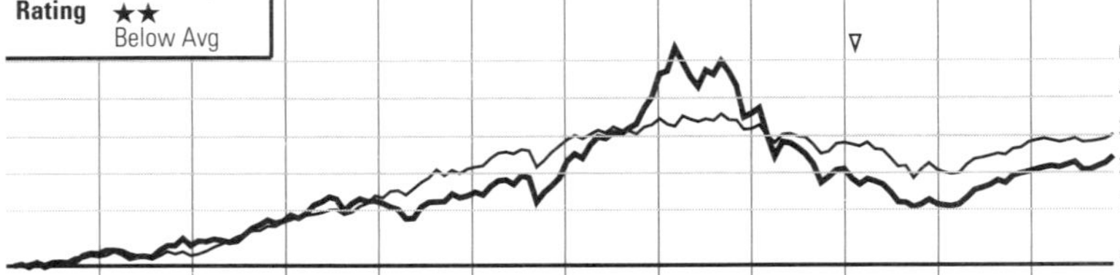

Performance Quartile (within Category)

1993	1994	1995	1996	1997	1998	1999	2000	2001	2002	2003	12-04	History
21.92	22.98	27.44	29.34	30.48	36.22	76.67	53.27	32.00	22.95	31.17	37.62	NAV
15.67	8.92	27.25	11.65	10.82	33.75	121.90	-30.52	-39.93	-28.28	35.82	20.69	Total Return %
5.61	7.61	-10.28	-11.29	-22.53	5.18	100.86	-21.42	-28.05	-6.19	7.15	9.82	+/-S&P 500
4.48	11.08	-6.73	-5.83	-11.72	15.89	70.61	-18.77	-19.78	-0.87	-6.89	5.21	+/-Russ MG
0.09	2.36	7.13	0.00	0.00	0.00	0.00	0.00	0.00	0.00	0.00	0.00	Income Return %
15.58	6.56	20.12	11.65	10.82	33.75	121.90	-30.52	-39.93	-28.28	35.82	20.69	Capital Return %
44	8	76	75	86	13	8	92	94	57	47	6	Total Rtn % Rank Cat
0.02	0.52	1.64	0.00	0.00	0.00	0.00	0.00	0.00	0.00	0.00	0.00	Income $
0.55	0.38	0.16	1.28	1.96	4.30	3.33	0.00	0.00	0.00	0.00	0.00	Capital Gains $
1.36	1.25	1.23	1.12	1.04	1.08	0.95	0.88	0.90	0.90	1.02	1.03	Expense Ratio %
0.14	-0.32	0.02	-0.78	-0.61	-0.67	-0.67	-0.65	-0.55	-0.43	-0.46	-0.46	Income Ratio %
201	193	194	93	111	134	98	80	85	64	32	27	Turnover Rate %
259	354	499	722	573	728	4,435	6,267	3,209	1,626	1,884	1,767	Net Assets $mil

Performance 12-31-04

	1st Qtr	2nd Qtr	3rd Qtr	4th Qtr	Total
2000	11.57	-7.42	-1.54	-31.68	-30.52
2001	-32.66	8.42	-27.80	13.96	-39.93
2002	-9.09	-11.65	-13.00	2.64	-28.28
2003	0.04	16.59	4.63	11.28	35.82
2004	5.33	3.75	-3.82	14.84	20.69

Trailing	Total Return%	+/- S&P 500	+/- Russ MG	%Rank Cat	Growth of $10,000
3 Mo	14.84	5.61	0.90	21	11,484
6 Mo	10.45	3.26	1.44	16	11,045
1 Yr	20.69	9.82	5.21	6	12,069
3 Yr Avg	5.54	1.96	-0.62	33	11,756
5 Yr Avg	-13.27	-10.97	-9.91	90	4,907
10 Yr Avg	8.65	-3.42	-2.58	70	22,924
15 Yr Avg	—	—	—	—	—

Tax Analysis	Tax-Adj Rtn%	%Rank Cat	Tax-Cost Rat	%Rank Cat
3 Yr (estimated)	5.54	26	0.00	1
5 Yr (estimated)	-13.27	89	0.00	1
10 Yr (estimated)	7.70	52	0.87	17

Potential Capital Gain Exposure: -213% of assets

Rating and Risk

Time Period	Load-Adj Return %	Morningstar Rtn vs Cat	Morningstar Risk vs Cat	Morningstar Risk-Adj Rating
1 Yr	20.69			
3 Yr	5.54	+Avg	-Avg	★★★★
5 Yr	-13.27	-Avg	+Avg	★★
10 Yr	8.65	-Avg	+Avg	★★
Incept	11.31			

Other Measures	Standard Index S&P 500	Best Fit Index Russ MG
Alpha	2.5	0.3
Beta	0.82	0.78
R-Squared	66	87
Standard Deviation	16.02	
Mean	5.54	
Sharpe Ratio	0.26	

Portfolio Analysis 11-30-04

Share change since 10-04 Total Stocks:103	Sector	PE	YTD Ret%	% Assets
Ball	Goods	20.9	49.08	3.02
Kinder Morgan	Energy	21.1	28.39	2.84
Lamar Advertising A	Business	—	14.63	2.61
⊖ Starwood Hotels & Resort	Consumer	33.9	64.71	2.44
EOG Resources	Energy	16.5	55.21	2.27
Berkshire Hathaway B	Financial	20.9	4.30	2.27
Murphy Oil	Energy	16.5	24.71	2.05
⊖ Harman International Ind	Goods	48.4	71.77	2.00
⊖ T Rowe Price Group	Financial	25.6	33.16	2.00
⊖ Apollo Group A	Consumer	NMF	19.02	1.93
⊖ NVR	Consumer	12.2	65.11	1.80
Fisher Scientific Intern	Health	43.9	50.79	1.74
Advanced Micro Devices	Hardware	33.0	47.79	1.72
⊕ St. Jude Medical	Health	38.0	36.69	1.69
Yum Brands	Consumer	19.7	37.84	1.58
Paychex	Business	38.9	-7.06	1.55
Apple Computer	Hardware	NMF	201.36	1.55
Manpower	Business	18.2	3.24	1.48
⊖ EchoStar Communications	Media	NMF	0.85	1.45
Staples	Consumer	24.7	24.38	1.45

Current Investment Style

Market Cap	%
Giant	3.4
Large	28.2
Mid	66.2
Small	2.2
Micro	0.0
Avg $mil: 6,367	

Value Measures		Rel Category
Price/Earnings	21.34	0.97
Price/Book	3.01	1.00
Price/Sales	1.53	0.86
Price/Cash Flow	9.02	0.93
Dividend Yield %	0.44	1.02

Growth Measures	%	Rel Category
Long-Term Erngs	14.13	0.90
Book Value	10.85	1.08
Sales	9.56	1.11
Cash Flow	15.90	1.30
Historical Erngs	18.97	1.19

Profitability	%	Rel Category
Return on Equity	16.80	1.17
Return on Assets	8.16	1.14
Net Margin	10.79	1.12

Sector Weightings	% of Stocks	Rel S&P 500	3 Year High	3 Year Low
Info	19.03	0.89		
Software	4.11	0.96	5	2
Hardware	10.37	1.02	13	5
Media	3.52	0.92	7	3
Telecom	1.03	0.33	2	0
Service	56.36	1.21		
Health	16.36	1.31	23	14
Consumer	13.73	1.51	19	13
Business	16.90	4.17	19	14
Financial	9.37	0.45	21	9
Mfg	24.61	0.77		
Goods	12.42	1.33	12	1
Ind Mtrls	3.83	0.30	5	1
Energy	7.25	1.01	8	6
Utilities	1.11	0.38	1	0

Composition

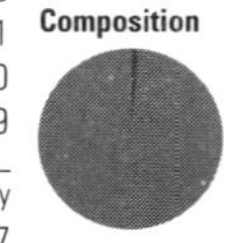

Cash	1.3
Stocks	98.7
Bonds	0.0
Other	0.0
Foreign (% of Stock)	6.6

Morningstar's Take by Bridget Hughes 11-10-04

After a strong run, risk has elevated a bit at Janus Enterprise, but we like the long-term prospects of this fund.

Janus Enterprise has had quite a year so far in 2004. Up 11.7% for the year to date through Nov. 9, 2004, the fund ranks inside the mid-growth category's best decile--on the heels of a 35.8% gain in 2003. Consumer-oriented stocks have been most beneficial this year: Top 10 holding Harman International Industries has advanced nearly 78% for in 2004, for example, while a smaller position in NAVTEQ has also done well. Both stocks produce goods that go into autos. Other strong consumer names include Mandalay Resort Group and Starwood Hotels & Resorts Worldwide.

While these consumer names and others have helped the fund lately, the positioning could also hurt if an economic stumble or inflationary pressures cause consumers to change their propensity to spend. Manager Jonathan Coleman doesn't think that's likely--a thought that goes into his bottom-up assessment of a company's prospects. The portfolio remains overweighted in consumer areas, and given Coleman's longer-term thinking and comparatively low turnover, we wouldn't expect that bias to abate overnight.

That said, Coleman is very cognizant of risk for this portfolio--one reason why he won't let position sizes grow to much more than 3% of assets--and he has worked to diversify the fund, specifically seeking ideas less tied to consumer spending. In that vein, he's added a couple of health-care names, such as Varian Medical Systems and Respironics. He has also taken profits in Harman and Starwood--and Mandalay Resort was taken out of the portfolio via its acquisition by MGM Mirage.

For the longer haul, we think this fund boasts advantages, including a deep research bench, low expenses, and a huge tax loss carryforward that means buy and hold shareholders here won't need to worry about taxable distributions for some time.

Address:	100 Fillmore St Denver CO 80206 800-525-3713
Web Address:	www.janus.com
Inception:	09-01-92
Advisor:	Janus
Subadvisor:	None
NTF Plans:	Fidelity Retail-NTF, Schwab OneSource

Minimum Purchase:	$2500	Add: $100	IRA: $500
Min Auto Inv Plan:	$500	Add: $100	
Sales Fees:	No-load		
Management Fee:	0.64%		
Actual Fees:	Mgt:0.64%	Dist:	
Expense Projections:	3Yr:$322	5Yr:$558	10Yr:$1236
Income Distrib:	Annually		

Janus Global Life Sci

Ticker	Load	NAV	Yield	Total Assets	Mstar Category
JAGLX	None	$17.99	0.0%	$1,213 mil	Specialty-Health

Governance and Management

Fiduciary Grade: C

Portfolio Manager(s)

Tom Malley has been running the fund since its January 1999 inception. He served as an assistant portfolio manager on Janus Mercury. Andy Acker, who has worked as an analyst on the fund since 1999, was recently promoted to assistant portfolio manager. The fund is supported by four analysts, but could have five by the end of 2005.

Strategy

Manager Tom Malley searches across the health-care category for fast-growing names and is often willing to pay up for his picks, even though he has toned things down a bit in recent years. Indeed, while the fund still invests in aggressive areas such as biotechnology, it has found picks in other places in recent years as well, such as the health-information, pharmaceutical, and medical-device subsectors.

Historical Profile

Return Below Avg
Risk Above Avg
Rating ★★ Below Avg

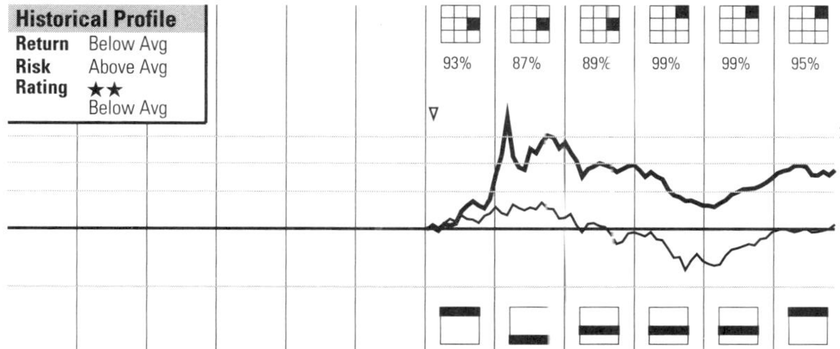

Investment Style: Equity Stock %

▼ Manager Change
∇ Partial Manager Change

Growth of $10,000
— Investment Values of Fund
— Investment Values of S&P 500

Performance Quartile (within Category)

1993	1994	1995	1996	1997	1998	1999	2000	2001	2002	2003	12-04	History
—	—	—	—	—	10.00	16.10	21.45	17.57	12.28	15.65	17.99	NAV
—	—	—	—	—	0.00*	61.00	33.34	-18.09	-30.11	27.44	14.95	Total Return %
—	—	—	—	—	—	39.96	42.44	-6.21	-8.02	-1.23	4.08	+/-S&P 500
—	—	—	—	—	—	65.03	-4.13	-5.43	-9.30	8.01	10.40	+/-DJ Hlthcare
—	—	—	—	—	—	0.00	0.10	0.00	0.00	0.00	0.00	Income Return %
—	—	—	—	—	—	61.00	33.24	-18.09	-30.11	27.44	14.95	Capital Return %
—	—	—	—	—	—	11	83	73	71	65	9	Total Rtn % Rank Cat
—	—	—	—	—	0.00	0.00	0.02	0.00	0.00	0.00	0.00	Income $
—	—	—	—	—	0.00	0.00	0.00	0.00	0.00	0.00	0.00	Capital Gains $
—	—	—	—	—	—	1.19	0.94	0.91	0.88	0.98	—	Expense Ratio %
—	—	—	—	—	—	-0.41	0.14	0.32	-0.42	-0.28	—	Income Ratio %
—	—	—	—	—	—	235	147	84	—	135	—	Turnover Rate %
—	—	—	—	—	—	601	3,992	2,418	1,278	1,273	1,213	Net Assets $mil

Performance 12-31-04

	1st Qtr	2nd Qtr	3rd Qtr	4th Qtr	Total
2000	17.58	7.08	12.73	-6.05	33.34
2001	-26.25	12.83	-7.51	6.42	-18.09
2002	-6.03	-14.54	-9.43	-3.91	-30.11
2003	2.04	10.14	3.70	9.36	27.44
2004	7.80	2.67	-4.16	8.37	14.95

Trailing	Total Return%	+/- S&P 500	+/- DJ Hlthcare	%Rank Cat	Growth of $10,000
3 Mo	8.37	-0.86	2.47	34	10,837
6 Mo	3.87	-3.32	2.87	38	10,387
1 Yr	14.95	4.08	10.40	9	11,495
3 Yr Avg	0.79	-2.79	1.16	50	10,239
5 Yr Avg	2.26	4.56	-1.25	80	11,182
10 Yr Avg	—	—	—	—	—
15 Yr Avg	—	—	—	—	—

Tax Analysis	Tax-Adj Rtn%	%Rank Cat	Tax-Cost Rat	%Rank Cat
3 Yr (estimated)	0.79	39	0.00	1
5 Yr (estimated)	2.25	73	0.01	3
10 Yr (estimated)	—	—	—	—

Potential Capital Gain Exposure: -58% of assets

Rating and Risk

Time Period	Load-Adj Return %	Morningstar Rtn vs Cat	Morningstar Risk vs Cat	Morningstar Risk-Adj Rating
1 Yr	14.95			
3 Yr	0.79	Avg	Avg	★★★
5 Yr	2.26	-Avg	+Avg	★★
10 Yr	—	—	—	—
Incept	10.29			

Other Measures	Standard Index S&P 500	Best Fit Index DJ Hlthcare
Alpha	-1.6	1.1
Beta	0.55	0.81
R-Squared	41	59

Standard Deviation	12.96
Mean	0.79
Sharpe Ratio	-0.05

Portfolio Analysis 11-30-04

Share change since 10-04 Total Stocks:66	Sector	PE	YTD Ret%	% Assets
⊖ Aetna	Financial	16.9	84.67	3.65
UnitedHealth Group	Health	23.8	51.38	3.59
Genzyme	Health	—	17.81	3.13
⊖ Roche Holding	Health	—	—	3.00
Gilead Sciences	Health	36.9	20.08	2.95
⊖ Caremark RX	Health	32.8	55.67	2.88
⊖ Amgen	Health	37.7	3.82	2.76
Fisher Scientific Intern	Health	43.9	50.79	2.57
⊖ Genentech	Health	78.6	16.36	2.48
⊖ MGI Pharma	Health	—	36.14	2.32
Invitrogen	Health	50.3	-3.98	2.31
⊖ Pfizer	Health	22.0	-22.31	2.30
Novartis	Health	—	—	2.29
⊖ Sanofi-Synthelabo	Health	—	—	2.13
⊖ Kinetic Concepts	Health	—	—	2.11
⊕ St. Jude Medical	Health	38.0	36.69	2.09
⊖ PacifiCare Health System	Health	21.5	67.22	1.93
Celgene	Health	95.6	18.18	1.89
⊖ Boston Scientific	Health	32.3	-3.29	1.89
⊖ Elan ADR	Health	—	295.50	1.84

Current Investment Style

Value Blnd Growth — Large Mid Small

Market Cap	%
Giant	26.7
Large	33.8
Mid	28.2
Small	9.4
Micro	1.9
Avg $mil: 10,507	

Value Measures		Rel Category
Price/Earnings	23.62	1.00
Price/Book	2.89	1.05
Price/Sales	2.21	0.78
Price/Cash Flow	9.94	0.91
Dividend Yield %	0.50	0.70

Growth Measures	%	Rel Category
Long-Term Erngs	15.53	0.96
Book Value	10.08	0.65
Sales	4.00	0.33
Cash Flow	20.52	1.11
Historical Erngs	2.50	0.26

Profitability	%	Rel Category
Return on Equity	9.34	0.96
Return on Assets	3.16	1.02
Net Margin	7.92	1.04

Industry Weightings	% of Stocks	Rel Cat
Biotech	31.5	0.9
Drugs	25.6	0.9
Mgd Care	11.9	2.0
Hospitals	0.0	0.0
Other HC Srv	0.7	0.6
Diagnostics	0.0	0.0
Equipment	19.9	1.3
Good/Srv	3.8	0.8
Other	6.7	1.1

Composition

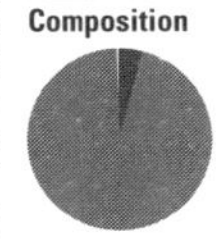

Cash	4.0
Stocks	95.3
Bonds	0.0
Other	0.6
Foreign (% of Stock)	18.8

Morningstar's Take by Dan Culloton 12-14-04

Janus Global Life Sciences isn't out of the woods yet.

Its performance has improved. The regulatory troubles of its advisor have begun to subside. And it still has one of the lowest expense ratios in the specialty health category. Nevertheless, this offering still has to prove it has a consistent strategy for achieving long-term success.

Manager Tom Malley is one of more-tenured managers in the health-care category (though his six years at the helm hardly make him a graybeard) and can talk in detail about the stocks this fund owns. In recent years, Malley also has made a concerted effort to pay closer attention to price and to keep this offering more balanced across market caps and industries (in its early days it relied heavily on small-cap biotechnology stocks). This has helped smooth the portfolio's volatility, as measured by standard deviation.

It can be hard to get a handle on Malley's investment style, though. He's not a buy-and-hold value investor. He bought Merck in the spring because it looked cheap, but sold the drug-maker after it pulled its pain-killer Vioxx from the market and got even cheaper. (The fund later repurchased the stock when Malley decided its price discounted the Vioxx controversy.) Unlike some growth investors, though, Malley doesn't always cut and run at the first sign of trouble or slipping momentum. For example, the fund kept its position in small, speculative specialty drug-maker Ligand Pharmaceuticals in August after an earnings disappointment and auditor resignation battered its shares. Malley thought the market was too pessimistic about the company's drug pipeline.

Flexibility? Inconsistency? You could make arguments either way. Whatever it is, the fund still has been a laggard longer than it has been a leader. It has finished four of the last six calendar years below the category average. That's not the record of a fund that has found a reliable formula for success.

Address:	100 Fillmore St Denver CO 80206 800-525-3713
Web Address:	www.janus.com
Inception:	12-31-98 *
Advisor:	Janus
Subadvisor:	None
NTF Plans:	Fidelity Retail-NTF, Schwab OneSource

Minimum Purchase:	$2500	Add: $100	IRA: $500
Min Auto Inv Plan:	$500	Add: $100	
Sales Fees:	No-load, 2.00%R		
Management Fee:	0.64%		
Actual Fees:	Mgt:0.64%	Dist:	
Expense Projections:	3Yr:$312	5Yr:$542	10Yr:$1201
Income Distrib:	Annually		

Janus Global Opps

Ticker	Load	NAV	Yield	Total Assets	Mstar Category
JGVAX	None	$14.24	0.2%	$219 mil	World Stock

Governance and Management

Fiduciary Grade: C

Portfolio Manager(s)

Jason Yee has been head of this fund since its inception in mid-2001. However, in July 2004, Janus placed him in charge of international flagship Janus Worldwide as well. He cut his teeth as an analyst at Janus from 1992 until 1996, after which he left the firm to work at a small money-management shop in Denver. He returned to Janus in 2000.

Strategy

Jason Yee won't buy stocks unless he can get them cheaply. He likes to grab a company when its stock is trading at a noticeable discount to his estimate of the firm's worth. This isn't bottom-of-the-barrel value investing, though: Yee also wants companies that boast strong free cash flows and impressive franchises. The fund invests across the globe and across market caps, but the portfolio is usually quite concentrated.

Historical Profile

Return Above Avg
Risk High
Rating ★★★★ Above Avg

Investment Style
Equity
Stock %: 87% (2001), 88% (2002), 88% (2003), 87% (12-04)

▼ Manager Change
▽ Partial Manager Change

Growth of $10,000
▬ Investment Values of Fund
— Investment Values of MSCI EAFE

Performance Quartile (within Category)

History

1993	1994	1995	1996	1997	1998	1999	2000	2001	2002	2003	12-04	History
—	—	—	—	—	—	—	—	10.70	8.96	12.37	14.24	NAV
—	—	—	—	—	—	—	—	7.29*	-15.92	38.41	15.33	Total Return %
—	—	—	—	—	—	—	—	—	0.02	-0.18	-4.92	+/-MSCI EAFE
—	—	—	—	—	—	—	—	—	3.97	5.30	0.61	+/-MSCI World
—	—	—	—	—	—	—	—	0.00	0.34	0.35	0.21	Income Return %
—	—	—	—	—	—	—	—	—	-16.26	38.06	15.12	Capital Return %
—	—	—	—	—	—	—	—	—	22	25	46	Total Rtn % Rank Cat
—	—	—	—	—	—	—	—	0.02	0.04	0.03	0.03	Income $
—	—	—	—	—	—	—	—	0.01	0.00	0.00	0.00	Capital Gains $
—	—	—	—	—	—	—	—	1.50	1.16	1.16	—	Expense Ratio %
—	—	—	—	—	—	—	—	0.64	0.40	0.27	—	Income Ratio %
—	—	—	—	—	—	—	—	—	84	31	—	Turnover Rate %
—	—	—	—	—	—	—	—	96	150	153	219	Net Assets $mil

Performance 12-31-04

	1st Qtr	2nd Qtr	3rd Qtr	4th Qtr	Total
2000	—	—	—	—	—
2001	—	—	-8.70	17.51	7.29 *
2002	8.32	-4.83	-21.31	3.65	-15.92
2003	-12.05	22.21	12.98	13.99	38.41
2004	5.17	3.54	-5.72	12.33	15.33

Trailing	Total Return%	+/- MSCI EAFE	+/- MSCI World	%Rank Cat	Growth of $10,000
3 Mo	12.33	-2.99	0.39	51	11,233
6 Mo	5.91	-9.09	-4.91	96	10,591
1 Yr	15.33	-4.92	0.61	46	11,533
3 Yr Avg	10.31	-1.58	3.36	26	13,423
5 Yr Avg	—	—	—	—	—
10 Yr Avg	—	—	—	—	—
15 Yr Avg	—	—	—	—	—

Tax Analysis	Tax-Adj Rtn%	%Rank Cat	Tax-Cost Rat	%Rank Cat
3 Yr (estimated)	10.19	21	0.11	15
5 Yr (estimated)	—	—	—	—
10 Yr (estimated)	—	—	—	—

Potential Capital Gain Exposure: 13% of assets

Rating and Risk

Time Period	Load-Adj Return %	Morningstar Rtn vs Cat	Morningstar Risk vs Cat	Morningstar Risk-Adj Rating
1 Yr	15.33			
3 Yr	10.31	+Avg	High	★★★★
5 Yr	—	—	—	—
10 Yr	—	—	—	—
Incept	10.96			

Other Measures	Standard Index S&P 500	Best Fit Index Mstar Mid Core
Alpha	-1.3	-3.3
Beta	1.03	1.11
R-Squared	78	85
Standard Deviation	20.13	
Mean	10.31	
Sharpe Ratio	0.45	

Portfolio Analysis 11-30-04

Share change since 10-04 Total Stocks:36	Sector	Country	% Assets
NIPPONKOA Insurance	Financial	Japan	4.75
British Sky Broadcasting	Media	U.K.	4.39
IAC/InterActiveCorp	Consumer	United States	4.02
Walt Disney	Media	United States	3.93
Smiths Grp	Ind Mtrls	U.K.	3.80
Nippon Broadcasting Syte	Media	Japan	3.64
J.P. Morgan Chase & Co.	Financial	United States	3.58
⊖ Tyco International	Ind Mtrls	United States	3.41
⊖ FKI Babcock	Business	U.K.	3.07
Health Management Associ	Health	United States	3.05
Mattel	Goods	United States	2.94
Berkshire Hathaway B	Financial	United States	2.85
Tenma	Ind Mtrls	Japan	2.84
☼ Ligand Pharmaceuticals	Health	United States	2.69
Interpublic Group of Com	Business	United States	2.69
Pfeiffer Vacuum Technolo	Ind Mtrls	Germany	2.65
Vivendi Universal	Media	France	2.47
Millea Hldgs	Financial	Japan	2.29
Tenet Healthcare	Health	United States	2.27
Takeda Pharma	Health	Japan	2.21

Current Investment Style

Value Blnd Growth; Large Mid Small

Market Cap	%
Giant	28.2
Large	32.6
Mid	29.8
Small	9.4
Micro	0.0
Avg $mil: 10,269	

Value Measures		Rel Category
Price/Earnings	17.84	1.13
Price/Book	1.03	0.46
Price/Sales	1.24	1.06
Price/Cash Flow	5.25	0.83
Dividend Yield %	1.71	0.91

Growth Measures	%	Rel Category
Long-Term Erngs	11.73	0.97
Book Value	2.22	1.00
Sales	-0.02	NMF
Cash Flow	0.72	0.12
Historical Erngs	14.98	1.75

Composition

Cash	12.3	Bonds	0.0
Stocks	86.7	Other	1.1
Foreign (% of Stock)			56.4

Sector Weightings	% of Stocks	Rel MSCI EAFE	3 Year High	3 Year Low
Info	26.59	1.60		
Software	2.90	2.69	5	2
Hardware	0.00	0.00	3	0
Media	23.69	10.39	24	7
Telecom	0.00	0.00	0	0
Service	44.45	0.99		
Health	13.38	1.84	13	0
Consumer	4.64	0.92	12	4
Business	8.94	1.64	18	9
Financial	17.49	0.65	21	10
Mfg	28.96	0.75		
Goods	13.06	0.96	16	7
Ind Mtrls	15.90	1.29	22	14
Energy	0.00	0.00	10	0
Utilities	0.00	0.00	0	0

Regional Exposure	% Stock		
UK/W. Europe	38	N. America	43
Japan	18	Latn America	1
Asia X Japan	0	Other	0

Country Exposure	% Stock		
United States	43	Netherlands	8
U.K.	18	Germany	4
Japan	18		

Morningstar's Take by Gareth Lyons 12-23-04

Behind-the-scenes developments diminish our enthusiasm for Janus Global Opportunities.

When this fund's manager, Jason Yee, was picked to run Janus Worldwide, we raised concerns that Yee would be distracted from his duties managing this much smaller fund. We also noted that a manager change could eventually be in the offing for Global Opportunities.

While those worries haven't entirely receded, it appears to be business as usual at this fund. Yee has indicated to us that he is committed to running both funds for the long term. And the fact that the manager has a significant amount of his personal wealth invested in this fund (he is its third-largest direct shareholder) suggests that his interests are aligned with shareholders'. Moreover, other managers, such as Oakmark's Bill Nygren and Legg Mason's Bill Miller, have been successful running core offerings as well as more concentrated vehicles. (Worldwide is a core offering, whereas this fund is more concentrated.)

While we don't doubt that Yee is a talented manager, shareholders of this fund have reason to gripe. Worldwide, which boasts more than $7 billion in assets, is the flagship in Janus' foreign suite, easily dwarfing this $220 million fund. Yee's obligation to his many new constituents is apt to mean that he won't be able to devote as much time to this tiny fund. We also can't ignore that Janus has typically dealt with similar situations by assigning another manager to the smaller fund or by merging both portfolios.

Our lingering worries here don't mean this fund has lost all of its charm, however. Yee is a talented manager, and this fund's smaller asset base grants him much greater flexibility to execute his go-anywhere strategy than he has at sibling Worldwide, where large caps will rule the roost. But the uncertainty does take the fund down a notch in our eyes. Potential investors may want to explore other options.

Address:	100 Fillmore St Denver CO 80206 800-525-3713
Web Address:	www.janus.com
Inception:	06-29-01 *
Advisor:	Janus
Subadvisor:	None
NTF Plans:	Fidelity Retail-NTF, Schwab OneSource

Minimum Purchase:	$2500	Add: $100	IRA: $500
Min Auto Inv Plan:	$100	Add: $100	
Sales Fees:	No-load, 2.00%R		
Management Fee:	0.64%		
Actual Fees:	Mgt:0.64%	Dist:	
Expense Projections:	3Yr:$368	5Yr:$638	10Yr:$1409
Income Distrib:	Annually		

Janus Growth & Income

Ticker	Load	NAV	Yield	Total Assets	Mstar Category
JAGIX	None	$32.19	0.5%	$5,422 mil	Large Growth

Governance and Management

Fiduciary Grade: C

Portfolio Manager(s)

David Corkins passed the torch to his assistant portfolio manager Minyoung Sohn on Jan. 1, 2004. This is Sohn's first portfolio manager assignment. He joined Janus as an analyst in 1998. David Corkins will be focusing on Janus Mercury, an aggressive growth fund, which he took over in February 2003. Janus reports that Sohn has been the firm's top analyst over the past few years.

Strategy

Minyoung Sohn did not make any strategic changes when taking over for David Corkins on Jan. 1, 2004. He continues to buy and hold companies with strong balance sheets that can deliver higher earnings or cash-flow growth than Wall Street expects. Turnover is about half the category average, and the fund has generally been more diversified than many of Janus' other growth offerings.

Historical Profile

Return High
Risk Below Avg
Rating ★★★★★ Highest

Investment Style: Equity — Stock %: 96% 90% 78% 83% 80% 79% 75% 96% 96%

▼ Manager Change
∇ Partial Manager Change

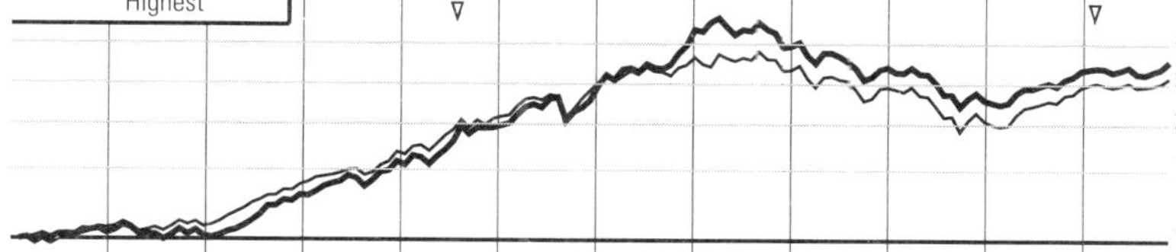

Growth of $10,000
— Investment Values of Fund
— Investment Values of S&P 500

Performance Quartile (within Category)

History	1993	1994	1995	1996	1997	1998	1999	2000	2001	2002	2003	12-04
NAV	14.69	13.88	16.67	19.05	23.15	29.10	41.94	35.35	29.97	23.34	28.91	32.19
Total Return %	6.70	-4.87	36.35	26.03	34.66	34.87	51.18	-11.41	-14.37	-21.51	24.65	11.89
+/-S&P 500	-3.36	-6.18	-1.18	3.09	1.31	6.30	30.14	-2.31	-2.49	0.58	-4.02	1.02
+/-Russ 1000Gr	3.83	-7.49	-0.83	2.91	4.17	-3.84	18.02	11.01	6.05	6.37	-5.10	5.59
Income Return %	1.17	0.65	7.33	0.58	0.37	0.34	0.34	0.55	0.85	0.65	0.68	0.52
Capital Return %	5.53	-5.52	29.02	25.45	34.29	34.53	50.84	-11.96	-15.22	-22.16	23.97	11.37
Total Rtn % Rank Cat	67	77	22	10	10	37	18	41	20	13	69	16
Income $	0.17	0.09	1.01	0.10	0.07	0.08	0.10	0.23	0.30	0.20	0.16	0.15
Capital Gains $	0.33	0.00	1.23	1.89	2.38	2.02	1.84	1.62	0.00	0.00	0.00	0.00
Expense Ratio %	1.28	1.22	1.17	1.03	0.96	0.96	0.90	0.88	0.86	0.88	0.91	—
Income Ratio %	1.13	1.26	1.11	0.70	0.30	0.33	0.37	0.49	0.96	0.73	0.67	—
Turnover Rate %	138	123	195	153	127	95	43	41	59	—	50	—
Net Assets $mil	514	456	632	1,101	2,005	3,504	7,493	8,349	7,148	5,277	5,977	5,422

Performance 12-31-04

	1st Qtr	2nd Qtr	3rd Qtr	4th Qtr	Total
2000	9.04	-8.29	0.24	-11.62	-11.41
2001	-11.82	5.24	-15.86	9.68	-14.37
2002	-0.23	-10.45	-16.37	5.05	-21.51
2003	-1.89	11.29	1.63	12.32	24.65
2004	1.56	0.95	-3.14	12.67	11.89

Trailing	Total Return%	+/- S&P 500	+/- Russ 1000Gr	%Rank Cat	Growth of $10,000
3 Mo	12.67	3.44	3.50	11	11,267
6 Mo	9.13	1.94	5.66	9	10,913
1 Yr	11.89	1.02	5.59	16	11,189
3 Yr Avg	3.06	-0.52	3.24	18	10,946
5 Yr Avg	-3.65	-1.35	5.64	17	8,303
10 Yr Avg	14.63	2.56	5.04	2	39,173
15 Yr Avg	—	—	—	—	—

Tax Analysis	Tax-Adj Rtn%	%Rank Cat	Tax-Cost Rat	%Rank Cat
3 Yr (estimated)	2.82	16	0.23	40
5 Yr (estimated)	-4.07	16	0.44	27
10 Yr (estimated)	12.93	2	1.48	48

Potential Capital Gain Exposure: 51% of assets

Rating and Risk

Time Period	Load-Adj Return %	Morningstar Rtn vs Cat	Morningstar Risk vs Cat	Morningstar Risk-Adj Rating
1 Yr	11.89			
3 Yr	3.06	+Avg	-Avg	★★★★
5 Yr	-3.65	+Avg	-Avg	★★★★
10 Yr	14.63	High	-Avg	★★★★★
Incept	13.69			

Other Measures	Standard Index S&P 500	Best Fit Index MSCI World
Alpha	-0.3	-3.1
Beta	0.88	0.89
R-Squared	93	94
Standard Deviation	14.13	
Mean	3.06	
Sharpe Ratio	0.12	

Portfolio Analysis 11-30-04

Share change since 10-04 Total Stocks:68	Sector	PE	YTD Ret%	% Assets
⊖ Tyco International	Ind Mtrls	25.1	35.41	5.29
ExxonMobil	Energy	13.9	28.04	3.93
Advanced Micro Devices	Hardware	33.0	47.79	3.70
Citigroup	Financial	15.3	2.72	3.39
⊖ UnitedHealth Group	Health	23.8	51.38	3.15
Roche Holding	Health	—	—	2.61
Microsoft	Software	36.1	8.95	2.58
British Sky Broadcasting	Media	—	—	2.32
Procter & Gamble	Goods	23.3	12.38	2.13
⊖ Caremark RX	Health	32.8	55.67	2.06
⊖ Aetna	Financial	16.9	84.67	2.06
Cisco Systems	Hardware	24.5	-20.26	2.00
Clear Channel Communicat	Media	23.5	-27.57	1.86
⊖ Maxim Integrated Product	Hardware	27.9	-13.87	1.83
⊖ Texas Instruments	Hardware	21.1	-15.90	1.81
⊖ Time Warner	Media	27.5	8.12	1.78
J.P. Morgan Chase & Co.	Financial	19.4	9.97	1.75
General Electric	Ind Mtrls	22.8	20.68	1.65
Rockwell Automation	Ind Mtrls	28.0	41.75	1.64
Suncor Energy	Energy	20.6	42.16	1.63

Current Investment Style

Value Blnd Growth — Large Mid Small

Market Cap	%
Giant	56.1
Large	30.3
Mid	13.0
Small	0.6
Micro	0.0
Avg $mil: 36,019	

Value Measures		Rel Category
Price/Earnings	18.41	0.87
Price/Book	3.19	0.99
Price/Sales	2.01	0.93
Price/Cash Flow	9.82	0.89
Dividend Yield %	1.01	1.31

Growth Measures	%	Rel Category
Long-Term Erngs	12.88	0.92
Book Value	5.14	0.40
Sales	5.78	0.68
Cash Flow	21.19	1.28
Historical Erngs	18.11	1.25

Profitability	%	Rel Category
Return on Equity	18.83	1.05
Return on Assets	9.76	1.04
Net Margin	12.03	0.98

Sector Weightings	% of Stocks	Rel S&P 500	3 Year High	3 Year Low
Info	30.96	1.44		
Software	5.73	1.33	6	3
Hardware	14.57	1.43	17	5
Media	10.09	2.63	16	10
Telecom	0.57	0.18	1	0
Service	34.22	0.74		
Health	11.24	0.90	15	7
Consumer	6.98	0.77	8	4
Business	2.30	0.57	6	2
Financial	13.70	0.66	29	14
Mfg	34.83	1.08		
Goods	12.72	1.36	13	9
Ind Mtrls	12.73	1.00	13	9
Energy	9.38	1.31	9	6
Utilities	0.00	0.00	1	0

Composition

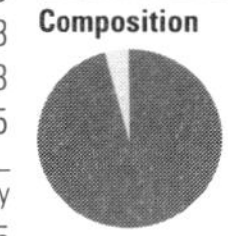

Cash	0.6
Stocks	95.8
Bonds	0.0
Other	3.7
Foreign (% of Stock)	17.2

Morningstar's Take by Dan McNeela 10-15-04

Janus Growth & Income has some hurdles to clear.

This fund has changed in a couple key ways. Most notably, Min Sohn was promoted from the analyst ranks at the beginning of 2004, when former manager David Corkins shifted over to run Janus Mercury. The fact that Sohn had been Janus' top performing analyst over the past few years is encouraging, but this is his first assignment as a manager and his total investment experience only dates back to 1998.

The other key development has been the evolution of the fund's asset allocation. Corkins traditionally only invested about 80% of the fund's assets in stocks, while cash and fixed-income investments served as ballast. But with interest rates at historic lows, Corkins moved increasingly toward stocks. Sohn has maintained that stock-heavy look and intends to stay that way until he sees better potential in the bond market. With that structure, the fund is likely to lose some of the stability that helped it survive the bear market.

That said, neither of those risks has caused problems with performance yet. With a modest loss of 1.4% year to date through Oct. 14, 2004 the fund has done better than more than 70% of its large-cap growth peers. Sohn hadn't covered any health-care stocks as an analyst, but he was wise enough to hold onto HMO stocks Aetna and United Health Group based on recommendations from Janus' research staff. The fund's overweight in semiconductor stocks hasn't hurt too much because its stock selection has been good.

We've also been encouraged by Sohn's restraint with the fund's sector weights. He's backing off of the fund's traditional bias in favor of media stocks, for example, because he doesn't have good enough reasons on a fundamental basis to be so highly exposed.

We're still cautious about this fund's prospects given Sohn's limited track record, but it's looking like a fund to watch.

Address:	100 Fillmore St Denver CO 80206 800-525-3713	Minimum Purchase:	$2500	Add: $100 IRA: $500
		Min Auto Inv Plan:	$500	Add: $100
		Sales Fees:	No-load	
Web Address:	www.janus.com	Management Fee:	0.62%	
Inception:	05-15-91	Actual Fees:	Mgt:0.62%	Dist:
Advisor:	Janus	Expense Projections:	3Yr:$281	5Yr:$488 10Yr:$1084
Subadvisor:	None	Income Distrib:	Quarterly	
NTF Plans:	Fidelity Retail-NTF, Schwab OneSource			

Janus High-Yield

Ticker	Load	NAV	Yield	SEC Yield	Total Assets	Mstar Category
JAHYX	None	$9.92	6.1%	5.57%	$556 mil	High Yield Bond

Governance and Management

Fiduciary Grade: C

Portfolio Manager(s)

Gibson Smith joined this fund in early December 2003. He has been with Janus since 2001 and has worked as an assistant portfolio manager on Janus Flexible Income and as a portfolio manager on Janus Short-Term Bond. He is supported by four analysts.

Strategy

This fund's profile has changed a bit under its new manager. Former manager Sandy Rufenacht was quite willing to hold large cash stakes, while Gibson Smith, who took over the fund in late 2003, plans to stay more fully invested. Smith has also trimmed the fund's exposure to the gaming sector, which was a favorite of Rufenacht's. Overall, the fund still looks a bit more conservative than its average peer, but not as conservative as it was with Rufenacht at the helm.

Historical Profile

Return Above Avg
Risk Low
Rating ★★★★ Above Avg

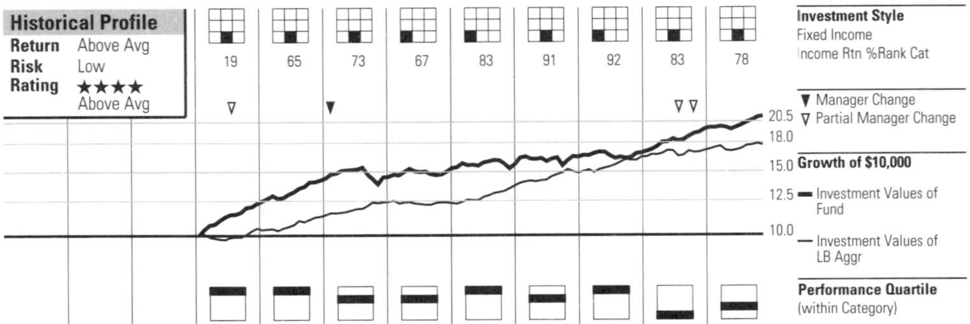

1993	1994	1995	1996	1997	1998	1999	2000	2001	2002	2003	12-04	History
—	—	10.00	11.23	11.39	10.61	10.28	9.69	9.37	8.97	9.71	9.92	NAV
—	—	0.00*	23.99	15.47	0.97	5.53	2.49	4.59	2.56	16.04	8.85	Total Return %
—	—	—	20.36	5.82	-7.72	6.35	-9.14	-3.85	-7.69	11.94	4.51	+/-LB Aggr
—	—	—	11.57	2.84	0.39	2.25	7.70	-1.19	-0.55	-11.89	-3.11	+/-CSFB Glb HY
—	—	—	10.11	8.80	8.21	8.76	8.57	8.08	6.95	7.51	6.46	Income Return %
—	—	—	13.88	6.67	-7.24	-3.23	-6.08	-3.49	-4.39	8.53	2.39	Capital Return %
—	—	—	1	10	44	37	6	38	15	94	69	Total Rtn % Rank Cat
—	—	0.00	0.97	0.95	0.90	0.89	0.85	0.76	0.63	0.65	0.61	Income $
—	—	0.00	0.11	0.56	0.00	0.00	0.00	0.00	0.00	0.00	0.01	Capital Gains $
—	—	—	1.00	1.00	0.96	1.00	1.00	0.99	0.96	0.95	—	Expense Ratio %
—	—	—	9.00	8.45	7.85	8.48	8.43	8.04	7.02	6.90	—	Income Ratio %
—	—	—	324	404	336	310	295	358	161	203	—	Turnover Rate %
—	—	—	238	357	295	275	301	433	668	666	556	Net Assets $mil

Performance 12-31-04

	1st Qtr	2nd Qtr	3rd Qtr	4th Qtr	Total
2000	1.84	1.73	1.24	-2.28	2.49
2001	3.35	-1.61	-2.46	5.46	4.59
2002	2.31	-1.54	-1.60	3.46	2.56
2003	4.02	4.83	1.64	4.70	16.04
2004	1.53	-0.44	4.51	3.03	8.85

Trailing	Total Return%	+/- LB Aggr	+/- CSFB Glb HY	%Rank Cat	Growth of $10,000
3 Mo	3.03	2.08	-1.53	90	10,303
6 Mo	7.68	3.50	-1.58	75	10,768
1 Yr	8.85	4.51	-3.11	69	10,885
3 Yr Avg	9.01	2.82	-4.87	75	12,954
5 Yr Avg	6.79	-0.92	-1.38	23	13,888
10 Yr Avg	—	—	—	—	—
15 Yr Avg	—	—	—	—	—

Tax Analysis	Tax-Adj Rtn%	%Rank Cat	Tax-Cost Rat	%Rank Cat
3 Yr (estimated)	6.39	61	2.40	22
5 Yr (estimated)	3.91	9	2.70	16
10 Yr (estimated)	—	—	—	—

Potential Capital Gain Exposure: -1% of assets

Rating and Risk

Time Period	Load-Adj Return %	Morningstar Rtn vs Cat	Morningstar Risk vs Cat	Morningstar Risk-Adj Rating
1 Yr	8.85			
3 Yr	9.01	Avg	Low	★★★
5 Yr	6.79	+Avg	Low	★★★★
10 Yr	—	—	—	—
Incept	8.69			

Other Measures	Standard Index LB Aggr	Best Fit Index CSFB Glb HY
Alpha	6.9	0.3
Beta	0.15	0.59
R-Squared	2	85

Standard Deviation	4.30
Mean	9.01
Sharpe Ratio	1.79

Morningstar's Take by Scott Berry 11-08-04

We're still in wait-and-see mode with Janus High Yield.

This fund has taken shareholders on quite a ride over the last few years. Not only did star manager Sandy Rufenacht leave to start his own firm, but his replacement Michael Buchanan lasted just six months before departing for greener pastures. Add in market-timing allegations, settlements with the SEC and New York Attorney General, and volatile relative returns, and you've got a recipe for disaster.

Fortunately disaster hasn't struck. The fund landed near the back of the high-yield pack in 2003, but its underperformance owed primarily to the defensive positioning that was in place when Rufenacht departed in July of that year. Since Gibson Smith took over in December 2003, the fund's performance has actually stabilized quite nicely. For the 12 months ended November 4, the fund gained 11.2% and ranked near the middle of the high yield pack. Its year-to-date return ranked just inside the group's best half.

Smith's efforts have focused on finding improving companies and properly weighting their bonds in the portfolio. For example, he was confident that the value of El Paso's assets more than covered the level of its debt, so he made it one of the fund's top holdings. As El Paso has made progress in its turnaround plan, its bonds have rallied sharply. Meanwhile, Smith has been concerned that rising interest rates could hamper returns, so he has kept the fund's duration (a measure of interest-rate risk) a bit short of its benchmark index. That move has yet to pay off, as interest rates have remained stubbornly low, but should help the fund hold its own if interest rates move higher.

We have no complaints about the work Smith has done here. We'd just like to see more of it before recommending this fund over others, given Janus' recent regulatory issues and given Smith's relatively short tenure.

Address:	100 Fillmore St Denver CO 80206 800-525-3713
Web Address:	www.janus.com
Inception:	12-29-95 *
Advisor:	Janus
Subadvisor:	None
NTF Plans:	Fidelity Retail-NTF, Schwab OneSource

Minimum Purchase:	$2500	Add: $100	IRA: $500
Min Auto Inv Plan:	$500	Add: $100	
Sales Fees:	No-load, 2.00%R		
Management Fee:	0.65% mx./0.55% mn.		
Actual Fees:	Mgt:0.59%	Dist:	
Expense Projections:	3Yr:$271	5Yr:$471	10Yr:$1049
Income Distrib:	Monthly		

Portfolio Analysis 11-30-04

Total Fixed-Income:231	Date of Maturity	Amount $000	Value $000	% Net Assets
Dow Jones Cdx Na Hy 3 Tr	12-29-09	17,450	17,712	3.21
Targeted Return Index Se	08-01-15	13,004	14,060	2.55
Mission Engy Hldg 13.5%	07-15-08	6,500	8,149	1.48
Reliant Engy 9.5%	07-15-13	6,050	6,942	1.26
Lyondell Chem 11.125%	07-15-12	5,150	6,090	1.10
Centennial Comms 10.125%	06-15-13	5,500	5,995	1.09
Nalco 8.875%	11-15-13	5,025	5,546	1.01
Owens-Brockway Glass Con	02-15-09	5,000	5,425	0.98
Crown Cork & Seal Fin 7%	12-15-06	5,100	5,381	0.98
Crown European Hldgs Sa	03-01-13	4,500	5,321	0.97
Tyco Intl Grp S A 5.8%	08-01-06	5,000	5,191	0.94
Tenneco Automotive 11.62	10-15-09	4,850	5,149	0.93
Venetian Casino Resort 1	06-15-10	4,500	5,130	0.93
Equistar Chemicals L P 6	02-15-06	5,000	5,125	0.93
Georgia Pac 9.5%	12-01-11	4,000	4,970	0.90
Hammons John Q Hotels L	05-15-12	4,350	4,948	0.90
Forest Oil 8%	12-15-11	3,900	4,417	0.80
Dex Media 8%	11-15-13	4,100	4,392	0.80
Ship Fin Intl 8.5%	12-15-13	4,250	4,383	0.79
Cch Ii 10.25%	09-15-10	4,150	4,337	0.79

Current Investment Style

Duration: Short Int Long; Quality: High Med Low

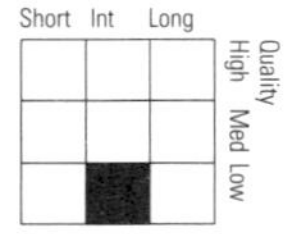

[1] figure provided by fund

Avg Eff Duration[1]	4.4 Yrs
Avg Eff Maturity	6.0 Yrs
Avg Credit Quality	B
Avg Wtd Coupon	8.22%
Avg Wtd Price	107.59% of par

Coupon Range	% of Bonds	Rel Cat
0% PIK	6.0	1.3
0% to 8%	42.1	1.1
8% to 11%	49.6	0.9
11% to 14%	8.4	1.2
More than 14%	0.0	0.0

1.00=Category Average

Credit Analysis		% bonds 11-30-04	
US Govt	0	BB	24
AAA	0	B	53
AA	0	Below B	13
A	0	NR/NA	9
BBB	1		

Sector Breakdown	% of assets
US Treasuries	0
TIPS	0
US Agency	0
Mortgage Pass-Throughs	0
Mortgage CMO	0
Mortgage ARM	0
US Corporate	93
Asset-Backed	0
Convertible	1
Municipal	0
Corporate Inflation-Protected	0
Foreign Corporate	3
Foreign Govt	0

Composition			
Cash	4.1	Bonds	94.8
Stocks	0.0	Other	1.2

Special Securities	
Restricted/Illiquid Secs	25
Exotic Mortgage-Backed	0
Emerging-Markets Secs	0
Options/Futures/Warrants	No

Janus Mercury

Ticker	Load	NAV	Yield	Total Assets	Mstar Category
JAMRX	None	$21.57	0.1%	$4,601 mil	Large Growth

Governance and Management

Fiduciary Grade: C

Portfolio Manager(s)

David Corkins took over for longtime manager Warren Lammert in late-February 2003. Corkins has a long and impressive record at Janus Growth & Income. In December 2003, he dropped his responsibilities on Growth & Income to focus on Mercury.

Strategy

This fund has traditionally sought rapid growers that are dominating their niches, and has paid little attention to price tags. Under new manager David Corkins, expect this fund to be more sensitive to valuations. At Janus Growth & Income, Corkins showed a willingness to buy into fast-growing stocks, but also restraint to sell them when their price multiples grew lofty. Corkins also pays close attention to firms' balance sheets--in addition to their income statements--which allows him to ferret out stocks with too many red flags.

Historical Profile

Return Average
Risk Above Avg
Rating ★★★ Neutral

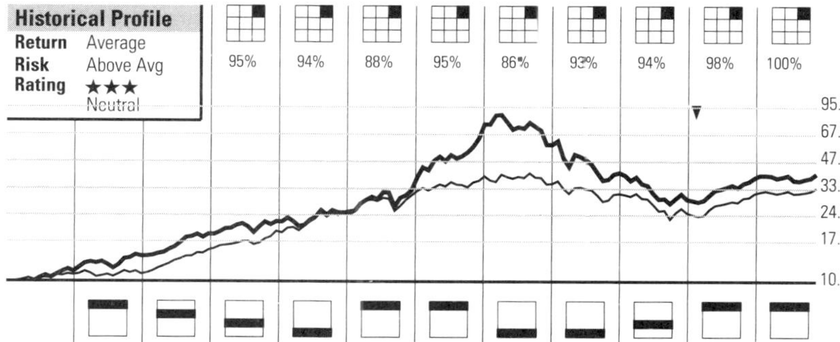

1993	1994	1995	1996	1997	1998	1999	2000	2001	2002	2003	12-04	History
11.98	13.61	16.04	16.52	16.50	24.11	43.81	29.57	20.79	14.76	19.50	21.57	NAV
19.80*	15.86	33.01	17.67	11.88	58.41	96.23	-22.75	-29.78	-29.00	32.11	10.77	Total Return %
—	14.55	-4.52	-5.27	-21.47	29.84	75.19	-13.65	-17.90	-6.91	3.44	-0.10	+/-S&P 500
—	13.24	-4.17	-5.45	-18.61	19.70	63.07	-0.33	-9.36	-1.12	2.36	4.47	+/-Russ 1000Gr
0.00	1.37	12.91	0.47	0.25	0.00	0.00	3.80	0.15	0.00	0.00	0.15	Income Return %
—	14.49	20.10	17.20	11.63	58.41	96.23	-26.55	-29.33	-29.00	32.11	10.62	Capital Return %
—	1	42	63	96	6	3	84	34	62	21	23	Total Rtn % Rank Cat
0.00	0.16	1.76	0.08	0.04	0.00	0.00	1.66	0.04	0.00	0.00	0.03	Income $
0.00	0.11	0.30	2.28	1.90	2.01	3.27	2.78	0.00	0.00	0.00	0.00	Capital Gains $
1.75	1.33	1.12	1.00	0.96	0.97	0.91	0.88	0.88	0.92	0.95	0.97	Expense Ratio %
-0.40	0.25	0.50	0.45	0.21	-0.33	-0.39	0.08	0.16	-0.07	-0.31	-0.26	Income Ratio %
151	283	201	177	157	105	89	71	83	97	54	43	Turnover Rate %
127	690	1,596	2,061	1,911	3,112	13,543	13,345	8,438	4,879	5,366	4,694	Net Assets $mil

Performance 12-31-04

	1st Qtr	2nd Qtr	3rd Qtr	4th Qtr	Total
2000	12.83	-14.46	0.64	-20.47	-22.75
2001	-24.30	9.39	-23.12	10.30	-29.78
2002	-5.34	-18.80	-12.39	5.43	-29.00
2003	-1.08	15.55	1.84	13.50	32.11
2004	2.56	0.45	-4.58	12.68	10.77

Trailing	Total Return%	+/- S&P 500	+/- Russ 1000Gr	%Rank Cat	Growth of $10,000
3 Mo	12.68	3.45	3.51	11	11,268
6 Mo	7.52	0.33	4.05	17	10,752
1 Yr	10.77	-0.10	4.47	23	11,077
3 Yr Avg	1.28	-2.30	1.46	30	10,389
5 Yr Avg	-10.84	-8.54	-1.55	79	5,634
10 Yr Avg	11.86	-0.21	2.27	12	30,672
15 Yr Avg	—	—	—	—	—

Tax Analysis	Tax-Adj Rtn%	%Rank Cat	Tax-Cost Rat	%Rank Cat
3 Yr (estimated)	1.27	25	0.01	2
5 Yr (estimated)	-11.47	78	0.71	44
10 Yr (estimated)	9.57	16	2.05	75

Potential Capital Gain Exposure: -113% of assets

Rating and Risk

Time Period	Load-Adj Return %	Morningstar Rtn vs Cat	Morningstar Risk vs Cat	Morningstar Risk-Adj Rating
1 Yr	10.77			
3 Yr	1.28	+Avg	Avg	★★★★
5 Yr	-10.84	-Avg	+Avg	★★
10 Yr	11.86	+Avg	+Avg	★★★
Incept	13.22			

Other Measures	Standard Index S&P 500	Best Fit Index Russ MG
Alpha	-2.1	-4.0
Beta	1.00	0.85
R-Squared	87	92
Standard Deviation	16.46	
Mean	1.28	
Sharpe Ratio	-0.01	

Portfolio Analysis 11-30-04

Share change since 10-04 Total Stocks:75	Sector	PE	YTD Ret%	% Assets
⊖ Liberty Media	Media	—	11.56	4.84
⊖ Tyco International	Ind Mtrls	25.1	35.41	4.16
Roche Holding	Health	—	—	3.69
⊖ Berkshire Hathaway B	Financial	20.9	4.30	3.62
UnitedHealth Group	Health	23.8	51.38	3.32
⊖ Canadian National Railwa	Business	23.9	47.10	3.22
⊖ Yahoo	Media	95.1	67.36	3.20
⊖ Time Warner	Media	27.5	8.12	3.06
⊖ Starwood Hotels & Resort	Consumer	33.9	64.71	2.92
Microsoft	Software	36.1	8.95	2.90
⊕ J.P. Morgan Chase & Co.	Financial	19.4	9.97	2.86
Samsung Electronics	Goods	—	—	2.56
Texas Instruments	Hardware	21.1	-15.90	2.32
⊕ Freddie Mac	Financial	10.6	28.75	2.12
⊖ FedEx	Business	27.9	46.40	2.01
⊖ Cisco Systems	Hardware	24.5	-20.26	1.92
Caremark RX	Health	32.8	55.67	1.75
⊕ Maxim Integrated Product	Hardware	27.9	-13.87	1.71
⊖ Comcast	Media	—	-13.77	1.68
⊖ Staples	Consumer	24.7	24.38	1.57

Current Investment Style

Value Blnd Growth — Large Mid Small

Market Cap	%
Giant	46.4
Large	39.1
Mid	14.3
Small	0.3
Micro	0.0
Avg $mil: 29,487	

Value Measures		Rel Category
Price/Earnings	18.87	0.89
Price/Book	2.42	0.75
Price/Sales	1.88	0.87
Price/Cash Flow	10.36	0.94
Dividend Yield %	0.84	1.09

Growth Measures	%	Rel Category
Long-Term Erngs	15.49	1.10
Book Value	5.01	0.39
Sales	9.82	1.15
Cash Flow	14.72	0.89
Historical Erngs	20.08	1.39

Profitability	%	Rel Category
Return on Equity	13.72	0.76
Return on Assets	7.45	0.80
Net Margin	8.66	0.70

Sector Weightings	% of Stocks	Rel S&P 500	3 Year High	3 Year Low
Info	32.61	1.52		
Software	3.91	0.91	10	4
Hardware	10.25	1.00	15	6
Media	18.11	4.72	21	16
Telecom	0.34	0.11	0	0
Service	47.72	1.03		
Health	15.16	1.21	23	14
Consumer	8.85	0.97	9	6
Business	8.62	2.13	9	3
Financial	15.09	0.73	25	14
Mfg	19.66	0.61		
Goods	8.21	0.88	8	1
Ind Mtrls	9.60	0.76	10	4
Energy	1.32	0.18	6	1
Utilities	0.53	0.18	1	0

Composition

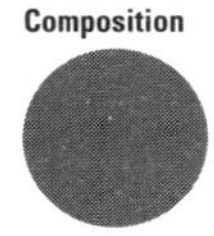

Cash	0.2
Stocks	99.8
Bonds	0.0
Other	0.0
Foreign (% of Stock)	16.1

Morningstar's Take by Dan McNeela 10-19-04

Janus Mercury is keeping an even keel by balancing optimism with risk aversion.

This fund isn't having the kind of year that makes investors jump for joy. Its modest 1.8% year-to-date loss through Oct. 18, 2004 is a bit better than Morningstar's large-cap growth category average, but its had some rough spots. The fund's tech holdings, including stakes in networking firm Cisco and chipmaker Texas Instruments, have not done well due to sector-wide weakness in revenue growth. Stock-specific issues have popped up with software firm Synopsis, which slashed earnings expectations, and pay TV broadcaster British Sky Broadcasting, which reported disappointing subscriber growth.

Despite those shortcomings, we think manager David Corkins has this fund on solid footing. He's held on to or bought more of his slumping hardware stocks because he likes their strong balance sheets and profit margins. Such patience has paid off for him in 2003. The silver lining with the individual stock misses is that neither was more than a 1% position in the fund, so Corkins limited the damage through portfolio construction.

In all, we see Corkins continuing to be opportunistic without overreaching. He took profits in his energy holdings after rising oil prices pushed valuation levels above his comfort levels. Similarly, he booked gains in security software firm Symantec and online auctioneer eBay when they reached his fair-value targets. In the short term, the fund would have been better off if it still owned those stocks, but we're encouraged to see it maintain its sell discipline.

Going forward, Corkins sees many firms struggling to increase revenues, but is encouraged that many companies are producing healthy cash flows and sell at reasonable prices. We think the fund should fare well in that environment.

Investors who want a proven growth manager with a good feel for downside risk should give this fund consideration.

Address:	100 Fillmore St Denver CO 80206 800-525-8983
Web Address:	www.janus.com
Inception:	05-03-93 *
Advisor:	Janus
Subadvisor:	None
NTF Plans:	Fidelity Retail-NTF, Schwab OneSource

Minimum Purchase:	$2500	Add: $100	IRA: $500
Min Auto Inv Plan:	$500	Add: $100	
Sales Fees:	No-load		
Management Fee:	0.64%		
Actual Fees:	Mgt:0.64%	Dist:	
Expense Projections:	3Yr:$303	5Yr:$526	10Yr:$1166
Income Distrib:	Annually		

Janus Mid Cap Val Inv

Analyst Pick

Ticker	Load	NAV	Yield	Total Assets	Mstar Category
JMCVX	None	$22.09	0.3%	$3,779 mil	Mid-Cap Value

Governance and Management

Fiduciary Grade: B

Portfolio Manager(s)

Tom Perkins of Perkins, Wolf, McDonnell & Company has run this fund since its August 1998 inception. He was joined by comanager Jeff Kautz, who had been an analyst at the Chicago-based firm since 1997, in February 2002. Five analysts back the duo. The firm is 30% owned by Janus, which has the option to buy an additional 14% annually. Bonuses for investment personnel are predicated on firm profitability.

Strategy

Lead manager Tom Perkins hunts for stocks trading at or near their historic lows. In particular, he looks for turnaround stories with strong cash flow, little to no debt, and proven management. The portfolio typically contains 85-90 stocks, although recent numbers are a bit higher, and individual positions are generally capped at about 3% of assets.

Historical Profile

Return High
Risk Average
Rating ★★★★★ Highest

Investment Style
Equity
Stock %

1998	1999	2000	2001	2002	2003	12-04
79%	91%	93%	84%	88%	90%	86%

▼ Manager Change
▽ Partial Manager Change

Growth of $10,000
▬ Investment Values of Fund
— Investment Values of S&P 500

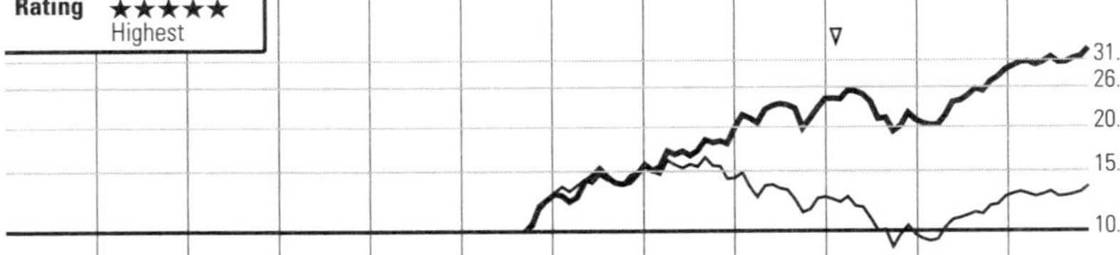

Performance Quartile (within Category)

1993	1994	1995	1996	1997	1998	1999	2000	2001	2002	2003	12-04	History
—	—	—	—	—	11.38	12.51	14.39	16.96	14.71	20.39	22.09	NAV
—	—	—	—	—	14.40*	21.56	27.34	20.52	-13.09	39.33	18.36	Total Return %
—	—	—	—	—	—	0.52	36.44	32.40	9.00	10.66	7.49	+/-S&P 500
—	—	—	—	—	—	21.67	8.16	18.19	-3.45	1.26	-5.35	+/-Russ MV
—	—	—	—	—	0.00	0.39	0.80	0.20	0.18	0.70	0.41	Income Return %
—	—	—	—	—	—	21.17	26.54	20.32	-13.27	38.63	17.95	Capital Return %
—	—	—	—	—	—	11	25	3	55	24	45	Total Rtn % Rank Cat
—	—	—	—	—	0.06	0.04	0.10	0.03	0.03	0.10	0.08	Income $
—	—	—	—	—	0.00	1.24	1.36	0.35	0.00	0.00	1.93	Capital Gains $
—	—	—	—	—	1.68	1.62	1.59	1.22	1.15	1.08	—	Expense Ratio %
—	—	—	—	—	-2.30	0.54	0.72	0.78	0.20	0.45	—	Income Ratio %
—	—	—	—	—	—	154	129	116	39	97	—	Turnover Rate %
—	—	—	—	—	23	25	51	265	948	1,747	3,278	Net Assets $mil

Performance 12-31-04

	1st Qtr	2nd Qtr	3rd Qtr	4th Qtr	Total
2000	9.27	-3.00	8.82	10.40	27.34
2001	2.92	13.37	-14.83	21.28	20.52
2002	5.54	-6.98	-17.66	7.51	-13.09
2003	-2.99	17.17	6.52	15.08	39.33
2004	5.30	3.03	-0.90	10.10	18.36

Trailing	Total Return%	+/- S&P 500	+/- Russ MV	%Rank Cat	Growth of $10,000
3 Mo	10.10	0.87	-3.36	73	11,010
6 Mo	9.10	1.91	-6.33	72	10,910
1 Yr	18.36	7.49	-5.35	45	11,836
3 Yr Avg	12.75	9.17	-2.81	33	14,333
5 Yr Avg	17.08	19.38	3.60	15	22,000
10 Yr Avg	—	—	—	—	—
15 Yr Avg	—	—	—	—	—

Tax Analysis	Tax-Adj Rtn%	%Rank Cat	Tax-Cost Rat	%Rank Cat
3 Yr (estimated)	11.94	29	0.72	58
5 Yr (estimated)	15.82	14	1.08	55
10 Yr (estimated)	—	—	—	—

Potential Capital Gain Exposure: 17% of assets

Rating and Risk

Time Period	Load-Adj Return %	Morningstar Rtn vs Cat	Morningstar Risk vs Cat	Morningstar Risk-Adj Rating
1 Yr	18.36			
3 Yr	12.75	+Avg	Avg	★★★★
5 Yr	17.08	High	Avg	★★★★★
10 Yr	—	—	—	—
Incept	19.13			

Other Measures	Standard Index S&P 500	Best Fit Index Mstar Mid Core
Alpha	9.2	0.2
Beta	0.89	0.95
R-Squared	81	95
Standard Deviation	16.62	
Mean	12.75	
Sharpe Ratio	0.69	

Portfolio Analysis 11-30-04

Share change since 10-04 Total Stocks:138

	Sector	PE	YTD Ret%	% Assets
⊕ Omnicare	Health	14.0	-14.07	1.67
⊕ Independence Community B	Financial	13.9	21.37	1.40
⊕ PNC Financial Services G	Financial	13.3	8.92	1.36
⊕ Lubrizol	Energy	22.0	17.03	1.32
Old Republic Internation	Financial	10.3	1.89	1.32
Washington Federal	Financial	15.1	7.15	1.32
⊕ Jacobs Engineering Group	Business	19.9	-0.46	1.30
⊕ State Street	Financial	15.3	-4.41	1.24
Magna Int'l	Ind Mtrls	12.9	5.09	1.15
CIT Group	Financial	13.2	29.28	1.13
⊕ Centurytel	Telecom	14.2	9.54	1.09
⊕ Manpower	Business	18.2	3.24	1.09
Alltel	Telecom	16.9	29.71	1.05
⊕ Liberty Media	Media	—	11.56	1.04
⊕ Cooper Cameron	Energy	40.2	15.47	1.03
⊖ Patterson-UTI Energy	Energy	33.3	18.55	1.00
⊕ Laidlaw Int'l	Ind Mtrls	—	77.82	0.97
Steris	Health	17.1	4.96	0.97
⊕ Newfield Exploration	Energy	12.5	32.58	0.95
Rayonier	Ind Mtrls	15.2	23.81	0.95

Current Investment Style

Value Blnd Growth; Large Mid Small

Market Cap	%
Giant	1.1
Large	22.6
Mid	63.4
Small	12.8
Micro	0.1
Avg $mil: 4,163	

Value Measures		Rel Category
Price/Earnings	16.55	1.07
Price/Book	1.95	1.02
Price/Sales	1.08	1.23
Price/Cash Flow	5.49	0.96
Dividend Yield %	1.24	0.87

Growth Measures	%	Rel Category
Long-Term Erngs	11.10	1.01
Book Value	8.46	1.50
Sales	7.00	1.46
Cash Flow	4.29	1.09
Historical Erngs	12.78	1.11

Profitability	%	Rel Category
Return on Equity	12.03	0.94
Return on Assets	6.90	1.14
Net Margin	10.66	1.21

Sector Weightings	% of Stocks	Rel S&P 500	3 Year High	3 Year Low
Info	16.62	0.77		
Software	2.32	0.54	6	2
Hardware	6.00	0.59	12	4
Media	4.77	1.24	5	1
Telecom	3.53	1.12	4	0
Service	53.87	1.16		
Health	11.71	0.94	14	9
Consumer	10.80	1.19	13	8
Business	8.71	2.15	10	6
Financial	22.65	1.09	30	21
Mfg	29.51	0.92		
Goods	3.21	0.34	6	2
Ind Mtrls	11.22	0.89	15	9
Energy	14.35	2.00	16	11
Utilities	0.73	0.25	2	0

Composition

Cash	13.8
Stocks	85.5
Bonds	0.0
Other	0.7
Foreign (% of Stock)	3.6

Morningstar's Take by Kunal Kapoor 11-01-04

Slow and steady it may be, but Janus Mid Cap Value has been off to the races lately.

After delivering a sterling 39% gain in 2003, this fund is at it again, jumping approximately 9% for the year to date though October 2004. The fund has been powered by picks in the energy sector, such as Patterson-UTI Energy, as well as a bunch of takeouts, the most recent of which was International Steel. All told, the fund has outpaced 97% of its mid-cap value peers for the trailing five years.

While it's stayed ahead of the pack, lead manager Tom Perkins and his colleagues use many of the same techniques as some of the category's other conservative managers. They place a premium on capital preservation and aren't afraid to raise cash when they can't identify opportunities. Currently, for instance, the fund is sitting on a cash stake of approximately 15% of assets. Moreover, like several other notable managers, they've lately been moving the portfolio up the market ladder as small- and mid-cap stocks have become relatively expensive. For example, the fund recently initiated a position in Tribune, the newspaper publisher whose business has been under a cloud lately.

In other ways, though, the fund is different from some of the category's other distinguished players. Key among them is its willingness to look beyond traditional value sectors such as financials. While a 24% stake in that sector soaks up the majority of this fund's assets, it is also willing to go into areas such as technology, where some of its peers won't venture. In particular, it gravitates toward industries such as semiconductors--as it is doing now--which exhibit cyclical characteristics.

This means that the fund can hit some bumps, as it did in 2002, but that it's also got a wide range. Thus, while it's unlikely to replicate it's massive absolute gains over the trailing five years anytime soon, it remains among the most competitive offerings in its area of specialty.

Address:	100 Fillmore St Denver CO 80206 800-525-3713
Web Address:	www.janus.com
Inception:	08-12-98 *
Advisor:	Janus
Subadvisor:	Perkins, Wolf, McDonnell and Co, LLC
NTF Plans:	Fidelity Retail-NTF, Schwab OneSource

Minimum Purchase:	$2500	Add: $100	IRA: $500
Min Auto Inv Plan:	$500	Add: $100	
Sales Fees:	No-load		
Management Fee:	0.64%		
Actual Fees:	Mgt:0.64%	Dist:	
Expense Projections:	3Yr:$340	5Yr:$590	10Yr:$1306
Income Distrib:	Annually		

Janus Olympus

Ticker	Load	NAV	Yield	Total Assets	Mstar Category
JAOLX	None	$28.63	0.0%	$2,424 mil	Large Growth

Governance and Management

Fiduciary Grade: C

Portfolio Manager(s)

Claire Young took over this portfolio from Scott Schoelzel in mid-1997. Prior to assuming control at this fund, she was an analyst with Janus.

Strategy

Manager Claire Young has typically concentrated on fast-growing firms from high-growth industries. In the past, she was not afraid to take a flier on companies without earnings, but now she steps a bit more lightly. In this more-moderate vein, she prefers firms with strong cash flow and strong balance sheets. Young has been known to make big sector bets, but her recent portfolios are more diversified, with an emphasis on financials, health-care, and consumer stocks.

Historical Profile

Return Below Avg
Risk Above Avg
Rating ★★ Below Avg

Investment Style: Equity Stock %: 93% 95% 87% 89% 86% 95% 91% 98% 97%

▼ Manager Change
∇ Partial Manager Change

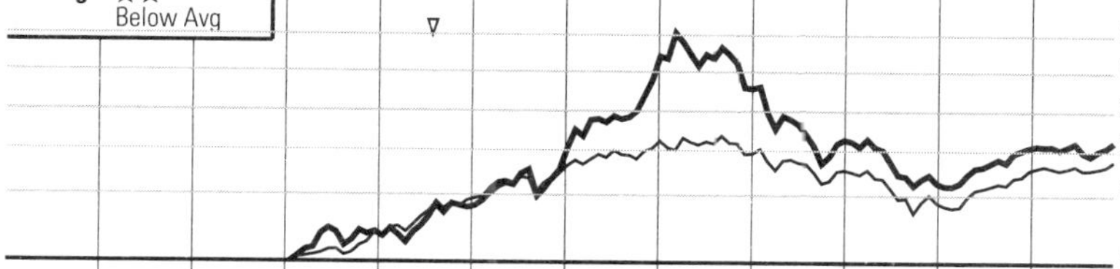

57.6 43.6 32.4 24.0 17.0 10.0

Growth of $10,000
— Investment Values of Fund
— Investment Values of S&P 500

Performance Quartile (within Category)

1993	1994	1995	1996	1997	1998	1999	2000	2001	2002	2003	12-04	History
—	—	12.00	14.48	17.58	27.58	53.26	41.15	27.35	20.00	26.33	28.63	NAV
—	—	0.00*	21.73	26.73	56.97	100.12	-21.63	-32.05	-28.19	31.65	8.74	Total Return %
—	—	—	-1.21	-6.62	28.40	79.08	-12.53	-20.17	-6.10	2.98	-2.13	+/-S&P 500
—	—	—	-1.39	-3.76	18.26	66.96	0.79	-11.53	-0.31	1.90	2.44	+/-Russ 1000Gr
—	—	—	1.08	0.28	0.07	0.05	0.44	0.26	0.00	0.00	0.00	Income Return %
—	—	—	20.65	26.45	56.90	100.07	-22.07	-32.31	-28.19	31.65	8.74	Capital Return %
—	—	—	31	50	7	2	81	88	55	24	39	Total Rtn % Rank Cat
—	—	0.00	0.13	0.04	0.01	0.01	0.23	0.01	0.00	0.00	0.00	Income $
—	—	0.00	0.00	0.71	0.00	1.78	0.39	0.00	0.00	0.00	0.00	Capital Gains $
—	—	—	1.15	1.03	1.01	0.93	0.90	0.89	0.91	0.98	1.03	Expense Ratio %
—	—	—	1.64	0.26	-0.21	0.06	0.51	0.34	-0.13	-0.14	-0.36	Income Ratio %
—	—	—	303	244	123	91	93	118	90	84	76	Turnover Rate %
—	—	—	413	629	1,288	6,174	6,165	3,437	2,024	2,778	2,424	Net Assets $mil

Performance 12-31-04

	1st Qtr	2nd Qtr	3rd Qtr	4th Qtr	Total
2000	11.10	-8.74	-0.02	-22.69	-21.63
2001	-26.29	3.46	-25.84	20.16	-32.05
2002	0.47	-16.19	-16.38	1.99	-28.19
2003	0.15	13.08	3.40	12.43	31.65
2004	0.91	2.60	-5.58	11.23	8.73

Trailing	Total Return%	+/- S&P 500	+/- Russ 1000Gr	%Rank Cat	Growth of $10,000
3 Mo	11.23	2.00	2.06	26	11,123
6 Mo	5.03	-2.16	1.56	47	10,503
1 Yr	8.74	-2.13	2.44	39	10,874
3 Yr Avg	0.92	-2.66	1.10	33	10,279
5 Yr Avg	-11.35	-9.05	-2.06	81	5,475
10 Yr Avg	—	—	—	—	—
15 Yr Avg	—	—	—	—	—

Tax Analysis	Tax-Adj Rtn%	%Rank Cat	Tax-Cost Rat	%Rank Cat
3 Yr (estimated)	0.92	28	0.00	1
5 Yr (estimated)	-11.45	77	0.11	7
10 Yr (estimated)	—	—	—	—

Potential Capital Gain Exposure: 0% of assets

Rating and Risk

Time Period	Load-Adj Return %	Morningstar Rtn vs Cat	Morningstar Risk vs Cat	Morningstar Risk-Adj Rating
1 Yr	8.74			
3 Yr	0.92	Avg	Avg	★★★
5 Yr	-11.35	-Avg	+Avg	★★
10 Yr	—	—	—	—
Incept	11.44			

Other Measures	Standard Index S&P 500	Best Fit Index Russ MG
Alpha	-2.3	-4.3
Beta	0.93	0.81
R-Squared	83	93
Standard Deviation	15.60	
Mean	0.92	
Sharpe Ratio	-0.03	

Portfolio Analysis 11-30-04

Share change since 10-04 Total Stocks:77	Sector	PE	YTD Ret%	% Assets
Yahoo	Media	95.1	67.36	3.64
Gap	Consumer	17.6	-8.63	3.43
⊖ Maxim Integrated Product	Hardware	27.9	-13.87	2.63
☼ Four Seasons Hotels	—	—	—	2.45
UnitedHealth Group	Health	23.8	51.38	2.34
Total SA ADR	Energy	17.0	23.39	2.16
Roche Holding	Health	—	—	2.09
Neurocrine Biosciences	Health	—	-9.61	1.94
Varian Medical Systems	Health	36.0	25.15	1.92
⊖ Microsoft	Software	36.1	8.95	1.92
Whole Foods Market	Consumer	45.4	43.11	1.75
⊖ Chicago Mercantile Excha	Financial	37.9	218.54	1.70
United Parcel Service B	Business	28.5	16.40	1.67
⊖ Ball	Goods	20.9	49.08	1.66
FedEx	Business	27.9	46.40	1.63
Reliant Energy	Utilities	—	85.46	1.62
Mitsubishi Tokyo Fin. Gr	Financial	—	—	1.59
⊖ Cisco Systems	Hardware	24.5	-20.26	1.59
⊕ Paychex	Business	38.9	-7.06	1.59
SAP	Software	—	—	1.56

Current Investment Style

Value Blnd Growth — Large Mid Small

Market Cap	%
Giant	30.4
Large	33.7
Mid	35.9
Small	0.0
Micro	0.0
Avg $mil: 17,410	

Value Measures		Rel Category
Price/Earnings	25.20	1.18
Price/Book	3.42	1.06
Price/Sales	2.05	0.95
Price/Cash Flow	10.89	0.99
Dividend Yield %	0.63	0.82

Growth Measures	%	Rel Category
Long-Term Erngs	15.38	1.09
Book Value	8.14	0.64
Sales	9.86	1.16
Cash Flow	18.92	1.14
Historical Erngs	15.94	1.10

Profitability	%	Rel Category
Return on Equity	17.43	0.97
Return on Assets	9.15	0.98
Net Margin	12.03	0.98

Sector Weightings	% of Stocks	Rel S&P 500	3 Year High	3 Year Low
Info	22.17	1.03		
Software	7.21	1.68	8	2
Hardware	9.11	0.89	24	6
Media	5.85	1.52	11	3
Telecom	0.00	0.00	1	0
Service	54.38	1.17		
Health	21.22	1.70	24	15
Consumer	13.29	1.46	16	9
Business	11.08	2.74	11	8
Financial	8.79	0.42	24	7
Mfg	23.44	0.73		
Goods	8.13	0.87	13	6
Ind Mtrls	4.50	0.36	6	2
Energy	9.10	1.27	9	3
Utilities	1.71	0.58	2	0

Composition

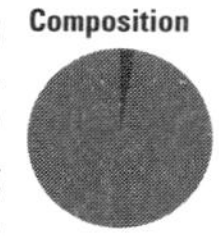

Cash	2.6
Stocks	97.4
Bonds	0.0
Other	0.0
Foreign (% of Stock)	12.6

Morningstar's Take by Dan McNeela 10-18-04

Janus Olympus has made some good moves, but it hasn't gotten too far.

One of the key questions for this fund is how well it has learned any lessons from its disappointing showings during the bear market. Manager Claire Young promised to keep the fund positioned as an aggressive growth offering, but yet pay more heed to valuation levels to keep its price risk in check.

The fund's performance in 2003 provided few insights to any progress because the market bounced back so strongly that the rising tide lifted many of the more-speculative stocks along with steadier fare. Shareholders had to be pleased that the fund gained 32% and topped Morningstar's large-growth category average by 3 percentage points, but the fund's strengthened valuation sensitivity wasn't put to the test.

In 2004, however, the uneven market has provided some useful data. Early in the year, Young became uneasy about valuation levels in the semiconductor area and worried about increased production capacity putting a dent in pricing. Those concerns were justified, as chip makers and chip-equipment firms have been the two worst-performing industries in this year's market.

But the fund hasn't fully benefited from that analysis because its stake in the hardware sector, which has dropped during the year from 21% to 10% of assets, came down slowly. Texas Instruments, for example, was still a top ten holding as of June 30, 2004. The fund has been able to make up ground elsewhere, with top holding Yahoo continuing to deliver. But its 2.6% year-to-date loss through Oct. 15, 2004 ranks in the middle of Morningstar's large-growth category.

Looking ahead, the fund is now counting heavily on healthcare stocks. Many of those holdings are drug and biotech stocks, which can be volatile depending on clinical trials for new therapies.

We think most investors will want to see more from this fund before committing to it.

Address:	100 Fillmore St Denver CO 80206 800-525-3713
Web Address:	www.janus.com
Inception:	12-29-95*
Advisor:	Janus
Subadvisor:	None
NTF Plans:	Fidelity Retail-NTF, Schwab OneSource

Minimum Purchase:	$2500	Add: $100	IRA: $500
Min Auto Inv Plan:	$500	Add: $100	
Sales Fees:	No-load		
Management Fee:	0.64%		
Actual Fees:	Mgt:0.64%	Dist:	
Expense Projections:	3Yr:$312	5Yr:$542	10Yr:$1201
Income Distrib:	Annually		

Janus Orion

Ticker	Load	NAV	Yield	Total Assets	Mstar Category
JORNX	None	$6.94	0.0%	$548 mil	Mid-Cap Growth

Governance and Management

Fiduciary Grade: C

Portfolio Manager(s)

This is Ron Sachs' first stint as a lead manager; he has been with the fund since its 2000 inception. Previously, he served as assistant manager on Janus Enterprise. Like all Janus managers, Sachs looks to Janus' analysts for research support and stock suggestions, although the analysts do not make buy and sell decisions.

Strategy

This offering will go just about anywhere in its search for promising investments, from small caps to blue chips. The portfolio only holds a few dozen names, making for a highly aggressive offering. Sachs looks for companies with pricing power that are growing and capable of generating high free cash flow.

Historical Profile

Return Average
Risk Average
Rating ★★★ Neutral

Investment Style
Equity
Stock %

2000	2001	2002	2003	12-04
96%	77%	86%	95%	95%

▼ Manager Change
▽ Partial Manager Change

Growth of $10,000
— Investment Values of Fund
— Investment Values of S&P 500

Performance Quartile (within Category)

1993	1994	1995	1996	1997	1998	1999	2000	2001	2002	2003	12-04	History
—	—	—	—	—	—	—	7.01	5.98	4.20	6.04	6.94	NAV
—	—	—	—	—	—	—	-29.69*	-14.69	-29.77	43.81	14.90	Total Return %
—	—	—	—	—	—	—	—	-2.81	-7.68	15.14	4.03	+/-S&P 500
—	—	—	—	—	—	—	—	5.46	-2.36	1.10	-0.58	+/-Russ MG
—	—	—	—	—	—	—	0.00	0.00	0.00	0.00	0.00	Income Return %
—	—	—	—	—	—	—	—	-14.69	-29.77	43.81	14.90	Capital Return %
—	—	—	—	—	—	—	—	35	65	15	36	Total Rtn % Rank Cat
—	—	—	—	—	—	—	0.02	0.00	0.00	0.00	0.00	Income $
—	—	—	—	—	—	—	0.00	0.00	0.00	0.00	0.00	Capital Gains $
—	—	—	—	—	—	—	1.12	1.03	1.04	1.08	1.08	Expense Ratio %
—	—	—	—	—	—	—	0.82	-0.06	-0.30	-0.43	-0.05	Income Ratio %
—	—	—	—	—	—	—	35	206	161	72	69	Turnover Rate %
—	—	—	—	—	—	—	879	688	391	541	548	Net Assets $mil

Performance 12-31-04

	1st Qtr	2nd Qtr	3rd Qtr	4th Qtr	Total
2000	—	—	-3.40	-27.22	-29.69 *
2001	-22.54	5.34	-14.86	22.79	-14.69
2002	-2.01	-16.21	-16.70	2.69	-29.77
2003	-3.10	23.59	4.17	15.27	43.81
2004	5.13	2.05	-3.70	11.22	14.90

Trailing	Total Return%	+/- S&P 500	+/- Russ MG	%Rank Cat	Growth of $10,000
3 Mo	11.22	1.99	-2.72	80	11,122
6 Mo	7.10	-0.09	-1.91	57	10,710
1 Yr	14.90	4.03	-0.58	36	11,490
3 Yr Avg	5.09	1.51	-1.07	37	11,606
5 Yr Avg	—	—	—	—	—
10 Yr Avg	—	—	—	—	—
15 Yr Avg	—	—	—	—	—

Tax Analysis	Tax-Adj Rtn%	%Rank Cat	Tax-Cost Rat	%Rank Cat
3 Yr (estimated)	5.09	31	0.00	1
5 Yr (estimated)	—	—	—	—
10 Yr (estimated)	—	—	—	—

Potential Capital Gain Exposure: -85% of assets

Rating and Risk

Time Period	Load-Adj Return %	Morningstar Rtn vs Cat	Morningstar Risk vs Cat	Morningstar Risk-Adj Rating
1 Yr	14.90			
3 Yr	5.09	Avg	Avg	★★★
5 Yr	—	—	—	—
10 Yr	—	—	—	—
Incept	-7.73			

Other Measures	Standard Index S&P 500	Best Fit Index S&P Mid 400
Alpha	1.6	-5.4
Beta	1.08	1.09
R-Squared	83	86
Standard Deviation	18.74	
Mean	5.09	
Sharpe Ratio	0.20	

Portfolio Analysis 11-30-04

Share change since 10-04 Total Stocks:40	Sector	PE	YTD Ret%	% Assets
Dade Behring Holdings	Health	35.9	56.69	7.92
⊖ Chicago Mercantile Excha	Financial	37.9	218.54	4.33
Roche Holding	Health	—	—	3.99
Sider De Tubarao	—	—	—	3.99
CapitalSource	Financial	—	18.40	3.93
Costco Wholesale	Consumer	25.6	31.15	3.87
Puma AG Rudolf Dassler S	Goods	—	—	3.83
LVMH Moet Hennessy L.V.	Goods	—	—	3.24
Companhia Siderurgica Na	Ind Mtrls	9.4	52.32	3.19
Molson	Goods	—	—	3.16
Hermes Int'l	Goods	—	—	3.03
Oriflame Cosmetics	Consumer	—	—	3.03
Aracruz Celulose SA ADR	Ind Mtrls	24.1	14.28	3.00
Berkshire Hathaway B	Financial	20.9	4.30	2.87
FedEx	Business	27.9	46.40	2.83
Univision Communications	Media	39.5	-26.25	2.83
⊕ Celgene	Health	95.6	18.18	2.65
Assurant	Financial	—	—	2.61
Time Warner	Media	27.5	8.12	2.53
EOG Resources	Energy	16.5	55.21	2.41

Current Investment Style

Market Cap	%
Giant	11.2
Large	31.3
Mid	47.0
Small	10.5
Micro	0.0

Avg $mil: 6,616

Value Measures		Rel Category
Price/Earnings	19.74	0.90
Price/Book	2.56	0.85
Price/Sales	1.62	0.92
Price/Cash Flow	8.93	0.92
Dividend Yield %	0.49	1.14

Growth Measures	%	Rel Category
Long-Term Erngs	16.98	1.08
Book Value	10.77	1.07
Sales	8.41	0.98
Cash Flow	19.64	1.61
Historical Erngs	17.49	1.10

Profitability	%	Rel Category
Return on Equity	18.29	1.27
Return on Assets	8.44	1.18
Net Margin	12.63	1.31

Sector Weightings	% of Stocks	Rel S&P 500	3 Year High	3 Year Low
Info	13.01	0.61		
Software	1.34	0.31	3	0
Hardware	3.13	0.31	10	1
Media	8.54	2.22	17	7
Telecom	0.00	0.00	2	0
Service	57.52	1.24		
Health	21.06	1.68	23	8
Consumer	12.91	1.42	23	7
Business	7.18	1.77	13	5
Financial	16.37	0.79	27	16
Mfg	29.48	0.92		
Goods	20.44	2.19	25	0
Ind Mtrls	6.51	0.51	9	4
Energy	2.53	0.35	8	2
Utilities	0.00	0.00	4	0

Composition

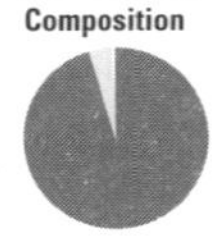

Cash	0.9
Stocks	95.1
Bonds	0.0
Other	4.0
Foreign (% of Stock)	33.1

Morningstar's Take by Dan McNeela 11-17-04

With Janus Orion striking a unique profile, we think it needs more time to prove itself.

This fund can be pretty difficult to pin down. Its portfolio has tended to land in Morningstar's mid-cap growth style box, but manager Ron Sachs' picks are an eclectic group. Warren Buffett's Berkshire Hathaway has been a top holding for a few years, but the fund also owns Israeli generic-drug maker Taro Pharmaceutical Industries. Sachs' penchant for companies based outside of the U.S. has become more pronounced in recent years; the current stake in foreign stocks reaches 40%. The fund remains fairly concentrated, as its recent roster of holdings lists fewer than 40 stocks.

The fund's unique approach isn't necessarily a bad thing, and in fact, it could turn out to be quite beneficial if Sachs proves correct. But evaluating the fund is tricky. Coming up with a relevant benchmark is problematic and its concentrated nature make performance swings inevitable. The fund posted an impressive 44% gain in 2003, but its results in other years have been mixed at best. Holding nearly 60% in tech and telecom stocks damaged the fund soon after its mid-2000 launch. Sachs sharply cut back on the fund's stakes in those areas in 2001, but the fund suffered through another tough year in 2002. In 2004, not owning much in the tech sector should have been an advantage, but the fund's 7.5% year-to-date gain through Nov. 16 is middling.

We like Sachs' approach. He's focused on finding firms with high growth potential, pricing power, the ability to generate excess free cash flow, and reasonable valuations. He has also shown discipline in trimming back his winners as they've reached his target prices, as he did this year with Harman International Industries.

This fund is also likely to benefit from Janus' push to expand its research staff and cover more stocks. But until it demonstrates that it can execute over longer time periods, investors should look for other options.

Address:	100 Fillmore St Denver CO 80206 800-295-2687
Web Address:	www.janus.com
Inception:	06-30-00 *
Advisor:	Janus
Subadvisor:	None
NTF Plans:	Fidelity Retail-NTF, Schwab OneSource

Minimum Purchase:	$2500	Add: $100	IRA: $500
Min Auto Inv Plan:	$500	Add: $100	
Sales Fees:	No-load		
Management Fee:	0.64%		
Actual Fees:	Mgt:0.64%	Dist:	
Expense Projections:	3Yr:$347	5Yr:$601	10Yr:$1329
Income Distrib:	Annually		

Janus Overseas

Ticker	Load	NAV	Yield	Total Assets	Mstar Category
JAOSX	None	$24.26	0.9%	$2,252 mil	Foreign Large Growth

Governance and Management

Fiduciary Grade: C

Portfolio Manager(s)

Things have changed here. Helen Young Hayes was lead skipper from the fund's 1994 inception until her retirement in mid-June 2003. It was on her watch that the fund amassed its stellar early record. Brent Lynn joined her as a comanager in December 2000 and has been an analyst with Janus since 1991. Still, Hayes' departure is a loss.

Strategy

Manager Brent Lynn scours the world for the fastest-growing companies. He emphasizes experienced management and high returns on capital. The fund often ends up concentrated by region, sector, or both. Price multiples for the portfolio have been on the high side at times. Janus recently implemented new systems to improve its fair-value pricing methods to deter market-timers.

Historical Profile

Return Above Avg
Risk High
Rating ★★★★ Above Avg

Investment Style: Equity Stock %: 85% 90% 90% 90% 85% 83% 90% 97% 99%

▼ Manager Change
∇ Partial Manager Change

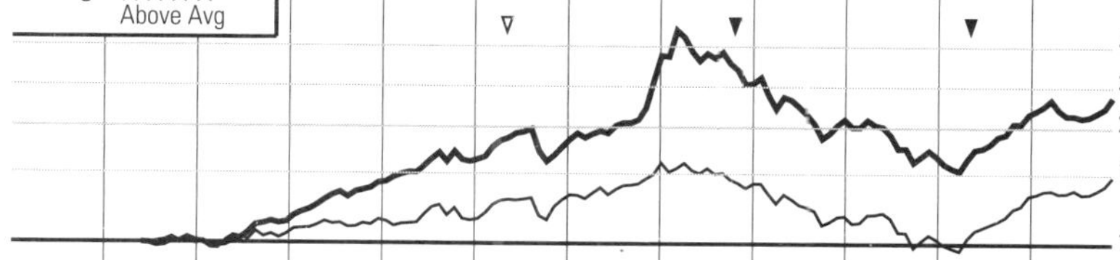

Growth of $10,000
▬ Investment Values of Fund
— Investment Values of MSCI EAFE

Performance Quartile (within Category)

1993	1994	1995	1996	1997	1998	1999	2000	2001	2002	2003	12-04	History
—	10.05	12.05	15.22	17.39	20.08	37.20	26.54	20.30	15.29	20.66	24.26	NAV
—	0.50*	22.05	28.83	18.23	16.03	86.07	-18.57	-23.11	-23.89	36.79	18.58	Total Return %
—	—	10.84	22.78	16.45	-3.90	59.04	-4.38	-1.69	-7.95	-1.80	-1.67	+/-MSCI EAFE
—	—	10.64	21.96	15.96	-2.66	58.09	-5.21	-1.72	-8.09	-2.63	-1.80	+/-MSCI Wd xUS
—	0.00	1.65	0.35	0.63	0.56	0.00	2.12	0.38	0.80	1.59	1.10	Income Return %
—	—	20.40	28.48	17.60	15.47	86.07	-20.69	-23.49	-24.69	35.20	17.48	Capital Return %
—	—	7	5	10	37	12	48	43	83	32	23	Total Rtn % Rank Cat
—	0.00	0.17	0.04	0.10	0.10	0.00	0.73	0.10	0.16	0.24	0.23	Income $
—	0.00	0.05	0.26	0.50	0.00	0.14	3.06	0.00	0.00	0.00	0.00	Capital Gains $
—	2.16	1.73	1.23	1.01	0.96	0.91	0.83	0.85	0.89	0.94	—	Expense Ratio %
—	-0.64	0.36	0.73	0.81	0.58	-0.03	0.22	0.77	0.69	1.21	—	Income Ratio %
—	181	188	71	72	105	92	62	65	63	104	—	Turnover Rate %
—	65	129	955	3,241	4,329	8,765	8,157	5,278	3,092	2,768	2,252	Net Assets $mil

Performance 12-31-04

	1st Qtr	2nd Qtr	3rd Qtr	4th Qtr	Total
2000	14.62	-11.42	-7.02	-13.74	-18.57
2001	-16.99	1.59	-20.82	15.16	-23.11
2002	-0.39	-10.48	-18.23	4.40	-23.89
2003	-10.33	18.67	10.69	16.13	36.79
2004	11.23	-10.92	2.34	16.93	18.58

Trailing	Total Return%	+/- MSCI EAFE	+/- MSCI Wd xUS	%Rank Cat	Growth of $10,000
3 Mo	16.93	1.61	1.78	3	11,693
6 Mo	19.68	4.68	4.31	2	11,968
1 Yr	18.58	-1.67	-1.80	23	11,858
3 Yr Avg	7.27	-4.62	-4.95	47	12,343
5 Yr Avg	-5.02	-3.89	-4.26	40	7,730
10 Yr Avg	11.99	6.37	6.05	7	31,031
15 Yr Avg	—	—	—	—	—

Tax Analysis	Tax-Adj Rtn%	%Rank Cat	Tax-Cost Rat	%Rank Cat
3 Yr (estimated)	6.86	49	0.38	67
5 Yr (estimated)	-5.85	38	0.87	52
10 Yr (estimated)	11.18	5	0.72	25

Potential Capital Gain Exposure: -25% of assets

Rating and Risk

Time Period	Load-Adj Return %	Morningstar Rtn vs Cat	Morningstar Risk vs Cat	Morningstar Risk-Adj Rating
1 Yr	18.58			
3 Yr	7.27	Avg	+Avg	★★★
5 Yr	-5.02	Avg	High	★★★
10 Yr	11.99	+Avg	High	★★★★
Incept	11.24			

Other Measures	Standard Index S&P 500	Best Fit Index DJ 60%
Alpha	-4.3	-8.6
Beta	1.04	1.82
R-Squared	86	87

Standard Deviation	18.93
Mean	7.27
Sharpe Ratio	0.31

Portfolio Analysis 11-30-04

Share change since 10-04 Total Stocks:79	Sector	Country	% Assets
Reliance Industries Ltd	Ind Mtrls	India	6.58
Samsung Electronics	Goods	Korea	4.07
⊕ Hellenic Org. of Footbal	Consumer	Greece	3.11
Aracruz Celulose SA ADR	Ind Mtrls	Brazil	2.74
Imerys	Ind Mtrls	France	2.45
Sanofi-Synthe abo	Health	France	2.42
British Sky Broadcasting	Media	U.K.	2.27
⊖ Companhia Vale Do Rio Do	Ind Mtrls	Brazil	2.09
LVMH Moet Hennessy L.V.	Goods	France	2.05
⊖ Grupo Televisa ADR	Media	Mexico	1.97
Hermes Int'l	Goods	France	1.96
⊖ Housing Development Fina	Financial	India	1.87
Millea Hldgs	Financial	Japan	1.86
⊖ Companhia Siderurgica Na	Ind Mtrls	Brazil	1.85
LG Electronics	Goods	Korea	1.80
LG Petrochemical	Ind Mtrls	Korea	1.78
ARM Hldgs	Hardware	U.K.	1.77
Amdocs	Software	United States	1.74
Lukoil ADR	Energy	Russia	1.73
Kookmin Bank	Financial	Korea	1.70

Current Investment Style

Style box: Value / Blnd / Growth × Large / Mid / Small (Large Growth)

Market Cap	%
Giant	37.6
Large	35.0
Mid	27.3
Small	0.1
Micro	0.0
Avg $mil: 10,013	

Value Measures		Rel Category
Price/Earnings	14.64	0.99
Price/Book	1.27	0.61
Price/Sales	1.22	1.16
Price/Cash Flow	3.37	0.61
Dividend Yield %	1.85	0.91

Growth Measures	%	Rel Category
Long-Term Erngs	16.80	1.41
Book Value	6.02	3.48
Sales	7.24	1.57
Cash Flow	6.71	0.89
Historical Erngs	7.26	0.87

Composition

Cash	0.7	Bonds	0.0
Stocks	99.3	Other	0.0
Foreign (% of Stock)			93.9

Sector Weightings	% of Stocks	Rel MSCI EAFE	3 Year High	3 Year Low
Info	19.45	1.17		
Software	3.43	3.18	5	1
Hardware	8.98	2.46	12	4
Media	6.01	2.64	10	2
Telecom	1.03	0.11	8	1
Service	37.66	0.84		
Health	3.67	0.51	11	1
Consumer	7.88	1.56	8	3
Business	5.16	0.95	8	5
Financial	20.95	0.78	28	11
Mfg	42.89	1.11		
Goods	14.22	1.04	23	12
Ind Mtrls	24.31	1.98	24	10
Energy	3.46	0.47	14	3
Utilities	0.90	0.17	1	0

Regional Exposure	% Stock		
UK/W. Europe	29	N. America	8
Japan	17	Latn America	9
Asia X Japan	34	Other	3

Country Exposure	% Stock		
Japan	17	U.K.	10
India	14	France	9
South Korea	11		

Morningstar's Take by Gareth Lyons 12-01-04

Janus Overseas has perked up, but we're not sold.

When Brent Lynn took over from this fund's longtime skipper, Helen Young Hayes, back in June of 2003, the young manager made some immediate changes. Lynn, who had worked under Hayes as comanager on this fund and before that as an analyst, promptly tilted the portfolio toward economically sensitive fare, snapping up shares of emerging-market names, such as Brazilian iron-ore producer Companhia Vale do Rio Doce and Indian conglomerate Reliance Industries.

The move has paid off. Industrial-material and other cyclical stocks, especially those from certain emerging markets, have been this year's biggest winners so far. As a result, this fund's 13.4% gain through November 29 outpaces the typical foreign large-growth offering. Given this fund's wicked bear-market performance, we're glad to see Lynn get off to a good start.

However, we're not ready to give this fund a ringing endorsement. True, Lynn pays close attention to valuations and is less likely to repeat his predecessor's mistake of overpaying for growth names. But his approach tacks on risk in other ways. Seven of the top-ten names in the portfolio hail from emerging-market countries, accounting for almost one fourth of assets. Granted, most of Lynn's picks are reasonably valued large firms that boast high trading volumes (and therefore liquidity) in their respective local markets. However, emerging-markets securities can freefall when political or global economic risks arise, even when company fundamentals look fine.

Of course, Lynn's bold style has significant upside potential, and it offers a refreshing contrast to the benchmark-focused strategies that seem to pervade this category. Nonetheless, Lynn's limited experience makes us wary of putting too much faith in the execution and risk management of his bold approach. We'd like to see this manager weather a full market cycle before endorsing this pioneering fund.

Address:	100 Fillmore St Denver CO 80206 800-525-3713
Web Address:	www.janus.com
Inception:	05-02-94 *
Advisor:	Janus
Subadvisor:	None
NTF Plans:	Fidelity Retail-NTF, Schwab OneSource

Minimum Purchase:	$2500	Add: $100	IRA: $500
Min Auto Inv Plan:	$500	Add: $100	
Sales Fees:	No-load, 2.00%R		
Management Fee:	0.64%		
Actual Fees:	Mgt:0.64%	Dist:	
Expense Projections:	3Yr:$296	5Yr:$515	10Yr:$1143
Income Distrib:	Annually		

Janus Sm Cap Val Instl

Ticker	Load	NAV	Yield	Total Assets	Mstar Category
JSIVX	Closed	$29.98	1.1%	$3,010 mil	Small Value

Governance and Management

Fiduciary Grade: B

Portfolio Manager(s)

After more than a decade of running funds for an insurance company, manager Bob Perkins cofounded his own investment company in 1980 and started this fund in 1985. His son Todd recently joined the team as comanager. Their firm is 30% owned by Janus, which has the option to buy an additional 14% annually. Bonuses for investment personnel are predicated on firm profitability.

Strategy

Managers Bob and Todd Perkins hunt for stocks that trade at or near their historic lows. To avoid buying the most troubled names, they insist that picks sport traits such as strong cash flow and debt-free balance sheets. The Perkins think such a profile suggests that company management can turn things around within four to six quarters. They have a soft spot for REITs (real estate investment trusts) and high dividend yields, but they also build big positions in fallen growth stocks. The portfolio typically contains 65 to 70 stocks, and individual positions are generally capped at about 3.5% of assets.

Historical Profile

Return Above Avg
Risk Above Avg
Rating ★★★★ Above Avg

Investment Style: Equity Stock %

94% | 84% | 91% | 93% | 89% | 88% | 88% | 83%

▼ Manager Change
▽ Partial Manager Change

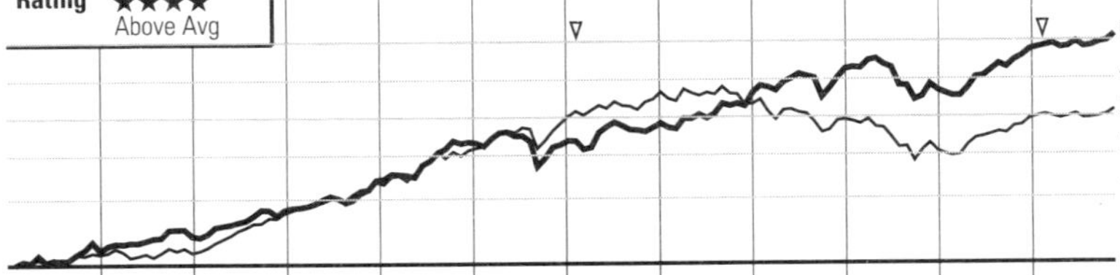

Growth of $10,000
— Investment Values of Fund
— Investment Values of S&P 500

Performance Quartile (within Category)

1993	1994	1995	1996	1997	1998	1999	2000	2001	2002	2003	12-04	History
13.99	12.75	14.57	16.48	19.94	19.32	21.67	25.47	28.15	22.81	31.09	29.98	NAV
16.28	6.70	26.09	25.60	33.06	1.83	14.69	27.16	20.42	-15.33	37.18	13.80	Total Return %
6.22	5.39	-11.44	2.66	-0.29	-26.74	-6.35	36.26	32.30	6.76	8.51	2.93	+/-S&P 500
-7.49	8.24	0.34	4.23	1.28	8.28	16.18	4.33	6.40	-3.90	-8.85	-8.45	+/-Russ 2000 VL
0.20	0.00	0.71	0.72	1.54	0.74	1.25	1.78	0.96	0.23	0.86	1.25	Income Return %
16.08	6.70	25.38	24.88	31.52	1.09	13.44	25.38	19.46	-15.56	36.32	12.55	Capital Return %
67	7	34	31	31	16	21	18	30	76	75	94	Total Rtn % Rank Cat
0.03	0.00	0.09	0.11	0.23	0.14	0.24	0.39	0.24	0.07	0.20	0.39	Income $
1.54	2.14	1.41	1.72	1.73	0.81	0.23	1.60	2.25	0.96	0.00	4.96	Capital Gains $
1.31	1.43	1.64	1.48	1.33	1.19	1.01	0.88	0.84	0.82	0.82	0.81	Expense Ratio %
0.18	-0.04	0.64	0.69	0.63	1.26	1.69	1.99	1.26	0.53	0.91	1.12	Income Ratio %
108	125	90	69	81	69	66	72	47	39	60	50	Turnover Rate %
16	18	32	36	61	144	525	1,003	1,517	1,282	1,559	1,464	Net Assets $mil

Performance 12-31-04

	1st Qtr	2nd Qtr	3rd Qtr	4th Qtr	Total
2000	3.78	0.22	10.34	10.80	27.16
2001	1.73	13.89	-16.71	24.78	20.42
2002	7.03	-5.48	-22.47	7.94	-15.33
2003	-4.69	16.97	7.16	14.83	37.18
2004	4.63	1.54	-0.67	7.83	13.80

Trailing	Total Return%	+/- S&P 500	+/- Russ 2000 VL	%Rank Cat	Growth of $10,000
3 Mo	7.83	-1.40	-5.37	97	10,783
6 Mo	7.11	-0.08	-6.26	93	10,711
1 Yr	13.80	2.93	-8.45	94	11,380
3 Yr Avg	9.74	6.16	-6.76	95	13,216
5 Yr Avg	15.14	17.44	-2.09	61	20,236
10 Yr Avg	17.42	5.35	2.25	8	49,822
15 Yr Avg	14.08	3.15	0.06	46	72,134

Tax Analysis	Tax-Adj Rtn%	%Rank Cat	Tax-Cost Rat	%Rank Cat
3 Yr (estimated)	8.39	94	1.23	70
5 Yr (estimated)	13.03	67	1.83	84
10 Yr (estimated)	14.92	8	2.13	75

Potential Capital Gain Exposure: 18% of assets

Rating and Risk

Time Period	Load-Adj Return %	Morningstar Rtn vs Cat	Morningstar Risk vs Cat	Morningstar Risk-Adj Rating
1 Yr	13.80			
3 Yr	9.74	Low	Avg	★★
5 Yr	15.14	Avg	Avg	★★★
10 Yr	17.42	High	+Avg	★★★★★
Incept	14.18			

Other Measures	Standard Index S&P 500	Best Fit Index Russ 2000 VL
Alpha	6.5	-4.5
Beta	0.91	0.89
R-Squared	69	93

Standard Deviation	18.01
Mean	9.74
Sharpe Ratio	0.47

Morningstar's Take by Kunal Kapoor 11-30-04

With small-cap value funds partying like its 1999, Janus Small Cap Value's defensive posture only cements our confidence in it.

Despite a sterling gain of 12.57% for the year to date through Nov. 29, 2004, this fund has been a relatively tepid performer of late. That's because managers Bob and Todd Perkins aren't nearly as enthusiastic about the investing environment as some of their peers, and have consciously taken steps to dial back the fund's risk. Perhaps most apparently, they've allowed cash to rise to approximately 18% of assets, as fewer and fewer investments have met their targeted risk/reward profiles. As such, the fund has lagged in what remains a surprisingly strong small-cap market.

We're not concerned by their defensiveness for a variety of reasons. First and foremost, we don't believe that this is a veiled attempt at market-timing. Rather, we can appreciate that the Perkins aren't going to stretch their valuation principles just to remain fully invested. Moreover, we think their prudence is well placed. Aggregate valuations for small-cap value funds are at or near historical highs, and numerous good small-cap funds have shut their doors for want of good investment opportunities. We even believe that it's prudent for shareholders of this and other small-cap value funds to tone down their expectations and rebalance their portfolios to ensure that they aren't overexposed to this recently hot asset class.

Meanwhile, if the rally in small stocks stalls, we think this fund will make up recently lost ground. Not only will the cash provide a cushion but with 30% of the portfolio's equity assets currently in mid-caps, the fund can play defense better than those rivals who are overcommitted to the tiniest and most speculative stocks As such, while the fund may continue to lag in the short term, we like its chances of navigating successfully through a tougher environment, as well as its long-term prospects.

Portfolio Analysis 11-30-04

Share change since 10-04 Total Stocks:99	Sector	PE	YTD Ret%	% Assets
Lubrizol	Energy	22.0	17.03	2.29
Steris	Health	17.1	4.96	2.13
Washington Federal	Financial	15.1	7.15	1.97
Rayonier	Ind Mtrls	15.2	23.81	1.90
Wolverine World Wide	Goods	19.2	55.69	1.89
Manor Care	Health	19.1	4.21	1.89
⊖ Forest Oil	Energy	20.7	11.03	1.83
Home Properties	Financial	42.6	13.35	1.78
First Niagara Financial	Financial	21.1	-4.68	1.74
Laidlaw Int'l	Ind Mtrls	—	77.82	1.66
⊕ Perrigo	Health	14.7	10.69	1.64
Emcor Group	Business	25.9	2.92	1.64
SuperValu	Consumer	12.4	23.24	1.62
⊕ Provident Financial Serv	Financial	—	3.84	1.61
Big Lots	Consumer	14.9	-14.64	1.59
Equity Lifestyle Propert	Financial	—	20.88	1.51
Brookline Bancorp	Financial	51.5	11.73	1.51
⊖ Harsco	Ind Mtrls	20.7	30.31	1.50
Old Republic Internation	Financial	10.3	1.89	1.49
Arch Coal	Energy	—	15.05	1.38

Current Investment Style

Market Cap	%
Giant	0.0
Large	0.0
Mid	33.4
Small	64.0
Micro	2.6
Avg $mil: 1,304	

Value Measures		Rel Category
Price/Earnings	18.95	1.19
Price/Book	1.77	1.07
Price/Sales	1.00	1.33
Price/Cash Flow	8.13	1.57
Dividend Yield %	1.58	1.32

Growth Measures	%	Rel Category
Long-Term Erngs	10.76	0.89
Book Value	6.43	1.48
Sales	3.96	1.27
Cash Flow	-1.12	NMF
Historical Erngs	2.75	0.57

Profitability	%	Rel Category
Return on Equity	9.36	1.03
Return on Assets	4.42	1.07
Net Margin	8.82	1.32

Sector Weightings	% of Stocks	Rel S&P 500	3 Year High	3 Year Low
Info	12.93	0.60		
Software	3.44	0.80	8	2
Hardware	5.87	0.58	13	3
Media	2.32	0.60	3	0
Telecom	1.30	0.41	2	0
Service	52.93	1.14		
Health	11.70	0.94	15	7
Consumer	9.20	1.01	10	3
Business	6.42	1.59	12	5
Financial	25.61	1.23	28	19
Mfg	34.15	1.06		
Goods	2.81	0.30	7	3
Ind Mtrls	17.55	1.39	22	17
Energy	13.79	1.93	14	10
Utilities	0.00	0.00	1	0

Composition

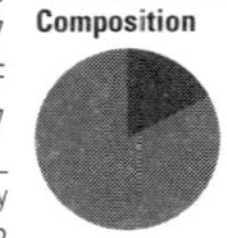

Cash	17.2
Stocks	82.8
Bonds	0.0
Other	0.0
Foreign (% of Stock)	0.4

Address:	100 Fillmore St Denver CO 80206 800-525-0020
Web Address:	www.janus.com
Inception:	02-14-85
Advisor:	Janus
Subadvisor:	Perkins, Wolf, McDonnell and Co, LLC
NTF Plans:	Federated Tr NTF, TD Waterhouse Ins NT

Minimum Purchase:	Closed	Add: —	IRA: —
Min Auto Inv Plan:	Closed	Add: —	
Sales Fees:	No-load		
Management Fee:	0.72%		
Actual Fees:	Mgt:0.72%	Dist:	
Expense Projections:	3Yr:$340	5Yr:$590	10Yr:$1306
Income Distrib:	Annually		

Janus Twenty

Ticker	Load	NAV	Yield	Total Assets	Mstar Category
JAVLX	Closed	$44.80	0.0%	$9,590 mil	Large Growth

Governance and Management

Fiduciary Grade: C

Portfolio Manager(s)

Before assuming control of Twenty in mid-1997, Scott Schoelzel managed Janus Olympus and Dreyfus Founders Growth. He also runs Janus Adviser Capital Appreciation and Janus Aspen Capital Appreciation, both of which are also large-growth funds, though they own several more stocks.

Strategy

Manager Scott Schoelzel has typically sought fast-growing firms that dominate their industries. During the bear market, however, the fund focused less on aggressive-growth firms and now boasts a more diversified portfolio, including both financial-services and energy stocks. That characteristic, to some extent, has continued even as the markets have performed better, but aggressive names have also become top positions. As the name of the fund indicates, it's typically concentrated in 20 to 30 stocks, and Schoelzel isn't afraid to make large individual stock bets. He's also willing to hold a substantial cash position.

Historical Profile

Return Above Avg
Risk Above Avg
Rating ★★★★ Above Avg

Investment Style: Equity Stock % — 97% 84% 79% 89% 99% 78% 77% 95% 97%

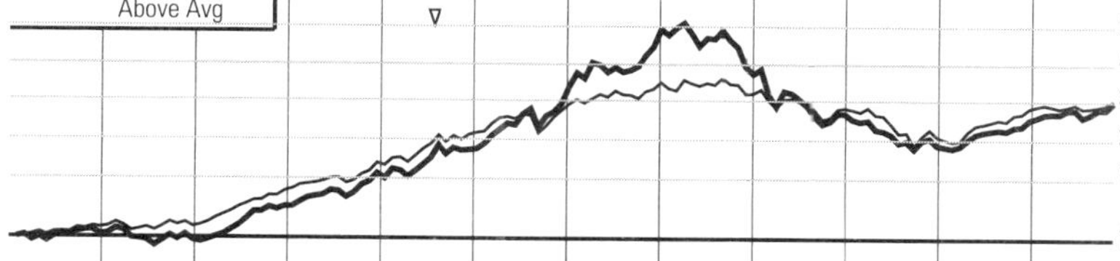

▼ Manager Change
∇ Partial Manager Change

Growth of $10,000
▬ Investment Values of Fund
— Investment Values of S&P 500

Performance Quartile (within Category)

History

	1993	1994	1995	1996	1997	1998	1999	2000	2001	2002	2003	12-04
NAV	24.42	22.71	25.67	27.47	30.99	53.30	83.43	54.80	38.46	29.01	36.17	44.80
Total Return %	3.43	-6.73	36.22	27.85	29.70	73.39	64.90	-32.42	-29.20	-24.02	25.31	23.89
+/-S&P 500	-6.63	-8.04	-1.31	4.91	-3.65	44.82	43.86	-23.32	-17.32	-1.93	-3.36	13.02
+/-Russ 1000Gr	0.56	-9.35	-0.96	4.73	-0.79	34.68	31.74	-10.00	-8.78	3.86	-4.44	17.59
Income Return %	1.04	0.28	10.04	0.71	0.36	0.45	0.35	0.00	0.61	0.56	0.60	0.03
Capital Return %	2.39	-7.01	26.18	27.14	29.34	72.94	64.55	-32.42	-29.81	-24.58	24.71	23.86
Total Rtn % Rank Cat	81	86	24	7	36	2	9	93	83	27	62	1
Income $	0.25	0.07	2.28	0.18	0.10	0.14	0.19	0.00	0.34	0.21	0.17	0.01
Capital Gains $	0.45	0.00	2.99	5.32	4.46	0.30	4.08	1.75	0.00	0.00	0.00	0.00
Expense Ratio %	1.05	1.02	0.99	0.92	0.91	0.91	0.87	0.85	0.84	0.83	0.88	0.89
Income Ratio %	0.87	0.57	0.62	0.67	0.33	0.39	0.40	-0.13	0.63	0.56	0.52	0.06
Turnover Rate %	99	102	147	137	123	54	40	27	50	53	44	14
Net Assets $mil	3,516	2,504	3,057	4,071	6,004	15,797	36,909	24,253	15,082	9,476	9,886	9,590

Performance 12-31-04

	1st Qtr	2nd Qtr	3rd Qtr	4th Qtr	Total
2000	5.51	-12.28	-2.10	-25.42	-32.42
2001	-24.60	6.75	-19.68	9.51	-29.20
2002	-5.72	-11.58	-11.67	3.18	-24.02
2003	-0.52	12.86	1.20	10.29	25.31
2004	5.53	3.62	0.33	12.93	23.89

Trailing	Total Return%	+/- S&P 500	+/- Russ 1000Gr	%Rank Cat	Growth of $10,000
3 Mo	12.93	3.70	3.76	10	11,293
6 Mo	13.30	6.11	9.83	1	11,330
1 Yr	23.89	13.02	17.59	1	12,389
3 Yr Avg	5.66	2.08	5.84	7	11,796
5 Yr Avg	-10.81	-8.51	-1.52	78	5,644
10 Yr Avg	13.81	1.74	4.22	4	36,459
15 Yr Avg	12.82	1.89	3.32	9	61,065

Tax Analysis	Tax-Adj Rtn%	%Rank Cat	Tax-Cost Rat	%Rank Cat
3 Yr (estimated)	5.50	6	0.15	26
5 Yr (estimated)	-11.05	75	0.27	16
10 Yr (estimated)	11.78	5	1.78	62

Potential Capital Gain Exposure: 87% of assets

Rating and Risk

Time Period	Load-Adj Return %	Morningstar Rtn vs Cat	Morningstar Risk vs Cat	Morningstar Risk-Adj Rating
1 Yr	23.89			
3 Yr	5.66	High	-Avg	★★★★★
5 Yr	-10.81	-Avg	+Avg	★★
10 Yr	13.81	High	+Avg	★★★★
Incept	13.65			

Other Measures	Standard Index S&P 500	Best Fit Index Morningstar Large Core TR
Alpha	2.5	3.2
Beta	0.82	0.83
R-Squared	78	78
Standard Deviation	14.74	
Mean	5.66	
Sharpe Ratio	0.29	

Portfolio Analysis 11-30-04

Share change since 10-04 Total Stocks:23	Sector	PE	YTD Ret%	% Assets
eBay	Consumer	81.6	80.07	18.74
UnitedHealth Group	Health	23.8	51.38	13.45
Roche Holding	Health	—	—	7.08
Bank of America	Financial	12.3	21.50	6.52
Genentech	Health	78.6	16.36	5.97
Nike B	Goods	23.6	33.94	5.89
⊖ Electronic Arts	Software	30.9	29.36	5.14
Wells Fargo	Financial	15.5	8.97	3.55
⊖ Procter & Gamble	Goods	23.3	12.38	3.06
Goldman Sachs Group	Financial	12.3	6.49	3.02
SLM	Financial	15.8	44.21	3.01
⊖ 3M Company	Ind Mtrls	23.5	-1.75	2.70
⊖ Countrywide Financial	Financial	9.0	48.15	2.65
Qualcomm	Hardware	42.0	58.20	2.59
Kohl's	Consumer	25.5	9.41	2.57
Yahoo	Media	95.1	67.36	2.01
Texas Instruments	Hardware	21.1	-15.90	1.96
AutoZone	Consumer	13.8	7.16	1.79
Amazon.com	Consumer	55.5	-15.83	1.37
⊖ Forest Laboratories	Health	18.0	-27.41	1.28

Current Investment Style

Value Blnd Growth — Large Mid Small

Market Cap	%
Giant	71.6
Large	25.5
Mid	2.9
Small	0.0
Micro	0.0
Avg $mil: 48,338	

Value Measures		Rel Category
Price/Earnings	23.63	1.11
Price/Book	5.07	1.57
Price/Sales	3.11	1.45
Price/Cash Flow	15.53	1.41
Dividend Yield %	0.73	0.95

Growth Measures	%	Rel Category
Long-Term Erngs	15.17	1.08
Book Value	13.56	1.07
Sales	11.99	1.41
Cash Flow	34.76	2.10
Historical Erngs	27.93	1.93

Profitability	%	Rel Category
Return on Equity	20.99	1.17
Return on Assets	12.64	1.35
Net Margin	16.97	1.38

Sector Weightings	% of Stocks	Rel S&P 500	3 Year High	Low
Info	13.14	0.61		
Software	5.27	1.23	13	5
Hardware	5.81	0.57	8	3
Media	2.06	0.54	19	2
Telecom	0.00	0.00	3	0
Service	74.90	1.61		
Health	30.57	2.45	32	11
Consumer	25.10	2.76	25	10
Business	0.00	0.00	0	0
Financial	19.23	0.93	27	19
Mfg	11.96	0.37		
Goods	9.19	0.98	10	2
Ind Mtrls	2.77	0.22	4	1
Energy	0.00	0.00	10	0
Utilities	0.00	0.00	0	0

Composition

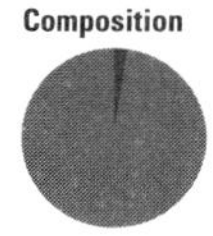

Cash	2.5
Stocks	97.5
Bonds	0.0
Other	0.0
Foreign (% of Stock)	3.4

Morningstar's Take by Bridget Hughes 10-14-04

Janus Twenty is a keeper.

We've come full circle on this large-growth offering. While generally supportive of this fund in the late 1990s and early 2000s, we regularly questioned whether or not it was getting too big for its concentrated, aggressive approach. The bear market proved it was indeed, the offering came crashing down, and we were disappointed. Things have changed, however, in three ways. First, the easy one: The fund is much, much smaller than it was at its peak, and with roughly $10 billion in assets, we think it can now effectively work its methods. Second, Janus' growth funds don't have the kind of stock overlap they once did. That too should make trading stocks easier.

The third change is much less tangible, but also extremely important. Simply put, manager Scott Schoelzel learned some lessons during the bear market. As a result, he has no plans to reopen the fund. He has also developed a more stringent sell discipline, which he won't specify for competitive reasons, to keep him from hanging on to stocks on their way down for too long. And he has built a broader portfolio. Sure, it remains extremely concentrated in its top picks. However, those same picks aren't highly correlated with each other, which means they shouldn't all tank at the same time and/or to the same degree. That's no accident, and while Twenty remains an aggressive pick (16% of assets in eBay!), this diversification should help control volatility and risk some.

One question is whether or not Schoelzel can provide enough reward buying a variety of large-cap stocks. The good news is that Janus has the analytic resources to do original research, and Schoelzel has enough experience and a strong track record. And since October 2002, the fund has performed well, even though its larger-cap bias was a headwind. Costs remain very reasonable, and the Janus organization is progressing nicely after getting mixed up in the fund-trading scandal.

Address:	100 Fillmore St Denver CO 80206 800-525-3713
Web Address:	www.janus.com
Inception:	04-30-85
Advisor:	Janus
Subadvisor:	None
NTF Plans:	Fidelity Retail-NTF, Schwab OneSource

Minimum Purchase:	Closed	Add: —	IRA: —
Min Auto Inv Plan:	Closed	Add: —	
Sales Fees:	No-load		
Management Fee:	0.64%		
Actual Fees:	Mgt:0.64%	Dist:	
Expense Projections:	3Yr:$278	5Yr:$482	10Yr:$1073
Income Distrib:	Annually		

Janus Venture

Ticker	Load	NAV	Yield	Total Assets	Mstar Category
JAVTX	Closed	$58.59	0.0%	$1,411 mil	Small Growth

Governance and Management

Fiduciary Grade: C

Portfolio Manager(s)

Will Bales has been on board since 1997. Former comanager Jonathan Coleman stepped down in late 2000 to become an assistant portfolio manager on Janus Fund. Coleman now runs Janus Enterprise.

Strategy

Manager Will Bales follows the typical Janus approach. He looks for well-managed, fast-growing companies with improving returns on invested capital. This once led to a very aggressive portfolio stuffed full of high P/E stocks, but now consistency in earnings and valuation are more important. Bales has been willing to sacrifice high growth rates in favor of diversification and stability.

Historical Profile

Return Average
Risk Above Avg
Rating ★★ Below Avg

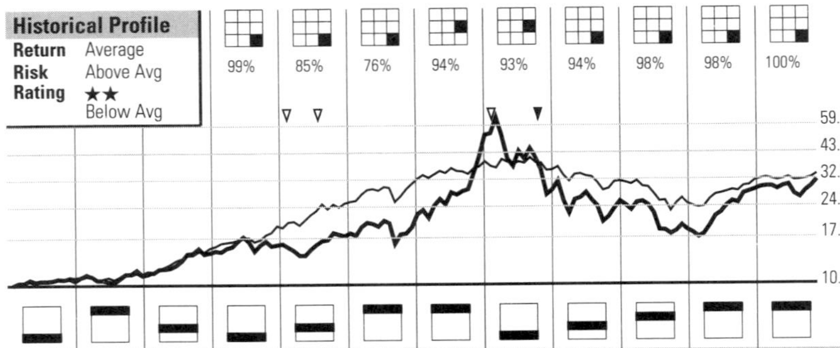

Investment Style
Equity
Stock %

▼ Manager Change
▽ Partial Manager Change

Growth of $10,000
— Investment Values of Fund
— Investment Values of S&P 500

Performance Quartile (within Category)

1993	1994	1995	1996	1997	1998	1999	2000	2001	2002	2003	12-04	History
48.88	48.68	54.10	53.06	50.05	57.14	121.67	49.94	43.98	32.00	49.84	58.59	NAV
9.08	5.46	26.46	8.02	12.61	23.22	140.71	-45.77	-11.93	-27.24	55.75	17.56	Total Return %
-0.98	4.15	-11.07	-14.92	-20.74	-5.35	119.67	-36.67	-0.05	-5.15	27.08	6.69	+/-S&P 500
-4.29	7.89	-4.58	-3.24	-0.34	21.99	97.62	-23.34	-2.70	3.02	7.21	3.25	+/-Russ 2000 Gr
1.07	0.06	7.41	0.00	0.14	0.01	0.00	0.00	0.00	0.00	0.00	0.00	Income Return %
8.01	5.40	19.05	8.02	12.47	23.21	140.71	-45.77	-11.93	-27.24	55.75	17.56	Capital Return %
82	18	73	88	71	7	7	99	54	48	12	20	Total Rtn % Rank Cat
0.53	0.03	3.61	0.00	0.07	0.00	0.00	0.00	0.00	0.00	0.00	0.00	Income $
4.37	2.84	3.85	5.28	9.29	4.41	14.26	16.38	0.00	0.00	0.00	0.00	Capital Gains $
0.97	0.96	0.91	0.88	0.92	0.94	0.92	0.86	0.86	0.87	0.93	0.90	Expense Ratio %
1.29	0.27	0.29	-0.33	0.11	-0.29	-0.55	-0.35	-0.36	-0.73	-0.67	-0.74	Income Ratio %
139	114	113	136	146	90	104	87	70	90	75	61	Turnover Rate %
1,779	1,496	1,790	1,705	1,234	1,246	2,876	1,487	1,175	743	1,408	1,411	Net Assets $mil

Performance 12-31-04

	1st Qtr	2nd Qtr	3rd Qtr	4th Qtr	Total
2000	-0.74	-16.10	-6.75	-30.17	-45.77
2001	-22.69	25.54	-27.67	25.44	-11.93
2002	-1.43	-11.03	-20.79	4.75	-27.24
2003	-4.44	26.81	11.22	15.56	55.75
2004	3.51	1.71	-6.33	19.21	17.56

Trailing	Total Return%	+/- S&P 500	+/- Russ 2000 Gr	%Rank Cat	Growth of $10,000
3 Mo	19.21	9.98	4.13	2	11,921
6 Mo	11.66	4.47	3.50	15	11,166
1 Yr	17.56	6.69	3.25	20	11,756
3 Yr Avg	10.03	6.45	4.24	19	13,321
5 Yr Avg	-8.65	-6.35	-5.08	86	6,361
10 Yr Avg	11.25	-0.82	4.13	41	29,040
15 Yr Avg	11.74	0.81	4.24	41	52,860

Tax Analysis	Tax-Adj Rtn%	%Rank Cat	Tax-Cost Rat	%Rank Cat
3 Yr (estimated)	10.03	14	0.00	1
5 Yr (estimated)	-9.55	85	0.99	42
10 Yr (estimated)	8.90	40	2.11	78

Potential Capital Gain Exposure: 23% of assets

Rating and Risk

Time Period	Load-Adj Return %	Morningstar Rtn vs Cat	Morningstar Risk vs Cat	Morningstar Risk-Adj Rating
1 Yr	17.56			
3 Yr	10.03	+Avg	+Avg	★★★★
5 Yr	-8.65	-Avg	+Avg	★★
10 Yr	11.25	Avg	+Avg	★★
Incept	13.90			

Other Measures	Standard Index S&P 500	Best Fit Index Russ 2000 Gr
Alpha	7.1	4.3
Beta	1.12	0.95
R-Squared	61	93

Standard Deviation	23.91
Mean	10.03
Sharpe Ratio	0.37

Morningstar's Take by Dan McNeela 12-16-04

Janus Venture is flashing its potential again, but it's got more work ahead.

This fund has put together a solid year in 2004. Its 14% year-to-date gain through Dec. 15 ranks in the top quartile of Morningstar's small-growth category. Once again, the fund caught fire amid a strong market rally. In the three-month period ending Nov. 30, 2004, it gained 21.1% while the category average added just 15.6%. A buyout of former top holding Artisan Components, a chip-design specialist, provided a welcome boost.

Manager Will Bales has also benefited from going off the beaten path. Few investors were initially interested in the June 2004 IPO of commercial real estate firm CB Richard Ellis, but the fund has already posted a better than 50% gain in it. Bales couldn't pass up the chance to buy the firm given its low price to cash flow ratio and its healthy growth prospects.

While it's encouraging to see the fund thrive during rallies, we think it has more to prove during tougher markets. Bales says he's learned lessons by struggling through the bear market, but other signs point to continued aggressiveness. In the three-year period ending Nov. 30, 2004, its standard deviation of returns (a common measure of volatility) is higher than nearly 80% of its category peers. Bales also made Infocrossing Inc, a private placement, a top holding. Bales says that Janus lawyers sign off on all such deals, but other funds have gotten into trouble with pricing these thinly traded securities in the past.

The fund has also been building its analyst resources by adding two researchers to the small-cap team in 2004. One was an internal hire while the other had experience with investment firm Robertson Stevens. Bales is still looking for a fifth analyst, however, to beef up the tech research.

The prevailing winds here are positive, although we'd like to see more stability from the fund and the team.

Address:	100 Fillmore St Denver CO 80206 800-525-3713	Minimum Purchase:	Closed	Add: —	IRA: —
		Min Auto Inv Plan:	Closed	Add: —	
		Sales Fees:	No-load		
Web Address:	www.janus.com	Management Fee:	0.64%		
Inception:	04-30-85	Actual Fees:	Mgt:0.64%	Dist:	
Advisor:	Janus	Expense Projections:	3Yr:$296	5Yr:$515	10Yr:$1143
Subadvisor:	None	Income Distrib:	Annually		

NTF Plans: Fidelity Retail-NTF, Schwab OneSource

Portfolio Analysis 11-30-04

Share change since 10-04 Total Stocks:134	Sector	PE	YTD Ret%	% Assets
⊖ Euronet Worldwide	Business	75.8	44.24	3.58
CB Richard Ellis Group	Financial	—	—	2.55
Infocrossing Inc Private	—	—	—	2.25
TIBCO Software	Software	83.0	97.05	2.15
Talx	Business	38.1	13.04	2.13
⊖ Centene	Financial	25.4	102.43	2.02
Ultimate Software Pp	—	—	—	1.72
K2	Goods	19.1	4.41	1.57
iPayment	Business	—	46.12	1.48
Lions Gate Entertainment	Software	—	137.05	1.47
Jarden	Goods	27.5	58.89	1.47
Marvel Enterprises	Goods	20.2	5.53	1.41
MGI Pharma	Health	—	36.14	1.38
Open Solutions	Business	—	47.50	1.33
⊕ Sonic Solutions	Software	31.1	46.67	1.32
Quiksilver	Goods	23.0	68.02	1.27
I-Flow	Health	—	30.96	1.26
Pharmion	Health	—	176.79	1.25
Western Oil Sands	Energy	—	—	1.23
Advisory Board	Business	33.4	5.89	1.21

Current Investment Style

Value Blnd Growth / Large Mid Small

Market Cap	%
Giant	0.0
Large	0.0
Mid	27.7
Small	50.9
Micro	21.4
Avg $mil:	819

Value Measures		Rel Category
Price/Earnings	26.80	1.23
Price/Book	2.79	1.06
Price/Sales	1.43	0.95
Price/Cash Flow	7.32	0.91
Dividend Yield %	0.08	0.26

Growth Measures	%	Rel Category
Long-Term Erngs	19.43	1.12
Book Value	3.39	0.53
Sales	12.44	1.93
Cash Flow	6.57	0.49
Historical Erngs	4.28	0.32

Profitability	%	Rel Category
Return on Equity	7.94	0.80
Return on Assets	3.78	0.86
Net Margin	4.54	0.66

Sector Weightings	% of Stocks	Rel S&P 500	3 Year High	3 Year Low
Info	22.16	1.03		
Software	9.57	2.23	10	0
Hardware	10.19	1.00	15	2
Media	0.00	0.00	7	0
Telecom	2.40	0.76	3	0
Service	61.51	1.33		
Health	13.35	1.07	25	12
Consumer	10.17	1.12	22	10
Business	26.10	6.44	28	18
Financial	11.89	0.57	12	5
Mfg	16.34	0.51		
Goods	8.56	0.92	9	3
Ind Mtrls	3.88	0.31	7	3
Energy	3.90	0.54	4	0
Utilities	0.00	0.00	0	0

Composition

Cash	0.1
Stocks	99.6
Bonds	0.0
Other	0.3
Foreign (% of Stock)	7.7

Janus Worldwide

Ticker	Load	NAV	Yield	Total Assets	Mstar Category
JAWWX	None	$41.41	0.8%	$7,119 mil	World Stock

Governance and Management

Fiduciary Grade: C

Portfolio Manager(s)

In July 2004, Jason Yee replaced Laurence Chang as manager of the fund. Yee, who also manages Janus Global Opportunities, cut his teeth as an analyst at Janus from 1992 until 1996. He left the firm to work at a small money-management shop in Denver, but returned to Janus in 2000.

Strategy

Jason Yee will not buy stocks unless he can get them at a bargain. He likes to grab a company when it's selling at a noticeable discount to his estimate of the stock's worth. This is not bottom-of-the-barrel value investing, though: Yee also wants companies that boast strong free cash flows and impressive franchises. At another fund, he has invested across the globe and across market caps, but that was with a much smaller asset base. It's unlikely he will have as much flexibility here. He aims to hold a portfolio of between 40 and 70 names with minimal exposure to emerging markets.

Historical Profile

Return Below Avg
Risk Average
Rating ★★ Below Avg

Investment Style Equity Stock %: 89% (1993), 97%, 87%, 91%, 90%, 85%, 85%, 99%, 91%

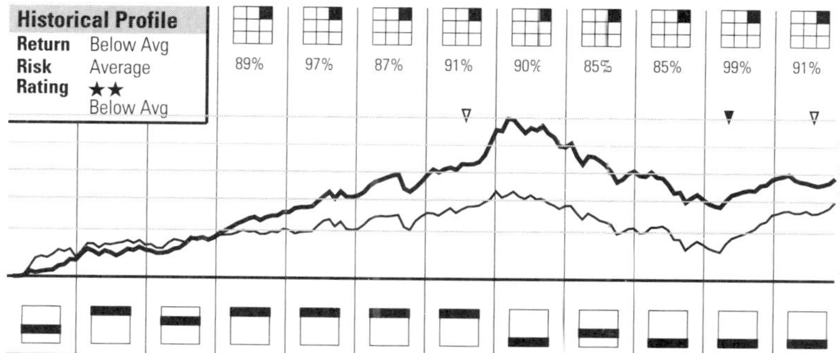

History

1993	1994	1995	1996	1997	1998	1999	2000	2001	2002	2003	12-04	History
25.03	24.39	28.40	33.69	37.78	47.36	76.43	56.83	43.84	32.13	39.54	41.41	NAV
28.41	3.61	21.90	26.40	20.48	25.87	64.37	-16.87	-22.88	-26.01	24.23	5.54	Total Return %
-4.15	-4.17	10.69	20.35	18.70	5.94	37.34	-2.68	-1.46	-10.07	-14.36	-14.71	+/-MSCI EAFE
5.91	-1.47	1.18	12.92	4.72	1.55	39.42	-3.68	-6.08	-6.12	-8.88	-9.18	+/-MSCI World
1.38	2.15	1.07	0.54	0.58	0.51	0.06	0.99	0.02	0.70	1.12	0.79	Income Return %
27.03	1.46	20.83	25.86	19.90	25.36	64.31	-17.86	-22.90	-26.71	23.11	4.75	Capital Return %
69	9	28	4	25	16	17	78	74	86	93	97	Total Rtn % Rank Cat
0.28	0.54	0.26	0.15	0.20	0.19	0.03	0.75	0.01	0.31	0.36	0.31	Income $
0.38	1.01	1.07	2.04	2.60	0.00	1.28	6.17	0.00	0.00	0.00	0.00	Capital Gains $
1.32	1.12	1.23	1.01	0.95	0.92	0.88	0.86	0.85	0.86	0.92	—	Expense Ratio %
0.92	0.42	0.99	0.73	0.65	0.47	0.07	0.13	0.53	0.62	0.99	—	Income Ratio %
124	158	142	80	79	86	68	58	78	73	108	—	Turnover Rate %
935	1,543	1,975	5,046	10,568	16,323	33,803	33,144	21,679	12,815	10,961	7,119	Net Assets $mil

Performance 12-31-04

	1st Qtr	2nd Qtr	3rd Qtr	4th Qtr	Total
2000	11.81	-8.45	-5.73	-13.86	-16.87
2001	-17.16	4.12	-20.80	12.91	-22.88
2002	-0.89	-12.57	-17.56	3.56	-26.01
2003	-8.37	16.34	3.01	13.14	24.23
2004	5.51	-8.39	-2.09	11.52	5.54

Trailing	Total Return%	+/- MSCI EAFE	+/- MSCI World	%Rank Cat	Growth of $10,000
3 Mo	11.52	-3.80	-0.42	71	11,152
6 Mo	9.18	-5.82	-1.64	69	10,918
1 Yr	5.54	-14.71	-9.18	97	10,554
3 Yr Avg	-1.01	-12.90	-7.96	98	9,700
5 Yr Avg	-9.06	-7.93	-6.61	93	6,220
10 Yr Avg	9.10	3.48	1.01	47	23,892
15 Yr Avg	—	—	—	—	—

Tax Analysis	Tax-Adj Rtn%	%Rank Cat	Tax-Cost Rat	%Rank Cat
3 Yr (estimated)	-1.33	97	0.32	43
5 Yr (estimated)	-9.66	91	0.66	45
10 Yr (estimated)	8.06	43	0.95	29

Potential Capital Gain Exposure: -76% of assets

Rating and Risk

Time Period	Load-Adj Return %	Morningstar Rtn vs Cat	Morningstar Risk vs Cat	Morningstar Risk-Adj Rating
1 Yr	5.54			
3 Yr	-1.01	Low	Avg	★
5 Yr	-9.06	Low	Avg	★★
10 Yr	9.10	Avg	Avg	★★★
Incept	11.28			

Other Measures	Standard Index S&P 500	Best Fit Index MSCI World
Alpha	-10.9	-6.3
Beta	0.92	0.98
R-Squared	89	92
Standard Deviation	15.18	
Mean	-1.01	
Sharpe Ratio	-0.16	

Portfolio Analysis 11-30-04

Share change since 10-04 Total Stocks:65	Sector	Country	% Assets
British Sky Broadcasting	Media	U.K.	5.65
IAC/InterActiveCorp	Consumer	United States	4.43
J.P. Morgan Chase & Co.	Financial	United States	3.92
Walt Disney	Media	United States	3.16
Tyco International	Ind Mtrls	United States	3.12
Diageo	Goods	U.K.	2.50
UnitedHealth Group	Health	United States	2.35
Nestle	Goods	Switzerland	2.28
Heineken	Goods	Netherlands	2.25
⊖ Reliance Industries Ltd	Ind Mtrls	India	2.11
Reed Elsevier	Media	U.K.	2.09
Smiths Grp	Ind Mtrls	U.K.	2.00
Grupo Televisa ADR	Media	Mexico	1.94
WPP Grp	Business	U.K.	1.94
Koninklijke Philips Elec	Goods	Netherlands	1.72
Citigroup	Financial	United States	1.68
Roche Holding	Health	Switzerland	1.68
Anheuser-Busch Companies	Goods	United States	1.61
Millea Hldgs	Financial	Japan	1.58
Berkshire Hathaway B	Financial	United States	1.57

Current Investment Style

Value Blnd Growth — Large Growth

Market Cap	%
Giant	53.5
Large	39.2
Mid	7.3
Small	0.0
Micro	0.0
Avg $mil: 28,181	

Value Measures		Rel Category
Price/Earnings	15.54	0.98
Price/Book	1.37	0.62
Price/Sales	1.40	1.20
Price/Cash Flow	4.96	0.78
Dividend Yield %	1.88	1.00

Growth Measures	%	Rel Category
Long-Term Erngs	12.69	1.05
Book Value	1.51	0.68
Sales	3.77	0.90
Cash Flow	10.90	1.86
Historical Erngs	17.30	2.02

Composition			
Cash	8.7	Bonds	0.0
Stocks	90.7	Other	0.6
Foreign (% of Stock)			67.2

Sector Weightings	% of Stocks	Rel MSCI EAFE	3 Year High	3 Year Low
Info	20.63	1.24		
Software	0.52	0.48	4	1
Hardware	0.00	0.00	12	0
Media	18.50	8.11	19	5
Telecom	1.61	0.17	4	1
Service	39.44	0.88		
Health	8.24	1.13	18	8
Consumer	7.51	1.49	8	3
Business	3.13	0.58	7	2
Financial	20.56	0.76	25	16
Mfg	39.93	1.03		
Goods	25.07	1.84	25	11
Ind Mtrls	11.79	0.96	23	9
Energy	2.98	0.41	10	3
Utilities	0.09	0.02	1	0

Regional Exposure	% Stock		
UK/W. Europe	42	N. America	33
Japan	14	Latn America	4
Asia X Japan	8	Other	0

Country Exposure	% Stock		
United States	33	Switzerland	8
U.K.	22	Netherlands	6
Japan	14		

Morningstar's Take by Gareth Lyons 12-20-04

Janus Worldwide remains a work in progress.

From a near-term perspective, the midyear arrival of new manager Jason Yee was poorly timed. Yee slashed this fund's huge emerging-markets stake in the third quarter, just as many of those names were regaining steam. Worst still, a flood of redemptions forced the manager to maintain a hefty cash stake, further damaging returns. Thus, the fund is set to post its fifth-consecutive year of subpar returns.

As hard to stomach as that record is, we view Yee's arrival as a long-term positive. The manager will use the same approach as the one he has successfully plied at his other charge, Janus Global Opportunities. (This offering has a larger-cap tilt, however.) He looks to invest in firms with strong competitive advantages and focused management teams, spreading the portfolio across about 60 names mostly from developed regions. To be sure, many rivals do the same. But Yee is a long-term and distinctly thrifty stock-picker, often waiting to buy shares of firms that are down on their luck or have depressed valuations. Given that this fund's abysmal five-year record owes largely to his predecessors' tendency to overpay for growth names, we think Yee's attention to valuation will provide this offering with the ballast it has sorely lacked in downturns. Moreover, we think Yee's contrarian bets have the potential to goose returns--his recent aggressive purchase of InterActiveCorp after its earnings shortfall has paid off nicely, for example.

Yee's abilities aside, we're less sanguine about the depth and quality of research that backs him up at this time. Yee's valuelike strategy requires a much more-robust research effort on individual names than what the analysts here have been used to. Granted, the manager explains that the team is adapting to the style shift and that more hires are on the way. Still, we'd rather watch this fund from the sidelines until the team gets rounded out and up to speed.

Address:	100 Fillmore St Denver CO 80206 800-525-3713
Web Address:	www.janus.com
Inception:	05-15-91
Advisor:	Janus
Subadvisor:	None
NTF Plans:	Fidelity Retail-NTF, Schwab OneSource

Minimum Purchase:	$2500	Add: $100	IRA: $500
Min Auto Inv Plan:	$500	Add: $100	
Sales Fees:	No-load, 2.00%R		
Management Fee:	0.60%		
Actual Fees:	Mgt:0.60%	Dist:	
Expense Projections:	3Yr:$281	5Yr:$488	10Yr:$1084
Income Distrib:	Annually		

Jensen J

Ticker	Load	NAV	Yield	Total Assets	Mstar Category
JENSX	12b-1 only	$24.35	0.7%	$2,834 mil	Large Growth

Governance and Management

Fiduciary Grade: A

Portfolio Manager(s)

Although fund founder Val Jensen stepped down in early March 2004, the fund has long been run by a team. Gary Hibler has been on board since the fund's 1992 inception. Robert Zagunis joined the team in 1993, Robert Millen joined in 2000, and Eric Schoenstein was promoted from analyst to manager in 2004. They're supported by two analysts, Winfield Evans and Gary Richards.

Strategy

The team screens nearly 10,000 publicly traded companies for those that have delivered returns on equity of at least 15% in each of the past 10 years. That whittles the pool of candidates down to 100 to 125 names. The managers then analyze those companies to determine which ones have the best prospects, and they buy those trading at discounts of at least 40% to their estimate of intrinsic value. That has resulted in a concentrated portfolio. Although turnover is low, management will sell a holding that doesn't deliver an ROE of at least 15% or reach full value. The fund is concentrated.

Historical Profile

Return High
Risk Low
Rating ★★★★★ Highest

Investment Style
Equity
Stock %

97%	95%	99%	92%	86%	93%	98%	99%	99%

▼ Manager Change
▽ Partial Manager Change

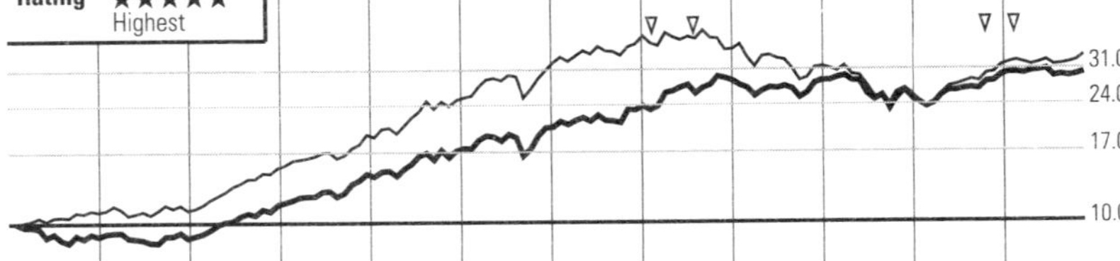

Growth of $10,000
— Investment Values of Fund
— Investment Values of S&P 500

Performance Quartile (within Category)

1993	1994	1995	1996	1997	1998	1999	2000	2001	2002	2003	12-04	History
9.27	8.96	11.26	13.49	16.14	18.61	21.67	22.70	22.62	20.07	23.13	24.35	NAV
-7.27	-1.77	27.61	21.06	22.99	16.70	16.71	20.04	0.03	-10.97	16.06	6.01	Total Return %
-17.33	-3.08	-9.92	-1.88	-10.36	-11.87	-4.33	29.14	11.91	11.12	-12.61	-4.86	+/-S&P 500
-10.14	-4.39	-9.57	-2.06	-7.50	-22.01	-16.45	42.46	20.45	16.91	-13.69	-0.29	+/-Russ 1000Gr
1.30	1.56	1.80	1.15	0.58	1.31	0.25	0.41	0.34	0.31	0.75	0.71	Income Return %
-8.57	-3.33	25.81	19.91	22.41	15.39	16.46	19.63	-0.31	-11.28	15.31	5.30	Capital Return %
100	54	78	38	70	89	88	1	2	2	99	64	Total Rtn % Rank Cat
0.13	0.14	0.16	0.13	0.08	0.21	0.05	0.08	0.08	0.07	0.15	0.16	Income $
0.00	0.00	0.00	0.00	0.37	0.00	0.00	3.07	0.00	0.00	0.00	0.00	Capital Gains $
0.89	1.13	1.20	1.20	1.32	1.02	0.96	0.94	0.95	1.00	0.90	0.88	Expense Ratio %
1.54	1.36	1.48	1.23	0.61	1.44	0.27	0.31	0.45	0.23	0.62	0.71	Income Ratio %
—	5	11	48	24	21	14	32	4	1	7	5	Turnover Rate %
9	9	11	13	18	23	27	40	118	1,051	1,718	2,547	Net Assets $mil

Performance 12-31-04

	1st Qtr	2nd Qtr	3rd Qtr	4th Qtr	Total
2000	9.84	5.96	-0.06	3.20	20.04
2001	-10.67	5.77	-6.54	13.26	0.03
2002	3.30	-12.43	-8.65	7.74	-10.97
2003	-5.40	9.70	1.22	10.49	16.06
2004	1.01	3.11	-5.05	7.19	6.01

Trailing	Total Return%	+/- S&P 500	+/- Russ 1000Gr	%Rank Cat	Growth of $10,000
3 Mo	7.19	-2.04	-1.98	93	10,719
6 Mo	1.78	-5.41	-1.69	89	10,178
1 Yr	6.01	-4.86	-0.29	64	10,601
3 Yr Avg	3.09	-0.49	3.27	18	10,956
5 Yr Avg	5.64	7.94	14.93	1	13,157
10 Yr Avg	13.03	0.96	3.44	6	34,036
15 Yr Avg	—	—	—	—	—

Tax Analysis	Tax-Adj Rtn%	%Rank Cat	Tax-Cost Rat	%Rank Cat
3 Yr (estimated)	2.87	16	0.21	36
5 Yr (estimated)	4.90	1	0.70	43
10 Yr (estimated)	12.39	4	0.57	9

Potential Capital Gain Exposure: 10% of assets

Rating and Risk

Time Period	Load-Adj Return %	Morningstar Rtn vs Cat	Morningstar Risk vs Cat	Morningstar Risk-Adj Rating
1 Yr	6.01			
3 Yr	3.09	+Avg	-Avg	★★★★
5 Yr	5.64	High	Low	★★★★★
10 Yr	13.03	High	Low	★★★★★
Incept	9.69			

Other Measures	Standard Index S&P 500	Best Fit Index Morningstar Large Core TR
Alpha	-0.1	0.6
Beta	0.78	0.80
R-Squared	81	83
Standard Deviation	13.41	
Mean	3.09	
Sharpe Ratio	0.13	

Morningstar's Take by Greg Carlson 12-23-04

Although management's disciplined approach isn't foolproof, Jensen Portfolio is a sound long-term investment.

This year has been modestly disappointing for this fund's shareholders. Because of a few high-profile missteps, such as Coca-Cola, Merck, and Pfizer, the fund has gained just 5% for the year to date through December 22, lagging nearly two thirds of its large-growth peers. Management's stringent investment criteria--the team only buys firms that have churned out returns on equity (ROE) of at least 15% in each of the past 10 years and sell at a 40% discount to their estimate of intrinsic value--has led to a compact portfolio of just 20 to 25 holdings, which courts substantial stock-specific risk.

One of the biggest sources of trouble for the fund this year was Merck, a longtime holding. On September 30, the firm was forced to recall its arthritis drug, Vioxx, after a study revealed potentially dangerous side effects. The fund's management team, which had already been concerned about Merck's prospects after two drugs in late-stage trials failed to pan out, decided to sell the stock that day. However, the damage was already done, as Merck had declined 30% for the year by the market's close. Merck's disappointing performance, in spite of the firm's long history of solid execution, shows that past is not necessarily prologue. Thus, the ROE screen used by this fund's management team doesn't mean its holdings will always continue to deliver the goods; fundamental analysis is an equally important part of the process.

Nevertheless, we wouldn't make too much of this bump in the road: The fund's long-term record is superb, and management's focus on steady growers has led to a very smooth ride. As such, our confidence in the team is unshaken. Its experience and prudent strategy, as well as the fund's modest costs, make this a fine core holding.

Portfolio Analysis 09-30-04

Share change since 06-04 Total Stocks:25	Sector	PE	YTD Ret%	% Assets
⊕ Stryker	Health	46.2	13.52	5.84
⊕ Omnicom Group	Business	21.6	-2.33	5.26
⊕ MBNA	Financial	14.0	15.53	5.24
⊕ Gen Elec	Ind Mtrls	22.8	20.68	5.08
⊕ Emerson Electric	Ind Mtrls	22.8	11.09	4.97
⊕ Pfizer	Health	22.0	-22.31	4.83
⊕ 3M Company	Ind Mtrls	23.5	-1.75	4.60
⊕ Procter & Gamble	Goods	23.3	12.38	4.38
⊕ Gannett	Media	17.1	-7.23	4.34
⊕ Abbott Laboratories	Health	22.1	2.61	4.16
⊕ State Street	Financial	15.3	-4.41	4.13
⊕ Medtronic	Health	30.7	2.68	4.07
⊕ McGraw-Hill Companies	Media	22.7	32.94	4.03
⊕ Patterson Companies	Health	37.8	35.62	3.99
⊕ Equifax	Business	17.6	15.19	3.98
⊕ Johnson & Johnson	Health	20.6	25.17	3.92
⊕ PepsiCo	Goods	22.5	13.82	3.63
⊕ Automatic Data Processin	Business	26.9	13.46	3.60
⊕ Fannie Mae	Financial	9.1	-2.33	3.54
⊕ Clorox	Goods	23.2	23.93	3.53

Current Investment Style

Value Blnd Growth; Large Mid Small

Market Cap	%
Giant	43.2
Large	47.2
Mid	8.1
Small	1.6
Micro	0.0
Avg $mil: 34,643	

Value Measures		Rel Category
Price/Earnings	18.60	0.87
Price/Book	4.06	1.26
Price/Sales	2.71	1.26
Price/Cash Flow	11.29	1.03
Dividend Yield %	1.64	2.13

Growth Measures	%	Rel Category
Long-Term Erngs	11.83	0.84
Book Value	19.78	1.56
Sales	7.42	0.87
Cash Flow	13.00	0.79
Historical Erngs	10.03	0.69

Profitability	%	Rel Category
Return on Equity	26.43	1.47
Return on Assets	12.65	1.35
Net Margin	15.14	1.23

Sector Weightings	% of Stocks	Rel S&P 500	3 Year High	3 Year Low
Info	8.48	0.39		
Software	0.00	0.00	2	0
Hardware	0.00	0.00	5	0
Media	8.48	2.21	8	2
Telecom	0.00	0.00	0	0
Service	59.34	1.28		
Health	30.49	2.44	31	22
Consumer	0.00	0.00	0	0
Business	15.77	3.89	18	15
Financial	13.08	0.63	23	12
Mfg	32.18	1.00		
Goods	17.35	1.86	21	12
Ind Mtrls	14.83	1.17	16	13
Energy	0.00	0.00	0	0
Utilities	0.00	0.00	0	0

Composition

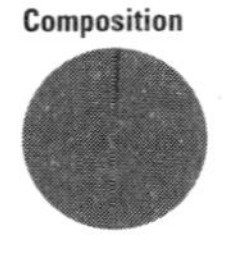

Cash	1.3
Stocks	98.8
Bonds	0.0
Other	0.0
Foreign (% of Stock)	0.0

Address: 2130 Pacwest Center, Portland OR 97204-3721, 800-992-4144
Web Address: www.jenseninvestment.com

Inception: 08-03-92
Advisor: Jensen Investment Management Inc.
Subadvisor: None

Minimum Purchase:	$2500	Add: $100	IRA: $2500
Min Auto Inv Plan:	$100	Add: $100	
Sales Fees:	0.25%B		
Management Fee:	0.50%, 0.05%A		
Actual Fees:	Mgt:0.50%	Dist:0.25%	
Expense Projections:	3Yr:$281	5Yr:$488	10Yr:$1084
Income Distrib:	Quarterly		

NTF Plans: Fidelity Retail-NTF, Schwab OneSource

Hancock Strategic Inc A

Ticker	Load	NAV	Yield	SEC Yield	Total Assets	Mstar Category
JHFIX	4.50%	$7.18	5.·%	3.41%	$1,540 mil	Multisector Bond

Governance and Management

Fiduciary Grade: C

Portfolio Manager(s)

Fred Cavanaugh has been with this fund since 1986. He has done well here and at John Hancock High-Yield, which he joined in 1998. Comanager Daniel Janis joined the team in October 1999.

Strategy

This multisector-bond fund owns a mix of high-yield bonds, foreign debt, and U.S. government securities. Comanagers Fred Cavanaugh and Daniel Janis generally make gradual changes to the fund's asset mix, and they've lately dialed down the fund's exposure to U.S. bonds in favor of foreign-debt issues. They've been upgrading the portfolio's average credit quality, as well.

Historical Profile

Return Above Avg
Risk Average
Rating ★★★★ Above Avg

Investment Style: Fixed Income — Income Rtn %Rank Cat: 13, 10, 23, 49, 35, 46, 37, 39, 50

▼ Manager Change
▽ Partial Manager Change

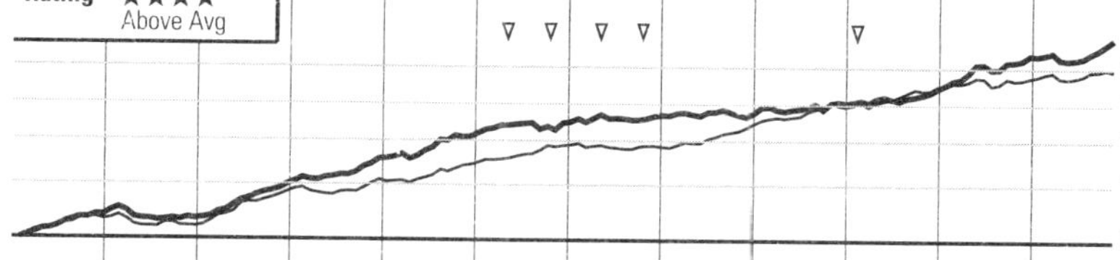

Performance Quartile (within Category)

1993	1994	1995	1996	1997	1998	1999	2000	2001	2002	2003	12-04	History
7.69	6.81	7.37	7.54	7.77	7.57	7.24	6.73	6.51	6.50	7.00	7.18	NAV
13.73	-3.05	18.71	11.68	12.68	5.41	3.35	1.14	4.90	7.30	16.89	8.75	Total Return %
3.98	-0.13	0.24	8.05	3.03	-3.28	4.17	-10.49	-3.54	-2.95	12.79	4.41	+/-LB Aggr
3.33	0.03	0.24	7.23	2.90	-1.90	3.18	-9.68	-3.19	-2.54	11.07	3.78	+/-LB. U.S. Univ. Bd
9.39	8.79	10.14	9.15	8.92	8.12	7.86	8.47	8.31	7.36	6.62	5.38	Income Return %
4.34	-11.84	8.57	2.53	3.76	-2.71	-4.51	-7.33	-3.41	-0.06	10.27	3.37	Capital Return %
62	19	44	39	7	13	46	57	43	39	48	40	Total Rtn % Rank Cat
0.67	0.65	0.66	0.65	0.65	0.61	0.57	0.59	0.54	0.46	0.42	0.37	Income $
0.00	0.00	0.00	0.00	0.04	0.00	0.00	0.00	0.00	0.00	0.15	0.04	Capital Gains $
1.58	1.32	1.09	1.03	1.00	0.92	0.89	0.91	0.93	0.93	0.95	0.90	Expense Ratio %
9.63	8.71	9.24	9.13	8.61	8.20	7.71	8.09	8.40	7.06	5.82	5.10	Income Ratio %
97	91	55	78	132	112	55	36	48	69	71	42	Turnover Rate %
339	318	354	407	445	512	549	507	505	517	647	735	Net Assets $mil

Performance 12-31-04

	1st Qtr	2nd Qtr	3rd Qtr	4th Qtr	Total
2000	1.20	0.29	-0.21	-0.14	1.14
2001	1.46	0.57	-0.31	3.12	4.90
2002	0.21	1.72	1.20	4.02	7.30
2003	4.54	7.11	0.96	3.40	16.89
2004	1.36	-3.25	4.68	5.94	8.75

Trailing	Total Return%	+/- LB Aggr	+/- LB. U.S. Univ. Bd	%Rank Cat	Growth of $10,000
3 Mo	5.94	4.99	4.66	9	10,594
6 Mo	10.90	6.72	6.11	12	11,090
1 Yr	8.75	4.41	3.78	40	10,875
3 Yr Avg	10.90	4.71	4.05	46	13,639
5 Yr Avg	7.67	-0.04	-0.21	40	14,470
10 Yr Avg	8.94	1.22	1.07	13	23,544
15 Yr Avg	8.37	0.67	—	30	33,392

Tax Analysis	Tax-Adj Rtn%	%Rank Cat	Tax-Cost Rat	%Rank Cat
3 Yr (estimated)	6.45	60	2.53	74
5 Yr (estimated)	3.70	60	2.79	70
10 Yr (estimated)	5.13	21	3.05	77

Potential Capital Gain Exposure: 2% of assets

Rating and Risk

Time Period	Load-Adj Return %	Morningstar Rtn vs Cat	Morningstar Risk vs Cat	Morningstar Risk-Adj Rating
1 Yr	3.86			
3 Yr	9.21	Avg	Avg	★★★
5 Yr	6.68	Avg	Avg	★★★
10 Yr	8.44	+Avg	Avg	★★★★
Incept	7.52			

Other Measures	Standard Index LB Aggr	Best Fit Index LB Credit
Alpha	5.5	4.9
Beta	0.79	0.68
R-Squared	46	58
Standard Deviation	5.48	
Mean	10.90	
Sharpe Ratio	1.76	

Portfolio Analysis 11-30-04

Total Fixed-Income:124	Date of Maturity	Amount $000	Value $000	% Net Assets
Canada Govt 8.75%	12-01-05	52,000	46,311	3.14
Australia (Commonwealth	09-15-09	52,000	44,469	3.01
Canada Govt 5.5%	06-01-09	49,000	44,253	3.00
Canada Govt 7%	12-01-06	45,000	40,760	2.76
US Treasury Bond 9.25%	02-15-16	27,600	39,002	2.64
Italy (Republic Of) 5.25	08-01-11	23,835	35,118	2.38
Canada Govt 5.75%	06-01-29	35,525	33,059	2.24
Canada Govt 6%	06-01-11	35,050	32,658	2.21
Canada Govt 5.5%	06-01-10	33,425	30,288	2.05
Spain (Kingdom Of) 4.2%	07-30-13	20,500	28,296	1.92
Spain (Kingdom Of) 5.35%	10-31-11	18,930	28,106	1.90
Koenigreich Norwegen 5%	05-15-15	158,000	27,878	1.89
US Treasury Note 6.125%	08-15-07	23,600	25,375	1.72
Sweden (Kingdom Of) 8%	08-15-07	146,500	24,633	1.67
Germany (Federal Republi	07-04-12	16,800	24,496	1.66
US Treasury Bond 8.125%	08-15-19	17,225	23,168	1.57
Colombia (Republic Of) 1	05-31-11	13,640	22,479	1.52
Venezuela (Republic Of)	03-05-08	14,500	22,451	1.52
Colombia Rep 10.375%	01-28-33	18,100	20,516	1.39
Italy (Republic Of) 4.75	02-01-13	14,250	20,410	1.38

Current Investment Style

Duration: Short Int Long — Quality: High Med Low

¹ figure provided by fund

Avg Eff Duration[1]	3.6 Yrs
Avg Eff Maturity	6.8 Yrs
Avg Credit Quality	AA
Avg Wtd Coupon	7.28%
Avg Wtd Price	105.45% of par

Coupon Range	% of Bonds	Rel Cat
0% PIK	0.0	0.0
0% to 6%	43.3	1.0
6% to 8%	19.9	0.7
8% to 10%	23.1	1.2
More than 10%	13.6	1.4

1.00=Category Average

Credit Analysis	% bonds 11-30-04		
US Govt	20	BB	15
AAA	34	B	11
AA	9	Below B	2
A	4	NR/NA	1
BBB	5		

Sector Breakdown	% of assets
US Treasuries	9
TIPS	0
US Agency	2
Mortgage Pass-Throughs	1
Mortgage CMO	0
Mortgage ARM	0
US Corporate	27
Asset-Backed	0
Convertible	0
Municipal	0
Corporate Inflation-Protected	0
Foreign Corporate	2
Foreign Govt	48

Composition			
Cash	10.3	Bonds	85.7
Stocks	1.5	Other	2.6

Special Securities	
Restricted/Illiquid Secs	2
Exotic Mortgage-Backed	0
Emerging-Markets Secs	6
Options/Futures/Warrants	No

Morningstar's Take by Dieter Bardy 11-10-04

Despite its recent sluggishness, John Hancock Strategic Income remains a strong option.

We're fans of this fund's sound strategy. Managers Fred Cavanaugh and Daniel Janis form an overview of where they think the U.S. economy is headed, and then direct the fund's three main sectors (corporate, emerging market, and U.S. government debt) toward that end. The two managers also lean on the support of six credit analysts at Hancock in selecting individual bonds, favoring companies with strong cash flows.

For some time now, however, Cavanaugh has been worried about the U.S. budget and current account deficits and as a result is predicting a further decline in the value of the U.S. dollar. Indeed, the fund's 51% weight in non-U.S. bonds is huge compared with its typical multisector bond rival's 14% stake. Most of that weighting, 49%, is staked in foreign sovereign debt, which is a form of higher-quality debt backed by non-U.S. governments. Still, 51% of the total assets are invested in nondollar bonds, with the bulk of that in Canadian and Euro bonds. If Cavanaugh's big picture view fails and the dollar rallies instead of falls, the fund may fall further than most because of the nondollar exposure.

Although the foreign bond stake has done well, it has not performed as well as high yield in particular, which has soared this year. Cavanaugh thinks that a lot of high yield bonds have become too pricey. The fund's 5.7% year-to-date gain through Nov. 5, 2004 is right in line with its typical peer's gain. We aren't put off by the fund's so-so showing, though. Cavanaugh has shown aptitude over longer periods, as the fund's trailing returns are all above average.

Cavanaugh has stuck to his strategy, which has proved correct over longer periods. Thus, we think there's reason for continued confidence in this offering. Its low costs are another reason why it's worth consideration.

Address:	101 Huntington Ave Boston MA 02199-7603 800-225-5291
Web Address:	www.jhfunds.com
Inception:	08-18-86
Advisor:	John Hancock Advisers, LLC
Subadvisor:	None
NTF Plans:	DATALynx NTF, Federated Tr NTF

Minimum Purchase:	$1000	Add: $0	IRA: $500
Min Auto Inv Plan:	$25	Add: $25	
Sales Fees:	4.50%L		
Management Fee:	0.37%		
Actual Fees:	Mgt:0.37%	Dist:0.30%	
Expense Projections:	3Yr:$739	5Yr:$952	10Yr:$1564
Income Distrib:	Monthly		

Julius Baer Intl Eqty A

Analyst Pick	Ticker	Load	NAV	Yield	Total Assets	Mstar Category
✔	BJBIX	12b-1 only	$31.61	1.4%	$9,983 mil	Foreign Large Blend

Governance and Management

Fiduciary Grade: B

Portfolio Manager(s)

Rudolph-Riad Younes and Richard Pell have worked for Bank Julius Baer and other firms in various investment-related capacities for many years. They've been running this fund since the spring of 1995, and have a team of five analysts. Though they work together, Younes handles the day-to-day management, while Pell focuses more on providing broader strategic oversight. They were named Morningstar's International Fund Managers of the Year for 2002.

Strategy

The managers consider sector selection and the outlook for the U.S. economy more than most peers, though they also do intensive company analysis. The result is a flexible strategy that incorporates both growth and value factors. They are willing to hold significant cash stakes, but not when the markets are rallying. Individual stock positions are typically less than 3% of assets. The fund's weightings can diverge quite sharply from those of the MSCI EAFE Index. The fund does very little currency hedging. It relies on a 2% redemption fee on short-term investors, rather than fair-value pricing, to deter market-timing.

Historical Profile

Return: High
Risk: Average
Rating: ★★★★★ Highest

Investment Style: Equity Stock %: 75% 90% 84% 93% 83% 89% 76% 71% 66%

▼ Manager Change
▽ Partial Manager Change

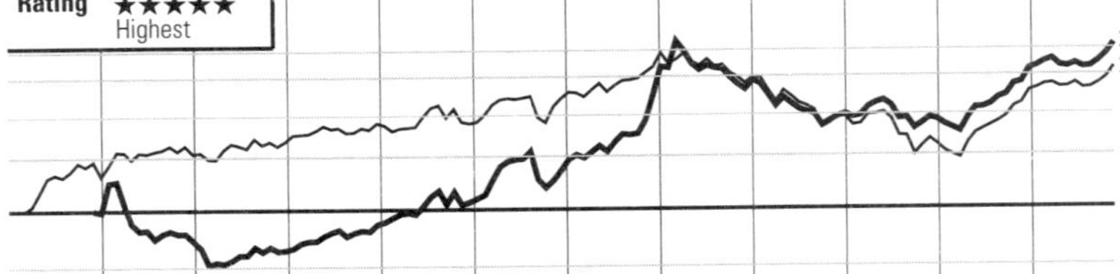

26.8 / 22.8 / 18.0 **Growth of $10,000** / 14.0 ▬ Investment Values of Fund — Investment Values of MSCI EAFE / 10.0 / 7.0

Performance Quartile (within Category)

1993	1994	1995	1996	1997	1998	1999	2000	2001	2002	2003	12-04	History
15.56	10.31	10.29	12.07	13.77	17.11	27.91	25.67	20.81	19.74	26.50	31.61	NAV
29.67*	-33.58	-0.19	17.66	15.33	27.07	76.58	-8.02	-18.93	-3.60	35.92	23.22	Total Return %
—	-41.36	-11.40	11.61	13.55	7.14	49.55	6.17	2.49	12.34	-2.67	2.97	+/-MSCI EAFE
—	-40.93	-11.60	10.79	13.06	8.38	48.60	5.34	2.46	12.20	-3.50	2.84	+/-MSCI Wd xUS
0.00	0.18	0.00	0.36	1.24	0.00	0.37	0.01	0.00	1.52	1.65	1.71	Income Return %
—	-33.76	-0.19	17.30	14.09	27.07	76.21	-8.03	-18.93	-5.12	34.27	21.51	Capital Return %
—	100	100	16	8	2	3	11	29	1	33	5	Total Rtn % Rank Cat
0.00	0.03	0.00	0.04	0.15	0.00	0.06	0.00	0.00	0.32	0.33	0.45	Income $
0.00	0.00	0.00	0.00	0.00	0.39	1.76	0.00	0.00	0.00	0.00	0.58	Capital Gains $
2.09	2.16	2.67	2.37	1.79	1.87	1.96	1.37	1.40	1.43	1.31	—	Expense Ratio %
-3.83	-1.26	-0.63	-0.58	0.00	-0.15	-0.48	0.32	0.36	0.49	0.83	—	Income Ratio %
—	169	116	67	94	134	73	72	89	93	114	—	Turnover Rate %
35	12	10	22	47	73	105	240	305	742	2,207	4,761	Net Assets $mil

Performance 12-31-04

	1st Qtr	2nd Qtr	3rd Qtr	4th Qtr	Total
2000	10.39	-8.80	-7.18	-1.57	-8.02
2001	-14.69	-2.01	-9.65	7.32	-18.93
2002	4.32	0.69	-13.08	5.59	-3.60
2003	-7.14	15.82	7.91	17.11	35.92
2004	6.30	-3.02	1.50	17.75	23.22

Trailing	Total Return%	+/- MSCI EAFE	+/- MSCI Wd xUS	%Rank Cat	Growth of $10,000
3 Mo	17.75	2.43	2.60	1	11,775
6 Mo	19.52	4.52	4.15	3	11,952
1 Yr	23.22	2.97	2.84	5	12,322
3 Yr Avg	17.31	5.42	5.09	2	16,144
5 Yr Avg	3.78	4.91	4.54	3	12,038
10 Yr Avg	13.85	8.23	7.91	1	36,587
15 Yr Avg	—	—	—	—	—

Tax Analysis	Tax-Adj Rtn%	%Rank Cat	Tax-Cost Rat	%Rank Cat
3 Yr (estimated)	16.52	2	0.67	73
5 Yr (estimated)	3.36	3	0.40	23
10 Yr (estimated)	13.22	1	0.55	9

Potential Capital Gain Exposure: 20% of assets

Rating and Risk

Time Period	Load-Adj Return %	Morningstar Rtn vs Cat	Morningstar Risk vs Cat	Morningstar Risk-Adj Rating
1 Yr	23.22			
3 Yr	17.31	High	Low	★★★★★
5 Yr	3.78	High	Avg	★★★★★
10 Yr	13.85	High	High	★★★★★
Incept	10.75			

Other Measures	Standard Index S&P 500	Best Fit Index MSCI Wd xUS
Alpha	6.7	6.4
Beta	0.81	0.82
R-Squared	91	91

Standard Deviation	15.48
Mean	17.31
Sharpe Ratio	1.04

Portfolio Analysis 07-31-04

Share change since 06-04 Total Stocks:267	Sector	Country	% Assets
BP	Energy	U.K.	2.02
Vodafone Grp	Telecom	U.K.	1.65
TOTAL	Energy	France	1.48
OTP Bank	Financial	Hungary	1.41
GlaxoSmithKline	Health	U.K.	1.23
Roche Holding	Health	Switzerland	1.20
Komercni banka	Financial	Czech Republic	1.18
⊕ Nomura Hldgs	Financial	Japan	1.16
Novartis	Health	Switzerland	1.09
Nestle	Goods	Switzerland	1.09
Royal Bank Of Scotland G	Financial	U.K.	1.08
Bk Pekao SA	Financial	Poland	0.83
Sberbank Rossii	Financial	Russia	0.79
⊕ Mitsubishi Tokyo Fin. Gr	Financial	Japan	0.78
⊕ E.ON	Utilities	Germany	0.77
⊕ Tesco	Consumer	U.K.	0.75
⊕ Toyota Motor	Goods	Japan	0.72
BNP Paribas	Financial	France	0.69
Metro AG Grp	Consumer	Germany	0.69
⊕ Matsushita Electric Indu	Ind Mtrls	Japan	0.69

Current Investment Style

Value Blnd Growth; Large Mid Small

Market Cap	%
Giant	47.3
Large	26.1
Mid	23.1
Small	3.4
Micro	0.1
Avg $mil: 17,384	

Value Measures		Rel Category
Price/Earnings	13.78	1.01
Price/Book	1.40	0.78
Price/Sales	0.60	0.66
Price/Cash Flow	5.48	1.11
Dividend Yield %	2.10	0.83

Growth Measures	%	Rel Category
Long-Term Erngs	10.72	1.00
Book Value	0.89	89.00
Sales	7.64	3.07
Cash Flow	2.24	0.40
Historical Erngs	-8.38	NMF

Composition			
Cash	31.9	Bonds	1.3
Stocks	65.7	Other	1.0
Foreign (% of Stock)			99.6

Sector Weightings	% of Stocks	Rel MSCI EAFE	3 Year High	3 Year Low
Info	12.21	0.74		
Software	0.00	0.00	1	0
Hardware	1.84	0.50	6	2
Media	3.20	1.40	6	2
Telecom	7.17	0.75	11	6
Service	48.63	1.09		
Health	9.26	1.28	11	3
Consumer	4.66	0.92	6	3
Business	3.93	0.72	11	3
Financial	30.78	1.14	39	19
Mfg	39.15	1.01		
Goods	17.13	1.25	18	12
Ind Mtrls	6.36	0.52	15	5
Energy	11.51	1.57	18	6
Utilities	4.15	0.78	8	1

Regional Exposure	% Stock		
UK/W. Europe	62	N. America	2
Japan	14	Latn America	1
Asia X Japan	3	Other	18

Country Exposure	% Stock		
U.K.	19	France	9
Japan	14	Switzerland	7
Germany	10		

Morningstar's Take by Gregg Wolper 11-22-04

Julius Baer International Equity's actions might seem contradictory, but the willingness to take them is a key to the fund's success.

In some ways, this fund's managers--Rudolph-Riad Younes and Richard Pell--show such originality that you'd swear they don't care what the indexes or their peers are doing. See, for example, the fund's longtime double-digit stake in Central European stocks or their current 3.5% position in Turkey. Yet Younes says he needs a good reason to veer too far away from the MSCI EAFE Index. That helps explain why the fund's top two holdings are index heavyweights BP and Total. Similarly, though the managers have a gloomy outlook for global stock markets, they (unlike some prominent rivals unable to find attractive picks) aren't letting cash build up. Instead, Younes and Pell have put excess cash in futures contracts that track major benchmarks such as Japan's Nikkei or Germany's DAX.

Younes explains such moves as risk-control measures. In short, he thinks it's never wise to fight too hard against the market's direction. Thus, if--for reasons he can't fathom--other investors are pushing markets higher, he won't sit out. The index futures allow the fund to participate in a general rise but are liquid enough to be dumped quickly if the tide turns.

Of course, attempts to read market direction are tough to pull off. But that's just a minor part of the managers' approach. And the fund's history argues in their favor: Its trailing 10-year return through October 31, 2004 tops the foreign large-blend category. This year through Nov. 19, it's is in the top decile. Younes partly credits an outsized emerging-markets stake (in particular, huge gains in those Turkish stocks) for this year's success.

In short, this fund has managed to win out by simultaneously defying the mainstream and jumping right in it. It wouldn't be advisable for every manager to copy these methods, but they certainly work here.

Address:	Julius Baer Investment Funds Indianapolis, Indiana 46204-1897 800-435-4659
Web Address:	www.us-funds.juliusbaer.com
Inception:	10-04-93*
Advisor:	Julius Baer Securities Inc.
Subadvisor:	None
NTF Plans:	Fidelity Retail-NTF, Schwab OneSource

Minimum Purchase:	$2500	Add: $1000	IRA: $100
Min Auto Inv Plan:	$2500	Add: $100	
Sales Fees:	0.25%B, 2.00%R		
Management Fee:	0.90%, 0.25%A		
Actual Fees:	Mgt:0.75%	Dist:0.25%	
Expense Projections:	3Yr:$600	5Yr:$1042	10Yr:$2270
Income Distrib:	Annually		

Kalmar Gr Val Sm Cp

Ticker	Load	NAV	Yield	Total Assets	Mstar Category
KGSCX	None	$16.17	0.0%	$372 mil	Small Growth

Governance and Management

Fiduciary Grade:

Portfolio Manager(s)

Ford Draper Jr. established Kalmar Investments in 1982, using this same strategy to manage separate accounts. Nine team members provide investment research. The three most senior members of the investment team all have more than 20 years of industry experience and at least 10 at Kalmar.

Strategy

Management invests in established, well-managed companies with above-average revenue and earnings growth, and it likes to buy them when they are cheap. This results in a portfolio of stocks that are reasonably priced relative to their earnings-growth rates. Management often can't find the growth it seeks in financial-services stocks, and its desire for profitability can limit its tech exposure.

Historical Profile

Return: Above Avg
Risk: Below Avg
Rating: ★★★★ Above Avg

Investment Style: Equity Stock %

1997	1998	1999	2000	2001	2002	2003	12-04
88%	90%	97%	88%	95%	90%	93%	91%

▼ Manager Change
▽ Partial Manager Change

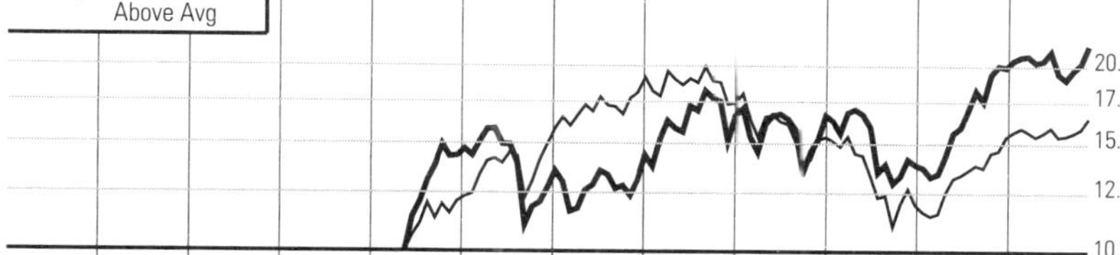

Growth of $10,000
— Investment Values of Fund
— Investment Values of S&P 500

Performance Quartile (within Category)

1993	1994	1995	1996	1997	1998	1999	2000	2001	2002	2003	12-04	History
—	—	—	—	13.70	12.65	13.41	12.95	12.95	10.81	14.80	16.17	NAV
—	—	—	—	47.53*	-7.66	6.01	15.70	0.00	-16.53	43.54	12.81	Total Return %
—	—	—	—	—	-36.23	-15.03	24.80	11.88	5.56	14.87	1.94	+/-S&P 500
—	—	—	—	—	-8.89	-37.08	38.13	9.23	13.73	-5.00	-1.50	+/-Russ 2000 Gr
—	—	—	—	0.00	0.00	0.00	0.00	0.00	0.00	0.00	0.00	Income Return %
—	—	—	—	—	-7.66	6.01	15.70	0.00	-16.53	43.54	12.81	Capital Return %
—	—	—	—	—	90	93	10	26	8	53	49	Total Rtn % Rank Cat
—	—	—	—	0.00	0.00	0.00	0.00	0.00	0.00	0.00	0.00	Income $
—	—	—	—	0.92	0.00	0.00	2.59	0.00	0.00	0.72	0.53	Capital Gains $
—	—	—	—	1.25	1.24	1.25	1.22	1.23	1.23	1.26	—	Expense Ratio %
—	—	—	—	-0.51	-0.52	-0.78	-0.82	-0.96	-1.03	-1.03	—	Income Ratio %
—	—	—	—	—	27	52	64	47	41	46	—	Turnover Rate %
—	—	—	—	227	222	195	196	207	217	270	372	Net Assets $mil

Performance 12-31-04

	1st Qtr	2nd Qtr	3rd Qtr	4th Qtr	Total
2000	13.42	5.72	2.98	-6.31	15.70
2001	-12.51	15.00	-19.34	23.22	0.00
2002	1.16	-5.19	-18.68	7.03	-16.53
2003	-3.24	18.64	10.07	13.59	43.54
2004	4.39	1.68	-6.68	13.88	12.81

Trailing	Total Return%	+/- S&P 500	+/- Russ 2000 Gr	%Rank Cat	Growth of $10,000
3 Mo	13.88	4.65	-1.20	49	11,388
6 Mo	6.27	-0.92	-1.89	66	10,627
1 Yr	12.81	1.94	-1.50	49	11,281
3 Yr Avg	10.57	6.99	4.78	14	13,518
5 Yr Avg	9.36	11.66	12.93	11	15,642
10 Yr Avg	—	—	—	—	—
15 Yr Avg	—	—	—	—	—

Tax Analysis	Tax-Adj Rtn%	%Rank Cat	Tax-Cost Rat	%Rank Cat
3 Yr (estimated)	10.14	13	0.39	35
5 Yr (estimated)	8.37	11	0.91	39
10 Yr (estimated)	—	—	—	—

Potential Capital Gain Exposure: 30% of assets

Rating and Risk

Time Period	Load-Adj Return %	Morningstar Rtn vs Cat	Morningstar Risk vs Cat	Morningstar Risk-Adj Rating
1 Yr	12.81			
3 Yr	10.57	+Avg	Avg	★★★★
5 Yr	9.36	+Avg	-Avg	★★★★
10 Yr	—	—	—	—
Incept	11.12			

Other Measures	Standard Index S&P 500	Best Fit Index Russ 2000
Alpha	7.6	0.1
Beta	0.93	0.90
R-Squared	59	91
Standard Deviation	20.20	
Mean	10.57	
Sharpe Ratio	0.46	

Portfolio Analysis 10-31-04

Share change since 09-04 Total Stocks:80	Sector	PE	YTD Ret%	% Assets
Pentair	Business	24.0	93.44	3.38
⊕ Acxiom	Business	32.3	42.18	2.46
Insight Enterprises	Consumer	15.3	9.15	2.33
Avocent	Hardware	NMF	11.20	2.26
⊕ Covance	Health	26.6	44.59	2.24
Ultra Petroleum	Energy	43.1	95.49	2.22
⊕ Petsmart	Consumer	32.1	49.86	2.13
MSC Industrial Direct Co	Business	28.4	32.26	2.02
Benchmark Electronics	Hardware	20.9	-2.04	1.96
⊕ Laureate Education	Consumer	32.0	53.14	1.93
⊕ Gamestop	Consumer	17.7	45.10	1.77
Barr Pharmaceuticals	Health	37.4	-11.23	1.75
Respironics	Health	27.6	20.24	1.39
ChoicePoint	Business	30.4	20.74	1.36
MacDermid	Ind Mtrls	19.4	5.95	1.31
⊕ Tekelec	Hardware	40.9	31.45	1.60
Aeroflex	Hardware	30.3	3.50	1.57
Navigant Consulting	Business	36.1	41.04	1.54
⊕ Carlisle Companies	Ind Mtrls	17.2	8.30	1.47
Alliance Data Systems	Business	35.1	71.53	1.46

Current Investment Style

Value Blnd Growth / Large Mid Small

Market Cap	%
Giant	0.0
Large	0.5
Mid	49.6
Small	42.7
Micro	7.2
Avg $mil: 1,351	

Value Measures		Rel Category
Price/Earnings	22.05	1.02
Price/Book	2.66	1.01
Price/Sales	1.30	0.87
Price/Cash Flow	12.46	1.56
Dividend Yield %	0.14	0.45

Growth Measures	%	Rel Category
Long-Term Erngs	17.17	0.99
Book Value	3.57	1.48
Sales	7.42	1.15
Cash Flow	34.25	2.53
Historical Erngs	12.93	0.96

Profitability	%	Rel Category
Return on Equity	12.45	1.26
Return on Assets	6.52	1.49
Net Margin	8.07	1.18

Sector Weightings	% of Stocks	Rel S&P 500	3 Year High	3 Year Low
Info	15.34	0.71		
Software	1.88	0.44	7	1
Hardware	13.00	1.27	14	8
Media	0.00	0.00	2	0
Telecom	0.46	0.15	1	0
Service	62.29	1.34		
Health	15.65	1.25	19	12
Consumer	19.87	2.19	28	19
Business	25.60	6.32	27	20
Financial	1.17	0.06	2	1
Mfg	22.37	0.70		
Goods	2.46	0.26	6	1
Ind Mtrls	12.63	1.00	14	10
Energy	7.28	1.02	10	4
Utilities	0.00	0.00	0	0

Composition

Cash	9.2
Stocks	90.8
Bonds	0.0
Other	0.0
Foreign (% of Stock)	2.0

Morningstar's Take by Dan McNeela 12-09-04

Kalmar Growth-with-Value Small Cap has a solid base of support.

This fund has a foundation that should produce reliable results. Its nine-person investment team of managers and analysts is both deep and experienced. The three most-senior members of the team each have at least 20 years of investment experience and more than a decade at Kalmar. Two recent hires came to fund with more than a dozen years of experience.

Knowing the ropes comes in handy because the fund likes to buy and hold for the long term. Ultra Petroleum looks like a timely stock to own given its nearly 100% gain in 2004, but that stock has been in the portfolio long enough for it to have appreciated eightfold. The fund's annual turnover rarely cracks the 50% mark. Much of the trading can be attributed to management's desire to trim its winners, which are pared back to keep stock-specific risk in check. Top holdings rarely exceed 2.5% of assets.

Those conservative traits don't mean that the fund is stuck on slow but steady growers, however. While the fund has never piled into tech stocks, the portfolio's growth characteristics match up well with its peers in Morningstar's small-cap growth category.

That said, the fund hasn't fared well in speculative markets, such as 1999. The vast majority of its holdings are already profitable, so investors aren't often asked to take a leap of faith.

In 2004 the fund is hovering near the middle of the pack. Profitable picks in energy and specialty retailers such as Petsmart have worked well, but disappointments in education firm DeVry and auto-parts firm Pep Boys have kept the fund from climbing the ranks.

Investors who want in here shouldn't wait too long. The fund is still small, but Kalmar runs more than $1 billion in separate accounts, and management has its capacity constraints in mind.

Address:	Kalmar Pooled Investment Trust Greenville, DE 19807 800-282-2319
Web Address:	www.kalmarinvestments.com
Inception:	04-11-97*
Advisor:	Kalmar Investments Inc
Subadvisor:	None
NTF Plans:	Schwab OneSource, Schwab Instl NTF

Minimum Purchase:	$10000	Add: $1000	IRA: $1000
Min Auto Inv Plan:	$10000	Add: $100	
Sales Fees:	No-load		
Management Fee:	1.00%, 0.15%A		
Actual Fees:	Mgt:1.00%	Dist:	
Expense Projections:	3Yr:$400	5Yr:$692	10Yr:$1523
Income Distrib:	Annually		

Legg Mason Opp Prim

Ticker	Load	NAV	Yield	Total Assets	Mstar Category
LMOPX	1.00%d	$15.67	0.0%	$3,817 mil	Mid-Cap Blend

Governance and Management

Fiduciary Grade: B

Portfolio Manager(s)

Bill Miller is widely regarded as one of the most-accomplished fund managers in the business. His Legg Mason Value Trust has beaten the S&P 500 in each of the past 13 calendar years. With more than a decade at that fund's helm, he brings a wealth of experience to this young offering.

Strategy

Bill Miller has free rein here. Although he seeks companies that are trading at discounts to his estimates of their intrinsic values, that often includes names that others might consider expensive. The fund holds between 20 and 40 positions, and it invests in both debt and equity instruments. Miller will also short stocks and other securities from time to time and can use derivatives.

Historical Profile

Return Above Avg
Risk High
Rating ★★★ Neutral

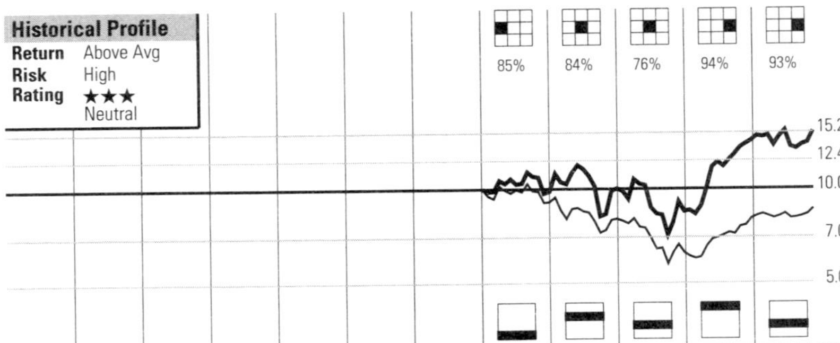

Investment Style
Equity
Stock %

▼ Manager Change
▽ Partial Manager Change

Growth of $10,000
— Investment Values of Fund
— Investment Values of S&P 500

Performance Quartile (within Category)

1993	1994	1995	1996	1997	1998	1999	2000	2001	2002	2003	12-04	History
—	—	—	—	—	—	10.00	9.65	9.80	8.23	13.77	15.67	NAV
—	—	—	—	—	—	0.00*	-1.68	1.94	-15.52	67.95	13.80	Total Return %
—	—	—	—	—	—	—	7.42	13.82	6.57	39.28	2.93	+/-S&P 500
—	—	—	—	—	—	—	-19.17	2.54	-0.99	32.36	-2.67	+/-S&P Mid 400
—	—	—	—	—	—	—	0.40	0.37	0.51	0.61	0.00	Income Return %
—	—	—	—	—	—	—	-2.08	1.57	-16.03	67.34	13.80	Capital Return %
—	—	—	—	—	—	—	78	36	52	3	71	Total Rtn % Rank Cat
—	—	—	—	—	—	0.00	0.04	0.04	0.05	0.05	0.00	Income $
—	—	—	—	—	—	0.00	0.14	0.00	0.00	0.00	0.00	Capital Gains $
—	—	—	—	—	—	1.99	1.98	1.89	1.94	1.90	—	Expense Ratio %
—	—	—	—	—	—	—	0.63	-0.45	0.99	0.00	—	Income Ratio %
—	—	—	—	—	—	—	26	60	44	27	—	Turnover Rate %
—	—	—	—	—	—	—	1,112	1,714	1,414	2,756	3,599	Net Assets $mil

Performance 12-31-04

	1st Qtr	2nd Qtr	3rd Qtr	4th Qtr	Total
2000	6.70	-2.72	5.78	-10.46	-1.68
2001	5.60	11.48	-29.49	22.81	1.94
2002	7.04	-18.78	-18.31	18.96	-15.52
2003	3.89	38.29	5.84	10.45	67.95
2004	3.70	3.57	-9.80	17.47	13.80

Trailing	Total Return%	+/- S&P 500	+/- S&P Mid 400	%Rank Cat	Growth of $10,000
3 Mo	17.47	8.24	5.32	3	11,747
6 Mo	5.95	-1.24	-3.84	90	10,595
1 Yr	13.80	2.93	-2.67	71	11,380
3 Yr Avg	17.32	13.74	6.81	6	16,148
5 Yr Avg	10.11	12.41	0.58	25	16,186
10 Yr Avg	—	—	—	—	—
15 Yr Avg	—	—	—	—	—

Tax Analysis	Tax-Adj Rtn%	%Rank Cat	Tax-Cost Rat	%Rank Cat
3 Yr (estimated)	17.18	4	0.12	14
5 Yr (estimated)	9.83	16	0.25	7
10 Yr (estimated)	—	—	—	—

Potential Capital Gain Exposure: 27% of assets

Rating and Risk

Time Period	Load-Adj Return %	Morningstar Rtn vs Cat	Morningstar Risk vs Cat	Morningstar Risk-Adj Rating
1 Yr	13.80			
3 Yr	17.32	High	High	★★★★
5 Yr	10.11	+Avg	High	★★★
10 Yr	—	—	—	—
Incept	10.10			

Other Measures	Standard Index S&P 500	Best Fit Index Mstar Mid Growth TR
Alpha	14.1	14.9
Beta	1.47	1.15
R-Squared	71	79
Standard Deviation	31.62	
Mean	17.32	
Sharpe Ratio	0.51	

Morningstar's Take by Christopher Traulsen 10-31-04

Legg Mason Opportunity Trust makes a very good case for itself in most respects.

Granted, this go-anywhere fund hasn't fared well in 2004. A stake in Level 3 Communications, along with big positions in Amazon.com and Interactive Corp., has sent the fund to a 1.7% loss for the year to date through Oct. 29. However, it has acquitted itself well since launching in late 1999. In that period, it has handily beaten its average mid-blend peer, and walloped the S&P 500 index. While it has been considerably more volatile than either benchmark, the added risk strikes us as a reasonable tradeoff for the upside potential.

The fund's performance flows from the compact portfolio put together by veteran fund manager Bill Miller. He holds just under 40 stocks in this funds, with about 50% of assets packed into the fund's top 10 holdings. That level of concentration is about the same as Legg Mason Value Trust's, Miller's far-more-conservative charge. Broadly speaking, Miller uses the same stock-picking philosophy here that he uses at Value Trust--looking for securities that are mispriced, often due to the market's misunderstanding of recent events or a company's true potential. But this fund goes places Value Trust can't. In the second quarter, Miller closed out a substantial short position in the Nasdaq 100 Trust. The fund also owns stakes in private equity partnerships and the debt and equity of troubled telecom firm Level 3 Communications.

We have one concern here: The fund now has over $3 billion in assets, and Miller indicates that he isn't going to recommend that the board close it to preserve its flexibility to invest in less-liquid securities. The board could take action on its own, but we think that's unlikely. This isn't necessarily a deal-breaker--especially given the fund's wide-ranging nature--but it means that investors should probably assume the fund's investment opportunities will be more limited than they are now as it continues to grow.

Portfolio Analysis 09-30-04

Share change since 03-04 Total Stocks:37	Sector	PE	YTD Ret%	% Assets
⊖ Tyco International	Ind Mtrls	25.1	35.41	8.22
⊖ AmeriCredit	Financial	14.3	53.48	7.08
Amazon.com	Consumer	55.5	-15.83	6.29
NII Holdings	Telecom	7.4	90.74	4.95
⊕ Iac / Interactivecorp	Consumer	43.1	-18.60	4.82
Providian Financial	Financial	14.3	41.50	4.79
Sepracor	Health	—	148.10	4.36
XM Satellite Radio Holdi	Media	—	43.10	3.44
Level 3 Comms 9.125%	—	—	—	3.40
VeriSign	Software	—	106.14	3.06
☼ Netflix	Consumer	39.3	-54.91	2.85
⊕ Level 3 Communications	Telecom	—	-40.53	2.79
Cendant	Business	13.6	6.52	2.46
AES	Utilities	30.9	44.81	2.46
⊕ Netease.com ADR	Business	41.4	43.34	2.34
Cott	Goods	22.2	-11.71	2.22
Friedman Billings Ramsey	Financial	9.0	-9.64	2.18
☼ UTStarcom	Hardware	12.7	-40.25	2.13
⊕ Yahoo	Media	95.1	67.36	2.09
☼ Arience Capital Limited	—	—	—	1.96

Current Investment Style

Value Blnd Growth; Large Mid Small

Market Cap	%
Giant	11.3
Large	16.7
Mid	62.1
Small	9.9
Micro	0.0
Avg $mil: 5,473	

Value Measures		Rel Category
Price/Earnings	19.66	1.16
Price/Book	1.77	0.82
Price/Sales	1.34	1.26
Price/Cash Flow	4.42	0.71
Dividend Yield %	0.09	0.09

Growth Measures	%	Rel Category
Long-Term Erngs	12.22	0.97
Book Value	2.23	0.32
Sales	6.21	1.10
Cash Flow	11.48	1.53
Historical Erngs	-9.71	NMF

Profitability	%	Rel Category
Return on Equity	12.25	0.89
Return on Assets	2.64	0.41
Net Margin	5.74	0.63

Sector Weightings	% of Stocks	Rel S&P 500	3 Year High	3 Year Low
Info	24.47	1.14		
Software	5.06	1.18	7	3
Hardware	2.31	0.23	11	2
Media	7.25	1.89	7	0
Telecom	9.85	3.13	17	9
Service	58.33	1.26		
Health	8.09	0.65	9	4
Consumer	18.95	2.09	19	12
Business	11.20	2.77	18	11
Financial	20.09	0.97	23	18
Mfg	17.21	0.54		
Goods	3.91	0.42	6	4
Ind Mtrls	10.64	0.84	11	5
Energy	0.00	0.00	4	0
Utilities	2.66	0.90	4	2

Composition

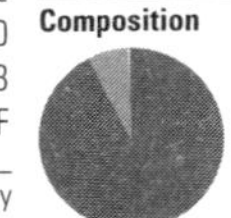

Cash	0.7
Stocks	92.5
Bonds	6.8
Other	0.0
Foreign (% of Stock)	5.5

Address:	100 Light Street Baltimore MD 21202 800-822-5544
Web Address:	www.leggmason.com
Inception:	12-30-99*
Advisor:	LMM LLC
Subadvisor:	Legg Mason Funds Management Inc.
NTF Plans:	N/A

Minimum Purchase:	$1000	Add: $100	IRA: $1000
Min Auto Inv Plan:	$1000	Add: $50	
Sales Fees:	1.00%D, 0.25%S		
Management Fee:	1.00% mx./0.75% mn.		
Actual Fees:	Mgt:0.76%	Dist:1.00%	
Expense Projections:	3Yr:$597	5Yr:$1026	10Yr:$2222
Income Distrib:	Annually		

Legg Mason Spec Invt Pr

Ticker	Load	NAV	Yield	Total Assets	Mstar Category
LMASX	12b-1 only	$46.48	0.0%	$3,860 mil	Mid-Cap Blend

Governance and Management

Fiduciary Grade: B

Portfolio Manager(s)

All-star manager Bill Miller has temporarily returned to this fund. He ran the fund from 1985 through early 2001, then handed the reins to Lisa Rapuano. Rapuano left for a hedge fund in January 2004, however, and a team led by Miller resumed control on an interim basis. The firm is now searching for a permanent replacement for Rapuano.

Strategy

The fund focuses on companies its managers think are trading cheaply relative to their prospects, based on qualitative research and estimates of the present value of their future free cash flow. The managers are willing to make fairly optimistic assumptions about growth, however, and the fund will hold more-expensive names than many value offerings. The fund has featured exceptionally large individual positions from time to time, and the volatile technology and telecom sectors have occasionally played prominent roles in the portfolio.

Historical Profile

Return Above Avg
Risk High
Rating ★★★ Neutral

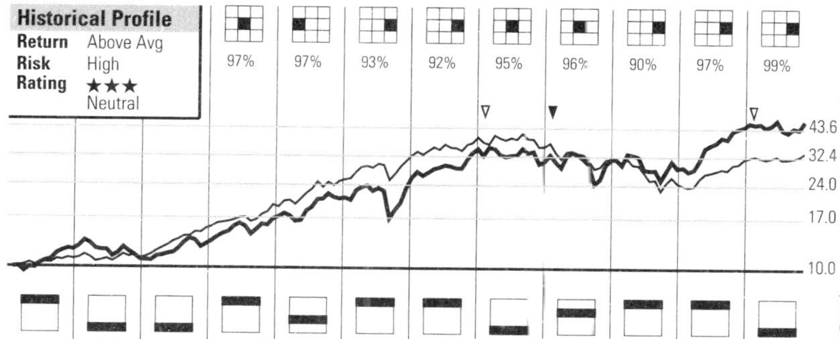

1993	1994	1995	1996	1997	1998	1999	2000	2001	2002	2003	12-04	History
22.14	19.03	22.81	27.83	32.27	36.70	40.15	33.94	33.73	29.63	44.49	46.48	NAV
24.13	-13.07	22.50	28.65	22.12	23.31	35.54	-12.00	2.23	-8.74	54.36	13.05	Total Return %
14.07	-14.38	-15.03	5.71	-11.23	-5.26	14.50	-2.90	14.14	13.35	25.69	2.18	+/-S&P 500
10.20	-9.48	-8.42	9.47	-10.12	4.20	20.82	-29.49	2.86	5.79	18.77	-3.42	+/-S&P Mid 400
0.17	0.00	0.16	0.00	0.00	0.00	0.00	0.00	0.00	0.00	0.00	0.00	Income Return %
23.96	-13.07	22.34	28.65	22.12	23.31	35.54	-12.00	2.26	-8.74	54.36	13.05	Capital Return %
13	95	83	9	71	10	17	92	34	10	5	79	Total Rtn % Rank Cat
0.03	0.00	0.03	0.00	0.00	0.00	0.00	0.00	0.00	0.00	0.00	0.00	Income $
0.14	0.23	0.44	1.41	1.49	2.66	8.04	1.52	1.00	1.20	1.22	3.69	Capital Gains $
2.00	1.94	1.93	1.96	1.92	1.86	1.84	1.80	1.79	1.79	1.83	1.78	Expense Ratio %
0.20	0.00	-0.20	0.00	-0.90	-1.10	-1.00	-1.20	-0.90	-1.00	-0.90	-1.30	Income Ratio %
32	17	28	36	29	30	48	29	37	36	18	15	Turnover Rate %
510	582	713	964	1,367	1,730	2,567	2,281	2,242	2,020	3,226	3,627	Net Assets $mil

Performance 12-31-04

	1st Qtr	2nd Qtr	3rd Qtr	4th Qtr	Total
2000	0.32	-6.86	2.77	-8.37	-12.00
2001	-6.22	14.34	-26.29	29.38	2.26
2002	5.90	-15.01	-10.61	13.44	-8.74
2003	-1.18	29.17	6.50	13.55	54.36
2004	3.53	3.43	-7.49	14.13	13.05

Trailing	Total Return%	+/- S&P 500	+/- S&P Mid 400	%Rank Cat	Growth of $10,000
3 Mo	14.13	4.90	1.98	15	11,413
6 Mo	5.58	-1.61	-4.21	92	10,558
1 Yr	13.05	2.18	-3.42	79	11,305
3 Yr Avg	16.78	13.20	6.27	6	15,926
5 Yr Avg	7.46	9.76	-2.07	54	14,330
10 Yr Avg	16.51	4.44	0.42	11	46,093
15 Yr Avg	14.91	3.98	0.25	4	80,421

Tax Analysis	Tax-Adj Rtn%	%Rank Cat	Tax-Cost Rat	%Rank Cat
3 Yr (estimated)	15.88	5	0.77	78
5 Yr (estimated)	6.68	48	0.73	30
10 Yr (estimated)	15.03	8	1.27	18

Potential Capital Gain Exposure: 41% of assets

Rating and Risk

Time Period	Load-Adj Return %	Morningstar Rtn vs Cat	Morningstar Risk vs Cat	Morningstar Risk-Adj Rating
1 Yr	13.05			
3 Yr	16.78	High	High	★★★★
5 Yr	7.46	Avg	High	★★
10 Yr	16.51	High	High	★★★
Incept	14.08			

Other Measures	Standard Index S&P 500	Best Fit Index Mstar Mid Growth TR
Alpha	13.3	13.9
Beta	1.21	0.97
R-Squared	70	83

Standard Deviation	25.49
Mean	16.78
Sharpe Ratio	0.61

Portfolio Analysis 09-30-04

Share change since 08-04 Total Stocks:39	Sector	PE	YTD Ret%	% Assets
⊕ Amazon.com	Consumer	55.5	-15.83	5.94
Providian Financial	Financial	14.3	41.50	5.87
⊕ Nextel Communications	Telecom	11.1	6.95	5.19
WellPoint Health Network	Health	—	—	4.88
⊕ Iac / Interactivecorp	Consumer	43.1	-18.60	4.48
☼ Bear Stearns Companies	Financial	10.9	29.25	4.19
⊖ Republic Services A	Business	21.8	32.45	3.98
⊖ Caremark RX	Health	32.8	55.67	3.54
CNET Networks	Media	NMF	64.66	3.46
⊕ NII Holdings	Telecom	7.4	90.74	3.42
Radian Group	Financial	11.9	9.40	3.36
XM Satellite Radio Holdi	Media	—	43.10	3.03
⊕ DeVry	Consumer	23.1	-30.92	2.77
Acxiom	Business	32.3	42.18	2.76
Sepracor	Health	—	148.10	2.69
⊕ Level 3 Communications	Telecom	—	-40.53	2.48
AmeriCredit	Financial	14.3	53.48	2.43
WPP Grp	Business	—	—	2.39
⊖ Pepsi Bottling Group	Goods	15.5	12.48	2.37
Symantec	Software	34.5	49.33	2.23

Current Investment Style

Value Blnd Growth — Large Mid Small

Market Cap	%
Giant	0.0
Large	36.9
Mid	50.1
Small	12.2
Micro	0.8
Avg $mil: 5,812	

Value Measures		Rel Category
Price/Earnings	17.56	1.04
Price/Book	[illegible].82	0.84
Price/Sales	[illegible].01	0.95
Price/Cash Flow	5.09	0.81
Dividend Yield %	0.26	0.26

Growth Measures	%	Rel Category
Long-Term Erngs	11.26	0.90
Book Value	8.63	1.22
Sales	6.33	1.12
Cash Flow	11.04	1.47
Historical Erngs	8.98	0.80

Profitability	%	Rel Category
Return on Equity	14.24	1.03
Return on Assets	4.35	0.67
Net Margin	6.42	0.71

Sector Weightings	% of Stocks	Rel S&P 500	3 Year High	3 Year Low
Info	23.63	1.10		
Software	4.55	1.06	9	5
Hardware	0.00	0.00	4	0
Media	6.59	1.72	7	2
Telecom	12.49	3.97	20	7
Service	69.13	1.49		
Health	17.29	1.38	17	13
Consumer	15.77	1.74	22	14
Business	16.60	4.10	22	16
Financial	19.47	0.94	26	17
Mfg	7.24	0.23		
Goods	7.24	0.78	7	0
Ind Mtrls	0.00	0.00	0	0
Energy	0.00	0.00	0	0
Utilities	0.00	0.00	2	0

Composition

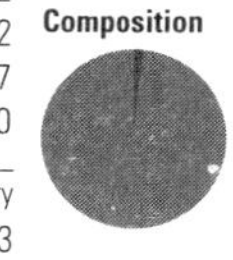

Cash	1.5
Stocks	98.5
Bonds	0.0
Other	0.0
Foreign (% of Stock)	2.4

Morningstar's Take by Christopher Traulsen 10-31-04

This fund's future management still isn't clear.

Legg Mason Special Investment has been run by a team headed by Bill Miller since its former manager, Lisa Rapuano, left Legg Mason in early 2004. Miller is a highly skilled manager who has built one of the best records in the business at Legg Mason Value Trust. He also managed this offering prior to Rapuano's tenure. However, the arrangement is temporary, and the firm is searching for a permanent replacement.

We expect the firm will ultimately hire someone whose style is a very close match with Miller's, and whoever gets the job will draw on the work of his research team. Even so, there will be differences in skill and personal preferences that will affect the fund under its new leader.

Aside from that uncertainty, the fund holds some appeal. It's volatile--to say the least--in large part because its managers have been unafraid to hold large positions in high-beta technology, Internet, and telecom stocks, and to concentrate the fund in relatively few sectors. Indeed, the fund has eschewed industrial and energy stocks, in no small part because Miller is a long-term investor who doesn't believe in buying firms that don't earn back their cost of capital over time.

That bet and big positions in sagging picks such as Amazon.com and Level 3 Communications have hurt the fund in 2004, leaving it in the category's bottom decile for the year to date through Oct. 29. But, however prone to such lapses it is, the fund has rewarded investors for sticking with it: Its 10-year return ranks in the category's top quartile and easily beats the S&P 500.

Nevertheless, until we know more about who will run this fund on a permanent basis and the strategy that person will employ, it's hard to recommend this offering. It's also worth noting that Legg Mason only offers this fund to individual investors in a level-load share class that is very costly to own over time. We think the firm should make a less-costly alternative available.

Address:	100 Light St Baltimore MD 21202 800-577-8589
Web Address:	www.leggmason.com
Inception:	12-30-85
Advisor:	Legg Mason Funds Management Inc.
Subadvisor:	None
NTF Plans:	DATALynx NTF, TD Waterhouse Ins NT

Minimum Purchase:	$1000	Add: $100	IRA: $1000
Min Auto Inv Plan:	$1000	Add: $50	
Sales Fees:	0.75%B, 0.25%S		
Management Fee:	0.69%		
Actual Fees:	Mgt:0.69%	Dist:1.00%	
Expense Projections:	3Yr:$560	5Yr:$964	10Yr:$2095
Income Distrib:	Annually		

Legg Mason Value Prim

Ticker	Load	NAV	Yield	Total Assets	Mstar Category
LMVTX	12b-1 only	$65.23	0.0%	$17,223 mil	Large Blend

Governance and Management

Fiduciary Grade: B

Portfolio Manager(s)

Longtime manager Bill Miller has vastly outperformed his average peer and the index during his tenure. Assistant manager Nancy Dennin, who focused mostly on administrative tasks, recently stepped down. Some of her duties are being taken on by David Nelson, manager of American Leading Companies. The firm has hired a new research director, Ira Malis, and chief strategist, Michael Mauboussin, along with three new analysts, and it plans to hire more.

Strategy

Bill Miller looks for companies that are trading cheaply relative to his estimates of what they're worth. This often leads him to beaten-down turnaround plays. Unlike many value managers, however, Miller is willing to make fairly optimistic assumptions about growth, and he doesn't shy away from owning companies in traditional growth sectors. In this portfolio, pricey Internet stocks rub elbows with bargain-priced financials and turnaround plays. Miller will also let favored names run, allowing top positions to soak up a large percentage of assets.

Historical Profile

Return High
Risk High
Rating ★★★★★ Highest

Investment Style: Equity Stock %

91%	91%	93%	99%	99%	99%	100%	98%	99%

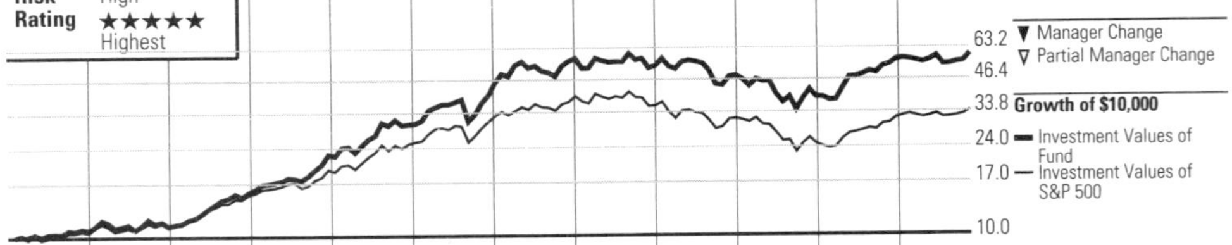

Performance Quartile (within Category)

History

1993	1994	1995	1996	1997	1998	1999	2000	2001	2002	2003	12-04	History
18.87	19.04	25.19	32.99	42.74	61.58	75.27	55.44	50.06	40.59	58.26	65.23	NAV
11.26	1.39	40.76	38.43	37.05	48.04	26.71	-7.14	-9.29	-18.92	43.53	11.96	Total Return %
1.20	0.08	3.23	15.49	3.70	19.47	5.67	1.96	2.59	3.17	14.86	1.09	+/-S&P 500
1.08	1.00	2.99	15.98	4.20	21.02	5.80	0.65	3.16	2.73	13.64	0.56	+/-Russ 1000
1.04	0.27	0.93	0.66	0.11	0.00	0.00	0.00	0.00	0.00	0.00	0.00	Income Return %
10.22	1.12	39.83	37.77	36.94	48.04	26.71	-7.14	-9.29	-18.92	43.53	11.96	Capital Return %
43	20	3	2	4	1	19	52	23	22	2	22	Total Rtn % Rank Cat
0.18	0.05	0.17	0.16	0.04	0.00	0.00	0.00	0.00	0.00	0.00	0.00	Income $
0.20	0.04	1.24	1.53	2.32	1.41	2.46	14.47	0.26	0.00	0.00	0.00	Capital Gains $
1.86	1.82	1.81	1.82	1.77	1.73	1.69	1.68	1.69	1.68	1.72	1.70	Expense Ratio %
1.10	0.50	0.50	0.80	0.40	-0.10	-0.40	-0.60	-0.50	-0.50	-0.40	-0.60	Income Ratio %
22	26	20	20	10	13	19	20	27	24	25	4	Turnover Rate %
914	933	1,340	1,976	3,683	8,079	12,540	10,597	9,788	7,218	10,738	11,947	Net Assets $mil

Performance 12-31-04

	1st Qtr	2nd Qtr	3rd Qtr	4th Qtr	Total
2000	-0.01	-3.31	1.78	-5.63	-7.14
2001	-3.08	7.33	-20.01	9.02	-9.29
2002	-3.66	-13.73	-13.96	13.38	-18.92
2003	-2.91	25.48	3.54	13.79	43.53
2004	-1.22	4.59	-5.80	15.04	11.96

Trailing	Total Return%	+/- S&P 500	+/- Russ 1000	%Rank Cat	Growth of $10,000
3 Mo	15.04	5.81	5.24	1	11,504
6 Mo	8.37	1.18	0.56	23	10,837
1 Yr	11.96	1.09	0.56	22	11,196
3 Yr Avg	9.22	5.64	4.95	3	13,029
5 Yr Avg	1.88	4.18	3.64	13	10,976
10 Yr Avg	18.58	6.51	6.42	1	54,969
15 Yr Avg	14.61	3.68	3.53	3	77,328

Tax Analysis	Tax-Adj Rtn%	%Rank Cat	Tax-Cost Rat	%Rank Cat
3 Yr (estimated)	9.22	2	0.00	1
5 Yr (estimated)	0.97	13	0.89	47
10 Yr (estimated)	17.34	1	1.05	32

Potential Capital Gain Exposure: 28% of assets

Rating and Risk

Time Period	Load-Adj Return %	Morningstar Rtn vs Cat	Morningstar Risk vs Cat	Morningstar Risk-Adj Rating
1 Yr	11.96			
3 Yr	9.22	High	High	★★★★★
5 Yr	1.88	+Avg	High	★★★★
10 Yr	18.58	High	High	★★★★★
Incept	17.01			

Other Measures	Standard Index S&P 500	Best Fit Index Russ 1000
Alpha	5.5	4.6
Beta	1.29	1.31
R-Squared	87	88
Standard Deviation	23.02	
Mean	9.22	
Sharpe Ratio	0.34	

Portfolio Analysis 09-30-04

Share change since 03-04 Total Stocks:34	Sector	PE	YTD Ret%	% Assets
Nextel Communications	Telecom	11.1	6.95	7.10
Tyco International	Ind Mtrls	25.1	35.41	7.06
UnitedHealth Group	Health	23.8	51.38	6.29
Amazon.com	Consumer	55.5	-15.83	6.09
⊕ J P Morgan Chase	Financial	19.4	9.97	5.47
⊕ Iac / Interactivecorp	Consumer	43.1	-18.60	4.68
⊕ eBay	Consumer	81.6	80.07	3.73
⊕ Eastman Kodak	Goods	—	27.90	3.71
⊕ AES	Utilities	30.9	44.81	3.52
⊖ MGIC Investment	Financial	12.7	21.42	3.42
⊖ Washington Mutual	Financial	13.9	10.05	2.91
Waste Management	Business	18.9	3.81	2.87
⊕ Citigroup	Financial	15.3	2.72	2.69
⊕ Home Depot	Consumer	19.0	21.47	2.65
Albertson's	Consumer	20.2	8.87	2.59
⊕ The Directv Group	Media	—	1.15	2.56
Electronic Arts	Software	30.9	29.36	2.49
⊕ Qwest Communications Int	Telecom	—	2.78	2.41
McKesson	Health	15.8	-1.41	2.26
Capital One Financial	Financial	12.5	37.61	2.25

Current Investment Style

Value Blnd Growth; Large Mid Small

Market Cap	%
Giant	29.3
Large	55.3
Mid	15.4
Small	0.0
Micro	0.0

Avg $mil: 24,222

Value Measures		Rel Category
Price/Earnings	16.75	0.99
Price/Book	2.17	0.83
Price/Sales	0.88	0.61
Price/Cash Flow	8.38	1.09
Dividend Yield %	0.82	0.55

Growth Measures	%	Rel Category
Long-Term Erngs	12.99	1.12
Book Value	5.69	0.73
Sales	7.17	1.25
Cash Flow	9.29	0.98
Historical Erngs	5.50	0.47

Profitability	%	Rel Category
Return on Equity	13.67	0.78
Return on Assets	8.53	0.99
Net Margin	9.59	0.84

Sector Weightings	% of Stocks	Rel S&P 500	3 Year High	3 Year Low
Info	22.81	1.06		
Software	4.06	0.94	5	0
Hardware	2.73	0.27	7	2
Media	6.43	1.67	7	3
Telecom	9.59	3.04	12	3
Service	62.79	1.35		
Health	12.96	1.04	16	13
Consumer	21.66	2.39	23	18
Business	6.83	1.69	10	6
Financial	21.34	1.03	34	21
Mfg	14.41	0.45		
Goods	3.74	0.40	6	3
Ind Mtrls	7.12	0.56	7	3
Energy	0.00	0.00	0	0
Utilities	3.55	1.20	4	2

Composition

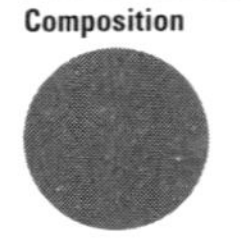

Cash	0.8
Stocks	99.2
Bonds	0.0
Other	0.0
Foreign (% of Stock)	2.2

Morningstar's Take by Christopher Traulsen 01-07-05

Legg Mason Value's 2004 showing helps illustrate its strengths.

We don't want to put too much emphasis on the fact that this fund just beat the S&P 500 index for the 14th straight year under manager Bill Miller. As we've said before, the fund has lagged the index over numerous 12-month periods during its streak--only none of them happened to match up with a calendar year. What matters is that Miller has delivered excellent long-term returns.

Still, it's worth looking at how the fund beat the index, as it helps shed some light on what sets Miller apart from other managers. As the fund's low turnover shows, he invests for the long term and, based on his team's research, he's often more willing to make more-optimistic assumptions about companies' prospects than are many value managers. Thus, while many shunned Tyco as having too many problems after its scandal in early 2002, Miller's team studied the business and determined that the market had oversold the firm realtive to their assessment of its future prospects. Miller follows up this research by holding significant positions in relatively few companies.

The resulting portfolio is concentrated and has little in common with its benchmark. In 2004, investors saw both the risks and the rewards of that trait. The fund badly lagged the index for most of the year as several top holdings slid. But Miller didn't try to rapidly adjust the portfolio; he stuck with the same stocks, which he thought remained good long-term investments. The market eventually agreed with him, and the fund surged past the index in the last two months of the year.

In a world where far too many managers deliver mediocre portfolios aimed at not taking big risks versus their benchmarks, Miller's approach is refreshing, and he and his team have shown they have the skill to pull it off with aplomb. However, we remain concerned with the fund's high overall expense ratio. The fund's board should ensure that retail investors are offered a cheaper alternative.

Address:	100 Light St Baltimore MD 21203 800-577-8589
Web Address:	www.leggmason.com
Inception:	04-16-82
Advisor:	Legg Mason Funds Management Inc.
Subadvisor:	None
NTF Plans:	DATALynx NTF, TD Waterhouse Ins NT

Minimum Purchase:	$1000	Add: $100	IRA: $1000
Min Auto Inv Plan:	$1000	Add: $50	
Sales Fees:	0.75%B, 0.20%S		
Management Fee:	0.66%		
Actual Fees:	Mgt:0.66%	Dist:0.95%	
Expense Projections:	3Yr:$536	5Yr:$923	10Yr:$2009
Income Distrib:	Annually		

LKCM Small Cap Equity Ins

Ticker	Load	NAV	Yield	Total Assets	Mstar Category
LKSCX	None	$21.46	0.0%	$344 mil	Small Blend

Governance and Management

Fiduciary Grade: A

Portfolio Manager(s)

Luther King founded Luther King Capital Management in 1979 and has managed this fund since its 1994 inception. Steve Purvis has comanaged the fund since January 1998, serving as the firm's director of research before that. They are supported by a team of 11 analysts, two of whom are dedicated to analyzing small-cap stocks.

Strategy

Managers Luther King and Steve Purvis like to invest in companies they'd like to own outright. This means that their holdings tend to have a unique niche or product, high returns on capital, and a strong balance sheet. They consider valuation important and will trim a stock if it's getting too expensive, but they won't buy a stock just because it's cheap. Although they consider themselves primarily bottom-up managers, they do use macroeconomic forecasts to help shape the portfolio.

Historical Profile

Return Average
Risk Low
Rating ★★★★ Above Avg

Investment Style: Equity, Stock %: 93% 94% 83% 79% 79% 86% 88% 95% 94%

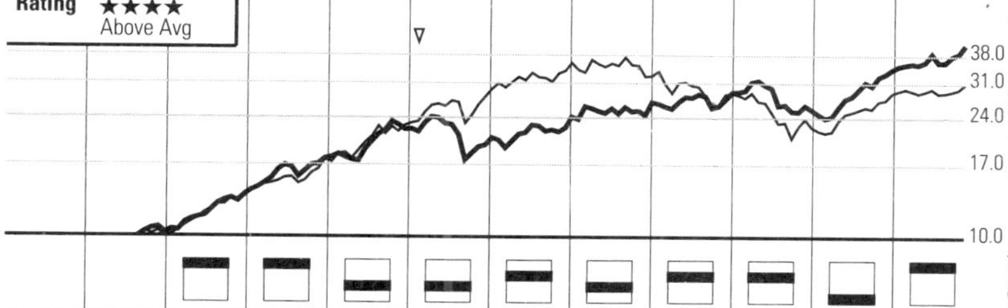

History	1993	1994	1995	1996	1997	1998	1999	2000	2001	2002	2003	12-04
NAV	—	10.50	13.84	16.20	16.89	15.72	18.08	17.00	17.29	15.24	19.54	21.46
Total Return %	—	5.00*	33.23	26.95	23.07	-6.26	16.82	11.37	7.50	-11.79	34.71	22.09
+/-S&P 500	—	—	-4.30	4.01	-10.28	-34.83	-4.22	20.47	19.38	10.30	6.04	11.22
+/-Russ 2000	—	—	4.78	10.46	0.71	-3.71	-4.44	14.39	5.01	8.69	-12.54	3.76
Income Return %	—	0.00	1.33	0.49	0.45	0.39	0.18	0.28	0.44	0.03	0.00	0.00
Capital Return %	—	—	31.90	26.46	22.62	-6.65	16.64	11.09	7.06	-11.82	34.71	22.09
Total Rtn % Rank Cat	—	—	17	23	70	58	41	58	50	26	84	21
Income $	—	0.00	0.14	0.07	0.07	0.07	0.03	0.05	0.07	0.01	0.00	0.00
Capital Gains $	—	0.00	0.00	1.02	2.64	0.05	0.25	3.10	0.92	0.01	1.00	2.40
Expense Ratio %	—	—	1.00	1.00	0.95	0.91	0.90	0.93	0.92	0.94	0.97	—
Income Ratio %	—	—	1.15	0.39	0.22	0.35	0.16	0.32	0.46	-0.19	-0.45	—
Turnover Rate %	—	—	53	66	34	35	48	79	62	52	43	—
Net Assets $mil	—	—	123	199	255	246	230	211	221	207	267	344

Performance 12-31-04

	1st Qtr	2nd Qtr	3rd Qtr	4th Qtr	Total
2000	6.42	-0.05	-2.24	7.11	11.37
2001	-4.59	8.51	-7.33	12.05	7.50
2002	7.98	-4.28	-15.67	1.21	-11.79
2003	-4.92	16.15	8.14	12.80	34.71
2004	4.35	7.60	-1.82	10.75	22.09

Trailing	Total Return%	+/- S&P 500	+/- Russ 2000	%Rank Cat	Growth of $10,000
3 Mo	10.75	1.52	-3.34	84	11,075
6 Mo	8.73	1.54	-2.10	79	10,873
1 Yr	22.09	11.22	3.76	21	12,209
3 Yr Avg	13.20	9.62	1.72	40	14,506
5 Yr Avg	11.67	13.97	5.06	54	17,365
10 Yr Avg	14.75	2.68	3.21	34	39,585
15 Yr Avg	—	—	—	—	—

Tax Analysis	Tax-Adj Rtn%	%Rank Cat	Tax-Cost Rat	%Rank Cat
3 Yr (estimated)	12.35	38	0.75	51
5 Yr (estimated)	10.12	52	1.39	68
10 Yr (estimated)	13.02	25	1.51	32

Potential Capital Gain Exposure: 37% of assets

Rating and Risk

Time Period	Load-Adj Return %	Morningstar Rtn vs Cat	Morningstar Risk vs Cat	Morningstar Risk-Adj Rating
1 Yr	22.09			
3 Yr	13.20	Avg	Low	★★★★
5 Yr	11.67	Avg	Low	★★★
10 Yr	14.75	Avg	-Avg	★★★★
Incept	14.58			

Other Measures	Standard Index S&P 500	Best Fit Index Mstar Small Core
Alpha	10.2	0.8
Beta	0.72	0.81
R-Squared	56	92
Standard Deviation	16.24	
Mean	13.20	
Sharpe Ratio	0.74	

Portfolio Analysis 09-30-04

Share change since 06 04 Total Stocks:89

Share change	Holding	Sector	PE	YTD Ret%	% Assets
⊖	Kirby	Business	21.8	27.24	3.07
⊕	Texas Regional Bancshare	Financial	16.7	34.08	2.08
	EGL	Business	30.2	70.02	1.93
	Lindsay Manufacturing	Ind Mtrls	29.9	3.38	1.92
	Landstar System	Business	37.0	93.59	1.63
	Reliance Steel and Alumi	Ind Mtrls	33.9	18.18	1.66
	Mobile Mini	Ind Mtrls	35.5	67.55	1.66
	Tractor Supply	Consumer	24.8	-4.58	1.60
	Cullen/Frost Bankers	Financial	18.4	22.60	1.43
⊕	Captiva Software	Software	41.7	-19.65	1.46
	Millennium Chemicals	Ind Mtrls	—	—	1.45
⊕	P.F. Chang's China Bistr	Consumer	62.4	10.75	1.43
	Province Healthcare	Health	23.2	39.69	1.42
	Harris	Hardware	27.4	64.22	1.40
	Hydril	Energy	28.3	89.55	1.37
⊕	Hughes Supply	Business	16.1	31.56	1.34
	Denbury Resources	Energy	19.5	97.34	1.29
	United Natural Foods	Consumer	37.4	73.21	1.29
	Waste Connections	Business	20.4	36.02	1.29
	Triad Hospitals	Health	30.3	11.84	1.28

Current Investment Style

Value Blnd Growth; Large Mid Small

Market Cap	%
Giant	0.0
Large	0.0
Mid	22.1
Small	60.2
Micro	17.7

Avg $mil: 970

Value Measures		Rel Category
Price/Earnings	18.38	1.10
Price/Book	2.39	1.05
Price/Sales	1.04	1.09
Price/Cash Flow	8.09	1.38
Dividend Yield %	1.03	1.24

Growth Measures	%	Rel Category
Long-Term Erngs	16.08	1.19
Book Value	7.15	1.27
Sales	7.44	1.73
Cash Flow	11.68	2.36
Historical Erngs	9.83	1.32

Profitability	%	Rel Category
Return on Equity	10.23	0.98
Return on Assets	4.68	0.94
Net Margin	5.92	0.81

Sector Weightings	% of Stocks	Rel S&P 500	3 Year High	3 Year Low
Info	14.91	0.69		
Software	5.49	1.28	5	0
Hardware	5.33	0.52	10	2
Media	1.70	0.44	7	2
Telecom	2.39	0.76	2	0
Service	52.24	1.13		
Health	7.35	0.59	13	7
Consumer	12.81	1.41	14	9
Business	16.77	4.14	20	15
Financial	15.31	0.74	16	12
Mfg	32.86	1.02		
Goods	5.55	0.59	9	5
Ind Mtrls	18.88	1.49	25	14
Energy	8.43	1.18	12	7
Utilities	0.00	0.00	0	0

Composition

Cash	5.9
Stocks	94.1
Bonds	0.0
Other	0.0
Foreign (% of Stock)	1.7

Morningstar's Take by David Kathman 11-22-04

LKCM Small Cap Equity continues to quietly impress.

There's nothing flashy about this fund. Lead manager Luther King has been at the helm since its inception a decade ago, and comanager Steve Purvis has been on board since 1998, before which he was an analyst under King. The fund has beaten the small-blend category by a modest amount over its lifetime, but more importantly, it has done so with an appealing steadiness. It has been notably less volatile than most of its small-blend peers and has only lost money in one year, 2002, when its 11.8% loss was still better than the small-blend average.

King and Purvis employ a fairly low-key strategy that can't be easily pigeonholed. They look for quality small-cap names with high returns on capital, strong balance sheets, and competitive advantages, preferably stocks they can hold for a long time. They're very aware of valuation but are not really value investors, as the fund's average valuations are all somewhat higher than the small-blend average.

The fund has been having a strong year in 2004, with double-digit returns that ranked near the small-blend category's top 10% as of mid-November. Part of this outperformance has been due to good sector and industry weightings. The fund has been underweight relative to its peers in tech stocks, which have mostly struggled, and a big bet on transport stocks such as Kirby, EGL, and Landstar System (all among the top 10 holdings) has paid off handsomely. A higher than usual number of holdings have also been acquired at a premium this year, boosting returns.

We don't expect the fund to always perform as well as it has this year, but we do expect it to continue its steady course, putting up respectable returns with a lot less volatility than most of its peers. Add in a low expense ratio for its category and a generally shareholder-friendly culture, and there's plenty to like here.

Address:	73 Tremont Street Boston MA 01082 800-688-5526
Web Address:	www.lkcm.com
Inception:	07-14-94*
Advisor:	King Luther Capital Managment Corp Adv
Subadvisor:	None
NTF Plans:	N/A

Minimum Purchase:	$10000	Add: $1000	IRA: $10000
Min Auto Inv Plan:	$10000	Add: $100	
Sales Fees:	No-load, 1.00%R		
Management Fee:	0.75%, 0.06%A		
Actual Fees:	Mgt:0.75%	Dist:	
Expense Projections:	3Yr:$309	5Yr:$536	10Yr:$1189
Income Distrib:	Annually		

Longleaf Partners

Ticker	Load	NAV	Yield	Total Assets	Mstar Category
LLPFX	Closed	$31.32	0.5%	$8,192 mil	Large Value

Governance and Management

Fiduciary Grade: A

Portfolio Manager(s)

Mason Hawkins and Staley Cates have been at the helm since 1987 and 1994, respectively. John Buford was named comanager in 1999. The team members keep all of their own invested assets in this fund and its siblings.

Strategy

This fund takes value seriously. Its comanagers scour the markets for companies that trade at discounts of 40% or more to the team's estimates of their intrinsic value, using discounted cash-flow analysis, asset values, or sales of comparable firms to determine the latter. The team isn't afraid to take sizable positions, and the fund typically holds 20 to 25 names. The fund rarely finds stocks that meet its criteria in growth sectors, such as technology.

Historical Profile

Return High
Risk Average
Rating ★★★★★ Highest

Investment Style: Equity Stock %

80%	100%	96%	98%	100%	83%	83%	85%	78%

▼ Manager Change
▽ Partial Manager Change

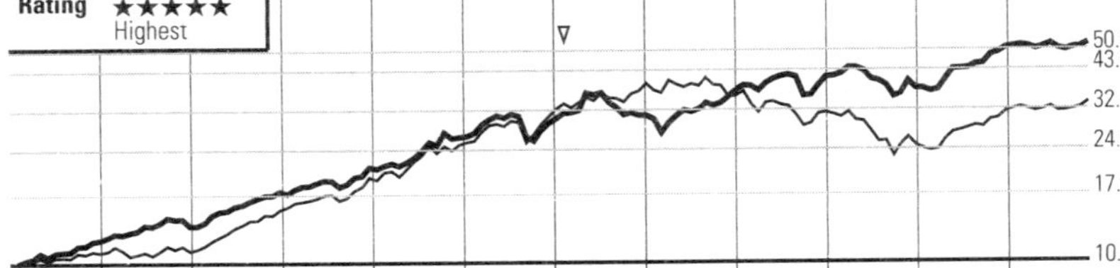

Growth of $10,000
▬ Investment Values of Fund
— Investment Values of S&P 500

Performance Quartile (within Category)

History

1993	1994	1995	1996	1997	1998	1999	2000	2001	2002	2003	12-04	History
16.92	17.13	21.15	22.85	25.98	24.39	20.49	22.71	24.51	22.24	29.98	31.32	NAV
22.23	8.96	27.48	21.02	28.25	14.28	2.18	20.60	10.34	-8.34	34.80	7.14	Total Return %
12.17	7.65	-10.05	-1.92	-5.10	-14.29	-18.86	29.70	22.22	13.75	6.13	-3.73	+/-S&P 500
4.16	10.94	-10.88	-0.62	-6.93	-1.35	-5.17	13.59	15.93	7.18	4.77	-9.35	+/-Russ 1000 VI
0.64	0.95	1.40	1.81	0.94	1.15	1.42	0.80	0.87	0.35	0.00	0.50	Income Return %
21.59	8.01	26.08	19.21	27.31	13.13	0.76	19.80	9.47	-8.69	34.80	6.64	Capital Return %
4	1	85	39	40	39	62	11	5	4	10	97	Total Rtn % Rank Cat
0.09	0.16	0.24	0.38	0.21	0.25	0.29	0.15	0.20	0.09	0.00	0.15	Income $
0.95	1.14	0.44	2.38	3.11	4.81	4.23	1.72	0.33	0.14	0.00	0.63	Capital Gains $
1.26	1.17	1.01	0.95	0.94	0.93	0.92	0.93	0.94	0.91	0.91	—	Expense Ratio %
0.63	1.18	1.45	1.61	0.81	1.12	1.16	0.75	0.89	0.17	0.32	—	Income Ratio %
19	27	13	33	38	44	50	20	18	20	7	—	Turnover Rate %
397	754	1,876	2,300	2,605	3,688	3,631	3,757	4,535	5,052	7,669	8,192	Net Assets $mil

Performance 12-31-04

	1st Qtr	2nd Qtr	3rd Qtr	4th Qtr	Total
2000	-5.42	8.46	4.85	12.12	20.60
2001	-0.40	11.32	-13.62	15.21	10.34
2002	7.10	-8.15	-12.36	6.32	-8.34
2003	-1.03	16.67	3.97	12.28	34.80
2004	1.20	1.85	-2.98	7.14	7.14

Trailing	Total Return%	+/- S&P 500	+/- Russ 1000 VI	%Rank Cat	Growth of $10,000
3 Mo	7.14	-2.09	-3.24	92	10,714
6 Mo	3.95	-3.24	-8.13	98	10,395
1 Yr	7.14	-3.73	-9.35	97	10,714
3 Yr Avg	9.80	6.22	1.23	7	13,238
5 Yr Avg	11.99	14.29	6.72	4	17,616
10 Yr Avg	15.07	3.00	1.24	4	40,703
15 Yr Avg	14.48	3.55	2.45	1	76,023

Tax Analysis	Tax-Adj Rtn%	%Rank Cat	Tax-Cost Rat	%Rank Cat
3 Yr (estimated)	9.53	5	0.25	17
5 Yr (estimated)	11.28	2	0.63	34
10 Yr (estimated)	13.00	3	1.80	51

Potential Capital Gain Exposure: 27% of assets

Rating and Risk

Time Period	Load-Adj Return %	Morningstar Rtn vs Cat	Morningstar Risk vs Cat	Morningstar Risk-Adj Rating
1 Yr	7.14			
3 Yr	9.80	High	-Avg	★★★★★
5 Yr	11.99	High	Avg	★★★★★
10 Yr	15.07	High	+Avg	★★★★★
Incept	14.47			

Other Measures	Standard Index S&P 500	Best Fit Index S&P Mid 400
Alpha	6.7	1.5
Beta	0.73	0.75
R-Squared	69	74
Standard Deviation	14.31	
Mean	9.80	
Sharpe Ratio	0.59	

Morningstar's Take by Christopher Traulsen 10-31-04

Longleaf Partners deserves and requires a long-term commitment.

This closed fund is having a difficult 2004. For the year to date through Oct. 29, 2004, it's up just 0.63%. The fund's average mid-value peer is up 7.14%, and the average large-blend fund is up 2% (the fund remains in the mid-value category, but its last few portfolios have landed in large-blend).

That short-term underperformance helps point to some potential pitfalls. Despite its Morningstar style box position, the managers are disciplined value investors who try to seek out companies with quality management that are trading well below the team's estimates of their intrinsic values. This often leads them to invest in companies that may face significant near-term issues. They recently added to the fund's position in Philips Electronics, for example, believing it had been oversold based on weakness in the semiconductor sector. Such companies can fall further before they turn around. The managers also hold just 20-35 stocks in the fund, so every pick has a significant impact.

In 2004, Level 3 Communications has hurt the fund badly, but the managers believe their case for investing in the company is intact. They like the demand growth for the firm's broadband capacity, and think it's extremely undervalued. More recently, insurer Aon was hurt by Eliot Spitzer's investigation into contingent commissions. Manager Staley Cates notes, however, that the commissions are not nearly as important to Aon's business as they are to some other firms', and that even after removing the commissions from the firm's value, Aon still looks cheap.

That willingness to wait out bad news and focus on the long term are key traits of this fund, and they've served it extremely well in the long-term--its 10-year return is excellent. For investors to get those results, however, they need to be willing to wait out periods like the current one--or worse. We believe doing so will prove worthwhile in the long haul.

Address:	6410 Poplar Memphis TN 38119 800-445-9469
Web Address:	www.LongleafPartners.com
Inception:	04-08-87
Advisor:	Southeastern Asset Management Inc.
Subadvisor:	None
NTF Plans:	N/A

Minimum Purchase:	Closed	Add: —	IRA: —
Min Auto Inv Plan:	Closed	Add: —	
Sales Fees:	No-load		
Management Fee:	1.00% mx./0.75% mn., 0.10%A		
Actual Fees:	Mgt:0.77%	Dist:	
Expense Projections:	3Yr:$298	5Yr:$518	10Yr:$1150
Income Distrib:	Annually		

Portfolio Analysis 09-30-04

Share change since 06-04 Total Stocks:22	Sector	PE	YTD Ret%	% Assets
FedEx	Business	27.9	46.40	6.01
⊕ Philips Elec(Kon)	Goods	—	—	5.50
Aon	Financial	10.8	2.17	5.25
Walt Disney	Media	24.3	20.21	5.20
Yum Brands	Consumer	19.7	37.84	5.02
⊕ General Motors	Goods	7.2	-21.48	4.64
Vivendi Universal	Media	—	—	4.60
⊕ NIPPONKOA Insurance	Financial	—	—	4.45
Comcast	Media	—	-13.77	4.45
⊕ The Directv Group	Media	—	1.15	4.28
Hilton Hotels	Consumer	36.1	33.34	4.25
Telephone and Data Syste	Telecom	39.5	24.11	3.78
Pioneer Natural Resource	Energy	15.3	10.60	3.72
Waste Management	Business	18.9	3.81	3.47
TrizecHahn	Financial	—	—	2.65
Diageo	Goods	—	—	2.62
Level 3 Communications	Telecom	—	-40.53	2.62
Knight Ridder	Media	16.8	-11.83	2.43
Vivendi Universal ADR	Media	—	32.08	1.33
⊖ Marriott International A	Consumer	25.6	37.22	0.74

Current Investment Style

Value Blnd Growth / Large Mid Small

Market Cap	%
Giant	11.8
Large	64.5
Mid	23.6
Small	0.0
Micro	0.0
Avg $mil: 13,948	

Value Measures		Rel Category
Price/Earnings	15.55	1.03
Price/Book	1.74	0.77
Price/Sales	0.70	0.59
Price/Cash Flow	7.36	1.15
Dividend Yield %	1.10	0.54

Growth Measures	%	Rel Category
Long-Term Erngs	10.88	1.05
Book Value	0.38	0.07
Sales	-2.41	NMF
Cash Flow	-0.16	NMF
Historical Erngs	13.76	1.16

Profitability	%	Rel Category
Return on Equity	12.16	0.77
Return on Assets	3.79	0.48
Net Margin	4.38	0.43

Sector Weightings	% of Stocks	Rel S&P 500	3 Year High	3 Year Low
Info	37.46	1.74		
Software	0.00	0.00	0	0
Hardware	0.00	0.00	0	0
Media	29.27	7.62	30	11
Telecom	8.19	2.60	14	4
Service	40.74	0.88		
Health	0.00	0.00	0	0
Consumer	12.80	1.41	22	13
Business	12.13	3.00	16	12
Financial	15.81	0.76	17	12
Mfg	21.80	0.68		
Goods	17.04	1.83	18	10
Ind Mtrls	0.00	0.00	10	0
Energy	4.76	0.66	8	5
Utilities	0.00	0.00	0	0

Composition

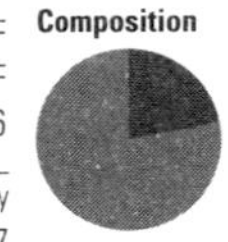

Cash	21.9
Stocks	78.1
Bonds	0.0
Other	0.0
Foreign (% of Stock)	27.8

Longleaf Partners Intl

Ticker	Load	NAV	Yield	Total Assets	Mstar Category
LLINX	Closed	$15.55	0.0%	$2,362 mil	Foreign Large Value

Governance and Management

Fiduciary Grade: B

Portfolio Manager(s)

Comanagers Mason Hawkins and Staley Cates and assistant manager Andrew McDermott have run this fund since its inception. Hawkins and Cates are veteran managers of Longleaf Partners' domestic offerings. McDermott is based in Japan, which allows the team to keep close tabs on its Asian holdings. One of the team's analysts, Jim Thompson, works out of London and provides research for the fund's U.K. and European holdings.

Strategy

This fund's managers only buy companies that trade at discounts of 40% or more to their estimates of their intrinsic values. They also pay scant attention to country and sector weightings. The fund holds 20 to 30 names and eschews pricey sectors. Although it carries substantial issue- and country-specific risk, its limited valuation risk should help moderate volatility. The managers hedge the economic exposure of the fund's holdings to foreign currency.

Historical Profile

Return Average
Risk Above Avg
Rating ★★★ Neutral

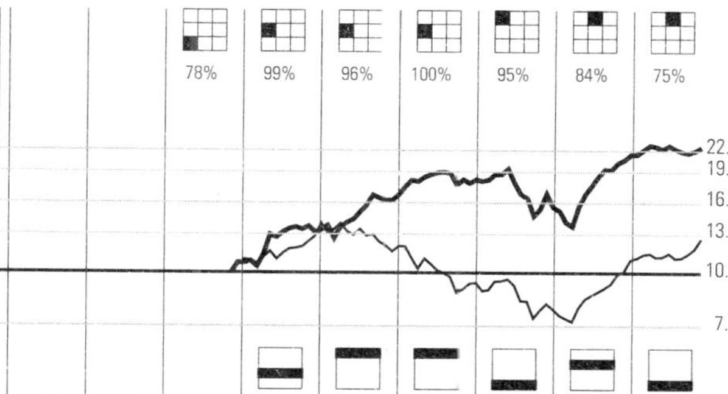

Investment Style
Equity
Stock %

▼ Manager Change
▽ Partial Manager Change

Growth of $10,000
— Investment Values of Fund
— Investment Values of MSCI EAFE

Performance Quartile (within Category)

1993	1994	1995	1996	1997	1998	1999	2000	2001	2002	2003	12-04	History
—	—	—	—	—	9.97	12.02	12.06	12.34	9.97	14.11	15.55	NAV
—	—	—	—	—	9.02*	24.37	25.93	10.47	-16.52	41.52	10.21	Total Return %
—	—	—	—	—	—	-2.66	40.12	31.89	-0.58	2.93	-10.04	+/-MSCI EAFE
—	—	—	—	—	—	-3.61	39.29	31.86	-0.72	2.10	-10.17	+/-MSCI Wd xUS
—	—	—	—	—	0.00	0.57	3.80	1.15	0.00	0.00	0.00	Income Return %
—	—	—	—	—	—	23.80	22.13	9.32	-16.52	41.52	10.21	Capital Return %
—	—	—	—	—	—	54	1	1	84	33	100	Total Rtn % Rank Cat
—	—	—	—	—	0.01	0.06	0.38	0.13	0.00	0.00	0.00	Income $
—	—	—	—	—	0.00	0.33	2.63	0.85	0.32	0.00	0.00	Capital Gains $
—	—	—	—	—	1.75	1.75	1.79	1.82	1.80	1.68	—	Expense Ratio %
—	—	—	—	—	0.10	0.60	3.36	1.17	-0.68	-0.68	—	Income Ratio %
—	—	—	—	—	—	50	69	32	16	10	—	Turnover Rate %
—	—	—	—	—	75	294	403	834	1,016	1,924	2,362	Net Assets $mil

Performance 12-31-04

	1st Qtr	2nd Qtr	3rd Qtr	4th Qtr	Total
2000	2.08	10.11	9.62	2.21	25.93
2001	9.12	6.00	-7.67	3.44	10.47
2002	3.57	-5.32	-19.59	5.88	-16.52
2003	-11.84	30.72	10.97	10.67	41.52
2004	6.52	-0.20	-4.67	8.74	10.21

Trailing	Total Return%	+/- MSCI EAFE	+/- MSCI Wd xUS	%Rank Cat	Growth of $10,000
3 Mo	8.74	-6.58	-6.41	95	10,874
6 Mo	3.67	-11.33	-11.70	100	10,367
1 Yr	10.21	-10.04	-10.17	100	11,021
3 Yr Avg	9.20	-2.69	-3.02	94	13,022
5 Yr Avg	12.62	13.75	13.38	1	18,117
10 Yr Avg	—	—	—	—	—
15 Yr Avg	—	—	—	—	—

Tax Analysis	Tax-Adj Rtn%	%Rank Cat	Tax-Cost Rat	%Rank Cat
3 Yr (estimated)	8.86	91	0.31	26
5 Yr (estimated)	10.32	3	2.04	97
10 Yr (estimated)	—	—	—	—

Potential Capital Gain Exposure: 21% of assets

Rating and Risk

Time Period	Load-Adj Return %	Morningstar Rtn vs Cat	Morningstar Risk vs Cat	Morningstar Risk-Adj Rating
1 Yr	10.21			
3 Yr	9.20	Low	+Avg	★
5 Yr	12.62	High	+Avg	★★★★★
10 Yr	—	—	—	—
Incept	15.64			

Other Measures	Standard Index S&P 500	Best Fit Index MSCI World
Alpha	-1.9	3.4
Beta	0.99	1.06
R-Squared	71	74
Standard Deviation	20.25	
Mean	9.20	
Sharpe Ratio	0.39	

Morningstar's Take by Christopher Traulsen 11-29-04

Longleaf Partners International can pay a price for its individuality, but it should be worth it.

This closed fund is up 5.1% for the year to date through November 26. That's solid enough in absolute terms, but the performance of other foreign large-value funds is far better: The typical fund in the category is up 17%.

A big part of the problem is the fund's cash stake, which has ranged between 25% and 30% of assets for much of the year. The fund's policy of hedging its economic exposure to foreign currency has also dented the fund's performance relative to unhedged peers. With the dollar weakening against major currencies, the fund hasn't benefited from foreign-currency gains to the same extent as many of its rivals. At 43% of the fund's equity exposure, the fund's position in Japan is about twice the category norm. With European equities vastly outperforming Japanese issues in 2004, that slant has also worked against the fund.

That alone should be enough to suggest that the fund doesn't look much like its peers. Investors here shouldn't expect that to change. The managers are deep-value investors who go wherever they find bargains, regardless of the fund's country weights. They will hold cash when they can't find securities that meet their criteria. And (to their credit, in our view) they're willing to hold companies through near-term dips. Canadian insurer Fairfax Financial, for example, has slumped under pressure from a large short interest in 2004. The managers don't think the shorts' concerns are warranted. Further, they've known the firm's CEO for 25 years and think he's a top-rate manager.

Given its style, this fund will post returns that will deviate wildly from category norms at times. Over time, however, it has proven the strength of its approach by delivering a top flight five-year return. It probably shouldn't be one's only source of foreign-stock exposure, but investors in this fund have every reason to stay put if they can withstand its risks.

Address:	6410 Poplar Memphis TN 38119 800-445-9469
Web Address:	www.LongleafPartners.com
Inception:	10-26-98 *
Advisor:	Southeastern Asset Management Inc.
Subadvisor:	None
NTF Plans:	N/A

Minimum Purchase:	Closed	Add: —		IRA: —	
Min Auto Inv Plan:	Closed	Add: —			
Sales Fees:	No-load				
Management Fee:	1.50% mx./1.25% mn., 0.10%A				
Actual Fees:	Mgt:1.50%	Dist:			
Expense Projections:	3Yr:$585	5Yr: —		10Yr: —	
Income Distrib:	Annually				

Portfolio Analysis 09-30-04

Share change since 06-04 Total Stocks:23	Sector	Country	% Assets
NIPPONKOA Insurance	Financial	Japan	6.74
Renault	Goods	France	5.51
Shaw Communications	Media	Canada	5.49
Vivendi Universal	Media	France	5.03
☼ Olympus	Goods	Japan	5.02
Millea Hldgs	Financial	Japan	4.56
Nippon Broadcasting Syte	Media	Japan	4.24
Yum Brands	Consumer	United States	4.15
Nippon Telegraph & Telep	Telecom	Japan	3.42
Bil International Limite	—	—	3.12
Fairfax Financial Hldgs	Financial	Canada	3.09
Philips Electronics NV A	Goods	Netherlands	2.96
⊕ Philips Elec(Kon	Goods	Netherlands	2.94
Ezaki Glico	Goods	Japan	2.74
NTT DoCoMo	Telecom	Japan	2.68
Sky Perfect Communicatio	Media	Japan	2.58
Adolph Coors B	Goods	United States	2.53
TrizecHahn	Financial	Canada	2.15
☼ Willis Group Holdings	Business	Bermuda	1.39
News Corporation ADR	Media	Australia	1.32

Current Investment Style

Value Blnd Growth — Large Mid Small

Market Cap	%
Giant	20.7
Large	54.3
Mid	24.6
Small	0.0
Micro	0.4
Avg $mil: 9,282	

Value Measures		Rel Category
Price/Earnings	15.78	1.17
Price/Book	0.54	0.33
Price/Sales	0.73	0.89
Price/Cash Flow	2.39	0.54
Dividend Yield %	1.90	0.68

Growth Measures	%	Rel Category
Long-Term Erngs	7.26	0.74
Book Value	1.32	2.87
Sales	-1.92	NMF
Cash Flow	9.93	3.22
Historical Erngs	16.10	5.81

Composition

Cash	25.0	Bonds	0.0
Stocks	75.0	Other	0.0
Foreign (% of Stock)			91.1

Sector Weightings	% of Stocks	Rel MSCI EAFE	3 Year High	3 Year Low
Info	36.44	2.19		
Software	0.00	0.00	5	0
Hardware	0.00	0.00	0	0
Media	27.96	12.26	39	25
Telecom	8.48	0.88	11	0
Service	31.97	0.71		
Health	0.00	0.00	2	0
Consumer	6.17	1.22	8	5
Business	2.77	0.51	3	0
Financial	23.03	0.85	31	23
Mfg	31.58	0.82		
Goods	31.58	2.31	32	13
Ind Mtrls	0.00	0.00	4	0
Energy	0.00	0.00	0	0
Utilities	0.00	0.00	0	0

Regional Exposure	% Stock		
UK/W. Europe	24	N. America	25
Japan	45	Latn America	3
Asia X Japan	4	Other	0

Country Exposure	% Stock		
Japan	45	United States	9
Canada	15	Netherlands	8
France	15		

Longleaf Partners Sm-Cap

Ticker	Load	NAV	Yield	Total Assets	Mstar Category
LLSCX	Closed	$29.85	1.3%	$2,361 mil	Small Value

Governance and Management

Fiduciary Grade: A

Portfolio Manager(s)

Staley Cates and Mason Hawkins have comanaged the fund since 1991. John Buford was named comanager in 1999, but he has been at the firm since 1990. The team is required to limit its personal investments to this fund and other Longleaf offerings (as are all of the advisor's employees).

Strategy

This fund's comanagers scour the market for small-cap companies trading at discounts of 40% or more to the team's estimates of their intrinsic values. To arrive at this value, the team uses several methods. Much of the time, it projects future free cash flow out eight years, assuming very low growth after that period, then discounts the terminal value and flows back to the present. The team will also look for firms selling at steep discounts to the difference between their net assets or the sales prices of comparable businesses. Management will take sizable positions, and the fund typically holds just 20 to 30 names.

Historical Profile

Return Average
Risk Below Avg
Rating ★★★ Neutral

Investment Style Equity Stock %: 100% 100% 94% 99% 100% 93% 78% 87% 68%

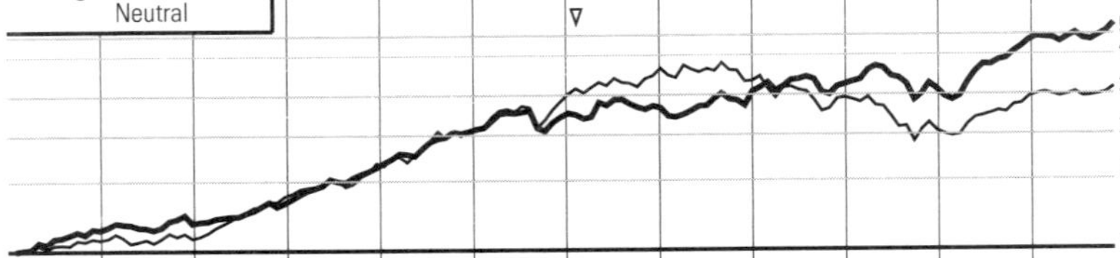

Performance Quartile (within Category)

1993	1994	1995	1996	1997	1998	1999	2000	2001	2002	2003	12-04	History
13.49	13.28	14.46	17.86	22.18	21.95	20.20	22.62	21.68	20.33	28.81	29.85	NAV
19.84	3.70	18.57	30.64	29.04	12.71	4.05	12.80	5.45	-3.74	43.85	14.78	Total Return %
9.78	2.39	-18.96	7.70	-4.31	-15.86	-16.99	21.90	17.33	18.35	15.18	3.91	+/-S&P 500
-3.93	5.24	-7.18	9.27	-2.74	19.16	5.54	-10.03	-8.57	7.69	-2.18	-7.47	+/-Russ 2000 VL
0.00	0.00	0.89	0.16	1.01	0.84	0.40	0.24	1.15	2.42	2.14	1.61	Income Return %
19.84	3.70	17.68	30.48	28.03	11.87	3.65	12.56	4.30	-6.16	41.71	13.17	Capital Return %
34	28	77	6	62	1	41	72	87	20	35	91	Total Rtn % Rank Cat
0.00	0.00	0.12	0.02	0.18	0.17	0.08	0.05	0.24	0.53	0.44	0.43	Income $
0.17	0.70	1.17	1.00	0.69	2.77	2.54	0.11	1.84	0.02	0.00	2.70	Capital Gains $
1.45	1.38	1.30	1.23	1.09	1.01	0.97	0.98	0.96	0.95	0.95	—	Expense Ratio %
-0.45	-0.22	0.84	0.18	1.18	0.87	0.38	0.24	1.14	2.43	1.89	—	Income Ratio %
14	20	33	28	17	53	47	22	40	17	4	—	Turnover Rate %
85	100	136	252	915	1,351	1,431	1,477	1,635	1,914	2,365	2,361	Net Assets $mil

Performance 12-31-04

	1st Qtr	2nd Qtr	3rd Qtr	4th Qtr	Total
2000	-4.95	6.77	4.93	5.93	12.80
2001	0.35	9.16	-9.28	6.10	5.45
2002	11.16	-4.52	-16.30	8.36	-3.74
2003	-4.97	26.50	4.46	14.55	43.85
2004	1.53	3.62	-1.95	11.27	14.78

Trailing	Total Return%	+/- S&P 500	+/- Russ 2000 VL	%Rank Cat	Growth of $10,000
3 Mo	11.27	2.04	-1.93	74	11,127
6 Mo	9.10	1.91	-4.27	88	10,910
1 Yr	14.78	3.91	-7.47	91	11,478
3 Yr Avg	16.70	13.12	0.20	33	15,893
5 Yr Avg	13.58	15.88	-3.65	75	18,902
10 Yr Avg	16.05	3.98	0.88	34	44,305
15 Yr Avg	11.62	0.69	-2.40	84	52,015

Tax Analysis	Tax-Adj Rtn%	%Rank Cat	Tax-Cost Rat	%Rank Cat
3 Yr (estimated)	15.44	34	1.08	64
5 Yr (estimated)	12.31	75	1.12	58
10 Yr (estimated)	14.20	26	1.59	34

Potential Capital Gain Exposure: 31% of assets

Rating and Risk

Time Period	Load-Adj Return %	Morningstar Rtn vs Cat	Morningstar Risk vs Cat	Morningstar Risk-Adj Rating
1 Yr	14.78			
3 Yr	16.70	+Avg	-Avg	★★★★
5 Yr	13.58	-Avg	-Avg	★★
10 Yr	16.05	Avg	Low	★★★★
Incept	12.88			

Other Measures	Standard Index S&P 500	Best Fit Index Mstar Mid Value
Alpha	13.4	2.7
Beta	0.85	0.93
R-Squared	65	71
Standard Deviation	18.38	
Mean	16.70	
Sharpe Ratio	0.84	

Portfolio Analysis 09-30-04

Share change since 06-04 Total Stocks:16	Sector	PE	YTD Ret%	% Assets
Level 3 Comms Cv 6%	—	—	—	7.03
Texas Industries	Ind Mtrls	15.5	69.88	6.07
Shaw Communications	Media	—	19.27	5.95
Adolph Coors B	Goods	16.0	36.53	5.40
Neiman-Marcus	Consumer	—	—	5.08
☼ Hilb Rogal & Hobbs Compa	Financial	15.0	14.30	4.75
Hilton Hotels	Consumer	36.1	33.34	4.73
IHOP	Consumer	27.1	11.84	4.66
NCR	Hardware	26.7	78.43	4.36
PepsiAmericas	Goods	16.1	25.93	4.11
Fairfax Financial Hldgs	Financial	12.8	-2.65	4.06
☼ Hasbro	Goods	19.3	-7.90	3.89
⊖ Forest City Enterprises	Financial	49.5	22.42	3.50
⊕ Jacuzzi Brands	Ind Mtrls	82.3	22.71	3.37
Level 3 Communications	Telecom	—	-40.53	2.88
Ruddick	Consumer	15.0	23.66	2.73
Level 3 Comms 9.125%	—	—	—	2.58
Deltic Timber	Ind Mtrls	38.4	40.58	2.43

Current Investment Style

Market Cap	%
Giant	0.0
Large	9.5
Mid	52.4
Small	38.2
Micro	0.0

Avg $mil: 1,974

Value Measures		Rel Category
Price/Earnings	17.19	1.08
Price/Book	1.77	1.07
Price/Sales	0.77	1.03
Price/Cash Flow	6.49	1.25
Dividend Yield %	0.55	0.46

Growth Measures	%	Rel Category
Long-Term Erngs	8.98	0.74
Book Value	4.15	0.96
Sales	5.28	1.69
Cash Flow	16.92	7.80
Historical Erngs	2.16	0.45

Profitability	%	Rel Category
Return on Equity	7.79	0.85
Return on Assets	2.70	0.65
Net Margin	3.55	0.53

Sector Weightings	% of Stocks	Rel S&P 500	3 Year High	3 Year Low
Info	19.41	0.90		
Software	0.00	0.00	0	0
Hardware	6.41	0.63	8	0
Media	8.76	2.28	13	6
Telecom	4.24	1.35	14	0
Service	43.42	0.94		
Health	0.00	0.00	0	0
Consumer	25.31	2.79	28	19
Business	0.00	0.00	0	0
Financial	18.11	0.87	31	18
Mfg	37.17	1.16		
Goods	19.72	2.11	20	7
Ind Mtrls	17.45	1.38	29	16
Energy	0.00	0.00	0	0
Utilities	0.00	0.00	0	0

Composition

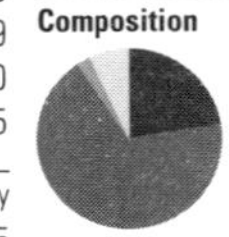

Cash	22.4
Stocks	68.0
Bonds	2.6
Other	7.0
Foreign (% of Stock)	14.7

Morningstar's Take by Christopher Traulsen 11-29-04

Longleaf Partners Small Cap merits patience.

This offering, long closed to new investors, is having a solid year in absolute terms. Its 12.8% return for the year to date through Nov. 26, 2004, also is in keeping with the fund's stated goal of generating a return of 10% over and above the rate of inflation. Still, its return is relatively poor compared with other small-value funds, ranking in the category's bottom 20% for the period.

Such a short-term showing by itself doesn't mean much, particularly given the long-term approach taken by the fund's managers. However, it has been something of a larger pattern here recently, as the fund's five-year return also ranks in the small-value category's worst decile. Part of the problem this year has been the fund's large cash stake. The managers trimmed back on some of their winners and haven't found many compelling new investments. But the fund has also been dinged by a large position in the convertible debt and a smaller position in the common stock of struggling Level 3 Communications.

We're not overly worried about either problem. The managers have held cash at their offerings before and generated good long-term results. We are somewhat concerned by the problems at Level 3, as this fund has exhibited a pattern in recent years of big positions taking a bite out of returns. Some notable bombs at the top of the portfolio have included Safety Kleen, Fleming Companies, and USG. The managers have had much success running portfolios with such large positions over the years, so we're loath to suggest changes are in order, but it's clear that such positions increase the risks at this fund.

These risks make this fund inappropriate for investors who don't share the managers' commitment to long-term investing. Given that the advisor has demonstrated an ability to execute its style well over the long term, however, we continue to think this is a fine holding for investors who have the necessary patience.

Address:	6410 Poplar Memphis TN 38119 800-445-9469
Web Address:	www.LongleafPartners.com
Inception:	12-28-88
Advisor:	Southeastern Asset Management Inc.
Subadvisor:	None
NTF Plans:	N/A

Minimum Purchase:	Closed	Add: —	IRA: —
Min Auto Inv Plan:	Closed	Add: —	
Sales Fees:	No-load		
Management Fee:	1.00% mx./0.75% mn., 0.10%A		
Actual Fees:	Mgt:0.83%	Dist:	
Expense Projections:	3Yr:$321	5Yr:$557	10Yr:$1234
Income Distrib:	Annually		

Loomis Sayles Bond Ret

Analyst Pick

Ticker	Load	NAV	Yield	SEC Yield	Total Assets	Mstar Category
LSBRX	12b-1 only	$13.80	5.7%	4.33%	$3,077 mil	Multisector Bond

Governance and Management

Fiduciary Grade: B

Portfolio Manager(s)

Dan Fuss has managed this fund since 1991 and is widely acknowledged to be one of the best in the business. Kathleen Gaffney joined him in 1997 and works on several other Loomis Sayles bond portfolios.

Strategy

This fund is about as aggressive as bond funds come. Comanagers Dan Fuss and Kathleen Gaffney typically keep close to one third of assets in a mix of domestic junk bonds and emerging-markets credits. Their strategy resembles that of a value-biased stock manager, and they often load up on bonds in out-of-favor sectors.

Historical Profile

Return High
Risk High
Rating ★★★★★ Highest

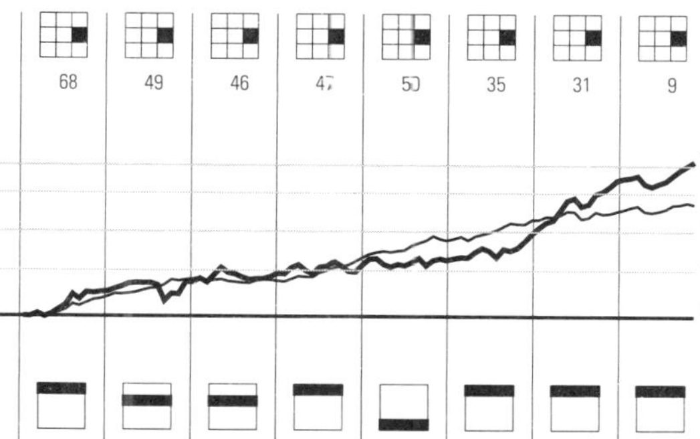

1993	1994	1995	1996	1997	1998	1999	2000	2001	2002	2003	12-04	History
—	—	—	—	12.82	11.95	11.52	11.06	10.43	10.99	13.31	13.80	NAV
—	—	—	—	12.36*	4.51	4.23	4.09	2.29	13.18	28.83	11.02	Total Return %
—	—	—	—	—	-4.18	5.05	-7.54	-6.15	2.93	24.73	6.68	+/-LB Aggr
—	—	—	—	2.58	-2.80	4.06	-6.73	-5.80	3.34	23.01	6.05	+/-LB. U.S. Univ. Bd
—	—	—	—	6.88	7.37	7.99	8.22	8.11	7.51	7.19	7.11	Income Return %
—	—	—	—	5.48	-2.86	-3.76	-4.13	-5.82	5.67	21.64	3.91	Capital Return %
—	—	—	—	9	26	38	15	76	8	9	9	Total Rtn % Rank Cat
—	—	—	—	0.83	0.92	0.93	0.92	0.87	0.76	0.77	0.92	Income $
—	—	—	—	0.22	0.52	0.00	0.00	0.00	0.00	0.00	0.00	Capital Gains $
—	—	—	—	1.00	1.00	1.00	1.00	1.00	1.00	1.00	1.00	Expense Ratio %
—	—	—	—	7.09	7.13	7.90	8.10	8.28	7.15	6.35	5.24	Income Ratio %
—	—	—	—	41	24	33	17	20	22	35	42	Turnover Rate %
—	—	—	—	33	56	61	79	63	71	180	344	Net Assets $mil

Performance 12-31-04

	1st Qtr	2nd Qtr	3rd Qtr	4th Qtr	Total
2000	4.17	-1.08	0.71	0.31	4.09
2001	0.36	-0.59	0.00	2.53	2.29
2002	1.32	3.19	0.06	8.19	13.18
2003	6.69	11.04	1.87	6.75	28.83
2004	2.24	-3.59	6.60	5.66	11.02

Trailing	Total Return%	+/- LB Aggr	+/- LB. U.S. Univ. Bd	%Rank Cat	Growth of $10,000
3 Mo	5.66	4.71	4.38	15	10,566
6 Mo	12.63	8.45	7.84	7	11,263
1 Yr	11.02	6.68	6.05	9	11,102
3 Yr Avg	17.42	11.23	10.57	5	16,189
5 Yr Avg	11.50	3.79	3.62	4	17,234
10 Yr Avg	—	—	—	—	—
15 Yr Avg	—	—	—	—	—

Tax Analysis	Tax-Adj Rtn%	%Rank Cat	Tax-Cost Rat	%Rank Cat
3 Yr (estimated)	14.60	5	2.40	62
5 Yr (estimated)	8.51	2	2.68	60
10 Yr (estimated)	—	—	—	—

Potential Capital Gain Exposure: 4% of assets

Rating and Risk

Time Period	Load-Adj Return %	Morningstar Rtn vs Cat	Morningstar Risk vs Cat	Morningstar Risk-Adj Rating
1 Yr	11.02			
3 Yr	17.42	High	High	★★★★★
5 Yr	11.50	High	High	★★★★★
10 Yr	—	—	—	—
Incept	9.78			

Other Measures	Standard Index LB Aggr	Best Fit Index LB Credit
Alpha	10.6	9.2
Beta	1.04	0.99
R-Squared	37	57
Standard Deviation	8.43	
Mean	17.42	
Sharpe Ratio	1.92	

Morningstar's Take by Paul Herbert 11-16-04

Going its own way has once again given Loomis Sayles Bond an edge.

This fund wins points for its unique strategy. Managers Dan Fuss and Kathleen Gaffney seek to provide a mix of appreciation and income, and they'll look across the credit spectrum and around the world to find attractively priced bonds and currencies. Instead of trying to match an index's returns, they're more concerned with making money for shareholders. The fund has posted impressive gains during its 13-year history.

Sticking to their convictions has paid off lately. Coming into 2004, Fuss and Gaffney were bearish on interest rates and on the U.S. dollar versus certain currencies, but fell behind the pack when market yields continued to fall and the dollar held its own in the year's first few months. But they stuck to their guns, and when rates reversed course, their cautious nature, which includes holding substantial high-yield and non-U.S positions, bore fruit. With default rates falling and the greenback depreciating relative to the Canadian, New Zealand, and Scandinavian currencies, the fund has now gained a cool 8.4% so far this year.

Fuss and Gaffney expect the same trends that have taken hold in recent months to persist. Reflecting their position that rates will tick upward as the U.S. economy improves and the Treasury's borrowing needs grow, more than half of the portfolio was recently devoted to bonds with maturities of less than five years. And high-yield bonds continue to look attractive to the managers because many issuers have repaired their financial positions and could be due for upgrades. Many junk bonds are trading more richly these days after a strong run during the past two years, but we take some comfort in the fact that the duo specifically targets bonds selling at discounts.

This fund's shareholders should brace for a bumpy ride, but in all we think this fund continues to be a standout.

Portfolio Analysis 09-30-04

Total Fixed-Income:232	Date of Maturity	Amount $000	Value $000	% Net Assets
Intl Bk Recon Dev Mtns B	08-20-07	152,375	85,953	3.23
FNMA 2.29%	02-19-09	145,900	85,566	3.21
Mexico United Mexican S	12-20-12	895,400	74,331	2.79
US Treasury Note 1.625%	02-28-06	75,000	74,235	2.79
Manitoba Prov Cda 5.75%	06-02-08	74,125	62,570	2.35
Sweden (Kingdom Of) 6.5%	05-05-08	394,045	59,505	2.23
FNMA	10-29-07	103,925	57,567	2.16
British Columbia Prov Cd	06-09-08	66,745	56,806	2.13
Canada Govt 4.5%	09-01-07	69,350	56,465	2.12
Canada Govt 4.25%	09-01-08	69,120	55,718	2.09
Inter American Developme	05-11-09	297,000	51,723	1.94
Canada Govt 6%	06-01-08	52,500	44,836	1.68
Ontario Prov Cda 3.5%	09-08-06	52,020	41,430	1.55
Lucent Tech 6.45%	03-15-29	49,920	40,435	1.52
Cerro Negro Fin 144A 7.9	12-01-20	38,705	37,737	1.42
FHLMC 2.875%	05-15-07	35,000	34,867	1.31
US Treasury Note 1.625%	10-31-05	35,000	34,781	1.31
Loews 3.125%	09-15-07	35,029	34,285	1.29
FNMA 5.25%	01-15-09	31,665	33,725	1.27
Brazil Federative Rep 8.	01-20-34	37,005	32,990	1.24

Current Investment Style

Duration: Short Int Long; Quality: High Med Low

¹ figure provided by fund

Avg Eff Duration¹	6.6 Yrs
Avg Eff Maturity	11.0 Yrs
Avg Credit Quality	A
Avg Wtd Coupon	5.46%
Avg Wtd Price	82.16% of par

Coupon Range	% of Bonds	Rel Cat
0% PIK	10.5	3.2
0% to 6%	48.7	1.1
6% to 8%	37.3	1.4
8% to 10%	13.6	0.7
More than 10%	0.5	0.0

1.00=Category Average

Credit Analysis		% bonds 09-30-04	
US Govt	18	BB	11
AAA	17	B	17
AA	9	Below B	4
A	5	NR/NA	1
BBB	17		

Sector Breakdown	% of assets
US Treasuries	5
TIPS	0
US Agency	6
Mortgage Pass-Throughs	4
Mortgage CMO	0
Mortgage ARM	0
US Corporate	42
Asset-Backed	3
Convertible	2
Municipal	0
Corporate Inflation-Protected	0
Foreign Corporate	11
Foreign Govt	15

Composition			
Cash	11.2	Bonds	84.6
Stocks	0.8	Other	3.3

Special Securities	
Restricted/Illiquid Secs	6
Exotic Mortgage-Backed	0
Emerging-Markets Secs	4
Options/Futures/Warrants	No

Address:	399 Boylston Street Boston MA 02116 800-633-3330
Web Address:	www.loomissayles.com
Inception:	01-01-97 *
Advisor:	Loomis, Sayles & Company LP
Subadvisor:	None
NTF Plans:	Fidelity Retail-NTF, Accutrade NTF

Minimum Purchase:	$2500	Add: $50	IRA: $2500
Min Auto Inv Plan:	$2500	Add: $50	
Sales Fees:	0.25%B, 2.00%R		
Management Fee:	0.60%		
Actual Fees:	Mgt:0.60%	Dist:0.25%	
Expense Projections:	3Yr:$333	5Yr:$583	10Yr:$1218
Income Distrib:	Quarterly		

Lord Abbett Affiliated A

Ticker	Load	NAV	Yield	Total Assets	Mstar Category
LAFFX	5.75%	$14.78	1.3%	$19,501 mil	Large Value

Governance and Management

Fiduciary Grade: C

Portfolio Manager(s)

Eli Salzmann has worked on the fund since 1997 and took over as lead manager in 1998. He is assisted by Bob Morris, the firm's chief investment officer for equities, who has worked on the fund since 1991, as well as Tom Hudson (a 22-year veteran here), Stan Dinsky, and Ken Fuller.

Strategy

Eli Salzmann and other senior Lord Abbett managers hunt for companies that are cheap relative to their normalized earnings and where insiders are buying more shares. They also use company-specific analysis to gauge the strength of an industry: Looking for inflection points, they will overweight certain sectors, based in part on their view of macroeconomic conditions.

Historical Profile

Return Average
Risk Average
Rating ★★★ Neutral

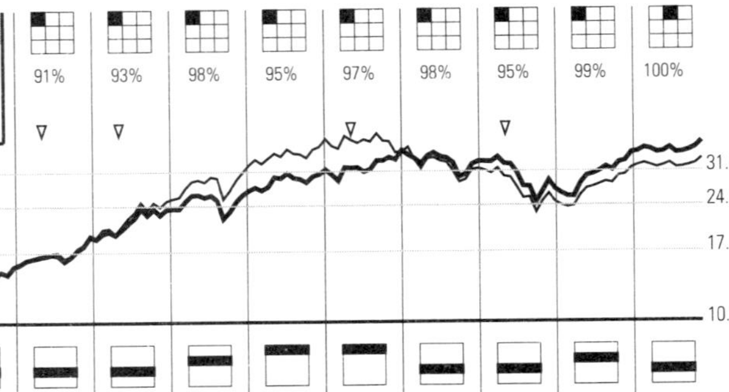

Investment Style
Equity
Stock %

▼ Manager Change
▽ Partial Manager Change

Growth of $10,000
— Investment Values of Fund
— Investment Values of S&P 500

Performance Quartile (within Category)

1993	1994	1995	1996	1997	1998	1999	2000	2001	2002	2003	12-04	History
10.67	9.99	11.59	12.58	13.97	14.74	15.20	15.76	13.69	10.53	13.55	14.78	NAV
13.23	3.95	31.70	20.14	25.16	14.42	16.88	15.24	-7.94	-18.79	30.89	12.60	Total Return %
3.17	2.64	-5.83	-2.80	-8.19	-14.15	-4.16	24.34	3.94	3.30	2.22	1.73	+/-S&P 500
-4.84	5.93	-6.66	-1.50	-10.02	-1.21	9.53	8.23	-2.35	-3.27	0.86	-3.89	+/-Russ 1000 VI
3.27	3.02	3.08	2.64	2.44	1.74	1.66	1.61	1.54	1.51	1.91	1.49	Income Return %
9.96	0.93	28.62	17.50	22.72	12.68	15.22	13.63	-9.48	-20.30	28.98	11.11	Capital Return %
54	11	67	51	74	38	8	22	75	52	28	53	Total Rtn % Rank Cat
0.33	0.32	0.30	0.30	0.30	0.24	0.24	0.24	0.24	0.21	0.20	0.20	Income $
0.60	0.77	1.19	1.03	1.39	0.95	1.76	1.39	0.57	0.41	0.00	0.25	Capital Gains $
0.63	0.63	0.63	0.66	0.65	0.63	0.74	0.79	0.79	0.85	0.84	—	Expense Ratio %
2.95	2.91	2.90	2.61	2.15	1.64	1.36	1.62	1.28	1.08	1.17	—	Income Ratio %
45	51	54	47	46	56	62	52	77	60	43	—	Turnover Rate %
4,157	4,082	5,307	6,292	7,730	8,594	9,704	10,658	10,292	8,883	12,600	15,002	Net Assets $mil

Performance 12-31-04

	1st Qtr	2nd Qtr	3rd Qtr	4th Qtr	Total
2000	1.59	-3.13	8.61	7.82	15.24
2001	-9.47	5.32	-13.97	12.22	-7.94
2002	3.15	-10.96	-19.74	10.16	-18.79
2003	-5.46	18.25	2.90	13.78	30.89
2004	2.47	1.10	-1.93	10.82	12.60

Trailing	Total Return%	+/- S&P 500	+/- Russ 1000 VI	%Rank Cat	Growth of $10,000
3 Mo	10.82	1.59	0.44	13	11,082
6 Mo	8.69	1.50	-3.39	57	10,869
1 Yr	12.60	1.73	-3.89	53	11,260
3 Yr Avg	6.17	2.59	-2.40	44	11,968
5 Yr Avg	4.89	7.19	-0.38	39	12,696
10 Yr Avg	12.89	0.82	-0.94	17	33,617
15 Yr Avg	11.53	0.60	-0.50	21	51,390

Tax Analysis	Tax-Adj Rtn%	%Rank Cat	Tax-Cost Rat	%Rank Cat
3 Yr (estimated)	3.14	69	0.92	61
5 Yr (estimated)	2.30	56	1.31	69
10 Yr (estimated)	9.90	36	2.08	69

Potential Capital Gain Exposure: 20% of assets

Rating and Risk

Time Period	Load-Adj Return %	Morningstar Rtn vs Cat	Morningstar Risk vs Cat	Morningstar Risk-Adj Rating
1 Yr	6.12			
3 Yr	4.10	Avg	+Avg	★★
5 Yr	3.66	Avg	Avg	★★★
10 Yr	12.23	Avg	Avg	★★★
Incept	—			

Other Measures	Standard Index S&P 500	Best Fit Index Russ 1000 VI
Alpha	2.5	-2.6
Beta	1.06	1.07
R-Squared	96	97
Standard Deviation	17.32	
Mean	6.17	
Sharpe Ratio	0.28	

Portfolio Analysis 11-30-04

Share change since 10-04 Total Stocks:93	Sector	PE	YTD Ret%	% Assets
ExxonMobil	Energy	13.9	28.04	5.24
⊖ Deere & Company	Ind Mtrls	15.7	16.26	3.04
⊕ J.P. Morgan Chase & Co.	Financial	19.4	9.97	2.77
⊕ International Paper	Ind Mtrls	—	-0.20	2.48
⊖ Motorola	Hardware	28.7	37.93	2.44
⊕ General Electric	Ind Mtrls	22.8	20.68	2.39
⊖ Walt Disney	Media	24.3	20.21	2.19
⊕ Verizon Communications	Telecom	32.4	20.25	2.10
⊖ EMC	Hardware	41.5	15.09	2.05
⊕ Kraft Foods	Goods	20.3	13.15	2.03
⊕ DuPont De Nemours E.I.	Ind Mtrls	22.3	10.42	1.91
⊕ Citigroup	Financial	15.3	2.72	1.82
⊕ Wyeth	Health	17.0	2.73	1.77
⊕ PepsiCo	Goods	22.5	13.82	1.61
⊕ Comcast	Media	—	-13.77	1.60
⊖ Xerox	Ind Mtrls	20.2	23.26	1.59
⊖ American International G	Financial	16.2	-0.53	1.59
⊕ Alcoa	Ind Mtrls	18.8	-15.75	1.54
Merrill Lynch & Company	Financial	12.6	3.12	1.51
⊕ Novartis AG ADR	Health	23.9	12.04	1.50

Current Investment Style

Value Blnd Growth; Large Mid Small

Market Cap	%
Giant	42.1
Large	54.2
Mid	3.7
Small	0.0
Micro	0.0
Avg $mil: 40,382	

Value Measures		Rel Category
Price/Earnings	18.17	1.21
Price/Book	2.70	1.19
Price/Sales	1.50	1.26
Price/Cash Flow	8.17	1.28
Dividend Yield %	1.67	0.82

Growth Measures	%	Rel Category
Long-Term Erngs	10.56	1.01
Book Value	5.88	1.04
Sales	1.82	0.43
Cash Flow	3.62	0.69
Historical Erngs	7.77	0.66

Profitability	%	Rel Category
Return on Equity	14.35	0.90
Return on Assets	6.59	0.84
Net Margin	8.94	0.88

Sector Weightings	% of Stocks	Rel S&P 500	3 Year High	Low
Info	21.20	0.99		
Software	1.71	0.40	3	0
Hardware	8.96	0.88	10	5
Media	7.11	1.85	10	7
Telecom	3.42	1.09	4	2
Service	35.34	0.76		
Health	10.30	0.82	11	5
Consumer	3.83	0.42	9	4
Business	4.60	1.14	10	3
Financial	16.61	0.80	22	17
Mfg	43.46	1.35		
Goods	9.60	1.03	10	6
Ind Mtrls	24.66	1.95	25	16
Energy	8.36	1.17	11	6
Utilities	0.84	0.28	8	1

Composition

Cash	0.0
Stocks	100.0
Bonds	0.0
Other	0.0
Foreign (% of Stock)	4.5

Morningstar's Take by Greg Carlson 12-23-04

Although one element of management's approach is offbeat, Lord Abbett Affiliated is a fine long-term holding.

This fund's management team employs a somewhat unorthodox strategy. While lead manager Eli Salzmann and his team buy large-cap stocks based on their own bottom-up analysis, they're also guided by the macroeconomic views of Lord Abbett's economist, Milton Ezrati, who joined the firm in 2000. As a result of his often-bullish calls, the fund typically sports a bigger stake in pricier, more economically sensitive sectors, such as tech, than its typical large-value rival.

Such bets can lead to uneven relative performance: A shift away from defensive names, such as utilities, in mid-2001 proved costly in the latter half of the bear market. Conversely, the fund thrived in last year's rally, outpacing more than two thirds of its rivals.

That said, this is more than just a bull-market vehicle, and Salzmann and company have proven their ability to make solid picks. Their timely purchase of beaten-down tech shares in mid-1998, and a subsequent sale late in 1999 (due to rising inventories and weakening balance sheets) just before the sector peaked, led to fine showings in both 1999 and 2000. All told, the fund's long-term returns land in the category's top quartile. It has also beaten the vast majority of large-blend offerings as well as the S&P 500 Index. What's more, the deep, experienced team responsible for much of that record remains in place: Salzmann and two other members have worked on the fund for at least seven years.

It's worth noting that the fund's growth tilt has made for modestly higher volatility. Also, we're disappointed that its expense ratio has crept upward despite an increase in assets. But it's still much cheaper than its typical broker-sold rival.

This offering won't serve to counterbalance an aggressive-growth fund, but it's a solid core holding.

Address:	90 Hudson Street Jersey City NJ 07302 800-201-6984
Web Address:	www.lordabbett.com
Inception:	05-01-34
Advisor:	Lord Abbett and Co. LLC
Subadvisor:	None
NTF Plans:	Federated Tr NTF, Fidelity Instl-NTF

Minimum Purchase:	$250	Add: $0	IRA: $250
Min Auto Inv Plan:	$250	Add: $50	
Sales Fees:	5.75%L, 0.25%S		
Management Fee:	0.50% mx./0.30% mn.		
Actual Fees:	Mgt:0.31%	Dist:0.35%	
Expense Projections:	3Yr:$834	5Yr:$1024	10Yr:$1575
Income Distrib:	Quarterly		

MainStay MAP I

Ticker	Load	NAV	Yield	Total Assets	Mstar Category
MUBFX	None	$34.20	0.3%	$1,122 mil	Mid-Cap Blend

Governance and Management

Fiduciary Grade:

Portfolio Manager(s)

The portfolio is split between Markston International and Jennison Associates. Michael Mullarkey, Roger Lob, and Chris Mullarkey each manage separate pieces of Markston's part. Michael Mullarkey runs most of it; Lob handles most of the rest. Chris Mullarkey, who joined in October 2001, gets a small slice. Mark DeFranco and Brian Gillott, who run Jennison's part, comanage Prudential's Jennison Equity Opportunity.

Strategy

This fund owns small, medium, and large companies. One subadvisor, Markston, looks closely at insider transactions, management changes, and stock buybacks in assembling the portfolio. It also considers the effects of broad themes in the economy. The result is an eclectic mix of value and growth names. The other subadvisor, Jennison, tries to buy companies it thinks offer at least three times as much upside potential as downside risk. This leads it to firms trading cheaply relative to measures such as earnings, assets, or EBITDA (earnings before interest, taxes, depreciation, and amortization).

Historical Profile

Return: Above Avg
Risk: Below Avg
Rating: ★★★★ Above Avg

Investment Style: Equity, Stock %

1993	1994	1995	1996	1997	1998	1999	2000	2001	2002	2003	12-04
89%	86%	94%	96%	96%	79%	88%	90%	88%			

▼ Manager Change
▽ Partial Manager Change

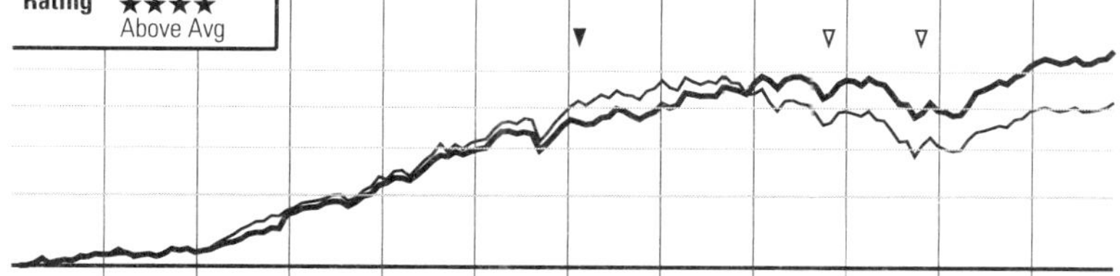

Growth of $10,000
— Investment Values of Fund
— Investment Values of S&P 500

Performance Quartile (within Category)

History	1993	1994	1995	1996	1997	1998	1999	2000	2001	2002	2003	12-04
NAV	18.13	16.67	19.36	20.66	22.73	24.58	26.25	27.31	27.75	22.03	30.56	34.20
Total Return %	8.74	2.80	32.61	24.02	28.35	24.25	12.18	16.88	2.36	-19.81	38.72	16.69
+/-S&P 500	-1.32	1.49	-4.92	1.08	-5.00	-4.32	-8.86	25.98	14.24	2.28	10.05	5.82
+/-S&P Mid 400	-5.19	6.39	1.69	4.84	-3.89	5.14	-2.54	-0.61	2.96	-5.28	3.13	0.22
Income Return %	1.85	2.06	2.62	1.98	1.41	1.57	0.45	0.11	0.24	0.59	0.00	0.40
Capital Return %	6.89	0.74	29.99	22.04	26.94	22.68	11.73	16.77	2.12	-20.40	38.72	16.29
Total Rtn % Rank Cat	80	17	33	33	32	8	66	32	34	78	30	41
Income $	0.36	0.37	0.43	0.36	0.29	0.33	0.11	0.03	0.07	0.16	0.00	0.12
Capital Gains $	3.21	1.59	2.21	2.86	3.41	2.96	1.14	3.16	0.14	0.06	0.00	1.31
Expense Ratio %	1.04	1.07	0.81	0.74	0.82	0.70	0.88	1.00	1.00	1.08	1.10	—
Income Ratio %	1.76	2.03	2.30	1.82	1.18	1.10	0.39	0.37	0.62	0.88	0.08	—
Turnover Rate %	20	39	39	53	58	41	32	40	19	77	61	—
Net Assets $mil	49	44	60	73	94	57	63	69	97	123	208	307

Performance 12-31-04

	1st Qtr	2nd Qtr	3rd Qtr	4th Qtr	Total
2000	8.72	-2.03	5.26	4.25	16.88
2001	-3.59	8.89	-14.65	14.24	2.36
2002	1.48	-10.67	-15.77	5.02	-19.81
2003	-3.04	20.27	4.40	13.94	38.72
2004	3.99	2.08	-0.99	11.03	16.70

Trailing	Total Return%	+/- S&P 500	+/- S&P Mid 400	%Rank Cat	Growth of $10,000
3 Mo	11.03	1.80	-1.12	62	11,103
6 Mo	9.93	2.74	0.14	43	10,993
1 Yr	16.69	5.82	0.22	41	11,669
3 Yr Avg	9.08	5.50	-1.43	57	12,979
5 Yr Avg	9.20	11.50	-0.33	33	15,528
10 Yr Avg	16.41	4.34	0.32	13	45,699
15 Yr Avg	13.68	2.75	-0.98	16	68,432

Tax Analysis	Tax-Adj Rtn%	%Rank Cat	Tax-Cost Rat	%Rank Cat
3 Yr (estimated)	8.70	51	0.35	40
5 Yr (estimated)	8.35	29	0.78	34
10 Yr (estimated)	14.15	16	1.94	64

Potential Capital Gain Exposure: 20% of assets

Rating and Risk

Time Period	Load-Adj Return %	Morningstar Rtn vs Cat	Morningstar Risk vs Cat	Morningstar Risk-Adj Rating
1 Yr	16.69			
3 Yr	9.08	Avg	Avg	★★★
5 Yr	9.20	Avg	-Avg	★★★★
10 Yr	16.41	+Avg	-Avg	★★★★★
Incept	—			

Other Measures	Standard Index S&P 500	Best Fit Index Wil 4500
Alpha	5.5	-1.6
Beta	0.94	0.90
R-Squared	87	91
Standard Deviation	16.36	
Mean	9.08	
Sharpe Ratio	0.48	

Portfolio Analysis 10-31-04

Share change since 09-04 Total Stocks:278	Sector	PE	YTD Ret%	% Assets
Duke Energy	Utilities	—	30.21	2.59
Tyco International	Ind Mtrls	25.1	35.41	2.49
DuPont De Nemours E.I.	Ind Mtrls	22.3	10.42	1.74
⊖ Metropolitan Life Insura	Financial	11.1	21.76	1.58
Monsanto Company	Ind Mtrls	54.5	96.09	1.51
Boston Scientific	Health	32.3	-3.29	1.50
Harris	Hardware	27.4	64.22	1.50
Northrop Grumman	Ind Mtrls	18.3	15.68	1.31
Symbol Technologies	Hardware	54.7	2.58	1.30
⊕ Schlumberger	Energy	40.7	23.84	1.20
Genentech	Health	78.6	16.36	1.19
Citigroup	Financial	15.3	2.72	1.14
American Express	Financial	20.3	17.60	1.11
Microsoft	Software	36.1	8.95	1.09
Principal Financial Grou	Financial	16.0	25.56	1.08
⊕ Medco Health Solutions	Health	—	22.39	1.05
Popular	Financial	16.4	31.94	1.03
Bk Of New York	Financial	18.5	3.52	1.03
Devon Energy	Energy	9.0	36.78	1.00
⊕ Radio One D	Media	—	—	1.00

Current Investment Style

Value Blnd Growth; Large Mid Small

Market Cap	%
Giant	17.0
Large	35.4
Mid	35.8
Small	10.2
Micro	1.6
Avg $mil: 9,248	

Value Measures		Rel Category
Price/Earnings	18.99	1.12
Price/Book	1.99	0.92
Price/Sales	0.97	0.92
Price/Cash Flow	7.14	1.14
Dividend Yield %	1.18	1.18

Growth Measures	%	Rel Category
Long-Term Erngs	11.83	0.94
Book Value	2.80	0.40
Sales	3.87	0.68
Cash Flow	-0.24	NMF
Historical Erngs	1.04	0.09

Profitability	%	Rel Category
Return on Equity	9.41	0.68
Return on Assets	5.24	0.80
Net Margin	7.21	0.79

Sector Weightings	% of Stocks	Rel S&P 500	3 Year High	3 Year Low
Info	17.74	0.83		
Software	4.74	1.10	6	3
Hardware	6.62	0.65	17	5
Media	4.80	1.25	8	4
Telecom	1.58	0.50	5	1
Service	44.61	0.96		
Health	11.48	0.92	19	5
Consumer	5.47	0.60	11	4
Business	6.43	1.59	8	3
Financial	21.23	1.02	24	14
Mfg	37.65	1.17		
Goods	2.47	0.26	5	2
Ind Mtrls	19.69	1.55	22	15
Energy	10.77	1.50	15	6
Utilities	4.72	1.59	5	0

Composition

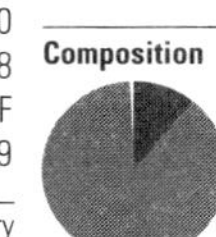

Cash	10.7
Stocks	88.3
Bonds	0.5
Other	0.6
Foreign (% of Stock)	3.6

Morningstar's Take by Gregg Wolper 11-03-04

Mainstay MAP is full of surprises, and is a fund worthy of attention.

This fund's portfolio isn't quite what you'd expect from a mid-cap blend fund. Its high stakes in the industrial-materials sector (about 22% of the portfolio), energy (12%), and utilities (5%) are more reminiscent of a hardcore value strategy. All three weightings are far above the mid-blend category average. But does that make this a conventional mid-value fund that should be in that category instead of mid-cap blend? Not quite. If that were the case, one would expect a low stake in the growth-oriented information-technology sectors, but this fund actually has a slight overweighting there.

The explanation is that each of this fund's subadvisors--Markston International and Jennison Associates--uses a flexible approach that includes many traditional value components, but is by no means limited to such considerations. Markston, for example, focuses on the trading patterns of company insiders as a key factor in making its decisions. For example, during the first half of the fund's 2004 fiscal year, Markston bought Duke Energy and trimmed Yahoo, partly because of insider buying at the former and selling at the latter. Another pleasant surprise, meanwhile, is this fund's modest turnover rate, which has consistently been below the category norm.

Performance has been solid, too. Jennison was awarded roughly half the portfolio in late 2002; the fund beat two thirds of its category rivals in 2003 and is slightly ahead of the midpoint for the year to date through Nov. 1, 2004. Prior to that, the fund racked up a very worthy record under Markston's sole direction. True, performance under the dual-advisor format isn't long enough or outstanding enough to pound the table. All told, though, there's a lot to like.

Address:	MainStay Funds Parsippany, NJ 07054 800-624-6782
Web Address:	www.mainstayfunds.com
Inception:	01-21-71
Advisor:	New York Life Investment Management LLC
Subadvisor:	Multiple
NTF Plans:	Federated Tr NTF

Minimum Purchase:	$5000000	Add: $0	IRA: $0
Min Auto Inv Plan:	$0	Add: —	
Sales Fees:	No-load		
Management Fee:	0.75% mx./0.70% mn.		
Actual Fees:	Mgt:0.75%	Dist:	
Expense Projections:	3Yr:$350	5Yr:$606	10Yr:$1340
Income Distrib:	Annually		

Mairs & Power Growth

Ticker	Load	NAV	Yield	Total Assets	Mstar Category
MPGFX	None	$70.33	1.0%	$2,056 mil	Large Blend

Governance and Management

Fiduciary Grade: A

Portfolio Manager(s)

William Frels succeeded long-time manager George Maris III in June 2004. Frels has been a comanager here since December 1999 and has delivered strong results at Mairs & Power Balanced Fund since 1992.

Strategy

Manager Bill Frels and the investment team at Mairs & Power buy what they know. They look for well-managed companies with strong market share in their industries, and they keep the portfolio in about 35 companies, most of which are located in or around the firm's home state, Minnesota. And once a stock is added to the fund, it usually stays. The turnover rate is microscopic.

Historical Profile

Return High
Risk Below Avg
Rating ★★★★★ Highest

Investment Style: Equity Stock % — 100% 100% 100% | 100% 100% 98% 98% 97%

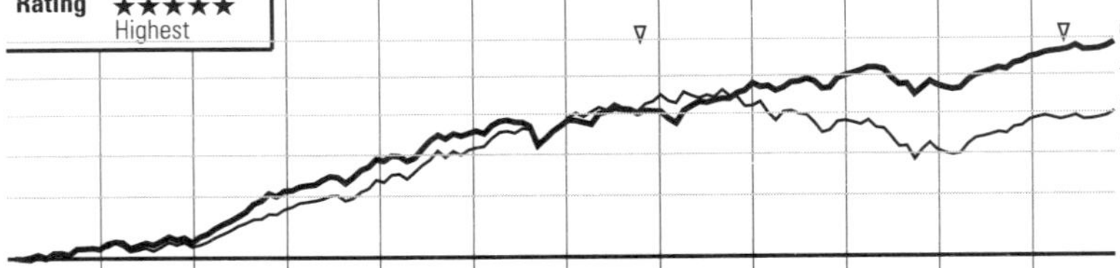

▼ Manager Change
∇ Partial Manager Change

Growth of $10,000
▬ Investment Values of Fund
— Investment Values of S&P 500

Performance Quartile (within Category)

1993	1994	1995	1996	1997	1998	1999	2000	2001	2002	2003	12-04	History
19.42	19.69	28.02	34.74	43.34	46.34	46.45	53.41	54.36	49.26	60.90	70.33	NAV
13.06	5.66	47.70	27.76	28.68	9.36	7.16	26.48	6.48	-8.12	26.33	17.99	Total Return %
3.00	4.35	10.17	4.82	-4.67	-19.21	-13.88	35.58	18.36	13.97	-2.34	7.12	+/-S&P 500
2.88	5.27	9.93	5.31	-4.17	-17.66	-13.75	34.27	18.93	13.53	-3.56	6.59	+/-Russ 1000
1.40	1.68	1.43	1.27	1.44	0.83	1.01	1.18	0.96	0.83	1.08	1.12	Income Return %
11.66	3.98	46.27	26.49	27.24	8.53	6.15	25.30	5.52	-8.95	25.25	16.87	Capital Return %
31	2	1	7	51	90	91	1	2	2	59	2	Total Rtn % Rank Cat
0.25	0.33	0.28	0.36	0.50	0.36	0.47	0.54	0.51	0.45	0.53	0.68	Income $
0.62	0.49	0.76	0.70	0.85	0.68	2.74	4.82	2.00	0.24	0.77	0.82	Capital Gains $
0.98	0.99	0.99	0.89	0.84	0.82	0.79	0.78	0.76	0.78	0.75	—	Expense Ratio %
1.15	1.74	1.00	1.18	0.98	0.97	0.83	1.06	0.97	0.93	1.05	—	Income Ratio %
4	5	4	3	5	2	6	15	8	1	2	—	Turnover Rate %
39	42	71	150	413	555	547	582	677	850	1,307	2,056	Net Assets $mil

Performance 12-31-04

	1st Qtr	2nd Qtr	3rd Qtr	4th Qtr	Total
2000	0.66	6.92	3.05	14.05	26.48
2001	-6.14	7.80	-5.72	11.62	6.48
2002	6.75	-8.38	-12.84	7.77	-8.12
2003	-2.56	13.43	3.34	10.60	26.33
2004	4.88	5.17	-2.89	10.17	17.99

Trailing	Total Return%	+/- S&P 500	+/- Russ 1000	%Rank Cat	Growth of $10,000
3 Mo	10.17	0.94	0.37	26	11,017
6 Mo	6.98	-0.21	-0.83	51	10,698
1 Yr	17.99	7.12	6.59	2	11,799
3 Yr Avg	11.05	7.47	6.78	1	13,695
5 Yr Avg	13.02	15.32	14.78	1	18,441
10 Yr Avg	18.03	5.96	5.87	1	52,472
15 Yr Avg	16.55	5.62	5.47	1	99,468

Tax Analysis	Tax-Adj Rtn%	%Rank Cat	Tax-Cost Rat	%Rank Cat
3 Yr (estimated)	10.51	1	0.49	41
5 Yr (estimated)	11.98	1	0.92	49
10 Yr (estimated)	16.90	1	0.96	26

Potential Capital Gain Exposure: 30% of assets

Rating and Risk

Time Period	Load-Adj Return %	Morningstar Rtn vs Cat	Morningstar Risk vs Cat	Morningstar Risk-Adj Rating
1 Yr	17.99			
3 Yr	11.05	High	Low	★★★★★
5 Yr	13.02	High	-Avg	★★★★★
10 Yr	18.03	High	-Avg	★★★★★
Incept	12.24			

Other Measures	Standard Index S&P 500	Best Fit Index Russ 1000
Alpha	7.7	7.2
Beta	0.73	0.74
R-Squared	86	87
Standard Deviation	12.97	
Mean	11.05	
Sharpe Ratio	0.75	

Portfolio Analysis 11-30-04

Share change since 10-04 Total Stocks:38	Sector	PE	YTD Ret%	% Assets
Target	Consumer	22.3	36.14	5.03
⊕ Wells Fargo	Financial	15.5	8.97	4.91
⊕ Medtronic	Health	30.7	2.68	4.10
TCF Financial	Financial	13.3	28.60	3.99
Pentair	Business	24.0	93.44	3.97
⊕ 3M Company	Ind Mtrls	23.5	-1.75	3.95
⊕ US Bancorp	Financial	14.2	10.46	3.69
⊕ Valspar	Goods	19.7	2.74	3.44
Donaldson	Business	25.1	11.03	3.41
⊕ General Mills	Goods	19.4	12.56	3.38
Ecolab	Ind Mtrls	28.6	29.72	3.38
Graco	Ind Mtrls	24.8	49.29	3.37
⊕ SuperValu	Consumer	12.4	23.24	3.20
Johnson & Johnson	Health	20.6	25.17	3.15
⊕ Emerson Electric	Ind Mtrls	22.8	11.09	3.14
⊕ Pfizer	Health	22.0	-22.31	3.13
Toro	Ind Mtrls	20.6	76.07	3.02
Hormel Foods	Goods	18.2	23.44	2.94
Gen Elec	Ind Mtrls	22.8	20.68	2.92
⊕ Bemis	Goods	18.5	19.23	2.88

Current Investment Style

Value Blnd Growth — Large Mid Small

Market Cap	%
Giant	30.3
Large	26.5
Mid	35.3
Small	8.0
Micro	0.0
Avg $mil: 13,759	

Value Measures		Rel Category
Price/Earnings	19.22	1.13
Price/Book	3.13	1.19
Price/Sales	1.45	1.01
Price/Cash Flow	10.88	1.42
Dividend Yield %	1.60	1.08

Growth Measures	%	Rel Category
Long-Term Erngs	11.38	0.98
Book Value	10.48	1.35
Sales	3.24	0.56
Cash Flow	9.15	0.97
Historical Erngs	9.98	0.85

Profitability	%	Rel Category
Return on Equity	18.77	1.07
Return on Assets	10.47	1.21
Net Margin	11.63	1.02

Sector Weightings	% of Stocks	Rel S&P 500	3 Year High	3 Year Low
Info	3.93	0.18		
Software	0.00	0.00	0	0
Hardware	2.83	0.28	3	1
Media	0.00	0.00	0	0
Telecom	1.10	0.35	2	0
Service	54.22	1.17		
Health	17.27	1.38	23	17
Consumer	8.48	0.93	9	7
Business	11.69	2.89	13	8
Financial	16.78	0.81	20	15
Mfg	41.83	1.30		
Goods	13.43	1.44	16	13
Ind Mtrls	28.40	2.24	28	22
Energy	0.00	0.00	0	0
Utilities	0.00	0.00	0	0

Composition

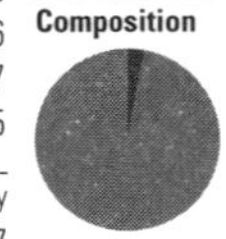

Cash	3.0
Stocks	97.0
Bonds	0.0
Other	0.0
Foreign (% of Stock)	0.0

Morningstar's Take by Kerry O'Boyle 12-20-04

A management succession has changed little at the standout Mairs & Power Growth.

As expected, long-time comanager William Frels has taken the lead role at this fund as of June 2004. Former day-to-day manager George Mairs III has stepped down at age 76 due to the firm's mandatory retirement policy. Frels has been with the firm for more than a decade, successfully running sibling offering Mairs & Power Balanced since 1992. Shareholders won't be entirely without Mairs' 40 years of experience, however. He continues to serve as an active member of the fund's six-member investment committee.

The committee is charged with maintaining a list of the 15 most attractive stocks in its investment universe. Names are culled from a local watch list that includes mainly small- and mid-cap stocks of companies based in the firm's home state of Minnesota and a national list of high-quality large caps. In July, Frels added a name from each. Intel was added to the portfolio as a stable grower selling at an attractive price after the stock dropped 35% during the first half of 2004. Also new to the fund is SurModics, a Twin Cities specialty chemical company that provides materials for increasingly popular drug-coated stents and is run by the former CEO of Medtronic.

The fund's mix of national stalwarts and local heroes has served shareholders well. It ranks in the top percentile of the large-blend category for the trailing three-, five-, and 10-year periods through Dec. 17, 2004. Still, investors should keep future expectations in check. The fund has benefited from its all-cap bias, as smaller companies have generally outperformed their larger rivals over the past five years. A rally in mega-cap stocks could leave the fund short, as it did in 1998 and 1999.

Little has changed in style or execution with the switch to Frels. Below-average volatility, low costs, and a stringent buy-and-hold mentality make this an attractive option.

Address:	332 Minnesota St Ste W-1520 St Paul MN 55101 800-304-7404
Web Address:	www.mairsandpower.com
Inception:	11-07-58
Advisor:	Mairs & Power
Subadvisor:	None
NTF Plans:	N/A

Minimum Purchase:	$2500	Add: $100	IRA: $1000
Min Auto Inv Plan:	$2500	Add: $100	
Sales Fees:	No-load		
Management Fee:	0.60%		
Actual Fees:	Mgt:0.60%	Dist:	
Expense Projections:	3Yr:$241	5Yr:$418	10Yr:$933
Income Distrib:	Semi-Annually		

Managers Special Equity

Ticker	Load	NAV	Yield	Total Assets	Mstar Category
MGSEX	None	$90.41	0.0%	$3,653 mil	Small Growth

Governance and Management

Fiduciary Grade: C

Portfolio Manager(s)

Tom Hoffman, director of research for Managers Funds, oversees five subadvisors: Andy Knuth of Westport Select Cap joined in 1985, while Bob Kern of Fremont U.S. Micro-Cap joined in 1997. A team from Skyline Special Equities was hired in 2000--lead manager Bill Dutton is stepping back, but other experienced team members are taking over. Donald Smith of Donald Smith & Co. joined in 2002, and Essex Investment Management (a firm that also runs a slice of Managers Capital Appreciation) joined in 2003, although the impending departure of lead manager Craig Lewis means the firm may not be retained.

Strategy

Five subadvisors each run 20% of the fund's assets: Andy Knuth of Westport Asset Management buys modestly priced firms with solid growth prospects. Essex Investment Management, led by the soon-to-depart Craig Lewis, invests in companies with accelerating earnings. Micro-cap duties are handled by Bob Kern of Kern Capital Management, who favors firms with innovative products. A team from Skyline Asset Management seeks out small companies that trade cheaply yet possess strong earnings growth potential. Deep-value manager Donald Smith of Donald Smith & Co. buys stocks with very low price/book ratios.

Performance 12-31-04

	1st Qtr	2nd Qtr	3rd Qtr	4th Qtr	Total
2000	13.59	-0.76	-2.13	-11.67	-2.56
2001	-13.50	16.23	-23.74	19.91	-8.07
2002	0.96	-10.21	-19.67	7.14	-21.98
2003	-6.37	20.73	9.57	15.05	42.50
2004	4.08	0.83	-3.96	14.28	15.19

Trailing	Total Return%	+/- S&P 500	+/- Russ 2000 Gr	%Rank Cat	Growth of $10,000
3 Mo	14.28	5.05	-0.80	42	11,428
6 Mo	9.76	2.57	1.60	30	10,976
1 Yr	15.19	4.32	0.88	32	11,519
3 Yr Avg	8.59	5.01	2.80	27	12,805
5 Yr Avg	2.78	5.08	6.35	32	11,469
10 Yr Avg	13.93	1.86	6.81	14	36,845
15 Yr Avg	12.96	2.03	5.46	25	62,211

Tax Analysis	Tax-Adj Rtn%	%Rank Cat	Tax-Cost Rat	%Rank Cat
3 Yr (estimated)	8.59	22	0.00	1
5 Yr (estimated)	1.98	29	0.78	35
10 Yr (estimated)	12.60	13	1.17	31

Potential Capital Gain Exposure: 25% of assets

Historical Profile

Return Above Avg
Risk Average
Rating ★★★★ Above Avg

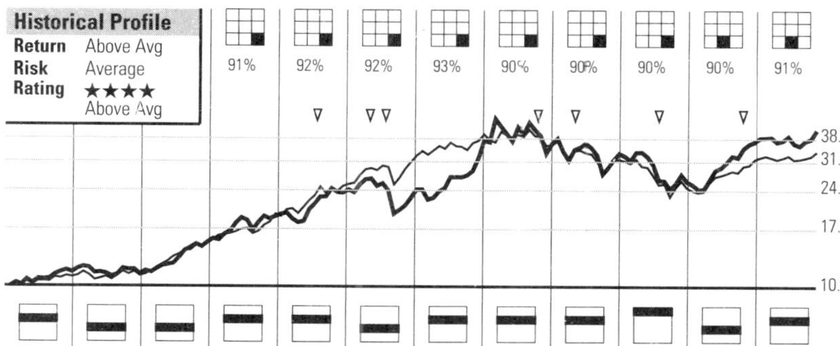

Investment Style
Equity
Stock %

▼ Manager Change
∇ Partial Manager Change

Growth of $10,000
— Investment Values of Fund
— Investment Values of S&P 500

Performance Quartile (within Category)

1993	1994	1995	1996	1997	1998	1999	2000	2001	2002	2003	12-04	History
38.90	36.79	43.34	50.95	61.17	61.22	91.42	76.30	70.60	55.08	78.49	90.41	NAV
17.35	-1.99	33.94	24.75	24.45	0.20	54.11	-2.56	-8.07	-21.98	42.50	15.19	Total Return %
7.29	-3.30	-3.59	1.81	-8.90	-28.37	33.07	6.54	3.81	0.11	13.83	4.32	+/-S&P 500
3.98	0.44	2.90	13.49	11.50	-1.03	11.02	19.37	1.16	8.28	-6.04	0.88	+/-Russ 2000 Gr
0.03	0.00	0.00	0.00	0.14	0.00	0.00	0.00	0.00	0.00	0.00	0.00	Income Return %
17.32	-1.99	33.94	24.75	24.31	0.20	54.11	-2.56	-8.07	-21.98	42.50	15.19	Capital Return %
45	57	56	29	29	65	47	41	44	24	58	32	Total Rtn % Rank Cat
0.01	0.00	0.00	0.00	0.07	0.00	0.00	0.00	0.00	0.00	0.00	0.00	Income $
3.37	1.34	5.66	3.07	2.07	0.07	2.82	11.77	0.00	0.00	0.00	0.00	Capital Gains $
1.26	1.37	1.44	1.43	1.35	1.34	1.31	1.26	1.29	1.31	1.43	—	Expense Ratio %
0.07	-0.06	-0.16	-0.10	0.17	-0.26	-0.47	-0.16	-0.27	-0.56	-0.72	—	Income Ratio %
45	66	65	56	49	64	89	69	52	67	64	—	Turnover Rate %
99	110	118	271	720	957	1,545	2,125	2,312	2,016	3,290	3,428	Net Assets $mil

Rating and Risk

Time Period	Load-Adj Return %	Morningstar Rtn vs Cat	Morningstar Risk vs Cat	Morningstar Risk-Adj Rating
1 Yr	15.19			
3 Yr	8.59	+Avg	Avg	★★★★
5 Yr	2.78	Avg	Avg	★★★
10 Yr	13.93	+Avg	-Avg	★★★★
Incept	14.22			

Other Measures	Standard Index S&P 500	Best Fit Index Russ 2000
Alpha	5.2	-2.1
Beta	1.05	0.94
R-Squared	75	97
Standard Deviation	19.97	
Mean	8.59	
Sharpe Ratio	0.37	

Portfolio Analysis 11-30-04

Share change since 10-04 Total Stocks:327	Sector	PE	YTD Ret%	% Assets
AK Steel Holding	Ind Mtrls	—	183.73	2.20
Reliant Energy	Utilities	—	85.46	1.99
Toys R Us	Goods	28.3	61.95	1.68
MI Developments	Financial	—	—	1.67
ITT Educational Services	Consumer	32.8	1.24	1.52
⊖ Dillard's	Consumer	35.0	64.46	1.45
Felcor Lodging Trust	Financial	—	32.22	1.05
Visteon	Ind Mtrls	—	-3.79	1.04
Mer Star Hospitality	Consumer	—	28.26	0.96
⊕ Corinthian Colleges	Consumer	21.3	-32.10	0.85
⊖ Kerzner International	Consumer	24.5	54.13	0.83
⊕ Triad Hospitals	Health	30.3	11.84	0.78
Hibernia	Financial	15.2	29.44	0.70
Ross Stores	Consumer	22.6	9.82	0.70
Pogo Producing	Energy	10.6	0.87	0.69
Sierra Pacific Resources	Utilities	—	43.05	0.67
Downey Financial	Financial	17.8	16.51	0.64
Emmis Communications A	Media	—	-29.06	0.62
Avista Corporation	Utilities	29.0	0.39	0.60
Eclipsys	Software	—	75.52	0.59

Current Investment Style

Value Blnd Growth — Large Mid Small

Market Cap	%
Giant	0.0
Large	0.1
Mid	41.8
Small	47.9
Micro	10.3
Avg $mil: 1,240	

Value Measures		Rel Category
Price/Earnings	18.86	0.87
Price/Book	1.81	0.69
Price/Sales	0.74	0.49
Price/Cash Flow	5.22	0.65
Dividend Yield %	0.53	1.71

Growth Measures	%	Rel Category
Long-Term Erngs	13.95	0.81
Book Value	1.96	0.30
Sales	2.52	0.39
Cash Flow	21.09	1.56
Historical Erngs	6.36	0.47

Profitability	%	Rel Category
Return on Equity	3.11	0.32
Return on Assets	2.41	0.55
Net Margin	3.50	0.51

Sector Weightings	% of Stocks	Rel S&P 500	3 Year High	3 Year Low
Info	17.64	0.82		
Software	4.93	1.15	7	3
Hardware	10.04	0.98	16	9
Media	2.15	0.56	6	2
Telecom	0.52	0.17	3	0
Service	54.59	1.18		
Health	9.40	0.75	14	9
Consumer	16.72	1.84	22	15
Business	13.30	3.28	15	12
Financial	15.17	0.73	16	12
Mfg	27.76	0.86		
Goods	3.16	0.34	4	1
Ind Mtrls	16.46	1.30	17	9
Energy	4.02	0.56	4	2
Utilities	4.12	1.39	4	1

Composition

Cash	8.9
Stocks	91.1
Bonds	0.0
Other	0.0
Foreign (% of Stock)	3.3

Morningstar's Take by Greg Carlson 12-15-04

Managers Special Equity doesn't make the grade.

This small-growth fund has long been a standout, thanks to a solid roster of subadvisors overseen by Tom Hoffman, director of research for Managers Funds. However, several recent developments have shaken our confidence.

Most importantly, the fund's expense ratio has risen even as its asset base has grown dramatically. That's due in part to the fund's management fee schedule, which features no breakpoints as assets increase. Hoffman also cited an influx of investors accessing the fund through discount brokers' no-transaction fee programs as a factor--Managers pays a fee to be included on such platforms and is passing along that cost to all shareholders.

In addition, two of the fund's five subadvisors face significant issues. Craig Lewis, lead manager for Essex Investment Management, which was hired one year ago after the firing of scandal-tarred firm Pilgrim Baxter, is leaving Essex after several years of poor performance. Hoffman is re-evaluating Essex and may seek a replacement for the firm. Also, subadvisor Bob Kern, who runs Fremont U.S. Micro-Cap has $1.8 billion under management. Although Kern's sleeve of this fund's portfolio isn't solely dedicated to micro-caps, we're concerned that his ability to maneuver among lightly traded fare could be constrained by future growth. Indeed, while the retail share class of his other charge remains closed to new investors, that fund's institutional shares remain open as does this offering, and there are no plans to close either.

All told, investors interested in small-cap funds run by multiple managers--a model that tends to confer more capacity by spreading the asset load more evenly--should check out more-attractive options such as Vanguard Explorer and Masters' Select Smaller Companies.

Address:	800 Connecticut Avenue Norwalk CT 06854 800-835-3879
Web Address:	www.managersfunds.com
Inception:	06-01-84
Advisor:	Managers Funds LLC
Subadvisor:	Multiple
NTF Plans:	Fidelity Retail-NTF, Schwab OneSource

Minimum Purchase:	$2000	Add: $100	IRA: $1000
Min Auto Inv Plan:	$100	Add: $100	
Sales Fees:	No-load		
Management Fee:	0.90%		
Actual Fees:	Mgt:0.90%	Dist:	
Expense Projections:	3Yr:$460	5Yr:$796	10Yr:$1745
Income Distrib:	Annually		

Marsico 21st Century

Ticker	Load	NAV	Yield	Total Assets	Mstar Category
MXXIX	12b-1 only	$12.01	0.0%	$323 mil	Large Growth

Governance and Management

Fiduciary Grade: A

Portfolio Manager(s)

Cory Gilchrist has been with Marsico Capital Management since May 2000, working in various capacities but primarily on the shop's successful International Opportunities. Prior to Marsico, Gilchrist worked at Invista Capital Management, serving on a team that managed international-equity funds.

Strategy

As is the case with the other Marsico funds, manager Cory Gilchrist uses macroeconomic themes to determine the portfolio's overall positioning. From there, he focuses largely on three types of companies: rapidly growing firms that are hitting on all cylinders, steadier-growth companies, and otherwise-promising companies that have suffered short-term setbacks. Unlike Marsico's other U.S.-stock funds, however, this one buys stocks of any market capitalization.

Historical Profile

Return High
Risk Above Avg
Rating ★★★★★ Highest

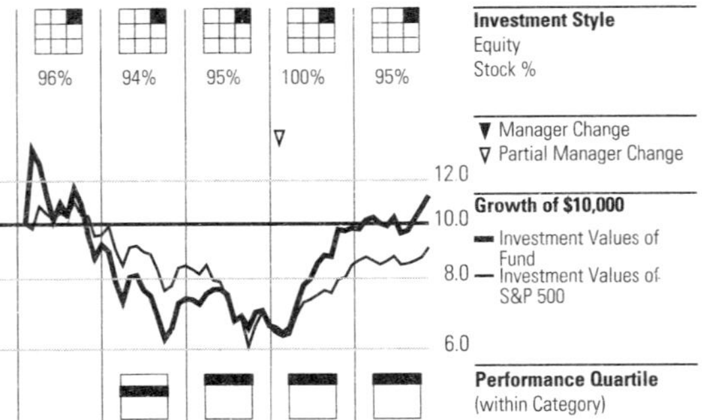

1993	1994	1995	1996	1997	1998	1999	2000	2001	2002	2003	12-04	History
—	—	—	—	—	—	—	9.19	7.37	6.60	9.82	12.01	NAV
—	—	—	—	—	—	—	-8.10*	-19.80	-10.45	48.79	22.30	Total Return %
—	—	—	—	—	—	—	—	-7.92	11.64	20.12	11.43	+/-S&P 500
—	—	—	—	—	—	—	—	0.62	17.43	19.04	16.00	+/-Russ 1000Gr
—	—	—	—	—	—	—	0.00	0.00	0.00	0.00	0.00	Income Return %
—	—	—	—	—	—	—	—	-19.80	-10.45	48.79	22.30	Capital Return %
—	—	—	—	—	—	—	—	48	1	3	1	Total Rtn % Rank Cat
—	—	—	—	—	—	—	0.00	0.00	0.00	0.00	0.00	Income $
—	—	—	—	—	—	—	0.00	0.00	0.00	0.00	0.00	Capital Gains $
—	—	—	—	—	—	—	1.50	1.50	1.60	1.55	1.50	Expense Ratio %
—	—	—	—	—	—	—	-0.92	-0.76	-0.99	-1.05	-0.48	Income Ratio %
—	—	—	—	—	—	—	267	399	388	236	191	Turnover Rate %
—	—	—	—	—	—	—	99	69	54	162	323	Net Assets $mil

Performance 12-31-04

	1st Qtr	2nd Qtr	3rd Qtr	4th Qtr	Total
2000	—	-15.07	-0.18	-15.38	-8.10*
2001	-20.67	4.80	-18.06	17.73	-19.80
2002	2.04	-0.40	-12.68	0.92	-10.45
2003	-0.91	22.17	9.39	12.36	48.79
2004	4.48	-0.10	-0.49	17.75	22.30

Trailing	Total Return%	+/- S&P 500	+/- Russ 1000Gr	%Rank Cat	Growth of $10,000
3 Mo	17.75	8.52	8.58	1	11,775
6 Mo	17.17	9.98	13.70	1	11,717
1 Yr	22.30	11.43	16.00	1	12,230
3 Yr Avg	17.68	14.10	17.86	1	16,297
5 Yr Avg	—	—	—	—	—
10 Yr Avg	—	—	—	—	—
15 Yr Avg	—	—	—	—	—

Tax Analysis	Tax-Adj Rtn%	%Rank Cat	Tax-Cost Rat	%Rank Cat
3 Yr (estimated)	17.68	1	0.00	1
5 Yr (estimated)	—	—	—	—
10 Yr (estimated)	—	—	—	—

Potential Capital Gain Exposure: 5% of assets

Rating and Risk

Time Period	Load-Adj Return %	Morningstar Rtn vs Cat	Morningstar Risk vs Cat	Morningstar Risk-Adj Rating
1 Yr	22.30			
3 Yr	17.68	High	+Avg	★★★★★
5 Yr	—	—	—	—
10 Yr	—	—	—	—
Incept	3.80			

Other Measures	Standard Index S&P 500	Best Fit Index Wil 4500
Alpha	14.4	6.8
Beta	0.83	0.87
R-Squared	62	76

Standard Deviation	18.42
Mean	17.68
Sharpe Ratio	0.90

Morningstar's Take by Bridget Hughes 10-18-04

Marsico 21st Century continues its hot streak, but we're not shying away from it.

This fund has topped the charts during nearly all of its 4.5 years of existence. Compared with the average large-growth fund, its annualized return of 0.61% beats the loss suffered by the typical large-growth fund. To be sure, its all-cap approach--and more specifically its inclusion of small- and mid-cap names--has helped, as smaller stocks have generally performed better over the period. But the fund also handily beats the average small- and mid- growth funds.

We generally get nervous after a fund has posted such a strong run relative to its peers. Indeed, if large caps take off, this fund will likely fall behind the large-growth pack. Still, we think this fund is flexible enough to adapt to different environments. Manager Cory Gilchrist says that while the fund is roughly evenly split among small, mid- and large caps, he has lately found more to like in the mid- and large-cap areas. And fund family founder Tom Marsico, who with his team often comes up with top-down themes that shape all the portfolios managed by Marsico Capital Management (MCM), has proved adept at navigating different types of markets. (Gilchrist has been a manager here only since February 2003, but an analyst at MCM since May 2000.)

Further demonstrating the fund's flexible methods is the typical composition that combines steady-growth ideas and more-aggressive growth picks with companies undergoing some kind of meaningful change or enduring a temporary setback. These days, Gilchrist and his colleagues are beginning to add to more-aggressive names, such as Harman International, after moving away from them in the past year or so.

There are risks here. The fund's concentrated portfolio means, for example, that misses in just a few stocks can have a marked impact. But we think flexibility and MCM's strong research team argue persuasively in its favor.

Address:	Marsico Investment Fund Milwaukee, WI 53201-3210 888-860-8686
Web Address:	www.marsicofunds.com
Inception:	02-01-00*
Advisor:	Marsico Capital Management, LLC
Subadvisor:	None
NTF Plans:	Fidelity Retail-NTF, Schwab OneSource

Minimum Purchase:	$2500	Add: $100	IRA: $1000
Min Auto Inv Plan:	$1000	Add: $50	
Sales Fees:	0.25%B, 2.00%R		
Management Fee:	0.85%, 0.12%A		
Actual Fees:	Mgt:0.85%	Dist:0.25%	
Expense Projections:	3Yr:$497	5Yr:$866	10Yr:$1902
Income Distrib:	Annually		

Portfolio Analysis 09-30-04

Share change since 03-04 Total Stocks:40	Sector	PE	YTD Ret%	% Assets
⊕ Countrywide Financial	Financial	9.0	48.15	5.20
⊕ Wynn Resorts	Consumer	—	138.92	4.71
⊕ Qualcomm	Hardware	42.0	58.20	4.46
⊕ UCBH Holdings	Financial	19.5	18.04	4.29
⊕ Royal Caribbean Cruises	Goods	36.9	58.33	4.28
⊕ UnitedHealth Group	Health	23.8	51.38	3.70
⊕ Harman International Ind	Goods	48.4	71.77	3.55
☼ Petsmart	Consumer	32.1	49.86	3.42
⊕ Genentech	Health	78.6	16.36	3.04
⊖ Brunswick	Goods	18.1	57.47	2.99
⊕ South Financial Group	Financial	15.7	19.71	2.93
⊖ Jefferies Group	Financial	15.5	23.25	2.91
⊕ Government Properties Tr	Financial	—	—	2.88
☼ eBay	Consumer	81.6	80.07	2.82
⊕ Wright Medical Group	Health	39.3	-6.25	2.72
☼ Dell	Hardware	34.0	24.01	2.65
☼ FedEx	Business	27.9	46.40	2.56
☼ Getty Images	Business	37.9	37.34	2.51
☼ Crown Castle Internation	Telecom	—	50.86	2.49
⊕ Shangri-La Asia Ltd	Consumer	—	—	2.48

Current Investment Style

Value Blnd Growth — Large Mid Small

Market Cap	%
Giant	19.3
Large	31.3
Mid	37.4
Small	9.0
Micro	3.0
Avg $mil: 7,941	

Value Measures		Rel Category
Price/Earnings	19.16	0.90
Price/Book	2.83	0.88
Price/Sales	2.11	0.98
Price/Cash Flow	12.45	1.13
Dividend Yield %	0.52	0.68

Growth Measures	%	Rel Category
Long-Term Erngs	14.20	1.01
Book Value	8.69	0.68
Sales	9.85	1.16
Cash Flow	5.63	0.34
Historical Erngs	28.43	1.96

Profitability	%	Rel Category
Return on Equity	14.30	0.80
Return on Assets	7.86	0.84
Net Margin	12.07	0.98

Sector Weightings	% of Stocks	Rel S&P 500	3 Year High	Low
Info	13.46	0.63		
Software	2.41	0.56	14	0
Hardware	7.82	0.77	17	3
Media	0.67	0.17	13	0
Telecom	2.56	0.81	6	0
Service	64.59	1.39		
Health	9.73	0.78	25	4
Consumer	23.18	2.55	29	8
Business	6.21	1.53	19	0
Financial	25.47	1.23	33	4
Mfg	21.94	0.68		
Goods	16.83	1.80	22	3
Ind Mtrls	5.11	0.40	18	0
Energy	0.00	0.00	8	0
Utilities	0.00	0.00	4	0

Composition

Cash	2.7
Stocks	95.4
Bonds	0.0
Other	1.9
Foreign (% of Stock)	5.9

Marsico Focus

Analyst Pick

Ticker	Load	NAV	Yield	Total Assets	Mstar Category
MFOCX	12b-1 only	$16.61	0.0%	$3,237 mil	Large Growth

Governance and Management

Fiduciary Grade: A

Portfolio Manager(s)

Before forming his own firm in late 1997, Tom Marsico built a terrific record at Janus Twenty. Marsico has a staff of 17 analysts and traders. He is also a large shareholder in each of the four funds the shop offers. More than 70% of the fund's board is independent; all the independent trustees have money invested in the fund.

Strategy

Tom Marsico combines top-down analysis with bottom-up stock-picking. He fills the bulk of the portfolio with steady-growth stocks that he intends to hold for the long haul, but he has owned more-explosive growth names in tech and telecom. He also reserves a portion of the portfolio for relatively inexpensive firms that stand to benefit from a catalyst. Marsico limits the portfolio to a small number of stocks, typically about 25.

Historical Profile

Return Above Avg
Risk Average
Rating ★★★★ Above Avg

Investment Style: Equity, Stock %

1998	1999	2000	2001	2002	2003	12-04
88%	96%	95%	99%	96%	100%	100%

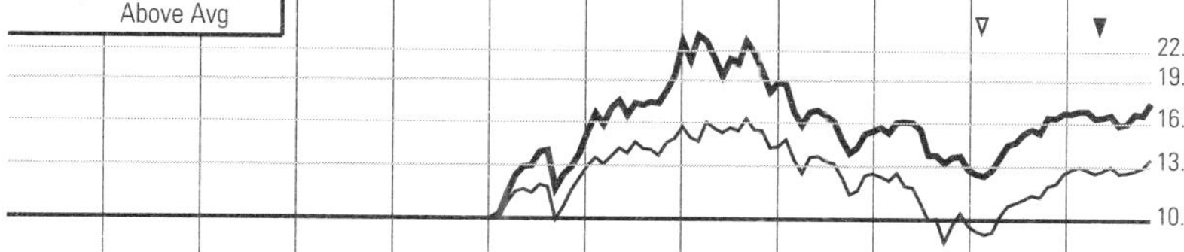

Performance Quartile (within Category)

1993	1994	1995	1996	1997	1998	1999	2000	2001	2002	2003	12-04	History
—	—	—	—	10.00	15.13	23.45	17.23	13.60	11.33	14.87	16.61	NAV
—	—	—	—	0.00*	51.30	55.27	-17.91	-20.81	-16.69	31.24	11.70	Total Return %
—	—	—	—	—	22.73	34.23	-8.81	-6.93	5.40	2.57	0.83	+/-S&P 500
—	—	—	—	—	12.59	22.11	4.51	-0.39	11.19	1.49	5.40	+/-Russ 1000Gr
—	—	—	—	—	0.00	0.00	0.00	0.00	0.00	0.00	0.00	Income Return %
—	—	—	—	—	51.30	55.27	-17.91	-20.81	-16.69	31.24	11.70	Capital Return %
—	—	—	—	—	9	14	69	52	6	26	17	Total Rtn % Rank Cat
—	—	—	—	0.00	0.00	0.00	0.00	0.00	0.00	0.00	0.00	Income $
—	—	—	—	0.00	0.00	0.04	1.96	0.04	0.00	0.00	0.00	Capital Gains $
—	—	—	—	—	1.56	1.31	1.27	1.30	1.35	1.34	1.30	Expense Ratio %
—	—	—	—	—	-0.27	-0.43	-0.69	-0.36	-0.68	-0.59	-0.36	Income Ratio %
—	—	—	—	—	170	173	176	127	117	90	84	Turnover Rate %
—	—	—	—	2	1,204	3,257	2,325	1,401	1,349	2,641	3,237	Net Assets $mil

Performance 12-31-04

	1st Qtr	2nd Qtr	3rd Qtr	4th Qtr	Total
2000	0.21	-8.30	2.88	-13.17	-17.91
2001	-18.63	4.85	-16.53	11.20	-20.81
2002	4.49	-3.45	-14.87	-3.00	-16.69
2003	-0.09	14.22	4.33	10.23	31.24
2004	1.01	-1.93	0.68	12.00	11.70

Trailing	Total Return%	+/- S&P 500	+/- Russ 1000Gr	%Rank Cat	Growth of $10,000
3 Mo	12.00	2.77	2.83	16	11,200
6 Mo	12.76	5.57	9.29	1	11,276
1 Yr	11.70	0.83	5.40	17	11,170
3 Yr Avg	6.89	3.31	7.07	4	12,213
5 Yr Avg	-4.51	-2.21	4.78	23	7,939
10 Yr Avg	—	—	—	—	—
15 Yr Avg	—	—	—	—	—

Tax Analysis	Tax-Adj Rtn%	%Rank Cat	Tax-Cost Rat	%Rank Cat
3 Yr (estimated)	6.89	3	0.00	1
5 Yr (estimated)	-4.93	20	0.44	27
10 Yr (estimated)	—	—	—	—

Potential Capital Gain Exposure: 18% of assets

Rating and Risk

Time Period	Load-Adj Return %	Morningstar Rtn vs Cat	Morningstar Risk vs Cat	Morningstar Risk-Adj Rating
1 Yr	11.70			
3 Yr	6.89	High	-Avg	★★★★★
5 Yr	-4.51	+Avg	Avg	★★★★
10 Yr	—	—	—	—
Incept	9.31			

Other Measures	Standard Index S&P 500	Best Fit Index Russ 2000
Alpha	4.0	-1.0
Beta	0.71	0.64
R-Squared	61	80
Standard Deviation	14.65	
Mean	6.89	
Sharpe Ratio	0.38	

Portfolio Analysis 09-30-04

Share change since 03-04 Total Stocks:34	Sector	PE	YTD Ret%	% Assets
⊕ UnitedHealth Group	Health	23.8	51.38	9.29
⊕ Qualcomm	Hardware	42.0	58.20	6.21
⊕ Genentech	Health	78.6	16.36	5.79
⊖ SLM	Financial	15.8	44.21	5.48
⊕ Countrywide Financial	Financial	9.0	48.15	5.46
⊕ Gen Elec	Ind Mtrls	22.8	20.68	4.98
Citigroup	Financial	15.3	2.72	4.14
⊕ Lowe's Companies	Consumer	22.1	4.25	3.94
⊕ FedEx	Business	27.9	46.40	3.50
☼ eBay	Consumer	81.6	80.07	3.46
⊖ Caterpillar	Ind Mtrls	17.6	19.75	3.43
⊕ Procter & Gamble	Goods	23.3	12.38	3.38
⊕ Dell	Hardware	34.0	24.01	3.02
☼ Microsoft	Software	36.1	8.95	2.94
⊖ Boston Scientific	Health	32.3	-3.29	2.87
☼ Zimmer Holdings	Health	54.0	13.81	2.87
Medtronic	Health	30.7	2.68	2.64
⊕ Electronic Arts	Software	30.9	29.36	2.58
⊖ Wal-Mart Stores	Consumer	23.4	0.51	2.49
⊕ Nike B	Goods	23.6	33.94	2.30

Current Investment Style

Value Blnd Growth — Large Mid Small

Market Cap	%
Giant	45.7
Large	45.5
Mid	8.8
Small	0.0
Micro	0.0
Avg $mil: 44,290	

Value Measures		Rel Category
Price/Earnings	18.96	0.89
Price/Book	3.44	1.07
Price/Sales	2.11	0.98
Price/Cash Flow	12.68	1.15
Dividend Yield %	0.81	1.05

Growth Measures	%	Rel Category
Long-Term Erngs	14.15	1.01
Book Value	17.09	1.34
Sales	10.67	1.25
Cash Flow	6.60	0.40
Historical Erngs	28.81	1.99

Profitability	%	Rel Category
Return on Equity	22.15	1.23
Return on Assets	13.19	1.41
Net Margin	15.23	1.24

Sector Weightings	% of Stocks	Rel S&P 500	3 Year High	Low
Info	16.99	0.79		
Software	5.52	1.28	9	0
Hardware	10.22	1.00	23	0
Media	0.00	0.00	9	0
Telecom	1.25	0.40	5	0
Service	64.43	1.39		
Health	23.47	1.88	32	18
Consumer	18.35	2.02	19	7
Business	3.50	0.86	5	1
Financial	19.11	0.92	24	11
Mfg	18.59	0.58		
Goods	10.18	1.09	23	7
Ind Mtrls	8.41	0.66	18	3
Energy	0.00	0.00	0	0
Utilities	0.00	0.00	0	0

Composition

Cash	0.0
Stocks	100.0
Bonds	0.0
Other	0.0
Foreign (% of Stock)	2.3

Morningstar's Take by Bridget Hughes 10-18-04

Marsico Focus is in bullish mode.

Considering even this fund's manager, Tom Marsico, concedes that the low-inflation, low-interest-rate environment he sees for the U.S. economy means growth will be hard to come by in the near term, a bullish take may seem somewhat surprising. But to Marsico's way of thinking, the corollary to that low-rate outlook is tempting stock valuations. That is, when one compares earnings yields with, say, the 10-year Treasury yield, it's much easier to make a bullish case for stocks. That view extends even to racier growth areas, where prices have come down in recent months amid a tech-led correction. As such, Marsico reports putting money to work in some traditional growth names, such as Qualcomm and Dell, while whittling the fund's cash stake down to 1% of assets.

Marsico is hardly loading up on tech, however. In fact, absent an obvious trend in one sector or another, the top-down ideas that have regularly proved successful here are playing second-fiddle to stock-picking. Take top holding UnitedHealth Group, for example. Sure, Marsico knows demographic trends work in this managed-care company's favor. But he's really enamored with the way the company harnesses technology to achieve cost leadership and thinks the stock still looks cheap, pointing out its attractive cash-flow yield. And while Qualcomm is no bargain, Marsico likes its prospects as the world embraces third-generation (3G) wireless technology. It also boasts high margins on its royalties business that translate into strong cash-flow generation.

It's tough to argue with Marsico's results, which have been strong over the long haul. That doesn't mean there aren't risks to his approach, and his charges have suffered dry spells and meaningful setbacks from time to time. Further, while this offering is home to less than $3 billion, Marsico is responsible for more money now than ever, which could prove a challenge. For now, though, we're sticking by the fund.

Address:	Marsico Investment Fund Milwaukee, WI 53201-3210 888-860-8686
Web Address:	www.marsicofunds.com
Inception:	12-31-97 *
Advisor:	Marsico Capital Management, LLC
Subadvisor:	None
NTF Plans:	Fidelity Retail-NTF, Schwab OneSource

Minimum Purchase:	$2500	Add: $100	IRA: $1000
Min Auto Inv Plan:	$1000	Add: $50	
Sales Fees:	0.25%B, 2.00%R		
Management Fee:	0.85%		
Actual Fees:	Mgt:0.85%	Dist:0.25%	
Expense Projections:	3Yr:$425	5Yr:$734	10Yr:$1613
Income Distrib:	Annually		

Marsico Growth

Ticker	Load	NAV	Yield	Total Assets	Mstar Category
MGRIX	12b-1 only	$17.66	0.0%	$1,637 mil	Large Growth

Governance and Management

Fiduciary Grade: A

Portfolio Manager(s)

Before forming his firm in late 1997, Tom Marsico built a great record at Janus Twenty. Marsico has a staff of 17 analysts and traders. He is a large shareholder in each of the four funds the shop offers. All but one of the independent trustees have money invested in the fund.

Strategy

Manager Tom Marsico combines top-down analysis with bottom-up stock-picking to build this portfolio. He holds about 10 more names here than at his other charge, Marsico Focus, but the fund is still quite concentrated. Marsico primarily buys growth stocks, but he'll also look at cheaper names that he thinks have a catalyst for a turnaround.

Historical Profile

Return Above Avg
Risk Average
Rating ★★★★ Above Avg

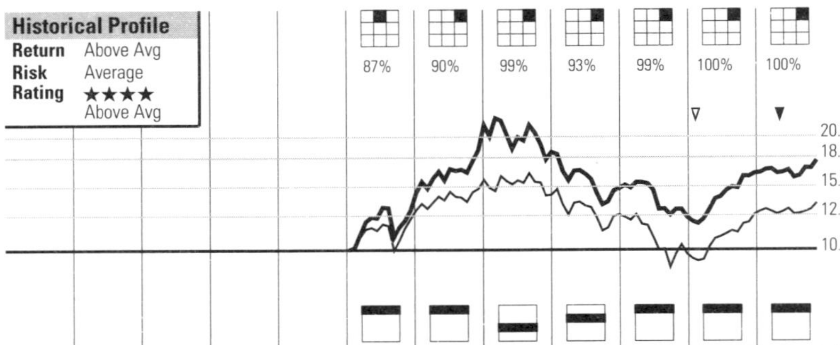

Investment Style
Equity
Stock %

▼ Manager Change
▽ Partial Manager Change

Growth of $10,000
— Investment Values of Fund
— Investment Values of S&P 500

Performance Quartile (within Category)

1993	1994	1995	1996	1997	1998	1999	2000	2001	2002	2003	12-04	History
—	—	—	—	10.00	14.34	21.86	17.67	14.06	11.70	15.44	17.66	NAV
—	—	—	—	0.00*	43.40	53.31	-15.85	-20.34	-16.79	31.97	14.38	Total Return %
—	—	—	—	—	14.83	32.27	-6.75	-8.46	5.30	3.30	3.51	+/-S&P 500
—	—	—	—	—	4.69	20.15	6.57	0.08	11.09	2.22	8.08	+/-Russ 1000Gr
—	—	—	—	—	0.00	0.00	0.00	0.00	0.00	0.00	0.00	Income Return %
—	—	—	—	—	43.40	53.31	-15.85	-20.34	-16.79	31.97	14.38	Capital Return %
—	—	—	—	—	15	15	61	50	6	22	6	Total Rtn % Rank Cat
—	—	—	—	0.00	0.00	0.00	0.00	0.00	0.00	0.00	0.00	Income $
—	—	—	—	0.00	0.00	0.11	0.70	0.02	0.00	0.00	0.00	Capital Gains $
—	—	—	—	—	1.51	1.43	1.30	1.33	1.37	1.38	1.30	Expense Ratio %
—	—	—	—	—	-0.14	-0.46	-0.55	-0.53	-0.49	-0.62	-0.34	Income Ratio %
—	—	—	—	—	141	137	137	120	111	91	73	Turnover Rate %
—	—	—	—	18	374	1,048	830	604	622	1,019	1,637	Net Assets $mil

Performance 12-31-04

	1st Qtr	2nd Qtr	3rd Qtr	4th Qtr	Total
2000	2.84	-10.05	2.97	-11.65	-15.85
2001	-16.24	4.05	-17.47	10.75	-20.34
2002	3.84	-4.79	-14.53	-1.52	-16.79
2003	-0.85	15.00	5.62	9.58	31.97
2004	2.66	-0.69	1.33	10.72	14.38

Trailing	Total Return%	+/- S&P 500	+/- Russ 1000Gr	%Rank Cat	Growth of $10,000
3 Mo	10.72	1.49	1.55	33	11,072
6 Mo	12.20	5.01	8.73	2	11,220
1 Yr	14.38	3.51	8.08	6	11,438
3 Yr Avg	7.90	4.32	8.08	2	12,562
5 Yr Avg	-3.38	-1.08	5.91	16	8,420
10 Yr Avg	—	—	—	—	—
15 Yr Avg	—	—	—	—	—

Tax Analysis	Tax-Adj Rtn%	%Rank Cat	Tax-Cost Rat	%Rank Cat
3 Yr (estimated)	7.90	2	0.00	1
5 Yr (estimated)	-3.54	14	0.17	10
10 Yr (estimated)	—	—	—	—

Potential Capital Gain Exposure: 17% of assets

Rating and Risk

Time Period	Load-Adj Return %	Morningstar Rtn vs Cat	Morningstar Risk vs Cat	Morningstar Risk-Adj Rating
1 Yr	14.38			
3 Yr	7.90	High	-Avg	★★★★★
5 Yr	-3.38	+Avg	Avg	★★★★
10 Yr	—	—	—	—
Incept	9.19			

Other Measures	Standard Index S&P 500	Best Fit Index S&P Mid 400
Alpha	4.9	-0.5
Beta	0.69	0.77
R-Squared	63	80
Standard Deviation	14.00	
Mean	7.90	
Sharpe Ratio	0.47	

Portfolio Analysis 09-30-04

Share change since 03-04 Total Stocks:46	Sector	PE	YTD Ret%	% Assets
⊕ UnitedHealth Group	Health	23.8	51.38	8.09
⊕ Genentech	Health	78.6	16.36	5.29
⊕ Qualcomm	Hardware	42.0	58.20	5.06
⊕ Gen Elec	Ind Mtrls	22.8	20.68	4.95
⊕ Countrywide Financial	Financial	9.0	48.15	4.72
⊖ SLM	Financial	15.8	44.21	3.40
Citigroup	Financial	15.3	2.72	3.35
Caterpillar	Ind Mtrls	17.6	19.75	3.17
Wynn Resorts	Consumer	—	138.92	3.13
☼ eBay	Consumer	81.6	80.07	3.12
⊕ FedEx	Business	27.9	46.40	3.06
⊕ Wal-Mart Stores	Consumer	23.4	0.51	2.92
⊕ Boston Scientific	Health	32.3	-3.29	2.86
⊕ Dell	Hardware	34.0	24.01	2.79
⊕ Lowe's Companies	Consumer	22.1	4.25	2.78
☼ Microsoft	Software	36.1	8.95	2.75
⊕ Procter & Gamble	Goods	23.3	12.38	2.61
⊕ Electronic Arts	Software	30.9	29.36	2.39
⊕ Samsung Electronics	Goods	—	—	2.18
Merrill Lynch & Company	Financial	12.6	3.12	2.17

Current Investment Style

Value Blnd Growth; Large Mid Small

Market Cap	%
Giant	42.9
Large	46.2
Mid	10.7
Small	0.1
Micro	0.0

Avg $mil: 38,543

Value Measures		Rel Category
Price/Earnings	18.43	0.87
Price/Book	3.31	1.02
Price/Sales	1.99	0.93
Price/Cash Flow	12.37	1.13
Dividend Yield %	0.79	1.03

Growth Measures	%	Rel Category
Long-Term Erngs	14.08	1.00
Book Value	15.50	1.22
Sales	10.01	1.17
Cash Flow	5.73	0.35
Historical Erngs	23.78	1.64

Profitability	%	Rel Category
Return on Equity	19.91	1.11
Return on Assets	11.30	1.21
Net Margin	14.00	1.14

Sector Weightings	% of Stocks	Rel S&P 500	3 Year High	3 Year Low
Info	15.22	0.71		
Software	5.14	1.20	9	0
Hardware	8.81	0.86	22	1
Media	0.00	0.00	8	0
Telecom	1.27	0.40	4	0
Service	60.59	1.31		
Health	22.13	1.77	28	17
Consumer	19.93	2.19	22	10
Business	3.06	0.76	8	2
Financial	15.47	0.75	21	9
Mfg	24.20	0.75		
Goods	11.13	1.19	24	7
Ind Mtrls	13.07	1.03	14	3
Energy	0.00	0.00	1	0
Utilities	0.00	0.00	0	0

Composition

Cash	0.0
Stocks	100.0
Bonds	0.0
Other	0.0
Foreign (% of Stock)	2.2

Morningstar's Take by Bridget Hughes 10-19-04

Is Marsico Growth getting its tech mojo back?

Yes, and no. Manager Tom Marsico recently added to some technology stocks, especially those that he thinks cheapened through 2004, like Dell and Electronic Arts. He also is a fan of stocks boasting strong secular growth drivers, such as current favorite Qualcomm. Marsico likes the wireless-equipment firm's growth prospects as the world embraces third-generation (3G) wireless technology. It also boasts high margins on its royalties business that translate into strong cash-flow generation.

Marsico has also played technology in a more esoteric way. He likes companies that are using technology to better their business. For example, top holding UnitedHealth Group harnesses technology (and its scale) to achieve cost leadership. (It also doesn't hurt that the stock is cheap in Marsico's view.) Other indirect plays on tech include FedEx and eBay.

Overall, however, technology officially remains at a low weighting in the portfolio. Marsico still isn't excited about corporate IT spending, which puts a damper on the outlook for many tech names. That said, he recognizes that corporate balance sheets are as healthy as perhaps they've ever been, and CEOs could be keeping their powder dry until political and economic uncertainties subside.

The upshot for the portfolio is a diversified set of investment theses. While Marsico continues to hang on to firms that will be able to grow in the low-inflation environment he foresees, like UnitedHealth and SLM, he's also starting to emphasize more-aggressive growth picks that he thinks are cheap considering multi-year forecasts. This kind of positioning could mute performance if a narrow section of the market takes off, but we think it's smart and helps diversify a concentrated portfolio. And Marsico has regularly adopted this kind of split to good effect over the long haul.

Address:	Marsico Investment Fund Milwaukee, WI 53201-3210 888-860-8686
Web Address:	www.marsicofunds.com
Inception:	12-31-97*
Advisor:	Marsico Capital Management, LLC
Subadvisor:	None
NTF Plans:	Fidelity Retail-NTF, Schwab OneSource

Minimum Purchase:	$2500	Add: $100	IRA: $1000
Min Auto Inv Plan:	$1000	Add: $50	
Sales Fees:	0.25%B, 2.00%R		
Management Fee:	0.85%		
Actual Fees:	Mgt:0.85%	Dist:0.25%	
Expense Projections:	3Yr:$434	5Yr:$750	10Yr:$1646
Income Distrib:	Annually		

Marsico Intl Opp

Ticker	Load	NAV	Yield	Total Assets	Mstar Category
MIOFX	12b-1 only	$12.01	0.0%	$147 mil	Foreign Large Growth

Governance and Management

Fiduciary Grade: B

Portfolio Manager(s)

This is James Gendelman's first stint as a portfolio manager. He previously spent 13 years at Goldman Sachs, primarily in a sales and product development role that focused on launching Goldman's international offerings. He has one analyst working closely with him on this fund, but has ready access to Marsico's other analysts, who truly search for good ideas globally. Gendelman also contributes to the portfolios of Marsico's U.S.-based funds.

Strategy

Like other Marsico funds, this offering is run in a concentrated format. The fund has a blue-chip orientation and can lean toward fast-growing firms. James Gendelman considers three types of firms for the portfolio: core-growth stocks, aggressive-growth stocks, and firms undergoing life-cycle changes, such as a major restructuring. The fund has a redemption fee to deter market-timers.

Historical Profile

Return High
Risk Average
Rating ★★★★★ Highest

Investment Style	2000	2001	2002	2003	12-04
Equity Stock %	74%	94%	86%	99%	99%

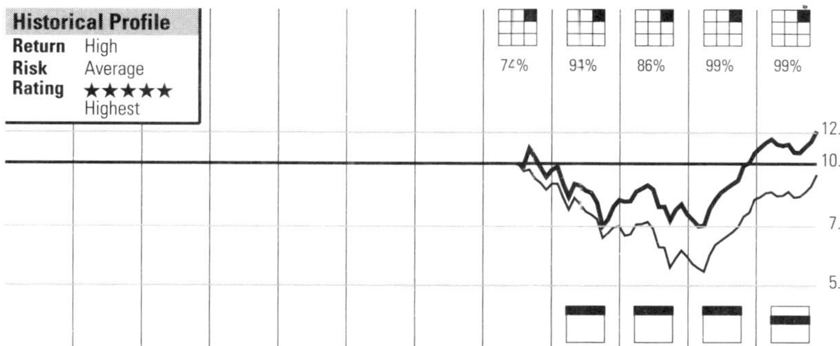

▼ Manager Change
▽ Partial Manager Change

Growth of $10,000
— Investment Values of Fund
— Investment Values of MSCI EAFE

Performance Quartile (within Category)

1993	1994	1995	1996	1997	1998	1999	2000	2001	2002	2003	12-04	History
—	—	—	—	—	—	—	9.33	7.86	7.25	10.26	12.01	NAV
—	—	—	—	—	—	—	-3.52*	-15.65	-7.76	41.52	17.06	Total Return %
—	—	—	—	—	—	—	—	5.77	8.18	2.93	-3.19	+/-MSCI EAFE
—	—	—	—	—	—	—	—	5.74	8.04	2.10	-3.32	+/-MSCI Wd xUS
—	—	—	—	—	—	—	0.00	0.10	0.00	0.00	0.00	Income Return %
—	—	—	—	—	—	—	—	-15.75	-7.76	41.52	17.06	Capital Return %
—	—	—	—	—	—	—	—	13	1	17	31	Total Rtn % Rank Cat
—	—	—	—	—	—	—	0.04	0.01	0.00	0.00	0.00	Income $
—	—	—	—	—	—	—	0.27	0.00	0.00	0.00	0.00	Capital Gains $
—	—	—	—	—	—	—	1.60	1.60	1.60	1.68	1.60	Expense Ratio %
—	—	—	—	—	—	—	0.33	0.05	-0.25	0.18	0.07	Income Ratio %
—	—	—	—	—	—	—	190	543	192	211	105	Turnover Rate %
—	—	—	—	—	—	—	14	20	21	38	147	Net Assets $mil

Performance 12-31-04

	1st Qtr	2nd Qtr	3rd Qtr	4th Qtr	Total
2000	—	—	3.60	-6.87	-3.52 *
2001	-14.15	3.62	-18.31	16.07	-15.65
2002	4.96	1.21	-16.17	3.57	-7.76
2003	-6.21	20.74	7.06	16.72	41.52
2004	8.19	-2.88	-1.39	12.98	17.06

Trailing	Total Return%	+/- MSCI EAFE	+/- MSCI Wd xUS	%Rank Cat	Growth of $10,000
3 Mo	12.98	-2.34	-2.17	84	11,298
6 Mo	11.41	-3.59	-3.96	70	11,141
1 Yr	17.06	-3.19	-3.32	31	11,706
3 Yr Avg	15.18	3.29	2.96	3	15,280
5 Yr Avg	—	—	—	—	—
10 Yr Avg	—	—	—	—	—
15 Yr Avg	—	—	—	—	—

Tax Analysis	Tax-Adj Rtn%	%Rank Cat	Tax-Cost Rat	%Rank Cat
3 Yr (estimated)	15.18	1	0.00	1
5 Yr (estimated)	—	—	—	—
10 Yr (estimated)	—	—	—	—

Potential Capital Gain Exposure: 13% of assets

Rating and Risk

Time Period	Load-Adj Return %	Morningstar Rtn vs Cat	Morningstar Risk vs Cat	Morningstar Risk-Adj Rating
1 Yr	17.06			
3 Yr	15.18	High	Avg	★★★★★
5 Yr	—	—	—	—
10 Yr	—	—	—	—
Incept	4.96			

Other Measures	Standard Index S&P 500	Best Fit Index MSCI EAFE
Alpha	4.2	4.2
Beta	0.88	0.88
R-Squared	89	89

Standard Deviation	16.73
Mean	15.18
Sharpe Ratio	0.83

Portfolio Analysis 09-30-04

Share change since 03-04 Total Stocks:50	Sector	Country	% Assets
⊕ HSBC Hldgs	Financial	U.K.	4.30
⊕ UBS	Financial	Switzerland	4.20
⊕ Roche Holding	Health	Switzerland	4.12
☼ Renault	Goods	France	4.10
⊕ Reed Elsevier	Media	U.K.	3.33
☼ Tyco Intl	Ind Mtrls	Bermuda	3.29
⊕ Samsung Electronics	Goods	Korea	3.11
☼ InterContinental Hotels	Consumer	U.K.	2.91
⊕ Emi Grp	Goods	U.K.	2.89
⊕ NTL	Telecom	United States	2.77
⊕ TOTAL	Energy	France	2.69
⊕ Synthes-Stratec	Health	Switzerland	2.63
☼ Grupo Televisa ADR	Media	Mexico	2.34
☼ Vodafone Grp	Telecom	U.K.	2.24
⊖ Sogecable	Media	Spain	2.21
⊖ Nissan Motor	Goods	Japan	2.18
☼ Royal Bank Of Scotland G	Financial	U.K.	2.17
⊕ SAP	Software	Germany	2.16
⊕ Mitsubishi Tokyo Fin. Gr	Financial	Japan	2.14
☼ KDDI	Telecom	Japan	2.14

Current Investment Style

Value Blnd Growth / Large Mid Small

Market Cap	%
Giant	50.0
Large	34.7
Mid	14.1
Small	1.3
Micro	0.0
Avg $mil: 20,713	

Value Measures		Rel Category
Price/Earnings	13.39	0.90
Price/Book	1.25	0.60
Price/Sales	1.18	1.12
Price/Cash Flow	4.28	0.78
Dividend Yield %	1.99	0.98

Growth Measures	%	Rel Category
Long-Term Erngs	12.08	1.01
Book Value	4.68	2.71
Sales	5.11	1.11
Cash Flow	8.38	1.11
Historical Erngs	13.90	1.67

Composition			
Cash	0.0	Bonds	0.0
Stocks	99.3	Other	0.7
Foreign (% of Stock)			95.8

Sector Weightings	% of Stocks	Rel MSCI EAFE	3 Year High	3 Year Low
Info	28.37	1.71		
Software	2.25	2.08	4	0
Hardware	4.38	1.20	9	2
Media	11.83	5.19	13	2
Telecom	9.91	1.03	10	0
Service	42.73	0.96		
Health	8.74	1.20	9	0
Consumer	10.56	2.10	13	1
Business	3.46	0.64	24	3
Financial	19.97	0.74	30	11
Mfg	28.90	0.75		
Goods	21.61	1.58	39	19
Ind Mtrls	1.79	0.15	9	0
Energy	5.50	0.75	8	1
Utilities	0.00	0.00	2	0

Regional Exposure	% Stock		
UK/W. Europe	52	N. America	7
Japan	16	Latn America	7
Asia X Japan	16	Other	2

Country Exposure	% Stock		
U.K.	21	France	8
Japan	16	Germany	4
Switzerland	15		

Morningstar's Take by Bridget Hughes 12-01-04

The Marsico approach travels well.

On Marsico International Opportunities, manager Jim Gendelman uses the same strategy that successful U.S. investor Tom Marsico has used for decades. The upshot for this portfolio is a fund that's more flexible than its foreign large-growth peers, typically with a mix of different-sized stocks and the inclusion of so-called value stocks in addition to growth picks. Gendelman also invests based on themes, which are often based on macroeconomic ideas. Finally, like Marsico, Gendelman concentrates his picks in a compact portfolio. In short, it's one of the group's more-eclectic funds.

While that can sometimes make it tougher for investors to use the fund in a carefully planned portfolio, it also gives the fund a better chance to perform well in a variety of market climates. Indeed, the fund's healthy stash of mid-cap stocks has certainly helped over the past several years, as smaller names have paced global markets. Since its mid-2000 inception, the fund has been among the best-performing in its category.

Lately, Gendelman has been more enamored with larger companies--the fund's average market cap has crept up--and with more-aggressive growth stocks, such as recent buys, Ericsson, Reuters, Research in Motion, and ARM Holdings. While several of these holdings have performed well lately, foreign large-growth funds have generally been laggards over the past three years. Moving more aggressively into such stocks could prove good timing as market leadership changes.

Of course, there are risks. With a concentrated portfolio, blowups in just a few names can have a marked impact on performance. And Research in Motion, among others in the portfolio, looks expensive on traditional valuations metrics.

Given some heightened risk here, we'd couple the fund with a more-docile fund, such as Tweedy, Browne Global Value, but we think this is a good foreign large-growth choice.

Address:	Marsico Investment Fund Milwaukee, WI 53201-3210 888-860-8686
Web Address:	www.marsicofunds.com
Inception:	06-30-00 *
Advisor:	Marsico Capital Management, LLC
Subadvisor:	None
NTF Plans:	Fidelity Retail-NTF, Schwab OneSource

Minimum Purchase:	$2500	Add: $100	IRA: $1000
Min Auto Inv Plan:	$1000	Add: $50	
Sales Fees:	0.25%B, 2.00%R		
Management Fee:	0.85%		
Actual Fees:	Mgt:0.85%	Dist:0.25%	
Expense Projections:	3Yr:$639	5Yr:$1142	10Yr:$2525
Income Distrib:	Annually		

Masters' Select Equity

Ticker	Load	NAV	Yield	Total Assets	Mstar Category
MSEFX	Closed	$15.26	0.0%	$855 mil	Large Blend

Governance and Management

Fiduciary Grade: A

Portfolio Manager(s)

Christopher Davis of Davis NY Venture and Glen Bickerstaff of TCW Galileo Select Equities each invest 20% of assets in large-cap stocks. Mason Hawkins of Longleaf Partners and Bill Miller of Legg Mason Value each devote 20% of assets to stocks of all sizes. Dick Weiss of Strong Advisor Common Stock and Bill D'Alonzo of Brandywine both put 10% of the fund into small- and mid-cap names. Bickerstaff will step down at the end of 2004, leaving the fund in the hands of comanagers Craig Blum and Steve Burlingame.

Strategy

Litman/Gregory Fund Advisors selects six equity shops to run this fund. These managers pick their best stocks, up to 15 each, to include in the portfolio. Although each subadvisor makes big bets on individual positions, the overall fund isn't too concentrated.

Historical Profile

Return High
Risk Above Avg
Rating ★★★★★ Highest

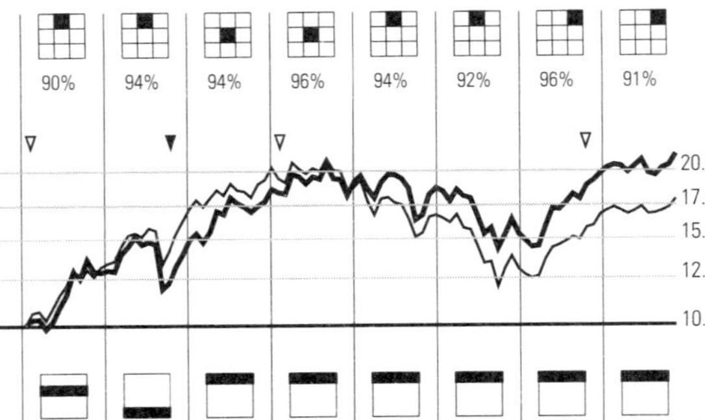

Investment Style
Equity
Stock %

▼ Manager Change
▽ Partial Manager Change

Growth of $10,000
▬ Investment Values of Fund
— Investment Values of S&P 500

Performance Quartile (within Category)

1993	1994	1995	1996	1997	1998	1999	2000	2001	2002	2003	12-04	History
—	—	—	10.00	11.84	13.57	14.38	12.98	12.59	10.19	13.44	15.26	NAV
—	—	—	0.00*	29.11	14.90	26.45	3.17	-2.55	-19.06	31.89	13.54	Total Return %
—	—	—	—	-4.24	-13.67	5.41	12.27	9.33	3.03	3.22	2.67	+/-S&P 500
—	—	—	—	-3.74	-12.12	5.54	10.96	9.90	2.59	2.00	2.14	+/-Russ 1000
—	—	—	—	0.31	0.27	0.12	0.00	0.00	0.00	0.00	0.00	Income Return %
—	—	—	—	28.80	14.63	26.33	3.17	-2.55	-19.06	31.89	13.54	Capital Return %
—	—	—	—	48	76	20	16	6	23	11	12	Total Rtn % Rank Cat
—	—	—	0.00	0.03	0.03	0.02	0.00	0.00	0.00	0.00	0.00	Income $
—	—	—	0.00	1.05	0.00	2.68	1.76	0.06	0.00	0.00	0.00	Capital Gains $
—	—	—	—	1.47	1.38	1.26	1.24	1.26	1.25	1.23	—	Expense Ratio %
—	—	—	—	0.12	0.30	-0.12	-0.35	-0.36	-0.30	-0.39	—	Income Ratio %
—	—	—	—	145	135	116	130	95	94	84	—	Turnover Rate %
—	—	—	—	297	406	449	469	508	431	610	855	Net Assets $mil

Performance 12-31-04

	1st Qtr	2nd Qtr	3rd Qtr	4th Qtr	Total
2000	7.23	-1.23	-0.92	-1.68	3.17
2001	-6.86	11.08	-18.76	15.94	-2.55
2002	-0.87	-11.30	-14.00	7.04	-19.06
2003	-5.50	18.38	4.91	12.37	31.89
2004	3.50	2.88	-3.77	10.82	13.54

Trailing	Total Return%	+/- S&P 500	+/- Russ 1000	%Rank Cat	Growth of $10,000
3 Mo	10.82	1.59	1.02	16	11,082
6 Mo	6.64	-0.55	-1.17	62	10,664
1 Yr	13.54	2.67	2.14	12	11,354
3 Yr Avg	6.62	3.04	2.35	9	12,120
5 Yr Avg	4.03	6.33	5.79	7	12,184
10 Yr Avg	—	—	—	—	—
15 Yr Avg	—	—	—	—	—

Tax Analysis	Tax-Adj Rtn%	%Rank Cat	Tax-Cost Rat	%Rank Cat
3 Yr (estimated)	6.62	6	0.00	1
5 Yr (estimated)	3.45	6	0.56	30
10 Yr (estimated)	—	—	—	—

Potential Capital Gain Exposure: 20% of assets

Rating and Risk

Time Period	Load-Adj Return %	Morningstar Rtn vs Cat	Morningstar Risk vs Cat	Morningstar Risk-Adj Rating
1 Yr	13.54			
3 Yr	6.62	High	+Avg	★★★★★
5 Yr	4.03	High	+Avg	★★★★★
10 Yr	—	—	—	—
Incept	10.89			

Other Measures	Standard Index S&P 500	Best Fit Index Wil 4500
Alpha	3.0	-4.6
Beta	1.03	0.99
R-Squared	89	92

Standard Deviation	17.54
Mean	6.62
Sharpe Ratio	0.30

Morningstar's Take by Todd Trubey 12-06-04

Masters' Select Equity has shuttered its doors.

As of Oct. 4, 2004, this fund isn't taking money from most new investors. On that date Litman/Gregory Advisors announced that the fund's asset base had crossed the $750-million mark, the preannounced level for the fund's closing. This is a very modest level for a fund that invests across the market-cap spectrum. However, the advisor believes that staying nimble is especially important for this offering given that each of its subadvisors runs a portfolio of no more than 15 stocks.

We applaud this move. Asset growth can hamper a stock-picker's ability to execute trades without affecting securities' prices and can weigh on performance. We are fans of firms that acknowledge this potential difficulty and plan accordingly. This is one of many examples of how Litman/Gregory stands out as a fiduciary.

It has been a busy time for this fund's shareholders. TCW Investment Management, one of this fund's subadvisors, announced at the end of September that Glen Bickerstaff, a stock-picker for this fund, will step aside from portfolio management at the end of 2004. Craig Blum and Steve Burlingame--comanagers of the TCW-run portion of this fund since Crawford's departure--will take control of TCW's slice of the fund beginning in 2005. As of now, Litman/Gregory is sticking with TCW.

This change is cause for mild concern, but not much more. Blum and Burlingame can't lay claim to a long track record of success running focused portfolios the way Bickerstaff or other managers here can. Nonetheless, the fund's advisor has managed transitions like this one well before. It wisely sat tight after the retirement of Shelby Davis of Davis/Selected in the mid-1990s, for one. Plus, Bickerstaff is staying on at TCW and will oversee his successors' progress.

In all, we aren't alarmed by the manager change and continue to be fans of this strong fund.

Address:	2020 E. Financial Way Glendora CA 91741 800-960-0188	Minimum Purchase:	Closed	Add: —	IRA: —
Web Address:	www.mastersselect.com	Min Auto Inv Plan:	Closed	Add: —	
Inception:	12-31-96*	Sales Fees:	No-load		
Advisor:	Litman Gregory Fund Advisors LLC	Management Fee:	1.10%, 0.10%A		
Subadvisor:	Multiple	Actual Fees:	Mgt:1.10%	Dist:	
NTF Plans:	N/A	Expense Projections:	3Yr:$398	5Yr:$690	10Yr:$1521
		Income Distrib:	Annually		

Portfolio Analysis 09-30-04

Share change since 06-04 Total Stocks:79	Sector	PE	YTD Ret%	% Assets
⊖ Tyco International	Ind Mtrls	25.1	35.41	4.60
☼ J P Morgan Chase	Financial	19.4	9.97	3.27
⊕ Iac / Interactivecorp	Consumer	43.1	-18.60	2.34
Capital One Financial	Financial	12.5	37.61	2.21
⊕ Yahoo!	Media	95.1	67.36	2.18
Eastman Kodak	Goods	—	27.90	2.14
⊕ Comcast	Media	—	-13.77	2.08
⊕ eBay	Consumer	81.6	80.07	2.07
American International G	Financial	16.2	-0.53	2.06
⊕ Progressive	Financial	11.7	1.63	1.95
American Express	Financial	20.3	17.60	1.94
☼ EOG Resources	Energy	16.5	55.21	1.92
MGIC Investment	Financial	12.7	21.42	1.90
Waste Management	Business	18.9	3.81	1.87
⊖ Aon	Financial	10.8	2.17	1.85
⊕ Home Depot	Consumer	19.0	21.47	1.82
FedEx	Business	27.9	46.40	1.81
Berkshire Hathaway A	Financial	—	—	1.77
Republic Services A	Business	21.8	32.45	1.74
⊕ Amazon.com	Consumer	55.5	-15.83	1.73

Current Investment Style

Value Blnd Growth — Large Mid Small

Market Cap	%
Giant	31.9
Large	28.5
Mid	29.9
Small	7.7
Micro	2.1
Avg $mil: 12,914	

Value Measures		Rel Category
Price/Earnings	17.52	1.03
Price/Book	2.10	0.80
Price/Sales	1.18	0.82
Price/Cash Flow	5.11	0.67
Dividend Yield %	0.77	0.52

Growth Measures	%	Rel Category
Long-Term Erngs	12.57	1.09
Book Value	12.25	1.58
Sales	3.99	0.70
Cash Flow	-0.22	NMF
Historical Erngs	8.86	0.75

Profitability	%	Rel Category
Return on Equity	12.75	0.73
Return on Assets	7.03	0.81
Net Margin	10.10	0.88

Sector Weightings	% of Stocks	Rel S&P 500	3 Year High	3 Year Low
Info	23.28	1.08		
Software	2.22	0.52	4	1
Hardware	6.81	0.67	9	6
Media	12.09	3.15	12	5
Telecom	2.16	0.69	3	1
Service	55.25	1.19		
Health	6.02	0.48	8	6
Consumer	13.33	1.47	15	13
Business	9.42	2.33	14	7
Financial	26.48	1.28	30	26
Mfg	21.48	0.67		
Goods	10.14	1.09	10	6
Ind Mtrls	6.41	0.51	8	5
Energy	4.93	0.69	8	3
Utilities	0.00	0.00	1	0

Composition

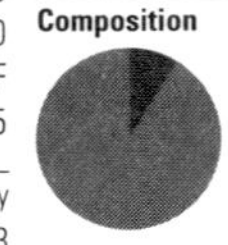

Cash	8.8
Stocks	91.2
Bonds	0.0
Other	0.0
Foreign (% of Stock)	6.8

Masters' Select Intl

Ticker	Load	NAV	Yield	Total Assets	Mstar Category
MSILX	Closed	$16.89	0.4%	$1,137 mil	Foreign Large Blend

Governance and Management

Fiduciary Grade: A

Portfolio Manager(s)

There have been a few changes over time, but this fund continues to sport an impressive roster of managers: Artisan International's Mark Yockey; Marshall International Stock's Dan Jaworski; Oakmark International's David Herro; Ted Tyson, formerly of American Century and Harbor International Growth; and Bill Fries of Thornburg International Value. Each now manages 20% of the portfolio.

Strategy

The five managers follow diverse styles, but each runs 20% of the fund and contributes eight to 15 stock picks to the portfolio. Advisor Litman/Gregory has been diligent in fighting market-timers. Years ago, it implemented a 2% redemption fee on shares held fewer than six months; it has turned away substantial amounts of money from platforms that wanted permission not to enforce the redemption fee; and it has always been aggressive about finding and getting rid of timers. The firm, which has used fair-value pricing for specific securities for some time, is also researching the possibility of using broader fair value pricing.

Historical Profile

Return Above Avg
Risk Above Avg
Rating ★★★★ Above Avg

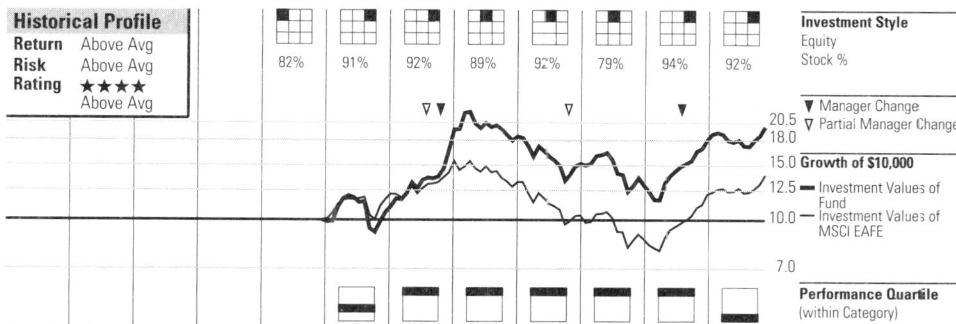

1993	1994	1995	1996	1997	1998	1999	2000	2001	2002	2003	12-04	History
—	—	—	—	9.88	10.95	18.67	15.31	12.53	10.70	14.83	16.89	NAV
—	—	—	—	-1.20*	11.74	75.01	-5.01	-17.94	-14.33	38.86	14.37	Total Return %
—	—	—	—	—	-8.19	47.98	9.18	3.48	1.61	0.27	-5.88	+/-MSCI EAFE
—	—	—	—	—	-6.95	47.03	8.35	3.45	1.47	-0.56	-6.01	+/-MSCI Wd xUS
—	—	—	—	0.00	0.89	0.31	0.25	0.22	0.27	0.25	0.47	Income Return %
—	—	—	—	—	10.85	74.70	-5.26	-18.16	-14.60	38.61	13.90	Capital Return %
—	—	—	—	—	68	3	6	16	24	15	86	Total Rtn % Rank Cat
—	—	—	—	0.00	0.09	0.03	0.05	0.03	0.03	0.03	0.07	Income $
—	—	—	—	0.00	0.00	0.38	2.34	0.00	0.00	0.00	0.00	Capital Gains $
—	—	—	—	1.77	1.55	1.29	1.18	1.19	1.13	1.10	—	Expense Ratio %
—	—	—	—	0.42	0.87	0.01	0.47	0.52	0.47	0.69	—	Income Ratio %
—	—	—	—	—	74	100	149	174	141	110	—	Turnover Rate %
—	—	—	—	46	95	218	276	278	336	732	1,137	Net Assets $mil

Performance 12-31-04

	1st Qtr	2nd Qtr	3rd Qtr	4th Qtr	Total
2000	13.82	-7.81	-4.59	-5.11	-5.01
2001	-13.52	0.00	-16.09	13.08	-17.94
2002	5.99	-2.64	-20.80	4.82	-14.33
2003	-10.28	23.65	7.58	16.35	38.86
2004	4.32	-4.14	-0.07	14.44	14.37

Trailing	Total Return%	+/- MSCI EAFE	+/- MSCI Wd xUS	%Rank Cat	Growth of $10,000
3 Mo	14.44	-0.88	-0.71	41	11,444
6 Mo	14.37	-0.63	-1.00	41	11,437
1 Yr	14.37	-5.88	-6.01	86	11,437
3 Yr Avg	10.80	-1.09	-1.42	27	13,603
5 Yr Avg	1.18	2.31	1.94	8	10,604
10 Yr Avg	—	—	—	—	—
15 Yr Avg	—	—	—	—	—

Tax Analysis	Tax-Adj Rtn%	%Rank Cat	Tax-Cost Rat	%Rank Cat
3 Yr (estimated)	10.68	20	0.11	12
5 Yr (estimated)	0.24	8	0.93	64
10 Yr (estimated)	—	—	—	—

Potential Capital Gain Exposure: 17% of assets

Rating and Risk

Time Period	Load-Adj Return %	Morningstar Rtn vs Cat	Morningstar Risk vs Cat	Morningstar Risk-Adj Rating
1 Yr	14.37			
3 Yr	10.80	+Avg	+Avg	★★★
5 Yr	1.18	+Avg	+Avg	★★★★
10 Yr	—	—	—	—
Incept	10.65			

Other Measures	Standard Index S&P 500	Best Fit Index MSCI Wd xUS
Alpha	-1.3	-1.7
Beta	1.05	1.06
R-Squared	90	91
Standard Deviation	19.11	
Mean	10.80	
Sharpe Ratio	0.50	

Portfolio Analysis 09-30-04

Share change since 06-04 Total Stocks:61	Sector	Country	% Assets
⊕ Tesco	Consumer	U.K.	5.91
⊕ EnCana	Energy	Canada	3.73
⊕ Kingfisher	Consumer	U.K.	3.36
⊕ Precision Drilling	Energy	Canada	3.05
⊕ Sinopec	Energy	Hong Kong	2.96
⊕ Telekomunikasi Indonesia	Telecom	Indonesia	2.74
Talisman Energy	Energy	Canada	2.42
Ericsson AB (publ)	Hardware	Sweden	2.22
Petroleo Brasileiro ADR	Energy	Brazil	2.06
⊕ Antena 3 de Television	Media	Spain	2.02
⊕ Toyota Motor	Goods	Japan	1.78
Baycorp Advantage Ltd	Financial	Australia	1.75
GlaxoSmithKline	Health	U.K.	1.72
Altadis	Goods	Spain	1.72
⊖ Ansell Ltd	Ind Mtrls	Australia	1.66
⊕ Australia & New Zealand	Financial	Australia	1.65
⊕ Portugal Telecom, SGPS	Telecom	Portugal	1.63
Wal-Mart de Mexico	Consumer	Mexico	1.63
BOUYGUES	Business	France	1.61
⊕ Umicore Grp	Ind Mtrls	Belgium	1.60

Current Investment Style

Value Blnd Growth; Large Mid Small

Market Cap	%
Giant	37.8
Large	31.7
Mid	22.3
Small	6.1
Micro	2.2
Avg $mil: 9,365	

Value Measures		Rel Category
Price/Earnings	15.67	1.14
Price/Book	2.15	1.19
Price/Sales	0.97	1.07
Price/Cash Flow	6.83	1.39
Dividend Yield %	1.88	0.74

Growth Measures	%	Rel Category
Long-Term Erngs	14.68	1.36
Book Value	2.01	201.00
Sales	3.98	1.60
Cash Flow	8.16	1.45
Historical Erngs	5.58	1.00

Composition

Cash	6.1	Bonds	0.0
Stocks	92.5	Other	1.5
Foreign (% of Stock)			100.0

Sector Weightings	% of Stocks	Rel MSCI EAFE	3 Year High	3 Year Low
Info	19.70	1.19		
Software	0.00	0.00	10	0
Hardware	4.20	1.15	6	0
Media	7.68	3.37	16	3
Telecom	7.82	0.81	8	0
Service	39.16	0.88		
Health	4.87	0.67	8	3
Consumer	14.01	2.78	14	6
Business	4.12	0.76	6	0
Financial	16.16	0.60	24	11
Mfg	41.13	1.06		
Goods	16.78	1.23	42	17
Ind Mtrls	8.99	0.73	25	6
Energy	15.36	2.09	15	3
Utilities	0.00	0.00	0	0

Regional Exposure	% Stock		
UK/W. Europe	55	N. America	11
Japan	9	Latn America	7
Asia X Japan	17	Other	1

Country Exposure	% Stock		
U.K.	23	Australia	6
Canada	11	Germany	5
Japan	9		

Morningstar's Take by William Samuel Rocco 11-10-04

Masters' Select International's recent closure is encouraging as well as unsurprising.

Litman/Gregory Fund Advisors has long made it clear that it would close this offering once its asset base hit $1 billion. The fund, which began 2004 with more than $700 million in assets and had roughly $950 million in assets at midyear, hit that mark late last month, and Litman/Gregory shut the doors to most new investors on Oct. 27.

It's heartening when an advisor is transparent about how large it will allow a fund to get, and then follows through. But that's certainly not the only reason to be pleased with the closure here. All sorts of offerings have trouble executing their strategies when their asset bases get too big, and this multimanager fund is more sensitive to asset bloat than most. Each of its five managers invests in just eight to 15 stocks and most of them pay significant attention to smaller-cap names. By closing at a very reasonable size--more than 40 foreign large-cap offerings are bigger--this fund ensured its managers can continue to implement their strategies as they always have.

There's considerable reason for shareholders to be pleased that the five managers will be able to stick to their styles. Though the fund is lagging this year, it produced top-quartile results in five of its first six calendar years. Overall, it has earned a 6.8% annualized gain since opening in late 1997, while the average foreign large-blend offering has posted a 0.3% annualized return during that span.

The fund also has a below-average expense ratio for a no-load offering in its group. And the closure is just one example of the fundholder friendliness of the fund and its advisor, as the fund's Fiduciary Grade attests. In short, shareholders are likely to be happy here, as long as they know that the fund is somewhat more volatile than most of its peers, due to its issue focus and other distinctions.

Address:	2020 E. Financial Way Glendora CA 91741 800-960-0188
Web Address:	www.mastersselect.com
Inception:	12-01-97 *
Advisor:	Litman Gregory Fund Advisors LLC
Subadvisor:	Multiple
NTF Plans:	N/A

Minimum Purchase:	Closed	Add: —	IRA: —
Min Auto Inv Plan:	Closed	Add: —	
Sales Fees:	No-load, 2.00%R		
Management Fee:	1.10%, 0.10%A		
Actual Fees:	Mgt:1.10%	Dist: —	
Expense Projections:	3Yr:$401	5Yr:$707	10Yr:$1575
Income Distrib:	Annually		

Masters' Select Small Co

Analyst Pick

Ticker	Load	NAV	Yield	Total Assets	Mstar Category
MSSFX	None	$13.84	0.0%	$162 mil	Small Growth

Governance and Management

Fiduciary Grade: A

Portfolio Manager(s)

Five managers with experience running concentrated small-cap funds call the shots here. Former Morningstar Fund Manager of the Year Bob Rodriguez of FPA Capital leads a strong roster that also includes John Rogers of Ariel, Bill D'Alonzo of Brandywine, Dick Weiss of Strong Advisor Common Stock and David Anthony of Ranger Investment Management. Previously, Anthony was CIO of John McStay Investment Counsel, advisor to the Brazos funds.

Strategy

Litman/Gregory Advisors divvies up assets equally among five subadvisors, and each picks eight to 15 stocks according to his own investing style. Broadly speaking, Rodriguez and Rogers are value managers, D'Alonzo and Anthony favor growth stocks, and Weiss falls in between, but all have the flexibility to invest in stocks that don't neatly fall into one bucket or the other. Litman/Gregory isn't dogmatic about the fund's market-cap limits, so there will be a number of smaller mid-caps here. As of June 30, 2004, though, more than half of the fund was devoted to stocks with market caps below $1.3 billion.

Historical Profile

Return
Risk
Rating Not Rated

Investment Style
Equity
Stock %

90% 89%

▼ Manager Change
▽ Partial Manager Change

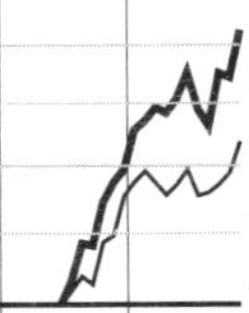

Growth of $10,000
— Investment Values of Fund
— Investment Values of S&P 500

Performance Quartile (within Category)

1993	1994	1995	1996	1997	1998	1999	2000	2001	2002	2003	12-04	History
—	—	—	—	—	—	—	—	—	—	11.79	13.84	NAV
—	—	—	—	—	—	—	—	—	—	—	21.01	Total Return %
—	—	—	—	—	—	—	—	—	—	—	10.14	+/-S&P 500
—	—	—	—	—	—	—	—	—	—	—	6.70	+/-Russ 2000 Gr
—	—	—	—	—	—	—	—	—	—	0.00	0.00	Income Return %
—	—	—	—	—	—	—	—	—	—	—	21.01	Capital Return %
—	—	—	—	—	—	—	—	—	—	—	11	Total Rtn % Rank Cat
—	—	—	—	—	—	—	—	—	—	0.00	0.00	Income $
—	—	—	—	—	—	—	—	—	—	0.13	0.43	Capital Gains $
—	—	—	—	—	—	—	—	—	—	1.65	—	Expense Ratio %
—	—	—	—	—	—	—	—	—	—	-1.33	—	Income Ratio %
—	—	—	—	—	—	—	—	—	—	—	—	Turnover Rate %
—	—	—	—	—	—	—	—	—	—	51	162	Net Assets $mil

Performance 12-31-04

	1st Qtr	2nd Qtr	3rd Qtr	4th Qtr	Total
2000	—	—	—	—	—
2001	—	—	—	—	—
2002	—	—	—	—	—
2003	—	—	8.00	10.34	—*
2004	8.23	4.55	-0.07	7.03	21.01

Trailing	Total Return%	+/- S&P 500	+/- Russ 2000 Gr	%Rank Cat	Growth of $10,000
3 Mo	7.03	-2.20	-8.05	99	10,703
6 Mo	6.95	-0.24	-1.21	59	10,695
1 Yr	21.01	10.14	6.70	11	12,101
3 Yr Avg	—	—	—	—	—
5 Yr Avg	—	—	—	—	—
10 Yr Avg	—	—	—	—	—
15 Yr Avg	—	—	—	—	—

Tax Analysis	Tax-Adj Rtn%	%Rank Cat	Tax-Cost Rat	%Rank Cat
3 Yr (estimated)	—	—	—	—
5 Yr (estimated)	—	—	—	—
10 Yr (estimated)	—	—	—	—

Potential Capital Gain Exposure: 14% of assets

Rating and Risk

Time Period	Load-Adj Return %	Morningstar Rtn vs Cat	Morningstar Risk vs Cat	Morningstar Risk-Adj Rating
1 Yr	21.01			
3 Yr	—	—	—	—
5 Yr	—	—	—	—
10 Yr	—	—	—	—
Incept	27.52			

Other Measures	Standard Index S&P 500	Best Fit Index
Alpha	—	—
Beta	—	—
R-Squared	—	—
Standard Deviation	—	
Mean	—	
Sharpe Ratio	—	

Portfolio Analysis 09-30-04

Share change since 06-04 Total Stocks:72	Sector	PE	YTD Ret%	% Assets
⊕ Ceradyne	Ind Mtrls	37.3	151.95	2.71
⊕ Big Lots	Consumer	14.9	-14.64	2.01
☆ Hansen Natural	Consumer	28.7	332.42	1.97
⊕ Quicksilver Resources	Energy	69.9	127.74	1.93
⊖ LifeCell	Health	12.7	64.84	1.78
⊕ RSA Security	Software	39.8	40.77	1.59
⊕ Journal Register	Media	7.6	-6.62	1.57
☆ Stratasys	Software	44.3	24.07	1.55
⊕ Autobytel	Consumer	24.0	-33.70	1.55
National Oilwell	Energy	36.9	57.83	1.54
☆ Andrew	Hardware	—	17.60	1.54
Rowan Companies	Energy	—	11.78	1.52
☆ Armor Holdings	Business	24.6	78.72	1.48
⊖ Caesars Entertainment	Consumer	62.6	95.97	1.47
⊕ Salix Pharmaceuticals	Health	—	16.34	1.46
⊕ Witness Systems	Software	—	88.35	1.42
☆ Greater Bay Bancorp	Financial	17.4	-0.15	1.42
General Binding	Ind Mtrls	38.7	-27.44	1.41
⊕ Markel	Financial	21.8	43.58	1.41
⊕ Janus Capital Group	Financial	3.8	2.71	1.41

Current Investment Style

Value Blnd Growth; Large Mid Small

Market Cap	%
Giant	0.0
Large	0.0
Mid	36.9
Small	48.0
Micro	15.1

Avg $mil: 1,096

Value Measures		Rel Category
Price/Earnings	21.38	0.98
Price/Book	2.31	0.88
Price/Sales	1.25	0.83
Price/Cash Flow	7.81	0.98
Dividend Yield %	0.21	0.68

Growth Measures	%	Rel Category
Long-Term Erngs	14.56	0.84
Book Value	5.89	0.91
Sales	3.00	0.46
Cash Flow	2.91	0.21
Historical Erngs	12.74	0.94

Profitability	%	Rel Category
Return on Equity	12.74	1.29
Return on Assets	5.62	1.28
Net Margin	8.19	1.20

Sector Weightings	% of Stocks	Rel S&P 500	3 Year High	3 Year Low
Info	22.91	1.07		
Software	11.45	2.66	—	—
Hardware	5.64	0.55	—	—
Media	5.82	1.52	—	—
Telecom	0.00	0.00	—	—
Service	45.27	0.98		
Health	11.42	0.91	—	—
Consumer	16.70	1.84	—	—
Business	9.35	2.31	—	—
Financial	7.80	0.38	—	—
Mfg	31.83	0.99		
Goods	5.43	0.58	—	—
Ind Mtrls	10.15	0.80	—	—
Energy	16.25	2.27	—	—
Utilities	0.00	0.00	—	—

Composition

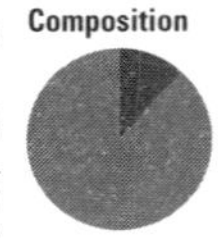

Cash	11.5
Stocks	88.5
Bonds	0.0
Other	0.0
Foreign (% of Stock)	2.9

Morningstar's Take by Todd Trubey 12-10-04

We think Masters' Select Smaller Companies achieves its high goal.

Litman/Gregory Advisor aims to provide one-stop access to a range of top small-cap stock pickers. The fund divides assets evenly between two value gurus, two growth skippers, and a blend manager. All five have long, superior track records. The fund has always been a small-growth fund, but that's partly because value managers Bob Rodriguez and John Rogers hold heavy cash. The fund is meant to be style-neutral and should be over the long term.

While constraints exist, the managers have fairly free rein, so the fund can look quite different from most peers. Each subadvisor must choose between eight and 15 stocks, generally firms with market caps below $1.3 billion. A portfolio of 60 to 80 holdings results. Now at 72 stocks, the fund has about half the holdings of the typical small-blend or small-growth peer. The managers keep the portfolio diversified through sectors, but weightings can be unusual. For instance, the fund's current 6% media and 16% energy stakes more than double the small-blend and small-growth category averages. Such quirky, compact funds often have higher risk/reward profiles than most peers.

To date, investors have certainly seen the reward part of that equation. Energy has been the top sector in small-caps this year, so the big stake has helped. Some of the fund's best stocks, moreover, have been energy stocks. Quicksilver Resources (a favorite at Dick Weiss' Strong Capital management) and National Oilwell (a key holding at Bob Rodriguez's First Pacific Advisors) have gained 110% and 52% year to date through Dec. 6, 2004.

Rounding out the fine picture here is excellent fiduciary attention. Litman/Gregory generally keeps costs reasonable, closes funds early, and provides excellent information to shareowners. This is a worthy choice.

Address:	2020 E. Financial Way Glendora CA 91741 800-960-0188
Web Address:	www.mastersselect.com
Inception:	06-30-03
Advisor:	Litman Gregory Fund Advisors LLC
Subadvisor:	Multiple
NTF Plans:	N/A

Minimum Purchase:	$5000	Add: $250	IRA: $1000
Min Auto Inv Plan:	$2500	Add: $100	
Sales Fees:	No-load, 2.00%R		
Management Fee:	1.14%		
Actual Fees:	Mgt:1.14%	Dist:	
Expense Projections:	3Yr:$553	5Yr: —	10Yr: —
Income Distrib:	Annually		

Masters' Select Value

Ticker	Load	NAV	Yield	Total Assets	Mstar Category
MSVFX	None	$14.90	0.0%	$306 mil	Large Value

Governance and Management

Fiduciary Grade: A

Portfolio Manager(s)

This fund's group of managers is a value all-star team. Mason Hawkins of Longleaf Partners, Bill Miller of Legg Mason Value, Bill Nygren of Oakmark Select, and David Winters of Mutual Shares each invest 25% of assets in undervalued stocks.

Strategy

Litman/Gregory Advisors has selected four value managers to run different portions of this fund. Each picks eight to 15 favorite stocks to include in the portfolio. Because all four are value managers and look for companies trading at a discount to their intrinsic or transaction value, it is likely that some picks will overlap. Due to the fund's small asset base, investors might expect it to hold more small-cap stocks than the managers hold elsewhere.

Historical Profile

Return Above Avg
Risk Average
Rating ★★★★ Above Avg

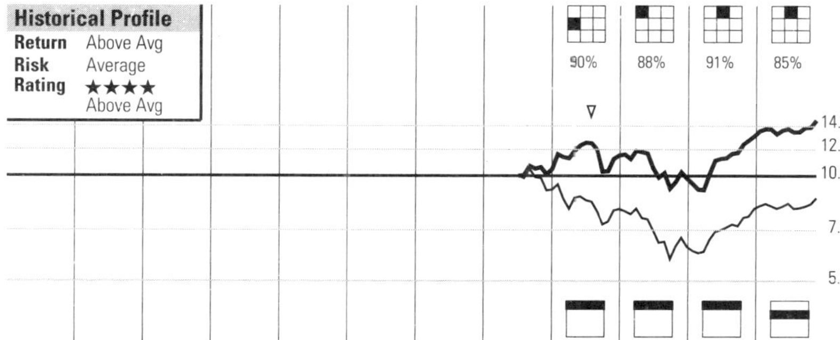

Investment Style
Equity
Stock %

▼ Manager Change
▽ Partial Manager Change

Growth of $10,000
▬ Investment Values of Fund
— Investment Values of S&P 500

Performance Quartile (within Category)

1993	1994	1995	1996	1997	1998	1999	2000	2001	2002	2003	12-04	History
—	—	—	—	—	—	—	10.45	11.43	9.81	12.99	14.90	NAV
—	—	—	—	—	—	—	4.50*	9.64	-14.17	32.42	14.70	Total Return %
—	—	—	—	—	—	—	—	21.52	7.92	3.75	3.83	+/-S&P 500
—	—	—	—	—	—	—	—	15.23	1.35	2.39	-1.79	+/-Russ 1000 VI
—	—	—	—	—	—	—	0.00	0.01	0.00	0.00	0.00	Income Return %
—	—	—	—	—	—	—	—	9.63	-14.17	32.42	14.70	Capital Return %
—	—	—	—	—	—	—	—	5	19	17	27	Total Rtn % Rank Cat
—	—	—	—	—	—	—	0.00	0.00	0.00	0.00	0.00	Income $
—	—	—	—	—	—	—	0.00	0.03	0.00	0.00	0.00	Capital Gains $
—	—	—	—	—	—	—	—	1.35	1.29	1.28	—	Expense Ratio %
—	—	—	—	—	—	—	—	-0.04	0.55	0.35	—	Income Ratio %
—	—	—	—	—	—	—	—	33	54	22	—	Turnover Rate %
—	—	—	—	—	—	—	56	160	138	181	306	Net Assets $mil

Performance 12-31-04

	1st Qtr	2nd Qtr	3rd Qtr	4th Qtr	Total
2000	—	—	4.80	-0.29	4.50 *
2001	7.56	10.95	-17.42	11.34	9.64
2002	3.15	-10.94	-12.57	6.86	-14.17
2003	-7.34	22.99	4.03	11.69	32.42
2004	4.70	0.15	0.88	8.44	14.70

Trailing	Total Return%	+/- S&P 500	+/- Russ 1000 VI	%Rank Cat	Growth of $10,000
3 Mo	8.44	-0.79	-1.94	70	10,844
6 Mo	9.40	2.21	-2.66	46	10,940
1 Yr	14.70	3.83	-1.79	27	11,470
3 Yr Avg	9.24	5.66	0.67	10	13,036
5 Yr Avg	—	—	—	—	—
10 Yr Avg	—	—	—	—	—
15 Yr Avg	—	—	—	—	—

Tax Analysis	Tax-Adj Rtn%	%Rank Cat	Tax-Cost Rat	%Rank Cat
3 Yr (estimated)	9.24	6	0.00	1
5 Yr (estimated)	—	—	—	—
10 Yr (estimated)	—	—	—	—

Potential Capital Gain Exposure: 19% of assets

Rating and Risk

Time Period	Load-Adj Return %	Morningstar Rtn vs Cat	Morningstar Risk vs Cat	Morningstar Risk-Adj Rating
1 Yr	14.70			
3 Yr	9.24	+Avg	Avg	★★★★
5 Yr	—	—	—	—
10 Yr	—	—	—	—
Incept	9.32			

Other Measures	Standard Index S&P 500	Best Fit Index DJ 60%
Alpha	5.8	-5.3
Beta	0.93	1.59
R-Squared	82	87
Standard Deviation	16.77	
Mean	9.24	
Sharpe Ratio	0.47	

Portfolio Analysis 09-30-04

Share change since 06-04 Total Stocks:45	Sector	PE	YTD Ret%	% Assets
⊕ Home Depot	Consumer	19.0	21.47	4.50
⊖ Providian Financial	Financial	14.3	41.50	3.77
Washington Mutual	Financial	13.9	10.05	3.62
⊖ Tyco International	Ind Mtrls	25.1	35.41	3.10
Capital One Financial	Financial	12.5	37.61	2.99
⊕ Iac / Interactivecorp	Consumer	43.1	-18.60	2.89
Telephone and Data Syste	Telecom	39.5	24.11	2.86
Kt&G	Goods	—	—	2.65
Eastman Kodak	Goods	—	27.90	2.61
⊕ Berkshire Hathaway B	Financial	20.9	4.30	2.45
☼ J P Morgan Chase	Financial	19.4	9.97	2.41
Waste Management	Business	18.9	3.81	2.07
Aon	Financial	10.8	2.17	1.98
Hilton Hotels	Consumer	36.1	33.34	1.90
Unumprovident	Financial	—	16.09	1.90
First Data	Business	18.8	3.72	1.85
⊕ Time Warner	Media	27.5	8.12	1.73
⊕ Comcast	Media	—	-13.77	1.73
⊕ General Motors	Goods	7.2	-21.48	1.72
Limited Brands	Consumer	16.0	37.88	1.71

Current Investment Style

Value Blnd Growth; Large Mid Small

Market Cap	%
Giant	21.3
Large	44.2
Mid	34.6
Small	0.0
Micro	0.0
Avg $mil: 15,250	

Value Measures		Rel Category
Price/Earnings	15.69	1.04
Price/Book	1.65	0.73
Price/Sales	1.00	0.84
Price/Cash Flow	7.61	1.19
Dividend Yield %	1.18	0.58

Growth Measures	%	Rel Category
Long-Term Erngs	13.04	1.25
Book Value	8.42	1.49
Sales	1.72	0.41
Cash Flow	2.52	0.48
Historical Erngs	2.87	0.24

Profitability	%	Rel Category
Return on Equity	11.81	0.74
Return on Assets	7.06	0.90
Net Margin	7.96	0.78

Sector Weightings	% of Stocks	Rel S&P 500	3 Year High	3 Year Low
Info	20.77	0.97		
Software	0.00	0.00	0	0
Hardware	0.00	0.00	2	0
Media	10.70	2.79	16	8
Telecom	10.07	3.20	11	6
Service	57.39	1.24		
Health	1.88	0.15	2	2
Consumer	18.28	2.01	20	13
Business	11.03	2.72	13	11
Financial	26.20	1.26	37	26
Mfg	21.84	0.68		
Goods	11.34	1.22	12	6
Ind Mtrls	8.96	0.71	10	4
Energy	0.00	0.00	2	0
Utilities	1.54	0.52	2	0

Composition

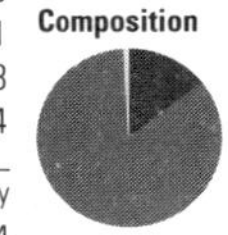

Cash	14.2
Stocks	84.7
Bonds	0.0
Other	1.1
Foreign (% of Stock)	11.4

Morningstar's Take by Todd Trubey 12-01-04

Masters' Select Value Fund remains an interesting proposition for value investors.

The idea behind this unusual fund is that you can outperform the pack by combining into one portfolio the top picks of some of the best concentrated-value managers. In this case, Masters' Select Value combines eight to 15 favorite picks from four topnotch managers, including former Morningstar Manager of the Year winners Bill Miller of Legg Mason and Bill Nygren of Harris Associates, the advisor to the Oakmark Funds.

One thing to consider, however, is whether a fund such as this one is likely to outperform its subadvisors' own funds. So far in 2004, at least, Masters' Select Value has. For the year to date ending Nov. 30, 2004, the fund has gained more than 11%, better than any of the individual funds run by its managers. One of the reasons for this is that the fund has been particularly light on struggling technology stocks, which have dragged down the returns of Legg Mason Value Trust, for instance. Bigger stakes in stocks such as Korean tobacco firm KT&G, which Mutual Series' David Winters has made a top-10 position here, have also helped.

We also think this fund has some of the necessary components to outperform over the long haul. First, its recent asset base of $260 million is relatively small, giving its managers more flexibility to trade nimbly and take meaningful positions in smaller names. Second, its advisor has committed to closing the fund at $1 billion, a conservative level for a fund that invests across the market-cap spectrum. Finally, declining expenses should help it as well.

This fund might be due for a breather, given how successful it has been since its 2001 inception, but we think it's a long-term winner.

Address:	2020 E. Financial Way Glendora CA 91741 800-960-0188
Web Address:	www.mastersselect.com
Inception:	06-30-00 *
Advisor:	Litman Gregory Fund Advisors LLC
Subadvisor:	Multiple
NTF Plans:	N/A

Minimum Purchase:	$5000	Add: $250	IRA: $1000
Min Auto Inv Plan:	$2500	Add: $100	
Sales Fees:	No-load, 2.00%R		
Management Fee:	1.10%		
Actual Fees:	Mgt:1.08%	Dist:	
Expense Projections:	3Yr:$540	5Yr: —	10Yr: —
Income Distrib:	Annually		

Matrix Advisors Value

Ticker	Load	NAV	Yield	Total Assets	Mstar Category
MAVFX	None	$54.41	0.8%	$294 mil	Large Blend

Governance and Management

Fiduciary Grade: B

Portfolio Manager(s)

David Katz has led the management team here since Matrix inherited the fund from Management Asset Corporation in July 1996. Katz is backed by two research analysts as well as one of the firm's other partners, Steve Roukis. Four partners sit on the firm's investment committee.

Strategy

This fund's flexible mandate allows it to buy both large- and small-capitalization names. Manager David Katz looks for stocks that sell at a discount to their intrinsic value of one third or more, but he's willing to delve deeply into pricey sectors such as technology. He sets sell targets and sticks to them, but he often repurchases favorites if they temporarily slip.

Historical Profile

Return High
Risk High
Rating ★★★★ Above Avg

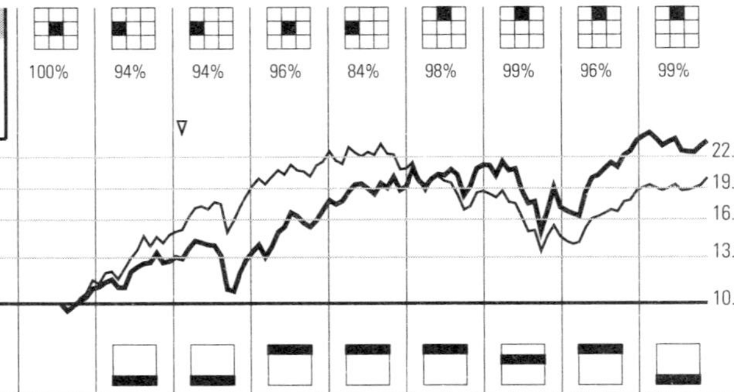

Investment Style
Equity
Stock %

▼ Manager Change
▽ Partial Manager Change

Growth of $10,000
▬ Investment Values of Fund
— Investment Values of S&P 500

Performance Quartile (within Category)

History

1993	1994	1995	1996	1997	1998	1999	2000	2001	2002	2003	12-04	History
—	—	—	26.33	30.86	30.94	40.77	43.11	47.23	37.22	53.59	54.41	NAV
—	—	—	9.93*	17.85	2.90	32.85	7.96	12.35	-20.74	44.59	3.90	Total Return %
—	—	—	—	-15.50	-25.67	11.81	17.06	24.23	1.35	15.92	-6.97	+/-S&P 500
—	—	—	—	-15.00	-24.12	11.94	15.75	24.80	0.91	14.70	-7.50	+/-Russ 1000
—	—	—	0.00	0.65	0.30	0.00	0.37	0.35	0.18	0.57	0.79	Income Return %
—	—	—	—	17.20	2.60	32.85	7.59	12.00	-20.92	44.02	3.12	Capital Return %
—	—	—	—	91	98	10	11	1	34	2	96	Total Rtn % Rank Cat
—	—	—	0.33	0.17	0.09	0.00	0.15	0.15	0.08	0.21	0.42	Income $
—	—	—	0.00	0.00	0.70	0.32	0.78	1.03	0.14	0.00	0.81	Capital Gains $
—	—	—	—	1.42	1.23	1.25	0.99	0.99	0.99	0.99	0.99	Expense Ratio %
—	—	—	—	0.44	0.45	0.10	0.31	0.60	0.29	0.54	0.51	Income Ratio %
—	—	—	—	129	68	33	40	55	45	30	17	Turnover Rate %
—	—	—	8	9	9	13	30	51	67	225	294	Net Assets $mil

Performance 12-31-04

	1st Qtr	2nd Qtr	3rd Qtr	4th Qtr	Total
2000	4.93	1.66	0.34	0.86	7.96
2001	-0.30	6.51	-10.55	18.27	12.35
2002	1.91	-14.52	-20.30	14.16	-20.74
2003	-4.67	25.14	4.64	15.84	44.59
2004	1.05	-0.24	-7.07	10.91	3.90

Trailing	Total Return%	+/- S&P 500	+/- Russ 1000	%Rank Cat	Growth of $10,000
3 Mo	10.91	1.68	1.11	15	11,091
6 Mo	3.07	-4.12	-4.74	94	10,307
1 Yr	3.90	-6.97	-7.50	96	10,390
3 Yr Avg	5.99	2.41	1.72	11	11,907
5 Yr Avg	7.63	9.93	9.39	2	14,443
10 Yr Avg	—	—	—	—	—
15 Yr Avg	—	—	—	—	—

Tax Analysis	Tax-Adj Rtn%	%Rank Cat	Tax-Cost Rat	%Rank Cat
3 Yr (estimated)	5.60	10	0.37	31
5 Yr (estimated)	7.17	1	0.43	23
10 Yr (estimated)	—	—	—	—

Potential Capital Gain Exposure: 12% of assets

Rating and Risk

Time Period	Load-Adj Return %	Morningstar Rtn vs Cat	Morningstar Risk vs Cat	Morningstar Risk-Adj Rating
1 Yr	3.90			
3 Yr	5.99	High	High	★★★
5 Yr	7.63	High	High	★★★★★
10 Yr	—	—	—	—
Incept	11.66			

Other Measures	Standard Index S&P 500	Best Fit Index Russ 1000
Alpha	2.3	1.3
Beta	1.41	1.43
R-Squared	91	92

Standard Deviation	23.92
Mean	5.99
Sharpe Ratio	0.19

Morningstar's Take by Gareth Lyons 12-21-04

Matrix Advisors Value remains a decent option despite its recent stumble.

After a category-topping 2003, this fund has struck out this year: Its gain of 1.1% for the year to date through Dec. 20 ranks next to last in the large-blend category. The slump owes primarily to the portfolio's overweight in technology stocks, which, after zooming in 2003, have taken a beating in recent months because of fears of shrinking growth prospects. The fund's exposure to drug stocks has hurt badly, too, amid regulatory concerns.

Despite the setback, manager David Katz is sticking to buying companies that trade at a steep discount to his estimate of their intrinsic value. He has added to his favorite, albeit troubled, picks in the technology and financial sectors. Citing intact fundamentals, he has scooped up more shares of Novellus Systems and Symbol Technologies, bringing the fund's tech weighting up to 23% of assets--nearly twice the category average.

Katz's hard-charging moves won't suit everyone, especially those in search of benchmarklike performance. That the portfolio is concentrated in approximately 40 names courts stock-specific risks, too. However, Katz has earned our confidence by paying strict attention to company fundamentals as well as valuations. His willingness to weather short-term volatility in his picks will make for bumpy going, but Katz's patient approach usually pays off. As a complement to a more diversified holding within an overall investment portfolio, we think this fund has strong appeal.

The fund also scores well on the fiduciary front. Katz's considerable personal stake in the fund shows that he's aligned with shareholders. The fund's board is also attuned to its constituents' interests. In September 2003, it wisely voted to suspend the fund's slated inclusion to the scandal-tainted Strong lineup--arguably the most prescient decision to benefit this fund.

Portfolio Analysis 10-31-04

Share change since 09-04 Total Stocks:37	Sector	PE	YTD Ret%	% Assets
MedImmune	Health	—	6.82	4.76
Symbol Technologies	Hardware	54.7	2.58	4.19
Morgan Stanley	Financial	14.2	-2.25	3.92
Microsoft	Software	36.1	8.95	3.87
Guidant	Health	35.0	20.55	3.80
American Power Conversio	Ind Mtrls	22.1	-10.99	3.74
⊕ American International G	Financial	16.2	-0.53	3.62
Novellus Systems	Hardware	31.6	-29.98	3.62
Walt Disney	Media	24.3	20.21	3.49
Gen Elec	Ind Mtrls	22.8	20.68	3.48
⊕ Pfizer	Health	22.0	-22.31	3.46
Citigroup	Financial	15.3	2.72	3.43
Wyeth	Health	17.0	2.73	3.40
Merrill Lynch & Company	Financial	12.6	3.12	3.39
CVS	Consumer	21.1	25.61	3.36
Bank of America	Financial	12.3	21.50	3.34
Nokia ADR	Hardware	18.1	-6.14	3.27
Gap	Consumer	17.6	-8.63	3.25
Baxter International	Health	32.9	15.22	3.23
Bk Of New York	Financial	18.5	3.52	3.08

Current Investment Style

Value Blnd Growth / Large Mid Small

Market Cap	%
Giant	48.9
Large	22.8
Mid	26.3
Small	2.0
Micro	0.0
Avg $mil: 28,806	

Value Measures		Rel Category
Price/Earnings	18.07	1.07
Price/Book	2.30	0.88
Price/Sales	1.80	1.25
Price/Cash Flow	7.36	0.96
Dividend Yield %	1.33	0.90

Growth Measures	%	Rel Category
Long-Term Erngs	12.17	1.05
Book Value	10.36	1.33
Sales	3.04	0.53
Cash Flow	1.18	0.12
Historical Erngs	7.65	0.65

Profitability	%	Rel Category
Return on Equity	13.04	0.75
Return on Assets	8.92	1.03
Net Margin	10.63	0.93

Sector Weightings	% of Stocks	Rel S&P 500	3 Year High	3 Year Low
Info	29.13	1.36		
Software	3.90	0.91	4	0
Hardware	19.12	1.87	24	17
Media	6.11	1.59	6	2
Telecom	0.00	0.00	5	0
Service	59.02	1.27		
Health	20.50	1.64	24	15
Consumer	9.94	1.09	14	8
Business	1.48	0.37	11	1
Financial	27.10	1.31	30	23
Mfg	11.85	0.37		
Goods	2.36	0.25	4	0
Ind Mtrls	7.28	0.57	9	4
Energy	2.21	0.31	4	0
Utilities	0.00	0.00	0	0

Composition

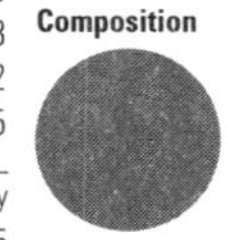

Cash	0.9
Stocks	99.1
Bonds	0.0
Other	0.0
Foreign (% of Stock)	3.3

Address:	747 Third Avenue New York NY 10017 800-366-6223
Web Address:	
Inception:	07-01-96*
Advisor:	Matrix Asset Advisors, Inc.
Subadvisor:	None
NTF Plans:	Fidelity Retail-NTF, Schwab OneSource

Minimum Purchase:	$1000	Add: $100	IRA: $500
Min Auto Inv Plan:	$500	Add: $100	
Sales Fees:	No-load, 1.00%R		
Management Fee:	1.00%		
Actual Fees:	Mgt:0.66%	Dist:	
Expense Projections:	3Yr:$350	5Yr:$606	10Yr:$1340
Income Distrib:	Annually		

Matthews Pacific Tiger

Analyst Pick	Ticker	Load	NAV	Yield	Total Assets	Mstar Category
✔	MAPTX	None	$15.90	0.6%	$855 mil	Pacific/Asia ex-Japan Stk

Governance and Management

Fiduciary Grade: B

Portfolio Manager(s)

Paul Matthews has been running Asian money more than 20 years, and Mark Headley has one of the broadest resumes of any Asia hand. Because the firm boasts seven Asia offerings, they have a variety of Asia specialists to consult.

Strategy

Paul Matthews and Mark Headley focus on firms with robust long-term earnings prospects and moderate valuations. They pay attention to all of emerging Asia, consider companies of all sizes, and are not afraid to run a focused portfolio. To combat market-timing, the fund levies a 2% redemption fee on shares held 90 days or less, and it uses fair-value pricing whenever necessary.

Historical Profile

Return Above Avg
Risk Above Avg
Rating ★★★★ Above Avg

Investment Style: Equity Stock %: 95% 92% 98% 98% 98% 100% 100% 100% 100%

▼ Manager Change ▽ Partial Manager Change

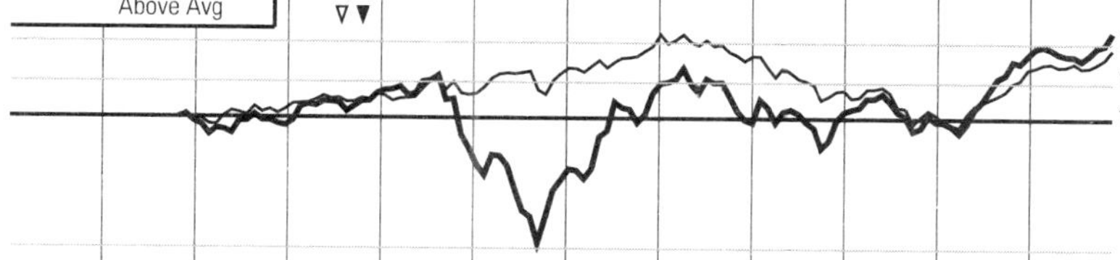

Performance Quartile (within Category)

1993	1994	1995	1996	1997	1998	1999	2000	2001	2002	2003	12-04	History
—	9.47	9.76	12.12	7.15	6.84	12.32	8.20	8.81	8.24	13.15	15.90	NAV
—	-5.08*	3.06	24.18	-40.89	-2.86	83.01	-24.00	7.91	-6.47	60.15	23.34	Total Return %
—	—	-8.15	18.13	-42.67	-22.79	55.98	-9.81	29.33	9.47	21.56	3.09	+/-MSCI EAFE
—	—	-3.78	14.85	4.72	4.31	23.59	13.88	12.05	4.58	19.38	9.11	+/-MSCIAC FExJ
—	0.00	0.00	0.00	0.05	0.20	2.77	3.35	0.13	0.00	0.54	0.73	Income Return %
—	—	3.06	24.18	-40.94	-3.06	80.24	-27.35	7.78	-6.47	59.61	22.61	Capital Return %
—	—	48	15	84	12	24	53	15	22	26	3	Total Rtn % Rank Cat
—	0.02	0.00	0.00	0.01	0.01	0.19	0.41	0.01	0.00	0.04	0.10	Income $
—	0.00	0.00	0.00	0.02	0.06	0.00	0.84	0.03	0.00	0.00	0.21	Capital Gains $
—	—	2.17	1.90	1.90	1.90	1.90	1.81	1.90	1.79	1.75	1.48	Expense Ratio %
—	—	0.36	0.32	0.27	0.30	3.35	1.56	0.67	-0.17	1.04	0.95	Income Ratio %
—	—	93	125	71	73	99	52	64	57	28	15	Turnover Rate %
—	1	3	33	37	52	119	71	87	107	456	855	Net Assets $mil

Performance 12-31-04

	1st Qtr	2nd Qtr	3rd Qtr	4th Qtr	Total
2000	11.44	-7.06	-11.51	-17.08	-24.00
2001	0.12	6.46	-21.62	29.17	7.91
2002	10.10	-2.06	-18.84	6.87	-6.47
2003	-7.65	25.10	20.80	14.75	60.15
2004	4.64	-4.94	6.65	16.27	23.34

Trailing	Total Return%	+/- MSCI EAFE	+/- MSCIAC FExJ	%Rank Cat	Growth of $10,000
3 Mo	16.27	0.95	4.55	12	11,627
6 Mo	24.00	9.00	6.66	7	12,400
1 Yr	23.34	3.09	9.11	3	12,334
3 Yr Avg	22.70	10.81	10.03	8	18,473
5 Yr Avg	8.66	9.79	11.82	7	15,148
10 Yr Avg	7.38	1.76	9.58	10	20,381
15 Yr Avg	—	—	—	—	—

Tax Analysis	Tax-Adj Rtn%	%Rank Cat	Tax-Cost Rat	%Rank Cat
3 Yr (estimated)	22.47	6	0.19	41
5 Yr (estimated)	7.79	7	0.80	73
10 Yr (estimated)	6.83	10	0.51	68

Potential Capital Gain Exposure: 24% of assets

Rating and Risk

Time Period	Load-Adj Return %	Morningstar Rtn vs Cat	Morningstar Risk vs Cat	Morningstar Risk-Adj Rating
1 Yr	23.34			
3 Yr	22.70	+Avg	+Avg	★★★★
5 Yr	8.66	+Avg	+Avg	★★★★
10 Yr	7.38	+Avg	+Avg	★★★★
Incept	6.61			

Other Measures	Standard Index S&P 500	Best Fit Index MSCIAC FExJ
Alpha	10.9	9.8
Beta	0.94	0.94
R-Squared	67	86

Standard Deviation	21.79
Mean	22.70
Sharpe Ratio	0.99

Morningstar's Take by William Samuel Rocco 10-04-04

Emerging Asia fans who ignore Matthews Pacific Tiger are making a mistake.

Topnotch management gives this fund a superior foundation. Mark Headley has been involved with Asian investments for more than 15 years, including eight years as a manager here. Paul Matthews is even more experienced. He has been running Asia money for 22 years and managing this fund for 10 years. Headley and Matthews are assisted by five veteran investment professionals, and they are looking to add a well-tested India analyst in the coming months. In short, the fund boasts one of the deepest and most seasoned teams in the its category.

The fund also has relatively low costs. Fees have declined in recent years as assets have grown, and for the nine months ending May 31, it had an annualized expense ratio of 1.49%--nearly 40 basis points lower than that of the average retail, no-load fund in its group. Headley and Matthews tend to move at a measured pace, and that limits trading costs, which are high in emerging markets and aren't included in expense ratios.

The two managers provide one of the more distinctive portfolios in the group. They make full use of their country range and readily consider smaller-cap stocks as they pursue growth opportunities. Indeed, the fund now has significantly more exposure to India and Thailand than its peers, and its average market cap is about half the group norm.

Finally, the fund, which has prospered as Asia's emerging markets have rebounded in recent months due to good picks in Korea and Hong Kong, has consistently thrived in rallies. And while it often lags in sell-offs, it doesn't always do so and tends to do well in mixed conditions. Overall, it has earned exceptional long-term returns without incurring a lot more volatility than most funds in its wild group.

For all these reasons, this fund is worth a long look from emerging Asia fans.

Address:	c/o First Data Investor Service Group IN King Of Prussia PA 19406 800-789-2742
Web Address:	www.matthewsfunds.com
Inception:	09-13-94 *
Advisor:	Matthews International Capital Mgt LLC
Subadvisor:	None
NTF Plans:	Fidelity Retail-NTF, Schwab OneSource

Minimum Purchase:	$2500	Add: $250	IRA: $500
Min Auto Inv Plan:	$2500	Add: $100	
Sales Fees:	No-load, 2.00%R		
Management Fee:	1.00% mx./0.90% mn., 0.15%A		
Actual Fees:	Mgt:1.00%	Dist:	
Expense Projections:	3Yr:$584	5Yr:$1010	10Yr:$2195
Income Distrib:	Annually		

Portfolio Analysis 08-31-04

Share change since 05-04 Total Stocks:51	Sector	Country	% Assets
⊕ Dah Sing Financial Grp	Financial	Hong Kong	4.50
Hana Bank	Financial	Korea	3.95
⊖ Advcd Info Serv	Telecom	Thailand	3.86
Giordano International L	Goods	Hong Kong	3.84
Bangkok Bk	Financial	Thailand	3.74
AMOREPACIFIC	Goods	Korea	3.71
⊕ Hon Hai Precision Indust	Business	Taiwan	3.65
⊖ DBS Grp Hldgs Ltd	Financial	Singapore	3.56
Swire Pacific	Ind Mtrls	Hong Kong	3.44
Fraser & Neave Ltd	Ind Mtrls	Singapore	3.21
Venture Manufacturing Lt	Hardware	Singapore	3.20
Internet Auction	Consumer	Korea	3.01
⊕ Lenovo Grp	Hardware	Hong Kong	2.72
⊕ Samsung Electronics	Goods	Korea	2.25
⊕ TravelSky Technology Ltd	Business	Hong Kong	2.22
Hite Brewery	Goods	Korea	2.02
Nongshim	Ind Mtrls	Korea	2.01
PICC Property & Casualty	Financial	Hong Kong	1.96
⊕ Shangri-La Asia Ltd	Consumer	Hong Kong	1.95
COSCO Pacific Ltd	Business	Hong Kong	1.92

Current Investment Style

Market Cap	%
Giant	24.4
Large	25.1
Mid	41.5
Small	8.9
Micro	0.0
Avg $mil: 2,611	

Value Measures		Rel Category
Price/Earnings	11.96	1.02
Price/Book	1.82	1.08
Price/Sales	1.48	1.16
Price/Cash Flow	5.57	0.98
Dividend Yield %	2.25	0.72

Growth Measures	%	Rel Category
Long-Term Erngs	14.00	0.70
Book Value	6.83	1.07
Sales	6.93	0.51
Cash Flow	16.29	1.76
Historical Erngs	11.10	0.92

Composition

Cash	0.0	Bonds	0.0
Stocks	100.0	Other	0.0
Foreign (% of Stock)			100.0

Sector Weightings	% of Stocks	Rel MSCI EAFE	3 Year High	3 Year Low
Info	19.00	1.14		
Software	1.82	1.69	2	0
Hardware	6.78	1.86	18	5
Media	2.45	1.07	9	2
Telecom	7.95	0.83	18	7
Service	49.17	1.10		
Health	5.21	0.72	6	0
Consumer	9.40	1.87	12	6
Business	9.09	1.67	9	5
Financial	25.47	0.94	32	18
Mfg	31.82	0.82		
Goods	20.14	1.47	20	14
Ind Mtrls	8.67	0.70	11	4
Energy	0.00	0.00	0	0
Utilities	3.01	0.56	5	3

Regional Exposure	% Stock		
UK/W. Europe	0	N. America	0
Japan	0	Latn America	0
Asia X Japan	100	Other	0

Country Exposure	% Stock		
Hong Kong	33	Thailand	9
South Korea	26	India	7
Singapore	13		

Merger Fund

Ticker	Load	NAV	Yield	Total Assets	Mstar Category
MERFX	Closed	$15.42	0.0%	$1,651 mil	Conservative Allocation

Governance and Management

Fiduciary Grade: A

Portfolio Manager(s)

No retail mutual fund manager has been doing merger arbitrage exclusively longer than comanagers Fred Green and Bonnie Smith. They have been at the fund's helm since its inception in 1989. Their firm, Westchester Capital Management, has been doing merger arbitrage for private and institutional accounts since 1980.

Strategy

This fund uses a merger-arbitrage strategy, buying the stock of acquisition targets and occasionally shorting the acquirer's stock. If the deal closes, the fund makes money. The fund can also invest in corporate reorganizations, and in certain circumstances it will use options and invest in corporate bonds. The offering's fixed-income positions are usually small, though. Before investing, management researches the strategic rationale behind the merger. It shoots for a 10% to 15% gain on its investments.

Historical Profile

Return Average
Risk Average
Rating ★★★ Neutral

Investment Style
Equity
Stock %: 94% 93% 93% 47% 52% 64% 75%

▼ Manager Change
▽ Partial Manager Change

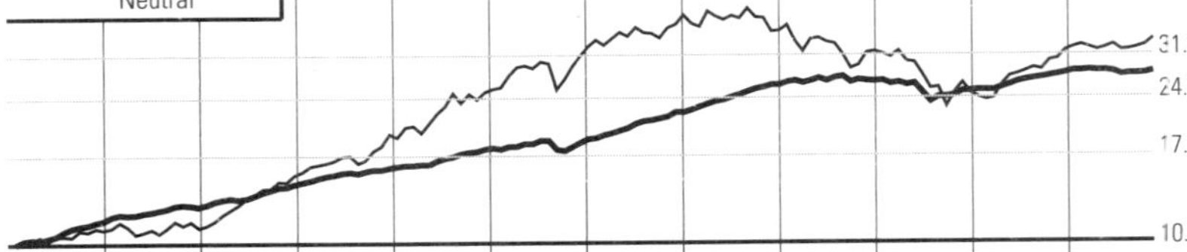

Performance Quartile (within Category)

1993	1994	1995	1996	1997	1998	1999	2000	2001	2002	2003	12-04	History
12.96	13.17	14.13	14.11	14.15	13.58	14.72	15.52	14.77	13.73	15.21	15.42	NAV
17.69	7.13	14.15	9.95	11.65	5.35	17.39	17.58	2.01	-5.67	11.04	2.71	Total Return %
7.63	5.82	-23.38	-12.99	-21.70	-23.22	-3.65	26.68	13.89	16.42	-17.63	-8.16	+/-S&P 500
6.93	8.36	-4.01	1.06	-2.45	-6.38	9.53	10.79	-1.21	-1.65	-6.62	-6.30	+/-DJ 40%
0.00	0.00	0.58	1.32	0.21	1.56	0.54	0.93	1.35	1.37	0.26	0.01	Income Return %
17.69	7.13	13.57	8.63	11.44	3.79	16.85	16.65	0.66	-7.04	10.78	2.70	Capital Return %
6	1	92	61	74	86	6	7	27	74	63	84	Total Rtn % Rank Cat
0.00	0.00	0.08	0.19	0.03	0.22	0.07	0.14	0.21	0.20	0.04	0.00	Income $
1.10	0.71	0.83	1.24	1.58	1.10	1.15	1.65	0.85	0.00	0.00	0.20	Capital Gains $
2.19	1.58	1.41	1.36	1.36	1.33	1.38	1.34	1.34	1.38	1.37	1.37	Expense Ratio %
-0.57	-0.03	0.57	1.36	0.13	1.36	0.54	1.57	2.23	1.36	0.34	-0.68	Income Ratio %
186	390	290	277	271	355	387	419	384	258	309	257	Turnover Rate %
27	171	246	474	436	346	635	1,042	980	823	1,345	1,651	Net Assets $mil

Performance 12-31-04

	1st Qtr	2nd Qtr	3rd Qtr	4th Qtr	Total
2000	5.03	4.20	4.90	2.41	17.58
2001	1.10	1.21	-0.82	0.52	2.01
2002	-0.74	-5.87	-2.46	3.51	-5.67
2003	0.29	5.08	2.56	2.73	11.04
2004	1.64	-0.97	-1.37	3.46	2.71

Trailing	Total Return%	+/- S&P 500	+/- DJ 40%	%Rank Cat	Growth of $10,000
3 Mo	3.46	-5.77	-1.94	66	10,346
6 Mo	2.04	-5.15	-4.45	91	10,204
1 Yr	2.71	-8.16	-6.30	84	10,271
3 Yr Avg	2.47	-1.11	-4.71	87	10,759
5 Yr Avg	5.23	7.53	-1.07	19	12,903
10 Yr Avg	8.38	-3.69	-0.77	42	22,361
15 Yr Avg	8.73	-2.20	-0.07	34	35,095

Tax Analysis	Tax-Adj Rtn%	%Rank Cat	Tax-Cost Rat	%Rank Cat
3 Yr (estimated)	2.09	77	0.37	10
5 Yr (estimated)	3.57	19	1.58	69
10 Yr (estimated)	6.03	44	2.17	56

Potential Capital Gain Exposure: -2% of assets

Rating and Risk

Time Period	Load-Adj Return %	Morningstar Rtn vs Cat	Morningstar Risk vs Cat	Morningstar Risk-Adj Rating
1 Yr	2.71			
3 Yr	2.47	-Avg	Avg	★★
5 Yr	5.23	+Avg	Avg	★★★★
10 Yr	8.38	Avg	-Avg	★★★
Incept	8.65			

Other Measures	Standard Index S&P 500	Best Fit Index Merrill Lynch Convert
Alpha	0.4	-3.3
Beta	0.25	0.62
R-Squared	42	66

Standard Deviation	5.91
Mean	2.47
Sharpe Ratio	0.18

Portfolio Analysis 09-30-04

Total Stocks:46 Share change since 06-30-04	Sectors	P/E Ratio	YTD Return %	% Net Assets
⊖ AT&T Wireless Services	Telecom	—	—	5.33
Dreyers G Ice Crea	Goods	—	—	4.93
⊕ WellPoint Health Networks	Health	—	—	4.74
⊕ Chelsea Property Group	Financial	—	—	4.07
⊕ Mandalay Resort Group	Consumer	22.7	0.11	3.89
⊕ InVision Technologies	Business	—	—	3.83
⊕ ILEX Oncology	Health	—	—	3.73
⊕ Price Communications	Telecom	—	-4.52	3.62
⊕ Cox Communications A	Media	—	—	3.21

Total Fixed-Income:5	Date of Maturity	Amount $000	Value $000	% Net Assets
Roadway 8.25%	12-01-08	27,195	31,104	1.70
Adelphia Comms 10.25%	06-15-11	15,000	14,175	0.77
Adelphia Comms 9.375%	11-15-09	13,342	12,341	0.67
Digitalnet 9%	07-15-10	9,490	11,056	0.60
Adelphia Comms 9.25%		11,695	10,409	0.57
Adelphia Comms Cv 6%	02-15-06	27,125	7,595	0.41
Adelphia Comms Cv 3.25%	05-01-21	21,458	5,794	0.32
Tnp Enterprises Cv		50	5,671	0.31

Equity Style
Style: Growth
Size: Mid-Cap

Value Measures		Rel Category
Price/Earnings	26.37	1.60
Price/Book	1.73	0.73
Price/Sales	1.37	1.05
Price/Cash Flow	4.67	0.67
Dividend Yield %	0.62	0.36

Growth Measures	%	Rel Category
Long-Term Erngs	15.35	1.37
Book Value	11.23	2.05
Sales	7.33	1.60
Cash Flow	8.99	1.34
Historical Erngs	-15.24	NMF

Market Cap %			
Giant	0.0	Small	42.9
Large	23.0	Micro	1.4
Mid	32.6	Avg $mil:	3,017

Fixed-Income Style
Duration: —
Quality: —

Avg Eff Duration[1]	—
Avg Eff Maturity	—
Avg Credit Quality	—
Avg Wtd Coupon	—

[1] figure provided by fund

Sector Weightings	% of Stocks	Rel S&P 500	3 Year High	3 Year Low
Info	34.02	1.58		
Software	3.73	0.87	12	0
Hardware	5.72	0.56	7	0
Media	9.72	2.53	10	0
Telecom	14.85	4.71	32	4
Service	48.35	1.04		
Health	19.29	1.54	25	4
Consumer	8.39	0.92	17	3
Business	7.30	1.80	13	0
Financial	13.37	0.64	25	6
Mfg	17.63	0.55		
Goods	7.68	0.82	15	2
Ind Mtrls	6.77	0.53	23	3
Energy	0.51	0.07	12	0
Utilities	2.67	0.90	10	0

Composition

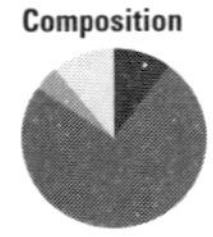

Cash	10.1
Stocks	74.6
Bonds	4.3
Other	11.0
Foreign (% of Stock)	5.5

Morningstar's Take by Dan Culloton 12-30-04

Merger Fund had an off year but still has value.

This risk arbitrage fund shoots for annual gains of 10% and has achieved that in most of the calendar years since its 1989 inception. Last year it didn't, because it needs mergers that avoid the regulatory, legal, or financial pitfalls that can delay or doom deals. Though deal volume was up in 2004, there were a number of controversial transactions that caused the fund to fall in two of four quarters.

Despite the difficulty, managers Fred Green and Bonnie Smith stuck to their strategy and eked out a gain for the year. No merger is a cinch, so there is usually a spread between the share prices of the parties involved that reflects the market's view of deal's chances of closing. This fund exploits that difference by buying the shares of the acquisition target and shorting the stock of its suitor. If the deals get done, the fund makes money.

Of course, it's not always that simple. Those spreads wax and wane with the market's outlook for the deal and it takes a seasoned hand to know which deals offer the best risk/reward tradeoff. Last year put Green and Smith's decades of expertise to the test. A lot of deals, such as the combination of HMOs Anthem and Wellpoint, General Electric's takeover of bomb detector firm Invision Technologies, and Lockheed Martin's bid for Titan, ran into trouble. The fund stuck with those mergers, though, after studying their terms and motivations and most worked.

Green and Smith's experience and a flurry of recent deals, such as the mergers of Sprint and Nextel, and Johnson & Johnson's and Guidant, bode well for the fund's chances of achieving its objectives of steady absolute returns.

Be careful, though: The offering's expense ratio is high for the moderate-allocation category, even though it lowered its management fee late last year. The portfolio also realizes a lot of short-term capital gains as it jumps in and out of deals. It's a good diversifier, but only for tax-sheltered portfolios.

Address:	Merger Fund Valhalla, NY 10595 800-343-8959
Web Address:	
Inception:	01-31-89
Advisor:	Westchester Capital Management Inc
Subadvisor:	None
NTF Plans:	Fidelity Retail-NTF, Schwab OneSource

Minimum Purchase:	Closed	Add: —	IRA: —
Min Auto Inv Plan:	Closed	Add: —	
Sales Fees:	0.20%B		
Management Fee:	1.00%		
Actual Fees:	Mgt:1.00%	Dist:0.20%	
Expense Projections:	3Yr:$437	5Yr:$755	10Yr:$1657
Income Distrib:	Annually		

Meridian Growth

Ticker	Load	NAV	Yield	Total Assets	Mstar Category
MERDX	None	$37.24	0.0%	$1,252 mil	Mid-Cap Growth

Governance and Management

Fiduciary Grade: B

Portfolio Manager(s)

Rick Aster has been at the helm since the fund's 1984 inception. He is the founder of the fund's advisor, Aster Investment Management Company. Over the past two years, Aster has brought aboard two analysts to assist in stock-picking here and at sibling Meridian Value.

Strategy

This fund takes a kinder, gentler approach to growth investing. Manager Rick Aster looks for small- and mid-cap names growing their earnings at least 15% a year. He won't pay up for that growth, however, which gives the fund price multiples below the mid-growth averages. Aster employs a buy-and-hold style, and won't necessarily dump picks that have drifted into large-cap territory. He keeps a compact portfolio of fewer than 50 holdings and often concentrates his picks in a handful of sectors.

Historical Profile

Return High
Risk Below Avg
Rating ★★★★★ Highest

Investment Style: Equity, Stock %

77%	100%	88%	100%	100%	100%	95%	98%	98%

▼ Manager Change
∇ Partial Manager Change

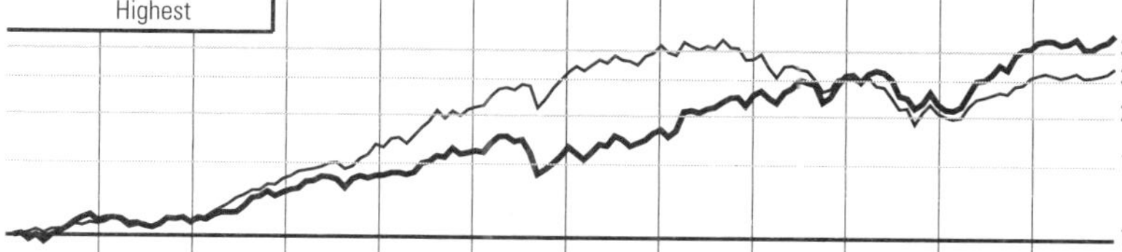

Growth of $10,000
— Investment Values of Fund
— Investment Values of S&P 500

Performance Quartile (within Category)

1993	1994	1995	1996	1997	1998	1999	2000	2001	2002	2003	12-04	History
25.87	25.12	29.90	30.08	30.73	24.29	25.40	28.06	28.79	22.98	33.03	37.24	NAV
13.05	0.55	22.43	11.19	19.23	3.09	13.33	28.20	14.76	-17.82	47.90	14.47	Total Return %
2.99	-0.76	-15.10	-11.75	-14.12	-25.48	-7.71	37.30	26.64	4.27	19.23	3.60	+/-S&P 500
1.86	2.71	-11.55	-6.29	-3.31	-14.77	-37.96	39.95	34.91	9.59	5.19	-1.01	+/-Russ MG
1.30	0.69	1.23	1.26	1.11	0.46	0.62	9.85	0.00	0.20	1.00	0.00	Income Return %
11.75	-0.14	21.20	9.93	18.12	2.63	12.71	18.35	14.76	-18.02	46.90	14.47	Capital Return %
51	29	92	76	49	86	89	3	1	12	8	39	Total Rtn % Rank Cat
0.30	0.17	0.31	0.36	0.32	0.14	0.15	2.44	0.00	0.06	0.23	0.00	Income $
0.15	0.70	0.54	2.76	4.81	6.50	1.78	1.86	2.34	0.61	0.69	0.56	Capital Gains $
1.47	1.22	1.06	0.96	0.96	0.95	1.01	1.09	1.04	1.06	0.95	0.88	Expense Ratio %
-0.01	0.38	1.18	0.99	1.23	0.76	0.49	0.31	-0.26	1.18	-0.47	-0.21	Income Ratio %
61	43	29	34	37	38	1	28	42	26	27	19	Turnover Rate %
160	257	375	378	332	231	138	152	208	317	482	1,252	Net Assets $mil

Performance 12-31-04

	1st Qtr	2nd Qtr	3rd Qtr	4th Qtr	Total
2000	13.62	2.04	8.23	2.17	28.20
2001	-5.49	17.91	-14.72	20.75	14.76
2002	1.60	-3.90	-18.51	3.28	-17.82
2003	-2.00	20.96	7.48	16.09	47.90
2004	5.78	1.26	-3.76	11.04	14.47

Trailing	Total Return%	+/- S&P 500	+/- Russ MG	%Rank Cat	Growth of $10,000
3 Mo	11.04	1.81	-2.90	83	11,104
6 Mo	6.87	-0.32	-2.14	60	10,687
1 Yr	14.47	3.60	-1.01	39	11,447
3 Yr Avg	11.63	8.05	5.47	3	13,911
5 Yr Avg	15.40	17.70	18.76	1	20,466
10 Yr Avg	14.52	2.45	3.29	9	38,798
15 Yr Avg	15.21	4.28	4.21	2	83,628

Tax Analysis	Tax-Adj Rtn%	%Rank Cat	Tax-Cost Rat	%Rank Cat
3 Yr (estimated)	11.06	3	0.51	61
5 Yr (estimated)	13.51	1	1.64	70
10 Yr (estimated)	12.06	9	2.15	62

Potential Capital Gain Exposure: 24% of assets

Rating and Risk

Time Period	Load-Adj Return %	Morningstar Rtn vs Cat	Morningstar Risk vs Cat	Morningstar Risk-Adj Rating
1 Yr	14.47			
3 Yr	11.63	High	Avg	★★★★★
5 Yr	15.40	High	-Avg	★★★★★
10 Yr	14.52	+Avg	Low	★★★★★
Incept	14.60			

Other Measures	Standard Index S&P 500	Best Fit Index Russ 2000
Alpha	8.3	1.3
Beta	0.97	0.88
R-Squared	69	91
Standard Deviation	19.70	
Mean	11.63	
Sharpe Ratio	0.53	

Portfolio Analysis 01-31-04

Share change since 12-03 Total Stocks:48	Sector	PE	YTD Ret%	% Assets
⊖ Andrew	Hardware	—	17.60	3.22
⊕ DeVry	Consumer	23.1	-30.92	2.82
⊕ Regis	Consumer	18.1	17.22	2.76
⊕ Laboratory Corp of Ameri	Health	19.1	34.83	2.76
⊕ Davita	Health	19.0	52.04	2.71
⊕ Mercury General	Financial	12.2	32.38	2.71
United Rentals	Consumer	—	-1.87	2.63
Plantronics	Hardware	23.7	27.33	2.62
⊕ Renal Care Group	Health	22.6	31.03	2.56
Tektronix	Hardware	17.0	-3.86	2.54
⊕ Granite Construction	Business	19.8	15.25	2.52
⊕ Republic Services A	Business	21.8	32.45	2.51
⊕ Kemet	Hardware	—	-34.62	2.51
⊕ Synopsys	Software	19.8	-42.26	2.44
Vishay Intertechnology	Hardware	21.3	-34.41	2.43
Symbol Technologies	Hardware	54.7	2.58	2.42
⊕ Silicon Valley Bancshare	Financial	50.6	24.26	2.41
⊕ Applebee's International	Consumer	19.8	1.09	2.37
⊕ Ruby Tuesday	Consumer	14.5	-8.32	2.31
⊕ Cost Plus	Consumer	18.2	-21.63	2.30

Current Investment Style

Value Blnd Growth / Large Mid Small

Market Cap	%
Giant	0.0
Large	0.6
Mid	75.8
Small	23.6
Micro	0.0
Avg $mil: 2,232	

Value Measures		Rel Category
Price/Earnings	24.94	1.14
Price/Book	2.65	0.88
Price/Sales	1.65	0.93
Price/Cash Flow	10.38	1.07
Dividend Yield %	0.27	0.63

Growth Measures	%	Rel Category
Long-Term Erngs	14.94	0.95
Book Value	4.13	0.41
Sales	0.81	0.09
Cash Flow	4.29	0.35
Historical Erngs	3.37	0.21

Profitability	%	Rel Category
Return on Equity	10.39	0.72
Return on Assets	5.75	0.80
Net Margin	3.49	0.36

Sector Weightings	% of Stocks	Rel S&P 500	3 Year High	3 Year Low
Info	31.76	1.48		
Software	8.84	2.06	9	6
Hardware	20.80	2.04	21	14
Media	0.00	0.00	0	0
Telecom	2.12	0.67	2	1
Service	59.31	1.28		
Health	14.27	1.14	17	12
Consumer	25.92	2.85	37	26
Business	8.93	2.20	16	9
Financial	10.19	0.49	10	4
Mfg	8.93	0.28		
Goods	6.81	0.73	7	2
Ind Mtrls	2.12	0.17	6	2
Energy	0.00	0.00	0	0
Utilities	0.00	0.00	0	0

Composition

Cash	2.1
Stocks	97.9
Bonds	0.0
Other	0.0
Foreign (% of Stock)	0.0

Morningstar's Take by Christopher Davis 11-16-04

Although Meridian Growth has gotten even more appealing as a long-term holding, keep your nearer-term expectations in check.

This offering's size has grown considerably in recent years, with its assets rising from around $200 million at the end of 2001 to more than $1.2 billion today. We like to see costs decline as assets rise, and that's fortunately been the case here. The fund's expense ratio now weighs in at 0.88%, down from an already modest 1.04% in 2001, making it one of the most reasonably priced actively managed mid-growth offerings around.

Lower costs give manager Rick Aster an even bigger long-term advantage over the competition. That adds to the allure of the fund's sparkling record--all of the fund's long-term returns rank in the category's top 10% or better. And it's done so without exposing shareholders to much downside volatility. The fund's 17% drop in 2002 marked its first calendar-year loss since 1987.

To be sure, the fund takes some significant risks. The portfolio is relatively compact, with less than 50 holdings. Aster places no limits on sector concentration either, as the fund's large hardware, software, and consumer services stakes makes clear. He moderates the risks of a concentrated portfolio by avoiding more-speculative names and by paying close attention to valuation. Aster has also avoided potholes with deft stock-picking. For instance, winning picks like Mercury General and Autodesk have pushed the fund to a 12% gain for the year to date through Nov. 15, 2004, a top-quartile showing in its category.

That said, the fund's below-average market cap has given it a tailwind in recent years as small caps have ruled the roost. In a market more favorable to large caps, the fund may look weak relative to its peers--witness the fund's sluggish showings in the mid- and late 1990s when large caps dominated. However, we think experienced management, a sound strategy, and modest costs give the fund a long-term edge.

Address:	60 E Sir Francis Drake Blvd Larkspur CA 94939 800-446-6662
Web Address:	
Inception:	08-01-84
Advisor:	Aster Investment Management CO Inc
Subadvisor:	None
NTF Plans:	N/A

Minimum Purchase:	$1000	Add: $50	IRA: $1000
Min Auto Inv Plan:	$1000	Add: $50	
Sales Fees:	No-load		
Management Fee:	1.00% mx./0.75% mn.		
Actual Fees:	Mgt:0.81%	Dist: —	
Expense Projections:	3Yr:$326	5Yr:$565	10Yr:$1253
Income Distrib:	Annually		

Meridian Value

Ticker	Load	NAV	Yield	Total Assets	Mstar Category
MVALX	None	$38.09	0.7%	$2,134 mil	Mid-Cap Blend

Governance and Management

Fiduciary Grade: B

Portfolio Manager(s)

At the end of 2003, Jamie England took over from longtime manager Kevin O'Boyle after being the sole analyst for two years. Like O'Boyle, England manages the fund on a day-to-day basis. Rick Aster is the successful manager of Meridian Growth. Larry Cardisco joined in 2003 as an analyst after three years at Bank of America. In January 2004, Meridian hired Jim O'Connor, a recent MBA graduate and sell-side analyst, as another analyst.

Strategy

Since taking the helm in January 2004, Jamie England has stuck to the strategy he inherited from his predecessor, Kevin O'Boyle. England screens for companies that have had two or three disappointing quarters in a row, thinking that such firms are often punished too harshly. He'll then invest in those firms that are market leaders and boast good returns on invested capital and sound financials. The fund employs a multi-cap approach, though it's tilted toward small- and mid-cap fare. Because of its size, though, the fund's initial purchases in small- and micro-cap names are usually limited to 1% of assets.

Historical Profile

Return Above Avg
Risk Below Avg
Rating ★★★★★ Highest

Investment Style: Equity Stock %

94%	100%	80%	100%	100%	100%	95%	95%	98%

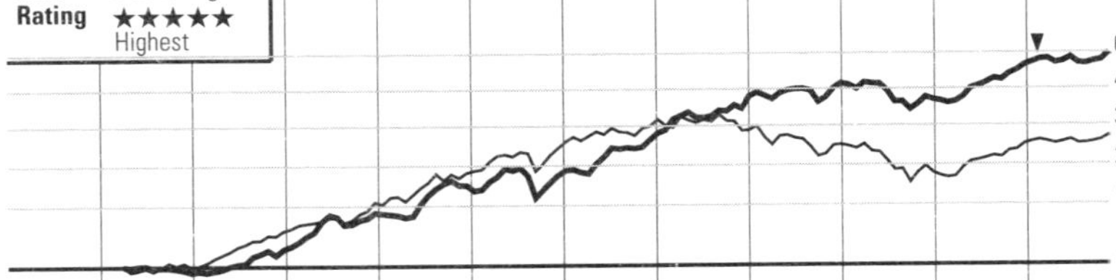

▼ Manager Change
▽ Partial Manager Change

Growth of $10,000
— Investment Values of Fund
— Investment Values of S&P 500

Performance Quartile (within Category)

1993	1994	1995	1996	1997	1998	1999	2000	2001	2002	2003	12-04	History
—	9.62	11.91	14.85	15.86	18.32	22.69	29.11	32.42	28.09	37.84	38.09	NAV
—	-3.80*	23.80	32.29	21.37	18.94	38.28	37.14	11.70	-13.36	34.71	15.10	Total Return %
—	—	-13.73	9.35	-11.98	-9.63	17.24	46.24	23.58	8.73	6.04	4.23	+/-S&P 500
—	—	-7.12	13.11	-10.87	-0.17	23.56	19.65	12.30	1.17	-0.88	-1.37	+/-S&P Mid 400
—	0.00	0.00	4.85	2.23	0.00	3.73	4.84	0.13	0.00	0.00	0.75	Income Return %
—	—	23.80	27.44	19.14	18.94	34.55	32.30	11.57	-13.36	34.71	14.35	Capital Return %
—	—	76	5	74	22	12	3	15	32	46	62	Total Rtn % Rank Cat
—	0.00	0.00	0.58	0.33	0.00	0.68	1.09	0.04	0.00	0.00	0.28	Income $
—	0.00	0.00	0.27	1.90	0.47	1.68	0.68	0.04	0.00	0.00	5.11	Capital Gains $
—	—	2.78	2.55	2.51	2.16	1.63	1.41	1.10	1.12	1.11	1.09	Expense Ratio %
—	—	-0.58	-1.36	-1.96	-1.35	-0.65	0.39	0.60	-0.22	-0.12	0.01	Income Ratio %
—	—	77	125	144	133	124	86	77	54	60	81	Turnover Rate %
—	1	1	5	9	18	35	286	1,135	1,185	1,508	2,134	Net Assets $mil

Performance 12-31-04

	1st Qtr	2nd Qtr	3rd Qtr	4th Qtr	Total
2000	16.09	-1.75	5.92	13.51	37.14
2001	-2.34	8.97	-10.65	17.46	11.70
2002	0.62	-6.99	-14.83	8.71	-13.36
2003	-1.64	14.55	5.21	13.63	34.71
2004	5.60	0.98	-3.52	11.88	15.10

Trailing	Total Return%	+/- S&P 500	+/- S&P Mid 400	%Rank Cat	Growth of $10,000
3 Mo	11.88	2.65	-0.27	42	11,188
6 Mo	7.94	0.75	-1.85	78	10,794
1 Yr	15.10	4.23	-1.37	62	11,510
3 Yr Avg	10.34	6.76	-0.17	38	13,434
5 Yr Avg	15.53	17.83	6.00	4	20,581
10 Yr Avg	21.00	8.93	4.91	1	67,275
15 Yr Avg	—	—	—	—	—

Tax Analysis	Tax-Adj Rtn%	%Rank Cat	Tax-Cost Rat	%Rank Cat
3 Yr (estimated)	9.60	38	0.67	74
5 Yr (estimated)	14.55	4	0.85	38
10 Yr (estimated)	19.34	1	1.37	26

Potential Capital Gain Exposure: 19% of assets

Rating and Risk

Time Period	Load-Adj Return %	Morningstar Rtn vs Cat	Morningstar Risk vs Cat	Morningstar Risk-Adj Rating
1 Yr	15.10			
3 Yr	10.34	Avg	-Avg	★★★★
5 Yr	15.53	High	-Avg	★★★★★
10 Yr	21.00	High	Avg	★★★★★
Incept	18.71			

Other Measures	Standard Index S&P 500	Best Fit Index Wil 4500
Alpha	7.0	0.2
Beta	0.81	0.82
R-Squared	80	93
Standard Deviation	14.84	
Mean	10.34	
Sharpe Ratio	0.61	

Portfolio Analysis 01-31-04

Share change since 12-03 Total Stocks:80

	Sector	PE	YTD Ret%	% Assets
SAFECO	Financial	10.9	36.61	2.78
Omnicare	Health	14.0	-14.07	2.60
⊖ Storage Technology	Hardware	20.8	22.76	2.08
⊕ ServiceMaster	Consumer	22.0	22.67	2.07
Davita	Health	19.0	52.04	2.01
⊖ Kimberly-Clark	Goods	17.8	16.12	1.97
Lamar Advertising A	Business	—	14.63	1.85
National-Oilwell	Energy	36.9	57.83	1.83
American Power Conversio	Ind Mtrls	22.1	-10.99	1.83
Waste Management	Business	18.9	3.81	1.81
Valero Energy	Energy	7.0	97.64	1.77
Arch Coal	Energy	—	15.05	1.73
Newmont Mining	Ind Mtrls	45.6	-8.02	1.70
⊕ EchoStar Communications	Media	NMF	0.85	1.67
⊕ Furniture Brands Interna	Goods	14.4	-12.81	1.65
Yellow Roadway	Business	—	—	1.61
Boston Scientific	Health	32.3	-3.29	1.55
⊖ Burlington Resources	Energy	10.9	58.50	1.53
⊕ American Greetings	Media	17.1	16.18	1.50
Serono Sa	Health	25.8	-6.19	1.49

Current Investment Style

Market Cap	%
Giant	3.2
Large	21.2
Mid	55.1
Small	20.5
Micro	0.0

Avg $mil: 4,246

Value Measures		Rel Category
Price/Earnings	20.38	1.20
Price/Book	2.36	1.09
Price/Sales	1.12	1.06
Price/Cash Flow	8.97	1.44
Dividend Yield %	1.05	1.05

Growth Measures	%	Rel Category
Long-Term Erngs	11.16	0.89
Book Value	0.55	0.08
Sales	2.57	0.45
Cash Flow	2.00	0.27
Historical Erngs	1.32	0.12

Profitability	%	Rel Category
Return on Equity	9.83	0.71
Return on Assets	3.37	0.52
Net Margin	6.14	0.68

Sector Weightings	% of Stocks	Rel S&P 500	3 Year High	3 Year Low
Info	20.50	0.95		
Software	6.42	1.49	6	2
Hardware	6.72	0.66	14	6
Media	6.11	1.59	7	3
Telecom	1.25	0.40	7	1
Service	44.34	0.96		
Health	19.00	1.52	26	18
Consumer	8.04	0.89	18	6
Business	9.73	2.40	10	6
Financial	7.57	0.36	9	5
Mfg	35.15	1.09		
Goods	11.98	1.28	14	7
Ind Mtrls	15.02	1.19	18	8
Energy	8.15	1.14	11	3
Utilities	0.00	0.00	3	0

Composition

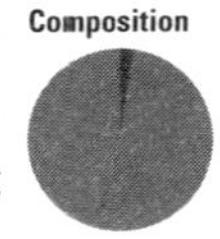

Cash	2.3
Stocks	97.7
Bonds	0.0
Other	0.0
Foreign (% of Stock)	9.8

Morningstar's Take by Christopher Davis 11-01-04

Whether Meridian Value's future will be as good as its past remains an open question.

Since taking the helm of this offering in January 2004, skipper Jamie England continues to follow the strategy employed by former manager Kevin O'Boyle. Using the approach developed by founder Rick Aster in 1994, England looks for depressed stocks that have suffered several consecutive quarters of earnings disappointments but have catalysts in place to drive a turnaround. Like O'Boyle, England has favored a mix of smaller and larger names. He recently scooped up small-cap retailer Christopher & Banks, for instance, which he says is regaining its footing after a string of poor merchandising decisions led to subpar earnings. And he also added large-cap Kraft Foods on the grounds that new product launches and more-stable commodity prices should reinvigorate the company.

England hasn't gotten off to a terrific start--the fund has delivered lackluster results this year--but that's far too short of a period to assess his stock-picking abilities. That said, we're not sure whether England can follow in his predecessor's footsteps. The fund's $2.1 billion asset base is by no means excessive for a mid-cap offering, but it makes it difficult for the fund to invest large sums in small- and micro-cap stocks, which where a major driver of its outsized gains in much of O'Boyle's tenure.

To be sure, O'Boyle was able to overcome the hurdle posed by a large asset base, so England's task isn't impossible. And there's some cause for optimism here. Prior to coming aboard this year, England worked closely with O'Boyle as an analyst for two years, so he's well acquainted with the fund's strategy and presumably supplied research for some of O'Boyle's winners.

Thus far, we haven't seen anything from England that should send current shareholders to the exits. However, until he proves his mettle, we think others should look elsewhere.

Address:	60 E Sir Francis Drake Blvd Larkspur CA 94939 800-446-6662
Web Address:	
Inception:	02-10-94 *
Advisor:	Aster Investment Management CO Inc
Subadvisor:	None
NTF Plans:	N/A

Minimum Purchase:	$1000	Add: $50	IRA: $1000
Min Auto Inv Plan:	$1000	Add: $50	
Sales Fees:	No-load		
Management Fee:	1.00%		
Actual Fees:	Mgt:1.00%	Dist: —	
Expense Projections:	3Yr:$358	5Yr:$620	10Yr:$1369
Income Distrib:	Annually		

Merrill Basic Value I

Ticker	Load	NAV	Yield	Total Assets	Mstar Category
MABAX	5.25%	$31.82	1.3%	$8,738 mil	Large Value

Governance and Management

Fiduciary Grade: B

Portfolio Manager(s)

Kevin Rendino, who previously worked as an analyst on this fund for nine years, took over management responsibilities in July 1999. Merrill Lynch Focus Value manager Robert Martorelli helps as comanager. Their analyst team includes Harry Radovich, Geri Gunn-Hertig, Carrie King, John Arege, and Michelle Smith.

Strategy

Manager Kevin Rendino looks for stocks that appear cheap relative to the market on a range of valuation measures, and he favors those with above-average dividend yields. He likes to buy stocks that have recently been battered but that offer good long-term growth prospects. He doesn't pay close attention to the sector weights of a benchmark and often holds more in tech stocks than the typical large-value offering.

Historical Profile

Return Average
Risk Above Avg
Rating ★★★ Neutral

Investment Style: Equity, Stock %

84% 88% 89% 92% 90% 94% 94% 95% 96%

▼ Manager Change
▽ Partial Manager Change

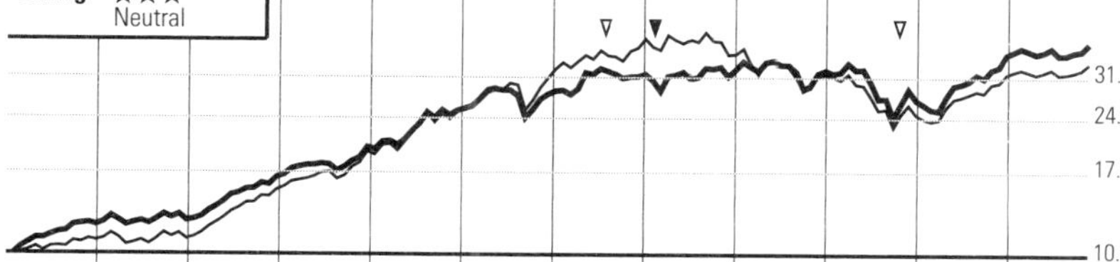

Growth of $10,000
— Investment Values of Fund
— Investment Values of S&P 500

Performance Quartile (within Category)

History

	1993	1994	1995	1996	1997	1998	1999	2000	2001	2002	2003	12-04
NAV	23.37	22.35	28.31	31.00	37.08	38.02	38.15	32.32	29.28	23.36	30.56	31.82
Total Return %	22.26	1.97	32.90	17.81	29.48	11.66	11.06	3.17	-0.51	-16.79	32.70	10.48
+/-S&P 500	12.20	0.66	-4.63	-5.13	-3.87	-16.91	-9.98	12.27	11.37	5.30	4.03	-0.39
+/-Russ 1000 Vl	4.19	3.95	-5.46	-3.83	-5.70	-3.97	3.71	-3.84	5.08	-1.27	2.67	-6.01
Income Return %	3.51	3.03	3.43	2.91	2.57	2.25	1.96	1.78	1.27	1.19	1.71	1.42
Capital Return %	18.75	-1.06	29.47	14.90	26.91	9.41	9.10	1.39	-1.78	-17.98	30.99	9.06
Total Rtn % Rank Cat	3	22	55	73	29	54	25	78	30	37	16	76
Income $	0.70	0.69	0.76	0.80	0.78	0.81	0.72	0.65	0.40	0.34	0.40	0.43
Capital Gains $	0.75	0.78	0.57	1.39	2.23	2.41	3.38	5.76	3.05	0.67	0.00	1.37
Expense Ratio %	0.54	0.53	0.59	0.56	0.55	0.54	0.55	0.56	0.56	0.81	0.60	0.56
Income Ratio %	3.48	2.76	3.19	2.88	2.54	2.14	1.95	1.68	1.60	0.94	1.48	1.36
Turnover Rate %	21	22	12	14	13	18	16	28	38	38	32	33
Net Assets $mil	2,181	2,318	3,230	4,374	5,215	5,426	5,014	4,263	3,988	3,105	3,758	4,232

Performance 12-31-04

	1st Qtr	2nd Qtr	3rd Qtr	4th Qtr	Total
2000	-1.21	-1.51	6.40	-0.35	3.17
2001	-0.94	3.88	-14.11	12.57	-0.51
2002	4.54	-11.34	-19.62	11.69	-16.79
2003	-6.42	18.16	3.72	15.70	32.70
2004	2.55	1.75	-2.47	8.55	10.48

Trailing	Total Return%	+/- S&P 500	+/- Russ 1000 Vl	%Rank Cat	Growth of $10,000
3 Mo	8.55	-0.68	-1.83	69	10,855
6 Mo	5.87	-1.32	-6.21	93	10,587
1 Yr	10.48	-0.39	-6.01	76	11,048
3 Yr Avg	6.85	3.27	-1.72	32	12,199
5 Yr Avg	4.60	6.90	-0.67	42	12,522
10 Yr Avg	12.15	0.08	-1.68	34	31,477
15 Yr Avg	11.01	0.08	-1.02	36	47,911

Tax Analysis	Tax-Adj Rtn%	%Rank Cat	Tax-Cost Rat	%Rank Cat
3 Yr (estimated)	3.97	58	0.92	61
5 Yr (estimated)	1.55	63	1.87	93
10 Yr (estimated)	9.33	48	1.99	64

Potential Capital Gain Exposure: 29% of assets

Rating and Risk

Time Period	Load-Adj Return %	Morningstar Rtn vs Cat	Morningstar Risk vs Cat	Morningstar Risk-Adj Rating
1 Yr	4.68			
3 Yr	4.94	Avg	+Avg	★★★
5 Yr	3.48	Avg	+Avg	★★★
10 Yr	11.55	Avg	Avg	★★★
Incept	13.66			

Other Measures	Standard Index S&P 500	Best Fit Index Russ 1000 Vl
Alpha	3.1	-2.3
Beta	1.12	1.13
R-Squared	95	96

Standard Deviation	18.49
Mean	6.85
Sharpe Ratio	0.30

Portfolio Analysis 09-30-04

Share change since 06-04 Total Stocks:77	Sector	PE	YTD Ret%	% Assets
ExxonMobil	Energy	13.9	28.04	5.06
Wells Fargo	Financial	15.5	8.97	4.30
☼ J P Morgan Chase	Financial	19.4	9.97	3.02
Citigroup	Financial	15.3	2.72	2.82
⊖ Raytheon	Ind Mtrls	38.1	32.20	2.71
⊕ Morgan Stanley	Financial	14.2	-2.25	2.06
American International G	Financial	16.2	-0.53	2.03
⊕ Bank of America	Financial	12.3	21.50	1.97
⊕ Viacom B	Media	36.1	-17.44	1.97
Kimberly-Clark	Goods	17.8	16.12	1.88
⊕ Alcoa	Ind Mtrls	18.8	-15.75	1.76
⊖ GlobalSantaFe	Energy	NMF	34.38	1.74
Gen Elec	Ind Mtrls	22.8	20.68	1.67
⊖ Diamond Offshore Drillin	Energy	—	97.23	1.58
⊕ Hewlett-Packard	Hardware	18.9	-7.28	1.57
SBC Communications	Telecom	15.4	3.74	1.57
⊕ IBM	Hardware	20.2	7.19	1.54
⊖ DuPont De Nemours E.I.	Ind Mtrls	22.3	10.42	1.54
⊖ Honeywell International	Ind Mtrls	20.5	8.21	1.53
⊖ Comcast	Media	—	-13.77	1.51

Current Investment Style

Value Blnd Growth; Large Mid Small

Market Cap	%
Giant	44.6
Large	45.7
Mid	9.7
Small	0.0
Micro	0.0
Avg $mil: 36,264	

Value Measures		Rel Category
Price/Earnings	15.83	1.05
Price/Book	2.08	0.92
Price/Sales	1.25	1.05
Price/Cash Flow	6.83	1.07
Dividend Yield %	2.03	1.00

Growth Measures	%	Rel Category
Long-Term Erngs	7.07	0.97
Book Value	2.40	0.43
Sales	1.87	0.45
Cash Flow	17.66	3.38
Historical Erngs	10.50	0.89

Profitability	%	Rel Category
Return on Equity	13.38	0.84
Return on Assets	6.66	0.85
Net Margin	7.77	0.76

Sector Weightings	% of Stocks	Rel S&P 500	3 Year High	3 Year Low
Info	24.31	1.13		
Software	0.51	0.12	1	1
Hardware	12.38	1.21	15	12
Media	7.63	1.99	9	6
Telecom	3.79	1.20	4	3
Service	35.56	0.77		
Health	5.40	0.43	5	4
Consumer	2.07	0.23	4	2
Business	0.00	0.00	1	0
Financial	28.09	1.35	29	23
Mfg	40.12	1.25		
Goods	10.03	1.08	12	7
Ind Mtrls	14.34	1.13	17	13
Energy	14.68	2.05	19	14
Utilities	1.07	0.36	1	0

Composition

Cash	3.7
Stocks	96.3
Bonds	0.0
Other	0.0
Foreign (% of Stock)	5.5

Morningstar's Take by Karen Papalois 12-07-04

Investors should stick with Merrill Lynch Basic Value.

This fund is having a difficult 2004. Its 7.18% gain through Dec. 7, 2004, lands in the large-value category's bottom third. Despite that, it still has appeal. For one, the fund charges 36% less than the typical large-value fund with a front-end sales charge, and its other share classes are reasonably priced too. That gives it an instant head start over its peers.

The fund's strategy requires patience, though. That's because portfolio manager Kevin Rendino is willing to delve into volatile areas such as hardware stocks when he thinks they're cheap. On average, the portfolio has kept 13% of assets in the sector since taking over in 1999. That's more than double the norm for large-value funds. The fund's heavy hardware stake propelled it to the category's top quartile in 2003 as chip stocks rallied that year.

The fund's attention to valuation has helped ease the downside of its aggressive inclinations. Rendino favors stocks trading at less than two thirds the industry average on a price/earnings and price/cash flow basis. Still, tech stocks generally court aggressive price multiples and the fund has experienced a bumpier ride (as measured by standard deviation) than most of its peers because of it.

Other facets of the fund's strategy help mitigate its risks too. Rendino keeps a diversified portfolio of approximately 80 stocks with less than the category in its top 10 holdings. That helps minimize the effect of huge stock declines. Also, the fund has a longer-than-average holding period--about three years, judging from its turnover ratio. That helps keep a lid on transaction costs that can arise with higher turnover strategies.

Rendino's approach has worked well over his tenure. The fund's reasonable expenses and consistent strategy also are appealing. Investors who can stick around through thick and thin should be well served over time.

Address:	P O Box 9011 Princeton NJ 08543 800-995-6526
Web Address:	www.mlim.ml.com
Inception:	07-05-77
Advisor:	Fund Asset Management LP
Subadvisor:	Merrill Lynch Asset Management
NTF Plans:	N/A

Minimum Purchase:	$1000	Add: $50	IRA: $100
Min Auto Inv Plan:	$1000	Add: $50	
Sales Fees:	5.25%L		
Management Fee:	0.60% mx./0.40% mn.		
Actual Fees:	Mgt:0.40%	Dist:	
Expense Projections:	3Yr:$770	5Yr:$951	10Yr:$1474
Income Distrib:	Semi-Annually		

Merrill Global Alloc A

Analyst Pick	Ticker	Load	NAV	Yield	Total Assets	Mstar Category
✔	MDLOX	5.25%	$16.47	2.6%	$9,768 mil	World Allocation

Governance and Management

Fiduciary Grade: C

Portfolio Manager(s)

Dennis Stattman has been at the helm since the fund's 1989 inception, making him one of the category's longest-serving managers. Veteran analyst Dan Chamby became associate manager in 2004. They are supported by analysts Karene Morley Wescott, James Wei, Catherine Brady Rauscher, and Lisa O'Donnell.

Strategy

The fund invests in out-of-favor stocks and bonds that its managers think will rebound. For example, it loaded up on emerging-markets bonds in 1998 when few others would touch them. And in 2002 it moved into equities (particularly technology stocks) and corporate bonds when the near-term outlook for them was bleak. The portfolio's broad diversification takes the edge off its contrarian bent. It owns hundreds of securities, limits individual positions, and keeps its equity stake close to 60%, which mutes the effects of stock, sector, or geographic region blowups.

Historical Profile

Return Above Avg
Risk Above Avg
Rating ★★★ Neutral

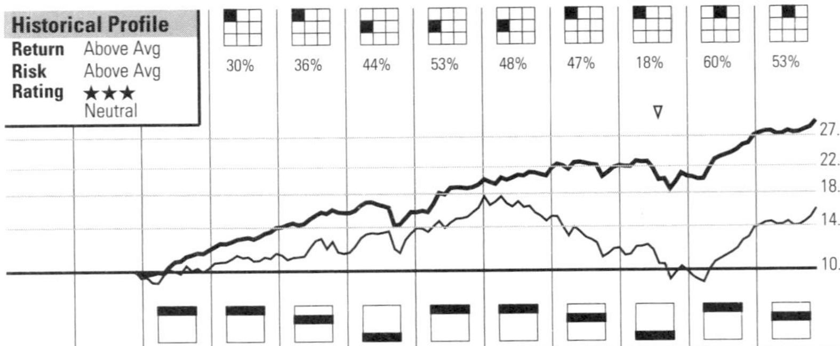

Investment Style
Equity
Stock %

▼ Manager Change
▽ Partial Manager Change

Growth of $10,000
— Investment Values of Fund
— Investment Values of MSCI EAFE

Performance Quartile (within Category)

1993	1994	1995	1996	1997	1998	1999	2000	2001	2002	2003	12-04	History
—	12.24	13.87	14.54	14.13	12.60	14.01	13.10	12.83	11.41	14.97	16.47	NAV
—	-2.35*	23.29	15.96	11.12	0.37	27.75	8.57	1.88	-7.96	35.98	14.27	Total Return %
—	—	12.08	9.91	9.34	-19.56	0.72	22.76	23.30	7.98	-2.61	-5.98	+/-MSCI EAFE
—	—	3.49	5.30	-0.78	-11.95	10.42	10.24	4.68	-1.19	8.60	1.30	+/-DJ 60%
—	0.00	6.25	6.20	7.54	3.74	7.02	2.52	3.88	3.15	4.45	2.90	Income Return %
—	—	17.04	9.76	3.58	-3.37	20.73	6.05	-2.00	-11.11	31.53	11.37	Capital Return %
—	—	25	25	50	84	1	20	42	76	11	48	Total Rtn % Rank Cat
—	0.22	0.76	0.85	1.08	0.52	0.87	0.35	0.50	0.40	0.50	0.43	Income $
—	0.30	0.43	0.65	0.94	1.05	1.13	1.69	0.01	0.00	0.00	0.18	Capital Gains $
—	1.69	1.16	1.10	1.08	1.10	1.16	1.13	1.19	1.19	1.18	1.13	Expense Ratio %
—	4.46	5.63	5.04	4.38	4.40	4.61	3.11	2.92	2.85	2.28	1.54	Income Ratio %
—	57	37	51	55	50	27	54	45	58	45	43	Turnover Rate %
—	98	304	1,091	1,454	1,269	1,275	1,441	2,053	2,034	2,586	3,652	Net Assets $mil

Performance 12-31-04

	1st Qtr	2nd Qtr	3rd Qtr	4th Qtr	Total
2000	1.28	2.04	1.70	3.29	8.57
2001	-0.69	4.61	-9.70	8.60	1.88
2002	3.43	-5.65	-14.26	10.00	-7.96
2003	-1.93	18.05	5.57	11.25	35.98
2004	3.34	0.13	0.98	9.37	14.27

Trailing	Total Return%	+/- MSCI EAFE	+/- DJ 60%	%Rank Cat	Growth of $10,000
3 Mo	9.37	-5.95	0.52	60	10,937
6 Mo	10.44	-4.56	0.66	61	11,044
1 Yr	14.27	-5.98	1.30	48	11,427
3 Yr Avg	12.67	0.78	2.38	30	14,303
5 Yr Avg	9.61	10.74	4.51	20	15,822
10 Yr Avg	12.41	6.79	2.78	25	32,214
15 Yr Avg	—	—	—	—	—

Tax Analysis	Tax-Adj Rtn%	%Rank Cat	Tax-Cost Rat	%Rank Cat
3 Yr (estimated)	9.32	57	1.21	75
5 Yr (estimated)	6.48	35	1.80	84
10 Yr (estimated)	8.79	34	2.70	91

Potential Capital Gain Exposure: 17% of assets

Rating and Risk

Time Period	Load-Adj Return %	Morningstar Rtn vs Cat	Morningstar Risk vs Cat	Morningstar Risk-Adj Rating
1 Yr	8.27			
3 Yr	10.66	Avg	High	★★
5 Yr	8.43	+Avg	+Avg	★★★
10 Yr	11.81	+Avg	+Avg	★★★★
Incept	11.31			

Other Measures	Standard Index S&P 500	Best Fit Index Russ 1000 VI
Alpha	3.2	5.1
Beta	0.74	0.80
R-Squared	88	93

Standard Deviation	13.74
Mean	12.67
Sharpe Ratio	0.83

Morningstar's Take by Karen Papalois 12-22-04

The world is Merrill Lynch Global Allocation's playground.

Portfolio manager Dennis Stattman isn't afraid to deviate from his peers or benchmark. His macroeconomic views drive the fund's positioning. The fund's cash stake hasn't dropped below 10% of assets since 1999 and it currently stands at about 25% of assets (that's roughly 10 percentage points more than the average for world-allocation funds). Stattman has avoided long-term Treasury bonds because he thinks their yields are bound to rise, which would hurt their prices. That avoidance has hurt the fund's relative performance this year, though, because long-term interest rates have stayed low even though the economy has been improving, monetary policy tightening, and commodity prices rising.

Stattman is bearish about the U.S. dollar too. Thus, he's shifted assets toward international investments such as European bonds and Asian equities. In Asia, Stattman is finding a combination of reasonable valuations and earnings growth. Overall, the fund has maintained its tilt toward economically sensitive equities.

Stattman's willingness to go against the grain gives the fund an edge over peers and has worked over time. For example, a heavy equity position boosted returns in 2003. Likewise, the fund added Latin American Brady Bonds in 1995 and REITs in 1996, before they all rallied.

The fund has kept a lid on volatility by spreading risks among 500 holdings in different asset classes, sectors, and regions. Despite having persistently high cash stakes in recent years, the fund lands in the category's top quartile for the trailing five years through the end of November 2004. And over Stattman's 15-year tenure, the fund's older B shares have returned an annualized 11.33%, which beats the category average. Overall, this fund's experienced manager and proven track record give us confidence in its flexible style. It remains a favorite.

Address:	P O Box 9011 Princeton NJ 08543 800-995-6526
Web Address:	www.mlim.ml.com
Inception:	10-21-94 *
Advisor:	Merrill Lynch Investment Managers, LLC
Subadvisor:	Merrill Lynch Asset Management UK Ltd
NTF Plans:	Federated Tr NTF, Fidelity Instl-NTF

Minimum Purchase:	$1000	Add: $50	IRA: $100
Min Auto Inv Plan:	$1000	Add: $50	
Sales Fees:	0.02%D, 0.25%S		
Management Fee:	0.75% mx./0.60% mn.		
Actual Fees:	Mgt:0.75%	Dist:0.25%	
Expense Projections:	3Yr:$880	5Yr:$1140	10Yr:$1882
Income Distrib:	Semi-Annually		

Portfolio Analysis 09-30-04

Total Stocks:396 Share change since 06-30-04	Sectors	P/E Ratio	YTD Return %	% Net Assets
Gen Elec	Ind Mtrls	22.8	-3.01	1.06
⊕ Microsoft	Software	36.1	0.04	1.03
⊖ Millea Hldgs	Financial	—	—	0.97
⊖ Mitsui Sumitomo Insurance	Financial	—	—	0.84
⊕ Pfizer	Health	22.0	-2.75	0.78
NIPPONKOA Insurance	Financial	—	—	0.77
Reliance Industries Ltd	Ind Mtrls	—	—	0.72
⊖ Computer Associates Inter	Software	—	-9.56	0.70
El Paso	Energy	—	0.00	0.69

Total Fixed-Income:70	Date of Maturity	Amount $000	Value $000	% Net Assets
European Invest Bk 6.125%	12-07-05	60,200	110,437	1.18
Metromedia Intl Grp	09-30-07	132,057	83,196	0.89
US Treasury Note 4.75%	05-15-14	77,250	81,088	0.87
Land Nordrhein-Westfalen	02-16-07	51,000	65,452	0.70
European Invest Bk 3.55%	04-15-08	51,850	64,785	0.69
Kreditanstalt Fur Wiedera	06-07-06	34,250	61,127	0.65
Abn Amro Bk N V N Y Brh 4	11-05-17	70,713	58,692	0.63
Foster Wheeler Llc	09-15-11	55,594	57,818	0.62

Current Investment Style

Value Blnd Growth / Large Mid Small (Large Blend)

Market Cap	%
Giant	42.9
Large	32.2
Mid	16.9
Small	7.2
Micro	0.8
Avg $mil: 16,461	

Value Measures		Rel Category
Price/Earnings	15.05	1.08
Price/Book	1.08	0.57
Price/Sales	0.70	0.65
Price/Cash Flow	4.42	0.79
Dividend Yield %	2.76	0.97

Growth Measures	%	Rel Category
Long-Term Erngs	10.98	1.07
Book Value	2.24	0.85
Sales	0.78	0.20
Cash Flow	1.64	0.31
Historical Erngs	10.34	1.61

Composition

Cash	26.3	Bonds	12.7
Stocks	53.0	Other	8.0
Foreign (% of Stock)			47.8

Sector Weightings	% of Stocks	Rel MSCI EAFE	3 Year High	3 Year Low
Info	19.40	1.17		
Software	4.74	4.39	5	1
Hardware	4.44	1.22	8	4
Media	2.45	1.07	2	1
Telecom	7.77	0.81	11	7
Service	39.18	0.88		
Health	7.71	1.06	11	7
Consumer	5.14	1.02	5	3
Business	3.75	0.69	4	3
Financial	22.58	0.84	27	20
Mfg	41.41	1.07		
Goods	9.39	0.69	10	8
Ind Mtrls	16.37	1.33	19	14
Energy	13.07	1.78	14	11
Utilities	2.58	0.48	5	2

Regional Exposure	% Stock		
UK/W. Europe	15	N. America	54
Japan	13	Latn America	3
Asia X Japan	14	Other	1

Country Exposure	% Stock		
United States	52	South Korea	4
Japan	13	India	4
U.K.	5		

Metro West Low Dur M

Ticker	Load	NAV	Yield	SEC Yield	Total Assets	Mstar Category
MWLDX	12b-1 only	$9.43	4.0%	—	$595 mil	Short-Term Bond

Governance and Management

Fiduciary Grade: A

Portfolio Manager(s)

The fund's management team, which includes Tad Rivelle, Laird Landmann, and Stephen Kane, has put up good since-inception numbers here. Prior to founding Metropolitan West, the team had a strong record with Hotchkis & Wiley in the mid-1990s. This fund opened in March 1997.

Strategy

Managers Tad Rivelle, Laird Landmann, Stephen Kane, and David Lippman don't typically make big macroeconomic bets but instead try to boost returns by identifying undervalued corners of the bond market. The fund's duration (a measure of interest-rate sensitivity) is kept within a year of the Merrill Lynch 1-3 Year U.S. Treasury Index's. The fund typically takes on more issue-specific and credit risk than its average category peer, although its limit on new purchases has been reduced to 2.5% of assets.

Historical Profile

Return Average
Risk Above Avg
Rating ★★★ Neutral

Investment Style: Fixed Income — Income Rtn %Rank Cat

1997	1998	1999	2000	2001	2002	2003	12-04
100	7	2	1	3	5	2	9

▼ Manager Change
∇ Partial Manager Change

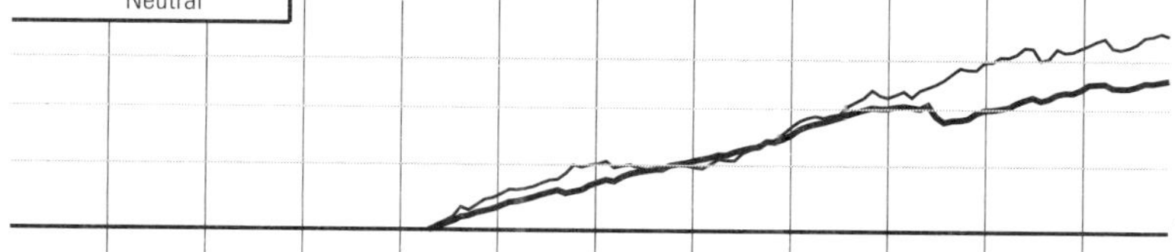

Growth of $10,000
— Investment Values of Fund
— Investment Values of LB Aggr

Performance Quartile (within Category)

History

1993	1994	1995	1996	1997	1998	1999	2000	2001	2002	2003	12-04	History
—	—	—	—	10.17	10.16	10.02	9.91	9.98	9.41	9.50	9.43	NAV
—	—	—	—	6.83*	6.64	6.23	7.32	7.60	-0.40	5.95	3.27	Total Return %
—	—	—	—	—	-2.05	7.05	-4.31	-0.84	-10.65	1.85	-1.07	+/-LB Aggr
—	—	—	—	—	-0.99	4.14	-1.59	-1.43	-8.52	2.60	1.42	+/-LB 1-5 YR
—	—	—	—	0.00	6.65	7.19	8.43	6.94	5.41	4.96	4.02	Income Return %
—	—	—	—	—	-0.01	-0.96	-1.11	0.66	-5.81	0.99	-0.75	Capital Return %
—	—	—	—	—	36	1	61	40	99	4	8	Total Rtn % Rank Cat
—	—	—	—	0.49	0.66	0.71	0.81	0.67	0.53	0.46	0.37	Income $
—	—	—	—	0.01	0.01	0.05	0.00	0.00	0.00	0.00	0.00	Capital Gains $
—	—	—	—	—	0.58	0.58	0.58	0.58	0.58	0.58	0.58	Expense Ratio %
—	—	—	—	—	6.72	6.61	7.22	8.08	6.21	5.40	4.47	Income Ratio %
—	—	—	—	—	—	73	126	53	26	65	94	Turnover Rate %
—	—	—	—	78	210	338	140	333	327	320	319	Net Assets $mil

Performance 12-31-04

	1st Qtr	2nd Qtr	3rd Qtr	4th Qtr	Total
2000	1.61	1.42	2.30	1.80	7.32
2001	3.07	1.76	2.17	0.41	7.60
2002	0.33	-2.43	-0.92	2.70	-0.40
2003	0.83	2.78	0.85	1.38	5.95
2004	1.64	-1.24	1.41	1.45	3.27

Trailing	Total Return%	+/- LB Aggr	+/- LB 1-5 YR	%Rank Cat	Growth of $10,000
3 Mo	1.45	0.50	1.30	7	10,145
6 Mo	2.89	-1.29	1.01	10	10,289
1 Yr	3.27	-1.07	1.42	8	10,327
3 Yr Avg	2.91	-3.28	-1.50	65	10,899
5 Yr Avg	4.71	-3.00	-1.50	61	12,588
10 Yr Avg	—	—	—	—	—
15 Yr Avg	—	—	—	—	—

Tax Analysis	Tax-Adj Rtn%	%Rank Cat	Tax-Cost Rat	%Rank Cat
3 Yr (estimated)	1.15	71	1.71	87
5 Yr (estimated)	2.43	81	2.18	97
10 Yr (estimated)	—	—	—	—

Potential Capital Gain Exposure: -10% of assets

Rating and Risk

Time Period	Load-Adj Return %	Morningstar Rtn vs Cat	Morningstar Risk vs Cat	Morningstar Risk-Adj Rating
1 Yr	3.27			
3 Yr	2.91	Avg	+Avg	★★★
5 Yr	4.71	Avg	+Avg	★★★
10 Yr	—	—	—	—
Incept	5.58			

Other Measures	Standard Index LB Aggr	Best Fit Index CSFB Glb HY
Alpha	0.5	-2.6
Beta	0.22	0.35
R-Squared	10	52
Standard Deviation	3.06	
Mean	2.91	
Sharpe Ratio	0.50	

Portfolio Analysis 09-30-04

Total Fixed-Income: 153	Date of Maturity	Amount $000	Value $000	% Net Assets
FHLMC 5.5%	10-15-19	12,000	12,394	1.94
Georgia Pwr Cap Tr Vi FR	11-01-42	10,860	11,196	1.76
Msstr 2004-1 4a1	03-25-32	10,000	10,190	1.60
MCI		564	9,439	1.48
Metris Master Tr 2000-3	09-20-09	8,970	8,950	1.40
FNMA 5%	10-25-19	8,690	8,829	1.38
Wamu Mtg Cert 2004-Ar10	07-25-44	8,572	8,556	1.34
Mastr Asset Tr 2002-6 CM	10-25-32	8,297	8,430	1.32
General Mtrs Accep FRN	09-23-08	8,363	8,346	1.31
Lb Abs Mfh Tr 2001-B FRN	05-15-41	527,236	8,239	1.29
Washington Mutual 2003-M	03-25-18	8,222	8,170	1.28
Indymac Mbs 2004-Ar8 CMO	11-25-34	8,040	8,046	1.26
Air 2 Us 1999 8.027%	10-01-20	9,433	7,884	1.24
US Treasury Note 3.625%	07-15-09	7,719	7,815	1.23
FHLMC 2%	11-28-05	7,638	7,635	1.20
Qwest Cap Fdg 7.75%	08-15-06	7,250	7,313	1.15
Conseco Fin Secs 1999-H	03-15-24	6,892	7,158	1.12
Indymac Mbs 2004-Ar7 CMO	09-25-34	7,030	7,031	1.10
Arg Fdg FRN	03-20-07	7,000	7,012	1.10
GNMA FRN	07-20-34	6,842	6,945	1.09

Current Investment Style

Duration: Short Int Long — Quality: High Med Low

1 figure provided by fund

Avg Eff Duration[1]	1.4 Yrs
Avg Eff Maturity	2.8 Yrs
Avg Credit Quality	AA
Avg Wtd Coupon	5.24%
Avg Wtd Price	93.90% of par

Coupon Range	% of Bonds	Rel Cat
0% PIK	9.5	1.9
0% to 6%	53.2	0.7
6% to 8%	35.5	1.5
8% to 10%	11.0	4.0
More than 10%	0.3	0.4

1.00=Category Average

Credit Analysis		% bonds 09-30-04	
US Govt	30	BB	2
AAA	22	B	5
AA	9	Below B	2
A	15	NR/NA	0
BBB	14		

Sector Breakdown	% of assets
US Treasuries	1
TIPS	0
US Agency	3
Mortgage Pass-Throughs	7
Mortgage CMO	13
Mortgage ARM	0
US Corporate	18
Asset-Backed	30
Convertible	0
Municipal	0
Corporate Inflation-Protected	0
Foreign Corporate	1
Foreign Govt	0

Composition			
Cash	27.1	Bonds	71.4
Stocks	1.5	Other	0.0

Special Securities	
Restricted/Illiquid Secs	4
Exotic Mortgage-Backed	1
Emerging-Markets Secs	0
Options/Futures/Warrants	No

Morningstar's Take by Scott Berry 10-14-04

Despite its subpar three- and five-year trailing returns, we think Metropolitan West Low Duration makes a good case for itself.

With the exception of a brutal two-month stretch in mid-2002, this fund has delivered solid results. In fact, since its inception in early 1997, it has outperformed more than 75% of its short-term bond category peers. The fund's early success isn't captured by its three- and five-year trailing returns, however, with both of those measures landing in the category's bottom third.

The fund has recovered much of the ground it lost in mid-2002 though. Many of the corporate bonds that collapsed that year ultimately recovered most if not all of their value in late 2002 and 2003. More recently, the fund has benefited from the added yield provided by its asset-backed securities and corporate bond holdings. And although the fund's defensive interest-rate positioning has cost it some ground in recent weeks, it should offer added protection if interest rates move higher, as many predict they will. Overall, the fund has returned 1.96% for the year to date through Oct. 12, 2004, while its average category peer has gained 1.35%.

We think the fund's improved performance will eventually shine through to its three- and five-year trailing returns, as will its skilled management and reasonable expense ratio. The fund's management team could have caved under pressure in 2002 but stuck to its guns, allowing the fund to participate in many issue-specific recoveries. Post-bankrupt MCI stock remains in the fund, but its volatility has moderated since the company announced a roughly 10% cash dividend. The holding sticks out like a sore thumb here, but management isn't willing to sell the position until it can get what it considers a fair price.

Overall, we think short-term bond investors will like what they find here. This fund isn't immune to rising interest rates, but its added yield, below-average expense ratio, and defensive positioning should provide it some protection.

Address:	11766 Wilshire Blvd Los Angeles CA 90025 800-241-4671
Web Address:	
Inception:	03-31-97 *
Advisor:	Metropolitan West Asset Mangement LLC
Subadvisor:	None
NTF Plans:	Fidelity Retail-NTF, Schwab OneSource

Minimum Purchase:	$5000	Add: $0	IRA: $1000
Min Auto Inv Plan:	$0	Add: —	
Sales Fees:	0.19%B		
Management Fee:	0.30%		
Actual Fees:	Mgt:0.30%	Dist:0.19%	
Expense Projections:	3Yr:$199	5Yr:$351	10Yr:$793
Income Distrib:	Monthly		

Metro West Total Ret

Analyst Pick

Ticker	Load	NAV	Yield	SEC Yield	Total Assets	Mstar Category
MWTRX	12b-1 only	$9.82	6.0%	—	$1,311 mil	Intermediate-Term Bond

Governance and Management

Fiduciary Grade: A

Portfolio Manager(s)

The fund's management team of Stephen Kane, Laird Landmann, and Tad Rivelle delivered solid returns at Hotchkis & Wiley and Pimco before starting this fund in 1997. David Lippman joined the team in 2001.

Strategy

This fund attempts to outperform its peers through duration bets, yield-curve adjustments, sector rotation, and issue selection. Management argues that there are issue and sector-level inefficiencies in the bond market because information is not always widely disseminated. As of late, that has meant above-average stakes in corporate bonds and asset-backed securities. Management is not shy about holding large positions or taking on credit risk, although the fund follows a policy of putting no more than 2.5% of assets in a single purchase.

Historical Profile

Return Above Avg
Risk High
Rating ★★★★ Above Avg

Investment Style: Fixed Income, Income Rtn %Rank Cat

▼ Manager Change
▽ Partial Manager Change

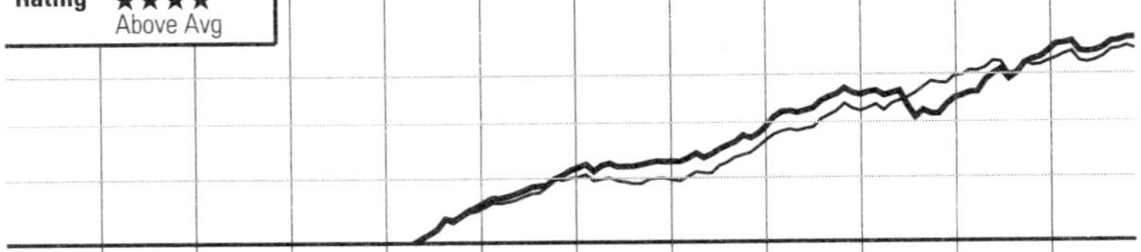

Growth of $10,000
— Investment Values of Fund
— Investment Values of LB Aggr

Performance Quartile (within Category)

History

	1993	1994	1995	1996	1997	1998	1999	2000	2001	2002	2003	12-04
Income Rtn %Rank Cat					100	3	1	1	2	2	1	2
NAV	—	—	—	—	10.51	10.65	10.05	10.11	10.15	9.30	9.92	9.82
Total Return %	—	—	—	—	11.88*	9.96	1.72	10.18	9.18	-0.95	13.88	5.15
+/-LB Aggr	—	—	—	—	—	1.27	2.54	-1.45	0.74	-11.20	9.78	0.81
+/-LB 5-10YR	—	—	—	—	—	-0.18	4.60	-2.26	0.36	-13.98	7.91	-0.15
Income Return %	—	—	—	—	0.00	7.10	7.42	9.48	7.81	7.17	6.96	6.15
Capital Return %	—	—	—	—	—	2.86	-5.70	0.70	1.37	-8.12	6.92	-1.00
Total Rtn % Rank Cat	—	—	—	—	—	3	3	50	12	99	1	10
Income $	—	—	—	—	0.54	0.72	0.76	0.91	0.76	0.70	0.63	0.59
Capital Gains $	—	—	—	—	0.11	0.15	0.01	0.00	0.10	0.04	0.00	0.00
Expense Ratio %	—	—	—	—	—	0.65	0.65	0.65	0.65	0.65	0.65	0.65
Income Ratio %	—	—	—	—	—	7.39	6.92	7.68	9.16	7.14	7.40	5.62
Turnover Rate %	—	—	—	—	—	—	136	128	205	78	90	165
Net Assets $mil	—	—	—	—	15	83	187	278	621	568	483	479

Performance 12-31-04

	1st Qtr	2nd Qtr	3rd Qtr	4th Qtr	Total
2000	2.29	1.16	3.88	2.50	10.18
2001	4.37	0.79	4.01	-0.22	9.18
2002	-0.21	-2.82	-2.30	4.54	-0.95
2003	1.66	6.49	1.77	3.36	13.88
2004	2.80	-2.68	2.81	2.23	5.15

Trailing	Total Return%	+/- LB Aggr	+/- LB 5-10YR	%Rank Cat	Growth of $10,000
3 Mo	2.23	1.28	1.25	4	10,223
6 Mo	5.10	0.92	-0.47	12	10,510
1 Yr	5.15	0.81	-0.15	10	10,515
3 Yr Avg	5.85	-0.34	-2.20	35	11,860
5 Yr Avg	7.37	-0.34	-1.70	27	14,270
10 Yr Avg	—	—	—	—	—
15 Yr Avg	—	—	—	—	—

Tax Analysis	Tax-Adj Rtn%	%Rank Cat	Tax-Cost Rat	%Rank Cat
3 Yr (estimated)	3.29	55	2.42	93
5 Yr (estimated)	4.36	58	2.80	95
10 Yr (estimated)	—	—	—	—

Potential Capital Gain Exposure: -7% of assets

Rating and Risk

Time Period	Load-Adj Return %	Morningstar Rtn vs Cat	Morningstar Risk vs Cat	Morningstar Risk-Adj Rating
1 Yr	5.15			
3 Yr	5.85	+Avg	High	★★★
5 Yr	7.37	+Avg	High	★★★★
10 Yr	—	—	—	—
Incept	7.76			

Other Measures	Standard Index LB Aggr	Best Fit Index CSFB Glb HY
Alpha	1.4	-3.8
Beta	0.64	0.70
R-Squared	24	60
Standard Deviation	5.88	
Mean	5.85	
Sharpe Ratio	0.77	

Morningstar's Take by Scott Berry 10-18-04

Metropolitan West Total Return has struggled to stand out recently, but we think investors should stay the course.

It's been a surprisingly quiet period for this fund. After stumbling badly in 2002 and rallying hard in 2003, this fund has simply kept pace with its average intermediate bond peer in 2004. The fund's defensive interest-rate positioning worked in its favor when rates jumped in the spring but held it back when rates retreated over the summer. Overall, the fund has returned 3.1% for the year to date through Oct. 13, while its average category peer has climbed 3.2%.

Management has not only been defensive on interest rates but has also been a bit wary of taking on too much credit risk. The fund continues to own a stash of corporate bonds and continues to have more credit risk than its average peer, but in recent months management has looked to seek shelter in asset-backed securities and other higher-quality debt, arguing that riskier issues aren't offering enough yield to make them attractive.

Despite its relatively defensive profile, the fund continues to pump out a lot of income thanks to the added yield offered by its asset-backed holdings and its still-sizable corporate bond stake. The fund's SEC yield recently stood at 5.48%, for example, while its average peer's checked in at just 3.81%. We don't like to overemphasize yield, as it can often mask poor total returns, but in this case the fund has delivered both good long-term total returns and an attractive yield. In fact, its since-inception total return ranks in the category's top 10%, while its annual income return percentage typically ranks near the top of the charts.

This fund's credit risk should not be overlooked, but we think investors who can stomach a little added risk should like what they find here. The fund's experienced management, good track record, and reasonable expense ratio make it one of our Analyst Picks.

Address:	11766 Wilshire Blvd Los Angeles CA 90025 800-241-4671
Web Address:	
Inception:	03-31-97 *
Advisor:	Metropolitan West Asset Mangement LLC
Subadvisor:	None
NTF Plans:	Fidelity Retail-NTF, Schwab OneSource

Minimum Purchase:	$5000	Add: $0	IRA: $1000
Min Auto Inv Plan:	$0	Add: —	
Sales Fees:	0.21%B		
Management Fee:	0.35%		
Actual Fees:	Mgt:0.35%	Dist:0.21%	
Expense Projections:	3Yr:$215	5Yr:$376	10Yr:$844
Income Distrib:	Monthly		

Portfolio Analysis 09-30-04

Total Fixed-Income:223	Date of Maturity	Amount $000	Value $000	% Net Assets
US Treasury Bond 5.375%	02-15-31	68,394	73,288	5.21
FNMA 0.05%		36,900	37,488	2.66
US Treasury Note 3%	07-15-12	28,455	33,202	2.36
FNMA 0.05%		33,060	32,719	2.32
MCI		1,953	32,704	2.32
US Treasury Bond 8.75%	05-15-17	18,505	26,114	1.86
Short-Term Asset Receiva	06-11-18	22,250	22,271	1.58
Air 2 Us 1999 8.027%	10-01-20	25,614	21,409	1.52
Citigroup Mtg Ln Tr FRN	05-25-34	19,094	18,642	1.32
Lb Commrcl Mtg Tr 2000-C	08-15-26	15,155	17,538	1.25
Metris Master Tr 2000-1	08-20-08	17,275	17,241	1.22
Duke Fdg I 144A		17,000	17,183	1.22
Ingress 7.38%	03-30-40	16,895	16,628	1.18
Fmac Ln Recv Tr 1998-B C	11-15-20	22,283	16,503	1.17
U S West Cap Fdg 6.375%	07-15-08	17,590	16,315	1.16
Conseco Manu Hsg Pt 2000	05-01-31	15,832	16,284	1.16
General Mtrs 8.375%	07-15-33	14,958	15,927	1.13
Ford Mtr 7.45%	07-16-31	15,907	15,642	1.11
Ford Motor Cr 7.25%	10-25-11	14,379	15,582	1.11
Calpine Generating 144A	04-01-10	16,200	15,471	1.10

Current Investment Style

Duration: Short Int Long; Quality: High Med Low

[1] figure provided by fund

Avg Eff Duration[1]	3.9 Yrs
Avg Eff Maturity	7.4 Yrs
Avg Credit Quality	AA
Avg Wtd Coupon	5.45%
Avg Wtd Price	95.51% of par

Coupon Range	% of Bonds	Rel Cat
0% PIK	4.8	1.2
0% to 6%	41.7	0.7
6% to 8%	42.3	1.5
8% to 10%	15.0	2.6
More than 10%	1.1	0.9

1.00=Category Average

Credit Analysis		% bonds 09-30-04	
US Govt	37	BB	5
AAA	8	B	12
AA	10	Below B	2
A	8	NR/NA	0
BBB	17		

Sector Breakdown	% of assets
US Treasuries	8
TIPS	2
US Agency	1
Mortgage Pass-Throughs	11
Mortgage CMO	7
Mortgage ARM	0
US Corporate	21
Asset-Backed	25
Convertible	0
Municipal	0
Corporate Inflation-Protected	0
Foreign Corporate	3
Foreign Govt	0

Composition			
Cash	22.1	Bonds	75.0
Stocks	2.5	Other	0.5

Special Securities	
Restricted/Illiquid Secs	10
Exotic Mortgage-Backed	2
Emerging-Markets Secs	0
Options/Futures/Warrants	No

MFS Mass Inv Grth Stk A

Ticker	Load	NAV	Yield	Total Assets	Mstar Category
MIGFX	5.75%	$12.36	0.4%	$8,972 mil	Large Growth

Governance and Management

Fiduciary Grade: C

Portfolio Manager(s)

Stephen Pesek, this fund's manager since early 1999, has produced reasonable returns at this offering, although it lagged in the early 2000s' bear market. Irfan Ali joined this offering in October 2003 when the fund switched to a sleeve structure. He's running one third of its assets in the same style as his aggressive MFS Strategic Growth. Former analyst Gregory Locraft also joined in October 2003 and manages 12% of the fund's assets.

Strategy

This fund moved to a sleeve structure in October 2003. Longtime manager Stephen Pesek now runs about two thirds of the fund's assets. He looks for blue-chip companies with strong earnings growth in expanding sectors of the economy. Meanwhile Irfan Ali is running one third of the fund's portfolio in the same manner as his gutsy MFS Strategic Growth. Gregory Locraft, who recently was promoted from analyst, will eventually take over one third of the fund's assets from Pesek, but for now, Locraft is only investing a sliver of the fund.

Historical Profile

Return Average
Risk Average
Rating ★★★ Neutral

Investment Style: Equity Stock %

1993	1994	1995	1996	1997	1998	1999	2000	2001	2002	2003	12-04
	91%	93%	81%	96%	92%	93%	94%	98%	97%		

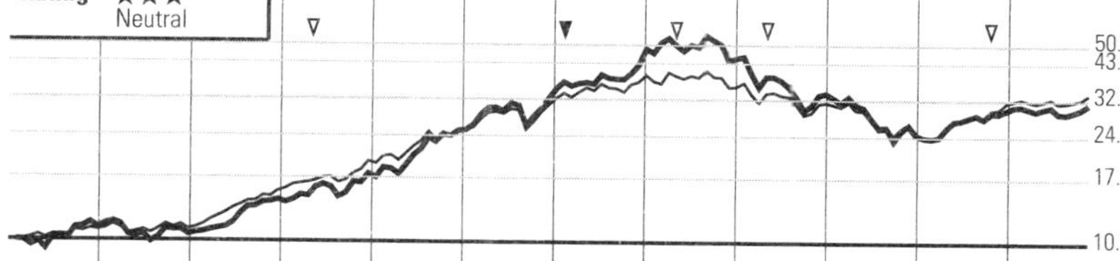

▼ Manager Change
▽ Partial Manager Change

Growth of $10,000
— Investment Values of Fund
— Investment Values of S&P 500

Performance Quartile (within Category)

1993	1994	1995	1996	1997	1998	1999	2000	2001	2002	2003	12-04	History
11.40	9.55	10.63	9.98	12.42	15.91	20.33	17.14	12.89	9.23	11.32	12.36	NAV
14.46	-6.73	28.34	22.84	48.15	40.00	38.76	-7.22	-24.80	-28.39	22.64	9.63	Total Return %
4.40	-8.04	-9.19	-0.10	14.80	11.43	17.72	1.83	-12.92	-6.30	-6.03	-1.24	+/-S&P 500
11.59	-9.35	-8.84	-0.28	17.66	1.29	5.60	15.23	-4.38	-0.51	-7.11	3.33	+/-Russ 1000Gr
0.00	0.00	0.00	0.00	0.07	0.05	0.00	1.22	0.00	0.00	0.00	0.44	Income Return %
14.46	-6.73	28.34	22.84	48.08	39.95	38.76	-8.44	-24.80	-28.39	22.64	9.19	Capital Return %
35	86	76	24	1	20	39	25	71	56	82	31	Total Rtn % Rank Cat
0.00	0.00	0.00	0.00	0.01	0.01	0.00	0.25	0.00	0.00	0.00	0.05	Income $
1.99	1.08	1.61	3.10	2.26	1.39	1.62	1.48	0.00	0.00	0.00	0.00	Capital Gains $
0.71	0.72	0.73	0.72	0.71	0.79	0.87	0.85	0.94	0.94	0.95	—	Expense Ratio %
-0.19	-0.06	-0.08	-0.05	0.05	0.15	-0.08	-0.15	-0.03	-0.14	0.01	—	Income Ratio %
52	56	46	107	93	62	174	26[illegible]	73	227	283	—	Turnover Rate %
1,133	966	1,123	1,241	1,750	3,609	7,964	9,695	8,425	5,864	7,260	5,588	Net Assets $mil

Performance 12-31-04

	1st Qtr	2nd Qtr	3rd Qtr	4th Qtr	Total
2000	9.35	-5.31	3.75	-13.64	-7.22
2001	-21.00	5.54	-21.62	15.09	-24.80
2002	-2.72	-15.87	-14.79	2.67	-28.39
2003	-1.84	14.79	1.15	7.60	22.64
2004	1.15	1.48	-4.04	11.30	9.63

Trailing	Total Return%	+/- S&P 500	+/- Russ 1000Gr	%Rank Cat	Growth of $10,000
3 Mo	11.30	2.07	2.13	24	11,130
6 Mo	6.80	-0.39	3.33	24	10,680
1 Yr	9.63	-1.24	3.33	31	10,963
3 Yr Avg	-1.26	-4.84	-1.08	61	9,627
5 Yr Avg	-7.65	-5.35	1.64	53	6,717
10 Yr Avg	11.79	-0.28	2.20	12	30,481
15 Yr Avg	11.[illegible]4	0.21	1.64	20	48,759

Tax Analysis	Tax-Adj Rtn%	%Rank Cat	Tax-Cost Rat	%Rank Cat
3 Yr (estimated)	-3.23	76	0.04	7
5 Yr (estimated)	-9.18	60	0.48	29
10 Yr (estimated)	8.60	26	2.28	84

Potential Capital Gain Exposure: -55% of assets

Rating and Risk

Time Period	Load-Adj Return %	Morningstar Rtn vs Cat	Morningstar Risk vs Cat	Morningstar Risk-Adj Rating
1 Yr	3.33			
3 Yr	-3.19	-Avg	-Avg	★★
5 Yr	-8.74	Avg	Avg	★★★
10 Yr	11.13	+Avg	Avg	★★★★
Incept	10.73			

Other Measures	Standard Index S&P 500	Best Fit Index Russ 1000Gr
Alpha	-4.6	-1.2
Beta	0.95	0.92
R-Squared	93	95
Standard Deviation	14.65	
Mean	-1.26	
Sharpe Ratio	-0.18	

Portfolio Analysis 08-31-04

Share change since 07-04 Total Stocks:171	Sector	PE	YTD Ret%	% Assets
Johnson & Johnson	Health	20.6	25.17	3.88
⊖ Microsoft	Software	36.1	8.95	3.25
⊖ Pfizer	Health	22.0	-22.31	2.89
⊖ Cisco Systems	Hardware	24.5	-20.26	2.79
⊕ Amgen	Health	37.7	3.82	2.38
⊕ Genzyme	Health	—	17.81	2.21
⊕ American International G	Financial	16.2	-0.53	2.18
⊖ Dell	Hardware	34.0	24.01	2.10
⊖ Medtronic	Health	30.7	2.68	2.06
⊕ Wyeth	Health	17.0	2.73	1.99
⊖ Tyco International	Ind Mtrls	25.1	35.41	1.95
Abbott Laboratories	Health	22.1	2.61	1.94
⊖ Target	Consumer	22.3	36.14	1.92
⊕ Citigroup	Financial	15.3	2.72	1.89
⊖ IBM	Hardware	20.2	7.19	1.84
⊖ Comcast A	Media	81.0	1.49	1.69
⊕ Procter & Gamble	Goods	23.3	12.38	1.68
⊖ Gen Elec	Ind Mtrls	22.8	20.68	1.67
⊕ PepsiCo	Goods	22.5	13.82	1.64
⊕ Kohl's	Consumer	25.5	9.41	1.51

Current Investment Style

Value Blnd Growth / Large Mid Small

Market Cap	%
Giant	47.9
Large	40.6
Mid	11.1
Small	0.1
Micro	0.3
Avg $mil: 34,354	

Value Measures		Rel Category
Price/Earnings	22.39	1.05
Price/Book	3.22	1.00
Price/Sales	2.23	1.04
Price/Cash Flow	10.59	0.96
Dividend Yield %	0.75	0.97

Growth Measures	%	Rel Category
Long-Term Erngs	14.08	1.00
Book Value	11.09	0.87
Sales	9.05	1.06
Cash Flow	24.50	1.48
Historical Erngs	9.07	0.63

Profitability	%	Rel Category
Return on Equity	18.68	1.04
Return on Assets	9.19	0.98
Net Margin	12.36	1.00

Sector Weightings	% of Stocks	Rel S&P 500	3 Year High	3 Year Low
Info	34.92	1.62		
Software	9.60	2.23	11	6
Hardware	15.25	1.50	19	8
Media	8.19	2.13	10	4
Telecom	1.88	0.60	2	0
Service	47.26	1.02		
Health	23.18	1.85	27	14
Consumer	13.65	1.50	17	9
Business	4.59	1.13	8	2
Financial	5.84	0.28	17	8
Mfg	17.81	0.55		
Goods	9.48	1.02	13	6
Ind Mtrls	6.79	0.54	13	6
Energy	1.54	0.22	4	1
Utilities	0.00	0.00	0	0

Composition

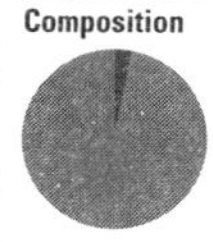

Cash	2.9
Stocks	97.1
Bonds	0.0
Other	0.0
Foreign (% of Stock)	5.3

Morningstar's Take by Dan Culloton 10-15-04

Massachusetts Investors Growth Stock is still trying to prove itself.

It has been about one year since this fund's manager--Stephen Pesek--divvied up this portfolio's assets with two colleagues in a new multimanager format. The results have been mixed. The fund's 0.18% annualized loss over the trailing 12-months ending Oct. 14, 2004 (which roughly covers the period since MFS Strategic Growth manager Irfan Ali and analyst Greg Locraft took over portions of this fund), is in the middle of the large-growth pack. That's too short a time to judge the new arrangement, but it's a sign of improvement for a fund that had lagged its peers in three of the previous four calendar years.

The new regime has not produced a dramatic change in the overall portfolio. The fund still focuses on established large-cap companies in traditional growth sectors, such as software, media and health care. Its best-performing picks, however, have come from elsewhere, such as industrial conglomerate Tyco International and retailer Target. Meanwhile hardware and media stocks, such as Cisco Systems and Comcast have been a brake on returns.

Ultimately, the three managers each will run about one third of the portfolio. Pesek will pursue blue-chip growth stocks that appear reasonably priced. Locraft will use a similar approach. Ali will add some spice by targeting fast growing, and often pricier, equities, just as he does at MFS Strategic Growth.

This fund still offers reasonably priced exposure to growth stocks. It also has an admirable long-term record and risk profile. Much of that history was written before any of the current managers arrived here, though, and it's not clear how the multimanager set up will work over the long haul. There are positive signs, but investors should still tread carefully around this fund until it shows it's capable of consistent above-average results.

Address:	500 Boylston St Boston MA 02116 800-637-2929
Web Address:	www.mfs.com
Inception:	01-01-35
Advisor:	MFS Investment Management
Subadvisor:	None
NTF Plans:	DATALynx NTF, Federated Tr NTF

Minimum Purchase:	$1000	Add: $50	IRA: $250
Min Auto Inv Plan:	$50	Add: $50	
Sales Fees:	5.75%L, 0.25%S, 2.00%R		
Management Fee:	0.33%, 0.02%A		
Actual Fees:	Mgt:0.33%	Dist:0.35%	
Expense Projections:	3Yr:$837	5Yr:$1029	10Yr:$1586
Income Distrib:	Annually		

MFS Mass Inv Trust A

Ticker	Load	NAV	Yield	Total Assets	Mstar Category
MITTX	5.75%	$17.26	0.9%	$6,111 mil	Large Blend

Governance and Management

Fiduciary Grade: C

Portfolio Manager(s)

John Laupheimer has managed this portfolio since 1993. Comanager Brooks Taylor, who joined the fund in January 2001, left the offering in January 2004 for MFS' value-investing team. Former analyst Kevin Beatty was named to the fund in July 2004. The managers are supported by MFS' team of 30-plus analysts.

Strategy

John Laupheimer and Kevin Beatty favor large-cap stocks that offer both above-average growth rates and below-average valuations. This strategy has often left the portfolio light on tech stocks. The managers are significantly more valuation-conscious than many of their colleagues at MFS.

Historical Profile

Return Average
Risk Below Avg
Rating ★★★ Neutral

Investment Style: Equity Stock % — 93% 97% 93% 99% 95% 97% 95% 98% 98%

▼ Manager Change
▽ Partial Manager Change

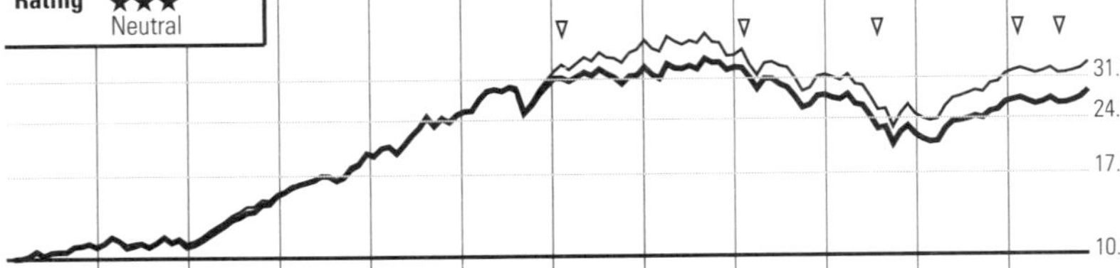

Growth of $10,000
— Investment Values of Fund
— Investment Values of S&P 500

Performance Quartile (within Category)

1993	1994	1995	1996	1997	1998	1999	2000	2001	2002	2003	12-04	History
11.50	10.07	12.71	14.46	17.52	20.25	20.95	20.02	16.58	12.87	15.62	17.26	NAV
10.03	-1.02	39.34	25.90	31.69	22.95	6.96	-0.34	-16.24	-22.00	22.14	11.51	Total Return %
-0.03	-2.33	1.81	2.96	-1.66	-5.62	-14.08	8.76	-4.36	0.09	-6.53	0.64	+/-S&P 500
-0.15	-1.41	1.57	3.45	-1.16	-4.07	-13.95	7.45	-3.79	-0.35	-7.75	0.11	+/-Russ 1000
3.17	2.16	2.51	1.61	1.26	0.91	0.49	0.17	0.25	0.40	0.71	0.96	Income Return %
6.86	-3.18	36.83	24.29	30.43	22.04	6.47	-0.51	-16.49	-22.40	21.43	10.55	Capital Return %
51	62	6	14	33	50	91	26	85	42	89	27	Total Rtn % Rank Cat
0.39	0.25	0.25	0.20	0.18	0.16	0.10	0.04	0.05	0.07	0.09	0.15	Income $
1.67	1.07	1.03	1.32	1.27	1.05	0.58	0.82	0.14	0.00	0.00	0.00	Capital Gains $
0.68	0.71	0.70	0.74	0.74	0.73	0.88	0.87	0.91	0.92	0.94	—	Expense Ratio %
3.04	2.20	2.13	1.51	1.09	0.86	0.55	0.38	0.47	0.58	0.72	—	Income Ratio %
41	87	54	47	44	54	62	68	77	55	76	—	Turnover Rate %
1,626	1,535	2,074	2,681	4,296	7,142	8,530	7,644	5,732	3,565	3,753	3,485	Net Assets $mil

Performance 12-31-04

	1st Qtr	2nd Qtr	3rd Qtr	4th Qtr	Total
2000	1.90	-1.21	1.88	-2.83	-0.34
2001	-12.71	2.71	-13.65	8.20	-16.24
2002	0.37	-12.93	-16.16	6.45	-22.00
2003	-4.35	13.67	1.72	10.44	22.14
2004	0.34	1.92	-1.63	10.85	11.51

Trailing	Total Return%	+/- S&P 500	+/- Russ 1000	%Rank Cat	Growth of $10,000
3 Mo	10.85	1.62	1.05	16	11,085
6 Mo	9.04	1.85	1.23	15	10,904
1 Yr	11.51	0.64	0.11	27	11,151
3 Yr Avg	2.04	-1.54	-2.23	67	10,625
5 Yr Avg	-2.38	-0.08	-0.62	51	8,865
10 Yr Avg	10.42	-1.65	-1.74	52	26,945
15 Yr Avg	9.72	-1.21	-1.36	57	40,206

Tax Analysis	Tax-Adj Rtn%	%Rank Cat	Tax-Cost Rat	%Rank Cat
3 Yr (estimated)	-0.20	81	0.24	20
5 Yr (estimated)	-3.89	69	0.38	20
10 Yr (estimated)	8.42	53	1.23	42

Potential Capital Gain Exposure: -1% of assets

Rating and Risk

Time Period	Load-Adj Return %	Morningstar Rtn vs Cat	Morningstar Risk vs Cat	Morningstar Risk-Adj Rating
1 Yr	5.10			
3 Yr	0.04	-Avg	-Avg	★★
5 Yr	-3.52	-Avg	-Avg	★★★
10 Yr	9.77	Avg	-Avg	★★★
Incept	9.22			

Other Measures	Standard Index S&P 500	Best Fit Index S&P 500
Alpha	-1.4	-1.4
Beta	0.92	0.92
R-Squared	98	98
Standard Deviation	14.28	
Mean	2.04	
Sharpe Ratio	0.05	

Portfolio Analysis 08-31-04

Share change since 07-04 Total Stocks:90	Sector	PE	YTD Ret%	% Assets
⊖ Johnson & Johnson	Health	20.6	25.17	4.00
⊖ Microsoft	Software	36.1	8.95	3.20
⊖ Gen Elec	Ind Mtrls	22.8	20.68	2.87
⊖ BP PLC ADR	Energy	20.7	22.07	2.62
⊖ Citigroup	Financial	15.3	2.72	2.45
⊖ United Technologies	Ind Mtrls	18.6	10.72	2.44
⊖ American International G	Financial	16.2	-0.53	2.41
⊖ Fannie Mae	Financial	9.1	-2.33	2.39
⊖ Cisco Systems	Hardware	24.5	-20.26	2.19
⊖ Tyco International	Ind Mtrls	25.1	35.41	2.03
⊕ Bank of America	Financial	12.3	21.50	1.98
⊖ Lockheed Martin	Ind Mtrls	19.9	9.97	1.87
⊖ Praxair	Ind Mtrls	21.0	17.32	1.56
⊕ Colgate-Palmolive	Goods	20.3	4.14	1.55
⊖ American Express	Financial	20.3	17.60	1.50
⊕ Dell	Hardware	34.0	24.01	1.50
⊖ Target	Consumer	22.3	36.14	1.44
⊖ PepsiCo	Goods	22.5	13.82	1.40
⊖ Dow Chemical	Ind Mtrls	16.6	22.83	1.39
⊖ United Parcel Service B	Business	28.5	16.40	1.33

Current Investment Style (Value Blnd Growth; Large Mid Small)

Market Cap	%
Giant	52.6
Large	43.5
Mid	3.9
Small	0.0
Micro	0.0
Avg $mil: 44,089	

Value Measures		Rel Category
Price/Earnings	18.97	1.12
Price/Book	3.13	1.19
Price/Sales	1.87	1.30
Price/Cash Flow	10.21	1.33
Dividend Yield %	1.27	0.86

Growth Measures	%	Rel Category
Long-Term Erngs	12.48	1.08
Book Value	8.90	1.15
Sales	6.75	1.18
Cash Flow	13.12	1.39
Historical Erngs	15.15	1.28

Profitability	%	Rel Category
Return on Equity	19.01	1.09
Return on Assets	8.63	1.00
Net Margin	10.69	0.93

Sector Weightings	% of Stocks	Rel S&P 500	3 Year High	3 Year Low
Info	21.39	1.00		
Software	4.26	0.99	6	4
Hardware	9.23	0.90	10	7
Media	5.32	1.39	10	5
Telecom	2.58	0.82	5	2
Service	39.89	0.86		
Health	15.46	1.24	16	13
Consumer	5.83	0.64	9	6
Business	3.56	0.88	6	3
Financial	15.04	0.72	23	16
Mfg	38.72	1.21		
Goods	10.65	1.14	10	6
Ind Mtrls	17.81	1.41	18	9
Energy	8.19	1.14	9	6
Utilities	2.07	0.70	3	1

Composition

Cash	1.9
Stocks	98.1
Bonds	0.0
Other	0.0
Foreign (% of Stock)	10.5

Morningstar's Take by Laura Pavlenko Lutton 12-21-04

This is a reasonable--but not dazzling--core fund.

MFS Massachusetts Investors Trust got a new comanager in July 2004. Kevin Beatty, a former analyst at MFS, replaced Brooks Taylor, who left this large-blend offering in January 2004 for MFS Total Return. Beatty is picking stocks for this offering with longtime manager John Laupheimer. The fund previously was run in sleeves, but now Laupheimer and Beatty are making buy and sell decisions in concert.

Since Beatty's arrival, the team has made a few tweaks. For example, the managers have reduced the number of holdings in the fund to 90, down from 120 under the previous sleeve structure. But the fund is unchanged at its core: Laupheimer and Beatty still seek blue-chip stocks that are trading at reasonable valuations. The managers keep risk in check by limiting top stock bets to 4% of assets, and while the sector weights do vary from the S&P 500 Index norm, they're not extreme. Thus, this fund has sported low volatility, and we expect that to continue under the new management structure.

Given this fund's strategy, its relative performance will hinge on Laupheimer and Beatty's stock-picking skills. Unfortunately, the fund has struggled at times under Laupheimer's guidance. To be sure, the fund has done well in 2004. Its 10.09% gain for the year to date through Dec. 20 lands it in the peer group's top quartile. But the fund also finished three of the last five calendar years in the large-blend category's bottom quartile. What's more, this is Beatty's first time running a public mutual fund, so it's difficult to predict how he'll do here.

Over the long run, this offering has been a mediocre yet competitive player. That makes it tough to get excited about the fund, but at the same time, we don't hate it either. If your investment choices are limited, this offering is acceptable. Otherwise, we'd go with a cheap index fund.

Address:	500 Boylston St Boston MA 02116 800-637-2929
Web Address:	www.mfs.com
Inception:	07-15-24
Advisor:	MFS Investment Management
Subadvisor:	None
NTF Plans:	DATALynx NTF, Federated Tr NTF

Minimum Purchase:	$1000	Add: $50	IRA: $250
Min Auto Inv Plan:	$1000	Add: $50	
Sales Fees:	5.75%L, 0.25%S, 2.00%R		
Management Fee:	0.33%, 0.02%A		
Actual Fees:	Mgt:0.33%	Dist:0.35%	
Expense Projections:	3Yr:$837	5Yr:$1029	10Yr:$1586
Income Distrib:	Annually		

MFS Strategic Value A

Ticker	Load	NAV	Yield	Total Assets	Mstar Category
MSVTX	5.75%	$16.08	0.7%	$1,562 mil	Large Value

Governance and Management

Fiduciary Grade: D

Portfolio Manager(s)

Ken Enright has managed this fund since its March 1998 inception, and he was joined by former analyst Alan T. Langsner in July 2004. Katrina Mead was also named on the fund in July 2004, but she does not pick stocks. Rather, she focuses on risk-management tasks. In addition to this offering, the trio also comanage MFS Total Return and MFS Capital Opportunities.

Strategy

Ken Enright and Alan Langsner consider companies of all sizes when looking for firms selling at a discount to the overall market. In addition to traditional valuation measures, the managers look for catalysts such as corporate restructuring efforts and progressive-minded management.

Historical Profile
Return Above Avg
Risk High
Rating ★★★★ Above Avg

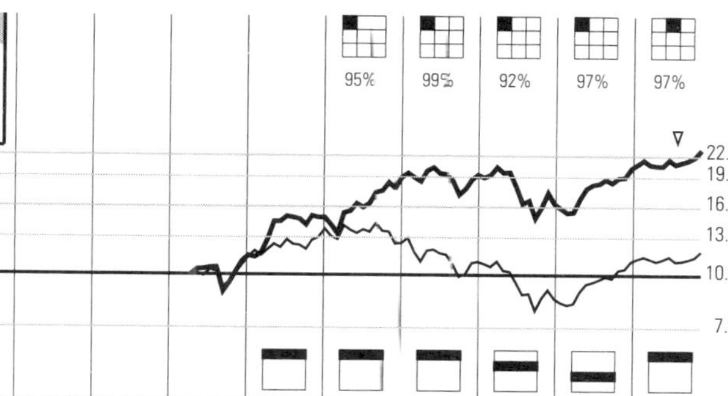

1993	1994	1995	1996	1997	1998	1999	2000	2001	2002	2003	12-04	History
—	—	—	—	—	11.00	11.13	13.33	13.58	11.17	14.20	16.08	NAV
—	—	—	—	—	15.68*	29.66	31.17	1.88	-17.69	27.22	17.94	Total Return %
—	—	—	—	—	—	8.62	40.27	13.75	4.40	-1.45	7.07	+/-S&P 500
—	—	—	—	—	—	22.31	24.16	7.47	-2.17	-2.81	1.45	+/-Russ 1000 VI
—	—	—	—	—	0.00	0.79	0.55	0.00	0.01	0.09	0.82	Income Return %
—	—	—	—	—	—	28.87	30.62	1.83	-17.70	27.13	17.12	Capital Return %
—	—	—	—	—	—	1	2	20	44	55	8	Total Rtn % Rank Cat
—	—	—	—	—	0.04	0.09	0.06	0.00	0.00	0.01	0.12	Income $
—	—	—	—	—	0.50	2.95	1.16	0.00	0.01	0.00	0.54	Capital Gains $
—	—	—	—	—	1.25	1.27	1.26	1.50	1.46	1.45	1.29	Expense Ratio %
—	—	—	—	—	1.22	0.45	-0.62	0.39	0.29	0.41	0.33	Income Ratio %
—	—	—	—	—	—	131	142	63	78	65	63	Turnover Rate %
—	—	—	—	—	1	—	—	151	253	563	800	Net Assets $mil

Performance 12-31-04

	1st Qtr	2nd Qtr	3rd Qtr	4th Qtr	Total
2000	3.23	3.74	11.91	9.44	31.17
2001	-2.55	5.54	-13.42	14.41	1.88
2002	5.38	-12.45	-19.09	10.27	-17.69
2003	-5.55	20.38	1.42	10.33	27.22
2004	2.54	3.37	-0.33	11.65	17.94

Trailing	Total Return%	+/- S&P 500	+/- Russ 1000 VI	%Rank Cat	Growth of $10,000
3 Mo	11.65	2.42	1.27	7	11,165
6 Mo	11.28	4.09	-0.80	16	11,128
1 Yr	17.94	7.07	1.45	8	11,794
3 Yr Avg	7.29	3.71	-1.28	27	12,350
5 Yr Avg	10.54	12.84	5.27	6	16,504
10 Yr Avg	—	—	—	—	—
15 Yr Avg	—	—	—	—	—

Tax Analysis	Tax-Adj Rtn%	%Rank Cat	Tax-Cost Rat	%Rank Cat
3 Yr (estimated)	4.88	48	0.29	20
5 Yr (estimated)	8.41	8	0.76	40
10 Yr (estimated)	—	—	—	—

Potential Capital Gain Exposure: 14% of assets

Rating and Risk

Time Period	Load-Adj Return %	Morningstar Rtn vs Cat	Morningstar Risk vs Cat	Morningstar Risk-Adj Rating
1 Yr	11.16			
3 Yr	5.19	Avg	+Avg	★★★
5 Yr	9.24	High	High	★★★★
10 Yr	—	—	—	—
Incept	13.28			

Other Measures	Standard Index S&P 500	Best Fit Index Russ 1000 VI
Alpha	3.6	-1.8
Beta	1.12	1.13
R-Squared	91	93
Standard Deviation	18.93	
Mean	7.29	
Sharpe Ratio	0.32	

Morningstar's Take by Laura Pavlenko Lutton 12-08-04

New managers have been added to MFS Strategic Value, but our view of the fund is unchanged.

In July 2004, Alan Langsner and Katrina Mead joined this large-value offering as comanagers. Of the two arrivals, Langsner's is more notable. He was promoted from MFS' analyst ranks to run this offering alongside veteran Ken Enright, who had managed this fund solo since its 1998 inception. Enright and Langsner are doing the stock-picking, while Mead is focusing on cash- and risk-management issues.

As has been the case, Enright and Langsner are running a relatively concentrated portfolio of 45 to 60 value stocks, primarily large caps. They're opportunistic, often buying companies with operating problems or poor short-term outlooks. In recent months, Enright and Langsner have doubled the fund's stake in pharmaceutical stocks to a hefty 15% of assets. For example, they added to the fund's already large position in Merck after the shares plunged amid controversy with its Vioxx pain-reliever drug. The managers think Merck's future earnings will be stronger than the market expects.

For the most part, this fund's bold moves have been on the mark. The managers typically find a number of telecom and energy stocks meet their investment criteria, and large weights in those sectors have helped deliver top-decile returns in 1999, 2000, and so far in 2004. (Recently, however, the managers have trimmed the fund's energy holdings as many have reached their price targets.) In fact, the fund has ended just one calendar year below the large-value category's midpoint since inception, and its 10.2% annualized return is one of the best five-year records in the category.

This fund's strategy may yield the occasional hiccup in short-term performance, but overall, we like this offering's potential. We're also pleased that it recently lowered its expenses to 1.29%, which is now below the category average.

Address:	500 Boylston St Boston MA 02116 800-225-2606
Web Address:	www.mfs.com
Inception:	03-17-98*
Advisor:	MFS Investment Management
Subadvisor:	None
NTF Plans:	DATALynx NTF, Federated Tr NTF

Minimum Purchase:	$1000	Add: $50	IRA: $250
Min Auto Inv Plan:	$50	Add: $50	
Sales Fees:	5.75%L, 0.25%S, 2.00%R		
Management Fee:	0.75%		
Actual Fees:	Mgt:0.65%	Dist:0.35%	
Expense Projections:	3Yr:$1101	5Yr:$1507	10Yr:$2639
Income Distrib:	Annually		

Portfolio Analysis 08-31-04

Share change since 07-04 Total Stocks:54	Sector	PE	YTD Ret%	% Assets
Sprint	Telecom	—	55.24	4.70
⊖ Verizon Communications	Telecom	32.4	20.25	4.17
Microsoft	Software	36.1	8.95	3.79
Johnson & Johnson	Health	20.6	25.17	3.67
⊕ Viacom B	Media	36.1	-17.44	3.45
GlobalSantaFe	Energy	NMF	34.38	2.98
⊕ Comcast	Media	—	-13.77	2.95
Wyeth	Health	17.0	2.73	2.89
⊕ Nokia ADR	Hardware	18.1	-6.14	2.87
Lockheed Martin	Ind Mtrls	19.9	9.97	2.34
Merck	Health	11.4	-27.76	2.67
Noble	Energy	51.7	39.02	2.61
Freddie Mac	Financial	10.6	28.75	2.45
⊕ Bank of America	Financial	12.3	21.50	2.39
Mellon Financial	Financial	16.2	-0.78	2.32
Owens-Illinois	Ind Mtrls	—	90.50	2.28
Allstate	Financial	12.8	23.12	2.21
Companhia Vale Do Rio Do	Ind Mtrls	6.5	61.38	2.17
⊕ Nortel Networks	Hardware	—	-17.97	2.12
Vodafone Group PLC ADR	Telecom	—	11.74	2.06

Current Investment Style

Value Blnd Growth — Large Mid Small

Market Cap	%
Giant	44.7
Large	29.4
Mid	23.6
Small	2.3
Micro	0.0
Avg $mil: 26,940	

Value Measures		Rel Category
Price/Earnings	17.06	1.14
Price/Book	1.93	0.85
Price/Sales	1.02	0.86
Price/Cash Flow	5.69	0.89
Dividend Yield %	1.57	0.77

Growth Measures	%	Rel Category
Long-Term Erngs	11.72	1.13
Book Value	1.08	0.19
Sales	2.35	0.56
Cash Flow	0.89	0.17
Historical Erngs	9.03	0.76

Profitability	%	Rel Category
Return on Equity	12.40	0.78
Return on Assets	6.20	0.79
Net Margin	8.45	0.83

Sector Weightings	% of Stocks	Rel S&P 500	3 Year High	3 Year Low
Info	30.97	1.44		
Software	6.24	1.45	7	1
Hardware	5.11	0.50	5	0
Media	8.45	2.20	9	5
Telecom	11.17	3.55	14	9
Service	35.08	0.76		
Health	13.70	1.10	16	7
Consumer	2.24	0.25	14	2
Business	0.57	0.14	1	0
Financial	18.57	0.89	22	18
Mfg	33.95	1.06		
Goods	5.48	0.59	6	0
Ind Mtrls	13.99	1.10	18	10
Energy	11.51	1.61	18	12
Utilities	2.97	1.00	8	3

Composition

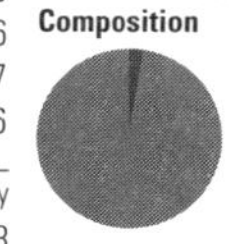

Cash	2.3
Stocks	97.4
Bonds	0.0
Other	0.4
Foreign (% of Stock)	9.7

MFS Total Return A

Ticker	Load	NAV	Yield	Total Assets	Mstar Category
MSFRX	4.75%	$16.00	2.4%	$11,507 mil	Moderate Allocation

Governance and Management

Fiduciary Grade: C

Portfolio Manager(s)

David Calabro, who has been on board here since 1995, will step down as lead manager on Dec. 31, 2004, and will retire from MFS at the end of February 2005. Brooks Taylor, who has been running Calabro's sleeve of this offering since February 2004, will take over as lead manager. Taylor is one of five equity managers, several of whom are very experienced, picking value stocks for the fund. Michael Roberge took the reins of the fund's fixed-income subportfolio in 2002 and is assisted by Bill Adams and Bill Douglas. The two remaining managers, Ed Baldini and Katrina Mead, assist with risk-management tasks.

Strategy

This fund maintains a 60/40 mix between stocks and bonds. The equity portion is made up of value stocks selling at discounts to the S&P 500 or to industry peers. The bond portfolio generally has a strong bias toward investment-grade corporate issues and largely eschews big duration and credit plays. Overall, this is a plain-vanilla balanced fund.

Historical Profile

Return Above Avg
Risk Below Avg
Rating ★★★★ Above Avg

Investment Style: Equity Stock % — 54% 52% 47% 55% 58% 55% 50% 58% 58%

▼ Manager Change
▽ Partial Manager Change

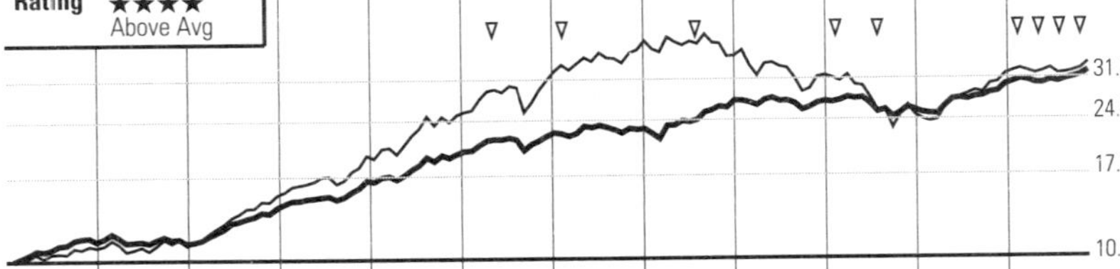

Growth of $10,000
— Investment Values of Fund
-- Investment Values of S&P 500

Performance Quartile (within Category)

1993	1994	1995	1996	1997	1998	1999	2000	2001	2002	2003	12-04	History
13.34	12.44	14.41	14.79	15.82	14.96	13.88	15.41	14.48	13.27	15.10	16.00	NAV
15.15	-2.64	26.91	14.60	20.67	11.92	2.31	19.03	-0.63	-5.56	16.85	11.35	Total Return %
5.09	-3.95	-10.62	-8.34	-12.68	-16.65	-18.73	28.13	11.25	16.53	-11.82	0.48	+/-S&P 500
3.42	-0.69	2.14	3.26	1.47	-0.47	-10.54	14.59	-0.79	4.98	-7.21	0.18	+/-DJ 60%
4.76	4.13	5.21	4.38	4.10	3.88	3.25	3.49	3.13	2.91	2.79	2.59	Income Return %
10.39	-6.77	21.70	10.22	16.57	8.04	-0.94	15.54	-3.76	-8.47	14.06	8.76	Capital Return %
19	57	43	44	44	58	84	3	19	7	78	15	Total Rtn % Rank Cat
0.57	0.54	0.63	0.62	0.59	0.60	0.48	0.47	0.47	0.42	0.37	0.39	Income $
0.21	0.01	0.66	1.06	1.37	2.07	0.94	0.55	0.35	0.00	0.00	0.39	Capital Gains $
0.84	0.85	0.87	0.91	0.93	0.90	0.89	0.90	0.88	0.92	0.90	0.89	Expense Ratio %
4.51	4.26	4.82	4.35	3.84	3.44	3.45	3.36	3.09	2.84	2.45	2.37	Income Ratio %
95	91	102	140	143	126	151	112	96	86	71	65	Turnover Rate %
1,735	1,825	2,356	2,707	3,263	3,811	3,629	3,795	4,541	4,772	6,205	6,845	Net Assets $mil

Performance 12-31-04

	1st Qtr	2nd Qtr	3rd Qtr	4th Qtr	Total
2000	1.96	2.27	7.61	6.07	19.03
2001	-2.93	2.55	-5.39	5.51	-0.63
2002	2.48	-4.06	-8.20	4.62	-5.56
2003	-2.55	10.21	1.18	7.52	16.85
2004	2.38	0.16	1.48	7.00	11.35

Trailing	Total Return%	+/- S&P 500	+/- DJ 60%	%Rank Cat	Growth of $10,000
3 Mo	7.00	-2.23	-0.48	49	10,700
6 Mo	8.58	1.39	1.05	14	10,858
1 Yr	11.35	0.48	0.18	15	11,135
3 Yr Avg	7.11	3.53	-0.15	14	12,288
5 Yr Avg	7.76	10.06	2.52	5	14,531
10 Yr Avg	11.31	-0.76	0.82	15	29,197
15 Yr Avg	10.18	-0.75	0.23	25	42,810

Tax Analysis	Tax-Adj Rtn%	%Rank Cat	Tax-Cost Rat	%Rank Cat
3 Yr (estimated)	4.22	36	1.10	75
5 Yr (estimated)	5.12	8	1.50	73
10 Yr (estimated)	8.03	29	2.47	91

Potential Capital Gain Exposure: 13% of assets

Rating and Risk

Time Period	Load-Adj Return %	Morningstar Rtn vs Cat	Morningstar Risk vs Cat	Morningstar Risk-Adj Rating
1 Yr	6.06			
3 Yr	5.38	Avg	-Avg	★★★★
5 Yr	6.72	+Avg	-Avg	★★★★★
10 Yr	10.77	+Avg	Low	★★★★
Incept	11.10			

Other Measures	Standard Index S&P 500	Best Fit Index Russ 1000 VI
Alpha	4.3	1.8
Beta	0.49	0.51
R-Squared	84	91

Standard Deviation	8.47
Mean	7.11
Sharpe Ratio	0.68

Morningstar's Take by Laura Pavlenko Lutton 12-07-04

MFS Total Return's lead manager is retiring, but that's no reason to panic.

David Calabro, who heads a large team of managers on this offering, is leaving MFS on Feb. 28, 2005. Brooks Taylor, one of a handful of equity managers on this moderate-allocation offering, will succeed Calabro as lead manager as of Jan. 1, 2005.

We're sorry to see Calabro go. He's helped manage this fund for nearly a decade, and since he came aboard, the fund has outperformed its typical category peer by more than 2 percentage points annually. What's more, Calabro is the second veteran value investor to leave MFS in less than a year. Lisa Nurme, an accomplished stock-picker, retired from the firm in May 2004.

Taylor, Calabro's replacement on this fund, is relatively new to the offering. He joined the management team in February 2004 and then took over the sleeve of the portfolio that Calabro previously managed. Prior to this assignment, Taylor spent three years running a portion of MFS' flagship large-blend fund, MFS Massachusetts Investors Trust. During Taylor's tenure on that offering, returns were relatively poor.

Normally, Taylor's relative inexperience would give us pause, but he's joined on this fund by a number of proven equity managers, including Ken Enright of MFS Strategic Value. Also, Taylor has no plans to change this fund's investment approach. It will maintain its staid 60%/40% stock/bond mix, and the stock portion of the fund will continue to invest in a well-diversified group of value stocks. Meanwhile, the bond portfolio should continue to behave much like the Lehman Brothers Aggregate Bond Index.

In the end, we think investors remain in reasonably good hands here. The fund should continue to perform well when value stocks are leading the market, as has been the case in 2004. This is a sensible choice for investors seeking a reserved hybrid fund.

Portfolio Analysis 08-31-04

Total Stocks:263 (Share change since 07-31-04)	Sectors	P/E Ratio	YTD Return %	% Net Assets
⊕ Bank of America	Financial	12.3	-3.85	1.98
Citigroup	Financial	15.3	0.08	1.98
⊕ Sprint	Telecom	—	-2.86	1.60
⊖ Verizon Communications	Telecom	32.4	-3.79	1.51
⊖ Johnson & Johnson	Health	20.6	-0.85	1.21
⊕ Viacom B	Media	36.1	5.11	1.21
BP PLC ADR	Energy	20.7	-2.40	1.02
⊕ Comcast	Media	—	-36.67	1.00
⊖ Lockheed Martin	Ind Mtrls	19.9	-0.81	0.99

Total Fixed-Income:417	Date of Maturity	Amount $000	Value $000	% Net Assets
FNMA 5.25%	04-15-07	124,940	132,377	1.23
US Treasury Bond 6.25%	08-15-23	108,762	126,338	1.18
US Treasury Note 7%	07-15-06	96,977	105,186	0.98
FHLMC 4.875%	11-15-13	83,650	85,640	0.80
US Treasury Note 4.75%	11-15-08	79,739	84,825	0.79
US Treasury Note 4.75%	05-15-14	65,936	69,199	0.64
US Treasury Note 3%	07-15-12	51,942	57,387	0.53
FHLMC 5.5%	07-15-06	47,114	49,660	0.46
GNMA 6%	03-15-34	45,185	46,971	0.44

Equity Style
Style: Value
Size: Large-Cap

Value Measures		Rel Category
Price/Earnings	15.48	0.93
Price/Book	2.15	0.88
Price/Sales	1.21	0.92
Price/Cash Flow	6.19	0.85
Dividend Yield %	2.00	1.27

Growth Measures	%	Rel Category
Long-Term Erngs	10.41	0.90
Book Value	4.90	0.85
Sales	3.91	0.75
Cash Flow	9.21	1.15
Historical Erngs	12.42	1.15

Market Cap %			
Giant	43.6	Small	1.5
Large	38.6	Micro	0.1
Mid	16.1	Avg $mil:	30,365

Fixed-Income Style
Duration: Interm-Term
Quality: High

Avg Eff Duration[1]	4.7 Yrs
Avg Eff Maturity	15.2 Yrs
Avg Credit Quality	AA
Avg Wtd Coupon	5.76%

[1]figure provided by fund as of 08-31-04

Sector Weightings	% of Stocks	Rel S&P 500	3 Year High	3 Year Low
Info	20.05	0.93		
Software	2.27	0.53	3	0
Hardware	3.16	0.31	5	2
Media	7.02	1.83	8	6
Telecom	7.60	2.41	9	6
Service	41.01	0.88		
Health	9.05	0.72	11	7
Consumer	3.54	0.39	7	2
Business	1.93	0.48	2	2
Financial	26.49	1.28	27	23
Mfg	38.93	1.21		
Goods	7.56	0.81	8	6
Ind Mtrls	16.06	1.27	17	12
Energy	10.89	1.52	16	12
Utilities	4.42	1.49	7	5

Composition

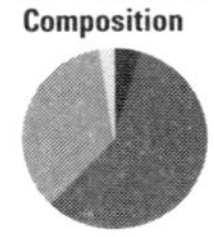

Cash	4.5
Stocks	57.6
Bonds	35.4
Other	2.5
Foreign (% of Stock)	10.0

Address:	500 Boylston St Boston MA 02116 800-637-2929
Web Address:	www.mfs.com
Inception:	10-06-70
Advisor:	MFS Investment Management
Subadvisor:	None
NTF Plans:	DATALynx NTF, Federated Tr NTF

Minimum Purchase:	$1000	Add: $50	IRA: $250
Min Auto Inv Plan:	$50	Add: $50	
Sales Fees:	4.75%L, 0.25%S, 2.00%R		
Management Fee:	0.35% mx./0.34% mn., 0.02%A		
Actual Fees:	Mgt:0.35%	Dist:0.35%	
Expense Projections:	3Yr:$757	5Yr:$965	10Yr:$1564
Income Distrib:	Monthly		

MFS Utilities A

Ticker	Load	NAV	Yield	Total Assets	Mstar Category
MMUFX	4.75%	$10.99	1.2%	$1,486 mil	Specialty-Utilities

Governance and Management

Fiduciary Grade: C

Portfolio Manager(s)

Maura Shaughnessy has run this fund since its 1992 inception, before which she spent a year as an analyst for MFS. Previously she was an analyst for Harvard Management and the Federal Reserve. She has access to numerous MFS analysts who cover the subsectors and geographical areas this fund deals with. Shaughnessy also comanaged MFS Total Return from 1995 to 1999 and MFS Capital Opportunities from 1999 to October 2002.

Strategy

Manager Maura Shaughnessy emphasizes diversification, so the portfolio usually has sizable exposure to telecom, energy, and media stocks in addition to traditional electric and gas utilities. She's not shy about venturing abroad, often putting as much as 30% of assets in international stocks. A sizable bond stake cushions against volatility over the long haul and helps bolster the fund's yield. She maintains a portfolio of roughly 60 names, and top holdings are capped at 5% of assets.

Historical Profile

Return Above Avg
Risk Average
Rating ★★★★ Above Avg

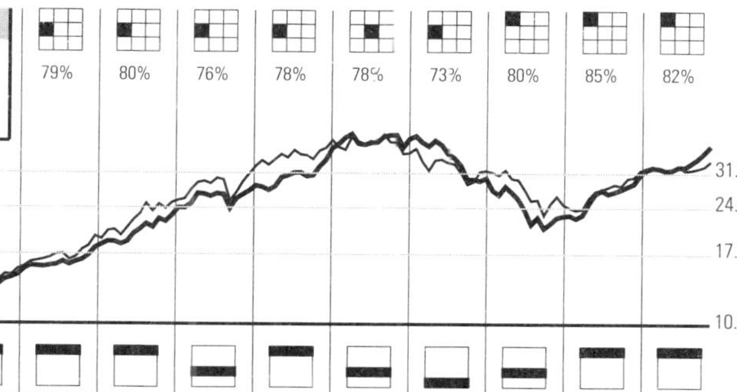

Investment Style
Equity
Stock %

▼ Manager Change
▽ Partial Manager Change

Growth of $10,000
— Investment Values of Fund
— Investment Values of S&P 500

Performance Quartile (within Category)

1993	1994	1995	1996	1997	1998	1999	2000	2001	2002	2003	12-04	History
7.54	6.84	8.48	8.98	9.99	10.81	12.76	11.87	8.72	6.43	8.58	10.99	NAV
19.56	-5.01	32.47	20.06	31.55	17.79	31.79	7.06	-25.02	-24.33	35.96	29.88	Total Return %
9.50	-6.32	-5.06	-2.88	-1.80	-10.78	10.75	16.16	-13.14	-2.24	7.29	19.01	+/-S&P 500
9.93	10.28	0.49	10.96	8.55	-1.09	37.81	-43.70	1.25	-0.95	6.57	-0.36	+/-DOWJNS UTIL
5.54	4.41	4.64	4.31	3.53	2.98	2.29	3.90	1.75	2.02	2.20	1.54	Income Return %
14.02	-9.42	27.83	15.75	28.02	14.81	29.50	3.16	-26.77	-26.35	33.76	28.34	Capital Return %
20	1	13	9	7	65	24	56	34	59	2	8	Total Rtn % Rank Cat
0.37	0.33	0.31	0.35	0.31	0.29	0.24	0.49	0.21	0.17	0.14	0.13	Income $
0.21	0.00	0.21	0.79	1.39	0.61	1.09	1.22	0.00	0.00	0.00	0.00	Capital Gains $
0.65	0.65	0.83	1.08	1.10	1.05	1.05	0.98	1.03	1.11	1.19	—	Expense Ratio %
4.57	4.58	4.30	4.37	3.27	2.60	1.88	4.11	1.95	2.10	2.11	—	Income Ratio %
119	115	152	137	153	124	137	113	110	80	144	—	Turnover Rate %
45	41	52	65	324	706	728	921	721	391	502	666	Net Assets $mil

Performance 12-31-04

	1st Qtr	2nd Qtr	3rd Qtr	4th Qtr	Total
2000	10.91	-6.21	5.75	-2.67	7.06
2001	-5.23	-5.37	-17.19	0.97	-25.02
2002	-5.87	-16.06	-12.64	9.62	-24.33
2003	0.78	20.17	0.65	11.52	35.96
2004	4.78	1.12	6.25	15.38	29.76

Trailing	Total Return%	+/- S&P 500	+/- DOWJNS UTIL	%Rank Cat	Growth of $10,000
3 Mo	15.38	6.15	0.91	4	11,538
6 Mo	22.58	15.39	-0.17	4	12,258
1 Yr	29.88	19.01	-0.36	8	12,988
3 Yr Avg	10.14	6.56	1.25	7	13,361
5 Yr Avg	1.41	3.71	-6.08	28	10,725
10 Yr Avg	13.29	1.22	2.29	1	34,827
15 Yr Avg	—	—	—	—	—

Tax Analysis	Tax-Adj Rtn%	%Rank Cat	Tax-Cost Rat	%Rank Cat
3 Yr (estimated)	7.60	16	0.71	30
5 Yr (estimated)	-1.11	41	1.53	57
10 Yr (estimated)	9.72	6	2.68	100

Potential Capital Gain Exposure: -30% of assets

Rating and Risk

Time Period	Load-Adj Return %	Morningstar Rtn vs Cat	Morningstar Risk vs Cat	Morningstar Risk-Adj Rating
1 Yr	23.71			
3 Yr	8.37	+Avg	Avg	★★★★
5 Yr	0.43	Avg	Avg	★★★
10 Yr	12.74	High	Avg	★★★★★
Incept	11.81			

Other Measures	Standard Index S&P 500	Best Fit Index DJ 60%
Alpha	7.0	-3.6
Beta	0.86	1.50
R-Squared	64	72
Standard Deviation	17.61	
Mean	10.14	
Sharpe Ratio	0.50	

Portfolio Analysis 08-31-04

Share change since 07-04 Total Stocks:87	Sector	PE	YTD Ret%	% Assets
⊖ Exelon	Utilities	16.1	37.55	3.36
Entergy	Utilities	21.1	22.14	3.26
⊕ Vodafone Grp	Telecom	—	—	2.47
⊖ PPL	Utilities	12.0	26.14	2.37
⊕ PG & E	Utilities	3.7	19.84	2.30
⊕ Comcast	Media	—	-13.77	2.22
⊕ America Movil SA ADR	Telecom	23.2	92.36	2.08
⊕ AES	Utilities	30.9	44.81	1.82
Enagas	Energy	—	—	1.79
Cinergy	Utilities	20.5	12.63	1.77
Sprint	Telecom	—	55.24	1.72
⊕ AGL Resources	Utilities	14.8	18.81	1.71
Equitable Resources	Energy	13.0	45.53	1.68
Constellation Energy Gro	Utilities	10.2	14.80	1.68
⊕ TXU	Utilities	NMF	177.67	1.65
⊕ E.ON	Utilities	—	—	1.55
⊖ Dominion Resources	Utilities	22.2	10.49	1.51
⊕ Halliburton	Energy	47.7	53.28	1.46
⊖ MDU Resources Group	Utilities	15.0	15.27	1.37
⊕ Enel	Utilities	—	—	1.36

Current Investment Style

Value Blnd Growth / Large Mid Small

Market Cap	%
Giant	19.7
Large	38.4
Mid	41.4
Small	0.5
Micro	0.1
Avg $mil: 10,458	

Value Measures		Rel Category
Price/Earnings	15.96	1.05
Price/Book	1.57	0.89
Price/Sales	1.13	1.10
Price/Cash Flow	5.52	1.00
Dividend Yield %	2.32	0.78

Growth Measures	%	Rel Category
Long-Term Erngs	8.03	1.33
Book Value	-3.39	NMF
Sales	3.44	0.85
Cash Flow	2.78	1.15
Historical Erngs	0.91	0.84

Profitability	%	Rel Category
Return on Equity	8.20	0.73
Return on Assets	2.65	0.83
Net Margin	7.38	0.94

Industry Weightings	% of Stocks	Rel Cat
Telecom Srv	8.3	0.7
Electric Utls	44.2	0.7
Nat Gas Utls	8.8	0.9
Wireless Srv	5.3	1.0
Energy	15.0	1.8
Media	10.2	5.8
Network Eq	0.0	0.0
Water	0.0	0.0
Other	8.2	4.1

Composition

Cash	11.5
Stocks	81.8
Bonds	5.7
Other	1.0
Foreign (% of Stock)	34.1

Morningstar's Take by David Kathman 12-29-04

Deft stock picking has kept MFS Utilities near the top of its class in 2004.

In many ways, this offering looks different from most other utilities funds. Its weighting of foreign stocks is twice as big as its average peer's, and manager Maura Shaughnessy is also more willing than her peers to venture beyond the utility and telecom sectors. About 25% of the portfolio consists of media and energy stocks, which make up less than 10% of the average utilities fund. Shaughnessy also invests up to 20% of assets in utility bonds and convertibles, though that stake is now about 13% due to valuation concerns.

Overall, these unusual features have not resulted in much of a net benefit in 2004. The fund's big foreign stake has included some big winners, such as Mexican wireless firm America Movil, but also some so-so performers such as Vodafone. While the fund's energy holdings have done quite well, with such stocks as Halliburton gaining more than 50%, its media stocks have been a drag on performance, with top-10 holding Comcast one of the worst offenders.

However, the fund has still ranked among the category's top 20% in 2004, and the main driver has been the core utilities portion of the portfolio. Utilities have had a great run, and stalwarts such as top-holdings Exelon and Entergy have gained more than 20% for the year. Shaughnessy has also made some very successful bets on smaller, riskier utilities, though in many cases she feels the market has overstated the risks. These include a number of firms that recently came out of bankruptcy, such as TXU, NRG Energy, and Northwestern.

In fact, the fund's utility positions have done so well that Shaughnessy has trimmed many of them and is having trouble finding reasonably priced new ideas. That could crimp performance in the short term, but we're reassured by the fund's stellar long-term record under Shaughnessy. This remains a good utilities option for investors with patience and a long time horizon.

Address:	500 Boylston St Boston MA 02116 800-637-2929
Web Address:	www.mfs.com
Inception:	02-14-92
Advisor:	MFS Investment Management
Subadvisor:	None
NTF Plans:	DATALynx NTF, Federated Tr NTF

Minimum Purchase:	$1000	Add: $50	IRA: $250
Min Auto Inv Plan:	$50	Add: $50	
Sales Fees:	4.75%L, 0.25%S, 2.00%R		
Management Fee:	0.60%, 0.02%A		
Actual Fees:	Mgt:0.55%	Dist:0.25%	
Expense Projections:	3Yr:$809	5Yr:$1066	10Yr:$1802
Income Distrib:	Monthly		

Morgan Stan Ins US R/E A

Analyst Pick

Ticker	Load	NAV	Yield	Total Assets	Mstar Category
MSUSX	None	$23.21	1.8%	$1,251 mil	Specialty-Real Estate

Governance and Management

Fiduciary Grade:

Portfolio Manager(s)

Lead manager Ted Bigman has been managing REIT money since the mid-1980s. Comanager Doug Funke, who had comanaged the fund since 1999, left the firm in mid-2004. Five analysts give the fund solid coverage of the industry. The same team also runs Morgan Stanley Real Estate using an identical strategy.

Strategy

This fund targets companies that trade at discounts to their assessment of underlying asset values. Management is willing to load up in specific subsectors when it uncovers large discrepancies between stock prices and intrinsic values. The fund generally focuses on the largest, most-liquid REITs and on residential, retail, and commercial properties. The fund tends to emphasize offices and apartments, while carrying minimal exposure to smaller subsectors such as health care.

Historical Profile

Return Above Avg
Risk Average
Rating ★★★★ Above Avg

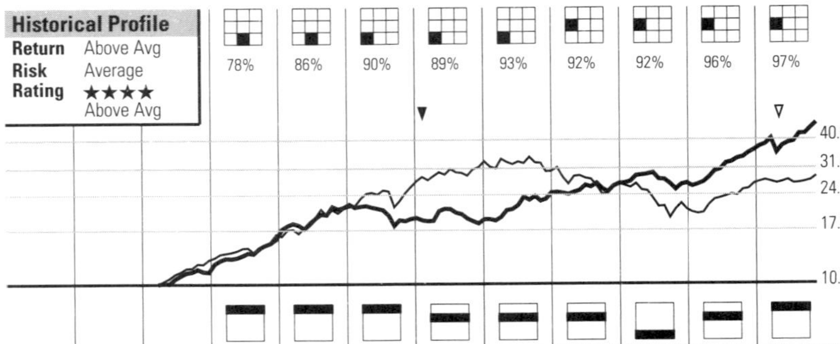

Investment Style
Equity
Stock %

▼ Manager Change
▽ Partial Manager Change

Growth of $10,000
▬ Investment Values of Fund
— Investment Values of S&P 500

Performance Quartile (within Category)

1993	1994	1995	1996	1997	1998	1999	2000	2001	2002	2003	12-04	History
—	—	11.42	14.41	15.38	12.71	11.84	14.50	14.63	13.55	17.92	23.21	NAV
—	—	21.07*	39.56	27.62	-12.29	-1.48	29.65	9.27	0.18	37.61	37.28	Total Return %
—	—	—	16.62	-5.73	-40.86	-22.52	38.75	21.15	22.27	8.94	26.41	+/-S&P 500
—	—	—	2.52	7.95	4.71	1.09	-1.39	-3.09	-3.42	1.55	3.46	+/-Wil REIT
—	—	0.00	3.44	3.04	3.26	5.28	4.83	4.04	3.61	3.58	2.38	Income Return %
—	—	—	36.12	24.58	-15.55	-6.76	24.82	5.23	-3.43	34.03	34.90	Capital Return %
—	—	—	12	8	14	27	29	43	85	35	10	Total Rtn % Rank Cat
—	—	0.24	0.39	0.43	0.49	0.66	0.56	0.57	0.52	0.48	0.42	Income $
—	—	0.43	1.01	2.42	0.33	0.04	0.23	0.61	0.60	0.18	0.86	Capital Gains $
—	—	1.00	1.00	1.00	1.00	1.00	1.00	1.00	0.99	1.00	—	Expense Ratio %
—	—	4.04	3.08	2.72	3.33	6.52	4.13	4.19	3.49	3.08	—	Income Ratio %
—	—	—	171	135	117	47	31	33	47	17	—	Turnover Rate %
—	—	69	210	361	259	311	585	662	—	897	1,103	Net Assets $mil

Performance 12-31-04

	1st Qtr	2nd Qtr	3rd Qtr	4th Qtr	Total
2000	2.11	12.29	9.34	3.41	29.65
2001	-1.59	9.10	-3.32	5.27	9.27
2002	7.79	2.78	-10.05	0.53	0.18
2003	0.96	13.07	11.11	8.49	37.61
2004	11.55	-4.11	9.16	17.56	37.28

Trailing	Total Return%	+/- S&P 500	+/- Wil REIT	%Rank Cat	Growth of $10,000
3 Mo	17.56	8.33	0.87	18	11,756
6 Mo	28.33	21.14	2.07	9	12,833
1 Yr	37.28	26.41	3.46	10	13,728
3 Yr Avg	23.69	20.11	0.13	45	18,924
5 Yr Avg	21.80	24.10	-0.87	30	26,806
10 Yr Avg	—	—	—	—	—
15 Yr Avg	—	—	—	—	—

Tax Analysis	Tax-Adj Rtn%	%Rank Cat	Tax-Cost Rat	%Rank Cat
3 Yr (estimated)	21.71	37	1.60	45
5 Yr (estimated)	19.55	27	1.85	57
10 Yr (estimated)	—	—	—	—

Potential Capital Gain Exposure: 43% of assets

Rating and Risk

Time Period	Load-Adj Return %	Morningstar Rtn vs Cat	Morningstar Risk vs Cat	Morningstar Risk-Adj Rating
1 Yr	37.28			
3 Yr	23.69	Avg	Avg	★★★
5 Yr	21.80	+Avg	Avg	★★★★
10 Yr	—	—	—	—
Incept	17.75			

Other Measures	Standard Index S&P 500	Best Fit Index Wil REIT
Alpha	21.8	1.3
Beta	0.37	0.94
R-Squared	15	98
Standard Deviation	17.24	
Mean	23.69	
Sharpe Ratio	1.31	

Portfolio Analysis 09-30-04

Share change since 06-04 Total Stocks:59	Sector	PE	YTD Ret%	% Assets
⊕ Simon Property Group	Financial	37.3	46.10	8.29
⊕ Brookfield Properties	Financial	22.1	32.89	6.17
⊖ Rouse	Financial	—	—	5.66
AvalonBay Communities	Financial	58.1	65.02	5.46
⊖ Starwood Hotels & Resort	Consumer	33.9	64.71	5.10
Archstone-Smith Trust	Financial	52.6	48.79	5.06
⊕ Boston Properties	Financial	23.9	40.60	4.48
Federal Realty Investmen	Financial	37.8	40.53	3.66
⊕ Arden Realty	Financial	52.1	32.27	3.57
⊖ Public Storage	Financial	43.5	33.22	3.38
⊖ ProLogis Trust	Financial	25.1	41.03	3.36
⊕ AMB Property	Financial	39.1	28.55	3.30
⊕ Host Marriott	Financial	—	40.88	3.27
⊕ Vornado Realty Trust	Financial	30.8	46.53	3.26
⊖ Equity Office Properties	Financial	45.9	9.06	3.05
⊕ Regency Centers	Financial	27.3	46.22	2.50
⊖ Apartment Investment & M	Financial	—	20.31	2.47
⊕ Hilton Hotels	Consumer	36.1	33.34	2.37
⊖ Taubman Centers	Financial	—	51.72	2.34
Shurgard Storage Centers	Financial	NMF	23.92	2.20

Current Investment Style

Value Blnd Growth / Large Mid Small

Market Cap	%
Giant	0.0
Large	25.1
Mid	67.1
Small	6.7
Micro	1.2
Avg $mil: 4,374	

Value Measures		Rel Category
Price/Earnings	15.80	1.10
Price/Book	2.11	1.05
Price/Sales	3.43	0.92
Price/Cash Flow	12.54	1.04
Dividend Yield %	4.09	0.84

Growth Measures	%	Rel Category
Long-Term Erngs	6.97	0.99
Book Value	-0.71	NMF
Sales	0.10	0.06
Cash Flow	-6.18	NMF
Historical Erngs	-5.23	NMF

Profitability	%	Rel Category
Return on Equity	9.39	0.91
Return on Assets	6.74	0.88
Net Margin	19.74	0.91

Sector Weightings	% of Stocks	Rel S&P 500	3 Year High	3 Year Low
Info	0.00	0.00		
Software	0.00	0.00	0	0
Hardware	0.00	0.00	0	0
Media	0.00	0.00	0	0
Telecom	0.00	0.00	0	0
Service	100.00	2.16		
Health	0.00	0.00	0	0
Consumer	7.95	0.88	8	7
Business	0.00	0.00	0	0
Financial	92.05	4.43	93	92
Mfg	0.00	0.00		
Goods	0.00	0.00	0	0
Ind Mtrls	0.00	0.00	0	0
Energy	0.00	0.00	0	0
Utilities	0.00	0.00	0	0

Composition

Cash	1.7
Stocks	97.3
Bonds	0.0
Other	1.0
Foreign (% of Stock)	0.0

Morningstar's Take by Dan McNeela 12-23-04

Morgan Stanley Institutional U.S. Real Estate lost an important cog, but the team's overall strength should allow it to prevail.

This investment team lost a key member when comanager Doug Funke left Morgan Stanley in mid-2004. Funke joined the team as an analyst in 1995 and earned a promotion to comanager in 1999. He'll be missed, but management is well equipped to put up good numbers. Most importantly, manager Ted Bigman, a comanager since the fund's 1995 inception, is still at the helm. Bigman fortuitously made a nice hire in 2003, bringing on an analyst with 15 years of experience. All told, this team of six investment professionals still has its bases covered.

On the performance front, the fund continues to churn out solid results, proving that 2002 was a rare miss. The fund's 37.2% year-to-date gain through Dec. 22, 2004, ranks in the category's best decile. This year the team has not only been in the right subsectors, but it has also picked the right stocks. Starwood Hotels & Resorts Worldwide has been one of the best picks in its industry as has apartment REIT AvalonBay Communities.

The fund stands out from the crowd with its strategy as well. Few of its peers are as committed to a net asset value method of finding good buys. With that philosophy in place, management eschews macroeconomic calls to build the portfolio as it focuses on buying real estate stocks that are selling below the underlying value of their properties. Management's overweight position in hotels hasn't stemmed from a forecast of a strong economy; instead, those stocks looked to be selling at a sizable discount to their replacement value, so management bought.

With many real estate investors wondering how much longer the current rally can last, it's also worth noting that the fund played better defense than its peers did during the downturn of 1998 and 1999. The big rally won't last forever, but this fund has staying power.

Address:	1221 Avenue of the Americas New York NY 10020 800-548-7786
Web Address:	www.morganstanley.com/im
Inception:	02-27-95*
Advisor:	Morgan Stanley Investment Mgt Inc.
Subadvisor:	None
NTF Plans:	N/A

Minimum Purchase:	$500000	Add: $1000	IRA: $0
Min Auto Inv Plan:	$0	Add: —	
Sales Fees:	No-load		
Management Fee:	0.80%, 0.15%A		
Actual Fees:	Mgt:0.80%	Dist:	
Expense Projections:	3Yr:$325	5Yr:$563	10Yr:$1248
Income Distrib:	Quarterly		

Muhlenkamp

Ticker	Load	NAV	Yield	Total Assets	Mstar Category
MUHLX	None	$78.97	0.1%	$1,985 mil	Mid-Cap Value

Governance and Management

Fiduciary Grade:

Portfolio Manager(s)

Ron Muhlenkamp founded Muhlenkamp & Co. in 1977 to manage private accounts for individuals and institutions. He launched this fund in 1988.

Strategy

This fund's picks are derived from a combination of macroeconomic analysis and bottom-up individual stock assessment. Manager Ron Muhlenkamp will give the fund more or less cyclical exposure depending on his outlook for GDP growth, interest rates, and other top-down factors. Returns on equity and valuations drive the stock selection. The fund is managed in a low-turnover, tax-efficient manner.

Historical Profile

Return High
Risk High
Rating ★★★★ Above Avg

Investment Style: Equity Stock %

100%	87%	89%	97%	96%	97%	95%	94%	95%

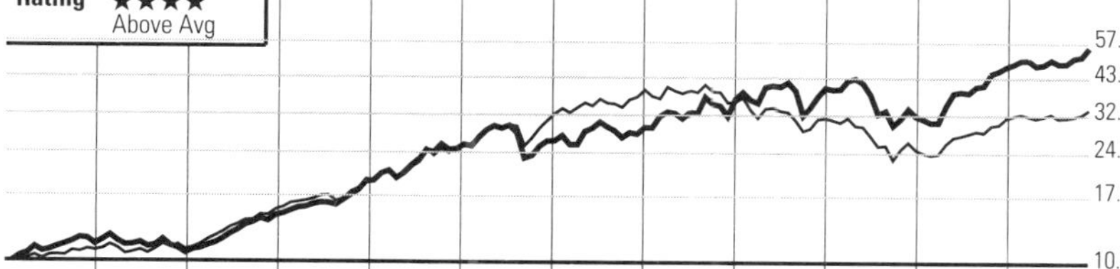

Performance Quartile (within Category)

1993	1994	1995	1996	1997	1998	1999	2000	2001	2002	2003	12-04	History
17.86	16.23	21.26	27.52	36.55	37.65	41.11	48.96	53.56	42.89	63.51	78.97	NAV
18.13	-7.19	32.96	29.98	33.30	3.22	11.40	25.30	9.35	-19.92	48.08	24.51	Total Return %
8.07	-8.50	-4.57	7.04	-0.05	-25.35	-9.64	34.40	21.23	2.17	19.41	13.64	+/-S&P 500
2.51	-5.06	-1.98	9.72	-1.07	-1.86	11.51	6.12	7.02	-10.28	10.01	0.80	+/-Russ MV
0.63	0.39	1.23	0.53	0.47	0.21	0.00	0.00	0.00	0.00	0.00	0.17	Income Return %
17.50	-7.58	31.73	29.45	32.83	3.01	11.40	25.30	9.35	-19.92	48.08	24.34	Capital Return %
59	82	22	6	21	48	42	33	37	82	10	8	Total Rtn % Rank Cat
0.10	0.07	0.20	0.11	0.13	0.08	0.00	0.00	0.00	0.00	0.00	0.11	Income $
0.00	0.28	0.12	0.00	0.00	0.00	0.80	2.33	0.00	0.00	0.00	0.00	Capital Gains $
1.30	1.57	1.35	1.56	1.33	1.32	1.38	1.28	1.17	1.17	1.18	—	Expense Ratio %
0.70	0.70	1.10	0.58	0.53	0.21	-0.26	-0.20	-0.14	-0.10	-0.04	—	Income Ratio %
14	26	23	17	14	27	15	32	11	11	9	—	Turnover Rate %
12	17	24	42	125	195	177	266	539	601	1,157	1,985	Net Assets $mil

Performance 12-31-04

	1st Qtr	2nd Qtr	3rd Qtr	4th Qtr	Total
2000	13.16	-0.24	6.70	4.02	25.30
2001	-3.06	13.94	-20.43	24.41	9.35
2002	6.16	-10.64	-21.53	7.57	-19.92
2003	-4.90	27.51	5.17	16.11	48.08
2004	5.57	0.21	1.59	15.85	24.51

Trailing	Total Return%	+/- S&P 500	+/- Russ MV	%Rank Cat	Growth of $10,000
3 Mo	15.85	6.62	2.39	5	11,585
6 Mo	17.69	10.50	2.26	2	11,769
1 Yr	24.51	13.64	0.80	8	12,451
3 Yr Avg	13.87	10.29	-1.69	21	14,765
5 Yr Avg	15.13	17.43	1.65	22	20,228
10 Yr Avg	18.28	6.21	2.56	5	53,594
15 Yr Avg	15.26	4.33	1.56	1	84,174

Tax Analysis	Tax-Adj Rtn%	%Rank Cat	Tax-Cost Rat	%Rank Cat
3 Yr (estimated)	13.85	13	0.02	2
5 Yr (estimated)	14.89	19	0.21	12
10 Yr (estimated)	18.00	1	0.24	1

Potential Capital Gain Exposure: 31% of assets

Rating and Risk

Time Period	Load-Adj Return %	Morningstar Rtn vs Cat	Morningstar Risk vs Cat	Morningstar Risk-Adj Rating
1 Yr	24.51			
3 Yr	13.87	+Avg	High	★★★
5 Yr	15.13	+Avg	High	★★★
10 Yr	18.28	High	High	★★★★
Incept	15.04			

Other Measures	Standard Index S&P 500	Best Fit Index S&P Mid 400
Alpha	10.3	1.2
Beta	1.18	1.27
R-Squared	78	91
Standard Deviation	23.06	
Mean	13.87	
Sharpe Ratio	0.55	

Portfolio Analysis 09-30-04

Share change since 06-04 Total Stocks:72	Sector	PE	YTD Ret%	% Assets
⊕ Countrywide Financial	Financial	9.0	48.15	5.73
NVR	Consumer	12.2	65.11	5.01
Centex	Consumer	8.9	23.40	5.00
Fidelity National Financ	Financial	10.2	32.24	4.32
Black & Decker	Ind Mtrls	16.4	81.42	3.98
Capital One Financial	Financial	12.5	37.61	3.17
Tyco International	Ind Mtrls	25.1	35.41	2.98
Meritage Homes	Consumer	14.0	69.96	2.81
Fannie Mae	Financial	9.1	-2.33	2.79
⊕ Patterson-UTI Energy	Energy	33.3	18.55	2.64
Mohawk Industries	Goods	16.1	29.36	2.55
Cendant	Business	13.6	6.52	2.53
Citigroup	Financial	15.3	2.72	2.47
Johnson & Johnson	Health	20.6	25.17	2.46
⊕ Allstate	Financial	12.8	23.12	2.45
⊕ Masco	Ind Mtrls	17.2	36.23	2.39
⊕ Nabors Industries	Energy	28.9	23.59	2.38
Polaris Industries	Goods	24.1	56.60	2.11
Altria Group	Goods	13.3	18.38	2.11
⊕ Winnebago Industries	Ind Mtrls	17.6	14.48	2.09

Current Investment Style

Market Cap	%
Giant	19.3
Large	25.4
Mid	38.4
Small	13.3
Micro	3.6
Avg $mil: 8,412	

Value Measures		Rel Category
Price/Earnings	11.51	0.75
Price/Book	2.02	1.05
Price/Sales	0.87	0.99
Price/Cash Flow	4.39	0.77
Dividend Yield %	1.05	0.73

Growth Measures	%	Rel Category
Long-Term Erngs	12.40	1.13
Book Value	15.83	2.81
Sales	10.53	2.20
Cash Flow	42.45	10.75
Historical Erngs	25.57	2.23

Profitability	%	Rel Category
Return on Equity	23.51	1.85
Return on Assets	12.58	2.07
Net Margin	10.85	1.24

Sector Weightings	% of Stocks	Rel S&P 500	3 Year High	3 Year Low
Info	3.63	0.17		
Software	0.00	0.00	3	0
Hardware	3.05	0.30	7	3
Media	0.00	0.00	1	0
Telecom	0.58	0.18	1	0
Service	51.70	1.11		
Health	4.51	0.36	5	2
Consumer	18.44	2.03	22	18
Business	2.72	0.67	6	3
Financial	26.03	1.25	27	15
Mfg	44.68	1.39		
Goods	11.81	1.27	14	12
Ind Mtrls	19.51	1.54	20	13
Energy	10.90	1.52	13	7
Utilities	2.46	0.83	5	1

Composition

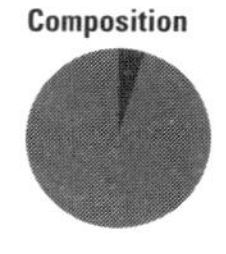

Cash	4.6
Stocks	95.4
Bonds	0.0
Other	0.0
Foreign (% of Stock)	2.3

Morningstar's Take by Jeffrey Ptak 11-01-04

A sensible strategy and capable management continue to give reason to recommend Muhlenkamp.

Manager and namesake Ron Muhlenkamp is one of an increasingly rare breed in the mutual fund world: an investor who unabashedly pays heed to macroeconomic currents. In particular, Muhlenkamp tries to estimate the required return on stocks in view of prevailing inflation rates and the 30-year Treasury yield. That estimate--which recently stood at 8% before taxes and inflation--governs the stock-selection process.

Muhlenkamp aims to invest in firms that can deliver superior pretax nominal returns at a discount to the P/E multiple implied by his required return estimate (which works out to roughly 17 or 18 times earnings by his most recent projection). Thus, the portfolio's aggregate return on equity measure typically well exceeds the S&P 500 Index's while its overall P/E ratio skirts the index's.

While that might seem too good to be true, it's a reflection of Muhlenkamp's opportunistic and free-wheeling approach. Not one to be hemmed into a style-box, Muhlenkamp invests practically wherever opportunities reside--including areas mired in negative sentiment. That go-anywhere ethos extends even to traditional growth realms: Muhlenkamp recently scooped-up shares of drugmaker Johnson & Johnson. And since Muhlenkamp is market-cap agnostic, the portfolio is splayed across stocks of all sizes.

Of course, this approach wouldn't amount to much without deft stock picking. But Muhlenkamp has shown a steady hand in that regard as well, consistently topping the fund's peers while racking up a fine long-term record. All that said, the fund's wide wingspan might deter those seeking a cookie-cutter option. Also, Muhlenkamp's penchant for smaller and, at times, more- controversial fare has made for above-average volatility.

Those caveats aside, we think the fund remains a fine option.

Address:	3000 Stonewood, Suite 310 Wexford PA 15090-8388 800-860-3863
Web Address:	www.muhlenkamp.com
Inception:	11-17-88
Advisor:	Muhlenkamp & CO Inc
Subadvisor:	None
NTF Plans:	Fidelity Retail-NTF, Schwab OneSource

Minimum Purchase:	$1500	Add: $50	IRA: $1500
Min Auto Inv Plan:	$200	Add: $50	
Sales Fees:	No-load		
Management Fee:	1.00%		
Actual Fees:	Mgt:1.00%	Dist:	
Expense Projections:	3Yr:$375	5Yr:$649	10Yr:$1432
Income Distrib:	Annually		

Mutual Beacon A

Ticker	Load	NAV	Yield	Total Assets	Mstar Category
TEBIX	5.75%	$15.87	2.0%	$5,671 mil	Mid-Cap Value

Governance and Management

Fiduciary Grade: C

Portfolio Manager(s)

Comanager Larry Sondike stepped down in late 2001. David Winters, who has been with the advisor for 14 years, remains. He was joined by new hire Matt Haynes on Aug. 1, 2001. Haynes has eight years of experience managing value-oriented global portfolios for Morgan Stanley. The firm has recently added another distressed debt analyst and a stock analyst.

Strategy

This fund tries to sniff out bargains among unloved and downtrodden companies. In addition to equity investments in traditional value arenas, such as industrials and financials, it also buys distressed credits. Turnarounds and restructurings are common in the portfolio, and the managers will actively try to influence companies to improve their businesses. The fund often carries an ample cash cushion and invests a large portion of its portfolio in foreign securities.

Historical Profile

Return Below Avg
Risk Low
Rating ★★★ Neutral

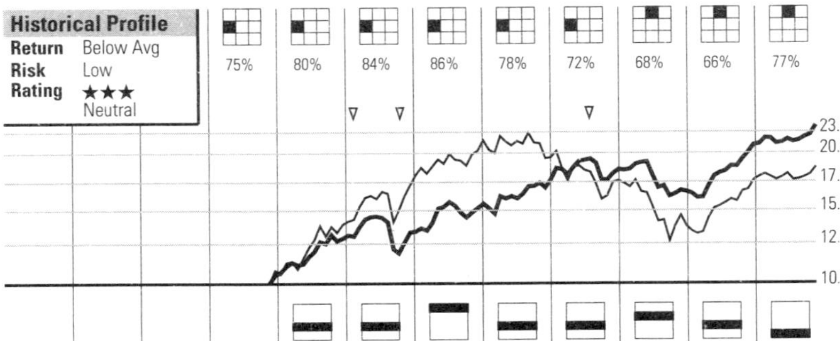

Investment Style
Equity
Stock %

▼ Manager Change
▽ Partial Manager Change

Growth of $10,000
— Investment Values of Fund
— Investment Values of S&P 500

Performance Quartile (within Category)

1993	1994	1995	1996	1997	1998	1999	2000	2001	2002	2003	12-04	History
—	—	—	12.98	14.09	13.09	13.81	13.34	13.01	11.27	14.33	15.87	NAV
—	—	—	6.32*	22.52	2.02	16.40	13.89	5.78	-11.41	28.99	14.13	Total Return %
—	—	—	—	-10.83	-26.55	-4.64	22.99	17.66	10.68	0.32	3.26	+/-S&P 500
—	—	—	—	-11.85	-3.06	16.51	-5.29	3.45	-1.77	-9.08	-9.58	+/-Russ MV
—	—	—	0.00	3.95	2.89	1.63	2.89	1.16	1.23	1.69	2.26	Income Return %
—	—	—	—	18.57	-0.87	14.77	11.00	4.62	-12.64	27.30	11.87	Capital Return %
—	—	—	—	75	52	19	69	52	42	75	84	Total Rtn % Rank Cat
—	—	—	0.33	0.51	0.40	0.21	0.39	0.15	0.16	0.19	0.32	Income $
—	—	—	0.75	1.26	0.87	1.19	1.86	0.94	0.11	0.00	0.15	Capital Gains $
—	—	—	—	1.09	1.11	1.13	1.16	1.14	1.15	1.21	—	Expense Ratio %
—	—	—	—	1.58	1.89	1.18	1.20	1.12	1.53	1.13	—	Income Ratio %
—	—	—	67	55	65	68	62	55	52	50	—	Turnover Rate %
—	—	—	97	751	950	761	759	979	922	1,304	1,466	Net Assets $mil

Performance 12-31-04

	1st Qtr	2nd Qtr	3rd Qtr	4th Qtr	Total
2000	4.13	-1.19	6.99	3.47	13.89
2001	2.77	8.31	-10.18	5.80	5.78
2002	2.92	-5.85	-10.83	2.52	-11.41
2003	-3.11	14.21	3.72	12.38	28.99
2004	3.63	-0.53	1.16	9.46	14.13

Trailing	Total Return%	+/- S&P 500	+/- Russ MV	%Rank Cat	Growth of $10,000
3 Mo	9.46	0.23	-4.00	82	10,946
6 Mo	10.72	3.53	-4.71	53	11,072
1 Yr	14.13	3.26	-9.58	84	11,413
3 Yr Avg	9.26	5.68	-6.30	71	13,043
5 Yr Avg	9.46	11.76	-4.02	68	15,714
10 Yr Avg	—	—	—	—	—
15 Yr Avg	—	—	—	—	—

Tax Analysis	Tax-Adj Rtn%	%Rank Cat	Tax-Cost Rat	%Rank Cat
3 Yr (estimated)	6.37	85	0.70	56
5 Yr (estimated)	6.29	79	1.74	88
10 Yr (estimated)	—	—	—	—

Potential Capital Gain Exposure: 30% of assets

Rating and Risk

Time Period	Load-Adj Return %	Morningstar Rtn vs Cat	Morningstar Risk vs Cat	Morningstar Risk-Adj Rating
1 Yr	7.57			
3 Yr	7.12	-Avg	Low	★★
5 Yr	8.17	-Avg	Low	★★★
10 Yr	—	—	—	—
Incept	10.68			

Other Measures	Standard Index S&P 500	Best Fit Index Mstar Mid Value
Alpha	6.3	-1.2
Beta	0.57	0.67
R-Squared	69	88
Standard Deviation	11.20	
Mean	9.26	
Sharpe Ratio	0.71	

Morningstar's Take by Christopher Traulsen 10-28-04

Mutual Beacon isn't much like its peers, but that's a big part of its appeal.

This fund doesn't look much like other equity funds or its typical mid-value peer. As of Sept. 30, 2004, the fund devoted just 77% of its assets to stocks, with 13% in cash and about 10% in bonds. It also held about 39% of its equity portfolio in non-North American stocks, and had a significant overweight in consumer goods.

That wide-ranging portfolio stems from the managers' emphasis on risk control. They don't feel compelled to stick to a particular style box square or asset class. To keep the fund diversified and reduce price-risk, they invest in undervalued equities, distressed debt, and merger-arbitrage. The team also invests overseas if that's where the opportunities are and often holds sizable cash stakes.

The fund has had many successes over the years. One of the more recent ones is International Steel Group. Although the stock is down a bit this year, the fund bought its private equity in 2002 because the managers thought its restructuring plan looked promising. They were right. The fund's total cost for its ISG stake was $17.2 million, and it's now worth $130.3 million.

Over the years, the fund has outperformed the S&P 500/Barra Value Index--a reasonable benchmark for this fund--with much less volatility. Indeed, its diversification and penchant for holding cash have made it one of the least volatile funds in its category. It does tend to lag when equities lead they way, though, so it isn't for investors seeking to keep pace with the market over short periods of time.

We do have one concern. The fund's advisor has experienced significant turnover in its investment personnel in recent years. In 2004, Tim Rankin, an analyst and assistant manager of Mutual Shares, left to join a hedge fund. The advisor needs to improve its ability to retain talent for this fund to remain an appealing investment.

Address:	51 John F Kennedy Pkwy Short Hills NJ 07078 800-342-5236
Web Address:	www.franklintempleton.com
Inception:	11-01-96 *
Advisor:	Franklin Mutual Advisers, LLC
Subadvisor:	None
NTF Plans:	DATALynx NTF, Federated Tr NTF

Minimum Purchase:	$1000	Add: $50	IRA: $250
Min Auto Inv Plan:	$50	Add: $25	
Sales Fees:	5.75%L, 2.00%R		
Management Fee:	0.60% mx./0.54% mn., 0.15%A		
Actual Fees:	Mgt:0.60%	Dist:0.35%	
Expense Projections:	3Yr:$937	5Yr:$1202	10Yr:$1957
Income Distrib:	Semi-Annually		

Portfolio Analysis 09-30-04

Share change since 12-03 Total Stocks:137	Sector	PE	YTD Ret%	% Assets
⊕ White Mountains Insuranc	Financial	41.1	40.75	3.79
Altadis	Goods	—	—	2.36
Washington Post	Media	27.8	25.21	2.06
⊕ Newmont Mining	Ind Mtrls	45.6	-8.02	2.03
International Steel Grp	—	—	—	2.02
British American Tobacco	Goods	—	—	1.72
☼ Freeport-McMoRan Copper	Ind Mtrls	—	-6.50	1.69
⊕ Brascan	Ind Mtrls	36.0	80.66	1.64
⊕ Carlsberg	Goods	—	—	1.56
⊕ NTL	Telecom	—	4.60	1.47
Berkshire Hathaway B	Financial	20.9	4.30	1.33
⊕ Florida East Coast Inds	Business	30.8	36.92	1.32
⊕ Imperial Tobacco Grp	Goods	—	—	1.23
Impala Platinum Hldgs Lt	Ind Mtrls	—	—	1.22
⊕ Reynolds American	Goods	—	43.11	1.21
Berkshire Hathaway A	Financial	—	—	1.21
⊕ Orkla	Goods	—	—	1.15
Liberty Media	Media	—	11.56	1.14
Diageo	Goods	—	—	1.12
⊕ Altria Group	Goods	13.3	18.38	1.08

Current Investment Style

Value Blnd Growth; Large Mid Small

Market Cap	%
Giant	14.7
Large	37.3
Mid	39.8
Small	7.0
Micro	1.3
Avg $mil: 8,208	

Value Measures		Rel Category
Price/Earnings	16.14	1.05
Price/Book	2.02	1.05
Price/Sales	1.37	1.56
Price/Cash Flow	6.07	1.06
Dividend Yield %	2.14	1.50

Growth Measures	%	Rel Category
Long-Term Erngs	11.30	1.03
Book Value	3.48	0.62
Sales	2.94	0.62
Cash Flow	4.66	1.18
Historical Erngs	6.69	0.58

Profitability	%	Rel Category
Return on Equity	12.27	0.96
Return on Assets	5.14	0.85
Net Margin	8.25	0.94

Sector Weightings	% of Stocks	Rel S&P 500	3 Year High	Low
Info	14.31	0.67		
Software	0.00	0.00	1	0
Hardware	0.15	0.01	0	0
Media	9.39	2.45	12	9
Telecom	4.77	1.51	7	3
Service	36.55	0.79		
Health	4.33	0.35	7	4
Consumer	0.87	0.10	8	1
Business	2.69	0.66	8	3
Financial	28.66	1.38	32	22
Mfg	49.14	1.53		
Goods	24.84	2.66	25	18
Ind Mtrls	18.62	1.47	19	13
Energy	3.87	0.54	5	2
Utilities	1.81	0.61	3	1

Composition

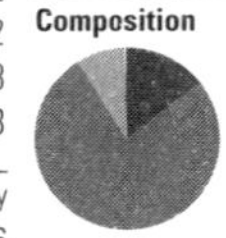

Cash	14.3
Stocks	76.7
Bonds	8.4
Other	0.6
Foreign (% of Stock)	40.4

Mutual Discovery A

Ticker	Load	NAV	Yield	Total Assets	Mstar Category
TEDIX	5.75%	$24.08	1.9%	$5,887 mil	World Stock

Governance and Management

Fiduciary Grade: C

Portfolio Manager(s)

Franklin, Mutual's corporate parent, has been implicated in the mutual fund trading scandal. Although evidence against the firm so far doesn't rise to the level of malfeasance seen elsewhere, these charges detract from the firm's appeal. Mutual's managers are independent, but the funds are distributed through Franklin. We will be watching Franklin closely and will keep investors apprised of new developments and any impact on this fund.

Strategy

The managers hunt for bargain-basement stocks of all sizes, particularly in Europe and the United States. They also look to buy the debt of distressed companies and are active participants on creditors' committees as these firms restructure. Historically the managers hedged all foreign-currency exposure back into the dollar, but they have recently been removing some of the hedge on a tactical basis.

Historical Profile

Return: High
Risk: Low
Rating: ★★★★★ Highest

Investment Style: Equity Stock %

1996	1997	1998	1999	2000	2001	2002	2003	12-04
80%	81%	80%	85%	68%	75%	71%	75%	82%

▼ Manager Change
∇ Partial Manager Change

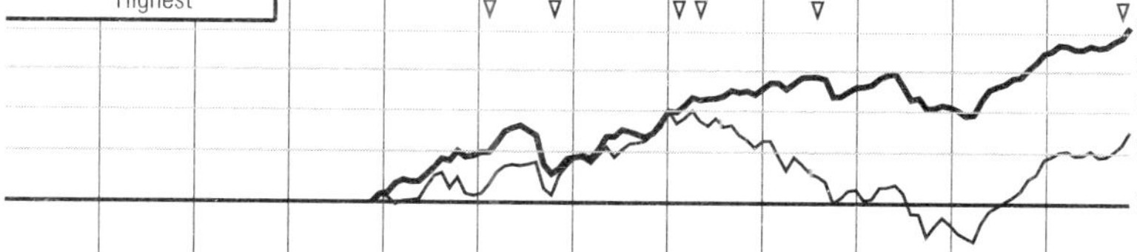

Growth of $10,000
— Investment Values of Fund
— Investment Values of MSCI EAFE

Performance Quartile (within Category)

1993	1994	1995	1996	1997	1998	1999	2000	2001	2002	2003	12-04	History
—	—	—	17.16	18.83	17.19	21.00	18.33	18.08	16.06	20.66	24.08	NAV
—	—	—	4.86*	22.47	-2.37	26.38	12.26	0.86	-9.39	31.13	18.93	Total Return %
—	—	—	—	20.69	-22.30	-0.65	26.45	22.28	6.55	-7.46	-1.32	+/-MSCI EAFE
—	—	—	—	6.71	-26.69	1.43	25.45	17.66	10.50	-1.98	4.21	+/-MSCI World
—	—	—	0.00	4.53	2.25	2.07	2.70	1.51	1.43	2.35	2.25	Income Return %
—	—	—	—	17.94	-4.62	24.31	9.56	-0.35	-10.82	28.78	16.68	Capital Return %
—	—	—	—	18	92	67	3	3	10	65	17	Total Rtn % Rank Cat
—	—	—	0.28	0.77	0.42	0.35	0.55	0.28	0.26	0.38	0.46	Income $
—	—	—	1.07	1.36	0.81	0.32	4.04	0.62	0.08	0.00	0.00	Capital Gains $
—	—	—	—	1.33	1.35	1.38	1.37	1.37	1.39	1.46	—	Expense Ratio %
—	—	—	—	1.39	1.46	0.98	1.30	1.57	1.53	1.20	—	Income Ratio %
—	—	—	80	58	84	88	75	59	41	46	—	Turnover Rate %
—	—	—	68	698	863	845	880	913	927	1,438	2,108	Net Assets $mil

Performance 12-31-04

	1st Qtr	2nd Qtr	3rd Qtr	4th Qtr	Total
2000	7.14	-0.34	3.10	1.97	12.26
2001	-0.16	6.42	-9.68	5.10	0.86
2002	4.59	-3.88	-10.69	0.92	-9.39
2003	-3.92	15.46	4.80	12.79	31.13
2004	3.97	0.04	2.25	11.83	18.93

Trailing	Total Return%	+/- MSCI EAFE	+/- MSCI World	%Rank Cat	Growth of $10,000
3 Mo	11.83	-3.49	-0.11	64	11,183
6 Mo	14.34	-0.66	3.52	20	11,434
1 Yr	18.93	-1.32	4.21	17	11,893
3 Yr Avg	12.22	0.33	5.27	17	14,132
5 Yr Avg	9.86	10.99	12.31	4	16,003
10 Yr Avg	—	—	—	—	—
15 Yr Avg	—	—	—	—	—

Tax Analysis	Tax-Adj Rtn%	%Rank Cat	Tax-Cost Rat	%Rank Cat
3 Yr (estimated)	9.24	28	0.71	75
5 Yr (estimated)	6.43	8	1.97	98
10 Yr (estimated)	—	—	—	—

Potential Capital Gain Exposure: 26% of assets

Rating and Risk

Time Period	Load-Adj Return %	Morningstar Rtn vs Cat	Morningstar Risk vs Cat	Morningstar Risk-Adj Rating
1 Yr	12.09			
3 Yr	10.02	+Avg	Low	★★★★
5 Yr	8.57	High	Low	★★★★★
10 Yr	—	—	—	—
Incept	11.26			

Other Measures	Standard Index S&P 500	Best Fit Index Mstar Mid Value
Alpha	4.1	1.4
Beta	0.60	0.68
R-Squared	79	85
Standard Deviation	11.77	
Mean	12.22	
Sharpe Ratio	0.93	

Portfolio Analysis 09-30-04

Share change since 12-03 Total Stocks:153	Sector	Country	% Assets
⊕ British American Tobacco	Goods	U.K.	2.91
⊕ Altadis	Goods	Spain	2.10
⊕ Imperial Tobacco Grp	Goods	U.K.	1.93
⊕ Berkshire Hathaway B	Financial	United States	1.80
⊕ White Mountains Insuranc	Financial	United States	1.76
⊕ NTL	Telecom	United States	1.75
⊕ Orkla	Goods	Norway	1.70
⊕ Carlsberg	Goods	Denmark	1.70
⊕ Newmont Mining	Ind Mtrls	United States	1.65
International Steel Grp	—	—	1.58
⊕ Allied Irish Banks	Financial	Ireland	1.58
⊕ Florida East Coast Inds	Business	United States	1.55
⊕ Potlatch	Ind Mtrls	United States	1.46
⊕ Anglo American	Ind Mtrls	U.K.	1.45
Berkshire Hathaway A	Financial	United States	1.43
⊕ Brascan	Ind Mtrls	Canada	1.26
Diageo	Goods	U.K.	1.25
SES GLOBAL	Telecom	Luxembourg	1.22
⊕ Kt&G	Goods	Korea	1.19
⊖ Pargesa Holding	Financial	Switzerland	1.12

Current Investment Style

Value Blnd Growth / Large Mid Small

Market Cap	%
Giant	19.4
Large	40.4
Mid	33.9
Small	6.0
Micro	0.3
Avg $mil: 9,613	

Value Measures		Rel Category
Price/Earnings	14.36	0.91
Price/Book	2.03	0.91
Price/Sales	1.12	0.96
Price/Cash Flow	6.21	0.98
Dividend Yield %	2.23	1.19

Growth Measures	%	Rel Category
Long-Term Erngs	11.47	0.95
Book Value	2.22	1.00
Sales	5.16	1.23
Cash Flow	3.24	0.55
Historical Erngs	4.05	0.47

Composition

Cash	7.3	Bonds	7.9
Stocks	82.5	Other	2.4
Foreign (% of Stock)			65.9

Sector Weightings	% of Stocks	Rel MSCI EAFE	3 Year High	3 Year Low
Info	13.21	0.80		
Software	0.75	0.69	1	1
Hardware	0.13	0.04	0	0
Media	5.24	2.30	8	5
Telecom	7.09	0.74	7	1
Service	31.21	0.70		
Health	3.33	0.46	5	3
Consumer	1.42	0.28	8	1
Business	4.28	0.79	10	4
Financial	22.18	0.82	25	22
Mfg	55.59	1.44		
Goods	29.72	2.18	30	24
Ind Mtrls	20.25	1.65	20	13
Energy	3.51	0.48	5	3
Utilities	2.11	0.39	4	2

Regional Exposure	% Stock		
UK/W. Europe	47	N. America	41
Japan	3	Latn America	2
Asia X Japan	5	Other	2

Country Exposure	% Stock		
United States	34	France	6
U.K.	16	Switzerland	5
Canada	7		

Morningstar's Take by Terence Geenty 12-29-04

We're concerned, but not alarmed, about this fund's recent manager departure.

Mutual Discovery's assistant manager, Timothy Rankin, left the firm in October 2004 and was replaced by one of the fund's analysts, David Segal. Segal will be joining the fund's longtime lead manager David Winters.

This personnel shuffling will not affect the fund's investment strategy. Winters and Segal will continue to look for securities that they believe are cheap relative to the firm's assets and cash flows. They also look far and wide--at companies of all sizes, for distressed debt and merger arbitrage opportunities--for what they perceive to represent the best risk-reward payoff. Thus, the fund has an average market capitalization that is less than half that of the world-stock category norm and a higher allocation to bonds than any other offering in the group. Winters also anticipates participating in more arbitrage opportunities with the pick-up in recent mergers and acquisitions.

This unusual approach has made the fund a top performer in its category. Its year-to-date gain of 16.98% through December 20 beats its typical rival's by more than four percentage points. Additionally, this fund has posted a top-decile annualized return over the trailing five-year period with much less volatility. Still, this fund does tend to lag its peers in big growth markets which was the case in 1998, 1999, and 2003, but we think that's a reasonable trade-off.

Our main concern with this offering is manager turnover at Mutual. This fund's parent company has had a difficult time retaining talent since Franklin bought it out in 1996. There was another departure this year when Mutual European's assistant manager, Matthew Haynes, left. For now, Mutual has kept enough key people in place to maintain its core competencies, but we're keeping watch for signs to the contrary.

Address:	51 John F Kennedy Pkwy Short Hills NJ 07078 800-342-5236
Web Address:	www.franklintempleton.com
Inception:	11-01-96*
Advisor:	Franklin Mutual Advisers, LLC
Subadvisor:	None
NTF Plans:	DATALynx NTF, Federated Tr NTF

Minimum Purchase:	$1000	Add: $50	IRA: $250
Min Auto Inv Plan:	$50	Add: $50	
Sales Fees:	5.75%L, 2.00%R		
Management Fee:	0.80% mx./0.73% mn., 0.15%A		
Actual Fees:	Mgt:0.80%	Dist:0.35%	
Expense Projections:	3Yr:$1010	5Yr:$1327	10Yr:$2221
Income Distrib:	Semi-Annually		

Mutual European A

Analyst Pick	Ticker	Load	NAV	Yield	Total Assets	Mstar Category
✔	TEMIX	5.75%	$19.50	2.7%	$1,450 mil	Europe Stock

Governance and Management

Fiduciary Grade: C

Portfolio Manager(s)

David Winters, a Mutual Series veteran who also runs Mutual Discovery, is the lead manager here. Philippe Brugere-Trelat, who was an analyst at Mutual from 1984 to 1994, joined Winters as an assistant manager in December 2004.

Strategy

This fund favors dirt-cheap firms. It normally hedges much or all of its foreign-currency exposure, which is quite rare for a Europe-stock offering. The manager also invests in the debt of bankrupt or distressed companies when he spies value, and he dabbles in arbitrage plays.

Historical Profile

Return Above Avg
Risk Low
Rating ★★★★ Above Avg

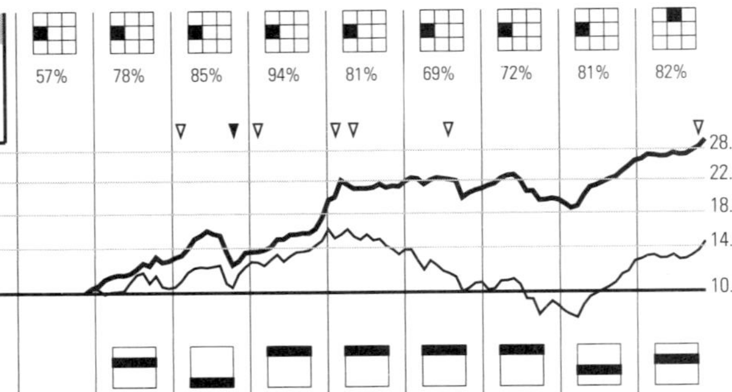

1993	1994	1995	1996	1997	1998	1999	2000	2001	2002	2003	12-04	History
—	—	—	11.38	12.57	12.47	16.75	15.36	14.27	12.83	16.58	19.50	NAV
—	—	—	5.41*	22.70	4.07	46.05	14.07	-5.05	-8.05	32.34	21.18	Total Return %
—	—	—	—	20.92	-15.86	19.02	28.26	16.37	7.89	-6.25	0.93	+/-MSCI EAFE
—	—	—	—	-1.10	-24.43	30.12	22.47	14.85	10.33	-6.20	0.30	+/-MSCI Eur
—	—	—	0.00	7.13	2.41	3.64	2.92	1.80	1.46	2.95	3.24	Income Return %
—	—	—	—	15.57	1.66	42.41	11.15	-6.85	-9.51	29.39	17.94	Capital Return %
—	—	—	—	37	87	13	2	7	25	67	29	Total Rtn % Rank Cat
—	—	—	0.05	0.81	0.30	0.45	0.48	0.28	0.21	0.38	0.53	Income $
—	—	—	0.02	0.56	0.36	0.89	3.16	0.04	0.10	0.00	0.02	Capital Gains $
—	—	—	—	1.37	1.40	1.39	1.38	1.40	1.40	1.43	—	Expense Ratio %
—	—	—	—	1.84	1.68	1.36	1.56	1.88	1.53	1.84	—	Income Ratio %
—	—	—	—	98	98	127	112	52	30	52	—	Turnover Rate %
—	—	—	17	93	171	177	233	256	304	417	545	Net Assets $mil

Performance 12-31-04

	1st Qtr	2nd Qtr	3rd Qtr	4th Qtr	Total
2000	11.70	-2.64	0.58	4.28	14.07
2001	-1.89	4.03	-12.86	6.76	-5.05
2002	7.64	-1.39	-13.52	0.17	-8.05
2003	-4.52	16.29	6.07	12.36	32.34
2004	3.98	1.65	1.96	12.45	21.18

Trailing	Total Return%	+/- MSCI EAFE	+/- MSCI Eur	%Rank Cat	Growth of $10,000
3 Mo	12.45	-2.87	-3.47	88	11,245
6 Mo	14.65	-0.35	-2.67	68	11,465
1 Yr	21.18	0.93	0.30	29	12,118
3 Yr Avg	13.82	1.93	2.84	32	14,745
5 Yr Avg	9.82	10.95	9.76	13	15,974
10 Yr Avg	—	—	—	—	—
15 Yr Avg	—	—	—	—	—

Tax Analysis	Tax-Adj Rtn%	%Rank Cat	Tax-Cost Rat	%Rank Cat
3 Yr (estimated)	10.59	40	0.91	84
5 Yr (estimated)	6.16	20	2.17	95
10 Yr (estimated)	—	—	—	—

Potential Capital Gain Exposure: 27% of assets

Rating and Risk

Time Period	Load-Adj Return %	Morningstar Rtn vs Cat	Morningstar Risk vs Cat	Morningstar Risk-Adj Rating
1 Yr	14.21			
3 Yr	11.60	Avg	Low	★★★
5 Yr	8.52	+Avg	Low	★★★★
10 Yr	—	—	—	—
Incept	14.21			

Other Measures	Standard Index S&P 500	Best Fit Index Mstar Small Value
Alpha	5.5	1.1
Beta	0.62	0.63
R-Squared	77	85

Standard Deviation	12.44
Mean	13.82
Sharpe Ratio	1.01

Portfolio Analysis 09-30-04

Share change since 12-03 Total Stocks:90	Sector	Country	% Assets
⊕ British American Tobacco	Goods	U.K.	3.39
⊕ NTL	Telecom	United States	3.39
⊕ Altadis	Goods	Spain	2.92
⊕ Orkla	Goods	Norway	2.48
⊕ Allied Irish Banks	Financial	Ireland	2.39
White Mountains Insuranc	Financial	United States	2.39
⊕ Anglo American	Ind Mtrls	U.K.	2.03
⊕ Imperial Tobacco Grp	Goods	U.K.	2.00
⊕ Carlsberg	Goods	Denmark	1.99
☼ Seton House Finance Limi	—	—	1.91
⊕ Nestle	Goods	Switzerland	1.76
Diageo	Goods	U.K.	1.70
⊕ Groupe Danone	Goods	France	1.66
⊖ Givaudan	Ind Mtrls	Switzerland	1.57
Cadbury Schweppes	Goods	U.K.	1.47
☼ Heineken Hldg Nv	Goods	Netherlands	1.43
Almanij Grp	Financial	Belgium	1.41
☼ Schindler-Hldg Ag	Ind Mtrls	Switzerland	1.40
SES GLOBAL	Telecom	Luxembourg	1.39
Berkshire Hathaway A	Financial	United States	1.39

Current Investment Style

Value Blnd Growth — Large Mid Small (style box: Large Blend)

Market Cap	%
Giant	13.0
Large	37.4
Mid	38.8
Small	10.5
Micro	0.3
Avg $mil: 7,124	

Value Measures		Rel Category
Price/Earnings	12.82	0.95
Price/Book	2.11	1.04
Price/Sales	0.87	0.96
Price/Cash Flow	6.70	1.25
Dividend Yield %	2.76	1.05

Growth Measures	%	Rel Category
Long-Term Erngs	10.57	0.95
Book Value	0.56	0.21
Sales	3.98	1.37
Cash Flow	-1.46	NMF
Historical Erngs	-0.29	NMF

Composition			
Cash	12.8	Bonds	4.9
Stocks	81.8	Other	0.6
Foreign (% of Stock)			90.6

Sector Weightings	% of Stocks	Rel MSCI EAFE	3 Year High	3 Year Low
Info	11.28	0.68		
Software	0.00	0.00	1	0
Hardware	0.00	0.00	0	0
Media	1.42	0.62	5	1
Telecom	9.86	1.03	10	1
Service	31.45	0.70		
Health	1.14	0.16	1	0
Consumer	2.26	0.45	7	1
Business	6.78	1.25	22	7
Financial	21.27	0.79	24	21
Mfg	57.26	1.48		
Goods	31.65	2.32	32	24
Ind Mtrls	21.83	1.77	22	12
Energy	2.78	0.38	3	1
Utilities	1.00	0.19	3	1

Regional Exposure	% Stock		
UK/W. Europe	87	N. America	11
Japan	0	Latn America	0
Asia X Japan	0	Other	2

Country Exposure	% Stock		
U.K.	22	Ireland	9
Switzerland	10	France	8
United States	9		

Morningstar's Take by Terence Geenty 12-29-04

A manager change doesn't diminish the appeal of this fund, but it does raise a few questions.

Mutual European's assistant portfolio manager Matt Haynes left the firm in November 2004. Remaining at the helm is the fund's longtime lead manager David Winters. Philippe Brugere-Trelat, who was an analyst at the firm from 1984 to 1994, joined Winters in late December. Since Brugere-Trelat is familiar with the investment process here, we expect a smooth transition.

Winters continues to use the same approach he always has. He looks for securities that he believes are cheap relative to the value of the firm's assets and cash flows. Additionally, he invests in small-, mid-, and large-cap companies, distressed debt, and merger arbitrage opportunities. And when there aren't attractive valuations to be found, the fund's cash stake can build: Cash was 12% of assets as of Sept. 30, 2004. Winters hasn't found many distressed-debt deals recently but thinks that the sudden increase in mergers and acquisitions will provide new arbitrage opportunities.

Despite the high allocation to cash, the fund has turned in a year-to-date gain of 19.32% through December 21, which is slightly ahead of the Europe stock category norm. Strong returns from tobacco holdings British American Tobacco , Altadis, and Imperial Tobacco Group are largely behind these results. Over longer periods, this fund has delivered above-average returns with very little volatility. We think this fund's risk-reward ratio makes it an attractive way to gain exposure to European companies.

Our main concern with this offering is manager turnover at Mutual. This fund's parent company has had difficulty retaining talent since Franklin bought it out in 1996. There was another departure this year when Mutual Discovery's assistant manager, Timothy Rankin, left. For now, Mutual has kept enough key people to maintain its core competencies, but we'll watch for signs to the contrary.

Address:	51 John F Kennedy Pkwy Short Hills NJ 07078 800-342-5236
Web Address:	www.franklintempleton.com
Inception:	11-01-96*
Advisor:	Franklin Mutual Advisers, LLC
Subadvisor:	None
NTF Plans:	DATALynx NTF, Federated Tr NTF

Minimum Purchase:	$1000	Add: $50	IRA: $250
Min Auto Inv Plan:	$50	Add: $50	
Sales Fees:	5.75%L, 2.00%R		
Management Fee:	0.80% mx./0.73% mn., 0.15%A		
Actual Fees:	Mgt:0.80%	Dist:0.35%	
Expense Projections:	3Yr:$1001	5Yr:$1312	10Yr:$2190
Income Distrib:	Semi-Annually		

Mutual Financial Svcs A

Ticker	Load	NAV	Yield	Total Assets	Mstar Category
TFSIX	5.75%	$20.47	1.1%	$661 mil	Specialty-Financial

Governance and Management

Fiduciary Grade: C

Portfolio Manager(s)

Former manager Ray Garea left Mutual Series at the end of September 2001. Jeff Diamond and Josh Ross were named to replace him, but Ross left in January 2002, and Diamond left in December 2003. Todd Jonasz and John Wimsatt took the helm in December 2003. Then Wimsatt left in December 2004 and was replaced by Charles Lahr, a financials analyst who has been with the firm since 2003.

Strategy

Like its Mutual Series siblings, this fund rummages through the bargain bins. Management scours the markets for financials firms trading cheaply on various measures and is willing to load the boat with sectors and companies that others shun. That keeps the fund out of many big-cap, mainstream financials. The fund will also hold sizable cash stakes and invest in foreign equities, distressed debt, and private placements.

Historical Profile

Return Above Avg
Risk Below Avg
Rating ★★★★ Above Avg

Investment Style Equity Stock %: 85% (1998), 87% (1999), 78% (2000), 80% (2001), 74% (2002), 84% (2003), 87% (2004)

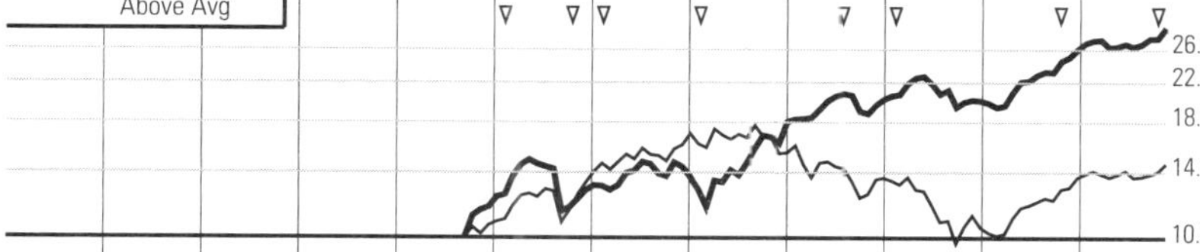

Performance Quartile (within Category)

History

	1993	1994	1995	1996	1997	1998	1999	2000	2001	2002	2003	12-04
NAV	—	—	—	—	12.28	12.87	13.07	16.35	16.66	15.95	20.08	20.47
Total Return %	—	—	—	—	23.93*	5.84	4.35	31.90	11.85	-0.57	29.79	15.17
+/-S&P 500	—	—	—	—	—	-22.73	-16.69	41.00	23.73	21.52	1.12	4.30
+/-DJ Finance	—	—	—	—	—	-1.67	2.83	4.93	18.23	11.78	-2.44	1.78
Income Return %	—	—	—	—	0.00	1.01	1.07	1.51	1.09	1.32	1.12	1.25
Capital Return %	—	—	—	—	—	4.83	3.28	30.39	10.76	-1.89	28.67	13.92
Total Rtn % Rank Cat	—	—	—	—	—	54	16	23	12	12	55	26
Income $	—	—	—	—	0.02	0.12	0.14	0.19	0.17	0.22	0.18	0.25
Capital Gains $	—	—	—	—	0.09	0.00	0.22	0.57	1.41	0.43	0.43	2.33
Expense Ratio %	—	—	—	—	1.35	1.35	1.42	1.59	1.45	1.44	1.48	—
Income Ratio %	—	—	—	—	1.02	1.42	0.82	1.30	1.03	1.12	0.93	—
Turnover Rate %	—	—	—	—	—	137	82	54	83	40	26	—
Net Assets $mil	—	—	—	—	77	165	108	131	168	179	264	297

Performance 12-31-04

	1st Qtr	2nd Qtr	3rd Qtr	4th Qtr	Total
2000	-1.84	2.78	22.09	7.07	31.90
2001	2.14	11.38	-7.50	6.29	11.85
2002	8.40	-0.22	-10.95	3.24	-0.57
2003	-2.45	13.28	4.49	12.41	29.79
2004	4.93	-2.06	2.81	9.01	15.17

Trailing	Total Return%	+/- S&P 500	+/- DJ Finance	%Rank Cat	Growth of $10,000
3 Mo	9.01	-0.22	0.06	55	10,901
6 Mo	12.08	4.89	1.81	34	11,208
1 Yr	15.17	4.30	1.78	26	11,517
3 Yr Avg	14.12	10.54	4.59	24	14,862
5 Yr Avg	17.00	19.30	7.67	14	21,924
10 Yr Avg	—	—	—	—	—
15 Yr Avg	—	—	—	—	—

Tax Analysis	Tax-Adj Rtn%	%Rank Cat	Tax-Cost Rat	%Rank Cat
3 Yr (estimated)	10.32	33	1.40	71
5 Yr (estimated)	13.67	20	1.70	77
10 Yr (estimated)	—	—	—	—

Potential Capital Gain Exposure: 25% of assets

Rating and Risk

Time Period	Load-Adj Return %	Morningstar Rtn vs Cat	Morningstar Risk vs Cat	Morningstar Risk-Adj Rating
1 Yr	8.55			
3 Yr	11.89	+Avg	-Avg	★★★★
5 Yr	15.63	+Avg	-Avg	★★★★
10 Yr	—	—	—	—
Incept	15.16			

Other Measures	Standard Index S&P 500	Best Fit Index Russ MV
Alpha	11.1	2.7
Beta	0.58	0.69
R-Squared	65	85
Standard Deviation	12.24	
Mean	14.12	
Sharpe Ratio	1.05	

Portfolio Analysis 09-30-04

Share change since 12-03 Total Stocks:73	Sector	PE	YTD Ret%	% Assets
⊖ White Mountains Insuranc	Financial	41.1	40.75	3.26
⊖ Sovereign Bancorp	Financial	16.4	-4.54	3.20
⊕ Allied Irish Banks	Financial	—	—	3.01
⊕ Saxon Capital	Financial	—	—	2.96
⊕ Old Republic Internation	Financial	10.3	1.89	2.39
☼ Hanmi Financial	Financial	23.1	84.24	2.33
☼ State Natl Bancshares	Financial	—	—	2.32
Euronext	Financial	—	—	2.19
⊖ First Community Bancorp	Financial	19.1	20.73	2.19
⊕ Bank of Ireland	Financial	—	—	2.00
☼ Occum Acquisition	—	—	—	1.91
☼ BNP Paribas	Financial	—	—	1.87
⊕ iStar Financial	Financial	29.3	24.56	1.87
⊖ Danske Bank Grp	Financial	—	—	1.35
☼ Bimini Mortgage Manageme	Financial	—	—	1.35
⊕ Bank Mutual	Financial	34.9	8.58	1.74
☼ Conseco	Financial	—	-8.49	1.63
☼ Centennial Bk Hldgs	—	—	—	1.62
Berkshire Hathaway A	Financial	—	—	1.60
☼ Deutsche Boerse	Financial	—	—	1.53

Current Investment Style (Value Blnd Growth; Large Mid Small)

Market Cap	%
Giant	2.7
Large	17.5
Mid	38.9
Small	21.3
Micro	19.6
Avg $mil: 2,176	

Value Measures		Rel Category
Price/Earnings	14.06	1.08
Price/Book	1.28	0.67
Price/Sales	1.68	0.90
Price/Cash Flow	1.11	0.30
Dividend Yield %	2.24	1.09

Growth Measures	%	Rel Category
Long-Term Erngs	10.76	0.92
Book Value	7.62	0.78
Sales	-2.48	NMF
Cash Flow	0.20	0.01
Historical Erngs	9.49	0.48

Profitability	%	Rel Category
Return on Equity	14.82	0.92
Return on Assets	9.46	0.91
Net Margin	18.96	1.07

Industry Weightings	% of Stocks	Rel Cat
Intl Banks	0.0	0.0
Banks	21.2	1.0
Real Estate	6.0	2.2
Sec Mgmt	2.6	0.2
S & Ls	25.5	2.5
Prop & Reins	23.3	1.3
Life Ins	8.8	2.3
Misc. Ins	5.4	1.5
Other	7.1	0.5

Composition

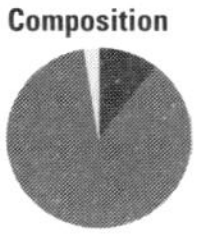

Cash	10.3
Stocks	87.1
Bonds	0.0
Other	2.5
Foreign (% of Stock)	21.4

Morningstar's Take by Christopher Traulsen 01-05-05

Mutual Financial Services needs to prove itself all over again.

This fund has undergone yet another manager change. In mid-December 2004, comanager John Wimsatt left the firm. That still leaves Todd Jonasz, who had run the fund with Wimsatt since December 2003, at the helm. He's joined by Charles Lahr, who has been with the firm since 2003.

We don't expect any changes to the fund's style. Like all Mutual Series funds, this one uses a unique approach, spreading its assets across undervalued equities, both in the U.S. and overseas, distressed debt, and merger-arbitrage plays. The fund also typically holds anywhere from 10% to 20% of assets in cash, depending on the opportunities available to the portfolio managers.

That style has been hugely successful here. The fund has delivered excellent longer-term returns relative to its financials peers. Moreover, its standard deviation--a measure of volatility--has been much lower than the category norm. In the latter regard, the fund has been helped by its diversification across asset classes and limited price risk.

Nevertheless, we're increasingly concerned by the manager turnover at this fund and at Mutual Series in general. This fund has seen four managers leave since mid-2001, and the firm as a whole--once vaunted--has now lost most of the investment talent that was responsible for its rise. The sole remaining portfolio manager with a link to the firm's past is David Winters, who joined in 1996. Of the rest, two joined in 2000, one in 2001, two in 2002, and one in 2003.

Given its unique style, this fund may well be able to overcome the challenge presented by the loss of talent. But at this point, it has to prove its worth. More importantly, Franklin Resources, which owns Mutual Series, needs to do something to retain people. When you lose as many managers as Mutual has in such a short time, it's clear that something isn't working.

Address:	51 John F Kennedy Pkwy Short Hills NJ 07078 800-342-5236
Web Address:	www.franklintempleton.com
Inception:	08-19-97 *
Advisor:	Franklin Mutual Advisers, LLC
Subadvisor:	None
NTF Plans:	DATALynx NTF, Federated Tr NTF

Minimum Purchase:	$1000	Add: $50	IRA: $250
Min Auto Inv Plan:	$50	Add: $50	
Sales Fees:	5.75%L, 0.10%S, 2.00%R		
Management Fee:	0.80% mx./0.73% mn., 0.15%A		
Actual Fees:	Mgt:0.80%	Dist:0.35%	
Expense Projections:	3Yr:$1016	5Yr:$1336	10Yr:$2242
Income Distrib:	Semi-Annually		

Mutual Qualified A

Ticker	Load	NAV	Yield	Total Assets	Mstar Category
TEQIX	5.75%	$19.41	1.6%	$4,495 mil	Mid-Cap Value

Governance and Management

Fiduciary Grade: B

Portfolio Manager(s)

Manager Ray Garea left this fund at the end of July 2001. Jeff Diamond replaced him but left in December 2003. Anne Gudefin, an expert in European securities and the fund's assistant manager under Diamond, has been named manager. Shawn Tumulty, a distressed-debt analyst, has been named assistant manager. Several other managers have departed the Mutual Series complex in recent years.

Strategy

This deep-value offering hunts for bargains amid the market's rubble. Its management uses methods such as discounted cash flow and sum-of-the-parts analysis to identify firms it thinks are undervalued. In addition to domestic equities, management is also fond of foreign conglomerates, distressed credits, and merger-arbitrage plays. The fund usually holds 130 to 150 equity positions and will have significant cash positions when management can't find securities that meet its criteria.

Historical Profile

Return Average
Risk Low
Rating ★★★ Neutral

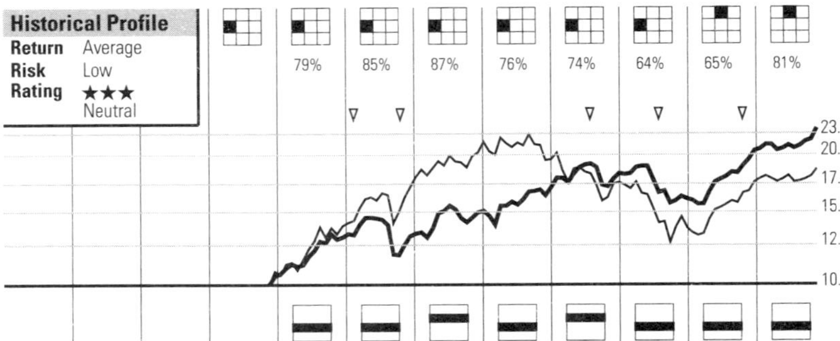

Investment Style
Equity
Stock %

1996	1997	1998	1999	2000	2001	2002	2003	12-04
	79%	85%	87%	76%	74%	64%	65%	81%

▼ Manager Change
▽ Partial Manager Change

Growth of $10,000
▬ Investment Values of Fund
— Investment Values of S&P 500

Performance Quartile (within Category)

1993	1994	1995	1996	1997	1998	1999	2000	2001	2002	2003	12-04	History
—	—	—	16.23	18.14	16.42	16.87	16.56	16.44	13.91	17.80	19.41	NAV
—	—	—	6.21*	24.44	0.15	13.27	13.81	7.85	-13.00	29.98	16.27	Total Return %
—	—	—	—	-8.91	-28.42	-7.77	22.91	19.73	9.09	1.31	5.40	+/-S&P 500
—	—	—	—	-9.93	-4.93	13.38	-5.37	5.52	-3.36	-8.09	-7.44	+/-Russ MV
—	—	—	0.00	3.74	2.16	1.42	3.00	0.84	1.29	1.89	1.82	Income Return %
—	—	—	—	20.70	-2.01	11.85	10.81	7.01	-14.29	28.09	14.45	Capital Return %
—	—	—	—	58	61	29	70	44	54	68	56	Total Rtn % Rank Cat
—	—	—	0.41	0.60	0.39	0.23	0.49	0.14	0.21	0.26	0.32	Income $
—	—	—	0.82	1.40	1.33	1.48	1.98	1.27	0.22	0.00	0.93	Capital Gains $
—	—	—	—	1.11	1.11	1.11	1.13	1.14	1.15	1.20	—	Expense Ratio %
—	—	—	—	1.48	1.66	0.97	1.08	0.94	1.46	0.99	—	Income Ratio %
—	—	—	65	53	67	60	55	53	51	50	—	Turnover Rate %
—	—	—	55	452	571	474	444	485	454	627	696	Net Assets $mil

Performance 12-31-04

	1st Qtr	2nd Qtr	3rd Qtr	4th Qtr	Total
2000	2.79	0.64	7.75	2.10	13.81
2001	2.78	10.07	-10.53	6.54	7.85
2002	3.41	-6.26	-12.32	2.37	-13.00
2003	-2.80	14.63	3.44	12.78	29.98
2004	3.37	-0.35	2.08	10.58	16.27

Trailing	Total Return%	+/- S&P 500	+/- Russ MV	%Rank Cat	Growth of $10,000
3 Mo	10.58	1.35	-2.88	63	11,058
6 Mo	12.87	5.68	-2.56	25	11,287
1 Yr	16.27	5.40	-7.44	56	11,627
3 Yr Avg	9.55	5.97	-6.01	69	13,147
5 Yr Avg	10.05	12.35	-3.43	64	16,142
10 Yr Avg	—	—	—	—	—
15 Yr Avg	—	—	—	—	—

Tax Analysis	Tax-Adj Rtn%	%Rank Cat	Tax-Cost Rat	%Rank Cat
3 Yr (estimated)	6.42	84	0.92	75
5 Yr (estimated)	6.89	71	1.71	87
10 Yr (estimated)	—	—	—	—

Potential Capital Gain Exposure: 32% of assets

Rating and Risk

Time Period	Load-Adj Return %	Morningstar Rtn vs Cat	Morningstar Risk vs Cat	Morningstar Risk-Adj Rating
1 Yr	9.58			
3 Yr	7.41	-Avg	Low	★★
5 Yr	8.75	Avg	Low	★★★
10 Yr	—	—	—	—
Incept	10.62			

Other Measures	Standard Index S&P 500	Best Fit Index Mstar Mid Value
Alpha	6.5	-1.6
Beta	0.63	0.73
R-Squared	73	91
Standard Deviation	12.02	
Mean	9.55	
Sharpe Ratio	0.69	

Portfolio Analysis 09-30-04

Share change since 12-03 Total Stocks:145	Sector	PE	YTD Ret%	% Assets
White Mountains Insuranc	Financial	41.1	40.75	4.40
International Steel Grp	—	—	—	2.08
⊕ Altadis	Goods	—	—	2.05
⊕ Newmont Mining	Ind Mtrls	45.6	-8.02	2.02
Sovereign Bancorp	Financial	16.4	-4.54	1.96
☼ Freeport-McMoRan Copper	Ind Mtrls	—	-6.50	1.65
⊕ Allied Irish Banks	Financial	—	—	1.62
⊕ NTL	Telecom	—	4.60	1.51
Washington Post	Media	27.8	25.21	1.46
⊕ Saxon Capital	Financial	—	—	1.38
⊕ British American Tobacco	Goods	—	—	1.38
⊕ Orkla	Goods	—	—	1.37
Liberty Media	Media	—	11.56	1.29
⊕ Florida East Coast Inds	Business	30.8	36.92	1.28
☼ Kkr Finl 144A	—	—	—	1.27
⊕ Groupe Danone	Goods	—	—	1.25
⊕ EW Scripps	Media	20.0	3.37	1.15
Republic Services A	Business	21.8	32.45	1.14
⊕ Reynolds American	Goods	—	43.11	1.12
Canary Wharf Grp	Financial	—	—	1.07

Current Investment Style

Market Cap	%
Giant	14.3
Large	30.8
Mid	41.7
Small	11.5
Micro	1.6
Avg $mil: 7,262	

Value Measures		Rel Category
Price/Earnings	15.80	1.03
Price/Book	1.87	0.97
Price/Sales	1.22	1.39
Price/Cash Flow	2.19	0.38
Dividend Yield %	1.86	1.30

Growth Measures	%	Rel Category
Long-Term Erngs	10.54	0.96
Book Value	1.81	0.32
Sales	0.34	0.07
Cash Flow	4.24	1.07
Historical Erngs	5.68	0.49

Profitability	%	Rel Category
Return on Equity	12.34	0.97
Return on Assets	5.15	0.85
Net Margin	7.90	0.90

Sector Weightings	% of Stocks	Rel S&P 500	3 Year High	3 Year Low
Info	14.59	0.68		
Software	0.00	0.00	1	0
Hardware	0.15	0.01	1	0
Media	8.56	2.23	13	9
Telecom	5.88	1.87	6	1
Service	47.27	1.02		
Health	7.19	0.58	8	6
Consumer	2.17	0.24	10	2
Business	5.91	1.46	10	6
Financial	32.00	1.54	34	22
Mfg	38.14	1.19		
Goods	17.13	1.84	17	11
Ind Mtrls	14.80	1.17	15	10
Energy	3.90	0.54	7	4
Utilities	2.31	0.78	4	2

Composition

Cash	9.4
Stocks	80.5
Bonds	9.8
Other	0.3
Foreign (% of Stock)	38.1

Morningstar's Take by Christopher Traulsen 10-29-04

Mutual Qualified is more flexible than its siblings, which may give it an edge.

At $4.1 billion in assets, this fund isn't svelte, but it is the smallest of the three big domestic Mutual Series funds. That should give it slightly more ability to descend down the market-cap ladder. Its prospectus also now permits it to invest up to 50% of its assets in foreign securities.

That flexibility should come in handy given the wide-ranging style employed by all the Mutual Series offerings. Like its siblings, this fund seeks undervalued equities across the market-cap spectrum, It also invests in distressed debt and merger-arbitrage. As of Sept. 30, the fund held just 81% of its assets in equities. The remainder of the fund's assets is in cash and bonds.

That style has produced very solid risk-adjusted results over the years. The fund is one of the least-volatile offerings in the mid-value category, thanks to its diversification across asset classes and attention to value. It has also soundly beaten the S&P 500/Barra Value index over time--a reasonable benchmark for a go-anywhere value offering like this.

One of the fund's recent successes is International Steel Group. Although the stock is down a bit this year, the fund bought its private equity in 2002 because its restructuring plan looked promising. That was a good call. The fund's total cost for its shares in ISG is $13.8 million, and its stake is now worth $104.9 million.

The fund does tend to lag when equities lead they way, so it isn't for investors seeking to keep pace with the market over short-periods of time. We're also concerned that the fund's advisor has experienced significant turnover in its investment personnel in recent years. This fund's former manager left at the end of 2003, and Tim Rankin, another high-level investment professional, left this year. The advisor needs to improve its ability to retain talent for this fund to remain an appealing investment.

Address:	51 John F Kennedy Pkwy Short Hills NJ 07078 800-342-5236
Web Address:	www.franklintempleton.com
Inception:	11-01-96*
Advisor:	Franklin Mutual Advisers, LLC
Subadvisor:	None
NTF Plans:	DATALynx NTF, Federated Tr NTF

Minimum Purchase:	$1000	Add: $50	IRA: $250
Min Auto Inv Plan:	$50	Add: $50	
Sales Fees:	5.75%L, 2.00%R		
Management Fee:	0.60% mx./0.54% mn., 0.15%A		
Actual Fees:	Mgt:0.60%	Dist:0.35%	
Expense Projections:	3Yr:$934	5Yr:$1197	10Yr:$1946
Income Distrib:	Semi-Annually		

Mutual Shares A

Ticker	Load	NAV	Yield	Total Assets	Mstar Category
TESIX	5.75%	$22.94	1.3%	$12,401 mil	Large Value

Governance and Management

Fiduciary Grade: C

Portfolio Manager(s)

Larry Sondike stepped down in fall 2002. David Winters, who has been with the advisor for 14 years, has since taken the reins. He's joined by assistant manager Deborah Turner. Tim Rankin had also been an assistant manager until stepping down in 2004. The firm recently hired another distressed debt analyst, who has experience analyzing the capital structures of cable and telecom companies, and a stock analyst focused on the industrials sector.

Strategy

This deep-value fund tries to ferret out gems among the market's rubble. Its management uses a variety of methods to value companies, including discounted cash-flow and sum-of-the-parts analyses. In addition to domestic equities, that has led it into a stack of mispriced foreign conglomerates and distressed credits. The fund holds about 125 stocks and frequents the financials and industrials arenas.

Historical Profile

Return Above Avg
Risk Low
Rating ★★★★ Above Avg

Investment Style
Equity
Stock %: 75% 76% 77% 81% 77% 71% 59% 64% 71%

▼ Manager Change
▽ Partial Manager Change

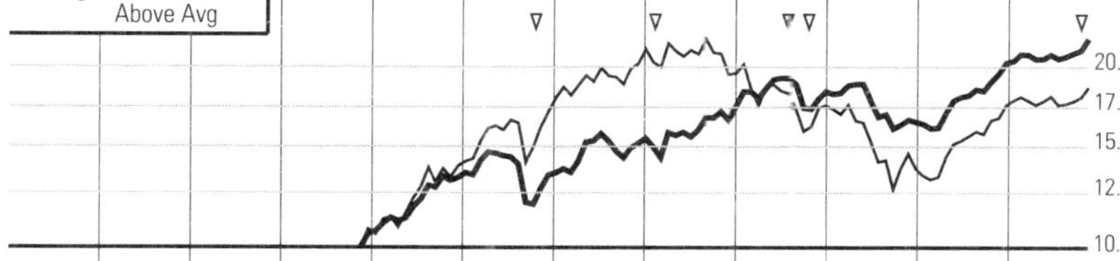

Growth of $10,000
▬ Investment Values of Fund
— Investment Values of S&P 500

Performance Quartile (within Category)

1993	1994	1995	1996	1997	1998	1999	2000	2001	2002	2003	12-04	History
—	—	—	18.56	21.26	19.49	20.38	19.73	19.37	16.78	20.89	22.94	NAV
—	—	—	6.66*	26.03	0.01	14.63	13.42	5.94	-11.20	26.18	13.44	Total Return %
—	—	—	—	-7.32	-28.56	-6.41	22.52	17.82	10.89	-2.49	2.57	+/-S&P 500
—	—	—	—	-9.15	-15.62	7.28	6.41	11.53	4.32	-3.85	-3.05	+/-Russ 1000 VI
—	—	—	0.00	2.69	2.19	1.78	3.19	0.92	1.02	1.57	1.49	Income Return %
—	—	—	—	23.34	-2.18	12.85	10.23	5.02	-12.22	24.61	11.95	Capital Return %
—	—	—	—	66	90	13	30	10	6	66	41	Total Rtn % Rank Cat
—	—	—	0.47	0.49	0.46	0.34	0.63	0.13	0.19	0.26	0.31	Income $
—	—	—	1.16	1.58	1.29	1.58	2.51	1.35	0.26	0.00	0.42	Capital Gains $
—	—	—	—	1.07	1.08	1.10	1.11	1.12	1.14	1.19	—	Expense Ratio %
—	—	—	—	1.58	1.78	1.23	1.34	1.05	1.44	0.93	—	Income Ratio %
—	—	—	58	50	69	66	63	53	51	55	—	Turnover Rate %
—	—	—	77	1,038	1,515	1,365	1,285	1,573	1,551	2,337	2,946	Net Assets $mil

Performance 12-31-04

	1st Qtr	2nd Qtr	3rd Qtr	4th Qtr	Total
2000	2.26	-1.66	7.75	4.67	13.42
2001	3.14	8.30	-11.03	6.59	5.94
2002	2.43	-5.98	-10.18	2.66	-11.20
2003	-2.26	12.82	2.45	11.70	26.18
2004	3.21	0.04	0.56	9.26	13.44

Trailing	Total Return%	+/- S&P 500	+/- Russ 1000 VI	%Rank Cat	Growth of $10,000
3 Mo	9.26	0.03	-1.12	46	10,926
6 Mo	9.87	2.68	-2.21	37	10,987
1 Yr	13.44	2.57	-3.05	41	11,344
3 Yr Avg	8.32	4.74	-0.25	16	12,709
5 Yr Avg	8.84	11.14	3.57	11	15,274
10 Yr Avg	—	—	—	—	—
15 Yr Avg	—	—	—	—	—

Tax Analysis	Tax-Adj Rtn%	%Rank Cat	Tax-Cost Rat	%Rank Cat
3 Yr (estimated)	5.51	39	0.66	44
5 Yr (estimated)	5.78	22	1.65	86
10 Yr (estimated)	—	—	—	—

Potential Capital Gain Exposure: 25% of assets

Rating and Risk

Time Period	Load-Adj Return %	Morningstar Rtn vs Cat	Morningstar Risk vs Cat	Morningstar Risk-Adj Rating
1 Yr	6.92			
3 Yr	6.21	Avg	Low	★★★★
5 Yr	7.56	+Avg	Low	★★★★
10 Yr	—	—	—	—
Incept	10.25			

Other Measures	Standard Index S&P 500	Best Fit Index Mstar Mid Value
Alpha	5.4	-1.5
Beta	0.55	0.63
R-Squared	74	88
Standard Deviation	10.35	
Mean	8.32	
Sharpe Ratio	0.68	

Portfolio Analysis 09-30-04

Share change since 12-03 Total Stocks:130	Sector	PE	YTD Ret%	% Assets
⊕ White Mountains Insuranc	Financial	41.1	40.75	3.43
⊕ British American Tobacco	Goods	—	—	3.29
⊕ Berkshire Hathaway B	Financial	20.9	4.30	2.62
⊕ Altadis	Goods	—	—	2.37
Washington Post	Media	27.8	25.21	1.96
Diageo	Goods	—	—	1.80
⊕ Reynolds American	Goods	—	43.11	1.69
⊕ Newmont Mining	Ind Mtrls	45.6	-8.02	1.67
International Steel Grp	—	—	—	1.66
⊕ Florida East Coast Inds	Business	30.8	36.92	1.41
☼ Freeport-McMoRan Copper	Ind Mtrls	—	-6.50	1.37
Imperial Tobacco Grp	Goods	—	—	1.35
Nestle	Goods	—	—	1.34
☼ Opti Canada	—	—	—	1.30
Berkshire Hathaway A	Financial	—	—	1.23
⊕ Orkla	Goods	—	—	1.21
⊕ Allied Irish Banks	Financial	—	—	1.14
Sovereign Bancorp	Financial	16.4	-4.54	1.14
Liberty Media	Media	—	11.56	1.12
⊕ NTL	Telecom	—	4.60	1.12

Current Investment Style

Value Blnd Growth — Large Mid Small

Market Cap	%
Giant	19.1
Large	36.2
Mid	38.8
Small	5.1
Micro	0.7
Avg $mil: 10,013	

Value Measures		Rel Category
Price/Earnings	15.27	1.02
Price/Book	2.17	0.96
Price/Sales	1.24	1.04
Price/Cash Flow	2.97	0.47
Dividend Yield %	1.96	0.96

Growth Measures	%	Rel Category
Long-Term Erngs	11.14	1.07
Book Value	1.47	0.26
Sales	2.57	0.61
Cash Flow	4.44	0.85
Historical Erngs	8.29	0.70

Profitability	%	Rel Category
Return on Equity	13.43	0.85
Return on Assets	5.45	0.70
Net Margin	6.05	0.59

Sector Weightings	% of Stocks	Rel S&P 500	3 Year High	3 Year Low
Info	13.91	0.65		
Software	0.00	0.00	1	0
Hardware	0.16	0.02	0	0
Media	9.15	2.38	15	9
Telecom	4.60	1.46	5	1
Service	40.81	0.88		
Health	5.76	0.46	10	5
Consumer	1.66	0.18	10	1
Business	4.64	1.15	8	5
Financial	28.75	1.38	30	21
Mfg	45.28	1.41		
Goods	27.17	2.91	27	16
Ind Mtrls	13.35	1.05	13	7
Energy	2.67	0.37	5	2
Utilities	2.09	0.71	4	2

Composition

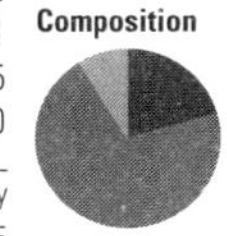

Cash	20.3
Stocks	70.7
Bonds	8.8
Other	0.2
Foreign (% of Stock)	39.6

Morningstar's Take by Christopher Traulsen 10-28-04

Mutual Shares is good at what it does, but we have a concern about its advisor.

This fund has a lot in its favor. Unlike many equity offerings, it's designed to emphasize risk control. Its managers don't feel compelled to stick to a particular style box square or asset class. They invest in undervalued equities, distressed debt, and merger arbitrage. The team also invests overseas if that's where the opportunities are and often holds sizable cash stakes.

The resulting portfolio doesn't look much like other equity funds' or its typical mid-value peer's. As of Sept. 30, 2004, the fund devoted just 71% of its assets to stocks, with 20% in cash, and about 9% in bonds. It also held about 35% of its equity portfolio in non-North American stocks and had a significant overweight in consumer-goods stocks.

The fund has had many successes over the years. One of the more recent ones is International Steel Group. Although the stock is down a bit this year, the fund bought in to its private equity in 2002 because the managers thought its restructuring plan looked promising. They were right. The fund's total cost for its shares in ISG is $29.7 million, and its stake is now worth $225.8 million.

Over the years, the fund has outperformed the S&P 500/Barra Value index--a reasonable benchmark for a fund like this, with much less volatility than the index. Indeed, its diversification and penchant for holding cash have made it one of the least volatile funds in its category. It does tend to lag when equities lead the way, though, so it isn't for investors seeking to keep pace with the market over short periods of time.

We do have one concern. The fund's advisor has experienced significant turnover in its investment personnel in recent years. In 2004, assistant manager Tim Rankin left to join a hedge fund. His departure isn't particularly noteworthy, but we're worried that the firm is having trouble retaining talent. The advisor needs to address this issue for this fund to remain an appealing investment.

Address:	51 John F Kennedy Pkwy Short Hills NJ 07078 800-342-5236
Web Address:	www.franklintempleton.com
Inception:	11-01-96*
Advisor:	Franklin Mutual Advisers, LLC
Subadvisor:	None
NTF Plans:	DATALynx NTF, Federated Tr NTF

Minimum Purchase:	$1000 Add: $50 IRA: $250
Min Auto Inv Plan:	$50 Add: $50
Sales Fees:	5.75%L, 2.00%R
Management Fee:	0.60% mx./0.51% mn., 0.15%A
Actual Fees:	Mgt:0.59% Dist:0.35%
Expense Projections:	3Yr:$931 5Yr:$1192 10Yr:$1935
Income Distrib:	Semi-Annually

N/I Numeric Inv Sm CapVl

Ticker	Load	NAV	Yield	Total Assets	Mstar Category
NISVX	Closed	$19.30	0.4%	$258 mil	Small Value

Governance and Management

Fiduciary Grade: B

Portfolio Manager(s)

All N/I Numeric Investors' funds are team-managed, but Arup Datta, who joined the firm in 1993 as a quantitative analyst and who helped develop the firm's models, serves as lead manager. Sharing day-to-day management responsibilities with Datta is Joe Schirripa, who arrived in April 2003. Datta and Schirripa are supported by Numeric's CIO, Langdon Wheeler, and one research analyst.

Strategy

Four quantitative models are used to build this broadly diversified portfolio. Because it is a value offering, management takes most of its cues from the shop's fair-value model, which seeks out companies trading at a discount to their industry peers and that sell at a relatively low price/cash-flow ratio. The other models identify companies that avoid sketchy accounting, boast increasing earnings or price momentum, and are not magnets for short-sellers. The fund's sector weightings mimic those of the Russell 2000 Value Index. Portfolio turnover is high but may moderate as the earnings-trend model is used more sparingly.

Historical Profile

Return High
Risk Average
Rating ★★★★★ Highest

Investment Style: Equity, Stock %: 95% (1999), 96% (2000), 97% (2001), 96% (2002), 99% (2003), 97% (12-04)

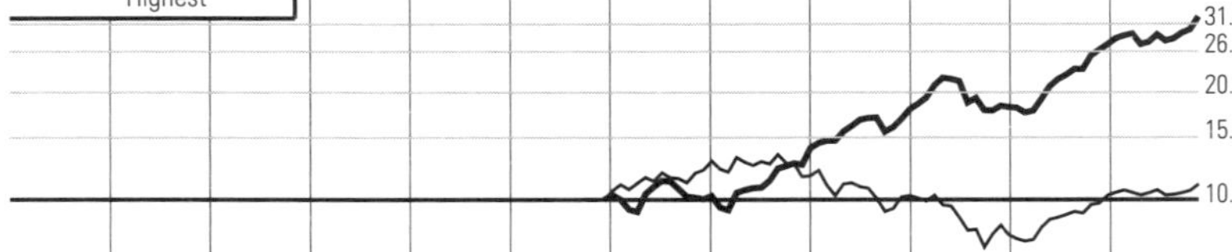

▼ Manager Change
▽ Partial Manager Change

Growth of $10,000
— Investment Values of Fund
— Investment Values of S&P 500

Performance Quartile (within Category)

History

1993	1994	1995	1996	1997	1998	1999	2000	2001	2002	2003	12-04	History
—	—	—	—	—	12.37	10.83	14.52	15.69	14.46	19.19	19.30	NAV
—	—	—	—	—	3.08*	-0.63	35.61	27.89	1.44	49.52	23.80	Total Return %
—	—	—	—	—	—	-21.67	44.71	39.77	23.53	20.85	12.93	+/-S&P 500
—	—	—	—	—	—	0.86	12.78	13.87	12.87	3.49	1.55	+/-Russ 2000 VL
—	—	—	—	—	0.00	0.79	1.32	0.12	0.00	0.64	0.43	Income Return %
—	—	—	—	—	—	-1.42	34.29	27.77	1.44	48.88	23.37	Capital Return %
—	—	—	—	—	—	60	4	13	5	24	22	Total Rtn % Rank Cat
—	—	—	—	—	0.00	0.10	0.14	0.02	0.00	0.09	0.08	Income $
—	—	—	—	—	0.00	1.32	0.00	2.58	1.41	2.24	3.76	Capital Gains $
—	—	—	—	—	—	1.00	1.00	1.67	1.73	1.55	—	Expense Ratio %
—	—	—	—	—	—	1.15	1.35	0.17	-0.35	0.33	—	Income Ratio %
—	—	—	—	—	—	—	256	277	276	268	—	Turnover Rate %
—	—	—	—	—	—	11	20	46	114	198	258	Net Assets $mil

Performance 12-31-04

	1st Qtr	2nd Qtr	3rd Qtr	4th Qtr	Total
2000	2.03	3.44	14.70	12.02	35.61
2001	4.75	14.27	-7.42	15.41	27.89
2002	16.70	2.68	-17.02	2.02	1.44
2003	-2.28	22.36	6.65	17.25	49.52
2004	7.03	-0.54	1.01	15.13	23.80

Trailing	Total Return%	+/- S&P 500	+/- Russ 2000 VL	%Rank Cat	Growth of $10,000
3 Mo	15.13	5.90	1.93	6	11,513
6 Mo	16.28	9.09	2.91	5	11,628
1 Yr	23.80	12.93	1.55	22	12,380
3 Yr Avg	23.37	19.79	6.87	5	18,777
5 Yr Avg	26.63	28.93	9.40	1	32,560
10 Yr Avg	—	—	—	—	—
15 Yr Avg	—	—	—	—	—

Tax Analysis	Tax-Adj Rtn%	%Rank Cat	Tax-Cost Rat	%Rank Cat
3 Yr (estimated)	17.84	14	4.48	100
5 Yr (estimated)	21.68	2	3.91	100
10 Yr (estimated)	—	—	—	—

Potential Capital Gain Exposure: 14% of assets

Rating and Risk

Time Period	Load-Adj Return %	Morningstar Rtn vs Cat	Morningstar Risk vs Cat	Morningstar Risk-Adj Rating
1 Yr	23.80			
3 Yr	23.37	High	Avg	★★★★★
5 Yr	26.63	High	Avg	★★★★★
10 Yr	—	—	—	—
Incept	21.89			

Other Measures	Standard Index S&P 500	Best Fit Index Mstar Small Value
Alpha	20.4	4.8
Beta	0.73	0.93
R-Squared	47	90
Standard Deviation	19.46	
Mean	23.37	
Sharpe Ratio	1.14	

Portfolio Analysis 10-31-04

Share change since 09-04 Total Stocks:181	Sector	PE	YTD Ret%	% Assets
⊖ Overseas Shipholding Gro	Business	9.6	64.92	1.52
LandAmerica Financial Gr	Financial	6.8	4.33	1.43
Vintage Petroleum	Energy	—	90.70	1.38
Pacific Capital Bancorp	Financial	16.7	26.15	1.35
MAF Bancorp	Financial	13.7	9.05	1.34
Omega Healthcare Investo	Financial	NMF	35.67	1.31
Tanger Factory Outlet Ce	Financial	64.8	38.12	1.31
Walter Industries	Ind Mtrls	—	155.04	1.30
☼ Highwoods Properties	Financial	—	16.86	1.28
⊕ Avista Corporation	Utilities	29.0	0.39	1.27
RPM International	Goods	14.0	23.68	1.26
Nash-Finch	Consumer	29.5	72.72	1.24
⊕ Westcorp	Financial	12.4	27.32	1.24
SL Green Realty	Financial	16.8	53.52	1.23
Silgan Holdings	Goods	16.4	44.83	1.23
IPC Holdings	Financial	10.5	14.38	1.22
CBL & Associates Propert	Financial	16.8	41.69	1.22
⊕ UGI	Utilities	17.1	25.02	1.21
⊕ Assured Guaranty	Financial	—	—	1.19
⊕ Brown Shoe	Consumer	12.6	-20.37	1.19

Current Investment Style

Value Blnd Growth / Large Mid Small

Market Cap	%
Giant	0.0
Large	0.0
Mid	30.2
Small	48.6
Micro	21.2

Avg $mil: 887

Value Measures		Rel Category
Price/Earnings	13.66	0.86
Price/Book	1.75	1.05
Price/Sales	0.63	0.84
Price/Cash Flow	4.70	0.91
Dividend Yield %	1.53	1.28

Growth Measures	%	Rel Category
Long-Term Erngs	12.21	1.01
Book Value	4.29	0.99
Sales	2.62	0.84
Cash Flow	6.08	2.80
Historical Erngs	14.07	2.93

Profitability	%	Rel Category
Return on Equity	10.96	1.20
Return on Assets	4.34	1.05
Net Margin	8.60	1.29

Sector Weightings	% of Stocks	Rel S&P 500	3 Year High	Low
Info	10.24	0.48		
Software	2.49	0.58	3	0
Hardware	4.76	0.47	8	4
Media	1.92	0.50	3	0
Telecom	1.07	0.34	2	0
Service	56.20	1.21		
Health	4.41	0.35	6	3
Consumer	9.11	1.00	15	7
Business	9.39	2.32	12	5
Financial	33.29	1.60	35	23
Mfg	33.56	1.04		
Goods	4.26	0.46	11	4
Ind Mtrls	16.67	1.32	24	15
Energy	7.15	1.00	8	2
Utilities	5.48	1.85	6	4

Composition

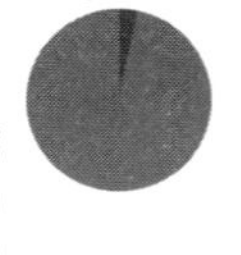

Cash	3.3
Stocks	96.7
Bonds	0.0
Other	0.0
Foreign (% of Stock)	0.0

Morningstar's Take by Greg Carlson 11-23-04

The closed N/I Numeric Investors Small Cap Value has become even more attractive.

Like most quantitative stock-pickers, the team that runs this fund tweaks its models--which are designed to beat the Russell 2000 Value Index through stock selection--as their effectiveness flags. However, lead manager Arup Datta and company are making significant changes this time. First, they're adding a model that gauges the amount of short-selling in a stock. That measure, used successfully in Numeric's two small-growth offerings since mid-2003, should help management steer clear of small-cap stocks whose prices are being driven down by short-sellers. The firm's earnings momentum model is making way for the new short-selling model as well as a model that gauges stock-price momentum. The team is also altering its valuation model to measure the cash that firms generate, which they believe will help in identifying fallen growth stocks that enter their universe.

At first blush, this may look like a case of fixing what ain't broke: The team has generated superb results since the fund's 1998 inception. However, the firm deserves kudos for its refusal to rest on its laurels; Numeric has a history of making solid additions to its quant models, such as the 2001 implementation of an earnings-quality measure that has juiced returns. And the performance of the earnings momentum model has been spotty in recent years, which is why its weighting is being dialed back. That move may provide an ancillary benefit: Because that model has led to more trading than the other measures, management expects portfolio turnover--which has typically exceeded 250% annually--to moderate. That ought to lead to lower trading costs here; the fund paid out a substantial 0.61% of its average net assets in brokerage commissions in fiscal 2003.

All told, we continue to have confidence in this fund's management team. Its shareholders are a fortunate group.

Address:	400 Bellevue Pkwy Ste 100 Wilmington DE 19809 800-686-3742
Web Address:	www.numeric.com
Inception:	11-30-98*
Advisor:	Numeric Investors LP
Subadvisor:	None
NTF Plans:	N/A

Minimum Purchase:	Closed	Add: —	IRA: —
Min Auto Inv Plan:	Closed	Add: —	
Sales Fees:	No-load, 2.00%R		
Management Fee:	1.35%, 0.50%A		
Actual Fees:	Mgt:1.35%	Dist:	
Expense Projections:	3Yr:$610	5Yr:$1054	10Yr:$2289
Income Distrib:	Annually		

Needham Growth

Ticker	Load	NAV	Yield	Total Assets	Mstar Category
NEEGX	12b-1 only	$31.17	0.0%	$288 mil	Small Growth

Governance and Management

Fiduciary Grade: C

Portfolio Manager(s)

Vincent Gallagher and Jim Kloppenburg became comanagers on April 22, 2003. Gallagher has managed Needham Small Cap Growth since May 2002, and Kloppenburg has managed Needham Aggressive Growth since September 2001. Most research comes from Needham's team of more than 40 analysts.

Strategy

The fund's simple mandate is to garner positive, aftertax returns. Its method is to seek growth at a reasonable price, mainly in four sectors in the small- and mid-cap range. The managers focus on Needham's four main research areas: technology, health, consumer, and business services. They may also use techniques often found in hedge funds, such as options and short sales to dampen losses and taxes.

Historical Profile

Return Above Avg
Risk Average
Rating ★★★★ Above Avg

Investment Style: Equity, Stock %: 66% (1996), 77% (1997), 97% (1998), 97% (1999), 86% (2000), 85% (2001), 94% (2002), 81% (2003), 92% (12-04)

▼ Manager Change
∇ Partial Manager Change

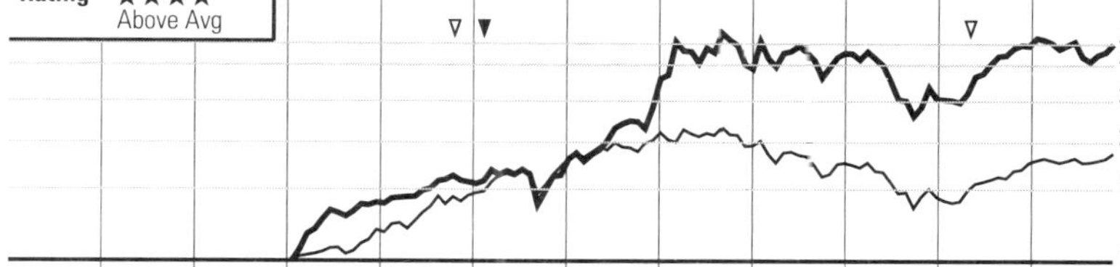

Growth of $10,000
▬ Investment Values of Fund
— Investment Values of S&P 500

Performance Quartile (within Category)

History

1993	1994	1995	1996	1997	1998	1999	2000	2001	2002	2003	12-04	History
—	—	10.00	14.49	14.42	17.27	26.47	24.77	27.78	19.92	29.35	31.17	NAV
—	—	0.00*	51.56	15.66	19.85	79.72	7.40	12.15	-28.29	47.34	6.20	Total Return %
—	—	—	28.62	-17.69	-8.72	58.68	16.50	24.03	-6.20	18.67	-4.67	+/-S&P 500
—	—	—	40.30	2.71	18.62	36.63	29.83	21.38	1.97	-1.20	-8.11	+/-Russ 2000 Gr
—	—	—	0.00	0.36	0.04	0.00	0.00	0.00	0.00	0.00	0.00	Income Return %
—	—	—	51.56	15.30	19.81	79.72	7.40	12.15	-28.29	47.34	6.20	Capital Return %
—	—	—	2	60	10	27	22	10	57	33	80	Total Rtn % Rank Cat
—	—	0.00	0.00	0.05	0.01	0.00	0.00	0.00	0.00	0.00	0.00	Income $
—	—	0.00	0.67	2.34	0.00	3.32	4.15	0.00	0.00	0.00	0.00	Capital Gains $
—	—	—	2.50	2.50	2.50	2.50	2.19	1.87	1.75	1.77	—	Expense Ratio %
—	—	—	-1.27	0.37	-1.72	-1.63	-1.07	1.04	-1.01	-1.38	—	Income Ratio %
—	—	—	569	724	586	145	187	150	78	42	—	Turnover Rate %
—	—	—	14	22	18	42	77	345	290	364	288	Net Assets $mil

Performance 12-31-04

	1st Qtr	2nd Qtr	3rd Qtr	4th Qtr	Total
2000	22.44	2.04	6.11	-18.98	7.40
2001	1.61	16.25	-20.54	19.48	12.15
2002	1.22	-19.31	-22.57	13.38	-28.29
2003	-2.61	23.61	14.22	7.16	47.34
2004	2.21	0.87	-9.12	13.35	6.20

Trailing	Total Return%	+/- S&P 500	+/- Russ 2000 Gr	%Rank Cat	Growth of $10,000
3 Mo	13.35	4.12	-1.73	62	11,335
6 Mo	3.01	-4.18	-5.15	90	10,301
1 Yr	6.20	-4.67	-8.11	80	10,620
3 Yr Avg	3.91	0.33	-1.88	58	11,219
5 Yr Avg	6.21	8.51	9.78	20	13,515
10 Yr Avg	—	—	—	—	—
15 Yr Avg	—	—	—	—	—

Tax Analysis	Tax-Adj Rtn%	%Rank Cat	Tax-Cost Rat	%Rank Cat
3 Yr (estimated)	3.91	52	0.00	1
5 Yr (estimated)	5.66	18	0.52	25
10 Yr (estimated)	—	—	—	—

Potential Capital Gain Exposure: 8% of assets

Rating and Risk

Time Period	Load-Adj Return %	Morningstar Rtn vs Cat	Morningstar Risk vs Cat	Morningstar Risk-Adj Rating
1 Yr	6.20			
3 Yr	3.91	Avg	+Avg	★★★
5 Yr	6.21	+Avg	Avg	★★★★
10 Yr	—	—	—	—
Incept	19.81			

Other Measures	Standard Index S&P 500	Best Fit Index Mstar Small Growth
Alpha	0.8	0.9
Beta	1.26	0.86
R-Squared	73	92
Standard Deviation	23.58	
Mean	3.91	
Sharpe Ratio	0.11	

Portfolio Analysis 12-31-04

Share change since 1-04 Total Stocks:73	Sector	PE	YTD Ret%	% Assets
Ceradyne	Ind Mtrls	37.3	151.95	5.32
Talisman Energy	Energy	15.2	44.37	4.24
⊖ Seagate Technology	Hardware	22.3	-5.50	3.77
Motorola	Hardware	28.7	37.93	3.76
Scientific-Atlanta	Hardware	20.4	21.07	3.46
National Semiconductor	Hardware	17.1	-8.80	3.45
Comcast A	Media	81.0	1.49	2.91
Thermo Electron	Health	27.2	19.80	2.74
Kronos	Software	37.8	29.08	2.68
Conmed	Health	21.1	19.41	2.48
Lucent Tech Cv 8%	—	—	—	2.33
Chesapeake Energy	Energy	13.1	22.90	2.31
GlobalSantaFe	Energy	NMF	34.38	2.26
Johnson & Johnson	Health	20.6	25.17	2.22
CarMax	Consumer	29.6	0.39	2.01
Analogic	Health	63.5	9.95	1.80
Hyperion Solutions	Software	40.7	54.68	1.79
Merck	Health	11.4	-27.76	1.69
Iron Mountain	Business	33.7	15.67	1.60
ViaSat	Hardware	33.9	26.80	1.43

Current Investment Style

Value Blnd Growth; Large Mid Small

Market Cap	%
Giant	7.5
Large	12.7
Mid	32.6
Small	25.4
Micro	21.8
Avg $mil: 2,379	

Value Measures		Rel Category
Price/Earnings	24.61	1.13
Price/Book	2.30	0.87
Price/Sales	1.59	1.06
Price/Cash Flow	9.12	1.14
Dividend Yield %	0.48	1.55

Growth Measures	%	Rel Category
Long-Term Erngs	15.93	0.92
Book Value	1.79	0.28
Sales	-0.82	NMF
Cash Flow	11.42	0.84
Historical Erngs	17.20	1.27

Profitability	%	Rel Category
Return on Equity	10.59	1.07
Return on Assets	5.56	1.27
Net Margin	7.85	1.15

Sector Weightings	% of Stocks	Rel S&P 500	3 Year High	3 Year Low
Info	53.08	2.47		
Software	7.80	1.81	12	7
Hardware	42.15	4.13	50	32
Media	3.13	0.82	5	1
Telecom	0.00	0.00	3	0
Service	28.30	0.61		
Health	19.56	1.56	20	6
Consumer	3.54	0.39	10	3
Business	5.20	1.28	6	1
Financial	0.00	0.00	3	0
Mfg	18.62	0.58		
Goods	0.69	0.07	1	0
Ind Mtrls	7.76	0.61	14	5
Energy	10.17	1.42	23	7
Utilities	0.00	0.00	1	0

Composition

Cash	3.3
Stocks	92.4
Bonds	0.0
Other	4.3
Foreign (% of Stock)	4.6

Morningstar's Take by Todd Trubey 12-13-04

We think the glory days are over for Needham Growth.

Peter Trapp ran this fund from 1998 to 2003 with a lot of flair, but that's now sorely lacking here. This all-cap growth fund allows its manager a lot of freedom, like the ability to short stocks (that is: bet that they'll drop). When Trapp left in spring 2003, 25% of the fund's assets were spread across 30 short positions, and 20% of assets were in 12 energy firms. Those stances clearly stood out from small- and mid-growth peers at the time. Comanagers Vincent Gallagher and Jim Kloppenberg now have only 5% of assets in six short positions and 10% of assets in four energy stocks. Versus peers, the fund looks much more standard.

The new duo say they're returning the fund to its roots. It began as a retail alternative to the firm's hedge funds. Needham uses a growth-at-a-reasonable price approach emphasizing four areas--tech, health, consumer, and business services. So the peel-back in energy stocks is part of a plan to re-emphasize the shop's core areas. The managers also recently cut the number of holdings down to 81 (from 170 when Trapp left). That's fine, but while the fund retains the risks of shorting (theoretically, unlimited losses are possible), it doesn't now seem to get much advantage. After stocks have run so far, one would expect a valuation-conscious shop to find more than six overpriced stocks. In the hands of a wizard, this fund was worth its high 1.77% expense ratio. Managed as it is now, it's not.

So it might be wise for investors to explore similar alternatives from more seasoned managers. While Bill Miller is most famous for beating the S&P 500 index annually with Legg Mason Value Trust, his go-anywhere, do-anything Legg Mason Opportunity has done even better since 1999. And in nearly 10-years at Leuthold Core Investment, Steve Leuthold has shown real talent mixing long- and short-stock positions with bonds.

Address:	445 Park Ave New York NY 10022 800-625-7071
Web Address:	www.needhamfunds.com
Inception:	12-26-95*
Advisor:	Needham Investment Management, LLC
Subadvisor:	None
NTF Plans:	Fidelity Retail-NTF, Schwab OneSource

Minimum Purchase:	$5000	Add: $500	IRA: $1500
Min Auto Inv Plan:	$5000	Add: $100	
Sales Fees:	0.25%B, 2.00%R		
Management Fee:	1.25%		
Actual Fees:	Mgt:1.25%	Dist:0.25%	
Expense Projections:	3Yr:$557	5Yr:$959	10Yr:$2084
Income Distrib:	Annually		

Neuberger Ber Fasciano In

Ticker	Load	NAV	Yield	Total Assets	Mstar Category
NBFSX	None	$42.86	0.0%	$479 mil	Small Growth

Governance and Management

Fiduciary Grade: B

Portfolio Manager(s)

Seasoned. Michael Fasciano started this offering on his own back in 1987. He sold his firm to Neuberger Berman, which is now part of Lehman Brothers, in January 2001 and is backed by that firm's research staff. He has one dedicated analyst.

Strategy

Manager Michael Fasciano seeks companies with clean balance sheets and the ability to increase earnings by 15% to 25% a year. The fund's turnover tends to be fairly low, as Fasciano typically has a three- to five-year time horizon for each of his picks.

Historical Profile

Return Above Avg
Risk Low
Rating ★★★★ Above Avg

Investment Style: Equity, Stock %: 100% 96% 50% 83% 100% 99% 96% 91% 92%

▼ Manager Change
▽ Partial Manager Change

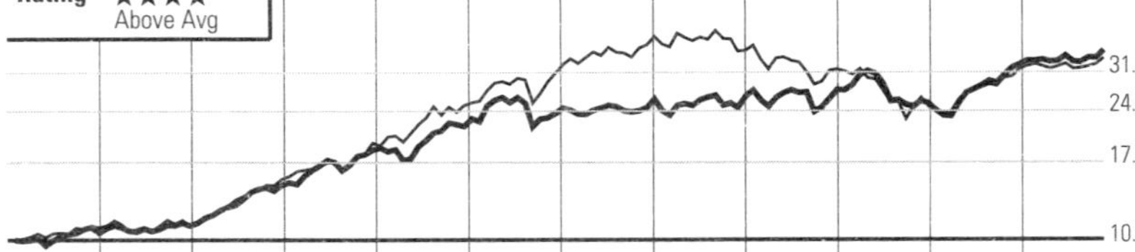

Growth of $10,000
— Investment Values of Fund
— Investment Values of S&P 500

Performance Quartile (within Category)

History	1993	1994	1995	1996	1997	1998	1999	2000	2001	2002	2003	12-04
NAV	17.68	17.18	21.18	26.20	30.31	31.19	32.72	32.98	33.33	30.44	39.29	42.86
Total Return %	8.08	3.68	31.12	26.54	21.51	7.19	6.16	1.70	4.46	-8.67	29.72	12.55
+/-S&P 500	-1.98	2.37	-6.41	3.60	-11.84	-21.38	-14.88	10.80	16.34	13.42	1.05	1.68
+/-Russ 2000 Gr	-5.29	6.11	0.08	15.28	8.56	5.96	-36.93	24.13	13.69	21.59	-18.82	-1.76
Income Return %	0.00	0.00	0.00	0.00	0.00	0.10	1.25	0.90	0.00	0.00	0.00	0.00
Capital Return %	8.08	3.68	31.12	26.54	21.51	7.09	4.91	0.80	4.46	-8.67	29.72	12.55
Total Rtn % Rank Cat	85	27	62	23	35	35	93	31	19	1	95	50
Income $	0.00	0.00	0.00	0.00	0.00	0.03	0.39	0.29	0.00	0.00	0.00	0.00
Capital Gains $	1.00	1.14	1.34	0.59	1.49	1.25	0.00	0.00	1.08	0.00	0.19	1.34
Expense Ratio %	1.70	1.70	1.70	1.50	1.40	1.30	1.20	1.20	1.58	1.36	1.24	1.22
Income Ratio %	-0.30	-0.30	-0.60	-0.30	-0.40	0.24	1.80	0.80	-1.03	-0.48	-0.36	-0.52
Turnover Rate %	43	99	38	46	41	50	20	29	3	24	24	17
Net Assets $mil	17	18	24	34	56	233	398	237	199	214	318	456

Performance 12-31-04

	1st Qtr	2nd Qtr	3rd Qtr	4th Qtr	Total
2000	-4.03	3.66	-3.53	5.98	1.70
2001	-6.49	11.54	-13.37	15.60	4.46
2002	10.44	-5.49	-13.19	0.79	-8.67
2003	-8.02	19.46	4.16	13.34	29.72
2004	3.13	2.71	-1.35	7.70	12.55

Trailing	Total Return%	+/- S&P 500	+/- Russ 2000 Gr	%Rank Cat	Growth of $10,000
3 Mo	7.70	-1.53	-7.38	98	10,770
6 Mo	6.25	-0.94	-1.91	66	10,625
1 Yr	12.55	1.68	-1.76	50	11,255
3 Yr Avg	10.07	6.49	4.28	19	13,335
5 Yr Avg	7.21	9.51	10.78	17	14,164
10 Yr Avg	12.51	0.44	5.39	24	32,502
15 Yr Avg	11.67	0.74	4.17	44	52,366

Tax Analysis	Tax-Adj Rtn%	%Rank Cat	Tax-Cost Rat	%Rank Cat
3 Yr (estimated)	9.80	15	0.25	25
5 Yr (estimated)	6.84	14	0.35	16
10 Yr (estimated)	11.76	16	0.67	9

Potential Capital Gain Exposure: 25% of assets

Rating and Risk

Time Period	Load-Adj Return %	Morningstar Rtn vs Cat	Morningstar Risk vs Cat	Morningstar Risk-Adj Rating
1 Yr	12.55			
3 Yr	10.07	+Avg	Low	★★★★
5 Yr	7.21	+Avg	Low	★★★★
10 Yr	12.51	+Avg	Low	★★★★
Incept	12.29			

Other Measures	Standard Index S&P 500	Best Fit Index Mstar Small Value
Alpha	7.3	-4.8
Beta	0.65	0.80
R-Squared	50	88

Standard Deviation	15.11
Mean	10.07
Sharpe Ratio	0.58

Portfolio Analysis 12-31-04

Share change since 11-04 Total Stocks:72	Sector	PE	YTD Ret%	% Assets
Landstar System	Business	37.0	93.59	3.71
⊕ OM Group	Ind Mtrls	—	23.79	2.75
⊕ MSC Industrial Direct Co	Business	28.4	32.26	2.54
⊕ International Speedway A	Goods	29.0	18.96	2.49
⊕ Assured Guaranty	Financial	—	—	2.36
⊕ G & K Services A	Consumer	25.0	18.36	2.34
⊕ HCC Insurance Holdings	Financial	17.0	5.19	2.28
⊕ ScanSource	Ind Mtrls	25.8	36.26	2.18
⊕ Spartech	Ind Mtrls	18.3	11.97	2.17
⊕ Idex	Ind Mtrls	24.1	48.09	2.05
⊕ Plantronics	Hardware	23.7	27.33	1.98
⊕ Emmis Communications A	Media	—	-29.06	1.97
⊖ Pulitzer	Media	30.8	21.92	1.95
⊕ K-V Pharmaceutical A	Health	23.6	-13.53	1.91
⊕ Meredith	Media	22.7	12.08	1.82
⊕ Young Innovations	Health	24.3	-5.85	1.80
⊕ Journal Register	Media	7.6	-6.62	1.76
⊕ Apria HealthCare Group	Health	13.9	15.74	1.70
⊕ Stericycle	Business	29.3	-1.61	1.68
⊕ Snap-on	Ind Mtrls	25.6	9.99	1.64

Current Investment Style

Value Blnd Growth / Large Mid Small

Market Cap	%
Giant	0.0
Large	0.0
Mid	38.6
Small	50.9
Micro	10.5
Avg $mil: 1,168	

Value Measures		Rel Category
Price/Earnings	18.62	0.86
Price/Book	2.55	0.97
Price/Sales	0.99	0.66
Price/Cash Flow	9.56	1.19
Dividend Yield %	0.66	2.13

Growth Measures	%	Rel Category
Long-Term Erngs	13.69	0.79
Book Value	-1.17	NMF
Sales	3.06	0.47
Cash Flow	7.41	0.55
Historical Erngs	13.42	0.99

Profitability	%	Rel Category
Return on Equity	16.44	1.67
Return on Assets	9.65	2.20
Net Margin	11.73	1.71

Sector Weightings	% of Stocks	Rel S&P 500	3 Year High	3 Year Low
Info	15.31	0.71		
Software	0.00	0.00	0	0
Hardware	3.61	0.35	7	4
Media	11.16	2.91	22	11
Telecom	0.54	0.17	1	0
Service	54.94	1.18		
Health	12.99	1.04	18	12
Consumer	10.88	1.20	14	10
Business	17.38	4.29	17	13
Financial	13.69	0.66	15	11
Mfg	29.75	0.93		
Goods	3.74	0.40	6	3
Ind Mtrls	23.13	1.83	24	14
Energy	2.88	0.40	3	0
Utilities	0.00	0.00	0	0

Composition

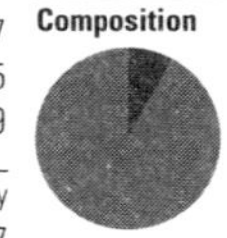

Cash	7.8
Stocks	92.2
Bonds	0.0
Other	0.0
Foreign (% of Stock)	2.3

Morningstar's Take by Andrew Gogerty 12-15-04

Neuberger Berman Fasciano is still a solid choice.

This fund has been competitive thus far in 2004: Its 10% gain for the year to date through December 13 outpaces the 8.7% return posted by the typical small-growth offering. The fund has benefited from an increased stake in top-10 holding Plantronics which manufactures headsets and wireless products. The stock is up more than 26% this year and manger Michael Fasciano remains attracted to the company's leading market share, low debt, and strong cash flow.

Fasciano only invests in companies that have a proven earnings history and demonstrated profitability. This tack leads the fund to hold moderate growth names and largely avoid speculative sectors such as technology. Fasciano thinks most of the companies in that sector lack a consistent earnings history and typically have products with short-term life cycles. Not surprisingly, the fund has lagged during rallies fueled by aggressive growth stocks--its returns in 2003 trailed 96% of its peers'.

Over time, however, shareholders have benefited from the fund's focus on financial health. Its long-term returns rank in the category's top quartile. And investors have been able to sleep at night--the fund's volatility is one of the category's lowest. This profile was highlighted during the recent market downturn: Performance was relatively flat from March 2000 through March 2003, while the typical small-growth offering shed 48% of its value.

As such, we remain fans of this offering. Fasciano has remained true to his investment discipline regardless of the market environment. Plus, the fund's expense ratio has declined as assets have grown--its current levy of 1.22% is well below the 1.65% charged by its typical no-load category peer. That, combined with the fund's attractive risk/reward profile trumps concerns over temporary underperformance.

Address:	605 Third Ave 2nd FL New York NY 10158-0006 800-877-9700
Web Address:	www.nb.com
Inception:	11-10-88
Advisor:	Neuberger Berman Management Inc.
Subadvisor:	None
NTF Plans:	Fidelity Retail-NTF, Schwab OneSource

Minimum Purchase:	$1000	Add: $100	IRA: $250
Min Auto Inv Plan:	$100	Add: $100	
Sales Fees:	No-load		
Management Fee:	0.85% mx./0.73% mn.		
Actual Fees:	—	Dist:	
Expense Projections:	3Yr:$393	5Yr:$681	10Yr:$1500
Income Distrib:	Annually		

Neuberger Ber Genesis Inv

Ticker	Load	NAV	Yield	Total Assets	Mstar Category
NBGNX	Closed	$29.84	0.0%	$7,935 mil	Small Blend

Governance and Management

Fiduciary Grade: B

Portfolio Manager(s)

Judy Vale has managed this fund since February 1994, and comanager Bob D'Alelio joined her in August 1997. Kevin O'Brien was a comanager from December 2001 to mid-2003, when he left to help run a hedge fund. Vale and D'Alelio have two analysts working directly with them, and they can also draw on ideas from Neuberger Berman's shared analyst team.

Strategy

Managers Judy Vale and Bob D'Alelio try to own companies that dominate a competitive niche, generate good free cash flow, and are able to grow internally regardless of what the economy does. They try to keep the portfolio's P/E ratio below that of the Russell 2000, though they'll pay up more for stocks in faster-growing industries. They can't buy stocks with market caps above $1.5 billion, but some of the stocks in the portfolio have grown bigger than that.

Historical Profile

Return High
Risk Low
Rating ★★★★★ Highest

Investment Style: Equity Stock % — 95% 94% 93% 92% 93% 95% 93% 94% 94%

▼ Manager Change
▽ Partial Manager Change

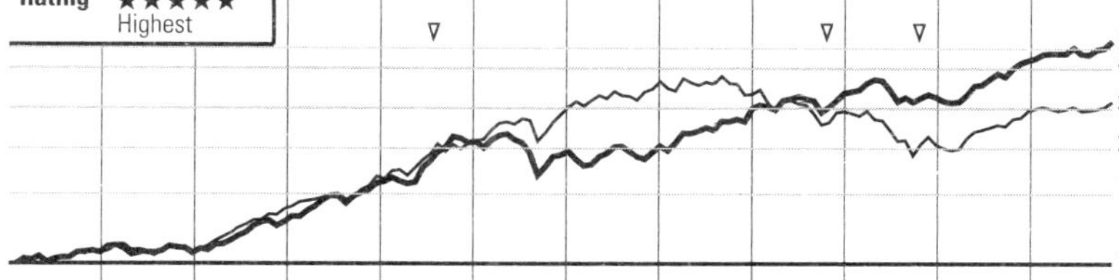

Growth of $10,000
— Investment Values of Fund
— Investment Values of S&P 500

Performance Quartile (within Category)

1993	1994	1995	1996	1997	1998	1999	2000	2001	2002	2003	12-04	History
8.26	7.80	9.38	12.03	16.03	14.44	14.94	18.67	20.33	19.66	25.88	29.84	NAV
13.89	-1.82	27.31	29.86	34.89	-6.95	4.04	32.51	12.11	-2.96	31.70	18.76	Total Return %
3.83	-3.13	-10.22	6.92	1.54	-35.52	-17.00	41.61	23.99	19.13	3.03	7.89	+/-S&P 500
-4.99	0.00	-1.14	13.37	12.53	-4.40	-17.22	35.53	9.62	17.52	-15.55	0.43	+/-Russ 2000
0.13	0.00	0.00	0.00	0.00	0.75	0.55	0.00	0.00	0.00	0.00	0.00	Income Return %
13.76	-1.82	27.31	29.86	34.89	-7.70	3.49	32.51	12.11	-2.96	31.70	18.76	Capital Return %
67	54	46	16	16	65	74	7	34	3	92	51	Total Rtn % Rank Cat
0.01	0.00	0.00	0.00	0.00	0.12	0.08	0.00	0.00	0.00	0.00	0.00	Income $
0.75	0.31	0.55	0.15	0.19	0.34	0.00	1.04	0.58	0.07	0.01	0.89	Capital Gains $
1.65	1.36	1.35	1.28	1.16	1.11	1.17	1.21	1.11	1.10	1.08	1.05	Expense Ratio %
0.15	-0.20	-0.16	-0.18	-0.08	0.72	0.61	-0.02	-0.07	-0.05	-0.31	-0.38	Income Ratio %
54	63	37	21	18	18	33	—	19	19	17	23	Turnover Rate %
125	108	119	299	1,246	1,195	736	841	1,081	1,054	1,301	1,539	Net Assets $mil

Performance 12-31-04

	1st Qtr	2nd Qtr	3rd Qtr	4th Qtr	Total
2000	10.17	4.19	4.72	10.22	32.51
2001	-0.86	10.32	-11.17	15.39	12.11
2002	7.77	-5.02	-8.60	3.73	-2.96
2003	-3.36	13.53	6.17	13.07	31.70
2004	5.18	4.52	-1.37	9.54	18.76

Trailing	Total Return%	+/- S&P 500	+/- Russ 2000	%Rank Cat	Growth of $10,000
3 Mo	9.54	0.31	-4.55	93	10,954
6 Mo	8.04	0.85	-2.79	85	10,804
1 Yr	18.76	7.89	0.43	51	11,876
3 Yr Avg	14.92	11.34	3.44	24	15,177
5 Yr Avg	17.66	19.96	11.05	10	22,550
10 Yr Avg	17.15	5.08	5.61	6	48,688
15 Yr Avg	14.34	3.41	3.25	16	74,640

Tax Analysis	Tax-Adj Rtn%	%Rank Cat	Tax-Cost Rat	%Rank Cat
3 Yr (estimated)	14.71	18	0.18	13
5 Yr (estimated)	16.90	8	0.65	26
10 Yr (estimated)	16.37	3	0.67	7

Potential Capital Gain Exposure: 37% of assets

Rating and Risk

Time Period	Load-Adj Return %	Morningstar Rtn vs Cat	Morningstar Risk vs Cat	Morningstar Risk-Adj Rating
1 Yr	18.76			
3 Yr	14.92	+Avg	Low	★★★★
5 Yr	17.66	High	Low	★★★★★
10 Yr	17.15	High	-Avg	★★★★★
Incept	14.50			

Other Measures	Standard Index S&P 500	Best Fit Index S&P Mid 400
Alpha	11.9	6.1
Beta	0.63	0.76
R-Squared	60	87

Standard Deviation	13.89
Mean	14.92
Sharpe Ratio	0.99

Portfolio Analysis 12-31-04

Share change since 11-04 Total Stocks:130	Sector	PE	YTD Ret%	% Assets
⊕ Church & Dwight Company	Goods	18.5	28.24	2.75
Zebra Technologies	Hardware	33.1	27.20	2.61
XTO Energy	Energy	20.5	56.85	2.39
Alberto-Culver	Goods	32.8	16.43	2.34
AptarGroup	Goods	20.5	36.72	2.24
United Defense Industrie	Ind Mtrls	14.2	48.21	2.13
Engineered Support Syste	Business	22.8	7.62	1.96
Mentor	Health	25.0	44.90	1.87
⊕ Henry Schein	Health	23.1	3.05	1.86
Patterson Companies	Health	37.8	35.62	1.71
East West Bancorp	Financial	28.3	57.37	1.63
National Oilwell	Energy	36.9	57.83	1.56
Idexx Laboratories	Health	27.0	17.96	1.56
Fair Isaac	Business	23.5	12.17	1.52
R. H. Donnelley	Business	36.8	48.22	1.36
United Stationers	Ind Mtrls	16.0	12.90	1.36
Dentsply International	Health	23.9	24.96	1.33
Regis	Consumer	18.1	17.22	1.33
⊕ Pharmaceutica Product D	Health	41.7	53.10	1.31
Simpson Manufacturing	Ind Mtrls	15.8	37.98	1.30

Current Investment Style

Value Blnd Growth / Large Mid Small

Market Cap	%
Giant	0.0
Large	2.5
Mid	61.8
Small	34.2
Micro	1.4

Avg $mil: 1,956

Value Measures		Rel Category
Price/Earnings	20.72	1.20
Price/Book	3.06	1.54
Price/Sales	1.83	1.93
Price/Cash Flow	9.02	1.54
Dividend Yield %	0.64	0.77

Growth Measures	%	Rel Category
Long-Term Erngs	14.73	1.09
Book Value	15.97	2.83
Sales	11.15	2.59
Cash Flow	9.38	3.92
Historical Erngs	7.22	2.31

Profitability	%	Rel Category
Return on Equity	17.87	1.71
Return on Assets	9.51	1.92
Net Margin	2.58	1.72

Sector Weightings	% of Stocks	Rel S&P 500	3 Year High	3 Year Low
Info	8.38	0.39		
Software	2.00	0.47	2	1
Hardware	5.55	0.54	10	5
Media	0.83	0.22	3	1
Telecom	0.00	0.00	0	0
Service	50.43	1.09		
Health	21.73	1.74	24	15
Consumer	6.14	0.68	12	6
Business	10.07	2.49	12	9
Financial	12.49	0.60	19	12
Mfg	41.19	1.28		
Goods	8.68	0.93	10	6
Ind Mtrls	15.96	1.26	18	12
Energy	16.55	2.31	17	7
Utilities	0.00	0.00	0	0

Composition

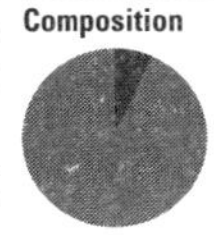

Cash	6.4
Stocks	93.6
Bonds	0.0
Other	0.0
Foreign (% of Stock)	2.3

Morningstar's Take by David Kathman 11-23-04

This fund's cautious nature has served shareholders well.

Neuberger Berman Genesis isn't your average small-cap offering. Managers Judy Vale and Bob D'Alelio prefer to find stocks they like and then stick with them for the long term, so that the fund has a turnover ratio under 20%, among the lowest in the small-blend category. The stocks they like tend to be dominant niche players with good free cash flow, usually from steady but relatively unexciting businesses. Baking-soda maker Church & Dwight and Zebra Technologies, which makes bar-code printers and readers, are prime examples which have been top holdings for years.

On top of this cautious overall approach, Vale and D'Alelio also tend to be cautious in their outlook for the general U.S. economy. They expect GDP growth to be subpar in the coming years, and so they've shunned the cyclical stocks that so many of their fellow managers are piling into. The fund is underweight in tech stocks and consumer cyclicals, as well as financials that are sensitive to interest rates.

Instead, Vale and D'Alelio have the fund heavily invested in steady stocks and others that can grow regardless of what the broader economy does. They have a big bet on energy stocks such as XTO Energy, because they think supply and demand will keep oil prices high. They are also overweight in small-cap defense stocks such as United Defense Industries.

This strategy has helped the fund achieve outstanding top-decile returns over the past decade relative to its small-blend peers. The only times it has trailed its peer group was in the frothy bull markets of 1998 to 1999 and 2003, and even then its returns were good in absolute terms. Unfortunately for new investors, the fund has been closed since December 2001 and is not likely to reopen any time soon. Investors lucky enough to already own the fund have every reason to hang on to this long-term winner.

Address:	605 Third Ave 2nd FL New York NY 10158-0006 800-877-9700
Web Address:	www.nb.com
Inception:	09-27-88
Advisor:	Neuberger Berman Management Inc.
Subadvisor:	Neuberger Berman, LLC
NTF Plans:	Schwab OneSource, Federated Tr NTF

Minimum Purchase:	Closed	Add: —	IRA: —
Min Auto Inv Plan:	Closed	Add: —	
Sales Fees:	No-load		
Management Fee:	0.85% mx./0.65% mn.		
Actual Fees:	Mgt:0.81%	Dist:	
Expense Projections:	3Yr:$474	5Yr:$818	10Yr:$1791
Income Distrib:	Annually		

Northeast Investors

Analyst Pick

Ticker	Load	NAV	Yield	SEC Yield	Total Assets	Mstar Category
NTHEX	None	$7.87	7.1%	—	$1,565 mil	High Yield Bond

Governance and Management

Fiduciary Grade: A

Portfolio Manager(s)

Bruce Monrad and Ernest Monrad have extensive experience. Ernest Monrad has been with the fund since 1960, and Bruce Monrad since 1993. As the fund's long-term performance shows, they have done quite well. Both invest heavily in the fund themselves, so their interests are aligned with those of the fund's shareholders.

Strategy

Managers Bruce Monrad and Ernest Monrad hold a core of domestic high-yield bonds, but they will dabble in emerging-markets debt and individual stocks. Sector allocations and issue selection largely determine the fund's relative performance. In 2001 and 2002, the fund's avoidance of the telecommunications and cable sectors helped it avoid a number of high-profile blowups. More recently, though, issue-specific recoveries in a few of the fund's largest holdings have helped it rally past its typical peer.

Historical Profile

Return Above Avg
Risk Below Avg
Rating ★★★★ Above Avg

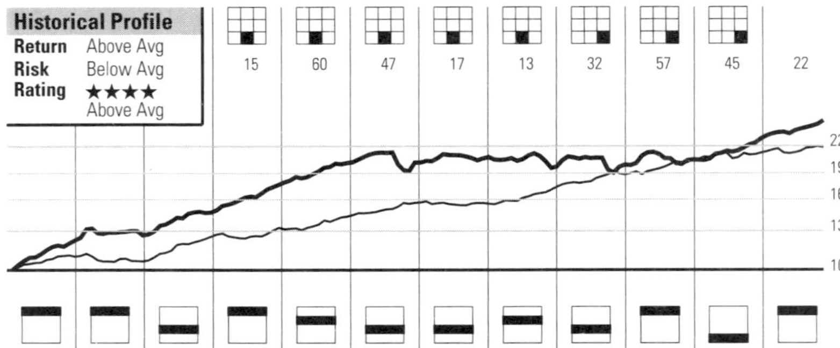

Investment Style
Fixed Income
Income Rtn %Rank Cat

▼ Manager Change
∇ Partial Manager Change

Growth of $10,000
— Investment Values of Fund
— Investment Values of LB Aggr

Performance Quartile (within Category)

1993	1994	1995	1996	1997	1998	1999	2000	2001	2002	2003	12-04	History
10.29	9.55	10.16	11.12	11.65	10.47	9.77	8.17	7.43	7.05	7.41	7.87	NAV
23.60	2.20	17.27	20.16	13.89	-0.25	3.50	-6.05	1.33	3.23	14.35	14.38	Total Return %
13.85	5.12	-1.20	16.53	4.24	-8.94	4.32	-17.68	-7.11	-7.02	10.25	10.04	+/-LB Aggr
4.69	3.17	-0.12	7.74	1.26	-0.83	0.22	-0.84	-4.45	0.12	-13.58	2.42	+/-CSFB Glb HY
11.29	9.87	10.76	10.20	8.91	8.86	10.56	11.32	11.08	8.61	8.79	7.77	Income Return %
12.31	-7.67	6.51	9.96	4.98	-9.11	-7.06	-17.37	-9.75	-5.38	5.56	6.61	Capital Return %
8	3	51	6	29	59	58	40	65	11	96	5	Total Rtn % Rank Cat
1.00	0.98	0.99	1.00	0.96	1.00	1.06	1.06	0.87	0.62	0.60	0.56	Income $
0.00	0.00	0.00	0.00	0.00	0.18	0.00	0.00	0.00	0.00	0.00	0.00	Capital Gains $
1.21	1.06	1.02	0.66	0.64	0.61	0.61	0.61	0.65	0.70	0.65	0.67	Expense Ratio %
10.53	9.37	9.77	9.41	8.65	8.73	9.99	10.84	11.10	8.61	7.97	7.92	Income Ratio %
76	73	41	32	33	64	27	4	22	18	13	40	Turnover Rate %
549	555	805	1,355	2,161	2,314	1,854	1,318	1,292	1,730	1,761	1,565	Net Assets $mil

Performance 12-31-04

	1st Qtr	2nd Qtr	3rd Qtr	4th Qtr	Total
2000	-1.53	0.24	1.92	-6.61	-6.05
2001	6.12	-0.47	-7.03	3.19	1.33
2002	5.79	1.14	-5.69	2.30	3.23
2003	0.59	5.07	2.14	5.92	14.35
2004	4.07	1.25	2.95	5.44	14.38

Trailing	Total Return%	+/- LB Aggr	+/- CSFB Glb HY	%Rank Cat	Growth of $10,000
3 Mo	5.44	4.49	0.88	15	10,544
6 Mo	8.55	4.37	-0.71	52	10,855
1 Yr	14.38	10.04	2.42	5	11,438
3 Yr Avg	10.53	4.34	-3.35	48	13,503
5 Yr Avg	5.15	-2.56	-3.02	57	12,854
10 Yr Avg	7.85	0.13	-0.77	18	21,291
15 Yr Avg	8.97	1.27	-1.12	21	36,275

Tax Analysis	Tax-Adj Rtn%	%Rank Cat	Tax-Cost Rat	%Rank Cat
3 Yr (estimated)	7.35	37	2.88	54
5 Yr (estimated)	1.53	53	3.44	60
10 Yr (estimated)	4.03	17	3.54	65

Potential Capital Gain Exposure: -35% of assets

Rating and Risk

Time Period	Load-Adj Return %	Morningstar Rtn vs Cat	Morningstar Risk vs Cat	Morningstar Risk-Adj Rating
1 Yr	14.38			
3 Yr	10.53	Avg	-Avg	★★★
5 Yr	5.15	Avg	-Avg	★★★
10 Yr	7.85	+Avg	-Avg	★★★★
Incept	5.94			

Other Measures	Standard Index LB Aggr	Best Fit Index CSFB Glb HY
Alpha	9.8	1.6
Beta	-0.12	0.61
R-Squared	1	52
Standard Deviation	5.72	
Mean	10.53	
Sharpe Ratio	1.62	

Portfolio Analysis 09-30-04

Total Fixed-Income:98	Date of Maturity	Amount $000	Value $000	% Net Assets
Trump Atlantic City Asso	05-01-06	90,530	73,839	4.05
Advantica Restrnt Grp 11	01-15-08	58,769	60,973	3.34
Illinois Pwr 11.5%	12-15-10	50,000	59,250	3.25
Venetian Casino Resort 1	06-15-10	50,000	57,875	3.17
Midwest Generation 8.75%	05-01-34	50,000	54,500	2.99
Harrahs Oper 7.875%	12-15-05	48,941	51,694	2.84
Mgm Mirage 9.75%	06-01-07	37,857	42,069	2.31
Park Pl Entmt 7.875%	12-15-05	39,164	41,220	2.26
Charter Comms Oper 144A	04-30-12	40,000	39,900	2.19
Orion Pwr Hldgs 12%	05-01-10	29,000	36,250	1.99
Brazil Federative Rep 14	10-15-09	26,366	34,012	1.87
Anr Pipe 8.875%	03-15-10	29,630	33,334	1.83
Owens Ill 8.1%	05-15-07	30,000	31,500	1.73
Us West Comms 5.625%	11-15-08	30,127	29,524	1.62
Houghton Mifflin 8.25%	02-01-11	27,220	28,445	1.56
Hollywood Pk 9.25%	02-15-07	27,307	27,990	1.54
Forest Oil 8%	06-15-08	24,655	27,244	1.49
Crown European Hldgs Sa	03-01-11	23,000	25,645	1.41
Lyondell Chem 11.125%	07-15-12	20,000	23,200	1.27
Husky Oil FRN	08-15-28	20,000	23,147	1.27

Current Investment Style

Duration: Short Int Long
Quality: High Med Low

1 figure provided by fund

Avg Eff Duration[1]	—
Avg Eff Maturity	—
Avg Credit Quality	B
Avg Wtd Coupon	9.19%
Avg Wtd Price	102.40% of par

Coupon Range	% of Bonds	Rel Cat
0% PIK	2.3	0.5
0% to 8%	27.2	0.7
8% to 11%	49.0	0.9
11% to 14%	21.6	3.2
More than 14%	2.3	11.7

1.00=Category Average

Credit Analysis		% bonds 09-30-04	
US Govt	0	BB	30
AAA	0	B	37
AA	0	Below B	20
A	4	NR/NA	8
BBB	1		

Sector Breakdown	% of assets
US Treasuries	0
TIPS	0
US Agency	0
Mortgage Pass-Throughs	0
Mortgage CMO	0
Mortgage ARM	0
US Corporate	83
Asset-Backed	0
Convertible	2
Municipal	0
Corporate Inflation-Protected	0
Foreign Corporate	2
Foreign Govt	3

Composition			
Cash	9.3	Bonds	79.3
Stocks	8.1	Other	3.3

Special Securities	
Restricted/Illiquid Secs	7
Exotic Mortgage-Backed	0
Emerging-Markets Secs	Trace
Options/Futures/Warrants	No

Morningstar's Take by Scott Berry 11-12-04

Seasoned management and a low expense ratio make Northeast Investors an appealing choice.

It's hard to find more experienced high-yield bond managers than Ernest and Bruce Monrad. Ernest has been managing this fund since 1960, while Bruce has joined the effort since 1993. That gives them a combined 56 years of experience with this fund. The average tenure for the high-yield bond category is less than five years.

That experience has served shareholders well here. We wouldn't typically highlight 10- and 15-year trailing returns, given that few managers last that long, but for this fund those measures are relevant. And for each of those periods, the fund lands in high-yield bond category's top quartile.

Over the years, the Monrads have successfully navigated a number of tricky market environments. A move into shorter-term high-yield bonds allowed it to hold up better than most of its peers when the bond market slumped in 1994, while a general avoidance of the telecom sector spared the fund some pain when that area of the market crumbled in 2000 and 2001. Of course, the Monrads are not infallible. The fund failed to fully participate in a high-yield rally in 2003, as a large cash stake and a big default weighed on its return.

More recently, the two have been on their game. For the year to date through Nov. 11, 2004, the fund gained 10.6% and ranked near the very top of the charts. Good issue selection has been the main driver of returns, as top-five holdings Trump Atlantic City and Advantica Restaurant Group (Denny's) have both rallied nicely. The Monrads have found fewer opportunities though, and have recently shifted into relatively defensive short-term issues to guard against a tougher environment.

With an expense ratio of just 0.65%, we think investors are paying a discount here for premium high-yield management. This fund remains one of our high-yield Analyst Picks.

Address:	50 Congress St Boston MA 02109 800-225-6704
Web Address:	www.northeastinvestors.com
Inception:	08-01-50
Advisor:	Northeast Investors Trust
Subadvisor:	None
NTF Plans:	N/A

Minimum Purchase:	$1000	Add: $0	IRA: $500
Min Auto Inv Plan:	$1000	Add: $50	
Sales Fees:	No-load		
Management Fee:	0.50%		
Actual Fees:	Mgt:0.50%	Dist:	
Expense Projections:	3Yr:$208	5Yr:$362	10Yr:$810
Income Distrib:	Quarterly		

Northern Technology

Ticker	Load	NAV	Yield	Total Assets	Mstar Category
NTCHX	None	$11.82	0.0%	$333 mil	Specialty-Technology

Governance and Management

Fiduciary Grade:

Portfolio Manager(s)

John Leo, who managed this fund since its 1996 inception and leads Northern's growth research team, stepped down in July 2004. George Gilbert, an experienced tech analyst, has comanaged this offering since 1997 and is now lead manager. He is assisted by Deborah Koch, who joined Northern in 2003 and currently comanages Northern Mid Cap Growth. Prior to joining Northern, Koch briefly comanaged tech offerings at both Strong and Scudder.

Strategy

Management focuses on companies with strong positions in large and growing markets. Big companies have typically dominated the portfolio, but management is also willing to look at smaller firms with niche dominance. When managers find several compelling buys in one subsector, they're not afraid to load up.

Historical Profile

Return Average
Risk Average
Rating ★★★ Neutral

Investment Style
Equity
Stock %

1996	1997	1998	1999	2000	2001	2002	2003	12-04
100%	98%	97%	98%	88%	99%	98%	99%	99%

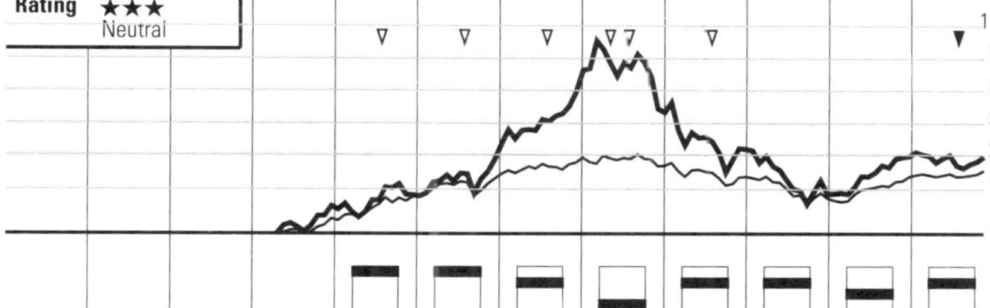

1993	1994	1995	1996	1997	1998	1999	2000	2001	2002	2003	12-04	History
—	—	—	13.11	14.35	25.58	51.76	19.03	12.47	7.40	11.47	11.82	NAV
—	—	—	32.53*	16.68	83.02	134.48	-38.43	-34.47	-40.66	55.00	3.05	Total Return %
—	—	—	—	-16.67	54.45	113.44	-29.33	-22.59	-18.57	26.33	-7.82	+/-S&P 500
—	—	—	—	-3.29	28.42	18.08	-22.21	-18.38	-7.33	2.86	-8.68	+/-PSE Tech 100
—	—	—	0.00	0.00	0.00	0.00	0.00	0.00	0.00	0.00	0.00	Income Return %
—	—	—	—	16.68	83.02	134.48	-38.43	-34.47	-40.66	55.00	3.05	Capital Return %
—	—	—	—	17	9	43	81	46	36	51	50	Total Rtn % Rank Cat
—	—	—	0.00	0.00	0.00	0.00	0.00	0.00	0.00	0.00	0.00	Income $
—	—	—	0.15	0.90	0.67	5.74	12.51	0.00	0.00	0.00	0.00	Capital Gains $
—	—	—	—	1.25	1.25	1.23	1.25	1.25	1.25	1.25	1.25	Expense Ratio %
—	—	—	—	-0.75	-0.96	-0.87	-1.05	-0.74	-0.96	-0.90	-0.92	Income Ratio %
—	—	—	—	68	75	61	156	180	76	62	61	Turnover Rate %
—	—	—	34	81	228	1,810	1,195	609	288	423	333	Net Assets $mil

Performance 12-31-04

	1st Qtr	2nd Qtr	3rd Qtr	4th Qtr	Total
2000	27.14	-14.44	0.67	-43.78	-38.43
2001	-31.58	9.91	-33.75	31.54	-34.47
2002	-8.02	-24.15	-24.37	12.46	-40.66
2003	-0.13	22.33	11.39	13.90	55.00
2004	0.44	0.95	-9.89	12.79	3.05

Trailing	Total Return%	+/- S&P 500	+/- PSE Tech 100	%Rank Cat	Growth of $10,000
3 Mo	12.79	3.56	-1.73	92	11,279
6 Mo	1.63	-5.56	-4.30	67	10,163
1 Yr	3.05	-7.82	-8.68	50	10,305
3 Yr Avg	-1.77	-5.35	-6.03	41	9,478
5 Yr Avg	-17.49	-15.19	-13.16	57	3,824
10 Yr Avg	—	—	—	—	—
15 Yr Avg	—	—	—	—	—

Tax Analysis	Tax-Adj Rtn%	%Rank Cat	Tax-Cost Rat	%Rank Cat
3 Yr (estimated)	-1.77	34	0.00	1
5 Yr (estimated)	-19.53	59	2.47	93
10 Yr (estimated)	—	—	—	—

Potential Capital Gain Exposure: -301% of assets

Rating and Risk

Time Period	Load-Adj Return %	Morningstar Rtn vs Cat	Morningstar Risk vs Cat	Morningstar Risk-Adj Rating
1 Yr	3.05			
3 Yr	-1.77	Avg	-Avg	★★★★
5 Yr	-17.49	Avg	Avg	★★★
10 Yr	—	—	—	—
Incept	11.23			

Other Measures	Standard Index S&P 500	Best Fit Index PSE Tech 100
Alpha	-4.6	-5.6
Beta	1.63	1.05
R-Squared	78	96
Standard Deviation	28.40	
Mean	-1.77	
Sharpe Ratio	-0.11	

Portfolio Analysis 12-31-04

Share change since 09-04 Total Stocks:69	Sector	PE	YTD Ret%	% Assets
⊖ eBay	Consumer	81.6	80.07	4.77
⊖ Yahoo	Media	95.1	67.36	4.68
Ericsson Telephone ADR B	Hardware	—	77.91	4.68
⊕ Juniper Networks	Hardware	NMF	45.56	4.00
⊖ EMC	Hardware	41.5	15.09	3.68
Dell	Hardware	34.0	24.01	3.49
⊖ Qualcomm	Hardware	42.0	58.20	3.27
Accenture	Business	21.7	2.58	3.25
⊖ Electronic Arts	Software	30.9	29.36	2.94
⊕ Broadcom	Hardware	66.4	-5.12	2.80
Microsoft	Software	36.1	8.95	2.59
Oracle	Software	25.4	3.70	2.58
Cisco Systems	Hardware	24.5	-20.26	2.43
⊖ First Data	Business	18.8	3.72	2.40
⊕ Veritas Software	Software	23.7	-22.88	2.20
⊖ Motorola	Hardware	28.7	37.93	2.11
Micron Technology	Hardware	46.2	-8.32	2.09
⊖ Flextronics International	Hardware	—	-6.62	1.94
Intel	Hardware	19.8	-26.56	1.87
Nokia ADR	Hardware	18.1	-6.14	1.86

Current Investment Style

Value Blnd Growth — Large Mid Small

Market Cap	%
Giant	37.8
Large	42.3
Mid	14.4
Small	4.9
Micro	0.6
Avg $mil: 23,502	

Value Measures		Rel Category
Price/Earnings	30.48	1.10
Price/Book	4.08	1.22
Price/Sales	3.33	1.12
Price/Cash Flow	11.58	0.92
Dividend Yield %	0.29	1.53

Growth Measures	%	Rel Category
Long-Term Erngs	15.81	0.93
Book Value	5.06	1.22
Sales	4.22	1.39
Cash Flow	17.71	1.10
Historical Erngs	12.02	0.98

Profitability	%	Rel Category
Return on Equity	14.36	1.26
Return on Assets	8.69	1.36
Net Margin	12.90	1.24

Industry Weightings	% of Stocks	Rel Cat
Software	19.8	0.9
Hardware	20.3	1.6
Networking Eq	8.4	1.2
Semis	11.7	0.7
Semi Equip	2.0	0.5
Comp/Data Sv	6.2	1.3
Telecom	0.2	0.1
Health Care	0.0	0.0
Other	31.4	1.3

Composition

Cash	0.5
Stocks	99.4
Bonds	0.0
Other	0.1
Foreign (% of Stock)	12.3

Morningstar's Take by Laura Pavlenko Lutton 12-09-04

We'd take a more-cautious approach to Northern Technology.

It's been about five months since longtime manager John Leo stepped down from to focus on his duties as head of Northern's growth-equity research team. George Gilbert, who had comanaged the fund with Leo since 1997, is now the lead manager here. Gilbert is assisted by Deborah Koch, a former technology analyst and comanager of Northern Mid Cap Growth.

Gilbert brings some excellent experience to the table. He's been a career-long technology analyst and fund manager, and he and Koch are maintaining the fund's approach to picking tech stocks. They're looking for technology companies with high growth potential. For example, the managers recently cut back the fund's position in Amazon.com because they thought growth prospects at other Internet firms, including Google and Shopping.com, were superior.

Since they've been on their own here, Gilbert and Koch have produced competitive returns, but that record is far too short to be meaningful. Instead, we'd focus on Gilbert's results with Leo. That pair produced consistently strong results in a variety of market conditions for tech. Since 1997, the fund has ended just one calendar year in the technology category's bottom half.

While good stock-picking certainly contributed to this fund's past success and will likely carry through with Gilbert, Leo was especially accomplished at top-down calls. For example, he pushed the fund into Internet stocks in 1998, just as that area was taking off. The fund also correctly shifted its emphasis toward consumers in 2001. Without Leo's guidance on sector calls, the fund's returns may suffer going forward.

We don't think the manager change here is reason enough to sell, but we're not as enthusiastic about this offering as we once were.

Address:	Northern Funds Chicago, IL 60607 800-595-9111
Web Address:	www.northernfunds.com
Inception:	04-01-96 *
Advisor:	Northern Trust Investments, Nat. Assoc.
Subadvisor:	None
NTF Plans:	Fidelity Retail-NTF, Schwab OneSource

Minimum Purchase:	$2500	Add: $50	IRA: $500
Min Auto Inv Plan:	$250	Add: $50	
Sales Fees:	No-load		
Management Fee:	1.10%, 0.15%A		
Actual Fees:	Mgt:1.00%	Dist: —	
Expense Projections:	3Yr:$447	5Yr:$824	10Yr:$1802
Income Distrib:	Annually		

Oak Value

Analyst Pick

Ticker	Load	NAV	Yield	Total Assets	Mstar Category
OAKVX	None	$30.74	0.0%	$262 mil	Large Blend

Governance and Management

Fiduciary Grade:

Portfolio Manager(s)

This management team was dealt a blow in July 2003, when comanager and CEO George Brumley died in a plane crash. Comanager and chief investment officer David Carr remains on the fund. Longtime analysts Larry Coats and Matt Sauer were promoted to comanager roles after having served on the fund's investment committee for several years.

Strategy

Like Warren Buffett, management looks for companies with understandable business models, sustainable cash flows, and strong management teams. But it won't buy such a company unless it's selling at a discount to the team's estimate of its intrinsic value. Insurance, media, and consumer-products stocks have traditionally been the managers' favorites.

Historical Profile

Return High
Risk Above Avg
Rating ★★★★★ Highest

Investment Style: Equity Stock %

100% 88% 97% 95% 95% 100% 100% 98% 99%

▼ Manager Change
▽ Partial Manager Change

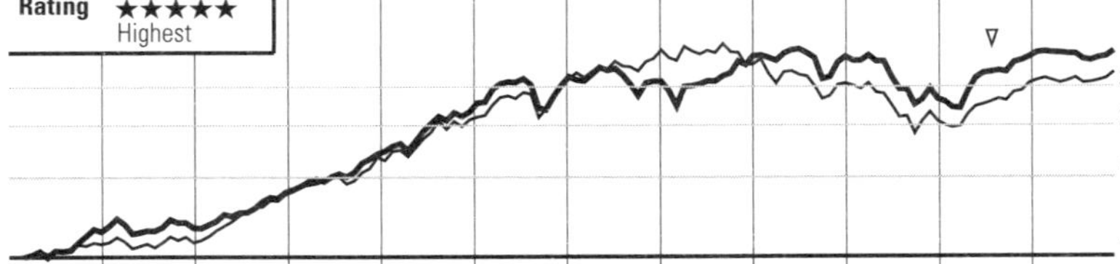

Growth of $10,000
- Investment Values of Fund
- Investment Values of S&P 500

Performance Quartile (within Category)

1993	1994	1995	1996	1997	1998	1999	2000	2001	2002	2003	12-04	History
11.99	10.99	14.06	17.49	23.19	27.29	25.52	29.49	29.08	21.55	28.47	30.74	NAV
22.05*	-1.51	28.84	28.99	37.70	18.93	-3.12	18.17	-0.47	-24.34	32.11	7.97	Total Return %
—	-2.82	-8.69	6.05	4.35	-9.64	-24.16	27.27	11.41	-2.25	3.44	-2.90	+/-S&P 500
—	-1.90	-8.93	6.54	4.85	-8.09	-24.03	25.96	11.98	-2.69	2.22	-3.43	+/-Russ 1000
0.00	0.00	0.00	0.00	0.00	0.41	0.29	0.11	0.00	0.00	0.00	0.00	Income Return %
—	-1.51	28.84	28.99	37.70	18.52	-3.41	18.06	-0.47	-24.34	32.11	7.97	Capital Return %
—	68	80	6	2	64	98	3	4	77	10	76	Total Rtn % Rank Cat
0.00	0.00	0.00	0.00	0.00	0.09	0.08	0.03	0.00	0.00	0.00	0.00	Income $
0.22	0.81	0.10	0.63	0.81	0.19	0.91	0.55	0.27	0.52	0.00	0.00	Capital Gains $
2.19	1.89	1.89	1.90	1.59	1.22	1.10	1.13	1.22	1.23	1.36	1.25	Expense Ratio %
-0.81	-0.58	-0.53	-0.43	-0.16	0.41	0.27	0.28	-0.12	-0.36	-0.33	-0.52	Income Ratio %
—	91	104	58	22	15	38	22	52	63	28	24	Turnover Rate %
4	8	13	29	140	561	470	329	320	220	250	262	Net Assets $mil

Performance 12-31-04

	1st Qtr	2nd Qtr	3rd Qtr	4th Qtr	Total
2000	-3.33	3.76	5.33	11.85	18.17
2001	-2.95	7.86	-17.86	15.76	-0.47
2002	0.93	-13.31	-16.65	3.76	-24.34
2003	-5.89	26.13	0.82	10.39	32.11
2004	2.77	-0.82	-2.52	8.69	8.00

Trailing	Total Return%	+/- S&P 500	+/- Russ 1000	%Rank Cat	Growth of $10,000
3 Mo	8.66	-0.57	-1.14	71	10,866
6 Mo	5.93	-1.26	-1.88	75	10,593
1 Yr	7.97	-2.90	-3.43	76	10,797
3 Yr Avg	2.57	-1.01	-1.70	58	10,791
5 Yr Avg	4.89	7.19	6.65	5	12,696
10 Yr Avg	12.84	0.77	0.68	8	33,468
15 Yr Avg	—	—	—	—	—

Tax Analysis	Tax-Adj Rtn%	%Rank Cat	Tax-Cost Rat	%Rank Cat
3 Yr (estimated)	2.43	45	0.14	12
5 Yr (estimated)	4.66	3	0.22	12
10 Yr (estimated)	12.31	5	0.47	6

Potential Capital Gain Exposure: 27% of assets

Rating and Risk

Time Period	Load-Adj Return %	Morningstar Rtn vs Cat	Morningstar Risk vs Cat	Morningstar Risk-Adj Rating
1 Yr	7.97			
3 Yr	2.57	Avg	+Avg	★★★
5 Yr	4.89	High	+Avg	★★★★★
10 Yr	12.84	High	+Avg	★★★★★
Incept	12.35			

Other Measures	Standard Index S&P 500	Best Fit Index Russ 1000
Alpha	-0.8	-1.5
Beta	0.98	1.00
R-Squared	84	86
Standard Deviation	16.49	
Mean	2.57	
Sharpe Ratio	0.07	

Morningstar's Take by Dan McNeela 11-03-04

Oak Value's patience should pay off in the long run.

This fund continues to commit to investing for the long haul. Management prides itself on being very selective about the type of stocks it owns. Before buying in, the investment team must be comfortable that a company's business model is sturdy enough to withstand competitive pressures and deliver above-average returns on capital.

As a result, the fund holds very few stocks (just 22 as of June 30, 2004). Management invests in companies it likes when they're selling at attractive prices, but new ideas don't pop up overnight. The fund added just three stocks in the 12-month period ending June 2004: AutoZone, Cadbury Schweppes and Cox Communications. The fund's turnover has averaged less than 40% annually.

Being so selective can have its drawbacks, because the fund invests heavily in the firms it prizes. For example, drug maker Merck, which checked in at nearly 3% of assets as of June 30, has lost 40% of its value in the past three months after it was forced pull arthritis drug Vioxx off the shelves. Management has also been a big believer in the ability of cable operators to make good on their huge capital expenditures, but thus far the fund has not been rewarded. Management continues to believe that cable operators are meeting expectations, however, so it is holding firm.

It's also worth noting that while the fund's performance relative to its mid-blend peers is sagging, the fund's primary hunting ground includes equal portions of large- and mid-cap stocks. Not owning many small-cap stocks has been a major headwind in recent years. Relative to the S&P 500, however, the fund has an edge over the trailing three-year, five-year, and 10-year periods.

Given that the three comanagers have been on the team for at least 10 years and that concentrated funds are expected to have ups and downs, we are still firmly in this fund's corner.

Portfolio Analysis 06-30-04

Share change since 03-04 Total Stocks:22	Sector	PE	YTD Ret%	% Assets
⊕ Zale	Goods	13.1	12.29	7.00
⊖ Constellation Brands A	Goods	19.9	41.24	6.54
Berkshire Hathaway B	Financial	20.9	4.30	6.31
Comcast	Media	—	-13.77	6.26
Ambac Financial Group	Financial	12.7	19.13	5.61
Time Warner	Media	27.5	8.12	5.32
Cendant	Business	13.6	6.52	5.22
⊕ XL Capital	Financial	20.1	2.80	5.18
⊕ EW Scripps	Media	20.0	3.37	5.00
Equifax	Business	17.6	15.19	4.88
⊕ AutoZone	Consumer	13.8	7.16	4.83
⊕ Cadbury Schweppes PLC AD	Goods	30.6	29.68	4.69
PartnerRe	Financial	—	9.36	4.44
Berkshire Hathaway A	Financial	—	—	4.05
Dow Jones & Company	Media	32.0	-11.70	3.94
IMS Health	Business	19.3	-6.32	3.65
⊖ Cox Communications A	Media	—	—	3.28
AFLAC	Financial	21.6	11.20	3.23
Certegy	Business	21.2	8.92	2.86
Hewlett-Packard	Hardware	18.9	-7.28	2.35

Current Investment Style

Value Blnd Growth; Large Mid Small

Market Cap	%
Giant	18.0
Large	30.0
Mid	44.1
Small	7.9
Micro	0.0
Avg $mil: 10,075	

Value Measures		Rel Category
Price/Earnings	14.06	0.83
Price/Book	2.03	0.77
Price/Sales	1.34	0.93
Price/Cash Flow	4.64	0.60
Dividend Yield %	0.60	0.41

Growth Measures	%	Rel Category
Long-Term Erngs	13.45	1.16
Book Value	9.45	1.22
Sales	14.96	2.61
Cash Flow	32.43	3.43
Historical Erngs	19.52	1.66

Profitability	%	Rel Category
Return on Equity	22.84	1.31
Return on Assets	7.10	0.82
Net Margin	10.94	0.96

Sector Weightings	% of Stocks	Rel S&P 500	3 Year High	3 Year Low
Info	26.44	1.23		
Software	0.00	0.00	0	0
Hardware	2.37	0.23	8	2
Media	24.07	6.27	31	20
Telecom	0.00	0.00	0	0
Service	53.16	1.15		
Health	0.00	0.00	12	0
Consumer	7.23	0.80	7	0
Business	16.80	4.15	20	14
Financial	29.13	1.40	39	25
Mfg	20.40	0.64		
Goods	20.40	2.19	20	9
Ind Mtrls	0.00	0.00	0	0
Energy	0.00	0.00	0	0
Utilities	0.00	0.00	0	0

Composition

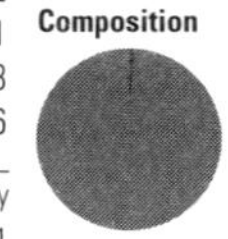

Cash	1.1
Stocks	98.9
Bonds	0.0
Other	0.0
Foreign (% of Stock)	6.7

Address:	3100 Tower Blvd Durham NC 27707 800-622-2474
Web Address:	
Inception:	01-18-93 *
Advisor:	Oak Value Capital Management, Inc
Subadvisor:	None
NTF Plans:	Fidelity Retail-NTF, Schwab OneSource

Minimum Purchase:	$2500	Add: $100	IRA: $1000
Min Auto Inv Plan:	$2500	Add: $100	
Sales Fees:	No-load		
Management Fee:	0.90%, 0.10%A		
Actual Fees:	Mgt:0.90%	Dist:	
Expense Projections:	3Yr:$390	5Yr:$676	10Yr:$1489
Income Distrib:	Semi-Annually		

Oakmark Equity & Inc I

Ticker	Load	NAV	Yield	Total Assets	Mstar Category
OAKBX	None	$23.50	0.8%	$8,705 mil	Moderate Allocation

Governance and Management

Fiduciary Grade: B

Portfolio Manager(s)

Clyde McGregor has managed the fund since its inception and is a large shareholder in the fund. Edward Studzinski joined him in March 2000. McGregor became an analyst with Harris Associates, the fund's advisor, in the early 1980s, and Studzinski joined Harris as an analyst in 1995. McGregor and Studzinski make decisions related to the bond portfolio themselves and can cull ideas from Harris' teams of analysts.

Strategy

Management keeps the fund's stock/bond mix close to 60/40, but bottom-up stock-picking drives the fund's asset allocation. On the stock side, the managers target value stocks, with an emphasis on cash-rich companies, and it keeps the portfolio concentrated. On the bond side, it invests most of the fund's assets in Treasuries, while holding small positions in corporate, high-yield, and non-U.S. government bonds.

Historical Profile

Return High
Risk Below Avg
Rating ★★★★★ Highest

Investment Style: Equity Stock % — 59% (2003), 53% (12-04)

▼ Manager Change
▽ Partial Manager Change

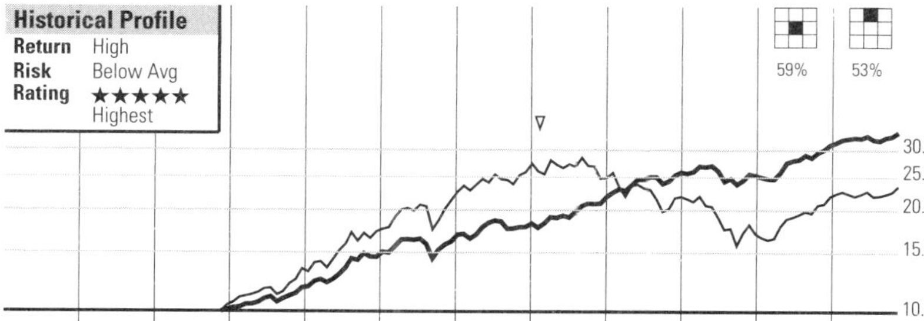

Growth of $10,000
— Investment Values of Fund
— Investment Values of S&P 500

Performance Quartile (within Category)

1993	1994	1995	1996	1997	1998	1999	2000	2001	2002	2003	12-04	History
—	—	10.24	11.55	13.76	15.03	14.40	15.96	18.53	17.99	22.02	23.50	NAV
—	—	2.40*	15.29	26.56	12.38	7.90	19.89	18.01	-2.14	23.21	10.36	Total Return %
—	—	—	-7.65	-6.79	-16.19	-13.14	28.99	29.39	19.95	-5.46	-0.51	+/-S&P 500
—	—	—	3.95	7.36	-0.01	-4.95	15.45	17.35	8.40	-0.85	-0.81	+/-DJ 60%
—	—	0.00	1.17	2.04	1.54	3.00	1.69	0.37	1.30	0.77	0.91	Income Return %
—	—	—	14.12	24.52	10.84	4.90	18.20	17.04	-3.44	22.44	9.45	Capital Return %
—	—	—	40	6	55	67	2	1	3	23	24	Total Rtn % Rank Cat
—	—	0.00	0.12	0.24	0.21	0.45	0.24	0.15	0.24	0.14	0.20	Income $
—	—	0.00	0.13	0.59	0.20	1.36	1.00	0.04	0.00	0.00	0.59	Capital Gains $
—	—	—	2.50	1.50	1.31	1.18	1.24	0.98	0.96	0.93	0.92	Expense Ratio %
—	—	—	1.21	2.38	2.39	2.65	3.04	2.07	1.71	1.07	0.78	Income Ratio %
—	—	—	66	53	46	81	87	124	73	48	72	Turnover Rate %
—	—	6	15	41	59	58	75	1,099	2,614	5,172	8,129	Net Assets $mil

Performance 12-31-04

	1st Qtr	2nd Qtr	3rd Qtr	4th Qtr	Total
2000	4.38	-0.13	9.93	4.63	19.89
2001	4.14	8.06	-2.84	7.93	18.01
2002	4.19	-3.19	-8.57	6.12	-2.14
2003	-2.28	13.20	2.01	9.19	23.21
2004	4.18	1.87	-1.07	5.11	10.36

Trailing	Total Return%	+/- S&P 500	+/- DJ 60%	%Rank Cat	Growth of $10,000
3 Mo	5.11	-4.12	-2.37	88	10,511
6 Mo	3.98	-3.21	-3.55	90	10,398
1 Yr	10.36	-0.51	-0.81	24	11,036
3 Yr Avg	9.99	6.41	2.73	2	13,306
5 Yr Avg	13.49	15.79	8.25	1	18,827
10 Yr Avg	—	—	—	—	—
15 Yr Avg	—	—	—	—	—

Tax Analysis	Tax-Adj Rtn%	%Rank Cat	Tax-Cost Rat	%Rank Cat
3 Yr (estimated)	9.47	2	0.47	32
5 Yr (estimated)	12.67	1	0.72	29
10 Yr (estimated)	—	—	—	—

Potential Capital Gain Exposure: 13% of assets

Rating and Risk

Time Period	Load-Adj Return %	Morningstar Rtn vs Cat	Morningstar Risk vs Cat	Morningstar Risk-Adj Rating
1 Yr	10.36			
3 Yr	9.99	High	Avg	★★★★★
5 Yr	13.49	High	-Avg	★★★★★
10 Yr	—	—	—	—
Incept	14.32			

Other Measures	Standard Index S&P 500	Best Fit Index S&P Mid 400
Alpha	7.1	3.2
Beta	0.52	0.55
R-Squared	74	85

Standard Deviation	9.76
Mean	9.99
Sharpe Ratio	0.89

Morningstar's Take by William Samuel Rocco 01-05-05

Oakmark Equity & Income has a lot going for it, but that doesn't mean it can shine every year.

This fund's appeal begins with its firm and managers. Oakmark is a fundholder-friendly shop, with an excellent board of trustees and corporate culture. The fund relies on the same proven value discipline as its five siblings. Clyde McGregor, who has been at the helm since the fund opened in late 1995, has been with advisor Harris Associates for more than 20 years, while Ed Studzinski, who became a comanager in early 2000, joined Harris roughly 10 years ago and boasts nearly two decades of investment experience.

Due to the family's strict value style, the fund sports a distinctive portfolio. McGregor and Studzinski like to run a fairly focused portfolio and readily buy bargains in bunches, so the fund usually owns about one third the category norm of 140 or so equities, and it often sports sizable stakes in individual sectors. And the duo's all-cap style means the fund's average market cap is typically much smaller than the group norm.

McGregor and Studzinski have executed their miserly approach skillfully over the short term and longer stretches. The fund gained 10% and beat three fourths of its moderate-allocation peers in 2004. The managers' style has been in favor--smaller-cap and value names have led the way this year--but their stock selection also has been good. And the fund posted topnotch results in the first four years of this decade for essentially the same reasons.

The fund also had some success in the mid-1990s, so it has crushed its average peer since opening in late 1995. That long-term performance and the fund's other strengths make us confident in its long-term prospects. But it's crucial to note that the fund's miserly all-cap equity style was a burden in the late-1990s large-growth-led rallies, and it's likely to be so again the next time such issues lead the way.

Address:	Harris Associates LP Chicago IL 60602-3790 800-625-6275
Web Address:	www.oakmark.com
Inception:	11-01-95*
Advisor:	Harris Associates LP
Subadvisor:	None
NTF Plans:	Fidelity Retail-NTF

Minimum Purchase:	$1000	Add: $100	IRA: $1000
Min Auto Inv Plan:	$500	Add: $100	
Sales Fees:	No-load, 2.00%R		
Management Fee:	0.75% mx./0.65% mn.		
Actual Fees:	Mgt:0.73%	Dist:	
Expense Projections:	3Yr:$296	5Yr:$515	10Yr:$1143
Income Distrib:	Annually		

Portfolio Analysis 07-31-04

Total Stocks:54 Share change since 06-30-04	Sectors	P/E Ratio	YTD Return %	% Net Assets
Burlington Resources	Energy	10.9	-4.28	3.62
XTO Energy	Energy	20.5	-6.16	3.10
First Data	Business	18.8	-2.70	2.84
General Dynamics	Ind Mtrls	17.5	-2.95	2.61
⊕ Diageo PLC ADR	Goods	17.5	-3.90	2.57
Nestle SA ADR	Goods	21.6	-3.56	2.32
Safeco	Financial	10.9	-4.90	2.27
Abbott Laboratories	Health	22.1	0.92	2.10
RR Donnelley & Sons	Business	24.2	-5.38	1.91

Total Fixed-Income:40	Date of Maturity	Amount $000	Value $000	% Net Assets
US Treasury Note 5%	08-15-11	400,000	429,891	5.34
US Treasury Note 2.75%	08-15-07	400,000	398,906	4.95
US Treasury Note 2.25%	04-30-06	400,000	398,844	4.95
US Treasury Note 2.375%	08-31-06	400,000	398,516	4.95
US Treasury Note 1.625%	02-28-06	400,000	395,922	4.92
US Treasury Note 3.375%	01-15-07	254,642	272,058	3.38
US Treasury Note 1.875%	12-31-05	200,000	198,977	2.47
US Treasury Note 3%	02-15-09	200,000	197,992	2.46
US Treasury Note 4%	02-15-14	100,000	99,227	1.23

Equity Style
Style: Blend
Size: Large-Cap

Value Measures		Rel Category
Price/Earnings	16.58	1.00
Price/Book	2.59	1.06
Price/Sales	1.19	0.90
Price/Cash Flow	7.80	1.07
Dividend Yield %	1.04	0.66

Growth Measures	%	Rel Category
Long-Term Erngs	11.43	0.98
Book Value	8.53	1.49
Sales	7.69	1.48
Cash Flow	14.71	1.84
Historical Erngs	10.32	0.95

Market Cap %			
Giant	18.1	Small	5.8
Large	39.9	Micro	0.1
Mid	36.3	Avg $mil:	12,632

Fixed-Income Style
Duration: —
Quality: —

Avg Eff Duration[1]	—
Avg Eff Maturity	—
Avg Credit Quality	—
Avg Wtd Coupon	2.59%

[1]figure provided by fund

Composition

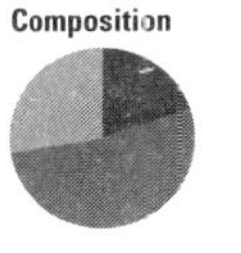

Cash	19.7
Stocks	52.6
Bonds	27.7
Other	0.0
Foreign (% of Stock)	10.3

Sector Weightings	% of Stocks	Rel S&P 500	3 Year High	3 Year Low
Info	7.08	0.33		
Software	2.30	0.53	—	—
Hardware	0.82	0.08	—	—
Media	3.96	1.03	—	—
Telecom	0.00	0.00	—	—
Service	47.39	1.02		
Health	14.79	1.18	—	—
Consumer	10.94	1.20	—	—
Business	13.65	3.37	—	—
Financial	8.01	0.39	—	—
Mfg	45.52	1.42		
Goods	12.36	1.32	—	—
Ind Mtrls	18.44	1.46	—	—
Energy	14.72	2.06	—	—
Utilities	0.00	0.00	—	—

Oakmark Global I

Analyst Pick	Ticker	Load	NAV	Yield	Total Assets	Mstar Category
✔	OAKGX	None	$21.81	0.5%	$1,568 mil	World Stock

Governance and Management

Fiduciary Grade: A

Portfolio Manager(s)

Michael Welsh has been with Harris Associates since 1992 and comanages Oakmark International and Oakmark International Small Cap; he has run the overseas portion since the fund's August 1999 start. He's supported by six analysts. Clyde McGregor, comanager of Oakmark Equity & Income, replaced Greg Jackson as this fund's domestic manager in October 2003 and is supported by a deep and talented pool of U.S. analysts.

Strategy

This fund's managers buy stocks that trade at discounts to their estimates of the stocks' intrinsic value. The managers take an all-cap approach, they aren't afraid to build big positions in individual names, sectors, and countries, and they run a focused portfolio. Though the fund is normally unhedged, the managers will hedge some of their currency exposure when they see extreme risk in a particular currency. A portion of the fund's British pound exposure has been hedged since July 2004, for example.

Historical Profile

Return High
Risk Above Avg
Rating ★★★★★ Highest

Investment Style Equity Stock %

1999	2000	2001	2002	2003	2004
91%	92%	90%	97%	91%	99%

▼ Manager Change
▽ Partial Manager Change

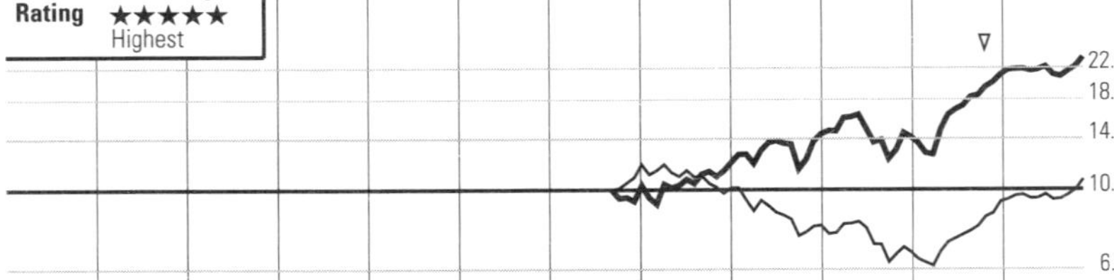

Growth of $10,000
— Investment Values of Fund
— Investment Values of MSCI EAFE

Performance Quartile (within Category)

1993	1994	1995	1996	1997	1998	1999	2000	2001	2002	2003	12-04	History
—	—	—	—	—	—	9.97	11.31	13.26	12.98	19.28	21.81	NAV
—	—	—	—	—	—	-0.20*	15.84	20.05	-2.11	48.98	15.63	Total Return %
—	—	—	—	—	—	—	30.03	41.47	13.83	10.39	-4.62	+/-MSCI EAFE
—	—	—	—	—	—	—	29.03	36.85	17.78	15.87	0.91	+/-MSCI World
—	—	—	—	—	—	0.00	1.75	0.02	0.00	0.01	0.54	Income Return %
—	—	—	—	—	—	—	14.09	20.03	-2.11	48.97	15.09	Capital Return %
—	—	—	—	—	—	—	2	1	3	7	43	Total Rtn % Rank Cat
—	—	—	—	—	—	0.01	0.17	0.00	0.00	0.00	0.10	Income $
—	—	—	—	—	—	0.00	0.05	0.29	0.00	0.05	0.37	Capital Gains $
—	—	—	—	—	—	1.75	1.75	1.75	1.55	1.28	1.26	Expense Ratio %
—	—	—	—	—	—	0.98	0.54	0.00	-0.01	0.00	0.47	Income Ratio %
—	—	—	—	—	—	—	147	114	86	42	16	Turnover Rate %
—	—	—	—	—	—	31	28	76	230	1,168	1,535	Net Assets $mil

Performance 12-31-04

	1st Qtr	2nd Qtr	3rd Qtr	4th Qtr	Total
2000	0.80	3.18	5.21	5.86	15.84
2001	-0.71	15.76	-16.69	25.37	20.05
2002	10.86	-6.60	-17.70	14.87	-2.11
2003	-10.55	33.51	9.55	13.88	48.98
2004	3.89	1.40	-2.86	13.00	15.64

Trailing	Total Return%	+/- MSCI EAFE	+/- MSCI World	%Rank Cat	Growth of $10,000
3 Mo	13.00	-2.32	1.06	34	11,300
6 Mo	9.77	-5.23	-1.05	62	10,977
1 Yr	15.63	-4.62	0.91	43	11,563
3 Yr Avg	19.03	7.14	12.08	2	16,864
5 Yr Avg	18.59	19.72	21.04	1	23,455
10 Yr Avg	—	—	—	—	—
15 Yr Avg	—	—	—	—	—

Tax Analysis	Tax-Adj Rtn%	%Rank Cat	Tax-Cost Rat	%Rank Cat
3 Yr (estimated)	18.84	2	0.16	22
5 Yr (estimated)	18.18	1	0.35	22
10 Yr (estimated)	—	—	—	—

Potential Capital Gain Exposure: 24% of assets

Rating and Risk

Time Period	Load-Adj Return %	Morningstar Rtn vs Cat	Morningstar Risk vs Cat	Morningstar Risk-Adj Rating
1 Yr	15.63			
3 Yr	19.03	High	High	★★★★★
5 Yr	18.59	High	+Avg	★★★★★
10 Yr	—	—	—	—
Incept	17.02			

Other Measures	Standard Index S&P 500	Best Fit Index Russ 1000 VI
Alpha	5.9	8.9
Beta	1.10	1.19
R-Squared	78	82
Standard Deviation	23.26	
Mean	19.03	
Sharpe Ratio	0.77	

Morningstar's Take by William Samuel Rocco 12-21-04

Don't be fooled by this year's result; this fund is no ordinary world-stock offering.

Oakmark Global has failed to distinguish itself in 2004. It does have more international exposure than most of its rivals--and overseas stocks have outperformed this year--but some of its key foreign names have been sluggish. GlaxoSmithKline and Nestle, which are roughly 4% of assets each, have managed only low-single-digit returns. Meanwhile, a few domestic stocks have disappointed. Thus, despite the strength of overseas picks like Bulgari and domestic selections like Burlington Resources, the fund has posted a thoroughly average 13% gain for the year to date.

Middling results are the exception here, though. Indeed, the fund, which opened in late 1999, earned top-decile results in each of its first four calendar years.

Not surprisingly, a distinctive style lies behind these topnotch results. Michael Welsh and Clyde McGregor rely on Oakmark's penurious philosophy as they seek attractive bargains of all sizes across the globe, so the fund normally has a pronounced value bias and more exposure to smaller caps than most of its peers. And the duo goes wherever the best bargains are, readily buys stocks in bunches, and runs a focused portfolio. Thus, the country and sector weights usually stand out here, and the fund typically owns about one third the group norm of 130 to 140 names.

Still, it's important to recognize that this strategy comes with real risks. The all-cap-value orientation has been a boon in the early 2000s, but it's likely to be a burden the next time blue-chip growth stocks lead the way. And though Welsh and McGregor have put their freedom and focus to good use so far, both court volatility. Thus, while the duo's success here and elsewhere makes us optimistic about this fund's long-term prospects, investors should expect some bumps along the way.

Address:	Harris Associates LP Chicago IL 60602-3790 800-625-6275
Web Address:	www.oakmark.com
Inception:	08-04-99 *
Advisor:	Harris Associates LP
Subadvisor:	None
NTF Plans:	Fidelity Retail-NTF

Minimum Purchase:	$1000	Add: $100	IRA: $1000
Min Auto Inv Plan:	$500	Add: $100	
Sales Fees:	No-load, 2.00%R		
Management Fee:	1.00% mx./0.90% mn.		
Actual Fees:	Mgt:0.93%	Dist:	
Expense Projections:	3Yr:$406	5Yr:$702	10Yr:$1545
Income Distrib:	Annually		

Portfolio Analysis 06-30-04

Share change since 05-04 Total Stocks:45	Sector	Country	% Assets
Diageo	Goods	U.K.	5.14
First Data	Business	United States	4.84
Takeda Chemical Industri	Health	Japan	4.33
GlaxoSmithKline	Health	U.K.	4.22
Bk Of Ireland (The Gover	Financial	Ireland	4.05
Nestle	Goods	Switzerland	3.88
Euronext	Financial	France	3.85
Burlington Resources	Energy	United States	3.83
eFunds	Business	United States	3.18
Laboratory Corp of Ameri	Health	United States	2.90
Vivendi Universal	Media	France	2.73
Equifax	Business	United States	2.68
Julius Baer Holding Ltd	Financial	Switzerland	2.65
Akzo Nobel	Ind Mtrls	Netherlands	2.61
Cadbury Schweppes	Goods	U.K.	2.52
TJX Companies	Consumer	United States	2.46
Bulgari	Goods	Italy	2.40
Lonza Grp	Health	Switzerland	2.40
Waste Management	Business	United States	2.39
Henkel Grp	Ind Mtrls	Germany	2.37

Current Investment Style

Market Cap	%
Giant	26.6
Large	32.8
Mid	35.4
Small	4.9
Micro	0.3
Avg $mil: 10,799	

Value Measures		Rel Category
Price/Earnings	15.51	0.98
Price/Book	2.72	1.23
Price/Sales	1.65	1.41
Price/Cash Flow	6.84	1.08
Dividend Yield %	1.78	0.95

Growth Measures	%	Rel Category
Long-Term Erngs	12.84	1.07
Book Value	1.37	0.62
Sales	-4.64	NMF
Cash Flow	3.33	0.57
Historical Erngs	3.24	0.38

Composition

Cash	6.3	Bonds	0.0
Stocks	93.7	Other	0.0
Foreign (% of Stock)			64.9

Sector Weightings	% of Stocks	Rel MSCI EAFE	3 Year High	3 Year Low
Info	12.37	0.74		
Software	2.45	2.27	12	1
Hardware	0.65	0.18	7	0
Media	7.33	3.21	17	6
Telecom	1.94	0.20	3	0
Service	56.51	1.26		
Health	14.00	1.93	19	4
Consumer	2.79	0.55	11	0
Business	21.28	3.91	31	20
Financial	18.44	0.68	19	4
Mfg	31.13	0.81		
Goods	16.46	1.20	17	7
Ind Mtrls	11.16	0.91	13	5
Energy	3.51	0.48	4	0
Utilities	0.00	0.00	0	0

Regional Exposure	% Stock		
UK/W. Europe	48	N. America	35
Japan	7	Latn America	3
Asia X Japan	6	Other	1

Country Exposure	% Stock		
United States	35	Japan	7
U.K.	13	France	7
Switzerland	11		

Oakmark I

Analyst Pick

Ticker	Load	NAV	Yield	Total Assets	Mstar Category
OAKMX	None	$41.77	0.4%	$7,222 mil	Large Value

Governance and Management

Fiduciary Grade: B

Portfolio Manager(s)

Bill Nygren has worked for Harris Associates, advisor to the Oakmark funds, for two decades. He makes the final decisions about the portfolio, and he has also run Oakmark Select with aplomb. Comanager Kevin Grant assists Nygren.

Strategy

This traditionally was one of the purest value funds around, but manager Bill Nygren has recently found more fallen growth stocks that meet his valuation criteria. He buys stocks that are trading at discounts to their estimated private market values. To estimate companies' intrinsic values, Nygren and his colleagues use discounted cash-flow analysis and look at comparable transactions, among many factors. The fund has migrated from its former mid-cap home into large-cap territory, as many of Nygren's recent purchases have fallen into the latter area.

Historical Profile

Return Above Avg
Risk Above Avg
Rating ★★★★ Above Avg

Investment Style: Equity Stock %

93% 90% [illegible]7% 89% 91% 90% 94% 91% 92%

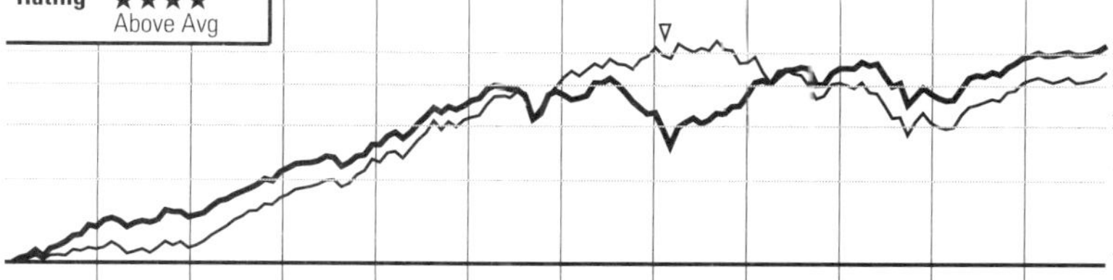

38.0 31.0 24.0 17.0 10.0

▼ Manager Change
▽ Partial Manager Change

Growth of $10,000
— Investment Values of Fund
— Investment Values of S&P 500

Performance Quartile (within Category)

1993	1994	1995	1996	1997	[illegible]998	1999	200[illegible]	200[illegible]	2002	2003	12-04	History
23.93	22.97	29.75	32.35	40.41	3[illegible].82	27.20	29.99	35.2[illegible]	30.08	37.54	41.77	NAV
30.50	3.31	34.42	16.20	32.59	[illegible].73	-10.47	11.78	18.2[illegible]	-14.41	25.30	11.73	Total Return %
20.44	2.00	-3.11	-6.74	-0.76	-2[illegible].84	-31.51	20.88	30.1[illegible]	7.68	-3.37	0.86	+/-S&P 500
12.43	5.29	-3.94	-5.44	-2.59	-1[illegible].90	-17.82	4.77	23.8[illegible]	1.11	-4.73	-4.76	+/-Russ 1000 VI
1.20	0.97	1.24	1.16	1.24	[illegible].21	0.73	1.42	0.6[illegible]	0.32	0.47	0.45	Income Return %
29.30	2.34	33.18	15.04	31.35	[illegible].52	-11.20	10.36	17.6[illegible]	-14.73	24.83	11.28	Capital Return %
1	15	38	82	10	87	97	39	1	21	74	63	Total Rtn % Rank Cat
0.23	0.23	0.28	0.34	0.40	[illegible].44	0.26	0.39	0.20	0.11	0.14	0.17	Income $
0.77	1.47	0.84	1.87	1.98	[illegible].63	4.73	0.00	0.00	0.00	0.00	0.00	Capital Gains $
1.32	1.22	1.17	1.18	1.08	1.08	1.11	1.21	1.15	1.17	1.14	1.05	Expense Ratio %
0.94	1.19	1.27	1.13	1.19	1.22	1.02	1.42	0.73	0.38	0.48	0.47	Income Ratio %
18	29	18	24	—	43	13	50	57	44	21	19	Turnover Rate %
1,214	1,627	3,302	4,195	7,301	7,[illegible]58	3,818	2,206	3,644	3,789	5,509	7,156	Net Assets $mil

Performance 12-31-04

	1st Qtr	2nd Qtr	3rd Qtr	4th Qtr	Total
2000	-8.97	2.58	6.10	12.82	11.78
2001	7.37	9.25	-9.01	10.82	18.29
2002	4.17	-8.36	-16.60	7.51	-14.41
2003	-4.09	16.95	0.33	11.35	25.30
2004	1.44	2.23	-0.64	8.44	11.73

Trailing	Total Return%	+/- S&P 500	+/- Russ 1000 VI	%Rank Cat	Growth of $10,000
3 Mo	8.44	-0.79	-1.94	70	10,844
6 Mo	7.74	0.55	-4.34	69	10,774
1 Yr	11.73	0.86	-4.76	63	11,173
3 Yr Avg	6.22	2.64	-2.35	43	11,984
5 Yr Avg	9.64	11.94	4.37	7	15,843
10 Yr Avg	11.79	-0.28	-2.04	41	30,481
15 Yr Avg	—	—	—	—	—

Tax Analysis	Tax-Adj Rtn%	%Rank Cat	Tax-Cost Rat	%Rank Cat
3 Yr (estimated)	6.07	30	0.14	10
5 Yr (estimated)	9.38	6	0.24	13
10 Yr (estimated)	10.34	27	1.30	23

Potential Capital Gain Exposure: 20% of assets

Rating and Risk

Time Period	Load-Adj Return %	Morningstar Rtn vs Cat	Morningstar Risk vs Cat	Morningstar Risk-Adj Rating
1 Yr	11.73			
3 Yr	6.22	Avg	-Avg	★★★
5 Yr	9.64	High	+Avg	★★★★★
10 Yr	11.79	Avg	+Avg	★★★
Incept	16.74			

Other Measures	Standard Index S&P 500	Best Fit Index Russ 1000 VI
Alpha	2.8	-1.4
Beta	0.87	0.88
R-Squared	89	91
Standard Deviation	14.63	
Mean	6.22	
Sharpe Ratio	0.33	

Portfolio Analysis 06-30-04

Share change since 03-04 Total Stocks:56	Sector	PE	YTD Ret%	% Assets
Washington Mutual	Financial	13.9	10.05	2.78
⊕ McDonald's	Consumer	19.7	31.48	2.43
First Data	Business	18.8	3.72	2.39
H & R Block	Consumer	14.5	-9.99	2.28
Yum Brands	Consumer	19.7	37.84	2.27
Black & Decker	Ind Mtrls	16.4	81.42	2.26
Masco	Ind Mtrls	17.2	36.23	2.22
⊕ Time Warner	Media	27.5	8.12	2.21
⊕ Liberty Media	Media	—	11.56	2.15
Home Depot	Consumer	19.0	21.47	2.13
⊕ Anheuser-Busch Companies	Goods	18.1	-1.95	2.05
⊕ Walt Disney	Media	24.3	20.21	2.04
Limited Brands	Consumer	16.0	37.88	2.03
⊕ Wal-Mart Stores	Consumer	23.4	0.51	2.02
⊕ Gap	Consumer	17.6	-8.63	2.01
⊕ Comcast	Media	—	-13.77	2.01
Fortune Brands	Goods	16.5	9.86	1.97
⊕ Baxter International	Health	32.9	15.22	1.96
⊕ Citigroup	Financial	15.3	2.72	1.95
⊕ Fannie Mae	Financial	9.1	-2.33	1.92

Current Investment Style

Value Blnd Growth — Large Mid Small

Market Cap	%
Giant	22.4
Large	64.0
Mid	13.6
Small	0.0
Micro	0.0

Avg $mil: 23,545

Value Measures		Rel Category
Price/Earnings	16.61	1.11
Price/Book	2.55	1.12
Price/Sales	1.32	1.11
Price/Cash Flow	8.35	1.31
Dividend Yield %	1.32	0.75

Growth Measures	%	Rel Category
Long-Term Erngs	11.45	1.10
Book Value	6.88	1.22
Sales	7.59	1.81
Cash Flow	13.[illegible]2	2.51
Historical Erngs	10.50	0.89

Profitability	%	Rel Category
Return on Equity	18.87	1.19
Return on Assets	5.68	0.75
Net Margin	9.47	0.93

Sector Weightings	% of Stocks	Rel S&P 500	3 Year High	3 Year Low
Info	16.35	0.76		
Software	0.00	0.00	0	0
Hardware	1.78	0.17	2	1
Media	12.95	3.37	17	6
Telecom	1.62	0.51	5	1
Service	52.13	1.12		
Health	12.28	0.98	15	7
Consumer	18.46	2.03	20	17
Business	7.51	1.85	12	6
Financial	13.88	0.67	16	11
Mfg	31.50	0.98		
Goods	16.77	1.80	20	15
Ind Mtrls	10.80	0.85	11	9
Energy	3.93	0.55	6	2
Utilities	0.00	0.00	4	0

Composition

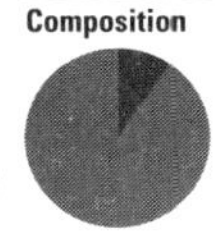

Cash	9.7
Stocks	90.3
Bonds	0.0
Other	0.0
Foreign (% of Stock)	1.8

Morningstar's Take by Kunal Kapoor 10-17-04

Oakmark Fund is a good match for most portfolios.

This fund continues to warm up to some of the stocks it wouldn't even have dreamed of owning five years ago. During the past quarter, for example, media conglomerate Viacom found a place in the portfolio. It's the latest of many sliding blue chips that the fund owns, reflecting manager Bill Nygren's view that many "above-average" businesses are now trading at average prices. It's also the latest among a growing arsenal of media holdings, a sector Nygren says offers some of the best opportunities available. That's good news for shareholders, as Nygren has a strong record of investing in such businesses.

A group where the fund hasn't had much recent success, however, is among pharmaceutical stocks. Most recently, the fund was hurt by Merck, whose shares slid after the firm pulled arthritis drug Vioxx off the market. Nygren says that the market's reaction was justified given the accompanying drop in revenues, but that the stock remains a value.

To be sure, one of the risks of being a value investor is that one can move too early into sagging stocks. However, we think that in general this fund is protected by the margin of safety that Nygren builds into each pick, as well as his willingness to add to positions on the way down when appropriate. Moreover, Nygren strives for solid aftertax returns, a positive for taxable investors.

These points aside, though, this fund is beginning to look very different than some of the other value funds it is otherwise commonly associated with. Few rivals have embraced blue chips with the vigor that it has. As such, while we think the fund will continue delivering, we wouldn't be shocked to see its performance veer from other value rivals'.

Address:	Harris Associates LP Chicago IL 60602-3790 800-625-6275
Web Address:	www.oakmark.com
Inception:	08-05-91
Advisor:	Harris Associates LP
Subadvisor:	None
NTF Plans:	Fidelity Retail-NTF, Schwab OneSource

Minimum Purchase:	$1000	Add: $100	IRA: $1000
Min Auto Inv Plan:	$500	Add: $100	
Sales Fees:	No-load, 2.00%R		
Management Fee:	1.00% mx./0.75% mn.		
Actual Fees:	Mgt:0.91%	Dist:	
Expense Projections:	3Yr:$362	5Yr:$628	10Yr:$1386
Income Distrib:	Annually		

Oakmark International I

Ticker	Load	NAV	Yield	Total Assets	Mstar Category
OAKIX	None	$21.13	1.3%	$4,989 mil	Foreign Large Value

Governance and Management

Fiduciary Grade: B

Portfolio Manager(s)

This fund (which is now closed to new investors buying through broker/dealers and third-party intermediaries but is still open to new investors buying directly from Oakmark) is run by David Herro and Michael Welsh. Herro has been at the helm since the fund opened in late 1992. Michael Welsh joined him in November 1995. They also run Oakmark International Small Cap. Six analysts support them.

Strategy

The managers invest in stocks that trade at a discount of at least 40% to their estimates of intrinsic value. (Willingness to invest in fallen growth stocks can push the fund into the blend or growth column of the Morningstar style box. Many such firms see earnings and cash flow fall along with their stocks, so they still have high price multiples--although they look cheap on an intrinsic value basis.) They readily consider emerging-markets and smaller-cap names, and the fund's sector and country weights often look quite different from its peers'. To combat market-timers, the fund has a 2% redemption fee.

Historical Profile

Return High
Risk High
Rating ★★★★ Above Avg

Investment Style: Equity Stock %

1993	1994	1995	1996	1997	1998	1999	2000	2001	2002	2003	12-04
90%	93%	97%	96%	96%	95%	92%	95%	96%			

▼ Manager Change
▽ Partial Manager Change

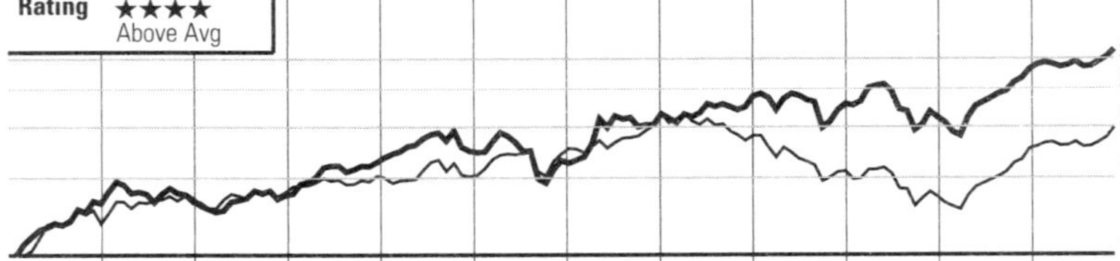

Growth of $10,000
— Investment Values of Fund
— Investment Values of MSCI EAFE

Performance Quartile (within Category)

1993	1994	1995	1996	1997	1998	1999	2000	2001	2002	2003	12-04	History
14.79	12.41	12.38	15.68	12.83	10.91	14.70	15.46	14.49	13.14	18.02	21.13	NAV
53.58	-9.06	8.32	28.02	3.32	-7.00	39.47	12.50	-5.13	-8.46	38.04	19.09	Total Return %
21.02	-16.84	-2.89	21.97	1.54	-26.93	12.44	26.69	16.29	7.48	-0.55	-1.16	+/-MSCI EAFE
21.37	-16.41	-3.09	21.15	1.05	-25.69	11.49	25.86	16.26	7.34	-1.38	-1.29	+/-MSCI Wd xUS
0.82	0.00	0.00	1.31	3.67	1.90	4.46	3.45	1.07	0.87	0.83	1.48	Income Return %
52.76	-9.06	8.32	26.71	-0.35	-8.90	35.01	9.05	-6.20	-9.33	37.21	17.61	Capital Return %
1	100	82	1	79	98	16	5	7	27	59	74	Total Rtn % Rank Cat
0.08	0.00	0.00	0.16	0.58	0.24	0.49	0.51	0.16	0.13	0.11	0.27	Income $
0.15	1.06	1.04	0.00	2.86	0.78	0.00	0.50	0.00	0.00	0.00	0.05	Capital Gains $
1.26	1.37	1.40	1.32	1.26	1.32	1.29	1.30	1.30	1.31	1.25	1.20	Expense Ratio %
1.55	1.44	1.40	1.45	2.09	1.95	1.94	1.87	1.40	1.34	1.03	1.40	Income Ratio %
21	55	27	42	61	43	54	64	58	24	34	21	Turnover Rate %
1,108	1,080	786	1,233	1,238	797	785	818	964	1,656	3,509	4,677	Net Assets $mil

Performance 12-31-04

	1st Qtr	2nd Qtr	3rd Qtr	4th Qtr	Total
2000	-0.20	7.09	-1.97	7.39	12.50
2001	-8.73	9.99	-19.39	17.24	-5.13
2002	11.46	-2.23	-22.93	8.99	-8.46
2003	-11.72	25.43	7.70	15.75	38.04
2004	3.61	1.82	-0.16	13.07	19.09

Trailing	Total Return%	+/- MSCI EAFE	+/- MSCI Wd xUS	%Rank Cat	Growth of $10,000
3 Mo	13.07	-2.25	-2.08	84	11,307
6 Mo	12.89	-2.11	-2.48	81	11,289
1 Yr	19.09	-1.16	-1.29	74	11,909
3 Yr Avg	14.59	2.70	2.37	46	15,047
5 Yr Avg	9.94	11.07	10.70	5	16,061
10 Yr Avg	11.56	5.94	5.62	4	29,860
15 Yr Avg	—	—	—	—	—

Tax Analysis	Tax-Adj Rtn%	%Rank Cat	Tax-Cost Rat	%Rank Cat
3 Yr (estimated)	14.18	36	0.36	31
5 Yr (estimated)	9.08	4	0.78	38
10 Yr (estimated)	9.65	8	1.71	86

Potential Capital Gain Exposure: 25% of assets

Rating and Risk

Time Period	Load-Adj Return %	Morningstar Rtn vs Cat	Morningstar Risk vs Cat	Morningstar Risk-Adj Rating
1 Yr	19.09			
3 Yr	14.59	Avg	+Avg	★★★
5 Yr	9.94	High	High	★★★★
10 Yr	11.56	High	High	★★★★
Incept	12.40			

Other Measures	Standard Index S&P 500	Best Fit Index MSCI Wd xUS
Alpha	1.9	1.4
Beta	1.08	1.10
R-Squared	89	89
Standard Deviation	20.66	
Mean	14.59	
Sharpe Ratio	0.65	

Morningstar's Take by William Samuel Rocco 11-15-04

Investors who look beyond Oakmark International's current style box and recent results will find a strict and strong bargain hunter.

Oakmark International's portfolio lands in the large-blend section of the international style box, and it has resided there or in the large-growth section for several quarters. But that's not because David Herro and Michael Welsh have become growth-at-a-reasonable-price investors.

Instead, it's due to the fact that Herro and Welsh remain dedicated to finding companies that are trading at big discounts to their intrinsic values--rather than simply focusing on firms with low price multiples--and they've been finding lots of opportunities among fallen growth stocks. The fund's health-care stake is still more than twice the foreign-large-value norm of 6%, for example, as the duo continue to believe that GlaxoSmithKline and the fund's other drug names are fetching bargains with good prospects.

The fund hasn't reaped a lot of benefits from its fallen growth picks yet. Its drug stocks posted restrained gains last year, and most of them have been sluggish thus far in 2004. Thus, the fund posted so-so returns in 2003, and it's on pace to do so again this year.

But these recent results are average rather than bad, and Herro and Welsh have executed their wide-ranging value style deftly over time. Indeed, although their open-mindedness has backfired at times--and led to more volatility than the group norm--the fund has earned a 12% annualized gain since opening in late 1992, while its typical peer has posted an 8% annualized return during that period.

Those returns are impressive, and the fund remains a good option for bold value fans with long horizons. But such investors need to be sure they can handle the risks that come with the fund's go-anywhere style, and they should note that the fund expects to make a small distribution early next month.

Address:	Harris Associates LP Chicago IL 60602-3790 800-625-6275
Web Address:	www.oakmark.com
Inception:	09-30-92
Advisor:	Harris Associates LP
Subadvisor:	None
NTF Plans:	Fidelity Retail-NTF, Schwab OneSource

Minimum Purchase:	$1000	Add: $100	IRA: $1000
Min Auto Inv Plan:	$500	Add: $100	
Sales Fees:	No-load, 2.00%R		
Management Fee:	1.00% mx./0.85% mn.		
Actual Fees:	Mgt:0.96%	Dist:	
Expense Projections:	3Yr:$397	5Yr:$686	10Yr:$1511
Income Distrib:	Annually		

Portfolio Analysis 06-30-04

Share change since 05-04 Total Stocks:58	Sector	Country	% Assets
GlaxoSmithKline	Health	U.K.	3.91
⊕ Diageo	Goods	U.K.	3.53
Bk Of Ireland (The Gover	Financial	Ireland	3.31
Euronext	Financial	France	3.31
Novartis	Health	Switzerland	2.95
Takeda Chemical Industri	Health	Japan	2.83
Bayer Motoren Werk	Goods	Germany	2.80
⊕ Nestle	Goods	Switzerland	2.80
⊕ Publicis Groupe	Business	France	2.58
Cadbury Schweppes	Goods	U.K.	2.57
⊕ Akzo Nobel	Ind Mtrls	Netherlands	2.53
Reed Elsevier	Media	U.K.	2.48
⊕ Lonza Grp	Health	Switzerland	2.41
Australia & New Zealand	Financial	Australia	2.39
Signet Grp	Goods	U.K.	2.36
SK Telecom	Telecom	Korea	2.33
⊕ Deutsche Boerse	Financial	Germany	2.30
Associated British Ports	Business	U.K.	2.28
⊖ Grupo Televisa ADR	Media	Mexico	2.24
⊖ Givaudan	Ind Mtrls	Switzerland	2.16

Current Investment Style

Style box: Value / Blnd / Growth; Large / Mid / Small

Market Cap	%
Giant	35.7
Large	26.6
Mid	32.5
Small	5.2
Micro	0.0
Avg $mil: 10,515	

Value Measures		Rel Category
Price/Earnings	14.02	1.04
Price/Book	2.22	1.35
Price/Sales	1.07	1.30
Price/Cash Flow	6.73	1.52
Dividend Yield %	2.79	1.00

Growth Measures	%	Rel Category
Long-Term Erngs	11.18	1.14
Book Value	1.62	3.52
Sales	-0.42	NMF
Cash Flow	-3.69	NMF
Historical Erngs	-0.79	NMF

Composition

Cash	3.5	Bonds	0.0
Stocks	96.5	Other	0.0
Foreign (% of Stock)			99.4

Sector Weightings	% of Stocks	Rel MSCI EAFE	3 Year High	Low
Info	13.24	0.80		
Software	0.00	0.00	0	0
Hardware	0.64	0.18	76	1
Media	9.91	4.35	14	0
Telecom	2.69	0.28	4	0
Service	43.09	0.96		
Health	11.61	1.60	16	0
Consumer	1.51	0.30	5	0
Business	8.38	1.54	14	0
Financial	21.59	0.80	24	10
Mfg	43.67	1.13		
Goods	25.95	1.90	27	0
Ind Mtrls	16.01	1.30	23	0
Energy	1.71	0.23	2	0
Utilities	0.00	0.00	0	0

Regional Exposure	% Stock		
UK/W. Europe	77	N. America	1
Japan	7	Latn America	4
Asia X Japan	10	Other	1

Country Exposure	% Stock		
U.K.	26	Japan	7
Switzerland	16	Germany	7
France	13		

Oakmark Intl Small Cap I

Ticker	Load	NAV	Yield	Total Assets	Mstar Category
OAKEX	Closed	$20.03	1.3%	$862 mil	Foreign Small/Mid Value

Governance and Management

Fiduciary Grade: A

Portfolio Manager(s)

The fund boasts a deep and talented management team, consisting of two managers and six analysts. David Herro and Michael Welsh have served as comanagers since the fund opened in November 1995. Chad Clark, a longtime analyst on the fund, will replace Welsh as comanager on Jan. 28, 2005, but the latter will remain on board as an analyst here (and as comanager on two other Oakmark funds).

Strategy

The fund's managers invest in stocks that trade at discounts of at least 40% of their estimates of their intrinsic values. They sell stocks that get within 10% of their estimates. The fund frequently carries a large emerging-markets stake, and it has an unusual portfolio makeup. The fund has a 2% redemption fee on shares held for less than three months. A pricing committee meets when conditions warrant, putting fair-value pricing into effect.

Performance 12-31-04

	1st Qtr	2nd Qtr	3rd Qtr	4th Qtr	Total
2000	-4.96	0.93	-4.00	-1.02	-8.86
2001	3.22	3.58	-11.35	19.19	12.98
2002	10.19	2.51	-22.25	8.04	-5.12
2003	-12.24	29.18	14.12	17.81	52.41
2004	6.54	2.92	3.69	13.41	28.95

Trailing	Total Return%	+/- MSCI EAFE	+/- MSCI Wd xUS	%Rank Cat	Growth of $10,000
3 Mo	13.41	-1.91	-1.74	71	11,341
6 Mo	17.60	2.60	2.23	16	11,760
1 Yr	28.95	8.70	8.57	39	12,895
3 Yr Avg	23.09	11.20	10.87	37	18,650
5 Yr Avg	13.94	15.07	14.70	16	19,204
10 Yr Avg	—	—	—	—	—
15 Yr Avg	—	—	—	—	—

Tax Analysis	Tax-Adj Rtn%	%Rank Cat	Tax-Cost Rat	%Rank Cat
3 Yr (estimated)	22.32	37	0.63	45
5 Yr (estimated)	12.78	16	1.02	52
10 Yr (estimated)	—	—	—	—

Potential Capital Gain Exposure: 32% of assets

Historical Profile

Return Above Avg
Risk High
Rating ★★★★ Above Avg

Investment Style: Equity Stock %

1996	1997	1998	1999	2000	2001	2002	2003	12-04
99%	94%	89%	96%	93%	96%	94%	95%	

▼ Manager Change
∇ Partial Manager Change

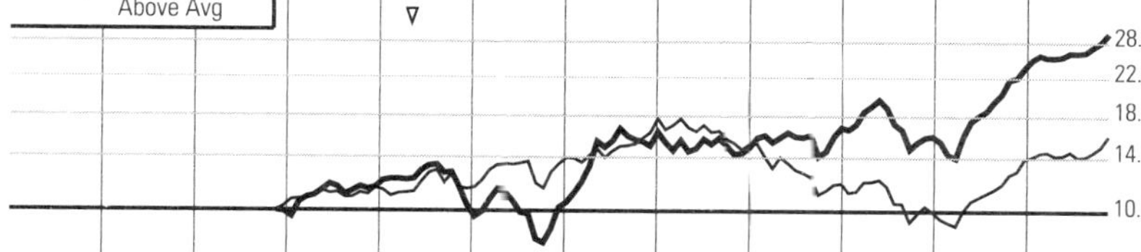

Growth of $10,000
— Investment Values of Fund
— Investment Values of MSCI EAFE

Performance Quartile (within Category)

History

1993	1994	1995	1996	1997	1998	1999	2000	2001	2002	2003	12-04	History
—	—	9.63	11.59	8.09	3.62	12.50	10.55	11.53	10.62	16.06	20.03	NAV
—	—	-3.70*	25.01	-19.91	3.20	53.77	-8.86	12.93	-5.12	52.41	28.95	Total Return %
—	—	—	18.96	-21.69	-13.73	26.74	5.33	34.40	10.82	13.82	8.70	+/-MSCI EAFE
—	—	—	18.14	-22.18	-3.49	25.79	4.50	34.37	10.68	12.99	8.57	+/-MSCI Wd xUS
—	—	0.00	0.81	0.48	.53	1.32	2.72	1.52	0.79	1.10	1.69	Income Return %
—	—	—	24.20	-20.39	.67	52.45	-11.58	11.46	-5.91	51.31	27.26	Capital Return %
—	—	—	1	78	11	18	80	1	75	39	39	Total Rtn % Rank Cat
—	—	0.00	0.08	0.06	.20	0.11	0.34	0.16	0.09	0.12	0.27	Income $
—	—	0.00	0.36	1.34	.00	0.59	0.49	0.14	0.27	0.00	0.38	Capital Gains $
—	—	—	2.50	1.93	.96	1.79	1.76	1.74	1.64	1.57	1.49	Expense Ratio %
—	—	—	0.65	1.23	2.17	2.31	1.98	1.83	1.28	0.99	0.72	Income Ratio %
—	—	—	27	63	69	126	40	49	42	30	29	Turnover Rate %
—	—	7	47	50	56	129	84	190	368	598	862	Net Assets $mil

Rating and Risk

Time Period	Load-Adj Return %	Morningstar Rtn vs Cat	Morningstar Risk vs Cat	Morningstar Risk-Adj Rating
1 Yr	28.95			
3 Yr	23.09	Avg	High	★★★
5 Yr	13.94	+Avg	High	★★★★
10 Yr	—	—	—	—
Incept	13.17			

Other Measures	Standard Index S&P 500	Best Fit Index MSCI EAFE
Alpha	10.2	10.2
Beta	1.03	1.03
R-Squared	82	82
Standard Deviation	21.70	
Mean	23.09	
Sharpe Ratio	1.01	

Morningstar's Take by William Samuel Rocco 12-14-04

Next month's partial manager change shouldn't cause any worries.

Harris Associates just announced that Michael Welsh will give up his comanager position on Oakmark International Small Cap on Jan. 28, 2005 and that Chad Clark will take his place.

Welsh has played a key role in this closed fund's success, but we're sanguine about the upcoming switch for several reasons. Welsh is staying with the firm, so he'll continue to serve as an analyst on this fund as well as a comanager of Oakmark International and Oakmark Global. Clark, who has been at the firm since 1995, has been a major contributor to the fund as an analyst. And the rest of the deep and talented team remains in place, including David Herro, who has comanaged this fund since its late-1995 inception and also serves as the firm's chief investment officer of international equities.

Not surprisingly, the fund's distinctive strategy isn't going to change one bit. Although some foreign small/mid-value funds are all-cap offerings, and others have moved up the market-cap ladder as their asset bases have grown, this one, which closed to new investors 2 and a half years ago will remain strict about its market-cap range. The fund, which has significantly fewer overall holdings and more assets in its top 10 names than its average peer, will continue to sport a relatively concentrated portfolio. And it will continue to have big stakes in selected sectors and nations.

The fund has been more volatile than most of its peers over time--due to the variety of risks that come with its daring style--but it has also delivered superior long-term returns, as Herro and the rest of the team have repeatedly demonstrated real stock-picking talent.

All told, we think the fund will remain a great supplement to many foreign large-blend and large-growth offerings after next month's partial manager change.

Portfolio Analysis 07-31-04

Share change since 06-04 Total Stocks: 62

Share change	Holding	Sector	Country	% Assets
	Grupo Aeroportuario ADR	Business	Mexico	3.88
⊖	Neopost	Ind Mtrls	France	3.80
⊕	Julius Baer Holding Ltd	Financial	Switzerland	3.66
⊕	Gurit-Heberlein	Ind Mtrls	Switzerland	3.53
	Ansell Ltd	Ind Mtrls	Australia	3.43
	Kobenhavns Lufthavne AS	Business	Denmark	3.16
⊖	Baycorp Advantage Ltd	Financial	Australia	3.10
	Schindler Holding Ltd	Ind Mtrls	Switzerland	2.97
	Interpump Grp	Ind Mtrls	Italy	2.72
⊕	Morse	Business	U.K.	2.65
	Bulgari	Goods	Italy	2.43
⊕	Dogan Sirketler Grubu Ho	Media	Turkey	2.41
	Pargesa Holding	Financial	Switzerland	2.39
	Carpetright	Consumer	U.K.	2.12
	Pfeiffer Vacuum Technolo	Ind Mtrls	Germany	2.09
	Campari	Goods	Italy	2.07
⊕	Geest	Goods	U.K.	2.04
⊖	Santen Pharmaceutical	Health	Japan	1.93
	Jyske Bank	Financial	Denmark	1.93
	Baron de Ley Grp	Goods	Spain	1.91

Current Investment Style

Market Cap	%
Giant	0.0
Large	2.5
Mid	51.5
Small	42.5
Micro	3.5
Avg $mil: 860	

Value Measures		Rel Category
Price/Earnings	14.75	1.09
Price/Book	2.00	1.23
Price/Sales	0.86	1.28
Price/Cash Flow	7.08	1.37
Dividend Yield %	2.39	0.89

Growth Measures	%	Rel Category
Long-Term Erngs	9.31	0.79
Book Value	-2.38	NMF
Sales	-0.15	NMF
Cash Flow	-1.32	NMF
Historical Erngs	-9.22	NMF

Composition

Cash	5.4	Bonds	0.0
Stocks	94.6	Other	0.0
Foreign (% of Stock)			100.0

Sector Weightings	% of Stocks	Rel MSCI EAFE	3 Year High	3 Year Low
Info	8.13	0.49		
Software	1.98	1.83	4	0
Hardware	0.00	0.00	3	0
Media	6.15	2.70	7	0
Telecom	0.00	0.00	0	0
Service	43.42	0.97		
Health	4.77	0.66	6	0
Consumer	2.56	0.51	14	2
Business	23.42	4.31	28	18
Financial	12.67	0.47	24	8
Mfg	48.45	1.25		
Goods	16.21	1.19	18	5
Ind Mtrls	32.24	2.62	39	26
Energy	0.00	0.00	0	0
Utilities	0.00	0.00	0	0

Regional Exposure % Stock

UK/W. Europe	68	N. America	0
Japan	8	Latn America	4
Asia X Japan	18	Other	2

Country Exposure % Stock

Switzerland	16	Italy	9
France	14	Japan	8
U.K.	10		

Address:	Harris Associates LP, Chicago IL 60602-3790, 800-625-6275
Web Address:	www.oakmark.com
Inception:	11-01-95*
Advisor:	Harris Associates LP
Subadvisor:	None
NTF Plans:	Fidelity Retail-NTF, Schwab OneSource

Minimum Purchase:	Closed	Add: —	IRA: —
Min Auto Inv Plan:	Closed	Add: —	
Sales Fees:	No-load, 2.00%R		
Management Fee:	1.25% mx./1.10% mn.		
Actual Fees:	Mgt:1.23%	Dist:	
Expense Projections:	3Yr:$496	5Yr:$855	10Yr:$ 867
Income Distrib:	Annually		

Oakmark Select I

Ticker	Load	NAV	Yield	Total Assets	Mstar Category
OAKLX	Closed	$33.35	0.7%	$5,837 mil	Large Value

Governance and Management

Fiduciary Grade: B

Portfolio Manager(s)

Lead manager Bill Nygren has two decades of investment experience, including a stint as research director for Harris Associates, advisor to the Oakmark Funds. He also serves as lead manager of Oakmark Fund, which remains open to new investors. Comanager Henry Berghoef is also experienced but plays a subordinate role. Berghoef is the director of research for Harris Associates.

Strategy

Management looks for companies trading at significant discounts to what a rational businessperson would pay for them. Although there is no question that Bill Nygren is a value manager, he has historically been willing to invest in nontraditional value areas, including biotechnology. The portfolio is very concentrated, typically holding only 15 to 20 stocks. Top positions usually approach 10% of net assets but at times have reached 15% or more of assets.

Historical Profile

Return High
Risk Average
Rating ★★★★★ Highest

Investment Style
Equity
Stock %

1996	1997	1998	1999	2000	2001	2002	2003	12-04
92%	88%	100%	90%	92%	93%	91%	93%	

▼ Manager Change
▽ Partial Manager Change

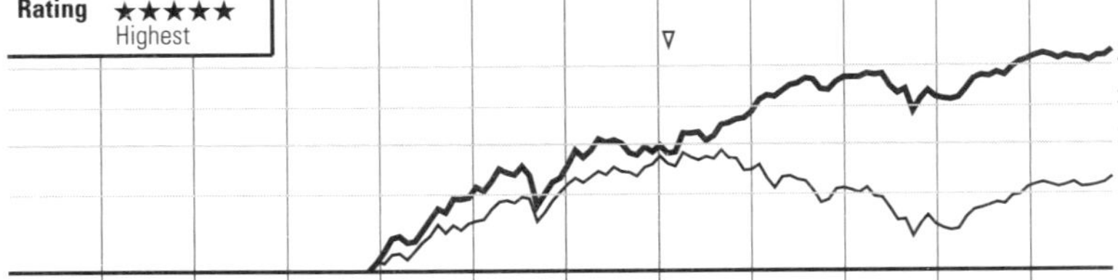

Growth of $10,000
— Investment Values of Fund
— Investment Values of S&P 500

Performance Quartile (within Category)

1993	1994	1995	1996	1997	1998	1999	2000	2001	2002	2003	12-04	History
—	—	—	11.42	17.52	19.54	18.42	21.65	27.24	23.82	30.62	33.35	NAV
—	—	—	14.20*	55.02	16.21	14.49	25.81	26.06	-12.47	29.00	9.73	Total Return %
—	—	—	—	21.67	-12.36	-6.55	34.91	37.94	9.62	0.33	-1.14	+/-S&P 500
—	—	—	—	19.84	0.58	7.14	18.80	31.65	3.05	-1.03	-6.76	+/-Russ 1000 VI
—	—	—	0.00	0.00	0.28	1.01	0.47	0.23	0.08	0.43	0.79	Income Return %
—	—	—	—	55.02	15.93	13.48	25.34	25.83	-12.55	28.57	8.94	Capital Return %
—	—	—	—	1	25	14	6	1	9	40	83	Total Rtn % Rank Cat
—	—	—	0.00	0.00	0.05	0.20	0.09	0.05	0.02	0.10	0.24	Income $
—	—	—	0.00	0.17	0.71	3.72	1.36	0.00	0.00	0.00	0.00	Capital Gains $
—	—	—	—	1.12	1.22	1.16	1.17	1.08	1.07	1.02	1.00	Expense Ratio %
—	—	—	—	-0.11	0.17	0.98	0.76	0.26	0.09	0.23	0.50	Income Ratio %
—	—	—	—	—	56	67	69	21	32	20	14	Turnover Rate %
—	—	—	50	982	1,298	1,581	2,102	4,684	4,080	5,631	5,734	Net Assets $mil

Performance 12-31-04

	1st Qtr	2nd Qtr	3rd Qtr	4th Qtr	Total
2000	8.96	-5.23	12.78	8.04	25.81
2001	10.76	9.26	-3.82	8.30	26.06
2002	2.53	-8.09	-15.58	10.02	-12.47
2003	-0.50	16.20	0.04	11.53	29.00
2004	2.45	-1.53	1.00	7.69	9.73

Trailing	Total Return%	+/- S&P 500	+/- Russ 1000 VI	%Rank Cat	Growth of $10,000
3 Mo	7.69	-1.54	-2.69	83	10,769
6 Mo	8.77	1.58	-3.31	55	10,877
1 Yr	9.73	-1.14	-6.76	83	10,973
3 Yr Avg	7.40	3.82	-1.17	25	12,388
5 Yr Avg	14.46	16.76	9.19	1	19,646
10 Yr Avg	—	—	—	—	—
15 Yr Avg	—	—	—	—	—

Tax Analysis	Tax-Adj Rtn%	%Rank Cat	Tax-Cost Rat	%Rank Cat
3 Yr (estimated)	7.25	17	0.14	10
5 Yr (estimated)	13.97	1	0.43	23
10 Yr (estimated)	—	—	—	—

Potential Capital Gain Exposure: 36% of assets

Rating and Risk

Time Period	Load-Adj Return %	Morningstar Rtn vs Cat	Morningstar Risk vs Cat	Morningstar Risk-Adj Rating
1 Yr	9.73			
3 Yr	7.40	+Avg	Avg	★★★★
5 Yr	14.46	High	Avg	★★★★★
10 Yr	—	—	—	—
Incept	20.64			

Other Measures	Standard Index S&P 500	Best Fit Index Russ 1000
Alpha	4.1	3.5
Beta	0.87	0.89
R-Squared	81	82
Standard Deviation	15.68	
Mean	7.40	
Sharpe Ratio	0.39	

Portfolio Analysis 09-30-04

Share change since 06-04 Total Stocks:20	Sector	PE	YTD Ret%	% Assets
⊖ Washington Mutual	Financial	13.9	10.05	16.23
⊖ H & R Block	Consumer	14.5	-9.99	7.58
Yum Brands	Consumer	19.7	37.84	6.78
First Data	Business	18.8	3.72	6.16
Time Warner	Media	27.5	8.12	4.46
Limited Brands	Consumer	16.0	37.88	4.43
Xerox	Ind Mtrls	20.2	23.26	4.27
Dun & Bradstreet	Business	19.8	17.63	4.19
Moody's	Business	32.5	44.06	4.15
⊖ Mattel	Goods	16.1	3.54	3.87
⊖ Burlington Resources	Energy	10.9	58.50	3.83
⊖ Toys R Us	Goods	28.3	61.95	3.82
Chiron	Health	33.2	-41.51	3.72
IMS Health	Business	19.3	-6.32	3.60
⊕ Gap	Consumer	17.6	-8.63	3.41
Knight Ridder	Media	16.8	-11.83	3.09
Bristol-Myers Squibb	Health	17.7	-7.27	3.00
⊖ Office Depot	Consumer	16.4	3.89	2.84
⊖ Janus Capital Group	Financial	3.8	2.71	2.08
⊖ Sprint	Telecom	—	55.24	1.11

Current Investment Style

Value Blnd Growth / Large Mid Small

Market Cap	%
Giant	8.1
Large	54.4
Mid	37.5
Small	0.0
Micro	0.0
Avg $mil: 13,725	

Value Measures		Rel Category
Price/Earnings	16.09	1.07
Price/Book	2.04	0.90
Price/Sales	1.35	1.13
Price/Cash Flow	8.45	1.32
Dividend Yield %	1.51	0.74

Growth Measures	%	Rel Category
Long-Term Erngs	11.52	1.11
Book Value	11.18	1.98
Sales	3.28	0.78
Cash Flow	10.89	2.09
Historical Erngs	18.78	1.59

Profitability	%	Rel Category
Return on Equity	24.45	1.54
Return on Assets	11.95	1.53
Net Margin	14.56	1.43

Sector Weightings	% of Stocks	Rel S&P 500	3 Year High	3 Year Low
Info	9.35	0.44		
Software	0.00	0.00	0	0
Hardware	0.00	0.00	0	0
Media	8.15	2.12	9	4
Telecom	1.20	0.38	9	1
Service	73.61	1.59		
Health	7.25	0.58	7	4
Consumer	27.04	2.98	30	24
Business	19.54	4.82	24	16
Financial	19.78	0.95	24	17
Mfg	17.05	0.53		
Goods	8.30	0.89	8	4
Ind Mtrls	4.61	0.36	5	3
Energy	4.14	0.58	5	4
Utilities	0.00	0.00	0	0

Composition

Cash	7.4
Stocks	92.6
Bonds	0.0
Other	0.0
Foreign (% of Stock)	0.0

Morningstar's Take by Kunal Kapoor 11-09-04

Oakmark Select is reopening to new investors.

After a steady trickle of outflows during the past six months, manager Bill Nygren says that it's time to reopen this fund. Nygren, who has long placed a premium on strong aftertax returns and has minimized capital gains distributions to shareholders, says that further net redemptions would have forced him to realize some gains, and the reopening is thus aimed at stabilizing flows. While we'll be watching carefully to see what kind of reaction this elicits among investors, we're encouraged that the opening is limited at this stage, and only investors who go directly through Oakmark can access the fund.

Meanwhile, it would be a mistake to put too much weight on the fund's short-term underperformance, as some investors are clearly doing. While occasional missteps are likely to be par for the course, what differentiates this fund is Nygren's focus on investing only in firms where he identifies a significant discount to his estimate of their intrinsic value. This discipline can act as a risk-control mechanism by limiting a stock's downside when Nygren's thesis doesn't play out as planned. For instance, while much has been made of the travails of top holding Washington Mutual in 2004, it's worth pointing out that its stock is actually up 2.6% for the year to date. Moreover, Nygren has increasingly moved this portfolio into large-cap territory, a factor that has hurt the fund versus purer mid-cap rivals. In fact, a move to Morningstar's large-cap value category at the end of this month is likely in the cards for this fund.

All told, we remain fans of this mutual fund. The nature of a concentrated portfolio means that short-term volatility is inevitable, but for those who stay the course, the rewards should show. We're adding the fund back to our Analyst Picks list now that it has reopened.

Address:	Harris Associates LP Chicago IL 60602-3790 800-625-6275
Web Address:	www.oakmark.com
Inception:	11-01-96*
Advisor:	Harris Associates LP
Subadvisor:	None
NTF Plans:	Fidelity Retail-NTF, Schwab OneSource

Minimum Purchase:	Closed	Add: —	IRA: —
Min Auto Inv Plan:	Closed	Add: —	
Sales Fees:	No-load, 2.00%R		
Management Fee:	1.00% mx./0.75% mn.		
Actual Fees:	Mgt:0.87%	Dist:	
Expense Projections:	3Yr:$325	5Yr:$563	10Yr:$1248
Income Distrib:	Annually		

Oppenheimer Cap Inc A

Ticker	Load	NAV	Yield	Total Assets	Mstar Category
OPPEX	5.75%	$12.46	3.9%	$3,101 mil	Moderate Allocation

Governance and Management

Fiduciary Grade: B

Portfolio Manager(s)

Mike Levine has managed the fund since June 1999, taking over lead manager duties after longtime manager John Doney's retirement at the beginning of 2001. Levine focuses mainly on the fund's stock and convertible picks, plus asset allocation; a team led by Angelo Manioudakis handles the bond portion. Three analysts plus an intern help Levine with research.

Strategy

The fund invests in a mix of value-oriented stocks, mostly high-quality bonds, convertible securities, and REITs. The fund's equity stake has tended to be about 65% of assets, but manager Mike Levine has trimmed that to about 40% of late. Even so, the fund still tends to be more equity-sensitive than its peers due to a 30% stake in convertibles. Levine has broadened the fund's sector mix a bit since taking the helm, but it continues to be overweight in financial stocks relative to its peers.

Historical Profile

Return Above Avg
Risk Above Avg
Rating ★★★★ Above Avg

Investment Style
Equity Stock %

58%	58%	53%	59%	68%	64%	40%	36%	38%

▼ Manager Change
▽ Partial Manager Change

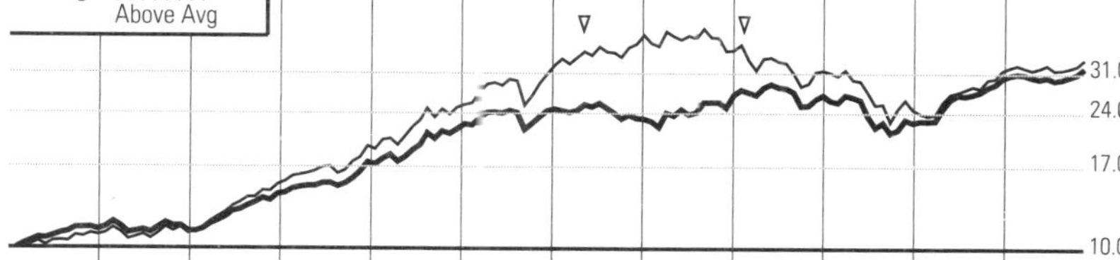

Growth of $10,000
— Investment Values of Fund
— Investment Values of S&P 500

Performance Quartile (within Category)

1993	1994	1995	1996	1997	1998	1999	2000	2001	2002	2003	12-04	History
10.02	9.14	10.92	12.18	14.45	4.25	11.81	12.74	11.89	9.52	12.14	12.46	NAV
14.57	-2.79	27.92	20.06	29.68	0.32	-6.25	16.82	-0.19	-16.16	33.47	10.28	Total Return %
4.51	-4.10	-9.61	-2.88	-3.67	- 8.25	-27.29	25.92	11.69	5.93	4.80	-0.59	+/-S&P 500
2.84	-0.84	3.15	8.72	10.48	2.07	-19.10	12.33	-0.35	-5.62	9.41	-0.89	+/-DJ 60%
5.24	4.88	5.35	4.47	4.12	3.44	3.46	4.13	3.82	4.10	5.45	4.17	Income Return %
9.33	-7.67	22.57	15.59	25.56	6.88	-9.71	12.69	-4.01	-20.26	28.02	6.11	Capital Return %
25	60	33	8	3	70	96	4	13	85	2	26	Total Rtn % Rank Cat
0.48	0.48	0.48	0.48	0.49	0.49	0.49	0.48	0.43	0.48	0.51	0.50	Income $
0.17	0.13	0.24	0.40	0.79	1.17	1.07	0.51	0.33	0.00	0.00	0.39	Capital Gains $
0.79	0.90	0.96	0.89	0.88	0.87	0.89	0.93	0.91	0.98	0.93	0.89	Expense Ratio %
5.12	4.72	5.15	4.51	3.97	3.47	3.51	3.78	3.2[illegible]	4.48	5.41	3.85	Income Ratio %
59	30	46	43	24	18	40	37	74	148	141	52	Turnover Rate %
1,861	1,714	2,074	2,353	2,988	3,260	2,619	2,427	2,377	1,802	2,276	2,609	Net Assets $mil

Performance 12-31-04

	1st Qtr	2nd Qtr	3rd Qtr	4th Qtr	Total
2000	3.93	-0.94	8.24	4.83	16.82
2001	-0.07	5.09	-11.36	7.23	-0.19
2002	0.07	-12.71	-10.28	6.99	-16.16
2003	1.12	18.21	2.03	9.44	33.47
2004	2.08	-1.63	0.46	9.31	10.28

Trailing	Total Return%	+/- S&P 500	+/- DJ 60%	%Rank Cat	Growth of $10,000
3 Mo	9.31	0.08	1.83	8	10,931
6 Mo	9.82	2.63	2.29	6	10,982
1 Yr	10.28	-0.59	-0.89	26	11,028
3 Yr Avg	7.26	3.68	0.00	12	12,340
5 Yr Avg	7.55	9.85	2.31	6	14,390
10 Yr Avg	11.48	-0.59	0.99	13	29,646
15 Yr Avg	9.83	-1.10	-0.12	37	40,815

Tax Analysis	Tax-Adj Rtn%	%Rank Cat	Tax-Cost Rat	%Rank Cat
3 Yr (estimated)	3.35	52	1.72	96
5 Yr (estimated)	4.24	11	1.92	92
10 Yr (estimated)	8.28	22	2.29	84

Potential Capital Gain Exposure: 17% of assets

Rating and Risk

Time Period	Load-Adj Return %	Morningstar Rtn vs Cat	Morningstar Risk vs Cat	Morningstar Risk-Adj Rating
1 Yr	3.94			
3 Yr	5.16	Avg	High	★★★
5 Yr	6.28	+Avg	+Avg	★★★★
10 Yr	10.82	+Avg	+Avg	★★★★
Incept	13.19			

Other Measures	Standard Index S&P 500	Best Fit Index DJ 60%
Alpha	4.2	-4.7
Beta	0.73	1.27
R-Squared	74	81

Standard Deviation	13.58
Mean	7.26
Sharpe Ratio	0.44

Portfolio Analysis 09-30-04

Total Stocks:56 Share change since 07-31-04	Sectors	P/E Ratio	YTD Return %	% Net Assets
⊕ Kinder Morgan Management	Energy	30.7	0.39	4.10
Kinder Morgan	Energy	21.1	-1.97	3.42
⊕ Altria Group	Goods	13.3	0.82	3.17
CSK Auto	Consumer	39.6	-7.65	2.69
⊕ Citigroup	Financial	15.3	0.08	2.47
Everest Re Group	Financial	9.5	-2.39	2.31
Washington Mutual	Financial	13.9	-2.55	1.36
⊖ Raytheon	Ind Mtrls	38.1	-5.87	1.36
⊕ Bank of America	Financial	12.3	-3.85	1.23

Total Fixed-Income:322	Date of Maturity	Amount $000	Value $000	% Net Assets
Liberty Media 3.25%	03-15-31	118,500	107,983	3.36
FNCL 7%	10-01-34	82,593	87,574	2.72
El Paso Cv	02-28-21	117,500	60,513	1.88
Tyco Intl Grp S A Cv 2.75	01-15-18	38,750	54,492	1.70
Tyco Intl Grp S A 144A Cv	01-15-18	36,000	50,625	1.57
FNCL 6.5%	10-01-34	37,445	39,282	1.22
FNCI 5.5%	10-01-19	37,943	39,212	1.22
Charter Comms Hldgs	04-01-11	50,000	38,750	1.21
Liberty Media 4%	11-15-29	46,500	33,073	1.03

Equity Style
Style: Value
Size: Large-Cap

Fixed-Income Style
Duration: —
Quality: —

Value Measures		Rel Category
Price/Earnings	13.16	0.79
Price/Book	1.91	0.78
Price/Sales	1.20	0.91
Price/Cash Flow	3.74	0.52
Dividend Yield %	2.13	1.36

Growth Measures	%	Rel Category
Long-Term Erngs	11.33	0.97
Book Value	5.28	0.92
Sales	1.58	0.31
Cash Flow	35.33	4.41
Historical Erngs	12.98	1.20

Avg Eff Duration [1]	—
Avg Eff Maturity	—
Avg Credit Quality	—
Avg Wtd Coupon	4.62%

[1] figure provided by fund

Market Cap %			
Giant	35.1	Small	12.9
Large	18.4	Micro	0.1
Mid	33.5	Avg $mil:	13,977

Sector Weightings	% of Stocks	Rel S&P 500	3 Year High	3 Year Low
Info	5.41	0.25		
Software	0.52	0.12	2	0
Hardware	0.81	0.08	2	0
Media	1.36	0.35	1	0
Telecom	2.72	0.86	6	0
Service	48.62	1.05		
Health	4.61	0.37	7	2
Consumer	9.30	1.02	12	0
Business	1.82	0.45	2	0
Financial	32.89	1.58	61	33
Mfg	45.99	1.43		
Goods	8.37	0.90	11	0
Ind Mtrls	9.56	0.75	10	4
Energy	26.34	3.68	30	13
Utilities	1.72	0.58	7	0

Composition

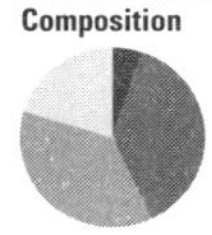

Cash	5.2
Stocks	37.8
Bonds	36.6
Other	20.3
Foreign (% of Stock)	2.4

Morningstar's Take by David Kathman 12-20-04

Oppenheimer Capital Income shouldn't be mistaken for a core balanced fund, but it offers some appeal for adventurous investors.

The main thing setting this offering apart from its peers is its asset allocation. While the fund's fixed-income weighting is similar to that in the typical moderate-allocation fund, its 43% stock weighting (as of mid-December) is well below the 59% category average. The main reason for this discrepancy is the fund's large 29% weighting in convertible securities, which have characteristics of both stocks and bonds.

That big convertible stake makes this fund tough to classify easily. Its stock portfolio is fairly conservative, with valuations well below the category average, and cheap stocks such as Altria and Citigroup among the top holdings. Manager Mike Levine also keeps sector weightings on the cautious side, with very few tech stocks but overweights in financials and energy relative to the category average. Yet because convertibles are more volatile than straight bonds, this fund has given investors a bumpier ride than its average peer. Its standard deviation (a common measure of volatility) is among the highest 10% in the moderate-allocation category over the five-plus years that Levine has been in charge.

However, for investors who can stand the volatility, Levine has put up some impressive returns during his tenure. The fund ranked among the moderate-allocation category's top 5% in both 2000 and 2003, and it's among the top 10% in the category over the trailing five years. The one blemish on this record is a bottom-quartile finish in 2002, when a number of stock and convertible holdings tanked.

This fund's volatility and big performance swings make it a dubious choice for cautious investors looking for a hybrid fund to anchor their portfolio. However, it should have more appeal for those with a long time horizon who are willing to take on more risk in exchange for total return.

Address:	6803 South Tucson Way Centennial CO 80112-3924 800-525-7048
Web Address:	
Inception:	12-01-70
Advisor:	OppenheimerFunds, Inc.
Subadvisor:	None
NTF Plans:	DATALynx NTF, Federated Tr NTF

Minimum Purchase:	$1000	Add: $50	IRA: $500
Min Auto Inv Plan:	$500	Add: $50	
Sales Fees:	5.75%L, 0.23%S		
Management Fee:	0.75% mx./0.50% mn.		
Actual Fees:	Mgt:0.53%	Dist:0.23%	
Expense Projections:	3Yr:$843	5Yr:$1040	10Yr:$ 608
Income Distrib:	Quarterly		

Oppenheimer Develop MktA ✔ Analyst Pick

Ticker	Load	NAV	Yield	Total Assets	Mstar Category
ODMAX	5.75%	$26.88	1.4%	$2,875 mil	Diversified Emerging Mkts

Governance and Management

Fiduciary Grade: B

Portfolio Manager(s)

Mark Madden, who ran Pioneer Emerging Markets from mid-1994 through mid-2004, joined longtime manager Rajeev Bhaman as a comanager in August 2004. Bhaman, who is a comanager of Oppenheimer Global, transitioned off this fund on Dec. 1, 2004, and Madden took sole control of the portfolio on that date. Oppenheimer hired a new senior Asia analyst with lots of experience in China as well as two junior international analysts in the summer of 2004, so Madden has 15 international experts to call on for support (including the firm's other overseas managers).

Strategy

Manager Mark Madden favors good businesses that are reasonably priced and growing nicely. He likes them to have superior products and operate in businesses with barriers to entry. He considers smaller firms as readily as larger ones. The fund has a 2% redemption fee on shares held fewer than 30 days and uses fair-value pricing in certain circumstances.

Historical Profile

Return High
Risk Above Avg
Rating ★★★★★ Highest

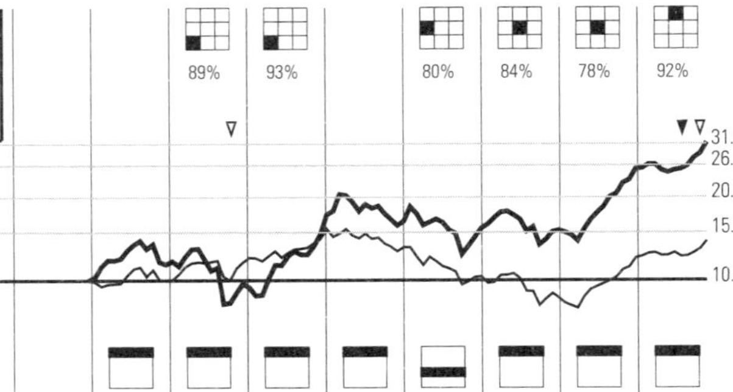

Investment Style
Equity
Stock %

▼ Manager Change
▽ Partial Manager Change

Growth of $10,000
— Investment Values of Fund
— Investment Values of MSCI EAFE

Performance Quartile (within Category)

1993	1994	1995	1996	1997	1998	1999	2000	2001	2002	2003	12-04	History
—	—	—	10.15	11.01	8.70	15.72	14.30	13.28	12.87	20.61	26.88	NAV
—	—	—	1.50*	14.09	-19.36	82.30	-5.26	-5.73	-1.60	65.24	33.00	Total Return %
—	—	—	—	12.31	-39.29	55.27	8.93	15.69	14.34	26.65	12.75	+/-MSCI EAFE
—	—	—	—	27.54	8.31	18.21	26.64	-1.05	6.37	13.65	10.55	+/-MSCI EmrMkt
—	—	—	0.00	0.88	0.91	1.43	1.25	1.38	1.48	4.80	1.79	Income Return %
—	—	—	—	13.21	-20.27	80.87	-6.51	-7.11	-3.08	60.44	31.21	Capital Return %
—	—	—	—	2	15	25	1	72	20	15	5	Total Rtn % Rank Cat
—	—	—	0.00	0.09	0.10	0.12	0.20	0.20	0.20	0.62	0.37	Income $
—	—	—	0.00	0.46	0.07	0.00	0.39	0.00	0.00	0.00	0.13	Capital Gains $
—	—	—	—	1.94	2.18	2.37	1.96	1.69	1.77	1.76	1.52	Expense Ratio %
—	—	—	—	1.45	0.87	1.11	1.56	1.76	1.91	1.42	1.64	Income Ratio %
—	—	—	—	27	78	37	22	16	10	6	15	Turnover Rate %
—	—	—	7	33	27	62	131	196	342	859	2,410	Net Assets $mil

Performance 12-31-04

	1st Qtr	2nd Qtr	3rd Qtr	4th Qtr	Total
2000	17.05	-7.07	-7.54	-5.80	-5.26
2001	-3.29	2.39	-23.16	23.90	-5.73
2002	14.01	-5.61	-18.82	12.65	-1.60
2003	-8.39	25.87	17.05	22.43	65.24
2004	3.78	-4.67	10.50	21.66	33.00

Trailing	Total Return%	+/- MSCI EAFE	+/- MSCI EmrMkt	%Rank Cat	Growth of $10,000
3 Mo	21.66	6.34	4.85	1	12,166
6 Mo	34.43	19.43	8.98	2	13,443
1 Yr	33.00	12.75	10.55	5	13,300
3 Yr Avg	29.32	17.43	9.78	11	21,627
5 Yr Avg	14.07	15.20	11.98	1	19,313
10 Yr Avg	—	—	—	—	—
15 Yr Avg	—	—	—	—	—

Tax Analysis	Tax-Adj Rtn%	%Rank Cat	Tax-Cost Rat	%Rank Cat
3 Yr (estimated)	25.84	15	0.75	82
5 Yr (estimated)	11.85	4	0.78	81
10 Yr (estimated)	—	—	—	—

Potential Capital Gain Exposure: 31% of assets

Rating and Risk

Time Period	Load-Adj Return %	Morningstar Rtn vs Cat	Morningstar Risk vs Cat	Morningstar Risk-Adj Rating
1 Yr	25.35			
3 Yr	26.79	+Avg	+Avg	★★★★
5 Yr	12.73	High	+Avg	★★★★★
10 Yr	—	—	—	—
Incept	14.95			

Other Measures	Standard Index S&P 500	Best Fit Index MSCI EmrMkt
Alpha	16.1	9.1
Beta	1.01	0.97
R-Squared	74	87

Standard Deviation	23.63
Mean	29.32
Sharpe Ratio	1.20

Morningstar's Take by William Samuel Rocco 12-02-04

Oppenheimer Developing Markets' smooth manager transition is now complete.

Mark Madden, former manager of Pioneer Emerging Markets, joined this fund as Rajeev Bhaman's comanager in August 2004. Oppenheimer made it clear at that time that Bhaman would stay on board for a few months as Madden became fully familiar with the portfolio, strategy, and processes here. That process is complete, and Madden took charge of the fund on Dec. 1.

The smooth nature of this transition isn't the only reason we're sanguine about this change. Bhaman, who was named a comanager on Oppenheimer Global this summer, will continue to research and invest in emerging markets for that world-stock offering and thus will remain a valuable resource for Madden. Moreover, Oppenheimer recently hired one senior and two junior international analysts, raising the total number of investment professionals on its global team to 15. Thus, Madden has considerable overall support.

Meanwhile, the iconoclastic value style Madden used at Pioneer Emerging Markets is similar to this fund's strategy. Madden, like Bhaman, goes wherever the best bargains are and lets his country and sector weights fall where they may. And Madden earned good overall results during his 10 years at his former charge, while this fund posted superior results over the few months he ran it with Bhaman in 2004. Thus, we believe Madden has the temperament as well as the talent to execute this fund's distinctive discipline well.

In short, we expect this fund to remain one of the more distinctive and attractive offerings in its group. Interested investors should note that Oppenheimer just lowered the minimum initial investment back down to $5,000 here and that the fund is expected to make a tiny distribution next week.

Address:	6803 South Tucson Way Centennial CO 80112-3924 800-525-7048
Web Address:	www.oppenheimerfunds.com
Inception:	11-18-96 *
Advisor:	OppenheimerFunds, Inc.
Subadvisor:	None
NTF Plans:	DATALynx NTF, Federated Tr NTF

Minimum Purchase:	$5000	Add: $50	IRA: $5000
Min Auto Inv Plan:	$5000	Add: $50	
Sales Fees:	5.75%L, 0.24%S, 2.00%R		
Management Fee:	1.00% mx./0.85% mn.		
Actual Fees:	Mgt:0.91%	Dist:0.24%	
Expense Projections:	3Yr:$1028	5Yr:$1356	10Yr:$2283
Income Distrib:	Annually		

Portfolio Analysis 07-31-04

Share change since 06-04 Total Stocks:108	Sector	Country	% Assets
Embraer-Empresa Brasilei	Ind Mtrls	Brazil	3.42
SK	Energy	Korea	2.88
Grupo Televisa ADR	Media	Mexico	2.68
Corporacion Geo	Consumer	Mexico	2.24
Gpo Fin Inbursa Sa	Financial	Mexico	2.05
Tele Norte Leste Partici	Telecom	Brazil	1.92
Cemig Cia Energ Mg	—	Brazil	1.92
Housing Development Fina	Financial	India	1.81
Companhia Vale Do Rio Do	Ind Mtrls	Brazil	1.73
SK Telecom Co ADR	Telecom	Korea	1.69
HCL Technologies Ltd	Software	India	1.65
SM Prime Hldgs	Financial	Philippines	1.64
Bco Bradesco Sa	—	Brazil	1.62
Companhia Brasileira de	Consumer	Brazil	1.59
⊕ HSBC Hldgs	Financial	U.K.	1.56
Unibanco Uniao de Bancos	Financial	Brazil	1.53
Old Mutual	Financial	U.K.	1.51
⊕ BenQ	Goods	Taiwan	1.51
SINOTRANS LTD	Business	China	1.49
ITC Ltd	Goods	India	1.46

Current Investment Style

Market Cap	%
Giant	14.1
Large	43.5
Mid	30.4
Small	9.1
Micro	3.0
Avg $mil: 2,527	

Value Measures		Rel Category
Price/Earnings	10.66	1.17
Price/Book	1.55	1.00
Price/Sales	0.78	0.94
Price/Cash Flow	3.12	0.71
Dividend Yield %	3.31	1.20

Growth Measures	%	Rel Category
Long-Term Erngs	21.37	1.10
Book Value	7.30	2.10
Sales	4.00	0.34
Cash Flow	7.29	0.98
Historical Erngs	2.64	0.38

Composition

Cash	2.7	Bonds	0.0
Stocks	92.0	Other	5.2
Foreign (% of Stock)			99.9

Sector Weightings	% of Stocks	Rel MSCI EAFE	3 Year High	3 Year Low
Info	18.77	1.13		
Software	2.82	2.61	4	1
Hardware	0.26	0.07	2	0
Media	6.57	2.88	19	5
Telecom	9.12	0.95	10	3
Service	42.44	0.95		
Health	3.02	0.42	11	3
Consumer	11.75	2.33	19	10
Business	6.78	1.25	17	7
Financial	20.89	0.77	27	19
Mfg	38.78	1.00		
Goods	16.08	1.18	17	8
Ind Mtrls	16.29	1.32	16	2
Energy	4.58	0.62	10	4
Utilities	1.83	0.34	2	0

Regional Exposure	% Stock		% Stock
UK/W. Europe	10	N. America	0
Japan	0	Latn America	28
Asia X Japan	50	Other	12

Country Exposure	% Stock		% Stock
India	18	Mexico	11
Brazil	16	South Africa	7
South Korea	12		

Oppenheimer Glob A

Analyst Pick

Ticker	Load	NAV	Yield	Total Assets	Mstar Category
OPPAX	5.75%	$60.77	0.6%	$12,989 mil	World Stock

Governance and Management

Fiduciary Grade: B

Portfolio Manager(s)

Bill Wilby, who has managed this fund since 1992, has assumed managerial duties at Oppenheimer and is slowly transitioning off this fund. He is currently comanaging the fund with his chosen successor, Rajeev Bhaman, who has run Oppenheimer Developing Markets since late 1996 and has compiled a stellar record. Oppenheimer also recently hired a new senior Asia analyst, and the managers interact frequently with other portfolio managers of the strong Global Equity team, including George Evans, Frank Jennings, Mark Madden, and Dominic Freud.

Strategy

Manager Bill Wilby employs a theme-based strategy focusing on companies most likely to benefit from mass affluence, new technologies, restructuring, and aging. He is long-term oriented and keeps the portfolio well-diversified. Rajeev Bhaman, who will eventually take over the portfolio, applies a similar investment discipline. Oppenheimer uses fair-value pricing selectively to deter market-timers, and the firm also has a 2% redemption fee in place on its foreign and global funds.

Historical Profile

Return: Above Avg
Risk: Above Avg
Rating: ★★★★ Above Avg

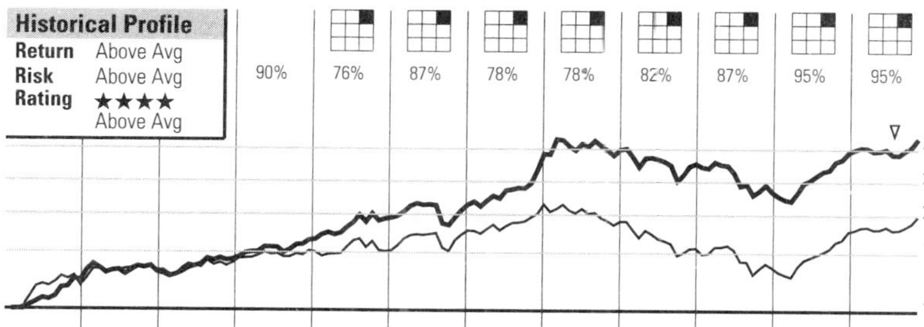

Investment Style: Equity Stock %

▼ Manager Change
▽ Partial Manager Change

Growth of $10,000
— Investment Values of Fund
— Investment Values of MSCI EAFE

Performance Quartile (within Category)

1993	1994	1995	1996	1997	1998	1999	2000	2001	2002	2003	12-04	History
36.85	31.94	34.89	39.03	41.00	42.60	62.55	52.98	46.73	36.24	51.50	60.77	NAV
42.63	-3.11	16.58	17.52	21.82	12.71	58.48	4.06	-11.30	-22.45	43.07	18.67	Total Return %
10.07	-10.89	5.37	11.47	20.04	-7.22	31.45	18.25	9.62	-6.51	4.48	-1.58	+/-MSCI EAFE
20.13	-8.19	-4.14	4.04	6.06	-11.61	33.53	17.25	5.00	-2.56	9.96	3.95	+/-MSCI World
0.88	0.00	0.75	1.52	2.12	0.95	0.84	0.00	0.00	0.00	0.92	0.66	Income Return %
41.75	-3.11	15.83	16.00	19.70	11.76	57.64	4.06	-11.80	-22.45	42.15	18.01	Capital Return %
10	66	59	40	20	55	25	11	29	73	13	19	Total Rtn % Rank Cat
0.25	0.00	0.24	0.53	0.83	0.39	0.36	0.00	0.00	0.00	0.34	0.34	Income $
3.37	3.75	2.05	1.38	5.74	2.99	4.12	11.96	0.00	0.00	0.00	0.00	Capital Gains $
1.18	1.15	1.20	1.17	1.13	1.14	1.16	1.03	1.12	1.23	1.23	1.15	Expense Ratio %
0.84	0.38	0.90	0.62	0.74	0.96	0.37	0.41	0.42	0.18	0.59	0.48	Income Ratio %
87	78	84	103	66	65	68	62	36	27	46	22	Turnover Rate %
1,662	1,849	2,183	2,610	3,239	3,428	5,206	6,154	5,807	4,681	6,651	9,721	Net Assets $mil

Performance 12-31-04

	1st Qtr	2nd Qtr	3rd Qtr	4th Qtr	Total
2000	13.45	-3.26	-1.70	-3.54	4.06
2001	-14.38	7.34	-17.77	16.71	-11.80
2002	1.52	-9.19	-18.18	2.81	-22.45
2003	-7.89	21.09	9.65	16.99	43.07
2004	4.31	-1.06	-0.96	16.10	18.67

Trailing	Total Return%	+/- MSCI EAFE	+/- MSCI World	%Rank Cat	Growth of $10,000
3 Mo	16.10	0.78	4.16	7	11,610
6 Mo	14.99	-0.01	4.17	16	11,499
1 Yr	18.67	-1.58	3.95	19	11,867
3 Yr Avg	9.61	-2.28	2.66	32	13,169
5 Yr Avg	3.86	4.99	6.31	15	12,085
10 Yr Avg	13.68	8.06	5.59	6	36,045
15 Yr Avg	11.90	7.67	5.31	1	54,007

Tax Analysis	Tax-Adj Rtn%	%Rank Cat	Tax-Cost Rat	%Rank Cat
3 Yr (estimated)	7.31	41	0.14	19
5 Yr (estimated)	1.65	23	0.96	63
10 Yr (estimated)	11.29	7	1.51	58

Potential Capital Gain Exposure: 25% of assets

Rating and Risk

Time Period	Load-Adj Return %	Morningstar Rtn vs Cat	Morningstar Risk vs Cat	Morningstar Risk-Adj Rating
1 Yr	11.85			
3 Yr	7.46	Avg	+Avg	★★★
5 Yr	2.64	+Avg	+Avg	★★★★
10 Yr	13.00	High	Avg	★★★★★
Incept	12.68			

Other Measures	Standard Index S&P 500	Best Fit Index DJ 60%
Alpha	-2.1	-6.5
Beta	1.02	1.80
R-Squared	91	93
Standard Deviation	18.40	
Mean	9.61	
Sharpe Ratio	0.45	

Portfolio Analysis 09-30-04

Share change since 07-04 Total Stocks:147	Sector	Country	% Assets
Vodafone Grp	Telecom	U.K.	3.66
Sirius Satellite Radio	Media	United States	2.90
⊕ Ericsson AB (publ)	Hardware	Sweden	2.15
H&M Hennes & Mauritz	Consumer	Sweden	2.01
⊕ Royal Bank Of Scotland G	Financial	U.K.	1.97
⊕ Sanofi-Synthelabo	Health	France	1.88
J.P. Morgan Chase & Co.	Financial	United States	1.84
Reckitt Benckiser	Goods	U.K.	1.84
KDDI	Telecom	Japan	1.56
Transocean	Energy	United States	1.21
Roche Holding	Health	Switzerland	1.20
HSBC Hldgs	Financial	U.K.	1.05
Technip	Energy	France	1.05
Wachovia	Financial	United States	1.05
Dixons Grp	Consumer	U.K.	1.04
GlobalSantaFe	Energy	United States	1.02
Infosys Technologies Ltd	Software	India	1.02
⊖ Qualcomm	Hardware	United States	1.01
SAP	Software	Germany	0.99
⊕ Gilead Sciences	Health	United States	0.98

Current Investment Style

Value Blnd Growth — Large Mid Small

Market Cap	%
Giant	43.2
Large	34.7
Mid	21.4
Small	0.6
Micro	0.0
Avg $mil:	19,407

Value Measures		Rel Category
Price/Earnings	16.36	1.04
Price/Book	2.41	1.09
Price/Sales	1.61	1.38
Price/Cash Flow	6.29	0.99
Dividend Yield %	1.67	0.89

Growth Measures	%	Rel Category
Long-Term Erngs	11.95	0.99
Book Value	-4.40	NMF
Sales	4.12	0.98
Cash Flow	13.19	2.25
Historical Erngs	12.73	1.49

Composition

Cash	4.4	Bonds	0.0
Stocks	95.4	Other	0.2
Foreign (% of Stock)			60.4

Sector Weightings	% of Stocks	Rel MSCI EAFE	3 Year High	3 Year Low
Info	33.17	2.00		
Software	5.48	5.07	15	5
Hardware	11.44	3.13	12	6
Media	8.17	3.58	10	4
Telecom	8.08	0.84	9	1
Service	42.94	0.96		
Health	13.85	1.91	23	14
Consumer	7.71	1.53	8	3
Business	2.50	0.46	3	1
Financial	18.88	0.70	20	14
Mfg	23.90	0.62		
Goods	11.26	0.82	16	11
Ind Mtrls	3.30	0.27	7	3
Energy	8.55	1.16	9	5
Utilities	0.79	0.15	1	0

Regional Exposure	% Stock		
UK/W. Europe	37	N. America	42
Japan	9	Latn America	3
Asia X Japan	9	Other	0

Country Exposure	% Stock		
United States	40	France	7
U.K.	16	Sweden	4
Japan	9		

Morningstar's Take by Dan Lefkovitz 12-23-04

Oppenheimer Global's manager transition is worth watching but not panicking over.

Bill Wilby, longtime manager of this long-stellar fund, reports that he will be stepping down as manager sometime in 2005 or early 2006. Since August, Wilby has been splitting his time between managing the Global fund and serving as the senior investment officer of Oppenheimer Funds. He has been sharing portfolio management duties on this fund with Rajeev Bhaman, who formerly managed Oppenheimer Developing Markets and will become the sole manager of the Global portfolio upon Wilby's departure.

One cause for concern is that Bhaman's previous experience was on an emerging-markets fund, whereas this portfolio is concentrated largely in developed markets. As of November 30, this fund had 42% in the U.S., 36% in Europe, 8% in Japan, and the small remainder in emerging markets.

Nevertheless, we are heartened by the fact that Bhaman has an outstanding record. In his nearly eight years managing Developing Markets, the fund gained an average of 15% per year, trouncing the emerging-markets category average of 5%. We are encouraged that Wilby is grooming his successor over a substantial period of time and giving fundholders ample notice of his departure.

This transition is important because Oppenheimer Global has been so outstanding for so long. Wilby's long-term oriented, contrarian investing style has contributed to the fund's 14% average annual gain since he became manager in late 1992, a record that bests its world-stock rivals by a wide margin. It's illustrative that several of the top contributors to the fund's above-average 2004 gains, such as Qualcomm and Sanofi-Aventis, have been in the portfolio for years. And it's encouraging that Bhaman also uses a patient, low-turnover style. So while no manager transition is completely seamless, this fine fund looks to be in good shape.

Address:	6803 South Tucson Way Centennial CO 80112-3924 800-525-7048
Web Address:	www.oppenheimerfunds.com
Inception:	12-22-69
Advisor:	OppenheimerFunds, Inc.
Subadvisor:	None
NTF Plans:	DATALynx NTF, Federated Tr NTF

Minimum Purchase:	$1000	Add: $50	IRA: $500
Min Auto Inv Plan:	$500	Add: $50	
Sales Fees:	5.75%L, 0.23%S, 2.00%R		
Management Fee:	0.80% mx./0.61% mn.		
Actual Fees:	Mgt:0.67%	Dist:0.23%	
Expense Projections:	3Yr:$943	5Yr:$1212	10Yr:$1978
Income Distrib:	Annually		

Oppenheimer Glob Oppor A

Ticker	Load	NAV	Yield	Total Assets	Mstar Category
OPGIX	5.75%	$33.25	0.0%	$3,457 mil	World Stock

Governance and Management

Fiduciary Grade: B

Portfolio Manager(s)

Frank Jennings has earned a terrific record since coming on-board in October 1995. Prior to this post, he was managing director of global equities for Mitchell Hutchins Asset Management for three years. In August 2004, Jennings named senior analyst Randy Dishmon his comanager.

Strategy

This fund's portfolio can run the gamut of stocks and bonds, U.S. and foreign equities, and large-caps and small-caps. Manager Frank Jennings and his comanager Randy Dishmon are long-term investors, and stock-picking is informed by several themes, such as mass affluence, new technologies, corporate restructuring, and aging. Oppenheimer uses fair-value pricing selectively to deter market-timers, and the firm also has a 2% redemption fee in place on its foreign and global funds. The fund can hedge currency.

Historical Profile

Return Above Avg
Risk High
Rating ★★★ Neutral

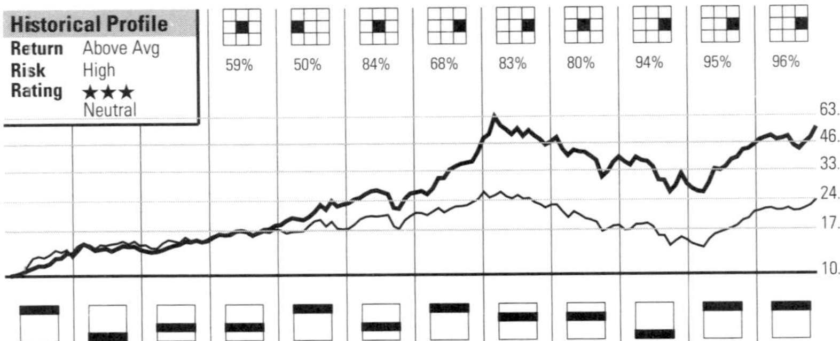

Investment Style
Equity
Stock %

▼ Manager Change
∇ Partial Manager Change

Growth of $10,000
▬ Investment Values of Fund
— Investment Values of MSCI EAFE

Performance Quartile (within Category)

1993	1994	1995	1996	1997	1998	1999	2000	2001	2002	2003	12-04	History
15.47	13.53	14.60	15.00	17.44	16.64	29.12	27.04	22.59	16.28	25.60	33.25	NAV
39.49	-4.70	17.37	15.31	28.25	12.83	86.57	-4.23	-16.32	-26.99	57.25	29.88	Total Return %
6.93	-12.48	6.16	9.26	26.47	-7.10	59.54	9.96	5.10	-11.05	18.66	9.63	+/-MSCI EAFE
16.99	-9.78	-3.35	1.83	12.49	-11.49	61.62	8.96	0.48	-7.10	24.14	15.16	+/-MSCI World
1.73	2.61	2.99	2.77	4.36	2.31	2.30	0.18	0.07	1.02	0.00	0.00	Income Return %
37.76	-7.31	14.38	12.54	23.89	10.52	84.27	-4.41	-16.39	-28.01	57.25	29.88	Capital Return %
19	84	56	59	2	54	5	28	49	88	1	1	Total Rtn % Rank Cat
0.20	0.40	0.40	0.40	0.65	0.40	0.38	0.05	0.02	0.23	0.00	0.00	Income $
0.48	0.82	0.83	1.38	1.07	2.56	1.32	0.81	0.02	0.00	0.00	0.00	Capital Gains $
1.56	1.49	1.63	1.52	1.43	1.36	1.33	1.20	1.22	1.40	1.36	1.19	Expense Ratio %
2.68	2.44	3.09	2.65	2.47	1.62	2.51	0.72	0.38	-0.17	-0.48	-0.20	Income Ratio %
91	87	135	208	90	117	98	48	53	39	61	52	Turnover Rate %
113	125	109	124	187	257	789	1,540	1,353	916	1,329	2,027	Net Assets $mil

Performance 12-31-04

	1st Qtr	2nd Qtr	3rd Qtr	4th Qtr	Total
2000	16.28	-3.66	-7.97	-7.10	-4.23
2001	-14.72	3.82	-24.98	25.99	-16.32
2002	-0.40	-10.44	-25.26	9.52	-26.99
2003	-9.15	29.14	15.45	16.10	57.25
2004	10.82	-0.74	-7.21	27.25	29.88

Trailing	Total Return%	+/- MSCI EAFE	+/- MSCI World	%Rank Cat	Growth of $10,000
3 Mo	27.25	11.93	15.31	1	12,725
6 Mo	18.08	3.08	7.26	3	11,808
1 Yr	29.88	9.63	15.16	1	12,988
3 Yr Avg	14.25	2.36	7.30	9	14,913
5 Yr Avg	3.63	4.76	6.08	17	11,952
10 Yr Avg	15.88	10.26	7.79	1	43,660
15 Yr Avg	—	—	—	—	—

Tax Analysis	Tax-Adj Rtn%	%Rank Cat	Tax-Cost Rat	%Rank Cat
3 Yr (estimated)	11.83	14	0.17	24
5 Yr (estimated)	2.11	20	0.29	19
10 Yr (estimated)	13.10	2	1.82	78

Potential Capital Gain Exposure: 15% of assets

Rating and Risk

Time Period	Load-Adj Return %	Morningstar Rtn vs Cat	Morningstar Risk vs Cat	Morningstar Risk-Adj Rating
1 Yr	22.41			
3 Yr	12.02	+Avg	High	★★★
5 Yr	2.41	+Avg	High	★★★
10 Yr	15.20	High	High	★★★★
ncept	13.37			

Other Measures	Standard Index S&P 500	Best Fit Index Wil 4500
Alpha	-1.1	-2.0
Beta	1.48	1.56
R-Squared	78	88
Standard Deviation	30.89	
Mean	14.25	
Sharpe Ratio	0.42	

Portfolio Analysis 09-30-04

Share change since 07-04 Total Stocks:88	Sector	Country	% Assets
Advanced Micro Devices	Hardware	United States	8.13
Sirius Satellite Radio	Media	United States	7.78
Nektar Therapeutics	Health	United States	6.39
National Semiconductor	Hardware	United States	3.42
Porsche	Goods	Germany	2.39
⊖ Ericsson AB (publ)	Hardware	Sweden	2.06
H. Lundbeck	Health	Denmark	2.00
Alexion Pharmaceuticals	Health	United States	1.85
H&M Hennes & Mauritz	Consumer	Sweden	1.82
⊖ UCB Grp	Health	Belgium	1.77
Affymetrix	Health	United States	1.69
⊖ Cree	Hardware	United States	1.69
⊖ Gn Store Nord	Goods	Denmark	1.67
Electrocomponents	Business	U.K.	1.66
⊖ Siemens	Hardware	Germany	1.62
Musashino Bank, Ltd	Financial	Japan	1.60
⊖ Novozymes	Ind Mtrls	Denmark	1.49
Nintendo	Goods	Japan	1.35
Autonomy	Software	U.K.	1.26
JDS Uniphase	Hardware	United States	1.24

Current Investment Style

Value Blnd Growth — Mid Growth (Large / Mid / Small)

Market Cap	%
Giant	12.6
Large	17.4
Mid	48.2
Small	16.5
Micro	5.3
Avg $mil: 3,756	

Value Measures		Rel Category
Price/Earnings	18.68	1.18
Price/Book	2.45	1.10
Price/Sales	1.53	1.31
Price/Cash Flow	7.12	1.12
Dividend Yield %	0.95	0.51

Growth Measures	%	Rel Category
Long-Term Erngs	10.78	0.90
Book Value	-12.94	NMF
Sales	3.01	0.72
Cash Flow	4.64	0.79
Historical Erngs	8.21	0.96

Composition

Cash	3.7	Bonds	0.0
Stocks	96.3	Other	0.1
Foreign (% of Stock)			48.7

Sector Weightings	% of Stocks	Rel MSCI EAFE	3 Year High	3 Year Low
Info	37.67	2.27		
Software	3.42	3.17	7	0
Hardware	22.85	6.26	40	23
Media	9.64	4.23	13	5
Telecom	1.76	0.18	2	0
Service	46.64	1.04		
Health	23.13	3.19	24	13
Consumer	4.74	0.94	12	0
Business	3.18	0.58	9	1
Financial	15.59	0.58	18	9
Mfg	15.70	0.41		
Goods	12.90	0.94	17	7
Ind Mtrls	2.80	0.23	5	1
Energy	0.00	0.00	3	0
Utilities	0.00	0.00	0	0

Regional Exposure % Stock

UK/W. Europe	36	N. America	51
Japan	12	Latn America	0
Asia X Japan	1	Other	0

Country Exposure % Stock

United States	51	Sweden	7
Japan	12	Denmark	5
Germany	8		

Morningstar's Take by Dan Lefkovitz 12-20-04

Loyalty is usually rewarded at Oppenheimer Global Opportunities.

Frank Jennings and his recently named comanager Randy Dishmon buy stocks of companies whose long-term potential they believe in, and as the fund's moderate turnover rate indicates, they are willing to stand by their picks for years waiting for this potential to be realized. What's more, Jennings has never paid much heed to indices and traditionally places big bets. As of Nov. 30, 2004, Advanced Micro Devices, Nektar Therapeutics, and Sirius Satellite Radio each consumed over 6% of assets. A quarter of the portfolio was allocated to both the information technology and health-care sectors.

Due to their long-term perspective, Jennings and Dishmon are often willing to ride out bad press and changes in sentiment about their holdings. For example, Jennings bought Sirius in 1999 because he believed in the future of satellite radio, and he has stuck with it ever since, despite various criticisms of the company over the years, including recent questions over its stock-price valuation.

This loyalty has paid off. Sirius's 142% gain for the year to date through Dec. 17 has been a crucial driver of the fund's 2004 performance, as have similarly controversial holdings AMD and Ericsson. The fund has gained an eye-popping 27% for the year to date, compared with a 12% return for the average fund in the world stock category. Jennings' long-term record is just as impressive. In his nine years as manager, the fund has gained an average of 15.5% per year, nearly double the return of its typical peer.

But fundholders should be prepared for significant volatility along the way. The fund's big sector and stock bets leave it vulnerable to industry- and issue-specific risk. Its healthy dose of small-caps is another source of volatility. That said, investors who, like the managers, maintain a long-time horizon, should be rewarded.

Address:	6803 South Tucson Way Centennial CO 80112-3924 800-525-7048
Web Address:	www.oppenheimerfunds.com
Inception:	10-22-90
Advisor:	OppenheimerFunds, Inc.
Subadvisor:	None
NTF Plans:	DATALynx NTF, Federated Tr NTF

Minimum Purchase:	$1000	Add: $50	IRA: $500	
Min Auto Inv Plan:	$500	Add: $50		
Sales Fees:	5.75%L, 0.24%S, 2.00%R			
Management Fee:	0.80% mx./0.65% mn.			
Actual Fees:	Mgt:0.73%	Dist:0.24%		
Expense Projections:	3Yr:$981	5Yr:$1277	10Yr:$2116	
Income Distrib:	Annually			

Oppenheimer Main St Sm A

Ticker	Load	NAV	Yield	Total Assets	Mstar Category
OPMSX	5.75%	$20.08	0.0%	$2,607 mil	Small Blend

Governance and Management

Fiduciary Grade: B

Portfolio Manager(s)

Mark Zavanelli has managed this fund since its August 1999 inception, becoming lead manager after Chuck Albers retired in September 2003. Zavanelli first joined the Main Street team in 1998 as an analyst, although he had previously helped develop the team's quantitative models as a consultant. Nikos Monoyios, who has been part of the Main Street team for more than 20 years, is comanager.

Strategy

Managers Mark Zavanelli and Nikos Monoyios use bottom-up quantitative models to look for stocks with market caps less than $2.5 billion that rank highly on a combination of valuation, price/earnings momentum, quality, and other factors such as stock buybacks and mergers. They also use top-down models, which lead them to adjust the fund's average market cap, sector weightings, and other macro factors. The fund typically holds more than 1,000 different stocks.

Historical Profile

Return Average
Risk Above Avg
Rating ★★★ Neutral

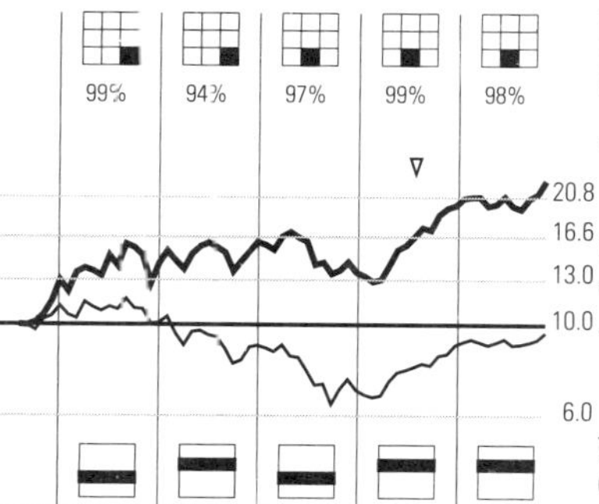

1993	1994	1995	1996	1997	1998	1999	2000	2001	2002	2003	12-04	History
—	—	—	—	—	—	12.84	13.36	15.08	12.67	18.56	20.08	NAV
—	—	—	—	—	—	28.65*	10.15	12.93	-15.98	46.49	19.18	Total Return %
—	—	—	—	—	—	—	19.25	24.81	6.11	17.82	8.31	+/-S&P 500
—	—	—	—	—	—	—	13.17	10.44	4.50	-0.76	0.85	+/-Russ 2000
—	—	—	—	—	—	0.00	0.00	0.00	0.00	0.00	0.00	Income Return %
—	—	—	—	—	—	—	10.15	12.93	-15.98	46.49	19.18	Capital Return %
—	—	—	—	—	—	—	65	23	57	30	47	Total Rtn % Rank Cat
—	—	—	—	—	—	0.00	0.00	0.00	0.00	0.00	0.00	Income $
—	—	—	—	—	—	0.02	0.79	0.01	0.00	0.00	1.96	Capital Gains $
—	—	—	—	—	—	—	1.50	1.28	1.36	1.36	1.17	Expense Ratio %
—	—	—	—	—	—	—	-0.82	-0.60	-0.59	-0.59	-0.42	Income Ratio %
—	—	—	—	—	—	—	108	181	117	117	130	Turnover Rate %
—	—	—	—	—	—	74	205	381	492	867	1,417	Net Assets $mil

Performance 12-31-04

	1st Qtr	2nd Qtr	3rd Qtr	4th Qtr	Total
2000	7.17	7.34	4.74	-8.57	10.15
2001	-3.29	16.25	-15.05	18.24	12.93
2002	3.18	-2.83	-16.86	0.80	-15.98
2003	-4.03	21.55	9.07	15.14	46.49
2004	5.01	0.15	-1.08	14.55	19.17

Trailing	Total Return%	+/- S&P 500	+/- Russ 2000	%Rank Cat	Growth of $10,000
3 Mo	14.55	5.32	0.46	15	11,455
6 Mo	13.31	6.12	2.48	17	11,331
1 Yr	19.18	8.31	0.85	47	11,918
3 Yr Avg	13.62	10.04	2.14	33	14,668
5 Yr Avg	12.78	15.08	6.17	47	18,246
10 Yr Avg	—	—	—	—	—
15 Yr Avg	—	—	—	—	—

Tax Analysis	Tax-Adj Rtn%	%Rank Cat	Tax-Cost Rat	%Rank Cat
3 Yr (estimated)	10.88	59	0.47	33
5 Yr (estimated)	10.66	49	0.71	29
10 Yr (estimated)	—	—	—	—

Potential Capital Gain Exposure: 23% of assets

Rating and Risk

Time Period	Load-Adj Return %	Morningstar Rtn vs Cat	Morningstar Risk vs Cat	Morningstar Risk-Adj Rating
1 Yr	12.32			
3 Yr	11.40	Avg	Avg	★★★
5 Yr	11.45	Avg	+Avg	★★★
10 Yr	—	—	—	—
Incept	15.77			

Other Measures	Standard Index S&P 500	Best Fit Index Russ 2000
Alpha	10.5	3.1
Beta	0.88	0.87
R-Squared	61	96

Standard Deviation	19.23
Mean	13.62
Sharpe Ratio	0.64

Portfolio Analysis 09-30-04

Share change since 07-04 Total Stocks:1291	Sector	PE	YTD Ret%	% Assets
FMC	Ind Mtrls	16.8	41.52	0.38
Joy Global	Ind Mtrls	41.0	67.83	0.36
⊕ Cal Dive International	Energy	23.4	68.95	0.35
⊖ Cimarex Energy	Energy	12.3	42.00	0.34
⊖ Carpenter Technology	Ind Mtrls	22.4	99.59	0.34
⊖ Louisiana-Pacific	Ind Mtrls	4.9	51.48	0.33
Websense	Software	47.4	73.28	0.33
Jack In The Box	Consumer	16.9	72.61	0.32
⊖ AmerUs Group	Financial	10.9	30.70	0.31
⊖ OMI	Business	8.8	91.70	0.31
Pacific Capital Bancorp	Financial	16.7	26.15	0.31
⊖ Penn National Gaming	Goods	34.8	161.89	0.31
EGL	Business	30.2	70.02	0.31
⊕ Anixter International	Ind Mtrls	21.0	46.40	0.30
Potlatch	Ind Mtrls	16.3	55.31	0.30
⊕ TIBCO Software	Software	83.0	97.05	0.30
InfoSpace	Telecom	—	106.29	0.30
⊖ Briggs & Stratton	Ind Mtrls	14.4	25.63	0.30
⊕ Nautilus Group	Consumer	29.8	76.14	0.30
Genlyte Group	Ind Mtrls	22.7	46.76	0.30

Current Investment Style

Value Blnd Growth / Large Mid Small

Market Cap	%
Giant	0.0
Large	0.3
Mid	31.0
Small	57.4
Micro	11.4
Avg $mil: 1,065	

Value Measures		Rel Category
Price/Earnings	16.77	0.97
Price/Book	2.17	1.09
Price/Sales	0.76	0.80
Price/Cash Flow	5.43	0.93
Dividend Yield %	0.67	0.81

Growth Measures	%	Rel Category
Long-Term Erngs	14.40	1.06
Book Value	5.14	0.91
Sales	4.14	1.03
Cash Flow	13.53	2.74
Historical Erngs	8.16	1.09

Profitability	%	Rel Category
Return on Equity	11.64	1.11
Return on Assets	5.98	1.21
Net Margin	8.19	1.12

Sector Weightings	% of Stocks	Rel S&P 500	3 Year High	3 Year Low
Info	18.42	0.86		
Software	7.42	1.73	8	3
Hardware	8.00	0.78	13	5
Media	1.14	0.30	3	0
Telecom	1.86	0.59	3	0
Service	48.08	1.04		
Health	11.53	0.92	15	11
Consumer	11.37	1.25	19	11
Business	11.32	2.80	12	9
Financial	13.86	0.67	18	14
Mfg	33.49	1.04		
Goods	6.37	0.68	9	6
Ind Mtrls	17.98	1.42	18	11
Energy	7.91	1.10	8	4
Utilities	1.23	0.42	1	0

Composition

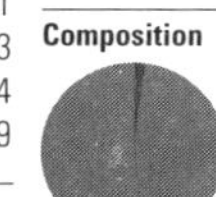

Cash	2.1
Stocks	97.9
Bonds	0.0
Other	0.1
Foreign (% of Stock)	2.8

Morningstar's Take by David Kathman 11-22-04

Oppenheimer Main Street Small Cap continues to be an appealingly steady option.

Like the other Main Street funds, this one uses quantitative models in an effort to gain a modest edge over its peer group without taking on excessive risk. For the most part, it has met that goal; in slightly more than five years since its inception, the fund's returns have ranked among the top one third of small-cap blend funds. It has achieved these results by following a steady middle course, never finishing in either top or the bottom quartile of its category in any calendar year.

The models behind this performance have their roots in a system originated 30 years ago by quant pioneer Chuck Albers, recently retired from the Main Street team. Managers Mark Zavanelli and Nikos Monoyios each worked on the system for more than a decade and are constantly tweaking it to reflect new market trends. For example, they recently adjusted the model to downplay momentum factors in the fourth quarter of each year, based on recent changes in the market's behavior.

The fund sparkled in 2003, when a heavy weighting in micro-caps and cyclical tech stocks helped it outpace the small-blend category with a 46.5% return. When the market abruptly soured on such speculative fare in early 2004, the models were slow to react, causing the fund to temporarily fall far behind its peers. But the revamped portfolio came back strong in the third quarter to surpass the category for the year to date as of mid-November, illustrating the value and resiliency of the fund's flexible models.

Given the experience and track record of the Main Street team, we expect such solid performance to continue. Although it's never likely to be among the category leaders, this fund can be a good anchor for the small-cap portion of a portfolio.

Address:	6803 South Tucson Way Centennial CO 80112-3924 800-525-7048
Web Address:	www.oppenheimerfunds.com
Inception:	08-02-99 *
Advisor:	OppenheimerFunds, Inc.
Subadvisor:	None
NTF Plans:	DATALynx NTF, Federated Tr NTF

Minimum Purchase:	$1000	Add: $50	IRA: $500	
Min Auto Inv Plan:	$500	Add: $50		
Sales Fees:	5.75%L			
Management Fee:	0.75% mx./0.60% mn.			
Actual Fees:	Mgt:0.70%	Dist:0.25%		
Expense Projections:	3Yr:$984	5Yr:$1282	10Yr:$2127	
Income Distrib:	Annually			

Oppenheimer Main Street A

Ticker	Load	NAV	Yield	Total Assets	Mstar Category
MSIGX	5.75%	$35.46	1.2%	$12,724 mil	Large Blend

Governance and Management

Fiduciary Grade: B

Portfolio Manager(s)

Lead manager Nikos Monoyios worked for more than 20 years with this fund's original manager, Chuck Albers, first at Guardian Park Avenue and then here until Albers' retirement at the end of 2003. Comanager Marc Reinganum is a former finance professor who has been the team's director of quantitative research since September 2002. Monoyios also manages Oppenheimer Main Street Opportunity.

Strategy

Managers Nikos Monoyios and Marc Reinganum use bottom-up quantitative models to look for stocks that rank highly on a combination of quality, valuation, momentum, and other factors such as stock buybacks and mergers. They also use top-down models that lead them to adjust the fund's market capitalization and other macro factors, but they won't make huge sector bets. Individual stocks are given weights in the portfolio no more than 0.60% above or below their weights in the benchmark.

Historical Profile

Return Average
Risk Below Avg
Rating ★★★ Neutral

Investment Style: Equity Stock %

1993	1994	1995	1996	1997	1998	1999	2000	2001	2002	2003	12-04
69%	81%	94%	91%	96%	96%	98%	99%	99%			

▼ Manager Change
▽ Partial Manager Change

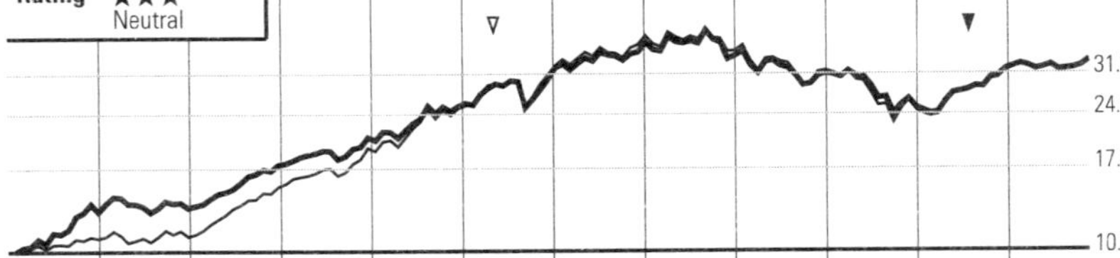

Performance Quartile (within Category)

1993	1994	1995	1996	1997	1998	1999	2000	2001	2002	2003	12-04	History
21.76	20.98	26.89	28.74	33.39	39.91	42.00	36.43	32.50	26.00	32.80	35.46	NAV
35.38	-1.53	30.77	15.70	26.59	25.19	17.12	-7.94	-10.46	-19.42	26.95	9.39	Total Return %
25.32	-2.84	-6.76	-7.24	-6.76	-3.38	-3.92	1.16	1.42	2.67	-1.72	-1.48	+/-S&P 500
25.20	-1.92	-7.00	-6.75	-6.26	-1.83	-3.79	-0.15	1.99	2.23	-2.94	-2.01	+/-Russ 1000
1.55	2.04	2.04	1.50	1.40	0.75	0.08	0.28	0.18	0.59	0.77	1.26	Income Return %
33.83	-3.57	28.73	14.20	25.19	24.44	17.04	-8.22	-10.64	-20.01	26.18	8.13	Capital Return %
1	68	69	90	61	41	68	56	29	25	52	62	Total Rtn % Rank Cat
0.28	0.44	0.43	0.40	0.40	0.25	0.03	0.12	0.07	0.19	0.20	0.41	Income $
1.99	0.00	0.08	1.98	2.50	1.50	4.48	2.10	0.05	0.00	0.00	0.00	Capital Gains $
1.46	1.28	1.07	0.99	0.94	0.90	0.91	0.90	0.86	0.99	0.97	0.93	Expense Ratio %
1.02	2.46	2.31	1.55	1.29	0.83	0.50	0.54	0.47	0.52	0.87	0.75	Income Ratio %
283	199	101	93	62	81	72	73	76	78	94	76	Turnover Rate %
164	1,269	2,466	3,590	4,849	6,525	8,694	7,953	7,426	6,042	7,549	7,997	Net Assets $mil

Performance 12-31-04

	1st Qtr	2nd Qtr	3rd Qtr	4th Qtr	Total
2000	4.00	-2.95	0.94	-9.64	-7.94
2001	-10.38	4.50	-11.49	8.01	-10.46
2002	1.23	-8.78	-16.49	4.50	-19.42
2003	-3.31	14.00	3.04	11.77	26.95
2004	2.01	0.57	-1.99	8.79	9.39

Trailing	Total Return%	+/- S&P 500	+/- Russ 1000	%Rank Cat	Growth of $10,000
3 Mo	8.79	-0.44	-1.01	68	10,879
6 Mo	6.63	-0.56	-1.18	62	10,663
1 Yr	9.39	-1.48	-2.01	62	10,939
3 Yr Avg	3.82	0.24	-0.45	30	11,190
5 Yr Avg	-1.60	0.70	0.16	40	9,225
10 Yr Avg	9.99	-2.08	-2.17	59	25,914
15 Yr Avg	13.92	2.99	2.84	4	70,632

Tax Analysis	Tax-Adj Rtn%	%Rank Cat	Tax-Cost Rat	%Rank Cat
3 Yr (estimated)	1.48	61	0.30	25
5 Yr (estimated)	-3.20	55	0.45	24
10 Yr (estimated)	8.15	59	1.09	34

Potential Capital Gain Exposure: 9% of assets

Rating and Risk

Time Period	Load-Adj Return %	Morningstar Rtn vs Cat	Morningstar Risk vs Cat	Morningstar Risk-Adj Rating
1 Yr	3.10			
3 Yr	1.79	Avg	-Avg	★★★
5 Yr	-2.76	Avg	-Avg	★★★
10 Yr	9.34	-Avg	-Avg	★★★
Incept	13.88			

Other Measures	Standard Index S&P 500	Best Fit Index MSCI World
Alpha	0.4	-2.3
Beta	0.85	0.86
R-Squared	97	97
Standard Deviation	13.41	
Mean	3.82	
Sharpe Ratio	0.18	

Morningstar's Take by David Kathman 12-06-04

Despite some recent stumbles, Oppenheimer Main Street remains an appealing long-term option for the core of a portfolio.

This fund uses a set of quantitative models in an effort to stay slightly ahead of the S&P 500 over the long term without too much volatility. These models rank stocks according to valuation, momentum, and quality criteria, and also identify style elements, such as size and credit quality, that are expected to outperform. Managers Nikos Monoyios and Marc Reinganum are constantly refining the models to reflect new research and adapt to changes in market behavior.

The fund has had a bit of an off year in 2004. Though it's still comfortably ahead of both the S&P 500 Index and the large-blend category since the current team took over nearly seven years ago, it has lagged both of those benchmarks over the past year. The main reason for this underperformance is the fund's recent heavy tilt toward mega-cap stocks, now about 70% of the portfolio. The models began indicating in the spring that mega-caps looked attractive, but instead they continued to substantially trail smaller stocks into the fall.

We're not worried, though, because the fund's strategy is a long-term one, and the managers are very seasoned. Monoyios has been part of the team since the late 1970s, when he joined original manager Chuck Albers on Guardian Park Avenue. That fund substantially outperformed the S&P 500 over a 26-year period before the team came to Oppenheimer in 1998. Reinganum only became comanager in late 2003 when Albers retired, but he had advised the team for more than a decade before that.

Investors in a fund like this shouldn't be too worried about the inevitable short-term performance fluctuations. What matters here is stability and long-term results, and on both of those counts this fund has done a fine job.

Portfolio Analysis 09-30-04

Share change since 07-04 Total Stocks:445	Sector	PE	YTD Ret%	% Assets
⊕ General Electric	Ind Mtrls	22.8	20.68	4.42
⊖ ExxonMobil	Energy	13.9	28.04	4.05
⊕ Pfizer	Health	22.0	-22.31	3.34
⊕ Microsoft	Software	36.1	8.95	3.31
Citigroup	Financial	15.3	2.72	3.22
⊕ Bank of America	Financial	12.3	21.50	2.50
Johnson & Johnson	Health	20.6	25.17	2.21
J.P. Morgan Chase & Co.	Financial	19.4	9.97	2.15
⊖ American International G	Financial	16.2	-0.53	2.15
⊕ Intel	Hardware	19.8	-26.56	2.02
⊕ Procter & Gamble	Goods	23.3	12.38	1.84
Wal-Mart Stores	Consumer	23.4	0.51	1.82
⊕ IBM	Hardware	20.2	7.19	1.80
⊕ ChevronTexaco	Energy	7.7	25.57	1.77
⊕ Cisco Systems	Hardware	24.5	-20.26	1.71
Altria Group	Goods	13.3	18.38	1.54
⊕ Home Depot	Consumer	19.0	21.47	1.45
⊕ Verizon Communications	Telecom	32.4	20.25	1.37
⊖ Wells Fargo	Financial	15.5	8.97	1.35
⊖ Dell	Hardware	34.0	24.01	1.32

Current Investment Style

Value Blnd Growth; Large Mid Small

Market Cap	%
Giant	69.7
Large	21.0
Mid	8.2
Small	1.1
Micro	0.0
Avg $mil: 61,066	

Value Measures		Rel Category
Price/Earnings	15.66	0.92
Price/Book	2.72	1.04
Price/Sales	1.56	1.08
Price/Cash Flow	7.74	1.01
Dividend Yield %	1.75	1.18

Growth Measures	%	Rel Category
Long-Term Erngs	11.03	0.95
Book Value	10.56	1.36
Sales	6.49	1.13
Cash Flow	12.60	1.33
Historical Erngs	14.01	1.19

Profitability	%	Rel Category
Return on Equity	19.90	1.14
Return on Assets	10.65	1.23
Net Margin	13.33	1.17

Sector Weightings	% of Stocks	Rel S&P 500	3 Year High	3 Year Low
Info	24.28	1.13		
Software	5.04	1.17	6	3
Hardware	11.65	1.14	13	4
Media	2.92	0.76	3	1
Telecom	4.67	1.48	5	3
Service	47.08	1.01		
Health	13.39	1.07	14	10
Consumer	8.81	0.97	15	8
Business	1.58	0.39	5	1
Financial	23.30	1.12	26	20
Mfg	28.63	0.89		
Goods	8.88	0.95	13	8
Ind Mtrls	10.21	0.81	12	6
Energy	9.12	1.27	11	7
Utilities	0.42	0.14	5	0

Composition

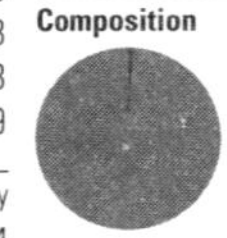

Cash	1.0
Stocks	98.9
Bonds	0.0
Other	0.0
Foreign (% of Stock)	0.6

Address:	6803 South Tucson Way Centennial CO 80112-3924 800-525-7048
Web Address:	www.oppenheimerfunds.com
Inception:	02-03-88
Advisor:	OppenheimerFunds, Inc.
Subadvisor:	None
NTF Plans:	DATALynx NTF, Federated Tr NTF

Minimum Purchase:	$1000	Add: $50	IRA: $500
Min Auto Inv Plan:	$500	Add: $50	
Sales Fees:	5.75%L, 0.24%S		
Management Fee:	0.65% mx./0.45% mn.		
Actual Fees:	Mgt:0.46%	Dist:0.24%	
Expense Projections:	3Yr:$872	5Yr:$1091	10Yr:$1718
Income Distrib:	Annually		

Oppenheimer Quest Bal A

Ticker	Load	NAV	Yield	Total Assets	Mstar Category
QVGIX	5.75%	$18.04	0.1%	$7,651 mil	Moderate Allocation

Governance and Management

Fiduciary Grade: B

Portfolio Manager(s)

Colin Glinsman has been at the helm of this fund since December 1992. He makes all the calls on both the stock and bond portions of the portfolio, but he is assisted by 20 Oppenheimer Capital stock analysts and three bond analysts, none of whom is exclusive to this fund.

Strategy

Aggressive. The fund's equity stake can range from 50%-75% of assets, but lately it has been at the high end of that range. Manager Colin Glinsman maintains a concentrated portfolio of 30-35 stocks, which he chooses through a bottom-up process that looks at a company's long-term cash flow and earnings potential. On the fixed-income side, Glinsman owns mostly corporate bonds, and he's willing to make duration (a measure of interest-rate sensitivity) bets according to where he thinks bond prices and interest rates are heading.

Performance 12-31-04

	1st Qtr	2nd Qtr	3rd Qtr	4th Qtr	Total
2000	0.85	-0.25	1.78	5.43	7.94
2001	4.76	2.30	-5.10	1.48	3.20
2002	-2.06	-14.73	-13.51	10.87	-19.92
2003	-0.15	15.38	3.91	9.06	30.56
2004	3.73	0.73	-0.00	5.56	10.29

Trailing	Total Return%	+/- S&P 500	+/- DJ 60%	%Rank Cat	Growth of $10,000
3 Mo	5.56	-3.67	-1.92	80	10,556
6 Mo	5.56	-1.63	-1.97	71	10,556
1 Yr	10.29	-0.58	-0.88	25	11,029
3 Yr Avg	4.86	1.28	-2.40	46	11,530
5 Yr Avg	5.13	7.43	-0.11	15	12,842
10 Yr Avg	13.77	1.70	3.28	2	36,331
15 Yr Avg	—	—	—	—	—

Tax Analysis	Tax-Adj Rtn%	%Rank Cat	Tax-Cost Rat	%Rank Cat
3 Yr (estimated)	2.52	65	0.28	19
5 Yr (estimated)	3.06	18	0.81	34
10 Yr (estimated)	10.90	5	1.95	61

Potential Capital Gain Exposure: 7% of assets

Historical Profile

Return Above Avg
Risk High
Rating ★★★★ Above Avg

Investment Style: Equity Stock %

68%	71%	57%	51%	61%	60%	69%	69%	68%

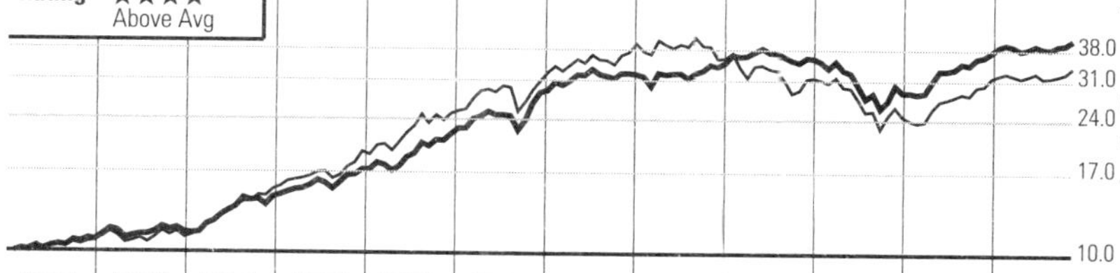

Performance Quartile (within Category)

1993	1994	1995	1996	1997	1998	1999	2000	2001	2002	2003	12-04	History
9.87	9.27	11.12	11.69	13.26	14.80	15.79	16.19	16.01	12.63	16.37	18.04	NAV
11.77	1.13	28.41	17.95	31.01	28.17	11.23	7.94	3.20	-19.92	30.56	10.29	Total Return %
1.71	-0.18	-9.12	-4.99	-2.34	-0.40	-9.81	17.04	15.08	2.17	1.89	-0.58	+/-S&P 500
0.04	3.08	3.64	6.61	11.81	15.78	-1.62	3.50	3.04	-9.38	6.50	-0.88	+/-DJ 60%
3.09	3.02	2.66	2.15	1.65	1.88	2.00	3.30	1.65	1.28	0.79	0.08	Income Return %
8.68	-1.89	25.75	15.80	29.36	26.29	9.23	4.64	1.55	-21.20	29.77	10.21	Capital Return %
44	11	27	14	1	3	47	16	9	96	4	25	Total Rtn % Rank Cat
0.31	0.29	0.24	0.24	0.19	0.25	0.29	0.52	0.27	0.20	0.10	0.01	Income $
1.70	0.42	0.50	1.15	1.79	1.92	0.38	0.30	0.44	0.00	0.00	0.00	Capital Gains $
1.90	1.86	1.99	1.90	1.58	1.55	1.51	1.45	1.45	1.51	1.38	—	Expense Ratio %
2.66	3.16	2.60	2.03	1.68	2.07	1.81	2.24	2.24	1.20	1.60	—	Income Ratio %
192	113	130	124	89	165	58	105	88	108	92	—	Turnover Rate %
29	29	40	51	88	191	1,019	1,053	1,989	1,733	2,359	3,253	Net Assets $mil

Rating and Risk

Time Period	Load-Adj Return %	Morningstar Rtn vs Cat	Morningstar Risk vs Cat	Morningstar Risk-Adj Rating
1 Yr	3.95			
3 Yr	2.81	-Avg	High	★★
5 Yr	3.90	+Avg	+Avg	★★★
10 Yr	13.10	High	High	★★★★★
Incept	11.89			

Other Measures	Standard Index S&P 500	Best Fit Index Russ 1000
Alpha	1.5	0.8
Beta	0.93	0.94
R-Squared	87	87
Standard Deviation	15.67	
Mean	4.86	
Sharpe Ratio	0.22	

Portfolio Analysis 09-30-04

Total Stocks:30 Share change since 07-31-04	Sectors	P/E Ratio	YTD Return %	% Net Assets
⊕ ConocoPhillips	Energy	9.0	-1.42	4.85
Sanofi-Aventis ADR	Health	23.0	-5.12	4.54
⊕ Wal-Mart Stores	Consumer	23.4	1.46	4.40
Royal Caribbean Cruises	Goods	36.9	-3.75	3.76
⊕ The Directv Group	Media	—	-3.23	3.67
⊕ Alcan	Ind Mtrls	53.1	-4.77	3.10
Inco Ltd	Ind Mtrls	59.5	-6.17	3.01
⊖ International Paper	Ind Mtrls	—	-2.38	3.00
⊕ Texas Instruments	Hardware	21.1	-9.14	2.93

Total Fixed-Income:44	Date of Maturity	Amount $000	Value $000	% Net Assets
US Treasury Note 2.625%	03-15-09	65,155	63,445	0.87
Jpmorgan & Chase 5.25%	05-30-07	46,725	49,132	0.68
Alcoa 4.25%	08-15-07	44,705	45,953	0.63
Chevrontexaco Cap 3.5%	09-17-07	43,790	44,230	0.61
Coca Cola Enterprises 5.2	05-15-07	41,139	43,277	0.60
General Mls 2.625%	10-24-06	43,810	43,198	0.60
Amer Express 5.5%	09-12-06	41,100	43,064	0.59
Intl Lease Fin Mtn Be 4%	01-17-06	41,660	42,337	0.58
Wachovia 4.95%	11-01-06	40,680	42,272	0.58

Equity Style
Style: Blend
Size: Large-Cap

Value Measures		Rel Category
Price/Earnings	15.04	0.91
Price/Book	2.21	0.91
Price/Sales	1.15	0.87
Price/Cash Flow	7.06	0.97
Dividend Yield %	1.02	0.65

Growth Measures	%	Rel Category
Long-Term Erngs	11.91	1.02
Book Value	-0.11	NMF
Sales	8.74	1.69
Cash Flow	-3.18	NMF
Historical Erngs	11.39	1.05

Market Cap %			
Giant	49.9	Small	0.0
Large	30.5	Micro	0.0
Mid	19.6	Avg $mil:	28,030

Fixed-Income Style
Duration: —
Quality: —

Avg Eff Duration[1]	—
Avg Eff Maturity	—
Avg Credit Quality	—
Avg Wtd Coupon	4.86%

[1] figure provided by fund

Sector Weightings	% of Stocks	Rel S&P 500	3 Year High	3 Year Low
Info	23.26	1.08		
Software	1.05	0.24	5	0
Hardware	16.78	1.65	19	7
Media	5.43	1.41	9	1
Telecom	0.00	0.00	9	0
Service	42.78	0.92		
Health	12.45	1.00	15	0
Consumer	12.88	1.42	14	2
Business	1.83	0.45	8	0
Financial	15.62	0.75	40	16
Mfg	33.96	1.06		
Goods	5.55	0.59	16	2
Ind Mtrls	14.36	1.13	20	3
Energy	14.05	1.96	14	0
Utilities	0.00	0.00	8	0

Composition

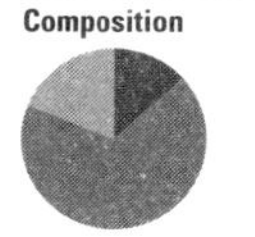

Cash	13.2
Stocks	67.7
Bonds	19.1
Other	0.0
Foreign (% of Stock)	22.6

Morningstar's Take by David Kathman 12-13-04

Oppenheimer Quest Balanced offers impressive long-term results, though with a few caveats attached.

This fund mixes aggressive asset allocation with rather tame security selection. The portfolio contains a mixture of stocks and bonds, and for the past couple of years manager Colin Glinsman has kept the stock allocation around 70%, near the 75% upper limit specified by the prospectus. That's higher than the 60% stock weighting of the average moderate-allocation fund, and it has helped the fund to handily outperform the category during a period of rising stock prices.

One drawback of this stock-heavy portfolio is the fact that it increases the fund's volatility relative to its peers. Adding to this volatility is the concentrated nature of the fund. Glinsman typically holds about 30 stocks and 40 bonds, many fewer than the average moderate-allocation fund, and the fund's standard deviation (a common measure of volatility) is correspondingly higher.

Moderating this volatility to some degree is the mildly conservative nature of the fund's stock and bond holdings. Its valuations are below the category average, thanks in part to beaten-down stocks such as Pfizer and Fannie Mae. Although the fund is overweight in hardware stocks, these are mostly big names with relatively modest valuations, such as Dell and Intel. The duration of the bond portfolio remains low, around two years.

The long-term results of this strategy have been outstanding, with 10-year returns in the moderate-allocation category's top 5%. The fund's one off year was 2002, when several stock picks imploded, but it has returned to the category's top tier in the two years since then. Our one sticking point here remains expenses, which have come down recently but are still above the category average for comparable share classes. This is a fine fund for investors who can handle the volatility, but it would be even more attractive if it were cheaper.

Address:	6803 South Tucson Way Centennial CO 80112-3924 800-525-7048
Web Address:	www.oppenheimerfunds.com
Inception:	11-01-91
Advisor:	OppenheimerFunds, Inc.
Subadvisor:	Opcap Advisors LLC
NTF Plans:	DATALynx NTF, Federated Tr NTF

Minimum Purchase:	$1000	Add: $50	IRA: $500
Min Auto Inv Plan:	$500	Add: $50	
Sales Fees:	5.75%L, 0.25%S		
Management Fee:	0.85% mx./0.50% mn.		
Actual Fees:	Mgt:0.79%	Dist:0.25%	
Expense Projections:	3Yr:$975	5Yr:$1267	10Yr:$2095
Income Distrib:	Quarterly		

Oppenheimer Quest Intl A

Ticker	Load	NAV	Yield	Total Assets	Mstar Category
QIVAX	5.75%	$18.90	0.1%	$421 mil	Foreign Large Blend

Governance and Management

Fiduciary Grade: B

Portfolio Manager(s)

Dominic Freud is taking over this portfolio on Jan. 1, 2005 from Elisa Mazen of subadvisor Oppenheimer Capital. Freud joined Oppenheimer Funds in March 2003 from SLS, a hedge fund where he had his first portfolio-management experience. Before that, he ran the European equities desk at SG Cowen and served as an equity analyst at Bank Paribas. He took over the newly created Oppenheimer International Value in August 2003. He is supported by a couple of senior analysts, as well as the deeply experienced global equity team of portfolio managers.

Strategy

Manager Dominic Freud is a bottom-up value investor. His ideal companies have significant market shares and strong balance sheets but are trading close to their book values due to short-term problems. Freud aims for a low-volatility, low-turnover portfolio that shines during bear markets. To discourage frequent trading, Oppenheimer levies a 2% redemption fee on all shares redeemed within 30 days of purchase. Freud will typically hedge roughly 15% of the fund's foreign currency exposure as a means of dampening volatility.

Historical Profile

Return: Above Avg
Risk: Low
Rating: ★★★★ Above Avg

Investment Style: Equity Stock %

93%	86%	93%	96%	97%	92%	94%	99%	99%

▼ Manager Change
▽ Partial Manager Change

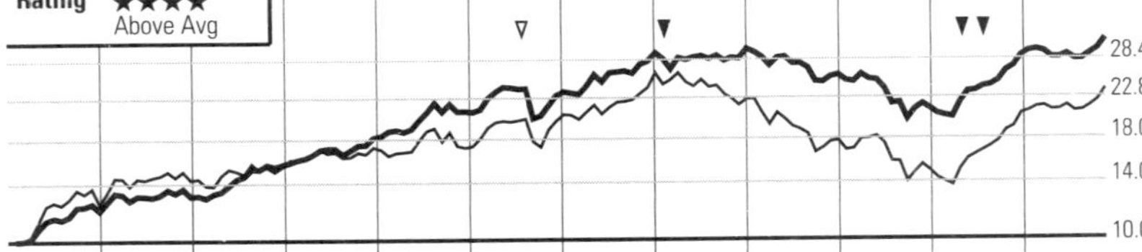

Growth of $10,000
▬ Investment Values of Fund
— Investment Values of MSCI EAFE

Performance Quartile (within Category)

	1993	1994	1995	1996	1997	1998	1999	2000	2001	2002	2003	12-04	History
	13.74	12.98	14.30	16.06	17.62	18.52	18.55	17.35	14.91	12.27	16.59	18.90	NAV
	25.42	3.41	20.74	16.29	14.61	12.31	24.99	2.21	-14.06	-17.71	35.21	14.10	Total Return %
	-7.14	-4.37	9.53	10.24	12.83	-7.62	-2.04	16.40	7.36	-1.77	-3.38	-6.15	+/-MSCI EAFE
	-6.79	-3.94	9.33	9.42	12.34	-6.38	-2.99	15.57	7.33	-1.91	-4.21	-6.28	+/-MSCI Wd xUS
	0.24	0.00	1.01	0.04	0.16	0.49	1.18	0.00	0.00	0.00	0.00	0.17	Income Return %
	25.18	3.41	19.73	16.25	14.45	11.82	23.81	2.21	-14.06	-17.71	35.21	13.93	Capital Return %
	93	22	2	28	8	64	90	1	6	63	36	87	Total Rtn % Rank Cat
	0.03	0.00	0.13	0.01	0.03	0.09	0.22	0.00	0.00	0.00	0.00	0.03	Income $
	0.58	1.23	1.24	0.55	0.76	1.11	4.24	1.57	0.00	0.00	0.00	0.00	Capital Gains $
	1.76	1.95	1.88	1.88	1.73	1.76	1.75	1.70	1.71	1.66	1.59	—	Expense Ratio %
	0.04	-0.23	0.77	0.19	0.17	0.09	-0.11	0.47	0.12	0.09	0.51	—	Income Ratio %
	46	1	76	48	32	59	78	104	71	75	150	—	Turnover Rate %
	143	147	161	195	266	299	359	300	241	187	245	324	Net Assets $mil

Performance 12-31-04

	1st Qtr	2nd Qtr	3rd Qtr	4th Qtr	Total
2000	-2.86	1.00	-2.64	7.00	2.21
2001	-9.11	1.08	-9.91	3.83	-14.06
2002	0.27	-7.89	-16.27	6.42	-17.71
2003	-5.05	16.48	5.90	15.45	35.21
2004	2.41	-1.77	0.36	13.01	14.10

Trailing	Total Return%	+/- MSCI EAFE	+/- MSCI Wd xUS	%Rank Cat	Growth of $10,000
3 Mo	13.01	-2.31	-2.14	85	11,301
6 Mo	13.41	-1.59	-1.96	65	11,341
1 Yr	14.10	-6.15	-6.28	87	11,410
3 Yr Avg	8.28	-3.61	-3.94	69	12,695
5 Yr Avg	2.20	3.33	2.96	4	11,149
10 Yr Avg	9.68	4.06	3.74	8	25,193
15 Yr Avg	—	—	—	—	—

Tax Analysis	Tax-Adj Rtn%	%Rank Cat	Tax-Cost Rat	%Rank Cat
3 Yr (estimated)	6.14	81	0.02	3
5 Yr (estimated)	0.63	6	0.37	21
10 Yr (estimated)	7.57	11	1.34	68

Potential Capital Gain Exposure: 16% of assets

Rating and Risk

Time Period	Load-Adj Return %	Morningstar Rtn vs Cat	Morningstar Risk vs Cat	Morningstar Risk-Adj Rating
1 Yr	7.54			
3 Yr	6.16	-Avg	Low	★★
5 Yr	1.00	+Avg	Low	★★★★★
10 Yr	9.03	+Avg	Low	★★★★★
Incept	8.33			

Other Measures	Standard Index S&P 500	Best Fit Index MSCI World
Alpha	-2.0	2.7
Beta	0.86	0.91
R-Squared	93	95
Standard Deviation	15.04	
Mean	8.28	
Sharpe Ratio	0.46	

Portfolio Analysis 09-30-04

Share change since 07-04 Total Stocks:58	Sector	Country	% Assets
Takeda Pharma	Health	Japan	4.01
⊕ TOTAL	Energy	France	4.01
BP	Energy	U.K.	3.37
Rio Tinto	Ind Mtrls	U.K.	3.26
Tesco	Consumer	U.K.	3.19
⊖ Barclays	Financial	U.K.	2.98
⊕ The Swatch Grp Ltd	Goods	Switzerland	2.98
Dassault Systemes	Software	France	2.93
⊕ Deutsche Telekom	Telecom	Germany	2.93
Pernod Ricard	Goods	France	2.82
⊕ SKF	Ind Mtrls	Sweden	2.77
☼ Shire Pharmaceuticals Gr	Health	U.K.	2.68
Vodafone Grp	Telecom	U.K.	2.64
⊕ Banco Popolare di Verona	Financial	Italy	2.54
Sanofi-Synthelabo	Health	France	2.43
⊕ Deutsche Boerse	Financial	Germany	2.36
⊕ NTT DoCoMo	Telecom	Japan	2.35
Novartis	Health	Switzerland	2.19
Luxottica Grp	Health	Italy	1.98
⊕ BNP Paribas	Financial	France	1.95

Current Investment Style

Value Blnd Growth / Large Mid Small

Market Cap	%
Giant	53.2
Large	24.1
Mid	20.3
Small	2.4
Micro	0.0
Avg $mil: 19,920	

Value Measures		Rel Category
Price/Earnings	14.31	1.04
Price/Book	1.91	1.06
Price/Sales	1.00	1.10
Price/Cash Flow	6.96	1.41
Dividend Yield %	2.16	0.85

Growth Measures	%	Rel Category
Long-Term Erngs	9.84	0.91
Book Value	0.23	23.00
Sales	2.14	0.86
Cash Flow	7.98	1.42
Historical Erngs	7.62	1.36

Composition

Cash	0.7	Bonds	0.0
Stocks	99.3	Other	0.0
Foreign (% of Stock)			98.7

Sector Weightings	% of Stocks	Rel MSCI EAFE	3 Year High	Low
Info	15.72	0.95		
Software	2.95	2.73	3	0
Hardware	3.14	0.86	8	1
Media	1.66	0.73	3	0
Telecom	7.97	0.83	10	3
Service	43.04	0.96		
Health	15.23	2.10	15	3
Consumer	6.14	1.22	10	1
Business	1.96	0.36	5	1
Financial	19.71	0.73	35	20
Mfg	41.24	1.07		
Goods	16.37	1.20	26	9
Ind Mtrls	16.42	1.33	21	13
Energy	8.45	1.15	11	2
Utilities	0.00	0.00	6	0

Regional Exposure	% Stock		
UK/W. Europe	74	N. America	5
Japan	18	Latn America	0
Asia X Japan	4	Other	0

Country Exposure	% Stock		
U.K.	25	Germany	11
France	21	Switzerland	7
Japan	18		

Morningstar's Take by Dan Lefkovitz 12-29-04

Oppenheimer Quest International Value is going through another uncertain transition.

Oppenheimer Funds announced that it will manage this fund in-house as of January 1. Dominic Freud, who has overseen Oppenheimer International Value since August 2003, will replace Elisa Mazen of subadvisor Oppenheimer Capital--which is owned by Allianz and is distinct from Oppenheimer Funds. The fund has had a turbulent history, including both manager and strategy changes. Bill Wilby, director of equities for Oppenheimer Funds, says the move was prompted partly by dissatisfaction with the fund's performance and partly because Oppenheimer's own global equity team has improved its capabilities in value investing, thanks in large part to its hiring of Freud in March 2003.

Freud says he will make the Quest International portfolio nearly identical to International Value, and the two funds will eventually merge. This will have four major effects, all reflective of Freud's investment style. First, the fund is likely to become more of a strict value offering. (International Value lands in Morningstar's foreign large-value category, while the Quest fund is categorized as foreign large blend.) Second, the fund's turnover rate should come down. Third, the refashioned portfolio is apt to contain more stocks than before. Fourth, the fund will likely hold more small caps, though the Quest fund's asset size will prevent some smaller stock purchases.

Freud is a long-term investor, so it's unfair to judge him on his relatively short record on International Value. That fund's 31% return from Aug. 1, 2003, through Nov. 30, 2004, is roughly in line with the foreign large-value category average. Largely based on our confidence in Oppenheimer's global equity team, we'd advise current fundholders to adopt a wait-and-see approach, but we'll require more time to become comfortable with Freud before recommending the fund to new investors.

Address:	6803 South Tucson Way Centennial CO 80112-3924 800-525-7048
Web Address:	www.oppenheimerfunds.com
Inception:	07-02-90
Advisor:	OppenheimerFunds, Inc.
Subadvisor:	Opcap Advisors LLC
NTF Plans:	DATALynx NTF, Federated Tr NTF

Minimum Purchase:	$1000	Add: $50	IRA: $500
Min Auto Inv Plan:	$500	Add: $50	
Sales Fees:	5.75%L, 0.25%S, 2.00%R		
Management Fee:	0.75% mx./0.55% mn.		
Actual Fees:	Mgt:0.75%	Dist:0.25%	
Expense Projections:	3Yr:$1083	5Yr:$1450	10Yr:$2478
Income Distrib:	Annually		

Pax World Balanced

Analyst Pick	Ticker	Load	NAV	Yield	Total Assets	Mstar Category
✔	PAXWX	12b-1 only	$23.22	0.9%	$1,465 mil	Moderate Allocation

Governance and Management

Fiduciary Grade: B

Portfolio Manager(s)

Chris Brown has more than a decade of experience as an investment professional and he has run this fund skillfully since taking the wheel in early 1998. He also serves as a senior vice president and portfolio manager with H.G. Wellington. He is supported by one analyst/assistant manager in Portsmouth as well as H.G. Wellington's team of New York-based analysts.

Strategy

This fund's social screens lend it a propensity for services, retail, health-care, and tech stocks, which readily pass environmental and other screens. Manager Chris Brown amplifies those tendencies with growth-oriented stock selection. He readily considers smaller-cap and international names.

Historical Profile

Return Above Avg
Risk Below Avg
Rating ★★★★★ Highest

Investment Style
Equity
Stock %

58% 53% 64% 66% 58% 56% 60% 70% 71%

▼ Manager Change
▽ Partial Manager Change

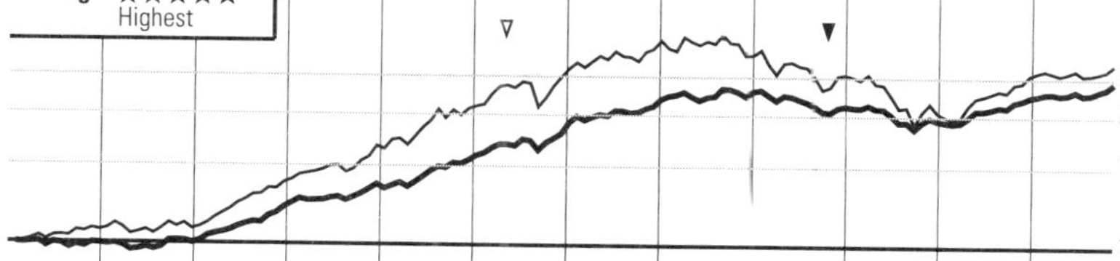

Growth of $10,000
— Investment Values of Fund
— Investment Values of S&P 500

Performance Quartile (within Category)

1993	1994	1995	1996	1997	1998	1999	2000	2001	2002	2003	12-04	History
13.55	13.39	16.33	16.56	18.52	21.64	23.40	22.41	19.91	17.82	20.68	23.22	NAV
-1.05	2.65	29.19	10.36	25.12	24.62	17.23	5.66	-9.09	-8.86	17.27	13.39	Total Return %
-11.11	1.34	-8.34	-12.58	-8.23	-3.95	-3.81	14.76	2.79	13.23	-11.40	2.52	+/-S&P 500
-12.78	4.60	4.42	-0.98	5.92	12.23	4.38	1.22	-9.25	1.68	-6.79	2.22	+/-DJ 60%
3.54	3.73	5.97	3.40	3.06	2.54	2.13	2.26	2.12	1.65	1.16	1.06	Income Return %
-4.59	-1.08	23.22	6.96	22.06	22.08	15.10	3.40	-11.21	-10.51	16.11	12.33	Capital Return %
100	6	20	84	10	8	16	26	83	22	73	4	Total Rtn % Rank Cat
0.50	0.50	0.79	0.55	0.50	0.47	0.46	0.53	0.47	0.33	0.21	0.22	Income $
0.07	0.00	0.14	0.89	1.65	0.88	1.41	1.75	0.00	0.00	0.00	0.00	Capital Gains $
0.94	0.98	0.97	0.89	0.91	0.95	0.89	0.96	0.93	0.95	0.99	—	Expense Ratio %
3.63	3.66	3.44	3.24	2.67	2.33	2.05	2.14	2.27	1.74	1.09	—	Income Ratio %
22	25	28	35	14	29	21	26	38	37	19	—	Turnover Rate %
464	388	477	518	629	838	1,070	1,228	1,162	1,035	1,226	1,465	Net Assets $mil

Performance 12-31-04

	1st Qtr	2nd Qtr	3rd Qtr	4th Qtr	Total
2000	4.96	-3.30	5.68	-1.49	5.66
2001	-5.85	0.71	-7.62	3.78	-9.09
2002	0.70	-6.08	-8.87	5.75	-8.86
2003	-1.12	8.17	1.93	7.57	17.27
2004	2.51	1.56	0.05	8.86	13.39

Trailing	Total Return%	+/- S&P 500	+/- DJ 60%	%Rank Cat	Growth of $10,000
3 Mo	8.86	-0.37	1.38	11	10,886
6 Mo	8.91	1.72	1.38	11	10,891
1 Yr	13.39	2.52	2.22	4	11,339
3 Yr Avg	6.62	3.04	-0.64	20	12,120
5 Yr Avg	3.09	5.39	-2.15	32	11,643
10 Yr Avg	11.74	-0.33	1.25	10	30,345
15 Yr Avg	9.93	-1.00	-0.02	32	41,376

Tax Analysis	Tax-Adj Rtn%	%Rank Cat	Tax-Cost Rat	%Rank Cat
3 Yr (estimated)	6.12	15	0.47	32
5 Yr (estimated)	2.13	26	0.93	41
10 Yr (estimated)	9.95	10	1.60	37

Potential Capital Gain Exposure: 23% of assets

Rating and Risk

Time Period	Load-Adj Return %	Morningstar Rtn vs Cat	Morningstar Risk vs Cat	Morningstar Risk-Adj Rating
1 Yr	13.39			
3 Yr	6.62	+Avg	-Avg	★★★★
5 Yr	3.09	+Avg	-Avg	★★★★
10 Yr	11.74	+Avg	-Avg	★★★★★
Incept	—			

Other Measures	Standard Index S&P 500	Best Fit Index Russ 1000
Alpha	3.8	3.4
Beta	0.51	0.52
R-Squared	90	91
Standard Deviation	8.56	
Mean	6.62	
Sharpe Ratio	0.62	

Portfolio Analysis 12-31-04

Total Stocks:78 Share change since 11-30-04	Sectors	P/E Ratio	YTD Return %	% Net Assets
EMC	Hardware	41.5	-8.00	1.98
Amgen	Health	37.7	-0.58	1.76
America Movil SA ADR	Telecom	23.2	-8.52	1.70
Caremark RX	Health	32.8	6.57	1.62
Starbucks	Consumer	60.4	-7.97	1.60
Dell	Hardware	34.0	-2.52	1.59
Cemex SA de CV ADR	Ind Mtrls	18.1	-2.99	1.50
Staples	Consumer	24.7	-3.44	1.50
Apache	Energy	11.4	-3.20	1.47

Total Fixed-Income:113	Date of Maturity	Amount $000	Value $000	% Net Assets
Cit Grp 5.5%	11-30-07	10,000	10,475	0.72
Bristol Myers Squibb 5.75	10-01-11	8,400	9,009	0.62
FNMA FRN	02-17-09	7,324	7,391	0.51
FHLMC 4.125%	08-19-08	7,000	6,964	0.48
FHLBA 3.25%	05-12-09	6,000	5,998	0.41
Natl Fuel Gas 6.303%	05-27-08	5,500	5,913	0.40
Vodafone Airtouch 7.75%	02-15-10	5,000	5,809	0.40
Pentair 7.85%	10-15-09	5,000	5,720	0.39
FNMA 5%	04-01-18	5,500	5,593	0.38

Equity Style
Style: Growth
Size: Large-Cap

Fixed-Income Style
Duration: —
Quality: —

Value Measures		Rel Category
Price/Earnings	20.79	1.25
Price/Book	3.08	1.26
Price/Sales	1.57	1.19
Price/Cash Flow	10.31	1.42
Dividend Yield %	0.96	0.61
Growth Measures	**%**	**Rel Category**
Long-Term Erngs	12.53	1.08
Book Value	11.17	1.95
Sales	7.74	1.49
Cash Flow	21.00	2.62
Historical Erngs	9.95	0.92

Avg Eff Duration[1]	—
Avg Eff Maturity	—
Avg Credit Quality	—
Avg Wtd Coupon	4.20%

[1]figure provided by fund

Market Cap %			
Giant 27.2		Small	2.9
Large 32.8		Micro	0.3
Mid 36.9		Avg $mil:	14,780

Sector Weightings	% of Stocks	Rel S&P 500	3 Year High	Low
Info	23.91	1.11		
Software	8.39	1.95	8	5
Hardware	6.21	0.61	8	2
Media	4.39	1.14	9	4
Telecom	4.92	1.56	11	4
Service	45.35	0.98		
Health	18.10	1.45	23	18
Consumer	9.36	1.03	16	9
Business	9.68	2.39	10	5
Financial	8.21	0.40	9	4
Mfg	30.75	0.96		
Goods	10.09	1.08	15	8
Ind Mtrls	6.56	0.52	7	1
Energy	9.90	1.38	10	4
Utilities	4.20	1.42	14	4

Composition

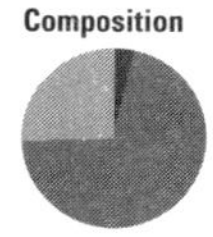

Cash	3.5
Stocks	70.8
Bonds	25.6
Other	0.1
Foreign (% of Stock)	14.6

Morningstar's Take by William Samuel Rocco 11-13-04

Pax World Balanced continues to take advantage of its flexibility.

This fund has a broader asset-allocation range than the category norm. Most moderate-allocation managers keep their equity positions close to 60% of assets--and that is the neutral weight here--but manager Chris Brown has the freedom to differ significantly from that level when he sees fit. In fact, he has kept the fund's equity weighting near 70% of assets for the past 12 months or so because he has been optimistic about the stock market and wary of rising interest rates.

Moreover, while most of his peers focus on domestic blue chips, Brown, who follows a growth-at-a-reasonable-price approach, often makes sizable investments in overseas and smaller-cap issues. Indeed, the Mexican firms America Movil and Cemex and the mid-caps Fisher Scientific International and Corn Products International are all top holdings here. Overall, the fund now has 14% of its equity portfolio in foreign names and 40% of its equity portfolio in smaller-cap issues.

Brown has put his freedom to good use since taking charge in April 1998. The fund thrived the rest of that year and in 1999, thanks to his decision to go heavy on stocks and to his growth bias. It held up fairly well in the early 2000s sell-offs, because he shifted toward bonds and smaller caps, which held up better than giant caps. And it has prospered this year, fueled by both its foreign picks and its smaller-cap names.

The fund can disappoint. It lagged in 2003, despite its big stock stake, as some health-care and other picks tanked. But, during Brown's tenure, it has suffered less volatility than the group norm. That's due to his commitment to issue diversification and conservative bonds as well as the general accuracy of his composition calls.

This fund is still one of the best choices in its group.

Address:	222 State Street Portsmouth NH 03801-3852 800-767-1729
Web Address:	
Inception:	11-30-71
Advisor:	Pax World Management Corp.
Subadvisor:	None
NTF Plans:	Fidelity Retail-NTF, Schwab OneSource

Minimum Purchase:	$250	Add: $50	IRA: $250
Min Auto Inv Plan:	$250	Add: $50	
Sales Fees:	0.27%B		
Management Fee:	0.75% mx./0.50% mn.		
Actual Fees:	Mgt:0.49%	Dist:0.27%	
Expense Projections:	3Yr:$297	5Yr:$515	10Yr:$1141
Income Distrib:	Semi-Annually		

Payden Core Bond

Ticker	Load	NAV	Yield	SEC Yield	Total Assets	Mstar Category
PYCBX	None	$10.61	3.7%	3.78%	$583 mil	Intermediate-Term Bond

Governance and Management

Fiduciary Grade: A

Portfolio Manager(s)

Lead manager Brian Matthews works with a roster of sector specialists, each of whom leads a team of analysts.

Strategy

This fund benchmarks itself against the Lehman Brothers Aggregate Bond Index, and it sticks to investment-grade sectors. Duration is typically kept within one-half year of the bogy's, with plus or minus one year being about as extreme as it gets. Diversification and issue selection are cornerstones of the fund's approach.

Historical Profile

Return Above Avg
Risk Above Avg
Rating ★★★★ Above Avg

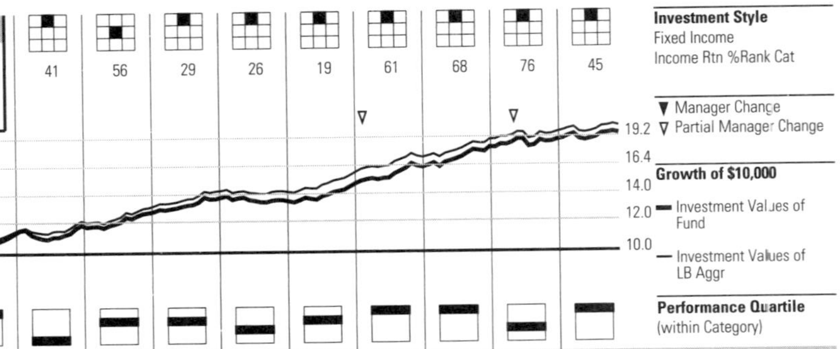

1993	1994	1995	1996	1997	1998	1999	2000	2001	2002	2003	12-04	History
10.00	9.06	10.23	9.76	9.97	10.07	9.25	9.54	9.91	10.59	10.60	10.61	NAV
0.00*	-4.70	19.71	1.75	9.00	8.07	-2.28	10.33	9.55	11.52	4.03	4.51	Total Return %
—	-1.78	1.24	-1.88	-0.65	-0.62	-1.46	-1.30	1.11	1.27	-0.07	0.17	+/-LB Aggr
—	-0.19	-1.72	-0.94	-0.43	-2.07	0.60	-2.11	0.73	-1.51	-1.94	-0.79	+/-LB 5-10YR
—	4.84	6.39	6.31	6.20	6.17	6.07	6.98	5.60	4.49	3.24	3.82	Income Return %
—	-9.54	13.32	-4.56	2.80	1.90	-8.35	3.35	3.95	7.03	0.79	0.69	Capital Return %
—	69	22	88	49	37	72	45	7	3	57	25	Total Rtn % Rank Cat
0.00	0.47	0.56	0.63	0.59	0.60	0.59	0.63	0.52	0.44	0.34	0.40	Income $
0.00	0.00	0.00	0.00	0.05	0.08	0.00	0.00	0.00	0.00	0.07	0.06	Capital Gains $
—	0.49	0.45	0.45	0.45	0.44	0.50	0.50	0.50	0.55	0.51	—	Expense Ratio %
—	5.25	6.20	6.41	6.03	6.12	6.06	6.59	5.63	4.50	3.21	—	Income Ratio %
—	—	252	197	317	156	67	161	787	582	303	—	Turnover Rate %
—	2	31	37	119	244	153	86	155	284	488	583	Net Assets $mil

Performance 12-31-04

	1st Qtr	2nd Qtr	3rd Qtr	4th Qtr	Total
2000	1.92	0.79	2.99	4.28	10.33
2001	2.79	0.26	5.60	0.66	9.55
2002	0.09	4.40	5.16	1.50	11.52
2003	1.33	2.96	-0.58	0.29	4.03
2004	3.15	-2.72	3.31	0.81	4.51

Trailing	Total Return%	+/- LB Aggr	+/- LB 5-10YR	%Rank Cat	Growth of $10,000
3 Mo	0.81	-0.14	-0.17	63	10,081
6 Mo	4.15	-0.03	-1.42	38	10,415
1 Yr	4.51	0.17	-0.79	25	10,451
3 Yr Avg	6.63	0.44	-1.42	14	12,124
5 Yr Avg	7.94	0.23	-1.13	11	14,653
10 Yr Avg	7.47	-0.25	-0.99	22	20,553
15 Yr Avg	—	—	—	—	—

Tax Analysis	Tax-Adj Rtn%	%Rank Cat	Tax-Cost Rat	%Rank Cat
3 Yr (estimated)	5.08	7	1.45	34
5 Yr (estimated)	5.99	5	1.81	37
10 Yr (estimated)	5.17	13	2.14	45

Potential Capital Gain Exposure: 1% of assets

Rating and Risk

Time Period	Load-Adj Return %	Morningstar Rtn vs Cat	Morningstar Risk vs Cat	Morningstar Risk-Adj Rating
1 Yr	4.51			
3 Yr	6.63	+Avg	+Avg	★★★★
5 Yr	7.94	+Avg	+Avg	★★★★
10 Yr	7.47	+Avg	+Avg	★★★★
Incept	6.30			

Other Measures	Standard Index LB Aggr	Best Fit Index LB Aggr
Alpha	-0.2	-0.2
Beta	1.13	1.13
R-Squared	98	98
Standard Deviation	5.20	
Mean	6.63	
Sharpe Ratio	1.02	

Morningstar's Take by Eric Jacobson 10-28-04

Even when Payden Core Bond is being aggressive, it's still cautious.

The fund set itself apart from the competition in 2004 by taking a stand on the economy and interest rates shared by few others. Although comanager Brian Matthews and his colleagues believe the Fed will continue to raise short-term rates, they don't think the economy is on the explosive track over which many others seem to fret. As such, they expect long-term yields to stay in a range, and have been willing to take on more interest-rate risk than many others. The fund thus fell behind when yields spiked in late-March and April 2004, but has otherwise thrived as rates have been steady or fallen. Largely as a result, the fund's 4% year-to-date return through Oct. 27, 2004, places in the intermediate-bond category's best quartile.

That relative success isn't really due to an overzealous bet. Rather, Matthews and team took the fund's duration (a measure of interest-rate sensitivity) only around one-tenth of a year longer than the Lehman Brothers Aggregate Bond Index. What's made a big difference, however, is that so many other managers were convinced rates had nowhere to go but up, and pulled in their fangs.

A look at the rest of the fund shows it to be cautious overall. For one thing, it stays out of high-yield bonds. And when it comes to the midquality issues the fund does hold, they're typically spread across a list of positions under 1%. And though the fund has an overweighting in mortgages, for example, Matthews notes they've been quick to shift into Treasuries when mortgages look expensive and risky.

No fund is risk-free, including this one. In fact, its volatility has historically been a tad high for the category. Overall, however, Matthews and company have kept a laser focus on risk, trying to prevent big or permanent losses. Add a very low expense ratio--set to drop to 0.44%--to that comparatively modest profile and a great record, and you've got a winner.

Address:	333 S Grand Ave Los Angeles CA 90071 800-572-9336
Web Address:	www.payden.com
Inception:	12-31-93*
Advisor:	Payden & Rygel
Subadvisor:	None
NTF Plans:	Schwab OneSource, Fidelity Instl-NTF

Minimum Purchase:	$5000	Add: $1000	IRA: $2000
Min Auto Inv Plan:	$5000	Add: $250	
Sales Fees:	No-load		
Management Fee:	0.28% mx./0.25% mn., 0.06%A		
Actual Fees:	Mgt:0.28%	Dist:	
Expense Projections:	3Yr:$161	5Yr:$280	10Yr:$629
Income Distrib:	Monthly		

Portfolio Analysis 09-30-04

Total Fixed-Income:109	Date of Maturity	Amount $000	Value $000	% Net Assets
FNMA 5%	10-01-18	49,980	50,761	7.26
FNMA 6.5%	10-01-33	47,076	49,371	7.06
US Treasury Note 2.5%	05-31-06	33,120	33,134	4.74
FHLMC 4.5%	09-01-19	22,790	22,637	3.25
US Treasury Note 3.125%	05-15-07	21,440	21,621	3.09
Federal Republic Of Germ	07-04-14	14,980	18,997	2.72
GNMA 5.5%	07-15-33	16,682	17,005	2.43
FHLMC 1.875%	02-15-06	12,827	12,712	1.82
Nomura Asset Secs CMO 6.	03-15-30	11,400	12,490	1.79
Ford Mtr 7.45%	07-16-31	11,070	10,854	1.55
Puma Global Tr S-1 FRN	08-09-35	10,705	10,705	1.53
Morgan Stanley Cap 2004-	05-25-34	10,161	10,161	1.45
FNMA 3%	08-15-07	10,030	9,987	1.43
First Natl Nt Tr 2003-1	08-15-08	9,650	9,664	1.38
Bk One Oneseries 2004-1a	10-15-11	8,600	8,525	1.22
US Treasury Bond 6.25%	08-15-23	7,280	8,501	1.22
Liberty Media 5.7%	05-15-13	8,390	8,295	1.19
General Mtrs 8.375%	07-15-33	7,170	7,613	1.09
US Treasury Note 3.375%	09-15-09	6,442	6,443	0.92
Cwabs FRN	05-25-33	6,400	6,400	0.92

Current Investment Style

Duration: Short Int Long; Quality: High Med Low

[1] figure provided by fund

Avg Eff Duration[1]	3.7 Yrs
Avg Eff Maturity	5.9 Yrs
Avg Credit Quality	AAA
Avg Wtd Coupon	4.53%
Avg Wtd Price	104.12% of par

Coupon Range	% of Bonds	Rel Cat
0% PIK	5.4	1.3
0% to 6%	68.0	1.1
6% to 8%	29.9	1.0
8% to 10%	2.0	0.4
More than 10%	0.0	0.0

1.00=Category Average

Credit Analysis		% bonds 09-30-04	
US Govt	57	BB	0
AAA	10	B	0
AA	3	Below B	0
A	9	NR/NA	0
BBB	21		

Sector Breakdown	% of assets
US Treasuries	11
TIPS	0
US Agency	5
Mortgage Pass-Throughs	23
Mortgage CMO	8
Mortgage ARM	0
US Corporate	26
Asset-Backed	12
Convertible	0
Municipal	0
Corporate Inflation-Protected	0
Foreign Corporate	1
Foreign Govt	3

Composition			
Cash	10.9	Bonds	89.1
Stocks	0.0	Other	0.0

Special Securities	
Restricted/Illiquid Secs	1
Exotic Mortgage-Backed	0
Emerging-Markets Secs	Trace
Options/Futures/Warrants	No

Payden Emerging Mkts Bond

Ticker	Load	NAV	Yield	SEC Yield	Total Assets	Mstar Category
PYEMX	None	$12.23	5.8%	6.08%	$34 mil	Emerging Markets Bond

Governance and Management

Fiduciary Grade: A

Portfolio Manager(s)

Country and corporate allocations are managed by Payden's global policy committee and Kristin Ceva, who leads the emerging-markets team and now has day-to-day responsibility for the portfolio.

Strategy

Conservativsm is the name of the game here: The fund invests primarily in higher-quality dollar-denominated sovereign debt with a small stake in corporate credits. Country and corporate allocations are determined by top-down analysis of sovereign risk and key macroeconomic factors. Management doesn't make major bets on individual countries.

Historical Profile
Return Below Avg
Risk Low
Rating ★★ Below Avg

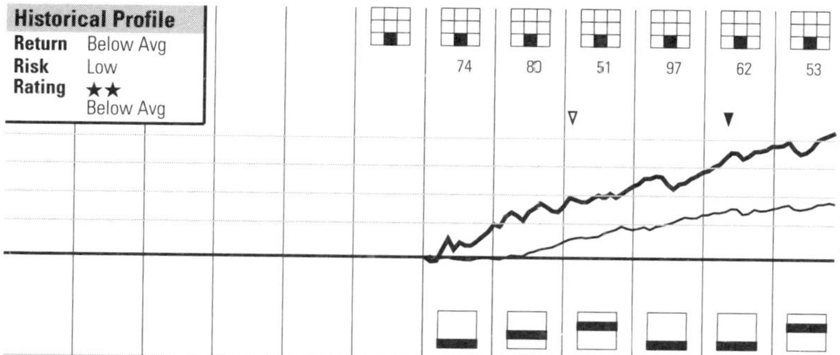

Investment Style
Fixed Income
Income Rtn %Rank Cat

▼ Manager Change
▽ Partial Manager Change

Growth of $10,000
— Investment Values of Fund
— Investment Values of LB Aggr

Performance Quartile (within Category)

1993	1994	1995	1996	1997	1998	1999	2000	2001	2002	2003	12-04	History
—	—	—	—	—	9.90	10.90	10.96	11.23	11.61	11.50	12.23	NAV
—	—	—	—	—	-1.00*	23.55	12.49	13.82	9.74	18.38	13.13	Total Return %
—	—	—	—	—	—	24.37	0.86	5.38	-0.51	14.28	8.79	+/-LB Aggr
—	—	—	—	—	—	6.74	-0.33	6.22	0.95	-5.94	1.87	+/-
—	—	—	—	—	—	10.59	10.25	11.10	6.19	7.26	6.36	Income Return %
—	—	—	—	—	—	12.96	2.24	2.72	3.55	11.12	6.77	Capital Return %
—	—	—	—	—	—	76	67	23	86	100	31	Total Rtn % Rank Cat
—	—	—	—	—	0.00	1.01	1.07	1.17	0.68	0.81	0.71	Income $
—	—	—	—	—	0.00	0.21	0.21	0.00	0.00	1.38	0.00	Capital Gains $
—	—	—	—	—	—	0.80	0.80	0.80	0.80	0.86	—	Expense Ratio %
—	—	—	—	—	—	9.91	9.56	9.83	7.39	6.55	—	Income Ratio %
—	—	—	—	—	—	225	146	191	134	187	—	Turnover Rate %
—	—	—	—	—	7	12	55	30	91	58	34	Net Assets $mil

Performance 12-31-04

	1st Qtr	2nd Qtr	3rd Qtr	4th Qtr	Total
2000	7.86	0.45	3.34	0.46	12.49
2001	2.83	4.46	-1.46	7.53	13.82
2002	5.25	-3.68	0.99	7.18	9.74
2003	5.35	7.33	1.06	3.60	18.38
2004	2.81	-6.52	9.99	7.02	13.13

Trailing	Total Return%	+/- LB Aggr	+/-	%Rank Cat	Growth of $10,000
3 Mo	7.02	6.07	3.77	15	10,702
6 Mo	17.71	13.53	5.87	19	11,771
1 Yr	13.13	8.79	1.87	31	11,313
3 Yr Avg	13.69	7.50	-0.90	93	14,695
5 Yr Avg	13.48	5.77	0.67	77	18,819
10 Yr Avg	—	—	—	—	—
15 Yr Avg	—	—	—	—	—

Tax Analysis	Tax-Adj Rtn%	%Rank Cat	Tax-Cost Rat	%Rank Cat
3 Yr (estimated)	9.96	93	3.28	70
5 Yr (estimated)	9.37	77	3.62	56
10 Yr (estimated)	—	—	—	—

Potential Capital Gain Exposure: 15% of assets

Rating and Risk

Time Period	Load-Adj Return %	Morningstar Rtn vs Cat	Morningstar Risk vs Cat	Morningstar Risk-Adj Rating
1 Yr	13.13			
3 Yr	13.69	Low	Low	★
5 Yr	13.48	-Avg	Low	★★
10 Yr	—	—	—	—
Incept	14.79			

Other Measures	Standard Index LB Aggr	Best Fit Index
Alpha	6.9	1.3
Beta	1.09	0.83
R-Squared	33	71
Standard Deviation	9.13	
Mean	13.69	
Sharpe Ratio	1.37	

Morningstar's Take by Arijit Dutta 12-14-04

Payden Emerging Markets Bond has chosen to strike a more flamboyant pose, but we're not sold on it.

This fund is currently being more emphatic with its bets, which is a bit of a departure from the caution it has tended to show in recent times. While it was late to buy into Brazilian debt (and therefore missed a big part of the rally in that country's debt in 2003), the fund is now solidly overweighted in that country. A similar emphasis on Venezuela, Mexico and Colombia has led to a pretty big tilt (about 60% of the portfolio) toward Latin America. The resultant portfolio is therefore among the most concentrated in the emerging-markets bond category. The fund has also boosted its corporate bond holdings to 20% of assets and has a 10% exposure to local currencies, both close to historical highs for the fund. While its 37% stake in bonds rated B or below is near the category norm, the number exceeds those of the category's more conservative subset--a club where the fund has typically belonged.

Management has dedicated this selective and bolder stance to general improvement in the status of this asset class. It believes that credit upgrades in countries like Brazil, Turkey and Russia should continue at least in the near term. Moreover, management is also banking on interest rates to remain within a benevolent range--neither threatening a major slowdown in these countries, nor sparking inflation worries.

While the fund could use some daring (its lukewarm approach has generated quite unattractive risk-adjusted relative returns), now may not be the best time. Emerging-markets bonds have had an extended runup already. Should there be a correction, the fund's concentration could prove a handicap.

Overall, this fund has to demonstrate it can thrive on a bolder approach. Meanwhile, investors have more appealing choices.

Address:	333 S Grand Ave Los Angeles CA 90071 800-572-9336
Web Address:	www.payden.com
Inception:	12-16-98*
Advisor:	Payden & Rygel
Subadvisor:	None
NTF Plans:	Schwab OneSource, Fidelity Instl-NTF

Minimum Purchase:	$5000	Add: $1000	IRA: $2000
Min Auto Inv Plan:	$5000	Add: $250	
Sales Fees:	No-load		
Management Fee:	0.45%		
Actual Fees:	Mgt:0.45%	Dist:	
Expense Projections:	3Yr:$288	5Yr:$500	10Yr:$1112
Income Distrib:	Monthly		

Portfolio Analysis 09-30-04

Total Fixed-Income:34	Date of Maturity	Amount $000	Value $000	% Net Assets
Russian Federation FRN	03-31-30	2,250	2,164	8.24
Brazil Federative Rep 11	08-17-40	1,610	1,805	6.87
Brazil Federative Rep 14	10-15-09	950	1,226	4.67
Brazil Federative Rep 10	05-15-27	1,050	1,113	4.24
Russian Federation 3%	05-14-06	1,100	1,075	4.09
Panama Rep 9.625%	02-08-11	900	1,033	3.93
Peru (Republic Of) 4.5%	03-07-17	1,175	1,033	3.33
United Mexican Sts Mtn B	08-15-31	900	1,024	3.90
United Mexican Sts Mtn B	09-24-22	800	902	3.43
Ukraine (Republic Of) 11	03-15-07	770	841	3.20
Bulgaria (Republic Of) 8	01-15-15	650	803	3.06
Venezuela Rep 9.25%	09-15-27	775	764	2.91
Uruguay Rep 7.5%	03-15-15	725	642	2.44
Russian Federation 11%	07-24-18	475	619	2.36
Colombia Rep 11.75%	02-25-20	500	611	2.33
Philippines Rep 8.375%	03-12-09	550	589	2.24
Philippines Rep 9.875%	01-15-19	570	587	2.24
Venezuela Rep 8.5%	10-08-14	600	587	2.23
Republic Of Turkey 11.87	01-15-30	400	552	2.10
Colombia Rep 10%	01-23-12	450	499	1.90

Current Investment Style

Duration: Short Int Long; Quality: High Med Low (style box: Int duration, Low quality)

[1] figure provided by fund

Avg Eff Duration[1]	5.4 Yrs
Avg Eff Maturity	14.6 Yrs
Avg Credit Quality	BB
Avg Wtd Coupon	8.98%
Avg Wtd Price	108.74% of par

Coupon Range	% of Bonds	Rel Cat
0% PIK	0.0	0.0
0% to 6%	17.2	0.7
6% to 8%	11.9	0.6
8% to 10%	34.8	1.3
More than 10%	36.1	1.3

1.00=Category Average

Credit Analysis		% bonds 09-30-04	
US Govt	0	BB	38
AAA	3	B	37
AA	0	Below B	0
A	0	NR/NA	0
BBB	23		

Sector Breakdown	% of assets
US Treasuries	—
TIPS	—
US Agency	—
Mortgage Pass-Throughs	—
Mortgage CMO	—
Mortgage ARM	—
US Corporate	—
Asset-Backed	—
Convertible	—
Municipal	—
Corporate Inflation-Protected	—
Foreign Corporate	—
Foreign Govt	—

Composition			
Cash	5.3	Bonds	94.7
Stocks	0.0	Other	0.0

Special Securities	
Restricted/Illiquid Secs	4
Exotic Mortgage-Backed	0
Emerging-Markets Secs	—
Options/Futures/Warrants	No

Payden Limited Maturity

Analyst Pick

Ticker	Load	NAV	Yield	SEC Yield	Total Assets	Mstar Category
PYLMX	None	$9.90	1.7%	2.10%	$359 mil	Ultrashort Bond

Governance and Management

Fiduciary Grade: A

Portfolio Manager(s)

Payden & Rygel uses a team approach to managing its funds, but this portfolio falls under the main responsibility of James Sarni.

Strategy

This fund works the quiet end of the ultrashort category and keeps its duration between about one third and three fourths of a year. It sticks mostly with high-quality securities and spreads its assets among several sectors, including mortgages, asset-backeds, corporates, and government bonds.

Historical Profile

Return Below Avg
Risk Below Avg
Rating ★★ Below Avg

Investment Style
Fixed Income
Income Rtn %Rank Cat

1996	1997	1998	1999	2000	2001	2002	2003	2004
89	83	36	14	53	42	61	68	69

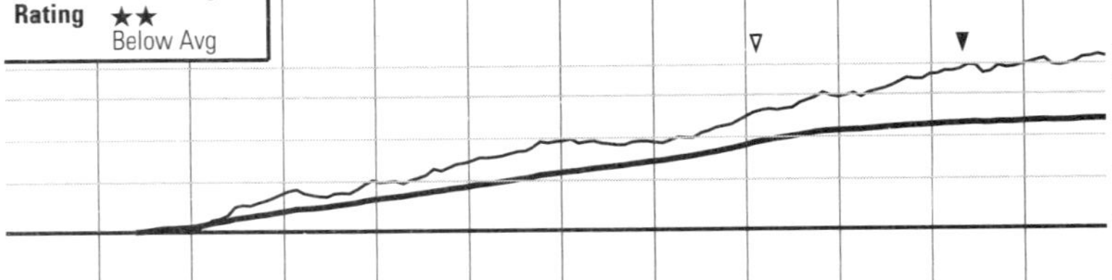

▼ Manager Change
▽ Partial Manager Change

20.5
18.0
15.0 **Growth of $10,000**
12.5 — Investment Values of Fund
10.0 — Investment Values of LB Aggr

Performance Quartile (within Category)

1993	1994	1995	1996	1997	1998	1999	2000	2001	2002	2003	12-04	**History**
—	9.96	10.07	10.05	10.05	10.06	9.95	10.02	10.06	10.02	9.96	9.90	NAV
—	2.40*	7.08	5.15	5.53	5.82	4.67	7.01	6.22	2.39	1.20	1.09	Total Return %
—	—	-11.39	1.52	-4.12	-2.87	5.49	-4.62	-2.22	-7.86	-2.90	-3.25	+/-LB Aggr
—	—	1.10	0.06	-0.04	0.45	-0.48	0.68	2.73	0.59	0.02	-0.71	+/-6 Month CD
—	0.00	5.96	5.35	5.53	5.72	5.79	6.27	5.26	2.79	1.80	1.70	Income Return %
—	—	1.12	-0.20	0.00	0.10	-1.12	0.74	0.96	-0.40	-0.60	-0.61	Capital Return %
—	—	68	88	89	15	38	29	29	67	73	52	Total Rtn % Rank Cat
—	0.28	0.58	0.53	0.54	0.56	0.57	0.61	0.52	0.28	0.18	0.17	Income $
—	0.00	0.00	0.00	0.00	0.00	0.00	0.00	0.05	0.00	0.00	0.00	Capital Gains $
—	0.41	0.33	0.30	0.30	0.29	0.38	0.40	0.40	0.40	0.40	—	Expense Ratio %
—	4.74	5.59	5.45	5.52	5.58	5.56	6.04	5.50	2.76	1.60	—	Income Ratio %
—	—	166	217	135	91	60	103	112	115	91	—	Turnover Rate %
—	16	16	53	138	115	90	167	187	205	298	359	Net Assets $mil

Performance 12-31-04

	1st Qtr	2nd Qtr	3rd Qtr	4th Qtr	Total
2000	1.35	1.51	1.87	2.10	7.01
2001	2.14	1.49	1.74	0.72	6.22
2002	0.39	0.84	0.68	0.46	2.39
2003	0.42	0.47	0.13	0.17	1.20
2004	0.47	-0.12	0.52	0.21	1.09

Trailing	Total Return%	+/- LB Aggr	+/- 6 Month CD	%Rank Cat	Growth of $10,000
3 Mo	0.21	-0.74	-0.42	77	10,021
6 Mo	0.73	-3.45	-0.40	69	10,073
1 Yr	1.09	-3.25	-0.71	52	10,109
3 Yr Avg	1.56	-4.63	-0.03	67	10,475
5 Yr Avg	3.55	-4.16	0.65	64	11,906
10 Yr Avg	4.59	-3.13	0.43	80	15,664
15 Yr Avg	—	—	—	—	—

Tax Analysis	Tax-Adj Rtn%	%Rank Cat	Tax-Cost Rat	%Rank Cat
3 Yr (estimated)	0.79	48	0.76	26
5 Yr (estimated)	2.14	50	1.36	53
10 Yr (estimated)	2.75	72	1.76	32

Potential Capital Gain Exposure: -1% of assets

Rating and Risk

Time Period	Load-Adj Return %	Morningstar Rtn vs Cat	Morningstar Risk vs Cat	Morningstar Risk-Adj Rating
1 Yr	1.09			
3 Yr	1.56	Avg	-Avg	★★★
5 Yr	3.55	Avg	Low	★★★
10 Yr	4.59	-Avg	-Avg	★★
Incept	4.53			

Other Measures	Standard Index LB Aggr	Best Fit Index LB 1-5 YR
Alpha	-0.2	-0.2
Beta	0.08	0.14
R-Squared	71	75
Standard Deviation	0.44	
Mean	1.56	
Sharpe Ratio	0.40	

Morningstar's Take by Eric Jacobson 10-31-04

Splitting the hairs of Payden Limited Maturity may make sense to some investors in search of an ultrashort offering.

In general, Morningstar analysts are skeptical about comparing funds against tiny peer groups. It's not uncommon for managers to complain that we've unfairly maligned them by putting them in a peer group with funds that don't hold exactly the same kinds of portfolios they do. Such arguments sometimes just split hairs over small differences, and they're usually made in an effort to divert attention from an otherwise poor record. What's more, we don't often buy such pitches, because we know that most investors aren't looking to hold, for example, multiple funds, each dedicated to a narrow, similar slice of the bond market.

In the case of this fund, however, we do see some room for such differentiation. That's not so much because we think it's necessary for investors to slice and dice among shades of ultrashort funds, but rather because we know that there are many who want to stretch beyond money-market territory, but who are also adamant about keeping a nearly lock-tight grip on risk.

If those are the criteria, this fund has perhaps 10 or fewer legitimate peers against which to compare. Its duration, a measure of rate sensitivity, is typically among the shortest of any category peer. And though the fund holds corporates, asset-backeds and mortgages, it keeps a tighter rein on credit and bond-structure risk than the majority of those rivals, as well. As such, it's also among the category's least volatile offerings.

What makes such a profile potentially worthwhile is that even though the fund's returns have been modest compared with the overall category, they've been competitive with the handful of similar funds, and have handily outpaced the average money market fund over long time periods. A low expense ratio has no doubt been a big help too.

Address:	333 S Grand Ave Los Angeles CA 90071 800-572-9336
Web Address:	www.payden.com
Inception:	04-29-94 *
Advisor:	Payden & Rygel
Subadvisor:	None
NTF Plans:	Schwab OneSource, Fidelity Instl-NTF

Minimum Purchase:	$5000	Add: $1000	IRA: $2000
Min Auto Inv Plan:	$2500	Add: $250	
Sales Fees:	No-load		
Management Fee:	0.28% mx./0.25% mn., 0.06%A		
Actual Fees:	Mgt:0.28%	Dist:	
Expense Projections:	3Yr:$144	5Yr:$257	10Yr:$587
Income Distrib:	Monthly		

Portfolio Analysis 09-30-04

Total Fixed-Income:97	Date of Maturity	Amount $000	Value $000	% Net Assets
Regions Auto Rec Tr 2003	01-15-08	9,000	8,972	2.60
Citibank Cr Cd Mstr Tr 1	11-15-06	8,750	8,803	2.55
Ford Credit Auto Tr 2002	09-15-06	8,000	8,085	2.34
Discover Card Mstr Tr I	07-15-07	7,000	7,099	2.06
Cap Auto Recv Abn 2004-1	05-15-06	7,000	6,972	2.02
Morgan Stanley Cap 2004-	08-25-34	6,913	6,915	2.00
New Century He Tr 2004-3	11-25-34	6,000	6,000	1.74
Structured Asset Adj 200	09-25-34	5,859	5,910	1.71
Whole Auto Ln Tr 2002-1	08-15-06	5,636	5,646	1.63
Bmw Veh Own Tr 2003-A 1.	02-25-07	5,624	5,612	1.63
Granite Mtg Plc 2004-3 F	09-20-44	5,500	5,500	1.59
Asset Backed Fdg 2004-Op	04-25-34	5,230	5,233	1.52
Chase Man Auto Owner Tr	02-15-08	5,052	5,099	1.48
Impac Cmb Tr 2004-7 CMO	11-25-34	4,802	4,804	1.39
FHLMC CMO 5%	03-15-13	4,678	4,752	1.38
Bear Stearns Arm Tr 2004	06-25-34	4,689	4,695	1.36
Cap One Auto Tr 2001-A 5	05-15-08	4,538	4,616	1.34
Morgan Stanley Cap 2004-	05-25-34	4,434	4,434	1.28
Nissan Auto Recv Gr Tr 2	07-15-06	4,450	4,432	1.28
First Franklin Mtg 2004-	11-25-34	4,230	4,230	1.22

Current Investment Style

Duration: Short Int Long
Quality: High Med Low

[1] figure provided by fund

Avg Eff Duration[1]	0.5 Yrs
Avg Eff Maturity	1.5 Yrs
Avg Credit Quality	AA
Avg Wtd Coupon	2.54%
Avg Wtd Price	100.22% of par

Coupon Range	% of Bonds	Rel Cat
0% PIK	20.0	1.0
0% to 6%	88.8	1.1
6% to 8%	11.2	0.8
8% to 10%	0.0	0.0
More than 10%	0.0	0.0

1.00=Category Average

Credit Analysis		% bonds 09-30-04	
US Govt	4	BB	0
AAA	58	B	0
AA	11	Below B	0
A	13	NR/NA	0
BBB	14		

Sector Breakdown	% of assets
US Treasuries	0
TIPS	0
US Agency	0
Mortgage Pass-Throughs	2
Mortgage CMO	19
Mortgage ARM	0
US Corporate	22
Asset-Backed	32
Convertible	0
Municipal	7
Corporate Inflation-Protected	0
Foreign Corporate	1
Foreign Govt	0

Composition			
Cash	17.5	Bonds	82.5
Stocks	0.0	Other	0.0

Special Securities	
Restricted/Illiquid Secs	3
Exotic Mortgage-Backed	0
Emerging-Markets Secs	0
Options/Futures/Warrants	No

PBHG Mid Cap PBHG

Ticker	Load	NAV	Yield	Total Assets	Mstar Category
PBMCX	None	$18.54	0.0%	$437 mil	Mid-Cap Blend

Governance and Management

Fiduciary Grade: F

Portfolio Manager(s)

Jerome Heppelmann took the reins of this fund, PBHG Small Cap, PBHG Focused, and the value portion of PBHG Strategic Small Company in June 1999. Prior to June 1999, Heppelmann was an analyst at Pilgrim Baxter. James Bell III, formerly an analyst, was named comanager in May 2004.

Strategy

Like PBHG's growth funds, this fund emphasizes stocks that have upside earnings-surprise potential and improving profits, as well as solid fundamentals. Manager Jerome Heppelmann is not willing to pay up for growth, however, so he looks for names that aren't too expensive relative to industry peers. Although Heppelmann will load up on an area where he finds good stocks, the fund has exposure to most industries and generally keeps sector weights within 10 percentage points of the S&P Midcap 400 Index's.

Historical Profile

Return Above Avg
Risk Average
Rating ★★★★ Above Avg

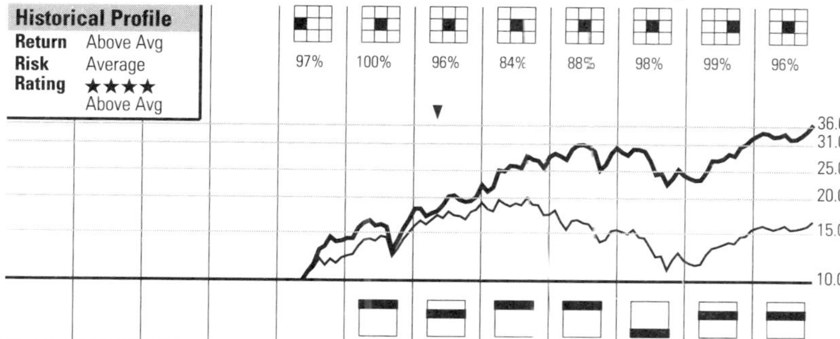

1993	1994	1995	1996	1997	1998	1999	2000	2001	2002	2003	12-04	History
—	—	—	—	13.44	15.64	12.26	14.77	15.92	12.77	17.18	18.54	NAV
—	—	—	—	41.48*	27.84	21.72	26.17	7.79	-19.79	34.53	18.01	Total Return %
—	—	—	—	—	-0.73	0.68	35.27	19.67	2.30	5.86	7.14	+/-S&P 500
—	—	—	—	—	8.73	7.00	8.68	8.39	-5.26	-1.06	1.54	+/-S&P Mid 400
—	—	—	—	0.00	0.00	0.01	0.25	0.00	0.00	0.00	0.00	Income Return %
—	—	—	—	—	27.84	21.71	25.92	7.79	-19.79	34.53	18.01	Capital Return %
—	—	—	—	—	3	44	9	23	77	48	26	Total Rtn % Rank Cat
—	—	—	—	0.00	0.00	0.00	0.03	0.00	0.00	0.00	0.00	Income $
—	—	—	—	0.69	1.13	6.28	0.64	0.00	0.00	0.00	1.66	Capital Gains $
—	—	—	—	—	1.47	1.33	1.44	1.35	1.31	1.40	1.37	Expense Ratio %
—	—	—	—	—	-0.17	0.01	-0.15	0.40	-0.15	-0.33	-0.48	Income Ratio %
—	—	—	—	—	—	733	743	248	237	195	144	Turnover Rate %
—	—	—	—	40	113	35	158	465	310	454	430	Net Assets $mil

Performance 12-31-04

	1st Qtr	2nd Qtr	3rd Qtr	4th Qtr	Total
2000	12.72	3.55	5.66	2.31	26.17
2001	-2.23	12.88	-18.53	19.88	7.79
2002	-1.13	-8.83	-17.56	7.95	-19.79
2003	-3.76	17.01	3.89	14.99	34.53
2004	4.37	-0.33	-1.46	15.12	18.01

Trailing	Total Return%	+/- S&P 500	+/- S&P Mid 400	%Rank Cat	Growth of $10,000
3 Mo	15.12	5.89	2.97	8	11,512
6 Mo	13.45	6.26	3.66	10	11,345
1 Yr	18.01	7.14	1.54	26	11,801
3 Yr Avg	8.39	4.81	-2.12	65	12,734
5 Yr Avg	11.61	13.91	2.08	15	17,319
10 Yr Avg	—	—	—	—	—
15 Yr Avg	—	—	—	—	—

Tax Analysis	Tax-Adj Rtn%	%Rank Cat	Tax-Cost Rat	%Rank Cat
3 Yr (estimated)	7.75	59	0.59	65
5 Yr (estimated)	10.82	12	0.71	29
10 Yr (estimated)	—	—	—	—

Potential Capital Gain Exposure: 17% of assets

Rating and Risk

Time Period	Load-Adj Return %	Morningstar Rtn vs Cat	Morningstar Risk vs Cat	Morningstar Risk-Adj Rating
1 Yr	18.01			
3 Yr	8.39	Avg	Avg	★★★
5 Yr	11.61	+Avg	Avg	★★★★
10 Yr	—	—	—	—
Incept	19.06			

Other Measures	Standard Index S&P 500	Best Fit Index Mstar Mid Core
Alpha	4.9	-4.2
Beta	0.97	1.01
R-Squared	84	93

Standard Deviation	17.21
Mean	8.39
Sharpe Ratio	0.41

Portfolio Analysis 09-30-04

Share change since 06-04 Total Stocks:90	Sector	PE	YTD Ret%	% Assets
⊖ Intuit	Software	25.7	-16.74	2.80
⊕ Veritas Software	Software	23.7	-22.88	2.16
⊕ Lincare Holdings	Health	16.1	41.79	1.86
⊕ Friedman Billings Ramsey	Financial	9.0	-9.64	1.72
El Paso	Energy	—	29.51	1.69
⊕ Federated Investors B	Financial	17.0	5.00	1.67
☼ Cincinnati Financial	Financial	14.5	14.24	1.63
☼ Tribune	Media	20.6	-17.47	1.62
⊖ Host Marriott	Financial	—	40.88	1.61
☼ Sysco	Consumer	26.0	3.69	1.60
⊖ Westwood One	Media	25.8	-21.28	1.53
⊖ BMC Software	Software	—	-0.27	1.52
☼ Fiserv	Business	21.3	1.64	1.51
⊖ Dun & Bradstreet	Business	19.8	17.63	1.50
☼ Citrix Systems	Software	34.1	15.60	1.45
⊖ Satyam Computer Services	Software	—	—	1.42
⊖ XL Capital	Financial	20.1	2.80	1.41
⊖ American Financial Realt	Financial	—	1.39	1.39
⊕ CB Richard Ellis Group	Financial	—	—	1.39
⊖ Citadel Broadcasting	Media	—	-27.67	1.39

Current Investment Style

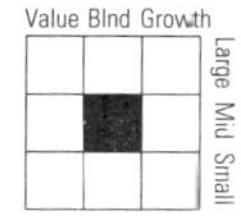

Market Cap	%
Giant	0.0
Large	23.7
Mid	69.9
Small	6.4
Micro	0.0
Avg $mil: 4,494	

Value Measures		Rel Category
Price/Earnings	17.50	1.03
Price/Book	1.35	0.85
Price/Sales	1.14	1.08
Price/Cash Flow	5.36	0.95
Dividend Yield %	1.30	1.30

Growth Measures	%	Rel Category
Long-Term Erngs	12.95	1.03
Book Value	8.56	1.21
Sales	8.33	1.47
Cash Flow	1.52	0.26
Historical Erngs	11.63	1.03

Profitability	%	Rel Category
Return on Equity	11.67	0.85
Return on Assets	6.86	1.05
Net Margin	9.96	1.10

Sector Weightings	% of Stocks	Rel S&P 500	3 Year High	3 Year Low
Info	28.14	1.31		
Software	11.87	2.76	13	2
Hardware	5.72	0.56	10	2
Media	10.54	2.74	12	6
Telecom	0.01	0.00	1	0
Service	53.45	1.15		
Health	7.62	0.61	17	5
Consumer	9.92	1.09	17	5
Business	9.08	2.24	15	6
Financial	26.83	1.29	27	18
Mfg	18.41	0.57		
Goods	0.99	0.11	9	1
Ind Mtrls	4.19	0.33	7	3
Energy	11.23	1.57	14	5
Utilities	2.00	0.68	8	1

Composition

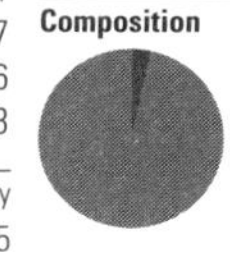

Cash	3.6
Stocks	96.4
Bonds	0.0
Other	0.0
Foreign (% of Stock)	2.8

Morningstar's Take by Christopher Davis 10-31-04

Thanks to reforms at its advisor, investors can again appreciate PBHG Mid Cap's virtues.

In November 2003, we recommended that investors consider selling this and other PBHG funds. Advisor Pilgrim Baxter & Associates and its founders, Gary Pilgrim and Harold Baxter, had been charged with fraud and breach of fiduciary duty for engaging in and facilitating frequent trades of the PBHG mutual funds that clearly violated the funds' prospectuses. Since then, Pilgrim and Baxter have resigned and the firm has settled with regulators. In addition, PBHG has also implemented measures to prevent trading abuses from taking place again, including adding redemption fees, instituting a portfolio-holdings disclosure policy, and curbing fund managers' abilities to trade in PBHG funds. Thus, we think it's safe again to evaluate each PBHG fund on its merits.

We regard this offering as one of the few PBHG funds worth considering. Manager Jerome Heppelmann has delivered commendable results since taking charge of the fund in June 1999. Indeed, the fund has returned 11% annually since his start, 3 percentage points better than its typical mid-blend rival.

Admittedly, the fund has been a disappointment in recent years. A raft of cable holdings torpedoed returns in 2002, and the fund delivered middling relative results in 2003. It appears to be back in the saddle this year, though, thanks to a passel of strong-performing energy holdings. More importantly, the strategy underlying Heppelmann's strong record remains intact. He continues to seek companies with strong long-term growth rates and near-term momentum while avoiding stocks with excessive valuations. Further, the fund is still relatively small, enabling Heppelmann to freely roam the market-cap spectrum, a driver of past success. Tax efficiency here hasn't been great due to high turnover, so investors in taxable accounts may want to steer clear. Others, however, will find this offering holds appeal.

Address:	PBHG Funds Kansas City, MO 64121-9534 800-433-0051
Web Address:	www.pbhgfunds.com
Inception:	04-30-97 *
Advisor:	Liberty Ridge Capital, Inc.
Subadvisor:	None
NTF Plans:	Fidelity Retail-NTF, Schwab OneSource

Minimum Purchase:	$2500	Add: $0	IRA: $2000
Min Auto Inv Plan:	$500	Add: $25	
Sales Fees:	No-load		
Management Fee:	0.85%, 0.15%A		
Actual Fees:	Mgt:0.85%	Dist:	
Expense Projections:	3Yr:$421	5Yr:$729	10Yr:$1601
Income Distrib:	Annually		

PIMCO CommRealRetStrA

Analyst Pick

Ticker	Load	NAV	Yield	Total Assets	Mstar Category
PCRAX	5.50%	$14.78	5.3%	$6,306 mil	Specialty-Natural Res

Governance and Management

Fiduciary Grade: B

Portfolio Manager(s)

Manager John Brynjolfsson has managed this fund since inception. He has also managed PIMCO Real Return since 1997. That fund mostly invests in TIPS. He is a member of the PIMCO management team that won Morningstar's Fixed-Income Manager of the Year honors in 1998 and 2000.

Strategy

In contrast to most natural-resources funds that invest in the stocks of companies that produce commodities, this fund invests in derivative instruments that seek to replicate the performance of the Dow Jones-AIG Commodity Index. Because the fund can gain full exposure to the index with only a small portion of assets, the remaining assets are invested in TIPS, which serve as collateral for the derivatives. Through the investment in TIPS, the managers hope to recoup the expenses of running the fund and even hope to best the bogy.

Historical Profile

Return
Risk
Rating Not Rated

Investment Style: Equity Stock % — 0% 0% 0%

▼ Manager Change
▽ Partial Manager Change

Growth of $10,000
— Investment Values of Fund
— Investment Values of S&P 500

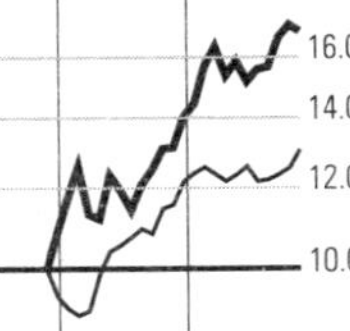

Performance Quartile (within Category)

	1993	1994	1995	1996	1997	1998	1999	2000	2001	2002	2003	12-04	History
	—	—	—	—	—	—	—	—	—	11.56	13.62	14.78	NAV
	—	—	—	—	—	—	—	—	—	8.33*	29.09	15.78	Total Return %
	—	—	—	—	—	—	—	—	—	—	0.42	4.91	+/-S&P 500
	—	—	—	—	—	—	—	—	—	—	-4.92	-8.79	+/-GS NATR RES
	—	—	—	—	—	—	—	—	—	0.00	10.13	5.99	Income Return %
	—	—	—	—	—	—	—	—	—	—	18.96	9.79	Capital Return %
	—	—	—	—	—	—	—	—	—	—	53	94	Total Rtn % Rank Cat
	—	—	—	—	—	—	—	—	—	0.77	1.16	0.80	Income $
	—	—	—	—	—	—	—	—	—	0.00	0.14	0.18	Capital Gains $
	—	—	—	—	—	—	—	—	—	—	1.24	1.24	Expense Ratio %
	—	—	—	—	—	—	—	—	—	—	-55.21	39.56	Income Ratio %
	—	—	—	—	—	—	—	—	—	—	492	290	Turnover Rate %
	—	—	—	—	—	—	—	—	—	—	286	1,412	Net Assets $mil

Performance 12-31-04

	1st Qtr	2nd Qtr	3rd Qtr	4th Qtr	Total
2000	—	—	—	—	—
2001	—	—	—	—	—
2002	—	—	—	—	8.33 *
2003	3.98	5.44	4.70	12.45	29.09
2004	16.61	-7.43	10.17	-2.64	15.78

Trailing	Total Return%	+/- S&P 500	+/- GS NATR RES	%Rank Cat	Growth of $10,000
3 Mo	-2.64	-11.87	-7.46	88	9,736
6 Mo	7.26	0.07	-7.93	87	10,726
1 Yr	15.78	4.91	-8.79	94	11,578
3 Yr Avg	—	—	—	—	—
5 Yr Avg	—	—	—	—	—
10 Yr Avg	—	—	—	—	—
15 Yr Avg	—	—	—	—	—

Tax Analysis	Tax-Adj Rtn%	%Rank Cat	Tax-Cost Rat	%Rank Cat
3 Yr (estimated)	—	—	—	—
5 Yr (estimated)	—	—	—	—
10 Yr (estimated)	—	—	—	—

Potential Capital Gain Exposure: -3% of assets

Rating and Risk

Time Period	Load-Adj Return %	Morningstar Rtn vs Cat	Morningstar Risk vs Cat	Morningstar Risk-Adj Rating
1 Yr	9.42			
3 Yr	—	—	—	—
5 Yr	—	—	—	—
10 Yr	—	—	—	—
Incept	22.58			

Other Measures	Standard Index S&P 500	Best Fit Index
Alpha	—	—
Beta	—	—
R-Squared	—	—
Standard Deviation	—	
Mean	—	
Sharpe Ratio	—	

Portfolio Analysis 09-30-04

Share change since 06-04 Total Stocks:0	Sector	PE	YTD Ret%	% Assets
⊕ US Treasury Note 3%	—	—	—	16.63
⊕ US Treasury Note 2%	—	—	—	16.56
⊖ US Treasury Note 3.625%	—	—	—	13.45
⊕ US Treasury Bond 3.875%	—	—	—	8.63
⊖ US Treasury Note 3.375%	—	—	—	7.66
⊕ US Treasury Note 3.5%	—	—	—	5.99
⊕ US Treasury Note 3.875%	—	—	—	5.98
⊕ US Treasury Bond 3.625%	—	—	—	4.67
⊕ US Treasury Note 1.875%	—	—	—	3.75
⊕ US Treasury Note 4.25%	—	—	—	3.58
☼ EuroDollar (Fut)	—	—	—	3.35
⊕ US Treasury Note (Fut)	—	—	—	3.03
☼ US Treasury Bond 2.375%	—	—	—	2.42
⊕ US Treasury Bond 3.375%	—	—	—	0.51
⊕ US Treasury Note 3.375%	—	—	—	0.36
⊕ Brazil (Federative Repub	—	—	—	0.34
⊕ Canada Govt 3%	—	—	—	0.28
⊕ France (Republic Of) 3.1	—	—	—	0.22
☼ Petroleos Mexicanos 9.25	—	—	—	0.15
⊖ FHLMC CMO 7.5%	—	—	—	0.14

Current Investment Style

Value Blnd Growth — Large Mid Small

Market Cap	%
Giant	—
Large	—
Mid	—
Small	—
Micro	—
Avg $mil:	—

Value Measures		Rel Category
Price/Earnings	—	—
Price/Book	—	—
Price/Sales	—	—
Price/Cash Flow	—	—
Dividend Yield %	—	—

Growth Measures	%	Rel Category
Long-Term Erngs	—	—
Book Value	—	—
Sales	—	—
Cash Flow	—	—
Historical Erngs	—	—

Profitability	%	Rel Category
Return on Equity	—	—
Return on Assets	—	—
Net Margin	—	—

Industry Weightings	% of Stocks	Rel Cat
Oil & Gas	—	—
Oil/Gas Products	—	—
Oil & Gas Srv	—	—
Pipelines	—	—
Utilities	—	—
Hard Commd	—	—
Soft Commd	—	—
Misc. Indstrl	—	—
Other	—	—

Composition

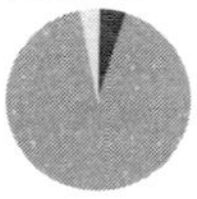

Cash	4.9
Stocks	0.0
Bonds	92.0
Other	3.2
Foreign (% of Stock)	0.0

Morningstar's Take by Karen Papalois 12-22-04

Don't fret over PIMCO Commodity Real Return's relative weakness this year.

This offering's 15% year-to-date return through Dec. 27, 2004, lands in the bottom 10% of the natural-resources category. But we don't expect it to behave like its peers because it follows a unique strategy. Most offerings buy shares of companies involved in the production of raw goods, but this fund has exposure to the actual price of commodities by using derivatives to mimic the Dow Jones-AIG Commodity Index.

Treasury Inflation Protected Securities (TIPS) affect the fund's performance too. Because only a fraction of assets are needed to get 100% exposure to the index, the fund parks the rest in a portfolio of TIPS. The TIPS introduce an element of interest-rate risk into the picture because they generally lose value when interest rates rise.

Over time, TIPS should add to the fund's returns and act as another hedge against inflation. Still, it's possible that commodity prices and TIPS may gain or lose value concurrently, thereby increasing the fund's short-term volatility. For example, a downturn in the TIPS market caused the fund to lose more than the index in April 2004 (the fund lost 6.2% compared with the index's loss of 1.8%). Notably, this strategy isn't tax-efficient, either, because the TIPS and derivatives generate taxable income and capital gains distributions.

Commodities are volatile, but the index's diversification helps mitigate commodity-specific dangers. It caps exposure to a single type of commodity at 33% of assets, so the fund's energy stake is limited. That leaves room for other raw goods such as metals, livestock, and grains.

Diversification will help, but the fund could still get hit hard. The unpredictable nature of commodity prices means that the fund could lose ground as quickly as it has gained. Investors with long time horizons will be well served by buying slowly, preferably in a tax-sheltered account.

Address:	PIMCO Funds Stamford, CT 06902 800-426-0107
Web Address:	www.pimcofunds.com
Inception:	11-29-02*
Advisor:	PA Fund Management LLC
Subadvisor:	First Quadrant

Minimum Purchase:	$5000	Add: $100	IRA: $2500
Min Auto Inv Plan:	$2500	Add: $100	
Sales Fees:	5.50%L, 0.25%S, 2.00%R		
Management Fee:	0.49%, 0.50%A		
Actual Fees:	Mgt:0.49%	Dist:0.25%	
Expense Projections:	3Yr:$922	5Yr:$1194	10Yr:$1967
Income Distrib:	Quarterly		

NTF Plans: Federated Tr NTF, TD Waterhouse Ins NT

PIMCO Emerg Mkts Bd A

Analyst Pick

Ticker	Load	NAV	Yield	SEC Yield	Total Assets	Mstar Category
PAEMX	3.75%	$10.86	3.9%	3.08%	$1,674 mil	Emerging Markets Bond

Governance and Management

Fiduciary Grade: B

Portfolio Manager(s)

After a 15-year stint at the International Monetary Fund, Mohamed El-Erian headed to the investment-management business, taking over this offering in 1999. He has tremendous resources at his disposal, including two comanagers in Munich, one in Singapore, and two in PIMCO's California office. He also gets macroeconomic direction for the fund's investment-grade credits from PIMCO analysts.

Strategy

Unlike some of its large peers, this fund isn't afraid to avoid countries completely whose debt comprises a good deal of the market. Management sometimes overweights countries it favors and attempts to hedge such moves by shorting the bonds of neighboring countries that it believes to be relatively weak. In addition to shorting bonds (effectively betting that they will decline in value), the fund also utilizes derivatives, including credit-default swaps.

Historical Profile

Return: Average
Risk: Above Avg
Rating: ★★★ Neutral

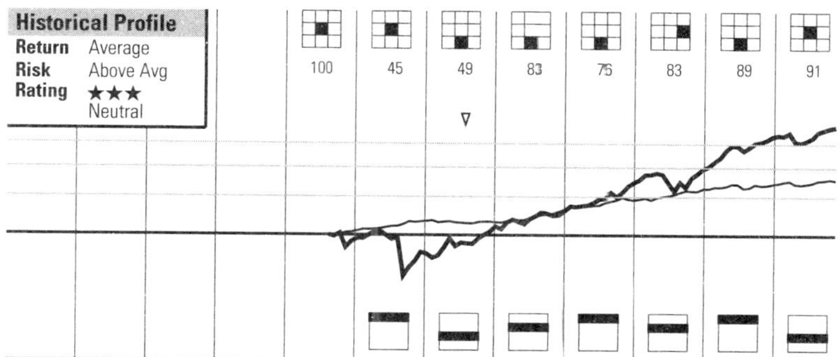

Investment Style: Fixed Income — Income Rtn %Rank Cat: 100 45 49 83 75 83 89 91

▼ Manager Change
▽ Partial Manager Change

Growth of $10,000
— Investment Values of Fund
— Investment Values of LB Aggr

Performance Quartile (within Category)

1993	1994	1995	1996	1997	1998	1999	2000	2001	2002	2003	12-04	History
—	—	—	—	9.29	7.36	8.31	8.21	9.10	9.25	10.51	10.86	NAV
—	—	—	—	-2.97*	-12.10	26.10	14.14	27.63	12.37	32.02	11.79	Total Return %
—	—	—	—	—	-20.79	26.92	2.51	19.19	2.12	27.92	7.45	+/-LB Aggr
—	—	—	—	—	-6.80	9.29	1.32	20.03	3.58	7.70	0.53	+/-
—	—	—	—	0.00	8.94	12.11	10.24	9.83	7.54	6.05	4.28	Income Return %
—	—	—	—	—	-21.04	13.99	3.90	17.80	4.83	25.97	7.51	Capital Return %
—	—	—	—	—	11	60	31	3	45	24	61	Total Rtn % Rank Cat
—	—	—	—	0.26	0.80	0.85	0.81	0.77	0.66	0.54	0.44	Income $
—	—	—	—	0.15	0.05	0.00	0.40	0.50	0.25	1.08	0.40	Capital Gains $
—	—	—	—	—	1.26	1.25	1.29	1.26	1.25	1.27	1.25	Expense Ratio %
—	—	—	—	—	6.93	10.26	10.59	9.08	7.47	6.99	4.44	Income Ratio %
—	—	—	—	—	—	315	328	902	617	388	461	Turnover Rate %
—	—	—	—	—	—	—	—	5	42	215	239	Net Assets $mil

Performance 12-31-04

	1st Qtr	2nd Qtr	3rd Qtr	4th Qtr	Total
2000	6.10	0.64	4.52	2.27	14.14
2001	4.56	5.90	2.01	12.99	27.63
2002	7.24	-6.98	-3.65	16.91	12.37
2003	10.36	10.33	2.59	5.68	32.02
2004	3.12	-6.32	9.50	5.67	11.78

Trailing	Total Return%	+/- LB Aggr	+/-	%Rank Cat	Growth of $10,000
3 Mo	5.67	4.72	2.42	81	10,567
6 Mo	15.71	11.53	3.87	59	11,571
1 Yr	11.79	7.45	0.53	61	11,179
3 Yr Avg	18.37	12.18	3.78	40	16,585
5 Yr Avg	19.29	11.58	6.48	13	24,156
10 Yr Avg	—	—	—	—	—
15 Yr Avg	—	—	—	—	—

Tax Analysis	Tax-Adj Rtn%	%Rank Cat	Tax-Cost Rat	%Rank Cat
3 Yr (estimated)	12.55	78	3.70	82
5 Yr (estimated)	13.19	23	4.38	85
10 Yr (estimated)	—	—	—	—

Potential Capital Gain Exposure: 5% of assets

Rating and Risk

Time Period	Load-Adj Return %	Morningstar Rtn vs Cat	Morningstar Risk vs Cat	Morningstar Risk-Adj Rating
1 Yr	7.59			
3 Yr	16.87	Avg	+Avg	★★
5 Yr	18.38	+Avg	+Avg	★★★★
10 Yr	—	—	—	—
Incept	13.15			

Other Measures	Standard Index LB Aggr	Best Fit Index
Alpha	11.7	-2.4
Beta	1.13	1.49
R-Squared	14	91

Standard Deviation	15.04
Mean	18.37
Sharpe Ratio	1.14

Morningstar's Take by Arijit Dutta 12-13-04

PIMCO Emerging Markets Bond is bold, and not lacking in wisdom either.

Manager Mohamed El-Erian has made some inspired calls against the grain of prevailing market sentiment since he took charge in mid-1999. In late 2002, he overweighted Brazil, a market then distressed by deep political concerns. The move was based on his confidence in the fundamental soundness of Brazil's economy and turned out to be very profitable. The fund also staged a timely and complete exodus from Argentina prior to that country's debt default in 2001--a daring feat considering the country's bonds comprised 22% of the JP Morgan EMBI Plus index at the time. PIMCO has formidable research resources and has cultivated information networks around the globe, all of which inform El-Erian's judgment while making such calls.

The fund's self-assured style is also evident in some of its current positions. El-Erian has continued to avoid Turkey (the country's bonds take up 6.6% of the index), as he is not convinced by that debt-laden economy's case. He has also avoided corporate bonds and exposure to local currencies, which have been favored by many in 2004. These decisions have hurt relative performance--the fund lags more than 70% of its peers in the emerging-markets bond category so far this year.

The fund's great long-term record overwhelms this hiccup, however. Under El-Erian, the fund has returned 20.7% annually on average, beating all but one fund in the category. He operates mainly by favoring countries that he believes show sustainable improvement in macroeconomic fundamentals, and he tries to avoid getting swayed by short-term setbacks.

So should investors, though caution is indeed warranted due to the extended rally in this asset class. The category looks set to have its sixth straight year of double-digit returns. Shareholders should stay on guard, lest there be a correction, but will be hard-pressed to find a better fund than this.

Portfolio Analysis 09-30-04

Total Fixed-Income:109	Date of Maturity	Amount $000	Value $000	% Net Assets
Russian Federation FRN	03-31-30	174,058	167,861	8.19
Brazil (Federative Repub	04-15-14	126,756	126,162	6.16
Ecuador (Republic Of) 8%	08-15-30	81,417	66,253	3.23
Banque Centrale De Tunis	04-25-12	38,887	44,380	2.17
Brazil (Federative Repub	04-15-12	44,941	41,916	2.04
Brazil Federative Rep 11	01-11-12	36,239	41,765	2.04
Brazil (Federative Repub	04-15-09	37,028	36,357	1.77
US Treasury Note (Fut)	12-20-04	31,700	35,211	1.72
Brazil Federative Rep 11	08-17-40	30,331	34,039	1.66
Cabinet Ministers Ukrain	03-04-11	32,300	31,896	1.56
Mexico-United Mexican St	12-30-19	25,665	29,515	1.44
Brazil (Federative Repub	04-15-06	27,801	27,772	1.35
Pemex Project Fdg Master	10-15-09	25,103	25,976	1.27
United Mexican Sts Mtn B	01-16-13	22,986	24,262	1.18
Brazil Federative Rep 10	05-15-27	22,550	24,016	1.17
United Mexican Sts Mtn B	01-14-11	19,142	22,488	1.10
Brazil Federative Rep 12	03-06-30	17,365	21,533	1.05
Peru (Republic Of) 4.5%	03-07-17	23,864	21,369	1.04
Panama Rep 9.375%	07-23-12	18,233	20,740	1.01
United Mexican Sts Mtn B	09-24-22	17,380	19,639	0.96

Current Investment Style

Duration: Short Int Long — Quality: High Med Low

[1] figure provided by fund

Avg Eff Duration[1]	4.7 Yrs
Avg Eff Maturity	7.5 Yrs
Avg Credit Quality	BBB
Avg Wtd Coupon	7.02%
Avg Wtd Price	104.09% of par

Coupon Range	% of Bonds	Rel Cat
0% PIK	1.5	0.4
0% to 6%	34.0	1.3
6% to 8%	31.7	1.7
8% to 10%	19.3	0.7
More than 10%	14.9	0.6

1.00=Category Average

Credit Analysis		% bonds 09-30-04	
US Govt	3	BB	37
AAA	14	B	5
AA	0	Below B	4
A	3	NR/NA	0
BBB	34		

Sector Breakdown	% of assets
US Treasuries	—
TIPS	—
US Agency	—
Mortgage Pass-Throughs	—
Mortgage CMO	—
Mortgage ARM	—
US Corporate	—
Asset-Backed	—
Convertible	—
Municipal	—
Corporate Inflation-Protected	—
Foreign Corporate	—
Foreign Govt	—

Composition			
Cash	35.8	Bonds	62.1
Stocks	0.0	Other	2.1

Special Securities	
Restricted/Illiquid Secs	5
Exotic Mortgage-Backed	0
Emerging-Markets Secs	—
Options/Futures/Warrants	Yes

Address:	PIMCO Funds Stamford, CT 06902 888-877-4626
Web Address:	www.pimcofunds.com
Inception:	07-31-97*
Advisor:	PA Fund Management LLC
Subadvisor:	First Quadrant
NTF Plans:	Federated Tr NTF, TD Waterhouse Ins NT

Minimum Purchase:	$5000	Add: $100	IRA: $1000
Min Auto Inv Plan:	$1000	Add: $50	
Sales Fees:	3.75%L, 0.25%S, 2.00%R		
Management Fee:	0.45%, 0.55%A		
Actual Fees:	Mgt:0.45%	Dist:0.25%	
Expense Projections:	3Yr:$757	5Yr:$1036	10Yr:$1830
Income Distrib:	Monthly		

PIMCO Foreign Bond D

Analyst Pick

Ticker	Load	NAV	Yield	SEC Yield	Total Assets	Mstar Category
PFODX	None	$10.47	2.3%	2.06%	$1,710 mil	World Bond

Governance and Management

Fiduciary Grade: B

Portfolio Manager(s)

Sudi Mariappa took over this fund in November 2000, but he works with the same global research group as did his predecessor, Lee Thomas. Before his arrival at PIMCO in mid-2000, Mariappa worked for Merrill Lynch.

Strategy

Management invests the bulk of its assets overseas, primarily in government-issued bonds. It hedges most of its currency exposure back into the dollar, so the fund offers little in the way of currency diversification. Although management avoids big bets, it will make modest adjustments to the fund's country and currency weights based on its macroeconomic outlook.

Historical Profile

Return Average
Risk Low
Rating ★★★ Neutral

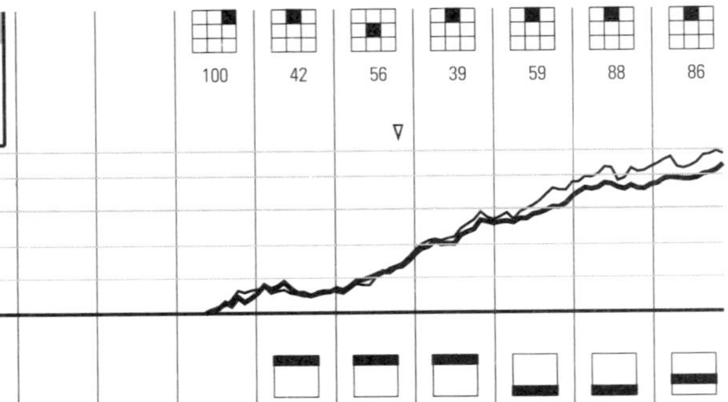

Investment Style
Fixed Income
Income Rtn %Rank Cat

▼ Manager Change
▽ Partial Manager Change

Growth of $10,000
▬ Investment Values of Fund
— Investment Values of LB Aggr

Performance Quartile (within Category)

1993	1994	1995	1996	1997	1998	1999	2000	2001	2002	2003	12-04	History
—	—	—	—	—	10.57	9.97	10.10	10.46	10.58	10.39	10.47	NAV
—	—	—	—	—	4.82*	1.11	9.38	8.48	7.23	3.10	6.17	Total Return %
—	—	—	—	—	—	1.93	-2.25	0.04	-3.02	-1.00	1.83	+/-LB Aggr
—	—	—	—	—	—	6.18	12.01	12.02	-14.76	-15.42	-5.97	+/-SB Wld Govt
—	—	—	—	—	0.00	5.44	5.76	4.62	3.57	2.92	2.37	Income Return %
—	—	—	—	—	—	-4.33	3.62	3.86	3.66	0.18	3.80	Capital Return %
—	—	—	—	—	—	20	18	8	79	88	73	Total Rtn % Rank Cat
—	—	—	—	—	0.42	0.56	0.56	0.46	0.37	0.30	0.24	Income $
—	—	—	—	—	0.35	0.15	0.21	0.02	0.25	0.21	0.31	Capital Gains $
—	—	—	—	—	—	0.95	1.16	0.99	0.95	0.95	0.96	Expense Ratio %
—	—	—	—	—	—	4.82	5.77	5.26	4.09	3.31	2.52	Income Ratio %
—	—	—	—	—	280	376	330	417	434	589	711	Turnover Rate %
—	—	—	—	—	5	9	19	45	112	157	202	Net Assets $mil

Performance 12-31-04

	1st Qtr	2nd Qtr	3rd Qtr	4th Qtr	Total
2000	1.97	1.61	1.96	3.53	9.38
2001	3.34	-0.52	3.88	1.58	8.48
2002	0.22	2.19	1.94	2.72	7.23
2003	1.99	1.34	-0.40	0.15	3.10
2004	1.89	-0.41	1.65	2.94	6.17

Trailing	Total Return%	+/- LB Aggr	+/- SB Wld Govt	%Rank Cat	Growth of $10,000
3 Mo	2.94	1.99	-7.70	77	10,294
6 Mo	4.63	0.45	-9.64	81	10,463
1 Yr	6.17	1.83	-5.97	73	10,617
3 Yr Avg	5.49	-0.70	-11.99	80	11,739
5 Yr Avg	6.85	-0.86	-1.92	66	13,927
10 Yr Avg	—	—	—	—	—
15 Yr Avg	—	—	—	—	—

Tax Analysis	Tax-Adj Rtn%	%Rank Cat	Tax-Cost Rat	%Rank Cat
3 Yr (estimated)	3.67	81	1.73	46
5 Yr (estimated)	4.73	61	1.98	50
10 Yr (estimated)	—	—	—	—

Potential Capital Gain Exposure: 6% of assets

Rating and Risk

Time Period	Load-Adj Return %	Morningstar Rtn vs Cat	Morningstar Risk vs Cat	Morningstar Risk-Adj Rating
1 Yr	6.17			
3 Yr	5.49	-Avg	Low	★★
5 Yr	6.85	Avg	Low	★★★
10 Yr	—	—	—	—
Incept	5.95			

Other Measures	Standard Index LB Aggr	Best Fit Index SB Wld Govt
Alpha	2.4	1.4
Beta	0.33	0.17
R-Squared	41	45
Standard Deviation	2.36	
Mean	5.49	
Sharpe Ratio	1.78	

Morningstar's Take by Lynn Russell 11-29-04

This fund is more attractive than its recent ranking would suggest.

PIMCO Foreign Bond has looked pretty dismal compared to its world-bond rivals over the past few years. The fund's year-to-date gain of 5.4% through Nov. 23, 2004, trails more than two thirds of its world-bond category peers', while the fund's three-year trailing return lands in the category's bottom quartile.

But that's exactly what we would expect from this offering. Unlike some of its more adventurous world-bond rivals, this fund avoids significant country and credit risk, and takes on limited currency risk. Manager Sudi Mariappa sticks primarily to high-quality government debt from developed countries and hedges the fund's foreign-currency exposure back into the dollar. He relies on a combination of small interest-rate, yield-curve and sector moves as well as complex derivatives tactics to add value, while keeping the fund's overall risk close to that of the its benchmark's, the J.P. Morgan non-U.S. Government Index.

So it's no surprise that as the dollar has weakened against most major currencies recently and emerging-market bonds have soared, the fund's returns have lagged those of its more daring rivals. The tradeoff for those relatively muted returns has been a much calmer ride for investors. The fund typically endures less than half of the month-to-month volatility of its average rival.

Investors looking for currency exposure won't find it here--although they may want to take a look at the recently introduced unhedged version of this fund. But for those more cautious investors who want to add exposure to international fixed-income markets to their portfolios without taking on significant credit risk--or the volatility of currency fluctuations--this is an appealing option. Experienced management that can rely on the deep research resources of PIMCO is another plus.

Address:	PIMCO Funds Stamford, CT 06902 888-877-4626	Minimum Purchase:	$5000	Add: $100	IRA: $1000
		Min Auto Inv Plan:	$1000	Add: $50	
		Sales Fees:	No-load, 0.25%S, 2.00%R		
Web Address:	www.pimcofunds.com	Management Fee:	0.25%, 0.70%A		
Inception:	04-08-98*	Actual Fees:	Mgt:0.25%	Dist:0.25%	
Advisor:	PA Fund Management LLC	Expense Projections:	3Yr:$306	5Yr:$531	10Yr:$1178
Subadvisor:	First Quadrant	Income Distrib:	Monthly		
NTF Plans:	Fidelity Retail-NTF, Schwab OneSource				

Portfolio Analysis 09-30-04

Total Fixed-Income:238	Date of Maturity	Amount $000	Value $000	% Net Assets
EuroDollar (Fut)	09-19-05	204,000	197,860	8.28
US Treasury Note (Fut)	12-20-04	150,900	169,951	7.11
Germany (Federal Republi	07-04-27	75,260	118,478	4.96
EuroDollar (Fut)	06-13-05	118,250	114,963	4.81
Japan (Government Of) 0.	12-20-07	9,054,000	82,285	3.44
Germany (Federal Republi	01-04-12	53,000	71,255	2.98
Japan (Government Of) 1.	09-20-13	6,760,000	62,868	2.63
France (Republic Of) 5.2	04-25-08	47,000	62,745	2.62
U.K. Treasury Stock 5%	03-07-12	32,300	59,205	2.48
Spain (Kingdom Of) 5.15%	07-30-09	37,730	50,815	2.13
France (Republic Of) 4%	04-25-09	31,050	39,832	1.67
U.K. Treasury 5%	03-07-08	21,600	39,430	1.65
Germany (Federal Republi	01-04-11	28,400	38,631	1.62
France (Republic Of) 4%	10-25-09	30,070	38,563	1.61
Germany (Federal Republi	07-04-10	26,300	35,702	1.49
U.K. Treasury Stock 8%	09-27-13	15,450	34,391	1.44
US Treasury Note 3.5%	01-15-11	29,819	33,759	1.41
Germany (Federal Republi	01-04-14	25,500	32,439	1.36
Canada Govt 6%	06-01-08	34,300	29,279	1.22
Japan (Government Of) 1.	09-20-11	2,960,000	27,599	1.15

Current Investment Style

Duration: Short Int Long
Quality: High Med Low

¹ figure provided by fund

Avg Eff Duration¹	4.8 Yrs
Avg Eff Maturity	8.7 Yrs
Avg Credit Quality	AAA
Avg Wtd Coupon	4.05%
Avg Wtd Price	100.13% of par

Coupon Range	% of Bonds	Rel Cat
0% PIK	1.3	0.9
0% to 6%	80.7	1.1
6% to 8%	17.4	0.9
8% to 10%	1.9	0.4
More than 10%	0.0	0.0

1.00=Category Average

Credit Analysis		% bonds 09-30-04	
US Govt	0	BB	1
AAA	77	B	0
AA	17	Below B	0
A	2	NR/NA	0
BBB	3		

Sector Breakdown	% of assets
US Treasuries	—
TIPS	—
US Agency	—
Mortgage Pass-Throughs	—
Mortgage CMO	—
Mortgage ARM	—
US Corporate	—
Asset-Backed	—
Convertible	—
Municipal	—
Corporate Inflation-Protected	—
Foreign Corporate	—
Foreign Govt	—

Composition			
Cash	27.4	Bonds	64.0
Stocks	0.0	Other	8.7

Special Securities	
Restricted/Illiquid Secs	1
Exotic Mortgage-Backed	0
Emerging-Markets Secs	—
Options/Futures/Warrants	Yes

PIMCO High-Yield A

Analyst Pick

Ticker	Load	NAV	Yield	SEC Yield	Total Assets	Mstar Category
PHDAX	3.75%	$9.97	6.4%	5.32%	$7,303 mil	High Yield Bond

Governance and Management

Fiduciary Grade: B

Portfolio Manager(s)

Lead manager Ray Kennedy has been with PIMCO since 1996 and became comanager of this fund in early 2002. He worked alongside veteran manager Ben Trosky for several years and took over this offering when Trosky retired at the end of 2002.

Strategy

Unlike most high-yield funds, which concentrate on single B issues, this portfolio emphasizes slightly higher-quality BBs and has even been known to stash 30% or more in the investment-grade arena. Furthermore, it casts a wider net than most, sometimes holding small weightings in mortgage-backed securities or just about anything else that looks particularly attractive. It generally buys no bonds rated below B.

Historical Profile

Return Average
Risk Average
Rating ★★★ Neutral

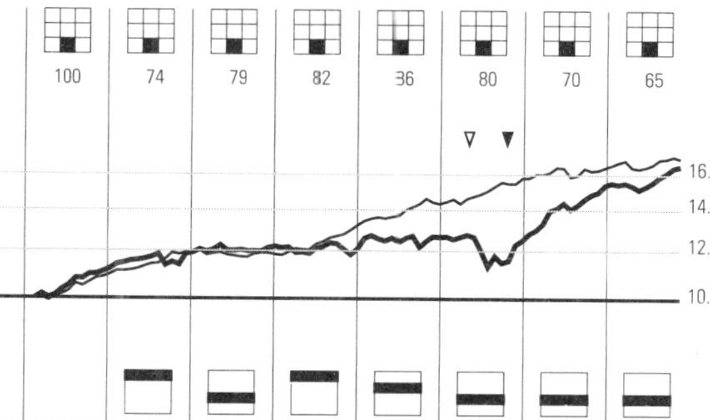

Investment Style
Fixed Income
Income Rtn %Rank Cat

▼ Manager Change
∇ Partial Manager Change

Growth of $10,000
▬ Investment Values of Fund
— Investment Values of LB Aggr

Performance Quartile (within Category)

1993	1994	1995	1996	1997	1998	1999	2000	2001	2002	2003	12-04	History
—	—	—	—	11.54	11.31	10.68	9.71	9.36	8.52	9.77	9.97	NAV
—	—	—	—	12.67*	6.12	2.39	-0.84	4.59	-1.23	23.20	9.02	Total Return %
—	—	—	—	—	-2.57	3.21	-12.47	-3.85	-11.48	19.10	4.68	+/-LB Aggr
—	—	—	—	—	5.54	-0.89	4.37	-1.19	-4.34	-4.73	-2.94	+/-CSFB Glb HY
—	—	—	—	0.00	8.20	8.16	8.57	8.44	7.83	8.08	6.76	Income Return %
—	—	—	—	—	-2.08	-5.77	-9.41	-3.85	-9.06	15.12	2.26	Capital Return %
—	—	—	—	—	6	74	12	38	56	57	66	Total Rtn % Rank Cat
—	—	—	—	0.91	0.91	0.89	0.88	0.79	0.71	0.67	0.64	Income $
—	—	—	—	0.09	0.00	0.00	0.00	0.00	0.00	0.00	0.00	Capital Gains $
—	—	—	—	0.92	0.90	0.90	0.90	0.90	0.90	0.90	0.90	Expense Ratio %
—	—	—	—	8.28	8.02	7.94	8.23	8.62	7.83	8.18	6.86	Income Ratio %
—	—	—	—	67	37	39	39	53	96	129	105	Turnover Rate %
—	—	—	—	65	113	203	185	417	673	1,373	1,165	Net Assets $mil

Performance 12-31-04

	1st Qtr	2nd Qtr	3rd Qtr	4th Qtr	Total
2000	-2.28	1.54	1.85	-1.87	-0.84
2001	3.90	-1.27	-1.77	3.79	4.59
2002	0.01	-5.01	-4.39	8.74	-1.23
2003	6.50	8.10	1.44	5.50	23.20
2004	0.82	-1.22	5.14	4.12	9.02

Trailing	Total Return%	+/- LB Aggr	+/- CSFB Glb HY	%Rank Cat	Growth of $10,000
3 Mo	4.12	3.17	-0.44	56	10,412
6 Mo	9.47	5.29	0.21	24	10,947
1 Yr	9.02	4.68	-2.94	66	10,902
3 Yr Avg	9.88	3.69	-4.00	61	13,266
5 Yr Avg	6.59	-1.12	-1.58	26	13,759
10 Yr Avg	—	—	—	—	—
15 Yr Avg	—	—	—	—	—

Tax Analysis	Tax-Adj Rtn%	%Rank Cat	Tax-Cost Rat	%Rank Cat
3 Yr (estimated)	5.65	73	2.62	36
5 Yr (estimated)	2.74	30	2.87	23
10 Yr (estimated)	—	—	—	—

Potential Capital Gain Exposure: 2% of assets

Rating and Risk

Time Period	Load-Adj Return %	Morningstar Rtn vs Cat	Morningstar Risk vs Cat	Morningstar Risk-Adj Rating
1 Yr	4.93			
3 Yr	8.49	-Avg	+Avg	★★
5 Yr	5.78	Avg	-Avg	★★★
10 Yr	—	—	—	—
Incept	6.25			

Other Measures	Standard Index LB Aggr	Best Fit Index CSFB Glb HY
Alpha	7.4	-5.6
Beta	0.27	1.19
R-Squared	2	86
Standard Deviation	8.71	
Mean	9.88	
Sharpe Ratio	0.98	

Morningstar's Take by Eric Jacobson 11-19-04

PIMCO High Yield's 2004 troubles have been modest and aren't a deal-breaker, but they are instructive.

This venerable fund has fallen behind a tad in 2004, turning in a 7.8% year-to-date gain that puts it into the high-yield category's bottom half. In the past modest lethargy has typically been attributable to the fund's less aggressive mandate. When the overall high-yield market rallies, the junkiest junk often leads the way. On the other hand, this fund's conservatism has held it in good stead overall, keeping it out of deeper trouble during some of the market's darkest days.

This year the problems have been different. For one, the fund at one point built a 7% stake in emerging markets. Although manager Ray Kennedy says that the position has turned out to be neutral over the course of the year thus far, a springtime slump brought volatility.

Asset flows have also been an issue. The fund took in a lot of money in 2003, and Kennedy added some index-based securities to sop up cash until he could deploy it. The springtime sell-off affected U.S. high-yield bonds too, though, and with hedge funds trading heavily in the same index securities Kennedy was using, they were hit unusually hard. They too have since recovered, and Kennedy has decided to avoid them in the future.

The biggest problem, however, was that in the wake of regulator accusations against PIMCO in February--which were later dropped--some investors fled the portfolio, driving its assets down to $6.3 billion. And although it's now back to more than $7.4 billion, the rapid outflows hurt returns.

As we've noted, the margin of weakness here is modest, and we remain fans of PIMCO, Kennedy and their credit staff. And in light of its cautious style, we're not convinced the fund's overall size is necessarily a problem. We do expect, though, that rapid flows could occur again. If they do, we'd like to see PIMCO consider much more definitive measures to try and mitigate such troubles.

Address:	PIMCO Funds Stamford, CT 06902 888-877-4626	Minimum Purchase:	$5000	Add: $100	IRA: $1000
Web Address:	www.pimcofunds.com	Min Auto Inv Plan:	$1000	Add: $50	
Inception:	01-13-97*	Sales Fees:	3.75%L, 0.25%S, 2.00%R		
Advisor:	PA Fund Management LLC	Management Fee:	0.25%, 0.40%A		
Subadvisor:	First Quadrant	Actual Fees:	Mgt:0.25%	Dist:0.25%	
		Expense Projections:	3Yr:$651	5Yr:$855	10Yr:$1441
		Income Distrib:	Monthly		
NTF Plans:	Federated Tr NTF, TD Waterhouse Ins NT				

Portfolio Analysis 09-30-04

Total Fixed-Income:413	Date of Maturity	Amount $000	Value $000	% Net Assets
EuroDollar (Fut)	09-19-05	1,466,500	1,422,358	16.41
EuroDollar (Fut)	06-13-05	383,000	372,353	4.30
Brazil (Federative Repub	04-15-14	114,984	114,445	1.32
Midwest Gen Ergy 2000 8.	01-02-16	95,755	102,218	1.18
Russian Federation FRN	03-31-30	92,898	89,591	1.03
Aes 144A 8.75%	05-15-13	71,365	80,821	0.93
Targeted Return Index Se	08-01-15	66,320	71,454	0.82
Qwest Cap Fdg 7.25%	02-15-11	77,975	69,983	0.81
US Treasury Note 2.5%	09-30-06	70,000	69,871	0.81
Csc Hldgs 7.625%	04-01-11	59,073	62,544	0.72
Williams Cos 7.875%	09-01-21	55,329	61,692	0.71
Mandalay Resort Grp 9.37	02-15-10	52,722	60,894	0.70
Mci 6.688%	05-01-09	60,638	58,591	0.68
Hca 6.75%	07-15-13	54,408	57,937	0.67
Pseg Engy Hldgs 8.5%	06-15-11	50,610	57,316	0.66
Aes Ironwood 8.857%	11-30-25	51,117	57,251	0.66
Hanover Equip Tr 8.5%	09-01-08	51,295	55,399	0.64
Nextel Comms 6.875%	10-31-13	51,635	53,959	0.62
Nrg Engy 144A 8%	12-15-13	49,390	53,156	0.61
At&T 7.3%	11-15-11	46,645	52,417	0.60

Current Investment Style

Duration
Short Int Long
Quality High Med Low

[1] figure provided by fund

Avg Eff Duration[1]	4.3 Yrs
Avg Eff Maturity	6.2 Yrs
Avg Credit Quality	BB
Avg Wtd Coupon	7.98%
Avg Wtd Price	106.63% of par

Coupon Range	% of Bonds	Rel Cat
0% PIK	2.3	0.5
0% to 8%	48.0	1.3
8% to 11%	49.8	0.9
11% to 14%	2.2	0.3
More than 14%	0.0	0.0

1.00=Category Average

Credit Analysis		% bonds 09-30-04	
US Govt	0	BB	38
AAA	9	B	43
AA	0	Below B	4
A	0	NR/NA	0
BBB	6		

Sector Breakdown	% of assets
US Treasuries	1
TIPS	0
US Agency	0
Mortgage Pass-Throughs	0
Mortgage CMO	0
Mortgage ARM	0
US Corporate	60
Asset-Backed	3
Convertible	1
Municipal	0
Corporate Inflation-Protected	0
Foreign Corporate	4
Foreign Govt	3

Composition			
Cash	27.2	Bonds	68.8
Stocks	0.0	Other	3.9

Special Securities	
Restricted/Illiquid Secs	10
Exotic Mortgage-Backed	0
Emerging-Markets Secs	3
Options/Futures/Warrants	Yes

PIMCO Low Duration Instl

Ticker	Load	NAV	Yield	SEC Yield	Total Assets	Mstar Category
PTLDX	None	$10.20	2.1%	1.89%	$14,266 mil	Short-Term Bond

Governance and Management

Fiduciary Grade: B

Portfolio Manager(s)

Bill Gross has led this fund since its 1987 inception. He and his team at Pimco won Morningstar's 1998 and 2000 fixed-income manager-of-the-year honors.

Strategy

This fund sticks primarily to short-term bonds, investing in a mix of corporates, mortgage-backed securities (with short durations), and Treasuries. Manager Bill Gross makes occasional adjustments to the fund's duration, but he doesn't stray far from that of the Merrill Lynch U.S. Treasury 1-3 Year Index. He will also occasionally dabble in lower-quality bonds.

Historical Profile

Return High
Risk Average
Rating ★★★★★ Highest

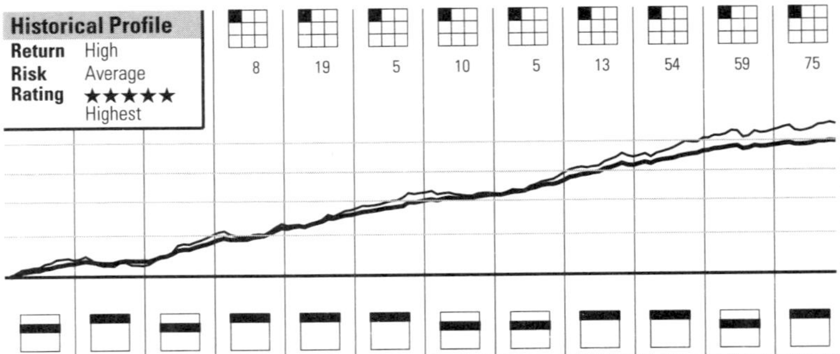

Investment Style
Fixed Income
Income Rtn %Rank Cat

▼ Manager Change
▽ Partial Manager Change

Growth of $10,000
▬ Investment Values of Fund
— Investment Values of LB Aggr

Performance Quartile (within Category)

1993	1994	1995	1996	1997	1998	1999	2000	2001	2002	2003	12-04	History
10.22	9.67	10.11	10.05	10.19	10.17	9.84	9.90	10.07	10.27	10.24	10.20	NAV
7.78	0.63	11.93	6.14	8.23	7.16	2.97	7.70	8.01	7.66	2.97	2.39	Total Return %
-1.97	3.55	-6.54	2.51	-1.42	-1.53	3.79	-3.93	-0.43	-2.59	-1.13	-1.95	+/-LB Aggr
0.68	1.34	-0.95	1.47	1.10	-0.47	0.88	-1.21	-1.02	-0.46	-0.38	0.54	+/-LB 1-5 YR
6.50	6.15	7.02	6.68	6.50	6.73	6.30	7.03	6.15	4.20	2.82	2.14	Income Return %
1.28	-5.52	4.91	-0.54	1.73	0.43	-3.33	0.67	1.86	3.46	0.15	0.25	Capital Return %
30	17	30	8	5	9	33	48	25	9	31	16	Total Rtn % Rank Cat
0.64	0.61	0.66	0.66	0.63	0.67	0.62	0.67	0.59	0.41	0.29	0.22	Income $
0.10	0.00	0.02	0.00	0.03	0.06	0.00	0.00	0.01	0.14	0.05	0.06	Capital Gains $
0.45	0.43	0.41	0.42	0.43	0.43	0.43	0.43	0.43	0.43	0.43	0.43	Expense Ratio %
7.21	6.05	6.46	6.88	6.46	6.39	6.36	6.40	6.86	5.30	3.43	2.01	Income Ratio %
68	43	77	209	240	309	245	82	348	569	218	247	Turnover Rate %
2,127	2,216	2,497	2,814	2,783	3,137	3,744	3,684	4,190	5,980	9,210	9,550	Net Assets $mil

Performance 12-31-04

	1st Qtr	2nd Qtr	3rd Qtr	4th Qtr	Total
2000	1.35	1.75	2.25	2.14	7.70
2001	2.99	1.38	3.35	0.08	8.01
2002	1.00	2.37	2.06	2.03	7.66
2003	1.39	1.36	-0.01	0.22	2.97
2004	1.16	-0.65	1.31	0.56	2.39

Trailing	Total Return%	+/- LB Aggr	+/- LB 1-5 YR	%Rank Cat	Growth of $10,000
3 Mo	0.56	-0.39	0.41	16	10,056
6 Mo	1.87	-2.31	-0.01	28	10,187
1 Yr	2.39	-1.95	0.54	16	10,239
3 Yr Avg	4.31	-1.88	-0.10	14	11,350
5 Yr Avg	5.72	-1.99	-0.49	15	13,206
10 Yr Avg	6.48	-1.24	-0.03	6	18,736
15 Yr Avg	6.86	-0.84	0.14	5	27,054

Tax Analysis	Tax-Adj Rtn%	%Rank Cat	Tax-Cost Rat	%Rank Cat
3 Yr (estimated)	2.90	8	1.35	56
5 Yr (estimated)	3.80	13	1.82	68
10 Yr (estimated)	4.15	9	2.19	78

Potential Capital Gain Exposure: -1% of assets

Rating and Risk

Time Period	Load-Adj Return %	Morningstar Rtn vs Cat	Morningstar Risk vs Cat	Morningstar Risk-Adj Rating
1 Yr	2.39			
3 Yr	4.31	+Avg	Avg	★★★★
5 Yr	5.72	+Avg	Avg	★★★★
10 Yr	6.48	High	Avg	★★★★★
Incept	7.20			

Other Measures	Standard Index LB Aggr	Best Fit Index LB. U.S. Univ. Bd
Alpha	0.8	0.5
Beta	0.43	0.44
R-Squared	85	85

Standard Deviation	2.08
Mean	4.31
Sharpe Ratio	1.44

Morningstar's Take by Eric Jacobson 10-30-04

Key to the greatness of Pimco--and its Low Duration fund--is how it keeps a handle on risk.

When many investors think of Pimco, they think of manager Bill Gross and the market-slaying moves he's famed for making, whether they involve loading up on Treasuries at just the right time or making a prescient interest-rate bet.

As meaningful as such efforts can occasionally be, however, it's his ability to keep his funds from spinning out of control that has arguably been the foundation of their long-term success. That's especially critical for a fund of this type. With a mandate for low volatility, one bad mistake could easily wreck its reputation.

It's therefore reassuring that Pimco has expended so much energy on making certain that its managers, including skipper Gross, understand just what risks they're taking on. Over the past year, for example, he's had a strong taste for foreign bonds. That was particularly notable at the end of March when non-U.S. bonds accounted for roughly one third of the fund's rate sensitivity (and were almost fully hedged). Still, that represents a fairly modest exposure, given the fund's overall duration (a measure of interest-rate sensitivity) at the time was only 1.6 years. Pimco also uses numerous tools to model and measure the amount of risk such positions represent and just how divergent the fund's returns are likely to be if a bet is misplaced. And though it's common for fund companies to brag about the sophistication of such analytical tools, it's clear that Pimco's are second to none.

Of course, long-term success is the best evidence of their utility, and that's what this fund has enjoyed. Its three-, five- and 10-year returns are topnotch, and Gross has handily avoided blowups. Although we generally view the fund's lettered, retail shares as pricey, it's a stellar option for investors with access to its low-cost institutional classes.

Portfolio Analysis 09-30-04

Total Fixed-Income:1444	Date of Maturity	Amount $000	Value $000	% Net Assets
EuroDollar (Fut)	09-19-05	3,658,500	3,548,379	15.31
EuroDollar (Fut)	06-13-05	3,553,500	3,454,712	14.91
US Treasury Note 3.625%	01-15-08	523,087	573,823	2.48
FNMA 5.5%		530,200	537,325	2.32
Euro Dollar (Fut)	12-13-04	527,750	515,585	2.22
US Treasury Note 3.875%	01-15-09	320,034	360,376	1.55
EuroDollar (Fut)	12-19-05	296,500	286,864	1.24
US Treasury Note 3.375%	01-15-07	222,841	238,153	1.03
FNMA CMO 5%	04-25-33	108,594	109,510	0.47
Dg Fdg Tr Pfd 144A		10	103,544	0.45
FHLMC CMO 6.5%	07-25-43	97,780	103,402	0.45
FNMA 5%		93,000	94,482	0.41
Cwabs CMO	10-25-21	91,006	91,063	0.39
Pacific Gas & Elec FRN	04-03-06	90,000	90,089	0.39
France Telecom Sa 7.2%	03-01-06	66,900	71,490	0.31
Mellon Residential 2000-	06-15-30	50,875	50,661	0.22
Cwmbs CMO 6.5%	06-25-33	49,462	50,543	0.22
Bear Stearns Arm Tr 2003	01-25-34	48,846	49,349	0.21
Structured Asset Mtg 200	09-19-32	49,198	49,015	0.21
FNMA 5%	06-01-18	47,234	48,104	0.21

Current Investment Style

Duration: Short Int Long
Quality: High Med Low

[1] figure provided by fund

Avg Eff Duration[1]	1.7 Yrs
Avg Eff Maturity	1.9 Yrs
Avg Credit Quality	AAA
Avg Wtd Coupon	4.57%
Avg Wtd Price	103.88% of par

Coupon Range	% of Bonds	Rel Cat
0% PIK	4.7	1.0
0% to 6%	87.2	1.2
6% to 8%	12.2	0.5
8% to 10%	0.6	0.2
More than 10%	0.0	0.0

1.00=Category Average

Credit Analysis	% bonds 09-30-04		
US Govt	11	BB	1
AAA	79	B	0
AA	0	Below B	0
A	2	NR/NA	0
BBB	7		

Sector Breakdown	% of assets
US Treasuries	0
TIPS	5
US Agency	0
Mortgage Pass-Throughs	10
Mortgage CMO	5
Mortgage ARM	0
US Corporate	2
Asset-Backed	1
Convertible	0
Municipal	0
Corporate Inflation-Protected	0
Foreign Corporate	0
Foreign Govt	0

Composition			
Cash	76.0	Bonds	23.3
Stocks	0.0	Other	0.7

Special Securities	
Restricted/Illiquid Secs	1
Exotic Mortgage-Backed	0
Emerging-Markets Secs	Trace
Options/Futures/Warrants	Yes

Address:	PIMCO Funds Stamford, CT 06902 800-927-4648
Web Address:	www.pimcofunds.com
Inception:	05-11-87
Advisor:	PA Fund Management LLC
Subadvisor:	First Quadrant
NTF Plans:	N/A

Minimum Purchase:	$5000000	Add: $0	IRA: $0
Min Auto Inv Plan:	$0	Add: —	
Sales Fees:	No-load		
Management Fee:	0.25%, 0.18%A		
Actual Fees:	Mgt:0.25%	Dist:	
Expense Projections:	3Yr:$138	5Yr:$241	10Yr:$542
Income Distrib:	Monthly		

PIMCO RCM Glob Tech Instl

Analyst Pick

Ticker	Load	NAV	Yield	Total Assets	Mstar Category
DRGTX	None	$36.31	0.0%	$606 mil	Specialty-Technology

Governance and Management

Fiduciary Grade:

Portfolio Manager(s)

Seasoned. Huachen Chen and Walter Price have been running institutional tech money together for more than 10 years and have managed this fund since its late-1995 inception. Chen left Allianz, apparently frustrated by internal politics, early in 2003, but continued to work on the fund as an independent contractor. He returned as a comanager in early 2004, however, having reconciled whatever differences he had with Allianz.

Strategy

This fund cuts a broad swath across the technology sector. It is typically well diversified across subsectors and market-cap ranges. Management splits the fund into three categories: emerging stocks, which include more-speculative issues; core blue chips; and opportunistic value plays. The fund is required to own securities in at least three countries, but, despite its global name, it has typically invested the bulk of its assets in U.S. companies. Management will hold cash and use options and shorts to give the fund a defensive cast at times and will also use ETFs to manage near-term sector exposures.

Historical Profile

Return: High
Risk: Average
Rating: ★★★★ Above Avg

Investment Style: Equity, Stock %

1996	1997	1998	1999	2000	2001	2002	2003	12-04
80%	96%	96%	79%	93%	88%	95%	95%	

▼ Manager Change
▽ Partial Manager Change

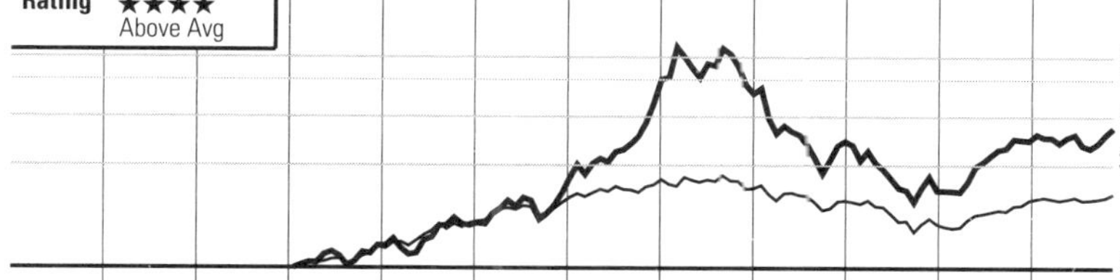

Performance Quartile (within Category)

History

1993	1994	1995	1996	1997	1998	1999	2000	2001	2002	2003	12-04	History
—	—	10.04	12.60	13.69	21.47	59.21	50.32	30.54	18.21	30.79	36.31	NAV
—	—	0.40*	26.41	27.08	61.06	182.95	-14.33	-39.31	-40.37	69.08	17.93	Total Return %
—	—	—	3.47	-6.27	32.49	161.91	-5.23	-27.43	-18.28	40.41	7.06	+/-S&P 500
—	—	—	6.38	7.11	6.46	66.55	1.89	-23.72	-7.04	16.94	6.20	+/-PSE Tech 100
—	—	—	0.90	0.00	0.00	0.00	0.00	0.00	0.00	0.00	0.00	Income Return %
—	—	—	25.51	27.08	61.06	182.95	-14.33	-39.31	-40.37	69.08	17.93	Capital Return %
—	—	—	18	3	35	12	7	60	34	18	5	Total Rtn % Rank Cat
—	—	0.00	0.09	0.00	0.00	0.00	0.00	0.00	0.00	0.00	0.00	Income $
—	—	0.00	0.00	2.21	0.57	1.38	0.43	0.00	0.00	0.00	0.00	Capital Gains $
—	—	—	1.73	1.75	1.75	1.50	1.21	1.56	1.29	1.36	1.36	Expense Ratio %
—	—	—	-1.34	-1.15	-0.99	-1.02	-0.23	-0.15	-0.85	-0.92	-1.16	Income Ratio %
—	—	—	156	189	266	119	451	386	343	237	206	Turnover Rate %
—	—	1	5	7	18	197	366	200	81	194	237	Net Assets $mil

Performance 12-31-04

	1st Qtr	2nd Qtr	3rd Qtr	4th Qtr	Total
2000	26.79	-6.99	10.83	-34.45	-14.33
2001	-34.12	-1.48	-33.31	40.22	-39.31
2002	-9.95	-24.80	-21.95	12.83	-40.37
2003	-1.43	37.05	15.33	8.53	69.08
2004	3.09	3.37	-8.93	21.52	17.93

Trailing	Total Return%	+/- S&P 500	+/- PSE Tech 100	%Rank Cat	Growth of $10,000
3 Mo	21.52	12.29	7.00	5	12,152
6 Mo	10.67	3.48	4.74	6	11,067
1 Yr	17.93	7.06	6.20	5	11,793
3 Yr Avg	5.94	2.36	1.68	5	11,890
5 Yr Avg	-9.17	-6.87	-4.84	13	6,182
10 Yr Avg	—	—	—	—	—
15 Yr Avg	—	—	—	—	—

Tax Analysis	Tax-Adj Rtn%	%Rank Cat	Tax-Cost Rat	%Rank Cat
3 Yr (estimated)	5.94	4	0.00	1
5 Yr (estimated)	-9.23	9	0.07	9
10 Yr (estimated)	—	—	—	—

Potential Capital Gain Exposure: -64% of assets

Rating and Risk

Time Period	Load-Adj Return %	Morningstar Rtn vs Cat	Morningstar Risk vs Cat	Morningstar Risk-Adj Rating
1 Yr	17.93			
3 Yr	5.94	High	Avg	★★★★★
5 Yr	-9.17	High	Avg	★★★★
10 Yr	—	—	—	—
Incept	18.29			

Other Measures	Standard Index S&P 500	Best Fit Index PSE Tech 100
Alpha	3.3	2.0
Beta	1.64	1.07
R-Squared	72	91

Standard Deviation	32.13
Mean	5.94
Sharpe Ratio	0.14

Morningstar's Take by Christopher Traulsen 01-05-05

A pending merger could force some small changes at PIMCO RCM Global Technology, but nothing that should endanger its appeal relative to peers.

Pending shareholder approval, the former PIMCO PEA Innovation will merge into this fund. Even if the merger is not approved, that offering is now being run by the RCM team as a clone of this fund. The boost in assets under management is not insignificant: Innovation had roughly $840 million in assets at last count. Managers Huachen Chen and Walter Price were recently running about $1.1 billion in the Global Tech style, with about $606 million in this offering.

The merger will likely limit RCM Global Tech's ability to invest in micro-caps. However, such firms typically have not been a large part of the fund's strategy. It had less than 5% of assets in micro-caps recently, so we don't think the increased asset size will notably impact the fund's performance. There may also be a silver lining: The merger could help cut the expense ratio by allowing the fund to benefit from economies of scale. We won't know if this is the case for sure, however, until the official proxy is filed.

In any case, we continue to think investors here have one of the better tech funds around. It features an experienced management team that has shown a particular aptitude for running tech money, offers reasonably broad exposure to the technology sector, and has built a fabulous record relative to its peers. It's worth noting that the fund has begun to invest small portions of its assets outside of the tech sector, but its managers expect it to remain a tech fund at its core. Our bigger caveat is simply this: We don't think most investors need a technology fund. Such offerings are extremely volatile and tend to be expensive to own, and also attract erratic fund flows. If you want one, though, this is a great choice.

Address:	840 Newport Center Dr, Newport Beach CA 92660, 800-426-0107
Web Address:	www.pimcoadvisors.com
Inception:	12-27-95*
Advisor:	PA Fund Management LLC
Subadvisor:	RCM Capital Management LLC
NTF Plans:	N/A

Minimum Purchase:	$5000000	Add: $250	IRA: $2000
Min Auto Inv Plan:	$0	Add: —	
Sales Fees:	No-load		
Management Fee:	0.95%		
Actual Fees:	—	Dist:	
Expense Projections:	3Yr:$384	5Yr:$665	10Yr:$1466
Income Distrib:	Annually		

Portfolio Analysis 11-30-04

Share change since 10-04 Total Stocks:61	Sector	PE	YTD Ret%	% Assets
NCR	Hardware	26.7	78.43	5.70
Apple Computer	Hardware	NMF	201.36	5.55
⊖ Marvel Technology	Hardware	NMF	87.03	5.15
⊖ Research In Motion Ltd	Hardware	—	146.66	5.05
⊕ VeriSign	Software	—	106.14	4.59
⊖ Yahoo	Media	95.1	67.36	3.98
⊕ Autodesk	Software	46.6	209.62	3.42
⊖ Comverse Technology	Hardware	—	39.00	3.40
⊕ eBay	Consumer	81.6	80.07	3.19
Shanda Interactive Enter	Business	—	—	3.09
⊕ McAfee	Software	18.2	92.35	3.04
⊖ Google	Business	—	—	3.00
⊖ Mercury Interactive	Software	60.5	-6.35	2.99
⊕ Johnson & Johnson	Health	20.6	25.17	2.60
⊖ Citrix Systems	Software	34.1	15.60	2.44
Symantec	Software	34.5	49.33	2.39
Tyco International	Ind Mtrls	25.1	35.41	2.26
NetEase.com ADR	Business	41.4	43.34	2.18
Trend Micro	Software	—	—	1.95
☼ Broadcom	Hardware	66.4	-5.12	1.66

Current Investment Style

Value Blnd Growth; Large Mid Small

Market Cap	%
Giant	24.3
Large	18.7
Mid	48.5
Small	7.5
Micro	1.0
Avg $mil: 9,535	

Value Measures		Rel Category
Price/Earnings	38.78	1.40
Price/Book	4.64	1.39
Price/Sales	3.62	1.21
Price/Cash Flow	11.62	0.93
Dividend Yield %	0.11	0.58

Growth Measures	%	Rel Category
Long-Term Erngs	17.24	1.02
Book Value	-0.24	NMF
Sales	2.51	0.83
Cash Flow	26.53	1.64
Historical Erngs	-8.54	NMF

Profitability	%	Rel Category
Return on Equity	10.78	0.94
Return on Assets	5.71	0.90
Net Margin	9.41	0.90

Industry Weightings	% of Stocks	Rel Cat
Software	27.2	1.3
Hardware	14.7	1.1
Networking Eq	4.2	0.6
Semis	7.9	0.5
Semi Equip	0.0	0.0
Comp/Data Sv	2.0	0.4
Telecom	3.2	1.4
Health Care	8.9	1.4
Other	31.9	1.3

Composition

Cash	3.8
Stocks	95.5
Bonds	0.0
Other	0.7
Foreign (% of Stock)	16.0

PIMCO Real Ret A

Ticker	Load	NAV	Yield	SEC Yield	Total Assets	Mstar Category
PRTNX	3.00%	$11.49	3.4%	1.31%	$12,578 mil	Long Government

Governance and Management

Fiduciary Grade: B

Portfolio Manager(s)

John Brynjolfsson has managed this fund since its 1997 inception. He is a member of the PIMCO management team that won Morningstar's Fixed-Income Manager of the Year honors in 1998 and 2000.

Strategy

Manager John Brynjolfsson invests the majority of this fund's assets in Treasury inflation-protected securities (TIPS), although he will occasionally venture into corporate and foreign inflation-indexed bonds. Because the principal on these bonds is adjusted to keep up with changes in the consumer price index (or some other price index), they provide a unique inflation hedge. He will often buy TIPS through forward contracts, as well, which only require a modest amount of cash to purchase, and therefore permit the fund to use the remainder to invest in short-term corporates.

Historical Profile

Return Average
Risk Below Avg
Rating ★★★★ Above Avg

Investment Style
Fixed Income
Income Rtn %Rank Cat

100	65	7	7	31	73	64	47

▼ Manager Change
▽ Partial Manager Change

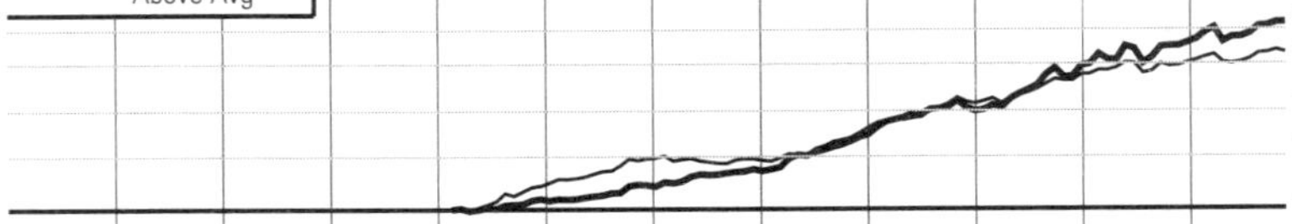

Growth of $10,000
— Investment Values of Fund
— Investment Values of LB Aggr

Performance Quartile (within Category)

1993	1994	1995	1996	1997	1998	1999	2000	2001	2002	2003	12-04	History
—	—	—	—	9.80	9.77	9.63	10.03	10.18	11.26	11.25	11.49	NAV
—	—	—	—	3.68*	4.81	5.29	13.01	8.24	16.54	8.02	8.71	Total Return %
—	—	—	—	—	-3.88	6.11	1.38	-0.20	6.29	3.92	4.37	+/-LB Aggr
—	—	—	—	—	-8.60	14.02	-7.28	3.90	-0.45	5.41	0.77	+/-LB LTGvtBd
—	—	—	—	0.00	5.09	6.64	7.82	5.86	4.23	3.51	3.59	Income Return %
—	—	—	—	—	-0.28	-1.35	5.19	2.38	12.31	4.51	5.12	Capital Return %
—	—	—	—	—	88	7	87	13	65	14	32	Total Rtn % Rank Cat
—	—	—	—	0.42	0.49	0.63	0.73	0.57	0.42	0.39	0.40	Income $
—	—	—	—	0.14	0.00	0.02	0.08	0.10	0.15	0.51	0.32	Capital Gains $
—	—	—	—	0.90	0.92	0.90	0.93	0.94	0.90	0.91	0.90	Expense Ratio %
—	—	—	—	6.14	4.06	5.37	6.57	7.03	3.03	3.96	2.84	Income Ratio %
—	—	—	—	160	967	154	253	202	237	191	308	Turnover Rate %
—	—	—	—	—	5	13	53	426	1,264	1,821	2,952	Net Assets $mil

Performance 12-31-04

	1st Qtr	2nd Qtr	3rd Qtr	4th Qtr	Total
2000	4.29	2.23	2.49	3.42	13.01
2001	5.18	1.88	2.41	-1.37	8.24
2002	1.28	6.10	7.58	0.80	16.54
2003	2.08	3.69	0.63	1.40	8.02
2004	5.13	-3.07	3.74	2.83	8.71

Trailing	Total Return%	+/- LB Aggr	+/- LB LTGvtBd	%Rank Cat	Growth of $10,000
3 Mo	2.83	1.88	1.26	26	10,283
6 Mo	6.68	2.50	-1.41	54	10,668
1 Yr	8.71	4.37	0.77	32	10,871
3 Yr Avg	11.02	4.83	2.00	30	13,684
5 Yr Avg	10.85	3.14	0.63	29	16,737
10 Yr Avg	—	—	—	—	—
15 Yr Avg	—	—	—	—	—

Tax Analysis	Tax-Adj Rtn%	%Rank Cat	Tax-Cost Rat	%Rank Cat
3 Yr (estimated)	7.65	38	2.05	78
5 Yr (estimated)	7.60	55	2.34	82
10 Yr (estimated)	—	—	—	—

Potential Capital Gain Exposure: % of assets

Rating and Risk

Time Period	Load-Adj Return %	Morningstar Rtn vs Cat	Morningstar Risk vs Cat	Morningstar Risk-Adj Rating
1 Yr	5.44			
3 Yr	9.90	Avg	-Avg	★★★★
5 Yr	10.18	Avg	-Avg	★★★★
10 Yr	—	—	—	—
Incept	8.13			

Other Measures	Standard Index LB Aggr	Best Fit Index LB LTGvtBd
Alpha	2.4	4.6
Beta	1.49	0.62
R-Squared	78	83
Standard Deviation	7.96	
Mean	11.02	
Sharpe Ratio	1.23	

Portfolio Analysis 09-30-04

Total Fixed-Income:131	Date of Maturity	Amount $000	Value $000	% Net Assets
US Treasury Note 3.875%	01-15-09	1,664,500	1,874,318	11.14
US Treasury Note 3%	07-15-12	1,580,944	1,751,082	10.40
US Treasury Note 3.375%	01-15-07	1,585,202	1,694,123	10.07
US Treasury Note 3.625%	01-15-08	1,497,960	1,643,252	9.76
US Treasury Bond 3.875%	04-15-29	1,087,583	1,442,917	8.57
US Treasury Bond 3.625%	04-15-28	961,632	1,220,447	7.25
US Treasury Note 2%	01-15-14	1,026,013	1,050,902	6.24
US Treasury Note 3.5%	01-15-11	889,897	1,007,496	5.99
US Treasury Note 4.25%	01-15-10	849,217	985,855	5.86
US Treasury Note (Fut)	12-20-04	749,900	844,575	5.02
EuroDollar (Fut)	06-13-05	609,250	592,313	3.52
US Treasury Note 1.875%	07-15-13	525,643	534,740	3.18
US Treasury Note 3.375%	01-15-12	279,420	316,695	1.88
US Treasury Bond 2.375%	01-15-25	214,332	223,350	1.33
US Treasury Bond 3.375%	04-15-32	112,366	142,498	0.85
US Treasury Note 2%	07-15-14	89,230	91,238	0.54
France (Republic Of) 3.1	07-25-12	53,826	74,174	0.44
Germany (Federal Republi	01-04-11	42,500	57,811	0.34
Pylon Ltd Frn 18dec08 Se	12-18-08	40,700	52,508	0.31
Phoenix Quake 144A FRN	07-03-08	50,550	52,411	0.31

Current Investment Style

Duration: Short Int Long — Quality: High Med Low

[1] figure provided by fund

Avg Eff Duration[1]	6.1 Yrs
Avg Eff Maturity	11.4 Yrs
Avg Credit Quality	AAA
Avg Wtd Coupon	3.26%
Avg Wtd Price	113.50% of par

Coupon Range	% of Bonds	Rel Cat
0% PIK	1.1	0.0
0% to 6%	98.1	1.2
6% to 8%	1.6	0.1
8% to 10%	0.2	0.1
More than 10%	0.1	0.2

1.00=Category Average

Credit Analysis		% bonds 09-30-04	
US Govt	91	BB	2
AAA	4	B	0
AA	0	Below B	0
A	1	NR/NA	0
BBB	2		

Sector Breakdown	% of assets
US Treasuries	2
TIPS	85
US Agency	0
Mortgage Pass-Throughs	0
Mortgage CMO	0
Mortgage ARM	0
US Corporate	3
Asset-Backed	0
Convertible	0
Municipal	1
Corporate Inflation-Protected	0
Foreign Corporate	0
Foreign Govt	2

Composition			
Cash	6.2	Bonds	88.8
Stocks	0.0	Other	5.0

Special Securities	
Restricted/Illiquid Secs	2
Exotic Mortgage-Backed	0
Emerging-Markets Secs	Trace
Options/Futures/Warrants	Yes

Morningstar's Take by Eric Jacobson 12-30-04

PIMCO Real Return is behaving in a very PIMCO way.

That may sound trite, but we mean it. For one thing, this fund has always distinguished itself from rivals focused on inflation-protected Treasuries (TIPS) who have chosen to go the plain-vanilla route. Maturity-spectrum plays are common among that crowd, but that's about it. But while this fund has decidedly not gone overboard on risk with its bets, it has been willing to span the globe. Eurozone bonds (mostly hedged), emerging-market issues, mortgages, and even munis have all played a role here at one time or another.

Manager John Brynjolfsson also employs a classic PIMCO strategy of eking out extra returns by using forward purchase contracts to get much of its bond exposure. Buy investing the cash necessary to back such transactions in ultrashort securities, the fund can pocket their returns, minus financing costs. Most of the time that's a very low-risk, profitable tool that helps give the fund an advantage over many rivals.

As of late, Brynjolfsson's most interesting tactic has involved interest-rate positioning. Based on his outlook for the TIPS market itself, he's keeping the rate sensitivity of his TIPS holdings in line with, or just short of, its benchmark. Owing to an overall concern about inflation, however, he's also been using short Treasury futures and interest-rate swaps to eliminate some sensitivity to the conventional Treasury market.

Taken together, those factors have been a big help both over the past several months, and over the much longer term. The fund's year-to-date return beats all but one true peer. Its long-term record is equally impressive.

One needs to be comfortable giving much latitude to a manager to own this fund, and missteps are possible when so many bets are in play at once. The fund has thus far done a terrific job at managing such risks, and producing great returns, though, making it a compelling option.

Address:	PIMCO Funds Stamford, CT 06902 888-877-4626
Web Address:	www.pimcofunds.com
Inception:	01-29-97 *
Advisor:	PA Fund Management LLC
Subadvisor:	First Quadrant
NTF Plans:	Federated Tr NTF, Schwab Instl NTF

Minimum Purchase:	$5000	Add: $100	IRA: $2500
Min Auto Inv Plan:	$2500	Add: $100	
Sales Fees:	3.00%L, 0.25%S, 2.00%R		
Management Fee:	0.25%, 0.40%A		
Actual Fees:	Mgt:0.25%	Dist:0.25%	
Expense Projections:	3Yr:$578	5Yr:$784	10Yr:$1375
Income Distrib:	Monthly		

PIMCO Total Ret Instl

Ticker	Load	NAV	Yield	SEC Yield	Total Assets	Mstar Category
PTTRX	None	$10.67	2.3%	2.14%	$77,547 mil	Intermediate-Term Bond

Governance and Management

Fiduciary Grade: B

Portfolio Manager(s)

Bill Gross and Pimco's extensive team of analysts and traders, who jointly received Morningstar's manager-of-the-year honors in 1998 and 2000, are widely acknowledged to be among the best in the business.

Strategy

Manager Bill Gross couples Pimco's long-term macroeconomic outlook with its take on short-term cyclical factors to determine this fund's sector weightings and duration. Although Gross will focus heavily on certain sectors, he doesn't make huge interest-rate bets against the Lehman Brothers Aggregate Index. (Such plays are typically plus or minus 20% of the index's duration.) However, he will occasionally invest in nonindex sectors of the market such as high-yield, developed-markets international, and emerging-markets debt.

Historical Profile

Return High
Risk Above Avg
Rating ★★★★★ Highest

Investment Style: Fixed Income — Income Rtn %Rank Cat

16	36	23	36	22	45	60	68	90

▼ Manager Change
∇ Partial Manager Change

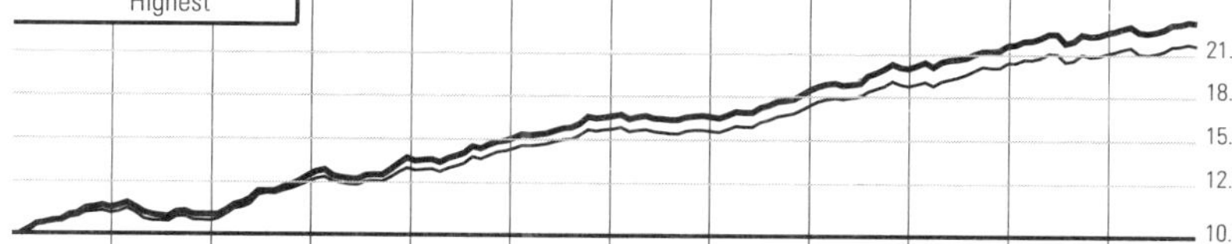

Growth of $10,000
— Investment Values of Fund
— Investment Values of LB Aggr

Performance Quartile (within Category)

1993	1994	1995	1996	1997	1998	1999	2000	2001	2002	2003	12-04	History
10.64	9.69	10.72	10.50	10.60	10.54	9.90	10.39	10.46	10.67	10.71	10.67	NAV
12.52	-3.58	19.79	4.69	10.17	9.77	-0.28	12.09	9.48	10.20	5.56	5.15	Total Return %
2.77	-0.66	1.32	1.06	0.52	1.08	0.54	0.46	1.04	-0.05	1.46	0.81	+/-LB Aggr
0.28	0.93	-1.64	2.00	0.74	-0.37	2.60	-0.35	0.66	-2.83	-0.41	-0.15	+/-LB 5-10YR
6.89	5.53	7.54	6.65	6.48	6.29	5.94	6.89	5.88	4.68	3.48	2.43	Income Return %
5.63	-9.11	12.25	-1.96	3.69	3.48	-6.22	5.20	3.60	5.52	2.08	2.72	Capital Return %
18	45	21	17	14	3	22	9	8	11	27	11	Total Rtn % Rank Cat
0.71	0.57	0.71	0.69	0.66	0.65	0.61	0.66	0.59	0.48	0.37	0.26	Income $
0.55	0.00	0.12	0.00	0.27	0.42	0.00	0.00	0.30	0.35	0.18	0.33	Capital Gains $
0.43	0.41	0.41	0.42	0.43	0.43	0.43	0.43	0.43	0.43	0.43	0.43	Expense Ratio %
7.07	6.27	6.72	6.85	6.60	6.06	5.91	6.25	6.57	5.16	4.17	2.73	Income Ratio %
90	177	98	221	173	206	154	223	418	445	234	273	Turnover Rate %
4,576	6,555	10,035	12,237	14,791	20,126	23,380	29,500	33,260	39,854	42,077	44,845	Net Assets $mil

Performance 12-31-04

	1st Qtr	2nd Qtr	3rd Qtr	4th Qtr	Total
2000	2.21	1.82	2.87	4.69	12.09
2001	2.86	-0.27	6.49	0.22	9.48
2002	0.65	3.33	3.43	2.45	10.20
2003	2.08	2.83	-0.18	0.75	5.56
2004	2.70	-2.18	3.25	1.38	5.15

Trailing	Total Return%	+/- LB Aggr	+/- LB 5-10YR	%Rank Cat	Growth of $10,000
3 Mo	1.38	0.43	0.40	18	10,138
6 Mo	4.67	0.49	-0.90	20	10,467
1 Yr	5.15	0.81	-0.15	11	10,515
3 Yr Avg	6.95	0.76	-1.10	9	12,233
5 Yr Avg	8.46	0.75	-0.61	4	15,009
10 Yr Avg	8.54	0.82	0.08	2	22,693
15 Yr Avg	8.69	0.99	0.37	2	34,901

Tax Analysis	Tax-Adj Rtn%	%Rank Cat	Tax-Cost Rat	%Rank Cat
3 Yr (estimated)	4.82	10	1.99	74
5 Yr (estimated)	5.95	6	2.31	80
10 Yr (estimated)	5.70	4	2.62	94

Potential Capital Gain Exposure: 0% of assets

Rating and Risk

Time Period	Load-Adj Return %	Morningstar Rtn vs Cat	Morningstar Risk vs Cat	Morningstar Risk-Adj Rating
1 Yr	5.15			
3 Yr	6.95	High	Avg	★★★★★
5 Yr	8.46	High	+Avg	★★★★★
10 Yr	8.54	High	+Avg	★★★★★
Incept	8.89			

Other Measures	Standard Index LB Aggr	Best Fit Index LB. U.S. Univ. Bd
Alpha	0.8	-0.1
Beta	0.98	1.03
R-Squared	95	97
Standard Deviation	4.61	
Mean	6.95	
Sharpe Ratio	1.22	

Portfolio Analysis 09-30-04

Total Fixed-Income 5732	Date of Maturity	Amount $000	Value $000	% Net Assets
US Treasury Note (Fut)	12-20-04	—	—	10.17
EuroDollar (Fut)	06-13-05	—	—	8.47
FNMA 5%		7,258,400	7,279,043	6.04
EuroDollar (Fut)	09-19-05	6,112,001	5,928,029	4.92
US Treasury Note 2.5%	09-30-06	4,473,301	4,465,082	3.70
FNMA 5.5%		2,902,900	2,941,909	2.44
Euro Dollar (Fut)	12-13-04	2,804,250	2,739,612	2.27
US Treasury Note 3.875%	01-15-09	1,636,463	1,842,748	1.53
EuroDollar (Fut)	12-19-05	1,396,750	1,351,356	1.12
US Treasury Note 4.25%	01-15-10	1,046,239	1,214,577	1.01
US Treasury Note 3.625%	01-15-08	1,017,432	1,116,116	0.93
US Treasury Note 3.5%	01-15-11	984,551	1,114,658	0.92
FNMA 5%	03-01-34	605,405	600,772	0.50
US Treasury Note 3%	07-15-12	459,257	508,681	0.42
US Treasury Bond 5.375%	02-15-31	297,400	318,683	0.26
US Treasury Note 3.375%	01-15-07	269,824	288,364	0.24
United Mexican Sts Mtn B	08-15-31	246,890	281,455	0.23
US Treasury Bond 6.25%	05-15-30	175,600	208,470	0.17
Golden St Tob Securitiza	06-01-33	186,615	176,637	0.15
MI Mtg Investors 2004-Wm	01-25-35	131,124	131,197	0.11

Current Investment Style

Duration: Short Int Long — Quality: High Med Low

¹figure provided by fund

Avg Eff Duration¹	4.3 Yrs
Avg Eff Maturity	6.0 Yrs
Avg Credit Quality	AAA
Avg Wtd Coupon	3.72%
Avg Wtd Price	106.05% of par

Coupon Range	% of Bonds	Rel Cat
0% PIK	1.9	0.5
0% to 6%	80.7	1.3
6% to 8%	14.6	0.5
8% to 10%	4.1	0.7
More than 10%	0.7	0.6

1.00=Category Average

Credit Analysis	% bonds 09-30-04		
US Govt	37	BB	1
AAA	52	B	0
AA	1	Below B	1
A	2	NR/NA	0
BBB	6		

Sector Breakdown	% of assets
US Treasuries	5
TIPS	6
US Agency	0
Mortgage Pass-Throughs	16
Mortgage CMO	4
Mortgage ARM	0
US Corporate	3
Asset-Backed	1
Convertible	0
Municipal	2
Corporate Inflation-Protected	0
Foreign Corporate	0
Foreign Govt	1

Composition			
Cash	55.7	Bonds	34.0
Stocks	0.0	Other	10.3

Special Securities	
Restricted/Illiquid Secs	Trace
Exotic Mortgage-Backed	0
Emerging-Markets Secs	Trace
Options/Futures/Warrants	Yes

Morningstar's Take by Eric Jacobson 10-28-04

Bill Gross' successful 2004 decisions help explain how he attempts to pursue return while mitigating risk.

At first glance, his sector bets might appear to support the iconic image of Gross as a market gunslinger. By the end of this year's first quarter, for example, PIMCO Total Return had some 22% of its assets devoted to bonds outside of the United States. On the other hand, Gross has largely eschewed corporate bonds, maintaining a large underweighting relative to the fund's benchmark, the Lehman Brothers Aggregate Bond Index. So even though Gross missed out on some of corporates' gains--while they helped fuel many competitors--the fund has performed quite well thanks largely to its foreign bonds. Its 4.6% institutional share gains place in the intermediate-bond category's best decile--an extension of the fund's stellar record.

PIMCO makes a good argument, however, that investors shouldn't overestimate the impact of its foreign holdings. For one thing, thanks to hedging, this fund rarely takes on more than a few percentage points of nondollar exposure, which typically lends the bulk of volatility to such positions. In addition, the large early-2004 foreign stake was skewed to short maturities. As such, the portfolio's overall rate sensitivity was actually low relative to the benchmark. (Now that Gross has shifted to longer foreign bonds, they consume less of the fund.) Finally, PIMCO's analytics suggest that while its foreign-bond bets are important to the fund's success, they aren't likely to have nearly as much an impact as some of its other plays, such as interest-rate positioning, for example.

The bottom line is that while Bill Gross has the flexibility, and arguably the fortitude, to place more unusual bets than most, risk has always been part of the PIMCO calculus. That doesn't mean this fund can't underperform, but it does help explain how it has avoided many of the market's worst potholes. All in all, it remains one of our favorites.

Address:	PIMCO Funds Stamford, CT 06902 800-927-4648
Web Address:	www.pimcofunds.com
Inception:	05-11-87
Advisor:	PA Fund Management LLC
Subadvisor:	First Quadrant
NTF Plans:	N/A

Minimum Purchase:	$5000000	Add: $0	IRA: $0
Min Auto Inv Plan:	$0	Add: —	
Sales Fees:	No-load		
Management Fee:	0.25%, 0.18%A		
Actual Fees:	Mgt:0.25%	Dist:	
Expense Projections:	3Yr:$138	5Yr:$241	10Yr:$542
Income Distrib:	Monthly		

Pioneer A

Ticker	Load	NAV	Yield	Total Assets	Mstar Category
PIODX	5.75%	$42.06	0.8%	$7,242 mil	Large Blend

Governance and Management

Fiduciary Grade: C

Portfolio Manager(s)

John Carey is a veteran manager and has been with Pioneer since 1979. He has been running the show here since 1986. In 2001, he was joined by assistant portfolio manager Walter Hunnewell. Carey has also put up solid numbers at his other charge, Pioneer Equity-Income.

Strategy

John Carey uses a patient, growth-at-a-reasonable-price approach. He looks for blue-chip companies that have been beaten down but have some catalyst for increased earnings. Along with healthy operating margins, Carey favors firms whose rates of return on equity surpass those of industry peers. He sticks with what he buys, too, as the fund has one of the category's lowest turnover rates.

Historical Profile

Return Average
Risk Below Avg
Rating ★★★ Neutral

Investment Style
Equity
Stock %

98% | 99% | 99% | 99% | 100% | 100% | 99% | 99% | 100%

▼ Manager Change
▽ Partial Manager Change

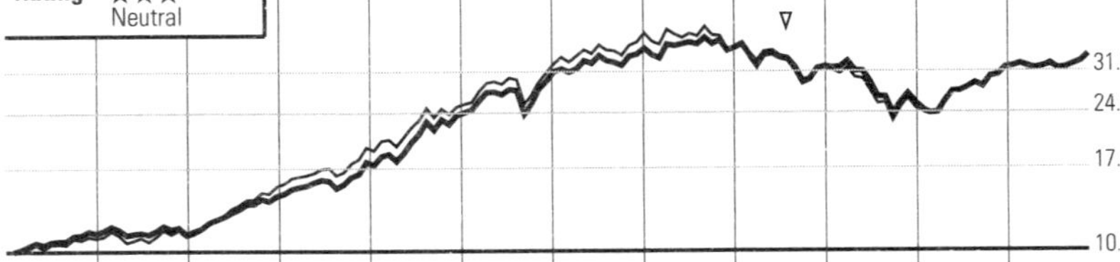

Growth of $10,000
— Investment Values of Fund
— Investment Values of S&P 500

Performance Quartile (within Category)

1993	1994	1995	1996	1997	1998	1999	2000	2001	2002	2003	12-04	History
23.25	21.32	24.36	26.89	34.95	43.33	47.60	44.26	38.87	30.76	38.00	42.06	NAV
14.22	-0.58	26.64	19.70	38.47	29.09	15.54	0.12	-11.13	-20.26	24.58	11.63	Total Return %
4.16	-1.89	-10.89	-3.24	5.12	0.52	-5.50	9.22	0.75	1.83	-4.09	0.76	+/-S&P 500
4.04	-0.97	-11.13	-2.75	5.62	2.07	-5.37	7.91	1.32	1.39	-5.31	0.23	+/-Russ 1000
2.20	2.12	2.30	1.54	1.15	0.59	0.40	0.26	0.37	0.66	0.92	0.89	Income Return %
12.02	-2.70	24.34	18.16	37.32	28.50	15.14	-0.14	-11.50	-20.92	23.66	10.74	Capital Return %
28	56	88	66	2	13	74	25	36	30	72	26	Total Rtn % Rank Cat
0.47	0.49	0.49	0.37	0.31	0.20	0.17	0.12	0.16	0.26	0.28	0.34	Income $
0.83	1.30	2.09	1.82	1.89	1.49	2.22	3.24	0.30	0.00	0.00	0.00	Capital Gains $
0.95	0.94	0.94	0.99	1.03	1.08	1.09	1.11	1.13	1.11	1.09	—	Expense Ratio %
2.04	2.13	2.02	1.42	0.93	0.53	0.40	0.31	0.44	0.76	0.86	—	Income Ratio %
12	20	31	25	17	9	10	20	6	7	6	—	Turnover Rate %
2,042	2,011	2,446	2,896	3,992	5,395	6,637	6,644	6,146	4,586	5,371	5,627	Net Assets $mil

Performance 12-31-04

	1st Qtr	2nd Qtr	3rd Qtr	4th Qtr	Total
2000	2.50	1.29	-1.03	-2.56	0.12
2001	-9.01	3.80	-14.02	9.44	-11.13
2002	3.40	-12.24	-18.18	7.40	-20.26
2003	-5.99	14.45	2.69	12.75	24.58
2004	0.48	1.55	-0.26	9.69	11.63

Trailing	Total Return%	+/- S&P 500	+/- Russ 1000	%Rank Cat	Growth of $10,000
3 Mo	9.69	0.46	-0.11	35	10,969
6 Mo	9.41	2.22	1.60	11	10,941
1 Yr	11.63	0.76	0.23	26	11,163
3 Yr Avg	3.51	-0.07	-0.76	35	11,090
5 Yr Avg	-0.27	2.03	1.49	26	9,866
10 Yr Avg	11.94	-0.13	-0.22	18	30,892
15 Yr Avg	10.36	-0.57	-0.72	34	43,871

Tax Analysis	Tax-Adj Rtn%	%Rank Cat	Tax-Cost Rat	%Rank Cat
3 Yr (estimated)	1.18	66	0.30	25
5 Yr (estimated)	-1.99	33	0.56	30
10 Yr (estimated)	9.97	30	1.18	40

Potential Capital Gain Exposure: 37% of assets

Rating and Risk

Time Period	Load-Adj Return %	Morningstar Rtn vs Cat	Morningstar Risk vs Cat	Morningstar Risk-Adj Rating
1 Yr	5.21			
3 Yr	1.48	-Avg	Avg	★★
5 Yr	-1.44	Avg	-Avg	★★★
10 Yr	11.28	Avg	-Avg	★★★★
Incept	12.45			

Other Measures	Standard Index S&P 500	Best Fit Index S&P 500
Alpha	0.0	0.0
Beta	0.97	0.97
R-Squared	97	97
Standard Deviation	15.36	
Mean	3.51	
Sharpe Ratio	0.14	

Morningstar's Take by Sonya Morris 12-10-04

Pioneer Fund remains a fine choice.

Longtime manager John Carey employs a strategy that's unlikely to suit daring types. Carey sifts through the large-cap universe for names that he believes are cheap relative to his estimate of their future earnings growth. He pays close attention to valuations, favoring stocks trading near historically low multiples or at a discount to the broader market.

That said, Carey isn't a total chicken. For instance, he'll sometimes scoop up out-of-favor names if he believes the conditions are ripe for an earnings pickup. For example, this year, he bought shares of apparel retailer Gap on weakness when disappointing same-store sales felled the stock. Despite that adversity, Carey argues, the company still boasts a solid franchise overseen by a capable management team.

Carey also possesses an increasingly scarce commodity among managers: patience. Indeed, the portfolio's ultralow 6% turnover rate is indicative of Carey's buy-and-hold style. In fact, the fund still has a position in Walgreen, the first name Carey added to the portfolio when he took the reins here 18 years ago.

Of course, you can wait an eternity to draw water from stone and still come up dry. But Carey has shown a deft stock-picking touch during his tenure. For example, the fund's 10-year trailing return surpasses more than 80% of its large-blend rivals.

This strategy does have drawbacks. For instance, because Carey tends to shun pricier fare, the fund can have less exposure to the tech sector than its rivals. That means it can look like an also-ran in go-go growth climates, as evidenced by the fund's lackluster 1999 and 2003 campaigns. However, wide diversification--stock positions can't exceed 4.5% of assets and sector weightings are capped at 25%--has tempered volatility, making it a particularly appealing choice for conservative investors.

Portfolio Analysis 12-31-04

Share change since 11-04 Total Stocks:141	Sector	PE	YTD Ret%	% Assets
⊕ ExxonMobil	Energy	13.9	28.04	2.40
⊕ ChevronTexaco	Energy	7.7	25.57	2.34
⊕ Target	Consumer	22.3	36.14	2.16
McGraw-Hill Companies	Media	22.7	32.94	2.03
Norfolk Southern	Business	—	55.12	1.87
⊕ Johnson & Johnson	Health	20.6	25.17	1.82
T Rowe Price Group	Financial	25.6	33.16	1.81
John Wiley & Sons A	Media	24.9	35.06	1.68
Rio Tinto	Ind Mtrls	—	—	1.63
SBC Communications	Telecom	15.4	3.74	1.60
⊕ PACCAR	Ind Mtrls	15.6	47.28	1.52
Walgreen	Consumer	31.6	6.03	1.51
National City	Financial	9.6	14.90	1.49
General Dynamics	Ind Mtrls	17.5	17.40	1.44
⊕ Microsoft	Software	36.1	8.95	1.38
⊕ Deere & Company	Ind Mtrls	15.7	16.26	1.37
⊕ United Technologies	Ind Mtrls	18.6	10.72	1.32
Chubb	Financial	12.9	15.43	1.25
⊕ Gannett	Media	17.1	-7.23	1.24
Becton, Dickinson and Co	Health	24.4	39.74	1.20

Current Investment Style

Value Blnd Growth — Large Mid Small

Market Cap	%
Giant	35.6
Large	52.5
Mid	11.9
Small	0.0
Micro	0.0
Avg $mil: 30,511	

Value Measures		Rel Category
Price/Earnings	17.34	1.02
Price/Book	3.07	1.17
Price/Sales	1.50	1.04
Price/Cash Flow	8.62	1.12
Dividend Yield %	1.56	1.05

Growth Measures	%	Rel Category
Long-Term Erngs	10.42	0.90
Book Value	10.17	1.31
Sales	7.11	1.24
Cash Flow	6.14	0.65
Historical Erngs	12.63	1.07

Profitability	%	Rel Category
Return on Equity	20.40	1.17
Return on Assets	10.14	1.17
Net Margin	12.38	1.08

Sector Weightings	% of Stocks	Rel S&P 500	3 Year High	3 Year Low
Info	20.80	0.97		
Software	3.00	0.70	4	3
Hardware	8.79	0.86	13	8
Media	5.39	1.40	6	5
Telecom	3.62	1.15	7	3
Service	42.95	0.33		
Health	11.82	0.95	13	10
Consumer	7.73	0.85	9	6
Business	7.32	1.81	9	7
Financial	16.08	0.77	18	14
Mfg	36.24	1.13		
Goods	10.02	1.07	14	8
Ind Mtrls	16.33	1.29	17	10
Energy	8.01	1.12	10	6
Utilities	1.88	0.64	2	1

Composition

Cash	0.0
Stocks	100.0
Bonds	0.0
Other	0.0
Foreign (% of Stock)	5.8

Address:	60 State St., 19th Floor, Boston MA 02109, 800-225-6292
Web Address:	www.pioneerfunds.com
Inception:	02-10-28
Advisor:	Pioneer Investment Management, Inc.
Subadvisor:	None
NTF Plans:	DATALynx NTF, Federated Tr NTF

Minimum Purchase:	$1000	Add: $100	IRA: $250
Min Auto Inv Plan:	$0	Add: —	
Sales Fees:	5.75%L		
Management Fee:	0.50%		
Actual Fees:	Mgt:0.50%	Dist:0.25%	
Expense Projections:	3Yr:$902	5Yr:$1141	10Yr:$1827
Income Distrib:	Quarterly		

Pioneer High Yield A

Ticker	Load	NAV	Yield	SEC Yield	Total Assets	Mstar Category
TAHYX	4.50%	$11.61	6.2%	3.88%	$8,091 mil	High Yield Bond

Governance and Management

Fiduciary Grade: C

Portfolio Manager(s)

Margie Patel has run this fund since its inception in 1998. The fund started out as Third Avenue High Yield, but it was sold to Pioneer in early 2000. Patel works with a team of 18 Pioneer equity analysts.

Strategy

This high-yield fund is less diversified than most and owns a large chunk of convertible bonds, which typically account for close to 60% of the portfolio. Manager Margie Patel favors convertibles, arguing that they provide the fund exposure to sectors of the market that typically don't issue a lot of high-yield fare. They also provide added total-return potential and added liquidity. In the high-yield market, she prefers to invest in stable companies and has largely avoided the telecom sector. However, many of the fund's convertibles are from the volatile technology sector.

Historical Profile

Return Above Avg
Risk Above Avg
Rating ★★★★ Above Avg

Investment Style
Fixed Income
Income Rtn %Rank Cat

1998	1999	2000	2001	2002	2003	12-04
100	85	32	45	34	67	78

▼ Manager Change
▽ Partial Manager Change

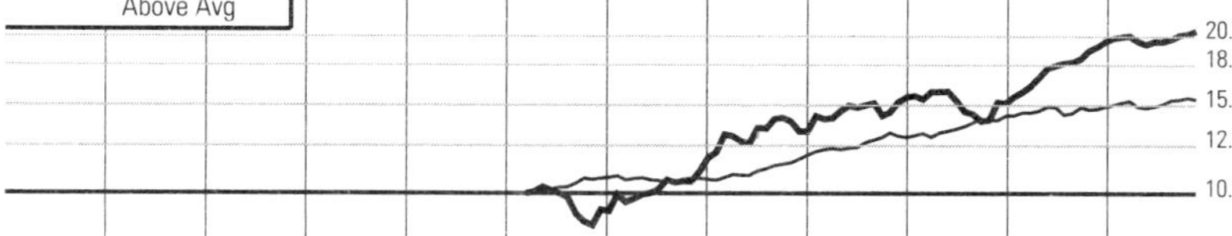

Growth of $10,000
— Investment Values of Fund
— Investment Values of LB Aggr

Performance Quartile (within Category)

History

1993	1994	1995	1996	1997	1998	1999	2000	2001	2002	2003	12-04	History
—	—	—	—	—	8.89	10.39	10.35	10.98	9.70	11.94	11.61	NAV
—	—	—	—	—	-6.69*	27.09	12.81	16.74	-2.70	32.13	6.75	Total Return %
—	—	—	—	—	—	27.91	1.18	8.30	-12.95	28.03	2.41	+/-LB Aggr
—	—	—	—	—	—	23.81	18.02	10.96	-5.81	4.20	-5.21	+/-CSFB Glb HY
—	—	—	—	—	0.00	7.88	10.49	10.52	9.34	8.14	6.44	Income Return %
—	—	—	—	—	—	19.21	2.32	6.22	-12.04	23.99	0.31	Capital Return %
—	—	—	—	—	—	1	2	2	68	6	94	Total Rtn % Rank Cat
—	—	—	—	—	0.44	0.68	1.04	1.04	0.98	0.76	0.74	Income $
—	—	—	—	—	0.00	0.15	0.34	0.00	0.00	0.01	0.35	Capital Gains $
—	—	—	—	—	1.90	1.90	0.95	0.96	1.10	1.06	—	Expense Ratio %
—	—	—	—	—	6.22	7.31	8.96	9.54	9.13	7.30	—	Income Ratio %
—	—	—	—	—	38	38	57	24	29	38	—	Turnover Rate %
—	—	—	—	—	8	9	61	572	1,505	3,614	3,642	Net Assets $mil

Performance 12-31-04

	1st Qtr	2nd Qtr	3rd Qtr	4th Qtr	Total
2000	10.38	3.92	4.55	-5.95	12.81
2001	6.17	4.94	-3.63	8.72	16.74
2002	2.42	-3.77	-8.98	8.45	-2.70
2003	8.01	9.79	3.14	8.03	32.13
2004	2.76	-2.50	2.94	3.50	6.75

Trailing	Total Return%	+/- LB Aggr	+/- CSFB Glb HY	%Rank Cat	Growth of $10,000
3 Mo	3.50	2.55	-1.06	79	10,350
6 Mo	6.54	2.36	-2.72	95	10,654
1 Yr	6.75	2.41	-5.21	94	10,675
3 Yr Avg	11.13	4.94	-2.75	36	13,724
5 Yr Avg	12.56	4.85	4.39	2	18,068
10 Yr Avg	—	—	—	—	—
15 Yr Avg	—	—	—	—	—

Tax Analysis	Tax-Adj Rtn%	%Rank Cat	Tax-Cost Rat	%Rank Cat
3 Yr (estimated)	6.26	63	2.91	56
5 Yr (estimated)	7.70	2	3.43	59
10 Yr (estimated)	—	—	—	—

Potential Capital Gain Exposure: 8% of assets

Rating and Risk

Time Period	Load-Adj Return %	Morningstar Rtn vs Cat	Morningstar Risk vs Cat	Morningstar Risk-Adj Rating
1 Yr	1.94			
3 Yr	9.44	Avg	+Avg	★★★
5 Yr	11.53	High	+Avg	★★★★★
10 Yr	—	—	—	—
Incept	10.97			

Other Measures	Standard Index LB Aggr	Best Fit Index Merrill Lynch Convert
Alpha	11.2	2.4
Beta	-0.23	0.97
R-Squared	1	76
Standard Deviation	9.27	
Mean	11.13	
Sharpe Ratio	1.06	

Portfolio Analysis 06-30-04

Total Fixed-Income:90	Date of Maturity	Amount $000	Value $000	% Net Assets
Tesoro Pete 9.625%	04-01-12	237,380	266,459	3.48
Conexant Sys Cv 4%	02-01-07	221,715	212,292	2.77
Texas Inds 10.25%	06-15-11	185,535	206,872	2.70
Freeport-Mcmoran Copper		199	178,354	2.33
Sci Sys Cv 3%	03-15-07	183,695	171,755	2.24
Crown European Hldgs Sa	03-01-11	156,371	170,444	2.22
Ivax Cv 4.5%	05-15-08	169,355	167,661	2.19
Bowater 6.5%	06-15-13	177,140	166,648	2.17
Interpublic Grp Cos 7.25	08-15-11	150,125	160,601	2.10
Corning Cv 3.5%	11-01-08	112,309	158,075	2.06
Lnr Ppty 7.25%	10-15-13	154,195	150,340	1.96
Crescent Real Estate Equ	04-15-09	129,130	134,941	1.76
Millennium Chemicals 144	11-15-23	83,580	129,967	1.70
Interpublic Grp Cos Cv 4	03-15-23	93,775	127,534	1.66
Freeport-Mcmoran Copper	02-11-11	89,900	125,411	1.64
Drs Tech 6.875%	11-01-13	124,888	121,766	1.59
Jlg Inds 8.375%	06-15-12	113,585	115,573	1.51
Human Genome Sciences Cv	03-15-07	123,019	115,330	1.50
Forest City Enterprises	06-01-15	108,230	108,771	1.42
Inco Cv 3.5%	03-14-52	73,450	106,962	1.40

Current Investment Style
Duration: Short Int Long
Quality: High Med Low

¹ figure provided by fund

Avg Eff Duration¹	4.6 Yrs
Avg Eff Maturity	6.9 Yrs
Avg Credit Quality	B
Avg Wtd Coupon	6.17%
Avg Wtd Price	103.73% of par

Coupon Range	% of Bonds	Rel Cat
0% PIK	0.0	0.0
0% to 8%	57.9	1.5
8% to 11%	41.8	0.8
11% to 14%	0.2	0.0
More than 14%	0.0	0.0

1.00=Category Average

Credit Analysis		% bonds 06-30-04	
US Govt	0	BB	27
AAA	0	B	38
AA	0	Below B	7
A	0	NR/NA	18
BBB	9		

Sector Breakdown	% of assets
US Treasuries	0
TIPS	0
US Agency	0
Mortgage Pass-Throughs	0
Mortgage CMO	0
Mortgage ARM	0
US Corporate	52
Asset-Backed	0
Convertible	45
Municipal	0
Corporate Inflation-Protected	0
Foreign Corporate	2
Foreign Govt	0

Composition			
Cash	0.8	Bonds	53.3
Stocks	0.2	Other	45.6

Special Securities	
Restricted/Illiquid Secs	13
Exotic Mortgage-Backed	0
Emerging-Markets Secs	0
Options/Futures/Warrants	No

Morningstar's Take by Scott Berry 11-15-04

We don't think investors should be overly concerned about Pioneer High Yield's disappointing near-term results.

The high-yield bond market has continued to deliver solid gains in 2004, but this fund has fallen off the pace set by its category rivals. The fund started the year strong, but price erosion in its convertible securities weighed on returns in the second quarter. The fund has rallied since then, but its 4.9% gain for the year to date through Nov. 12, 2004, ranked near the back of the pack.

This fund is not a typical high-yield bond fund, so we don't expect typical results here. Rather than sticking with plain-vanilla low-quality corporate bonds, manager Margie Patel bulks up on convertible securities to the tune of 40% to 60% of net assets. She argues that convertible issues often provide more upside potential and less downside risk than many conventional high-yield issues. That certainly looked to be the case in 1999, 2000, and 2001, when convertible issues powered the fund to double-digit gains. However, as the fund's recent results can illustrate, convertible securities can make this fund a bit unpredictable.

Patel has managed the fund's risks well over the long-term, though, and has actually played more defense than offense in recent months. She has trimmed the fund's convertible bond stake, arguing that convertibles have gone from cheap to very risky, and has bulked up on higher-quality plain-vanilla junk bonds, arguing that lower-rated issues aren't offering enough yield or total return potential to compensate for their added risk. The fund's defensive leanings might limit its total return potential, but should cushion the fund against a market downturn.

We think Patel has done a marvelous job with this fund, and think investors comfortable with its risks could be quite happy here. However, those looking for a more traditional high-yield bond fund may want to look elsewhere, given the fund's large convertible bond exposure.

Address:	60 State Street 19th Floor Boston MA 02109 800-225-6292
Web Address:	www.pioneerfunds.com
Inception:	02-12-98*
Advisor:	Pioneer Investment Management, Inc.
Subadvisor:	None
NTF Plans:	DATALynx NTF, Federated Tr NTF

Minimum Purchase:	$1000	Add: $1000	IRA: $500
Min Auto Inv Plan:	$1000	Add: $200	
Sales Fees:	4.50%L, 0.25%S		
Management Fee:	0.70% mx./0.30% mn.		
Actual Fees:	Mgt:0.63%	Dist:0.25%	
Expense Projections:	3Yr:$803	5Yr:$1078	10Yr:$1862
Income Distrib:	Monthly		

Putnam Capital Opport A

Ticker	Load	NAV	Yield	Total Assets	Mstar Category
PCOAX	5.25%	$12.02	0.0%	$1,098 mil	Small Blend

Governance and Management

Fiduciary Grade: C

Portfolio Manager(s)

Managers Joe Joseph and Gerry Moore, both Putnam veterans, have been at the helm since February 1999 and August 2000, respectively. Joseph helps run other offerings for the family, including Putnam International Capital Opportunities. Tinh Bui, who invests all of his deferred compensation in this offering, has helped with stock selection since July 2002. John Ferry joined the management team in December 2003.

Strategy

This fund's managers buy small- and mid-cap stocks that look cheap based on the firms' expected earnings growth. This go-anywhere mandate has prompted the fund to shift among the squares in the lower two rows of Morningstar's style box. Sometimes the managers are in the right place at the right time, but not always.

Historical Profile

Return Below Avg
Risk High
Rating ★ Lowest

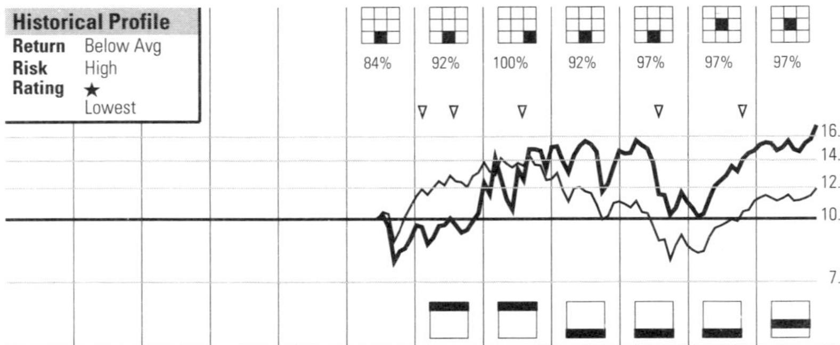

Investment Style
Equity
Stock %

▼ Manager Change
▽ Partial Manager Change

Growth of $10,000
— Investment Values of Fund
— Investment Values of S&P 500

Performance Quartile (within Category)

1993	1994	1995	1996	1997	1998	1999	2000	2001	2002	2003	12-04	History
—	—	—	—	—	8.10	10.29	10.65	10.33	7.62	10.15	12.02	NAV
—	—	—	—	—	-3.47*	27.04	21.93	-2.08	-24.84	33.20	18.42	Total Return %
—	—	—	—	—	—	6.00	31.03	9.80	-2.75	4.53	7.55	+/-S&P 500
—	—	—	—	—	—	5.78	24.95	-4.57	-4.36	-14.05	0.09	+/-Russ 2000
—	—	—	—	—	0.00	0.00	0.00	0.00	0.00	0.00	0.00	Income Return %
—	—	—	—	—	—	27.04	21.93	-2.08	-24.84	33.20	18.42	Capital Return %
—	—	—	—	—	—	20	23	89	92	89	53	Total Rtn % Rank Cat
—	—	—	—	—	0.03	0.00	0.00	0.00	0.00	0.00	0.00	Income $
—	—	—	—	—	0.00	0.00	1.80	0.10	0.15	0.00	0.00	Capital Gains $
—	—	—	—	—	—	1.15	1.24	1.17	1.10	1.17	1.19	Expense Ratio %
—	—	—	—	—	—	0.30	-0.67	-0.40	-0.31	-0.01	0.10	Income Ratio %
—	—	—	—	—	—	272	273	220	120	91	134	Turnover Rate %
—	—	—	—	—	51	81	165	258	365	472	428	Net Assets $mil

Performance 12-31-04

	1st Qtr	2nd Qtr	3rd Qtr	4th Qtr	Total
2000	2.33	5.22	12.09	1.02	21.93
2001	-13.05	19.11	-24.66	25.50	-2.08
2002	6.10	-11.68	-25.41	7.54	-24.84
2003	-6.56	20.51	5.48	12.15	33.20
2004	4.14	1.51	-1.40	13.61	18.42

Trailing	Total Return%	+/- S&P 500	+/- Russ 2000	%Rank Cat	Growth of $10,000
3 Mo	13.61	4.38	-0.48	34	11,361
6 Mo	12.02	4.83	1.19	27	11,202
1 Yr	18.42	7.55	0.09	53	11,842
3 Yr Avg	5.84	2.26	-5.64	94	11,856
5 Yr Avg	7.20	9.50	0.59	80	14,157
10 Yr Avg	—	—	—	—	—
15 Yr Avg	—	—	—	—	—

Tax Analysis	Tax-Adj Rtn%	%Rank Cat	Tax-Cost Rat	%Rank Cat
3 Yr (estimated)	3.77	96	0.17	12
5 Yr (estimated)	4.65	91	1.32	64
10 Yr (estimated)	—	—	—	—

Potential Capital Gain Exposure: 20% of assets

Rating and Risk

Time Period	Load-Adj Return %	Morningstar Rtn vs Cat	Morningstar Risk vs Cat	Morningstar Risk-Adj Rating
1 Yr	12.21			
3 Yr	3.95	Low	+Avg	★
5 Yr	6.05	-Avg	High	★
10 Yr	—	—	—	—
Incept	7.85			

Other Measures	Standard Index S&P 500	Best Fit Index S&P Mid 400
Alpha	2.5	-5.7
Beta	1.12	1.23
R-Squared	78	94
Standard Deviation	20.35	
Mean	5.84	
Sharpe Ratio	0.22	

Morningstar's Take by Laura Pavlenko Lutton 11-30-04

We think investors have stronger options elsewhere than Putnam Capital Opportunities.

This is not a typical small-blend fund. To be sure, the fund's strategy is fairly straightforward. The management team, led by Putnam veteran Joe Joseph, looks for cheap companies with improving returns on capital and reasonable financial leverage. These criteria lead the managers to a mix of value and growth stocks, thus making this offering's blend designation appropriate.

Where the fund differs significantly from its typical category peer is in its market-cap hunting ground. This offering owns virtually no micro-cap stocks, but it does hold names with up to $4 billion in market-cap--stocks solidly in the mid-cap camp. Thus, the fund at times looks more like a mid-blend offering than the average small-blend fund.

Unfortunately, this fund's mandate hasn't served it well in recent years. For three calendar years beginning in 2001, value-oriented micro-caps led the market, yet this offering leaned toward mid-cap growth stocks. The fund therefore finished all three calendar years in the small-blend group's bottom quartile and sunk its long-term record.

Things are going better in 2004 now that the micro-cap rally has subsided. Sizable gains among the fund's top holdings, including chemical maker Georgia Gulf, have helped lift the offering 15.17% for the year to date through Nov. 29. That return isn't stellar, but it's near the category average and the fund's best relative showing since 2000.

This fund's struggles relative to its category average are somewhat understandable, but we're not ready to excuse its poor returns. In fact, relative to other funds with similar strategies, this offering's record is mediocre at best. That suggests that the managers' stock-picking has missed the mark at times, which is troubling. Therefore, until the stock-picking improves here, we see little reason to invest.

Address:	One Post Office Square Boston MA 02109 800-225-1581
Web Address:	www.putnaminvestments.com
Inception:	06-01-98*
Advisor:	Putnam Investment Management Co.
Subadvisor:	None
NTF Plans:	Federated Tr NTF, Fidelity Instl-NTF

Minimum Purchase:	$500	Add: $50	IRA: $500
Min Auto Inv Plan:	$500	Add: $25	
Sales Fees:	5.25%L, 0.25%S, 2.00%R		
Management Fee:	0.65% mx./0.38% mn.		
Actual Fees:	Mgt:0.59%	Dist:0.25%	
Expense Projections:	3Yr:$883	5Yr:$1145	10Yr:$1892
Income Distrib:	Annually		

Portfolio Analysis 09-30-04

Share change since 06-04 Total Stocks:121	Sector	PE	YTD Ret%	% Assets
⊕ Terex	Ind Mtrls	24.3	67.31	2.90
⊕ Georgia Gulf	Ind Mtrls	20.4	73.99	2.64
⊕ BMC Software	Software	—	-0.27	2.51
⊕ Citrix Systems	Software	34.1	15.60	2.50
⊖ SuperValu	Consumer	12.4	23.24	2.43
⊕ NVR	Consumer	12.2	65.11	2.34
⊕ Renaissance Re Holdings	Financial	41.6	7.39	2.14
Michaels Stores	Consumer	22.9	36.87	1.93
Denbury Resources	Energy	19.5	97.34	1.88
Autoliv	Ind Mtrls	16.9	30.63	1.85
⊕ Manor Care	Health	19.1	4.21	1.76
Providian Financial	Financial	14.3	41.50	1.67
Coinstar	Business	26.6	48.15	1.61
⊕ Hasbro	Goods	19.3	-7.90	1.60
Rent-A-Center	Consumer	13.7	-11.67	1.56
Yankee Candle Company	Ind Mtrls	20.9	21.41	1.53
Cabot Oil & Gas A	Energy	18.1	51.42	1.50
Health Net	Health	15.4	-11.71	1.37
Storage Technology	Hardware	20.8	22.76	1.35
⊖ CR Bard	Health	26.6	58.94	1.27

Current Investment Style

Value Blnd Growth; Large Mid Small

Market Cap	%
Giant	0.0
Large	0.0
Mid	57.6
Small	40.6
Micro	1.8

Avg $mil: 1,787

Value Measures		Rel Category
Price/Earnings	13.76	0.80
Price/Book	2.19	1.10
Price/Sales	0.87	0.92
Price/Cash Flow	4.66	0.80
Dividend Yield %	1.07	1.29

Growth Measures	%	Rel Category
Long-Term Erngs	12.04	0.89
Book Value	8.06	1.43
Sales	6.68	1.55
Cash Flow	13.01	2.63
Historical Erngs	16.73	2.24

Profitability	%	Rel Category
Return on Equity	18.07	1.73
Return on Assets	8.70	1.75
Net Margin	12.65	1.73

Sector Weightings	% of Stocks	Rel S&P 500	3 Year High	3 Year Low
Info	13.69	0.64		
Software	6.17	1.43	8	2
Hardware	6.10	0.60	16	6
Media	0.00	0.00	7	0
Telecom	1.42	0.45	3	0
Service	55.26	1.19		
Health	10.18	0.81	14	6
Consumer	13.54	1.49	15	9
Business	7.37	1.82	16	6
Financial	24.17	1.16	24	14
Mfg	31.03	0.97		
Goods	2.81	0.30	9	3
Ind Mtrls	18.35	1.45	18	11
Energy	7.24	1.01	7	1
Utilities	2.63	0.89	4	2

Composition

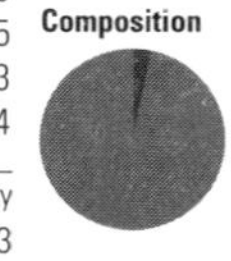

Cash	3.1
Stocks	96.8
Bonds	0.0
Other	0.0
Foreign (% of Stock)	0.0

Putnam Fund for Gr&Inc A

Ticker	Load	NAV	Yield	Total Assets	Mstar Category
PGRWX	5.25%	$19.40	1.2%	$18,274 mil	Large Value

Governance and Management

Fiduciary Grade: C

Portfolio Manager(s)

Hugh Mullin leads the fund's management team and has been on board here since 1996. Mullin is assisted by Chris Miller (who joined in 2000) and David King (who runs the successful Putnam New Value Fund and has been a manager here since 1993). These experienced managers have Putnam's deep and talented pool of analysts at their disposal.

Strategy

The fund's three managers follow a plain-vanilla investing style. They look for fundamentally strong blue-chip companies that are trading below the managers' estimates of their fair values. Additionally, they pay ample attention to diversification and stick with larger-cap names.

Historical Profile

Return Below Avg
Risk Average
Rating ★★ Below Avg

Investment Style: Equity — Stock %: 92% | 100% | 96% | 99% | 98% | 96% | 95% | 99% | 98%

▼ Manager Change
▽ Partial Manager Change

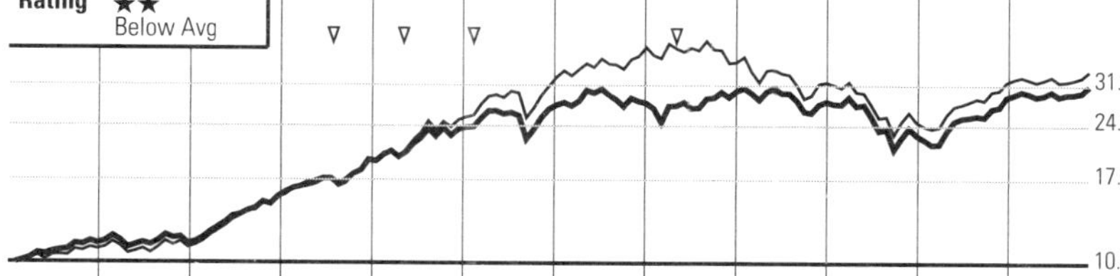

Growth of $10,000
— Investment Values of Fund
— Investment Values of S&P 500

Performance Quartile (within Category)

1993	1994	1995	1996	1997	1998	1999	2000	2001	2002	2003	12-04	History
13.60	12.72	16.19	18.02	19.54	20.49	18.75	19.53	1?.72	14.14	17.70	19.40	NAV
14.45	-0.28	36.54	21.81	24.16	15.18	1.26	7.94	-6.37	-19.13	27.22	10.97	Total Return %
4.39	-1.59	-0.99	-1.13	-9.19	-13.39	-19.78	17.04	5.51	2.96	-1.45	0.10	+/-S&P 500
-3.62	1.70	-1.82	0.17	-11.02	-0.45	-6.09	0.93	-0.78	-3.61	-2.81	-5.52	+/-Russ 1000 VI
4.11	2.97	3.18	2.59	2.57	1.88	1.99	1.35	1.44	1.19	1.80	1.30	Income Return %
10.34	-3.25	33.36	19.22	21.59	13.30	-0.73	6.59	-?.81	-20.32	25.42	9.67	Capital Return %
47	45	19	29	81	33	65	59	66	56	55	71	Total Rtn % Rank Cat
0.52	0.40	0.40	0.42	0.46	0.37	0.41	0.25	0.28	0.21	0.25	0.23	Income $
0.54	0.44	0.72	1.24	2.38	1.60	1.64	0.42	0.30	0.00	0.00	0.00	Capital Gains $
0.93	0.95	0.89	0.92	0.86	0.84	0.79	0.81	0.82	0.86	0.90	—	Expense Ratio %
3.18	3.18	3.20	2.59	1.95	1.27	1.32	1.38	1.14	1.33	1.53	—	Income Ratio %
64	49	58	41	64	79	50	52	37	30	33	—	Turnover Rate %
5,327	5,848	8,611	12,305	17,298	20,760	21,090	20,229	19,023	14,196	14,702	12,739	Net Assets $mil

Performance 12-31-04

	1st Qtr	2nd Qtr	3rd Qtr	4th Qtr	Total
2000	-1.76	-1.39	6.84	4.29	7.94
2001	-5.29	4.27	-10.99	6.52	-6.37
2002	2.71	-11.59	-18.60	9.40	-19.13
2003	-5.65	18.13	0.70	13.36	27.22
2004	2.42	1.16	-1.54	8.77	10.96

Trailing	Total Return%	+/- S&P 500	+/- Russ 1000 VI	%Rank Cat	Growth of $10,000
3 Mo	8.77	-0.46	-1.61	62	10,877
6 Mo	7.10	-0.09	-4.98	77	10,710
1 Yr	10.97	0.10	-5.52	71	11,097
3 Yr Avg	4.51	0.93	-4.06	65	11,415
5 Yr Avg	2.90	5.20	-2.37	62	11,537
10 Yr Avg	10.76	-1.31	-3.07	62	27,786
15 Yr Avg	10.26	-0.67	-1.77	56	43,278

Tax Analysis	Tax-Adj Rtn%	%Rank Cat	Tax-Cost Rat	%Rank Cat
3 Yr (estimated)	2.14	79	0.50	34
5 Yr (estimated)	1.11	69	0.68	36
10 Yr (estimated)	8.25	68	1.73	46

Potential Capital Gain Exposure: 17% of assets

Rating and Risk

Time Period	Load-Adj Return %	Morningstar Rtn vs Cat	Morningstar Risk vs Cat	Morningstar Risk-Adj Rating
1 Yr	5.14			
3 Yr	2.65	-Avg	Avg	★★
5 Yr	1.80	-Avg	Avg	★★
10 Yr	10.16	-Avg	Avg	★★
Incept	7.76			

Other Measures	Standard Index S&P 500	Best Fit Index Russ 1000 VI
Alpha	0.9	-3.9
Beta	1.01	1.03
R-Squared	97	98
Standard Deviation	16.22	
Mean	4.51	
Sharpe Ratio	0.19	

Portfolio Analysis 09-30-04

Share change since 06-04 Total Stocks:194	Sector	PE	YTD Ret%	% Assets
⊕ ExxonMobil	Energy	13.9	28.04	4.78
⊖ Citigroup	Financial	15.3	2.72	3.73
⊕ Gen Elec	Ind Mtrls	22.8	20.68	3.24
⊖ Pfizer	Health	22.0	-22.31	2.88
⊕ Bank of America	Financial	12.3	21.50	2.54
⊖ American International G	Financial	16.2	-0.53	2.43
⊕ J P Morgan Chase	Financial	19.4	9.97	2.30
⊕ Altria Group	Goods	13.3	18.38	1.96
⊖ Fannie Mae	Financial	9.1	-2.33	1.87
⊖ Hewlett-Packard	Hardware	18.9	-7.28	1.79
⊖ US Bancorp	Financial	14.2	10.46	1.78
⊖ Tyco International	Ind Mtrls	25.1	35.41	1.75
⊕ Coca-Cola	Goods	21.9	-16.12	1.66
⊕ Johnson & Johnson	Health	20.6	25.17	1.66
⊕ ChevronTexaco	Energy	7.7	25.57	1.65
⊖ Wells Fargo	Financial	15.5	8.97	1.59
⊖ Verizon Communications	Telecom	32.4	20.25	1.58
⊖ Dov/ Chemical	Ind Mtrls	16.6	22.83	1.44
⊖ Frecdie Mac	Financial	10.6	28.75	1.43
⊖ Abbott Laboratories	Health	22.1	2.61	1.40

Current Investment Style

Value Blnd Growth — Large Mid Small

Market Cap	%
Giant	55.3
Large	35.1
Mid	9.5
Small	0.1
Micro	0.0
Avg $mil: 46,502	

Value Measures		Rel Category
Price/Earnings	14.29	0.95
Price/Book	2.32	1.02
Price/Sales	1.15	0.97
Price/Cash Flow	5.67	0.89
Dividend Yield %	2.08	1.02

Growth Measures	%	Rel Category
Long-Term Erngs	10.76	1.03
Book Value	9.81	1.74
Sales	5.34	1.27
Cash Flow	7.22	1.38
Historical Erngs	14.68	1.24

Profitability	%	Rel Category
Return on Equity	18.29	1.15
Return on Assets	9.42	1.20
Net Margin	11.03	1.08

Sector Weightings	% of Stocks	Rel S&P 500	3 Year High	Low
Info	9.86	0.46		
Software	0.43	0.10	2	0
Hardware	4.41	0.43	6	3
Media	2.18	0.57	3	2
Telecom	2.84	0.90	5	3
Service	48.13	1.04		
Health	10.76	0.86	14	10
Consumer	6.11	0.67	7	4
Business	2.65	0.65	3	2
Financial	28.61	1.38	33	28
Mfg	42.01	1.31		
Goods	9.27	0.99	12	9
Ind Mtrls	20.03	1.58	20	12
Energy	9.26	1.29	1[illegible]	7
Utilities	3.45	1.17	6	3

Composition

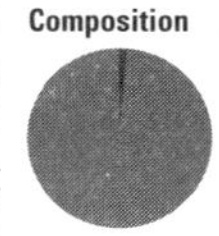

Cash	1.2
Stocks	98.3
Bonds	0.0
Other	0.5
Foreign (% of Stock)	0.3

Morningstar's Take by Laura Pavlenko Lutton 12-21-04

It's hard to get excited about Putnam Fund for Growth & Income.

This offering is a lumbering giant. At $18 billion in assets, it is one of the largest funds in the large-value category and one of Putnam's flagship offerings. Managers Hugh Mullin, David King, and Chris Miller have a straightforward approach, investing in large- and mega-cap stocks that appear undervalued based on their fair value estimates. They don't make any sudden moves or take on extraordinary risk. The fund's turnover is very low, and key holdings in this portfolio are very similar to those at the top of the Russell 1000 Value Index.

In recent years, this fund's staid approach has produced mediocre results. The fund hasn't ended any calendar year since 1999 in the large-value category's top half, and it's on track to do the same in 2004: The fund's 9.36% gain for the year to date through Dec. 20, 2004, is slimmer than two thirds of its peers. Many of the fund's pharmaceutical stocks have disappointed this year, particularly Pfizer, a top holding that's down about 28% so far in 2004 on news that its painkiller Celebrex may increase heart risk in patients.

The fund's lackluster results also can be explained, at least in part, by the fund's lack of mid-cap holdings; smaller-cap names have generally outperformed large since 2000. But when comparing this offering's returns to other mega-cap-heavy funds in the category, its returns are competitive, but not inspiring. That indicates that stock-picking hasn't been as sharp as it could have been.

Should large-cap stocks take off, this offering's relative returns should perk up a bit. That said, this is merely a serviceable option for investors seeking exposure to a steady portfolio of large-cap value names. We think there are more compelling options available. Within the Putnam family, we think Putnam New Value is a better--albiet much riskier--choice.

Address:	One Post Office Sq Boston MA 02109 800-225-1581
Web Address:	www.putnaminvestments.com
Inception:	11-06-57
Advisor:	Putnam Investment Management Co.
Subadvisor:	None
NTF Plans:	Federated Tr NTF, Fidelity Instl-NTF

Minimum Purchase:	$500	Add: $50	IRA: $500
Min Auto Inv Plan:	$500	Add: $25	
Sales Fees:	5.25%L, 2.00%R		
Management Fee:	0.65% mx./0.32% mn.		
Actual Fees:	Mgt:0.43%	Dist:0.25%	
Expense Projections:	3Yr:$797	5Yr:$997	10Yr:$1575
Income Distrib:	Quarterly		

Putnam Investors A

Ticker	Load	NAV	Yield	Total Assets	Mstar Category
PINVX	5.75%	$12.59	0.1%	$4,383 mil	Large Blend

Governance and Management

Fiduciary Grade: C

Portfolio Manager(s)

This fund is run by Putnam's U.S. core team, which took over the fund in April 2002. James Wiess, who also runs Putnam Tax Smart Equity, has taken the lead here and manages the fund along with Richard Cervone and James Yu. Joshua Brooks, the new chief investment officer of Putnam's global core investing group, joined in January 2004 but doesn't participate in day-to-day management.

Strategy

This fund went through a major strategic overhaul in 2002, and Putnam set this up to be its flagship large-blend offering. The firm's team of U.S. core managers now picks stocks for the offering, taking analyst recommendations and quantitative analysis into account. Management is much more concerned with valuation and less interested in finding catalysts for growth than the previous managers, who were part of the large-growth team. Sector bets should be relatively tame.

Historical Profile

Return Below Avg
Risk Above Avg
Rating ★★ Below Avg

Investment Style: Equity Stock %: 94% 100% 97% 100% 99% 95% 95% 99% 98%

▼ Manager Change
▽ Partial Manager Change

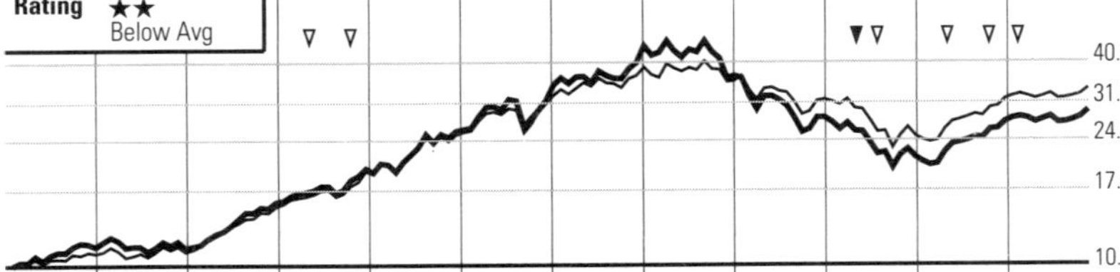

Growth of $10,000
▬ Investment Values of Fund
— Investment Values of S&P 500

Performance Quartile (within Category)

1993	1994	1995	1996	1997	1998	1999	2000	2001	2002	2003	12-04	History
8.16	7.14	8.61	9.21	11.24	14.82	19.15	15.36	11.55	8.80	11.18	12.59	NAV
17.87	-3.19	37.55	21.40	34.49	35.52	30.14	-18.50	-24.80	-23.81	27.62	12.76	Total Return %
7.81	-4.50	0.02	-1.54	1.14	6.95	9.10	-9.40	-12.92	-1.72	-1.05	1.89	+/-S&P 500
7.69	-3.58	-0.22	-1.05	1.64	8.50	9.23	-10.71	-12.35	-2.16	-2.27	1.36	+/-Russ 1000
0.91	0.00	1.19	0.63	0.46	0.00	0.00	0.00	0.00	0.00	0.55	0.14	Income Return %
16.96	-3.19	36.36	20.77	34.03	35.52	30.14	-18.50	-24.80	-23.81	27.07	12.62	Capital Return %
14	84	12	51	9	2	14	98	96	74	45	16	Total Rtn % Rank Cat
0.07	0.00	0.09	0.05	0.04	0.00	0.00	0.00	0.00	0.00	0.05	0.02	Income $
1.31	0.73	1.12	1.17	1.08	0.38	0.13	0.26	0.00	0.00	0.00	0.00	Capital Gains $
0.90	0.99	0.99	1.03	1.00	0.95	0.89	0.87	0.89	0.98	1.06	1.05	Expense Ratio %
0.84	0.88	1.03	0.69	0.50	0.03	-0.14	-0.25	-0.06	0.06	0.49	0.32	Income Ratio %
134	100	97	128	95	59	75	65	94	130	82	66	Turnover Rate %
829	766	1,022	1,324	1,943	4,218	7,903	7,311	5,064	3,026	2,863	2,287	Net Assets $mil

Performance 12-31-04

	1st Qtr	2nd Qtr	3rd Qtr	4th Qtr	Total
2000	3.34	-5.66	-1.50	-15.13	-18.50
2001	-20.31	6.37	-19.66	10.42	-24.80
2002	-3.64	-12.40	-15.90	7.32	-23.81
2003	-4.43	15.93	3.18	11.63	27.62
2004	2.06	1.23	-2.34	11.76	12.76

Trailing	Total Return%	+/- S&P 500	+/- Russ 1000	%Rank Cat	Growth of $10,000
3 Mo	11.76	2.53	1.96	7	11,176
6 Mo	9.15	1.96	1.34	14	10,915
1 Yr	12.76	1.89	1.36	16	11,276
3 Yr Avg	3.11	-0.47	-1.16	45	10,962
5 Yr Avg	-7.65	-5.35	-5.89	97	6,717
10 Yr Avg	10.28	-1.79	-1.88	56	26,605
15 Yr Avg	9.85	-1.08	-1.23	54	40,926

Tax Analysis	Tax-Adj Rtn%	%Rank Cat	Tax-Cost Rat	%Rank Cat
3 Yr (estimated)	1.03	68	0.07	6
5 Yr (estimated)	-8.83	98	0.11	6
10 Yr (estimated)	8.45	53	1.08	34

Potential Capital Gain Exposure: -43% of assets

Rating and Risk

Time Period	Load-Adj Return %	Morningstar Rtn vs Cat	Morningstar Risk vs Cat	Morningstar Risk-Adj Rating
1 Yr	6.28			
3 Yr	1.10	-Avg	Avg	★★
5 Yr	-8.73	Low	+Avg	★
10 Yr	9.63	-Avg	+Avg	★★
Incept	9.48			

Other Measures	Standard Index S&P 500	Best Fit Index Russ 1000
Alpha	-0.4	-1.1
Beta	1.00	1.01
R-Squared	97	97
Standard Deviation	15.74	
Mean	3.11	
Sharpe Ratio	0.11	

Portfolio Analysis 09-30-04

Share change since 06-04 Total Stocks:157	Sector	PE	YTD Ret%	% Assets
⊖ Microsoft	Software	36.1	8.95	5.24
⊖ Citigroup	Financial	15.3	2.72	4.17
⊖ ExxonMobil	Energy	13.9	28.04	3.80
⊖ Johnson & Johnson	Health	20.6	25.17	3.15
⊖ Pfizer	Health	22.0	-22.31	2.94
⊕ Cisco Systems	Hardware	24.5	-20.26	2.52
⊕ Altria Group	Goods	13.3	18.38	2.43
⊖ US Bancorp	Financial	14.2	10.46	2.31
⊕ Lowe's Companies	Consumer	22.1	4.25	2.23
⊖ Intel	Hardware	19.8	-26.56	2.08
⊕ Fannie Mae	Financial	9.1	-2.33	2.03
⊕ Commerce Bancorp NJ	Financial	19.8	23.89	1.95
⊖ Tyco International	Ind Mtrls	25.1	35.41	1.84
⊖ Freddie Mac	Financial	10.6	28.75	1.80
⊖ Capital One Financial	Financial	12.5	37.61	1.80
⊕ ACE	Financial	9.6	5.26	1.63
⊕ Everest Re Group	Financial	9.5	6.40	1.61
⊖ Lockheed Martin	Ind Mtrls	19.9	9.97	1.60
⊕ Cardinal Health	Health	16.9	-4.73	1.45
⊖ MBNA	Financial	14.0	15.53	1.34

Current Investment Style

Market Cap	%
Giant	47.0
Large	34.3
Mid	18.7
Small	0.0
Micro	0.0
Avg $mil: 35,028	

Value Measures		Rel Category
Price/Earnings	14.52	0.86
Price/Book	2.43	0.93
Price/Sales	1.34	0.93
Price/Cash Flow	6.24	0.81
Dividend Yield %	1.34	0.91

Growth Measures	%	Rel Category
Long-Term Erngs	12.94	1.12
Book Value	15.09	1.94
Sales	9.50	1.66
Cash Flow	18.84	1.99
Historical Erngs	20.20	1.71

Profitability	%	Rel Category
Return on Equity	19.71	1.13
Return on Assets	11.87	1.38
Net Margin	13.84	1.21

Sector Weightings	% of Stocks	Rel S&P 500	3 Year High	3 Year Low
Info	18.75	0.87		
Software	7.51	1.75	8	6
Hardware	8.42	0.83	17	5
Media	2.40	0.63	6	2
Telecom	0.42	0.13	4	0
Service	60.41	1.30		
Health	16.24	1.30	20	15
Consumer	12.58	1.39	13	9
Business	2.58	0.64	4	3
Financial	29.01	1.40	29	20
Mfg	20.85	0.65		
Goods	5.96	0.64	9	5
Ind Mtrls	8.33	0.66	11	5
Energy	6.47	0.90	8	1
Utilities	0.09	0.03	3	0

Composition

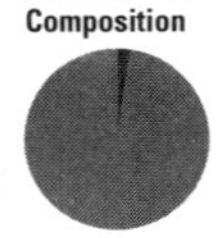

Cash	2.0
Stocks	98.0
Bonds	0.0
Other	0.0
Foreign (% of Stock)	2.5

Morningstar's Take by Laura Pavlenko Lutton 12-22-04

The jury is still out on Putnam Investors.

It's been nearly three years since Putnam overhauled its investment process for U.S. large-blend offerings, and that strategy has been employed at this fund since May 2002. Here the managers work closely with Putnam's pool of stock researchers to find companies that they think are undervalued based on the firms' future earnings potential. The managers also use computer models to help them identify lesser-known stocks that may also fit their investment criteria. Finally, they draw on key picks from Putnam's sector portfolios.

The resulting portfolio maintains a risk profile that's similar to that of the S&P 500 Index. Thus, the fund's sector bets aren't too extreme versus the benchmark, and the fund is relatively well diversified across about 150 stocks. In the end, the fund's relative performance should be based on the managers' stock selection.

We like the idea behind this portfolio's strategy because it harnesses resources available at a big investment firm such as Putnam: a deep bench of managers, dozens of stock analysts, and sophisticated quantitative analysis tools. The risk controls in place here should also prevent style drift.

That said, we have some reservations that prevent us from suggesting this offering over a proven fund in the category. First, there has been considerable manager turnover since the fund switched to this blend investment strategy in May 2002. Two key managers--Kevin Divney and Paul Marrkand--left the fund in 2003 to employ this same investment process at Putnam Vista, a troubled mid-cap growth fund.

In addition, the offering hasn't consistently beaten its benchmark. It trailed the S&P 500 bogy during 2003, for example. Granted, the fund has outperformed thus far in 2004, but we haven't seen enough from the current managers to suggest they're topnotch stock-pickers.

Address:	One Post Office Sq Boston MA 02109 800-225-1581
Web Address:	
Inception:	12-01-25
Advisor:	Putnam Investment Management Co.
Subadvisor:	None
NTF Plans:	Federated Tr NTF, Fidelity Instl-NTF

Minimum Purchase:	$500	Add: $50	IRA: $500
Min Auto Inv Plan:	$500	Add: $25	
Sales Fees:	5.75%L, 0.25%S, 2.00%R		
Management Fee:	0.65% mx./0.38% mn.		
Actual Fees:	Mgt:0.48%	Dist:0.25%	
Expense Projections:	3Yr:$892	5Yr:$1125	10Yr:$1792
Income Distrib:	Annually		

Putnam Voyager A

Ticker	Load	NAV	Yield	Total Assets	Mstar Category
PVOYX	5.25%	$16.61	0.0%	$13,588 mil	Large Growth

Governance and Management

Fiduciary Grade: C

Portfolio Manager(s)

Brian O'Toole, Putnam's head of large-growth investing, is the lead manager of this fund. O'Toole joined Putnam in June 2002, after a stint in a similar system with Citigroup. Walter Pearson and David Santos are team members.

Strategy

This fund takes a diversified approach to growth investing. In trying to top the Russell 1000 Growth Index, it stays fairly sector-neutral and relies on its stock-picking to get a leg up. The fund isn't swinging for the fences, as it looks for modest gains to compound over time. Putnam combines detailed quantitative analysis with in-depth analyst research to feed teams of portfolio managers with extensive information. The fund's risk tolerances are carefully monitored by internal systems.

Historical Profile

Return Below Avg
Risk Average
Rating ★★★ Neutral

Investment Style Equity Stock %: 96% (1993), 100%, 95%, 100%, 100%, 97%, 95%, 98%, 99%

▼ Manager Change ▽ Partial Manager Change

Growth of $10,000
— Investment Values of Fund
— Investment Values of S&P 500

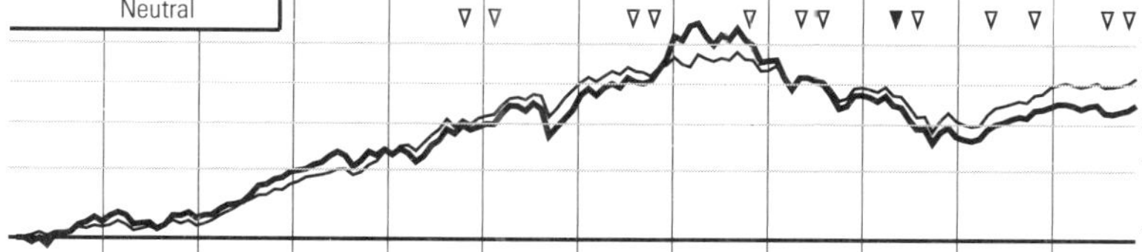

Performance Quartile (within Category)

1993	1994	1995	1996	1997	1998	1999	2000	2001	2002	2003	12-04	History
11.99	11.52	15.25	16.12	19.05	21.92	30.96	23.30	17.30	12.71	15.85	16.61	NAV
18.40	0.44	40.15	12.80	25.98	24.06	56.13	-16.78	-22.46	-26.53	24.70	4.79	Total Return %
8.34	-0.87	2.62	-10.14	-7.37	-4.51	35.09	-7.68	-10.58	-4.44	-3.97	-6.08	+/-S&P 500
15.53	-2.18	2.97	-10.32	-4.51	-14.65	22.97	5.64	-2.04	1.35	-5.05	-1.51	+/-Russ 1000Gr
0.00	0.00	0.00	0.00	0.00	0.00	0.00	0.00	0.18	0.00	0.00	0.00	Income Return %
18.40	0.44	40.15	12.80	25.98	24.06	56.13	-16.78	-22.54	-26.53	24.70	4.79	Capital Return %
19	28	11	90	55	77	13	66	59	44	68	76	Total Rtn % Rank Cat
0.00	0.00	0.00	0.00	0.00	0.00	0.00	0.00	0.04	0.00	0.00	0.00	Income $
0.46	0.51	0.86	1.09	1.21	1.59	2.98	2.60	0.75	0.00	0.00	0.00	Capital Gains $
1.12	1.10	1.07	1.03	1.02	0.96	0.90	0.86	0.38	0.96	1.02	1.04	Expense Ratio %
-0.14	-0.18	0.17	-0.10	0.00	-0.20	-0.25	-0.37	0.33	0.21	0.10	-0.04	Income Ratio %
65	58	65	58	60	60	85	77	140	91	62	46	Turnover Rate %
2,884	3,469	5,986	8,633	11,755	15,570	24,363	21,539	15,953	11,026	12,095	8,522	Net Assets $mil

Performance 12-31-04

	1st Qtr	2nd Qtr	3rd Qtr	4th Qtr	Total
2000	10.30	-8.52	-3.33	-14.69	-16.78
2001	-19.06	6.57	-18.81	10.71	-22.46
2002	-0.87	-15.92	-16.16	5.13	-26.53
2003	-1.49	12.54	3.48	8.71	24.70
2004	0.95	0.50	-5.04	8.78	4.79

Trailing	Total Return%	+/- S&P 500	+/- Russ 1000Gr	%Rank Cat	Growth of $10,000
3 Mo	8.78	-0.45	-0.39	72	10,878
6 Mo	3.30	-3.89	-0.17	73	10,330
1 Yr	4.79	-6.08	-1.51	76	10,479
3 Yr Avg	-1.35	-4.93	-1.17	62	9,600
5 Yr Avg	-9.13	-6.83	0.16	66	6,196
10 Yr Avg	9.10	-2.97	-0.49	47	23,892
15 Yr Avg	10.64	-0.29	1.14	29	45,570

Tax Analysis	Tax-Adj Rtn%	%Rank Cat	Tax-Cost Rat	%Rank Cat
3 Yr (estimated)	-3.11	75	0.01	2
5 Yr (estimated)	-10.74	73	0.70	43
10 Yr (estimated)	7.21	51	1.21	34

Potential Capital Gain Exposure: -22% of assets

Rating and Risk

Time Period	Load-Adj Return %	Morningstar Rtn vs Cat	Morningstar Risk vs Cat	Morningstar Risk-Adj Rating
1 Yr	-0.71			
3 Yr	-3.10	-Avg	-Avg	★★
5 Yr	-10.11	-Avg	Avg	★★★
10 Yr	8.52	Avg	Avg	★★★
Incept	12.04			

Other Measures	Standard Index S&P 500	Best Fit Index Russ 1000Gr
Alpha	-4.7	-1.3
Beta	0.95	0.93
R-Squared	95	98
Standard Deviation	14.56	
Mean	-1.35	
Sharpe Ratio	-0.19	

Morningstar's Take by Dan McNeela 10-15-04

Putnam Voyager has more steps to take to win back investor confidence.

Wholesale changes on Putnam's large-cap growth team put a new team in place here in 2002, with lead manager Brian O'Toole signing on. His task was to bring back some accountability to the investment process and start delivering consistent outperformance through a variety of market environments.

The fund seems to have addressed many of its issues. O'Toole's philosophy fits well with Putnam's new emphasis on risk controls. The fund continues to use a mix of quantitative and fundamental analysis to form its portfolio, but it rejects big sector bets, leaving stock-picking as the primary path to gains. The emphasis is on high-quality growth stocks, which O'Toole believes will rise to the top in most markets.

We feel the changes are enough to prevent major disappointments, but we're less optimistic that all the pieces are in place to give the fund an edge over it peers. The fund has been less than stellar on the performance front. It lagged both the category average and its benchmark by a considerable margin in 2003.

In 2004, its modest overweight in tech and its underweight in energy again puts it behind both of those measuring sticks. While the team found a number of winners among software stocks and benefited from sticking with a sizeable stake in Qualcomm, its research wasn't sharp enough to keep it away from other trouble spots. The fund sold Career Education, for example, after allegations of fraudulent recruiting practices sent the stock spiraling downward. Management also threw in the towel on financial services firm State Street after being optimistic early in the year.

We recognize that the fund has made progress, but until we see more evidence that it has an advantage to exploit, we'd look elsewhere.

Address:	One Post Office Sq Boston MA 02109 800-225-1581
Web Address:	
Inception:	04-01-69
Advisor:	Putnam Investment Management Co.
Subadvisor:	None
NTF Plans:	Federated Tr NTF, Fidelity Instl-NTF

Minimum Purchase:	$500	Add: $50	IRA: $500
Min Auto Inv Plan:	$500	Add: $25	
Sales Fees:	5.25%L, 2.00%R		
Management Fee:	0.70% mx./0.37% mn.		
Actual Fees:	Mgt:0.49%	Dist:0.25%	
Expense Projections:	3Yr:$881	5Yr:$1106	10Yr:$1751
Income Distrib:	Annually		

Portfolio Analysis 09-30-04

Share change since 06-04 Total Stocks:137	Sector	PE	YTD Ret%	% Assets
⊖ Pfizer	Health	22.0	-22.31	5.61
⊖ Microsoft	Software	36.1	8.95	4.90
⊕ Johnson & Johnson	Health	20.6	25.17	3.72
⊖ Wal-Mart Stores	Consumer	23.4	0.51	3.03
⊖ Cisco Systems	Hardware	24.5	-20.26	2.70
⊕ Procter & Gamble	Goods	23.3	12.38	2.61
⊕ Qualcomm	Hardware	42.0	58.20	2.41
⊖ Intel	Hardware	19.8	-26.56	2.35
⊖ Home Depot	Consumer	19.0	21.47	2.29
⊖ Dell	Hardware	34.0	24.01	2.16
⊕ Adobe Systems	Software	34.2	60.76	1.95
⊕ Amerada Hess	Energy	10.1	57.47	1.82
⊖ Peps Co	Goods	22.5	13.82	1.77
⊕ Boeing	Ind Mtrls	14.7	24.86	1.77
⊕ UnitedHealth Group	Health	23.8	51.38	1.65
⊖ American International G	Financial	16.2	-0.53	1.63
⊖ 3M Company	Ind Mtrls	23.5	-1.75	1.51
⊖ Gen Elec	Ind Mtrls	22.8	20.68	1.46
⊖ Symantec	Software	34.5	49.33	1.46
⊖ Oracle	Software	25.4	3.70	1.37

Current Investment Style

Value Blnd Growth — Large Mid Small

Market Cap	%
Giant	54.0
Large	31.0
Mid	14.8
Small	0.1
Micro	0.0

Avg $mil: 43,021

Value Measures		Rel Category
Price/Earnings	18.65	0.88
Price/Book	3.25	1.01
Price/Sales	1.63	0.76
Price/Cash Flow	10.11	0.92
Dividend Yield %	0.94	1.22

Growth Measures	%	Rel Category
Long-Term Erngs	13.08	0.93
Book Value	17.40	1.37
Sales	9.62	1.13
Cash Flow	13.64	0.82
Historical Erngs	9.88	0.68

Profitability	%	Rel Category
Return on Equity	22.01	1.23
Return on Assets	11.55	1.23
Net Margin	13.47	1.09

Sector Weightings	% of Stocks	Rel S&P 500	3 Year High	3 Year Low
Info	26.83	1.25		
Software	10.36	2.41	10	6
Hardware	15.10	1.48	22	12
Media	0.76	0.20	5	1
Telecom	0.61	0.19	4	0
Service	50.35	1.09		
Health	23.52	1.88	30	18
Consumer	16.66	1.83	18	10
Business	1.26	0.31	4	1
Financial	8.91	0.43	16	9
Mfg	22.82	0.71		
Goods	10.89	1.17	11	6
Ind Mtrls	8.08	0.64	10	6
Energy	3.23	0.45	5	0
Utilities	0.62	0.21	3	0

Composition

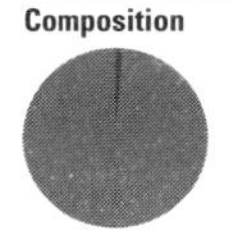

Cash	1.2
Stocks	98.8
Bonds	0.0
Other	0.0
Foreign (% of Stock)	0.0

Royce Opportunity Inv

Ticker	Load	NAV	Yield	Total Assets	Mstar Category
RYPNX	None	$13.31	0.0%	$2,017 mil	Small Value

Governance and Management

Fiduciary Grade: B

Portfolio Manager(s)

Buzz Zaino has managed this fund since April 1998. Zaino brings his own brand of value to this fund, after a 17-year stint with Lehman Brothers and a tour with Trust Company of the West. Zaino added William Hench, an accountant with sell-side experience, as an assistant portfolio manager in 2004.

Strategy

Manager Buzz Zaino looks for stocks that fit into one of four categories: undervalued asset plays, turnaround stories, undervalued growth, and high potential growth. In each area, Zaino's holdings must meet his quantitative definition of a value stock based on P/E or price/sales ratios. This fund is loaded with micro-cap stocks. Position sizes typically don't exceed 1% of assets.

Historical Profile

Return Above Avg
Risk High
Rating ★★★ Neutral

Investment Style: Equity Stock %

1997	1998	1999	2000	2001	2002	2003	12-04
94%	92%	97%	95%	93%	95%	93%	93%

▼ Manager Change
▽ Partial Manager Change

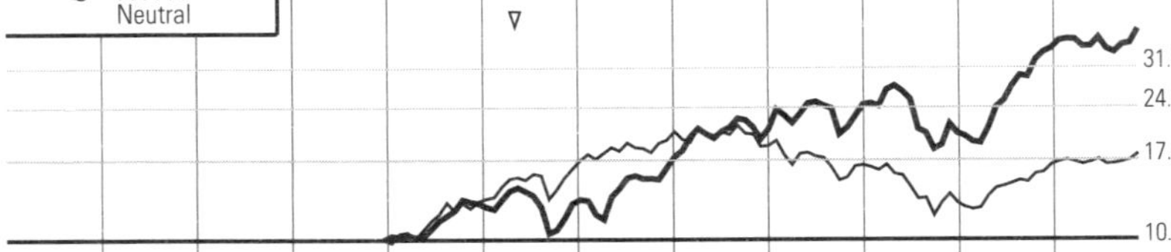

Growth of $10,000
— Investment Values of Fund
— Investment Values of S&P 500

Performance Quartile (within Category)

1993	1994	1995	1996	1997	1998	1999	2000	2001	2002	2003	12-04	History
—	—	—	5.26	5.92	6.02	7.19	7.78	9.01	7.37	12.14	13.31	NAV
—	—	—	5.20*	20.83	4.91	32.34	19.85	17.32	-17.01	72.87	17.51	Total Return %
—	—	—	—	-12.52	-23.66	11.30	28.95	29.20	5.08	44.20	6.64	+/-S&P 500
—	—	—	—	-10.95	11.36	33.83	-2.98	3.30	-5.58	26.84	-4.74	+/-Russ 2000 VL
—	—	—	0.00	1.52	0.00	0.00	0.00	0.00	0.00	0.00	0.00	Income Return %
—	—	—	—	19.31	4.91	32.34	19.85	17.32	-17.01	72.87	17.51	Capital Return %
—	—	—	—	89	7	9	47	49	84	2	79	Total Rtn % Rank Cat
—	—	—	0.00	0.08	0.00	0.00	0.00	0.00	0.00	0.00	0.00	Income $
—	—	—	0.00	0.36	0.18	0.74	0.81	0.11	0.11	0.58	0.93	Capital Gains $
—	—	—	—	0.99	1.25	1.46	1.24	1.19	1.17	1.15	—	Expense Ratio %
—	—	—	—	1.23	-0.16	-0.07	0.00	-0.19	-0.49	-0.65	—	Income Ratio %
—	—	—	—	77	120	122	56	44	46	55	—	Turnover Rate %
—	—	—	18	22	33	60	297	526	636	1,310	1,622	Net Assets $mil

Performance 12-31-04

	1st Qtr	2nd Qtr	3rd Qtr	4th Qtr	Total
2000	20.45	-1.73	7.52	-5.83	19.85
2001	4.24	14.67	-19.03	21.22	17.32
2002	10.10	-5.95	-27.76	10.94	-17.01
2003	-6.11	31.94	16.43	19.86	72.87
2004	6.01	1.01	-4.46	14.86	17.51

Trailing	Total Return%	+/- S&P 500	+/- Russ 2000 VL	%Rank Cat	Growth of $10,000
3 Mo	14.86	5.63	1.66	8	11,486
6 Mo	9.74	2.55	-3.63	79	10,974
1 Yr	17.51	6.64	-4.74	79	11,751
3 Yr Avg	19.02	15.44	2.52	17	16,860
5 Yr Avg	18.84	21.14	1.61	21	23,704
10 Yr Avg	—	—	—	—	—
15 Yr Avg	—	—	—	—	—

Tax Analysis	Tax-Adj Rtn%	%Rank Cat	Tax-Cost Rat	%Rank Cat
3 Yr (estimated)	17.84	15	0.99	58
5 Yr (estimated)	17.30	22	1.30	64
10 Yr (estimated)	—	—	—	—

Potential Capital Gain Exposure: 28% of assets

Rating and Risk

Time Period	Load-Adj Return %	Morningstar Rtn vs Cat	Morningstar Risk vs Cat	Morningstar Risk-Adj Rating
1 Yr	17.51			
3 Yr	19.02	+Avg	High	★★★
5 Yr	18.84	+Avg	High	★★★
10 Yr	—	—	—	—
Incept	19.29			

Other Measures	Standard Index S&P 500	Best Fit Index Russ 2000
Alpha	15.9	5.3
Beta	1.26	1.21
R-Squared	63	96

Standard Deviation	28.67
Mean	19.02
Sharpe Ratio	0.62

Portfolio Analysis 09-30-04

Share change since 06-04 Total Stocks:281	Sector	PE	YTD Ret%	% Assets
⊖ Hexcel	Ind Mtrls	—	95.68	0.96
⊕ Titanium Metals	Ind Mtrls	—	129.86	0.91
⊖ Oregon Steel Mills	Ind Mtrls	19.7	249.23	0.90
⊖ Warnaco Group	Goods	—	35.42	0.89
⊖ IMC Global	Ind Mtrls	—	—	0.83
⊖ Volt Information Science	Business	—	30.04	0.81
⊖ Esterline Technologies	Hardware	23.7	22.42	0.79
⊖ Belden CDT	Hardware	—	29.62	0.78
⊖ Flowserve	Ind Mtrls	24.5	31.90	0.78
⊖ Timken	Ind Mtrls	22.3	32.66	0.77
⊖ BE Aerospace	Ind Mtrls	—	115.56	0.72
⊖ Regal-Beloit	Ind Mtrls	25.0	32.66	0.72
⊖ Spartech	Ind Mtrls	18.3	11.97	0.71
⊖ TRC Companies	Business	18.5	-19.28	0.70
⊖ Longs Drug Stores	Consumer	32.5	14.18	0.66
⊖ Terex	Ind Mtrls	24.3	67.31	0.66
⊖ Symmetricom	Telecom	—	33.38	0.65
⊖ Emmis Communications A	Media	—	-29.06	0.64
⊖ McGrath RentCorp	Consumer	19.2	64.24	0.64
⊖ Baldor Electric	Ind Mtrls	27.8	23.37	0.63

Current Investment Style

Value Blnd Growth / Large Mid Small

Market Cap	%
Giant	0.0
Large	0.1
Mid	6.8
Small	52.3
Micro	40.8

Avg $mil: 437

Value Measures		Rel Category
Price/Earnings	15.16	0.95
Price/Book	1.46	0.88
Price/Sales	0.61	0.81
Price/Cash Flow	5.69	1.10
Dividend Yield %	0.34	0.28

Growth Measures	%	Rel Category
Long-Term Erngs	15.55	1.23
Book Value	1.50	0.35
Sales	1.36	0.43
Cash Flow	-7.19	NMF
Historical Erngs	1.73	0.36

Profitability	%	Rel Category
Return on Equity	2.18	0.24
Return on Assets	1.12	0.27
Net Margin	1.04	0.16

Sector Weightings	% of Stocks	Rel S&P 500	3 Year High	3 Year Low
Info	31.75	1.48		
Software	4.73	1.10	6	4
Hardware	20.72	2.03	28	20
Media	4.94	1.29	5	3
Telecom	1.36	0.43	2	1
Service	24.66	0.53		
Health	2.51	0.20	6	3
Consumer	8.71	0.96	12	9
Business	10.13	2.50	12	10
Financial	3.31	0.16	4	1
Mfg	43.59	1.36		
Goods	6.44	0.69	7	4
Ind Mtrls	32.64	2.58	33	24
Energy	4.31	0.60	6	4
Utilities	0.20	0.07	1	0

Composition

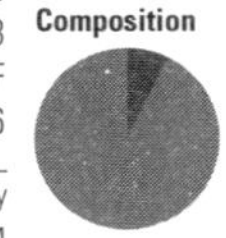

Cash	7.5
Stocks	92.5
Bonds	0.0
Other	0.0
Foreign (% of Stock)	1.5

Morningstar's Take by Todd Trubey 11-29-04

Royce Opportunity's story remains largely intact.

In small-cap specialist Royce's broad lineup, this fund has the headiest risk/reward profile. Manager Buzz Zaino seeks opportunities in four areas: undervalued assets, undervalued growth, turnarounds, and high potential growth. Sowing seeds in unloved firms often leads to periods of poor relative performance, as in 2004 and 2002. But the harvest can be tremendous: witness a 73% gain in 2003.

Zaino, an experienced realist, knows this fund will run hot and cold. After the 2003 campaign he knew performance-chasers would want to hop on board so he closed the fund from March 12, 2004, to Sept. 20, 2004. With the fund now in net redemptions, he believes the cooling-off period worked.

With $1.8 billion in assets, though, the fund is among the largest open small-cap funds and one must wonder how it will handle its girth. On the plus side, the fund doesn't depend on big bets from individual stocks. Now with 283 stocks and only 8.3% of assets in the top 10 holdings, it's long been among the most diversified small value category members. Zaino and other Royce managers also say micro-cap stocks aren't as attractive as larger small-caps. And yet this fund's average market cap of $437 million is lower than 90% of small-value peers. The fund has heavily used microcaps but now has less staked to them (41% of assets) than ever before on Zaino's watch.

On balance, though, Zaino can still make the contrarian moves that have driven the fund's success despite the fund's size. While he tends to invest heavily in tech and industrial firms, he shifts to out-of-favor industries within them. This summer, for instance, he bought software firms with solid balance sheets as they fell. A similar play in 2002 on aerospace firms has paid off nicely.

This might not be the top choice for a new purchase, but it remains an attractive holding.

Address:	1414 Ave of the Americas New York NY 10019 800-221-4268	Minimum Purchase:	$2000	Add: $50	IRA: $500
Web Address:	www.roycefunds.com	Min Auto Inv Plan:	$500	Add: $50	
Inception:	11-19-96 *	Sales Fees:	No-load, 1.00%R		
Advisor:	Royce & Associates, LLC	Management Fee:	1.00%		
Subadvisor:	None	Actual Fees:	Mgt:1.00%	Dist: —	
		Expense Projections:	3Yr:$365	5Yr:$633	10Yr:$1398
		Income Distrib:	Annually		
NTF Plans:	Bidwell & Co. NTF, ETrade No Load ETF				

Royce Premier Inv

Analyst Pick	Ticker	Load	NAV	Yield	Total Assets	Mstar Category
✔	RYPRX	None	$15.12	0.0%	$3,039 mil	Small Blend

Governance and Management

Fiduciary Grade: B

Portfolio Manager(s)

Chuck Royce is one of the best and most experienced small-value managers in the business. He has managed Pennsylvania Mutual for nearly 30 years and has earned a reputation for low-risk investing. Whitney George has done well with Royce Low-Priced Stock.

Strategy

This Royce offering has comfortably sat in the small-blend style box for more than five years, although it does have a hefty weighting in smaller mid-caps. Chuck Royce and comanager Whitney George have been more willing to pay up for well-positioned companies in this concentrated portfolio. It is focused on the larger companies in the small-cap arena.

Historical Profile

Return: Above Avg
Risk: Low
Rating: ★★★★ Above Avg

Investment Style: Equity Stock %

100% | 87% | 91% | 91% | 89% | 87% | 91% | 82% | 86%

▼ Manager Change
∇ Partial Manager Change

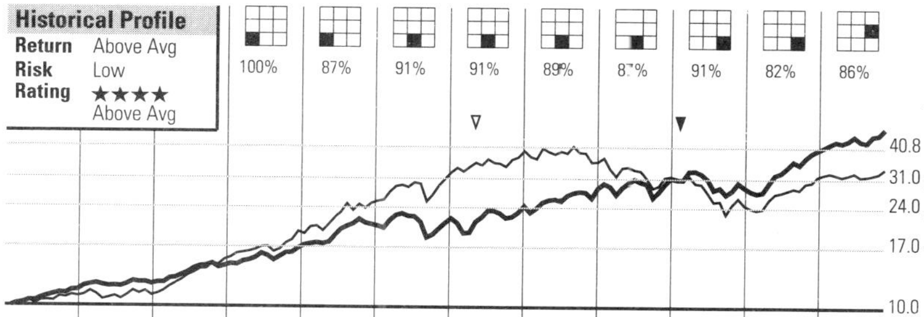

Performance Quartile (within Category)

1993	1994	1995	1996	1997	1998	1999	2000	2001	2002	2003	12-04	History
6.41	6.48	7.12	7.81	8.70	9.14	9.56	9.83	10.54	9.39	12.90	15.12	NAV
19.02	3.28	17.81	18.13	18.41	6.74	11.49	17.12	9.61	-7.75	38.74	22.82	Total Return %
8.96	1.97	-19.72	-4.81	-14.94	-21.83	-9.55	26.22	21.49	14.34	10.07	11.95	+/-S&P 500
0.14	5.10	-10.64	1.64	-3.95	9.29	-9.77	20.14	7.12	12.73	-8.51	4.49	+/-Russ 2000
0.36	0.78	1.42	1.40	1.13	0.57	0.11	0.31	0.00	0.00	0.00	0.00	Income Return %
18.66	2.50	16.39	16.73	17.28	6.17	11.38	16.81	9.61	-7.75	38.74	22.82	Capital Return %
41	14	82	72	88	6	53	34	44	12	65	16	Total Rtn % Rank Cat
0.02	0.05	0.09	0.10	0.09	0.05	0.01	0.03	0.00	0.00	0.00	0.00	Income $
0.14	0.09	0.42	0.49	0.46	0.09	0.58	1.27	0.23	0.34	0.13	0.71	Capital Gains $
1.50	1.38	1.25	1.25	1.24	1.23	1.23	1.20	1.19	1.17	1.16	—	Expense Ratio %
0.68	1.19	1.48	1.25	1.20	0.55	0.11	0.34	-0.04	-0.40	-0.29	—	Income Ratio %
85	38	39	34	18	46	48	40	41	33	26	—	Turnover Rate %
36	202	302	317	534	572	568	674	799	854	1,772	2,863	Net Assets $mil

Performance 12-31-04

	1st Qtr	2nd Qtr	3rd Qtr	4th Qtr	Total
2000	3.35	1.01	8.82	3.10	17.12
2001	-5.29	14.39	-14.84	18.80	9.61
2002	6.07	-6.62	-12.55	6.49	-7.75
2003	-4.05	18.42	7.50	13.58	38.74
2004	7.91	4.67	0.34	8.37	22.82

Trailing	Total Return%	+/- S&P 500	+/- Russ 2000	%Rank Cat	Growth of $10,000
3 Mo	8.37	-0.86	-5.72	96	10,837
6 Mo	8.74	1.55	-2.09	78	10,874
1 Yr	22.82	11.95	4.49	16	12,282
3 Yr Avg	16.27	12.69	4.79	17	15,718
5 Yr Avg	15.08	17.38	8.47	31	20,184
10 Yr Avg	14.75	2.68	3.21	35	39,585
15 Yr Avg	—	—	—	—	—

Tax Analysis	Tax-Adj Rtn%	%Rank Cat	Tax-Cost Rat	%Rank Cat
3 Yr (estimated)	15.60	13	0.58	41
5 Yr (estimated)	13.93	26	1.00	48
10 Yr (estimated)	13.28	18	1.28	24

Potential Capital Gain Exposure: 29% of assets

Rating and Risk

Time Period	Load-Adj Return %	Morningstar Rtn vs Cat	Morningstar Risk vs Cat	Morningstar Risk-Adj Rating
1 Yr	22.82			
3 Yr	16.27	+Avg	Low	★★★★
5 Yr	15.08	+Avg	-Avg	★★★★
10 Yr	14.75	Avg	Low	★★★★
Incept	14.22			

Other Measures	Standard Index S&P 500	Best Fit Index Mstar Small Core
Alpha	12.9	3.5
Beta	0.81	0.81
R-Squared	71	93
Standard Deviation	16.56	
Mean	16.27	
Sharpe Ratio	0.91	

Portfolio Analysis 09-30-04

Share change since 06-04 Total Stocks:59	Sector	PE	YTD Ret%	% Assets
⊕ Florida Rock Industries	Ind Mtrls	21.2	68.98	2.87
⊕ Simpson Manufacturing	Ind Mtrls	15.8	37.98	2.86
⊕ Endo Pharmaceutical Hldg	Health	32.4	8.52	2.73
⊕ Alleghany	Financial	14.7	30.77	2.69
⊕ Nu Skin Enterprises A	Health	22.1	50.57	2.60
⊕ Ensign Resource Service	Energy	—	—	2.56
⊕ Erie Indemnity A	Financial	17.9	25.69	2.39
⊕ Unit	Energy	22.0	62.25	2.23
⊕ Lincoln Electric Holding	Ind Mtrls	16.5	42.65	2.17
⊕ Glamis Gold Ltd	Ind Mtrls	NMF	0.23	2.11
⊕ Ritchie Bros. Auctioneer	Consumer	29.5	26.17	2.05
⊕ Polo Ralph Lauren	Goods	20.3	48.73	2.03
⊕ Perot Systems	Business	20.9	18.92	2.02
⊕ EGL	Business	30.2	70.02	1.96
⊕ Goldcorp	Ind Mtrls	26.4	-3.78	1.90
⊕ Trican Well Service Ltd	Energy	—	—	1.85
Winnebago Industries	Ind Mtrls	17.6	14.48	1.83
⊕ Dionex	Health	28.0	23.14	1.78
⊕ Timberland	Goods	15.7	20.36	1.74
⊕ Cabot Microelectronics	Hardware	20.5	-18.22	1.72

Current Investment Style

Value Blnd Growth / Large Mid Small

Market Cap	%
Giant	0.0
Large	1.6
Mid	57.5
Small	40.9
Micro	0.0
Avg $mil: 1,593	

Value Measures		Rel Category
Price/Earnings	19.58	1.13
Price/Book	2.67	1.34
Price/Sales	1.61	1.69
Price/Cash Flow	8.47	1.45
Dividend Yield %	0.51	0.61

Growth Measures	%	Rel Category
Long-Term Erngs	14.88	1.10
Book Value	10.02	1.78
Sales	7.37	1.71
Cash Flow	16.63	3.37
Historical Erngs	8.14	1.09

Profitability	%	Rel Category
Return on Equity	15.04	1.44
Return on Assets	9.73	1.96
Net Margin	11.38	1.56

Sector Weightings	% of Stocks	Rel S&P 500	3 Year High	3 Year Low
Info	9.61	0.45		
Software	0.90	0.21	2	1
Hardware	6.85	0.67	11	6
Media	0.00	0.00	1	0
Telecom	1.86	0.59	2	1
Service	46.64	1.01		
Health	15.98	1.28	22	12
Consumer	7.62	0.84	10	5
Business	13.25	3.27	20	13
Financial	9.79	0.47	13	7
Mfg	43.75	1.36		
Goods	5.69	0.61	7	4
Ind Mtrls	26.65	2.10	27	21
Energy	11.41	1.59	12	6
Utilities	0.00	0.00	0	0

Composition

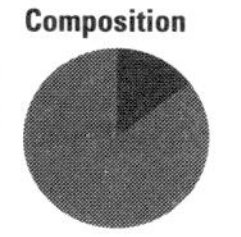

Cash	14.2
Stocks	85.8
Bonds	0.0
Other	0.0
Foreign (% of Stock)	11.4

Morningstar's Take by Todd Trubey 12-01-04

Royce Premier's success is no surprise.

Royce believes micro-caps and small caps allow different investment strategies. The shop's micro-caps funds usually own hundreds of stocks, because tiny firms are risky and hard to know. Small firms above the $500 million market-cap range are less volatile and more understandable, allowing more concentration in them. So this fund aims to buy and hold about 60 such firms with good balance sheets and high returns on capital.

Today's portfolio, managed by Chuck Royce and Whitney George, has an enticing mix of old and new. Eight of its 60 stocks were held in Royce's Low-Priced Stock, Micro-Cap, or Total Return funds in 1997. Two of these, Simpson Manufacturing and Florida Rock Industries, are top-five holdings with 30%-plus gains this year. But George has also succeeded outside the shop's historical favorites in gold, steel, and energy stocks.

So this fund nicely blends spice and safety. It lends the comfort of seasoned small-cap experts who know their holdings well. Yet the fund's compact size and opportunism keep it from being too tame. The fund's risk/reward profile has embodied this mix: Over the trailing five- and 10-year periods the fund has had superior returns and low volatility versus small-blend peers.

The fund's success has brought heavy inflows. It has grown from $800 million in 2001 to $2.9 billion now, and an $800 million slice of Pennsylvania Mutual mirrors this fund. Nearly $4 billion is a ton of money to invest in just 60 small firms. The top 10 positions here soak up 2% of net assets, or roughly $80 million, each. That's 10% of an $800 million firm, meaning that establishing or liquidating a position can be difficult and costly. That's a key reason why the fund nows own larger firms: Half the assets are in firms Morningstar considers mid-caps, so be careful when pairing this fund with a mid-cap fund.

Meanwhile, this great fund remains an Analyst Pick.

Address:	1414 Ave of the Americas New York NY 10019 800-221-4268
Web Address:	www.roycefunds.com
Inception:	12-31-91
Advisor:	Royce & Associates, LLC.
Subadvisor:	None
NTF Plans:	Accutrade NTF, Bidwell & Co. NTF

Minimum Purchase:	$2000	Add: $50	IRA: $500
Min Auto Inv Plan:	$500	Add: $50	
Sales Fees:	No-load, 1.00%R		
Management Fee:	1.00%		
Actual Fees:	Mgt:1.00%	Dist: —	
Expense Projections:	3Yr:$368	5Yr:$638	10Yr:$1409
Income Distrib:	Annually		

Royce Special Equity Inv

Ticker	Load	NAV	Yield	Total Assets	Mstar Category
RYSEX	Closed	$19.61	0.9%	$1,003 mil	Small Value

Governance and Management

Fiduciary Grade: A

Portfolio Manager(s)

Charlie Dreifus, a senior portfolio manager at Royce Associates, runs the show, poring over balance sheets and conducting nearly all of the fund's bottom-up research. Dreifus worked at Lazard Freres and Oppenheimer for about 30 years, managing money using a similar approach to the one he now employs.

Strategy

Eschewing sector considerations, manager Charlie Dreifus zeroes in on stocks trading at a steep discount to his estimate of intrinsic value regardless of industry. A balance-sheet skeptic, Dreifus insists on crystal-clear financial reporting from potential picks and has a strong preference for companies with high returns on invested capital and plenty of cash on hand.

Historical Profile

Return Above Avg
Risk Low
Rating ★★★★★ Highest

Investment Style: Equity, Stock %: 96% 96% 92% 92% 84% 82% 87%

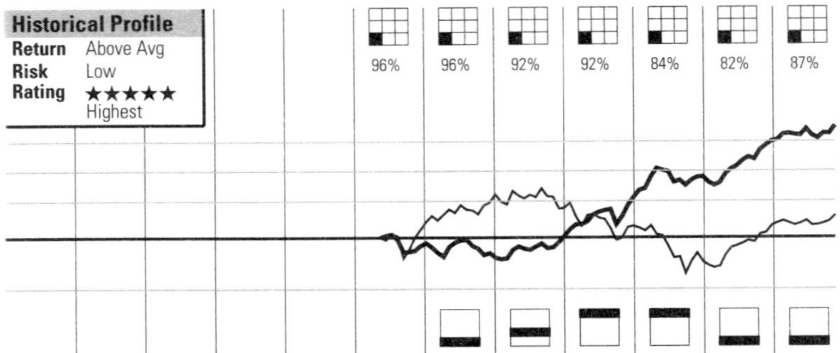

1993	1994	1995	1996	1997	1998	1999	2000	2001	2002	2003	12-04	History
—	—	—	—	—	9.30	8.31	9.55	12.37	14.24	17.97	19.61	NAV
—	—	—	—	—	-6.84*	-9.64	16.30	30.75	15.32	27.64	13.91	Total Return %
—	—	—	—	—	—	-30.68	25.40	42.63	37.41	-1.03	3.04	+/-S&P 500
—	—	—	—	—	—	-8.15	-6.53	16.73	26.75	-18.39	-8.34	+/-Russ 2000 VL
—	—	—	—	—	0.00	1.02	1.32	1.17	0.20	0.32	1.02	Income Return %
—	—	—	—	—	—	-10.66	14.98	29.58	15.12	27.32	12.89	Capital Return %
—	—	—	—	—	—	91	60	7	1	98	94	Total Rtn % Rank Cat
—	—	—	—	—	0.02	0.10	0.11	0.11	0.03	0.05	0.18	Income $
—	—	—	—	—	0.00	0.00	0.00	0.00	0.00	0.15	0.67	Capital Gains $
—	—	—	—	—	—	1.49	1.49	1.49	1.20	1.19	—	Expense Ratio %
—	—	—	—	—	—	0.96	1.38	0.87	0.27	0.35	—	Income Ratio %
—	—	—	—	—	—	57	61	124	41	22	—	Turnover Rate %
—	—	—	—	—	3	3	3	6	394	748	848	Net Assets $mil

Performance 12-31-04

	1st Qtr	2nd Qtr	3rd Qtr	4th Qtr	Total
2000	5.54	-0.00	1.14	8.96	16.30
2001	8.38	9.08	-8.50	20.87	30.75
2002	15.20	3.72	-9.00	6.06	15.32
2003	-4.21	12.39	4.70	13.25	27.64
2004	5.40	3.27	-3.02	7.91	13.91

Trailing	Total Return%	+/- S&P 500	+/- Russ 2000 VL	%Rank Cat	Growth of $10,000
3 Mo	7.91	-1.32	-5.29	96	10,791
6 Mo	4.65	-2.54	-8.72	97	10,465
1 Yr	13.91	3.04	-8.34	94	11,391
3 Yr Avg	18.80	15.22	2.30	19	16,767
5 Yr Avg	20.59	22.89	3.36	12	25,501
10 Yr Avg	—	—	—	—	—
15 Yr Avg	—	—	—	—	—

Tax Analysis	Tax-Adj Rtn%	%Rank Cat	Tax-Cost Rat	%Rank Cat
3 Yr (estimated)	18.24	12	0.47	28
5 Yr (estimated)	20.04	6	0.46	23
10 Yr (estimated)	—	—	—	—

Potential Capital Gain Exposure: 23% of assets

Rating and Risk

Time Period	Load-Adj Return %	Morningstar Rtn vs Cat	Morningstar Risk vs Cat	Morningstar Risk-Adj Rating
1 Yr	13.91			
3 Yr	18.80	+Avg	Low	★★★★★
5 Yr	20.59	+Avg	Low	★★★★★
10 Yr	—	—	—	—
Incept	12.68			

Other Measures	Standard Index S&P 500	Best Fit Index Mstar Small Core
Alpha	16.1	8.8
Beta	0.49	0.59
R-Squared	40	73
Standard Deviation	13.76	
Mean	18.80	
Sharpe Ratio	1.28	

Portfolio Analysis 09-30-04

Share change since 06-04 Total Stocks:72	Sector	PE	YTD Ret%	% Assets
⊕ Borders Group	Consumer	14.1	17.47	3.60
⊕ Banta	Business	18.3	12.31	3.02
Lubrizol	Energy	22.0	17.03	2.69
⊕ Lancaster Colony	Goods	18.9	-2.92	2.57
⊕ Schweitzer-Mauduit Inter	Ind Mtrls	14.4	16.25	2.46
⊕ Bio-Rad Laboratories	Health	22.1	-0.52	2.43
⊕ Hilb Rogal & Hobbs Compa	Financial	15.0	14.30	2.40
⊕ Bandag A	Ind Mtrls	—	—	2.38
⊕ BJ's Wholesale Club	Consumer	16.6	26.87	2.25
⊕ American Woodmark	Goods	22.4	59.21	2.21
⊕ Briggs & Stratton	Ind Mtrls	14.4	25.63	2.16
⊕ CEC Entertainment	Consumer	18.3	26.52	2.02
⊕ A Schulman	Ind Mtrls	20.9	3.23	2.01
⊕ Universal	Goods	9.2	11.91	1.97
⊕ National Presto Industri	Goods	20.1	29.69	1.97
Hooker Furniture	Goods	15.7	12.39	1.83
⊖ Bob Evans Farms	Consumer	14.9	-18.04	1.83
⊕ Lawson Products	Ind Mtrls	21.3	54.52	1.82
⊕ CSS Industries	Media	12.8	3.64	1.65
⊕ Dress Barn	Consumer	17.9	17.41	1.53

Current Investment Style

Value Blnd Growth; Large Mid Small

Market Cap	%
Giant	0.0
Large	0.0
Mid	16.8
Small	51.4
Micro	31.9
Avg $mil: 661	

Value Measures		Rel Category
Price/Earnings	14.43	0.90
Price/Book	1.87	1.13
Price/Sales	0.72	0.96
Price/Cash Flow	7.71	1.49
Dividend Yield %	1.24	1.03

Growth Measures	%	Rel Category
Long-Term Erngs	11.73	0.97
Book Value	11.20	2.59
Sales	7.04	2.25
Cash Flow	0.65	0.30
Historical Erngs	5.90	1.23

Profitability	%	Rel Category
Return on Equity	14.33	1.57
Return on Assets	8.34	2.01
Net Margin	6.09	0.91

Sector Weightings	% of Stocks	Rel S&P 500	3 Year High	3 Year Low
Info	1.90	0.09		
Software	0.00	0.00	1	0
Hardware	0.00	0.00	0	0
Media	1.90	0.49	2	2
Telecom	0.00	0.00	0	0
Service	42.86	0.92		
Health	4.82	0.39	5	2
Consumer	26.56	2.93	27	15
Business	8.72	2.15	11	7
Financial	2.76	0.13	3	0
Mfg	55.24	1.72		
Goods	26.83	2.88	44	27
Ind Mtrls	24.66	1.95	28	20
Energy	3.75	0.52	5	1
Utilities	0.00	0.00	0	0

Composition

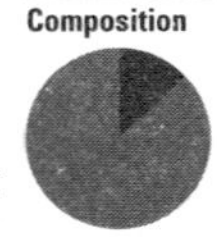

Cash	13.0
Stocks	87.0
Bonds	0.0
Other	0.0
Foreign (% of Stock)	0.0

Morningstar's Take by Todd Trubey 11-22-04

In a world of index-hugging funds and concerns over relative returns, Royce Special Equity stands out nicely.

The fund's name fits: it's special. It's got a compact portfolio of unusually small stocks: Of the 124 small value funds, only five others have portfolios with fewer than 75 stocks and an average market cap under $700 million. And the fund's focus on absolute returns makes it behave differently. In 2002 when stocks fell across all styles and market-cap ranges, this fund led its category with a 15% return, beating the runner-up by 11 percentage points.

Lead manager Charlie Dreifus's process goes to extremes to avoid losses--and aims only for decent returns. After screening for cheap stocks, Dreifus derives an enterprise value for the firm using conservative merger and acquisition style analysis. He thereby aims to buy a piece of the firm for less than its worth. He then gauges whether a firm's involved in a good business, one that can grow over time. Finally, he grades the firm's financial reporting to decide whether its accounting is nicely conservative or not. All told, only one in 10 firms he researches lands in the portfolio.

This approach is why the fund's portfolio is so quirky. While most compact funds seek high-return holdings, this one seeks low-risk ones. In other words, over three decades Dreifus has never found more than 80 stocks safe enough to hold simultaneously. Plus, the fund mainly holds cash cows with high returns on capital, such as consumer-oriented and manufacturing stocks. Certain types of firms, such as technology, telecom, and utilities firms rarely make the cut.

Earlier this year the fund closed to new investors, before Dreifus felt it had reached its capacity. The main reason was that he found fewer screaming bargains than previously and cash was building. The fund thus retains its rare, stellar risk/reward profile for its lucky owners.

Address:	1414 Ave of the Americas New York NY 10019 800-221-4268
Web Address:	www.roycefunds.com
Inception:	05-01-98*
Advisor:	Royce & Associates, LLC
Subadvisor:	None
NTF Plans:	Bidwell & Co. NTF, Dreyfus LION-NTF

Minimum Purchase:	Closed	Add: —	IRA: —		
Min Auto Inv Plan:	Closed	Add: —			
Sales Fees:	No-load, 1.00%R				
Management Fee:	1.00%				
Actual Fees:	Mgt:1.00%	Dist: —			
Expense Projections:	3Yr:$378	5Yr:$654	10Yr:$1443		
Income Distrib:	Annually				

Royce Total Return Inv

Ticker	Load	NAV	Yield	Total Assets	Mstar Category
RYTRX	None	$12.26	0.9%	$4,430 mil	Small Value

Governance and Management

Fiduciary Grade: B

Portfolio Manager(s)

Consistent. Chuck Royce has run this fund since its 1993 inception. He has been chief investment officer with Royce Funds for 28 years.

Strategy

An emphasis on dividend-paying stocks is just one of the ways this fund maintains its low-risk profile. Chuck Royce thinks the dividend provides a cushion during market downturns. Although the fund spreads its bets across many holdings, it does not seek diversification across all industries. Financials and industrial stocks have been its favorites.

Historical Profile

Return Average
Risk Low
Rating ★★★★ Above Avg

Investment Style: Equity, Stock %: 82% 68% 76% 83% 96% 90% 90% 81% 87%

▼ Manager Change
▽ Partial Manager Change

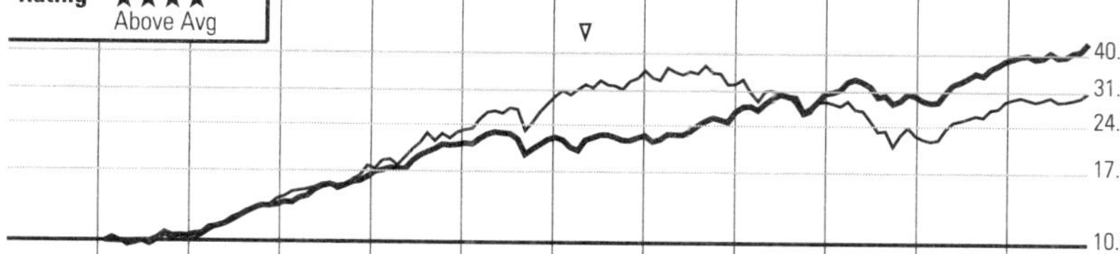

Performance Quartile (within Category)

1993	1994	1995	1996	1997	1998	1999	2000	2001	2002	2003	12-04	History
5.00	5.12	5.76	6.29	7.52	7.56	7.15	7.77	8.59	8.37	10.69	12.26	NAV
0.00*	5.12	26.86	25.48	23.70	4.75	1.55	19.43	14.78	-1.60	29.99	17.52	Total Return %
—	3.81	-10.67	2.54	-9.65	-23.82	-19.49	28.53	26.66	20.49	1.32	6.65	+/-S&P 500
—	6.66	1.11	4.11	-8.08	11.20	3.04	-3.40	0.76	9.83	-16.04	-4.73	+/-Russ 2000 VL
—	2.72	2.54	2.78	1.78	1.99	2.13	2.11	1.36	0.88	1.11	1.11	Income Return %
—	2.40	24.32	22.70	21.92	2.76	-0.58	17.32	13.42	-2.48	28.88	16.41	Capital Return %
—	19	31	33	82	8	48	49	59	12	92	78	Total Rtn % Rank Cat
0.00	0.14	0.13	0.16	0.11	0.15	0.16	0.15	0.11	0.08	0.09	0.12	Income $
0.00	0.00	0.60	0.73	0.15	0.16	0.35	0.57	0.21	0.01	0.08	0.17	Capital Gains $
0.29	1.96	1.67	1.25	1.25	1.25	1.25	1.25	1.24	1.20	1.18	—	Expense Ratio %
-0.29	0.49	2.42	2.50	3.15	2.75	2.32	2.08	1.14	1.01	1.27	—	Income Ratio %
—	88	68	111	26	66	39	24	24	22	20	—	Turnover Rate %
—	—	3	6	121	244	249	277	511	980	2,285	3,584	Net Assets $mil

Performance 12-31-04

	1st Qtr	2nd Qtr	3rd Qtr	4th Qtr	Total
2000	1.00	2.23	10.69	4.49	19.43
2001	1.27	12.57	-12.58	15.17	14.78
2002	9.14	-3.37	-11.86	5.85	-1.60
2003	-4.30	16.00	4.86	11.66	29.99
2004	4.31	1.98	0.09	10.37	17.52

Trailing	Total Return%	+/- S&P 500	+/- Russ 2000 VL	%Rank Cat	Growth of $10,000
3 Mo	10.37	1.14	-2.83	85	11,037
6 Mo	10.47	3.28	-2.90	69	11,047
1 Yr	17.52	6.65	-4.73	78	11,752
3 Yr Avg	14.55	10.97	-1.95	58	15,031
5 Yr Avg	15.56	17.86	-1.67	51	20,608
10 Yr Avg	15.75	3.68	0.58	41	43,173
15 Yr Avg	—	—	—	—	—

Tax Analysis	Tax-Adj Rtn%	%Rank Cat	Tax-Cost Rat	%Rank Cat
3 Yr (estimated)	13.95	47	0.52	31
5 Yr (estimated)	14.31	54	1.08	56
10 Yr (estimated)	13.61	41	1.85	58

Potential Capital Gain Exposure: 22% of assets

Rating and Risk

Time Period	Load-Adj Return %	Morningstar Rtn vs Cat	Morningstar Risk vs Cat	Morningstar Risk-Adj Rating
1 Yr	17.52			
3 Yr	14.55	Avg	Low	★★★
5 Yr	15.56	Avg	Low	★★★
10 Yr	15.75	Avg	Low	★★★★★
Incept	14.67			

Other Measures	Standard Index S&P 500	Best Fit Index Mstar Small Core
Alpha	11.4	3.6
Beta	0.66	0.68
R-Squared	69	95
Standard Deviation	13.41	
Mean	14.55	
Sharpe Ratio	0.99	

Morningstar's Take by Todd Trubey 11-29-04

Royce Total Return's main strength remains defense.

In small-cap expert Royce's stable, this fund has had the tamest risk/reward profile. Indeed, based on standard deviation (a measure of volatility), it's the most placid small-value category member over the past decade. It really stood out in 2002, when it lost 1.6% while its average peer lost 9.6%. But its tendency to own dull, high-quality stocks holds it back in small-cap rallies, as its bottom quintile finishes in 1997 and 2003 show.

The key issue here, as at many Royce funds, is whether the fund's massive asset base will hurt it. With $4 billion in assets, the fund is the largest actively managed small-cap fund open to new investors. As it's ballooned, its style has shifted. In late 2000 it held $511 million across 200 stocks with an average market cap of $500 million. It now holds more than 400 stocks with an average market cap of $1.2 billion. Over that time its micro-cap stake has been cut in half while its mid-cap stake has doubled to 45% of assets.

The driving force behind the fund's behavior, though, has been its mandate to invest at least 80% of assets in dividend-paying stocks. That keeps the fund heavily tilted toward small firms with dependable cash flows, typically financial, industrial, energy, and utility firms. Such firms hold up well in downturns, during which time their dividend yield works nicely. And yield is a conscious focus: Longtime manager Chuck Royce recently added Treasury bonds to the portfolio.

This fund will probably remain open for some time. Royce generally shutters funds briefly to stanch performance-chasers' "hot money" rather than close long-term to preserve style indefinitely. Also, Chuck Royce suggests that this fund isn't near capacity. We think the fund's continually more diffuse look and higher mid-cap weight may bring returns down slightly, so it's no longer a small-value pick. That said, for a defensive small-cap fund, it's tough to beat.

Address:	1414 Ave of the Americas New York NY 10019 800-221-4268	Minimum Purchase:	$2000	Add: $50	IRA: $500
Web Address:	www.roycefunds.com	Min Auto Inv Plan:	$500	Add: $50	
Inception:	12-15-93*	Sales Fees:	No-load, 1.00%R		
Advisor:	Royce & Associates, LLC	Management Fee:	0.99%		
Subadvisor:	None	Actual Fees:	Mgt:0.99%	Dist: —	
		Expense Projections:	3Yr:$372	5Yr:$644	10Yr:$1420
		Income Distrib:	Quarterly		
NTF Plans:	Accutrade NTF, Bidwell & Co. NTF				

Portfolio Analysis 09-30-04

Share change since 06-04 Total Stocks:402	Sector	PE	YTD Ret%	% Assets
US Treasury Note 3.25%	—	—	—	2.71
US Treasury Note 5.625%	—	—	—	1.27
Erie Indemnity A	Financial	17.9	25.69	0.66
⊕ Alleghany	Financial	14.7	30.77	0.61
Rayonier	Ind Mtrls	15.2	23.81	0.60
Expeditors International	Business	42.3	49.04	0.58
⊕ Brady A	Ind Mtrls	26.2	56.54	0.58
⊕ Invacare	Health	18.1	14.72	0.57
⊕ Commerce Group MA	Financial	9.8	58.71	0.56
⊕ Florida Rock Industries	Ind Mtrls	21.2	68.98	0.56
⊕ Bob Evans Farms	Consumer	14.9	-18.04	0.55
⊕ Reynolds & Reynolds	Media	16.1	-7.18	0.55
⊕ T Rowe Price Group	Financial	25.6	33.16	0.54
Ritchie Bros. Auctioneer	Consumer	29.5	26.17	0.54
⊕ La-Z-Boy	Goods	—	-24.88	0.54
⊕ Federated Investors B	Financial	17.0	5.00	0.53
Nuveen Investment	Financial	22.6	51.57	0.53
⊕ Clarcor	Ind Mtrls	21.5	25.62	0.52
⊖ Tidewater	Energy	48.3	21.49	0.52
TSX Grp	Financial	—	—	0.52

Current Investment Style

Value Blnd Growth; Large Mid Small

Market Cap	%
Giant	0.0
Large	1.4
Mid	44.8
Small	41.7
Micro	12.2
Avg $mil: 1,269	

Value Measures		Rel Category
Price/Earnings	16.48	1.03
Price/Book	1.89	1.14
Price/Sales	1.02	1.36
Price/Cash Flow	7.11	1.37
Dividend Yield %	1.68	1.40

Growth Measures	%	Rel Category
Long-Term Erngs	11.70	0.96
Book Value	8.26	1.91
Sales	5.54	1.77
Cash Flow	12.08	5.57
Historical Erngs	3.52	0.73

Profitability	%	Rel Category
Return on Equity	13.15	1.44
Return on Assets	7.11	1.71
Net Margin	10.51	1.57

Sector Weightings	% of Stocks	Rel S&P 500	3 Year High	3 Year Low
Info	5.85	0.27		
Software	0.07	0.02	1	0
Hardware	4.09	0.40	6	4
Media	1.36	0.35	1	1
Telecom	0.33	0.10	1	0
Service	47.52	1.02		
Health	5.69	0.46	6	4
Consumer	7.03	0.77	7	4
Business	12.22	3.02	17	10
Financial	22.58	1.09	23	23
Mfg	46.62	1.45		
Goods	10.14	1.09	11	10
Ind Mtrls	26.03	2.05	23	25
Energy	7.25	1.01	7	3
Utilities	3.20	1.08	4	2

Composition

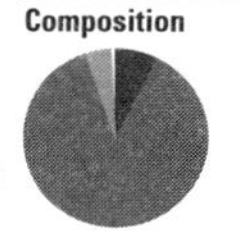

Cash	7.3
Stocks	87.2
Bonds	4.6
Other	0.9
Foreign (% of Stock)	5.0

RS Diversified Growth

Ticker	Load	NAV	Yield	Total Assets	Mstar Category
RSDGX	Closed	$22.69	0.0%	$956 mil	Small Growth

Governance and Management

Fiduciary Grade: C

Portfolio Manager(s)

Manager John Wallace built an outstanding record in his nearly five years at Oppenheimer Main Street Income & Growth and has run this fund since its inception in late 1996. Comanager John Seabern has been with the fund since March 1998.

Strategy

Managers John Wallace and John Seabern look for rapidly growing firms boasting strong earnings momentum that they think can at least double in price over the next two years. They favor companies with growth catalysts, such as new products or management. Although the managers' process is bottom-up, they will load up on fast-moving sectors such as technology if the bulk of the opportunities are there. They trade around positions frequently, giving the fund extremely high turnover. To limit stock-specific risk, they keep individual positions small and trim stocks that fall more than 15% below the fund's cost.

Historical Profile

Return Below Avg
Risk Above Avg
Rating ★★ Below Avg

Investment Style: Equity Stock % — 96% 97% 94% 97% 98% 95% 98% 100% 99%

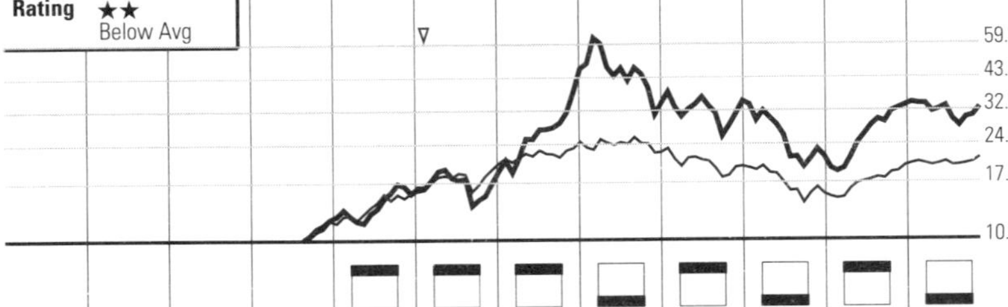

History	1993	1994	1995	1996	1997	1998	1999	2000	2001	2002	2003	12-04
NAV	—	—	—	12.42	14.04	15.89	32.99	22.83	23.26	14.16	22.36	22.69
Total Return %	—	—	—	24.20*	29.45	16.28	150.21	-26.91	1.88	-39.12	57.91	1.48
+/-S&P 500	—	—	—	—	-3.90	-12.29	129.17	-17.81	13.76	-17.03	29.24	-9.39
+/-Russ 2000 Gr	—	—	—	—	16.50	15.05	107.12	-4.48	11.11	-8.86	9.37	-12.83
Income Return %	—	—	—	0.00	0.00	0.00	0.00	0.00	0.00	0.00	0.00	0.00
Capital Return %	—	—	—	—	29.45	16.28	150.21	-26.91	1.88	-39.12	57.91	1.48
Total Rtn % Rank Cat	—	—	—	—	16	17	4	94	22	86	10	93
Income $	—	—	—	0.00	0.00	0.00	0.00	0.00	0.00	0.00	0.00	0.00
Capital Gains $	—	—	—	0.00	1.93	0.39	5.48	1.23	0.00	0.00	0.00	0.00
Expense Ratio %	—	—	—	2.28	1.94	1.89	1.84	1.51	1.52	1.50	1.48	—
Income Ratio %	—	—	—	-1.05	-1.20	-1.29	-1.40	-1.01	-1.03	-1.11	-0.92	—
Turnover Rate %	—	—	—	—	370	403	473	383	255	223	305	—
Net Assets $mil	—	—	—	60	80	69	305	523	852	572	1,098	956

Performance 12-31-04

	1st Qtr	2nd Qtr	3rd Qtr	4th Qtr	Total
2000	25.46	-19.81	-5.15	-23.41	-26.91
2001	-11.13	18.78	-29.38	36.66	1.88
2002	-8.30	-19.50	-24.93	9.85	-39.12
2003	-10.24	36.03	11.45	16.04	57.91
2004	1.34	-2.07	-9.78	13.34	1.48

Trailing	Total Return%	+/- S&P 500	+/- Russ 2000 Gr	%Rank Cat	Growth of $10,000
3 Mo	13.34	4.11	-1.74	62	11,334
6 Mo	2.25	-4.94	-5.91	93	10,225
1 Yr	1.48	-9.39	-12.83	93	10,148
3 Yr Avg	-0.82	-4.40	-6.61	85	9,756
5 Yr Avg	-6.19	-3.89	-2.62	78	7,265
10 Yr Avg	—	—	—	—	—
15 Yr Avg	—	—	—	—	—

Tax Analysis	Tax-Adj Rtn%	%Rank Cat	Tax-Cost Rat	%Rank Cat
3 Yr (estimated)	-0.82	82	0.00	1
5 Yr (estimated)	-6.58	74	0.42	19
10 Yr (estimated)	—	—	—	—

Potential Capital Gain Exposure: -11% of assets

Rating and Risk

Time Period	Load-Adj Return %	Morningstar Rtn vs Cat	Morningstar Risk vs Cat	Morningstar Risk-Adj Rating
1 Yr	1.48			
3 Yr	-0.82	-Avg	High	★★
5 Yr	-6.19	-Avg	+Avg	★★
10 Yr	—	—	—	—
Incept	15.64			

Other Measures	Standard Index S&P 500	Best Fit Index Russ 2000 Gr
Alpha	-3.5	-6.2
Beta	1.48	1.17
R-Squared	70	91
Standard Deviation	27.30	
Mean	-0.82	
Sharpe Ratio	-0.08	

Portfolio Analysis 09-30-04

Share change since 06-04 Total Stocks:137

	Sector	PE	YTD Ret%	% Assets
⊖ Scientific Games	Hardware	27.8	40.48	1.52
⊖ Commercial Metals	Ind Mtrls	11.5	67.69	1.49
⊖ Simpson Manufacturing	Ind Mtrls	15.8	37.98	1.42
⊕ Sonic Solutions	Software	31.1	46.67	1.40
⊕ Multimedia Games	Consumer	12.8	-23.29	1.33
⊖ Landstar System	Business	37.0	93.59	1.32
⊕ ValueClick	Business	32.4	46.97	1.31
☼ InfoSpace	Telecom	—	106.29	1.29
⊕ PC Mall	Consumer	NMF	37.89	1.22
☼ J2 Global Communications	Telecom	19.8	39.17	1.21
⊕ 24/7 Real Media	Business	—	-35.37	1.15
⊖ Nextel Partners A	Telecom	—	45.28	1.13
⊖ Corillian	Software	18.3	-22.40	1.12
⊖ Jos A. Bank Clothiers	Consumer	18.6	52.96	1.12
⊕ Southern Union	Utilities	18.5	36.84	1.04
⊕ QLT	Health	26.1	-14.70	1.03
☼ Digitas	Business	22.4	2.47	1.03
⊕ Magellan Health Services	Health	3.1	—	1.03
⊖ Credence Systems	Hardware	—	-30.47	1.03
⊕ Cal Dive International	Energy	23.4	68.95	1.01

Current Investment Style

Value Blnd Growth; Large Mid Small

Market Cap	%
Giant	0.0
Large	0.9
Mid	21.9
Small	51.1
Micro	26.0
Avg $mil: 789	

Value Measures		Rel Category
Price/Earnings	19.80	0.91
Price/Book	2.84	1.08
Price/Sales	1.43	0.95
Price/Cash Flow	6.60	0.82
Dividend Yield %	0.13	0.42

Growth Measures	%	Rel Category
Long-Term Erngs	19.99	1.16
Book Value	6.76	1.05
Sales	5.60	0.87
Cash Flow	8.38	0.62
Historical Erngs	15.95	1.18

Profitability	%	Rel Category
Return on Equity	11.01	1.12
Return on Assets	5.50	1.25
Net Margin	9.32	1.36

Sector Weightings	% of Stocks	Rel S&P 500	3 Year High	3 Year Low
Info	30.01	1.40		
Software	9.05	2.10	17	8
Hardware	15.32	1.50	20	7
Media	1.03	0.27	3	0
Telecom	4.61	1.46	5	1
Service	47.71	1.03		
Health	15.33	1.23	21	12
Consumer	11.18	1.23	15	6
Business	14.49	3.58	20	10
Financial	6.71	0.32	12	4
Mfg	22.28	0.69		
Goods	2.61	0.28	7	1
Ind Mtrls	10.10	0.80	14	4
Energy	8.51	1.19	9	4
Utilities	1.06	0.36	1	0

Composition

Cash	0.9
Stocks	99.1
Bonds	0.0
Other	0.0
Foreign (% of Stock)	4.5

Morningstar's Take by Christopher Traulsen 12-15-04

RS Diversified Growth's appeal isn't eliminated by market-timing charges at RS.

Without admitting or denying them, this closed fund's advisor recently settled charges that it permitted several entities to market-time its flagship offering, RS Emerging Growth. The settlement suggests that RS executives agreed to the scheme in exchange for long-term assets. It appears that RS violated that fund's prospectus by allowing the trades (the prospectus does not limit rapid trading outright, but it does limit the number of exchanges investors may make between RS funds), while earning fatter management fees for itself. It also suggests there were serious flaws in the firm's compliance program.

However, we believe the terms of the settlement and voluntary actions taken by RS go a long way toward ensuring that this kind of thing can't happen again. The firm has brought in a new chief operating officer and general counsel, completely revamped its compliance procedures, and brought in a new chief compliance officer and several new compliance staffers. The funds have also named independent cochairs to their board of directors. Finally, the settlement provides for regular third-party inspections of the funds' compliance procedures. CEO Randy Hecht, who had a hand in approving the deals, remains onboard, though his duties are severely curtailed.

This fund itself is going through a rough period in 2004. It's up just 0.4% for the year to date through Dec. 14, while its average peer is up about 9.6%. Comanager John Wallace has an excellent long-term record here, but we're concerned about the fund's inconsistent results in recent years. He and comanager John Seabern have taken some steps recently to even out performance, including cutting down sector bets and cutting the fund's exposure to individual issues. It's too soon to see if that will make much of a difference, but based on Wallace's past, we'd give this fund the benefit of the doubt for now.

Address:	388 Market St. San Francisco CA 94104 800-766-3863
Web Address:	www.RSInvestments.com
Inception:	08-01-96 *
Advisor:	RS Investment Management LP
Subadvisor:	None
NTF Plans:	Fidelity Retail-NTF, Schwab OneSource

Minimum Purchase:	Closed	Add: —	IRA: —
Min Auto Inv Plan:	Closed	Add: —	
Sales Fees:	0.25%B		
Management Fee:	1.00%		
Actual Fees:	Mgt:1.00%	Dist:0.25%	
Expense Projections:	3Yr:$508	5Yr:$876	10Yr:$1911
Income Distrib:	Annually		

RS Emerging Growth

Ticker	Load	NAV	Yield	Total Assets	Mstar Category
RSEGX	Closed	$32.36	0.0%	$1,411 mil	Small Growth

Governance and Management

Fiduciary Grade: C

Portfolio Manager(s)

Jim Callinan was named Morningstar's 1999 Domestic Stock Fund Manager of the Year. He has delivered strong results since taking the helm in 1996, and he also blew past the competition during an earlier stint at Putnam OTC Emerging Growth. He's supported by a team of analysts, including Wendell Laidley, a software analyst formerly of First Boston, and Greg Miliotes, a health-care analyst formerly of Robertson Stephens.

Strategy

Jim Callinan and his team of analysts look for companies growing revenues or earnings at 20% or better per year. Among those, the team prefers firms with proprietary advantages that give them an edge over their rivals, strong management teams, and high or improving margins. The fund often puts more than half of its assets into the technology sector. It typically holds well more than 100 names, and individual position sizes are relatively small.

Historical Profile

Return Average
Risk High
Rating ★★ Below Avg

Investment Style: Equity, Stock %

1996	1997	1998	1999	2000	2001	2002	2003	12-04
90%	98%	100%	100%	86%	100%	96%	98%	97%

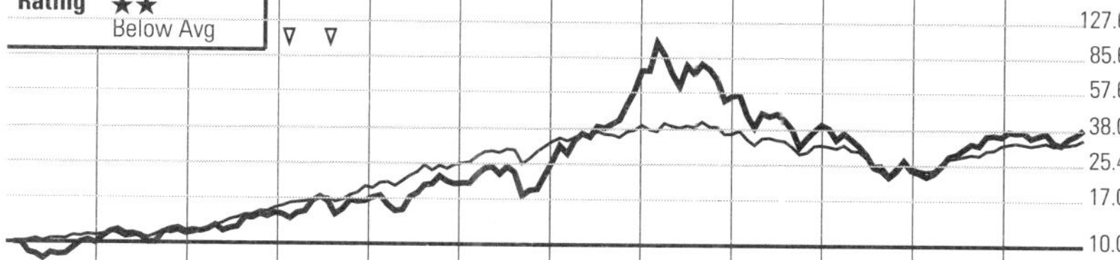

Performance Quartile (within Category)

1993	1994	1995	1996	1997	1998	1999	2000	2001	2002	2003	12-04	History
17.98	17.32	19.21	20.07	18.71	22.95	60.67	44.02	32.00	19.15	28.10	32.36	NAV
7.22	7.96	20.31	21.53	18.54	28.02	182.56	-25.04	-27.31	-40.16	46.74	15.16	Total Return %
-2.84	6.65	-17.22	-1.41	-14.81	-0.55	161.52	-15.34	-15.43	-18.07	18.07	4.29	+/-S&P 500
-6.15	10.39	-10.73	10.27	5.59	26.79	139.47	-2.61	-18.08	-9.90	-1.80	0.85	+/-Russ 2000 Gr
0.00	0.00	0.00	0.00	0.00	0.00	0.00	0.00	0.00	0.00	0.00	0.00	Income Return %
7.22	7.96	20.31	21.53	18.54	28.02	182.56	-25.04	-27.31	-40.16	46.74	15.16	Capital Return %
89	8	87	42	48	4	3	92	88	90	36	32	Total Rtn % Rank Cat
0.00	0.00	0.00	0.00	0.00	0.00	0.00	0.00	0.00	0.00	0.00	0.00	Income $
0.00	2.10	1.58	3.19	5.02	0.88	3.31	1.44	0.00	0.00	0.00	0.00	Capital Gains $
1.54	1.60	1.64	1.60	1.50	1.47	1.51	1.29	1.37	1.53	1.49	—	Expense Ratio %
-0.61	-1.27	-0.99	-0.83	-0.68	-1.03	-1.19	-0.82	-0.79	-1.35	-1.39	—	Income Ratio %
—	274	147	270	462	291	177	157	148	166	190	—	Turnover Rate %
170	176	159	210	249	394	3,577	3,869	2,498	1,310	1,636	1,411	Net Assets $mil

Performance 12-31-04

	1st Qtr	2nd Qtr	3rd Qtr	4th Qtr	Total
2000	19.40	-11.02	-4.11	-26.42	-25.04
2001	-29.69	16.70	-31.26	28.88	-27.31
2002	-9.16	-21.33	-22.61	8.19	-40.16
2003	-3.50	24.13	10.64	10.72	46.74
2004	5.55	-1.08	-5.56	16.78	15.16

Trailing	Total Return%	+/- S&P 500	+/- Russ 2000 Gr	%Rank Cat	Growth of $10,000
3 Mo	16.78	7.55	1.70	8	11,678
6 Mo	10.29	3.10	2.13	24	11,029
1 Yr	15.16	4.29	0.85	32	11,516
3 Yr Avg	0.37	-3.21	-5.42	78	10,111
5 Yr Avg	-11.24	-8.94	-7.67	90	5,509
10 Yr Avg	13.20	1.13	6.08	20	34,551
15 Yr Avg	13.61	2.68	6.11	10	67,803

Tax Analysis	Tax-Adj Rtn%	%Rank Cat	Tax-Cost Rat	%Rank Cat
3 Yr (estimated)	0.37	75	0.00	1
5 Yr (estimated)	-11.45	89	0.24	11
10 Yr (estimated)	10.91	22	2.02	70

Potential Capital Gain Exposure: -93% of assets

Rating and Risk

Time Period	Load-Adj Return %	Morningstar Rtn vs Cat	Morningstar Risk vs Cat	Morningstar Risk-Adj Rating
1 Yr	15.16			
3 Yr	0.37	-Avg	+Avg	★★
5 Yr	-11.24	-Avg	High	★
10 Yr	13.20	+Avg	High	★★
Incept	16.74			

Other Measures	Standard Index S&P 500	Best Fit Index Mstar Small Growth
Alpha	-2.4	-2.5
Beta	1.37	0.98
R-Squared	69	96
Standard Deviation	25.58	
Mean	0.37	
Sharpe Ratio	-0.04	

Portfolio Analysis 09-30-04

Share change since 06-04 Total Stocks:140	Sector	PE	YTD Ret%	% Assets
⊕ InfoSpace	Telecom	—	106.29	2.67
⊕ Altiris	Software	58.4	-2.88	1.78
⊕ Navigant Consulting	Business	36.1	41.04	1.44
⊕ Deckers Outdoor	Goods	25.3	129.22	1.42
⊕ Tessera Technologies	Hardware	—	97.82	1.30
⊖ ValueClick	Business	32.4	46.97	1.27
⊕ Urban Outfitters	Consumer	42.4	139.68	1.25
⊕ FormFactor	Hardware	—	37.07	1.23
⊕ Alexion Pharmaceuticals	Health	—	48.15	1.23
⊕ Unit	Energy	22.0	62.25	1.21
⊕ M-Systems Flash Disk Pio	Hardware	—	14.32	1.20
⊕ CNET Networks	Media	NMF	64.66	1.20
⊕ Grant Prideco	Energy	77.8	53.99	1.18
⊕ Angiotech Pharmaceutical	Health	—	-19.77	1.15
⊕ bebe stores	Consumer	38.8	134.46	1.14
⊕ WebEx Communications	Software	14.8	18.07	1.12
⊕ Patterson-UTI Energy	Energy	33.3	18.55	1.11
⊖ UTI Worldwide	Business	48.3	80.36	1.08
⊖ Magma Design Automation	Hardware	89.1	-46.40	1.04
⊕ Rigel Pharmaceuticals	Health	0.9	27.19	1.02

Current Investment Style

Value Blnd Growth / Large Mid Small

Market Cap	%
Giant	1.0
Large	2.0
Mid	17.4
Small	62.0
Micro	17.5
Avg $mil: 929	

Value Measures		Rel Category
Price/Earnings	24.79	1.14
Price/Book	3.11	1.18
Price/Sales	2.60	1.73
Price/Cash Flow	7.74	0.97
Dividend Yield %	0.04	0.13

Growth Measures	%	Rel Category
Long-Term Erngs	21.46	1.24
Book Value	4.69	0.73
Sales	6.88	1.07
Cash Flow	5.87	0.43
Historical Erngs	12.91	0.95

Profitability	%	Rel Category
Return on Equity	5.82	0.59
Return on Assets	3.51	0.80
Net Margin	8.40	1.23

Sector Weightings	% of Stocks	Rel S&P 500	3 Year High	3 Year Low
Info	30.28	1.41		
Software	6.68	1.55	13	7
Hardware	18.04	1.77	23	16
Media	1.86	0.48	6	1
Telecom	3.70	1.17	4	0
Service	54.98	1.19		
Health	19.21	1.54	33	19
Consumer	13.21	1.45	17	11
Business	14.96	3.69	17	10
Financial	7.60	0.37	11	5
Mfg	14.74	0.46		
Goods	4.92	0.53	6	1
Ind Mtrls	3.71	0.29	4	0
Energy	6.11	0.85	6	0
Utilities	0.00	0.00	1	0

Composition

Cash	3.4
Stocks	96.6
Bonds	0.0
Other	0.0
Foreign (% of Stock)	5.8

Morningstar's Take by Christopher Traulsen 12-14-04

The recent market-timing scandal at the company is cause for considerable concern, but not panic, for owners of RS Emerging Growth.

Without admitting or denying them, this fund's advisor recently settled charges that it permitted several entities to market-time this offering. The settlement suggests that RS executives agreed to the scheme in exchange for long-term assets. It appears that RS violated the fund's prospectus by allowing the trades (the prospectus does not limit rapid trading outright, but it does limit the number of exchanges investors may make between RS funds), while earning fatter management fees for itself. It also suggests there were serious flaws in the firm's compliance program.

That said, we believe the terms of the settlement and voluntary actions taken by RS go a long way toward ensuring that this kind of thing can't happen again. The firm has brought in a new chief operating officer and general counsel, completely revamped its compliance procedures, and brought in a new chief compliance officer and several new compliance staffers. The funds have also named independent cochairs to their board of directors. Finally, the settlement provides for regular third-party inspections of the funds' compliance procedures. CEO Randy Hecht, who had a hand in approving the deals, remains onboard, though his duties are severely curtailed.

This closed fund otherwise holds some appeal, but for a very limited audience. Jim Callinan is an experienced manager who has delivered good long-term returns relative to his peers. However, Callinan's emphasis on emerging companies in fast-changing industries exposes the fund to enormous business risk and price risk, as its horrible bear-market losses show. Still, the fund continues to shine in up markets, and offers investors exposure to a slate of young, rapidly growing companies. If you want to speculate on such issues with a small part of your portfolio, this fund is worth holding.

Address:	388 Market St. San Francisco CA 94104 800-766-3863
Web Address:	www.RSInvestments.com
Inception:	11-30-87
Advisor:	RS Investment Management LP
Subadvisor:	None
NTF Plans:	Fidelity Retail-NTF, Schwab OneSource

Minimum Purchase:	Closed	Add: —	IRA: —		
Min Auto Inv Plan:	Closed	Add: —			
Sales Fees:	0.25%B				
Management Fee:	1.00%				
Actual Fees:	Mgt:1.00%	Dist:0.25%			
Expense Projections:	3Yr:$508	5Yr:$876	10Yr:$1911		
Income Distrib:	Annually				

RS MidCap Opport

Ticker	Load	NAV	Yield	Total Assets	Mstar Category
RSMOX	12b-1 only	$12.18	0.0%	$209 mil	Mid-Cap Growth

Governance and Management

Fiduciary Grade: D

Portfolio Manager(s)

John Wallace has one of the better long-term records of any manager. He fared extremely well at Oppenheimer Total Return and Oppenheimer Main St Growth & Income from 1990 through 1995 and had great success at RS Diversified Growth in the late 1990s. Longtime analyst Jay Sherwood was named comanager in early 2003.

Strategy

Manager John Wallace seeks fast-growing companies with strong earnings growth that he thinks can double in price within 18 months. He sets upside price targets on his buys and starts selling stocks when they get within 10% of those targets. He's also quick to trim names that drop more than 15% below the fund's cost. The fund's price multiples are below the category average, and Wallace spreads his picks across roughly 80 to 100 names. The fund's turnover is extremely high.

Historical Profile

Return Average
Risk Average
Rating ★★★ Neutral

Investment Style
Equity
Stock %

1996	1997	1998	1999	2000	2001	2002	2003	12-04
88%	91%	77%	96%	89%	87%	91%	91%	98%

▼ Manager Change
∇ Partial Manager Change

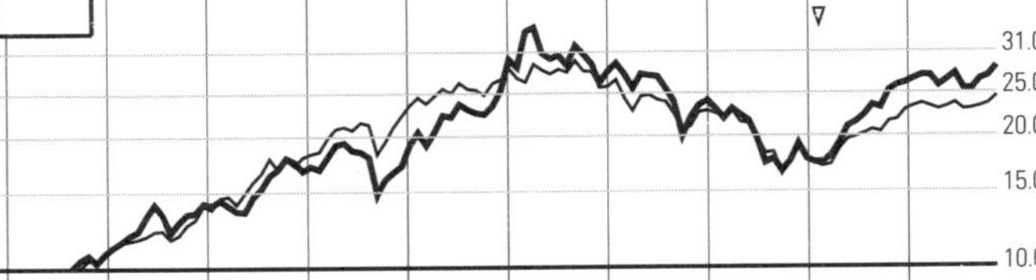

Growth of $10,000
▬ Investment Values of Fund
— Investment Values of S&P 500

Performance Quartile (within Category)

1993	1994	1995	1996	1997	1998	1999	2000	2001	2002	2003	12-04	History
—	—	11.24	13.62	13.52	14.04	15.92	11.65	9.92	7.30	10.84	12.18	NAV
—	—	12.40*	24.16	22.39	11.65	56.12	-6.28	-14.01	-26.41	48.49	12.36	Total Return %
—	—	—	1.22	-10.96	-16.92	35.08	2.82	-2.13	-4.32	19.82	1.49	+/-S&P 500
—	—	—	6.68	-0.15	-6.21	4.83	5.47	6.14	1.00	5.78	-3.12	+/-Russ MG
—	—	0.00	0.18	0.28	1.43	0.33	0.12	0.85	0.00	0.00	0.00	Income Return %
—	—	—	23.98	22.11	10.22	55.79	-6.40	-14.86	-26.41	48.49	12.36	Capital Return %
—	—	—	15	34	68	45	53	33	45	8	55	Total Rtn % Rank Cat
—	—	0.00	0.02	0.04	0.19	0.05	0.02	0.10	0.00	0.00	0.00	Income $
—	—	0.00	0.32	3.04	0.77	5.06	3.14	0.00	0.00	0.00	0.00	Capital Gains $
—	—	—	1.71	1.30	1.30	1.59	1.39	1.47	1.53	1.53	—	Expense Ratio %
—	—	—	0.18	0.45	1.00	0.31	-0.14	0.87	-0.60	-0.76	—	Income Ratio %
—	—	—	212	236	212	408	542	409	401	253	—	Turnover Rate %
—	—	136	310	298	184	227	198	156	89	141	209	Net Assets $mil

Performance 12-31-04

	1st Qtr	2nd Qtr	3rd Qtr	4th Qtr	Total
2000	18.15	-13.56	0.43	-8.63	-6.28
2001	-8.50	6.38	-26.63	20.41	-14.01
2002	-4.23	-14.63	-15.54	6.57	-26.41
2003	1.51	19.30	7.81	13.75	48.49
2004	3.78	0.98	-2.99	10.53	12.36

Trailing	Total Return%	+/- S&P 500	+/- Russ MG	%Rank Cat	Growth of $10,000
3 Mo	10.53	1.30	-3.41	88	11,053
6 Mo	7.22	0.03	-1.79	55	10,722
1 Yr	12.36	1.49	-3.12	55	11,236
3 Yr Avg	7.08	3.50	0.92	19	12,278
5 Yr Avg	-0.21	2.09	3.15	28	9,895
10 Yr Avg	—	—	—	—	—
15 Yr Avg	—	—	—	—	—

Tax Analysis	Tax-Adj Rtn%	%Rank Cat	Tax-Cost Rat	%Rank Cat
3 Yr (estimated)	7.08	16	0.00	1
5 Yr (estimated)	-2.03	31	1.82	75
10 Yr (estimated)	—	—	—	—

Potential Capital Gain Exposure: -2% of assets

Rating and Risk

Time Period	Load-Adj Return %	Morningstar Rtn vs Cat	Morningstar Risk vs Cat	Morningstar Risk-Adj Rating
1 Yr	12.36			
3 Yr	7.08	+Avg	+Avg	★★★★
5 Yr	-0.21	Avg	Avg	★★★
10 Yr	—	—	—	—
Incept	12.08			

Other Measures	Standard Index S&P 500	Best Fit Index Mstar Small Growth
Alpha	3.7	3.9
Beta	1.07	0.71
R-Squared	77	94
Standard Deviation	19.69	
Mean	7.08	
Sharpe Ratio	0.29	

Portfolio Analysis 09-30-04

Share change since 06-04 Total Stocks:100	Sector	PE	YTD Ret%	% Assets
⊕ XM Satellite Radio Holdi	Media	—	43.10	1.57
⊕ Nextel Partners A	Telecom	—	45.28	1.56
⊕ Career Education	Consumer	20.6	-0.62	1.53
⊕ Adobe Systems	Software	34.2	60.76	1.51
⊕ Gilead Sciences	Health	36.9	20.08	1.49
⊕ Kinetic Concepts	Health	—	—	1.48
⊕ Tellabs	Hardware	38.1	2.14	1.46
☼ Plantronics	Hardware	23.7	27.33	1.43
⊖ Valeant Pharmaceuticals	Health	—	6.22	1.43
☼ Research In Motion Ltd	Hardware	—	146.66	1.35
⊕ Polo Ralph Lauren	Goods	20.3	48.73	1.32
☼ Rockwell Collins	Ind Mtrls	23.6	32.97	1.29
⊕ AmeriCredit	Financial	14.3	53.48	1.28
⊕ CapitalSource	Financial	—	18.40	1.24
Assurant	Financial	—	—	1.23
⊕ Lamar Advertising A	Business	—	14.63	1.22
Providian Financial	Financial	14.3	41.50	1.20
Ryder System	Business	15.7	41.93	1.19
⊕ Friedman Billings Ramsey	Financial	9.0	-9.64	1.19
Newfield Exploration	Energy	12.5	32.58	1.18

Current Investment Style

Value Blnd Growth / Large Mid Small

Market Cap	%
Giant	2.0
Large	20.6
Mid	76.7
Small	0.7
Micro	0.0
Avg $mil: 5,037	

Value Measures		Rel Category
Price/Earnings	20.82	0.95
Price/Book	2.71	0.90
Price/Sales	1.60	0.90
Price/Cash Flow	5.12	0.53
Dividend Yield %	0.30	0.70

Growth Measures	%	Rel Category
Long-Term Erngs	15.70	1.00
Book Value	6.41	0.64
Sales	9.12	1.06
Cash Flow	8.90	0.73
Historical Erngs	7.21	0.45

Profitability	%	Rel Category
Return on Equity	11.80	0.82
Return on Assets	4.70	0.66
Net Margin	7.68	0.80

Sector Weightings	% of Stocks	Rel S&P 500	3 Year High	3 Year Low
Info	27.00	1.26		
Software	2.49	0.58	13	2
Hardware	18.09	1.77	19	2
Media	2.49	0.65	7	1
Telecom	3.93	1.25	5	1
Service	50.05	1.08		
Health	18.90	1.51	30	13
Consumer	10.81	1.19	18	11
Business	10.90	2.69	11	3
Financial	9.44	0.45	12	6
Mfg	22.96	0.71		
Goods	3.18	0.34	8	2
Ind Mtrls	7.75	0.61	17	2
Energy	11.55	1.61	12	5
Utilities	0.48	0.16	3	0

Composition

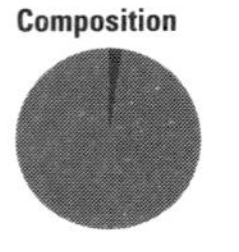

Cash	2.5
Stocks	97.5
Bonds	0.0
Other	0.0
Foreign (% of Stock)	4.0

Morningstar's Take by Christopher Traulsen 11-12-04

RS MidCap Opportunities' appeal is dented, but not eliminated by, the market-timing charges at RS.

Without admitting or denying them, this fund's advisor recently settled charges that it permitted several entities to market-time its flagship offering, RS Emerging Growth. The settlement suggests that RS executives agreed to the scheme in exchange for the investment of long-term assets into Emerging Growth. Although RS MidCap Opportunities doesn't appear to have been involved in the deals, the charges are serious. It appears that RS violated Emerging Growth's prospectus by allowing the trades, while earning fatter management fees by virtue of the deals. It also suggests there were serious flaws in the firm's compliance program.

Nevertheless, we believe the terms of the settlement and voluntary actions taken by RS go a long way toward ensuring that this kind of thing can't happen again. The firm has brought in a new chief operating officer and general counsel, completely revamped its compliance procedures, and hired a new chief compliance officer and several new compliance staffers. The funds have also named independent cochairs to their board of directors. Finally, the settlement provides for regular third-party inspections of the funds' compliance procedures for a number of years.

This fund itself is otherwise an attractive offering. It features an experienced management team and has delivered strong risk-adjusted returns relative to other mid-growth funds. It has held its own in 2004, with an energy stake helping it deliver a 6.9% return through November 11, about even with the category median.

We have removed this fund from our Analyst Picks in light of the charges against its advisor. It's also worth noting that CEO Randy Hecht, who had some involvement in the approval of the deals, remains on board, though his duties are severely curtailed. We still think this is a solid fund, but we'll be keeping an eye on compliance at RS.

Address:	388 Market St. San Francisco CA 94104 800-766-3863
Web Address:	www.RSInvestments.com
Inception:	07-12-95*
Advisor:	RS Investment Management LP
Subadvisor:	None
NTF Plans:	Fidelity Retail-NTF, Schwab OneSource

Minimum Purchase:	$5000	Add: $100	IRA: $1000
Min Auto Inv Plan:	$5000	Add: $100	
Sales Fees:	0.25%B		
Management Fee:	1.00%, 0.25%A		
Actual Fees:	Mgt:1.00%	Dist:0.25%	
Expense Projections:	3Yr:$492	5Yr:$856	10Yr:$1881
Income Distrib:	Annually		

Salomon Bros Investors O

Ticker	Load	NAV	Yield	Total Assets	Mstar Category
SAIFX	Closed	$20.52	1.6%	$1,911 mil	Large Value

Governance and Management

Fiduciary Grade: C

Portfolio Manager(s)

Former lead manager John Cunningham, who had led the fund since autumn 1998, left advisor Salomon Brothers Asset Management in August 2004. Filling his shoes as lead manager is Mark McAllister, who had served as comanager since April 2000. McAllister also is lead manager for Smith Barney Large Cap Value and SB Capital & Income. Robert Feitler, a veteran Salomon Brothers analyst/manager specializing in financials, was named comanager at the same time.

Strategy

Management looks for stocks selling at substantial discounts to the S&P 500 Index, their industries, or both. Favored companies have estimated earnings that exceed the market's, good management, and a catalyst to drive up share prices. As a result, the portfolio is a mix of down-and-out growth stocks and true-blue value holdings.

Historical Profile

Return Average
Risk High
Rating ★★★ Neutral

Investment Style
Equity
Stock %

95% 94% 86% 88% 97% 92% 96% 95%

▼ Manager Change
▽ Partial Manager Change

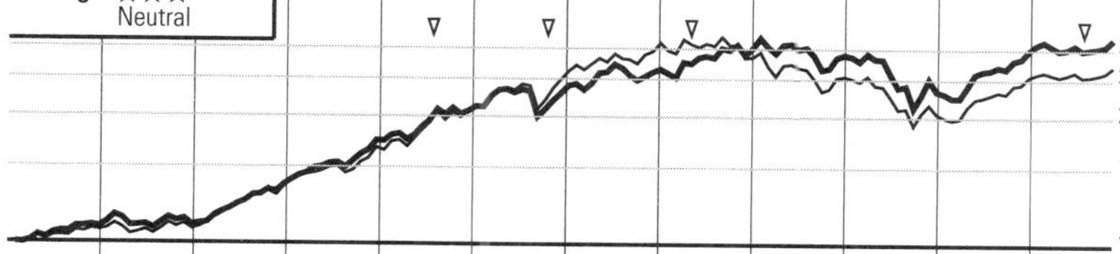

Growth of $10,000
— Investment Values of Fund
— Investment Values of S&P 500

Performance Quartile (within Category)

1993	1994	1995	1996	1997	1998	1999	2000	2001	2002	2003	12-04	History
15.60	13.63	16.63	18.90	21.13	22.05	20.69	20.38	18.94	14.66	19.04	20.52	NAV
15.19	-0.80	34.99	30.40	26.47	15.44	11.73	15.24	-4.19	-21.57	32.01	10.83	Total Return %
5.13	-2.11	-2.54	7.46	-6.88	-13.13	-9.31	24.34	7.69	0.52	3.34	-0.04	+/-S&P 500
-2.88	1.18	-3.37	8.76	-8.71	-0.19	4.38	8.23	1.40	-6.05	1.98	-5.66	+/-Russ 1000 VI
2.06	2.26	1.63	1.53	1.05	1.13	1.05	1.38	0.96	1.07	1.85	1.78	Income Return %
13.13	-3.06	33.36	28.87	25.42	14.31	10.68	13.86	-5.15	-22.64	30.16	9.05	Capital Return %
40	55	32	2	61	31	21	23	49	73	19	72	Total Rtn % Rank Cat
0.33	0.34	0.22	0.25	0.20	0.23	0.22	0.27	0.19	0.20	0.27	0.34	Income $
2.52	1.49	1.48	2.33	2.42	2.00	3.71	3.08	0.42	0.00	0.00	0.23	Capital Gains $
0.68	0.69	0.69	0.76	0.69	0.63	0.63	0.73	0.74	0.63	0.67	—	Expense Ratio %
1.90	1.75	1.67	1.36	1.15	1.15	1.16	1.12	0.98	1.37	1.60	—	Income Ratio %
79	66	86	58	62	74	66	75	43	44	34	—	Turnover Rate %
386	348	429	518	609	651	661	700	611	493	757	790	Net Assets $mil

Performance 12-31-04

	1st Qtr	2nd Qtr	3rd Qtr	4th Qtr	Total
2000	4.75	4.25	4.06	1.41	15.24
2001	-3.21	2.63	-12.76	10.56	-4.19
2002	0.82	-12.92	-20.16	11.89	-21.57
2003	-4.42	19.87	1.68	13.33	32.01
2004	2.83	0.70	-1.75	8.95	10.83

Trailing	Total Return%	+/- S&P 500	+/- Russ 1000 VI	%Rank Cat	Growth of $10,000
3 Mo	8.95	-0.28	-1.43	57	10,895
6 Mo	7.03	-0.16	-5.05	78	10,703
1 Yr	10.83	-0.04	-5.66	72	11,083
3 Yr Avg	4.69	1.11	-3.88	63	11,474
5 Yr Avg	4.85	7.15	-0.42	40	12,672
10 Yr Avg	13.79	1.72	-0.04	9	36,395
15 Yr Avg	11.90	0.97	-0.13	16	54,007

Tax Analysis	Tax-Adj Rtn%	%Rank Cat	Tax-Cost Rat	%Rank Cat
3 Yr (estimated)	4.05	57	0.61	41
5 Yr (estimated)	3.45	43	1.34	70
10 Yr (estimated)	11.13	12	2.34	82

Potential Capital Gain Exposure: 21% of assets

Rating and Risk

Time Period	Load-Adj Return %	Morningstar Rtn vs Cat	Morningstar Risk vs Cat	Morningstar Risk-Adj Rating
1 Yr	10.83			
3 Yr	4.69	Avg	High	★★
5 Yr	4.85	Avg	+Avg	★★★
10 Yr	13.79	+Avg	High	★★★★
Incept	—			

Other Measures	Standard Index S&P 500	Best Fit Index Russ 1000
Alpha	1.1	0.2
Beta	1.17	1.19
R-Squared	93	94
Standard Deviation	19.27	
Mean	4.69	
Sharpe Ratio	0.17	

Morningstar's Take by Gregg Wolper 11-13-04

Keep an eye on Salomon Brothers Investors Value.

In August 2004, Jack Cunningham, who had been the fund's lead manager for nearly six years, left Salomon Brothers Asset Management to become chief investment officer at Seligman. Cunningham's departure is a blow, for he not only had final say over this fund's buy and sell calls, but he also was head of the team of analysts and managers who provide research for Salomon Brothers (and some Smith Barney) equity mutual funds. Moreover, the fund's performance during his tenure was excellent, even taking into account a subpar 2002. Its annualized return from October 1998 through July 2004 beat the large-value average by about two percentage points.

Though the change hurts, the fund has not been left bereft. Mark McAllister, now the lead manager, had served as the fund's sole comanager since April 2000. He is assisted by newly named comanager Bob Feitler, a longtime member of the Salomon Brothers manager/analyst group, and still can rely on the other members of that group. McAllister said he plans to keep intact the fund's style--a flexible value approach that focuses on larger companies but also delves into the mid-cap range. He did expect to make some minor moves, however, such as raising the energy and financials stakes a bit. (Their underweighting partly explains why the fund's year-to-date return through Nov. 12, 2004, lags roughly three fourths of the category.)

With Cunningham gone, this fund now has to prove it still deserves high marks. But don't count it out. After all, it was in a similar position when Cunningham succeeded a longtime manager who left for another firm, and shareholders who stuck with it were well served in the long run.

Address:	399 Park Avenue New York NY 10022 800-446-1013	Minimum Purchase:	Closed	Add: —	IRA: —
		Min Auto Inv Plan:	Closed	Add: —	
		Sales Fees:	No-load		
Web Address:	www.sbam.com	Management Fee:	0.65% mx./0.45% mn., 0.05%A		
Inception:	09-01-58	Actual Fees:	Mgt:0.53%	Dist:	
Advisor:	Salomon Brothers Asset Management Inc.	Expense Projections:	3Yr:$214	5Yr:$373	10Yr:$835
Subadvisor:	None	Income Distrib:	Quarterly		
NTF Plans:	TD Waterhouse Ins NT				

Portfolio Analysis 09-30-04

Share change since 08-04 Total Stocks:82	Sector	PE	YTD Ret%	% Assets
Bank of America	Financial	12.3	21.50	2.80
Pfizer	Health	22.0	-22.31	2.68
Altria Group	Goods	13.3	18.38	2.34
⊕ ChevronTexaco	Energy	7.7	25.57	2.19
Total SA ADR	Energy	17.0	23.39	2.15
BP PLC ADR	Energy	20.7	22.07	1.91
American International G	Financial	16.2	-0.53	1.86
Microsoft	Software	36.1	8.95	1.82
Nokia ADR	Hardware	18.1	-6.14	1.82
Verizon Communications	Telecom	32.4	20.25	1.81
Kroger	Consumer	66.5	-5.24	1.71
Kimberly-Clark	Goods	17.8	16.12	1.67
McDonald's	Consumer	19.7	31.48	1.67
Honeywell International	Ind Mtrls	20.5	8.21	1.65
Nortel Networks	Hardware	—	-17.97	1.57
Hewlett-Packard	Hardware	18.9	-7.28	1.54
SBC Communications	Telecom	15.4	3.74	1.52
⊕ Royal Dutch Petroleum AD	Energy	—	14.31	1.52
Lockheed Martin	Ind Mtrls	19.9	9.97	1.51
Wyeth	Health	17.0	2.73	1.49

Current Investment Style

Value Blnd Growth — Large Mid Small

Market Cap	%
Giant	48.1
Large	38.8
Mid	13.1
Small	0.0
Micro	0.0

Avg $mil: 37,020

Value Measures		Rel Category
Price/Earnings	16.19	1.08
Price/Book	2.09	0.92
Price/Sales	1.15	0.97
Price/Cash Flow	5.44	0.85
Dividend Yield %	2.21	1.08

Growth Measures	%	Rel Category
Long-Term Erngs	10.07	0.97
Book Value	-2.29	NMF
Sales	-1.40	NMF
Cash Flow	-6.10	NMF
Historical Erngs	2.76	0.23

Profitability	%	Rel Category
Return on Equity	14.33	0.90
Return on Assets	7.62	0.97
Net Margin	9.48	0.93

Sector Weightings	% of Stocks	Rel S&P 500	3 Year High	3 Year Low
Info	25.93	1.21		
Software	2.23	0.52	3	0
Hardware	9.87	0.97	18	9
Media	7.05	1.84	7	1
Telecom	6.78	2.15	9	5
Service	40.43	0.87		
Health	9.73	0.78	11	7
Consumer	5.77	0.64	13	6
Business	0.81	0.20	1	0
Financial	24.12	1.16	33	24
Mfg	33.63	1.05		
Goods	6.37	0.68	8	3
Ind Mtrls	10.41	0.82	11	7
Energy	12.58	1.76	13	8
Utilities	4.27	1.44	5	0

Composition

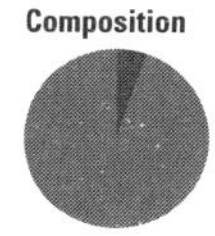

Cash	5.1
Stocks	94.9
Bonds	0.0
Other	0.0
Foreign (% of Stock)	12.9

Schwab 1000 Inv

Ticker	Load	NAV	Yield	Total Assets	Mstar Category
SNXFX	None	$34.59	1.4%	$6,783 mil	Large Blend

Governance and Management

Fiduciary Grade: C

Portfolio Manager(s)

Larry Mano handles the day-to-day management of the fund. He took over here from long-time manager Geri Hom earlier in 2004. Mano has been with Schwab since 1998 and also manages other index offerings at Schwab, including Schwab Total Stock Marketand Schwab International Index. Jeffery Mortimer, who joined Schwab in 1997, is head of equities at the firm. He oversees all of Schwab's equity offerings.

Strategy

This fund emulates Schwab's index of the largest 1,000 U.S. stocks, and has more mid-cap exposure than S&P 500 Index funds. But unlike index funds that track the broader Wilshire 5000, this fund has very little small-cap exposure. Management uses trading strategies like harvesting losses to offset realized gains in order to keep taxes at a minimum. The fund hasn't made a capital-gains distribution since its inception.

Historical Profile

Return Above Avg
Risk Average
Rating ★★★★ Above Avg

Investment Style: Equity Stock %

1993	1994	1995	1996	1997	1998	1999	2000	2001	2002	2003	12-04
100%	100%	99%	99%	99%	99%	99%	100%	100%			

▼ Manager Change
▽ Partial Manager Change

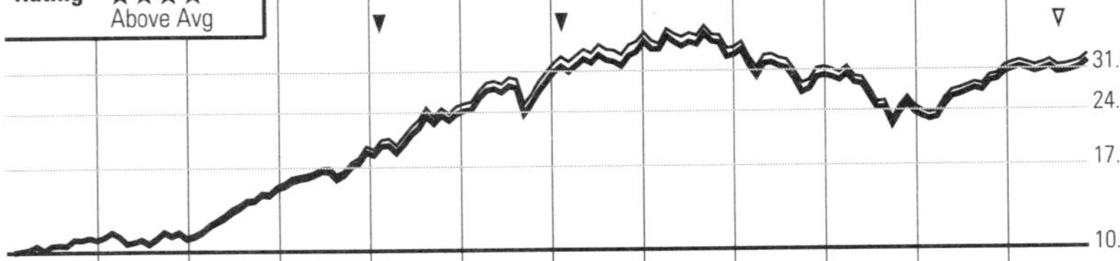

Growth of $10,000
— Investment Values of Fund
— Investment Values of S&P 500

Performance Quartile (within Category)

1993	1994	1995	1996	1997	1998	1999	2000	2001	2002	2003	12-04	History
12.85	12.57	16.94	20.34	26.56	33.51	40.28	36.73	31.95	24.86	31.65	34.59	NAV
9.63	-0.11	36.60	21.58	31.92	27.16	21.00	-8.21	-12.26	-21.19	28.74	10.82	Total Return %
-0.43	-1.42	-0.93	-1.36	-1.43	-1.41	-0.04	0.89	-0.38	0.90	0.07	-0.05	+/-S&P 500
-0.55	-0.50	-1.17	-0.87	-0.93	0.14	0.09	-0.42	0.19	0.46	-1.15	-0.58	+/-Russ 1000
2.15	2.05	1.83	1.53	1.29	0.95	0.77	0.60	0.74	1.01	1.38	1.50	Income Return %
7.48	-2.16	34.77	20.05	30.63	26.21	20.23	-8.81	-13.00	-22.20	27.36	9.32	Capital Return %
57	51	27	47	31	31	38	58	53	37	28	35	Total Rtn % Rank Cat
0.26	0.26	0.23	0.26	0.26	0.25	0.26	0.24	0.27	0.32	0.34	0.48	Income $
0.00	0.00	0.00	0.00	0.00	0.00	0.00	0.00	0.00	0.00	0.00	0.00	Capital Gains $
0.45	0.51	0.54	0.49	0.47	0.46	0.46	0.47	0.46	0.46	0.54	—	Expense Ratio %
2.21	2.06	2.03	1.66	1.33	1.02	0.78	0.63	0.78	1.04	0.74	—	Income Ratio %
1	3	2	2	2	2	3	9	8	9	5	—	Turnover Rate %
529	554	1,063	1,909	2,823	4,184	5,311	4,731	4,163	3,191	4,211	4,524	Net Assets $mil

Performance 12-31-04

	1st Qtr	2nd Qtr	3rd Qtr	4th Qtr	Total
2000	3.57	-3.76	0.35	-8.24	-8.21
2001	-12.58	6.45	-15.39	11.44	-12.26
2002	0.81	-13.10	-16.61	7.88	-21.19
2003	-3.02	15.26	2.88	11.95	28.74
2004	1.90	1.27	-1.90	9.47	10.82

Trailing	Total Return%	+/- S&P 500	+/- Russ 1000	%Rank Cat	Growth of $10,000
3 Mo	9.48	0.25	-0.32	40	10,948
6 Mo	7.40	0.21	-0.41	38	10,740
1 Yr	10.82	-0.05	-0.58	35	11,082
3 Yr Avg	3.99	0.41	-0.28	28	11,245
5 Yr Avg	-1.96	0.34	-0.20	44	9,058
10 Yr Avg	11.81	-0.26	-0.35	21	30,536
15 Yr Avg	—	—	—	—	—

Tax Analysis	Tax-Adj Rtn%	%Rank Cat	Tax-Cost Rat	%Rank Cat
3 Yr (estimated)	3.51	25	0.46	38
5 Yr (estimated)	-2.35	38	0.40	21
10 Yr (estimated)	11.36	8	0.40	4

Potential Capital Gain Exposure: 6% of assets

Rating and Risk

Time Period	Load-Adj Return %	Morningstar Rtn vs Cat	Morningstar Risk vs Cat	Morningstar Risk-Adj Rating
1 Yr	10.82			
3 Yr	3.99	+Avg	Avg	★★★★
5 Yr	-1.96	Avg	Avg	★★★
10 Yr	11.81	+Avg	Avg	★★★★
Incept	10.89			

Other Measures	Standard Index S&P 500	Best Fit Index Russ 1000
Alpha	0.4	-0.3
Beta	0.97	0.98
R-Squared	100	100
Standard Deviation	15.21	
Mean	3.99	
Sharpe Ratio	0.17	

Portfolio Analysis 09-30-04

Share change since 06-04 Total Stocks:985	Sector	PE	YTD Ret%	% Assets
⊖ Gen Elec	Ind Mtrls	22.8	20.68	2.95
⊖ ExxonMobil	Energy	13.9	28.04	2.67
⊖ Microsoft	Software	36.1	8.95	2.52
⊖ Pfizer	Health	22.0	-22.31	1.97
⊖ Citigroup	Financial	15.3	2.72	1.93
⊖ Wal-Mart Stores	Consumer	23.4	0.51	1.93
⊖ American International G	Financial	16.2	-0.53	1.50
⊕ Bank of America	Financial	12.3	21.50	1.49
⊖ Johnson & Johnson	Health	20.6	25.17	1.41
⊖ IBM	Hardware	20.2	7.19	1.22
⊕ J P Morgan Chase	Financial	19.4	9.97	1.19
⊖ Procter & Gamble	Goods	23.3	12.38	1.18
⊖ Intel	Hardware	19.8	-26.56	1.09
⊖ Cisco Systems	Hardware	24.5	-20.26	1.03
⊕ ChevronTexaco	Energy	7.7	25.57	0.97
⊖ Verizon Communications	Telecom	32.4	20.25	0.92
⊖ Wells Fargo	Financial	15.5	8.97	0.85
Berkshire Hathaway A	Financial	—	—	0.85
⊖ Coca-Cola	Goods	21.9	-16.12	0.82
⊕ Altria Group	Goods	13.3	18.38	0.81

Current Investment Style

Value Blnd Growth / Large Mid Small

Market Cap	%
Giant	45.8
Large	33.5
Mid	19.9
Small	0.7
Micro	0.0
Avg $mil: 33,035	

Value Measures		Rel Category
Price/Earnings	16.66	0.98
Price/Book	2.55	0.97
Price/Sales	1.43	0.99
Price/Cash Flow	7.41	0.96
Dividend Yield %	1.63	1.10

Growth Measures	%	Rel Category
Long-Term Erngs	11.16	0.97
Book Value	7.09	0.91
Sales	4.99	0.87
Cash Flow	7.35	0.78
Historical Erngs	11.83	1.00

Profitability	%	Rel Category
Return on Equity	17.68	1.01
Return on Assets	9.03	1.05
Net Margin	11.86	1.04

Sector Weightings	% of Stocks	Rel S&P 500	3 Year High	3 Year Low
Info	21.31	0.99		
Software	4.16	0.97	5	4
Hardware	9.20	0.90	11	8
Media	4.49	1.17	5	4
Telecom	3.46	1.10	4	3
Service	48.94	1.05		
Health	12.59	1.01	15	13
Consumer	9.55	1.05	10	9
Business	4.41	1.09	5	4
Financial	22.39	1.08	23	20
Mfg	29.73	0.93		
Goods	8.66	0.93	10	8
Ind Mtrls	11.10	0.88	11	10
Energy	7.00	0.98	7	5
Utilities	2.97	1.00	3	3

Composition

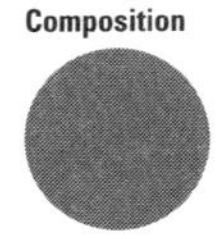

Cash	0.0
Stocks	100.0
Bonds	0.0
Other	0.0
Foreign (% of Stock)	0.0

Morningstar's Take by Sonya Morris 12-10-04

Though hardly the cream of the index-fund crop, Schwab 1000 is worth considering for a taxable account.

This fund charts a middle course between index funds tied to the S&P 500 and so-called total-market index funds that track the Wilshire 5000. By holding the 1,000 largest U.S. stocks by market capitalization, the fund has more mid-cap names than the S&P 500 and much less small-cap exposure than the Wilshire 5000.

The slice of mid-caps has helped the Schwab index slightly outpace the S&P 500 over the trailing three- and five-year periods. But because of its dearth of smaller-cap stocks, the index has lagged the Wilshire 5000 in years when small caps excelled. However, on balance, the fund hasn't looked all that different from either the S&P 500 or Wilshire 5000 over the long haul.

So the choice between this fund and competing S&P 500-tracking or Wilshire 5000-tracking index offerings boils down to cost: the lower the better. By that standard, this fund fails to distinguish itself. Its 0.54% expense ratio is triple that of Vanguard 500 Index and dwarfs Fidelity Spartan Total Market's 0.10% levy. That might not seem like much, but successful indexing is predicated on beating active managers at the cost line, a battle of inches in which every basis point counts.

That said, investors shouldn't dismiss this fund for taxable accounts. Indeed, its 11.1% 10-year annualized aftertax return ranks near the top of the large-blend category. Credit that success to prior manager Geri Hom's ability to harvest tax losses to offset gains. Thanks to her dexterity, the fund has not distributed a capital gain since its inception. And while Hom left the fund earlier this year, we don't expect her successor, Larry Mano (who has been an analyst and manager at Schwab since 1998) to miss a beat.

Thus, while this certainly wouldn't be our first choice of index funds, it'll do in a pinch, especially in taxable accounts.

Address:	101 Montgomery St San Francisco CA 94104 800-435-4000
Web Address:	www.schwab.com
Inception:	04-02-91
Advisor:	Charles Schwab
Subadvisor:	None
NTF Plans:	Schwab OneSource, Schwab Instl NTF

Minimum Purchase:	$2500	Add: $500	IRA: $1000
Min Auto Inv Plan:	$2500	Add: $100	
Sales Fees:	No-load, 0.75%R		
Management Fee:	0.30% mx./0.22% mn.		
Actual Fees:	Mgt:0.23%	Dist:	
Expense Projections:	3Yr:$156	5Yr:$276	10Yr:$624
Income Distrib:	Annually		

Scudder Flag Communic A

Ticker	Load	NAV	Yield	Total Assets	Mstar Category
TISHX	5.75%	$16.80	0.0%	$367 mil	Specialty-Communications

Governance and Management

Fiduciary Grade: C

Portfolio Manager(s)

Bruce Behrens has been at the helm since 1984. Comanager Liam Burke stepped down in May 2002 after becoming manager in 1997. His replacement, Patrick O'Brien, hadn't managed a telecom-focused portfolio before, but he had 10 years of experience as a portfolio manager and analyst. According to a recent shareholder report, management invests in the fund. Its compensation is reportedly tied to assets under management.

Strategy

The comanagers seek communications companies with strong business models, healthy cash flows, and savvy management teams. They're long-term investors--evident in the fund's low turnover rate--and they will load up on favorite holdings. Regional bells have tended to dominate, although difficult competitive conditions have increasingly forced management to turn its gaze elsewhere. New sources of ideas have included foreign services names along with opportunistic plays on beaten-down names.

Historical Profile

Return Average
Risk Average
Rating ★★★ Neutral

Investment Style: Equity Stock %

1993	1994	1995	1996	1997	1998	1999	2000	2001	2002	2003	12-04
98%	98%	92%	93%	96%	95%	97%	96%	96%			

▼ Manager Change
▽ Partial Manager Change

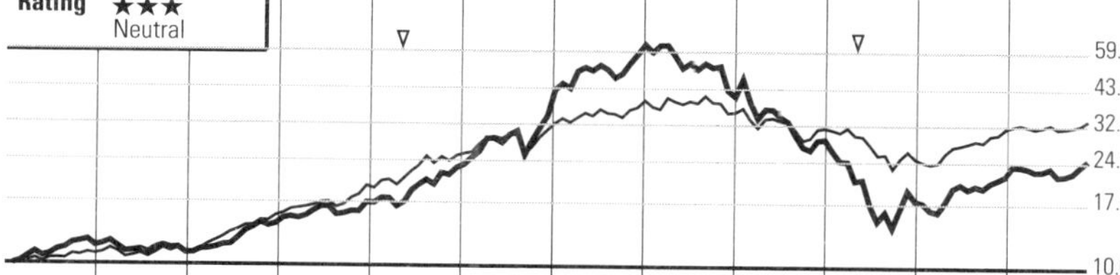

Growth of $10,000
— Investment Values of Fund
— Investment Values of S&P 500

Performance Quartile (within Category)

History

1993	1994	1995	1996	1997	1998	1999	2000	2001	2002	2003	12-04	History
13.73	12.33	14.87	15.60	19.37	34.23	43.65	26.37	18.58	11.28	13.86	16.80	NAV
18.09	-6.57	33.44	13.46	37.36	85.30	45.47	-34.52	-29.54	-39.29	22.87	21.21	Total Return %
8.03	-7.88	-4.09	-9.48	4.01	56.73	24.43	-25.42	-17.66	-17.20	-5.80	10.34	+/-S&P 500
2.20	-1.42	-7.08	13.35	-3.28	33.48	27.06	5.75	-16.77	-4.74	15.54	2.51	+/-DJ Telecom
3.49	2.61	3.65	2.58	2.62	0.65	0.64	0.11	0.00	0.00	0.00	0.00	Income Return %
14.60	-9.18	29.79	10.88	34.74	84.65	44.83	-34.63	-29.54	-39.29	22.87	21.21	Capital Return %
100	83	29	38	1	1	71	64	50	59	89	55	Total Rtn % Rank Cat
0.42	0.35	0.44	0.38	0.40	0.13	0.21	0.05	0.00	0.00	0.00	0.00	Income $
0.28	0.15	1.01	0.84	1.50	1.18	5.43	2.50	0.00	0.00	0.00	0.00	Capital Gains $
0.92	0.92	0.93	1.14	1.11	1.05	0.96	1.05	1.24	1.62	1.34	—	Expense Ratio %
3.12	3.14	2.85	1.74	1.07	0.48	0.62	0.09	-0.22	-0.20	0.13	—	Income Ratio %
14	23	24	20	26	14	17	11	14	43	62	—	Turnover Rate %
469	436	492	506	623	1,251	2,115	1,435	730	303	286	285	Net Assets $mil

Performance 12-31-04

	1st Qtr	2nd Qtr	3rd Qtr	4th Qtr	Total
2000	-0.41	-13.63	-3.60	-21.03	-34.52
2001	-16.31	1.31	-21.96	6.48	-29.54
2002	-16.58	-29.94	-16.67	24.64	-39.29
2003	-8.95	25.71	-3.10	10.79	22.87
2004	6.57	0.00	-3.79	18.23	21.21

Trailing	Total Return%	+/- S&P 500	+/- DJ Telecom	%Rank Cat	Growth of $10,000
3 Mo	18.23	9.00	10.01	37	11,823
6 Mo	13.74	6.55	-1.15	58	11,374
1 Yr	21.21	10.34	2.51	55	12,121
3 Yr Avg	-3.30	-6.88	2.58	76	9,042
5 Yr Avg	-16.04	-13.74	-0.68	71	4,172
10 Yr Avg	8.87	-3.20	4.42	57	23,393
15 Yr Avg	8.29	-2.64	—	50	33,024

Tax Analysis	Tax-Adj Rtn%	%Rank Cat	Tax-Cost Rat	%Rank Cat
3 Yr (estimated)	-5.19	79	0.00	1
5 Yr (estimated)	-17.30	85	0.33	28
10 Yr (estimated)	6.76	43	1.35	34

Potential Capital Gain Exposure: -116% of assets

Rating and Risk

Time Period	Load-Adj Return %	Morningstar Rtn vs Cat	Morningstar Risk vs Cat	Morningstar Risk-Adj Rating
1 Yr	14.24			
3 Yr	-5.19	-Avg	Avg	★★
5 Yr	-17.03	-Avg	Avg	★★
10 Yr	8.22	Avg	Avg	★★★
Incept	11.86			

Other Measures	Standard Index S&P 500	Best Fit Index Russ 1000Gr
Alpha	-6.0	-0.4
Beta	1.60	1.55
R-Squared	77	78
Standard Deviation	27.76	
Mean	-3.30	
Sharpe Ratio	-0.17	

Portfolio Analysis 09-30-04

Share change since 06-04 Total Stocks:34	Sector	PE	YTD Ret%	% Assets
American Tower A	Telecom	—	70.06	6.82
Telefonica SA ADR	Telecom	36.4	31.63	6.34
Western Wireless A	Telecom	—	59.59	5.85
Freddie Mac	Financial	10.6	28.75	5.76
R. H. Donnelley	Business	36.8	48.22	5.59
⊖ Telefonos de Mexico SA A	Telecom	11.6	20.14	4.97
Nextel Communications	Telecom	11.1	6.95	4.70
☼ Pagesjaunes, Paris	—	—	—	4.66
⊖ Vodafone Group PLC ADR	Telecom	—	11.74	4.19
Cincinnati Bell	Telecom	1.2	-17.82	3.70
Crown Castle Internation	Telecom	—	50.86	3.20
Adtran	Hardware	17.1	-37.70	3.17
WellPoint Health Network	Health	—	—	3.13
Capital One Financial	Financial	12.5	37.61	2.92
Electronic Data Systems	Business	—	-3.82	2.59
☼ Gray Television	Media	—	—	2.54
NII Holdings	Telecom	7.4	90.74	2.50
Cablevision Systems A	Media	—	6.46	2.46
Adelphia Comms Cv 6%	—	—	—	2.12
Comcast	Media	—	-13.77	2.12

Current Investment Style

Value Blnd Growth — Large Mid Small

Market Cap	%
Giant	30.6
Large	17.9
Mid	40.3
Small	10.0
Micro	1.2
Avg $mil: 8,342	

Value Measures		Rel Category
Price/Earnings	16.73	0.79
Price/Book	1.78	0.88
Price/Sales	1.28	0.85
Price/Cash Flow	4.28	0.79
Dividend Yield %	0.30	0.28

Growth Measures	%	Rel Category
Long-Term Erngs	9.44	0.71
Book Value	-1.66	NMF
Sales	2.80	4.52
Cash Flow	10.47	1.10
Historical Erngs	38.60	14.09

Profitability	%	Rel Category
Return on Equity	8.59	0.80
Return on Assets	6.16	1.54
Net Margin	5.29	0.88

Industry Weightings	% of Stocks	Rel Cat
Telecom Srv	18.9	0.8
Wireless Srv	35.2	1.1
Network Eq	4.3	0.3
Semis	0.0	0.0
Big Media	0.0	0.0
Cable TV	6.6	2.4
Other Media	5.5	2.7
Soft/Hardwr	1.5	0.4
Other	27.9	2.1

Composition

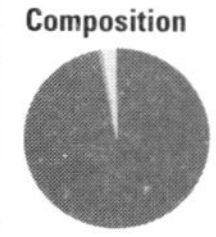

Cash	0.4
Stocks	96.5
Bonds	1.0
Other	2.1
Foreign (% of Stock)	26.2

Morningstar's Take by Jeffrey Ptak 01-07-05

While this isn't a bad option, it's not our first choice in the telecom field.

Manager Bruce Behrens stands out from his typical communications-category peer in a few respects. For one thing, he tends to view his universe through a value manager's lens, sizing up bargains by weighing a firm's stock price versus an estimate of its intrinsic worth rather than comparing its price multiples with industry or historic norms. In addition, Behrens isn't shy about adding nontelecom picks to the mix, particularly when bargains are scarce.

The fund's portfolio reflects Behrens' distinctive approach. To wit, its aggregate valuation measures uniformly skirt the category norms, with picks tending to cluster in the fixed line and wireless service areas as opposed to pricier realms, like the wireless equipment subsector. Behrens has also increasingly looked abroad for opportunities, with recent picks including Mexican wireless carrier America Movil, where competitive and regulatory conditions are often more benign. Finally, roughly 18% of assets were recently invested in health-care, financial, and industrial names such as insurer Leucadia National.

We think Behrens strategy has merit, particularly for cautious types skittish about courting heavy price risk. But execution has been spotty, with the gravest breakdown coming during a dreadful 2000 to 2002 stretch when the fund shed 72% of its value. Behrens has since rectified the mistakes that led to that dismal showing, but performance has continued to lag, with the fund's returns hovering near the group's midpoint in each of the past six calendar years. And while the fund's 21.2% return last year is respectable, that showing owed at least in part to surging non-telecom picks like R. H. Donnelley and Wellpoint. That's not to take anything away from Behrens and his team. But we'd need to see more evidence of consistently deft stock selection in the telecom arena in order to recommend this fund.

Address:	One South Street Baltimore MD 21202 800-621-1048
Web Address:	www.scudder.com
Inception:	01-18-84
Advisor:	Investment Company Capital Corp.
Subadvisor:	Alex. Brown Investment Management
NTF Plans:	DATALynx NTF, Federated Tr NTF

Minimum Purchase:	$2000	Add: $100	IRA: $1000
Min Auto Inv Plan:	$250	Add: $100	
Sales Fees:	5.75%L		
Management Fee:	1.00% mx./0.65% mn.		
Actual Fees:	Mgt:0.85%	Dist:0.25%	
Expense Projections:	3Yr:$1086	5Yr:$1466	10Yr:$2527
Income Distrib:	Annually		

Scudder Flag Val Bldr A

Ticker	Load	NAV	Yield	Total Assets	Mstar Category
FLVBX	5.75%	$24.28	1.7%	$676 mil	Moderate Allocation

Governance and Management

Fiduciary Grade: C

Portfolio Manager(s)

Despite various name changes, this fund has been managed by Hoby Buppert since its 1992 inception. Deutsche Asset Management, the advisor to the Scudder funds, recently acquired Flag Investors, but the existing subadvisory relationship with Alex. Brown Investment Management, Buppert's employer since 1980, is still intact. Buppert also took over large-blend offering Scudder Flag Equity Partners in June 2002.

Strategy

Manager Hoby Buppert traditionally allocates two thirds of the fund's portfolio to stocks and one third to bonds. On the stock side, he favors firms with good long-term growth prospects that are trading at a discount to his estimate of their intrinsic value. Generous free cash flow, high returns on equity, and moderate P/E are important criteria. On the bond side, Buppert buys mostly midgrade bonds as well as some high-yield credits, many of them issued by the same companies he holds on the stock side.

Historical Profile

Return Average
Risk High
Rating ★★★ Neutral

Investment Style
Equity
Stock %: 68% 58% 64% 70% 70% 68% 68% 73% 71%

▼ Manager Change
▽ Partial Manager Change

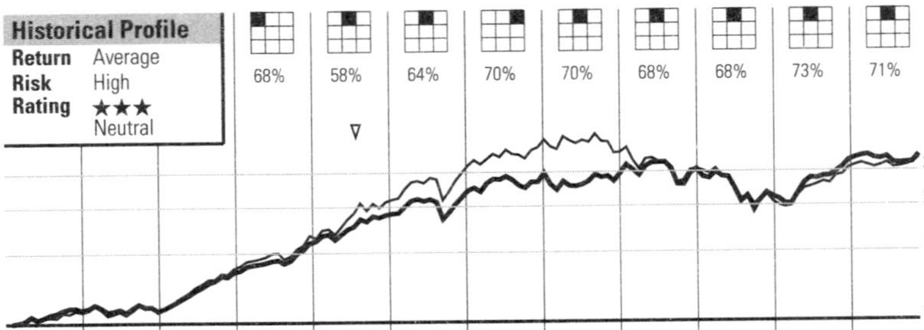

Growth of $10,000
▬ Investment Values of Fund
— Investment Values of S&P 500

Performance Quartile (within Category)

History

1993	1994	1995	1996	1997	1998	1999	2000	2001	2002	2003	12-04	History
11.53	11.12	13.99	16.98	20.06	22.82	24.75	22.09	22.36	17.75	22.73	24.28	NAV
11.76	-0.37	32.75	24.64	22.67	18.52	13.81	-0.49	3.20	-18.88	30.74	8.74	Total Return %
1.70	-1.68	-4.78	1.70	-10.68	-10.05	-7.23	8.61	15.08	3.21	2.07	-2.13	+/-S&P 500
0.03	1.58	7.98	13.30	3.47	6.13	0.96	-4.93	3.04	-8.34	6.68	-2.43	+/-DJ 60%
3.08	3.03	3.42	2.60	2.67	2.86	2.32	2.12	1.69	1.80	2.33	1.82	Income Return %
8.68	-3.40	29.33	22.04	20.00	15.66	11.49	-2.61	1.51	-20.68	28.41	6.92	Capital Return %
46	23	6	2	25	23	29	56	9	95	3	49	Total Rtn % Rank Cat
0.33	0.35	0.37	0.36	0.45	0.56	0.52	0.51	0.37	0.40	0.41	0.41	Income $
0.05	0.02	0.36	0.06	0.28	0.33	0.64	1.97	0.05	0.00	0.00	0.00	Capital Gains $
1.35	1.35	1.35	1.31	1.27	1.14	1.12	1.09	1.11	1.09	1.11	1.15	Expense Ratio %
2.88	3.14	3.07	2.72	2.51	2.49	2.64	2.06	2.13	1.86	2.38	1.77	Income Ratio %
—	8	18	15	13	7	10	26	8	12	12	13	Turnover Rate %
120	136	184	251	408	610	716	569	572	388	434	483	Net Assets $mil

Performance 12-31-04

	1st Qtr	2nd Qtr	3rd Qtr	4th Qtr	Total
2000	-5.98	-2.41	5.42	2.88	-0.49
2001	-1.40	9.94	-15.08	12.12	3.20
2002	-2.19	-11.89	-12.45	7.53	-18.88
2003	-5.24	21.18	1.43	12.25	30.74
2004	3.93	-1.49	-4.33	11.02	8.74

Trailing	Total Return%	+/- S&P 500	+/- DJ 60%	%Rank Cat	Growth of $10,000
3 Mo	11.02	1.79	3.54	1	11,102
6 Mo	6.21	-0.98	-1.32	56	10,621
1 Yr	8.74	-2.13	-2.43	49	10,874
3 Yr Avg	4.87	1.29	-2.39	46	11,533
5 Yr Avg	3.44	5.74	-1.80	29	11,842
10 Yr Avg	12.48	0.41	1.99	8	32,416
15 Yr Avg	—	—	—	—	—

Tax Analysis	Tax-Adj Rtn%	%Rank Cat	Tax-Cost Rat	%Rank Cat
3 Yr (estimated)	2.07	73	0.73	51
5 Yr (estimated)	1.08	40	1.12	51
10 Yr (estimated)	10.42	8	1.25	14

Potential Capital Gain Exposure: 30% of assets

Rating and Risk

Time Period	Load-Adj Return %	Morningstar Rtn vs Cat	Morningstar Risk vs Cat	Morningstar Risk-Adj Rating
1 Yr	2.49			
3 Yr	2.82	-Avg	High	★★
5 Yr	2.22	Avg	High	★★★
10 Yr	11.82	+Avg	High	★★★★
Incept	10.91			

Other Measures	Standard Index S&P 500	Best Fit Index DJ 60%
Alpha	1.6	-8.7
Beta	0.89	1.53
R-Squared	80	86
Standard Deviation	15.63	
Mean	4.87	
Sharpe Ratio	0.23	

Portfolio Analysis 09-30-04

Total Stocks:44 Share change since 06-30-04	Sectors	P/E Ratio	YTD Return %	% Net Assets
Cendant	Business	13.6	-3.64	5.79
WellPoint Health Networks	Health	—	—	4.68
American Financial Realty	Financial	—	-6.24	4.30
Tyco International	Ind Mtrls	25.1	-0.92	4.20
First Data	Business	18.8	-2.70	4.11
Citigroup	Financial	15.3	0.08	3.31
⊕ Kinder Morgan Management	Energy	30.7	0.39	2.87
Allied Waste Industries	Business	—	-2.37	2.46
⊖ Consol Energy	Energy	32.2	-7.53	2.38

Total Fixed-Income:43	Date of Maturity	Amount $000	Value $000	% Net Assets
Millipore 7.5%	04-01-07	9,050	9,663	1.54
Tenet Healthcare 6.5%	06-01-12	9,350	8,368	1.33
Marriott Intl 7.875%	09-15-09	5,700	6,590	1.05
Cendant 6.875%	08-15-06	5,475	5,836	0.93
Calenergy 7.63%	10-15-07	5,000	5,543	0.88
Clear Channel Comms 6%	11-01-06	5,200	5,460	0.87
Blyth 7.9%	10-01-09	4,500	5,097	0.81
Jefferies Grp 7.5%	08-15-07	4,000	4,443	0.71
Raychem 7.2%	10-15-08	3,815	4,372	0.70

Equity Style
Style: Blend
Size: Large-Cap

Value Measures		Rel Category
Price/Earnings	14.83	0.89
Price/Book	1.77	0.73
Price/Sales	1.09	0.83
Price/Cash Flow	3.54	0.49
Dividend Yield %	2.74	1.75

Growth Measures	%	Rel Category
Long-Term Erngs	13.21	1.14
Book Value	12.85	2.24
Sales	8.02	1.55
Cash Flow	20.10	2.51
Historical Erngs	37.95	3.50

Market Cap %			
Giant	23.7	Small	8.5
Large	38.0	Micro	2.8
Mid	27.1	Avg $mil:	11,688

Composition

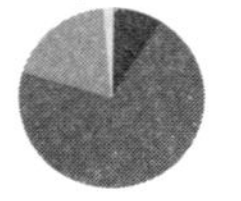

Cash	9.1
Stocks	70.6
Bonds	18.9
Other	1.5
Foreign (% of Stock)	0.8

Fixed-Income Style
Duration: Interm-Term
Quality: Medium

Avg Eff Duration [1]	3.7 Yrs
Avg Eff Maturity	5.2 Yrs
Avg Credit Quality	BBB
Avg Wtd Coupon	6.87%

[1]figure provided by fund as of 09-30-04

Sector Weightings	% of Stocks	Rel S&P 500	3 Year High	3 Year Low
Info	12.03	0.56		
Software	0.00	0.00	0	0
Hardware	2.04	0.20	3	2
Media	9.04	2.35	11	8
Telecom	0.95	0.30	2	1
Service	67.16	1.45		
Health	14.56	1.16	17	10
Consumer	2.93	0.32	4	3
Business	18.28	4.51	29	18
Financial	31.39	1.51	31	21
Mfg	20.82	0.65		
Goods	2.14	0.23	4	1
Ind Mtrls	10.52	0.83	14	10
Energy	8.16	1.14	8	2
Utilities	0.00	0.00	1	0

Morningstar's Take by Greg Carlson 12-23-04

Scudder Flag Value Builder's recent so-so record masks its solid potential, but investors shouldn't send new money here.

This fund's returns, relative to its typical moderate-allocation peer, often follow a feast-or-famine pattern: In eight of its 11 full years of operation, the fund has landed in the category's top or bottom quartile. That owes to manager Hoby Buppert's bold approach. He typically stashes at least two thirds of the fund's assets in stocks--the category norm is 60%--and the remainder in midgrade and high-yield corporate bonds. As a result, when equities post subpar returns, the fund may lag its typical peer.

What's more, Buppert runs a concentrated stock portfolio: More than 51% of the fund's equity allocation (roughly 36% of its total assets) is stashed in the top 10 stock holdings, which magnifies the effect of stock-specific events. In 2004 one of Buppert's top picks, waste collector Allied Waste Industries, declined 36% through Dec. 22. As such, even though the fund has thrived in the recent stock rally, its 7.65% gain through Dec. 22, 2004, lands in the category's bottom half.

Because of the fund's high sensitivity to equities and Buppert's concentrated style, its mediocre 2004 showing and three-year return aren't indicative of its merit. Buppert has racked up a fine long-term record since taking the helm at the fund's 1992 inception, outgunning more than 90% of his rivals. True, this offering isn't for the meek; due to its makeup, it's more volatile than most of its competitors. But Buppert has made the bumps worthwhile during his fine tenure.

Unfortunately, due to ethical issues at the fund's advisor, we can't recommend it right now. Deutsche Asset Management's revelation that it allowed several of its foreign-stock offerings to be market-timed is troubling. As such, investors shouldn't send new money to any of Scudder's funds.

Address:	One South Street Baltimore MD 21202 800-621-1048
Web Address:	www.scudder.com
Inception:	06-15-92
Advisor:	Investment Company Capital Corp.
Subadvisor:	Alex. Brown Investment Management
NTF Plans:	DATALynx NTF, Federated Tr NTF

Minimum Purchase:	$2000	Add: $100	IRA: $1000
Min Auto Inv Plan:	$250	Add: $100	
Sales Fees:	5.75%L		
Management Fee:	1.00% mx./0.70% mn.		
Actual Fees:	Mgt:0.75%	Dist:0.25%	
Expense Projections:	3Yr:$790	5Yr:$1039	10Yr:$1752
Income Distrib:	Quarterly		

Scudder Hi-Yld T/F AARP

Ticker	Load	NAV	Yield	SEC Yield	Total Assets	Mstar Category
SHYFX	None	$12.79	5.2%	4.38%	$812 mil	High Yield Muni

Governance and Management

Fiduciary Grade: C

Portfolio Manager(s)

Lead manager Phil Condon has run this fund since 1987, with very good returns. He was joined by Rebecca Wilson in 1998. The pair is backed by a team of seven analysts, five of whom have more than 15 years experience.

Strategy

Phil Condon tries to give shareholders extra yield, focusing on mid- to low-rated credits and those with no ratings at all. The fund's duration is kept within a narrow range of a self-selected peer group as well as the Lehman Brothers Municipal Bond Index. Overall, however, the fund--which maintains a pretty large stake in high-quality munis--sports a relatively conservative profile when compared with other high-yield muni funds.

Historical Profile

Return Above Avg
Risk Above Avg
Rating ★★★★ Above Avg

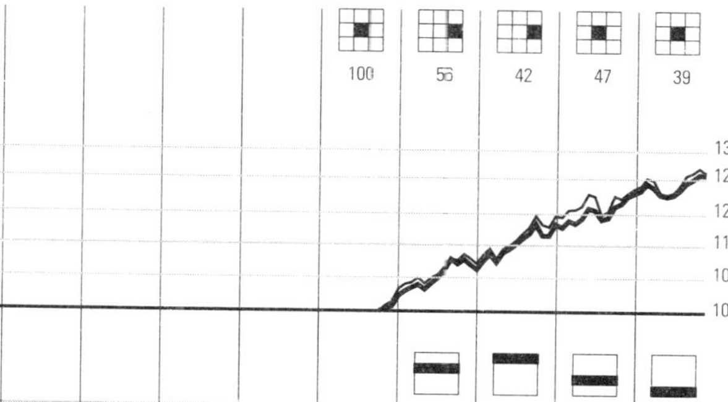

Investment Style
Fixed Income
Income Rtn %Rank Cat

▼ Manager Change
▽ Partial Manager Change

Growth of $10,000
— Investment Values of Fund
— Investment Values of LB Muni

Performance Quartile (within Category)

1993	1994	1995	1996	1997	1998	1999	2000	2001	2002	2003	12-04	History
—	—	—	—	—	—	—	12.37	12.35	12.76	12.84	12.79	NAV
—	—	—	—	—	—	—	3.00*	5.34	9.13	6.10	4.96	Total Return %
—	—	—	—	—	—	—	—	0.21	-0.47	0.79	0.48	+/-LB Muni
—	—	—	—	—	—	—	—	0.72	-1.04	0.40	0.81	+/-LB Muni 10YR
—	—	—	—	—	—	—	0.00	5.57	5.74	5.36	5.27	Income Return %
—	—	—	—	—	—	—	—	-0.23	3.39	0.74	-0.31	Capital Return %
—	—	—	—	—	—	—	—	28	2	59	82	Total Rtn % Rank Cat
—	—	—	—	—	—	—	0.17	0.57	0.69	0.67	0.66	Income $
—	—	—	—	—	—	—	0.00	0.00	0.00	0.01	0.01	Capital Gains $
—	—	—	—	—	—	—	—	0.79	0.77	0.77	0.76	Expense Ratio %
—	—	—	—	—	—	—	—	5.58	5.50	5.47	5.28	Income Ratio %
—	—	—	—	—	—	—	62	12	21	16	44	Turnover Rate %
—	—	—	—	—	—	—	1	12	29	44	51	Net Assets $mil

Performance 12-31-04

	1st Qtr	2nd Qtr	3rd Qtr	4th Qtr	Total
2000	—	—	—	3.00	3.00 *
2001	2.22	1.31	2.79	-1.05	5.34
2002	1.43	3.60	3.85	0.00	9.13
2003	0.14	2.57	0.70	2.58	6.10
2004	1.11	-1.42	3.08	2.16	4.96

Trailing	Total Return%	+/- LB Muni	+/- LB Muni 10YR	%Rank Cat	Growth of $10,000
3 Mo	2.16	0.91	1.33	63	10,216
6 Mo	5.31	0.12	0.31	73	10,531
1 Yr	4.96	0.48	0.81	82	10,496
3 Yr Avg	6.72	0.28	0.08	34	12,155
5 Yr Avg	—	—	—	—	—
10 Yr Avg	—	—	—	—	—
15 Yr Avg	—	—	—	—	—

Tax Analysis	Tax-Adj Rtn%	%Rank Cat	Tax-Cost Rat	%Rank Cat
3 Yr (estimated)	6.71	21	0.01	34
5 Yr (estimated)	—	—	—	—
10 Yr (estimated)	—	—	—	—

Potential Capital Gain Exposure: 4% of assets

Rating and Risk

Time Period	Load-Adj Return %	Morningstar Rtn vs Cat	Morningstar Risk vs Cat	Morningstar Risk-Adj Rating
1 Yr	4.96			
3 Yr	6.72	+Avg	+Avg	★★★★
5 Yr	—	—	—	—
10 Yr	—	—	—	—
Incept	6.72			

Other Measures	Standard Index LB Aggr	Best Fit Index LB Muni CA
Alpha	1.4	1.8
Beta	0.76	0.71
R-Squared	88	89
Standard Deviation	4.08	
Mean	6.72	
Sharpe Ratio	1.33	

Portfolio Analysis 09-30-04

Total Fixed-Income:214	Date of Maturity	Amount $000	Value $000	% Net Assets
Bma 12yr Swap Flt		55,500	55,500	5.62
Libor 10yr Swap Flt		37,450	37,450	3.79
Libor 12yr Swap		27,000	27,000	2.73
Libor 10yr Swap Fl		25,500	25,500	2.58
Massachusetts St 6%	11-01-10	16,000	18,556	1.88
San Joaquin Hills Calif	01-01-12	15,000	17,908	1.81
Golden St Tob Securitiza	06-01-39	17,750	17,183	1.74
Golden St Tob Securitiza	06-01-38	15,110	15,772	1.60
Bma 12yr Swap Fl		14,700	14,700	1.49
Washington St Pub Pwr Sp	07-01-12	10,000	11,935	1.21
Denver Colo City & Cnty	11-15-13	9,775	11,924	1.21
Maryland St Econ Dev 7.6	12-01-22	12,000	11,905	1.21
California St 5%	02-01-20	11,105	11,754	1.19
Travis Cnty Tex Health F	11-15-15	10,000	11,707	1.19
Berkeley Cnty S C Sch Di	01-15-17	8,970	10,158	1.03

Current Investment Style

Duration: Short Int Long; Quality: High Med Low

[1]Avg Eff Duration	5.7 Yrs
Avg Eff Maturity	10.0 Yrs
Avg Credit Quality	A
Avg Wtd Coupon	6.51%
Avg Wtd Price	108.57% of par

[1]figure provided by fund

Credit Analysis	% bonds 09-30-04		
US Govt	0	BB	4
AAA	33	B	3
AA	8	Below B	0
A	16	NR/NA	19
BBB	17		

Top 5 States	% bonds		
CA	18.2	WA	5.7
TX	10.6	PA	5.2
MA	8.7		

Composition			
Cash	0.9	Bonds	81.5
Stocks	0.0	Other	17.6

Special Securities	
Restricted/Illiquid Secs	Trace
Options/Futures/Warrants	No

Sector Weightings	% of Bonds	Rel Cat
General Obligation	22.5	1.50
Utilities	13.4	1.55
Health	16.0	1.21
Water/Waste	3.4	0.49
Housing	1.1	0.14
Education	3.5	1.13
Transportation	9.0	1.18
COP/Lease	2.7	1.89
Industrial	28.4	0.79
Misc Revenue	0.0	—
Demand	0.0	0.00

Morningstar's Take by Eric Jacobson 01-05-05

Scudder High-Yield Tax-Free's conservatism anchors its appeal, but a caution flag warns against new voyages right now.

It might be tempting to look at this fund's 2004 performance and assume that it has lost a step. After all, it was a great year for credit-sensitive bonds of all kinds, and while the 5% return for the fund's AARP class looked pretty good relative to many investment-grade portfolios, it was a relatively modest showing compared with other high-yield municipal offerings: It placed the fund in the category's bottom quartile. A slightly higher level of interest-rate related volatility has also hurt the fund a tad.

The fact is, however, that this is one of the most low-key offerings in the high-yield muni category, so its 2004 lethargy isn't surprising. Nearly every one of its high-yield rivals holds a larger stake in bonds rated BBB and lower or in those that carry no ratings at all. Comanager Phil Condon has also steered clear of the relatively large sector specific bets favored by some of his intrepid rivals. A handful of funds have been big buyers of bonds backed by the tobacco industry master settlement agreement in recent years, while others have plowed headlong into shaky airline credits.

Although some funds are content to present themselves as cautious and forgo competing on the return front, though, that hasn't been the case over the long term here. Despite this fund's recent relative weakness, its S share returns of five years and longer remain terrific.

Nevertheless, we can't lend an unqualified endorsement here. Although Scudder's parent, Deutsche Bank, appears to have made strides addressing issues raised by the mutual fund timing scandal, the company hasn't yet settled accounts with regulators. So although we like this fund's management, and don't see any reason to flee, we can't recommend that investors send new money right now.

Address:	Deutsche Asset Management Boston MA 02110 800-253-2277
Web Address:	
Inception:	10-02-00*
Advisor:	Deutsche Investment Mgt Americas Inc.
Subadvisor:	None
NTF Plans:	N/A

Minimum Purchase:	$1000	Add: $0	IRA: $500
Min Auto Inv Plan:	$50	Add: $50	
Sales Fees:	No-load		
Management Fee:	0.65% mx./0.57% mn.		
Actual Fees:	Mgt:0.64%	Dist:	
Expense Projections:	3Yr:$284	5Yr:$493	10Yr:$1096
Income Distrib:	Monthly		

Scudder Interm T/A F AARP

Ticker	Load	NAV	Yield	SEC Yield	Total Assets	Mstar Category
SMTTX	None	$11.46	3.8%	2.74%	$865 mil	Muni National Interm

Governance and Management

Fiduciary Grade: D

Portfolio Manager(s)

Phil Condon and Ashton Goodfield have made a good team here and at other Scudder offerings, such as Managed Municipal Bonds. Goodfield has been on board since 1990, while Condon joined her in 1998.

Strategy

Management tries to add value by focusing on undervalued bonds of various maturity and coupon structures. The managers prefer noncallable bonds as well as high-rated bonds, and they have kept duration within a tight range of the fund's typical peer.

Historical Profile

Return Above Avg
Risk Average
Rating ★★★★ Above Avg

Investment Style
Fixed Income
Income Rtn %Rank Cat

2000	2001	2002	2003	2004
100	24	29	15	27

▼ Manager Change
▽ Partial Manager Change

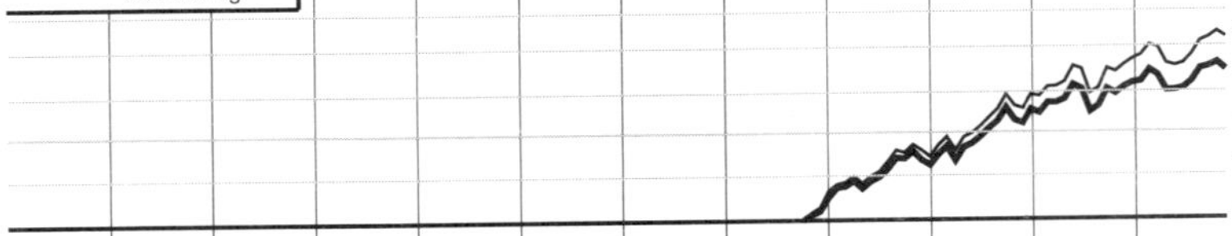

Growth of $10,000
▬ Investment Values of Fund
— Investment Values of LB Muni

Performance Quartile (within Category)

History

1993	1994	1995	1996	1997	1998	1999	2000	2001	2002	2003	12-04	History
—	—	—	—	—	—	—	11.17	11.20	11.61	11.58	11.46	NAV
—	—	—	—	—	—	—	3.38*	4.86	8.49	3.97	2.93	Total Return %
—	—	—	—	—	—	—	—	-0.27	-1.11	-1.34	-1.55	+/-LB Muni
—	—	—	—	—	—	—	—	0.24	-1.68	-1.73	-1.22	+/-LB Muni 10YR
—	—	—	—	—	—	—	0.00	4.63	4.29	4.20	3.85	Income Return %
—	—	—	—	—	—	—	—	0.23	4.20	-0.23	-0.92	Capital Return %
—	—	—	—	—	—	—	—	25	54	59	45	Total Rtn % Rank Cat
—	—	—	—	—	—	—	0.13	0.51	0.47	0.48	0.44	Income $
—	—	—	—	—	—	—	0.00	0.00	0.05	0.00	0.01	Capital Gains $
—	—	—	—	—	—	—	—	0.73	0.68	0.69	0.70	Expense Ratio %
—	—	—	—	—	—	—	—	4.64	4.42	4.20	3.95	Income Ratio %
—	—	—	—	—	—	—	21	21	18	13	21	Turnover Rate %
—	—	—	—	—	—	—	—	2	5	7	8	Net Assets $mil

Performance 12-31-04

	1st Qtr	2nd Qtr	3rd Qtr	4th Qtr	Total
2000	—	—	—	3.38	3.38 *
2001	2.49	0.53	2.74	-0.94	4.86
2002	0.62	3.63	4.31	-0.26	8.49
2003	1.00	2.03	-0.03	0.92	3.97
2004	1.07	-1.94	3.26	0.57	2.93

Trailing	Total Return%	+/- LB Muni	+/- LB Muni 10YR	%Rank Cat	Growth of $10,000
3 Mo	0.57	-0.68	-0.26	66	10,057
6 Mo	3.85	-1.34	-1.15	47	10,385
1 Yr	2.93	-1.55	-1.22	45	10,293
3 Yr Avg	5.10	-1.34	-1.54	55	11,609
5 Yr Avg	—	—	—	—	—
10 Yr Avg	—	—	—	—	—
15 Yr Avg	—	—	—	—	—

Tax Analysis	Tax-Adj Rtn%	%Rank Cat	Tax-Cost Rat	%Rank Cat
3 Yr (estimated)	5.06	36	0.04	13
5 Yr (estimated)	—	—	—	—
10 Yr (estimated)	—	—	—	—

Potential Capital Gain Exposure: 6% of assets

Rating and Risk

Time Period	Load-Adj Return %	Morningstar Rtn vs Cat	Morningstar Risk vs Cat	Morningstar Risk-Adj Rating
1 Yr	2.93			
3 Yr	5.10	+Avg	Avg	★★★★
5 Yr	—	—	—	—
10 Yr	—	—	—	—
Incept	5.56			

Other Measures	Standard Index LB Aggr	Best Fit Index LB Muni 10YR
Alpha	-1.1	-0.7
Beta	0.98	0.85
R-Squared	98	99
Standard Deviation	4.90	
Mean	5.10	
Sharpe Ratio	0.77	

Portfolio Analysis 09-30-04

Total Fixed-Income:171	Date of Maturity	Amount $000	Value $000	% Net Assets
Libor Swap 5yr Flt	03-03-10	37,500	37,500	5.74
California St Dept Wtr R	05-01-15	10,000	11,428	1.75
Tobacco Settlement Fing	06-01-18	10,000	10,971	1.68
North Slope Boro Alaska	06-30-06	11,150	10,757	1.65
Indianapolis Ind Loc Pub	02-01-14	8,000	9,708	1.49
Fulton Dekalb Ga Hosp Au	01-01-16	8,500	9,450	1.45
Massachusetts St 5.75%	06-01-09	8,340	9,422	1.44
Houston Tex Wtr & Swr Sy	12-01-15	8,250	9,327	1.43
King & Snohomish Cntys W	12-01-15	8,000	9,230	1.41
Wisconsin St 5.25%	05-01-16	7,705	8,553	1.31
Foothill / Eastern Trans	01-01-09	7,275	8,388	1.28
Hoffman Estates III Tax	05-15-06	8,500	8,061	1.23
California St Dept Wtr R	05-01-16	7,000	7,992	1.22
Chicago III	01-01-14	11,570	7,897	1.21
Brownsville Tex Util Sys	09-01-14	6,500	7,852	1.20

Current Investment Style

Duration: Short Int Long; Quality: High Med Low

[1]Avg Eff Duration	5.3 Yrs
Avg Eff Maturity	6.6 Yrs
Avg Credit Quality	AAA
Avg Wtd Coupon	4.79%
Avg Wtd Price	108.82% of par

[1]figure provided by fund

Credit Analysis	% bonds 09-30-04		
US Govt	0	BB	0
AAA	75	B	0
AA	14	Below B	0
A	8	NR/NA	0
BBB	3		

Top 5 States	% bonds		
TX	13.6	IL	7.4
CA	12.7	MI	6.8
NY	10.4		

Composition			
Cash	2.5	Bonds	97.5
Stocks	0.0	Other	0.0

Special Securities	
Restricted/Illiquid Secs	0
Options/Futures/Warrants	No

Sector Weightings	% of Bonds	Rel Cat
General Obligation	36.8	1.04
Utilities	15.4	1.39
Health	6.6	0.89
Water/Waste	18.7	1.89
Housing	0.0	0.00
Education	13.8	0.98
Transportation	2.0	0.36
COP/Lease	0.0	0.00
Industrial	6.3	0.70
Misc Revenue	0.0	0.00
Demand	0.4	0.91

Morningstar's Take by Eric Jacobson 01-05-05

We're comfortable with Scudder Intermediate Tax/AMT Free, if not the storm from which its advisor has yet to emerge.

This portfolio is a prototype for the basic, cautious style of Scudder muni skipper Phil Condon and his colleagues. As a group they generally try to keep their funds' durations (a measure of interest-rate sensitivity) in line with indexes and select peer groups, although they do make adjustments if they believe those benchmarks don't adequately reflect the rate risk inherent in their holdings. This fund also sticks almost entirely to high-quality bonds, as well. Although Condon and comanager Ashton Goodfield do have some flexibility to spread the risk across maturities, they don't generally go too far out on that spectrum given the fund's intermediate mandate.

At one time or another, each of those features of caution has been a mild hindrance. In 2004, for example, several intermediate muni funds that bet on longer maturity bonds earned more generous returns. Those that took on more credit risk or made larger bets on risky sectors also had an advantage depending on their timing. Still, the fund's overall record remains sound. Its long-term returns have been middling versus the category, but its volatility has also been moderate.

But while we're fans of this fund's overall style and management--and don't believe that shareholders who came aboard with the merger of Scudder Municipal Bond have anything to worry about--we're less sanguine about many of its share classes and Scudder's regulatory hurdles. Its AARP and S classes (the latter only available through planners) are reasonably priced, but its other retail classes are too costly for us. And although it appears Scudder has dealt well with concerns raised by last year's market-timing scandal, the firm has yet to come to terms with regulators or resolve all of the outstanding questions that remain. As such, we still can't suggest sending new money here.

Address:	Deutsche Asset Management Boston MA 02110 800-253-2277
Web Address:	www.scudder.com
Inception:	10-02-00 *
Advisor:	Deutsche Investment Mgt Americas Inc.
Subadvisor:	None
NTF Plans:	N/A

Minimum Purchase:	$1000	Add: $50	IRA: $500
Min Auto Inv Plan:	$50	Add: $50	
Sales Fees:	No-load		
Management Fee:	0.55% mx./0.40% mn., 0.15%A		
Actual Fees:	—	Dist:	
Expense Projections:	3Yr:$237	5Yr:$411	10Yr:$918
Income Distrib:	Monthly		

Security Cap US Real Est

Analyst Pick

Ticker	Load	NAV	Yield	Total Assets	Mstar Category
SUSIX	12b-1 only	$17.82	2.8%	$304 mil	Specialty-Real Estate

Governance and Management

Fiduciary Grade:

Portfolio Manager(s)

Security Capital Research & Management is the fund's advisor. In September 2003, Bank One agreed to acquire Security Capital from GE Real Estate. Bank One then merged with J.P. Morgan Chase in 2004. Security Capital expects to remain autonomous, though. Ken Statz, Kevin Bedell, and Anthony Manno have been at the helm since the fund's late-1996 inception. Before that, they spent many years in the real estate industry.

Strategy

Management uses a valuation matrix, which includes a discounted cash-flow model and NAVs to set price targets on its universe of stocks. Management selects those with the best rate-of-return prospects given current prices relative to the targets. The portfolio typically holds 20 to 25 stocks, and its top 10 holdings generally account for more than half of its assets.

Historical Profile

Return: Average
Risk: Above Avg
Rating: ★★★★ Above Avg

Investment Style: Equity, Stock %

100% | 93% | 87% | 90% | 92% | 100% | 98% | 98%

▼ Manager Change
▽ Partial Manager Change

Growth of $10,000
— Investment Values of Fund
— Investment Values of S&P 500

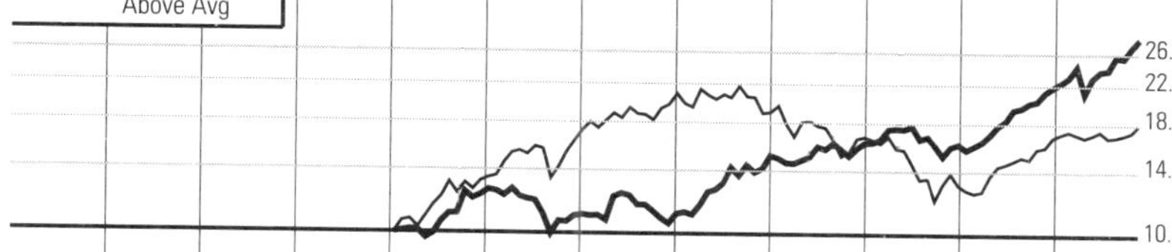

Performance Quartile (within Category)

1993	1994	1995	1996	1997	1998	1999	2000	2001	2002	2003	12-04	History
—	—	—	10.38	11.95	9.82	9.37	12.14	12.16	11.27	14.46	17.82	NAV
—	—	—	3.80*	25.17	-11.94	0.58	35.84	7.04	-0.43	35.02	36.81	Total Return %
—	—	—	—	-8.18	-40.51	-20.46	44.94	18.92	21.66	6.35	25.94	+/-S&P 500
—	—	—	—	5.50	5.06	3.15	4.80	-5.32	-4.03	-1.04	2.99	+/-Wil REIT
—	—	—	—	5.08	4.02	5.33	5.75	4.78	4.72	5.40	3.73	Income Return %
—	—	—	—	20.09	-15.96	-4.75	30.09	2.26	-5.15	29.62	33.08	Capital Return %
—	—	—	—	22	10	16	1	79	89	63	12	Total Rtn % Rank Cat
—	—	—	0.00	0.52	0.46	0.51	0.53	0.57	0.56	0.60	0.53	Income $
—	—	—	0.00	0.48	0.29	0.00	0.00	0.24	0.29	0.07	1.35	Capital Gains $
—	—	—	—	0.94	1.00	1.20	1.35	1.24	1.21	1.18	—	Expense Ratio %
—	—	—	—	4.08	4.75	4.18	5.02	4.96	3.41	2.59	—	Income Ratio %
—	—	—	—	104	109	50	91	91	75	67	—	Turnover Rate %
—	—	—	10	117	91	46	116	160	205	298	304	Net Assets $mil

Performance 12-31-04

	1st Qtr	2nd Qtr	3rd Qtr	4th Qtr	Total
2000	4.66	12.40	9.80	5.17	35.84
2001	-3.93	9.18	-1.42	3.51	7.04
2002	7.48	1.62	-9.56	0.81	-0.43
2003	1.31	11.62	9.84	8.71	35.02
2004	11.36	-2.28	7.26	17.21	36.81

Trailing	Total Return%	+/- S&P 500	+/- Wil REIT	%Rank Cat	Growth of $10,000
3 Mo	17.21	7.98	0.52	27	11,721
6 Mo	25.72	18.53	-0.54	44	12,572
1 Yr	36.81	25.94	2.99	12	13,681
3 Yr Avg	22.52	18.94	-1.04	61	18,392
5 Yr Avg	21.74	24.04	-0.93	34	26,740
10 Yr Avg	—	—	—	—	—
15 Yr Avg	—	—	—	—	—

Tax Analysis	Tax-Adj Rtn%	%Rank Cat	Tax-Cost Rat	%Rank Cat
3 Yr (estimated)	19.93	65	2.11	73
5 Yr (estimated)	19.19	37	2.09	73
10 Yr (estimated)	—	—	—	—

Potential Capital Gain Exposure: 40% of assets

Rating and Risk

Time Period	Load-Adj Return %	Morningstar Rtn vs Cat	Morningstar Risk vs Cat	Morningstar Risk-Adj Rating
1 Yr	36.81			
3 Yr	22.52	Avg	Avg	★★★
5 Yr	21.74	Avg	+Avg	★★★★
10 Yr	—	—	—	—
Incept	15.03			

Other Measures	Standard Index S&P 500	Best Fit Index Wil REIT
Alpha	20.7	-0.1
Beta	0.36	0.96
R-Squared	14	97

Standard Deviation	17.63
Mean	22.52
Sharpe Ratio	1.21

Morningstar's Take by Dan McNeela 12-28-04

Despite several changes, Security Capital U.S. Real Estate Fund's key selling points remain intact.

Pending a proxy vote, the fund will be reorganized on Feb. 18, 2005. That vote follows the acquisition of Security Capital by Bank One in late 2003 and the subsequent Bank One merger with J.P. Morgan Chase in mid-2004.

If approved, the fund will be renamed under the JP Morgan brand and new investors who don't meet the minimums for the institutional share class will have to pay a load to access the fund. Current investors will still be able to purchase additional shares of the fund without paying a load, even after the reorganization takes place. The fund's expense ratio is being capped at its current level of 1.18% until Oct. 31, 2006. Most importantly, however, Security Capital Research & Management, now a subsidiary of J.P. Morgan, is being retained to run the fund. All the key members of that team remain in place.

The value added by Security Capital has been plain to see in 2004. With its distinctive philosophy of discounted cash flow analysis and portfolio construction, the fund has plucked a number of winners from this year's buoyant real estate market. Its two top picks in the apartment subsector, AvalonBay Communities and Archstone-Smith Trust, are both up more than 45% in 2004 through late December. Management also kept a neutral stake in the regional mall subsector, even as it's been taking profits after a multiyear run. In all, the fund's 35.5% year-to-date gain through Dec. 23, 2004, ranks in the category's top decile.

Investing in real estate funds won't always be this profitable, so investors should take care to keep their overall exposure to the sector in check. But this experienced group has shown that it can deliver for investors. This fund remains one of our favorites in the real estate category.

Address:	11 South Lasalle Street Chicago IL 60603 888-732-8748	Minimum Purchase:	$1000 Add: $100 IRA: $500
Web Address:	www.securitycapital.com	Min Auto Inv Plan:	$100 Add: $100
Inception:	12-20-96*	Sales Fees:	0.25%B
Advisor:	Security Capital Research & Mgt Inc.	Management Fee:	0.60%, 0.02%A
Subadvisor:	None	Actual Fees:	Mgt:0.60% Dist:0.25%
		Expense Projections:	3Yr:$385 5Yr:$667 10Yr:$1472
		Income Distrib:	Quarterly
NTF Plans:	Fidelity Retail-NTF, Schwab OneSource		

Portfolio Analysis 09-30-04

Share change since 12-03 Total Stocks:25	Sector	PE	YTD Ret%	% Assets
⊕ Macerich	Financial	43.9	48.39	6.43
⊕ AMB Property	Financial	39.1	28.55	5.96
⊕ Equity Residential	Financial	90.2	29.50	5.88
⊖ SL Green Realty	Financial	16.8	53.52	5.88
⊖ AvalonBay Communities	Financial	58.1	65.02	5.43
⊖ Federal Realty Invest Tr	Financial	37.8	40.53	5.36
⊖ Corporate Office Propert	Financial	NMF	45.17	5.12
⊕ Public Storage	Financial	43.5	33.22	4.9
⊕ Starwood Hotels & Resort	Consumer	33.9	64.71	4.89
⊕ Simon Property Group	Financial	37.3	46.10	4.76
⊖ Mack-Cali Realty	Financial	24.4	17.29	4.62
⊕ Apartment Investment & M	Financial	—	20.31	4.21
⊖ Reckson Associates Realt	Financial	11.5	43.02	4.14
⊖ Archstone-Smith Trust	Financial	52.6	48.79	4.12
☼ Regency Centers	Financial	27.3	46.22	3.00
Camden Property Trust	Financial	62.7	21.60	2.93
☼ Host Marriott	Financial	—	40.88	2.83
⊖ Fairmont Hotels & Resort	Consumer	51.6	28.01	2.68
⊖ Shurgard Storage Centers	Financial	NMF	23.92	2.68
☼ Brandywine Realty Trust	Financial	22.1	16.65	2.15

Current Investment Style

Value Blnd Growth / Large Mid Small

Market Cap	%
Giant	0.0
Large	15.8
Mid	70.4
Small	13.8
Micro	0.0
Avg $mil: 3,099	

Value Measures		Rel Category
Price/Earnings	15.21	1.06
Price/Book	1.95	0.97
Price/Sales	3.81	1.02
Price/Cash Flow	13.32	1.11
Dividend Yield %	4.54	0.93

Growth Measures	%	Rel Category
Long-Term Erngs	6.51	0.92
Book Value	0.10	0.67
Sales	2.50	1.51
Cash Flow	-9.36	NMF
Historical Erngs	-10.57	NMF

Profitability	%	Rel Category
Return on Equity	8.24	0.80
Return on Assets	5.50	0.72
Net Margin	19.28	0.89

Sector Weightings	% of Stocks	Rel S&P 500	3 Year High	3 Year Low
Info	0.00	0.00		
Software	0.00	0.00	0	0
Hardware	0.00	0.00	0	0
Media	0.00	0.00	0	0
Telecom	0.00	0.00	0	0
Service	100.00	2.16		
Health	0.00	0.00	0	0
Consumer	7.70	0.85	12	6
Business	0.00	0.00	0	0
Financial	92.30	4.45	94	88
Mfg	0.00	0.00		
Goods	0.00	0.00	0	0
Ind Mtrls	0.00	0.00	0	0
Energy	0.00	0.00	0	0
Utilities	0.00	0.00	0	0

Composition

Cash	1.6
Stocks	98.3
Bonds	0.0
Other	0.0
Foreign (% of Stock)	2.7

Selected American S

Analyst Pick

Ticker	Load	NAV	Yield	Total Assets	Mstar Category
SLASX	12b-1 only	$36.87	0.7%	$7,344 mil	Large Blend

Governance and Management

Fiduciary Grade: A

Portfolio Manager(s)

Comanager Chris Davis has been here since 1991, and he plans to stick around the family-run firm. Comanager Ken Feinberg began as a financial-stock analyst with the firm in 1994 and became comanager in 1998. Davis' family owns the firm and invests heavily in the funds. Other employees are also significant owners, and the bonus plan here is set up with an eye toward long-term outperformance.

Strategy

Management tries to buy great companies whose shares are temporarily depressed, estimating a firm's intrinsic value based on managers' own earnings analysis, which tries to assess a firm's true cash earnings. They then look at those earnings relative to a return on adjusted invested capital. The idea is to figure out how well the company has historically allocated its capital.

Historical Profile

Return High
Risk Below Avg
Rating ★★★★★ Highest

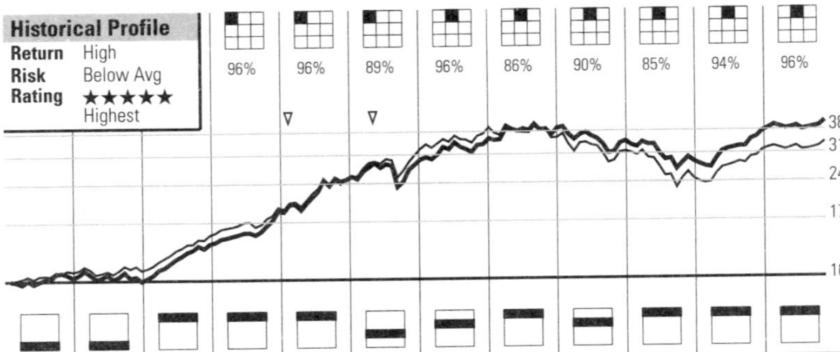

1993	1994	1995	1996	1997	1998	1999	2000	2001	2002	2003	12-04	History
14.59	13.09	17.68	21.53	27.18	31.16	35.80	35.33	30.99	25.51	33.17	36.87	NAV
5.42	-3.20	38.09	30.73	37.32	16.27	20.32	9.33	-11.17	-17.06	30.90	11.97	Total Return %
-4.64	-4.51	0.56	7.79	3.97	-12.30	-0.72	18.43	0.71	5.03	2.23	1.10	+/-S&P 500
-4.76	-3.59	0.32	8.28	4.47	-10.75	-0.59	17.12	1.28	4.59	1.01	0.57	+/-Russ 1000
1.58	1.52	1.69	1.03	0.97	0.55	0.48	0.38	0.41	0.65	0.84	0.80	Income Return %
3.84	-4.72	36.40	29.70	36.35	15.72	19.84	8.95	-11.58	-17.71	30.06	11.17	Capital Return %
89	85	9	5	3	71	47	9	36	14	14	22	Total Rtn % Rank Cat
0.26	0.22	0.22	0.18	0.21	0.15	0.15	0.14	0.14	0.20	0.21	0.27	Income $
3.22	0.82	0.15	1.30	2.04	0.26	1.44	3.46	0.24	0.00	0.00	0.00	Capital Gains $
1.01	1.26	1.09	1.03	0.96	0.94	0.93	0.92	0.94	0.93	0.93	—	Expense Ratio %
1.37	1.42	1.42	0.87	0.62	0.52	0.24	0.52	0.45	0.61	0.80	—	Income Ratio %
79	23	27	29	26	20	21	22	20	19	8	—	Turnover Rate %
452	528	925	1,378	2,218	2,905	3,703	5,703	5,563	4,353	5,976	6,664	Net Assets $mil

Performance 12-31-04

	1st Qtr	2nd Qtr	3rd Qtr	4th Qtr	Total
2000	9.06	-2.21	1.23	1.26	9.33
2001	-9.71	2.91	-14.06	11.23	-11.17
2002	-0.97	-9.78	-13.22	6.96	-17.06
2003	-5.21	17.74	2.32	14.63	30.90
2004	3.80	0.46	-0.98	8.44	11.97

Trailing	Total Return%	+/- S&P 500	+/- Russ 1000	%Rank Cat	Growth of $10,000
3 Mo	8.44	-0.79	-1.36	75	10,844
6 Mo	7.38	0.19	-0.43	38	10,738
1 Yr	11.97	1.10	0.57	22	11,197
3 Yr Avg	6.73	3.15	2.46	8	12,158
5 Yr Avg	3.38	5.68	5.14	8	11,808
10 Yr Avg	15.14	3.07	2.98	3	40,951
15 Yr Avg	12.90	1.97	1.82	6	61,718

Tax Analysis	Tax-Adj Rtn%	%Rank Cat	Tax-Cost Rat	%Rank Cat
3 Yr (estimated)	6.45	7	0.26	22
5 Yr (estimated)	2.65	8	0.71	38
10 Yr (estimated)	14.01	2	0.98	27

Potential Capital Gain Exposure: 27% of assets

Rating and Risk

Time Period	Load-Adj Return %	Morningstar Rtn vs Cat	Morningstar Risk vs Cat	Morningstar Risk-Adj Rating
1 Yr	11.97			
3 Yr	6.73	High	-Avg	★★★★★
5 Yr	3.38	High	-Avg	★★★★★
10 Yr	15.14	High	Avg	★★★★★
Incept	—			

Other Measures	Standard Index S&P 500	Best Fit Index MSCI World
Alpha	3.3	1.3
Beta	0.87	0.89
R-Squared	91	95

Standard Deviation	14.48
Mean	6.73
Sharpe Ratio	0.37

Portfolio Analysis 09-30-04

Share change since 06-04 Total Stocks:62	Sector	PE	YTD Ret%	% Assets
American Express	Financial	20.3	17.60	6.72
American International G	Financial	16.2	-0.53	4.98
Altria Group	Goods	13.3	18.38	4.40
Berkshire Hathaway A	Financial	—	—	4.37
Tyco International	Ind Mtrls	25.1	35.41	4.16
⊕ HSBC Hldgs	Financial	—	—	3.75
☼ J P Morgan Chase	Financial	19.4	9.97	3.43
Wells Fargo	Financial	15.5	8.97	3.27
⊕ Comcast	Media	—	-13.77	3.21
Progressive	Financial	11.7	1.63	3.21
Citigroup	Financial	15.3	2.72	3.08
Golden West Financial	Financial	15.3	19.45	2.99
Costco Wholesale	Consumer	25.6	31.15	2.97
Sealed Air	Goods	20.4	-1.61	2.60
ConocoPhillips	Energy	9.0	35.60	2.54
⊕ Occidental Petroleum	Energy	10.1	41.27	2.11
Devon Energy	Energy	9.0	36.78	1.96
⊕ CenterPoint Properties	Financial	65.7	32.93	1.90
Lexmark International	Hardware	20.0	8.09	1.78
Loews	Financial	—	43.59	1.70

Current Investment Style

Value Blnd Growth / Large Mid Small

Market Cap	%
Giant	50.7
Large	32.5
Mid	16.8
Small	0.0
Micro	0.0
Avg $mil: 31,514	

Value Measures		Rel Category
Price/Earnings	14.04	0.83
Price/Book	2.28	0.87
Price/Sales	1.43	0.99
Price/Cash Flow	5.58	0.73
Dividend Yield %	1.73	1.17

Growth Measures	%	Rel Category
Long-Term Erngs	10.51	0.91
Book Value	12.33	1.59
Sales	8.07	1.41
Cash Flow	12.39	1.31
Historical Erngs	17.86	1.51

Profitability	%	Rel Category
Return on Equity	18.46	1.05
Return on Assets	11.23	1.30
Net Margin	13.67	1.19

Sector Weightings	% of Stocks	Rel S&P 500	3 Year High	Low
Info	8.99	0.42		
Software	1.16	0.27	2	0
Hardware	2.19	0.21	8	2
Media	5.18	1.35	5	1
Telecom	0.46	0.15	0	0
Service	65.72	1.42		
Health	4.08	0.33	8	3
Consumer	6.15	0.68	9	5
Business	4.15	1.02	8	4
Financial	51.34	2.47	56	44
Mfg	25.29	0.79		
Goods	10.47	1.12	14	5
Ind Mtrls	5.69	0.45	13	5
Energy	9.13	1.28	9	4
Utilities	0.00	0.00	0	0

Composition

Cash	3.7
Stocks	96.3
Bonds	0.0
Other	0.0
Foreign (% of Stock)	12.5

Morningstar's Take by Kunal Kapoor 12-29-04

Selected American Shares embodies the best in a core mutual fund holding.

As numerous studies have demonstrated, mutual fund investors have done a lot worse than published returns may indicate. That's because investors are notorious for buying and selling funds at precisely the wrong time. There's a tendency among investors to buy funds after they've done well, and to sell them when they're underperforming. Unfortunately, this tendency also exists among professional money managers, who all too often invest with the rear-view mirror in plain sight.

On both those scores, we think this fund is different, and thus, compelling. First, it tends to be run on a fairly even keel, so extreme performances are rare. In general, the fund is more steady than flashy, so it's easier for investors to own, which hopefully translates into longer holding periods than is typical. At the management level, too, comanagers Chris Davis and Ken Feinberg have a long holding period and never adjust the portfolio to simply own issues that are driving the market at any one moment in time.

Viewed in that light, 2004's performance is all the more remarkable. With more than half its equity assets in financials, many may have expected this fund to give up some ground. After all, the financial media have been abuzz with stories about how financials are going to suffer in a rising-rate environment, and many professionals have been reducing their exposure to the sector. While they may yet be proven right, the reality is that the fund owns a diverse bunch of financials which have contributed nicely to its 12% gain for the year to date through Dec. 28, 2004. Moreover, the fund has done itself a favor by largely staying away from the drug stocks that have hurt many peers. However, the falling valuations in that sector have to be intriguing to this fund's management, even if they haven't bitten yet.

We continue to think very highly of this fund.

Address:	2949 E. Elvira Road Tucson AZ 85706 800-243-1575
Web Address:	www.selectedfunds.com
Inception:	02-28-33
Advisor:	Davis Selected Advisers LP
Subadvisor:	Davis Selected Advisers - NY, Inc.
NTF Plans:	Fidelity Retail-NTF, Schwab OneSource

Minimum Purchase:	$1000	Add: $25	IRA: $1000
Min Auto Inv Plan:	$1000	Add: $25	
Sales Fees:	0.25%B		
Management Fee:	0.65% mx./0.49% mn.		
Actual Fees:	Mgt:0.56%	Dist:0.25%	
Expense Projections:	3Yr:$300	5Yr:$520	10Yr:$1155
Income Distrib:	Annually		

Selected Special Shares S

Analyst Pick

Ticker	Load	NAV	Yield	Total Assets	Mstar Category
SLSSX	12b-1 only	$12.44	0.4%	$110 mil	Mid-Cap Blend

Governance and Management

Fiduciary Grade: A

Portfolio Manager(s)

Chris Davis and Ken Feinberg, listed as this fund's managers, have plenty of experience managing money, but they aren't the only ones running this fund. They delegate a fair amount of authority to the fund's analysts. The day-to-day management here is overseen by Davis, Feinberg, and four of the firm's senior analysts.

Strategy

This fund's managers look for great companies trading at modest prices. They focus on stocks that aren't liquid enough to be large holdings in sibling fund Selected American Shares. That means the fund will hold mid-caps and less-liquid large caps. Overall, the fund's average market cap tends to be well above the group norm.

Historical Profile

Return Below Avg
Risk Above Avg
Rating ★★ Below Avg

Investment Style: Equity Stock %: 98% 98% 97% 100% 72% 98% 94% 97% 95%

▼ Manager Change
∇ Partial Manager Change

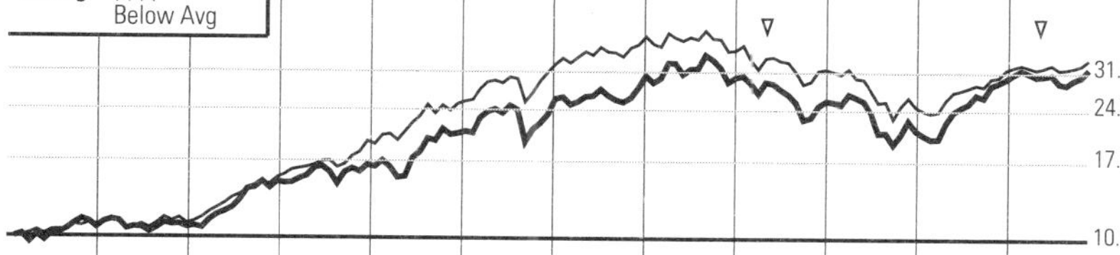

Growth of $10,000
- Investment Values of Fund
- Investment Values of S&P 500

Performance Quartile (within Category)

1993	1994	1995	1996	1997	1998	1999	2000	2001	2002	2003	12-04	History
10.20	9.02	10.80	10.89	13.03	14.76	16.17	13.68	10.50	8.61	11.70	12.44	NAV
10.70	-2.46	34.24	11.86	26.90	24.52	16.83	-1.10	-14.41	-17.62	41.40	11.34	Total Return %
0.64	-3.77	-3.29	-11.08	-6.45	-4.05	-4.21	8.00	-2.53	4.47	12.73	0.47	+/-S&P 500
-3.23	1.13	3.32	-7.32	-5.34	5.41	2.11	-18.59	-13.81	-3.09	5.81	-5.13	+/-S&P Mid 400
0.00	0.00	0.00	0.00	0.00	0.00	0.00	0.00	0.00	0.00	0.00	0.43	Income Return %
10.70	-2.46	34.24	11.86	26.90	24.52	16.83	-1.10	-14.41	-17.62	41.40	10.91	Capital Return %
74	58	22	88	47	6	53	77	94	63	20	90	Total Rtn % Rank Cat
0.00	0.00	0.00	0.00	0.00	0.00	0.00	0.00	0.00	0.00	0.00	0.05	Income $
1.30	0.93	1.26	1.18	0.62	1.32	0.97	2.24	1.21	0.04	0.47	0.52	Capital Gains $
1.24	1.41	1.48	1.33	1.28	1.25	1.17	1.15	1.15	1.17	1.21	—	Expense Ratio %
-0.07	-0.27	-0.58	-0.66	-0.61	-0.58	-0.59	-0.25	-0.20	-0.46	-0.39	—	Income Ratio %
100	99	127	98	51	41	44	35	117	46	46	—	Turnover Rate %
53	47	60	62	75	94	107	97	73	60	96	91	Net Assets $mil

Performance 12-31-04

	1st Qtr	2nd Qtr	3rd Qtr	4th Qtr	Total
2000	9.15	-3.97	6.49	-11.40	-1.10
2001	-10.08	2.57	-18.14	13.36	-14.41
2002	4.67	-11.28	-19.08	9.64	-17.62
2003	-5.34	23.31	6.77	13.46	41.40
2004	3.93	-0.90	-3.40	11.91	11.34

Trailing	Total Return%	+/- S&P 500	+/- S&P Mid 400	%Rank Cat	Growth of $10,000
3 Mo	11.91	2.68	-0.24	40	11,191
6 Mo	8.10	0.91	-1.69	75	10,810
1 Yr	11.34	0.47	-5.13	90	11,134
3 Yr Avg	9.05	5.47	-1.46	57	12,968
5 Yr Avg	1.89	4.19	-7.64	84	10,981
10 Yr Avg	11.77	-0.30	-4.32	78	30,427
15 Yr Avg	9.98	-0.95	-4.68	80	41,659

Tax Analysis	Tax-Adj Rtn%	%Rank Cat	Tax-Cost Rat	%Rank Cat
3 Yr (estimated)	8.33	55	0.66	73
5 Yr (estimated)	0.46	86	1.40	68
10 Yr (estimated)	9.75	66	1.81	56

Potential Capital Gain Exposure: 30% of assets

Rating and Risk

Time Period	Load-Adj Return %	Morningstar Rtn vs Cat	Morningstar Risk vs Cat	Morningstar Risk-Adj Rating
1 Yr	11.34			
3 Yr	9.05	Avg	+Avg	★★★
5 Yr	1.89	-Avg	Avg	★★
10 Yr	11.77	-Avg	+Avg	★★
Incept	—			

Other Measures	Standard Index S&P 500	Best Fit Index S&P Mid 400
Alpha	5.5	-2.3
Beta	1.10	1.14
R-Squared	84	93
Standard Deviation	19.61	
Mean	9.05	
Sharpe Ratio	0.40	

Portfolio Analysis 09-30-04

Share change since 06-04 Total Stocks:64	Sector	PE	YTD Ret%	% Assets
Gpe Bruxelles Lam	Ind Mtrls	—	—	4.58
Lagardere SCA	Media	—	—	4.26
AutoNation	Consumer	14.3	4.57	3.93
AutoZone	Consumer	13.8	7.16	3.61
Tyco International	Ind Mtrls	25.1	35.41	3.20
Tiffany	Goods	22.6	-28.79	3.12
⊖ Golden West Financial	Financial	15.3	19.45	2.80
Premcor	Energy	11.0	62.27	2.75
Microsoft	Software	36.1	8.95	2.69
Reynolds & Reynolds	Media	16.1	-7.18	2.65
Sigma-Aldrich	Ind Mtrls	18.4	6.99	2.56
⊕ Hughes Supply	Business	16.1	31.56	2.56
⊕ Hunter Douglas Grp	Goods	—	—	2.44
AmerisourceBergen	Health	14.3	4.69	2.29
Garmin	Hardware	25.3	12.63	2.24
⊕ Nokia ADR	Hardware	18.1	-6.14	2.21
Sempra Energy	Utilities	10.0	25.57	2.15
☼ J P Morgan Chase	Financial	19.4	9.97	1.99
Aramark	Consumer	18.9	-2.53	1.93
WPP Group PLC ADR	Business	35.2	12.32	1.91

Current Investment Style

Value Blnd Growth; Large Mid Small

Market Cap	%
Giant	17.4
Large	28.8
Mid	51.2
Small	2.7
Micro	0.0

Avg $mil: 8,786

Value Measures		Rel Category
Price/Earnings	15.15	0.90
Price/Book	1.91	0.88
Price/Sales	0.72	0.68
Price/Cash Flow	7.20	1.15
Dividend Yield %	1.11	1.11

Growth Measures	%	Rel Category
Long-Term Erngs	12.08	0.96
Book Value	9.21	1.31
Sales	9.06	1.60
Cash Flow	7.93	1.06
Historical Erngs	12.20	1.08

Profitability	%	Rel Category
Return on Equity	15.17	1.10
Return on Assets	7.84	1.20
Net Margin	12.32	1.36

Sector Weightings	% of Stocks	Rel S&P 500	3 Year High	3 Year Low
Info	23.64	1.10		
Software	2.84	0.66	7	3
Hardware	12.23	1.20	16	5
Media	7.29	1.90	9	4
Telecom	1.28	0.41	3	0
Service	44.33	0.96		
Health	6.04	0.48	13	2
Consumer	16.95	1.87	20	7
Business	7.48	1.85	18	6
Financial	13.86	0.67	22	14
Mfg	32.02	1.00		
Goods	13.03	1.40	17	10
Ind Mtrls	10.91	0.86	11	1
Energy	5.60	0.78	7	3
Utilities	2.48	0.84	2	0

Composition

Cash	5.0
Stocks	94.9
Bonds	0.0
Other	0.1
Foreign (% of Stock)	29.9

Morningstar's Take by Kunal Kapoor 10-28-04

You can't put Selected Special Shares in a box.

This fund's makeup is inconsistent with that of the typical mid-cap blend fund. It currently invests just 53% of its assets in true mid-caps, and when the percentage changes in the future, it's unlikely to be by much. Moreover, those looking for a clearly defined growth or value strategy aren't going to find one. This fund borrows from both styles, investing in what it perceives to be temporarily depressed firms as well as steady growers on the opposite end of the spectrum. Shareholders can only be sure about what they won't get here: Momentum or distressed stocks, which fall on the far ends of the growth and value spectrums. All told, the portfolio sports an average market cap of $8.9 billion--the group average is $6.1 billion--and moderate growth and value characteristics.

Among these apparent inconsistencies, though, lies a portfolio that's consistent on many fronts. First, there is tremendous management continuity, with the team overseeing this fund boasting years of experience among it. And execution is very consistent: The goal is to buy stocks with underestimated "owner earnings," or earnings adjusted for factors such as option expenses, which are a real cost to shareholders. That leads management to firms such as Autozone, which has a razor-sharp focus on return on equity, and picks such as Cardinal Health, which has been under a cloud due to an SEC investigation, the impact of which this fund's management believes the market is overestimating. (A jump in the stock in late October 2004 seems to have vindicated that thesis, although it's still early to come to a conclusion.)

Those comfortable with the fund's makeup have a good one on their hands. While the fund's trailing three-year relative return is only so-so, it includes a period where the portfolio was undergoing a transition to the current team. In fact, those who look at sibling--and near clone--Davis Opportunity, which the team has managed since inception, will see a more compelling three- and five-year record.

Address:	2949 E. Elvira Road Tucson AZ 85706 800-243-1575
Web Address:	www.selectedfunds.com
Inception:	05-01-39
Advisor:	Davis Selected Advisers LP
Subadvisor:	Davis Selected Advisers - NY, Inc.
NTF Plans:	Fidelity Retail-NTF, Schwab OneSource

Minimum Purchase:	$1000	Add: $25	IRA: $1000
Min Auto Inv Plan:	$1000	Add: $25	
Sales Fees:	0.25%B		
Management Fee:	0.70% mx./0.60% mn.		
Actual Fees:	Mgt:0.69%	Dist:0.25%	
Expense Projections:	3Yr:$384	5Yr:$665	10Yr:$1466
Income Distrib:	Annually		

Sentinel Small Company A

Ticker	Load	NAV	Yield	Total Assets	Mstar Category
SAGWX	Closed	$7.47	0.0%	$1,395 mil	Small Growth

Governance and Management

Fiduciary Grade: C

Portfolio Manager(s)

Chuck Schwartz became manager of this fund in September 2004 after the departure of Scott Brayman. Schwartz had been an analyst for this fund since 1999, covering technology, telecom, aerospace/defense, and auto-parts stocks, and has been with Sentinel since 1996. Analyst Betsy Pecor covers consumer and health-care stocks; she used to work on this fund and moved back here from Sentinel's mid-cap team in October 2004. Sentinel plans to hire another analyst for the fund by early 2005.

Strategy

Manager Chuck Schwartz, like his predecessor Scott Brayman, looks for small-cap companies with strong management teams that are generating excess return on capital. He wants to own the stocks of companies that have strong competitive positions within their industries, scalable business models, and recurring revenue streams. His focus on returns on capital leads him to firms that are labor-intensive rather than capital-intensive (and, therefore, have fairly low book values). He wants to buy these companies at a discount to what a private buyer would pay.

Historical Profile

Return Above Avg
Risk Low
Rating ★★★★★ Highest

Investment Style
Equity
Stock %

83% 94% 91% 96% 93% 87% 86% 86% 89%

▼ Manager Change
▽ Partial Manager Change

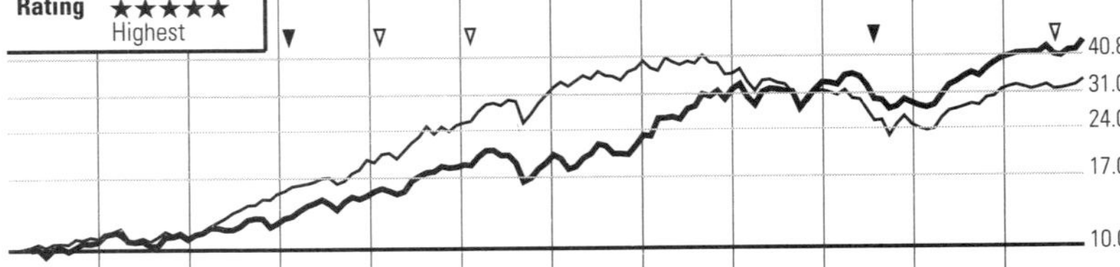

Growth of $10,000
— Investment Values of Fund
— Investment Values of S&P 500

Performance Quartile (within Category)

1993	1994	1995	1996	1997	1998	1999	2000	2001	2002	2003	12-04	History
5.72	4.80	4.40	5.29	5.62	5.38	5.43	5.65	5.87	5.04	6.87	7.47	NAV
11.70*	0.08	12.48	21.30	21.20	7.17	15.11	39.12	4.81	-14.14	38.09	15.98	Total Return %
—	-1.23	-25.05	-1.64	-12.15	-21.40	-5.93	48.22	16.69	7.95	9.42	5.11	+/-S&P 500
—	2.51	-18.56	10.04	8.25	5.94	-27.98	61.55	14.04	16.12	-10.45	1.67	+/-Russ 2000 Gr
0.00	0.00	0.54	0.16	0.36	0.00	0.00	0.00	0.00	0.00	0.00	0.00	Income Return %
—	0.08	11.94	21.14	20.84	7.17	15.11	39.12	4.81	-14.14	38.09	15.98	Capital Return %
—	43	97	44	36	36	85	1	18	3	76	27	Total Rtn % Rank Cat
0.00	0.00	0.03	0.01	0.02	0.00	0.00	0.00	0.00	0.00	0.00	0.00	Income $
1.48	0.91	0.96	0.04	0.75	0.61	0.72	1.74	0.05	0.00	0.09	0.49	Capital Gains $
1.52	1.58	1.56	1.47	1.34	1.31	1.31	1.25	1.21	1.22	1.20	—	Expense Ratio %
-1.01	-0.74	0.26	0.23	0.38	-0.07	-0.14	-0.03	-0.06	-0.27	-0.29	—	Income Ratio %
61	46	79	60	45	45	43	87	58	54	36	—	Turnover Rate %
109	90	90	102	116	114	114	171	227	317	689	1,083	Net Assets $mil

Performance 12-31-04

	1st Qtr	2nd Qtr	3rd Qtr	4th Qtr	Total
2000	13.08	6.84	9.30	5.35	39.12
2001	-10.97	11.93	-12.97	20.85	4.81
2002	5.28	-7.28	-15.71	4.35	-14.14
2003	-1.59	18.55	4.25	13.53	38.09
2004	3.93	4.76	-2.81	9.60	15.98

Trailing	Total Return%	+/- S&P 500	+/- Russ 2000 Gr	%Rank Cat	Growth of $10,000
3 Mo	9.60	0.37	-5.48	96	10,960
6 Mo	6.52	-0.67	-1.64	63	10,652
1 Yr	15.98	5.11	1.67	27	11,598
3 Yr Avg	11.20	7.62	5.41	13	13,750
5 Yr Avg	14.93	17.23	18.50	4	20,052
10 Yr Avg	15.13	3.06	8.01	12	40,915
15 Yr Avg	—	—	—	—	—

Tax Analysis	Tax-Adj Rtn%	%Rank Cat	Tax-Cost Rat	%Rank Cat
3 Yr (estimated)	8.67	21	0.59	42
5 Yr (estimated)	11.51	4	1.97	76
10 Yr (estimated)	11.89	14	2.31	84

Potential Capital Gain Exposure: 20% of assets

Rating and Risk

Time Period	Load-Adj Return %	Morningstar Rtn vs Cat	Morningstar Risk vs Cat	Morningstar Risk-Adj Rating
1 Yr	10.18			
3 Yr	9.32	+Avg	Low	★★★★
5 Yr	13.75	High	Low	★★★★★
10 Yr	14.54	+Avg	Low	★★★★★
Incept	13.21			

Other Measures	Standard Index S&P 500	Best Fit Index Mstar Small Core
Alpha	8.0	-0.7
Beta	0.77	0.79
R-Squared	69	92
Standard Deviation	15.48	
Mean	11.20	
Sharpe Ratio	0.64	

Portfolio Analysis 09-30-04

Share change since 08-04 Total Stocks:92	Sector	PE	YTD Ret%	% Assets
☼ iShares S&P SmallCap 600	—	—	—	4.76
⊕ Performance Food Group	Consumer	20.8	-25.60	1.74
⊕ Church & Dwight Company	Goods	18.5	28.24	1.68
Superior Energy Services	Energy	39.7	63.94	1.66
Fred's	Consumer	19.2	-43.61	1.65
Biosite	Health	28.6	112.57	1.62
Bisys Group	Business	23.1	10.55	1.61
Teleflex	Ind Mtrls	18.3	9.45	1.56
⊕ Bob Evans Farms	Consumer	14.9	-18.04	1.49
⊖ Perot Systems	Business	20.9	18.92	1.47
⊕ HCC Insurance Holdings	Financial	17.0	5.19	1.44
Hain Celestial Group	Goods	28.5	-10.94	1.43
⊕ Regis	Consumer	18.1	17.22	1.40
⊕ Healthcare Realty Trust	Financial	24.4	21.93	1.33
⊖ Sourcecorp	Business	12.0	-24.91	1.22
Ceridian	Business	22.1	-12.70	1.22
⊖ ICU Medical	Health	25.5	-20.27	1.18
⊕ Timberland	Goods	15.7	20.36	1.18
Waste Connections	Business	20.4	36.02	1.16
⊖ Clarcor	Ind Mtrls	21.5	25.62	1.14

Current Investment Style

Value Blnd Growth — Large Mid Small

Market Cap	%
Giant	0.0
Large	0.0
Mid	31.8
Small	63.1
Micro	5.2
Avg $mil: 1,052	

Value Measures		Rel Category
Price/Earnings	19.17	0.88
Price/Book	2.23	0.85
Price/Sales	1.21	0.81
Price/Cash Flow	9.12	1.14
Dividend Yield %	0.75	2.42

Growth Measures	%	Rel Category
Long-Term Erngs	14.20	0.82
Book Value	12.13	1.88
Sales	9.37	1.45
Cash Flow	11.79	0.87
Historical Erngs	11.32	0.84

Profitability	%	Rel Category
Return on Equity	11.99	1.21
Return on Assets	6.45	1.47
Net Margin	9.22	1.35

Sector Weightings	% of Stocks	Rel S&P 500	3 Year High	Low
Info	12.36	0.58		
Software	7.16	1.67	7	1
Hardware	3.45	0.34	7	3
Media	1.71	0.45	4	1
Telecom	0.04	0.01	7	0
Service	60.82	1.31		
Health	16.34	1.31	19	8
Consumer	13.55	1.49	14	3
Business	17.54	4.33	21	0
Financial	13.39	0.64	25	9
Mfg	26.83	0.84		
Goods	8.64	0.93	23	7
Ind Mtrls	11.47	0.91	17	11
Energy	6.53	0.91	12	5
Utilities	0.19	0.06	6	0

Composition

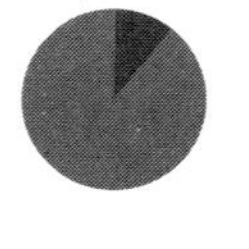

Cash	10.7
Stocks	89.4
Bonds	0.0
Other	0.0
Foreign (% of Stock)	0.0

Morningstar's Take by David Kathman 12-14-04

The new manager of Sentinel Small Company has a lot to live up to.

This fund suffered a major blow in September when most of its management team bolted to start a new money-management firm. Longtime manager Scott Brayman, analyst David O'Neil, and trader Deborah Healy all joined the exodus, leaving only analyst Chuck Schwartz, now promoted to portfolio manager. Sentinel has moved one former analyst back to this fund from the mid-cap team and plans to hire another by early 2005, but it will be a while before the team is fully settled in.

These moves are a tough break for Sentinel, as Brayman had built this fund into one of the stars of the small-growth category in his nine years at the helm. He guided the fund to returns in the category's top 10% over that period, with very low volatility relative to its peers. In June 2004, Sentinel closed the fund to new investors after its asset base tripled in two years.

Schwartz had worked with Brayman as an analyst since 1999, so the fact that he is staying on to manage the fund provides some continuity. He is very familiar with the moderate growth style that has served the fund so well, and he hasn't made any major changes in strategy so far. He has trimmed some of the fund's less-liquid positions, reduced cash, and brought sector weightings more in line with the S&P 600 index by adding more economically sensitive names.

However, Schwartz has never run an actively managed mutual fund before, so he definitely has to prove himself here. He has comanaged the Sentinel Growth Index since 1999, but that's a passively managed quantitative fund with one twentieth the asset base of this one.

The fund got off to a slow start in its first few months under Schwartz, but he deserves time to show what he can do. However, current investors may want to look into other options if they bought the fund specifically for Brayman's expertise and track record.

Address:	National Life Dr Montpelier VT 05604 800-282-3863
Web Address:	www.sentinelfunds.com
Inception:	03-01-93*
Advisor:	Sentinel Advisors, Co.
Subadvisor:	None
NTF Plans:	DATALynx NTF, Fidelity Instl-NTF

Minimum Purchase:	Closed	Add: —	IRA: —
Min Auto Inv Plan:	Closed	Add: —	
Sales Fees:	5.00%L		
Management Fee:	0.59%		
Actual Fees:	Mgt:0.59%	Dist:0.29%	
Expense Projections:	3Yr:$862	5Yr:$1127	10Yr:$1882
Income Distrib:	Annually		

Sequoia

Ticker	Load	NAV	Yield	Total Assets	Mstar Category
SEQUX	Closed	$154.27	0.0%	$3,749 mil	Large Value

Governance and Management

Fiduciary Grade:

Portfolio Manager(s)

Bill Ruane has been a manager of this fund since its 1970 inception. Robert Goldfarb was named comanager in 1998, but he has been with the fund for more than 30 years. Nine analysts back up the comanagers.

Strategy

Comanagers Bill Ruane and Robert Goldfarb aren't afraid to play favorites. The fund typically holds anywhere between 10 and 20 stocks. When its high standards aren't met, it holds as much as 30% of assets in Treasuries. Companies with top-quality management, long-lasting competitive advantages, and simple businesses qualify for entry into the portfolio.

Historical Profile

Return High
Risk Average
Rating ★★★★★ Highest

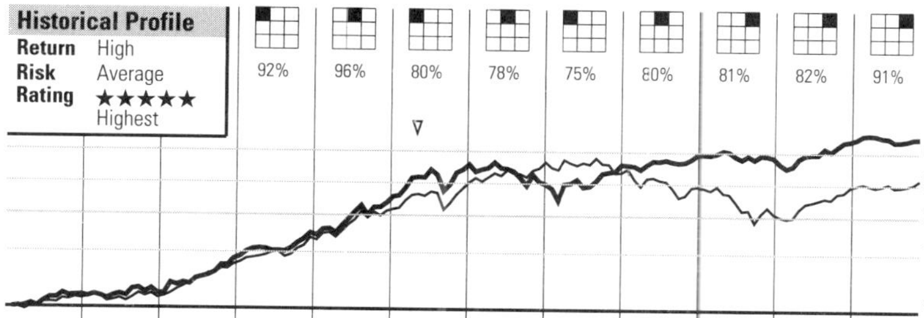

Investment Style
Equity
Stock %

▼ Manager Change
▽ Partial Manager Change

Growth of $10,000
— Investment Values of Fund
— Investment Values of S&P 500

Performance Quartile (within Category)

1993	1994	1995	1996	1997	1998	1999	2000	2001	2002	2003	12-04	History
54.84	55.59	78.13	88.44	125.63	160.70	127.27	122.09	130.24	126.63	147.61	154.27	NAV
10.78	3.34	41.38	21.74	43.20	35.25	-16.54	20.06	10.52	-2.64	17.12	4.51	Total Return %
0.72	2.03	3.85	-1.20	9.85	6.68	-37.58	29.16	22.40	19.45	-11.55	-6.36	+/-S&P 500
-7.29	5.32	3.02	0.10	8.02	19.62	-23.89	13.05	16.11	12.88	-12.91	-11.98	+/-Russ 1000 Vl
1.18	0.76	0.56	0.48	0.12	0.29	0.55	1.31	0.81	0.01	0.00	0.00	Income Return %
9.60	2.58	40.82	21.26	43.08	34.96	-17.09	18.75	9.71	-2.65	17.12	4.51	Capital Return %
73	15	3	31	1	1	99	12	4	1	99	99	Total Rtn % Rank Cat
0.65	0.42	0.31	0.38	0.11	0.37	0.86	1.66	0.97	0.01	0.00	0.00	Income $
7.20	0.66	0.08	6.10	0.88	8.02	6.59	28.51	3.38	0.16	0.61	0.00	Capital Gains $
1.00	1.00	1.00	1.00	1.00	1.00	1.00	1.00	1.00	1.00	1.00	—	Expense Ratio %
1.10	0.80	0.50	0.40	0.10	0.30	0.60	1.20	0.80	-0.30	-0.50	—	Income Ratio %
24	32	15	23	8	21	12	36	7	8	3	—	Turnover Rate %
1,512	1,548	2,186	2,581	3,673	5,002	3,898	3,944	3,925	4,372	—	3,749	Net Assets $mil

Performance 12-31-04

	1st Qtr	2nd Qtr	3rd Qtr	4th Qtr	Total
2000	0.09	-2.64	13.62	8.43	20.06
2001	-4.06	7.85	-1.36	8.29	10.52
2002	0.96	-2.54	-2.76	1.74	-2.64
2003	-7.42	11.73	2.57	10.39	17.12
2004	6.00	-2.77	-2.33	3.83	4.51

Trailing	Total Return%	+/- S&P 500	+/- Russ 1000 VI	%Rank Cat	Growth of $10,000
3 Mo	3.83	-5.40	-6.55	100	10,383
6 Mo	1.41	-5.78	-10.67	100	10,141
1 Yr	4.51	-6.36	-11.98	99	10,451
3 Yr Avg	6.02	2.44	-2.55	46	11,917
5 Yr Avg	9.60	11.90	4.33	7	15,814
10 Yr Avg	15.97	3.90	2.14	2	44,000
15 Yr Avg	14.29	3.36	2.26	3	74,152

Tax Analysis	Tax-Adj Rtn%	%Rank Cat	Tax-Cost Rat	%Rank Cat
3 Yr (estimated)	5.98	31	0.04	3
5 Yr (estimated)	8.43	8	1.07	57
10 Yr (estimated)	14.80	1	1.01	9

Potential Capital Gain Exposure: 0% of assets

Rating and Risk

Time Period	Load-Adj Return %	Morningstar Rtn vs Cat	Morningstar Risk vs Cat	Morningstar Risk-Adj Rating
1 Yr	4.51			
3 Yr	6.02	Avg	Low	★★★★
5 Yr	9.60	High	-Avg	★★★★★
10 Yr	15.97	High	+Avg	★★★★★
Incept	14.92			

Other Measures	Standard Index S&P 500	Best Fit Index S&P Mid 400
Alpha	3.6	0.2
Beta	0.44	0.49
R-Squared	42	54
Standard Deviation	10.68	
Mean	6.02	
Sharpe Ratio	0.44	

Portfolio Analysis 06-30-04

Share change since 03-03 Total Stocks:18	Sector	PE	YTD Ret%	% Assets
⊖ Berkshire Hathaway A	Financial	—	—	36.87
⊖ Progressive	Financial	11.7	1.63	13.12
⊖ Fifth Third Bancorp	Financial	14.1	-17.89	9.88
⊖ TJX Companies	Consumer	17.0	14.80	7.98
⊖ Mohawk Industries	Goods	16.1	29.36	6.95
⊖ Fastenal	Business	—	24.64	3.39
⊖ Expeditors International	Business	42.3	49.04	2.58
⊕ Walgreen	Consumer	31.6	6.03	2.22
⊖ Ethan Allen Interiors	Goods	17.8	3.98	1.83
☼ Brown & Brown	Financial	24.9	34.53	1.80
☼ Idexx Laboratories	Health	27.0	17.96	1.31
⊖ Tiffany	Goods	22.6	-28.79	1.24
⊕ Danaher	Ind Mtrls	25.8	25.29	0.58
⊕ Harley-Davidson	Goods	20.5	28.70	0.53
☼ Patterson Cos	—	—	—	0.13
⊖ Mercantile Bankshares	Financial	18.7	17.95	0.09
⊖ Costco Wholesale	Consumer	25.6	31.15	0.05
☼ Berkshire Hathaway B	Financial	20.9	4.30	0.01

Current Investment Style

Value Blnd Growth — Large Mid Small

Market Cap	%
Giant	0.0
Large	64.1
Mid	32.4
Small	3.4
Micro	0.0

Avg $mil: 11,145

Value Measures		Rel Category
Price/Earnings	16.60	1.10
Price/Book	3.30	1.45
Price/Sales	1.43	1.20
Price/Cash Flow	4.22	0.66
Dividend Yield %	0.76	0.37

Growth Measures	%	Rel Category
Long-Term Erngs	13.59	1.31
Book Value	18.76	3.33
Sales	13.77	3.28
Cash Flow	47.79	9.16
Historical Erngs	25.79	2.18

Profitability	%	Rel Category
Return on Equity	—	—
Return on Assets	—	—
Net Margin	—	—

Sector Weightings	% of Stocks	Rel S&P 500	3 Year High	3 Year Low
Info	0.00	0.00		
Software	0.00	0.00	0	0
Hardware	0.00	0.00	0	0
Media	0.00	0.00	0	0
Telecom	0.00	0.00	0	0
Service	87.68	1.89		
Health	1.44	0.12	1	0
Consumer	11.33	1.25	11	9
Business	6.61	1.63	8	7
Financial	68.30	3.29	76	68
Mfg	12.32	0.38		
Goods	11.68	1.25	12	3
Ind Mtrls	0.64	0.05	3	1
Energy	0.00	0.00	0	0
Utilities	0.00	0.00	0	0

Composition

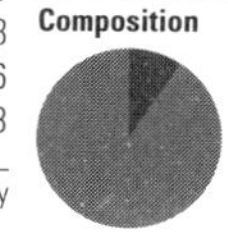

Cash	9.4
Stocks	90.6
Bonds	0.0
Other	0.0
Foreign (% of Stock)	0.0

Morningstar's Take by Dan McNeela 12-27-04

A couple of years of underperformance doesn't tarnish Sequoia's appeal.

Staying focused on the long term isn't always easy or fun. Management's preference for companies that have high returns on capital, strong free cash flow, dependable management teams, and a sustainable competitive advantage leads to a very select group of holdings here. It has also led to a top-heavy portfolio, with the five largest holdings consuming 75% of the fund's assets.

When one or two of those fall behind the pace, the fund won't look too good. Lately the laggards have been Berkshire Hathaway, which suffered more than $1 billion in losses from a series of hurricanes in Florida, and Fifth Third Bancorp, which lost ground steadily throughout the year. The fund's modest 4.8% year-to-date gain through Dec. 23, 2004, is nearly 6 percentage points behind the S&P 500. With just a few days left in the year, the fund is headed for its second consecutive finish in the bottom tier of our large-cap value category.

Management has never boasted about its short-term prognosticating abilities, however. It stakes its reputation on finding durable companies that will appreciate over time. Indeed, both Berkshire Hathaway and Fifth Third have been big winners for investors in past years.

Despite the fund's long history of success, it's not resting on its laurels. The fund's reserve of cash and bonds is down from 33% of assets in mid-2000 to just 9% as of June 30, 2004. Another long-term trend has been management's willingness to relax its valuation criteria when it finds a company that has great long-term growth potential. Management regretted missing out on great firms that it passed up for price reasons. Recent purchases such as insurer Brown & Brown and pet diagnostics firm Idexx Laboratories both trade at lofty multiples.

Although the fund is taking on more price risk now, investors in this closed fund have plenty of reasons to keep the faith here.

Address:	767 Fifth Ave New York NY 10153-4798 800-686-6884
Web Address:	www.sequoiafund.com
Inception:	07-15-70
Advisor:	Ruane Cunniff & Company
Subadvisor:	None
NTF Plans:	N/A

Minimum Purchase:	Closed	Add: —	IRA: —
Min Auto Inv Plan:	Closed	Add: —	
Sales Fees:	No-load		
Management Fee:	1.00%		
Actual Fees:	Mgt:0.98%	Dist:	
Expense Projections:	3Yr:$325	5Yr:$563	10Yr:$1248
Income Distrib:	Annually		

Skyline Spec Equities

Ticker	Load	NAV	Yield	Total Assets	Mstar Category
SKSEX	None	$28.64	0.0%	$567 mil	Small Value

Governance and Management

Fiduciary Grade: B

Portfolio Manager(s)

Manager Bill Dutton has been at the helm since the fund's early-1987 inception and will step down as lead manager at the end of 2004. Mike Maloney, who was named comanager in March 2001, will become lead manager. Maloney will be assisted by the fund's other two comanagers, Bill Fiedler and Mark Odegard. The team conducts its own research, assisted by three analysts.

Strategy

This fund's managers look for small companies that are trading at significant discounts to the overall market and that enjoy strong earnings prospects. They set target prices for every purchase and sell holdings when they meet them. Although the fund used to concentrate almost exclusively on consumer, financial, and industrial issues, it began paying more attention to tech, energy, and real estate names in early 2000.

Historical Profile

Return: Average
Risk: Average
Rating: ★★★ Neutral

Investment Style: Equity, Stock %

1996	1997	1998	1999	2000	2001	2002	2003	12-04
92%	93%	94%	95%	95%	94%	100%	93%	96%

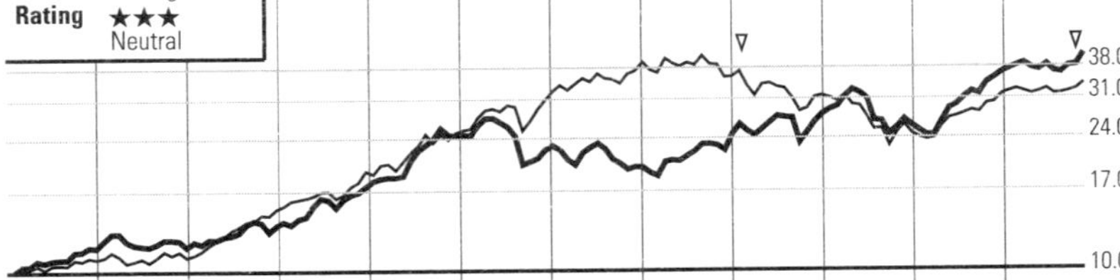

Performance Quartile (within Category)

History

	1993	1994	1995	1996	1997	1998	1999	2000	2001	2002	2003	12-04
NAV	17.83	15.64	16.79	18.16	21.66	19.78	15.90	19.75	22.50	20.86	27.78	28.64
Total Return %	22.84	-1.15	13.82	30.37	35.43	-7.17	-13.29	24.21	13.92	-7.29	40.71	16.61
+/-S&P 500	12.78	-2.46	-23.71	7.43	2.08	-35.74	-34.33	33.31	25.80	14.80	12.04	5.74
+/-Russ 2000 VL	-0.93	0.39	-11.93	9.00	3.65	-0.72	-11.80	1.38	-0.10	4.14	-5.32	-5.64
Income Return %	0.00	0.00	0.00	0.00	0.00	0.00	0.00	0.00	0.00	0.00	0.00	0.00
Capital Return %	22.84	-1.15	13.82	30.37	35.43	-7.17	-13.29	24.21	13.92	-7.29	40.71	16.61
Total Rtn % Rank Cat	17	62	92	8	17	58	100	25	62	36	51	86
Income $	0.00	0.00	0.00	0.00	0.00	0.00	0.00	0.00	0.00	0.00	0.00	0.00
Capital Gains $	3.14	1.93	1.00	3.61	2.89	0.32	1.23	0.00	0.00	0.00	1.56	3.69
Expense Ratio %	1.48	1.49	1.51	1.51	1.48	1.47	1.48	1.51	1.49	1.48	1.48	—
Income Ratio %	-0.54	-0.49	0.35	-0.32	-0.41	-0.50	-0.32	-0.32	-0.16	-0.26	-0.26	—
Turnover Rate %	104	82	71	130	62	68	81	92	93	81	52	—
Net Assets $mil	228	203	175	219	467	446	223	287	374	383	527	567

Performance 12-31-04

	1st Qtr	2nd Qtr	3rd Qtr	4th Qtr	Total
2000	3.77	3.76	8.18	6.64	24.21
2001	-0.86	13.38	-15.77	20.32	13.92
2002	11.87	-1.39	-20.91	6.27	-7.29
2003	-6.23	21.93	7.21	14.79	40.71
2004	6.08	-0.98	-0.99	12.13	16.61

Trailing	Total Return%	+/- S&P 500	+/- Russ 2000 VL	%Rank Cat	Growth of $10,000
3 Mo	12.13	2.90	-1.07	65	11,213
6 Mo	11.02	3.83	-2.35	61	11,102
1 Yr	16.61	5.74	-5.64	86	11,661
3 Yr Avg	15.01	11.43	-1.49	52	15,213
5 Yr Avg	16.57	18.87	-0.66	42	21,525
10 Yr Avg	13.29	1.22	-1.88	77	34,827
15 Yr Avg	14.92	3.99	0.90	31	80,526

Tax Analysis	Tax-Adj Rtn%	%Rank Cat	Tax-Cost Rat	%Rank Cat
3 Yr (estimated)	13.62	51	1.21	69
5 Yr (estimated)	15.73	39	0.72	35
10 Yr (estimated)	11.63	77	1.47	25

Potential Capital Gain Exposure: 27% of assets

Rating and Risk

Time Period	Load-Adj Return %	Morningstar Rtn vs Cat	Morningstar Risk vs Cat	Morningstar Risk-Adj Rating
1 Yr	16.61			
3 Yr	15.01	Avg	Avg	★★★
5 Yr	16.57	Avg	Avg	★★★
10 Yr	13.29	-Avg	Avg	★★
Incept	14.38			

Other Measures	Standard Index S&P 500	Best Fit Index Russ 2000 VL
Alpha	11.7	-0.1
Beta	0.89	0.91
R-Squared	65	94

Standard Deviation	18.96
Mean	15.01
Sharpe Ratio	0.73

Morningstar's Take by Laura Pavlenko Lutton 11-28-04

Skyline Special Equities' well-regarded lead manager is taking a backseat, but we see reason to stick around.

Bill Dutton, who has run this fund since its inception, will step down from his role as lead manager on Jan. 1, 2005. Mike Maloney, who has been sharing lead-manager tasks with Dutton over the past year, will become the fund's top manager. Dutton will help with stock-picking on a weekly basis.

We're sad to see Dutton take a lesser role here. He has helped deliver impressive results: The fund's annualized return since early 1989 outpaces the averages for the small-value category and the S&P 500 index by more than 2 percentage points.

That said, Dutton has had a deep bench of managers backing him for years. Maloney, Bill Fiedler, and Mark Odegard were named managers here in 2001 after working as analysts, and we expect they will do a fine job executing this fund's strategy. They will continue to seek undervalued companies with strong growth potential. Historically, the fund has invested heavily in consumer, financial, and industrial materials stocks.

This fund's penchant for just a few sectors explains its somewhat lumpy short-term performance. The offering held few technology stocks in 1999, for example, and it turned in one of the steepest losses in the category that year. Since then, the managers have diversified the portfolio a bit, but it still makes notable sector and industry bets. In 2004, the managers have held few banks and REITs because their price tags seem too rich, and that stance has held back returns. The fund's 12.71% gain for the year to date through Nov. 26 is one of the slimmer returns in the category.

This fund may have the occasional hiccup, and its expenses are steep. But this offering remains an interesting option among open small-value funds, in our opinion.

Address:	311 South Wacker Drive Chicago IL 60606 800-458-5222
Web Address:	
Inception:	04-23-87
Advisor:	Skyline Asset Management, LP
Subadvisor:	None
NTF Plans:	Fidelity Retail-NTF, Schwab OneSource

Minimum Purchase:	$1000	Add: $100	IRA: $1000
Min Auto Inv Plan:	$1000	Add: $50	
Sales Fees:	No-load		
Management Fee:	1.50% mx./1.35% mn.		
Actual Fees:	Mgt:1.47%	Dist:	
Expense Projections:	3Yr:$468	5Yr:$808	10Yr:$1768
Income Distrib:	Annually		

Portfolio Analysis 11-30-04

Share change since 10-04 Total Stocks:71	Sector	PE	YTD Ret%	% Assets
Airgas	Ind Mtrls	21.8	24.36	2.92
CBRL Group	Consumer	17.7	10.68	2.59
Davita	Health	19.0	52.04	2.47
Pentair	Business	24.0	93.44	2.25
Spartech	Ind Mtrls	18.3	11.97	2.12
iStar Financial	Financial	29.3	24.56	1.89
⊕ Commerce Bancshares	Financial	15.5	9.60	1.84
Triad Hospitals	Health	30.3	11.84	1.80
⊖ Delphi Financial Group	Financial	12.4	29.22	1.78
Benchmark Electronics	Hardware	20.9	-2.04	1.77
⊕ Crane	Ind Mtrls	—	-4.91	1.74
⊖ School Specialty	Ind Mtrls	18.3	13.38	1.73
Westcorp	Financial	12.4	27.32	1.71
Laidlaw Int'l	Ind Mtrls	—	77.82	1.70
Newfield Exploration	Energy	12.5	32.58	1.67
⊕ Cytec Industries	Ind Mtrls	22.4	35.27	1.67
Shaw Group	Ind Mtrls	—	31.06	1.66
Tech Data	Ind Mtrls	17.5	14.39	1.64
Minerals Technologies	Ind Mtrls	19.1	12.97	1.64
Flowserve	Ind Mtrls	24.5	31.90	1.62

Current Investment Style

Value Blnd Growth; Large Mid Small

Market Cap	%
Giant	0.0
Large	0.0
Mid	46.7
Small	50.2
Micro	3.2
Avg $mil: 1,439	

Value Measures		Rel Category
Price/Earnings	16.25	1.02
Price/Book	1.79	1.08
Price/Sales	0.74	0.99
Price/Cash Flow	7.03	1.35
Dividend Yield %	0.89	0.74

Growth Measures	%	Rel Category
Long-Term Erngs	12.68	1.05
Book Value	8.07	1.86
Sales	3.52	1.12
Cash Flow	49.45	22.79
Historical Erngs	10.49	2.18

Profitability	%	Rel Category
Return on Equity	12.97	1.42
Return on Assets	5.73	1.38
Net Margin	7.68	1.15

Sector Weightings	% of Stocks	Rel S&P 500	3 Year High	3 Year Low
Info	6.59	0.31		
Software	0.00	0.00	1	0
Hardware	5.66	0.55	8	3
Media	0.93	0.24	1	0
Telecom	0.00	0.00	0	0
Service	53.37	1.15		
Health	6.02	0.48	8	5
Consumer	6.89	0.76	19	7
Business	18.33	4.53	18	10
Financial	22.13	1.07	29	22
Mfg	40.02	1.25		
Goods	1.10	0.12	8	1
Ind Mtrls	35.96	2.84	37	21
Energy	2.96	0.41	4	2
Utilities	0.00	0.00	0	0

Composition

Cash	4.3
Stocks	95.7
Bonds	0.0
Other	0.0
Foreign (% of Stock)	1.1

Smith Barney Aggr Grth A

Ticker	Load	NAV	Yield	Total Assets	Mstar Category
SHRAX	5.00%	$95.17	0.0%	$8,907 mil	Large Growth

Governance and Management

Fiduciary Grade: D

Portfolio Manager(s)

Very seasoned. Richie Freeman is one of the longest-tenured managers in the large-growth group, having managed this offering since its inception in 1983.

Strategy

Manager Richard Freeman looks for dynamic small- and mid-cap companies that are growing their earnings by 20% per year. Once he finds a stock he likes, Freeman sticks with it: The fund's turnover is among the lowest in the large-growth category. Given Freeman's buy-and-hold strategy and the success of his long-held picks, the fund's average market cap falls into large-cap territory.

Historical Profile

Return High
Risk Above Avg
Rating ★★★★ Above Avg

Investment Style Equity Stock %: 97% 99% 94% 91% 87% 90% 93% 94% 98%

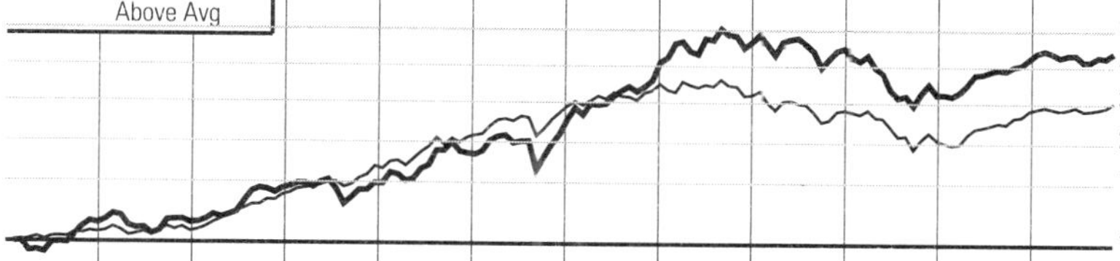

Performance Quartile (within Category)

1993	1994	1995	1996	1997	1998	1999	2000	2001	2002	2003	12-04	History
26.80	25.50	31.49	31.52	38.56	51.09	82.78	98.61	93.68	63.00	86.04	95.17	NAV
21.10	-1.65	35.75	2.73	28.58	35.05	63.74	19.12	-5.00	-32.75	36.57	10.61	Total Return %
11.04	-2.96	-1.78	-20.21	-4.77	6.48	42.70	28.22	6.88	-10.66	7.90	-0.26	+/-S&P 500
18.23	-4.27	-1.43	-20.39	-1.91	-3.66	30.58	41.54	15.42	-4.87	6.82	4.31	+/-Russ 1000Gr
0.00	0.00	0.00	0.00	0.00	0.00	0.00	0.00	0.00	0.00	0.00	0.00	Income Return %
21.10	-1.65	35.75	2.73	28.58	35.05	63.74	19.12	-5.00	-32.75	36.57	10.61	Capital Return %
13	54	26	99	42	37	10	1	3	84	12	24	Total Rtn % Rank Cat
0.00	0.00	0.00	0.00	0.00	0.00	0.00	0.00	0.00	0.00	0.00	0.00	Income $
0.00	0.86	2.88	0.81	1.96	0.88	0.72	0.00	0.00	0.00	0.00	0.00	Capital Gains $
1.34	1.42	1.37	1.30	1.21	1.21	1.18	1.14	1.17	1.21	1.22	1.19	Expense Ratio %
-1.01	-1.23	-1.05	-0.97	-0.93	-0.97	-0.89	-0.66	-0.80	-0.88	-0.86	-0.82	Income Ratio %
13	11	44	13	6	7	8	1	—	1	1	5	Turnover Rate %
188	174	294	269	340	472	956	1,728	2,211	1,854	2,788	3,425	Net Assets $mil

Performance 12-31-04

	1st Qtr	2nd Qtr	3rd Qtr	4th Qtr	Total
2000	19.79	2.55	3.07	-5.92	19.12
2001	-10.32	15.59	-22.35	18.03	-5.00
2002	-5.90	-25.52	-12.63	9.83	-32.75
2003	2.19	17.04	3.09	10.76	36.57
2004	5.00	-1.27	-1.65	8.49	10.61

Trailing	Total Return%	+/- S&P 500	+/- Russ 1000Gr	%Rank Cat	Growth of $10,000
3 Mo	8.49	-0.74	-0.68	76	10,849
6 Mo	6.70	-0.49	3.23	25	10,670
1 Yr	10.61	-0.26	4.31	24	11,061
3 Yr Avg	0.53	-3.05	0.71	38	10,160
5 Yr Avg	2.83	5.13	12.12	2	11,497
10 Yr Avg	16.38	4.31	6.79	1	45,581
15 Yr Avg	14.30	3.37	4.80	2	74,249

Tax Analysis	Tax-Adj Rtn%	%Rank Cat	Tax-Cost Rat	%Rank Cat
3 Yr (estimated)	-1.18	53	0.00	1
5 Yr (estimated)	1.78	2	0.00	1
10 Yr (estimated)	15.22	1	0.49	7

Potential Capital Gain Exposure: 24% of assets

Rating and Risk

Time Period	Load-Adj Return %	Morningstar Rtn vs Cat	Morningstar Risk vs Cat	Morningstar Risk-Adj Rating
1 Yr	5.08			
3 Yr	-1.18	Avg	High	★★
5 Yr	1.78	High	+Avg	★★★★★
10 Yr	15.79	High	+Avg	★★★★★
Incept	14.18			

Other Measures	Standard Index S&P 500	Best Fit Index Russ 1000Gr
Alpha	-2.8	1.4
Beta	1.16	1.15
R-Squared	83	88

Standard Deviation	19.60
Mean	0.53
Sharpe Ratio	-0.04

Morningstar's Take by Kerry O'Boyle 10-15-04

Savvy stock-picking and a disciplined approach make Smith Barney Aggressive Growth a standout.

Investors should check the fund's portfolio holdings to make sure they like what they see, because they'll likely be seeing those names for a long time. Turnover here is microscopic. While manager Richie Freeman looks for fast-growing companies--especially midsized firms with lots of room to grow--he's also conscious of valuation, preferring to buy stocks on the cheap. And unless there are significant changes in the fundamentals of a firm's business, he'll stick with those picks through thick and thin. For example, the fund has owned Imclone Systems through all of its travails since 2000 to good effect.

Freeman's most recent additions to the portfolio have been prescient. He initiated positions in Anadarko Petroleum and Biogen IDEC in November 2003 and quickly boosted both into the fund's top 10 holdings. Those picks have stood out as the fund has bested more than 80% of its rivals thus far in 2004's turbulent market. Anadarko is part of the fund's 10% stake in surging energy stocks--three times that of its typical peer--which has helped to keep it ahead of the pack.

Freeman's style does entail quite a bit of risk, however. More than 50% of assets are devoted to the fund's top 10 holdings, making it susceptible to individual blowups. That risk was highlighted during the fund's disastrous year in 2002--when a number of top picks imploded. And recently, flu-vaccine maker Chiron dropped more than 30% on news that one of its plants had been shut down. Moreover, the fund is vulnerable to sector risk with its big stakes in health-care, media, and energy stocks.

Over time, though, Freeman's disciplined stock-picking has overcome near-term volatility. The fund's long-term record is superb. While we remain disappointed at the relatively high price tag for an $8 billion fund, it remains a solid option.

Portfolio Analysis 09-30-04

Share change since 08-04 Total Stocks:76	Sector	PE	YTD Ret%	% Assets
UnitedHealth Group	Health	23.8	51.38	9.00
Lehman Brothers Holdings	Financial	11.7	14.22	6.56
Anadarko Petroleum	Energy	10.9	28.27	6.16
Biogen IDEC	Health	—	81.50	5.23
Forest Laboratories	Health	18.0	-27.41	4.39
Amgen	Health	37.7	3.82	4.21
Weatherford International	Energy	27.8	42.50	3.99
Chiron	Health	33.2	-41.51	3.97
Genzyme	Health	—	17.81	3.95
Comcast	Media	—	-13.77	3.92
Tyco International	Ind Mtrls	25.1	35.41	3.38
Time Warner	Media	27.5	8.12	2.96
Merrill Lynch & Company	Financial	12.6	3.12	2.67
L-3 Communications Holdi	Hardware	20.6	43.54	2.60
Imclone Systems	Health	38.5	16.19	2.45
Micron Technology	Hardware	46.2	-8.32	2.02
Cablevision Systems A	Media	—	6.46	1.94
Liberty Media	Media	—	11.56	1.81
NASDAQ 100 Trust Shares	—	—	—	1.72
Motorola	Hardware	28.7	37.93	1.65

Current Investment Style

Market Cap	%
Giant	21.8
Large	42.7
Mid	29.4
Small	4.4
Micro	1.7

Avg $mil: 15,303

Value Measures		Rel Category
Price/Earnings	19.25	0.91
Price/Book	1.74	0.54
Price/Sales	2.20	1.02
Price/Cash Flow	9.73	0.89
Dividend Yield %	0.36	0.47

Growth Measures	%	Rel Category
Long-Term Erngs	13.91	0.99
Book Value	12.54	0.99
Sales	4.50	0.53
Cash Flow	7.40	0.45
Historical Erngs	18.56	1.28

Profitability	%	Rel Category
Return on Equity	11.46	0.64
Return on Assets	4.76	0.51
Net Margin	4.56	0.37

Sector Weightings	% of Stocks	Rel S&P 500	3 Year High	3 Year Low
Info	29.66	1.38		
Software	1.85	0.43	2	1
Hardware	12.62	1.24	18	12
Media	14.16	3.69	16	12
Telecom	1.03	0.33	3	1
Service	55.24	1.19		
Health	41.81	3.34	51	38
Consumer	0.53	0.06	1	0
Business	0.51	0.13	1	0
Financial	12.39	0.60	17	12
Mfg	15.10	0.47		
Goods	0.00	0.00	0	0
Ind Mtrls	3.49	0.28	5	3
Energy	11.61	1.62	12	1
Utilities	0.00	0.00	0	0

Composition

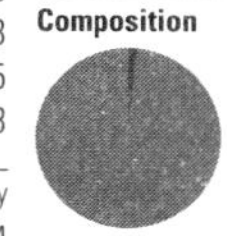

Cash	1.6
Stocks	98.4
Bonds	0.0
Other	0.0
Foreign (% of Stock)	0.9

Address:	125 Broad Street New York NY 10004 800-451-2010
Web Address:	www.smithbarney.com
Inception:	10-24-83
Advisor:	Smith Barney Fund Management, LLC
Subadvisor:	None
NTF Plans:	Fidelity Instl-NTF

Minimum Purchase:	$1000	Add: $50	IRA: $250
Min Auto Inv Plan:	$25	Add: $25	
Sales Fees:	5.00%L		
Management Fee:	0.80%, 0.20%A		
Actual Fees:	Mgt:0.80%	Dist:0.25%	
Expense Projections:	3Yr:$868	5Yr:$1137	10Yr:$1903
Income Distrib:	Annually		

Sound Shore

Analyst Pick

Ticker	Load	NAV	Yield	Total Assets	Mstar Category
SSHFX	None	$36.70	0.3%	$1,698 mil	Large Value

Governance and Management

Fiduciary Grade: A

Portfolio Manager(s)

Managers Harry Burn and Gibbs Kane founded their firm in 1978 and have led this fund since its inception in May 1985. John DeGulis, an analyst here since 1995, recently also took on portfolio-management duties. The firm's profit-sharing plan is invested in the fund.

Strategy

Management seeks beaten-down stocks with solid fundamentals. It screens a universe of 1,250 U.S. equities to identify stocks trading at large discounts to their historic price multiples. Once the list is narrowed, the team scrutinizes a firm's competitive position by speaking with company management, competitors, and customers. The team then prepares detailed financial and valuation models. The upshot is a portfolio of 40 or so mid- and large-cap companies.

Historical Profile
Return: Above Avg
Risk: Above Avg
Rating: ★★★★ Above Avg

Investment Style: Equity Stock %: 92% 97% 98% 93% 95% 97% 94% 93%

▼ Manager Change
▽ Partial Manager Change

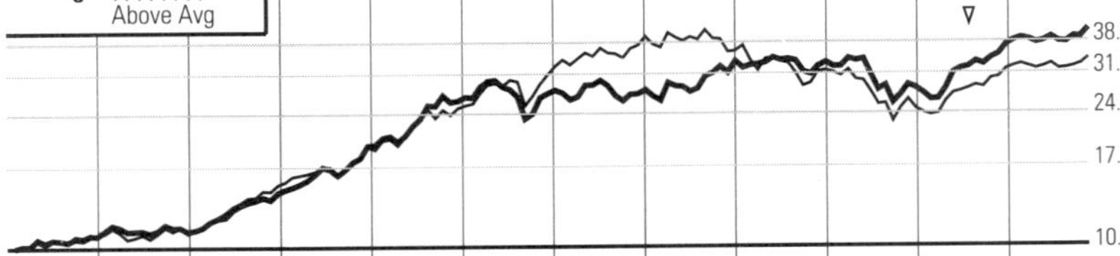

Growth of $10,000
— Investment Values of Fund
— Investment Values of S&P 500

Performance Quartile (within Category)

1993	1994	1995	1996	1997	1998	1999	2000	2001	2002	2003	12-04	History
16.50	15.46	18.16	21.71	28.57	29.62	29.47	33.70	30.58	25.81	33.51	36.70	NAV
11.97	0.30	29.87	33.27	36.40	4.40	0.05	20.18	-0.81	-15.43	31.74	15.34	Total Return %
1.91	-1.01	-7.66	10.33	3.05	-24.17	-20.99	29.28	11.07	6.66	3.07	4.47	+/-S&P 500
-6.10	2.28	-8.49	11.63	1.22	-11.23	-7.30	13.17	4.78	0.09	1.71	-1.15	+/-Russ 1000 VI
0.86	1.33	1.38	0.70	0.57	0.73	0.57	0.48	0.30	0.17	0.20	0.30	Income Return %
11.11	-1.03	28.49	32.57	35.83	3.67	-0.52	19.70	-1.11	-15.60	31.54	15.04	Capital Return %
64	37	73	1	2	87	72	12	31	28	21	21	Total Rtn % Rank Cat
0.14	0.22	0.21	0.13	0.12	0.21	0.17	0.14	0.10	0.05	0.05	0.10	Income $
1.54	0.87	1.67	2.35	0.89	0.00	0.00	1.56	2.76	0.00	0.44	1.85	Capital Gains $
1.27	1.22	1.15	1.15	1.08	0.99	0.98	0.98	0.98	0.98	0.98	—	Expense Ratio %
0.88	1.32	1.41	0.70	0.62	0.77	0.50	0.44	0.32	0.17	0.18	—	Income Ratio %
91	76	53	69	53	44	41	98	104	72	62	—	Turnover Rate %
58	57	68	131	1,304	1,965	1,184	1,052	1,047	759	1,016	1,698	Net Assets $mil

Performance 12-31-04

	1st Qtr	2nd Qtr	3rd Qtr	4th Qtr	Total
2000	4.68	-5.71	12.81	7.92	20.18
2001	-2.05	2.75	-7.18	6.18	-0.81
2002	2.49	-10.23	-16.36	9.90	-15.43
2003	-6.94	21.73	2.81	13.11	31.74
2004	3.55	1.46	0.09	9.69	15.34

Trailing	Total Return%	+/- S&P 500	+/- Russ 1000 VI	%Rank Cat	Growth of $10,000
3 Mo	9.69	0.46	-0.69	36	10,969
6 Mo	9.78	2.59	-2.30	40	10,978
1 Yr	15.34	4.47	-1.15	21	11,534
3 Yr Avg	8.72	5.14	0.15	12	12,851
5 Yr Avg	8.90	11.20	3.63	11	15,316
10 Yr Avg	14.21	2.14	0.38	7	37,761
15 Yr Avg	12.78	1.85	0.75	7	60,741

Tax Analysis	Tax-Adj Rtn%	%Rank Cat	Tax-Cost Rat	%Rank Cat
3 Yr (estimated)	8.25	9	0.43	29
5 Yr (estimated)	8.01	9	0.82	43
10 Yr (estimated)	12.81	4	1.23	19

Potential Capital Gain Exposure: 21% of assets

Rating and Risk

Time Period	Load-Adj Return %	Morningstar Rtn vs Cat	Morningstar Risk vs Cat	Morningstar Risk-Adj Rating
1 Yr	15.34			
3 Yr	8.72	+Avg	+Avg	★★★★
5 Yr	8.90	+Avg	Avg	★★★★
10 Yr	14.21	High	+Avg	★★★★
Incept	13.47			

Other Measures	Standard Index S&P 500	Best Fit Index Mstar Mid Value
Alpha	5.2	-6.0
Beta	0.97	1.05
R-Squared	83	89
Standard Deviation	17.42	
Mean	8.72	
Sharpe Ratio	0.43	

Morningstar's Take by Kunal Kapoor 12-30-04

Sound Shore Fund just keeps on ticking.

There's nothing complicated about this fund's strategy. The experienced management team here prefers to invest in firms whose stocks prices are temporarily depressed. The aim is to identify companies with real long-term earnings growth potential even if their short-term results are a little choppy. Media holdings such as Time Warner and Liberty Media fit the bill. In fact, at approximately 8% of assets, the fund's media stake is approaching twice the group norm. Additionally, the fund has a penchant for identifying firms whose stocks are cheap largely because Wall Street misunderstands their business models. A case in point is Direct TV, whose ability to win new customers is being underestimated, according to comanager Gibb Kane.

The result is a fund that's delivered over the long haul without much ado: Its trailing five- and 10-year returns trump the majority of its rivals and the S&P 500 Index. But the case for this fund runs deeper than just performance. We assigned it a fiduciary grade of A because we think management's incentives are appropriately aligned with fundholders' interests. For instance, instead of trying to grow by launching a suite of funds, Sound Shore Management Inc., the fund's advisor, has stuck to the same discipline for its one fund and separately managed accounts. What's more, the fund has always been reasonably priced and the firm doesn't really market it. Taken together, these factors help allay concerns that management, which consists of the firm's principal owners, may put firm profitability ahead of fundholders' interests.

As with most truly active funds, it will underperform from time to time--witness its relative struggles in the late 1990s. In particular, the fund may be vulnerable if mega-caps bounce back. But for those looking to put some money away for a college or retirement fund, such short-term events shouldn't be of concern.

Address:	P.O.Box 446 Portland, ME 04112 800-551-1980
Web Address:	www.soundshorefund.com
Inception:	05-03-85
Advisor:	Sound Shore Management Inc
Subadvisor:	None
NTF Plans:	Fidelity Retail-NTF, Schwab OneSource

Minimum Purchase:	$10000	Add: $0	IRA: $2000
Min Auto Inv Plan:	$10000	Add: $50	
Sales Fees:	No-load		
Management Fee:	0.75%, 0.10%A		
Actual Fees:	Mgt:0.75%	Dist:	
Expense Projections:	3Yr:$315	5Yr:$548	10Yr:$1216
Income Distrib:	Semi-Annually		

Portfolio Analysis 09-30-04

Share change since 06-04 Total Stocks:36	Sector	PE	YTD Ret%	% Assets
⊕ Berkshire Hathaway A	Financial	—	—	4.49
⊕ Freddie Mac	Financial	10.6	28.75	4.16
⊕ Countrywide Financial	Financial	9.0	48.15	3.31
⊕ US Bancorp	Financial	14.2	10.46	3.25
⊕ Liberty Media	Media	—	11.56	3.22
⊕ Halliburton	Energy	47.7	53.28	3.14
⊕ Cigna	Health	8.4	42.87	3.11
⊕ Devon Energy	Energy	9.0	36.78	3.09
⊕ El Paso	Energy	—	29.51	3.09
⊕ Centurytel	Telecom	14.2	9.54	3.05
Aetna	Financial	16.9	84.67	3.03
⊕ Tyco International	Ind Mtrls	25.1	35.41	2.95
⊕ Ambac Financial Group	Financial	12.7	19.13	2.92
⊕ Chubb	Financial	12.9	15.43	2.84
⊕ Comerica	Financial	14.8	12.87	2.81
⊖ Marathon Oil	Energy	—	17.07	2.78
⊕ Interpublic Group of Com	Business	—	-14.10	2.77
Laboratory Corp of Ameri	Health	19.1	34.83	2.74
⊕ Baxter International	Health	32.9	15.22	2.73
⊕ SPX	Ind Mtrls	13.7	-30.17	2.69

Current Investment Style

Value Blnd Growth / Large Mid Small

Market Cap	%
Giant	21.7
Large	51.3
Mid	26.9
Small	0.0
Micro	0.0

Avg $mil: 14,411

Value Measures		Rel Category
Price/Earnings	13.97	0.93
Price/Book	1.61	0.71
Price/Sales	0.78	0.66
Price/Cash Flow	5.15	0.81
Dividend Yield %	1.27	0.62

Growth Measures	%	Rel Category
Long-Term Erngs	11.72	1.13
Book Value	5.15	0.91
Sales	5.64	1.34
Cash Flow	0.57	0.11
Historical Erngs	32.66	2.76

Profitability	%	Rel Category
Return on Equity	11.31	0.71
Return on Assets	5.68	0.73
Net Margin	9.01	0.88

Sector Weightings	% of Stocks	Rel S&P 500	3 Year High	3 Year Low
Info	17.32	0.81		
Software	0.00	0.00	0	0
Hardware	5.57	0.55	8	0
Media	8.06	2.10	8	3
Telecom	3.69	1.17	10	3
Service	52.92	1.14		
Health	13.99	1.12	25	14
Consumer	4.66	0.51	8	2
Business	5.54	1.37	19	4
Financial	28.73	1.38	29	20
Mfg	29.76	0.93		
Goods	2.17	0.23	3	0
Ind Mtrls	11.77	0.93	16	8
Energy	15.82	2.21	16	2
Utilities	0.00	0.00	6	0

Composition

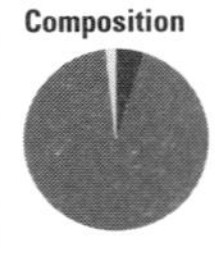

Cash	5.0
Stocks	93.3
Bonds	0.0
Other	1.7
Foreign (% of Stock)	2.2

SSgA Yield Plus

Analyst Pick	Ticker	Load	NAV	Yield	SEC Yield	Total Assets	Mstar Category
✓	SSYPX	12b-1 only	$9.96	1.2%	2.09%	$265 mil	Ultrashort Bond

Governance and Management

Fiduciary Grade: C

Portfolio Manager(s)

Mike O'Hara took over the day-to-day lead management of this fund in February 2003. He has the assistance of a team of portfolio managers with sector-specific research duties. O'Hara joined SSgA in 2002 and specializes in structured securities.

Strategy

This is a conservative portfolio. When he took over early in 2003, manager Mike O'Hara shifted the portfolio from a focus on corporate bonds to asset-backed securities. Although O'Hara has added a bit more mid-quality securities to the mix, he emphasizes high-quality bonds and keeps duration short, typically at about 90 days, in an effort to ensure stability.

Historical Profile

Return Below Avg
Risk Low
Rating ★★ Below Avg

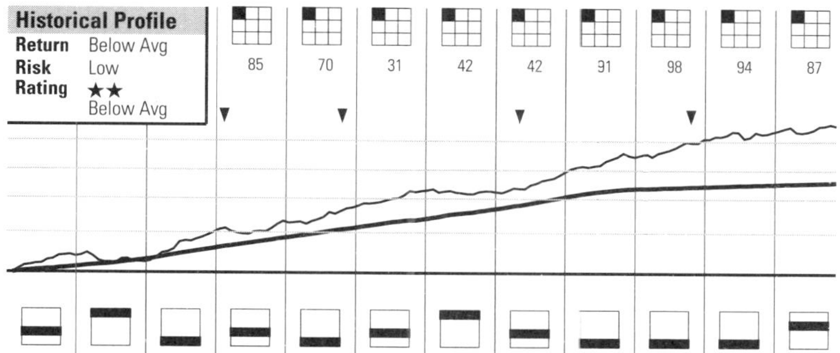

1993	1994	1995	1996	1997	1998	1999	2000	2001	2002	2003	12-04	History
10.00	9.96	10.01	10.00	9.99	9.90	9.91	9.94	9.96	9.93	9.94	9.96	NAV
3.44	4.10	6.56	5.49	5.54	4.83	5.52	6.68	4.53	1.35	1.14	1.44	Total Return %
-6.31	7.02	-11.91	1.86	-4.11	-3.86	6.34	-4.95	-3.91	-8.90	-2.96	-2.90	+/-LB Aggr
0.16	-0.90	0.58	0.40	-0.03	-0.54	0.37	0.35	1.04	-0.45	-0.04	-0.36	+/-6 Month CD
3.55	4.43	6.05	5.59	5.65	5.76	5.43	6.37	4.33	1.65	1.04	1.24	Income Return %
-0.11	-0.33	0.51	-0.10	-0.11	-0.93	0.09	0.31	0.20	-0.30	0.10	0.20	Capital Return %
73	6	80	73	86	57	3	64	85	83	76	33	Total Rtn % Rank Cat
0.35	0.43	0.59	0.55	0.55	0.56	0.52	0.61	0.42	0.16	0.10	0.12	Income $
0.00	0.01	0.00	0.00	0.00	0.00	0.00	0.00	0.00	0.00	0.00	0.00	Capital Gains $
0.38	0.35	0.38	0.36	0.38	0.41	0.41	0.42	0.48	0.53	0.58	0.57	Expense Ratio %
3.54	3.82	5.64	5.59	5.42	5.66	5.29	5.90	5.31	2.17	1.18	1.08	Income Ratio %
138	143	200	97	92	249	167	162	86	80	71	32	Turnover Rate %
1,235	1,210	1,381	1,002	704	788	542	258	215	262	267	265	Net Assets $mil

Performance 12-31-04

	1st Qtr	2nd Qtr	3rd Qtr	4th Qtr	Total
2000	1.58	1.41	1.72	1.82	6.68
2001	1.62	1.22	1.03	0.59	4.53
2002	0.28	0.35	0.40	0.32	1.35
2003	0.27	0.46	0.24	0.17	1.14
2004	0.36	0.27	0.34	0.46	1.44

Trailing	Total Return%	+/- LB Aggr	+/- 6 Month CD	%Rank Cat	Growth of $10,000
3 Mo	0.46	-0.49	-0.17	32	10,046
6 Mo	0.80	-3.38	-0.33	57	10,080
1 Yr	1.44	-2.90	-0.36	33	10,144
3 Yr Avg	1.31	-4.88	-0.28	81	10,398
5 Yr Avg	3.01	-4.70	0.11	88	11,598
10 Yr Avg	4.29	-3.43	0.13	88	15,220
15 Yr Avg	—	—	—	—	—

Tax Analysis	Tax-Adj Rtn%	%Rank Cat	Tax-Cost Rat	%Rank Cat
3 Yr (estimated)	0.83	44	0.47	7
5 Yr (estimated)	1.88	69	1.10	13
10 Yr (estimated)	2.59	84	1.63	11

Potential Capital Gain Exposure: -1% of assets

Rating and Risk

Time Period	Load-Adj Return %	Morningstar Rtn vs Cat	Morningstar Risk vs Cat	Morningstar Risk-Adj Rating
1 Yr	1.44			
3 Yr	1.31	-Avg	Low	★★
5 Yr	3.01	-Avg	Low	★★
10 Yr	4.29	-Avg	Low	★★
Incept	4.20			

Other Measures	Standard Index LB Aggr	Best Fit Index LB Muni 20YR
Alpha	-0.1	-0.2
Beta	0.01	0.01
R-Squared	3	6
Standard Deviation	0.29	
Mean	1.31	
Sharpe Ratio	-0.28	

Portfolio Analysis 12-31-04

Total Fixed-Income:66	Date of Maturity	Amount $000	Value $000	% Net Assets
Permanent Fing Plc 2002-	12-10-07	10,000	10,009	3.77
Citibank Ccmt 2001-A2 FR	02-07-08	9,000	9,008	3.39
Granite Mtg Plc 2002-1 F	07-20-19	6,562	6,571	2.47
Cap Auto Recv Abn 2002-3	02-15-09	6,000	6,008	2.26
Arms Ii Global Fd 3 2004	01-10-35	5,119	5,124	1.93
Structured Asset Inv 200	04-25-33	5,000	5,054	1.90
Access Grp 144A FRN	04-25-23	4,954	5,018	1.89
Natl City Ccmt 2002-1 FR	01-15-09	5,000	5,014	1.89
Amer Express Master 2001	11-15-08	5,000	5,008	1.88
Residential Asset Sec 20	06-25-31	5,000	5,008	1.88
Holmes Financing 7 Plc 2	01-15-08	5,000	5,008	1.88
Citigroup Ccm Mtg 2004-	07-15-18	5,000	5,005	1.88
Holmes Financing 3 Plc 2	01-16-07	5,000	5,005	1.88
Gracechurch Cd Fdg 2003-	08-15-08	5,000	5,004	1.88
Chase Cc Master Tr 2000-	06-15-07	5,000	5,001	1.88
Permanent Fing Plc 2004-	06-10-11	5,000	5,000	1.88
Providian Master Tr 2000	04-15-09	5,000	4,998	1.88
Jp Morgan Com Mtg 2004-F	04-16-19	4,979	4,985	1.88
Mmca Whs Tr 2003-2 FRN	10-15-08	4,800	4,825	1.82
Ge Busn Ln Tr 2003-2 FRN	11-15-31	4,775	4,812	1.81

Current Investment Style

Duration: Short Int Long; Quality: High Med Low

[1] figure provided by fund

Avg Eff Duration[1]	—
Avg Eff Maturity	—
Avg Credit Quality	—
Avg Wtd Coupon	2.54%
Avg Wtd Price	98.43% of par

Coupon Range	% of Bonds	Rel Cat
0% PIK	1.6	0.1
0% to 6%	93.3	1.1
6% to 8%	6.7	0.5
8% to 10%	0.0	0.0
More than 10%	0.0	0.0

1.00=Category Average

Credit Analysis	% bonds 12-31-04		
US Govt	—	BB	—
AAA	—	B	—
AA	—	Below B	—
A	—	NR/NA	—
BBB	—		

Sector Breakdown	% of assets
US Treasuries	0
TIPS	0
US Agency	0
Mortgage Pass-Throughs	1
Mortgage CMO	18
Mortgage ARM	0
US Corporate	3
Asset-Backed	7[illegible]
Convertible	0
Municipal	0
Corporate Inflation-Protected	0
Foreign Corporate	0
Foreign Govt	0

Composition			
Cash	7.0	Bonds	93.0
Stocks	0.0	Other	0.0

Special Securities	
Restricted/Illiquid Secs	2
Exotic Mortgage-Backed	2
Emerging-Markets Secs	0
Options/Futures/Warrants	No

Morningstar's Take by Lynn Russell 10-25-04

Don't let this fund's lack of stars obscure its virtues.

In a category that takes on very limited interest rate risk, SSgA Yield Plus Fund takes on less than most. Lead manager Mike O'Hara usually keeps the fund's duration (a measure of interest rate sensitivity) at a quarter of a year or less. This year, it's been closer to an exceptionally short one-tenth of a year. Moreover, roughly 90% of the portfolio is invested in floating rate notes, which demonstrate relatively limited volatility when rates move up.

Not surprisingly, the fund's returns usually lag well behind its rivals' when falling interest rates fuel bond market rallies, as they have over the past several years. However, the fund shines when rates spike. In fact, it rose to the top of the ultrashort category when rates jumped in 1994 and 1999. More recently, it lost less than its peers when rates moved up in July 2003, and was one of the few funds to stay in the black when rates jumped this past April.

The fund also differs from many of its peers in its investment focus. When O'Hara took the helm in 2003, he shifted the fund's focus to mortgage and asset-backed securities (bonds backed by assets such as credit card receivables) from corporate bonds. He keeps the credit quality fairly high, but the fund's performance may not always mirror that of the overall ultrashort category, given its narrow focus.

Investors looking for a relatively quiet place for their short-term stash should give this fund a look. The fund is not a perfect substitute for a money market fund--its NAV can fluctuate--but it is an attractive alternative. The fund's NAV hasn't dropped by more than $.09 (just less than 1%) in any one year since inception, nor has the fund posted a negative quarter over that period. One caveat, however: While the fund's expense ratio remains a bit below its category's average, it has consistently moved upward over the past several years.

Address:	SSgA Funds Boston, MA 02110 800-647-7327
Web Address:	www.ssgafunds.com
Inception:	11-09-92
Advisor:	SSGA Funds Management, Inc.
Subadvisor:	Tuckerman Group LLC
NTF Plans:	Fidelity Retail-NTF, Schwab OneSource

Minimum Purchase:	$1000	Add: $100	IRA: $250
Min Auto Inv Plan:	$1000	Add: $100	
Sales Fees:	0.09%B, 0.08%S		
Management Fee:	0.25%, 0.06%A		
Actual Fees:	Mgt:0.25%	Dist:0.17%	
Expense Projections:	3Yr:$186	5Yr:$324	10Yr:$726
Income Distrib:	Monthly		

State St Res Aurora A

Ticker	Load	NAV	Yield	Total Assets	Mstar Category
SSRAX	5.75%	$40.48	0.0%	$3,753 mil	Small Blend

Governance and Management

Fiduciary Grade: D

Portfolio Manager(s)

The fund has had problems with manager turnover of late, and shareholders should brace themselves for yet another change after this fund becomes part of the BlackRock family during the first quarter of 2005. Wayne Archambo, who has managed BlackRock Mid Cap Value and BlackRock Small Cap Value since January 2002, will take over. Returns at both funds have been mediocre during his limited tenure. He employs a quick-trading style, and turnover at both funds exceeds 200%.

Strategy

In August 2004, MetLife announced that it sold its State Street Research division to BlackRock Inc. As a result, this fund will become part of the BlackRock family (pending shareholder approval) during the first quarter of 2005. Although BlackRock asserts that this offering's approach will not change, it plans to expand this fund's investment universe to include mid-cap stocks. BlackRock's Wayne Archambo will take over the fund upon the merger.

Historical Profile

Return: Average
Risk: Above Avg
Rating: ★★★ Neutral

Investment Style: Equity Stock %

1995	1996	1997	1998	1999	2000	2001	2002	2003	12-04
		71%	82%	86%	86%	94%	97%	99%	97%

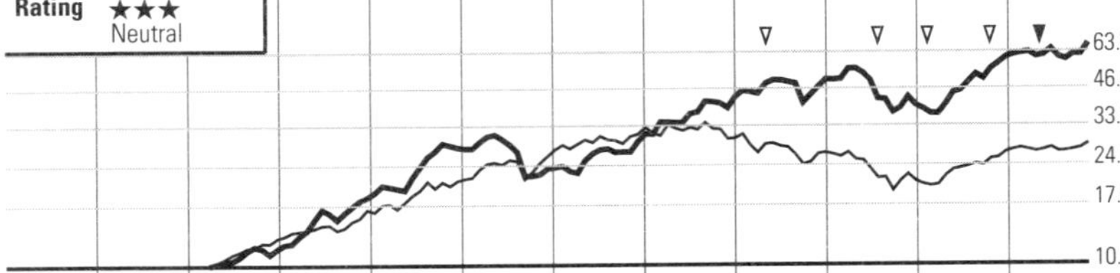

Performance Quartile (within Category)

1993	1994	1995	1996	1997	1998	1999	2000	2001	2002	2003	12-04	History
—	—	10.91	13.53	19.61	16.63	22.21	27.93	32.35	25.80	38.61	40.48	NAV
—	—	20.62*	56.57	46.59	-15.20	33.55	37.02	15.83	-19.79	49.73	14.95	Total Return %
—	—	—	33.63	13.24	-43.77	12.51	46.12	27.71	2.30	21.06	4.08	+/-S&P 500
—	—	—	40.08	24.23	-12.65	12.29	40.04	13.34	0.69	2.48	-3.38	+/-Russ 2000
—	—	0.00	0.00	0.00	0.00	0.00	0.00	0.00	0.00	0.00	0.00	Income Return %
—	—	—	56.57	46.59	-15.20	33.55	37.02	15.83	-19.79	49.73	14.95	Capital Return %
—	—	—	2	2	93	10	3	21	75	18	80	Total Rtn % Rank Cat
—	—	0.09	0.00	0.00	0.00	0.00	0.00	0.00	0.00	0.00	0.00	Income $
—	—	0.50	3.48	0.22	0.00	0.00	2.31	0.00	0.15	0.02	3.84	Capital Gains $
—	—	1.45	1.45	1.34	1.39	1.46	1.40	1.43	1.48	1.55	1.40	Expense Ratio %
—	—	1.05	-0.56	0.17	0.09	0.30	0.42	0.08	-0.73	-0.69	-0.57	Income Ratio %
—	—	—	125	25	68	65	77	26	42	48	33	Turnover Rate %
—	—	6	1	198	132	187	742	1,693	1,437	2,039	2,336	Net Assets $mil

Performance 12-31-04

	1st Qtr	2nd Qtr	3rd Qtr	4th Qtr	Total
2000	10.36	7.47	10.74	4.33	37.02
2001	2.83	11.98	-17.57	22.03	15.83
2002	9.40	-9.47	-23.75	6.22	-19.79
2003	-7.05	22.02	10.32	19.67	49.73
2004	4.35	2.41	-4.29	12.39	14.95

Trailing	Total Return%	+/- S&P 500	+/- Russ 2000	%Rank Cat	Growth of $10,000
3 Mo	12.39	3.16	-1.70	61	11,239
6 Mo	7.57	0.38	-3.26	89	10,757
1 Yr	14.95	4.08	-3.38	80	11,495
3 Yr Avg	11.35	7.77	-0.13	64	13,806
5 Yr Avg	16.98	19.28	10.37	14	21,906
10 Yr Avg	—	—	—	—	—
15 Yr Avg	—	—	—	—	—

Tax Analysis	Tax-Adj Rtn%	%Rank Cat	Tax-Cost Rat	%Rank Cat
3 Yr (estimated)	8.55	80	0.57	40
5 Yr (estimated)	14.45	23	1.00	48
10 Yr (estimated)	—	—	—	—

Potential Capital Gain Exposure: 29% of assets

Rating and Risk

Time Period	Load-Adj Return %	Morningstar Rtn vs Cat	Morningstar Risk vs Cat	Morningstar Risk-Adj Rating
1 Yr	8.34			
3 Yr	9.17	-Avg	+Avg	★★
5 Yr	15.61	+Avg	+Avg	★★★★
10 Yr	—	—	—	—
Incept	20.81			

Other Measures	Standard Index S&P 500	Best Fit Index Russ 2000
Alpha	8.0	-0.3
Beta	1.15	1.03
R-Squared	72	95
Standard Deviation	22.84	
Mean	11.35	
Sharpe Ratio	0.44	

Portfolio Analysis 10-31-04

Share change since 09-04 Total Stocks:228	Sector	PE	YTD Ret%	% Assets
Wabtec	Ind Mtrls	29.8	25.35	1.39
Technitrol	Ind Mtrls	42.6	-12.25	1.27
Veeco Instruments	Hardware	—	-25.18	1.19
Argosy Gaming	Consumer	24.0	79.68	1.08
Agrium	Ind Mtrls	—	3.13	1.06
OMI	Business	8.8	91.70	1.03
Trinity Industries	Ind Mtrls	—	11.40	0.97
Martin Marietta Material	Ind Mtrls	20.6	16.14	0.95
EGL	Business	30.2	70.02	0.86
Allegheny Technologies	Ind Mtrls	—	66.41	0.85
Hanover Compressor	Energy	—	26.73	0.83
GATX	Consumer	11.0	9.01	0.82
Roper Industries	Ind Mtrls	31.4	24.26	0.82
Reader's Digest Associat	Media	46.5	-3.75	0.81
Heidrick & Struggles Int	Business	—	57.20	0.78
Stewart Enterprises	Consumer	—	23.06	0.77
Valeant Pharmaceuticals	Health	—	6.22	0.77
Province Healthcare	Health	23.2	39.69	0.77
United States Steel	Ind Mtrls	—	47.19	0.76
Peabody Energy	Energy	35.4	96.04	0.75

Current Investment Style

Value Blnd Growth — Large Mid Small

Market Cap	%
Giant	0.0
Large	0.0
Mid	23.1
Small	59.9
Micro	17.0
Avg $mil: 894	

Value Measures		Rel Category
Price/Earnings	17.94	1.04
Price/Book	1.81	0.91
Price/Sales	0.81	0.85
Price/Cash Flow	6.24	1.07
Dividend Yield %	0.72	0.87

Growth Measures	%	Rel Category
Long-Term Erngs	13.18	0.97
Book Value	1.53	0.27
Sales	0.80	0.19
Cash Flow	-0.95	NMF
Historical Erngs	-6.47	NMF

Profitability	%	Rel Category
Return on Equity	5.20	0.50
Return on Assets	2.04	0.41
Net Margin	2.98	0.41

Sector Weightings	% of Stocks	Rel S&P 500	3 Year High	3 Year Low
Info	16.73	0.78		
Software	1.57	0.37	2	0
Hardware	11.28	1.11	18	11
Media	2.56	0.67	4	3
Telecom	1.32	0.42	1	1
Service	39.70	0.86		
Health	6.09	0.49	6	2
Consumer	12.20	1.34	14	7
Business	12.09	2.99	13	10
Financial	9.32	0.45	9	4
Mfg	43.59	1.36		
Goods	6.00	0.64	8	3
Ind Mtrls	29.25	2.31	37	28
Energy	7.13	1.00	9	5
Utilities	1.21	0.41	1	0

Composition

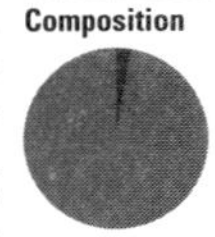

Cash	2.6
Stocks	97.4
Bonds	0.0
Other	0.0
Foreign (% of Stock)	1.4

Morningstar's Take by Sonya Morris 11-23-04

State Street Research Aurora's upcoming transformation raises too many doubts to recommend it.

Change is on the way for this fund. In August, MetLife announced that it had sold its State Street Research division to BlackRock Inc. Consequently, this fund is slated to be subsumed into the BlackRock family (pending shareholder approval) in early 2005.

Manager Paul Haagensen, who has managed this offering since early 2003, will not stay on after the merger. The baton will pass to BlackRock's Wayne Archambo, who has skippered BlackRock Small Cap Value and BlackRock Mid Cap Value since January 2002. His record at both funds, while not particularly inspiring, is too short to be meaningful. Furthermore, Archambo trades frequently. His charges' turnover ratios both top 150%, dwarfing this fund's--meaning that trading costs are likely to tick up here. In fact, brokerage commissions as a percentage of assets at both Archambo's funds have been roughly 100 basis points higher than this fund's over the past few years.

And expenses here are already above average for front-load small-blend funds. What's worse, the expense ratio has risen even as assets have increased. Although BlackRock has said it will not increase expenses after the merger, we think it has room to cut costs here.

Finally, we recently voiced concern that the fund's asset size may limit its maneuverability in the small-cap arena. To sidestep that problem, BlackRock plans to broaden this fund's universe to include mid-cap stocks, but that could pose its own set of problems, as shareholders who purchased this fund to fill out the small-cap slot of their portfolio will now get an offering that skews toward larger stocks instead.

All told, current shareholders and new investors are better served elsewhere.

Address:	One Financial Ctr Boston MA 02111 800-882-0052
Web Address:	www.ssrfunds.com
Inception:	02-13-95 *
Advisor:	State Street Research & Management Co.
Subadvisor:	None
NTF Plans:	DATALynx NTF, Federated Tr NTF

Minimum Purchase:	$2500	Add: $50	IRA: $2000
Min Auto Inv Plan:	$2500	Add: $50	
Sales Fees:	5.75%L, 0.25%S		
Management Fee:	0.85%		
Actual Fees:	Mgt:0.85%	Dist:0.30%	
Expense Projections:	3Yr:$1004	5Yr:$1317	10Yr:$2200
Income Distrib:	Annually		

Strong Adv Common Stk Z

Ticker	Load	NAV	Yield	Total Assets	Mstar Category
STCSX	Closed	$22.65	0.0%	$1,325 mil	Mid-Cap Blend

Governance and Management

Fiduciary Grade: F

Portfolio Manager(s)

Dick Weiss has been on board since 1991. He owns a small stake in Strong Capital Management. Ann Miletti was named comanager of the fund in October 2001 after serving as an associate manager for several years. A team of analysts assists them.

Strategy

Dick Weiss and Ann Miletti search for stocks with strong growth prospects that are trading at discounts to their estimates of private-market value. They are more flexible about valuations when making sell decisions.

Historical Profile

Return Average
Risk Average
Rating ★★★ Neutral

Investment Style
Equity
Stock %

1993	1994	1995	1996	1997	1998	1999	2000	2001	2002	2003	12-04
90%	89%	88%	91%	86%	85%	86%	94%	95%			

▼ Manager Change
∇ Partial Manager Change

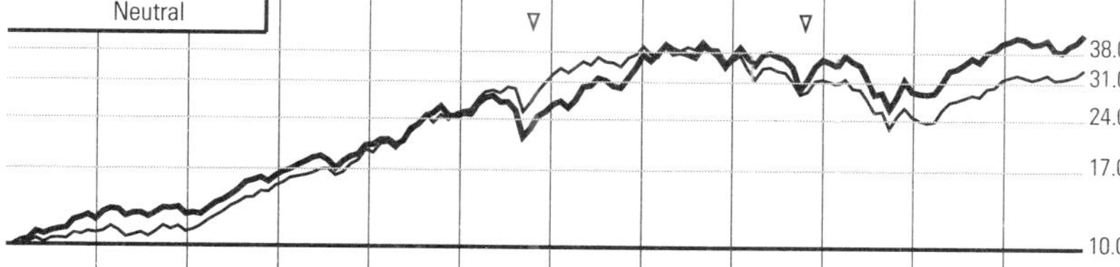

Growth of $10,000
— Investment Values of Fund
— Investment Values of S&P 500

Performance Quartile (within Category)

History

1993	1994	1995	1996	1997	1998	1999	2000	2001	2002	2003	12-04	History
17.94	16.74	19.77	20.24	21.02	21.06	25.21	20.16	19.78	15.97	22.15	22.65	NAV
25.38	-0.49	32.41	20.47	24.04	6.60	40.35	-1.20	-1.70	-19.26	38.70	9.96	Total Return %
15.32	-1.80	-5.12	-2.47	-9.31	-21.97	19.31	7.90	10.18	2.83	10.03	-0.91	+/-S&P 500
11.45	3.10	1.49	1.29	-8.20	-12.51	25.63	-18.69	-1.10	-4.73	3.11	-6.51	+/-S&P Mid 400
0.43	0.25	0.71	0.59	0.20	0.00	0.00	0.21	0.00	0.00	0.00	0.00	Income Return %
24.95	-0.74	31.70	19.88	23.84	6.60	40.35	-1.41	-1.70	-19.26	38.70	9.96	Capital Return %
10	42	37	47	61	65	8	77	53	75	30	94	Total Rtn % Rank Cat
0.06	0.04	0.12	0.11	0.04	0.00	0.00	0.04	0.00	0.00	0.00	0.00	Income $
0.87	1.07	2.21	3.35	3.86	1.32	4.03	4.46	0.04	0.00	0.00	1.65	Capital Gains $
1.40	1.30	1.20	1.20	1.20	1.20	1.20	1.20	1.30	1.30	1.40	—	Expense Ratio %
0.20	0.30	0.50	0.30	0.00	0.00	-0.10	-0.10	-0.10	-0.30	-0.40	—	Income Ratio %
81	83	92	91	117	103	80	95	89	65	42	—	Turnover Rate %
762	790	1,061	1,244	1,565	1,440	1,733	1,719	1,703	1,476	1,437	1,187	Net Assets $mil

Performance 12-31-04

	1st Qtr	2nd Qtr	3rd Qtr	4th Qtr	Total
2000	7.06	-6.19	3.24	-4.72	-1.20
2001	-5.26	5.97	-20.06	22.48	-1.70
2002	2.68	-14.77	-17.97	12.46	-19.26
2003	-1.06	18.04	4.66	13.47	38.70
2004	2.89	-0.61	-3.66	11.62	9.96

Trailing	Total Return%	+/- S&P 500	+/- S&P Mid 400	%Rank Cat	Growth of $10,000
3 Mo	11.62	2.39	-0.53	48	11,162
6 Mo	7.53	0.34	-2.26	83	10,753
1 Yr	9.96	-0.91	-6.51	94	10,996
3 Yr Avg	7.18	3.60	-3.33	75	12,312
5 Yr Avg	3.64	5.94	-5.89	78	11,957
10 Yr Avg	13.47	1.40	-2.62	52	35,384
15 Yr Avg	15.71	4.78	1.05	1	89,241

Tax Analysis	Tax-Adj Rtn%	%Rank Cat	Tax-Cost Rat	%Rank Cat
3 Yr (estimated)	6.81	70	0.35	40
5 Yr (estimated)	2.30	78	1.29	64
10 Yr (estimated)	10.60	61	2.53	88

Potential Capital Gain Exposure: 28% of assets

Rating and Risk

Time Period	Load-Adj Return %	Morningstar Rtn vs Cat	Morningstar Risk vs Cat	Morningstar Risk-Adj Rating
1 Yr	9.96			
3 Yr	7.18	-Avg	+Avg	★★
5 Yr	3.64	-Avg	+Avg	★★
10 Yr	13.47	Avg	Avg	★★★
Incept	15.71			

Other Measures	Standard Index S&P 500	Best Fit Index Russ MG
Alpha	3.5	1.2
Beta	1.15	0.96
R-Squared	89	93

Standard Deviation	19.69
Mean	7.18
Sharpe Ratio	0.30

Portfolio Analysis 09-30-04

Share change since 06-04 Total Stocks:68	Sector	PE	YTD Ret%	% Assets
⊖ Noble	Energy	51.7	39.02	2.33
⊖ Burlington Resources	Energy	10.9	58.50	2.15
⊖ Apache	Energy	11.4	25.41	2.14
⊖ Smith International	Energy	34.2	31.05	2.02
⊖ SanDisk	Hardware	15.7	-18.40	1.99
⊖ Cox Communications A	Media	—	—	1.82
Cablevision Systems A	Media	—	6.46	1.81
MedImmune	Health	—	6.82	1.77
⊖ Pactiv	Goods	23.0	5.82	1.71
⊖ EOG Resources	Energy	16.5	55.21	1.68
Alcoa	Ind Mtrls	18.8	-15.75	1.68
⊕ Business Objects SA ADR	Software	68.1	-26.93	1.67
⊖ Republic Services A	Business	21.8	32.45	1.64
⊖ International Flavors &	Goods	20.3	24.89	1.63
⊖ Sprint	Telecom	—	55.24	1.62
⊖ Roper Industries	Ind Mtrls	31.4	24.26	1.60
⊖ City National	Financial	17.4	16.08	1.59
⊖ Ryder System	Business	15.7	41.93	1.57
⊖ Carlisle Companies	Ind Mtrls	17.2	8.30	1.56
⊖ Affiliated Computer Serv	Business	14.7	10.52	1.52

Current Investment Style

Value Blnd Growth — Large Mid Small

Market Cap	%
Giant	1.5
Large	22.9
Mid	69.6
Small	6.0
Micro	0.0
Avg $mil: 4,838	

Value Measures		Rel Category
Price/Earnings	17.97	1.06
Price/Book	2.06	0.95
Price/Sales	0.99	0.93
Price/Cash Flow	6.80	1.09
Dividend Yield %	0.72	0.72

Growth Measures	%	Rel Category
Long-Term Erngs	12.85	1.02
Book Value	6.02	0.85
Sales	2.66	0.47
Cash Flow	9.55	1.29
Historical Erngs	8.54	0.77

Profitability	%	Rel Category
Return on Equity	10.95	0.79
Return on Assets	4.90	0.75
Net Margin	7.68	0.85

Sector Weightings	% of Stocks	Rel S&P 500	3 Year High	3 Year Low
Info	28.07	1.31		
Software	4.58	1.07	8	2
Hardware	12.34	1.21	12	4
Media	9.44	2.46	9	6
Telecom	1.71	0.54	5	2
Service	46.42	1.00		
Health	13.27	1.06	17	10
Consumer	10.74	1.18	15	7
Business	10.41	2.57	11	8
Financial	12.00	0.58	14	10
Mfg	25.51	0.79		
Goods	6.15	0.66	12	6
Ind Mtrls	6.99	0.55	12	7
Energy	12.37	1.73	15	10
Utilities	0.00	0.00	2	0

Composition

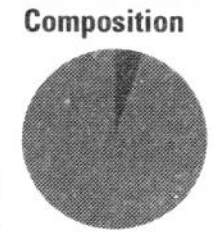

Cash	5.0
Stocks	94.9
Bonds	0.0
Other	0.1
Foreign (% of Stock)	7.5

Morningstar's Take by Kerry O'Boyle 11-03-04

Given its recent turmoil, Strong Advisor Common Stock lacks appeal.

Following its settlement with regulators over improper trading practices and the announcement of its acquisition by Wells Fargo, Strong and its sprawling fund complex are to undergo a major overhaul. The Strong brand will virtually disappear as the shop attempts to put the trading scandal behind it and restore faith in its badly tarnished culture. Pending a shareholder vote, this fund will change its name to Wells Fargo Common Stock.

While the plan is for the fund's strategy to remain intact under the continued guidance of veteran manager Dick Weiss, the merger is a source of uncertainty. Analysis of past fund-company mergers shows that potential benefits--lower fees, economies of scale, and improved research capabilities--often prove illusory. It remains to be seen whether the independent-minded survivors of Midwest-based Strong will be able to thrive under the direction of a giant California bank.

As it is, things haven't been going all that great here the past few years. The fund's trailing three- and five-year returns are distinctly subpar versus its mid-blend peers. Weiss' tendency to own big stakes in media stocks--the worst-performing sector of the market since 1999--has hurt. Plus, the fund's large asset base makes it difficult to hold the sizeable positions in favored small-cap stocks that helped it boost returns during the 1990s.

Granted, Weiss is widely respected within the industry for his stock-picking skills, and the fund is likely to benefit greatly should media stocks stage a comeback. But uncertainty surrounding the merger gives us pause. And although Wells Fargo has remained unblemished by the scandal and done a decent job of retaining some of Strong's top talent, until it shows a willingness to cut into the hefty expense ratio that has been rising here of late, we think that investors can do better elsewhere.

Address:	100 Heritage Reserve Menomonee Falls WI 53051 800-368-3863
Web Address:	www.strong-funds.com
Inception:	12-29-89
Advisor:	Strong Capital Management Inc.
Subadvisor:	None
NTF Plans:	Fidelity Retail-NTF, Schwab OneSource

Minimum Purchase:	Closed	Add: —	IRA: —
Min Auto Inv Plan:	Closed	Add: —	
Sales Fees:	No-load		
Management Fee:	0.75% mx./0.70% mn.		
Actual Fees:	Mgt:0.75%	Dist:	
Expense Projections:	3Yr:$375	5Yr:$649	10Yr:$1432
Income Distrib:	Annually		

Strong Opportunity Inv

Ticker	Load	NAV	Yield	Total Assets	Mstar Category
SOPFX	None	$46.40	0.0%	$2,547 mil	Mid-Cap Blend

Governance and Management

Fiduciary Grade: F

Portfolio Manager(s)

Dick Weiss has been a comanager or sole manager here since 1991. He owns a small stake in Strong Capital Management. Ann Miletti was promoted to comanager in October 2001. A team of analysts assists them.

Strategy

Dick Weiss and Ann Miletti search for stocks that are trading at discounts to their estimates of their private market values. They use the same strategy on the sell side, shedding stocks when they reach their price targets. Management's price targets are generous enough, however, that the fund's price multiples are substantially higher than its average peer's. They also keep the fund diversified by sector, giving it larger weightings than its typical peer in growth areas such as technology.

Historical Profile

Return Average
Risk Average
Rating ★★★ Neutral

Investment Style
Equity
Stock %

90% | 90% | 83% | 88% | 85% | 82% | 86% | 96% | 94%

▼ Manager Change
▽ Partial Manager Change

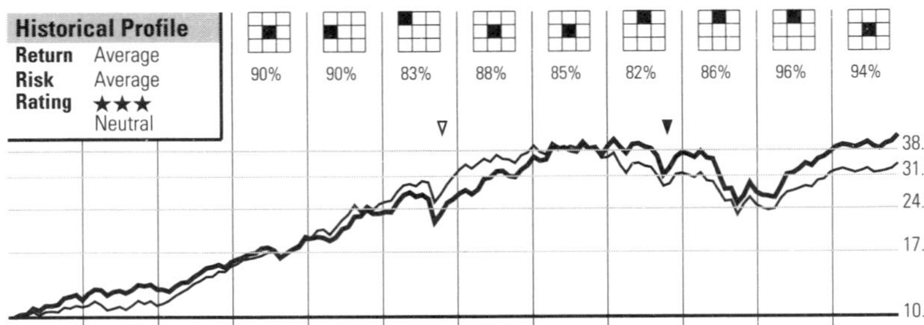

Growth of $10,000
▬ Investment Values of Fund
— Investment Values of S&P 500

Performance Quartile (within Category)

1993	1994	1995	1996	1997	1998	1999	2000	2001	2002	2003	12-04	History
28.23	27.71	33.35	35.26	37.41	38.62	44.69	42.35	39.29	28.70	39.45	46.40	NAV
21.19	3.18	27.27	18.14	23.45	15.49	33.39	8.57	-4.80	-26.95	37.46	17.62	Total Return %
11.13	1.87	-10.26	-4.80	-9.90	-13.08	12.35	17.67	7.08	-4.86	8.79	6.75	+/-S&P 500
7.26	6.77	-3.65	-1.04	-8.79	-3.62	18.67	-8.92	-4.20	-12.42	1.87	1.15	+/-S&P Mid 400
0.25	0.48	0.78	0.77	0.30	0.14	0.22	0.43	0.17	0.00	0.00	0.00	Income Return %
20.94	2.70	26.49	17.37	23.15	15.35	33.17	8.14	-4.97	-26.95	37.46	17.62	Capital Return %
29	13	55	66	65	34	21	56	72	90	33	30	Total Rtn % Rank Cat
0.06	0.13	0.21	0.25	0.10	0.05	0.08	0.17	0.07	0.00	0.00	0.00	Income $
1.57	1.28	1.63	3.82	5.75	4.47	6.35	5.64	0.95	0.00	0.00	0.00	Capital Gains $
1.40	1.40	1.30	1.30	1.20	1.20	1.20	1.20	1.40	1.40	1.40	—	Expense Ratio %
0.20	0.50	0.70	0.60	0.30	0.20	0.20	0.50	0.02	-0.20	-0.40	—	Income Ratio %
109	59	92	103	94	86	81	87	88	71	60	—	Turnover Rate %
444	806	1,328	1,770	1,925	2,038	2,537	3,337	3,664	2,507	2,709	2,406	Net Assets $mil

Performance 12-31-04

	1st Qtr	2nd Qtr	3rd Qtr	4th Qtr	Total
2000	7.88	-2.51	1.45	1.77	8.57
2001	-5.31	5.24	-20.09	19.56	-4.80
2002	0.94	-16.59	-20.53	9.17	-26.95
2003	-4.32	21.41	5.85	11.79	37.46
2004	4.97	3.02	-1.48	10.40	17.62

Trailing	Total Return%	+/- S&P 500	+/- S&P Mid 400	%Rank Cat	Growth of $10,000
3 Mo	10.40	1.17	-1.75	78	11,040
6 Mo	8.77	1.58	-1.02	65	10,877
1 Yr	17.62	6.75	1.15	30	11,762
3 Yr Avg	5.70	2.12	-4.81	87	11,809
5 Yr Avg	4.07	6.37	-5.46	77	12,208
10 Yr Avg	13.31	1.24	-2.78	55	34,889
15 Yr Avg	12.67	1.74	-1.99	52	59,858

Tax Analysis	Tax-Adj Rtn%	%Rank Cat	Tax-Cost Rat	%Rank Cat
3 Yr (estimated)	5.70	80	0.00	1
5 Yr (estimated)	3.31	72	0.73	30
10 Yr (estimated)	11.18	52	1.88	60

Potential Capital Gain Exposure: 25% of assets

Rating and Risk

Time Period	Load-Adj Return %	Morningstar Rtn vs Cat	Morningstar Risk vs Cat	Morningstar Risk-Adj Rating
1 Yr	17.62			
3 Yr	5.70	-Avg	+Avg	★★
5 Yr	4.07	-Avg	Avg	★★
10 Yr	13.31	Avg	Avg	★★★
Incept	15.23			

Other Measures	Standard Index S&P 500	Best Fit Index Russ 1000
Alpha	2.1	1.3
Beta	1.16	1.18
R-Squared	89	90
Standard Deviation	19.71	
Mean	5.70	
Sharpe Ratio	0.22	

Portfolio Analysis 09-30-04

Share change since 06-04 Total Stocks:69	Sector	PE	YTD Ret%	% Assets
⊖ Weatherford Internationa	Energy	27.8	42.50	2.51
⊖ Apache	Energy	11.4	25.41	2.22
⊖ Praxair	Ind Mtrls	21.0	17.32	2.20
⊖ GlobalSantaFe	Energy	NMF	34.38	1.96
⊕ SanDisk	Hardware	15.7	-18.40	1.84
Comcast	Media	—	-13.77	1.84
⊖ W.W. Grainger	Business	22.0	42.69	1.83
⊖ VeriSign	Software	—	106.14	1.78
Molex Cl A	Hardware	—	—	1.77
⊖ Cox Communications A	Media	—	—	1.70
⊖ Waters	Health	27.6	41.10	1.68
⊖ Devon Energy	Energy	9.0	36.78	1.67
⊕ Barrick Gold	Ind Mtrls	—	7.68	1.65
⊖ Sprint	Telecom	—	55.24	1.64
⊖ Genzyme	Health	—	17.81	1.64
⊖ American Standard Compan	Business	18.2	23.10	1.61
⊖ Ensco International	Energy	51.8	17.23	1.58
XL Capital	Financial	20.1	2.80	1.54
⊖ ConocoPhillips	Energy	9.0	35.60	1.52
⊖ Dollar Tree Stores	Consumer	17.3	-4.32	1.49

Current Investment Style

Value Blnd Growth / Large Mid Small

Market Cap	%
Giant	2.0
Large	44.0
Mid	50.7
Small	3.2
Micro	0.1
Avg $mil: 8,066	

Value Measures		Rel Category
Price/Earnings	18.25	1.08
Price/Book	2.06	0.95
Price/Sales	1.05	0.99
Price/Cash Flow	7.34	1.17
Dividend Yield %	0.60	0.60

Growth Measures	%	Rel Category
Long-Term Erngs	11.92	0.95
Book Value	4.41	0.63
Sales	6.35	1.12
Cash Flow	-4.89	NMF
Historical Erngs	15.93	1.42

Profitability	%	Rel Category
Return on Equity	11.75	0.85
Return on Assets	5.10	0.78
Net Margin	6.52	0.72

Sector Weightings	% of Stocks	Rel S&P 500	3 Year High	3 Year Low
Info	28.01	1.30		
Software	4.07	0.95	5	1
Hardware	9.13	0.90	17	7
Media	11.51	3.00	13	10
Telecom	3.30	1.05	4	2
Service	46.35	1.00		
Health	7.20	0.58	14	7
Consumer	15.37	1.69	15	8
Business	12.78	3.16	13	3
Financial	11.00	0.53	13	8
Mfg	25.64	0.80		
Goods	2.99	0.32	10	3
Ind Mtrls	8.69	0.69	15	9
Energy	12.45	1.74	13	9
Utilities	1.51	0.51	2	1

Composition

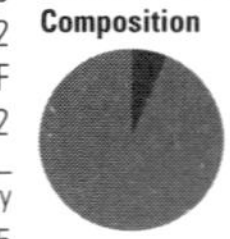

Cash	6.2
Stocks	93.8
Bonds	0.0
Other	0.0
Foreign (% of Stock)	3.0

Morningstar's Take by Kerry O'Boyle 11-03-04

Lackluster performance and major firmwide changes raise doubts about Strong Opportunity.

Following its settlement with regulators over improper trading practices and the announcement of its acquisition by Wells Fargo, Strong and its sprawling fund complex are to undergo a major overhaul. The Strong brand will virtually disappear as the shop attempts to put the trading scandal behind it and restore faith in its badly tarnished culture. Pending a shareholder vote, this fund will change its name to Wells Fargo Opportunity.

While the plan is for the fund's strategy to remain intact under the continued guidance of veteran manager Dick Weiss, the merger is a source of uncertainty. Past analyses of fund-company mergers show that potential benefits--lower fees, economies of scale, and improved research capabilities--often prove illusory. It remains to be seen whether the independently minded survivors of Midwest-based Strong will be able to thrive under the direction of a giant California bank.

As it is, things haven't been going all that great here the past few years. The fund's trailing three- and five-year returns are distinctly subpar versus its mid-blend peers. Weiss' penchant for owning big stakes in media stocks--the worst performing sector of the market since 1999--has hurt. Plus, the fund's significant holdings in large-cap stocks have been a drag too, as smaller companies have dominated during that period.

Granted, Weiss is widely respected within the industry for his stock-picking skills, and the fund is likely to benefit greatly should media stocks stage a comeback. But uncertainty surrounding the merger gives us pause. Wells Fargo has remained unblemished by the scandal and done a decent job of retaining some of Strong's top talent, but until it shows a willingness to cut into the hefty expense ratio at this $2 billion offering, we think that investors can do better elsewhere.

Address:	100 Heritage Reserve Menomonee Falls WI 53051 800-368-1030
Web Address:	www.strong-funds.com
Inception:	12-31-85
Advisor:	Strong Capital Management Inc.
Subadvisor:	None
NTF Plans:	Fidelity Retail-NTF, Schwab OneSource

Minimum Purchase:	$2500	Add: $100	IRA: $1000
Min Auto Inv Plan:	$2500	Add: $100	
Sales Fees:	No-load		
Management Fee:	0.75% mx./0.70% mn.		
Actual Fees:	Mgt:0.75%	Dist:	
Expense Projections:	3Yr:$381	5Yr:$660	10Yr:$1455
Income Distrib:	Annually		

Strong S/T Muni Bond Inv

Ticker	Load	NAV	Yield	SEC Yield	Total Assets	Mstar Category
STSMX	None	$9.84	3.1%	2.71%	$507 mil	Muni National Short

Governance and Management

Fiduciary Grade: F

Portfolio Manager(s)

Lyle Fitterer, who also leads two other short-term muni funds, joined this portfolio in March 2000 after stints at several of Strong's short-term taxable offerings. He works with a team of five analysts.

Strategy

Manager Lyle Fitterer sticks primarily with short-term municipal bonds. Like his predecessor, he favors mid-quality bonds and isn't afraid to throw the occasional high-yield security into the mix. Fitterer doesn't make big interest-rate bets, and the fund's duration is typically shorter than the category average. He limits new BBB purchases to 1% of assets or less, and BB purchases to 0.5% of assets or less.

Historical Profile

Return: High
Risk: Average
Rating: ★★★★★ Highest

Investment Style
Fixed Income
Income Rtn %Rank Cat: 7, 8, 7, 8, 14, 10, 6, 3, 4

▼ Manager Change
▽ Partial Manager Change

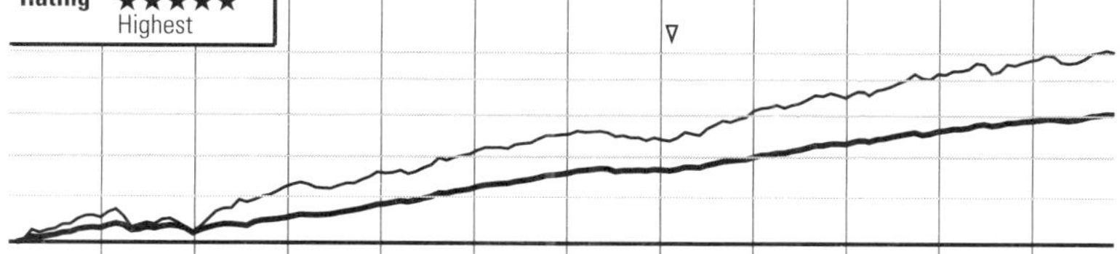

Growth of $10,000
— Investment Values of Fund
— Investment Values of LB Muni

Performance Quartile (within Category)

History

1993	1994	1995	1996	1997	1998	1999	2000	2001	2002	2003	12-04	History
10.36	9.73	9.77	9.74	9.92	9.97	9.63	9.64	9.70	9.79	9.84	9.84	NAV
6.76	-1.61	5.37	4.87	6.93	5.55	1.17	5.05	5.17	5.08	4.02	3.21	Total Return %
-5.52	3.56	-12.09	0.44	-2.26	-0.93	3.23	-6.63	0.04	-4.52	-1.29	-1.27	+/-LB Muni
0.54	-2.29	-3.50	0.43	1.45	0.34	-0.79	-1.18	-1.42	-1.64	1.34	1.43	+/-LB Muni 3YR
4.42	4.45	4.96	5.16	5.03	5.03	4.67	4.93	4.55	4.14	3.50	3.16	Income Return %
2.34	-6.06	0.41	-0.29	1.90	0.52	-3.50	0.12	0.62	0.94	0.52	0.05	Capital Return %
43	77	100	9	7	2	35	67	28	54	4	1	Total Rtn % Rank Cat
0.44	0.45	0.47	0.49	0.48	0.49	0.46	0.46	0.43	0.39	0.34	0.31	Income $
0.07	0.01	0.00	0.00	0.00	0.00	0.00	0.00	0.00	0.00	0.00	0.00	Capital Gains $
0.60	0.70	0.80	0.70	0.70	0.60	0.60	0.60	0.60	0.60	0.60	0.70	Expense Ratio %
4.20	4.50	4.80	5.10	5.00	4.80	4.70	4.80	4.50	4.10	4.10	3.10	Income Ratio %
142	273	227	—	26	16	23	49	74	68	84	69	Turnover Rate %
216	161	133	145	181	264	282	312	511	126	528	499	Net Assets $mil

Performance 12-31-04

	1st Qtr	2nd Qtr	3rd Qtr	4th Qtr	Total
2000	1.09	0.89	1.66	1.33	5.05
2001	1.59	1.28	1.67	0.52	5.17
2002	0.92	1.99	1.61	0.47	5.08
2003	0.94	1.81	0.53	0.69	4.02
2004	0.76	-0.22	1.72	0.92	3.21

Trailing	Total Return%	+/- LB Muni	+/- LB Muni 3YR	%Rank Cat	Growth of $10,000
3 Mo	0.92	-0.33	0.73	1	10,092
6 Mo	2.66	-2.53	0.56	4	10,266
1 Yr	3.21	-1.27	1.43	1	10,321
3 Yr Avg	4.10	-2.34	0.39	11	11,281
5 Yr Avg	4.50	-2.70	-0.28	27	12,462
10 Yr Avg	4.63	-2.43	-0.34	20	15,724
15 Yr Avg	—	—	—	—	—

Tax Analysis	Tax-Adj Rtn%	%Rank Cat	Tax-Cost Rat	%Rank Cat
3 Yr (estimated)	4.10	8	0.00	1
5 Yr (estimated)	4.50	20	0.00	1
10 Yr (estimated)	4.63	17	0.00	1

Potential Capital Gain Exposure: 0% of assets

Rating and Risk

Time Period	Load-Adj Return %	Morningstar Rtn vs Cat	Morningstar Risk vs Cat	Morningstar Risk-Adj Rating
1 Yr	3.21			
3 Yr	4.10	High	-Avg	★★★★★
5 Yr	4.50	+Avg	Avg	★★★★
10 Yr	4.63	High	Avg	★★★★★
Incept	4.49			

Other Measures	Standard Index LB Aggr	Best Fit Index LB Muni 3YR
Alpha	1.2	1.3
Beta	0.29	0.58
R-Squared	79	81
Standard Deviation	1.62	
Mean	4.10	
Sharpe Ratio	1.70	

Portfolio Analysis 09-30-04

Total Fixed-Income:222	Date of Maturity	Amount $000	Value $000	% Net Assets
Bexar Cnty Tex 5.75%	08-15-22	9,000	9,788	2.03
Tobacco Settlement Fing	06-01-07	7,500	7,988	1.66
Golden St Tob Securitza	06-01-20	7,000	7,236	1.50
Chicago Ill Tran Auth 4.	06-01-08	5,910	6,028	1.25
Illinois Health Facs Aut	12-01-22	5,500	5,699	1.18
Matagorda Cnty Tex Nav D	11-01-29	5,450	5,661	1.17
Tobacco Settlement Fing	06-01-11	5,390	5,646	1.17
Hazelwood Mo Indl Dev Au	08-01-18	5,500	5,466	1.13
New York St Urban Dev 5%	01-01-27	5,000	5,419	1.12
Forest Cnty Potawatomie	12-01-09	5,165	5,275	1.09
Munimae Tr FRN	08-24-09	5,165	5,242	1.09
Calif Statewide 35 Day	12-01-28	5,200	5,200	1.08
Missouri Higher Ed Ln Au	05-01-39	4,950	4,950	1.03
Fullerton Calif Redev Ag	04-01-34	4,500	4,770	0.99
Sayre Pa Health Care Fac	12-01-12	4,455	4,733	0.98

Current Investment Style

Duration: Short Int Long
Quality: High Med Low

[1]Avg Eff Duration	1.7 Yrs
Avg Eff Maturity	1.8 Yrs
Avg Credit Quality	A
Avg Wtd Coupon	4.88%
Avg Wtd Price	102.27% of par

[1]figure provided by fund

Credit Analysis	% bonds 09-30-04		
US Govt	0	BB	5
AAA	30	B	1
AA	14	Below B	1
A	23	NR/NA	0
BBB	26		

Top 5 States	% bonds		
NY	10.0	CA	6.7
TX	8.3	WI	6.7
PA	7.5		

Composition			
Cash	20.2	Bonds	79.7
Stocks	0.0	Other	0.1

Special Securities	
Restricted/Illiquid Secs	Trace
Options/Futures/Warrants	No

Sector Weightings	% of Bonds	Rel Cat
General Obligation	15.5	0.44
Utilities	9.7	1.04
Health	13.4	1.86
Water/Waste	6.6	0.63
Housing	11.9	1.59
Education	4.5	0.52
Transportation	6.2	1.45
COP/Lease	2.0	1.29
Industrial	30.3	2.00
Misc Revenue	0.0	—
Demand	0.0	0.00

Morningstar's Take by Andrew Gogerty 12-27-04

A clearer future should encourage Strong Short-Term Municipal Bond shareholders to stick around.

This fund is likely to be flying under a Wells Fargo banner in early 2005, but we don't expect many other changes here. Manager Lyle Fitterer (who took control here in March 2000) will remain at the helm. And even with smaller sibling Short-Term High-Yield Municipal merging into this fund (pending shareholder approval), we don't expect Fitterer's investment approach will change, given the sucess he has had here.

Fitterer focuses on security selection and income to drive performance. But he doesn't bulk up on individual issues. Instead, he aims to keep the fund's assets broadly diversified. This ploy has kept volatility (as measured by standard deviation) down but hasn't hampered performance. This year, for example, the fund's stake in hospital bonds bolstered returns, as the industry continued to ride a high-yield rally. Overall, the fund's 3.1% year-to-date gain through Dec. 23, 2004, tops the short-term muni category. And while not as eye-popping, Fitterer's record since coming aboard is also strong: The fund's 4.5% annualized gain has outpaced the category gain of 3.9%.

Investors should remain mindful, however, that the fund's performance has also been driven by its credit profile. It currently holds more than 32% of assets in bonds rated BBB and below, almost four times the 9% invested in these credit tiers by its typical peer. And while this approach contributes to a higher yield for the fund, it exposes the portfolio to issue- and sector-specific credit problems, which can add ot its volatility.

Overall, though, we think shareholders have reason enough to stick around given the fund's success with Fitterer at the helm. And moving under the Wells Fargo umbrella will help the fund move beyond its family's recent scandal.

Address:	100 Heritage Reserve Menomonee Falls WI 53051 800-368-1030
Web Address:	www.strong-funds.com
Inception:	12-31-91
Advisor:	Strong Capital Management Inc.
Subadvisor:	None
NTF Plans:	Fidelity Retail-NTF, Schwab OneSource

Minimum Purchase:	$2500	Add: $100	IRA: $1000
Min Auto Inv Plan:	$2500	Add: $100	
Sales Fees:	No-load		
Management Fee:	0.25% mx./0.20% mn.		
Actual Fees:	Mgt:0.25%	Dist:	
Expense Projections:	3Yr:$192	5Yr:$335	10Yr:$750
Income Distrib:	Monthly		

T. Rowe Price Balanced

Ticker	Load	NAV	Yield	Total Assets	Mstar Category
RPBAX	None	$19.70	2.3%	$2,333 mil	Moderate Allocation

Governance and Management

Fiduciary Grade: B

Portfolio Manager(s)

Rich Whitney has steered this fund since 1991. He sets the fund's security mix and runs the fund's domestic stock portfolio. Ray Mills, who runs T. Rowe Price International Growth & Income manages the fund's slice of foreign stocks. Ned Notzon of T. Rowe Price Spectrum Income selects investment-grade bonds, while Mark Vaselkiv of T. Rowe Price High Yield also plies his specialty here.

Strategy

The fund strives to be a one-stop shop for investors. It offers a relatively stock-heavy neutral allocation of 65% equities and 35% bonds/cash. Manager Rich Whitney relies heavily on T. Rowe's other managers and analysts to assemble the domestic-stock portfolio, employing the firm's trademark growth-at-a-reasonable-price approach. He and fixed-income expert Ned Notzon add spice by placing 12% to 15% of assets in foreign stocks and up to 8% in high-yield bonds. The managers also keep the fund well-diversified among issues and sectors, and they aren't afraid to look for bonds overseas as well.

Historical Profile

Return: Above Avg
Risk: Below Avg
Rating: ★★★★ Above Avg

Investment Style Equity Stock %

1993	1994	1995	1996	1997	1998	1999	2000	2001	2002	2003	12-04
59%	59%	59%	64%	59%	60%	59%	65%	64%			

▼ Manager Change
▽ Partial Manager Change

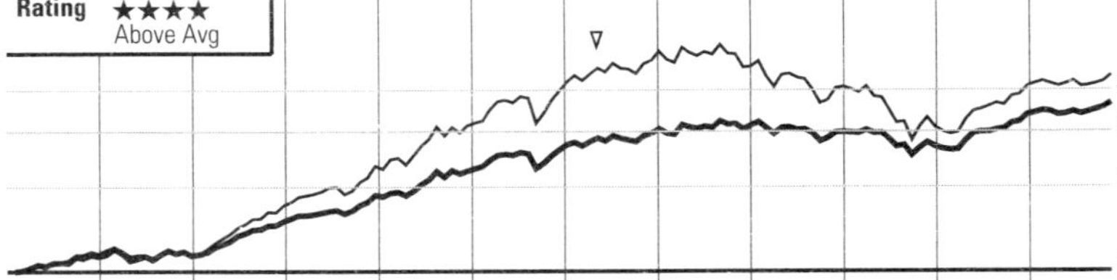

Growth of $10,000
— Investment Values of Fund
— Investment Values of S&P 500

Performance Quartile (within Category)

1993	1994	1995	1996	1997	1998	1999	2000	2001	2002	2003	12-04	History
12.02	11.14	13.22	14.48	16.54	18.59	19.69	19.17	17.49	15.51	18.41	19.70	NAV
13.35	-2.05	24.88	14.57	18.97	15.97	10.26	2.09	-3.98	-8.54	21.71	10.32	Total Return %
3.29	-3.36	-12.65	-8.37	-14.38	-12.60	-10.78	11.19	7.90	13.55	-6.96	-0.55	+/-S&P 500
1.62	-0.10	0.11	3.23	-0.23	3.58	-2.59	-2.35	-4.14	2.00	-2.35	-0.85	+/-DJ 60%
3.59	3.63	4.30	3.84	3.71	3.18	2.94	2.72	2.79	2.72	2.73	2.52	Income Return %
9.76	-5.68	20.58	10.73	15.26	12.79	7.32	-0.63	-6.77	-11.26	18.98	7.80	Capital Return %
37	43	63	45	58	36	56	39	40	21	34	25	Total Rtn % Rank Cat
0.39	0.43	0.47	0.50	0.53	0.52	0.54	0.53	0.52	0.47	0.42	0.46	Income $
0.11	0.20	0.17	0.13	0.12	0.04	0.23	0.40	0.38	0.03	0.00	0.12	Capital Gains $
1.00	1.00	0.95	0.87	0.81	0.78	0.79	0.79	0.83	0.79	0.78	—	Expense Ratio %
3.45	3.72	3.87	3.70	3.36	3.04	2.80	2.75	2.84	2.88	2.50	—	Income Ratio %
9	33	13	22	16	12	21	17	36	49	38	—	Turnover Rate %
341	392	608	876	1,219	1,650	2,091	1,896	1,791	1,582	2,049	2,333	Net Assets $mil

Performance 12-31-04

	1st Qtr	2nd Qtr	3rd Qtr	4th Qtr	Total
2000	2.54	-1.00	1.22	-0.66	2.09
2001	-5.05	2.60	-6.87	5.83	-3.98
2002	1.32	-5.40	-9.66	5.62	-8.54
2003	-1.94	11.64	1.97	9.02	21.71
2004	2.01	-0.10	1.08	7.10	10.32

Trailing	Total Return%	+/- S&P 500	+/- DJ 60%	%Rank Cat	Growth of $10,000
3 Mo	7.10	-2.13	-0.38	46	10,710
6 Mo	8.26	1.07	0.73	19	10,826
1 Yr	10.32	-0.55	-0.85	25	11,032
3 Yr Avg	7.08	3.50	-0.18	14	12,278
5 Yr Avg	3.78	6.08	-1.46	25	12,038
10 Yr Avg	10.11	-1.96	-0.38	33	26,198
15 Yr Avg	9.86	-1.07	-0.09	34	40,982

Tax Analysis	Tax-Adj Rtn%	%Rank Cat	Tax-Cost Rat	%Rank Cat
3 Yr (estimated)	6.02	16	0.99	68
5 Yr (estimated)	2.53	22	1.20	56
10 Yr (estimated)	8.62	19	1.35	20

Potential Capital Gain Exposure: 27% of assets

Rating and Risk

Time Period	Load-Adj Return %	Morningstar Rtn vs Cat	Morningstar Risk vs Cat	Morningstar Risk-Adj Rating
1 Yr	10.32			
3 Yr	7.08	+Avg	Avg	★★★★
5 Yr	3.78	+Avg	-Avg	★★★★
10 Yr	10.11	Avg	-Avg	★★★★
Incept	10.07			

Other Measures	Standard Index S&P 500	Best Fit Index MSCI World
Alpha	4.1	2.7
Beta	0.58	0.59
R-Squared	94	97
Standard Deviation	9.44	
Mean	7.08	
Sharpe Ratio	0.61	

Portfolio Analysis 09-30-04

Total Stocks:351 Share change since 06-30-04	Sectors	P/E Ratio	YTD Return %	% Net Assets
Gen Elec	Ind Mtrls	22.8	-3.01	1.95
ExxonMobil	Energy	13.9	-2.75	1.54
Pfizer	Health	22.0	-2.75	1.30
⊕ Bank of America	Financial	12.3	-3.85	1.24
Microsoft	Software	36.1	0.04	1.22
Citigroup	Financial	15.3	0.08	1.17
American International Gr	Financial	16.2	2.25	0.90
Wal-Mart Stores	Consumer	23.4	1.46	0.89
Procter & Gamble	Goods	23.3	2.21	0.72

Total Fixed-Income:418	Date of Maturity	Amount $000	Value $000	% Net Assets
T. Rowe Price Instl High		14,166	154,404	7.17
US Treasury Note 1.625%	02-28-06	28,000	27,711	1.29
US Treasury Bond 5.375%	02-15-31	18,995	20,348	0.94
US Treasury Note 4.625%	05-15-06	19,000	19,656	0.91
US Treasury Bond 6.5%	11-15-26	16,000	19,337	0.90
US Treasury Note 3.25%	08-15-07	16,500	16,681	0.77
GNMA 5.5%	02-20-34	15,141	15,397	0.71
US Treasury Note 4.75%	11-15-08	13,019	13,804	0.64
US Treasury Note 4.25%	08-15-14	13,000	13,134	0.61

Equity Style
Style: Blend
Size: Large-Cap

Value Measures		Rel Category
Price/Earnings	15.29	0.92
Price/Book	2.40	0.98
Price/Sales	1.18	0.89
Price/Cash Flow	7.60	1.05
Dividend Yield %	1.82	1.16

Growth Measures	%	Rel Category
Long-Term Erngs	10.75	0.92
Book Value	5.83	1.02
Sales	4.12	0.80
Cash Flow	4.94	0.62
Historical Erngs	9.43	0.87

Market Cap %			
Giant	51.3	Small	0.4
Large	36.5	Micro	0.1
Mid	11.8	Avg $mil:	37,411

Fixed-Income Style
Duration: Interm-Term
Quality: High

Avg Eff Duration [1]	4.9 Yrs
Avg Eff Maturity	8.0 Yrs
Avg Credit Quality	AA
Avg Wtd Coupon	5.59%

[1]figure provided by fund as of 09-30-04

Sector Weightings	% of Stocks	Rel S&P 500	3 Year High	3 Year Low
Info	18.54	0.86		
Software	4.12	0.96	4	3
Hardware	7.15	0.70	9	6
Media	3.67	0.96	4	4
Telecom	3.60	1.14	6	4
Service	44.34	0.96		
Health	10.64	0.85	15	11
Consumer	7.89	0.87	9	7
Business	3.81	0.94	4	3
Financial	22.00	1.06	22	18
Mfg	37.11	1.16		
Goods	8.70	0.93	10	9
Ind Mtrls	16.06	1.27	16	13
Energy	8.72	1.22	9	7
Utilities	3.63	1.23	4	2

Composition

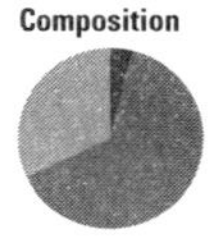

Cash	3.7
Stocks	64.3
Bonds	31.5
Other	0.5
Foreign (% of Stock)	23.1

Morningstar's Take by Greg Carlson 12-22-04

T. Rowe Price Balanced is a fine option for one-stop shopping.

This offering is on a roll: It's on pace to beat at least 60% of its rivals for the fifth-straight year. That streak is due in part to management's wide-ranging tastes. Rich Whitney, who has set the fund's security mix and run its domestic-equity portfolio since 1991, tends to hold a sizable slug of foreign stocks: They recently consumed nearly 15% of the fund's assets, more than double that of its typical rival. Whitney will also hold up to an 8% stake in high-yield debt, as well as a smattering of bonds.

Those areas have had stretches of outperformance in recent years, although there have been notable exceptions: Foreign developed-markets stocks (the fund holds relatively few emerging-markets names) fared worse than their domestic counterparts in 2000 and 2001, while high-yield bonds lagged investment-grade issues in each year of stocks' bear market. However, Whitney has made measured shifts that have helped boost returns. For example, he increased the fund's exposure to foreign stocks in 2002, just as they began to benefit from a weakening dollar.

However, the fund's foreign stake can weigh on returns when those names stall: In 1995 and 1997, for example, the MSCI EAFE Index lagged the Wilshire 5000 Index (a proxy for the broad U.S. stock market by more than 25 percentage points, and this offering landed in the category's bottom half.

Despite forays into more-volatile asset classes, this offering never veers far off course: Its stock/bond split stays in a narrow range (equities typically consume 60% to 65% of assets), and the portfolio is diversified across more than 700 securities. The result has been a relatively smooth ride. A solid long-term record and modest expenses burnish the fund's appeal.

This is a fine long-term holding.

Address:	100 E Pratt St Baltimore MD 21202 800-638-5660
Web Address:	www.troweprice.com
Inception:	12-29-39
Advisor:	T. Rowe Price Associates, Inc.
Subadvisor:	None
NTF Plans:	N/A

Minimum Purchase:	$2500	Add: $100	IRA: $1000
Min Auto Inv Plan:	$50	Add: $50	
Sales Fees:	No-load		
Management Fee:	0.47%		
Actual Fees:	Mgt:0.47%	Dist:	
Expense Projections:	3Yr:$243	5Yr:$422	10Yr:$942
Income Distrib:	Quarterly		

T. Rowe Price BlChpGr

Ticker	Load	NAV	Yield	Total Assets	Mstar Category
TRBCX	None	$30.92	0.5%	$8,321 mil	Large Growth

Governance and Management

Fiduciary Grade: B

Portfolio Manager(s)

Larry Puglia has been at the helm since the fund's June 1993 inception. T. Rowe Price's deep bench of analysts assists him. Puglia says he keeps a substantial portion of his 401(k) invested in this offering.

Strategy

Manager Larry Puglia seeks stocks with sustainable earnings growth, strong management, and leading market positions. Although the fund lands in the large-growth category, the portfolio is well diversified, split between lower-priced financials and growth-oriented tech and health-care stocks. Puglia pays close attention to valuation, which makes the fund one of its group's more-temperate options. Turnover here is modest.

Historical Profile

Return Above Avg
Risk Below Avg
Rating ★★★★ Above Avg

Investment Style Equity Stock %: 89% 93% 95% 96% 95% 98% 100% 100% 100%

▼ Manager Change
▽ Partial Manager Change

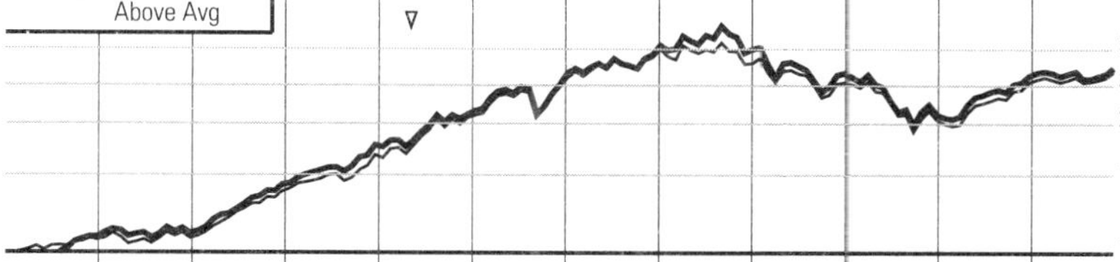

Growth of $10,000
— Investment Values of Fund
— Investment Values of S&P 500

Performance Quartile (within Category)

History

1993	1994	1995	1996	1997	1998	1999	2000	2001	2002	2003	12-04	History
11.24	11.11	15.09	19.06	24.17	30.60	36.34	33.85	28.97	21.95	28.45	30.92	NAV
14.32*	0.80	37.90	27.75	27.56	28.84	20.00	-2.53	-14.42	-24.23	29.75	9.25	Total Return %
—	-0.51	0.37	4.81	-5.79	0.27	-1.04	6.57	-2.54	-2.14	1.08	-1.62	+/-S&P 500
—	-1.82	0.72	4.63	-2.93	-9.87	-13.16	19.89	6.00	3.65	0.00	2.95	+/-Russ 1000Gr
0.00	0.98	1.35	0.93	0.63	0.46	0.10	0.00	0.00	0.00	0.14	0.56	Income Return %
—	-0.18	36.55	26.82	26.93	28.38	19.90	-2.53	-14.42	-24.23	29.61	8.69	Capital Return %
—	23	18	8	45	61	84	13	20	29	35	34	Total Rtn % Rank Cat
0.05	0.11	0.15	0.14	0.12	0.11	0.03	0.00	0.00	0.00	0.03	0.16	Income $
0.14	0.11	0.08	0.08	0.02	0.39	0.33	1.62	0.00	0.00	0.00	0.00	Capital Gains $
1.25	1.25	1.25	1.12	0.95	0.91	0.91	0.91	0.96	0.96	0.95	—	Expense Ratio %
0.80	1.05	1.27	0.87	0.86	0.43	0.10	-0.09	-0.06	0.00	0.10	—	Income Ratio %
89	75	38	26	24	34	41	51	48	46	33	—	Turnover Rate %
25	39	146	540	2,345	4,330	6,709	7,113	6,242	4,482	6,317	7,290	Net Assets $mil

Performance 12-31-04

	1st Qtr	2nd Qtr	3rd Qtr	4th Qtr	Total
2000	6.30	0.54	1.00	-9.71	-2.53
2001	-17.19	8.10	-15.84	13.61	-14.42
2002	-1.28	-15.80	-15.41	7.76	-24.23
2003	-1.28	15.51	1.92	11.65	29.75
2004	1.86	1.04	-3.07	9.52	9.25

Trailing	Total Return%	+/- S&P 500	+/- Russ 1000Gr	%Rank Cat	Growth of $10,000
3 Mo	9.52	0.29	0.35	57	10,952
6 Mo	6.15	-1.04	2.68	33	10,615
1 Yr	9.25	-1.62	2.95	34	10,925
3 Yr Avg	2.41	-1.17	2.59	21	10,741
5 Yr Avg	-2.17	0.13	7.12	10	8,961
10 Yr Avg	12.03	-0.04	2.44	10	31,142
15 Yr Avg	—	—	—	—	—

Tax Analysis	Tax-Adj Rtn%	%Rank Cat	Tax-Cost Rat	%Rank Cat
3 Yr (estimated)	2.33	19	0.08	14
5 Yr (estimated)	-2.40	8	0.24	15
10 Yr (estimated)	11.70	5	0.29	4

Potential Capital Gain Exposure: 13% of assets

Rating and Risk

Time Period	Load-Adj Return %	Morningstar Rtn vs Cat	Morningstar Risk vs Cat	Morningstar Risk-Adj Rating
1 Yr	9.25			
3 Yr	2.41	+Avg	Avg	★★★★
5 Yr	-2.17	+Avg	-Avg	★★★★
10 Yr	12.03	+Avg	-Avg	★★★★★
Incept	11.74			

Other Measures	Standard Index S&P 500	Best Fit Index Russ 1000
Alpha	-1.1	-1.8
Beta	1.03	1.04
R-Squared	98	98
Standard Deviation	16.11	
Mean	2.41	
Sharpe Ratio	0.06	

Morningstar's Take by Christopher Davis 10-15-04

Fortunately, T. Rowe Price Blue Chip Growth hasn't fallen far from the family tree.

It's not surprising that conservative offerings such as T. Rowe Price Equity-Income employ cautious, price-conscious styles. But that ethos is also shared by growth funds such as this one. Longtime manager Larry Puglia pays attention to valuation and spreads his bets across the major market sectors, ensuring his portfolio isn't dominated by pricey, volatile growth sectors such as technology or health care. Moreover, Puglia favors the tried and true, gravitating toward market leaders with strong management and sustainable earnings that generate copious free cash flow and boast high returns on invested capital. As such, the portfolio's average market cap is about 30% higher than the large-growth category average.

These days, Puglia is finding a handful of new names meeting his criteria. He added SAP to the portfolio in 2004's first half; he likes it for its market-leading position among enterprise software providers, impressive management and sound balance sheet. Puglia also scooped up Juniper Networks, pointing to the networking company's growing market share, surprising earnings strength, and its decision to implement a share-repurchase program.

Pugila's relatively cautious tack won't always work in his favor--1999 is a case in point--but its worth has been proved over time, as the fund's fine long-term record makes clear. Further, his temperate approach has led to volatility well below the large-growth norm.

If we have got one beef here, it's the fund's 0.96% expense ratio. That's by no means exorbitant, but it's what it charged in 1997, when it was about one third of its current size. It's also notably more expensive than the smaller, similarly managed T. Rowe Price Growth Stock. That caveat aside, we think it's a fine core growth offering.

Address:	C/O T Rowe Price Associates Inc Baltimore MD 21202 800-638-5660
Web Address:	www.troweprice.com
Inception:	06-30-93*
Advisor:	T. Rowe Price Associates, Inc.
Subadvisor:	None
NTF Plans:	N/A

Minimum Purchase:	$2500	Add: $100	IRA: $1000
Min Auto Inv Plan:	$50	Add: $50	
Sales Fees:	No-load		
Management Fee:	0.62%		
Actual Fees:	Mgt:0.62%	Dist:	
Expense Projections:	3Yr:$303	5Yr:$525	10Yr:$1166
Income Distrib:	Annually		

Portfolio Analysis 09-30-04

Share change since 06-04 Total Stocks:136	Sector	PE	YTD Ret%	% Assets
⊖ Citigroup	Financial	15.3	2.72	3.43
UnitedHealth Group	Health	23.8	51.38	3.30
⊕ Microsoft	Software	36.1	8.95	3.23
⊕ Gen Elec	Ind Mtrls	22.8	20.68	2.96
⊖ Pfizer	Health	22.0	-22.31	2.46
⊖ American International G	Financial	16.2	-0.53	2.16
⊕ Danaher	Ind Mtrls	25.8	25.29	2.09
⊕ Dell	Hardware	34.0	24.01	1.81
⊕ Tyco International	Ind Mtrls	25.1	35.41	1.78
⊕ Home Depot	Consumer	19.0	21.47	1.66
⊕ Wal-Mart Stores	Consumer	23.4	0.51	1.65
Target	Consumer	22.3	36.14	1.59
⊕ Cisco Systems	Hardware	24.5	-20.26	1.58
⊕ Schlumberger	Energy	40.7	23.84	1.48
⊕ State Street	Financial	15.3	-4.41	1.44
⊕ Amgen	Health	37.7	3.82	1.44
⊕ International Game Tech	Consumer	28.1	-2.49	1.38
⊕ United Parcel Service B	Business	28.5	16.40	1.35
⊕ WellPoint Health Network	Health	—	—	1.34
⊕ Baker Hughes	Energy	30.3	34.28	1.29

Current Investment Style

Value Blnd Growth — Large Mid Small

Market Cap	%
Giant	47.7
Large	45.7
Mid	6.7
Small	0.0
Micro	0.0
Avg $mil: 42,138	

Value Measures		Rel Category
Price/Earnings	18.77	0.88
Price/Book	3.08	0.95
Price/Sales	2.13	0.99
Price/Cash Flow	9.85	0.90
Dividend Yield %	0.98	1.27

Growth Measures	%	Rel Category
Long-Term Erngs	13.88	0.99
Book Value	13.69	1.08
Sales	9.10	1.07
Cash Flow	8.14	0.49
Historical Erngs	15.02	1.04

Profitability	%	Rel Category
Return on Equity	18.68	1.04
Return on Assets	11.05	1.18
Net Margin	13.69	1.11

Sector Weightings	% of Stocks	Rel S&P 500	3 Year High	3 Year Low
Info	24.84	1.16		
Software	6.79	1.58	7	2
Hardware	10.14	0.99	11	8
Media	6.37	1.66	10	6
Telecom	1.54	0.49	4	1
Service	54.75	1.18		
Health	16.95	1.36	24	17
Consumer	11.35	1.25	12	8
Business	4.74	1.17	9	4
Financial	21.71	1.05	27	22
Mfg	20.41	0.64		
Goods	4.72	0.51	5	4
Ind Mtrls	10.54	0.83	11	5
Energy	5.15	0.72	5	3
Utilities	0.00	0.00	0	0

Composition

Cash	0.1
Stocks	99.9
Bonds	0.0
Other	0.0
Foreign (% of Stock)	2.9

T. Rowe Price Cap Apprec

Ticker	Load	NAV	Yield	Total Assets	Mstar Category
PRWCX	None	$19.49	1.5%	$4,952 mil	Moderate Allocation

Governance and Management

Fiduciary Grade: B

Portfolio Manager(s)

Steve Boesel, who ran T. Rowe Price Growth & Income for many years before stepping back in 2001, took the reins here after Rich Howard left in September 2001. Howard had managed this offering since 1989. Boesel has been at T. Rowe Price since 1973.

Strategy

Steve Boesel took over here in August 2001. He fills approximately 60% of the portfolio with cheap stocks he thinks have been overly punished by the market. He favors stocks with relatively high yields and relatively cheap valuations. Boesel prefers to allocate about 25% of assets to convertible bonds, focusing on those that are trading far from their conversion premium. However, that number can fluctuate based on the relative attractiveness of various asset classes. Finally, the fund isn't an enthusiastic investor in traditional fixed income.

Historical Profile

Return High
Risk Below Avg
Rating ★★★★★ Highest

Investment Style: Equity Stock %: 51% 53% 49% 54% 58% 60% 59% 64% 64%

▼ Manager Change
∇ Partial Manager Change

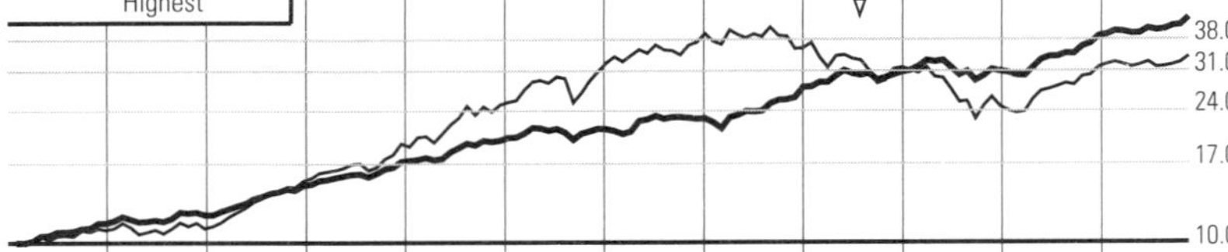

Performance Quartile (within Category)

History

1993	1994	1995	1996	1997	1998	1999	2000	2001	2002	2003	12-04	History
12.66	12.10	13.67	14.47	14.71	13.22	12.51	13.95	14.64	14.21	17.50	19.49	NAV
15.66	3.80	22.57	16.82	16.20	5.77	7.07	22.17	10.26	0.54	25.47	15.29	Total Return %
5.60	2.49	-14.96	-6.12	-17.15	-22.80	-13.97	31.27	22.14	22.63	-3.20	4.42	+/-S&P 500
3.93	5.75	-2.20	5.48	-3.00	-6.62	-5.78	17.73	10.10	11.08	1.41	4.12	+/-DJ 60%
1.58	2.76	3.64	4.39	3.46	3.40	3.78	3.60	2.72	1.91	1.83	1.66	Income Return %
14.08	1.04	18.93	12.43	12.74	2.37	3.29	18.57	7.54	-1.37	23.64	13.63	Capital Return %
16	2	79	22	82	89	71	2	3	2	12	1	Total Rtn % Rank Cat
0.18	0.35	0.44	0.60	0.50	0.50	0.50	0.45	0.38	0.28	0.26	0.29	Income $
0.33	0.69	0.72	0.90	1.58	1.82	1.13	0.82	0.35	0.23	0.06	0.39	Capital Gains $
1.09	1.10	0.97	0.76	0.66	0.62	0.88	0.87	0.86	0.85	0.83	—	Expense Ratio %
2.37	2.91	3.28	4.07	3.17	3.04	3.44	3.22	2.85	2.39	1.85	—	Income Ratio %
39	44	47	44	48	53	28	32	25	18	18	—	Turnover Rate %
536	655	864	960	1,060	1,004	856	914	1,405	1,853	2,937	4,952	Net Assets $mil

Performance 12-31-04

	1st Qtr	2nd Qtr	3rd Qtr	4th Qtr	Total
2000	0.72	3.65	7.66	8.70	22.17
2001	3.15	5.77	-4.14	5.43	10.26
2002	7.72	-4.57	-7.91	6.20	0.54
2003	-2.89	13.04	1.99	12.06	25.47
2004	2.91	2.17	1.74	7.78	15.29

Trailing	Total Return%	+/- S&P 500	+/- DJ 60%	%Rank Cat	Growth of $10,000
3 Mo	7.78	-1.45	0.30	26	10,778
6 Mo	9.65	2.46	2.12	7	10,965
1 Yr	15.29	4.42	4.12	1	11,529
3 Yr Avg	13.30	9.72	6.04	1	14,544
5 Yr Avg	14.40	16.70	9.16	1	19,594
10 Yr Avg	13.95	1.88	3.46	1	36,910
15 Yr Avg	12.46	1.53	2.51	3	58,206

Tax Analysis	Tax-Adj Rtn%	%Rank Cat	Tax-Cost Rat	%Rank Cat
3 Yr (estimated)	12.36	1	0.83	58
5 Yr (estimated)	12.87	1	1.34	65
10 Yr (estimated)	11.29	3	2.33	87

Potential Capital Gain Exposure: 20% of assets

Rating and Risk

Time Period	Load-Adj Return %	Morningstar Rtn vs Cat	Morningstar Risk vs Cat	Morningstar Risk-Adj Rating
1 Yr	15.29			
3 Yr	13.30	High	Avg	★★★★★
5 Yr	14.40	High	Avg	★★★★★
10 Yr	13.95	High	Low	★★★★★
Incept	13.14			

Other Measures	Standard Index S&P 500	Best Fit Index Mstar Mid Value
Alpha	10.2	3.0
Beta	0.57	0.63
R-Squared	79	91
Standard Deviation	10.63	
Mean	13.30	
Sharpe Ratio	1.13	

Morningstar's Take by Kunal Kapoor 01-05-05

T. Rowe Price Capital Appreciation is the perfect antidote for investors' nerves.

By nature, investors are an uneasy bunch. That's particularly true when it comes to hanging tough in downturns. As such, there's a tendency among investors to want to bail out of funds at the worst possible time. Still, this may not be a concern for many right now, especially in light of the strong returns stocks posted in 2003 and 2004. In fact, as mutual fund flows indicate, the reverse is now true: Investors are shoveling money into the equity markets once again.

But that's what worries us. Stocks, for one, aren't cheap by historical standards, with few pockets for contrarian investors to currently point to. And with rates likely to continue rising, the bond market is hardly a panacea. In fact, even the convertible market is increasingly drawing skepticism. As such, the reality is that investors likely have a tough environment ahead of them in the years to come, with the likelihood of smaller gains than what the past two years have delivered.

For those reasons, and because of this offering's fundamental strengths, we think it holds appeal. Manager Steve Boesel is a cautious investor and favors firms with ample free cash flows which pay out hefty dividends. And he's not afraid to diverge from his peers. For instance, as a safeguard against rising rates, the fund currently has minimal exposure to intermediate- and long-term bonds, unlike most category rivals. And Boesel has also been dialing back its convertible stake for more than a year. In fact, cash now accounts for more than 20% of assets.

Such caution may slow the fund a bit, but it also provides it with good--and prudent--protection in the event of a downturn. In the meantime, the fund continues to hum along thanks to some solid stock-picking. In fact, it finished 2004 atop the moderate-allocation category, adding another feather to its cap.

Address:	100 East Pratt St Baltimore MD 21202 800-638-5660
Web Address:	www.troweprice.com
Inception:	06-30-86
Advisor:	T. Rowe Price Associates, Inc.
Subadvisor:	None
NTF Plans:	N/A

Minimum Purchase:	$2500	Add: $100	IRA: $1000
Min Auto Inv Plan:	$50	Add: $50	
Sales Fees:	No-load		
Management Fee:	0.62%		
Actual Fees:	Mgt:0.62%	Dist:	
Expense Projections:	3Yr:$265	5Yr:$460	10Yr:$1025
Income Distrib:	Annually		

Portfolio Analysis 09-30-04

Total Stocks:81 Share change since 06-30-04	Sectors	P/E Ratio	YTD Return %	% Net Assets
Newmont Mining	Ind Mtrls	45.6	-4.44	2.48
⊕ Microsoft	Software	36.1	0.04	2.33
Amerada Hess	Energy	10.1	-2.65	1.94
⊕ Marsh & McLennan Companie	Financial	13.4	-6.57	1.72
Nucor	Ind Mtrls	9.6	-7.60	1.61
Ryder System	Business	15.7	-3.43	1.46
FirstEnergy	Utilities	15.2	-3.16	1.34
⊕ Potash Corp./Saskatchewan	Ind Mtrls	—	-9.87	1.34
⊕ Qwest Communications Inte	Telecom	—	-2.70	1.29

Total Fixed-Income:5	Date of Maturity	Amount $000	Value $000	% Net Assets
Roche Hldgs 144A Cv	07-25-21	86,000	53,249	1.26
General Mls Cv	10-28-22	57,500	40,372	0.96
Corning Cv	11-08-15	38,500	30,610	0.73
Lucent Tech Cv 8%	08-01-31	27,700	30,136	0.71
Liberty Media 3.25%	03-15-31	26,700	23,773	0.56
Loews 3.125%	09-15-07	24,100	23,634	0.56
Newell Finl Tr I Cv		520	22,565	0.53
Amerisource Health Cv 5%	12-01-07	20,000	21,488	0.51
Teck Cominco Cv 3.75%	07-15-06	18,600	18,423	0.44

Equity Style
Style: Value
Size: Large-Cap

Value Measures		Rel Category
Price/Earnings	15.32	0.92
Price/Book	2.17	0.89
Price/Sales	1.08	0.82
Price/Cash Flow	6.29	0.87
Dividend Yield %	1.75	1.11

Growth Measures	%	Rel Category
Long-Term Erngs	10.17	0.87
Book Value	3.47	0.60
Sales	2.31	0.45
Cash Flow	2.45	0.31
Historical Erngs	3.66	0.34

Market Cap %			
Giant	21.8	Small	3.3
Large	46.3	Micro	0.8
Mid	27.8	Avg $mil:	15,851

Fixed-Income Style
Duration: —
Quality: —

Avg Eff Duration [1]	—
Avg Eff Maturity	—
Avg Credit Quality	—
Avg Wtd Coupon	—

[1]figure provided by fund

Sector Weightings	% of Stocks	Rel S&P 500	3 Year High	3 Year Low
Info	17.12	0.80		
Software	3.71	0.86	4	0
Hardware	2.30	0.23	4	1
Media	6.13	1.60	11	6
Telecom	4.98	1.58	6	3
Service	35.02	0.75		
Health	7.93	0.63	9	6
Consumer	4.27	0.47	13	4
Business	5.74	1.42	6	3
Financial	17.08	0.82	17	8
Mfg	47.87	1.49		
Goods	6.83	0.73	7	3
Ind Mtrls	21.60	1.70	24	19
Energy	10.98	1.53	20	11
Utilities	8.46	2.86	10	6

Composition

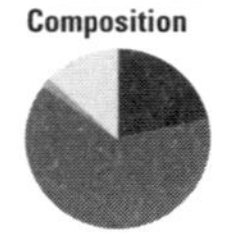

Cash	21.2
Stocks	63.8
Bonds	1.4
Other	13.6
Foreign (% of Stock)	5.5

T. Rowe Price Div Growth

Ticker	Load	NAV	Yield	Total Assets	Mstar Category
PRDGX	None	$22.92	1.1%	$755 mil	Large Blend

Governance and Management

Fiduciary Grade: B

Portfolio Manager(s)

Tom Huber replaced Bill Stromberg as the fund's day-to-day manager in March 2000. Huber has been an analyst at T. Rowe Price since 1994. A seven-member advisory committee, including Stromberg, works on the fund.

Strategy

Manager Tom Huber looks for reasonably priced stocks of companies that deliver increasing dividends. He is drawn to market leaders with high returns on equity and capital. Although Huber's focus on stocks with increasing dividends gives the fund a value bent, the fund's broad-based portfolio places it in the large-blend camp. Like many T. Rowe managers, Huber moves cautiously and keeps turnover low.

Historical Profile

Return Above Avg
Risk Low
Rating ★★★★ Above Avg

Investment Style: Equity Stock %

1993	1994	1995	1996	1997	1998	1999	2000	2001	2002	2003	12-04
	80%	85%	81%	85%	87%	93%	94%	97%	98%		

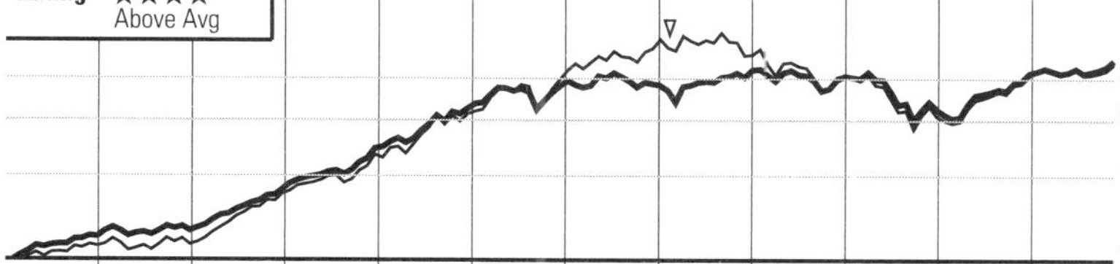

Performance Quartile (within Category)

1993	1994	1995	1996	1997	1998	1999	2000	2001	2002	2003	12-04	History
11.48	11.04	13.81	16.37	20.13	22.01	20.21	21.88	20.79	16.76	20.72	22.92	NAV
19.41	2.16	31.75	25.36	30.77	15.04	-2.82	10.06	-3.64	-18.47	25.17	11.90	Total Return %
9.35	0.85	-5.78	2.42	-2.58	-13.53	-23.86	19.16	8.24	3.62	-3.50	1.03	+/-S&P 500
9.23	1.77	-6.02	2.91	-2.08	-11.98	-23.73	17.85	8.81	3.18	-4.72	0.50	+/-Russ 1000
2.93	3.00	3.30	2.66	2.73	2.33	2.07	1.45	1.29	0.97	1.38	1.21	Income Return %
16.48	-0.84	28.45	22.70	28.04	12.71	-4.89	8.61	-4.93	-19.44	23.79	10.69	Capital Return %
11	16	62	15	40	75	98	8	9	20	68	23	Total Rtn % Rank Cat
0.29	0.34	0.36	0.36	0.44	0.46	0.45	0.29	0.28	0.20	0.23	0.25	Income $
0.15	0.34	0.33	0.51	0.75	0.63	0.72	0.05	0.00	0.00	0.00	0.00	Capital Gains $
1.00	1.00	1.10	1.10	0.80	0.77	0.77	0.81	0.82	0.83	0.83	—	Expense Ratio %
2.60	3.11	2.92	2.53	2.42	2.26	2.01	1.43	1.31	1.08	1.25	—	Income Ratio %
51	71	56	43	39	37	38	36	35	20	17	—	Turnover Rate %
41	54	85	209	747	1,338	1,028	751	692	531	695	755	Net Assets $mil

Performance 12-31-04

	1st Qtr	2nd Qtr	3rd Qtr	4th Qtr	Total
2000	-0.69	3.15	3.32	3.98	10.06
2001	-6.58	4.13	-9.59	9.57	-3.64
2002	2.41	-11.10	-16.41	7.13	-18.47
2003	-4.66	15.49	1.96	11.49	25.17
2004	1.35	1.38	-0.71	9.67	11.90

Trailing	Total Return%	+/- S&P 500	+/- Russ 1000	%Rank Cat	Growth of $10,000
3 Mo	9.67	0.44	-0.13	36	10,967
6 Mo	8.90	1.71	1.09	17	10,890
1 Yr	11.90	1.03	0.50	23	11,190
3 Yr Avg	4.52	0.94	0.25	23	11,418
5 Yr Avg	3.90	6.20	5.66	7	12,108
10 Yr Avg	11.33	-0.74	-0.83	35	29,250
15 Yr Avg	—	—	—	—	—

Tax Analysis	Tax-Adj Rtn%	%Rank Cat	Tax-Cost Rat	%Rank Cat
3 Yr (estimated)	4.08	20	0.42	35
5 Yr (estimated)	3.40	6	0.48	25
10 Yr (estimated)	10.09	28	1.11	36

Potential Capital Gain Exposure: 28% of assets

Rating and Risk

Time Period	Load-Adj Return %	Morningstar Rtn vs Cat	Morningstar Risk vs Cat	Morningstar Risk-Adj Rating
1 Yr	11.90			
3 Yr	4.52	+Avg	-Avg	★★★★
5 Yr	3.90	High	-Avg	★★★★★
10 Yr	11.33	Avg	Low	★★★★
Incept	11.18			

Other Measures	Standard Index S&P 500	Best Fit Index Russ 1000 VI
Alpha	1.0	-3.3
Beta	0.91	0.92
R-Squared	98	98
Standard Deviation	14.42	
Mean	4.52	
Sharpe Ratio	0.22	

Morningstar's Take by Christopher Davis 01-07-05

T. Rowe Price Dividend Growth continues to offer more of the same, and that's a good thing.

Earlier this year, this offering moved from the large-value to the large-blend categories. The shift would have raised our ire if it reflected a change in manager Tom Huber's strategy. But that's not the case. Huber's focus on companies that are increasing their dividends and can continue to do so remains unchanged, explaining why holdings that sport relatively low dividend yields such as Microsoft rub elbows with the likes of higher-yielding fare such as St. Paul Travelers. So unlike other dividend-focused offerings that concentrate in income-rich, value-oriented areas, Huber can move further afield. As such, the fund has long straddled the line between the large-value and large-blend slots of the style box.

The flexibility of Huber's strategy was on display in 2004. Earlier this year, for instance, he scooped up aerospace heavyweight Lockheed Martin which he says is well-managed, growing earnings at a healthy clip, and has aggressively raised its dividend. He also built up the fund's weighting in media giant Viacom, pointing to the company's valuable portfolio of assets, network TV, cable, and radio platforms, ample free cash flow, and recently-instituted dividend.

Huber's approach won't shine in every market. In 2003's speculative environment, for example, his preference for stable businesses with sound balance sheets--the sort most capable of increasing their dividends--put a lid on returns. However, the fund has held its ground in choppier environments and has been considerably less volatile than its rivals and the S&P 500 Index. All told, the fund's long-term returns nicely outpace most large-blend funds while its volatility is markedly lower.

Simply put, those seeking a steady core holding will find this offering a worthwhile choice.

Portfolio Analysis 09-30-04

Share change since 06-04 Total Stocks:112	Sector	PE	YTD Ret%	% Assets
Citigroup	Financial	15.3	2.72	2.54
⊖ Pfizer	Health	22.0	-22.31	2.47
ExxonMobil	Energy	13.9	28.04	2.23
⊖ Gen Elec	Ind Mtrls	22.8	20.68	2.03
⊖ Vodafone Group PLC ADR	Telecom	—	11.74	1.77
Microsoft	Software	36.1	8.95	1.63
Target	Consumer	22.3	36.14	1.63
US Bancorp	Financial	14.2	10.46	1.53
XL Capital	Financial	20.1	2.80	1.33
Home Depot	Consumer	19.0	21.47	1.33
Tyco International	Ind Mtrls	25.1	35.41	1.32
⊕ State Street	Financial	15.3	-4.41	1.32
Diamond Offshore Drillin	Energy	—	97.23	1.31
⊖ Verizon Communications	Telecom	32.4	20.25	1.23
Viacom B	Media	36.1	-17.44	1.23
American International G	Financial	16.2	-0.53	1.22
Lockheed Martin	Ind Mtrls	19.9	9.97	1.21
Altria Group	Goods	13.3	18.38	1.13
⊕ Wyeth	Health	17.0	2.73	1.13
Waste Management	Business	18.9	3.81	1.13

Current Investment Style

Value Blnd Growth — Large Mid Small

Market Cap	%
Giant	42.1
Large	35.5
Mid	22.5
Small	0.0
Micro	0.0
Avg $mil: 29,023	

Value Measures		Rel Category
Price/Earnings	16.75	0.99
Price/Book	2.58	0.98
Price/Sales	1.60	1.11
Price/Cash Flow	7.82	1.02
Dividend Yield %	1.82	1.23

Growth Measures	%	Rel Category
Long-Term Erngs	11.69	1.01
Book Value	7.82	1.01
Sales	6.30	1.10
Cash Flow	2.80	0.30
Historical Erngs	9.24	0.78

Profitability	%	Rel Category
Return on Equity	16.84	0.96
Return on Assets	9.07	1.05
Net Margin	10.71	0.94

Sector Weightings	% of Stocks	Rel S&P 500	3 Year High	3 Year Low
Info	19.40	0.90		
Software	1.85	0.43	2	2
Hardware	5.46	0.54	6	4
Media	6.59	1.72	7	4
Telecom	5.50	1.75	6	4
Service	50.05	1.08		
Health	9.58	0.77	14	10
Consumer	7.59	0.84	10	8
Business	8.68	2.14	9	8
Financial	24.20	1.17	28	24
Mfg	30.56	0.95		
Goods	7.84	0.84	9	6
Ind Mtrls	12.67	1.00	13	8
Energy	8.73	1.22	9	7
Utilities	1.32	0.45	1	1

Composition

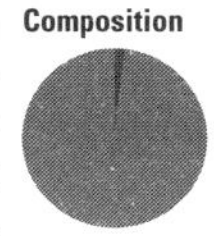

Cash	1.9
Stocks	98.1
Bonds	0.0
Other	0.0
Foreign (% of Stock)	5.6

Address:	T. Rowe Price Associates, Inc. Baltimore MD 21202 800-638-5660
Web Address:	www.troweprice.com
Inception:	12-31-92
Advisor:	T. Rowe Price Associates, Inc.
Subadvisor:	None
NTF Plans:	N/A

Minimum Purchase:	$2500	Add: $100	IRA: $1000
Min Auto Inv Plan:	$50	Add: $50	
Sales Fees:	No-load		
Management Fee:	0.52%		
Actual Fees:	Mgt:0.52%	Dist:	
Expense Projections:	3Yr:$265	5Yr:$460	10Yr:$1025
Income Distrib:	Quarterly		

T. Rowe Price Emg Mkt St

Analyst Pick

Ticker	Load	NAV	Yield	Total Assets	Mstar Category
PRMSX	None	$19.41	0.2%	$753 mil	Diversified Emerging Mkts

Governance and Management

Fiduciary Grade: B

Portfolio Manager(s)

This fund is run by a deep and experienced team of managers based in London and various emerging markets.

Strategy

Chris Alderson and his comanagers hunt for companies that have strong earnings growth and are leaders in their industries. They're not averse to accumulating substantial stakes in growth industries, but they build them slowly and avoid the raciest issues. Management may use a wide range of hedging tools to protect against adverse currency movements or to generate added returns.

Historical Profile

Return Average
Risk Above Avg
Rating ★★★ Neutral

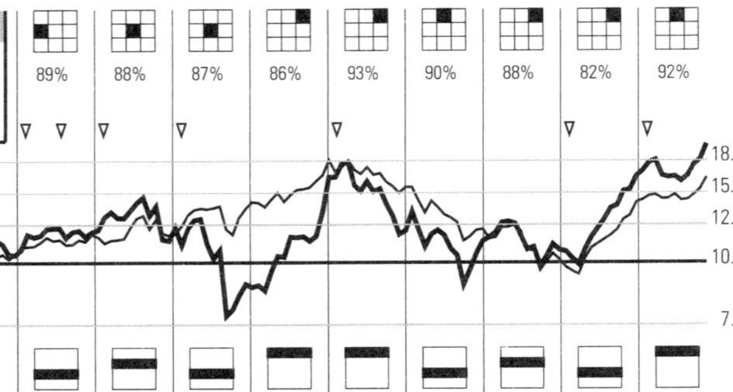

Investment Style
Equity
Stock %

▼ Manager Change
▽ Partial Manager Change

Growth of $10,000
▬ Investment Values of Fund
— Investment Values of MSCI EAFE

Performance Quartile (within Category)

1993	1994	1995	1996	1997	1998	1999	2000	2001	2002	2003	12-04	History
—	—	10.76	11.69	11.68	8.28	15.52	11.43	10.77	10.22	15.47	19.41	NAV
—	—	7.70*	11.82	1.23	-28.75	87.44	-26.35	-5.69	-4.92	52.30	26.98	Total Return %
—	—	—	5.77	-0.55	-48.68	60.41	-12.16	15.73	11.02	13.71	6.73	+/-MSCI EAFE
—	—	—	7.89	14.68	-1.08	23.35	5.55	-1.01	3.05	0.71	4.53	+/-MSCI EmrMkt
—	—	0.00	0.37	0.00	0.34	0.00	0.00	0.09	0.19	0.88	0.26	Income Return %
—	—	—	11.45	1.23	-29.09	87.44	-26.35	-5.78	-5.11	51.42	26.72	Capital Return %
—	—	—	57	40	59	16	20	71	40	61	20	Total Rtn % Rank Cat
—	—	0.01	0.04	0.00	0.04	0.00	0.00	0.01	0.02	0.09	0.04	Income $
—	—	0.00	0.30	0.15	0.00	0.00	0.00	0.00	0.00	0.00	0.18	Capital Gains $
—	—	1.75	1.75	1.75	1.75	1.75	1.50	1.58	1.51	1.43	—	Expense Ratio %
—	—	0.54	0.44	0.21	0.46	-0.14	-0.12	0.19	0.41	1.12	—	Income Ratio %
—	—	—	42	84	54	59	56	70	70	66	—	Turnover Rate %
—	—	17	73	124	72	124	152	155	170	439	753	Net Assets $mil

Performance 12-31-04

	1st Qtr	2nd Qtr	3rd Qtr	4th Qtr	Total
2000	8.89	-10.30	-12.20	-14.12	-26.35
2001	-8.66	6.71	-24.51	28.18	-5.69
2002	11.14	-7.60	-15.73	9.87	-4.92
2003	-7.93	22.85	13.93	18.18	52.30
2004	9.63	-8.96	6.80	19.13	26.98

Trailing	Total Return%	+/- MSCI EAFE	+/- MSCI EmrMkt	%Rank Cat	Growth of $10,000
3 Mo	19.13	3.81	2.32	12	11,913
6 Mo	27.23	12.23	1.78	31	12,723
1 Yr	26.98	6.73	4.53	20	12,698
3 Yr Avg	22.51	10.62	2.97	37	18,387
5 Yr Avg	5.01	6.14	2.92	35	12,769
10 Yr Avg	—	—	—	—	—
15 Yr Avg	—	—	—	—	—

Tax Analysis	Tax-Adj Rtn%	%Rank Cat	Tax-Cost Rat	%Rank Cat
3 Yr (estimated)	22.30	30	0.17	24
5 Yr (estimated)	4.90	30	0.10	17
10 Yr (estimated)	—	—	—	—

Potential Capital Gain Exposure: 26% of assets

Rating and Risk

Time Period	Load-Adj Return %	Morningstar Rtn vs Cat	Morningstar Risk vs Cat	Morningstar Risk-Adj Rating
1 Yr	26.98			
3 Yr	22.51	Avg	Avg	★★★
5 Yr	5.01	Avg	+Avg	★★★
10 Yr	—	—	—	—
Incept	7.79			

Other Measures	Standard Index S&P 500	Best Fit Index MSCI EmrMkt
Alpha	10.0	2.7
Beta	0.99	0.99
R-Squared	77	99
Standard Deviation	21.58	
Mean	22.51	
Sharpe Ratio	0.99	

Portfolio Analysis 09-30-04

Share change since 06-04 Total Stocks:157	Sector	Country	% Assets
⊖ Samsung Electronics	Goods	Korea	2.95
⊕ America Movil SA ADR	Telecom	Mexico	2.82
Petroleo Brasileiro Sa P	Energy	Brazil	2.79
⊕ Vimpel-Communications AD	Telecom	Russia	1.80
Cathay Finl Hldg	Financial	Taiwan	1.59
Wal-Mart de Mexico	Consumer	Mexico	1.57
Impala Platinum Hldgs Lt	Ind Mtrls	South Africa	1.55
Naspers Ltd	Media	South Africa	1.49
Mobile TeleSystems ADR	Telecom	Russia	1.41
⊕ Makhteshim-Agan Industri	Ind Mtrls	Israel	1.36
☼ ChinaTrust Financial Hld	Financial	Taiwan	1.36
⊖ PetroKazakhstan	Energy	United States	1.27
⊖ Kookmin Bank	Financial	Korea	1.25
Lukoil ADR	Energy	Russia	1.22
Zee Telefilms Ltd	Media	India	1.21
Sanlam Ltd	Financial	South Africa	1.21
⊕ Teva Pharmaceutical Indu	Health	Israel	1.19
S-Oil	Energy	Korea	1.16
Bk Hapoalim B.M.	Financial	Israel	1.14
☼ Hyundai Motor	—	Korea	1.10

Current Investment Style

Value Blnd Growth (Large / Mid / Small)

Market Cap	%
Giant	22.4
Large	28.3
Mid	40.7
Small	6.2
Micro	2.4
Avg $mil: 3,765	

Value Measures		Rel Category
Price/Earnings	10.18	1.12
Price/Book	1.34	0.86
Price/Sales	0.89	1.07
Price/Cash Flow	3.21	0.73
Dividend Yield %	2.99	1.09

Growth Measures	%	Rel Category
Long-Term Erngs	17.85	0.92
Book Value	8.22	2.37
Sales	10.23	0.88
Cash Flow	9.32	1.25
Historical Erngs	-0.93	NMF

Composition

Cash	2.3	Bonds	0.0
Stocks	92.0	Other	5.7
Foreign (% of Stock)			97.0

Sector Weightings	% of Stocks	Rel MSCI EAFE	3 Year High	3 Year Low
Info	26.22	1.58		
Software	1.66	1.54	3	1
Hardware	3.38	0.93	9	2
Media	5.94	2.61	6	1
Telecom	15.24	1.59	18	11
Service	32.62	0.73		
Health	1.33	0.18	4	1
Consumer	5.81	1.15	7	3
Business	3.98	0.73	6	4
Financial	21.50	0.80	25	18
Mfg	41.17	1.06		
Goods	13.72	1.00	22	14
Ind Mtrls	15.21	1.24	17	7
Energy	11.64	1.58	12	4
Utilities	0.60	0.11	1	0

Regional Exposure	% Stock		% Stock
UK/W. Europe	3	N. America	3
Japan	0	Latn America	20
Asia X Japan	45	Other	29

Country Exposure	% Stock		% Stock
South Korea	17	South Africa	9
Taiwan	10	Mexico	9
Brazil	10		

Morningstar's Take by Arijit Dutta 12-22-04

T. Rowe Price Emerging Markets Stock remains a sensible way to play emerging markets.

Although many emerging-markets funds focus on either top-down analysis or bottom-up stock-picking, this fund's managers try to strike a balance between the two. They begin their process by using macroeconomic screens to determine the portfolio's country allocations, and then proceed to pick stocks.

This balanced approach has contributed to a solid long-term performance. The fund's five-year trailing returns rank in the category's 28th percentile, and since its 1995 inception the fund has outperformed two thirds of its peers. This year's 22.3% return (through Dec. 20) is in the same vein. While the fund's significant underweight in industrial materials (a bet on slowing Chinese demand) did not pan out as expected, managers more than made up the ground with strong telecom and financials picks.

The fund's long-term risk profile is also solid, thanks in part to the managers' moderate approach to growth investing. While they like to buy companies with sustainable competitive advantages and strong growth prospects, they don't go overboard in their tolerance of high valuations. For example, they departed from pricey telecom stocks in 1999 and moved out of pricey Indian automakers in early 2004. Both moves proved timely and protected the fund from losses. Management further controls risk by limiting exposure to markets that may appear lucrative from a macro standpoint but lack depth and liquidity. For instance, the fund has a less than 1% stake in Argentina and none in Pakistan, although management recognizes the reforms in those markets.

While they may not always get their macro calls right, a portfolio well diversified across countries and sectors has shielded investors well. This is a solid emerging-markets fund.

Address:	100 E Pratt St Baltimore MD 21202 800-638-5660
Web Address:	www.troweprice.com
Inception:	03-31-95*
Advisor:	T. Rowe Price Associates, Inc.
Subadvisor:	None
NTF Plans:	N/A

Minimum Purchase:	$2500	Add: $100	IRA: $1000
Min Auto Inv Plan:	$50	Add: $50	
Sales Fees:	No-load, 2.00%R		
Management Fee:	1.07%		
Actual Fees:	Mgt:1.07%	Dist:	
Expense Projections:	3Yr:$452	5Yr:$782	10Yr:$1713
Income Distrib:	Annually		

T. Rowe Price Eq-Inc

Analyst Pick	Ticker	Load	NAV	Yield	Total Assets	Mstar Category
✔	PRFDX	None	$26.59	1.5%	$18,291 mil	Large Value

Governance and Management

Fiduciary Grade: B

Portfolio Manager(s)

Seasoned. Brian Rogers has managed this offering since its 1985 inception. He's backed by T. Rowe Price's deep bench of analysts. In January 2004, Rogers became T. Rowe Price's chief investment officer. He says he invests a large portion of his assets in the fund.

Strategy

This offering employs a true-blue approach to value investing. Longtime manager Brian Rogers strives to keep the fund's yield at least 25% higher than that of the S&P 500 Index, and he looks for companies trading cheaply relative to their historic price multiples. This strategy often leads him to load up on traditional value sectors, such as energy and industrial cyclicals, although he's willing to delve into growth-oriented areas such as health care, technology, and telecom when the price is right.

Historical Profile

Return Above Avg
Risk Average
Rating ★★★★ Above Avg

Investment Style
Equity
Stock %

1993	1994	1995	1996	1997	1998	1999	2000	2001	2002	2003	12-04
	86%	89%	93%	93%	92%	94%	96%	96%	94%		

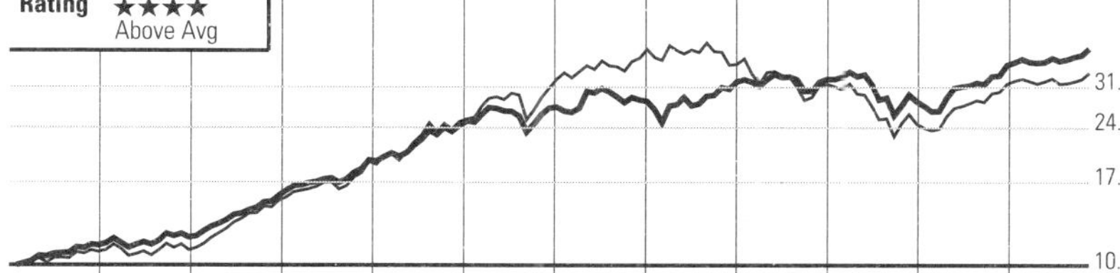

▼ Manager Change
▽ Partial Manager Change

Growth of $10,000
— Investment Values of Fund
— Investment Values of S&P 500

Performance Quartile (within Category)

1993	1994	1995	1996	1997	1998	1999	2000	2001	2002	2003	12-04	History
16.65	15.98	20.01	22.54	26.07	26.32	24.81	24.67	23.65	19.79	24.16	26.59	NAV
14.84	4.53	33.35	20.40	28.82	9.23	3.82	13.12	1.64	-13.04	25.78	15.05	Total Return %
4.78	3.22	-4.18	-2.54	-4.53	-19.34	-17.22	22.22	13.52	9.05	-2.89	4.18	+/-S&P 500
-3.23	6.51	-5.01	-1.24	-6.36	-6.40	-3.53	6.11	7.23	2.48	-4.25	-1.44	+/-Russ 1000 VI
3.52	3.61	4.15	3.30	2.99	2.40	2.04	2.12	1.49	1.54	1.99	1.76	Income Return %
11.32	0.92	29.20	17.10	25.83	6.83	1.78	11.00	0.15	-14.58	23.79	13.29	Capital Return %
45	8	50	47	34	71	54	31	21	12	69	23	Total Rtn % Rank Cat
0.54	0.59	0.65	0.65	0.66	0.61	0.53	0.51	0.36	0.36	0.39	0.42	Income $
0.72	0.81	0.54	0.84	2.14	1.49	1.97	2.64	1.01	0.45	0.27	0.72	Capital Gains $
0.91	0.88	0.85	0.81	0.79	0.77	0.77	0.78	0.80	0.79	0.78	—	Expense Ratio %
3.23	3.63	3.69	3.08	2.67	2.26	1.95	2.01	1.53	1.72	1.80	—	Income Ratio %
31	36	21	25	24	23	22	22	17	15	12	—	Turnover Rate %
2,848	3,204	5,215	7,818	12,771	13,495	12,321	10,187	10,128	8,954	12,167	15,947	Net Assets $mil

Performance 12-31-04

	1st Qtr	2nd Qtr	3rd Qtr	4th Qtr	Total
2000	-2.92	0.16	6.88	8.85	13.12
2001	-2.81	5.76	-8.28	7.81	1.64
2002	4.62	-7.93	-17.33	9.21	-13.04
2003	-6.02	16.82	1.49	12.90	25.78
2004	1.91	2.59	0.72	9.25	15.05

Trailing	Total Return%	+/- S&P 500	+/- Russ 1000 VI	%Rank Cat	Growth of $10,000
3 Mo	9.25	0.02	-1.13	46	10,925
6 Mo	10.05	2.86	-2.03	34	11,005
1 Yr	15.05	4.18	-1.44	23	11,505
3 Yr Avg	7.96	4.38	-0.61	19	12,583
5 Yr Avg	7.67	9.97	2.40	17	14,470
10 Yr Avg	13.00	0.93	-0.83	16	33,946
15 Yr Avg	11.94	1.01	-0.09	15	54,297

Tax Analysis	Tax-Adj Rtn%	%Rank Cat	Tax-Cost Rat	%Rank Cat
3 Yr (estimated)	6.87	20	1.01	65
5 Yr (estimated)	6.05	20	1.50	79
10 Yr (estimated)	10.79	16	1.96	62

Potential Capital Gain Exposure: 8% of assets

Rating and Risk

Time Period	Load-Adj Return %	Morningstar Rtn vs Cat	Morningstar Risk vs Cat	Morningstar Risk-Adj Rating
1 Yr	15.05			
3 Yr	7.96	+Avg	Avg	★★★★
5 Yr	7.67	+Avg	Avg	★★★★
10 Yr	13.00	+Avg	-Avg	★★★★
Incept	13.53			

Other Measures	Standard Index S&P 500	Best Fit Index Russ 1000 VI
Alpha	4.4	-0.3
Beta	0.92	0.95
R-Squared	92	97
Standard Deviation	15.56	
Mean	7.96	
Sharpe Ratio	0.43	

Portfolio Analysis 09-30-04

Share change since 06-04 Total Stocks:117	Sector	PE	YTD Ret%	% Assets
⊕ J P Morgan Chase	Financial	19.4	9.97	2.22
Gen Elec	Ind Mtrls	22.8	20.68	2.10
⊕ ChevronTexaco	Energy	7.7	25.57	2.01
⊖ ExxonMobil	Energy	13.9	28.04	1.97
Honeywell International	Ind Mtrls	20.5	8.21	1.63
⊕ Bank of America	Financial	12.3	21.50	1.63
⊕ Merck	Health	11.4	-27.76	1.55
⊖ Amerada Hess	Energy	10.1	57.47	1.53
⊕ Marsh & McLennan Compani	Financial	13.4	-29.80	1.50
⊕ Viacom B	Media	36.1	-17.44	1.47
⊕ Royal Dutch Petroleum AD	Energy	—	14.31	1.45
⊖ Verizon Communications	Telecom	32.4	20.25	1.42
⊕ New York Times A	Media	20.8	-13.42	1.34
Bristol-Myers Squibb	Health	17.7	-7.27	1.33
⊕ Comcast A	Media	81.0	1.49	1.33
Johnson & Johnson	Health	20.6	25.17	1.32
Union Pacific	Business	19.6	-1.28	1.28
Wyeth	Health	17.0	2.73	1.17
⊕ Dow Jones & Company	Media	32.0	-11.70	1.14
⊕ International Paper	Ind Mtrls	—	-0.20	1.14

Current Investment Style

Value Blnd Growth

Market Cap	%
Giant	37.1
Large	38.7
Mid	23.7
Small	0.5
Micro	0.0
Avg $mil: 26,568	

Value Measures		Rel Category
Price/Earnings	15.84	1.05
Price/Book	2.30	1.01
Price/Sales	1.31	1.10
Price/Cash Flow	7.10	1.11
Dividend Yield %	2.31	1.13

Growth Measures	%	Rel Category
Long-Term Erngs	9.65	0.93
Book Value	3.79	0.67
Sales	2.69	0.64
Cash Flow	29.18	5.59
Historical Erngs	6.71	0.57

Profitability	%	Rel Category
Return on Equity	13.57	1.04
Return on Assets	7.42	0.95
Net Margin	9.32	0.91

Sector Weightings	% of Stocks	Rel S&P 500	3 Year High	Low
Info	18.93	0.88		
Software	1.09	0.25	1	0
Hardware	3.79	0.37	4	2
Media	8.40	2.19	8	4
Telecom	5.65	1.79	8	6
Service	38.15	0.82		
Health	10.28	0.82	11	8
Consumer	4.62	0.51	6	5
Business	3.40	0.84	6	3
Financial	19.85	0.96	20	18
Mfg	42.93	1.34		
Goods	12.27	1.32	15	11
Ind Mtrls	15.15	1.20	17	15
Energy	10.94	1.53	12	10
Utilities	4.57	1.54	5	2

Composition

Cash	4.2
Stocks	94.0
Bonds	0.0
Other	1.8
Foreign (% of Stock)	4.4

Morningstar's Take by Christopher Davis 12-27-04

T. Rowe Price Equity-Income Fund has been hunting for value in unusual places, but that's likely to work in its favor eventually.

Investing can make for some strange bedfellows. When Brian Rogers, the veteran skipper of this offering, met with a group of Morningstar analysts in our Chicago offices in early 2004, he pointed out his portfolio more closely resembled that of large-growth sibling T. Rowe Price Blue Chip Growth than it had at any time in recent memory. Although one would be hard-pressed to confuse the two offerings, many of Blue Chip Growth skipper Larry Puglia's favorites also appear attractive according to Rogers' criteria. General Electric, a top holding at Equity-Income and Blue Chip Growth, boasts a handsome dividend yield and is historically cheap--two characteristics Rogers prizes. Yet Puglia likes the company for its steady earnings growth and ample free cash flow.

GE is a less-than-traditional holding for a value manager, but Rogers has gravitated to a number of beaten-down growth-oriented names in recent years. For instance, he owns a passel of big-cap drugmakers such as Merck, Wyeth, and Johnson & Johnson, which once were staples in many large-growth portfolios. More recently, he built a small stake in biotech drugmaker MedImmune. The stock has languished amid disappointing sales of FluMist, an intranasal influenza vaccine. However, Rogers surmises the market is undervaluing the long-term potential of the firm's currently available drugs, as well as its pipeline of new products.

Rogers' picks often don't pan out quickly--the fund's health-care investments have suffered greatly this year, for example--but they have paid off handsomely over time. Indeed, all of the fund's long-term returns land in or near the large-value group's top 20%. Moreover, its volatility has been well below the category average, thanks to Rogers' income-oriented approach. All in all, we consider this one of the best choices in the large-value category.

Address:	100 E Pratt St Baltimore MD 21202 800-638-5660
Web Address:	www.troweprice.com
Inception:	10-31-85
Advisor:	T. Rowe Price Associates, Inc.
Subadvisor:	None
NTF Plans:	N/A

Minimum Purchase:	$2500	Add: $100	IRA: $1000
Min Auto Inv Plan:	$50	Add: $50	
Sales Fees:	No-load		
Management Fee:	0.57%		
Actual Fees:	Mgt:0.57%	Dist:	
Expense Projections:	3Yr:$249	5Yr:$433	10Yr:$966
Income Distrib:	Quarterly		

T. Rowe Price Fincl Svcs

Analyst Pick	Ticker	Load	NAV	Yield	Total Assets	Mstar Category
	PRISX	None	$23.50	0.7%	$412 mil	Specialty-Financial

Governance and Management

Fiduciary Grade: B

Portfolio Manager(s)

Michael Holton is a longtime T. Rowe Price analyst who specialized in financial-services issues for a couple of years before becoming this fund's manager in November 2002. He receives the support of several analysts. Holton invests in this fund through his firm's 401(k) plan.

Strategy

Like his predecessor, Anna Dopkin, manager Michael Holton seeks well-established companies with strong management, above-average earnings-growth rates, and strong market share. The fund's various managers have also invested with a long-term time horizon, which has kept turnover low. The portfolio tends to be well-diversified by subsector but is fairly concentrated in individual issues, with about 50 stocks.

Historical Profile

Return: Average
Risk: Average
Rating: ★★★ Neutral

Investment Style: Equity Stock %

1996	1997	1998	1999	2000	2001	2002	2003	12-04
88%	87%	97%	96%	88%	86%	100%	99%	99%

▼ Manager Change
▽ Partial Manager Change

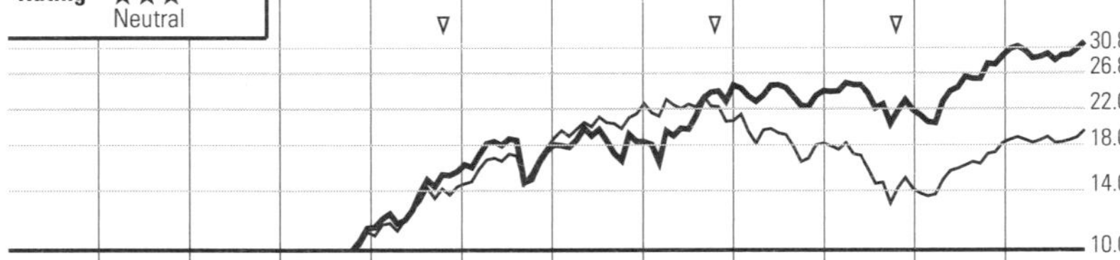

Growth of $10,000
— Investment Values of Fund
— Investment Values of S&P 500

Performance Quartile (within Category)

1993	1994	1995	1996	1997	1998	1999	2000	2001	2002	2003	12-04	History
—	—	—	11.31	15.56	16.82	16.12	21.38	18.84	16.75	21.86	23.50	NAV
—	—	—	13.40*	41.44	11.55	1.70	36.76	-3.13	-10.10	35.08	13.42	Total Return %
—	—	—	—	8.09	-17.02	-19.34	45.86	8.75	11.99	6.41	2.55	+/-S&P 500
—	—	—	—	-7.50	4.04	0.18	9.82	3.25	2.25	2.85	0.03	+/-DJ Finance
—	—	—	0.00	0.88	1.03	0.59	0.56	0.70	0.69	1.37	0.78	Income Return %
—	—	—	—	40.56	10.52	1.11	36.20	-3.83	-10.79	33.71	12.64	Capital Return %
—	—	—	—	79	38	28	10	32	38	34	42	Total Rtn % Rank Cat
—	—	—	0.03	0.10	0.16	0.10	0.09	0.15	0.13	0.23	0.17	Income $
—	—	—	0.00	0.33	0.34	0.85	0.55	1.68	0.06	0.51	1.10	Capital Gains $
—	—	—	1.25	1.25	1.19	1.14	1.00	0.97	1.00	0.97	—	Expense Ratio %
—	—	—	1.71	1.15	0.94	0.50	0.69	0.69	0.80	1.16	—	Income Ratio %
—	—	—	6	46	47	37	33	55	50	51	—	Turnover Rate %
—	—	—	30	177	224	159	337	309	265	371	412	Net Assets $mil

Performance 12-31-04

	1st Qtr	2nd Qtr	3rd Qtr	4th Qtr	Total
2000	6.20	0.88	22.76	3.99	36.76
2001	-8.61	9.57	-10.74	8.38	-3.13
2002	4.46	-5.49	-15.54	7.81	-10.10
2003	-6.81	21.59	4.90	13.64	35.08
2004	2.88	-1.78	-0.54	12.85	13.42

Trailing	Total Return%	+/- S&P 500	+/- DJ Finance	%Rank Cat	Growth of $10,000
3 Mo	12.85	3.62	3.90	14	11,285
6 Mo	12.24	5.05	1.97	30	11,224
1 Yr	13.42	2.55	0.03	42	11,342
3 Yr Avg	11.26	7.68	1.73	39	13,773
5 Yr Avg	12.78	15.08	3.45	33	18,246
10 Yr Avg	—	—	—	—	—
15 Yr Avg	—	—	—	—	—

Tax Analysis	Tax-Adj Rtn%	%Rank Cat	Tax-Cost Rat	%Rank Cat
3 Yr (estimated)	10.38	32	0.79	46
5 Yr (estimated)	11.59	32	1.06	54
10 Yr (estimated)	—	—	—	—

Potential Capital Gain Exposure: 27% of assets

Rating and Risk

Time Period	Load-Adj Return %	Morningstar Rtn vs Cat	Morningstar Risk vs Cat	Morningstar Risk-Adj Rating
1 Yr	13.42			
3 Yr	11.26	Avg	+Avg	★★★
5 Yr	12.78	Avg	Avg	★★★
10 Yr	—	—	—	—
Incept	15.65			

Other Measures	Standard Index S&P 500	Best Fit Index DJ Finance
Alpha	7.6	1.4
Beta	0.99	1.04
R-Squared	84	94
Standard Deviation	18.09	
Mean	11.26	
Sharpe Ratio	0.55	

Portfolio Analysis 09-30-04

Share change since 06-04 Total Stocks:46	Sector	PE	YTD Ret%	% Assets
J P Morgan Chase	Financial	19.4	9.97	5.08
⊕ Lehman Brothers Holdings	Financial	11.7	14.22	4.99
Radian Group	Financial	11.9	9.40	4.84
⊕ Bank of New York	Financial	18.5	3.52	4.70
Mellon Financial	Financial	16.2	-0.78	4.46
Citigroup	Financial	15.3	2.72	4.13
⊕ MGIC Investment	Financial	12.7	21.42	4.11
Freddie Mac	Financial	10.6	28.75	4.11
Morgan Stanley	Financial	14.2	-2.25	4.10
⊕ Merrill Lynch & Company	Financial	12.6	3.12	3.83
⊕ Ameritrade Holding	Financial	20.3	0.79	3.71
⊕ Legg Mason	Financial	22.3	43.56	3.44
US Bancorp	Financial	14.2	10.46	3.37
⊖ Comerica	Financial	14.8	12.87	3.26
⊕ State Street	Financial	15.3	-4.41	3.19
⊖ Franklin Resources	Financial	26.0	34.62	3.15
Goldman Sachs Group	Financial	12.3	6.49	2.70
Ohio Casualty	Financial	14.4	33.70	2.65
Principal Financial Grou	Financial	16.0	25.56	2.47
⊕ Royal Bank Of Scotland G	Financial	—	—	2.30

Current Investment Style

Value Blnd Growth; Large Mid Small

Market Cap	%
Giant	32.3
Large	37.5
Mid	21.8
Small	8.4
Micro	0.0
Avg $mil: 16,537	

Value Measures		Rel Category
Price/Earnings	12.86	0.99
Price/Book	1.83	0.96
Price/Sales	1.81	0.97
Price/Cash Flow	5.10	1.37
Dividend Yield %	1.60	0.78

Growth Measures	%	Rel Category
Long-Term Erngs	13.24	1.13
Book Value	9.24	0.94
Sales	-1.90	NMF
Cash Flow	6.37	0.45
Historical Erngs	16.69	0.84

Profitability	%	Rel Category
Return on Equity	14.96	0.93
Return on Assets	11.74	1.13
Net Margin	17.32	0.98

Industry Weightings	% of Stocks	Rel Cat
Intl Banks	10.4	0.8
Banks	11.5	0.5
Real Estate	0.0	0.0
Sec Mgmt	39.1	2.5
S & Ls	3.0	0.3
Prop & Reins	14.1	1.0
Life Ins	5.7	1.8
Misc. Ins	7.3	2.0
Other	8.9	0.6

Composition

Cash	1.0
Stocks	99.0
Bonds	0.0
Other	0.0
Foreign (% of Stock)	3.4

Morningstar's Take by Laura Pavlenko Lutton 12-23-04

T. Rowe Price Financial Services is a sensible choice among financials funds.

This fund takes a diversified approach to the sector. Manager Michael Holton spreads the fund's assets across all of the major industries in the sector, investing in about 50 firms that he thinks have the best growth prospects, strong market shares, and reasonable stock prices.

Holton isn't afraid to make significant subsector bets when his stock-by-stock research points to a group of attractive stocks. Heading into 2004, for example, Holton sold names that had been winners in recent years, including regional banks, and loaded up on stocks that he thought would perform better as the economy strengthened and interest rates ticked up, namely securities processors, asset managers, and brokerage firms.

Many a talented manager has been tripped up by poorly timing subsector bets, and that initially was the case here. For the most part, Holton's move into economically sensitive stocks was too early: At midyear, the fund was struggling near the bottom of the financials category. Since then, however, the fund has made up ground. Several picks, including mortgage-insurer MGIC Investment, have turned in strong returns, and the fund avoided many of the insurance stocks that here hit this fall by regulatory concerns. Thus, the fund's 13.03% return for the year to date through Dec. 22, 2004, is above the financials group norm and strong relative to more-diversified funds in the category.

Since Holton has been here for just two years, it's difficult to predict whether he'll consistently be in the right place at the right time. But we have reason to believe he'll be successful over the long term. The former financials analyst is backed by a deep bench of researchers at T. Rowe Price who have helped previous managers build impressively consistent winning long-term record. In short, we think this fund has a lot going for it--so much so we've made it an Analyst Pick.

Address:	100 E Pratt Street Baltimore MD 21202 800-638-5660
Web Address:	www.troweprice.com
Inception:	09-30-96 *
Advisor:	T. Rowe Price Associates, Inc.
Subadvisor:	None
NTF Plans:	N/A

Minimum Purchase:	$2500	Add: $100	IRA: $1000
Min Auto Inv Plan:	$50	Add: $50	
Sales Fees:	No-load		
Management Fee:	0.67%		
Actual Fees:	Mgt:0.67%	Dist:	
Expense Projections:	3Yr:$309	5Yr:$536	10Yr:$1190
Income Distrib:	Annually		

T. Rowe Price Glob Tech

Ticker	Load	NAV	Yield	Total Assets	Mstar Category
PRGTX	None	$5.50	0.0%	$92 mil	Specialty-Technology

Governance and Management

Fiduciary Grade: B

Portfolio Manager(s)

Rob Gensler, who took over here in January 2002, has been a telecom analyst with T. Rowe Price for seven years and has been lead manager of the excellent T. Rowe Price Media & Telecommunications since January 2000. He is supported by one of the industry's largest staffs of technology and related analysts.

Strategy

This fund offers a broad mix of technology, telecommunications-service, and media stocks. In addition, management devotes a significant chunk of assets to foreign stocks. Manager Rob Gensler, who took over in January 2002, emphasizes companies with strong free cash flow, sound balance sheets, and improving positions in their industries. He also pays more attention to a stock's valuation than many other tech managers.

Historical Profile

Return High
Risk Below Avg
Rating ★★★★★ Highest

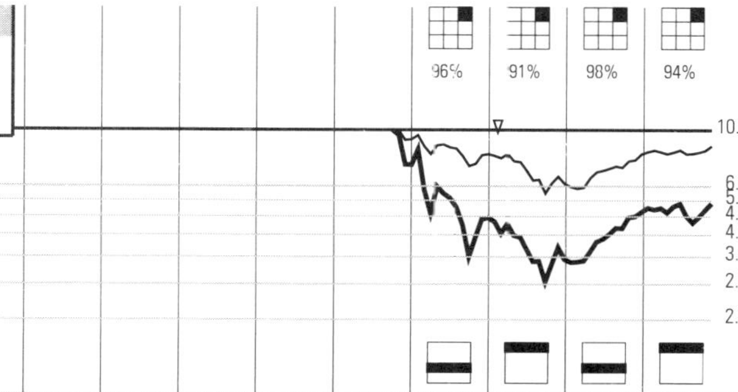

Investment Style
Equity
Stock %

▼ Manager Change
∇ Partial Manager Change

Growth of $10,000
— Investment Values of Fund
— Investment Values of S&P 500

Performance Quartile (within Category)

1993	1994	1995	1996	1997	1998	1999	2000	2001	2002	2003	12-04	History
—	—	—	—	—	—	—	7.43	4.75	3.33	4.99	5.50	NAV
—	—	—	—	—	—	—	-25.70*	-36.07	-29.89	49.85	10.22	Total Return %
—	—	—	—	—	—	—	—	-24.19	-7.80	21.18	-0.65	+/-S&P 500
—	—	—	—	—	—	—	—	-20.48	3.44	-2.29	-1.51	+/-PSE Tech 100
—	—	—	—	—	—	—	0.00	0.00	0.00	0.00	0.00	Income Return %
—	—	—	—	—	—	—	—	-36.07	-29.89	49.85	10.22	Capital Return %
—	—	—	—	—	—	—	—	51	6	62	23	Total Rtn % Rank Cat
—	—	—	—	—	—	—	0.00	0.00	0.00	0.00	0.00	Income $
—	—	—	—	—	—	—	0.00	0.00	0.00	0.00	0.00	Capital Gains $
—	—	—	—	—	—	—	—	1.50	1.50	1.50	—	Expense Ratio %
—	—	—	—	—	—	—	—	-1.08	-1.15	-1.17	—	Income Ratio %
—	—	—	—	—	—	—	—	189	211	151	—	Turnover Rate %
—	—	—	—	—	—	—	131	84	55	85	92	Net Assets $mil

Performance 12-31-04

	1st Qtr	2nd Qtr	3rd Qtr	4th Qtr	Total
2000	—	—	—	-25.70	-25.70 *
2001	-33.78	14.02	-39.39	39.71	-36.07
2002	-5.05	-19.73	-24.03	21.09	-29.89
2003	-1.20	20.36	9.60	14.98	49.85
2004	3.21	3.88	-10.47	14.82	10.22

Trailing	Total Return%	+/- S&P 500	+/- PSE Tech 100	%Rank Cat	Growth of $10,000
3 Mo	14.82	5.59	0.30	59	11,482
6 Mo	2.80	-4.39	-3.13	53	10,280
1 Yr	10.22	-0.65	-1.51	23	11,022
3 Yr Avg	5.01	1.43	0.75	7	11,580
5 Yr Avg	—	—	—	—	—
10 Yr Avg	—	—	—	—	—
15 Yr Avg	—	—	—	—	—

Tax Analysis	Tax-Adj Rtn%	%Rank Cat	Tax-Cost Rat	%Rank Cat
3 Yr (estimated)	5.01	5	0.00	1
5 Yr (estimated)	—	—	—	—
10 Yr (estimated)	—	—	—	—

Potential Capital Gain Exposure: -85% of assets

Rating and Risk

Time Period	Load-Adj Return %	Morningstar Rtn vs Cat	Morningstar Risk vs Cat	Morningstar Risk-Adj Rating
1 Yr	10.22			
3 Yr	5.01	High	-Avg	★★★★★
5 Yr	—	—	—	—
10 Yr	—	—	—	—
Incept	-13.12			

Other Measures	Standard Index S&P 500	Best Fit Index PSE Tech 100
Alpha	1.6	0.9
Beta	1.56	0.96
R-Squared	84	95
Standard Deviation	27.59	
Mean	5.01	
Sharpe Ratio	0.13	

Portfolio Analysis 09-30-04

Share change since 06-04 Total Stocks:55	Sector	PE	YTD Ret%	% Assets
⊕ Dell	Hardware	34.0	24.01	9.77
⊕ Red Hat	Software	70.6	-28.88	6.72
☼ Samsung Electnc	—	—	—	3.92
Cisco Systems	Hardware	24.5	-20.26	3.84
⊕ Infosys Technologies Ltd	Software	—	—	3.59
Intel	Hardware	19.8	-26.56	3.25
⊕ Veritas Software	Software	23.7	-22.88	3.11
⊕ Qualcomm	Hardware	42.0	58.20	2.92
☼ Texas Instruments	Hardware	21.1	-15.90	2.92
⊕ Xilinx	Hardware	25.2	-22.82	2.86
⊖ Ericsson AB (publ)	Hardware	—	—	2.71
⊕ Oracle	Software	25.4	3.70	2.32
⊖ Yahoo	Media	95.1	67.36	2.16
⊖ eBay	Consumer	81.6	80.07	2.06
⊕ Mercury Interactive	Software	60.5	-6.35	1.96
⊕ AMIS Holdings	Hardware	—	—	1.94
⊖ ChoicePoint	Business	30.4	20.74	1.86
⊕ Corning	Hardware	—	12.85	1.80
⊖ International Game Tech	Consumer	28.1	-2.49	1.79
☼ Nokia	Hardware	—	—	1.72

Current Investment Style

Value Blnd Growth — Large Mid Small

Market Cap	%
Giant	34.5
Large	24.7
Mid	25.7
Small	11.6
Micro	3.6

Avg $mil: 10,297

Value Measures		Rel Category
Price/Earnings	25.48	0.92
Price/Book	3.82	1.14
Price/Sales	3.67	1.23
Price/Cash Flow	13.55	1.08
Dividend Yield %	0.[illegible]4	0.74

Growth Measures	%	Rel Category
Long-Term Erngs	18.89	1.12
Book Value	7.[illegible]3	1.43
Sales	6.74	2.22
Cash Flow	13.23	0.82
Historical Erngs	18.88	1.55

Profitability	%	Rel Category
Return on Equity	17.75	1.55
Return on Assets	10.86	1.70
Net Margin	15.60	1.49

Industry Weightings	% of Stocks	Rel Cat
Software	26.4	1.3
Hardware	13.1	1.0
Networking Eq	8.8	1.2
Semis	24.1	1.5
Semi Equip	0.0	0.0
Comp/Data Sv	1.6	0.3
Telecom	0.0	0.0
Health Care	0.0	0.0
Other	26.0	1.1

Composition

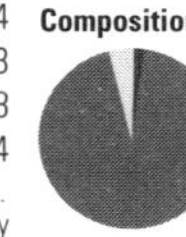

Cash	2.4
Stocks	93.7
Bonds	0.0
Other	3.9
Foreign (% of Stock)	15.8

Morningstar's Take by Jeffrey Ptak 01-07-05

T. Rowe Price Global Technology Fund is a good choice for dedicated tech exposure.

Investors familiar with manager Rob Gensler's work at T. Rowe Price Media & Telecom will note some similarities with this offering. True, this fund's mandate is far narrower than that of Gensler's other charge, where he has the full run of the tech, telecom, and media sectors. Yet, Gensler employs the same growth-at-a-reasonable price ethos here, focusing on firms propelled by secular, as opposed to cyclical, growth trends.

That approach has typically translated to a blue-chip-leaning portfolio, including top holdings Dell, Qualcomm, and Cisco. In particular, Gensler favors firms growing free cash at a faster clip than industry peers through some combination of product differentiation or margin expansion. And he isn't shy about making bets. For instance, he has continued to underweight semi-equipment issues on the conviction that the consolidation of that industry's end-markets will stoke heavy competitive pressure, stifling growth.

As one might expect, Gensler's taste for more established firms pushes the portfolio's aggregate price multiples modestly above the specialty-tech category norms. Gensler compensates, however, by aggressively trimming positions as they approach his estimates. Thus, the fund has been no more volatile than the group norm. Meanwhile, Gensler has posted sterling relative returns during his tenure: The fund's 3.9% annualized gain since his January 2002 arrival, while disappointing in absolute terms, bests virtually all comers.

That said, investors should keep their expectations in check. The fund can look sluggish when smaller, more speculative fare rules the roost, as evidenced by the fund's middling 2003 campaign (though it did post a stellar absolute return that year). However, given Gensler's impressive track record elsewhere and his auspicious start here, we think this fund is an option well worth considering.

Address:	100 East Pratt Street Baltimore MD 21202 800-638-5660
Web Address:	www.troweprice.com
Inception:	10-02-00 *
Advisor:	T. Rowe Price Associates, Inc.
Subadvisor:	None
NTF Plans:	Federated Tr NTF

Minimum Purchase:	$2500	Add: $100	IRA: $1000
Min Auto Inv Plan:	$50	Add: $50	
Sales Fees:	No-load		
Management Fee:	0.77%		
Actual Fees:	Mgt:0.77%	Dist:	
Expense Projections:	3Yr:$509	5Yr:$897	10Yr:$1985
Income Distrib:	Annually		

T. Rowe Price GNMA

Ticker	Load	NAV	Yield	SEC Yield	Total Assets	Mstar Category
PRGMX	None	$9.66	4.5%	3.93%	$1,356 mil	Intermediate Government

Governance and Management

Fiduciary Grade: B

Portfolio Manager(s)

Connie Bavely joined this fund in October 2000 and has delivered solid results during her tenure. She also contributes on T. Rowe Price New Income, a more diversified offering.

Strategy

Manager Connie Bavely searches for inefficiencies in the GNMA market, looking for situations in which investors have made faulty assumptions about the likely prepayment of certain bonds. She also tries to add value when rates are falling by selectively investing in GNMA CMOs and project loans. She will also venture into Treasuries when opportunities present themselves. The fund recently held a small stake (0.50% of assets) in inflation-protected Treasury securities, for example.

Historical Profile

Return Above Avg
Risk Below Avg
Rating ★★★★ Above Avg

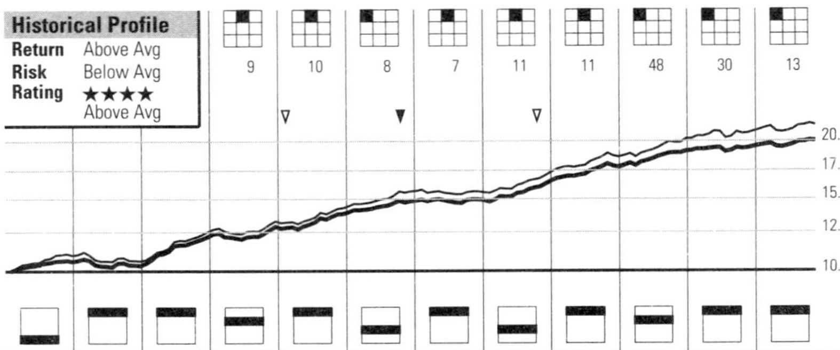

Investment Style
Fixed Income
Income Rtn %Rank Cat

▼ Manager Change
∇ Partial Manager Change

Growth of $10,000
— Investment Values of Fund
— Investment Values of LB Aggr

Performance Quartile (within Category)

1993	1994	1995	1996	1997	1998	1999	2000	2001	2002	2003	12-04	History
9.72	8.88	9.74	9.37	9.58	9.57	8.99	9.34	9.48	9.89	9.73	9.66	NAV
6.13	-1.64	17.81	3.12	9.48	6.56	0.21	10.93	7.69	9.03	2.36	3.82	Total Return %
-3.62	1.28	-0.66	-0.51	-0.17	-2.13	1.03	-0.70	-0.75	-1.22	-1.74	-0.52	+/-LB Aggr
-4.53	1.74	-0.53	0.35	-0.11	-3.29	2.44	-2.31	0.46	-2.47	0.00	0.34	+/-LB Govt
7.25	7.22	7.87	6.90	7.11	6.68	6.45	6.83	6.20	4.61	4.00	4.54	Income Return %
-1.12	-8.86	9.94	-3.78	2.37	-0.12	-6.24	4.10	1.49	4.42	-1.64	-0.72	Capital Return %
83	12	23	43	13	74	25	53	18	50	25	25	Total Rtn % Rank Cat
0.69	0.68	0.68	0.65	0.65	0.62	0.60	0.60	0.56	0.43	0.39	0.43	Income $
0.00	0.00	0.00	0.00	0.00	0.00	0.00	0.00	0.00	0.00	0.00	0.00	Capital Gains $
0.79	0.77	0.76	0.74	0.74	0.70	0.71	0.71	0.70	0.70	0.70	0.69	Expense Ratio %
7.65	6.93	7.50	7.04	6.98	6.67	6.36	6.61	6.39	3.68	3.68	3.23	Income Ratio %
94	92	121	114	116	121	87	64	71	386	386	302	Turnover Rate %
917	752	896	928	1,063	1,146	1,089	1,091	1,139	1,408	1,315	1,356	Net Assets $mil

Performance 12-31-04

	1st Qtr	2nd Qtr	3rd Qtr	4th Qtr	Total
2000	2.02	1.79	2.88	3.84	10.93
2001	2.64	1.00	4.16	-0.26	7.69
2002	0.91	3.56	3.12	1.18	9.03
2003	0.89	0.84	0.00	0.60	2.36
2004	1.58	-1.13	2.27	1.07	3.82

Trailing	Total Return%	+/- LB Aggr	+/- LB Govt	%Rank Cat	Growth of $10,000
3 Mo	1.07	0.12	0.58	18	10,107
6 Mo	3.36	-0.82	-0.25	37	10,336
1 Yr	3.82	-0.52	0.34	25	10,382
3 Yr Avg	5.03	-1.16	-0.67	30	11,586
5 Yr Avg	6.72	-0.99	-0.76	28	13,843
10 Yr Avg	6.99	-0.73	-0.47	19	19,653
15 Yr Avg	7.02	-0.68	-0.46	17	27,668

Tax Analysis	Tax-Adj Rtn%	%Rank Cat	Tax-Cost Rat	%Rank Cat
3 Yr (estimated)	3.41	20	1.54	58
5 Yr (estimated)	4.70	22	1.89	67
10 Yr (estimated)	4.57	19	2.26	80

Potential Capital Gain Exposure: 1% of assets

Rating and Risk

Time Period	Load-Adj Return %	Morningstar Rtn vs Cat	Morningstar Risk vs Cat	Morningstar Risk-Adj Rating
1 Yr	3.82			
3 Yr	5.03	+Avg	-Avg	★★★★
5 Yr	6.72	+Avg	-Avg	★★★★
10 Yr	6.99	+Avg	-Avg	★★★★
Incept	7.22			

Other Measures	Standard Index LB Aggr	Best Fit Index LB Mort
Alpha	0.7	-0.4
Beta	0.61	0.99
R-Squared	88	97
Standard Deviation	2.93	
Mean	5.03	
Sharpe Ratio	1.27	

Morningstar's Take by Scott Berry 12-09-04

T. Rowe Price GNMA's plain-vanilla approach serves investors well.

This fund doesn't have any tricks up its sleeve. Manager Connie Bavely sticks with bonds that are backed by the full faith and credit of the US government and avoids making large bets on the overall direction of interest rates. That approach has kept the fund out of too much trouble, but hasn't prevented it from delivering solid long-term results. In fact, the fund's long-term returns rank in the intermediate government category's best third and also compare favorably to those of its average intermediate government mortgage subgroup peer.

The fund's success has continued in 2004. Its positioning wasn't spot on during certain periods of the year, but the fund has performed well enough to rank in the mortgage subgroup's best half. Manager Connie Bavely has kept the fund defensively positioned for much of the year in an effort to protect it from rising interest rates, and that stance held the fund back a bit when rates trended down over the summer. On the plus side, though, the fund's Ginnie Mae project loans have performed relatively well, as has its small stake (0.5% of assets) in Treasury Inflation-Protected Securities. Overall, the fund returned 3.2% for the year to date through Nov. 30, while its average subgroup peer climbed 2.9%.

In addition to a solid record and proven management, we like this fund for its good shareholder communication. The fund's shareholder reports include detailed commentary about performance and strategy, as well as an outlook for the fund and for the overall market. Good communication doesn't directly impact performance, but it reflects a shareholder-friendly approach and inspires confidence in the fund and the firm.

The fund faces stiff competition from its no-load Ginnie Mae peers, but we think it more than earns its keep.

Address:	100 E Pratt St Baltimore MD 21202 800-638-5660	Minimum Purchase:	$2500	Add: $100 IRA: $1000
		Min Auto Inv Plan:	$50	Add: $50
		Sales Fees:	No-load	
Web Address:	www.troweprice.com	Management Fee:	0.47%	
Inception:	11-26-85	Actual Fees:	Mgt:0.47%	Dist:
Advisor:	T. Rowe Price Associates, Inc.	Expense Projections:	3Yr:$224	5Yr:$390 10Yr:$871
Subadvisor:	None	Income Distrib:	Monthly	
NTF Plans:	N/A			

Portfolio Analysis 09-30-04

Total Fixed-Income:2723	Date of Maturity	Amount $000	Value $000	% Net Assets
GNMA 5%	10-20-33	74,808	74,348	5.30
GNMA 5.5%	02-20-34	57,534	58,510	4.17
GNMA 6%	02-20-34	55,746	57,731	4.11
GNMA 6%	08-20-34	39,847	41,253	2.94
GNMA 5.5%	02-15-18	37,466	39,035	2.78
GNMA 5.5%	01-20-34	37,830	38,472	2.74
GNMA 6%	04-15-34	34,345	35,621	2.54
GNMA 5.5%		34,500	35,018	2.49
GNMA 5.5%	04-20-34	33,929	34,504	2.46
GNMA 6%	09-20-34	31,803	32,925	2.35
GNMA 6.5%		31,208	32,885	2.34
GNMA 5%	08-20-33	32,539	32,338	2.30
GNMA 5%	07-20-33	30,359	30,172	2.15
GNMA 6%	04-15-34	27,782	28,814	2.05
GNMA 6%	12-20-33	27,020	27,981	1.99
GNMA CMO 5.5%	10-20-30	25,900	26,702	1.90
GNMA 5%	09-15-33	24,224	24,135	1.72
GNMA 6.73%	05-15-40	19,379	21,676	1.54
GNMA 6%	07-20-34	18,870	19,536	1.39
GNMA 5%	09-20-33	18,549	18,434	1.31

Current Investment Style

Duration: Short Int Long
Quality: High Med Low

¹ figure provided by fund

Avg Eff Duration¹	3.0 Yrs
Avg Eff Maturity	4.7 Yrs
Avg Credit Quality	AAA
Avg Wtd Coupon	5.88%
Avg Wtd Price	103.39% of par

Coupon Range	% of Bonds	Rel Cat
0% PIK	0.1	0.0
0% to 6%	77.8	1.0
6% to 8%	20.9	1.0
8% to 10%	1.0	0.5
More than 10%	0.3	0.2

1.00=Category Average

Credit Analysis		% bonds 09-30-04	
US Govt	100	BB	0
AAA	0	B	0
AA	0	Below B	0
A	0	NR/NA	0
BBB	0		

Sector Breakdown	% of assets
US Treasuries	0
TIPS	0
US Agency	0
Mortgage Pass-Throughs	88
Mortgage CMO	7
Mortgage ARM	0
US Corporate	0
Asset-Backed	0
Convertible	0
Municipal	0
Corporate Inflation-Protected	0
Foreign Corporate	0
Foreign Govt	0

Composition			
Cash	5.0	Bonds	95.0
Stocks	0.0	Other	0.0

Special Securities	
Restricted/Illiquid Secs	0
Exotic Mortgage-Backed	0
Emerging-Markets Secs	0
Options/Futures/Warrants	No

T. Rowe Price Grth & Inc

Ticker	Load	NAV	Yield	Total Assets	Mstar Category
PRGIX	None	$22.51	1.1%	$1,904 mil	Large Blend

Governance and Management

Fiduciary Grade: B

Portfolio Manager(s)

Anna Dopkin took over management of this fund from Robert Sharps in October 2002. Dopkin has been a T. Rowe Price analyst covering the financial-services sector for six years, and she managed T. Rowe Price Financial Services for nearly three years, becoming sole manager in December 2000. Under her guidance, that fund performed well enough to warrant inclusion in our Fund Analyst Picks for the financials category.

Strategy

In the past, this fund emphasized stocks with sizable yields and histories of growing dividends. Nowadays, management is focusing on reasonably priced companies with high ROEs and earnings growth. It includes both growth and value stocks in the portfolio, as opposed to its previous value orientation. The goal is also to have a dividend yield higher than that of the S&P 500.

Historical Profile

Return Average
Risk Average
Rating ★★★ Neutral

Investment Style: Equity Stock %: 86% 87% 91% 94% 84% 96% 96% 98% 98%

▼ Manager Change
▽ Partial Manager Change

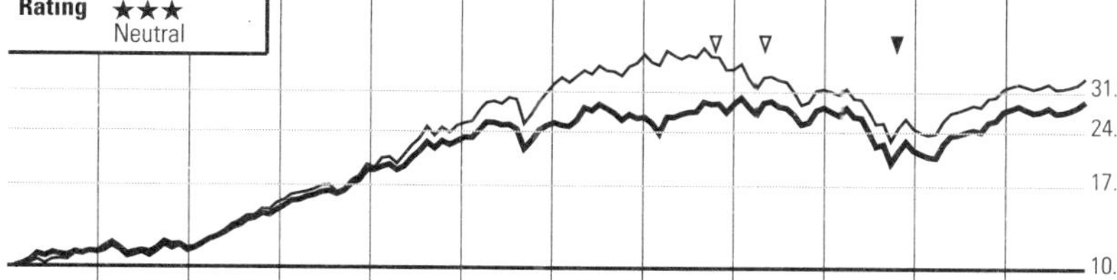

Growth of $10,000
- Investment Values of Fund
- Investment Values of S&P 500

Performance Quartile (within Category)

1993	1994	1995	1996	1997	1998	1999	2000	2001	2002	2003	12-04	History
16.57	15.63	19.18	22.63	26.36	26.25	24.44	24.44	22.82	17.11	21.72	22.51	NAV
12.96	-0.15	30.92	25.64	23.53	9.96	3.78	8.96	-2.17	-23.84	28.22	10.82	Total Return %
2.90	-1.46	-6.61	2.70	-9.82	-18.61	-17.26	18.06	9.71	-1.75	-0.45	-0.05	+/-S&P 500
2.78	-0.54	-6.85	3.19	-9.32	-17.06	-17.13	16.75	10.28	-2.19	-1.67	-0.58	+/-Russ 1000
3.06	3.00	3.85	2.69	2.50	2.08	1.96	1.40	1.09	0.71	1.11	1.20	Income Return %
9.90	-3.15	27.07	22.95	21.03	7.88	1.82	7.56	-3.26	-24.55	27.11	9.62	Capital Return %
32	51	68	14	79	89	95	10	6	74	34	35	Total Rtn % Rank Cat
0.47	0.49	0.59	0.51	0.56	0.53	0.51	0.34	0.26	0.16	0.19	0.26	Income $
0.48	0.42	0.60	0.90	0.97	2.13	2.25	1.83	0.78	0.15	0.00	1.27	Capital Gains $
0.83	0.81	0.84	0.82	0.78	0.77	0.77	0.77	0.81	0.81	0.82	—	Expense Ratio %
2.91	3.08	3.31	2.53	2.22	2.03	1.78	1.35	1.08	0.84	1.02	—	Income Ratio %
22	26	26	14	16	20	20	80	66	45	41	—	Turnover Rate %
1,171	1,229	1,748	2,489	3,447	3,563	3,440	2,989	2,394	1,675	1,970	1,904	Net Assets $mil

Performance 12-31-04

	1st Qtr	2nd Qtr	3rd Qtr	4th Qtr	Total
2000	0.13	3.28	5.18	0.17	8.96
2001	-6.70	5.31	-10.75	11.55	-2.17
2002	-0.43	-14.19	-17.93	8.60	-23.84
2003	-4.62	15.91	1.70	14.04	28.22
2004	1.29	0.96	-1.40	9.91	10.82

Trailing	Total Return%	+/- S&P 500	+/- Russ 1000	%Rank Cat	Growth of $10,000
3 Mo	9.91	0.68	0.11	31	10,991
6 Mo	8.37	1.18	0.56	23	10,837
1 Yr	10.82	-0.05	-0.58	35	11,082
3 Yr Avg	2.66	-0.92	-1.61	56	10,819
5 Yr Avg	2.90	5.20	4.66	10	11,537
10 Yr Avg	10.34	-1.73	-1.82	54	26,750
15 Yr Avg	9.80	-1.13	-1.28	56	40,648

Tax Analysis	Tax-Adj Rtn%	%Rank Cat	Tax-Cost Rat	%Rank Cat
3 Yr (estimated)	1.96	54	0.68	57
5 Yr (estimated)	1.82	11	1.05	55
10 Yr (estimated)	8.57	51	1.60	61

Potential Capital Gain Exposure: 25% of assets

Rating and Risk

Time Period	Load-Adj Return %	Morningstar Rtn vs Cat	Morningstar Risk vs Cat	Morningstar Risk-Adj Rating
1 Yr	10.82			
3 Yr	2.66	Avg	+Avg	★★★
5 Yr	2.90	+Avg	Avg	★★★★
10 Yr	10.34	Avg	-Avg	★★★
Incept	11.07			

Other Measures	Standard Index S&P 500	Best Fit Index Russ 1000
Alpha	-0.9	-1.6
Beta	1.05	1.06
R-Squared	98	98
Standard Deviation	16.44	
Mean	2.66	
Sharpe Ratio	0.08	

Portfolio Analysis 09-30-04

Share change since 06-04 Total Stocks:113	Sector	PE	YTD Ret%	% Assets
Gen Elec	Ind Mtrls	22.8	20.68	2.97
⊕ Microsoft	Software	36.1	8.95	2.27
⊖ Citigroup	Financial	15.3	2.72	2.08
⊖ Transocean	Energy	56.3	76.55	1.72
⊖ US Bancorp	Financial	14.2	10.46	1.65
United Parcel Service B	Business	28.5	16.40	1.62
⊖ Lockheed Martin	Ind Mtrls	19.9	9.97	1.42
⊕ Potash Corp./Saskatchewa	Ind Mtrls	—	94.19	1.41
St. Paul Travelers Compa	Financial	30.8	-3.15	1.32
Altria Group	Goods	13.3	18.38	1.30
Wyeth	Health	17.0	2.73	1.30
⊖ Baker Hughes	Energy	30.3	34.28	1.30
⊕ Marsh & McLennan Compani	Financial	13.4	-29.80	1.27
⊕ State Street	Financial	15.3	-4.41	1.25
Time Warner	Media	27.5	8.12	1.24
BP PLC ADR	Energy	20.7	22.07	1.21
⊕ Viacom B	Media	36.1	-17.44	1.18
⊖ Verizon Communications	Telecom	32.4	20.25	1.17
Duke Energy	Utilities	—	30.21	1.17
News Corporation ADR A	Media	—	6.65	1.12

Current Investment Style

Value Blnd Growth / Large Mid Small

Market Cap	%
Giant	41.1
Large	48.4
Mid	10.5
Small	0.0
Micro	0.0
Avg $mil: 32,574	

Value Measures		Rel Category
Price/Earnings	17.19	1.01
Price/Book	2.47	0.94
Price/Sales	1.64	1.14
Price/Cash Flow	8.02	1.04
Dividend Yield %	1.69	1.14

Growth Measures	%	Rel Category
Long-Term Erngs	12.14	1.05
Book Value	4.37	0.56
Sales	4.79	0.83
Cash Flow	-0.10	NMF
Historical Erngs	9.33	0.79

Profitability	%	Rel Category
Return on Equity	15.51	0.89
Return on Assets	8.57	0.99
Net Margin	10.79	0.94

Sector Weightings	% of Stocks	Rel S&P 500	3 Year High	Low
Info	22.52	1.05		
Software	3.72	0.87	4	1
Hardware	8.67	0.85	9	5
Media	6.95	1.81	8	5
Telecom	3.18	1.01	6	3
Service	44.49	0.96		
Health	8.68	0.69	20	9
Consumer	6.29	0.69	8	6
Business	5.46	1.35	7	5
Financial	24.06	1.16	30	24
Mfg	32.99	1.03		
Goods	7.45	0.80	9	3
Ind Mtrls	14.46	1.14	15	9
Energy	8.59	1.20	9	6
Utilities	2.49	0.84	2	0

Composition

Cash	1.7
Stocks	98.3
Bonds	0.0
Other	0.0
Foreign (% of Stock)	6.5

Morningstar's Take by Kunal Kapoor 10-01-04

With two years under its current manager in the books, T. Rowe Price Growth & Income now exits the honeymoon phase and confronts reality.

Since taking over here in October 2002, manager Anna Dopkin has brought much change to this once-lackluster fund. In particular, she has clarified what the fund is about and how it fits in T. Rowe's lineup. That's meant adding more growth stocks, such as Cisco Systems, to the portfolio and firmly pushing the fund into blend territory. As such, it now looks and behaves somewhat differently than offerings such as T. Rowe Price Equity Income.

Now comes the hard part. With the portfolio positioned to her liking, Dopkin must compete with some of the most accomplished managers in the industry and a tough-to-beat index, the S&P 500. After all, this is a category populated with funds such as Selected American and Fidelity Contrafund, and one that will soon welcome a PRIMECAP-managed offering, too. These funds are helmed by some of the most experienced managers in the industry. Moreover, with Fidelity putting pressure on index-fund pricing, it's going to get tougher for active funds to gain an edge.

But we think this fund is capable of carving out its own niche. For starters, it has the advantage of a small asset base, which allows Dopkin to build sizable positions in midsized companies. More importantly, we like Dopkin's background and detail-oriented approach. Indeed, her background as a financials analyst is an asset here because it's a sector that's likely to absorb at least a fifth of this fund's assets on an ongoing basis. Finally, we believe that T. Rowe's contrarian approach to investing is a positive and differentiating factor.

To be sure, the ultimate test of this approach can only be evaluated after the fund builds a five-year record under Dopkin's tutelage. But we like what we've seen thus far, and think that the fund's current momentum should persist. Given the resources at Dopkin's disposal, she should be able to execute over longer periods.

Address:	100 East Pratt St Baltimore MD 21202 800-638-5660
Web Address:	www.troweprice.com
Inception:	12-21-82
Advisor:	T. Rowe Price Associates, Inc.
Subadvisor:	None
NTF Plans:	N/A

Minimum Purchase:	$2500	Add: $100	IRA: $1000
Min Auto Inv Plan:	$50	Add: $50	
Sales Fees:	No-load		
Management Fee:	0.57%		
Actual Fees:	Mgt:0.57%	Dist:	
Expense Projections:	3Yr:$262	5Yr:$455	10Yr:$1014
Income Distrib:	Quarterly		

T. Rowe Price Gr Stk

Ticker	Load	NAV	Yield	Total Assets	Mstar Category
PRGFX	None	$26.67	0.6%	$8,723 mil	Large Growth

Governance and Management

Fiduciary Grade: B

Portfolio Manager(s)

Bob Smith has been at the helm of this offering since 1997. He's supported by T. Rowe Price's deep analyst bench domestically and overseas. Smith says he splits about 70% of his personal investment holdings between this fund and his other charge, T. Rowe Price Global Stock, which he has helped run since 1995.

Strategy

Manager Bob Smith uses a growth-at-a-reasonable-price approach, paying particular attention to financially sound companies with strong management teams and ample free cash flows. His growth leanings push the fund into the large-growth camp, but the fund is more diversified by sector than its typical peer. Smith also pays more attention to foreign blue chips than most of his rivals do: The fund often has 10%-15% of assets invested abroad, considerably above the category norm.

Historical Profile

Return: Above Avg
Risk: Average
Rating: ★★★★★ Highest

Investment Style: Equity Stock %

1996	1997	1998	1999	2000	2001	2002	2003	12-04
96%	92%	93%	96%	93%	95%	99%	97%	97%

▼ Manager Change
▽ Partial Manager Change (1997: ▽ ▽)

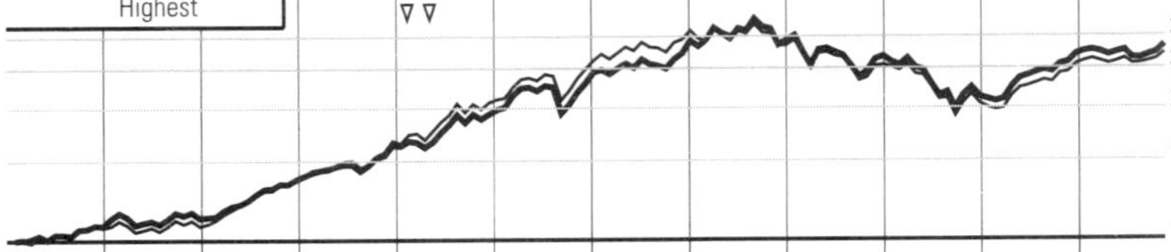

Growth of $10,000
— Investment Values of Fund
— Investment Values of S&P 500

Performance Quartile (within Category)

History

1993	1994	1995	1996	1997	1998	1999	2000	2001	2002	2003	12-04	History
20.42	18.75	23.35	26.18	28.99	32.07	33.27	27.20	24.18	18.58	24.33	26.67	NAV
15.56	0.89	30.97	21.70	26.57	27.41	22.15	0.27	-9.79	-23.00	31.23	10.24	Total Return %
5.50	-0.42	-6.56	-1.24	-6.78	-1.16	1.11	9.37	2.09	-0.91	2.56	-0.63	+/-S&P 500
12.69	-1.73	-6.21	-1.42	-3.92	-11.30	-11.01	22.69	10.63	4.88	1.48	3.94	+/-Russ 1000Gr
0.75	0.88	1.23	0.81	0.76	0.86	0.31	0.21	0.29	0.17	0.27	0.62	Income Return %
14.81	0.01	29.74	20.89	25.81	26.55	21.84	0.06	-10.08	-23.17	30.96	9.62	Capital Return %
28	23	59	32	51	68	80	7	7	20	26	26	Total Rtn % Rank Cat
0.14	0.18	0.23	0.19	0.20	0.25	0.10	0.07	0.08	0.04	0.05	0.15	Income $
0.99	1.66	0.97	2.06	3.87	4.27	5.42	6.28	0.27	0.00	0.00	0.00	Capital Gains $
0.82	0.81	0.80	0.77	0.75	0.74	0.74	0.73	0.77	0.77	0.76	—	Expense Ratio %
0.86	0.91	1.09	0.74	0.75	0.67	0.31	0.20	0.34	0.23	0.29	—	Income Ratio %
35	54	42	49	41	55	56	74	64	47	35	—	Turnover Rate %
2,051	2,068	2,762	3,431	3,988	5,041	5,672	5,428	4,685	3,728	5,645	8,174	Net Assets $mil

Performance 12-31-04

	1st Qtr	2nd Qtr	3rd Qtr	4th Qtr	Total
2000	8.60	-0.42	1.08	-8.28	0.27
2001	-14.96	8.86	-14.81	14.39	-9.79
2002	-1.41	-14.97	-15.15	8.25	-23.00
2003	-1.61	16.36	2.59	11.74	31.23
2004	1.52	1.01	-3.17	11.02	10.24

Trailing	Total Return%	+/- S&P 500	+/- Russ 1000Gr	%Rank Cat	Growth of $10,000
3 Mo	11.02	1.79	1.85	28	11,102
6 Mo	7.50	0.31	4.03	18	10,750
1 Yr	10.24	-0.63	3.94	26	11,024
3 Yr Avg	3.66	0.08	3.84	15	11,139
5 Yr Avg	0.15	2.45	9.44	5	10,075
10 Yr Avg	12.21	0.14	2.62	9	31,646
15 Yr Avg	11.33	0.40	1.83	17	50,025

Tax Analysis	Tax-Adj Rtn%	%Rank Cat	Tax-Cost Rat	%Rank Cat
3 Yr (estimated)	3.54	12	0.12	21
5 Yr (estimated)	-0.93	6	1.08	64
10 Yr (estimated)	10.16	13	1.83	65

Potential Capital Gain Exposure: 18% of assets

Rating and Risk

Time Period	Load-Adj Return %	Morningstar Rtn vs Cat	Morningstar Risk vs Cat	Morningstar Risk-Adj Rating
1 Yr	10.24			
3 Yr	3.66	+Avg	Avg	★★★★
5 Yr	0.15	High	Avg	★★★★★
10 Yr	12.21	+Avg	-Avg	★★★★★
Incept	9.39			

Other Measures	Standard Index S&P 500	Best Fit Index Russ 1000
Alpha	0.1	-0.6
Beta	1.02	1.03
R-Squared	97	98
Standard Deviation	16.13	
Mean	3.66	
Sharpe Ratio	0.14	

Portfolio Analysis 09-30-04

Share change since 06-04 Total Stocks:119	Sector	PE	YTD Ret%	% Assets
⊕ Microsoft	Software	36.1	8.95	3.44
⊕ Citigroup	Financial	15.3	2.72	3.27
⊕ Gen Elec	Ind Mtrls	22.8	20.68	2.63
⊖ UnitedHealth Group	Health	23.8	51.38	2.56
⊕ American International G	Financial	16.2	-0.53	2.25
⊕ Pfizer	Health	22.0	-22.31	1.79
⊕ Wal-Mart Stores	Consumer	23.4	0.51	1.70
⊕ Dell	Hardware	34.0	24.01	1.64
⊕ WellPoint Health Network	Health	—	—	1.61
⊖ Target	Consumer	22.3	36.14	1.61
⊕ State Street	Financial	15.3	-4.41	1.56
⊕ Danaher	Ind Mtrls	25.8	25.29	1.55
⊕ Tyco International	Ind Mtrls	25.1	35.41	1.53
⊕ American Express	Financial	20.3	17.60	1.50
⊕ Home Depot	Consumer	19.0	21.47	1.41
⊕ International Game Tech	Consumer	28.1	-2.49	1.39
⊕ Baker Hughes	Energy	30.3	34.28	1.39
⊕ Accenture	Business	21.7	2.58	1.32
⊕ Liberty Media	Media	—	11.56	1.31
⊕ Nextel Communications	Telecom	11.1	6.95	1.31

Current Investment Style

Value Blnd Growth; Large Mid Small

Market Cap	%
Giant	47.3
Large	45.4
Mid	7.3
Small	0.0
Micro	0.0
Avg $mil: 40,498	

Value Measures		Rel Category
Price/Earnings	18.09	0.85
Price/Book	2.83	0.88
Price/Sales	1.90	0.88
Price/Cash Flow	8.29	0.75
Dividend Yield %	0.98	1.27

Growth Measures	%	Rel Category
Long-Term Erngs	14.27	1.02
Book Value	10.66	0.84
Sales	9.57	1.12
Cash Flow	13.52	0.82
Historical Erngs	16.67	1.15

Profitability	%	Rel Category
Return on Equity	18.51	1.03
Return on Assets	10.48	1.12
Net Margin	12.52	1.02

Sector Weightings	% of Stocks	Rel S&P 500	3 Year High	3 Year Low
Info	27.85	1.30		
Software	7.49	1.74	8	4
Hardware	8.18	0.80	9	4
Media	9.32	2.43	11	7
Telecom	2.86	0.91	4	2
Service	54.61	1.18		
Health	13.97	1.12	22	13
Consumer	14.49	1.60	15	11
Business	6.49	1.60	12	6
Financial	19.66	0.95	23	19
Mfg	17.54	0.55		
Goods	4.81	0.52	8	5
Ind Mtrls	7.85	0.62	8	4
Energy	4.88	0.68	5	4
Utilities	0.00	0.00	0	0

Composition

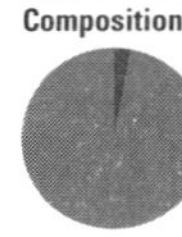

Cash	2.8
Stocks	97.2
Bonds	0.0
Other	0.0
Foreign (% of Stock)	9.4

Morningstar's Take by Christopher Davis 10-15-04

T. Rowe Price Growth Stock's commitment to its strategy should continue to serve long-term investors well.

In the late 1990s, some pundits dismissed T. Rowe Price's conservative ethos as hopelessly old fashioned. And indeed, it did put the firm out of step with investors' infatuation with racy technology and Internet names during the period. This offering, in fact, lagged the S&P 500 Index and ranked in the large-growth category's bottom third in 1999. But these days, T. Rowe's one-time critics are noticeably quiet, and this fund is one of the reasons why. Not only did it suffer much smaller losses than its rivals in the 2000-02 bear market, but it also delivered peer-beating gains in 2003's spirited rally.

The fund's success amid different environments stems from manager Bob Smith's valuation-sensitive, against-the-grain approach. Smith's avoidance of so-called new economy fare in the late 1990s helped pave the way to the fund's stronger 2003 campaign, as picks such as Cisco Systems and Yahoo rallied sharply off their lows.

So far this year, the fund has continued to outpace the competition. In late 2003, Smith began to tilt the portfolio toward larger-cap names, which he thought looked cheap relative to other areas of the market. With big-cap favorites such as Microsoft and General Electric notching relatively strong gains, that shift has begun to bear fruit, contributing to the fund's top-quartile showing for the year to date through Oct. 11, 2004.

While Smith's price-conscious approach can be a liability in racy markets, it has been well acquitted over time, as evidenced by the fund's stellar long-term record. All in all, we think this fund's seasoned management, sound strategy, and modest costs make it a fine choice for a core growth offering.

Address:	100 E Pratt St, Baltimore MD 21202, 800-638-5660
Web Address:	www.troweprice.com
Inception:	04-11-50
Advisor:	T. Rowe Price Associates, Inc.
Subadvisor:	None
NTF Plans:	N/A

Minimum Purchase:	$2500	Add: $100	IRA: $1000
Min Auto Inv Plan:	$50	Add: $50	
Sales Fees:	No-load		
Management Fee:	0.57%		
Actual Fees:	Mgt:0.57%	Dist:	
Expense Projections:	3Yr:$243	5Yr:$422	10Yr:$942
Income Distrib:	Annually		

T. Rowe Price Health Sci

Analyst Pick	Ticker	Load	NAV	Yield	Total Assets	Mstar Category
✔	PRHSX	None	$23.11	0.0%	$1,331 mil	Specialty-Health

Governance and Management

Fiduciary Grade: B

Portfolio Manager(s)

Kris Jenner, a physician by training, has been at the fund's helm since February 2000. Prior to that, he served as T. Rowe Price's biotechnology analyst for two years. Four analysts support Jenner in running the portfolio. Jenner says he keeps his entire retirement account invested in this offering.

Strategy

Kris Jenner emphasizes smaller-cap pharmaceutical and biotech stocks, which he thinks have the brightest long-term growth prospects in the health-care sector. Recognizing that such names are often quite volatile, Jenner has also given the fund considerable exposure to big-cap drugmakers and health-care service companies. Even so, with a hefty biotech stake and a market cap far below the category average, the fund is more adventuresome than most diversified health-care offerings.

Historical Profile

Return: Above Avg
Risk: Above Avg
Rating: ★★★ Neutral

Investment Style: Equity Stock %

1996	1997	1998	1999	2000	2001	2002	2003	12-04
96%	91%	92%	95%	94%	98%	99%	98%	96%

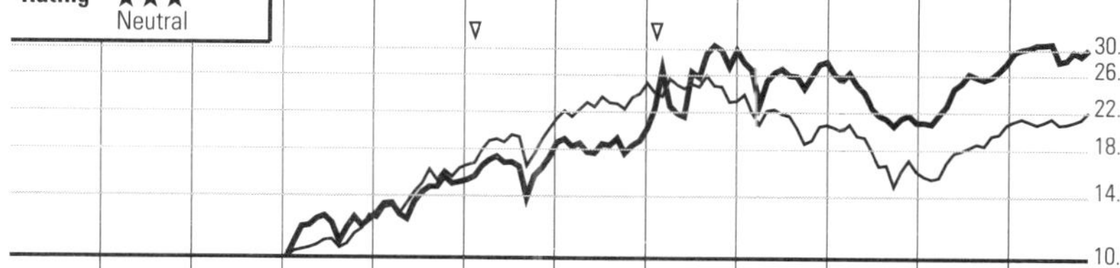

▼ Manager Change
▽ Partial Manager Change

Growth of $10,000
— Investment Values of Fund
— Investment Values of S&P 500

Performance Quartile (within Category)

History

1993	1994	1995	1996	1997	1998	1999	2000	2001	2002	2003	12-04	History
—	—	10.00	12.27	13.66	16.01	15.93	21.70	20.08	14.51	19.95	23.11	NAV
—	—	0.00*	26.75	19.41	22.37	7.97	52.19	-5.97	-27.74	37.49	15.84	Total Return %
—	—	—	3.81	-13.94	-6.20	-13.07	61.29	5.91	-5.65	8.82	4.97	+/-S&P 500
—	—	—	8.20	-17.47	-16.72	12.00	14.72	6.64	-6.93	18.06	11.29	+/-DJ Hlthcare
—	—	—	0.00	0.00	0.00	0.00	0.00	0.00	0.00	0.00	0.00	Income Return %
—	—	—	26.75	19.41	22.37	7.97	52.19	-5.97	-27.74	37.49	15.84	Capital Return %
—	—	—	1	59	53	52	49	27	63	24	7	Total Rtn % Rank Cat
—	—	0.00	0.00	0.00	0.00	0.00	0.00	0.00	0.00	0.00	0.00	Income $
—	—	0.00	0.40	0.97	0.66	1.26	2.48	0.31	0.00	0.00	0.00	Capital Gains $
—	—	—	1.35	1.18	1.16	1.11	0.98	1.02	1.04	1.00	—	Expense Ratio %
—	—	—	-0.32	-0.21	-0.25	-0.25	-0.22	-0.60	-0.64	-0.64	—	Income Ratio %
—	—	—	133	104	86	82	111	75	63	45	—	Turnover Rate %
—	—	—	194	271	317	303	972	961	678	1,028	1,331	Net Assets $mil

Performance 12-31-04

	1st Qtr	2nd Qtr	3rd Qtr	4th Qtr	Total
2000	12.81	20.03	15.21	-2.44	52.19
2001	-25.39	21.37	-9.82	15.15	-5.97
2002	-5.88	-16.93	-9.24	1.82	-27.74
2003	4.34	18.43	1.90	9.20	37.49
2004	8.62	2.31	-4.24	8.86	15.84

Trailing	Total Return%	+/- S&P 500	+/- DJ Hlthcare	%Rank Cat	Growth of $10,000
3 Mo	8.86	-0.37	2.96	27	10,886
6 Mo	4.24	-2.95	3.24	35	10,424
1 Yr	15.84	4.97	11.29	7	11,584
3 Yr Avg	4.80	1.22	5.17	20	11,510
5 Yr Avg	10.50	12.80	6.99	25	16,474
10 Yr Avg	—	—	—	—	—
15 Yr Avg	—	—	—	—	—

Tax Analysis	Tax-Adj Rtn%	%Rank Cat	Tax-Cost Rat	%Rank Cat
3 Yr (estimated)	4.80	15	0.00	1
5 Yr (estimated)	9.74	25	0.69	47
10 Yr (estimated)	—	—	—	—

Potential Capital Gain Exposure: 22% of assets

Rating and Risk

Time Period	Load-Adj Return %	Morningstar Rtn vs Cat	Morningstar Risk vs Cat	Morningstar Risk-Adj Rating
1 Yr	15.84			
3 Yr	4.80	+Avg	Avg	★★★★
5 Yr	10.50	+Avg	+Avg	★★★
10 Yr	—	—	—	—
Incept	14.15			

Other Measures	Standard Index S&P 500	Best Fit Index DJ Hlthcare
Alpha	2.1	5.7
Beta	0.74	1.04
R-Squared	52	69

Standard Deviation	16.01
Mean	4.80
Sharpe Ratio	0.22

Portfolio Analysis 09-30-04

Share change since 06-04 Total Stocks:129	Sector	PE	YTD Ret%	% Assets
⊕ Gilead Sciences	Health	36.9	20.08	6.97
UnitedHealth Group	Health	23.8	51.38	5.93
⊕ Anthem	Health	17.4	53.33	5.26
⊖ Imclone Systems	Health	38.5	16.19	3.63
⊖ Amgen	Health	37.7	3.82	3.42
⊕ Cephalon	Health	—	5.10	3.18
Biogen IDEC	Health	—	81.50	2.36
Wyeth	Health	17.0	2.73	2.10
⊖ Pfizer	Health	22.0	-22.31	2.09
⊕ Elan ADR	Health	—	295.50	1.97
⊕ Genentech	Health	78.6	16.36	1.83
⊕ Medicines	Health	92.3	-2.24	1.81
⊕ Neurocrine Biosciences	Health	—	-9.61	1.72
⊕ Onyx Pharmaceuticals	Health	—	14.74	1.64
MGI Pharma	Health	—	36.14	1.61
⊕ Fisher Scientific Intern	Health	43.9	50.79	1.52
⊕ Eli Lilly & Company	Health	24.3	-17.55	1.21
⊖ Boston Scientific	Health	32.3	-3.29	1.20
⊕ Guidant	Health	35.0	20.55	1.19
⊕ Forest Laboratories	Health	18.0	-27.41	1.17

Current Investment Style

Value Blnd Growth — Large Mid Small

Market Cap	%
Giant	13.9
Large	34.0
Mid	29.1
Small	15.7
Micro	7.4
Avg $mil: 6 070	

Value Measures		Rel Category
Price/Earnings	23.32	1.01
Price/Book	2.32	1.02
Price/Sales	2.45	0.87
Price/Cash Flow	8.39	0.83
Dividend Yield %	0.28	0.39

Growth Measures	%	Rel Category
Long-Term Erngs	16.78	1.04
Book Value	15.36	0.98
Sales	15.31	1.30
Cash Flow	13.36	0.72
Historical Erngs	10.39	1.16

Profitability	%	Rel Category
Return on Equity	9.53	0.98
Return on Assets	-1.15	NMF
Net Margin	6.34	0.79

Industry Weightings	% of Stocks	Rel Cat
Biotech	49.7	1.4
Drugs	16.8	0.6
Mgd Care	7.6	1.3
Hospitals	1.8	1.1
Other HC Srv	1.4	1.2
Diagnostics	1.4	1.4
Equipment	11.1	0.7
Good/Srv	8.7	1.8
Other	1.6	0.3

Composition

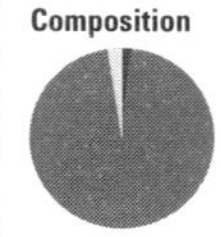

Cash	1.4
Stocks	96.0
Bonds	0.0
Other	2.5
Foreign (% of Stock)	5.7

Morningstar's Take by Christopher Davis 01-02-05

T. Rowe Price Health Sciences' ability to navigate choppy waters makes it a favorite.

While investor wariness of large-cap drug stocks has grown stronger in recent months thanks to the controversy surrounding blockbuster arthritis treatments Vioxx and Celebrex, manager Kris Jenner has consistently de-emphasized the role such names play in the portfolio all along. Jenner has long been skeptical of the industry's growth prospects, instead favoring a mix of established and emerging biotech firms such as Amgen, Gilead Sciences, and Imclone Systems, which he says boast more robust drug pipelines and are developing innovative treatments for ailments overlooked by the giants. As a result, the fund sports a hefty biotech stake--it accounts for about half of its assets--and an average market cap well below the health-care category norm.

That approach makes the fund more adventuresome than most of its rivals--biotech stocks are notoriously volatile while smaller health-care firms' prospects typically hinge on just a small number of products. Despite those risks, Jenner has posted relatively strong results when his aggressive style has been out of favor, as in 2001 and 2002. The fund has delivered the goods in more-hospitable environments. Rallying biotech picks such as Biogen Idec, along with managed-care holdings such as Anthem, propelled the fund to a 16% gain in 2004, a top decile showing in the category. Its three- and five-year returns rank in or near its group's top quartile.

All in all, this offering is an attractive package. Jenner has proved a capable manager. His skills, coupled with T. Rowe's analytical expertise and the fund's moderate expenses, should continue to give the fund an edge. Jenner's focus on smaller companies also makes the fund a better diversifier for investors' portfolios. This offering may look relatively sluggish in a more hospitable environment for large cap health-care stocks, but we think this offering holds long-term appeal.

Address:	100 E Pratt St Baltimore MD 21202 800-638-5660
Web Address:	www.troweprice.com
Inception:	12-29-95 *
Advisor:	T. Rowe Price Associates, Inc.
Subadvisor:	None
NTF Plans:	N/A

Minimum Purchase:	$2500	Add: $100	IRA: $1000
Min Auto Inv Plan:	$50	Add: $50	
Sales Fees:	No-load		
Management Fee:	0.67%		
Actual Fees:	Mgt:0.67%	Dist:	
Expense Projections:	3Yr:$318	5Yr:$552	10Yr:$1225
Income Distrib:	Annually		

T. Rowe Price Hi-Yld

Ticker	Load	NAV	Yield	SEC Yield	Total Assets	Mstar Category
PRHYX	Closed	$7.20	7.6%	6.37%	$4,263 mil	High Yield Bond

Governance and Management

Fiduciary Grade: B

Portfolio Manager(s)

Mark Vaselkiv took over this fund in 1996, and it has performed very well on his watch. He is backed by seven credit analysts and three traders. The team works closely with T. Rowe Price's equity-research staff.

Strategy

Manager Mark Vaselkiv keeps this fund well diversified, which reduces its issue-specific risk. Vaselkiv also tends to favor less-speculative bonds than many of his peers, although he has the flexibility to dip into beaten-down issues and sectors. In 2003, for example, he has increased the fund's exposure to CCC rated issues, which gave the fund a lift during the market's rally. More recently, he has shifted back into BB and B rated issues.

Historical Profile

Return High
Risk Below Avg
Rating ★★★★★ Highest

Investment Style
Fixed Income
Income Rtn %Rank Cat

39	27	37	49	46	49	36	24	16

▼ Manager Change
∇ Partial Manager Change

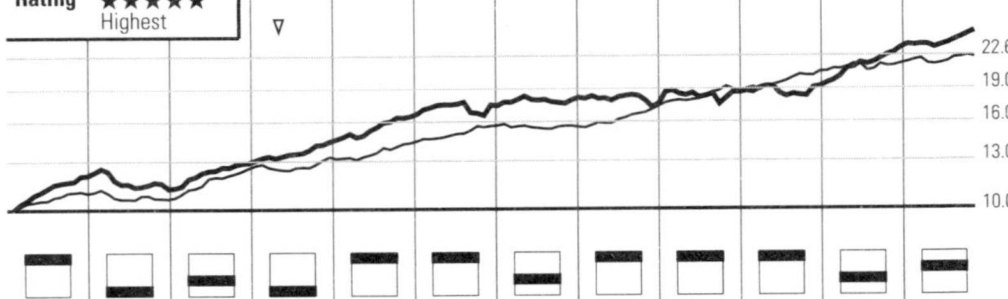

Growth of $10,000
— Investment Values of Fund
— Investment Values of LB Aggr

Performance Quartile (within Category)

1993	1994	1995	1996	1997	1998	1999	2000	2001	2002	2003	12-04	History
9.22	7.75	8.19	8.34	8.74	8.36	7.94	6.94	6.67	6.27	7.06	7.20	NAV
21.82	-8.00	15.77	11.58	14.46	4.46	4.18	-3.25	6.10	3.08	22.53	10.34	Total Return %
12.07	-5.08	-2.70	7.95	4.81	-4.23	5.00	-14.88	-2.34	-7.17	18.43	6.00	+/-LB Aggr
2.91	-7.03	-1.62	-0.84	1.83	3.88	0.90	1.96	0.32	-0.03	-5.40	-1.62	+/-CSFB Glb HY
10.28	8.52	9.99	9.58	9.45	9.08	9.47	10.03	10.32	9.24	9.44	8.00	Income Return %
11.54	-16.52	5.78	2.00	5.01	-4.62	-5.29	-13.28	-4.22	-6.16	13.09	2.34	Capital Return %
14	98	75	83	20	11	51	20	21	11	64	37	Total Rtn % Rank Cat
0.82	0.75	0.74	0.75	0.76	0.76	0.76	0.76	0.69	0.59	0.57	0.55	Income $
0.00	0.00	0.00	0.00	0.00	0.00	0.00	0.00	0.00	0.00	0.00	0.01	Capital Gains $
0.89	0.85	0.88	0.85	0.84	0.81	0.82	0.83	0.82	0.83	0.81	0.78	Expense Ratio %
9.85	8.99	9.27	8.89	9.15	8.78	8.93	9.60	10.16	9.56	9.09	8.07	Income Ratio %
104	107	74	100	111	130	96	76	80	71	60	74	Turnover Rate %
1,622	1,040	1,227	1,325	1,572	1,704	1,682	1,447	1,577	1,940	3,197	3,486	Net Assets $mil

Performance 12-31-04

	1st Qtr	2nd Qtr	3rd Qtr	4th Qtr	Total
2000	-0.59	0.83	0.60	-4.06	-3.25
2001	5.36	-1.79	-3.51	6.27	6.10
2002	2.32	-2.76	-1.02	4.67	3.08
2003	5.44	7.36	2.28	5.83	22.53
2004	1.75	-0.43	4.19	4.52	10.35

Trailing	Total Return%	+/- LB Aggr	+/- CSFB Glb HY	%Rank Cat	Growth of $10,000
3 Mo	4.52	3.57	-0.04	41	10,452
6 Mo	8.90	4.72	-0.36	37	10,890
1 Yr	10.34	6.00	-1.62	37	11,034
3 Yr Avg	11.70	5.51	-2.18	27	13,937
5 Yr Avg	7.42	-0.29	-0.75	10	14,303
10 Yr Avg	8.69	0.97	0.07	10	23,009
15 Yr Avg	8.61	0.91	-1.48	35	34,518

Tax Analysis	Tax-Adj Rtn%	%Rank Cat	Tax-Cost Rat	%Rank Cat
3 Yr (estimated)	8.31	22	3.03	65
5 Yr (estimated)	3.81	10	3.36	55
10 Yr (estimated)	4.96	7	3.43	51

Potential Capital Gain Exposure: -3% of assets

Rating and Risk

Time Period	Load-Adj Return %	Morningstar Rtn vs Cat	Morningstar Risk vs Cat	Morningstar Risk-Adj Rating
1 Yr	10.34			
3 Yr	11.70	+Avg	-Avg	★★★★
5 Yr	7.42	+Avg	-Avg	★★★★
10 Yr	8.69	High	-Avg	★★★★★
Incept	9.21			

Other Measures	Standard Index LB Aggr	Best Fit Index CSFB Glb HY
Alpha	10.1	0.0
Beta	0.05	0.83
R-Squared	0	96
Standard Deviation	5.83	
Mean	11.70	
Sharpe Ratio	1.78	

Portfolio Analysis 09-30-04

Total Fixed-Income:442	Date of Maturity	Amount $000	Value $000	% Net Assets
Quebecor Media 11.125%	07-15-11	32,249	37,248	0.92
Venetian Casino Resort 1	06-15-10	30,878	35,510	0.88
Rockwood Special Group B	07-16-14	35,000	35,000	0.87
Williams Cos 8.125%	03-15-12	30,340	34,891	0.87
Georgia Pac 9.375%	02-01-13	28,425	33,470	0.83
Qwest Svcs 144A 13.5%	12-15-10	25,774	30,188	0.75
Gencorp 9.5%	08-15-13	27,100	28,726	0.71
Jorgensen Earle M 9.75%	06-01-12	24,745	27,529	0.68
Universal City Dev Partn	04-01-10	23,550	27,436	0.68
Amerigas Partners Lp/Ap	05-20-11	23,365	25,760	0.64
Aes 8.875%	02-15-11	21,050	23,523	0.58
Nextel Comms 6.875%	10-31-13	22,725	23,520	0.58
Jostens 12.75%	05-01-10	19,921	22,262	0.55
Warner Music Grp 144A 7.	04-15-14	21,200	21,889	0.54
Synagro Tech 9.5%	04-01-09	19,980	21,279	0.53
Csc Hldgs 144A 6.75%	04-15-12	21,050	21,155	0.53
Nrg Engy 144A 8%	12-15-13	19,740	21,122	0.52
R H Donnelley Fin 10.875	12-15-12	17,150	20,794	0.52
Plastipak Hldgs 10.75%	09-01-11	18,425	20,544	0.51
Refco Fin Hldgs 144A 9%	08-01-12	19,325	20,358	0.51

Current Investment Style

Duration: Short Int Long; Quality: High Med Low

¹ figure provided by fund

Avg Eff Duration¹	3.4 Yrs
Avg Eff Maturity	7.3 Yrs
Avg Credit Quality	B
Avg Wtd Coupon	8.97%
Avg Wtd Price	106.95% of par

Coupon Range	% of Bonds	Rel Cat
0% PIK	3.7	0.8
0% to 8%	26.1	0.7
8% to 11%	62.3	1.1
11% to 14%	11.2	1.6
More than 14%	0.5	2.3

1.00=Category Average

Credit Analysis		% bonds 09-30-04	
US Govt	0	BB	20
AAA	0	B	69
AA	0	Below B	11
A	0	NR/NA	0
BBB	0		

Sector Breakdown	% of assets
US Treasuries	0
TIPS	0
US Agency	0
Mortgage Pass-Throughs	0
Mortgage CMO	0
Mortgage ARM	0
US Corporate	92
Asset-Backed	0
Convertible	0
Municipal	0
Corporate Inflation-Protected	0
Foreign Corporate	4
Foreign Govt	0

Composition			
Cash	3.1	Bonds	94.1
Stocks	2.1	Other	0.7

Special Securities	
Restricted/Illiquid Secs	22
Exotic Mortgage-Backed	0
Emerging-Markets Secs	0
Options/Futures/Warrants	No

Morningstar's Take by Scott Berry 11-05-04

T. Rowe Price High-Yield remains closed to new investors, but it continues to get the job done.

This fund has delivered solid results since the first of the year. Returns in the high-yield bond group have been tightly bunched for much of the year, but good performances by a number of this fund's larger holdings, including Dex Media and Allegheny Energy, have helped push this fund past its average peer. For the year to date through Nov. 12, 2004, the fund gained 8.47%, while its average high-yield rival returned 7.94%.

Solid performance is nothing new here. In fact, the fund's three-year trailing return lands in the category's top third, while its five- and 10-year results rank in the group's best quartile. That success owes to Mark Vaselkiv's skilled management and the fund's below-average costs. Vaselkiv has been at the helm here for more than eight years and has guided the fund with a steady hand through a variety of market environments. The fund held up better than most during the high-yield market's slump in 2000, for example, and nearly kept pace with its average peer during the market's rally in 2003. On the expense front, the fund's 0.78% expense ratio provides the fund a sustainable advantage over its average no-load peer, which charges 0.94%.

We also like this fund for its relatively low volatility and competitive yield. Vaselkiv, backed by a team of 10 analysts, has the flexibility to bulk up on riskier higher-yielding CCC bonds or more interest-rate sensitive BB issues, but he sticks primarily with B rated issues. Those issues have provided an ample yield for shareholders, while Vaselkiv's skilled issue selection has kept the fund out of too much trouble.

This fund's returns could taper off if interest rates move higher or defaults pick up, but we expect Vaselkiv and his team will continue to deliver good relative returns. Potential investors will need to look elsewhere, though, because the fund closed to new investors in early 2004.

Address:	100 E Pratt St Baltimore MD 21202 800-638-5660
Web Address:	www.troweprice.com
Inception:	12-31-84
Advisor:	T. Rowe Price Associates, Inc.
Subadvisor:	None
NTF Plans:	Federated Tr NTF

Minimum Purchase:	Closed	Add: —	IRA: —
Min Auto Inv Plan:	Closed	Add: —	
Sales Fees:	No-load, 1.00%R		
Management Fee:	0.62%		
Actual Fees:	Mgt:0.62%	Dist:	
Expense Projections:	3Yr:$259	5Yr:$450	10Yr:$1002
Income Distrib:	Monthly		

T. Rowe Price Intl Bd

Analyst Pick

Ticker	Load	NAV	Yield	SEC Yield	Total Assets	Mstar Category
RPIBX	None	$10.69	2.3%	2.13%	$1,727 mil	World Bond

Governance and Management

Fiduciary Grade: B

Portfolio Manager(s)

Ian Kelson is the lead manager at this fund, backed by comanagers Chris Rothery and Mike Conelius. Kelson joined T. Rowe Price in 2000 as head of fixed-income investment. Rothery has been with the fund since 1994; Conelius has been around since 1995. The three also manage T. Rowe Price Emerging Markets Bond, which has a solid long-term record.

Strategy

This fund provides investors with diversification from U.S. markets. The managers establish duration positioning and country exposure relative to the J.P. Morgan Non-U.S. Dollar Global Government Bond Index. The fund will venture into emerging-markets and high-yield corporate debt, but management stashes the bulk of its assets in government bonds from developed countries.

Historical Profile

Return Above Avg
Risk Above Avg
Rating ★★★ Neutral

Investment Style: Fixed Income — Income Rtn %Rank Cat

65	66	52	82	75	61	70	90	83

▼ Manager Change
∇ Partial Manager Change

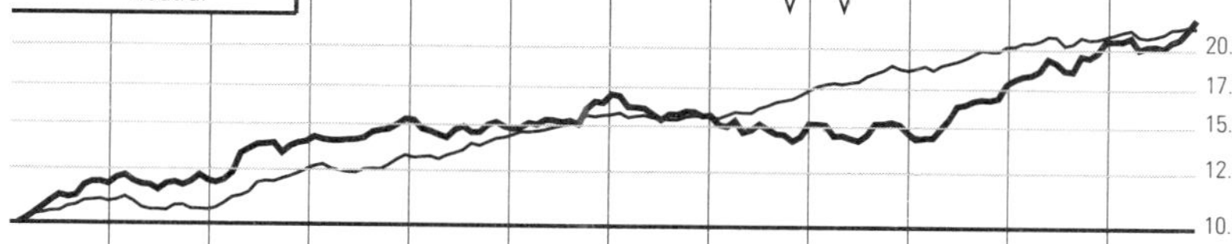

Growth of $10,000
▬ Investment Values of Fund
— Investment Values of LB Aggr

Performance Quartile (within Category)

1993	1994	1995	1996	1997	1998	1999	2000	2001	2002	2003	12-04	History
10.34	9.34	10.46	10.46	9.58	10.46	9.16	8.47	7.86	9.29	10.25	10.69	NAV
20.03	-1.84	20.31	7.14	-3.17	15.03	-7.86	-3.13	-3.41	21.80	18.78	11.41	Total Return %
10.28	1.08	1.84	3.51	-12.82	6.34	-7.04	-14.76	-11.85	11.55	14.68	7.07	+/-LB Aggr
4.91	-7.83	0.76	3.06	1.09	-2.76	-2.79	-0.50	0.13	-0.19	0.26	-0.73	+/-SB Wld Govt
7.36	5.95	6.86	5.92	5.16	5.47	3.76	4.39	3.90	3.25	2.78	2.50	Income Return %
12.67	-7.79	13.45	1.22	-8.33	9.56	-11.62	-7.52	-7.31	18.55	16.00	8.91	Capital Return %
7	27	31	72	85	15	83	82	84	9	23	19	Total Rtn % Rank Cat
0.68	0.60	0.62	0.60	0.53	0.51	0.38	0.39	0.32	0.25	0.25	0.25	Income $
0.46	0.21	0.12	0.11	0.02	0.00	0.11	0.00	0.00	0.00	0.50	0.44	Capital Gains $
0.99	0.98	0.90	0.87	0.86	0.88	0.90	0.91	0.95	0.93	0.91	—	Expense Ratio %
6.58	6.07	6.10	5.86	5.38	5.19	3.93	4.76	3.98	3.01	2.58	—	Income Ratio %
396	345	237	234	156	129	95	161	108	114	39	—	Turnover Rate %
745	738	1,016	969	826	926	779	753	762	1,058	1,303	1,658	Net Assets $mil

Performance 12-31-04

	1st Qtr	2nd Qtr	3rd Qtr	4th Qtr	Total
2000	-1.99	-1.30	-4.07	4.39	-3.13
2001	-4.70	-1.82	7.04	-3.55	-3.41
2002	-1.89	13.56	2.72	6.44	21.80
2003	3.65	5.05	2.76	6.16	18.78
2004	1.41	-3.23	2.96	10.25	11.41

Trailing	Total Return%	+/- LB Aggr	+/- SB Wld Govt	%Rank Cat	Growth of $10,000
3 Mo	10.25	9.30	-0.39	15	11,025
6 Mo	13.52	9.34	-0.75	16	11,352
1 Yr	11.41	7.07	-0.73	19	11,141
3 Yr Avg	17.25	11.06	-0.23	17	16,119
5 Yr Avg	8.57	0.86	-0.20	30	15,085
10 Yr Avg	7.15	-0.57	-0.18	52	19,949
15 Yr Avg	8.26	0.56	-0.40	13	32,887

Tax Analysis	Tax-Adj Rtn%	%Rank Cat	Tax-Cost Rat	%Rank Cat
3 Yr (estimated)	14.94	14	1.97	62
5 Yr (estimated)	6.55	30	1.86	42
10 Yr (estimated)	4.94	52	2.06	34

Potential Capital Gain Exposure: 15% of assets

Rating and Risk

Time Period	Load-Adj Return %	Morningstar Rtn vs Cat	Morningstar Risk vs Cat	Morningstar Risk-Adj Rating
1 Yr	11.41			
3 Yr	17.25	+Avg	+Avg	★★★★
5 Yr	8.57	+Avg	+Avg	★★★
10 Yr	7.15	Avg	+Avg	★★★
Incept	8.22			

Other Measures	Standard Index LB Aggr	Best Fit Index SB Wld Govt
Alpha	9.5	0.1
Beta	1.24	0.98
R-Squared	40	99
Standard Deviation	9.79	
Mean	17.25	
Sharpe Ratio	1.64	

Morningstar's Take by Lynn Russell 12-13-04

T. Rowe Price International Bond offers fixed-income investors a lot of diversification, but it comes with a lot of volatility.

This fund's fortunes are driven in large part by fluctuations in the dollar. Unlike some of its world-bond competitors, the fund avoids U.S. securities and doesn't typically hedge its foreign currency exposure back into the greenback. As a growing trade deficit and slow U.S. economic growth contributed to a continued decline in the dollar, the fund has profited, gaining 9.3% for the year to date through Dec. 11.

That's a drop from last year's spectacular gain of 19%, but it's good enough to land in the world-bond category's top third. But while the fund has notched three years of very strong gains, those returns have come on top of three straight years of losses. Overall the fund has delivered just average long-term trailing returns--10-year trailing returns slip just below the category midpoint--while enduring more month-to-month volatility than its average peer due to its exposure to currency fluctuations.

But while the fund takes on a ton of currency risk, it limits country and credit risk. The fund has the flexibility to invest in high-yield and emerging-markets bonds, for example, but lead manager Ian Kelson sticks primarily to sovereign debt from developed countries. More than 90% of assets are currently in securities rated AA or better, and the fund holds just a dash of investment-grade emerging-markets debt.

While most investors don't need an unhedged international-bond fund, those few who value the diversification benefits of the fund's currency exposure should find this fund appealing. Given its experienced management, high-quality portfolio, and below-average costs, we think this is a good choice for those investors who can handle its sometimes very bumpy ride.

Address:	100 E Pratt St Baltimore MD 21202 800-638-5660	Minimum Purchase:	$2500	Add: $100	IRA: $1000
		Min Auto Inv Plan:	$50	Add: $50	
		Sales Fees:	No-load, 2.00%R		
Web Address:	www.troweprice.com	Management Fee:	0.67%		
Inception:	09-10-86	Actual Fees:	Mgt:0.67%	Dist:	
Advisor:	T. Rowe Price Associates, Inc.	Expense Projections:	3Yr:$290	5Yr:$504	10Yr:$1120
Subadvisor:	None	Income Distrib:	Monthly		
NTF Plans:	N/A				

Portfolio Analysis 09-30-04

Total Fixed-Income:60	Date of Maturity	Amount $000	Value $000	% Net Assets
Germany (Federal Republi	07-04-07	46,800	62,914	4.42
Spain (Kingdom Of) 6%	01-31-08	34,200	46,493	3.26
Japan (Government Of) 1.	06-20-11	4,923,001	45,690	3.21
Italy (Republic Of) 6%	11-01-07	33,800	45,677	3.21
Italy (Republic Of) 6%	05-01-31	29,400	43,281	3.04
Portugal (Republic Of) 3	07-17-06	28,000	34,995	2.46
France (Republic Of) 5%	01-12-06	26,100	33,458	2.35
U.K. Treasury Stock 4.25	06-07-32	19,600	33,363	2.34
France (Republic Of) 5%	04-25-12	24,750	33,214	2.33
Germany (Federal Republi	01-04-31	21,500	30,211	2.12
Belgium (Kingdom Of) 4.2	09-28-13	22,500	28,522	2.00
Japan (Government Of) 1.	03-20-12	3,050,000	28,269	1.99
Austria (Republic Of) 5.	01-15-10	18,750	25,622	1.80
Germany (Federal Republi	01-05-06	19,350	25,083	1.76
Japan (Government Of) 1.	12-20-13	2,771,800	24,999	1.76
France (Republic Of) 5.7	10-25-32	16,672	24,228	1.70
Federal Republic Of Germ	01-04-12	16,260	21,821	1.53
Japan (Government Of) 1%	12-20-12	2,432,200	21,678	1.52
Ireland (Republic Of) 3.	04-18-09	16,300	20,247	1.42
Japan (Government Of) 1.	09-20-12	2,200,000	19,827	1.39

Current Investment Style

Duration: Short Int Long; Quality: High Med Low

	■	

[1] figure provided by fund

Avg Eff Duration[1]	4.5 Yrs
Avg Eff Maturity	6.4 Yrs
Avg Credit Quality	AA
Avg Wtd Coupon	4.79%
Avg Wtd Price	99.15% of par

Coupon Range	% of Bonds	Rel Cat
0% PIK	0.0	0.0
0% to 6%	92.0	1.2
6% to 8%	5.0	0.3
8% to 10%	1.9	0.3
More than 10%	1.1	0.6

1.00=Category Average

Credit Analysis	% bonds 09-30-04		
US Govt	0	BB	0
AAA	56	B	0
AA	38	Below B	0
A	5	NR/NA	0
BBB	1		

Sector Breakdown	% of assets
US Treasuries	—
TIPS	—
US Agency	—
Mortgage Pass-Throughs	—
Mortgage CMO	—
Mortgage ARM	—
US Corporate	—
Asset-Backed	—
Convertible	—
Municipal	—
Corporate Inflation-Protected	—
Foreign Corporate	—
Foreign Govt	—

Composition			
Cash	28.1	Bonds	71.7
Stocks	0.0	Other	0.2

Special Securities	
Restricted/Illiquid Secs	0
Exotic Mortgage-Backed	0
Emerging-Markets Secs	—
Options/Futures/Warrants	No

T. Rowe Price Intl Disc

Ticker	Load	NAV	Yield	Total Assets	Mstar Category
PRIDX	None	$32.63	0.0%	$1,002 mil	Foreign Small/Mid Growth

Governance and Management

Fiduciary Grade: B

Portfolio Manager(s)

Justin Thomson ran small-cap money for LGT Asset Management for several years before taking the helm at this fund in June 1998. A handful of seasoned Rowe Price-Fleming International managers serve as his comanagers.

Strategy

Manager Justin Thomson focuses on firms with market caps between $250 million and $3 billion that enjoy rapid earnings growth, robust sales growth, and strong returns on equity. The firm has frequently employed fair-value pricing in an effort to limit any potential damage to long-term shareholders from short-term fund traders.

Historical Profile

Return Above Avg
Risk Average
Rating ★★★★ Above Avg

Investment Style: Equity, Stock %: 88% 91% 96% 90% 89% 95% 92% 96% 93%

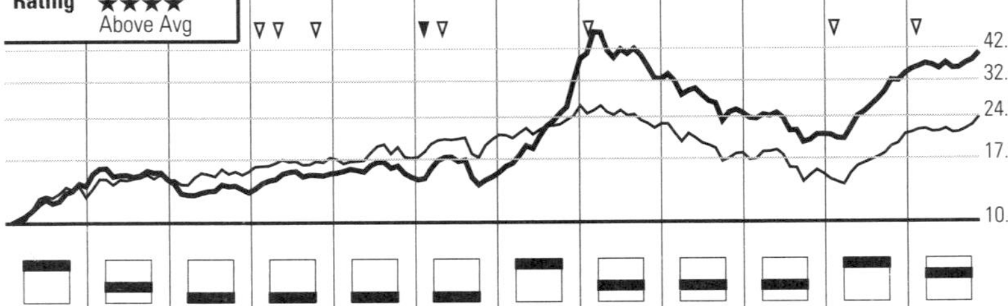

	1993	1994	1995	1996	1997	1998	1999	2000	2001	2002	2003	12-04	History
	17.41	15.14	14.36	16.22	15.05	15.65	36.77	25.45	19.18	16.06	26.40	32.63	NAV
	49.85	-7.63	-4.36	13.87	-5.67	6.12	155.03	-15.60	-24.64	-16.27	65.29	23.76	Total Return %
	17.29	-15.41	-15.57	7.82	-7.45	-13.81	128.00	-1.41	-3.22	-0.33	26.70	3.51	+/-MSCI EAFE
	17.64	-14.98	-15.77	7.00	-7.94	-12.57	127.05	-2.24	-3.25	-0.47	25.87	3.38	+/-MSCI Wd xUS
	0.60	0.34	0.66	0.49	0.00	0.07	0.00	0.00	0.00	0.00	0.50	0.04	Income Return %
	49.25	-7.97	-5.02	13.38	-5.67	6.05	155.03	-15.60	-24.64	-16.27	64.79	23.72	Capital Return %
	1	67	100	100	89	94	3	55	52	60	19	49	Total Rtn % Rank Cat
	0.07	0.06	0.10	0.07	0.00	0.01	0.00	0.00	0.00	0.00	0.08	0.01	Income $
	0.02	0.87	0.02	0.06	0.25	0.30	2.81	5.83	0.00	0.00	0.06	0.03	Capital Gains $
	1.50	1.50	1.50	1.45	1.41	1.47	1.42	1.27	1.38	1.44	1.41	1.32	Expense Ratio %
	0.81	0.38	0.55	0.40	0.13	0.25	-0.17	0.15	0.25	0.06	0.46	0.28	Income Ratio %
	72	57	44	52	73	34	98	81	59	94	116	106	Turnover Rate %
	392	437	303	322	228	193	687	765	486	370	705	1,002	Net Assets $mil

Performance 12-31-04

	1st Qtr	2nd Qtr	3rd Qtr	4th Qtr	Total
2000	24.20	-12.96	-4.91	-17.90	-15.60
2001	-12.30	-0.22	-19.26	6.67	-24.64
2002	-1.30	-2.85	-18.05	6.57	-16.27
2003	-3.49	25.03	18.27	15.82	65.29
2004	8.60	0.59	-0.45	13.80	23.76

Trailing	Total Return%	+/- MSCI EAFE	+/- MSCI Wd xUS	%Rank Cat	Growth of $10,000
3 Mo	13.80	-1.52	-1.35	69	11,380
6 Mo	13.29	-1.71	-2.08	67	11,329
1 Yr	23.76	3.51	3.38	49	12,376
3 Yr Avg	19.65	7.76	7.43	25	17,129
5 Yr Avg	1.73	2.86	2.49	24	10,895
10 Yr Avg	11.72	6.10	5.78	57	30,291
15 Yr Avg	9.13	4.90	4.72	1	37,082

Tax Analysis	Tax-Adj Rtn%	%Rank Cat	Tax-Cost Rat	%Rank Cat
3 Yr (estimated)	19.55	21	0.08	23
5 Yr (estimated)	0.26	31	1.45	94
10 Yr (estimated)	10.42	57	1.16	85

Potential Capital Gain Exposure: 6% of assets

Rating and Risk

Time Period	Load-Adj Return %	Morningstar Rtn vs Cat	Morningstar Risk vs Cat	Morningstar Risk-Adj Rating
1 Yr	23.76			
3 Yr	19.65	+Avg	Avg	★★★★
5 Yr	1.73	+Avg	Avg	★★★★
10 Yr	11.72	Avg	Avg	★★★
Incept	10.92			

Other Measures	Standard Index S&P 500	Best Fit Index MSCI Wd xUS
Alpha	7.8	7.4
Beta	0.94	0.95
R-Squared	82	82

Standard Deviation	19.27
Mean	19.65
Sharpe Ratio	0.96

Morningstar's Take by Arijit Dutta 11-22-04

T. Rowe Price International Discovery can play a useful role.

This is a genuine small-cap vehicle. The fund stands apart by being among the most small-cap focused in the foreign small/mid-growth category. As recently as 2003, it had 60% of assets in small- and micro-cap stocks, far exceeding the category norm of 37%.

This fund is also uncommonly bold in playing emerging markets. The fund has about a 15% stake, almost twice the category average. The fund has favored emerging markets such as India, where the legal and competitive climates make it easier for smaller companies to thrive and not be stifled by large corporations. It has therefore avoided countries with otherwise-lucrative markets, such as Russia and Brazil, that lack these characteristics. And the fund has also tapped into growth in emerging economies by indirect means. For example, the fund owns Cairns Energy, a British oil exploration company with operations in South Asia (Cairns' stock has risen 275% thus far in 2004).

Under current lead manager Justin Thomson (who has led the team since 1998), the fund has managed these twin risks well. Most notably, during the global recession of 2000-2002, the fund managed not to lose much more than the category norm, even with its oversized load of smaller companies. Partly offsetting the fund's aggressive positioning is its diversification across stocks. With close to 200 holdings, it is among the most diversified in the category.

In addition to its reliable performance, the fund also has some of the lowest fees among the overtly small-cap focused funds in the category. An experienced management team based in London, Tokyo, and Singapore inspires confidence that it will continue to be a good pick.

This fund is risky, but with its sensibly executed strategy, we think it can ably support a core foreign holding.

Address:	100 E Pratt St Baltimore MD 21202 800-638-5660
Web Address:	www.troweprice.com
Inception:	12-30-88
Advisor:	T. Rowe Price Associates, Inc.
Subadvisor:	None
NTF Plans:	N/A

Minimum Purchase:	$2500	Add: $100	IRA: $1000
Min Auto Inv Plan:	$50	Add: $50	
Sales Fees:	No-load, 2.00%R		
Management Fee:	1.07%		
Actual Fees:	Mgt:1.07%	Dist:	
Expense Projections:	3Yr:$446	5Yr:$771	10Yr:$1691
Income Distrib:	Annually		

Portfolio Analysis 09-30-04

Share change since 06-04 Total Stocks:215	Sector	Country	% Assets
⊖ Aristocrat Leisure Ltd	Consumer	Australia	1.81
K & S Ag	Ind Mtrls	Germany	1.75
Spir Communication	Media	France	1.21
⊕ IDS Scheer	Business	Germany	1.18
UCB Grp	Health	Belgium	1.12
Sorin	Health	Italy	1.11
⊕ GfK	Business	Germany	1.10
Dis Deutscher Restricted	—	—	1.10
Cairn Energy	Energy	U.K.	1.01
3i Grp	Financial	U.K.	0.97
⊕ Benfield Grp Ltd	Business	U.K.	0.94
Rapala VMC	Goods	Finland	0.92
⊕ Marlborough Stirling	Software	U.K.	0.90
☼ OMC Card	Financial	Japan	0.87
⊕ Eidos	Software	U.K.	0.87
Merchant Retail Grp	Consumer	U.K.	0.86
☼ Germanos Restricted	—	—	0.83
Teleca	Business	Sweden	0.83
⊖ Neopost	Ind Mtrls	France	0.80
Ipsos	Business	France	0.80

Current Investment Style

Value Blnd Growth (style box: Small Growth)

Market Cap	%
Giant	0.0
Large	3.2
Mid	45.5
Small	38.8
Micro	12.4
Avg $mil: 760	

Value Measures		Rel Category
Price/Earnings	14.78	1.07
Price/Book	2.04	1.07
Price/Sales	0.93	1.13
Price/Cash Flow	5.70	1.14
Dividend Yield %	1.94	0.85

Growth Measures	%	Rel Category
Long-Term Erngs	432.14	9.34
Book Value	-3.40	NMF
Sales	5.90	0.94
Cash Flow	4.14	0.89
Historical Erngs	-2.93	NMF

Composition

Cash	3.9	Bonds	0.3
Stocks	93.4	Other	2.4
Foreign (% of Stock)			99.3

Sector Weightings	% of Stocks	Rel MSCI EAFE	3 Year High	3 Year Low
Info	14.06	0.85		
Software	4.60	4.26	10	5
Hardware	1.99	0.55	5	1
Media	3.86	1.69	4	0
Telecom	3.61	0.38	6	1
Service	51.75	1.16		
Health	10.77	1.48	17	6
Consumer	11.86	2.35	12	7
Business	14.88	2.74	17	13
Financial	14.24	0.53	16	6
Mfg	34.20	0.88		
Goods	11.75	0.86	27	12
Ind Mtrls	19.35	1.57	20	8
Energy	2.76	0.38	3	0
Utilities	0.34	0.06	1	0

Regional Exposure	% Stock		
UK/W. Europe	49	N. America	1
Japan	24	Latn America	1
Asia X Japan	25	Other	0

Country Exposure	% Stock		
Japan	24	France	6
U.K.	14	Australia	6
Germany	8		

T. Rowe Price Intl Stk

Ticker	Load	NAV	Yield	Total Assets	Mstar Category
PRITX	None	$12.93	1.2%	$5,260 mil	Foreign Large Growth

Governance and Management

Fiduciary Grade: B

Portfolio Manager(s)

A seasoned team of professionals from Rowe Price-Fleming International--one of the most respected international investment houses--runs this fund. It includes Mark Bickford-Smith, David J.L. Warren, and James B.M. Seddon, each of whom has been on the fund for more than nine years and boasts more than 17 years of industry experience. Long-time comanager John Ford took a leave of absence in March 2004.

Strategy

Management focuses on large caps with good earnings growth and moderate prices. It is no surprise, given the fund's enormous asset base, that managers move slowly and pay attention to diversification. T. Rowe Price applies fair-value pricing to the fund.

Historical Profile

Return Average
Risk Average
Rating ★★★ Neutral

Investment Style: Equity Stock %: 92% | 95% | 94% | 94% | 92% | 96% | 96% | 97% | 95%

▼ Manager Change ∇ Partial Manager Change

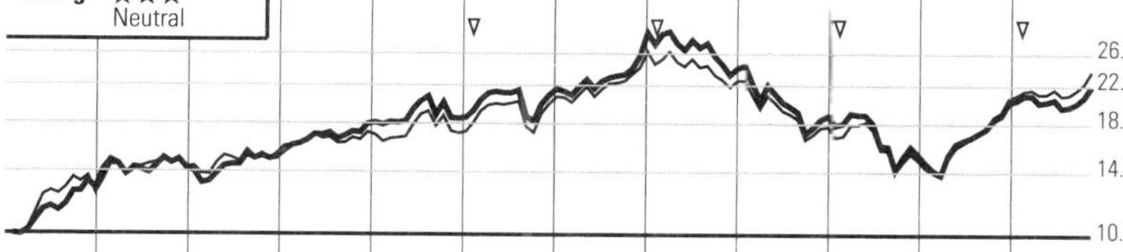

Growth of $10,000
— Investment Values of Fund
— Investment Values of MSCI EAFE

Performance Quartile (within Category)

1993	1994	1995	1996	1997	1998	1999	2000	2001	2002	2003	12-04	History
12.16	11.32	12.23	13.80	13.42	14.99	19.03	14.52	10.99	8.88	11.49	12.93	NAV
40.11	-0.76	11.39	15.99	2.70	16.14	34.60	-17.09	-22.02	-18.18	31.28	13.89	Total Return %
7.55	-8.54	0.18	9.94	0.92	-3.79	7.57	-2.90	-0.60	-2.24	-7.31	-6.36	+/-MSCI EAFE
7.90	-8.11	-0.02	9.12	0.43	-2.55	6.62	-3.73	-0.63	-2.38	-8.14	-6.49	+/-MSCI Wd xUS
1.01	0.99	1.59	1.47	1.45	1.64	0.87	0.47	2.07	1.00	1.46	1.31	Income Return %
39.10	-1.75	9.80	14.52	1.25	14.50	33.73	-17.56	-24.09	-19.18	29.82	12.58	Capital Return %
39	48	38	36	73	35	80	43	36	34	65	60	Total Rtn % Rank Cat
0.09	0.12	0.18	0.18	0.20	0.22	0.13	0.09	0.30	0.11	0.13	0.15	Income $
0.20	0.62	0.20	0.20	0.55	0.35	0.91	1.18	0.03	0.00	0.03	0.00	Capital Gains $
1.01	0.96	0.91	0.88	0.85	0.85	0.85	0.84	0.90	0.92	0.95	0.92	Expense Ratio %
1.52	1.11	1.56	1.58	1.33	1.50	1.05	0.55	2.14	0.96	1.39	1.22	Income Ratio %
30	23	18	12	16	12	18	38	17	22	25	28	Turnover Rate %
4,290	5,787	6,703	9,341	9,721	10,142	12,674	9,735	6,507	4,434	5,208	5,221	Net Assets $mil

Performance 12-31-04

	1st Qtr	2nd Qtr	3rd Qtr	4th Qtr	Total
2000	0.47	-4.45	-8.10	-6.03	-17.09
2001	-15.50	-0.98	-15.14	9.83	-22.02
2002	1.27	-4.94	-21.64	8.47	-18.18
2003	-10.14	19.92	6.17	14.74	31.28
2004	3.74	-2.01	-1.97	14.29	13.89

Trailing	Total Return%	+/- MSCI EAFE	+/- MSCI Wd xUS	%Rank Cat	Growth of $10,000
3 Mo	14.29	-1.03	-0.86	35	11,429
6 Mo	12.04	-2.96	-3.33	57	11,204
1 Yr	13.89	-6.36	-6.49	60	11,389
3 Yr Avg	6.95	-4.94	-5.27	53	12,233
5 Yr Avg	-4.58	-3.45	-3.82	32	7,910
10 Yr Avg	5.07	-0.55	-0.87	62	16,398
15 Yr Avg	5.78	1.55	1.37	29	23,230

Tax Analysis	Tax-Adj Rtn%	%Rank Cat	Tax-Cost Rat	%Rank Cat
3 Yr (estimated)	6.45	53	0.47	76
5 Yr (estimated)	-5.41	33	0.87	52
10 Yr (estimated)	4.01	49	1.01	55

Potential Capital Gain Exposure: 10% of assets

Rating and Risk

Time Period	Load-Adj Return %	Morningstar Rtn vs Cat	Morningstar Risk vs Cat	Morningstar Risk-Adj Rating
1 Yr	13.89			
3 Yr	6.95	Avg	+Avg	★★★
5 Yr	-4.58	Avg	Avg	★★★★
10 Yr	5.07	Avg	-Avg	★★★
Incept	10.82			

Other Measures	Standard Index S&P 500	Best Fit Index MSCI EAFE
Alpha	-4.8	-4.8
Beta	1.05	1.05
R-Squared	98	98
Standard Deviation	17.81	
Mean	6.95	
Sharpe Ratio	0.32	

Portfolio Analysis 09-30-04

Share change since 06-04 Total Stocks:175	Sector	Country	% Assets
⊖ GlaxoSmithKline	Health	U.K.	3.23
⊖ TOTAL	Energy	France	2.58
⊖ Royal Bank Of Scotland G	Financial	U.K.	2.45
⊖ Vodafone Grp	Telecom	U.K.	2.40
⊕ UBS	Financial	Switzerland	1.80
⊖ Nestle	Goods	Switzerland	1.65
⊖ Shell Transport & Tradin	Energy	U.K.	1.59
⊖ Kingfisher	Consumer	U.K.	1.41
⊖ Eni	Energy	Italy	1.36
⊖ Sanofi-Synthelabo	Health	France	1.23
⊕ AstraZeneca	Health	U.K.	1.22
⊖ Adecco	Business	Switzerland	1.18
⊖ BNP Paribas	Financial	France	1.11
⊖ Securitas	Business	Sweden	1.09
⊖ Canon	Goods	Japan	1.07
⊖ ING Groep	Financial	Netherlands	1.02
⊖ Nokia	Hardware	Finland	0.97
⊖ UniCredito Italiano Grp	Financial	Italy	0.96
⊖ France Telecom	Telecom	France	0.96
⊖ Credit Agricole	Financial	France	0.95

Current Investment Style

Value Blnd Growth / Large Mid Small

Market Cap	%
Giant	56.7
Large	31.9
Mid	11.1
Small	0.3
Micro	0.0

Avg $mil: 22,780

Value Measures		Rel Category
Price/Earnings	14.15	0.95
Price/Book	2.11	1.01
Price/Sales	1.04	0.99
Price/Cash Flow	4.35	0.79
Dividend Yield %	2.31	1.13

Growth Measures	%	Rel Category
Long-Term Erngs	10.47	0.88
Book Value	1.19	0.69
Sales	2.97	0.64
Cash Flow	8.46	1.12
Historical Erngs	8.10	0.97

Composition

Cash	3.4	Bonds	0.0
Stocks	95.4	Other	1.2
Foreign (% of Stock)			99.4

Sector Weightings	% of Stocks	Rel MSCI EAFE	3 Year High	3 Year Low
Info	19.82	1.19		
Software	1.39	1.29	1	0
Hardware	4.24	1.16	7	4
Media	4.87	2.14	5	2
Telecom	9.32	0.97	11	8
Service	46.32	1.04		
Health	9.01	1.24	15	9
Consumer	6.96	1.38	8	4
Business	6.45	1.19	9	5
Financial	23.90	0.89	24	21
Mfg	33.86	0.88		
Goods	15.36	1.12	17	14
Ind Mtrls	8.63	0.70	9	5
Energy	8.24	1.12	12	5
Utilities	1.63	0.30	2	1

Regional Exposure	% Stock		
UK/W. Europe	65	N. America	1
Japan	22	Latn America	3
Asia X Japan	7	Other	2

Country Exposure	% Stock		
U.K.	23	Switzerland	6
Japan	22	Italy	5
France	15		

Morningstar's Take by Arijit Dutta 11-19-04

T. Rowe Price International Stock is not really a fund you'd recognize in a crowd.

The fund has struggled against mediocrity. After flirting with top-third rankings in the foreign large-growth category during the 2001-2002 bear market, it fell behind the average peer as markets took off in 2003. In 2004, markets have been largely favorable to this fund's valuation-wary take on growth investing. Yet, International Stock's 8.44% return through Nov. 12 falls short of the category median of 9.42%. The fund's 3- and 5-year trailing returns reflect the same tendency to relegate to the category's middle.

Uninspired stock selection is largely to blame. The fund's long-term performance speaks to an inability to consistently add value through stock-picking. The fund misread the political risk surrounding Russian oil giant Yukos, for example. The sharp drop in British food-service provider Compass Group, over earnings concerns, was another bad surprise.

In many ways, T. Rowe's international team is a work in progress. T. Rowe took control of Rowe Price Fleming in 2000, and it had to assemble its analyst staff from scratch although it retained its portfolio managers. It takes a while to make a team mesh, and this may be why stock selection has been poor. T. Rowe is focusing its efforts on improving results overseas, and it could be that enough time has passed that it is ready to turn the corner.

Still, this is only a middling fund and there are more attractive options out there.

Address:	100 E Pratt St Baltimore MD 21202 800-638-5660
Web Address:	www.troweprice.com
Inception:	05-09-80
Advisor:	T. Rowe Price Associates, Inc.
Subadvisor:	None
NTF Plans:	N/A

Minimum Purchase:	$2500	Add: $100	IRA: $1000
Min Auto Inv Plan:	$50	Add: $50	
Sales Fees:	No-load, 2.00%R		
Management Fee:	0.67%		
Actual Fees:	Mgt:0.67%	Dist:	
Expense Projections:	3Yr:$303	5Yr:$525	10Yr:$1166
Income Distrib:	Annually		

T. Rowe Price Latin Amer

Analyst Pick

Ticker	Load	NAV	Yield	Total Assets	Mstar Category
PRLAX	None	$15.95	1.3%	$310 mil	Latin America Stock

Governance and Management

Fiduciary Grade: B

Portfolio Manager(s)

Gonzalo Pangaro replaced Benedict Thomas as manager at the end of January 2004. Pangaro had worked with Thomas as comanager from March 2000 through December 2002. Pangaro has the support of two analysts who work exclusively on Latin American stocks and an analyst covering global telecommunications--an important sector in Latin America.

Strategy

Management looks for reasonably priced blue chips that it thinks will improve earnings year after year. The fund will build big positions in individual growth industries, such as telecom, but management does this and everything else at a moderate pace. Turnover is well below average here.

Historical Profile

Return Above Avg
Risk Below Avg
Rating ★★★★ Above Avg

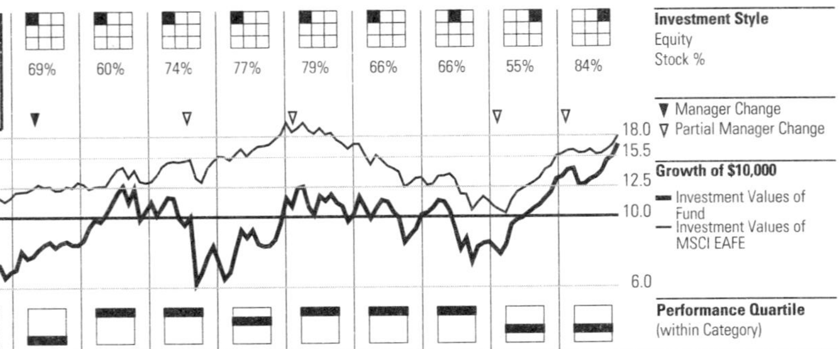

1993	1994	1995	1996	1997	1998	1999	2000	2001	2002	2003	12-04	History
10.05	8.45	6.81	8.26	10.77	6.81	10.81	9.56	9.17	7.51	11.69	15.95	NAV
0.50*	-15.92	-18.70	23.35	31.88	-35.43	59.38	-11.20	-0.23	-18.10	57.92	38.35	Total Return %
—	-23.70	-29.91	17.30	30.10	-55.36	32.35	2.99	21.19	-2.16	19.33	18.10	+/-MSCI EAFE
—	-14.93	-3.67	4.48	3.54	2.63	3.90	7.18	4.01	6.69	-9.14	3.58	+/-MSCI EMF LA
—	0.00	0.71	1.62	1.45	1.30	0.59	0.37	1.57	0.00	2.13	1.80	Income Return %
—	-15.92	-19.41	21.73	30.43	-36.73	58.79	-11.57	-1.80	-18.10	55.79	36.55	Capital Return %
—	75	34	100	17	17	40	1	1	1	67	53	Total Rtn % Rank Cat
0.00	0.00	0.06	0.11	0.12	0.14	0.04	0.04	0.15	0.00	0.16	0.21	Income $
0.00	0.00	0.00	0.03	0.00	0.00	0.00	0.00	0.20	0.00	0.00	0.00	Capital Gains $
—	1.99	1.82	1.66	1.47	1.53	1.62	1.46	1.49	1.53	1.55	1.41	Expense Ratio %
—	-0.35	0.76	1.29	1.30	1.35	1.05	0.42	1.40	1.88	1.55	2.22	Income Ratio %
—	12	19	22	33	19	43	28	30	21	27	35	Turnover Rate %
—	164	150	211	433	182	268	207	177	129	201	310	Net Assets $mil

Performance 12-31-04

	1st Qtr	2nd Qtr	3rd Qtr	4th Qtr	Total
2000	8.79	-6.63	-4.83	-8.14	-11.20
2001	-2.93	12.93	-25.57	22.28	-0.23
2002	10.91	-18.58	-21.26	15.18	-18.10
2003	-2.13	22.04	9.81	20.40	57.92
2004	7.61	-7.47	14.69	21.15	38.35

Trailing	Total Return%	+/- MSCI EAFE	+/- MSCI EMF LA	%Rank Cat	Growth of $10,000
3 Mo	21.15	5.83	1.34	67	12,115
6 Mo	38.94	23.94	-0.70	67	13,894
1 Yr	38.35	18.10	3.58	53	13,835
3 Yr Avg	21.40	9.51	2.21	47	17,892
5 Yr Avg	9.65	10.78	3.89	19	15,851
10 Yr Avg	7.99	2.37	2.84	17	21,569
15 Yr Avg	—	—	—	—	—

Tax Analysis	Tax-Adj Rtn%	%Rank Cat	Tax-Cost Rat	%Rank Cat
3 Yr (estimated)	21.00	40	0.33	50
5 Yr (estimated)	9.07	10	0.53	90
10 Yr (estimated)	7.45	17	0.50	34

Potential Capital Gain Exposure: 23% of assets

Rating and Risk

Time Period	Load-Adj Return %	Morningstar Rtn vs Cat	Morningstar Risk vs Cat	Morningstar Risk-Adj Rating
1 Yr	38.35			
3 Yr	21.40	Avg	-Avg	★★★
5 Yr	9.65	High	-Avg	★★★★★
10 Yr	7.99	—	—	—
Incept	5.61			

Other Measures	Standard Index S&P 500	Best Fit Index MSCI EMF LA
Alpha	7.8	3.3
Beta	1.21	0.90
R-Squared	64	98
Standard Deviation	29.16	
Mean	21.40	
Sharpe Ratio	0.69	

Portfolio Analysis 09-30-04

Share change since 06-04 Total Stocks:36	Sector	Country	% Assets
Petroleo Brasileiro Sa P	Energy	Brazil	13.17
⊕ America Movil SA ADR	Telecom	Mexico	10.83
Wal-Mart de Mexico	Consumer	Mexico	5.76
☼ Bco Itau Hldg F	—	Brazil	5.25
⊖ Telefonos de Mexico SA A	Telecom	Mexico	4.74
Grupo Televisa ADR	Media	Mexico	4.55
⊕ Companhia Vale Do Rio Do	Ind Mtrls	Brazil	3.53
☼ Companhia Vale Do Rio Do	Ind Mtrls	United States	3.42
⊕ Tele Norte Leste Partici	Telecom	Brazil	2.79
⊖ CEMEX	Ind Mtrls	Mexico	2.69
⊕ Petroleo Brasileiro ADR	Energy	Brazil	2.61
☼ Bco Bradesco Sa	—	Brazil	2.28
⊖ Companhia de Bebidas das	Goods	United States	2.17
⊕ Gpo Fin Banorte	Financial	Mexico	2.17
⊖ Gpo Modelo Sa De C	Goods	Mexico	2.11
⊕ Votorantim Celulose e Pa	Ind Mtrls	Brazil	2.11
⊖ Cemig Cia Energ Mg	—	Brazil	2.06
Tenaris SA	Ind Mtrls	Luxembourg	2.05
Grupo Aeroportuario ADR	Business	Mexico	1.79
⊕ Telesp Celular Participa	Telecom	Brazil	1.75

Current Investment Style

Value Blnd Growth; Large Mid Small

Market Cap	%
Giant	46.4
Large	30.1
Mid	22.9
Small	0.6
Micro	0.0
Avg $mil: 8,232	

Value Measures		Rel Category
Price/Earnings	11.60	0.96
Price/Book	2.08	1.10
Price/Sales	1.43	1.40
Price/Cash Flow	9.21	1.01
Dividend Yield %	1.10	1.00

Growth Measures	%	Rel Category
Long-Term Erngs	13.70	0.66
Book Value	12.77	2.18
Sales	10.83	0.73
Cash Flow	-12.95	NMF
Historical Erngs	17.38	1.64

Composition

Cash	5.1	Bonds	0.0
Stocks	83.8	Other	11.1
Foreign (% of Stock)			93.3

Sector Weightings	% of Stocks	Rel MSCI EAFE	3 Year High	3 Year Low
Info	32.11	1.93		
Software	0.00	0.00	0	0
Hardware	0.00	0.00	0	0
Media	5.60	2.46	8	4
Telecom	26.51	2.76	49	27
Service	17.34	0.39		
Health	0.00	0.00	0	0
Consumer	9.79	1.94	19	0
Business	2.78	0.51	6	0
Financial	4.77	0.18	23	0
Mfg	50.56	1.31		
Goods	5.86	0.43	26	6
Ind Mtrls	24.13	1.96	27	9
Energy	19.41	2.64	19	0
Utilities	1.16	0.22	4	0

Regional Exposure (% Stock)

UK/W. Europe	2	N. America	6
Japan	0	Latn America	91
Asia X Japan	0	Other	1

Country Exposure (% Stock)

Mexico	43	Chile	3
Brazil	43	Luxembourg	2
United States	6		

Morningstar's Take by Bridget Hughes 12-22-04

T. Rowe Price Latin America is the lone Analyst Pick in its category, but that's hardly a recommendation to load up.

Despite a management change in early 2004, this fund remains our only favorite from the Latin America-stock category. To a large extent, that's because of T. Rowe Price's steady and moderate approach. The firm's consistent and ingrained method--a growth-at-a-reasonable-price strategy used at the shop's other international funds--means that manager changes can be less of an issue, even though we were fans of previous manager Benedict Thomas. Further, we appreciate T. Rowe Price's cautious approach, which includes paying attention to valuations and typically turning to higher-quality firms, particularly in a category that's already as risky as the Latin America group. We're also pleased that the fund's expense ratio is one of the lowest in this small category.

While we like the fund better than its peers, we believe most investors should probably take a pass on the category. As a group, Latin America funds are highly volatile, making them harder to own for the long haul. The volatility comes from the risks inherent in the politically charged region, whose stock markets have regularly produced wild swings in performance. And given that the investable universe of the region is comparatively small, the funds are typically beholden to two countries, Mexico and Brazil, and a small, typically concentrated stash of stocks. Indeed, even this moderate fund owns just 40 or so names, with regularly big stakes in Latin index anchors Petrobras, American Movil, and Telmex.

We're more emphatic about that guidance now. The category has produced very strong results in the past two years. This fund, for example, has more than doubled since 2002's fourth quarter. Although there have been some positive fundamental developments in the region, that could also mean one of Latin America's periodic dry spells is just around the corner.

Address:	100 E Pratt St, Baltimore MD 21202, 800-638-5660
Web Address:	www.troweprice.com
Inception:	12-29-93*
Advisor:	T. Rowe Price Associates, Inc.
Subadvisor:	None
NTF Plans:	N/A

Minimum Purchase:	$2500	Add: $100	IRA: $1000
Min Auto Inv Plan:	$50	Add: $50	
Sales Fees:	No-load, 2.00%R		
Management Fee:	1.07%		
Actual Fees:	Mgt:1.07%	Dist:	
Expense Projections:	3Yr:$490	5Yr:$845	10Yr:$1845
Income Distrib:	Annually		

T. Rowe Price Med & Tele

Analyst Pick

Ticker	Load	NAV	Yield	Total Assets	Mstar Category
PRMTX	None	$28.43	0.0%	$877 mil	Specialty-Communications

Governance and Management

Fiduciary Grade: B

Portfolio Manager(s)

Manager Rob Gensler started in January 2000, after former manager Brian Stansky left to run a hedge fund. He had worked as an analyst covering the telecom-services and -equipment areas since 1995, and he worked with Stansky on this fund. He is supported by roughly a dozen analysts throughout the world. Gensler reportedly invests his entire 401(k) account in the fund. His compensation is based, in part, on the fund's performance.

Strategy

Manager Rob Gensler seeks to buy communications- and media-related companies positioned to benefit from secular trends. He looks for firms trading at discounts to comparable industry peers, but he will pay more for those he thinks are dominant. Strong management and substantial leads over competitors are qualities that pique his interest. Gensler will look at peer averages in calibrating the fund's subsector weightings. He also has been increasingly willing to look abroad for opportunities, particularly in areas characterized by less-onerous competition.

Historical Profile

Return: High
Risk: Average
Rating: ★★★★★ Highest

Investment Style: Equity Stock %

93% 92% 88% 83% 93% 98% 97% 97%

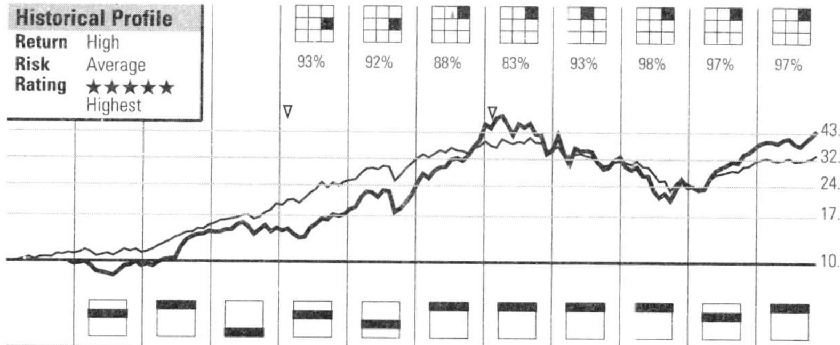

▼ Manager Change
∇ Partial Manager Change

Growth of $10,000
— Investment Values of Fund
— Investment Values of S&P 500

Performance Quartile (within Category)

History

1993	1994	1995	1996	1997	1998	1999	2000	2001	2002	2003	12-04	History
13.57	13.44	17.99	15.22	17.40	22.54	39.99	21.65	20.15	14.43	22.51	28.43	NAV
-2.16*	-0.90	43.29	1.78	28.05	35.14	93.09	-25.11	-6.93	-28.39	55.99	26.30	Total Return %
—	-2.21	5.76	-21.16	-5.30	6.57	72.05	-16.01	4.95	-6.30	27.32	15.43	+/-S&P 500
—	4.25	2.77	1.67	-12.59	-16.68	74.68	15.16	5.84	6.16	48.66	7.60	+/-DJ Telecom
0.00	0.05	0.52	0.00	0.20	0.00	0.00	0.93	0.00	0.00	0.00	0.00	Income Return %
—	-0.95	42.77	1.78	27.85	35.14	93.09	-26.04	-6.93	-28.39	55.99	26.30	Capital Return %
—	50	1	87	50	56	8	22	4	17	33	19	Total Rtn % Rank Cat
0.01	0.01	0.07	0.00	0.03	0.00	0.00	0.37	0.00	0.00	0.00	0.00	Income $
0.00	0.00	1.13	3.09	2.02	0.86	3.22	8.60	0.00	0.00	0.00	0.00	Capital Gains $
1.30	1.35	1.25	1.22	1.21	1.03	0.93	0.94	1.08	1.15	1.10	—	Expense Ratio %
0.24	-0.15	-0.25	-0.55	-0.06	-0.38	-0.24	1.07	-0.39	-0.31	-0.51	—	Income Ratio %
—	134	119	103	39	49	58	198	241	185	124	—	Turnover Rate %
203	201	269	213	134	246	930	798	675	421	665	877	Net Assets $mil

Performance 12-31-04

	1st Qtr	2nd Qtr	3rd Qtr	4th Qtr	Total
2000	9.83	-8.63	-10.42	-16.69	-25.11
2001	-14.73	17.33	-16.76	11.76	-6.93
2002	-10.92	-23.18	-10.37	16.75	-28.39
2003	-2.49	27.01	5.82	19.04	55.99
2004	6.31	3.76	-3.22	18.31	26.30

Trailing	Total Return%	+/- S&P 500	+/- DJ Telecom	%Rank Cat	Growth of $10,000
3 Mo	18.31	9.08	10.09	32	11,831
6 Mo	14.50	7.31	-0.39	47	11,450
1 Yr	26.30	15.43	7.60	19	12,630
3 Yr Avg	12.16	8.58	18.04	1	14,110
5 Yr Avg	-0.33	1.97	15.03	15	9,836
10 Yr Avg	16.96	4.89	12.51	1	47,904
15 Yr Avg	—	—	—	—	—

Tax Analysis	Tax-Adj Rtn%	%Rank Cat	Tax-Cost Rat	%Rank Cat
3 Yr (estimated)	12.16	1	0.00	1
5 Yr (estimated)	-1.98	15	1.66	91
10 Yr (estimated)	14.41	1	2.18	83

Potential Capital Gain Exposure: -4% of assets

Rating and Risk

Time Period	Load-Adj Return %	Morningstar Rtn vs Cat	Morningstar Risk vs Cat	Morningstar Risk-Adj Rating
1 Yr	26.30			
3 Yr	12.16	High	Avg	★★★★★
5 Yr	-0.33	+Avg	+Avg	★★★★
10 Yr	16.96	High	Avg	★★★★★
Incept	14.68			

Other Measures	Standard Index S&P 500	Best Fit Index Russ 1000Gr
Alpha	8.6	14.0
Beta	1.38	1.35
R-Squared	82	85

Standard Deviation	26.10
Mean	12.16
Sharpe Ratio	0.42

Morningstar's Take by Jeffrey Ptak 01-05-05

This fund has passed an important milestone.

T. Rowe Price Media & Telecom manager Rob Gensler is no stranger to success. In fact, the fund has topped at least two thirds of its specialty-communications category peers in every rolling one-year period since he took the helm in January 2000, a remarkable feat. What's more, he's racked up those results in a variety of market climates, traversing the hills and valleys that have spanned the telecom sector's bear market meltdown and subsequent rebound in 2003.

But last year's campaign found the fund in an unfamiliar position: protecting gains. Indeed, Gensler had shown a knack for defense thanks in part to the fund's wide mandate as well as his penchant for market-dominant players trading at sane valuations. But many of his picks, such as Spanish cable firm Sogecable, rang up big returns in 2003, forcing Gensler to tread more carefully in managing price risk.

Nevertheless, he appears to have managed the transition with ease. True, some of the fund's 2003 winners, such as slot-machine maker International Game Tech, fell in 2004 before Gensler could salt away all of the fund's gains. But he deftly maneuvered elsewhere, trimming the fund's stake in emerging-markets wireless carrier Millicom International Cellular, for instance, before it swooned in 2004's third quarter. Meanwhile, surging picks such as wireless-device maker Research in Motion also juiced returns.

Although Gensler has proved deft in keeping price risk at bay, the fund can be a rocky ride. In particular, Gensler's taste for firms boasting copious free cash flow growth conferred by dominant competitive positions often finds him paying a slight premium. That has spurred volatility, as such names tend to be more sensitive to short-term events that might call the long-term growth thesis into question. But we like the fund's broad charter, and Gensler has executed his strategy with aplomb. It's a fine choice.

Address:	100 E Pratt St Baltimore MD 21202 800-638-5660	Minimum Purchase:	$2500	Add: $100 IRA: $1000
Web Address:	www.troweprice.com	Min Auto Inv Plan:	$50	Add: $50
Inception:	10-14-93*	Sales Fees:	No-load	
Advisor:	T. Rowe Price Associates, Inc.	Management Fee:	0.67%	
Subadvisor:	None	Actual Fees:	Mgt:0.67%	Dist:
NTF Plans:	N/A	Expense Projections:	3Yr:$365	5Yr:$633 10Yr:$1398
		Income Distrib:	Annually	

Portfolio Analysis 09-30-04

Share change since 06-04 Total Stocks:65	Sector	PE	YTD Ret%	% Assets
⊕ America Movil SA ADR	Telecom	23.2	92.36	6.19
⊖ Sogecable	Media	—	—	4.44
Vodafone Group PLC ADR	Telecom	—	11.74	4.32
Vodafone Grp	Telecom	—	—	3.96
⊕ Time Warner	Media	27.5	8.12	3.78
⊖ Crown Castle International	Telecom	—	50.86	2.77
⊖ International Game Tech	Consumer	28.1	-2.49	2.72
⊖ Western Wireless Cl A	Telecom	—	59.59	2.57
⊕ News Corporation ADR A	Media	—	6.65	2.48
⊖ Viacom B	Media	36.1	-17.44	2.45
⊕ SK Telecom Co ADR	Telecom	8.9	25.54	2.41
⊖ Grupo Televisa ADR	Media	25.8	65.69	2.40
⊖ Yahoo	Media	95.1	67.36	2.34
☼ Singapore Telecom	Telecom	—	—	2.30
☼ Liberty Media	Media	—	11.56	2.16
⊖ American Tower A	Telecom	—	70.06	2.03
⊖ SpectraSite	Telecom	—	66.62	2.02
Nextel Communications	Telecom	11.1	6.95	1.97
⊕ Fox Entertainment Group	Media	—	7.24	1.97
⊖ eBay	Consumer	81.6	80.07	1.96

Current Investment Style

Value Blnd Growth — Large Mid Small

Market Cap	%
Giant	35.5
Large	25.2
Mid	31.3
Small	7.4
Micro	0.6

Avg $mil: 11,665

Value Measures		Rel Category
Price/Earnings	22.70	1.08
Price/Book	2.07	1.02
Price/Sales	2.38	1.58
Price/Cash Flow	8.78	1.62
Dividend Yield %	0.30	0.28

Growth Measures	%	Rel Category
Long-Term Erngs	16.6	1.25
Book Value	-2.25	NMF
Sales	8.83	14.24
Cash Flow	14.88	1.56
Historical Erngs	18.88	6.89

Profitability	%	Rel Category
Return on Equity	10.40	0.97
Return on Assets	4.06	1.01
Net Margin	4.35	0.72

Industry Weightings	% of Stocks	Rel Cat
Telecom Srv	0.0	0.0
Wireless Srv	27.1	0.9
Network Eq	4.6	0.3
Semis	0.0	0.0
Big Media	24.5	7.2
Cable TV	9.1	3.3
Other Media	2.3	1.1
Soft/Hardwr	6.5	1.6
Other	25.9	2.0

Composition

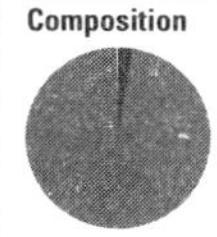

Cash	2.5
Stocks	96.8
Bonds	0.0
Other	0.8
Foreign (% of Stock)	44.5

T. Rowe Price Mid Gr

Ticker	Load	NAV	Yield	Total Assets	Mstar Category
RPMGX	Closed	$49.88	0.0%	$13,208 mil	Mid-Cap Growth

Governance and Management

Fiduciary Grade: B

Portfolio Manager(s)

Brian Berghuis has run this offering since its June 1992 inception. He is assisted by comanager John Wakeman, and the two draw ideas from T. Rowe's deep analyst bench.

Strategy

Manager Brian Berghuis looks for companies with sound business models that are growing rapidly. But unlike some other mid-growth managers, he pays close attention to valuations: The fund's average P/E is well below that of its typical rival. He also keeps the fund well-diversified across sectors and does not let individual positions in the portfolio become too significant.

Historical Profile

Return High
Risk Below Avg
Rating ★★★★★ Highest

Investment Style: Equity Stock %: 90% 92% 92% 92% 96% 94% 95% 94% 94%

▼ Manager Change
▽ Partial Manager Change

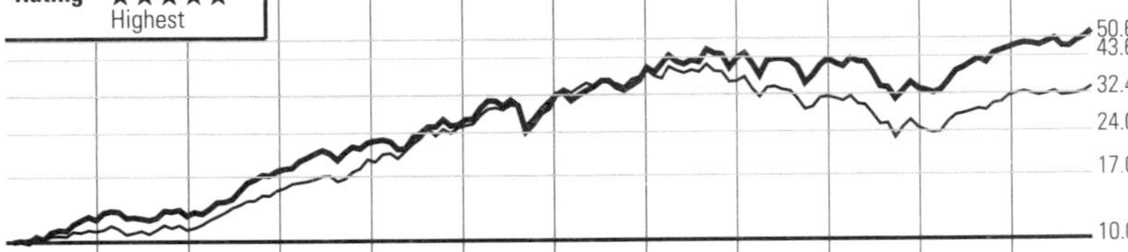

Growth of $10,000
— Investment Values of Fund
— Investment Values of S&P 500

Performance Quartile (within Category)

History

1993	1994	1995	1996	1997	1998	1999	2000	2001	2002	2003	12-04	History
15.18	14.85	20.13	24.43	28.60	34.08	40.13	39.79	39.40	31.04	42.90	49.88	NAV
26.24	0.29	40.95	24.84	18.33	22.00	23.78	7.43	-0.98	-21.22	38.21	18.39	Total Return %
16.18	-1.02	3.42	1.90	-15.02	-6.57	2.74	16.53	10.90	0.87	9.54	7.52	+/-S&P 500
15.05	2.45	6.97	7.36	-4.21	4.14	-27.51	19.18	19.17	6.19	-4.50	2.91	+/-Russ MG
0.00	0.00	0.00	0.00	0.00	0.00	0.00	0.00	0.00	0.00	0.00	0.00	Income Return %
26.24	0.29	40.95	24.84	18.33	22.00	23.78	7.43	-0.98	-21.22	38.21	18.39	Capital Return %
8	34	20	12	53	32	84	28	7	25	32	12	Total Rtn % Rank Cat
0.00	0.00	0.00	0.00	0.00	0.00	0.00	0.00	0.00	0.00	0.00	0.00	Income $
0.30	0.37	0.79	0.69	0.30	0.73	1.88	3.27	0.00	0.00	0.00	0.90	Capital Gains $
1.25	1.25	1.25	1.04	0.95	0.91	0.87	0.86	0.89	0.88	0.87	—	Expense Ratio %
-0.12	0.02	-0.01	-0.11	-0.14	-0.14	-0.09	-0.09	-0.35	-0.50	-0.44	—	Income Ratio %
62	49	58	38	43	47	53	54	43	36	30	—	Turnover Rate %
64	101	264	1,021	1,839	3,310	5,243	6,589	6,739	5,713	9,869	12,651	Net Assets $mil

Performance 12-31-04

	1st Qtr	2nd Qtr	3rd Qtr	4th Qtr	Total
2000	9.97	-3.83	5.61	-3.81	7.43
2001	-13.24	14.37	-17.71	21.27	-0.98
2002	0.53	-10.96	-18.88	8.49	-21.22
2003	-1.32	19.62	4.20	12.36	38.21
2004	3.36	4.22	-2.14	12.32	18.39

Trailing	Total Return%	+/- S&P 500	+/- Russ MG	%Rank Cat	Growth of $10,000
3 Mo	12.32	3.09	-1.62	63	11,232
6 Mo	9.91	2.72	0.90	20	10,991
1 Yr	18.39	7.52	2.91	12	11,839
3 Yr Avg	8.83	5.25	2.67	12	12,890
5 Yr Avg	6.52	8.82	9.88	11	13,714
10 Yr Avg	15.73	3.66	4.50	5	43,098
15 Yr Avg	—	—	—	—	—

Tax Analysis	Tax-Adj Rtn%	%Rank Cat	Tax-Cost Rat	%Rank Cat
3 Yr (estimated)	8.74	9	0.08	13
5 Yr (estimated)	6.12	9	0.38	17
10 Yr (estimated)	15.04	4	0.60	11

Potential Capital Gain Exposure: 30% of assets

Rating and Risk

Time Period	Load-Adj Return %	Morningstar Rtn vs Cat	Morningstar Risk vs Cat	Morningstar Risk-Adj Rating
1 Yr	18.39			
3 Yr	8.83	+Avg	Avg	★★★★
5 Yr	6.52	+Avg	-Avg	★★★★
10 Yr	15.73	High	-Avg	★★★★★
Incept	16.57			

Other Measures	Standard Index S&P 500	Best Fit Index Russ MG
Alpha	5.3	3.0
Beta	1.02	0.88
R-Squared	86	95
Standard Deviation	17.92	
Mean	8.83	
Sharpe Ratio	0.42	

Portfolio Analysis 09-30-04

Share change since 06-04 Total Stocks:149	Sector	PE	YTD Ret%	% Assets
⊖ BJ Svcs	Energy	21.8	30.07	1.61
ChoicePoint	Business	30.4	20.74	1.54
⊕ MedImmune	Health	—	6.82	1.42
⊕ Potash Corp./Saskatchewa	Ind Mtrls	—	94.19	1.41
Murphy Oil	Energy	16.5	24.71	1.37
Rockwell Collins	Ind Mtrls	23.6	32.97	1.37
⊖ Smith International	Energy	34.2	31.05	1.33
Harris	Hardware	27.4	64.22	1.30
Brunswick	Goods	18.1	57.47	1.29
Omnicare	Health	14.0	-14.07	1.25
McAfee	Software	18.2	92.35	1.15
Certegy	Business	21.2	8.92	1.14
Roper Industries	Ind Mtrls	31.4	24.26	1.14
DST Systems	Business	15.3	24.81	1.13
⊕ Gilead Sciences	Health	36.9	20.08	1.08
Alliant Techsystems	Ind Mtrls	16.7	13.19	1.06
Manpower	Business	18.2	3.24	1.06
⊕ Manor Care	Health	19.1	4.21	1.05
⊖ Western Wireless Cl A	Telecom	—	59.59	1.04
Laboratory Corp of Ameri	Health	19.1	34.83	1.04

Current Investment Style

Value Blnd Growth — Large Mid Small

Market Cap	%
Giant	0.0
Large	11.7
Mid	83.1
Small	4.8
Micro	0.4
Avg $mil: 3,910	

Value Measures		Rel Category
Price/Earnings	22.11	1.01
Price/Book	2.94	0.98
Price/Sales	1.71	0.97
Price/Cash Flow	11.05	1.14
Dividend Yield %	0.28	0.65

Growth Measures	%	Rel Category
Long-Term Erngs	15.58	0.99
Book Value	9.13	0.91
Sales	9.97	1.16
Cash Flow	5.14	0.42
Historical Erngs	11.31	0.71

Profitability	%	Rel Category
Return on Equity	14.98	1.04
Return on Assets	6.77	0.94
Net Margin	8.83	0.92

Sector Weightings	% of Stocks	Rel S&P 500	3 Year High	3 Year Low
Info	23.07	1.07		
Software	5.82	1.35	6	4
Hardware	10.11	0.99	11	8
Media	4.17	1.09	4	2
Telecom	2.97	0.94	3	1
Service	53.80	1.16		
Health	18.37	1.47	23	18
Consumer	10.31	1.14	15	10
Business	17.12	4.23	23	17
Financial	8.00	0.39	12	7
Mfg	23.14	0.72		
Goods	2.15	0.23	2	1
Ind Mtrls	11.09	0.88	11	5
Energy	9.90	1.38	10	7
Utilities	0.00	0.00	0	0

Composition

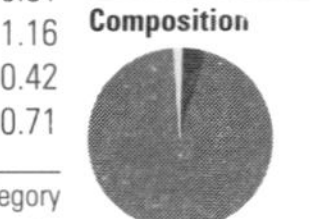

Cash	4.6
Stocks	94.1
Bonds	0.0
Other	1.4
Foreign (% of Stock)	4.3

Morningstar's Take by Kunal Kapoor 11-05-04

It's not flashy, but T. Rowe Price Mid-Cap Growth is all substance.

This fund is among our favorites in the mid-cap growth category. While its long-term performance is superb, it's manager Brian Berghuis's process that is its key selling point. Like many of his rivals, Berghuis is looking for growing companies, but gains an edge by employing a consistent valuation discipline and long-term approach. This tack allows him to separate a firm's long-term potential from the short-term noise surrounding it, an increasingly important asset in a crowded market. For example, while the fund has recently benefited from a rise in shares of MedImmune, the reasons why Berghuis favors the stock are different from the market's--and longer-term in nature. Thus, while the firm's shares have rallied lately because of expectations that a vaccine shortage will boost the firm's FluMist product, Berghuis says that the real long-term value lies in Numax, a respiratory drug in Phase 3 trials.

A diversified portfolio is another asset here. While rivals often concentrate resources in sectors such as technology and biotech, this fund casts a wide net. As such, it holds its own even when those sectors are out of favor, as they have been for much of 2004. The fund's near-11% gain for 2004 through Nov. 4, for example, owes in large part to energy and industrial material picks, such as BJ Services and Nucor. Ever the cautious one, Berghuis is responding by trimming holdings in these areas, lowering the portfolio's overall economic sensitivity. Those moves, however, are somewhat offset by growing positions in economically sensitive technology stocks.

This contrarian streak means that the fund won't always look this good, but we have confidence in the persistence of Berghuis' strategy. And with a quality organization behind him, the fund should be in good stead over the long haul.

Address:	100 E Pratt St Baltimore MD 21202 800-638-5660
Web Address:	www.troweprice.com
Inception:	06-30-92
Advisor:	T. Rowe Price Associates, Inc.
Subadvisor:	None
NTF Plans:	N/A

Minimum Purchase:	Closed	Add: —	IRA: —
Min Auto Inv Plan:	Closed	Add: —	
Sales Fees:	No-load		
Management Fee:	0.67%		
Actual Fees:	Mgt:0.67%	Dist:	
Expense Projections:	3Yr:$278	5Yr:$482	10Yr:$1073
Income Distrib:	Annually		

T. Rowe Price Mid Val

Analyst Pick

Ticker	Load	NAV	Yield	Total Assets	Mstar Category
TRMCX	None	$22.99	0.4%	$5,042 mil	Mid-Cap Value

Governance and Management

Fiduciary Grade: B

Portfolio Manager(s)

Dave Wallack took charge in January 2001. Before that, he was the fund's natural-resources stock analyst, and he has been on its investment committee, which oversees and supervises the portfolio manager, since the fund's 1996 inception. Wallack is assisted by T. Rowe's large analyst staff.

Strategy

Manager Dave Wallack looks for reasonably priced companies with experienced management teams that are market leaders in their industries. He's also drawn to firms with the financial flexibility to invest in new products and acquire companies. And he likes firms that posses value drivers, such as divestitures of underperforming businesses and stock buybacks. Wallack tends to focus on smaller mid-caps, giving the fund a market cap considerably below the mid-value norm.

Historical Profile

Return High
Risk Average
Rating ★★★★★ Highest

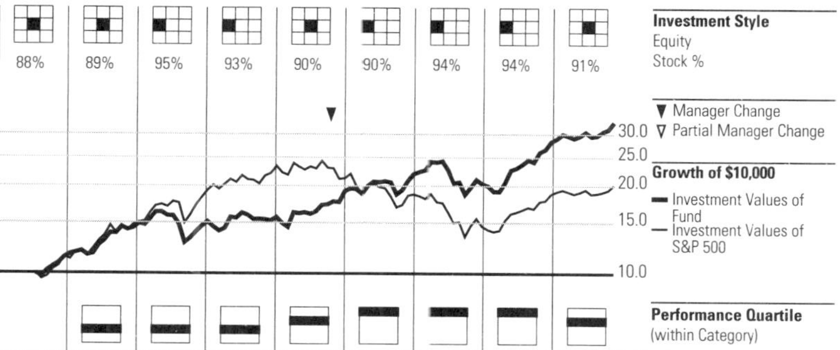

History

1993	1994	1995	1996	1997	1998	1999	2000	2001	2002	2003	12-04	History
—	—	—	11.56	14.47	13.66	13.37	15.64	16.40	15.00	20.34	22.99	NAV
—	—	—	16.30*	27.11	1.39	3.52	22.75	14.36	-7.38	39.00	20.56	Total Return %
—	—	—	—	-6.24	-27.18	-17.52	31.85	26.24	14.71	10.33	9.69	+/-S&P 500
—	—	—	—	-7.26	-3.69	3.63	3.57	12.03	2.26	0.93	-3.15	+/-Russ MV
—	—	—	0.00	0.69	1.31	1.68	1.27	0.83	0.73	0.87	0.49	Income Return %
—	—	—	—	26.42	0.08	1.84	21.48	13.53	-8.11	38.13	20.07	Capital Return %
—	—	—	—	51	57	62	40	21	13	25	33	Total Rtn % Rank Cat
—	—	—	0.07	0.08	0.19	0.23	0.17	0.13	0.12	0.13	0.10	Income $
—	—	—	0.00	0.14	0.76	0.51	0.56	1.31	0.07	0.36	1.40	Capital Gains $
—	—	—	1.25	1.25	1.08	1.04	0.99	0.98	0.96	0.91	—	Expense Ratio %
—	—	—	2.10	1.18	1.24	1.60	1.33	0.95	0.98	0.91	—	Income Ratio %
—	—	—	4	16	32	27	32	58	51	50	—	Turnover Rate %
—	—	—	49	218	221	212	282	503	991	1,867	4,541	Net Assets $mil

Performance 12-31-04

	1st Qtr	2nd Qtr	3rd Qtr	4th Qtr	Total
2000	3.74	-1.08	7.73	11.04	22.75
2001	-2.11	9.60	-9.12	17.29	14.36
2002	10.12	-6.48	-17.29	8.74	-7.38
2003	-5.87	20.18	4.83	17.20	39.00
2004	4.62	3.05	0.32	11.46	20.56

Trailing	Total Return%	+/- S&P 500	+/- Russ MV	%Rank Cat	Growth of $10,000
3 Mo	11.46	2.23	-2.00	49	11,146
6 Mo	11.82	4.63	-3.61	38	11,182
1 Yr	20.56	9.69	-3.15	33	12,056
3 Yr Avg	15.78	12.20	0.22	9	15,520
5 Yr Avg	16.85	19.15	3.37	16	21,784
10 Yr Avg	—	—	—	—	—
15 Yr Avg	—	—	—	—	—

Tax Analysis	Tax-Adj Rtn%	%Rank Cat	Tax-Cost Rat	%Rank Cat
3 Yr (estimated)	14.74	9	0.90	73
5 Yr (estimated)	15.42	16	1.22	64
10 Yr (estimated)	—	—	—	—

Potential Capital Gain Exposure: 16% of assets

Rating and Risk

Time Period	Load-Adj Return %	Morningstar Rtn vs Cat	Morningstar Risk vs Cat	Morningstar Risk-Adj Rating
1 Yr	20.56			
3 Yr	15.78	High	Avg	★★★★★
5 Yr	16.85	High	Avg	★★★★★
10 Yr	—	—	—	—
Incept	15.39			

Other Measures	Standard Index S&P 500	Best Fit Index Russ MV
Alpha	12.1	-0.1
Beta	0.95	1.03
R-Squared	84	93
Standard Deviation	17.90	
Mean	15.78	
Sharpe Ratio	0.81	

Portfolio Analysis 09-30-04

Share change since 06-04 Total Stocks:126	Sector	PE	YTD Ret%	% Assets
⊕ Diamond Offshore Drillin	Energy	—	97.23	2.99
☆ Mattel	Goods	16.1	3.54	1.76
⊕ TECO Energy	Utilities	—	12.72	1.59
⊕ Campbell Soup	Goods	18.0	14.22	1.49
⊕ St. Paul Travelers Compa	Financial	30.8	-3.15	1.45
⊕ MedImmune	Health	—	6.82	1.31
⊕ Dow Jones & Company	Media	32.0	-11.70	1.31
⊕ Tenet Healthcare	Health	—	-31.59	1.26
⊕ CSX	Business	21.2	12.91	1.25
⊕ NiSource	Utilities	14.2	8.45	1.23
⊕ Entercom Communications	Media	21.2	-32.23	1.21
⊕ Novellus Systems	Hardware	31.6	-29.98	1.21
⊕ Cablevision Systems A	Media	—	6.46	1.19
⊕ Charles Schwab	Financial	32.9	1.77	1.18
⊕ AmerisourceBergen	Health	14.3	4.69	1.17
⊖ Grant Prideco	Energy	77.8	53.99	1.16
⊕ Duke Energy	Utilities	—	30.21	1.15
⊕ Union Pacific	Business	19.6	-1.28	1.13
⊕ Molex Cl A	Hardware	—	—	1.12
Genworth Financial	Financial	—	—	1.12

Current Investment Style

Market Cap	%
Giant	0.0
Large	26.1
Mid	66.6
Small	7.2
Micro	0.1

Avg $mil: 4,625

Value Measures		Rel Category
Price/Earnings	18.12	1.18
Price/Book	1.73	0.90
Price/Sales	0.94	1.07
Price/Cash Flow	5.81	1.01
Dividend Yield %	1.46	1.02

Growth Measures	%	Rel Category
Long-Term Erngs	11.06	1.00
Book Value	-1.90	NMF
Sales	1.84	0.38
Cash Flow	-7.63	NMF
Historical Erngs	3.15	0.27

Profitability	%	Rel Category
Return on Equity	9.98	0.78
Return on Assets	4.57	0.75
Net Margin	6.60	0.75

Sector Weightings	% of Stocks	Rel S&P 500	3 Year High	3 Year Low
Info	22.67	1.05		
Software	4.59	1.07	5	1
Hardware	4.19	0.41	8	4
Media	11.01	2.87	11	4
Telecom	2.88	0.91	4	1
Service	44.60	0.96		
Health	8.36	0.67	10	4
Consumer	4.82	0.53	7	4
Business	9.21	2.27	10	4
Financial	22.21	1.07	24	18
Mfg	32.74	1.02		
Goods	6.23	0.67	12	4
Ind Mtrls	10.57	0.83	21	10
Energy	7.19	1.00	11	6
Utilities	8.75	2.96	13	7

Composition

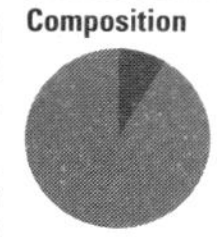

Cash	8.5
Stocks	91.4
Bonds	0.0
Other	0.1
Foreign (% of Stock)	4.0

Morningstar's Take by Christopher Davis 11-01-04

T. Rowe Price Mid-Cap Value is a top-flight choice, but keep your expectations in check.

This offering continues to excel. Through Oct. 28, 2004, the fund is up 10% for the year to date, placing in the mid-value group's top quartile. That puts manager Dave Wallack on pace to deliver his fourth consecutive peer-beating performance since taking the helm in January 2001.

In his tenure here, Wallack has proved an adept stock-picker. In early 2001, for instance, he scooped up beaten-down insurers such as Aetna and Safeco, both of which rebounded smartly later in the year and throughout 2002. And he deftly built stakes in electric utilities such as FirstEnergy and TXU in 2002 believing they had been improperly linked with energy traders such as Enron. His picks in the sector rallied in 2003 and are up nicely this year (he reports recently selling TXU, though). Wallack also ramped up the fund's weighting in out-of-favor energy stocks such as Diamond Offshore Drilling in 2003 in time for the sector's recent run.

These days, Wallack says the best bargains to be had are among poor-performing publishing stocks such as Tribune and radio broadcaster Entercom Communications. The companies are market leaders, he argues, and notes their managements have been buying back shares. Wallack concedes Internet advertising and satellite radio pose competitive threats to traditional media firms, but he believes such concerns are overblown. Media stocks are rarely this cheap, he says, and will benefit from bigger ad budgets from the likes of Coca-Cola.

To be sure, the fund's below-average market cap has given it a tailwind in recent years as small caps have ruled the roost. In a market more favorable to large caps, the fund may look more sluggish relative to its peers. That said, we think talented management, along with moderate costs and strong analyst support, give this offering a long-term edge.

Address:	T Rowe Price Associates Inc Baltimore MD 21202 800-638-5660
Web Address:	www.troweprice.com
Inception:	06-28-96*
Advisor:	T. Rowe Price Associates, Inc.
Subadvisor:	None
NTF Plans:	N/A

Minimum Purchase:	$2500	Add: $100	IRA: $1000
Min Auto Inv Plan:	$50	Add: $50	
Sales Fees:	No-load		
Management Fee:	0.67%		
Actual Fees:	Mgt:0.67%	Dist:	
Expense Projections:	3Yr:$290	5Yr:$504	10Yr:$1120
Income Distrib:	Annually		

T. Rowe Price New Amer

Analyst Pick

Ticker	Load	NAV	Yield	Total Assets	Mstar Category
PRWAX	None	$33.14	0.0%	$952 mil	Large Growth

Governance and Management

Fiduciary Grade: B

Portfolio Manager(s)

Joseph Milano took the reins here in July 2002 from interim manager Robert Smith. In May 2002, Smith had replaced Marc Baylin, who oversaw the fund's transition to a pure large-growth fund in 2000. Baylin took over for Jack LaPorte, who had managed the fund since its 1985 inception. There is some continuity here, though; Baylin and Milano both worked on the fund as analysts for several years.

Strategy

Before 2000, this fund avoided technology and stayed in services industries such as telecommunications, retail, and financials. The fund's mandate changed to growth in 2000, however, opening it up to tech. It looks for low-debt, high-growth companies trading at discounts to historical price multiples and future cash flows. Manager Joe Milano says that his primary areas of interest are IT services, technology, media, retail, and health care, although he's been willing to look for ideas just about anywhere.

Historical Profile

Return Above Avg
Risk Above Avg
Rating ★★★★ Above Avg

Investment Style
Equity
Stock %

96% 95% 99% 91% 94% 92% 100% 99% 98%

▼ Manager Change
▽ Partial Manager Change

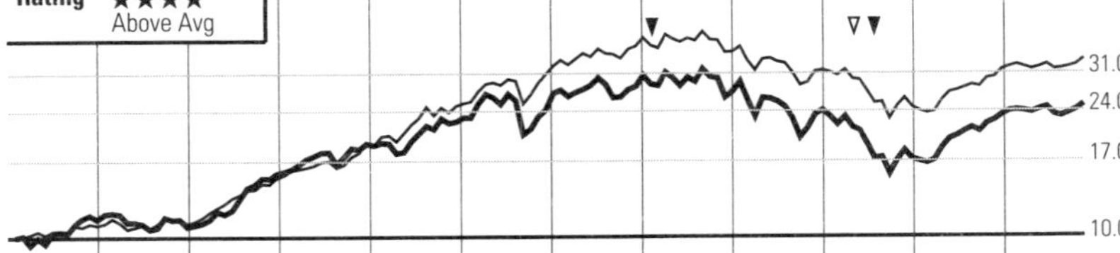

Growth of $10,000
— Investment Values of Fund
— Investment Values of S&P 500

Performance Quartile (within Category)

1993	1994	1995	1996	1997	1998	1999	2000	2001	2002	2003	12-04	History
28.04	25.42	34.91	38.37	44.19	47.79	48.06	35.77	30.87	22.06	29.83	33.14	NAV
17.44	-7.43	44.31	20.01	21.10	17.89	12.76	-10.53	-11.89	-28.54	35.22	11.10	Total Return %
7.38	-8.74	6.78	-2.93	-12.25	-10.68	-8.28	-1.43	-0.01	-6.45	6.55	0.23	+/-S&P 500
14.57	-10.05	7.13	-3.11	-9.39	-20.82	-20.40	11.89	8.53	-0.66	5.47	4.80	+/-Russ 1000Gr
0.00	0.00	0.00	0.00	0.00	0.00	0.00	0.00	0.00	0.00	0.00	0.00	Income Return %
17.44	-7.43	44.31	20.01	21.10	17.89	12.76	-10.53	-11.89	-28.54	35.22	11.10	Capital Return %
21	91	7	46	78	87	93	38	10	57	14	21	Total Rtn % Rank Cat
0.00	0.00	0.00	0.00	0.00	0.00	0.00	0.00	0.00	0.00	0.00	0.00	Income $
1.13	0.53	1.75	3.49	2.20	3.84	5.40	7.52	0.64	0.00	0.00	0.00	Capital Gains $
1.23	1.14	1.07	1.01	0.96	0.95	0.94	0.93	0.99	0.99	0.98	—	Expense Ratio %
-0.39	-0.27	-0.46	-0.39	-0.34	-0.49	-0.43	-0.33	-0.36	-0.42	-0.34	—	Income Ratio %
44	31	56	37	43	46	40	81	52	61	62	—	Turnover Rate %
619	646	1,028	1,440	1,758	2,064	1,826	1,519	1,183	761	921	952	Net Assets $mil

Performance 12-31-04

	1st Qtr	2nd Qtr	3rd Qtr	4th Qtr	Total
2000	2.23	-3.58	0.30	-9.49	-10.53
2001	-15.60	10.70	-21.78	20.57	-11.89
2002	-4.37	-17.07	-18.75	10.91	-28.54
2003	-0.86	18.24	3.09	11.89	35.22
2004	2.72	2.48	-3.89	9.81	11.10

Trailing	Total Return%	+/- S&P 500	+/- Russ 1000Gr	%Rank Cat	Growth of $10,000
3 Mo	9.81	0.58	0.64	51	10,981
6 Mo	5.54	-1.65	2.07	39	10,554
1 Yr	11.10	0.23	4.80	21	11,110
3 Yr Avg	2.39	-1.19	2.57	22	10,734
5 Yr Avg	-3.28	-0.98	6.01	15	8,464
10 Yr Avg	8.96	-3.11	-0.63	49	23,587
15 Yr Avg	9.69	-1.24	0.19	46	40,041

Tax Analysis	Tax-Adj Rtn%	%Rank Cat	Tax-Cost Rat	%Rank Cat
3 Yr (estimated)	2.39	18	0.00	1
5 Yr (estimated)	-4.03	15	0.78	47
10 Yr (estimated)	7.56	45	1.28	38

Potential Capital Gain Exposure: 21% of assets

Rating and Risk

Time Period	Load-Adj Return %	Morningstar Rtn vs Cat	Morningstar Risk vs Cat	Morningstar Risk-Adj Rating
1 Yr	11.10			
3 Yr	2.39	+Avg	+Avg	★★★★
5 Yr	-3.28	+Avg	Avg	★★★★
10 Yr	8.96	Avg	+Avg	★★★
Incept	11.45			

Other Measures	Standard Index S&P 500	Best Fit Index Russ 1000
Alpha	-1.2	-1.9
Beta	1.12	1.13
R-Squared	95	95
Standard Deviation	17.78	
Mean	2.39	
Sharpe Ratio	0.06	

Morningstar's Take by Kunal Kapoor 10-13-04

T. Rowe Price New America Growth gets the nod as our newest Analyst Pick.

For a fund to rank among our favorites in a category, we have to be convinced of its all-around merits. That's why investors may be a bit surprised to see us pick this offering ahead of several established funds with more experienced management, including a couple at T. Rowe Price. But we think this fund will stand out over the long haul in a competitive category.

Our confidence stems from manager Joe Milano's flexible approach. While many of his peers stick to owning only the largest stocks around, Milano has put a framework in place that lets the fund venture out of this subset of stocks. During his still-short tenure here, he's demonstrated a willingness and ability to look outside traditional growth areas such as technology and biotech to unearth atypical picks such as top-three holding ChoicePoint. And when he has looked in those areas, he has taken a bit of a contrarian approach. For instance, Milano reports a recent affinity for semiconductor stocks, which have thus far had a tough 2004. The result is a portfolio aggressive enough to hold its own in up markets, but one that retains some ability to play defense in tougher climates. Couple that with an asset base of less than $1 billion, and it makes for a compelling investment thesis.

Naturally, there is a downside here, too. Some of the very things that endear this fund to us--such as its ability to span the market-cap spectrum--could hold it back if there's a more focused large-cap rally. And investors should remember that at the end of the day this is a true growth fund, so short-term volatility is likely to be par for the course. Nevertheless, this is a compelling long-term investment, especially for those who are investing for such goals as college savings.

Portfolio Analysis 09-30-04

Share change since 06-04 Total Stocks:101	Sector	PE	YTD Ret%	% Assets
United Parcel Service B	Business	28.5	16.40	3.03
Dell	Hardware	34.0	24.01	3.03
⊖ ChoicePoint	Business	30.4	20.74	2.83
⊖ Microsoft	Software	36.1	8.95	2.32
⊕ Cisco Systems	Hardware	24.5	-20.26	2.23
⊕ International Game Tech	Consumer	28.1	-2.49	2.11
Intuit	Software	25.7	-16.74	2.00
Lockheed Martin	Ind Mtrls	19.9	9.97	1.96
⊕ CDW	Consumer	25.4	15.52	1.92
Gen Elec	Ind Mtrls	22.8	20.68	1.89
⊖ Smith International	Energy	34.2	31.05	1.85
⊖ Medtronic	Health	30.7	2.68	1.83
⊕ Getty Images	Business	37.9	37.34	1.75
Amgen	Health	37.7	3.82	1.56
⊕ Pfizer	Health	22.0	-22.31	1.53
⊕ Sysco	Consumer	26.0	3.69	1.52
American International G	Financial	16.2	-0.53	1.52
UnitedHealth Group	Health	23.8	51.38	1.52
⊖ Family Dollar Stores	Consumer	20.2	-12.00	1.51
⊖ Wal-Mart Stores	Consumer	23.4	0.51	1.50

Current Investment Style

Value Blnd Growth — Large Mid Small

Market Cap	%
Giant	28.6
Large	35.1
Mid	34.6
Small	1.7
Micro	0.0
Avg $mil: 17,407	

Value Measures		Rel Category
Price/Earnings	21.14	0.99
Price/Book	3.01	0.93
Price/Sales	2.19	1.02
Price/Cash Flow	13.28	1.21
Dividend Yield %	0.57	0.74

Growth Measures	%	Rel Category
Long-Term Erngs	15.38	1.09
Book Value	13.77	1.08
Sales	9.49	1.11
Cash Flow	7.08	0.43
Historical Erngs	13.57	0.94

Profitability	%	Rel Category
Return on Equity	17.66	0.98
Return on Assets	9.53	1.02
Net Margin	12.13	0.99

Sector Weightings	% of Stocks	Rel S&P 500	3 Year High	3 Year Low
Info	26.05	1.21		
Software	8.57	1.99	9	5
Hardware	12.19	1.20	12	9
Media	3.52	0.92	11	4
Telecom	1.77	0.56	3	1
Service	63.06	1.36		
Health	18.25	1.46	23	18
Consumer	16.69	1.84	18	15
Business	16.46	4.06	20	15
Financial	11.66	0.56	14	11
Mfg	10.89	0.34		
Goods	1.32	0.14	3	0
Ind Mtrls	4.43	0.35	4	2
Energy	5.14	0.72	6	4
Utilities	0.00	0.00	0	0

Composition

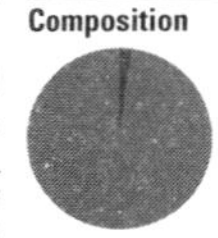

Cash	2.0
Stocks	98.0
Bonds	0.0
Other	0.0
Foreign (% of Stock)	1.4

Address:	100 E Pratt St Baltimore MD 21202 800-638-5660	Minimum Purchase:	$2500 Add: $100 IRA: $1000
Web Address:	www.troweprice.com	Min Auto Inv Plan:	$50 Add: $50
Inception:	09-30-85	Sales Fees:	No-load
Advisor:	T. Rowe Price Associates, Inc.	Management Fee:	0.67%
Subadvisor:	None	Actual Fees:	Mgt:0.67% Dist:
NTF Plans:	N/A	Expense Projections:	3Yr:$312 5Yr:$542 10Yr:$1201
		Income Distrib:	Annually

T. Rowe Price New Asia

Analyst Pick

Ticker	Load	NAV	Yield	Total Assets	Mstar Category
PRASX	None	$10.04	0.0%	$997 mil	Pacific/Asia ex-Japan Stk

Governance and Management

Fiduciary Grade: B

Portfolio Manager(s)

Frances Dydasco handles the fund's day-to-day operations, with help from Rowe Price-Fleming International's bevy of London-based veterans. Dydasco is based in Singapore.

Strategy

Frances Dydasco and her colleagues follow a moderate-growth strategy, favoring industry leaders with strong earnings prospects and reasonable prices. They generally avoid huge sector wagers.

Historical Profile

Return Average
Risk Average
Rating ★★★ Neutral

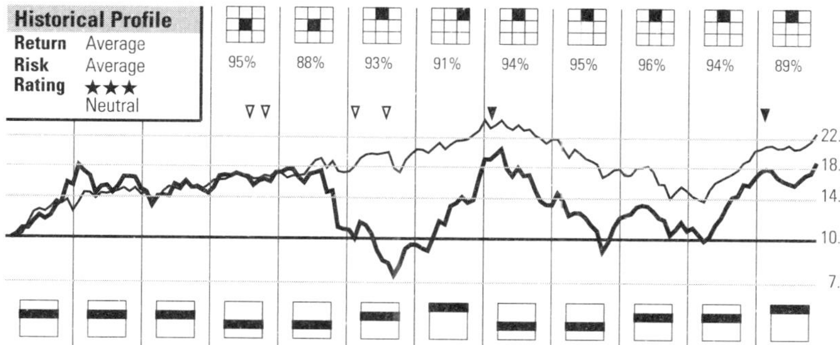

1993	1994	1995	1996	1997	1998	1999	2000	2001	2002	2003	12-04	History
11.10	8.01	8.22	9.26	5.74	5.01	9.97	6.90	6.21	5.59	8.51	10.04	NAV
78.84	-19.19	3.75	13.51	-37.13	-11.11	99.88	-30.79	-10.00	-9.36	53.54	18.60	Total Return %
46.28	-26.97	-7.46	7.46	-38.91	-31.04	72.85	-16.60	11.42	6.58	14.95	-1.65	+/-MSCI EAFE
-20.24	-0.07	-3.09	4.18	8.48	-3.94	40.46	7.09	-5.86	1.69	12.77	4.37	+/-MSCIAC FExJ
0.55	0.63	1.12	0.73	0.86	1.57	0.80	0.00	0.00	0.64	1.07	0.00	Income Return %
78.29	-19.82	2.63	12.78	-37.99	-12.68	99.08	-30.79	-10.00	-10.00	52.47	18.60	Capital Return %
40	40	34	57	72	45	10	75	63	29	35	7	Total Rtn % Rank Cat
0.04	0.07	0.09	0.06	0.08	0.09	0.04	0.00	0.00	0.04	0.06	0.00	Income $
0.19	0.89	0.00	0.01	0.00	0.00	0.00	0.00	0.00	0.00	0.01	0.05	Capital Gains $
1.29	1.22	1.15	1.11	1.10	1.29	1.21	1.08	1.22	1.17	1.17	1.09	Expense Ratio %
1.02	0.85	0.97	0.66	0.76	2.33	0.87	0.41	0.49	0.53	1.06	1.12	Income Ratio %
40	63	64	42	42	68	70	52	49	72	72	72	Turnover Rate %
2,234	1,988	1,880	2,182	782	622	1,375	800	639	543	885	997	Net Assets $mil

Performance 12-31-04

	1st Qtr	2nd Qtr	3rd Qtr	4th Qtr	Total
2000	8.73	-14.11	-15.90	-11.88	-30.79
2001	-8.26	-1.58	-23.76	30.74	-10.00
2002	9.50	-3.09	-17.60	3.66	-9.36
2003	-8.05	20.43	20.03	15.52	53.54
2004	5.99	-9.87	6.64	16.41	18.60

Trailing	Total Return%	+/- MSCI EAFE	+/- MSCIAC FExJ	%Rank Cat	Growth of $10,000
3 Mo	16.41	1.09	4.69	10	11,641
6 Mo	24.14	9.14	6.80	5	12,414
1 Yr	18.60	-1.65	4.37	7	11,860
3 Yr Avg	18.18	6.29	5.51	17	16,506
5 Yr Avg	0.56	1.69	3.72	56	10,283
10 Yr Avg	3.06	-2.56	5.26	38	13,518
15 Yr Avg	—	—	—	—	—

Tax Analysis	Tax-Adj Rtn%	%Rank Cat	Tax-Cost Rat	%Rank Cat
3 Yr (estimated)	17.89	17	0.25	53
5 Yr (estimated)	0.41	53	0.15	41
10 Yr (estimated)	2.76	38	0.29	53

Potential Capital Gain Exposure: 22% of assets

Rating and Risk

Time Period	Load-Adj Return %	Morningstar Rtn vs Cat	Morningstar Risk vs Cat	Morningstar Risk-Adj Rating
1 Yr	18.60			
3 Yr	18.18	Avg	+Avg	★★★★
5 Yr	0.56	Avg	Avg	★★★
10 Yr	3.06	Avg	Avg	★★★
Incept	7.03			

Other Measures	Standard Index S&P 500	Best Fit Index MSCIAC FExJ
Alpha	7.5	5.0
Beta	0.88	1.00
R-Squared	59	96
Standard Deviation	21.15	
Mean	18.18	
Sharpe Ratio	0.80	

Morningstar's Take by Arijit Dutta 10-15-04

T. Rowe Price New Asia remains a very sensible option.

Its modest-growth approach has again proved to be the right recipe. Following the fund's 53% return in 2003, manager Frances Dydasco trimmed or sold outright a lot of her cyclical manufacturing holdings in India, Thailand and Hong Kong. Dydasco moved these assets to companies that are less dependent on economic cycles and have more-reasonable valuations, including consumer goods, media, and financials. She has also trimmed back on China in 2004, as she expects a further correction in those stocks. These defensive moves have helped: For the year to date through Oct. 13, 2004, the fund is up 2.94%--comfortably ahead of the Pacific /Asia ex-Japan category average of 2.43%.

That's typical of how the fund has performed over the long term--outpacing the average peer at a fair-to-modest clip. While its fortunes have swung along with those of this very-volatile category, it has not landed in the category's bottom quartile in more than a decade. This fund's low expense ratio gives us confidence that it will stay out of the cellar for most of the next 10 years.

Besides attention to price, diversification has helped to steady the fund. It has more holdings than most peers, and its concentration in its top 10 holdings is also among the lowest in the group. However, these country allocations come about largely via bottom-up stock selection.

We continue to view this fund favorably.

Address:	100 E Pratt St Baltimore MD 21202 800-638-5660	Minimum Purchase:	$2500	Add: $100 IRA: $1000
Web Address:	www.troweprice.com	Min Auto Inv Plan:	$50	Add: $50
Inception:	09-28-90	Sales Fees:	No-load, 2.00%R	
Advisor:	T. Rowe Price Associates, Inc.	Management Fee:	0.82%	
Subadvisor:	None	Actual Fees:	Mgt:0.82%	Dist:
NTF Plans:	N/A	Expense Projections:	3Yr:$372	5Yr:$644 10Yr:$1420
		Income Distrib:	Annually	

Portfolio Analysis 09-30-04

Share change since 06-04 Total Stocks:132	Sector	Country	% Assets
⊖ Samsung Electronics	Goods	Korea	4.96
⊖ Cathay Finl Hldg	Financial	Taiwan	2.01
⊖ Kookmin Bank	Financial	Korea	1.87
⊖ Taiwan Semiconductor Mfg	Hardware	Taiwan	1.62
⊖ Zee Telefilms Ltd	Media	India	1.57
⊕ DBS Grp Hldgs Ltd	Financial	Singapore	1.55
⊖ HDFC Bank Ltd	Financial	India	1.55
⊖ Swire Pacific	Ind Mtrls	Hong Kong	1.51
☼ Hyundai Motor	—	Korea	1.49
☼ Cheung Kong (hldgs) Ltd	Financial	Hong Kong	1.49
☼ ChinaTrust Financial Hld	Financial	Taiwan	1.47
⊖ AMOREPACIFIC	Goods	Korea	1.40
⊖ CNOOC Ltd	Energy	Hong Kong	1.39
☼ Samsung Electnc	—	Korea	1.34
⊕ Kotak Mahindra Bank Ltd	Financial	India	1.34
⊖ SK Telecom	Telecom	Korea	1.33
⊖ Henderson Land Developme	Financial	Hong Kong	1.30
⊕ LG Chem	Ind Mtrls	Korea	1.26
⊖ S-Oil	Energy	Korea	1.23
⊕ Taishin Financial Hldgs	Ind Mtrls	Taiwan	1.22

Current Investment Style

Value Blnd Growth; Large Mid Small

Market Cap	%
Giant	23.5
Large	33.8
Mid	29.1
Small	12.3
Micro	1.4

Avg $mil: 2,930

Value Measures		Rel Category
Price/Earnings	11.61	0.99
Price/Book	1.32	0.79
Price/Sales	0.87	0.68
Price/Cash Flow	3.40	0.60
Dividend Yield %	2.57	0.82

Growth Measures	%	Rel Category
Long-Term Erngs	16.79	0.83
Book Value	6.85	1.07
Sales	8.62	0.64
Cash Flow	7.97	0.86
Historical Erngs	10.67	0.89

Composition

Cash	1.7	Bonds	0.0
Stocks	88.7	Other	9.6
Foreign (% of Stock)			100.0

Sector Weightings	% of Stocks	Rel MSCI EAFE	3 Year High	Low
Info	19.03	1.15		
Software	0.70	0.65	2	0
Hardware	6.83	1.87	9	3
Media	5.90	2.59	6	1
Telecom	5.60	0.58	14	6
Service	45.70	1.02		
Health	1.60	0.22	2	0
Consumer	6.43	1.28	6	4
Business	7.01	1.29	11	7
Financial	30.66	1.14	38	23
Mfg	35.27	0.91		
Goods	20.21	1.48	23	20
Ind Mtrls	7.87	0.64	13	6
Energy	5.34	0.73	5	0
Utilities	1.85	0.35	2	0

Regional Exposure % Stock

UK/W. Europe	1	N. America	0
Japan	0	Latn America	1
Asia X Japan	99	Other	0

Country Exposure % Stock

South Korea	25	Taiwan	15
Hong Kong	20	Malaysia	9
India	17		

T. Rowe Price New Era

Ticker	Load	NAV	Yield	Total Assets	Mstar Category
PRNEX	None	$33.68	0.7%	$2,161 mil	Specialty-Natural Res

Governance and Management

Fiduciary Grade: B

Portfolio Manager(s)

Charlie Ober has called the shots since 1997 and was an analyst on the fund from 1980 to 1997. He leads a three-member team that follows natural-resources stocks.

Strategy

Management looks for companies selling below its estimates of their private market values. It has typically limited its energy exposure to less than 60% of assets, but management will now permit the portfolio's energy stake to increase to 80%. The remainder of the portfolio is diversified across other natural-resources subsectors and includes nonresource names that management expects to do well during inflationary periods.

Historical Profile

Return Average
Risk Below Avg
Rating ★★★★ Above Avg

Investment Style
Equity
Stock %

92% 95% 96% 96% 97% 96% 99% 94% 90%

▼ Manager Change
▽ Partial Manager Change

Growth of $10,000
— Investment Values of Fund
— Investment Values of S&P 500

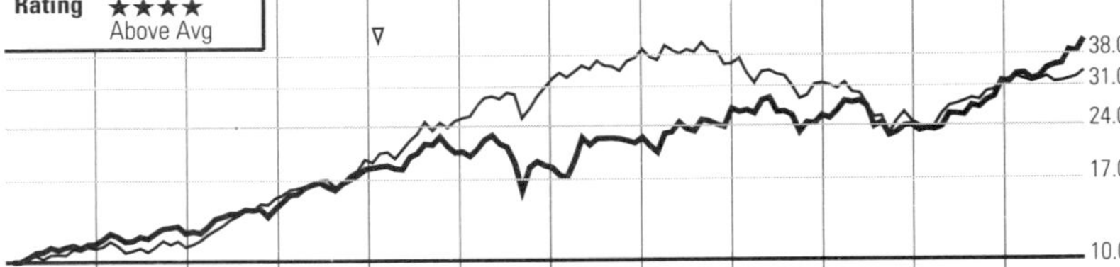

Performance Quartile (within Category)

1993	1994	1995	1996	1997	1998	1999	2000	2001	2002	2003	12-04	History
20.35	20.15	22.65	26.06	25.95	19.78	21.80	24.30	22.24	20.63	27.22	33.68	NAV
15.33	5.17	20.76	24.25	10.96	-9.88	21.22	20.37	-4.35	-6.34	33.20	30.09	Total Return %
5.27	3.86	-16.77	1.31	-22.39	-38.45	0.18	29.47	7.53	15.75	4.53	19.22	+/-S&P 500
—	—	—	—	-5.98	14.79	-6.00	4.56	11.24	6.92	-0.81	5.52	+/-GS NATR RES
2.01	1.87	2.38	1.68	1.42	1.54	1.52	1.33	1.11	0.90	1.21	0.84	Income Return %
13.32	3.30	18.38	22.57	9.54	-11.42	19.70	19.04	-5.46	-7.24	31.99	29.25	Capital Return %
87	10	64	70	28	3	77	67	26	56	31	36	Total Rtn % Rank Cat
0.38	0.38	0.48	0.38	0.37	0.40	0.30	0.29	0.27	0.20	0.25	0.23	Income $
1.03	0.87	1.20	1.71	2.54	3.17	1.82	1.51	0.68	0.00	0.00	1.46	Capital Gains $
0.80	0.80	0.79	0.76	0.74	0.75	0.74	0.72	0.72	0.72	0.72	—	Expense Ratio %
1.92	1.87	2.00	1.53	1.33	1.27	1.29	1.29	1.11	1.03	1.13	—	Income Ratio %
25	25	23	29	28	23	32	29	18	11	18	—	Turnover Rate %
753	979	1,090	1,468	1,493	997	1,082	1,195	1,070	985	1,334	2,161	Net Assets $mil

Performance 12-31-04

	1st Qtr	2nd Qtr	3rd Qtr	4th Qtr	Total
2000	2.52	2.91	5.26	8.38	20.37
2001	-3.13	0.89	-12.21	11.47	-4.35
2002	9.80	-3.56	-17.20	6.82	-6.34
2003	-2.76	10.57	4.42	18.65	33.20
2004	4.96	3.19	12.21	7.04	30.09

Trailing	Total Return%	+/- S&P 500	+/- GS NATR RES	%Rank Cat	Growth of $10,000
3 Mo	7.04	-2.19	2.22	33	10,704
6 Mo	20.12	12.93	4.93	25	12,012
1 Yr	30.09	19.22	5.52	36	13,009
3 Yr Avg	17.52	13.94	4.39	43	16,231
5 Yr Avg	13.32	15.62	6.13	41	18,687
10 Yr Avg	13.01	0.94	—	44	33,976
15 Yr Avg	10.39	-0.54	—	23	44,050

Tax Analysis	Tax-Adj Rtn%	%Rank Cat	Tax-Cost Rat	%Rank Cat
3 Yr (estimated)	16.88	45	0.54	60
5 Yr (estimated)	12.22	44	0.97	78
10 Yr (estimated)	10.96	50	1.81	100

Potential Capital Gain Exposure: 42% of assets

Rating and Risk

Time Period	Load-Adj Return %	Morningstar Rtn vs Cat	Morningstar Risk vs Cat	Morningstar Risk-Adj Rating
1 Yr	30.09			
3 Yr	17.52	Avg	-Avg	★★★
5 Yr	13.32	Avg	Low	★★★
10 Yr	13.01	Avg	-Avg	★★★★
Incept	—			

Other Measures	Standard Index S&P 500	Best Fit Index GS NATR RES
Alpha	14.7	4.9
Beta	0.72	0.91
R-Squared	44	96
Standard Deviation	19.07	
Mean	17.52	
Sharpe Ratio	0.86	

Portfolio Analysis 09-30-04

Share change since 06-04 Total Stocks:91	Sector	PE	YTD Ret%	% Assets
⊕ Newmont Mining	Ind Mtrls	45.6	-8.02	3.08
⊕ Murphy Oil	Energy	16.5	24.71	2.94
⊕ BP PLC ADR	Energy	20.7	22.07	2.68
⊕ ExxonMobil	Energy	13.9	28.04	2.59
⊖ Nucor	Ind Mtrls	9.6	89.07	2.40
⊕ Royal Dutch Petroleum AD	Energy	—	14.31	2.40
⊕ BHP Billiton Ltd	Ind Mtrls	—	—	2.33
⊕ Potash Corp./Saskatchewa	Ind Mtrls	—	94.19	2.29
⊕ Baker Hughes	Energy	30.3	34.28	2.28
⊕ ConocoPhillips	Energy	9.0	35.60	2.10
☼ Teck Cominco Ltd Teck Co	—	—	—	2.07
⊕ Total SA ADR	Energy	17.0	23.39	1.99
⊕ Devon Energy	Energy	9.0	36.78	1.97
⊕ Schlumberger	Energy	40.7	23.84	1.82
Diamond Offshore Drillin	Energy	—	97.23	1.77
Transocean	Energy	56.3	76.55	1.71
⊖ Amerada Hess	Energy	10.1	57.47	1.66
⊕ BJ Svcs	Energy	21.8	30.07	1.62
⊕ International Paper	Ind Mtrls	—	-0.20	1.57
⊕ Agrium	Ind Mtrls	—	3.13	1.50

Current Investment Style

Value Blnd Growth; Large Mid Small

Market Cap	%
Giant	22.9
Large	34.0
Mid	36.9
Small	5.8
Micro	0.4

Avg $mil: 12,542

Value Measures		Rel Category
Price/Earnings	16.84	1.03
Price/Book	2.46	1.03
Price/Sales	1.19	0.99
Price/Cash Flow	9.68	1.22
Dividend Yield %	1.24	1.10

Growth Measures	%	Rel Category
Long-Term Erngs	9.87	0.92
Book Value	4.93	0.92
Sales	9.29	0.98
Cash Flow	1.48	0.22
Historical Erngs	19.83	0.95

Profitability	%	Rel Category
Return on Equity	11.79	0.94
Return on Assets	5.31	0.99
Net Margin	8.38	0.90

Industry Weightings	% of Stocks	Rel Cat
Oil & Gas	38.6	0.9
Oil/Gas Products	0.0	0.0
Oil & Gas Srv	20.6	0.8
Pipelines	0.0	0.0
Utilities	0.0	0.0
Hard Commd	12.7	1.4
Soft Commd	10.7	2.5
Misc. Indstrl	4.1	0.7
Other	13.2	1.7

Composition

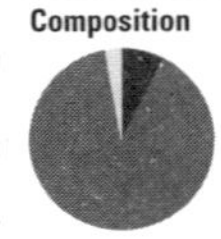

Cash	7.5
Stocks	89.7
Bonds	0.0
Other	2.8
Foreign (% of Stock)	24.1

Morningstar's Take by Sonya Morris 12-29-04

Though it's not a must-own, T. Rowe Price New Era is a fine fund for heady times.

Natural-resource funds have been on fire in 2004. And while this fund has racked up an impressive 28% gain through Dec. 27, 2004, we're not surprised that it's not leading the charge. Through the sector's ups and downs, this fund has taken a steady approach that has dampened volatility yet yielded solid long-term returns.

Manager Charlie Ober is a patient investor (as evidenced by the fund's ultralow 13% turnover rate) who spreads assets over a wide variety of natural-resource names including energy, metals, chemicals, and forest products. Ober typically anchors the portfolio in large integrated oil firms, such as BP and ExxonMobil, which tend to be insulated from oil-price swings because of their diverse revenue streams. But Ober also has a contrarian bent, opting for areas that are unloved or undiscovered, and he's not afraid to invest in the earliest stages of an up cycle.

Presently, the fund sports a 56% energy weighting, which is one of the lowest in the category. That said, Ober is still bullish on energy even though he thinks that oil prices may slide further. But Ober also sees opportunity beyond energy. For instance, lately he has been attracted to the forest-products and chemical sectors, where he's seeing early signs of an upturn. As a result, he has ratcheted up the fund's exposure to names like International Paper and Dow Chemical.

Because this fund spans a variety of natural-resource subsectors, it can provide diversification to a portfolio at a reasonable price. (Its 0.72% expense ratio is one of the lowest in the category.) However, many investors may already have sufficient exposure to the sector through their other holdings, and in any case, investors shouldn't expect a repeat of the robust returns seen in 2004. With easing oil prices, this category could be due to cool off, and investors would be wise to rein in their expectations.

Address:	100 E Pratt St Baltimore MD 21202 800-638-5660
Web Address:	www.troweprice.com
Inception:	01-20-69
Advisor:	T. Rowe Price Associates, Inc.
Subadvisor:	None
NTF Plans:	N/A

Minimum Purchase:	$2500	Add: $100	IRA: $1000
Min Auto Inv Plan:	$50	Add: $50	
Sales Fees:	No-load		
Management Fee:	0.57%		
Actual Fees:	Mgt:0.57%	Dist:	
Expense Projections:	3Yr:$230	5Yr:$401	10Yr:$894
Income Distrib:	Annually		

T. Rowe Price New Horiz

Ticker	Load	NAV	Yield	Total Assets	Mstar Category
PRNHX	None	$29.24	0.0%	$5,831 mil	Small Growth

Governance and Management

Fiduciary Grade: B

Portfolio Manager(s)

Stability has been the name of the game at this fund. Jack Laporte has run it since 1987. T. Rowe Price's staff of 30 to 35 sector analysts also contributes ideas.

Strategy

Jack Laporte scours the small-cap universe for companies with strong and predictable earnings growth and then typically lets his winners run. With nearly 300 names and broad industry diversification, this fund covers more territory than most peers.

Historical Profile

Return Above Avg
Risk Average
Rating ★★★ Neutral

Investment Style: Equity Stock %

98%	97%	96%	95%	94%	98%	98%	99%	98%

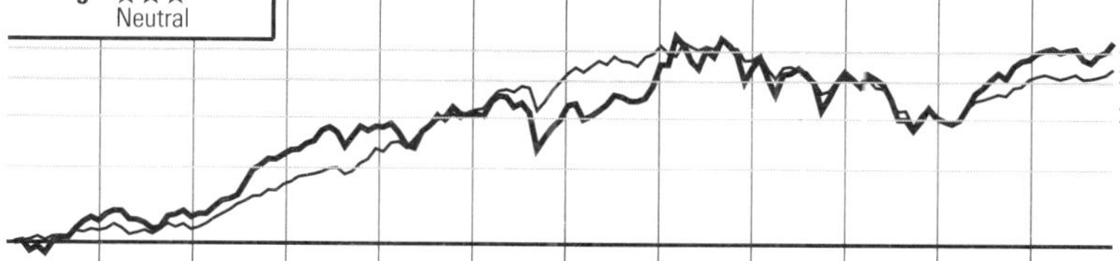

▼ Manager Change
▽ Partial Manager Change

Growth of $10,000
▬ Investment Values of Fund
— Investment Values of S&P 500

Performance Quartile (within Category)

1993	1994	1995	1996	1997	1998	1999	2000	2001	2002	2003	12-04	History
16.16	14.76	20.50	21.77	23.30	23.34	27.53	23.89	22.63	16.61	24.80	29.24	NAV
22.01	0.30	55.44	17.03	9.77	6.25	32.52	-1.86	-2.84	-26.60	49.31	17.90	Total Return %
11.95	-1.01	17.91	-5.91	-23.58	-22.32	11.48	7.24	9.04	-4.51	20.64	7.03	+/-S&P 500
8.64	2.73	24.40	5.77	-3.18	5.02	-10.57	20.57	6.39	3.66	0.77	3.59	+/-Russ 2000 Gr
0.00	0.00	0.00	0.00	0.00	0.00	0.00	0.00	0.00	0.00	0.00	0.00	Income Return %
22.01	0.30	55.44	17.03	9.77	6.25	32.52	-1.86	-2.84	-26.60	49.31	17.90	Capital Return %
34	42	7	63	82	37	69	39	31	45	25	19	Total Rtn % Rank Cat
0.00	0.00	0.00	0.00	0.00	0.00	0.00	0.00	0.00	0.00	0.00	0.00	Income $
2.70	1.43	2.41	2.19	0.58	1.27	3.02	3.14	0.56	0.00	0.00	0.00	Capital Gains $
0.93	0.93	0.90	0.90	0.88	0.89	0.90	0.88	0.91	0.92	0.91	—	Expense Ratio %
-0.50	-0.50	-0.23	-0.41	-0.57	-0.65	-0.66	-0.51	-0.77	-0.81	-0.75	—	Income Ratio %
49	44	56	41	45	41	45	47	27	24	29	—	Turnover Rate %
1,640	1,648	2,855	4,363	5,104	5,228	6,022	6,122	5,583	3,359	4,960	5,831	Net Assets $mil

Performance 12-31-04

	1st Qtr	2nd Qtr	3rd Qtr	4th Qtr	Total
2000	14.38	-3.37	3.32	-14.06	-1.86
2001	-16.95	20.06	-25.15	30.18	-2.84
2002	-1.50	-15.48	-19.16	9.06	-26.60
2003	-1.57	24.53	6.58	14.29	49.31
2004	7.66	-0.30	-4.06	14.49	17.90

Trailing	Total Return%	+/- S&P 500	+/- Russ 2000 Gr	%Rank Cat	Growth of $10,000
3 Mo	14.49	5.26	-0.59	39	11,449
6 Mo	9.84	2.65	1.68	29	10,984
1 Yr	17.90	7.03	3.59	19	11,790
3 Yr Avg	8.92	5.34	3.13	25	12,922
5 Yr Avg	4.26	6.56	7.83	27	12,319
10 Yr Avg	13.23	1.16	6.11	19	34,643
15 Yr Avg	13.24	2.31	5.74	22	64,565

Tax Analysis	Tax-Adj Rtn%	%Rank Cat	Tax-Cost Rat	%Rank Cat
3 Yr (estimated)	8.92	20	0.00	1
5 Yr (estimated)	3.57	24	0.66	29
10 Yr (estimated)	11.63	17	1.41	41

Potential Capital Gain Exposure: 38% of assets

Rating and Risk

Time Period	Load-Adj Return %	Morningstar Rtn vs Cat	Morningstar Risk vs Cat	Morningstar Risk-Adj Rating
1 Yr	17.90			
3 Yr	8.92	+Avg	Avg	★★★★
5 Yr	4.26	+Avg	Avg	★★★
10 Yr	13.23	+Avg	Avg	★★★
Incept	11.51			

Other Measures	Standard Index S&P 500	Best Fit Index Russ 2000 Gr
Alpha	5.5	3.3
Beta	1.16	0.90
R-Squared	78	96
Standard Deviation	21.75	
Mean	8.92	
Sharpe Ratio	0.35	

Portfolio Analysis 09-30-04

Share change since 06-04 Total Stocks:261	Sector	PE	YTD Ret%	% Assets
⊕ Apollo Group A	Consumer	NMF	19.02	4.74
Henry Schein	Health	23.1	3.05	2.59
NII Holdings	Telecom	7.4	90.74	1.83
⊖ Davita	Health	19.0	52.04	1.79
Omnicare	Health	14.0	-14.07	1.68
Toll Brothers	Consumer	17.3	72.56	1.65
O'Reilly Automotive	Consumer	21.6	16.83	1.36
Oshkosh Truck	Ind Mtrls	20.5	34.70	1.35
Coventry Health Care	Health	15.5	23.46	1.35
⊖ Tuesday Morning	Consumer	21.2	1.26	1.28
Laureate Education	Consumer	32.0	53.14	1.21
School Specialty	Ind Mtrls	18.3	13.38	1.17
Station Casinos	Consumer	77.1	81.31	1.14
Roper Industries	Ind Mtrls	31.4	24.26	1.08
FMC Technologies	Energy	23.4	38.20	0.99
Corporate Executive Boar	Business	54.1	44.20	0.97
⊖ Western Wireless Cl A	Telecom	—	59.59	0.97
P.F. Chang's China Bistr	Consumer	62.4	10.75	0.96
Actuant A	Ind Mtrls	50.7	44.06	0.95
Nextel Partners A	Telecom	—	45.28	0.93

Current Investment Style

Value Blnd Growth / Large Mid Small

Market Cap	%
Giant	0.0
Large	6.6
Mid	45.5
Small	39.9
Micro	8.1
Avg $mil: 1,561	

Value Measures		Rel Category
Price/Earnings	20.35	0.94
Price/Book	2.64	1.00
Price/Sales	1.65	1.10
Price/Cash Flow	9.40	1.17
Dividend Yield %	0.09	0.29

Growth Measures	%	Rel Category
Long-Term Erngs	17.23	1.00
Book Value	11.05	1.71
Sales	13.33	2.06
Cash Flow	17.05	1.26
Historical Erngs	15.59	1.15

Profitability	%	Rel Category
Return on Equity	14.01	1.42
Return on Assets	4.48	1.02
Net Margin	8.00	1.17

Sector Weightings	% of Stocks	Rel S&P 500	3 Year High	3 Year Low
Info	24.29	1.13		
Software	8.84	2.06	9	7
Hardware	7.76	0.76	12	7
Media	3.30	0.86	5	3
Telecom	4.39	1.39	4	0
Service	60.37	1.30		
Health	19.88	1.59	23	20
Consumer	22.08	2.43	23	19
Business	9.46	2.34	19	9
Financial	8.95	0.43	9	4
Mfg	15.33	0.48		
Goods	1.06	0.11	3	1
Ind Mtrls	8.60	0.68	9	4
Energy	5.67	0.79	9	5
Utilities	0.00	0.00	0	0

Composition

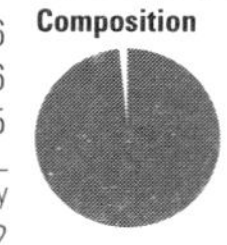

Cash	0.4
Stocks	98.2
Bonds	0.8
Other	0.6
Foreign (% of Stock)	0.7

Morningstar's Take by Kerry O'Boyle 12-15-04

T. Rowe Price New Horizons is one of the more-reliable funds in the small-growth category.

For consistent performance year in and year out, this offering is tough to beat. It's seldom near the top of the heap of small-growth funds, and even rarer near the bottom. But over the long haul, its steady returns have landed it in the top quartile for all the major trailing periods through Dec. 14, 2004.

Longtime manager Jack Laporte looks for reasonably priced companies early in their growth cycle that he can then own for the long haul. With the support of T. Rowe Price's experienced research staff, he roots out steady growers with strong management teams, that he thinks can deliver consistent results for many years.

Apollo Group, by far the largest position in the fund after its recent reacquisition of fellow holding University of Phoenix, is a case in point. Public for nearly a decade, Laporte has owned it in the portfolio the entire time. And despite the shadow hanging over for-profit education companies, he continues to believe in the superior culture at the conservatively run firm.

Still, a $16 billion company like Apollo makes for an odd fit in a small-growth offering, and points to one of the fund's drawbacks. Laporte's buy-and-hold philosophy--plus an asset base of more than $5 billion--leads it to invest significantly more in mid-cap stocks than its typical peer. While he consciously fights against style creep working its way into the portfolio, the fund can sometimes find itself out of step with offerings more focused on smaller stocks.

In the end, though, Laporte has proven himself to be a savvy, contrarian stock-picker who can deliver. His continued faith in homebuilders like Toll Brothers and Ryland--up 66% and 30%, respectively--has paid off again in 2004, despite worries about rising interest rates. And LaPorte added to the fund's tech holdings on weakness during the third quarter. Given his record, the fund remains a top choice for growth investors.

Address:	100 E Pratt St Baltimore MD 21202 800-638-5660
Web Address:	www.troweprice.com
Inception:	06-03-60
Advisor:	T. Rowe Price Associates, Inc.
Subadvisor:	None
NTF Plans:	N/A

Minimum Purchase:	$2500	Add: $100	IRA: $1000
Min Auto Inv Plan:	$50	Add: $50	
Sales Fees:	No-load		
Management Fee:	0.67%		
Actual Fees:	Mgt:0.67%	Dist:	
Expense Projections:	3Yr:$290	5Yr:$504	10Yr:$1120
Income Distrib:	Annually		

T. Rowe Price Pers Inc

Analyst Pick	Ticker	Load	NAV	Yield	Total Assets	Mstar Category
✓	PRSIX	None	$14.84	2.4%	$371 mil	Conservative Allocation

Governance and Management

Fiduciary Grade: B

Portfolio Manager(s)

Lead manager Ned Notzon, who sets the fund's security mix, fills the same role at four other T. Rowe Price funds and runs the investment-grade bond slice of T. Rowe Price Balanced. The managers of this fund's subportfolios include Larry Puglia of T. Rowe Price Blue Chip Growth, Stephen Boesel of T. Rowe Price Capital Appreciation, Greg McCrickard of T. Rowe Price Small-Cap Stock, Ray Mills of T. Rowe Price International Growth & Income, Daniel Shackelford of T. Rowe Price New Income, and Mark Vaselkiv of T. Rowe Price High-Yield.

Strategy

The fund is designed to provide one-stop exposure to most asset classes. Each stock or bond component mirrors one of T. Rowe Price's offerings. The stock portfolio, which typically consumes 35% to 45% of the fund's assets, is divided among large-growth, large-value, small-cap, and international components. The fund's bond stake includes domestic investment-grade and high-yield issues, and sometimes international bonds. An investment committe headed by lead manager Ned Notzon determines the fund's asset allocation.

Performance 12-31-04

	1st Qtr	2nd Qtr	3rd Qtr	4th Qtr	Total
2000	1.62	1.14	1.83	1.83	6.58
2001	-2.88	2.76	-3.63	4.96	0.95
2002	1.33	-2.79	-5.97	4.32	-3.37
2003	-0.59	9.20	1.94	7.15	18.58
2004	2.45	0.00	1.14	6.10	9.95

Trailing	Total Return%	+/- S&P 500	+/- DJ 40%	%Rank Cat	Growth of $10,000
3 Mo	6.10	-3.13	0.70	11	10,610
6 Mo	7.31	0.12	0.82	14	10,731
1 Yr	9.95	-0.92	0.94	11	10,995
3 Yr Avg	8.00	4.42	0.82	10	12,597
5 Yr Avg	6.27	8.57	-0.03	11	13,554
10 Yr Avg	9.81	-2.26	0.66	14	25,493
15 Yr Avg	—	—	—	—	—

Tax Analysis	Tax-Adj Rtn%	%Rank Cat	Tax-Cost Rat	%Rank Cat
3 Yr (estimated)	6.91	11	1.01	52
5 Yr (estimated)	4.93	11	1.26	46
10 Yr (estimated)	7.82	4	1.81	30

Potential Capital Gain Exposure: 14% of assets

Historical Profile

Return: Above Avg
Risk: Average
Rating: ★★★★★ Highest

Investment Style: Equity Stock %

1995	1996	1997	1998	1999	2000	2001	2002	2003	12-04
42%	38%	38%	43%	40%	39%	43%	44%	46%	

▼ Manager Change
▽ Partial Manager Change

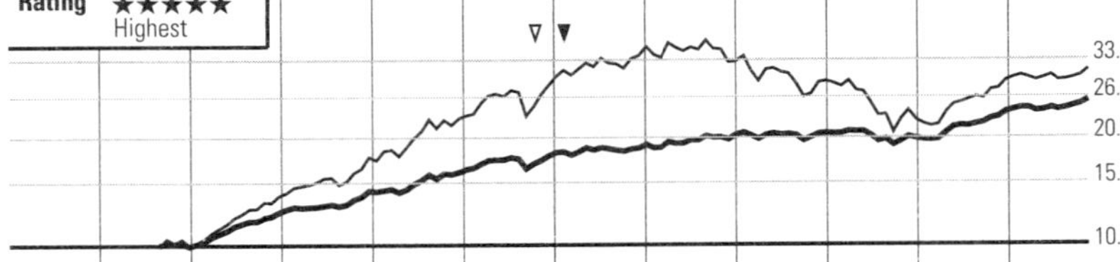

Growth of $10,000
▬ Investment Values of Fund
— Investment Values of S&P 500

Performance Quartile (within Category)

1993	1994	1995	1996	1997	1998	1999	2000	2001	2002	2003	12-04	History
—	9.88	11.70	11.56	12.45	13.27	13.03	13.18	12.81	12.00	13.87	14.84	NAV
—	0.80*	24.71	11.79	15.01	11.50	5.17	6.58	0.95	-3.37	18.58	9.95	Total Return %
—	—	-12.82	-11.15	-18.34	-17.07	-15.87	15.68	12.83	18.72	-10.09	-0.92	+/-S&P 500
—	—	6.55	2.90	0.91	-0.23	-2.69	-0.21	-2.27	0.65	0.92	0.94	+/-DJ 40%
—	0.00	4.95	4.16	4.66	4.00	4.05	4.13	3.69	3.00	2.69	2.55	Income Return %
—	—	19.76	7.63	10.35	7.50	1.12	2.45	-2.74	-6.37	15.89	7.40	Capital Return %
—	—	16	34	41	39	51	23	38	53	11	11	Total Rtn % Rank Cat
—	0.20	0.48	0.47	0.53	0.49	0.53	0.53	0.48	0.38	0.32	0.35	Income $
—	0.00	0.10	0.98	0.28	0.10	0.37	0.16	0.00	0.00	0.01	0.04	Capital Gains $
—	—	0.95	0.95	0.95	0.95	0.90	0.90	0.90	1.02	0.80	0.71	Expense Ratio %
—	—	4.71	4.31	4.38	4.13	3.91	4.06	4.04	2.54	2.89	2.36	Income Ratio %
—	—	50	34	45	31	49	45	80	116	109	98	Turnover Rate %
—	—	26	33	66	213	206	228	251	259	341	371	Net Assets $mil

Rating and Risk

Time Period	Load-Adj Return %	Morningstar Rtn vs Cat	Morningstar Risk vs Cat	Morningstar Risk-Adj Rating
1 Yr	9.95			
3 Yr	8.00	High	+Avg	★★★★★
5 Yr	6.27	+Avg	Avg	★★★★
10 Yr	9.81	+Avg	Avg	★★★★★
Incept	9.47			

Other Measures	Standard Index S&P 500	Best Fit Index DJ 60%
Alpha	5.4	0.4
Beta	0.40	0.70
R-Squared	85	96
Standard Deviation	6.84	
Mean	8.00	
Sharpe Ratio	0.98	

Portfolio Analysis 09-30-04

Total Stocks:689 Share change since 06-30-04	Sectors	P/E Ratio	YTD Return %	% Net Assets
⊖ Nucor	Ind Mtrls	9.6	-7.60	0.78
⊕ Tyco International	Ind Mtrls	25.1	-0.92	0.73
⊕ American International Gr	Financial	16.2	2.25	0.64
⊕ Citigroup	Financial	15.3	0.08	0.62
⊕ UnitedHealth Group	Health	23.8	-0.59	0.60
⊕ Microsoft	Software	36.1	0.04	0.59
⊕ Gen Elec	Ind Mtrls	22.8	-3.01	0.54
⊕ Baker Hughes	Energy	30.3	-3.45	0.53
⊕ Lockheed Martin	Ind Mtrls	19.9	-0.81	0.51

Total Fixed-Income:321	Date of Maturity	Amount $000	Value $000	% Net Assets
T. Rowe Price Instl High		2,778	30,277	8.62
US Treasury Note 2.375%	08-31-06	8,600	8,566	2.44
US Treasury Note 3.25%	08-15-07	5,685	5,747	1.64
US Treasury Note 3.5%	11-15-06	4,465	4,542	1.29
FHLMC 4.625%	02-15-07	1,885	2,435	0.69
FHLMC 5%	10-01-18	1,713	1,742	0.50
US Treasury Bond 6.375%	08-15-27	1,375	1,642	0.47
US Treasury Bond 6.25%	05-15-30	1,335	1,584	0.45
GNMA 5%	07-15-33	1,342	1,337	0.38

Equity Style
Style: Blend
Size: Large-Cap

Value Measures		Rel Category
Price/Earnings	15.98	0.97
Price/Book	2.41	1.02
Price/Sales	1.22	0.94
Price/Cash Flow	6.81	0.98
Dividend Yield %	1.81	1.04

Growth Measures	%	Rel Category
Long-Term Erngs	11.59	1.04
Book Value	6.11	1.11
Sales	4.23	0.93
Cash Flow	5.96	0.89
Historical Erngs	8.58	0.91

Market Cap %			
Giant	36.0	Small	5.7
Large	40.1	Micro	0.8
Mid	17.4	Avg $mil:	19,439

Composition

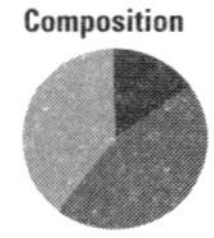

Cash	14.9
Stocks	45.5
Bonds	39.1
Other	0.5
Foreign (% of Stock)	20.5

Fixed-Income Style
Duration: Interm-Term
Quality: Medium

Avg Eff Duration [1]	4.2 Yrs
Avg Eff Maturity	6.9 Yrs
Avg Credit Quality	A
Avg Wtd Coupon	4.79%

[1] figure provided by fund as of 09-30-04

Sector Weightings	% of Stocks	Rel S&P 500	3 Year High	3 Year Low
Info	16.91	0.79		
Software	3.50	0.81	4	2
Hardware	6.44	0.63	7	4
Media	4.30	1.12	5	4
Telecom	2.67	0.85	4	3
Service	47.14	1.02		
Health	11.16	0.89	14	11
Consumer	8.59	0.95	9	7
Business	6.35	1.57	9	6
Financial	21.04	1.01	25	21
Mfg	35.95	1.12		
Goods	9.87	1.06	12	10
Ind Mtrls	16.11	1.27	16	11
Energy	7.53	1.05	8	6
Utilities	2.44	0.82	3	2

Morningstar's Take by Greg Carlson 12-22-04

T. Rowe Price Personal Strategy Income offers more diversification, and a better management team, than most of its rivals.

This offering covers a lot of ground. Ned Notzon, the fund's lead manager since November 1998, spreads the fund's assets among domestic stocks of all sizes, as well as foreign equities, investment-grade and high-yield debt, and, occasionally, foreign bonds. He chairs a committee that sizes up relative valuations and macroeconomic conditions, and makes minor adjustments to the fund's asset allocation based on the committee's recommendations.

Casting such a wide net would strain the resources of many firms, but T. Rowe Price uses some of its best fund managers to choose this fund's securities. Three of the firm's skippers run portions of the domestic-stock portfolio; each one has managed money in his or her current style for T. Rowe for more than a decade. What's more, the three skippers who cover the remaining asset classes have at least 4.5 years on the job. And there's no weak link in the bunch: All six have beaten the majority of their peers at their current charges, while providing less turbulent returns.

Notzon, too, is a proven veteran. In addition to this offering, he sets the security mix for four other T. Rowe funds, and has run the investment-grade bond slice of another offering for more than 13 years. It's worth noting that this fund's stock weighting will typically be higher than the conservative-allocation group norm of 35%; Notzon currently holds a 46% stake in equities, which is near the top of the fund's range. That bias may hurt when stocks suffer--witness the fund's middling showing in 2002--but it still held up better than its typical peer during the bear market.

All told, this fund has beaten more than 75% of its rivals on Notzon's watch, and volatility has been modest. Given the breadth and depth of its management team, as well as its reasonable expenses, it's a fine choice.

Address:	C/O T Rowe Price Associates Inc Baltimore MD 21202 800-638-5660
Web Address:	www.troweprice.com
Inception:	07-29-94*
Advisor:	T. Rowe Price Associates, Inc.
Subadvisor:	None
NTF Plans:	N/A

Minimum Purchase:	$2500	Add: $100	IRA: $1000
Min Auto Inv Plan:	$50	Add: $50	
Sales Fees:	No-load		
Management Fee:	0.47%		
Actual Fees:	Mgt:0.47%	Dist:	
Expense Projections:	3Yr:$262	5Yr:$472	10Yr:$1076
Income Distrib:	Quarterly		

T. Rowe Price Real Est

Ticker	Load	NAV	Yield	Total Assets	Mstar Category
TRREX	None	$17.90	3.3%	$640 mil	Specialty-Real Estate

Governance and Management

Fiduciary Grade: B

Portfolio Manager(s)

David Lee has managed this fund since its October 1997 inception. Lee had been T. Rowe Price's real estate analyst prior to that. T. Rowe's hotel analyst adds some expertise.

Strategy

Manager David Lee has a large-cap, low-turnover strategy. With the Wilshire Real Estate Securities Index as its benchmark, the fund will own both REITs and REOCs (real estate operating companies). Ideal candidates for the fund will have proven management teams that are in the process of repositioning or redeveloping their assets.

Historical Profile

Return Above Avg
Risk Average
Rating ★★★★ Above Avg

Investment Style
Equity
Stock %

1997	1998	1999	2000	2001	2002	2003	12-04
97%	93%	93%	93%	89%	98%	99%	

▼ Manager Change
▽ Partial Manager Change

Growth of $10,000
— Investment Values of Fund
— Investment Values of S&P 500

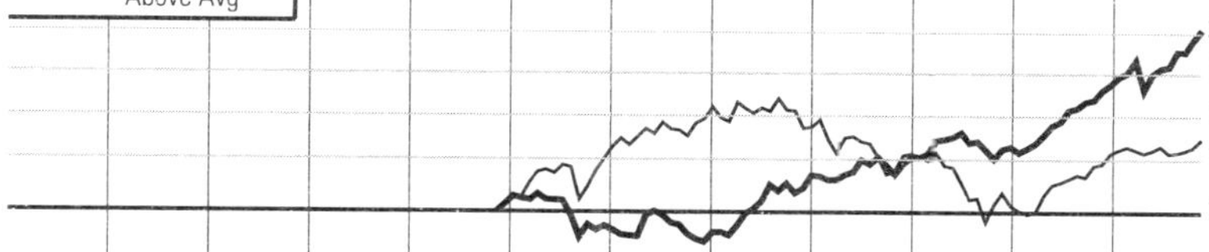

Performance Quartile (within Category)

1993	1994	1995	1996	1997	1998	1999	2000	2001	2002	2003	12-04	History
—	—	—	—	10.69	8.68	8.11	10.19	10.54	10.62	13.65	17.90	NAV
—	—	—	—	7.82*	-14.86	-1.23	31.92	8.87	5.38	34.84	36.82	Total Return %
—	—	—	—	—	-43.43	-22.27	41.02	20.75	27.47	6.17	25.95	+/-S&P 500
—	—	—	—	—	2.14	1.34	0.88	-3.49	1.78	-1.22	3.00	+/-Wil REIT
—	—	—	—	0.00	4.18	5.28	5.90	5.30	4.72	5.66	4.46	Income Return %
—	—	—	—	—	-19.04	-6.51	26.02	3.57	0.66	29.18	32.36	Capital Return %
—	—	—	—	—	34	25	12	47	32	66	11	Total Rtn % Rank Cat
—	—	—	—	0.09	0.44	0.45	0.47	0.53	0.49	0.59	0.60	Income $
—	—	—	—	0.00	0.00	0.00	0.00	0.00	0.00	0.00	0.07	Capital Gains $
—	—	—	—	—	1.00	1.00	1.00	1.00	1.00	1.00	—	Expense Ratio %
—	—	—	—	—	4.07	4.22	4.61	4.09	4.07	3.49	—	Income Ratio %
—	—	—	—	—	57	27	19	37	10	4	—	Turnover Rate %
—	—	—	—	7	28	25	54	69	132	290	640	Net Assets $mil

Performance 12-31-04

	1st Qtr	2nd Qtr	3rd Qtr	4th Qtr	Total
2000	3.46	12.34	8.97	4.16	31.92
2001	-2.25	10.02	-2.57	3.90	8.87
2002	8.45	3.97	-7.78	1.35	5.38
2003	1.78	11.04	9.90	8.57	34.84
2004	12.11	-3.71	8.18	17.15	36.82

Trailing	Total Return%	+/- S&P 500	+/- Wil REIT	%Rank Cat	Growth of $10,000
3 Mo	17.15	7.92	0.46	29	11,715
6 Mo	26.74	19.55	0.48	23	12,674
1 Yr	36.82	25.95	3.00	11	13,682
3 Yr Avg	24.81	21.23	1.25	24	19,442
5 Yr Avg	22.80	25.10	0.13	12	27,925
10 Yr Avg	—	—	—	—	—
15 Yr Avg	—	—	—	—	—

Tax Analysis	Tax-Adj Rtn%	%Rank Cat	Tax-Cost Rat	%Rank Cat
3 Yr (estimated)	22.83	20	1.59	44
5 Yr (estimated)	20.68	13	1.73	47
10 Yr (estimated)	—	—	—	—

Potential Capital Gain Exposure: 27% of assets

Rating and Risk

Time Period	Load-Adj Return %	Morningstar Rtn vs Cat	Morningstar Risk vs Cat	Morningstar Risk-Adj Rating
1 Yr	36.82			
3 Yr	24.81	+Avg	-Avg	★★★★
5 Yr	22.80	+Avg	Avg	★★★★
10 Yr	—	—	—	—
Incept	13.84			

Other Measures	Standard Index S&P 500	Best Fit Index Wil REIT
Alpha	23.0	2.6
Beta	0.33	0.92
R-Squared	13	99

Standard Deviation	16.97
Mean	24.81
Sharpe Ratio	1.40

Portfolio Analysis 09-30-04

Share change since 06-04 Total Stocks:45	Sector	PE	YTD Ret%	% Assets
⊕ Simon Property Group	Financial	37.3	46.10	4.87
⊕ Vornado Realty Trust	Financial	30.8	46.53	4.43
⊕ Boston Properties	Financial	23.9	40.60	4.12
⊕ Equity Residential	Financial	90.2	29.50	3.66
⊕ ProLogis Trust	Financial	25.1	41.03	3.49
⊕ Archstone-Smith Trust	Financial	52.6	48.79	3.41
⊕ Equity Office Properties	Financial	45.9	9.06	3.20
SL Green Realty	Financial	16.8	53.52	3.07
⊕ AMB Property	Financial	39.1	28.55	3.05
⊕ Starwood Hotels & Resort	Consumer	33.9	64.71	2.96
⊕ Regency Centers	Financial	27.3	46.22	2.94
⊕ CarrAmerica Realty	Financial	48.2	18.32	2.88
⊕ AvalonBay Communities	Financial	58.1	65.02	2.85
⊕ Weingarten Realty	Financial	31.5	42.37	2.74
⊕ Kimco Realty	Financial	23.4	35.56	2.62
⊕ Camden Property Trust	Financial	62.7	21.60	2.61
⊖ General Growth Propertie	Financial	26.6	35.96	2.57
⊕ Essex Property Trust	Financial	31.3	36.36	2.49
⊕ EastGroup Properties	Financial	41.0	25.21	2.32
⊕ Duke Realty	Financial	33.1	16.66	2.30

Current Investment Style

Value Blnd Growth — Large Mid Small

Market Cap	%
Giant	0.0
Large	16.2
Mid	74.1
Small	8.5
Micro	1.2
Avg $mil: 3,555	

Value Measures		Rel Category
Price/Earnings	14.61	1.02
Price/Book	2.19	1.09
Price/Sales	3.96	1.06
Price/Cash Flow	13.34	1.11
Dividend Yield %	4.61	0.94

Growth Measures	%	Rel Category
Long-Term Erngs	6.50	0.92
Book Value	1.38	9.20
Sales	2.90	1.75
Cash Flow	-6.98	NMF
Historical Erngs	-1.73	NMF

Profitability	%	Rel Category
Return on Equity	9.93	0.96
Return on Assets	7.37	0.96
Net Margin	22.64	1.04

Sector Weightings	% of Stocks	Rel S&P 500	3 Year High	Low
Info	0.00	0.00		
Software	0.00	0.00	0	0
Hardware	0.00	0.00	0	0
Media	0.00	0.00	0	0
Telecom	0.00	0.00	0	0
Service	100.00	2.16		
Health	0.00	0.00	0	0
Consumer	5.33	0.59	5	3
Business	0.00	0.00	0	0
Financial	94.67	4.56	97	95
Mfg	0.00	0.00		
Goods	0.00	0.00	0	0
Ind Mtrls	0.00	0.00	0	0
Energy	0.00	0.00	0	0
Utilities	0.00	0.00	0	0

Composition

Cash	1.3
Stocks	98.7
Bonds	0.0
Other	0.0
Foreign (% of Stock)	0.0

Morningstar's Take by Dan McNeela 12-29-04

Avoiding the flash pays off for T. Rowe Price Real Estate.

During this heady real estate rally, many off-beat strategies have had their day in the sun. Some managers emphasized high-dividend payers or small-cap REITs, while a couple dove into homebuilders. This fund hasn't needed to make such moves to get ahead. Manager David Lee is well versed in T. Rowe's philosophy of sticking to long-term drivers of returns. He refrains from making big subsector bets, preferring to buy and hold high-quality stocks. The fund's turnover ratio in 2003 was just 4%.

Even so, the fund's returns since its 1997 inception have been compelling. Only once have its annual returns slipped into the category's bottom half. That happened in 2003, when the fund's 35% gain lagged the category average.

Lee responded to that minor defeat by keeping the fund on a steady course, and his persistence paid off in 2004. The real estate rally has continued unabated, but leadership in the sector has transferred to larger REITs. Lee's stock-picking has also been on target. While office REITs have generally underperformed, the fund's sizeable stake in SL Green rose by 50%, as the Manhattan office market boomed.

Lee also resisted the temptation to sell out of the shopping-center area, as many managers fear the impact of Wal-Mart's expansion plans. Lee banked on shopping-center REITs that had built-in barriers to such competition and watched as Federal Realty Investment Trust and Pan Pacific Retail Properties continued to post strong gains.

As much as we like the fund's long-term prospects, investors should recognize that real estate has been a frothy area over the past couple years. This type of fund makes more sense as a diversifier and should be kept to a modest portion of a portfolio. Claims of a real estate bubble may be overstated, but the value proposition certainly seems less advantageous at present.

Address:	100 E Pratt St Baltimore MD 21202 800-638-5660
Web Address:	www.troweprice.com
Inception:	10-31-97 *
Advisor:	T. Rowe Price Associates, Inc.
Subadvisor:	None
NTF Plans:	N/A

Minimum Purchase:	$2500	Add: $100	IRA: $1000
Min Auto Inv Plan:	$50	Add: $50	
Sales Fees:	No-load, 1.00%R		
Management Fee:	0.62%		
Actual Fees:	Mgt:0.62%	Dist:	
Expense Projections:	3Yr:$294	5Yr:$528	10Yr:$1201
Income Distrib:	Quarterly		

T. Rowe Price SciTech

Ticker	Load	NAV	Yield	Total Assets	Mstar Category
PRSCX	None	$19.10	0.0%	$4,519 mil	Specialty-Technology

Governance and Management

Fiduciary Grade: B

Portfolio Manager(s)

Longtime manager Chip Morris stepped down from this fund in January 2002. Michael Sola, who has been with T. Rowe since 1995, replaced Morris. Sola is a onetime networking and software analyst who has also managed T. Rowe Price Developing Technologies since its August 2000 inception.

Strategy

Manager Mike Sola aims to provide broad exposure to technology, with less volatility than most tech funds. The idea is to outperform with stock picks rather than industry bets. He holds 75 to 85 names to reduce issue-specific risk and will favor industry leaders over racier fare. Sola is also well aware of the limitations the fund's large asset base imposes on him. In addition to refraining from outsized industry bets (which are hard to unwind quickly at a fund of this size), he favors blue chips and keeps turnover relatively low for a tech fund.

Historical Profile

Return Average
Risk Average
Rating ★★★ Neutral

Investment Style: Equity, Stock %: 96% 92% 96% 96% 96% 95% 95% 98% 98%

▼ Manager Change
▽ Partial Manager Change

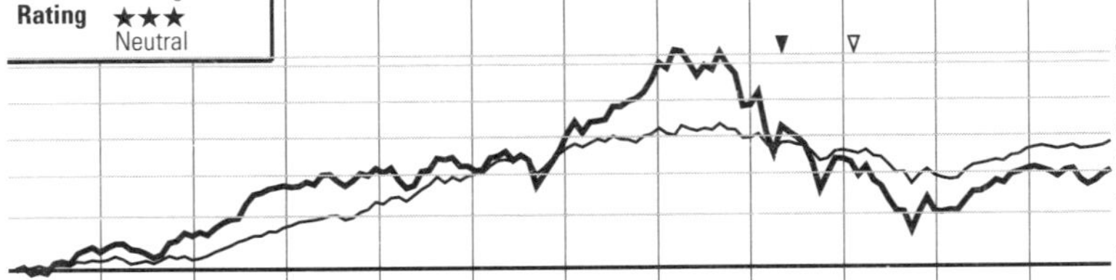

Growth of $10,000
— Investment Values of Fund
— Investment Values of S&P 500

Performance Quartile (within Category)

1993	1994	1995	1996	1997	1998	1999	2000	2001	2002	2003	12-04	History
18.95	21.64	29.12	29.71	27.26	37.67	63.71	35.57	20.92	12.43	18.80	19.10	NAV
24.25	15.79	55.53	14.23	1.71	42.35	100.99	-34.19	-41.19	-40.58	51.25	1.60	Total Return %
14.19	14.48	18.00	-8.71	-31.64	13.78	79.95	-25.09	-29.31	-18.49	22.58	-9.27	+/-S&P 500
5.20	-5.08	7.82	-5.80	-18.26	-12.25	-15.41	-17.97	-25.60	-7.25	-0.89	-10.13	+/-PSE Tech 100
0.00	0.00	0.00	0.00	0.00	0.00	0.00	0.00	0.00	0.00	0.00	0.00	Income Return %
24.25	15.79	55.53	14.23	1.71	42.35	100.99	-34.19	-41.19	-40.58	51.25	1.60	Capital Return %
60	54	13	76	95	69	68	56	62	36	57	58	Total Rtn % Rank Cat
0.00	0.00	0.00	0.00	0.00	0.00	0.00	0.00	0.00	0.00	0.00	0.00	Income $
2.51	0.30	4.54	3.60	2.87	0.99	10.72	7.28	0.00	0.00	0.00	0.00	Capital Gains $
1.25	1.11	1.01	0.97	0.94	0.94	0.87	0.86	1.00	1.11	1.09	—	Expense Ratio %
-0.68	-0.58	-0.15	-0.33	-0.44	-0.61	-0.26	-0.55	-0.73	-0.87	-0.73	—	Income Ratio %
163	113	130	126	134	109	128	134	144	61	48	—	Turnover Rate %
500	915	2,285	3,292	3,538	4,696	12,271	8,892	5,209	2,839	4,391	3,911	Net Assets $mil

Performance 12-31-04

	1st Qtr	2nd Qtr	3rd Qtr	4th Qtr	Total
2000	11.57	-12.79	-0.11	-32.29	-34.19
2001	-37.76	16.85	-40.28	35.40	-41.19
2002	-7.17	-27.75	-26.23	20.10	-40.58
2003	1.05	20.70	8.31	14.49	51.25
2004	-2.66	2.73	-11.33	14.58	1.60

Trailing	Total Return%	+/- S&P 500	+/- PSE Tech 100	%Rank Cat	Growth of $10,000
3 Mo	14.58	5.35	0.06	64	11,458
6 Mo	1.60	-5.59	-4.33	67	10,160
1 Yr	1.60	-9.27	-10.13	58	10,160
3 Yr Avg	-2.99	-6.57	-7.25	51	9,130
5 Yr Avg	-18.78	-16.48	-14.45	61	3,534
10 Yr Avg	6.21	-5.86	-12.81	79	18,266
15 Yr Avg	11.23	0.30	-7.24	80	49,355

Tax Analysis	Tax-Adj Rtn%	%Rank Cat	Tax-Cost Rat	%Rank Cat
3 Yr (estimated)	-2.99	46	0.00	1
5 Yr (estimated)	-19.35	58	0.70	50
10 Yr (estimated)	4.23	79	1.86	46

Potential Capital Gain Exposure: -131% of assets

Rating and Risk

Time Period	Load-Adj Return %	Morningstar Rtn vs Cat	Morningstar Risk vs Cat	Morningstar Risk-Adj Rating
1 Yr	1.60			
3 Yr	-2.99	Avg	-Avg	★★★
5 Yr	-18.78	Avg	Avg	★★★
10 Yr	6.21	-Avg	Avg	★★
Incept	11.29			

Other Measures	Standard Index S&P 500	Best Fit Index PSE Tech 100
Alpha	-5.9	-6.8
Beta	1.74	1.09
R-Squared	83	97

Standard Deviation	29.17
Mean	-2.99
Sharpe Ratio	-0.15

Morningstar's Take by Christopher Traulsen 01-05-05

T. Rowe Price Science & Technology's manager has more to prove, but we like his reforms.

Manager Michael Sola has now been at the helm of this fund for just about three years. Since taking over on Jan. 16, 2002, he has compiled a respectable record given the technology sector's general fate. The fund is down 4.9% per year on an annualized basis in that period, which is slightly better than the average tech fund's 5.2% annualized loss.

The fund did post slightly subpar showings in both 2003 and 2004, however. In 2003, Sola refused to participate in the most speculative stocks that led the rally, holding the fund back a bit, and in 2004, the fund was hurt again by its limited exposure to arguably pricey names such as Ebay and Apple Computer, as well as by a slight overweight in semiconductor and semiconductor-capital-equipment companies. Sola simply thought the former were too expensive given their prospects. He continues to believe the latter have better growth in front of them than the market is giving them credit for.

The fund's recent underperformance notwithstanding, we like what Sola has done here since taking the helm. He has cut back on the type of industry bets that hurt the fund late in the tenure of previous manager Chip Morris. That's a sensible move given that its asset base makes it extremely difficult for Sola to unwind such bets if they don't work out. Instead, Sola is focused on making good longer-term investments and appears to keep a fairly close eye on valuations, both of which should help even out the fund's performance.

Sola hasn't been here long enough to truly judge his abilities, but from what we've seen thus far, we think he has the fund moving in the right direction. We also like its below-average expense ratio. We don't think most investors need a tech fund, but if you want one, this offering merits a look.

Address:	100 E Pratt St, Baltimore MD 21202, 800-638-5660
Web Address:	www.troweprice.com
Inception:	09-30-87
Advisor:	T. Rowe Price Associates, Inc.
Subadvisor:	None
NTF Plans:	N/A

Minimum Purchase:	$2500	Add: $100	IRA: $1000
Min Auto Inv Plan:	$50	Add: $50	
Sales Fees:	No-load		
Management Fee:	0.67%		
Actual Fees:	Mgt:0.67%	Dist:	
Expense Projections:	3Yr:$347	5Yr:$601	10Yr:$1329
Income Distrib:	Annually		

Portfolio Analysis 09-30-04

Share change since 06-04 Total Stocks:71

	Sector	PE	YTD Ret%	% Assets
⊖ Microsoft	Software	36.1	8.95	5.56
⊕ Cisco Systems	Hardware	24.5	-20.26	5.55
⊖ Dell	Hardware	34.0	24.01	4.47
⊕ Intel	Hardware	19.8	-26.56	4.03
⊕ Veritas Software	Software	23.7	-22.88	3.46
⊕ Analog Devices	Hardware	24.2	-18.69	3.31
⊕ Oracle	Software	25.4	3.70	3.12
⊕ Mercury Interactive	Software	60.5	-6.35	2.93
⊕ IBM	Hardware	20.2	7.19	2.48
⊖ Yahoo	Media	95.1	67.36	2.30
⊕ Maxim Integrated Product	Hardware	27.9	-13.87	2.28
⊕ Red Hat	Software	70.6	-28.88	2.00
⊖ QLogic	Hardware	25.3	-28.78	1.93
⊖ Cadence Design Systems	Software	NMF	-23.19	1.87
⊕ Xilinx	Hardware	25.2	-22.82	1.86
⊖ Applied Materials	Hardware	20.7	-23.80	1.86
⊖ SAP AG ADR	Software	42.7	6.80	1.71
⊕ Novellus Systems	Hardware	31.6	-29.98	1.67
⊕ Viacom B	Media	36.1	-17.44	1.52
Samsung Electronics	Goods	—	—	1.50

Current Investment Style

Market Cap	%
Giant	39.8
Large	28.8
Mid	31.0
Small	0.3
Micro	0.0
Avg $mil: 21,271	

Value Measures		Rel Category
Price/Earnings	23.19	0.84
Price/Book	3.01	0.90
Price/Sales	3.26	1.09
Price/Cash Flow	13.46	1.08
Dividend Yield %	0.22	1.16

Growth Measures	%	Rel Category
Long-Term Erngs	15.80	0.93
Book Value	4.76	0.96
Sales	5.64	1.86
Cash Flow	13.34	0.83
Historical Erngs	12.75	1.04

Profitability	%	Rel Category
Return on Equity	15.01	1.31
Return on Assets	8.52	1.34
Net Margin	14.01	1.34

Industry Weightings	% of Stocks	Rel Cat
Software	29.5	1.4
Hardware	13.1	1.0
Networking Eq	8.8	1.2
Semis	21.1	1.3
Semi Equip	5.3	1.2
Comp/Data Sv	4.5	0.9
Telecom	0.3	0.1
Health Care	2.0	0.3
Other	15.4	0.6

Composition

Cash	1.2
Stocks	98.1
Bonds	0.0
Other	0.6
Foreign (% of Stock)	8.1

T. Rowe Price Sm Stk

Ticker	Load	NAV	Yield	Total Assets	Mstar Category
OTCFX	Closed	$31.82	0.0%	$6,827 mil	Small Blend

Governance and Management

Fiduciary Grade: B

Portfolio Manager(s)

Greg McCrickard has managed this offering since September 1992. Before becoming the fund's manager, he worked as an analyst at T. Rowe Price for six years. McCrickard is assisted by T. Rowe's large analyst staff, most notably the fund's longtime analyst Curt Organt.

Strategy

Manager Greg McCrickard divides this portfolio into two sections. The first half is composed of value issues, for which he uses discounted cash-flow analysis to help identify cheap stocks. With the other half of the portfolio, McCrickard concentrates on out-of-favor growth stocks. McCrickard is a buy-and-hold manager: The fund's turnover is lower than average.

Historical Profile

Return Average
Risk Average
Rating ★★★★ Above Avg

Investment Style: Equity Stock %

90% | 89% | 90% | 91% | 91% | 91% | 95% | 92% | 91%

▼ Manager Change
▽ Partial Manager Change

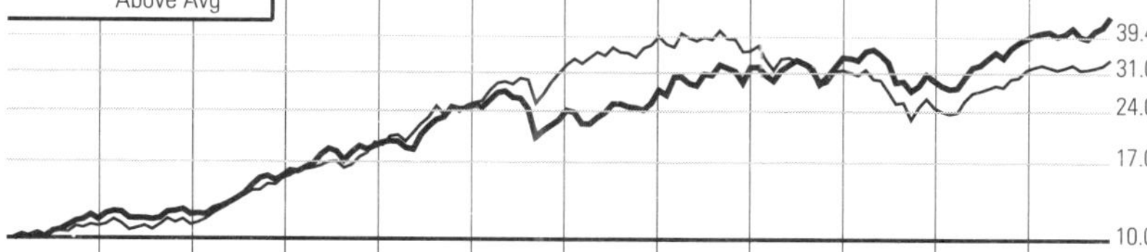

Growth of $10,000
— Investment Values of Fund
— Investment Values of S&P 500

Performance Quartile (within Category)

1993	1994	1995	1996	1997	1998	1999	2000	2001	2002	2003	12-04	History
15.39	13.80	16.32	18.07	22.20	20.79	22.80	23.87	25.34	21.50	27.98	31.82	NAV
18.40	0.08	33.85	21.05	28.81	-3.46	14.66	16.49	6.81	-14.21	32.35	18.77	Total Return %
8.34	-1.23	-3.68	-1.89	-4.54	-32.03	-6.38	25.59	18.69	7.88	3.68	7.90	+/-S&P 500
-0.48	1.90	5.40	4.56	6.45	-0.91	-6.60	19.51	4.32	6.27	-14.90	0.44	+/-Russ 2000
0.00	0.19	0.87	0.55	0.22	0.45	0.38	0.61	0.42	0.04	0.00	0.00	Income Return %
18.40	-0.11	32.98	20.50	28.59	-3.91	14.28	15.88	6.39	-14.25	32.35	18.77	Capital Return %
48	32	15	53	33	39	45	36	53	37	90	51	Total Rtn % Rank Cat
0.00	0.03	0.12	0.09	0.04	0.10	0.08	0.14	0.10	0.01	0.00	0.00	Income $
1.58	1.56	2.01	1.58	1.01	0.50	0.89	2.46	0.05	0.23	0.46	1.39	Capital Gains $
1.20	1.11	1.11	1.07	1.02	1.01	0.96	0.94	0.98	0.96	0.96	—	Expense Ratio %
-0.01	0.24	0.74	0.56	0.33	0.46	0.47	0.63	0.45	0.04	-0.10	—	Income Ratio %
41	42	58	31	23	26	42	16	27	19	22	—	Turnover Rate %
205	197	279	416	816	1,153	1,740	2,255	3,158	3,298	4,937	6,371	Net Assets $mil

Performance 12-31-04

	1st Qtr	2nd Qtr	3rd Qtr	4th Qtr	Total
2000	9.34	1.85	4.17	0.42	16.49
2001	-8.59	14.80	-14.69	19.31	6.81
2002	4.18	-6.78	-17.55	7.15	-14.21
2003	-4.84	16.57	4.95	13.68	32.35
2004	4.75	2.32	-1.53	12.54	18.77

Trailing	Total Return%	+/- S&P 500	+/- Russ 2000	%Rank Cat	Growth of $10,000
3 Mo	12.54	3.31	-1.55	59	11,254
6 Mo	10.81	3.62	-0.02	52	11,081
1 Yr	18.77	7.90	0.44	51	11,877
3 Yr Avg	10.48	6.90	-1.00	75	13,485
5 Yr Avg	10.91	13.21	4.30	58	16,782
10 Yr Avg	14.51	2.44	2.97	39	38,764
15 Yr Avg	12.39	1.46	1.30	56	57,665

Tax Analysis	Tax-Adj Rtn%	%Rank Cat	Tax-Cost Rat	%Rank Cat
3 Yr (estimated)	10.00	68	0.43	30
5 Yr (estimated)	10.02	53	0.80	35
10 Yr (estimated)	12.99	26	1.33	26

Potential Capital Gain Exposure: 26% of assets

Rating and Risk

Time Period	Load-Adj Return %	Morningstar Rtn vs Cat	Morningstar Risk vs Cat	Morningstar Risk-Adj Rating
1 Yr	18.77			
3 Yr	10.48	-Avg	-Avg	★★★
5 Yr	10.91	Avg	-Avg	★★★
10 Yr	14.51	Avg	Avg	★★★★
Incept	13.74			

Other Measures	Standard Index S&P 500	Best Fit Index Mstar Small Core
Alpha	7.2	-2.8
Beta	0.87	0.91
R-Squared	69	97
Standard Deviation	17.30	
Mean	10.48	
Sharpe Ratio	0.53	

Portfolio Analysis 09-30-04

Share change since 06-04 Total Stocks:285	Sector	PE	YTD Ret%	% Assets
National Oilwell	Energy	36.9	57.83	1.35
Airgas	Ind Mtrls	21.8	24.36	1.19
Grant Prideco	Energy	77.8	53.99	1.15
Armor Holdings	Ind Mtrls	24.6	78.72	1.07
⊕ Iron Mountain	Business	33.7	15.67	1.03
⊖ Kronos	Software	37.8	29.08	1.00
FMC Technologies	Energy	23.4	38.20	1.00
⊕ Westamerica Bancorp	Financial	18.9	19.63	0.97
Brunswick	Goods	18.1	57.47	0.96
Minerals Technologies	Ind Mtrls	19.1	12.97	0.96
⊕ Chittenden	Financial	14.7	9.58	0.94
Ohio Casualty	Financial	14.4	33.70	0.89
Harsco	Ind Mtrls	20.7	30.31	0.89
Noble Energy	Energy	14.7	39.34	0.86
⊕ Knight Transportation	Business	29.7	45.15	0.85
Citizens Banking MI	Financial	19.6	8.81	0.84
Henry Schein	Health	23.1	3.05	0.83
AnnTaylor Stores	Consumer	15.3	-17.19	0.83
⊕ Sunrise Senior Living	Health	18.4	19.67	0.82
Forest Oil	Energy	20.7	11.03	0.81

Current Investment Style

Value Blnd Growth — Large / Mid / Small

Market Cap	%
Giant	0.0
Large	0.0
Mid	33.3
Small	57.6
Micro	9.1

Avg $mil: 1,082

Value Measures		Rel Category
Price/Earnings	19.78	1.14
Price/Book	2.14	1.08
Price/Sales	1.27	1.34
Price/Cash Flow	5.85	1.00
Dividend Yield %	0.60	0.72

Growth Measures	%	Rel Category
Long-Term Erngs	13.95	1.03
Book Value	7.47	1.32
Sales	5.78	1.34
Cash Flow	4.95	1.00
Historical Erngs	6.47	0.87

Profitability	%	Rel Category
Return on Equity	10.26	0.98
Return on Assets	3.60	0.73
Net Margin	7.78	1.06

Sector Weightings	% of Stocks	Rel S&P 500	3 Year High	3 Year Low
Info	17.33	0.81		
Software	6.24	1.45	7	4
Hardware	8.81	0.86	10	7
Media	1.38	0.36	2	1
Telecom	0.90	0.29	1	0
Service	52.79	1.14		
Health	11.03	0.88	11	7
Consumer	9.12	1.00	11	9
Business	14.00	3.46	15	13
Financial	18.64	0.90	21	17
Mfg	29.88	0.93		
Goods	4.10	0.44	9	4
Ind Mtrls	16.99	1.34	17	14
Energy	8.30	1.16	8	4
Utilities	0.49	0.17	2	0

Composition

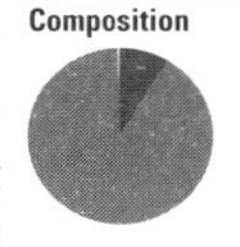

Cash	8.5
Stocks	90.9
Bonds	0.0
Other	0.7
Foreign (% of Stock)	0.1

Morningstar's Take by Kunal Kapoor 11-30-04

T. Rowe Price Small-Cap Stock goes about its business in a quiet but effective manner.

As easy as it may look right now, investing in small caps is no simple task. While the typical fund in the small-cap blend category has delivered an astounding 12.99% return for the trailing five-year period through Nov. 29, 2004, investors should not assume that the category is without risks. Small caps can seemingly do no wrong right now, but they have been notoriously volatile and unpredictable over other time periods.

That's why we're fans of manager Greg McCrickard's measured approach, which gives equal consideration to growth and valuation characteristics of potential investments. Unlike many of his rivals, McCrickard prefers to invest in firms that chart a steady and realistic growth trajectory, rather than those that embrace risk to grow at unsustainably high short-term rates. The result is a well-balanced portfolio that gets help from many quarters. For instance, the fund has been boosted by an 8% energy position in 2004, as well as some well-reasoned picks in the information technology area, where stocks such as top-three holding Kronos have bucked an otherwise tough environment for tech firms. All told, the fund's 16.37% year-to-date gain is enough to put it in the category's top half.

That steady performance is what investors are likely to find here over the long haul. With the fund eschewing more-speculative investments, it's never going to be a barn burner. To be sure, as with other small-cap funds, investors would do well to tone down their expectations here. With the small-cap rally getting a little long in the tooth, it's unlikely that funds playing in the space can keep up their torrid pace. As such, while it's important to maintain a targeted allocation of the fund, investors shouldn't forget to rebalance their portfolio weightings if their allocation of this offering is above desired levels.

Address:	T Rowe Price Associates Inc Baltimore MD 21202 800-638-5660	Minimum Purchase: Min Auto Inv Plan: Sales Fees:	Closed Closed No-load	Add: — Add: —	IRA: —
Web Address:	www.troweprice.com	Management Fee:	0.65%		
Inception:	06-01-56	Actual Fees:	—	Dist:	
Advisor:	T. Rowe Price Associates, Inc.	Expense Projections:	3Yr:$306	5Yr:$531	10Yr:$1178
Subadvisor:	None	Income Distrib:	Annually		
NTF Plans:	N/A				

T. Rowe Price Sm Val

Ticker	Load	NAV	Yield	Total Assets	Mstar Category
PRSVX	Closed	$35.68	0.4%	$5,077 mil	Small Value

Governance and Management

Fiduciary Grade: B

Portfolio Manager(s)

Manager Preston Athey has been managing director of this fund's investment-advisory committee since 1991. He has been managing investments at the company since 1982. He taps T. Rowe's large analyst staff for research.

Strategy

As straightforward as its name. Manager Preston Athey tends to look at much smaller stocks than his peers do, and he buys stocks that are trading cheaply based on value measures appropriate to their particular industry. Athey lets his winners run, keeping turnover very low, but he'll generally finance new acquisitions by selling stakes in companies that have run up in terms of market capitalization and valuation.

Historical Profile

Return Above Avg
Risk Low
Rating ★★★★ Above Avg

Investment Style: Equity Stock %

84% 87% 94% 90% 90% 90% 93% 92% 92%

▼ Manager Change
▽ Partial Manager Change

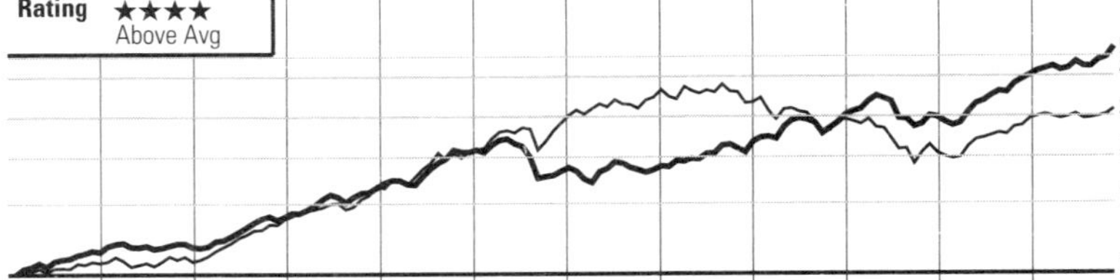

Growth of $10,000
▬ Investment Values of Fund
— Investment Values of S&P 500

Performance Quartile (within Category)

1993	1994	1995	1996	1997	1998	1999	2000	2001	2002	2003	12-04	History
14.68	13.40	16.53	19.56	23.40	18.97	17.62	19.14	22.66	21.94	29.39	35.68	NAV
23.30	-1.38	29.29	24.61	27.92	-12.47	1.19	19.77	21.94	-1.76	36.43	25.69	Total Return %
13.24	-2.69	-8.24	1.67	-5.43	-41.04	-19.85	28.87	33.82	20.33	7.76	14.82	+/-S&P 500
-0.47	0.16	3.54	3.24	-3.86	-6.02	2.68	-3.06	7.92	9.67	-9.60	3.44	+/-Russ 2000 VL
0.81	0.95	1.34	1.39	1.02	1.07	0.90	1.14	0.89	0.62	0.55	0.54	Income Return %
22.49	-2.33	27.95	23.22	26.90	-13.54	0.29	18.63	21.05	-2.38	35.88	25.15	Capital Return %
9	65	18	39	67	82	50	48	24	13	77	8	Total Rtn % Rank Cat
0.10	0.14	0.18	0.23	0.20	0.25	0.17	0.20	0.17	0.14	0.12	0.16	Income $
0.35	0.92	0.61	0.80	1.39	1.20	1.35	1.68	0.48	0.18	0.41	1.08	Capital Gains $
1.05	0.97	0.98	0.94	0.87	0.87	0.92	0.90	0.89	0.89	0.88	—	Expense Ratio %
0.91	0.93	1.59	1.28	1.01	1.02	0.84	1.06	0.88	0.66	0.48	—	Income Ratio %
12	21	18	15	15	17	7	14	17	12	10	—	Turnover Rate %
454	408	936	1,410	2,088	1,632	1,262	1,361	2,012	2,395	3,295	4,462	Net Assets $mil

Performance 12-31-04

	1st Qtr	2nd Qtr	3rd Qtr	4th Qtr	Total
2000	3.46	5.92	7.04	2.10	19.77
2001	2.25	16.40	-10.67	14.69	21.94
2002	10.72	-0.20	-17.05	7.18	-1.76
2003	-4.15	17.59	6.63	13.51	36.43
2004	6.81	3.41	1.23	12.42	25.69

Trailing	Total Return%	+/- S&P 500	+/- Russ 2000 VL	%Rank Cat	Growth of $10,000
3 Mo	12.42	3.19	-0.78	56	11,242
6 Mo	13.80	6.61	0.43	22	11,380
1 Yr	25.69	14.82	3.44	8	12,569
3 Yr Avg	18.99	15.41	2.49	18	16,847
5 Yr Avg	19.73	22.03	2.50	15	24,605
10 Yr Avg	16.21	4.14	1.04	23	44,920
15 Yr Avg	14.73	3.80	0.71	39	78,552

Tax Analysis	Tax-Adj Rtn%	%Rank Cat	Tax-Cost Rat	%Rank Cat
3 Yr (estimated)	18.41	11	0.49	30
5 Yr (estimated)	18.69	13	0.87	43
10 Yr (estimated)	14.72	13	1.28	17

Potential Capital Gain Exposure: 42% of assets

Rating and Risk

Time Period	Load-Adj Return %	Morningstar Rtn vs Cat	Morningstar Risk vs Cat	Morningstar Risk-Adj Rating
1 Yr	25.69			
3 Yr	18.99	+Avg	-Avg	★★★★
5 Yr	19.73	+Avg	Low	★★★★
10 Yr	16.21	+Avg	Low	★★★★
Incept	14.18			

Other Measures	Standard Index S&P 500	Best Fit Index Russ 2000 VL
Alpha	15.9	5.0
Beta	0.71	0.79
R-Squared	57	96
Standard Deviation	16.65	
Mean	18.99	
Sharpe Ratio	1.07	

Portfolio Analysis 09-30-04

Share change since 06-04 Total Stocks:257	Sector	PE	YTD Ret%	% Assets
Landstar System	Business	37.0	93.59	1.91
East West Bancorp	Financial	28.3	57.37	1.40
Proassurance	Financial	17.1	21.65	1.24
Kilroy Realty	Financial	40.1	37.63	1.14
⊕ Aaron Rents	Consumer	17.7	86.63	1.11
⊕ Raven Industries	Hardware	17.3	51.97	1.08
⊕ Texas Regional Bancshare	Financial	16.7	34.08	1.08
Carpenter Technology	Ind Mtrls	22.4	99.59	1.02
Tetra Technologies	Energy	36.7	16.75	0.97
Sun Communities	Financial	—	10.92	0.93
Rare Hospitality Interna	Consumer	22.3	30.36	0.92
Encore Acquisition	Energy	14.4	41.62	0.92
⊕ JLG Industries	Ind Mtrls	42.8	29.07	0.90
First Republic Bank	Financial	21.5	49.90	0.87
UCBH Holdings	Financial	19.5	18.04	0.85
⊕ Whiting Petroleum	Energy	—	64.40	0.84
Markel	Financial	21.8	43.58	0.84
⊖ Overseas Shipholding Gro	Business	9.6	64.92	0.82
Ruby Tuesday	Consumer	14.5	-8.32	0.82
⊖ Ultra Petroleum	Energy	43.1	95.49	0.80

Current Investment Style

Value Blnd Growth; Large Mid Small

Market Cap	%
Giant	0.0
Large	0.0
Mid	14.9
Small	58.4
Micro	26.7
Avg $mil: 643	

Value Measures		Rel Category
Price/Earnings	17.75	1.11
Price/Book	1.97	1.19
Price/Sales	1.06	1.41
Price/Cash Flow	4.03	0.78
Dividend Yield %	1.03	0.86

Growth Measures	%	Rel Category
Long-Term Erngs	13.40	1.10
Book Value	5.98	1.38
Sales	4.94	1.58
Cash Flow	9.99	4.60
Historical Erngs	2.98	0.62

Profitability	%	Rel Category
Return on Equity	9.74	1.07
Return on Assets	4.23	1.02
Net Margin	8.06	1.20

Sector Weightings	% of Stocks	Rel S&P 500	3 Year High	Low
Info	12.00	0.56		
Software	3.09	0.72	3	2
Hardware	5.82	0.57	6	4
Media	2.75	0.72	3	2
Telecom	0.34	0.11	0	0
Service	52.82	1.14		
Health	5.41	0.43	6	5
Consumer	11.34	1.25	14	11
Business	12.16	3.00	14	12
Financial	23.91	1.15	28	24
Mfg	35.18	1.10		
Goods	3.60	0.39	7	4
Ind Mtrls	21.60	1.70	22	17
Energy	7.60	1.06	8	5
Utilities	2.38	0.80	3	2

Composition

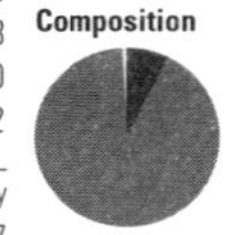

Cash	7.3
Stocks	91.7
Bonds	0.2
Other	0.8
Foreign (% of Stock)	1.6

Morningstar's Take by Kunal Kapoor 11-08-04

T. Rowe Price Small-Cap Value's manager is again sounding the alarm, and investors should pay attention.

In early 2003, we followed manager Preston Athey's advice and warned that the outperformance of small-cap value funds could not continue indefinitely. We even advised investors to rebalance their portfolios so that their allocations to this fund would not be above a targeted amount. The advice hasn't proven prescient thus far: After delivering a solid 36% gain in 2003, the fund is up an additional 18.24% for the year to date through Nov. 5, 2004.

But we're sticking to our message, as is Athey. It's not that this isn't a topnotch fund or that we don't expect it to continue to outperform over the long haul. It is, and we do. Rather, we continue to believe that markets moves in cycles and that different segments rotate in and out of favor. Thus, just as most investors left small-value funds for dead in the late 1990s, they may now be ignoring more large-cap-focused funds to their peril. As Athey points out in his latest report to shareholders: "Just as trees do not grow to the sky, periods of great relative performance for our sector inevitably end. In my opinion, small-cap stocks overall are fairly valued, but at the margin I find other sectors of the market more attractive. Given this outlook, I encourage shareholders to review their mix of fund holdings; if the Small-Cap Value Fund has grown to be too large a portion of your assets, consider trimming it back and redeploying the money."

It's a candid message and another reason why we like this fund as part of a diversified portfolio. Over the years, Athey has made a habit of communicating candidly with shareholders, and in our view, that's a signal that he takes his responsibility to fundholders very seriously. We appreciate that he doesn't take his--or the fund's--reputation for granted.

Address:	100 E. Pratt Street New York NY 10154 800-638-5660
Web Address:	www.troweprice.com
Inception:	06-30-88
Advisor:	T. Rowe Price Associates, Inc.
Subadvisor:	None
NTF Plans:	N/A

Minimum Purchase:	Closed	Add: —	IRA: —
Min Auto Inv Plan:	Closed	Add: —	
Sales Fees:	No-load, 1.00%R		
Management Fee:	0.67%		
Actual Fees:	Mgt:0.67%	Dist:	
Expense Projections:	3Yr:$281	5Yr:$488	10Yr:$1084
Income Distrib:	Annually		

T. Rowe Price Spect Grth

Ticker	Load	NAV	Yield	Total Assets	Mstar Category
PRSGX	None	$16.87	0.7%	$2,605 mil	Large Blend

Governance and Management

Fiduciary Grade: B

Portfolio Manager(s)

A five-member committee meets once a month to steer this fund. The committee is led by Ned Notzon and includes fund managers Brian Rogers (who's also T. Rowe Price's CIO), Jack Laporte, Steve Boesel, and Mary Miller.

Strategy

Diversification is the name of the game here. This fund invests in 11 T. Rowe Price funds that range from small to large cap, value to growth, and domestic to international. It overweights areas of the market that are undervalued and skimps on those that look expensive.

Historical Profile

Return Above Avg
Risk Above Avg
Rating ★★★★ Above Avg

Investment Style: Equity — Stock %: 92% | 62% | 95% | 72% | 96% | 97% | 97% | 97%

▼ Manager Change
▽ Partial Manager Change

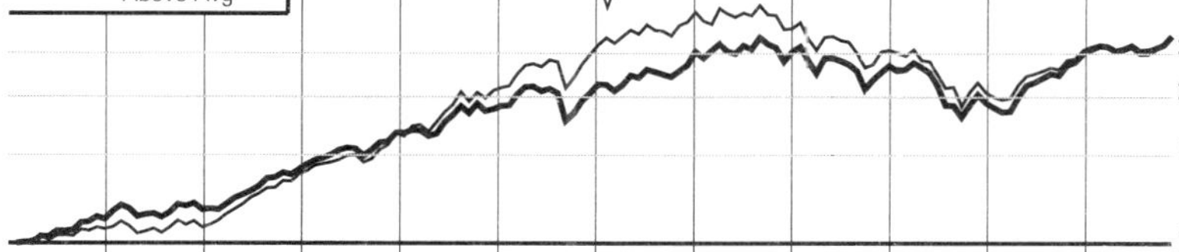

Growth of $10,000
— Investment Values of Fund
— Investment Values of S&P 500

Performance Quartile (within Category)

1993	1994	1995	1996	1997	1998	1999	2000	2001	2002	2003	12-04	History
11.87	11.13	13.49	15.13	15.93	16.45	17.71	15.72	14.04	11.13	14.80	16.87	NAV
20.98	1.40	29.96	20.53	17.40	13.62	21.20	-0.11	-7.83	-19.66	34.09	15.16	Total Return %
10.92	0.09	-7.57	-2.41	-15.95	-14.95	0.16	8.99	4.05	2.43	5.42	4.29	+/-S&P 500
10.80	1.01	-7.81	-1.92	-15.45	-13.40	0.29	7.68	4.62	1.99	4.20	3.76	+/-Russ 1000
1.52	1.43	1.89	1.48	1.32	1.13	1.03	0.68	1.02	0.57	0.90	0.81	Income Return %
19.46	-0.03	28.07	19.05	16.08	12.49	20.17	-0.79	-8.85	-20.23	33.19	14.35	Capital Return %
7	19	73	58	92	81	36	26	17	27	7	6	Total Rtn % Rank Cat
0.16	0.17	0.21	0.20	0.20	0.18	0.17	0.12	0.16	0.08	0.10	0.12	Income $
0.72	0.73	0.76	0.93	1.60	1.37	1.91	1.85	0.28	0.07	0.02	0.05	Capital Gains $
0.00	0.00	0.00	0.00	0.00	0.00	0.00	0.00	0.00	0.00	0.00	—	Expense Ratio %
1.57	1.60	1.81	1.58	1.26	1.09	0.85	0.70	1.05	0.68	0.75	—	Income Ratio %
7	21	7	3	20	18	20	12	6	4	2	—	Turnover Rate %
582	879	1,358	2,104	2,605	2,768	3,031	2,889	2,373	1,739	2,237	2,605	Net Assets $mil

Performance 12-31-04

	1st Qtr	2nd Qtr	3rd Qtr	4th Qtr	Total
2000	4.69	-1.02	0.93	-4.47	-0.11
2001	-11.83	7.58	-15.43	14.90	-7.83
2002	1.64	-12.54	-16.83	8.67	-19.66
2003	-4.94	18.81	4.22	13.93	34.09
2004	3.85	0.33	-1.23	11.91	15.16

Trailing	Total Return%	+/- S&P 500	+/- Russ 1000	%Rank Cat	Growth of $10,000
3 Mo	11.91	2.68	2.11	7	11,191
6 Mo	10.53	3.34	2.72	4	11,053
1 Yr	15.16	4.29	3.76	6	11,516
3 Yr Avg	7.45	3.87	3.18	6	12,406
5 Yr Avg	2.70	5.00	4.46	11	11,425
10 Yr Avg	11.21	-0.86	-0.95	38	26,936
15 Yr Avg	—	—	—	—	—

Tax Analysis	Tax-Adj Rtn%	%Rank Cat	Tax-Cost Rat	%Rank Cat
3 Yr (estimated)	7.08	4	0.34	29
5 Yr (estimated)	1.76	11	0.92	49
10 Yr (estimated)	9.44	39	1.59	61

Potential Capital Gain Exposure: 23% of assets

Rating and Risk

Time Period	Load-Adj Return %	Morningstar Rtn vs Cat	Morningstar Risk vs Cat	Morningstar Risk-Adj Rating
1 Yr	15.16			
3 Yr	7.45	High	+Avg	★★★★★
5 Yr	2.70	+Avg	+Avg	★★★★
10 Yr	11.21	Avg	Avg	★★★
Incept	10.83			

Other Measures	Standard Index S&P 500	Best Fit Index MSCI World
Alpha	3.9	1.7
Beta	0.96	0.98
R-Squared	89	92
Standard Deviation	16.35	
Mean	7.45	
Sharpe Ratio	0.38	

Portfolio Analysis 09-30-04

Share change since 06-04 Total Stocks:0	Sector	PE	YTD Ret%	% Assets
⊕ T. Rowe Price New Horizo	—	—	—	16.43
⊖ T. Rowe Price Equity-Inc	—	—	—	16.18
⊕ T. Rowe Price Growth Sto	—	—	—	14.44
⊕ T. Rowe Price Blue Chip	—	—	—	14.44
⊖ T. Rowe Price Internatio	—	—	—	10.05
⊖ T. Rowe Price Mid-Cap Va	—	—	—	7.96
⊕ T. Rowe Price Intl Gr &	—	—	—	6.04
⊕ T. Rowe Price Value	—	—	—	5.08
T. Rowe Price Emerging M	—	—	—	4.26
⊖ T. Rowe Price Growth & I	—	—	—	4.04
⊖ T. Rowe Price New Era	—	—	—	1.08

Morningstar's Take by Christopher Davis 11-30-04

Investing can be complicated, but T. Rowe Price Spectrum Growth makes it easy.

No wonder so many investors find building their portfolios a complex endeavor. There's the first challenge of piecing together a well-diversified group of funds. Second, investors must sift through thousands of funds to unearth solid, low-cost options for their portfolios. Finally, they also need to periodically rebalance a portfolio to ensure no one fund dominates it.

This fund of funds greatly simplifies the process. By investing in 11 different T. Rowe offerings, its portfolio spans market caps, investment styles, sectors, and domestic and overseas markets. As such, investors can get all the equity exposure they need right here.

One-stop diversification isn't the fund's only appealing trait. With all of its underlying holdings sporting solid to terrific long-term records, investors get access to strong lineup of funds. Also important is that each fund sports moderate costs--a T. Rowe trademark--which should help the funds maintain their edge over the long haul.

An added attraction is an oversight committee that rebalances the portfolio regularly and modestly tweaks it toward areas of the market it believes are most attractive. With large-growth stocks lagging their large-value counterparts for several years running, for instance, lead manager Ned Notzon reports the committee has been increasing the fund's exposure to the large-growth T. Rowe Price Growth Stock and Blue Chip Growth funds. That move has yet to pay off, but past shifts have worked nicely. With small caps rallying in recent years, the committee's decision to favor small-growth offering T. Rowe Price New Horizons was on the mark. For those services, the fund charges no additional fees on top of those levied by its underlying holdings.

All in all, we think this fund gives investors plenty to like.

Address:	100 E Pratt St, Baltimore MD 21202, 800-638-5660		
Web Address:	www.troweprice.com		
Inception:	06-29-90		
Advisor:	T. Rowe Price Associates, Inc.		
Subadvisor:	None		
NTF Plans:	N/A		

Minimum Purchase:	$2500	Add: $100	IRA: $1000
Min Auto Inv Plan:	$50	Add: $50	
Sales Fees:	No-load		
Management Fee:	0.00%		
Actual Fees:	Mgt:0.00%	Dist:	
Expense Projections:	3Yr:$281	5Yr:$488	10Yr:$1084
Income Distrib:	Annually		

Current Investment Style

Value Blnd Growth — Large Mid Small

Market Cap	%
Giant	32.4
Large	33.1
Mid	24.9
Small	8.1
Micro	1.5

Avg $mil: 14,084

Value Measures		Rel Category
Price/Earnings	16.85	0.99
Price/Book	2.32	0.89
Price/Sales	1.32	0.92
Price/Cash Flow	6.78	0.88
Dividend Yield %	1.61	1.09

Growth Measures	%	Rel Category
Long-Term Erngs	12.54	1.08
Book Value	3.25	0.42
Sales	4.47	0.78
Cash Flow	2.85	0.30
Historical Erngs	8.72	0.74

Profitability	%	Rel Category
Return on Equity	15.49	0.89
Return on Assets	5.26	0.73
Net Margin	10.24	0.90

Sector Weightings	% of Stocks	Rel S&P 500	3 Year High	Low
Info	22.02	1.02		
Software	4.46	1.04	4	2
Hardware	6.23	0.61	8	4
Media	6.49	1.69	7	5
Telecom	4.84	1.54	6	4
Service	49.13	1.06		
Health	12.60	1.01	17	11
Consumer	10.43	1.15	11	6
Business	6.28	1.55	11	6
Financial	19.82	0.95	23	18
Mfg	28.85	0.90		
Goods	7.50	0.80	9	8
Ind Mtrls	11.51	0.91	15	7
Energy	7.85	1.10	10	7
Utilities	1.99	0.67	4	1

Composition

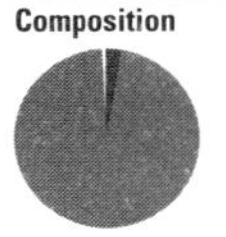

Cash	2.6
Stocks	96.5
Bonds	0.1
Other	0.7
Foreign (% of Stock)	23.9

T. Rowe Price Spect Inc

Analyst Pick

Ticker	Load	NAV	Yield	SEC Yield	Total Assets	Mstar Category
RPSIX	None	$12.09	4.0%	3.66%	$4,489 mil	Multisector Bond

Governance and Management

Fiduciary Grade: B

Portfolio Manager(s)

Ned Notzon has been at the helm since late 1998. He serves on an investment team that meets once a month to determine the fund's allocations to various sectors of the market. While he is looking to add value by shifting assets from fund to fund, his portfolio adjustments tend to be quite small.

Strategy

The fund can invest in up to nine other T. Rowe Price funds to gain exposure to virtually all sectors of the bond market. The idea is to beat the returns of the Lehman Brothers Aggregate Index without adding volatility. Included among the holdings is a small stake in stock fund T. Rowe Price Equity-Income. Manager Ned Notzon and his team will slightly adjust the fund's holdings if they see a sector as particularly under- or overvalued.

Historical Profile

Return Above Avg
Risk Below Avg
Rating ★★★★ Above Avg

Investment Style
Fixed Income
Income Rtn %Rank Cat: 87 85 80 86 87 85 86 86 80

▼ Manager Change
▽ Partial Manager Change

Growth of $10,000
— Investment Values of Fund
— Investment Values of LB Aggr

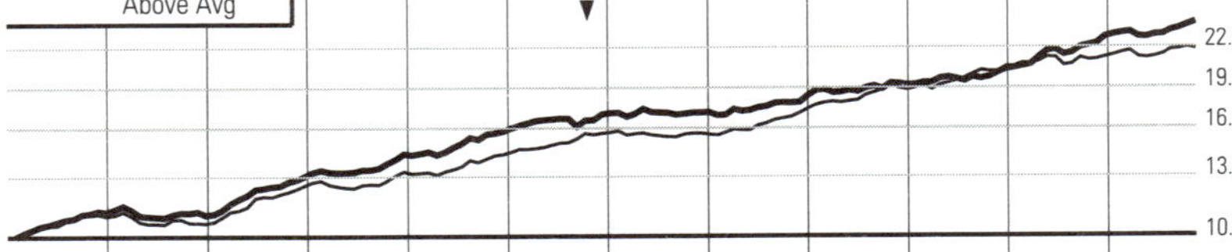

Performance Quartile (within Category)

1993	1994	1995	1996	1997	1998	1999	2000	2001	2002	2003	12-04	History
11.11	10.11	11.24	11.20	11.66	11.50	10.71	10.77	10.59	10.76	11.77	12.09	NAV
12.37	-1.93	19.42	7.65	12.19	6.58	0.26	7.40	4.50	6.96	14.96	8.06	Total Return %
2.62	0.99	0.95	4.02	2.54	-2.11	1.08	-4.23	-3.94	-3.29	10.86	3.72	+/-LB Aggr
1.97	1.15	0.95	3.20	2.41	-0.73	0.09	-3.42	-3.59	-2.88	9.14	3.09	+/-LB. U.S. Univ. Bd
6.67	6.36	7.32	6.55	6.53	6.40	6.17	6.73	6.06	5.28	4.77	4.27	Income Return %
5.70	-8.29	12.10	1.10	5.66	0.18	-5.91	0.67	-1.56	1.68	10.19	3.79	Capital Return %
91	4	31	87	10	9	77	4	48	44	56	52	Total Rtn % Rank Cat
0.69	0.69	0.72	0.71	0.71	0.72	0.69	0.70	0.63	0.55	0.50	0.49	Income $
0.19	0.10	0.06	0.15	0.15	0.18	0.13	0.00	0.02	0.00	0.06	0.11	Capital Gains $
0.00	0.00	0.00	0.00	0.00	0.00	0.00	0.77	0.00	0.80	0.00	—	Expense Ratio %
6.19	6.48	6.43	6.46	6.21	6.22	5.95	6.03	1.05	5.17	4.47	—	Income Ratio %
14	23	20	18	14	13	19	19	6	14	4	—	Turnover Rate %
584	625	987	1,356	2,022	2,574	2,548	2,471	2,465	2,713	3,533	4,489	Net Assets $mil

Performance 12-31-04

	1st Qtr	2nd Qtr	3rd Qtr	4th Qtr	Total
2000	1.37	0.72	2.04	3.10	7.40
2001	1.20	0.48	1.17	1.59	4.50
2002	1.14	1.51	0.13	4.05	6.96
2003	2.09	6.52	1.02	4.65	14.96
2004	2.02	-1.23	2.79	4.34	8.06

Trailing	Total Return%	+/- LB Aggr	+/- LB. U.S. Univ. Bd	%Rank Cat	Growth of $10,000
3 Mo	4.34	3.39	3.06	44	10,434
6 Mo	7.25	3.07	2.46	61	10,725
1 Yr	8.06	3.72	3.09	52	10,806
3 Yr Avg	9.94	3.75	3.09	57	13,288
5 Yr Avg	8.32	0.61	0.44	27	14,912
10 Yr Avg	8.68	0.96	0.81	15	22,988
15 Yr Avg	—	—	—	—	—

Tax Analysis	Tax-Adj Rtn%	%Rank Cat	Tax-Cost Rat	%Rank Cat
3 Yr (estimated)	7.99	36	1.77	15
5 Yr (estimated)	6.11	16	2.04	14
10 Yr (estimated)	6.08	9	2.39	15

Potential Capital Gain Exposure: 7% of assets

Rating and Risk

Time Period	Load-Adj Return %	Morningstar Rtn vs Cat	Morningstar Risk vs Cat	Morningstar Risk-Adj Rating
1 Yr	8.06			
3 Yr	9.94	Avg	-Avg	★★★
5 Yr	8.32	+Avg	-Avg	★★★★
10 Yr	8.68	+Avg	-Avg	★★★★
Incept	8.70			

Other Measures	Standard Index LB Aggr	Best Fit Index LB Credit
Alpha	5.7	5.1
Beta	0.56	0.51
R-Squared	35	50
Standard Deviation	4.37	
Mean	9.94	
Sharpe Ratio	1.98	

Portfolio Analysis 09-30-04

Total Fixed-Income:0	Date of Maturity	Amount $000	Value $000	% Net Assets
T. Rowe Price New Income		104,223	947,384	22.82
T. Rowe Price High-Yield		121,079	851,186	20.50
T. Rowe Price Equity-Inc		25,600	639,223	15.40
Price T Rowe Intl Bond		54,267	548,644	13.22
T. Rowe Price GNMA		51,122	494,352	11.91
T. Rowe Price Short-Term		78,370	373,827	9.00
T. Rowe Price U.S. Treas		8,128	96,725	2.33
T Rowe Price Emerging Ma		6,846	86,669	2.09
T. Rowe Price Corporate		7,126	69,761	1.68

Morningstar's Take by Scott Berry 11-03-04

Despite lackluster near-term results, we think T. Rowe Price Spectrum Income makes a good case for itself.

This fund of funds has struggled to stand out in recent years. Its underlying holdings have performed well, with top five holdings High-Yield, Equity-Income, and International Bond delivering solid returns. However, the fund's investment-grade bond exposure looks to be holding it back a bit. Much of that exposure comes in the form of New Income and GNMA, which have outperformed their average category peers in recent years, but which have delivered lower absolute returns. Overall, the fund's one- and three-year trailing returns land near the midpoint of the multisector-bond category.

The fund looks much better compared with Morningstar's intermediate-bond category. The fund's exposures to high-yield bonds, emerging-markets issues, and individual stocks make it a better fit for Morningstar's multisector bond category, but with the fund playing the role of a core bond holding in many portfolios, it's worth comparing it to both groups. Its volatility has been in line with the intermediate-bond category norm, while its long-term returns rank in the group's best quartile. Actually, the fund's 10-year trailing returns rank in the top quartile of both categories.

We like this fund for its solid long-term record but we also like it for its structure. Unlike many funds of funds that charge an extra management fee on top of the costs of the underlying funds, this fund simply bears its pro-rata share of the expenses of the underlying funds, which are reasonably priced to start with. The resulting expense ratio provides the fund a sustainable advantage over its average peer.

This fund may not pack as big a punch as many of its multisector peers, but we think it's a good pick for bond investors looking for limited exposure to dividend-paying stocks and high-yield bonds.

Address:	100 E Pratt St Baltimore MD 21202 800-638-5660	Minimum Purchase:	$2500	Add: $100 IRA: $1000
Web Address:	www.troweprice.com	Min Auto Inv Plan:	$50	Add: $50
Inception:	06-29-90	Sales Fees:	No-load	
Advisor:	T. Rowe Price Associates, Inc.	Management Fee:	0.00%	
Subadvisor:	None	Actual Fees:	Mgt:0.00%	Dist:
		Expense Projections:	3Yr:$249	5Yr:$433 10Yr:$966
		Income Distrib:	Monthly	
NTF Plans:	N/A			

Current Investment Style

Duration: Short Int Long; Quality: High Med Low

¹figure provided by fund

Avg Eff Duration¹	—
Avg Eff Maturity	—
Avg Credit Quality	—
Avg Wtd Coupon	—
Avg Wtd Price	101.95% of par

Coupon Range	% of Bonds	Rel Cat
0% PIK	3.0	0.9
0% to 6%	49.1	1.1
6% to 8%	23.1	0.9
8% to 10%	17.9	0.9
More than 10%	9.8	1.0

1.00=Category Average

Credit Analysis	% bonds 09-30-04		
US Govt	0	BB	0
AAA	0	B	0
AA	0	Below B	0
A	0	NR/NA	100
BBB	0		

Sector Breakdown	% of assets
US Treasuries	5
TIPS	0
US Agency	2
Mortgage Pass-Throughs	25
Mortgage CMO	6
Mortgage ARM	0
US Corporate	42
Asset-Backed	4
Convertible	0
Municipal	1
Corporate Inflation-Protected	0
Foreign Corporate	2
Foreign Govt	1

Composition			
Cash	8.8	Bonds	59.8
Stocks	15.4	Other	16.0

Special Securities	
Restricted/Illiquid Secs	6
Exotic Mortgage-Backed	0
Emerging-Markets Secs	Trace
Options/Futures/Warrants	No

T. Rowe Price T/F Hi-Yld

Analyst Pick

Ticker	Load	NAV	Yield	SEC Yield	Total Assets	Mstar Category
PRFHX	None	$11.79	5.1%	4.34%	$1,218 mil	High Yield Muni

Governance and Management

Fiduciary Grade: B

Portfolio Manager(s)

Jim Murphy leads the effort here. He joined T. Rowe Price from Prudential in early 2001 and has led the fund since that time. He is supported by T. Rowe Price muni veteran Mary Miller and a team of six credit analysts.

Strategy

This fund hunts for opportunity on two fronts. First, its credit-research department ferrets out good yield in lower-quality credits. The fund typically keeps significantly more than half of its assets in such bonds. It also makes occasional, slight changes to duration (a measure of interest-rate sensitivity) to take advantage of management's interest-rate outlook. To dampen risk, the fund spreads assets across more than 300 issues.

Historical Profile

Return Above Avg
Risk Above Avg
Rating ★★★★ Above Avg

Investment Style: Fixed Income — Income Rtn %Rank Cat

51	39	31	30	20	30	38	42	36

▼ Manager Change
∇ Partial Manager Change

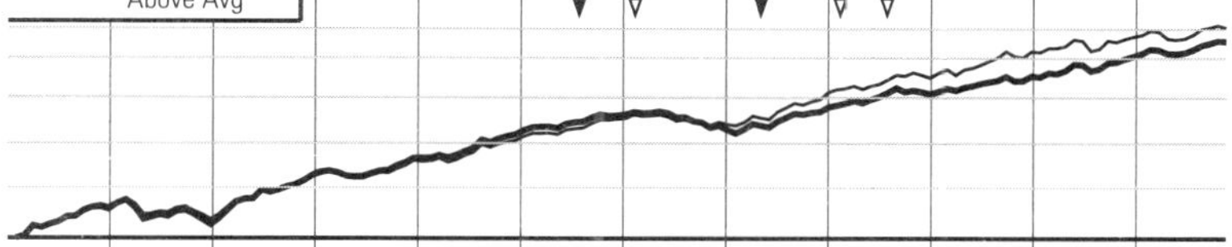

Growth of $10,000
— Investment Values of Fund
— Investment Values of LB Muni

Performance Quartile (within Category)

1993	1994	1995	1996	1997	1998	1999	2000	2001	2002	2003	12-04	History
12.46	11.16	12.24	12.12	12.62	12.57	11.30	11.52	11.39	11.46	11.64	11.79	NAV
12.98	-4.38	16.60	4.97	10.17	5.55	-5.10	8.14	4.66	6.38	7.10	6.65	Total Return %
0.70	0.79	-0.86	0.54	0.98	-0.93	-3.04	-3.54	-0.47	-3.22	1.79	2.17	+/-LB Muni
0.21	0.39	-0.57	0.43	0.93	-1.21	-3.86	-2.62	0.04	-3.79	1.40	2.50	+/-LB Muni 10YR
6.46	5.99	6.69	5.88	5.88	5.48	5.32	6.09	5.89	5.76	5.46	5.31	Income Return %
6.52	-10.37	9.91	-0.91	4.29	0.07	-10.42	2.05	-1.23	0.62	1.64	1.34	Capital Return %
23	41	32	31	25	33	66	7	53	39	29	33	Total Rtn % Rank Cat
0.75	0.72	0.73	0.70	0.69	0.68	0.65	0.67	0.66	0.64	0.61	0.60	Income $
0.23	0.04	0.00	0.00	0.00	0.06	0.00	0.00	0.00	0.00	0.00	0.00	Capital Gains $
0.81	0.79	0.79	0.75	0.74	0.72	0.71	0.71	0.72	0.71	0.71	0.71	Expense Ratio %
6.58	5.95	6.29	6.07	5.86	5.59	5.28	5.54	5.89	5.72	5.56	5.33	Income Ratio %
35	59	60	39	37	24	39	57	15	33	31	26	Turnover Rate %
953	802	983	1,033	1,200	1,345	1,132	1,084	1,089	1,119	1,136	1,218	Net Assets $mil

Performance 12-31-04

	1st Qtr	2nd Qtr	3rd Qtr	4th Qtr	Total
2000	2.05	0.88	2.43	2.54	8.14
2001	2.25	1.36	1.73	-0.73	4.66
2002	1.23	2.39	2.45	0.18	6.38
2003	0.81	3.19	0.63	2.31	7.10
2004	2.25	-1.01	3.32	1.99	6.65

Trailing	Total Return%	+/- LB Muni	+/- LB Muni 10YR	%Rank Cat	Growth of $10,000
3 Mo	1.99	0.74	1.16	77	10,199
6 Mo	5.37	0.18	0.37	67	10,537
1 Yr	6.65	2.17	2.50	33	10,665
3 Yr Avg	6.71	0.27	0.07	37	12,151
5 Yr Avg	6.58	-0.62	-0.46	21	13,752
10 Yr Avg	6.39	-0.67	-0.69	26	18,578
15 Yr Avg	6.66	-0.33	-0.42	34	26,304

Tax Analysis	Tax-Adj Rtn%	%Rank Cat	Tax-Cost Rat	%Rank Cat
3 Yr (estimated)	6.71	20	0.00	1
5 Yr (estimated)	6.58	17	0.00	1
10 Yr (estimated)	6.38	13	0.01	15

Potential Capital Gain Exposure: 6% of assets

Rating and Risk

Time Period	Load-Adj Return %	Morningstar Rtn vs Cat	Morningstar Risk vs Cat	Morningstar Risk-Adj Rating
1 Yr	6.65			
3 Yr	6.71	+Avg	Avg	★★★★
5 Yr	6.58	+Avg	+Avg	★★★★
10 Yr	6.39	+Avg	+Avg	★★★★
Incept	7.84			

Other Measures	Standard Index LB Aggr	Best Fit Index LB Muni 20YR
Alpha	2.0	1.5
Beta	0.65	0.60
R-Squared	89	90
Standard Deviation	3.46	
Mean	6.71	
Sharpe Ratio	1.56	

Portfolio Analysis 09-30-04

Total Fixed-Income:381	Date of Maturity	Amount $000	Value $000	% Net Assets
Mississippi Busn Fin 5.9	05-01-22	14,325	14,465	1.24
North Carolina Eastr Mun	01-01-26	10,125	11,199	0.96
Oregon St Dept Administr	11-01-20	10,000	10,763	0.92
California St 5.5%	11-01-33	10,140	10,742	0.92
California St Dept Wtr R	05-01-14	9,000	10,266	0.88
Sacramento Calif City Fi	01-01-30	10,000	10,081	0.86
Golden St Tob Securitiza	06-01-33	9,100	9,436	0.81
Maryland St Econ Dev 6%	07-01-34	8,250	8,526	0.73
Golden St Tob Securitiza	06-01-38	8,000	8,342	0.71
Clark Cnty Nev Indl Dev	03-01-38	7,545	8,089	0.69
New York N Y 6.25%	08-01-09	6,720	7,281	0.62
Hodge La Util Sys 7.45%	03-01-24	6,250	7,257	0.62
Gulf Coast Waste Disp Au	04-01-36	6,750	7,117	0.61
Bucks Cnty Pa Indl Dev A	05-01-29	7,625	7,107	0.61
Tooele Cnty Utah Hazardo	11-01-26	7,000	7,073	0.61

Current Investment Style

Duration: Short Int Long — Quality: High Med Low

[1]Avg Eff Duration	5.5 Yrs
Avg Eff Maturity	17.1 Yrs
Avg Credit Quality	BBB
Avg Wtd Coupon	6.04%
Avg Wtd Price	102.85% of par

[1]figure provided by fund

Credit Analysis	% bonds 09-30-04		
US Govt	0	BB	4
AAA	13	B	5
AA	4	Below B	0
A	16	NR/NA	30
BBB	28		

Top 5 States	% bonds		
CA	13.0	PA	5.1
NY	8.9	NJ	4.9
TX	7.8		

Composition			
Cash	0.1	Bonds	99.9
Stocks	0.0	Other	0.0

Special Securities	
Restricted/Illiquid Secs	Trace
Options/Futures/Warrants	No

Sector Weightings	% of Bonds	Rel Cat
General Obligation	14.4	0.96
Utilities	12.8	1.49
Health	14.7	1.12
Water/Waste	11.2	1.61
Housing	6.7	0.85
Education	3.3	1.06
Transportation	4.2	0.54
COP/Lease	1.0	0.72
Industrial	31.7	0.88
Misc Revenue	0.0	—
Demand	0.0	0.00

Morningstar's Take by Scott Berry 01-03-05

T. Rowe Price Tax-Free High-Yield is one of our favorite high-yield muni funds.

This fund may not have stood head and shoulders above the crowd in 2004, but it turned in a solid showing nonetheless. Manager Jim Murphy shied away from airline issues and tobacco bonds, which led the market higher, but held a number of utility and hospital bonds, which performed quite well in their own right. The fund also profited from a bet on California bonds, which paid off when the state was upgraded by Moody's, and issue-specific recoveries in the toll road sector. Overall, the fund gained 6.6% for the year ending Dec. 31, while its average high yield muni peer returned 6.3%.

The fund also boasts a strong long-term record. In fact, its three-, five-, and 10-year trailing returns all rank in the category's top third. Further, the fund has been quite consistent, with its annual returns landing in the group's top half in eight of the last 10 calendar years.

That success owes much to the quality of T. Rowe Price's municipal-bond group and the fund's below-average costs. Murphy, who has led the effort here since early 2001, is backed by six credit analysts, but can also tap the managers of T. Rowe Price's state-specific and national investment-grade offerings for ideas and opportunities. Meanwhile, the fund's 0.71% expense ratio provides it a sustainable advantage over its average category peer, which charges 1.24% per year.

This fund has a lot going for it, but its risk profile should not be overlooked. It may not hold sizeable stakes in the market's riskiest sectors, but with more than 65% of its assets in bonds rated BBB and below (including nonrated issues), it takes on plenty of risk. And that risk could result in a sometimes bumpy ride for shareholders.

That said, we think investors looking for a proven high-yield muni fund have come to the right place.

Address:	100 E Pratt St Baltimore MD 21202 800-638-5660
Web Address:	www.troweprice.com
Inception:	03-01-85
Advisor:	T. Rowe Price Associates, Inc.
Subadvisor:	None
NTF Plans:	N/A

Minimum Purchase:	$2500	Add: $100	IRA: $1000
Min Auto Inv Plan:	$50	Add: $50	
Sales Fees:	No-load		
Management Fee:	0.62%		
Actual Fees:	Mgt:0.62%	Dist:	
Expense Projections:	3Yr:$227	5Yr:$395	10Yr:$883
Income Distrib:	Monthly		

T. Rowe Price T/F Inc

Ticker	Load	NAV	Yield	SEC Yield	Total Assets	Mstar Category
PRTAX	None	$10.06	4.3%	3.39%	$1,732 mil	Muni National Long

Governance and Management

Fiduciary Grade: B

Portfolio Manager(s)

Mary Miller was recently named T. Rowe Price's director of fixed income but has no plans to leave this fund, which she has managed with much success since early 1997. Miller is backed by a team of eight analysts.

Strategy

Manager Mary Miller maintains a cautious stance but seeks out pockets of opportunity. She doesn't venture far from the duration of an internally selected peer group, though she will make modest adjustments depending on her view on the direction of market yields. Miller usually focuses on higher-rated credits but will park some assets in mid-rated bonds when they offer compelling yields.

Historical Profile
Return: Above Avg
Risk: Below Avg
Rating: ★★★★ Above Avg

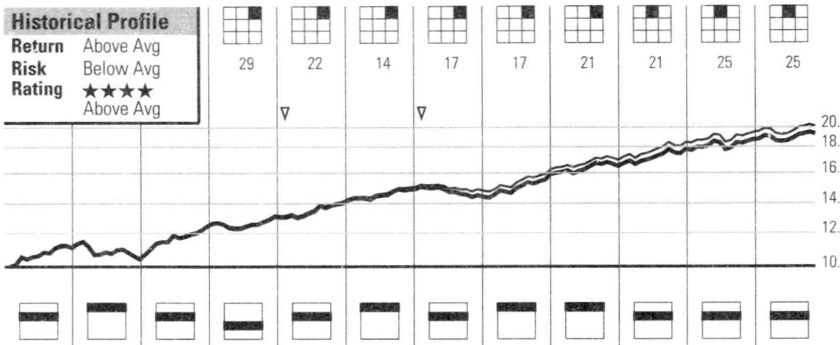

Investment Style
Fixed Income
Income Rtn %Rank Cat: 29, 22, 14, 17, 17, 21, 21, 25, 25

▼ Manager Change
▽ Partial Manager Change

Growth of $10,000
— Investment Values of Fund
— Investment Values of LB Muni

Performance Quartile (within Category)

1993	1994	1995	1996	1997	1998	1999	2000	2001	2002	2003	12-04	History
9.90	8.80	9.80	9.59	9.94	9.97	9.09	9.68	9.62	10.02	10.07	10.06	NAV
12.77	-5.46	17.69	3.26	9.32	5.96	-3.91	12.29	4.38	9.23	5.11	4.33	Total Return %
0.49	-0.29	0.23	-1.17	0.13	-0.52	-1.85	0.61	-0.75	-0.37	-0.20	-0.15	+/-LB Muni
-1.61	1.88	-3.28	-1.20	-1.52	-0.86	0.77	-2.95	-0.49	-0.80	-1.22	-2.23	+/-LB Muni 20YR
5.87	5.47	6.07	5.36	5.53	5.23	5.07	5.57	5.07	4.98	4.58	4.40	Income Return %
6.90	-10.93	11.62	-2.10	3.79	0.73	-8.98	6.72	-0.69	4.25	0.53	-0.07	Capital Return %
43	22	37	52	39	22	31	22	25	33	36	31	Total Rtn % Rank Cat
0.54	0.53	0.52	0.51	0.52	0.51	0.49	0.49	0.48	0.47	0.45	0.43	Income $
0.18	0.04	0.00	0.00	0.00	0.04	0.01	0.00	0.00	0.00	0.00	0.00	Capital Gains $
0.61	0.59	0.59	0.58	0.57	0.55	0.55	0.55	0.54	0.54	0.55	0.54	Expense Ratio %
5.98	5.40	5.80	5.49	5.41	5.31	5.06	5.24	5.25	4.95	4.78	4.47	Income Ratio %
77	71	49	49	41	36	34	44	29	28	24	26	Turnover Rate %
1,500	1,254	1,397	1,345	1,385	1,481	1,328	1,396	1,328	1,401	1,488	1,451	Net Assets $mil

Performance 12-31-04

	1st Qtr	2nd Qtr	3rd Qtr	4th Qtr	Total
2000	3.27	1.25	2.29	4.99	12.29
2001	1.97	0.63	2.77	-1.02	4.38
2002	0.90	3.32	4.69	0.09	9.23
2003	1.04	2.44	0.03	1.52	5.11
2004	1.57	-2.10	3.66	1.21	4.32

Trailing	Total Return%	+/- LB Muni	+/- LB Muni 20YR	%Rank Cat	Growth of $10,000
3 Mo	1.21	-0.04	-0.77	45	10,121
6 Mo	4.92	-0.27	-1.83	46	10,492
1 Yr	4.33	-0.15	-2.23	31	10,433
3 Yr Avg	6.20	-0.24	-1.43	22	11,978
5 Yr Avg	7.02	-0.18	-1.52	16	14,039
10 Yr Avg	6.62	-0.44	-1.33	17	18,984
15 Yr Avg	6.66	-0.33	-0.99	25	26,304

Tax Analysis	Tax-Adj Rtn%	%Rank Cat	Tax-Cost Rat	%Rank Cat
3 Yr (estimated)	6.20	13	0.00	1
5 Yr (estimated)	7.02	10	0.00	1
10 Yr (estimated)	6.61	11	0.01	5

Potential Capital Gain Exposure: 7% of assets

Rating and Risk

Time Period	Load-Adj Return %	Morningstar Rtn vs Cat	Morningstar Risk vs Cat	Morningstar Risk-Adj Rating
1 Yr	4.33			
3 Yr	6.20	+Avg	-Avg	★★★★
5 Yr	7.02	+Avg	-Avg	★★★★
10 Yr	6.62	+Avg	-Avg	★★★★
Incept	6.81			

Other Measures	Standard Index LB Aggr	Best Fit Index LB Muni
Alpha	-0.2	-0.2
Beta	1.00	1.00
R-Squared	99	99
Standard Deviation	5.05	
Mean	6.20	
Sharpe Ratio	0.97	

Portfolio Analysis 09-30-04

Total Fixed-Income:341	Date of Maturity	Amount $000	Value $000	% Net Assets
Triborough Brdg & Tunl A	01-01-17	18,275	21,050	1.23
South Carolina St Pub Sv	01-01-22	17,750	19,064	1.11
New York N Y City Transi	02-01-29	16,640	18,321	1.07
New York St Urban Dev 5.	01-01-21	15,600	17,064	1.00
Washington St 5.7%	10-01-15	14,000	16,192	0.95
New Hampshire St Busn Fi	05-01-21	14,500	15,880	0.93
Burlington Kans Pollutio	06-01-31	15,000	15,823	0.92
California St Pub Wks Br	06-01-28	14,810	15,242	0.89
California St Econ Recov	07-01-16	14,000	14,991	0.88
Metropolitan Transn Auth	07-01-21	12,750	14,345	0.84
District Columbia 5.125%	06-01-17	12,720	13,790	0.81
Tacoma Wash Solid Waste	12-01-17	12,080	13,238	0.77
King Cnty Wash Pub Hosp	09-01-20	10,950	12,836	0.75
California Statewide Cmn	04-01-34	12,500	12,443	0.73
Houston Tex Higher Ed Fi	11-15-29	11,450	12,077	0.71

Current Investment Style

Duration: Short Int Long — Quality: High Med Low

[1]Avg Eff Duration	5.3 Yrs
Avg Eff Maturity	14.2 Yrs
Avg Credit Quality	AA
Avg Wtd Coupon	5.45%
Avg Wtd Price	106.93% of par

[1]figure provided by fund

Credit Analysis	% bonds 09-30-04		
US Govt	0	BB	1
AAA	47	B	1
AA	22	Below B	0
A	18	NR/NA	3
BBB	8		

Top 5 States	% bonds		
NY	17.8	IL	5.2
CA	13.3	WA	5.0
TX	6.1		

Composition			
Cash	0.1	Bonds	99.9
Stocks	0.0	Other	0.0

Special Securities	
Restricted/Illiquid Secs	0
Options/Futures/Warrants	No

Sector Weightings	% of Bonds	Rel Cat
General Obligation	25.6	0.98
Utilities	14.3	1.08
Health	14.2	1.80
Water/Waste	12.8	1.15
Housing	6.8	0.95
Education	8.9	0.77
Transportation	3.5	0.47
COP/Lease	2.4	1.16
Industrial	11.4	0.88
Misc Revenue	0.0	0.00
Demand	0.0	0.00

Morningstar's Take by Scott Berry 12-09-04

Above-average returns and below-average volatility make T. Rowe Price Tax-Free Income an appealing choice.

This fund boasts a solid long-term record. Manager Mary Miller, who has been at the helm since 1997, has kept the fund on an even keel by avoiding large interest-rate bets and by steering clear of lower-rated bonds. Meanwhile, the fund's build-in expense advantage has combined with Miller's skilled management to help the fund cruise past its average muni national long-term category peer. In fact, the fund's calendar-year returns have landed in the group's best half in each of the past seven years, while its three-, five-, and 10-year trailing returns all rank in the category's best quartile.

The fund's success has continued in 2004. Its California and New York holdings have performed well, while its modestly short duration (a measure of interest-rate sensitivity) has limited volatility. Wary of rising interest rates, Miller has targeted a duration that is 0% to 5% short of the Lehman Brothers Municipal Index. Though interest rates have remained stubbornly low, that stance helped the fund weather a bond-market downturn better than most in late March and April. And should rates trend higher, a shorter duration should provide some cushion for the portfolio. Overall, the fund has gained 3.6% for the year to date through December 7 and has outperformed roughly two thirds of its category peers.

The fund's returns are likely to look even better to investors who are subject to the Alternative Minimum Tax or AMT. For those investors, the income from certain municipal bonds is actually taxable. However, unlike many of its peers, this fund avoids such issues. As a result, its income is 100% AMT tax-free.

We think this fund has a lot to offer. Its reasonable costs, proven management, solid long-term record, and AMT-friendly portfolio make it an easy fund for us to recommend.

Address:	100 East Pratt Street Baltimore MD 21202 800-638-5660
Web Address:	www.troweprice.com
Inception:	10-26-76
Advisor:	T. Rowe Price Associates, Inc.
Subadvisor:	None
NTF Plans:	N/A

Minimum Purchase:	$2500	Add: $100	IRA: $1000
Min Auto Inv Plan:	$50	Add: $50	
Sales Fees:	No-load		
Management Fee:	0.47%		
Actual Fees:	Mgt:0.47%	Dist:	
Expense Projections:	3Yr:$173	5Yr:$302	10Yr:$677
Income Distrib:	Monthly		

T. Rowe Price T/F Sh-Int

Analyst Pick

Ticker	Load	NAV	Yield	SEC Yield	Total Assets	Mstar Category
PRFSX	None	$5.44	2.7%	2.23%	$571 mil	Muni National Short

Governance and Management

Fiduciary Grade: B

Portfolio Manager(s)

Charlie Hill has run this fund since early 1995 and has had much success. He is backed by the firm's strong credit-research department. He also manages T. Rowe Price Tax-Free Intermediate and two of T. Rowe Price's single-state municipal bond funds.

Strategy

Manager Charlie Hill generally keeps interest-rate and credit risk under wraps. Duration (a measure of interest-rate sensitivity) stays close to its benchmark index, and most of the fund's assets are stashed in credits rated AA or higher. But that doesn't mean Hill can't hunt for opportunity. He believes the best way to outperform over time is to avoid big duration bets and to seek out incrementally higher-yielding bonds. By prospectus, he can fill up to 5% of assets with lower-rated or nonrated issues.

Historical Profile

Return: Above Avg
Risk: Average
Rating: ★★★★ Above Avg

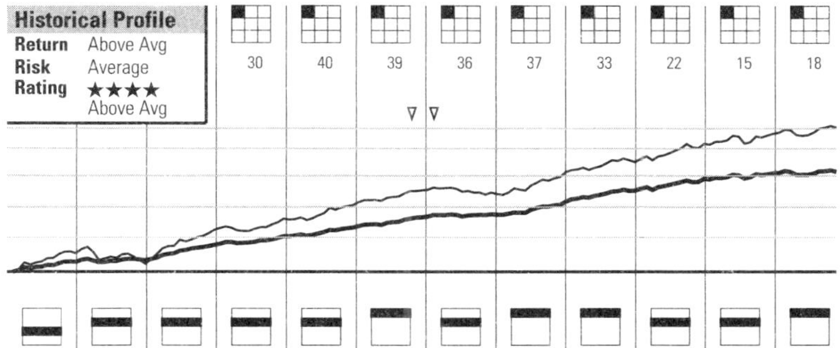

Investment Style: Fixed Income
Income Rtn %Rank Cat

▼ Manager Change
▽ Partial Manager Change

Growth of $10,000
— Investment Values of Fund
— Investment Values of LB Muni

Performance Quartile (within Category)

1993	1994	1995	1996	1997	1998	1999	2000	2001	2002	2003	12-04	History
5.38	5.18	5.36	5.34	5.36	5.38	5.21	5.33	5.42	5.53	5.50	5.44	NAV
6.32	0.33	8.11	4.01	5.30	4.97	0.99	6.76	5.81	6.16	2.78	1.61	Total Return %
-5.96	5.50	-9.35	-0.42	-3.89	-1.51	3.05	-4.92	0.68	-3.44	-2.53	-2.87	+/-LB Muni
0.10	-0.35	-0.76	-0.43	-0.18	-0.24	-0.97	0.53	-0.78	-0.56	0.10	-0.17	+/-LB Muni 3YR
4.40	4.10	4.58	4.37	4.33	4.21	4.04	4.38	4.12	3.71	3.14	2.70	Income Return %
1.92	-3.77	3.53	-0.36	0.97	0.76	-3.05	2.38	1.69	2.45	-0.36	-1.09	Capital Return %
52	26	37	33	37	19	38	16	2	35	30	22	Total Rtn % Rank Cat
0.23	0.22	0.23	0.23	0.23	0.22	0.21	0.22	0.22	0.20	0.17	0.15	Income $
0.00	0.00	0.00	0.00	0.03	0.02	0.01	0.00	0.00	0.02	0.01	0.00	Capital Gains $
0.63	0.60	0.59	0.57	0.56	0.54	0.53	0.53	0.53	0.52	0.52	0.51	Expense Ratio %
4.61	4.18	4.19	4.39	4.30	4.23	4.06	4.07	4.27	3.92	3.54	3.03	Income Ratio %
38	51	93	70	84	77	40	41	41	30	30	41	Turnover Rate %
534	451	451	439	439	458	417	405	447	560	582	571	Net Assets $mil

Performance 12-31-04

	1st Qtr	2nd Qtr	3rd Qtr	4th Qtr	Total
2000	1.06	1.47	1.65	2.41	6.76
2001	2.37	1.20	1.90	0.23	5.81
2002	0.36	2.62	2.19	0.86	6.16
2003	0.44	1.34	0.58	0.39	2.78
2004	0.68	-1.34	1.78	0.49	1.61

Trailing	Total Return%	+/- LB Muni	+/- LB Muni 3YR	%Rank Cat	Growth of $10,000
3 Mo	0.49	-0.76	0.30	17	10,049
6 Mo	2.28	-2.91	0.18	17	10,228
1 Yr	1.61	-2.87	-0.17	22	10,161
3 Yr Avg	3.50	-2.94	-0.21	30	11,087
5 Yr Avg	4.60	-2.60	-0.18	23	12,522
10 Yr Avg	4.63	-2.43	-0.34	22	15,724
15 Yr Avg	4.85	-2.14	—	50	20,348

Tax Analysis	Tax-Adj Rtn%	%Rank Cat	Tax-Cost Rat	%Rank Cat
3 Yr (estimated)	3.46	25	0.04	57
5 Yr (estimated)	4.58	15	0.02	40
10 Yr (estimated)	4.59	20	0.04	50

Potential Capital Gain Exposure: 2% of assets

Rating and Risk

Time Period	Load-Adj Return %	Morningstar Rtn vs Cat	Morningstar Risk vs Cat	Morningstar Risk-Adj Rating
1 Yr	1.61			
3 Yr	3.50	+Avg	+Avg	★★★★
5 Yr	4.60	+Avg	Avg	★★★★
10 Yr	4.63	+Avg	Avg	★★★★
Incept	5.30			

Other Measures	Standard Index LB Aggr	Best Fit Index LB Muni
Alpha	-0.7	-0.7
Beta	0.55	0.55
R-Squared	94	94
Standard Deviation	2.80	
Mean	3.50	
Sharpe Ratio	0.77	

Portfolio Analysis 09-30-04

Total Fixed-Income:17?	Date of Maturity	Amount $000	Value $000	% Net Assets
Jea Fla St Johns Riv Pwr	10-01-09	8,000	8,832	1.51
Puerto Rico Comwlth 5%	07-01-28	8,000	8,700	1.49
Massachusetts Mun Whsl E	07-01-07	7,995	8,594	1.47
Maryland St 5.25%	07-15-06	8,000	8,486	1.45
Maryland St Dept Transn	02-01-09	7,370	8,261	1.41
Louisiana St 5.5%	04-15-07	7,000	7,595	1.30
Jefferson Cnty Ala Swr	02-01-40	6,405	7,313	1.25
Savannah Ga Econ Dev Aut	10-01-29	5,880	7,011	1.20
Northeast Md Waste Disp	04-01-11	6,000	6,647	1.14
California St Pub Wks Br	06-01-07	6,000	6,418	1.10
Pennsylvania St 5%	09-15-06	6,000	6,358	1.09
California St Dept Wtr R	05-01-09	5,725	6,354	1.09
San Antonio Tex 5%	08-01-10	5,745	6,337	1.08
Florida St Brd Ed Lotter	07-01-08	5,185	5,760	0.98
Florida St Div Bd Fin De	07-01-09	5,000	5,724	0.98

Current Investment Style

Duration: Short Int Long; Quality: High Med Low

¹Avg Eff Duration	2.9 Yrs
Avg Eff Maturity	3.7 Yrs
Avg Credit Quality	AA
Avg Wtd Coupon	5.21%
Avg Wtd Price	108.25% of par

¹figure provided by fund

Credit Analysis	% bonds 09-30-04		
US Govt	0	BB	0
AAA	51	B	0
AA	31	Below B	0
A	13	NR/NA	2
BBB	4		

Top 5 States	% bonds		
FL	11.4	MD	8.0
NY	9.3	TX	6.5
CA	8.1		

Composition			
Cash	7.5	Bonds	92.5
Stocks	0.0	Other	0.0

Special Securities	
Restricted/Illiquid Secs	0
Options/Futures/Warrants	No

Sector Weightings	% of Bonds	Rel Cat
General Obligation	46.7	1.33
Utilities	16.7	1.80
Health	3.0	0.42
Water/Waste	6.8	0.65
Housing	0.4	0.06
Education	1.4	0.17
Transportation	13.8	3.25
COP/Lease	3.5	2.23
Industrial	7.5	0.50
Misc Revenue	0.0	—
Demand	0.0	0.00

Morningstar's Take by Scott Berry 12-17-04

T. Rowe Price Tax-Free Short-Intermediate remains one of our favorites, but it could struggle if interest rates move higher.

This fund continues to deliver. For the year to date through Dec. 16, 2004, it gained 1.5% and outperformed more than 70% of its muni national short-term rivals. Over the past year, the fund has benefited from its increased exposure to California, which was upgraded by Moody's earlier in the year, and has profited from its added interest-rate sensitivity, which pushed the fund higher over the summer months and gave it an added lift in early December.

The fund's added rate sensitivity is not the result of a bet that interest rates will go lower, but rather reflects the added sensitivity of the fund's benchmark index. Manager Charlie Hill has actually kept the fund more defensive than its benchmark to guard against rising interest rates. But with a benchmark that is slightly more rate-sensitive than the category as a whole, the fund's duration (a measure of interest-rate sensitivity) has remained longer than that of its average peer. That added sensitivity has worked in the fund's favor in recent years, but could hamper performance if interest rates trend higher. For example, when bond yields spiked in April 2004, this fund dropped 1.5%, while its average category peer dipped 0.9%.

We remain confident in this fund's long-term prospects though, given its reasonable expense ratio and skilled management. The fund's expense ratio, which checks in at just 0.51%, provides it a built-in head start each year, while manager Charlie Hill's portfolio adjustments have paid off more often than not. The fund profited from Hill's move into utility issues in 2003, for example.

We think this fund continues to make a strong case for itself and believe it remains a fine choice for investors looking for a conservative core municipal bond fund. Those investors that can't afford to lose principal, though, may want to consider other options.

Address:	100 East Pratt St, Baltimore MD 21202, 800-638-5660
Web Address:	www.troweprice.com
Inception:	12-23-83
Advisor:	T. Rowe Price Associates, Inc.
Subadvisor:	None
NTF Plans:	N/A

Minimum Purchase:	$2500	Add: $100	IRA: $1000
Min Auto Inv Plan:	$50	Add: $50	
Sales Fees:	No-load		
Management Fee:	0.42%		
Actual Fees:	Mgt:0.42%	Dist:	
Expense Projections:	3Yr:$164	5Yr:$285	10Yr:$640
Income Distrib:	Monthly		

T. Rowe Price US Try L/T

Analyst Pick

Ticker	Load	NAV	Yield	SEC Yield	Total Assets	Mstar Category
PRULX	None	$11.86	4.3%	4.08%	$232 mil	Long Government

Governance and Management

Fiduciary Grade: B

Portfolio Manager(s)

Although his 2003 appointment marks the first mutual fund management assignment for new skipper Brian Brennan, he brings 16 years of experience to the table. Much of that time was spent managing fixed-income assets in separate accounts. And though he now has prime responsibility for this portfolio, Brennan will continue to receive support from colleagues Jerome Clark, Cheryl Mickel, and Dan Shackelford.

Strategy

Management stores at least 85% of assets in Treasuries. Although the rest of the portfolio is typically composed of GNMA mortgages, management will also hold other bonds that are fully backed by the U.S. government. The fund's duration (a measure of interest-rate sensitivity) is typically kept within a range of nine to 11 years, though generally hews close to the midpoint. As such, the fund can be subject to dramatic fluctuations when interest rates change. In general, though, the bulk of management effort is spent on yield-curve and government-subsector selections.

Historical Profile

Return Average
Risk Average
Rating ★★★ Neutral

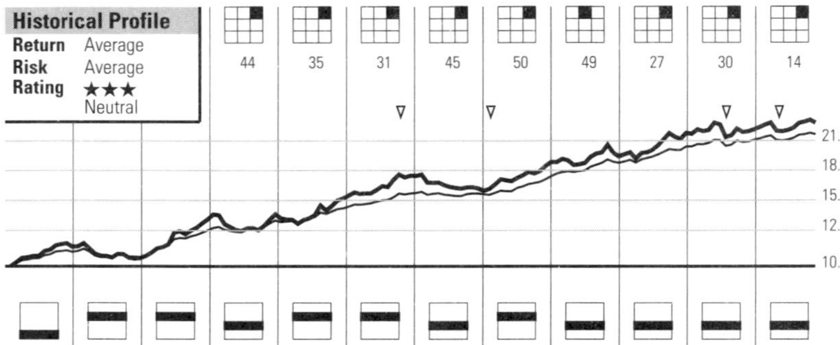

Investment Style
Fixed Income
Income Rtn %Rank Cat

▼ Manager Change
▽ Partial Manager Change

Growth of $10,000
▬ Investment Values of Fund
— Investment Values of LB Aggr

Performance Quartile (within Category)

1993	1994	1995	1996	1997	1998	1999	2000	2001	2002	2003	12-04	History
10.71	9.41	11.36	10.43	11.27	11.98	10.22	11.50	11.29	12.28	11.74	11.86	NAV
12.93	-5.75	28.60	-2.37	14.73	12.82	-8.75	19.10	3.39	15.13	2.10	5.79	Total Return %
3.18	-2.83	10.13	-6.00	5.08	4.13	-7.93	7.47	-5.05	4.88	-2.00	1.45	+/-LB Aggr
-4.49	1.98	-2.30	-1.53	-0.39	-0.59	-0.02	-1.19	-0.95	-1.86	-0.51	-2.15	+/-LB LTGvtBd
6.75	6.56	7.20	5.77	6.25	5.72	5.34	6.21	5.30	5.16	4.45	4.47	Income Return %
6.18	-12.31	21.40	-8.14	8.48	7.10	-14.09	12.89	-1.91	9.97	-2.35	1.32	Capital Return %
82	29	40	67	44	44	60	48	65	75	66	68	Total Rtn % Rank Cat
0.68	0.68	0.66	0.64	0.63	0.63	0.62	0.62	0.60	0.57	0.53	0.51	Income $
0.29	0.01	0.00	0.00	0.00	0.07	0.11	0.00	0.00	0.10	0.26	0.03	Capital Gains $
0.80	0.80	0.80	0.80	0.80	0.67	0.66	0.64	0.63	0.66	0.68	0.67	Expense Ratio %
6.75	6.17	7.05	6.05	6.22	5.71	5.30	5.89	5.51	5.13	4.54	4.31	Income Ratio %
165	59	99	60	68	81	74	22	31	49	66	52	Turnover Rate %
57	58	71	73	207	310	324	315	306	297	245	232	Net Assets $mil

Performance 12-31-04

	1st Qtr	2nd Qtr	3rd Qtr	4th Qtr	Total
2000	7.31	0.82	2.73	7.16	19.10
2001	0.97	-1.54	6.63	-2.46	3.39
2002	-1.33	5.46	10.53	0.10	15.13
2003	1.09	4.13	-2.50	-0.52	2.10
2004	4.25	-4.44	5.13	1.01	5.79

Trailing	Total Return%	+/- LB Aggr	+/- LB LTGvtBd	%Rank Cat	Growth of $10,000
3 Mo	1.01	0.06	-0.56	87	10,101
6 Mo	6.20	2.02	-1.89	63	10,620
1 Yr	5.79	1.45	-2.15	68	10,579
3 Yr Avg	7.54	1.35	-1.48	78	12,437
5 Yr Avg	8.90	1.19	-1.32	74	15,316
10 Yr Avg	8.55	0.83	-1.11	40	22,714
15 Yr Avg	8.00	0.30	-1.15	56	31,722

Tax Analysis	Tax-Adj Rtn%	%Rank Cat	Tax-Cost Rat	%Rank Cat
3 Yr (estimated)	5.53	78	1.87	62
5 Yr (estimated)	6.76	74	1.97	46
10 Yr (estimated)	6.18	40	2.18	67

Potential Capital Gain Exposure: 9% of assets

Rating and Risk

Time Period	Load-Adj Return %	Morningstar Rtn vs Cat	Morningstar Risk vs Cat	Morningstar Risk-Adj Rating
1 Yr	5.79			
3 Yr	7.54	-Avg	Avg	★★★
5 Yr	8.90	-Avg	Avg	★★
10 Yr	8.55	Avg	Avg	★★★
Incept	8.15			

Other Measures	Standard Index LB Aggr	Best Fit Index LB Long Tr
Alpha	-3.1	-0.1
Beta	1.99	0.83
R-Squared	96	100
Standard Deviation	9.34	
Mean	7.54	
Sharpe Ratio	0.67	

Portfolio Analysis 09-30-04

Total Fixed-Income:114	Date of Maturity	Amount $000	Value $000	% Net Assets
US Treasury Bond 8.875%	02-15-19	28,225	40,767	17.28
US Treasury Bond 7.125%	02-15-23	31,400	40,025	16.97
US Treasury Bond 7.625%	02-15-25	21,375	28,883	12.24
US Treasury Bond 6.25%	08-15-23	18,500	21,602	9.16
US Treasury Bond 6%	02-15-26	14,500	16,530	7.01
US Treasury Bond 7.875%	02-15-21	7,650	10,350	4.39
US Treasury Bond 8.75%	05-15-17	6,255	8,825	3.74
US Treasury Bond 6.25%	05-15-30	6,525	7,744	3.28
US Treasury Note 2%	07-15-14	6,531	6,678	2.83
US Treasury Bond 2.375%	01-15-25	5,225	5,443	2.31
US Treasury Note 1.875%	07-15-13	3,197	3,252	1.38
US Treasury Bond 5.375%	02-15-31	2,750	2,946	1.25
GNMA CMO 6.5%	05-20-28	2,755	2,867	1.22
GNMA CMO 5.5%	02-20-30	2,550	2,652	1.12
GNMA 6%	01-15-18	1,377	1,453	0.62
GNMA CMO	10-16-33	1,500	1,405	0.60
GNMA CMO	03-16-30	1,250	1,260	0.53
GNMA 5.5%	01-01-33	1,200	1,217	0.52
GNMA 6%	11-15-17	1,047	1,106	0.47
GNMA 6%	08-15-16	617	651	0.28

Current Investment Style

Duration: Short Int Long — Quality: High Med Low

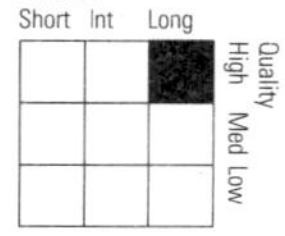

[1] figure provided by fund

Avg Eff Duration[1]	8.9 Yrs
Avg Eff Maturity	15.0 Yrs
Avg Credit Quality	AAA
Avg Wtd Coupon	6.95%
Avg Wtd Price	126.04% of par

Coupon Range	% of Bonds	Rel Cat
0% PIK	0.0	0.0
0% to 6%	22.8	0.3
6% to 8%	53.0	4.6
8% to 10%	24.2	7.4
More than 10%	0.0	0.1

1.00=Category Average

Credit Analysis	% bonds 09-30-04		
US Govt	100	BB	0
AAA	0	B	0
AA	0	Below B	0
A	0	NR/NA	0
BBB	0		

Sector Breakdown	% of assets
US Treasuries	80
TIPS	1
US Agency	0
Mortgage Pass-Throughs	5
Mortgage CMO	3
Mortgage ARM	0
US Corporate	0
Asset-Backed	0
Convertible	0
Municipal	0
Corporate Inflation-Protected	0
Foreign Corporate	0
Foreign Govt	0

Composition			
Cash	9.8	Bonds	90.2
Stocks	0.0	Other	0.0

Special Securities	
Restricted/Illiquid Secs	0
Exotic Mortgage-Backed	—
Emerging-Markets Secs	0
Options/Futures/Warrants	No

Morningstar's Take by Eric Jacobson 01-07-05

If T. Rowe Price U.S. Treasury Long-Term produced any bigger returns, we'd find it difficult to consider.

That might seem counterintuitive following two years of moderate, single-digit gains. For most, the idea of getting more return is such a fundamental goal as to need no explanation. Other than long-term Treasuries, though, there are few areas that as cleanly illustrate the investing tradeoff between risk and return. Whether through the use of longer bonds, or derivatives that help approximate extra interest-rate risk, there's nearly always a Treasury holding one can buy with more risk and return potential.

The problem, though, is that at a certain point the exercise becomes counterproductive. In large part, that's a function of the maturity spectrum. The longer the Treasury bond, the more return you stand to enjoy, mostly from income. At a point usually beyond 10 years, though, the extra income one can earn over shorter bonds levels off. As such, very long bonds with much more rate sensitivity than say, a 10-year issue, may generate bigger short-term gains and losses, but whose additional long-term returns come with a massive additional amount of risk.

We make that point because this fund has staked out a sweet spot along the maturity spectrum. Although management works to pick individual bonds, and also uses some inflation-indexed bonds and mortgages, the main purpose of this fund is to offer exposure to the long-term part of the Treasury market, without taking on excessive risk.

It's against that backdrop that we caution investors to recognize why this fund isn't the top returning entrant in its category. Those that are carry levels of rate sensitivity that can trigger 20%-plus short-term gains, but also losses equally severe. Over the long haul, such offerings haven't earned enough return for most people to be willing to assume their risks.

Address:	100 E Pratt St Baltimore MD 21202 800-638-5660
Web Address:	www.troweprice.com
Inception:	09-29-89
Advisor:	T. Rowe Price Associates, Inc.
Subadvisor:	None
NTF Plans:	N/A

Minimum Purchase:	$2500	Add: $100	IRA: $1000
Min Auto Inv Plan:	$50	Add: $50	
Sales Fees:	No-load		
Management Fee:	0.37%		
Actual Fees:	Mgt:0.37%	Dist:	
Expense Projections:	3Yr:$214	5Yr:$373	10Yr:$835
Income Distrib:	Monthly		

T. Rowe Price Value

Ticker	Load	NAV	Yield	Total Assets	Mstar Category
TRVLX	None	$22.90	0.8%	$2,577 mil	Large Value

Governance and Management

Fiduciary Grade: B

Portfolio Manager(s)

John Linehan took charge on March 31, 2003. He joined T. Rowe Price in 1998 as an analyst covering the paper, energy, and airline industries and has been a member of the fund's investment committee since 2001. Linehan also helped run the firm's institutional large-value accounts since 1999 with Brian Rogers and Steve Boesel.

Strategy

Like former manager Brian Rogers, John Linehan seeks stocks that appear cheap relative to historical standards. But unlike Rogers, who was apt to own firms with shakier fundamentals, Linehan favors high-quality names. And because he runs the fund as a pure large-value portfolio, its average market cap should continue to rise. Linehan also devotes a small slice of the portfolio to overseas names in hopes of exploiting valuation disparities that often arise between U.S. companies and their foreign counterparts.

Historical Profile

Return Above Avg
Risk Above Avg
Rating ★★★★ Above Avg

Investment Style: Equity, Stock %: 90% 90% 95% 93% 93% 95% 97% 96% 95%

▼ Manager Change
▽ Partial Manager Change

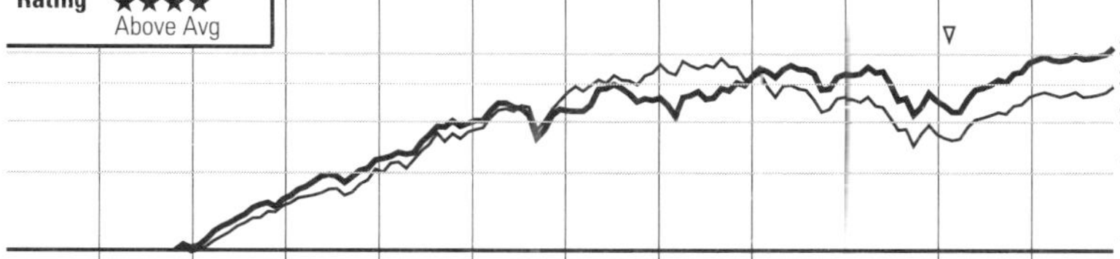

Growth of $10,000
— Investment Values of Fund
— Investment Values of S&P 500

Performance Quartile (within Category)

1993	1994	1995	1996	1997	1998	1999	2000	2001	2002	2003	12-04	History
—	10.24	13.21	15.76	18.24	18.31	17.50	19.15	18.88	15.56	20.01	22.90	NAV
—	3.10*	39.85	28.51	29.25	6.85	9.16	15.75	1.60	-16.58	30.00	15.36	Total Return %
—	—	2.32	5.57	-4.10	-21.72	-11.88	24.85	13.48	5.51	1.33	4.49	+/-S&P 500
—	—	1.49	6.87	-5.93	-8.78	1.81	8.74	7.19	-1.06	-0.03	-1.13	+/-Russ 1000 VI
—	0.00	2.56	2.00	1.35	1.12	1.19	1.31	0.89	0.79	1.29	0.90	Income Return %
—	—	37.29	26.51	27.90	5.73	7.97	14.44	0.71	-17.37	28.71	14.46	Capital Return %
—	—	5	5	30	82	32	21	22	36	33	20	Total Rtn % Rank Cat
—	0.07	0.26	0.26	0.21	0.20	0.21	0.23	0.17	0.15	0.20	0.18	Income $
—	0.00	0.82	0.91	1.83	0.96	2.20	0.84	0.40	0.04	0.01	0.00	Capital Gains $
—	1.10	1.10	1.10	1.05	0.98	0.92	0.91	0.94	0.95	0.97	—	Expense Ratio %
—	3.16	2.03	1.71	1.26	1.06	1.14	1.38	0.93	1.01	1.06	—	Income Ratio %
—	31	90	68	67	72	68	56	42	30	31	—	Turnover Rate %
—	—	47	198	546	775	851	989	1,322	1,140	1,480	2,463	Net Assets $mil

Performance 12-31-04

	1st Qtr	2nd Qtr	3rd Qtr	4th Qtr	Total
2000	0.40	-1.20	5.82	10.27	15.75
2001	-0.57	5.72	-13.11	11.25	1.60
2002	4.98	-11.05	-18.66	9.82	-16.58
2003	-7.20	17.80	3.82	14.54	30.00
2004	1.65	3.24	-0.62	10.61	15.36

Trailing	Total Return%	+/- S&P 500	+/- Russ 1000 VI	%Rank Cat	Growth of $10,000
3 Mo	10.61	1.38	0.23	18	11,061
6 Mo	9.92	2.73	-2.16	36	10,992
1 Yr	15.36	4.49	-1.13	20	11,536
3 Yr Avg	7.75	4.17	-0.82	21	12,510
5 Yr Avg	8.03	10.33	2.76	16	14,714
10 Yr Avg	14.83	2.76	1.00	5	39,862
15 Yr Avg	—	—	—	—	—

Tax Analysis	Tax-Adj Rtn%	%Rank Cat	Tax-Cost Rat	%Rank Cat
3 Yr (estimated)	7.35	15	0.37	25
5 Yr (estimated)	7.23	14	0.74	39
10 Yr (estimated)	12.79	4	1.78	49

Potential Capital Gain Exposure: 14% of assets

Rating and Risk

Time Period	Load-Adj Return %	Morningstar Rtn vs Cat	Morningstar Risk vs Cat	Morningstar Risk-Adj Rating
1 Yr	15.36			
3 Yr	7.75	+Avg	+Avg	★★★★
5 Yr	8.03	+Avg	+Avg	★★★★
10 Yr	14.83	High	High	★★★★★
Incept	14.78			

Other Measures	Standard Index S&P 500	Best Fit Index Russ 1000 VI
Alpha	4.1	-1.1
Beta	1.05	1.08
R-Squared	91	95
Standard Deviation	17.74	
Mean	7.75	
Sharpe Ratio	0.36	

Portfolio Analysis 09-30-04

Share change since 06-04 Total Stocks:114	Sector	PE	YTD Ret%	% Assets
⊕ Gen Elec	Ind Mtrls	22.8	20.68	2.62
⊕ J P Morgan Chase	Financial	19.4	9.97	1.79
⊕ Total SA ADR	Energy	17.0	23.39	1.58
⊕ Bank of America	Financial	12.3	21.50	1.50
⊕ Microsoft	Software	36.1	8.95	1.36
⊕ Liberty Media	Media	—	11.56	1.32
⊕ Marsh & McLennan Compani	Financial	13.4	-29.80	1.28
⊖ Nucor	Ind Mtrls	9.6	89.07	1.28
⊕ Union Pacific	Business	19.6	-1.28	1.28
⊕ Comcast	Media	—	-13.77	1.26
⊕ International Paper	Ind Mtrls	—	-0.20	1.22
⊕ Honeywell International	Ind Mtrls	20.5	8.21	1.20
⊕ St. Paul Travelers Compa	Financial	30.8	-3.15	1.19
Lockheed Martin	Ind Mtrls	19.9	9.97	1.19
US Bancorp	Financial	14.2	10.46	1.18
⊕ Royal Dutch Petroleum AD	Energy	—	14.31	1.17
⊕ Principal Financial Grou	Financial	16.0	25.56	1.16
⊕ DuPont De Nemours E.I.	Ind Mtrls	22.3	10.42	1.16
⊕ Merck	Health	11.4	-27.76	1.16
Baker Hughes	Energy	30.3	34.28	1.14

Current Investment Style

Value Blnd Growth / Large Mid Small

Market Cap	%
Giant	33.9
Large	40.4
Mid	24.9
Small	0.8
Micro	0.0
Avg $mil: 22,417	

Value Measures		Rel Category
Price/Earnings	15.63	1.04
Price/Book	2.08	0.92
Price/Sales	1.11	0.93
Price/Cash Flow	6.58	1.03
Dividend Yield %	1.94	0.95

Growth Measures	%	Rel Category
Long-Term Erngs	10.84	1.04
Book Value	2.56	0.45
Sales	1.69	0.40
Cash Flow	1.26	0.24
Historical Erngs	6.11	0.52

Profitability	%	Rel Category
Return on Equity	14.07	0.89
Return on Assets	6.72	0.86
Net Margin	8.33	0.82

Sector Weightings	% of Stocks	Rel S&P 500	3 Year High	3 Year Low
Info	18.54	0.86		
Software	1.88	0.44	2	0
Hardware	3.81	0.37	6	3
Media	10.04	2.61	11	9
Telecom	2.81	0.89	5	2
Service	41.02	0.88		
Health	8.30	0.66	10	8
Consumer	5.47	0.60	10	5
Business	4.52	1.12	6	4
Financial	22.73	1.09	23	18
Mfg	40.43	1.26		
Goods	10.56	1.13	11	7
Ind Mtrls	18.18	1.43	21	15
Energy	8.43	1.18	8	7
Utilities	3.26	1.10	3	2

Composition

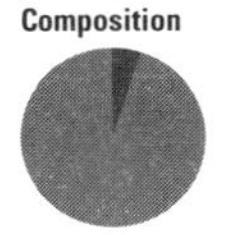

Cash	4.8
Stocks	94.8
Bonds	0.0
Other	0.4
Foreign (% of Stock)	8.5

Morningstar's Take by Christopher Davis 01-07-05

This offering has a lot going for it, but it faces a tough competitor from within its own family.

Since coming aboard in early 2003, T. Rowe Price Value manager John Linehan has slowly put his imprint on the portfolio. While former manager Brian Rogers gave the fund an all-cap flavor, Linehan has gradually pushed the fund into large-cap territory (though its average market cap still remains below the category average). Moreover, Rogers often gravitated to stocks that were inexpensive but also had shaky fundamentals. Linehan, by contrast, is more likely to emphasize higher-quality names with strong balance sheets.

There's nothing inherently wrong with those changes, but they do put the fund in closer competition with Rogers' longtime charge, T. Rowe Price Equity-Income. However, Equity-Income's mandate is to focus on higher-yielding stocks, and Linehan is bound by no such limitation. So while there is considerable overlap between Equity-Income and Value--the funds share about 65% of their portfolios in common--Linehan has the freedom to buy cheap stocks that pay little or nothing in the way of dividends. Harley Davidson featured a paltry yield when Linehan scooped up the stock in mid-2004, but he liked its market-leading position and relatively low price tag.

Linehan has fared well since taking charge. From his March 2003 start through December 2004, the fund topped the large-value average by four percentage points annually. We also think Linehan's continued success is likely: He was an experienced analyst prior to taking the helm here and has been a comanager of the company's institutional large-value accounts.

With a slightly less conservative strategy than Equity-Income, this offering could hold more appeal for investors willing to take on more risk. However, we think its sibling's veteran management and superior long-term record make it a better choice for most large-value investors.

Address:	100 E Pratt St Baltimore MD 21202 800-638-5660
Web Address:	www.troweprice.com
Inception:	09-30-94*
Advisor:	T. Rowe Price Associates, Inc.
Subadvisor:	None
NTF Plans:	N/A

Minimum Purchase:	$2500	Add: $100	IRA: $1000
Min Auto Inv Plan:	$50	Add: $50	
Sales Fees:	No-load		
Management Fee:	0.67%		
Actual Fees:	Mgt:0.67%	Dist:	
Expense Projections:	3Yr:$309	5Yr:$536	10Yr:$1190
Income Distrib:	Annually		

TCW Galileo Opportunity N

Ticker	Load	NAV	Yield	Total Assets	Mstar Category
TGONX	None	$13.73	0.0%	$73 mil	Small Blend

Governance and Management

Fiduciary Grade: C

Portfolio Manager(s)

Manager Diane Jaffee has been on board since November 1995. She has six dedicated analysts assisting her with stock selection. Before becoming a money manager, Jaffee had worked as a research analyst since 1982, and she is a seasoned stock-picker. Former comanager William Church departed this offering in 2003 to run a hedge fund for TCW.

Strategy

Manager Diane Jaffee and her team screen for stocks that look cheap based on a variety of metrics, including price/earnings, price/cash-flow, and price/book ratios. The team also looks for companies that are trading at discounts to their private market values. If a stock looks cheap based on any of these criteria, the managers follow up with more fundamental research, looking for some catalyst for growth, such as a new management team or product line. All new positions comprise 0.25% of assets when they're added to the portfolio.

Historical Profile

Return Average
Risk Above Avg
Rating ★★★ Neutral

Investment Style
Equity
Stock %

89% 98% 88% 99% 94% 100% 100% 93% 92%

▼ Manager Change
∇ Partial Manager Change

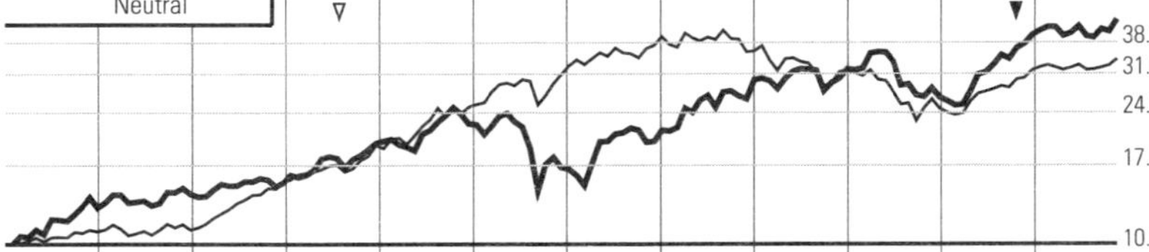

Growth of $10,000
— Investment Values of Fund
— Investment Values of S&P 500

Performance Quartile (within Category)

1993	1994	1995	1996	1997	1998	1999	2000	2001	2002	2003	12-04	History
7.32	7.12	8.04	8.79	7.95	5.93	7.66	10.32	10.41	8.66	12.92	13.73	NAV
31.57	3.89	15.56	25.18	11.30	-25.38	29.07	39.12	7.22	-16.81	50.17	13.56	Total Return %
21.51	2.58	-21.97	2.24	-22.05	-53.95	8.03	48.22	19.10	5.28	21.50	2.69	+/-S&P 500
12.69	5.71	-12.89	8.69	-11.06	-22.83	7.81	42.14	4.73	3.67	2.92	-4.77	+/-Russ 2000
0.00	0.00	0.00	0.00	0.00	0.00	0.00	0.00	0.00	0.00	0.00	0.00	Income Return %
31.57	3.89	15.56	25.18	11.30	-25.38	29.07	39.12	7.22	-16.81	50.17	13.56	Capital Return %
1	9	90	34	95	98	19	2	51	62	18	89	Total Rtn % Rank Cat
0.00	0.00	0.00	0.00	0.00	0.00	0.00	0.00	0.00	0.00	0.00	0.00	Income $
2.51	0.47	0.19	1.23	1.75	0.00	0.00	0.30	0.63	0.00	0.08	0.92	Capital Gains $
1.63	1.47	1.43	1.39	1.38	1.46	1.59	1.61	1.59	1.31	1.50	—	Expense Ratio %
-1.10	-0.66	-0.28	-0.46	-0.53	-0.67	-0.67	-0.52	-0.68	-0.43	-0.51	—	Income Ratio %
167	152	148	182	159	124	150	164	111	42	56	—	Turnover Rate %
19	34	40	45	53	23	21	22	20	19	26	41	Net Assets $mil

Performance 12-31-04

	1st Qtr	2nd Qtr	3rd Qtr	4th Qtr	Total
2000	15.35	8.65	3.08	7.68	39.12
2001	-5.70	13.86	-13.36	15.26	7.22
2002	10.85	-5.29	-19.67	-1.37	-16.81
2003	-4.73	23.76	9.11	16.74	50.17
2004	5.19	0.59	-1.98	9.49	13.56

Trailing	Total Return%	+/- S&P 500	+/- Russ 2000	%Rank Cat	Growth of $10,000
3 Mo	9.49	0.26	-4.60	94	10,949
6 Mo	7.33	0.14	-3.50	91	10,733
1 Yr	13.56	2.69	-4.77	89	11,356
3 Yr Avg	12.36	8.78	0.88	54	14,185
5 Yr Avg	16.17	18.47	9.56	22	21,158
10 Yr Avg	12.62	0.55	1.08	67	32,821
15 Yr Avg	14.15	3.22	3.06	20	72,801

Tax Analysis	Tax-Adj Rtn%	%Rank Cat	Tax-Cost Rat	%Rank Cat
3 Yr (estimated)	11.94	46	0.37	26
5 Yr (estimated)	15.26	17	0.78	34
10 Yr (estimated)	10.90	61	1.53	34

Potential Capital Gain Exposure: 22% of assets

Rating and Risk

Time Period	Load-Adj Return %	Morningstar Rtn vs Cat	Morningstar Risk vs Cat	Morningstar Risk-Adj Rating
1 Yr	13.56			
3 Yr	12.36	Avg	+Avg	★★★
5 Yr	16.17	+Avg	Avg	★★★★
10 Yr	12.62	Avg	+Avg	★★
Incept	13.61			

Other Measures	Standard Index S&P 500	Best Fit Index Russ 2000 VL
Alpha	9.3	-3.6
Beta	0.98	1.01
R-Squared	61	91
Standard Deviation	21.09	
Mean	12.36	
Sharpe Ratio	0.53	

Portfolio Analysis 11-30-04

Share change since 10-04 Total Stocks:117	Sector	PE	YTD Ret%	% Assets
⊖ Eclipsys	Software	—	75.52	3.88
Lindsay Manufacturing	Ind Mtrls	29.9	3.38	2.49
Too	Consumer	30.8	44.91	2.21
Solectron	Hardware	—	-9.81	1.75
⊖ Calgon Carbon	Ind Mtrls	48.2	48.97	1.75
United Surgical Partners	Health	34.1	24.55	1.72
Wind River Systems	Software	—	54.68	1.71
Kirby	Business	21.8	27.24	1.61
Warnaco Group	Goods	—	35.42	1.61
AGCO	Ind Mtrls	12.1	8.69	1.57
⊖ Agrium	Ind Mtrls	—	3.13	1.39
Wabtec	Ind Mtrls	29.8	25.35	1.36
NetIQ	Software	—	-7.85	1.31
Avista Corporation	Utilities	29.0	0.39	1.28
Darden Restaurants	Consumer	20.1	32.28	1.27
Shaw Group	Ind Mtrls	—	31.06	1.23
Bank Mutual	Financial	34.9	8.58	1.20
Spanish Broadcasting Sys	Media	—	0.10	1.19
Fuelcell Energy	Ind Mtrls	—	-23.96	1.16
THQ	Software	32.1	35.66	1.15

Current Investment Style

Value Blnd Growth / Large Mid Small

Market Cap	%
Giant	0.0
Large	0.6
Mid	31.5
Small	52.8
Micro	15.1

Avg $mil: 1,013

Value Measures		Rel Category
Price/Earnings	21.09	1.22
Price/Book	1.69	0.85
Price/Sales	0.78	0.82
Price/Cash Flow	6.99	1.19
Dividend Yield %	0.71	0.86

Growth Measures	%	Rel Category
Long-Term Erngs	17.76	1.31
Book Value	0.34	0.06
Sales	2.30	0.53
Cash Flow	-6.89	NMF
Historical Erngs	3.11	0.42

Profitability	%	Rel Category
Return on Equity	1.15	0.11
Return on Assets	1.69	0.34
Net Margin	3.00	0.41

Sector Weightings	% of Stocks	Rel S&P 500	3 Year High	3 Year Low
Info	22.40	1.04		
Software	10.38	2.41	11	3
Hardware	7.86	0.77	11	3
Media	3.27	0.85	4	1
Telecom	0.89	0.28	1	0
Service	39.46	0.85		
Health	11.66	0.93	16	8
Consumer	10.18	1.12	11	7
Business	3.08	0.76	8	3
Financial	14.54	0.70	15	6
Mfg	38.12	1.19		
Goods	6.51	0.70	7	1
Ind Mtrls	23.45	1.85	37	23
Energy	5.65	0.79	22	6
Utilities	2.51	0.85	3	1

Composition

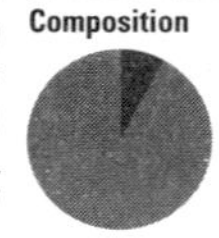

Cash	7.8
Stocks	92.2
Bonds	0.0
Other	0.0
Foreign (% of Stock)	2.8

Morningstar's Take by Terence Geenty 11-29-04

TCW Galileo Opportunity remains a solid offering.

Manager Diane Jaffee has been at the helm of this small-blend offering since late 1995. She looks for cheap companies that have improving fundamentals or are in a weak period of their earnings cycle. Jaffee starts by screening stocks based on a variety of valuation characteristics, then follows this up with a more qualitative evaluation of the remaining companies' growth potential.

This approach tends to keep the fund from loading up on pricey technology and health-care stocks. Jaffee didn't add notably to the fund's hardware position as valuations dipped this year, because she didn't see strong cash flows that would signal improved growth prospects. That doesn't mean the fund avoids these areas altogether, though. Jaffee increased the fund's stake in software stocks in late 2003 because she thought those companies would grow as businesses upgraded their computer systems. Some of her picks, including top holdings Eclipsys and Wind River Systems, have nearly doubled in value since, and have raised this fund's stake in the software sector to double the small-blend average.

Still, these moves haven't kept the fund's 9.83% year-to-date gain from lagging the category norm by 5 percentage points through Nov. 24, 2004. The fund has been hurt in part by its relatively slim stake in financial services stocks.

Disappointing short-term results shouldn't concern investors, in our opinion. Jaffe and her team have proven to be effective stock-pickers over time. She has produced respectable results during her tenure here and has delivered strong performance at her large-cap charges, TCW Galileo Diversified Value and TCW Galileo Dividend Focused. Plus, this fund's modest asset base should keep it nimble enough to navigate the small-cap space.

We think experienced management and a proven strategy make this a decent option.

Address:	865 S Figueroa St Los Angeles CA 90017 800-386-3829
Web Address:	www.tcw.com
Inception:	03-31-88
Advisor:	TCW Investment Management Co.
Subadvisor:	None
NTF Plans:	Fidelity Retail-NTF, Schwab OneSource

Minimum Purchase:	$2000	Add: $250	IRA: $500
Min Auto Inv Plan:	$2000	Add: $100	
Sales Fees:	No-load, 0.25%S		
Management Fee:	0.90%		
Actual Fees:	Mgt:0.90%	Dist:0.25%	
Expense Projections:	3Yr:$563	5Yr:$970	10Yr:$2105
Income Distrib:	Annually		

TCW Galileo Select Eq I

Ticker	Load	NAV	Yield	Total Assets	Mstar Category
TGCEX	None	$19.5€	0.0%	$4,192 mil	Large Growth

Governance and Management

Fiduciary Grade: C

Portfolio Manager(s)

Longtime manager Glen Bickerstaff will be stepping down as senior portfolio manager on Jan. 1, 2005. He will continue to serve in a supervisory role on the fund, but day-to-day management will be turned over to Craig Blum and Steve Burlingame. Blum and Burlingame have worked closely with Bickerstaff since 2002 but will have only one year of portfolio management experience at the time they take over.

Strategy

Glen Bickerstaff and comanagers Craig Blum and Steve Burlingame use a combination of top-down and bottom-up analysis. They first look for major secular trends and then focus on businesses that they think will benefit. Bickerstaff and his team also want to see companies with unique business models or market niches and favor those with lots of free cash flow. They stick with their holdings over the long haul, so the fund's turnover is fairly low.

Historical Profile

Return: High
Risk: High
Rating: ★★★★ Above Avg

Investment Style: Equity, Stock %: 100% | 100% | 98% | 100% | 100% | 100% | 100% | 99% | 96%

▼ Manager Change
▽ Partial Manager Change

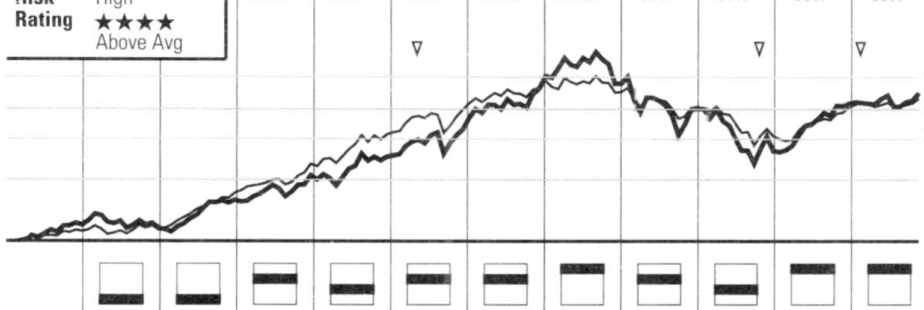

Growth of $10,000
— Investment Values of Fund
— Investment Values of S&P 500

Performance Quartile (within Category)

History

1993	1994	1995	1996	1997	1998	1999	2000	2001	2002	2003	12-04	History
11.81	10.93	13.77	16.39	14.22	16.91	23.19	20.52	16.57	11.54	17.34	19.58	NAV
18.77*	-7.04	26.45	20.59	22.70	37.97	42.95	-6.21	-19.25	-30.36	50.26	12.92	Total Return %
—	-8.35	-11.08	-2.35	-10.65	9.40	21.91	2.89	-7.37	-8.27	21.59	2.05	+/-S&P 500
—	-9.66	-10.73	-2.53	-7.79	-0.74	9.79	16.21	1.17	-2.48	20.51	6.62	+/-Russ 1000Gr
0.00	0.41	0.47	0.15	0.00	0.00	0.00	0.00	0.00	0.00	0.00	0.00	Income Return %
—	-7.45	25.98	20.44	22.70	37.97	42.95	-6.21	-19.25	-30.36	50.26	12.92	Capital Return %
—	89	81	42	73	26	32	21	46	74	3	9	Total Rtn % Rank Cat
0.03	0.05	0.05	0.02	0.00	0.00	0.00	0.00	0.00	0.00	0.00	0.00	Income $
0.00	0.00	0.00	0.20	5.76	2.45	0.92	1.32	0.00	0.00	0.00	0.00	Capital Gains $
1.00	0.91	0.85	0.82	0.83	0.86	0.88	0.85	0.87	0.86	0.89	—	Expense Ratio %
0.55	0.44	0.48	0.18	0.08	-0.14	-0.39	-0.31	-0.52	-0.56	-0.56	—	Income Ratio %
—	—	54	40	39	104	48	52	12	3	22	—	Turnover Rate %
56	123	190	232	117	222	310	572	1,139	992	2,096	2,799	Net Assets $mil

Performance 12-31-04

	1st Qtr	2nd Qtr	3rd Qtr	4th Qtr	Total
2000	16.47	0.15	-1.71	-18.69	-6.21
2001	-21.78	10.34	-25.75	26.01	-19.25
2002	-0.66	-21.93	-19.22	11.18	-30.36
2003	4.51	20.07	7.53	11.37	50.26
2004	-0.12	7.16	-5.44	11.57	12.92

Trailing	Total Return%	+/- S&P 500	+/- Russ 1000Gr	%Rank Cat	Growth of $10,000
3 Mo	11.57	2.34	2.40	20	11,157
6 Mo	5.50	-1.69	2.03	40	10,550
1 Yr	12.92	2.05	6.62	9	11,292
3 Yr Avg	5.72	2.14	5.90	7	11,816
5 Yr Avg	-2.20	0.10	7.09	10	8,947
10 Yr Avg	12.69	0.62	3.10	7	33,026
15 Yr Avg	—	—	—	—	—

Tax Analysis	Tax-Adj Rtn%	%Rank Cat	Tax-Cost Rat	%Rank Cat
3 Yr (estimated)	5.72	5	0.00	1
5 Yr (estimated)	-2.52	9	0.33	20
10 Yr (estimated)	11.29	7	1.24	36

Potential Capital Gain Exposure: 15% of assets

Rating and Risk

Time Period	Load-Adj Return %	Morningstar Rtn vs Cat	Morningstar Risk vs Cat	Morningstar Risk-Adj Rating
1 Yr	12.92			
3 Yr	5.72	High	High	★★★★
5 Yr	-2.20	+Avg	High	★★★
10 Yr	12.69	High	+Avg	★★★★
Incept	11.55			

Other Measures	Standard Index S&P 500	Best Fit Index PSE Tech 100
Alpha	2.2	1.6
Beta	1.36	0.83
R-Squared	85	94
Standard Deviation	23.90	
Mean	5.72	
Sharpe Ratio	0.18	

Portfolio Analysis 11-30-04

Share change since 10-04 Total Stocks: 27	Sector	PE	YTD Ret%	% Assets
Progressive	Financial	11.7	1.63	8.48
Yahoo	Media	95.1	67.36	7.76
eBay	Consumer	81.6	80.07	7.58
Network Appliance	Hardware	67.5	62.52	6.24
Qualcomm	Hardware	42.0	58.20	5.69
Amazon.com	Consumer	55.5	-15.83	5.04
Genentech	Health	78.6	16.36	4.78
XM Satellite Radio Holdi	Media	—	43.10	4.58
Maxim Integrated Product	Hardware	27.9	-13.87	4.09
Dell	Hardware	34.0	24.01	3.77
Starbucks	Consumer	60.4	88.06	3.75
Amgen	Health	37.7	3.82	3.32
Symantec	Software	34.5	49.33	3.10
⊕ Apollo Group A	Consumer	NMF	19.02	2.98
Xilinx	Hardware	25.2	-22.82	2.36
⊕ Electronic Arts	Software	30.9	29.36	2.72
AFLAC	Financial	21.6	11.20	2.30
Pixar	Media	29.3	23.55	2.07
Walgreen	Consumer	31.6	6.03	1.90
Applied Materials	Hardware	20.7	-23.80	1.82

Current Investment Style

Value Blnd Growth; Large Mid Small

Market Cap	%
Giant	41.6
Large	50.1
Mid	8.3
Small	0.0
Micro	0.0
Avg $mil: 29,873	

Value Measures		Rel Category
Price/Earnings	29.83	1.40
Price/Book	5.08	1.57
Price/Sales	3.83	1.78
Price/Cash Flow	14.76	1.34
Dividend Yield %	0.27	0.35

Growth Measures	%	Rel Category
Long-Term Erngs	17.11	1.22
Book Value	20.36	1.60
Sales	16.15	1.90
Cash Flow	30.28	1.83
Historical Erngs	37.44	2.59

Profitability	%	Rel Category
Return on Equity	17.25	0.96
Return on Assets	10.29	1.10
Net Margin	17.13	1.39

Sector Weightings	% of Stocks	Rel S&P 500	3 Year High	3 Year Low
Info	48.72	2.27		
Software	6.09	1.42	12	0
Hardware	27.55	2.70	36	24
Media	15.08	3.93	15	2
Telecom	0.00	0.00	0	0
Service	47.61	1.03		
Health	8.47	0.68	25	8
Consumer	24.08	2.65	24	6
Business	0.00	0.00	7	0
Financial	15.06	0.73	26	15
Mfg	3.67	0.11		
Goods	1.89	0.20	2	0
Ind Mtrls	1.78	0.14	3	2
Energy	0.00	0.00	0	0
Utilities	0.00	0.00	0	0

Composition

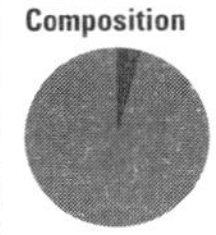

Cash	4.4
Stocks	95.6
Bonds	0.0
Other	0.0
Foreign (% of Stock)	0.0

Morningstar's Take by Terence Geenty 10-15-04

We don't think the manager change here eliminates this fund's appeal, but it raises some big questions.

Senior manager Glen Bickerstaff will be stepping down at TCW Galileo Select Equities on Jan. 1, 2005. Replacing him are co-managers Craig Blum and Steve Burlingame.

This represents a significant change for this fund. Bickerstaff has led this charge for more than six years with very strong results. Since taking the helm in May 1998, this fund has posted returns that beat more than 90% of its large-growth rivals. Bickerstaff has built that record using a compact portfolio of 30 positions or fewer, and he hasn't hesitated to load up on companies he likes. (As of Aug. 31, 2004, auto-insurer Progressive accounted for nearly 9% of assets.) The fund's turnover is also low, so once a name is in the fund, it tends to stay there. Thus, stock-picking is key here.

In that regard, it's difficult to assess the capabilities of Blum and Burlingame at this juncture. Both have worked closely with Bickerstaff since 2002, but each will have only one year of experience as a portfolio manager at the time Bickerstaff steps down. Further, neither Blum nor Burlingame was available for an interview at the time of this write-up.

That said, we don't expect this fund to change much. Bickerstaff will continue to work at TCW in a supervisory role, and will meet with the management team to provide guidance and advice. Additionally, Blum and Burlingame are well versed in the investment process here, and a TCW spokesman says they are committed to maintaining a consistent approach throughout this transition. Finally, given the fund's typically low turnover and focus on strong long-term holdings, any changes here are likely to be gradual.

While it's cause for concern, we don't think Bickerstaff's impending departure is reason to sell this fund. However, it's hard to recommend this fund until we learn more about Blum and Burlingame's abilities.

Address:	865 S Figueroa St Los Angeles CA 90017 800-386-3829
Web Address:	www.tcw.com
Inception:	03-01-93 *
Advisor:	TCW Investment Management Co.
Subadvisor:	None
NTF Plans:	N/A

Minimum Purchase:	$2000	Add: $250	IRA: $500
Min Auto Inv Plan:	$2000	Add: $100	
Sales Fees:	No-load		
Management Fee:	0.75%		
Actual Fees:	Mgt:0.75%	Dist:	
Expense Projections:	3Yr:$284	5Yr:$493	10Yr:$1096
Income Distrib:	Annually		

TCW Galileo Tot Ret Bd I

Ticker	Load	NAV	Yield	SEC Yield	Total Assets	Mstar Category
TGLMX	None	$9.61	4.7%	5.30%	$254 mil	Intermediate-Term Bond

Governance and Management

Fiduciary Grade: B

Portfolio Manager(s)

Jeffrey Gundlach, who has primary responsibility for this portfolio, has been managing it since its 1993 inception. He has been with TCW since 1985. He's supported by TCW CIO Philip Barach and mortgage-backed securities specialist Frederick Horton.

Strategy

Management keeps this mortgage-backed securities fund's duration at about two thirds of the way between the (shorter) Lehman Brothers Mortgage Backed Securities Index and the Lehman Brothers Aggregate Bond Index, which is the benchmark for most core bond funds. That design is intended to help keep the fund competitive with both basic government mortgage funds and intermediate-term bond portfolios. In that pursuit, the fund buys lots of out-of-index sectors such as CMOs, private-label CMOs, ARMs, and inverse floaters.

Historical Profile

Return High
Risk Below Avg
Rating ★★★★★ Highest

Investment Style
Fixed Income
Income Rtn %Rank Cat

3 1 1 1 18 14 2 1 8

▼ Manager Change
▽ Partial Manager Change

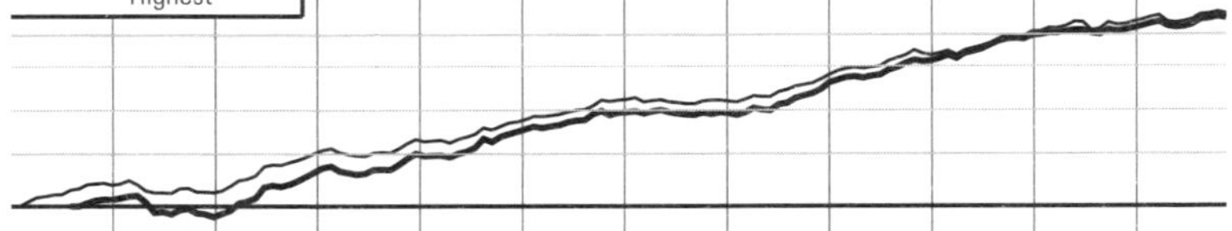

Growth of $10,000
— Investment Values of Fund
— Investment Values of LB Aggr

Performance Quartile (within Category)

1993	1994	1995	1996	1997	1998	1999	2000	2001	2002	2003	12-04	History
10.07	8.73	9.79	9.56	9.84	9.58	8.84	9.39	9.65	9.96	9.58	9.61	NAV
3.51*	-6.18	20.80	5.08	11.93	7.23	-0.46	13.58	9.41	11.04	3.06	5.19	Total Return %
—	-3.26	2.33	1.45	2.28	-1.46	0.36	1.95	0.97	0.79	-1.04	0.85	+/-LB Aggr
—	-1.67	-0.63	2.39	2.50	-2.91	2.42	1.14	0.59	-1.99	-2.91	-0.11	+/-LB 5-10YR
0.00	7.49	8.24	7.34	8.27	10.04	7.54	7.00	6.58	7.72	6.99	4.85	Income Return %
—	-13.67	12.56	-2.26	3.66	-2.81	-8.00	6.58	2.83	3.32	-3.93	0.34	Capital Return %
—	90	13	12	2	62	26	1	9	3	82	10	Total Rtn % Rank Cat
0.28	0.73	0.69	0.70	0.76	0.95	0.70	0.60	0.60	0.72	0.68	0.46	Income $
0.00	0.00	0.00	0.00	0.05	0.00	0.00	0.00	0.00	0.00	0.00	0.00	Capital Gains $
0.65	0.65	0.68	0.68	0.67	0.70	0.69	0.77	0.74	0.70	0.51	0.44	Expense Ratio %
5.37	8.03	7.88	7.15	7.77	8.52	6.62	6.63	6.31	7.78	5.76	4.73	Income Ratio %
—	—	24	39	16	28	28	8	11	26	60	33	Turnover Rate %
25	63	77	114	78	92	90	83	79	127	144	176	Net Assets $mil

Performance 12-31-04

	1st Qtr	2nd Qtr	3rd Qtr	4th Qtr	Total
2000	2.18	1.49	3.75	5.57	13.58
2001	2.46	0.69	4.97	1.03	9.41
2002	0.98	3.93	4.22	1.52	11.04
2003	1.01	1.19	0.20	0.63	3.06
2004	2.67	-2.01	3.39	1.12	5.19

Trailing	Total Return%	+/- LB Aggr	+/- LB 5-10YR	%Rank Cat	Growth of $10,000
3 Mo	1.12	0.17	0.14	32	10,112
6 Mo	4.56	0.38	-1.01	23	10,456
1 Yr	5.19	0.85	-0.11	10	10,519
3 Yr Avg	6.38	0.19	-1.67	19	12,039
5 Yr Avg	8.39	0.68	-0.68	5	14,960
10 Yr Avg	8.54	0.82	0.08	2	22,693
15 Yr Avg	—	—	—	—	—

Tax Analysis	Tax-Adj Rtn%	%Rank Cat	Tax-Cost Rat	%Rank Cat
3 Yr (estimated)	3.99	29	2.25	90
5 Yr (estimated)	5.84	6	2.35	83
10 Yr (estimated)	5.57	5	2.74	97

Potential Capital Gain Exposure: 1% of assets

Rating and Risk

Time Period	Load-Adj Return %	Morningstar Rtn vs Cat	Morningstar Risk vs Cat	Morningstar Risk-Adj Rating
1 Yr	5.19			
3 Yr	6.38	+Avg	Low	★★★★
5 Yr	8.39	High	-Avg	★★★★★
10 Yr	8.54	High	Avg	★★★★★
Incept	7.09			

Other Measures	Standard Index LB Aggr	Best Fit Index LB 1-5 YR GOVT
Alpha	1.7	2.3
Beta	0.66	1.12
R-Squared	81	86
Standard Deviation	3.35	
Mean	6.38	
Sharpe Ratio	1.52	

Portfolio Analysis 11-30-04

Total Fixed-Income:81	Date of Maturity	Amount $000	Value $000	% Net Assets
FNMA 2.375%	12-15-05	10,000	9,942	3.82
FHLMC CMO 3%	01-15-21	10,000	9,858	3.79
FHLMC CMO 4.5%	07-15-23	8,000	7,471	2.87
FHLMC CMO 7%	05-15-32	6,890	7,461	2.87
FNMA CMO 4%	09-25-17	7,419	7,276	2.80
FNMA FRN	04-01-33	7,097	7,079	2.72
GNMA 7%	08-20-34	6,556	6,970	2.68
FNMA 5.5%	07-01-33	6,663	6,746	2.59
FHLMC CMO 4%	09-15-18	7,000	6,355	2.44
FNMA 4%	03-01-19	6,499	6,342	2.44
FNMA FRN	02-01-33	5,419	5,482	2.11
FNMA FRN	02-01-33	5,131	5,208	2.00
GNMA FRN	07-20-34	5,151	5,116	1.97
FHLMC FRN	11-01-34	5,049	5,063	1.95
FHLMC CMO	09-15-33	5,736	4,915	1.89
FNMA 5.5%	02-01-23	4,769	4,892	1.88
FNMA CMO 4.5%	05-25-34	4,992	4,876	1.87
Structured Asset Secs 20	04-25-33	4,799	4,834	1.86
Mastr Asset Tr 2003-8 CM	09-25-33	4,699	4,741	1.82
FNMA FRN	01-01-33	4,563	4,621	1.78

Current Investment Style

Duration
Short Int Long
Quality High Med Low

[1] figure provided by fund

Avg Eff Duration[1]	3.9 Yrs
Avg Eff Maturity	4.3 Yrs
Avg Credit Quality	AAA
Avg Wtd Coupon	3.96%
Avg Wtd Price	97.82% of par

Coupon Range	% of Bonds	Rel Cat
0% PIK	26.3	6.5
0% to 6%	80.3	1.3
6% to 8%	16.5	0.6
8% to 10%	1.9	0.3
More than 10%	1.2	1.1

1.00=Category Average

Credit Analysis	% bonds 11-30-04		
US Govt	0	BB	0
AAA	100	B	0
AA	0	Below B	0
A	0	NR/NA	0
BBB	0		

Sector Breakdown	% of assets
US Treasuries	0
TIPS	0
US Agency	4
Mortgage Pass-Throughs	37
Mortgage CMO	47
Mortgage ARM	0
US Corporate	0
Asset-Backed	0
Convertible	0
Municipal	0
Corporate Inflation-Protected	0
Foreign Corporate	0
Foreign Govt	0

Composition			
Cash	12.0	Bonds	88.0
Stocks	0.0	Other	0.0

Special Securities	
Restricted/Illiquid Secs	0
Exotic Mortgage-Backed	0
Emerging-Markets Secs	0
Options/Futures/Warrants	No

Morningstar's Take by Eric Jacobson 10-25-04

TCW Galileo Total Return Bond is successfully running a slow, deliberate strategy.

We don't suggest that the execution here is in any way simplistic. In fact, the fund's setup itself requires some explanation. Manager Jeffrey Gundlach's goal here is to hit a sweet spot between bond funds that benchmark themselves off of the market-standard Lehman Brothers Aggregate benchmark--by keeping the fund's rate sensitivity closer to that bogy--and those focusing on GNMA funds--by filling the fund up with mortgages. His hope is to beat both groups over the long term.

That's no easy feat, as it requires buying just the right securities, and Gundlach's long-term success relies quite a bit on understanding the vagaries and nuances of the mortgage market. As such, this is no plain-vanilla fund. Its holdings range from simple mortgages to a smattering of complex derivatives. The good news is that Gundlach's been working with them for years and has demonstrated a strong rein on risk while also focusing on unloved bonds that offer lots of value.

That's what his latest tactic involves. Although market yields have actually fallen a bit in the past year, many investors--and the mortgage models they use--remain convinced that rising rates and lower prepayments are on the way. That's been the state of the market for some time, though, and Gundlach has responded by holding bonds that are priced accordingly, but that are currently prepaying at higher speeds than the models suggest. Such issues have generated above-market yields, thus helping inch up the fund's income and total returns. Its 6% gain for the past 12 months has thus beaten that of the average intermediate-bond fund, as well as the Lehman Aggregate.

Such techniques are emblematic of the fund's historical style, and they've helped it earn a terrific record of top-quartile long-term returns. An ultracompetitive expense ratio only sweetens the deal. The fund may lag when mortgage funds do (as in 2003), but it's a winner overall.

Address:	865 S Figueroa St Los Angeles CA 90017 800-386-3829
Web Address:	www.tcw.com
Inception:	06-18-93 *
Advisor:	TCW Investment Management Co.
Subadvisor:	None
NTF Plans:	N/A

Minimum Purchase:	$2000	Add: $250	IRA: $500
Min Auto Inv Plan:	$2000	Add: $100	
Sales Fees:	No-load		
Management Fee:	0.50%		
Actual Fees:	Mgt:0.50%	Dist:	
Expense Projections:	3Yr:$221	5Yr:$384	10Yr:$859
Income Distrib:	Monthly		

TCW Galileo Value Added I

Ticker	Load	NAV	Yield	Total Assets	Mstar Category
TGSVX	None	$13.88	0.0%	$39 mil	Small Blend

Governance and Management

Fiduciary Grade: C

Portfolio Manager(s)

Experienced. Nicholas Galluccio and Susan Suvall have been running money together for nearly 20 years. They are also in charge of TCW Galileo Value Opportunities, which they run in a similar style. They've garnered topnotch returns at that offering since its inception in 1997. Four analysts assist Galluccio and Suvall.

Strategy

At this offering, comanagers Nicholas Galluccio and Susan Suvall use an approach that's similar to one they use at their other charge. The duo breaks up the portfolio into four categories: companies trading below liquidation value, turnaround stories, busted-growth stocks, and emerging-growth stocks. Like many money managers, they want to see high free cash flow and a strong balance sheet. They often delve into nontraditional value sectors, such as technology. They are committed to keeping the portfolio in the small-cap space and will sell a holding if its market cap gets too high.

Historical Profile

Return Low
Risk High
Rating ★ Lowest

Investment Style
Equity
Stock %

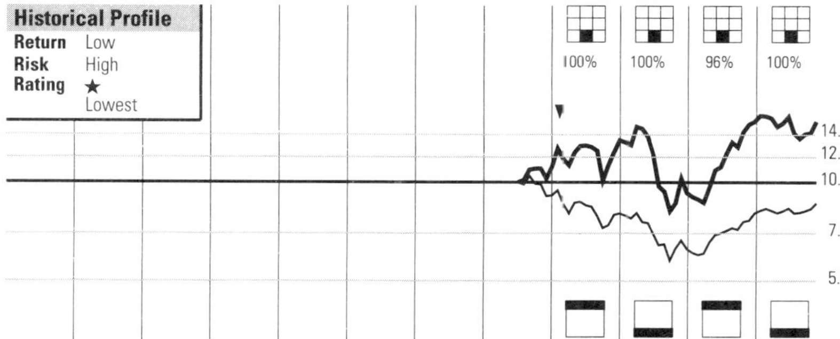

▼ Manager Change
▽ Partial Manager Change

Growth of $10,000
— Investment Values of Fund
— Investment Values of S&P 500

Performance Quartile (within Category)

1993	1994	1995	1996	1997	1998	1999	2000	2001	2002	2003	12-04	History
—	—	—	—	—	—	—	10.87	13.03	9.05	14.70	13.88	NAV
—	—	—	—	—	—	—	11.14*	20.14	-30.54	63.76	4.50	Total Return %
—	—	—	—	—	—	—	—	32.02	-8.45	35.09	-6.37	+/-S&P 500
—	—	—	—	—	—	—	—	17.65	-10.06	16.51	-13.83	+/-Russ 2000
—	—	—	—	—	—	—	0.00	0.26	0.00	0.00	0.00	Income Return %
—	—	—	—	—	—	—	—	19.88	-30.54	63.76	4.50	Capital Return %
—	—	—	—	—	—	—	—	13	96	4	99	Total Rtn % Rank Cat
—	—	—	—	—	—	—	0.00	0.03	0.00	0.00	0.00	Income $
—	—	—	—	—	—	—	0.24	0.00	0.00	0.12	1.46	Capital Gains $
—	—	—	—	—	—	—	1.55	1.58	1.56	1.61	—	Expense Ratio %
—	—	—	—	—	—	—	0.00	-0.85	-1.14	-1.16	—	Income Ratio %
—	—	—	—	—	—	—	32	77	72	68	—	Turnover Rate %
—	—	—	—	—	—	—	1	11	22	39	39	Net Assets $mil

Performance 12-31-04

	1st Qtr	2nd Qtr	3rd Qtr	4th Qtr	Total
2000	—	—	9.92	1.31	11.14 *
2001	1.01	14.66	-21.52	32.18	20.14
2002	9.75	-17.62	-32.34	13.55	-30.54
2003	-6.63	28.28	14.76	19.13	63.76
2004	2.31	1.00	-11.13	13.79	4.50

Trailing	Total Return%	+/- S&P 500	+/- Russ 2000	%Rank Cat	Growth of $10,000
3 Mo	13.79	4.56	-0.30	30	11,379
6 Mo	1.13	-6.06	-9.70	98	10,113
1 Yr	4.50	-6.37	-13.83	99	10,450
3 Yr Avg	5.93	2.35	-5.55	94	11,887
5 Yr Avg	—	—	—	—	—
10 Yr Avg	—	—	—	—	—
15 Yr Avg	—	—	—	—	—

Tax Analysis	Tax-Adj Rtn%	%Rank Cat	Tax-Cost Rat	%Rank Cat
3 Yr (estimated)	5.08	92	0.80	54
5 Yr (estimated)	—	—	—	—
10 Yr (estimated)	—	—	—	—

Potential Capital Gain Exposure: 19% of assets

Rating and Risk

Time Period	Load-Adj Return %	Morningstar Rtn vs Cat	Morningstar Risk vs Cat	Morningstar Risk-Adj Rating
1 Yr	4.50			
3 Yr	5.93	Low	High	★
5 Yr	—	—	—	—
10 Yr	—	—	—	—
Incept	10.69			

Other Measures	Standard Index S&P 500	Best Fit Index Russ 2000
Alpha	3.1	-7.4
Beta	1.58	1.40
R-Squared	72	92
Standard Deviation	30.65	
Mean	5.93	
Sharpe Ratio	0.15	

Portfolio Analysis 11-30-04

Share change since 10-04 Total Stocks:174	Sector	PE	YTD Ret%	% Assets
⊖ MKS Instruments	Hardware	17.3	-36.03	1.96
⊖ Kemet	Hardware	—	-34.62	1.87
⊖ Vishay Intertechnology	Hardware	21.3	-34.41	1.78
⊖ Belden CDT	Hardware	—	29.62	1.67
⊖ Mykrolis	Hardware	19.6	-11.88	1.50
⊖ MacDermid	Ind Mtrls	19.4	5.95	1.28
⊖ Bisys Group	Business	23.1	10.55	1.25
⊖ Pride International	Energy	—	10.19	1.21
⊖ Integrated Device Techno	Hardware	82.9	-32.67	1.10
⊖ Forest Oil	Energy	20.7	11.03	1.10
⊖ Merix	Hardware	—	-53.04	1.06
⊖ FEI	Hardware	59.0	-6.67	1.05
⊖ Varian Semiconductor Equ	Hardware	28.4	-15.87	1.04
⊖ Brooks Automation	Hardware	—	-27.46	1.04
⊖ Coherent	Health	—	27.90	1.02
⊖ Exar	Hardware	54.4	-17.26	1.01
⊖ Electro Scientific Indus	Hardware	15.4	-16.98	1.00
⊖ LeCroy	Ind Mtrls	26.9	29.09	0.99
⊖ Remec	Hardware	—	-15.67	0.99
⊖ ATMI	Hardware	31.4	-2.93	0.97

Current Investment Style

Value Blnd Growth (Large / Mid / Small)

Market Cap	%
Giant	0.0
Large	0.0
Mid	15.4
Small	61.1
Micro	23.4
Avg $mil: 718	

Value Measures		Rel Category
Price/Earnings	23.37	1.35
Price/Book	1.69	0.85
Price/Sales	0.94	0.99
Price/Cash Flow	6.14	1.05
Dividend Yield %	0.50	0.60

Growth Measures	%	Rel Category
Long-Term Erngs	16.61	1.23
Book Value	-0.26	NMF
Sales	-1.20	NMF
Cash Flow	12.07	2.44
Historical Erngs	-2.51	NMF

Profitability	%	Rel Category
Return on Equity	3.72	0.36
Return on Assets	1.43	0.29
Net Margin	1.29	0.18

Sector Weightings	% of Stocks	Rel S&P 500	3 Year High	3 Year Low
Info	40.81	1.90		
Software	5.11	1.19	8	4
Hardware	32.49	3.19	41	28
Media	2.88	0.75	5	1
Telecom	0.33	0.10	1	0
Service	31.67	0.68		
Health	6.70	0.54	7	3
Consumer	9.41	1.04	13	7
Business	8.36	2.06	10	6
Financial	7.20	0.35	7	3
Mfg	27.51	0.86		
Goods	5.61	0.60	6	3
Ind Mtrls	18.06	1.43	19	16
Energy	3.84	0.54	10	3
Utilities	0.00	0.00	0	0

Composition

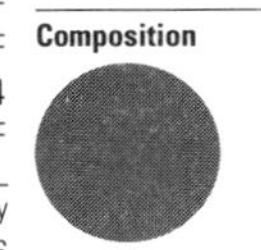

Cash	0.4
Stocks	99.6
Bonds	0.0
Other	0.0
Foreign (% of Stock)	0.5

Morningstar's Take by Terence Geenty 11-29-04

TCW Galileo Value Added's recent poor performance shouldn't scare off investors.

This fund's 1.02% loss for the year to date through Nov. 23, 2004, ranks near the very bottom in the small-blend category. The fund was hurt by its oversized stake in hardware stocks, which has been one of the worst performing sectors in 2004. (More than 30% of the portfolio was allocated there while the group norm is 8%.)

This recent bet on hardware stocks has been painful, but it's understandable given the fund's strategy. Managers Nick Galluccio and Susan Suvall look for companies that they believe have been punished more than their fundamentals justify, and they often buy growth companies that are experiencing cyclical weakness. Such out-of-favor positions can take some time to turn around, however, and the managers are happy to buy more of a stock if it continues to fall.

This has been the case in 2004. Galluccio and Suvall added to many of the fund's hardware holdings as stock prices in the sector slid. Thus, 13 of the fund's top 20 holdings as of Sept. 30 were hardware stocks. That willingness to wait out near-term difficulties and load up on individual sectors have made this offering one of the most volatile in its category.

Still, the managers' bets often have been correct. For example, the fund soared in 2003 as the market reversed course and favored many of the beaten-up growth stocks Galluccio and Suvall held then. Additionally, the managers are experienced, having run assets in this style for nearly two decades.

This fund isn't for investors seeking a well-diversified small-blend option. But for adventurous types who are willing to sit tight through the downturns, we think this remains a decent choice.

Address:	865 S Figueroa St Los Angeles CA 90017 800-386-3829
Web Address:	www.tcw.com
Inception:	06-14-00 *
Advisor:	TCW Investment Management Co.
Subadvisor:	None
NTF Plans:	N/A

Minimum Purchase:	$2000	Add: $250	IRA: $500
Min Auto Inv Plan:	$2000	Add: $100	
Sales Fees:	No-load		
Management Fee:	1.00%		
Actual Fees:	Mgt:1.00%	Dist:	
Expense Projections:	3Yr:$517	5Yr:$892	10Yr:$1994
Income Distrib:	Annually		

TCW Galileo Val Opport I

Analyst Pick

Ticker	Load	NAV	Yield	Total Assets	Mstar Category
TGVOX	None	$22.33	0.0%	$1,218 mil	Mid-Cap Blend

Governance and Management

Fiduciary Grade: B

Portfolio Manager(s)

Experienced. Susan Suvall has run money for TCW for the past 20 years. She and Nicholas Galluccio have run this fund since its inception in 1997. Four analysts assist with stock research and selection.

Strategy

Comanagers Susan Suvall and Nicholas Galluccio start with quantitative screens, looking at a firm's projected earnings over the next two years. The duo break up the portfolio into three categories: companies trading below liquidation value, turnaround stories, and busted-growth stocks. Like many money managers, they want to see high free cash flows and strong balance sheets. They often delve into nontraditional value sectors, such as technology, and keep the portfolio fairly concentrated with about 55-60 holdings.

Historical Profile

Return Above Avg
Risk High
Rating ★★★★ Above Avg

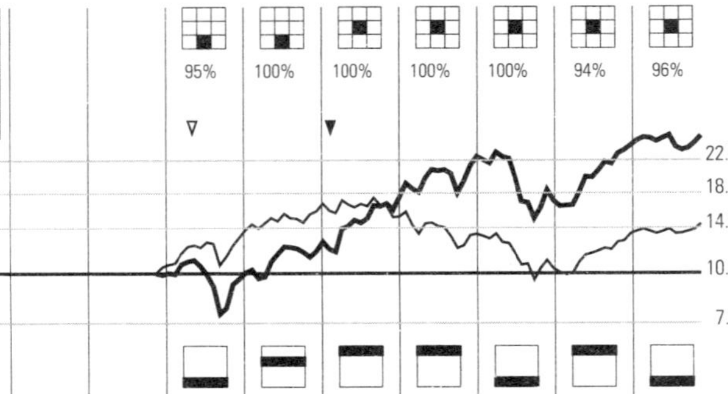

Investment Style
Equity
Stock %

▼ Manager Change
∇ Partial Manager Change

22.8
18.0 **Growth of $10,000**
14.0 — Investment Values of Fund
10.0 — Investment Values of S&P 500
7.0

Performance Quartile (within Category)

1993	1994	1995	1996	1997	1998	1999	2000	2001	2002	2003	12-04	History
—	—	—	—	10.01	10.04	11.28	14.24	18.86	13.72	20.44	22.33	NAV
—	—	—	—	-1.46*	0.30	25.06	38.26	33.65	-27.25	48.98	10.72	Total Return %
—	—	—	—	—	-28.27	4.02	47.36	45.53	-5.16	20.31	-0.15	+/-S&P 500
—	—	—	—	—	-18.81	10.34	20.77	34.25	-12.72	13.39	-5.75	+/-S&P Mid 400
—	—	—	—	0.00	0.00	0.00	0.55	0.00	0.00	0.00	0.00	Income Return %
—	—	—	—	—	0.30	25.06	37.71	33.65	-27.25	48.98	10.72	Capital Return %
—	—	—	—	—	85	37	2	1	91	7	92	Total Rtn % Rank Cat
—	—	—	—	0.01	0.00	0.00	0.06	0.00	0.00	0.00	0.00	Income $
—	—	—	—	0.00	0.00	1.21	1.24	0.16	0.00	0.00	0.30	Capital Gains $
—	—	—	—	—	1.16	1.18	1.15	1.02	0.95	0.98	—	Expense Ratio %
—	—	—	—	—	0.05	-0.10	0.41	-0.04	-0.34	-0.24	—	Income Ratio %
—	—	—	—	—	—	140	137	76	85	54	—	Turnover Rate %
—	—	—	—	—	28	32	72	520	294	659	902	Net Assets $mil

Performance 12-31-04

	1st Qtr	2nd Qtr	3rd Qtr	4th Qtr	Total
2000	9.93	4.19	12.62	7.18	38.26
2001	3.23	16.67	-14.69	30.09	33.65
2002	3.18	-16.60	-25.69	13.76	-27.25
2003	-3.13	22.05	10.30	14.25	48.98
2004	5.43	2.09	-9.05	13.10	10.72

Trailing	Total Return%	+/- S&P 500	+/- S&P Mid 400	%Rank Cat	Growth of $10,000
3 Mo	13.10	3.87	0.95	24	11,310
6 Mo	2.87	-4.32	-6.92	98	10,287
1 Yr	10.72	-0.15	-5.75	92	11,072
3 Yr Avg	6.27	2.69	-4.24	83	12,001
5 Yr Avg	17.26	19.56	7.73	3	22,169
10 Yr Avg	—	—	—	—	—
15 Yr Avg	—	—	—	—	—

Tax Analysis	Tax-Adj Rtn%	%Rank Cat	Tax-Cost Rat	%Rank Cat
3 Yr (estimated)	6.19	77	0.08	10
5 Yr (estimated)	16.57	3	0.59	20
10 Yr (estimated)	—	—	—	—

Potential Capital Gain Exposure: 16% of assets

Rating and Risk

Time Period	Load-Adj Return %	Morningstar Rtn vs Cat	Morningstar Risk vs Cat	Morningstar Risk-Adj Rating
1 Yr	10.72			
3 Yr	6.27	-Avg	High	★★
5 Yr	17.26	High	High	★★★★★
10 Yr	—	—	—	—
Incept	15.37			

Other Measures	Standard Index S&P 500	Best Fit Index Russ MG
Alpha	2.8	-0.1
Beta	1.37	1.17
R-Squared	84	91
Standard Deviation	24.21	
Mean	6.27	
Sharpe Ratio	0.20	

Morningstar's Take by Terence Geenty 10-31-04

TCW Galileo Value Opportunities makes a solid case for itself, but it isn't for everyone.

Managers Susan Suvall and Nicholas Galluccio have run money together for the past two decades. They consider themselves opportunistic value buyers and look to acquire companies at a 40% discount to their perceived intrinsic value. This approach could have them courting traditional value fare or beaten-up growth stocks alike.

They build the fund's portfolio based on a bottom-up process that leads them to areas of the market they believe are the most undervalued. This can sometimes result in significant sector bets. For example, this fund had a 20% allocation to hardware stocks as of Sept. 30, which is nearly 3 times the average mid-cap blend weight. Also, Suvall and Galluccio opt for a concentrated portfolio so that they have more time to research each of the companies they invest in.

Their bets have yet to pay off in 2004. The fund's year-to-date returns through Oct. 27 land in the bottom quartile of the group. Poor performance from hardware stocks Novellus Systems, Vishay Intertechnology and Teradyne have hurt the fund. Still, Suvall sees good value in these companies and believes they will benefit from improvements in capital expenditures.

Taking big stakes in out-of-favor areas has made this fund one of the most volatile offerings in its category over the last five years. But this risk has not been without its reward. Indeed, this fund has produced annual returns since inception that are nearly double its average rival's. Additionally, it has performed well in a variety of market environments.

Conservative investors aren't likely to feel comfortable in a fund like this but we think it makes a fine pick for those willing to tolerate above-average volatility.

Portfolio Analysis 11-30-04

Share change since 10-04 Total Stocks:56	Sector	PE	YTD Ret%	% Assets
Health Net	Health	15.4	-11.71	2.84
Assurant	Financial	—	—	2.78
Novellus Systems	Hardware	31.6	-29.98	2.76
Vishay Intertechnology	Hardware	21.3	-34.41	2.66
Teradyne	Hardware	19.5	-32.93	2.64
⊕ Hillenbrand Industries	Health	17.8	-8.85	2.57
Transocean	Energy	56.3	76.55	2.56
Veritas Software	Software	23.7	-22.88	2.52
Darden Restaurants	Consumer	20.1	32.28	2.42
⊕ North Fork Bancorporatio	Financial	15.4	10.24	2.33
Interpublic Group of Com	Business	—	-14.10	2.20
Talbots	Consumer	14.2	-10.34	2.17
⊕ Varian	Health	24.8	-1.56	2.16
Andrew	Hardware	—	17.60	2.16
⊕ SunGard Data Systems	Business	17.5	2.24	2.10
Jones Apparel Group	Goods	14.8	4.84	2.09
Alliant Techsystems	Ind Mtrls	16.7	13.19	2.09
Edwards Lifesciences	Health	—	37.17	2.06
⊕ Tiffany	Goods	22.6	-28.79	2.02
Thermo Electron	Health	27.2	19.80	2.01

Current Investment Style

Value Blnd Growth / Large Mid Small

Market Cap	%
Giant	0.0
Large	13.0
Mid	75.9
Small	11.1
Micro	0.0
Avg $mil: 3,716	

Value Measures		Rel Category
Price/Earnings	19.23	1.14
Price/Book	2.09	0.96
Price/Sales	1.01	0.95
Price/Cash Flow	9.79	1.57
Dividend Yield %	0.58	0.58

Growth Measures	%	Rel Category
Long-Term Erngs	12.07	0.96
Book Value	6.88	0.98
Sales	3.12	0.55
Cash Flow	-8.14	NMF
Historical Erngs	3.26	0.29

Profitability	%	Rel Category
Return on Equity	10.53	0.76
Return on Assets	5.56	0.85
Net Margin	7.62	0.84

Sector Weightings	% of Stocks	Rel S&P 500	3 Year High	3 Year Low
Info	29.62	1.38		
Software	4.26	0.99	7	2
Hardware	21.09	2.07	27	20
Media	4.27	1.11	12	3
Telecom	0.00	0.00	0	0
Service	50.87	1.10		
Health	17.96	1.44	18	5
Consumer	7.06	0.78	12	5
Business	11.76	2.90	12	6
Financial	14.09	0.68	15	8
Mfg	19.50	0.61		
Goods	4.26	0.46	9	4
Ind Mtrls	8.36	0.66	14	8
Energy	6.88	0.96	11	4
Utilities	0.00	0.00	0	0

Composition

Cash	3.6
Stocks	96.4
Bonds	0.0
Other	0.0
Foreign (% of Stock)	1.8

Address:	865 S Figueroa St, Los Angeles CA 90017, 800-386-3829	Minimum Purchase:	$2000	Add: $250 IRA: $500
Web Address:	www.tcw.com	Min Auto Inv Plan:	$2000	Add: $100
Inception:	11-03-97*	Sales Fees:	No-load	
Advisor:	TCW Investment Management Co.	Management Fee:	0.80%	
Subadvisor:	None	Actual Fees:	Mgt:0.80%	Dist:
NTF Plans:	N/A	Expense Projections:	3Yr:$312	5Yr:$542 10Yr:$1201
		Income Distrib:	Annually	

Templeton Devel Mkts A

Ticker	Load	NAV	Yield	Total Assets	Mstar Category
TEDMX	5.75%	$18.52	1.4%	$2,807 mil	Diversified Emerging Mkts

Governance and Management

Fiduciary Grade: D

Portfolio Manager(s)

Lead manager Mark Mobius is a veteran of emerging-markets investing. He has been running this fund since 1991 and has run a similar closed-end fund, Templeton Emerging Markets, since 1987. Mobius is supported by comanagers Tom Wu and Dennis Lim and a large analyst staff that is spread across the globe.

Strategy

Mark Mobius, Tom Wu, and Dennis Lim are buy-and-hold investors who focus on firms that appear cheap relative to their assets, or relative to their long-term earnings. They are willing to make significant sector and country bets at times and to hold hundreds of issues. The analytical team for their emerging-markets group works separately from the staff of Templeton's other foreign and world-stock funds.

Historical Profile

Return Average
Risk Below Avg
Rating ★★★ Neutral

Investment Style: Equity Stock %: 82% 83% 91% 87% 81% 88% 92% 92% 99%

▼ Manager Change
▽ Partial Manager Change

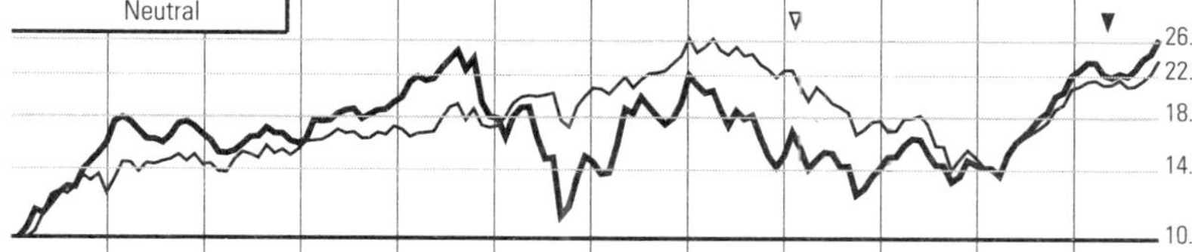

Growth of $10,000
- Investment Values of Fund
- Investment Values of MSCI EAFE

Performance Quartile (within Category)

1993	1994	1995	1996	1997	1998	1999	2000	2001	2002	2003	12-04	History
15.26	13.42	13.01	15.40	12.94	10.30	15.61	10.59	9.88	10.00	14.99	18.52	NAV
74.49	-8.58	0.36	22.51	-9.41	-18.72	51.55	-31.85	-5.76	1.68	53.14	25.45	Total Return %
41.93	-16.36	-10.85	16.46	-11.19	-38.65	24.52	-17.66	15.66	17.62	14.55	5.20	+/-MSCI EAFE
2.83	0.14	7.27	18.58	4.04	8.95	-12.54	0.05	-1.08	9.65	1.55	3.00	+/-MSCI EmrMkt
0.62	0.79	1.50	1.35	1.01	1.48	0.00	0.40	0.97	0.50	2.53	1.71	Income Return %
73.87	-9.37	-1.14	21.16	-10.42	-20.20	51.55	-32.25	-6.73	1.18	50.61	23.74	Capital Return %
67	55	44	18	81	12	90	61	72	9	56	35	Total Rtn % Rank Cat
0.06	0.12	0.20	0.18	0.16	0.19	0.00	0.06	0.10	0.05	0.25	0.26	Income $
0.12	0.43	0.25	0.34	0.84	0.05	0.00	0.00	0.00	0.00	0.00	0.00	Capital Gains $
2.20	2.11	2.10	2.03	1.96	2.11	2.02	2.09	2.09	2.24	2.17	—	Expense Ratio %
0.57	1.08	1.66	1.16	0.99	1.40	0.45	0.56	0.56	0.96	1.85	—	Income Ratio %
16	19	10	12	30	38	46	69	61	49	49	—	Turnover Rate %
1,392	2,001	2,148	3,307	3,457	2,182	2,955	1,540	1,228	1,174	1,880	2,306	Net Assets $mil

Performance 12-31-04

	1st Qtr	2nd Qtr	3rd Qtr	4th Qtr	Total
2000	-7.16	-9.14	-11.97	-8.23	-31.85
2001	-6.36	7.89	-18.09	13.88	-5.76
2002	11.44	-3.65	-12.88	8.70	1.68
2003	-5.19	20.81	12.19	19.17	53.14
2004	6.50	-5.05	7.25	15.67	25.45

Trailing	Total Return%	+/- MSCI EAFE	+/- MSCI EmrMkt	%Rank Cat	Growth of $10,000
3 Mo	15.67	0.35	-1.14	72	11,567
6 Mo	24.06	9.06	-1.39	65	12,406
1 Yr	25.45	5.20	3.00	35	12,545
3 Yr Avg	25.01	13.12	5.47	18	19,536
5 Yr Avg	4.64	5.77	2.55	41	12,546
10 Yr Avg	5.58	-0.04	4.60	36	17,211
15 Yr Avg	—	—	—	—	—

Tax Analysis	Tax-Adj Rtn%	%Rank Cat	Tax-Cost Rat	%Rank Cat
3 Yr (estimated)	21.97	33	0.48	55
5 Yr (estimated)	2.99	53	0.41	58
10 Yr (estimated)	4.25	51	0.68	75

Potential Capital Gain Exposure: 5% of assets

Rating and Risk

Time Period	Load-Adj Return %	Morningstar Rtn vs Cat	Morningstar Risk vs Cat	Morningstar Risk-Adj Rating
1 Yr	18.24			
3 Yr	22.56	Avg	Low	★★★
5 Yr	3.41	Avg	Low	★★★
10 Yr	4.96	Avg	-Avg	★★★
Incept	6.66			

Other Measures	Standard Index S&P 500	Best Fit Index MSCI EmrMkt
Alpha	14.0	8.0
Beta	0.81	0.80
R-Squared	72	90

Standard Deviation	18.57
Mean	25.01
Sharpe Ratio	1.29

Portfolio Analysis 09-30-04

Share change since 06-04 Total Stocks:132	Sector	Country	% Assets
Anglo American	Ind Mtrls	U.K.	3.10
⊕ Samsung Electronics	Goods	Korea	2.67
China Mobile	Telecom	Hong Kong	2.35
SABMiller	Goods	U.K.	2.31
Kimberly-Clark de Mexico	Ind Mtrls	Mexico	2.28
Remgro Ltd	Ind Mtrls	South Africa	2.10
Inbev	Goods	Belgium	1.98
Taiwan Cellular	Telecom	Taiwan	1.89
Companhia de Bebidas das	Goods	United States	1.87
Fraser & Neave Ltd	Ind Mtrls	Singapore	1.79
Keppel	Business	Singapore	1.77
BA Holding Ag	Financial	Austria	1.70
⊕ Daewoo Shipbuilding & Ma	Ind Mtrls	Korea	1.66
Mol Magyar Olaj- Es Gazi	Energy	Hungary	1.57
⊖ Telefonos de Mexico SA A	Telecom	Mexico	1.54
⊕ Cheung Kong (Hldgs) Ltd	Financial	Hong Kong	1.45
Banco Bradesco S.A. (ADR	Financial	United States	1.44
☼ Singapore Telecommunicat	Telecom	Singapore	1.41
Kangwon Land	Consumer	Korea	1.39
⊕ Samsung Heavy Industries	Ind Mtrls	Korea	1.34

Current Investment Style

Market Cap	%
Giant	22.0
Large	41.0
Mid	34.2
Small	2.8
Micro	0.0
Avg $mil: 5,707	

Value Measures		Rel Category
Price/Earnings	10.87	1.19
Price/Book	1.51	0.97
Price/Sales	0.88	1.06
Price/Cash Flow	4.64	1.06
Dividend Yield %	3.39	1.23

Growth Measures	%	Rel Category
Long-Term Erngs	13.45	0.69
Book Value	7.61	2.19
Sales	5.70	0.49
Cash Flow	6.50	0.87
Historical Erngs	3.75	0.54

Composition

Cash	0.9	Bonds	0.0
Stocks	98.8	Other	0.3
Foreign (% of Stock)			96.2

Sector Weightings	% of Stocks	Rel MSCI EAFE	3 Year High	3 Year Low
Info	18.17	1.09		
Software	0.03	0.03	1	0
Hardware	2.83	0.78	3	1
Media	0.59	0.26	1	0
Telecom	14.72	1.53	18	11
Service	26.30	0.59		
Health	1.84	0.25	3	2
Consumer	5.89	1.17	6	2
Business	7.60	1.40	8	7
Financial	10.97	0.41	15	10
Mfg	55.51	1.44		
Goods	22.20	1.63	23	18
Ind Mtrls	22.59	1.84	27	18
Energy	8.63	1.17	14	8
Utilities	2.09	0.39	6	2

Regional Exposure	% Stock		
UK/W. Europe	16	N. America	4
Japan	0	Latn America	7
Asia X Japan	58	Other	15

Country Exposure	% Stock		
South Korea	17	U.K.	7
Hong Kong	14	Singapore	7
Taiwan	13		

Morningstar's Take by Dieter Bardy 12-02-04

Templeton Developing Markets would be more attractive if not for its steep price.

This fund follows a sensible approach to investing in emerging markets. Longtime manager Mark Mobius has much experience in this area and has been at the helm of the fund since its 1991 inception. He is supported by two comanagers, Tom Wu and Dennis Lim, in addition to the rest of Templeton's 34-person team of global analysts. Mobius favors companies that are trading at a discount to his estimate of their value and frequently ventures into beaten-down industries and countries. Over time, this approach has led to 25% less volatility (as measured by standard deviation) than the MSCI Emerging Markets Index, while results have been competitive as well. For example, the fund has placed in the top half of its peer group for the trailing three- and five-year periods, while investors who have stuck around for the past 10 years have outdistanced the category average by more than 15 percentage points.

The fund's recent moves are a further example of its restrained approach. For example, it has been selling winning picks in the oil and gas industries such as Lukoil and adding to positions in consumer-oriented stocks such as China Mobil and Telefonos de Mexico. Mobius likes these stocks because he sees basic consumer industries as an avenue of future growth in emerging markets.

Unfortunately, the fund costs too much. While its 2.17% expense ratio is near the category's 2.13% average, we think its $2.5 billion size, which is five times larger than typical rivals', should result in more cost savings here. As such, we would not invest in this fund until it gets cheaper. Investors are better off choosing its closed-end sibling, Templeton Emerging Markets. Its slightly lower expenses and stable asset base (which is easier to manage) make it a more compelling option.

Address:	Broward Financial Centre Fort Lauderdale FL 33394-3091 800-342-5236
Web Address:	www.franklintempleton.com
Inception:	10-16-91
Advisor:	Templeton Asset Management Limited
Subadvisor:	None
NTF Plans:	DATALynx NTF, Federated Tr NTF

Minimum Purchase:	$1000	Add: $50	IRA: $250
Min Auto Inv Plan:	$50	Add: $50	
Sales Fees:	5.75%L, 2.00%R		
Management Fee:	1.25%, 0.15%A		
Actual Fees:	Mgt:1.25%	Dist:0.35%	
Expense Projections:	3Yr:$1215	5Yr:$1672	10Yr:$2934
Income Distrib:	Annually		

Templeton Foreign A

Ticker	Load	NAV	Yield	Total Assets	Mstar Category
TEMFX	5.75%	$12.30	1.8%	$18,056 mil	Foreign Large Value

Governance and Management

Fiduciary Grade: C

Portfolio Manager(s)

Jeff Everett has been with Templeton since 1989. He took over this fund from longtime manager Mark Holowesko at the beginning of 2001 and also manages Templeton World Fund.

Strategy

This fund favors firms whose stocks are cheap relative to their assets, cash flow, and earnings potential. The managers dip freely into emerging markets and make large sector and country bets. They're devoted enough to their deep-value discipline to weather dry spells; for example, the fund badly lagged the category average in 1998. The managers generally don't hedge currencies. Templeton imposes a 2% redemption fee on shares held less than 30 days.

Historical Profile

Return Average
Risk Below Avg
Rating ★★★ Neutral

Investment Style
Equity
Stock %

70%	66%	91%	82%	84%	83%	74%	80%	87%

▼ Manager Change
▽ Partial Manager Change

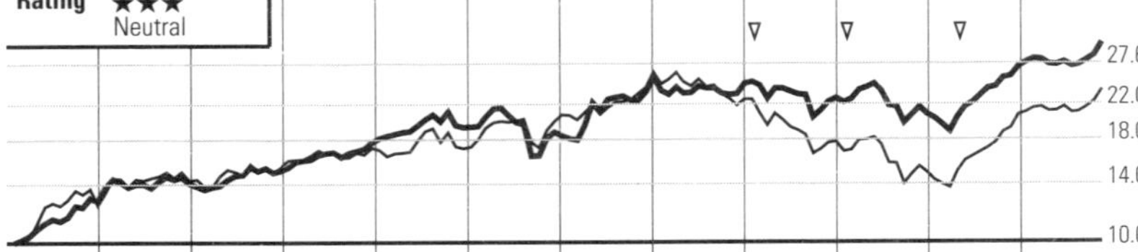

Growth of $10,000
— Investment Values of Fund
— Investment Values of MSCI EAFE

Performance Quartile (within Category)

1993	1994	1995	1996	1997	1998	1999	2000	2001	2002	2003	12-04	History
9.43	8.82	9.18	10.36	9.95	8.39	11.22	10.34	9.25	8.31	10.64	12.30	NAV
36.76	0.38	11.15	18.00	6.65	-4.89	39.21	-3.67	-7.92	-8.64	30.51	18.14	Total Return %
4.20	-7.40	-0.06	11.95	4.87	-24.82	12.18	10.52	13.50	7.30	-8.08	-2.11	+/-MSCI EAFE
4.55	-6.97	-0.26	11.13	4.38	-23.58	11.23	9.69	13.47	7.16	-8.91	-2.24	+/-MSCI Wd xUS
1.79	1.67	2.87	3.02	3.15	2.61	3.77	2.06	2.45	1.51	2.31	2.14	Income Return %
34.97	-1.29	8.28	14.98	3.50	-7.50	35.44	-5.73	-10.37	-10.15	28.20	16.00	Capital Return %
56	76	57	42	53	89	17	58	12	30	93	85	Total Rtn % Rank Cat
0.13	0.16	0.25	0.28	0.32	0.26	0.31	0.23	0.25	0.14	0.19	0.23	Income $
0.14	0.52	0.36	0.18	0.85	0.77	0.09	0.21	0.00	0.00	0.00	0.02	Capital Gains $
1.12	1.14	1.15	1.12	1.08	1.12	1.13	1.15	1.18	1.16	1.22	1.23	Expense Ratio %
2.11	1.84	2.81	3.09	3.28	2.79	2.92	2.14	2.54	1.63	1.79	1.58	Income Ratio %
21	37	22	16	37	38	26	45	21	34	33	25	Turnover Rate %
3,529	5,306	7,312	11,082	14,014	10,862	13,170	10,743	8,748	8,115	12,040	15,182	Net Assets $mil

Performance 12-31-04

	1st Qtr	2nd Qtr	3rd Qtr	4th Qtr	Total
2000	-5.61	0.57	-3.94	5.65	-3.67
2001	-8.03	3.89	-13.46	11.36	-7.92
2002	4.65	-0.52	-16.41	4.97	-8.64
2003	-9.27	17.77	9.23	11.81	30.51
2004	4.04	-1.36	0.92	14.07	18.14

Trailing	Total Return%	+/- MSCI EAFE	+/- MSCI Wd xUS	%Rank Cat	Growth of $10,000
3 Mo	14.07	-1.25	-1.08	55	11,407
6 Mo	15.11	0.11	-0.26	46	11,511
1 Yr	18.14	-2.11	-2.24	85	11,814
3 Yr Avg	12.10	0.21	-0.12	75	14,087
5 Yr Avg	4.55	5.68	5.31	51	12,492
10 Yr Avg	8.75	3.13	2.81	57	23,136
15 Yr Avg	9.01	4.78	4.60	67	36,475

Tax Analysis	Tax-Adj Rtn%	%Rank Cat	Tax-Cost Rat	%Rank Cat
3 Yr (estimated)	9.16	91	0.68	67
5 Yr (estimated)	2.36	63	0.93	48
10 Yr (estimated)	6.43	78	1.55	82

Potential Capital Gain Exposure: 20% of assets

Rating and Risk

Time Period	Load-Adj Return %	Morningstar Rtn vs Cat	Morningstar Risk vs Cat	Morningstar Risk-Adj Rating
1 Yr	11.35			
3 Yr	9.91	-Avg	Low	★★
5 Yr	3.32	-Avg	Low	★★★
10 Yr	8.11	Avg	Avg	★★★
Incept	13.18			

Other Measures	Standard Index S&P 500	Best Fit Index MSCI Wd xUS
Alpha	1.6	1.3
Beta	0.85	0.86
R-Squared	93	93

Standard Deviation	15.29
Mean	12.10
Sharpe Ratio	0.71

Portfolio Analysis 09-30-04

Share change since 06-04 Total Stocks:169	Sector	Country	% Assets
Cheung Kong (hldgs) Ltd	Financial	Hong Kong	2.93
⊕ Hutchison Whampoa Ltd	Telecom	Hong Kong	2.15
Nintendo	Goods	Japan	2.06
⊕ BP PLC ADR	Energy	U.K.	2.03
Nippon Telegraph & Telep	Telecom	Japan	1.99
Royal Dutch Petroleum	Energy	Netherlands	1.97
Sony	Goods	Japan	1.93
⊕ GlaxoSmithKline	Health	U.K.	1.77
☼ Sanofi-Synthelabo	Health	France	1.74
BASF	Ind Mtrls	Germany	1.55
⊕ Swiss Re	Financial	Switzerland	1.53
Repsol YPF	Energy	Spain	1.43
⊕ Novartis	Health	Switzerland	1.39
Telefonos de Mexico SA A	Telecom	Mexico	1.39
CLP Hldgs Ltd	Utilities	Hong Kong	1.30
⊕ ACE	Financial	United States	1.30
UPM-Kymmene	Ind Mtrls	Finland	1.29
⊕ BCE	Telecom	Canada	1.28
Hitachi, Ltd	Hardware	Japan	1.22
⊕ Shell Transport & Tradin	Energy	U.K.	1.14

Current Investment Style

Value Blnd Growth — Large / Mid / Small

Market Cap	%
Giant	47.5
Large	40.4
Mid	12.1
Small	0.0
Micro	0.0
Avg $mil: 16,893	

Value Measures		Rel Category
Price/Earnings	13.08	0.97
Price/Book	1.62	0.98
Price/Sales	0.93	1.13
Price/Cash Flow	4.76	1.08
Dividend Yield %	3.21	1.15

Growth Measures	%	Rel Category
Long-Term Erngs	10.20	1.04
Book Value	-0.69	NMF
Sales	2.56	1.83
Cash Flow	7.48	2.43
Historical Erngs	0.77	0.28

Composition

Cash	8.7	Bonds	0.3
Stocks	87.3	Other	3.7
Foreign (% of Stock)			96.3

Sector Weightings	% of Stocks	Rel MSCI EAFE	3 Year High	3 Year Low
Info	17.81	1.07		
Software	1.67	1.55	3	1
Hardware	2.30	0.63	4	2
Media	3.43	1.50	3	1
Telecom	10.41	1.08	11	8
Service	36.20	0.81		
Health	7.99	1.10	8	1
Consumer	2.06	0.41	2	1
Business	3.78	0.69	6	4
Financial	22.37	0.83	28	21
Mfg	46.01	1.19		
Goods	10.41	0.76	12	7
Ind Mtrls	18.40	1.50	28	18
Energy	10.25	1.39	12	6
Utilities	6.95	1.30	9	6

Regional Exposure	% Stock		
UK/W. Europe	50	N. America	7
Japan	15	Latn America	2
Asia X Japan	26	Other	0

Country Exposure	% Stock		
U.K.	20	South Korea	6
Japan	15	Netherlands	5
Hong Kong	13		

Morningstar's Take by Dieter Bardy 11-30-04

Templeton Foreign isn't going to blow out the competition in any single year, but it won't disappoint, either.

This fund hasn't been as hot as some of its foreign large-value peers thus far in 2004. For the year-to-date period through Nov. 26, its 14% gain is slightly off its typical peer's 17% rise. This is in contrast to the fund's long-term record. Since manager Jeff Everett took over in 2001, the fund has earned a more level 6% annually, versus its average peer's 4.6% annualized gain. In particular, the fund has better protected investors' money during market downturns that beat up competitors.

Everett looks for companies with steady growth prospects over the next three to five years that are selling at big discounts to his estimate of their intrinsic values. And because Everett often buys on bad news (like when he added Shell Trading and Transport to the portfolio after its reserves restatement), it can take time for his thesis to pan out. The fund's low turnover suggests that Everett holds on to his selections for an average of four years--conviction is key to the fund's appeal, in our opinion.

One mark against the fund, however, are its expenses. At 1.23%, they are below the category norm, but with more than $16 billion in assets, the fund's fees could be lower, especially considering that this fund is twice as large as its nearest category rival. Also irksome is the fact that the fund's expenses are 10% higher today than they were a few years ago, when assets stood at $13 billion.

These concerns aside, this fund adds valuable international exposure to investor's portfolios. Considering that the fund has delivered pleasing results with less volatility than typical rivals is an added bonus.

Address:	500 E Broward Blvd Fort Lauderdale FL 33394 800-342-5236
Web Address:	www.franklintempleton.com
Inception:	10-05-82
Advisor:	Templeton Global Advisors Limited
Subadvisor:	None
NTF Plans:	DATALynx NTF, Federated Tr NTF

Minimum Purchase:	$1000	Add: $50	IRA: $250
Min Auto Inv Plan:	$50	Add: $50	
Sales Fees:	5.75%L, 2.00%R		
Management Fee:	0.75% mx./0.60% mn., 0.15%A		
Actual Fees:	Mgt:0.61%	Dist:0.25%	
Expense Projections:	3Yr:$940	5Yr:$1207	10Yr:$1967
Income Distrib:	Annually		

Templeton Growth A

Ticker	Load	NAV	Yield	Total Assets	Mstar Category
TEPLX	5.75%	$22.89	1.8%	$22,248 mil	World Stock

Governance and Management

Fiduciary Grade: C

Portfolio Manager(s)

Murdo Murchison replaced lead manager Mark Holowesko in January 2001. He has managed Templeton's offshore portfolios since 1993. He's supported by comanager Jeff Everett. Former comanager Dale Winner left in Feb. 2004, to spend more time on his other fund, Templeton Global Long-Short.

Strategy

This fund favors firms whose stocks are cheap relative to their underlying assets, cash flow, and earnings potential. It keeps approximately 40% of its assets in the U.S. and the rest overseas. The fund frequently invests in emerging markets, and its manager doesn't hedge currencies. To deter market-timers, Templeton imposes a 2% redemption fee on all shares held fewer than 30 days.

Historical Profile

Return: Above Avg
Risk: Below Avg
Rating: ★★★★ Above Avg

Investment Style: Equity Stock %

77%	74%	86%	88%	87%	84%	74%	84%	89%

▼ Manager Change
▽ Partial Manager Change

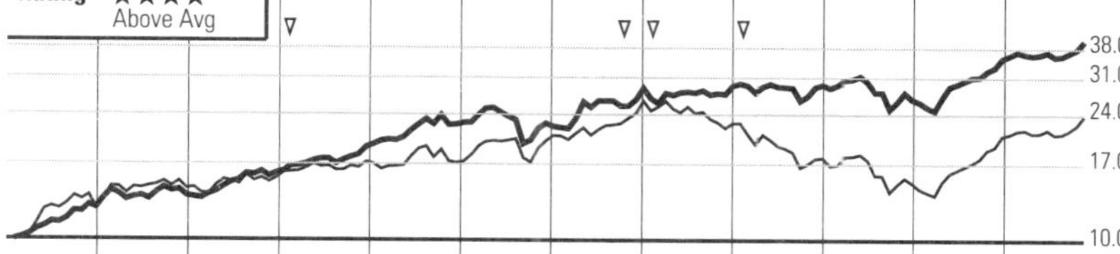

Growth of $10,000
— Investment Values of Fund
— Investment Values of MSCI EAFE

Performance Quartile (within Category)

1993	1994	1995	1996	1997	1998	1999	2000	2001	2002	2003	12-04	History
17.62	16.23	17.35	19.54	19.40	16.37	19.96	18.39	18.00	15.93	20.67	22.89	NAV
32.70	0.82	19.83	20.55	16.18	-2.48	30.44	1.74	0.54	-9.48	32.85	17.00	Total Return %
0.14	-6.96	8.62	14.50	14.40	-22.41	3.41	15.93	21.96	6.46	-5.74	-3.25	+/-MSCI EAFE
10.20	-4.26	-0.89	7.07	0.42	-26.80	5.49	14.93	17.34	10.41	-0.26	2.28	+/-MSCI World
1.91	1.68	2.75	2.83	2.87	2.09	3.30	1.87	2.20	2.00	2.85	2.03	Income Return %
30.79	-0.86	17.08	17.72	13.31	-4.57	27.14	-0.13	-1.66	-11.48	30.00	14.97	Capital Return %
50	45	41	21	40	92	55	15	4	11	56	35	Total Rtn % Rank Cat
0.27	0.29	0.44	0.49	0.54	0.41	0.53	0.37	0.40	0.36	0.45	0.42	Income $
1.12	1.29	1.61	0.81	2.88	2.04	0.69	1.42	0.06	0.00	0.00	0.78	Capital Gains $
1.03	1.10	1.12	1.09	1.08	1.08	1.12	1.11	1.15	1.10	1.13	1.10	Expense Ratio %
2.10	1.76	2.40	2.87	2.81	2.53	2.60	1.83	2.11	1.85	2.05	1.75	Income Ratio %
29	27	35	20	42	48	32	51	24	56	32	25	Turnover Rate %
4,625	5,476	7,308	9,614	12,660	12,238	14,413	12,795	12,108	11,049	15,024	18,461	Net Assets $mil

Performance 12-31-04

	1st Qtr	2nd Qtr	3rd Qtr	4th Qtr	Total
2000	-3.51	1.04	-1.95	6.43	1.74
2001	-4.68	4.16	-9.26	11.58	0.54
2002	3.50	-1.56	-16.96	6.99	-9.48
2003	-7.47	20.22	4.97	13.78	32.85
2004	3.05	1.46	-0.32	12.27	17.00

Trailing	Total Return%	+/- MSCI EAFE	+/- MSCI World	%Rank Cat	Growth of $10,000
3 Mo	12.27	-3.05	0.33	55	11,227
6 Mo	11.91	-3.09	1.09	38	11,191
1 Yr	17.00	-3.25	2.28	35	11,700
3 Yr Avg	12.06	0.17	5.11	18	14,072
5 Yr Avg	7.55	8.68	10.00	10	14,390
10 Yr Avg	11.88	6.26	3.79	16	30,727
15 Yr Avg	11.44	7.21	4.85	14	50,771

Tax Analysis	Tax-Adj Rtn%	%Rank Cat	Tax-Cost Rat	%Rank Cat
3 Yr (estimated)	8.80	31	0.97	91
5 Yr (estimated)	4.86	12	1.35	85
10 Yr (estimated)	8.83	27	2.15	95

Potential Capital Gain Exposure: 21% of assets

Rating and Risk

Time Period	Load-Adj Return %	Morningstar Rtn vs Cat	Morningstar Risk vs Cat	Morningstar Risk-Adj Rating
1 Yr	10.27			
3 Yr	9.87	+Avg	-Avg	★★★★
5 Yr	6.29	+Avg	-Avg	★★★★
10 Yr	11.22	+Avg	-Avg	★★★★
Incept	13.88			

Other Measures	Standard Index S&P 500	Best Fit Index MSCI World
Alpha	1.4	6.3
Beta	0.87	0.91
R-Squared	91	91
Standard Deviation	15.91	
Mean	12.06	
Sharpe Ratio	0.68	

Portfolio Analysis 09-30-04

Share change since 06-04 Total Stocks:100	Sector	Country	% Assets
Germany (Federa Republi	—	Germany	2.35
⊕ GlaxoSmithKline	Health	U.K.	2.14
⊕ Shell Transport & Tradin	Energy	U.K.	2.07
AT&T Wireless Services	Telecom	United States	1.93
☼ BP PLC ADR	Energy	U.K.	1.93
E.ON	Utilities	Germany	1.83
Eni	Energy	Italy	1.64
⊕ Nestle	Goods	Switzerland	1.62
⊕ BCE	Telecom	Canada	1.48
Cheung Kong (hldgs) Ltd	Financial	Hong Kong	1.47
National Grid Transco	Utilities	U.K.	1.42
Nintendo	Goods	Japan	1.41
⊕ British Sky Broadcasting	Media	U.K.	1.36
⊕ Royal Bank Of Scotland G	Financial	U.K.	1.36
Novartis	Health	Switzerland	1.34
BAE Systems	Ind Mtrls	U.K.	1.31
☼ Sanofi-Synthelabo	Health	France	1.28
KT ADR	Telecom	Korea	1.23
⊕ Nomura Hldgs	Financial	Japan	1.21
⊕ Unilever NV	Goods	Netherlands	1.20

Current Investment Style

Value Blnd Growth / Large Mid Small

Market Cap	%
Giant	39.8
Large	47.5
Mid	12.1
Small	0.5
Micro	0.0
Avg $mil: 20,513	

Value Measures		Rel Category
Price/Earnings	14.91	0.94
Price/Book	1.85	0.83
Price/Sales	0.89	0.76
Price/Cash Flow	5.69	0.89
Dividend Yield %	2.47	1.31

Growth Measures	%	Rel Category
Long-Term Erngs	8.86	0.74
Book Value	1.79	0.81
Sales	3.80	0.91
Cash Flow	7.05	1.20
Historical Erngs	1.48	0.17

Sector Weightings	% of Stocks	Rel MSCI EAFE	3 Year High	3 Year Low
Info	21.70	1.31		
Software	0.86	0.80	2	0
Hardware	2.24	0.61	3	1
Media	6.07	2.66	6	0
Telecom	12.53	1.31	14	9
Service	35.05	0.78		
Health	13.64	1.88	14	6
Consumer	2.43	0.48	7	2
Business	5.54	1.02	7	3
Financial	13.44	0.50	25	13
Mfg	43.25	1.12		
Goods	10.92	0.80	13	8
Ind Mtrls	16.51	1.34	20	16
Energy	8.89	1.21	11	6
Utilities	6.93	1.30	10	6

Composition			
Cash	6.9	Bonds	3.5
Stocks	89.0	Other	0.6
Foreign (% of Stock)			74.6

Regional Exposure	% Stock		
UK/W. Europe	52	N. America	29
Japan	8	Latn America	1
Asia X Japan	10	Other	0

Country Exposure	% Stock		
United States	25	Switzerland	7
U.K.	24	Netherlands	5
Japan	8		

Morningstar's Take by Dieter Bardy 12-13-04

Seldom the category killer, Templeton Growth approaches investing with an eye to the long term.

This fund's strategy isn't particularly unique, but management's depth of analysis and patience separate it from competitors. Like all Templeton funds, the portfolio is a mix of companies that are currently trading cheaply relative to their five-year projected earnings-growth rates. The fund favors firms with strong balance sheets and healthy free cash flows, and manager Murdo Murchison often gets excited about companies when the crowd isn't.

Murchison, who has managed this fund since January 2001 and also worked on it for eight years prior under the tutelage of former manager Mark Holowesko, has lately been attracted to health-care and media stocks. Among the latter, Murchison likes British Sky Broadcasting; its stock has suffered because of hefty upcoming capital expenditures, but Murchison believes that they will only solidify the firm's long-term standing.

Still, while the fund has been flying high lately--it's up more than 14.4% for the year-to-date period through Dec. 7, 2004--investors should keep its success in perspective. The recent market has rewarded most value-based investment styles, so a slowdown is entirely possible. That said, Murchison had no problem filling out the portfolio with new ideas and we have confidence in the fund's long-term abilities.

Overall, the fund is a solid option. Its experienced management and patient approach are keys to its appeal. Further, at 1.1%, its expense ratio is well below the world-stock average of 1.6%. Investors who aren't afraid to wait out tough periods (such as 1998 when it trailed peers by a wide margin) will be well rewarded over the long haul.

Address:	500 East Broward Blvd Fort Lauderdale FL 33394 800-342-5236
Web Address:	www.franklintempleton.com
Inception:	11-29-54
Advisor:	Templeton Global Advisors Limited
Subadvisor:	None
NTF Plans:	DATALynx NTF, Federated Tr NTF

Minimum Purchase:	$1000	Add: $50	IRA: $250
Min Auto Inv Plan:	$50	Add: $50	
Sales Fees:	5.75%L		
Management Fee:	0.63% mx./0.54% mn.		
Actual Fees:	Mgt:0.61%	Dist:0.25%	
Expense Projections:	3Yr:$913	5Yr:$1161	10Yr:$1871
Income Distrib:	Annually		

Templeton World A

Ticker	Load	NAV	Yield	Total Assets	Mstar Category
TEMWX	5.75%	$17.75	1.7%	$8,179 mil	World Stock

Governance and Management

Fiduciary Grade: C

Portfolio Manager(s)

Jeff Everett, a Templeton manager since 1996, is well versed in the company gospel. He assisted former manager Mark Holowesko for seven years. He uses Templeton's extensive team of analysts and the firm's centralized buy list. Managers here generally don't hedge currencies. To deter market-timers, Franklin Templeton imposes a 2% redemption fee on shares held less than 30 days.

Strategy

Like its siblings, Templeton World generally favors cheap stocks. Management here makes significant sector bets and is willing to commit as much as 25% of assets to emerging markets. The fund also holds on to stocks for the long haul, shunning calls to follow market trends.

Historical Profile

Return Above Avg
Risk Below Avg
Rating ★★★★ Above Avg

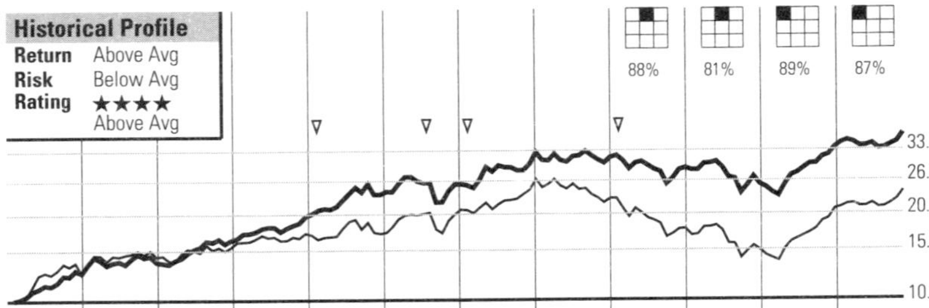

Investment Style
Equity
Stock %

▼ Manager Change
▽ Partial Manager Change

Growth of $10,000
▬ Investment Values of Fund
— Investment Values of MSCI EAFE

Performance Quartile (within Category)

1993	1994	1995	1996	1997	1998	1999	2000	2001	2002	2003	12-04	History
15.71	14.17	14.91	16.55	16.82	15.93	18.69	16.48	14.86	12.89	16.87	17.75	NAV
33.60	0.88	21.55	21.45	19.23	6.01	28.12	-3.99	-8.10	-12.15	33.38	15.63	Total Return %
1.04	-6.90	10.34	15.40	17.45	-13.92	1.09	10.20	13.32	3.79	-5.21	-4.62	+/-MSCI EAFE
11.10	-4.20	0.83	7.97	3.47	-18.31	3.17	9.20	8.70	7.74	0.27	0.91	+/-MSCI World
2.08	1.81	2.64	2.93	2.73	2.14	2.42	1.46	1.62	1.10	2.32	1.93	Income Return %
31.52	-0.93	18.91	18.52	16.50	3.87	25.70	-5.45	-9.72	-13.25	31.06	13.70	Capital Return %
47	43	30	18	28	72	62	27	16	17	54	43	Total Rtn % Rank Cat
0.27	0.28	0.37	0.43	0.44	0.36	0.38	0.27	0.27	0.16	0.30	0.32	Income $
1.37	1.46	1.88	1.04	2.60	1.39	1.09	1.15	0.00	0.00	0.00	1.26	Capital Gains $
1.02	1.04	1.05	1.03	1.03	1.04	1.04	1.07	1.09	1.08	1.11	1.11	Expense Ratio %
2.13	1.67	2.18	2.66	2.58	2.34	1.99	1.52	1.79	1.15	1.40	1.32	Income Ratio %
24	31	34	22	39	43	36	47	25	45	44	38	Turnover Rate %
4,986	5,020	5,988	7,160	8,682	8,724	9,957	8,448	7,060	5,744	7,110	7,786	Net Assets $mil

Performance 12-31-04

	1st Qtr	2nd Qtr	3rd Qtr	4th Qtr	Total
2000	-1.34	-1.95	0.55	-1.30	-3.99
2001	-8.68	2.59	-13.54	13.45	-8.10
2002	3.30	-3.00	-18.07	7.00	-12.15
2003	-8.77	19.81	7.59	13.41	33.38
2004	4.15	-1.20	-0.98	13.48	15.63

Trailing	Total Return%	+/- MSCI EAFE	+/- MSCI World	%Rank Cat	Growth of $10,000
3 Mo	13.48	-1.84	1.54	25	11,348
6 Mo	12.37	-2.63	1.55	32	11,237
1 Yr	15.63	-4.62	0.91	43	11,563
3 Yr Avg	10.65	-1.24	3.70	25	13,547
5 Yr Avg	3.64	4.77	6.09	16	11,957
10 Yr Avg	11.07	5.45	2.98	24	28,574
15 Yr Avg	10.28	6.05	3.69	34	43,396

Tax Analysis	Tax-Adj Rtn%	%Rank Cat	Tax-Cost Rat	%Rank Cat
3 Yr (estimated)	7.45	40	0.96	90
5 Yr (estimated)	1.24	25	1.14	77
10 Yr (estimated)	8.12	40	2.08	93

Potential Capital Gain Exposure: 22% of assets

Rating and Risk

Time Period	Load-Adj Return %	Morningstar Rtn vs Cat	Morningstar Risk vs Cat	Morningstar Risk-Adj Rating
1 Yr	8.98			
3 Yr	8.49	Avg	Avg	★★★
5 Yr	2.41	+Avg	-Avg	★★★★
10 Yr	10.42	+Avg	-Avg	★★★★
Incept	13.74			

Other Measures	Standard Index S&P 500	Best Fit Index MSCI World
Alpha	-0.4	4.7
Beta	0.93	0.99
R-Squared	90	92

Standard Deviation	16.96
Mean	10.65
Sharpe Ratio	0.55

Portfolio Analysis 09-30-04

Share change since 06-04 Total Stocks:123	Sector	Country	% Assets
Cheung Kong (hldgs) Ltd	Financial	Hong Kong	3.56
☼ Sanofi-Synthelabo	Health	France	2.35
☼ BP PLC ADR	Energy	U.K.	2.18
Royal Dutch Petroleum	Energy	Netherlands	2.11
⊕ Hutchison Whampoa Ltd	Telecom	Hong Kong	2.06
Nippon Telegraph & Telep	Telecom	Japan	1.74
⊕ Vodafone Group Plc	—	—	1.60
Nintendo	Goods	Japan	1.57
⊕ GlaxoSmithKline	Health	U.K.	1.55
AmerisourceBergen	Health	United States	1.54
⊕ Swiss Re	Financial	Switzerland	1.51
⊕ Novartis	Health	Switzerland	1.36
Kookmin Bank	Financial	Korea	1.33
ACE	Financial	United States	1.31
Nomura Hldgs	Financial	Japan	1.29
⊖ Dow Chemical	Ind Mtrls	United States	1.27
Tenet Healthcare	Health	United States	1.22
Merrill Lynch & Company	Financial	United States	1.22
Rodamco Europe Inc	—	Netherlands	1.19
⊕ The Directv Group	Media	United States	1.17

Current Investment Style

Value Blnd Growth — Large Mid Small

Market Cap	%
Giant	43.9
Large	36.3
Mid	19.3
Small	0.2
Micro	0.2
Avg $mil: 17,970	

Value Measures		Rel Category
Price/Earnings	13.28	0.84
Price/Book	1.61	0.73
Price/Sales	0.84	0.72
Price/Cash Flow	5.17	0.81
Dividend Yield %	2.60	1.38

Growth Measures	%	Rel Category
Long-Term Erngs	10.39	0.86
Book Value	-0.26	NMF
Sales	4.83	1.15
Cash Flow	5.90	1.01
Historical Erngs	5.91	0.69

Sector Weightings	% of Stocks	Rel MSCI EAFE	3 Year High	3 Year Low
Info	16.72	1.01		
Software	3.98	3.69	6	3
Hardware	1.11	0.30	4	1
Media	4.78	2.10	5	0
Telecom	6.85	0.71	12	7
Service	45.33	1.01		
Health	14.37	1.98	14	7
Consumer	0.59	0.12	4	1
Business	4.33	0.80	6	3
Financial	26.04	0.96	31	24
Mfg	37.95	0.98		
Goods	9.24	0.68	15	8
Ind Mtrls	13.41	1.09	16	12
Energy	10.05	1.37	10	5
Utilities	5.25	0.98	7	3

Regional Exposure	% Stock		
UK/W. Europe	43	N. America	25
Japan	10	Latn America	1
Asia X Japan	22	Other	0

Composition			
Cash	7.8	Bonds	0.9
Stocks	86.9	Other	4.4
Foreign (% of Stock)	75.0		

Country Exposure	% Stock		
United States	25	Hong Kong	10
U.K.	19	South Korea	6
Japan	10		

Morningstar's Take by Dieter Bardy 12-28-04

Templeton World Fund proves that patience pays off.

A volatile year for world-stock markets hasn't left this fund untouched. The first half of 2004 was tough for the fund, but currency gains and good stock-picking helped in the second half. For the year-to-date period through Dec. 23, 2004, the fund has gained 14.4%, which is in line with its peers. More importantly, the fund has placed in the top quartile for the trailing three-, five-, and 10-year periods.

The fund's strategy keeps it from slipping and losing focus. Lead manager Jeff Everett looks for temporarily underpriced shares of firms with strong three- to five-year earnings outlooks. Frequently, he finds the best deals where others are selling. For example, big-cap pharmaceutical issues got a lot of negative press in 2004, but in typical Templeton fashion, Everett added to favorites such as GlaxoSmithKlin. He feels the stock was needlessly hit by problems that didn't affect it and likes the firm's diversified product line--no one drug contributes more than 10% to its total sales.

Another difference here is the fund's regional exposure. Because the fund only invests where it finds undervalued opportunities, fewer ideas have surfaced in the U.S., where stocks, according to Everett, continue to look overvalued relative to other markets around the world. Only 24% of the fund is in the U.S., compared with its typical rival's 45% weight. Meanwhile, it currently holds 28% of its assets in Asia, roughly 50 percentage points greater than its typical peer. Nevertheless, this is a fairly normal profile here: an underweight in the U.S., with overweights in other areas around the globe.

All in all, this fund deserves a look. Its experienced management, low fees, and patient approach distinguish its record.

Address:	500 E Broward Blvd Fort Lauderdale FL 33394 800-342-5236
Web Address:	www.franklintempleton.com
Inception:	01-17-78
Advisor:	Templeton Global Advisors Limited
Subadvisor:	None
NTF Plans:	DATALynx NTF, Federated Tr NTF

Minimum Purchase:	$1000	Add: $50	IRA: $250
Min Auto Inv Plan:	$50	Add: $50	
Sales Fees:	5.75%L		
Management Fee:	0.63% mx./0.54% mn., 0.15%A		
Actual Fees:	Mgt:0.62%	Dist:0.25%	
Expense Projections:	3Yr:$908	5Yr:$1151	10Yr:$1849
Income Distrib:	Annually		

The Fairholme Fund

Ticker	Load	NAV	Yield	Total Assets	Mstar Category
FAIRX	None	$22.77	0.3%	$235 mil	Mid-Cap Blend

Governance and Management

Fiduciary Grade:

Portfolio Manager(s)

Bruce Berkowitz started this fund in December 1999 as an outgrowth of his separate-accounts practice. Previously, he worked for Salomon Smith Barney and Lehman Brothers. Larry Pitkowsky was named comanager to start 2002. Keith Trauner is the fund's sole analyst.

Strategy

Managers Bruce Berkowitz and Larry Pitkowsky have adopted the principles of legendary value investor Benjamin Graham. They only buy stocks when they can forecast high enough levels of free cash flow to compensate for the risk of owning the stock. The fund will retreat to bonds or cash when management is not satisfied with potential investment opportunities.

Historical Profile

Return High
Risk Low
Rating ★★★★★ Highest

Investment Style: Equity Stock % — 87% (2000), 77% (2001), 70% (2002), 80% (2003), 80% (12-04)

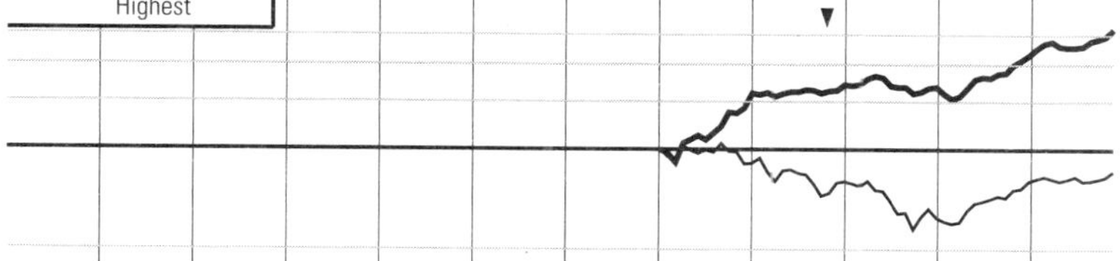

▼ Manager Change
▽ Partial Manager Change

Growth of $10,000
— Investment Values of Fund
— Investment Values of S&P 500

Performance Quartile (within Category)

1993	1994	1995	1996	1997	1998	1999	2000	2001	2002	2003	12-04	History
—	—	—	—	—	—	10.21	14.68	15.47	15.09	18.70	22.77	NAV
—	—	—	—	—	—	2.20*	46.54	6.18	-1.58	23.96	24.93	Total Return %
—	—	—	—	—	—	—	55.64	18.06	20.51	-4.71	14.06	+/-S&P 500
—	—	—	—	—	—	—	29.05	6.78	12.95	-11.63	8.46	+/-S&P Mid 400
—	—	—	—	—	—	—	0.36	0.20	0.20	0.00	0.32	Income Return %
—	—	—	—	—	—	—	46.18	5.98	-1.78	23.96	24.61	Capital Return %
—	—	—	—	—	—	—	1	26	2	96	3	Total Rtn % Rank Cat
—	—	—	—	—	—	0.00	0.04	0.03	0.03	0.00	0.06	Income $
—	—	—	—	—	—	0.00	0.25	0.09	0.10	0.01	0.53	Capital Gains $
—	—	—	—	—	—	—	1.00	1.00	1.00	1.00	—	Expense Ratio %
—	—	—	—	—	—	—	0.46	0.24	0.05	-0.13	—	Income Ratio %
—	—	—	—	—	—	—	39	29	48	13	—	Turnover Rate %
—	—	—	—	—	—	—	17	26	41	69	235	Net Assets $mil

Performance 12-31-04

	1st Qtr	2nd Qtr	3rd Qtr	4th Qtr	Total
2000	4.31	2.35	20.73	13.69	46.54
2001	-2.04	3.20	-0.94	6.04	6.18
2002	4.07	-4.72	-4.95	4.43	-1.58
2003	-6.03	13.82	2.91	12.62	23.96
2004	9.63	-3.71	5.72	11.94	24.93

Trailing	Total Return%	+/- S&P 500	+/- S&P Mid 400	%Rank Cat	Growth of $10,000
3 Mo	11.94	2.71	-0.21	40	11,194
6 Mo	18.35	11.16	8.56	1	11,835
1 Yr	24.93	14.06	8.46	3	12,493
3 Yr Avg	15.09	11.51	4.58	8	15,244
5 Yr Avg	18.85	21.15	9.32	2	23,714
10 Yr Avg	—	—	—	—	—
15 Yr Avg	—	—	—	—	—

Tax Analysis	Tax-Adj Rtn%	%Rank Cat	Tax-Cost Rat	%Rank Cat
3 Yr (estimated)	14.81	8	0.24	28
5 Yr (estimated)	18.45	1	0.34	10
10 Yr (estimated)	—	—	—	—

Potential Capital Gain Exposure: 23% of assets

Rating and Risk

Time Period	Load-Adj Return %	Morningstar Rtn vs Cat	Morningstar Risk vs Cat	Morningstar Risk-Adj Rating
1 Yr	24.93			
3 Yr	15.09	High	Low	★★★★★
5 Yr	18.85	High	Low	★★★★★
10 Yr	—	—	—	—
Incept	19.32			

Other Measures	Standard Index S&P 500	Best Fit Index Mstar Mid Value
Alpha	12.4	5.5
Beta	0.47	0.57
R-Squared	48	66
Standard Deviation	11.52	
Mean	15.09	
Sharpe Ratio	1.20	

Portfolio Analysis 08-31-04

Share change since 05-04 Total Stocks:21	Sector	PE	YTD Ret%	% Assets
Leucadia National	Ind Mtrls	34.4	51.53	15.63
⊕ MCI	Telecom	—	—	13.00
Berkshire Hathaway B	Financial	20.9	4.30	7.84
⊕ Berkshire Hathaway A	Financial	—	—	7.06
Alleghany	Financial	14.7	30.77	4.26
Penn West Petroleum Ltd	Energy	—	—	3.68
⊖ Miscellaneous Investment	—	—	—	3.23
Mercury General	Financial	12.2	32.38	3.11
HomeFed	Financial	—	—	2.72
Gladstone Capital	Financial	20.0	12.85	2.14
White Mtns Ins Grp	Financial	41.1	40.75	2.10
EchoStar Communications	Media	NMF	0.85	2.01
⊕ Duke Energy	Utilities	—	30.21	1.98
Markel	Financial	21.8	43.58	1.97
Gladstone Commercial	Financial	—	4.44	1.95
JZ Equity Partners	Financial	—	—	1.43
Rinker Grp Ltd	Ind Mtrls	—	—	1.42
Health Management Associ	Health	16.6	-4.89	1.41
Ethan Allen Interiors	Goods	17.8	3.98	1.39
Capital Southwest	Financial	—	27.62	0.75

Current Investment Style

Market Cap	%
Giant	11.7
Large	13.9
Mid	62.0
Small	4.2
Micro	8.1
Avg $mil: 4,589	

Value Measures		Rel Category
Price/Earnings	17.42	1.03
Price/Book	1.56	0.72
Price/Sales	0.77	0.73
Price/Cash Flow	0.79	0.13
Dividend Yield %	0.49	0.49

Growth Measures	%	Rel Category
Long-Term Erngs	12.49	1.00
Book Value	11.15	1.58
Sales	-1.92	NMF
Cash Flow	70.93	9.47
Historical Erngs	10.16	0.90

Profitability	%	Rel Category
Return on Equity	10.02	0.73
Return on Assets	20.33	3.12
Net Margin	26.83	2.96

Sector Weightings	% of Stocks	Rel S&P 500	3 Year High	3 Year Low
Info	20.34	0.95		
Software	0.00	0.00	0	0
Hardware	0.00	0.00	4	0
Media	3.38	0.88	4	0
Telecom	16.96	5.38	17	0
Service	47.95	1.03		
Health	1.85	0.15	4	0
Consumer	0.00	0.00	4	0
Business	0.00	0.00	0	0
Financial	46.10	2.22	79	46
Mfg	31.71	0.99		
Goods	1.81	0.19	8	2
Ind Mtrls	22.25	1.76	24	8
Energy	5.06	0.71	5	0
Utilities	2.59	0.88	3	0

Composition

Cash	13.9
Stocks	73.9
Bonds	0.0
Other	0.3
Foreign (% of Stock)	8.4

Morningstar's Take by Dan McNeela 11-03-04

The Fairholme Fund has just passed another field test.

Investors who've come to know this fund may have raised an eyebrow in the wake of New York Attorney General Eliot Spitzer's recent investigation into insurance firms. After all, about one third of the fund's assets in stocks is invested in firms whose primary business is insurance. Spitzer's complaint, which alleged bid rigging, sent the stock price of insurance broker Marsh & McLennan and several other insurers reeling.

The fund, however, escaped unharmed, as none of its insurers have been implicated in the investigation. It also avoided the scandal because its property and casualty insurers and reinsurance giant Berkshire Hathaway aren't big players in the commercial insurance business.

Dodging that bullet, however, doesn't dismiss the potential risk of having significant industry concentration. Manager Bruce Berkowitz acknowledges that its not always possible to root out unethical business practices that may lead to a blow-up, but Fairholme works hard to gain insight. It prefers management teams with the integrity to admit to internal problems and lumpy earnings. Berkowitz also looks for a long paper trail of history that reflects positively on management. Berkowitz has so much experience with insurers that White Mountain Insurance Group (a current holding) appointed him to their board of directors in 2004.

Given the fund's style, investors should expect some years when performance sags relative to various benchmarks. But those risks haven't yet been an issue. In 2004, the fund has powered to a very strong year-to-date return of 13% through November 2. In addition to getting solid gains from its insurers, top-holding Leucadia National has soared by more than 25% this year.

This unique offering continues to show an ability to root out hidden gems in various corners of the market. We give it our endorsement.

Address:	51 JFK Parkway Short Hills NJ 07078 866-202-2263
Web Address:	www.fairholmefunds.com
Inception:	12-29-99*
Advisor:	Fairholme Capital Management, LLC.
Subadvisor:	None
NTF Plans:	N/A

Minimum Purchase:	$2500	Add: $1000	IRA: $1000
Min Auto Inv Plan:	$2500	Add: $100	
Sales Fees:	No-load, 2.00%R		
Management Fee:	1.00%, 0.50%A		
Actual Fees:	Mgt:0.50%	Dist: —	
Expense Projections:	3Yr:$318	5Yr:$552	10Yr:$1225
Income Distrib:	Annually		

Third Avenue Intl Value

Ticker	Load	NAV	Yield	Total Assets	Mstar Category
TAVIX	None	$18.41	1.2%	$369 mil	Foreign Small/Mid Value

Governance and Management

Fiduciary Grade: B

Portfolio Manager(s)

Amit Wadhwaney has been the fund's skipper since its inception. Before this, Wadhwaney hadn't run a retail mutual fund. But he has considerable experience at Third Avenue, having been a senior analyst for many years in support of the firm's domestic charges (including Third Avenue Value and Third Avenue Small-Cap Value). As with all Third Avenue funds, he can draw on fellow managers and analysts for ideas and research support.

Strategy

Manager Amit Wadhwaney is a value hound. He looks for companies that are trading at big discounts to their private or liquidation values, scrutinizing each firm's balance sheet to get a fix on the sum of its parts. Though Wadhwaney has targeted small-cap stocks thus far, he views the fund as an all-cap product and is willing to venture into larger fare. He pays no heed to benchmarks, so sector bets are common, and the portfolio is more focused than the norm. Though foreign-currency exposure is generally unhedged, management can use instruments such as out-of-the-money put options to hedge out positions.

Historical Profile

Return Average
Risk Low
Rating ★★★ Neutral

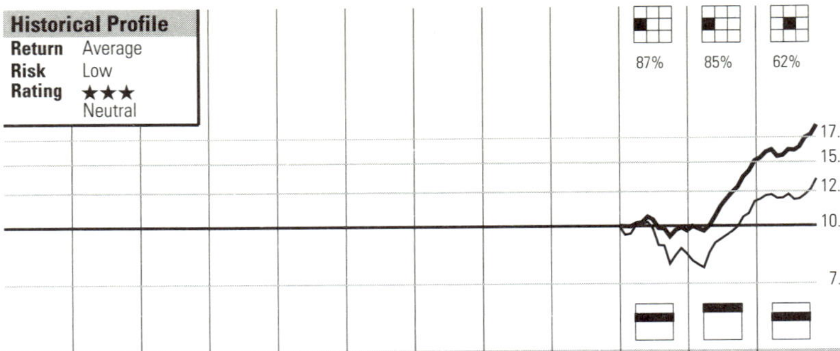

Investment Style
Equity
Stock %

▼ Manager Change
▽ Partial Manager Change

Growth of $10,000
— Investment Values of Fund
— Investment Values of MSCI EAFE

Performance Quartile (within Category)

1993	1994	1995	1996	1997	1998	1999	2000	2001	2002	2003	12-04	History
—	—	—	—	—	—	—	—	10.00	9.63	14.59	18.41	NAV
—	—	—	—	—	—	—	—	0.00*	-2.87	54.68	27.70	Total Return %
—	—	—	—	—	—	—	—	—	13.07	16.09	7.45	+/-MSCI EAFE
—	—	—	—	—	—	—	—	—	12.93	15.26	7.32	+/-MSCI Wd xUS
—	—	—	—	—	—	—	—	—	0.82	3.08	1.51	Income Return %
—	—	—	—	—	—	—	—	—	-3.69	51.60	26.19	Capital Return %
—	—	—	—	—	—	—	—	—	35	21	43	Total Rtn % Rank Cat
—	—	—	—	—	—	—	—	0.00	0.08	0.30	0.22	Income $
—	—	—	—	—	—	—	—	0.00	0.00	0.00	0.00	Capital Gains $
—	—	—	—	—	—	—	—	—	1.75	1.75	—	Expense Ratio %
—	—	—	—	—	—	—	—	—	0.34	0.52	—	Income Ratio %
—	—	—	—	—	—	—	—	—	—	4	—	Turnover Rate %
—	—	—	—	—	—	—	—	—	26	140	369	Net Assets $mil

Performance 12-31-04

	1st Qtr	2nd Qtr	3rd Qtr	4th Qtr	Total
2000	—	—	—	—	—
2001	—	—	—	—	0.00 *
2002	1.60	2.46	-10.09	3.77	-2.87
2003	-0.21	16.86	12.64	17.75	54.68
2004	7.13	-0.00	7.81	10.58	27.70

Trailing	Total Return%	+/- MSCI EAFE	+/- MSCI Wd xUS	%Rank Cat	Growth of $10,000
3 Mo	10.58	-4.74	-4.57	96	11,058
6 Mo	19.21	4.21	3.84	1	11,921
1 Yr	27.70	7.45	7.32	43	12,770
3 Yr Avg	24.26	12.37	12.04	29	19,186
5 Yr Avg	—	—	—	—	—
10 Yr Avg	—	—	—	—	—
15 Yr Avg	—	—	—	—	—

Tax Analysis	Tax-Adj Rtn%	%Rank Cat	Tax-Cost Rat	%Rank Cat
3 Yr (estimated)	23.65	27	0.49	29
5 Yr (estimated)	—	—	—	—
10 Yr (estimated)	—	—	—	—

Potential Capital Gain Exposure: 23% of assets

Rating and Risk

Time Period	Load-Adj Return %	Morningstar Rtn vs Cat	Morningstar Risk vs Cat	Morningstar Risk-Adj Rating
1 Yr	27.70			
3 Yr	24.26	Avg	Low	★★★
5 Yr	—	—	—	—
10 Yr	—	—	—	—
Incept	24.25			

Other Measures	Standard Index S&P 500	Best Fit Index MSCI Pac xJp
Alpha	15.8	7.4
Beta	0.57	0.77
R-Squared	66	78
Standard Deviation	13.42	
Mean	24.26	
Sharpe Ratio	1.72	

Morningstar's Take by William Samuel Rocco 11-12-04

The distinctive Third Avenue International Value has had a great start and enjoys superior long-term prospects, but that doesn't mean it's perfect.

Third Avenue International Value takes its family's cheap-and-safe strategy abroad, and Amit Wadhwaney is just as open-minded and unconcerned with benchmarks as the firm's domestic managers. Thus, little-followed and unpopular stocks are common here, as are atypical sector and country weights.

Top holding Toll NZ, a New Zealand railroad operator, isn't owned by any of the fund's peers. No. 2 name Aker Kvaerner Ogep Asa, a Norwegian firm in the energy-services and engineering-and-construction businesses, has also escaped the attention of the fund's rivals. And the fund's New Zealand and Norway positions are much bigger than the category norms, while its financials stake is the group's largest.

Wadhwaney has executed this distinctive discipline deftly so far. After posting limited losses in a rough 2002, the fund surged to a 55% gain in 2003's rally. And it's up an impressive 20% for the year to date, due to big gains from Toll NZ and other picks. Overall, the fund has posted a 21.5% annualized returns since opening at the end of 2001, while its typical peer has generated a 13.8% annualized return over that period.

Moreover, Wadhwaney, a Third Avenue veteran, has had longer-term success running private and other accounts. The firm has generated superior results, using a like-minded style, on its domestic funds. And the fund's low turnover should enhance tax efficiency.

In short, there are ample grounds to be confident about the fund over the long term. That said, interested investors need to understand that it is likely to struggle when blue-chip or growth stocks dominate; that its penchant for building big positions in individual issues, countries, and sectors will backfire at times; and that it won't post superior results every year.

Address:	622 Third Avenue New York NY 10017 800-443-1021
Web Address:	www.thirdavenuefunds.com
Inception:	12-31-01 *
Advisor:	Third Avenue Management LLC
Subadvisor:	None
NTF Plans:	Fidelity Retail-NTF, Schwab OneSource

Minimum Purchase:	$2500	Add: $1000	IRA: $500
Min Auto Inv Plan:	$2500	Add: $200	
Sales Fees:	No-load, 2.00%R		
Management Fee:	1.25%		
Actual Fees:	Mgt:1.25%	Dist:	
Expense Projections:	3Yr:$1304	5Yr:$2188	10Yr:$4454
Income Distrib:	Annually		

Portfolio Analysis 10-31-04

Share change since 07-04 Total Stocks:41	Sector	Country	% Assets
⊕ Toll Nz	Business	New Zealand	6.85
⊕ Aker Kvaerner Ogep Asa	Energy	Norway	3.69
⊕ Zinifex	Ind Mtrls	Australia	3.61
⊕ Hutchison Whampoa Ltd	Telecom	Hong Kong	3.35
⊕ Telecom Corp. of New Zea	Telecom	New Zealand	2.61
⊕ Geac Computer	Software	Canada	2.52
⊕ Oslo Bors Asa	Media	Norway	2.49
⊕ Rubicon Ltd	Ind Mtrls	New Zealand	2.32
Ganger Rolf	Business	Norway	2.24
⊕ Brit Insurance Hldgs	Financial	U.K.	2.15
⊕ Compagnie Gen. de Geophy	Ind Mtrls	France	2.07
⊕ Canfor	Ind Mtrls	Canada	2.00
Chuan Hup Hldgs Ltd	Business	Singapore	1.90
⊕ Asatsu-DK	Business	Japan	1.88
⊕ Dundee Precious Metals	Financial	Canada	1.72
Smedvig	Energy	Norway	1.59
⊕ Guoco Grp Ltd	Financial	Hong Kong	1.50
⊕ Noranda	Ind Mtrls	Canada	1.23
Agrium	Ind Mtrls	Canada	1.15
Ichiyoshi Securities	Financial	Japan	1.12

Current Investment Style

Value Blnd Growth — Large Mid Small

Market Cap	%
Giant	7.8
Large	14.9
Mid	36.7
Small	36.1
Micro	4.4
Avg $mil: 1,276	

Value Measures		Rel Category
Price/Earnings	12.44	0.92
Price/Book	1.10	0.67
Price/Sales	1.06	1.58
Price/Cash Flow	5.48	1.06
Dividend Yield %	2.47	0.91

Growth Measures	%	Rel Category
Long-Term Erngs	10.04	0.82
Book Value	0.26	2.36
Sales	6.17	3.12
Cash Flow	-0.82	NMF
Historical Erngs	-0.71	NMF

Composition

Cash	37.5	Bonds	0.0
Stocks	62.5	Other	0.0
Foreign (% of Stock)			98.8

Sector Weightings	% of Stocks	Rel MSCI EAFE	3 Year High	Low
Info	17.57	1.06		
Software	4.04	3.74	11	2
Hardware	0.00	0.00	0	0
Media	3.99	1.75	5	0
Telecom	9.54	0.99	20	0
Service	47.40	1.06		
Health	0.00	0.00	0	0
Consumer	0.00	0.00	0	0
Business	27.16	4.99	28	15
Financial	20.24	0.75	42	20
Mfg	35.04	0.91		
Goods	2.23	0.16	3	0
Ind Mtrls	22.96	1.87	28	17
Energy	9.85	1.34	10	0
Utilities	0.00	0.00	0	0

Regional Exposure	% Stock		
UK/W. Europe	32	N. America	18
Japan	6	Latn America	3
Asia X Japan	41	Other	0

Country Exposure	% Stock		
New Zealand	19	Hong Kong	9
Norway	19	Singapore	6
Canada	17		

Third Avenue RealEst Val

Analyst Pick	Ticker	Load	NAV	Yield	Total Assets	Mstar Category
✔	TAREX	None	$26.96	0.7%	$1,548 mil	Specialty-Real Estate

Governance and Management

Fiduciary Grade: A

Portfolio Manager(s)

Lead manager Mike Winer has run this fund since its 1998 inception. He has extensive real estate industry experience, including stints in development and distressed situations. He's supported by senior analyst Jason Wolf, who joined the fund in April 2004 with an impressive and varied resume in the real estate industry.

Strategy

Like other Third Avenue offerings, this one seeks companies that trade at a discount to management's estimate of net asset value (NAV). The manager favors REOCs (real estate operating companies) over REITs because the former can reinvest cash flow back into the business for growth. The fund often stashes more than 60% of assets in its top-10 holdings, which means it's among the most concentrated in the category.

Historical Profile

Return Above Avg
Risk Low
Rating ★★★★★ Highest

Investment Style
Equity
Stock %: 76% 93% 82% 86% 85% 95% 73%

▼ Manager Change
▽ Partial Manager Change

Growth of $10,000
— Investment Values of Fund
— Investment Values of S&P 500

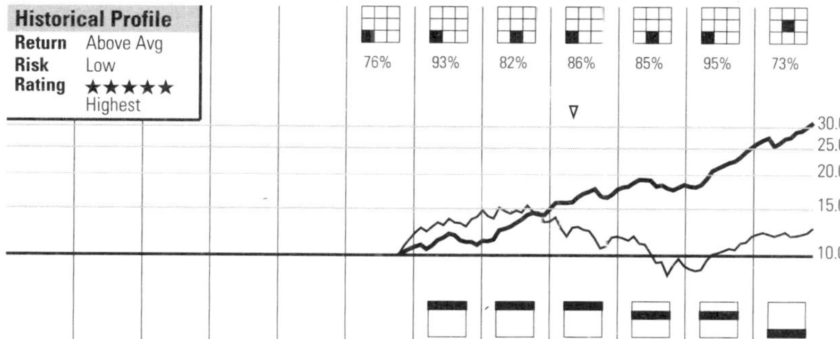

Performance Quartile (within Category)

1993	1994	1995	1996	1997	1998	1999	2000	2001	2002	2003	12-04	History
—	—	—	—	—	10.65	10.89	13.68	15.78	15.96	21.38	26.96	NAV
—	—	—	—	—	7.47*	5.17	30.91	18.20	4.24	37.34	28.16	Total Return %
—	—	—	—	—	—	-15.87	40.01	30.08	26.33	8.67	17.29	+/-S&P 500
—	—	—	—	—	—	7.74	-0.13	5.84	0.64	1.28	-5.66	+/-Wil REIT
—	—	—	—	—	0.00	2.37	2.49	1.37	1.12	2.83	0.84	Income Return %
—	—	—	—	—	—	2.80	28.42	16.83	3.12	34.51	27.32	Capital Return %
—	—	—	—	—	—	3	19	6	43	41	85	Total Rtn % Rank Cat
—	—	—	—	—	0.10	0.25	0.27	0.19	0.18	0.45	0.18	Income $
—	—	—	—	—	0.00	0.06	0.29	0.20	0.30	0.08	0.26	Capital Gains $
—	—	—	—	—	1.87	1.87	1.50	1.50	1.22	1.19	—	Expense Ratio %
—	—	—	—	—	3.20	3.20	3.89	2.79	0.93	3.51	—	Income Ratio %
—	—	—	—	—	5	5	23	20	21	11	—	Turnover Rate %
—	—	—	—	—	3	10	27	77	346	787	1,548	Net Assets $mil

Performance 12-31-04

	1st Qtr	2nd Qtr	3rd Qtr	4th Qtr	Total
2000	9.46	6.38	8.91	3.23	30.91
2001	5.56	8.17	-1.98	5.62	18.20
2002	5.96	2.09	-6.50	3.06	4.24
2003	-0.13	15.24	6.04	12.53	37.34
2004	8.23	-0.78	7.01	11.52	28.16

Trailing	Total Return%	+/- S&P 500	+/- Wil REIT	%Rank Cat	Growth of $10,000
3 Mo	11.52	2.29	-5.17	96	11,152
6 Mo	19.34	12.15	-6.92	93	11,934
1 Yr	28.16	17.29	-5.66	85	12,816
3 Yr Avg	22.42	18.84	-1.74	64	18,347
5 Yr Avg	23.21	25.51	0.54	8	28,394
10 Yr Avg	—	—	—	—	—
15 Yr Avg	—	—	—	—	—

Tax Analysis	Tax-Adj Rtn%	%Rank Cat	Tax-Cost Rat	%Rank Cat
3 Yr (estimated)	21.55	40	0.71	2
5 Yr (estimated)	22.10	3	0.90	5
10 Yr (estimated)	—	—	—	—

Potential Capital Gain Exposure: 26% of assets

Rating and Risk

Time Period	Load-Adj Return %	Morningstar Rtn vs Cat	Morningstar Risk vs Cat	Morningstar Risk-Adj Rating
1 Yr	28.16			
3 Yr	22.42	Avg	Low	★★★★
5 Yr	23.21	High	Low	★★★★★
10 Yr	—	—	—	—
Incept	20.37			

Other Measures	Standard Index S&P 500	Best Fit Index Wil REIT
Alpha	20.0	8.5
Beta	0.35	0.54
R-Squared	30	71

Standard Deviation	11.39
Mean	22.42
Sharpe Ratio	1.87

Morningstar's Take by William Samuel Rocco 12-22-04

We remain keen on this fund, despite its asset growth and subpar showing this year.

Third Avenue Real Estate Value, which began 2004 with roughly $800 million in assets, now has more than $1.9 billion in assets. The growth in assets is partly due to performance--the fund is up 26% since January 1--but it's also due to substantial inflows, and cash was 25% of assets this fall.

This asset growth is significant--and means the fund can't make meaningful investments in tiny real estate plays like it used to--but we remain bullish about the long-term prospects here for several reasons. First, manager Mike Winer says that Third Avenue plans to take steps in early 2005 to slow inflows and that the firm will do more if these steps aren't enough and the asset base or cash stake becomes a persistent problem.

Second, the fund's style is relatively well-suited to a sizable asset base. Winer has a bigger universe than most of his peers because he doesn't focus on domestic REITs like most of them do. He favors real estate operating companies over REITS and readily considers retailers and agricultural firms with major property holdings, as well as overseas real estate plays. He also moves at a far slower pace than most of his rivals, as the fund's turnover rate, which has been low from the get-go, attests.

We're not too worried about the bottom-quartile year-to-date results return, either. The 26% gain is excellent in absolute terms and the underperformance has far more to do with the cash than Winer's picks (which have generally been terrific). And though cash may well be a reoccurring issue here, due to Winer's dedication to the firm's careful and miserly strategy, other Third Avenue funds have faced the same and delivered strong risk-adjusted returns over time. The fact that this fund's overall record is great adds to our confidence.

This fund has evolved, but we still think it's a great option for flexible real estate fans.

Address:	622 Third Avenue New York NY 10017 800-443-1021
Web Address:	www.thirdavenuefunds.com
Inception:	09-17-98*
Advisor:	Third Avenue Management LLC
Subadvisor:	None
NTF Plans:	Fidelity Retail-NTF, Schwab OneSource

Minimum Purchase:	$1000	Add: $1000	IRA: $500
Min Auto Inv Plan:	$1000	Add: $200	
Sales Fees:	No-load, 1.00%R		
Management Fee:	0.90%		
Actual Fees:	Mgt:0.90%	Dist:	
Expense Projections:	3Yr:$446	5Yr:$771	10Yr:$1691
Income Distrib:	Annually		

Portfolio Analysis 10-31-04

Share change since 07-04 Total Stocks:41	Sector	PE	YTD Ret%	% Assets
⊕ St. Joe	Financial	57.6	74.18	8.78
⊕ Forest City Enterprises	Financial	49.5	22.42	8.36
LNR Property	Financial	21.7	27.19	7.33
Catellus Development	Financial	—	34.01	5.85
Brascan	Ind Mtrls	36.0	80.66	5.48
Vornado Realty Trust	Financial	30.8	46.53	3.83
ProLogis Trust	Financial	25.1	41.03	3.40
⊕ PS Business Parks A	Financial	64.2	12.41	3.22
Kmart Hldg	Consumer	37.1	313.15	2.62
Brookfield Properties	Financial	22.1	32.89	2.57
⊕ British Land	Financial	—	—	2.06
Trammell Crow	Financial	27.3	36.68	1.93
⊕ American Financial Realt	Financial	—	1.39	1.83
☼ Thomas Properties Group	Financial	—	—	1.44
☼ Fairmont Hotels & Resort	Consumer	51.6	28.01	1.21
Avatar Holdings	Financial	15.3	30.25	1.14
Consolidated-Tomoka Land	Financial	17.8	32.47	1.12
One Liberty Properties	Financial	21.3	11.08	1.02
☼ UNITE Grp	Financial	—	—	0.92
⊕ Tejon Ranch	Ind Mtrls	—	-0.51	0.85

Current Investment Style

Value Blnd Growth / Large Mid Small

Market Cap	%
Giant	0.0
Large	11.5
Mid	61.7
Small	15.2
Micro	11.6
Avg $mil: 2,157	

Value Measures		Rel Category
Price/Earnings	16.53	1.15
Price/Book	1.97	0.98
Price/Sales	2.55	0.69
Price/Cash Flow	9.98	0.83
Dividend Yield %	2.26	0.46

Growth Measures	%	Rel Category
Long-Term Erngs	8.65	1.23
Book Value	3.62	24.13
Sales	-1.78	NMF
Cash Flow	3.99	0.59
Historical Erngs	3.39	4.40

Profitability	%	Rel Category
Return on Equity	12.69	1.23
Return on Assets	7.30	0.95
Net Margin	17.27	0.80

Sector Weightings	% of Stocks	Rel S&P 500	3 Year High	3 Year Low
Info	0.00	0.00		
Software	0.00	0.00	0	0
Hardware	0.00	0.00	0	0
Media	0.00	0.00	0	0
Telecom	0.00	0.00	0	0
Service	91.10	1.96		
Health	0.00	0.00	0	0
Consumer	5.80	0.64	6	0
Business	0.00	0.00	2	0
Financial	85.30	4.11	96	85
Mfg	8.90	0.28		
Goods	0.00	0.00	0	0
Ind Mtrls	8.90	0.70	9	3
Energy	0.00	0.00	0	0
Utilities	0.00	0.00	0	0

Composition

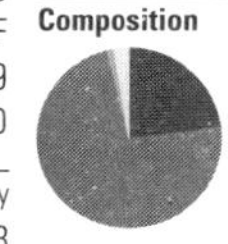

Cash	22.9
Stocks	73.1
Bonds	1.2
Other	2.7
Foreign (% of Stock)	19.0

Third Avenue Sm-Cap Val

Analyst Pick

Ticker	Load	NAV	Yield	Total Assets	Mstar Category
TASCX	None	$22.57	0.4%	$889 mil	Small Blend

Governance and Management

Fiduciary Grade: A

Portfolio Manager(s)

Curtis Jensen became this fund's sole manager when comanager Marty Whitman stepped down in mid-2001. Jensen has been on the fund since its inception, however, and shares Whitman's commitment to value investing. Whitman remains at the firm, and Jensen continues to work closely with him. The firm has lost two distressed debt analysts in recent years, but it has replaced them.

Strategy

Curtis Jensen does things a bit differently at this fund than firm founder Marty Whitman does at sibling Third Avenue Value. He still tries to invest in companies with strong balance sheets at less than half of what he thinks they're worth. This usually means purchasing companies at a significant discount to net asset value, or less than 10 times peak earnings. Like Whitman, Jensen uses a tax-efficient, buy-and-hold strategy. But at this fund, he focuses mostly on small caps and runs a somewhat more-concentrated portfolio. Also, unlike Third Avenue Value, this fund does not usually buy distressed debt.

Historical Profile

Return Above Avg
Risk Below Avg
Rating ★★★★ Above Avg

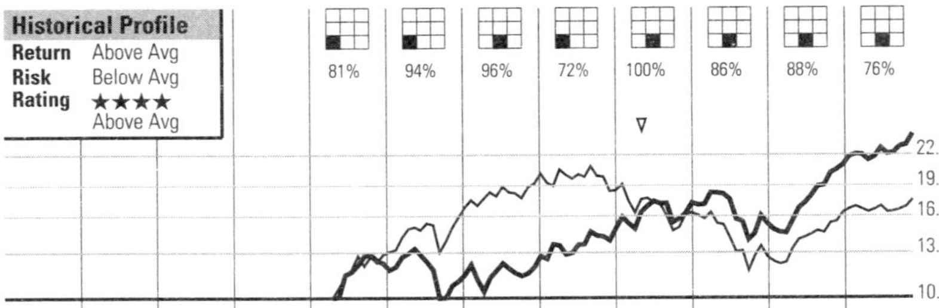

Investment Style
Equity
Stock %

▼ Manager Change
▽ Partial Manager Change

Growth of $10,000
— Investment Values of Fund
— Investment Values of S&P 500

Performance Quartile (within Category)

1993	1994	1995	1996	1997	1998	1999	2000	2001	2002	2003	12-04	History
—	—	—	—	11.64	11.23	12.40	13.59	15.37	13.56	18.75	22.57	NAV
—	—	—	—	17.02*	-2.77	11.29	17.18	15.26	-10.89	39.08	21.27	Total Return %
—	—	—	—	—	-31.34	-9.75	26.28	27.14	11.20	10.41	10.40	+/-S&P 500
—	—	—	—	—	-0.22	-9.97	20.20	12.77	9.59	-8.17	2.94	+/-Russ 2000
—	—	—	—	0.00	0.76	0.87	1.71	0.86	0.90	0.18	0.49	Income Return %
—	—	—	—	—	-3.53	10.42	15.47	14.40	-11.79	38.90	20.78	Capital Return %
—	—	—	—	—	33	53	33	24	23	63	30	Total Rtn % Rank Cat
—	—	—	—	0.06	0.09	0.10	0.21	0.12	0.14	0.03	0.09	Income $
—	—	—	—	0.00	0.00	0.00	0.69	0.17	0.00	0.08	0.08	Capital Gains $
—	—	—	—	1.65	1.28	1.28	1.30	1.23	1.17	1.17	—	Expense Ratio %
—	—	—	—	1.44	0.72	0.72	1.43	1.16	1.03	0.21	—	Income Ratio %
—	—	—	—	—	6	10	19	18	19	22	—	Turnover Rate %
—	—	—	—	106	144	127	141	364	395	602	889	Net Assets $mil

Performance 12-31-04

	1st Qtr	2nd Qtr	3rd Qtr	4th Qtr	Total
2000	6.21	0.53	5.14	4.38	17.18
2001	-0.29	16.68	-11.13	11.48	15.26
2002	5.99	-3.68	-20.46	9.75	-10.89
2003	-5.24	18.60	10.37	12.13	39.08
2004	5.87	3.73	0.97	9.37	21.27

Trailing	Total Return%	+/- S&P 500	+/- Russ 2000	%Rank Cat	Growth of $10,000
3 Mo	9.37	0.14	-4.72	95	10,937
6 Mo	10.44	3.25	-0.39	61	11,044
1 Yr	21.27	10.40	2.94	30	12,127
3 Yr Avg	14.55	10.97	3.07	28	15,031
5 Yr Avg	15.21	17.51	8.60	29	20,298
10 Yr Avg	—	—	—	—	—
15 Yr Avg	—	—	—	—	—

Tax Analysis	Tax-Adj Rtn%	%Rank Cat	Tax-Cost Rat	%Rank Cat
3 Yr (estimated)	14.26	22	0.25	18
5 Yr (estimated)	14.49	23	0.62	24
10 Yr (estimated)	—	—	—	—

Potential Capital Gain Exposure: 30% of assets

Rating and Risk

Time Period	Load-Adj Return %	Morningstar Rtn vs Cat	Morningstar Risk vs Cat	Morningstar Risk-Adj Rating
1 Yr	21.27			
3 Yr	14.55	+Avg	-Avg	★★★★
5 Yr	15.21	+Avg	-Avg	★★★★
10 Yr	—	—	—	—
Incept	12.95			

Other Measures	Standard Index S&P 500	Best Fit Index Mstar Mid Core
Alpha	11.1	1.6
Beta	0.91	0.98
R-Squared	75	89
Standard Deviation	17.90	
Mean	14.55	
Sharpe Ratio	0.74	

Portfolio Analysis 10-31-04

Share change since 07-04 Total Stocks:73	Sector	PE	YTD Ret%	% Assets
Brascan	Ind Mtrls	36.0	80.66	3.51
Kmart Hldg	Consumer	37.1	313.15	2.76
TimberWest Forest	Ind Mtrls	—	—	2.74
LNR Property	Financial	21.7	27.19	2.56
Forest City Enterprises	Financial	49.5	22.42	2.17
⊕ St. Joe	Financial	57.6	74.18	2.16
⊕ Pogo Producing	Energy	10.6	0.87	2.16
⊕ CommScope	Hardware	16.3	15.74	2.08
⊕ Whiting Petroleum	Energy	—	64.40	2.00
Fording Canadian Coal Tr	Energy	—	—	1.97
E-L Financial	Financial	—	—	1.87
⊕ Superior Industries Inte	Ind Mtrls	12.6	-32.12	1.78
Agrium	Ind Mtrls	—	3.13	1.76
Trinity Industries	Ind Mtrls	—	11.40	1.62
Precision Drilling	Energy	17.5	43.77	1.58
⊕ St. Mary Land & Explorat	Energy	14.8	46.85	1.40
⊕ Electro Scientific Indus	Hardware	15.4	-16.98	1.35
Leucadia National	Ind Mtrls	34.4	51.53	1.34
⊕ K-Swiss	Goods	17.7	22.24	1.29
⊕ Arch Capital Group	Financial	9.1	-2.91	1.28

Current Investment Style

Value Blnd Growth — Large Mid Small

Market Cap	%
Giant	0.0
Large	7.3
Mid	39.1
Small	39.2
Micro	14.4
Avg $mil: 1,262	

Value Measures		Rel Category
Price/Earnings	17.19	0.99
Price/Book	1.67	0.84
Price/Sales	1.32	1.39
Price/Cash Flow	5.87	1.00
Dividend Yield %	1.55	1.87

Growth Measures	%	Rel Category
Long-Term Erngs	13.13	0.97
Book Value	0.77	0.14
Sales	-0.68	NMF
Cash Flow	12.34	2.50
Historical Erngs	0.75	0.10

Profitability	%	Rel Category
Return on Equity	8.84	0.85
Return on Assets	4.85	0.98
Net Margin	9.37	1.28

Sector Weightings	% of Stocks	Rel S&P 500	3 Year High	3 Year Low
Info	17.63	0.82		
Software	2.78	0.65	3	0
Hardware	14.85	1.46	32	15
Media	0.00	0.00	0	0
Telecom	0.00	0.00	0	0
Service	36.60	0.79		
Health	3.61	0.29	5	3
Consumer	6.94	0.76	7	1
Business	2.01	0.50	5	1
Financial	24.04	1.16	37	24
Mfg	45.76	1.42		
Goods	4.16	0.45	4	1
Ind Mtrls	28.43	2.24	31	26
Energy	13.17	1.84	13	2
Utilities	0.00	0.00	0	0

Composition

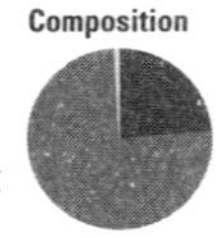

Cash	23.4
Stocks	75.6
Bonds	0.0
Other	1.0
Foreign (% of Stock)	19.4

Morningstar's Take by Christopher Traulsen 12-01-04

We think Third Avenue Small Cap Value holds considerable appeal.

This fund has much to offer, in our view. Its advisor uses a well-defined, time-tested style, and doesn't veer from its convictions about the right way to invest. Like his colleagues, manager Curtis Jensen (the heir apparent to firm founder Marty Whitman) looks for securities that are both safe and cheap. No equity security, of course, can offer safety from market risk, but that's not what Jensen means--he defines safe as being readily understandable and having a rock-solid balance sheet. This often leads Jensen to asset-rich companies trading well below his estimates of their net asset values.

In 2004, Jensen simply hasn't been able to find much that meets his criteria. Given that he pulled money out of the fund's technology stake during and after the 2003 tech rally, the lack of qualifying opportunities has left the fund with a high cash stake for much of the year. As of Sept. 30, 2004, it stood near 25% of assets.

Despite that large cash stake, the fund has outpaced both the small-blend and small-value category averages thus far in 2004. A prescient move into Kmart has helped a lot, but the fund has also drawn strength from an array of other picks including Brascan, LNR Property, and Whiting Petroleum. Such picks have allowed the fund to succeed even though it had significant exposure to the weak technology hardware sector.

The fund has also fared well for investors over the long term. It has handily beat the average small-blend fund and edged the average small-value fund since its inception, with less volatility (as measured by standard deviation) than either. The fund could well be held back by its large cash stake if the market shoots up, but we'd rather the fund stuck to its disciplined, time-tested process than chase short-term gains. For investors who can wait out the occasional lean spell, we think this a good value-oriented small-cap fund.

Address:	622 Third Avenue New York NY 10017 800-443-1021
Web Address:	www.thirdavenuefunds.com
Inception:	04-01-97 *
Advisor:	Third Avenue Management LLC
Subadvisor:	None
NTF Plans:	Fidelity Retail-NTF, Schwab OneSource

Minimum Purchase:	$1000	Add: $1000	IRA: $500
Min Auto Inv Plan:	$1000	Add: $200	
Sales Fees:	No-load, 1.00%R		
Management Fee:	0.90%		
Actual Fees:	Mgt:0.90%	Dist:	
Expense Projections:	3Yr:$372	5Yr:$644	10Yr:$1420
Income Distrib:	Annually		

Third Avenue Value

Ticker	Load	NAV	Yield	Total Assets	Mstar Category
TAVFX	None	$51.70	1.5%	$3,646 mil	Small Blend

Governance and Management

Fiduciary Grade: A

Portfolio Manager(s)

Marty Whitman is a premier value manager and is an expert in bankruptcies and distressed securities. He has been managing mutual funds since 1986 and is supported by a staff of 11 analysts and portfolio managers.

Strategy

Manager Marty Whitman sniffs out bargains among beaten-down and unloved companies. He tries to buy asset plays at discounts of at least 20% to NAV and earnings-driven companies at no more than 10 times peak earnings. Although he wants to buy cheap companies, he also wants them to be safe. The strength of a company's balance sheet is thus a key factor in his investment decisions. Whitman also keeps a significant percentage of the fund's assets in distressed debt. He uses a buy-and-hold style and manages the fund with a careful eye to tax efficiency.

Historical Profile

Return Above Avg
Risk Low
Rating ★★★★ Above Avg

Investment Style: Equity Stock %

1993	1994	1995	1996	1997	1998	1999	2000	2001	2002	2003	12-04
61%	54%	90%	97%	84%	81%	78%	84%	71%			

▼ Manager Change
▽ Partial Manager Change

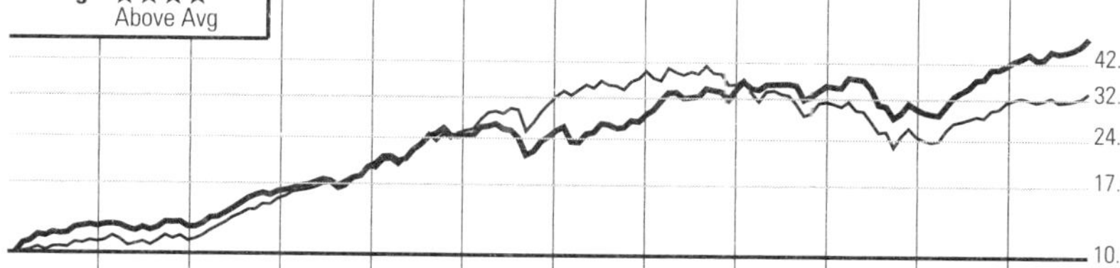

Growth of $10,000
— Investment Values of Fund
— Investment Values of S&P 500

Performance Quartile (within Category)

History

1993	1994	1995	1996	1997	1998	1999	2000	2001	2002	2003	12-04	History
17.62	16.97	21.80	25.86	31.46	32.29	35.99	36.22	36.43	30.47	41.45	51.70	NAV
23.66	-1.46	31.73	21.92	23.87	3.92	12.82	20.76	2.82	-15.19	37.09	26.60	Total Return %
13.60	-2.77	-5.80	-1.02	-9.48	-24.65	-8.22	29.86	14.70	6.90	8.42	15.73	+/-S&P 500
4.78	0.36	3.28	5.43	1.51	6.47	-8.44	23.78	0.33	5.29	-10.16	8.27	+/-Russ 2000
1.79	1.41	2.39	2.63	1.59	1.28	0.00	2.10	1.70	1.08	1.03	1.87	Income Return %
21.87	-2.87	29.34	19.29	22.28	2.64	12.82	18.66	1.12	-16.27	36.06	24.73	Capital Return %
12	49	27	47	63	10	48	26	74	50	76	6	Total Rtn % Rank Cat
0.26	0.25	0.41	0.57	0.41	0.40	0.00	0.68	0.62	0.39	0.32	0.78	Income $
0.25	0.14	0.15	0.14	0.16	0.00	0.42	6.16	0.19	0.04	0.00	0.00	Capital Gains $
1.42	1.16	1.25	1.21	1.13	1.08	1.10	1.09	1.07	1.07	1.11	—	Expense Ratio %
1.45	1.85	2.24	2.67	2.10	1.44	1.27	1.41	1.31	0.90	1.23	—	Income Ratio %
17	5	15	14	10	24	5	30	21	19	11	—	Turnover Rate %
138	180	329	645	1,676	1,600	1,379	1,940	2,654	2,233	3,098	3,646	Net Assets $mil

Performance 12-31-04

	1st Qtr	2nd Qtr	3rd Qtr	4th Qtr	Total
2000	17.48	-3.30	5.34	0.91	20.76
2001	-0.28	4.26	-10.75	10.80	2.82
2002	6.07	-7.40	-19.40	7.14	-15.19
2003	-4.63	18.55	9.75	10.47	37.09
2004	8.95	2.21	1.26	12.27	26.60

Trailing	Total Return%	+/- S&P 500	+/- Russ 2000	%Rank Cat	Growth of $10,000
3 Mo	12.27	3.04	-1.82	63	11,227
6 Mo	13.68	6.49	2.85	14	11,368
1 Yr	26.60	15.73	8.27	6	12,660
3 Yr Avg	13.75	10.17	2.27	32	14,718
5 Yr Avg	12.82	15.12	6.21	45	18,278
10 Yr Avg	15.60	3.53	4.06	23	42,617
15 Yr Avg	—	—	—	—	—

Tax Analysis	Tax-Adj Rtn%	%Rank Cat	Tax-Cost Rat	%Rank Cat
3 Yr (estimated)	13.25	28	0.44	31
5 Yr (estimated)	11.47	44	1.20	58
10 Yr (estimated)	14.54	11	0.92	17

Potential Capital Gain Exposure: 43% of assets

Rating and Risk

Time Period	Load-Adj Return %	Morningstar Rtn vs Cat	Morningstar Risk vs Cat	Morningstar Risk-Adj Rating
1 Yr	26.60			
3 Yr	13.75	+Avg	-Avg	★★★★
5 Yr	12.82	Avg	Low	★★★
10 Yr	15.60	+Avg	Low	★★★★
Incept	16.95			

Other Measures	Standard Index S&P 500	Best Fit Index S&P Mid 400
Alpha	10.3	3.5
Beta	0.88	0.95
R-Squared	75	88

Standard Deviation	17.31
Mean	13.75
Sharpe Ratio	0.72

Portfolio Analysis 10-31-04

Share change since 07-04 Total Stocks:84	Sector	PE	YTD Ret%	% Assets
⊕ Kmart Hldg	Consumer	37.1	313.15	8.86
⊕ Toyota Industries	Goods	—	—	5.98
⊕ St. Joe	Financial	57.6	74.18	3.82
Millea Holdings ADR	Financial	—	11.80	3.70
⊕ Brascan	Ind Mtrls	36.0	80.66	3.38
Tejon Ranch	Ind Mtrls	—	-0.51	3.24
MBIA	Financial	11.3	8.57	2.72
Forest City Enterprises	Financial	49.5	22.42	2.56
Japanese Yen/Usd Swap	—	—	—	2.55
☼ Usg 9.25%	—	—	—	2.51
⊕ Legg Mason	Financial	22.3	43.56	2.44
Mitsui Sumitomo Insuranc	Financial	—	—	2.35
⊕ Hutchison Whampoa Ltd	Telecom	—	—	2.03
AVX	Hardware	75.0	-23.37	2.02
Radian Group	Financial	11.9	9.40	2.00
Investor	Financial	—	—	1.78
Hm Prods Intl 9.625%	—	—	—	1.49
Alexander & Baldwin	Business	18.4	29.05	1.34
Nabors Industries	Energy	28.9	23.59	1.30
American Power Conversio	Ind Mtrls	22.1	-10.99	1.27

Current Investment Style

Value Blnd Growth — Large Mid Small

Market Cap	%
Giant	12.3
Large	21.5
Mid	48.1
Small	14.9
Micro	3.1
Avg $mil: 4,365	

Value Measures		Rel Category
Price/Earnings	16.83	0.97
Price/Book	1.44	0.72
Price/Sales	0.98	1.03
Price/Cash Flow	5.12	0.88
Dividend Yield %	0.92	1.11

Growth Measures	%	Rel Category
Long-Term Erngs	12.34	0.91
Book Value	2.85	0.51
Sales	-5.34	NMF
Cash Flow	14.81	3.00
Historical Erngs	13.14	1.76

Profitability	%	Rel Category
Return on Equity	10.20	0.98
Return on Assets	5.30	1.07
Net Margin	8.90	1.22

Sector Weightings	% of Stocks	Rel S&P 500	3 Year High	3 Year Low
Info	7.58	0.35		
Software	0.00	0.00	0	0
Hardware	4.80	0.47	31	5
Media	0.00	0.00	0	0
Telecom	2.78	0.88	3	1
Service	65.98	1.42		
Health	2.30	0.18	5	2
Consumer	12.31	1.36	12	0
Business	1.92	0.47	3	2
Financial	49.45	2.38	55	39
Mfg	26.45	0.82		
Goods	8.97	0.96	10	1
Ind Mtrls	13.64	1.08	17	13
Energy	2.95	0.41	3	0
Utilities	0.89	0.30	2	0

Composition

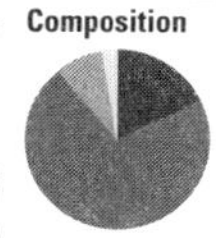

Cash	17.6
Stocks	71.1
Bonds	8.4
Other	2.9
Foreign (% of Stock)	31.8

Morningstar's Take by Christopher Traulsen 11-30-04

Third Avenue Value is showing why it pays to be patient.

In terms of portfolio moves, this fund is about as exciting as watching paint dry. In an era when so many managers appear determined to trade rapidly to justify their existence, manager Marty Whitman just keeps doing very little, very well. The fund's turnover in fiscal 2003 clocked in at a measly 11%, and it has averaged just 15% over the last 10 years. In contrast, the typical small-blend fund has a turnover rate of 81% (65% if you throw out some oddball funds that have high turnover rates due to a heavy reliance on futures and options).

Whitman buys companies that have rock-solid balance sheets and are significantly undervalued, meaning that if there's no material deterioration of the former, he tends to sit on them until they become grossly overvalued or they're acquired by another firm. That helps keep transactions costs down and makes the fund tax-efficient.

Over the long-term the fund has made its style pay off nicely for shareholders. It has delivered superior long-term returns, with less volatility than the category norm. In 2004, a big position in Kmart common stock, which Whitman acquired for the fund by buying up Kmart debt as the firm headed for bankruptcy, has led it to a 23.5% return. Whitman also helped the fund's cause by slashing its hedged position in the Japanese yen, enabling the fund to benefit from the dollar's weakness.

Investors here shouldn't always expect such performance. With its offbeat sector concentrations, significant exposure to distressed debt, and sizable foreign stake, the fund's returns can deviate substantially from category norms--sometimes in the wrong direction. Investors thus need to share Whitman's patient approach and have a long enough time horizon to stick with the fund for the long haul. For those who are prepared to make that commitment, we think this is a strong choice.

Address:	622 Third Avenue New York NY 10017 800-443-1021
Web Address:	www.thirdavenuefunds.com
Inception:	11-01-90
Advisor:	Third Avenue Management LLC
Subadvisor:	None
NTF Plans:	Fidelity Retail-NTF, Schwab OneSource

Minimum Purchase:	$1000	Add: $1000	IRA: $500
Min Auto Inv Plan:	$1000	Add: $200	
Sales Fees:	No-load, 1.00%R		
Management Fee:	0.90%		
Actual Fees:	Mgt:0.90%	Dist:	
Expense Projections:	3Yr:$340	5Yr:$590	10Yr:$1306
Income Distrib:	Annually		

Thompson Plumb Growth

Ticker	Load	NAV	Yield	Total Assets	Mstar Category
THPGX	None	$46.78	0.9%	$1,525 mil	Large Blend

Governance and Management

Fiduciary Grade:

Portfolio Manager(s)

John C. Thompson runs the fund. Thompson has worked closely for years with his father, John W. Thompson, who served as the fund's first manager and who continues to consult with his son on the management of the fund. The Thompsons have dissolved their relationship with Thomas G. Plumb and established a separate asset management firm, Thompson Investment Management.

Strategy

The managers like to buy companies that are reasonably priced relative to historical earnings growth. They are willing to exploit the fund's all-cap mandate and will include smaller-cap stocks in the portfolio when they find attractive values. They will also make significant sector bets.

Historical Profile

Return High
Risk High
Rating ★★★★ Above Avg

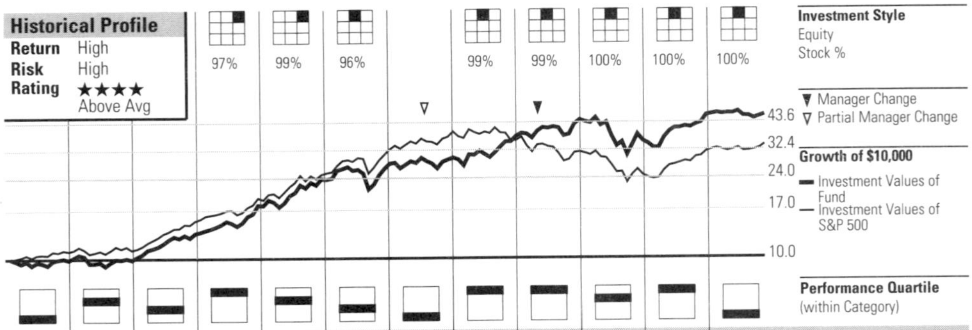

1993	1994	1995	1996	1997	1998	1999	2000	2001	2002	2003	12-04	History
21.01	19.23	24.54	30.17	36.44	39.35	40.27	40.78	44.31	34.91	45.89	46.78	NAV
1.60	0.43	30.49	33.05	32.37	18.41	6.44	25.68	19.13	-20.42	31.86	4.14	Total Return %
-8.46	-0.88	-7.04	10.11	-0.98	-10.16	-14.60	34.78	31.01	1.67	3.19	-6.73	+/-S&P 500
-8.58	0.04	-7.28	10.60	-0.48	-8.61	-14.47	33.47	31.58	1.23	1.97	-7.26	+/-Russ 1000
0.00	0.00	0.00	0.00	0.00	0.00	0.00	0.00	0.06	0.56	0.40	0.96	Income Return %
1.60	0.43	30.49	33.05	32.37	18.41	6.44	25.68	19.07	-20.98	31.46	3.18	Capital Return %
96	44	71	4	27	66	92	1	1	31	11	96	Total Rtn % Rank Cat
0.00	0.00	0.00	0.00	0.00	0.00	0.00	0.00	0.02	0.25	0.14	0.44	Income $
0.00	1.86	0.55	2.47	3.36	3.50	1.56	9.35	4.03	0.11	0.00	0.55	Capital Gains $
1.93	2.00	2.00	1.58	1.52	1.41	1.32	1.29	1.20	1.11	1.07	—	Expense Ratio %
-0.54	-0.49	-0.31	-0.27	-0.41	-0.19	-0.34	-0.09	0.11	0.68	0.47	—	Income Ratio %
99	117	87	102	78	67	79	64	63	74	41	—	Turnover Rate %
—	—	13	24	47	72	78	85	328	512	1,000	1,525	Net Assets $mil

Performance 12-31-04

	1st Qtr	2nd Qtr	3rd Qtr	4th Qtr	Total
2000	3.15	0.29	8.26	12.22	25.68
2001	-1.96	11.01	-7.84	18.79	19.13
2002	2.30	-17.65	-18.94	16.53	-20.42
2003	-7.36	23.81	0.85	14.00	31.86
2004	1.26	2.58	-7.41	8.27	4.16

Trailing	Total Return%	+/- S&P 500	+/- Russ 1000	%Rank Cat	Growth of $10,000
3 Mo	8.27	-0.96	-1.53	78	10,827
6 Mo	0.25	-6.94	-7.56	99	10,025
1 Yr	4.14	-6.73	-7.26	96	10,414
3 Yr Avg	3.00	-0.58	-1.27	48	10,927
5 Yr Avg	10.35	12.65	12.11	1	16,363
10 Yr Avg	16.83	4.76	4.67	2	47,374
15 Yr Avg	—	—	—	—	—

Tax Analysis	Tax-Adj Rtn%	%Rank Cat	Tax-Cost Rat	%Rank Cat
3 Yr (estimated)	2.66	40	0.33	28
5 Yr (estimated)	8.41	1	1.76	86
10 Yr (estimated)	14.74	1	1.79	72

Potential Capital Gain Exposure: 8% of assets

Rating and Risk

Time Period	Load-Adj Return %	Morningstar Rtn vs Cat	Morningstar Risk vs Cat	Morningstar Risk-Adj Rating
1 Yr	4.14			
3 Yr	3.00	Avg	High	★★
5 Yr	10.35	High	High	★★★★★
10 Yr	16.83	High	High	★★★★★
Incept	13.36			

Other Measures	Standard Index S&P 500	Best Fit Index S&P 500
Alpha	-0.5	-0.5
Beta	1.31	1.31
R-Squared	88	88
Standard Deviation	21.95	
Mean	3.00	
Sharpe Ratio	0.07	

Portfolio Analysis 09-30-04

Share change since 06-04 Total Stocks:57	Sector	PE	YTD Ret%	% Assets
⊕ Fannie Mae	Financial	9.1	-2.33	7.77
⊕ Viacom B	Media	36.1	-17.44	6.26
⊕ Microsoft	Software	36.1	8.95	5.77
⊕ Pfizer	Health	22.0	-22.31	5.41
⊖ First Data	Business	18.8	3.72	4.85
⊖ Freddie Mac	Financial	10.6	28.75	4.36
⊕ ExxonMobil	Energy	13.9	28.04	3.43
⊕ Coca-Cola	Goods	21.9	-16.12	3.35
⊖ Johnson & Johnson	Health	20.6	25.17	3.33
Tyco International	Ind Mtrls	25.1	35.41	3.10
⊕ ChevronTexaco	Energy	7.7	25.57	3.06
⊕ Time Warner	Media	27.5	8.12	2.98
⊕ Clear Channel Communicat	Media	23.5	-27.57	2.60
☼ State Street	Financial	15.3	-4.41	2.56
⊕ Cincinnati Financial	Financial	14.5	14.24	2.53
General Mills	Goods	19.4	12.56	2.50
⊕ Cardinal Health	Health	16.9	-4.73	2.29
⊕ McKesson	Health	15.8	-1.41	2.25
⊕ Morgan Stanley	Financial	14.2	-2.25	2.23
⊕ Fifth Third Bancorp	Financial	14.1	-17.89	2.12

Current Investment Style

Value Blnd Growth / Large Mid Small

Market Cap	%
Giant	65.2
Large	22.5
Mid	10.9
Small	1.2
Micro	0.1
Avg $mil: 49,575	

Value Measures		Rel Category
Price/Earnings	14.83	0.88
Price/Book	2.06	0.79
Price/Sales	1.09	0.76
Price/Cash Flow	6.59	0.86
Dividend Yield %	1.49	1.01

Growth Measures	%	Rel Category
Long-Term Erngs	12.63	1.09
Book Value	8.99	1.16
Sales	10.85	1.89
Cash Flow	15.83	1.67
Historical Erngs	21.28	1.80

Profitability	%	Rel Category
Return on Equity	18.36	1.05
Return on Assets	10.18	1.18
Net Margin	12.77	1.12

Sector Weightings	% of Stocks	Rel S&P 500	3 Year High	3 Year Low
Info	23.00	1.07		
Software	6.46	1.50	7	3
Hardware	2.62	0.26	10	2
Media	13.92	3.63	14	8
Telecom	0.00	0.00	10	0
Service	56.52	1.22		
Health	17.69	1.42	25	18
Consumer	5.39	0.59	10	5
Business	7.63	1.88	11	7
Financial	25.81	1.24	26	15
Mfg	20.46	0.64		
Goods	8.76	0.94	10	0
Ind Mtrls	5.20	0.41	10	5
Energy	6.50	0.91	7	0
Utilities	0.00	0.00	0	0

Composition

Cash	0.1
Stocks	99.9
Bonds	0.0
Other	0.0
Foreign (% of Stock)	0.1

Morningstar's Take by Andrew Gogerty 11-22-04

Thompson Plumb Growth may hit the occasional bump, but it remains a strong choice.

Lead manager John C. Thompson likes to move against the grain. Believing that the market overreacts to declines in earnings growth, he looks for battered growth stocks trading at a discount relative to their historical earnings. He analyzes a potential company's balance sheet and ability to generate substantial free-cash flows, as these traits often lead good companies to reignite their earnings growth. Because Thompson devotes almost half of the fund's assets to its top 10 holdings, his bets on the market's fallen angels can be quite large.

The result of this compact, contrarian style is uneven performance. Volatility has been consistently in the upper echelon of the large-blend category, as the fund's sector and individual picks tend to take time to pan out. The fund largely avoided tech stocks in 1999 to its relative detriment, but it was rewarded handsomely in 2000 and 2001 when the sector faltered. Recently, the fund's large stakes in media and health-care stocks have held back returns. Thompson thinks this is only temporary, as media giant Viacom and drug distributor Cardinal Health generate substantial cash flows and possess wide profit margins in their respective sectors. He has also been buying up Freddie Mac since its mid-2003 sell off, believing that the firm's accounting issues do not affect its business fundamentals or ability to generate cash. In part, Freddie's 19% gain for the year to date through Nov. 18, 2004, has been a bright spot for the fund.

All told, Thompson has employed this strategy well. The fund has handily beaten its large-blend peers and the S&P 500 Index over the past decade. While this fund will not consistently top the charts and may well end up closer to the bottom at times, it is a compelling option for long-term investors willing to ride out the occasional rough patch.

Address:	1200 John Q. Hammons Drive Madison WI 53717 800-999-0887
Web Address:	www.thompsonplumb.com
Inception:	02-10-92
Advisor:	Thompson Investment Management, LLC
Subadvisor:	None
NTF Plans:	Fidelity Retail-NTF, CommonWealth NTF

Minimum Purchase:	$2500	Add: $100	IRA: $2000
Min Auto Inv Plan:	$1000	Add: $50	
Sales Fees:	No-load		
Management Fee:	1.00% mx./0.90% mn.		
Actual Fees:	Mgt:0.96%	Dist:	
Expense Projections:	3Yr:$381	5Yr:$660	10Yr:$1455
Income Distrib:	Annually		

Thornburg Intl Value A

Ticker	Load	NAV	Yield	Total Assets	Mstar Category
TGVAX	4.50%	$20.40	0.3%	$1,513 mil	Foreign Large Blend

Governance and Management

Fiduciary Grade: A

Portfolio Manager(s)

William Fries has been at the helm since the fund's 1998 inception. He has run Thornburg Value with excellent results since its origin in 1995. He is assisted by four analysts, who have a lot of say in assembling the fund's portfolio. Thornburg has a shareholder-friendly Web site that provides manager commentary on each holding and that replays the fund's quarterly teleconferences.

Strategy

Manager William Fries looks for investments in every corner of the market: large and small caps as well as growth and value stocks. He maintains about 50% of the portfolio in a diversified group of blue-chip stocks that pays dividends, primarily in the financial and consumer sectors. The rest of the fund goes to stocks selling below their earnings prospects and to rapidly growing industry leaders. This last group tends to occupy a smaller portion of assets than do the other two sleeves. Fries keeps the portfolio concentrated, holding between 40 and 50 stocks. He likes to buy when his picks are down.

Historical Profile

Return High
Risk Below Avg
Rating ★★★★★ Highest

Investment Style: Equity Stock % — 85% 81% 81% 84% 94% 92%

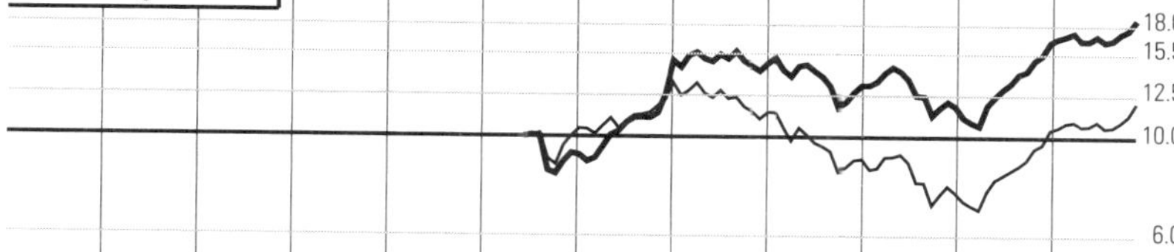

▼ Manager Change
∇ Partial Manager Change

Growth of $10,000
— Investment Values of Fund
— Investment Values of MSCI EAFE

Performance Quartile (within Category)

1993	1994	1995	1996	1997	1998	1999	2000	2001	2002	2003	12-04	History
—	—	—	—	—	10.80	17.29	15.63	13.87	12.42	17.39	20.40	NAV
—	—	—	—	—	-9.32*	63.40	-1.57	-10.53	-10.45	40.02	17.73	Total Return %
—	—	—	—	—	—	36.37	12.62	10.89	5.49	1.43	-2.52	+/-MSCI EAFE
—	—	—	—	—	—	35.42	11.79	10.86	5.35	0.60	-2.65	+/-MSCI Wd xUS
—	—	—	—	—	0.00	2.75	8.33	0.78	0.00	0.00	0.41	Income Return %
—	—	—	—	—	—	60.65	-9.90	-11.31	-10.45	40.02	17.32	Capital Return %
—	—	—	—	—	—	6	2	2	7	11	47	Total Rtn % Rank Cat
—	—	—	—	—	0.03	0.30	1.41	0.12	0.00	0.00	0.07	Income $
—	—	—	—	—	0.00	0.00	0.00	0.00	0.00	0.00	0.00	Capital Gains $
—	—	—	—	—	—	1.63	1.53	1.54	1.57	1.59	1.49	Expense Ratio %
—	—	—	—	—	—	1.07	2.61	0.22	0.19	0.44	0.88	Income Ratio %
—	—	—	—	—	—	58	86	61	28	58	36	Turnover Rate %
—	—	—	—	—	—	39	79	68	78	299	944	Net Assets $mil

Performance 12-31-04

	1st Qtr	2nd Qtr	3rd Qtr	4th Qtr	Total
2000	4.34	-1.11	-3.31	-1.35	-1.57
2001	-6.40	2.82	-17.09	12.13	-10.53
2002	6.71	-3.45	-16.86	4.55	-10.45
2003	-9.42	20.98	9.85	16.32	40.02
2004	4.95	-1.66	1.28	12.64	17.73

Trailing	Total Return%	+/- MSCI EAFE	+/- MSCI Wd xUS	%Rank Cat	Growth of $10,000
3 Mo	12.64	-2.68	-2.51	93	11,264
6 Mo	14.08	-0.92	-1.29	49	11,408
1 Yr	17.73	-2.52	-2.65	47	11,773
3 Yr Avg	13.86	1.97	1.64	6	14,761
5 Yr Avg	5.38	6.51	6.14	2	12,995
10 Yr Avg	—	—	—	—	—
15 Yr Avg	—	—	—	—	—

Tax Analysis	Tax-Adj Rtn%	%Rank Cat	Tax-Cost Rat	%Rank Cat
3 Yr (estimated)	12.08	10	0.04	5
5 Yr (estimated)	3.63	2	0.76	51
10 Yr (estimated)	—	—	—	—

Potential Capital Gain Exposure: 17% of assets

Rating and Risk

Time Period	Load-Adj Return %	Morningstar Rtn vs Cat	Morningstar Risk vs Cat	Morningstar Risk-Adj Rating
1 Yr	12.44			
3 Yr	12.13	+Avg	-Avg	★★★★
5 Yr	4.42	High	-Avg	★★★★★
10 Yr	—	—	—	—
Incept	9.68			

Other Measures	Standard Index S&P 500	Best Fit Index MSCI EAFE
Alpha	3.1	3.1
Beta	0.87	0.87
R-Squared	88	88
Standard Deviation	16.48	
Mean	13.86	
Sharpe Ratio	0.77	

Portfolio Analysis 10-31-04

Share change since 09-04 Total Stocks:56	Sector	Country	% Assets
UBS	Financial	Switzerland	2.96
Tesco	Consumer	U.K.	2.36
Petroleo Brasileiro ADR	Energy	Brazil	2.33
Novartis AG ADR	Health	Switzerland	2.35
⊕ Mitsubishi Tokyo Fin. Gr	Financial	Japan	2.36
⊕ Lloyds TSB Grp	Financial	U.K.	2.54
☆ Shaw Communications	Media	Canada	2.51
Kingfisher	Consumer	U.K.	2.45
⊕ Burberry Grp	Consumer	U.K.	2.41
⊕ Euronext	Financial	France	2.37
Givaudan	Ind Mtrls	Switzerland	2.32
Vodafone Group PLC ADR	Telecom	U.K.	2.28
Adidas-Salomon	Goods	Germany	2.25
Bank of Fukuoka	Financial	Japan	2.23
Rogers Comms CI B	Media	Canada	2.18
Fraport	Business	Germany	2.16
⊕ FamilyMart	Consumer	Japan	2.15
Portugal Telecom, SGPS	Telecom	Portugal	2.14
Canon	Goods	Japan	2.11
Barclays	Financial	U.K.	2.07

Current Investment Style

Market Cap	%
Giant	43.7
Large	26.1
Mid	27.9
Small	0.9
Micro	1.4
Avg $mil: 13,283	

Value Measures		Rel Category
Price/Earnings	13.57	0.99
Price/Book	1.30	0.72
Price/Sales	1.04	1.14
Price/Cash Flow	5.24	1.07
Dividend Yield %	2.23	0.88

Growth Measures	%	Rel Category
Long-Term Erngs	11.16	1.04
Book Value	13.93	1393.00
Sales	8.89	3.57
Cash Flow	13.98	2.49
Historical Erngs	14.81	2.65

Composition

Cash	8.1	Bonds	0.0
Stocks	91.9	Other	0.0
Foreign (% of Stock)			96.1

Sector Weightings	% of Stocks	Rel MSCI EAFE	3 Year High	3 Year Low
Info	18.78	1.13		
Software	3.72	3.44	4	0
Hardware	0.46	0.13	15	0
Media	7.00	3.07	9	[illegible]
Telecom	7.60	0.79	14	[illegible]
Service	53.56	1.20		
Health	8.00	1.10	20	5
Consumer	14.27	2.83	17	5
Business	6.07	1.12	6	0
Financial	25.22	0.93	25	5
Mfg	27.65	0.72		
Goods	14.76	1.08	40	15
Ind Mtrls	5.15	0.42	22	5
Energy	5.32	0.72	13	3
Utilities	2.42	0.45	3	0

Regional Exposure	% Stock		
UK/W. Europe	54	N. America	9
Japan	11	Latn America	9
Asia X Japan	16	Other	1

Country Exposure	% Stock		
U.K.	25	Switzerland	9
Japan	11	South Korea	6
Germany	10		

Morningstar's Take by William Samuel Rocco 11-21-04

Don't be fooled by its so-so 2004 results: This is a first-rate overseas option.

Thornburg International Value has been a ho-hum relative performer in 2004's choppy conditions. Petrobras and its other energy stocks have prospered, as have some other issues, including two financials picks--UBS and Barclays--that Bill Fries picked up this summer. But a variety of holdings have posted lackluster results or worse. Top-25 holdings Novartis and News Corporation have earned sluggish gains, for example, while the Bermuda-domiciled insurer ACE has declined since its midyear purchase and the Taiwanese integrated circuit tester ASE Text struggled before it was sold. Thus, the fund sits in the middle of its group for the year to date with an 11.5% gain.

But average results are unusual here. Due to HSBC Holdings and other names, the fund surged 40% and beat 89% of its foreign large-blend peers in 2003's global rally. And it produced top-decile returns in the up-and-down conditions that prevailed in its first four calendar years. As a result, it has earned an 8% annualized gain since opening in May 1998, whereas its typical peer has suffered a 2% annualized loss over that period.

Not surprisingly, there's a distinctive style behind these distinguished results. Fries readily buys stocks in bunches and ventures outside the developed world. He recently bought the global billing software power Amdocs and has maintained a sizable stake in Infosys, and the fund has far more software and emerging-markets exposure than its average peer. He also continues to pay more attention to smaller caps and focuses on 40 to 50 issues, so the fund's average market cap and total number of names remains well below the group norm.

Of course, this atypical style has its risks--and the fund isn't for the faint of heart--but we believe patient and risk-tolerant investors will be happy here.

Address:	119 E Marcy St Santa Fe NM 87501 800-847-0200
Web Address:	www.thornburg.com
Inception:	05-28-98 *
Advisor:	Thornburg Investment Management Inc.
Subadvisor:	None
NTF Plans:	DATALynx NTF, Federated Tr NTF

Minimum Purchase:	$5000	Add: $100	IRA: $2000
Min Auto Inv Plan:	$5000	Add: $100	
Sales Fees:	4.50%L, 1.00%R		
Management Fee:	0.88% mx./0.68% mn.		
Actual Fees:	Mgt:0.88%	Dist:0.25%	
Expense Projections:	3Yr:$953	5Yr:$1317	10Yr:$2337
Income Distrib:	Annually		

Thornburg Ltd-Tm A

Ticker	Load	NAV	Yield	SEC Yield	Total Assets	Mstar Category
LTMFX	1.50%	$13.78	2.8%	2.07%	$1,433 mil	Muni National Short

Governance and Management

Fiduciary Grade: A

Portfolio Manager(s)

George Strickland joined Brian McMahon on this fund in 1991 and took over as sole manager in 2001. He currently leads Thornburg's municipal-bond team. The firm's other muni funds, which use a similar strategy, tend to have more-mixed results than this one.

Strategy

Manager George Strickland ladders this fund's portfolio among bonds with maturities between one and 10 years. When the shorter bonds mature, they fall off the ladder, and he replaces them with longer ones. The fund's income return is usually above average for the short-term muni category, but its often-longer-than-average duration adds volatility relative to the group.

Historical Profile

Return Above Avg
Risk Above Avg
Rating ★★★★ Above Avg

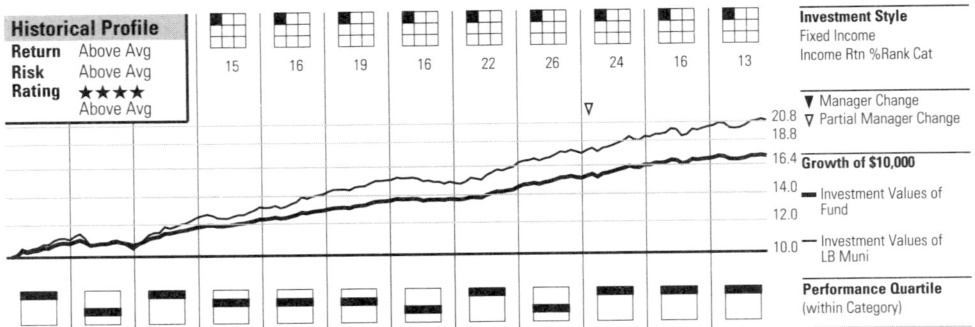

1993	1994	1995	1996	1997	1998	1999	2000	2001	2002	2003	12-04	History
13.75	12.92	13.55	13.45	13.55	13.59	13.05	13.33	13.41	13.90	13.93	13.78	NAV
8.81	-1.49	9.97	3.97	5.47	4.78	0.33	6.81	4.82	7.34	3.25	1.74	Total Return %
-3.47	3.68	-7.49	-0.46	-3.72	-1.70	2.39	-4.87	-0.31	-2.26	-2.06	-2.74	+/-LB Muni
2.59	-2.17	1.10	-0.47	-0.01	-0.43	-1.63	0.58	-1.77	0.62	0.57	-0.04	+/-LB Muni 3YR
4.98	4.67	5.02	4.70	4.70	4.48	4.40	4.58	4.25	3.63	3.03	2.79	Income Return %
3.83	-6.16	4.95	-0.73	0.77	0.30	-4.07	2.23	0.57	3.71	0.22	-1.05	Capital Return %
15	71	13	37	29	33	60	14	52	11	17	18	Total Rtn % Rank Cat
0.65	0.63	0.63	0.62	0.62	0.59	0.59	0.59	0.56	0.48	0.42	0.38	Income $
0.00	0.00	0.00	0.00	0.00	0.00	0.00	0.00	0.00	0.00	0.00	0.00	Capital Gains $
1.01	0.95	0.97	0.97	0.96	0.97	0.96	0.96	0.99	0.95	0.93	0.91	Expense Ratio %
5.03	4.60	5.83	4.66	4.65	4.50	4.35	4.48	4.36	3.83	3.20	2.85	Income Ratio %
19	16	23	21	23	25	22	34	25	20	16	21	Turnover Rate %
912	1,019	917	915	856	822	743	645	678	904	1,040	1,038	Net Assets $mil

Performance 12-31-04

	1st Qtr	2nd Qtr	3rd Qtr	4th Qtr	Total
2000	1.13	1.22	1.74	2.56	6.81
2001	2.08	0.91	2.20	-0.43	4.82
2002	0.50	3.14	2.92	0.61	7.34
2003	0.86	1.48	0.51	0.37	3.25
2004	1.00	-1.39	1.80	0.33	1.74

Trailing	Total Return%	+/- LB Muni	+/- LB Muni 3YR	%Rank Cat	Growth of $10,000
3 Mo	0.33	-0.92	0.14	34	10,033
6 Mo	2.14	-3.05	0.04	22	10,214
1 Yr	1.74	-2.74	-0.04	18	10,174
3 Yr Avg	4.08	-2.36	0.37	13	11,275
5 Yr Avg	4.77	-2.43	-0.01	14	12,624
10 Yr Avg	4.82	-2.24	-0.15	10	16,012
15 Yr Avg	5.20	-1.79	—	9	21,391

Tax Analysis	Tax-Adj Rtn%	%Rank Cat	Tax-Cost Rat	%Rank Cat
3 Yr (estimated)	3.56	20	0.00	1
5 Yr (estimated)	4.46	23	0.00	1
10 Yr (estimated)	4.66	15	0.00	1

Potential Capital Gain Exposure: 4% of assets

Rating and Risk

Time Period	Load-Adj Return %	Morningstar Rtn vs Cat	Morningstar Risk vs Cat	Morningstar Risk-Adj Rating
1 Yr	0.21			
3 Yr	3.56	+Avg	+Avg	★★★★
5 Yr	4.46	+Avg	+Avg	★★★★
10 Yr	4.66	+Avg	+Avg	★★★★
Incept	6.01			

Other Measures	Standard Index LB Aggr	Best Fit Index LB Muni NY
Alpha	-0.4	-0.4
Beta	0.61	0.63
R-Squared	95	95
Standard Deviation	3.11	
Mean	4.08	
Sharpe Ratio	0.88	

Portfolio Analysis 11-30-04

Total Fixed-Income:610	Date of Maturity	Amount $000	Value $000	% Net Assets
New York St Dorm Auth 5%	12-15-05	15,100	15,383	1.09
Albuquerque N Mex Arpt	07-01-14	15,300	15,300	1.08
Chicago Ill Pk Dist 6.6%	11-15-14	11,900	12,376	0.87
Forsyth Mont Pollution C	10-01-32	11,440	12,299	0.87
Harris Cnty Tex Hosp Dis	02-15-11	10,000	11,171	0.79
Birmingham-Carraway Ala	08-15-09	10,000	10,925	0.77
Michigan St Hosp Fin Aut	11-15-33	10,000	10,730	0.76
Rhode Island Ref Bd Auth	10-01-06	10,085	10,564	0.75
Wilsonville Ala Indl Dev	06-01-19	8,955	9,186	0.65
Metropolitan Transn Auth	11-15-07	8,000	8,533	0.60
Central Platte Vy Met Di	12-01-31	7,985	8,446	0.60
Kentucky Econ Dev Fin Au	10-01-10	7,830	8,294	0.59
Kentucky Econ Dev Fin Au	10-01-09	7,400	7,777	0.55
Dade Cnty Fla Solid Wast	10-01-07	7,000	7,669	0.54
Louisiana St Correctiona	12-15-08	7,135	7,654	0.54

Current Investment Style

Duration: Short Int Long; Quality: High Med Low

[1]Avg Eff Duration	2.9 Yrs
Avg Eff Maturity	3.9 Yrs
Avg Credit Quality	AA
Avg Wtd Coupon	4.93%
Avg Wtd Price	105.79% of par

[1]figure provided by fund

Credit Analysis	% bonds 11-30-04		
US Govt	0	BB	0
AAA	59	B	0
AA	25	Below B	0
A	9	NR/NA	1
BBB	6		

Top 5 States	% bonds		
IL	12.0	FL	5.0
TX	11.3	WA	4.8
NY	7.3		

Composition			
Cash	6.1	Bonds	93.9
Stocks	0.0	Other	0.0

Special Securities	
Restricted/Illiquid Secs	0
Options/Futures/Warrants	No

Sector Weightings	% of Bonds	Rel Cat
General Obligation	18.1	0.51
Utilities	15.4	1.66
Health	16.1	2.23
Water/Waste	5.8	0.55
Housing	4.9	0.65
Education	11.7	1.34
Transportation	5.5	1.28
COP/Lease	2.6	1.68
Industrial	19.8	1.31
Misc Revenue	0.0	—
Demand	0.0	0.00

Morningstar's Take by Lynn Russell 12-22-04

A consistent strategy and experienced management make Thornburg Limited Term Muni a respectable option--we just wish it were cheaper.

This fund falls into the muni national short category, but it is one of the longer-term funds in that group. Manager George Strickland sticks to investment grade-securities and spreads the fund's holdings relatively evenly over a maturity range of one to 10 years. That approach typically results in a longer duration (a measure of interest-rate sensitivity) and more interest-rate risk than the category norm.

The fund's added rate sensitivity worked in its favor as rates trended lower for most of the past decade, but it can leave the fund more vulnerable than most to rising interest rates. While the fund has typically finished in the top half of its category, it fell behind its peers when rates spiked in 1994 and 1999, for example. And even though Strickland had overweighted holdings at the shorter end of the fund's maturity ladder coming into 2004, the fund lost 1.39% in the second quarter of 2004, compared with the loss of 1.10% for its typical muni short rival.

Even with those hiccups, the fund's five- and 10-year trailing returns rank in the muni short category's top 15%, although the fund may face some challenges in repeating that stellar performance if rates continue to trend higher. Meanwhile, the fund's yield has consistently ranked in the group's top third thanks to its stash of higher-yielding intermediate-term bonds.

Experienced management and a solid total-return track record make this fund attractive for investors who are comfortable with its added interest-rate risk. But at 0.93%, the expense ratio for the fund's A shares is well above the category average for that share class and too high to make them a compelling choice. However, those investors who have access to the fund's I shares, which charge a more competitive 0.57%, may find the fund more attractive.

Address:	119 E Marcy St Ste 201 Santa Fe NM 87501 800-847-0200
Web Address:	www.thornburg.com
Inception:	09-28-84
Advisor:	Thornburg Investment Management Inc.
Subadvisor:	None
NTF Plans:	DATALynx NTF, Federated Tr NTF

Minimum Purchase:	$5000	Add: $100	IRA: $0
Min Auto Inv Plan:	$5000	Add: $100	
Sales Fees:	1.50%L, 0.25%S		
Management Fee:	0.50% mx./0.23% mn., 0.12%A		
Actual Fees:	Mgt:0.45%	Dist:0.25%	
Expense Projections:	3Yr:$463	5Yr:$693	10Yr:$1356
Income Distrib:	Monthly		

Thornburg Value A

Ticker	Load	NAV	Yield	Total Assets	Mstar Category
TVAFX	4.50%	$30.88	1.0%	$2,035 mil	Large Blend

Governance and Management

Fiduciary Grade: B

Portfolio Manager(s)

William Fries has been at the helm since the fund's 1995 inception. He has also run Thornburg International Value with excellent results since its origin in 1998. He is assisted by nine analysts, who have a lot of say in assembling the fund's portfolio. Thornburg has a shareholder-friendly Web site that provides manager commentary on each holding and that replays the fund's quarterly teleconferences.

Strategy

William Fries divides holdings into three groups: basic value (or stocks selling below their earnings power), consistent earners (blue-chip stocks selling below their historical price multiples), and emerging franchises (rapidly growing companies establishing leadership in their industries). The final group occupies a smaller portion of this fund's assets than the other two. Fries keeps the portfolio concentrated, holding between 40 and 50 stocks. He likes to buy when his picks are down, but he's not afraid to let them run.

Historical Profile

Return Average
Risk Below Avg
Rating ★★★ Neutral

Investment Style Equity Stock %: 92% | 91% | 82% | 94% | 93% | 95% | 93% | 95% | 95%

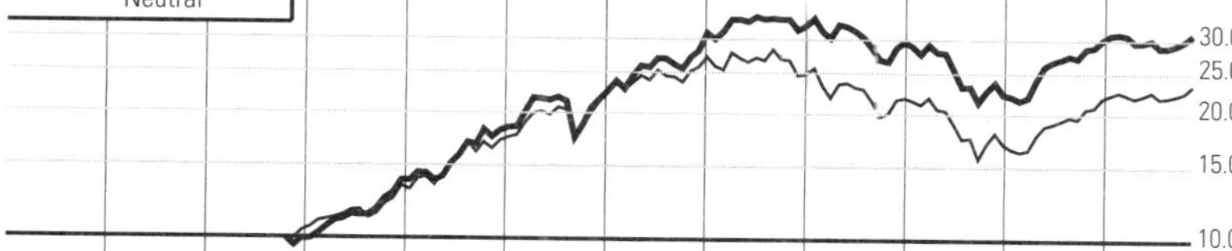

▼ Manager Change
▽ Partial Manager Change

Growth of $10,000
— Investment Values of Fund
— Investment Values of S&P 500

Performance Quartile (within Category)

1993	1994	1995	1996	1997	1998	1999	2000	2001	2002	2003	12-04	History
—	—	11.83	15.59	19.24	23.36	31.37	31.40	28.73	21.59	29.10	30.88	NAV
—	—	-0.53*	37.82	33.70	22.25	37.44	3.96	-8.11	-24.85	34.99	7.20	Total Return %
—	—	—	14.88	0.35	-6.32	16.40	13.06	3.77	-2.76	6.32	-3.67	+/-S&P 500
—	—	—	15.37	0.85	-4.77	16.53	11.75	4.34	-3.20	5.10	-4.20	+/-Russ 1000
—	—	0.00	2.43	1.18	0.77	1.06	3.26	0.40	0.00	0.19	1.05	Income Return %
—	—	—	35.39	32.52	21.48	36.38	0.70	-8.51	-24.85	34.80	6.15	Capital Return %
—	—	—	2	11	53	6	14	18	81	6	82	Total Rtn % Rank Cat
—	—	0.05	0.28	0.18	0.15	0.25	1.01	0.13	0.00	0.04	0.30	Income $
—	—	0.00	0.37	1.35	0.00	0.39	0.25	0.00	0.00	0.00	0.00	Capital Gains $
—	—	—	1.55	1.61	1.61	1.44	1.38	1.37	1.40	1.43	1.37	Expense Ratio %
—	—	—	2.48	1.35	0.96	0.62	2.31	0.07	0.00	0.66	0.69	Income Ratio %
—	—	—	60	79	100	63	72	72	76	83	69	Turnover Rate %
—	—	7	15	80	234	506	936	1,233	793	1,051	1,084	Net Assets $mil

Performance 12-31-04

	1st Qtr	2nd Qtr	3rd Qtr	4th Qtr	Total
2000	7.44	1.63	-1.38	-3.45	3.96
2001	-6.41	4.03	-14.45	10.33	-8.11
2002	-1.57	-12.62	-16.11	4.15	-24.85
2003	-1.48	21.39	1.98	10.69	34.99
2004	2.23	-2.41	-2.55	10.26	7.20

Trailing	Total Return%	+/- S&P 500	+/- Russ 1000	%Rank Cat	Growth of $10,000
3 Mo	10.26	1.03	0.46	24	11,026
6 Mo	7.45	0.26	-0.36	37	10,745
1 Yr	7.20	-3.67	-4.20	82	10,720
3 Yr Avg	2.84	-0.74	-1.43	52	10,876
5 Yr Avg	0.77	3.07	2.53	19	10,391
10 Yr Avg	—	—	—	—	—
15 Yr Avg	—	—	—	—	—

Tax Analysis	Tax-Adj Rtn%	%Rank Cat	Tax-Cost Rat	%Rank Cat
3 Yr (estimated)	1.13	67	0.14	12
5 Yr (estimated)	-0.54	21	0.38	20
10 Yr (estimated)	—	—	—	—

Potential Capital Gain Exposure: 2% of assets

Rating and Risk

Time Period	Load-Adj Return %	Morningstar Rtn vs Cat	Morningstar Risk vs Cat	Morningstar Risk-Adj Rating
1 Yr	2.38			
3 Yr	1.27	-Avg	Avg	★★
5 Yr	-0.16	+Avg	-Avg	★★★★
10 Yr	—	—	—	—
Incept	12.83			

Other Measures	Standard Index S&P 500	Best Fit Index Russ 1000
Alpha	-0.6	-1.3
Beta	0.97	0.98
R-Squared	91	93
Standard Deviation	15.67	
Mean	2.84	
Sharpe Ratio	0.09	

Portfolio Analysis 11-30-04

Share change since 10-04 Total Stocks:46	Sector	PE	YTD Ret%	% Assets
Bank of New York	Financial	18.5	3.52	3.40
General Electric	Ind Mtrls	22.8	20.68	3.22
ExxonMobil	Energy	13.9	28.04	3.17
Citigroup	Financial	15.3	2.72	3.01
⊕ Cardinal Health	Health	16.9	-4.73	2.85
Southwest Airlines	Business	38.5	0.99	2.74
Union Pacific	Business	19.6	-1.28	2.65
⊖ Unocal	Energy	11.4	19.85	2.63
Nextel Communications	Telecom	11.1	6.95	2.62
Pfizer	Health	22.0	-22.31	2.62
UnitedHealth Group	Health	23.8	51.38	2.58
Bank of America	Financial	12.3	21.50	2.55
Alltel	Telecom	16.9	29.71	2.54
NII Holdings	Telecom	7.4	90.74	2.47
St. Paul Travelers Compa	Financial	30.8	-3.15	2.45
⊕ Fox Entertainment Group	Media	—	7.24	2.40
American International G	Financial	16.2	-0.53	2.37
Texas Instruments	Hardware	21.1	-15.90	2.31
Health Management Associ	Health	16.6	-4.89	2.30
T Rowe Price Group	Financial	25.6	33.16	2.29

Current Investment Style

Value Blnd Growth — Large Mid Small

Market Cap	%
Giant	35.7
Large	42.2
Mid	15.7
Small	6.3
Micro	0.0
Avg $mil: 27,803	

Value Measures		Rel Category
Price/Earnings	16.44	0.97
Price/Book	2.43	0.93
Price/Sales	1.48	1.03
Price/Cash Flow	6.47	0.84
Dividend Yield %	1.33	0.90

Growth Measures	%	Rel Category
Long-Term Erngs	12.55	1.09
Book Value	10.27	1.32
Sales	3.95	1.56
Cash Flow	17.36	1.84
Historical Erngs	13.28	1.13

Profitability	%	Rel Category
Return on Equity	17.35	0.99
Return on Assets	3.02	1.05
Net Margin	11.96	1.05

Sector Weightings	% of Stocks	Rel S&P 500	3 Year High	3 Year Low
Info	29.51	1.37		
Software	4.23	0.98	7	3
Hardware	5.16	0.51	7	0
Media	11.19	2.91	11	5
Telecom	8.93	2.83	9	0
Service	57.06	1.23		
Health	17.02	1.36	21	12
Consumer	6.51	0.72	10	4
Business	9.36	2.31	11	2
Financial	24.17	1.16	35	24
Mfg	13.42	0.42		
Goods	3.59	0.38	11	3
Ind Mtrls	3.70	0.29	6	0
Energy	6.13	0.86	11	6
Utilities	0.00	0.00	7	0

Composition

Cash	1.3
Stocks	94.6
Bonds	1.5
Other	2.0
Foreign (% of Stock)	4.7

Morningstar's Take by William Samuel Rocco 11-21-04

Thornburg Value remains more interesting and appealing than its peers.

This fund's charms begin with its exceptional portfolio. Bill Fries makes full use of the sector spectrum and isn't afraid to buy stocks in bunches, so the fund's sector weights normally stand out. He considers mid-cap and small-cap names, such as top-20 holding NII Holdings and midyear purchase Linen 'N Things, which keep the fund's average market cap well below the category norm. And while most active large-blend managers own about 150 stocks, Fries focuses on 40 to 50 issues.

This distinctive and concentrated style means that stock selection is paramount here, and several picks have been off the mark this year. Fries sold Seagate Technologies in April, once he realized that the quality of its disk drives wasn't giving it the pricing power he expected, but that stock suffered big losses early in the year. A few other names caused some damage before Fries sold them this spring and summer, including Hewlett Packard. And some remaining holdings, such as Pfizer, have struggled. Thus, the fund is mired in the large-blend group's bottom decile for the year to date with a 2% gain.

But Fries' stock selection has generally been quite good. The fund earned top-quintile results in six of its first eight calendar years, in fact, thriving in all sorts of market conditions. It returned an impressive 35% in 2003's global rally, fueled by Caremark RX and other good picks. And it posted a 4% gain in a challenging 2000. Overall, it has gained an average of 13% per year since opening in late 1995, while the typical large-blend offering has returned an average of 5% per year over that period.

In short, this fund is still a terrific choice for investors seeking a distinctive offering.

Address:	119 E Marcy St Santa Fe NM 87501 800-847-0200
Web Address:	www.thornburg.com
Inception:	10-02-95*
Advisor:	Thornburg Investment Management Inc.
Subadvisor:	None
NTF Plans:	DATALynx NTF, Federated Tr NTF

Minimum Purchase:	$5000	Add: $100	IRA: $2000
Min Auto Inv Plan:	$5000	Add: $100	
Sales Fees:	4.50%L, 0.25%S, 1.00%R		
Management Fee:	0.88% mx./0.68% mn., 0.12%A		
Actual Fees:	Mgt:0.82%	Dist:0.25%	
Expense Projections:	3Yr:$882	5Yr:$1196	10Yr:$2086
Income Distrib:	Quarterly		

TIAA-CREF Equity Index

Ticker	Load	NAV	Yield	Total Assets	Mstar Category
TCEIX	None	$8.59	1.6%	$357 mil	Large Blend

Governance and Management

Fiduciary Grade: B

Portfolio Manager(s)

This fund is team-managed. TIAA-CREF has plenty of experience in the indexing arena.

Strategy

This offering tracks the performance of the Russell 3000 Index, which comprises the 3,000 largest publicly traded U.S. stocks. Although that benchmark excludes the tiniest of companies, it still provides broad exposure to stocks of all market caps. For liquidity reasons, the fund doesn't own every one of the smaller companies in the index, instead holding a representative sample.

Historical Profile

Return: Above Avg
Risk: Average
Rating: ★★★★ Above Avg

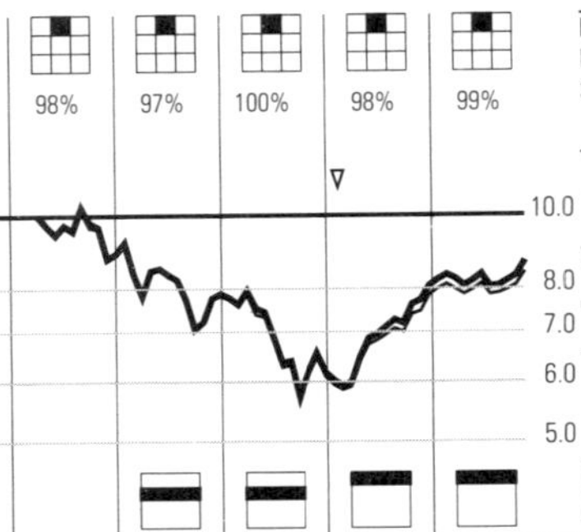

	1993	1994	1995	1996	1997	1998	1999	2000	2001	2002	2003	12-04	History
	—	—	—	—	—	—	—	9.19	8.05	6.23	7.90	8.59	NAV
	—	—	—	—	—	—	—	-10.93*	-11.62	-21.52	30.66	11.68	Total Return %
	—	—	—	—	—	—	—	—	0.26	0.57	1.99	0.81	+/-S&P 500
	—	—	—	—	—	—	—	—	0.83	0.13	0.77	0.28	+/-Russ 1000
	—	—	—	—	—	—	—	0.00	0.68	1.09	1.43	1.80	Income Return %
	—	—	—	—	—	—	—	—	-12.30	-22.61	29.23	9.88	Capital Return %
	—	—	—	—	—	—	—	—	41	39	16	25	Total Rtn % Rank Cat
	—	—	—	—	—	—	—	0.06	0.06	0.09	0.09	0.14	Income $
	—	—	—	—	—	—	—	0.00	0.01	0.00	0.15	0.09	Capital Gains $
	—	—	—	—	—	—	—	—	0.26	0.26	0.26	—	Expense Ratio %
	—	—	—	—	—	—	—	—	1.12	1.40	1.49	—	Income Ratio %
	—	—	—	—	—	—	—	—	6	4	17	—	Turnover Rate %
	—	—	—	—	—	—	—	67	97	140	338	357	Net Assets $mil

Performance 12-31-04

	1st Qtr	2nd Qtr	3rd Qtr	4th Qtr	Total
2000	—	-2.89	0.79	-9.00	-10.93 *
2001	-12.19	6.82	-15.55	11.57	-11.62
2002	0.87	-13.05	-17.00	7.81	-21.52
2003	-3.05	16.06	3.42	12.28	30.66
2004	2.15	1.36	-1.96	10.01	11.68

Trailing	Total Return%	+/- S&P 500	+/- Russ 1000	%Rank Cat	Growth of $10,000
3 Mo	10.01	0.78	0.21	30	11,001
6 Mo	7.85	0.66	0.04	31	10,785
1 Yr	11.68	0.81	0.28	25	11,168
3 Yr Avg	4.62	1.04	0.35	22	11,451
5 Yr Avg	—	—	—	—	—
10 Yr Avg	—	—	—	—	—
15 Yr Avg	—	—	—	—	—

Tax Analysis	Tax-Adj Rtn%	%Rank Cat	Tax-Cost Rat	%Rank Cat
3 Yr (estimated)	3.88	22	0.71	59
5 Yr (estimated)	—	—	—	—
10 Yr (estimated)	—	—	—	—

Potential Capital Gain Exposure: 12% of assets

Rating and Risk

Time Period	Load-Adj Return %	Morningstar Rtn vs Cat	Morningstar Risk vs Cat	Morningstar Risk-Adj Rating
1 Yr	11.68			
3 Yr	4.62	+Avg	Avg	★★★★
5 Yr	—	—	—	—
10 Yr	—	—	—	—
Incept	-2.16			

Other Measures	Standard Index S&P 500	Best Fit Index Russ 1000
Alpha	1.0	0.3
Beta	0.99	1.00
R-Squared	99	100
Standard Deviation	15.56	
Mean	4.62	
Sharpe Ratio	0.21	

Portfolio Analysis 09-30-04

Share change since 06-04 Total Stocks:2882

	Sector	PE	YTD Ret%	% Assets
⊖ General Electric	Ind Mtrls	22.8	20.68	2.91
⊖ ExxonMobil	Energy	13.9	28.04	2.60
⊖ Microsoft	Software	36.1	8.95	2.08
⊖ Pfizer	Health	22.0	-22.31	1.92
⊖ Citigroup	Financial	15.3	2.72	1.87
⊕ Bank of America	Financial	12.3	21.50	1.45
⊖ Johnson & Johnson	Health	20.6	25.17	1.37
⊖ American International G	Financial	16.2	-0.53	1.28
⊖ IBM	Hardware	20.2	7.19	1.19
⊕ J.P. Morgan Chase & Co.	Financial	19.4	9.97	1.16
⊖ Procter & Gamble	Goods	23.3	12.38	1.14
⊖ Wal-Mart Stores	Consumer	23.4	0.51	1.12
⊖ Intel	Hardware	19.8	-26.56	1.06
⊖ Cisco Systems	Hardware	24.5	-20.26	1.00
⊕ ChevronTexaco	Energy	7.7	25.57	0.95
⊖ Verizon Communications	Telecom	32.4	20.25	0.89
⊖ Wells Fargo	Financial	15.5	8.97	0.82
⊖ Altria Group	Goods	13.3	18.38	0.79
⊖ Dell	Hardware	34.0	24.01	0.74
⊖ Home Depot	Consumer	19.0	21.47	0.72

Current Investment Style

Value Blnd Growth / Large Mid Small

Market Cap	%
Giant	42.4
Large	30.8
Mid	19.3
Small	6.0
Micro	1.5
Avg $mil: 24,566	

Value Measures		Rel Category
Price/Earnings	16.62	0.98
Price/Book	2.49	0.95
Price/Sales	1.37	0.95
Price/Cash Flow	7.14	0.93
Dividend Yield %	1.63	1.10

Growth Measures	%	Rel Category
Long-Term Erngs	11.26	0.97
Book Value	6.56	0.84
Sales	4.58	0.80
Cash Flow	5.94	0.63
Historical Erngs	11.32	0.96

Profitability	%	Rel Category
Return on Equity	16.99	0.97
Return on Assets	8.55	0.99
Net Margin	11.51	1.01

Sector Weightings	% of Stocks	Rel S&P 500	3 Year High	3 Year Low
Info	20.99	0.98		
Software	3.95	0.92	5	4
Hardware	9.64	0.95	11	8
Media	3.96	1.03	4	4
Telecom	3.44	1.09	4	3
Service	48.57	1.05		
Health	13.29	1.06	16	13
Consumer	8.82	0.97	9	8
Business	4.65	1.15	5	4
Financial	21.81	1.05	22	20
Mfg	30.45	0.95		
Goods	8.30	0.89	9	8
Ind Mtrls	11.94	0.94	12	10
Energy	7.04	0.98	7	6
Utilities	3.17	1.07	3	3

Composition

Cash	0.3
Stocks	99.4
Bonds	0.0
Other	0.3
Foreign (% of Stock)	0.0

Morningstar's Take by Christopher Davis 01-07-05

TIAA-CREF Equity Index isn't the cheapest option on the block, but it still holds plenty of appeal.

In August 2004, Fidelity Investments challenged low-cost index funds like this one by dropping the expense ratios of five equity index offerings, including this fund's nearest competitor, Fidelity Spartan U.S. Equity Index, to a mere 0.10%. That price tag is less than half the 0.26% levy this offering charges. Even so, the Fidelity fund is out of reach for many investors: Its minimum required initial investment is $10,000 and requires another $1,000 for subsequent investments.

In addition to being more accessible, this fund is still plenty cheap by the standards of the large-blend category. With the typical fund in the group charging 1.26% annually, this one has a percentage point head start on its competitors. That lead grows even wider once its rivals' higher transaction costs, which are the result of much higher turnover, enter into the picture.

To be sure, the fund, whose bogy is the Russell 3000 Index, isn't an exact substitute for the Fidelity and Vanguard offerings, which track the Wilshire 5000 Index. The Wilshire benchmark does include some more of the market's smallest names. However, the differences between the indexes are slight, as both provide exposure to thousands of stocks across market caps, investment styles, and sectors. Thus, the fund's returns should closely approximate those of the broad market, a feat most active large-cap managers have historically failed to achieve.

One caveat: Because the fund features higher mid- and small-cap stakes than its typical peer, it may not fare as well if large caps return to favor. Nonetheless, given its highly diversified portfolio and low costs, we think long-term investors will find this offering a fine choice.

Address:	730 Third Ave New York NY 10017 800-223-1200	Minimum Purchase:	$2500	Add: $50	IRA: $2000
		Min Auto Inv Plan:	$50	Add: $50	
Web Address:	www.tiaa-cref.org	Sales Fees:	No-load		
Inception:	04-03-00 *	Management Fee:	0.26%		
Advisor:	Teachers Advisors, Inc.	Actual Fees:	Mgt:0.26%	Dist:	
Subadvisor:	None	Expense Projections:	3Yr:$84	5Yr:$146	10Yr:$331
NTF Plans:	N/A	Income Distrib:	Annually		

TIAA-CREF Growth & Inc

Ticker	Load	NAV	Yield	Total Assets	Mstar Category
TIGIX	None	$12.20	1.4%	$538 mil	Large Blend

Governance and Management

Fiduciary Grade: B

Portfolio Manager(s)

TIAA-CREF dismissed managers Carlton Martin and Sachie Makishi in February 2003, naming Hans Erikson and Bill Riegel as their interim replacements. Erikson is one of TIAA-CREF's two senior managing directors of quantitative investing. Riegel is a member of TIAA-CREF's value team and was recently named the firm's head of domestic actively managed portfolios.

Strategy

Like its equity fund siblings, this offering blends fundamental stock analysis with quantitative investing techniques. Focusing on financially strong companies with high rates of return on invested capital, management makes sizable bets versus its bogy, choosing 40 to 80 names meeting its criteria. To minimize risk relative to the index, management uses quantitative models to fill the remainder of the portfolio, giving the aggregate fund similar characteristics to the benchmark, including closely aligned sector and market-cap exposure.

Historical Profile

Return Below Avg
Risk Average
Rating ★★ Below Avg

Investment Style: Equity, Stock %

1997	1998	1999	2000	2001	2002	2003	12-04
100%	99%	98%	99%	99%	98%	99%	100%

▼ Manager Change
∇ Partial Manager Change

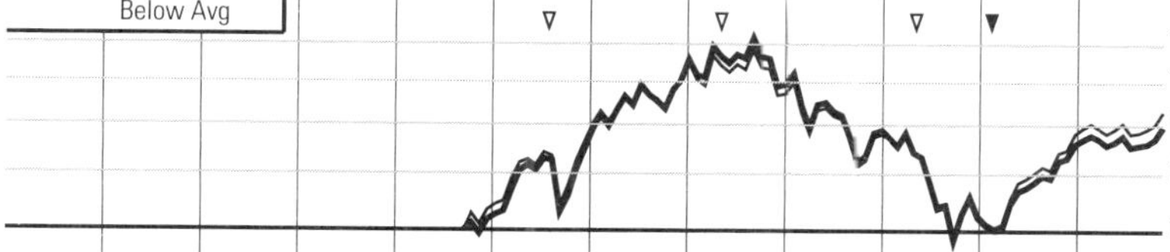

Performance Quartile (within Category)

1993	1994	1995	1996	1997	1998	1999	2000	2001	2002	2003	12-04	History
—	—	—	—	10.32	13.33	15.93	14.05	12.07	9.09	11.30	12.20	NAV
—	—	—	—	5.08*	30.51	24.46	-7.33	-13.37	-23.86	25.83	9.55	Total Return %
—	—	—	—	—	1.94	3.42	1.77	-1.49	-1.77	-2.84	-1.32	+/-S&P 500
—	—	—	—	—	3.49	3.55	0.46	-0.92	-2.21	-4.06	-1.85	+/-Russ 1000
—	—	—	—	0.00	0.98	0.84	0.70	0.72	0.87	1.36	1.52	Income Return %
—	—	—	—	—	29.53	23.62	-8.03	-14.09	-24.73	24.47	8.03	Capital Return %
—	—	—	—	—	9	25	54	69	74	64	60	Total Rtn % Rank Cat
—	—	—	—	0.04	0.10	0.11	0.11	0.10	0.10	0.12	0.17	Income $
—	—	—	—	0.00	0.03	0.53	0.61	0.00	0.00	0.00	0.00	Capital Gains $
—	—	—	—	—	0.43	0.43	0.43	0.43	0.43	0.43	—	Expense Ratio %
—	—	—	—	—	0.97	0.82	0.72	0.84	0.99	1.21	—	Income Ratio %
—	—	—	—	—	71	39	21	70	112	141	—	Turnover Rate %
—	—	—	—	62	233	542	665	638	497	552	538	Net Assets $mil

Performance 12-31-04

	1st Qtr	2nd Qtr	3rd Qtr	4th Qtr	Total
2000	4.17	-2.48	-0.60	-8.23	-7.33
2001	-12.86	5.43	-14.73	10.59	-13.37
2002	-0.91	-14.22	-16.54	7.32	-23.86
2003	-3.81	14.10	3.00	11.30	25.83
2004	1.63	1.00	-2.45	9.39	9.55

Trailing	Total Return%	+/- S&P 500	+/- Russ 1000	%Rank Cat	Growth of $10,000
3 Mo	9.39	0.16	-0.41	42	10,939
6 Mo	6.72	-0.47	-1.09	60	10,672
1 Yr	9.55	-1.32	-1.85	60	10,955
3 Yr Avg	1.62	-1.96	-2.65	73	10,494
5 Yr Avg	-3.37	-1.07	-1.61	72	8,425
10 Yr Avg	—	—	—	—	—
15 Yr Avg	—	—	—	—	—

Tax Analysis	Tax-Adj Rtn%	%Rank Cat	Tax-Cost Rat	%Rank Cat
3 Yr (estimated)	1.17	66	0.44	37
5 Yr (estimated)	-3.95	70	0.60	32
10 Yr (estimated)	—	—	—	—

Potential Capital Gain Exposure: -15% of assets

Rating and Risk

Time Period	Load-Adj Return %	Morningstar Rtn vs Cat	Morningstar Risk vs Cat	Morningstar Risk-Adj Rating
1 Yr	9.55			
3 Yr	1.62	Avg	Avg	★★★
5 Yr	-3.37	-Avg	Avg	★★
10 Yr	—	—	—	—
Incept	5.08			

Other Measures	Standard Index S&P 500	Best Fit Index S&P 500
Alpha	-1.9	-1.9
Beta	0.98	0.98
R-Squared	99	99
Standard Deviation	15.05	
Mean	1.62	
Sharpe Ratio	0.02	

Portfolio Analysis 09-30-04

Share change since 06-04 Total Stocks:342	Sector	PE	YTD Ret%	% Assets
⊖ ExxonMobil	Energy	13.9	28.04	3.63
⊖ General Electric	Ind Mtrls	22.8	20.68	3.48
⊕ Microsoft	Software	36.1	8.95	2.80
⊖ Procter & Gamble	Goods	23.3	12.38	2.31
⊖ Pfizer	Health	22.0	-22.31	2.22
⊖ Citigroup	Financial	15.3	2.72	2.20
⊕ Wal-Mart Stores	Consumer	23.4	0.51	2.19
⊕ Bank of America	Financial	12.3	21.50	1.70
⊖ American International G	Financial	16.2	-0.53	1.69
⊕ Johnson & Johnson	Health	20.6	25.17	1.59
⊖ Dell	Hardware	34.0	24.01	1.58
⊖ United Technologies	Ind Mtrls	18.6	10.72	1.44
⊖ US Bancorp	Financial	14.2	10.46	1.40
⊖ PepsiCo	Goods	22.5	13.82	1.36
⊕ J.P. Morgan Chase & Co.	Financial	19.4	9.97	1.34
⊕ Cisco Systems	Hardware	24.5	-20.26	1.32
⊖ Fannie Mae	Financial	9.1	-2.33	1.29
⊖ IBM	Hardware	20.2	7.19	1.27
⊖ American Express	Financial	20.3	17.60	1.23
⊖ Intel	Hardware	19.8	-26.56	1.21

Current Investment Style

Value Blnd Growth; Large Mid Small

Market Cap	%
Giant	58.0
Large	31.0
Mid	10.5
Small	0.4
Micro	0.0
Avg $mil: 48,009	

Value Measures		Rel Category
Price/Earnings	16.77	0.99
Price/Book	2.64	1.01
Price/Sales	1.45	1.01
Price/Cash Flow	3.11	1.06
Dividend Yield %	1.65	1.11

Growth Measures	%	Rel Category
Long-Term Erngs	11.14	0.96
Book Value	6.77	0.87
Sales	4.57	0.80
Cash Flow	7.04	0.74
Historical Erngs	12.00	1.02

Profitability	%	Rel Category
Return on Equity	18.31	1.05
Return on Assets	9.53	1.10
Net Margin	12.28	1.07

Sector Weightings	% of Stocks	Rel S&P 500	3 Year High	3 Year Low
Info	22.13	1.03		
Software	4.23	0.98	7	4
Hardware	10.40	1.02	12	8
Media	3.69	0.96	4	3
Telecom	3.81	1.21	4	2
Service	47.40	1.02		
Health	12.65	1.01	17	13
Consumer	9.35	1.03	9	2
Business	3.74	0.92	5	2
Financial	21.66	1.04	22	19
Mfg	30.48	0.95		
Goods	8.71	0.93	12	3
Ind Mtrls	12.42	0.98	14	11
Energy	6.66	0.93	9	6
Utilities	2.69	0.91	3	1

Composition

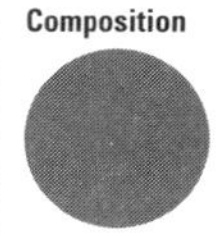

Cash	0.0
Stocks	100.0
Bonds	0.0
Other	0.0
Foreign (% of Stock)	0.5

Morningstar's Take by Christopher Davis 10-05-04

We're skeptical of TIAA-CREF Growth & Income's prospects.

This offering's future remains uncertain. In February 2004, TIAA-CREF gave managers Carlton Martin and Sachie Makishi the heave-ho, assigning Hans Erikson and Bill Riegel to run the portfolio on an interim basis. Nothing has changed since, as the firm has yet to name a permanent successor.

That said, investors shouldn't expect any significant changes in strategy once the permanent team is put in place. All TIAA-CREF funds use quantitative models designed to keep their portfolio's sector weightings and other characteristics aligned with those of their benchmark--in this case, the S&P 500 index. The new management team will attempt to add value on the margins by making a relatively small number of stock-specific bets against the S&P.

It wasn't always that way here. Until recent years, for instance, management had greater latitude to emphasize, or tread lightly in, particular areas of the market. That was a boon to returns in the late 1990s when management's reliance on economically-sensitive tech holdings paid off. But it backfired from 2000 to 2002, as the tech sector was ravaged by a steep downturn in capital spending, contributing to the fund's poor showing during the bear market. In 2003, TIAA-CREF instituted the current sector-neutral approach. However, the fund has continued to struggle in that guise, with the portfolio's defensive posture weighing last year amid a rally in smaller, more speculative fare and a clutch of struggling tech holdings doing a number on returns in 2004.

While there's nothing inherently wrong with the strategy in place here, we need to be convinced management can execute it successfully. So far, it has fallen well shy on that count. As such, despite the fund's laudably low 0.43% expense ratio--which will at least give its new managers a fighting chance once they arrive--investors should head elsewhere for the time being.

Address:	730 Third Ave New York NY 10017 800-223-1200
Web Address:	www.tiaa-cref.org
Inception:	09-01-97 *
Advisor:	Teachers Advisors, Inc.
Subadvisor:	None
NTF Plans:	N/A

Minimum Purchase:	$2500	Add: $50	IRA: $2000
Min Auto Inv Plan:	$50	Add: $50	
Sales Fees:	No-load		
Management Fee:	0.43%		
Actual Fees:	Mgt:0.43%	Dist:	
Expense Projections:	3Yr:$138	5Yr:$241	10Yr:$542
Income Distrib:	Quarterly		

TIAA-CREF Growth Eqty

Ticker	Load	NAV	Yield	Total Assets	Mstar Category
TIGEX	None	$9.17	0.7%	$568 mil	Large Growth

Governance and Management

Fiduciary Grade: B

Portfolio Manager(s)

Greg Luttrell and Susan Cordes took the helm of this offering in November 2002. The pair also runs newly launched TIAA-CREF Mid-Cap Growth. Comanager David Fording joined in April 2002 and primarily focuses on mid-cap stocks and cyclical growth industries, such as media. Luttrell emphasizes large caps and follows tech and health care most closely. The managers draw on TIAA-CREF's experienced analysts.

Strategy

This fund is closely tied to its Russell 1000 Growth benchmark, using a strategy that blends fundamental stock analysis with quantitative investing techniques. Focusing on companies with strong cash flows and high rates of return on invested capital, managers Greg Luttrell and David Fording make more-sizable bets versus their bogy, choosing 50 or so names that meet their criteria. To minimize the fund's risk, comanager Susan Cordes uses quantitative models to fill out the remainder, giving the portfolio similar characteristics to the benchmark, including closely aligned sector and market-cap exposure.

Historical Profile

Return Below Avg
Risk Above Avg
Rating ★★ Below Avg

Investment Style
Equity
Stock %

1997	1998	1999	2000	2001	2002	2003	12-04
100%	96%	98%	99%	98%	100%	100%	100%

▼ Manager Change
▽ Partial Manager Change

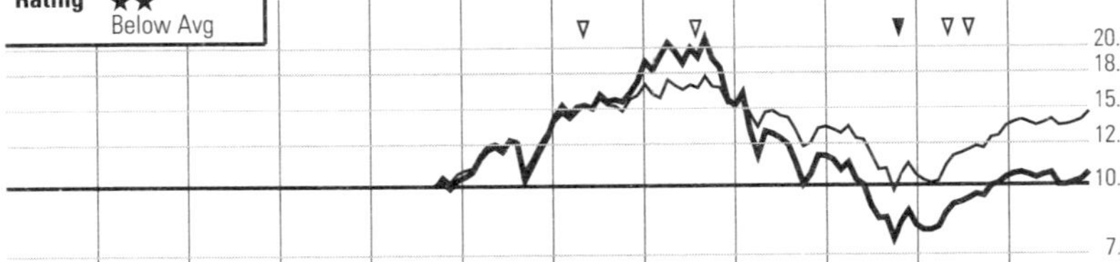

Growth of $10,000
▬ Investment Values of Fund
— Investment Values of S&P 500

Performance Quartile (within Category)

History

1993	1994	1995	1996	1997	1998	1999	2000	2001	2002	2003	12-04	History
—	—	—	—	10.12	13.65	17.19	12.87	9.85	6.84	8.70	9.17	NAV
—	—	—	—	4.89*	35.97	33.00	-20.29	-23.02	-30.12	28.05	6.16	Total Return %
—	—	—	—	—	7.40	11.96	-11.19	-11.14	-8.03	-0.62	-4.71	+/-S&P 500
—	—	—	—	—	-2.74	-0.16	2.13	-2.60	-2.24	-1.70	-0.14	+/-Russ 1000Gr
—	—	—	—	0.00	0.25	0.14	0.00	0.00	0.44	0.86	0.76	Income Return %
—	—	—	—	—	35.72	32.86	-20.29	-23.02	-30.56	27.19	5.40	Capital Return %
—	—	—	—	—	33	56	78	62	71	45	63	Total Rtn % Rank Cat
—	—	—	—	0.03	0.02	0.02	0.00	0.00	0.04	0.06	0.07	Income $
—	—	—	—	0.16	0.08	0.93	0.85	0.06	0.00	0.00	0.00	Capital Gains $
—	—	—	—	—	0.45	0.45	0.45	0.45	0.45	0.45	—	Expense Ratio %
—	—	—	—	—	0.37	0.16	0.00	0.15	0.40	0.72	—	Income Ratio %
—	—	—	—	—	50	70	42	38	50	73	—	Turnover Rate %
—	—	—	—	64	297	696	786	657	422	550	568	Net Assets $mil

Performance 12-31-04

	1st Qtr	2nd Qtr	3rd Qtr	4th Qtr	Total
2000	9.83	-2.60	-5.27	-21.34	-20.29
2001	-22.69	9.05	-21.11	15.74	-23.02
2002	-3.45	-20.08	-15.66	7.39	-30.12
2003	-0.88	13.57	3.25	10.18	28.05
2004	1.15	0.91	-4.62	9.04	6.16

Trailing	Total Return%	+/- S&P 500	+/- Russ 1000Gr	%Rank Cat	Growth of $10,000
3 Mo	9.04	-0.19	-0.13	67	10,904
6 Mo	4.01	-3.18	0.54	63	10,401
1 Yr	6.16	-4.71	-0.14	63	10,616
3 Yr Avg	-1.69	-5.27	-1.51	67	9,502
5 Yr Avg	-10.23	-7.93	-0.94	76	5,830
10 Yr Avg	—	—	—	—	—
15 Yr Avg	—	—	—	—	—

Tax Analysis	Tax-Adj Rtn%	%Rank Cat	Tax-Cost Rat	%Rank Cat
3 Yr (estimated)	-1.93	62	0.24	41
5 Yr (estimated)	-10.61	72	0.42	26
10 Yr (estimated)	—	—	—	—

Potential Capital Gain Exposure: -56% of assets

Rating and Risk

Time Period	Load-Adj Return %	Morningstar Rtn vs Cat	Morningstar Risk vs Cat	Morningstar Risk-Adj Rating
1 Yr	6.16			
3 Yr	-1.69	Avg	Avg	★★★
5 Yr	-10.23	-Avg	+Avg	★★
10 Yr	—	—	—	—
Incept	1.38			

Other Measures	Standard Index S&P 500	Best Fit Index Russ 1000Gr
Alpha	-5.1	-1.4
Beta	1.04	1.03
R-Squared	94	99

Standard Deviation	15.94
Mean	-1.69
Sharpe Ratio	-0.20

Portfolio Analysis 09-30-04

Share change since 06-04 Total Stocks:115	Sector	PE	YTD Ret%	% Assets
⊖ Procter & Gamble	Goods	23.3	12.38	3.72
⊖ Pfizer	Health	22.0	-22.31	3.37
⊕ American International G	Financial	16.2	-0.53	2.95
⊖ Microsoft	Software	36.1	8.95	2.86
⊕ Dell	Hardware	34.0	24.01	2.72
⊕ American Express	Financial	20.3	17.60	2.63
⊕ Qualcomm	Hardware	42.0	58.20	2.59
⊕ Medtronic	Health	30.7	2.68	2.45
⊕ Johnson & Johnson	Health	20.6	25.17	2.43
⊖ Cisco Systems	Hardware	24.5	-20.26	2.25
⊕ Wal-Mart Stores	Consumer	23.4	0.51	2.20
⊕ PepsiCo	Goods	22.5	13.82	2.13
⊕ St. Jude Medical	Health	38.0	36.69	1.90
⊕ Motorola	Hardware	28.7	37.93	1.83
⊕ United Technologies	Ind Mtrls	18.6	10.72	1.77
⊕ 3M Company	Ind Mtrls	23.5	-1.75	1.73
⊕ eBay	Consumer	81.6	80.07	1.70
⊕ Eli Lilly & Company	Health	24.3	-17.55	1.63
⊕ Target	Consumer	22.3	36.14	1.51
⊕ Gillette	Goods	27.6	23.94	1.48

Current Investment Style

Value Blnd Growth; Large Mid Small

Market Cap	%
Giant	49.4
Large	38.3
Mid	12.2
Small	0.1
Micro	0.0

Avg $mil: 36,640

Value Measures		Rel Category
Price/Earnings	21.49	1.01
Price/Book	3.19	0.99
Price/Sales	2.12	0.99
Price/Cash Flow	12.56	1.14
Dividend Yield %	0.80	1.04

Growth Measures	%	Rel Category
Long-Term Erngs	14.26	1.01
Book Value	14.42	1.13
Sales	8.75	1.03
Cash Flow	10.67	0.64
Historical Erngs	11.68	0.81

Profitability	%	Rel Category
Return on Equity	20.71	1.15
Return on Assets	10.58	1.13
Net Margin	13.20	1.07

Sector Weightings	% of Stocks	Rel S&P 500	3 Year High	3 Year Low
Info	27.36	1.27		
Software	6.96	1.62	9	7
Hardware	16.11	1.58	20	13
Media	3.55	0.92	5	3
Telecom	0.74	0.23	1	0
Service	53.77	1.16		
Health	24.69	1.98	29	25
Consumer	13.17	1.45	14	10
Business	5.25	1.30	5	3
Financial	10.66	0.51	11	7
Mfg	18.86	0.59		
Goods	11.74	1.26	12	7
Ind Mtrls	5.84	0.46	9	5
Energy	1.28	0.18	2	1
Utilities	0.00	0.00	0	0

Composition

Cash	0.0
Stocks	100.0
Bonds	0.0
Other	0.0
Foreign (% of Stock)	2.5

Morningstar's Take by Christopher Davis 10-15-04

TIAA-CREF Growth Equity plays a game of inches that we're not convinced it can win.

This offering bears close resemblance to its Russell 1000 Growth benchmark in a number of important respects. Its sector weightings line up with those of the index, as do its portfolio's average price multiples and growth rates. That's by design: Like all TIAA-CREF's actively managed equity offerings, the fund uses quantitative models designed to keep its sector exposure and other portfolio characteristics from deviating far from its bogy's.

As such, the fund's success is largely dependent upon the stock-picking skills of managers Greg Luttrell and David Fording. In building their portfolio, the managers modestly overweight stocks with the characteristics they prize most highly, namely strong free cash flows and high returns on capital. While the lion's share of management's favorites are drawn from their Russell bogy, that's not always the case. In late 2004, for instance, Luttrell and Fording pared the fund's weighting in index constituent Intel in favor of overseas rival Taiwan Semiconductor Manufacturing, which it thought was more reasonably valued.

With low costs--the fund's 0.45% expense ratio is among the lowest price tags of any actively managed large-growth offering--the managers have a big head start over the competition and only a modest hurdle to overcome in beating its bogy. But they haven't been able to translate that advantage into meaningful outperformance. Despite 2004 winners such as eBay, wayward bets on names such as Novellus Systems and Inuit has kept the fund even with its benchmark and in the middle of the large-growth pack this year. And in 2003, management's first full year at the helm, the fund posted middling results and trailed its bogy by 1.7 percentage points.

We do think this fund has potential, but we need to see a consistent record of outperformance before we'll endorse it.

Address:	730 Third Ave New York NY 10017 800-223-1200
Web Address:	www.tiaa-cref.org
Inception:	09-01-97 *
Advisor:	Teachers Advisors, Inc.
Subadvisor:	None
NTF Plans:	N/A

Minimum Purchase:	$2500	Add: $50	IRA: $2000
Min Auto Inv Plan:	$50	Add: $50	
Sales Fees:	No-load		
Management Fee:	0.45%		
Actual Fees:	Mgt:0.45%	Dist:	
Expense Projections:	3Yr:$144	5Yr:$252	10Yr:$567
Income Distrib:	Annually		

TIAA-CREF High-Yield Bd

Ticker	Load	NAV	Yield	SEC Yield	Total Assets	Mstar Category
TCHYX	None	$9.48	6.9%	5.91%	$279 mil	High Yield Bond

Governance and Management

Fiduciary Grade: B

Portfolio Manager(s)

This fund is managed by TIAA-CREF's high-yield team (formed in 1995). The group, led by Kevin Lorenz, manages roughly $2 billion in high-yield assets and has this fund off to a solid start.

Strategy

Management focuses on cash-flow analysis and looks for companies that are self-financing. That approach hasn't prevented the fund from hitting a few bumps in the road, but it generally steers it to more-mature sectors of the high-yield market, such as radio and printing. The fund is also domestic-oriented.

Historical Profile

Return Average
Risk Above Avg
Rating ★★★ Neutral

Investment Style
Fixed Income
Income Rtn %Rank Cat: 100 (2000), 49 (2001), 46 (2002), 36 (2003), 44 (12-04)

▼ Manager Change
▽ Partial Manager Change

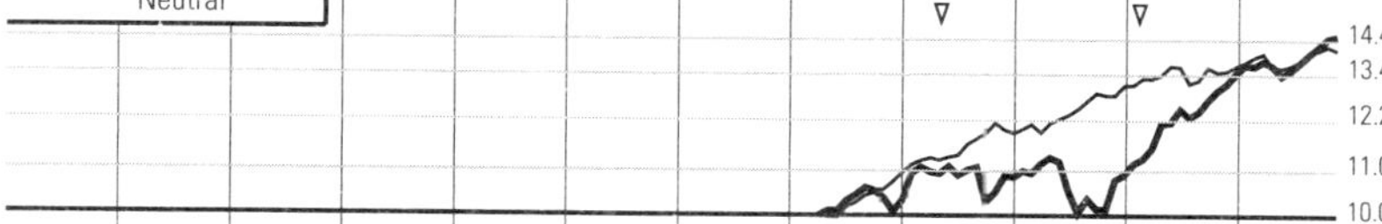

Growth of $10,000
▬ Investment Values of Fund
— Investment Values of LB Aggr

Performance Quartile (within Category)

1993	1994	1995	1996	1997	1998	1999	2000	2001	2002	2003	12-04	History
—	—	—	—	—	—	—	9.41	8.94	8.20	9.32	9.48	NAV
—	—	—	—	—	—	—	3.19*	4.88	0.45	23.23	9.16	Total Return %
—	—	—	—	—	—	—	—	-3.56	-9.80	19.13	4.82	+/-LB Aggr
—	—	—	—	—	—	—	—	-0.90	-2.66	-4.70	-2.80	+/-CSFB Glb HY
—	—	—	—	—	—	—	0.00	10.34	8.94	9.07	7.29	Income Return %
—	—	—	—	—	—	—	—	-5.46	-8.49	14.16	1.87	Capital Return %
—	—	—	—	—	—	—	—	34	35	57	65	Total Rtn % Rank Cat
—	—	—	—	—	—	—	0.71	0.93	0.77	0.72	0.66	Income $
—	—	—	—	—	—	—	0.00	0.00	0.00	0.00	0.00	Capital Gains $
—	—	—	—	—	—	—	—	0.34	0.34	0.34	—	Expense Ratio %
—	—	—	—	—	—	—	—	9.97	9.17	8.13	—	Income Ratio %
—	—	—	—	—	—	—	37	75	74	42	—	Turnover Rate %
—	—	—	—	—	—	—	64	92	104	227	279	Net Assets $mil

Performance 12-31-04

	1st Qtr	2nd Qtr	3rd Qtr	4th Qtr	Total
2000	—	3.09	2.04	-1.91	3.19 *
2001	6.00	-0.69	-5.36	5.27	4.88
2002	2.76	-5.57	-3.50	7.28	0.45
2003	5.64	8.35	1.82	5.74	23.23
2004	2.57	-1.84	5.00	3.26	9.16

Trailing	Total Return%	+/- LB Aggr	+/- CSFB Glb HY	%Rank Cat	Growth of $10,000
3 Mo	3.26	2.31	-1.30	85	10,326
6 Mo	8.43	4.25	-0.83	57	10,843
1 Yr	9.16	4.82	-2.80	65	10,916
3 Yr Avg	10.56	4.37	-3.32	46	13,514
5 Yr Avg	—	—	—	—	—
10 Yr Avg	—	—	—	—	—
15 Yr Avg	—	—	—	—	—

Tax Analysis	Tax-Adj Rtn%	%Rank Cat	Tax-Cost Rat	%Rank Cat
3 Yr (estimated)	7.36	37	2.89	55
5 Yr (estimated)	—	—	—	—
10 Yr (estimated)	—	—	—	—

Potential Capital Gain Exposure: 3% of assets

Rating and Risk

Time Period	Load-Adj Return %	Morningstar Rtn vs Cat	Morningstar Risk vs Cat	Morningstar Risk-Adj Rating
1 Yr	9.16			
3 Yr	10.56	Avg	+Avg	★★★
5 Yr	—	—	—	—
10 Yr	—	—	—	—
Incept	8.33			

Other Measures	Standard Index LB Aggr	Best Fit Index CSFB Glb HY
Alpha	8.5	-5.2
Beta	0.16	1.20
R-Squared	1	94
Standard Deviation	8.47	
Mean	10.56	
Sharpe Ratio	1.09	

Portfolio Analysis 09-30-04

Total Fixed-Income:236	Date of Maturity	Amount $000	Value $000	% Net Assets
Qwest 144A 8.875%	03-15-12	3,000	3,300	1.29
Fisher Comms 144A 8.625%	09-15-14	2,250	2,340	0.92
Keystone Automotive Oper	11-01-13	2,000	2,150	0.84
Panamsat 144A 9%	08-15-14	2,000	2,080	0.82
Coinmach 9%	02-01-10	2,000	2,075	0.81
Broder Bros 11.25%	10-15-10	2,000	2,000	0.78
Ftd 7.75%	02-15-14	2,000	1,995	0.78
Primedia 7.625%	04-01-08	2,000	1,975	0.77
Case New Holland 144A 9.	08-01-11	1,750	1,960	0.77
Chesapeake Engy 6.875%	01-15-16	1,870	1,954	0.77
Georgia Pac 9.5%	12-01-11	1,500	1,856	0.73
Qwest 144A 7.875%	09-01-11	1,750	1,816	0.71
Liberty Grp Oper 9.375%	02-01-08	1,750	1,763	0.69
Georgia Pac 8.875%	02-01-10	1,500	1,755	0.69
Lyondell Chem 10.5%	06-01-13	1,500	1,733	0.68
Autonation 9%	08-01-08	1,500	1,725	0.68
Graphic Packaging Intl 9	08-15-13	1,500	1,714	0.67
Directv Hldgs 8.375%	03-15-13	1,500	1,706	0.67
At&T 7.3%	11-15-11	1,500	1,678	0.66
Park Pl Entmt 7%	04-15-13	1,500	1,669	0.65

Current Investment Style
Duration: Short Int Long
Quality: High Med Low
¹ figure provided by fund

Avg Eff Duration¹	4.1 Yrs
Avg Eff Maturity	7.0 Yrs
Avg Credit Quality	B
Avg Wtd Coupon	8.57%
Avg Wtd Price	107.54% of par

Coupon Range	% of Bonds	Rel Cat
0% PIK	0.8	0.2
0% to 8%	38.0	1.0
8% to 11%	57.8	1.1
11% to 14%	4.2	0.6
More than 14%	0.0	0.0

1.00=Category Average

Credit Analysis		% bonds 09-30-04	
US Govt	0	BB	37
AAA	0	B	61
AA	0	Below B	2
A	0	NR/NA	0
BBB	0		

Sector Breakdown	% of assets
US Treasuries	0
TIPS	0
US Agency	0
Mortgage Pass-Throughs	0
Mortgage CMO	0
Mortgage ARM	0
US Corporate	88
Asset-Backed	0
Convertible	0
Municipal	0
Corporate Inflation-Protected	0
Foreign Corporate	4
Foreign Govt	0

Composition			
Cash	8.3	Bonds	91.7
Stocks	0.0	Other	0.0

Special Securities	
Restricted/Illiquid Secs	18
Exotic Mortgage-Backed	0
Emerging-Markets Secs	0
Options/Futures/Warrants	No

Morningstar's Take by Lynn Russell 11-11-04

TIAA-CREF High-Yield Bond may not shoot out the lights, but it's not likely to shoot investors in the foot either.

This fund doesn't usually top the charts, but it has continued to post consistently solid returns since its inception. The fund got off to a quite respectable start in 2000 and held up quite well compared with its category as high-yield bonds took a beating over the next couple of years. And while the fund lagged during 2003's roaring rally, its rather nice gain of 23% wasn't far off the high-yield category's midpoint. The high-yield market has continued strong in 2004, although it has slowed its scorching pace, and the fund is again right at the middle of the pack for the year to date through Nov. 11.

The fund's resilience in the face of bear markets and somewhat laggardly performance in strong rallies results from its relatively moderate approach to investing in junk bonds. The fund's management team, led by Kevin Lorenz, starts with fundamental credit analysis, analyzes worst-case scenarios, and looks for seasoned companies they believe can stay afloat during down markets. The fund generally sticks to the higher-quality end of the high-yield risk spectrum.

The downside of those higher-quality standards is that the fund tends to be more sensitive to interest-rate fluctuations than many of its more aggressive rivals. For instance, the fund took more of a hit in the second quarter of 2004 when rates moved up sharply but was also able to make up that lost ground when rates moved back down later in the year. If interest rates move higher, though, as many predict they will, this fund could once again find itself struggling to keep pace with the category as whole.

That said, we think this fund's experienced management, moderate strategy, rock-bottom expenses, and competitive yield make it an appealing choice for more-conservative long-term investors.

Address:	730 Third Ave New York NY 10017 800-223-1200
Web Address:	www.tiaa-cref.org
Inception:	04-03-00 *
Advisor:	Teachers Advisors, Inc.
Subadvisor:	None
NTF Plans:	N/A

Minimum Purchase:	$2500	Add: $50	IRA: $2000
Min Auto Inv Plan:	$50	Add: $50	
Sales Fees:	No-load		
Management Fee:	0.34%		
Actual Fees:	Mgt:0.34%	Dist:	
Expense Projections:	3Yr:$109	5Yr:$191	10Yr:$431
Income Distrib:	Monthly		

TIAA-CREF Intl Equity

Ticker	Load	NAV	Yield	Total Assets	Mstar Category
TIINX	None	$10.67	1.6%	$362 mil	Foreign Large Blend

Governance and Management

Fiduciary Grade: B

Portfolio Manager(s)

Chris Semenuk has worked at TIAA-CREF since 1995 and has been at the helm since the fund's September 1997 launch. Yumiko Miura also joined the company in 1995 but only came aboard here in June 2002 after running CREF's Japanese-equity account. Semenuk says his pension is invested in the fund, but Miura reports she invests in index and money market funds instead of this offering.

Strategy

This offering blends fundamental stock analysis with quantitative-investing techniques. Managers Chris Semenuk and Yumiko Miura make a relatively small number of sizable stock-specific bets versus its MSCI EAFE bogy while quantitative managers use optimizing models to fill out the remainder of the portfolio. The idea is to give the fund similar risk characteristics to the index, including comparable volatility and similar industry, region, and market-cap exposure, making management's stock-picking the overwhelming factor in determining its success. The fund doesn't hedge its currency exposure.

Historical Profile

Return Average
Risk Above Avg
Rating ★★★ Neutral

Investment Style: Equity, Stock %: 99% 95% 98% 97% 99% 90% 99% 99%

▼ Manager Change
▽ Partial Manager Change

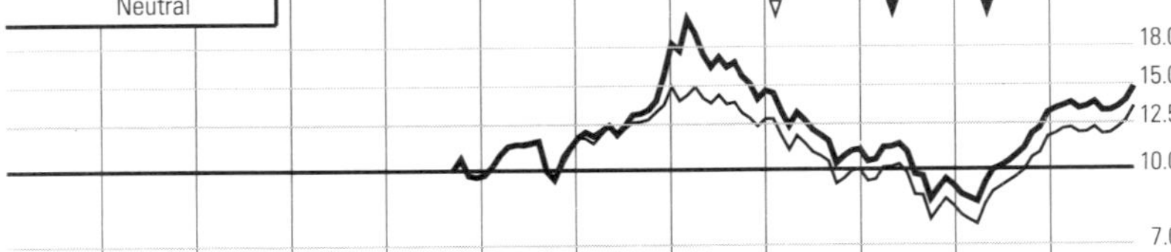

Performance Quartile (within Category)

1993	1994	1995	1996	1997	1998	1999	2000	2001	2002	2003	12-04	History
—	—	—	—	8.92	10.54	16.08	10.75	8.07	6.68	9.24	10.67	NAV
—	—	—	—	-2.30*	19.27	55.83	-19.99	-24.29	-15.73	40.83	17.37	Total Return %
—	—	—	—	—	-0.66	28.80	-5.80	-2.87	0.21	2.24	-2.88	+/-MSCI EAFE
—	—	—	—	—	0.58	27.85	-6.63	-2.90	0.07	1.41	-3.01	+/-MSCI Wd xUS
—	—	—	—	0.00	1.10	1.04	0.55	0.63	1.47	2.49	1.87	Income Return %
—	—	—	—	—	18.17	54.79	-20.54	-24.92	-17.20	38.34	15.50	Capital Return %
—	—	—	—	—	20	14	79	73	37	8	50	Total Rtn % Rank Cat
—	—	—	—	0.00	0.10	0.11	0.09	0.07	0.12	0.17	0.17	Income $
—	—	—	—	0.00	0.00	0.23	2.00	0.00	0.00	0.00	0.00	Capital Gains $
—	—	—	—	—	0.49	0.49	0.49	0.49	0.49	0.49	—	Expense Ratio %
—	—	—	—	—	1.23	1.03	0.49	1.10	1.47	1.96	—	Income Ratio %
—	—	—	—	—	27	74	138	113	78	162	—	Turnover Rate %
—	—	—	—	48	119	256	275	262	219	287	362	Net Assets $mil

Performance 12-31-04

	1st Qtr	2nd Qtr	3rd Qtr	4th Qtr	Total
2000	4.85	-10.56	-8.62	-6.64	-19.99
2001	-15.35	-1.87	-14.67	6.81	-24.29
2002	0.99	-2.09	-20.18	6.77	-15.73
2003	-7.49	18.12	9.04	18.18	40.83
2004	4.76	0.31	-2.27	14.27	17.37

Trailing	Total Return%	+/- MSCI EAFE	+/- MSCI Wd xUS	%Rank Cat	Growth of $10,000
3 Mo	14.27	-1.05	-0.88	47	11,427
6 Mo	11.69	-3.31	-3.68	90	11,169
1 Yr	17.37	-2.88	-3.01	50	11,737
3 Yr Avg	11.68	-0.21	-0.54	18	13,929
5 Yr Avg	-3.34	-2.21	-2.58	58	8,438
10 Yr Avg	—	—	—	—	—
15 Yr Avg	—	—	—	—	—

Tax Analysis	Tax-Adj Rtn%	%Rank Cat	Tax-Cost Rat	%Rank Cat
3 Yr (estimated)	10.98	17	0.63	68
5 Yr (estimated)	-4.60	62	1.30	80
10 Yr (estimated)	—	—	—	—

Potential Capital Gain Exposure: -4% of assets

Rating and Risk

Time Period	Load-Adj Return %	Morningstar Rtn vs Cat	Morningstar Risk vs Cat	Morningstar Risk-Adj Rating
1 Yr	17.37			
3 Yr	11.68	+Avg	Avg	★★★★
5 Yr	-3.34	Avg	High	★★★
10 Yr	—	—	—	—
Incept	5.99			

Other Measures	Standard Index S&P 500	Best Fit Index MSCI EAFE
Alpha	-0.1	-0.1
Beta	0.99	0.99
R-Squared	99	99
Standard Deviation	17.33	
Mean	11.68	
Sharpe Ratio	0.60	

Portfolio Analysis 06-30-04

Share change since 12-03 Total Stocks:419	Sector	Country	% Assets
⊕ Royal Bank Of Scotland G	Financial	U.K.	3.72
⊕ Tesco	Consumer	U.K.	2.89
☼ Compass Grp	Consumer	U.K.	2.71
⊕ Reckitt Benckiser	Goods	U.K.	2.46
☼ Holcim	Ind Mtrls	Switzerland	2.38
☼ UBS Ag (Reg)	Financial	Switzerland	2.20
⊕ Reed Elsevier	Media	U.K.	2.19
⊖ E.On	Utilities	Germany	1.95
⊕ GlaxoSmithKline	Health	U.K.	1.82
⊖ Vinci	Business	France	1.79
☼ STMicroelectronics	Hardware	France	1.55
☼ The Swatch Grp	Goods	Switzerland	1.55
⊕ Royal Dutch Petroleum	Energy	Netherlands	1.37
⊕ Toyota Motor	Goods	Japan	1.30
⊕ Zurich Financial Service	Financial	Switzerland	1.28
⊖ HSBC Hldgs	Financial	U.K.	1.25
⊖ BP PLC ADR	Energy	U.K.	1.23
⊖ Novartis	Health	Switzerland	1.17
⊖ Celesio	Health	Germany	1.07
☼ DEPFA Bank	Financial	Germany	1.07

Current Investment Style (Value Blnd Growth; Large Mid Small)

Market Cap	%
Giant	45.0
Large	37.9
Mid	16.7
Small	0.4
Micro	0.0

Avg $mil: 18,072

Value Measures		Rel Category
Price/Earnings	14.75	1.08
Price/Book	1.87	1.04
Price/Sales	0.65	0.71
Price/Cash Flow	5.34	1.09
Dividend Yield %	2.16	0.85

Growth Measures	%	Rel Category
Long-Term Erngs	10.03	0.93
Book Value	0.26	26.00
Sales	1.16	0.47
Cash Flow	7.47	1.33
Historical Erngs	10.84	1.94

Composition

Cash	0.0	Bonds	0.0
Stocks	99.0	Other	1.0

Foreign (% of Stock) 100.0

Sector Weightings	% of Stocks	Rel MSCI EAFE	3 Year High	3 Year Low
Info	14.17	0.85		
Software	1.47	1.36	2	0
Hardware	4.50	1.23	7	4
Media	2.86	1.25	3	1
Telecom	5.34	0.56	8	5
Service	48.45	1.08		
Health	8.29	1.14	15	7
Consumer	10.06	2.00	10	2
Business	4.93	0.91	10	5
Financial	25.17	0.93	25	16
Mfg	37.38	0.97		
Goods	14.01	1.03	23	13
Ind Mtrls	13.85	1.13	14	11
Energy	5.71	0.78	9	5
Utilities	3.81	0.71	5	1

Regional Exposure	% Stock		
UK/W. Europe	68	N. America	0
Japan	25	Latn America	0
Asia X Japan	7	Other	0

Country Exposure	% Stock		
Japan	25	France	10
U.K.	24	Germany	9
Switzerland	13		

Morningstar's Take by Christopher Davis 12-01-04

TIAA-CREF International Equity's full potential hasn't been realized.

This offering resembles its MSCI EAFE Index benchmark in a number of important respects. Its sector weightings and regional exposure align fairly closely to that of the index, as do its portfolio's average price multiples and growth rates. That's by design: Like all of TIAA-CREF's actively managed equity offerings, the fund uses quantitative models designed to keep its portfolio characteristics from deviating far from its bogy's.

As such, the fund's success is largely dependent upon the stock-picking skills of managers Chris Semenuk and Yumiko Miura, who cover European and Asian stocks respectively. The pair overweights stocks with strong free cash flows, high returns on capital, and moderate valuations. While most of the managers' favorites hail from their bogy, position sizes of individual holdings can deviate sharply. Top holdings Vinci, Fiat, and Holcim, for instance, have miniscule weightings in the index.

With low costs--the fund's 0.49% expense ratio is among the lowest price tags of any actively managed foreign large-blend offering--the managers have a big head start over the competition and only a modest hurdle to overcome in beating their bogy. Management has generally translated that cost advantage into outperformance. While the fund has lagged the EAFE by more than two percentage points this year, it fared relatively well in 2003 and 2002, when management first adopted its sector- and region-neutral approach.

That said, we're bothered by the ongoing weakness in Miura's picks. Semenuk has continually made up for lost ground as Miura's favorites have disappointed, whether it was Sony in 2003 or Shin-Etsu Chemical in 2004. But we need to be confident in both managers' abilities to give it the nod. Thus, despite the fund's low costs and sensible strategy, we think investors can find better options elsewhere.

Address:	730 Third Ave, New York NY 10017, 800-223-1200
Web Address:	www.tiaa-cref.org
Inception:	09-01-97 *
Advisor:	Teachers Advisors, Inc.
Subadvisor:	None
NTF Plans:	N/A

Minimum Purchase:	$2500	Add: $50	IRA: $2000
Min Auto Inv Plan:	$50	Add: $50	
Sales Fees:	No-load		
Management Fee:	0.49%		
Actual Fees:	Mgt:0.49%	Dist: —	
Expense Projections:	3Yr:$157	5Yr:$274	10Yr:$616
Income Distrib:	Annually		

TIAA-CREF Managed Alloc

Ticker	Load	NAV	Yield	Total Assets	Mstar Category
TIMAX	None	$11.13	3.4%	$497 mil	Moderate Allocation

Governance and Management

Fiduciary Grade: B

Portfolio Manager(s)

Jim Fleischmann and Ed Grzybowski oversee equity and fixed-income research, respectively, at TIAA-CREF. They make the fund's asset-allocation decisions.

Strategy

The fund invests in other TIAA-CREF funds, particularly Growth Equity, Large-Cap Value, Small-Cap Equity, International Equity, Bond Plus, and High-Yield Bond. It dropped TIAA-CREF Growth & Income from the portfolio when it added the value and small-cap funds to its menu in May 2003, but its prospectus says it can still use the Growth & Income fund. The offering typically stashes 60% of its assets in equities and 40% in bonds, although that distribution can vary by as much as 15 percentage points.

Historical Profile

Return Average
Risk Average
Rating ★★★ Neutral

Investment Style
Equity
Stock %

33% 57% 60% 63% 59% 61% 60%

▼ Manager Change
∇ Partial Manager Change

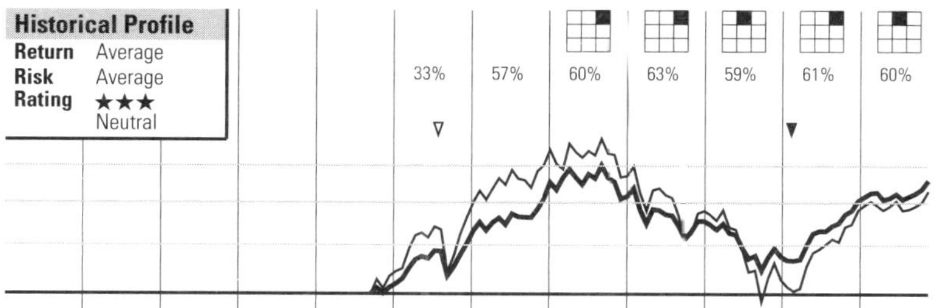

Growth of $10,000
— Investment Values of Fund
— Investment Values of S&P 500

Performance Quartile (within Category)

1993	1994	1995	1996	1997	1998	1999	2000	2001	2002	2003	12-04	History
—	—	—	—	10.01	11.79	13.59	12.20	10.50	8.87	10.41	11.13	NAV
—	—	—	—	3.77*	21.24	19.20	-4.94	-8.52	-12.09	22.44	10.69	Total Return %
—	—	—	—	—	-7.33	-1.84	4.16	3.36	10.00	-6.23	-0.18	+/-S&P 500
—	—	—	—	—	8.85	6.35	-9.38	-8.68	-1.55	-1.62	-0.48	+/-DJ 60%
—	—	—	—	0.00	3.27	3.30	3.53	2.30	3.26	4.92	3.71	Income Return %
—	—	—	—	—	17.97	15.90	-8.47	-10.82	-15.35	17.52	6.98	Capital Return %
—	—	—	—	—	15	11	88	81	53	28	20	Total Rtn % Rank Cat
—	—	—	—	0.17	0.32	0.38	0.47	0.28	0.34	0.43	0.38	Income $
—	—	—	—	0.00	0.00	0.05	0.26	0.38	0.03	0.00	0.00	Capital Gains $
—	—	—	—	—	0.00	0.00	0.00	0.00	0.00	0.00	—	Expense Ratio %
—	—	—	—	—	2.80	5.19	2.87	3.34	2.68	2.56	—	Income Ratio %
—	—	—	—	—	5	4	1	3	12	37	—	Turnover Rate %
—	—	—	—	59	163	244	331	319	287	398	497	Net Assets $mil

Performance 12-31-04

	1st Qtr	2nd Qtr	3rd Qtr	4th Qtr	Total
2000	4.88	-1.77	-1.27	-6.55	-4.94
2001	-9.43	3.39	-8.49	6.75	-8.52
2002	-0.97	-8.40	-7.86	5.18	-12.09
2003	-1.07	10.97	2.88	8.41	22.44
2004	3.07	-0.54	0.22	7.74	10.69

Trailing	Total Return%	+/- S&P 500	+/- DJ 60%	%Rank Cat	Growth of $10,000
3 Mo	7.74	-1.49	0.26	28	10,774
6 Mo	7.98	0.79	0.45	22	10,798
1 Yr	10.69	-0.18	-0.48	20	11,069
3 Yr Avg	6.01	2.43	-1.25	27	11,914
5 Yr Avg	0.71	3.01	-4.53	67	10,360
10 Yr Avg	—	—	—	—	—
15 Yr Avg	—	—	—	—	—

Tax Analysis	Tax-Adj Rtn%	%Rank Cat	Tax-Cost Rat	%Rank Cat
3 Yr (estimated)	4.55	31	1.38	87
5 Yr (estimated)	-0.83	71	1.53	75
10 Yr (estimated)	—	—	—	—

Potential Capital Gain Exposure: -1% of assets

Rating and Risk

Time Period	Load-Adj Return %	Morningstar Rtn vs Cat	Morningstar Risk vs Cat	Morningstar Risk-Adj Rating
1 Yr	10.69			
3 Yr	6.01	+Avg	Avg	★★★★
5 Yr	0.71	-Avg	Avg	★★★
10 Yr	—	—	—	—
Incept	6.19			

Other Measures	Standard Index S&P 500	Best Fit Index Russ 1000
Alpha	3.0	2.6
Beta	0.58	0.59
R-Squared	94	94
Standard Deviation	9.46	
Mean	6.01	
Sharpe Ratio	0.49	

Portfolio Analysis 06-30-04

Total Stocks:0 Share change since 12-31-03	Sectors	P/E Ratio	YTD Return %	% Net Assets
⊕ TIAA-CREF Inst'l Large-Cap	—	—	—	20.94
⊕ TIAA-CREF Growth Equity	—	—	—	19.31
⊕ TIAA-CREF International E	—	—	—	12.03
⊕ TIAA-CREF Equity Index	—	—	—	3.91
⊕ TIAA-CREF Inst'l Small-Cap	—	—	—	3.36
⊕ TIAA-CREF Inst'l Real Esta	—	—	—	0.99

Total Fixed-Income:3	Date of Maturity	Amount $000	Value $000	% Net Assets
TIAA-CREF Bond Plus		15,554	157,872	35.14
TIAA-CREF High-Yield Bond		1,239	11,209	2.49
TIAA-CREF Short-Term Bond		688	7,246	1.61

Morningstar's Take by Christopher Davis 12-27-04

A weak link at TIAA-CREF Managed Allocation Fund undermines its appeal.

One of the biggest challenges investors face is building broadly diversified portfolios. This offering resolves that dilemma by spreading its portfolio across eight TIAA-CREF offerings, which invest in large and small caps, growth and value stocks, at home and abroad, and in bonds of all stripes.

Another obstacle investors must overcome is costs. But with TIAA-CREF funds' expense ratios far below those of their category peers, that hurdle is much easier to clear. What's more, because TIAA-CREF is charging no fee on top of the expenses of the fund's investments, it has an even bigger advantage over costlier rivals.

Unfortunately, while low expenses give the fund's underlying holdings a decided advantage over the competition, they still don't guarantee success. TIAA-CREF Growth Equity, which accounts for 20% of this fund's assets, is living proof. Like all actively managed TIAA-CREF equity offerings, that fund ties its sector weightings and other portfolio characteristics to its benchmark, in that case the Russell 1000 Growth Index, making management's stock-picking abilities the primary determinant of success. That fund's team has continued to fall short of the mark, however, leading to middling results relative to the fund's large-growth peers and to its bogy.

There are some things to like here, however. For one, the fund's fixed-income investments, most notably TIAA-CREF Bond Plus, have been strong performers. Also, relatively new holdings like TIAA-CREF Institutional Large-Cap Value and TIAA-CREF Institutional Small-Cap Equity have gotten off to strong starts.

This isn't a bad choice for investors seeking to shop in one stop for stock and bond exposure. But TIAA-CREF's mixed success in developing solid actively managed equity funds makes us wary of giving this offering our wholehearted endorsement.

Address:	730 Third Ave New York NY 10017 800-223-1200
Web Address:	www.tiaa-cref.org
Inception:	09-01-97*
Advisor:	Teachers Advisors, Inc.
Subadvisor:	None
NTF Plans:	N/A

Minimum Purchase:	$2500	Add: $50	IRA: $2000
Min Auto Inv Plan:	$50	Add: $50	
Sales Fees:	No-load		
Management Fee:	0.00%		
Actual Fees:	Mgt:0.00%	Dist:	
Expense Projections:	3Yr:$125	5Yr:$219	10Yr:$493
Income Distrib:	Quarterly		

Equity Style
Style: Blend
Size: Large-Cap

Value Measures		Rel Category
Price/Earnings	17.12	1.03
Price/Book	2.30	0.94
Price/Sales	1.24	0.94
Price/Cash Flow	7.71	1.06
Dividend Yield %	1.72	1.10
Growth Measures	**%**	**Rel Category**
Long-Term Erngs	10.98	0.94
Book Value	5.33	0.93
Sales	3.96	0.76
Cash Flow	-1.59	NMF
Historical Erngs	11.14	1.03

Market Cap %			
Giant	45.2	Small	6.3
Large	31.0	Micro	1.5
Mid	16.1	Avg $mil:	23,540

Composition

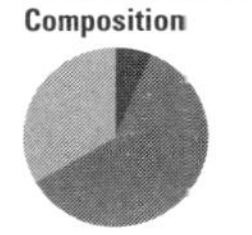

Cash	6.3
Stocks	60.1
Bonds	33.5
Other	0.2
Foreign (% of Stock)	21.9

Fixed-Income Style
Duration: Interm-Term
Quality: High

Avg Eff Duration[1]	4.5 Yrs
Avg Eff Maturity	6.3 Yrs
Avg Credit Quality	AAA
Avg Wtd Coupon	5.58%

[1]figure provided by fund as of 06-30-04

Sector Weightings	% of Stocks	Rel S&P 500	3 Year High	3 Year Low
Info	20.59	0.96		
Software	3.63	0.84	6	4
Hardware	10.21	1.00	15	10
Media	3.73	0.97	4	3
Telecom	3.02	0.96	4	3
Service	50.30	1.08		
Health	13.90	1.11	20	13
Consumer	7.87	0.87	10	6
Business	5.22	1.29	5	3
Financial	23.31	1.12	24	14
Mfg	29.12	0.91		
Goods	9.14	0.98	12	9
Ind Mtrls	11.03	0.87	11	10
Energy	5.54	0.77	6	5
Utilities	3.41	1.15	3	[illegible]

TIAA-CREF Short-Term Bd

Ticker	Load	NAV	Yield	SEC Yield	Total Assets	Mstar Category
TCSTX	None	$10.55	2.9%	3.13%	$239 mil	Short-Term Bond

Governance and Management

Fiduciary Grade: B

Portfolio Manager(s)

John Cerra replaced recently promoted Lisa Black in September 2003. Black is now group managing director in the fixed-income department, and Cerra reports to her. Cerra is a TIAA-CREF veteran who worked in the bond group from 1989 to 1995 and then worked in public project loan and asset-backed securities and derivatives areas. Besides managing this fund, he also leads the team that runs TIAA-CREF Bond Plus.

Strategy

The fund tries to outpace the Lehman Brothers 1-5 Year Govt/Credit Index through issue selection and sector rotation, and it largely shuns mortgage-backed securities. Manager John Cerra sticks mainly with investment-grade bonds and avoids making interest-rate bets. But because its benchmark's duration is longer than its average rival's, this fund also typically sports more interest-rate sensitivity--on both the up side and the down side--than the average short-term government offering.

Historical Profile

Return Above Avg
Risk Above Avg
Rating ★★★★ Above Avg

Investment Style
Fixed Income
Income Rtn %Rank Cat

2000	2001	2002	2003	12-04
100	37	41	46	44

▼ Manager Change
▽ Partial Manager Change

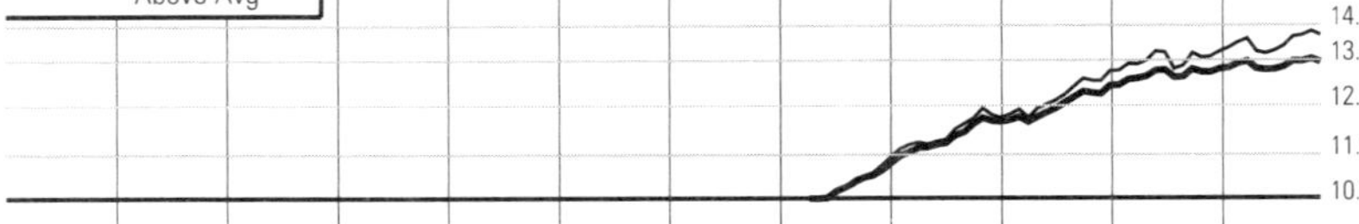

Growth of $10,000
▬ Investment Values of Fund
— Investment Values of LB Aggr

Performance Quartile (within Category)

1993	1994	1995	1996	1997	1998	1999	2000	2001	2002	2003	12-04	History
—	—	—	—	—	—	—	10.23	10.48	10.76	10.69	10.55	NAV
—	—	—	—	—	—	—	7.73*	9.09	7.81	3.51	1.72	Total Return %
—	—	—	—	—	—	—	—	0.65	-2.44	-0.59	-2.62	+/-LB Aggr
—	—	—	—	—	—	—	—	0.06	-0.31	0.16	-0.13	+/-LB 1-5 YR
—	—	—	—	—	—	—	0.00	5.72	4.42	3.05	2.86	Income Return %
—	—	—	—	—	—	—	—	3.37	3.39	0.46	-1.14	Capital Return %
—	—	—	—	—	—	—	—	1	7	20	37	Total Rtn % Rank Cat
—	—	—	—	—	—	—	0.49	0.57	0.45	0.32	0.30	Income $
—	—	—	—	—	—	—	0.05	0.09	0.06	0.12	0.02	Capital Gains $
—	—	—	—	—	—	—	—	0.30	0.30	0.30	—	Expense Ratio %
—	—	—	—	—	—	—	—	5.36	4.32	3.00	—	Income Ratio %
—	—	—	—	—	—	—	387	132	158	176	—	Turnover Rate %
—	—	—	—	—	—	—	30	61	149	210	239	Net Assets $mil

Performance 12-31-04

	1st Qtr	2nd Qtr	3rd Qtr	4th Qtr	Total
2000	—	1.60	2.81	3.13	7.73*
2001	3.25	1.01	4.10	0.49	9.09
2002	-0.06	2.89	3.56	1.24	7.81
2003	1.48	1.77	0.16	0.06	3.51
2004	1.59	-1.71	1.68	0.18	1.72

Trailing	Total Return%	+/- LB Aggr	+/- LB 1-5 YR	%Rank Cat	Growth of $10,000
3 Mo	0.18	-0.77	0.03	58	10,018
6 Mo	1.87	-2.31	-0.01	28	10,187
1 Yr	1.72	-2.62	-0.13	37	10,172
3 Yr Avg	4.32	-1.87	-0.09	14	11,353
5 Yr Avg	—	—	—	—	—
10 Yr Avg	—	—	—	—	—
15 Yr Avg	—	—	—	—	—

Tax Analysis	Tax-Adj Rtn%	%Rank Cat	Tax-Cost Rat	%Rank Cat
3 Yr (estimated)	2.87	9	1.39	60
5 Yr (estimated)	—	—	—	—
10 Yr (estimated)	—	—	—	—

Potential Capital Gain Exposure: 0% of assets

Rating and Risk

Time Period	Load-Adj Return %	Morningstar Rtn vs Cat	Morningstar Risk vs Cat	Morningstar Risk-Adj Rating
1 Yr	1.72			
3 Yr	4.32	+Avg	+Avg	★★★★
5 Yr	—	—	—	—
10 Yr	—	—	—	—
Incept	6.25			

Other Measures	Standard Index LB Aggr	Best Fit Index LB 1-5 YR
Alpha	0.0	-0.1
Beta	0.60	1.01
R-Squared	91	98

Standard Deviation	2.81
Mean	4.32
Sharpe Ratio	1.06

Portfolio Analysis 09-30-04

Total Fixed-Income:155	Date of Maturity	Amount $000	Value $000	% Net Assets
FNMA 5.25%	06-15-06	20,000	20,836	8.68
FHLMC 2.875%	05-15-07	14,500	14,438	6.02
FHLMC 1.875%	02-15-06	12,750	12,634	5.26
US Treasury Note 3.5%	08-15-09	9,000	9,053	3.77
US Treasury Note 3.125%	09-15-08	8,500	8,493	3.54
FNMA 4.375%	10-15-06	8,000	8,244	3.44
US Treasury Note 3.625%	07-15-09	6,875	6,958	2.90
US Treasury Note 2.625%	11-15-06	6,550	6,547	2.73
US Treasury Bond 11.75%	02-15-10	6,000	6,214	2.59
FFCB 2.25%	09-01-06	6,000	5,945	2.48
US Treasury Note 3.875%	01-15-09	5,197	5,851	2.44
US Treasury Note 2.25%	02-15-07	5,550	5,491	2.29
US Treasury Note 7%	07-15-06	5,000	5,389	2.25
US Treasury Note 2.625%	05-15-08	5,100	5,025	2.09
Wal Mart Stores 3.375%	10-01-08	5,000	4,966	2.07
FNMA 5%	01-15-07	3,500	3,657	1.52
US Treasury Note 3.25%	08-15-08	3,450	3,466	1.44
US Treasury Note 3%	02-15-09	2,250	2,227	0.93
US Treasury Note 3.25%	01-15-09	2,050	2,051	0.85
US Treasury Note 3.125%	05-15-07	2,000	2,017	0.84

Current Investment Style
Duration: Short Int Long
Quality: High Med Low

1 figure provided by fund

Avg Eff Duration[1]	2.5 Yrs
Avg Eff Maturity	2.7 Yrs
Avg Credit Quality	AA
Avg Wtd Coupon	4.21%
Avg Wtd Price	101.94% of par

Coupon Range	% of Bonds	Rel Cat
0% PIK	0.3	0.1
0% to 6%	91.3	1.3
6% to 8%	5.8	0.3
8% to 10%	0.2	0.1
More than 10%	2.7	3.2

1.00=Category Average

Credit Analysis	% bonds 09-30-04		
US Govt	30	BB	0
AAA	31	B	0
AA	11	Below B	0
A	14	NR/NA	1
BBB	13		

Sector Breakdown	% of assets
US Treasuries	26
TIPS	2
US Agency	27
Mortgage Pass-Throughs	1
Mortgage CMO	1
Mortgage ARM	0
US Corporate	35
Asset-Backed	0
Convertible	0
Municipal	0
Corporate Inflation-Protected	0
Foreign Corporate	2
Foreign Govt	0

Composition			
Cash	4.6	Bonds	95.4
Stocks	0.0	Other	0.0

Special Securities	
Restricted/Illiquid Secs	4
Exotic Mortgage-Backed	0
Emerging-Markets Secs	0
Options/Futures/Warrants	No

Morningstar's Take by Lynn Russell 10-20-04

This fund may have slowed down a bit, but we're still fans.

TIAA-CREF Short-Term Bond Fund got off to a very strong start, racking up three years in a row of top-quartile returns. In addition to benefiting from its low costs, the fund fund has profited from its longer-than-average duration (a measure of interest-rate sensitivity). With interest rates generally trending lower since the fund's inception in 2000, the fund has had a nice wind at its back.

The fund's above-average sensitivity to interest rate moves isn't due to interest rate bets by its managers. They typically keep the fund's duration close to that of its benchmark, the Lehman Brothers 1-5 Year Government/Credit Index and look to add value by taking advantage of short-term market dislocations and by making small sector bets. But that Index tends to be more rate sensitive than the average short-term bond offering.

That relatively long duration has been less of an advantage as yields have bounced up more recently. The fund lost more than its average short-term rival when rates jumped in July of 2003 and again in April 2004. But even with those hits, the fund managed to outpace most of its peers both last year and so far in 2004. Solid security selection in corporate bonds boosted returns in both years, while the fund's low costs also played a key role in keeping the fund ahead of its peers. At just 0.30%, the fund's expense ratio is less than half that of its average peer and checks in as one of the lowest in the category.

Overall, we like this fund for its ultralow costs, experienced management, and moderate approach. Although the fund's higher level of interest rate risk could be more of a headwind if rates move up dramatically, its ultralow expense ratio gives it a sustainable advantage that should prove difficult for its higher-cost competitors to overcome over the long term.

Address:	730 Third Ave New York NY 10017 800-223-1200
Web Address:	www.tiaa-cref.org
Inception:	04-03-00*
Advisor:	Teachers Advisors, Inc.
Subadvisor:	None
NTF Plans:	N/A

Minimum Purchase:	$2500	Add: $50	IRA: $2000
Min Auto Inv Plan:	$50	Add: $50	
Sales Fees:	No-load		
Management Fee:	0.30%		
Actual Fees:	Mgt:0.30%	Dist:	
Expense Projections:	3Yr:$97	5Yr:$169	10Yr:$381
Income Distrib:	Monthly		

TIAA-CREF Soc Choice Eq

Ticker	Load	NAV	Yield	Total Assets	Mstar Category
TCSCX	None	$9.19	1.3%	$119 mil	Large Blend

Governance and Management

Fiduciary Grade: B

Portfolio Manager(s)

This fund is run by an experienced team from TIAA-CREF's quantitative group. The same team has done a fine job overseeing TIAA-CREF Equity Index.

Strategy

This fund aims to replicate the performance of the Russell 3000 Index while screening out companies that don't pass certain social screens. To do so, it eliminates all the alcohol, tobacco, gambling, weapons, and nuclear-energy companies in the Russell 3000 Index as well as the firms with poor product safety, employee relations, and environmental track records. The result is an investment universe of 2,400 names, which mirrors the Kinder, Lydenberg, Domini Broad Market Social Index. Management then buys all the larger firms in the universe while holding a representative sampling of the smaller companies.

Historical Profile

Return Above Avg
Risk Average
Rating ★★★★ Above Avg

Investment Style: Equity, Stock %

▼ Manager Change
∇ Partial Manager Change

Growth of $10,000
— Investment Values of Fund
— Investment Values of S&P 500

Performance Quartile (within Category)

1993	1994	1995	1996	1997	1998	1999	2000	2001	2002	2003	12-04	History
—	—	—	—	—	—	—	9.57	8.28	6.47	8.28	9.19	NAV
—	—	—	—	—	—	—	-9.99*	-12.75	-20.71	29.87	12.46	Total Return %
—	—	—	—	—	—	—	—	-0.87	1.38	1.20	1.59	+/-S&P 500
—	—	—	—	—	—	—	—	-0.30	0.94	-0.02	1.06	+/-Russ 1000
—	—	—	—	—	—	—	0.00	0.67	1.14	1.89	1.47	Income Return %
—	—	—	—	—	—	—	—	-13.42	-21.85	27.98	10.99	Capital Return %
—	—	—	—	—	—	—	—	62	33	20	18	Total Rtn % Rank Cat
—	—	—	—	—	—	—	0.06	0.06	0.09	0.12	0.12	Income $
—	—	—	—	—	—	—	0.02	0.01	0.00	0.00	0.00	Capital Gains $
—	—	—	—	—	—	—	—	0.27	0.27	0.27	—	Expense Ratio %
—	—	—	—	—	—	—	—	1.09	1.33	1.46	—	Income Ratio %
—	—	—	—	—	—	—	5	10	27	15	—	Turnover Rate %
—	—	—	—	—	—	—	39	65	68	70	119	Net Assets $mil

Performance 12-31-04

	1st Qtr	2nd Qtr	3rd Qtr	4th Qtr	Total
2000	—	-2.33	-1.24	-6.69	-9.99 *
2001	-12.23	4.17	-13.37	10.16	-12.75
2002	0.72	-13.07	-16.41	8.34	-20.71
2003	-3.09	16.43	2.88	11.89	29.87
2004	2.78	1.53	-2.31	10.32	12.46

Trailing	Total Return%	+/- S&P 500	+/- Russ 1000	%Rank Cat	Growth of $10,000
3 Mo	10.32	1.09	0.52	23	11,032
6 Mo	7.77	0.58	-0.04	32	10,777
1 Yr	12.46	1.59	1.06	18	11,246
3 Yr Avg	5.01	1.43	0.74	18	11,580
5 Yr Avg	—	—	—	—	—
10 Yr Avg	—	—	—	—	—
15 Yr Avg	—	—	—	—	—

Tax Analysis	Tax-Adj Rtn%	%Rank Cat	Tax-Cost Rat	%Rank Cat
3 Yr (estimated)	4.48	18	0.50	42
5 Yr (estimated)	—	—	—	—
10 Yr (estimated)	—	—	—	—

Potential Capital Gain Exposure: 1% of assets

Rating and Risk

Time Period	Load-Adj Return %	Morningstar Rtn vs Cat	Morningstar Risk vs Cat	Morningstar Risk-Adj Rating
1 Yr	12.46			
3 Yr	5.01	+Avg	Avg	★★★★
5 Yr	—	—	—	—
10 Yr	—	—	—	—
Incept	-1.98			

Other Measures	Standard Index S&P 500	Best Fit Index Russ 1000
Alpha	1.4	0.7
Beta	0.98	0.99
R-Squared	99	99
Standard Deviation	15.54	
Mean	5.01	
Sharpe Ratio	0.24	

Morningstar's Take by William Samuel Rocco 11-21-04

Socially responsible investors will find a lot to like at TIAA-CREF Social Choice Equity.

This fund sports one of the most diversified socially responsible investing portfolios around. The fact that it is a large-blend offering means that it naturally offers more balanced sector exposure than most of its large-growth and large-value peers. Since it tracks the Russell 3000 Index--minus those firms that fail its social screens--it has more exposure to smaller caps than the majority of its large-blend and other counterparts. And although it holds only a representative sample of the smaller firms in the Russell 3000 that pass it screens, it still owns more issues than all of its SRI peers and it normally devotes only about 20% of its assets to its top 10 names.

The fund also stands out from a cost perspective. Its 0.27% expense ratio is roughly 50 points lower than the expense ratio for the typical SRI index offering that focuses on large caps and is available to retail investors. And the fund has an even bigger cost edge relative to its actively managed peers. The average actively run large-cap screened offering has an expense ratio of nearly 1.50%.

Meanwhile, the fund has much more than a distinctive portfolio and an exceptional expense ratio going for it. It is on pace to beat most of its SRI and category peers for the third straight year. And although that has a lot to do with its smaller-cap weighting--a stake will be a burden when giant caps dominate--its overall diversification should help it avoid major trouble, and its low costs give it a big edge year in and year out. Thus, we expect this fund to post attractive returns over time, while its portfolio breadth should keep volatility under wraps.

For all these reasons, we believe it is worth a long look from SRI fans seeking a core domestic holding.

Portfolio Analysis 09-30-04

Share change since 06-04 Total Stocks:915	Sector	PE	YTD Ret%	% Assets
⊕ Microsoft	Software	36.1	8.95	2.43
⊕ Johnson & Johnson	Health	20.6	25.17	2.29
⊕ J.P. Morgan Chase & Co.	Financial	19.4	9.97	2.07
⊕ American International G	Financial	16.2	-0.53	2.01
⊕ Procter & Gamble	Goods	23.3	12.38	1.77
⊕ IBM	Hardware	20.2	7.19	1.73
⊕ Wells Fargo	Financial	15.5	8.97	1.43
⊕ Intel	Hardware	19.8	-26.56	1.34
⊕ Coca-Cola	Goods	21.9	-16.12	1.22
⊕ Verizon Communications	Telecom	32.4	20.25	1.20
⊕ Cisco Systems	Hardware	24.5	-20.26	1.17
⊕ PepsiCo	Goods	22.5	13.82	1.14
⊕ Merck	Health	11.4	-27.76	1.12
⊕ SBC Communications	Telecom	15.4	3.74	1.12
⊕ Fannie Mae	Financial	9.1	-2.33	1.09
⊕ American Express	Financial	20.3	17.60	1.05
⊕ 3M Company	Ind Mtrls	23.5	-1.75	1.04
⊕ Wachovia	Financial	14.3	16.80	1.02
Home Depot	Consumer	19.0	21.47	1.00
⊕ Dell	Hardware	34.0	24.01	0.96

Current Investment Style

Value Blnd Growth; Large Mid Small

Market Cap	%
Giant	38.6
Large	36.6
Mid	18.1
Small	4.6
Micro	2.1
Avg $mil: 21,649	

Value Measures		Rel Category
Price/Earnings	13.75	0.99
Price/Book	2.50	0.95
Price/Sales	1.34	0.93
Price/Cash Flow	7.09	0.92
Dividend Yield %	1.60	1.08

Growth Measures	%	Rel Category
Long-Term Erngs	11.58	1.00
Book Value	4.21	0.54
Sales	4.67	0.81
Cash Flow	7.26	0.77
Historical Erngs	14.66	1.24

Profitability	%	Rel Category
Return on Equity	17.60	1.01
Return on Assets	9.61	1.11
Net Margin	12.77	1.12

Sector Weightings	% of Stocks	Rel S&P 500	3 Year High	Low
Info	22.30	1.04		
Software	3.68	0.86	5	4
Hardware	10.62	1.04	12	8
Media	4.07	1.06	5	3
Telecom	3.93	1.25	5	3
Service	50.86	1.10		
Health	13.32	1.07	16	13
Consumer	8.42	0.93	8	7
Business	4.45	1.10	5	4
Financial	24.67	1.19	25	22
Mfg	26.84	0.84		
Goods	8.31	0.89	10	8
Ind Mtrls	8.45	0.67	9	6
Energy	6.22	0.87	6	4
Utilities	3.86	1.30	5	4

Composition

Cash	1.1
Stocks	98.9
Bonds	0.0
Other	0.0
Foreign (% of Stock)	0.0

Address:	730 Third Ave New York NY 10017 800-223-1200
Web Address:	www.tiaa-cref.org
Inception:	04-03-00 *
Advisor:	Teachers Advisors, Inc.
Subadvisor:	None
NTF Plans:	N/A

Minimum Purchase:	$2500	Add: $50	IRA: $2000
Min Auto Inv Plan:	$50	Add: $50	
Sales Fees:	No-load		
Management Fee:	0.27%		
Actual Fees:	Mgt:0.27%	Dist:	
Expense Projections:	3Yr:$87	5Yr:$152	10Yr:$343
Income Distrib:	Annually		

TIAA-CREF Tax-Exempt Bd

Ticker	Load	NAV	Yield	SEC Yield	Total Assets	Mstar Category
TCTEX	None	$10.93	3.5%	3.15%	$194 mil	Muni National Long

Governance and Management

Fiduciary Grade: B

Portfolio Manager(s)

Peter Scola and Carmen Failla have comanaged this fund since its inception. Although TIAA-CREF doesn't have a large presence in the municipal-bond fund world, the firm does boast considerable analytical heft, although it focuses primarily on taxable fixed-income instruments.

Strategy

Unlike the typical member of the muni-national long-term category, which achieves its long-term orientation by investing in bonds across the maturity spectrum, this offering invests almost exclusively in bonds that will mature over the next eight to 12 years; the fund's benchmark, the Lehman Brothers 10-Year Municipal Index, is composed of such bonds. More typical of their peers, managers Peter Scola and Carmen Failla emphasize high-quality debt, attempting to ferret out undervalued issues.

Historical Profile

Return Above Avg
Risk Above Avg
Rating ★★★★ Above Avg

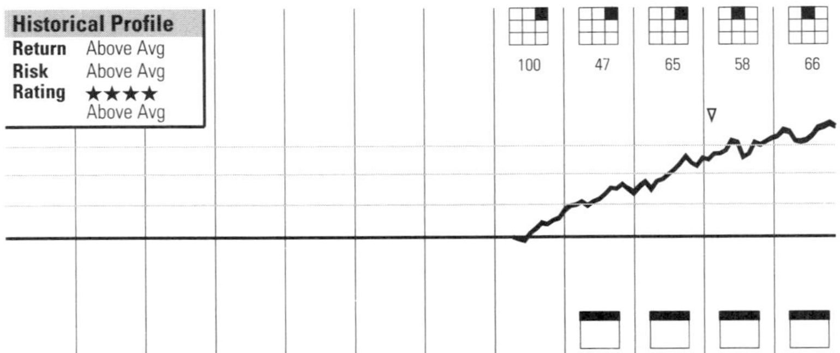

1993	1994	1995	1996	1997	1998	1999	2000	2001	2002	2003	12-04	History
—	—	—	—	—	—	—	10.46	10.38	10.92	10.92	10.93	NAV
—	—	—	—	—	—	—	7.64*	4.99	10.70	5.87	4.58	Total Return %
—	—	—	—	—	—	—	—	-0.14	1.10	0.56	0.10	+/-LB Muni
—	—	—	—	—	—	—	—	0.12	0.67	-0.46	-1.98	+/-LB Muni 20YR
—	—	—	—	—	—	—	0.00	4.62	4.23	3.87	3.61	Income Return %
—	—	—	—	—	—	—	—	0.37	6.47	2.00	0.97	Capital Return %
—	—	—	—	—	—	—	—	11	3	14	22	Total Rtn % Rank Cat
—	—	—	—	—	—	—	0.38	0.47	0.43	0.42	0.39	Income $
—	—	—	—	—	—	—	0.03	0.12	0.12	0.21	0.09	Capital Gains $
—	—	—	—	—	—	—	—	0.30	0.30	0.30	—	Expense Ratio %
—	—	—	—	—	—	—	—	4.48	4.06	3.79	—	Income Ratio %
—	—	—	—	—	—	—	136	298	264	157	—	Turnover Rate %
—	—	—	—	—	—	—	2	4	146	168	194	Net Assets $mil

Performance 12-31-04

	1st Qtr	2nd Qtr	3rd Qtr	4th Qtr	Total
2000	—	1.14	2.47	3.86	7.64 *
2001	2.56	0.73	3.08	-1.41	4.99
2002	1.16	4.40	5.29	-0.44	10.70
2003	1.26	3.32	-0.03	1.24	5.87
2004	1.92	-2.38	4.19	0.88	4.58

Trailing	Total Return%	+/- LB Muni	+/- LB Muni 20YR	%Rank Cat	Growth of $10,000
3 Mo	0.88	-0.37	-1.10	78	10,088
6 Mo	5.11	-0.08	-1.64	38	10,511
1 Yr	4.58	0.10	-1.98	22	10,458
3 Yr Avg	7.02	0.58	-0.61	6	12,257
5 Yr Avg	—	—	—	—	—
10 Yr Avg	—	—	—	—	—
15 Yr Avg	—	—	—	—	—

Tax Analysis	Tax-Adj Rtn%	%Rank Cat	Tax-Cost Rat	%Rank Cat
3 Yr (estimated)	6.67	6	0.33	78
5 Yr (estimated)	—	—	—	—
10 Yr (estimated)	—	—	—	—

Potential Capital Gain Exposure: 3% of assets

Rating and Risk

Time Period	Load-Adj Return %	Morningstar Rtn vs Cat	Morningstar Risk vs Cat	Morningstar Risk-Adj Rating
1 Yr	4.58			
3 Yr	7.02	+Avg	+Avg	★★★★
5 Yr	—	—	—	—
10 Yr	—	—	—	—
Incept	7.10			

Other Measures	Standard Index LB Aggr	Best Fit Index LB Muni 10YR
Alpha	-0.2	0.3
Beta	1.16	1.01
R-Squared	99	100

Standard Deviation	5.93
Mean	7.02
Sharpe Ratio	0.96

Portfolio Analysis 09-30-04

Total Fixed-Income:103	Date of Maturity	Amount $000	Value $000	% Net Assets
Brazos River Auth 4.9%	10-01-15	5,055	5,587	2.96
California St Dept Wtr R	05-01-12	4,435	5,021	2.66
California St 5.25%	12-01-12	4,340	4,859	2.57
Tobacco Settlement Fing	06-01-12	4,000	4,350	2.30
Puerto Rico Pub Bldgs Au	07-01-10	3,800	4,252	2.25
Port Seattle Wash 5.5%	09-01-17	3,345	3,894	2.06
New York St Dorm Auth 5.	11-15-23	3,400	3,764	1.99
Snohomish Cnty Wash Pub	12-01-12	3,000	3,393	1.80
Anderson Ind Sch Bldg 5.	07-15-14	2,865	3,238	1.71
New Jersey St Tpk Auth 5	05-01-13	2,895	3,224	1.71
Puerto Rico Comwlth 5.5%	07-01-10	2,800	3,133	1.66
Carbon Cnty Pa Indl Dev	05-01-10	2,840	3,073	1.63
New York St Twy Auth 5.5	04-01-12	2,650	3,001	1.59
Nassau Cnty N Y Interim	11-15-13	2,660	2,981	1.58
New York St Environmenta	03-15-14	2,670	2,964	1.57

Current Investment Style

Duration: Short Int Long; Quality: High Med Low

Avg Eff Duration[1]	6.6 Yrs
Avg Eff Maturity	8.8 Yrs
Avg Credit Quality	AA
Avg Wtd Coupon	5.34%
Avg Wtd Price	111.09% of par

[1]figure provided by fund

Credit Analysis	% bonds 09-30-04		
US Govt	0	BB	0
AAA	44	B	0
AA	14	Below B	0
A	22	NR/NA	2
BBB	17		

Top 5 States	% bonds		
NY	16.8	WA	8.2
CA	15.1	PR	6.5
TX	9.1		

Composition			
Cash	0.0	Bonds	100.0
Stocks	0.0	Other	0.0

Special Securities	
Restricted/Illiquid Secs	0
Options/Futures/Warrants	No

Sector Weightings	% of Bonds	Rel Cat
General Obligation	46.6	1.78
Utilities	13.7	1.03
Health	2.5	0.32
Water/Waste	6.8	0.62
Housing	1.1	0.16
Education	11.9	1.03
Transportation	6.1	0.81
COP/Lease	1.6	0.78
Industrial	9.6	0.74
Misc Revenue	0.0	0.00
Demand	0.0	0.00

Morningstar's Take by Lynn Russell 12-14-04

TIAA-CREF Tax-Exempt Bond continues to post solidly competitive returns.

This fund is on track to land in the muni-long-bond category's top quartile for the fourth year in a row, with a gain of 4.5% for the year to date through Dec. 13. The fund gets a head start over its competition with the advantage of ultralow costs. At just 0.30% the fund's expense ratio is less than half that of its average no-load competitor.

But this fund isn't just about costs. Solid sector and security selection have also boosted returns. Managers Peter Scola and Carmen Failla use a value-oriented approach, looking for bonds that they believe are cheap relative to the rest of the market. For instance, although the fund had earlier eliminated its exposure to California general obligation bonds, when their prices dropped earlier this year, they not only added them back to the portfolio but also overweighted them. The state was upgraded during the year, and the bonds rebounded strongly. An overweight in Puerto Rican securities also added to the bottom line.

We also like this fund for its straightforward approach. While the managers are willing to make modest sector and state wagers and tend to hold more midquality bonds than many of their peers, they avoid betting on interest rates. They typically keep the fund's duration (a measure of interest-rate sensitivity) close to that of its benchmark, the Lehman Brothers 10-Year Municipal Index. But the fund does concentrate much of its portfolio in the eight- to 10-year maturity range, which has been more volatile than other areas of the maturity spectrum. That's meant a slightly bumpier ride for investors than with the average muni long fund.

Overall, we like this fund for its low costs and experienced management. It's still relatively young, but the fund has gotten off to a good start, and those low costs give it a long-term competitive advantage.

Address:	730 Third Ave New York NY 10017 800-223-1200
Web Address:	www.tiaa-cref.org
Inception:	04-03-00 *
Advisor:	Teachers Advisors, Inc.
Subadvisor:	None
NTF Plans:	N/A

Minimum Purchase:	$2500	Add: $50	IRA: $2000
Min Auto Inv Plan:	$50	Add: $50	
Sales Fees:	No-load		
Management Fee:	0.30%		
Actual Fees:	Mgt:0.30%	Dist:	
Expense Projections:	3Yr:$97	5Yr:$169	10Yr:$381
Income Distrib:	Monthly		

Tocqueville Sm Cap Value

Ticker	Load	NAV	Yield	Total Assets	Mstar Category
TSCVX	12b-1 only	$17.92	0.0%	$84 mil	Small Value

Governance and Management

Fiduciary Grade: D

Portfolio Manager(s)

Jean-Pierre Conreur has been at the helm since the fund's inception in 1994. He is assisted by one dedicated analyst, and he also draws on Tocqueville's team of about a dozen analysts. Conreur has a substantial portion of his personal assets invested in this fund.

Strategy

Manager Jean-Pierre Conreur buys out-of-favor growth stocks trading at value prices. He looks for strong fundamentals, such as low long-term debt, strong management, and high insider ownership. That said, he's not afraid to invest in companies that are losing money--as long as they're investing in growth. The portfolio also makes large commitments to its top holdings, and Conreur lets his winners run long after a typical value manager would have sold.

Historical Profile

Return: Average
Risk: High
Rating: ★ Lowest

Investment Style: Equity Stock %

1995	1996	1997	1998	1999	2000	2001	2002	2003	12-04
92%	93%	97%	98%	100%	94%	100%	98%	97%	

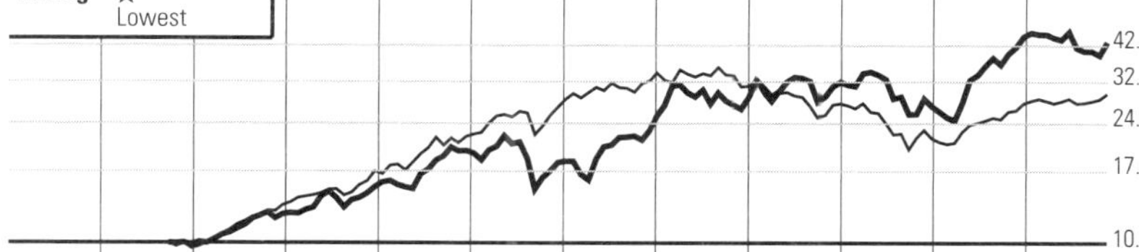

▼ Manager Change
▽ Partial Manager Change

Growth of $10,000
— Investment Values of Fund
— Investment Values of S&P 500

Performance Quartile (within Category)

1993	1994	1995	1996	1997	1998	1999	2000	2001	2002	2003	12-04	History
—	10.04	11.60	13.00	14.30	13.50	16.19	15.02	15.33	12.89	18.45	17.92	NAV
—	2.71*	23.21	25.03	23.37	-5.59	38.66	14.40	11.64	-15.92	65.69	0.78	Total Return %
—	—	-14.32	2.09	-9.98	-34.16	17.62	23.50	23.52	6.17	37.02	-10.09	+/-S&P 500
—	—	-2.54	3.66	-8.41	0.86	40.15	-8.43	-2.38	-4.49	19.66	-21.47	+/-Russ 2000 VL
—	0.00	0.00	0.00	0.00	0.00	0.00	0.00	0.00	0.00	0.00	0.00	Income Return %
—	—	23.21	25.03	23.37	-5.59	38.66	14.40	11.64	-15.92	65.69	0.78	Capital Return %
—	—	51	37	83	41	7	68	70	79	6	99	Total Rtn % Rank Cat
—	0.03	0.00	0.00	0.00	0.00	0.00	0.00	0.00	0.00	0.00	0.00	Income $
—	0.19	0.77	1.46	1.73	0.00	2.40	3.32	1.38	0.00	2.82	0.66	Capital Gains $
—	2.08	2.50	2.36	1.75	1.67	1.52	1.45	1.52	1.44	1.36	—	Expense Ratio %
—	0.85	-0.53	-1.18	-0.81	-1.12	-0.87	-0.63	-0.69	-0.62	-0.48	—	Income Ratio %
—	—	88	107	95	62	72	87	47	25	65	—	Turnover Rate %
—	7	10	13	21	23	33	31	45	54	85	84	Net Assets $mil

Performance 12-31-04

	1st Qtr	2nd Qtr	3rd Qtr	4th Qtr	Total
2000	25.32	-3.84	-7.48	2.61	14.40
2001	0.20	15.48	-16.40	15.40	11.64
2002	6.52	-4.04	-22.40	6.00	-15.92
2003	-9.85	38.90	7.81	22.74	65.69
2004	1.46	1.98	-13.15	12.15	0.78

Trailing	Total Return%	+/- S&P 500	+/- Russ 2000 VL	%Rank Cat	Growth of $10,000
3 Mo	12.15	2.92	-1.05	64	11,215
6 Mo	-2.59	-9.78	-15.96	100	9,741
1 Yr	0.78	-10.09	-21.47	99	10,078
3 Yr Avg	11.98	8.40	-4.52	82	14,042
5 Yr Avg	12.39	14.69	-4.84	84	17,932
10 Yr Avg	16.13	4.06	0.96	26	44,611
15 Yr Avg	—	—	—	—	—

Tax Analysis	Tax-Adj Rtn%	%Rank Cat	Tax-Cost Rat	%Rank Cat
3 Yr (estimated)	10.85	81	1.01	60
5 Yr (estimated)	10.03	87	2.10	90
10 Yr (estimated)	13.65	39	2.14	78

Potential Capital Gain Exposure: 20% of assets

Rating and Risk

Time Period	Load-Adj Return %	Morningstar Rtn vs Cat	Morningstar Risk vs Cat	Morningstar Risk-Adj Rating
1 Yr	0.78			
3 Yr	11.98	-Avg	High	★
5 Yr	12.39	-Avg	High	★
10 Yr	16.13	+Avg	High	★★
Incept	15.74			

Other Measures	Standard Index S&P 500	Best Fit Index Russ 2000
Alpha	9.0	-0.2
Beta	1.25	1.14
R-Squared	62	83
Standard Deviation	27.26	
Mean	11.98	
Sharpe Ratio	0.39	

Portfolio Analysis 09-30-04

Share change since 06-04 Total Stocks:34	Sector	PE	YTD Ret%	% Assets
Visteon	Ind Mtrls	—	-3.79	5.78
Del Monte Foods	Goods	15.3	5.96	5.52
⊖ Magnetek	Ind Mtrls	—	4.70	5.21
Timken	Ind Mtrls	22.3	32.68	5.18
Schering-Plough	Health	—	21.56	5.02
Vicor	Ind Mtrls	—	15.68	3.99
Hercules	Ind Mtrls	—	21.72	3.75
Powerwave Technologies	Hardware	—	9.56	3.65
Westell Technologies	Hardware	13.6	7.77	3.40
⊖ Input/Output	Energy	—	96.01	3.39
Global Industries	Energy	—	61.60	3.25
Longs Drug Stores	Consumer	32.5	14.18	3.18
Corn Products Internatio	Goods	19.2	57.18	3.03
⊖ Paxar	Goods	23.3	65.45	2.98
Baldor Electric	Ind Mtrls	27.8	23.37	2.80
3Com	Hardware	—	-48.96	2.78
Tower Automotive	Ind Mtrls	—	-65.01	2.75
Priority Healthcare	Health	18.2	-9.44	2.65
A Schulman	Ind Mtrls	20.9	3.23	2.31
Federal Signal	Ind Mtrls	21.7	3.06	2.45

Current Investment Style

Value Blnd Growth / Large Mid Small

Market Cap	%
Giant	0.0
Large	5.2
Mid	24.3
Small	53.9
Micro	16.6

Avg $mil: 920

Value Measures		Rel Category
Price/Earnings	24.33	1.52
Price/Book	1.57	0.95
Price/Sales	0.31	0.41
Price/Cash Flow	4.63	0.89
Dividend Yield %	0.95	0.79

Growth Measures	%	Rel Category
Long-Term Erngs	2.33	1.02
Book Value	-0.61	NMF
Sales	-1.58	NMF
Cash Flow	-25.60	NMF
Historical Erngs	-8.61	NMF

Profitability	%	Rel Category
Return on Equity	0.21	0.02
Return on Assets	0.15	0.04
Net Margin	-2.65	NMF

Sector Weightings	% of Stocks	Rel S&P 500	3 Year High	3 Year Low
Info	18.63	0.87		
Software	5.09	1.18	5	2
Hardware	13.54	1.33	21	5
Media	0.00	0.00	0	0
Telecom	0.00	0.00	0	0
Service	23.29	0.50		
Health	13.73	1.10	14	7
Consumer	5.36	0.59	7	4
Business	4.20	1.04	11	4
Financial	0.00	0.00	1	0
Mfg	58.07	1.81		
Goods	11.85	1.27	19	10
Ind Mtrls	39.40	3.11	44	38
Energy	6.82	0.95	12	3
Utilities	0.00	0.00	0	0

Composition

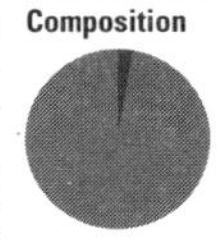

Cash	2.6
Stocks	97.4
Bonds	0.0
Other	0.0
Foreign (% of Stock)	0.0

Morningstar's Take by Laura Pavlenko Lutton 11-23-04

There's reason to be patient with Tocqueville Small Cap Value.

This fund has been showing its wild side. After an eye-popping, peer-beating 65.7% gain in 2003, the fund has followed this year with a loss. It's down 5.26% for the year to date through Nov. 19, 2004, while the average small-value fund has posted a mid-teens gain for the period. This fund is no stranger to broad swings in performance: Over the past seven calendar years, the fund has ended two years in the category's top decile and four years in the peer group's bottom third.

While the volatility here has been difficult to stomach at times, it's understandable given this offering's strategy. Manager Jean-Pierre Conreur is a deep-value investor who buys the market's unloved stocks. He places relatively hefty bets on distressed companies that have a plan to improve operations and grow considerably within five years. For example, this fall he added ailing appliance maker Maytag to the portfolio because he thinks the firm's profits will grow nicely as it improves its distribution in the coming years.

The fund also gets some added kick from its relatively concentrated portfolio. Conreur typically owns just three dozen stocks, and he loads up on sectors where he finds several stocks that meet his investment criteria. Lately he has tied considerable assets to technology, health-care, and industrial-materials stocks relative to the average small-value fund. As one would expect, the fund soars when these picks are in style. But when tech and health-care stocks are dragging, which has been the case in 2004, the fund slumps badly.

Conreur's approach may be unusual, but we think he has done a reasonably good job executing his strategy. And investors who have stuck with this fund have done reasonably well: The offering's 10-year record is in the peer group's top half. Thus, we think this fund has merit, but those seeking a plain-vanilla small-value offering should look elsewhere.

Address:	Tocqueville Trust New York, NY 10019 800-697-3863
Web Address:	www.tocqueville.com
Inception:	08-03-94 *
Advisor:	Tocqueville Asset Management LP
Subadvisor:	None
NTF Plans:	Schwab OneSource, Accutrade NTF

Minimum Purchase:	$1000	Add: $100	IRA: $250
Min Auto Inv Plan:	$1000	Add: $100	
Sales Fees:	0.25%B, 2.00%R		
Management Fee:	0.75% mx./0.65% mn., 0.15%A		
Actual Fees:	Mgt:0.75%	Dist:0.25%	
Expense Projections:	3Yr:$431	5Yr:$745	10Yr:$1635
Income Distrib:	Annually		

Torray

Ticker	Load	NAV	Yield	Total Assets	Mstar Category
TORYX	None	$41.08	0.5%	$1,735 mil	Large Blend

Governance and Management

Fiduciary Grade:

Portfolio Manager(s)

Comanagers Bob Torray and Doug Eby have plenty of experience and a great record. Torray founded his own firm in 1972, and he has guided the fund since its late-1990 inception. Eby came aboard in January 1992. Both are substantially personally invested in their fund.

Strategy

The managers jump into companies when they trade at fire-sale prices and then hang on for the long haul. A buy-and-hold style leads them mostly to larger companies that they think have sustainable competitive advantages. The fund tends to concentrate more assets in individual holdings than its peers do, and it also takes sizable sector positions. The fund is run in a tax-efficient manner.

Historical Profile

Return Above Avg
Risk Above Avg
Rating ★★★★ Above Avg

Investment Style: Equity, Stock %: 96% | 99% | 100% | 100% | 97% | 99% | 98% | 98% | 100%

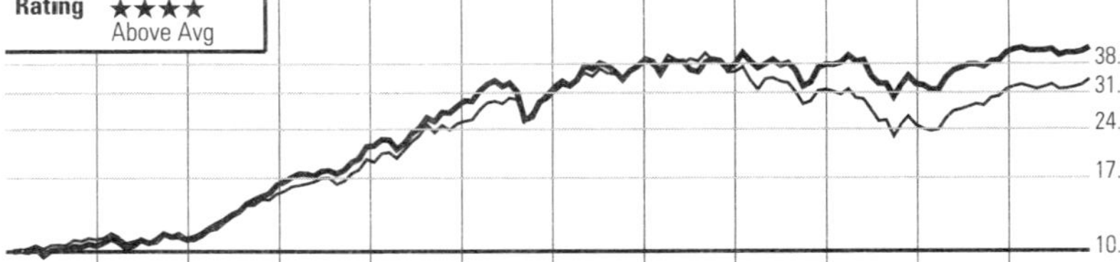

▼ Manager Change
▽ Partial Manager Change

Growth of $10,000
— Investment Values of Fund
— Investment Values of S&P 500

Performance Quartile (within Category)

1993	1994	1995	1996	1997	1998	1999	2000	2001	2002	2003	12-04	History
14.27	13.76	20.11	25.22	33.85	36.48	44.31	39.79	37.53	32.24	39.98	41.08	NAV
6.37	2.46	50.37	29.09	37.12	8.19	24.03	-3.38	-0.52	-13.04	25.19	6.90	Total Return %
-3.69	1.15	12.84	6.15	3.77	-20.38	2.99	5.72	11.36	9.05	-3.48	-3.97	+/-S&P 500
-3.81	2.07	12.60	6.64	4.27	-18.83	3.12	4.41	11.93	8.61	-4.70	-4.50	+/-Russ 1000
0.89	1.50	1.56	0.93	0.52	0.41	0.20	0.58	0.47	0.55	1.07	0.53	Income Return %
5.48	0.96	48.81	28.16	36.60	7.78	23.83	-3.96	-0.99	-13.59	24.12	6.37	Capital Return %
84	14	1	6	4	91	27	37	5	4	68	84	Total Rtn % Rank Cat
0.12	0.21	0.21	0.19	0.13	0.14	0.07	0.25	0.18	0.21	0.34	0.21	Income $
0.22	0.65	0.32	0.53	0.58	0.00	0.79	2.80	1.76	0.21	0.00	1.38	Capital Gains $
1.25	1.25	1.25	1.25	1.13	1.09	1.07	1.06	1.07	1.07	1.11	—	Expense Ratio %
0.94	1.51	1.31	0.87	0.47	0.42	0.18	0.64	0.45	0.58	0.62	—	Income Ratio %
29	37	23	21	12	26	33	45	38	23	37	—	Turnover Rate %
20	23	51	117	609	1,461	1,896	1,822	1,641	1,368	1,655	1,735	Net Assets $mil

Performance 12-31-04

	1st Qtr	2nd Qtr	3rd Qtr	4th Qtr	Total
2000	-1.89	-5.79	7.95	-3.17	-3.38
2001	-3.02	1.81	-13.68	16.72	-0.52
2002	6.66	-13.53	-13.77	9.35	-13.04
2003	-3.75	16.73	0.81	10.53	25.19
2004	1.44	1.00	-2.66	7.19	6.90

Trailing	Total Return%	+/- S&P 500	+/- Russ 1000	%Rank Cat	Growth of $10,000
3 Mo	7.19	-2.04	-2.61	91	10,719
6 Mo	4.34	-2.85	-3.47	89	10,434
1 Yr	6.90	-3.97	-4.50	84	10,690
3 Yr Avg	5.18	1.60	0.91	17	11,636
5 Yr Avg	2.27	4.57	4.03	12	11,188
10 Yr Avg	14.86	2.79	2.70	3	39,966
15 Yr Avg	—	—	—	—	—

Tax Analysis	Tax-Adj Rtn%	%Rank Cat	Tax-Cost Rat	%Rank Cat
3 Yr (estimated)	4.68	16	0.48	40
5 Yr (estimated)	1.42	11	0.83	44
10 Yr (estimated)	14.04	2	0.71	15

Potential Capital Gain Exposure: 17% of assets

Rating and Risk

Time Period	Load-Adj Return %	Morningstar Rtn vs Cat	Morningstar Risk vs Cat	Morningstar Risk-Adj Rating
1 Yr	6.90			
3 Yr	5.18	+Avg	Avg	★★★★
5 Yr	2.27	+Avg	+Avg	★★★★
10 Yr	14.86	High	+Avg	★★★★★
Incept	14.04			

Other Measures	Standard Index S&P 500	Best Fit Index Russ 1000
Alpha	1.7	1.1
Beta	0.93	0.94
R-Squared	89	89

Standard Deviation	15.62
Mean	5.18
Sharpe Ratio	0.25

Portfolio Analysis 12-31-04

Share change since 11-04 Total Stocks:39	Sector	PE	YTD Ret%	% Assets
⊖ Amgen	Health	37.7	3.82	6.02
⊖ Franklin Resources	Financial	26.0	34.62	5.74
⊖ Cardinal Health	Health	16.9	-4.73	5.59
⊖ Illinois Tool Works	Ind Mtrls	22.1	11.75	4.61
First Data	Business	18.8	3.72	4.51
⊖ Ambac Financial Group	Financial	12.7	19.13	4.26
⊕ Univision Communications	Media	39.5	-26.25	4.22
⊖ Anheuser-Busch Companies	Goods	18.1	-1.95	4.21
Markel	Financial	21.8	43.58	4.18
⊖ Automatic Data Processin	Business	26.9	13.46	3.87
Walt Disney	Media	24.3	20.21	3.50
J.P. Morgan Chase & Co.	Financial	19.4	9.97	3.23
⊖ United Technologies	Ind Mtrls	18.6	10.72	3.18
⊖ The Directv Group	Media	—	1.15	2.88
General Electric	Ind Mtrls	22.8	20.68	2.79
Abbott Laboratories	Health	22.1	2.61	2.78
Honeywell International	Ind Mtrls	20.5	8.21	2.63
⊖ SBC Communications	Telecom	15.4	3.74	2.57
Emerson Electric	Ind Mtrls	22.8	11.09	2.42
Allied Capital	Financial	11.6	0.82	2.36

Current Investment Style

Value Blnd Growth / Large Mid Small

Market Cap	%
Giant	30.9
Large	55.5
Mid	12.6
Small	1.0
Micro	0.0
Avg $mil: 25,758	

Value Measures		Rel Category
Price/Earnings	19.62	1.16
Price/Book	2.38	0.91
Price/Sales	1.71	1.19
Price/Cash Flow	8.04	1.05
Dividend Yield %	1.32	0.89

Growth Measures	%	Rel Category
Long-Term Erngs	12.30	1.06
Book Value	9.99	1.29
Sales	8.27	1.44
Cash Flow	70.84	7.49
Historical Erngs	10.19	0.86

Profitability	%	Rel Category
Return on Equity	15.12	0.86
Return on Assets	7.43	0.86
Net Margin	14.07	1.23

Sector Weightings	% of Stocks	Rel S&P 500	3 Year High	3 Year Low
Info	20.84	0.97		
Software	0.00	0.00	2	0
Hardware	1.94	0.19	9	1
Media	16.33	4.25	17	11
Telecom	2.57	0.82	3	0
Service	55.04	1.19		
Health	16.60	1.33	24	14
Consumer	2.22	0.24	2	0
Business	8.38	2.07	12	4
Financial	27.84	1.34	34	19
Mfg	24.13	0.75		
Goods	4.21	0.45	15	4
Ind Mtrls	19.26	1.52	22	14
Energy	0.09	0.01	0	0
Utilities	0.57	0.19	1	0

Composition

Cash	0.0
Stocks	100.0
Bonds	0.0
Other	0.0
Foreign (% of Stock)	2.1

Morningstar's Take by Christopher Traulsen 12-29-04

Torray's sensible approach serves investors well.

Comanagers Douglas Eby and Robert Torray take a much longer-term view than many of their large-blend competitors do. This is evident from the fund's annual turnover, which typically ranges from 20% to 40%, well below the category norm. That helps keep transaction costs down and limit the fund's taxable distributions. Because they usually hold companies for so long, the managers look for high-quality companies that are generating cash and have long histories of success. They try to buy them on the cheap, but once a company is in the fund, it's in for the long haul.

The fund is also fairly concentrated. It usually has just 30 to 40 holdings in the portfolio, compared with more than 200 for its average rival. It also currently emphasizes just four economic sectors: industrials, media, health care, and financials.

These traits tend to make the fund a bit more volatile than its average peer, but not markedly so. In 2004, however, the risks of the fund's style have been on display. Energy, in which the fund has no investments, has soared, while drugmakers and media, two of the fund's larger areas of emphasis, have stumbled badly. As a result, the fund has lagged its average peer in 2004: Its return for the year to date through December 28 is 6.8%--good in absolute terms, but a bottom-quintile showing relative to its large-blend peers.

That doesn't concern us much, though. The managers use a sensible style and focus on doing what they know best rather than chasing short-term performance. Over time, they have more than proved their style works. The fund owns a sterling long-term record, besting the S&P 500 by 2.7 percentage points per year over the past decade and beating 97% of its large-value peers over the same period.

This fund could be cheaper given its size, but that's a relatively minor quibble. We think it remains a fine choice.

Address:	Torray Fund Bethesda, MD 20817 800-626-9769
Web Address:	www.torray.com
Inception:	12-18-90
Advisor:	The Torray Corporation
Subadvisor:	None
NTF Plans:	N/A

Minimum Purchase:	$10000	Add: $500	IRA: $10000
Min Auto Inv Plan:	$0	Add: —	
Sales Fees:	No-load		
Management Fee:	1.00%		
Actual Fees:	Mgt:1.00%	Dist:	
Expense Projections:	3Yr:$342	5Yr:$593	10Yr:$1310
Income Distrib:	Quarterly		

Turner Midcap Growth

Analyst Pick

Ticker	Load	NAV	Yield	Total Assets	Mstar Category
TMGFX	None	$24.43	0.0%	$999 mil	Mid-Cap Growth

Governance and Management

Fiduciary Grade: B

Portfolio Manager(s)

Lead manager Chris McHugh has run the fund successfully since its 1996 inception. He started as an analyst with Turner Investment Partners in 1990 and has been a member of its technology sector team since then. He is backed by Turner's 10 sector analysts.

Strategy

Like other Turner funds, this one hunts for stocks that exhibit accelerating earnings growth and positive price trends. Management will pay a premium for its high-momentum picks. That leads it to high-P/E stocks in racy areas, such as tech and telecom. It's pretty finicky about staying in mid-cap territory, and it keeps its sector weightings in line with the Russell Midcap Growth Index's.

Historical Profile

Return Below Avg
Risk High
Rating ★★ Below Avg

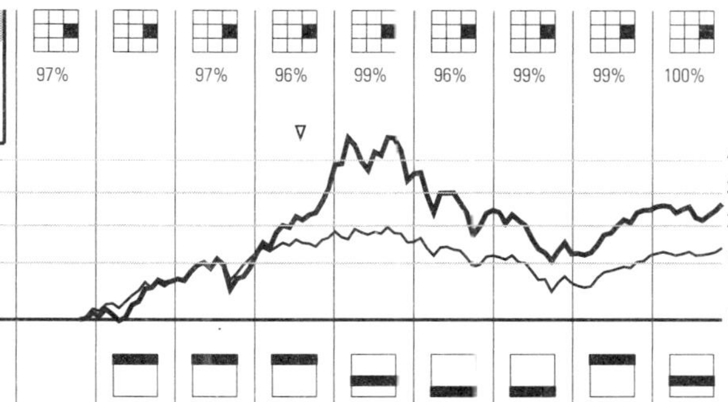

Investment Style
Equity
Stock %

▼ Manager Change
▽ Partial Manager Change

Growth of $10,000
— Investment Values of Fund
— Investment Values of S&P 500

Performance Quartile
(within Category)

1993	1994	1995	1996	1997	1998	1999	2000	2001	2002	2003	12-04	History
—	—	—	10.22	13.84	17.51	36.45	30.59	21.91	14.71	22.00	24.43	NAV
—	—	—	3.33*	40.56	26.52	125.45	-8.00	-28.38	-32.86	49.56	11.05	Total Return %
—	—	—	—	7.21	-2.05	104.41	1.10	-16.50	-10.77	20.89	0.18	+/-S&P 500
—	—	—	—	18.02	8.66	74.16	3.75	-8.23	-5.45	6.85	-4.43	+/-Russ MG
—	—	—	0.00	0.00	0.00	0.00	0.00	0.00	0.00	0.00	0.00	Income Return %
—	—	—	—	40.56	26.52	125.45	-8.00	-28.38	-32.86	49.56	11.05	Capital Return %
—	—	—	—	3	24	7	58	77	80	6	65	Total Rtn % Rank Cat
—	—	—	0.00	0.00	0.00	0.00	0.00	0.00	0.00	0.00	0.00	Income $
—	—	—	0.11	0.50	0.00	2.70	3.07	0.00	0.00	0.00	0.00	Capital Gains $
—	—	—	—	1.25	1.23	1.03	1.03	1.04	1.05	1.15	—	Expense Ratio %
—	—	—	—	-0.62	-0.79	-0.58	-0.72	-0.77	-0.81	-0.87	—	Income Ratio %
—	—	—	—	—	304	291	307	335	260	209	—	Turnover Rate %
—	—	—	2	13	35	333	937	749	652	877	998	Net Assets $mil

Performance 12-31-04

	1st Qtr	2nd Qtr	3rd Qtr	4th Qtr	Total
2000	19.59	-6.08	13.63	-27.91	-8.00
2001	-29.78	19.69	-32.32	25.92	-28.38
2002	-3.83	-19.55	-18.70	6.75	-32.86
2003	1.09	19.44	10.02	12.59	49.56
2004	3.23	-0.22	-7.37	16.39	11.05

Trailing	Total Return%	+/- S&P 500	+/- Russ MG	%Rank Cat	Growth of $10,000
3 Mo	16.39	7.16	2.45	8	11,639
6 Mo	7.81	0.62	-1.20	49	10,781
1 Yr	11.05	0.18	-4.43	65	11,105
3 Yr Avg	3.70	0.12	-2.46	51	11,152
5 Yr Avg	-5.98	-3.68	-2.62	66	7,347
10 Yr Avg	—	—	—	—	—
15 Yr Avg	—	—	—	—	—

Tax Analysis	Tax-Adj Rtn%	%Rank Cat	Tax-Cost Rat	%Rank Cat
3 Yr (estimated)	3.70	45	0.00	1
5 Yr (estimated)	-6.64	63	0.70	31
10 Yr (estimated)	—	—	—	—

Potential Capital Gain Exposure: -37% of assets

Rating and Risk

Time Period	Load-Adj Return %	Morningstar Rtn vs Cat	Morningstar Risk vs Cat	Morningstar Risk-Adj Rating
1 Yr	11.05			
3 Yr	3.70	Avg	+Avg	★★★
5 Yr	-5.98	-Avg	High	★★
10 Yr	—	—	—	—
Incept	14.44			

Other Measures	Standard Index S&P 500	Best Fit Index Mstar Mid Growth TR
Alpha	0.5	0.9
Beta	1.22	1.03
R-Squared	74	95
Standard Deviation	22.56	
Mean	3.70	
Sharpe Ratio	0.10	

Portfolio Analysis 12-31-04

Share change since 11-04 Total Stocks:120	Sector	PE	YTD Ret%	% Assets
Juniper Networks	Hardware	NMF	45.56	2.13
Coach	Goods	37.4	49.40	1.95
Marriott International A	Consumer	25.6	37.22	1.68
⊕ Apple Computer	Hardware	NMF	201.36	1.68
⊖ VeriSign	Software	—	106.14	1.54
☼ Wellpoint	Health	17.4	53.33	1.49
Yum Brands	Consumer	19.7	37.84	1.43
☼ CR Bard	Health	26.6	58.94	1.42
Fisher Scientific Intern	Health	43.9	50.79	1.40
Lam Research	Hardware	21.5	-10.50	1.38
Polycom	Hardware	45.9	19.47	1.35
PMC-Sierra	Hardware	38.2	-44.03	1.33
T Rowe Price Group	Financial	25.6	33.16	1.28
⊕ Comverse Technology	Hardware	—	39.00	1.26
⊖ Monster Worldwide	Business	54.6	53.19	1.25
Bed Bath & Beyond	Consumer	27.6	-8.12	1.23
E*Trade Financial	Financial	13.7	18.18	1.23
Marvell Technology	Hardware	NMF	87.03	1.22
Rockwell Automation	Ind Mtrls	28.0	41.75	1.18
Chico's FAS	Consumer	33.3	23.22	1.18

Current Investment Style

Value Blnd Growth — Large Mid Small

Market Cap	%
Giant	0.0
Large	25.6
Mid	67.0
Small	7.4
Micro	0.0
Avg $mil: 4,874	

Value Measures		Rel Category
Price/Earnings	26.86	1.22
Price/Book	3.57	1.19
Price/Sales	2.10	1.19
Price/Cash Flow	7.13	0.74
Dividend Yield %	0.22	0.51

Growth Measures	%	Rel Category
Long-Term Erngs	16.32	1.04
Book Value	4.34	0.43
Sales	6.28	0.73
Cash Flow	6.56	0.54
Historical Erngs	12.25	0.77

Profitability	%	Rel Category
Return on Equity	12.43	0.86
Return on Assets	6.40	0.89
Net Margin	7.69	0.80

Sector Weightings	% of Stocks	Rel S&P 500	3 Year High	3 Year Low
Info	30.74	1.43		
Software	9.10	2.12	11	5
Hardware	17.33	1.70	25	12
Media	1.87	0.49	5	1
Telecom	2.44	0.77	2	0
Service	54.53	1.18		
Health	18.43	1.47	26	16
Consumer	14.72	1.62	20	10
Business	12.19	3.01	14	7
Financial	9.19	0.44	10	4
Mfg	14.74	0.46		
Goods	4.46	0.48	6	3
Ind Mtrls	4.89	0.39	7	2
Energy	5.39	0.75	8	3
Utilities	0.00	0.00	2	0

Composition

Cash	0.0
Stocks	99.9
Bonds	0.0
Other	0.1
Foreign (% of Stock)	1.1

Morningstar's Take by Karen Wallace 11-16-04

Turner Midcap Growth sticks to its strategy through thick and thin.

On a relative basis, this fund's year-to-date returns are subpar. The fund has gained about 5% through Nov. 15, 2004, which lands in the mid-growth category's bottom quartile. But the fund can be expected to lag when growthy fare is out of favor, so we're not too concerned about this relative underperformance in a year when value stocks are leading the way.

Manager Chris McHugh, who has been at the helm since the fund's 1996 inception, seeks out companies that offer high growth rates and favorable momentum characteristics, so the fund always has exposure to areas in which expectations are strong. Although he won't take sector bets versus the Russell Midcap Growth Index, holding some of the raciest names in the tech area makes the fund a bold offering.

For example, he believes blue-chip semiconductor firms such as Intel will increase their spending forecasts for 2005, which should boost the fortunes of equipment firms such as portfolio holding Lam Research. That stock has stumbled this year, but McHugh will hold on to stocks despite a sizable correction when he believes they continue to have good earnings potential. In the case of Lam, the stock continued to meet and exceed management's specifications for earnings-growth rates, so the team took advantage of the price dip to add to its position.

Overall, although the fund's performance can be volatile, its style is consistent. That could make the fund a good complement to a more conservative, diversified portfolio. Investors should be aware that it can post steep losses when its style is out of favor (such as in 2002, when it shed one third of its value) but it tends to race to the front of the pack when growth stocks rally: In 2003, it soared 50%. Compared with similarly aggressive funds, this one's experienced management and strong long-term record make it an appealing option.

Address:	Turner Funds Berwyn PA 19312 800-224-6312
Web Address:	www.turnerinvestments.com
Inception:	10-01-96 *
Advisor:	Turner Investment Partners, Inc.
Subadvisor:	None
NTF Plans:	Fidelity Retail-NTF, Schwab OneSource

Minimum Purchase:	$2500	Add: $50	IRA: $2000
Min Auto Inv Plan:	$100	Add: $50	
Sales Fees:	No-load		
Management Fee:	0.75%, 0.12%A		
Actual Fees:	Mgt:0.75%	Dist:	
Expense Projections:	3Yr:$340	5Yr:$590	10Yr:$1306
Income Distrib:	Annually		

Turner Small Cap Growth

Ticker	Load	NAV	Yield	Total Assets	Mstar Category
TSCEX	Closed	$23.97	0.0%	$264 mil	Small Growth

Governance and Management

Fiduciary Grade: A

Portfolio Manager(s)

Bill McVail ran BlackRock Small Cap Growth successfully for nearly five years. He also runs Preferred Small Cap Growth. His specialty at Turner is the consumer-discretionary sector. Chris McHugh, Jason Schrotberger, and Frank Sustersic also serve as members of the fund's management team. Turner's employee retirement plan is among the largest owners of several of its funds.

Strategy

Manager Bill McVail looks at earnings momentum and technical factors to pick rapidly growing companies. He doesn't ignore valuation, but it clearly takes a backseat. As risky as that seems, he also requires strong fundamentals, limits individual positions to 2% of assets, and keeps the fund sector neutral with respect to the Russell 2000 Growth Index.

Historical Profile

Return Above Avg
Risk Above Avg
Rating ★★★ Neutral

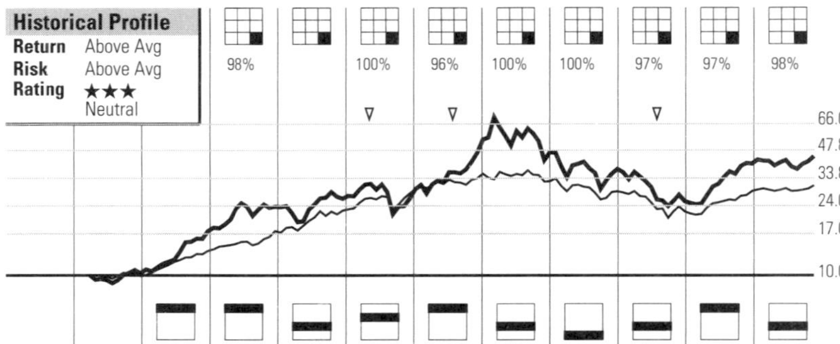

1993	1994	1995	1996	1997	1998	1999	2000	2001	2002	2003	12-04	History
—	10.98	17.37	21.86	24.62	26.72	41.49	24.73	20.07	13.44	21.42	23.97	NAV
—	9.80*	68.16	28.85	14.97	8.53	85.04	-14.38	-18.84	-33.03	59.38	11.90	Total Return %
—	—	30.63	5.91	-18.38	-20.04	64.00	-5.28	-6.96	-10.94	30.71	1.03	+/-S&P 500
—	—	37.12	17.59	2.02	7.30	41.95	8.05	-9.61	-2.77	10.84	-2.41	+/-Russ 2000 Gr
—	0.00	0.00	0.00	0.00	0.00	0.00	0.00	0.00	0.00	0.00	0.00	Income Return %
—	—	68.16	28.85	14.97	8.53	85.04	-14.38	-18.84	-33.03	59.38	11.90	Capital Return %
—	—	1	16	63	31	23	74	78	75	10	54	Total Rtn % Rank Cat
—	0.00	0.00	0.00	0.00	0.00	0.00	0.00	0.00	0.00	0.00	0.00	Income $
—	0.00	1.04	0.51	0.48	0.00	7.18	10.47	0.00	0.00	0.00	0.00	Capital Gains $
—	1.09	1.25	1.25	1.24	1.25	1.25	1.25	1.25	1.25	1.25	1.25	Expense Ratio %
—	-0.27	-0.68	-0.88	-0.84	-0.99	-0.98	-0.94	-0.96	-0.99	-0.79	-0.95	Income Ratio %
—	174	183	149	131	168	224	203	176	188	188	151	Turnover Rate %
—	5	17	74	153	189	379	368	286	147	228	264	Net Assets $mil

Performance 12-31-04

	1st Qtr	2nd Qtr	3rd Qtr	4th Qtr	Total
2000	16.32	-4.54	-2.78	-20.69	-14.38
2001	-26.81	21.22	-28.67	28.24	-13.84
2002	-3.59	-17.42	-21.03	6.50	-33.03
2003	-3.05	27.78	13.39	13.45	53.38
2004	3.41	0.95	-4.61	12.38	11.90

Trailing	Total Return%	+/- S&P 500	+/- Russ 2000 Gr	%Rank Cat	Growth of $10,000
3 Mo	12.38	3.15	-2.70	79	11,238
6 Mo	7.20	0.01	-0.96	58	10,720
1 Yr	11.90	1.03	-2.41	54	11,190
3 Yr Avg	6.10	2.52	0.31	42	11,944
5 Yr Avg	-3.66	-1.36	-0.09	66	8,299
10 Yr Avg	15.30	3.23	8.18	11	41,523
15 Yr Avg	—	—	—	—	—

Tax Analysis	Tax-Adj Rtn%	%Rank Cat	Tax-Cost Rat	%Rank Cat
3 Yr (estimated)	6.10	38	0.00	1
5 Yr (estimated)	-5.79	71	2.21	83
10 Yr (estimated)	13.06	12	1.94	63

Potential Capital Gain Exposure: -36% of assets

Rating and Risk

Time Period	Load-Adj Return %	Morningstar Rtn vs Cat	Morningstar Risk vs Cat	Morningstar Risk-Adj Rating
1 Yr	11.90			
3 Yr	6.10	Avg	+Avg	★★★
5 Yr	-3.66	Avg	+Avg	★★
10 Yr	15.30	+Avg	+Avg	★★★
Incept	14.94			

Other Measures	Standard Index S&P 500	Best Fit Index Russ 2000 Gr
Alpha	3.0	0.3
Beta	1.25	1.01
R-Squared	70	96
Standard Deviation	24.22	
Mean	6.10	
Sharpe Ratio	0.20	

Morningstar's Take by Karen Wallace 12-14-04

Turner Small Cap Growth is behaving predictably, and that's a feather in its cap.

After assets in this fund and related accounts topped $1 billion recently, Turner Investment Partners closed this fund to new investors on July 31, 2004. We applaud this move: Manager Bill McVail and his colleagues purchase and sell shares based on quickly changing information about firms' earnings expectations, a practice that becomes difficult to execute if assets become unwieldy. Fund firms often place a higher priority on raking in fees from a swelling asset base than on ensuring that a popular fund can operate efficiently. In this regard, Turner has done right by its shareholders.

The popularity of Turner's funds stems from a strict adherence to a somewhat-predictable, growth-oriented strategy, which has its benefits and drawbacks. McVail and his cohorts seek small-cap stocks offering rapid earnings growth and favorable momentum characteristics, and they always maintain exposure to growth areas. The fund really revs up when the stock market is rising, such as during the late 1990s and 2003. It stalls in dodgy conditions, however: Witness its double-digit annual losses during the 2000 to 2002 period.

It has been business as usual for the fund in 2004. Several of its top holdings have done well this year. Online retailer Overstock.com, for example, has gained more than 270% for the year to date through Dec. 13, 2004. And top holding Immocor, which makes automated systems and devices for blood transfusions and blood testing, has shot up nearly 150% through the same period. Each stock has helped lately but also carries a rich price tag.

In all, we like this fund's bold convictions, but investors should not expect a smooth ride here. Indeed, shareholders would be wise to devote just a small portion of their portfolios to this spicy side dish.

Address:	Turner Funds Berwyn PA 19312 800-224-6312	Minimum Purchase: Min Auto Inv Plan: Sales Fees:	Closed Closed No-load	Add: — Add: —	IRA: —
Web Address:	www.turnerinvestments.com	Management Fee:	1.00%, 0.12%A		
Inception:	02-07-94 *	Actual Fees:	Mgt:0.99%	Dist:	
Advisor:	Turner Investment Partners, Inc.	Expense Projections:	3Yr:$397	5Yr:$693	10Yr:$1537
Subadvisor:	None	Income Distrib:	Annually		
NTF Plans:	Fidelity Retail-NTF, Schwab OneSource				

Portfolio Analysis 12-31-04

Share change since 11-04 Total Stocks:131	Sector	PE	YTD Ret%	% Assets
⊕ Immucor	Health	95.1	159.44	1.92
F5 Networks	Hardware	46.9	94.10	1.46
Genesis HealthCare	Health	—	—	1.41
⊕ Scientific Games	Hardware	27.8	40.48	1.25
MGI Pharma	Health	—	36.14	1.24
ResMed	Health	30.4	23.01	1.24
Advanced Medical Optics	Health	—	109.36	1.23
East West Bancorp	Financial	28.3	57.37	1.21
Powerwave Technologies	Hardware	—	9.56	1.20
Overstock.com	Business	—	247.26	1.18
Trimble Navigation	Hardware	25.2	33.08	1.16
Sierra Health Services	Health	14.7	100.77	1.14
⊕ Eyetech Pharmaceuticals	Health	—	—	1.12
Amerigroup	Financial	24.7	77.40	1.11
Navigant Consulting	Business	36.1	41.04	1.10
⊕ Witness Systems	Software	—	88.35	1.06
P.F. Chang's China Bistr	Consumer	62.4	10.75	1.05
⊖ Avid Technology	Software	30.9	28.65	1.01
Insight Enterprises	Consumer	15.3	9.15	0.99
Affiliated Managers Grou	Financial	28.2	46.01	0.98

Current Investment Style

Value Blnd Growth — Large Mid Small

Market Cap	%
Giant	0.0
Large	0.0
Mid	27.1
Small	66.3
Micro	6.6
Avg $mil: 1,086	

Value Measures		Rel Category
Price/Earnings	26.68	1.23
Price/Book	3.45	1.31
Price/Sales	1.68	1.12
Price/Cash Flow	11.23	1.40
Dividend Yield %	0.12	0.39

Growth Measures	%	Rel Category
Long-Term Erngs	17.02	0.98
Book Value	2.05	0.32
Sales	5.86	0.91
Cash Flow	9.96	0.74
Historical Erngs	11.61	0.86

Profitability	%	Rel Category
Return on Equity	8.83	0.89
Return on Assets	4.00	0.91
Net Margin	4.04	0.59

Sector Weightings	% of Stocks	Rel S&P 500	3 Year High	3 Year Low
Info	29.54	1.37		
Software	7.92	1.84	13	4
Hardware	16.67	1.63	27	9
Media	2.03	0.53	4	1
Telecom	2.92	0.93	4	0
Service	53.61	1.16		
Health	19.06	1.52	24	17
Consumer	9.02	0.99	18	7
Business	14.99	3.70	17	9
Financial	10.54	0.51	16	3
Mfg	16.87	0.53		
Goods	2.92	0.31	6	1
Ind Mtrls	9.91	0.78	15	4
Energy	4.04	0.56	7	2
Utilities	0.00	0.00	0	0

Composition

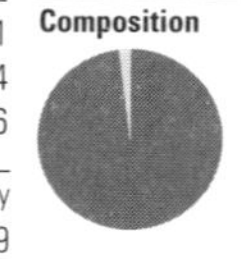

Cash	0.0
Stocks	97.9
Bonds	0.0
Other	2.1
Foreign (% of Stock)	2.2

Tweedy, Browne American

Analyst Pick

Ticker	Load	NAV	Yield	Total Assets	Mstar Category
TWEBX	None	$25.37	1.5%	$712 mil	Mid-Cap Value

Governance and Management

Fiduciary Grade: A

Portfolio Manager(s)

Longtime managers William Browne, Christopher Browne, and John Spears are old-school value investors who follow the disciplines of Ben Graham and Warren Buffett. They also manage the respected Tweedy, Browne Global Value. The three, along with many other Tweedy, Browne personnel, have sizable personal investments in the funds.

Strategy

The fund's managers buy stocks that are trading at discounts to their assessments of companies' private-market values. They also look for stocks with insider buying, citing empirical studies that show such stocks outperform. This is a mid-cap fund on average, but management buys stocks of all sizes.

Historical Profile

Return Below Avg
Risk Below Avg
Rating ★★★ Neutral

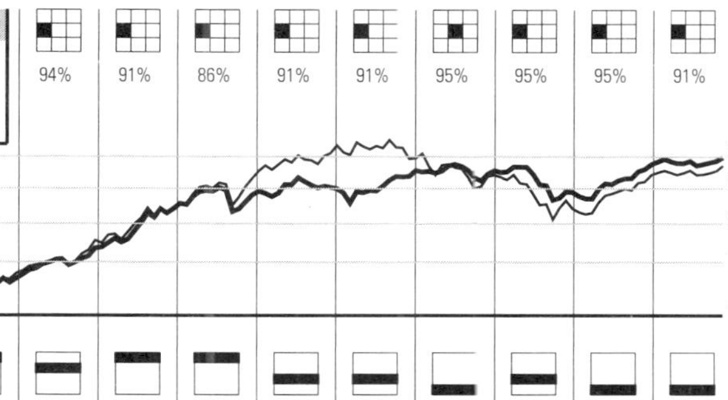

Investment Style: Equity Stock %

▼ Manager Change
▽ Partial Manager Change

Growth of $10,000
— Investment Values of Fund
— Investment Values of S&P 500

Performance Quartile (within Category)

1993	1994	1995	1996	1997	1998	1999	2000	2001	2002	2003	12-04	History
9.94	9.82	13.25	15.64	21.11	22.74	22.37	24.42	23.42	19.45	23.87	25.37	NAV
-0.60*	-0.56	36.21	22.45	38.87	9.59	2.00	14.45	-0.08	-14.91	23.24	9.42	Total Return %
—	-1.87	-1.32	-0.49	5.52	-18.98	-19.04	23.55	11.80	7.18	-5.43	-1.45	+/-S&P 500
—	1.57	1.27	2.19	4.50	4.51	2.11	-4.73	-2.41	-5.27	-14.83	-14.29	+/-Russ MV
—	0.64	1.08	1.29	1.07	0.67	1.21	0.46	0.33	0.43	0.51	1.63	Income Return %
—	-1.20	35.13	21.16	37.80	8.92	0.79	13.99	-0.41	-15.34	22.73	7.79	Capital Return %
—	40	16	29	3	21	64	66	76	68	95	97	Total Rtn % Rank Cat
0.00	0.06	0.11	0.17	0.17	0.14	0.28	0.10	0.08	0.10	0.10	0.39	Income $
0.00	0.00	0.02	0.42	0.43	0.25	0.53	1.08	0.90	0.37	0.00	0.36	Capital Gains $
—	2.26	1.74	1.39	1.39	1.39	1.39	1.37	1.36	1.36	1.36	1.38	Expense Ratio %
—	0.64	1.25	1.13	0.92	0.69	0.55	1.13	0.40	0.23	0.59	1.09	Income Ratio %
—	—	4	9	16	6	16	19	10	6	8	3	Turnover Rate %
3	36	168	278	721	1,160	1,026	956	977	717	751	712	Net Assets $mil

Performance 12-31-04

	1st Qtr	2nd Qtr	3rd Qtr	4th Qtr	Total
2000	-2.24	0.50	11.47	4.50	14.45
2001	-1.92	6.85	-9.65	5.53	-0.08
2002	2.82	-5.36	-17.42	5.88	-14.91
2003	-4.73	11.39	4.55	11.08	23.24
2004	2.14	0.29	-1.06	7.98	9.42

Trailing	Total Return%	+/- S&P 500	+/- Russ MV	%Rank Cat	Growth of $10,000
3 Mo	7.98	-1.25	-5.48	92	10,798
6 Mo	6.83	-0.36	-8.60	89	10,683
1 Yr	9.42	-1.45	-14.29	97	10,942
3 Yr Avg	4.69	1.11	-10.87	97	11,474
5 Yr Avg	5.58	7.88	-7.90	91	13,119
10 Yr Avg	13.01	0.94	-2.71	59	33,976
15 Yr Avg	—	—	—	—	—

Tax Analysis	Tax-Adj Rtn%	%Rank Cat	Tax-Cost Rat	%Rank Cat
3 Yr (estimated)	4.18	95	0.49	40
5 Yr (estimated)	4.80	91	0.74	36
10 Yr (estimated)	12.14	33	0.77	8

Potential Capital Gain Exposure: 39% of assets

Rating and Risk

Time Period	Load-Adj Return %	Morningstar Rtn vs Cat	Morningstar Risk vs Cat	Morningstar Risk-Adj Rating
1 Yr	9.42			
3 Yr	4.69	Low	-Avg	★★
5 Yr	5.58	-Avg	Low	★★
10 Yr	13.01	Avg	-Avg	★★★
Incept	11.57			

Other Measures	Standard Index S&P 500	Best Fit Index Russ MV
Alpha	1.6	-6.8
Beta	0.70	0.76
R-Squared	78	89
Standard Deviation	12.34	
Mean	4.69	
Sharpe Ratio	0.27	

Morningstar's Take by Bridget Hughes 10-31-04

Here's a 2-star fund we highly recommend.

Tweedy, Browne American Value's performance over the past five years has taken a toll on its Morningstar Rating for funds. The Star rating is a purely quantitative measure of how a fund has performed on a risk-adjusted basis within its assigned Morningstar category. While this fund is certainly helped by the incredible stability of its NAV compared with other mid-value funds, its comparatively weak returns since 1999 have hurt, even turning its once superior 10-year record into a merely middling one. All told, Morningstar's algorithms, which consider an offering's three-, five-, and 10-year records in varying weights, give this fund 2 stars.

That's the bad news, but we think it makes sense to consider this offering's record in a different context. Unlike most rivals in the mid-value grouping, Tweedy, Browne American Value takes a more-flexible approach, regularly building a portfolio that includes large and small caps, as well as mid-caps. It also typically invests 10% to 20% of assets overseas. Using its Graham-and-Dodd-inspired approach, its aim is to "beat the market," or the S&P 500 Index. On that score, the fund can still claim victory: Its three-, five-, and 10-year results all surpass the index's. Throw in how stable it has been compared with that bogy, and you're looking at very compelling testimony in favor of this fund.

One thing is clear, however: Owning this fund takes as much patience as its portfolio managers exercise in investing in a compact portfolio of around 50 or 60 stocks. That's because it can endure periods of weakness, even compared with the S&P 500. (Over the past year, for example, it has trailed that bogy by one percentage point; in the late 1990s, it fell well behind.)

Its stable nature certainly makes it easier to hang on, however, and we think over the long haul, it will continue to do well, giving it one of the fund world's better risk/reward profiles.

Address:	350 Park Ave New York NY 10022 800-432-4789
Web Address:	www.tweedy.com
Inception:	12-08-93 *
Advisor:	Tweedy, Browne Company LLC
Subadvisor:	None
NTF Plans:	N/A

Minimum Purchase:	$2500	Add: $250	IRA: $500
Min Auto Inv Plan:	$2500	Add: $250	
Sales Fees:	No-load		
Management Fee:	1.25%		
Actual Fees:	Mgt:1.25%	Dist:	
Expense Projections:	3Yr:$431	5Yr:$745	10Yr:$1635
Income Distrib:	Annually		

Portfolio Analysis 09-30-04

Share change since 08-04 Total Stocks:58	Sector	PE	YTD Ret%	% Assets
American Express	Financial	20.3	17.60	5.38
Popular	Financial	16.4	31.94	4.95
MBIA	Financial	11.3	8.57	3.99
Hollinger International	Media	—	17.75	3.85
Federated Investors B	Financial	17.0	5.00	3.67
Transatlantic Holdings	Financial	16.7	-3.74	3.67
Freddie Mac	Financial	10.6	28.75	3.64
⊕ ABN Amro Holding NV ADR	Financial	12.3	19.09	3.48
PNC Financial Services G	Financial	13.3	8.92	3.37
Proquest	Business	15.7	0.85	3.25
Torchmark	Financial	13.2	26.55	3.21
Comcast	Media	—	-13.77	3.15
Wells Fargo	Financial	15.5	8.97	3.12
⊕ Nestle SA ADR	Goods	21.6	7.65	2.97
Pfizer	Health	22.0	-22.31	2.62
National Western Life In	Financial	9.0	7.57	2.60
Heineken Hldg Nv	Goods	—	—	2.37
American National Insura	Financial	15.2	27.12	2.32
Schering-Plough	Health	—	21.56	2.28
Bristol-Myers Squibb	Health	17.7	-7.27	2.06

Current Investment Style

Value Blnd Growth / Large Mid Small

Market Cap	%
Giant	32.7
Large	11.5
Mid	36.0
Small	17.6
Micro	2.2
Avg $mil: 8,148	

Value Measures		Rel Category
Price/Earnings	13.91	0.90
Price/Book	1.65	0.86
Price/Sales	1.32	1.50
Price/Cash Flow	5.45	0.95
Dividend Yield %	1.79	1.25

Growth Measures	%	Rel Category
Long-Term Erngs	12.37	1.12
Book Value	10.97	1.95
Sales	6.01	1.26
Cash Flow	2.75	0.70
Historical Erngs	10.96	0.95

Profitability	%	Rel Category
Return on Equity	16.48	1.29
Return on Assets	9.72	1.60
Net Margin	13.32	1.52

Sector Weightings	% of Stocks	Rel S&P 500	3 Year High	3 Year Low
Info	8.34	0.39		
Software	0.00	0.00	0	0
Hardware	0.00	0.00	0	0
Media	7.69	2.00	8	4
Telecom	0.65	0.21	1	0
Service	72.86	1.57		
Health	9.49	0.76	13	9
Consumer	3.49	0.38	7	3
Business	8.48	2.09	9	6
Financial	51.40	2.48	52	48
Mfg	18.79	0.58		
Goods	12.87	1.38	16	11
Ind Mtrls	5.92	0.47	10	6
Energy	0.00	0.00	0	0
Utilities	0.00	0.00	0	0

Composition

Cash	9.1
Stocks	90.9
Bonds	0.0
Other	0.0
Foreign (% of Stock)	18.4

Tweedy, Browne Glob Val

Analyst Pick	Ticker	Load	NAV	Yield	Total Assets	Mstar Category
✔	TBGVX	None	$23.19	1.2%	$5,663 mil	Foreign Small/Mid Value

Governance and Management

Fiduciary Grade: A

Portfolio Manager(s)

The fund has been around since 1993, and lead managers Christopher Browne, William Browne, and John Spears are experienced investors. They also run Tweedy, Browne American Value, a similar U.S.-focused offering. The managers have lots of their own money invested here.

Strategy

Like sibling Tweedy, Browne American Value, this fund looks for stocks that are cheaper than the private market values the fund's managers assign them. The fund often ends up concentrated in admittedly wide-ranging financials, industrial-cyclicals, and service industries. In an effort to dampen volatility, the team hedges virtually all of its currency exposure back into the U.S. dollar. The managers tend to shop across the market-cap spectrum for their picks, but they usually stay away from emerging markets because they find it difficult to hedge their developing-markets currency exposure.

Historical Profile

Return Average
Risk Below Avg
Rating ★★★ Neutral

Investment Style: Equity Stock %

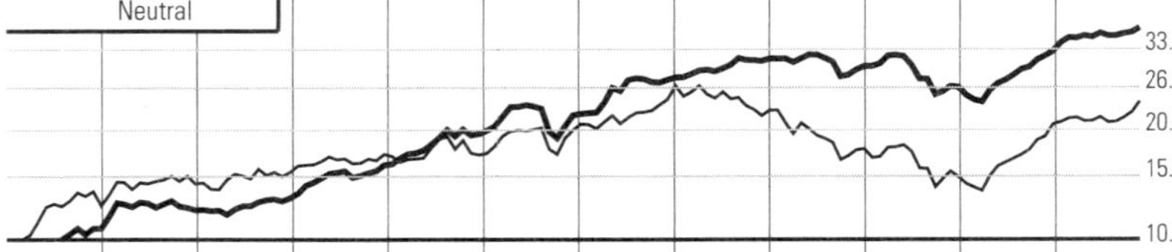

▼ Manager Change
▽ Partial Manager Change

Growth of $10,000
— Investment Values of Fund
— Investment Values of MSCI EAFE

Performance Quartile (within Category)

1993	1994	1995	1996	1997	1998	1999	2000	2001	2002	2003	12-04	History
	91%	88%	93%	89%	90%	87%	86%	87%	85%			Equity Stock %
11.54	11.88	12.95	14.45	16.39	16.82	20.21	19.98	18.53	15.81	19.55	23.19	NAV
15.40*	4.36	10.70	20.23	22.96	10.99	25.28	12.39	-4.67	-12.14	24.93	20.01	Total Return %
—	-3.42	-0.51	14.18	21.18	-8.94	-1.75	26.58	16.75	3.80	-13.66	-0.24	+/-MSCI EAFE
—	-2.99	-0.71	13.36	20.69	-7.70	-2.70	25.75	16.72	3.66	-14.49	-0.37	+/-MSCI Wd xUS
0.00	0.00	0.00	4.27	6.03	2.31	1.54	1.02	0.92	1.08	1.27	1.39	Income Return %
—	4.36	10.70	15.96	16.93	8.68	23.74	11.37	-5.59	-13.22	23.66	18.62	Capital Return %
—	60	25	40	1	6	56	1	21	89	100	68	Total Rtn % Rank Cat
0.00	0.00	0.00	0.55	0.87	0.38	0.26	0.21	0.18	0.20	0.20	0.27	Income $
0.00	0.16	0.20	0.57	0.49	0.99	0.59	2.52	0.33	0.27	0.00	0.00	Capital Gains $
—	1.73	1.65	1.60	1.58	1.42	1.41	1.38	1.38	1.37	1.37	1.39	Expense Ratio %
—	0.00	1.08	1.15	0.73	1.05	1.26	1.10	1.06	1.22	1.17	1.08	Income Ratio %
—	—	16	17	20	16	23	18	12	7	8	8	Turnover Rate %
158	566	802	1,211	1,985	2,492	3,142	3,564	3,834	4,132	4,899	5,663	Net Assets $mil

Performance 12-31-04

	1st Qtr	2nd Qtr	3rd Qtr	4th Qtr	Total
2000	4.40	1.33	5.38	0.82	12.39
2001	-2.30	4.76	-12.62	6.59	-4.67
2002	6.80	-5.81	-16.47	4.57	-12.14
2003	-8.67	14.40	8.41	10.28	24.93
2004	8.59	3.06	-0.27	7.53	20.01

Trailing	Total Return%	+/- MSCI EAFE	+/- MSCI Wd xUS	%Rank Cat	Growth of $10,000
3 Mo	7.53	-7.79	-7.62	100	10,753
6 Mo	7.23	-7.77	-8.14	96	10,723
1 Yr	20.01	-0.24	-0.37	68	12,001
3 Yr Avg	9.62	-2.27	-2.60	100	13,173
5 Yr Avg	7.14	8.27	7.90	76	14,118
10 Yr Avg	12.38	6.76	6.44	13	32,128
15 Yr Avg	—	—	—	—	—

Tax Analysis	Tax-Adj Rtn%	%Rank Cat	Tax-Cost Rat	%Rank Cat
3 Yr (estimated)	9.03	97	0.54	32
5 Yr (estimated)	5.92	76	1.14	69
10 Yr (estimated)	10.74	13	1.46	62

Potential Capital Gain Exposure: 28% of assets

Rating and Risk

Time Period	Load-Adj Return %	Morningstar Rtn vs Cat	Morningstar Risk vs Cat	Morningstar Risk-Adj Rating
1 Yr	20.01			
3 Yr	9.62	Low	-Avg	★
5 Yr	7.14	-Avg	Low	★★★
10 Yr	12.38	+Avg	-Avg	★★★★
Incept	12.43			

Other Measures	Standard Index S&P 500	Best Fit Index Mstar Mid Value
Alpha	0.9	-1.8
Beta	0.69	0.76
R-Squared	78	79

Standard Deviation	13.33
Mean	9.62
Sharpe Ratio	0.62

Portfolio Analysis 09-30-04

Share change since 08-04 Total Stocks:153	Sector	Country	% Assets
⊕ Abn-Amro Hldgs Nv	Financial	Netherlands	3.38
⊕ Nestle	Goods	Switzerland	2.96
Axel Springer Verlag	Media	Germany	2.94
KONE	Business	Finland	2.90
CNP Assurances	Financial	France	2.67
Trinity Mirror	Media	U.K.	2.65
Heineken Hldg Nv	Goods	Netherlands	2.53
⊖ Merck KGaA	Health	Germany	2.45
Hollinger International	Media	United States	2.00
Altadis	Goods	Spain	1.88
Telegraaf Hldg	Media	Netherlands	1.87
Novartis	Health	Switzerland	1.86
Pfizer	Health	United States	1.80
Diageo	Goods	U.K.	1.65
Jardine Strategic Hldgs	Consumer	Singapore	1.55
⊖ Randstad Holding	Business	Netherlands	1.54
Sika	Business	Switzerland	1.43
Almanij Grp	Financial	Belgium	1.41
Sanyo Shinpan Finance	Financial	Japan	1.36
Schering-Plough	Health	United States	1.35

Current Investment Style

Value Blnd Growth / Large Mid Small

Market Cap	%
Giant	21.9
Large	22.7
Mid	37.4
Small	16.2
Micro	1.8
Avg $mil: 5,125	

Value Measures		Rel Category
Price/Earnings	14.08	1.04
Price/Book	1.57	0.96
Price/Sales	0.75	1.12
Price/Cash Flow	6.39	1.24
Dividend Yield %	2.82	1.04

Growth Measures	%	Rel Category
Long-Term Erngs	11.17	0.91
Book Value	2.63	23.91
Sales	0.30	0.15
Cash Flow	-0.22	NMF
Historical Erngs	-1.69	NMF

Composition

Cash	12.2	Bonds	0.0
Stocks	84.9	Other	2.8
Foreign (% of Stock)			91.4

Sector Weightings	% of Stocks	Rel MSCI EAFE	3 Year High	3 Year Low
Info	19.95	1.20		
Software	0.00	0.00	0	0
Hardware	0.71	0.19	2	0
Media	19.24	8.44	20	15
Telecom	0.00	0.00	0	0
Service	44.16	0.99		
Health	12.62	1.74	16	12
Consumer	2.82	0.56	5	2
Business	9.78	1.80	11	5
Financial	18.94	0.70	24	17
Mfg	35.88	0.93		
Goods	21.66	1.59	23	18
Ind Mtrls	13.52	1.10	19	13
Energy	0.01	0.00	0	0
Utilities	0.69	0.13	1	0

Regional Exposure	% Stock		
UK/W. Europe	72	N. America	10
Japan	8	Latn America	2
Asia X Japan	8	Other	0

Country Exposure	% Stock		
Netherlands	18	U.K.	10
Switzerland	15	United States	8
Germany	10		

Morningstar's Take by Bridget Hughes 11-18-04

Investors should stick with Tweedy, Browne Global Value.

At first glance, this fund's recent performance looks weak. Over the past three years through Nov. 17, 2004, its 9.5% annualized return lands near the foreign small/mid-value category's bottom.

But gauging relative performance for this fund isn't that simple. That's because it's a misfit in any category. For one, it invests across the market-cap spectrum. So while its average market cap suggests placement in its current group, that statistic is regularly among the very largest in the group, because the portfolio almost always has a big chunk of assets in large-cap stocks (a disadvantage during the 2000s). Further, it always hedges the vast majority of its foreign-currency exposure, unlike virtually all of its peers. That cuts down on volatility here, but can also have a big impact on relative returns, both positively and negatively (lately, negatively).

But Tweedy, Browne Global Value's stability is a big point in its favor. The fund is among the least volatile among foreign-stock funds of any kind. That can make it easier for shareholders to hang on during tough times and more likely to reach their financial goals. And in a different light, even its recent returns look competitive. Its three-year results come close to those of the MSCI EAFE Index, beat those of the MSCI EAFE Hedged Index, and far exceed those of the S&P 500 Index (which means an investor's decision to allocate dollars to this fund and away from U.S. stocks was a good one). The fund also beat out the typical foreign large-value offering by a good margin. Considering this fund can easily be used as a core international holding, we think those comparisons are appropriate and reflect Browne, Browne, and Spears' skills as portfolio managers and the efficacy of their long-used approach.

Global Value's consistent approach, low volatility, and healthy long-term returns keep this fund on our Analyst Picks list.

Address:	350 Park Ave New York NY 10022 800-432-4789
Web Address:	www.tweedy.com
Inception:	06-15-93 *
Advisor:	Tweedy, Browne Company LLC
Subadvisor:	None
NTF Plans:	N/A

Minimum Purchase:	$2500	Add: $250	IRA: $500
Min Auto Inv Plan:	$2500	Add: $250	
Sales Fees:	No-load, 2.00%R		
Management Fee:	1.25%, 0.09%A		
Actual Fees:	Mgt:1.25%	Dist:	
Expense Projections:	3Yr:$434	5Yr:$750	10Yr:$1646
Income Distrib:	Annually		

UMB Scout WorldWide

Ticker	Load	NAV	Yield	Total Assets	Mstar Category
UMBWX	None	$24.10	0.7%	$1,023 mil	Foreign Large Blend

Governance and Management

Fiduciary Grade: C

Portfolio Manager(s)

Manager James Moffett has managed this fund since its inception in 1993. He relies on internal research from two internationally focused analysts dedicated to the fund as well as some insights from UMB's domestic-stock analysts. He also consults Wall Street research.

Strategy

James Moffett combines top-down country and sector analysis with bottom-up stock selection. He looks for positive macroeconomic trends to determine country weightings. He typically maintains a small weighting in emerging markets. He favors companies with good balance sheets that have stable long-term growth potential and prefers market leaders that can benefit from demographic trends. He invests primarily in U.S.-traded ADRs. The fund considers using fair value pricing when it deems it appropriate, and it imposes a 2% redemption fee on shares sold within two months after purchase.

Historical Profile

Return High
Risk Low
Rating ★★★★★ Highest

Investment Style: Equity Stock %

78%	84%	73%	85%	80%	85%	85%	91%

▼ Manager Change
▽ Partial Manager Change

Growth of $10,000
— Investment Values of Fund
— Investment Values of MSCI EAFE

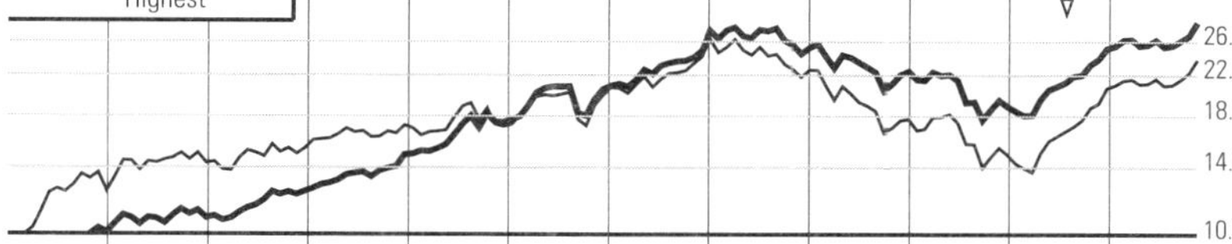

Performance Quartile (within Category)

1993	1994	1995	1996	1997	1998	1999	2000	2001	2002	2003	12-04	History
10.68	10.84	12.08	13.94	16.02	18.56	23.77	21.24	18.67	15.58	20.58	24.10	NAV
5.73*	3.82	14.66	18.35	18.35	17.96	31.43	-8.17	-11.00	-15.85	33.10	18.02	Total Return %
—	-3.96	3.45	12.30	16.57	-1.97	4.40	6.02	10.42	0.09	-5.49	-2.23	+/-MSCI EAFE
—	-3.53	3.25	11.48	16.08	-0.73	3.45	5.19	10.39	-0.05	-6.32	-2.36	+/-MSCI Wd xUS
0.00	1.60	2.04	1.92	1.75	1.97	1.16	0.20	1.08	0.73	0.87	0.83	Income Return %
—	2.22	12.62	16.43	16.60	15.99	30.27	-8.37	-12.08	-16.58	32.23	17.19	Capital Return %
—	17	19	14	1	26	62	12	3	38	49	45	Total Rtn % Rank Cat
0.03	0.17	0.22	0.23	0.24	0.31	0.21	0.05	0.23	0.14	0.14	0.17	Income $
0.00	0.07	0.12	0.11	0.22	0.02	0.36	0.56	0.01	0.00	0.00	0.00	Capital Gains $
0.85	0.85	0.85	0.85	0.86	0.87	0.86	0.91	1.12	1.12	1.14	1.10	Expense Ratio %
1.43	1.87	1.97	2.40	1.93	2.01	1.69	1.29	1.04	0.77	1.16	0.87	Income Ratio %
—	24	27	5	18	3	8	8	11	13	12	12	Turnover Rate %
6	18	24	41	57	108	268	307	358	354	593	1,023	Net Assets $mil

Performance 12-31-04

	1st Qtr	2nd Qtr	3rd Qtr	4th Qtr	Total
2000	1.60	-1.23	-5.20	-3.47	-8.17
2001	-9.51	2.75	-12.92	9.92	-11.00
2002	-0.32	-4.08	-17.60	6.81	-15.85
2003	-4.11	15.07	5.74	14.07	33.10
2004	4.52	-0.21	-0.33	13.53	18.02

Trailing	Total Return%	+/- MSCI EAFE	+/- MSCI Wd xUS	%Rank Cat	Growth of $10,000
3 Mo	13.53	-1.79	-1.62	72	11,353
6 Mo	13.15	-1.85	-2.22	72	11,315
1 Yr	18.02	-2.23	-2.36	45	11,802
3 Yr Avg	9.75	-2.14	-2.47	44	13,219
5 Yr Avg	1.56	2.69	2.32	5	10,805
10 Yr Avg	10.40	4.78	4.46	3	26,896
15 Yr Avg	—	—	—	—	—

Tax Analysis	Tax-Adj Rtn%	%Rank Cat	Tax-Cost Rat	%Rank Cat
3 Yr (estimated)	9.43	38	0.29	32
5 Yr (estimated)	1.17	4	0.38	22
10 Yr (estimated)	9.69	3	0.64	13

Potential Capital Gain Exposure: 20% of assets

Rating and Risk

Time Period	Load-Adj Return %	Morningstar Rtn vs Cat	Morningstar Risk vs Cat	Morningstar Risk-Adj Rating
1 Yr	18.02			
3 Yr	9.75	Avg	Low	★★★
5 Yr	1.56	High	Low	★★★★★
10 Yr	10.40	High	Low	★★★★★
Incept	10.06			

Other Measures	Standard Index S&P 500	Best Fit Index MSCI Wd xUS
Alpha	-0.5	-0.9
Beta	0.85	0.86
R-Squared	95	95
Standard Deviation	14.88	
Mean	9.75	
Sharpe Ratio	0.57	

Portfolio Analysis 09-30-04

Share change since 06-04 Total Stocks:70	Sector	Country	% Assets
⊕ Canon ADR	Goods	Japan	2.87
⊕ OMV Aktiengesellschaft	Energy	Austria	2.44
⊕ Novo Nordisk ADR	Health	Denmark	2.40
⊕ BHP Billiton ADR	Ind Mtrls	Australia	2.15
⊕ Potash Corp./Saskatchewa	Ind Mtrls	Canada	2.00
⊕ Coles Myer ADR	Consumer	Australia	1.98
⊕ Imperial Oil Ltd	Energy	Canada	1.81
⊕ EnCana	Energy	Canada	1.78
⊕ Portugal Telecom SA ADR	Telecom	Portugal	1.72
⊕ Imperial Chemical Indust	Ind Mtrls	U.K.	1.72
⊕ BP PLC ADR	Energy	U.K.	1.70
⊕ Nobel Biocare Holding	Health	Switzerland	1.68
⊕ Vodafone Group PLC ADR	Telecom	U.K.	1.67
⊕ Sociedad Quimica y Miner	Ind Mtrls	United States	1.67
⊕ Norsk Hydro ASA ADR	Energy	Norway	1.65
⊕ CLP Holdings Limited (AD	Utilities	United States	1.65
⊕ SAP AG ADR	Software	Germany	1.59
⊕ Total SA ADR	Energy	France	1.59
⊕ Mettler-Toledo Internati	Health	United States	1.58
⊕ Aracruz Celulose SA ADR	Ind Mtrls	Brazil	1.57

Current Investment Style (Value Blnd Growth; Large Mid Small)

Market Cap	%
Giant	40.8
Large	37.1
Mid	22.1
Small	0.0
Micro	0.0
Avg $mil: 15,762	

Value Measures		Rel Category
Price/Earnings	15.06	1.10
Price/Book	2.34	1.30
Price/Sales	1.30	1.43
Price/Cash Flow	6.02	1.22
Dividend Yield %	1.80	0.71

Growth Measures	%	Rel Category
Long-Term Erngs	6.59	0.61
Book Value	6.96	696.00
Sales	5.60	2.25
Cash Flow	19.21	3.42
Historical Erngs	27.63	4.94

Composition

Cash	9.0	Bonds	0.0
Stocks	91.0	Other	0.0
Foreign (% of Stock)			85.5

Sector Weightings	% of Stocks	Rel MSCI EAFE	3 Year High	Low
Info	18.44	1.11		
Software	1.81	1.68	2	1
Hardware	8.78	2.41	15	8
Media	0.00	0.00	3	0
Telecom	7.85	0.82	11	7
Service	26.84	0.60		
Health	13.47	1.86	16	8
Consumer	3.78	0.75	8	3
Business	3.89	0.72	4	2
Financial	5.70	0.21	9	4
Mfg	54.73	1.42		
Goods	14.43	1.06	22	14
Ind Mtrls	21.19	1.72	27	12
Energy	16.00	2.18	16	10
Utilities	3.11	0.58	3	0

Regional Exposure	% Stock		
UK/W. Europe	52	N. America	21
Japan	12	Latn America	3
Asia X Japan	10	Other	2

Country Exposure	% Stock		
United States	15	Australia	6
U.K.	13	Canada	6
Japan	12		

Morningstar's Take by Gregg Wolper 11-15-04

Now that it has addressed one of its few flaws, UMB Scout WorldWide is even more appealing than it was before.

This offering traditionally had kept roughly 15% of its assets in cash. That was rare in the fund world. A few managers will raise their cash stakes to that level (or even higher) if they can't find enough stocks that meet their standards, but even they don't do so permanently. However, manager Jim Moffett says this fund recently reversed its policy: It is now almost fully invested and will stay that way except in unusual circumstances. He says his firm is less concerned now about having money on-hand for redemptions--the main reason for the cash stake--now that international investing is much more accepted among the public. And even if he needed to raise cash, he notes that there are many big, heavily traded stocks in the portfolio that could easily be sold if necessary.

Although a cash cushion can help the fund when markets drop, it acts as a drag when the reverse is true. Thus, this fund's change is welcome. Indeed, some investors might have crossed the fund off their lists before. Now it's very hard to do that. Using a low-turnover strategy that focuses on established companies but not necessarily the biggest fish, Moffett has amassed a fine long-term record. Indeed, the fund's trailing 10-year return through Oct. 31, 2004 (Moffett has been at the helm all the while), tops 97% of the foreign large-blend category and comfortably beats the MSCI EAFE Index as well. So far in 2004, through Nov. 12, the fund is slightly ahead of the group's midpoint. Moffett credits an overweighting in energy in particular, though some picks in the health-care arena--a sector he has added to lately--have also helped. Conversely, some tech plays have hurt.

All told, there is good reason to check this fund out.

Address:	803 W Michigan St Milwaukee WI 53233 800-996-2862
Web Address:	www.umb.com
Inception:	09-14-93*
Advisor:	Scout Investment Advisors, Inc.
Subadvisor:	None
NTF Plans:	Fidelity Retail-NTF, Schwab OneSource

Minimum Purchase:	$1000	Add: $100	IRA: $250
Min Auto Inv Plan:	$1000	Add: $50	
Sales Fees:	No-load, 2.00%R		
Management Fee:	1.10% mx./0.90% mn.		
Actual Fees:	Mgt:1.00%	Dist: —	
Expense Projections:	3Yr:$280	5Yr:$480	10Yr:$1070
Income Distrib:	Semi-Annually		

USAA Income

Ticker	Load	NAV	Yield	SEC Yield	Total Assets	Mstar Category
USAIX	None	$12.42	4.4%	3.93%	$1,753 mil	Intermediate-Term Bond

Governance and Management

Fiduciary Grade: B

Portfolio Manager(s)

Margaret Didi Weinblatt has been at the helm since February 2000. She also manages USAA GNMA, which she took over in May 2002. Before joining the fund, she was a comanager at Neuberger Berman Limited Maturity Bond from 1986 to 1995.

Strategy

Like its typical peer, this offering invests across the major sectors of the taxable-bond market, usually holding a mix of Treasuries, agency bonds, mortgage-backed securities, and corporate debt. The fund will hold a handful of preferred stocks and REITs though. Further, management doesn't strictly manage the portfolio's duration (a measure of interest-rate risk) against an index, preferring to look instead to a self-selected peer group.

Historical Profile

Return Above Avg
Risk Above Avg
Rating ★★★★ Above Avg

Investment Style
Fixed Income
Income Rtn %Rank Cat

19 11 8 17 12 8 17 22 19

▼ Manager Change
∇ Partial Manager Change

Growth of $10,000
Investment Values of Fund
Investment Values of LB Aggr

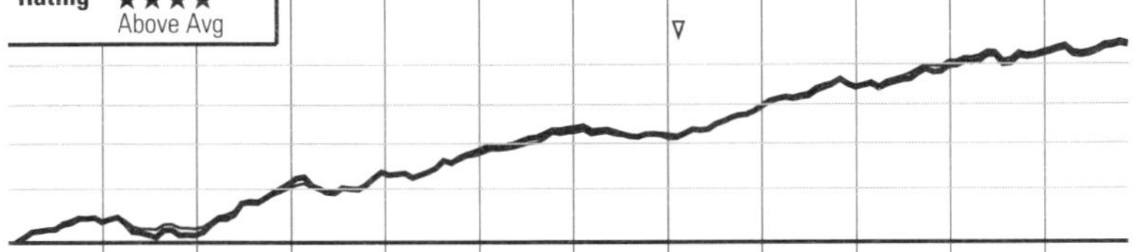

Performance Quartile (within Category)

1993	1994	1995	1996	1997	1998	1999	2000	2001	2002	2003	12-04	History
12.71	11.19	13.00	12.31	12.78	12.56	11.30	11.96	12.06	12.40	12.42	12.42	NAV
9.91	-5.22	24.47	1.33	11.05	8.75	-3.85	13.34	7.58	8.63	4.90	4.52	Total Return %
0.16	-2.30	6.00	-2.30	1.40	0.06	-3.03	1.71	-0.86	-1.62	0.80	0.18	+/-LB Aggr
-2.33	-0.71	3.04	-1.36	1.62	-1.39	-0.97	0.90	-1.24	-4.40	-1.07	-0.78	+/-LB 5-10YR
7.20	7.00	7.75	6.59	6.98	6.80	6.27	7.26	6.82	5.68	4.74	4.49	Income Return %
2.71	-12.22	16.72	-5.26	4.07	1.95	-10.12	6.08	0.76	2.95	0.16	0.03	Capital Return %
61	82	1	94	6	18	94	1	48	46	36	25	Total Rtn % Rank Cat
0.88	0.86	0.84	0.83	0.83	0.84	0.76	0.79	0.79	0.67	0.58	0.55	Income $
0.25	0.00	0.00	0.00	0.00	0.46	0.03	0.00	0.00	0.00	0.00	0.00	Capital Gains $
0.41	0.41	0.41	0.40	0.39	0.38	0.38	0.42	0.41	0.55	0.50	0.52	Expense Ratio %
7.00	6.98	7.27	6.64	6.76	6.62	6.31	6.78	6.63	5.89	4.79	4.36	Income Ratio %
45	25	31	81	58	47	54	25	43	60	61	28	Turnover Rate %
1,946	1,612	1,893	1,928	1,722	1,769	1,319	1,339	1,547	1,736	1,757	1,753	Net Assets $mil

Performance 12-31-04

	1st Qtr	2nd Qtr	3rd Qtr	4th Qtr	Total
2000	3.28	2.20	3.50	3.75	13.34
2001	3.60	1.06	4.21	-1.40	7.58
2002	-0.37	3.27	4.38	1.14	8.63
2003	1.51	3.04	-0.35	0.65	4.90
2004	2.64	-2.60	3.29	1.22	4.52

Trailing	Total Return%	+/- LB Aggr	+/- LB 5-10YR	%Rank Cat	Growth of $10,000
3 Mo	1.22	0.27	0.24	25	10,122
6 Mo	4.55	0.37	-1.02	23	10,455
1 Yr	4.52	0.18	-0.78	25	10,452
3 Yr Avg	6.00	-0.19	-2.05	29	11,910
5 Yr Avg	7.75	0.04	-1.32	14	14,524
10 Yr Avg	7.84	0.12	-0.62	9	21,272
15 Yr Avg	7.81	0.11	-0.51	20	30,895

Tax Analysis	Tax-Adj Rtn%	%Rank Cat	Tax-Cost Rat	%Rank Cat
3 Yr (estimated)	4.15	23	1.75	57
5 Yr (estimated)	5.51	11	2.08	60
10 Yr (estimated)	5.19	12	2.46	80

Potential Capital Gain Exposure: 1% of assets

Rating and Risk

Time Period	Load-Adj Return %	Morningstar Rtn vs Cat	Morningstar Risk vs Cat	Morningstar Risk-Adj Rating
1 Yr	4.52			
3 Yr	6.00	+Avg	+Avg	★★★★
5 Yr	7.75	+Avg	+Avg	★★★★
10 Yr	7.84	High	High	★★★★
Incept	9.28			

Other Measures	Standard Index LB Aggr	Best Fit Index LB 5-10YR
Alpha	-0.4	-0.1
Beta	1.04	0.70
R-Squared	95	97
Standard Deviation	4.83	
Mean	6.00	
Sharpe Ratio	0.97	

Portfolio Analysis 12-31-04

Total Fixed-Income:203	Date of Maturity	Amount $000	Value $000	% Net Assets
FNMA 5%	06-01-33	41,092	40,873	2.35
US Treasury Bond 5.25%	11-15-28	35,771	37,504	2.16
US Treasury Note 3.375%	01-15-12	32,254	36,724	2.11
US Treasury Note 4%	02-15-14	30,000	29,596	1.70
US Treasury Note 3.875%	01-15-09	26,127	29,292	1.69
Household Fin 6.375%	10-15-11	25,200	27,869	1.60
Lombardy Region 5.804%	10-25-32	25,000	26,672	1.54
Phillips Pete 8.75%	05-25-10	21,000	25,656	1.48
Landesbank Baden-Wurttem	04-01-12	20,000	22,456	1.29
GNMA 5%	08-15-33	21,878	21,932	1.26
GNMA 6%	09-15-28	20,143	20,961	1.21
Prologis Pfd		339	20,363	1.17
Citibank Ccmt 2003-A4 FR	03-20-09	20,000	20,039	1.15
Washington Mut 8.25%	04-01-10	17,000	19,911	1.15
New Jersey St Tpk Auth 4	01-01-16	20,000	19,317	1.11
Clorox 6.125%	02-01-11	17,000	18,587	1.07
Daimler Chrysler North A	06-15-10	15,000	17,357	1.00
Pan Pacific Retail Pptys	04-15-11	15,000	17,213	0.99
Chase Cc Master Tr 2002-	10-15-09	17,000	17,048	0.98
Kellogg 6.6%	04-01-11	15,000	16,825	0.97

Current Investment Style
Duration: Short Int Long
Quality: High Med Low

[1] figure provided by fund

Avg Eff Duration[1]	4.2 Yrs
Avg Eff Maturity	6.0 Yrs
Avg Credit Quality	AA
Avg Wtd Coupon	5.16%
Avg Wtd Price	104.61% of par

Coupon Range	% of Bonds	Rel Cat
0% PIK	4.8	1.2
0% to 6%	62.5	1.0
6% to 8%	31.7	1.1
8% to 10%	4.8	0.8
More than 10%	0.9	0.8

1.00=Category Average

Credit Analysis		% bonds 12-31-04	
US Govt	0	BB	0
AAA	38	B	0
AA	12	Below B	1
A	22	NR/NA	0
BBB	26		

Sector Breakdown	% of assets
US Treasuries	4
TIPS	4
US Agency	0
Mortgage Pass-Throughs	13
Mortgage CMO	1
Mortgage ARM	0
US Corporate	52
Asset-Backed	11
Convertible	1
Municipal	4
Corporate Inflation-Protected	0
Foreign Corporate	3
Foreign Govt	0

Composition			
Cash	5.6	Bonds	84.5
Stocks	1.4	Other	8.4

Special Securities	
Restricted/Illiquid Secs	9
Exotic Mortgage-Backed	0
Emerging-Markets Secs	0
Options/Futures/Warrants	No

Morningstar's Take by Dieter Bardy 10-08-04

USAA Income's many appealing traits should sit well with yield-hungry investors.

Solid returns have been the norm here. For the year-to-date period through Oct. 7, 2004, the fund has earned 2.9% compared with the average intermediate-term bond fund's gain of 2.5%. Its longer trailing returns are equally attractive.

The fund owes its success to manager Didi Weinblatt, who has managed the fund since February 2000 in a style similar to her predecessor's. She slowly adjusts the fund's portfolio based on her view of the economy. For example, as she expects interest rates to rise, Weinblatt has moved into defensive mode by buying floaters (securities with interest payments that are adjusted based on prevailing short-term market rates). She has also set the fund's duration a bit shorter than its index, the Lehman Brothers Aggregate Bond Index. It currently stands at 4.2 years, which is slightly more cautious than typical rival's 4.4 year sensitivity.

One quirk that separates this fund from its typical rivals is a stash of preferred REITs. Weinblatt likes these securities because they are senior to common stock holders and pay a healthy yield. The fund's current 8.7% stake in these names helps maintain its above average 4.4% yield. Nevertheless, these holdings have contributed to the fund's above-average volatility. For example, they were a drag on returns in April and May, but since then have been a catalyst for gains.

Last but not least, part of the fund's allure comes from its below-average expenses. Despite the fact that fees have ticked up in recent years, its 0.50% costs are almost half as large as its typical rival's.

All in all, this fund has a fair number of competitive advantages. An attractive above-average yield, below-average costs, and experienced management are key parts of its appeal.

Address:	9800 Fredericksburg Road San Antonio TX 78288-0227 800-382-8722
Web Address:	www.usaa.com
Inception:	03-04-74
Advisor:	USAA Investment Management Company
Subadvisor:	None
NTF Plans:	Dreyfus LION-NTF, Pershing NTF

Minimum Purchase:	$3000	Add: $50	IRA: $250
Min Auto Inv Plan:	$0	Add: $20	
Sales Fees:	No-load		
Management Fee:	0.24%		
Actual Fees:	Mgt:0.19%	Dist:	
Expense Projections:	3Yr:$160	5Yr:$280	10Yr:$628
Income Distrib:	Monthly		

USAA Income Stock

Ticker	Load	NAV	Yield	Total Assets	Mstar Category
USISX	None	$16.66	1.5%	$1,994 mil	Large Value

Governance and Management

Fiduciary Grade: C

Portfolio Manager(s)

Rob Soucy is a highly experienced manager from Grantham, Mayo, Van Otterloo, and Company (GMO) who took charge of this offering in July 2003. GMO is a well-regarded institutional asset management shop where Soucy and his colleagues run a number of funds with superior long-term records. GMO also subadvises (and Soucy is a comanager of) Vanguard U.S. Value, which has a short but impressive record.

Strategy

Quantitative models pick the fund's stocks. About half of the portfolio consists of stocks chosen using a dividend-discount model with a focus on profitability and retained earnings. Other models focus on stocks that are cheap relative to normalized earnings and companies with improving fundamentals and share-price trends. Soucy gives dividend-paying stocks greater weight, with the goal of producing a yield larger than the Russell 1000 Index's. Management keeps the fund's sector weightings reasonably close to those of the Russell 1000 Value Index while limiting individual holdings to 5% of assets.

Historical Profile

Return Average
Risk Below Avg
Rating ★★★ Neutral

Investment Style: Equity Stock %

82% 83% 86% 91% 92% 96% 94% 96% 98%

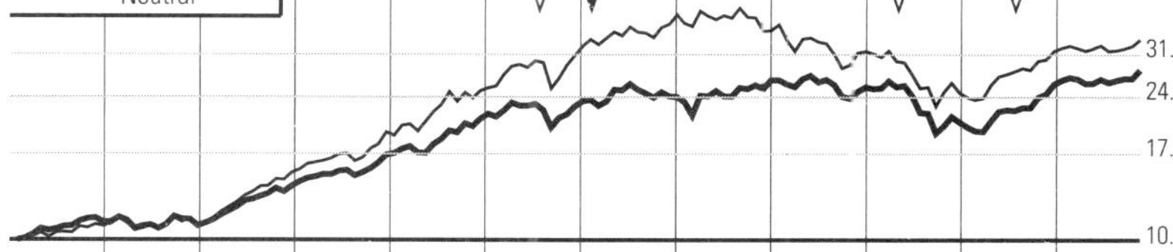

▼ Manager Change
∇ Partial Manager Change

Growth of $10,000
— Investment Values of Fund
— Investment Values of S&P 500

Performance Quartile (within Category)

History

1993	1994	1995	1996	1997	1998	1999	2000	2001	2002	2003	12-04	History
14.13	13.06	15.67	16.95	19.55	19.57	17.83	18.63	16.83	12.37	15.27	16.66	NAV
11.56	-0.70	28.62	18.70	26.99	8.10	2.46	10.83	-4.18	-19.00	25.76	12.02	Total Return %
1.50	-2.01	-8.91	-4.24	-6.36	-20.47	-18.58	19.93	7.70	3.09	-2.91	1.15	+/-S&P 500
-6.51	1.28	-9.74	-2.94	-8.19	-7.53	-4.89	3.82	1.41	-3.48	-4.27	-4.47	+/-Russ 1000 VI
5.38	5.46	6.06	5.17	4.76	3.70	2.87	3.14	2.38	1.82	2.03	1.70	Income Return %
6.18	-6.16	22.56	13.53	22.23	4.40	-0.41	7.69	-6.56	-20.82	23.73	10.32	Capital Return %
67	52	79	64	55	77	61	43	49	55	69	61	Total Rtn % Rank Cat
0.71	0.75	0.77	0.78	0.78	0.70	0.55	0.55	0.44	0.30	0.25	0.26	Income $
0.19	0.22	0.27	0.74	1.02	0.73	1.66	0.51	0.55	1.00	0.00	0.17	Capital Gains $
0.70	0.73	0.75	0.72	0.68	0.65	0.65	0.67	0.67	0.82	0.81	0.79	Expense Ratio %
5.43	5.25	5.34	4.84	4.73	3.85	3.06	2.97	2.57	2.14	2.10	1.66	Income Ratio %
27	25	35	32	35	22	34	13	18	94	142	54	Turnover Rate %
1,130	1,172	1,586	1,928	2,398	2,491	2,284	1,992	1,869	1,439	1,779	1,994	Net Assets $mil

Performance 12-31-04

	1st Qtr	2nd Qtr	3rd Qtr	4th Qtr	Total
2000	0.90	-0.35	4.52	5.45	10.83
2001	-3.96	2.87	-8.29	5.75	-4.18
2002	3.69	-8.65	-20.13	7.07	-19.00
2003	-5.63	14.09	1.37	15.24	25.76
2004	3.12	-0.14	0.47	8.26	12.02

Trailing	Total Return%	+/- S&P 500	+/- Russ 1000 VI	%Rank Cat	Growth of $10,000
3 Mo	8.26	-0.97	-2.12	74	10,826
6 Mo	8.78	1.59	-3.30	55	10,878
1 Yr	12.02	1.15	-4.47	61	11,202
3 Yr Avg	4.50	0.92	-4.07	66	11,412
5 Yr Avg	3.92	6.22	-1.35	51	12,120
10 Yr Avg	10.04	-2.03	-3.79	77	26,032
15 Yr Avg	9.50	-1.43	-2.53	72	39,013

Tax Analysis	Tax-Adj Rtn%	%Rank Cat	Tax-Cost Rat	%Rank Cat
3 Yr (estimated)	3.24	68	1.21	74
5 Yr (estimated)	2.46	54	1.40	74
10 Yr (estimated)	7.76	78	2.07	68

Potential Capital Gain Exposure: 12% of assets

Rating and Risk

Time Period	Load-Adj Return %	Morningstar Rtn vs Cat	Morningstar Risk vs Cat	Morningstar Risk-Adj Rating
1 Yr	12.02			
3 Yr	4.50	Avg	-Avg	★★★
5 Yr	3.92	Avg	-Avg	★★★
10 Yr	10.04	-Avg	-Avg	★★★
Incept	10.09			

Other Measures	Standard Index S&P 500	Best Fit Index Russ 1000 VI
Alpha	1.1	-3.4
Beta	0.90	0.94
R-Squared	89	96
Standard Deviation	14.86	
Mean	4.50	
Sharpe Ratio	0.21	

Portfolio Analysis 12-31-04

Share change since 11-04 Total Stocks:257	Sector	PE	YTD Ret%	% Assets
⊕ ExxonMobil	Energy	13.9	28.04	4.79
SBC Communications	Telecom	15.4	3.74	3.35
⊕ Verizon Communications	Telecom	32.4	20.25	3.14
⊕ Altria Group	Goods	13.3	18.38	3.12
⊕ Home Depot	Consumer	19.0	21.47	2.81
⊕ Dell	Hardware	34.0	24.01	2.59
⊕ Pfizer	Health	22.0	-22.31	2.58
⊕ Fannie Mae	Financial	9.1	-2.33	2.00
Washington Mutual	Financial	13.9	10.05	1.97
⊕ General Motors	Goods	7.2	-21.48	1.75
⊕ ChevronTexaco	Energy	7.7	25.57	1.72
BellSouth	Telecom	12.7	1.94	1.69
⊕ Merck	Health	11.4	-27.76	1.43
AT&T	Telecom	—	-0.63	1.39
Johnson & Johnson	Health	20.6	25.17	1.39
Cigna	Health	8.4	42.87	1.27
⊕ MBNA	Financial	14.0	15.53	1.23
Ford Motor	Goods	9.9	-6.00	1.21
Allstate	Financial	12.8	23.12	1.19
Eastman Kodak	Goods	—	27.90	1.17

Current Investment Style

Value Blnd Growth — Large Mid Small

Market Cap	%
Giant	39.7
Large	35.4
Mid	23.9
Small	1.0
Micro	0.0

Avg $mil: 27,583

Value Measures		Rel Category
Price/Earnings	13.72	0.91
Price/Book	2.14	0.94
Price/Sales	0.81	0.68
Price/Cash Flow	5.52	0.87
Dividend Yield %	2.28	1.12

Growth Measures	%	Rel Category
Long-Term Erngs	9.49	0.91
Book Value	6.40	1.13
Sales	2.32	0.55
Cash Flow	-2.28	NMF
Historical Erngs	7.80	0.66

Profitability	%	Rel Category
Return on Equity	18.17	1.14
Return on Assets	8.62	1.10
Net Margin	11.12	1.09

Sector Weightings	% of Stocks	Rel S&P 500	3 Year High	3 Year Low
Info	14.32	0.67		
Software	0.00	0.00	2	0
Hardware	4.14	0.41	6	3
Media	0.00	0.00	4	0
Telecom	10.18	3.23	11	4
Service	49.69	1.07		
Health	10.34	0.83	10	1
Consumer	10.97	1.21	11	2
Business	3.70	0.91	4	1
Financial	24.68	1.19	32	24
Mfg	35.99	1.12		
Goods	13.31	1.43	13	8
Ind Mtrls	5.87	0.46	21	6
Energy	10.96	1.53	16	6
Utilities	5.85	1.98	14	4

Composition

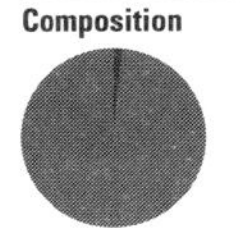

Cash	1.6
Stocks	98.4
Bonds	0.0
Other	0.0
Foreign (% of Stock)	0.0

Morningstar's Take by Christopher Davis 11-30-04

USAA Income Stock's future looks bright.

Manager Rob Soucy employs a quantitatively driven, three-pronged strategy at this offering by utilizing models that scour the Russell 1000 Index. Two attempt to identify companies trading at a large discount to their intrinsic values and with relatively low P/E ratios and the third model seeks those with attractive momentum characteristics. That approach is similar to the one he has used at other offerings, such as Fund Analyst Pick Vanguard U.S. Value and a number of funds under the banner of the fund's subadvisor, GMO. Soucy modestly tweaks his approach here to accommodate the fund's income mandate by adjusting his models to give dividend-paying stocks greater weight, with the goal of producing a yield larger than that of the Russell 1000.

The momentum piece of Soucy's strategy sets the fund apart from its large-value rivals. Momentum investing is typically the province of aggressive-growth offerings, but Soucy argues that it keeps the fund in the game when racier fare dominates, as in 2003. Meanwhile, Soucy's focus on stocks trading at low valuations has proved beneficial in more difficult environments: It helped bolster returns in the 2001 and 2002 bear market at Soucy's Vanguard charge, for instance. The added focus on dividend payers here is likely to lend added ballast in choppy markets.

While Soucy's tenure has been short, we believe he'll do just fine here. He's quite experienced, helping deliver excellent long-term results elsewhere. At Vanguard U.S. Value, for example, Soucy has topped his typical large-value rival by four percentage points annually since the fund's July 2000 inception (though its smaller-cap bent helped it in much of the period). We like this fund's prospects, though we'd note the similarly managed Vanguard offering is considerably cheaper.

Address:	9800 Fredericksburg Road San Antonio TX 78288-0227 800-382-8722
Web Address:	www.usaa.com
Inception:	05-04-87
Advisor:	USAA Investment Management Company
Subadvisor:	Grantham Mayo Van Otterloo & Co. LLC
NTF Plans:	Dreyfus LION-NTF, Pershing NTF

Minimum Purchase:	$3000	Add: $50	IRA: $250
Min Auto Inv Plan:	$0	Add: $50	
Sales Fees:	No-load		
Management Fee:	0.50%		
Actual Fees:	Mgt:0.45%	Dist:	
Expense Projections:	3Yr:$259	5Yr:$450	10Yr:$1002
Income Distrib:	Quarterly		

USAA Tax Ex Interm-Term

Analyst Pick

Ticker	Load	NAV	Yield	SEC Yield	Total Assets	Mstar Category
USATX	None	$13.34	4.3%	3.24%	$2,676 mil	Muni National Interm

Governance and Management

Fiduciary Grade: B

Portfolio Manager(s)

Cliff Gladson has been at the helm since 1993. He has also run USAA Tax Exempt Short-Term Fund for nearly as long and took charge of USAA NY Bond Fund in 1999. Gladson recently named Regina Shafer comanager in June 2003. Shafer has been a fixed-income analyst for USAA since 1995 and has run several of the firm's muni money market funds since 1999. Gladson says he's grooming Shafer as his successor.

Strategy

Manager Cliff Gladson employs an income-oriented approach, giving this fund one of the muni-national intermediate-term bond category's plumpest yields. While Gladson favors securities with healthy yields, he won't buy longer-duration or lower-quality credits unless he believes they are undervalued. In the past, he has been more adventuresome on duration and credit quality than his typical rival, but he has given the portfolio an increasingly conservative cast in recent years.

Historical Profile

Return: High
Risk: Below Avg
Rating: ★★★★★ Highest

Investment Style: Fixed Income — Income Rtn %Rank Cat: 4, 2, 2, 1, 2, 2, 3, 2, 5

▼ Manager Change
▽ Partial Manager Change

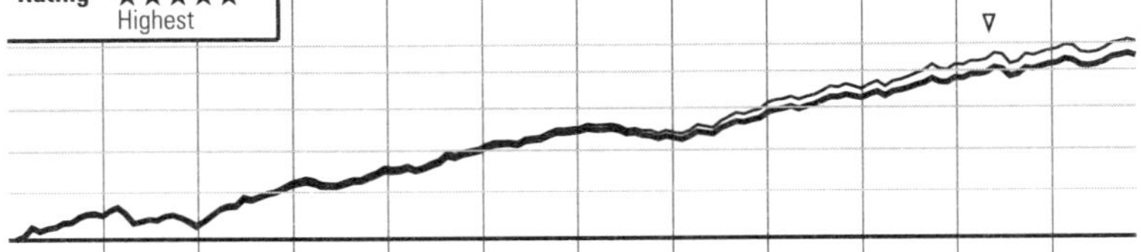

Growth of $10,000
- Investment Values of Fund
- Investment Values of LB Muni

Performance Quartile (within Category)

1993	1994	1995	1996	1997	1998	1999	2000	2001	2002	2003	12-04	History
13.26	12.02	13.08	12.92	13.38	13.50	12.47	12.97	13.00	13.33	13.38	13.34	NAV
11.47	-4.03	15.07	4.49	9.39	6.32	-2.56	9.83	5.55	7.69	5.17	4.27	Total Return %
-0.81	1.14	-2.39	0.06	0.20	-0.16	-0.50	-1.85	0.42	-1.91	-0.14	-0.21	+/-LB Muni
-1.30	0.74	-2.10	-0.05	0.15	-0.44	-1.32	-0.93	0.93	-2.48	-0.53	0.12	+/-LB Muni 10YR
5.70	5.32	6.07	5.67	5.69	5.40	5.28	5.66	5.35	5.09	4.78	4.39	Income Return %
5.77	-9.35	9.00	-1.18	3.70	0.92	-7.84	4.17	0.20	2.60	0.39	-0.12	Capital Return %
35	61	30	13	6	9	58	36	6	77	11	6	Total Rtn % Rank Cat
0.70	0.69	0.71	0.72	0.72	0.71	0.70	0.69	0.68	0.65	0.62	0.58	Income $
0.13	0.03	0.00	0.00	0.00	0.00	0.00	0.00	0.00	0.00	0.00	0.02	Capital Gains $
0.42	0.40	0.40	0.38	0.37	0.37	0.36	0.36	0.36	0.45	0.49	0.51	Expense Ratio %
5.85	5.30	5.63	5.54	5.65	5.42	5.21	5.39	5.41	5.06	4.86	4.58	Income Ratio %
74	69	72	28	23	8	12	10	9	12	15	23	Turnover Rate %
1,661	1,416	1,673	1,711	1,936	2,252	2,147	2,230	2,397	2,564	2,601	2,676	Net Assets $mil

Performance 12-31-04

	1st Qtr	2nd Qtr	3rd Qtr	4th Qtr	Total
2000	2.29	1.39	2.16	3.66	9.83
2001	2.27	0.78	2.65	-0.24	5.55
2002	0.69	2.96	3.61	0.26	7.69
2003	1.25	2.00	0.37	1.46	5.17
2004	1.39	-1.52	3.39	1.01	4.27

Trailing	Total Return%	+/- LB Muni	+/- LB Muni 10YR	%Rank Cat	Growth of $10,000
3 Mo	1.01	-0.24	0.18	17	10,101
6 Mo	4.43	-0.76	-0.57	22	10,443
1 Yr	4.27	-0.21	0.12	6	10,427
3 Yr Avg	5.70	-0.74	-0.94	25	11,809
5 Yr Avg	6.48	-0.72	-0.56	17	13,688
10 Yr Avg	6.43	-0.63	-0.65	10	18,648
15 Yr Avg	6.49	-0.50	-0.59	14	25,682

Tax Analysis	Tax-Adj Rtn%	%Rank Cat	Tax-Cost Rat	%Rank Cat
3 Yr (estimated)	5.69	13	0.01	4
5 Yr (estimated)	6.48	9	0.00	1
10 Yr (estimated)	6.43	4	0.00	1

Potential Capital Gain Exposure: 5% of assets

Rating and Risk

Time Period	Load-Adj Return %	Morningstar Rtn vs Cat	Morningstar Risk vs Cat	Morningstar Risk-Adj Rating
1 Yr	4.27			
3 Yr	5.70	High	-Avg	★★★★★
5 Yr	6.48	High	-Avg	★★★★★
10 Yr	6.43	High	Avg	★★★★★
Incept	7.97			

Other Measures	Standard Index LB Aggr	Best Fit Index LB Muni
Alpha	0.2	0.2
Beta	0.82	0.82
R-Squared	98	98
Standard Deviation	4.13	
Mean	5.70	
Sharpe Ratio	1.06	

Portfolio Analysis 12-31-04

Total Fixed-Income:513	Date of Maturity	Amount $000	Value $000	% Net Assets
New York St Urban Dev 5.	01-01-17	34,475	38,424	1.43
Brazos River Auth 5.375%	04-01-19	32,925	33,647	1.25
Puerto Rico Pub Fin 5.75	08-01-27	30,000	33,525	1.25
Washington D C Conventio	10-01-18	30,000	32,027	1.19
New York N Y 5.5%	08-01-15	26,625	29,326	1.09
Puerto Rico Hsg Bk & Fin	12-01-06	22,200	23,528	0.88
California St 5%	12-01-15	20,000	21,896	0.82
Chicago Ill O Hare Intl	01-01-07	21,235	21,672	0.81
Sales Tax Asset Receivab	10-15-23	20,000	21,314	0.79
Mississippi Hosp Equip &	12-01-15	19,850	20,910	0.78
Chicago Ill Brd Ed	12-01-13	29,925	20,769	0.77
Port Corpus Christi Tex	04-01-18	19,050	19,695	0.73
San Joaquin Hills Calif	01-01-08	16,795	19,365	0.72
Seattle Wash Mun Lt & Pw	08-01-21	19,165	19,276	0.72
Plano Tex Indpt Sch Dist	02-15-19	17,475	18,569	0.69

Current Investment Style

Duration: Short Int Long — Quality: High Med Low

[1]Avg Eff Duration	4.7 Yrs
Avg Eff Maturity	8.7 Yrs
Avg Credit Quality	AA
Avg Wtd Coupon	5.08%
Avg Wtd Price	105.43% of par

[1]figure provided by fund

Credit Analysis	% bonds 12-31-04		
US Govt	0	BB	0
AAA	45	B	0
AA	22	Below B	3
A	16	NR/NA	0
BBB	14		

Top 5 States	% bonds		
NY	19.8	IL	8.1
TX	11.8	PR	5.2
CA	9.5		

Composition			
Cash	0.4	Bonds	99.5
Stocks	0.0	Other	0.1

Special Securities	
Restricted/Illiquid Secs	0
Options/Futures/Warrants	No

Sector Weightings	% of Bonds	Rel Cat
General Obligation	22.4	0.63
Utilities	10.6	0.96
Health	13.7	1.85
Water/Waste	3.9	0.40
Housing	10.2	1.74
Education	17.6	1.26
Transportation	1.9	0.34
COP/Lease	0.8	0.51
Industrial	18.4	2.05
Misc Revenue	0.0	0.00
Demand	0.6	1.41

Morningstar's Take by Christopher Davis 01-05-05

USAA Tax-Exempt Intermediate Term Fund continues to show why we regard it as one of the elite.

This offering has continued to deliver strong results relative to its intermediate-term municipal-bond rivals. In fact, its 4% gain in 2004 topped its typical peer by 1.1 percentage points. Manager Cliff Gladson shortened the fund's duration (a measure of interest-rate sensitivity) dramatically in 2003, a stance that enabled it to hold up relatively well in early 2004, when bond investors were spooked by the prospect of rising rates. Good issue selection, though, proved a larger driver of performance. The fund's outsized stake in hospital bonds, for instance, continued to pay off nicely after boosting returns in 2003 as well.

Gladson has delivered similarly good results over the long haul. The fund's three-, five-, and 10-year marks all rank in the category's top third or better. Those returns have been consistent as well: Only once in Gladson's 11-year tenure did the fund land in its group's bottom quartile. USAA's veteran team of analysts further boosts our confidence here.

While we're confident in Gladson's abilities, we'd note that some past success was earned with the benefit of rock-bottom costs. Unfortunately, the fund's expenses have moved upward considerably in recent years. To be sure, its 0.51% expense ratio isn't excessive, but it's near the average for a no-load, intermediate-term bond offering. Consequently, the fund can no longer rely as heavily on a cost advantage to push it ahead of rivals.

All in all, we still consider this a fine choice for those seeking long-term bond exposure. But those with short time horizons may want to consider sibling USAA Tax-Exempt Short Term as an alternative. With interest rates likely to rise sooner or later, that fund's portfolio is less likely to take a short-term hit.

Address:	9800 Fredericksburg Road San Antonio TX 78288-0227 800-382-8722
Web Address:	www.usaa.com
Inception:	03-19-82
Advisor:	USAA Investment Management Company
Subadvisor:	None
NTF Plans:	Dreyfus LION-NTF, Pershing NTF

Minimum Purchase:	$3000	Add: $50	IRA: $0
Min Auto Inv Plan:	$0	Add: —	
Sales Fees:	No-load		
Management Fee:	0.28%		
Actual Fees:	—	Dist:	
Expense Projections:	3Yr:$164	5Yr:$285	10Yr:$640
Income Distrib:	Monthly		

USAA Tax Ex Long-Term

Ticker	Load	NAV	Yield	SEC Yield	Total Assets	Mstar Category
USTEX	None	$14.18	4.5%	3.49%	$2,282 mil	Muni National Long

Governance and Management

Fiduciary Grade: B

Portfolio Manager(s)

Bob Pariseau took the reins in November 1999. He has also run USAA California Bond and USAA Virginia Bond since 1995. Pariseau and colleague Cliff Gladson lead a team of three veteran muni-bond analysts. Pariseau keeps more than one third of his assets invested in this and other USAA funds.

Strategy

Even though manager Bob Pariseau has tempered the fund's income focus, he still isn't afraid to make some relatively bold moves to boost yield. He has brought the fund's credit profile more closely in line with the category average, but he still takes on a bit more credit risk than his typical peer. Though he sticks with investment-grade debt, Pariseau often finds bargains in issues rated A and BBB.

Historical Profile

Return High
Risk Average
Rating ★★★★★ Highest

Investment Style: Fixed Income — Income Rtn %Rank Cat: 3, 5, 2, 2, 3, 6, 12, 14, 17

▼ Manager Change
▽ Partial Manager Change

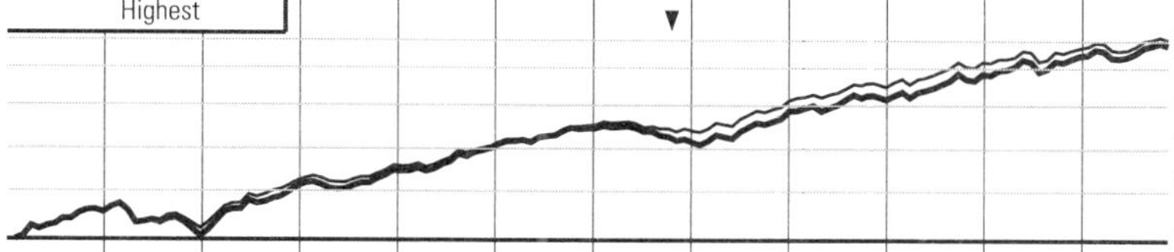

Growth of $10,000
— Investment Values of Fund
— Investment Values of LB Muni

Performance Quartile (within Category)

1993	1994	1995	1996	1997	1998	1999	2000	2001	2002	2003	12-04	History
14.18	12.22	13.63	13.42	13.99	14.04	12.60	13.33	13.18	13.76	14.05	14.18	NAV
12.51	-7.93	18.58	4.47	10.38	5.97	-5.00	12.11	4.33	9.70	7.02	5.60	Total Return %
0.23	-2.76	1.12	0.04	1.19	-0.51	-2.94	0.43	-0.80	0.10	1.71	1.12	+/-LB Muni
-1.87	-0.59	-2.39	0.01	-0.46	-0.85	-0.32	-3.13	-0.54	-0.33	0.69	-0.96	+/-LB Muni 20YR
6.30	5.64	6.77	5.94	5.96	5.62	5.58	6.06	5.53	5.20	4.84	4.61	Income Return %
6.21	-13.57	11.81	-1.47	4.42	0.35	-10.58	6.05	-1.20	4.50	2.18	0.99	Capital Return %
56	76	23	16	10	22	60	27	27	18	5	4	Total Rtn % Rank Cat
0.84	0.78	0.80	0.79	0.78	0.77	0.76	0.74	0.72	0.67	0.65	0.63	Income $
0.56	0.09	0.00	0.00	0.00	0.00	0.00	0.00	0.00	0.00	0.00	0.00	Capital Gains $
0.39	0.38	0.38	0.37	0.37	0.36	0.36	0.36	0.36	0.45	0.54	0.56	Expense Ratio %
6.35	5.69	6.23	5.99	5.95	5.65	5.44	5.77	5.72	5.25	4.90	4.63	Income Ratio %
88	109	163	53	41	35	30	29	47	40	29	23	Turnover Rate %
2,014	1,661	1,910	1,873	2,002	2,173	1,910	2,071	2,075	2,229	2,238	2,282	Net Assets $mil

Performance 12-31-04

	1st Qtr	2nd Qtr	3rd Qtr	4th Qtr	Total
2000	2.71	1.34	2.55	5.03	12.11
2001	2.00	0.24	2.60	-0.54	4.33
2002	0.73	3.59	5.30	-0.16	9.70
2003	1.71	2.78	0.33	2.04	7.02
2004	1.70	-2.05	4.31	1.64	5.60

Trailing	Total Return%	+/- LB Muni	+/- LB Muni 20YR	%Rank Cat	Growth of $10,000
3 Mo	1.64	0.39	-0.34	14	10,164
6 Mo	6.01	0.82	-0.74	6	10,601
1 Yr	5.60	1.12	-0.96	4	10,560
3 Yr Avg	7.43	0.99	-0.20	2	12,399
5 Yr Avg	7.72	0.52	-0.82	4	14,504
10 Yr Avg	7.16	0.10	-0.79	5	19,968
15 Yr Avg	6.82	-0.17	-0.83	15	26,902

Tax Analysis	Tax-Adj Rtn%	%Rank Cat	Tax-Cost Rat	%Rank Cat
3 Yr (estimated)	7.43	2	0.00	1
5 Yr (estimated)	7.72	3	0.00	1
10 Yr (estimated)	7.16	3	0.00	1

Potential Capital Gain Exposure: 8% of assets

Rating and Risk

Time Period	Load-Adj Return %	Morningstar Rtn vs Cat	Morningstar Risk vs Cat	Morningstar Risk-Adj Rating
1 Yr	5.60			
3 Yr	7.43	High	Avg	★★★★★
5 Yr	7.72	High	Avg	★★★★★
10 Yr	7.16	High	Avg	★★★★★
Incept	8.90			

Other Measures	Standard Index LB Aggr	Best Fit Index LB Muni 20YR
Alpha	0.7	-0.1
Beta	1.06	0.98
R-Squared	98	98

Standard Deviation	5.45
Mean	7.43
Sharpe Ratio	1.13

Portfolio Analysis 12-31-04

Total Fixed-Income:233	Date of Maturity	Amount $000	Value $000	% Net Assets
Mashantucket Western Peq	09-01-27	64,950	66,937	2.96
Michigan St Hosp Fin Aut	11-15-26	43,000	49,897	2.21
Regl Transn Auth 6.5%	07-01-30	37,550	48,364	2.14
District Columbia 5.5%	06-01-29	37,580	40,689	1.80
St Paul Minn Hsg & Redev	11-01-17	39,675	40,026	1.77
South Carolina Jobs-Econ	11-15-26	30,000	31,983	1.41
New Jersey St Tpk Auth 5	01-01-27	30,020	31,619	1.40
Maine St Tpk Auth 5.75%	07-01-28	27,750	31,079	1.37
Regl Transn Auth 5.75%	06-01-20	23,980	28,605	1.26
Texas St Vets Ld 3rd Vet	08-01-35	24,280	25,794	1.14
New York St Dorm Auth 6%	08-15-16	21,500	25,289	1.12
Bell Cnty Tex Health Fac	07-01-19	19,500	24,194	1.07
Clark Cnty Nev 5.5%	07-01-25	21,000	22,833	1.01
Univ Tex Perm Univ 5.25%	07-01-19	19,985	21,885	0.97
New Jersey Econ Dev Auth	07-01-31	20,000	21,348	0.94

Current Investment Style

Duration: Short Int Long — Quality: High Med Low

[1]Avg Eff Duration	5.5 Yrs
Avg Eff Maturity	15.3 Yrs
Avg Credit Quality	AA
Avg Wtd Coupon	5.47%
Avg Wtd Price	108.84% of par

[1]figure provided by fund

Credit Analysis	% bonds 12-31-04		
US Govt	0	BB	0
AAA	50	B	0
AA	13	Below B	4
A	15	NR/NA	0
BBB	13		

Top 5 States	% bonds		
NY	18.7	CA	4.8
TX	16.8	NJ	4.3
IL	8.6		

Composition			
Cash	0.0	Bonds	100.0
Stocks	0.0	Other	0.0

Special Securities	
Restricted/Illiquid Secs	Trace
Options/Futures/Warrants	No

Sector Weightings	% of Bonds	Rel Cat
General Obligation	35.1	1.34
Utilities	2.8	0.21
Health	17.1	2.17
Water/Waste	8.7	0.79
Housing	0.9	0.12
Education	15.6	1.35
Transportation	6.4	0.85
COP/Lease	0.6	0.27
Industrial	12.8	0.99
Misc Revenue	0.0	0.00
Demand	0.0	0.00

Morningstar's Take by Christopher Davis 12-15-04

USAA Tax-Exempt Long-Term continues to show why it's a fine choice.

This offering is on pace to close the year with an impressive lead over its long-term municipal-bond rivals. Indeed, its 5.5% gain for the year to date through Dec. 14, 2004, places it ahead of 97% of its peers. Manager Bob Pariseau shortened the fund's duration (a measure of interest-rate sensitivity) dramatically in 2003, a stance that enabled it to hold up relatively well in early 2004, when bond investors were spooked by the prospect of rising rates. Good issue selection, though, has been the biggest driver of performance. The fund's outsized stake in hospital bonds, for instance, has continued to pay off nicely.

Peer-beating performance is nothing new for Pariseau. All of the fund's long-term returns land in the category's top decile. Performance has also been consistently good: The fund has landed in its group's top third or higher in each of the five calendar years Pariseau has been at the helm. He's also delivered fine results at his longer-tenured charges, such as USAA California Bond and USAA Virginia Bond. USAA's veteran team of analysts further boosts our confidence here.

While we're confident in Pariseau's abilities, we'd note that some past success was earned with the benefit of rock-bottom costs. However, the fund's costs have risen considerably in recent years. True, its 0.56% expense ratio isn't excessive, but it's closer to the average for a no-load long-term muni-bond offering. As such, the fund can no longer rely as heavily on a cost advantage to push it ahead of rivals.

All told, though, we still think this is a worthwhile choice for long-term investors. But those with shorter time horizons may want to consider sibling USAA Tax-Exempt Intermediate Term as an alternative. Interest rates are bound to rise sooner or later, and that fund is likely to take less of a short-term hit.

Address:	9800 Fredericksburg Road San Antonio TX 78288-0227 800-382-8722
Web Address:	www.usaa.com
Inception:	03-19-82
Advisor:	USAA Investment Management Company
Subadvisor:	None
NTF Plans:	Dreyfus LION-NTF, Pershing NTF

Minimum Purchase:	$3000	Add: $50	IRA: $0
Min Auto Inv Plan:	$0	Add: —	
Sales Fees:	No-load		
Management Fee:	0.28%		
Actual Fees:	Mgt:0.28%	Dist:	
Expense Projections:	3Yr:$179	5Yr:$313	10Yr:$701
Income Distrib:	Monthly		

USAA Tax Ex Short-Term

Analyst Pick

Ticker	Load	NAV	Yield	SEC Yield	Total Assets	Mstar Category
USSTX	None	$10.76	2.5%	2.08%	$1,319 mil	Muni National Short

Governance and Management

Fiduciary Grade: B

Portfolio Manager(s)

Clifford Gladson has a good record at this fund and at USAA Tax Exempt Intermediate-Term. Gladson named Regina Shafer comanager in June 2003. Shafer has been a fixed-income analyst for USAA since 1995 and has run several of the firm's muni money market funds since 1999. Gladson says he's grooming Shafer as his successor. Three veteran analysts assist, and fellow muni manager Bob Pariseau completes the team.

Strategy

Less is more at this fund. Manager Clifford Gladson maintains a short and steady duration and keeps trading to a minimum. Gladson eschews explicit interest-rate bets and searches for income instead. He looks for the most income he can find for the duration risk, often in lower-rated investment-grade bonds.

Historical Profile

Return Above Avg
Risk Average
Rating ★★★★ Above Avg

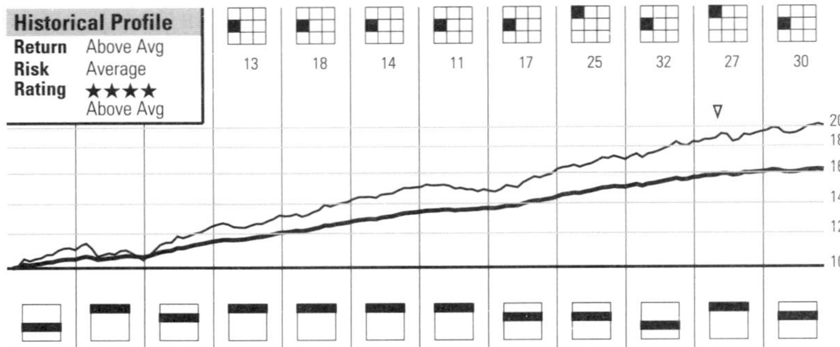

Investment Style
Fixed Income
Income Rtn %Rank Cat

▼ Manager Change
▽ Partial Manager Change

Growth of $10,000
▬ Investment Values of Fund
— Investment Values of LB Muni

Performance Quartile (within Category)

1993	1994	1995	1996	1997	1998	1999	2000	2001	2002	2003	12-04	History
10.70	10.33	10.65	10.62	10.74	10.77	10.47	10.60	10.69	10.85	10.87	10.76	NAV
5.52	0.82	8.11	4.43	5.85	5.02	1.78	6.03	5.10	4.97	2.97	1.52	Total Return %
-6.76	5.99	-9.35	0.00	-3.34	-1.46	3.84	-5.65	-0.03	-4.63	-2.34	-2.96	+/-LB Muni
-0.70	0.14	-0.76	-0.01	0.37	-0.19	-0.18	-0.20	-1.49	-1.75	0.29	-0.26	+/-LB Muni 3YR
4.47	4.34	4.96	4.70	4.69	4.73	4.63	4.74	4.25	3.45	2.79	2.54	Income Return %
1.05	-3.52	3.15	-0.27	1.16	0.29	-2.85	1.29	0.85	1.52	0.18	-1.02	Capital Return %
71	16	34	16	23	18	16	40	36	56	24	30	Total Rtn % Rank Cat
0.46	0.46	0.50	0.49	0.49	0.50	0.49	0.49	0.44	0.36	0.30	0.27	Income $
0.00	0.00	0.00	0.00	0.00	0.00	0.00	0.00	0.00	0.00	0.00	0.00	Capital Gains $
0.43	0.43	0.42	0.42	0.41	0.39	0.38	0.38	0.38	0.46	0.54	0.56	Expense Ratio %
4.75	4.25	4.50	4.73	4.60	4.57	4.55	4.48	4.60	3.90	3.25	2.60	Income Ratio %
138	102	103	36	28	8	7	19	19	20	14	22	Turnover Rate %
955	811	777	786	937	1,005	988	1,003	1,122	1,226	1,367	1,319	Net Assets $mil

Performance 12-31-04

	1st Qtr	2nd Qtr	3rd Qtr	4th Qtr	Total
2000	1.05	1.30	1.64	1.92	6.03
2001	1.96	1.10	1.74	0.21	5.10
2002	0.51	1.97	1.95	0.45	4.97
2003	0.93	1.09	0.47	0.45	2.97
2004	0.70	-0.85	1.28	0.40	1.51

Trailing	Total Return%	+/- LB Muni	+/- LB Muni 3YR	%Rank Cat	Growth of $10,000
3 Mo	0.40	-0.85	0.21	21	10,040
6 Mo	1.68	-3.51	-0.42	50	10,168
1 Yr	1.52	-2.96	-0.26	30	10,152
3 Yr Avg	3.14	-3.30	-0.57	44	10,972
5 Yr Avg	4.10	-3.10	-0.68	46	12,225
10 Yr Avg	4.56	-2.50	-0.41	29	15,619
15 Yr Avg	4.76	-2.23	—	58	20,088

Tax Analysis	Tax-Adj Rtn%	%Rank Cat	Tax-Cost Rat	%Rank Cat
3 Yr (estimated)	3.14	35	0.00	1
5 Yr (estimated)	4.10	40	0.00	1
10 Yr (estimated)	4.56	22	0.00	1

Potential Capital Gain Exposure: 1% of assets

Rating and Risk

Time Period	Load-Adj Return %	Morningstar Rtn vs Cat	Morningstar Risk vs Cat	Morningstar Risk-Adj Rating
1 Yr	1.52			
3 Yr	3.14	Avg	Avg	★★★
5 Yr	4.10	Avg	Avg	★★★
10 Yr	4.56	+Avg	Avg	★★★★
Incept	5.63			

Other Measures	Standard Index LB Aggr	Best Fit Index LB Muni 3YR
Alpha	0.0	0.2
Beta	0.35	0.68
R-Squared	92	92

Standard Deviation	1.76
Mean	3.14
Sharpe Ratio	1.01

Portfolio Analysis 12-31-04

Total Fixed-Income:238	Date of Maturity	Amount $000	Value $000	% Net Assets
Albuquerque N Mex Edl Fa	10-15-16	22,865	22,865	1.74
Converse Cnty Wyo Pollut	07-01-06	22,485	22,485	1.71
Texas St Pub Fin Auth 5%	12-15-08	20,000	21,817	1.66
Muskogee Okla Indl Tr Po	06-01-27	21,600	21,600	1.64
Amer Falls Idaho Reservo	02-01-25	19,885	19,885	1.51
Long Island Pwr Auth	06-01-06	20,360	19,717	1.50
Hillsborough Cnty Fla In	05-15-18	19,390	19,605	1.49
Ohio St Air Quality Dev	09-01-30	18,000	18,000	1.37
Chicago Ill Brd Ed	12-01-09	20,000	17,110	1.30
Texas St Tpk Auth 5%	06-01-08	15,000	16,192	1.23
Louisiana Pub Facs Auth	09-01-28	16,000	16,000	1.22
Farmington N Mex Pollutn	04-01-33	16,000	15,862	1.21
Brazos Riv Tex Hbr Nav D	05-15-33	15,000	15,598	1.19
New York N Y City Indl D	05-01-29	15,000	15,000	1.14
Lincoln Cnty Wyo Pollutn	01-01-06	15,000	14,773	1.12

Current Investment Style

Duration: Short Int Long — Quality: High Mod Low

[1]Avg Eff Duration	1.6 Yrs
Avg Eff Maturity	1.8 Yrs
Avg Credit Quality	A
Avg Wtd Coupon	3.35%
Avg Wtd Price	101.60% of par

[1]figure provided by fund

Credit Analysis	% bonds 12-31-04		
US Govt	0	BB	0
AAA	22	B	0
AA	36	Below B	2
A	17	NR/NA	0
BBB	23		

Top 5 States	% bonds		
NY	13.6	OH	5.4
TX	13.6	CA	5.0
LA	5.7		

Composition			
Cash	9.0	Bonds	91.0
Stocks	0.0	Other	0.0

Special Securities	
Restricted/Illiquid Secs	0
Options/Futures/Warrants	No

Sector Weightings	% of Bonds	Rel Cat
General Obligation	27.3	0.78
Utilities	7.8	0.84
Health	9.6	1.32
Water/Waste	3.0	0.29
Housing	3.1	0.42
Education	6.5	0.75
Transportation	2.2	0.51
COP/Lease	3.1	1.96
Industrial	37.1	2.45
Misc Revenue	0.0	—
Demand	0.2	0.27

Morningstar's Take by Christopher Davis 01-07-05

We still like USAA Tax Exempt Short-Term, but climbing costs threaten to dim its appeal.

Predicting the precise timing of interest-rate shifts is difficult to get right. But few investors dispute that interest rates are likely to rise in the near future. An improving economy and a less-accommodative Federal reserve should eventually push rates upward, sending bond prices down. To protect this fund from that scenario, manager Cliff Gladson has aggressively shortened its duration (a measure of interest-rate sensitivity) in recent years. It stands at just 1.6 years, considerably less than the typical short-term municipal-bond fund.

That cautious stance enabled the fund to hold up better than its rivals when interest rates spiked in March and April 2004, contributing to its 3% gain in 2004, a top-quartile showing in the category. A slug of strong-performing midgrade bonds, such as its hospital-related issues, also helped push the fund into its group's top quartile for the year. The fund's interest-rate posture and midgrade bond stake also boosted returns in 2003.

Admittedly, Gladson hasn't executed his strategy perfectly. In 2002, Gladson's move to shorten the fund's duration proved premature, as interest rates continued to slide. The fund also takes more credit risk than its typical rival, an approach that can backfire at times, as in 2002. As a result, the fund posted middling relative returns for the year.

All told, though, Gladson has turned in solid results over time here. He has also proved his worth at his longtime charge, USAA Tax Exempt Intermediate-Term. That said, the fund's biggest competitive advantage--low costs--has evaporated in recent years. Its expense ratio climbed from 0.38% in 2001 to 0.56% in 2003, about average for a no-load short-term muni fund. Skilled management makes this fund a good choice, but higher costs make it less likely it will be a great one.

Address:	9800 Fredericksburg Road San Antonio TX 78288-0227 800-382-8722
Web Address:	www.usaa.com
Inception:	03-19-82
Advisor:	USAA Investment Management Company
Subadvisor:	None
NTF Plans:	Dreyfus LION-NTF, Pershing NTF

Minimum Purchase:	$3000	Add: $50	IRA: $0
Min Auto Inv Plan:	$0	Add: —	
Sales Fees:	No-load		
Management Fee:	0.28%		
Actual Fees:	Mgt:0.28%	Dist:	
Expense Projections:	3Yr:$179	5Yr:$313	10Yr:$701
Income Distrib:	Monthly		

Van Kampen Comstock A

Ticker	Load	NAV	Yield	Total Assets	Mstar Category
ACSTX	5.75%	$18.51	1.2%	$14,490 mil	Large Value

Governance and Management

Fiduciary Grade: D

Portfolio Manager(s)

Robert Baker has been at the helm since July 1994. He's assisted by two comanagers: Jason Leder since 1995 and Kevin Holt since 1999.

Strategy

Robert Baker likes to take advantage of troubled situations. To this end, he employs a bottom-up contrarian approach and uses varied valuation criteria for stock selection to dive headfirst into extremely beaten-down issues. The fund typically has a huge overweighting in utilities stocks and a sizable one in energy fare. Baker keeps about 115 names in the portfolio and caps top holdings at 5% of assets.

Historical Profile

Return Above Avg
Risk Above Avg
Rating ★★★★ Above Avg

Investment Style: Equity Stock %

97%	89%	92%	91%	89%	83%	95%	92%	94%

▼ Manager Change ∇ Partial Manager Change

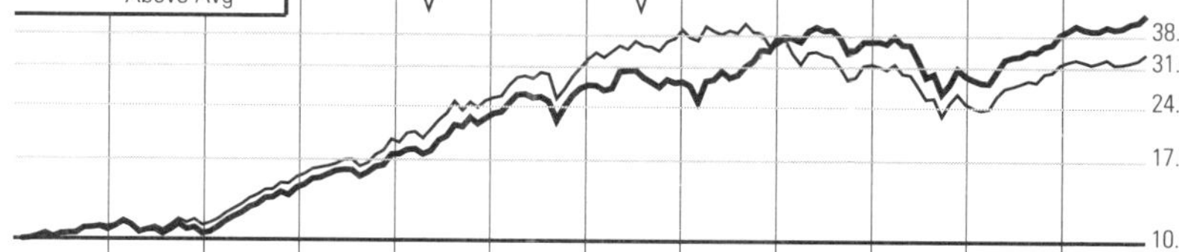

Growth of $10,000
— Investment Values of Fund
— Investment Values of S&P 500

Performance Quartile (within Category)

1993	1994	1995	1996	1997	1998	1999	2000	2001	2002	2003	12-04	History
16.39	12.40	14.54	14.78	16.20	16.39	14.80	17.23	15.68	12.34	15.95	18.51	NAV
9.09	-3.67	36.15	22.34	29.92	20.12	2.38	31.91	-1.79	-19.59	30.98	17.57	Total Return %
-0.97	-4.98	-1.38	-0.60	-3.43	-8.45	-18.66	41.01	10.09	2.50	2.31	6.70	+/-S&P 500
-8.98	-1.69	-2.21	0.70	-5.26	4.49	-4.97	24.90	3.80	-4.07	0.95	1.08	+/-Russ 1000 VI
1.75	2.00	2.23	1.81	1.74	1.80	1.81	2.19	1.34	1.09	1.50	1.39	Income Return %
7.34	-5.67	33.92	20.53	28.18	18.32	0.57	29.72	-3.13	-20.68	29.48	16.18	Capital Return %
84	81	23	23	26	7	62	2	37	60	27	10	Total Rtn % Rank Cat
0.30	0.32	0.27	0.26	0.25	0.28	0.29	0.31	0.23	0.17	0.18	0.22	Income $
2.12	3.05	1.96	2.59	2.57	2.67	1.65	1.65	1.00	0.14	0.00	0.00	Capital Gains $
0.96	1.01	0.96	1.00	0.94	0.91	0.89	0.93	0.87	0.89	0.90	—	Expense Ratio %
1.82	1.93	1.82	1.71	1.71	1.59	1.73	2.10	1.30	1.33	1.40	—	Income Ratio %
50	136	151	176	114	102	72	89	62	52	40	—	Turnover Rate %
981	872	1,078	1,241	1,532	1,756	1,797	2,509	3,797	4,195	6,734	10,592	Net Assets $mil

Performance 12-31-04

	1st Qtr	2nd Qtr	3rd Qtr	4th Qtr	Total
2000	0.44	2.12	11.47	15.36	31.91
2001	-1.70	7.51	-13.50	7.44	-1.79
2002	3.49	-13.96	-19.33	11.95	-19.59
2003	-4.53	18.45	3.44	11.97	30.98
2004	3.43	1.57	2.27	9.43	17.57

Trailing	Total Return%	+/- S&P 500	+/- Russ 1000 VI	%Rank Cat	Growth of $10,000
3 Mo	9.43	0.20	-0.95	42	10,943
6 Mo	11.91	4.72	-0.17	11	11,191
1 Yr	17.57	6.70	1.08	10	11,757
3 Yr Avg	7.38	3.80	-1.19	26	12,381
5 Yr Avg	9.91	12.21	4.64	6	16,039
10 Yr Avg	15.62	3.55	1.79	3	42,690
15 Yr Avg	12.81	1.88	0.78	6	60,984

Tax Analysis	Tax-Adj Rtn%	%Rank Cat	Tax-Cost Rat	%Rank Cat
3 Yr (estimated)	4.70	50	0.55	37
5 Yr (estimated)	6.98	15	1.51	79
10 Yr (estimated)	11.19	11	3.26	96

Potential Capital Gain Exposure: 15% of assets

Rating and Risk

Time Period	Load-Adj Return %	Morningstar Rtn vs Cat	Morningstar Risk vs Cat	Morningstar Risk-Adj Rating
1 Yr	10.81			
3 Yr	5.28	Avg	+Avg	★★★
5 Yr	8.62	+Avg	+Avg	★★★★
10 Yr	14.94	High	+Avg	★★★★★
Incept	12.17			

Other Measures	Standard Index S&P 500	Best Fit Index Russ 1000 VI
Alpha	3.8	-1.4
Beta	1.06	1.08
R-Squared	91	93
Standard Deviation	17.97	
Mean	7.38	
Sharpe Ratio	0.34	

Portfolio Analysis 09-30-04

Share change since 02-04 Total Stocks:94	Sector	PE	YTD Ret%	% Assets
⊕ Sprint	Telecom	—	55.24	4.83
⊕ Halliburton	Energy	47.7	53.28	4.26
⊕ Freddie Mac	Financial	10.6	28.75	3.74
⊕ International Paper	Ind Mtrls	—	-0.20	3.57
⊕ Verizon Communications	Telecom	32.4	20.25	3.50
⊕ GlaxoSmithKline PLC ADR	Health	18.3	5.55	3.45
⊕ SBC Communications	Telecom	15.4	3.74	3.02
⊕ Bristol-Myers Squibb	Health	17.7	-7.27	2.96
⊕ Georgia-Pacific Group	Ind Mtrls	14.4	24.12	2.54
⊕ Dow Chemical	Ind Mtrls	16.6	22.83	2.49
⊕ Bank of America	Financial	12.3	21.50	2.39
⊕ Kimberly-Clark	Goods	17.8	16.12	2.14
⊕ Citigroup	Financial	15.3	2.72	2.04
⊕ Wells Fargo	Financial	15.5	8.97	1.99
⊖ Schlumberger	Energy	40.7	23.84	1.90
⊕ Alcoa	Ind Mtrls	18.8	-15.75	1.84
⊕ DuPont De Nemours E.I.	Ind Mtrls	22.3	10.42	1.70
⊖ TXU	Utilities	NMF	177.67	1.62
⊕ Clear Channel Communicat	Media	23.5	-27.57	1.57
⊕ Altria Group	Goods	13.3	18.38	1.37

Current Investment Style

Value Blnd Growth — Large Mid Small

Market Cap	%
Giant	41.5
Large	49.0
Mid	8.9
Small	0.6
Micro	0.0
Avg $mil:	32,474

Value Measures		Rel Category
Price/Earnings	15.55	1.03
Price/Book	2.07	0.91
Price/Sales	1.05	0.88
Price/Cash Flow	5.70	0.89
Dividend Yield %	2.27	1.11

Growth Measures	%	Rel Category
Long-Term Erngs	10.59	1.02
Book Value	1.72	0.30
Sales	3.41	0.81
Cash Flow	4.30	0.82
Historical Erngs	13.12	1.11

Profitability	%	Rel Category
Return on Equity	14.21	0.90
Return on Assets	5.74	0.73
Net Margin	7.77	0.76

Sector Weightings	% of Stocks	Rel S&P 500	3 Year High	Low
Info	20.14	0.94		
Software	0.47	0.11	[illegible]	0
Hardware	3.07	0.30	14	3
Media	4.53	1.18	5	1
Telecom	12.07	3.83	12	4
Service	38.21	0.82		
Health	12.08	0.97	14	6
Consumer	4.08	0.45	12	4
Business	0.85	0.21	3	1
Financial	21.20	1.02	22	16
Mfg	41.65	1.30		
Goods	8.17	0.88	8	4
Ind Mtrls	13.63	1.08	14	5
Energy	13.92	1.94	18	13
Utilities	5.93	2.00	12	4

Composition

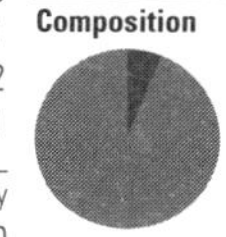

Cash	5.9
Stocks	94.1
Bonds	0.0
Other	0.0
Foreign (% of Stock)	11.1

Morningstar's Take by Terence Geenty 12-27-04

Van Kampen Comstock Fund is a solid offering for long-term investors.

This fund's experienced management team, led by Robert Baker, sticks to a simple strategy: It buys the stocks of out-of-favor companies that are in difficult business situations and holds them until the business environment improves. This often leads the fund to invest in cyclical fare like industrial-material stocks when they are experiencing periods of low demand. This long-term perspective keeps the fund's annual turnover rate near 50%--a two-year holding period--which is well below the category average of about 80%.

This process heightens the fund's short-term volatility, however. That's because picks can take time to turn around and management is happy to add to positions if prices fall. For example, the fund initiated a position in Halliburton when the oil-service industry was experiencing weak demand, then added to its position when the stock subsequently sunk due to fear about potential asbestos liabilities. Moreover, the fund carries sizable sector bets, which can also increase volatility. As of Sept. 30, 2004, for example, the fund's telecom stake was nearly three times the large-value category norm's.

Still, such conviction drives returns here. An overweight position in telecom and energy stocks, for example, is largely behind the fund's 15.6% year-to-date gain through December 17. Returns over longer periods have been equally impressive--the fund's five- and 10-year returns rank in the group's top decile. Plus, management's willingness to break with convention makes this portfolio less correlated with the S&P 500 than the typical large-value offering.

This fund may struggle over shorter periods, but it remains a good option for investors who are setting money aside for a long-term goal. Its modest expense ratio adds to this fund's overall appeal.

Address:	1221 Avenue of Americas New York NY 10020 800-421-5666
Web Address:	
Inception:	10-07-68
Advisor:	Van Kampen Asset Management, Inc.
Subadvisor:	None
NTF Plans:	Federated Tr NTF, Fidelity Instl-NTF

Minimum Purchase:	$1000	Add: $25	IRA: $500
Min Auto Inv Plan:	$25	Add: $25	
Sales Fees:	5.75%L, 0.25%S		
Management Fee:	0.50% mx./0.35% mn.		
Actual Fees:	Mgt:0.40%	Dist:0.24%	
Expense Projections:	3Yr:$837	5Yr:$1029	10Yr:$1586
Income Distrib:	Quarterly		

Van Kampen Eq and Inc A

Ticker	Load	NAV	Yield	Total Assets	Mstar Category
ACEIX	5.75%	$8.62	2.1%	$12,419 mil	Moderate Allocation

Governance and Management

Fiduciary Grade: D

Portfolio Manager(s)

Lead manager James Gilligan has been at the helm since January 1990. James Roeder, Vincent Vizachero, and Tom Bastian joined him as comanagers in May 1999, April 2002, and May 2003, respectively. Comanager Paul O'Brien has overseen the straight bond portion of the fund since March 2002. Although Van Kampen and parent firm Morgan Stanley have suffered from portfolio-manager turnover, we don't think that's a concern here: Gilligan is too valued to be allowed to leave.

Strategy

This fund usually devotes 55% to 65% of assets to stocks, 25% to 35% to convertible and straight bonds, and 5% to 10% to cash. (Weightings will vary, depending on manager Jim Gilligan's assessment of relative valuation and earnings momentum.) The fixed-income portion serves to provide stability and current income; dramatic credit and interest-rate bets aren't part of the strategy. Management prefers convertibles, when reasonably priced, to straight debt. The stock portion of the fund is devoted primarily to temporarily out-of-favor firms with strong cash flows.

Historical Profile

Return Above Avg
Risk Average
Rating ★★★★ Above Avg

Investment Style: Equity Stock %: 68% 64% 60% 62% 60% 57% 57% 63% 64%

▼ Manager Change
▽ Partial Manager Change

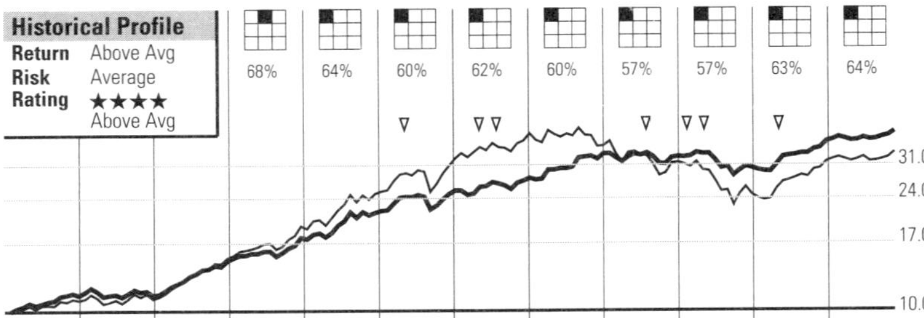

Performance Quartile (within Category)

1993	1994	1995	1996	1997	1998	1999	2000	2001	2002	2003	12-04	History
5.55	5.16	6.31	6.74	7.24	7.82	7.64	8.07	7.46	6.62	7.90	8.62	NAV
16.00	-1.98	32.60	15.55	24.13	16.99	9.95	20.19	-2.23	-8.32	22.16	11.77	Total Return %
5.94	-3.29	-4.93	-7.39	-9.22	-11.58	-11.09	29.29	9.65	13.77	-6.51	0.90	+/-S&P 500
4.27	-0.03	7.83	4.21	4.93	4.60	-2.90	15.75	-2.39	2.22	-1.90	0.60	+/-DJ 60%
3.32	3.40	3.69	2.51	2.55	2.46	2.38	2.70	2.56	2.29	2.56	2.34	Income Return %
12.68	-5.38	28.91	13.04	21.58	14.53	7.57	17.49	-4.79	-10.61	19.60	9.43	Capital Return %
13	43	7	36	15	29	57	2	24	19	30	13	Total Rtn % Rank Cat
0.17	0.19	0.19	0.16	0.17	0.18	0.18	0.20	0.20	0.17	0.17	0.18	Income $
0.23	0.10	0.32	0.37	0.92	0.45	0.74	0.86	0.21	0.07	0.00	0.01	Capital Gains $
1.06	1.02	0.95	0.97	0.86	0.85	0.82	0.82	0.82	0.82	0.83	—	Expense Ratio %
3.33	3.60	3.43	2.50	2.09	2.31	2.43	2.62	2.60	2.34	2.18	—	Income Ratio %
101	92	92	99	86	61	81	85	92	53	49	—	Turnover Rate %
187	240	357	472	638	819	1,068	1,636	2,261	2,833	5,192	7,741	Net Assets $mil

Performance 12-31-04

	1st Qtr	2nd Qtr	3rd Qtr	4th Qtr	Total
2000	6.47	1.07	9.15	2.33	20.19
2001	-5.76	4.94	-6.15	5.34	-2.23
2002	3.20	-5.52	-11.22	5.91	-8.32
2003	-2.70	12.83	1.69	9.42	22.16
2004	2.05	0.65	0.77	7.98	11.77

Trailing	Total Return%	+/- S&P 500	+/- DJ 60%	%Rank Cat	Growth of $10,000
3 Mo	7.98	-1.25	0.50	22	10,798
6 Mo	8.81	1.62	1.28	12	10,881
1 Yr	11.77	0.90	0.60	13	11,177
3 Yr Avg	7.77	4.19	0.51	9	12,517
5 Yr Avg	8.03	10.33	2.79	5	14,714
10 Yr Avg	13.66	1.59	3.17	3	35,981
15 Yr Avg	12.00	1.07	2.05	5	54,736

Tax Analysis	Tax-Adj Rtn%	%Rank Cat	Tax-Cost Rat	%Rank Cat
3 Yr (estimated)	4.71	30	0.91	63
5 Yr (estimated)	5.16	7	1.49	73
10 Yr (estimated)	10.45	7	2.25	81

Potential Capital Gain Exposure: 14% of assets

Rating and Risk

Time Period	Load-Adj Return %	Morningstar Rtn vs Cat	Morningstar Risk vs Cat	Morningstar Risk-Adj Rating
1 Yr	5.34			
3 Yr	5.67	+Avg	Avg	★★★★
5 Yr	6.75	+Avg	Avg	★★★★
10 Yr	12.99	High	Avg	★★★★★
Incept	11.04			

Other Measures	Standard Index S&P 500	Best Fit Index Russ 1000 VI
Alpha	4.7	1.6
Beta	0.60	0.62
R-Squared	87	94
Standard Deviation	10.24	
Mean	7.77	
Sharpe Ratio	0.63	

Morningstar's Take by Todd Trubey 12-01-04

Despite the shortcomings of its parent firm, this fund's manager makes it a fine option.

Van Kampen Equity & Income's poor Fiduciary Grade should make it clear that we don't think highly of Van Kampen's governance practices. For example, in the past, Van Kampen has failed to close popular offerings, such as Van Kampen Emerging Growth, before they grew too large. Also, the firm would not disclose to Morningstar the nature of management's incentives, such as the structure of fund manager compensation and the significance of each manager's investment in the funds he or she oversees.

Nevertheless, a case can certainly be made for owning this fund, due to the experience, disciplined strategy, and superb record of Jim Gilligan, the lead manager since 1990. The bulk of this fund's assets--typically 55% to 65%--are invested in equities, and the remainder in convertible bonds, straight bonds, and cash. He doesn't maintain constant weightings, but rather shifts asset classes opportunistically. For instance, in the bear market he let stocks fall from 62% of assets in early 2000 to 52% in September 2002. Then he started increasing the stock weighting, believing that earnings were finally more likely to improve--just as stocks bottomed out.

Gilligan has shown a discerning eye for stocks, too: He typically opts for firms in out-of-favor industries, but he will also buy firms in pricey sectors if they boast improving earnings and relatively cheap prices. For example, Gilligan held a 20% stake in tech names such as software maker Oracle when that sector rallied furiously in 1999. However, early in 2000, as tech shares peaked, he began selling them in favor of beaten-down fare, particularly financial-services names, which proved to be a boon that year. Thus, this fund's long-term returns land in the moderate-allocation category's top decile, and its volatility has been modest.

For those willing to look past Van Kampen's lapses, this offering is a good choice.

Portfolio Analysis 09-30-04

Total Stocks:73 Share change since 02-29-04	Sectors	P/E Ratio	YTD Return %	% Net Assets
⊕ BP PLC ADR	Energy	20.7	-2.40	2.19
⊕ J P Morgan Chase	Financial	19.4	-1.99	2.14
⊕ Bristol-Myers Squibb	Health	17.7	-2.90	2.13
⊕ Schlumberger	Energy	40.7	-5.20	1.95
⊕ Time Warner	Media	27.5	-3.91	1.65
⊕ Bayer AG ADR	Ind Mtrls	—	-7.86	1.59
⊕ ExxonMobil	Energy	13.9	-2.75	1.49
⊖ Chubb	Financial	12.9	-0.36	1.48
⊕ Honda Motor ADR	Goods	12.2	-0.04	1.41

Total Fixed-Income:207	Date of Maturity	Amount $000	Value $000	% Net Assets
US Treasury Note 1.875%	01-31-06	292,000	290,358	2.64
US Treasury Note 3.875%	02-15-13	193,800	192,649	1.75
US Treasury Note 4.75%	11-15-08	114,000	120,876	1.10
US Treasury Note 6.5%	02-15-10	55,000	63,125	0.57
Halliburton Cv 3.125%	07-15-23	50,000	57,188	0.52
US Treasury Note 3.5%	11-15-06	55,000	55,982	0.51
Nortel Networks Cv 4.25%	09-01-08	57,236	55,519	0.51
US Treasury Bond 8.125%	08-15-21	39,000	54,100	0.49
El Paso Cv	02-28-21	100,000	51,500	0.47

Equity Style
Style: Value
Size: Large-Cap

Value Measures		Rel Category
Price/Earnings	15.30	0.92
Price/Book	2.08	0.85
Price/Sales	1.20	0.91
Price/Cash Flow	6.00	0.83
Dividend Yield %	1.91	1.22

Growth Measures	%	Rel Category
Long-Term Erngs	10.72	0.92
Book Value	2.27	0.40
Sales	4.60	0.89
Cash Flow	8.88	1.11
Historical Erngs	14.71	1.36

Market Cap %			
Giant	43.1	Small	0.0
Large	50.6	Micro	0.0
Mid	6.3	Avg $mil:	35,787

Fixed-Income Style
Duration: Interm-Term
Quality: High

Avg Eff Duration [1]	4.8 Yrs
Avg Eff Maturity	3.6 Yrs
Avg Credit Quality	AAA
Avg Wtd Coupon	4.52%

[1]figure provided by fund as of 09-30-04

Sector Weightings	% of Stocks	Rel S&P 500	3 Year High	3 Year Low
Info	14.76	0.69		
Software	1.93	0.45	3	1
Hardware	2.20	0.22	5	0
Media	5.91	1.54	6	1
Telecom	4.72	1.50	6	2
Service	45.40	0.98		
Health	11.31	0.90	13	9
Consumer	4.93	0.54	7	5
Business	8.29	2.05	9	5
Financial	20.87	1.01	27	21
Mfg	39.85	1.24		
Goods	8.47	0.91	10	5
Ind Mtrls	12.74	1.01	17	11
Energy	14.02	1.96	17	10
Utilities	4.62	1.56	6	2

Composition

Cash	5.1
Stocks	64.4
Bonds	17.7
Other	12.8
Foreign (% of Stock)	15.2

Address:	1221 Avenue of Americas, New York NY 10020, 800-421-5666
Web Address:	
Inception:	08-03-60
Advisor:	Van Kampen Asset Management, Inc.
Subadvisor:	None
NTF Plans:	Federated Tr NTF, Fidelity Instl-NTF

Minimum Purchase:	$1000	Add: $25	IRA: $500
Min Auto Inv Plan:	$25	Add: $25	
Sales Fees:	5.75%L, 0.25%S		
Management Fee:	0.50% mx./0.35% mn.		
Actual Fees:	Mgt:0.36%	Dist:0.25%	
Expense Projections:	3Yr:$825	5Yr:$1009	10Yr:$1541
Income Distrib:	Quarterly		

Van Kampen Glob Val Eq A

Ticker	Load	NAV	Yield	Total Assets	Mstar Category
MGEAX	5.75%	$11.62	0.0%	$344 mil	World Stock

Governance and Management

Fiduciary Grade: C

Portfolio Manager(s)

Frances Campion has run an identical fund, Morgan Stanley Institutional Global Value, since its 1992 inception. Campion has four comanagers: Paul Boyne, Emilio Alvarez, Martin Moorman, and Doug McGraw. The London-based quintet has 21 analysts and managers to call on for support.

Strategy

The managers look for stocks trading at low P/E ratios with good franchises, healthy balance sheets, and strong management teams. As a result, the portfolio's price multiples are typically below those of its world-stock peers. The management team is willing to make significant sector and regional bets in its search for bargains. To deter market-timers, Van Kampen imposes a 2% redemption fee on all A shares redeemed within 60 days of purchase.

Historical Profile

Return Average
Risk Below Avg
Rating ★★★ Neutral

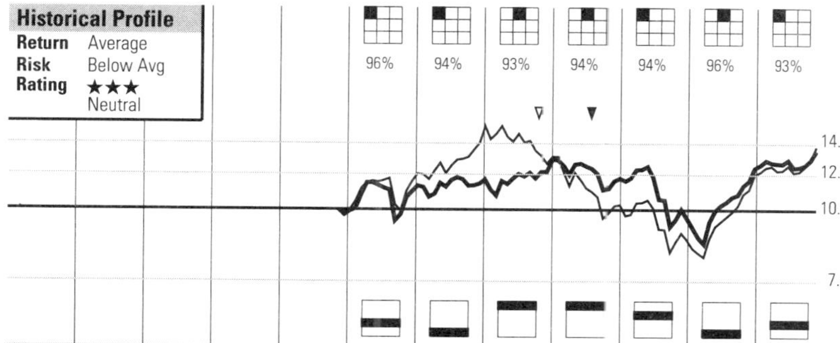

Investment Style
Equity
Stock %

▼ Manager Change
∇ Partial Manager Change

Growth of $10,000
— Investment Values of Fund
— Investment Values of MSCI EAFE

Performance Quartile (within Category)

1993	1994	1995	1996	1997	1998	1999	2000	2001	2002	2003	12-04	History
—	—	—	—	9.91	11.14	10.81	10.93	9.84	8.06	10.28	11.62	NAV
—	—	—	—	-0.74*	13.49	3.32	10.60	-9.04	-18.09	28.80	13.04	Total Return %
—	—	—	—	—	-6.44	-23.71	24.79	12.38	-2.15	-9.79	-7.21	+/-MSCI EAFE
—	—	—	—	—	-10.83	-21.63	23.79	7.76	1.80	-4.31	-1.68	+/-MSCI World
—	—	—	—	0.00	0.91	0.00	0.00	0.90	0.00	1.20	0.00	Income Return %
—	—	—	—	—	12.58	3.32	10.60	-9.94	-18.09	27.60	13.04	Capital Return %
—	—	—	—	—	53	97	8	20	38	76	68	Total Rtn % Rank Cat
—	—	—	—	0.02	0.09	0.00	0.00	0.10	0.00	0.10	0.00	Income $
—	—	—	—	0.00	0.01	0.68	0.98	0.00	0.00	0.00	0.00	Capital Gains $
—	—	—	—	—	1.70	1.65	1.66	1.64	1.60	1.67	1.64	Expense Ratio %
—	—	—	—	—	0.88	0.44	0.53	0.60	0.26	0.88	0.66	Income Ratio %
—	—	—	—	—	—	40	47	33	34	24	43	Turnover Rate %
—	—	—	—	55	77	67	72	59	49	56	94	Net Assets $mil

Performance 12-31-04

	1st Qtr	2nd Qtr	3rd Qtr	4th Qtr	Total
2000	-0.83	3.64	-2.16	9.98	10.60
2001	-7.32	4.24	-11.17	5.99	-9.04
2002	4.47	-3.70	-21.82	4.13	-18.09
2003	-11.79	20.96	5.47	14.45	28.80
2004	2.72	1.33	-2.43	11.30	13.04

Trailing	Total Return%	+/- MSCI EAFE	+/- MSCI World	%Rank Cat	Growth of $10,000
3 Mo	11.30	-4.02	-0.64	74	11,130
6 Mo	8.60	-6.40	-2.22	79	10,860
1 Yr	13.04	-7.21	-1.68	68	11,304
3 Yr Avg	6.04	-5.85	-0.91	61	11,924
5 Yr Avg	3.71	4.84	6.16	16	11,998
10 Yr Avg	—	—	—	—	—
15 Yr Avg	—	—	—	—	—

Tax Analysis	Tax-Adj Rtn%	%Rank Cat	Tax-Cost Rat	%Rank Cat
3 Yr (estimated)	3.85	71	0.12	17
5 Yr (estimated)	1.92	21	0.56	39
10 Yr (estimated)	—	—	—	—

Potential Capital Gain Exposure: 9% of assets

Rating and Risk

Time Period	Load-Adj Return %	Morningstar Rtn vs Cat	Morningstar Risk vs Cat	Morningstar Risk-Adj Rating
1 Yr	6.54			
3 Yr	3.97	-Avg	Avg	★★
5 Yr	2.49	+Avg	-Avg	★★★★
10 Yr	—	—	—	—
Incept	3.89			

Other Measures	Standard Index S&P 500	Best Fit Index MSCI EAFE
Alpha	-5.0	-5.0
Beta	0.97	0.97
R-Squared	93	93
Standard Deviation	16.82	
Mean	6.04	
Sharpe Ratio	0.28	

Portfolio Analysis 09-30-04

Share change since 02-04 Total Stocks:92	Sector	Country	% Assets
⊕ GlaxoSmithKline	Health	U.K.	2.58
⊕ Reed Elsevier	Media	U.K.	2.27
⊕ Royal Dutch Petroleum AD	Energy	Netherlands	2.02
⊕ Wyeth	Health	United States	2.01
⊕ Altria Group	Goods	United States	1.94
⊕ IBM	Hardware	United States	1.93
☼ Citigroup	Financial	United States	1.90
⊕ Nestle	Goods	Switzerland	1.83
⊕ Royal Bank Of Scotland G	Financial	U.K.	1.80
⊖ Eni	Energy	Italy	1.75
⊕ Vodafone Grp	Telecom	U.K.	1.70
⊕ Boeing	Ind Mtrls	United States	1.58
⊕ Northrop Grumman	Ind Mtrls	United States	1.56
⊕ Takeda Pharma	Health	Japan	1.55
⊕ Verizon Communications	Telecom	United States	1.52
⊖ Cadbury Schweppes	Goods	U.K.	1.50
☼ Sanofi-Synthelabo	Health	France	1.42
⊕ TOTAL	Energy	France	1.41
⊖ Allied Domecq	Goods	U.K.	1.37
⊕ Pfizer	Health	United States	1.31

Current Investment Style

Value Blnd Growth / Large Mid Small

Market Cap	%
Giant	55.3
Large	38.7
Mid	5.3
Small	0.8
Micro	0.0
Avg $mil: 32,941	

Value Measures		Rel Category
Price/Earnings	13.98	0.89
Price/Book	2.15	0.97
Price/Sales	1.20	1.03
Price/Cash Flow	5.98	0.94
Dividend Yield %	2.44	1.30

Growth Measures	%	Rel Category
Long-Term Erngs	8.73	0.73
Book Value	3.30	1.49
Sales	2.57	0.61
Cash Flow	9.31	1.59
Historical Erngs	5.14	0.60

Composition

Cash	5.5	Bonds	0.0
Stocks	93.5	Other	1.0
Foreign (% of Stock)			59.5

Sector Weightings	% of Stocks	Rel MSCI EAFE	3 Year High	Low
Info	16.89	1.02		
Software	0.00	0.00	0	0
Hardware	3.83	1.05	8	4
Media	4.48	1.96	5	3
Telecom	8.58	0.89	9	5
Service	39.29	0.88		
Health	13.91	1.92	14	8
Consumer	4.45	0.88	8	4
Business	3.08	0.57	4	3
Financial	17.85	0.66	24	18
Mfg	43.81	1.13		
Goods	18.41	1.35	2[illegible]	16
Ind Mtrls	15.70	1.28	2[illegible]	15
Energy	7.27	0.99	7	3
Utilities	2.43	0.45	3	0

Regional Exposure	% Stock		
UK/W. Europe	45	N. America	40
Japan	11	Latn America	0
Asia X Japan	3	Other	1

Country Exposure	% Stock		
United States	40	France	6
U.K.	22	Switzerland	6
Japan	11		

Morningstar's Take by William Samuel Rocco 01-03-05

Despite its subpar results of late, we're keen on Van Kampen Global Value Equity's long-term prospects.

This fund returned about two percentage points less than the group norm in 2004. And it lagged in 2003's rally. Thus, despite posting relatively limited losses in 2002, the fund has earned unexceptional three-year returns.

These uninspiring results should be evaluated in light of market conditions the past few years and certain aspects of the fund's reserved value style. Large-cap stocks have lagged smaller-cap names by a sizable margin in recent years, and emerging-markets issues have been hot for some time. But Frances Campion and her team focus on giant caps and pay very limited attention to emerging-markets opportunities as they pursue cheap stocks with good franchises. The fund, in fact, normally has one of the heftiest average market caps and one of the smallest developing-nations stakes in the category.

Meanwhile, Campion and her team have earned stong long-term results with their value discipline at their other charge, Morgan Stanley Institutional Global Value. Indeed, thanks to several top-quartile showings in the 1990s and very early 2000s, that fund has posted a 12% annualized gain since opening in mid-1992, whereas the typical world-stock offering has earned an 8% annualized gain during that period. And that fund has kept volatility well under control, due to the value orientation, issue diversification, and conservative market-cap and geographic biases of the team's discipline.

In short, the success Campion and her team have earned at their other offering makes us optimistic about this fund's future.

Address:	1221 Avenue of the Americas New York NY 10020 800-421-5666
Web Address:	www.vankampen.com
Inception:	10-24-97 *
Advisor:	Van Kampen Asset Management, Inc.
Subadvisor:	Morgan Stanley Investment Mgt Inc.
NTF Plans:	Federated Tr NTF, Fidelity Instl-NTF

Minimum Purchase:	$1000	Add: $25	IRA: $500
Min Auto Inv Plan:	$25	Add: $25	
Sales Fees:	5.75%L, 0.25%S, 2.00%R		
Management Fee:	1.00% mx./0.90% mn., 0.25%A		
Actual Fees:	Mgt:1.00%	Dist:0.25%	
Expense Projections:	3Yr:$1065	5Yr:$1420	10Yr:$2417
Income Distrib:	Annually		

Van Kampen Growth & IncA

Ticker	Load	NAV	Yield	Total Assets	Mstar Category
ACGIX	5.75%	$20.19	1.1%	$7,172 mil	Large Value

Governance and Management

Fiduciary Grade: D

Portfolio Manager(s)

James Gilligan is the constant at this fund; he has been at the helm since 1990. James Roeder, Vincent Vizachero, and Tom Bastian joined him as comanagers in May 1999, April 2002, and May 2003, respectively. This group also manages Van Kampen Equity & Income and Morgan Stanley Balanced Growth. While Van Kampen and parent firm Morgan Stanley have suffered from portfolio manager turnover, we don't think that's a concern here: Gilligan is too valuable to be allowed to leave.

Strategy

Lead manager James Gilligan looks for beaten-down companies with a catalyst for change. He is willing to hold on to his winners, and the fund has several positions with lofty valuations. He's also willing to make significant sector bets. The portfolio usually contains between 80 and 100 names.

Historical Profile

Return Average
Risk Below Avg
Rating ★★★★ Above Avg

Investment Style: Equity Stock %

84% | 87% | 87% | 90% | 86% | 91% | 92% | 95% | 95%

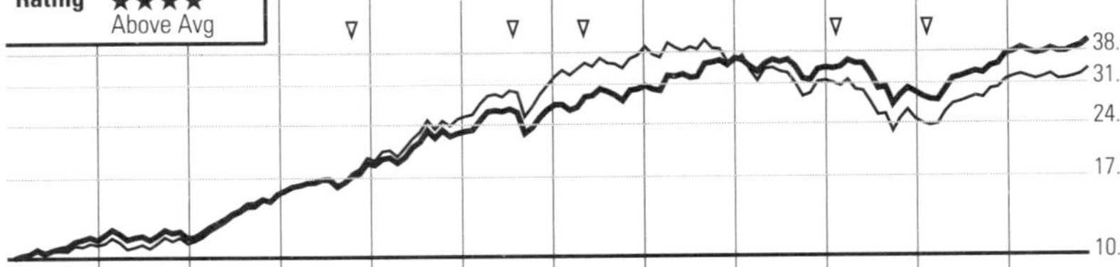

Performance Quartile (within Category)

History

1993	1994	1995	1996	1997	1998	1999	2000	2001	2002	2003	12-04	History
13.00	11.37	14.21	15.39	16.62	18.33	17.74	18.73	17.01	14.29	18.04	20.19	NAV
16.33	-1.66	35.67	18.05	24.49	18.44	12.70	19.02	-6.06	-14.71	27.57	13.94	Total Return %
6.27	-2.97	-1.86	-4.89	-8.86	-10.13	-8.34	28.12	5.82	7.38	-1.10	3.07	+/-S&P 500
-1.74	0.32	-2.69	-3.59	-10.69	2.81	5.35	12.01	-0.47	0.81	-2.46	-2.55	+/-Russ 1000 VI
2.14	2.31	2.40	1.70	1.50	1.20	1.04	1.13	1.09	1.05	1.17	1.28	Income Return %
14.19	-3.97	33.27	16.35	22.99	17.24	11.66	17.89	-7.15	-15.76	26.40	12.66	Capital Return %
34	65	25	71	78	11	18	13	64	23	52	35	Total Rtn % Rank Cat
0.27	0.29	0.27	0.24	0.23	0.20	0.19	0.20	0.20	0.18	0.17	0.23	Income $
1.57	1.13	0.90	1.09	2.25	1.11	2.63	2.12	0.37	0.07	0.00	0.11	Capital Gains $
1.16	1.16	1.15	1.04	0.94	0.92	0.88	0.88	0.82	0.85	0.86	—	Expense Ratio %
2.15	2.25	2.24	1.68	1.33	1.13	1.11	1.23	1.29	1.05	1.24	—	Income Ratio %
134	102	108	110	94	76	93	97	115	66	61	—	Turnover Rate %
213	205	399	580	778	929	1,018	1,365	1,744	2,071	3,647	5,728	Net Assets $mil

Performance 12-31-04

	1st Qtr	2nd Qtr	3rd Qtr	4th Qtr	Total
2000	6.53	-1.29	10.12	2.78	19.02
2001	-8.33	6.24	-10.06	7.25	-6.06
2002	4.64	-8.49	-17.70	8.21	-14.71
2003	-4.99	16.19	2.37	12.89	27.57
2004	1.76	1.47	0.31	10.01	13.94

Trailing	Total Return%	+/- S&P 500	+/- Russ 1000 VI	%Rank Cat	Growth of $10,000
3 Mo	10.01	0.78	-0.37	29	11,001
6 Mo	10.35	3.16	-1.73	29	11,035
1 Yr	13.94	3.07	-2.55	35	11,394
3 Yr Avg	7.43	3.85	-1.14	25	12,399
5 Yr Avg	6.75	9.05	1.48	23	13,862
10 Yr Avg	13.94	1.87	0.11	9	36,878
15 Yr Avg	12.31	1.38	0.28	10	57,053

Tax Analysis	Tax-Adj Rtn%	%Rank Cat	Tax-Cost Rat	%Rank Cat
3 Yr (estimated)	4.84	48	0.47	32
5 Yr (estimated)	4.48	32	0.96	51
10 Yr (estimated)	11.04	14	1.97	63

Potential Capital Gain Exposure: 17% of assets

Rating and Risk

Time Period	Load-Adj Return %	Morningstar Rtn vs Cat	Morningstar Risk vs Cat	Morningstar Risk-Adj Rating
1 Yr	7.39			
3 Yr	5.33	Avg	-Avg	★★★
5 Yr	5.49	Avg	-Avg	★★★★
10 Yr	13.27	+Avg	-Avg	★★★★
Incept	9.90			

Other Measures	Standard Index S&P 500	Best Fit Index Russ 1000 VI
Alpha	4.0	-0.5
Beta	0.88	0.91
R-Squared	91	96

Standard Deviation	14.77
Mean	7.43
Sharpe Ratio	0.41

Portfolio Analysis 09-30-04

Share change since 02-04 Total Stocks:73	Sector	PE	YTD Ret%	% Assets
⊕ BP PLC ADR	Energy	20.7	22.07	3.27
⊕ J P Morgan Chase	Financial	19.4	9.97	3.20
⊕ Bristol-Myers Squibb	Health	17.7	-7.27	3.17
⊕ Schlumberger	Energy	40.7	23.84	2.83
⊕ Time Warner	Media	27.5	8.12	2.40
⊕ Bayer AG ADR	Ind Mtrls	—	17.55	2.36
⊕ ExxonMobil	Energy	13.9	28.04	2.21
⊖ Chubb	Financial	12.9	15.43	2.21
⊕ Honda Motor ADR	Goods	12.2	16.92	2.05
⊕ Citigroup	Financial	15.3	2.72	2.03
⊕ Royal Dutch Petroleum AD	Energy	—	14.31	2.03
⊕ Norfolk Southern	Business	—	55.12	1.98
⊕ ConocoPhillips	Energy	9.0	35.60	1.98
⊕ Lehman Brothers Holdings	Financial	11.7	14.22	1.97
⊕ Kimberly-Clark	Goods	17.8	16.12	1.93
⊕ Schering-Plough	Health	—	21.56	1.90
⊕ Roche Holding AG ADR	Health	41.8	16.45	1.89
⊕ Merrill Lynch & Company	Financial	12.6	3.12	1.76
⊕ Walt Disney	Media	24.3	20.21	1.71
⊕ Bausch & Lomb	Health	22.2	25.26	1.63

Current Investment Style

Value Blnd Growth; Large Mid Small

Market Cap	%
Giant	43.1
Large	50.5
Mid	6.3
Small	0.0
Micro	0.0
Avg $mil: 35,895	

Value Measures		Rel Category
Price/Earnings	15.28	1.02
Price/Book	2.08	0.92
Price/Sales	1.20	1.01
Price/Cash Flow	5.99	0.94
Dividend Yield %	1.92	0.94

Growth Measures	%	Rel Category
Long-Term Erngs	10.71	1.03
Book Value	2.28	0.40
Sales	4.58	1.09
Cash Flow	8.86	1.70
Historical Erngs	14.74	1.24

Profitability	%	Rel Category
Return on Equity	13.34	0.84
Return on Assets	5.93	0.76
Net Margin	7.89	0.77

Sector Weightings	% of Stocks	Rel S&P 500	3 Year High	3 Year Low
Info	14.73	0.69		
Software	1.94	0.45	3	2
Hardware	2.22	0.22	5	0
Media	5.84	1.52	6	1
Telecom	4.73	1.50	6	2
Service	45.41	0.98		
Health	11.33	0.91	13	8
Consumer	4.88	0.54	7	5
Business	8.21	2.03	10	5
Financial	20.99	1.01	26	21
Mfg	39.87	1.24		
Goods	8.46	0.91	9	5
Ind Mtrls	12.75	1.01	16	12
Energy	14.02	1.96	18	10
Utilities	4.64	1.57	6	2

Composition

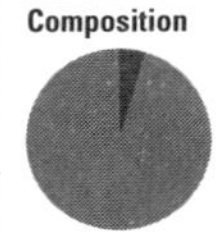

Cash	4.7
Stocks	95.3
Bonds	0.0
Other	0.0
Foreign (% of Stock)	15.2

Morningstar's Take by Todd Trubey 12-01-04

Van Kampen Growth & Income's charms outweigh our dim opinion of its advisor.

This fund's poor Fiduciary Grade should make it clear that we don't think highly of Van Kampen's governance practices. In the past, Van Kampen has failed to close popular offerings, such as Van Kampen Emerging Growth, before they grew too large. Also, the firm would not disclose to Morningstar the nature of its management incentives--including the structure of fund manager compensation and the significance of each manager's investment in shares of the funds they oversee.

Despite our concerns, this offering earns our endorsement due to its manager's proven record and its consistently executed strategy. Jim Gilligan, who has run the fund since its 1990 inception, believes that most industries are cyclical. In other words, all areas of the market suffer through poor earnings cycles and fall out of favor. So he and his team look in downtrodden industries to find top firms that have internal or external catalysts that will boost profits when the cycle picks up.

This approach means that although he is a value investor, Gilligan will buy firms in pricey sectors if they boast improving earnings and relatively cheap prices. This fund's price multiples are typically a bit higher than those of its large-value peers. For example, Gilligan held a 20% stake in tech names, such as software maker Oracle, when that sector rallied furiously in 1999. However, as tech shares peaked in early 2000, he began selling them in favor of beaten-down fare, particularly financial-services names such as insurer Allstate. As a result, the fund finished in the category's top quintile both years. All told, the fund boasts an outstanding risk/reward profile, topping 90% of its peers over Gilligan's 14-year tenure with below-average volatility.

For investors willing to overlook Van Kampen's less-than-shareholder-friendly ways, this fund is still a worthy holding.

Address:	1221 Avenue of Americas New York NY 10020 800-421-5666
Web Address:	www.vankampen.com
Inception:	08-01-46
Advisor:	Van Kampen Asset Management, Inc.
Subadvisor:	None
NTF Plans:	Federated Tr NTF, Fidelity Instl-NTF

Minimum Purchase:	$1000	Add: $25	IRA: $500
Min Auto Inv Plan:	$25	Add: $25	
Sales Fees:	5.75%L, 0.25%S		
Management Fee:	0.50% mx./0.35% mn.		
Actual Fees:	Mgt:0.38%	Dist:0.25%	
Expense Projections:	3Yr:$840	5Yr:$1035	10Yr:$1597
Income Distrib:	Quarterly		

Vanguard 500 Index

Analyst Pick

Ticker	Load	NAV	Yield	Total Assets	Mstar Category
VFINX	None	$111.64	1.8%	$106,579 mil	Large Blend

Governance and Management

Fiduciary Grade: B

Portfolio Manager(s)

Gus Sauter has run index money for more than a decade and is as good as anyone in the business at adding value at the margins.

Strategy

The core of the fund's strategy is simple: Gus Sauter buys and holds the stocks that compose the S&P 500 Index. Sauter attempts to add value on the margins by opportunistically buying futures contracts, among other techniques, and he actively tries to reduce trading costs.

Historical Profile

Return Above Avg
Risk Average
Rating ★★★★ Above Avg

Investment Style: Equity Stock %

100%	99%	98%	99%	99%	98%	99%	99%	100%

▼ Manager Change
∇ Partial Manager Change

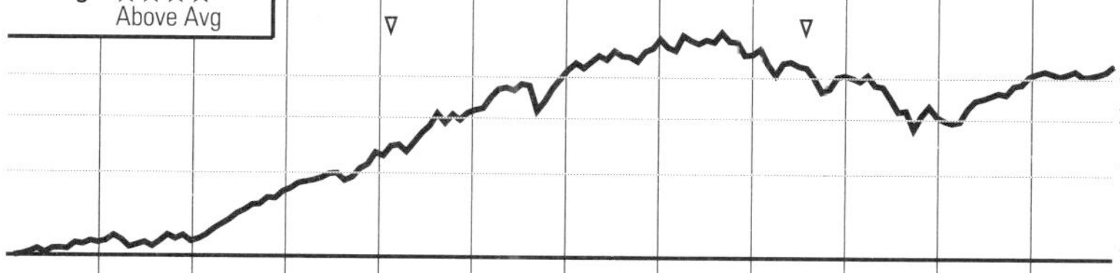

Growth of $10,000
— Investment Values of Fund
— Investment Values of S&P 500

Performance Quartile (within Category)

1993	1994	1995	1996	1997	1998	1999	2000	2001	2002	2003	12-04	History
43.83	42.97	57.60	69.17	90.07	113.95	135.33	121.86	105.89	81.15	102.67	111.64	NAV
9.89	1.18	37.45	22.88	33.19	28.62	21.07	-9.06	-12.02	-22.15	28.50	10.74	Total Return %
-0.17	-0.13	-0.08	-0.06	-0.16	0.05	0.03	0.04	-0.14	-0.06	-0.17	-0.13	+/-S&P 500
-0.29	0.79	-0.32	0.43	0.34	1.60	0.16	-1.27	0.43	-0.50	-1.39	-0.66	+/-Russ 1000
2.79	2.70	2.86	2.24	1.92	1.49	1.25	0.96	1.05	1.29	1.77	1.91	Income Return %
7.10	-1.52	34.59	20.64	31.27	27.13	19.82	-10.02	-13.07	-23.44	26.73	8.83	Capital Return %
52	23	13	29	14	16	38	64	46	45	29	36	Total Rtn % Rank Cat
1.13	1.17	1.22	1.28	1.32	1.33	1.41	1.30	1.28	1.36	1.43	1.95	Income $
0.03	0.20	0.13	0.25	0.59	0.42	1.00	0.00	0.00	0.00	0.00	0.00	Capital Gains $
0.19	0.19	0.20	0.20	0.19	0.18	0.18	0.18	0.18	0.18	0.18	—	Expense Ratio %
2.65	2.72	2.38	2.04	1.66	1.35	1.13	0.98	1.14	1.43	1.61	—	Income Ratio %
6	6	4	5	5	6	6	9	4	7	2	—	Turnover Rate %
8,273	9,356	17,372	30,332	49,358	74,229	104,652	88,240	73,151	56,224	75,342	84,167	Net Assets $mil

Performance 12-31-04

	1st Qtr	2nd Qtr	3rd Qtr	4th Qtr	Total
2000	2.25	-2.62	-0.93	-7.81	-9.06
2001	-11.90	5.82	-14.72	10.65	-12.02
2002	0.24	-13.43	-17.22	8.39	-22.15
2003	-3.19	15.39	2.60	12.12	28.50
2004	1.66	1.68	-1.91	9.21	10.74

Trailing	Total Return%	+/- S&P 500	+/- Russ 1000	%Rank Cat	Growth of $10,000
3 Mo	9.21	-0.02	-0.59	48	10,921
6 Mo	7.13	-0.06	-0.68	44	10,713
1 Yr	10.74	-0.13	-0.66	36	11,074
3 Yr Avg	3.47	-0.11	-0.80	36	11,078
5 Yr Avg	-2.38	-0.08	-0.62	52	8,865
10 Yr Avg	12.00	-0.07	-0.16	17	31,058
15 Yr Avg	10.82	-0.11	-0.26	24	46,695

Tax Analysis	Tax-Adj Rtn%	%Rank Cat	Tax-Cost Rat	%Rank Cat
3 Yr (estimated)	3.04	31	0.42	35
5 Yr (estimated)	-2.80	44	0.43	23
10 Yr (estimated)	11.32	8	0.61	10

Potential Capital Gain Exposure: 4% of assets

Rating and Risk

Time Period	Load-Adj Return %	Morningstar Rtn vs Cat	Morningstar Risk vs Cat	Morningstar Risk-Adj Rating
1 Yr	10.74			
3 Yr	3.47	Avg	Avg	★★★
5 Yr	-2.38	Avg	Avg	★★★
10 Yr	12.00	+Avg	Avg	★★★★
Incept	12.39			

Other Measures	Standard Index S&P 500	Best Fit Index S&P 500
Alpha	-0.1	-0.1
Beta	1.00	1.00
R-Squared	100	100
Standard Deviation	15.55	
Mean	3.47	
Sharpe Ratio	0.14	

Morningstar's Take by Jeffrey Ptak 10-04-04

Although it has been supplanted as cost king, Vanguard 500 Index remains a favorite.

In August 2004, Fidelity announced that it was slashing the fees it charges on five of its stock index funds, including its Spartan 500 Index, to a paltry 0.10%. A few days later, E*Trade did Fidelity one basis point better, trimming the expense ratio on its E*Trade S&P 500 Index to a minuscule 0.09%. That puts this fund in an unfamiliar position--playing second fiddle to cheaper rivals.

To be sure, cost is the paramount concern for investors in index funds, which use their expense advantage to grind past pricier rivals. That would seem to make the choices of the cheaper funds easy. But there's a catch--Fidelity and E*Trade have made those cost cuts by extending fee waivers that can be rescinded at virtually any time. If, for instance, the Fidelity offering fails to gather sufficient assets to naturally achieve further economies of scale, management could rescind the waiver, thereby allowing expenses to float higher. In that case, investors who thought they were getting the cheapest game in town would instead be paying a premium.

By contrast, Vanguard achieves this fund's low price tag by operating at cost. Thus, investors here don't bear the risk of expenses potentially spiking at management's whim. And while there's no question that Fidelity and E*Trade's moves are laudable and turn up the heat on Vanguard, we don't think the cost difference is material enough for current investors here to consider jumping ship. That's especially true of longtime shareholders in taxable accounts, who could see any cost savings swamped by the negative tax consequences of selling fund shares.

That said, with the sudden emergence of cheaper alternatives to this fund, prospective investors in tax-sheltered accounts unquestionably face a more difficult choice than they did before. But in view of the aforementioned risk of future expense hikes, we still think this is their best bet.

Portfolio Analysis 09-30-04

Share change since 06-04 Total Stocks:504	Sector	PE	YTD Ret%	% Assets
⊕ Gen Elec	Ind Mtrls	22.8	20.68	3.39
⊕ ExxonMobil	Energy	13.9	28.04	3.01
⊕ Microsoft	Software	36.1	8.95	2.88
⊖ Pfizer	Health	22.0	-22.31	2.21
⊕ Citigroup	Financial	15.3	2.72	2.19
⊖ Wal-Mart Stores	Consumer	23.4	0.51	2.16
⊕ American International G	Financial	16.2	-0.53	1.69
⊕ Bank of America	Financial	12.3	21.50	1.69
⊕ Johnson & Johnson	Health	20.6	25.17	1.60
⊕ IBM	Hardware	20.2	7.19	1.37
⊕ J P Morgan Chase	Financial	19.4	9.97	1.35
⊖ Procter & Gamble	Goods	23.3	12.38	1.32
⊖ Intel	Hardware	19.8	-26.56	1.23
⊕ Cisco Systems	Hardware	24.5	-20.26	1.17
⊕ ChevronTexaco	Energy	7.7	25.57	1.09
⊕ Verizon Communications	Telecom	32.4	20.25	1.04
⊕ Wells Fargo	Financial	15.5	8.97	0.96
⊕ Coca-Cola	Goods	21.9	-16.12	0.93
⊕ Altria Group	Goods	13.3	18.38	0.92
⊖ Dell	Hardware	34.0	24.01	0.85

Current Investment Style

Value Blnd Growth / Large Mid Small

Market Cap	%
Giant	52.1
Large	37.5
Mid	10.3
Small	0.1
Micro	0.0
Avg $mil: 44,991	

Value Measures		Rel Category
Price/Earnings	16.60	0.98
Price/Book	2.61	1.00
Price/Sales	1.43	0.99
Price/Cash Flow	7.51	0.98
Dividend Yield %	1.68	1.14

Growth Measures	%	Rel Category
Long-Term Erngs	11.06	0.96
Book Value	7.13	0.92
Sales	4.74	0.83
Cash Flow	7.10	0.75
Historical Erngs	11.54	0.98

Profitability	%	Rel Category
Return on Equity	18.29	1.05
Return on Assets	9.34	1.08
Net Margin	11.96	1.05

Sector Weightings	% of Stocks	Rel S&P 500	3 Year High	3 Year Low
Info	21.40	1.00		
Software	4.48	1.04	5	4
Hardware	9.55	0.94	11	8
Media	3.68	0.96	4	3
Telecom	3.69	1.17	5	3
Service	46.44	1.00		
Health	12.94	1.04	16	13
Consumer	8.90	0.98	10	9
Business	3.92	0.97	4	3
Financial	20.68	1.00	21	19
Mfg	32.15	1.00		
Goods	9.31	1.00	10	9
Ind Mtrls	12.61	1.00	13	11
Energy	7.35	1.03	8	6
Utilities	2.88	0.97	3	3

Composition

Cash	0.5
Stocks	99.5
Bonds	0.0
Other	0.0
Foreign (% of Stock)	0.0

Address:	P O Box 2600, Valley Forge PA 19482, 800-662-7447
Web Address:	www.vanguard.com
Inception:	08-31-76
Advisor:	Vanguard Advisers, Inc.
Subadvisor:	None
NTF Plans:	N/A

Minimum Purchase:	$3000	Add: $100	IRA: $1000
Min Auto Inv Plan:	$3000	Add: $50	
Sales Fees:	No-load		
Management Fee:	0.16%		
Actual Fees:	Mgt:0.16%	Dist: —	
Expense Projections:	3Yr:$58	5Yr:$101	10Yr:$230
Income Distrib:	Quarterly		

Vanguard Asset Alloc

Ticker	Load	NAV	Yield	Total Assets	Mstar Category
VAAPX	None	$24.56	2.0%	$10,473 mil	Moderate Allocation

Governance and Management

Fiduciary Grade: B

Portfolio Manager(s)

This fund boasts a seasoned team. Tom Loeb and William Fouse have run this fund with distinction since its 1988 inception. They've been at Mellon Capital Management Corp., this fund's advisor, for 20 years, and both had more than one decade of investment-management experience before joining Mellon. Fouse originally designed the fund's quantitative model in the early 1970s.

Strategy

Unlike many moderate-allocation offerings, this fund doesn't keep a fairly static asset mix. Instead, management frequently shifts the fund's asset mix based on a quantitative model designed to gauge the relative attractiveness of stocks, bonds, and cash, and it can invest the entire portfolio in a single asset class. The stock segment tracks the S&P 500 Index, while the bond segment tracks the Lehman Brothers Long Term Treasury Index. Management sometimes uses futures to get some of its stock and bond equity exposure; these instruments register as cash in Morningstar's composition section.

Historical Profile

Return: High
Risk: Above Avg
Rating: ★★★★ Above Avg

Investment Style: Equity Stock %

1993	1994	1995	1996	1997	1998	1999	2000	2001	2002	2003	12-04
47%	40%	47%	40%	44%	54%	63%	70%	83%			

▼ Manager Change
▽ Partial Manager Change

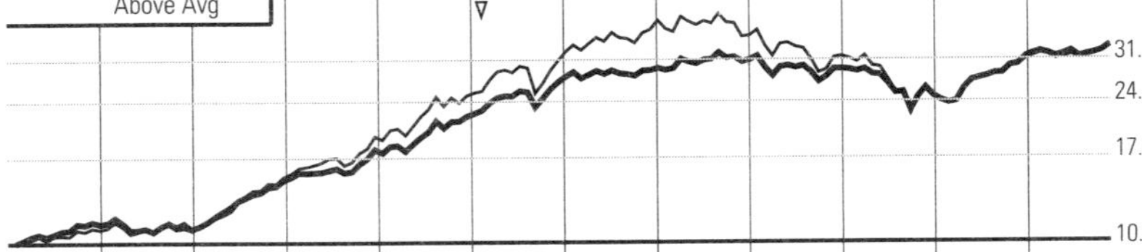

Growth of $10,000
— Investment Values of Fund
— Investment Values of S&P 500

Performance Quartile (within Category)

1993	1994	1995	1996	1997	1998	1999	2000	2001	2002	2003	12-04	History
14.45	13.54	17.05	17.94	21.05	24.38	23.80	23.67	21.81	18.08	22.56	24.56	NAV
13.49	-2.32	35.45	15.73	27.32	25.40	5.21	4.91	-5.30	-15.38	26.42	11.09	Total Return %
3.43	-3.63	-2.08	-7.21	-6.03	-3.17	-15.83	14.01	6.58	6.71	-2.25	0.22	+/-S&P 500
1.76	-0.37	10.68	4.39	8.12	13.01	-7.64	0.47	-5.46	-4.84	2.36	-0.08	+/-DJ 60%
3.55	3.98	4.92	4.26	4.15	3.63	3.64	4.33	2.59	1.82	1.55	2.14	Income Return %
9.94	-6.30	30.53	11.47	23.17	21.77	1.57	0.58	-7.89	-17.20	24.87	8.95	Capital Return %
36	49	2	35	5	6	76	30	53	80	9	17	Total Rtn % Rank Cat
0.48	0.57	0.66	0.72	0.74	0.76	0.88	1.02	0.61	0.40	0.28	0.36	Income $
0.53	0.00	0.61	1.05	1.01	1.18	0.96	0.27	0.00	0.00	0.00	0.00	Capital Gains $
0.49	0.50	0.49	0.47	0.49	0.49	0.49	0.44	0.44	0.42	0.43	0.38	Expense Ratio %
4.07	3.68	4.41	4.17	3.96	3.80	3.49	4.18	3.16	2.19	1.34	1.79	Income Ratio %
31	51	34	47	10	60	11	29	77	54	43	34	Turnover Rate %
1,126	1,126	1,791	2,597	4,099	6,974	8,597	8,889	7,750	6,513	8,445	9,724	Net Assets $mil

Performance 12-31-04

	1st Qtr	2nd Qtr	3rd Qtr	4th Qtr	Total
2000	5.63	-0.61	1.14	-1.20	4.91
2001	-9.29	5.20	-8.26	8.18	-5.30
2002	-0.09	-8.40	-15.57	9.51	-15.38
2003	-3.32	15.29	3.09	10.02	26.42
2004	2.39	0.09	0.00	8.39	11.09

Trailing	Total Return%	+/- S&P 500	+/- DJ 60%	%Rank Cat	Growth of $10,000
3 Mo	8.39	-0.84	0.91	17	10,839
6 Mo	8.39	1.20	0.86	16	10,839
1 Yr	11.09	0.22	-0.08	17	11,109
3 Yr Avg	5.92	2.34	-1.34	29	11,883
5 Yr Avg	3.38	5.68	-1.86	30	11,808
10 Yr Avg	12.01	-0.06	1.52	10	31,086
15 Yr Avg	10.86	-0.07	0.91	11	46,949

Tax Analysis	Tax-Adj Rtn%	%Rank Cat	Tax-Cost Rat	%Rank Cat
3 Yr (estimated)	5.35	21	0.54	37
5 Yr (estimated)	2.44	24	0.91	40
10 Yr (estimated)	9.97	9	1.82	52

Potential Capital Gain Exposure: 16% of assets

Rating and Risk

Time Period	Load-Adj Return %	Morningstar Rtn vs Cat	Morningstar Risk vs Cat	Morningstar Risk-Adj Rating
1 Yr	11.09			
3 Yr	5.92	+Avg	High	★★★
5 Yr	3.38	+Avg	+Avg	★★★
10 Yr	12.01	High	+Avg	★★★★
Incept	11.72			

Other Measures	Standard Index S&P 500	Best Fit Index S&P 500
Alpha	2.5	2.5
Beta	0.87	0.87
R-Squared	96	96
Standard Deviation	13.99	
Mean	5.92	
Sharpe Ratio	0.33	

Portfolio Analysis 09-30-04

Total Stocks:500 Share change since 03-31-04	Sectors	P/E Ratio	YTD Return %	% Net Assets
⊕ Gen Elec	Ind Mtrls	22.8	-3.01	2.84
⊕ ExxonMobil	Energy	13.9	-2.75	2.52
⊕ Microsoft	Software	36.1	0.04	2.41
⊕ Pfizer	Health	22.0	-2.75	1.85
⊕ Citigroup	Financial	15.3	0.08	1.83
⊕ Wal-Mart Stores	Consumer	23.4	1.46	1.81
⊕ American International Gr	Financial	16.2	2.25	1.42
⊕ Bank of America	Financial	12.3	-3.85	1.41
⊕ Johnson & Johnson	Health	20.6	-0.85	1.34

Total Fixed-Income:17	Date of Maturity	Amount $000	Value $000	% Net Assets
US Treasury Bond 6.25%	05-15-30	85,460	101,430	1.05
US Treasury Bond 10.625%	08-15-15	56,400	87,578	0.90
US Treasury Bond 7.125%	02-15-23	67,560	86,118	0.89
US Treasury Bond 6.25%	08-15-23	73,000	85,239	0.88
US Treasury Bond 8.125%	08-15-19	52,825	72,288	0.75
US Treasury Bond 7.625%	11-15-22	50,000	66,766	0.69
US Treasury Bond 8.75%	08-15-20	44,525	64,478	0.67
US Treasury Bond 6.125%	11-15-27	48,380	56,151	0.58
US Treasury Bond 6%	02-15-26	49,000	55,860	0.58

Equity Style
Style: Blend
Size: Large-Cap

Fixed-Income Style
Duration: —
Quality: —

Value Measures		Rel Category
Price/Earnings	16.61	1.00
Price/Book	2.62	1.07
Price/Sales	1.43	1.08
Price/Cash Flow	7.52	1.04
Dividend Yield %	1.68	1.07

Growth Measures	%	Rel Category
Long-Term Erngs	11.06	0.95
Book Value	7.13	1.24
Sales	4.76	0.92
Cash Flow	7.10	0.89
Historical Erngs	11.55	1.07

Market Cap %			
Giant	52.2	Small	0.1
Large	37.4	Micro	0.0
Mid	10.3	Avg $mil:	45,024

Avg Eff Duration [1]	—
Avg Eff Maturity	—
Avg Credit Quality	—
Avg Wtd Coupon	—

[1]figure provided by fund

Sector Weightings	% of Stocks	Rel S&P 500	3 Year High	3 Year Low
Info	21.40	1.00		
Software	4.48	1.04	5	4
Hardware	9.54	0.94	11	8
Media	3.69	0.96	4	3
Telecom	3.69	1.17	5	3
Service	46.47	1.00		
Health	12.95	1.04	16	13
Consumer	8.90	0.98	10	9
Business	3.93	0.97	4	3
Financial	20.69	1.00	21	19
Mfg	32.12	1.00		
Goods	9.33	1.00	10	9
Ind Mtrls	12.60	0.99	13	11
Energy	7.33	1.02	7	6
Utilities	2.86	0.97	3	3

Composition

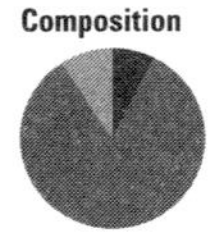

Cash	7.3
Stocks	83.3
Bonds	9.4
Other	0.0
Foreign (% of Stock)	0.0

Morningstar's Take by William Samuel Rocco 11-14-04

Flexible S&P 500 fans should check out Vanguard Asset Allocation, especially if they're risk-averse.

The large-blend category is the logical place to look for S&P 500 vehicles. After all, that category includes Vanguard 500 Index and several dozen lesser-known index funds that track that benchmark, as well as roughly one dozen enhanced index offerings that strive to outperform that bogy in one respect or another.

But S&P 500 index enthusiasts ignore this moderate-allocation fund at their own peril. The fund aims to earn S&P 500-like returns over time with less volatility than the index, and it has met that goal. It has an 10.6% annualized gain over the past 15 years and a 15-year standard deviation of 12.1, while the S&P 500 Index has an 10.7% annualized return over the past 15 years and a 15-year standard deviation of 16.2.

Managers Tom Loeb and William Fouse have achieved this feat by making generally skillful use of their freedom to make decisive asset-allocation calls. For example, the duo's decision to raise the portfolio's bond stake to 60% in late 1999 and to keep it pretty high enabled the fund to post a nice gain in 2000 as the S&P 500 Index sank. And the fund has posted superior results thus far in 2004, as they've kept the fund's equity stake at 80% of assets for most of this year before boosting it a bit this fall.

The fund isn't perfect, of course. It really struggles when Loeb and Fouse's asset calls are off the mark. Moreover, it's less tax efficient than Vanguard 500 Index--due to its higher turnover and bond exposure--and it's pricier than that offering (though its 0.43% expense ratio is quite attractive by most measures). But we think its attractive risk/reward profile and Loeb and Fouse's proven talents make it worth a long look from investors seeking a vehicle like the S&P 500 Index.

Address:	P.O. Box 2600 Valley Forge PA 19482 800-662-7447
Web Address:	www.vanguard.com
Inception:	11-03-88
Advisor:	Mellon Capital Management Corporation
Subadvisor:	None
NTF Plans:	N/A

Minimum Purchase:	$3000	Add: $100	IRA: $1000
Min Auto Inv Plan:	$3000	Add: $50	
Sales Fees:	No-load		
Management Fee:	0.40%		
Actual Fees:	Mgt:0.40%	Dist: —	
Expense Projections:	3Yr:$173	5Yr:$302	10Yr:$677
Income Distrib:	Semi-Annually		

Vanguard Bal Idx

Ticker	Load	NAV	Yield	Total Assets	Mstar Category
VBINX	None	$19.45	2.6%	$7,284 mil	Moderate Allocation

Governance and Management

Fiduciary Grade: B

Portfolio Manager(s)

Gus Sauter, who has been here since the fund's 1992 inception, leads the experienced indexing group that runs the fund's equity side. Chris Alwine handles the duties on the bond front. Although Alwine only came aboard in 2002, he's hardly a newcomer, having been a longtime member of the bond indexing team (the efforts of which he leverages fully here). Both managers boast impressive track records at their various other charges.

Strategy

The fund's equities stake, comprising 60% of its assets, mimics the Wilshire 5000 Index (which tracks all publicly traded companies). The bond stake takes up the other 40% of assets and mirrors the Lehman Brothers Aggregate Index of all investment-grade taxable domestic bonds. Management does not make asset-allocation bets.

Historical Profile

Return Above Avg
Risk Average
Rating ★★★★ Above Avg

Investment Style
Equity
Stock %

58% 57% 58% 59% 58% 59% 58% 60% 60%

▼ Manager Change
▽ Partial Manager Change

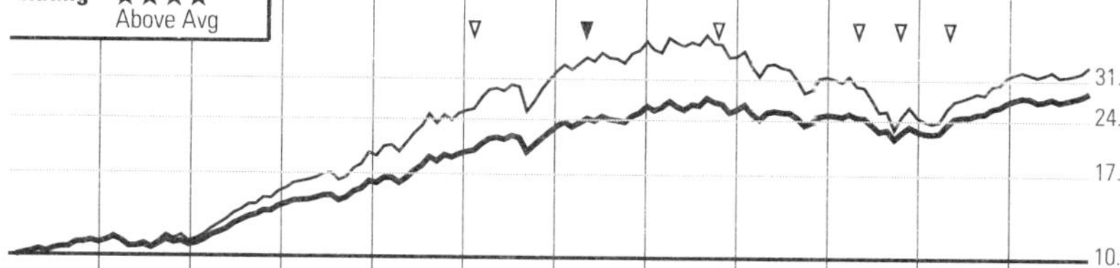

Growth of $10,000
— Investment Values of Fund
— Investment Values of S&P 500

Performance Quartile (within Category)

1993	1994	1995	1996	1997	1998	1999	2000	2001	2002	2003	12-04	History
10.91	10.34	12.77	13.92	16.29	18.48	20.22	19.08	17.86	15.65	18.27	19.45	NAV
10.00	-1.56	28.64	13.95	22.24	17.85	13.61	-2.04	-3.02	-9.52	19.87	9.33	Total Return %
-0.06	-2.87	-8.89	-8.99	-11.11	-10.72	-7.43	7.06	8.86	12.57	-8.80	-1.54	+/-S&P 500
-1.73	0.39	3.87	2.61	3.04	5.46	0.76	-6.48	-3.18	1.02	-4.19	-1.84	+/-DJ 60%
3.83	3.72	4.41	3.89	3.87	3.36	3.19	3.24	3.17	2.95	2.91	2.76	Income Return %
6.17	-5.28	24.23	10.06	18.37	14.49	10.42	-5.28	-6.19	-12.47	16.96	6.57	Capital Return %
70	34	24	52	29	26	30	68	30	28	48	40	Total Rtn % Rank Cat
0.39	0.40	0.45	0.49	0.53	0.54	0.58	0.65	0.60	0.52	0.45	0.38	Income $
0.03	0.00	0.05	0.12	0.14	0.14	0.14	0.10	0.03	0.00	0.00	0.00	Capital Gains $
0.20	0.20	0.20	0.20	0.20	0.21	0.20	0.22	0.22	0.22	0.22	—	Expense Ratio %
3.53	3.86	3.85	3.69	3.56	3.29	3.18	3.30	3.26	3.14	2.68	—	Income Ratio %
25	16	16	37	18	25	29	28	33	40	27	—	Turnover Rate %
367	403	590	826	1,260	2,004	3,128	3,586	3,117	2,990	3,895	4,674	Net Assets $mil

Performance 12-31-04

	1st Qtr	2nd Qtr	3rd Qtr	4th Qtr	Total
2000	3.30	-2.07	1.44	-4.54	-2.04
2001	-6.00	4.67	-7.82	6.92	-3.02
2002	0.67	-6.55	-8.58	5.20	-9.52
2003	-1.28	10.75	2.13	7.35	19.87
2004	2.63	-0.21	0.22	6.52	9.33

Trailing	Total Return%	+/- S&P 500	+/- DJ 60%	%Rank Cat	Growth of $10,000
3 Mo	6.52	-2.71	-0.96	60	10,652
6 Mo	6.75	-0.44	-0.78	45	10,675
1 Yr	9.33	-1.54	-1.84	40	10,933
3 Yr Avg	5.84	2.26	-1.42	30	11,856
5 Yr Avg	2.41	4.71	-2.83	41	11,264
10 Yr Avg	10.45	-1.62	-0.04	27	27,018
15 Yr Avg	—	—	—	—	—

Tax Analysis	Tax-Adj Rtn%	%Rank Cat	Tax-Cost Rat	%Rank Cat
3 Yr (estimated)	4.87	28	0.92	64
5 Yr (estimated)	1.28	37	1.10	50
10 Yr (estimated)	8.97	16	1.34	19

Potential Capital Gain Exposure: 12% of assets

Rating and Risk

Time Period	Load-Adj Return %	Morningstar Rtn vs Cat	Morningstar Risk vs Cat	Morningstar Risk-Adj Rating
1 Yr	9.33			
3 Yr	5.84	+Avg	-Avg	★★★★
5 Yr	2.41	Avg	Avg	★★★
10 Yr	10.45	+Avg	Avg	★★★★
Incept	9.57			

Other Measures	Standard Index S&P 500	Best Fit Index Russ 1000
Alpha	2.9	2.5
Beta	0.55	0.56
R-Squared	95	96

Standard Deviation	8.83
Mean	5.84
Sharpe Ratio	0.51

Portfolio Analysis 09-30-04

Total Stocks:3523 Share change since 06-30-04	Sectors	P/E Ratio	YTD Return %	% Net Assets
⊕ Gen Elec	Ind Mtrls	22.8	-3.01	1.57
⊕ ExxonMobil	Energy	13.9	-2.75	1.40
⊕ Microsoft	Software	36.1	0.04	1.33
⊕ Pfizer	Health	22.0	-2.75	1.02
⊕ Citigroup	Financial	15.3	0.08	1.01
⊕ Wal-Mart Stores	Consumer	23.4	1.46	1.01
⊕ Bank of America	Financial	12.3	-3.85	0.78
⊕ American International Gr	Financial	16.2	2.25	0.78
⊕ Johnson & Johnson	Health	20.6	-0.85	0.74

Total Fixed-Income:2651	Date of Maturity	Amount $000	Value $000	% Net Assets
US Treasury Note 7%	07-15-06	43,425	46,797	0.69
US Treasury Note 4.375%	08-15-12	41,850	43,125	0.64
US Treasury Note 6.5%	10-15-06	37,050	39,881	0.59
US Treasury Bond 8.875%	02-15-19	26,475	38,240	0.57
US Treasury Note 1.875%	12-31-05	34,225	34,048	0.50
US Treasury Note 3.25%	01-15-09	31,775	31,785	0.47
US Treasury Bond 7.625%	11-15-22	22,350	29,844	0.44
US Treasury Note 4.875%	02-15-12	26,845	28,603	0.42
US Treasury Note 5.625%	05-15-08	24,410	26,557	0.39

Equity Style
Style: Blend
Size: Large-Cap

Value Measures		Rel Category
Price/Earnings	16.78	1.01
Price/Book	2.48	1.02
Price/Sales	1.34	1.02
Price/Cash Flow	7.09	0.98
Dividend Yield %	1.54	0.98

Growth Measures	%	Rel Category
Long-Term Erngs	11.38	0.98
Book Value	5.34	1.10
Sales	4.55	0.88
Cash Flow	5.03	0.75
Historical Erngs	11.25	1.04

Market Cap %			
Giant	40.5	Small	6.8
Large	30.5	Micro	2.5
Mid	19.8	Avg $mil:	21,905

Composition

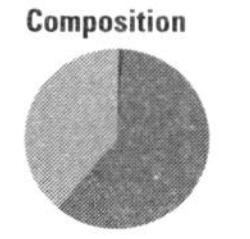

Cash	1.3
Stocks	59.8
Bonds	39.0
Other	0.0
Foreign (% of Stock)	0.0

Fixed-Income Style
Duration: Interm-Term
Quality: High

Avg Eff Duration[1]	4.5 Yrs
Avg Eff Maturity	7.3 Yrs
Avg Credit Quality	AAA
Avg Wtd Coupon	5.67%

[1]figure provided by fund as of 09-30-04

Sector Weightings	% of Stocks	Rel S&P 500	3 Year High	3 Year Low
Info	20.67	0.96		
Software	4.17	0.97	5	4
Hardware	9.00	0.88	11	7
Media	4.25	1.11	5	4
Telecom	3.25	1.03	4	3
Service	49.25	1.06		
Health	12.54	1.00	15	13
Consumer	9.50	1.05	10	9
Business	5.25	1.30	5	5
Financial	21.96	1.06	23	20
Mfg	30.10	0.94		
Goods	8.57	0.92	11	9
Ind Mtrls	11.42	0.90	11	10
Energy	7.21	1.01	7	6
Utilities	2.90	0.98	3	3

Morningstar's Take by Jeffrey Ptak 01-09-05

Vanguard Balanced Index is a good, if somewhat boring, choice.

In evaluating a mutual fund, two of the most critical considerations are the prudence of the underlying strategy and whether the investment personnel charged with implementing that approach have the goods to pull it off. In this fund's case, that means weighing both the merit of a wholly passive strategy--this offering's stock and bond sleeves are both indexed--and the ability of comanagers Gus Sauter and Chris Alwine to keep pace with their bogies.

On the latter count, we have few concerns. Both Sauter and Alwine have been able to keep their other charges, including Vanguard Total Stock Market Index and Vanguard Short-Term Bond Index, apace with their benchmarks over the long haul. With respect to this fund's strategy--which finds Sauter indexing the Wilshire 5000 Index (a proxy for all U.S. stocks) and Alwine tracking the Lehman Aggregate Index (a popular measure of the U.S. investment-grade bond market)--investors needn't lose any sleep for a simple reason: The fund is dirt cheap. Indexing depends on low costs to be successful, as index funds aim to replicate the gross returns earned by active managers while nudging ahead after expenses are factored in. This fund's 0.22% expense ratio--which is a fraction of the moderate-allocation category norm--makes that strategy all the more viable.

For those reasons, we think the fund remains a fine choice to anchor a portfolio. Investors should of course be mindful of the risks here. In fact, many observers believe that the going will be tough for U.S. stock and bond markets in the years ahead, a trend that doesn't augur well given this fund's mandate (which requires it to be fully invested at all times). However, the fund has prospered through a variety of market climates in the past--witness its fine long-term record. As such, it should suit those with a long time horizon.

Address:	P O Box 2600 Valley Forge PA 19482 800-662-7447
Web Address:	www.vanguard.com
Inception:	11-09-92
Advisor:	Vanguard Advisers, Inc.
Subadvisor:	None
NTF Plans:	N/A

Minimum Purchase:	$3000	Add: $100	IRA: $1000
Min Auto Inv Plan:	$3000	Add: $50	
Sales Fees:	No-load		
Management Fee:	0.17%		
Actual Fees:	Mgt:0.17%	Dist: —	
Expense Projections:	3Yr:$71	5Yr:$124	10Yr:$280
Income Distrib:	Quarterly		

Vanguard Calv Soc Idx

Ticker	Load	NAV	Yield	Total Assets	Mstar Category
VCSIX	None	$8.02	1.5%	$346 mil	Large Growth

Governance and Management

Fiduciary Grade: B

Portfolio Manager(s)

Vanguard index guru Gus Sauter has managed the fund since its May 2000 launch. The social screening behind the Calvert Social Index, the fund's bogy, is conducted by a social research team at Calvert Asset Management, the socially responsible investing industry's largest money manager. Among other things, the team relies on publicly available information, as well as conversations with company management and advocacy groups.

Strategy

This offering tracks the Calvert Social Index, which is a group of more than 600 companies that pass Calvert's social screens. The screens avoid alcoholic beverage and tobacco makers, as well as firms with poor labor practices and environmental track records. Those criteria have typically led to sizable weightings in the tech and health-care sectors, explaining the fund's slight growth tilt. Index turnover has been quite modest over time.

Historical Profile

Return Above Avg
Risk Above Avg
Rating ★★★★ Above Avg

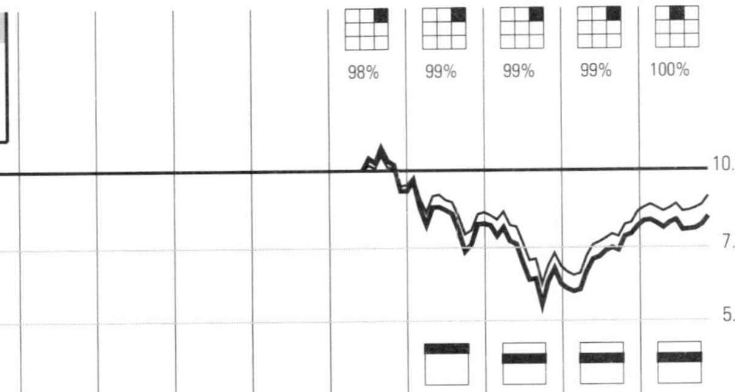

Investment Style
Equity
Stock %

▼ Manager Change
▽ Partial Manager Change

Growth of $10,000
— Investment Values of Fund
— Investment Values of S&P 500

Performance Quartile (within Category)

1993	1994	1995	1996	1997	1998	1999	2000	2001	2002	2003	12-04	History
—	—	—	—	—	—	—	9.09	7.76	5.82	7.52	8.02	NAV
—	—	—	—	—	—	—	-8.98*	-14.08	-24.24	30.45	8.27	Total Return %
—	—	—	—	—	—	—	—	-2.20	-2.15	1.78	-2.60	+/-S&P 500
—	—	—	—	—	—	—	—	6.34	3.64	0.70	1.97	+/-Russ 1000Gr
—	—	—	—	—	—	—	0.00	0.55	0.77	1.20	1.60	Income Return %
—	—	—	—	—	—	—	—	-14.63	-25.01	29.25	6.67	Capital Return %
—	—	—	—	—	—	—	—	19	29	31	43	Total Rtn % Rank Cat
—	—	—	—	—	—	—	0.03	0.05	0.06	0.07	0.12	Income $
—	—	—	—	—	—	—	0.01	0.00	0.00	0.00	0.00	Capital Gains $
—	—	—	—	—	—	—	0.25	0.25	0.25	0.25	0.25	Expense Ratio %
—	—	—	—	—	—	—	0.98	0.70	0.82	1.18	1.17	Income Ratio %
—	—	—	—	—	—	—	3	10	18	14	8	Turnover Rate %
—	—	—	—	—	—	—	62	99	98	203	332	Net Assets $mil

Performance 12-31-04

	1st Qtr	2nd Qtr	3rd Qtr	4th Qtr	Total
2000	—	—	-1.13	-12.97	-8.98 *
2001	-14.52	7.08	-17.43	13.68	-14.08
2002	-1.68	-15.20	-17.62	10.31	-24.24
2003	-2.58	16.23	3.03	11.81	30.45
2004	1.20	1.71	-4.01	9.58	8.27

Trailing	Total Return%	+/- S&P 500	+/- Russ 1000Gr	%Rank Cat	Growth of $10,000
3 Mo	9.58	0.35	0.41	56	10,958
6 Mo	5.19	-2.00	1.72	44	10,519
1 Yr	8.27	-2.60	1.97	43	10,827
3 Yr Avg	2.28	-1.30	2.46	23	10,700
5 Yr Avg	—	—	—	—	—
10 Yr Avg	—	—	—	—	—
15 Yr Avg	—	—	—	—	—

Tax Analysis	Tax-Adj Rtn%	%Rank Cat	Tax-Cost Rat	%Rank Cat
3 Yr (estimated)	1.92	22	0.35	60
5 Yr (estimated)	—	—	—	—
10 Yr (estimated)	—	—	—	—

Potential Capital Gain Exposure: 2% of assets

Rating and Risk

Time Period	Load-Adj Return %	Morningstar Rtn vs Cat	Morningstar Risk vs Cat	Morningstar Risk-Adj Rating
1 Yr	8.27			
3 Yr	2.28	+Avg	+Avg	★★★★
5 Yr	—	—	—	—
10 Yr	—	—	—	—
Incept	-3.81			

Other Measures	Standard Index S&P 500	Best Fit Index Russ 1000
Alpha	-1.3	-2.0
Beta	1.09	1.10
R-Squared	97	97
Standard Deviation	17.09	
Mean	2.28	
Sharpe Ratio	0.05	

Portfolio Analysis 09-30-04

Share change since 06-04 Total Stocks:640	Sector	PE	YTD Ret%	% Assets
⊕ Microsoft	Software	36.1	8.95	4.43
⊕ Pfizer	Health	22.0	-22.31	3.61
⊕ Bank of America	Financial	12.3	21.50	2.75
⊕ Johnson & Johnson	Health	20.6	25.17	2.61
⊕ American International G	Financial	16.2	-0.53	2.43
⊕ IBM	Hardware	20.2	7.19	2.30
⊕ J P Morgan Chase	Financial	19.4	9.97	2.21
⊕ Procter & Gamble	Goods	23.3	12.38	2.17
⊕ Intel	Hardware	19.8	-26.56	2.01
⊕ Cisco Systems	Hardware	24.5	-20.26	1.91
⊕ Wells Fargo	Financial	15.5	8.97	1.57
⊕ Home Depot	Consumer	19.0	21.47	1.36
⊕ SBC Communications	Telecom	15.4	3.74	1.34
⊕ Dell	Hardware	34.0	24.01	1.24
⊕ Merck	Health	11.4	-27.76	1.14
⊕ Amgen	Health	37.7	3.82	1.12
⊕ Time Warner	Media	27.5	8.12	1.11
⊕ Qualcomm	Hardware	42.0	58.20	0.99
⊕ Medtronic	Health	30.7	2.68	0.98
⊕ Wachovia	Financial	14.3	16.80	0.96

Current Investment Style

Value Blnd Growth — Large Mid Small

Market Cap	%
Giant	47.4
Large	30.7
Mid	20.4
Small	1.6
Micro	0.0
Avg $mil: 31,242	

Value Measures		Rel Category
Price/Earnings	17.30	0.81
Price/Book	2.67	0.83
Price/Sales	1.81	0.84
Price/Cash Flow	7.50	0.68
Dividend Yield %	1.38	1.79

Growth Measures	%	Rel Category
Long-Term Erngs	12.17	0.87
Book Value	9.62	0.76
Sales	6.05	0.71
Cash Flow	13.20	0.80
Historical Erngs	14.33	0.99

Profitability	%	Rel Category
Return on Equity	18.17	1.01
Return on Assets	10.34	1.10
Net Margin	13.78	1.12

Sector Weightings	% of Stocks	Rel S&P 500	3 Year High	3 Year Low
Info	29.41	1.37		
Software	6.22	1.45	8	6
Hardware	15.26	1.50	19	13
Media	4.11	1.07	4	3
Telecom	3.82	1.21	4	3
Service	57.92	1.25		
Health	16.31	1.30	21	16
Consumer	8.57	0.94	9	8
Business	5.15	1.27	6	5
Financial	27.89	1.34	30	26
Mfg	12.67	0.39		
Goods	6.26	0.67	6	4
Ind Mtrls	4.90	0.39	5	3
Energy	0.94	0.13	1	1
Utilities	0.57	0.19	1	1

Composition

Cash	0.1
Stocks	99.9
Bonds	0.0
Other	0.0
Foreign (% of Stock)	0.2

Morningstar's Take by Greg Carlson 12-22-04

For socially conscious investors who can handle a few bumps, Vanguard Calvert Social Index makes a fine centerpiece for a portfolio.

This fund tracks an index constructed by the advisor to the Calvert Funds, which applies its social screens to the 1,000 largest U.S. companies. Because those screens tend to exclude companies with poor environmental records, many firms in sectors such as industrials and energy don't make the cut. That leaves the fund with hefty stakes in pricier areas such as tech and health care, more so than other socially screened index funds, including its most-prominent rival, Domini Social Equity.

The differences between this fund's portfolio and the Domini fund's owe to both varying index construction and social-screening rules. Domini puts together a 400-stock index that includes half of the companies in the S&P 500 Index. To plug the holes left by the names that the social screens exclude, Domini also throws in a clutch of SRI-compliant non-S&P 500 Index stocks. In that way, the Domini portfolio's sector weightings better approximate the S&P's. Calvert, meanwhile, doesn't aim to mimic any major large-cap index, explaining this portfolio's larger divergences from the S&P 500 and Russell 1000 bogies.

To be sure, this fund's growth tilt has made for slightly higher volatility than the Domini offering and can weigh when pricier fare falls from grace. However, all told, this fund and the Domini offering have moved in near-lockstep in recent years, as evidenced by the tight correlation of their returns.

Where does that leave investors trying to choose between this fund and the Domini offering? Those seeking a more quintessentially core offering are likely to be happier at the Domini fund given its middle-of-the-fairway approach. But for others who are less finicky about short-term bumps along the way, we think this fund's 0.25% expense ratio--which is a fraction of the Domini offering's--makes it well worth considering.

Address:	PO Box 2600 Valley Forge PA 19482 800-662-7447
Web Address:	www.vanguard.com
Inception:	05-31-00*
Advisor:	Vanguard Advisers, Inc.
Subadvisor:	None
NTF Plans:	N/A

Minimum Purchase:	$3000	Add: $100	IRA: $1000
Min Auto Inv Plan:	$3000	Add: $50	
Sales Fees:	No-load		
Management Fee:	0.21%		
Actual Fees:	Mgt:0.12%	Dist: —	
Expense Projections:	3Yr:$80	5Yr:$141	10Yr:$318
Income Distrib:	Annually		

Vanguard Cap Opp

Ticker	Load	NAV	Yield	Total Assets	Mstar Category
VHCOX	Closed	$30.77	0.2%	$8,548 mil	Mid-Cap Growth

Governance and Management

Fiduciary Grade: B

Portfolio Manager(s)

The fund's three skippers--Howard Schow, Theo Kolokotrones, and Joel Fried--employ an unusual team structure. Although they share ideas, each independently manages a portion of the fund's assets. Their strong record at Vanguard Primecap speaks for itself. They were named Morningstar's Domestic Equity Managers of the Year for 2003.

Strategy

The fund's managers follow a contrarian-growth approach. They look for swiftly growing firms but like to buy their stocks on the cheap, when they're out of favor. The fund often has outsized sector weightings because many of the managers' favorites are clustered in a few industries.

Historical Profile

Return Above Avg
Risk Average
Rating ★★★★ Above Avg

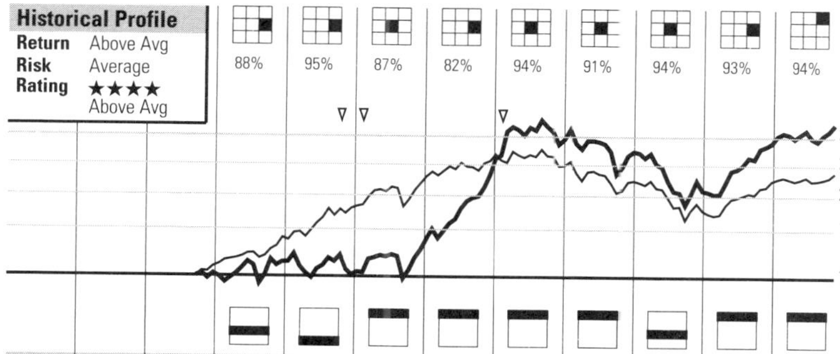

1993	1994	1995	1996	1997	1998	1999	2000	2001	2002	2003	12-04	History
—	—	9.82	11.13	10.20	12.49	24.02	26.22	23.61	17.00	25.41	30.77	NAV
—	—	-1.79*	13.41	-7.93	31.98	97.77	18.04	-9.68	-27.94	49.55	21.65	Total Return %
—	—	—	-9.53	-41.28	3.41	76.73	27.14	2.20	-5.85	20.88	10.78	+/-S&P 500
—	—	—	-4.07	-30.47	14.12	46.48	29.79	10.47	-0.53	6.84	6.17	+/-Russ MG
—	—	0.00	0.07	0.40	0.15	0.28	0.67	0.27	0.06	0.08	0.28	Income Return %
—	—	—	13.34	-8.33	31.83	97.49	17.37	-9.95	-28.00	49.47	21.37	Capital Return %
—	—	—	71	98	15	17	11	21	54	6	3	Total Rtn % Rank Cat
—	—	0.03	0.01	0.05	0.02	0.04	0.16	0.07	0.01	0.01	0.07	Income $
—	—	0.00	0.00	0.00	0.90	0.59	1.92	0.00	0.00	0.00	0.07	Capital Gains $
—	—	0.47	0.50	0.49	0.94	0.75	0.62	0.60	0.58	0.59	0.52	Expense Ratio %
—	—	1.29	0.11	0.27	0.18	0.31	0.64	0.28	0.07	0.05	0.06	Income Ratio %
—	—	—	128	195	103	22	15	20	14	14	10	Turnover Rate %
—	—	81	117	63	206	2,367	5,056	4,846	3,275	5,455	6,962	Net Assets $mil

Performance 12-31-04

	1st Qtr	2nd Qtr	3rd Qtr	4th Qtr	Total
2000	30.89	-0.54	0.80	-10.05	18.04
2001	-7.89	6.42	-23.85	21.01	-9.68
2002	-1.52	-20.73	-18.29	12.97	-27.94
2003	-2.59	23.25	8.72	14.57	49.55
2004	7.67	3.47	-3.78	13.48	21.65

Trailing	Total Return%	+/- S&P 500	+/- Russ MG	%Rank Cat	Growth of $10,000
3 Mo	13.48	4.25	-0.46	38	11,348
6 Mo	9.19	2.00	0.18	31	10,919
1 Yr	21.65	10.78	6.17	3	12,165
3 Yr Avg	9.44	5.86	3.28	9	13,108
5 Yr Avg	6.92	9.22	10.28	9	13,973
10 Yr Avg	—	—	—	—	—
15 Yr Avg	—	—	—	—	—

Tax Analysis	Tax-Adj Rtn%	%Rank Cat	Tax-Cost Rat	%Rank Cat
3 Yr (estimated)	9.02	8	0.06	10
5 Yr (estimated)	6.34	9	0.54	24
10 Yr (estimated)	—	—	—	—

Potential Capital Gain Exposure: 23% of assets

Rating and Risk

Time Period	Load-Adj Return %	Morningstar Rtn vs Cat	Morningstar Risk vs Cat	Morningstar Risk-Adj Rating
1 Yr	20.43			
3 Yr	9.08	+Avg	+Avg	★★★★
5 Yr	6.92	+Avg	Avg	★★★★
10 Yr	—	—	—	—
Incept	15.10			

Other Measures	Standard Index S&P 500	Best Fit Index PSE Tech 100
Alpha	5.7	5.2
Beta	1.29	0.77
R-Squared	87	94

Standard Deviation	22.86
Mean	9.44
Sharpe Ratio	0.36

Portfolio Analysis 09-30-04

Share change since 03-04 Total Stocks:122	Sector	PE	YTD Ret%	% Assets
Biogen IDEC	Health	—	81.50	4.80
⊖ Research In Motion Ltd	Hardware	—	146.66	4.44
FedEx	Business	27.9	46.40	3.53
⊖ Symantec	Software	34.5	49.33	3.06
The Directv Group	Media	—	1.15	2.64
Sprint	Telecom	—	55.24	2.63
⊕ Monsanto Company	Ind Mtrls	54.5	96.09	2.36
Murphy Oil	Energy	16.5	24.71	2.29
Micron Technology	Hardware	46.2	-8.32	2.04
ConocoPhillips	Energy	9.0	35.60	2.03
Applied Biosystems Group	Health	24.5	1.81	1.98
⊕ Novartis AG ADR	Health	23.9	12.04	1.94
Thomas & Betts	Hardware	19.1	34.34	1.93
⊕ VeriSign	Software	—	106.14	1.86
Corning	Hardware	—	12.85	1.82
Pfizer	Health	22.0	-22.31	1.74
Motorola	Hardware	28.7	37.93	1.59
Microsoft	Software	36.1	8.95	1.57
Nordstrom	Consumer	20.9	37.87	1.48
Pall	Health	23.0	9.51	1.46

Current Investment Style

Value Blnd Growth — Large Mid Small

Market Cap	%
Giant	11.0
Large	38.2
Mid	38.2
Small	10.6
Micro	2.0
Avg $mil: 8,055	

Value Measures		Rel Category
Price/Earnings	21.58	0.98
Price/Book	2.02	0.67
Price/Sales	1.45	0.82
Price/Cash Flow	9.02	0.93
Dividend Yield %	0.43	1.00

Growth Measures	%	Rel Category
Long-Term Erngs	12.74	0.81
Book Value	5.60	0.56
Sales	3.38	0.39
Cash Flow	49.63	4.07
Historical Erngs	15.65	0.98

Profitability	%	Rel Category
Return on Equity	8.51	0.59
Return on Assets	3.31	0.46
Net Margin	1.52	0.16

Sector Weightings	% of Stocks	Rel S&P 500	3 Year High	3 Year Low
Info	44.16	2.05		
Software	11.67	2.71	12	8
Hardware	26.36	2.58	29	19
Media	3.32	0.86	4	1
Telecom	2.81	0.89	3	1
Service	41.59	0.90		
Health	21.10	1.69	23	17
Consumer	11.38	1.25	15	10
Business	7.59	1.87	15	7
Financial	1.52	0.07	3	1
Mfg	14.24	0.44		
Goods	0.90	0.10	7	1
Ind Mtrls	4.08	0.32	6	3
Energy	9.26	1.29	10	7
Utilities	0.00	0.00	0	0

Composition

Cash	6.4
Stocks	93.6
Bonds	0.0
Other	0.0
Foreign (% of Stock)	8.6

Morningstar's Take by Jeffrey Ptak 11-04-04

Is Vanguard Capital Opportunity too big?

This fund's 11.7% return through Nov. 2, 2004, tops virtually all of its mid-blend category peers, as surging top picks such as Research in Motion have offset weakness in the semiconductor and biotech industries, favorite haunts of manager Primecap Management. Performance aside, some recent developments have put the issue of the fund's size into sharper focus. While Vanguard recently closed the fund to new investors, Primecap just launched its own series of offerings, one of which will clone this portfolio. Meanwhile, Vanguard has tapped Primecap to run a forthcoming large-blend offering that will share many names in common with this fund. Taken together, this poses the risk of heavier holdings overlap, which could make it more difficult for management to maneuver.

Fortunately, Primecap doesn't trade much and typically buys on weakness. That means the fund shouldn't be saddled with heavy transaction costs. And with three managers running sleeves of the portfolio independently, positions aren't necessarily built or trimmed in big chunks, which also relieves pressure.

But there's no ignoring the fact that the number of portfolio holdings has doubled since 1998 while its median market-cap has risen near large-cap territory. True, the fund has never been especially reliant on big stakes in individual names and the fund's stellar recent showings have been achieved with the current, broader portfolio. Yet, with roughly 40% of assets recently invested in names where the firm's holdings represented 5% or more of outstanding shares, odds are that Primecap will have to further expand the portfolio in the future to find capacity.

To its credit, Primecap has put groundwork in place to support the research demands that this transition will require. But asset bloat can humble even unquestionably savvy investors like the Primecap crew. As such, while we remain fans of the fund, investors should keep an eye on its size.

Address:	P O Box 2600 Valley Forge PA 19482 800-662-7447
Web Address:	www.vanguard.com
Inception:	08-14-95*
Advisor:	Primecap Management Co.
Subadvisor:	None
NTF Plans:	N/A

Minimum Purchase:	Closed	Add: —	IRA: —		
Min Auto Inv Plan:	Closed	Add: —			
Sales Fees:	No-load, 2.00%R				
Management Fee:	0.50% mx./0.15% mn.				
Actual Fees:	Mgt:0.50%	Dist: —			
Expense Projections:	3Yr:$300	5Yr:$324	10Yr:$726		
Income Distrib:	Annually				

Vanguard Capital Value

Ticker	Load	NAV	Yield	Total Assets	Mstar Category
VCVLX	None	$11.75	1.1%	$449 mil	Large Value

Governance and Management

Fiduciary Grade: B

Portfolio Manager(s)

David Fassnacht, who has been on board here since 2001, took over lead-manager responsibilities for this fund in June 2004, when Charles Freeman retired. Before assuming control, Fassnacht worked as an assistant portfolio manager on this fund and Vanguard Windsor.

Strategy

This fund is a diehard and opportunistic value hunter. Its managers favor stocks that have fallen hard and may hold sizable positions in individual names or sectors. While doing so, they look across the market-cap spectrum.

Historical Profile

Return Average
Risk High
Rating ★★★ Neutral

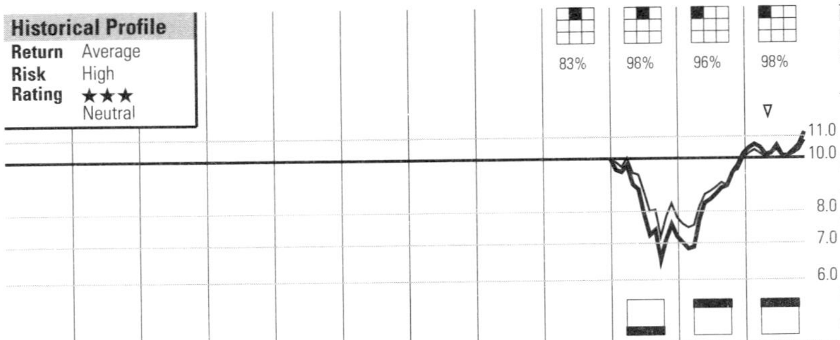

Investment Style
Equity
Stock %

▼ Manager Change
▽ Partial Manager Change

Growth of $10,000
— Investment Values of Fund
— Investment Values of S&P 500

Performance Quartile (within Category)

1993	1994	1995	1996	1997	1998	1999	2000	2001	2002	2003	12-04	History
—	—	—	—	—	—	—	—	10.26	7.31	10.30	11.75	NAV
—	—	—	—	—	—	—	—	2.60*	-28.07	41.74	15.38	Total Return %
—	—	—	—	—	—	—	—	—	-5.98	13.07	4.51	+/-S&P 500
—	—	—	—	—	—	—	—	—	-12.55	11.71	-1.11	+/-Russ 1000 VI
—	—	—	—	—	—	—	—	—	0.68	0.82	1.26	Income Return %
—	—	—	—	—	—	—	—	—	-28.75	40.92	14.12	Capital Return %
—	—	—	—	—	—	—	—	—	96	3	20	Total Rtn % Rank Cat
—	—	—	—	—	—	—	—	0.00	0.07	0.06	0.13	Income $
—	—	—	—	—	—	—	—	0.00	0.00	0.00	0.00	Capital Gains $
—	—	—	—	—	—	—	—	—	0.54	0.53	0.53	Expense Ratio %
—	—	—	—	—	—	—	—	—	0.77	0.82	0.95	Income Ratio %
—	—	—	—	—	—	—	—	—	40	40	40	Turnover Rate %
—	—	—	—	—	—	—	—	91	199	377	449	Net Assets $mil

Performance 12-31-04

	1st Qtr	2nd Qtr	3rd Qtr	4th Qtr	Total
2000	—	—	—	—	—
2001	—	—	—	—	2.60 *
2002	-2.63	-18.82	-17.63	10.48	-28.07
2003	-4.24	22.14	5.85	14.48	41.74
2004	2.62	0.66	-2.07	14.05	15.38

Trailing	Total Return%	+/- S&P 500	+/- Russ 1000 VI	%Rank Cat	Growth of $10,000
3 Mo	14.05	4.82	3.67	2	11,405
6 Mo	11.69	4.50	-0.39	13	11,169
1 Yr	15.38	4.51	-1.11	20	11,538
3 Yr Avg	5.56	1.98	-3.01	53	11,762
5 Yr Avg	—	—	—	—	—
10 Yr Avg	—	—	—	—	—
15 Yr Avg	—	—	—	—	—

Tax Analysis	Tax-Adj Rtn%	%Rank Cat	Tax-Cost Rat	%Rank Cat
3 Yr (estimated)	5.26	42	0.28	19
5 Yr (estimated)	—	—	—	—
10 Yr (estimated)	—	—	—	—

Potential Capital Gain Exposure: 14% of assets

Rating and Risk

Time Period	Load-Adj Return %	Morningstar Rtn vs Cat	Morningstar Risk vs Cat	Morningstar Risk-Adj Rating
1 Yr	15.38			
3 Yr	5.56	Avg	High	★★★
5 Yr	—	—	—	—
10 Yr	—	—	—	—
Incept	6.38			

Other Measures	Standard Index S&P 500	Best Fit Index Russ 1000
Alpha	1.9	1.0
Beta	1.18	1.19
R-Squared	94	95

Standard Deviation	19.33
Mean	5.56
Sharpe Ratio	0.22

Morningstar's Take by Christine Benz 01-05-05

We're standing by Vanguard Capital Value Fund.

Shareholders in this offering have had their patience tried over the past few years. Shortly after the fund made its debut, management bet heavily on some badly beleaguered companies only to see them fall further still. The fund's 28% loss in 2002, its first full calendar year, was far larger than its typical large-value peer's. A more significant worry for shareholders, however, was the departure of longtime lead manager Chuck Freeman, who retired in late June 2004.

Nonetheless, we think there's good reason to be sanguine about the fund's future prospects. Despite Freeman's departure, the team running the fund is still very experienced. The four most senior team members together have 63 years' worth of investment experience. David Fassnacht, who has assumed the lead-manager role, has worked at subadvisor Wellington Management for 13 years and has been an assistant portfolio manager on this fund since its inception.

We're also reassured by the consistency with which the team applies its contrarian strategy. True, calendar-year returns can be erratic when management is early into its picks (or, as was the case with some of their holdings in 2002, just plain wrong). But judging from the team's superior long-term record on Vanguard Windsor, where they run 70% of assets, their approach has served patient investors well. We also like the prospects for contrarian strategies in what may turn out to be a low-returning decade, as the team here is ready to pounce when it thinks the market is overreacting to a company's bad news. That strategy is particularly powerful given the fund's still-small asset base.

Investors and would-be investors should be prepared for periods of poor absolute and relative returns, but we think the fund is a reasonable choice for those who share management's contrarian streak.

Portfolio Analysis 09-30-04

Share change since 06-04 Total Stocks:85	Sector	PE	YTD Ret%	% Assets
Citigroup	Financial	15.3	2.72	4.81
⊖ Tyco International	Ind Mtrls	25.1	35.41	3.40
Comcast	Media	—	-13.77	3.23
⊕ Bank of America	Financial	12.3	21.50	2.87
⊕ Pactiv	Goods	23.0	5.82	2.67
Alcoa	Ind Mtrls	18.8	-15.75	2.67
Fannie Mae	Financial	9.1	-2.33	2.64
⊕ Wyeth	Health	17.0	2.73	2.61
Michelin Grp	Ind Mtrls	—	—	2.49
Renaissance Re Holdings	Financial	41.6	7.39	2.31
⊕ Sanofi-Aventis ADR	Health	23.0	9.75	2.26
⊕ Anthem	Health	17.4	53.33	2.23
Foot Locker	Consumer	17.6	15.99	2.20
⊖ Rinker Grp Ltd	Ind Mtrls	—	—	2.05
Petroleo Brasileiro Sa P	Energy	—	—	2.00
CIT Group	Financial	13.2	29.28	1.93
USF	Business	27.3	12.18	1.89
⊖ IBM	Hardware	20.2	7.19	1.88
☼ Fairchild Semiconductor	Hardware	34.3	-34.88	1.86
Ross Stores	Consumer	22.6	9.82	1.85

Current Investment Style

Value Blnd Growth — Large Mid Small

Market Cap	%
Giant	32.4
Large	24.6
Mid	34.9
Small	7.2
Micro	0.9
Avg $mil: 12,104	

Value Measures		Rel Category
Price/Earnings	12.91	0.86
Price/Book	1.93	0.85
Price/Sales	0.76	0.64
Price/Cash Flow	4.88	0.76
Dividend Yield %	1.24	0.61

Growth Measures	%	Rel Category
Long-Term Erngs	11.78	1.13
Book Value	7.52	1.33
Sales	5.68	1.35
Cash Flow	11.00	2.11
Historical Erngs	12.18	1.03

Profitability	%	Rel Category
Return on Equity	15.90	1.00
Return on Assets	8.64	1.10
Net Margin	10.56	1.03

Sector Weightings	% of Stocks	Rel S&P 500	3 Year High	3 Year Low
Info	20.51	0.95		
Software	1.72	0.40	2	0
Hardware	11.23	1.10	11	7
Media	5.91	1.54	10	4
Telecom	1.65	0.52	4	0
Service	53.42	1.15		
Health	13.01	1.04	14	9
Consumer	8.60	0.95	11	7
Business	6.39	1.58	12	6
Financial	25.42	1.22	31	25
Mfg	26.06	0.81		
Goods	4.83	0.52	5	2
Ind Mtrls	16.59	1.31	20	15
Energy	4.64	0.65	5	0
Utilities	0.00	0.00	0	0

Composition

Cash	0.1
Stocks	97.5
Bonds	0.0
Other	2.3
Foreign (% of Stock)	14.4

Address:	P.O. Box 2600 Valley Forge PA 19482 800-662-7447	Minimum Purchase:	$3000	Add: $100 IRA: $1000
Web Address:	www.vanguard.com	Min Auto Inv Plan:	$3000	Add: $50
Inception:	12-17-01 *	Sales Fees:	No-load	
Advisor:	Wellington Management Company, LLP	Management Fee:	0.42%	
Subadvisor:	None	Actual Fees:	Mgt:0.42%	Dist: —
		Expense Projections:	3Yr: —	5Yr: — 10Yr: —
		Income Distrib:	Annually	
NTF Plans:	N/A			

Vanguard Convertible Sec

Ticker	Load	NAV	Yield	Total Assets	Mstar Category
VCVSX	Closed	$13.29	2.8%	$941 mil	Convertibles

Governance and Management

Fiduciary Grade: B

Portfolio Manager(s)

In 1996 manager Larry Keele cofounded this fund's subadvisor Oaktree Capital Management. The shop specializes in convertibles, high-yield bonds, and distressed debt. He took on this fund in November 1996 and has been assisted since then by Andrew Watts. Stu Spangler and Steve Prado also serve as convertible analysts for the fund.

Strategy

Manager Larry Keele only invests in convertible bonds. He likes to make sure a firm's convertible has a solid structure and an attractive price before his group runs the company through a gauntlet of credit analysis. Upside potential for the stock is the last piece of analysis. Keele prefers to avoid convertible preferreds, equitylike converts, and "busted converts," which results in a portfolio of nearly 100% balanced convertible bonds.

Historical Profile

Return Above Avg
Risk Average
Rating ★★★ Neutral

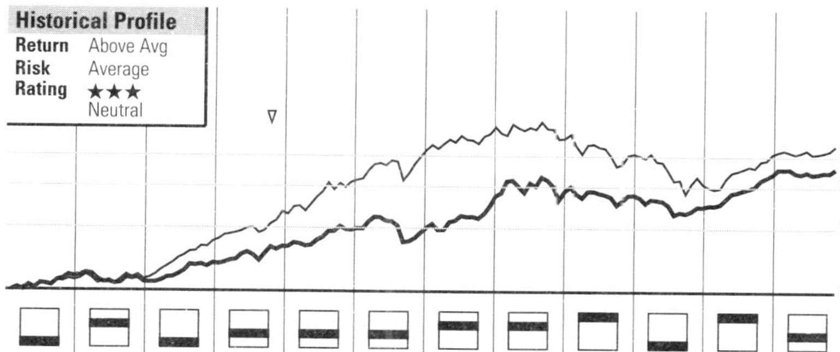

Investment Style
Equity
Stock %

▼ Manager Change
∇ Partial Manager Change

Growth of $10,000
— Investment Values of Fund
— Investment Values of S&P 500

Performance Quartile (within Category)

1993	1994	1995	1996	1997	1998	1999	2000	2001	2002	2003	12-04	History
11.91	10.55	11.62	11.63	11.82	11.34	13.46	12.96	12.00	10.41	13.23	13.29	NAV
13.54	-5.68	16.74	15.44	16.39	0.56	30.36	4.21	-3.10	-9.35	31.58	7.20	Total Return %
3.48	-6.99	-20.79	-7.50	-16.96	-28.01	9.32	13.31	8.78	12.74	2.91	-3.67	+/-S&P 500
-2.87	-0.84	-7.22	3.32	0.88	-11.65	-5.63	11.73	-0.19	-6.23	8.61	-1.11	+/-Merrill Lynch Convert
4.56	4.35	5.21	4.10	4.72	4.64	4.48	4.29	4.24	3.98	4.09	2.90	Income Return %
8.98	-10.03	11.53	11.34	11.67	-4.08	25.88	-0.08	-7.34	-13.33	27.49	4.30	Capital Return %
76	46	96	58	75	61	46	37	24	77	17	67	Total Rtn % Rank Cat
0.53	0.51	0.54	0.47	0.54	0.54	0.50	0.57	0.54	0.47	0.42	0.38	Income $
0.91	0.18	0.14	1.29	1.12	0.00	0.70	0.51	0.00	0.00	0.00	0.50	Capital Gains $
0.71	0.73	0.75	0.69	0.67	0.73	0.55	0.56	0.71	0.95	0.84	—	Expense Ratio %
4.44	4.68	4.63	3.43	4.29	4.36	4.30	4.19	4.21	4.27	3.82	—	Income Ratio %
81	52	46	97	182	186	162	182	156	118	127	—	Turnover Rate %
204	171	168	166	187	178	197	345	303	286	874	941	Net Assets $mil

Performance 12-31-04

	1st Qtr	2nd Qtr	3rd Qtr	4th Qtr	Total
2000	14.09	-2.22	2.51	-8.88	4.21
2001	-5.31	3.88	-9.26	8.57	-3.10
2002	-3.41	-4.61	-6.64	5.39	-9.35
2003	2.50	10.76	4.98	10.40	31.58
2004	4.54	-2.25	-0.38	5.30	7.20

Trailing	Total Return%	+/- S&P 500	+/- Merrill Lynch Convert	%Rank Cat	Growth of $10,000
3 Mo	5.30	-3.93	-1.06	96	10,530
6 Mo	4.91	-2.28	0.10	82	10,491
1 Yr	7.20	-3.67	-1.11	67	10,720
3 Yr Avg	8.54	4.96	-0.33	44	12,787
5 Yr Avg	5.25	7.55	2.26	30	12,915
10 Yr Avg	10.26	-1.81	-0.74	39	26,557
15 Yr Avg	9.99	-0.94	-0.57	50	41,716

Tax Analysis	Tax-Adj Rtn%	%Rank Cat	Tax-Cost Rat	%Rank Cat
3 Yr (estimated)	6.89	38	1.52	74
5 Yr (estimated)	3.33	28	1.82	41
10 Yr (estimated)	7.35	42	2.64	71

Potential Capital Gain Exposure: 6% of assets

Rating and Risk

Time Period	Load-Adj Return %	Morningstar Rtn vs Cat	Morningstar Risk vs Cat	Morningstar Risk-Adj Rating
1 Yr	7.20			
3 Yr	8.54	+Avg	Avg	★★★★
5 Yr	5.25	+Avg	Avg	★★★
10 Yr	10.26	Avg	Avg	★★★
Incept	9.04			

Other Measures	Standard Index S&P 500	Best Fit Index Merrill Lynch Convert
Alpha	5.9	-1.2
Beta	0.46	1.14
R-Squared	55	86
Standard Deviation	10.06	
Mean	8.54	
Sharpe Ratio	0.72	

Portfolio Analysis 09-30-04

Total Fixed-Income:24	Date of Maturity	Amount $000	Value $000	% Net Assets
Freeport-Mcmoran Copper		32	32,153	3.38
Schlumberger Cv 1.5%	06-01-23	27,035	29,603	3.11
Fisher Scientific Intl 3	03-01-24	27,455	29,480	3.10
Sealed Air 144A Cv 3%	06-30-33	26,000	25,968	2.73
Bj Svcs Cv 0.5%	04-24-22	29,380	25,597	2.69
Teva Pharma Fin Ii 0.25%	02-01-24	26,080	24,809	2.61
Cmnty Health Sys Cv 4.25	10-15-08	22,731	23,441	2.46
Disney Walt Cv 2.125%	04-15-23	22,415	23,003	2.42
Veeco Instrs Cv 4.125%	12-21-08	22,663	22,210	2.34
Hanover Compressor Cv 4.	01-15-14	16,760	20,657	2.17
Flextronics Intl Cv 1%	08-01-10	18,200	20,521	2.16
Sepracor 144A	10-15-24	21,165	20,504	2.16
Genzyme 1.25%	12-01-23	19,550	20,479	2.15
Graftech Intl 144A 1.625	01-15-24	16,355	17,643	1.86
Fluor 1.5%	02-15-24	16,570	17,295	1.82
Chesapeake Engy Pfd Cv 1		15	17,138	1.80
Cooper Cameron 1.5%	05-15-24	15,750	16,951	1.78
Cephalon Cv 2.5%	12-15-06	17,205	16,732	1.76
Mgi Pharma 144A 1.682%	03-02-24	20,515	16,720	1.76
Navistar Finl 4.75%	04-01-09	15,710	15,474	1.63

Investment Style	
Avg Eff Maturity	4.6 Yrs
Avg Credit Quality	BB
Avg Wtd Coupon	2.60%
Avg Wtd Price	102.30% of par

Coupon Range	% of Bonds	Rel Cat
0% PIK	9.8	0.8
0% to 8%	100.0	1.0
8% to 11%	0.0	0.0
11% to 14%	0.0	0.0
More than 14%	0.0	0.0

1.00=Category Average

Special Securities	
Restricted/ Illiquid Secs	30
Emerging-Markets Secs	0
Options/Futures/Warrants	No

Composition	
Cash	5.3
Stocks	0.4
Bonds	28.6
Convertibles	60.4
Other	5.3

Credit Analysis		% bonds 09-30-04	
US Govt	0	BB	7
AAA	0	B	27
AA	0	Below B	17
A	11	NR/NA	18
BBB	20		

Morningstar's Take by Gareth Lyons 12-23-04

Recently closed Vanguard Convertible Securities sticks to its knitting.

On May 14, this fund closed its doors to new investors. The move wasn't all that surprising. The fund has grown significantly. Assets went from $286 million at the end of 2002 to just short of $1 billion by spring of 2004. By many managers' accounts, opportunities are fewer, too. Fears of rising interest rates have diminished the appeal of all fixed-income securities. But other factors are at play in the converts arena. Issuance of new converts has slowed. With corporate profits ticking up, firms are more likely to raise capital through equity or straight-debt offerings, or by simply going to the bank. Moreover, slated legislative changes that will require firms to more accurately account for converts further muddy the supply outlook.

The difficult investment conditions haven't swayed manager Larry Keele from his disciplined approach, however. While many of his rivals put cash to work in straight bonds and/or equities, Keele invests exclusively in convertible issues. What's more, he limits both interest-rate and equity risk by focusing on "balanced converts," issues that have decent yields and reasonable equity exposure.

The converts-only mandate here means the fund does lose out on the potential benefits of a more-flexible approach. This year, many rival managers have goosed their returns by delving into high-yield bonds, for example. This fund isn't exactly risk free, either, as many of Keele's picks often reside below investment grade, where firms are prone to failure.

Keele's unwavering focus on his asset class and his strict attention to credit analysis has helped this fund avoid blowups that have wreaked havoc elsewhere in the converts' world, though. We think shareholders who wish to maintain their exposure to converts remain in good hands. A well-below-average expense ratio of 0.84% is an added bonus here.

Address:	PO Box 2600 V26 Valley Forge PA 19482 800-662-7447
Web Address:	www.vanguard.com
Inception:	06-17-86
Advisor:	The Vanguard Group, Inc.
Subadvisor:	Oaktree Capital Management, LLC
NTF Plans:	N/A

Minimum Purchase:	Closed	Add: —	IRA: —
Min Auto Inv Plan:	Closed	Add: —	
Sales Fees:	No-load		
Management Fee:	0.92%		
Actual Fees:	Mgt:0.92%	Dist: —	
Expense Projections:	3Yr:$303	5Yr:$525	10Yr:$1166
Income Distrib:	Quarterly		

Vanguard Dev Mkts Idx

Ticker	Load	NAV	Yield	Total Assets	Mstar Category
VDMIX	None	$9.20	2.1%	$1,198 mil	Foreign Large Blend

Governance and Management

Fiduciary Grade: B

Portfolio Manager(s)

Vanguard indexing expert Gus Sauter has managed this fund since its May 2000 inception. He also manages numerous other Vanguard funds, including Vanguard 500 Index and Vanguard Total International Stock Index.

Strategy

This is a passively managed fund of funds that invests all of its assets in Vanguard European Stock Index and Vanguard Pacific Stock Index. Its goal is to track the performance of the MSCI EAFE Index. It has minimal exposure to emerging markets.

Historical Profile

Return Above Avg
Risk Average
Rating ★★★★ Above Avg

Investment Style
Equity Stock %: 2000 98%, 2001 99%, 2002 96%, 2003 93%, 2004 98%

▼ Manager Change
∇ Partial Manager Change

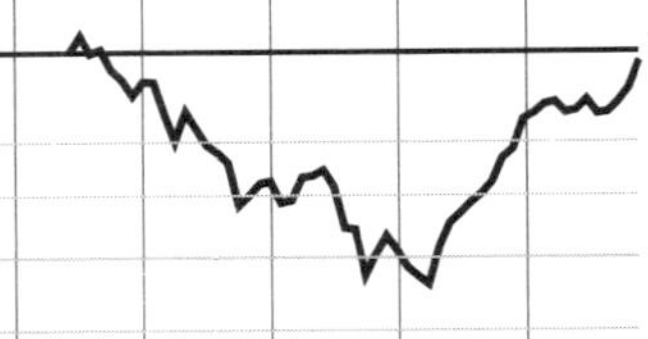

Growth of $10,000
— Investment Values of Fund
— Investment Values of MSCI EAFE

Performance Quartile (within Category)

History	1993	1994	1995	1996	1997	1998	1999	2000	2001	2002	2003	12-04
NAV	—	—	—	—	—	—	—	9.07	6.95	5.74	7.81	9.20
Total Return %	—	—	—	—	—	—	—	-7.79*	-22.05	-15.70	38.61	20.25
+/-MSCI EAFE	—	—	—	—	—	—	—	—	-0.63	0.24	0.02	0.00
+/-MSCI Wd xUS	—	—	—	—	—	—	—	—	-0.66	0.10	-0.81	-0.13
Income Return %	—	—	—	—	—	—	—	0.00	1.32	1.67	2.49	2.43
Capital Return %	—	—	—	—	—	—	—	—	-23.37	-17.37	36.12	17.82
Total Rtn % Rank Cat	—	—	—	—	—	—	—	—	54	36	17	17
Income $	—	—	—	—	—	—	—	0.15	0.12	0.12	0.14	0.19
Capital Gains $	—	—	—	—	—	—	—	0.00	0.00	0.00	0.00	0.00
Expense Ratio %	—	—	—	—	—	—	—	0.00	0.00	0.00	0.00	0.00
Income Ratio %	—	—	—	—	—	—	—	1.66	0.04	1.30	1.48	1.52
Turnover Rate %	—	—	—	—	—	—	—	8	3	5	7	4
Net Assets $mil	—	—	—	—	—	—	—	99	189	399	734	1,198

Performance 12-31-04

	1st Qtr	2nd Qtr	3rd Qtr	4th Qtr	Total
2000	—	—	-8.12	-2.93	-7.79 *
2001	-13.78	-1.02	-13.95	6.16	-22.05
2002	1.01	-2.28	-19.83	6.52	-15.70
2003	-8.19	19.35	8.11	17.00	38.61
2004	4.35	0.49	-0.49	15.23	20.25

Trailing	Total Return%	+/- MSCI EAFE	+/- MSCI Wd xUS	%Rank Cat	Growth of $10,000
3 Mo	15.23	-0.09	0.08	17	11,523
6 Mo	14.67	-0.33	-0.70	32	11,467
1 Yr	20.25	0.00	-0.13	17	12,025
3 Yr Avg	12.00	0.11	-0.22	15	14,049
5 Yr Avg	—	—	—	—	—
10 Yr Avg	—	—	—	—	—
15 Yr Avg	—	—	—	—	—

Tax Analysis	Tax-Adj Rtn%	%Rank Cat	Tax-Cost Rat	%Rank Cat
3 Yr (estimated)	11.30	14	0.63	68
5 Yr (estimated)	—	—	—	—
10 Yr (estimated)	—	—	—	—

Potential Capital Gain Exposure: -20% of assets

Rating and Risk

Time Period	Load-Adj Return %	Morningstar Rtn vs Cat	Morningstar Risk vs Cat	Morningstar Risk-Adj Rating
1 Yr	20.25			
3 Yr	12.00	+Avg	Avg	★★★★
5 Yr	—	—	—	—
10 Yr	—	—	—	—
Incept	0.21			

Other Measures	Standard Index S&P 500	Best Fit Index MSCI EAFE
Alpha	0.1	0.1
Beta	1.00	1.00
R-Squared	100	100

Standard Deviation	17.55
Mean	12.00
Sharpe Ratio	0.61

Portfolio Analysis 09-30-04

Share change since 06-04 Total Stocks:0	Sector	Country	% Assets
⊕ Vanguard European Stock	—	United States	69.44
⊕ Vanguard Pacific Stock I	—	United States	30.56

Current Investment Style

Market Cap	%
Giant	55.1
Large	31.8
Mid	12.6
Small	0.5
Micro	0.0
Avg $mil: 23,218	

Value Measures		Rel Category
Price/Earnings	13.87	1.01
Price/Book	1.75	0.97
Price/Sales	0.82	0.90
Price/Cash Flow	4.73	0.96
Dividend Yield %	2.80	1.10

Growth Measures	%	Rel Category
Long-Term Erngs	10.07	0.94
Book Value	-0.49	NMF
Sales	1.43	0.57
Cash Flow	3.03	0.54
Historical Erngs	5.56	0.99

Composition

Cash	0.2	Bonds	0.0
Stocks	98.2	Other	1.6

Foreign (% of Stock) 100.0

Sector Weightings	% of Stocks	Rel MSCI EAFE	3 Year High	3 Year Low
Info	14.78	0.89		
Software	0.72	0.67	1	0
Hardware	4.24	1.16	6	4
Media	2.37	1.04	3	2
Telecom	7.45	0.78	9	6
Service	44.87	1.00		
Health	8.38	1.15	11	8
Consumer	5.04	1.00	5	4
Business	4.77	0.88	6	4
Financial	26.68	0.99	27	21
Mfg	40.35	1.04		
Goods	13.91	1.02	16	14
Ind Mtrls	12.94	1.05	15	10
Energy	8.50	1.16	10	7
Utilities	5.00	0.93	5	4

Regional Exposure % Stock

UK/W. Europe	69	N. America	0
Japan	22	Latn America	0
Asia X Japan	8	Other	1

Country Exposure % Stock

U.K.	26	Switzerland	7
Japan	22	Germany	7
France	9		

Morningstar's Take by Gregg Wolper 11-11-04

Vanguard Developed Markets Index faces a serious challenge.

On the surface, everything is rosy here. This fund has been tearing up the track: Its year-to-date return through Nov. 11, 2004, is 12.2%, which puts it in the foreign large-blend category's top quartile. The fund also placed comfortably in the group's top half in 2002 and 2003 after landing in the middle in 2001, its first full calendar year.

But the story gets more complicated. A prominent rival that also tracks the MSCI EAFE Index, Fidelity Spartan International Index, drastically lowered its cost recently. That fund, which had an expense ratio of 47 basis points (i.e., 0.47%), now charges just 10 basis points. This fund's expense ratio, meanwhile, is 34 basis points. With index funds, such differences are crucial, for they can't make up ground with stock selection. Over the trailing three-year period, this fund is beating the Fidelity offering by 21 basis points annually. That divergence can be explained by the cost advantage this fund had enjoyed, as well as the ability of its manager, Gus Sauter, to pick up a basis point here and there with his well-developed index-tracking techniques. With the cost advantage now solidly in Fidelity's favor, it will be tougher for this fund to top its rival.

However, several things should be kept in mind. First, Fidelity's fee waiver, though unlikely to be removed anytime soon, could be eliminated at some point. Second, as the three-year figures show, even with the new cost arrangement in place this fund's return would have been roughly in line with the Fidelity fund's. Those factors--plus the fact that shareholders who switch might have to pay taxes or fees or both--means that despite the new situation, there's certainly no reason to abandon this fund.

Address:	PO Box 2600 Valley Forge PA 19482 800-662-7447
Web Address:	www.vanguard.com
Inception:	05-08-00 *
Advisor:	Vanguard Advisers, Inc.
Subadvisor:	None
NTF Plans:	N/A

Minimum Purchase:	$3000	Add: $100	IRA: $1000
Min Auto Inv Plan:	$3000	Add: $50	
Sales Fees:	No-load		
Management Fee:	0.31%		
Actual Fees:	Mgt:0.00%	Dist: —	
Expense Projections:	3Yr:$103	5Yr:$180	10Yr:$406
Income Distrib:	Annually		

Vanguard Dividend Growth

Ticker	Load	NAV	Yield	Total Assets	Mstar Category
VDIGX	None	$12.15	1.8%	$984 mil	Large Value

Governance and Management

Fiduciary Grade: B

Portfolio Manager(s)

Minerva Butler replaced former manager Mark Beckwith. Butler's experience includes stints as manager of both Fidelity Select Industrial Equipment and Fidelity Select Developing Communications, as well as analytical duties covering telecom, technology, wireless, and industrial materials for the firm. She signed on as analyst for Vanguard Wellington in September 1997.

Strategy

New manager Minerva Butler has cut the fund's utilities stake and emphasized diversification by spreading her bets across sectors. She prefers companies offering high dividend yields relative to the fund's new benchmark, the Russell 1000, along with attractive valuations and strong earnings growth. The fund will hold no more than 25% of assets in any one sector. Butler plans to maintain a portfolio of roughly 80 to 100 names.

Historical Profile

Return Below Avg
Risk Below Avg
Rating ★★ Below Avg

Investment Style
Equity
Stock %: 78% 83% 84% 88% 95% 95% 96% 97% 99%

▼ Manager Change
∇ Partial Manager Change

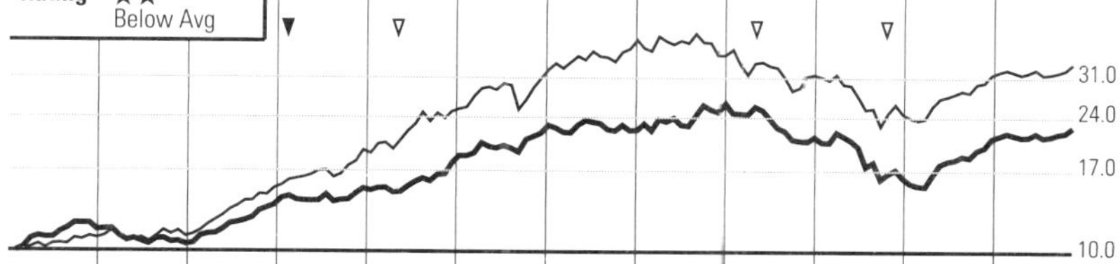

Growth of $10,000
— Investment Values of Fund
— Investment Values of S&P 500

Performance Quartile (within Category)

1993	1994	1995	1996	1997	1998	1999	2000	2001	2002	2003	12-04	History
11.63	9.94	12.68	12.74	14.98	16.54	14.33	15.66	11.88	8.79	11.15	12.15	NAV
15.06	-8.55	34.03	5.28	25.09	21.83	-2.96	18.77	-19.45	-23.16	29.20	11.02	Total Return %
5.00	-9.86	-3.50	-17.66	-8.26	-6.74	-24.00	27.87	-7.57	-1.07	0.53	0.15	+/-S&P 500
-3.01	-6.57	-4.33	-16.36	-10.09	6.20	-10.31	11.76	-13.86	-7.64	-0.83	-5.47	+/-Russ 1000 VI
5.20	5.22	5.74	4.49	4.79	4.02	3.17	3.83	2.44	3.24	2.17	1.98	Income Return %
9.86	-13.77	28.29	0.79	20.30	17.81	-6.13	14.94	-21.89	-26.40	27.03	9.04	Capital Return %
42	97	42	99	76	5	87	14	98	81	39	70	Total Rtn % Rank Cat
0.56	0.59	0.56	0.56	0.60	0.59	0.51	0.53	0.37	0.38	0.19	0.22	Income $
0.40	0.12	0.00	0.02	0.26	1.01	1.20	0.73	0.41	0.00	0.00	0.00	Capital Gains $
0.45	0.42	0.50	0.41	0.40	0.44	0.38	0.38	0.35	0.37	0.34	0.40	Expense Ratio %
4.70	4.82	5.43	4.88	4.63	4.30	3.51	3.13	2.76	2.85	3.57	1.84	Income Ratio %
—	46	35	35	38	41	55	47	48	27	104	23	Turnover Rate %
774	561	758	659	685	951	841	954	706	555	783	984	Net Assets $mil

Performance 12-31-04

	1st Qtr	2nd Qtr	3rd Qtr	4th Qtr	Total
2000	7.24	-3.60	13.62	1.12	18.77
2001	-6.83	-2.83	-12.45	1.62	-19.45
2002	3.12	-9.13	-18.74	0.91	-23.16
2003	-5.46	17.79	2.37	13.33	29.20
2004	2.06	1.32	-0.44	7.83	11.02

Trailing	Total Return%	+/- S&P 500	+/- Russ 1000 VI	%Rank Cat	Growth of $10,000
3 Mo	7.83	-1.40	-2.55	81	10,783
6 Mo	7.36	0.17	-4.72	74	10,736
1 Yr	11.02	0.15	-5.47	70	11,102
3 Yr Avg	3.29	-0.29	-5.28	79	11,020
5 Yr Avg	1.07	3.37	-4.20	84	10,547
10 Yr Avg	8.21	-3.86	-5.62	96	22,013
15 Yr Avg	—	—	—	—	—

Tax Analysis	Tax-Adj Rtn%	%Rank Cat	Tax-Cost Rat	%Rank Cat
3 Yr (estimated)	2.53	74	0.74	50
5 Yr (estimated)	-0.22	85	1.28	68
10 Yr (estimated)	6.25	95	1.81	51

Potential Capital Gain Exposure: -2% of assets

Rating and Risk

Time Period	Load-Adj Return %	Morningstar Rtn vs Cat	Morningstar Risk vs Cat	Morningstar Risk-Adj Rating
1 Yr	11.02			
3 Yr	3.29	-Avg	Avg	★★
5 Yr	1.07	-Avg	-Avg	★★
10 Yr	8.21	Low	-Avg	★★
Incept	7.85			

Other Measures	Standard Index S&P 500	Best Fit Index MSCI World
Alpha	0.0	-3.0
Beta	0.90	0.93
R-Squared	83	89
Standard Deviation	15.28	
Mean	3.29	
Sharpe Ratio	0.13	

Morningstar's Take by Paul Herbert 01-04-05

Vanguard Dividend Growth has looked out of place lately, but we think its time will come.

Financially sound companies have a home here. Manager Minerva Butler, who took the reins when Vanguard ditched the fund's former utilities-focused mandate in December 2002, does not simply look for stocks with long records of growing their dividends or those with high current yields. Rather, she seeks companies that have not paid out a dividend but have the potential to do so, and those who may have hit a snag in their dividend-growth plans, but possess the ability to resume distributing income. The unifying factor among the fund's holdings is big cash stores on balance sheets, records of earnings growth, and managements that are focused on returning money to shareholders.

The portfolio hasn't delivered standout performance, but we find that forgivable. It has turned in decent results since Butler took over, tracking the large-value category average from December 2002 through the end of 2004. But it has had the wind in its face during this period as the large-cap, higher-quality stocks it favors have trailed less-sturdy fare. When this trend reverses, the fund should be in good shape to go to the head of the class.

Lately, the fund has turned to the market's behemoths. Butler steadily added to Microsoft during 2004, encouraged by its progress on the regulatory front and the late-July announcement of its 100% dividend increase. She also ramped up the fund's weighting in General Electric, because she's optimistic that its power generation and aerospace businesses are picking up.

Vanguard investors have a tough choice when it comes to actively run large-value funds, as all have deep research resources and low costs. This fund is best for those seeking a bigger-cap, more-concentrated, lower-turnover vehicle.

Address:	PO Box 2600 Valley Forge PA 19482 800-662-7447
Web Address:	www.vanguard.com
Inception:	05-15-92
Advisor:	Wellington Management Company, LLP
Subadvisor:	None
NTF Plans:	N/A

Minimum Purchase:	$3000	Add: $100	IRA: $1000
Min Auto Inv Plan:	$3000	Add: $50	
Sales Fees:	No-load		
Management Fee:	0.35%		
Actual Fees:	Mgt:0.35%	Dist:	
Expense Projections:	3Yr:$119	5Yr:$208	10Yr:$468
Income Distrib:	Semi-Annually		

Portfolio Analysis 09-30-04

Share change since 06-04 Total Stocks:80	Sector	PE	YTD Ret%	% Assets
⊕ Gen Elec	Ind Mtrls	22.8	20.68	2.75
Microsoft	Software	36.1	8.95	2.59
Citigroup	Financial	15.3	2.72	2.55
⊕ Bank of America	Financial	12.3	21.50	2.46
⊕ Abbott Laboratories	Health	22.1	2.61	2.18
Marsh & McLennan Compani	Financial	13.4	-29.80	2.06
⊕ Pfizer	Health	22.0	-22.31	1.99
⊕ United Technologies	Ind Mtrls	18.6	10.72	1.94
Verizon Communications	Telecom	32.4	20.25	1.91
IBM	Hardware	20.2	7.19	1.88
⊕ Merrill Lynch & Company	Financial	12.6	3.12	1.86
General Dynamics	Ind Mtrls	17.5	17.40	1.80
⊕ Nokia ADR	Hardware	18.1	-6.14	1.73
ACE	Financial	9.6	5.26	1.77
Emerson Electric	Ind Mtrls	22.8	11.09	1.72
Altria Group	Goods	13.3	18.38	1.63
Baxter International	Health	32.9	15.22	1.64
⊕ General Mills	Goods	19.4	12.56	1.64
⊕ McDonald's	Consumer	19.7	31.48	1.59
ConocoPhillips	Energy	9.0	35.60	1.58

Current Investment Style

Value Blnd Growth — Large Mid Small

Market Cap	%
Giant	46.2
Large	42.2
Mid	11.5
Small	0.0
Micro	0.0
Avg $mil: 38,829	

Value Measures		Rel Category
Price/Earnings	15.25	1.01
Price/Book	2.71	1.19
Price/Sales	1.40	1.18
Price/Cash Flow	7.25	1.14
Dividend Yield %	2.20	1.08

Growth Measures	%	Rel Category
Long-Term Erngs	10.31	0.99
Book Value	5.02	0.89
Sales	6.01	1.43
Cash Flow	5.26	1.01
Historical Erngs	8.35	0.71

Profitability	%	Rel Category
Return on Equity	18.18	1.15
Return on Assets	8.90	1.14
Net Margin	10.82	1.06

Sector Weightings	% of Stocks	Rel S&P 500	3 Year High	3 Year Low
Info	16.39	0.76		
Software	3.37	0.78	3	0
Hardware	6.08	0.60	8	0
Media	3.18	0.83	3	0
Telecom	3.76	1.19	13	4
Service	41.97	0.90		
Health	14.42	1.15	19	0
Consumer	6.25	0.69	6	0
Business	3.61	0.89	4	0
Financial	17.69	0.85	21	0
Mfg	41.66	1.30		
Goods	8.62	0.92	9	0
Ind Mtrls	22.87	1.81	23	0
Energy	6.72	0.94	8	3
Utilities	3.45	1.17	86	3

Composition

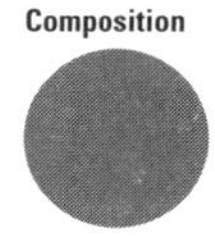

Cash	0.8
Stocks	99.3
Bonds	0.0
Other	0.0
Foreign (% of Stock)	6.4

Vanguard Em Mkt Idx

Ticker	Load	NAV	Yield	Total Assets	Mstar Category
VEIEX	None	$14.68	1.8%	$3,443 mil	Diversified Emerging Mkts

Governance and Management

Fiduciary Grade: B

Portfolio Manager(s)

Vanguard indexing guru Gus Sauter has managed this fund since its 1994 inception. He also manages numerous other Vanguard funds, including Vanguard 500 Index.

Strategy

This fund tracks a customized version of the MSCI Emerging Markets Free Index, which emphasizes the most-liquid emerging markets with the fewest barriers to foreign investment. Its bogy gives it heavy exposure to the major emerging markets but excludes a few markets, such as Russia. The occasionally major changes in the index sometimes make for more turnover here than at most passive index funds. In an effort to combat market-timing, the fund has a short-term redemption fee of 2% and also uses fair-value pricing on occasion. It does not hedge its currency exposure.

Historical Profile

Return Average
Risk Average
Rating ★★★ Neutral

Investment Style: Equity Stock %: 87% 83% 84% 85% 84% 85% 82% 88% 94%

▼ Manager Change
▽ Partial Manager Change

Growth of $10,000
— Investment Values of Fund
— Investment Values of MSCI EAFE

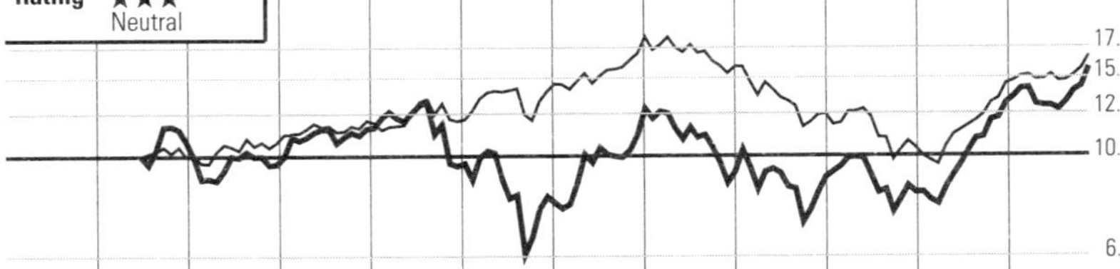

Performance Quartile (within Category)

1993	1994	1995	1996	1997	1998	1999	2000	2001	2002	2003	12-04	History
—	10.87	10.75	12.28	9.98	7.91	12.50	8.84	8.37	7.63	11.85	14.68	NAV
—	9.81*	0.56	15.83	-16.82	-18.12	61.57	-27.56	-2.88	-7.43	57.65	26.12	Total Return %
—	—	-10.65	9.78	-18.60	-38.05	34.54	-13.37	18.54	8.51	19.06	5.87	+/-MSCI EAFE
—	—	7.47	11.90	-3.37	9.55	-2.52	4.34	1.80	0.54	6.06	3.67	+/-MSCI EmrMkt
—	0.00	1.66	1.58	1.87	2.61	3.41	1.75	2.38	1.46	2.25	2.19	Income Return %
—	—	-1.10	14.25	-18.69	-20.73	58.16	-29.31	-5.26	-8.89	55.40	23.93	Capital Return %
—	—	41	34	93	10	69	26	46	66	29	28	Total Rtn % Rank Cat
—	0.07	0.18	0.17	0.23	0.26	0.27	0.22	0.21	0.12	0.17	0.26	Income $
—	0.04	0.00	0.00	0.00	0.00	0.00	0.00	0.00	0.00	0.00	0.00	Capital Gains $
—	0.60	0.60	0.60	0.57	0.61	0.58	0.59	0.57	0.57	0.53	0.48	Expense Ratio %
—	1.32	2.00	1.69	1.96	2.99	2.55	1.51	1.67	1.67	2.26	2.44	Income Ratio %
—	—	3	1	19	22	22	40	23	65	16	11	Turnover Rate %
—	83	234	637	681	577	1,138	1,019	801	896	1,873	3,140	Net Assets $mil

Performance 12-31-04

	1st Qtr	2nd Qtr	3rd Qtr	4th Qtr	Total
2000	-2.40	-6.89	-9.69	-11.72	-27.56
2001	-8.60	8.55	-22.03	25.55	-2.88
2002	10.39	-8.33	-17.12	10.37	-7.43
2003	-5.64	22.50	14.74	18.86	57.65
2004	7.85	-8.76	7.98	18.71	26.12

Trailing	Total Return%	+/- MSCI EAFE	+/- MSCI EmrMkt	%Rank Cat	Growth of $10,000
3 Mo	18.71	3.39	1.90	17	11,871
6 Mo	28.17	13.17	2.72	27	12,817
1 Yr	26.12	5.87	3.67	28	12,612
3 Yr Avg	22.55	10.66	3.01	36	18,405
5 Yr Avg	5.31	6.44	3.22	32	12,952
10 Yr Avg	5.20	-0.42	4.22	51	16,602
15 Yr Avg	—	—	—	—	—

Tax Analysis	Tax-Adj Rtn%	%Rank Cat	Tax-Cost Rat	%Rank Cat
3 Yr (estimated)	21.72	37	0.51	60
5 Yr (estimated)	4.47	35	0.69	75
10 Yr (estimated)	4.33	49	0.77	84

Potential Capital Gain Exposure: 20% of assets

Rating and Risk

Time Period	Load-Adj Return %	Morningstar Rtn vs Cat	Morningstar Risk vs Cat	Morningstar Risk-Adj Rating
1 Yr	25.49			
3 Yr	22.35	Avg	Avg	★★★
5 Yr	5.20	Avg	Avg	★★★
10 Yr	5.14	Avg	Avg	★★★
Incept	5.74			

Other Measures	Standard Index S&P 500	Best Fit Index MSCI EmrMkt
Alpha	10.2	2.4
Beta	0.99	1.01
R-Squared	74	99
Standard Deviation	22.01	
Mean	22.55	
Sharpe Ratio	0.97	

Morningstar's Take by Gregg Wolper 12-10-04

Be especially careful when deciding whether to buy Vanguard Emerging Markets Stock Index.

This offering has its attractions. Like other Vanguard index-tracking funds, it boasts low costs and a fine record of nearly matching (or even exceeding) its benchmark--in this case, a customized version of an MSCI emerging-markets index--over time. Moreover, its returns for the past two years are attention-getters: a 58% gain in 2003 followed by a 17.9% return for 2004 through Dec. 9. That 2003 return beat 71% of the diversified-emerging-markets category; this year's tops nearly as many.

Before jumping in, though, keep three things in mind. First, you're no doubt aware that emerging markets can be risky, but remember they're particularly risky after they've had a strong runup--and besides their strong gains of 2003 and 2004, they were outperforming developed markets for a couple of years before that. Even though all emerging markets don't necessarily move in lockstep with each other any more--so problems in one country or region may not sink the whole group--don't let recent performance obscure the dangers. Second, you may already have substantial emerging-markets exposure if you own a broad international fund. The typical such offering has about 8% or 10% in emerging markets, and some have more. Finally, be aware that this fund charges all shareholders an entry fee of 0.5% and an exit fee of 0.5% no matter how long they own it (short-term sellers must pay a higher exit fee).

All told, this is a reasonable way for investors to gain exposure to emerging markets. Besides the attributes named at the beginning, its trailing 10-year return lands in the middle of the category and its five-year gain is in the top half. However, it's not the slam-dunk recent years may make it appear.

Address:	PO Box 2600, Valley Forge PA 19482, 800-662-7447
Web Address:	www.vanguard.com
Inception:	05-04-94 *
Advisor:	Vanguard Advisers, Inc.
Subadvisor:	None
NTF Plans:	N/A

Minimum Purchase:	$3000	Add: $100	IRA: $1000
Min Auto Inv Plan:	$3000	Add: $50	
Sales Fees:	No-load, 2.00%R		
Management Fee:	0.30%, 0.50%A		
Actual Fees:	Mgt:0.30%	Dist: —	
Expense Projections:	3Yr:$276	5Yr:$407	10Yr:$789
Income Distrib:	Annually		

Portfolio Analysis 09-30-04

Share change since 06-04 Total Stocks:576	Sector	Country	% Assets
⊕ Samsung Electronics	Goods	Korea	6.07
⊕ Anglo American	Ind Mtrls	U.K.	4.02
⊕ China Mobile	Telecom	Hong Kong	1.80
⊖ Teva Pharmaceutical Indu	Health	Israel	1.79
⊕ Petroleo Brasileiro Sa -	Energy	Brazil	1.55
⊕ Taiwan Semiconductor Mfg	Hardware	Taiwan	1.42
⊕ Sasol Ltd	Ind Mtrls	South Africa	1.27
⊕ Standard Bank Investment	Financial	South Africa	1.24
⊕ Petroleo Brasileiro	Energy	Brazil	1.24
⊕ America Movil S.A. de C.	Telecom	Mexico	1.24
⊕ Kookmin Bank	Financial	Korea	1.13
⊕ Telefonos de Mexico	Telecom	Mexico	1.03
⊖ PetroChina	Energy	Hong Kong	1.02
⊕ POSCO	Ind Mtrls	Korea	0.96
☼ Cia Vale Rio Doce	—	Brazil	0.96
⊕ Hyundai Motor	Goods	Korea	0.95
⊕ Old Mutual	Financial	U.K.	0.94
⊕ Cia Vale Rio Doce	Ind Mtrls	Brazil	0.91
⊕ Reliance Industries Ltd	Ind Mtrls	India	0.85
⊖ CEMEX	Ind Mtrls	Mexico	0.81

Current Investment Style

Value Blnd Growth / Large Mid Small

Market Cap	%
Giant	39.4
Large	30.9
Mid	24.9
Small	3.8
Micro	1.0
Avg $mil: 7,131	

Value Measures		Rel Category
Price/Earnings	9.99	1.10
Price/Book	1.52	0.98
Price/Sales	0.85	1.02
Price/Cash Flow	4.35	1.00
Dividend Yield %	3.63	1.32

Growth Measures	%	Rel Category
Long-Term Erngs	17.70	0.91
Book Value	-16.22	NMF
Sales	10.26	0.88
Cash Flow	8.29	1.11
Historical Erngs	7.71	1.11

Composition

Cash	0.0	Bonds	0.0
Stocks	93.6	Other	6.4
Foreign (% of Stock)			99.2

Sector Weightings	% of Stocks	Rel MSCI EAFE	3 Year High	3 Year Low
Info	20.55	1.24		
Software	1.71	1.58	2	1
Hardware	5.39	1.48	9	5
Media	1.39	0.61	2	1
Telecom	12.06	1.26	16	11
Service	28.60	0.64		
Health	2.90	0.40	4	3
Consumer	3.81	0.76	4	2
Business	4.58	0.84	6	5
Financial	17.31	0.64	17	13
Mfg	50.86	1.32		
Goods	15.48	1.13	18	14
Ind Mtrls	23.64	1.92	28	23
Energy	9.41	1.28	9	2
Utilities	2.33	0.44	3	2

Regional Exposure	% Stock		
UK/W. Europe	5	N. America	1
Japan	0	Latn America	20
Asia X Japan	53	Other	21

Country Exposure	% Stock		
South Korea	19	Brazil	10
Taiwan	12	Hong Kong	9
South Africa	12		

Vanguard Energy

Ticker	Load	NAV	Yield	Total Assets	Mstar Category
VGENX	Closed	$40.00	1.3%	$5,242 mil	Specialty-Natural Res

Governance and Management

Fiduciary Grade: B

Portfolio Manager(s)

Karl Bandtel replaced longtime lead manager Ernst von Metzsch at the beginning of 2003. However, the management team here is seasoned. Bandtel has worked closely with von Metzsch for 11 years at Wellington Management (the fund's advisor). Bandtel is also supported by a team of analysts, many of whom have been with the firm for several years.

Strategy

This pure-energy fund has stakes in most subsectors, but it emphasizes large, integrated oil companies. Management looks to hang onto its picks for the long haul, seizing stocks it thinks are attractively valued often because bad news or a weak earnings report has prompted a sell-off. Management will devote a portion of the portfolio to overseas issues when they're considered cheaper than domestic fare. Unlike many other offerings in the category, this one steers clear of mining and other natural-resources stocks outside of energy.

Historical Profile

Return: Above Avg
Risk: Below Avg
Rating: ★★★★★ Highest

Investment Style
Equity
Stock %

1996	1997	1998	1999	2000	2001	2002	2003	2004
92%	94%	97%	96%	96%	97%	95%	91%	92%

▼ Manager Change
▽ Partial Manager Change

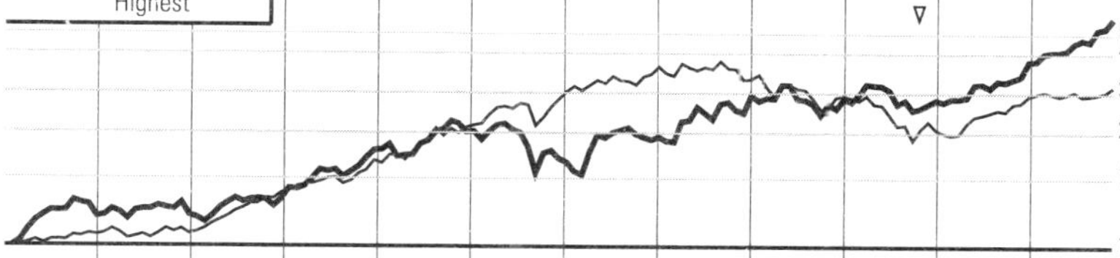

Growth of $10,000
— Investment Values of Fund
— Investment Values of S&P 500

Performance Quartile (within Category)

1993	1994	1995	1996	1997	1998	1999	2000	2001	2002	2003	12-04	History
15.06	14.29	17.31	22.54	24.14	18.42	21.92	28.07	25.29	23.20	29.85	40.00	NAV
26.42	-1.63	25.32	34.00	14.89	-20.53	20.98	36.43	-2.55	-0.62	33.80	36.65	Total Return %
16.36	-2.94	-12.21	11.06	-18.46	-49.10	-0.06	45.53	9.33	21.47	5.13	25.78	+/-S&P 500
—	—	—	—	-2.05	4.14	-6.24	20.62	13.04	12.64	-0.21	12.08	+/-GS NATR RES
2.18	1.60	1.96	1.39	1.43	1.45	1.93	1.64	1.43	1.44	1.68	1.77	Income Return %
24.24	-3.23	23.36	32.61	13.46	-21.98	19.05	34.79	-3.98	-2.06	32.12	34.88	Capital Return %
25	40	20	43	17	48	78	36	16	40	29	13	Total Rtn % Rank Cat
0.29	0.24	0.28	0.24	0.32	0.35	0.36	0.36	0.40	0.36	0.39	0.51	Income $
1.38	0.29	0.30	0.40	1.33	0.42	0.00	1.38	1.54	1.59	0.74	0.20	Capital Gains $
0.21	0.17	0.30	0.48	0.39	0.38	0.38	0.47	0.41	0.39	0.40	0.38	Expense Ratio %
2.47	1.87	1.66	1.55	1.36	1.36	1.36	1.63	1.52	1.57	1.56	1.79	Income Ratio %
37	41	13	21	15	19	19	18	24	28	23	26	Turnover Rate %
270	446	506	848	1,181	820	1,018	1,351	1,282	1,305	2,219	4,706	Net Assets $mil

Performance 12-31-04

	1st Qtr	2nd Qtr	3rd Qtr	4th Qtr	Total
2000	12.14	6.68	8.48	5.13	36.43
2001	-2.32	-0.29	-11.27	12.76	-2.55
2002	11.84	-4.40	-13.83	7.86	-0.62
2003	0.99	11.69	1.64	16.70	33.80
2004	7.31	7.13	10.80	7.28	36.65

Trailing	Total Return%	+/- S&P 500	+/- GS NATR RES	%Rank Cat	Growth of $10,000
3 Mo	7.28	-1.95	2.46	32	10,728
6 Mo	18.86	11.67	3.67	36	11,886
1 Yr	36.65	25.78	12.08	13	13,665
3 Yr Avg	22.03	18.45	8.90	31	18,172
5 Yr Avg	19.29	21.59	12.10	21	24,156
10 Yr Avg	16.18	4.11	—	20	44,804
15 Yr Avg	12.50	1.57	—	1	58,518

Tax Analysis	Tax-Adj Rtn%	%Rank Cat	Tax-Cost Rat	%Rank Cat
3 Yr (estimated)	20.68	25	1.11	80
5 Yr (estimated)	17.70	22	1.33	85
10 Yr (estimated)	14.65	20	1.32	74

Potential Capital Gain Exposure: 33% of assets

Rating and Risk

Time Period	Load-Adj Return %	Morningstar Rtn vs Cat	Morningstar Risk vs Cat	Morningstar Risk-Adj Rating
1 Yr	36.65			
3 Yr	22.03	+Avg	Low	★★★★
5 Yr	19.29	+Avg	-Avg	★★★★
10 Yr	16.18	+Avg	Avg	★★★★★
Incept	13.27			

Other Measures	Standard Index S&P 500	Best Fit Index GS NATR RES
Alpha	19.5	9.4
Beta	0.59	0.86
R-Squared	33	96
Standard Deviation	18.67	
Mean	22.03	
Sharpe Ratio	1.12	

Portfolio Analysis 09-30-04

Share change since 06-04 Total Stocks:62	Sector	PE	YTD Ret%	% Assets
⊕ ExxonMobil	Energy	13.9	28.04	5.45
⊕ Total SA ADR	Energy	17.0	23.39	4.43
⊕ ChevronTexaco	Energy	7.7	25.57	4.41
⊕ BP PLC ADR	Energy	20.7	22.07	3.31
⊕ ENI SpA ADR	Energy	14.3	36.69	3.37
⊕ ConocoPhillips	Energy	9.0	35.60	3.21
BG Grp	Utilities	—	—	2.71
Schlumberger	Energy	40.7	23.84	2.22
⊕ Transocean	Energy	56.3	76.55	2.06
⊕ Marathon Oil	Energy	—	17.07	2.01
⊕ Baker Hughes	Energy	30.3	34.28	1.96
⊕ GlobalSantaFe	Energy	NMF	34.38	1.89
⊕ Royal Dutch Petroleum AD	Energy	—	14.31	1.82
Shell Transport & Tradin	Energy	—	18.96	1.80
Unocal	Energy	11.4	19.85	1.80
Valero Energy	Energy	7.0	97.64	1.75
Burlington Resources	Energy	10.9	58.50	1.73
Statoil ASA ADR	Energy	—	—	1.71
BHP Billiton ADR	Ind Mtrls	27.0	34.11	1.69
Peabody Energy	Energy	35.4	96.04	1.65

Current Investment Style

Value Blnd Growth — Large / Mid / Small

Market Cap	%
Giant	41.9
Large	36.1
Mid	20.4
Small	1.6
Micro	0.0
Avg $mil: 23,934	

Value Measures		Rel Category
Price/Earnings	14.46	0.89
Price/Book	2.40	1.00
Price/Sales	0.96	0.80
Price/Cash Flow	5.96	0.75
Dividend Yield %	1.38	1.22

Growth Measures	%	Rel Category
Long-Term Erngs	8.06	0.75
Book Value	5.52	1.22
Sales	11.75	1.24
Cash Flow	12.96	1.93
Historical Erngs	25.29	1.26

Profitability	%	Rel Category
Return on Equity	17.46	1.39
Return on Assets	6.71	1.25
Net Margin	9.94	1.06

Industry Weightings	% of Stocks	Rel Cat
Oil & Gas	64.9	1.6
Oil/Gas Products	4.4	1.5
Oil & Gas Srv	18.8	0.7
Pipelines	0.6	0.5
Utilities	0.0	0.0
Hard Commd	2.7	0.3
Soft Commd	1.3	0.3
Misc. Indstrl	1.2	0.2
Other	6.0	0.8

Composition

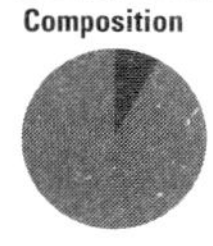

Cash	7.9
Stocks	92.1
Bonds	0.0
Other	0.0
Foreign (% of Stock)	40.3

Morningstar's Take by Sonya Morris 12-29-04

Shareholders at this newly closed fund should sit tight.

The natural-resources category has been on a tear lately, and investors have flooded these funds with cash. Vanguard Energy has seen assets balloon to $5.3 billion from $2.4 billion at the end of last year. Such fervent activity prompted Vanguard to close this fund to new investors in early December (it remains open to current shareholders and 401k participants) for what it terms a "temporary cooling off period." This is not an unusual move for Vanguard. For instance, they closed Vanguard Precious Metals when that sector's big gains lured investors in 2002. Such massive asset flows can be difficult to manage, and we think shuttering this fund is a prudent course that protects the interests of long-term shareholders.

Indeed, prudence is a watchword at this offering, which takes a measured approach to a volatile sector. Manager Karl Bandtel and the team of analysts at subadvisor Wellington Management typically keep a large slug of assets tucked away in large integrated oil companies like ExxonMobil and Total. In fact, Bandtel is currently stashing more assets into these mega-cap names, reflecting his cautious near-term view. Bandtel has a contrarian bent, and the popularity of the sector makes him wary, although he sees strong fundamentals for the sector over the long haul.

Despite its large stake in major oil stocks, which aren't typically high fliers, this fund has racked up solid returns while keeping volatility in check. This fund's year-to-date returns through Dec. 28, 2004, best 80% of category funds that concentrate primarily on energy stocks. And its long-term rankings are similarly strong.

Shareholders here have good reason to stick around, but given the sector's strong rally and the fund's growing stake of more staid integrated oil stocks, they may be wise to rein in their expectations.

Address:	PO Box 2600, Valley Forge PA 19482, 800-662-7447
Web Address:	www.vanguard.com
Inception:	05-23-84
Advisor:	Wellington Management Company, LLP
Subadvisor:	Wellington Management Company, LLP
NTF Plans:	N/A

Minimum Purchase:	Closed	Add: —	IRA: —
Min Auto Inv Plan:	Closed	Add: —	
Sales Fees:	No-load, 1.00%R		
Management Fee:	0.37%		
Actual Fees:	Mgt:0.37%	Dist: —	
Expense Projections:	3Yr:$128	5Yr:$224	10Yr:$505
Income Distrib:	Annually		

Vanguard Equity-Inc

Ticker	Load	NAV	Yield	Total Assets	Mstar Category
VEIPX	None	$23.50	2.4%	$3,843 mil	Large Value

Governance and Management

Fiduciary Grade: B

Portfolio Manager(s)

Seasoned. Wellington Management's John Ryan--who has been with this fund since January 2000 and runs roughly half of assets--boasts more than 20 years of investment experience. Gus Sauter and Joel Dickson, recent additions to the team, will use a quantitative-based approach in managing 30% of assets. Finally, John Levin--who runs the other 20%--has worked in investment management since 1963.

Strategy

The fund's assets are divided among three advisors who invest in stocks that are cheap and offer high dividend yields relative to the market. This line of attack often leads the team to pick up stocks that are temporarily under a cloud and hold them until they turn around. The upshot of this approach is that the fund tends to lag when growth stocks rule the roost, but it has been a steady performer over time. The fund's emphasis on cheap, high-yielding stocks, along with its broadly diversified portfolio, has kept volatility in check.

Historical Profile

Return: Above Avg
Risk: Below Avg
Rating: ★★★★ Above Avg

Investment Style: Equity — Stock %: 91% 91% 89% 92% 91% 95% 90% 95% 96%

▼ Manager Change
▽ Partial Manager Change

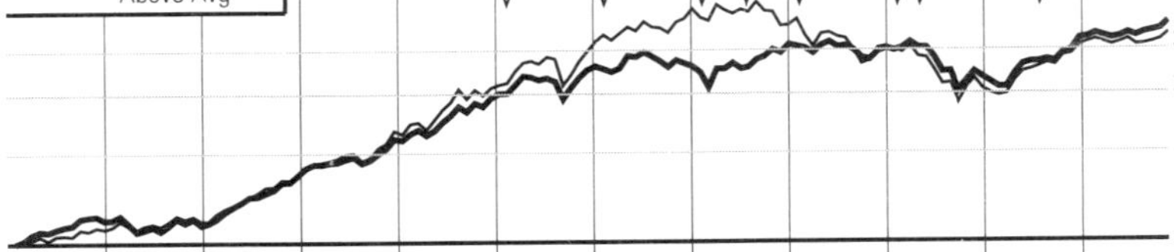

Growth of $10,000 (31.0, 24.0, 17.0, 10.0)
▬ Investment Values of Fund
— Investment Values of S&P 500

Performance Quartile (within Category)

History

1993	1994	1995	1996	1997	1998	1999	2000	2001	2002	2003	12-04	History
13.66	12.77	16.69	18.32	22.39	24.73	23.17	24.44	22.71	18.70	22.31	23.50	NAV
14.65	-1.59	37.34	17.39	31.17	17.34	-0.19	13.57	-2.34	-15.65	25.14	13.57	Total Return %
4.59	-2.90	-0.19	-5.55	-2.18	-11.23	-21.23	22.67	9.54	6.44	-3.53	2.70	+/-S&P 500
-3.42	0.39	-1.02	-4.25	-4.01	1.71	-7.54	6.56	3.25	-0.13	-4.89	-2.92	+/-Russ 1000 VI
4.80	4.32	4.77	3.89	3.70	2.89	2.65	2.66	2.10	2.13	3.10	2.69	Income Return %
9.85	-5.91	32.57	13.50	27.47	14.45	-2.84	10.91	-4.44	-17.78	22.04	10.88	Capital Return %
47	64	13	75	17	17	75	29	41	29	76	40	Total Rtn % Rank Cat
0.61	0.58	0.60	0.64	0.67	0.64	0.65	0.61	0.51	0.48	0.57	0.60	Income $
0.52	0.09	0.17	0.58	0.89	0.83	0.87	1.14	0.60	0.00	0.42	1.17	Capital Gains $
0.40	0.43	0.45	0.42	0.45	0.39	0.41	0.43	0.47	0.46	0.45	0.32	Expense Ratio %
4.39	4.41	4.27	3.69	3.25	2.80	2.59	2.59	2.26	2.21	2.61	2.61	Income Ratio %
15	18	31	21	22	23	18	36	31	21	55	36	Turnover Rate %
1,068	859	1,103	1,425	2,100	2,939	2,874	2,561	2,250	1,931	2,590	3,162	Net Assets $mil

Performance 12-31-04

	1st Qtr	2nd Qtr	3rd Qtr	4th Qtr	Total
2000	-1.54	0.12	7.37	7.30	13.57
2001	-4.97	3.68	-6.18	5.64	-2.34
2002	3.61	-8.58	-17.94	8.52	-15.65
2003	-5.73	15.74	0.40	14.24	25.14
2004	1.33	1.69	1.15	8.96	13.57

Trailing	Total Return%	+/- S&P 500	+/- Russ 1000 VI	%Rank Cat	Growth of $10,000
3 Mo	8.96	-0.27	-1.42	56	10,896
6 Mo	10.22	3.03	-1.86	31	11,022
1 Yr	13.57	2.70	-2.92	40	11,357
3 Yr Avg	6.23	2.65	-2.34	43	11,988
5 Yr Avg	5.86	8.16	0.59	29	13,294
10 Yr Avg	12.66	0.59	-1.17	25	32,938
15 Yr Avg	10.51	-0.42	-1.52	53	44,774

Tax Analysis	Tax-Adj Rtn%	%Rank Cat	Tax-Cost Rat	%Rank Cat
3 Yr (estimated)	5.07	45	1.09	69
5 Yr (estimated)	4.46	33	1.32	69
10 Yr (estimated)	10.75	18	1.70	44

Potential Capital Gain Exposure: 22% of assets

Rating and Risk

Time Period	Load-Adj Return %	Morningstar Rtn vs Cat	Morningstar Risk vs Cat	Morningstar Risk-Adj Rating
1 Yr	13.57			
3 Yr	6.23	Avg	-Avg	★★★
5 Yr	5.86	+Avg	-Avg	★★★★
10 Yr	12.66	+Avg	-Avg	★★★★
Incept	11.59			

Other Measures	Standard Index S&P 500	Best Fit Index Russ 1000 VI
Alpha	2.8	-1.6
Beta	0.88	0.91
R-Squared	92	98

Standard Deviation	14.61
Mean	6.23
Sharpe Ratio	0.34

Portfolio Analysis 09-30-04

Share change since 06-04 Total Stocks:170	Sector	PE	YTD Ret%	% Assets
⊕ Bank of America	Financial	12.3	21.50	3.42
⊕ Citigroup	Financial	15.3	2.72	3.30
ExxonMobil	Energy	13.9	28.04	2.84
⊕ Caterpillar	Ind Mtrls	17.6	19.75	2.23
⊕ J P Morgan Chase	Financial	19.4	9.97	1.96
⊕ Alcoa	Ind Mtrls	18.8	-15.75	1.72
⊕ Emerson Electric	Ind Mtrls	22.8	11.09	1.66
⊕ ConocoPhillips	Energy	9.0	35.60	1.64
⊕ Pfizer	Health	22.0	-22.31	1.63
⊕ Wells Fargo	Financial	15.5	8.97	1.48
⊕ Dow Chemical	Ind Mtrls	16.6	22.83	1.47
General Motors	Goods	7.2	-21.48	1.45
⊕ Wyeth	Health	17.0	2.73	1.45
⊕ SBC Communications	Telecom	15.4	3.74	1.43
⊖ SunTrust Banks	Financial	13.8	6.36	1.41
⊕ Abbott Laboratories	Health	22.1	2.61	1.23
⊖ BP PLC ADR	Energy	20.7	22.07	1.21
⊕ Morgan Stanley	Financial	14.2	-2.25	1.20
⊖ PNC Financial Services G	Financial	13.3	8.92	1.19
XL Capital	Financial	20.1	2.80	1.16

Current Investment Style (Value Blnd Growth; Large Mid Small)

Market Cap	%
Giant	41.6
Large	43.9
Mid	13.6
Small	0.9
Micro	0.0
Avg $mil: 31,471	

Value Measures		Rel Category
Price/Earnings	13.98	0.93
Price/Book	2.20	0.97
Price/Sales	1.11	0.93
Price/Cash Flow	5.79	0.91
Dividend Yield %	2.84	1.39

Growth Measures	%	Rel Category
Long-Term Erngs	9.48	0.91
Book Value	4.72	0.84
Sales	2.56	0.61
Cash Flow	0.66	0.13
Historical Erngs	8.91	0.75

Profitability	%	Rel Category
Return on Equity	16.72	1.05
Return on Assets	8.46	1.08
Net Margin	10.87	1.06

Sector Weightings	% of Stocks	Rel S&P 500	3 Year High	3 Year Low
Info	7.57	0.35		
Software	0.29	0.07	0	0
Hardware	1.25	0.12	3	1
Media	1.53	0.40	2	1
Telecom	4.50	1.43	9	4
Service	44.14	0.95		
Health	7.50	0.60	13	6
Consumer	2.44	0.27	3	2
Business	1.09	0.27	2	1
Financial	33.11	1.59	33	24
Mfg	48.29	1.50		
Goods	11.17	1.20	13	10
Ind Mtrls	19.68	1.55	20	14
Energy	10.65	1.49	14	11
Utilities	6.79	2.29	11	6

Composition

Cash	3.7
Stocks	96.3
Bonds	0.0
Other	0.0
Foreign (% of Stock)	4.2

Morningstar's Take by Jeffrey Ptak 01-06-05

This fund remains a fine choice.

Slow and steady is the rule at Vanguard Equity Income. A trio of managers employs variants of the same theme in picking stocks: seeking reasonably priced names that sport fat dividend yields. It's not the most original approach in the world, either in terms of the stock-picking ethos or the ground they tend to cover. Indeed, income-oriented strategies of this sort abound while the fund's above-average median-market cap makes it plain that management favors widely followed fare.

Two factors set the fund apart, however. First is the fund's paltry 0.32% expense ratio. Since costs consume income first, high expenses tend to hamstring income-oriented managers. That's not the case here. Second, while comanagers Jack Ryan (Wellington Management) and Jack Murphy (John Levin & Co.) trawl a very efficient part of the market, each tends to favor names in the throes of short-term weakness or areas that have fallen out of favor. To wit, Ryan scooped up shares of Abbott Labs recently on the conviction that the health-care firm's ailing drug and diagnostic units were on the mend. We think that sort of contrarian ethos has merit. (Vanguard's in-house Quantitative Equity Group also runs a sleeve of assets here, seeking stocks with above-average yields relative to industry and historical norms.)

The results have been solid, if unspectacular, as the fund has topped most of its large-value rivals over the long haul. Meanwhile, volatility has been below average thanks to the fund's diversification across issues and management's emphasis on sturdy franchises with solid balance sheets.

All told, we think this fund's prudent strategy, capable management, and low price tag make it an excellent core holding for the long haul. Moreover, it might be an especially timely choice given its mega-cap tilt, which held it back in recent years but could prove beneficial given that the small-cap rally has gotten long in the tooth.

Address:	P.O. Box 2600, Valley Forge PA 19482, 800-662-7447
Web Address:	www.vanguard.com
Inception:	03-21-88
Advisor:	The Vanguard Group, Inc.
Subadvisor:	Multiple
NTF Plans:	N/A

Minimum Purchase:	$3000	Add: $100	IRA: $1000
Min Auto Inv Plan:	$3000	Add: $50	
Sales Fees:	No-load		
Management Fee:	0.47%		
Actual Fees:	Mgt:0.47%	Dist: —	
Expense Projections:	3Yr:$148	5Yr:$258	10Yr:$579
Income Distrib:	Quarterly		

Vanguard Eur Stk Idx

Analyst Pick	Ticker	Load	NAV	Yield	Total Assets	Mstar Category
✔	VEURX	None	$25.99	2.2%	$11,271 mil	Europe Stock

Governance and Management

Fiduciary Grade: B

Portfolio Manager(s)

Vanguard indexing guru Gus Sauter has managed this fund since its 1990 inception. He also manages numerous other Vanguard funds, including Vanguard 500 Index and Vanguard Emerging Markets Stock Index.

Strategy

This fund tracks the MSCI Europe Index, a capitalization-weighted benchmark of the region's largest markets and stocks. Although the fund's sector weightings don't differ substantially from those of its typical peer, its larger-than-average portfolio dilutes its exposure to individual names. It does not own any stocks in the former Communist countries of central and eastern Europe. The fund does not hedge its currency exposure.

Historical Profile

Return: Average
Risk: Average
Rating: ★★★ Neutral

Investment Style: Equity Stock %: 98% 98% 95% 93% 98% 99% 96% 92% 98%

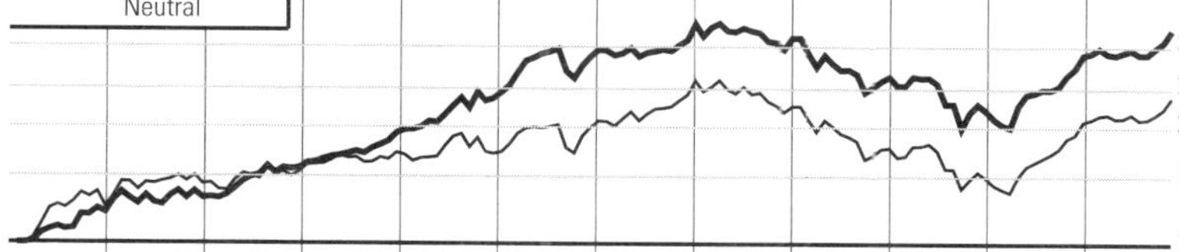

Performance Quartile (within Category)

History

1993	1994	1995	1996	1997	1998	1999	2000	2001	2002	2003	12-04	History
11.88	11.76	14.02	16.57	20.13	25.28	28.83	25.99	20.25	16.21	22.00	25.99	NAV
29.13	1.88	22.28	21.25	24.23	28.86	16.66	-8.21	-20.30	-17.95	38.70	20.86	Total Return %
-3.43	-5.90	11.07	15.20	22.45	8.93	-10.37	5.98	1.12	-2.01	0.11	0.61	+/-MSCI EAFE
-0.15	-0.40	0.66	0.16	0.43	0.36	0.73	0.19	-0.40	0.43	0.16	-0.02	+/-MSCI Eur
1.82	2.36	2.72	2.57	2.24	2.59	1.96	1.47	1.73	1.98	2.84	2.64	Income Return %
27.31	-0.48	19.56	18.68	21.99	26.27	14.68	-9.68	-22.03	-19.93	35.86	18.22	Capital Return %
58	92	10	82	17	13	82	66	42	58	37	32	Total Rtn % Rank Cat
0.17	0.28	0.32	0.36	0.37	0.52	0.50	0.42	0.45	0.40	0.46	0.58	Income $
0.00	0.06	0.04	0.06	0.08	0.14	0.15	0.05	0.00	0.00	0.00	0.00	Capital Gains $
0.32	0.32	0.35	0.35	0.31	0.29	0.29	0.29	0.30	0.33	0.32	0.27	Expense Ratio %
2.05	2.41	2.66	2.45	2.19	1.97	1.99	1.64	2.08	2.24	2.76	2.67	Income Ratio %
4	6	2	4	3	7	7	8	3	15	6	5	Turnover Rate %
601	715	1,017	1,595	2,432	4,479	6,106	5,611	4,405	3,998	6,252	9,220	Net Assets $mil

Performance 12-31-04

	1st Qtr	2nd Qtr	3rd Qtr	4th Qtr	Total
2000	0.13	-2.74	-7.46	1.85	-8.21
2001	-15.62	-1.87	-12.09	9.48	-20.30
2002	0.05	-4.05	-22.84	10.77	-17.95
2003	-9.25	22.30	3.89	20.30	38.70
2004	0.82	2.25	1.19	15.86	20.86

Trailing	Total Return%	+/- MSCI EAFE	+/- MSCI Eur	%Rank Cat	Growth of $10,000
3 Mo	15.86	0.54	-0.06	37	11,586
6 Mo	17.24	2.24	-0.08	34	11,724
1 Yr	20.86	0.61	-0.02	32	12,086
3 Yr Avg	11.21	-0.68	0.23	44	13,754
5 Yr Avg	0.12	1.25	0.06	52	10,060
10 Yr Avg	10.79	5.17	0.25	45	27,862
15 Yr Avg	—	—	—	—	—

Tax Analysis	Tax-Adj Rtn%	%Rank Cat	Tax-Cost Rat	%Rank Cat
3 Yr (estimated)	10.42	43	0.71	71
5 Yr (estimated)	-0.62	55	0.74	51
10 Yr (estimated)	9.87	10	0.83	17

Potential Capital Gain Exposure: 21% of assets

Rating and Risk

Time Period	Load-Adj Return %	Morningstar Rtn vs Cat	Morningstar Risk vs Cat	Morningstar Risk-Adj Rating
1 Yr	20.86			
3 Yr	11.21	Avg	Avg	★★★
5 Yr	0.12	Avg	Avg	★★★
10 Yr	10.79	Avg	Avg	★★★
Incept	9.41			

Other Measures	Standard Index S&P 500	Best Fit Index MSCI Eur
Alpha	-1.6	0.2
Beta	1.13	1.00
R-Squared	93	100
Standard Deviation	20.47	
Mean	11.21	
Sharpe Ratio	0.49	

Morningstar's Take by Gregg Wolper 12-09-04

Make sure to stay cool and collected when looking at Vanguard European Stock Index's more recent performance.

It's understandable if this offering's 2003 and 2004 returns cause excitement. In 2003, it posted a 38.7% gain that beat more than 60% of the Europe-stock category. And for year-to-date through Dec. 8, 2004, its 17% return tops two thirds of those rivals. Those rankings are nice, but it's the absolute returns that are truly eye-catching. At a time when many experts are predicting single-digit annual returns for stock funds, those sky-high numbers might seem to hint that this fund's got a magic touch.

Therefore, although this is indeed a worthwhile offering, it's important to put all of these figures in perspective. For example, the 2003 gain of nearly 39% is obviously abnormally high. It reflected the region's rebound after a bear market, and was further enhanced by currency translation from a sharp rise in European currencies against the U.S. dollar. The fund had never previously gained more than 30% in any calendar year since its 1990 inception. And the fund's 2004 return was much more mundane until just a couple of months ago. Then a sharp rally in the region's stock markets and, once again, its currencies, put the fund's returns into high gear. While many observers expect foreign currencies to continue gaining strength, that trend won't go on forever. When the tide turns, this fund's returns will lose that extra boost. Finally, a word on the rankings: The fund's five-year rank is merely middling (though its 10-year showing does beat 60% of the category).

All that said, this is still a suitable option for investors who want straightforward exposure to Western Europe's big companies. Its low expense ratio and minimal trading costs, and its proven ability to match its benchmark almost exactly, mark it as a solid fund. Just keep your expectations within reason.

Address:	PO Box 2600 Valley Forge PA 19482 800-662-7447
Web Address:	www.vanguard.com
Inception:	06-18-90
Advisor:	Vanguard Advisers, Inc.
Subadvisor:	None
NTF Plans:	N/A

Minimum Purchase:	$3000	Add: $100	IRA: $1000
Min Auto Inv Plan:	$3000	Add: $50	
Sales Fees:	No-load		
Management Fee:	0.23%		
Actual Fees:	Mgt:0.23%	Dist: —	
Expense Projections:	3Yr:$97	5Yr:$169	10Yr:$381
Income Distrib:	Annually		

Portfolio Analysis 09-30-04

Share change since 06-04 Total Stocks:548	Sector	Country	% Assets
⊕ BP	Energy	U.K.	3.53
⊕ HSBC Hldgs	Financial	U.K.	3.25
⊕ Vodafone Grp	Telecom	U.K.	2.69
⊕ GlaxoSmithKline	Health	U.K.	2.38
⊕ TOTAL	Energy	France	2.24
⊕ Novartis	Health	Switzerland	2.08
⊕ Royal Dutch Petroleum	Energy	Netherlands	2.01
⊕ Nestle	Goods	Switzerland	1.73
⊕ Royal Bank Of Scotland G	Financial	U.K.	1.51
⊕ UBS	Financial	Switzerland	1.41
⊕ Roche Holding	Health	Switzerland	1.36
⊕ Shell Transport & Tradin	Energy	U.K.	1.33
⊕ AstraZeneca	Health	U.K.	1.29
⊕ Sanofi-Synthelabo	Health	France	1.24
⊕ Nokia	Hardware	Finland	1.20
⊕ Barclays	Financial	U.K.	1.16
⊖ Telefonica	Telecom	Spain	1.15
⊕ Siemens	Hardware	Germany	1.10
⊕ ENI	Energy	Italy	1.09
⊕ HBOS	Financial	U.K.	0.98

Current Investment Style

Value Blnd Growth / Large Mid Small

Market Cap	%
Giant	56.4
Large	30.0
Mid	12.9
Small	0.7
Micro	0.0
Avg $mil: 30,896	

Value Measures		Rel Category
Price/Earnings	13.20	0.98
Price/Book	2.08	1.03
Price/Sales	0.84	0.92
Price/Cash Flow	5.33	0.99
Dividend Yield %	3.02	1.15

Growth Measures	%	Rel Category
Long-Term Ergs	9.82	0.88
Book Value	-2.49	NMF
Sales	1.76	0.60
Cash Flow	3.07	0.63
Historical Ergs	2.56	0.61

Composition

Cash	0.2	Bonds	0.0
Stocks	98.3	Other	1.5
Foreign (% of Stock)			100.0

Sector Weightings	% of Stocks	Rel MSCI EAFE	3 Year High	3 Year Low
Info	16.30	0.98		
Software	0.72	0.67	1	0
Hardware	4.04	1.11	6	4
Media	2.66	1.17	3	2
Telecom	8.88	0.93	11	7
Service	46.20	1.03		
Health	10.25	1.41	13	10
Consumer	4.91	0.97	5	4
Business	3.78	0.69	5	3
Financial	27.26	1.01	27	21
Mfg	37.50	0.97		
Goods	11.01	0.81	14	11
Ind Mtrls	9.68	0.79	14	8
Energy	11.74	1.60	14	9
Utilities	5.07	0.95	5	3

Regional Exposure	% Stock		
UK/W. Europe	100	N. America	0
Japan	0	Latn America	0
Asia X Japan	0	Other	0

Country Exposure	% Stock		
U.K.	37	Germany	10
France	14	Netherlands	7
Switzerland	10		

Vanguard Explorer

Analyst Pick	Ticker	Load	NAV	Yield	Total Assets	Mstar Category
✔	VEXPX	None	$74.57	0.0%	$9,576 mil	Small Growth

Governance and Management

Fiduciary Grade: B

Portfolio Manager(s)

There are five managers. Gus Sauter is arguably the biggest name in indexing, and Ed Antoian built a decent long-term record at Delaware before founding Chartwell Investment Partners. Jack Granahan (Granahan Investment Management) and Ken Abrams (Wellington Management Company) together run slightly more than half of the portfolio. Chris Darnell and Rob Soucy, from Grantham, Mayo & Van Otterloo, joined in 2000.

Strategy

Vanguard farms out this fund's assets to five subadvisors, each of which operates independently. One manager, Gus Sauter, uses a growth-indexing strategy. The other four seek to add value with stock-picking. Although each of the active managers uses a somewhat distinct approach, all focus on small-cap growth stocks. The overall portfolio has typically had less exposure to highly speculative issues than its typical peer has had, as most of the subadvisors pay close attention to valuations.

Historical Profile

Return Average
Risk Below Avg
Rating ★★★★ Above Avg

Investment Style
Equity
Stock %

89% 88% 90% 89% 88% 87% 90% 92% 94%

▼ Manager Change
▽ Partial Manager Change

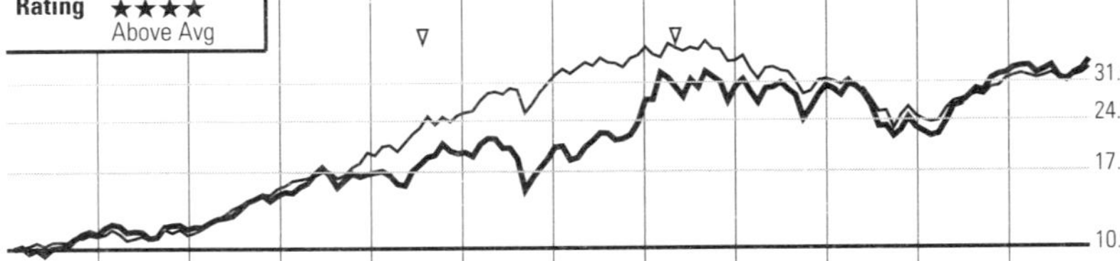

Growth of $10,000
▬ Investment Values of Fund
— Investment Values of S&P 500

Performance Quartile (within Category)

History

1993	1994	1995	1996	1997	1998	1999	2000	2001	2002	2003	12-04	History
45.11	42.86	49.95	53.83	55.30	56.71	68.62	60.09	60.32	45.49	65.62	74.57	NAV
15.41	0.54	26.60	14.04	14.57	3.52	37.26	9.22	0.56	-24.58	44.25	13.75	Total Return %
5.35	-0.77	-10.93	-8.90	-18.78	-25.05	16.22	18.32	12.44	-2.49	15.58	2.88	+/-S&P 500
2.04	2.97	-4.44	2.78	1.62	2.29	-5.83	31.65	9.79	5.68	-4.29	-0.56	+/-Russ 2000 Gr
0.32	0.38	0.56	0.54	0.46	0.36	0.41	0.36	0.17	0.01	0.00	0.00	Income Return %
15.09	0.16	26.04	13.50	14.11	3.16	36.85	8.86	0.39	-24.59	44.25	13.75	Capital Return %
57	40	72	68	65	48	64	20	25	33	48	43	Total Rtn % Rank Cat
0.14	0.17	0.24	0.27	0.25	0.20	0.23	0.25	0.11	0.01	0.00	0.00	Income $
5.17	2.26	4.00	2.83	5.85	0.30	8.03	13.91	0.00	0.00	0.00	0.07	Capital Gains $
0.73	0.70	0.68	0.63	0.62	0.62	0.74	0.71	0.72	0.70	0.72	—	Expense Ratio %
0.32	0.39	0.52	0.51	0.45	0.37	0.36	0.36	0.24	-0.01	-0.08	—	Income Ratio %
51	82	66	51	84	1	79	123	77	69	77	—	Turnover Rate %
848	1,122	1,648	2,264	2,541	2,464	3,136	4,488	4,648	3,508	6,126	8,230	Net Assets $mil

Performance 12-31-04

	1st Qtr	2nd Qtr	3rd Qtr	4th Qtr	Total
2000	15.97	-1.14	1.74	-6.37	9.22
2001	-10.30	14.42	-21.73	25.18	0.56
2002	1.33	-14.05	-18.47	6.22	-24.58
2003	-4.35	22.39	9.00	13.06	44.25
2004	5.01	-0.01	-5.18	14.26	13.75

Trailing	Total Return%	+/- S&P 500	+/- Russ 2000 Gr	%Rank Cat	Growth of $10,000
3 Mo	14.26	5.03	-0.82	43	11,426
6 Mo	8.34	1.15	0.18	48	10,834
1 Yr	13.75	2.88	-0.56	43	11,375
3 Yr Avg	7.36	3.78	1.57	33	12,374
5 Yr Avg	6.33	8.63	9.90	20	13,592
10 Yr Avg	12.32	0.25	5.20	28	31,957
15 Yr Avg	12.47	1.54	4.97	28	58,284

Tax Analysis	Tax-Adj Rtn%	%Rank Cat	Tax-Cost Rat	%Rank Cat
3 Yr (estimated)	7.36	28	0.00	1
5 Yr (estimated)	4.93	20	1.32	57
10 Yr (estimated)	10.45	26	1.66	53

Potential Capital Gain Exposure: 21% of assets

Rating and Risk

Time Period	Load-Adj Return %	Morningstar Rtn vs Cat	Morningstar Risk vs Cat	Morningstar Risk-Adj Rating
1 Yr	13.75			
3 Yr	7.36	Avg	Avg	★★★
5 Yr	6.33	+Avg	-Avg	★★★★
10 Yr	12.32	Avg	-Avg	★★★★
Incept	9.61			

Other Measures	Standard Index S&P 500	Best Fit Index Russ 2000 Gr
Alpha	4.0	1.8
Beta	1.10	0.88
R-Squared	74	99
Standard Deviation	20.65	
Mean	7.36	
Sharpe Ratio	0.29	

Morningstar's Take by Jeffrey Ptak 12-19-04

Vanguard Explorer is big--but not bloated.

The fund's management structure is interesting. Vanguard has flanked three stock-pickers with a pair of quantitative specialists--GMO and the firm's in-house Quantitative Equity Group. The latter gets only slightly more than a third of assets, but plays an important role in sopping up cash when the active managers can't put money to work fast enough. To wit, though Wellington's Ken Abrams hasn't received new inflows in over a year, Vanguard didn't have to close the fund since it could easily plough the money into the quantitative portfolios, which span hundreds of issues.

But there are limits, of course. Specifically, cash can't flow in unabated without gradually tapping out the active managers' capacity to invest it. In that case, Vanguard would be forced to either tip the balance toward the quantitative managers or add still more stock-pickers to spread the load. In either case, Vanguard would run the risk of altering the character of the portfolio, thereby throwing the fund's prospects into question.

That's not a purely esoteric possibility. The fund's growth in recent years has wrought change, as the portfolio is now nudging up against the mid-growth style box. What's more, its returns have also grown more correlated with large-cap stocks', making it a less-effective diversifier.

Yet, we don't think asset bloat is a near-term concern. The portfolio's ascent up the market-cap ladder bears watching. But it's not unprecedented, as the fund flirted with such levels in 1997, when it was a fraction of its current size. The other hallmarks of strained capacity, such as a swelling cash balance or difficult-to-trade positions in individual names, are also notably absent. Finally, while the fund has moved in tighter sync with the S&P 500, it's hardly alone. The same can be said of the broad-market Russell 2000 Index.

All told, the thesis for owning the fund remains intact.

Address:	PO Box 2600 Valley Forge PA 19482 800-662-7447	Minimum Purchase:	$3000	Add: $100 IRA: $1000
		Min Auto Inv Plan:	$3000	Add: $50
		Sales Fees:	No-load	
Web Address:	www.vanguard.com	Management Fee:	0.68%, 0.40%A	
Inception:	12-11-67	Actual Fees:	Mgt:0.68%	Dist: —
Advisor:	The Vanguard Group, Inc.	Expense Projections:	3Yr:$224	5Yr:$390 10Yr:$871
Subadvisor:	Multiple	Income Distrib:	Annually	
NTF Plans:	N/A			

Portfolio Analysis 09-30-04

Share change since 06-04 Total Stocks:951	Sector	PE	YTD Ret%	% Assets
⊕ Vanguard Small Cap VIPER	—	—	—	1.08
⊕ Bausch & Lomb	Health	22.2	25.26	0.64
⊖ Foot Locker	Consumer	17.6	15.99	0.62
⊖ Nextel Partners A	Telecom	—	45.28	0.60
⊕ MSC Industrial Direct Co	Business	28.4	32.26	0.58
⊕ Alliance Data Systems	Business	35.1	71.53	0.53
⊕ Urban Outfitters	Consumer	42.4	139.68	0.50
⊕ Cooper Companies	Health	28.4	49.92	0.49
⊕ Acxiom	Business	32.3	42.18	0.45
⊕ Ask Jeeves	Business	37.8	47.63	0.42
⊕ Maverick Tube	Ind Mtrls	7.2	57.40	0.42
⊕ Brunswick	Goods	18.1	57.47	0.40
⊖ Mentor	Health	25.0	44.90	0.38
⊕ Cal Dive International	Energy	23.4	68.95	0.38
⊖ Red Hat	Software	70.6	-28.88	0.37
⊕ Garmin	Hardware	25.3	12.63	0.35
⊕ Catalina Marketing	Business	—	48.90	0.34
⊖ Humana	Health	17.0	29.93	0.34
⊖ Sapient	Business	—	40.25	0.34
⊖ Cognizant Technology Sol	Business	62.5	85.50	0.33

Current Investment Style

Market Cap	%
Giant	0.0
Large	1.1
Mid	51.5
Small	41.8
Micro	5.7
Avg $mil: 1,518	

Value Measures		Rel Category
Price/Earnings	19.14	0.88
Price/Book	2.46	0.94
Price/Sales	1.12	0.75
Price/Cash Flow	7.45	0.93
Dividend Yield %	0.43	1.39

Growth Measures	%	Rel Category
Long-Term Erngs	15.82	0.91
Book Value	5.86	0.91
Sales	4.05	0.63
Cash Flow	13.35	0.99
Historical Erngs	12.76	0.94

Profitability	%	Rel Category
Return on Equity	11.61	1.18
Return on Assets	5.63	1.28
Net Margin	7.29	1.06

Sector Weightings	% of Stocks	Rel S&P 500	3 Year High	3 Year Low
Info	22.33	1.04		
Software	6.51	1.51	8	6
Hardware	11.58	1.14	18	10
Media	1.67	0.43	4	2
Telecom	2.57	0.82	3	1
Service	56.47	1.22		
Health	18.96	1.52	22	18
Consumer	13.78	1.52	16	12
Business	15.44	3.81	15	10
Financial	8.29	0.40	11	7
Mfg	21.19	0.66		
Goods	5.81	0.62	6	5
Ind Mtrls	9.44	0.75	9	5
Energy	5.82	0.81	6	4
Utilities	0.12	0.04	0	0

Composition

Cash	5.8
Stocks	93.8
Bonds	0.1
Other	0.3
Foreign (% of Stock)	1.1

Vanguard ExtMktIdx

Ticker	Load	NAV	Yield	Total Assets	Mstar Category
VEXMX	None	$31.36	0.9%	$8,972 mil	Mid-Cap Blend

Governance and Management

Fiduciary Grade: B

Portfolio Manager(s)

Experienced. Gus Sauter runs a number of index funds for Vanguard, and he's among the best in the business.

Strategy

This fund attempts to track the performance of the Wilshire 4500, a market-cap-weighted index that includes all publicly traded stocks that are not in the S&P 500 Index. Although the fund primarily holds small- and mid-cap issues, at times it has also owned sizable amounts of large companies that were not in the S&P 500. These issues, which include a number of speculative tech and biotech stocks, have been very volatile over the past few years.

Historical Profile

Return Average
Risk Above Avg
Rating ★★ Below Avg

Investment Style: Equity Stock %: 97% 97% 98% 98% 97% 99% 98% 99% 100%

▼ Manager Change
▽ Partial Manager Change

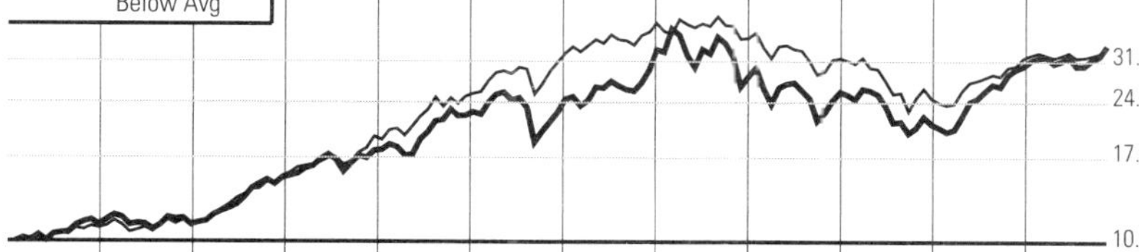

Performance Quartile (within Category)

1993	1994	1995	1996	1997	1998	1999	2000	2001	2002	2003	12-04	History
19.43	18.52	24.07	26.20	30.75	30.63	37.07	26.62	23.09	18.74	26.66	31.36	NAV
14.49	-1.76	33.80	17.65	26.69	8.35	36.22	-15.51	-9.17	-18.06	43.43	18.71	Total Return %
4.43	-3.07	-3.73	-5.29	-6.66	-20.22	15.18	-6.41	2.71	4.03	14.76	7.84	+/-S&P 500
0.56	1.83	2.88	-1.53	-5.55	-10.76	21.50	-33.00	-8.57	-3.53	7.84	2.24	+/-S&P Mid 400
1.33	1.45	1.62	1.43	1.39	1.23	1.10	0.73	0.82	0.78	1.14	1.07	Income Return %
13.16	-3.21	32.18	16.22	25.30	7.12	35.12	-16.24	-9.99	-18.84	42.29	17.64	Capital Return %
52	54	26	72	51	55	17	94	82	65	14	22	Total Rtn % Rank Cat
0.23	0.28	0.30	0.34	0.36	0.37	0.32	0.26	0.21	0.18	0.21	0.29	Income $
0.20	0.29	0.40	1.72	1.91	2.17	3.64	4.43	0.81	0.00	0.00	0.00	Capital Gains $
0.20	0.20	0.25	0.25	0.23	0.23	0.25	0.25	0.25	0.26	0.26	—	Expense Ratio %
1.48	1.51	1.51	1.42	1.30	1.21	1.04	0.81	0.83	0.88	1.01	—	Income Ratio %
13	19	15	22	15	27	26	33	20	17	8	—	Turnover Rate %
928	967	1,523	2,099	2,723	2,939	4,221	3,881	3,115	2,629	4,259	5,484	Net Assets $mil

Performance 12-31-04

	1st Qtr	2nd Qtr	3rd Qtr	4th Qtr	Total
2000	9.66	-8.66	3.79	-18.73	-15.51
2001	-15.77	14.30	-21.05	19.51	-9.17
2002	1.86	-10.03	-15.50	5.81	-18.06
2003	-3.30	21.30	7.51	13.73	43.43
2004	5.93	0.11	-1.84	14.04	18.71

Trailing	Total Return%	+/- S&P 500	+/- S&P Mid 400	%Rank Cat	Growth of $10,000
3 Mo	14.04	4.81	1.89	16	11,404
6 Mo	11.95	4.76	2.16	22	11,195
1 Yr	18.71	7.84	2.24	22	11,871
3 Yr Avg	11.74	8.16	1.23	21	13,952
5 Yr Avg	1.37	3.67	-8.16	86	10,704
10 Yr Avg	12.16	0.09	-3.93	66	31,505
15 Yr Avg	11.12	0.19	-3.54	76	48,628

Tax Analysis	Tax-Adj Rtn%	%Rank Cat	Tax-Cost Rat	%Rank Cat
3 Yr (estimated)	11.42	19	0.29	33
5 Yr (estimated)	0.18	89	1.17	57
10 Yr (estimated)	10.28	62	1.68	44

Potential Capital Gain Exposure: 15% of assets

Rating and Risk

Time Period	Load-Adj Return %	Morningstar Rtn vs Cat	Morningstar Risk vs Cat	Morningstar Risk-Adj Rating
1 Yr	18.71			
3 Yr	11.74	+Avg	+Avg	★★★★
5 Yr	1.37	-Avg	High	★★
10 Yr	12.16	Avg	+Avg	★★
Incept	12.30			

Other Measures	Standard Index S&P 500	Best Fit Index Wil 4500
Alpha	8.2	-0.2
Beta	0.94	1.01
R-Squared	78	100
Standard Deviation	17.82	
Mean	11.74	
Sharpe Ratio	0.59	

Morningstar's Take by Jeffrey Ptak 10-31-04

Though Vanguard Extended Market Index isn't the cheapest of its kind anymore, it remains a fine choice.

Fidelity has stolen some of its thunder. In August 2004, Fidelity announced it was slashing the fees it levies on five of its index funds, including Fidelity Spartan Extended Market Index, to a minuscule 0.10%. That's less than half the price tag of this fund's investor share class.

While it's true that this cost margin won't make for a huge disparity in returns over the long haul, every basis point counts in the index-fund arena, since such offerings rely on low costs to grind past pricier actively managed funds. And since this fund and the competing Fidelity offering are identical in terms of mandate--both track the Wilshire 4500 Index, which spans all publicly traded U.S. firm except for the large 500--low costs are paramount.

That said, we'd caution current investors in this fund to consider a few factors before making the jump to Fidelity. First, Fidelity's fee cut is possible only thanks to a fee waiver, which the firm can rescind at any time. Second, longtime shareholders of this fund in taxable accounts, who have amassed significant capital gains, would likely see any fee savings swamped by the tax costs triggered by a move.

Since investors in this fund's admiral share class as well as institutional shareholders--who together soak up over a third of total assets here--are paying roughly the same as Fidelity is now charging, they should stay put. However, current owners of this fund's investor shares who don't have hefty tax exposure, not to mention prospective buyers of the investor shares, would be remiss not to give the Fidelity fund a look.

That said, those who remain here should continue to reap the benefits, which include the fund's strong diversification potential, low expenses, and capable management.

Address:	P O Box 2600 Valley Forge PA 19482 800-662-7447			
Web Address:	www.vanguard.com			
Inception:	12-21-87			
Advisor:	Vanguard Advisers, Inc.			
Subadvisor:	None			
NTF Plans:	N/A			

Minimum Purchase:	$3000	Add: $100	IRA: $1000
Min Auto Inv Plan:	$3000	Add: $50	
Sales Fees:	No-load		
Management Fee:	0.23%		
Actual Fees:	Mgt:0.23%	Dist: —	
Expense Projections:	3Yr:$80	5Yr:$141	10Yr:$318
Income Distrib:	Annually		

Portfolio Analysis 09-30-04

Share change since 06-04 Total Stocks:3401	Sector	PE	YTD Ret%	% Assets
Berkshire Hathaway A	Financial	—	—	3.02
⊕ Genentech	Health	78.6	16.36	1.03
☆ Google	Business	—	—	0.93
⊖ Liberty Media	Media	—	11.56	0.80
⊖ The Directv Group	Media	—	1.15	0.76
⊕ Cox Communications A	Media	—	—	0.63
⊕ Kraft Foods	Goods	20.3	13.15	0.55
⊕ Amazon.com	Consumer	55.5	-15.83	0.52
⊖ Iac / Interactivecorp	Consumer	43.1	-18.60	0.49
⊖ Juniper Networks	Hardware	NMF	45.56	0.39
⊖ Fox Entertainment Group	Media	—	7.24	0.37
⊖ Genworth Financial	Financial	—	—	0.36
⊕ Washington Post	Media	27.8	25.21	0.28
⊖ UnionBanCal	Financial	13.1	14.77	0.28
⊕ XTO Energy	Energy	20.5	56.85	0.26
⊖ Murphy Oil	Energy	16.5	24.71	0.25
⊖ CIT Group	Financial	13.2	29.28	0.25
⊕ Vornado Realty Trust	Financial	30.8	46.53	0.25
⊖ Kmart Holding	Consumer	37.1	313.15	0.25
⊕ EW Scripps	Media	20.0	3.37	0.24

Current Investment Style

Value Blnd Growth; Large Mid Small

Market Cap	%
Giant	1.7
Large	6.6
Mid	51.2
Small	29.0
Micro	11.6
Avg $mil: 1,873	

Value Measures		Rel Category
Price/Earnings	17.69	1.05
Price/Book	2.03	0.94
Price/Sales	1.10	1.04
Price/Cash Flow	5.75	0.92
Dividend Yield %	1.07	1.07

Growth Measures	%	Rel Category
Long-Term Erngs	12.93	1.03
Book Value	4.18	0.59
Sales	4.04	0.71
Cash Flow	6.26	0.84
Historical Erngs	9.00	0.80

Profitability	%	Rel Category
Return on Equity	10.45	0.76
Return on Assets	4.89	0.75
Net Margin	8.76	0.97

Sector Weightings	% of Stocks	Rel S&P 500	3 Year High	3 Year Low
Info	17.84	0.83		
Software	3.14	0.73	5	3
Hardware	6.88	0.67	8	5
Media	6.05	1.58	6	5
Telecom	1.77	0.56	2	1
Service	58.00	1.25		
Health	10.95	0.88	13	11
Consumer	11.13	1.23	12	10
Business	9.33	2.30	10	8
Financial	26.59	1.28	30	26
Mfg	24.16	0.75		
Goods	5.89	0.63	7	6
Ind Mtrls	9.13	0.72	9	8
Energy	6.29	0.88	6	4
Utilities	2.85	0.96	3	3

Composition

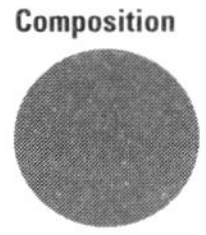

Cash	0.4
Stocks	99.6
Bonds	0.0
Other	0.0
Foreign (% of Stock)	0.0

Vanguard Global Equity

Ticker	Load	NAV	Yield	Total Assets	Mstar Category
VHGEX	None	$18.06	1.1%	$1,270 mil	World Stock

Governance and Management

Fiduciary Grade: B

Portfolio Manager(s)

Until Oct. 22, 2004, when a second subadvisor was added, Jeremy Hosking had been the sole manager of the fund since its inception in August 1995. He has been with Marathon Asset Management, the fund's original subadvisor, since 1986. Prior to that, he was a portfolio manager with GT Capital Management. The new subadvisor, which runs just a small portion of assets, is Acadian Asset Management. The managers from Acadian are John Chisholm, Ronald Frashure, and Brian Wolahan.

Strategy

Longtime sole subadvisor Marathon Asset Management was joined by Acadian Asset Management on Oct. 22, 2004, though for now Acadian runs just a tiny portion of the fund's assets. Marathon uses a fairly strict value discipline but will buy tech and telecom firms if their valuations and prospects are appealing. It's also willing to buy small- and mid-cap stocks. Acadian uses a quantitative strategy that looks at more than 20,000 securities. Vanguard uses fair-value pricing on occasion as well as other measures to combat market-timing.

Performance 12-31-04

	1st Qtr	2nd Qtr	3rd Qtr	4th Qtr	Total
2000	-1.20	0.86	-3.05	3.34	-0.17
2001	-4.28	6.37	-13.85	9.75	-3.73
2002	8.29	-1.75	-18.83	9.30	-5.61
2003	-4.34	18.92	9.58	15.93	44.51
2004	4.27	-0.50	0.31	15.38	20.09

Trailing	Total Return%	+/- MSCI EAFE	+/- MSCI World	%Rank Cat	Growth of $10,000
3 Mo	15.38	0.06	3.44	10	11,538
6 Mo	15.74	0.74	4.92	8	11,574
1 Yr	20.09	-0.16	5.37	12	12,009
3 Yr Avg	17.88	5.99	10.93	3	16,380
5 Yr Avg	9.50	10.63	11.95	5	15,742
10 Yr Avg	—	—	—	—	—
15 Yr Avg	—	—	—	—	—

Tax Analysis	Tax-Adj Rtn%	%Rank Cat	Tax-Cost Rat	%Rank Cat
3 Yr (estimated)	17.33	3	0.47	57
5 Yr (estimated)	8.31	4	1.09	73
10 Yr (estimated)	—	—	—	—

Potential Capital Gain Exposure: 25% of assets

Historical Profile

Return: High
Risk: Average
Rating: ★★★★★ Highest

Equity Stock %	91%	96%	94%	92%	95%	92%	93%	93%	97%

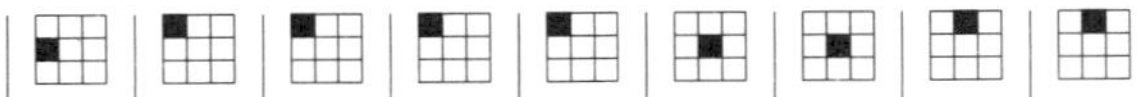

Investment Style
Equity
Stock %

▼ Manager Change
▽ Partial Manager Change

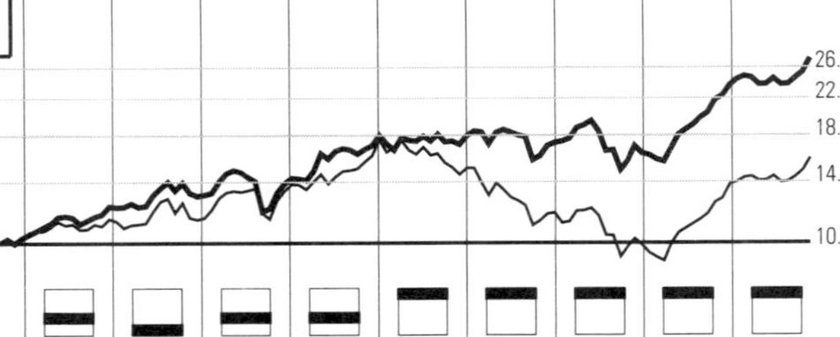

Growth of $10,000
▬ Investment Values of Fund
— Investment Values of MSCI EAFE

Performance Quartile (within Category)

1993	1994	1995	1996	1997	1998	1999	2000	2001	2002	2003	12-04	History
—	—	10.53	11.84	11.98	12.06	14.14	12.62	11.58	10.83	15.45	18.06	NAV
—	—	5.69*	15.59	6.91	9.39	25.95	-0.17	-3.73	-5.61	44.51	20.09	Total Return %
—	—	—	9.54	5.13	-10.54	-1.08	14.02	17.69	10.33	5.92	-0.16	+/-MSCI EAFE
—	—	—	2.11	-8.85	-14.93	1.00	13.02	13.07	14.28	11.40	5.37	+/-MSCI World
—	—	0.00	1.33	1.94	2.17	1.49	1.84	0.95	0.69	1.20	1.36	Income Return %
—	—	—	14.26	4.97	7.22	24.46	-2.01	-4.68	-6.30	43.31	18.73	Capital Return %
—	—	—	55	82	66	68	20	10	4	12	12	Total Rtn % Rank Cat
—	—	0.07	0.14	0.23	0.26	0.18	0.26	0.12	0.08	0.13	0.21	Income $
—	—	0.00	0.19	0.44	0.75	0.84	1.17	0.44	0.02	0.07	0.27	Capital Gains $
—	—	0.57	0.85	0.71	0.68	0.71	0.70	1.08	1.11	1.05	0.90	Expense Ratio %
—	—	2.04	1.53	1.67	1.47	1.39	1.88	1.10	0.86	1.14	1.47	Income Ratio %
—	—	—	29	24	34	36	31	27	14	13	19	Turnover Rate %
—	—	42	107	126	128	145	143	158	251	826	1,270	Net Assets $mil

Rating and Risk

Time Period	Load-Adj Return %	Morningstar Rtn vs Cat	Morningstar Risk vs Cat	Morningstar Risk-Adj Rating
1 Yr	20.09			
3 Yr	17.88	High	Avg	★★★★★
5 Yr	9.50	High	Avg	★★★★★
10 Yr	—	—	—	—
Incept	11.74			

Other Measures	Standard Index S&P 500	Best Fit Index DJ 60%
Alpha	6.3	1.9
Beta	0.92	1.64
R-Squared	88	92

Standard Deviation	18.06
Mean	17.88
Sharpe Ratio	0.92

Portfolio Analysis 09-30-04

Share change since 06-04 Total Stocks:306	Sector	Country	% Assets
⊕ Jardine Matheson Hldgs L	Ind Mtrls	Singapore	1.70
⊕ Costco Wholesale	Consumer	United States	1.47
⊕ Schering-Plough	Health	United States	1.39
⊕ Xerox	Ind Mtrls	United States	1.13
⊕ Berkshire Hathaway B	Financial	United States	1.11
⊕ Nextel Communications	Telecom	United States	1.09
⊕ Imperial Oil Ltd	Energy	Canada	1.06
⊕ Lucent Technologies	Hardware	United States	1.05
⊕ Jardine Strategic Hldgs	Consumer	Singapore	1.01
⊕ Moody's	Business	United States	0.96
⊕ IMS Health	Business	United States	0.96
⊕ Nortel Networks	Hardware	United States	0.94
⊕ Inco Ltd	Ind Mtrls	Canada	0.91
⊕ Hollinger International	Media	United States	0.89
⊕ Burlington Northern Sant	Business	United States	0.87
⊕ Liberty Media	Media	United States	0.87
⊕ Sun Microsystems	Hardware	United States	0.86
⊕ Alcan	Ind Mtrls	United States	0.86
⊕ Ayala	Ind Mtrls	Philippines	0.85
⊕ SBC Communications	Telecom	United States	0.85

Current Investment Style

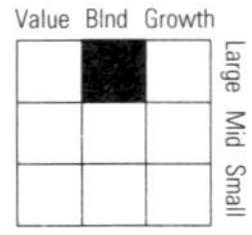

Market Cap	%
Giant	20.3
Large	42.3
Mid	32.6
Small	4.6
Micro	0.2
Avg $mil: 7,668	

Value Measures		Rel Category
Price/Earnings	15.05	0.95
Price/Book	1.80	0.81
Price/Sales	0.82	0.70
Price/Cash Flow	6.64	1.04
Dividend Yield %	5.97	3.18

Growth Measures	%	Rel Category
Long-Term Erngs	12.31	1.02
Book Value	-2.27	NMF
Sales	0.32	0.08
Cash Flow	3.63	0.62
Historical Erngs	7.85	0.92

Composition

Cash	3.1	Bonds	0.0
Stocks	96.8	Other	0.2
Foreign (% of Stock)			64.3

Sector Weightings	% of Stocks	Rel MSCI EAFE	3 Year High	3 Year Low
Info	23.04	1.39		
Software	0.38	0.35	0	0
Hardware	6.58	1.80	7	3
Media	8.60	3.77	10	6
Telecom	7.48	0.78	8	3
Service	41.76	0.93		
Health	5.12	0.71	6	3
Consumer	9.29	1.84	11	9
Business	11.14	2.05	14	11
Financial	16.21	0.60	16	12
Mfg	35.18	0.91		
Goods	10.17	0.74	15	10
Ind Mtrls	20.91	1.70	24	20
Energy	3.45	0.47	5	3
Utilities	0.65	0.12	1	1

Regional Exposure			% Stock
UK/W. Europe	28	N. America	39
Japan	11	Latn America	0
Asia X Japan	18	Other	4

Country Exposure			% Stock
United States	36	Hong Kong	5
U.K.	12	Singapore	4
Japan	11		

Morningstar's Take by Gregg Wolper 12-18-04

Vanguard Global Equity is again worth a look, though it has changed a bit.

This fine offering closed to new investors in December 2003. Marathon Asset Management, which at that time was the fund's sole subadvisor, had been inundated with new monies and was having trouble keeping up on the client-service front. So it decided to stop accepting new business, and Vanguard and Marathon jointly decided to close this fund as well. That was too bad for those shut out, for the fund had amassed an excellent long-term record, even though its value-oriented style fell out of favor during the late 1990s. But closing the fund made sense under the circumstances.

Vanguard reopened the fund on Oct. 22, 2004, albeit with a twist. In recognition of Marathon's situation, Vanguard added another subadvisor, Acadian Asset Management, which specializes in quantitative strategies. Initially, just 5% of the fund's assets was shifted to Acadian, but the bulk of any net inflows will go to the firm. Vanguard said it chose Acadian because it wanted to reopen the fund and had long considered Acadian a talented shop. Indeed, as of late October 2004, the separate accounts Acadian runs with a global-equity mandate had five- and 10-year returns that dwarfed the world-stock average for mutual funds. (Over the five-year period, Marathon had steered Vanguard Global Equity to even better returns than Acadian's, but Vanguard said diversification is one reason it added Acadian, so it would be wrong to expect identical performance from the two subadvisors.)

Bottom line: It's great to have this fund available again. Keep an eye on it, though, to see if its character changes if and when Acadian gets a bigger chunk of assets.

Address:	P O Box 2600 Valley Forge PA 19482 800-662-7447	Minimum Purchase:	$3000	Add: $100	IRA: $1000
Web Address:	www.vanguard.com	Min Auto Inv Plan:	$3000	Add: $50	
Inception:	08-14-95*	Sales Fees:	No-load		
Advisor:	The Vanguard Group, Inc.	Management Fee:	0.96%		
Subadvisor:	Multiple	Actual Fees:	Mgt:0.96%	Dist: —	
NTF Plans:	N/A	Expense Projections:	3Yr:$343	5Yr:$595	10Yr:$1317
		Income Distrib:	Annually		

Vanguard GNMA

Analyst Pick	Ticker	Load	NAV	Yield	SEC Yield	Total Assets	Mstar Category
✔	VFIIX	None	$10.44	4.6%	4.29%	$24,089 mil	Intermediate Government

Governance and Management

Fiduciary Grade: B

Portfolio Manager(s)

Seasoned. Paul Kaplan has been managing fixed-income funds for more than 15 years and has been at the helm of this offering since early 1994.

Strategy

This offering focuses exclusively on plain-vanilla GNMA pass-throughs, avoiding exotic mortgage-backed securities. Manager Paul Kaplan doesn't make big interest-rate bets either. He keeps the portfolio's duration (a measure of interest-rate sensitivity) close to those of similar funds and holds expenses down by keeping trading to a minimum.

Historical Profile

Return High
Risk Average
Rating ★★★★★ Highest

Investment Style: Fixed Income — Income Rtn %Rank Cat: 5, 6, 4, 3, 4, 2, 6, 8, 8

▼ Manager Change
▽ Partial Manager Change

Growth of $10,000
— Investment Values of Fund
— Investment Values of LB Aggr

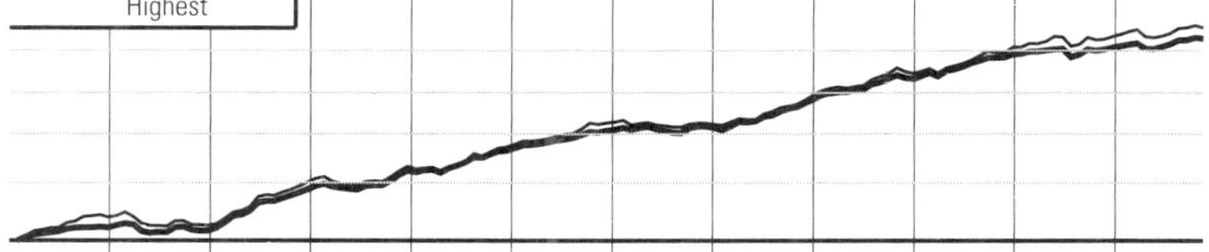

Performance Quartile (within Category)

1993	1994	1995	1996	1997	1998	1999	2000	2001	2002	2003	12-04	History
10.37	9.58	10.43	10.22	10.43	10.45	9.86	10.24	10.38	10.75	10.50	10.44	NAV
5.90	-0.95	17.04	5.24	9.47	7.14	0.78	11.22	7.94	9.68	2.49	4.13	Total Return %
-3.85	1.97	-1.43	1.61	-0.18	-1.55	1.60	-0.41	-0.50	-0.57	-1.61	-0.21	+/-LB Aggr
-4.76	2.43	-1.30	2.47	-0.12	-2.71	3.01	-2.02	0.7[illegible]	-1.82	0.13	0.65	+/-LB Govt
6.44	6.77	7.93	7.21	7.27	6.83	6.59	7.16	6.59	5.82	4.86	4.69	Income Return %
-0.54	-7.72	9.11	-1.97	2.20	0.31	-5.81	4.06	1.35	3.86	-2.37	-0.56	Capital Return %
87	5	37	5	16	60	12	42	12	39	23	17	Total Rtn % Rank Cat
0.65	0.68	0.73	0.73	0.72	0.69	0.67	0.68	0.66	0.59	0.51	0.48	Income $
0.00	0.01	0.00	0.00	0.00	0.01	0.00	0.00	0.00	0.02	0.00	0.00	Capital Gains $
0.29	0.28	0.30	0.29	0.27	0.31	0.30	0.27	0.27	0.25	0.22	0.20	Expense Ratio %
7.38	6.19	7.04	7.22	7.16	6.97	6.56	6.63	6.85	6.24	5.51	4.73	Income Ratio %
7	2	35	7	12	3	7	5	8	8	17	26	Turnover Rate %
7,073	5,778	6,908	7,399	8,725	10,993	12,548	13,911	15,531	21,792	19,408	18,858	Net Assets $mil

Performance 12-31-04

	1st Qtr	2nd Qtr	3rd Qtr	4th Qtr	Total
2000	2.16	1.95	3.16	3.52	11.22
2001	2.75	1.03	4.02	-0.04	7.94
2002	1.01	3.64	3.32	1.40	9.68
2003	1.04	1.00	-0.19	0.62	2.49
2004	1.59	-1.24	2.53	1.23	4.13

Trailing	Total Return%	+/- LB Aggr	+/- LB Govt	%Rank Cat	Growth of $10,000
3 Mo	1.23	0.28	0.74	12	10,123
6 Mo	3.79	-0.39	0.18	19	10,379
1 Yr	4.13	-0.21	0.65	17	10,413
3 Yr Avg	5.39	-0.80	-0.31	16	11,706
5 Yr Avg	7.04	-0.67	-0.44	15	14,052
10 Yr Avg	7.42	-0.30	-0.04	6	20,457
15 Yr Avg	7.49	-0.21	0.01	2	29,548

Tax Analysis	Tax-Adj Rtn%	%Rank Cat	Tax-Cost Rat	%Rank Cat
3 Yr (estimated)	3.47	19	1.82	83
5 Yr (estimated)	4.78	17	2.11	89
10 Yr (estimated)	4.83	9	2.41	98

Potential Capital Gain Exposure: 1% of assets

Rating and Risk

Time Period	Load-Adj Return %	Morningstar Rtn vs Cat	Morningstar Risk vs Cat	Morningstar Risk-Adj Rating
1 Yr	4.13			
3 Yr	5.39	+Avg	Avg	★★★★
5 Yr	7.04	+Avg	Avg	★★★★
10 Yr	7.42	High	-Avg	★★★★★
Incept	8.95			

Other Measures	Standard Index LB Aggr	Best Fit Index LB Mort
Alpha	0.5	-0.7
Beta	0.73	1.17
R-Squared	89	95
Standard Deviation	3.49	
Mean	5.39	
Sharpe Ratio	1.17	

Portfolio Analysis 09-30-04

Total Fixed-Income:34797	Date of Maturity	Amount $000	Value $000	% Net Assets
GNMA 6.5%	10-01-34	619,995	653,128	2.68
GNMA 6%	08-15-32	427,963	445,608	1.83
GNMA 5.5%	09-15-33	351,392	357,795	1.47
GNMA 6%	08-15-32	289,996	302,225	1.24
GNMA 5.5%	09-15-33	219,559	223,560	0.92
GNMA 5.5%	01-20-34	186,755	189,866	0.78
GNMA 5.5%	11-15-33	157,690	160,563	0.66
GNMA 5.5%	03-15-33	157,282	160,441	0.66
GNMA 5%	03-20-33	136,345	135,463	0.56
GNMA 5.5%	08-15-33	113,652	115,723	0.48
GNMA 6%	01-15-33	93,600	97,166	0.40
GNMA 6%	06-15-32	79,435	82,710	0.34
GNMA 5%	02-20-33	82,818	82,282	0.34
GNMA 5.5%	11-15-33	80,582	82,050	0.34
GNMA 5.5%	08-15-33	80,128	81,588	0.34
GNMA 5%	04-15-34	78,053	77,744	0.32
GNMA 5.5%	04-15-34	74,824	76,188	0.31
GNMA 5.5%	11-15-33	65,011	66,317	0.27
GNMA 5%	07-15-33	63,115	62,865	0.26
GNMA 5%	06-15-33	59,147	58,912	0.24

Current Investment Style

Duration: Short Int Long — Quality: High Med Low

[1] figure provided by fund

Avg Eff Duration[1]	3.1 Yrs
Avg Eff Maturity	4.7 Yrs
Avg Credit Quality	AAA
Avg Wtd Coupon	5.81%
Avg Wtd Price	102.95% of par

Coupon Range	% of Bonds	Rel Cat
0% PIK	0.0	0.0
0% to 6%	81.9	1.1
6% to 8%	17.7	0.8
8% to 10%	0.4	0.2
More than 10%	0.0	0.0

1.00=Category Average

Credit Analysis	% bonds 09-30-04		
US Govt	100	BB	0
AAA	0	B	0
AA	0	Below B	0
A	0	NR/NA	0
BBB	0		

Sector Breakdown	% of assets
US Treasuries	0
TIPS	0
US Agency	0
Mortgage Pass-Throughs	94
Mortgage CMO	0
Mortgage ARM	0
US Corporate	0
Asset-Backed	0
Convertible	0
Municipal	0
Corporate Inflation-Protected	0
Foreign Corporate	0
Foreign Govt	0

Composition			
Cash	5.9	Bonds	94.1
Stocks	0.0	Other	0.0

Special Securities	
Restricted/Illiquid Secs	0
Exotic Mortgage-Backed	—
Emerging-Markets Secs	0
Options/Futures/Warrants	No

Morningstar's Take by Lynn Russell 12-20-04

Low costs and consistency are just two of Vanguard GNMA's strong points.

This fund has long been one of our favorite core bond funds. For starters, we like its plain-vanilla approach. Longtime manager Paul Kaplan simply picks among various Ginnie Mae issues in an effort to add small increments of value. And perhaps just as importantly, he makes a point of avoiding moves that would risk losing the built-in head start that is provided by the fund's rock-bottom expense ratio. At just 0.20%, the fund's expense ratio provides the fund a huge sustainable advantage that is nearly impossible for its higher-cost competitors to overcome.

While this fund is hardly immune to the damage that can be done by rising interest rates, it has kept its balance better than most thanks largely to its expense advantage. The fund stayed well ahead of its category rivals when rates moved up sharply in 1994 and 1999, for example, and more recently it registered a narrower loss than its average peer when rates moved higher in April 2004. Overall, the fund's calendar-year returns have slipped below its intermediate-government category midpoint just once in the past decade and have more often landed in the group's top quartile.

That resilience and consistency have resulted in one of the best long-term records in the intermediate government category: The fund's five- and 10-year trailing returns through Dec. 17, 2004, land comfortably ahead of more than 80% of its intermediate-government peers. And the fund is equally impressive when compared with its rivals in the mortgage-focused subgroup, although it has displayed more month-to-month volatility relative to its mortgage peers.

Given the fund's experienced management, proven approach, attractive yield, and top-notch long-term record, we think it's hard to beat as a core bond holding.

Address:	PO Box 2600 Valley Forge PA 19482 800-662-7447
Web Address:	www.vanguard.com
Inception:	06-27-80
Advisor:	Wellington Management Company, LLP
Subadvisor:	None
NTF Plans:	N/A

Minimum Purchase:	$3000	Add: $100	IRA: $1000
Min Auto Inv Plan:	$3000	Add: $50	
Sales Fees:	No-load		
Management Fee:	0.19%		
Actual Fees:	Mgt:0.19%	Dist: —	
Expense Projections:	3Yr:$80	5Yr:$141	10Yr:$318
Income Distrib:	Monthly		

Vanguard Gr & Inc

Ticker	Load	NAV	Yield	Total Assets	Mstar Category
VQNPX	None	$30.61	1.4%	$7,222 mil	Large Blend

Governance and Management

Fiduciary Grade: B

Portfolio Manager(s)

John Cone took over as sole manager of this fund in July 2000. He had worked on quantitative models with former manager John Nagorniak since the early 1980s. Cone is one of five portfolio managers at the fund's adviser, Franklin Portfolio Associates. They are supported by one research analyst who focuses on valuation modeling and five IT analysts devoted to the firm's computerized model.

Strategy

Using a quantitative approach, management attempts to build a stock portfolio with risk comparable to that of the S&P 500 Index but that can outperform the index on an annual basis. Computer models rank a universe of 4,000 stocks on broad classifications of value, discounted cash flows, and earnings momentum. The models then build a portfolio with industry weights that are close to the index's, but the fund sports small overweights (versus the index) in attractive stocks and underweights those with poor risk/reward profiles.

Historical Profile

Return Above Avg
Risk Average
Rating ★★★★ Above Avg

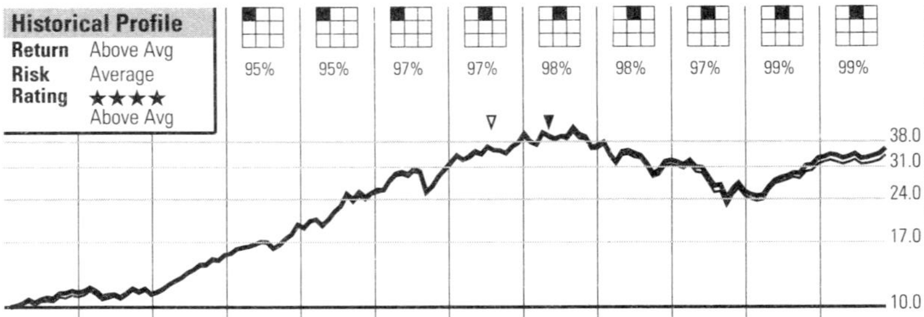

Investment Style
Equity
Stock %

▼ Manager Change
▽ Partial Manager Change

Growth of $10,000
— Investment Values of Fund
— Investment Values of S&P 500

Performance Quartile (within Category)

1993	1994	1995	1996	1997	1998	1999	2000	2001	2002	2003	12-04	History
16.45	15.56	19.95	22.23	26.19	30.76	37.08	32.06	28.20	21.75	27.94	30.61	NAV
13.83	-0.61	35.93	23.06	35.59	23.94	26.04	-8.97	-11.13	-21.92	30.15	11.11	Total Return %
3.77	-1.92	-1.60	0.12	2.24	-4.63	5.00	0.13	0.75	0.17	1.48	0.24	+/-S&P 500
3.65	-1.00	-1.84	0.61	2.74	-3.08	5.13	-1.18	1.32	-0.27	0.26	-0.29	+/-Russ 1000
2.41	2.44	2.71	2.05	1.97	1.29	1.08	0.97	0.94	1.01	1.57	1.51	Income Return %
11.42	-3.05	33.22	21.01	33.62	22.65	24.96	-9.94	-12.07	-22.93	28.58	9.60	Capital Return %
30	57	34	27	6	47	21	63	36	42	18	32	Total Rtn % Rank Cat
0.39	0.39	0.42	0.40	0.42	0.33	0.33	0.35	0.30	0.29	0.34	0.42	Income $
1.69	0.40	0.74	1.82	3.18	1.28	1.28	1.47	0.00	0.00	0.00	0.00	Capital Gains $
0.50	0.48	0.47	0.38	0.36	0.36	0.37	0.38	0.45	0.45	0.46	0.42	Expense Ratio %
2.22	2.50	2.25	1.97	1.74	1.27	1.04	1.02	1.02	1.02	1.39	1.35	Income Ratio %
85	71	59	75	66	47	54	65	41	70	88	79	Turnover Rate %
531	596	909	1,285	2,142	5,161	8,816	8,968	6,925	4,495	5,483	6,224	Net Assets $mil

Performance 12-31-04

	1st Qtr	2nd Qtr	3rd Qtr	4th Qtr	Total
2000	0.92	-2.91	1.62	-8.58	-8.97
2001	-12.51	7.49	-15.00	11.18	-11.13
2002	-0.07	-12.14	-16.04	5.91	-21.92
2003	-2.99	14.96	3.36	12.90	30.15
2004	2.18	1.34	-1.53	8.97	11.11

Trailing	Total Return%	+/- S&P 500	+/- Russ 1000	%Rank Cat	Growth of $10,000
3 Mo	8.97	-0.26	-0.83	61	10,897
6 Mo	7.31	0.12	-0.50	39	10,731
1 Yr	11.11	0.24	-0.29	32	11,111
3 Yr Avg	4.13	0.55	-0.14	27	11,291
5 Yr Avg	-1.80	0.50	-0.04	42	9,132
10 Yr Avg	12.46	0.39	0.30	11	32,358
15 Yr Avg	11.30	0.37	0.22	19	49,823

Tax Analysis	Tax-Adj Rtn%	%Rank Cat	Tax-Cost Rat	%Rank Cat
3 Yr (estimated)	3.77	23	0.35	29
5 Yr (estimated)	-2.36	38	0.57	30
10 Yr (estimated)	10.58	21	1.67	66

Potential Capital Gain Exposure: 3% of assets

Rating and Risk

Time Period	Load-Adj Return %	Morningstar Rtn vs Cat	Morningstar Risk vs Cat	Morningstar Risk-Adj Rating
1 Yr	11.11			
3 Yr	4.13	+Avg	Avg	★★★★
5 Yr	-1.80	Avg	Avg	★★★
10 Yr	12.46	+Avg	+Avg	★★★★
Incept	12.00			

Other Measures	Standard Index S&P 500	Best Fit Index Russ 1000
Alpha	0.6	0.0
Beta	0.94	0.95
R-Squared	99	99
Standard Deviation	14.87	
Mean	4.13	
Sharpe Ratio	0.19	

Portfolio Analysis 09-30-04

Share change since 06-04 Total Stocks:117	Sector	PE	YTD Ret%	% Assets
ExxonMobil	Energy	13.9	28.04	4.68
Johnson & Johnson	Health	20.6	25.17	3.20
⊖ Citigroup	Financial	15.3	2.72	3.08
⊕ IBM	Hardware	20.2	7.19	2.96
Wells Fargo	Financial	15.5	8.97	2.58
⊕ Home Depot	Consumer	19.0	21.47	2.49
⊕ Bank of America	Financial	12.3	21.50	2.07
⊕ ChevronTexaco	Energy	7.7	25.57	1.99
⊕ Walt Disney	Media	24.3	20.21	1.93
⊕ Kimberly-Clark	Goods	17.8	16.12	1.86
⊕ Qualcomm	Hardware	42.0	58.20	1.84
⊕ Intel	Hardware	19.8	-26.56	1.82
⊕ Allstate	Financial	12.8	23.12	1.79
⊕ Pfizer	Health	22.0	-22.31	1.77
⊕ General Dynamics	Ind Mtrls	17.5	17.40	1.75
⊕ Cendant	Business	13.6	6.52	1.75
⊖ Gen Elec	Ind Mtrls	22.8	20.68	1.71
American International G	Financial	16.2	-0.53	1.68
⊕ PNC Financial Services G	Financial	13.3	8.92	1.61
⊕ Harley-Davidson	Goods	20.5	28.70	1.59

Current Investment Style

Value Blnd Growth — Large Mid Small

Market Cap	%
Giant	51.0
Large	38.6
Mid	10.4
Small	0.0
Micro	0.0
Avg $mil: 44,060	

Value Measures		Rel Category
Price/Earnings	14.96	0.88
Price/Book	2.56	0.98
Price/Sales	1.30	0.90
Price/Cash Flow	6.57	0.86
Dividend Yield %	1.52	1.03

Growth Measures	%	Rel Category
Long-Term Erngs	10.91	0.94
Book Value	6.38	0.82
Sales	8.16	1.42
Cash Flow	14.46	1.53
Historical Erngs	14.99	1.27

Profitability	%	Rel Category
Return on Equity	19.63	1.12
Return on Assets	10.54	1.22
Net Margin	13.19	1.15

Sector Weightings	% of Stocks	Rel S&P 500	3 Year High	3 Year Low
Info	21.86	1.02		
Software	2.66	0.62	7	3
Hardware	12.12	1.19	12	7
Media	4.49	1.17	5	3
Telecom	2.59	0.82	5	3
Service	48.50	1.05		
Health	12.76	1.02	16	12
Consumer	8.28	0.91	11	8
Business	4.88	1.20	6	2
Financial	22.58	1.09	23	19
Mfg	29.64	0.92		
Goods	8.13	0.87	12	8
Ind Mtrls	11.26	0.89	13	9
Energy	8.53	1.19	9	6
Utilities	1.72	0.58	3	2

Composition

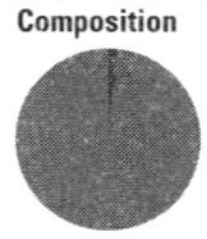

Cash	1.4
Stocks	98.6
Bonds	0.0
Other	0.0
Foreign (% of Stock)	0.0

Morningstar's Take by Jeffrey Ptak 10-06-04

Vanguard Growth & Income remains one of the best of its breed.

Vanguard is set to make manager John Cone's job a little easier. According to the fund's most recent semi-annual report, its expense ratio is slated to fall a few basis points to 0.43%.

True, that's not a huge markdown. But every basis point looms large here, owing to the grind-it-out nature of management's approach. Cone uses an array of computerized models to rank 4,000 stocks across roughly 40 factors, spanning valuation, growth, and "management signal" (such as insider trading) measures. After the models (which weight the valuation and growth factors equally) rank each stock, Cone and his team place a series of carefully calibrated bets on the top-rated names in particular industries. The idea is to mimic the bogy's risk profile while delivering up to 1.5% of excess returns per year. The end result is a portfolio of 150 or so names with sector weightings aligned with the S&P's, though the fund's typical holding also tends to be cheaper and faster-growing than the bogy's.

Given that big bets on individual stocks or sectors are frowned upon, the fund amasses its gains little bits at a time. That's why the fund's low expenses are such a key. Unburdened by a tall cost hurdle, Cone can let the models go about their work in the measured way envisioned. Further, low costs are vital by sheer virtue of the risk controls that Cone has put in place, which by definition don't confer the same outsized potential excess returns that a typical actively managed fund would.

This has paved the way for Cone's models to add value as intended: The fund's 0.9% annualized loss during his seven-year tenure--while not fabulous in absolute terms--is roughly 120 basis points superior to the S&P's. Meanwhile, the fund hasn't been excessively volatile either, giving it a fine risk/reward profile.

All told, it's a solid choice.

Address:	100 Vanguard Blvd Malvern PA 19355 800-662-7447
Web Address:	www.vanguard.com
Inception:	12-10-86
Advisor:	Franklin Portfolio Associates, LLC
Subadvisor:	Franklin Portfolio Associates, LLC
NTF Plans:	N/A

Minimum Purchase:	$3000	Add: $100	IRA: $1000
Min Auto Inv Plan:	$3000	Add: $50	
Sales Fees:	No-load		
Management Fee:	0.43%		
Actual Fees:	Mgt:0.43%	Dist: —	
Expense Projections:	3Yr:$144	5Yr:$252	10Yr:$567
Income Distrib:	Semi-Annually		

Vanguard Growth Equity

Analyst Pick	Ticker	Load	NAV	Yield	Total Assets	Mstar Category
✔	VGEQX	None	$9.66	0.1%	$787 mil	Large Growth

Governance and Management

Fiduciary Grade: B

Portfolio Manager(s)

A team from subadvisor Turner Investment Partners calls the shots here. Lead manager Robert Turner has run the fund since its 1992 inception and draws on the expertise of the firm's 10 sector analysts. Comanagers Chris McHugh, who also leads Turner Midcap Growth, and Mark Turner assist him.

Strategy

This fund's managers combine quantitative screens with fundamental and technical analysis to pick stocks. They think earnings expectations drive stock prices and pay close attention to earnings revisions and surprises. If one of the fund's holdings fails to meet its earnings or revenue targets, they are quick to sell it. They keep the fund sector-neutral relative to the Russell 1000 Growth Index, which gives it an above-average weighting in tech stocks.

Historical Profile

Return Average
Risk Above Avg
Rating ★★ Below Avg

Investment Style: Equity Stock % — 98% 98% 97% 98% 98% 99% 99% 100% 98%

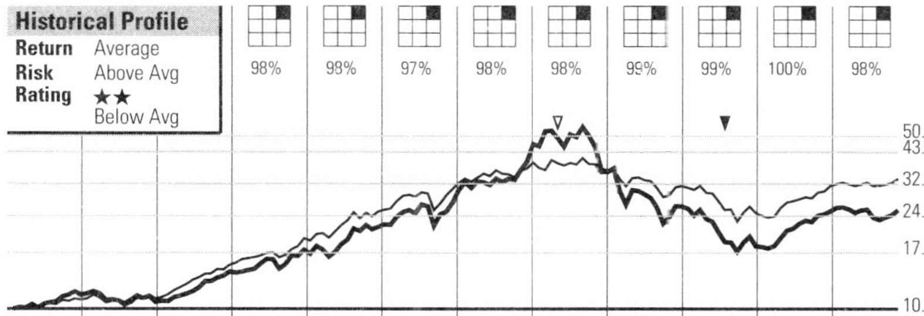

Performance Quartile (within Category)

History

	1993	1994	1995	1996	1997	1998	1999	2000	2001	2002	2003	12-04
NAV	12.89	11.92	14.53	12.76	11.71	14.44	17.27	13.28	9.64	6.64	9.18	9.66
Total Return %	15.38	-6.73	29.96	19.23	31.35	38.07	53.60	-23.10	-27.41	-30.94	38.56	5.35
+/-S&P 500	5.32	-8.04	-7.57	-3.71	-2.00	9.50	32.56	-14.00	-15.53	-8.85	9.89	-5.52
+/-Russ 1000Gr	12.51	-9.35	-7.22	-3.89	0.86	-0.64	20.44	-0.68	-6.99	-3.06	8.81	-0.95
Income Return %	0.77	0.79	0.79	0.04	0.00	0.00	0.00	0.00	0.00	0.19	0.30	0.12
Capital Return %	14.61	-7.52	29.17	19.19	31.35	38.07	53.60	-23.10	-27.41	-31.13	38.26	5.23
Total Rtn % Rank Cat	29	87	65	53	25	25	15	85	79	77	9	71
Income $	0.09	0.10	0.09	0.01	0.00	0.00	0.00	0.00	0.00	0.02	0.02	0.01
Capital Gains $	0.00	0.00	0.85	4.59	4.82	1.60	4.52	0.00	0.00	0.00	0.00	0.00
Expense Ratio %	1.00	0.95	0.94	1.06	1.02	1.00	0.92	0.72	0.59	0.43	0.42	0.61
Income Ratio %	0.80	0.86	0.78	0.03	-0.25	-0.42	-0.42	-0.19	-0.10	0.12	0.25	0.14
Turnover Rate %	88	165	178	178	178	250	328	303	357	273	220	162
Net Assets $mil	82	113	106	90	90	124	203	916	728	541	846	787

Performance 12-31-04

	1st Qtr	2nd Qtr	3rd Qtr	4th Qtr	Total
2000	13.26	-3.37	-1.16	-28.91	-23.10
2001	-26.13	10.09	-23.80	17.13	-27.41
2002	-3.11	-18.84	-16.49	5.18	-30.94
2003	0.30	17.42	6.39	10.58	38.56
2004	1.85	-0.21	-6.97	11.42	5.35

Trailing	Total Return%	+/- S&P 500	+/- Russ 1000Gr	%Rank Cat	Growth of $10,000
3 Mo	11.42	2.19	2.25	23	11,142
6 Mo	3.65	-3.54	0.18	68	10,365
1 Yr	5.35	-5.52	-0.95	71	10,535
3 Yr Avg	0.27	-3.31	0.45	42	10,081
5 Yr Avg	-10.86	-8.56	-1.57	79	5,628
10 Yr Avg	9.28	-2.79	-0.31	44	24,289
15 Yr Avg	—	—	—	—	—

Tax Analysis	Tax-Adj Rtn%	%Rank Cat	Tax-Cost Rat	%Rank Cat
3 Yr (estimated)	0.21	37	0.06	11
5 Yr (estimated)	-10.89	74	0.03	2
10 Yr (estimated)	5.82	73	3.17	98

Potential Capital Gain Exposure: -67% of assets

Rating and Risk

Time Period	Load-Adj Return %	Morningstar Rtn vs Cat	Morningstar Risk vs Cat	Morningstar Risk-Adj Rating
1 Yr	5.35			
3 Yr	0.27	Avg	+Avg	★★★
5 Yr	-10.86	-Avg	+Avg	★★
10 Yr	9.28	Avg	+Avg	★★
Incept	8.84			

Other Measures	Standard Index S&P 500	Best Fit Index Russ MG
Alpha	-3.1	-5.3
Beta	1.10	0.93
R-Squared	89	94
Standard Deviation	17.73	
Mean	0.27	
Sharpe Ratio	-0.06	

Portfolio Analysis 09-30-04

Share change since 06-04 Total Stocks:92	Sector	PE	YTD Ret%	% Assets
⊕ Cisco Systems	Hardware	24.5	-20.26	4.13
⊖ Dell	Hardware	34.0	24.01	2.90
⊕ Procter & Gamble	Goods	23.3	12.38	2.40
⊕ American Express	Financial	20.3	17.60	2.35
⊖ PepsiCo	Goods	22.5	13.82	2.20
⊕ Amgen	Health	37.7	3.82	2.03
⊕ Anthem	Health	17.4	53.33	1.96
⊖ American International G	Financial	16.2	-0.53	1.96
⊕ UnitedHealth Group	Health	23.8	51.38	1.82
⊖ Goldman Sachs Group	Financial	12.3	6.49	1.69
⊕ Caremark RX	Health	32.8	55.67	1.69
⊖ Time Warner	Media	27.5	8.12	1.68
⊕ Yahoo	Media	95.1	67.36	1.67
⊖ Genentech	Health	78.6	16.36	1.64
⊕ Boston Scientific	Health	32.3	-3.29	1.61
⊖ Applied Materials	Hardware	20.7	-23.80	1.61
⊖ Biogen IDEC	Health	—	81.50	1.58
☼ Medtronic	Health	30.7	2.68	1.52
⊖ SAP AG ADR	Software	42.7	6.80	1.47
⊖ First Data	Business	18.8	3.72	1.47

Current Investment Style

Market Cap	%
Giant	34.8
Large	44.6
Mid	20.6
Small	0.0
Micro	0.0
Avg $mil: 24,422	

Value Measures		Rel Category
Price/Earnings	23.12	1.09
Price/Book	3.11	0.96
Price/Sales	2.11	0.98
Price/Cash Flow	13.45	1.22
Dividend Yield %	0.39	0.51

Growth Measures	%	Rel Category
Long-Term Erngs	15.27	1.09
Book Value	5.22	0.41
Sales	9.32	1.09
Cash Flow	45.30	2.74
Historical Erngs	13.62	0.94

Profitability	%	Rel Category
Return on Equity	16.42	0.91
Return on Assets	8.68	0.93
Net Margin	9.72	0.79

Sector Weightings	% of Stocks	Rel S&P 500	3 Year High	3 Year Low
Info	32.09	1.49		
Software	6.27	1.46	9	3
Hardware	20.93	2.05	24	14
Media	4.89	1.27	6	3
Telecom	0.00	0.00	1	0
Service	51.10	1.10		
Health	23.70	1.90	28	24
Consumer	10.97	1.21	18	10
Business	7.13	1.76	10	2
Financial	9.30	0.45	10	6
Mfg	16.80	0.52		
Goods	7.61	0.82	10	7
Ind Mtrls	6.45	0.51	10	2
Energy	1.79	0.25	2	1
Utilities	0.95	0.32	1	0

Composition

Cash	1.7
Stocks	98.3
Bonds	0.0
Other	0.0
Foreign (% of Stock)	5.6

Morningstar's Take by Paul Herbert 10-19-04

It has taken its lumps lately, but there's still a place for Vanguard Growth Equity Fund.

This fund's recent performance leaves a lot to be desired. Specifically, manager Bob Turner's emphases within the tech and health-care areas have worked against the fund during the past few months. Leaning toward semiconductor-related stocks such as Analog Devices has hurt, for example, as the area has suffered due to slack demand. The fund has shed more than 5% through mid-October 2004, which places it near the back of the large-growth pack.

However, the fund's recent showing is not out of line with our expectations for it. Turner and his team look for companies that they expect will grow their profits at an accelerating rate. Such stocks often come with lofty price tags, and can fall from favor based on adverse news. Turner and his crew also keep the fund's sector weightings in line with the tech-heavy Russell 1000 Growth index's, meaning that the fund will always have a sizable stake in that volatile area. This also sets the fund up to perform nicely during growth rallies. Its relatively predictable performance makes it a suitable complement to a deep-value fund.

Turner, who is also one of his firm's lead tech analysts, hasn't backed down from some racy areas. He continues to favor chipmakers such as Texas Instruments, Xilinx, and Maxim Integrated Products, for instance. He thinks that their emphases on niche products will help them weather any downturn better than their peers. He also continues to overweight biotech stocks versus the index because of the pricing power firms such as Gilead enjoy.

This fund's aggressive, rapid-trading style has its drawbacks, but given factors such as its predictability and 0.42% expense ratio, we think it's an appealing option for investors' tax-deferred accounts.

Address:	P.O. Box 2600 Valley Forge PA 19482 800-662-7447
Web Address:	www.vanguard.com
Inception:	03-11-92
Advisor:	Turner Investment Partners, Inc.
Subadvisor:	None
NTF Plans:	Walnut St Secs NTF

Minimum Purchase:	$10000	Add: $100	IRA: $1000
Min Auto Inv Plan:	$100	Add: $50	
Sales Fees:	No-load		
Management Fee:	0.33%, 0.12%A		
Actual Fees:	Mgt:0.33%	Dist:	
Expense Projections:	3Yr:$113	5Yr:$197	10Yr:$443
Income Distrib:	Annually		

Vanguard Gr Idx

Ticker	Load	NAV	Yield	Total Assets	Mstar Category
VIGRX	None	$26.41	1.1%	$10,110 mil	Large Growth

Governance and Management

Fiduciary Grade: B

Portfolio Manager(s)

Gus Sauter, who has been here since the fund's November 1992 inception, runs all of Vanguard's equity index funds. Judging from the excellent results he has posted--the firm's index offerings generally have kept apace their benchmarks despite their expense hurdles--he could be the best in the business. Investors are in safe hands here.

Strategy

In 2003, the fund switched benchmarks, replacing the S&P/Barra Growth Index with the newly minted MSCI U.S. Prime Market Growth Index. This index represents growth stocks contained in the MSCI U.S. Prime Market 750 Index (which contains the 750 largest companies--in terms of free-float market capitalization--in the U.S.). MSCI defines style (growth versus value) using an eight-factor model that includes measures ranging from dividend yield to long-term historical sales per share. MSCI employs buffer zones to limit the migration of stocks between the growth and value camps. This should serve to limit turnover at the fund.

Historical Profile

Return Above Avg
Risk Average
Rating ★★★★ Above Avg

Investment Style: Equity, Stock %: 100% 99% 97% 100% 100% 98% 98% 100% 100%

▼ Manager Change
▽ Partial Manager Change

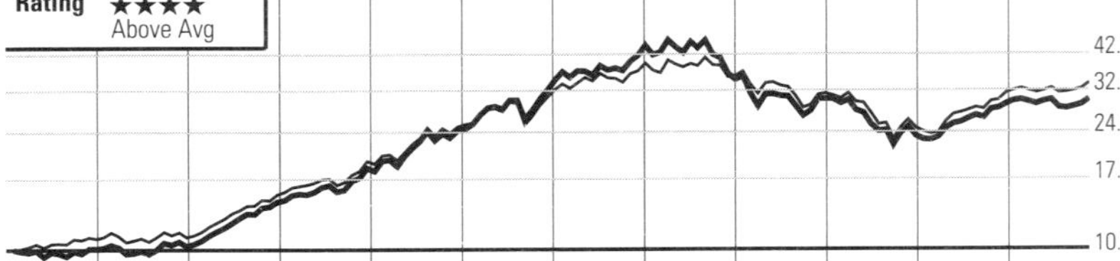

Growth of $10,000
— Investment Values of Fund
— Investment Values of S&P 500

Performance Quartile (within Category)

1993	1994	1995	1996	1997	1998	1999	2000	2001	2002	2003	12-04	History
10.20	10.28	13.97	16.90	22.53	31.67	39.43	30.57	26.42	19.95	24.92	26.41	NAV
1.53	2.89	38.06	23.74	36.34	42.20	28.76	-22.21	-12.93	-23.68	25.92	7.20	Total Return %
-8.53	1.58	0.53	0.80	2.99	13.63	7.72	-13.11	-1.05	-1.59	-2.75	-3.67	+/-S&P 500
-1.34	0.27	0.88	0.62	5.85	3.49	-4.40	0.21	7.49	4.20	-3.83	0.90	+/-Russ 1000Gr
2.06	2.07	1.96	1.59	1.37	0.98	0.72	0.32	0.61	0.86	0.88	1.19	Income Return %
-0.53	0.82	36.10	22.15	34.97	41.22	28.04	-22.53	-13.54	-24.54	25.04	6.01	Capital Return %
89	12	17	16	7	17	63	82	14	25	58	52	Total Rtn % Rank Cat
0.21	0.21	0.20	0.22	0.23	0.22	0.23	0.13	0.19	0.23	0.18	0.30	Income $
0.00	0.00	0.00	0.14	0.25	0.12	1.04	0.00	0.00	0.00	0.00	0.00	Capital Gains $
0.20	0.20	0.20	0.20	0.20	0.22	0.22	0.22	0.22	0.23	0.23	—	Expense Ratio %
2.10	2.08	1.71	1.57	1.19	0.92	0.64	0.33	0.67	0.97	0.77	—	Income Ratio %
36	28	24	29	26	29	33	33	31	23	44	—	Turnover Rate %
51	86	271	787	2,365	6,644	15,232	11,162	8,445	6,094	7,586	7,711	Net Assets $mil

Performance 12-31-04

	1st Qtr	2nd Qtr	3rd Qtr	4th Qtr	Total
2000	4.03	-1.39	-8.77	-16.88	-22.21
2001	-17.50	7.70	-13.26	12.97	-12.93
2002	-0.87	-16.30	-14.07	7.04	-23.68
2003	-0.91	11.57	3.24	10.33	25.92
2004	1.49	1.51	-4.88	9.40	7.20

Trailing	Total Return%	+/- S&P 500	+/- Russ 1000Gr	%Rank Cat	Growth of $10,000
3 Mo	9.40	0.17	0.23	59	10,940
6 Mo	4.06	-3.13	0.59	62	10,406
1 Yr	7.20	-3.67	0.90	52	10,720
3 Yr Avg	1.00	-2.58	1.18	32	10,303
5 Yr Avg	-6.94	-4.64	2.35	45	6,979
10 Yr Avg	11.52	-0.55	1.93	15	29,753
15 Yr Avg	—	—	—	—	—

Tax Analysis	Tax-Adj Rtn%	%Rank Cat	Tax-Cost Rat	%Rank Cat
3 Yr (estimated)	0.72	30	0.28	48
5 Yr (estimated)	-7.18	38	0.26	16
10 Yr (estimated)	10.99	9	0.48	7

Potential Capital Gain Exposure: -11% of assets

Rating and Risk

Time Period	Load-Adj Return %	Morningstar Rtn vs Cat	Morningstar Risk vs Cat	Morningstar Risk-Adj Rating
1 Yr	7.20			
3 Yr	1.00	+Avg	Avg	★★★★
5 Yr	-6.94	Avg	Avg	★★★
10 Yr	11.52	+Avg	Avg	★★★★
Incept	10.06			

Other Measures	Standard Index S&P 500	Best Fit Index Russ 1000Gr
Alpha	-2.4	1.0
Beta	0.94	0.93
R-Squared	94	98

Standard Deviation	14.77
Mean	1.00
Sharpe Ratio	-0.03

Morningstar's Take by Sonya Morris 10-15-04

Cheap and style-pure, Vanguard Growth Index is a fine choice.

In the indexing world, cheaper is always better because index funds rely on low costs to gain an edge over pricier actively managed rivals. That principle isn't lost on Vanguard Growth Index, whose 0.23% expense ratio is a fraction of the large-growth category norm.

But that's not the end of the story. This fund also keeps costs down by keeping turnover and, thus, transaction costs low. While such costs aren't reflected in a fund's expense ratio, they eat into returns all the same. (This fund's turnover rate was inflated in 2003 by Vanguard's switch to a new MSCI benchmark; we expect it to be much lower going forward.)

We also like the fund's style-purity. Unlike an actively managed growth fund that can stray from its roots in, say, chasing the latest hot trend, this fund is governed by a quantitative classification scheme. As such, it facilitates portfolio construction by providing unflagging exposure to growth stocks.

Of course, the downside to this strict approach is that it might fail to accurately reflect what active growth stock-pickers are holding. For instance, if the criteria for placing stocks in the growth camp were too strict, the index could end up treadling lightly in names that have caught the fancy of growth managers.

That said, we have high hopes for the fund's current bogy, which employs a more sophisticated multivariate approach. Further, since MSCI employs buffer zones to control migration between indexes, it does a better job of mimicking the holding patterns of active managers. Why does that matter? Because the name of the game is approximating the gross return of the typical active growth manager and then pulling ahead after costs are factored in. Thus, in more faithfully tracking the growth-stock universe, the MSCI bogy puts the fund in better position to consistently compete on cost, a battle it should win every time.

Address:	P O Box 2600 Valley Forge PA 19482 800-662-7447
Web Address:	www.vanguard.com
Inception:	11-02-92
Advisor:	Vanguard Advisers, Inc.
Subadvisor:	None
NTF Plans:	N/A

Minimum Purchase:	$3000	Add: $100	IRA: $1000
Min Auto Inv Plan:	$3000	Add: $50	
Sales Fees:	No-load		
Management Fee:	0.21%		
Actual Fees:	Mgt:0.21%	Dist: —	
Expense Projections:	3Yr:$71	5Yr:$124	10Yr:$280
Income Distrib:	Quarterly		

Portfolio Analysis 09-30-04

Share change since 06-04 Total Stocks:418	Sector	PE	YTD Ret%	% Assets
⊕ Microsoft	Software	36.1	8.95	5.14
⊕ Pfizer	Health	22.0	-22.31	4.46
⊕ Johnson & Johnson	Health	20.6	25.17	3.20
⊕ American International G	Financial	16.2	-0.53	2.88
⊖ Wal-Mart Stores	Consumer	23.4	0.51	2.82
⊖ IBM	Hardware	20.2	7.19	2.76
⊖ Procter & Gamble	Goods	23.3	12.38	2.53
⊕ Intel	Hardware	19.8	-26.56	2.48
⊖ Cisco Systems	Hardware	24.5	-20.26	2.34
⊖ Home Depot	Consumer	19.0	21.47	1.67
⊕ PepsiCo	Goods	22.5	13.82	1.59
⊖ Dell	Hardware	34.0	24.01	1.55
⊕ Amgen	Health	37.7	3.82	1.40
⊕ Qualcomm	Hardware	42.0	58.20	1.21
⊕ Medtronic	Health	30.7	2.68	1.20
⊕ Eli Lilly & Company	Health	24.3	-17.55	1.17
⊖ American Express	Financial	20.3	17.60	1.13
⊕ Coca-Cola	Goods	21.9	-16.12	1.09
⊕ UnitedHealth Group	Health	23.8	51.38	0.94
⊕ eBay	Consumer	81.6	80.07	0.87

Current Investment Style

Value Blnd Growth — Large Mid Small

Market Cap	%
Giant	47.4
Large	35.1
Mid	17.4
Small	0.1
Micro	0.0
Avg $mil: 38,350	

Value Measures		Rel Category
Price/Earnings	20.63	0.97
Price/Book	3.27	1.01
Price/Sales	1.96	0.91
Price/Cash Flow	10.25	0.93
Dividend Yield %	0.76	0.99

Growth Measures	%	Rel Category
Long-Term Erngs	14.01	1.00
Book Value	11.67	0.92
Sales	8.83	1.04
Cash Flow	15.90	0.96
Historical Erngs	12.29	0.85

Profitability	%	Rel Category
Return on Equity	19.97	1.11
Return on Assets	10.11	1.08
Net Margin	12.45	1.01

Sector Weightings	% of Stocks	Rel S&P 500	3 Year High	3 Year Low
Info	32.51	1.51		
Software	8.14	1.89	9	7
Hardware	18.05	1.77	21	12
Media	4.48	1.17	6	1
Telecom	1.84	0.58	3	0
Service	51.01	1.10		
Health	22.01	1.76	28	21
Consumer	13.73	1.51	15	12
Business	6.08	1.50	6	3
Financial	9.19	0.44	10	5
Mfg	16.47	0.51		
Goods	9.98	1.07	16	9
Ind Mtrls	3.17	0.25	10	3
Energy	3.20	0.45	3	0
Utilities	0.12	0.04	0	0

Composition

Cash	0.1
Stocks	99.9
Bonds	0.0
Other	0.0
Foreign (% of Stock)	0.1

Vanguard Health Care

Analyst Pick	Ticker	Load	NAV	Yield	Total Assets	Mstar Category
✔	VGHCX	None	$126.79	0.8%	$22,467 mil	Specialty-Health

Governance and Management

Fiduciary Grade: B

Portfolio Manager(s)

Ed Owens, who has been running the show since the fund's 1984 inception, may not be as daring as some of his rivals, but he's one of the best in the business. Three health-care analysts assist him.

Strategy

Ed Owens employs a measured, low-turnover approach. He maintains exposure to five areas of the health-care market: international stocks, pharmaceuticals, services, devices, and biotechnology. He then makes modest adjustments where he finds the best valuations. He likes to buy his stocks cheap and hold them for the long run.

Historical Profile

Return High
Risk Low
Rating ★★★★★ Highest

Investment Style: Equity Stock %

90%	90%	82%	91%	85%	89%	88%	93%	90%

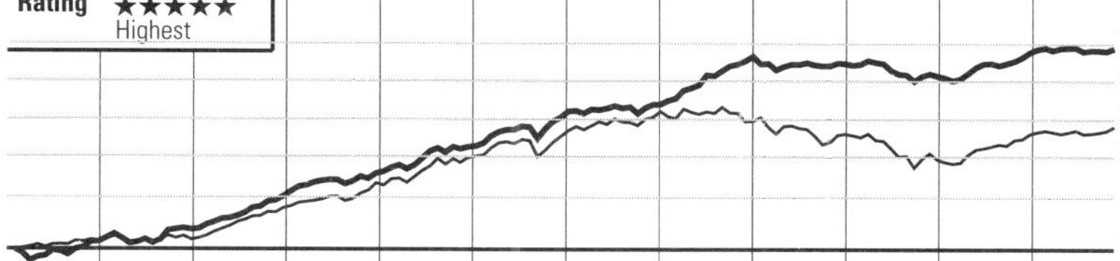

▼ Manager Change
∇ Partial Manager Change

Growth of $10,000
— Investment Values of Fund
— Investment Values of S&P 500

Performance Quartile (within Category)

History

1993	1994	1995	1996	1997	1998	1999	2000	2001	2002	2003	12-04	History
35.07	35.47	49.82	58.35	71.88	96.85	95.21	132.74	116.84	96.16	120.57	126.79	NAV
11.81	9.54	45.17	21.36	28.57	40.80	7.04	60.56	-6.87	-11.36	26.58	9.51	Total Return %
1.75	8.23	7.64	-1.58	-4.78	12.23	-14.00	69.66	5.01	10.73	-2.09	-1.36	+/-S&P 500
16.61	-1.24	-9.69	2.81	-8.31	1.71	11.07	23.09	5.74	9.45	7.15	4.96	+/-DJ Hlthcare
2.28	1.65	1.61	1.50	1.35	1.19	1.02	1.19	0.79	0.82	1.04	0.93	Income Return %
9.53	7.89	43.56	19.86	27.22	39.61	6.02	59.37	-7.66	-12.18	25.54	8.58	Capital Return %
8	34	72	15	45	6	54	34	29	3	70	43	Total Rtn % Rank Cat
0.76	0.57	0.57	0.74	0.78	0.84	0.97	1.07	1.03	0.96	1.00	1.11	Income $
1.97	2.31	1.02	1.29	2.14	3.08	7.14	15.93	5.46	6.53	0.10	4.00	Capital Gains $
0.22	0.19	0.40	0.45	0.38	0.40	0.36	0.39	0.34	0.31	0.29	0.28	Expense Ratio %
2.06	2.37	1.58	1.57	1.41	1.28	1.13	0.92	1.03	0.84	0.86	0.91	Income Ratio %
15	19	25	13	7	10	11	27	21	13	25	13	Turnover Rate %
609	708	1,473	2,662	4,466	9,268	10,421	18,467	16,241	13,752	17,645	19,606	Net Assets $mil

Performance 12-31-04

	1st Qtr	2nd Qtr	3rd Qtr	4th Qtr	Total
2000	14.75	16.25	9.48	9.94	60.56
2001	-12.60	5.66	-1.38	2.26	-6.87
2002	3.12	-9.32	-10.01	5.32	-11.36
2003	-2.62	15.98	0.29	11.76	26.58
2004	1.90	2.76	-2.75	7.54	9.51

Trailing	Total Return%	+/- S&P 500	+/- DJ Hlthcare	%Rank Cat	Growth of $10,000
3 Mo	7.54	-1.69	1.64	50	10,754
6 Mo	4.58	-2.61	3.58	33	10,458
1 Yr	9.51	-1.36	4.96	43	10,951
3 Yr Avg	7.11	3.53	7.48	12	12,288
5 Yr Avg	12.93	15.23	9.42	19	18,367
10 Yr Avg	20.15	8.08	5.32	1	62,696
15 Yr Avg	18.60	7.67	—	1	129,202

Tax Analysis	Tax-Adj Rtn%	%Rank Cat	Tax-Cost Rat	%Rank Cat
3 Yr (estimated)	5.83	12	0.86	89
5 Yr (estimated)	11.34	19	1.41	79
10 Yr (estimated)	18.48	1	1.39	53

Potential Capital Gain Exposure: 32% of assets

Rating and Risk

Time Period	Load-Adj Return %	Morningstar Rtn vs Cat	Morningstar Risk vs Cat	Morningstar Risk-Adj Rating
1 Yr	8.41			
3 Yr	6.75	+Avg	-Avg	★★★★
5 Yr	12.93	+Avg	Low	★★★★
10 Yr	20.15	High	Low	★★★★★
Incept	19.80			

Other Measures	Standard Index S&P 500	Best Fit Index DJ Hlthcare
Alpha	4.2	7.2
Beta	0.62	0.84
R-Squared	70	85
Standard Deviation	11.81	
Mean	7.11	
Sharpe Ratio	0.49	

Portfolio Analysis 09-30-04

Share change since 06-04 Total Stocks:103	Sector	PE	YTD Ret%	% Assets
Pfizer	Health	22.0	-22.31	5.76
⊕ Novartis	Health	—	—	3.02
Roche Holding	Health	—	—	2.99
☼ Sanofi-Aventis	Health	—	—	2.96
Eli Lilly & Company	Health	24.3	-17.55	2.84
⊖ Schering-Plough	Health	—	21.56	2.77
⊕ Cardinal Health	Health	16.9	-4.73	2.65
⊕ AstraZeneca	Health	—	—	2.59
Abbott Laboratories	Health	22.1	2.61	2.58
Amgen	Health	37.7	3.82	2.55
⊕ Forest Laboratories	Health	18.0	-27.41	2.38
CVS	Consumer	21.1	25.61	2.29
Genzyme	Health	—	17.81	2.08
Becton, Dickinson and Co	Health	24.4	39.74	2.07
Aetna	Financial	16.9	84.67	2.06
Wyeth	Health	17.0	2.73	1.98
⊕ Gilead Sciences	Health	36.9	20.08	1.94
McKesson	Health	15.8	-1.41	1.94
Medtronic	Health	30.7	2.68	1.79
Genentech	Health	78.6	16.36	1.59

Current Investment Style

Value Blnd Growth; Large Mid Small

Market Cap	%
Giant	39.5
Large	40.9
Mid	17.0
Small	2.5
Micro	0.0
Avg $mil: 21,893	

Value Measures		Rel Category
Price/Earnings	18.48	0.78
Price/Book	2.56	0.93
Price/Sales	1.07	0.38
Price/Cash Flow	9.40	0.86
Dividend Yield %	1.12	1.58

Growth Measures	%	Rel Category
Long-Term Erngs	13.35	0.83
Book Value	12.85	0.83
Sales	10.24	0.83
Cash Flow	9.09	0.49
Historical Erngs	7.14	0.75

Profitability	%	Rel Category
Return on Equity	16.53	1.69
Return on Assets	8.40	2.72
Net Margin	10.78	1.41

Industry Weightings	% of Stocks	Rel Cat
Biotech	17.5	0.5
Drugs	37.9	1.3
Mgd Care	4.7	0.8
Hospitals	2.4	1.4
Other HC Srv	0.1	0.1
Diagnostics	2.4	2.5
Equipment	14.2	0.9
Good/Srv	9.6	2.0
Other	11.4	1.9

Composition

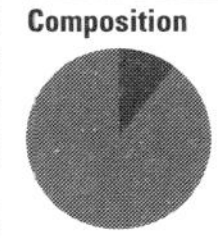

Cash	10.2
Stocks	89.8
Bonds	0.0
Other	0.0
Foreign (% of Stock)	30.0

Morningstar's Take by Christopher Davis 01-03-05

What Vanguard Health Care lacks in speed, it makes up for with endurance.

Many investors seem to regard sector funds as market-timing tools, but this offering demonstrates the appeal of investing for the long haul. For the trailing 10 years though Dec. 31, 2004, it returned 20% annually, which not only tops the health-care category but is also among the best showings of any mutual fund. Yet the fund's calendar-year returns rarely rank so highly. At the same time, it hasn't ended a year in the category's bottom quartile in more than a decade.

That consistent strength stems from manager Ed Owens' strategy. Owens doesn't make big bets on single stocks. He spreads his picks broadly across pharmaceutical, biotechnology, health-care services, and medical device stocks. He also keeps a chunk of the portfolio overseas. He employs a measured, valuation-conscious approach, slowly adjusting his holdings to reflect where he's finding the most-attractive valuations. In 2004, for instance, Owens continued to hike the fund's foreign and large-cap stakes, while tilting it away from drugmakers in favor of medical-equipment and services stocks.

The fund's wide-ranging portfolio means it can appear sluggish when one area of health care dominates. That was in the case in 2003, when biotech stocks surged. But with the sector on a more even footing in 2004, the fund turned in competitive returns. Overseas drug holdings like Novartis and Fujisawa Pharmaceutical posted strong gains, as did medical-equipment picks like Becton, Dickenson.

We'd concede this fund's mammoth $21.6 billion asset base will keep it from easily replicating its past success. However, we believe management's experience, consistent strategy, and rock-bottom costs give it a big edge over the competition. For health-care investors that can meet its $25,000 minimum, this offering is a worthwhile choice.

Address:	PO Box 2600 Valley Forge PA 19482 800-662-7447
Web Address:	www.vanguard.com
Inception:	05-23-84
Advisor:	Wellington Management Company, LLP
Subadvisor:	None
NTF Plans:	N/A

Minimum Purchase:	$25000	Add: $100	IRA: $25000
Min Auto Inv Plan:	$25000	Add: $50	
Sales Fees:	No-load, 1.00%R		
Management Fee:	0.15% mx./0.05% mn.		
Actual Fees:	Mgt:0.15%	Dist: —	
Expense Projections:	3Yr:$214	5Yr:$174	10Yr:$393
Income Distrib:	Annually		

Vanguard Hi-Yld Corp

Analyst Pick

Ticker	Load	NAV	Yield	SEC Yield	Total Assets	Mstar Category
VWEHX	None	$6.44	7.1%	5.80%	$9,598 mil	High Yield Bond

Governance and Management

Fiduciary Grade: B

Portfolio Manager(s)

This fund is subadvised by Wellington Management Company. Earl McEvoy has run this offering since 1984. He also runs Vanguard Long-Term Investment-Grade and the bond portion of Vanguard Wellesley Income's balanced portfolio, both of which have been strong performers.

Strategy

This fund invests mainly in higher-quality junk bonds, with the bulk of assets parked in BB and B rated credits, along with a smattering in investment-grade bonds. Manager Earl McEvoy's approach is predicated on error avoidance. He generally seeks out companies with steady-to-improving revenues and a relatively stable customer base. Although he's willing to bet on particular sectors, positions in individual issuers are kept relatively small to ward off blowups.

Historical Profile

Return Average
Risk Below Avg
Rating ★★★★ Above Avg

Investment Style: Fixed Income — Income Rtn %Rank Cat: 67, 48, 64, 77, 70, 72, 64, 58, 37

▼ Manager Change
∇ Partial Manager Change

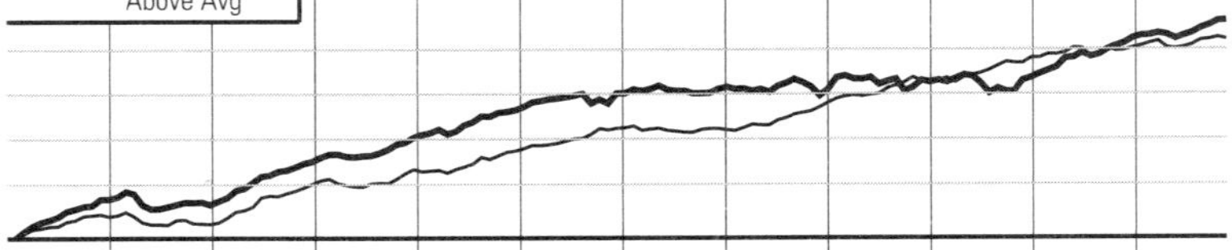

Growth of $10,000
— Investment Values of Fund
— Investment Values of LB Aggr

Performance Quartile (within Category)

1993	1994	1995	1996	1997	1998	1999	2000	2001	2002	2003	12-04	History
8.02	7.20	7.85	7.87	8.08	7.83	7.39	6.69	6.29	5.88	6.38	6.44	NAV
18.24	-1.71	19.15	9.55	11.91	5.62	2.49	-0.88	2.90	1.73	17.20	8.52	Total Return %
8.49	1.21	0.68	5.92	2.26	-3.07	3.31	-12.51	-5.54	-8.52	13.10	4.18	+/-LB Aggr
-0.67	-0.74	1.76	-2.87	-0.72	5.04	-0.79	4.33	-2.88	-1.38	-10.73	-3.44	+/-CSFB Glb HY
9.80	8.81	9.83	9.12	9.08	8.54	8.32	9.01	9.28	8.39	8.39	7.45	Income Return %
8.44	-10.52	9.32	0.43	2.83	-2.92	-5.83	-9.89	-6.38	-6.66	8.81	1.07	Capital Return %
55	30	17	95	79	6	72	13	54	22	92	76	Total Rtn % Rank Cat
0.70	0.68	0.68	0.69	0.69	0.66	0.63	0.64	0.60	0.51	0.48	0.46	Income $
0.00	0.00	0.00	0.00	0.00	0.03	0.00	0.00	0.00	0.00	0.00	0.00	Capital Gains $
0.34	0.32	0.34	0.34	0.29	0.28	0.29	0.28	0.27	0.27	0.26	0.23	Expense Ratio %
9.82	8.81	9.13	8.85	8.92	8.63	8.26	8.34	9.07	9.02	8.42	7.65	Income Ratio %
83	51	33	38	23	45	31	20	16	29	29	52	Turnover Rate %
2,530	2,121	2,900	3,563	4,571	5,380	5,699	5,270	5,160	5,433	7,095	7,317	Net Assets $mil

Performance 12-31-04

	1st Qtr	2nd Qtr	3rd Qtr	4th Qtr	Total
2000	-1.53	1.98	1.41	-2.66	-0.88
2001	4.20	-2.18	-2.71	3.77	2.90
2002	1.30	-1.84	-3.22	5.72	1.73
2003	4.27	5.98	1.31	4.69	17.20
2004	1.97	-1.01	4.30	3.07	8.51

Trailing	Total Return%	+/- LB Aggr	+/- CSFB Glb HY	%Rank Cat	Growth of $10,000
3 Mo	3.07	2.12	-1.49	89	10,307
6 Mo	7.51	3.33	-1.75	80	10,751
1 Yr	8.52	4.18	-3.44	76	10,852
3 Yr Avg	8.97	2.78	-4.91	76	12,940
5 Yr Avg	5.70	-2.01	-2.47	46	13,194
10 Yr Avg	7.63	-0.09	-0.99	20	20,861
15 Yr Avg	8.43	0.73	-1.66	49	33,670

Tax Analysis	Tax-Adj Rtn%	%Rank Cat	Tax-Cost Rat	%Rank Cat
3 Yr (estimated)	5.93	69	2.79	47
5 Yr (estimated)	2.46	38	3.07	35
10 Yr (estimated)	4.18	13	3.21	28

Potential Capital Gain Exposure: -10% of assets

Rating and Risk

Time Period	Load-Adj Return %	Morningstar Rtn vs Cat	Morningstar Risk vs Cat	Morningstar Risk-Adj Rating
1 Yr	8.52			
3 Yr	8.97	-Avg	-Avg	★★★
5 Yr	5.70	Avg	-Avg	★★★
10 Yr	7.63	+Avg	Low	★★★★
Incept	9.56			

Other Measures	Standard Index LB Aggr	Best Fit Index CSFB Glb HY
Alpha	6.5	-2.6
Beta	0.23	0.85
R-Squared	3	91
Standard Deviation	5.93	
Mean	8.97	
Sharpe Ratio	1.29	

Portfolio Analysis 09-30-04

Total Fixed-Income:344	Date of Maturity	Amount $000	Value $000	% Net Assets
US Treasury Note 6.625%	05-15-07	164,925	180,825	1.98
US Treasury Note 6.875%	05-15-06	115,200	123,282	1.35
Nextel Comms 9.5%	02-01-11	97,385	110,289	1.21
Xerox 9.75%	01-15-09	90,000	104,850	1.15
Qwest 144A 8.875%	03-15-12	93,455	103,034	1.13
At&T 7.3%	11-15-11	85,855	96,136	1.05
US Treasury Note 5.625%	05-15-08	88,060	95,807	1.05
Abitibi-Consolidated 8.5	08-01-10	83,635	91,058	1.00
Citizens Comms 9.25%	05-15-11	82,615	90,611	0.99
Mgm Mirage 8.5%	09-15-10	78,475	89,560	0.98
Quebecor Media 11.125%	07-15-11	75,700	87,434	0.96
Solectron 9.625%	02-15-09	77,575	85,914	0.94
Georgia Pac 9.375%	02-01-13	72,660	85,557	0.94
Insight Midwest L P / In	11-01-10	77,295	84,831	0.93
Host Marriott L P 7.125%	11-01-13	68,215	71,455	0.78
Aes 144A 9%	05-15-15	61,990	70,359	0.77
Case New Holland 144A 9.	08-01-11	61,450	68,978	0.76
US Treasury Note 5.5%	05-15-09	59,050	64,678	0.71
Bcp Caylux Hldgs Luxembo	06-15-14	59,480	64,238	0.70
Ucar Fin 10.25%	02-15-12	55,940	64,051	0.70

Current Investment Style

Duration: Short Int Long — Quality: High Med Low

¹figure provided by fund

Avg Eff Duration¹	3.9 Yrs
Avg Eff Maturity	6.5 Yrs
Avg Credit Quality	BB
Avg Wtd Coupon	8.54%
Avg Wtd Price	108.55% of par

Coupon Range	% of Bonds	Rel Cat
0% PIK	0.0	0.0
0% to 8%	37.0	1.0
8% to 11%	59.9	1.1
11% to 14%	3.1	0.5
More than 14%	0.0	0.0

1.00=Category Average

Credit Analysis	% bonds 09-30-04		
US Govt	6	BB	42
AAA	0	B	50
AA	0	Below B	0
A	0	NR/NA	1
BBB	1		

Sector Breakdown	% of assets
US Treasuries	6
TIPS	0
US Agency	0
Mortgage Pass-Throughs	0
Mortgage CMO	0
Mortgage ARM	0
US Corporate	85
Asset-Backed	1
Convertible	0
Municipal	0
Corporate Inflation-Protected	0
Foreign Corporate	7
Foreign Govt	0

Composition			
Cash	2.2	Bonds	97.8
Stocks	0.0	Other	0.0

Special Securities	
Restricted/Illiquid Secs	12
Exotic Mortgage-Backed	0
Emerging-Markets Secs	0
Options/Futures/Warrants	No

Morningstar's Take by Dieter Bardy 11-10-04

Vanguard High-Yield Corporate's low fees help it outrun the competition.

Low fees and a moderate strategy are the real highlights of this offering. Its 0.23% expense ratio is just a quarter of what its typical high-yield bond rival charges. This goes a long way toward giving the fund a yield advantage. Its trailing 12-month yield, at 7.3%, is among the category's highest. And its payout is consistently among the group's most attractive.

The fund's tremendous cost savings differentiate it from rival funds in other ways as well. Manager Earl McEvoy concentrates the fund's assets in issues among the upper tiers of the high-yield universe, instead of straying into lower and nonrated debt. This emphasis assists the fund in several ways. Besides the obvious benefit of reducing losses from single-issue blowups, this approach requires less effort to investigate issuers who are in or near default, and that helps the fund maintain its low fees.

However, the fund's middle-of-the-road approach has held it back during speculative high-yield rallies. Through Nov. 1, 2004, its year-to-date return is 7.1%, compared with its typical peer's 7.5% showing. But investors who have stuck around over the long haul have been well rewarded, as the fund's five-, 10- and 15-year trailing returns are all well entrenched in the top half in their peer group. What's more, investors who held this fund in a nontaxable account have brought home more of their earnings, partially due to McEvoy's longer-term approach to picking individual bonds.

The fund's many appealing aspects give us continued confidence in it. Investors must be aware that McEvoy does not try to shoot out the lights, but his tempered approach to high yield investing makes sense in this typically volatile category.

Address:	PO Box 2600 Valley Forge PA 19482 800-662-7447
Web Address:	www.vanguard.com
Inception:	12-27-78
Advisor:	Wellington Management Company, LLP
Subadvisor:	None
NTF Plans:	N/A

Minimum Purchase:	$3000	Add: $100	IRA: $1000
Min Auto Inv Plan:	$3000	Add: $50	
Sales Fees:	No-load, 1.00%R		
Management Fee:	0.24%		
Actual Fees:	Mgt:0.24%	Dist: —	
Expense Projections:	3Yr:$87	5Yr:$152	10Yr:$393
Income Distrib:	Monthly		

Vanguard Hi-Yld T/E

Analyst Pick

Ticker	Load	NAV	Yield	SEC Yield	Total Assets	Mstar Category
VWAHX	None	$10.83	4.7%	3.90%	$4,433 mil	Muni National Long

Governance and Management

Fiduciary Grade: B

Portfolio Manager(s)

Reid Smith took over day-to-day management of this fund in 1996. Bob Auwaerter sets the fund's duration range.

Strategy

The fund differs from many high-yield offerings in that its credit quality is fairly high. Management invests at least 80% of the fund's assets in municipal securities rated BBB and above. Management adjusts the fund's duration within a specified range, depending on its interest-rate outlook. Typically, the fund is less sensitive to rate changes than its average muni-national long-term peer.

Historical Profile

Return: High
Risk: Below Avg
Rating: ★★★★★ Highest

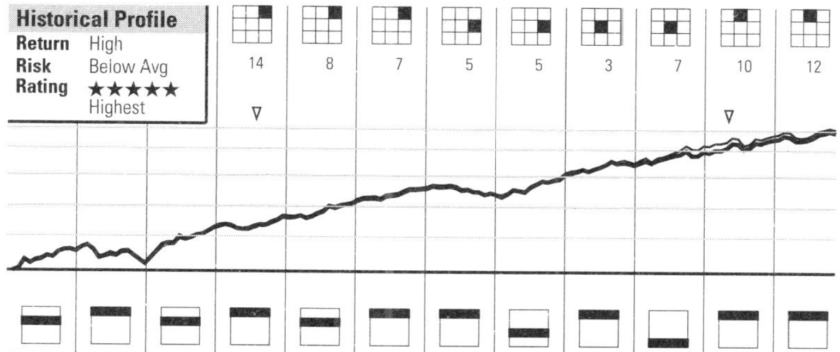

1993	1994	1995	1996	1997	1998	1999	2000	2001	2002	2003	12-04	History
11.01	9.66	10.76	10.63	10.93	10.97	10.04	10.50	10.48	10.67	10.81	10.83	NAV
12.66	-5.07	18.13	4.46	9.24	6.45	-3.38	10.73	5.34	7.30	6.35	4.98	Total Return %
0.38	0.10	0.67	0.03	0.05	-0.03	-1.32	-0.95	0.21	-2.30	1.04	0.50	+/-LB Muni
-1.72	2.27	-2.84	0.00	-1.60	-0.37	1.30	-4.51	0.47	-2.73	0.02	-1.58	+/-LB Muni 20YR
6.36	5.86	6.50	5.61	5.78	5.40	5.36	5.95	5.62	5.46	4.98	4.76	Income Return %
6.30	-10.93	11.63	-1.15	3.46	1.05	-8.74	4.78	-0.28	1.84	1.37	0.22	Capital Return %
47	16	30	16	45	5	17	62	6	77	8	12	Total Rtn % Rank Cat
0.65	0.63	0.61	0.59	0.60	0.58	0.57	0.58	0.58	0.56	0.52	0.50	Income $
0.21	0.17	0.00	0.00	0.05	0.07	0.00	0.00	0.00	0.00	0.00	0.00	Capital Gains $
0.20	0.20	0.21	0.20	0.19	0.20	0.18	0.19	0.19	0.17	0.17	0.15	Expense Ratio %
6.15	5.83	6.15	5.66	5.56	5.28	5.33	5.74	5.43	5.30	4.94	4.71	Income Ratio %
34	50	33	19	27	24	22	32	18	18	17	24	Turnover Rate %
1,904	1,573	1,988	2,039	2,320	2,767	2,753	3,143	2,650	2,669	2,668	2,764	Net Assets $mil

Performance 12-31-04

	1st Qtr	2nd Qtr	3rd Qtr	4th Qtr	Total
2000	2.58	1.36	2.71	3.68	10.73
2001	2.91	1.18	1.91	-0.72	5.34
2002	1.04	3.27	3.22	-0.37	7.30
2003	0.68	3.39	0.48	1.67	6.35
2004	1.44	-1.51	3.67	1.35	4.98

Trailing	Total Return%	+/- LB Muni	+/- LB Muni 20YR	%Rank Cat	Growth of $10,000
3 Mo	1.35	0.10	-0.63	34	10,135
6 Mo	5.07	-0.12	-1.68	39	10,507
1 Yr	4.98	0.50	-1.58	12	10,498
3 Yr Avg	6.21	-0.23	-1.42	21	11,981
5 Yr Avg	6.92	-0.28	-1.62	21	13,973
10 Yr Avg	6.84	-0.22	-1.11	11	19,379
15 Yr Avg	7.02	0.03	-0.63	8	27,668

Tax Analysis	Tax-Adj Rtn%	%Rank Cat	Tax-Cost Rat	%Rank Cat
3 Yr (estimated)	6.21	12	0.00	1
5 Yr (estimated)	6.92	11	0.00	1
10 Yr (estimated)	6.81	9	0.03	13

Potential Capital Gain Exposure: 3% of assets

Rating and Risk

Time Period	Load-Adj Return %	Morningstar Rtn vs Cat	Morningstar Risk vs Cat	Morningstar Risk-Adj Rating
1 Yr	4.98			
3 Yr	6.21	+Avg	Low	★★★★★
5 Yr	6.92	+Avg	Low	★★★★★
10 Yr	6.84	High	-Avg	★★★★★
Incept	7.51			

Other Measures	Standard Index LB Aggr	Best Fit Index LB Muni 20YR
Alpha	0.4	-0.2
Beta	0.87	0.81
R-Squared	94	94
Standard Deviation	4.51	
Mean	6.21	
Sharpe Ratio	1.09	

Portfolio Analysis 09-30-04

Total Fixed-Income:369	Date of Maturity	Amount $000	Value $000	% Net Assets
New Jersey St Tran 5.5%	02-01-09	61,405	61,594	1.42
Chicago Ill Wtr	11-01-31	60,000	60,000	1.39
California St Econ Recov	07-01-14	50,000	56,688	1.31
Massachusetts St Wtr Res	07-15-19	43,700	53,824	1.24
Memphis Tenn Elec Sys 5%	12-01-16	40,000	43,395	1.00
Minneapolis Minn Health	11-15-32	39,000	40,669	0.94
California Statewide Cmn	05-15-25	37,785	39,338	0.91
Puerto Rico Pub Fin 5.75	08-01-27	34,000	38,063	0.88
New Jersey Econ Dev Auth	04-01-31	30,500	37,556	0.87
Brazos Riv Tex Hbr Nav D	05-15-33	35,200	37,492	0.87
Puerto Rico Pub Bldgs Au	07-01-36	33,000	36,334	0.84
North Carolina Cap Facs	10-01-39	35,000	36,112	0.83
Loudoun Cnty Va Indl Dev	02-15-38	34,935	34,935	0.81
Maricopa Cnty Ariz Pollu	06-01-35	35,500	34,915	0.81
Connecticut St Dev Auth	09-01-28	33,250	34,773	0.80

Current Investment Style

Duration: Short Int Long; Quality: High Med Low

¹Avg Eff Duration	5.8 Yrs
Avg Eff Maturity	7.8 Yrs
Avg Credit Quality	AA
Avg Wtd Coupon	4.93%
Avg Wtd Price	104.31% of par

¹figure provided by fund

Credit Analysis	% bonds 09-30-04		
US Govt	0	BB	2
AAA	40	B	1
AA	17	Below B	0
A	14	NR/NA	7
BBB	18		

Top 5 States	% bonds		
CA	12.4	NJ	6.3
NY	8.5	MA	5.6
TX	7.8		

Composition			
Cash	0.4	Bonds	99.6
Stocks	0.0	Other	0.0

Special Securities	
Restricted/Illiquid Secs	0
Options/Futures/Warrants	No

Sector Weightings	% of Bonds	Rel Cat
General Obligation	20.4	0.78
Utilities	16.8	1.27
Health	8.2	1.04
Water/Waste	15.9	1.43
Housing	2.1	0.29
Education	5.1	0.44
Transportation	9.3	1.23
COP/Lease	1.4	0.67
Industrial	20.5	1.58
Misc Revenue	0.0	0.00
Demand	0.3	1.15

Morningstar's Take by Dieter Bardy 12-14-04

Vanguard High-Yield Tax-Exempt is a cheap and mild option in this often-risky part of the market.

This fund flaunts its huge cost advantage over other muni high-yield funds. At only 0.17%, the fund's expense ratio is fully one fifth the size of its typical rival's 0.94%. What's more, its low costs drive the fund's approach to picking high-yield municipal bonds. Instead of weighing down the portfolio with risky lower-rated issues, the fund targets higher-quality bonds (it holds 71% in credits rated A or better, versus 33% for its typical rival). Indeed, manager Reid Smith recognizes that the fund's cost advantage doesn't require extraordinary stretch to beat the competition.

The fund's long-term results plainly demonstrate how well the strategy works. While its returns for the year-to-date through Dec. 13, 2004, marginally lag its rivals', it stands out over the long haul. Its returns over the trailing five- and 10-year periods, for example, comfortably place in the top quartile of both the high-yield muni and muni-national long-term categories. Thus, over time, greater attention to risk and low expenses has worked wonders here.

The fund is sticking with its winning combination in the months to come, with one exception: interest rates. Smith is lengthening the fund's duration, a measure of how sensitive a fund is to interest changes, from defensive to a more neutral 7.3-year posture. He thinks that rising interest rates are being priced into the economy and that there's less chance of a big rate spike. So, he's looking more at bonds that should hold up better in a slowly rising rate environment, such as securities in the 6-7 year range and 20-21 year part of the market. The interest rates on those bonds has already moved higher in recent months, so future changes should be minimal.

The fund continues to be one of our favorites in the muni high-yield category. Its low costs and steady-eddy management make it difficult to beat. Tax-free investors should step right up.

Address:	PO Box 2600 Valley Forge PA 19482 800-662-7447
Web Address:	www.vanguard.com
Inception:	12-27-78
Advisor:	Vanguard Advisers, Inc.
Subadvisor:	None
NTF Plans:	N/A

Minimum Purchase:	$3000	Add: $100	IRA: $1000
Min Auto Inv Plan:	$3000	Add: $50	
Sales Fees:	No-load		
Management Fee:	0.15%		
Actual Fees:	Mgt:0.15%	Dist:	
Expense Projections:	3Yr:$55	5Yr:$96	10Yr:$217
Income Distrib:	Monthly		

Vanguard Infl-Prot Secs

Analyst Pick

Ticker	Load	NAV	Yield	SEC Yield	Total Assets	Mstar Category
VIPSX	None	$12.57	4.5%	1.21%	$7,718 mil	Intermediate Government

Governance and Management

Fiduciary Grade: B

Portfolio Manager(s)

Experienced. John Hollyer and Ken Volpert have worked in the investment industry since 1987 and 1982, respectively. Hollyer runs two other Vanguard funds, and Volpert is the firm's bond-index fund guru.

Strategy

The goal here is to provide inexpensive exposure to the inflation-protected bond market. Most of management's actions involve trying to identify undervalued issues along the inflation-protected bond-maturity spectrum. Historically, the fund has stuck exclusively with Treasury issues.

Historical Profile
Return High
Risk High
Rating ★★★★★ Highest

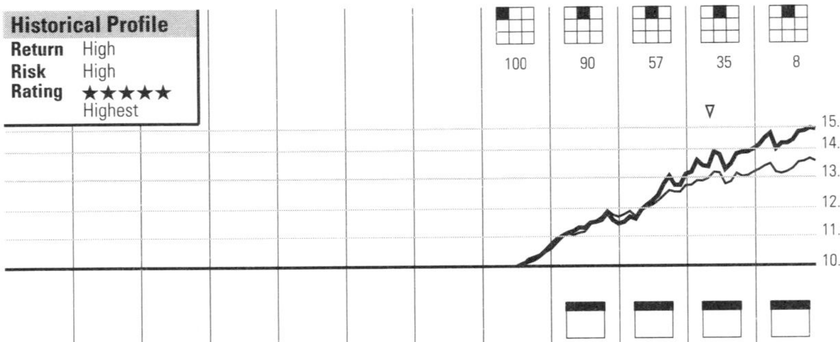

Investment Style
Fixed Income
Income Rtn %Rank Cat: 100 (2000), 90 (2001), 57 (2002), 35 (2003), 8 (12-04)

▼ Manager Change
▽ Partial Manager Change

Growth of $10,000
— Investment Values of Fund
— Investment Values of LB Aggr

Performance Quartile (within Category)

History

	1993	1994	1995	1996	1997	1998	1999	2000	2001	2002	2003	12-04
NAV	—	—	—	—	—	—	—	10.35	10.62	11.84	12.21	12.57
Total Return %	—	—	—	—	—	—	—	5.92*	7.61	16.61	8.00	8.27
+/-LB Aggr	—	—	—	—	—	—	—	—	-0.83	6.36	3.90	3.93
+/-LB Govt	—	—	—	—	—	—	—	—	0.38	5.11	5.64	4.79
Income Return %	—	—	—	—	—	—	—	0.00	4.37	4.39	3.85	4.70
Capital Return %	—	—	—	—	—	—	—	—	3.24	12.22	4.15	3.57
Total Rtn % Rank Cat	—	—	—	—	—	—	—	—	21	1	2	2
Income $	—	—	—	—	—	—	—	0.27	0.44	0.46	0.45	0.57
Capital Gains $	—	—	—	—	—	—	—	0.01	0.07	0.06	0.12	0.07
Expense Ratio %	—	—	—	—	—	—	—	—	0.25	0.25	0.22	0.18
Income Ratio %	—	—	—	—	—	—	—	—	6.38	3.92	4.55	3.46
Turnover Rate %	—	—	—	—	—	—	—	—	122	75	108	63
Net Assets $mil	—	—	—	—	—	—	—	148	772	2,988	4,557	7,182

Performance 12-31-04

	1st Qtr	2nd Qtr	3rd Qtr	4th Qtr	Total
2000	—	—	2.09	3.74	5.92 *
2001	4.63	1.58	2.42	-1.14	7.61
2002	1.51	5.77	7.96	0.60	16.61
2003	2.62	3.46	0.24	1.47	8.00
2004	5.00	-3.04	3.87	2.40	8.27

Trailing	Total Return%	+/- LB Aggr	+/- LB Govt	%Rank Cat	Growth of $10,000
3 Mo	2.40	1.45	1.91	5	10,240
6 Mo	6.36	2.18	2.75	5	10,636
1 Yr	8.27	3.93	4.79	2	10,827
3 Yr Avg	10.89	4.70	5.19	1	13,636
5 Yr Avg	—	—	—	—	—
10 Yr Avg	—	—	—	—	—
15 Yr Avg	—	—	—	—	—

Tax Analysis	Tax-Adj Rtn%	%Rank Cat	Tax-Cost Rat	%Rank Cat
3 Yr (estimated)	9.09	1	1.62	65
5 Yr (estimated)	—	—	—	—
10 Yr (estimated)	—	—	—	—

Potential Capital Gain Exposure: 1% of assets

Rating and Risk

Time Period	Load-Adj Return %	Morningstar Rtn vs Cat	Morningstar Risk vs Cat	Morningstar Risk-Adj Rating
1 Yr	8.27			
3 Yr	10.89	High	High	★★★★★
5 Yr	—	—	—	—
10 Yr	—	—	—	—
Incept	10.30			

Other Measures	Standard Index LB Aggr	Best Fit Index LB Long Tr
Alpha	2.5	4.7
Beta	1.44	0.61
R-Squared	77	83
Standard Deviation	7.75	
Mean	10.89	
Sharpe Ratio	1.24	

Portfolio Analysis 09-30-04

Total Fixed-Income:13	Date of Maturity	Amount $000	Value $000	% Net Assets
US Treasury Note 3%	07-15-12	1,064,950	1,242,402	18.03
US Treasury Bond 3.625%	04-15-28	583,925	867,768	12.60
US Treasury Note 1.875%	07-15-13	575,950	604,236	8.77
US Treasury Note 3.875%	01-15-09	415,025	539,740	7.83
US Treasury Bond 3.875%	04-15-29	349,250	533,838	7.75
US Treasury Note 2%	01-15-14	508,300	533,642	7.75
US Treasury Note 3.5%	01-15-11	427,425	526,618	7.64
US Treasury Bond 2.375%	01-15-25	486,950	509,695	7.40
US Treasury Note 3.375%	01-15-07	329,425	420,819	6.11
US Treasury Note 3.625%	01-15-08	296,750	381,654	5.54
US Treasury Bond 3.375%	04-15-32	96,100	130,037	1.89
US Treasury Note 4.25%	01-15-10	76,950	100,553	1.46
US Treasury Note 2%	07-15-14	8,775	9,015	0.13

Morningstar's Take by Eric Jacobson 12-27-04

For investors who understand something about the TIPS market they're getting into, Vanguard Inflation-Protected Securities is a terrific choice.

We view this fund as a plain-vanilla option for those in search of a TIPS (Treasury Inflation-Protected Securities) offering. It is actively managed, but skipper John Hollyer doesn't stray far from the market when making his bets. For much of this year, for example, he--like many bond managers--took a slightly cautious tack, expecting interest rates would rise, thus hurting nearly all bonds. He shied away from long issues and modestly trimmed the fund's overall interest-rate sensitivity.

But while that expectation has been largely defied--long-term yields are nearly back to their year-ago levels--Hollyer's bet wasn't that large. As such, the fund has performed well versus its TIPS-focused rivals and is nearly in line with Lehman Brothers TIPS index for the year to date through Dec. 23, 2004.

Of course, like other Vanguard bond funds, it's more than just its moderate nature that makes it shine: A tiny 0.19% (annualized) expense ratio gives the fund a huge advantage over its many more-costly rivals, particularly given the commodity nature of the TIPS market. What's more, that represents a nearly 25% price cut over the past three years.

Investors in the TIPS market should note the volatility that it can endure under certain circumstances. Market yields--for standard and inflation-protected Treasuries--have fallen far in recent years. As a result, TIPS prices have become much more volatile. To wit, April was the worst month ever for the Lehman TIPS index, and the range of its monthly gains and losses has widened substantially over the past four years. That doesn't mean investors should avoid TIPS. It does reinforce the notion, though, that TIPS aren't suitable as a substitute for the short-term slice of a portfolio, and by extension, neither is this or any TIPS fund.

Address:	PO Box 2600 Valley Forge PA 19482 800-662-7447	Minimum Purchase:	$3000	Add: $100 IRA: $1000
Web Address:	www.vanguard.com	Min Auto Inv Plan:	$3000	Add: $50
Inception:	06-29-00 *	Sales Fees:	No-load	
Advisor:	Vanguard Advisers, Inc.	Management Fee:	0.23%	
Subadvisor:	None	Actual Fees:	Mgt:0.23%	Dist: —
NTF Plans:	N/A	Expense Projections:	3Yr:$80	5Yr:$141 10Yr:$318
		Income Distrib:	Quarterly	

Current Investment Style

Duration: Short / Int / Long; Quality: High / Med / Low

¹ figure provided by fund

Avg Eff Duration¹	6.0 Yrs
Avg Eff Maturity	11.0 Yrs
Avg Credit Quality	AAA
Avg Wtd Coupon	3.12%
Avg Wtd Price	122.10% of par

Coupon Range	% of Bonds	Rel Cat
0% PIK	0.0	0.0
0% to 6%	100.0	1.3
6% to 8%	0.0	0.0
8% to 10%	0.0	0.0
More than 10%	0.0	0.0

1.00=Category Average

Credit Analysis		% bonds 09-30-04	
US Govt	100	BB	0
AAA	0	B	0
AA	0	Below B	0
A	0	NR/NA	0
BBB	0		

Sector Breakdown	% of assets
US Treasuries	8
TIPS	85
US Agency	0
Mortgage Pass-Throughs	0
Mortgage CMO	0
Mortgage ARM	0
US Corporate	0
Asset-Backed	0
Convertible	0
Municipal	0
Corporate Inflation-Protected	0
Foreign Corporate	0
Foreign Govt	0

Composition			
Cash	7.1	Bonds	92.9
Stocks	0.0	Other	0.0

Special Securities	
Restricted/Illiquid Secs	0
Exotic Mortgage-Backed	—
Emerging-Markets Secs	0
Options/Futures/Warrants	No

Vanguard Ins L/T TE Inv

Ticker	Load	NAV	Yield	SEC Yield	Total Assets	Mstar Category
VILPX	None	$12.82	4.5%	3.59%	$2,946 mil	Muni National Long

Governance and Management

Fiduciary Grade: B

Portfolio Manager(s)

Reid Smith has managed the fund since 1992 and is responsible for the day-to-day operations. Bob Auwaerter sets the fund's duration range.

Strategy

This fund invests at least 80% of its assets in municipal bonds that have principal and interest payments guaranteed by a third-party insurer. The fund's overall credit quality is very high. Management adjusts the fund's duration within a specified range, but it is generally less sensitive to interest-rate fluctuations than its average category peer. Management rotates between states and sectors based on assessments of relative value.

Historical Profile

Return High
Risk Above Avg
Rating ★★★★★ Highest

Investment Style: Fixed Income — Income Rtn %Rank Cat: 23, 17, 9, 10, 10, 20, 27, 23, 16

▼ Manager Change
▽ Partial Manager Change

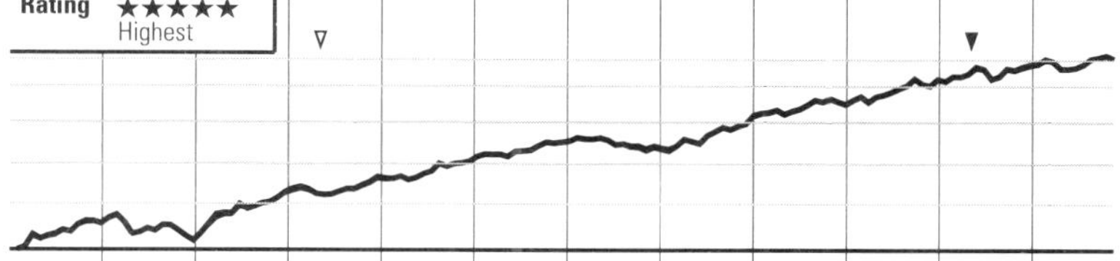

Growth of $10,000
- Investment Values of Fund
- Investment Values of LB Muni

Performance Quartile (within Category)

1993	1994	1995	1996	1997	1998	1999	2000	2001	2002	2003	12-04	History
12.81	11.23	12.60	12.34	12.62	12.65	11.65	12.54	12.37	12.91	12.93	12.82	NAV
13.09	-5.59	18.60	4.02	8.64	6.14	-2.91	13.61	4.30	10.03	5.77	3.93	Total Return %
0.81	-0.42	1.14	-0.41	-0.55	-0.34	-0.85	1.93	-0.83	0.43	0.46	-0.55	+/-LB Muni
-1.29	1.75	-2.37	-0.44	-2.20	-0.68	1.77	-1.63	-0.57	0.00	-0.56	-2.63	+/-LB Muni 20YR
5.99	5.61	6.14	5.46	5.58	5.32	5.22	5.70	5.08	4.89	4.61	4.61	Income Return %
7.10	-11.20	12.46	-1.44	3.06	0.82	-8.13	7.91	-0.78	5.14	1.16	-0.68	Capital Return %
33	24	22	27	64	13	9	7	29	12	17	43	Total Rtn % Rank Cat
0.71	0.70	0.67	0.67	0.67	0.66	0.64	0.65	0.62	0.59	0.58	0.58	Income $
0.18	0.17	0.00	0.07	0.08	0.07	0.00	0.00	0.08	0.08	0.12	0.02	Capital Gains $
0.20	0.20	0.21	0.20	0.19	0.20	0.19	0.19	0.19	0.17	0.17	0.15	Expense Ratio %
5.77	5.62	5.82	5.46	5.47	5.22	5.20	5.48	5.00	4.80	4.57	4.50	Income Ratio %
30	16	7	18	18	16	17	34	21	20	17	18	Turnover Rate %
2,162	1,738	2,017	1,949	2,091	2,268	2,153	2,439	1,847	1,962	1,944	1,875	Net Assets $mil

Performance 12-31-04

	1st Qtr	2nd Qtr	3rd Qtr	4th Qtr	Total
2000	3.75	1.48	2.27	5.52	13.61
2001	2.05	0.39	2.77	-0.93	4.30
2002	0.86	3.89	5.24	-0.22	10.03
2003	1.04	2.97	0.16	1.50	5.77
2004	1.23	-2.37	4.06	1.06	3.93

Trailing	Total Return%	+/- LB Muni	+/- LB Muni 20YR	%Rank Cat	Growth of $10,000
3 Mo	1.06	-0.19	-0.92	57	10,106
6 Mo	5.16	-0.03	-1.59	36	10,516
1 Yr	3.93	-0.55	-2.63	43	10,393
3 Yr Avg	6.55	0.11	-1.08	11	12,097
5 Yr Avg	7.46	0.26	-1.08	7	14,330
10 Yr Avg	7.07	0.01	-0.88	7	19,801
15 Yr Avg	7.05	0.06	-0.60	5	27,784

Tax Analysis	Tax-Adj Rtn%	%Rank Cat	Tax-Cost Rat	%Rank Cat
3 Yr (estimated)	6.42	9	0.12	31
5 Yr (estimated)	7.35	6	0.10	32
10 Yr (estimated)	6.96	7	0.10	42

Potential Capital Gain Exposure: 7% of assets

Rating and Risk

Time Period	Load-Adj Return %	Morningstar Rtn vs Cat	Morningstar Risk vs Cat	Morningstar Risk-Adj Rating
1 Yr	3.93			
3 Yr	6.55	High	+Avg	★★★★
5 Yr	7.46	High	+Avg	★★★★★
10 Yr	7.07	High	+Avg	★★★★★
Incept	8.29			

Other Measures	Standard Index LB Aggr	Best Fit Index LB Muni 10YR
Alpha	-0.6	-0.1
Beta	1.14	0.99
R-Squared	98	98
Standard Deviation	5.83	
Mean	6.55	
Sharpe Ratio	0.90	

Portfolio Analysis 09-30-04

Total Fixed-Income:290	Date of Maturity	Amount $000	Value $000	% Net Assets
New Jersey St Tran 5.5%	02-01-10	64,260	64,458	2.21
Louisville & Jefferson C	05-15-31	51,960	58,397	2.00
Puerto Rico Pub Fin 5.25	08-01-30	40,000	44,484	1.52
St Cloud Minn Health Car	05-01-26	37,665	41,420	1.42
New Jersey St Tpk Auth 6	01-01-13	30,000	36,401	1.25
New York N Y City Mun Wt	06-15-16	31,265	34,659	1.19
Monroe Cnty Mich Econ De	09-01-22	25,000	32,860	1.13
Maryland St Health & Hig	08-15-38	30,000	32,247	1.11
Regl Transn Auth 7.2%	11-01-20	24,000	31,689	1.09
California Infrasct & Ec	10-01-14	25,815	29,051	1.00
Metropolitan Transn Auth	11-01-34	29,000	29,000	0.99
Chicago Ill Pub Bldg Com	01-01-20	21,500	28,074	0.96
George L Smith Ii Ga Wor	07-01-20	24,740	26,952	0.92
California St Econ Recov	07-01-14	23,680	26,920	0.92
Chicago Ill 5.5%	01-01-38	24,845	26,740	0.92

Current Investment Style

Duration: Short Int Long — Quality: High Med Low

[1]Avg Eff Duration	6.4 Yrs
Avg Eff Maturity	8.2 Yrs
Avg Credit Quality	AAA
Avg Wtd Coupon	4.92%
Avg Wtd Price	107.29% of par

[1]figure provided by fund

Credit Analysis	% bonds 09-30-04		
US Govt	0	BB	0
AAA	94	B	0
AA	6	Below B	0
A	0	NR/NA	0
BBB	0		

Top 5 States	% bonds		
CA	10.8	NY	7.5
IL	8.4	NJ	6.9
TX	7.8		

Composition			
Cash	0.0	Bonds	100.0
Stocks	0.0	Other	0.0

Special Securities	
Restricted/Illiquid Secs	0
Options/Futures/Warrants	No

Sector Weightings	% of Bonds	Rel Cat
General Obligation	22.8	0.87
Utilities	14.1	1.06
Health	10.9	1.38
Water/Waste	25.5	2.30
Housing	1.4	0.20
Education	4.9	0.43
Transportation	11.0	1.46
COP/Lease	2.4	1.12
Industrial	7.1	0.55
Misc Revenue	0.0	0.00
Demand	0.0	0.00

Morningstar's Take by Dieter Bardy 12-14-04

Vanguard Insured Long-Term Tax Exempt's cost advantage makes it hard to beat.

The fund makes life difficult for rival funds. With an expense ratio of just 0.17%, the fund boasts a huge advantage over its typical muni-national long-term rival, which charges a 0.85% average. Low fees allow the fund to offer a competitive yield despite the fund's almost exclusive portfolio of high-quality bonds. In fact, the fund holds 94% of its assets in AAA rated debt, while its average peer holds just 60% of its assets in such high-quality bonds.

The fund continues to deliver competitive returns while holding above-average credit quality. For the year-to-date period through Dec. 13, 2004, the fund has gained 3.8%, outperforming its average category peers by a slight amount. Longer trailing periods are even more appealing, where the fund consistently places near the top decile of its category.

But that's not to say that all's rosy and perfect with this fund. Indeed, it's important to note that the fund has been more volatile (as measured by standard deviation) over its life than typical rivals. An unfortunate side effect of holding higher quality securities is greater than average sensitivity to interest rates. For example, when interest rates spiked in April 2004, the fund lost 2.7%.

Thus, it's particularly important for manager Reid Smith to keep a close eye on interest rates. Currently, he thinks that rising rates are already priced into the market, and doesn't expect any big rate spikes in the near term. Accordingly he shifted the fund away from a defensive duration (a measure interest-rate sensitivity) to a more neutral 7.3-year measure against its index, the Lehman Brothers 10-Year Municipal Bond Index.

All told, this fund represents a good bargain in a crowded category. Investors who want no credit risk, but are willing to put up with some added interest-rate risk, will have a hard time beating this option.

Address:	PO Box 2600 Valley Forge PA 19482 800-662-7447
Web Address:	www.vanguard.com
Inception:	10-01-84
Advisor:	Vanguard Advisers, Inc.
Subadvisor:	None
NTF Plans:	N/A

Minimum Purchase:	$3000	Add: $100	IRA: $1000
Min Auto Inv Plan:	$3000	Add: $50	
Sales Fees:	No-load		
Management Fee:	0.16%		
Actual Fees:	Mgt:0.16%	Dist:	
Expense Projections:	3Yr:$58	5Yr:$101	10Yr:$230
Income Distrib:	Monthly		

Vanguard Intm Bd Idx

Ticker	Load	NAV	Yield	SEC Yield	Total Assets	Mstar Category
VBIIX	None	$10.68	4.7%	4.36%	$4,628 mil	Intermediate-Term Bond

Governance and Management

Fiduciary Grade: B

Portfolio Manager(s)

Vanguard is the undisputed champ of indexing, and Ken Volpert has been the manager of this fund since its 1994 inception. Volpert's team, which includes six credit analysts, runs all of Vanguard's fixed-income index offerings, including the Short-Term Bond Index and Long-Term Bond Index as well as Total Bond Market Index.

Strategy

This fund's goal is to approximate the performance of the Lehman Brothers 5-10 Year Government/Credit Index, which is composed of U.S. Treasuries, agency debentures, and corporate bonds. Although the duration and other key characteristics of the index are carefully replicated, the fund does not hold every security in the index, and management selects specific corporate bonds based on fundamental credit research.

Historical Profile

Return High
Risk High
Rating ★★★★★ Highest

Investment Style
Fixed Income
Income Rtn %Rank Cat

1995	1996	1997	1998	1999	2000	2001	2002	2003	12-04
31	17	13	20	15	10	10	13	9	

▼ Manager Change
▽ Partial Manager Change

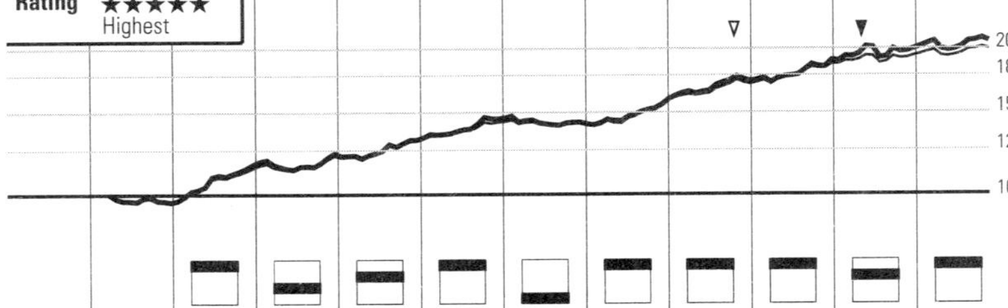

Growth of $10,000
▬ Investment Values of Fund
— Investment Values of LB Aggr

Performance Quartile (within Category)

1993	1994	1995	1996	1997	1998	1999	2000	2001	2002	2003	12-04	History
—	9.18	10.37	9.96	10.20	10.48	9.51	10.02	10.28	10.75	10.69	10.68	NAV
—	-2.88*	21.03	2.55	9.41	10.09	-3.00	12.78	9.28	10.85	5.65	5.22	Total Return %
—	—	2.56	-1.08	-0.24	1.40	-2.18	1.15	0.84	0.60	1.55	0.88	+/-LB Aggr
—	—	-0.40	-0.14	-0.02	-0.05	-0.12	0.34	0.46	-2.18	-0.32	-0.08	+/-LB 5-10YR
—	0.00	7.40	6.44	6.85	6.53	6.18	7.10	6.69	5.97	5.06	4.85	Income Return %
—	—	13.63	-3.89	2.56	3.56	-9.18	5.68	2.59	4.88	0.59	0.37	Capital Return %
—	—	11	70	35	2	85	4	10	5	26	9	Total Rtn % Rank Cat
—	0.53	0.66	0.65	0.66	0.65	0.63	0.65	0.65	0.60	0.53	0.51	Income $
—	0.00	0.03	0.00	0.00	0.07	0.03	0.00	0.00	0.01	0.12	0.05	Capital Gains $
—	0.18	0.20	0.20	0.20	0.20	0.20	0.21	0.21	0.21	0.20	—	Expense Ratio %
—	6.88	6.55	6.54	6.64	6.23	6.33	6.83	6.33	5.75	4.91	—	Income Ratio %
—	—	71	80	56	77	120	81	135	141	98	—	Turnover Rate %
—	71	346	457	687	1,102	1,449	1,642	2,096	2,415	2,749	3,501	Net Assets $mil

Performance 12-31-04

	1st Qtr	2nd Qtr	3rd Qtr	4th Qtr	Total
2000	2.35	1.21	3.54	5.15	12.78
2001	3.84	0.35	5.21	-0.33	9.28
2002	-0.67	3.36	5.77	2.08	10.85
2003	1.82	4.57	-0.74	-0.03	5.65
2004	3.77	-3.88	4.41	1.04	5.22

Trailing	Total Return%	+/- LB Aggr	+/- LB 5-10YR	%Rank Cat	Growth of $10,000
3 Mo	1.04	0.09	0.06	39	10,104
6 Mo	5.50	1.32	-0.07	7	10,550
1 Yr	5.22	0.88	-0.08	9	10,522
3 Yr Avg	7.21	1.02	-0.84	7	12,323
5 Yr Avg	8.72	1.01	-0.35	3	15,190
10 Yr Avg	8.22	0.50	-0.24	4	22,033
15 Yr Avg	—	—	—	—	—

Tax Analysis	Tax-Adj Rtn%	%Rank Cat	Tax-Cost Rat	%Rank Cat
3 Yr (estimated)	5.14	6	1.93	70
5 Yr (estimated)	6.35	2	2.18	69
10 Yr (estimated)	5.64	4	2.38	72

Potential Capital Gain Exposure: 3% of assets

Rating and Risk

Time Period	Load-Adj Return %	Morningstar Rtn vs Cat	Morningstar Risk vs Cat	Morningstar Risk-Adj Rating
1 Yr	5.22			
3 Yr	7.21	High	High	★★★★★
5 Yr	8.72	High	High	★★★★★
10 Yr	8.22	High	High	★★★★★
Incept	7.27			

Other Measures	Standard Index LB Aggr	Best Fit Index LB 5-10YR
Alpha	-1.1	-0.7
Beta	1.46	0.99
R-Squared	96	99
Standard Deviation	6.82	
Mean	7.21	
Sharpe Ratio	0.87	

Morningstar's Take by Dieter Bardy 10-28-04

Vanguard Intermediate-Term Bond Index's hands-off approach has worked like a charm this year.

In late March and April 2004, the whole bond market got hit by rising interest rates. This fund suffered more than most, losing 6% from mid-March through the end of June, because the index it tracks, the Lehman Brothers 5-10 year Government Credit Index, has no exposure to mortgage bonds, which fell less than Treasuries and corporates did. But interest rates soon fell, boosting returns: For the year-to-date through Oct. 25, 2004, the fund has gained 5.4%, which tops the benchmark's showing by 1.7% and also tops 95% of the intermediate-term bond fund group.

One main driver of those heady returns comes from the fund's interest-rate sensitivity. The fund's duration, a measure of such sensitivity, is tied to the index, meaning it is often more responsive to changes in interest rates than its typical rival is. That has been a help during much of the fund's lifetime, but if interest rates rise as many expect them to, we would expect this fund's 6-year measure to lead to bigger losses than its average peer's tamer 4.4-year measure would.

Another big contributor to this fund's consistent results is its low costs. At 0.20%, it is 80% cheaper than its typical rival. This advantage goes a long way in bond world where winners and losers are often only a few basis points apart.

Finally, one other way that the fund makes up basis points over its index is by carefully timing its new purchases. Since bond indexes are not reproducible because of their sheer scale and ever-changing nature, manager Ken Volpert can add some extra value by adeptly buying new issues as they enter the index.

We see no reason that this fund will not continue to deliver. Investors who are looking for an intermediate bond fund without mortgage debt exposure will like this fund's consistent record and inexpensive appeal.

Address:	PO Box 2600 Valley Forge PA 19482 800-662-7447		
Web Address:	www.vanguard.com		
Inception:	03-01-94*		
Advisor:	Vanguard Advisers, Inc.		
Subadvisor:	None		
NTF Plans:	N/A		

Minimum Purchase:	$3000	Add: $100	IRA: $1000
Min Auto Inv Plan:	$3000	Add: $50	
Sales Fees:	No-load		
Management Fee:	0.19%		
Actual Fees:	Mgt:0.19%	Dist: —	
Expense Projections:	3Yr:$68	5Yr:$118	10Yr:$268
Income Distrib:	Monthly		

Portfolio Analysis 09-30-04

Total Fixed-Income:679	Date of Maturity	Amount $000	Value $000	% Net Assets
US Treasury Note 4.25%	08-15-13	214,825	218,047	5.12
US Treasury Note 4.375%	08-15-12	209,275	215,652	5.07
US Treasury Bond 11.25%	02-15-15	115,125	183,193	4.30
US Treasury Note 4.875%	02-15-12	121,340	129,284	3.04
US Treasury Note 6.5%	02-15-10	81,625	93,639	2.20
US Treasury Bond 9.875%	11-15-15	41,425	61,795	1.45
US Treasury Bond 10.625%	08-15-15	36,250	56,289	1.32
FNMA 7.25%	01-15-10	44,800	51,965	1.22
US Treasury Note 5.75%	08-15-10	44,750	49,861	1.17
US Treasury Bond 12.75%	11-15-10	43,350	48,349	1.14
US Treasury Bond 9.25%	02-15-16	31,100	44,784	1.05
FNMA 6%	05-15-11	37,675	41,570	0.98
FHLMC 7%	03-15-10	35,000	40,221	0.94
FNMA 6.125%	03-15-12	32,910	36,651	0.86
FHLMC 6.875%	09-15-10	31,500	36,230	0.85
FNMA 4.625%	10-15-13	36,000	36,168	0.85
FHLMC 5.75%	01-15-12	32,575	35,491	0.83
US Treasury Bond 13.25%	05-15-14	24,025	34,146	0.80
Ford Motor Cr 7.25%	10-25-11	29,750	32,179	0.76
FHLMC 6%	06-15-11	26,500	29,253	0.69

Current Investment Style

Duration: Short Int Long; Quality: High Med Low (style box: Long duration, High quality)

[1] figure provided by fund

Avg Eff Duration[1]	6.0 Yrs
Avg Eff Maturity	7.6 Yrs
Avg Credit Quality	AA
Avg Wtd Coupon	6.55%
Avg Wtd Price	109.76% of par

Coupon Range	% of Bonds	Rel Cat
0% PIK	0.0	0.0
0% to 6%	47.9	0.7
6% to 8%	37.6	1.3
8% to 10%	5.6	1.0
More than 10%	8.8	7.7

1.00=Category Average

Credit Analysis	% bonds 09-30-04		
US Govt	45	BB	0
AAA	3	B	0
AA	4	Below B	0
A	22	NR/NA	0
BBB	26		

Sector Breakdown	% of assets
US Treasuries	28
TIPS	0
US Agency	16
Mortgage Pass-Throughs	0
Mortgage CMO	0
Mortgage ARM	0
US Corporate	51
Asset-Backed	1
Convertible	0
Municipal	0
Corporate Inflation-Protected	0
Foreign Corporate	2
Foreign Govt	0

Composition			
Cash	1.8	Bonds	98.1
Stocks	0.0	Other	0.1

Special Securities	
Restricted/Illiquid Secs	2
Exotic Mortgage-Backed	0
Emerging-Markets Secs	0
Options/Futures/Warrants	No

Vanguard IntTm Inv-Gr Fd

Ticker	Load	NAV	Yield	SEC Yield	Total Assets	Mstar Category
VFICX	None	$10.07	4.7%	4.32%	$4,645 mil	Intermediate-Term Bond

Governance and Management

Fiduciary Grade: B

Portfolio Manager(s)

Manager Bob Auwaerter is responsible for the fund's day-to-day management and has been with the fund since its 1993 inception. Until recently, Ian MacKinnon (former head of Vanguard's fixed-income group) set the fund's duration (a measure of interest-rate sensitivity) range. Auwaerter, his successor, has assumed that role. The team also includes an assistant portfolio manager, six credit analysts, and traders.

Strategy

Traditionally, this fund has invested mainly in midquality (A and BBB rated) investment-grade corporate bonds. A July 2004 modification will allow its managers to invest a bit more broadly though. The fund's duration (a measure of interest-rate sensitivity) is limited to a range of 4.75 to 6.25 years, which typically makes it a bit more sensitive to rate shifts than most of its intermediate-term bond peers. Comanager Bob Auwaerter also invests modestly in highly rated asset-backed securities when the outlook for corporates dims.

Performance 12-31-04

	1st Qtr	2nd Qtr	3rd Qtr	4th Qtr	Total
2000	1.99	0.62	3.71	4.00	10.70
2001	3.93	0.41	5.03	-0.16	9.42
2002	0.01	2.90	5.50	1.57	10.28
2003	1.97	4.01	-0.20	0.42	6.29
2004	3.12	-3.21	3.85	1.07	4.34

Trailing	Total Return%	+/- LB Aggr	+/- LB 5-10YR	%Rank Cat	Growth of $10,000
3 Mo	1.07	0.12	0.09	37	10,107
6 Mo	4.96	0.78	-0.61	15	10,496
1 Yr	4.75	0.41	-0.55	19	10,475
3 Yr Avg	7.08	0.89	-0.97	8	12,278
5 Yr Avg	8.26	0.55	-0.81	6	14,871
10 Yr Avg	7.98	0.26	-0.48	7	21,549
15 Yr Avg	—	—	—	—	—

Tax Analysis	Tax-Adj Rtn%	%Rank Cat	Tax-Cost Rat	%Rank Cat
3 Yr (estimated)	4.98	7	1.96	72
5 Yr (estimated)	5.84	7	2.24	74
10 Yr (estimated)	5.35	8	2.44	77

Potential Capital Gain Exposure: 3% of assets

Historical Profile

Return High
Risk High
Rating ★★★★★ Highest

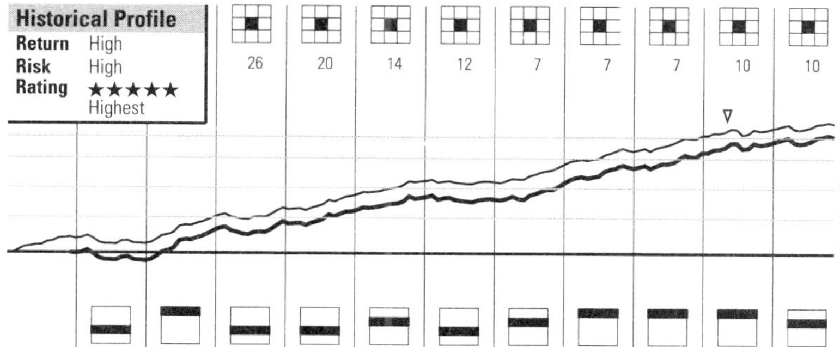

Investment Style
Fixed Income
Income Rtn %Rank Cat

▼ Manager Change
▽ Partial Manager Change

Growth of $10,000
▬ Investment Values of Fund
— Investment Values of LB Aggr

Performance Quartile (within Category)

1993	1994	1995	1996	1997	1998	1999	2000	2001	2002	2003	12-04	History
9.94	8.95	10.15	9.75	9.94	10.03	9.21	9.49	9.73	10.11	10.13	10.07	NAV
0.21*	-4.20	21.39	2.78	8.94	8.30	-1.53	10.70	9.42	10.28	6.29	4.75	Total Return %
—	-1.28	2.92	-0.85	-0.71	-0.39	-0.71	-0.93	0.98	0.03	2.19	0.41	+/-LB Aggr
—	0.31	-0.04	0.09	-0.49	-1.84	1.35	-1.74	0.60	-2.75	0.32	-0.55	+/-LB 5-10YR
0.00	5.97	7.60	6.49	6.75	6.53	6.40	7.42	6.88	6.19	5.31	4.79	Income Return %
—	-10.17	13.79	-3.71	2.19	1.77	-7.93	3.28	2.54	4.09	0.98	-0.04	Capital Return %
—	56	9	62	51	29	57	37	8	10	21	19	Total Rtn % Rank Cat
0.08	0.58	0.66	0.64	0.64	0.63	0.62	0.66	0.63	0.59	0.52	0.47	Income $
0.00	0.00	0.00	0.02	0.01	0.08	0.05	0.00	0.00	0.00	0.08	0.06	Capital Gains $
—	0.25	0.28	0.28	0.25	0.26	0.27	0.25	0.22	0.21	0.20	0.20	Expense Ratio %
—	5.11	6.46	6.70	6.61	6.51	6.25	6.60	7.17	6.99	5.87	4.90	Income Ratio %
—	74	97	78	85	69	71	67	85	118	84	55	Turnover Rate %
65	151	361	617	868	1,181	1,457	1,920	2,015	2,498	2,747	3,145	Net Assets $mil

Rating and Risk

Time Period	Load-Adj Return %	Morningstar Rtn vs Cat	Morningstar Risk vs Cat	Morningstar Risk-Adj Rating
1 Yr	4.75			
3 Yr	7.08	High	High	★★★★★
5 Yr	8.26	High	High	★★★★★
10 Yr	7.98	High	High	★★★★★
Incept	6.73			

Other Measures	Standard Index LB Aggr	Best Fit Index LB 5-10YR
Alpha	0.2	0.5
Beta	1.14	0.77
R-Squared	95	98
Standard Deviation	5.34	
Mean	7.08	
Sharpe Ratio	1.08	

Morningstar's Take by Dieter Bardy 10-08-04

Vanguard Intermediate Term Investment Grade's added flexibility hasn't altered its approach.

This fund underwent name and slight strategy changes in mid July 2004. The alteration gives manager Bob Auwaerter more flexibility to invest beyond corporate bonds, into sectors such as mortgages, U.S. agency bonds, and U.S. Treasury debt. We haven't seen evidence yet of Auwaerter using the extra flexibility, but we'll continue to watch for significant portfolio changes. Auwaerter argues that he will not make use of the added leeway except when he's struggling to find suitable corporate names.

Auwaerter has not, however, been sitting on his hands lately. He continues to position the fund more defensively because of his view that there will be further rates increases. Thus, he has reined in duration (a measure of interest-rate sensitivity). The fund's 4.7-year sensitivity is still longer than peer's 4.4-year average, but its duration will often be longer than its peers. Investors should remember that longer duration could lead to added volatility.

Over time, such moves have helped the fund achieve strong marks. Indeed, since Auwaerter began managing in 1993, the fund has earned an average 6.8% per year compared with its typical rival's 5.9%.

Ultra-low expenses remain this fund's biggest competitive advantage. Its expense ratio is only 0.20%, a levy that few rivals can match. Its typical rival charges almost five times as much at 0.98%. Additionally, it typically doesn't venture into lower-rated paper because its sizable cost advantage already gives it an above-average yield. Thus, risk-averse investors will find its higher credit quality appealing.

We continue to think this is a compelling intermediate-term core bond fund. Its low costs, solid long-term performance, and conservative strategy will benefit investors going forward. We'll continue to monitor its non-corporate sectors and update readers on any modifications to its look.

Portfolio Analysis 09-30-04

Total Fixed-Income:490	Date of Maturity	Amount $000	Value $000	% Net Assets
FHLMC CMO 4.5%	05-15-26	88,658	89,466	2.01
FNMA 5.375%	11-15-11	50,000	53,345	1.20
US Treasury Note 4.25%	08-15-14	49,710	50,223	1.13
US Treasury Note 4.75%	05-15-14	41,295	43,360	0.97
US Treasury Note 5%	08-15-11	37,400	40,193	0.90
Unilever Cap 7.125%	11-01-10	34,000	39,348	0.88
Cingular Wireless 6.5%	12-15-11	35,000	38,757	0.87
United Tech 6.35%	03-01-11	30,600	34,270	0.77
Wal Mart Stores 4.125%	02-15-11	34,000	34,037	0.76
FHLMC CMO 4.5%	06-15-28	31,487	31,384	0.70
FHLMC CMO 5%	04-15-16	27,808	28,297	0.63
Sara Lee 6.25%	09-15-11	25,000	27,747	0.62
Metlife 6.125%	12-01-11	25,000	27,267	0.61
General Elec Cap 5.875%	02-15-12	25,000	27,195	0.61
Pf Export Rec Tr 2001 6.	12-01-11	25,000	27,090	0.61
Usaa Cap 144A 4.64%	12-15-09	26,000	26,720	0.60
Washington Post 5.5%	02-15-09	24,350	25,983	0.58
Citigroup FRN	06-09-09	25,700	25,716	0.58
Bk One Oneseries 2003-3a	12-15-10	25,000	25,073	0.56
Target 5.375%	06-15-09	23,100	24,522	0.55

Current Investment Style

Duration: Short Int Long; Quality: High Med Low

[1] figure provided by fund

Avg Eff Duration[1]	5.0 Yrs
Avg Eff Maturity	6.5 Yrs
Avg Credit Quality	A
Avg Wtd Coupon	5.52%
Avg Wtd Price	105.83% of par

Coupon Range	% of Bonds	Rel Cat
0% PIK	2.0	0.5
0% to 6%	60.5	0.9
6% to 8%	35.8	1.2
8% to 10%	3.5	0.6
More than 10%	0.2	0.2

1.00=Category Average

Credit Analysis		% bonds 09-30-04	
US Govt	15	BB	2
AAA	12	B	1
AA	10	Below B	0
A	34	NR/NA	0
BBB	26		

Sector Breakdown	% of assets
US Treasuries	6
TIPS	0
US Agency	2
Mortgage Pass-Throughs	1
Mortgage CMO	4
Mortgage ARM	0
US Corporate	74
Asset-Backed	10
Convertible	0
Municipal	0
Corporate Inflation-Protected	0
Foreign Corporate	1
Foreign Govt	0

Composition			
Cash	1.8	Bonds	97.9
Stocks	0.0	Other	0.3

Special Securities	
Restricted/Illiquid Secs	12
Exotic Mortgage-Backed	0
Emerging-Markets Secs	0
Options/Futures/Warrants	No

Address:	PO Box 2600 Valley Forge PA 19482 800-662-7447
Web Address:	www.vanguard.com
Inception:	11-01-93*
Advisor:	Vanguard Advisers, Inc.
Subadvisor:	None
NTF Plans:	N/A

Minimum Purchase:	$3000	Add: $100	IRA: $1000
Min Auto Inv Plan:	$3000	Add: $50	
Sales Fees:	No-load		
Management Fee:	0.18%		
Actual Fees:	Mgt:0.18%	Dist: —	
Expense Projections:	3Yr:$64	5Yr:$113	10Yr:$255
Income Distrib:	Monthly		

Vanguard IntTm T/E

Analyst Pick

Ticker	Load	NAV	Yield	SEC Yield	Total Assets	Mstar Category
VWITX	None	$13.58	4.1%	3.14%	$12,085 mil	Muni National Interm

Governance and Management

Fiduciary Grade: B

Portfolio Manager(s)

Christopher Ryon has had day-to-day responsibilities for this fund since 1991. Ian MacKinnon, who as Vanguard's fixed-income director had set the fund's duration range, retired in June 2003. Bob Auwaerter replaced him.

Strategy

This fund invests in municipal securities from many states. It invests at least 75% of assets in bonds rated AAA, AA, or A. No more than 20% of assets can be invested in bonds rated BBB. Up to 5% can be invested in below-investment-grade bonds. Management makes modest duration bets within a specified range, depending on its interest-rate outlook. However, the fund's rate sensitivity tends to be below average.

Historical Profile

Return Above Avg
Risk Average
Rating ★★★★ Above Avg

Investment Style: Fixed Income, Income Rtn %Rank Cat: 19, 14, 11, 7, 17, 14, 15, 17, 14

▼ Manager Change
▽ Partial Manager Change

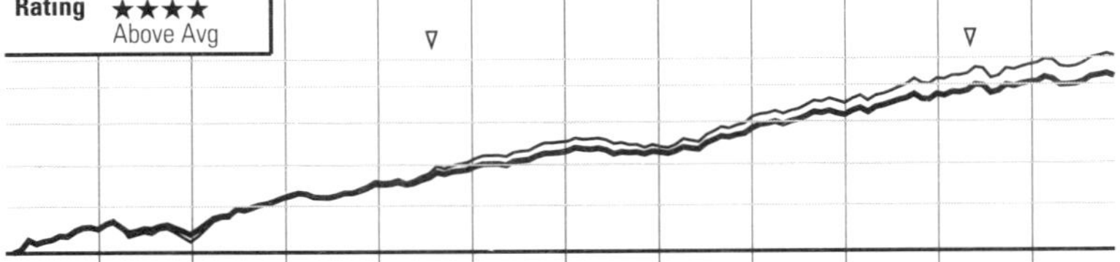

Growth of $10,000
- Investment Values of Fund
- Investment Values of LB Muni

Performance Quartile (within Category)

1993	1994	1995	1996	1997	1998	1999	2000	2001	2002	2003	12-04	History
13.52	12.39	13.36	13.23	13.42	13.48	12.77	13.27	13.27	13.66	13.70	13.58	NAV
11.55	-2.12	13.64	4.20	7.06	5.76	-0.50	9.24	5.05	7.91	4.46	3.23	Total Return %
-0.73	3.05	-3.82	-0.23	-2.13	-0.72	1.56	-2.44	-0.08	-1.69	-0.85	-1.25	+/-LB Muni
-1.22	2.65	-3.53	-0.34	-2.18	-1.00	0.74	-1.52	0.43	-2.26	-1.24	-0.92	+/-LB Muni 10YR
5.55	5.21	5.60	5.12	5.18	5.02	4.89	5.18	4.87	4.62	4.15	4.10	Income Return %
6.00	-7.33	8.04	-0.92	1.88	0.74	-5.39	4.06	0.18	3.29	0.31	-0.87	Capital Return %
31	23	52	27	73	34	8	49	17	70	32	30	Total Rtn % Rank Cat
0.70	0.69	0.68	0.67	0.67	0.66	0.64	0.65	0.63	0.60	0.56	0.55	Income $
0.08	0.16	0.01	0.00	0.05	0.04	0.00	0.00	0.03	0.04	0.00	0.00	Capital Gains $
0.20	0.20	0.21	0.20	0.19	0.21	0.18	0.18	0.19	0.17	0.17	0.14	Expense Ratio %
5.41	5.15	5.35	5.09	5.07	4.93	4.83	5.03	4.77	4.48	4.13	4.05	Income Ratio %
15	18	12	14	15	14	17	17	13	13	19	10	Turnover Rate %
5,238	4,585	5,770	6,123	6,891	7,896	7,920	8,925	6,653	7,338	6,970	6,897	Net Assets $mil

Performance 12-31-04

	1st Qtr	2nd Qtr	3rd Qtr	4th Qtr	Total
2000	1.83	1.59	2.11	3.42	9.24
2001	2.49	0.75	2.46	-0.71	5.05
2002	0.91	3.57	3.25	-0.00	7.91
2003	0.60	2.57	0.29	0.94	4.46
2004	1.22	-1.92	3.30	0.66	3.23

Trailing	Total Return%	+/- LB Muni	+/- LB Muni 10YR	%Rank Cat	Growth of $10,000
3 Mo	0.66	-0.59	-0.17	55	10,066
6 Mo	3.98	-1.21	-1.02	39	10,398
1 Yr	3.23	-1.25	-0.92	30	10,323
3 Yr Avg	5.18	-1.26	-1.46	48	11,636
5 Yr Avg	5.95	-1.25	-1.09	41	13,351
10 Yr Avg	5.94	-1.12	-1.14	31	17,807
15 Yr Avg	6.43	-0.56	-0.65	21	25,466

Tax Analysis	Tax-Adj Rtn%	%Rank Cat	Tax-Cost Rat	%Rank Cat
3 Yr (estimated)	5.16	29	0.02	7
5 Yr (estimated)	5.93	24	0.02	8
10 Yr (estimated)	5.91	18	0.03	15

Potential Capital Gain Exposure: 4% of assets

Rating and Risk

Time Period	Load-Adj Return %	Morningstar Rtn vs Cat	Morningstar Risk vs Cat	Morningstar Risk-Adj Rating
1 Yr	3.23			
3 Yr	5.18	+Avg	Avg	★★★★
5 Yr	5.95	+Avg	Avg	★★★★
10 Yr	5.94	+Avg	Avg	★★★★
Incept	6.54			

Other Measures	Standard Index LB Aggr	Best Fit Index LB Muni 10YR
Alpha	-0.7	-0.3
Beta	0.89	0.77
R-Squared	97	97

Standard Deviation	4.50
Mean	5.18
Sharpe Ratio	0.86

Portfolio Analysis 09-30-04

Total Fixed-Income:1066	Date of Maturity	Amount $000	Value $000	% Net Assets
California St Econ Recov	07-01-15	93,700	103,430	0.88
California St Dept Wtr R	05-01-16	77,880	88,469	0.75
Massachusetts St 5.5%	11-01-16	75,000	87,182	0.74
California Statewide Cmn	05-15-25	73,000	77,118	0.66
North Carolina Mun Pwr A	01-01-18	69,720	76,046	0.65
California St Dept Wtr R	05-01-15	61,875	70,620	0.60
Chicago Ill Wtr	11-01-31	70,000	70,000	0.59
Memphis Tenn Elec Sys 5%	12-01-09	60,140	66,178	0.56
Triborough Brdg & Tunl A	01-01-10	55,325	64,532	0.55
Brazos Riv Tex Hbr Nav D	05-15-33	58,000	61,777	0.52
Los Angeles Cnty Calif T	07-01-10	51,070	60,477	0.51
California Statewide Cmn	11-01-36	55,000	58,888	0.50
Massachusetts St 5.5%	11-01-16	50,000	58,122	0.49
New Jersey St Tpk Auth 6	01-01-09	50,000	57,822	0.49
Texas St Tpk Auth 5%	06-01-08	53,195	57,814	0.49

Current Investment Style

Duration: Short Int Long; Quality: High Med Low

[1]Avg Eff Duration	4.9 Yrs
Avg Eff Maturity	6.0 Yrs
Avg Credit Quality	AAA
Avg Wtd Coupon	5.15%
Avg Wtd Price	109.20% of par

[1]figure provided by fund

Credit Analysis	% bonds 09-30-04		
US Govt	0	BB	0
AAA	69	B	0
AA	21	Below B	0
A	6	NR/NA	0
BBB	3		

Top 5 States	% bonds		
NY	9.9	MA	7.4
CA	9.9	NJ	6.8
TX	9.2		

Composition			
Cash	2.5	Bonds	97.5
Stocks	0.0	Other	0.0

Special Securities	
Restricted/Illiquid Secs	0
Options/Futures/Warrants	No

Sector Weightings	% of Bonds	Rel Cat
General Obligation	44.3	1.26
Utilities	20.3	1.84
Health	2.8	0.38
Water/Waste	8.0	0.80
Housing	1.3	0.22
Education	3.4	0.24
Transportation	11.6	2.09
COP/Lease	1.0	0.66
Industrial	7.1	0.79
Misc Revenue	0.0	0.00
Demand	0.2	0.50

Morningstar's Take by Dieter Bardy 12-28-04

Vanguard Intermediate-Term Tax-Exempt is a great anchor for tax-averse investors' portfolios.

A couple of different things set this fund apart from other muni national intermediate bond funds. For one, the fund's 0.17% expense ratio is leagues apart from typical peers 0.75% measure. Besides saving investors money, the low fees also help drive the fund's careful approach to investing. Manager Chris Ryon fills up the portfolio with mostly higher-quality bonds, instead of wading through lower-rated fare in search of an extra few basis points of yield. Indeed, 97% of the fund's portfolio, as of Sept. 30, 2004, is in bonds rated A and better.

Low costs teamed with high-quality bonds are a potent mixture. The fund's 3% result through Dec. 20, 2004, is above average for the year-to-date period. Ryon attributes the fund's successes to specific yield curve positioning--in particular its ladder strategy (a way to structure the portfolio with equal bond weights in each maturity within a certain range), which helps guard against rising interest rates. Also, a large stake in California, which underwent a rating upgrade earlier in 2004, is another reason why the fund is beating many of its peers recently.

It's appealing that the fund has performed this well considering that it has had a defensive interest-rate stance for much of 2004. A bearish posture led to a slimmer loss than its rivals during rate spikes in early 2004, but then the market surprised, and rates trended downward for most of the rest of the year. Currently, the fund is keeping its defensive posture in place, given Ryon's view of more interest rates increases on the horizon.

The fund's solid long-term returns driven by its low costs are key to its lasting appeal. While it may experience absolute losses, like in April 2004 (albeit less than typical peer's loss) or throughout 1999, all but the most cautious investor should feel safe here.

Address:	PO Box 2600 Valley Forge PA 19482 800-662-7447
Web Address:	www.vanguard.com
Inception:	09-01-77
Advisor:	Vanguard Advisers, Inc.
Subadvisor:	None
NTF Plans:	N/A

Minimum Purchase:	$3000	Add: $100	IRA: $1000
Min Auto Inv Plan:	$3000	Add: $50	
Sales Fees:	No-load		
Management Fee:	0.15%		
Actual Fees:	Mgt:0.15%	Dist:	
Expense Projections:	3Yr:$61	5Yr:$107	10Yr:$243
Income Distrib:	Monthly		

Vanguard Intl Explorer

Ticker	Load	NAV	Yield	Total Assets	Mstar Category
VINEX	Closed	$16.34	1.4%	$1,865 mil	Foreign Small/Mid Growth

Governance and Management

Fiduciary Grade: B

Portfolio Manager(s)

Four regional portfolio managers (two on Europe, including the U.K., one on Japan, and one on Pacific/Asia ex-Japan) choose stocks, while team leader Matthew Dobbs determines the fund's regional allocation and portfolio structure. He and his comanagers meet at least weekly to talk about specific stocks and the regions. Besides this team of five, there are 13 analysts, making this bench one of the category's deepest.

Strategy

Like most at subadvisor Schroder, this fund's team takes a growth-at-a-reasonable-price approach, although it leans a bit more toward growth than value. At least two thirds of the portfolio's buys must have capitalizations of $1.5 billion or less, but the team isn't afraid to let its winners ride into the $4 billion to $5 billion range. That said, it does a better job than many of its peers at sticking with small companies. The fund invests almost exclusively in developed markets, but it has recently added more in emerging markets. Vanguard uses fair-value pricing.

Historical Profile

Return Above Avg
Risk Average
Rating ★★★★★ Highest

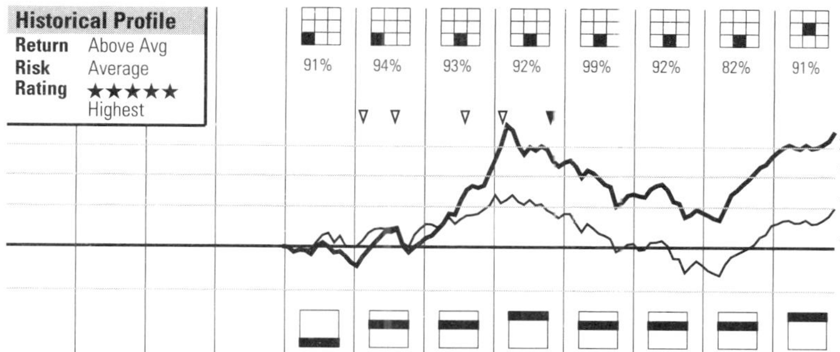

Investment Style
Equity
Stock %

▼ Manager Change
▽ Partial Manager Change

Growth of $10,000
— Investment Values of Fund
— Investment Values of MSCI EAFE

Performance Quartile (within Category)

1993	1994	1995	1996	1997	1998	1999	2000	2001	2002	2003	12-04	History
—	—	—	9.91	8.00	9.32	15.72	12.55	9.58	8.19	12.82	16.34	NAV
—	—	—	-0.82*	-14.13	25.98	90.29	-2.68	-22.52	-13.88	57.37	31.77	Total Return %
—	—	—	—	-15.91	6.05	63.26	11.51	-1.10	2.06	18.78	11.52	+/-MSCI EAFE
—	—	—	—	-16.40	7.29	62.31	10.68	-1.13	1.92	17.95	11.39	+/-MSCI Wd xUS
—	—	—	0.00	0.14	0.46	0.09	0.59	1.12	0.63	0.82	1.87	Income Return %
—	—	—	—	-14.27	25.52	90.20	-3.27	-23.64	-14.51	56.55	29.90	Capital Return %
—	—	—	—	100	33	42	13	41	38	28	5	Total Rtn % Rank Cat
—	—	—	0.01	0.01	0.04	0.01	0.09	0.14	0.06	0.07	0.24	Income $
—	—	—	0.00	0.50	0.70	1.96	2.61	0.00	0.00	0.00	0.29	Capital Gains $
—	—	—	—	1.50	1.50	1.50	1.50	1.50	1.04	0.73	0.57	Expense Ratio %
—	—	—	—	0.21	0.33	0.53	-0.26	0.15	1.13	1.52	1.96	Income Ratio %
—	—	—	—	32	82	81	86	48	40	60	21	Turnover Rate %
—	—	—	—	6	4	12	17	26	111	644	1,865	Net Assets $mil

Performance 12-31-04

	1st Qtr	2nd Qtr	3rd Qtr	4th Qtr	Total
2000	25.89	-12.43	-1.96	-9.95	-2.68
2001	-11.24	-0.99	-20.31	10.63	-22.52
2002	4.07	-0.50	-19.96	3.91	-13.88
2003	-5.98	27.66	14.95	14.06	57.37
2004	10.37	-0.00	0.42	18.88	31.77

Trailing	Total Return%	+/- MSCI EAFE	+/- MSCI Wd xUS	%Rank Cat	Growth of $10,000
3 Mo	18.88	3.56	3.73	17	11,888
6 Mo	19.39	4.39	4.02	9	11,939
1 Yr	31.77	11.52	11.39	5	13,177
3 Yr Avg	21.33	9.44	9.11	16	17,861
5 Yr Avg	6.13	7.26	6.89	8	13,465
10 Yr Avg	—	—	—	—	—
15 Yr Avg	—	—	—	—	—

Tax Analysis	Tax-Adj Rtn%	%Rank Cat	Tax-Cost Rat	%Rank Cat
3 Yr (estimated)	20.76	17	0.47	77
5 Yr (estimated)	4.61	15	1.43	91
10 Yr (estimated)	—	—	—	—

Potential Capital Gain Exposure: 21% of assets

Rating and Risk

Time Period	Load-Adj Return %	Morningstar Rtn vs Cat	Morningstar Risk vs Cat	Morningstar Risk-Adj Rating
1 Yr	31.77			
3 Yr	21.33	+Avg	Avg	★★★★
5 Yr	6.13	+Avg	Avg	★★★★★
10 Yr	—	—	—	—
Incept	13.20			

Other Measures	Standard Index S&P 500	Best Fit Index MSCI Wd xUS
Alpha	8.9	8.4
Beta	0.98	0.99
R-Squared	88	88
Standard Deviation	19.65	
Mean	21.33	
Sharpe Ratio	1.03	

Portfolio Analysis 09-30-04

Share change since 06-04 Total Stocks:234	Sector	Country	% Assets
☼ YIT	Business	Finland	1.25
⊕ Swedish Match	Goods	Sweden	0.97
⊕ Oriflame Cosmetics	—	Sweden	0.91
Hyundai Mobis	Ind Mtrls	Korea	0.91
⊕ Katokichi	Goods	Japan	0.87
⊕ Public Pwr	Utilities	Greece	0.87
⊕ Red Electrica de Espana	Utilities	Spain	0.86
⊕ Britannic Grp	Financial	U.K.	0.84
Eiffage	Business	France	0.84
⊕ Tokyo Ohka Kogyo	Ind Mtrls	Japan	0.83
⊕ Geberit	Consumer	Switzerland	0.82
⊕ SES GLOBAL	Telecom	Luxembourg	0.82
Nipro	Health	Japan	0.82
☼ Circle K Sunkus	—	Japan	0.79
⊕ Kuoni Grp	Business	Switzerland	0.79
DCC	—	Ireland	0.78
Andritz	Ind Mtrls	Austria	0.78
⊕ Groupe Bourbon	Consumer	France	0.76
Lindt & Sprungli	Goods	Switzerland	0.76
☼ Jelmoli Holding Ltd	Consumer	Switzerland	0.75

Current Investment Style

Value Blnd Growth — Large Mid Small

Market Cap	%
Giant	0.0
Large	3.2
Mid	52.2
Small	39.6
Micro	5.0
Avg $mil: 1,038	

Value Measures		Rel Category
Price/Earnings	13.43	0.97
Price/Book	1.43	0.75
Price/Sales	0.67	0.82
Price/Cash Flow	4.94	0.99
Dividend Yield %	2.68	1.18

Growth Measures	%	Rel Category
Long-Term Erngs	13.28	0.29
Book Value	4.74	1.21
Sales	3.21	0.51
Cash Flow	2.64	0.57
Historical Erngs	8.79	0.94

Composition

Cash	2.0	Bonds	0.0
Stocks	90.8	Other	7.2
Foreign (% of Stock)			99.9

Sector Weightings	% of Stocks	Rel MSCI EAFE	3 Year High	3 Year Low
Info	8.28	0.50		
Software	0.87	0.81	3	1
Hardware	2.88	0.79	4	2
Media	3.11	1.36	9	3
Telecom	1.42	0.15	3	1
Service	58.61	1.31		
Health	3.75	0.52	8	2
Consumer	15.85	3.14	17	12
Business	20.58	3.78	30	18
Financial	18.43	0.68	24	7
Mfg	33.12	0.86		
Goods	15.05	1.10	17	12
Ind Mtrls	13.08	1.06	18	10
Energy	2.12	0.29	3	0
Utilities	2.87	0.54	3	0

Regional Exposure	% Stock		
UK/W. Europe	69	N. America	0
Japan	21	Latn America	0
Asia X Japan	10	Other	0

Country Exposure	% Stock		
U.K.	26	Switzerland	6
Japan	21	Italy	5
France	6		

Morningstar's Take by Bridget Hughes 12-01-04

Vanguard International Explorer is a keeper, but adjust your expectations.

In some respects, this closed fund beat the odds in 2004. Through Nov. 30, it's up 23% and lands in the foreign small/mid-growth category's best quartile, helped by its emphasis on peripheral European markets, such as Denmark, Ireland, and Greece, and its stock selection in Japan. But the fund's strong showing came despite a surge of investor inflows that caused the management team to increase the number of names in its portfolio, hold a bit more cash than usual earlier in the year, and manage a much bigger fund in perennially illiquid international small-cap markets.

There continues to be much to like about the offering. Importantly, it has one of the largest staffs assigned specifically to international small-cap research, including 13 analysts and five portfolio managers. And they're more experienced than many of the new entrants in these markets. We think level of coverage and perspective gives the fund an advantage in looking for higher-quality small-cap companies. Further, the fund is by far the cheapest offering in its category.

Still, there are clear implications of the increased size. Although the portfolio had been fairly diffuse with around 150 names in the early 2000s, it's much bigger now at more than 250 stocks. While the fund had in the past regularly stashed 2.5% to 3% of assets in top holdings, it's been rare lately to see a company command more than a 1% stake. This means more of the team's picks will have to outperform to have a meaningful impact on returns. It could mean cooler returns going forward, particularly relative to nimbler peers.

We'd still hold the fund, though, particularly now. With international small-caps more richly priced now than they've been in several years, this more diversified and conservatively run portfolio could be the best defense. And it should stay competitive in up markets, as well.

Address:	PO Box 2600 Valley Forge PA 19482 800-662-7447
Web Address:	www.vanguard.com
Inception:	11-04-96 *
Advisor:	Schroder Investment Mgt N. America Inc.
Subadvisor:	None
NTF Plans:	N/A

Minimum Purchase:	Closed	Add: —	IRA: —		
Min Auto Inv Plan:	Closed	Add: —			
Sales Fees:	No-load, 2.00%R				
Management Fee:	0.60%, 0.18%A				
Actual Fees:	Mgt:0.59%	Dist: —			
Expense Projections:	3Yr:$233	5Yr:$406	10Yr:$906		
Income Distrib:	Annually				

Vanguard Intl Gr

Ticker	Load	NAV	Yield	Total Assets	Mstar Category
VWIGX	None	$18.86	1.7%	$9,609 mil	Foreign Large Blend

Governance and Management

Fiduciary Grade: B

Portfolio Manager(s)

Richard Foulkes has been at the helm since this fund's 1981 inception. However, in February 2003 Vanguard turned over one fifth of the fund's assets to Baillie Gifford, an Edinburgh-based firm with about $30 billion in assets under management. Although James Anderson has been designated the Baillie Gifford manager, the firm uses a team-management approach. Its Guardian Baillie Gifford International has mediocre returns.

Strategy

Long-term manager Richard Foulkes of Schroder follows a moderate-growth approach that emphasizes blue chips in developed markets. He looks for core growth issues trading on the cheap, but he'll also commit about one third of assets to opportunistic value plays. The fund's other subadvisor, Baillie Gifford, focuses on firms with sustainable competitive advantages. Although companies are also screened for value, quality is a priority. Vanguard employs fair-value pricing for its foreign-stock funds, but it uses this technique sparingly.

Historical Profile

Return: Above Avg
Risk: Average
Rating: ★★★★ Above Avg

Investment Style — Equity Stock %: 97% 91% 90% 92% 91% 94% 91% 84% 92%

▼ Manager Change
▽ Partial Manager Change

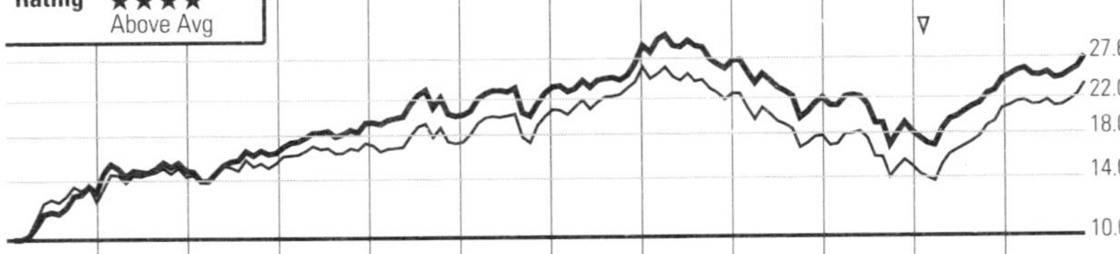

Growth of $10,000
— Investment Values of Fund
— Investment Values of MSCI EAFE

Performance Quartile (within Category)

History

	1993	1994	1995	1996	1997	1998	1999	2000	2001	2002	2003	12-04
NAV	13.51	13.43	15.02	16.46	16.39	18.77	22.49	18.87	15.01	12.16	16.13	18.86
Total Return %	44.74	0.76	14.89	14.65	4.12	16.93	26.34	-8.60	-18.92	-17.79	34.45	18.95
+/-MSCI EAFE	12.18	-7.02	3.68	8.60	2.34	-3.00	-0.69	5.59	2.50	-1.85	-4.14	-1.30
+/-MSCI Wd xUS	12.53	-6.59	3.48	7.78	1.85	-1.76	-1.64	4.76	2.47	-1.99	-4.97	-1.43
Income Return %	1.17	1.33	1.49	1.26	1.28	1.34	1.39	0.98	1.27	1.20	1.73	1.95
Capital Return %	43.57	-0.57	13.40	13.39	2.84	15.59	24.95	-9.58	-20.19	-18.99	32.72	17.00
Total Rtn % Rank Cat	11	46	17	38	68	29	86	13	29	64	40	33
Income $	0.11	0.18	0.20	0.19	0.21	0.22	0.26	0.22	0.24	0.18	0.21	0.32
Capital Gains $	0.00	0.00	0.21	0.55	0.52	0.16	0.90	1.42	0.04	0.00	0.00	0.00
Expense Ratio %	0.59	0.46	0.58	0.56	0.57	0.59	0.58	0.53	0.61	0.67	0.69	0.45
Income Ratio %	1.27	1.37	1.53	1.35	1.26	1.39	1.42	1.26	1.19	1.28	1.57	1.86
Turnover Rate %	51	28	31	22	22	37	37	48	48	40	59	45
Net Assets $mil	2,127	2,928	3,676	5,569	6,809	7,723	9,681	8,900	6,088	4,768	6,424	8,097

Performance 12-31-04

	1st Qtr	2nd Qtr	3rd Qtr	4th Qtr	Total
2000	6.05	-3.23	-9.92	-1.13	-8.60
2001	-11.98	-2.41	-16.04	12.42	-18.92
2002	0.40	-4.31	-20.80	8.06	-17.79
2003	-7.57	17.88	7.70	14.57	34.45
2004	6.20	-2.22	0.18	14.35	18.95

Trailing	Total Return%	+/- MSCI EAFE	+/- MSCI Wd xUS	%Rank Cat	Growth of $10,000
3 Mo	14.35	-0.97	-0.80	45	11,435
6 Mo	14.55	-0.45	-0.82	36	11,455
1 Yr	18.95	-1.30	-1.43	33	11,895
3 Yr Avg	9.55	-2.34	-2.67	49	13,147
5 Yr Avg	-0.52	0.61	0.24	19	9,743
10 Yr Avg	7.04	1.42	1.10	23	19,745
15 Yr Avg	6.30	2.07	1.89	46	25,003

Tax Analysis	Tax-Adj Rtn%	%Rank Cat	Tax-Cost Rat	%Rank Cat
3 Yr (estimated)	9.03	43	0.47	51
5 Yr (estimated)	-1.35	19	0.83	56
10 Yr (estimated)	5.99	22	0.98	36

Potential Capital Gain Exposure: 18% of assets

Rating and Risk

Time Period	Load-Adj Return %	Morningstar Rtn vs Cat	Morningstar Risk vs Cat	Morningstar Risk-Adj Rating
1 Yr	18.95			
3 Yr	9.55	Avg	+Avg	★★★
5 Yr	-0.52	+Avg	Avg	★★★★
10 Yr	7.04	+Avg	Avg	★★★★
Incept	12.56			

Other Measures	Standard Index S&P 500	Best Fit Index MSCI EAFE
Alpha	-2.2	-2.2
Beta	1.01	1.01
R-Squared	97	97
Standard Deviation	17.68	
Mean	9.55	
Sharpe Ratio	0.47	

Portfolio Analysis 09-30-04

Share change since 06-04 Total Stocks:189	Sector	Country	% Assets
⊕ Tesco	Consumer	U.K.	3.64
Vodafone Grp	Telecom	U.K.	2.49
Shell Transport & Tradin	Energy	U.K.	2.22
⊕ Royal Bank Of Scotland G	Financial	U.K.	2.18
Toyota Motor	Goods	Japan	1.91
Telecom Italia	Telecom	Italy	1.91
East Japan Railway	Business	Japan	1.75
Allied Irish Banks	Financial	Ireland	1.73
⊖ Mitsui & Co.	Ind Mtrls	Japan	1.70
Ricoh	Ind Mtrls	Japan	1.56
⊖ Nestle	Goods	Switzerland	1.46
TOTAL	Energy	France	1.44
⊕ Suez	Utilities	France	1.39
⊕ Kingfisher	Consumer	U.K.	1.30
⊖ Samsung Electronics	Goods	Korea	1.30
TPG	Business	Netherlands	1.25
⊕ Signet Grp	Goods	U.K.	1.24
⊕ Centrica	Utilities	U.K.	1.23
☼ Siemens	Hardware	Germany	1.17
BG Grp	Utilities	U.K.	1.08

Current Investment Style

Market Cap	%
Giant	50.8
Large	40.0
Mid	9.3
Small	0.0
Micro	0.0
Avg $mil: 19,878	

Value Measures		Rel Category
Price/Earnings	13.31	0.97
Price/Book	1.98	1.10
Price/Sales	0.77	0.85
Price/Cash Flow	6.01	1.22
Dividend Yield %	2.56	1.01

Growth Measures	%	Rel Category
Long-Term Erngs	10.48	0.97
Book Value	0.62	62.00
Sales	5.59	2.24
Cash Flow	4.79	0.85
Historical Erngs	11.42	2.04

Composition

Cash	5.9	Bonds	0.0
Stocks	91.9	Other	2.2
Foreign (% of Stock)			99.7

Sector Weightings	% of Stocks	Rel MSCI EAFE	3 Year High	3 Year Low
Info	13.87	0.84		
Software	0.45	0.42	1	0
Hardware	4.30	1.18	8	3
Media	1.77	0.78	6	2
Telecom	7.35	0.77	8	4
Service	39.25	0.88		
Health	3.78	0.52	8	4
Consumer	9.72	1.93	10	3
Business	7.55	1.39	9	5
Financial	18.20	0.67	29	17
Mfg	46.89	1.21		
Goods	19.15	1.40	21	15
Ind Mtrls	15.45	1.26	20	15
Energy	7.71	1.05	8	0
Utilities	4.58	0.86	5	2

Regional Exposure	% Stock		
UK/W. Europe	62	N. America	0
Japan	23	Latn America	1
Asia X Japan	12	Other	2

Country Exposure	% Stock		
U.K.	29	Switzerland	5
Japan	23	Italy	4
France	11		

Morningstar's Take by Dan Lefkovitz 11-30-04

We have confidence in at least 80% of Vanguard International Growth.

Longtime manager Richard Foulkes of subadvisor Schroder Investment Management divides the stocks in his portfolio into two categories: core and noncore. He selects core holdings on the basis of their growth potential and intends to hold them for three to five years. Noncore holdings are turned over more frequently and are selected as a result of top-down analyses. They typically occupy one third of the portfolio. Meanwhile, the team at Baillie Gifford, which Vanguard added in February 2003 to subadvise roughly 20% of the portfolio, looks for companies with sustainable competitive advantages.

Foulkes names top holding Tesco as a core holding, in addition to Telecom Italia and recently purchased Siemens. His underweighting of industrials stocks and lack of drug company shares are both results of top-down analyses, as is his Asia overweight. Foulkes is bearish on the European economy and is therefore putting a smaller share of his portfolio in European shares than are his peers in the foreign large-blend category.

Foulkes' positioning has contributed to slightly better-than-average results for 2004. The fund has gained 14% for the year to Nov. 26, despite holding few red-hot industrials names. Because Vanguard does not distinguish portfolio holdings between the two subadvisors, it's hard to say if Baillie Gifford helped or hurt this year. Guardian Baillie Gifford International, run by the same group that subadvises this fund, is having a good 2004, but its longer-term performance has been subpar.

Although Baillie Gifford has a mixed record, they only manage 20% of this fund. We have a high degree of confidence in the veteran Foulkes, who has steered this fund to top-quartile returns over the trailing 10-year period. His experience and consistent style, in addition to the fund's super-low expenses, make it a solid core foreign holding.

Address:	PO Box 2600 Valley Forge PA 19482 800-662-7447
Web Address:	www.vanguard.com
Inception:	09-30-81
Advisor:	The Vanguard Group, Inc.
Subadvisor:	Multiple
NTF Plans:	N/A

Minimum Purchase:	$3000	Add: $100	IRA: $1000
Min Auto Inv Plan:	$3000	Add: $50	
Sales Fees:	No-load		
Management Fee:	0.60%		
Actual Fees:	Mgt:0.60%	Dist: —	
Expense Projections:	3Yr:$214	5Yr:$373	10Yr:$835
Income Distrib:	Annually		

Vanguard Intl Value

Ticker	Load	NAV	Yield	Total Assets	Mstar Category
VTRIX	None	$30.93	1.6%	$2,663 mil	Foreign Large Blend

Governance and Management

Fiduciary Grade: B

Portfolio Manager(s)

The fund is managed by two separate subadvisors. Hansberger Global Investors, the sole subadvisor prior to April 2004, still manages about three fourths of the assets. It uses a team approach, but Ronald Holt and Aureole Foong are now primarily responsible for that firm's part of the fund. The Bernstein portion of the fund is also team-managed. Those chiefly responsible for its portion are Kevin Simms, Henry D'Auria, and Sharon Fay.

Strategy

The Hansberger managers follow a value strategy, although they don't look exclusively for cheap assets. They focus on companies whose shares are cyclically depressed or unusually cheap. The fund's sector and country weightings deviate from the MSCI All Country World ex-US Index's, but the managers do keep an eye on that bogy. The Bernstein managers seek to buy the greatest amount of long-term earnings for the most attractive price. Vanguard employs fair-value pricing at its international funds, but it uses the technique sparingly.

Historical Profile

Return: High
Risk: Above Avg
Rating: ★★★★ Above Avg

Investment Style: Equity Stock %: 97% 98% 98% 94% 92% 94% 92% 96% 91%

▼ Manager Change
∇ Partial Manager Change

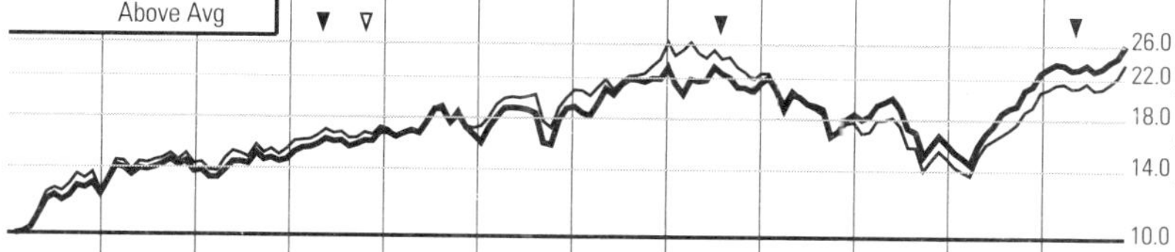

Growth of $10,000
— Investment Values of Fund
— Investment Values of MSCI EAFE

Performance Quartile (within Category)

History

1993	1994	1995	1996	1997	1998	1999	2000	2001	2002	2003	12-04	History
31.04	31.48	31.11	27.54	22.64	25.09	29.12	26.03	22.07	18.83	26.24	30.93	NAV
30.49	5.25	9.65	10.22	-4.58	19.46	21.77	-7.42	-14.05	-13.35	41.90	19.77	Total Return %
-2.07	-2.53	-1.56	4.17	-6.36	-0.47	-5.26	6.77	7.37	2.59	3.31	-0.48	+/-MSCI EAFE
-1.72	-2.10	-1.76	3.35	-6.85	0.77	-6.21	5.94	7.34	2.45	2.48	-0.61	+/-MSCI Wd xUS
3.34	1.81	2.54	2.67	2.57	4.76	2.63	2.53	1.15	1.31	2.44	1.83	Income Return %
27.15	3.44	7.11	7.55	-7.15	14.70	19.14	-9.95	-15.20	-14.66	39.46	17.94	Capital Return %
67	7	68	64	98	17	95	9	5	18	6	22	Total Rtn % Rank Cat
0.81	0.56	0.79	0.82	0.69	1.06	0.66	0.73	0.30	0.29	0.46	0.48	Income $
0.00	0.63	2.52	5.77	2.95	0.90	0.73	0.19	0.00	0.00	0.00	0.00	Capital Gains $
0.40	0.34	0.47	0.50	0.49	0.52	0.59	0.53	0.64	0.65	0.62	0.56	Expense Ratio %
1.76	1.71	2.29	2.50	2.36	2.77	2.54	1.94	1.93	1.80	2.46	1.99	Income Ratio %
39	40	47	82	37	39	41	78	37	26	27	74	Turnover Rate %
982	1,053	988	917	777	806	1,045	835	895	1,104	1,704	2,663	Net Assets $mil

Performance 12-31-04

	1st Qtr	2nd Qtr	3rd Qtr	4th Qtr	Total
2000	-5.72	6.32	-9.64	2.21	-7.42
2001	-12.22	2.89	-14.72	11.58	-14.05
2002	4.53	-1.60	-20.75	6.30	-13.35
2003	-9.51	20.77	10.40	17.60	41.90
2004	4.19	0.04	1.50	13.21	19.77

Trailing	Total Return%	+/- MSCI EAFE	+/- MSCI Wd xUS	%Rank Cat	Growth of $10,000
3 Mo	13.21	-2.11	-1.94	78	11,321
6 Mo	14.90	-0.10	-0.47	25	11,490
1 Yr	19.77	-0.48	-0.61	22	11,977
3 Yr Avg	13.77	1.88	1.55	7	14,726
5 Yr Avg	3.22	4.35	3.98	4	11,717
10 Yr Avg	6.99	1.37	1.05	24	19,653
15 Yr Avg	5.94	1.71	1.53	55	23,763

Tax Analysis	Tax-Adj Rtn%	%Rank Cat	Tax-Cost Rat	%Rank Cat
3 Yr (estimated)	13.21	6	0.49	53
5 Yr (estimated)	2.54	4	0.66	43
10 Yr (estimated)	4.66	52	2.18	90

Potential Capital Gain Exposure: 21% of assets

Rating and Risk

Time Period	Load-Adj Return %	Morningstar Rtn vs Cat	Morningstar Risk vs Cat	Morningstar Risk-Adj Rating
1 Yr	19.77			
3 Yr	13.77	High	+Avg	★★★★★
5 Yr	3.22	High	+Avg	★★★★★
10 Yr	6.99	+Avg	Avg	★★★
Incept	11.12			

Other Measures	Standard Index S&P 500	Best Fit Index MSCI EAFE
Alpha	1.9	1.9
Beta	0.98	0.98
R-Squared	94	94
Standard Deviation	18.01	
Mean	13.77	
Sharpe Ratio	0.70	

Portfolio Analysis 09-30-04

Share change since 06-04 Total Stocks:166	Sector	Country	% Assets
ENI	Energy	Italy	2.10
⊖ GlaxoSmithKline	Health	U.K.	1.88
⊕ Canon	Goods	Japan	1.86
⊕ Telefonica Moviles	Telecom	Spain	1.71
TOTAL	Energy	France	1.53
⊕ ING Groep	Financial	Netherlands	1.39
⊕ HSBC Hldgs	Financial	U.K.	1.39
E.On	Utilities	Germany	1.34
Petroleo Brasileiro ADR	Energy	Brazil	1.33
Vodafone Grp	Telecom	U.K.	1.33
⊕ Royal Bank Of Scotland G	Financial	U.K.	1.23
⊕ Sumitomo Tr And Bkg	Financial	Japan	1.23
⊕ Johnson Electric Hldgs L	Ind Mtrls	Hong Kong	1.22
⊕ Nestle	Goods	Switzerland	1.20
Societe Generale	Financial	France	1.19
DBS Grp Hldgs Ltd	Financial	Singapore	1.14
LG Chem	Ind Mtrls	Korea	1.14
⊕ HBOS	Financial	U.K.	1.13
⊕ Samsung Electronics	Goods	Korea	1.13
⊕ Sony	Goods	Japan	1.12

Current Investment Style

Market Cap	%
Giant	49.5
Large	36.5
Mid	13.6
Small	0.1
Micro	0.3
Avg $mil: 17,785	

Value Measures		Rel Category
Price/Earnings	12.45	0.91
Price/Book	1.76	0.98
Price/Sales	0.79	0.87
Price/Cash Flow	4.17	0.85
Dividend Yield %	2.56	1.01

Growth Measures	%	Rel Category
Long-Term Erngs	10.02	0.93
Book Value	.05	105.00
Sales	2.97	1.19
Cash Flow	5.89	1.05
Historical Erngs	.26	0.23

Composition			
Cash	7.4	Bonds	0.0
Stocks	91.4	Other	1.2
Foreign (% of Stock)			98.2

Sector Weightings	% of Stocks	Rel MSCI EAFE	3 Year High	3 Year Low
Info	10.79	0.65		
Software	0.00	0.00	0	0
Hardware	4.17	1.14	5	2
Media	0.26	0.11	3	0
Telecom	6.36	0.66	11	6
Service	45.31	1.01		
Health	8.39	1.16	9	8
Consumer	6.36	1.26	7	6
Business	4.27	0.78	7	4
Financial	26.29	0.97	26	17
Mfg	43.89	1.14		
Goods	16.60	1.22	20	15
Ind Mtrls	16.65	1.35	20	17
Energy	8.11	1.10	8	3
Utilities	2.53	0.47	3	2

Regional Exposure	% Stock		
UK/W. Europe	59	N. America	3
Japan	17	Latn America	3
Asia X Japan	16	Other	2

Country Exposure	% Stock		
U.K.	21	Germany	8
Japan	17	South Korea	6
France	13		

Morningstar's Take by Dan Lefkovitz 11-30-04

Caution continues to pay off for Vanguard International Value.

Hansberger Global Investors, which subadvises about three quarters of this fund's portfolio, has a disciplined, value-oriented style. Managers Ron Holt and Aureole Foong look for quality companies trading at discounts to "normalized" earnings. That is, they estimate what a company's earnings should look like at various points during the economic cycle. Then they buy shares that seem cheap and sell when one of their holdings is trading high. Meanwhile, a team from AllianceBernstein, which Vanguard brought on in April to manage roughly a quarter of the portfolio, focuses on companies generating high returns on equity.

Hansberger's Holt acknowledges that his cautious style has both helped and hurt in 2004. The fund benefited from a slew of industrial and materials names--many of them purchased in 2002, when they were trading below normalized earnings. But after these stocks soared, Holt and Foong scaled back, trimming exposure to names such as jet-engine maker Rolls Royce. That turned out to be premature, as industrials and materials have continued to rally. Similarly, Holt and Foong sold many of their small caps and mid-caps in 2003, which turned out to be too early.

Long term though, Hansberger's cautious strategy has worked. Over the trailing five-year period, the fund has beaten 90% of its competitors. And for the year through Nov. 26, the fund has gained 15.4%, well above the category average for foreign large-blend funds.

The newness of this fund's multimanager format raises some uncertainty. But the team from AllianceBernstein has compiled an impressive record on their International Value fund, and Hansberger has proved its worth. Super low expenses are another plus for a fund that makes a solid core foreign holding.

Address:	PO Box 2600 Valley Forge PA 19482 800-662-7447
Web Address:	www.vanguard.com
Inception:	05-16-83
Advisor:	The Vanguard Group, Inc.
Subadvisor:	Multiple
NTF Plans:	N/A

Minimum Purchase:	$3000	Add: $100	IRA: $1000
Min Auto Inv Plan:	$3000	Add: $50	
Sales Fees:	No-load		
Management Fee:	0.48% mx./0.11% mn.		
Actual Fees:	Mgt:0.48%	Dist: —	
Expense Projections:	3Yr:$205	5Yr:$357	10Yr:$798
Income Distrib:	Annually		

Vanguard LifeSt Cons Gr

Ticker	Load	NAV	Yield	Total Assets	Mstar Category
VSCGX	None	$15.26	2.8%	$3,650 mil	Conservative Allocation

Governance and Management

Fiduciary Grade: B

Portfolio Manager(s)

The fund's trustees oversee the percentage of assets allocated to each of the underlying funds, and they rarely make changes. All of the underlying funds are overseen by experienced and talented managers. Asset Allocation is run by savvy veterans Tom Loeb and William Fouse, for example, while Total Stock Market Index and Total International Stock Index are run by noted indexing guru Gus Sauter.

Strategy

This fund of funds invests at least 50% of assets in bonds, but that stake can go as high as 75%. That's because it invests about 25% of its assets in Vanguard Asset Allocation, which actively shifts between the S&P 500 Index and U.S. Treasury bonds based on projected long-term trends. The fund also invests approximately 30% in Total Bond Market Index, 20% in Total Stock Market Index, 20% in Short-Term Corporate, and 5% in Total International Stock Index.

Historical Profile

Return: Above Avg
Risk: Average
Rating: ★★★★ Above Avg

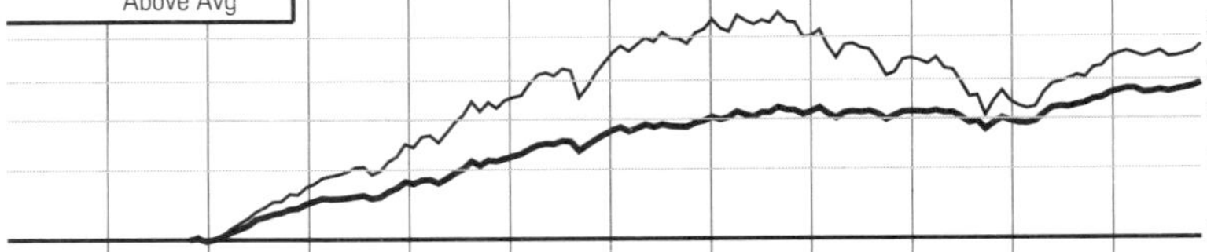

Investment Style: Equity Stock %

▼ Manager Change
▽ Partial Manager Change

Growth of $10,000
— Investment Values of Fund
— Investment Values of S&P 500

Performance Quartile (within Category)

1993	1994	1995	1996	1997	1998	1999	2000	2001	2002	2003	12-04	History
					32%	36%	31%	39%	39%	42%	46%	Equity Stock %
—	9.89	11.68	12.14	13.40	14.71	15.10	14.71	14.06	12.82	14.54	15.26	NAV
—	0.10*	24.35	10.36	16.81	15.88	7.86	3.12	-0.08	-5.37	17.22	8.02	Total Return %
—	—	-13.18	-12.58	-16.54	-12.69	-13.18	12.22	11.80	16.72	-11.45	-2.85	+/-S&P 500
—	—	6.19	1.47	2.71	4.15	0.00	-3.67	-3.30	-1.35	-0.44	-0.99	+/-DJ 40%
—	0.00	4.82	4.61	4.69	4.47	4.35	4.74	4.01	3.53	3.56	2.99	Income Return %
—	—	19.53	5.75	12.12	11.41	3.51	-1.62	-4.09	-8.90	13.66	5.03	Capital Return %
—	—	21	57	26	14	33	62	51	73	15	17	Total Rtn % Rank Cat
—	0.14	0.47	0.53	0.56	0.59	0.63	0.70	0.58	0.49	0.45	0.39	Income $
—	0.01	0.12	0.20	0.19	0.20	0.11	0.16	0.04	0.00	0.00	0.00	Capital Gains $
—	0.00	0.00	0.00	0.00	0.00	0.00	0.00	0.00	0.00	0.00	0.00	Expense Ratio %
—	7.07	5.14	4.86	4.61	4.32	4.34	4.73	3.78	3.79	2.92	2.74	Income Ratio %
—	—	1	2	1	3	5	9	14	12	5	5	Turnover Rate %
—	41	219	462	803	1,416	1,748	1,897	2,026	2,193	2,924	3,650	Net Assets $mil

Performance 12-31-04

	1st Qtr	2nd Qtr	3rd Qtr	4th Qtr	Total
2000	3.17	-0.51	1.33	-0.86	3.12
2001	-3.87	3.43	-4.10	4.78	-0.08
2002	0.43	-3.78	-6.74	5.02	-5.37
2003	-0.47	9.02	1.98	5.93	17.22
2004	2.48	-0.74	0.89	5.25	8.02

Trailing	Total Return%	+/- S&P 500	+/- DJ 40%	%Rank Cat	Growth of $10,000
3 Mo	5.25	-3.98	-0.15	23	10,525
6 Mo	6.19	-1.00	-0.30	22	10,619
1 Yr	8.02	-2.85	-0.99	17	10,802
3 Yr Avg	6.22	2.64	-0.96	23	11,984
5 Yr Avg	4.31	6.61	-1.99	37	12,349
10 Yr Avg	9.48	-2.59	0.33	18	24,737
15 Yr Avg	—	—	—	—	—

Tax Analysis	Tax-Adj Rtn%	%Rank Cat	Tax-Cost Rat	%Rank Cat
3 Yr (estimated)	5.02	22	1.13	62
5 Yr (estimated)	2.82	35	1.43	58
10 Yr (estimated)	7.59	8	1.73	24

Potential Capital Gain Exposure: 10% of assets

Rating and Risk

Time Period	Load-Adj Return %	Morningstar Rtn vs Cat	Morningstar Risk vs Cat	Morningstar Risk-Adj Rating
1 Yr	8.02			
3 Yr	6.22	+Avg	+Avg	★★★★
5 Yr	4.31	Avg	Avg	★★★
10 Yr	9.48	+Avg	Avg	★★★★
Incept	9.24			

Other Measures	Standard Index S&P 500	Best Fit Index DJ 60%
Alpha	3.5	-1.4
Beta	0.43	0.72
R-Squared	91	92
Standard Deviation	7.06	
Mean	6.22	
Sharpe Ratio	0.69	

Portfolio Analysis 09-30-04

Total Stocks:0 Share change since 06-30-04	Sectors	P/E Ratio	YTD Return %	% Net Assets
⊕ Vanguard Asset Allocation	—	—	—	24.97
⊕ Vanguard Total Stock Mkt	—	—	—	20.16
⊕ Vanguard Total Intl Stock	—	—	—	5.04

Total Fixed-Income:0	Date of Maturity	Amount $000	Value $000	% Net Assets
Vanguard Total Bond Marke		98,630	1,014,901	29.90
Vanguard Short-Term Inves		62,392	668,220	19.69

Morningstar's Take by William Samuel Rocco 11-13-04

One-stop shoppers should check out Vanguard LifeStrategy Conservative Growth.

The Vanguard LifeStrategy Series, which is designed for investors who lack the interest or the means to build diversified portfolios themselves, consists of four wide-ranging funds of funds that span the risk/reward spectrum. This is the second most-conservative member of the quartet. It's composed of two broad-based bond offerings, two exceptionally diversified equity index funds, and one asset-allocation offering. It has a fairly moderate equity range of 25% to 50% of assets.

It's important to note, though, that this fund tends to be moderately bolder than the typical conservative-allocation offering. The upper end of its equity range is 10 to 15 percentage points higher than the category average of 35%. Though this fund will only assume that equity-heavy posture if Vanguard Asset Allocation, one of its component funds, is all or nearly all in stocks, that offering has often been quite heavy on equities. Consequently, this fund has tended to overweight stocks relative to its rivals. On the flip side, this fund enjoys more issue and sector diversification than do most peers due to the breadth of its underlying offerings' portfolios.

The fact that this fund is modestly more adventurous than its average peer is reflected in its performance. It has suffered only a little more volatility than the group norm, as its ample diversification has partially offset the risks of its extra equity exposure. But it has regularly outperformed in stock rallies and outgained its typical rival by roughly 1.5 percentage points per year over the past decade, thanks to its equity bias and Vanguard Asset Allocation's generally good composition calls.

Investors who are attracted to this portfolio and its risk/reward profile should note that the underlying offerings are cheap and that this fund, unlike some of its rivals, only charges what its component funds charge.

Address:	PO Box 2600 Valley Forge PA 19482 800-662-7447
Web Address:	www.vanguard.com
Inception:	09-30-94 *
Advisor:	Vanguard Advisers, Inc.
Subadvisor:	None
NTF Plans:	N/A

Minimum Purchase:	$3000	Add: $100	IRA: $1000
Min Auto Inv Plan:	$3000	Add: $50	
Sales Fees:	No-load		
Management Fee:	—		
Actual Fees:	—	Dist:	
Expense Projections:	3Yr:$87	5Yr:$152	10Yr:$343
Income Distrib:	Quarterly		

Equity Style
Style: Blend
Size: Large-Cap

Value Measures		Rel Category
Price/Earnings	16.28	0.99
Price/Book	2.43	1.03
Price/Sales	1.30	1.00
Price/Cash Flow	6.91	0.99
Dividend Yield %	1.74	1.00

Growth Measures	%	Rel Category
Long-Term Erngs	11.16	1.00
Book Value	-14.54	NMF
Sales	4.23	0.93
Cash Flow	4.21	0.63
Historical Erngs	10.68	1.13

Market Cap %			
Giant	47.2	Small	3.1
Large	33.7	Micro	1.2
Mid	14.8	Avg $mil:	30,351

Fixed-Income Style
Duration: Interm-Term
Quality: High

Avg Eff Duration [1]	3.6 Yrs
Avg Eff Maturity	5.7 Yrs
Avg Credit Quality	AAA
Avg Wtd Coupon	5.11%

[1] figure provided by fund as of 09-30-04

Sector Weightings	% of Stocks	Rel S&P 500	3 Year High	3 Year Low
Info	20.51	0.95		
Software	3.94	0.92	5	4
Hardware	8.81	0.86	10	7
Media	3.76	0.98	4	4
Telecom	4.00	1.27	5	4
Service	47.34	1.02		
Health	12.25	0.98	14	12
Consumer	8.72	0.96	9	8
Business	4.58	1.13	5	4
Financial	21.79	1.05	22	20
Mfg	32.14	1.00		
Goods	9.58	1.03	11	10
Ind Mtrls	12.13	0.96	12	11
Energy	7.34	1.03	7	6
Utilities	3.09	1.04	3	3

Composition

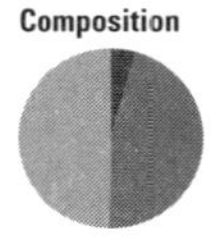

Cash	4.3
Stocks	45.8
Bonds	49.7
Other	0.1
Foreign (% of Stock)	10.7

Vanguard LifeSt Growth

Ticker	Load	NAV	Yield	Total Assets	Mstar Category
VASGX	None	$20.04	2.0%	$6,040 mil	Large Blend

Governance and Management

Fiduciary Grade: B

Portfolio Manager(s)

The fund's trustees oversee the percentage of assets allocated to each of the underlying funds, and they rarely make changes. All of the underlying funds are run by very experienced and talented managers. Asset Allocation is overseen by savvy veterans Tom Loeb and William Fouse, for example, while Total Stock Market Index and Total International Stock Index are run by noted indexing guru Gus Sauter.

Strategy

This fund of funds invests about 25% of assets in Vanguard Asset Allocation, which actively shifts between the S&P 500 Index and U.S. Treasury bonds based on projected long-term trends. As a result, this fund's equity allocation fluctuates within a fairly wide range of 65%-90% of assets. This fund also invests approximately 50% in Vanguard Total Stock Market Index, 15% in Vanguard Total International Stock Index, and 10% in Vanguard Total Bond Market index.

Historical Profile

Return Above Avg
Risk Below Avg
Rating ★★★★ Above Avg

Investment Style Equity Stock %

1995	1996	1997	1998	1999	2000	2001	2002	2003
100%	100%	60%	74%	59%	79%	78%	81%	85%

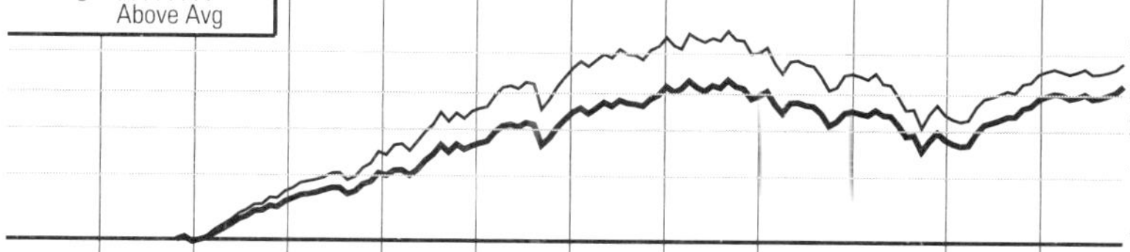

Performance Quartile (within Category)

1993	1994	1995	1996	1997	1998	1999	2000	2001	2002	2003	12-04	History
—	9.93	12.36	13.68	16.04	18.79	21.41	19.59	17.43	14.36	18.16	20.04	NAV
—	-0.10*	29.24	15.41	22.26	21.40	17.32	-5.44	-8.86	-15.84	28.52	12.58	Total Return %
—	—	-8.29	-7.53	-11.09	-7.17	-3.72	3.66	3.02	6.25	-0.15	1.71	+/-S&P 500
—	—	-8.53	-7.04	-10.59	-5.62	-3.59	2.35	3.59	5.81	-1.37	1.18	+/-Russ 1000
—	0.00	3.14	2.85	2.79	2.57	2.41	2.41	1.90	1.85	1.96	2.16	Income Return %
—	—	26.10	12.56	19.47	18.83	14.91	-7.85	-10.76	-17.69	26.56	10.42	Capital Return %
—	—	76	92	81	56	67	44	21	9	29	18	Total Rtn % Rank Cat
—	0.14	0.31	0.35	0.38	0.41	0.45	0.51	0.37	0.32	0.28	0.30	Income $
—	0.02	0.15	0.23	0.29	0.27	0.16	0.17	0.06	0.00	0.00	0.00	Capital Gains $
—	0.00	0.00	0.00	0.00	0.00	0.00	0.00	0.00	0.00	0.00	0.26	Expense Ratio %
—	7.06	3.67	3.18	2.84	2.53	2.50	4.73	1.53	2.12	1.79	1.79	Income Ratio %
—	—	1	—	1	2	1	9	7	7	2	5	Turnover Rate %
—	38	217	629	1,184	1,924	3,177	3,738	3.726	3,281	4,754	6,040	Net Assets $mil

Performance 12-31-04

	1st Qtr	2nd Qtr	3rd Qtr	4th Qtr	Total
2000	3.59	-2.76	-0.52	-5.64	-5.44
2001	-10.10	5.13	-11.81	9.36	-8.86
2002	0.75	-8.65	-14.91	7.47	-15.84
2003	-3.41	15.20	3.84	11.23	28.52
2004	2.86	0.38	-0.54	9.62	12.57

Trailing	Total Return%	+/- S&P 500	+/- Russ 1000	%Rank Cat	Growth of $10,000
3 Mo	9.62	0.39	-0.18	36	10,962
6 Mo	9.03	1.84	1.22	15	10,903
1 Yr	12.58	1.71	1.18	18	11,258
3 Yr Avg	6.79	3.21	2.52	8	12,178
5 Yr Avg	0.97	3.27	2.73	18	10,495
10 Yr Avg	10.55	-1.52	-1.61	49	27,264
15 Yr Avg	—	—	—	—	—

Tax Analysis	Tax-Adj Rtn%	%Rank Cat	Tax-Cost Rat	%Rank Cat
3 Yr (estimated)	6.16	8	0.59	49
5 Yr (estimated)	0.21	17	0.75	40
10 Yr (estimated)	9.39	40	1.05	32

Potential Capital Gain Exposure: 14% of assets

Rating and Risk

Time Period	Load-Adj Return %	Morningstar Rtn vs Cat	Morningstar Risk vs Cat	Morningstar Risk-Adj Rating
1 Yr	12.58			
3 Yr	6.79	High	-Avg	★★★★★
5 Yr	0.97	+Avg	-Avg	★★★★
10 Yr	10.55	Avg	Low	★★★
Incept	10.26			

Other Measures	Standard Index S&P 500	Best Fit Index MSCI World
Alpha	3.3	1.4
Beta	0.84	0.85
R-Squared	98	99

Standard Deviation	13.52
Mean	6.79
Sharpe Ratio	0.40

Portfolio Analysis 09-30-04

Share change since 06-04 Total Stocks:0	Sector	PE	YTD Ret%	% Assets
⊕ Vanguard Total Stock Mkt	—	—	—	50.0
⊕ Vanguard Asset Allocatio	—	—	—	24.96
⊕ Vanguard Total Intl Stoc	—	—	—	15.07
⊖ Vanguard Total Bond Mark	—	—	—	9.86

Current Investment Style

Market Cap	%
Giant	45.6
Large	32.3
Mid	16.4
Small	4.1
Micro	1.6

Avg $mil: 26,062

Value Measures		Rel Category
Price/Earnings	16.06	0.95
Price/Book	2.34	0.89
Price/Sales	1.23	0.85
Price/Cash Flow	6.63	0.86
Dividend Yield %	1.80	1.22

Growth Measures	%	Rel Category
Long-Term Erngs	11.19	0.97
Book Value	-15.75	NMF
Sales	3.56	0.69
Cash Flow	4.11	0.43
Historical Erngs	10.18	0.86

Profitability	%	Rel Category
Return on Equity	16.19	0.93
Return on Assets	7.86	0.91
Net Margin	10.81	0.94

Sector Weightings	% of Stocks	Rel S&P 500	3 Year High	Low
Info	20.08	0.93		
Software	3.66	0.85	4	3
Hardware	8.44	0.83	10	7
Media	3.74	0.97	4	4
Telecom	4.24	1.35	5	4
Service	47.53	1.02		
Health	11.88	0.95	14	12
Consumer	8.53	0.94	9	8
Business	4.82	1.19	5	5
Financial	22.30	1.07	23	21
Mfg	32.41	1.01		
Goods	9.83	1.05	12	10
Ind Mtrls	11.99	0.95	12	11
Energy	7.36	1.03	7	6
Utilities	3.23	1.09	3	3

Composition

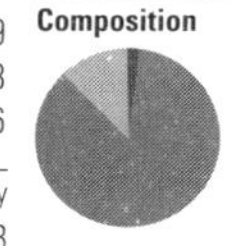

Cash	2.2
Stocks	85.4
Bonds	12.0
Other	0.4
Foreign (% of Stock)	17.2

Morningstar's Take by William Samuel Rocco 11-21-04

Vanguard LifeStrategy Growth delivers the goods.

This fund of funds is designed to provide broad equity-oriented exposure without too much risk. Thus, it parks 50% of its assets in Vanguard Total Stock Market Index and 15% of its assets in Vanguard Total International Stock Index, which combine to give it exceptionally broad exposure to domestic and overseas equities. To help keep volatility under control, the fund devotes 10% to Vanguard Total Bond Market Index. And it invests the remaining 25% of its portfolio in Vanguard Asset Allocation, which has the freedom to make bold composition calls and readily does so.

This fund has been rewarded for its range in recent years. The smaller-cap exposure it gets through Total Stock Market Index and the foreign exposure it gets from Total International Stock Index have been pluses thus far in 2004, as small and mid-caps have led the way here in the U.S., and overseas equities have outperformed. Its stake in Total Bond Market Index has also helped because that fund has gained much more than the typical large-blend offering. Thus, this fund is in its category top quintile for the year to date with a 8.3% return. It also posted superior results throughout the early 2000s, thanks to its smaller-cap stocks, its bonds, and Vanguard Asset Allocation's generally accurate composition calls.

Of course, it's important to note that this fund doesn't always shine. It posted subpar results during the late 1990s, and it's likely to do the same the next time domestic blue chips dominate. That said, it has kept pace with the typical large-blend offering since opening in late 1994 and it has suffered significantly less volatility than the group norm along the way. That risk/reward profile, plus the usual Vanguard low costs, makes us think this fund is a worthy option for those seeking a moderate equity vehicle.

Address:	PO Box 2600 Valley Forge PA 19482 800-662-7447
Web Address:	www.vanguard.com
Inception:	09-30-94 *
Advisor:	Vanguard Advisers, Inc.
Subadvisor:	None
NTF Plans:	N/A

Minimum Purchase:	$3000	Add: $100	IRA: $1000
Min Auto Inv Plan:	$3000	Add: $50	
Sales Fees:	No-load		
Management Fee:	—		
Actual Fees:	—	Dist:	
Expense Projections:	3Yr:$90	5Yr:$157	10Yr:$356
Income Distrib:	Semi-Annually		

Vanguard LifeSt Income

Ticker	Load	NAV	Yield	Total Assets	Mstar Category
VASIX	None	$13.53	3.3%	$1,654 mil	Conservative Allocation

Governance and Management

Fiduciary Grade: B

Portfolio Manager(s)

The fund's trustees oversee the percentage of assets allocated to each of the underlying funds, and they rarely make changes. All of the underlying funds are run by very experienced and talented managers. Savvy veterans Tom Loeb and William Fouse, for example, oversee Vanguard Asset Allocation while Vanguard Total Stock Market Index is run by noted indexing guru Gus Sauter.

Strategy

This fund of funds invests predominantly in bond funds, but its equity exposure can fluctuate between 5% and 30%. That's because it invests about 25% of assets in Vanguard Asset Allocation, which actively shifts between the S&P 500 Index and U.S. Treasury bonds based on projected long-term trends. The fund also invests approximately 50% in Vanguard Total Bond Market Index, 20% in Vanguard Short-Term Investment-Grade, and 5% in Vanguard Total Stock Market Index. The fund does not have any dedicated foreign-stock exposure.

Historical Profile

Return: Above Avg
Risk: Below Avg
Rating: ★★★★ Above Avg

Investment Style: Equity Stock %

18%	15%	16%	19%	20%	23%	26%

▼ Manager Change
▽ Partial Manager Change

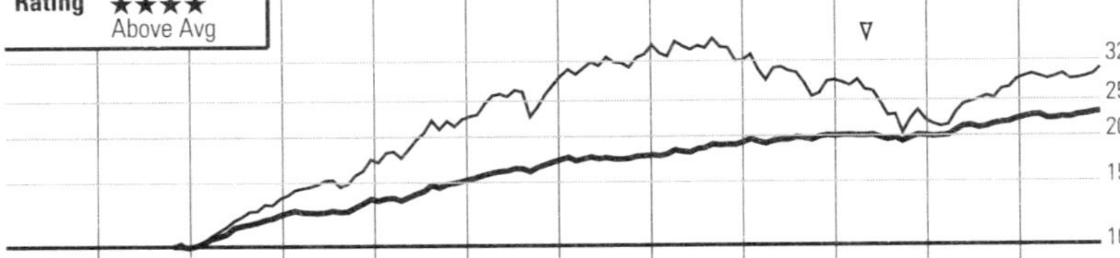

Growth of $10,000
— Investment Values of Fund
— Investment Values of S&P 500

Performance Quartile (within Category)

1993	1994	1995	1996	1997	1998	1999	2000	2001	2002	2003	12-04	History
—	9.88	11.54	11.55	12.43	13.22	12.82	13.01	12.86	12.32	13.20	13.53	NAV
—	0.20*	22.99	7.65	14.23	13.17	2.82	8.06	4.06	0.12	10.77	6.01	Total Return %
—	—	-14.54	-15.29	-19.12	-15.40	-18.22	17.16	15.94	22.21	-17.90	-4.86	+/-S&P 500
—	—	4.83	-1.24	0.13	1.44	-5.04	1.27	0.84	4.14	-6.89	-3.00	+/-DJ 40%
—	0.00	5.04	5.66	5.56	5.16	5.32	5.92	5.06	4.35	3.53	3.45	Income Return %
—	—	17.95	1.99	8.67	8.01	-2.50	2.14	-1.00	-4.23	7.24	2.56	Capital Return %
—	—	37	79	45	26	77	17	11	22	65	51	Total Rtn % Rank Cat
—	0.14	0.49	0.64	0.63	0.63	0.69	0.74	0.65	0.55	0.43	0.42	Income $
—	0.00	0.09	0.21	0.10	0.19	0.07	0.08	0.02	0.00	0.00	0.00	Capital Gains $
—	0.00	0.00	0.00	0.00	0.00	0.00	0.00	0.00	0.00	0.00	0.00	Expense Ratio %
—	7.31	5.76	5.66	5.54	5.24	5.37	5.84	4.87	4.64	3.53	3.31	Income Ratio %
—	—	4	22	6	3	11	17	4	10	4	4	Turnover Rate %
—	11	121	151	244	449	555	632	809	1,028	1,404	1,654	Net Assets $mil

Performance 12-31-04

	1st Qtr	2nd Qtr	3rd Qtr	4th Qtr	Total
2000	3.12	0.63	2.41	1.69	8.06
2001	-0.76	2.35	-0.13	2.60	4.06
2002	0.16	-1.18	-2.49	3.74	0.12
2003	0.08	6.20	1.01	3.18	10.77
2004	2.43	-1.41	1.75	3.17	6.01

Trailing	Total Return%	+/- S&P 500	+/- DJ 40%	%Rank Cat	Growth of $10,000
3 Mo	3.17	-6.06	-2.23	70	10,317
6 Mo	4.98	-2.21	-1.51	52	10,498
1 Yr	6.01	-4.86	-3.00	51	10,601
3 Yr Avg	5.54	1.96	-1.64	38	11,756
5 Yr Avg	5.74	8.04	-0.56	16	13,219
10 Yr Avg	8.81	-3.26	-0.34	31	23,264
15 Yr Avg	—	—	—	—	—

Tax Analysis	Tax-Adj Rtn%	%Rank Cat	Tax-Cost Rat	%Rank Cat
3 Yr (estimated)	4.17	35	1.30	73
5 Yr (estimated)	4.01	15	1.64	73
10 Yr (estimated)	6.67	31	1.97	44

Potential Capital Gain Exposure: 6% of assets

Rating and Risk

Time Period	Load-Adj Return %	Morningstar Rtn vs Cat	Morningstar Risk vs Cat	Morningstar Risk-Adj Rating
1 Yr	6.01			
3 Yr	5.54	+Avg	-Avg	★★★★
5 Yr	5.74	+Avg	-Avg	★★★★
10 Yr	8.81	+Avg	-Avg	★★★★
Incept	8.61			

Other Measures	Standard Index S&P 500	Best Fit Index DJ 60%
Alpha	3.5	0.6
Beta	0.22	0.40
R-Squared	59	71
Standard Deviation	4.40	
Mean	5.54	
Sharpe Ratio	0.95	

Portfolio Analysis 09-30-04

Total Stocks:0 Share change since 06-30-04	Sectors	P/E Ratio	YTD Return %	% Net Assets
⊕ Vanguard Asset Allocation	—	—	—	24.98
⊕ Vanguard Total Stock Mkt	—	—	—	4.95

Total Fixed-Income:0	Date of Maturity	Amount $000	Value $000	% Net Assets
Vanguard Total Bond Marke		76,573	787,934	49.98
Vanguard Short-Term Inves		29,332	314,144	19.93

Morningstar's Take by William Samuel Rocco 01-07-05

Vanguard LifeStrategy Income does more than honor its name.

This fund of funds has two intrinsic and significant advantages when it comes to yield: asset mix and low costs. It never devotes less than 70% of its assets to bonds--and it can invest as much as 95% of its assets in fixed-income securities---whereas most conservative-allocation offerings keep 50% to 60% of their assets in bonds. It doesn't tack its own fees on top of those of its underlying offerings. Those offerings are cheap, so it has an average weighted expense ratio of 0.25% while the typical offering in its category has an expense ratio of 1.35%. Not surprisingly, the fund normally pays out one of the best yields in its group.

The fund certainly isn't a one-trick pony, though. Thanks largely to its bond-heavy asset allocation, but also due to the exceptional issue, sector, and overall diversification of its underlying offerings, it has been significantly less volatile than most members of its rather tame category over time.

With three-, five-, and 10-year gains in the top third, the fund also looks pretty good from a long-term returns perspective. That outperformance is partly due to the fact that bonds handily outpaced stocks in three of the past five calendar years. But it's also due to the fact that the managers of Vanguard Asset Allocation, which makes up 25% of assets here, have generally put to good use their freedom to make dramatic composition calls.

While that is all encouraging, income seekers need to understand that the fund's bond-heavy stance makes it vulnerable to rising interest rates and slows it down in sustained equity rallies. It posted disappointing gains in both 1999 and 2003. Note also that the fund's overall conservatism means that solid results are more likely than superior results over the very long run.

Address:	PO Box 2600 Valley Forge PA 19482 800-662-7447
Web Address:	www.vanguard.com
Inception:	09-30-94*
Advisor:	Vanguard Advisers, Inc.
Subadvisor:	None
NTF Plans:	N/A

Minimum Purchase:	$3000	Add: $100	IRA: $1000
Min Auto Inv Plan:	$3000	Add: $50	
Sales Fees:	No-load		
Management Fee:	—		
Actual Fees:	—	Dist:	
Expense Projections:	3Yr:$87	5Yr:$152	10Yr:$343
Income Distrib:	Quarterly		

Equity Style
Style: Blend
Size: Large-Cap

Value Measures		Rel Category
Price/Earnings	16.64	1.01
Price/Book	2.59	1.09
Price/Sales	1.41	1.08
Price/Cash Flow	7.43	1.07
Dividend Yield %	1.65	0.95

Growth Measures	%	Rel Category
Long-Term Erngs	11.12	0.99
Book Value	6.98	1.27
Sales	4.72	1.03
Cash Flow	6.09	0.91
Historical Erngs	11.50	1.22

Market Cap %			
Giant	49.9	Small	1.4
Large	36.1	Micro	0.5
Mid	12.1	Avg $mil:	39,227

Composition

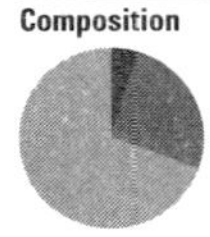

Cash	4.5
Stocks	25.8
Bonds	69.6
Other	0.1
Foreign (% of Stock)	0.0

Fixed-Income Style
Duration: Interm-Term
Quality: High

Avg Eff Duration [1]	4.0 Yrs
Avg Eff Maturity	6.3 Yrs
Avg Credit Quality	AAA
Avg Wtd Coupon	5.32%

[1]figure provided by fund as of 09-30-04

Sector Weightings	% of Stocks	Rel S&P 500	3 Year High	3 Year Low
Info	21.25	0.99		
Software	4.42	1.03	6	4
Hardware	9.43	0.92	11	8
Media	3.80	0.99	4	4
Telecom	3.60	1.14	5	3
Service	47.01	1.01		
Health	12.87	1.03	15	13
Consumer	9.02	0.99	10	9
Business	4.18	1.03	4	4
Financial	20.94	1.01	22	19
Mfg	31.74	0.99		
Goods	9.19	0.98	11	9
Ind Mtrls	12.38	0.98	12	11
Energy	7.31	1.02	7	6
Utilities	2.86	0.97	3	3

Vanguard LifeSt Mod Grth

Ticker	Load	NAV	Yield	Total Assets	Mstar Category
VSMGX	None	$17.91	2.5%	$7,002 mil	Moderate Allocation

Governance and Management

Fiduciary Grade: B

Portfolio Manager(s)

The fund's trustees oversee the percentage of assets allocated to each of the underlying funds, and they rarely make changes. All of the underlying funds are run by very experienced and talented managers. Asset Allocation is overseen by savvy veterans Tom Loeb and William Fouse, for example, while Total Stock Market Index and Total International Stock Index are run by noted indexing guru Gus Sauter.

Strategy

This fund of funds invests about 25% of assets in Vanguard Asset Allocation, which actively shifts between the S&P 500 Index and U.S. Treasury bonds based on projected long-term trends. The fund also invests approximately 35% in Total Stock Market Index, 30% in Total Bond Market Index, and 10% in Total International Stock Index. Its equity allocation can range from 45%-70% of assets.

Historical Profile

Return: Above Avg
Risk: Average
Rating: ★★★★ Above Avg

Investment Style: Equity Stock %

1997	1998	1999	2000	2001	2002	2003	12-04
46%	55%	45%	59%	59%	62%	66%	

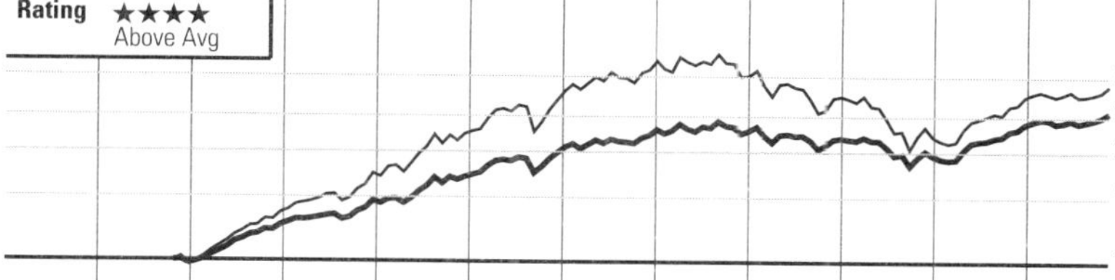

▼ Manager Change
▽ Partial Manager Change

Growth of $10,000
— Investment Values of Fund
— Investment Values of S&P 500

Performance Quartile (within Category)

1993	1994	1995	1996	1997	1998	1999	2000	2001	2002	2003	12-04	History
—	9.86	12.11	12.97	14.81	16.86	18.18	17.25	15.93	13.87	16.61	17.91	NAV
—	-0.70*	27.94	12.71	19.77	19.03	12.01	-0.88	-4.48	-10.32	22.40	10.57	Total Return %
—	—	-9.59	-10.23	-13.58	-9.54	-9.03	8.22	7.40	11.77	-6.27	-0.30	+/-S&P 500
—	—	3.17	1.37	0.57	6.64	-0.84	-5.32	-4.64	0.22	-1.66	-0.60	+/-DJ 60%
—	0.00	3.68	3.66	3.81	3.47	3.29	3.57	2.87	2.69	2.54	2.67	Income Return %
—	—	24.26	9.05	15.96	15.56	8.72	-4.45	-7.35	-13.01	19.86	7.90	Capital Return %
—	—	32	63	51	21	42	60	45	36	28	22	Total Rtn % Rank Cat
—	0.14	0.36	0.44	0.49	0.51	0.55	0.64	0.49	0.43	0.35	0.38	Income $
—	0.01	0.13	0.23	0.21	0.25	0.13	0.14	0.06	0.00	0.00	0.00	Capital Gains $
—	0.00	0.00	0.00	0.00	0.00	0.00	0.00	0.00	0.01	0.00	0.00	Expense Ratio %
—	7.10	4.42	3.98	3.72	3.43	3.47	3.59	2.69	2.98	2.39	2.36	Income Ratio %
—	—	1	3	2	5	3	12	16	15	5	6	Turnover Rate %
—	35	235	826	1,358	2,202	3,441	3,911	4,243	3,985	5,649	7,002	Net Assets $mil

Performance 12-31-04

	1st Qtr	2nd Qtr	3rd Qtr	4th Qtr	Total
2000	3.46	-1.59	0.44	-3.08	-0.88
2001	-7.01	4.25	-7.91	7.00	-4.48
2002	0.63	-6.11	-10.77	6.39	-10.32
2003	-2.23	12.23	2.85	8.46	22.40
2004	2.83	-0.29	0.36	7.45	10.57

Trailing	Total Return%	+/- S&P 500	+/- DJ 60%	%Rank Cat	Growth of $10,000
3 Mo	7.45	-1.78	-0.03	36	10,745
6 Mo	7.84	0.65	0.31	24	10,784
1 Yr	10.57	-0.30	-0.60	22	11,057
3 Yr Avg	6.67	3.09	-0.59	20	12,137
5 Yr Avg	2.82	5.12	-2.42	36	11,492
10 Yr Avg	10.22	-1.85	-0.27	31	26,461
15 Yr Avg	—	—	—	—	—

Tax Analysis	Tax-Adj Rtn%	%Rank Cat	Tax-Cost Rat	%Rank Cat
3 Yr (estimated)	5.78	17	0.83	58
5 Yr (estimated)	1.72	31	1.07	49
10 Yr (estimated)	8.73	18	1.35	20

Potential Capital Gain Exposure: 12% of assets

Rating and Risk

Time Period	Load-Adj Return %	Morningstar Rtn vs Cat	Morningstar Risk vs Cat	Morningstar Risk-Adj Rating
1 Yr	10.57			
3 Yr	6.67	+Avg	Avg	★★★★
5 Yr	2.82	Avg	Avg	★★★
10 Yr	10.22	+Avg	Avg	★★★★
Incept	9.88			

Other Measures	Standard Index S&P 500	Best Fit Index MSCI World
Alpha	3.5	2.1
Beta	0.63	0.64
R-Squared	96	97

Standard Deviation	10.23
Mean	6.67
Sharpe Ratio	0.52

Portfolio Analysis 09-30-04

Total Stocks:0 Share change since 06-30-04	Sectors	P/E Ratio	YTD Return %	% Net Assets
⊕ Vanguard Tota Stock Mkt	—	—	—	34.97
⊕ Vanguard Asset Allocation	—	—	—	24.93
⊕ Vanguard Tota Intl Stock	—	—	—	10.09

Total Fixed-Income:0	Date of Maturity	Amount $000	Value $000	% Net Assets
Vanguard Total Bond Marke		186,511	1,919,196	29.91

Equity Style
Style: Blend
Size: Large-Cap

Value Measures		Rel Category
Price/Earnings	16.13	0.97
Price/Book	2.37	0.97
Price/Sales	1.25	0.95
Price/Cash Flow	6.72	0.93
Dividend Yield %	1.78	1.13

Growth Measures	%	Rel Category
Long-Term Erngs	11.18	0.96
Book Value	-15.39	NMF
Sales	4.05	0.78
Cash Flow	4.14	0.52
Historical Erngs	10.35	0.95

Market Cap %			
Giant	46.1	Small	3.8
Large	32.8	Micro	1.4
Mid	15.8	Avg $mil:	27,487

Composition

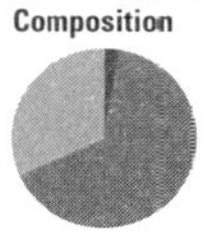

Cash	2.6
Stocks	65.5
Bonds	31.7
Other	0.1
Foreign (% of Stock)	15.0

Fixed-Income Style
Duration: Interm-Term
Quality: High

Avg Eff Duration [1]	4.8 Yrs
Avg Eff Maturity	7.7 Yrs
Avg Credit Quality	AAA
Avg Wtd Coupon	5.84%

[1]figure provided by fund as of 09-30-04

Sector Weightings	% of Stocks	Rel S&P 500	3 Year High	3 Year Low
Info	20.22	0.94		
Software	3.75	0.87	4	4
Hardware	8.57	0.84	10	7
Media	3.74	0.97	4	3
Telecom	4.16	1.32	5	4
Service	47.45	1.02		
Health	12.01	0.96	14	12
Consumer	8.59	0.95	9	8
Business	4.73	1.17	5	5
Financial	22.12	1.07	22	21
Mfg	32.32	1.01		
Goods	9.75	1.05	11	10
Ind Mtrls	12.04	0.95	12	11
Energy	7.35	1.03	7	6
Utilities	3.18	1.07	3	3

Morningstar's Take by William Samuel Rocco 11-14-04

Vanguard LifeStrategy Moderate Growth has real appeal as a stand-alone offering.

Investors who lack the means--or the desire--to construct a broad portfolio of offerings themselves should note that this fund of funds provides exceptional diversification in one package. It invests 30% of its assets in Vanguard Total Bond Market Index, which owns several thousand higher-quality U.S. government and corporate credits. And it divides its dedicated equity exposure between Vanguard Total Stock Market Index (35% of assets) and Vanguard Total International Stock Index (10% of assets), so it provides expansive exposure to domestic and overseas stocks.

Meanwhile, this fund devotes the final 25% of its assets to a moderate-allocation offering, Vanguard Asset Allocation, which has the leeway to make bold composition calls and readily does so. (That offering has kept 80%-90% of its assets in equities since the summer of 2003, and it completely avoided bonds for most of the 12 months prior to that.) Thus, one-stop shoppers need to understand that this fund's overall asset mix is subject to prompt and pronounced changes.

Investors who are comfortable with those sorts of asset-mix fluctuations and the risks that come with them will find quite a bit to like here. Indeed, while the average moderate-allocation has posted an 8.4% annualized return over the past 10 years, this fund has earned a 9.5% annualized gain, as Vanguard Asset Allocation's composition calls have generally been on the mark and the other underlying funds have been good performers. It has also kept volatility under control--and it never has had a bad calendar year--thanks to its diversification. And it pays out a relatively attractive yield, although it often sports an above-average equity stake, largely because its costs are quite low. (Its underlying funds are cheap, and it doesn't tack on its own fees like many funds of funds do.)

This fund is a terrific stand-alone offering.

Address:	PO Box 2600 Valley Forge PA 19482 800-662-7447
Web Address:	www.vanguard.com
Inception:	09-30-94 *
Advisor:	Vanguard Advisers, Inc.
Subadvisor:	None
NTF Plans:	N/A

Minimum Purchase:	$3000	Add: $100	IRA: $1000
Min Auto Inv Plan:	$3000	Add: $50	
Sales Fees:	No-load		
Management Fee:	—		
Actual Fees:	—	Dist:	
Expense Projections:	3Yr:$90	5Yr:$157	10Yr:$356
Income Distrib:	Semi-Annually		

Vanguard Long-Tm InvGrde

Analyst Pick

Ticker	Load	NAV	Yield	SEC Yield	Total Assets	Mstar Category
VWESX	None	$9.55	5.5%	5.29%	$4,881 mil	Long-Term Bond

Governance and Management

Fiduciary Grade: B

Portfolio Manager(s)

Seasoned. Earl McEvoy of esteemed subadvisor Wellington Management Company has managed this fund since March 1994. McEvoy also runs Vanguard High-Yield Corporate and the bond portion of Vanguard Wellesley Income's balanced portfolio, where he has posted impressive results.

Strategy

The fund invests mainly in high-quality corporate bonds, but it may also invest up to 20% of assets in Treasuries and other government securities. Starting in mid-2001, the fund could invest up to 5% of assets in high-yield debt, but it has barely endeavored to do so yet. The fund's duration is kept within 20% of the Lehman Brothers Long Credit A or Better Index's, meaning that it tends to be more sensitive to interest-rate shifts than many of its long-term bond peers. Over the past year or so, the fund's duration has ranged from 9.1 to 10.9 years.

Historical Profile

Return Above Avg
Risk High
Rating ★★★★ Above Avg

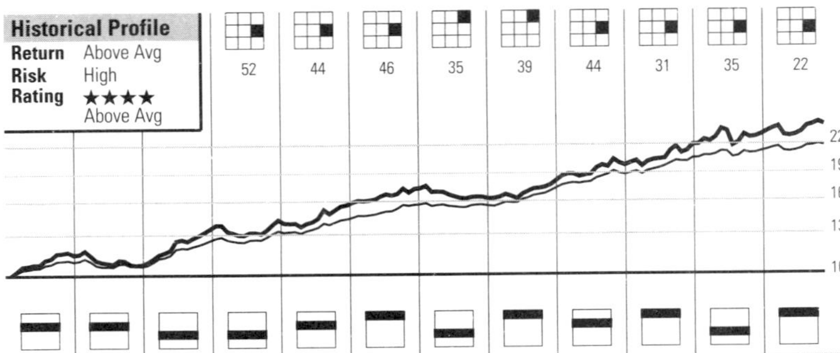

1993	1994	1995	1996	1997	1998	1999	2000	2001	2002	2003	12-04	History
9.22	8.05	9.48	8.79	9.26	9.29	8.11	8.45	8.68	9.23	9.27	9.55	NAV
14.49	-5.30	26.40	1.20	13.78	9.21	-6.23	11.76	9.57	13.22	6.26	8.94	Total Return %
4.74	-2.38	7.93	-2.43	4.13	0.52	-5.41	0.13	1.13	2.97	2.16	4.60	+/-LB Aggr
-1.67	1.80	-3.55	1.06	-0.74	-2.56	1.42	-4.40	2.29	-1.59	0.39	0.38	+/-LB LongTerm
7.45	6.95	8.05	6.79	7.21	6.56	6.25	7.30	6.86	6.60	5.85	5.77	Income Return %
7.04	-12.25	18.35	-5.59	6.57	2.65	-12.48	4.46	2.71	6.62	0.41	3.17	Capital Return %
50	40	53	63	32	9	75	8	26	10	63	17	Total Rtn % Rank Cat
0.64	0.62	0.63	0.62	0.61	0.59	0.56	0.57	0.56	0.56	0.53	0.52	Income $
0.26	0.07	0.00	0.15	0.07	0.21	0.06	0.00	0.00	0.00	0.00	0.00	Capital Gains $
0.31	0.30	0.32	0.31	0.28	0.32	0.30	0.30	0.30	0.32	0.31	0.28	Expense Ratio %
7.68	6.71	7.37	7.03	7.06	6.87	6.26	6.59	7.02	6.48	6.24	5.64	Income Ratio %
50	77	43	49	30	33	43	7	17	39	33	11	Turnover Rate %
3,168	2,552	3,356	3,412	3,637	4,153	3,724	3,704	3,550	3,753	3,851	4,213	Net Assets $mil

Performance 12-31-04

	1st Qtr	2nd Qtr	3rd Qtr	4th Qtr	Total
2000	2.64	0.31	3.41	4.97	11.76
2001	3.79	-0.10	4.72	0.90	9.57
2002	-0.59	4.29	7.96	1.16	13.22
2003	1.96	6.48	-2.18	0.04	6.26
2004	4.90	-5.01	6.48	2.67	8.94

Trailing	Total Return%	+/- LB Aggr	+/- LB LongTerm	%Rank Cat	Growth of $10,000
3 Mo	2.67	1.72	0.50	24	10,267
6 Mo	9.33	5.15	0.27	21	10,933
1 Yr	8.94	4.60	0.38	17	10,894
3 Yr Avg	9.44	3.25	-0.24	26	13,108
5 Yr Avg	9.92	2.21	-0.54	21	16,047
10 Yr Avg	9.11	1.39	-0.61	18	23,914
15 Yr Avg	9.03	1.33	-0.22	20	36,575

Tax Analysis	Tax-Adj Rtn%	%Rank Cat	Tax-Cost Rat	%Rank Cat
3 Yr (estimated)	7.15	21	2.09	61
5 Yr (estimated)	7.40	21	2.29	55
10 Yr (estimated)	6.28	18	2.59	69

Potential Capital Gain Exposure: 9% of assets

Rating and Risk

Time Period	Load-Adj Return %	Morningstar Rtn vs Cat	Morningstar Risk vs Cat	Morningstar Risk-Adj Rating
1 Yr	8.94			
3 Yr	9.44	+Avg	High	★★★
5 Yr	9.92	+Avg	High	★★★★
10 Yr	9.11	+Avg	+Avg	★★★★
Incept	9.14			

Other Measures	Standard Index LB Aggr	Best Fit Index LB LongTerm
Alpha	-2.0	0.0
Beta	2.14	0.98
R-Squared	90	98
Standard Deviation	10.53	
Mean	9.44	
Sharpe Ratio	0.77	

Portfolio Analysis 09-30-04

Total Fixed-Income:202	Date of Maturity	Amount $000	Value $000	% Net Assets
Illinois St 5.1%	06-01-33	113,900	107,893	2.37
Hartford Life 7.375%	03-01-31	57,500	68,679	1.51
Natl Rural Utils Coop Fi	03-01-32	50,000	64,830	1.42
Us Bk Natl Assn 6.3%	02-04-14	54,000	59,982	1.32
Intl Busn Machs 7%	10-30-25	50,000	58,450	1.28
Hydro-Quebec 9.4%	02-01-21	40,000	57,258	1.26
Wal Mart Stores 7.55%	02-15-30	45,000	57,015	1.25
Goldman Sachs Grp 6.125%	02-15-33	55,725	56,126	1.23
Intl Bk For Recon&Dev 7.	01-19-23	43,320	55,672	1.22
New York Life Ins 144A 5	05-15-33	52,775	53,167	1.17
Aluminum 6.75%	01-15-28	45,000	51,355	1.13
Liberty Mut Ins 144A 8.5	05-15-25	43,335	51,159	1.12
General Elec Cap 8.125%	05-15-12	42,000	50,988	1.12
Proc & Gambl Pft Shr Tr	01-01-21	35,000	47,496	1.04
Du Pont E I De Nemours 6	01-15-28	42,100	47,341	1.04
Dow Chem 7.375%	11-01-29	40,000	46,557	1.02
Royal Bk Scotland Grp 5%	10-01-14	46,025	46,416	1.02
General Elec Cap 6.75%	03-15-32	38,975	44,912	0.99
Caterpillar 6.625%	07-15-28	39,000	44,210	0.97
Bellsouth 6.875%	10-15-31	40,000	43,513	0.96

Current Investment Style

Duration: Short Int Long — Quality: High Med Low

1 figure provided by fund

Avg Eff Duration[1]	11.0 Yrs
Avg Eff Maturity	20.5 Yrs
Avg Credit Quality	A
Avg Wtd Coupon	6.83%
Avg Wtd Price	113.85% of par

Coupon Range	% of Bonds	Rel Cat
0% PIK	0.0	0.0
0% to 6%	22.6	0.6
6% to 8%	67.3	1.4
8% to 10%	10.1	0.7
More than 10%	0.0	0.0

1.00=Category Average

Credit Analysis	% bonds 09-30-04		
US Govt	0	BB	0
AAA	7	B	0
AA	29	Below B	0
A	50	NR/NA	1
BBB	13		

Sector Breakdown	% of assets
US Treasuries	0
TIPS	0
US Agency	0
Mortgage Pass-Throughs	0
Mortgage CMO	0
Mortgage ARM	0
US Corporate	89
Asset-Backed	1
Convertible	0
Municipal	3
Corporate Inflation-Protected	0
Foreign Corporate	4
Foreign Govt	0

Composition			
Cash	2.9	Bonds	97.1
Stocks	0.0	Other	0.0

Special Securities	
Restricted/Illiquid Secs	5
Exotic Mortgage-Backed	0
Emerging-Markets Secs	0
Options/Futures/Warrants	No

Morningstar's Take by Dieter Bardy 10-01-04

As recent performance shows, this fund is best approached with patience.

In July 2004, Vanguard Long-Term Corporate Bond underwent a name change to Vanguard Long-Term Investment-Grade. The prospectus language also changed in order to give manager Earl McEvoy flexibility to drift into other sectors such as mortgages, U.S. agency and/or U.S. Treasury debt. We don't think this change should worry investors. McEvoy argues that he will not invest there except in an extreme environment where there are no other suitable long-term corporate investments.

The Fund has had quite a volatile year. In anticipation of Federal Reserve rate increases, bond investors pushed prices down early in the year. As a result the fund lost 5.18% in April alone. But falling long-term rates have provided a strong tailwind in the months since. For the year-to-date period through Sept. 30, 2004, the fund is up 6.1% compared with its typical peer's 3.9% gain.

But it has behaved in much the way that we would have expected, given that it courts more interest-rate risk than its typical long-term bond peer. McEvoy manages duration (a measure of interest-rate sensitivity) around the Lehman Brothers Long Credit Index, which usually has a longer-than-average duration than the typical long-term bond fund. For example, the fund's duration currently stands at 11 years, which is almost twice as long as its typical rival's 6.3 years. So when interest rates rise, we expect to see this fund lag.

But even though this fund has had a bumpy ride this year, it has treated investors well over the long haul. Indeed, all of its returns over longer time periods rank in the category's top quartile. So while this fund may provide unsteady returns during times of rising interest rates, its skilled manager and rock-bottom costs make it a good choice for the long term.

Address:	PO Box 2600 Valley Forge PA 19482 800-662-7447
Web Address:	www.vanguard.com
Inception:	07-09-73
Advisor:	Wellington Management Company, LLP
Subadvisor:	None
NTF Plans:	N/A

Minimum Purchase:	$3000	Add: $100	IRA: $1000
Min Auto Inv Plan:	$3000	Add: $50	
Sales Fees:	No-load		
Management Fee:	0.29%		
Actual Fees:	Mgt:0.29%	Dist: —	
Expense Projections:	3Yr:$100	5Yr:$174	10Yr:$393
Income Distrib:	Monthly		

Vanguard Lg-Tm T/E

Analyst Pick	Ticker	Load	NAV	Yield	SEC Yield	Total Assets	Mstar Category
✔	VWLTX	None	$11.48	4.5%	3.56%	$1,954 mil	Muni National Long

Governance and Management

Fiduciary Grade: B

Portfolio Manager(s)

Christopher Ryon assumed day-to-day responsibilities for this fund in 1996. Ian MacKinnon, who as Vanguard's fixed-income director set the fund's duration range, retired in June 2003. He has since been replaced by Bob Auwaerter.

Strategy

This fund's strategy is fairly straightforward. Its duration (a measure of interest-rate sensitivity) is typically shorter than the category norm, and at least 75% of its assets are required to be invested in bonds rated A or better. Management attempts to add value by making modest duration shifts and rotating among states and sectors.

Historical Profile

Return High
Risk High
Rating ★★★★★ Highest

Investment Style: Fixed Income — Income Rtn %Rank Cat: 25, 23, 13, 12, 11, 17, 20, 21, 16

▼ Manager Change
▽ Partial Manager Change

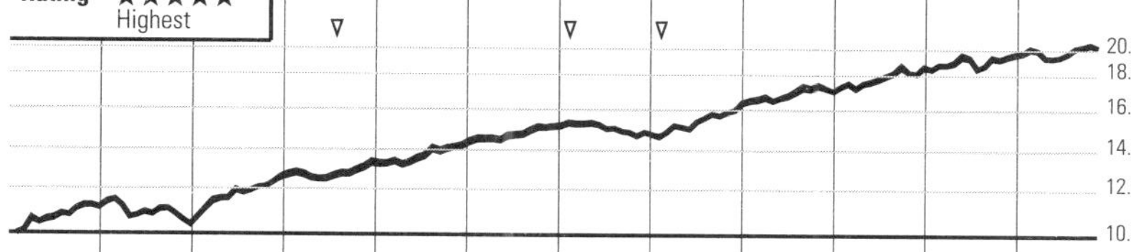

Growth of $10,000
— Investment Values of Fund
— Investment Values of LB Muni

Performance Quartile (within Category)

1993	1994	1995	1996	1997	1998	1999	2000	2001	2002	2003	12-04	History
11.29	9.88	11.09	10.95	11.29	11.26	10.31	11.07	10.98	11.48	11.54	11.48	NAV
13.45	-5.76	18.72	4.41	9.29	6.02	-3.53	13.32	4.54	10.12	5.21	4.12	Total Return %
1.17	-0.59	1.26	-0.02	0.10	-0.46	-1.47	1.64	-0.59	0.52	-0.10	-0.36	+/-LB Muni
-0.93	1.58	-2.25	-0.05	-1.55	-0.80	1.15	-1.92	-0.33	0.09	-1.12	-2.44	+/-LB Muni 20YR
5.98	5.57	6.21	5.41	5.51	5.24	5.14	5.68	5.16	4.99	4.65	4.61	Income Return %
7.47	-11.33	12.51	-1.00	3.78	0.78	-8.67	7.64	-0.62	5.13	0.56	-0.49	Capital Return %
23	28	21	17	42	20	21	8	21	8	32	35	Total Rtn % Rank Cat
0.62	0.61	0.60	0.59	0.59	0.58	0.57	0.57	0.56	0.54	0.52	0.52	Income $
0.21	0.16	0.00	0.02	0.06	0.12	0.00	0.00	0.03	0.05	0.00	0.00	Capital Gains $
0.20	0.20	0.21	0.20	0.19	0.21	0.18	0.19	0.19	0.17	0.17	0.15	Expense Ratio %
5.81	5.56	5.87	5.45	5.37	5.13	5.13	5.46	5.07	4.80	4.59	4.57	Income Ratio %
36	45	35	26	9	18	15	25	16	15	11	11	Turnover Rate %
1,104	920	1,114	1,142	1,291	1,537	1,487	1,746	1,187	1,248	1,146	1,127	Net Assets $mil

Performance 12-31-04

	1st Qtr	2nd Qtr	3rd Qtr	4th Qtr	Total
2000	3.46	1.57	2.30	5.42	13.32
2001	2.35	0.46	2.98	-1.26	4.54
2002	1.13	3.79	5.38	-0.45	10.12
2003	0.72	2.97	0.12	1.33	5.21
2004	1.38	-2.50	4.33	0.97	4.12

Trailing	Total Return%	+/- LB Muni	+/- LB Muni 20YR	%Rank Cat	Growth of $10,000
3 Mo	0.97	-0.28	-1.01	67	10,097
6 Mo	5.34	0.15	-1.41	26	10,534
1 Yr	4.12	-0.36	-2.44	35	10,412
3 Yr Avg	6.45	0.01	-1.18	14	12,062
5 Yr Avg	7.40	0.20	-1.14	8	14,290
10 Yr Avg	7.07	0.01	-0.88	6	19,801
15 Yr Avg	6.87	-0.12	-0.78	12	27,092

Tax Analysis	Tax-Adj Rtn%	%Rank Cat	Tax-Cost Rat	%Rank Cat
3 Yr (estimated)	6.42	9	0.03	9
5 Yr (estimated)	7.37	5	0.03	11
10 Yr (estimated)	7.01	5	0.06	25

Potential Capital Gain Exposure: 8% of assets

Rating and Risk

Time Period	Load-Adj Return %	Morningstar Rtn vs Cat	Morningstar Risk vs Cat	Morningstar Risk-Adj Rating
1 Yr	4.12			
3 Yr	6.45	+Avg	High	★★★★
5 Yr	7.40	High	High	★★★★★
10 Yr	7.07	High	+Avg	★★★★★
Incept	6.70			

Other Measures	Standard Index LB Aggr	Best Fit Index LB Muni
Alpha	-1.1	-1.1
Beta	1.23	1.23
R-Squared	97	97
Standard Deviation	6.29	
Mean	6.45	
Sharpe Ratio	0.82	

Portfolio Analysis 09-30-04

Total Fixed-Income:228	Date of Maturity	Amount $000	Value $000	% Net Assets
New York St Environmenta	06-15-20	37,090	40,316	2.12
Massachusetts St Wtr Res	07-15-19	32,000	39,413	2.07
Lower Colo Riv Auth 5.87	05-15-16	27,500	31,104	1.63
Texas Mun Pwr Agy	09-01-13	38,815	27,097	1.42
Met Govt Nashville & Dav	10-01-32	25,500	25,500	1.34
Manchester N H Arpt 5.62	01-01-30	23,000	25,012	1.31
Wisconsin St Clean Wtr 6	06-01-11	20,500	24,376	1.28
Philadelphia Pa Wtr & Wa	06-15-10	20,000	24,102	1.27
Chicago Ill Met Wtr Recl	01-01-11	20,000	23,766	1.25
San Bernardino Cnty Cali	08-01-24	18,000	23,467	1.23
Colorado Dept Transn 6%	06-15-12	20,000	23,252	1.22
Texas City Tex Indl Dev	10-01-20	17,000	22,360	1.18
Texas Mun Pwr Agy	09-01-17	39,235	22,029	1.16
Texas Wtr Dev Brd 6.4%	07-15-10	17,425	20,589	1.08
Detroit Mich Sew Disp 5.	07-01-29	18,000	20,378	1.07

Current Investment Style

Duration: Short Int Long; Quality: High Med Low

[1]Avg Eff Duration	6.3 Yrs
Avg Eff Maturity	8.0 Yrs
Avg Credit Quality	AAA
Avg Wtd Coupon	4.93%
Avg Wtd Price	106.88% of par

[1]figure provided by fund

Credit Analysis	% bonds 09-30-04		
US Govt	0	BB	0
AAA	75	B	0
AA	16	Below B	0
A	6	NR/NA	0
BBB	3		

Top 5 States	% bonds		
TX	13.0	CO	6.9
NY	11.6	MA	6.9
CA	10.7		

Composition			
Cash	0.0	Bonds	100.0
Stocks	0.0	Other	0.0

Special Securities	
Restricted/Illiquid Secs	0
Options/Futures/Warrants	No

Sector Weightings	% of Bonds	Rel Cat
General Obligation	31.1	1.19
Utilities	16.9	1.27
Health	3.6	0.46
Water/Waste	19.8	1.78
Housing	0.0	0.00
Education	9.9	0.86
Transportation	8.4	1.12
COP/Lease	2.1	1.00
Industrial	6.7	0.52
Misc Revenue	0.0	0.00
Demand	1.6	6.00

Morningstar's Take by Dieter Bardy 12-15-04

Vanguard Long-Term Tax-Exempt achieves great success thanks to its low fees.

This fund is all about low costs. Its expense ratio checks in at just 0.17%, while its average peer's clocks in at 0.85%. That advantage provides the fund a nearly insurmountable advantage and represents a vehicle to drive the fund's strategy. Indeed, manager Chris Ryon doesn't need to overreach for yield by purchasing higher-risk bonds, because the fund's low fees already provide a 65 basis-point advantage. Typically the fund holds upward of 75% of its assets in the highest-rated AAA bonds or better, while its average muni national long-term peer holds closer to 60% in such high-quality issues.

Thanks to its cost advantage, the fund doesn't sacrifice much in the way of return either. For the year-to-date period through Dec. 13, 2004, the fund returned 4%, while its typical rival gained just 3.8%. The fund's long-term returns look even more impressive. In fact, the fund's three-, five-, and 10-year trailing returns all rank in the category's upper reaches. Further, the fund has outperformed its average category peer each of the last 12 years.

However, the fund's interest-rate risk should not be overlooked. One of the trade-offs of holding higher quality bonds is added interest-rate sensitivity. Thus, when interest rates rise, this fund can suffer. For example, when rates spiked in April 2004, the fund lost 2.8%, while its typical peer dropped 2.4%. The fund's low expense ratio provides a cushion for the fund, but if rates trend higher, further losses are possible. When rates moved higher in 1994 and 1999, for example, the fund lost 5.8% and 3.5%, respectively.

That said, this fund remains a keeper for the long haul. This Analyst Pick's winning low-cost approach and experienced management make it a category favorite.

Address:	PO Box 2600 Valley Forge PA 19482 800-662-7447
Web Address:	www.vanguard.com
Inception:	09-01-77
Advisor:	Vanguard Advisers, Inc.
Subadvisor:	None
NTF Plans:	N/A

Minimum Purchase:	$3000	Add: $100	IRA: $1000
Min Auto Inv Plan:	$3000	Add: $50	
Sales Fees:	No-load		
Management Fee:	0.15%		
Actual Fees:	Mgt:0.15%	Dist:	
Expense Projections:	3Yr:$55	5Yr:$96	10Yr:$217
Income Distrib:	Monthly		

Vanguard Long-Tm US Try

Analyst Pick

Ticker	Load	NAV	Yield	SEC Yield	Total Assets	Mstar Category
VUSTX	None	$11.51	5.0%	4.60%	$1,866 mil	Long Government

Governance and Management

Fiduciary Grade: B

Portfolio Manager(s)

David Glocke assumed management responsibilities in May 2001. He joined the firm in 1997. Ian MacKinnon, the head of Vanguard's fixed-income group, had worked on the fund since its 1986 inception. However, Bob Auwaerter recently replaced MacKinnon, who retired on June 30. We expect Auwaerter--who is a veteran of the firm's fixed-income group--to ably succeed MacKinnon.

Strategy

Management invests primarily in long-term U.S. Treasury bonds. Most holdings won't mature for at least 10 years, and the fund strives to maintain an overall average maturity between 15 and 25 years. As a result, it tends to be more sensitive to interest-rate movements than its average peer. Management does not make big duration bets, however, and keeps that figure within a half year (approximately +/- 5%) of the Lehman Brothers Long-Term U.S. Treasury Index's. The fund can also invest in government-agency bonds, but that allocation hasn't exceeded 15% of assets in recent years.

Historical Profile

Return Above Avg
Risk Average
Rating ★★★★ Above Avg

Investment Style
Fixed Income
Income Rtn %Rank Cat

	1996	1997	1998	1999	2000	2001	2002	2003	12-04
Income Rtn %Rank Cat	38	12	16	36	35	34	11	19	3

▼ Manager Change
▽ Partial Manager Change

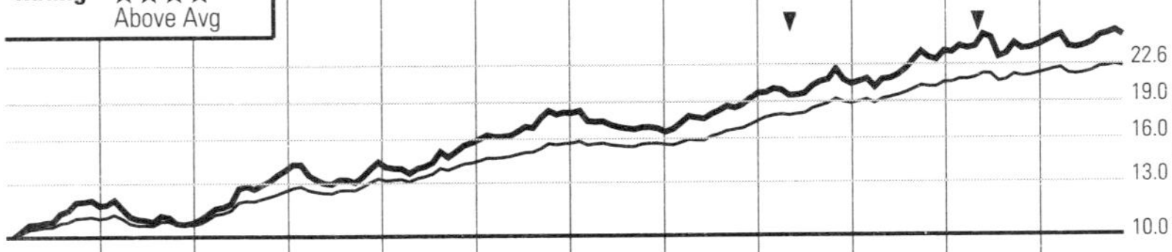

Growth of $10,000
▬ Investment Values of Fund
— Investment Values of LB Aggr

Performance Quartile (within Category)

1993	1994	1995	1996	1997	1998	1999	2000	2001	2002	2003	12-04	History
10.57	9.05	10.79	9.96	10.64	11.36	9.67	10.90	10.76	11.76	11.37	11.51	NAV
16.79	-7.04	30.09	-1.26	13.90	13.05	-8.66	19.72	4.31	16.67	2.68	7.12	Total Return %
7.04	-4.12	11.62	-4.89	4.25	4.36	-7.84	8.09	-4.13	6.42	-1.42	2.78	+/-LB Aggr
-0.63	0.69	-0.81	-0.42	-1.22	-0.36	0.07	-0.57	-0.03	-0.32	0.07	-0.82	+/-LB LTGvtBd
7.25	6.50	7.66	6.25	6.67	6.10	5.57	6.61	5.67	5.59	4.90	5.17	Income Return %
9.54	-13.54	22.43	-7.51	7.23	6.95	-14.23	13.11	-1.36	11.08	-2.22	1.95	Capital Return %
37	57	34	60	50	36	57	42	47	59	57	51	Total Rtn % Rank Cat
0.69	0.66	0.67	0.65	0.64	0.63	0.61	0.62	0.60	0.59	0.56	0.57	Income $
0.18	0.12	0.23	0.01	0.00	0.00	0.12	0.00	0.00	0.15	0.14	0.07	Capital Gains $
0.27	0.26	0.28	0.27	0.25	0.27	0.27	0.28	0.29	0.29	0.28	0.26	Expense Ratio %
7.26	6.44	7.02	6.57	6.66	6.38	5.69	5.98	6.00	5.52	5.19	4.81	Income Ratio %
170	7	85	105	31	18	22	43	49	64	100	64	Turnover Rate %
823	644	917	918	1,035	1,416	1,224	1,358	1,373	1,682	1,489	1,444	Net Assets $mil

Performance 12-31-04

	1st Qtr	2nd Qtr	3rd Qtr	4th Qtr	Total
2000	7.52	1.16	2.71	7.17	19.72
2001	1.47	-1.62	6.64	-2.02	4.31
2002	-1.49	5.97	11.64	0.12	16.67
2003	1.40	5.05	-2.57	-1.07	2.68
2004	5.24	-5.23	5.94	1.38	7.12

Trailing	Total Return%	+/- LB Aggr	+/- LB LTGvtBd	%Rank Cat	Growth of $10,000
3 Mo	1.38	0.43	-0.19	68	10,138
6 Mo	7.40	3.22	-0.69	41	10,740
1 Yr	7.12	2.78	-0.82	51	10,712
3 Yr Avg	8.67	2.48	-0.35	57	12,833
5 Yr Avg	9.89	2.18	-0.33	58	16,025
10 Yr Avg	9.25	1.53	-0.41	27	24,222
15 Yr Avg	8.73	1.03	-0.42	34	35,095

Tax Analysis	Tax-Adj Rtn%	%Rank Cat	Tax-Cost Rat	%Rank Cat
3 Yr (estimated)	6.48	67	2.02	72
5 Yr (estimated)	7.58	58	2.10	57
10 Yr (estimated)	6.64	34	2.39	80

Potential Capital Gain Exposure: 11% of assets

Rating and Risk

Time Period	Load-Adj Return %	Morningstar Rtn vs Cat	Morningstar Risk vs Cat	Morningstar Risk-Adj Rating
1 Yr	7.12			
3 Yr	8.67	Avg	Avg	★★★
5 Yr	9.89	Avg	Avg	★★★
10 Yr	9.25	+Avg	Avg	★★★★
Incept	8.67			

Other Measures	Standard Index LB Aggr	Best Fit Index LB Long Tr
Alpha	-3.4	0.0
Beta	2.31	0.97
R-Squared	95	100

Standard Deviation	10.98
Mean	8.67
Sharpe Ratio	0.67

Portfolio Analysis 09-30-04

Total Fixed-Income:21	Date of Maturity	Amount $000	Value $000	% Net Assets
US Treasury Bond 7.875%	02-15-21	241,581	326,852	17.68
US Treasury Bond 8.125%	08-15-19	182,523	249,772	13.51
US Treasury Bond 6.125%	08-15-29	212,000	247,080	13.37
US Treasury Bond 8.125%	05-15-21	116,875	161,798	8.75
US Treasury Bond 6.375%	08-15-27	101,650	121,376	6.57
US Treasury Bond 8.875%	02-15-19	59,663	86,175	4.66
US Treasury Bond 7.125%	02-15-23	59,000	75,207	4.07
Private Expt Fdg 7.25%	06-15-10	64,080	74,641	4.04
US Treasury Bond 6.875%	08-15-25	52,000	65,284	3.53
US Treasury Bond 6.25%	08-15-23	52,500	61,302	3.32
US Treasury Bond 6%	02-15-26	51,500	58,710	3.18
US Treasury Bond 6.625%	02-15-27	43,000	52,722	2.85
US Treasury Bond 6.125%	11-15-27	45,000	52,228	2.83
US Treasury Bond 6.5%	11-15-26	34,300	41,455	2.24
US Treasury Bond 5.5%	08-15-28	31,800	34,190	1.85
Private Expt Fdg 6.07%	04-30-11	29,000	32,142	1.74
US Treasury Bond 8.75%	05-15-17	22,000	31,041	1.68
US Treasury Bond 6.75%	08-15-26	20,585	25,558	1.38
Private Expt Fdg 6.67%	09-15-09	17,000	19,184	1.04
US Treasury Bond 8.75%	08-15-20	9,000	13,033	0.71

Current Investment Style

Duration: Short Int Long — Quality: High Med Low

¹ figure provided by fund

Avg Eff Duration¹	9.9 Yrs
Avg Eff Maturity	17.1 Yrs
Avg Credit Quality	AAA
Avg Wtd Coupon	7.24%
Avg Wtd Price	127.42% of par

Coupon Range	% of Bonds	Rel Cat
0% PIK	0.0	0.0
0% to 6%	5.0	0.1
6% to 8%	65.5	5.7
8% to 10%	29.5	9.0
More than 10%	0.0	0.0

1.00=Category Average

Credit Analysis		% bonds 09-30-04	
US Govt	92	BB	0
AAA	8	B	0
AA	0	Below B	0
A	0	NR/NA	0
BBB	0		

Sector Breakdown	% of assets
US Treasuries	92
TIPS	0
US Agency	7
Mortgage Pass-Throughs	0
Mortgage CMO	0
Mortgage ARM	0
US Corporate	0
Asset-Backed	0
Convertible	0
Municipal	0
Corporate Inflation-Protected	0
Foreign Corporate	0
Foreign Govt	0

Composition			
Cash	0.6	Bonds	99.4
Stocks	0.0	Other	0.0

Special Securities	
Restricted/Illiquid Secs	0
Exotic Mortgage-Backed	—
Emerging-Markets Secs	0
Options/Futures/Warrants	No

Morningstar's Take by Dieter Bardy 12-02-04

Vanguard Long-Term U.S. Treasury is not out of the woods yet, but we like its prospects.

As its name implies, the fund focuses on long-term U.S. government-debt obligations, primarily U.S. Treasuries and agencies. Yet, because of its focus on U.S. Treasury issues (which have no default risk), it is more interest-rate sensitive than other diversified bond funds. But, over the long haul, the fund has made solid gains, landing in the top quartile for the trailing 10-year period. Its longer maturity bonds gave the fund an edge over rivals.

Of course, the rate situation has been different lately. In 2004, the fund has survived the first two rounds of federal rate increases unscathed. For the year to date through Nov. 30, the fund advanced 4.8% compared with the typical long-term government fund's 2.8% gain. This is a big improvement from other years in which the fund faced rising rates, including 1999, when its sensitivity was a burden, leading it down 8.7% versus peers' 8.1% loss.

Although its recent showing is not much better than average, it is a solid gain for a fund that centers its interest-rate sensitivity near its index, the Lehman Brothers Long-Term U.S. Treasury Index. Its duration (a measure of interest-rate sensitivity) is 9.9 years, which is within the range of its typical category peer. But, again, longer-term bonds are often more volatile, so investors must be comfortable waiting out short-term swings.

Lately, manager David Glocke has kept his emphasis on bonds in the market's 15- to 20-year area. He feels this area offers the most reward for its level of relative risk. We think this is an appropriate response because it appears much of the anticipation in rate increases has already been priced into the long end of the market.

This remains a solid fund for investors who want a dedicated long-term U.S. Government fund. Vanguard's low expenses make it even better.

Address:	PO Box 2600 Valley Forge PA 19482 800-662-7447
Web Address:	www.vanguard.com
Inception:	05-19-86
Advisor:	Vanguard Advisers, Inc.
Subadvisor:	None
NTF Plans:	N/A

Minimum Purchase:	$3000	Add: $100	IRA: $1000
Min Auto Inv Plan:	$3000	Add: $50	
Sales Fees:	No-load		
Management Fee:	0.26%		
Actual Fees:	Mgt:0.26%	Dist: —	
Expense Projections:	3Yr:$93	5Yr:$163	10Yr:$368
Income Distrib:	Monthly		

Vanguard LtdTm T/E

Analyst Pick	Ticker	Load	NAV	Yield	SEC Yield	Total Assets	Mstar Category
✔	VMLTX	None	$10.92	2.9%	2.44%	$6,864 mil	Muni National Shor:

Governance and Management

Fiduciary Grade: B

Portfolio Manager(s)

Pam Wisehaupt-Tynan has managed the fund since the start of 1997. She has been with Vanguard since 1981 as an accountant and assistant portfolio manager. Broad interest-rate policy is set by Bob Auwaerter, who has led the firm's fixed-income group since the retirement of Vanguard veteran Ian McKinnon in June 2003.

Strategy

The fund invests in high-quality municipal issues with a combined average maturity of three to four years. At least three fourths of its bonds must be invested in the top three credit-rating categories. Management adjusts the fund's duration within a specified range, depending on its interest-rate outlook.

Historical Profile

Return Above Avg
Risk Average
Rating ★★★★ Above Avg

Investment Style
Fixed Income
Income Rtn %Rank Cat

1993	1994	1995	1996	1997	1998	1999	2000	2001	2002	2003	12-04
19	24	26	19	24	14	17	14	10			

▼ Manager Change
▽ Partial Manager Change

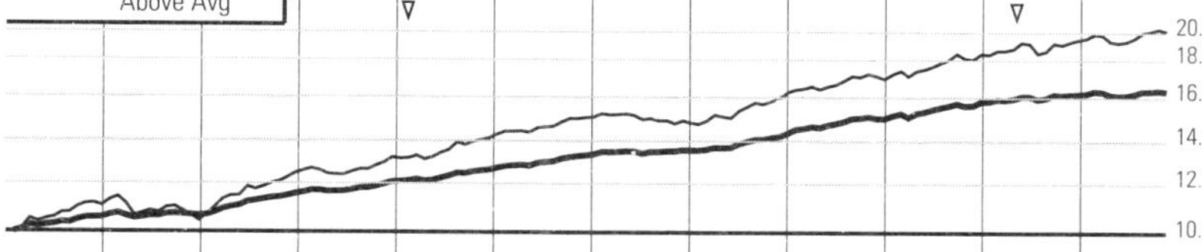

Growth of $10,000
— Investment Values of Fund
— Investment Values of LB Muni

Performance Quartile (within Category)

History

1993	1994	1995	1996	1997	1998	1999	2000	2001	2002	2003	12-04	History
10.82	10.37	10.76	10.71	10.77	10.85	10.55	10.73	10.85	11.11	11.07	10.92	NAV
6.31	0.07	8.57	4.08	5.10	5.12	1.47	6.35	5.58	6.31	2.79	1.53	Total Return %
-5.97	5.24	-8.89	-0.35	-4.09	-1.36	3.53	-5.33	0.45	-3.29	-2.52	-2.95	+/-LB Muni
0.09	-0.61	-0.30	-0.36	-0.38	-0.09	-0.49	0.12	-1.01	-0.41	0.11	-0.25	+/-LB Muni 3YR
4.48	4.31	4.76	4.53	4.51	4.35	4.29	4.58	4.48	3.87	3.15	2.90	Income Return %
1.83	-4.24	3.81	-0.45	0.59	0.77	-2.82	1.77	1.10	2.44	-0.36	-1.37	Capital Return %
57	39	27	28	51	14	27	29	7	31	29	28	Total Rtn % Rank Cat
0.47	0.46	0.48	0.48	0.47	0.46	0.46	0.47	0.47	0.41	0.35	0.32	Income $
0.02	0.00	0.00	0.00	0.00	0.00	0.00	0.00	0.00	0.00	0.00	0.00	Capital Gains $
0.20	0.20	0.21	0.21	0.19	0.21	0.18	0.18	0.19	0.17	0.17	0.14	Expense Ratio %
4.50	4.24	4.51	4.51	4.46	4.27	4.25	4.45	4.40	4.80	3.19	2.89	Income Ratio %
20	21	35	27	28	35	14	32	19	17	13	8	Turnover Rate %
1,818	1,630	1,683	1,789	2,023	2,391	2,569	2,932	2,104	2,773	3,256	3,494	Net Assets $mil

Performance 12-31-04

	1st Qtr	2nd Qtr	3rd Qtr	4th Qtr	Total
2000	1.01	1.32	1.69	2.18	6.35
2001	2.41	1.18	2.02	-0.13	5.58
2002	0.36	2.93	2.20	0.70	6.31
2003	0.64	1.34	0.58	0.20	2.79
2004	0.81	-1.27	1.64	0.36	1.53

Trailing	Total Return%	+/- LB Muni	+/- LB Muni 3YR	%Rank Cat	Growth of $10,000
3 Mo	0.36	-0.89	0.17	27	10,036
6 Mo	2.01	-3.18	-0.09	31	10,201
1 Yr	1.53	-2.95	-0.25	28	10,153
3 Yr Avg	3.52	-2.92	-0.19	27	11,094
5 Yr Avg	4.49	-2.71	-0.29	29	12,456
10 Yr Avg	4.67	-2.39	-0.30	15	15,784
15 Yr Avg	5.05	-1.94	—	17	20,938

Tax Analysis	Tax-Adj Rtn%	%Rank Cat	Tax-Cost Rat	%Rank Cat
3 Yr (estimated)	3.52	21	0.00	1
5 Yr (estimated)	4.49	21	0.00	1
10 Yr (estimated)	4.67	10	0.00	1

Potential Capital Gain Exposure: 1% of assets

Rating and Risk

Time Period	Load-Adj Return %	Morningstar Rtn vs Cat	Morningstar Risk vs Cat	Morningstar Risk-Adj Rating
1 Yr	1.53			
3 Yr	3.52	+Avg	Avg	★★★★
5 Yr	4.49	+Avg	Avg	★★★★
10 Yr	4.67	+Avg	Avg	★★★★
Incept	5.36			

Other Measures	Standard Index LB Aggr	Best Fit Index LB Muni 3YR
Alpha	-0.2	-0.1
Beta	0.47	0.96
R-Squared	88	96

Standard Deviation	2.44
Mean	3.52
Sharpe Ratio	0.89

Portfolio Analysis 09-30-04

Total Fixed-Income:603	Date of Maturity	Amount $000	Value $000	% Net Assets
Harris Cnty Tex Health F	02-15-31	119,080	119,080	1.72
Memphis Tenn Elec Sys 5%	12-01-08	58,050	63,510	0.92
Harris Cnty Tex Health F	12-01-32	58,300	58,300	0.84
Arapahoe Cnty Colo Cap I	08-31-26	280,005	57,513	0.83
North Carolina St 5%	03-01-09	50,000	55,016	0.79
Arapahoe Cnty Colo Cap I	08-31-15	114,235	54,681	0.79
Pennsylvania St 5.25%	02-01-08	50,000	54,681	0.79
Matagorda Cnty Tex Nav D	11-01-29	38,970	40,511	0.58
Texas St Tpk Auth 5%	06-01-08	36,300	39,452	0.57
Kent St Univ Ohio Univ R	05-01-31	38,755	38,755	0.56
New York N Y 5.25%	08-01-09	35,110	38,673	0.56
Cleveland Ohio Arpt Sys	01-01-31	38,500	38,500	0.55
Clark Cnty Nev Sch Dist	06-15-08	33,555	37,176	0.54
Amer Pub Engy Agy Neb Ga	02-01-14	34,896	34,896	0.50
Clark Cnty Nev Sch Dist	06-01-08	30,735	33,494	0.48

Current Investment Style

Duration: Short Int Long; Quality: High Med Low

¹Avg Eff Duration	2.3 Yrs
Avg Eff Maturity	2.5 Yrs
Avg Credit Quality	AA
Avg Wtd Coupon	4.46%
Avg Wtd Price	105.06% of par

¹figure provided by fund

Credit Analysis	% bonds 09-30-04		
US Govt	0	BB	0
AAA	58	B	0
AA	31	Below B	0
A	8	NR/NA	0
BBB	3		

Top 5 States	% bonds		
TX	11.3	OH	5.2
NY	8.3	CA	5.1
IL	5.8		

Composition			
Cash	8.8	Bonds	91.2
Stocks	0.0	Other	0.0

Special Securities	
Restricted/Illiquid Secs	0
Options/Futures/Warrants	No

Sector Weightings	% of Bonds	Rel Cat
General Obligation	50.8	1.44
Utilities	14.9	1.61
Health	3.0	0.41
Water/Waste	7.2	0.63
Housing	1.1	0.14
Education	4.2	0.43
Transportation	7.0	1.65
COP/Lease	0.0	0.00
Industrial	11.9	0.73
Misc Revenue	0.0	—
Demand	0.0	0.00

Morningstar's Take by Lynn Russell 12-22-04

Vanguard Limited-Term Tax-Exempt is one of our favorites.

It's easy to see why this fund has become the largest fund in the muni national short category. (Its sibling, Vanguard Short-Term Tax-Exempt, is next in line). The fund sports ultralow costs, experienced management, and a topnotch long-term record.

The fund's appeal starts with its ultralow expense ratio, which checks in at just 0.17%. The only offering that's less expensive in the category is this fund's Admiral share class, which has a higher minimum initial investment requirement. Given that almost unbeatable head start, manager Pam Wisehaupt-Tynan doesn't have to take many risks with the fund to keep returns competitive. She limits credit risk by keeping more than 90% of the fund's assets in bonds rated AA or AAA, and she limits interest-rate bets by keeping the fund's duration (a measure of interest-rate sensitivity) within a narrow range.

Expecting rising interest rates, Wisehaupt-Tynan kept the fund defensively positioned for much of the year. But with the fund's focus on bonds in a maturity range of one to six years, its duration has still run a bit longer than the category norm. As a result, the fund suffered more than its average muni-short peer when rates spiked in second quarter of 2004. As rates moved back down, the fund made up much of that lost ground. Additionally, good maturity selection has worked in the fund's favor. Overall, the fund gained 1.45% for the year to date through Dec. 21 to land in the category's top third.

That solid year-to-date performance is echoed by the fund's long-term record. The fund's five- and 10-year trailing returns land in the muni short category's top quartile. Given its above-average sensitivity to interest rates, the fund could suffer more than most if rates trend higher. However, given its low costs and strong track record, we think this fund is difficult to beat.

Address:	PO Box 2600 Valley Forge PA 19482 800-662-7447
Web Address:	www.vanguard.com
Inception:	08-31-87
Advisor:	Vanguard Advisers, Inc.
Subadvisor:	None
NTF Plans:	N/A

Minimum Purchase:	$3000	Add: $100	IRA: $1000
Min Auto Inv Plan:	$3000	Add: $50	
Sales Fees:	No-load		
Management Fee:	0.17%		
Actual Fees:	Mgt:0.17%	Dist:	
Expense Projections:	3Yr:$61	5Yr:$107	10Yr:$243
Income Distrib:	Monthly		

Vanguard Mid Cap Growth

Ticker	Load	NAV	Yield	Total Assets	Mstar Category
VMGRX	None	$16.05	0.0%	$512 mil	Mid-Cap Growth

Governance and Management

Fiduciary Grade: B

Portfolio Manager(s)

This fund is advised by Provident Investment Counsel. PIC's mid-cap management team is organized into four two-person teams--each one responsible for building a portfolio of 13-18 mid-growth stocks. Lead managers Evelyn Lapham and John Yoon oversee each team's buy-and-sell activity. The managers' pay is partly tied to the performance of the fund and team subportfolios compared with the Russell Midcap Growth Index.

Strategy

Management begins with a growth universe of about 300 companies, which the team whittles down based on rigorous fundamental research. It looks for companies with at least one catalyst for growth, such as a new or proprietary product, demographic trend, and improving cost structure. It emphasizes companies with high-quality managements that are committed to enhancing shareholder value, while also having extensive risk controls in place. For instance, it will start trimming a name that soaks up more than 3% of assets and will not make huge sector bets.

Historical Profile

Return Average
Risk Above Avg
Rating ★★★ Neutral

Investment Style
Equity
Stock %

1998	1999	2000	2001	2002	2003	12-04
99%	97%	93%	95%	94%	95%	97%

▼ Manager Change
▽ Partial Manager Change

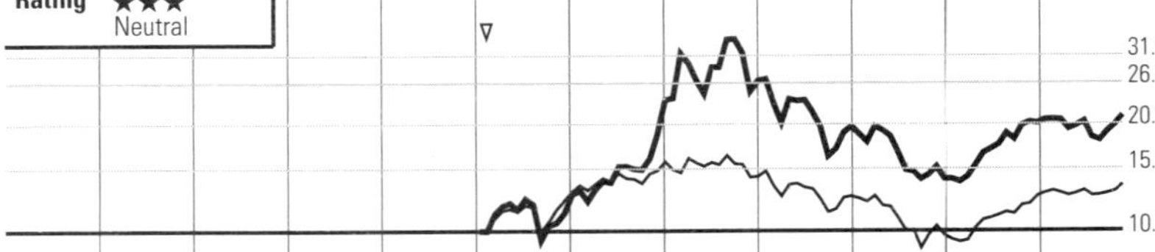

Growth of $10,000
— Investment Values of Fund
— Investment Values of S&P 500

Performance Quartile (within Category)

History

1993	1994	1995	1996	1997	1998	1999	2000	2001	2002	2003	12-04	History
—	—	—	—	10.00	12.63	22.09	18.92	14.12	10.09	14.41	16.05	NAV
—	—	—	—	0.00*	26.30	83.33	12.96	-25.37	-28.54	42.81	11.38	Total Return %
—	—	—	—	—	-2.27	62.29	22.06	-13.49	-6.45	14.14	0.51	+/-S&P 500
—	—	—	—	—	8.44	32.04	24.71	-5.22	-1.13	0.10	-4.10	+/-Russ MG
—	—	—	—	—	0.00	0.00	0.00	0.00	0.00	0.00	0.00	Income Return %
—	—	—	—	—	26.30	83.33	12.96	-25.37	-28.54	42.81	11.38	Capital Return %
—	—	—	—	—	24	24	17	70	59	18	63	Total Rtn % Rank Cat
—	—	—	—	0.00	0.00	0.00	0.00	0.00	0.00	0.00	0.00	Income $
—	—	—	—	0.00	0.00	0.94	6.71	0.00	0.00	0.00	0.00	Capital Gains $
—	—	—	—	—	1.04	1.39	2.14	1.39	1.24	0.48	0.34	Expense Ratio %
—	—	—	—	—	-0.43	-1.03	-1.76	-1.02	-1.02	-0.18	-0.05	Income Ratio %
—	—	—	—	—	167	174	206	149	221	106	102	Turnover Rate %
—	—	—	—	—	7	19	29	33	35	304	512	Net Assets $mil

Performance 12-31-04

	1st Qtr	2nd Qtr	3rd Qtr	4th Qtr	Total
2000	26.35	-2.44	19.65	-23.41	12.96
2001	-23.52	15.48	-30.22	21.10	-25.37
2002	0.07	-15.71	-15.45	0.20	-28.54
2003	1.39	19.45	6.38	10.85	42.81
2004	2.15	-1.09	-6.04	17.32	11.38

Trailing	Total Return%	+/- S&P 500	+/- Russ MG	%Rank Cat	Growth of $10,000
3 Mo	17.32	8.09	3.38	4	11,732
6 Mo	10.23	3.04	1.22	19	11,023
1 Yr	11.38	0.51	-4.10	63	11,138
3 Yr Avg	4.36	0.78	-1.80	45	11,366
5 Yr Avg	-0.85	1.45	2.51	31	9,582
10 Yr Avg	—	—	—	—	—
15 Yr Avg	—	—	—	—	—

Tax Analysis	Tax-Adj Rtn%	%Rank Cat	Tax-Cost Rat	%Rank Cat
3 Yr (estimated)	4.36	37	0.00	1
5 Yr (estimated)	-2.46	35	1.62	69
10 Yr (estimated)	—	—	—	—

Potential Capital Gain Exposure: 15% of assets

Rating and Risk

Time Period	Load-Adj Return %	Morningstar Rtn vs Cat	Morningstar Risk vs Cat	Morningstar Risk-Adj Rating
1 Yr	11.38			
3 Yr	4.36	Avg	+Avg	★★★
5 Yr	-0.85	Avg	+Avg	★★★
10 Yr	—	—	—	—
Incept	12.06			

Other Measures	Standard Index S&P 500	Best Fit Index Russ MG
Alpha	1.4	-1.5
Beta	1.01	0.99
R-Squared	62	89
Standard Deviation	20.23	
Mean	4.36	
Sharpe Ratio	0.15	

Morningstar's Take by Sonya Morris 11-10-04

Vanguard Mid-Cap Growth is a compelling choice, but it's not for the timid.

This offering departs from many of its mid-growth fund peers in a few respects. For starters, research and stock-picking duties are diffused among four pairs of analysts who assemble miniportfolios of 13-18 names apiece. Lead managers Evelyn Lapham and John Yoon run the combined portfolio and control risk by monitoring position sizes and sector bets. Each team seeks companies poised for strong earnings growth driven by catalysts such as new product cycles or broad demographic trends. For example, management recently added Marriott International to the portfolio when its research indicated an increase in business travel at a time of limited room supply.

Many growth funds seek to exploit catalysts, but this fund is more daring than most. First of all, management is willing to pay up if it thinks a company is primed for strong growth. Consequently, the fund's aggregate growth and valuation measures are higher than the mid-growth category norm. Furthermore, management won't shy away from making sector bets, although such wagers are capped at 1.5 times the weightings of the Russell Mid-Cap Growth Index.

The fund's strong growth bias means it often trails when value stocks rule the roost. That's certainly been the case this year, as it was in 2001 and 2002. Indeed, the ride here can be rocky at times. For example, during its worst three months, from July to September 2001, the fund lost 30% of its value, while soaring 67% during its best three-month stretch from December to February 2000. Long-term shareholders who weathered these ups and downs have been amply rewarded. The fund's average annual return since its Dec. 31, 1997, inception lands in the category's top decile.

For investors who can stomach occasional turbulence, this fund is an strong choice.

Portfolio Analysis 09-30-04

Share change since 06-04 Total Stocks:60	Sector	PE	YTD Ret%	% Assets
⊕ Royal Caribbean Cruises	Goods	36.9	58.33	3.43
⊕ Nextel Partners A	Telecom	—	45.28	2.73
⊕ Manpower	Business	18.2	3.24	2.46
☆ Precision Castparts	Ind Mtrls	26.0	44.97	2.42
⊕ Tektronix	Hardware	17.0	-3.86	2.29
⊕ MGI Pharma	Health	—	36.14	2.24
⊕ NII Holdings	Telecom	7.4	90.74	2.16
⊕ Brunswick	Goods	18.1	57.47	2.13
⊕ Cooper Companies	Health	28.4	49.92	2.09
⊕ Cognizant Technology Sol	Business	62.5	85.50	2.02
⊕ VeriSign	Software	—	106.14	1.99
⊕ Rockwell Automation	Ind Mtrls	28.0	41.75	1.98
⊕ Converse Technology	Hardware	—	39.00	1.98
⊕ Iron Mountain	Business	33.7	15.67	1.98
⊕ Protein Design Labs	Health	—	15.42	1.93
⊕ Thermo Electron	Health	27.2	19.80	1.91
⊕ Fossil	Goods	22.6	36.73	1.89
⊕ Monster Worldwide	Business	54.6	53.19	1.86
⊕ Jabil Circuit	Hardware	28.2	-9.61	1.84
⊕ Kinetic Concepts	Health	—	—	1.84

Current Investment Style

Value Blnd Growth — Large Mid Small

Market Cap	%
Giant	0.0
Large	15.1
Mid	82.0
Small	2.9
Micro	0.0
Avg $mil: 3,799	

Value Measures		Rel Category
Price/Earnings	25.13	1.14
Price/Book	2.93	0.98
Price/Sales	1.90	1.07
Price/Cash Flow	9.58	0.99
Dividend Yield %	0.21	0.49

Growth Measures	%	Rel Category
Long-Term Erngs	16.85	1.07
Book Value	7.17	0.71
Sales	7.76	0.90
Cash Flow	5.89	0.48
Historical Erngs	16.41	1.03

Profitability	%	Rel Category
Return on Equity	14.45	1.00
Return on Assets	7.40	1.03
Net Margin	10.41	1.08

Sector Weightings	% of Stocks	Rel S&P 500	3 Year High	3 Year Low
Info	26.79	1.25		
Software	8.29	1.93	14	5
Hardware	10.58	1.04	25	9
Media	2.87	0.75	6	2
Telecom	5.05	1.60	5	0
Service	45.73	0.99		
Health	19.39	1.55	27	15
Consumer	6.07	0.67	27	6
Business	16.19	4.00	17	10
Financial	4.08	0.20	11	2
Mfg	27.46	0.85		
Goods	11.37	1.22	11	0
Ind Mtrls	10.20	0.81	10	1
Energy	5.89	0.82	7	3
Utilities	0.00	0.00	0	0

Composition

Cash	3.2
Stocks	96.8
Bonds	0.0
Other	0.0
Foreign (% of Stock)	1.2

Address:	PO Box 2600 Valley Forge PA 19482 800-662-7447
Web Address:	www.vanguard.com
Inception:	12-31-97*
Advisor:	Provident Investment Counsel, Inc.
Subadvisor:	None
NTF Plans:	Schwab Instl NTF

Minimum Purchase:	$10000	Add: $250	IRA: $1000
Min Auto Inv Plan:	$2000	Add: $100	
Sales Fees:	No-load		
Management Fee:	0.62% mx./0.13% mn., 0.20%A		
Actual Fees:	Mgt:0.62%	Dist: —	
Expense Projections:	3Yr:$208	5Yr:$362	10Yr:$810
Income Distrib:	Annually		

Vanguard Mid Cap Idx

Analyst Pick	Ticker	Load	NAV	Yield	Total Assets	Mstar Category
✔	VIMSX	None	$15.64	1.0%	$8,485 mil	Mid-Cap Blend

Governance and Management

Fiduciary Grade: B

Portfolio Manager(s)

Experienced. Manager Gus Sauter (who has been here since the fund's May 1998 inception) and his team are among the best in the business in wringing out extra basis points via cagey trading and portfolio-construction techniques. Investors are in good hands.

Strategy

The fund's basic strategy had been to buy and hold the stocks that constitute the S&P Mid-Cap 400 Index. However, in 2003, Vanguard switched from the S&P index to the newly minted MSCI U.S. Mid-Cap 450 Index. Although the new benchmark won't shelter the fund from firms with limited operating histories like the S&P index did, it should help stem turnover. Because the new bogy pulls in a passel of large-cap names, the fund now sports a higher aggregate market cap. The new index, however, more closely approximates the group norm.

Historical Profile

Return: Above Avg
Risk: Average
Rating: ★★★★ Above Avg

Investment Style: Equity Stock %: 97% | 98% | 97% | 99% | 100% | 100% | 100%

▼ Manager Change
▽ Partial Manager Change

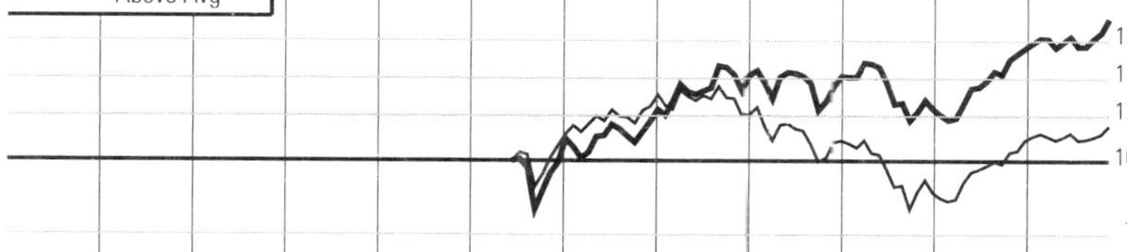

Growth of $10,000
— Investment Values of Fund
— Investment Values of S&P 500

Performance Quartile (within Category)

1993	1994	1995	1996	1997	1998	1999	2000	2001	2002	2003	12-04	History
—	—	—	—	—	10.79	11.29	12.21	11.81	9.88	13.13	15.64	NAV
—	—	—	—	—	8.35*	15.22	18.20	-0.50	-14.61	34.14	20.35	Total Return %
—	—	—	—	—	—	-5.82	27.30	11.38	7.48	5.47	9.48	+/-S&P 500
—	—	—	—	—	—	0.50	0.71	0.10	-0.08	-1.45	3.88	+/-S&P Mid 400
—	—	—	—	—	0.00	0.74	0.70	0.58	0.79	1.23	1.23	Income Return %
—	—	—	—	—	—	14.48	17.50	-1.08	-15.40	32.91	19.12	Capital Return %
—	—	—	—	—	—	58	26	45	41	54	15	Total Rtn % Rank Cat
—	—	—	—	—	0.05	0.08	0.08	0.07	0.09	0.12	0.16	Income $
—	—	—	—	—	0.05	0.94	0.98	0.25	0.13	0.00	0.00	Capital Gains $
—	—	—	—	—	0.25	0.25	0.25	0.25	0.26	0.26	—	Expense Ratio %
—	—	—	—	—	1.19	0.99	0.90	0.83	0.85	1.20	—	Income Ratio %
—	—	—	—	—	44	38	51	24	20	73	—	Turnover Rate %
—	—	—	—	—	206	605	1,614	2,049	2,267	3,610	5,234	Net Assets $mil

Performance 12-31-04

	1st Qtr	2nd Qtr	3rd Qtr	4th Qtr	Total
2000	13.02	-3.17	12.12	-3.67	18.20
2001	-10.80	13.20	-16.46	17.96	-0.50
2002	6.71	-9.35	-16.56	5.79	-14.61
2003	-4.45	16.31	6.28	13.57	34.14
2004	4.65	1.09	-0.94	14.84	20.35

Trailing	Total Return%	+/- S&P 500	+/- S&P Mid 400	%Rank Cat	Growth of $10,000
3 Mo	14.84	5.61	2.69	11	11,484
6 Mo	13.77	6.58	3.98	9	11,377
1 Yr	20.35	9.48	3.88	15	12,035
3 Yr Avg	11.30	7.72	0.79	27	13,787
5 Yr Avg	10.15	12.45	0.62	25	16,215
10 Yr Avg	—	—	—	—	—
15 Yr Avg	—	—	—	—	—

Tax Analysis	Tax-Adj Rtn%	%Rank Cat	Tax-Cost Rat	%Rank Cat
3 Yr (estimated)	10.88	26	0.38	43
5 Yr (estimated)	9.10	21	0.95	42
10 Yr (estimated)	—	—	—	—

Potential Capital Gain Exposure: 22% of assets

Rating and Risk

Time Period	Load-Adj Return %	Morningstar Rtn vs Cat	Morningstar Risk vs Cat	Morningstar Risk-Adj Rating
1 Yr	20.35			
3 Yr	11.30	+Avg	Avg	★★★★
5 Yr	10.15	+Avg	Avg	★★★★
10 Yr	—	—	—	—
Incept	11.28			

Other Measures	Standard Index S&P 500	Best Fit Index S&P Mid 400
Alpha	7.8	0.7
Beta	0.92	1.01
R-Squared	81	99

Standard Deviation	16.99
Mean	11.30
Sharpe Ratio	0.59

Portfolio Analysis 09-30-04

Share change since 06-04 Total Stocks:455	Sector	PE	YTD Ret%	% Assets
⊕ Apple Computer	Hardware	NMF	201.36	0.63
⊖ TXU	Utilities	NMF	177.67	0.78
⊕ PACCAR	Ind Mtrls	15.6	47.28	0.64
⊕ Xerox	Ind Mtrls	20.2	23.26	0.64
⊕ Valero Energy	Energy	7.0	97.64	0.58
⊕ J.C. Penney	Consumer	20.5	59.95	0.56
⊕ Cigna	Health	8.4	42.87	0.56
⊕ Monsanto Company	Ind Mtrls	54.5	96.09	0.55
⊕ Starwood Hotels & Resort	Consumer	33.9	64.71	0.54
⊕ Eaton	Ind Mtrls	18.5	36.07	0.51
⊕ Computer Sciences	Business	18.1	27.45	0.50
⊕ Phelps Dodge	Ind Mtrls	11.1	30.78	0.49
⊕ BJ Services	Energy	21.8	30.07	0.48
⊕ PPL	Utilities	12.0	26.14	0.47
⊕ Medco Health Solutions	Health	—	22.39	0.47
⊕ Georgia-Pacific Group	Ind Mtrls	14.4	24.12	0.47
⊕ Coach	Goods	37.4	49.40	0.45
⊕ Textron	Ind Mtrls	30.4	32.17	0.45
⊕ CIT Group	Financial	13.2	29.28	0.45
⊕ XTO Energy	Energy	20.5	56.85	0.45

Current Investment Style

Value Blnd Growth / Large Mid Small

Market Cap	%
Giant	0.0
Large	10.2
Mid	89.3
Small	0.5
Micro	0.0

Avg $mil: 4,939

Value Measures		Rel Category
Price/Earnings	16.68	0.99
Price/Book	2.22	1.02
Price/Sales	1.03	0.97
Price/Cash Flow	5.58	0.89
Dividend Yield %	1.20	1.20

Growth Measures	%	Rel Category
Long-Term Erngs	11.66	0.93
Book Value	4.93	0.70
Sales	5.09	0.90
Cash Flow	5.96	0.80
Historical Erngs	9.03	0.80

Profitability	%	Rel Category
Return on Equity	13.16	0.96
Return on Assets	6.67	1.02
Net Margin	9.78	1.08

Sector Weightings	% of Stocks	Rel S&P 500	3 Year High	3 Year Low
Info	16.60	0.77		
Software	2.60	0.60	5	3
Hardware	10.10	0.99	13	6
Media	2.48	0.65	4	2
Telecom	1.42	0.45	1	1
Service	48.11	1.04		
Health	10.01	0.80	14	10
Consumer	11.20	1.23	12	9
Business	6.53	1.61	12	7
Financial	20.37	0.98	20	18
Mfg	35.30	1.10		
Goods	7.75	0.83	9	8
Ind Mtrls	12.03	0.95	12	7
Energy	9.06	1.27	9	7
Utilities	6.46	2.18	7	6

Composition

Cash	0.3
Stocks	99.7
Bonds	0.0
Other	0.0
Foreign (% of Stock)	0.4

Morningstar's Take by Sonya Morris 10-25-04

Although competition is getting stiffer, this fund is still topnotch.

Although Vanguard Mid Capitalization Index bears the firm's trademark low expense ratio, it's no longer the low-cost leader. In August, Fidelity Investments lowered the expense ratios of five of its index funds, including mid-blend entrant Fidelity Spartan Extended Market Index, to an ultralow 0.10%. That's less than half this fund's price tag, which isn't chump change given that indexing's success depends on low costs.

But don't rush to cash out of this fund just yet. For one thing, Fidelity Spartan Extended Market Index isn't an easy substitute for this offering. Its bogy, the Wilshire 4500 Index, has a much wider wingspan, which may cause overlap with investors' other fund holdings. It also carries a much heavier small-cap stake, which could put off investors who prefer to tap active managers in that less efficient small-cap realm. In addition, Fidelity's fee cut, though laudable, isn't permanent: The firm can rescind the fee waiver anytime.

For those undeterred by these potential drawbacks, there are tax considerations as well. In particular, longtime shareholders of this fund who are considering a switch in a taxable account could see any cost savings wiped out by taxes triggered by the move. Others, like prospective investors or those without significant tax exposure, should at least give the Fidelity fund a look, as its cost margin over this offering is substantial.

Nevertheless, shareholders who decide to stay put here shouldn't feel like they're settling for second best. This offering still has one of the lowest expense ratios around, and manager Gus Sauter has proven quite adept at tracking the benchmark, which has been enough to lift the fund past the majority of its mid-blend rivals. In addition, thanks to a bogy switch last year (from the S&P Mid-Cap 400 to the MSCI U.S. Mid-Cap 450), this fund now provides purer exposure to the mid-cap space. It remains a strong contender.

Address:	P O Box 2600, Valley Forge PA 19482, 800-662-7447
Web Address:	www.vanguard.com
Inception:	05-21-98*
Advisor:	Vanguard Advisers, Inc.
Subadvisor:	None
NTF Plans:	N/A

Minimum Purchase:	$3000	Add: $100	IRA: $1000
Min Auto Inv Plan:	$3000	Add: $50	
Sales Fees:	No-load		
Management Fee:	0.23%		
Actual Fees:	Mgt:0.23%	Dist:	
Expense Projections:	3Yr:$80	5Yr:$141	10Yr:$318
Income Distrib:	Annually		

Vanguard Morgan Gr

Ticker	Load	NAV	Yield	Total Assets	Mstar Category
VMRGX	None	$16.32	0.6%	$5,171 mil	Large Growth

Governance and Management

Fiduciary Grade: B

Portfolio Manager(s)

All three of the fund's managers are highly experienced. In addition to his indexing duties, Gus Sauter (who arrived in May 1993) has done a fine job at Vanguard Strategic Equity. Wellington Management's Robert Rands (who took the helm in March 1994) has put up fine numbers at several accounts, and John Cone (who was added to the team in April 2000) has guided Vanguard Growth & Income to strong returns.

Strategy

Two of the fund's three managers, John Cone and Gus Sauter, use enhanced-index approaches. Based on a recent prospectus change, Cone now attempts to beat the Russell Midcap Growth Index, while Sauter tries to better the MSCI U.S. Prime Market Growth Index. Robert Rands, who manages 40% of the portfolio, looks for moderately priced growth stocks that have the potential to surge. Although it has a growth bias, the portfolio is still fairly well diversified across sectors and individual issues, typically courting less price risk than most funds in the category.

Historical Profile

Return Above Avg
Risk Average
Rating ★★★★ Above Avg

Investment Style: Equity Stock %

90%	91%	94%	91%	86%	96%	92%	95%	94%

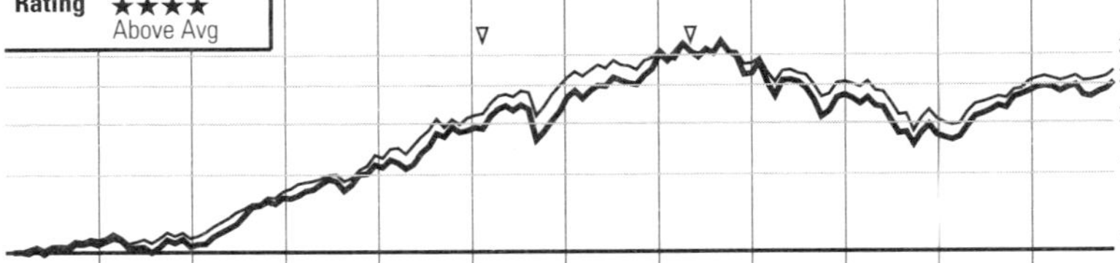

▼ Manager Change
▽ Partial Manager Change

Growth of $10,000
— Investment Values of Fund
— Investment Values of S&P 500

Performance Quartile (within Category)

1993	1994	1995	1996	1997	1998	1999	2000	2001	2002	2003	12-04	History
12.01	11.36	14.09	15.63	17.54	19.72	22.92	17.08	14.63	11.15	14.87	16.32	NAV
7.32	-1.67	35.98	23.30	30.81	22.26	34.10	-12.51	-13.60	-23.52	33.73	10.47	Total Return %
-2.74	-2.98	-1.55	0.36	-2.54	-6.31	13.06	-3.41	-1.72	-1.43	5.06	-0.40	+/-S&P 500
4.45	-4.29	-1.20	0.18	0.32	-16.45	0.94	9.91	6.82	4.36	3.98	4.17	+/-Russ 1000Gr
1.44	1.18	1.33	1.02	1.05	1.05	0.78	0.67	0.44	0.27	0.36	0.71	Income Return %
5.88	-2.85	34.65	22.28	29.76	21.21	33.32	-13.18	-14.04	-23.79	33.37	9.76	Capital Return %
65	54	24	20	29	81	54	47	17	24	16	25	Total Rtn % Rank Cat
0.18	0.14	0.15	0.14	0.16	0.18	0.15	0.15	0.08	0.04	0.04	0.11	Income $
1.35	0.31	1.16	1.53	2.52	1.43	3.08	2.95	0.05	0.00	0.00	0.00	Capital Gains $
0.49	0.50	0.48	0.51	0.48	0.44	0.42	0.40	0.41	0.48	0.50	0.44	Expense Ratio %
1.36	1.15	1.10	0.97	0.93	0.96	0.71	0.73	0.49	0.37	0.31	0.32	Income Ratio %
72	84	76	73	76	81	65	94	53	104	91	88	Turnover Rate %
1,135	1,075	1,471	2,054	2,795	3,555	5,066	4,661	3,493	2,576	3,789	4,563	Net Assets $mil

Performance 12-31-04

	1st Qtr	2nd Qtr	3rd Qtr	4th Qtr	Total
2000	7.02	-3.57	-1.74	-13.72	-12.51
2001	-14.17	9.92	-20.86	15.70	-13.60
2002	-1.85	-14.28	-14.78	6.67	-23.52
2003	-1.35	16.64	3.98	11.78	33.73
2004	2.69	1.38	-4.59	11.22	10.47

Trailing	Total Return%	+/- S&P 500	+/- Russ 1000Gr	%Rank Cat	Growth of $10,000
3 Mo	11.22	1.99	2.05	26	11,122
6 Mo	6.12	-1.07	2.65	34	10,612
1 Yr	10.47	-0.40	4.17	25	11,047
3 Yr Avg	4.16	0.58	4.34	12	11,301
5 Yr Avg	-3.11	-0.81	6.18	15	8,539
10 Yr Avg	11.87	-0.20	2.28	11	30,700
15 Yr Avg	10.58	-0.35	1.08	30	45,201

Tax Analysis	Tax-Adj Rtn%	%Rank Cat	Tax-Cost Rat	%Rank Cat
3 Yr (estimated)	4.01	10	0.14	24
5 Yr (estimated)	-4.04	16	0.96	58
10 Yr (estimated)	9.42	18	2.19	80

Potential Capital Gain Exposure: 4% of assets

Rating and Risk

Time Period	Load-Adj Return %	Morningstar Rtn vs Cat	Morningstar Risk vs Cat	Morningstar Risk-Adj Rating
1 Yr	10.47			
3 Yr	4.16	+Avg	Avg	★★★★
5 Yr	-3.11	+Avg	Avg	★★★★
10 Yr	11.87	+Avg	Avg	★★★★
Incept	11.01			

Other Measures	Standard Index S&P 500	Best Fit Index Russ MG
Alpha	0.7	-1.3
Beta	1.00	0.84
R-Squared	92	95
Standard Deviation	16.36	
Mean	4.16	
Sharpe Ratio	0.17	

Portfolio Analysis 09-30-04

Share change since 06-04 Total Stocks:315	Sector	PE	YTD Ret%	% Assets
⊕ Microsoft	Software	36.1	8.95	2.83
⊕ Yahoo	Media	95.1	67.36	2.12
⊕ American International G	Financial	16.2	-0.53	1.51
⊖ eBay	Consumer	81.6	80.07	1.34
⊕ Vanguard Growth VIPERs	—	—	—	1.29
⊖ Staples	Consumer	24.7	24.38	1.24
⊕ Pfizer	Health	22.0	-22.31	1.23
⊕ AstraZeneca PLC ADR	Health	27.2	-23.43	1.21
⊕ Apollo Group A	Consumer	NMF	19.02	1.19
⊕ Nextel Communications	Telecom	11.1	6.95	1.18
⊖ Cisco Systems	Hardware	24.5	-20.26	1.13
⊕ Dell	Hardware	34.0	24.01	1.09
⊕ Ericsson Telephone ADR B	Hardware	—	77.91	1.09
⊕ Guidant	Health	35.0	20.55	0.99
⊕ Eli Lilly & Company	Health	24.3	-17.55	0.94
⊖ Research In Motion Ltd	Hardware	—	146.66	0.92
⊕ Johnson & Johnson	Health	20.6	25.17	0.91
⊕ First Data	Business	18.8	3.72	0.87
⊕ Medtronic	Health	30.7	2.68	0.86
⊕ EMC	Hardware	41.5	15.09	0.79

Current Investment Style

Value Blnd Growth; Large Mid Small

Market Cap	%
Giant	29.8
Large	32.6
Mid	37.3
Small	0.3
Micro	0.0
Avg $mil: 16,604	

Value Measures		Rel Category
Price/Earnings	18.73	0.88
Price/Book	2.89	0.89
Price/Sales	1.53	0.71
Price/Cash Flow	8.61	0.78
Dividend Yield %	0.63	0.82

Growth Measures	%	Rel Category
Long-Term Erngs	14.43	1.03
Book Value	12.67	1.00
Sales	9.16	1.08
Cash Flow	10.64	0.64
Historical Erngs	18.55	1.28

Profitability	%	Rel Category
Return on Equity	17.96	1.00
Return on Assets	8.91	0.95
Net Margin	11.94	0.97

Sector Weightings	% of Stocks	Rel S&P 500	3 Year High	Low
Info	32.61	1.52		
Software	6.77	1.57	9	7
Hardware	15.41	1.51	20	9
Media	7.21	1.88	10	7
Telecom	3.22	1.02	3	1
Service	53.40	1.15		
Health	19.56	1.56	30	18
Consumer	15.23	1.68	16	11
Business	8.45	2.09	9	5
Financial	10.16	0.49	16	9
Mfg	13.99	0.44		
Goods	6.19	0.66	8	4
Ind Mtrls	4.25	0.34	5	3
Energy	3.52	0.49	4	2
Utilities	0.03	0.01	1	0

Composition

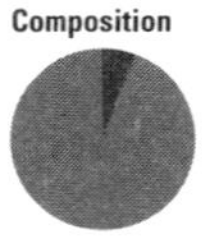

Cash	5.8
Stocks	93.8
Bonds	0.1
Other	0.3
Foreign (% of Stock)	9.1

Morningstar's Take by Jeffrey Ptak 10-17-04

Vanguard Morgan Growth quietly gets the job done.

Management of Vanguard Morgan Growth is split three ways. Wellington Management's Robert Rands handles the bulk of the stock picking chores, plying a multi-cap fundamental growth strategy. He's flanked by Franklin Portfolio Associates' manager John Cone and Vanguard's in-house quantitative team, both of whom use computerized models to ferret out reasonably priced, fast growing fare from the Russell Mid-Cap Growth and MSCI Investable Market Growth indexes respectively.

Since Cone and Vanguard's team keep industry weightings in line with their bogies, the fund's sector bets stem chiefly from Rand's bottom-up process. For his part, Rand typically favors areas propelled by secular forces, such as technology, new media, and e-tailers. Within those realms, he opts for firms with dominant market positions and clean balance sheets. For instance, he's a fan of wireless device-maker Research in Motion, which has forged lucrative ties with wireless carriers and should see explosive margin expansion on the service side of its business. While small- and mid-cap stock typically abound in Rand's sleeve of the portfolio, he reports finding better values in large-caps lately, including U.K. retailer GUS Plc.

That said, the fund continues to sport a pronounced smaller-cap bias. That has provided a tailwind in recent years as smaller firms have outpaced their larger counterparts. To be sure, management's valuation-conscious ethos would have seemed to place the fund on the outside of last year's rally looking in. Yet, Rands' deft semi-conductor and consumer discretionary picks have paved the way to solid showings last year and so far in 2004.

The fund's small-cap tilt can be a hindrance in large-cap dominated markets, as the fund's sluggish 1998 and 1999 campaigns attest. But its experienced managers, low costs, and proven approach make it a solid choice.

Address:	PO Box 2600 Valley Forge PA 19482 800-662-7447
Web Address:	www.vanguard.com
Inception:	12-31-68
Advisor:	The Vanguard Group, Inc.
Subadvisor:	Multiple
NTF Plans:	N/A

Minimum Purchase:	$3000	Add: $100	IRA: $1000
Min Auto Inv Plan:	$3000	Add: $50	
Sales Fees:	No-load		
Management Fee:	0.82%		
Actual Fees:	Mgt:0.39%	Dist: —	
Expense Projections:	3Yr:$154	5Yr:$269	10Yr:$604
Income Distrib:	Annually		

Vanguard Primecap

Ticker	Load	NAV	Yield	Total Assets	Mstar Category
VPMCX	Closed	$62.30	0.7%	$27,296 mil	Large Blend

Governance and Management

Fiduciary Grade: B

Portfolio Manager(s)

The fund's five managers employ an unusual management structure. Each manages a percentage of assets independently. They share ideas but make autonomous buy-and-sell decisions. Howard Schow, Theo Kolokotrones, and Joel Fried manage the lion's share of the fund's assets and have considerable experience. In addition, two managers were recently added: Mitchell Milias and Alfred Mordecai oversee 10% of assets each. Primecap has also beefed up its analyst ranks in recent years. The firm added four analysts in 2000 and 2001 and has hired two more in 2004, bringing the total to eight.

Strategy

The fund's managers follow a contrarian-growth approach. They look for swiftly growing firms, but they like to buy them on the cheap--usually when they're out of favor. They're particularly fond of companies with high unit growth. The fund often has outsized sector weightings because many of the managers' favorites are clustered in particular industries, such as hardware.

Historical Profile

Return: High
Risk: High
Rating: ★★★★ Above Avg

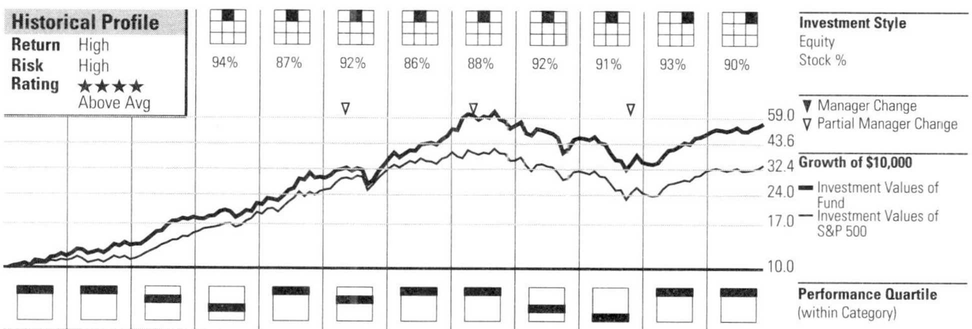

1993	1994	1995	1996	1997	1998	1999	2000	2001	2002	2003	12-04	History
18.42	19.98	26.23	30.08	39.57	47.66	62.07	60.38	51.52	38.66	53.04	62.30	NAV
18.03	11.41	35.48	18.31	36.83	25.41	41.34	4.47	-13.35	-24.56	37.75	18.31	Total Return %
7.97	10.10	-2.05	-4.63	3.48	-3.16	20.30	13.57	-1.47	-2.47	9.08	7.44	+/-S&P 500
7.85	11.02	-2.29	-4.14	3.98	-1.61	20.43	12.26	-0.90	-2.91	7.86	6.91	+/-Russ 1000
0.43	0.65	1.10	0.77	0.67	0.89	0.57	0.80	0.47	0.41	0.54	0.84	Income Return %
17.60	10.76	34.38	17.54	36.16	24.52	40.77	3.67	-13.82	-24.97	37.21	17.47	Capital Return %
14	1	38	74	4	40	5	14	69	79	4	1	Total Rtn % Rank Cat
0.07	0.12	0.22	0.20	0.20	0.35	0.27	0.49	0.28	0.21	0.21	0.45	Income $
0.59	0.41	0.59	0.73	1.30	1.52	4.65	4.05	0.53	0.00	0.00	0.00	Capital Gains $
0.67	0.64	0.58	0.59	0.51	0.51	0.51	0.48	0.50	0.49	0.51	0.46	Expense Ratio %
0.44	0.79	0.99	0.69	0.69	0.78	0.50	0.80	0.58	0.42	0.56	0.48	Income Ratio %
16	8	7	10	13	13	19	11	7	11	12	9	Turnover Rate %
791	1,534	3,237	4,204	8,186	11,210	17,912	21,762	18,096	12,999	18,356	22,998	Net Assets $mil

Performance 12-31-04

	1st Qtr	2nd Qtr	3rd Qtr	4th Qtr	Total
2000	19.54	-2.69	-3.52	-6.91	4.47
2001	-10.92	4.22	-21.68	19.17	-13.35
2002	1.34	-17.37	-17.39	9.05	-24.56
2003	-0.85	16.88	6.23	11.91	37.75
2004	5.17	3.42	-0.88	9.75	18.31

Trailing	Total Return%	+/- S&P 500	+/- Russ 1000	%Rank Cat	Growth of $10,000
3 Mo	9.75	0.52	-0.05	34	10,975
6 Mo	8.78	1.59	0.97	18	10,878
1 Yr	18.31	7.44	6.91	1	11,831
3 Yr Avg	7.13	3.55	2.86	6	12,295
5 Yr Avg	2.16	4.46	3.92	12	11,128
10 Yr Avg	15.78	3.71	3.62	2	43,285
15 Yr Avg	14.89	3.96	3.81	2	80,211

Tax Analysis	Tax-Adj Rtn%	%Rank Cat	Tax-Cost Rat	%Rank Cat
3 Yr (estimated)	6.59	6	0.17	15
5 Yr (estimated)	1.62	11	0.53	28
10 Yr (estimated)	14.73	2	0.91	23

Potential Capital Gain Exposure: 32% of assets

Rating and Risk

Time Period	Load-Adj Return %	Morningstar Rtn vs Cat	Morningstar Risk vs Cat	Morningstar Risk-Adj Rating
1 Yr	17.13			
3 Yr	6.77	High	High	★★★★
5 Yr	2.16	+Avg	High	★★★★
10 Yr	15.78	High	High	★★★★★
Incept	15.75			

Other Measures	Standard Index S&P 500	Best Fit Index Russ 1000
Alpha	3.5	2.7
Beta	1.09	1.10
R-Squared	93	94
Standard Deviation	18.20	
Mean	7.13	
Sharpe Ratio	0.32	

Portfolio Analysis 09-30-04

Share change since 06-04 Total Stocks:121	Sector	PE	YTD Ret%	% Assets
FedEx	Business	27.9	46.40	5.03
⊖ Biogen IDEC	Health	—	81.50	4.53
Guidant	Health	35.0	20.55	3.87
⊖ Adobe Systems	Software	34.2	60.76	3.56
ConocoPhillips	Energy	9.0	35.60	3.23
⊕ Novartis AG ADR	Health	23.9	12.04	2.80
The Directv Group	Media	—	1.15	2.37
⊕ Microsoft	Software	36.1	8.95	2.32
Micron Technology	Hardware	46.2	-8.32	2.11
Texas Instruments	Hardware	21.1	-15.90	2.02
Caterpillar	Ind Mtrls	17.6	19.75	1.87
⊕ Eli Lilly & Company	Health	24.3	-17.55	1.80
⊕ Pfizer	Health	22.0	-22.31	1.72
⊕ Potash Corp./Saskatchewa	Ind Mtrls	—	94.19	1.66
Dow Chemical	Ind Mtrls	16.6	22.83	1.58
Union Pacific	Business	19.6	-1.28	1.54
⊕ Qualcomm	Hardware	42.0	58.20	1.51
⊕ J P Morgan Chase	Financial	19.4	9.97	1.45
⊕ Motorola	Hardware	28.7	37.93	1.43
⊖ eBay	Consumer	81.6	80.07	1.37

Current Investment Style

Value Blnd Growth; Large Mid Small

Market Cap	%
Giant	27.1
Large	54.5
Mid	16.6
Small	1.6
Micro	0.2
Avg $mil: 21,061	

Value Measures		Rel Category
Price/Earnings	19.11	1.13
Price/Book	2.11	0.81
Price/Sales	1.33	0.92
Price/Cash Flow	8.56	1.11
Dividend Yield %	0.84	0.57

Growth Measures	%	Rel Category
Long-Term Erngs	11.53	1.00
Book Value	7.85	1.01
Sales	5.24	0.91
Cash Flow	5.63	0.60
Historical Erngs	10.21	0.87

Profitability	%	Rel Category
Return on Equity	11.10	0.63
Return on Assets	5.39	0.62
Net Margin	3.51	0.31

Sector Weightings	% of Stocks	Rel S&P 500	3 Year High	3 Year Low
Info	29.82	1.39		
Software	7.97	1.85	10	7
Hardware	16.19	1.59	19	14
Media	4.81	1.25	6	2
Telecom	0.85	0.27	2	1
Service	46.79	1.01		
Health	21.86	1.75	24	16
Consumer	7.38	0.81	9	7
Business	11.77	2.91	18	12
Financial	5.78	0.28	6	4
Mfg	23.38	0.73		
Goods	3.08	0.33	8	3
Ind Mtrls	11.43	0.90	11	7
Energy	8.87	1.24	10	7
Utilities	0.00	0.00	0	0

Composition

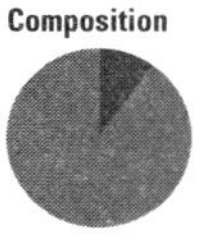

Cash	3.8
Stocks	9[illegible].3
Bonds	0.0
Other	0.0
Foreign (% of Stock)	3.8

Morningstar's Take by Jeffrey Ptak 10-07-04

Though the fund's managers are broadening their horizons, they're not losing focus.

Yes, Vanguard Primecap is on another tear. The fund has surged to a 10.1% gain for the year to date through Oct. 4, 2004, behind a clutch of strong-faring top picks, such as Biogen IDEC which has leapt 70% this year. This is the latest in a string of fine showings that management has posted in amassing a remarkable long-term record.

But that's only part of the story of what makes this fund special. In fact, it's management's deep commitment to the underlying investment process that truly sets it apart. Unlike many firms that pay lip service to original fundamental analysis while leaning heavily on sell-side research, Primecap pours itself into understanding each name and the industry it operates in, seeking those that offer superior unit growth potential. What's more, they've got nerve, typically waiting for stocks to sell off before stepping in, a tactic that finds them buying just as other investors are fleeing.

Nevertheless, the fund's success has largely coalesced around the efforts of a small core group--managers Joel Fried, Theo Kolokotrones, Mitch Milias, Al Mordecai, and Howard Schow. And with Primecap poised to launch its own suite of new funds (the firm is also being tapped to run a new Vanguard large-blend fund), the risk is that the firm's research efforts could be diluted as it tries to support a broader array of offerings.

But we're not too concerned. Primecap will be leveraging existing processes rather than starting from scratch. And while the firm has beefed up its analyst ranks in recent years, it hasn't skimped: Analysts are still given plenty of time to learn the ropes, which is vital given the premium that Primecap has placed on knowing their names in intimate detail. Further, analysts have been given the chance to buy into the firm over time, which invests them early on in its success while minimizing personnel turnover.

All told, this remains a terrific fund.

Address:	Po Box 2600 Valley Forge PA 19482 800-662-7447
Web Address:	www.vanguard.com
Inception:	11-01-84
Advisor:	Primecap Management Co.
Subadvisor:	None
NTF Plans:	N/A

Minimum Purchase:	Closed	Add: —	IRA: —
Min Auto Inv Plan:	Closed	Add: —	
Sales Fees:	No-load, 1.00%R		
Management Fee:	0.50% mx./0.15% mn.		
Actual Fees:	Mgt:0.47%	Dist: —	
Expense Projections:	3Yr:$271	5Yr:$274	10Yr:$616
Income Distrib:	Annually		

Vanguard REIT Index

Ticker	Load	NAV	Yield	Total Assets	Mstar Category
VGSIX	None	$18.79	4.7%	$5,998 mil	Specialty-Real Estate

Governance and Management

Fiduciary Grade: B

Portfolio Manager(s)

Gus Sauter is responsible for managing all of Vanguard's equity-index funds. He also oversees a few actively managed funds, which he runs using quantitative models. Over time, Vanguard has done a nice job of keeping its passively managed funds within striking distance of their bogies.

Strategy

This fund is designed to track the performance of the Morgan Stanley REIT Index, although the Wilshire REIT Index is a more common benchmark for real estate funds. Thus, the fund is beholden to the decisions that Morgan Stanley makes in adding or subtracting REITs from its index.

Historical Profile

Return Average
Risk Above Avg
Rating ★★★ Neutral

Investment Style: Equity, Stock %

1996	1997	1998	1999	2000	2001	2002	2003	12-04
93%	99%	95%	95%	94%	95%	94%	98%	98%

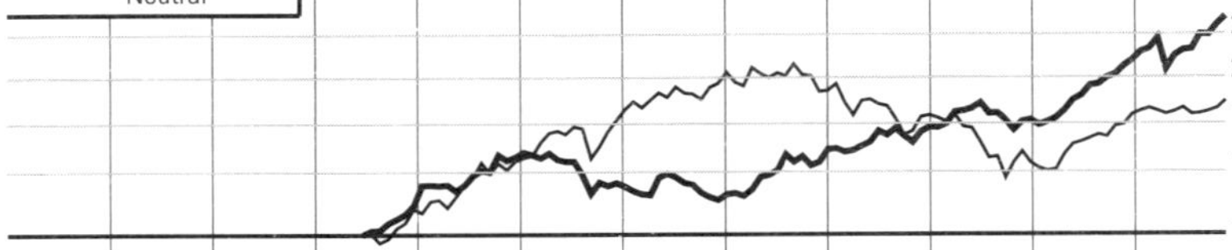

Performance Quartile (within Category)

1993	1994	1995	1996	1997	1998	1999	2000	2001	2002	2003	12-04	History
—	—	—	12.62	14.16	11.08	9.85	11.56	12.13	11.84	15.18	18.79	NAV
—	—	—	30.41*	18.76	-16.32	-4.04	26.35	12.35	3.75	35.65	30.76	Total Return %
—	—	—	—	-14.59	-44.89	-25.08	35.45	24.23	25.84	6.98	19.89	+/-S&P 500
—	—	—	—	-0.91	0.68	-1.47	-4.69	-0.01	0.15	-0.41	-3.06	+/-Wil REIT
—	—	—	0.00	4.77	4.81	6.21	6.72	7.19	6.40	6.74	5.92	Income Return %
—	—	—	—	13.99	-21.13	-10.25	19.63	5.16	-2.65	28.91	24.84	Capital Return %
—	—	—	—	88	55	58	67	18	52	59	65	Total Rtn % Rank Cat
—	—	—	0.34	0.59	0.67	0.67	0.64	0.81	0.76	0.78	0.88	Income $
—	—	—	0.04	0.18	0.14	0.11	0.18	0.00	0.00	0.00	0.07	Capital Gains $
—	—	—	—	0.36	0.24	0.26	0.33	0.33	0.28	0.27	0.24	Expense Ratio %
—	—	—	—	5.50	4.66	5.19	5.98	5.73	4.35	4.90	4.10	Income Ratio %
—	—	—	—	—	2	29	12	21	10	12	7	Turnover Rate %
—	—	—	469	1,278	924	875	1,094	1,230	1,784	3,051	4,663	Net Assets $mil

Performance 12-31-04

	1st Qtr	2nd Qtr	3rd Qtr	4th Qtr	Total
2000	2.56	10.51	7.49	3.71	26.35
2001	-0.50	10.66	-2.56	4.72	12.35
2002	8.08	4.78	-8.48	0.10	3.75
2003	1.01	12.27	9.47	9.27	35.65
2004	11.75	-5.95	8.13	15.06	30.76

Trailing	Total Return%	+/- S&P 500	+/- Wil REIT	%Rank Cat	Growth of $10,000
3 Mo	15.06	5.83	-1.63	71	11,506
6 Mo	24.41	17.22	-1.85	62	12,441
1 Yr	30.76	19.89	-3.06	65	13,076
3 Yr Avg	22.55	18.97	-1.01	60	18,405
5 Yr Avg	21.18	23.48	-1.49	52	26,131
10 Yr Avg	—	—	—	—	—
15 Yr Avg	—	—	—	—	—

Tax Analysis	Tax-Adj Rtn%	%Rank Cat	Tax-Cost Rat	%Rank Cat
3 Yr (estimated)	20.06	62	2.03	69
5 Yr (estimated)	18.52	59	2.20	76
10 Yr (estimated)	—	—	—	—

Potential Capital Gain Exposure: 30% of assets

Rating and Risk

Time Period	Load-Adj Return %	Morningstar Rtn vs Cat	Morningstar Risk vs Cat	Morningstar Risk-Adj Rating
1 Yr	30.76			
3 Yr	22.55	Avg	Avg	★★★
5 Yr	21.18	Avg	+Avg	★★★
10 Yr	—	—	—	—
Incept	14.62			

Other Measures	Standard Index S&P 500	Best Fit Index Wil REIT
Alpha	20.9	-0.1
Beta	0.33	0.96
R-Squared	12	100
Standard Deviation	17.42	
Mean	22.55	
Sharpe Ratio	1.23	

Morningstar's Take by Dan McNeela 12-23-04

Vanguard REIT Index provides diversified exposure, but it's nothing special.

This year has been a microcosm of the fund's long-running mediocrity. As always, it has delivered returns in-line with the Morgan Stanley REIT index. In 2004, that's meant a 30.8% year-to-date gain through Dec. 22. But relative to its peers in Morningstar's real estate category, it ranks just below the middle of the pack. Unless it inches ahead, it will fall below the category's midpoint for the seventh time in eight years.

As has typically been the case, this fund falls victim to its somewhat-restrictive mandate. In following its benchmark, the fund cannot own any real estate operating companies. Several funds with the freedom to invest in non-REIT stocks have gained a leg up this year by investing heavily in Starwood Hotels & Resorts Worldwide, which is up 64% as of late December.

Another important new difference is that the Morgan Stanley REIT index added several health-care REITs to its roster of holdings in 2002. That subsector amounts to about 6% of the fund. Most real estate funds snub health-care REITs because of their bondlike qualities. In 2004, health-care REITs have posted modest gains relative to other subsectors.

The news isn't all bad, though. Because REITs must pay out 90% of their income to shareholders, the fund's REIT mandate and its low expense ratio of 0.24% combine to give it a high yield of 4.6%. When real estate operating companies falter, as they did in 2001, the fund can shine. And while it hasn't climbed into the category's upper tiers often, the fund offers diversified REIT exposure and consistent--if middling--returns.

In all, we continue to think that this may be one part of the market where actively managed funds have proved their worth. Investors can't go too far astray with this index approach, but more successful options beckon.

Address:	PO Box 2600 Valley Forge PA 19482 800-662-7447
Web Address:	www.vanguard.com
Inception:	05-13-96 *
Advisor:	Vanguard Advisers, Inc.
Subadvisor:	None
NTF Plans:	N/A

Minimum Purchase:	$3000	Add: $100	IRA: $1000
Min Auto Inv Plan:	$3000	Add: $50	
Sales Fees:	No-load, 1.00%R		
Management Fee:	0.29%		
Actual Fees:	Mgt:0.26%	Dist: —	
Expense Projections:	3Yr:$90	5Yr:$157	10Yr:$356
Income Distrib:	Quarterly		

Portfolio Analysis 09-30-04

Share change since 06-04 Total Stocks:120	Sector	PE	YTD Ret%	% Assets
⊕ Simon Property Group	Financial	37.3	46.10	4.72
⊕ Equity Office Properties	Financial	45.9	9.06	4.65
⊕ Equity Residential	Financial	90.2	29.50	3.67
⊕ Vornado Realty Trust	Financial	30.8	46.53	3.33
⊕ Rouse	Financial	—	—	2.91
⊕ General Growth Propertie	Financial	26.6	35.96	2.86
⊕ ProLogis Trust	Financial	25.1	41.03	2.70
⊕ Public Storage	Financial	43.5	33.22	2.69
⊕ Archstone-Smith Trust	Financial	52.6	48.79	2.62
⊕ Boston Properties	Financial	23.9	40.60	2.53
⊕ Kimco Realty	Financial	23.4	35.56	2.41
⊕ Host Marriott	Financial	—	40.88	2.06
⊕ Duke Realty	Financial	33.1	16.66	1.99
⊕ AvalonBay Communities	Financial	58.1	65.02	1.82
⊕ Developers Diversified R	Financial	16.5	38.86	1.68
⊕ Health Care Property	Financial	23.8	14.48	1.45
⊕ Liberty Property Trust	Financial	22.9	17.74	1.43
⊕ Apartment Investment & M	Financial	—	20.31	1.38
⊕ Macerich	Financial	43.9	48.39	1.32
⊕ AMB Property	Financial	39.1	28.55	1.29

Current Investment Style

Value Blnd Growth; Large Mid Small

Market Cap	%
Giant	0.0
Large	13.3
Mid	66.0
Small	19.0
Micro	1.7
Avg $mil: 3,060	

Value Measures		Rel Category
Price/Earnings	13.72	0.96
Price/Book	1.93	0.96
Price/Sales	4.19	1.13
Price/Cash Flow	12.34	1.03
Dividend Yield %	5.41	1.11

Growth Measures	%	Rel Category
Long-Term Erngs	6.07	0.86
Book Value	1.24	8.27
Sales	3.30	1.99
Cash Flow	-5.87	NMF
Historical Erngs	-0.47	NMF

Profitability	%	Rel Category
Return on Equity	10.28	1.00
Return on Assets	8.15	1.06
Net Margin	23.41	1.08

Sector Weightings	% of Stocks	Rel S&P 500	3 Year High	3 Year Low
Info	0.00	0.00		
Software	0.00	0.00	0	0
Hardware	0.00	0.00	0	0
Media	0.00	0.00	0	0
Telecom	0.00	0.00	0	0
Service	100.00	2.16		
Health	0.00	0.00	0	0
Consumer	0.00	0.00	1	0
Business	0.00	0.00	0	0
Financial	100.00	4.82	100	99
Mfg	0.00	0.00		
Goods	0.00	0.00	0	0
Ind Mtrls	0.00	0.00	0	0
Energy	0.00	0.00	0	0
Utilities	0.00	0.00	0	0

Composition

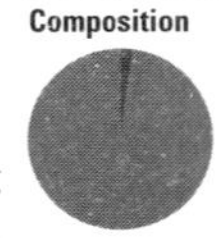

Cash	2.1
Stocks	97.9
Bonds	0.0
Other	0.0
Foreign (% of Stock)	0.0

Vanguard Selected Value

Analyst Pick

Ticker	Load	NAV	Yield	Total Assets	Mstar Category
VASVX	None	$18.07	1.4%	$2,300 mil	Mid-Cap Value

Governance and Management

Fiduciary Grade: B

Portfolio Manager(s)

Manager Jim Barrow took the fund's reins in March 1999. He has more than 30 years of investment experience and has built a fine long-term record as lead manager of Vanguard Windsor II. He is one of the more-seasoned hands in the mutual fund business. Comanager Mark Giambrone joined Barrow at this fund's helm in late 2002.

Strategy

Manager Jim Barrow and Mark Giambrone invest in stocks with very low valuations and high dividend yields. This often leads them to companies that are out of favor with most investors. The fund is fairly concentrated in individual issues, which means its performance swings will be more pronounced than some of its rivals. The managers sell stocks when their valuations get too high or fundamentals worsen.

Historical Profile

Return Above Avg
Risk Average
Rating ★★★★ Above Avg

Investment Style: Equity Stock %

1996	1997	1998	1999	2000	2001	2002	2003	12-04
92%	97%	100%	96%	89%	97%	97%	96%	95%

▼ Manager Change
▽ Partial Manager Change

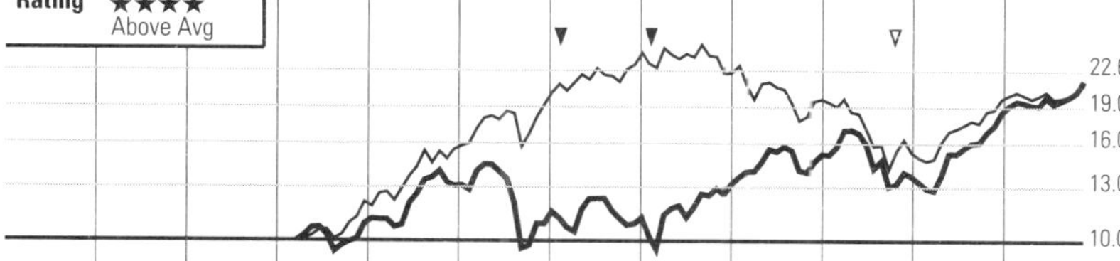

Growth of $10,000
▬ Investment Values of Fund
— Investment Values of S&P 500

Performance Quartile (within Category)

History

1993	1994	1995	1996	1997	1998	1999	2000	2001	2002	2003	12-04	History
—	—	—	10.91	12.28	10.39	9.94	11.43	12.97	11.46	15.23	18.07	NAV
—	—	—	10.81*	17.40	-11.77	-2.72	17.45	14.99	-9.79	35.21	20.38	Total Return %
—	—	—	—	-15.95	-40.34	-23.76	26.55	26.87	12.30	6.54	9.51	+/-S&P 500
—	—	—	—	-16.97	-16.85	-2.61	-1.73	12.66	-0.15	-2.86	-3.33	+/-Russ MV
—	—	—	0.00	0.46	0.65	1.54	2.41	1.49	1.85	2.27	1.71	Income Return %
—	—	—	—	16.94	-12.42	-4.26	15.04	13.50	-11.64	32.94	18.67	Capital Return %
—	—	—	—	89	94	80	54	20	30	43	35	Total Rtn % Rank Cat
—	—	—	0.06	0.05	0.08	0.16	0.24	0.17	0.24	0.26	0.26	Income $
—	—	—	0.11	0.46	0.33	0.00	0.00	0.00	0.00	0.00	0.00	Capital Gains $
—	—	—	0.75	0.74	0.65	0.73	0.63	0.70	0.74	0.78	0.60	Expense Ratio %
—	—	—	0.75	0.60	0.58	1.31	2.40	1.67	1.63	2.05	1.78	Income Ratio %
—	—	—	—	32	47	102	40	67	50	40	35	Turnover Rate %
—	—	—	106	191	149	187	196	995	1,094	1,422	2,300	Net Assets $mil

Performance 12-31-04

	1st Qtr	2nd Qtr	3rd Qtr	4th Qtr	Total
2000	1.21	-1.09	10.95	5.75	17.45
2001	6.12	9.89	-8.63	7.91	14.99
2002	11.95	-6.27	-18.22	5.13	-9.79
2003	-6.54	19.05	5.49	15.21	35.21
2004	4.79	2.69	-0.00	11.86	20.38

Trailing	Total Return%	+/- S&P 500	+/- Russ MV	%Rank Cat	Growth of $10,000
3 Mo	11.86	2.63	-1.60	39	11,186
6 Mo	11.86	4.67	-3.57	37	11,186
1 Yr	20.38	9.51	-3.33	35	12,038
3 Yr Avg	13.66	10.08	-1.90	22	14,683
5 Yr Avg	14.68	16.98	1.20	26	19,835
10 Yr Avg	—	—	—	—	—
15 Yr Avg	—	—	—	—	—

Tax Analysis	Tax-Adj Rtn%	%Rank Cat	Tax-Cost Rat	%Rank Cat
3 Yr (estimated)	12.69	24	0.52	42
5 Yr (estimated)	14.01	22	0.58	31
10 Yr (estimated)	—	—	—	—

Potential Capital Gain Exposure: 20% of assets

Rating and Risk

Time Period	Load-Adj Return %	Morningstar Rtn vs Cat	Morningstar Risk vs Cat	Morningstar Risk-Adj Rating
1 Yr	19.17			
3 Yr	13.28	+Avg	Avg	★★★★
5 Yr	14.68	+Avg	Avg	★★★★
10 Yr	—	—	—	—
Incept	9.37			

Other Measures	Standard Index S&P 500	Best Fit Index Mstar Mid Value
Alpha	10.3	-1.8
Beta	0.88	1.06
R-Squared	69	92

Standard Deviation	17.98
Mean	13.66
Sharpe Ratio	0.69

Portfolio Analysis 09-30-04

Share change since 06-04 Total Stocks:38	Sector	PE	YTD Ret%	% Assets
⊕ Marathon Oil	Energy	—	17.07	3.47
⊕ Brunswick	Goods	18.1	57.47	3.35
⊕ Weight Watchers Intl	Consumer	23.9	7.04	3.23
⊕ American Power Conversio	Ind Mtrls	22.1	-10.99	3.19
⊕ Kerr-McGee	Energy	20.9	28.52	3.16
⊕ Reynolds American	Goods	—	43.11	3.00
⊕ American Financial Realt	Financial	—	1.39	2.99
⊕ Triad Hospitals	Health	30.3	11.84	2.99
⊕ Wellchoice	Financial	18.2	54.78	2.97
⊕ Royal Caribbean Cruises	Goods	36.9	58.33	2.95
⊕ Stanley Works	Ind Mtrls	17.8	32.66	2.92
⊕ Dean Foods	Goods	19.5	0.24	2.91
⊕ Pinnacle West Capital	Utilities	15.3	16.10	2.89
⊕ Willis Group Holdings	Business	16.3	23.24	2.89
⊕ Radian Group	Financial	11.9	9.40	2.89
⊕ Goodrich	Ind Mtrls	25.3	12.87	2.73
⊕ UST, Inc.	Goods	22.4	42.18	2.65
⊕ Valeant Pharmaceuticals	Health	—	6.22	2.62
⊕ TCF Financial	Financial	13.3	28.60	2.61
⊕ Entergy	Utilities	21.1	22.14	2.60

Current Investment Style

Value Blnd Growth; Large Mid Small

Market Cap	%
Giant	0.0
Large	19.3
Mid	78.2
Small	2.5
Micro	0.0
Avg $mil: 4,601	

Value Measures		Rel Category
Price/Earnings	15.53	1.01
Price/Book	1.86	0.97
Price/Sales	0.89	1.01
Price/Cash Flow	5.43	0.95
Dividend Yield %	3.04	2.13

Growth Measures	%	Rel Category
Long-Term Erngs	9.97	0.91
Book Value	2.85	0.51
Sales	3.77	0.79
Cash Flow	0.02	0.01
Historical Erngs	-0.74	NMF

Profitability	%	Rel Category
Return on Equity	12.23	0.96
Return on Assets	4.79	0.79
Net Margin	5.48	0.62

Sector Weightings	% of Stocks	Rel S&P 500	3 Year High	3 Year Low
Info	0.00	0.00		
Software	0.00	0.00	0	0
Hardware	0.00	0.00	0	0
Media	0.00	0.00	0	0
Telecom	0.00	0.00	0	0
Service	48.84	1.05		
Health	8.57	0.69	10	5
Consumer	10.11	1.11	14	9
Business	4.80	1.19	8	2
Financial	25.36	1.22	27	19
Mfg	51.16	1.59		
Goods	15.63	1.68	18	15
Ind Mtrls	15.71	1.24	20	13
Energy	6.98	0.97	12	5
Utilities	12.84	4.34	16	7

Composition

Cash	4.9
Stocks	95.0
Bonds	0.0
Other	0.0
Foreign (% of Stock)	3.0

Morningstar's Take by Christine Benz 11-02-04

The mid-cap value category has long been home to some of the fund world's best stock-picker's funds. This is one of them.

With ranks that include celebrated bargain-hunters like Bill Nygren (Oakmark Select), Staley Cates and Mason Hawkins (Longleaf Partners), and Wally Weitz (Weitz Value), the mid-value category arguably has as much raw investment talent as any other group. We'd put this fund's managers, Jim Barrow and Mark Giambrone, in the category's top echelons, too, and that's why we recently elevated this fund to our roster of mid-value Analyst Picks.

To be sure, the managers' record both on this fund, which Barrow has run since early 1999, and on Vanguard Windsor II, where Barrow runs approximately 70% of assets, is impressive. By focusing on cheap valuations and high dividends, the team limited the fund's losses during the bear market, and also delivered above-average gains in 2003.

Even more important, we like the fund's prospects in what could be a low-returning environment for both stocks and bonds. Barrow and Giambrone focus on stocks that are cheap on an absolute basis, giving the fund room to make money no matter how overvalued the broad market is. (The fund's 10% year-to-date return, even as the S&P 500 has eked out only a small gain, is a case in point.) Moreover, the fund's dividend focus could be an important advantage if dividends become a bigger component of total return than they have been in the recent past. Finally, the fund's low expense ratio--it's the cheapest non-institutional fund in the category--will give it a leg up on its rivals in an environment of low absolute returns.

We also like the fund from the standpoint of usability: With a relatively pure focus on mid-caps, it's a good complement to large-cap-focused funds. Its $25,000 minimum may keep some investors out, but we think it's a fine choice.

Address:	PO Box 2600 Valley Forge PA 19482 800-662-7447
Web Address:	www.vanguard.com
Inception:	02-15-96 *
Advisor:	Barrow, Hanley, Mewhinney & Strauss Inc.
Subadvisor:	None
NTF Plans:	N/A

Minimum Purchase:	$25000	Add: $100	IRA: $25000
Min Auto Inv Plan:	$25000	Add: $50	
Sales Fees:	No-load, 1.00%R		
Management Fee:	0.69%		
Actual Fees:	Mgt:0.68%	Dist: —	
Expense Projections:	3Yr:$337	5Yr:$390	10Yr:$871
Income Distrib:	Annually		

Vanguard Sh-Tm Bd Idx

Analyst Pick

Ticker	Load	NAV	Yield	SEC Yield	Total Assets	Mstar Category
VBISX	None	$10.14	3.0%	3.24%	$5,264 mil	Short-Term Bond

Governance and Management

Fiduciary Grade: B

Portfolio Manager(s)

Chris Alwine assumed management duties in October 2002, but Ken Volpert, who runs Vanguard Total Bond Market Index, has been setting a good deal of the fund's strategy since its inception. Alwine is also no stranger to the fund, having successfully comanaged it from 1998-2000. More recently, he has served as manager of various Vanguard municipal-bond fund offerings, where he has racked up impressive results.

Strategy

The fund strives to approximate the returns of the Lehman Brothers 1-5 Year Government/Credit Index, which includes U.S. Treasury, government agency, and investment-grade corporate bonds. Mortgage-backed securities are not included in the index. Although the duration and other key characteristics of the index are carefully replicated, the fund does not hold every security in the index. The portfolio tends to hold a higher percentage of corporate bonds and fewer Treasuries than the index in an effort to pick up additional yield and return.

Historical Profile

Return Above Avg
Risk Above Avg
Rating ★★★★ Above Avg

Investment Style
Fixed Income
Income Rtn %Rank Cat

1996	1997	1998	1999	2000	2001	2002	2003	12-04
39	37	40	56	34	28	35	41	38

▼ Manager Change
▽ Partial Manager Change

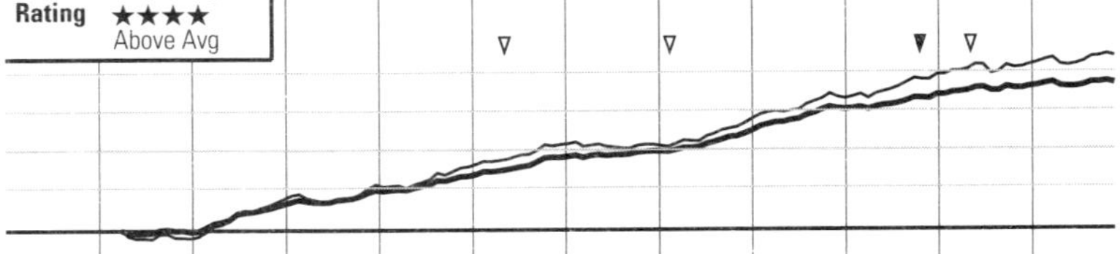

Growth of $10,000
— Investment Values of Fund
— Investment Values of LB Aggr

Performance Quartile (within Category)

1993	1994	1995	1996	1997	1998	1999	2000	2001	2002	2003	12-04	History
—	9.50	10.07	9.92	10.00	10.10	9.73	9.96	10.19	10.32	10.28	10.14	NAV
—	-0.37*	12.89	4.55	7.04	7.63	2.08	8.84	8.88	6.10	3.37	1.70	Total Return %
—	—	-5.58	0.92	-2.61	-1.06	2.90	-2.79	0.44	-4.15	-0.73	-2.64	+/-LB Aggr
—	—	0.01	-0.12	-0.09	0.00	-0.01	-0.07	-0.15	-2.02	0.02	-0.15	+/-LB 1-5 YR
—	0.00	6.76	6.00	6.19	5.90	5.49	6.35	5.85	4.53	3.23	2.99	Income Return %
—	—	6.13	-1.45	0.85	1.73	-3.41	2.49	3.03	1.57	0.14	-1.29	Capital Return %
—	—	19	41	23	3	60	15	2	36	23	38	Total Rtn % Rank Cat
—	0.46	0.62	0.59	0.60	0.57	0.54	0.60	0.57	0.45	0.33	0.30	Income $
—	0.00	0.00	0.00	0.00	0.07	0.03	0.00	0.07	0.02	0.06	0.01	Capital Gains $
—	0.18	0.20	0.20	0.20	0.20	0.20	0.21	0.21	0.22	0.20	—	Expense Ratio %
—	5.77	6.28	5.93	6.03	5.68	5.48	6.16	5.45	5.63	3.17	—	Income Ratio %
—	—	65	65	88	112	108	74	156	139	111	—	Turnover Rate %
—	77	208	327	446	709	1,156	1,287	1,680	2,553	3,041	3,795	Net Assets $mil

Performance 12-31-04

	1st Qtr	2nd Qtr	3rd Qtr	4th Qtr	Total
2000	1.39	1.64	2.72	2.82	8.84
2001	3.23	1.35	3.89	0.17	8.88
2002	-0.05	1.92	2.79	1.33	6.10
2003	1.15	1.77	0.30	0.12	3.37
2004	1.66	-1.80	1.76	0.11	1.42

Trailing	Total Return%	+/- LB Aggr	+/- LB 1-5 YR	%Rank Cat	Growth of $10,000
3 Mo	0.11	-0.84	-0.04	68	10,011
6 Mo	1.87	-2.31	-0.01	28	10,187
1 Yr	1.70	-2.64	-0.15	38	10,170
3 Yr Avg	3.71	-2.48	-0.70	31	11,155
5 Yr Avg	5.74	-1.97	-0.47	14	13,219
10 Yr Avg	6.26	-1.46	-0.25	11	18,353
15 Yr Avg	—	—	—	—	—

Tax Analysis	Tax-Adj Rtn%	%Rank Cat	Tax-Cost Rat	%Rank Cat
3 Yr (estimated)	2.32	23	1.34	55
5 Yr (estimated)	3.87	11	1.77	63
10 Yr (estimated)	4.07	10	2.06	59

Potential Capital Gain Exposure: 0% of assets

Rating and Risk

Time Period	Load-Adj Return %	Morningstar Rtn vs Cat	Morningstar Risk vs Cat	Morningstar Risk-Adj Rating
1 Yr	1.70			
3 Yr	3.71	+Avg	+Avg	★★★★
5 Yr	5.74	+Avg	+Avg	★★★★
10 Yr	6.26	+Avg	+Avg	★★★★
Incept	5.72			

Other Measures	Standard Index LB Aggr	Best Fit Index LB 1-5 YR
Alpha	-0.4	-0.5
Beta	0.57	0.93
R-Squared	91	95
Standard Deviation	2.62	
Mean	3.71	
Sharpe Ratio	0.90	

Portfolio Analysis 09-30-04

Total Fixed-Income:630	Date of Maturity	Amount $000	Value $000	% Net Assets
US Treasury Note 7%	07-15-06	214,335	230,980	4.42
US Treasury Note 2.75%	06-30-06	142,550	143,129	2.74
US Treasury Note 1.625%	02-28-06	137,550	136,132	2.60
US Treasury Note 2.5%	05-31-06	136,000	136,042	2.60
US Treasury Note 1.875%	12-31-05	132,250	131,568	2.52
US Treasury Note 6.5%	10-15-06	121,410	130,687	2.50
US Treasury Note 6.625%	05-15-07	116,825	128,088	2.45
US Treasury Note 6%	08-15-09	114,325	127,812	2.44
US Treasury Note 5.625%	05-15-08	110,325	120,030	2.29
US Treasury Note 6.125%	08-15-07	103,575	112,865	2.16
US Treasury Note 6.875%	05-15-06	102,925	110,146	2.11
US Treasury Note 3.25%	01-15-09	101,875	101,907	1.95
US Treasury Note 6.5%	02-15-10	80,475	92,320	1.76
US Treasury Note 3.125%	10-15-08	69,325	69,217	1.32
US Treasury Note 3.125%	09-15-08	64,700	64,660	1.24
US Treasury Note 5.75%	11-15-05	61,825	64,211	1.23
US Treasury Note 3.875%	05-15-09	53,600	54,890	1.05
FHLBA 5.125%	03-06-06	50,575	52,339	1.00
US Treasury Bond 13.25%	05-15-14	35,000	49,744	0.95
FHLBA 2.875%	09-15-06	49,000	49,038	0.94

Current Investment Style
Duration: Short Int Long
Quality: High Med Low

Avg Eff Duration[1]	2.5 Yrs
Avg Eff Maturity	2.8 Yrs
Avg Credit Quality	AAA
Avg Wtd Coupon	4.90%
Avg Wtd Price	104.70% of par

[1] figure provided by fund

Coupon Range	% of Bonds	Rel Cat
0% PIK	0.0	0.0
0% to 6%	69.5	1.0
6% to 8%	28.1	1.2
8% to 10%	1.4	0.5
More than 10%	1.0	1.2

1.00=Category Average

Credit Analysis	% bonds 09-30-04		
US Govt	67	BB	0
AAA	6	B	0
AA	5	Below B	0
A	13	NR/NA	0
BBB	10		

Sector Breakdown	% of assets
US Treasuries	42
TIPS	0
US Agency	23
Mortgage Pass-Throughs	0
Mortgage CMO	0
Mortgage ARM	0
US Corporate	29
Asset-Backed	0
Convertible	0
Municipal	0
Corporate Inflation-Protected	0
Foreign Corporate	2
Foreign Govt	0

Composition			
Cash	3.1	Bonds	96.9
Stocks	0.0	Other	0.0

Special Securities	
Restricted/Illiquid Secs	Trace
Exotic Mortgage-Backed	0
Emerging-Markets Secs	0
Options/Futures/Warrants	No

Morningstar's Take by Dieter Bardy 10-08-04

Vanguard Short-Term Bond Index is a solid capital preservation option.

Since the fund's inception more than a decade ago, it has only once had a losing year, in 1994. And it has also only once lagged its index, the Lehman Brothers 1-5 year Government/Credit Index, by more than 20 basis points over the past 10 years, in 2002. That year the fund stumbled because of poor performance from its lower-quality corporate-bond stake. To avoid a repeat of 2002, manager Chris Alwine has since paid more attention to diversification across issuers and reined in sector overweights. The fund continues to mimic the index in most other ways.

The only way that the fund now seeks to spice up shareholder returns is by opportunistically buying or selling bonds that will soon be added to or dropped from the index. For example, Alwine knows when the components of the index will change, so he is always looking to pick up paper that will soon be added to the index on the cheap. For instance, when a certain U.S. Treasury bond matures it is replaced in the index with a new issue. Alwine adds value by looking for an issue that is exactly the same from maturity and yield but also has a more reasonable price.

Lately, the fund's interest-rate stance has been relaxed to match its index's. Alwine increased the fund's duration (a measure of interest-rate sensitivity) in September to 2.5 years to match the index. This is slightly more aggressive than its typical short-term bond rival's 2.1-year duration, suggesting that the fund will feel pain if interest rates rise more quickly than anticipated.

But that is not to say that the fund is ill fated. Even though it may stumble when rates rise, as it did in 1999, over longer periods it has easily placed in the category's top quartile. True, the fund's ultralow fees play an important role. Its typical rival charges 0.68%, but this fund's 0.20% fees represent a bargain. All in all this is a compelling option for investors' short-term bond fund needs.

Address:	PO Box 2600 Valley Forge PA 19482 800-662-7447
Web Address:	www.vanguard.com
Inception:	03-01-94 *
Advisor:	Vanguard Advisers, Inc.
Subadvisor:	None
NTF Plans:	N/A

Minimum Purchase:	$3000	Add: $100	IRA: $1000
Min Auto Inv Plan:	$3000	Add: $50	
Sales Fees:	No-load		
Management Fee:	0.19%		
Actual Fees:	Mgt:0.19%	Dist: —	
Expense Projections:	3Yr:$68	5Yr:$118	10Yr:$268
Income Distrib:	Monthly		

Vanguard ShtTm Fed

Analyst Pick	Ticker	Load	NAV	Yield	SEC Yield	Total Assets	Mstar Category
✔	VSGBX	None	$10.41	2.8%	3.20%	$3,119 mil	Short Government

Governance and Management

Fiduciary Grade: B

Portfolio Manager(s)

John Hollyer has managed this offering since 1996. As with Vanguard's other bond funds, this offering's broad interest-rate policy is set by Bob Auwaerter, who has led the firm's fixed-income group since Vanguard veteran Ian MacKinnon retired at the end of June 2003.

Strategy

Unlike its sister fund, Vanguard Short-Term Treasury, which must keep 80% of its assets in Treasuries, this offering has no such restriction. In fact, management usually holds a very modest Treasury stake, preferring to hold agency bonds and mortgages. Duration is typically kept between 2.0 and 2.5 years.

Historical Profile

Return: Above Avg
Risk: Average
Rating: ★★★★ Above Avg

Investment Style: Fixed Income — Income Rtn %Rank Cat

	30	24	30	26	22	30	37	40	40

▼ Manager Change
∇ Partial Manager Change

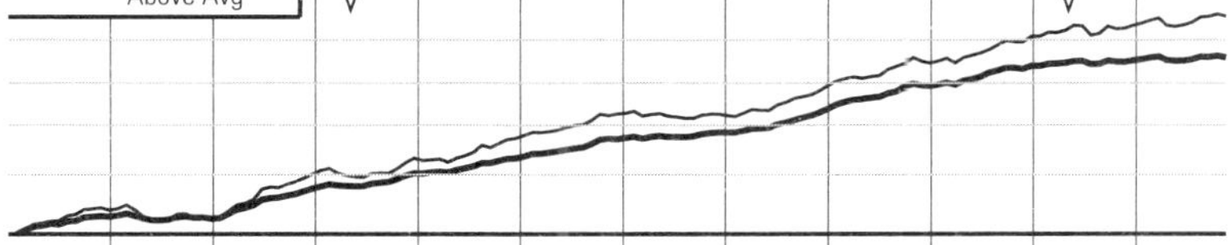

Growth of $10,000
— Investment Values of Fund
— Investment Values of LB Aggr

Performance Quartile (within Category)

1993	1994	1995	1996	1997	1998	1999	2000	2001	2002	2003	12-04	History
10.34	9.69	10.25	10.11	10.13	10.26	9.90	10.17	10.43	10.70	10.58	10.41	NAV
7.00	-0.94	12.26	4.75	6.46	7.22	2.07	9.18	8.61	7.61	1.99	1.36	Total Return %
-2.75	1.98	-6.21	1.12	-3.19	-1.47	2.89	-2.45	0.17	-2.64	-2.11	-2.98	+/-LB Aggr
0.12	-0.17	-0.40	0.15	-0.65	-0.43	0.11	0.09	-0.03	-0.08	-0.17	-0.18	+/-LB 1-5 YR GOVT
5.25	5.39	6.36	6.11	6.24	5.91	5.66	6.31	5.52	4.19	2.97	2.78	Income Return %
1.75	-6.33	5.90	-1.36	0.22	1.31	-3.59	2.87	3.09	3.42	-0.98	-1.42	Capital Return %
40	51	46	20	61	26	34	34	4	38	16	40	Total Rtn % Rank Cat
0.53	0.54	0.60	0.61	0.61	0.58	0.57	0.61	0.55	0.43	0.31	0.29	Income $
0.11	0.01	0.00	0.00	0.00	0.00	0.00	0.00	0.00	0.13	0.02	0.02	Capital Gains $
0.27	0.26	0.28	0.27	0.25	0.27	0.27	0.27	0.28	0.31	0.26	0.22	Expense Ratio %
5.88	4.98	5.53	5.93	6.09	6.04	5.68	5.64	6.10	5.07	3.90	2.86	Income Ratio %
70	49	57	74	57	94	107	93	169	80	136	81	Turnover Rate %
1,922	1,505	1,404	1,339	1,429	1,635	1,521	1,502	1,783	2,851	2,673	2,432	Net Assets $mil

Performance 12-31-04

	1st Qtr	2nd Qtr	3rd Qtr	4th Qtr	Total
2000	1.37	1.64	2.50	3.39	9.18
2001	3.24	1.12	3.74	0.29	8.61
2002	0.44	2.94	3.26	0.78	7.61
2003	0.83	0.95	0.12	0.08	1.99
2004	1.37	-1.50	1.38	0.12	1.36

Trailing	Total Return%	+/- LB Aggr	+/- LB 1-5 YR GOVT	%Rank Cat	Growth of $10,000
3 Mo	0.12	-0.83	0.05	65	10,012
6 Mo	1.50	-2.68	-0.15	50	10,150
1 Yr	1.36	-2.98	-0.18	40	10,136
3 Yr Avg	3.62	-2.57	-0.14	31	11,126
5 Yr Avg	5.69	-2.02	-0.09	24	13,188
10 Yr Avg	6.10	-1.62	-0.16	16	18,078
15 Yr Avg	6.29	-1.41	-0.22	25	24,968

Tax Analysis	Tax-Adj Rtn%	%Rank Cat	Tax-Cost Rat	%Rank Cat
3 Yr (estimated)	2.21	25	1.36	64
5 Yr (estimated)	3.90	17	1.69	64
10 Yr (estimated)	3.98	17	2.00	62

Potential Capital Gain Exposure: -1% of assets

Rating and Risk

Time Period	Load-Adj Return %	Morningstar Rtn vs Cat	Morningstar Risk vs Cat	Morningstar Risk-Adj Rating
1 Yr	1.36			
3 Yr	3.62	+Avg	Avg	★★★★
5 Yr	5.69	+Avg	Avg	★★★★
10 Yr	6.10	+Avg	Avg	★★★★
Incept	6.55			

Other Measures	Standard Index LB Aggr	Best Fit Index LB 1-5 YR GOVT
Alpha	-0.1	0.2
Beta	0.48	0.84
R-Squared	85	98
Standard Deviation	2.31	
Mean	3.62	
Sharpe Ratio	0.99	

Portfolio Analysis 09-30-04

Total Fixed-Income:82	Date of Maturity	Amount $000	Value $000	% Net Assets
FHLBA 5 125%	03-06-06	282,900	292,768	8.94
FNMA 5 25%	04-15-07	269,500	283,862	8.67
US Treasury Note 3.625%	07-15-09	275,000	278,267	8.50
FHLBA 2 875%	09-15-06	150,000	150,117	4.59
FNMA 5%	01-15-07	139,000	145,215	4.44
FHLMC 5.5%	07-15-06	129,000	135,046	4.13
FHLBA 2 5%	11-15-05	100,000	100,072	3.06
US Treasury Note 6.125%	08-15-07	90,000	98,072	3.00
FHLBA 2 375%	02-15-06	90,000	89,760	2.74
US Treasury Note 3.875%	05-15-09	75,000	76,805	2.35
US Treasury Note 4.375%	05-15-07	73,000	75,897	2.32
US Treasury Note 1.625%	02-28-06	67,000	66,309	2.03
Private Expt Fdg 5.53%	04-30-06	56,750	59,256	1.81
FNMA 5.75%	02-15-08	50,000	53,824	1.64
FNMA FRN	06-01-34	49,816	50,188	1.53
US Treasury Note 3.375%	12-15-08	48,500	48,803	1.49
Overseas Private Invt 2.	08-15-07	49,500	48,590	1.48
FNMA FRN	09-01-33	43,133	43,066	1.32
Overseas Private Invt	12-15-07	41,000	40,386	1.23
FNMA 6%	05-15-08	37,000	40,235	1.23

Current Investment Style

Duration: Short Int Long — Quality: High Med Low

[1] figure provided by fund

Avg Eff Duration[1]	2.1 Yrs
Avg Eff Maturity	2.3 Yrs
Avg Credit Quality	AAA
Avg Wtd Coupon	4.01%
Avg Wtd Price	102.82% of par

Coupon Range	% of Bonds	Rel Cat
0% PIK	9.1	0.9
0% to 6%	93.0	1.2
6% to 8%	7.0	0.4
8% to 10%	0.0	0.0
More than 10%	0.0	0.0

1.00=Category Average

Credit Analysis	% bonds 09-30-04		
US Govt	97	BB	0
AAA	3	B	0
AA	0	Below B	0
A	0	NR/NA	0
BBB	0		

Sector Breakdown	% of assets
US Treasuries	22
TIPS	0
US Agency	46
Mortgage Pass-Throughs	15
Mortgage CMO	2
Mortgage ARM	0
US Corporate	1
Asset-Backed	0
Convertible	0
Municipal	0
Corporate Inflation-Protected	0
Foreign Corporate	0
Foreign Govt	0

Composition			
Cash	13.7	Bonds	86.3
Stocks	0.0	Other	0.0

Special Securities	
Restricted/Illiquid Secs	0
Exotic Mortgage-Backed	—
Emerging-Markets Secs	0
Options/Futures/Warrants	No

Morningstar's Take by Lynn Russell 10-12-04

Vanguard Short-Term Federal demonstrates that a fund doesn't need to shoot out the lights to hit its targets.

This fund starts out with the major advantage of ultralow costs. At a measly 0.22%, the fund's expense ratio is a third of what its average no-load peer charges. Given that year-in, year-out head start, it's not surprising that the fund's annual returns are typically well into the top half of the short-government category. The fund doesn't often lead the pack, but has consistently outperformed its peers over the long term. Overall, it has racked up five- and ten-year trailing returns that land in the short-government category's top quartile, while enduring less month-to-month volatility than its average rival.

Even on its bad days, the fund often looks a bit better than many of its peers. Like most bond funds, it was stung when rates jumped in April. Even though manager John Hollyer had been keeping the fund's interest-rate risk on the defensive side of its range, the fund suffered its worst one-month loss ever, dropping 1.28%. But that loss was less than the average short-government fund's drop of 1.32%. And while the fund's relatively short duration (a measure of interest-rate sensitivity) has kept the fund from fully benefiting from falling rates over the past several months; its year-to-date gain of 1.53% through October 13 landed in the category's top half.

We think that this fund's super-low costs, experienced and long-tenured management, and consistent performance make it one of investors' best choices in the short-government category. Given the fund's primary focus on agency bonds, there could be some small bumps in the road as regulators have recently turned their attention to accounting policies at Fannie Mae. But it looks like the changes will be to improve the agency's credit quality, which is long-term good news for its bondholders. This fund is a keeper.

Address:	PO Box 2600 Valley Forge PA 19482 800-662-7447
Web Address:	www.vanguard.com
Inception:	12-31-87
Advisor:	Vanguard Advisers, Inc.
Subadvisor:	None
NTF Plans:	N/A

Minimum Purchase:	$3000	Add: $100	IRA: $1000
Min Auto Inv Plan:	$3000	Add: $50	
Sales Fees:	No-load		
Management Fee:	0.24%		
Actual Fees:	Mgt:0.24%	Dist: —	
Expense Projections:	3Yr:$100	5Yr:$174	10Yr:$393
Income Distrib:	Monthly		

Vanguard Sht-Tm Inv-Grade

Ticker	Load	NAV	Yield	SEC Yield	Total Assets	Mstar Category
VFSTX	None	$10.66	3.4%	3.25%	$18,250 mil	Short-Term Bond

Governance and Management

Fiduciary Grade: B

Portfolio Manager(s)

Seasoned and proven. Bob Auwaerter is responsible for the fund's day-to-day management and has been with the fund since 1984. He also has taken ownership for setting the fund's duration, a duty assumed from outgoing fixed-income chief Ian MacKinnon (whom Auwaerter succeeds). The team also includes an assistant portfolio manager, six credit analysts, and traders.

Strategy

Traditionally this fund has invested mainly in midquality (A and BBB rated) investment-grade corporate bonds. A July 2004 modification will allow its managers to invest a bit more broadly though. The fund's duration is limited to a range of 1.75 to 2.75 years, which typically makes it a bit less sensitive to rate shifts than most of its short-term bond peers. Comanager Bob Auwaerter can also invest in highly rated asset-backed securities because short-term corporate-bond supply can become scarce at times, he said.

Historical Profile

Return Above Avg
Risk Average
Rating ★★★★ Above Avg

Investment Style
Fixed Income
Income Rtn %Rank Cat

1993	1994	1995	1996	1997	1998	1999	2000	2001	2002	2003	12-04
26	25	16	12	7	5	4	14	23			

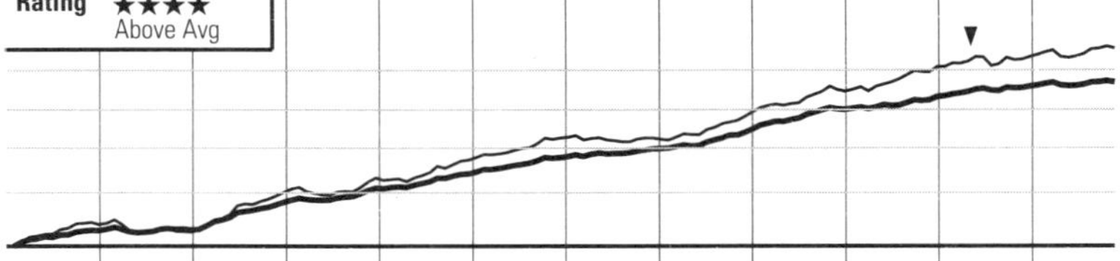

▼ Manager Change
▽ Partial Manager Change

Growth of $10,000
— Investment Values of Fund
— Investment Values of LB Aggr

20.5 / 17.5 / 15.0 / 12.5 / 10.0

Performance Quartile (within Category)

1993	1994	1995	1996	1997	1998	1999	2000	2001	2002	2003	12-04	History
10.90	10.30	10.91	10.75	10.81	10.84	10.53	10.65	10.82	10.79	10.80	10.66	NAV
7.07	-0.08	12.74	4.79	6.95	6.57	3.30	8.17	8.14	5.22	4.20	2.11	Total Return %
-2.68	2.84	-5.73	1.16	-2.70	-2.12	4.12	-3.46	-0.30	-5.03	0.10	-2.23	+/-LB Aggr
-0.03	0.63	-0.14	0.12	-0.18	-1.06	1.21	-0.74	-0.89	-2.90	0.85	0.26	+/-LB 1-5 YR
5.81	5.55	6.68	6.25	6.36	6.30	6.24	6.94	6.55	5.47	4.12	3.43	Income Return %
1.26	-5.63	6.06	-1.46	0.59	0.27	-2.94	1.23	1.59	-0.25	0.08	-1.32	Capital Return %
43	39	21	33	26	41	20	28	18	57	10	24	Total Rtn % Rank Cat
0.61	0.59	0.67	0.66	0.66	0.66	0.66	0.71	0.68	0.58	0.44	0.36	Income $
0.10	0.00	0.00	0.00	0.00	0.00	0.00	0.00	0.00	0.00	0.00	0.00	Capital Gains $
0.27	0.26	0.28	0.27	0.25	0.28	0.27	0.25	0.24	0.24	0.23	0.21	Expense Ratio %
6.33	5.48	5.66	6.23	6.18	6.17	6.08	6.21	6.76	6.18	5.27	3.80	Income Ratio %
71	61	69	62	45	45	46	52	54	69	59	33	Turnover Rate %
3,483	2,906	3,743	4,587	4,601	5,428	6,799	7,341	7,383	8,668	11,120	13,122	Net Assets $mil

Performance 12-31-04

	1st Qtr	2nd Qtr	3rd Qtr	4th Qtr	Total
2000	1.45	1.22	2.78	2.50	8.17
2001	3.18	1.25	3.34	0.17	8.14
2002	0.26	1.25	2.27	1.34	5.22
2003	1.39	1.89	0.39	0.46	4.20
2004	1.53	-1.30	1.50	0.39	2.11

Trailing	Total Return%	+/- LB Aggr	+/- LB 1-5 YR	%Rank Cat	Growth of $10,000
3 Mo	0.39	-0.56	0.24	28	10,039
6 Mo	1.90	-2.28	0.02	27	10,190
1 Yr	2.11	-2.23	0.26	24	10,211
3 Yr Avg	3.84	-2.35	-0.57	26	11,197
5 Yr Avg	5.54	-2.17	-0.67	20	13,094
10 Yr Avg	6.18	-1.54	-0.33	14	18,215
15 Yr Avg	6.52	-1.18	-0.20	18	25,791

Tax Analysis	Tax-Adj Rtn%	%Rank Cat	Tax-Cost Rat	%Rank Cat
3 Yr (estimated)	2.24	28	1.54	75
5 Yr (estimated)	3.50	25	1.93	81
10 Yr (estimated)	3.88	14	2.17	76

Potential Capital Gain Exposure: -1% of assets

Rating and Risk

Time Period	Load-Adj Return %	Morningstar Rtn vs Cat	Morningstar Risk vs Cat	Morningstar Risk-Adj Rating
1 Yr	2.11			
3 Yr	3.84	+Avg	Avg	★★★★
5 Yr	5.54	+Avg	Avg	★★★★
10 Yr	6.18	+Avg	Avg	★★★★
Incept	7.74			

Other Measures	Standard Index LB Aggr	Best Fit Index LB Credit
Alpha	0.5	0.4
Beta	0.40	0.33
R-Squared	76	84
Standard Deviation	2.03	
Mean	3.84	
Sharpe Ratio	1.22	

Portfolio Analysis 09-30-04

Total Fixed-Income:743	Date of Maturity	Amount $000	Value $000	% Net Assets
Morgan Stanley 144A FRN	03-01-07	187,920	197,104	1.10
Abn Amro Bk N V Amsterda	05-11-07	142,700	142,647	0.79
US Treasury Note 3.375%	09-15-09	120,000	120,000	0.67
Targeted Return Index Se	01-25-07	104,364	109,400	0.61
Bk One Chicago Ill Mtn B	03-26-07	94,009	99,841	0.56
Fifth Third Bk Cin Ohio	01-30-07	98,400	97,693	0.54
Bmw Floorplan Mstr Tr 20	10-17-08	97,500	97,500	0.54
Intl Busn Machs 4 875%	10-01-06	87,000	90,272	0.50
FHLBA 2.375%	02-15-06	87,285	87,052	0.48
Wells Fargo FRN	09-28-07	86,800	86,739	0.48
FHLMC FRN	07-01-33	82,032	81,432	0.45
General Elec Cap 5.375%	03-15-07	72,330	76,135	0.42
Monumental Global Fdg Ii	04-10-06	75,000	75,220	0.42
Brown Forman 2.125%	03-15-06	75,225	74,631	0.42
FNMA FRN	07-01-33	73,798	74,605	0.42
Daimlerchrysler Auto Tr	11-08-06	74,500	74,404	0.41
Ford Credit Auto Tr 2004	03-15-08	73,265	73,471	0.41
Natl City Auto Tr 2004-A	07-15-08	73,225	72,607	0.40
Wachovia Auto Tr 2004-A	06-20-08	71,300	71,719	0.40
FNMA FRN	06-01-33	71,759	71,647	0.40

Current Investment Style

Duration: Short Int Long
Quality: High Med Low

¹ figure provided by fund

Avg Eff Duration[1]	2.0 Yrs
Avg Eff Maturity	2.7 Yrs
Avg Credit Quality	AA
Avg Wtd Coupon	3.82%
Avg Wtd Price	101.75% of par

Coupon Range	% of Bonds	Rel Cat
0% PIK	14.0	2.8
0% to 6%	78.9	1.1
6% to 8%	17.5	0.8
8% to 10%	3.4	1.2
More than 10%	0.2	0.3

1.00=Category Average

Credit Analysis	% bonds 09-30-04		
US Govt	14	BB	2
AAA	23	B	0
AA	17	Below B	0
A	24	NR/NA	0
BBB	19		

Sector Breakdown	% of assets
US Treasuries	2
TIPS	0
US Agency	1
Mortgage Pass-Throughs	8
Mortgage CMO	5
Mortgage ARM	0
US Corporate	55
Asset-Backed	20
Convertible	0
Municipal	0
Corporate Inflation-Protected	0
Foreign Corporate	1
Foreign Govt	0

Composition			
Cash	8.8	Bonds	91.0
Stocks	0.0	Other	0.3

Special Securities	
Restricted/Illiquid Secs	12
Exotic Mortgage-Backed	0
Emerging-Markets Secs	0
Options/Futures/Warrants	No

Morningstar's Take by Dieter Bardy 10-12-04

Vanguard Short-Term Investment-Grade remains a good fit for income-oriented investors.

This fund underwent name and slight strategy changes in mid-July 2004. The alteration gives manager Bob Auwaerter more flexibility to invest beyond corporate bonds into sectors such as mortgages, U.S. agency bonds, and U.S. Treasury debt. We haven't seen evidence yet of Auwaerter using the extra flexibility, but we'll continue to watch for significant portfolio changes. Auwaerter argues that he will not make use of the added leeway except when he's struggling to find suitable corporate names.

However, this fund has always exhibited a different profile than its Vanguard corporate bond siblings. It has typically held a greater amount of securities in asset-backed securities (ABS), which are bonds backed by short-term cash flows such as credit-card receivables or car loans. Currently, Auwaerter prefers them to other corporate bonds, which he feels have become too rich. He views ABS as a high-quality alternative to short-term corporate debt. The most recent portfolio shows about 19% invested in senior-level ABS.

Apart from that, Auwaerter has not meaningfully changed the fund's interest-rate sensitivity. Duration, a measure of a fund's interest-rate sensitivity, has lengthened a bit to two years yet still remains on the short end of the short-term bond category's 2.1-year average. Thus, this fund should weather rising rates better than most.

Finally, one of the most attractive parts of this fund is its above-average yield. The fund's 3.5% payout is among the category's top quintile. It's able to maintain that payout rate partially because of the below average expenses. At 0.21% it is among the group's cheapest options. This enviable position--below-average expenses and an above-average yield--is a compelling reason to invest here.

Address:	PO Box 2600 Valley Forge PA 19482 800-662-7447
Web Address:	www.vanguard.com
Inception:	10-29-82
Advisor:	Vanguard Advisers, Inc.
Subadvisor:	None
NTF Plans:	N/A

Minimum Purchase:	$3000	Add: $100	IRA: $1000
Min Auto Inv Plan:	$3000	Add: $50	
Sales Fees:	No-load		
Management Fee:	0.21%		
Actual Fees:	Mgt:0.21%	Dist: —	
Expense Projections:	3Yr:$74	5Yr:$130	10Yr:$293
Income Distrib:	Monthly		

Vanguard Sht-Tm TE

Analyst Pick	Ticker	Load	NAV	Yield	SEC Yield	Total Assets	Mstar Category
✔	VWSTX	None	$15.63	1.9%	2.01%	$4,527 mil	Muni National Short

Governance and Management

Fiduciary Grade: B

Portfolio Manager(s)

Pam Wisehaupt-Tynan has managed the fund since the start of 1997 as well as its sibling, Vanguard Limited-Term Tax Exempt, which has an excellent record. She has been with Vanguard since 1981 as an accountant and assistant portfolio manager.

Strategy

The fund invests in high-quality municipal issues with a combined average maturity of one to two years. Management adjusts the fund's duration within a specified range, depending on its interest-rate outlook. The fund's short maturity and use of variable-rate notes make it look a lot like a tax-free money market fund, but with greater return potential and price volatility.

Historical Profile

Return Average
Risk Below Avg
Rating ★★★ Neutral

Investment Style: Fixed Income — Income Rtn %Rank Cat: 72, 60, 59, 64, 54, 45, 69, 67, 66

▼ Manager Change
▽ Partial Manager Change

Growth of $10,000
— Investment Values of Fund
— Investment Values of LB Muni

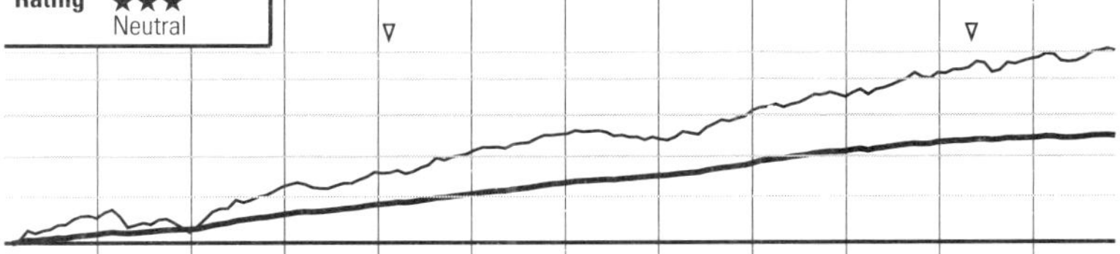

Performance Quartile (within Category)

History	1993	1994	1995	1996	1997	1998	1999	2000	2001	2002	2003	12-04
NAV	15.63	15.33	15.62	15.58	15.58	15.63	15.45	15.56	15.68	15.80	15.75	15.63
Total Return %	3.82	1.63	5.99	3.69	4.07	4.32	2.58	4.91	4.74	3.49	1.64	1.12
+/-LB Muni	-8.46	6.80	-11.47	-0.74	-5.12	-2.16	4.64	-6.77	-0.39	-6.11	-3.67	-3.36
+/-LB Muni 3YR	-2.40	0.95	-2.88	-0.75	-1.41	-0.89	0.62	-1.32	-1.85	-3.23	-1.04	-0.66
Income Return %	3.76	3.57	4.08	3.92	4.02	3.95	3.76	4.17	3.98	2.71	1.96	1.89
Capital Return %	0.06	-1.94	1.91	-0.23	0.05	0.37	-1.18	0.74	0.76	0.78	-0.32	-0.77
Total Rtn % Rank Cat	100	7	90	54	85	76	4	77	59	82	81	50
Income $	0.58	0.55	0.61	0.60	0.62	0.60	0.58	0.63	0.6[illegible]	0.42	0.31	0.29
Capital Gains $	0.02	0.00	0.00	0.00	0.01	0.01	0.00	0.00	0.00	0.00	0.00	0.00
Expense Ratio %	0.20	0.20	0.21	0.20	0.19	0.20	0.18	0.18	0.19	0.17	0.17	0.14
Income Ratio %	3.88	3.42	3.88	3.90	3.91	3.90	3.71	4.03	4.04	2.80	2.01	1.86
Turnover Rate %	46	27	32	33	34	36	56	45	47	53	25	10
Net Assets $mil	1,465	1,463	1,410	1,452	1,492	1,657	1,917	2,117	1,359	2,022	2,153	2,164

Performance 12-31-04

	1st Qtr	2nd Qtr	3rd Qtr	4th Qtr	Total
2000	0.91	1.17	1.23	1.51	4.91
2001	1.68	1.15	1.36	0.48	4.74
2002	0.32	1.48	1.00	0.64	3.49
2003	0.46	0.56	0.46	0.15	1.64
2004	0.46	-0.30	0.79	0.18	1.12

Trailing	Total Return%	+/- LB Muni	+/- LB Muni 3YR	%Rank Cat	Growth of $10,000
3 Mo	0.18	-1.07	-0.01	62	10,018
6 Mo	0.97	-4.22	-1.13	81	10,097
1 Yr	1.12	-3.36	-0.66	50	10,112
3 Yr Avg	2.08	-4.36	-1.63	79	10,637
5 Yr Avg	3.17	-4.03	-1.61	82	11,689
10 Yr Avg	3.64	-3.42	-1.33	80	14,298
15 Yr Avg	4.02	-2.97	—	91	18,061

Tax Analysis	Tax-Adj Rtn%	%Rank Cat	Tax-Cost Rat	%Rank Cat
3 Yr (estimated)	2.08	70	0.00	1
5 Yr (estimated)	3.17	79	0.00	1
10 Yr (estimated)	3.64	73	0.00	1

Potential Capital Gain Exposure: 0% of assets

Rating and Risk

Time Period	Load-Adj Return %	Morningstar Rtn vs Cat	Morningstar Risk vs Cat	Morningstar Risk-Adj Rating
1 Yr	1.12			
3 Yr	2.08	-Avg	-Avg	★★
5 Yr	3.17	-Avg	-Avg	★★
10 Yr	3.64	Avg	Low	★★★
Incept	4.92			

Other Measures	Standard Index LB Aggr	Best Fit Index LB Muni 3YR
Alpha	-0.2	-0.2
Beta	0.17	0.38
R-Squared	74	95
Standard Deviation	0.95	
Mean	2.08	
Sharpe Ratio	0.74	

Portfolio Analysis 09-30-04

Total Fixed-Income:357	Date of Maturity	Amount $000	Value $000	% Net Assets
Harris Cnty Tex Health F	12-01-32	97,175	97,175	2.02
New York St Twy Auth 2.2	10-06-05	68,000	68,387	1.42
Kenton Cnty Ky Arpt Brd	07-01-32	40,000	40,000	0.83
Amer Pub Engy Agy Neb Ga	02-01-14	36,371	36,371	0.76
California St Dept Wtr R	05-01-08	33,000	36,046	0.75
Atlanta Ga Arpt	01-01-30	35,300	35,300	0.74
Minnesota St 5%	08-01-07	30,685	33,142	0.69
New York N Y City Indl D	05-01-29	32,955	32,955	0.69
Chicago Ill Wtr	11-01-30	31,605	31,605	0.66
California St Econ Recov	07-01-07	29,000	31,285	0.65
Clark Cnty Nev Sch Dist	06-01-07	29,020	31,205	0.65
North Carolina St 5%	02-01-08	27,585	30,012	0.63
Missouri St 5%	10-01-06	27,505	29,201	0.61
Kentucky Econ Dev Fin Au	08-15-31	28,730	28,730	0.60
Massachusetts St 5%	02-01-06	27,500	28,653	0.60

Current Investment Style

Duration: Short Int Long — Quality: High Med Low

¹Avg Eff Duration	1.1 Yrs
Avg Eff Maturity	1.2 Yrs
Avg Credit Quality	AAA
Avg Wtd Coupon	3.73%
Avg Wtd Price	103.66% of par

¹figure provided by fund

Credit Analysis	% bonds 09-30-04		
US Govt	0	BB	0
AAA	67	B	0
AA	26	Below B	0
A	5	NR/NA	0
BBB	2		

Top 5 States	% bonds		
NY	10.1	CA	7.8
TX	9.7	IL	5.4
PA	8.5		

Composition			
Cash	26.4	Bonds	73.6
Stocks	0.0	Other	0.0

Special Securities	
Restricted/Illiquid Secs	0
Options/Futures/Warrants	No

Sector Weightings	% of Bonds	Rel Cat
General Obligation	42.1	1.20
Utilities	13.0	1.40
Health	3.7	0.51
Water/Waste	9.7	0.92
Housing	4.3	0.58
Education	6.8	0.78
Transportation	5.6	1.31
COP/Lease	0.0	0.00
Industrial	14.5	0.96
Misc Revenue	0.0	—
Demand	0.3	0.40

Morningstar's Take by Lynn Russell 12-21-04

Vanguard Short-Term Tax-Exempt is an attractive choice for conservative municipal bond investors.

The past year's interest-rate roller-coaster ride has underscored this fund's virtues. Like most fixed-income offerings, the fund was hit when rates jumped in April. The fund actually posted only its second negative calendar quarter in its 26-year history. However, it lost only a third as much as its average short-term muni peer. So though the fund struggled to keep pace when rates drifted lower over the summer months, it had a smaller hole to dig out of than many rivals. Overall, the fund gained 1.1% for the year to date through Dec. 20, 2004, matching the performance of its average peer.

That resilience in the face of climbing interest rates is due to the fund's relatively short duration (a measure of interest-rate sensitivity). Manager Pam Wisehaupt-Tynan keeps the portfolio's duration near the Lehman Brothers Three-Year Municipal Index. As a result, the fund typically exposes investors to much less interest-rate risk than all but a handful of competitors. As a result, the fund displays only a third of the month-to-month volatility of its typical competitor.

That shorter duration has held the fund back during bond-market rallies, though. The fund hasn't gotten as much benefit from falling interest rates as its longer-duration peers over the past decade, for example. Its focus on shorter maturity bonds has also meant a lower income return. Finally, though the fund typically shines when interest rates spike, it three-, five-, and 10-year trailing returns all land in category's bottom quartile.

Compared to tax-free money market funds, however, this offering looks much more appealing, with returns typically more than twice that of those funds. Unlike a money market fund, this fund's net asset value does fluctuate, but given its limited volatility, low costs, and experienced management, we think conservative investors will find this fund to their liking.

Address:	PO Box 2600 Valley Forge PA 19482 800-662-7447
Web Address:	www.vanguard.com
Inception:	09-01-77
Advisor:	Vanguard Advisers, Inc.
Subadvisor:	None
NTF Plans:	N/A

Minimum Purchase:	$3000	Add: $100	IRA: $1000
Min Auto Inv Plan:	$3000	Add: $50	
Sales Fees:	No-load		
Management Fee:	0.15%		
Actual Fees:	Mgt:0.15%	Dist: —	
Expense Projections:	3Yr:$55	5Yr:$96	10Yr:$217
Income Distrib:	Monthly		

Vanguard Short-Tm Trs

Ticker	Load	NAV	Yield	SEC Yield	Total Assets	Mstar Category
VFISX	None	$10.47	2.7%	2.86%	$3,507 mil	Short Government

Governance and Management

Fiduciary Grade: B

Portfolio Manager(s)

David Glocke assumed day-to-day management duties of this fund in May 2000. He is assisted by the head of Vanguard's fixed-income team, Bob Auwaerter, who has been setting the firm's interest-rate policy since Vanguard veteran Ian MacKinnon retired at the end of June 2003.

Strategy

Management is required to keep at least 80% of assets in Treasuries, and though it does hold agency bonds, it leaves the mortgage-backed market to its sibling, Vanguard Short-Term Federal. Manager David Glocke typically keeps the portfolio's duration between two and 2.5 years and avoids big interest-rate bets.

Historical Profile

Return: Above Avg
Risk: Average
Rating: ★★★★ Above Avg

Investment Style: Fixed Income — Income Rtn %Rank Cat: 47, 30, 48, 51, 35, 46, 51, 57, 47

▼ Manager Change
▽ Partial Manager Change

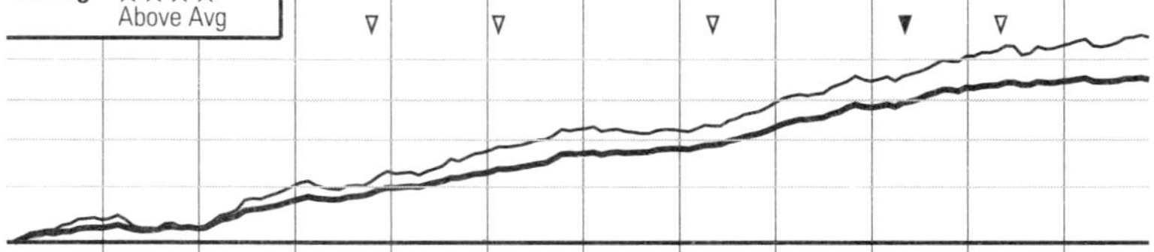

Growth of $10,000
— Investment Values of Fund
— Investment Values of LB Aggr

Performance Quartile (within Category)

History

1993	1994	1995	1996	1997	1998	1999	2000	2001	2002	2003	12-04	History
10.38	9.79	10.32	10.17	10.21	10.37	10.01	10.27	10.53	10.83	10.64	10.47	NAV
6.31	-0.48	12.11	4.39	6.51	7.36	1.85	8.83	7.80	8.02	2.38	1.03	Total Return %
-3.44	2.44	-6.36	0.76	-3.14	-1.33	2.67	-2.80	-0.64	-2.23	-1.72	-3.31	+/-LB Aggr
-0.57	0.29	-0.55	-0.21	-0.60	-0.29	-0.11	-0.26	-0.84	0.33	0.22	-0.51	+/-LB 1-5 YR GOVT
4.87	5.14	6.58	5.84	6.08	5.53	5.23	6.10	5.19	4.02	2.57	2.65	Income Return %
1.44	-5.62	5.53	-1.45	0.43	1.83	-3.38	2.73	2.61	4.00	-0.19	-1.62	Capital Return %
55	38	50	33	59	23	40	40	20	28	6	58	Total Rtn % Rank Cat
0.49	0.52	0.63	0.59	0.60	0.55	0.53	0.59	0.52	0.42	0.27	0.28	Income $
0.08	0.02	0.00	0.00	0.00	0.02	0.02	0.00	0.01	0.11	0.17	0.00	Capital Gains $
0.26	0.26	0.28	0.27	0.25	0.27	0.27	0.27	0.27	0.29	0.28	0.26	Expense Ratio %
5.12	4.64	5.33	6.14	5.77	5.80	5.27	5.27	5.91	4.82	3.70	2.52	Income Ratio %
71	86	126	93	86	83	132	124	296	102	165	125	Turnover Rate %
705	704	869	966	998	1,184	1,235	1,200	1,394	2,211	2,086	1,886	Net Assets $mil

Performance 12-31-04

	1st Qtr	2nd Qtr	3rd Qtr	4th Qtr	Total
2000	1.24	1.80	2.33	3.19	8.83
2001	2.85	0.83	3.92	0.02	7.80
2002	0.28	3.08	3.65	0.81	8.02
2003	0.78	1.17	0.25	0.17	2.38
2004	1.20	-1.34	1.16	0.02	1.03

Trailing	Total Return%	+/- LB Aggr	+/- LB 1-5 YR GOVT	%Rank Cat	Growth of $10,000
3 Mo	0.03	-0.92	-0.04	81	10,003
6 Mo	1.18	-3.00	-0.47	64	10,118
1 Yr	1.03	-3.31	-0.51	58	10,103
3 Yr Avg	3.77	-2.42	0.01	27	11,174
5 Yr Avg	5.56	-2.15	-0.22	29	13,107
10 Yr Avg	5.98	-1.74	-0.28	25	17,875
15 Yr Avg	—	—	—	—	—

Tax Analysis	Tax-Adj Rtn%	%Rank Cat	Tax-Cost Rat	%Rank Cat
3 Yr (estimated)	2.35	20	1.37	66
5 Yr (estimated)	3.80	22	1.67	61
10 Yr (estimated)	3.91	20	1.95	54

Potential Capital Gain Exposure: 0% of assets

Rating and Risk

Time Period	Load-Adj Return %	Morningstar Rtn vs Cat	Morningstar Risk vs Cat	Morningstar Risk-Adj Rating
1 Yr	1.03			
3 Yr	3.77	+Avg	Avg	★★★★
5 Yr	5.56	+Avg	Avg	★★★★
10 Yr	5.98	+Avg	Avg	★★★★
Incept	5.71			

Other Measures	Standard Index LB Aggr	Best Fit Index LB 1-5 YR GOVT
Alpha	0.1	0.3
Beta	0.48	0.87
R-Squared	79	96
Standard Deviation	2.40	
Mean	3.77	
Sharpe Ratio	1.01	

Morningstar's Take by Dieter Bardy 11-30-04

Vanguard Short-Term Treasury offers a cautious stance for risk-averse investors.

What you see is what you get with this fund. As its name suggests, its manager, David Glocke, buys mostly U.S. Treasury bonds with maturities of one to three years. Although he'll mix in a little agency debt on the margins, he won't hold any mortgage bonds--a key difference between this fund and the rest in the short-term government category.

That's not to say this is an index fund, though. Glocke tries to add value through timely shifts to the fund's interest-rate exposure. In early September 2004, the fund increased its interest sensitivity, but only to a small degree. Vanguard pushed the fund's duration, a measure of interest-rate sensitivity, up from two years to 2.18 years. This new average represents a neutral position for the fund relative to its benchmark, the Lehman Brothers 1-5 Year Treasury Index, and brings it closer to its typical short-term government category rival's 2.3 year average. Glocke has increased it because he feels that the market has priced in future short-term interest-rate hikes. Thus, unless there is a catalyst in the system that sparks an unexpected jump in rates, its more neutral position should help improve performance.

For most of 2004, the fund's previously bearish stance held it back. Indeed, the fund's 0.6% return for the year to date through Nov. 29, 2004, has been below its typical peer's 1.2% gain. Also, over time the fund has delivered solid performance, and its top quartile three-, five- and 10-year returns are testimony to that. Moreover, the fund's conservative stance has also led to a less volatile fund, as measured by standard deviation. The fund has been about 11% less volatile than its typical category rival over the long haul.

Even if interest rates rise further this year, we think that this fund is well-positioned. Investors who want safe, inexpensive exposure to U.S. government debt, without mortgages, will like this option.

Address:	PO Box 2600, Valley Forge PA 19482, 800-662-7447
Web Address:	www.vanguard.com
Inception:	10-28-91
Advisor:	Vanguard Advisers, Inc.
Subadvisor:	None
NTF Plans:	N/A

Minimum Purchase:	$3000	Add: $100	IRA: $1000
Min Auto Inv Plan:	$3000	Add: $50	
Sales Fees:	No-load		
Management Fee:	0.26%		
Actual Fees:	Mgt:0.26%	Dist: —	
Expense Projections:	3Yr:$93	5Yr:$163	10Yr:$368
Income Distrib:	Monthly		

Portfolio Analysis 09-30-04

Total Fixed-Income:43	Date of Maturity	Amount $000	Value $000	% Net Assets
US Treasury Note 7%	07-15-06	546,000	588,402	16.36
US Treasury Note 1.625%	10-31-05	540,000	536,539	14.92
US Treasury Note 6%	08-15-09	305,000	340,981	9.48
US Treasury Note 4%	06-15-09	312,875	321,920	8.95
US Treasury Note 6.875%	05-15-06	220,000	235,435	6.55
US Treasury Note 1.875%	01-31-06	200,000	198,750	5.53
US Treasury Note 2.25%	04-30-06	160,000	159,525	4.44
US Treasury Note 6.5%	10-15-06	125,000	134,551	3.74
US Treasury Note 3.125%	10-15-08	128,000	127,800	3.55
US Treasury Note 3.875%	05-15-09	75,000	76,805	2.14
US Treasury Note 5.625%	05-15-08	70,000	76,158	2.12
US Treasury Note 3.25%	08-15-08	65,000	65,315	1.82
US Treasury Note 3.375%	12-15-08	60,000	60,375	1.68
Private Expt Fdg 7.65%	05-15-06	55,000	59,286	1.65
US Treasury Note 5.875%	11-15-05	51,000	53,040	1.47
US Treasury Note 3.625%	07-15-09	50,000	50,594	1.41
US Treasury Note 1.875%	11-30-05	50,000	49,774	1.38
Private Expt Fdg 3.4%	02-15-08	45,000	45,095	1.25
Private Expt Fdg 5.53%	04-30-06	25,000	26,104	0.73
FHLBA 5.375%	02-15-06	20,000	20,750	0.58

Current Investment Style

Duration: Short Int Long; Quality: High Med Low

[1] figure provided by fund

Avg Eff Duration[1]	2.2 Yrs
Avg Eff Maturity	2.4 Yrs
Avg Credit Quality	AAA
Avg Wtd Coupon	4.53%
Avg Wtd Price	104.29% of par

Coupon Range	% of Bonds	Rel Cat
0% PIK	0.4	0.0
0% to 6%	68.1	0.9
6% to 8%	31.9	1.8
8% to 10%	0.0	0.0
More than 10%	0.0	0.0

1.00=Category Average

Credit Analysis	% bonds 09-30-04		
US Govt	96	BB	0
AAA	4	B	0
AA	0	Below B	0
A	0	NR/NA	0
BBB	0		

Sector Breakdown	% of assets
US Treasuries	86
TIPS	0
US Agency	4
Mortgage Pass-Throughs	1
Mortgage CMO	0
Mortgage ARM	0
US Corporate	1
Asset-Backed	0
Convertible	0
Municipal	0
Corporate Inflation-Protected	0
Foreign Corporate	0
Foreign Govt	0

Composition			
Cash	8.0	Bonds	92.0
Stocks	0.0	Other	0.0

Special Securities	
Restricted/Illiquid Secs	0
Exotic Mortgage-Backed	—
Emerging-Markets Secs	0
Options/Futures/Warrants	No

Vanguard SmCp Gr Idx

Ticker	Load	NAV	Yield	Total Assets	Mstar Category
VISGX	None	$15.16	0.1%	$1,473 mil	Small Growth

Governance and Management

Fiduciary Grade: B

Portfolio Manager(s)

Gus Sauter, who has been at the helm since this fund's May 1998 inception, is one of the most seasoned hands in the indexing business. He has been very successful guiding Vanguard's index lineup over a number of years.

Strategy

In 2003, this fund began to track a new bogy, the MSCI U.S. Small Cap Growth Index, which replaced the S&P Small Cap 600/Barra Growth Index. The S&P excluded companies with limited operating histories, making many startup tech firms off-limits, yet its over-reliance on price/book multiples to define "growth" made it an imperfect proxy for the small-growth universe. Because the new index's inclusion requirements are far less stringent and its classification methodology is far more robust (involving an eight-pronged classification model), it should offer a purer representation of small-growth stocks.

Historical Profile
Return Above Avg
Risk Below Avg
Rating ★★★★ Above Avg

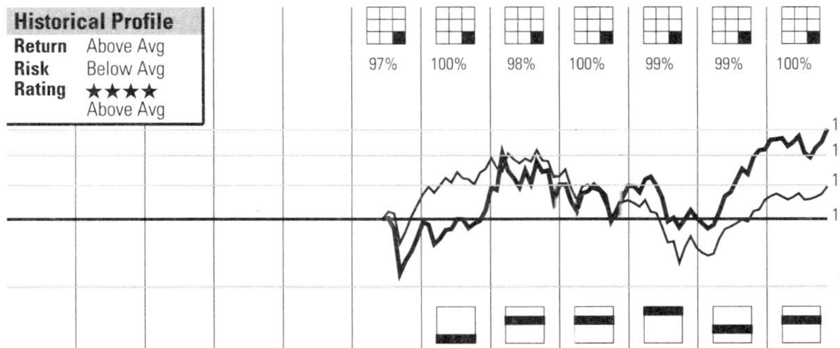

Investment Style
Equity
Stock %

▼ Manager Change
▽ Partial Manager Change

Growth of $10,000
— Investment Values of Fund
— Investment Values of S&P 500

Performance Quartile (within Category)

1993	1994	1995	1996	1997	1998	1999	2000	2001	2002	2003	12-04	History
—	—	—	—	—	9.53	11.38	10.97	10.87	9.17	13.08	15.16	NAV
—	—	—	—	—	-4.77*	19.80	1.59	-0.78	-15.41	42.88	16.06	Total Return %
—	—	—	—	—	—	-1.24	10.69	11.10	6.68	14.21	5.19	+/-S&P 500
—	—	—	—	—	—	-23.29	24.02	8.45	14.85	-5.66	1.75	+/-Russ 2000 Gr
—	—	—	—	—	0.00	0.37	0.03	0.14	0.23	0.24	0.15	Income Return %
—	—	—	—	—	—	19.43	1.56	-0.92	-15.64	42.64	15.91	Capital Return %
—	—	—	—	—	—	79	31	27	6	56	27	Total Rtn % Rank Cat
—	—	—	—	—	0.03	0.04	0.00	0.02	0.03	0.02	0.02	Income $
—	—	—	—	—	0.00	0.00	0.57	0.00	0.00	0.00	0.00	Capital Gains $
—	—	—	—	—	0.25	0.25	0.27	0.27	0.27	0.27	—	Expense Ratio %
—	—	—	—	—	0.63	0.33	0.03	0.11	0.24	0.21	—	Income Ratio %
—	—	—	—	—	—	82	136	74	61	108	—	Turnover Rate %
—	—	—	—	—	90	167	356	357	388	907	1,435	Net Assets $mil

Performance 12-31-04

	1st Qtr	2nd Qtr	3rd Qtr	4th Qtr	Total
2000	9.14	0.32	-0.88	-6.39	1.59
2001	-13.04	14.99	-17.50	20.27	-0.78
2002	3.59	-8.97	-14.63	5.09	-15.41
2003	-3.60	18.78	9.90	13.54	42.88
2004	6.04	1.08	-5.71	14.83	16.06

Trailing	Total Return%	+/- S&P 500	+/- Russ 2000 Gr	%Rank Cat	Growth of $10,000
3 Mo	14.83	5.60	-0.25	32	11,483
6 Mo	8.28	1.09	0.12	49	10,828
1 Yr	16.06	5.19	1.75	27	11,606
3 Yr Avg	11.94	8.36	6.15	9	14,027
5 Yr Avg	7.17	9.47	10.74	17	14,137
10 Yr Avg	—	—	—	—	—
15 Yr Avg	—	—	—	—	—

Tax Analysis	Tax-Adj Rtn%	%Rank Cat	Tax-Cost Rat	%Rank Cat
3 Yr (estimated)	11.87	8	0.06	7
5 Yr (estimated)	6.81	15	0.34	16
10 Yr (estimated)	—	—	—	—

Potential Capital Gain Exposure: 17% of assets

Rating and Risk

Time Period	Load-Adj Return %	Morningstar Rtn vs Cat	Morningstar Risk vs Cat	Morningstar Risk-Adj Rating
1 Yr	16.06			
3 Yr	11.94	+Avg	-Avg	★★★★
5 Yr	7.17	+Avg	-Avg	★★★★
10 Yr	—	—	—	—
Incept	7.50			

Other Measures	Standard Index S&P 500	Best Fit Index Russ 2000 Gr
Alpha	8.8	6.5
Beta	0.91	0.77
R-Squared	63	95
Standard Deviation	19.27	
Mean	11.94	
Sharpe Ratio	0.55	

Morningstar's Take by Sonya Morris 12-14-04

Vanguard Small-Cap Growth Index is a respectable, if not inspiring, option.

This fund has its merits. It's one of the cheapest small-growth funds around. Indeed, it's even cheaper than some competing ETF entrants. Plus, it's broadly diversified. And Gus Sauter, Vanguard's vaunted index-fund manager, has proven himself particularly adept at keeping up with a benchmark.

Furthermore, this fund's new bogy distinguishes it from its index brethren. The MSCI U.S. Small Cap Growth Index employs multiple variables to identify growth stocks. As a result, it should provide purer exposure to growth stocks than the fund's old benchmark, the S&P Small Cap 600/Barra Growth Index, which relies solely on the price/book ratio. In addition, the MSCI index should circumvent the technical reconstitution problems that have dogged the Russell 2000 Growth Index.

Still, these strengths may not be enough to lift this fund past its actively managed rivals. Indeed, active managers have had an easier time edging past indexes in the less efficient small-cap space. Also, given that small-cap stocks have been on an extended run, a cold streak could be in the offing. A tepid environment of this sort typically doesn't favor index funds, which must remain fully invested and can't take refuge in more stable parts of the market when trouble hits, as an active manager can.

That said, small-cap offerings have been flooded with assets recently, inhibiting their ability to execute their strategy. In fact, some of our favorite small-growth funds have closed to try to head off that problem. As a result, there are now fewer small-growth funds to choose from. Still, with a bit of work, investors can ferret out actively managed small-growth funds that still have some headroom. But, for those without the time or inclination to exercise such due diligence, this fund offers no-fuss exposure to small-growth stocks.

Portfolio Analysis 09-30-04

Share change since 06-04 Total Stocks:981	Sector	PE	YTD Ret%	% Assets
⊕ Cognizant Technology Sol	Business	62.5	85.50	0.60
⊕ Ultra Petroleum	Energy	43.1	95.49	0.56
⊕ American Tower A	Telecom	—	70.06	0.52
⊕ Davita	Health	19.0	52.04	0.47
⊕ Crown Castle International	Telecom	—	50.86	0.46
⊕ Cytyc	Health	41.3	99.21	0.41
⊖ Monster Worldwide	Business	54.6	53.19	0.40
⊕ NII Holdings	Telecom	7.4	90.74	0.39
⊕ Getty Images	Business	37.9	37.34	0.39
⊕ Covance	Health	26.6	44.59	0.38
⊕ Varco International	Energy	38.9	41.30	0.38
⊖ Polaris Industries	Goods	24.1	56.60	0.36
⊕ Grant Prideco	Energy	77.8	53.99	0.36
⊖ Certegy	Business	21.2	8.92	0.36
⊕ Navistar International	Ind Mtrls	17.5	-8.17	0.36
⊕ Western Wireless A	Telecom	—	59.59	0.35
⊕ International Rectifier	Hardware	23.6	-9.80	0.34
⊕ Cree	Hardware	33.7	126.57	0.34
⊖ Corporate Executive Boar	Business	54.1	44.20	0.34
⊕ SpectraSite	Telecom	—	66.62	0.34

Current Investment Style

Value Blnd Growth; Large Mid Small

Market Cap	%
Giant	0.0
Large	0.0
Mid	39.2
Small	52.5
Micro	8.3
Avg $mil: 1,163	

Value Measures		Rel Category
Price/Earnings	21.04	0.97
Price/Book	2.67	1.02
Price/Sales	1.33	0.89
Price/Cash Flow	7.31	0.91
Dividend Yield %	0.19	0.61

Growth Measures	%	Rel Category
Long-Term Erngs	17.22	1.00
Book Value	3.48	0.54
Sales	3.95	0.61
Cash Flow	11.74	0.87
Historical Erngs	10.52	0.78

Profitability	%	Rel Category
Return on Equity	10.92	1.11
Return on Assets	4.62	1.05
Net Margin	6.63	0.97

Sector Weightings	% of Stocks	Rel S&P 500	3 Year High	3 Year Low
Info	25.24	1.17		
Software	6.80	1.58	9	6
Hardware	12.68	1.24	17	6
Media	2.36	0.61	3	0
Telecom	3.40	1.08	3	0
Service	53.14	1.15		
Health	20.24	1.62	21	19
Consumer	12.61	1.39	20	12
Business	13.99	3.45	15	10
Financial	6.30	0.30	11	6
Mfg	21.62	0.67		
Goods	4.84	0.52	8	4
Ind Mtrls	10.11	0.80	16	7
Energy	6.56	0.92	7	3
Utilities	0.11	0.04	2	0

Composition

Cash	0.0
Stocks	100.0
Bonds	0.0
Other	0.0
Foreign (% of Stock)	0.0

Address:	P O Box 2600 Valley Forge PA 19482 800-662-7447
Web Address:	www.vanguard.com
Inception:	05-21-98*
Advisor:	Vanguard Advisers, Inc.
Subadvisor:	None
NTF Plans:	N/A

Minimum Purchase:	$3000	Add: $100	IRA: $1000
Min Auto Inv Plan:	$3000	Add: $50	
Sales Fees:	No-load		
Management Fee:	0.24%		
Actual Fees:	Mgt:0.24%	Dist: —	
Expense Projections:	3Yr:$87	5Yr:$152	10Yr:$343
Income Distrib:	Annually		

Vanguard SmCp Idx

Ticker	Load	NAV	Yield	Total Assets	Mstar Category
NAESX	None	$26.83	1.0%	$9,346 mil	Small Blend

Governance and Management

Fiduciary Grade: B

Portfolio Manager(s)

Index guru Gus Sauter has managed this fund since 1989, and there aren't many passive managers who are better than he is. He has done a superb job of adding value through effective trading techniques.

Strategy

Vanguard recently replaced this fund's old bogy, the Russell 2000 Index, with the MSCI U.S. Small Cap 1750 Index. The MSCI Index contains the smallest 1,750 of the top 2,500 publicly traded companies in the United States that are ranked by market capitalization. Because it pulls in a passel of mid-cap names (those that rank from 750th to 999th largest by market cap), its median market cap is a tad higher than that of the Russell Index.

Historical Profile

Return Below Avg
Risk Above Avg
Rating ★★ Below Avg

Investment Style: Equity, Stock %: 97% 97% 96% 98% 98% 99% 99% 99% 100%

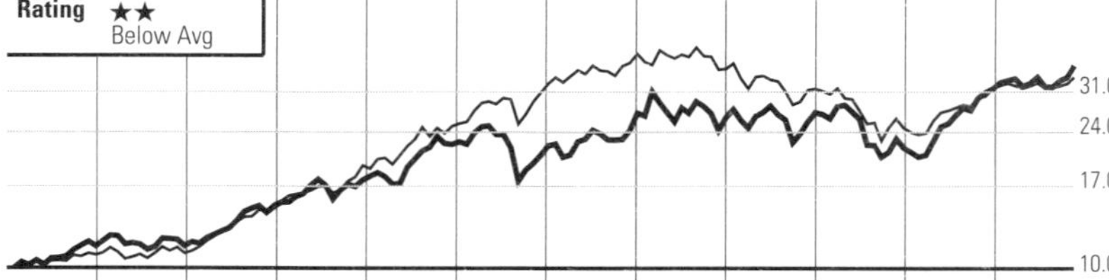

▼ Manager Change
▽ Partial Manager Change

Growth of $10,000
— Investment Values of Fund
— Investment Values of S&P 500

Performance Quartile (within Category)

1993	1994	1995	1996	1997	1998	1999	2000	2001	2002	2003	12-04	History
15.67	14.99	18.61	20.23	23.75	21.20	23.60	19.44	19.82	15.66	22.60	26.83	NAV
18.70	-0.51	28.74	18.12	24.59	-2.61	23.13	-2.67	3.10	-20.02	45.63	19.90	Total Return %
8.64	-1.82	-8.79	-4.82	-8.76	-31.18	2.09	6.43	14.98	2.07	16.96	9.03	+/-S&P 500
-0.18	1.31	0.29	1.63	2.23	-0.06	1.87	0.35	0.61	0.46	-1.62	1.57	+/-Russ 2000
1.28	1.40	1.53	1.46	1.36	1.29	1.27	1.11	1.16	0.97	1.30	1.17	Income Return %
17.42	-1.91	27.21	16.66	23.23	-3.90	21.86	-3.78	1.94	-20.99	44.33	18.73	Capital Return %
45	37	35	73	57	33	25	93	73	76	37	43	Total Rtn % Rank Cat
0.18	0.22	0.23	0.27	0.27	0.30	0.27	0.26	0.23	0.19	0.20	0.27	Income $
0.82	0.37	0.45	1.44	1.11	1.55	2.08	3.02	0.00	0.00	0.00	0.00	Capital Gains $
0.18	0.17	0.25	0.25	0.23	0.24	0.25	0.27	0.27	0.27	0.27	—	Expense Ratio %
1.47	1.50	1.58	1.51	1.38	1.39	1.25	1.17	1.16	1.11	1.17	—	Income Ratio %
26	25	28	28	29	35	42	49	39	32	39	—	Turnover Rate %
489	605	971	1,713	2,652	2,768	3,553	3,577	3,545	2,943	4,871	6,247	Net Assets $mil

Performance 12-31-04

	1st Qtr	2nd Qtr	3rd Qtr	4th Qtr	Total
2000	6.87	-3.16	0.87	-6.76	-2.67
2001	-6.48	15.02	-20.71	20.88	3.10
2002	3.99	-7.81	-21.37	6.10	-20.02
2003	-4.53	22.21	8.65	14.89	45.63
2004	6.59	1.00	-2.26	13.95	19.85

Trailing	Total Return%	+/- S&P 500	+/- Russ 2000	%Rank Cat	Growth of $10,000
3 Mo	13.95	4.72	-0.14	26	11,395
6 Mo	11.37	4.18	0.54	38	11,137
1 Yr	19.90	9.03	1.57	43	11,990
3 Yr Avg	11.77	8.19	0.29	61	13,963
5 Yr Avg	6.98	9.28	0.37	82	14,012
10 Yr Avg	12.28	0.21	0.74	75	31,844
15 Yr Avg	11.74	0.81	0.65	72	52,860

Tax Analysis	Tax-Adj Rtn%	%Rank Cat	Tax-Cost Rat	%Rank Cat
3 Yr (estimated)	11.40	52	0.33	23
5 Yr (estimated)	5.87	80	1.04	50
10 Yr (estimated)	10.60	69	1.50	31

Potential Capital Gain Exposure: 23% of assets

Rating and Risk

Time Period	Load-Adj Return %	Morningstar Rtn vs Cat	Morningstar Risk vs Cat	Morningstar Risk-Adj Rating
1 Yr	19.90			
3 Yr	11.77	Avg	+Avg	★★★
5 Yr	6.98	-Avg	+Avg	★★
10 Yr	12.28	-Avg	+Avg	★★
Incept	—			

Other Measures	Standard Index S&P 500	Best Fit Index Russ 2000
Alpha	8.4	0.6
Beta	1.03	0.96
R-Squared	70	100
Standard Deviation	20.70	
Mean	11.77	
Sharpe Ratio	0.51	

Morningstar's Take by Sonya Morris 12-02-04

It's not perfect, but investors could do worse than Vanguard Small Cap Index.

Experts have often questioned the efficacy of index funds in the less-efficient small-cap arena. This fund's performance doesn't appear to dispel those doubts, as its long-term returns trail the vast majority of its small-blend peers.

But that is not the whole story. First, the fund's relative performance is distorted by survivorship bias, since the category's relative rankings ignore the many poor-performing funds that were liquidated or merged away (a salient issue among small-caps where the attrition rate is especially high). Furthermore, until last year, this fund tracked the Russell 2000 Index, which has been dogged by technical headwinds connected to its annual reconstitution. Last year, however, Vanguard switched to a new MSCI benchmark, which should help alleviate that problem.

There's also a more prosaic issue to consider: Performance-chasing is endemic in the fund world. However, what makes that behavior pernicious in the small-cap world is the asset-bloat factor. That is, when investors flock to the small-cap manager with the hot hand, they're not only faced with the prospect of moderating returns when that manager's style cools off (as so often happens), but also with a manager whose flexibility has been limited by asset growth.

The challenge of finding talented small-cap managers that still have the headroom to take on more assets, like FPA Paramount's Eric Ende, isn't insurmountable. But investors have to do their homework. For those who lack the time or resolve to do that due diligence, this fund's low cost and wide diversification makes it a viable option. But we'd caution prospective investors here to consider that small-caps have reigned supreme in recent years, a trend that's likely to reverse itself before long. In view of that likelihood and the fact that index funds typically fare poorly in tepid climates, only those with long-time horizons need apply.

Address:	P O Box 2600 Valley Forge PA 19482 800-662-7447
Web Address:	www.vanguard.com
Inception:	10-03-60
Advisor:	Vanguard Advisers, Inc.
Subadvisor:	None
NTF Plans:	N/A

Minimum Purchase:	$3000	Add: $100	IRA: $1000
Min Auto Inv Plan:	$3000	Add: $50	
Sales Fees:	No-load		
Management Fee:	0.24%		
Actual Fees:	Mgt:0.24%	Dist:	
Expense Projections:	3Yr:$87	5Yr:$152	10Yr:$343
Income Distrib:	Annually		

Portfolio Analysis 09-30-04

Share change since 06-04 Total Stocks:1724	Sector	PE	YTD Ret%	% Assets
⊕ Cognizant Technology Sol	Business	62.5	85.50	0.29
⊕ Precision Castparts	Ind Mtrls	26.0	44.97	0.28
⊕ Peabody Energy	Energy	35.4	96.04	0.28
⊕ Ultra Petroleum	Energy	43.1	95.49	0.27
⊕ Newfield Exploration	Energy	12.5	32.58	0.26
⊕ American Tower A	Telecom	—	70.06	0.25
⊕ Pentair	Business	24.0	93.44	0.24
⊕ AmeriCredit	Financial	14.3	53.48	0.24
⊕ PacifiCare Health System	Health	21.5	67.22	0.23
⊕ Macerich	Financial	43.9	48.39	0.23
⊕ Ryder System	Business	15.7	41.93	0.22
⊕ Davita	Health	19.0	52.04	0.22
⊕ Crown Castle Internation	Telecom	—	50.86	0.22
⊕ Chelsea Property Group	Financial	—	—	0.21
⊕ American Capital Strateg	Financial	9.0	23.48	0.21
⊕ Mills	Financial	23.9	52.37	0.20
⊕ Boise Cascade	Ind Mtrls	—	-2.80	0.20
⊕ Alliant Energy	Utilities	—	19.44	0.20
⊕ Reliant Energy	Utilities	—	85.46	0.20
⊕ Catellus Development	Financial	—	34.01	0.20

Current Investment Style

Value Blnd Growth / Large Mid Small

Market Cap	%
Giant	0.0
Large	0.0
Mid	41.4
Small	51.5
Micro	7.1
Avg $mil: 1,199	

Value Measures		Rel Category
Price/Earnings	17.04	0.98
Price/Book	1.96	0.98
Price/Sales	0.96	1.01
Price/Cash Flow	5.30	0.91
Dividend Yield %	1.30	1.57

Growth Measures	%	Rel Category
Long-Term Erngs	12.55	0.93
Book Value	4.21	0.75
Sales	3.40	0.79
Cash Flow	4.07	0.82
Historical Erngs	5.64	0.76

Profitability	%	Rel Category
Return on Equity	10.51	1.01
Return on Assets	4.37	0.88
Net Margin	8.63	1.18

Sector Weightings	% of Stocks	Rel S&P 500	3 Year High	Low
Info	15.03	0.70		
Software	3.68	0.86	5	4
Hardware	7.60	0.75	10	8
Media	1.84	0.48	2	1
Telecom	1.91	0.61	2	1
Service	54.72	1.18		
Health	11.35	0.91	13	11
Consumer	10.15	1.12	12	9
Business	10.36	2.56	11	10
Financial	22.86	1.10	24	21
Mfg	30.25	0.94		
Goods	4.73	0.51	6	4
Ind Mtrls	14.81	1.17	15	12
Energy	6.29	0.88	6	4
Utilities	4.42	1.49	5	3

Composition

Cash	0.2
Stocks	99.8
Bonds	0.0
Other	0.0
Foreign (% of Stock)	0.0

Vanguard SmCp VI Idx

Ticker	Load	NAV	Yield	Total Assets	Mstar Category
VISVX	None	$13.97	1.6%	$3,100 mil	Small Value

Governance and Management

Fiduciary Grade: B

Portfolio Manager(s)

Index guru Gus Sauter, who has been in charge here since this fund's May 1998 inception, is among the best index managers around. He has been successful in keeping tracking error (the deviation of the fund's returns relative to the index's) extremely low on all the funds he manages and has even surpassed his bogies on occasion.

Strategy

Until recently, the fund tracked the S&P SmallCap 600/Barra Value Index by holding all of the stocks in the index. However, in May 2003, Vanguard replaced the S&P index with a new bogy developed by Morgan Stanley Capital International. The MSCI U.S. Small Cap Value Index consists of the cheapest stocks (as determined by its eight-pronged classification scheme) in the small-cap universe.

Historical Profile

Return Average
Risk Above Avg
Rating ★★★ Neutral

Investment Style: Equity Stock %: 97% (1998), 97% (1999), 100% (2000), 99% (2001), 100% (2002), 100% (2003), 100% (12-04)

▼ Manager Change
▽ Partial Manager Change

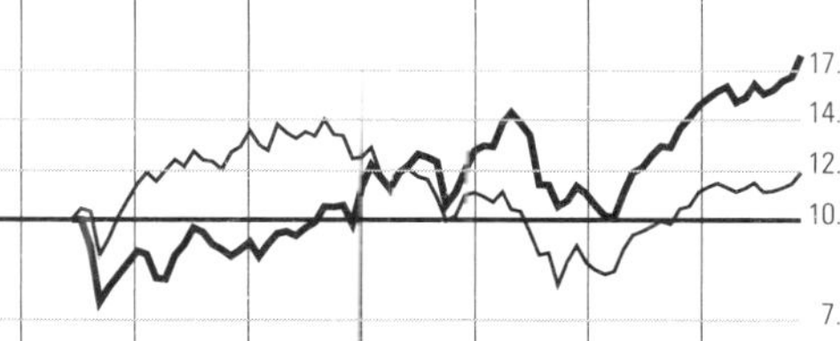

Growth of $10,000
— Investment Values of Fund
— Investment Values of S&P 500

Performance Quartile (within Category)

1993	1994	1995	1996	1997	1998	1999	2000	2001	2002	2003	12-04	History
—	—	—	—	—	8.74	8.45	9.65	10.29	8.52	11.49	13.97	NAV
—	—	—	—	—	-12.47*	3.35	21.88	13.70	-14.20	37.19	23.55	Total Return %
—	—	—	—	—	—	-17.69	30.98	25.58	7.89	8.52	12.68	+/-S&P 500
—	—	—	—	—	—	4.84	-0.95	-0.32	-2.77	-8.84	1.30	+/-Russ 2000 VL
—	—	—	—	—	0.00	0.80	1.00	0.71	0.90	2.32	1.96	Income Return %
—	—	—	—	—	—	2.55	20.88	12.99	-15.10	34.87	21.59	Capital Return %
—	—	—	—	—	—	43	37	64	73	74	25	Total Rtn % Rank Cat
—	—	—	—	—	0.06	0.07	0.08	0.07	0.09	0.20	0.23	Income $
—	—	—	—	—	0.00	0.50	0.50	0.55	0.28	0.00	0.00	Capital Gains $
—	—	—	—	—	0.25	0.25	0.27	0.27	0.27	0.27	—	Expense Ratio %
—	—	—	—	—	1.13	0.96	1.16	0.97	0.93	2.07	—	Income Ratio %
—	—	—	—	—	—	80	82	59	57	109	—	Turnover Rate %
—	—	—	—	—	113	204	317	802	1,176	1,730	2,947	Net Assets $mil

Performance 12-31-04

	1st Qtr	2nd Qtr	3rd Qtr	4th Qtr	Total
2000	3.06	2.01	7.76	7.58	21.88
2001	-0.78	13.25	-16.63	21.37	13.70
2002	10.41	-4.15	-22.50	4.62	-14.20
2003	-7.98	19.39	7.48	16.19	37.19
2004	7.14	0.89	1.13	13.03	23.55

Trailing	Total Return%	+/- S&P 500	+/- Russ 2000 VL	%Rank Cat	Growth of $10,000
3 Mo	13.03	3.80	-0.17	41	11,303
6 Mo	14.30	7.11	0.93	14	11,430
1 Yr	23.55	12.68	1.30	25	12,355
3 Yr Avg	13.30	9.72	-3.20	73	14,544
5 Yr Avg	15.05	17.35	-2.18	61	20,157
10 Yr Avg	—	—	—	—	—
15 Yr Avg	—	—	—	—	—

Tax Analysis	Tax-Adj Rtn%	%Rank Cat	Tax-Cost Rat	%Rank Cat
3 Yr (estimated)	12.48	65	0.72	42
5 Yr (estimated)	13.46	63	1.38	71
10 Yr (estimated)	—	—	—	—

Potential Capital Gain Exposure: 16% of assets

Rating and Risk

Time Period	Load-Adj Return %	Morningstar Rtn vs Cat	Morningstar Risk vs Cat	Morningstar Risk-Adj Rating
1 Yr	23.55			
3 Yr	13.30	-Avg	+Avg	★★
5 Yr	15.05	Avg	+Avg	★★★
10 Yr	—	—	—	—
Incept	9.50			

Other Measures	Standard Index S&P 500	Best Fit Index Russ 2000 VL
Alpha	10.2	-2.4
Beta	0.90	0.97
R-Squared	60	96
Standard Deviation	19.88	
Mean	13.30	
Sharpe Ratio	0.61	

Portfolio Analysis 09-30-04

Share change since 06-04 Total Stocks:954	Sector	PE	YTD Ret%	% Assets
⊕ Precision Castparts	Ind Mtrls	26.0	44.97	0.54
⊕ Peabody Energy	Energy	35.4	96.04	0.53
⊕ Pentair	Business	24.0	93.44	0.46
⊕ AmeriCredit	Financial	14.3	53.48	0.45
⊕ PacifiCare Health System	Health	21.5	67.22	0.44
⊕ Macerich	Financial	43.9	48.39	0.43
⊕ Ryder System	Business	15.7	41.93	0.43
⊕ Chelsea Property Group	Financial	—	—	0.41
⊕ American Capital Strateg	Financial	9.0	23.48	0.40
⊕ Mills	Financial	23.9	52.37	0.38
⊕ Boise Cascade	Ind Mtrls	—	-2.80	0.38
⊕ Alliant Energy	Utilities	—	19.44	0.38
⊕ Reliant Energy	Utilities	—	85.46	0.38
⊕ Catellus Development	Financial	—	34.01	0.38
⊕ Mack-Cali Realty	Financial	24.4	17.29	0.37
⊕ Louisiana-Pacific	Ind Mtrls	4.9	51.48	0.37
⊕ Webster Financial	Financial	13.3	12.57	0.36
⊕ Arrow Electronics	Hardware	14.5	5.01	0.36
⊕ Cummins	Ind Mtrls	12.3	74.61	0.35
⊕ Conseco	Financial	—	-8.49	0.35

Current Investment Style

Value Blnd Growth / Large Mid Small

Market Cap	%
Giant	0.0
Large	0.0
Mid	43.5
Small	50.5
Micro	6.0
Avg $mil: 1,235	

Value Measures		Rel Category
Price/Earnings	14.68	0.92
Price/Book	1.61	0.97
Price/Sales	0.77	1.03
Price/Cash Flow	4.31	0.83
Dividend Yield %	2.30	1.92

Growth Measures	%	Rel Category
Long-Term Erngs	9.82	0.81
Book Value	4.61	1.06
Sales	3.12	1.00
Cash Flow	0.63	0.29
Historical Erngs	3.61	0.75

Profitability	%	Rel Category
Return on Equity	10.16	1.11
Return on Assets	4.15	1.00
Net Margin	10.39	1.55

Sector Weightings	% of Stocks	Rel S&P 500	3 Year High	Low
Info	5.73	0.27		
Software	0.84	0.20	2	1
Hardware	2.98	0.29	9	3
Media	1.36	0.35	2	0
Telecom	0.55	0.17	1	0
Service	56.15	1.21		
Health	3.26	0.26	7	3
Consumer	7.92	0.87	14	7
Business	7.05	1.74	12	7
Financial	37.92	1.83	39	15
Mfg	38.11	1.19		
Goods	4.64	0.50	9	5
Ind Mtrls	19.08	1.51	23	18
Energy	6.05	0.84	10	4
Utilities	8.34	2.82	10	5

Composition

Cash	0.1
Stocks	99.9
Bonds	0.0
Other	0.0
Foreign (% of Stock)	0.1

Morningstar's Take by Sonya Morris 12-03-04

Vanguard Small Cap Value Index is a serviceable option.

Last year, this fund discarded its old benchmark, S&P Barra SmallCap 600 Index, in favor of the newly minted MSCI U.S. Small Cap Value Index. Shortcomings in the S&P methodology, specifically its exclusive reliance on price/book multiples to identify value stocks, were the impetus for the change, according to Vanguard. Since the MSCI index employs a variety of value metrics, it should produce a more representative picture of the small-value universe.

However, the new bogy is not without warts of its own. The fund holds far more financial stocks than its peers, primarily due to a large slug of REITs. Many active managers keep an eye on the fund's old bogy, which has a much lighter stake in REITs (the S&P index has a roughly 1% REITs stake versus 15% for MSCI).

The near-term concern is that a real estate downturn could drag this fund down. But the longer-term implications are more important to bear in mind. Specifically, Vanguard made the move to the new MSCI benchmark with an eye toward better mimicking the small-value universe. In so doing, the fund could more consistently replicate that universe's aggregate gross return and then wage the net-return battle at the cost line--where it would win almost every time. But the big financials stake could cause gross returns to deviate more widely from the small-value norm, undercutting its ability to compete on cost.

Nevertheless, the MSCI bogy's backtested annual returns correlate more tightly with the small-value category's average gross returns than its former S&P benchmark had. As such, we think the change represents a step in the right direction. While we're not ready to enthusiastically endorse it, the fund is a respectable option--especially for those unwilling to perform the due diligence necessary to ferret out talented small-value managers not already inundated with assets.

Address:	P O Box 2600 Valley Forge PA 19482 800-662-7447
Web Address:	www.vanguard.com
Inception:	05-21-98 *
Advisor:	Vanguard Advisers, Inc.
Subadvisor:	None
NTF Plans:	N/A

Minimum Purchase:	$3000	Add: $100	IRA: $1000
Min Auto Inv Plan:	$3000	Add: $50	
Sales Fees:	No-load		
Management Fee:	0.24%		
Actual Fees:	Mgt:0.24%	Dist: —	
Expense Projections:	3Yr:$87	5Yr:$152	10Yr:$343
Income Distrib:	Annually		

Vanguard STAR

Ticker	Load	NAV	Yield	Total Assets	Mstar Category
VGSTX	None	$18.74	2.4%	$10,763 mil	Moderate Allocation

Governance and Management

Fiduciary Grade: B

Portfolio Manager(s)

This fund of funds owns 11 actively managed offerings and boasts several well-known and talented managers, including Jim Barrow of Windsor II and Gus Sauter of indexing fame. Meanwhile, this fund's trustees oversee its asset allocation but rarely alter the lineup. Though no other changes are expected beyond the addition of two foreign-stock funds, a shareholder vote in May 2001 allows the board to add or subtract funds.

Strategy

This fund of funds invests in 11 Vanguard funds to build a diversified portfolio. The goal is a static asset allocation of 62% stocks, 25% intermediate- and long-term bonds, and 12% short-term bonds. The domestic-equity segment tends toward larger-cap value stocks, owing to its significant stake in deep-value funds Windsor and Windsor II. But it also invests in growth-oriented funds such as U.S. Growth and Explorer, the latter of which targets small caps. In May 2001, two foreign-stock funds--International Growth and International Value--were added to the overall stock segment.

Historical Profile

Return: Above Avg
Risk: Average
Rating: ★★★★ Above Avg

Investment Style: Equity Stock %: 60% 59% 58% 60% 58% 60% 58%

▼ Manager Change
∇ Partial Manager Change

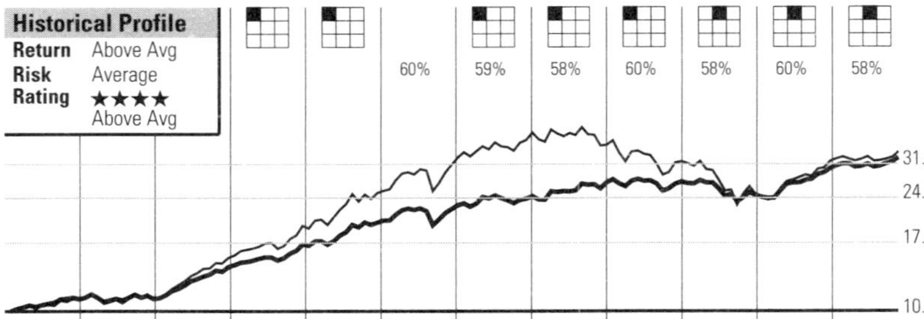

Growth of $10,000
— Investment Values of Fund
— Investment Values of S&P 500

Performance Quartile (within Category)

History

1993	1994	1995	1996	1997	1998	1999	2000	2001	2002	2003	12-04	History
13.41	12.61	15.03	15.86	17.38	17.96	18.21	17.81	16.44	14.35	17.20	18.74	NAV
10.88	-0.21	28.64	16.11	21.15	12.38	7.13	10.96	0.50	-9.87	22.70	11.60	Total Return %
0.82	-1.52	-8.89	-6.83	-12.20	-16.19	-13.91	20.06	12.38	12.22	-5.97	0.73	+/-S&P 500
-0.85	1.74	3.87	4.77	1.95	-0.01	-5.72	6.52	0.34	0.67	-1.36	0.43	+/-DJ 60%
3.68	3.92	4.73	3.96	3.75	3.36	3.42	3.74	3.27	2.94	2.73	2.57	Income Return %
7.20	-4.13	23.91	12.15	17.40	9.02	3.71	7.22	-2.77	-12.81	19.97	9.03	Capital Return %
58	21	25	32	38	56	71	9	15	31	27	13	Total Rtn % Rank Cat
0.47	0.52	0.59	0.59	0.59	0.58	0.61	0.64	0.55	0.48	0.39	0.39	Income $
0.40	0.25	0.57	0.98	1.20	0.98	0.40	1.65	0.87	0.00	0.00	0.00	Capital Gains $
0.00	0.00	0.00	0.00	0.00	0.00	0.00	0.00	0.00	0.00	0.00	0.00	Expense Ratio %
3.67	4.01	4.12	3.71	3.46	3.18	3.21	3.57	2.91	3.07	2.60	2.39	Income Ratio %
3	9	13	18	15	16	10	17	6	12	15	6	Turnover Rate %
3,628	3,766	4,842	5,863	7,355	8,083	8,087	8,119	8,242	7,217	9,134	10,763	Net Assets $mil

Performance 12-31-04

	1st Qtr	2nd Qtr	3rd Qtr	4th Qtr	Total
2000	3.80	-0.11	5.11	1.81	10.96
2001	-2.91	4.20	-7.41	7.29	0.50
2002	1.09	-6.20	-9.43	4.94	-9.87
2003	-1.81	12.12	2.75	8.48	22.70
2004	3.55	-0.22	0.40	7.59	11.60

Trailing	Total Return%	+/- S&P 500	+/- DJ 60%	%Rank Cat	Growth of $10,000
3 Mo	7.59	-1.64	0.11	32	10,759
6 Mo	8.02	0.83	0.49	22	10,802
1 Yr	11.60	0.73	0.43	13	11,160
3 Yr Avg	7.27	3.69	0.01	12	12,343
5 Yr Avg	6.60	8.90	1.36	9	13,765
10 Yr Avg	11.61	-0.46	1.12	12	29,994
15 Yr Avg	10.37	-0.56	0.42	21	43,930

Tax Analysis	Tax-Adj Rtn%	%Rank Cat	Tax-Cost Rat	%Rank Cat
3 Yr (estimated)	6.31	12	0.89	62
5 Yr (estimated)	4.83	9	1.66	83
10 Yr (estimated)	9.21	13	2.15	75

Potential Capital Gain Exposure: 22% of assets

Rating and Risk

Time Period	Load-Adj Return %	Morningstar Rtn vs Cat	Morningstar Risk vs Cat	Morningstar Risk-Adj Rating
1 Yr	11.60			
3 Yr	7.27	+Avg	Avg	★★★★
5 Yr	6.60	+Avg	Avg	★★★★
10 Yr	11.61	+Avg	Avg	★★★★
Incept	11.28			

Other Measures	Standard Index S&P 500	Best Fit Index DJ 60%
Alpha	4.2	-2.8
Beta	0.59	1.01
R-Squared	91	97
Standard Deviation	9.85	
Mean	7.27	
Sharpe Ratio	0.60	

Portfolio Analysis 09-30-04

Total Stocks:0 Share change since 06-30-04	Sectors	P/E Ratio	YTD Return %	% Net Assets
⊕ Vanguard Windsor II	—	—	—	16.15
⊕ Vanguard Windsor	—	—	—	8.81
⊕ Vanguard Primecap	—	—	—	6.98
⊕ Vanguard Morgan Growth	—	—	—	6.95
⊕ Vanguard U.S. Growth	—	—	—	6.89
⊕ Vanguard International Va	—	—	—	6.32
⊕ Vanguard International Gr	—	—	—	6.29
⊕ Vanguard Explorer	—	—	—	4.34

Total Fixed-Income:0	Date of Maturity	Amount $000	Value $000	% Net Assets
Vanguard Long-Term Invest		131,049	1,235,788	12.47
Vanguard GNMA		117,659	1,227,187	12.38
Vanguard Short-Term Inves		113,136	1,211,684	12.22

Morningstar's Take by William Samuel Rocco 11-14-04

Vanguard Star is a model fund of funds.

Instant diversification is the main attraction of funds of funds, and you'll find plenty of that at this one. It divides its domestic-equity stake, which is about 60% of assets, among one small-growth, one large-blend, two large-growth, and two large-value offerings. Even the underlying holdings that fall in the same category differ significantly from each other. For example, though both run large-value funds, the lead manager of Vanguard Windsor II is more interested in dividends and less interested in mid-caps than the lead manager of Vanguard Windsor.

What's more, this fund splits its foreign-equity position--which is about twice the moderate-allocation norm of 6% of assets--between Vanguard International Growth and Vanguard International Value. Also, it spreads its fixed-income stake across a long-term fund that focuses on corporate bonds but recently got the freedom to consider other investment-grade credits, an intermediate-term offering that favors GNMA-backed mortgage securities, and a short-term fund that recently expanded its purview to include Treasuries, agencies, and mortgages, as well as corporates.

This fund's attractions go beyond the breadth of its portfolio. It enjoys top-decile year-to-date results, as many of its underlying offerings have performed well in 2004's choppy climate. More importantly, it also boasts top-quintile longer-term returns, because all but one of its 11 holdings have thrived over time. And it has kept volatility under control along the way, largely due to its exceptional diversification. Meanwhile, it doesn't tack on its own fees as some funds of funds do and its underlying offerings are cheap, so it's also fetching from a cost perspective.

For all these reasons, this fund of funds is a first-rate choice for one-stop shoppers.

Address:	PO Box 2600 Valley Forge PA 19482 800-662-7447
Web Address:	www.vanguard.com
Inception:	03-29-85
Advisor:	Vanguard Advisers, Inc.
Subadvisor:	None
NTF Plans:	N/A

Minimum Purchase:	$1000	Add: $100	IRA: $1000
Min Auto Inv Plan:	$1000	Add: $50	
Sales Fees:	No-load		
Management Fee:	—		
Actual Fees:	—	Dist:	
Expense Projections:	3Yr:$119	5Yr:$208	10Yr:$468
Income Distrib:	Semi-Annually		

Equity Style
Style: Blend
Size: Large-Cap

Value Measures		Rel Category
Price/Earnings	15.72	0.95
Price/Book	2.28	0.93
Price/Sales	1.09	0.83
Price/Cash Flow	6.44	0.89
Dividend Yield %	1.54	0.98

Growth Measures	%	Rel Category
Long-Term Erngs	11.45	0.98
Book Value	6.29	1.10
Sales	5.87	1.13
Cash Flow	6.42	0.80
Historical Erngs	12.03	1.11

Market Cap %			
Giant	37.6	Small	3.3
Large	39.0	Micro	0.5
Mid	19.6	Avg $mil:	20,456

Composition

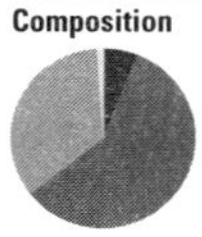

Cash	6.0
Stocks	58.4
Bonds	34.4
Other	1.1
Foreign (% of Stock)	24.4

Fixed-Income Style
Duration: Interm-Term
Quality: High

Avg Eff Duration [1]	5.9 Yrs
Avg Eff Maturity	9.9 Yrs
Avg Credit Quality	AA
Avg Wtd Coupon	5.56%

[1] figure provided by fund as of 09-30-04

Sector Weightings	% of Stocks	Rel S&P 500	3 Year High	3 Year Low
Info	19.57	0.91		
Software	3.70	0.86	4	2
Hardware	9.68	0.95	10	6
Media	3.54	0.92	5	4
Telecom	2.65	0.84	3	2
Service	49.08	1.06		
Health	14.24	1.14	15	11
Consumer	8.73	0.96	9	8
Business	6.75	1.67	7	7
Financial	19.36	0.93	23	19
Mfg	31.35	0.98		
Goods	9.20	0.99	11	9
Ind Mtrls	12.27	0.97	14	11
Energy	7.20	1.01	7	6
Utilities	2.68	0.91	5	3

Vanguard Strategic Eq

Ticker	Load	NAV	Yield	Total Assets	Mstar Category
VSEQX	None	$21.43	0.6%	$3,746 mil	Mid-Cap Blend

Governance and Management

Fiduciary Grade: B

Portfolio Manager(s)

Gus Sauter has managed this fund since its August 1998 inception. Though Sauter is best known for his prowess as an indexer, he has also been an active manager, having used quantitative stock-picking models for many years. Joel Dickson, who is a longtime member of Vanguard's vaunted quantitative equity group (the architect of the fund's underlying quantitative models) was added to the fold as comanager in January 2003.

Strategy

Comanagers Gus Sauter and Joel Dickson use quantitative models to build a portfolio with moderate valuations, strong earnings growth, and sector weightings similar to those of the MSCI U.S. Small and Mid-Cap 2200 Index. The models consider myriad factors, including revisions to analysts' earnings estimates and changes in insider ownership.

Historical Profile

Return Above Avg
Risk Below Avg
Rating ★★★★ Above Avg

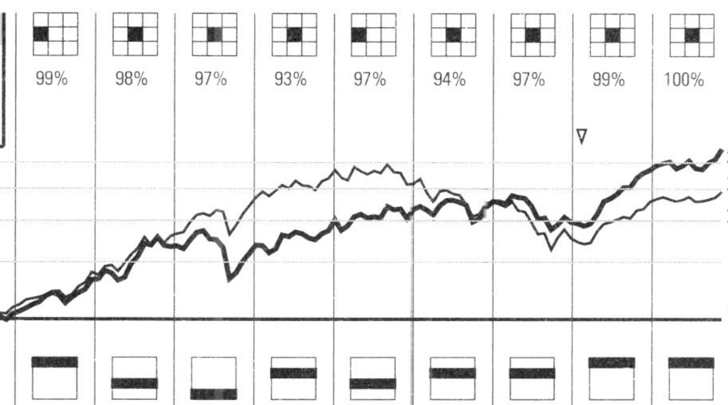

1993	1994	1995	1996	1997	1998	1999	2000	2001	2002	2003	12-04	History
—	—	10.76	12.56	14.60	14.53	16.76	14.58	15.23	13.10	18.71	21.43	NAV
—	—	7.76*	25.03	26.22	0.61	19.25	7.46	5.42	-13.14	43.83	20.49	Total Return %
—	—	—	2.09	-7.13	-27.96	-1.79	16.56	17.30	8.95	15.16	9.62	+/-S&P 500
—	—	—	5.85	-6.02	-18.50	4.53	-10.03	6.02	1.39	8.24	4.02	+/-S&P Mid 400
—	—	0.00	1.67	1.11	1.03	1.10	1.25	0.96	0.85	0.99	0.75	Income Return %
—	—	—	23.36	25.11	-0.42	18.15	6.21	4.46	-13.99	42.84	19.74	Capital Return %
—	—	—	25	56	84	50	59	28	28	12	14	Total Rtn % Rank Cat
—	—	0.08	0.18	0.14	0.15	0.16	0.21	0.14	0.13	0.13	0.14	Income $
—	—	0.00	0.71	1.08	0.00	0.37	3.03	0.00	0.00	0.00	0.96	Capital Gains $
—	—	0.06	0.38	0.40	0.43	0.46	0.49	0.54	0.50	0.50	0.45	Expense Ratio %
—	—	2.22	1.78	1.28	0.93	1.00	1.31	1.06	0.94	1.04	0.83	Income Ratio %
—	—	—	106	85	71	51	83	82	73	100	66	Turnover Rate %
—	—	75	153	474	535	626	745	879	914	1,980	3,746	Net Assets $mil

Performance 12-31-04

	1st Qtr	2nd Qtr	3rd Qtr	4th Qtr	Total
2000	2.21	0.00	4.90	0.23	7.46
2001	-3.70	10.76	-14.02	14.96	5.42
2002	4.46	-6.98	-15.07	5.24	-13.14
2003	-0.92	18.95	8.10	12.89	43.83
2004	5.93	0.76	-1.35	14.44	20.49

Trailing	Total Return%	+/- S&P 500	+/- S&P Mid 400	%Rank Cat	Growth of $10,000
3 Mo	14.44	5.21	2.29	13	11,444
6 Mo	12.89	5.70	3.10	14	11,289
1 Yr	20.49	9.62	4.02	14	12,049
3 Yr Avg	14.61	11.03	4.10	9	15,055
5 Yr Avg	11.27	13.57	1.74	17	17,057
10 Yr Avg	—	—	—	—	—
15 Yr Avg	—	—	—	—	—

Tax Analysis	Tax-Adj Rtn%	%Rank Cat	Tax-Cost Rat	%Rank Cat
3 Yr (estimated)	14.00	9	0.53	58
5 Yr (estimated)	9.57	17	1.53	75
10 Yr (estimated)	—	—	—	—

Potential Capital Gain Exposure: 20% of assets

Rating and Risk

Time Period	Load-Adj Return %	Morningstar Rtn vs Cat	Morningstar Risk vs Cat	Morningstar Risk-Adj Rating
1 Yr	20.49			
3 Yr	14.61	High	Avg	★★★★★
5 Yr	11.27	+Avg	-Avg	★★★★
10 Yr	—	—	—	—
Incept	14.21			

Other Measures	Standard Index S&P 500	Best Fit Index Wil 4500
Alpha	11.1	3.4
Beta	0.85	0.90
R-Squared	77	96
Standard Deviation	16.48	
Mean	14.61	
Sharpe Ratio	0.81	

Morningstar's Take by Sonya Morris 10-25-04

Vanguard Strategic Equity is a worthy competitor.

Vanguard's index pro Gus Sauter teams up with co-manager Joel Dickson on this actively managed offering. They employ a quantitative stock-picking model that churns through 3,500 stocks, assessing relative valuation, financial health, and growth prospects. The model then adds a twist by scouting for situations where investor sentiment (as indicated by trading momentum) doesn't square with a stock's fundamental characteristics. Based on those factors, stocks are ranked within industry groups, with the highest-rated stocks earning a spot in the portfolio.

Although management guards against unintended bets by keeping the fund's sector allocation and market-cap weightings neutral to the MSCI Small and Mid-Cap 2200 Index, the process does confer some biases. For example, because the model prefers cheap stocks and strong earnings, the portfolio's aggregate price/earnings multiple is below its benchmark's, while its aggregate return on equity is higher than its bogy's. Furthermore, because the MSCI index dips a little lower on the capitalization ladder, the fund's average market capitalization is roughly half the mid-blend category mean.

The model's preference for smaller, cheaper stocks means that it can look sluggish when pricier names or larger stocks are in favor, as in the late 1990s. However, over the long haul, this offering has proven its worth. Since its inception in August 1995, it has bested roughly 70% of its rivals. And thanks to its broad diversification, the ride here has been relatively smooth.

Finally, this fund works well along side a large-cap core holding. Indeed, this offering has far fewer holdings in common with the S&P 500 Index than the Vanguard Mid-Cap Index Fund since that fund changed its benchmark last year.

This fund is a fine choice to fill out the mid-cap slot of a portfolio.

Address:	P O Box 2600, Valley Forge PA 19482, 800-662-7447	Minimum Purchase:	$3000	Add: $100 IRA: $1000
Web Address:	www.vanguard.com	Min Auto Inv Plan:	$3000	Add: $50
Inception:	08-14-95 *	Sales Fees:	No-load	
Advisor:	Vanguard Advisers, Inc.	Management Fee:	0.48%	
Subadvisor:	None	Actual Fees:	Mgt:0.48%	Dist: —
NTF Plans:	N/A	Expense Projections:	3Yr:$160	5Yr:$280 10Yr:$628
		Income Distrib:	Annually	

Portfolio Analysis 09-30-04

Share change since 06-04 Total Stocks:388	Sector	PE	YTD Ret%	% Assets
⊕ Xerox	Ind Mtrls	20.2	23.26	1.12
⊖ PACCAR	Ind Mtrls	15.6	47.28	1.12
⊕ Eaton	Ind Mtrls	18.5	36.07	1.06
⊕ Georgia-Pacific Group	Ind Mtrls	14.4	24.12	1.04
⊕ DR Horton	Consumer	10.7	41.36	1.01
⊖ Phelps Dodge	Ind Mtrls	11.1	30.78	1.01
⊕ Sunoco	Energy	12.9	62.69	0.99
Monsanto Company	Ind Mtrls	54.5	96.09	0.99
Providian Financial	Financial	14.3	41.50	0.94
Textron	Ind Mtrls	30.4	32.17	0.94
⊕ MGM Mirage	Consumer	30.1	93.41	0.93
⊕ Huntington Bancshares	Financial	13.9	13.55	0.91
⊕ RadioShack	Consumer	15.3	7.97	0.88
☼ Selectron	Hardware	—	-9.81	0.88
⊖ Safeco	Financial	10.9	36.61	0.88
⊕ Ryder System	Business	15.7	41.93	0.85
⊕ Barnes & Noble	Consumer	14.5	36.25	0.84
Coventry Health Care	Health	15.5	23.46	0.83
⊕ Ball	Goods	20.9	49.08	0.83
⊕ Dade Behring Holdings	Health	35.9	56.69	0.82

Current Investment Style

Value Blnd Growth — Large Mid Small

Market Cap	%
Giant	0.0
Large	11.1
Mid	65.2
Small	22.6
Micro	1.2
Avg $mil: 2,792	

Value Measures		Rel Category
Price/Earnings	14.18	0.84
Price/Book	2.20	1.01
Price/Sales	0.93	0.88
Price/Cash Flow	3.72	0.60
Dividend Yield %	1.09	1.09

Growth Measures	%	Rel Category
Long-Term Erngs	12.28	0.98
Book Value	5.03	0.71
Sales	4.21	0.74
Cash Flow	10.39	1.39
Historical Erngs	15.84	1.41

Profitability	%	Rel Category
Return on Equity	14.81	1.07
Return on Assets	7.18	1.10
Net Margin	10.94	1.21

Sector Weightings	% of Stocks	Rel S&P 500	3 Year High	Low
Info	14.12	0.66		
Software	2.07	0.48	3	2
Hardware	7.84	0.77	11	4
Media	2.23	0.58	3	1
Telecom	1.98	0.63	2	1
Service	50.53	1.09		
Health	10.94	0.88	15	11
Consumer	11.06	1.22	14	11
Business	8.35	2.06	12	7
Financial	20.18	0.97	22	18
Mfg	35.37	1.10		
Goods	6.17	0.66	9	5
Ind Mtrls	16.26	1.28	16	11
Energy	7.10	0.99	7	1
Utilities	5.84	1.97	8	5

Composition

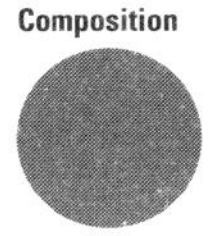

Cash	0.5
Stocks	99.5
Bonds	0.0
Other	0.0
Foreign (% of Stock)	0.0

Vanguard Tax-Mgd Bal

Analyst Pick	Ticker	Load	NAV	Yield	Total Assets	Mstar Category
✔	VTMFX	None	$18.49	2.6%	$561 mil	Conservative Allocation

Governance and Management

Fiduciary Grade: B

Portfolio Manager(s)

Gus Sauter, Vanguard's indexing guru, has managed the fund since its September 1994 inception. On the bond side, longtime manager Ian MacKinnon retired in June 2003. The fixed-income duties fell to Chris Ryon, who joined the team in 1996, and who has been handling the day-to-day management duties for some time.

Strategy

The fund invests half of its assets in stocks selected to match the key characteristics of the Russell 1000 Index, emphasizing those issues with low dividend yields. The bond portion consists of intermediate-term, high-quality municipal issues. The fund uses trading techniques, such as selling losers to offset gains, to minimize capital gains.

Historical Profile

Return Average
Risk High
Rating ★★★ Neutral

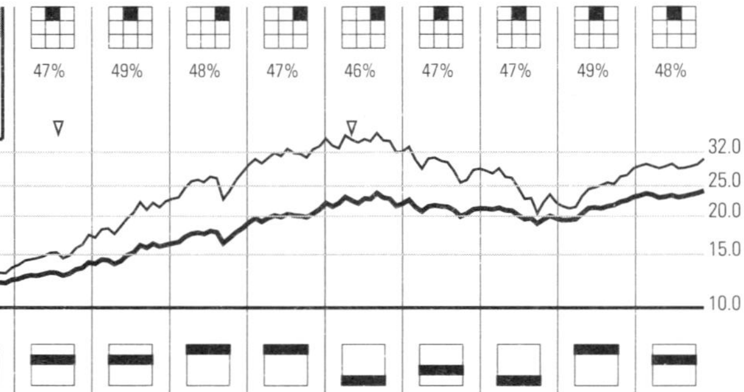

Investment Style: Equity Stock %

▼ Manager Change
▽ Partial Manager Change

Growth of $10,000
▬ Investment Values of Fund
— Investment Values of S&P 500

Performance Quartile (within Category)

1993	1994	1995	1996	1997	1998	1999	2000	2001	2002	2003	12-04	History
—	9.79	11.85	12.92	14.67	16.74	18.87	18.30	17.18	15.54	17.72	18.49	NAV
—	-1.40*	24.51	12.21	16.55	16.93	15.49	-0.50	-3.54	-7.08	17.05	7.16	Total Return %
—	—	-13.02	-10.73	-16.80	-11.64	-5.55	8.60	8.34	15.01	-11.62	-3.71	+/-S&P 500
—	—	6.35	3.32	2.45	5.20	7.63	-7.29	-6.76	-3.06	-0.61	-1.85	+/-DJ 40%
—	0.00	3.30	3.07	2.89	2.68	2.59	2.62	2.54	2.53	2.86	2.74	Income Return %
—	—	21.21	9.14	13.66	14.25	12.90	-3.12	-6.08	-9.61	14.19	4.42	Capital Return %
—	—	20	27	29	12	7	88	74	81	17	29	Total Rtn % Rank Cat
—	0.09	0.32	0.36	0.37	0.39	0.43	0.49	0.46	0.43	0.44	0.39	Income $
—	0.00	0.00	0.00	0.00	0.00	0.00	0.00	0.00	0.00	0.00	0.00	Capital Gains $
—	0.00	0.20	0.20	0.17	0.19	0.20	0.20	0.19	0.18	0.17	—	Expense Ratio %
—	2.88	3.06	3.04	2.77	2.63	2.52	2.61	2.64	2.69	2.58	—	Income Ratio %
—	—	5	5	7	7	13	15	21	24	16	—	Turnover Rate %
—	17	39	63	120	207	330	400	419	416	498	561	Net Assets $mil

Performance 12-31-04

	1st Qtr	2nd Qtr	3rd Qtr	4th Qtr	Total
2000	4.50	-1.12	0.62	-4.30	-0.50
2001	-5.52	3.78	-7.25	6.06	-3.54
2002	0.52	-5.41	-6.01	3.98	-7.08
2003	-0.58	9.04	1.80	6.06	17.05
2004	1.70	-0.39	0.51	5.25	7.16

Trailing	Total Return%	+/- S&P 500	+/- DJ 40%	%Rank Cat	Growth of $10,000
3 Mo	5.25	-3.98	-0.15	23	10,525
6 Mo	5.78	-1.41	-0.71	28	10,578
1 Yr	7.16	-3.71	-1.85	29	10,716
3 Yr Avg	5.24	1.66	-1.94	44	11,656
5 Yr Avg	2.27	4.57	-4.03	75	11,188
10 Yr Avg	9.42	-2.65	0.27	20	24,602
15 Yr Avg	—	—	—	—	—

Tax Analysis	Tax-Adj Rtn%	%Rank Cat	Tax-Cost Rat	%Rank Cat
3 Yr (estimated)	4.39	32	0.48	15
5 Yr (estimated)	1.93	54	0.33	3
10 Yr (estimated)	9.16	1	0.24	1

Potential Capital Gain Exposure: 27% of assets

Rating and Risk

Time Period	Load-Adj Return %	Morningstar Rtn vs Cat	Morningstar Risk vs Cat	Morningstar Risk-Adj Rating
1 Yr	6.09			
3 Yr	4.89	Avg	+Avg	★★★
5 Yr	2.27	-Avg	+Avg	★★
10 Yr	9.42	+Avg	High	★★★★
Incept	8.97			

Other Measures	Standard Index S&P 500	Best Fit Index Russ 1000
Alpha	2.6	2.3
Beta	0.42	0.43
R-Squared	89	90
Standard Deviation	6.97	
Mean	5.24	
Sharpe Ratio	0.56	

Portfolio Analysis 09-30-04

Total Stocks:569 Share change since 06-30-04	Sectors	P/E Ratio	YTD Return %	% Net Assets
⊕ Gen Elec	Ind Mtrls	22.8	-3.01	1.48
⊖ ExxonMobil	Energy	13.9	-2.75	1.36
⊕ Microsoft	Software	36.1	0.04	1.07
⊖ Pfizer	Health	22.0	-2.75	1.02
⊕ Citigroup	Financial	15.3	0.08	0.99
⊕ Bank of America	Financial	12.3	-3.85	0.74
Johnson & Johnson	Health	20.6	-0.85	0.72
⊕ American International Gr	Financial	16.2	2.25	0.72
⊕ IBM	Hardware	20.2	-3.63	0.64

Total Fixed-Income:135	Date of Maturity	Amount $000	Value $000	% Net Assets
South Carolina Transn Inf	10-01-13	5,700	6,460	1.23
Phoenix Ariz Civic Impt 5	07-01-15	5,525	6,261	1.19
Harris Cnty Tex Health Fa	02-15-31	5,700	5,700	1.08
Univ Tex Univ Revs 5.25%	08-15-18	4,900	5,570	1.06
Ohio St Wtr Dev Auth 5%	06-01-17	5,000	5,477	1.04
Salt Lake Cnty Utah Mun B	10-01-11	4,340	4,899	0.93
Indiana Mun Pwr Agy Pwr S	01-01-15	4,440	4,895	0.93
Georgia St 5.5%	07-01-14	4,000	4,658	0.88
California St Dept Wtr Re	05-01-14	4,065	4,637	0.88

Equity Style
Style: Blend
Size: Large-Cap

Value Measures		Rel Category
Price/Earnings	17.13	1.04
Price/Book	2.58	1.09
Price/Sales	1.39	1.07
Price/Cash Flow	7.37	1.06
Dividend Yield %	1.20	0.69

Growth Measures	%	Rel Category
Long-Term Erngs	11.98	1.07
Book Value	8.44	1.54
Sales	5.50	1.20
Cash Flow	9.98	1.49
Historical Erngs	13.33	1.41

Market Cap %			
Giant	44.2	Small	0.2
Large	30.2	Micro	0.0
Mid	25.4	Avg $mil:	30,124

Fixed-Income Style
Duration: Interm-Term
Quality: High

Avg Eff Duration [1]	5.1 Yrs
Avg Eff Maturity	6.2 Yrs
Avg Credit Quality	AAA
Avg Wtd Coupon	5.09%

[1]figure provided by fund as of 09-30-04

Sector Weightings	% of Stocks	Rel S&P 500	3 Year High	3 Year Low
Info	23.48	1.09		
Software	4.30	1.00	5	4
Hardware	11.43	1.12	13	9
Media	4.44	1.16	5	4
Telecom	3.31	1.05	4	3
Service	49.73	1.07		
Health	14.60	1.17	17	15
Consumer	11.23	1.24	12	11
Business	5.39	1.33	6	5
Financial	18.51	0.89	19	17
Mfg	26.79	0.83		
Goods	8.14	0.87	9	7
Ind Mtrls	9.61	0.76	10	8
Energy	7.88	1.10	8	7
Utilities	1.16	0.39	1	1

Composition

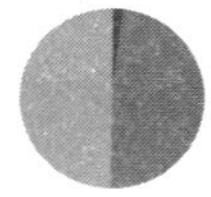

Cash	1.7
Stocks	48.4
Bonds	49.9
Other	0.0
Foreign (% of Stock)	0.0

Morningstar's Take by Jeffrey Ptak 01-07-05

Vanguard Tax-Managed Balanced Fund is as solid as they come.

Shareholders are soon slated to get an even better deal here. According to this fund's most recent semiannual report, the fund's expense ratio is slated to fall by five basis points to an ultra-low 0.12%. If that holds, it would make this fund the cheapest in Vanguard's stable, not to mention in the entire conservative-allocation category.

That move only burnishes this fund's considerable appeal, which turns on a prudent and well-executed tax-minimization strategy. Manager Gus Sauter constructs a sample of the Russell 1000 Index, underweighting that bogy's highest-yielding constituents (on the premise that it's preferable to forestall realization of capital gains than to receive dividend income that must be distributed to shareholders). On the bond side, which soaks up the other half of the portfolio, manager Chris Ryon spreads the fund's assets across a bevy of high-quality tax-exempt municipal bonds.

The 50/50 split might not suit aggressive investors seeking heavier stock exposure. They might seek an appropriate mix of Vanguard's Tax-Managed Capital Appreciation and Intermediate-Term Tax-Exempt Bond--which mirror the strategies used on the stock and bond sides of this offering. But investors shouldn't lose sight of the fact that this fund's hybrid structure provides a tax advantage in and of itself. Since the fund's expense ratio can be directed to the highest-taxed portion of its return stream first, investors are able to keep all of the tax-exempt muni income that the fund's bond portfolio throws off.

The results have been impressive. The fund's 10-year 9.2% annualized aftertax return through Dec. 31, 2004, tops virtually all rivals. Meanwhile, the fund's diversification and big bond stake have tamped down volatility, giving the fund a solid risk/reward profile.

It's a great option for a taxable account.

Address:	PO Box 2600 Valley Forge PA 19482 800-662-7447
Web Address:	www.vanguard.com
Inception:	09-06-94 *
Advisor:	Vanguard Advisers, Inc.
Subadvisor:	None
NTF Plans:	N/A

Minimum Purchase:	$10000	Add: $100	IRA: $10000
Min Auto Inv Plan:	$10000	Add: $50	
Sales Fees:	No-load, 2.00%R		
Management Fee:	0.15%		
Actual Fees:	Mgt:0.15%	Dist:	
Expense Projections:	3Yr:$58	5Yr:$101	10Yr:$230
Income Distrib:	Quarterly		

Vanguard Tx-Mgd App

Ticker	Load	NAV	Yield	Total Assets	Mstar Category
VMCAX	None	$28.05	1.3%	$3,095 mil	Large Growth

Governance and Management

Fiduciary Grade: B

Portfolio Manager(s)

Gus Sauter, Vanguard's index specialist, has proved one of the best index-fund managers in the business. He has done a great job of adding value through effective trading at a number of Vanguard's index offerings.

Strategy

Although this isn't an index fund, manager Gus Sauter uses a sampling technique to match the key characteristics of the Russell 1000 Index. Its returns have tended to correlate very tightly with those of its bogy. However, Sauter adds a twist by favoring the lowest-yielding stocks in the index to limit taxes, giving the fund a growth tilt relative to the index. To further minimize capital-gains distributions, Sauter may sell stocks at a loss to offset gains, liquidating the highest-cost shares first.

Historical Profile

Return Above Avg
Risk Average
Rating ★★★★ Above Avg

Investment Style
Equity
Stock %

1995	1996	1997	1998	1999	2000	2001	2002	2003	12-04
100%	100%	99%	99%	99%	99%	98%	100%	100%	

▼ Manager Change
▽ Partial Manager Change

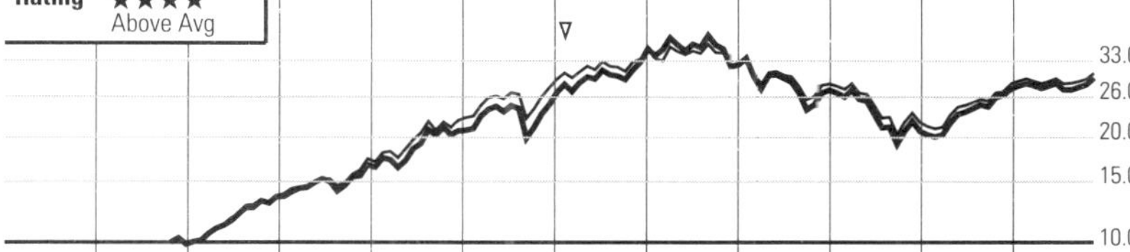

Growth of $10,000
▬ Investment Values of Fund
— Investment Values of S&P 500

Performance Quartile (within Category)

1993	1994	1995	1996	1997	1998	1999	2000	2001	2002	2003	12-04	History
—	9.95	13.28	15.95	20.18	25.68	34.17	30.59	25.73	19.49	25.43	28.05	NAV
—	-0.50*	34.38	20.93	27.29	27.90	33.55	-10.13	-15.34	-23.45	31.72	11.75	Total Return %
—	—	-3.15	-2.01	-6.06	-0.67	12.51	-1.03	-3.46	-1.36	3.05	0.88	+/-S&P 500
—	—	-2.80	-2.19	-3.20	-10.81	0.39	12.29	5.08	4.43	1.97	5.45	+/-Russ 1000Gr
—	0.00	0.90	0.83	0.75	0.64	0.48	0.35	0.56	0.80	1.22	1.44	Income Return %
—	—	33.48	20.10	26.54	27.26	33.07	-10.48	-15.90	-24.25	30.50	10.31	Capital Return %
—	—	35	39	47	66	55	36	24	24	24	17	Total Rtn % Rank Cat
—	0.04	0.09	0.11	0.12	0.13	0.12	0.12	0.17	0.21	0.24	0.37	Income $
—	0.00	0.00	0.00	0.00	0.00	0.00	0.00	0.00	0.00	0.00	0.00	Capital Gains $
—	0.20	0.20	0.20	0.17	0.19	0.19	0.19	0.18	0.17	0.17	—	Expense Ratio %
—	1.26	0.97	0.91	0.70	0.62	0.47	0.36	0.60	0.87	1.09	—	Income Ratio %
—	—	7	12	4	5	12	17	13	10	11	—	Turnover Rate %
—	70	254	517	893	1,479	2,378	2,643	1,678	1,154	1,466	1,596	Net Assets $mil

Performance 12-31-04

	1st Qtr	2nd Qtr	3rd Qtr	4th Qtr	Total
2000	7.43	-4.11	-0.48	-12.34	-10.13
2001	-14.61	7.12	-18.58	13.69	-15.34
2002	0.12	-14.64	-17.74	8.88	-23.45
2003	-2.31	16.02	3.49	12.30	31.72
2004	2.32	1.50	-2.61	10.49	11.75

Trailing	Total Return%	+/- S&P 500	+/- Russ 1000Gr	%Rank Cat	Growth of $10,000
3 Mo	10.49	1.26	1.32	38	11,049
6 Mo	7.60	0.41	4.13	17	10,760
1 Yr	11.75	0.88	5.45	17	11,175
3 Yr Avg	4.06	0.48	4.24	13	11,268
5 Yr Avg	-3.03	-0.73	6.26	15	8,574
10 Yr Avg	11.72	-0.35	2.13	14	30,291
15 Yr Avg	—	—	—	—	—

Tax Analysis	Tax-Adj Rtn%	%Rank Cat	Tax-Cost Rat	%Rank Cat
3 Yr (estimated)	3.36	13	0.34	59
5 Yr (estimated)	-3.31	12	0.29	18
10 Yr (estimated)	11.44	6	0.25	2

Potential Capital Gain Exposure: 19% of assets

Rating and Risk

Time Period	Load-Adj Return %	Morningstar Rtn vs Cat	Morningstar Risk vs Cat	Morningstar Risk-Adj Rating
1 Yr	10.63			
3 Yr	3.71	+Avg	Avg	★★★★
5 Yr	-3.03	+Avg	Avg	★★★★
10 Yr	11.72	+Avg	Avg	★★★★
Incept	11.28			

Other Measures	Standard Index S&P 500	Best Fit Index Russ 1000
Alpha	0.4	-0.3
Beta	1.04	1.06
R-Squared	99	99

Standard Deviation	16.43
Mean	4.06
Sharpe Ratio	0.16

Portfolio Analysis 09-30-04

Share change since 06-04 Total Stocks:556	Sector	PE	YTD Ret%	% Assets
⊕ Gen Elec	Ind Mtrls	22.8	20.68	3.06
ExxonMobil	Energy	13.9	28.04	2.79
⊕ Microsoft	Software	36.1	8.95	2.17
⊖ Pfizer	Health	22.0	-22.31	2.16
Citigroup	Financial	15.3	2.72	2.01
⊕ Bank of America	Financial	12.3	21.50	1.50
Johnson & Johnson	Health	20.6	25.17	1.49
⊖ American International G	Financial	16.2	-0.53	1.46
Wal-Mart Stores	Consumer	23.4	0.51	1.28
Intel	Hardware	19.8	-26.56	1.19
⊕ IBM	Hardware	20.2	7.19	1.17
⊖ Cisco Systems	Hardware	24.5	-20.26	1.16
Procter & Gamble	Goods	23.3	12.38	1.14
⊕ J P Morgan Chase	Financial	19.4	9.97	1.13
⊕ ChevronTexaco	Energy	7.7	25.57	0.88
⊕ Dell	Hardware	34.0	24.01	0.86
Verizon Communications	Telecom	32.4	20.25	0.84
PepsiCo	Goods	22.5	13.82	0.81
Wells Fargo	Financial	15.5	8.97	0.78
Altria Group	Goods	13.3	18.38	0.75

Current Investment Style

Value Blnd Growth — Large Mid Small

Market Cap	%
Giant	43.7
Large	30.1
Mid	25.9
Small	0.3
Micro	0.0
Avg $mil: 29,426	

Value Measures		Rel Category
Price/Earnings	17.15	0.81
Price/Book	2.56	0.79
Price/Sales	1.39	0.65
Price/Cash Flow	7.35	0.67
Dividend Yield %	1.18	1.53

Growth Measures	%	Rel Category
Long-Term Erngs	11.99	0.85
Book Value	8.59	0.68
Sales	5.44	0.64
Cash Flow	9.45	0.57
Historical Erngs	13.16	0.91

Profitability	%	Rel Category
Return on Equity	17.33	0.97
Return on Assets	9.08	0.97
Net Margin	11.51	0.94

Sector Weightings	% of Stocks	Rel S&P 500	3 Year High	3 Year Low
Info	23.74	1.10		
Software	4.30	1.00	5	4
Hardware	11.37	1.11	13	9
Media	4.65	1.21	5	4
Telecom	3.42	1.09	4	3
Service	49.37	1.06		
Health	14.79	1.18	18	15
Consumer	11.07	1.22	12	10
Business	5.32	1.31	6	5
Financial	18.19	0.88	19	16
Mfg	26.89	0.84		
Goods	7.86	0.84	9	6
Ind Mtrls	10.00	0.79	10	9
Energy	7.69	1.07	8	6
Utilities	1.34	0.45	1	1

Composition

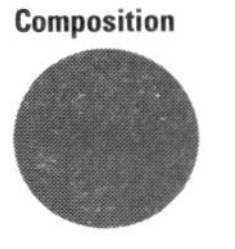

Cash	0.0
Stocks	100.0
Bonds	0.0
Other	0.0
Foreign (% of Stock)	0.0

Morningstar's Take by Sonya Morris 10-14-04

Vanguard Tax-Managed Capital Appreciation is a fine choice for a taxable account.

Vanguard indexing maven Gus Sauter takes a page out of the passive management playbook in running this fund. He constructs its portfolio to shadow the Russell 1000 Index. That tack serves to keep turnover and, thus, the risk of racking up highly taxed short-term capital gains nice and low.

But Sauter takes things a step further here. To further minimize capital gains, he sells high-cost share lots first to meet redemptions while also harvesting capital losses, which can be used to offset future capital gains. In addition, Sauter steers clear of high dividend-payers. Although dividends aren't subject to higher ordinary income tax rates any longer, Sauter prefers low-yielding fare since capital gain recognition can be forestalled indefinitely by continuing to hang onto a stock. By contrast, dividend income must be passed on to shareholders when received.

Given the emphasis on lower-yielding stocks, the tech and health-care sectors have typically figured prominently here. That bias gives the fund an edge when racier names prosper, as in 2003, but can weigh when growth stocks trail. It has also made the fund slightly more volatile than its Russell 1000 bogy, though its wide diversification has made the ride smoother than what investors would get at the typical large-growth offering.

Most relevant, the fund has achieved its aim of keeping a lid on taxes: Its 10-year annualized tax-adjusted return lands in the category's top decile. True, the fund owes a great deal of that success to its excellent pretax performance, a testament to the potency of indexing in the large-cap arena. But its 0.23% tax-cost ratio--which expresses the cost of taxes as a percentage similar to an expense ratio--is a fraction of Vanguard 500 Index's. The fund's very low 0.17% price tag seals the deal.

Tax-conscious investors will like what they get here.

Address:	PO Box 2600 Valley Forge PA 19482 800-662-7447
Web Address:	www.vanguard.com
Inception:	09-06-94 *
Advisor:	Vanguard Advisers, Inc.
Subadvisor:	None
NTF Plans:	N/A

Minimum Purchase:	$10000	Add: $100	IRA: $10000
Min Auto Inv Plan:	$10000	Add: $50	
Sales Fees:	No-load, 2.00%R		
Management Fee:	0.16%		
Actual Fees:	Mgt:0.16%	Dist: —	
Expense Projections:	3Yr:$170	5Yr:$96	10Yr:$217
Income Distrib:	Annually		

Vanguard Tx-Mgd Gr

Ticker	Load	NAV	Yield	Total Assets	Mstar Category
VTGIX	None	$26.36	1.8%	$2,615 mil	Large Blend

Governance and Management

Fiduciary Grade: B

Portfolio Manager(s)

Gus Sauter, Vanguard's chief investment officer, has shown himself to be one of the best indexers in the business. He has done a great job of adding value through effective trading techniques at a number of Vanguard's index offerings. Vanguard has also demonstrated its leadership in the tax-managed investing area, devising crafty trading strategies that put a dent in Uncle Sam's take.

Strategy

The fund tracks the S&P 500 Index. To minimize capital-gains distributions, manager Gus Sauter may sell stocks at a loss to offset gains, liquidating the highest-cost shares first. The fund also takes steps to deter market-timers, whose activity can lead to more selling, by imposing redemption fees on short-term investors, and by requiring a $10,000 minimum investment.

Historical Profile

Return Above Avg
Risk Average
Rating ★★★★ Above Avg

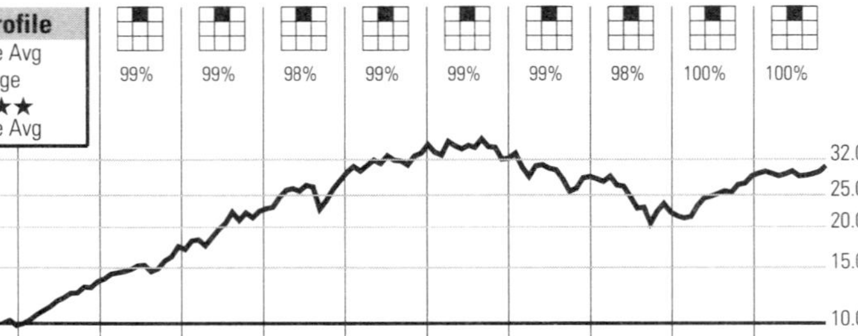

Investment Style
Equity
Stock %

▼ Manager Change
▽ Partial Manager Change

Growth of $10,000
▬ Investment Values of Fund
— Investment Values of S&P 500

Performance Quartile (within Category)

1993	1994	1995	1996	1997	1998	1999	2000	2001	2002	2003	12-04	History
—	9.77	13.16	15.89	20.88	26.55	31.81	28.66	24.93	19.15	24.23	26.36	NAV
—	-1.70*	37.53	23.03	33.31	28.67	21.12	-9.03	-11.93	-21.95	28.53	10.83	Total Return %
—	—	0.00	0.09	-0.04	0.10	0.08	0.07	-0.05	0.14	-0.14	-0.04	+/-S&P 500
—	—	-0.24	0.58	0.46	1.65	0.21	-1.24	0.52	-0.30	-1.36	-0.57	+/-Russ 1000
—	0.00	2.58	2.14	1.77	1.40	1.19	0.94	1.05	1.31	1.79	1.95	Income Return %
—	—	34.95	20.89	31.54	27.27	19.93	-9.97	-12.98	-23.26	26.74	8.88	Capital Return %
—	—	12	28	13	15	37	63	44	42	29	35	Total Rtn % Rank Cat
—	0.09	0.25	0.28	0.28	0.29	0.31	0.30	0.30	0.33	0.34	0.47	Income $
—	0.00	0.00	0.00	0.00	0.00	0.00	0.00	0.00	0.00	0.00	0.00	Capital Gains $
—	0.20	0.20	0.20	0.17	0.19	0.19	0.19	0.17	0.17	0.17	—	Expense Ratio %
—	2.82	2.37	2.04	1.62	1.32	1.11	0.96	1.44	1.44	1.63	—	Income Ratio %
—	—	6	7	2	4	4	5	5	9	5	—	Turnover Rate %
—	31	98	235	579	1,352	2,240	2,427	1,606	1,077	1,321	1,395	Net Assets $mil

Performance 12-31-04

	1st Qtr	2nd Qtr	3rd Qtr	4th Qtr	Total
2000	2.26	-2.65	-0.92	-7.78	-9.03
2001	-11.89	5.84	-14.66	10.68	-11.93
2002	0.24	-13.32	-17.10	8.36	-21.95
2003	-3.19	15.37	2.64	12.12	28.53
2004	1.70	1.71	-1.89	9.21	10.83

Trailing	Total Return%	+/- S&P 500	+/- Russ 1000	%Rank Cat	Growth of $10,000
3 Mo	9.21	-0.02	-0.59	48	10,921
6 Mo	7.15	-0.04	-0.66	43	10,715
1 Yr	10.83	-0.04	-0.57	35	11,083
3 Yr Avg	3.60	0.02	-0.67	33	11,119
5 Yr Avg	-2.29	0.01	-0.53	50	8,906
10 Yr Avg	12.09	0.02	-0.07	15	31,309
15 Yr Avg	—	—	—	—	—

Tax Analysis	Tax-Adj Rtn%	%Rank Cat	Tax-Cost Rat	%Rank Cat
3 Yr (estimated)	2.81	35	0.43	36
5 Yr (estimated)	-2.71	43	0.43	23
10 Yr (estimated)	11.51	7	0.52	8

Potential Capital Gain Exposure: 11% of assets

Rating and Risk

Time Period	Load-Adj Return %	Morningstar Rtn vs Cat	Morningstar Risk vs Cat	Morningstar Risk-Adj Rating
1 Yr	9.73			
3 Yr	3.25	Avg	Avg	★★★
5 Yr	-2.29	Avg	Avg	★★★
10 Yr	12.09	+Avg	Avg	★★★★
Incept	11.51			

Other Measures	Standard Index S&P 500	Best Fit Index S&P 500
Alpha	0.0	0.0
Beta	1.00	1.00
R-Squared	100	100
Standard Deviation	15.50	
Mean	3.60	
Sharpe Ratio	0.14	

Portfolio Analysis 09-30-04

Share change since 06-04 Total Stocks:503	Sector	PE	YTD Ret%	% Assets
⊕ Gen Elec	Ind Mtrls	22.8	20.68	3.40
⊖ ExxonMobil	Energy	13.9	28.04	3.02
⊕ Microsoft	Software	36.1	8.95	2.89
⊖ Pfizer	Health	22.0	-22.31	2.22
⊕ Citigroup	Financial	15.3	2.72	2.19
⊖ Wal-Mart Stores	Consumer	23.4	0.51	2.17
⊕ American International G	Financial	16.2	-0.53	1.70
⊕ Bank of America	Financial	12.3	21.50	1.69
⊕ Johnson & Johnson	Health	20.6	25.17	1.61
⊖ IBM	Hardware	20.2	7.19	1.38
⊕ J P Morgan Chase	Financial	19.4	9.97	1.36
⊖ Procter & Gamble	Goods	23.3	12.38	1.32
⊖ Intel	Hardware	19.8	-26.56	1.24
⊕ Cisco Systems	Hardware	24.5	-20.26	1.18
⊕ ChevronTexaco	Energy	7.7	25.57	1.10
⊕ Verizon Communications	Telecom	32.4	20.25	1.05
⊕ Wells Fargo	Financial	15.5	8.97	0.97
⊕ Coca-Cola	Goods	21.9	-16.12	0.93
⊕ Altria Group	Goods	13.3	18.38	0.93
⊖ Dell	Hardware	34.0	24.01	0.85

Current Investment Style

Value Blnd Growth / Large Mid Small

Market Cap	%
Giant	52.1
Large	37.5
Mid	10.3
Small	0.1
Micro	0.0
Avg $mil: 44,989	

Value Measures		Rel Category
Price/Earnings	16.60	0.98
Price/Book	2.62	1.00
Price/Sales	1.43	0.99
Price/Cash Flow	7.51	0.98
Dividend Yield %	1.68	1.14

Growth Measures	%	Rel Category
Long-Term Erngs	11.06	0.96
Book Value	7.14	0.92
Sales	4.74	0.83
Cash Flow	7.10	0.75
Historical Erngs	11.54	0.98

Profitability	%	Rel Category
Return on Equity	18.29	1.05
Return on Assets	9.34	1.08
Net Margin	11.96	1.05

Sector Weightings	% of Stocks	Rel S&P 500	3 Year High	3 Year Low
Info	21.41	1.00		
Software	4.48	1.04	5	4
Hardware	9.56	0.94	11	8
Media	3.68	0.96	4	3
Telecom	3.69	1.17	5	3
Service	46.44	1.00		
Health	12.94	1.04	16	13
Consumer	8.90	0.98	10	9
Business	3.92	0.97	4	3
Financial	20.68	1.00	21	19
Mfg	32.15	1.00		
Goods	9.31	1.00	10	9
Ind Mtrls	12.61	1.00	13	11
Energy	7.35	1.03	8	6
Utilities	2.88	0.97	3	3

Composition

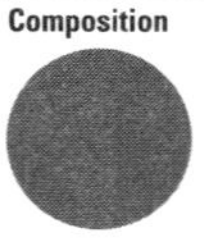

Cash	0.1
Stocks	99.9
Bonds	0.0
Other	0.0
Foreign (% of Stock)	0.0

Morningstar's Take by Jeffrey Ptak 10-05-04

This fund is cheap, boring, and pretty darn good at its job: keeping the taxman at bay.

If you guessed that Vanguard 500 Index Fund was the cheapest way to invest in the S&P 500 Index from Vanguard's mutual fund stable, you guessed wrong. That distinction belongs with this fund, which entered the year carrying a 0.17% price tag and is likely to exit it cheaper than that (its most recent semi-annual report pegged the expense ratio at 0.15%). Vanguard 500 will cost you a few basis points extra, weighing in at a still-paltry 0.18%.

This isn't a pure index fund, however. While manager Gus Sauter typically holds the 500 stocks in the index, he uses trading maneuvers to harvest capital losses that can be used to offset realized gains. Because tax rules prohibit deduction of realized losses when the same shares are repurchased within 30 days (the so-called "wash sale" rule), Sauter must wait a month before repurchasing shares of stocks that he has sold for loss-harvesting purposes. Thus, the fund courts the risk that its performance could deviate from the index should the price of the stock just sold dramatically rise or fall in the interim.

Yet, likely owing to the large-cap arena's efficiency, the fund hasn't run into any major problems over the long haul. In fact, its pretax returns have typically remained within five basis points of Vanguard 500's from one quarter to the next. The fund's long-term record attests to that tight correlation, as its 11.1% 10-year annualized return beats Vanguard 500's by an eyelash.

That changes a bit on an after-tax basis, however. This fund's 10.5% annualized aftertax return over the past decade tops its sibling's by more than 20 basis points per annum, reflecting Sauter's tax-minimization efforts. While that might not seem like much, it would translate to an extra $1,000 in earnings on a $10,000 investment in a taxable account over 10 years, which isn't chump change.

All told, it remains a solid choice.

Address:	PO Box 2600 Valley Forge PA 19482 800-662-7447
Web Address:	www.vanguard.com
Inception:	09-06-94 *
Advisor:	Vanguard Advisers, Inc.
Subadvisor:	None
NTF Plans:	N/A

Minimum Purchase:	$10000	Add: $100	IRA: $10000
Min Auto Inv Plan:	$10000	Add: $50	
Sales Fees:	No-load, 2.00%R		
Management Fee:	0.17%		
Actual Fees:	Mgt:0.17%	Dist: —	
Expense Projections:	3Yr:$170	5Yr:$96	10Yr:$217
Income Distrib:	Quarterly		

Vanguard Tax-Mgd Intl

Ticker	Load	NAV	Yield	Total Assets	Mstar Category
VTMGX	None	$10.33	2.0%	$968 mil	Foreign Large Blend

Governance and Management

Fiduciary Grade: B

Portfolio Manager(s)

Gus Sauter, Vanguard's index specialist, has proved to be one of the best passive managers in the business. He has done a great job adding value through effective trading at a number of Vanguard's index offerings.

Strategy

The fund uses a sampling technique to match the key characteristics of the MSCI EAFE Index, which tends to favor large-cap stocks. To minimize capital-gains distributions, manager Gus Sauter may sell stocks at a loss to offset gains, liquidating highest-cost shares first.

Historical Profile
Return Above Avg
Risk Average
Rating ★★★★ Above Avg

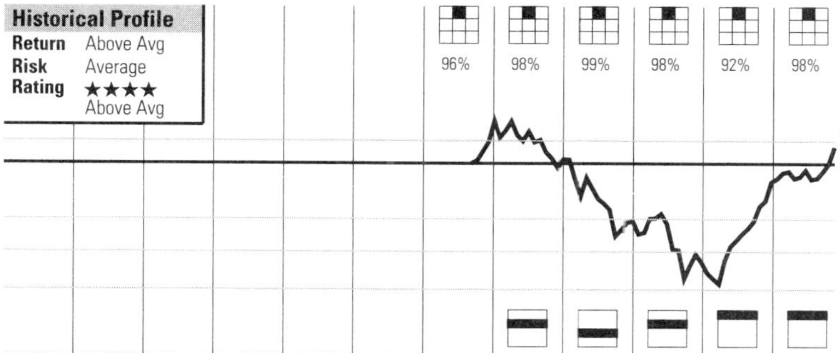

1993	1994	1995	1996	1997	1998	1999	2000	2001	2002	2003	12-04	History
—	—	—	—	—	—	11.96	10.14	7.79	6.43	8.76	10.33	NAV
—	—	—	—	—	—	20.01*	-14.29	-21.94	-15.62	38.67	20.25	Total Return %
—	—	—	—	—	—	—	-0.10	-0.52	0.32	0.08	0.00	+/-MSCI EAFE
—	—	—	—	—	—	—	-0.93	-0.55	0.18	-0.75	-0.13	+/-MSCI Wd xUS
—	—	—	—	—	—	0.00	0.92	1.23	1.80	2.38	2.31	Income Return %
—	—	—	—	—	—	—	-15.21	-23.17	-17.42	36.29	17.94	Capital Return %
—	—	—	—	—	—	—	32	52	35	16	17	Total Rtn % Rank Cat
—	—	—	—	—	—	0.04	0.11	0.13	0.14	0.15	0.20	Income $
—	—	—	—	—	—	0.00	0.00	0.00	0.00	0.00	0.00	Capital Gains $
—	—	—	—	—	—	0.35	0.35	0.35	0.31	0.28	—	Expense Ratio %
—	—	—	—	—	—	0.96	1.24	1.49	2.04	2.33	—	Income Ratio %
—	—	—	—	—	—	—	5	20	7	9	—	Turnover Rate %
—	—	—	—	—	—	135	241	327	334	514	825	Net Assets $mil

Performance 12-31-04

	1st Qtr	2nd Qtr	3rd Qtr	4th Qtr	Total
2000	-0.17	-4.02	-8.03	-2.74	-14.29
2001	-13.71	-1.03	-14.09	6.39	-21.94
2002	1.03	-2.16	-20.00	6.71	-15.62
2003	-8.24	19.32	8.10	17.16	38.67
2004	4.36	0.55	-0.54	15.23	20.25

Trailing	Total Return%	+/- MSCI EAFE	+/- MSCI Wd xUS	%Rank Cat	Growth of $10,000
3 Mo	15.22	-0.10	0.07	18	11,522
6 Mo	14.60	-0.40	-0.77	35	11,460
1 Yr	20.25	0.00	-0.13	17	12,025
3 Yr Avg	12.06	0.17	-0.16	14	14,072
5 Yr Avg	-1.20	-0.07	-0.44	27	9,414
10 Yr Avg	—	—	—	—	—
15 Yr Avg	—	—	—	—	—

Tax Analysis	Tax-Adj Rtn%	%Rank Cat	Tax-Cost Rat	%Rank Cat
3 Yr (estimated)	11.02	17	0.59	64
5 Yr (estimated)	-1.76	21	0.57	36
10 Yr (estimated)	—	—	—	—

Potential Capital Gain Exposure: 10% of assets

Rating and Risk

Time Period	Load-Adj Return %	Morningstar Rtn vs Cat	Morningstar Risk vs Cat	Morningstar Risk-Adj Rating
1 Yr	19.05			
3 Yr	11.68	+Avg	+Avg	★★★★
5 Yr	-1.20	+Avg	Avg	★★★★
10 Yr	—	—	—	—
Incept	2.30			

Other Measures	Standard Index S&P 500	Best Fit Index MSCI EAFE
Alpha	0.1	0.1
Beta	1.01	1.01
R-Squared	100	100
Standard Deviation	17.68	
Mean	12.06	
Sharpe Ratio	0.61	

Portfolio Analysis 09-30-04

Share change since 06-04 Total Stocks:1025	Sector	Country	% Assets
⊕ BP	Energy	U.K.	2.66
⊕ HSBC Hldgs	Financial	U.K.	2.28
⊖ Vodafone Grp	Telecom	U.K.	2.01
⊕ GlaxoSmithKline	Health	U.K.	1.67
⊕ TOTAL	Energy	France	1.56
⊕ Novartis	Health	Switzerland	1.45
⊕ Toyota Motor	Goods	Japan	1.44
⊕ Royal Dutch Petroleum	Energy	Netherlands	1.39
⊕ Nestle	Goods	Switzerland	1.20
⊕ Royal Bank Of Scotland G	Financial	U.K.	1.12
⊕ UBS	Financial	Switzerland	0.98
⊕ Roche Holding	Health	Switzerland	0.95
⊕ Shell Transport & Tradin	Energy	U.K.	0.93
⊕ AstraZeneca	Health	U.K.	0.90
⊕ Sanofi-Synthelabo	Health	France	0.87
⊕ Telefonica	Telecom	Spain	0.85
⊕ Barclays	Financial	U.K.	0.81
⊕ Siemens	Hardware	Germany	0.77
⊖ Nokia	Hardware	Finland	0.77
⊕ ENI	Energy	Italy	0.76

Current Investment Style

Value Blnd Growth / Large Mid Small

Market Cap	%
Giant	55.0
Large	31.7
Mid	12.8
Small	0.5
Micro	0.0

Avg $mil: 23,128

Value Measures		Rel Category
Price/Earnings	13.85	1.01
Price/Book	1.75	0.97
Price/Sales	0.82	0.90
Price/Cash Flow	4.70	0.96
Dividend Yield %	2.74	1.08

Growth Measures	%	Rel Category
Long-Term Erngs	10.08	0.94
Book Value	-0.53	NMF
Sales	1.47	0.59
Cash Flow	3.05	0.54
Historical Erngs	5.43	0.97

Composition

Cash	0.0	Bonds	0.0
Stocks	98.4	Other	1.6

Foreign (% of Stock) 100.0

Sector Weightings	% of Stocks	Rel MSCI EAFE	3 Year High	3 Year Low
Info	14.74	0.89		
Software	0.72	0.67	1	0
Hardware	4.21	1.15	5	4
Media	2.34	1.03	2	2
Telecom	7.47	0.78	9	6
Service	44.85	1.00		
Health	8.43	1.16	10	8
Consumer	5.05	1.00	5	5
Business	4.87	0.90	6	4
Financial	26.50	0.98	27	22
Mfg	40.42	1.05		
Goods	13.89	1.02	16	14
Ind Mtrls	12.98	1.06	13	11
Energy	8.50	1.16	12	8
Utilities	5.05	0.94	5	4

Regional Exposure % Stock

UK/W. Europe	70	N. America	0
Japan	22	Latn America	0
Asia X Japan	8	Other	0

Country Exposure % Stock

U.K.	26	Switzerland	7
Japan	22	Germany	7
France	9		

Morningstar's Take by Sonya Morris 12-06-04

Although Vanguard Tax-Managed International is a fine option, the competition is heating up.

Like its sibling, Vanguard Developed Markets Index, this fund is tethered to the MSCI EAFE Index. That strategy doesn't put the fund in select company--MSCI EAFE-conscious strategies abound in the foreign large-blend category. But it puts a twist on that familiar formula, as it's the only offering in its peer group with a tax-management mandate. Manager Gus Sauter employs tactics such as selling high-cost share lots to harvest losses that can be applied against future capital gains, in order to keep a lid on taxes.

Those efforts have generally paid off. On an after-tax basis, the fund has outpaced 66% of its rivals over the past five years. True, that success partly owes to the fund's strong relative pre-tax returns, which land in the category's top third. But Sauter has clearly wrung out savings over time, as evidenced by the fund's below-average 0.45% five-year tax-cost ratio (a measure that expresses taxes as a percentage).

That said, the case for this fund isn't a slam-dunk. Fidelity recently slashed the expense ratio on its EAFE-tracker, Fidelity Spartan International Index, to a paltry 0.10%, roughly a third of this fund's 0.28% price tag. That's a significant margin in the indexing realm where every basis point counts. Thus, the Fidelity offering's pretax returns are likely to nudge ahead of this fund's in the years ahead.

Nevertheless, we don't think investors should bail out on this offering. Fidelity's fee cut can be rescinded at any time. And a subsequent fee increase would place Fidelity shareholders in the unenviable position of having to weight the cost of sticking with a fund that's no longer the cheapest game in town versus incurring the not-inconsequential tax costs associated with heading elsewhere. Given that this fund is likely to remain very competitive after taxes, we simply don't see the upside to making a move.

Address:	PO Box 2600 Valley Forge PA 19482 800-662-7447
Web Address:	www.vanguard.com
Inception:	08-17-99 *
Advisor:	Vanguard Advisers, Inc.
Subadvisor:	None
NTF Plans:	N/A

Minimum Purchase:	$10000	Add: $100	IRA: $10000
Min Auto Inv Plan:	$10000	Add: $50	
Sales Fees:	No-load, 2.00%R		
Management Fee:	0.17%		
Actual Fees:	Mgt:0.17%	Dist: —	
Expense Projections:	3Yr:$214	5Yr:$174	10Yr:$393
Income Distrib:	Annually		

Vanguard Tax-Mgd SmCap R

Ticker	Load	NAV	Yield	Total Assets	Mstar Category
VTMSX	None	$21.25	0.8%	$1,297 mil	Small Blend

Governance and Management

Fiduciary Grade: B

Portfolio Manager(s)

Gus Sauter, Vanguard's index specialist, has proved to be one of the best passive managers in the business. He has done a great job of adding value through effective trading at a number of Vanguard's index offerings.

Strategy

Manager Gus Sauter uses a sampling technique to match the key characteristics of the S&P SmallCap 600 Index, which has lower turnover than the other popular small-cap benchmark, the Russell 2000. To ensure tax efficiency, Sauter emphasizes those stocks in the S&P index with low dividends. In addition, to minimize capital-gains distributions, Sauter may sell stocks at a loss to offset gains, and he liquidates highest-cost shares first.

Historical Profile

Return Average
Risk Average
Rating ★★★ Neutral

Investment Style
Equity
Stock %: 99% (1999), 99% (2000), 99% (2001), 100% (2002), 100% (2003), 100% (12-04)

▼ Manager Change
∇ Partial Manager Change

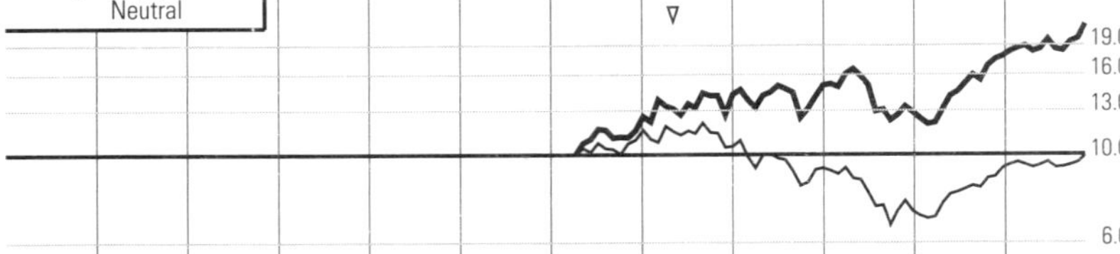

Growth of $10,000
▬ Investment Values of Fund
— Investment Values of S&P 500

Performance Quartile (within Category)

History

1993	1994	1995	1996	1997	1998	1999	2000	2001	2002	2003	12-04	History
—	—	—	—	—	—	12.61	14.23	14.92	12.67	17.44	21.25	NAV
—	—	—	—	—	—	26.28*	13.44	5.44	-14.44	38.51	22.84	Total Return %
—	—	—	—	—	—	—	22.54	17.32	7.65	9.84	11.97	+/-S&P 500
—	—	—	—	—	—	—	16.46	2.95	6.04	-8.74	4.51	+/-Russ 2000
—	—	—	—	—	—	0.00	0.59	0.60	0.64	0.86	0.99	Income Return %
—	—	—	—	—	—	—	12.85	4.84	-15.08	37.65	21.85	Capital Return %
—	—	—	—	—	—	—	51	63	41	67	16	Total Rtn % Rank Cat
—	—	—	—	—	—	0.05	0.07	0.09	0.10	0.11	0.17	Income $
—	—	—	—	—	—	0.00	0.00	0.00	0.00	0.00	0.00	Capital Gains $
—	—	—	—	—	—	0.19	0.20	0.20	0.17	0.17	—	Expense Ratio %
—	—	—	—	—	—	0.70	0.64	0.63	0.68	0.77	—	Income Ratio %
—	—	—	—	—	—	27	64	25	21	21	—	Turnover Rate %
—	—	—	—	—	—	194	368	568	601	929	1,282	Net Assets $mil

Performance 12-31-04

	1st Qtr	2nd Qtr	3rd Qtr	4th Qtr	Total
2000	6.26	1.19	4.79	0.66	13.44
2001	-7.38	13.58	-16.83	20.52	5.44
2002	6.84	-6.27	-18.41	4.72	-14.44
2003	-5.76	19.68	6.93	14.85	38.51
2004	6.19	3.67	-1.30	13.05	22.84

Trailing	Total Return%	+/- S&P 500	+/- Russ 2000	%Rank Cat	Growth of $10,000
3 Mo	13.05	3.82	-1.04	44	11,305
6 Mo	11.58	4.39	0.75	32	11,158
1 Yr	22.84	11.97	4.51	16	12,284
3 Yr Avg	13.33	9.75	1.85	37	14,556
5 Yr Avg	11.73	14.03	5.12	54	17,412
10 Yr Avg	—	—	—	—	—
15 Yr Avg	—	—	—	—	—

Tax Analysis	Tax-Adj Rtn%	%Rank Cat	Tax-Cost Rat	%Rank Cat
3 Yr (estimated)	12.70	33	0.22	16
5 Yr (estimated)	11.49	43	0.21	8
10 Yr (estimated)	—	—	—	—

Potential Capital Gain Exposure: 9% of assets

Rating and Risk

Time Period	Load-Adj Return %	Morningstar Rtn vs Cat	Morningstar Risk vs Cat	Morningstar Risk-Adj Rating
1 Yr	21.61			
3 Yr	12.95	Avg	Avg	★★★
5 Yr	11.73	Avg	Avg	★★★
10 Yr	—	—	—	—
Incept	14.63			

Other Measures	Standard Index S&P 500	Best Fit Index Mstar Small Core
Alpha	10.2	-1.1
Beta	0.89	0.99
R-Squared	62	98
Standard Deviation	19.27	
Mean	13.33	
Sharpe Ratio	0.63	

Portfolio Analysis 09-30-04

Share change since 06-04 Total Stocks:603	Sector	PE	YTD Ret%	% Assets
⊕ NVR	Consumer	12.2	65.11	0.76
⊕ MDC Holdings	Consumer	9.4	48.72	0.52
⊕ Polaris Industries	Goods	24.1	56.60	0.51
⊕ Yellow Roadway	Business	21.5	54.02	0.49
⊕ Cooper Companies	Health	28.4	49.92	0.48
⊕ Medicis Pharmaceuticals	Health	31.6	-1.23	0.48
⊕ Timken	Ind Mtrls	22.3	32.68	0.48
⊕ Massey Energy Company	Energy	—	69.03	0.48
⊕ Fossil	Goods	22.6	36.73	0.47
⊕ Roper Industries	Ind Mtrls	31.4	24.26	0.46
⊕ Florida Rock Industries	Ind Mtrls	21.2	68.98	0.46
⊕ Patina Oil & Gas	Energy	18.8	54.26	0.45
⊕ Briggs & Stratton	Ind Mtrls	14.4	25.63	0.45
⊕ New Century Financial	Financial	5.7	63.77	0.44
⊕ Global Payments	Business	31.3	24.66	0.44
⊕ Pharmaceutical Product D	Health	41.7	53.10	0.44
⊕ Oshkosh Truck	Ind Mtrls	20.5	34.70	0.44
⊕ South Financial Group	Financial	15.7	19.71	0.43
⊕ FLIR Systems	Ind Mtrls	27.4	74.77	0.43
⊕ First Bancorp	Financial	17.2	62.27	0.42

Current Investment Style

Value Blnd Growth — Large / Mid / Small

Market Cap	%
Giant	0.0
Large	0.0
Mid	21.0
Small	70.0
Micro	9.0
Avg $mil: 939	

Value Measures		Rel Category
Price/Earnings	17.32	1.00
Price/Book	2.01	1.01
Price/Sales	0.91	0.96
Price/Cash Flow	5.16	0.88
Dividend Yield %	0.91	1.10

Growth Measures	%	Rel Category
Long-Term Erngs	13.72	1.01
Book Value	7.74	1.37
Sales	5.77	1.34
Cash Flow	-0.23	NMF
Historical Erngs	7.39	0.99

Profitability	%	Rel Category
Return on Equity	11.31	1.08
Return on Assets	5.53	1.11
Net Margin	7.40	1.01

Sector Weightings	% of Stocks	Rel S&P 500	3 Year High	Low
Info	11.90	0.55		
Software	4.62	1.07	5	3
Hardware	6.38	0.63	10	6
Media	0.23	0.06	0	0
Telecom	0.67	0.21	1	0
Service	50.11	1.08		
Health	11.78	0.94	13	12
Consumer	11.80	1.30	17	12
Business	10.35	2.56	12	10
Financial	16.18	0.78	16	11
Mfg	38.00	1.18		
Goods	7.05	0.76	8	7
Ind Mtrls	20.72	1.64	21	17
Energy	6.69	0.93	7	6
Utiiities	3.54	1.20	4	3

Composition

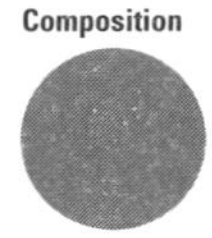

Cash	0.1
Stocks	99.9
Bonds	0.0
Other	0.0
Foreign (% of Stock)	0.0

Morningstar's Take by Sonya Morris 12-01-04

Vanguard Tax-Managed Small Cap is a solid choice for small-cap exposure in a taxable account.

Small cap stocks have been stellar in recent years. As a result, many small-cap funds are sitting on sizable taxable gains. Not so here. In fact, this fund hasn't made a capital gains distribution since its April 1992 inception, thanks to manager Gus Sauter's savvy tactics. Sauter augments the innate tax efficiency of indexing by employing tactics like selling high-cost share lots first and harvesting losses to offset future capital gains.

Although the small-cap realm has been less hospitable to indexing than other, more-efficient areas of the market, this fund has held its own. On a pre-tax basis, its five-year annualized returns are on par with the category average. And after taxes, the fund bests roughly 60% of its peers.

While those results aren't awe-inspiring, they're impressive when one considers that the five-year period includes a bear market, which typically doesn't favor passive strategies like this offering's.

Furthermore, actively managed funds were able to stockpile tax losses amid the downturn, which they have since used to offset recent gains, thereby boosting their tax efficiency to unusually high levels.

If one assumes that small-cap funds will continue to post gains over the long haul--an outcome which would see most small-cap funds deplete their loss carryforward reserves before long--this fund's tax efficient approach is likely to shine far brighter. On the other hand, leaner times for small caps--a distinct possibility given small stocks' lengthy run--could hinder this fund, given that active managers could replenish their loss reserves anew.

That said, this fund's bogy, the S&P Small Cap 600 Index has shown itself to be tough to beat before taxes over the past decade--a span that includes strong and tepid markets alike. On that basis, and given the fund's rock-bottom costs, we'd recommend it.

Address:	PO Box 2600 Valley Forge PA 19482 800-662-7447
Web Address:	www.vanguard.com
Inception:	03-25-99*
Advisor:	Vanguard Advisers, Inc.
Subadvisor:	None
NTF Plans:	N/A

Minimum Purchase:	$10000	Add: $100	IRA: $0
Min Auto Inv Plan:	$0	Add: —	
Sales Fees:	No-load, 2.00%R		
Management Fee:	0.14%		
Actual Fees:	Mgt:0.14%	Dist: —	
Expense Projections:	3Yr:$55	5Yr:$96	10Yr:$217
Income Distrib:	Annually		

Vanguard Total Bd Idx

Analyst Pick	Ticker	Load	NAV	Yield	SEC Yield	Total Assets	Mstar Category
✔	VBMFX	None	$10.27	4.3%	4.12%	$29,425 mil	Intermediate-Term Bond

Governance and Management

Fiduciary Grade: B

Portfolio Manager(s)

Nothing to worry about. Vanguard is the first name in indexing, and Ken Volpert has been the manager of this fund since 1992. Volpert's team, which includes eight credit analysts, runs all of Vanguard's fixed-income index funds, including Short-, Intermediate-, and Long-Term Bond Index.

Strategy

The fund strives to approximate the performance of the Lehman Brothers Aggregate Bond Index, which is a commonly used proxy for the broad, investment-grade U.S. bond market. The duration and other key characteristics of the index are carefully replicated, but the fund does not hold every security in the index. Instead, it tends to hold a higher percentage of short-term corporate bonds or asset-backed securities, and fewer short Treasuries than the index in an effort to pick up additional yield and return.

Historical Profile

Return Above Avg
Risk Average
Rating ★★★★ Above Avg

Investment Style: Fixed Income — Income Rtn %Rank Cat: 25 19 19 20 19 15 15 23 21

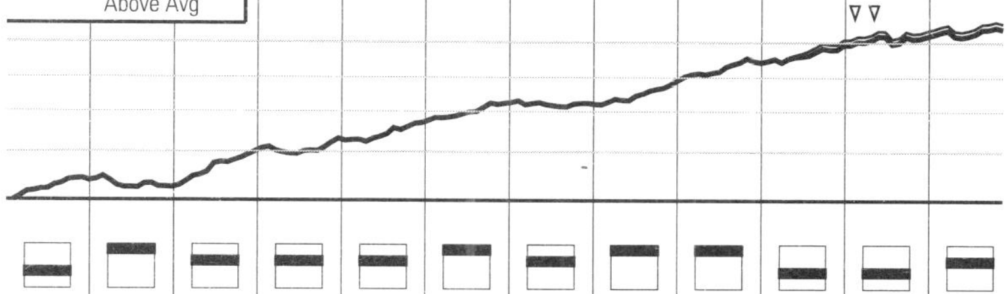

▼ Manager Change
▽ Partial Manager Change

Growth of $10,000
▬ Investment Values of Fund
— Investment Values of LB Aggr

Performance Quartile (within Category)

1993	1994	1995	1996	1997	1998	1999	2000	2001	2002	2003	12-04	History
10.06	9.17	10.14	9.84	10.09	10.27	9.56	9.96	10.15	10.38	10.31	10.27	NAV
9.68	-2.66	18.18	3.58	9.44	8.58	-0.76	11.39	8.43	8.26	3.97	4.24	Total Return %
-0.07	0.26	-0.29	-0.05	-0.21	-0.11	0.06	-0.24	-0.01	-1.99	-0.13	-0.10	+/-LB Aggr
-2.56	1.85	-3.25	0.89	0.01	-1.56	2.12	-1.05	-0.39	-4.77	-2.00	-1.06	+/-LB 5-10YR
6.66	6.37	7.31	6.51	6.76	6.36	6.19	6.99	6.53	5.77	4.67	4.42	Income Return %
3.02	-9.03	10.87	-2.93	2.68	2.22	-6.95	4.40	1.90	2.49	-0.70	-0.18	Capital Return %
68	20	42	36	33	20	35	20	22	56	58	35	Total Rtn % Rank Cat
0.64	0.62	0.65	0.64	0.65	0.62	0.62	0.65	0.63	0.57	0.47	0.45	Income $
0.12	0.00	0.00	0.00	0.00	0.04	0.02	0.00	0.00	0.01	0.00	0.02	Capital Gains $
0.18	0.18	0.20	0.20	0.20	0.20	0.20	0.22	0.22	0.22	0.22	—	Expense Ratio %
6.24	6.57	6.66	6.54	6.54	6.10	6.26	6.72	6.21	5.63	4.46	—	Income Ratio %
50	33	36	39	39	57	55	53	67	75	66	—	Turnover Rate %
1,540	1,731	2,405	2,953	5,129	7,765	9,477	11,180	14,116	16,676	17,032	19,479	Net Assets $mil

Performance 12-31-04

	1st Qtr	2nd Qtr	3rd Qtr	4th Qtr	Total
2000	2.42	1.48	3.07	3.98	11.39
2001	3.24	0.79	4.29	-0.08	8.43
2002	0.06	2.80	3.71	1.47	8.26
2003	1.30	2.57	-0.12	0.18	3.97
2004	2.71	-2.49	3.09	0.95	4.24

Trailing	Total Return%	+/- LB Aggr	+/- LB 5-10YR	%Rank Cat	Growth of $10,000
3 Mo	0.95	0.00	-0.03	48	10,095
6 Mo	4.07	-0.11	-1.50	43	10,407
1 Yr	4.24	-0.10	-1.06	35	10,424
3 Yr Avg	5.47	-0.72	-2.58	50	11,732
5 Yr Avg	7.22	-0.49	-1.85	34	14,170
10 Yr Avg	7.42	-0.30	-1.04	25	20,457
15 Yr Avg	7.43	-0.27	-0.89	35	29,301

Tax Analysis	Tax-Adj Rtn%	%Rank Cat	Tax-Cost Rat	%Rank Cat
3 Yr (estimated)	3.62	43	1.75	57
5 Yr (estimated)	5.02	31	2.05	58
10 Yr (estimated)	4.96	22	2.29	62

Potential Capital Gain Exposure: 2% of assets

Rating and Risk

Time Period	Load-Adj Return %	Morningstar Rtn vs Cat	Morningstar Risk vs Cat	Morningstar Risk-Adj Rating
1 Yr	4.24			
3 Yr	5.47	Avg	Avg	★★★
5 Yr	7.22	Avg	Avg	★★★★
10 Yr	7.42	+Avg	Avg	★★★★
Incept	7.37			

Other Measures	Standard Index LB Aggr	Best Fit Index LB. U.S. Univ. Bd
Alpha	-0.6	-1.4
Beta	0.97	1.01
R-Squared	98	99
Standard Deviation	4.41	
Mean	5.47	
Sharpe Ratio	0.94	

Morningstar's Take by Dieter Bardy 10-27-04

This well-rounded fund gets the job done.

Some might have lost faith in Vanguard Total Bond Market Index when it stumbled a few years ago, but we think recent improvements have put it on sound footing. In 2002 the fund trailed its index, the Lehman Brothers Aggregate Bond Index, by a remarkable amount--2.01 percentage points. Since then, manager Ken Volpert has taken steps to ensure that such a shortfall won't be repeated. He now aligns the issuers in the fund's portfolio more closely with the index's--94% of the issuers in the index are now included in the portfolio, compared with just 63% two years ago. This has improved the fund's trailing 12-month R-squared--a measure of how closely a fund tracks its benchmark--from 96 in late 2002 to 99.8 today. This is a big tracking improvement for an index fund.

The fund also trumps other bond index offerings because of its size. It continues to hold more of the individual issues in the index than any of its passive competitors. Greater issue diversification reduces the impact that a single issue's blowup will have on performance.

The fund has done a solid job for the year to date, outpacing 75% of its intermediate-term bond fund rivals through Oct. 25, 2004. A strong year for the index has kept the fund running ahead of its peers and strong attention to its strategy has kept the fund in line with the index. The fund has outdistanced its typical rival's 3.8% year-to-date gain with a 4.3% showing through Oct. 25, 2004. This follows its solid longer-term trailing results.

Finally, the fund's expense ratio of 0.22% is cheaper than that of other bond index funds and measurably cheaper than the average actively managed bond fund. This leaves more to pay out in yield than rival funds. Indeed, the fund's 4.4% trailing yield places in the top quartile of this large bond category. In a low-yield environment like today's, expenses matter. Investors will be well served by choosing this Analyst Pick.

Address:	PO Box 2600 Valley Forge PA 19482 800-662-7447	Minimum Purchase:	$3000 Add: $100 IRA: $1000
Web Address:	www.vanguard.com	Min Auto Inv Plan:	$3000 Add: $50
Inception:	12-11-86	Sales Fees:	No-load
Advisor:	Vanguard Advisers, Inc.	Management Fee:	0.20%
Subadvisor:	None	Actual Fees:	Mgt:0.20% Dist: —
NTF Plans:	N/A	Expense Projections:	3Yr:$71 5Yr:$124 10Yr:$280
		Income Distrib:	Monthly

Portfolio Analysis 09-30-04

Total Fixed-Income:8164	Date of Maturity	Amount $000	Value $000	% Net Assets
US Treasury Note 5.625%	05-15-08	619,745	674,264	2.41
US Treasury Note 4.375%	08-15-12	388,535	400,374	1.43
US Treasury Note 7%	07-15-06	346,775	373,706	1.33
US Treasury Note 4.875%	02-15-12	350,125	373,048	1.33
US Treasury Note 6.5%	10-15-06	331,375	356,695	1.27
US Treasury Bond 3.875%	08-15-17	223,465	318,753	1.14
US Treasury Note 1.875%	12-31-05	310,400	308,798	1.10
US Treasury Note 6.125%	08-15-07	281,100	306,312	1.09
US Treasury Bond 8.125%	08-15-21	188,475	261,332	0.93
US Treasury Note 6.5%	02-15-10	203,475	233,424	0.83
US Treasury Note 6%	08-15-09	199,905	223,488	0.80
US Treasury Note 2.75%	06-30-06	209,100	209,949	0.75
US Treasury Bond 8.125%	08-15-19	144,995	198,417	0.71
US Treasury Bond 9.25%	02-15-16	135,050	194,472	0.69
FHLMC 5.75%	04-15-08	177,055	190,987	0.68
US Treasury Note 3.25%	01-15-09	188,675	188,733	0.67
US Treasury Bond 7.625%	11-15-22	137,830	184,046	0.66
US Treasury Bond 8.875%	02-15-19	112,425	162,383	0.58
FNMA 5%	10-01-33	157,213	155,950	0.56
FHLMC 5%	10-01-33	146,386	145,255	0.52

Current Investment Style

Duration: Short Int Long — Quality: High Med Low

[1] figure provided by fund

Avg Eff Duration[1]	4.5 Yrs
Avg Eff Maturity	7.3 Yrs
Avg Credit Quality	AAA
Avg Wtd Coupon	5.75%
Avg Wtd Price	107.57% of par

Coupon Range	% of Bonds	Rel Cat
0% PIK	0.0	0.0
0% to 6%	62.4	1.0
6% to 8%	29.6	1.0
8% to 10%	7.6	1.3
More than 10%	0.4	0.3

1.00=Category Average

Credit Analysis	% bonds 09-30-04		
US Govt	71	BB	0
AAA	6	B	0
AA	3	Below B	0
A	10	NR/NA	0
BBB	10		

Sector Breakdown	% of assets
US Treasuries	[illegible]
TIPS	0
US Agency	9
Mortgage Pass-Throughs	34
Mortgage CMO	2
Mortgage ARM	0
US Corporate	22
Asset-Backed	3
Convertible	0
Municipal	0
Corporate Inflation-Protected	0
Foreign Corporate	1
Foreign Govt	0

Composition			
Cash	2.5	Bonds	97.4
Stocks	0.0	Other	0.0

Special Securities	
Restricted/Illiquid Secs	Trace
Exotic Mortgage-Backed	0
Emerging-Markets Secs	0
Options/Futures/Warrants	No

Vanguard Total Intl Stk

Analyst Pick	Ticker	Load	NAV	Yield	Total Assets	Mstar Category
✔	VGTSX	None	$12.60	2.0%	$8,516 mil	Foreign Large Blend

Governance and Management

Fiduciary Grade: B

Portfolio Manager(s)

Vanguard indexing expert Gus Sauter has managed this fund since its 1996 inception. He also manages its three component funds and many other Vanguard index funds.

Strategy

This fund of funds is made up of Vanguard's three regional index funds: Vanguard European Stock Index (roughly 60% of assets), Vanguard Pacific Stock Index (30%), and Vanguard Emerging Markets Stock Index (10%). It aims to track a customized index.

Historical Profile

Return Above Avg
Risk Average
Rating ★★★★ Above Avg

Investment Style: Equity Stock %

1996	1997	1998	1999	2000	2001	2002	2003	12-04
		94%	91%	0%	99%	95%	92%	98%

▼ Manager Change
▽ Partial Manager Change

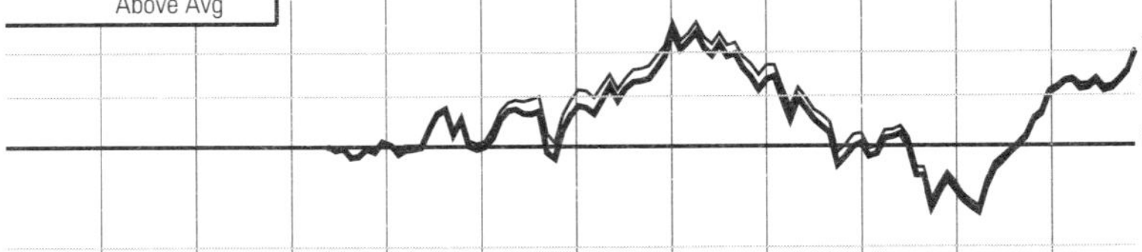

Performance Quartile (within Category)

History

1993	1994	1995	1996	1997	1998	1999	2000	2001	2002	2003	12-04	History
—	—	—	10.14	9.87	11.19	14.31	11.83	9.28	7.72	10.64	12.60	NAV
—	—	—	0.55*	-0.77	15.60	29.92	-15.61	-20.15	-15.08	40.34	20.84	Total Return %
—	—	—	—	-2.55	-4.33	2.89	-1.42	1.27	0.86	1.75	0.59	+/-MSCI EAFE
—	—	—	—	-3.04	-3.09	1.94	-2.25	1.24	0.72	0.92	0.46	+/-MSCI Wd xUS
—	—	—	0.00	1.68	2.13	1.88	1.40	1.39	1.69	2.46	2.40	Income Return %
—	—	—	—	-2.45	13.47	28.04	-17.01	-21.54	-16.77	37.88	18.44	Capital Return %
—	—	—	—	92	38	72	41	40	32	10	13	Total Rtn % Rank Cat
—	—	—	0.16	0.17	0.21	0.21	0.20	0.17	0.16	0.19	0.26	Income $
—	—	—	0.02	0.02	0.01	0.01	0.05	0.00	0.00	0.00	0.00	Capital Gains $
—	—	—	0.00	0.00	0.00	0.00	0.00	0.00	0.00	0.00	0.00	Expense Ratio %
—	—	—	1.51	2.19	2.18	2.04	1.68	0.05	2.24	1.75	1.54	Income Ratio %
—	—	—	—	6	2	1	3	2	5	2	3	Turnover Rate %
—	—	—	280	903	1,375	2,570	2,920	2,900	2,994	5,279	8,516	Net Assets $mil

Performance 12-31-04

	1st Qtr	2nd Qtr	3rd Qtr	4th Qtr	Total
2000	-0.21	-4.00	-8.34	-3.89	-15.61
2001	-13.27	0.10	-14.90	8.08	-20.15
2002	1.72	-2.75	-19.72	6.92	-15.08
2003	-7.90	19.55	8.71	17.25	40.34
2004	4.61	-0.36	0.27	15.62	20.84

Trailing	Total Return%	+/- MSCI EAFE	+/- MSCI Wd xUS	%Rank Cat	Growth of $10,000
3 Mo	15.62	0.30	0.47	9	11,562
6 Mo	15.93	0.93	0.56	16	11,593
1 Yr	20.84	0.59	0.46	13	12,084
3 Yr Avg	12.93	1.04	0.71	9	14,402
5 Yr Avg	-0.60	0.53	0.16	20	9,704
10 Yr Avg	—	—	—	—	—
15 Yr Avg	—	—	—	—	—

Tax Analysis	Tax-Adj Rtn%	%Rank Cat	Tax-Cost Rat	%Rank Cat
3 Yr (estimated)	12.23	9	0.62	67
5 Yr (estimated)	-1.26	18	0.66	43
10 Yr (estimated)	—	—	—	—

Potential Capital Gain Exposure: 16% of assets

Rating and Risk

Time Period	Load-Adj Return %	Morningstar Rtn vs Cat	Morningstar Risk vs Cat	Morningstar Risk-Adj Rating
1 Yr	20.84			
3 Yr	12.93	+Avg	+Avg	★★★★
5 Yr	-0.60	+Avg	Avg	★★★★
10 Yr	—	—	—	—
Incept	4.41			

Other Measures	Standard Index S&P 500	Best Fit Index MSCI Wd xUS
Alpha	0.9	0.5
Beta	1.01	1.02
R-Squared	100	100

Standard Deviation	17.77
Mean	12.93
Sharpe Ratio	0.66

Portfolio Analysis 09-30-04

Share change since 06-04 Total Stocks:0	Sector	Country	% Assets
⊕ Vanguard European Stock	—	United States	61.91
⊕ Vanguard Pacific Stock I	—	United States	27.24
⊕ Vanguard Emerging Mkts S	—	United States	10.80

Morningstar's Take by Gregg Wolper 11-12-04

A prominent rival has tried to outflank Vanguard Total International Stock Index, but this offering still has advantages on its side.

Fidelity recently cut the expense ratios on several index funds to a bare-bones 10 basis points (0.10%). One is--like this offering--an international index-tracker. Fidelity Spartan International Index used to have an expense ratio of 47 basis points, higher than this fund's 36-basis-point impost. Now the cost advantage is in Fidelity's favor.

That development is noteworthy. With index funds, such cost differentials are crucial, because they can't make up the difference with stock-picking or sector selection. (This fund's manager, Gus Sauter, does pick up a few basis points in returns here and there by exploiting technical tricks of the trade, but the payoff from such opportunities is limited.).

However, these two funds are not in fact identical. Unlike the Fidelity offering, this one does not try to equal the MSCI EAFE Index. Instead, it adds an emerging-markets component--currently about 11% of assets--to an EAFE core. This fund resembles the typical active foreign fund in that respect. Indeed, it makes sense for foreign funds to invest in emerging markets despite their higher volatility, for many global leaders in fields such as electronic products, semiconductors, and generic drugs are based in such places.

Partly because of stronger performance in emerging markets, this fund has beaten the Fidelity fund by 79 basis points annually over the trailing five-year period through Nov. 11, 2004. Of course, emerging markets won't always outperform, but this fund's greater breadth does make it a more compelling choice than a pure-EAFE fund for all but those particularly averse to emerging markets. That doesn't change with the new cost situation. Sauter's experience, and the potential tax costs or fees for shareholders thinking of switching, also argue in this fund's favor.

Address:	PO Box 2600 Valley Forge PA 19482 800-662-7447
Web Address:	www.vanguard.com
Inception:	04-29-96 *
Advisor:	Vanguard Advisers, Inc.
Subadvisor:	None
NTF Plans:	N/A

Minimum Purchase:	$3000	Add: $100	IRA: $1000
Min Auto Inv Plan:	$3000	Add: $50	
Sales Fees:	No-load		
Management Fee:	0.24%		
Actual Fees:	Mgt:0.24%	Dist:	
Expense Projections:	3Yr:$113	5Yr:$197	10Yr:$443
Income Distrib:	Annually		

Current Investment Style

Style box: Value Blnd Growth / Large Mid Small (Large Blend)

Market Cap	%
Giant	53.5
Large	31.7
Mid	13.9
Small	0.8
Micro	0.1
Avg $mil: 20,548	

Value Measures		Rel Category
Price/Earnings	13.38	0.98
Price/Book	1.73	0.96
Price/Sales	0.83	0.91
Price/Cash Flow	4.69	0.95
Dividend Yield %	2.87	1.13

Growth Measures	%	Rel Category
Long-Term Erngs	10.78	1.00
Book Value	-21.31	NMF
Sales	1.94	0.78
Cash Flow	3.41	0.61
Historical Erngs	5.57	1.00

Composition

Cash	0.3	Bonds	0.0
Stocks	97.6	Other	2.1
Foreign (% of Stock)			99.9

Sector Weightings	% of Stocks	Rel MSCI EAFE	3 Year High	Low
Info	15.37	0.93		
Software	0.82	0.76	1	0
Hardware	4.36	1.19	7	4
Media	2.27	1.00	3	2
Telecom	7.92	0.83	9	7
Service	43.18	0.97		
Health	7.81	1.08	11	8
Consumer	4.91	0.97	5	4
Business	4.75	0.87	6	4
Financial	25.71	0.95	26	21
Mfg	41.45	1.07		
Goods	14.08	1.03	16	14
Ind Mtrls	14.05	1.14	16	11
Energy	8.60	1.17	10	7
Utilities	4.72	0.88	5	4

Regional Exposure			% Stock
UK/W. Europe	63	N. America	0
Japan	20	Latn America	2
Asia X Japan	13	Other	2

Country Exposure			% Stock
U.K.	24	Switzerland	6
Japan	20	Germany	6
France	8		

Vanguard Tot Stk

Analyst Pick	Ticker	Load	NAV	Yield	Total Assets	Mstar Category
✓	VTSMX	None	$28.77	1.6%	$53,995 mil	Large Blend

Governance and Management

Fiduciary Grade: B

Portfolio Manager(s)

Few index fund managers are as experienced as Gus Sauter. Moreover, Vanguard's indexing team has proved remarkably adept at keeping up with benchmark indexes thanks to savvy trading decisions.

Strategy

The fund shadows the Wilshire 5000 Index, which includes nearly all publicly traded stocks. It would be impractical to own each smaller company in the index, so, among the tiniest firms, manager Gus Sauter selects a representative sample. In an effort to boost returns by a few basis points, Sauter uses various techniques, including securities lending.

Historical Profile

Return Above Avg
Risk Above Avg
Rating ★★★★ Above Avg

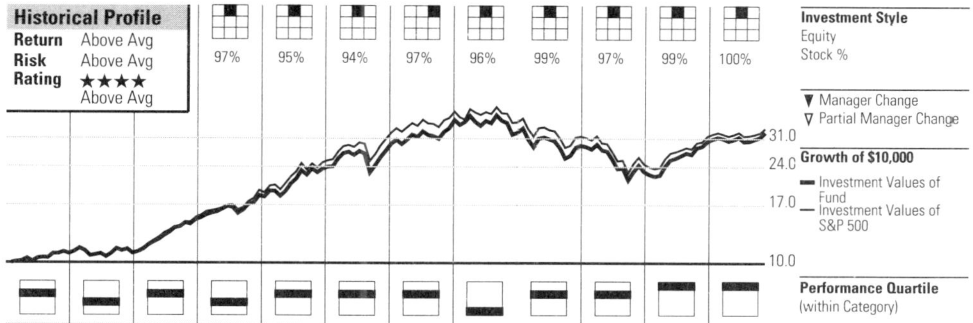

1993	1994	1995	1996	1997	1998	1999	2000	2001	2002	2003	12-04	History
11.69	11.37	15.04	17.77	22.64	27.42	33.22	29.26	25.74	20.07	25.99	28.77	NAV
10.62	-0.17	35.79	20.96	30.99	23.26	23.81	-10.57	-10.97	-20.96	31.35	12.52	Total Return %
0.56	-1.48	-1.74	-1.98	-2.36	-5.31	2.77	-1.47	0.91	1.13	2.68	1.65	+/-S&P 500
0.44	-0.56	-1.98	-1.49	-1.86	-3.76	2.90	-2.78	1.48	0.69	1.46	1.12	+/-Russ 1000
2.42	2.33	2.48	1.94	1.83	1.46	1.21	1.02	1.02	1.14	1.64	1.72	Income Return %
8.20	-2.50	33.31	19.02	29.16	21.80	22.60	-11.59	-11.99	-22.10	29.71	10.80	Capital Return %
47	52	35	56	38	49	28	83	34	35	12	18	Total Rtn % Rank Cat
0.26	0.27	0.28	0.29	0.32	0.33	0.33	0.34	0.30	0.29	0.33	0.45	Income $
0.03	0.03	0.09	0.11	0.27	0.13	0.32	0.14	0.00	0.00	0.00	0.00	Capital Gains $
0.20	0.20	0.25	0.22	0.20	0.20	0.20	0.20	0.20	0.20	0.20	—	Expense Ratio %
2.31	2.35	2.14	1.86	1.65	1.44	1.15	1.04	1.11	1.32	1.49	—	Income Ratio %
1	2	3	3	2	3	3	7	7	4	2	—	Turnover Rate %
512	786	1,571	3,531	5,093	9,308	18,133	16,856	15,781	14,254	24,059	31,718	Net Assets $mil

Performance 12-31-04

	1st Qtr	2nd Qtr	3rd Qtr	4th Qtr	Total
2000	3.84	-4.39	0.27	-10.17	-10.57
2001	-12.27	7.47	-15.93	12.32	-10.97
2002	0.97	-12.69	-16.84	7.82	-20.96
2003	-3.14	16.46	3.60	12.40	31.35
2004	2.58	1.28	-1.82	10.31	12.52

Trailing	Total Return%	+/- S&P 500	+/- Russ 1000	%Rank Cat	Growth of $10,000
3 Mo	10.31	1.08	0.51	23	11,031
6 Mo	8.29	1.10	0.48	24	10,829
1 Yr	12.52	1.65	1.12	18	11,252
3 Yr Avg	5.32	1.74	1.05	16	11,682
5 Yr Avg	-1.44	0.86	0.32	38	9,300
10 Yr Avg	11.81	-0.26	-0.35	20	30,536
15 Yr Avg	—	—	—	—	—

Tax Analysis	Tax-Adj Rtn%	%Rank Cat	Tax-Cost Rat	%Rank Cat
3 Yr (estimated)	4.93	14	0.37	31
5 Yr (estimated)	-1.86	32	0.43	23
10 Yr (estimated)	11.10	11	0.64	12

Potential Capital Gain Exposure: 12% of assets

Rating and Risk

Time Period	Load-Adj Return %	Morningstar Rtn vs Cat	Morningstar Risk vs Cat	Morningstar Risk-Adj Rating
1 Yr	12.52			
3 Yr	5.32	+Avg	Avg	★★★★
5 Yr	-1.44	Avg	+Avg	★★★
10 Yr	11.81	+Avg	+Avg	★★★★
Incept	10.93			

Other Measures	Standard Index S&P 500	Best Fit Index Russ 1000
Alpha	1.7	1.0
Beta	0.98	0.99
R-Squared	99	99
Standard Deviation	15.62	
Mean	5.32	
Sharpe Ratio	0.25	

Portfolio Analysis 09-30-04

Share change since 06-04 Total Stocks:3683	Sector	PE	YTD Ret%	% Assets
⊕ Gen Elec	Ind Mtrls	22.8	20.68	2.62
⊕ ExxonMobil	Energy	13.9	28.04	2.34
⊕ Microsoft	Software	36.1	8.95	2.22
⊕ Pfizer	Health	22.0	-22.31	1.71
⊕ Citigroup	Financial	15.3	2.72	1.69
⊕ Wal-Mart Stores	Consumer	23.4	0.51	1.68
⊕ American International G	Financial	16.2	-0.53	1.31
⊕ Bank of America	Financial	12.3	21.50	1.30
⊕ Johnson & Johnson	Health	20.6	25.17	1.24
⊕ IBM	Hardware	20.2	7.19	1.09
⊕ J P Morgan Chase	Financial	19.4	9.97	1.05
⊕ Procter & Gamble	Goods	23.3	12.38	1.03
⊕ Intel	Hardware	19.8	-26.56	0.95
⊕ Cisco Systems	Hardware	24.5	-20.26	0.90
⊕ ChevronTexaco	Energy	7.7	25.57	0.85
⊕ Verizon Communications	Telecom	32.4	20.25	0.81
⊕ Wells Fargo	Financial	15.5	8.97	0.74
⊕ Coca-Cola	Goods	21.9	-16.12	0.72
⊕ Altria Group	Goods	13.3	18.38	0.71
⊕ Dell	Hardware	34.0	24.01	0.66

Current Investment Style

Value Blnd Growth / Large Mid Small

Market Cap	%
Giant	40.6
Large	30.4
Mid	19.7
Small	6.7
Micro	2.6
Avg $mil: 21,918	

Value Measures		Rel Category
Price/Earnings	16.77	0.99
Price/Book	2.48	0.95
Price/Sales	1.34	0.93
Price/Cash Flow	7.08	0.92
Dividend Yield %	1.54	1.04

Growth Measures	%	Rel Category
Long-Term Erngs	11.38	0.98
Book Value	6.39	0.82
Sales	4.59	0.80
Cash Flow	6.07	0.64
Historical Erngs	11.25	0.95

Profitability	%	Rel Category
Return on Equity	16.66	0.95
Return on Assets	8.36	0.97
Net Margin	11.28	0.99

Sector Weightings	% of Stocks	Rel S&P 500	3 Year High	3 Year Low
Info	20.66	0.96		
Software	4.18	0.97	5	4
Hardware	8.99	0.88	11	7
Media	4.24	1.10	5	4
Telecom	3.25	1.03	4	3
Service	49.24	1.06		
Health	12.53	1.00	15	13
Consumer	9.50	1.05	10	9
Business	5.23	1.29	5	5
Financial	21.98	1.06	23	20
Mfg	30.09	0.94		
Goods	8.57	0.92	11	8
Ind Mtrls	11.41	0.90	11	10
Energy	7.22	1.01	7	6
Utilities	2.89	0.98	3	3

Composition

Cash	0.3
Stocks	99.6
Bonds	0.0
Other	0.0
Foreign (% of Stock)	0.0

Morningstar's Take by Jeffrey Ptak 12-23-04

Is it belt-tightening time for Vanguard Total Stock Market Index?

In August 2004, when Fidelity Investments slashed the fees on five of its index offerings, including Fidelity Spartan Total Market Index, the question quickly became whether Vanguard would respond in kind. But Vanguard has stood pat, in effect arguing that a fee cut would be untenable since the firm already operates at cost.

Vanguard's argument is at least partially valid. For instance, the firm's advisory fee--which covers the people and resources needed to assemble this fund's portfolio--amounted to roughly three cents on a $10,000 investment in 2003. Other costs, such as marketing and custody fees, are also peanuts.

Things get a bit fuzzier, however, at the "management and administrative" expense line. This rubric, which covers the back-office and shareholder servicing costs, accounted for roughly 17 basis points of the fund's 0.20% expense ratio in 2003. True, that levy didn't mark an increase over the prior year in percentage terms. But the mix of costs changed noticeably, with admin expenses jumping nearly $11 million over the prior year while shareholder-servicing costs barely budged.

Since Vanguard doesn't itemize the various types of admin expenses it incurs, it's difficult to say what's driving the uptick. It would seem that such costs--which can include the compensation of personnel as well as ongoing operating costs--are largely fixed. If that's the case, it stands to reason that asset growth should yield economies of scale and, thus, savings. Yet the opposite has occurred: Since 1999, admin expenses (stated in dollars) have doubled along with assets and they're on pace to rise further still in 2004.

To be sure, investors are hardly getting a raw deal here, as the fund's price tag already is already one of the lowest around (a trait that continues to burnish the fund's appeal). But given that indexing is a war of inches fought at the cost line, the expense trend here bears close watching.

Address:	P O Box 2600 Valley Forge PA 19482 800-662-7447
Web Address:	www.vanguard.com
Inception:	04-27-92
Advisor:	Vanguard Advisers, Inc.
Subadvisor:	None
NTF Plans:	N/A

Minimum Purchase:	$3000	Add: $100	IRA: $1000
Min Auto Inv Plan:	$3000	Add: $50	
Sales Fees:	No-load		
Management Fee:	0.18%		
Actual Fees:	Mgt:0.18%	Dist: —	
Expense Projections:	3Yr:$64	5Yr:$113	10Yr:$255
Income Distrib:	Quarterly		

Vanguard U.S. Gr

Ticker	Load	NAV	Yield	Total Assets	Mstar Category
VWUSX	None	$16.18	0.3%	$6,246 mil	Large Growth

Governance and Management

Fiduciary Grade: B

Portfolio Manager(s)

Alliance Capital ran the fund solo from June 2001 through mid-April 2004. Alan Levi and John Blundin run the fund for Alliance. They're backed by 25 analysts, and roughly 80% of each analyst's compensation is tied to his or her ability to identify strong stocks for the portfolio. In April 2004, Vanguard hired William Blair to run 25%-30% of the fund. The Blair team consists of John Jostrand, Rocky Barber, and Norbert Truderung.

Strategy

On the Alliance side, analysts assign stocks they cover a "buy," "sell," or "hold" rating based on projected growth and valuation. To ensure that the cream rises to the top, they must assign roughly equal numbers of sells and buys. The two managers then run the analysts' ratings, growth projections, and the stock's valuations through a computer screen and cull the top-ranking 150 for further review. From these, they select anywhere from 45-55 for the portfolio. The William Blair team seeks out 30-40 high-quality growth companies they think have the potential for strong long-term earnings growth.

Historical Profile

Return Low
Risk Above Avg
Rating ★ Lowest

Investment Style — Equity Stock %: 97% 96% 92% 98% 98% 98% 99% 100% 97%

▼ Manager Change
▽ Partial Manager Change

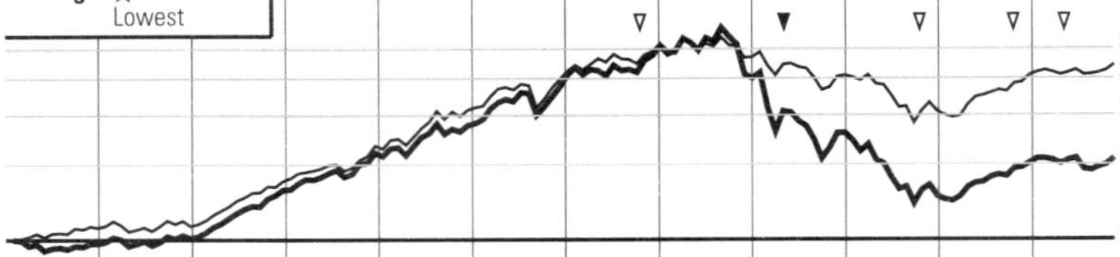

Growth of $10,000
— Investment Values of Fund
— Investment Values of S&P 500

Performance Quartile (within Category)

1993	1994	1995	1996	1997	1998	1999	2000	2001	2002	2003	12-04	History
14.93	15.33	20.35	23.74	28.70	37.49	43.53	27.65	18.85	12.06	15.16	16.18	NAV
-1.45	3.88	38.44	26.05	25.93	39.98	22.28	-20.17	-31.70	-35.80	26.10	7.03	Total Return %
-11.51	2.57	0.91	3.11	-7.42	11.41	1.24	-11.07	-19.82	-13.71	-2.57	-3.84	+/-S&P 500
-4.32	1.26	1.26	2.93	-4.56	1.27	-10.88	2.25	-11.28	-7.92	-3.65	0.73	+/-Russ 1000Gr
1.37	1.21	1.89	1.28	1.14	0.66	0.56	0.11	0.13	0.22	0.39	0.30	Income Return %
-2.82	2.67	36.55	24.77	24.79	39.32	21.72	-20.28	-31.83	-36.02	25.71	6.73	Capital Return %
97	8	16	10	55	21	79	78	88	92	56	53	Total Rtn % Rank Cat
0.21	0.18	0.29	0.26	0.27	0.19	0.21	0.05	0.04	0.04	0.05	0.05	Income $
0.00	0.00	0.57	1.62	0.89	2.31	2.02	7.45	0.00	0.00	0.00	0.00	Capital Gains $
0.49	0.52	0.44	0.43	0.42	0.41	0.39	0.36	0.44	0.50	0.55	0.53	Expense Ratio %
1.50	1.30	1.59	1.32	1.13	0.69	0.59	0.24	0.13	0.20	0.32	0.19	Income Ratio %
37	47	32	44	35	48	49	76	135	53	47	71	Turnover Rate %
1,847	2,109	3,624	5,532	8,055	13,624	19,068	16,232	9,180	5,030	6,086	5,411	Net Assets $mil

Performance 12-31-04

	1st Qtr	2nd Qtr	3rd Qtr	4th Qtr	Total
2000	5.17	0.15	1.03	-24.97	-20.17
2001	-31.03	7.45	-23.04	19.76	-31.70
2002	-7.80	-20.71	-16.55	5.23	-35.80
2003	-0.25	10.64	4.06	9.81	26.10
2004	1.91	1.42	-5.87	10.00	7.03

Trailing	Total Return%	+/- S&P 500	+/- Russ 1000Gr	%Rank Cat	Growth of $10,000
3 Mo	10.00	0.77	0.83	48	11,000
6 Mo	3.54	-3.65	0.07	70	10,354
1 Yr	7.03	-3.84	0.73	53	10,703
3 Yr Avg	-4.67	-8.25	-4.49	94	8,663
5 Yr Avg	-13.93	-11.63	-4.64	92	4,723
10 Yr Avg	5.92	-6.15	-3.67	90	17,774
15 Yr Avg	7.28	-3.65	-2.22	84	28,693

Tax Analysis	Tax-Adj Rtn%	%Rank Cat	Tax-Cost Rat	%Rank Cat
3 Yr (estimated)	-4.75	90	0.08	14
5 Yr (estimated)	-14.71	92	0.91	55
10 Yr (estimated)	4.64	84	1.21	34

Potential Capital Gain Exposure: -104% of assets

Rating and Risk

Time Period	Load-Adj Return %	Morningstar Rtn vs Cat	Morningstar Risk vs Cat	Morningstar Risk-Adj Rating
1 Yr	7.03			
3 Yr	-4.67	Low	+Avg	★
5 Yr	-13.93	Low	+Avg	★
10 Yr	5.92	Low	+Avg	★
Incept	—			

Other Measures	Standard Index S&P 500	Best Fit Index Russ 1000Gr
Alpha	-7.9	-4.2
Beta	1.10	1.09
R-Squared	88	94

Standard Deviation	16.94
Mean	-4.67
Sharpe Ratio	-0.36

Morningstar's Take by Christopher Traulsen 10-15-04

Vanguard U.S. Growth has steadied a bit, but it's still hard to make a convincing case for it.

When a team from Alliance took the helm here in mid-2001, it had its work cut out for it. The fund had floundered badly for several years under former subadvisor Lincoln Capital, underperforming the category in both bull and bear markets. But Alliance struggled out of the gate, and the fund lost 36% in 2002--a bottom-decile showing. The team had a better 2003, finishing just a bit behind their median peer in a red-hot market that didn't favor the managers' high-quality bias.

In April 2004, Vanguard opted to give a portion of the fund's assets (25%-30%) to a second subadvisor, William Blair. Like Alliance, that team has a bias toward higher-quality growth names. The combined portfolio carries valuations that are roughly in line with category averages (with the exception of price to sales, which is notably higher than the norm), and historical growth rates that are significantly higher than category averages.

The latter is somewhat encouraging, as it paints an overall picture of a portfolio that has delivered higher growth for a lower price than is the norm among large-growth funds. The managers have also made some nice picks in 2004, as picks such as eBay, Marvel Technologies, and Juniper Networks have soared. However, certain technology holdings, such as Broadcom, hurt it in the third quarter, and picks in other sectors, including Career Education and financials such as American International Group and Morgan Stanley, have also dinged the fund in 2004. In all, it has posted a loss of 4.02% for the year to date through Oct. 14, a slightly worse showing than its median peer.

Still, that and the fund's 2003 showing are improvements on the fund's awful prior record, and its low expenses are attractive. That said, given the wealth of strong funds in the large-growth category, this one needs to keep getting better to justify sending money here.

Address:	PO Box 2600 Valley Forge PA 19482 800-662-7447
Web Address:	www.vanguard.com
Inception:	01-06-59
Advisor:	The Vanguard Group, Inc.
Subadvisor:	Multiple
NTF Plans:	N/A

Minimum Purchase:	$3000	Add: $100	IRA: $1000
Min Auto Inv Plan:	$3000	Add: $50	
Sales Fees:	No-load		
Management Fee:	0.42% mx./0.10% mn.		
Actual Fees:	Mgt:0.42%	Dist: —	
Expense Projections:	3Yr:$141	5Yr:$246	10Yr:$555
Income Distrib:	Annually		

Portfolio Analysis 09-30-04

Share change since 06-04 Total Stocks:71	Sector	PE	YTD Ret%	% Assets
⊖ Dell	Hardware	34.0	24.01	3.64
⊖ Pfizer	Health	22.0	-22.31	3.37
⊖ eBay	Consumer	81.6	80.07	3.13
⊖ Marvell Technology	Hardware	NMF	87.03	3.11
⊕ Danaher	Ind Mtrls	25.8	25.29	3.07
⊖ American International G	Financial	16.2	-0.53	2.96
⊕ Symantec	Software	34.5	49.33	2.95
⊖ UnitedHealth Group	Health	23.8	51.38	2.90
⊖ Juniper Networks	Hardware	NMF	45.56	2.82
⊖ SAP AG ADR	Software	42.7	6.80	2.70
⊖ Harley-Davidson	Goods	20.5	28.70	2.53
⊕ Zimmer Holdings	Health	54.0	13.81	2.38
⊖ Citigroup	Financial	15.3	2.72	2.33
⊖ Broadcom	Hardware	66.4	-5.12	2.29
WellPoint Health Network	Health	—	—	2.17
⊖ Bed Bath & Beyond	Consumer	27.6	-8.12	2.15
⊖ Forest Laboratories	Health	18.0	-27.41	2.11
⊕ Yahoo	Media	95.1	67.36	1.99
⊖ Amgen	Health	37.7	3.82	1.94
⊖ Stryker	Health	46.2	13.52	1.85

Current Investment Style

Value Blnd Growth — Large Mid Small

Market Cap	%
Giant	36.6
Large	53.1
Mid	10.2
Small	0.0
Micro	0.0
Avg $mil: 30,204	

Value Measures		Rel Category
Price/Earnings	20.33	0.96
Price/Book	3.19	0.99
Price/Sales	2.55	1.19
Price/Cash Flow	10.04	0.91
Dividend Yield %	0.56	0.73

Growth Measures	%	Rel Category
Long-Term Erngs	15.47	1.10
Book Value	15.54	1.22
Sales	11.96	1.40
Cash Flow	25.12	1.52
Historical Erngs	21.06	1.46

Profitability	%	Rel Category
Return on Equity	19.18	1.07
Return on Assets	11.28	1.21
Net Margin	14.53	1.18

Sector Weightings	% of Stocks	Rel S&P 500	3 Year High	3 Year Low
Info	30.38	1.41		
Software	8.56	1.99	13	7
Hardware	19.17	1.88	21	10
Media	2.64	0.69	9	3
Telecom	0.01	0.00	4	0
Service	58.68	1.26		
Health	27.15	2.17	31	24
Consumer	11.72	1.29	13	7
Business	2.98	0.74	3	0
Financial	16.83	0.81	20	16
Mfg	10.94	0.34		
Goods	4.75	0.51	10	0
Ind Mtrls	5.28	0.42	8	3
Energy	0.91	0.13	3	0
Utilities	0.00	0.00	0	0

Composition

Cash	3.4
Stocks	96.7
Bonds	0.0
Other	0.0
Foreign (% of Stock)	5.5

Vanguard U.S. Value

Analyst Pick	Ticker	Load	NAV	Yield	Total Assets	Mstar Category
✔	VUVLX	None	$13.75	1.5%	$881 mil	Large Value

Governance and Management

Fiduciary Grade: B

Portfolio Manager(s)

Chris Darnell and Rob Soucy have comanaged the fund since its June 2000 inception. Both are highly experienced, and Darnell comanages a number of GMO funds with superior long-term records. Soucy handles the day-to-day management duties here. GMO's quantitative equity team also manages a number of other large-cap value funds under the GMO banner, where they've had success.

Strategy

Quantitative models pick the fund's stocks. About half of the portfolio consists of names with solid profits and returns on equity, as well as moderate valuations. Other slices of the portfolio contain stocks that are cheap relative to normalized earnings and companies with improving fundamentals and share-price trends. Because stocks are drawn from the broad-based Russell 3000 Index, the fund sports a noticeable tilt toward mid- and small-cap picks. Management keeps the fund's sector weightings reasonably close to those of the Russell 3000 Value Index while limiting the fund's stake in individual stocks.

Historical Profile

Return Above Avg
Risk Average
Rating ★★★★ Above Avg

Investment Style
Equity
Stock %: 92% (2000), 92% (2001), 94% (2002), 95% (2003), 93% (12-04)

▼ Manager Change
▽ Partial Manager Change

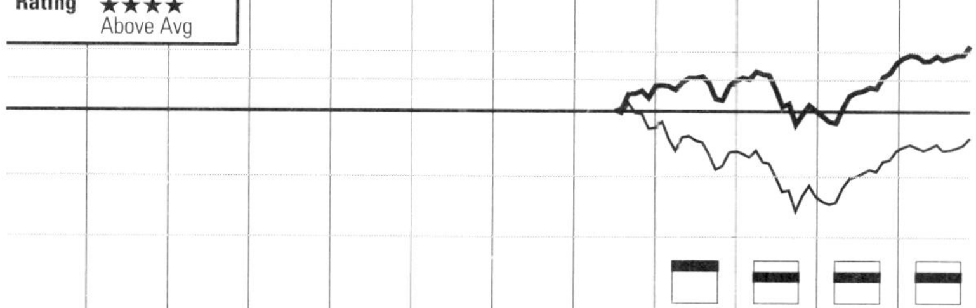

Performance Quartile (within Category)

1993	1994	1995	1996	1997	1998	1999	2000	2001	2002	2003	12-04	History
—	—	—	—	—	—	—	11.24	11.47	9.56	12.27	13.75	NAV
—	—	—	—	—	—	—	12.97*	2.94	-15.27	30.26	13.70	Total Return %
—	—	—	—	—	—	—	—	14.82	6.82	1.59	2.83	+/-S&P 500
—	—	—	—	—	—	—	—	8.53	0.25	0.23	-2.79	+/-Russ 1000 Vl
—	—	—	—	—	—	—	0.00	0.89	1.39	1.88	1.63	Income Return %
—	—	—	—	—	—	—	—	2.05	-16.66	28.38	12.07	Capital Return %
—	—	—	—	—	—	—	—	16	26	31	39	Total Rtn % Rank Cat
—	—	—	—	—	—	—	0.08	0.10	0.16	0.18	0.20	Income $
—	—	—	—	—	—	—	0.00	0.00	0.00	0.00	0.00	Capital Gains $
—	—	—	—	—	—	—	0.56	0.51	0.54	0.63	0.49	Expense Ratio %
—	—	—	—	—	—	—	2.08	1.67	1.36	1.72	1.61	Income Ratio %
—	—	—	—	—	—	—	18	54	46	50	56	Turnover Rate %
—	—	—	—	—	—	—	107	436	451	534	881	Net Assets $mil

Performance 12-31-04

	1st Qtr	2nd Qtr	3rd Qtr	4th Qtr	Total
2000	—	—	10.27	4.43	12.97*
2001	-2.14	6.64	-10.83	10.61	2.94
2002	5.14	-9.20	-17.72	7.86	-15.27
2003	-6.59	18.70	2.08	15.09	30.26
2004	3.91	0.00	0.55	8.83	13.70

Trailing	Total Return%	+/- S&P 500	+/- Russ 1000 Vl	%Rank Cat	Growth of $10,000
3 Mo	8.83	-0.40	-1.55	61	10,883
6 Mo	9.42	2.23	-2.66	45	10,942
1 Yr	13.70	2.83	-2.79	39	11,370
3 Yr Avg	7.86	4.28	-0.71	20	12,548
5 Yr Avg	—	—	—	—	—
10 Yr Avg	—	—	—	—	—
15 Yr Avg	—	—	—	—	—

Tax Analysis	Tax-Adj Rtn%	%Rank Cat	Tax-Cost Rat	%Rank Cat
3 Yr (estimated)	7.37	15	0.45	30
5 Yr (estimated)	—	—	—	—
10 Yr (estimated)	—	—	—	—

Potential Capital Gain Exposure: 14% of assets

Rating and Risk

Time Period	Load-Adj Return %	Morningstar Rtn vs Cat	Morningstar Risk vs Cat	Morningstar Risk-Adj Rating
1 Yr	13.70			
3 Yr	7.86	+Avg	Avg	★★★★
5 Yr	—	—	—	—
10 Yr	—	—	—	—
Incept	8.75			

Other Measures	Standard Index S&P 500	Best Fit Index Russ 1000 Vl
Alpha	4.4	-0.4
Beta	0.93	0.97
R-Squared	89	95
Standard Deviation	15.90	
Mean	7.86	
Sharpe Ratio	0.41	

Portfolio Analysis 09-30-04

Share change since 06-04 Total Stocks:368	Sector	PE	YTD Ret%	% Assets
⊕ SBC Communications	Telecom	15.4	3.74	3.34
⊕ Verizon Communications	Telecom	32.4	20.25	2.50
⊕ ExxonMobil	Energy	13.9	28.04	2.32
⊕ Altria Group	Goods	13.3	18.38	2.25
⊕ Home Depot	Consumer	19.0	21.47	1.99
⊕ Washington Mutual	Financial	13.9	10.05	1.78
⊕ American International G	Financial	16.2	-0.53	1.75
BellSouth	Telecom	12.7	1.94	1.60
⊕ General Motors	Goods	7.2	-21.48	1.59
J P Morgan Chase	Financial	19.4	9.97	1.57
⊕ Dell	Hardware	34.0	24.01	1.53
⊕ Pfizer	Health	22.0	-22.31	1.50
Fannie Mae	Financial	9.1	-2.33	1.30
⊕ Allstate	Financial	12.8	23.12	1.27
⊕ Ford Motor	Goods	9.9	-6.00	1.15
⊕ ChevronTexaco	Energy	7.7	25.57	1.07
⊕ Johnson & Johnson	Health	20.6	25.17	1.06
⊕ Merck	Health	11.4	-27.76	0.96
Cigna	Health	8.4	42.87	0.92
⊖ MBNA	Financial	14.0	15.53	0.92

Current Investment Style

Value Blnd Growth — Large / Mid / Small

Market Cap	%
Giant	30.9
Large	37.1
Mid	25.4
Small	6.0
Micro	0.6

Avg $mil: 17,816

Value Measures		Rel Category
Price/Earnings	12.69	0.84
Price/Book	1.90	0.84
Price/Sales	0.68	0.57
Price/Cash Flow	5.01	0.79
Dividend Yield %	2.20	1.08

Growth Measures	%	Rel Category
Long-Term Erngs	10.07	0.97
Book Value	3.61	0.64
Sales	3.03	0.72
Cash Flow	-2.50	NMF
Historical Erngs	8.09	0.68

Profitability	%	Rel Category
Return on Equity	16.96	1.07
Return on Assets	8.17	1.04
Net Margin	9.67	0.95

Sector Weightings	% of Stocks	Rel S&P 500	3 Year High	3 Year Low
Info	13.25	0.62		
Software	0.19	0.04	3	0
Hardware	3.05	0.30	7	3
Media	0.28	0.07	6	0
Telecom	9.73	3.09	10	7
Service	53.09	1.14		
Health	9.10	0.73	11	7
Consumer	12.80	1.41	13	7
Business	3.21	0.79	7	3
Financial	27.98	1.35	30	23
Mfg	33.66	1.05		
Goods	11.86	1.27	12	9
Ind Mtrls	7.49	0.59	13	7
Energy	7.93	1.11	8	3
Utilities	6.38	2.16	7	5

Composition

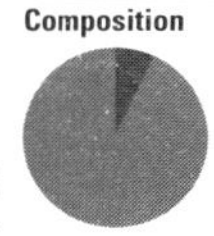

Cash	6.9
Stocks	93.1
Bonds	0.0
Other	0.0
Foreign (% of Stock)	0.0

Morningstar's Take by Jeffrey Ptak 01-04-05

Looking for love in all the wrong places?

Big moves into individual stocks or sectors typically don't comport with Vanguard U.S. Value's varied attack. Indeed, comanagers Chris Darnell and Rob Soucy spread assets across hundreds of stocks and a broad swath of industries in accordance with a phalanx of quantitative models that govern stock selection. Nevertheless, the portfolio tilted noticeably toward the oil patch in 2004, with additions including integrated producers such as ChevronTexaco and Occidental Petroleum.

That's a curious development at first blush given that, if anything, energy stocks got richer over the course of the year. In fact, management did its most aggressive buying in the heat of September's furious runup, a move that certainly seems at odds with the price-conscious ethos that's supposedly the fund's calling card. But, in truth, it's par for the course. Indeed, one of the quantitative models trawls for stocks exhibiting attractive price momentum relative to peers, making slightly pricier fare game. This, management argues, better acknowledges the fact that fundamentals sometimes take a backseat to sentiment.

Of course, the fund's other quantitative models--which home in on stocks that trade at a discount to management's estimate of intrinsic value or on a price/earnings basis--keep the fund from sticking out versus its large-value peers (its valuation measures skirt the group norms).

Yet it's the distinctively malleable nature of the process, conferred by traits like the previously mentioned momentum sleeve and the team's all-cap mandate, that steadied the fund through the bear market while paving the way to strong returns in the subsequent rally. Looking ahead, we're encouraged that the portfolio has shifted to emphasize larger fare, which has lagged amid the prolonged small-cap rally and now, in many cases, offers more tempting bargains. True, that doesn't guarantee success. But it's a mark of consistency, a trait that should continue to serve investors well.

Address:	P.O. Box 2600 Valley Forge PA 19482 800-662-7447
Web Address:	www.vanguard.com
Inception:	06-29-00*
Advisor:	Grantham Mayo Van Otterloo & Co. LLC
Subadvisor:	None
NTF Plans:	N/A

Minimum Purchase:	$3000	Add: $100	IRA: $1000
Min Auto Inv Plan:	$3000	Add: $50	
Sales Fees:	No-load		
Management Fee:	0.50%		
Actual Fees:	Mgt:0.46%	Dist: —	
Expense Projections:	3Yr:$164	5Yr:$285	10Yr:$640
Income Distrib:	Annually		

Vanguard Val Idx

Ticker	Load	NAV	Yield	Total Assets	Mstar Category
VIVAX	None	$21.35	2.1%	$5,473 mil	Large Value

Governance and Management

Fiduciary Grade: B

Portfolio Manager(s)

Gus Sauter runs more index money than anyone in the fund industry. And judging from his charges' fine record of meeting--and even narrowly surpassing--their benchmarks, one could reasonably argue that he's better at it than his rivals, too.

Strategy

This fund now tracks the MSCI U.S. Prime Market Value Index, which consists of the value stocks within a universe of the 750 largest U.S. companies (in terms of free-float market cap). MSCI classifies stocks as growth or value using an eight-factor model, and also employs "buffer zones" to limit the migration of stocks between the growth and value camps and, thus, turnover.

Historical Profile

Return Average
Risk Above Avg
Rating ★★★ Neutral

Investment Style
Equity
Stock %

99%	99%	99%	98%	98%	100%	100%	100%	100%

▼ Manager Change
▽ Partial Manager Change

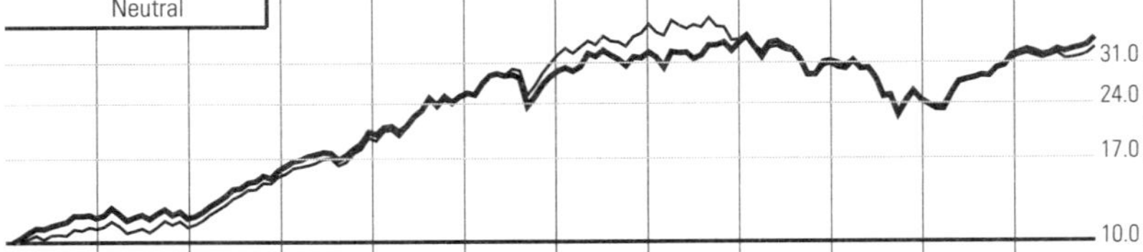

Growth of $10,000
— Investment Values of Fund
— Investment Values of S&P 500

Performance Quartile (within Category)

1993	1994	1995	1996	1997	1998	1999	2000	2001	2002	2003	12-04	History
11.73	11.12	14.80	17.02	20.85	22.51	22.89	22.87	18.90	14.65	18.95	21.35	NAV
18.25	-0.65	37.03	21.78	29.77	14.64	12.57	6.08	-11.88	-20.91	32.25	15.29	Total Return %
8.19	-1.96	-0.50	-1.16	-3.58	-13.93	-8.47	15.18	0.00	1.18	3.58	4.42	+/-S&P 500
0.18	1.33	-1.33	0.14	-5.41	-0.99	5.22	-0.93	-6.29	-5.39	2.22	-1.20	+/-Russ 1000 VI
3.73	3.30	3.64	2.62	2.22	1.77	1.66	1.60	1.44	1.68	2.56	2.44	Income Return %
14.52	-3.95	33.39	19.16	27.55	12.87	10.91	4.48	-13.32	-22.59	29.69	12.85	Capital Return %
20	51	14	30	26	36	19	67	92	69	18	21	Total Rtn % Rank Cat
0.38	0.38	0.40	0.38	0.37	0.36	0.36	0.36	0.32	0.32	0.37	0.46	Income $
0.06	0.16	0.00	0.57	0.75	0.99	1.96	0.98	0.98	0.00	0.00	0.00	Capital Gains $
0.20	0.20	0.20	0.20	0.20	0.22	0.22	0.22	0.22	0.23	0.23	—	Expense Ratio %
3.26	3.37	3.06	2.54	2.05	1.72	1.59	1.60	1.51	1.80	2.38	—	Income Ratio %
30	32	27	29	25	33	41	37	38	26	48	—	Turnover Rate %
190	297	496	1,016	1,796	2,421	3,378	3,450	3,018	2,197	2,921	3,592	Net Assets $mil

Performance 12-31-04

	1st Qtr	2nd Qtr	3rd Qtr	4th Qtr	Total
2000	0.17	-4.28	8.80	1.70	6.08
2001	-6.58	4.41	-16.26	7.89	-11.88
2002	1.32	-10.69	-20.45	9.88	-20.91
2003	-5.61	20.27	2.24	13.93	32.25
2004	2.12	1.56	1.24	9.80	15.29

Trailing	Total Return%	+/- S&P 500	+/- Russ 1000 VI	%Rank Cat	Growth of $10,000
3 Mo	9.80	0.57	-0.58	34	10,980
6 Mo	11.16	3.97	-0.92	18	11,116
1 Yr	15.29	4.42	-1.20	21	11,529
3 Yr Avg	6.44	2.86	-2.13	40	12,059
5 Yr Avg	2.43	4.73	-2.84	67	11,276
10 Yr Avg	12.16	0.09	-1.67	33	31,505
15 Yr Avg	—	—	—	—	—

Tax Analysis	Tax-Adj Rtn%	%Rank Cat	Tax-Cost Rat	%Rank Cat
3 Yr (estimated)	5.88	33	0.53	36
5 Yr (estimated)	1.34	66	1.06	57
10 Yr (estimated)	10.51	23	1.47	32

Potential Capital Gain Exposure: 3% of assets

Rating and Risk

Time Period	Load-Adj Return %	Morningstar Rtn vs Cat	Morningstar Risk vs Cat	Morningstar Risk-Adj Rating
1 Yr	15.29			
3 Yr	6.44	Avg	+Avg	★★★
5 Yr	2.43	Avg	+Avg	★★
10 Yr	12.16	Avg	+Avg	★★★
Incept	11.69			

Other Measures	Standard Index S&P 500	Best Fit Index Russ 1000 VI
Alpha	2.8	-2.5
Beta	1.07	1.10
R-Squared	95	98
Standard Deviation	17.62	
Mean	6.44	
Sharpe Ratio	0.29	

Portfolio Analysis 09-30-04

Share change since 06-04 Total Stocks:418	Sector	PE	YTD Ret%	% Assets
⊕ Gen Elec	Ind Mtrls	22.8	20.68	6.36
⊕ ExxonMobil	Energy	13.9	28.04	5.68
⊕ Citigroup	Financial	15.3	2.72	4.10
⊕ Bank of America	Financial	12.3	21.50	3.17
⊕ J P Morgan Chase	Financial	19.4	9.97	2.51
⊕ ChevronTexaco	Energy	7.7	25.57	2.06
⊕ Verizon Communications	Telecom	32.4	20.25	1.96
⊕ Wells Fargo	Financial	15.5	8.97	1.81
⊕ Altria Group	Goods	13.3	18.38	1.73
⊕ SBC Communications	Telecom	15.4	3.74	1.54
⊕ Merck	Health	11.4	-27.76	1.32
⊕ Time Warner	Media	27.5	8.12	1.27
⊕ Wachovia	Financial	14.3	16.80	1.11
⊕ Tyco International	Ind Mtrls	25.1	35.41	1.10
⊕ US Bancorp	Financial	14.2	10.46	0.98
⊕ Hewlett-Packard	Hardware	18.9	-7.28	0.98
⊕ ConocoPhillips	Energy	9.0	35.60	0.97
⊕ Viacom B	Media	36.1	-17.44	0.92
⊕ Wyeth	Health	17.0	2.73	0.90
⊕ BellSouth	Telecom	12.7	1.94	0.89

Current Investment Style

Value Blnd Growth / Large Mid Small

Market Cap	%
Giant	48.9
Large	35.3
Mid	15.7
Small	0.0
Micro	0.0
Avg $mil: 37,494	

Value Measures		Rel Category
Price/Earnings	13.93	0.93
Price/Book	2.15	0.95
Price/Sales	1.17	0.98
Price/Cash Flow	5.64	0.88
Dividend Yield %	2.50	1.23

Growth Measures	%	Rel Category
Long-Term Erngs	9.60	0.92
Book Value	5.01	0.89
Sales	3.18	0.76
Cash Flow	3.08	0.59
Historical Erngs	12.07	1.02

Profitability	%	Rel Category
Return on Equity	15.72	0.99
Return on Assets	8.33	1.06
Net Margin	11.49	1.13

Sector Weightings	% of Stocks	Rel S&P 500	3 Year High	3 Year Low
Info	11.31	0.53		
Software	0.19	0.04	1	0
Hardware	1.95	0.19	5	2
Media	3.93	1.02	7	3
Telecom	5.24	1.66	9	5
Service	43.63	0.94		
Health	4.85	0.39	7	2
Consumer	3.68	0.41	6	4
Business	1.73	0.43	3	2
Financial	33.37	1.61	36	31
Mfg	45.06	1.40		
Goods	7.65	0.82	9	3
Ind Mtrls	19.83	1.57	20	13
Energy	12.05	1.68	15	10
Utilities	5.53	1.87	6	5

Composition

Cash	0.0
Stocks	100.0
Bonds	0.0
Other	0.0
Foreign (% of Stock)	0.0

Morningstar's Take by Jeffrey Ptak 01-07-05

This fund is solid, if unspectacular.

Vanguard Value Index Fund does what any good index fund should: It offers broad and highly representative exposure to a class of securities--in this case, stocks deemed cheap by index-provider MSCI's eight-pronged classification methodology--at a very low cost.

But that doesn't mean you should buy it. In fact, perhaps the biggest dilemma facing prospective investors here is the bounty of other quality large-value options that Vanguard offers. To wit, those attracted by this fund's multicap format and style discipline might consider the computer-driven Vanguard U.S. Value Fund, which trawls the Russell 3000 Value Index for bargains. Or, for those with a stronger stomach, deep-value pro Jim Barrow's Vanguard Windsor II Fund beckons.

The irony, of course, is that these active managers take a page right out of indexing's playbook. They trade infrequently, stick doggedly to their investment discipline, and run inexpensive funds. Thus, it hardly seems coincidental that Vanguard's stock-pickers--or, for that matter, other managers unburdened by high costs and plying compelling strategies, like T. Rowe Price Equity-Income skipper Brian Rogers--have trounced their respective benchmarks over time.

Nevertheless, some investors might prefer this fund's predictability, which isn't dependent on a key manager's participation. Moreover, we think Vanguard's recent switch to a new benchmark that better represents what value managers actually own burnishes the fund's appeal. During the bear market, for instance, the fund only slightly outpaced its sibling, Vanguard Growth Index Fund, when both offerings tracked S&P Barra indexes. This was despite the fact that value stocks handily trumped their growth counterparts during that span, a fact that the S&P bogies failed to reflect. The fund's new MSCI bogy should rectify those weaknesses, thereby better facilitating portfolio construction. All told, it's a fine option.

Address:	P O Box 2600 Valley Forge PA 19482 800-662-7447
Web Address:	www.vanguard.com
Inception:	11-02-92
Advisor:	Vanguard Advisers, Inc.
Subadvisor:	None
NTF Plans:	N/A

Minimum Purchase:	$3000	Add: $100	IRA: $1000
Min Auto Inv Plan:	$3000	Add: $50	
Sales Fees:	No-load		
Management Fee:	0.20%		
Actual Fees:	Mgt:0.20%	Dist: —	
Expense Projections:	3Yr:$71	5Yr:$124	10Yr:$280
Income Distrib:	Quarterly		

Vanguard Wellesley Inc

Analyst Pick	Ticker	Load	NAV	Yield	Total Assets	Mstar Category
✔	VWINX	None	$21.58	3.9%	$10,896 mil	Conservative Allocation

Governance and Management

Fiduciary Grade: B

Portfolio Manager(s)

This fund boasts one of the most experienced management teams around. Earl McEvoy has been running the fixed-income portfolio for more than two decades. Jack Ryan, who also runs part of Vanguard Equity-Income, has been managing the equity portion of this fund since 1986. Both are senior vice presidents at Wellington Management.

Strategy

Comanager Jack Ryan, who runs the equity portion of the fund, is a yield-oriented contrarian. The fund typically has little exposure to growth-oriented sectors such as technology. The fund's bond stake (about 60% of assets) used to have a very long duration (a measure of interest-rate sensitivity), but Earl McEvoy, who runs the bond portion of the portfolio, now manages against a benchmark with a shorter duration, the Lehman Brothers Corporate A or Better Bond Index.

Historical Profile

Return High
Risk Average
Rating ★★★★★ Highest

Investment Style — Equity Stock %: 37% 36% 36% 40% 37% 36% 36% 39% 38%

▼ Manager Change
▽ Partial Manager Change

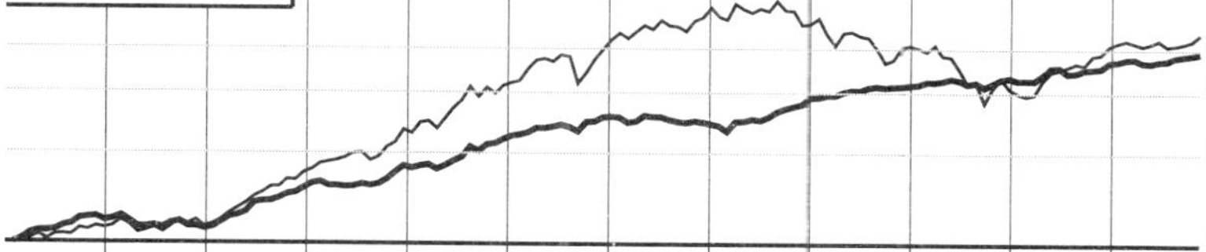

Performance Quartile (within Category)

1993	1994	1995	1996	1997	1998	1999	2000	2001	2002	2003	12-04	History
19.24	17.05	20.44	20.51	21.86	22.12	18.85	20.34	19.91	19.90	20.91	21.58	NAV
14.65	-4.44	28.91	9.42	20.19	11.84	-4.14	16.17	7.38	4.64	9.65	7.57	Total Return %
4.59	-5.75	-8.62	-13.52	-13.16	-16.73	-25.18	25.27	19.26	26.73	-19.02	-3.30	+/-S&P 500
3.89	-3.21	10.75	0.53	6.09	0.11	-12.00	9.38	4.16	8.66	-8.01	-1.44	+/-DJ 40%
6.42	5.92	6.84	5.82	6.01	5.31	5.20	5.74	5.06	4.65	4.44	4.08	Income Return %
8.23	-10.36	22.07	3.60	14.18	6.53	-9.34	10.43	2.32	-0.01	5.21	3.49	Capital Return %
35	49	2	65	12	35	95	10	5	10	72	23	Total Rtn % Rank Cat
1.14	1.11	1.14	1.16	1.20	1.13	1.12	1.06	1.00	0.91	0.87	0.66	Income $
0.40	0.24	0.28	0.60	1.44	1.14	1.25	0.40	0.86	0.00	0.00	0.04	Capital Gains $
0.33	0.34	0.34	0.31	0.31	0.31	0.30	0.31	0.33	0.30	0.31	0.26	Expense Ratio %
5.79	6.16	5.96	5.74	5.47	5.05	5.22	5.39	4.88	4.72	4.33	4.06	Income Ratio %
21	31	30	26	36	32	20	28	24	43	28	23	Turnover Rate %
6,011	5,681	7,181	7,013	7,646	8,498	6,976	6,558	6,495	7,484	8,439	9,268	Net Assets $mil

Performance 12-31-04

	1st Qtr	2nd Qtr	3rd Qtr	4th Qtr	Total
2000	1.41	0.79	6.85	6.37	16.17
2001	1.40	2.73	1.91	1.15	7.38
2002	2.01	1.09	-3.88	5.57	4.64
2003	-1.56	7.98	-1.32	4.54	9.65
2004	2.21	-1.41	3.10	3.55	7.57

Trailing	Total Return%	+/- S&P 500	+/- DJ 40%	%Rank Cat	Growth of $10,000
3 Mo	3.55	-5.68	-1.85	65	10,355
6 Mo	6.76	-0.43	0.27	18	10,676
1 Yr	7.57	-3.30	-1.44	23	10,757
3 Yr Avg	7.27	3.69	0.09	15	12,343
5 Yr Avg	9.02	11.32	2.72	6	15,400
10 Yr Avg	10.84	-1.23	1.69	1	27,988
15 Yr Avg	10.05	-0.88	1.25	23	42,058

Tax Analysis	Tax-Adj Rtn%	%Rank Cat	Tax-Cost Rat	%Rank Cat
3 Yr (estimated)	5.77	17	1.40	76
5 Yr (estimated)	6.93	6	1.92	84
10 Yr (estimated)	7.96	2	2.60	90

Potential Capital Gain Exposure: 11% of assets

Rating and Risk

Time Period	Load-Adj Return %	Morningstar Rtn vs Cat	Morningstar Risk vs Cat	Morningstar Risk-Adj Rating
1 Yr	7.57			
3 Yr	7.27	+Avg	Avg	★★★★
5 Yr	9.02	High	Avg	★★★★★
10 Yr	10.84	High	Avg	★★★★★
Incept	10.94			

Other Measures	Standard Index S&P 500	Best Fit Index Mstar Large Value
Alpha	5.2	4.1
Beta	0.23	0.27
R-Squared	37	56
Standard Deviation	6.00	
Mean	7.27	
Sharpe Ratio	0.99	

Portfolio Analysis 09-30-04

Total Stocks:55 Share change since 06-30-04	Sectors	P/E Ratio	YTD Return %	% Net Assets
ExxonMobil	Energy	13.9	-2.75	2.07
⊕ Bank of America	Financial	12.3	-3.85	1.92
⊕ Citigroup	Financial	15.3	0.08	1.72
Weyerhaeuser	Ind Mtrls	—	-0.03	1.29
ConocoPhillips	Energy	9.0	-1.42	1.29
⊕ FPL Group	Utilities	15.2	-3.01	1.28
⊕ Caterpillar	Ind Mtrls	17.6	-6.43	1.27
SBC Communications	Telecom	15.4	-3.12	1.26
National City	Financial	9.6	-3.68	1.10

Total Fixed-Income:332	Date of Maturity	Amount $000	Value $000	% Net Assets
Kreditanstalt Fur Wiedera	01-23-08	60,000	60,176	0.58
Wal Mart Stores 6.875%	08-10-09	50,000	56,781	0.55
Hydro-Quebec 6.3%	05-11-11	50,000	56,008	0.54
European Invt Bk 4.625%	05-15-14	54,000	55,662	0.54
Dow Chem 5.75%	12-15-08	50,000	53,455	0.52
Washington Post 5.5%	02-15-09	50,000	53,354	0.52
Household Fin 5.75%	01-30-07	48,000	50,733	0.49
Alcoa 6.5%	06-01-11	45,000	50,477	0.49
Illinois St 5.1%	06-01-33	52,000	49,258	0.48

Equity Style
Style: Value
Size: Large-Cap

Value Measures		Rel Category
Price/Earnings	13.11	0.80
Price/Book	2.27	0.96
Price/Sales	1.13	0.87
Price/Cash Flow	5.98	0.86
Dividend Yield %	3.12	1.79

Growth Measures	%	Rel Category
Long-Term Erngs	8.38	0.75
Book Value	6.70	1.22
Sales	3.53	0.77
Cash Flow	-3.38	NMF
Historical Erngs	10.11	1.07

Market Cap %			
Giant	43.7	Small	0.0
Large	50.9	Micro	0.0
Mid	5.3	Avg $mil:	39,524

Fixed-Income Style
Duration: Interm-Term
Quality: Medium

Avg Eff Duration [1]	5.3 Yrs
Avg Eff Maturity	7.7 Yrs
Avg Credit Quality	A
Avg Wtd Coupon	5.43%

[1]figure provided by fund as of 09-30-04

Sector Weightings	% of Stocks	Rel S&P 500	3 Year High	3 Year Low
Info	8.15	0.38		
Software	0.00	0.00	0	0
Hardware	0.00	0.00	0	0
Media	0.00	0.00	0	0
Telecom	8.15	2.59	15	8
Service	38.09	0.82		
Health	4.93	0.39	8	1
Consumer	0.00	0.00	3	0
Business	0.00	0.00	0	0
Financial	33.16	1.60	33	23
Mfg	53.76	1.67		
Goods	10.02	1.07	11	4
Ind Mtrls	18.76	1.48	22	15
Energy	15.44	2.16	19	11
Utilities	9.54	3.22	21	10

Composition

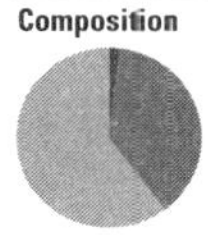

Cash	1.9
Stocks	37.6
Bonds	60.3
Other	0.2
Foreign (% of Stock)	5.2

Morningstar's Take by Jeffrey Ptak 01-06-05

This is a solid option, but only for those with a suitably long time horizon.

The objective of this conservative-allocation fund--whose portfolio is split roughly 60/40 between bonds and stocks--is straightforward: Seek yield. Management plays it safe in that regard. On the bond side, Earl McEvoy seeks intermediate- and long-maturity credits, keeping the portfolio's duration close to the Lehman Credit A or Better Index. Meanwhile, Jack Ryan favors stocks of dominant franchises that sport above-average dividend yields but trade at a discount to his estimate of fair value.

In aggregate, the portfolio sports a decidedly blue-chip look. The stock sleeve is anchored in industry giants like Bank of America and Exxon Mobil and picks typically cluster in typical value realms like the financial services and basic materials arenas. Similarly, the fund's bond portfolio is dominated by credits rated A or better, with the lion's share of assets in sturdy issuers like diversified money-center banks (Wachovia) and consumer staples (Procter & Gamble).

The fund has been a reliable performer over time, buoyed by the above-average yield that McEvoy's and Ryan's conservative, stay-the-course ethos has conferred. That picture shouldn't change much in the future thanks to the fund's paltry 0.26% expense ratio which consumes little of the income its holdings throw off.

But income will take the fund only so far. Yes, investors may gravitate to more stable, high yielding fare given forecasts for muted market returns. But the bond portfolio's sensitivity to interest-rate fluctuations shouldn't be ignored. To be sure, that attribute generally has been an asset over the past decade as rates have fallen. But the fund's subpar 1994, 1996, and 1999 campaigns (periods marked by rising rates) serve notice that the fund isn't an all-weather option. In view of the strong likelihood that rates will rise in the future, only investors with long time horizons need apply.

Address:	PO Box 2600 Valley Forge PA 19482 800-662-7447
Web Address:	www.vanguard.com
Inception:	07-01-70
Advisor:	Wellington Management Company, LLP
Subadvisor:	None
NTF Plans:	N/A

Minimum Purchase:	$3000	Add: $100	IRA: $1000
Min Auto Inv Plan:	$3000	Add: $50	
Sales Fees:	No-load		
Management Fee:	0.29%		
Actual Fees:	Mgt:0.29%	Dist: —	
Expense Projections:	3Yr:$100	5Yr:$174	10Yr:$393
Income Distrib:	Quarterly		

Vanguard Wellington

Analyst Pick	Ticker	Load	NAV	Yield	Total Assets	Mstar Category
✔	VWELX	None	$30.19	2.8%	$33,930 mil	Moderate Allocation

Governance and Management

Fiduciary Grade: B

Portfolio Manager(s)

This fund boasts an experienced management team. Paul Kaplan, who has run the fixed-income portion of the fund since 1999, has been with Wellington Management Company since 1978 and is a senior vice president and partner at the firm. Ed Bousa, who took over the equity portfolio at the end of 2002, did a solid job managing Putnam Equity Income from late 1992 through early 2000.

Strategy

On the stock side, Ed Bousa looks for dividend-paying companies with modest valuations and decent fundamentals. In that regard, his approach is similar to that of former manager Ernst von Metzsch. The fund is typically light on technology stocks and has plenty of exposure to value-oriented fare. Bond-portfolio manager Paul Kaplan emphasizes high-quality issues; historically, the fund's duration (a measure of interest-rate sensitivity) has been longer than its average peer's.

Historical Profile

Return: High
Risk: Average
Rating: ★★★★★ Highest

Investment Style: Equity Stock %

1993	1994	1995	1996	1997	1998	1999	2000	2001	2002	2003	12-04
62%	62%	60%	65%	63%	67%	65%	66%	65%			

▼ Manager Change
∇ Partial Manager Change

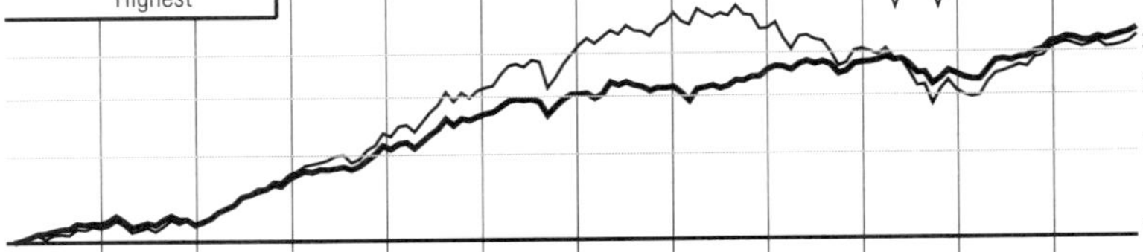

Growth of $10,000
— Investment Values of Fund
— Investment Values of S&P 500

Performance Quartile (within Category)

History	1993	1994	1995	1996	1997	1998	1999	2000	2001	2002	2003	12-04
NAV	20.40	19.39	24.43	26.15	29.45	29.35	27.96	28.21	27.26	24.56	28.81	30.19
Total Return %	13.52	-0.49	32.92	16.19	23.23	12.06	4.41	10.40	4.19	-6.90	20.75	11.17
+/-S&P 500	3.46	-1.80	-4.61	-6.75	-10.12	-16.51	-16.63	19.50	16.07	15.19	-7.92	0.30
+/-DJ 60%	1.79	1.46	8.15	4.85	4.03	-0.33	-8.44	5.96	4.03	3.64	-3.31	0.00
Income Return %	4.88	4.38	5.08	4.40	4.34	3.89	3.94	3.88	3.41	3.12	3.15	3.07
Capital Return %	8.64	-4.87	27.84	11.79	18.89	8.17	0.47	6.52	0.78	-10.02	17.60	8.10
Total Rtn % Rank Cat	36	25	5	30	22	58	79	10	7	12	42	16
Income $	0.92	0.88	0.97	1.06	1.12	1.13	1.14	1.07	0.95	0.84	0.77	0.59
Capital Gains $	0.38	0.03	0.28	1.11	1.57	2.44	1.50	1.48	1.12	0.00	0.00	0.91
Expense Ratio %	0.34	0.35	0.33	0.31	0.29	0.31	0.30	0.31	0.36	0.36	0.36	—
Income Ratio %	4.55	4.35	4.37	4.08	3.97	3.68	3.74	3.77	3.42	3.18	3.00	—
Turnover Rate %	34	32	24	30	27	29	22	33	33	25	28	—
Net Assets $mil	8,076	8,809	12,656	16,190	21,812	25,761	25,529	22,799	21,724	19,495	24,326	28,328

Performance 12-31-04

	1st Qtr	2nd Qtr	3rd Qtr	4th Qtr	Total
2000	-1.45	0.25	4.66	6.77	10.40
2001	-0.26	3.55	-5.68	6.96	4.19
2002	3.30	-4.58	-11.04	6.17	-6.90
2003	-3.35	12.55	1.37	9.50	20.75
2004	2.19	0.41	1.65	6.58	11.17

Trailing	Total Return%	+/- S&P 500	+/- DJ 60%	%Rank Cat	Growth of $10,000
3 Mo	6.58	-2.65	-0.90	59	10,658
6 Mo	8.34	1.15	0.81	17	10,834
1 Yr	11.17	0.30	0.00	16	11,117
3 Yr Avg	7.72	4.14	0.46	9	12,499
5 Yr Avg	7.53	9.83	2.29	6	14,376
10 Yr Avg	12.34	0.27	1.85	8	32,014
15 Yr Avg	10.85	-0.08	0.90	13	46,885

Tax Analysis	Tax-Adj Rtn%	%Rank Cat	Tax-Cost Rat	%Rank Cat
3 Yr (estimated)	6.55	10	1.09	75
5 Yr (estimated)	5.81	6	1.60	73
10 Yr (estimated)	9.97	9	2.11	71

Potential Capital Gain Exposure: 21% of assets

Rating and Risk

Time Period	Load-Adj Return %	Morningstar Rtn vs Cat	Morningstar Risk vs Cat	Morningstar Risk-Adj Rating
1 Yr	11.17			
3 Yr	7.72	+Avg	Avg	★★★★★
5 Yr	7.53	High	Avg	★★★★★
10 Yr	12.34	High	Avg	★★★★★
Incept	8.32			

Other Measures	Standard Index S&P 500	Best Fit Index Russ 1000 Vl
Alpha	4.7	1.7
Beta	0.58	0.61
R-Squared	87	93

Standard Deviation	10.00
Mean	7.72
Sharpe Ratio	0.64

Portfolio Analysis 09-30-04

Total Stocks:110 Share change since 06-30-04	Sectors	P/E Ratio	YTD Return %	% Net Assets
⊕ Citigroup	Financial	15.3	0.08	1.93
⊕ Bank of America	Financial	12.3	-3.85	1.43
⊕ IBM	Hardware	20.2	-3.63	1.38
Verizon Communications	Telecom	32.4	-3.79	1.37
⊕ Abbott Laboratories	Health	22.1	0.92	1.35
EnCana	Energy	11.3	-2.77	1.21
⊕ Total SA ADR	Energy	17.0	-4.33	1.17
Exelon	Utilities	16.1	-4.29	1.08
Weyerhaeuser	Ind Mtrls	—	-0.03	1.04

Total Fixed-Income:1439	Date of Maturity	Amount $000	Value $000	% Net Assets
US Treasury Note 2.75%	07-31-06	1,600,000	1,605,744	5.16
US Treasury Bond 6.25%	08-15-23	200,000	233,532	0.75
Household Fin 6.375%	10-15-11	75,000	82,768	0.27
Proc & Gambl Pft Shr Tr &	01-01-21	60,945	82,704	0.27
Aig Sunamerica Global Fin	05-10-11	60,000	66,422	0.21
Florida Windstorm Underwr	02-25-19	55,000	64,577	0.21
Metropolitan Life Ins 144	11-01-15	51,000	61,287	0.20
Merck 2.5%	03-30-07	60,000	59,260	0.19
Wachovia 5.625%	12-15-08	55,000	59,206	0.19

Equity Style
Style: Value
Size: Large-Cap

Value Measures		Rel Category
Price/Earnings	15.31	0.92
Price/Book	2.32	0.95
Price/Sales	1.38	1.05
Price/Cash Flow	6.74	0.93
Dividend Yield %	2.17	1.38

Growth Measures	%	Rel Category
Long-Term Erngs	10.37	0.89
Book Value	7.90	1.38
Sales	4.72	0.91
Cash Flow	9.30	1.16
Historical Erngs	12.21	1.13

Market Cap %			
Giant	46.1	Small	0.0
Large	46.1	Micro	0.0
Mid	7.8	Avg $mil:	37,577

Fixed-Income Style
Duration: Interm-Term
Quality: High

Avg Eff Duration [1]	4.8 Yrs
Avg Eff Maturity	7.1 Yrs
Avg Credit Quality	AA
Avg Wtd Coupon	5.57%

[1]figure provided by fund as of 09-30-04

Sector Weightings	% of Stocks	Rel S&P 500	3 Year High	3 Year Low
Info	15.37	0.72		
Software	1.44	0.33	1	0
Hardware	5.61	0.55	7	6
Media	2.77	0.72	3	1
Telecom	5.55	1.76	6	4
Service	39.38	0.85		
Health	10.41	0.83	11	9
Consumer	2.49	0.27	5	2
Business	8.17	2.02	10	8
Financial	18.31	0.88	20	16
Mfg	45.24	1.41		
Goods	6.78	0.73	9	7
Ind Mtrls	19.27	1.52	22	17
Energy	13.33	1.86	13	10
Utilities	5.86	1.98	8	6

Composition

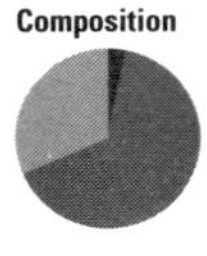

Cash	3.1
Stocks	65.4
Bonds	31.5
Other	0.0
Foreign (% of Stock)	13.3

Morningstar's Take by Christopher Traulsen 01-07-05

We continue to think highly of Vanguard Wellington.

This fund has much to offer. It's subadvised by venerable Wellington Management Company, a Boston-based firm with a reputation for strong research and an ability to retain key talent. Previous manager Ernst von Metzsch, who retired at the end of 2000, had been with the firm since the 1970s. Paul Kaplan, who helms the 35% or so of assets that the fund stashes in bonds, has been at the firm since 1978.

Since von Metzsch's retirement, the fund hasn't missed a beat. He was replaced by Edward Bousa, a veteran value manager who came to Wellington from Putnam in 2000. Like his predecessor, Bousa looks to buy giant- and large-cap companies with plump dividends on the cheap. That often leads him to favor integrated oil companies and industrials. The fund is also overweighted in dividend-rich telecom companies and utilities. In contrast, it's typically underweighted in areas such as technology, which tend to be pricey and offer little in the way of dividends.

The fund's style can hold the fund back when the priciest stocks lead the way--as was the case in 1999. However, it has held the fund in very good stead over time, particularly during the bear market that stretched from early 2000 through late 2002. In 2004, the fund once again served investors well, with its energy and industrials allocations contributing to the fund's top-quintile, 11% return.

The fund has grown quite large in recent years, clocking in at just less than $34 billion in assets recently. However, the fund's large-cap focus, tendency to keep positions small, and relatively low-turnover approach should help keep transactions costs reasonable. With its low costs, excellent record, and top-flight subadvisor, we continue to think this fund is an excellent choice for investors looking for a single fund to give them core exposure to stocks and bonds.

Address:	PO Box 2600 Valley Forge PA 19482 800-662-7447
Web Address:	www.vanguard.com
Inception:	07-01-29
Advisor:	Wellington Management Company, LLP
Subadvisor:	None
NTF Plans:	N/A

Minimum Purchase:	$3000	Add: $100	IRA: $1000
Min Auto Inv Plan:	$3000	Add: $50	
Sales Fees:	No-load		
Management Fee:	0.35%		
Actual Fees:	Mgt:0.35%	Dist: —	
Expense Projections:	3Yr:$116	5Yr:$202	10Yr:$456
Income Distrib:	Quarterly		

Vanguard Windsor

Ticker	Load	NAV	Yield	Total Assets	Mstar Category
VWNDX	None	$18.07	1.4%	$21,014 mil	Large Value

Governance and Management

Fiduciary Grade: B

Portfolio Manager(s)

Wellington Management runs roughly one third of the fund's assets. On June 30, 2004, David Fassnacht of Wellington took over lead-management responsibilities from Charles Freeman, who has been in charge since late 1995. Since mid-1999, Sanford C. Bernstein has managed 30% of the fund's assets. Bernstein is a value shop, but it takes a more diversified approach.

Strategy

Vanguard Windsor likes 'em cheap: Its advisor buys stocks when they've fallen hard. It readily adds to holdings on weakness that it still believes in, and is not shy about grabbing mid-cap names when they look attractive.

Historical Profile

Return Above Avg
Risk High
Rating ★★★ Neutral

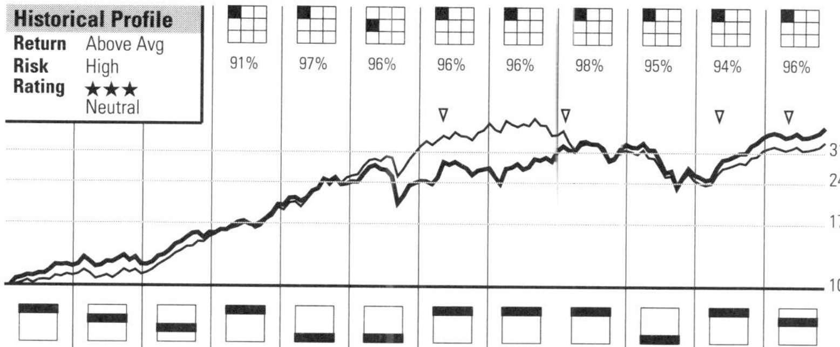

Investment Style
Equity
Stock %

▼ Manager Change
▽ Partial Manager Change

Growth of $10,000
— Investment Values of Fund
— Investment Values of S&P 500

Performance Quartile (within Category)

1993	1994	1995	1996	1997	1998	1999	2000	2001	2002	2003	12-04	History
13.91	12.59	14.53	16.59	16.98	15.57	15.17	15.29	15.64	12.00	16.26	18.07	NAV
19.37	-0.15	30.15	26.36	21.97	0.81	11.57	15.89	5.72	-22.25	37.01	13.38	Total Return %
9.31	-1.46	-7.38	3.42	-11.38	-27.76	-9.47	24.99	17.60	-0.16	8.34	2.51	+/-S&P 500
1.30	1.83	-8.21	4.72	-13.21	-14.82	4.22	8.88	11.31	-6.73	6.98	-3.11	+/-Russ 1000 VI
2.92	3.19	3.68	2.84	1.94	1.48	1.74	1.79	1.31	1.09	1.38	1.61	Income Return %
16.45	-3.34	26.47	23.52	20.03	-0.67	9.83	14.10	4.41	-23.34	35.63	11.77	Capital Return %
12	44	72	9	90	89	23	21	10	76	6	43	Total Rtn % Rank Cat
0.37	0.44	0.46	0.41	0.32	0.25	0.27	0.27	0.20	0.17	0.17	0.26	Income $
0.89	0.86	1.38	1.33	2.88	1.23	1.90	1.85	0.31	0.00	0.00	0.09	Capital Gains $
0.40	0.45	0.43	0.29	0.27	0.27	0.28	0.31	0.41	0.45	0.48	0.39	Expense Ratio %
2.68	3.11	3.01	2.75	1.89	1.31	1.56	1.75	1.37	1.16	1.27	1.32	Income Ratio %
25	34	32	34	61	48	56	41	33	30	23	28	Turnover Rate %
10,611	10,673	13,646	16,738	20,915	18,188	16,700	16,615	16,027	10,999	14,681	16,385	Net Assets $mil

Performance 12-31-04

	1st Qtr	2nd Qtr	3rd Qtr	4th Qtr	Total
2000	-0.40	-0.54	7.85	8.46	15.89
2001	-0.52	6.52	-12.74	14.35	5.72
2002	0.96	-13.36	-20.22	11.41	-22.25
2003	-3.75	18.77	4.77	14.39	37.01
2004	2.52	0.90	-1.68	11.46	13.38

Trailing	Total Return%	+/- S&P 500	+/- Russ 1000 VI	%Rank Cat	Growth of $10,000
3 Mo	11.46	2.23	1.08	9	11,146
6 Mo	9.60	2.41	-2.48	42	10,960
1 Yr	13.38	2.51	-3.11	43	11,338
3 Yr Avg	6.49	2.91	-2.08	40	12,076
5 Yr Avg	8.15	10.45	2.88	14	14,796
10 Yr Avg	12.81	0.74	-1.02	18	33,379
15 Yr Avg	11.38	0.45	-0.65	24	50,363

Tax Analysis	Tax-Adj Rtn%	%Rank Cat	Tax-Cost Rat	%Rank Cat
3 Yr (estimated)	6.09	30	0.38	26
5 Yr (estimated)	7.04	15	1.03	55
10 Yr (estimated)	10.30	28	2.22	76

Potential Capital Gain Exposure: 25% of assets

Rating and Risk

Time Period	Load-Adj Return %	Morningstar Rtn vs Cat	Morningstar Risk vs Cat	Morningstar Risk-Adj Rating
1 Yr	13.38			
3 Yr	6.49	Avg	+Avg	★★★
5 Yr	8.15	+Avg	+Avg	★★★★
10 Yr	12.81	+Avg	High	★★★
Incept	12.61			

Other Measures	Standard Index S&P 500	Best Fit Index Russ 1000
Alpha	2.8	2.0
Beta	1.12	1.13
R-Squared	97	97
Standard Deviation	18.19	
Mean	6.49	
Sharpe Ratio	0.28	

Portfolio Analysis 09-30-04

Share change since 06-04 Total Stocks:145	Sector	PE	YTD Ret%	% Assets
⊕ Citigroup	Financial	15.3	2.72	4.32
⊕ Bank of America	Financial	12.3	21.50	3.46
⊖ Tyco International	Ind Mtrls	25.1	35.41	3.39
⊕ Comcast	Media	—	-13.77	2.37
⊕ Wyeth	Health	17.0	2.73	2.34
⊕ Applied Materials	Hardware	20.7	-23.80	2.27
⊕ Alcoa	Ind Mtrls	18.8	-15.75	2.24
TJX Companies	Consumer	17.0	14.80	2.33
Fannie Mae	Financial	9.1	-2.33	2.32
⊕ Time Warner	Media	27.5	8.12	1.39
Microsoft	Software	36.1	8.95	1.75
⊕ Pfizer	Health	22.0	-22.31	1.74
Michelin Grp	Ind Mtrls	—	—	1.59
Petroleo Brasileiro ADR	Energy	—	42.37	1.57
⊕ Anthem	Health	17.4	53.33	1.56
⊕ Sanofi-Aventis ADR	Health	23.0	9.75	1.53
⊖ Vanguard Total Stock Mar	—	—	—	1.53
Health Net	Health	15.4	-11.71	1.37
Ross Stores	Consumer	22.6	9.82	1.35
⊖ Engelhard	Ind Mtrls	15.3	3.98	1.34

Current Investment Style

Value Blnd Growth — Large Mid Small

Market Cap	%
Giant	45.1
Large	31.0
Mid	22.7
Small	1.0
Micro	0.1

Avg $mil: 25,631

Value Measures		Rel Category
Price/Earnings	13.36	0.89
Price/Book	2.05	0.90
Price/Sales	0.93	0.78
Price/Cash Flow	5.21	0.82
Dividend Yield %	1.61	0.79

Growth Measures	%	Rel Category
Long-Term Erngs	11.15	1.07
Book Value	7.76	1.38
Sales	4.13	0.98
Cash Flow	10.13	1.94
Historical Erngs	13.90	1.17

Profitability	%	Rel Category
Return on Equity	16.30	1.03
Return on Assets	9.29	1.19
Net Margin	11.43	1.12

Sector Weightings	% of Stocks	Rel S&P 500	3 Year High	3 Year Low
Info	19.92	0.93		
Software	1.89	0.44	2	0
Hardware	9.73	0.95	10	7
Media	6.23	1.62	7	5
Telecom	2.07	0.66	4	1
Service	52.58	1.13		
Health	12.28	0.98	13	8
Consumer	7.13	0.79	12	7
Business	4.76	1.18	7	5
Financial	28.41	1.37	30	26
Mfg	27.51	0.86		
Goods	2.71	0.29	3	2
Ind Mtrls	14.47	1.14	20	14
Energy	8.69	1.21	9	4
Utilities	1.64	0.55	2	1

Composition

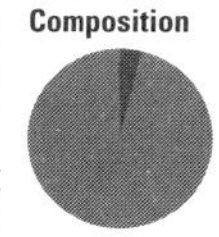

Cash	3.8
Stocks	95.9
Bonds	0.0
Other	0.3
Foreign (% of Stock)	9.6

Morningstar's Take by Christine Benz 12-21-04

We think it's well worth looking beneath the surface at Vanguard Windsor Fund.

At first glance, this venerable fund has a few warts. Its returns have long been streaky, falling into the category's top or bottom quartile in most calendar years. Perhaps the most significant strike against it, however, is that the fund underwent a significant management change in mid-2004, with longtime lead manager Chuck Freeman retiring after nearly nine years at the helm.

Investors who dig deeper, however, will actually find a comforting consistency. David Fassnacht, who took over from Freeman, has worked at lead advisor Wellington Management for 13 years. Fassnacht notes that the four senior Wellington investment professionals working on the fund boast a total of 63 years in the investment business, 57 of them on the Windsor fund. Meanwhile, a team from Sanford Bernstein has run roughly one third of the portfolio since 1999.

In addition, the fund's boom-and-bust performance pattern is easier to stomach when you realize that it springs from the consistent application of a disciplined strategy. Management buys stocks when everyone else hates them and eschews pockets of irrational exuberance. For example, in 2004, management skimped on the red-hot energy sector and initiated positions in the semiconductor industry, which got clobbered this past summer. Fassnacht has argued that Applied Materials, Windsor's biggest holding in the sector, is a high-quality company trading at a big discount to management's estimate of its intrinsic value.

As a result of such bold moves, year-to-year consistency will never be this fund's strong suit. (The fund is poised to finish around the category's midpoint in 2004, but that's a rarity.) Yet we believe that management's experience and time-tested approach, combined with low expenses, make this an attractive core holding.

Address:	PO Box 2600 Valley Forge PA 19482 800-662-7447
Web Address:	www.vanguard.com
Inception:	10-23-58
Advisor:	The Vanguard Group, Inc.
Subadvisor:	Multiple
NTF Plans:	N/A

Minimum Purchase:	$3000	Add: $100	IRA: $1000
Min Auto Inv Plan:	$3000	Add: $50	
Sales Fees:	No-load		
Management Fee:	0.43%		
Actual Fees:	Mgt:0.43%	Dist: —	
Expense Projections:	3Yr:$144	5Yr:$252	10Yr:$567
Income Distrib:	Semi-Annually		

Vanguard Windsor II

Ticker	Load	NAV	Yield	Total Assets	Mstar Category
VWNFX	None	$30.73	1.9%	$34,570 mil	Large Value

Governance and Management

Fiduciary Grade: B

Portfolio Manager(s)

Jim Barrow of subadvisor Barrow, Hanley, Mewhinney & Strauss handles approximately 70% of the assets here. He has been on the fund since its inception in 1985 and also manages the mid-cap oriented Vanguard Selected Value, where he has a strong record. Windor II's other advisors are Hotchkis and Wiley, Equinox Capital Management, Tukman Capital Management, and Vanguard's quantitative equity group.

Strategy

This is a true-blue value fund. Manager Jim Barrow searches for low-P/E, high-dividend-paying stocks. He isn't afraid to snap up a number of stocks in beaten-down sectors. Consequently, the fund sometimes has sector weightings that are very different from its average rival's.

Historical Profile

Return: Above Avg
Risk: Average
Rating: ★★★★ Above Avg

Investment Style: Equity Stock %

92%	93%	92%	93%	89%	92%	92%	98%	96%

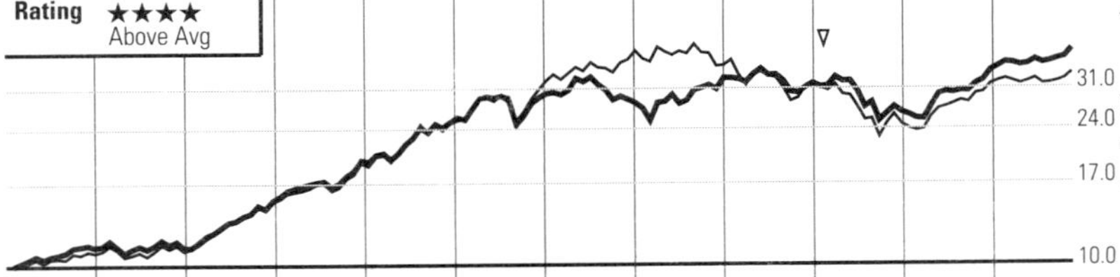

▼ Manager Change
∇ Partial Manager Change

Growth of $10,000
— Investment Values of Fund
— Investment Values of S&P 500

Performance Quartile (within Category)

1993	1994	1995	1996	1997	1998	1999	2000	2001	2002	2003	12-04	History
17.04	15.82	20.66	23.83	28.62	29.85	24.97	27.20	25.59	20.80	26.49	30.73	NAV
13.60	-1.17	38.83	24.18	32.37	16.36	-5.81	16.86	-3.40	-16.86	30.08	18.31	Total Return %
3.54	-2.48	1.30	1.24	-0.98	-12.21	-26.85	25.96	8.48	5.23	1.41	7.44	+/-S&P 500
-4.47	0.81	0.47	2.54	-2.81	0.73	-13.16	9.85	2.19	-1.34	0.05	1.82	+/-Russ 1000 VI
3.23	3.25	3.69	3.07	2.78	2.25	2.29	2.46	2.01	2.00	2.56	2.20	Income Return %
10.37	-4.42	35.14	21.11	29.59	14.11	-8.10	14.40	-5.41	-18.86	27.52	16.11	Capital Return %
51	61	7	16	11	24	95	19	46	38	33	6	Total Rtn % Rank Cat
0.51	0.55	0.58	0.63	0.66	0.64	0.68	0.61	0.55	0.51	0.53	0.58	Income $
0.50	0.47	0.69	1.16	2.19	2.67	2.50	1.24	0.15	0.00	0.00	0.00	Capital Gains $
0.39	0.39	0.39	0.39	0.37	0.41	0.37	0.37	0.40	0.42	0.43	0.36	Expense Ratio %
3.11	3.26	3.27	2.92	2.49	2.16	2.08	2.36	2.10	2.12	2.31	2.07	Income Ratio %
26	24	30	32	30	31	26	26	10	41	29	22	Turnover Rate %
7,616	7,959	11,013	15,700	24,376	31,538	26,902	25,083	22,429	17,739	22,766	29,016	Net Assets $mil

Performance 12-31-04

	1st Qtr	2nd Qtr	3rd Qtr	4th Qtr	Total
2000	-0.04	-0.62	10.56	6.40	16.86
2001	-2.72	4.58	-9.96	5.45	-3.40
2002	4.02	-8.68	-17.16	5.65	-16.86
2003	-4.23	18.80	0.43	13.84	30.08
2004	4.76	2.02	0.54	10.11	18.31

Trailing	Total Return%	+/- S&P 500	+/- Russ 1000 VI	%Rank Cat	Growth of $10,000
3 Mo	10.11	0.88	-0.27	26	11,011
6 Mo	10.70	3.51	-1.38	24	11,070
1 Yr	18.31	7.44	1.82	6	11,831
3 Yr Avg	8.56	4.98	-0.01	14	12,794
5 Yr Avg	7.63	9.93	2.36	18	14,443
10 Yr Avg	13.71	1.64	-0.12	10	36,140
15 Yr Avg	11.71	0.78	-0.32	17	52,648

Tax Analysis	Tax-Adj Rtn%	%Rank Cat	Tax-Cost Rat	%Rank Cat
3 Yr (estimated)	7.96	11	0.55	37
5 Yr (estimated)	6.68	16	0.88	47
10 Yr (estimated)	11.73	6	1.74	46

Potential Capital Gain Exposure: 27% of assets

Rating and Risk

Time Period	Load-Adj Return %	Morningstar Rtn vs Cat	Morningstar Risk vs Cat	Morningstar Risk-Adj Rating
1 Yr	18.31			
3 Yr	8.56	+Avg	Avg	★★★★
5 Yr	7.63	+Avg	Avg	★★★★
10 Yr	13.71	+Avg	Avg	★★★★
Incept	13.11			

Other Measures	Standard Index S&P 500	Best Fit Index Russ 1000 VI
Alpha	5.1	0.3
Beta	0.91	0.95
R-Squared	88	95
Standard Deviation	15.79	
Mean	8.56	
Sharpe Ratio	0.46	

Portfolio Analysis 09-30-04

Share change since 06-04 Total Stocks:277	Sector	PE	YTD Ret%	% Assets
⊕ Wells Fargo	Financial	15.5	8.97	2.96
⊕ Occidental Petroleum	Energy	10.1	41.27	2.94
⊖ ConocoPhillips	Energy	9.0	35.60	2.79
⊕ ChevronTexaco	Energy	7.7	25.57	2.65
⊕ Citigroup	Financial	15.3	2.72	2.54
⊕ J P Morgan Chase	Financial	19.4	9.97	2.53
⊕ Bank of America	Financial	12.3	21.50	2.51
⊖ Cendant	Business	13.6	6.52	2.40
⊖ Tyco International	Ind Mtrls	25.1	35.41	2.37
⊕ BP PLC ADR	Energy	20.7	22.07	2.27
⊕ Altria Group	Goods	13.3	18.38	2.14
⊕ Allstate	Financial	12.8	23.12	2.03
Imperial Tobacco Group P	Goods	29.1	44.30	1.85
⊕ Baxter International	Health	32.9	15.22	1.82
⊖ Carnival	Goods	26.2	46.74	1.75
SLM	Financial	15.8	44.21	1.72
⊖ Boeing	Ind Mtrls	14.7	24.86	1.70
Manulife Financial	Financial	19.3	45.67	1.69
⊕ Verizon Communications	Telecom	32.4	20.25	1.68
⊕ Vanguard Total Stock Mar	—	—	—	1.67

Current Investment Style

Value Blnd Growth / Large Mid Small

Market Cap	%
Giant	41.3
Large	48.0
Mid	10.5
Small	0.1
Micro	0.0

Avg $mil: 34,566

Value Measures		Rel Category
Price/Earnings	14.03	0.93
Price/Book	2.25	0.99
Price/Sales	1.05	0.88
Price/Cash Flow	5.59	0.88
Dividend Yield %	2.33	1.14

Growth Measures	%	Rel Category
Long-Term Erngs	9.88	0.95
Book Value	6.10	1.08
Sales	6.51	1.55
Cash Flow	6.76	1.30
Historical Erngs	12.11	1.02

Profitability	%	Rel Category
Return on Equity	16.26	1.02
Return on Assets	8.58	1.10
Net Margin	9.81	0.96

Sector Weightings	% of Stocks	Rel S&P 500	3 Year High	3 Year Low
Info	6.27	0.29		
Software	0.24	0.06	0	0
Hardware	1.60	0.16	3	2
Media	2.26	0.59	3	2
Telecom	2.17	0.69	4	2
Service	46.03	0.99		
Health	8.90	0.71	10	5
Consumer	3.95	0.44	6	4
Business	4.60	1.14	6	5
Financial	28.58	1.38	30	27
Mfg	47.71	1.49		
Goods	12.13	1.30	14	10
Ind Mtrls	15.56	1.23	17	12
Energy	12.56	1.75	13	10
Utilities	7.46	2.52	12	7

Composition

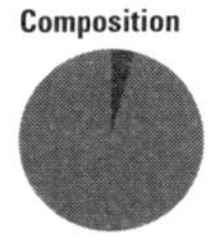

Cash	4.0
Stocks	96.0
Bonds	0.0
Other	0.0
Foreign (% of Stock)	5.3

Morningstar's Take by Christine Benz 12-27-04

There's much more to Vanguard Windsor II than its sizzling recent performance.

This offering posted a gain of 18% in 2004, landing in the top 10% of the large-cap value category. The energy sector was on fire last year, and this fund's top stock picks in the sector--including Occidental Petroleum, ConocoPhillips, and ChevronTexaco--accounted for a sizable percentage of the fund's outperformance The team also scored big gains in Tyco and Cendant, both of which exemplify management's willingness to wade into companies that are unloved or misunderstood.

Oftentimes a fund's strong recent returns are a reason to trim back on your holdings in it, not add to them. But we think this fund is an exception. For starters, lead manager Jim Barrow and his team, who are responsible for roughly 70% of the portfolio, look for stocks with low P/E ratios and high dividend yields; their steadfast application of that discipline keeps the fund from being too heavily exposed to overheating areas. In 1999, for example, the fund's valuation discipline prompted it to sit out the tech-stock frenzy. Although it dramatically underperformed its typical rival that year, it went on to hold up far better than its peers during the bear market.

The fund's focus on dividend-paying stocks could also help give it an edge if dividend income makes up a greater share of stocks' total returns than it has in the recent past. (That's a likely scenario if we're in for an era of limited price-multiple expansion.) The fund has one of the highest payouts of any plain-vanilla stock fund. That owes not only to its emphasis on high-yielding ugly-duckling stocks but also to its ultra-low expense ratio. (A fund's expense ratio is deducted directly from its dividend yield.)

In short, we think this offering is a terrific core holding. We're also big fans of the fund that Jim Barrow and his team run on their own, Vanguard Selected Value.

Address:	PO Box 2600 Valley Forge PA 19482 800-662-7447
Web Address:	www.vanguard.com
Inception:	06-24-85
Advisor:	Barrow, Hanley, Mewhinney & Strauss Inc.
Subadvisor:	None
NTF Plans:	N/A

Minimum Purchase:	$3000	Add: $100	IRA: $1000
Min Auto Inv Plan:	$3000	Add: $50	
Sales Fees:	No-load		
Management Fee:	—		
Actual Fees:	Mgt:0.39%	Dist: —	
Expense Projections:	3Yr:$128	5Yr:$224	10Yr:$505
Income Distrib:	Semi-Annually		

Wasatch Core Growth

Ticker	Load	NAV	Yield	Total Assets	Mstar Category
WGROX	Closed	$43.23	0.5%	$1,723 mil	Small Growth

Governance and Management

Fiduciary Grade: A

Portfolio Manager(s)

J.B. Taylor joined Wasatch as an analyst in 1996 and took over this fund's day-to-day operations at the start of 1999. Longtime Wasatch manager Sam Stewart oversees the fund. Stewart is also Wasatch's founder and deserves tremendous credit for the firm and its investors' success.

Strategy

Management seeks firms that will deliver consistent earnings-growth rates of between 15% and 25% during a three- to five-year time horizon. It also demands that a potential holding's trailing P/E ratio be less than or equal to its projection of the firm's sustainable earnings-growth rate. That tack has resulted in only minimal exposure to the tech sector and less volatility than the fund's typical peer.

Historical Profile

Return High
Risk Average
Rating ★★★★ Above Avg

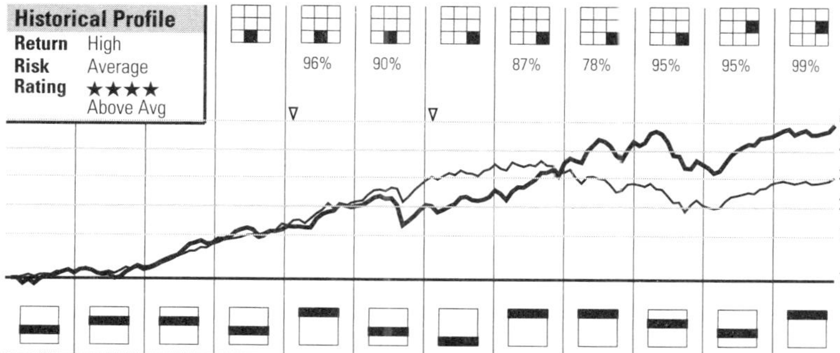

Investment Style
Equity
Stock %

▼ Manager Change
∇ Partial Manager Change

Growth of $10,000
▬ Investment Values of Fund
— Investment Values of S&P 500

Performance Quartile (within Category)

1993	1994	1995	1996	1997	1998	1999	2000	2001	2002	2003	12-04	**History**
15.14	11.61	15.96	17.19	20.22	19.57	22.80	28.71	34.60	26.68	36.92	43.23	NAV
11.12	2.68	40.42	16.54	27.55	1.56	19.35	37.39	28.82	-22.89	38.46	21.65	Total Return %
1.06	1.37	2.89	-6.40	-5.80	-27.01	-1.69	46.49	40.70	-0.80	9.79	10.78	+/-S&P 500
-2.25	5.11	9.38	5.28	14.60	0.33	-23.74	59.82	38.05	7.37	-10.08	7.34	+/-Russ 2000 Gr
0.00	0.00	0.43	0.44	0.17	0.00	0.00	0.00	0.00	0.00	0.08	0.60	Income Return %
11.12	2.68	39.99	16.10	27.38	1.56	19.35	37.39	28.82	-22.89	38.38	21.05	Capital Return %
73	31	30	63	21	57	80	2	2	28	74	9	Total Rtn % Rank Cat
0.00	0.00	0.05	0.07	0.03	0.00	0.00	0.00	0.00	0.00	0.02	0.22	Income $
1.37	3.94	0.29	1.31	1.62	0.72	0.48	2.32	2.14	0.00	0.00	1.32	Capital Gains $
1.50	1.50	1.50	1.50	1.50	1.44	1.44	1.38	1.32	1.29	1.25	1.21	Expense Ratio %
-0.55	-0.51	0.29	0.40	0.44	-0.50	-1.07	-0.86	-0.66	-0.02	-0.02	0.34	Income Ratio %
104	163	88	62	81	63	79	75	51	76	47	47	Turnover Rate %
16	8	62	90	69	39	57	30	32	32	1,455	1,723	Net Assets $mil

Performance 12-31-04

	1st Qtr	2nd Qtr	3rd Qtr	4th Qtr	Total
2000	-1.54	10.02	13.68	11.56	37.39
2001	0.84	30.74	-16.62	17.19	28.82
2002	10.14	-9.24	-26.37	4.75	-22.89
2003	-7.53	27.16	6.92	10.14	38.46
2004	9.07	-1.32	-3.17	16.72	21.65

Trailing	Total Return%	+/- S&P 500	+/- Russ 2000 Gr	%Rank Cat	Growth of $10,000
3 Mo	16.72	7.49	1.64	9	11,672
6 Mo	13.02	5.83	4.86	7	11,302
1 Yr	21.65	10.78	7.34	9	12,165
3 Yr Avg	9.11	5.53	3.32	23	12,990
5 Yr Avg	18.11	20.41	21.68	2	22,984
10 Yr Avg	19.25	7.18	12.13	3	58,155
15 Yr Avg	17.19	6.26	9.69	1	107,984

Tax Analysis	Tax-Adj Rtn%	%Rank Cat	Tax-Cost Rat	%Rank Cat
3 Yr (estimated)	8.85	20	0.24	24
5 Yr (estimated)	17.17	2	0.80	36
10 Yr (estimated)	17.91	2	1.12	28

Potential Capital Gain Exposure: 27% of assets

Rating and Risk

Time Period	Load-Adj Return %	Morningstar Rtn vs Cat	Morningstar Risk vs Cat	Morningstar Risk-Adj Rating
1 Yr	21.65			
3 Yr	9.11	+Avg	+Avg	★★★
5 Yr	18.11	High	-Avg	★★★★★
10 Yr	19.25	High	-Avg	★★★★★
Incept	15.39			

Other Measures	Standard Index S&P 500	Best Fit Index S&P Mid 400
Alpha	6.1	-3.2
Beta	1.11	1.31
R-Squared	63	88

Standard Deviation	23.27
Mean	9.11
Sharpe Ratio	0.34

Morningstar's Take by Kunal Kapoor 12-14-04

They don't come steadier than Wasatch Core Growth.

We like this fund's formula. While its managers are fans of growth stocks, they don't limit the fund's horizons to the tech and health-care sectors, and they invest more cautiously than many of their small-growth peers. We think this makes good sense because too many managers get caught up in owning the so-called "story" stocks. While they can be fun to own for a while, history has taught us that they are extremely volatile and tough to invest in successfully. So, this fund seeks out firms with more rational and steady growth prospects, targeting those that hum along at a 15% annual clip. This allows for a greater focus on firms' financials and improves the odds that the fund will successfully identify undervalued, but growing, long-term investments. In our estimate, that's a more effective and repeatable strategy, and a key reason why we like this fund.

The value of this approach has been on display in a choppy 2004, a year in which fundamentally oriented managers have seemingly gained an edge over rivals. For its part, this fund is up more than 18% for the year to date through Dec. 13, 2004, and leads 92% of its peers thanks to a broad mix of winners. In particular, the fund earns kudos for buying homebuilders when everyone else was abandoning them earlier in the year and for some good picks in the health-care area, where it keeps a fifth of its assets. That group's strong performance all but offsets any negative impact the fund could have felt from having absolutely no exposure to the energy sector, an area that Wasatch as a firm has never been too enthused about.

Still, as exciting as such short-term performance can be, what ultimately defines this fund is its ability to deliver over the long haul. We think it will keep doing just that, even if it doesn't always look this good.

Portfolio Analysis 06-30-04

Share change since 03-04 Total Stocks:82	Sector	PE	YTD Ret%	% Assets
⊖ Rent-A-Center	Consumer	13.7	-11.67	4.64
⊖ O'Reilly Automotive	Consumer	21.6	16.83	4.45
⊖ Copart	Business	24.9	58.55	3.97
⊕ Fidelity National Financ	Financial	10.2	32.24	3.90
⊕ AmeriCredit	Financial	14.3	53.48	3.59
⊖ SCP Pool	Goods	20.1	47.47	2.56
⊖ Amerigroup	Financial	24.7	77.40	2.35
⊕ Doral Financial	Financial	13.3	55.06	2.21
⊕ Dollar Tree Stores	Consumer	17.3	-4.32	2.04
⊖ Apria HealthCare Group	Health	13.9	15.74	1.95
MDC Holdings	Consumer	9.4	48.72	1.90
⊖ Commerce Bancorp NJ	Financial	19.8	23.89	1.88
⊕ Anworth Mortgage Asset	Financial	7.8	-14.09	1.79
Accredo Health	Health	18.3	-12.31	1.75
⊕ Waste Connections	Business	20.4	36.02	1.71
DR Horton	Consumer	10.7	41.36	1.71
⊖ Group 1 Automotive	Consumer	19.1	-12.96	1.63
⊕ Friedman Billings Ramsey	Financial	9.0	-9.64	1.62
Michael's Stores	Consumer	22.9	36.87	1.60
NVR	Consumer	12.2	65.11	1.55

Current Investment Style

Value Blnd Growth — Large Mid Small

Market Cap	%
Giant	0.0
Large	0.9
Mid	66.6
Small	30.7
Micro	1.8
Avg $mil: 1,912	

Value Measures		Rel Category
Price/Earnings	13.15	0.61
Price/Book	2.06	0.78
Price/Sales	1.04	0.69
Price/Cash Flow	7.26	0.91
Dividend Yield %	1.94	6.26

Growth Measures	%	Rel Category
Long-Term Erngs	13.62	0.79
Book Value	15.71	2.44
Sales	13.07	2.02
Cash Flow	17.59	1.30
Historical Erngs	13.48	1.37

Profitability	%	Rel Category
Return on Equity	13.06	1.83
Return on Assets	3.66	1.97
Net Margin	13.14	1.92

Sector Weightings	% of Stocks	Rel S&P 500	3 Year High	3 Year Low
Info	7.51	0.35		
Software	0.00	0.00	2	0
Hardware	6.42	0.63	8	1
Media	0.00	0.00	0	0
Telecom	1.09	0.35	1	0
Service	88.19	1.90		
Health	19.76	1.58	28	20
Consumer	22.91	2.52	31	23
Business	10.61	2.62	12	7
Financial	34.91	1.68	36	20
Mfg	4.30	0.13		
Goods	2.84	0.30	4	2
Ind Mtrls	1.46	0.12	1	0
Energy	0.00	0.00	0	0
Utilities	0.00	0.00	0	0

Composition

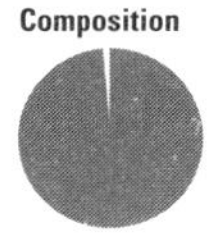

Cash	0.5
Stocks	98.6
Bonds	0.0
Other	0.8
Foreign (% of Stock)	3.0

Address:	Wasatch Funds Milwaukee,WI 53201-2172 800-551-1700
Web Address:	www.wasatchfunds.com
Inception:	11-28-86
Advisor:	Wasatch Advisors Inc.
Subadvisor:	None
NTF Plans:	Bidwell & Co. NTF, CommonWealth NTF

Minimum Purchase:	Closed	Add: —	IRA: —
Min Auto Inv Plan:	Closed	Add: —	
Sales Fees:	No-load, 2.00%R		
Management Fee:	1.00%, 0.28%A		
Actual Fees:	Mgt:1.00%	Dist:	
Expense Projections:	3Yr:$397	5Yr:$686	10Yr:$1511
Income Distrib:	Annually		

Wasatch Heritage Growth

Analyst Pick

Ticker	Load	NAV	Yield	Total Assets	Mstar Category
WAHGX	None	$11.14	0.0%	$202 mil	Mid-Cap Growth

Governance and Management

Fiduciary Grade:

Portfolio Manager(s)

This is the first time that Chris Bowen and Ryan Snow are managing a public portfolio. The former joined Wasatch in 2001, while the latter has an additional year at the firm under his belt. Most recently, Bowen has been a member of the team supporting Wasatch Core Growth, while Snow has been part of the crew at Wasatch Small Cap Growth.

Strategy

This fund plans to invest in companies that are between $3 billion and $20 billion in size. Managers Chris Bowen and Ryan Snow use the same fundamentally driven growth process that's popular at Wasatch. Although the managers occasionally buy high-priced stocks, investors can expect a more moderate growth approach here. Also, investors should expect the fund to own stocks that have grown too large for Wasatch's small-cap portfolios.

Historical Profile

Return
Risk
Rating Not Rated

Investment Style: Equity, Stock % 87%

▼ Manager Change
▽ Partial Manager Change

Growth of $10,000
— Investment Values of Fund
— Investment Values of S&P 500

Performance Quartile (within Category)

1993	1994	1995	1996	1997	1998	1999	2000	2001	2002	2003	12-04	History
—	—	—	—	—	—	—	—	—	—	—	11.14	NAV
—	—	—	—	—	—	—	—	—	—	—	—	Total Return %
—	—	—	—	—	—	—	—	—	—	—	—	+/-S&P 500
—	—	—	—	—	—	—	—	—	—	—	—	+/-Russ MG
—	—	—	—	—	—	—	—	—	—	—	—	Income Return %
—	—	—	—	—	—	—	—	—	—	—	—	Capital Return %
—	—	—	—	—	—	—	—	—	—	—	—	Total Rtn % Rank Cat
—	—	—	—	—	—	—	—	—	—	—	0.00	Income $
—	—	—	—	—	—	—	—	—	—	—	0.00	Capital Gains $
—	—	—	—	—	—	—	—	—	—	—	0.95	Expense Ratio %
—	—	—	—	—	—	—	—	—	—	—	-0.01	Income Ratio %
—	—	—	—	—	—	—	—	—	—	—	—	Turnover Rate %
—	—	—	—	—	—	—	—	—	—	—	202	Net Assets $mil

Performance 12-31-04

	1st Qtr	2nd Qtr	3rd Qtr	4th Qtr	Total
2000	—	—	—	—	—
2001	—	—	—	—	—
2002	—	—	—	—	—
2003	—	—	—	—	—
2004	—	—	-1.70	13.01	—*

Trailing	Total Return%	+/- S&P 500	+/- Russ MG	%Rank Cat	Growth of $10,000
3 Mo	13.01	3.78	-0.93	49	11,301
6 Mo	11.09	3.90	2.08	12	11,109
1 Yr	—	—	—	—	—
3 Yr Avg	—	—	—	—	—
5 Yr Avg	—	—	—	—	—
10 Yr Avg	—	—	—	—	—
15 Yr Avg	—	—	—	—	—

Tax Analysis	Tax-Adj Rtn%	%Rank Cat	Tax-Cost Rat	%Rank Cat
3 Yr (estimated)	—	—	—	—
5 Yr (estimated)	—	—	—	—
10 Yr (estimated)	—	—	—	—

Potential Capital Gain Exposure: 10% of assets

Rating and Risk

Time Period	Load-Adj Return %	Morningstar Rtn vs Cat	Morningstar Risk vs Cat	Morningstar Risk-Adj Rating
1 Yr	—			
3 Yr	—	—	—	—
5 Yr	—	—	—	—
10 Yr	—	—	—	—
Incept	11.43			

Other Measures	Standard Index S&P 500	Best Fit Index
Alpha	—	—
Beta	—	—
R-Squared	—	—
Standard Deviation	—	
Mean	—	
Sharpe Ratio	—	

Portfolio Analysis 06-30-04

Share change since 00-00 Total Stocks:65	Sector	PE	YTD Ret%	% Assets
Willis Group Holdings	Business	16.3	23.24	3.38
National Semiconductor	Hardware	17.1	-8.80	3.00
Fidelity National Financ	Financial	10.2	32.24	2.85
WellPoint Health Network	Health	—	—	2.76
NVR	Consumer	12.2	65.11	2.72
AutoZone	Consumer	13.8	7.16	2.53
Lennar	Consumer	10.7	19.45	2.37
Doral Financial	Financial	13.3	55.06	2.37
Harley-Davidson	Goods	20.5	28.70	2.36
DR Horton	Consumer	10.7	41.36	2.36
Pulte Homes	Consumer	9.8	36.77	2.36
Teva Pharmaceutical Indu	Health	—	5.89	2.30
Quest Diagnostics	Health	19.8	31.66	2.26
PacifiCare Health System	Health	21.5	67.22	2.21
TCF Financial	Financial	13.3	28.60	1.95
Bed Bath & Beyond	Consumer	27.6	-8.12	1.91
Countrywide Financial	Financial	9.0	48.15	1.87
Medtronic	Health	30.7	2.68	1.84
Dollar Tree Stores	Consumer	17.3	-4.32	1.80
Health Management Associ	Health	16.6	-4.89	1.70

Current Investment Style

Market Cap	%
Giant	5.0
Large	30.7
Mid	64.3
Small	0.0
Micro	0.0
Avg $mil: 7,445	

Value Measures		Rel Category
Price/Earnings	14.43	0.66
Price/Book	2.69	0.90
Price/Sales	1.33	0.75
Price/Cash Flow	8.82	0.91
Dividend Yield %	0.62	1.44

Growth Measures	%	Rel Category
Long-Term Erngs	14.55	0.92
Book Value	21.97	2.19
Sales	13.16	1.53
Cash Flow	54.66	4.48
Historical Erngs	32.27	2.03

Profitability	%	Rel Category
Return on Equity	24.16	1.68
Return on Assets	11.10	1.55
Net Margin	14.81	1.54

Sector Weightings	% of Stocks	Rel S&P 500	3 Year High	Low
Info	13.99	0.65		
Software	1.43	0.33	—	—
Hardware	9.17	0.90	—	—
Media	0.00	0.00	—	—
Telecom	3.39	1.08	—	—
Service	82.14	1.77		
Health	21.32	1.71	—	—
Consumer	29.46	3.24	—	—
Business	10.25	2.53	—	—
Financial	21.11	1.02	—	—
Mfg	3.88	0.12		
Goods	3.88	0.42	—	—
Ind Mtrls	0.00	0.00	—	—
Energy	0.00	0.00	—	—
Utilities	0.00	0.00	—	—

Composition

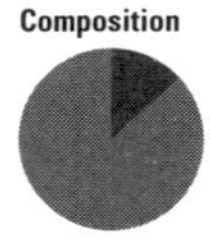

Cash	13.1
Stocks	86.8
Bonds	0.1
Other	0.0
Foreign (% of Stock)	8.9

Morningstar's Take by Kunal Kapoor 11-09-04

It's still very young, but Wasatch Heritage Growth is showing signs of what it may be capable of.

With almost five months under its belt, it's easier to assess this portfolio than it was a few months ago. With hefty stakes in the consumer services and health-care areas--perennial Wasatch favorites--this portfolio boasts below-average valuation metrics relative to the mid-cap growth category but more impressive growth characteristics. And a glance at the fund's makeup reveals a mix of approximately 65% mid-caps and 35% large caps, which together amount to an average market capitalization of approximately $7.4 billion, which is above the group norm of $4.8 billion.

This makeup suggests that investors are getting what they signed up for: A moderate growth portfolio that leans to mid-caps but that isn't shy about reaching up the cap ladder. As it relates to the former, it's likely that the fund will be more contrarian than many of its peers. For instance, at the time of its launch this summer, comanager Ryan Snow argued that investors were unfairly discounting the future growth prospects of homebuilders by focusing on the damage that rising interest rates may do to their businesses. The fund thus initiated positions in a handful of homebuilders during their summer swoon and has since benefited from their rebound. More recently, Snow says the fund has been attracted to a handful of semiconductor stocks such as Maxim Integrated Products and National Semiconductor, which have been somewhat beaten down.

This measured approach is likely to moderate some of the risks associated with investing in this part of the market. And despite the managers' relative inexperience, we're comfortable with the offering because they are backed by a quality research organization. While it's too soon to evaluate performance, our comfort with the strategy and organization give us the confidence to recommend this for long-term investors.

Address:	Wasatch Funds, Milwaukee,WI 53201-2172, 800-551-1700
Web Address:	www.wasatchfunds.com
Inception:	06-18-04
Advisor:	Wasatch Advisors Inc.
Subadvisor:	None
NTF Plans:	Fidelity Retail-NTF, Schwab OneSource

Minimum Purchase:	$2000	Add: $100	IRA: $1000
Min Auto Inv Plan:	$1000	Add: $50	
Sales Fees:	No-load, 2.00%R		
Management Fee:	0.70%		
Actual Fees:	Mgt:0.70%	Dist:	
Expense Projections:	3Yr:$283	5Yr: —	10Yr: —
Income Distrib:	Annually		

Wasatch Micro Cap

Ticker	Load	NAV	Yield	Total Assets	Mstar Category
WMICX	Closed	$6 93	0.0%	$574 mil	Small Growth

Governance and Management

Fiduciary Grade: B

Portfolio Manager(s)

Robert Gardiner has managed this offering since its inception in mid-1995. He was an analyst at Wasatch before the fund was launched and has been employed at the firm for more than 20 years. Dan Chace supports him as comanager. Though a few dedicated analysts form this fund's "team," all Wasatch funds pull from the same larger pool of analysts. The shop is close-knit and has never suffered a portfolio manager departure.

Strategy

Manager Robert Gardiner only considers firms with market capitalizations of less than $1 billion--up from $750 million before September 2003--for inclusion in this portfolio. He blends some of the market's fastest-growing firms with more-steadily growing names. These slower-growth names, which are usually growing earnings by at least 15%, have made this offering less volatile than its typical peer.

Historical Profile

Return High
Risk Average
Rating ★★★★★ Highest

Investment Style: Equity Stock %

1995	1996	1997	1998	1999	2000	2001	2002	2003	12-04
	99%	89%	89%	87%	80%	96%	92%	97%	

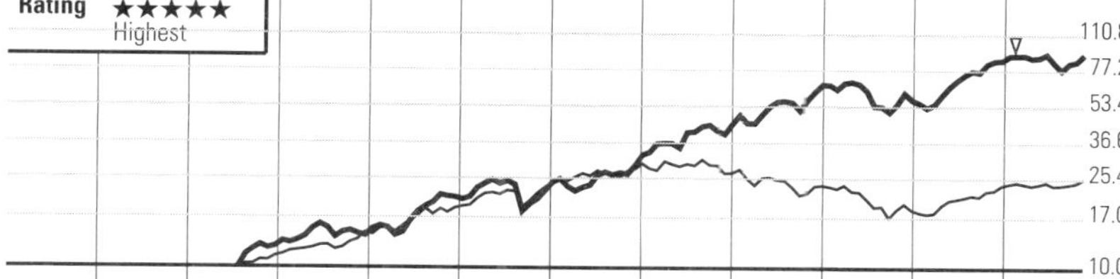

Performance Quartile (within Category)

History

1993	1994	1995	1996	1997	1998	1999	2000	2001	2002	2003	12-04	History
—	—	2.83	3.03	3.76	3.99	4.79	4.90	6.61	5.26	7.24	6.93	NAV
—	—	41.50*	13.66	35.32	18.98	32.86	37.53	49.99	-14.17	49.84	12.70	Total Return %
—	—	—	-9.28	1.97	-9.59	11.82	46.63	61.87	7.92	21.17	1.83	+/-S&P 500
—	—	—	2.40	22.37	17.75	-10.23	59.96	59.22	16.09	1.30	-1.61	+/-Russ 2000 Gr
—	—	0.00	0.00	0.00	0.00	0.00	0.00	0.00	0.00	0.00	0.00	Income Return %
—	—	—	13.66	35.32	18.98	32.86	37.53	49.99	-14.17	49.84	12.70	Capital Return %
—	—	—	73	6	14	68	1	1	3	23	50	Total Rtn % Rank Cat
—	—	0.00	0.00	0.00	0.00	0.00	0.00	0.00	0.00	0.00	0.00	Income $
—	—	0.00	0.18	0.33	0.36	0.42	1.55	0.60	0.34	0.59	1.06	Capital Gains $
—	—	2.50	2.50	2.50	2.50	2.46	2.38	2.32	2.28	2.24	2.19	Expense Ratio %
—	—	-0.76	-1.53	-1.64	-2.28	-2.22	-1.76	-1.76	-2.21	-2.13	-1.95	Income Ratio %
—	—	—	84	99	81	57	69	58	62	50	56	Turnover Rate %
—	—	46	82	121	154	168	243	473	368	562	574	Net Assets $mil

Performance 12-31-04

	1st Qtr	2nd Qtr	3rd Qtr	4th Qtr	Total
2000	12.94	11.83	7.93	0.88	37.53
2001	0.82	25.10	-8.58	30.08	49.99
2002	1.82	-7.73	-19.32	13.25	-14.17
2003	-4.37	27.44	8.89	12.92	49.84
2004	5.25	1.44	-8.80	15.73	12.70

Trailing	Total Return%	+/- S&P 500	+/- Russ 2000 Gr	%Rank Cat	Growth of $10,000
3 Mo	15.73	6.50	0.65	19	11,573
6 Mo	5.55	-1.64	-2.61	73	10,555
1 Yr	12.70	1.83	-1.61	50	11,270
3 Yr Avg	13.17	9.59	7.38	7	14,494
5 Yr Avg	24.49	26.79	28.06	1	29,900
10 Yr Avg	—	—	—	—	—
15 Yr Avg	—	—	—	—	—

Tax Analysis	Tax-Adj Rtn%	%Rank Cat	Tax-Cost Rat	%Rank Cat
3 Yr (estimated)	11.22	9	1.72	87
5 Yr (estimated)	21.08	1	2.74	92
10 Yr (estimated)	—	—	—	—

Potential Capital Gain Exposure: 30% of assets

Rating and Risk

Time Period	Load-Adj Return %	Morningstar Rtn vs Cat	Morningstar Risk vs Cat	Morningstar Risk-Adj Rating
1 Yr	12.70			
3 Yr	13.17	High	+Avg	★★★★
5 Yr	24.49	High	-Avg	★★★★★
10 Yr	—	—	—	—
Incept	27.69			

Other Measures	Standard Index S&P 500	Best Fit Index Russ 2000 Gr
Alpha	9.9	7.4
Beta	1.13	0.91
R-Squared	66	90

Standard Deviation	23.80
Mean	13.17
Sharpe Ratio	0.50

Portfolio Analysis 06-30-04

Share change since 03-04 Total Stocks:130	Sector	PE	YTD Ret%	% Assets
Amsurg	Health	14.6	16.76	3.58
O2Micro International	Hardware	28.6	-49.18	3.20
⊖ Big 5 Sporting Goods	Consumer	19.1	39.45	3.19
⊖ ICU Medical	Health	25.5	-20.27	2.34
⊖ PLX Technology	Hardware	—	17.51	2.35
ICON PLC ADR	Health	18.8	-11.95	1.99
⊖ O'Reilly Automotive	Consumer	21.6	16.83	1.98
⊕ AMN Healthcare Services	Health	25.5	-7.28	1.94
Guitar Center	Consumer	26.0	61.43	1.82
Cabot Microelectronics	Hardware	20.5	-18.22	1.80
Charles River Associates	Business	31.9	46.20	1.71
Home Capital Grp	Financial	—	—	1.65
⊖ Odyssey HealthCare	Health	10.5	-53.56	1.64
Bijou Brigitte Modische	Goods	—	—	1.55
⊖ Corvel	Financial	19.7	-29.15	1.47
⊕ Advanced Power Technolog	Hardware	—	-10.42	1.39
⊖ Excel Technology	Health	21.2	-20.88	1.38
⊕ Possis Medical	Health	20.2	-31.75	1.33
⊖ Resources Connection	Business	38.5	98.87	1.30
⊕ SM&A	Business	17.5	-27.09	1.30

Current Investment Style

Value Blnd Growth; Large Mid Small

Market Cap	%
Giant	0.0
Large	0.0
Mid	5.2
Small	50.3
Micro	44.5
Avg $mil: 396	

Value Measures		Rel Category
Price/Earnings	20.96	0.97
Price/Book	2.49	0.95
Price/Sales	1.44	0.96
Price/Cash Flow	8.61	1.07
Dividend Yield %	0.20	0.65

Growth Measures	%	Rel Category
Long-Term Erngs	17.66	1.02
Book Value	9.88	1.53
Sales	11.81	1.83
Cash Flow	6.30	0.47
Historical Erngs	16.45	1.22

Profitability	%	Rel Category
Return on Equity	14.35	1.45
Return on Assets	7.47	1.70
Net Margin	7.62	1.11

Sector Weightings	% of Stocks	Rel S&P 500	3 Year High	3 Year Low
Info	22.83	1.06		
Software	2.70	0.63	6	3
Hardware	20.13	1.97	24	17
Media	0.00	0.00	0	0
Telecom	0.00	0.00	0	0
Service	65.36	1.41		
Health	32.11	2.57	35	30
Consumer	13.26	1.46	14	9
Business	8.40	2.07	17	8
Financial	11.59	0.56	13	6
Mfg	11.81	0.37		
Goods	3.78	0.41	5	3
Ind Mtrls	7.40	0.58	7	2
Energy	0.63	0.09	1	-
Utilities	0.00	0.00	0	0

Composition

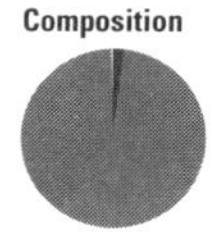

Cash	1.8
Stocks	97.4
Bonds	0.0
Other	0.8
Foreign (% of Stock)	14.9

Morningstar's Take by Jeffrey Ptak 12-20-04

Don't count out the excellent Wasatch Micro Cap.

The fund is in an unfamiliar position in 2004: below the majority of its small-growth competition. Indeed, while its 9.3% return for the year through Dec. 17 is fine in absolute terms, it trails the group norm.

The shortfall goes hand-in-glove with management's stock-picking style. Robert Gardiner and Dan Chace don't fuss over benchmark weightings, opting instead to put their chips down wherever opportunities may be. That's typically translated to above-average tech, healthcare, and consumer-related stakes, as such areas tend to teem with the mix of above-average growth and sane valuations that management craves. By contrast, since they're most enamored with firms dominant in niches propelled by secular forces rather than cyclical ones, they've tended to tread lightly in the financials and basic-materials realms. That profile has been a liability this year, as tech has lagged while areas more economically and commodity-sensitive have thrived.

That said, we aren't concerned about the underperformance. Management's approach hasn't changed an iota: It continues to hunt for firms, like ambulatory surgery center AmSurg, that churn out high returns on equity. And while the fund was stung by its chip-related tech holdings in the third-quarter when managers misjudged the momentum in capital spending, they're sticking to their guns, pointing to the proprietary nature of such firms' underlying business, which they believe will continue to confer plush margins.

Such conviction doesn't come cheap, as this fund's high expense ratio attests. But investors can take solace in the fact that Wasatch has invested heavily in the research process underpinning the approach here. Moreover, the firm has repeatedly shown the ability to ferret out obscure gems. We think that acumen, coupled with management's prudent approach and the fund's modest size (it remains closed), continue to recommend it.

Address:	Wasatch Funds Milwaukee,WI 53201-2172 800-551-1700
Web Address:	www.wasatchfunds.com
Inception:	06-19-95*
Advisor:	Wasatch Advisors Inc.
Subadvisor:	None
NTF Plans:	Bidwell & Co. NTF, CommonWealth NTF

Minimum Purchase:	Closed	Add: —	IRA: —
Min Auto Inv Plan:	Closed	Add: —	
Sales Fees:	No-load, 2.00%R		
Management Fee:	2.00%, 0.23%A		
Actual Fees:	Mgt:2.00%	Dist:	
Expense Projections:	3Yr:$700	5Yr:$1200	10Yr:$2575
Income Distrib:	Annually		

Wasatch Small Cap Growth

Ticker	Load	NAV	Yield	Total Assets	Mstar Category
WAAEX	Closed	$39.46	0.0%	$1,357 mil	Small Growth

Governance and Management

Fiduciary Grade: A

Portfolio Manager(s)

Jeff Cardon joined Wasatch as an analyst in 1980 and has been managing this offering since late 1986. All Wasatch funds share the same pool of analysts, and the firm's 10 portfolio managers often hold the same names across several funds. The firm is known for its close-knit management team and superb research, and it has never suffered a portfolio manager departure.

Strategy

Manager Jeff Cardon looks to buy firms with market caps of less than $1.5 billion that are growing their earnings by at least 20%. He does buy companies with growth rates that are significantly higher than 20%, but he blends them with steadier growers to keep a lid on volatility. He occasionally lets his winners run, which means the portfolio is sometimes home to mid- and large-cap names.

Historical Profile

Return Above Avg
Risk Average
Rating ★★★★ Above Avg

Investment Style: Equity Stock %

97%	99%	94%	95%	91%	80%	87%	94%	97%

▼ Manager Change
▽ Partial Manager Change

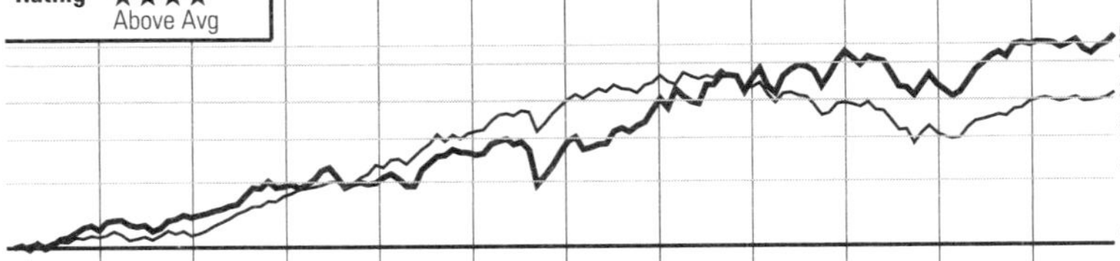

Growth of $10,000
— Investment Values of Fund
— Investment Values of S&P 500

Performance Quartile (within Category)

History

	1993	1994	1995	1996	1997	1998	1999	2000	2001	2002	2003	12-04
NAV	19.50	19.06	23.87	23.86	24.60	22.97	29.00	27.82	33.99	26.04	35.61	39.46
Total Return %	22.49	5.50	28.12	5.20	19.23	11.17	40.87	16.80	24.17	-23.39	37.43	13.36
+/-S&P 500	12.43	4.19	-9.41	-17.74	-14.12	-17.40	19.83	25.90	36.05	-1.30	8.76	2.49
+/-Russ 2000 Gr	9.12	7.93	-2.92	-6.06	6.28	9.94	-2.22	39.23	33.40	6.87	-11.11	-0.95
Income Return %	0.00	0.00	0.00	0.00	0.00	0.00	0.00	0.00	0.00	0.00	0.00	0.00
Capital Return %	22.49	5.50	28.12	5.20	19.23	11.17	40.87	16.80	24.17	-23.39	37.43	13.36
Total Rtn % Rank Cat	29	16	71	93	45	25	61	9	3	30	79	45
Income $	0.00	0.00	0.00	0.00	0.00	0.00	0.00	0.00	0.00	0.00	0.00	0.00
Capital Gains $	1.22	1.51	0.54	1.22	3.69	3.07	2.71	5.85	0.45	0.00	0.17	0.77
Expense Ratio %	1.50	1.50	1.47	1.50	1.50	1.48	1.44	1.38	1.36	1.31	1.25	1.20
Income Ratio %	-0.77	-0.67	-0.37	-0.65	-0.39	-0.60	-0.79	-0.84	-0.83	-1.25	-1.08	-0.91
Turnover Rate %	70	64	29	73	48	56	46	72	40	51	63	41
Net Assets $mil	29	56	294	219	172	157	182	240	934	786	1,258	1,357

Performance 12-31-04

	1st Qtr	2nd Qtr	3rd Qtr	4th Qtr	Total
2000	1.52	9.75	7.95	-2.89	16.80
2001	-10.89	24.93	-15.47	31.95	24.17
2002	-4.03	-12.63	-16.42	9.32	-23.39
2003	-5.88	25.79	5.19	10.35	37.43
2004	1.40	2.27	-5.39	15.53	13.36

Trailing	Total Return%	+/- S&P 500	+/- Russ 2000 Gr	%Rank Cat	Growth of $10,000
3 Mo	15.53	6.30	0.45	20	11,553
6 Mo	9.30	2.11	1.14	36	10,930
1 Yr	13.36	2.49	-0.95	45	11,336
3 Yr Avg	6.07	2.49	0.28	42	11,934
5 Yr Avg	11.60	13.90	15.17	7	17,311
10 Yr Avg	15.85	3.78	8.73	8	43,547
15 Yr Avg	16.25	5.32	8.75	4	95,696

Tax Analysis	Tax-Adj Rtn%	%Rank Cat	Tax-Cost Rat	%Rank Cat
3 Yr (estimated)	5.93	40	0.13	13
5 Yr (estimated)	10.59	6	0.91	39
10 Yr (estimated)	13.97	7	1.62	48

Potential Capital Gain Exposure: 31% of assets

Rating and Risk

Time Period	Load-Adj Return %	Morningstar Rtn vs Cat	Morningstar Risk vs Cat	Morningstar Risk-Adj Rating
1 Yr	13.36			
3 Yr	6.07	Avg	Avg	★★★
5 Yr	11.60	+Avg	Avg	★★★★
10 Yr	15.85	+Avg	Avg	★★★★
Incept	14.66			

Other Measures	Standard Index S&P 500	Best Fit Index Mstar Small Growth
Alpha	2.8	3.0
Beta	1.15	0.77
R-Squared	74	90

Standard Deviation	21.59
Mean	6.07
Sharpe Ratio	0.22

Portfolio Analysis 06-30-04

Share change since 03-04 Total Stocks:96	Sector	PE	YTD Ret%	% Assets
O'Reilly Automotive	Consumer	21.6	16.83	5.61
⊖ Amsurg	Health	14.6	16.76	2.99
⊕ Knight Transportation	Business	29.7	45.15	2.93
Techne	Health	28.3	2.80	2.92
⊕ Copart	Business	24.9	58.55	2.22
Amerigroup	Financial	24.7	77.40	2.06
⊖ Yankee Candle Company	Ind Mtrls	20.9	21.41	2.01
⊕ American Healthways	Health	41.8	38.42	1.96
⊕ Micrel	Hardware	28.3	-29.18	1.95
Nextel Partners A	Telecom	—	45.28	1.90
⊕ Cabot Microelectronics	Hardware	20.5	-18.22	1.89
⊕ Integrated Circuit Syste	Hardware	20.5	-26.60	1.87
O2Micro International	Hardware	28.6	-49.18	1.76
ICON PLC ADR	Health	18.8	-11.95	1.64
⊕ NVR	Consumer	12.2	65.11	1.63
⊖ Accredo Health	Health	18.3	-12.31	1.60
Chico's FAS	Consumer	33.3	23.22	1.60
⊖ Resources Connection	Business	38.5	98.87	1.60
Brown & Brown	Financial	24.9	34.53	1.54
⊖ Inveresk Research Group	Health	—	—	1.53

Current Investment Style

Value Blnd Growth / Large Mid Small

Market Cap	%
Giant	0.0
Large	0.7
Mid	39.0
Small	54.2
Micro	6.1
Avg $mil: 1,238	

Value Measures		Rel Category
Price/Earnings	21.50	0.99
Price/Book	3.05	1.16
Price/Sales	1.98	1.32
Price/Cash Flow	11.93	1.49
Dividend Yield %	0.24	0.77

Growth Measures	%	Rel Category
Long-Term Erngs	17.40	1.01
Book Value	19.39	3.01
Sales	20.79	3.22
Cash Flow	24.68	1.82
Historical Erngs	23.57	1.74

Profitability	%	Rel Category
Return on Equity	16.24	1.65
Return on Assets	9.07	2.07
Net Margin	10.76	1.57

Sector Weightings	% of Stocks	Rel S&P 500	3 Year High	3 Year Low
Info	19.50	0.91		
Software	2.84	0.66	6	3
Hardware	14.19	1.39	19	11
Media	0.41	0.11	2	0
Telecom	2.06	0.65	2	1
Service	75.29	1.62		
Health	28.71	2.30	38	29
Consumer	18.21	2.01	23	18
Business	17.58	4.34	19	15
Financial	10.79	0.52	11	2
Mfg	5.22	0.16		
Goods	1.55	0.17	2	0
Ind Mtrls	3.67	0.29	4	0
Energy	0.00	0.00	0	0
Utilities	0.00	0.00	0	0

Composition

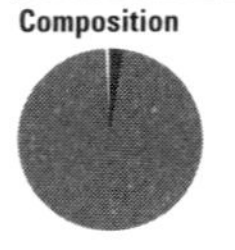

Cash	2.3
Stocks	96.8
Bonds	0.4
Other	0.5
Foreign (% of Stock)	6.2

Morningstar's Take by Kunal Kapoor 12-13-04

We like the way that Wasatch Small Cap Growth comes together.

To hear manager Jeff Cardon tell it, 2004 has been somewhat disappointing. Although the fund is up a more-than-respectable 9.48% for the year to date through Dec. 10 and leads more than half its small-growth rivals, Cardon feels the fund could have done better. That's because he says its investment style is suited to choppy and sideways markets such as the one we've been experiencing.

Still, it's worth noting that within the small-growth category, the level of risk a fund is willing to embrace has tended to dictate performance in 2004. Funds with lower risk thresholds have typically done best thanks to investments in areas such as energy, and funds with the largest appetite for risk have generally faltered because of commitments to lagging tech stocks. This fund falls somewhere in the middle of that spectrum and so does its performance. In fact, even among Wasatch's three small-growth offerings, the best performing is the most moderate of the bunch, Wasatch Core Growth, and the worst performing is the most aggressive, Wasatch Ultra Growth.

We continue to believe that shareholders in this fund own a very capable offering. While Cardon's predilection for sectors such as technology and health care--and lack of interest in areas such as energy--means that the fund will have some ups and downs, his ability to weave in fast-growing financials and consumer- and business-services stocks into the portfolio adds balance. Currently, for instance, while Cardon has upped the fund's stake in electronic technology stocks, he's also been putting money in picks such as Guitar Center, whose competitive position strengthened after its largest rival went bankrupt.

This balance sets the table for long-term outperformance, which we believe the fund will continue to deliver.

Address:	Wasatch Funds Milwaukee,WI 53201-2172 800-551-1700
Web Address:	www.wasatchfunds.com
Inception:	12-08-86
Advisor:	Wasatch Advisors Inc.
Subadvisor:	None
NTF Plans:	Bidwell & Co. NTF, CommonWealth NTF

Minimum Purchase:	Closed	Add: —	IRA: —
Min Auto Inv Plan:	Closed	Add: —	
Sales Fees:	No-load, 2.00%R		
Management Fee:	1.00%, 0.28%A		
Actual Fees:	Mgt:1.00%	Dist:	
Expense Projections:	3Yr:$397	5Yr:$686	10Yr:$1511
Income Distrib:	Annually		

Wasatch Small Cap Value

Ticker	Load	NAV	Yield	Total Assets	Mstar Category
WMCVX	Closed	$5.53	0.0%	$820 mil	Small Blend

Governance and Management

Fiduciary Grade: B

Portfolio Manager(s)

Jim Larkins and John Mazanec are responsible for the fund's day-to-day management. Larkins and Mazanec had worked as analysts before assuming their current positions. All Wasatch funds pull from the same pool of analysts, and the shop--which has never suffered a portfolio manager departure--is known for its close-knit, team-based management approach.

Strategy

Management won't buy firms with market caps greater than $2.5 billion (recently upped from $1.5 billion), but it has historically kept the portfolio's median market cap much smaller, typically less than $500 million. The managers look for either growth stocks that have stumbled or relatively undiscovered names that are selling at a discount to management's estimate of their growth rates.

Historical Profile

Return High
Risk Above Avg
Rating ★★★★★ Highest

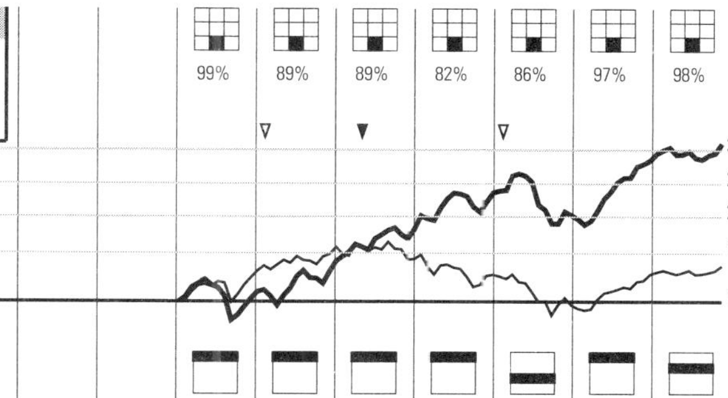

1993	1994	1995	1996	1997	1998	1999	2000	2001	2002	2003	12-04	History
—	—	—	—	2.01	2.18	2.69	3.15	4.10	3.43	5.30	5.53	NAV
—	—	—	—	0.50*	8.46	28.09	29.04	33.63	-16.34	54.57	21.58	Total Return %
—	—	—	—	—	-20.11	7.05	38.14	45.51	5.75	25.90	10.71	+/-S&P 500
—	—	—	—	—	11.01	6.83	32.06	31.14	4.14	7.32	3.25	+/-Russ 2000
—	—	—	—	—	0.00	0.00	0.00	0.00	0.00	0.00	0.00	Income Return %
—	—	—	—	—	8.46	28.09	29.04	33.63	-16.34	54.57	21.58	Capital Return %
—	—	—	—	—	5	20	11	2	60	10	27	Total Rtn % Rank Cat
—	—	—	—	0.00	0.00	0.00	0.00	0.00	0.00	0.00	0.00	Income $
—	—	—	—	0.00	0.00	0.09	0.31	0.10	0.00	0.00	0.78	Capital Gains $
—	—	—	—	—	1.95	1.95	1.95	1.92	1.81	1.78	1.73	Expense Ratio %
—	—	—	—	—	-1.02	-1.54	-1.02	-0.31	-0.44	-0.43	-0.26	Income Ratio %
—	—	—	—	—	114	106	67	41	69	69	56	Turnover Rate %
—	—	—	—	2	17	21	63	558	475	741	820	Net Assets $mil

Performance 12-31-04

	1st Qtr	2nd Qtr	3rd Qtr	4th Qtr	Total
2000	14.50	4.55	9.01	-1.11	29.04
2001	7.30	24.26	-10.48	11.95	33.63
2002	14.39	-4.90	-28.03	6.85	-16.34
2003	-4.37	25.91	11.86	14.75	54.57
2004	10.75	-2.90	-2.98	16.52	21.58

Trailing	Total Return%	+/- S&P 500	+/- Russ 2000	%Rank Cat	Growth of $10,000
3 Mo	16.52	7.29	2.43	6	11,652
6 Mo	13.05	5.86	2.22	18	11,305
1 Yr	21.58	10.71	3.25	27	12,158
3 Yr Avg	16.28	12.70	4.80	17	15,722
5 Yr Avg	22.07	24.37	15.46	2	27,105
10 Yr Avg	—	—	—	—	—
15 Yr Avg	—	—	—	—	—

Tax Analysis	Tax-Adj Rtn%	%Rank Cat	Tax-Cost Rat	%Rank Cat
3 Yr (estimated)	15.17	15	0.95	65
5 Yr (estimated)	20.62	2	1.19	58
10 Yr (estimated)	—	—	—	—

Potential Capital Gain Exposure: 28% of assets

Rating and Risk

Time Period	Load-Adj Return %	Morningstar Rtn vs Cat	Morningstar Risk vs Cat	Morningstar Risk-Adj Rating
1 Yr	21.58			
3 Yr	16.28	+Avg	High	★★★★
5 Yr	22.07	High	+Avg	★★★★★
10 Yr	—	—	—	—
Incept	20.82			

Other Measures	Standard Index S&P 500	Best Fit Index Russ 2000 VL
Alpha	13.2	-1.2
Beta	1.06	1.10
R-Squared	60	90

Standard Deviation	24.08
Mean	16.28
Sharpe Ratio	0.63

Portfolio Analysis 06-30-04

Share change since 03-04 Total Stocks:108	Sector	PE	YTD Ret%	% Assets
⊖ Mobile Mini	Ind Mtrls	35.5	67.55	2.98
⊕ Global Imaging Systems	Ind Mtrls	17.0	24.41	2.76
⊕ NBTY	Health	14.9	-10.61	2.62
⊕ Saxon Capital	Financial	—	—	2.58
⊕ AmeriCredit	Financial	14.3	53.48	2.47
⊕ Redwood Trust	Financial	4.8	40.90	2.25
⊕ Lithia Motors A	Consumer	11.4	7.69	1.99
⊕ Aftermarket Technology	Ind Mtrls	—	17.35	1.91
Newcastle Investment	Financial	12.4	26.67	1.91
⊖ Keystone Automotive Indu	Ind Mtrls	19.2	-8.39	1.86
⊕ Direct General	Financial	—	-2.53	1.82
⊖ HUB International Ltd	Financial	17.8	11.06	1.82
⊕ Commercial Capital Banco	Financial	22.4	44.94	1.76
⊕ Rent-A-Center	Consumer	13.7	-11.67	1.67
⊕ Friedman Billings Ramsey	Financial	9.0	-9.64	1.55
Fidelity National Financ	Financial	10.2	32.24	1.51
⊕ Doral Financial	Financial	13.3	55.06	1.40
AMN Healthcare Services	Health	25.5	-7.28	1.36
⊕ Supertex	Hardware	53.5	12.73	1.35
⊕ NVR	Consumer	12.2	65.11	1.33

Current Investment Style

Value Blnd Growth — Large Mid Small

Market Cap	%
Giant	0.0
Large	0.4
Mid	22.7
Small	42.9
Micro	34.0
Avg $mil: 634	

Value Measures		Rel Category
Price/Earnings	13.25	0.77
Price/Book	1.71	0.86
Price/Sales	0.72	0.76
Price/Cash Flow	5.70	0.97
Dividend Yield %	1.18	1.42

Growth Measures	%	Rel Category
Long-Term Erngs	12.71	0.94
Book Value	10.79	1.91
Sales	9.59	2.23
Cash Flow	11.25	2.28
Historical Erngs	9.61	1.29

Profitability	%	Rel Category
Return on Equity	15.22	1.46
Return on Assets	7.90	1.59
Net Margin	9.18	1.26

Sector Weightings	% of Stocks	Rel S&P 500	3 Year High	3 Year Low
Info	5.95	0.28		
Software	0.87	0.20	1	0
Hardware	3.71	0.36	6	1
Media	0.00	0.00	0	0
Telecom	1.37	0.43	2	0
Service	73.62	1.59		
Health	9.45	0.76	13	5
Consumer	21.04	2.32	27	21
Business	5.98	1.48	10	6
Financial	37.15	1.79	39	23
Mfg	20.44	0.64		
Goods	3.51	0.38	16	4
Ind Mtrls	13.71	1.08	14	8
Energy	3.22	0.45	3	0
Utilities	0.00	0.00	2	0

Composition

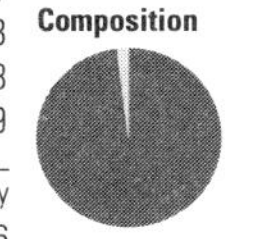

Cash	0.2
Stocks	98.0
Bonds	0.0
Other	1.8
Foreign (% of Stock)	5.1

Morningstar's Take by Jeffrey Ptak 12-05-04

Wasatch Small-Cap Value is daring to be different, and that's just fine.

Financial-services stocks have found few bigger fans than this closed fund's managers Jim Larkins and John Mazanec. In fact, the fund's recent 43% financials stake was more than twice the small-blend category norm. Management's enthusiasm doesn't appear to be widely held, however, as many small-cap managers report trimming their financials holdings amid concerns over rising interest rates.

While Larkins and Mazanec concur with the rising interest-rate thesis, they've found pockets of value. For instance, they're fans of commercial mortgage lenders, such as Newcastle Investment, which boast fat and stable dividend yields, thanks to the more predictable prepayment patterns of CMBS. Similarly, they've taken a shine to subprime REITS including Saxon Capital that boast high loan/value ratios (a measure of loan coverage). Management believes that, in addition to their plump yields, well-run subprime lenders should benefit from the improving consumer credit cycle.

Management's income focus is no accident. Larkins and Mazanec believe that demographics, such as aging baby boomers, will make stocks with histories of stable dividend payouts an even more popular refuge. This focus on secular growth drivers is a recurring part of the process here, as management typically aims for reasonably priced stocks likely to capitalize on such trends while mixing in a slug of contrarian deep-value plays.

We like the approach and management's execution, which has produced a string of strong campaigns. The fund has struggled of late due to its dearth of energy holdings and a raft of struggling retailer picks. But such missteps have proved infrequent. And while the fund is pricey, Wasatch has done a good job of closing the doors here before asset growth has gotten out of hand, thereby preserving management's ability to maneuver. All told, it's a fine choice.

Address:	Wasatch Funds Milwaukee,WI 53201-2172 800-551-1700
Web Address:	www.wasatchfunds.com
Inception:	12-17-97 *
Advisor:	Wasatch Advisors Inc.
Subadvisor:	None
NTF Plans:	Bidwell & Co. NTF, CommonWealth NTF

Minimum Purchase:	Closed	Add: —	IRA: —	
Min Auto Inv Plan:	Closed	Add: —		
Sales Fees:	No-load, 2.00%R			
Management Fee:	1.50%			
Actual Fees:	Mgt:1.50%	Dist:		
Expense Projections:	3Yr:$560	5Yr:$964	10Yr:$2095	
Income Distrib:	Annually			

Wasatch Ultra Growth

Ticker	Load	NAV	Yield	Total Assets	Mstar Category
WAMCX	Closed	$26.84	0.0%	$449 mil	Small Growth

Governance and Management

Fiduciary Grade: A

Portfolio Manager(s)

Lead manager Karey Barker has led this offering since its 1992 inception. Comanager Ajay Krishnan was an analyst on this fund before being elevated to his current position in early 2000.

Strategy

Management looks to buy firms with market capitalizations of no more than $5 billion that it thinks are capable of growing earnings by 25% or more annually. This approach has produced a portfolio that is almost entirely composed of names in the technology and health-care sectors. Management lets winners run and typically keeps about half of the fund's assets in its top 10 picks.

Historical Profile

Return Above Avg
Risk Above Avg
Rating ★★★★ Above Avg

Investment Style: Equity — Stock %: 100% 99% 85% 89% 90% 78% 84% 95% 96%

▼ Manager Change
▽ Partial Manager Change

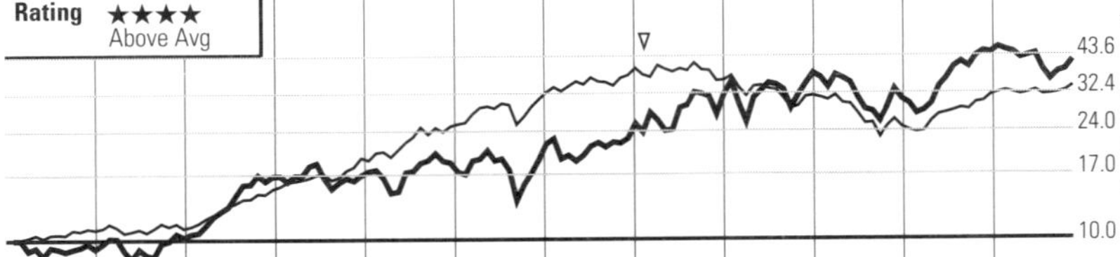

Growth of $10,000 — Investment Values of Fund; Investment Values of S&P 500 (43.6, 32.4, 24.0, 17.0, 10.0)

Performance Quartile (within Category)

1993	1994	1995	1996	1997	1998	1999	2000	2001	2002	2003	12-04	History
10.79	11.64	18.29	18.94	16.71	19.77	21.48	21.41	24.20	19.68	28.17	26.84	NAV
-2.97	8.11	58.77	3.57	-0.51	24.81	17.46	25.97	18.26	-18.68	44.52	-0.82	Total Return %
-13.03	6.80	21.24	-19.37	-33.86	-3.76	-3.58	35.07	30.14	3.41	15.85	-11.69	+/-S&P 500
-16.34	10.54	27.73	-7.69	-13.46	23.58	-25.63	48.40	27.49	11.58	-4.02	-15.13	+/-Russ 2000 Gr
0.00	0.00	0.00	0.00	0.00	0.00	0.00	0.00	0.00	0.00	0.00	0.00	Income Return %
-2.97	8.11	58.77	3.57	-0.51	24.81	17.46	25.97	18.26	-18.68	44.52	-0.82	Capital Return %
100	7	5	96	95	6	82	4	5	14	46	97	Total Rtn % Rank Cat
0.00	0.00	0.00	0.00	0.00	0.00	0.00	0.00	0.00	0.00	0.00	0.00	Income $
0.00	0.03	0.19	0.00	2.00	0.74	1.47	5.39	0.92	0.00	0.26	0.97	Capital Gains $
1.74	1.75	1.75	1.75	1.75	1.75	1.75	1.75	1.75	1.71	1.57	1.50	Expense Ratio %
-0.86	-1.19	-0.71	-1.27	-1.48	-1.54	-1.49	-1.19	-1.39	-1.67	-1.50	-1.39	Income Ratio %
113	213	46	121	103	91	77	135	123	78	76	67	Turnover Rate %
2	1	130	100	61	63	43	55	177	389	595	449	Net Assets $mil

Performance 12-31-04

	1st Qtr	2nd Qtr	3rd Qtr	4th Qtr	Total
2000	2.65	10.34	11.63	-0.38	25.97
2001	-19.85	36.42	-18.20	32.22	18.26
2002	-1.32	-16.58	-17.07	19.13	-18.68
2003	-8.74	29.29	9.52	11.84	44.52
2004	0.39	-1.41	-13.67	16.07	-0.82

Trailing	Total Return%	+/- S&P 500	+/- Russ 2000 Gr	%Rank Cat	Growth of $10,000
3 Mo	16.07	6.84	0.99	15	11,607
6 Mo	0.21	-6.98	-7.95	96	10,021
1 Yr	-0.82	-11.69	-15.13	97	9,918
3 Yr Avg	5.24	1.66	-0.55	48	11,656
5 Yr Avg	11.67	13.97	15.24	7	17,365
10 Yr Avg	15.33	3.26	8.21	10	41,632
15 Yr Avg	—	—	—	—	—

Tax Analysis	Tax-Adj Rtn%	%Rank Cat	Tax-Cost Rat	%Rank Cat
3 Yr (estimated)	4.91	45	0.31	29
5 Yr (estimated)	10.10	7	1.41	60
10 Yr (estimated)	13.76	9	1.36	37

Potential Capital Gain Exposure: 20% of assets

Rating and Risk

Time Period	Load-Adj Return %	Morningstar Rtn vs Cat	Morningstar Risk vs Cat	Morningstar Risk-Adj Rating
1 Yr	-0.82			
3 Yr	5.24	Avg	High	★★★
5 Yr	11.67	High	+Avg	★★★★
10 Yr	15.33	+Avg	+Avg	★★★★
Incept	13.63			

Other Measures	Standard Index S&P 500	Best Fit Index Mstar Small Growth
Alpha	2.5	2.4
Beta	1.33	0.94
R-Squared	63	87
Standard Deviation	27.13	
Mean	5.24	
Sharpe Ratio	0.14	

Portfolio Analysis 06-30-04

Share change since 03-04 Total Stocks:94	Sector	PE	YTD Ret%	% Assets
⊖ Accredo Health	Health	18.3	-12.31	8.78
⊕ UTStarcom	Hardware	12.7	-40.25	5.06
⊕ United Surgical Partners	Health	34.1	24.55	4.34
⊕ American Healthways	Health	41.8	38.42	3.68
⊕ O2Micro International	Hardware	28.6	-49.18	3.54
⊕ Wireless Facilities	Telecom	64.9	-36.47	3.48
⊕ Amsurg	Health	14.6	16.76	2.81
⊖ Cabot Microelectronics	Hardware	20.5	-18.22	2.37
⊕ Corinthian Colleges	Consumer	21.3	-32.10	2.25
⊖ Costar Group	Business	NMF	10.74	2.06
⊕ Cognizant Technology Sol	Business	62.5	85.50	2.05
⊖ Express Scripts	Health	22.3	15.07	2.02
⊕ O'Reilly Automotive	Consumer	21.6	16.83	1.88
⊕ Advisory Board	Business	33.4	5.89	1.68
⊕ Micrel	Hardware	28.3	-29.18	1.63
⊖ Odyssey HealthCare	Health	10.5	-53.56	1.56
⊖ Pediatrix Medical Group	Health	16.6	16.26	1.55
⊕ Dollar Tree Stores	Consumer	17.3	-4.32	1.54
⊖ AMN Healthcare Services	Health	25.5	-7.28	1.42
⊖ Centene	Financial	25.4	102.43	1.34

Current Investment Style (Value Blnd Growth; Large Mid Small)

Market Cap	%
Giant	0.0
Large	0.6
Mid	35.7
Small	47.4
Micro	16.3
Avg $mil: 1,003	

Value Measures		Rel Category
Price/Earnings	22.85	1.05
Price/Book	3.01	1.14
Price/Sales	1.70	1.13
Price/Cash Flow	10.20	1.27
Dividend Yield %	0.06	0.19

Growth Measures	%	Rel Category
Long-Term Erngs	21.41	1.24
Book Value	13.94	2.16
Sales	20.56	3.18
Cash Flow	18.57	1.37
Historical Erngs	26.20	1.94

Profitability	%	Rel Category
Return on Equity	12.32	1.25
Return on Assets	6.04	1.38
Net Margin	8.86	1.29

Sector Weightings	% of Stocks	Rel S&P 500	3 Year High	3 Year Low
Info	30.73	1.43		
Software	4.99	1.16	8	5
Hardware	20.11	1.97	33	18
Media	0.00	0.00	0	0
Telecom	5.63	1.79	6	3
Service	65.18	1.41		
Health	38.42	3.07	44	35
Consumer	7.10	0.78	10	3
Business	12.78	3.16	13	6
Financial	6.88	0.33	7	1
Mfg	4.09	0.13		
Goods	1.14	0.12	1	0
Ind Mtrls	2.95	0.23	4	2
Energy	0.00	0.00	0	0
Utilities	0.00	0.00	0	0

Composition

Cash	2.0
Stocks	96.4
Bonds	0.8
Other	0.8
Foreign (% of Stock)	7.9

Morningstar's Take by Kunal Kapoor 12-15-04

Wasatch Ultra Growth is proof that a highly concentrated and aggressive strategy can work in the small-cap growth space.

Many rivals have tried and failed to implement a strategy similar to the one that this fund executes. Simply put, it isn't easy to persevere with such an approach in this highly volatile part of the market. Yet, this fund just has carved out a very competitive long-term record, jumping more than 15% annually for the trailing 10-year period through Dec. 14, 2004.

There are a few reasons why the fund has carved out a successful niche and why it might continue to thrive. First, it hasn't gotten caught up in the dangerous earnings-momentum game. While it prizes fast growth, lead manager Karey Barker only pays up for stocks when she feels that they have the fundamentals in place to support their valuations. The approach isn't foolproof, but it insulates the fund from speculative stocks, a discipline that was of particular value when Internet stocks were ruling the roost in the late 1990s. Moreover, the fund isn't above playing contrarian and often feasts on stocks when their prices are pushed down because of temporary setbacks or plain-old market volatility. For instance, the fund got interested in semiconductor stocks this year during their fall swoon. Finally, the strategy is implemented successfully and consistently because Wasatch closed this fund and other accounts managed in this style at a very manageable level.

Of course, as the fund's lackluster showing in 2004 demonstrates--it's down more than 3% and trails 98% of its peers on a year-to-date basis--these safeguards don't mean that the fund will rise in a straight line. That's impossible, particularly because few companies grow without experiencing hiccups along the way. But management's ability to separate the hiccups from the fundamental problems is why we really think this fund is a worthwhile long-term holding.

Address:	Wasatch Funds Milwaukee,WI 53201-2172 800-551-1700
Web Address:	www.wasatchfunds.com
Inception:	08-17-92
Advisor:	Wasatch Advisors Inc.
Subadvisor:	None
NTF Plans:	Bidwell & Co. NTF, CommonWealth NTF

Minimum Purchase:	Closed	Add: —	IRA: —
Min Auto Inv Plan:	Closed	Add: —	
Sales Fees:	No-load, 2.00%R		
Management Fee:	1.25%, 0.28%A		
Actual Fees:	Mgt:1.25%	Dist:	
Expense Projections:	3Yr:$496	5Yr:$855	10Yr:$1867
Income Distrib:	Annually		

Weitz Hickory

Ticker	Load	NAV	Yield	Total Assets	Mstar Category
WEHIX	None	$32.86	0.7%	$344 mil	Small Blend

Governance and Management

Fiduciary Grade: A

Portfolio Manager(s)

Rick Lawson ran the fund from its 1993 inception through 2002. Firm founder Wally Weitz took his place at the end of 2002. Weitz has built great long-term records at Weitz Value and Weitz Partners Value. The firm has seven investment professionals, including a recently added small-cap analyst. The firm's analysts and managers are generalists and do not specialize in any one industry.

Strategy

Historically, the fund has emphasized out-of-favor stocks that its management thinks are cheap relative to the present value of their future cash flows, and it has frequently made large individual stock and sector bets. Together, these tendencies have led the fund's performance to deviate sharply from its peers'. Although the fund is valuation-conscious, it can provide an exceedingly bumpy ride. It changed managers at the end of 2002 and will likely be a bit less concentrated.

Historical Profile

Return Average
Risk High
Rating ★★★ Neutral

Investment Style: Equity Stock % — 90% 85% 97% 98% 96% 95% 92% 85%

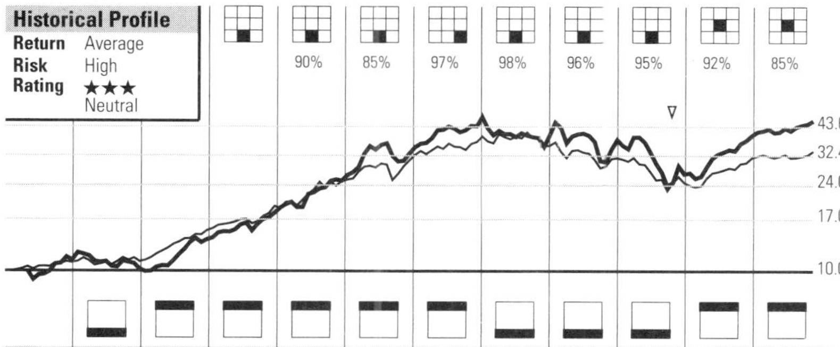

History

1993	1994	1995	1996	1997	1998	1999	2000	2001	2002	2003	12-04	History
13.36	10.61	14.66	18.80	23.70	30.98	39.65	27.55	26.26	18.42	26.99	32.86	NAV
21.59*	-17.34	40.49	35.36	39.17	33.01	36.67	-17.24	-4.65	-29.31	47.95	22.61	Total Return %
—	-18.65	2.96	12.42	5.82	4.44	15.63	-8.14	7.23	-7.22	19.28	11.74	+/-S&P 500
—	-15.52	12.04	18.87	16.81	35.56	15.41	-14.22	-7.14	-8.83	0.70	4.28	+/-Russ 2000
0.00	0.00	1.28	0.00	0.40	0.41	0.04	0.00	0.00	0.54	1.39	0.85	Income Return %
—	-17.34	39.21	35.36	38.77	32.60	36.63	-17.24	-4.65	-29.85	46.56	21.76	Capital Return %
—	100	7	9	13	1	8	99	93	95	25	17	Total Rtn % Rank Cat
0.00	0.00	0.14	0.00	0.07	0.10	0.01	0.00	0.00	0.14	0.25	0.23	Income $
0.05	0.45	0.07	1.04	1.91	0.45	2.56	5.29	0.01	0.00	0.00	0.00	Capital Gains $
—	1.50	1.50	1.50	1.50	1.46	1.30	1.23	1.22	1.25	1.32	1.30	Expense Ratio %
—	-2.90	-0.20	0.33	0.33	-0.13	0.48	-0.44	-0.27	-0.08	0.78	0.96	Income Ratio %
—	29	20	28	28	29	40	46	22	18	64	50	Turnover Rate %
2	3	5	10	22	539	913	466	339	195	235	344	Net Assets $mil

Performance 12-31-04

	1st Qtr	2nd Qtr	3rd Qtr	4th Qtr	Total
2000	-13.44	-6.09	-0.11	1.92	-17.24
2001	-7.84	10.56	-24.55	24.03	-4.65
2002	2.86	-14.48	-28.92	13.05	-29.31
2003	-2.44	25.28	3.43	17.04	47.95
2004	6.93	0.91	3.06	10.25	22.61

Trailing	Total Return%	+/- S&P 500	+/- Russ 2000	%Rank Cat	Growth of $10,000
3 Mo	10.25	1.02	-3.84	90	11,025
6 Mo	13.63	6.44	2.80	15	11,363
1 Yr	22.61	11.74	4.28	17	12,261
3 Yr Avg	8.64	5.06	-2.84	86	12,822
5 Yr Avg	0.24	2.54	-6.37	99	10,121
10 Yr Avg	17.15	5.08	5.61	5	48,688
15 Yr Avg	—	—	—	—	—

Tax Analysis	Tax-Adj Rtn%	%Rank Cat	Tax-Cost Rat	%Rank Cat
3 Yr (estimated)	8.32	82	0.29	21
5 Yr (estimated)	-0.59	98	0.83	37
10 Yr (estimated)	15.88	5	1.08	19

Potential Capital Gain Exposure: -18% of assets

Rating and Risk

Time Period	Load-Adj Return %	Morningstar Rtn vs Cat	Morningstar Risk vs Cat	Morningstar Risk-Adj Rating
1 Yr	22.61			
3 Yr	8.64	-Avg	High	★★
5 Yr	0.24	Low	High	★
10 Yr	17.15	High	+Avg	★★★★
Incept	14.36			

Other Measures	Standard Index S&P 500	Best Fit Index Wil 4500
Alpha	5.5	-4.3
Beta	1.24	1.24
R-Squared	67	75
Standard Deviation	25.19	
Mean	8.64	
Sharpe Ratio	0.29	

Portfolio Analysis 09-30-04

Share change since 06-04 Total Stocks:36	Sector	PE	YTD Ret%	% Assets
⊕ Fannie Mae	Financial	9.1	-2.33	5.82
Comcast	Media	—	-13.77	5.13
⊖ Redwood Trust	Financial	4.8	40.90	4.97
⊕ Caesars Entertainment	Consumer	62.6	85.97	4.83
⊕ Countrywide Financial	Financial	9.0	48.15	4.82
⊕ Berkshire Hathaway A	Financial	—	—	4.77
⊖ Cabela's	Consumer	—	—	4.71
⊕ Liberty Media	Media	—	11.56	4.67
Laboratory Corp of Ameri	Health	19.1	34.83	3.35
⊕ Harrah's Entertainment	Consumer	21.9	37.74	3.24
⊕ ITT Educational Services	Consumer	32.8	1.24	3.03
Freddie Mac	Financial	10.6	28.75	3.00
⊕ Liberty Media Internatio	Media	—	—	2.64
Charter Comms Hldgs 8.62	—	—	—	2.40
Host Marriott	Financial	—	40.88	2.36
☼ Iac / Interactivecorp	Consumer	43.1	-18.60	2.36
☼ Corinthian Colleges	Consumer	21.3	-32.10	2.29
☼ Cardinal Health	Health	16.9	-4.73	2.01
First Health Group	Health	14.2	-4.15	1.97
☼ Omnicare	Health	14.0	-14.07	1.30

Current Investment Style

Value Blnd Growth — Large Mid Small

Market Cap	%
Giant	11.7
Large	18.4
Mid	39.8
Small	23.3
Micro	6.8
Avg $mil: 4,199	

Value Measures		Rel Category
Price/Earnings	13.04	0.75
Price/Book	1.32	0.66
Price/Sales	0.77	0.81
Price/Cash Flow	4.56	0.78
Dividend Yield %	1.20	1.45

Growth Measures	%	Rel Category
Long-Term Erngs	13.49	1.00
Book Value	-1.77	NMF
Sales	7.91	1.84
Cash Flow	4.50	0.91
Historical Erngs	36.22	4.85

Profitability	%	Rel Category
Return on Equity	14.52	1.39
Return on Assets	8.40	1.69
Net Margin	8.41	1.15

Sector Weightings	% of Stocks	Rel S&P 500	3 Year High	3 Year Low
Info	21.32	0.99		
Software	0.00	0.00	0	0
Hardware	0.00	0.00	0	0
Media	18.25	4.75	23	12
Telecom	3.07	0.97	18	3
Service	76.72	1.65		
Health	13.14	1.05	13	2
Consumer	28.51	3.14	30	11
Business	1.95	0.48	10	0
Financial	33.12	1.60	34	25
Mfg	1.95	0.06		
Goods	1.95	0.21	8	2
Ind Mtrls	0.00	0.00	19	0
Energy	0.00	0.00	0	0
Utilities	0.00	0.00	0	0

Composition

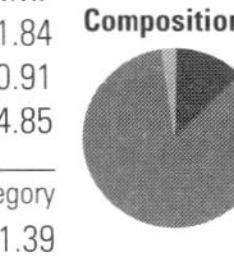

Cash	12.4
Stocks	85.2
Bonds	2.4
Other	0.0
Foreign (% of Stock)	0.0

Morningstar's Take by Christopher Traulsen 11-28-04

Weitz Hickory has changed, though it's still an acquired taste.

In our last analysis, we noted that manager Wally Weitz had, since taking the helm here in late 2002, taken steps to reduce the risks. He had reduced the fund's concentration in its top holdings, and cut positions in lower-quality stocks that had dented the portfolio in the bear market.

Nevertheless, the fund shouldn't be thought of as tame. It is still had 46% of assets packed into its top 10 holdings as of Sept. 30, 2004. The fund also owns many controversial companies, and is concentrated in relatively few sectors. Those are natural effects of Weitz's style. He attempts to buy companies at significant discounts to what a rational private buyer would pay for them, and such opportunities often arise because of near-term problems at a firm or industry-wide issues. In the third quarter, Weitz added new positions in IAC/Interactive Corp and Corinthian Colleges. The former has slumped over concerns about its growth and the health of its travel businesses, while the latter was dragged down by questions about its costs and the veracity of its placement claims.

The fund has delivered an excellent return thus far in 2004, thanks in part to large holdings such as Redwood Trust and Caesar's Entertainment. Its five-year showing is still lousy relative to other small-blend funds' (it still handily beats the S&P 500's return over that period, however), but we're encouraged by Weitz's presence and the changes he's made since taking the reins.

This fund can require patience. And although it currently lands in the small-blend category, it isn't for small-cap purists. It has ample exposure to mid- and large-caps, and its prospectus permits it to invest in companies of almost any size. Still, we think Weitz is an excellent investor. For those with the time to ride out some lean spells, the fund is well worth a look. Its small asset base is a plus, and its embedded tax losses should appeal to investors in taxable accounts.

Address:	1125 South 103 Street Omaha NE 68124-6008 800-232-4161
Web Address:	www.weitzfunds.com
Inception:	04-01-93*
Advisor:	Weitz Wallace R & Co.
Subadvisor:	None
NTF Plans:	Schwab OneSource, Schwab Instl NTF

Minimum Purchase:	$25000 Add: $5000 IRA: $25000
Min Auto Inv Plan:	$25000 Add: $5000
Sales Fees:	No-load
Management Fee:	1.00% mx./0.80% mn., 0.22%A
Actual Fees:	Mgt:1.00% Dist:
Expense Projections:	3Yr:$412 5Yr:$713 10Yr:$1568
Income Distrib:	Semi-Annually

Weitz Partners Value

Ticker	Load	NAV	Yield	Total Assets	Mstar Category
WPVLX	None	$23.90	0.3%	$2,893 mil	Mid-Cap Value

Governance and Management

Fiduciary Grade: A

Portfolio Manager(s)

Wally Weitz has been at the helm of this offering since its inception, and he also manages Weitz Hickory and Weitz Value. He owns Wallace Weitz & Co. and is a major shareholder in his firm's funds.

Strategy

Manager Wally Weitz looks for companies trading well below the price he thinks a rational private buyer would pay. To determine the latter, he relies mostly on discounted cash-flow analysis, often trying to look out 10 years or more. His price discipline and the need to project a business' long-term cash flows keep him out of expensive, unpredictable areas such as technology. Weitz will buy controversial names, though, as they're often among the cheapest. He'll also load up on individual sectors where he finds bargains and will hold cash when he can't find names that meet his criteria. Turnover here is low.

Historical Profile

Return Average
Risk Below Avg
Rating ★★★ Neutral

Investment Style: Equity Stock %

1996	1997	1998	1999	2000	2001	2002	2003	12-04
73%	75%	72%	77%	86%	77%	79%		

▼ Manager Change
∇ Partial Manager Change

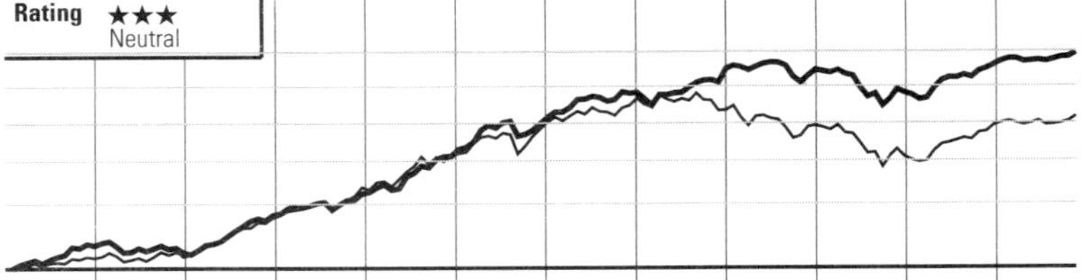

Growth of $10,000
▬ Investment Values of Fund
— Investment Values of S&P 500

Performance Quartile (within Category)

1993	1994	1995	1996	1997	1998	1999	2000	2001	2002	2003	12-04	History
10.00	8.28	10.39	11.52	15.45	17.68	20.02	21.51	20.87	17.15	21.48	23.90	NAV
23.03	-8.97	38.66	19.04	40.64	29.13	22.02	21.07	-0.86	-16.99	25.38	14.99	Total Return %
12.97	-10.28	1.13	-3.90	7.29	0.56	0.98	30.17	11.02	5.10	-3.29	4.12	+/-S&P 500
7.41	-6.84	3.72	-1.22	6.27	24.05	22.13	1.89	-3.19	-7.35	-12.69	-8.72	+/-Russ MV
0.00	0.00	2.86	0.55	0.00	1.08	0.28	2.63	0.98	0.24	0.11	0.39	Income Return %
23.03	-8.97	35.80	18.49	40.64	28.05	21.74	18.44	-1.84	-17.23	25.27	14.60	Capital Return %
28	90	5	54	1	2	10	44	80	77	89	72	Total Rtn % Rank Cat
0.00	0.00	0.24	0.06	0.00	0.17	0.05	0.50	0.21	0.05	0.02	0.08	Income $
1.01	0.82	0.85	0.79	0.53	1.67	1.23	1.88	0.26	0.13	0.00	0.70	Capital Gains $
—	1.29	1.27	1.23	1.24	1.25	1.24	1.19	1.13	1.08	1.08	1.13	Expense Ratio %
—	0.67	0.82	0.51	1.11	0.34	1.57	1.77	1.77	0.69	0.76	0.16	Income Ratio %
—	33	51	37	30	36	29	5	29	10	20	11	Turnover Rate %
—	51	74	95	134	292	1,143	1,948	2,978	2,993	2,811	2,893	Net Assets $mil

Performance 12-31-04

	1st Qtr	2nd Qtr	3rd Qtr	4th Qtr	Total
2000	-1.76	1.78	10.18	9.91	21.07
2001	-1.12	6.50	-11.03	5.81	-0.86
2002	-0.38	-13.30	-13.30	10.86	-16.99
2003	-4.31	18.16	0.21	10.66	25.38
2004	4.84	-1.28	2.35	8.55	14.99

Trailing	Total Return%	+/- S&P 500	+/- Russ MV	%Rank Cat	Growth of $10,000
3 Mo	8.55	-0.68	-4.91	89	10,855
6 Mo	11.10	3.91	-4.33	47	11,110
1 Yr	14.99	4.12	-8.72	72	11,499
3 Yr Avg	6.17	2.59	-9.39	89	11,968
5 Yr Avg	7.51	9.81	-5.97	81	14,363
10 Yr Avg	18.05	5.98	2.33	9	52,561
15 Yr Avg	14.99	4.06	1.29	4	81,265

Tax Analysis	Tax-Adj Rtn%	%Rank Cat	Tax-Cost Rat	%Rank Cat
3 Yr (estimated)	5.86	89	0.29	25
5 Yr (estimated)	6.50	78	0.94	46
10 Yr (estimated)	16.25	3	1.52	29

Potential Capital Gain Exposure: 19% of assets

Rating and Risk

Time Period	Load-Adj Return %	Morningstar Rtn vs Cat	Morningstar Risk vs Cat	Morningstar Risk-Adj Rating
1 Yr	14.99			
3 Yr	6.17	-Avg	Avg	★★
5 Yr	7.51	-Avg	-Avg	★★
10 Yr	18.05	+Avg	-Avg	★★★★★
Incept	15.63			

Other Measures	Standard Index S&P 500	Best Fit Index Russ 1000 VI
Alpha	2.8	-1.4
Beta	0.87	0.88
R-Squared	87	88
Standard Deviation	14.84	
Mean	6.17	
Sharpe Ratio	0.33	

Portfolio Analysis 09-30-04

Share change since 06-04 Total Stocks:40	Sector	PE	YTD Ret%	% Assets
⊕ Caesars Entertainment	Consumer	62.6	85.97	6.29
Comcast	Media	—	-13.77	5.71
Liberty Media	Media	—	11.56	5.19
⊖ Host Marriott	Financial	—	40.88	4.61
⊕ Countrywide Financial	Financial	9.0	48.15	4.39
Washington Post	Media	27.8	25.21	4.20
⊕ Fannie Mae	Financial	9.1	-2.33	4.05
Berkshire Hathaway B	Financial	20.9	4.30	3.57
Berkshire Hathaway A	Financial	—	—	3.48
Freddie Mac	Financial	10.6	28.75	3.34
Telephone and Data Syste	Telecom	39.5	24.11	3.21
Hilton Hotels	Consumer	36.1	33.34	3.07
⊖ Washington Mutual	Financial	13.9	10.05	3.05
⊖ Qwest Communications Int	Telecom	—	2.78	2.43
⊕ Redwood Trust	Financial	4.8	40.90	2.28
⊖ Citizens Communications	Telecom	60.2	34.09	2.20
☼ Cardinal Health	Health	16.9	-4.73	1.92
☼ Iac / Interactivecorp	Consumer	43.1	-18.60	1.69
⊕ Liberty Media Internatio	Media	—	—	1.61
⊖ GreenPoint Financial	Financial	—	—	1.35

Current Investment Style

Value Blnd Growth; Large Mid Small

Market Cap	%
Giant	17.4
Large	31.4
Mid	40.9
Small	9.2
Micro	1.2
Avg $mil: 9,949	

Value Measures		Rel Category
Price/Earnings	14.07	0.91
Price/Book	1.48	0.77
Price/Sales	0.91	1.03
Price/Cash Flow	4.79	0.84
Dividend Yield %	0.91	0.64

Growth Measures	%	Rel Category
Long-Term Erngs	12.66	1.15
Book Value	0.23	0.04
Sales	6.26	1.31
Cash Flow	1.24	0.31
Historical Erngs	31.16	2.71

Profitability	%	Rel Category
Return on Equity	10.71	0.84
Return on Assets	7.39	1.22
Net Margin	7.10	0.81

Sector Weightings	% of Stocks	Rel S&P 500	3 Year High	3 Year Low
Info	35.78	1.66		
Software	0.00	0.00	0	0
Hardware	0.00	0.00	0	0
Media	24.44	6.36	27	23
Telecom	11.34	3.60	18	11
Service	63.14	1.36		
Health	4.91	0.39	5	0
Consumer	16.41	1.81	17	7
Business	0.91	0.22	3	0
Financial	40.91	1.97	49	36
Mfg	1.07	0.03		
Goods	1.06	0.11	3	1
Ind Mtrls	0.01	0.00	1	0
Energy	0.00	0.00	0	0
Utilities	0.00	0.00	2	0

Composition

Cash	20.8
Stocks	78.8
Bonds	0.4
Other	0.0
Foreign (% of Stock)	0.0

Morningstar's Take by Christopher Traulsen 10-29-04

Weitz Partners Value's latest moves help show what its manager does best.

This fund ended the June quarter with 28% of assets in cash. But in the third quarter, Weitz found several companies that met his criteria, including drug distributor Cardinal Health, General Growth Properties (a REIT), and IAC/Interactive. He also added to Fannie Mae after it sold off on concerns regarding its accounting practices.

The purchases are typical of Weitz, who seeks companies selling cheaply relative to the net present value of their cash flows. In the case of Cardinal, the firm had sold off sharply amid an investigation into its accounting, a delay in filing its financial reports, and eroding margins. Despite these problems, Weitz thought the company was too cheap given its healthy free cash flows.

As a result of these purchases, the fund's cash stake stood at 17.8% on Sept 30. That's high, but Weitz has historically held large cash and/or bond stakes, and he's led the fund to a great 10-year return. Much of the fund's strength has been due to his willingness to buy into companies that have been oversold, then hang on and wait for the rest of the market to recognize their value. He bought into cable and telecom stocks when they were out of favor, for example, helping the fund to great returns in the late 1990s.

Weitz's style carries risks. His picks tend to concentrate in just a few sectors: media, telecom, and financials. His penchant for troubled companies can also burn the fund if he errs in his assumptions, and the fund's large cash stakes can hurt it in up markets. In 2004, the fund's cash and selected media and telecom picks have kept it back near the middle of the mid-value pack. The fund also lagged its peers during the bear market.

Thus, the fund isn't suitable for investors with short time horizons. Sibling Weitz Value is also better for tax-deferred accounts. However, we continue to think this is a fine choice for those with the time to wait out some lean patches.

Address:	1125 S 103rd St Omaha NE 68124-1071 800-232-4161
Web Address:	www.weitzfunds.com
Inception:	05-31-83
Advisor:	Weitz Wallace R & Co.
Subadvisor:	None
NTF Plans:	Fidelity Retail-NTF, Schwab OneSource

Minimum Purchase:	$25000	Add: $5000	IRA: $25000
Min Auto Inv Plan:	$25000	Add: $5000	
Sales Fees:	No-load		
Management Fee:	1.00% mx./0.80% mn., 0.20%A		
Actual Fees:	Mgt:0.99%	Dist:	
Expense Projections:	3Yr:$359	5Yr:$622	10Yr:$1375
Income Distrib:	Annually		

Weitz Value

Analyst Pick	Ticker	Load	NAV	Yield	Total Assets	Mstar Category
✔	WVALX	None	$37.70	0.5%	$4,502 mil	Mid-Cap Value

Governance and Management

Fiduciary Grade: A

Portfolio Manager(s)

Wally Weitz has been at the helm of this offering since its inception, and he also manages Weitz Hickory and Weitz Partners Value. He owns Wallace Weitz & Co. and is a major shareholder in his firm's funds. He is one of the best in the business. The firm's research staff includes six investment professionals.

Strategy

Manager Wally Weitz looks for companies trading well below the price he thinks a rational private buyer would pay. To determine the latter, he relies mostly on discounted cash-flow analysis, often trying to look out 10 years or more. His price discipline and the need to project a business' long-term cash flows keep him out of expensive, unpredictable areas such as technology. Weitz will buy controversial names, though, as they're often among the cheapest. He'll also load up on individual sectors where he finds bargains and will hold cash when he can't find names that meet his criteria. Turnover here is low.

Historical Profile

Return: Average
Risk: Below Avg
Rating: ★★★★ Above Avg

Investment Style: Equity, Stock %: 63% 82% 76% 81% 87% 76% 75%

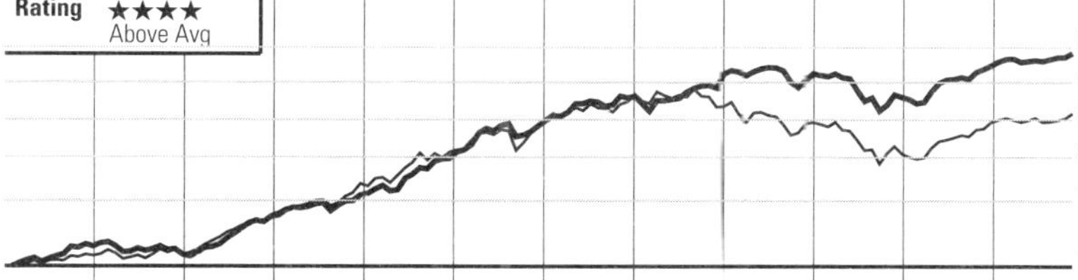

▼ Manager Change
▽ Partial Manager Change

Growth of $10,000
— Investment Values of Fund
— Investment Values of S&P 500

Performance Quartile (within Category)

1993	1994	1995	1996	1997	1998	1999	2000	2001	2002	2003	12-04	History
16.80	14.43	18.38	20.59	25.15	29.07	33.08	35.22	34.29	27.92	35.78	37.70	NAV
20.01	-9.82	38.37	18.70	38.93	28.95	20.97	19.62	0.24	-17.10	28.73	15.74	Total Return %
9.95	-11.13	0.84	-4.24	5.58	0.38	-0.07	28.72	12.12	4.99	0.06	4.87	+/-S&P 500
4.39	-7.69	3.43	-1.56	4.56	23.87	21.08	0.44	-2.09	-7.46	-9.34	-7.97	+/-Russ MV
0.16	0.00	2.93	0.68	1.59	0.73	1.30	1.56	1.06	0.58	0.55	0.59	Income Return %
19.85	-9.82	35.44	18.02	37.34	28.22	19.67	18.06	-0.82	-17.68	28.18	15.15	Capital Return %
53	92	7	58	2	3	12	47	75	78	77	61	Total Rtn % Rank Cat
0.02	0.00	0.42	0.13	0.31	0.17	0.37	0.49	0.37	0.20	0.15	0.21	Income $
0.59	0.73	1.08	1.10	2.61	3.01	1.67	3.42	0.67	0.32	0.00	3.30	Capital Gains $
1.35	1.41	1.42	1.35	1.29	1.27	1.26	1.19	1.11	1.06	1.08	1.11	Expense Ratio %
1.66	0.64	1.06	0.91	0.93	0.87	1.35	1.39	36.00	0.87	0.76	0.57	Income Ratio %
23	22	28	40	39	39	36	31	36	13	18	12	Turnover Rate %
107	108	149	261	366	1,197	2,680	3,317	4,150	4,308	4,063	4,502	Net Assets $mil

Performance 12-31-04

	1st Qtr	2nd Qtr	3rd Qtr	4th Qtr	Total
2000	-3.23	1.80	10.34	10.06	19.62
2001	-1.39	6.80	-11.08	7.04	0.24
2002	-0.12	-12.46	-14.89	11.39	-17.10
2003	-3.83	19.47	0.62	11.35	28.73
2004	5.59	-1.20	2.31	8.44	15.74

Trailing	Total Return%	+/- S&P 500	+/- Russ MV	%Rank Cat	Growth of $10,000
3 Mo	8.44	-0.79	-5.02	90	10,844
6 Mo	10.94	3.75	-4.49	51	11,094
1 Yr	15.74	4.87	-7.97	61	11,574
3 Yr Avg	7.29	3.71	-8.27	84	12,350
5 Yr Avg	8.17	10.47	-5.31	76	14,809
10 Yr Avg	18.08	6.01	2.36	7	52,694
15 Yr Avg	14.72	3.79	1.02	8	78,449

Tax Analysis	Tax-Adj Rtn%	%Rank Cat	Tax-Cost Rat	%Rank Cat
3 Yr (estimated)	6.48	83	0.75	61
5 Yr (estimated)	6.89	72	1.18	61
10 Yr (estimated)	16.01	5	1.75	38

Potential Capital Gain Exposure: 16% of assets

Rating and Risk

Time Period	Load-Adj Return %	Morningstar Rtn vs Cat	Morningstar Risk vs Cat	Morningstar Risk-Adj Rating
1 Yr	15.74			
3 Yr	7.29	-Avg	Avg	★★
5 Yr	8.17	-Avg	-Avg	★★★
10 Yr	18.08	High	-Avg	★★★★★
Incept	13.98			

Other Measures	Standard Index S&P 500	Best Fit Index Russ 1000 VI
Alpha	3.9	-0.5
Beta	0.89	0.91
R-Squared	85	88
Standard Deviation	15.39	
Mean	7.29	
Sharpe Ratio	0.39	

Portfolio Analysis 09-30-04

Share change since 06-04 Total Stocks:43	Sector	PE	YTD Ret%	% Assets
⊕ Caesars Entertainment	Consumer	62.6	85.97	6.36
Comcast	Media	—	-13.77	5.08
⊕ Liberty Media	Media	—	11.56	4.97
Berkshire Hathaway B	Financial	20.9	4.30	4.49
⊕ Countrywide Financial	Financial	9.0	48.15	4.41
⊖ Host Marriott	Financial	—	40.88	4.26
⊕ Fannie Mae	Financial	9.1	-2.33	3.88
Washington Post	Media	27.8	25.21	3.69
⊖ Citizens Communications	Telecom	60.2	34.09	3.39
Freddie Mac	Financial	10.6	28.75	3.39
⊕ Redwood Trust	Financial	4.8	40.90	2.90
Telephone and Data Syste	Telecom	39.5	24.11	2.85
⊖ Washington Mutual	Financial	13.9	10.05	2.81
Hilton Hotels	Consumer	36.1	33.34	2.52
Qwest Communications Int	Telecom	—	2.78	2.12
Berkshire Hathaway A	Financial	—	—	2.02
☼ Cardinal Health	Health	16.9	-4.73	1.94
☼ Iac / Interactivecorp	Consumer	43.1	-18.60	1.64
⊕ Liberty Media Internatio	Media	—	—	1.42
⊖ Alltel	Telecom	16.9	29.71	1.35

Current Investment Style

Value Blnd Growth / Large Mid Small

Market Cap	%
Giant	18.4
Large	30.9
Mid	39.8
Small	9.8
Micro	1.1
Avg $mil: 10,234	

Value Measures		Rel Category
Price/Earnings	13.71	0.89
Price/Book	1.48	0.77
Price/Sales	0.95	1.08
Price/Cash Flow	4.95	0.86
Dividend Yield %	1.11	0.78

Growth Measures	%	Rel Category
Long-Term Erngs	12.57	1.14
Book Value	0.58	0.10
Sales	5.83	1.43
Cash Flow	1.45	0.37
Historical Erngs	34.36	2.99

Profitability	%	Rel Category
Return on Equity	10.75	0.84
Return on Assets	7.07	1.16
Net Margin	7.59	0.86

Sector Weightings	% of Stocks	Rel S&P 500	3 Year High	3 Year Low
Info	35.80	1.67		
Software	0.00	0.00	0	0
Hardware	0.00	0.00	0	0
Media	22.91	5.97	26	21
Telecom	12.89	4.09	22	13
Service	63.22	1.36		
Health	5.19	0.42	5	0
Consumer	15.68	1.73	16	6
Business	0.50	0.12	1	0
Financial	41.85	2.02	53	39
Mfg	0.99	0.03		
Goods	0.98	0.11	3	1
Ind Mtrls	0.01	0.00	1	0
Energy	0.00	0.00	0	0
Utilities	0.00	0.00	2	0

Composition

Cash	24.3
Stocks	75.3
Bonds	0.4
Other	0.0
Foreign (% of Stock)	0.0

Morningstar's Take by Christopher Traulsen 10-29-04

Weitz Value's latest moves help show what its manager does best.

This fund ended the June quarter with 34% of assets in cash. But in the third quarter, Weitz found several companies that met his criteria, including drug distributor Cardinal Health, General Growth Properties (a REIT), and IAC/InterActiveCorp. He also added to Fannie Mae after it sold off on concerns regarding its accounting practices.

The purchases are typical of Weitz, who seeks companies selling cheaply relative to the net present value of their cash flows. In the case of Cardinal, the firm had sold off sharply amid an investigation into its accounting, a delay in filing its financial reports, and eroding margins. Despite these problems, Weitz thought the company was too cheap given its healthy free cash flows.

As a result of these purchases, the fund's cash stake stood at 21.8% on Sept 30. That's high, but Weitz has historically held large cash and/or bond stakes, and he's led the fund to a great 10-year return. Much of the fund's strength has been due to his willingness to buy into companies that have been oversold, then hang on and wait for the rest of the market to recognize their value. He bought into cable and telecom stocks when they were out of favor, for example, helping the fund to great returns in the late 1990s.

Weitz's style carries risks. His picks tend to concentrate in just a few sectors: media, telecom, and financials. His penchant for troubled companies can also burn the fund if he errs in his assumptions, and the fund's large cash stakes can hurt it in up markets. In 2004, the fund's cash and selected media and telecom picks have kept it back near the middle of the mid-value pack. The fund also lagged its peers during the bear market.

Thus, the fund isn't suitable for investors with short time horizons. Sibling Weitz Partners Value is also better for taxable accounts. However, we continue to think this is a fine choice for those with the time to wait out some lean patches.

Address:	1125 South 103 Street Omaha NE 68124-6008 800-232-4161
Web Address:	www.weitzfunds.com
Inception:	05-09-86
Advisor:	Weitz Wallace R & Co.
Subadvisor:	None
NTF Plans:	Fidelity Retail-NTF, Schwab OneSource

Minimum Purchase:	$25000	Add: $5000	IRA: $25000
Min Auto Inv Plan:	$25000	Add: $5000	
Sales Fees:	No-load		
Management Fee:	1.00% mx./0.80% mn., 0.22%A		
Actual Fees:	Mgt:0.96%	Dist:	
Expense Projections:	3Yr:$353	5Yr:$612	10Yr:$1352
Income Distrib:	Semi-Annually		

Westcore Midco Growth

Ticker	Load	NAV	Yield	Total Assets	Mstar Category
WTMGX	None	$7.48	0.0%	$194 mil	Mid-Cap Growth

Governance and Management

Fiduciary Grade: B

Portfolio Manager(s)

Todger Anderson has been at the helm since this fund's 1986 inception but is planning to retire within the next few years. Five industry analysts work on the fund and corresponding institutional accounts and make buy-and-sell decisions. William Chester, who became comanager in October 2002, will succeed him when he steps down.

Strategy

This fund reflects the advisor's institutional background. It delivers straightforward exposure to mid-cap growth stocks. Management looks for companies with at least 25% earnings-growth rates that are leaders in emerging industries and uses discounted cash-flow analysis to try to buy the ones that have significant upside ahead of them.

Historical Profile

Return Average
Risk Average
Rating ★★★ Neutral

Investment Style: Equity Stock %

87%	85%	84%	91%	86%	91%	95%	93%

▼ Manager Change
▽ Partial Manager Change

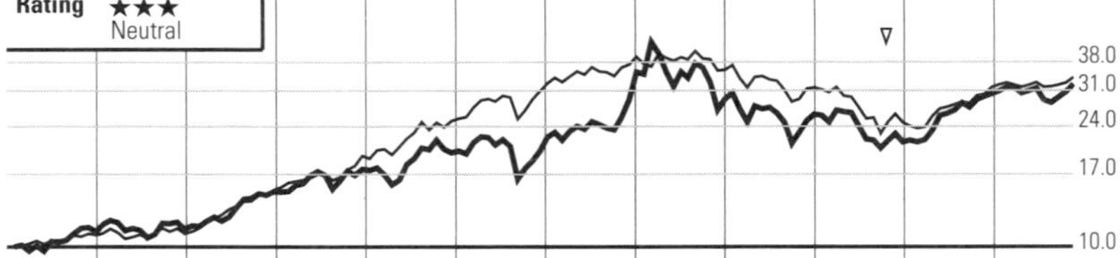

Growth of $10,000
— Investment Values of Fund
— Investment Values of S&P 500

Performance Quartile (within Category)

History

1993	1994	1995	1996	1997	1998	1999	2000	2001	2002	2003	12-04	History
16.79	16.08	19.76	20.06	19.66	18.92	20.06	6.41	5.74	4.71	6.65	7.48	NAV
17.47	-1.01	27.42	16.99	14.89	10.40	59.31	-17.51	-10.45	-17.94	41.19	12.48	Total Return %
7.41	-2.32	-10.11	-5.95	-18.46	-18.17	38.27	-8.41	1.43	4.15	12.52	1.61	+/-S&P 500
6.28	1.15	-6.56	-0.49	-7.65	-7.46	8.02	-5.76	9.70	9.47	-1.52	-3.00	+/-Russ MG
0.00	0.00	0.00	0.00	0.00	0.00	0.00	0.00	0.00	0.00	0.00	0.00	Income Return %
17.47	-1.01	27.42	16.99	14.89	10.40	59.31	-17.51	-10.45	-17.94	41.19	12.48	Capital Return %
38	45	76	48	69	72	42	82	24	13	24	54	Total Rtn % Rank Cat
0.00	0.00	0.00	0.00	0.00	0.00	0.00	0.00	0.00	0.00	0.00	0.00	Income $
1.03	0.53	0.72	3.02	3.24	2.50	8.85	9.96	0.00	0.00	0.00	0.00	Capital Gains $
0.83	0.84	0.94	1.08	1.14	1.13	1.15	1.15	1.15	1.15	1.15	1.14	Expense Ratio %
0.04	-0.09	-0.03	-0.42	-0.70	-0.71	-0.63	-0.81	-0.72	-0.75	-0.57	-0.62	Income Ratio %
56	52	50	63	61	76	116	118	191	67	49	53	Turnover Rate %
280	363	547	570	603	491	300	176	119	89	168	194	Net Assets $mil

Performance 12-31-04

	1st Qtr	2nd Qtr	3rd Qtr	4th Qtr	Total
2000	14.46	-12.46	3.08	-20.14	-17.51
2001	-15.29	11.05	-22.72	23.18	-10.45
2002	2.96	-10.66	-14.77	4.67	-17.94
2003	1.70	20.67	4.50	10.10	41.19
2004	4.81	-0.72	-6.36	15.43	12.48

Trailing	Total Return%	+/- S&P 500	+/- Russ MG	%Rank Cat	Growth of $10,000
3 Mo	15.43	6.20	1.49	15	11,543
6 Mo	8.09	0.90	-0.92	45	10,809
1 Yr	12.48	1.61	-3.00	54	11,248
3 Yr Avg	9.23	5.65	3.07	10	13,032
5 Yr Avg	-0.76	1.54	2.60	30	9,626
10 Yr Avg	11.23	-0.84	0.00	39	28,988
15 Yr Avg	13.01	2.08	2.01	10	62,626

Tax Analysis	Tax-Adj Rtn%	%Rank Cat	Tax-Cost Rat	%Rank Cat
3 Yr (estimated)	9.23	7	0.00	1
5 Yr (estimated)	-4.24	47	3.51	97
10 Yr (estimated)	7.35	61	3.49	98

Potential Capital Gain Exposure: 22% of assets

Rating and Risk

Time Period	Load-Adj Return %	Morningstar Rtn vs Cat	Morningstar Risk vs Cat	Morningstar Risk-Adj Rating
1 Yr	12.48			
3 Yr	9.23	High	Avg	★★★★★
5 Yr	-0.76	Avg	Avg	★★★
10 Yr	11.23	Avg	Avg	★★★
Incept	12.65			

Other Measures	Standard Index S&P 500	Best Fit Index Russ MG
Alpha	5.9	3.4
Beta	0.94	0.88
R-Squared	72	92
Standard Deviation	18.18	
Mean	9.23	
Sharpe Ratio	0.44	

Portfolio Analysis 11-30-04

Share change since 09-04 Total Stocks:64	Sector	PE	YTD Ret%	% Assets
Apache	Energy	11.4	25.41	2.48
Constellation Brands A	Goods	19.9	41.24	2.39
Intersil	Hardware	41.2	-32.28	2.17
Royal Caribbean Cruises	Goods	36.9	58.33	2.16
Mohawk Industries	Goods	16.1	29.36	2.13
Bed Bath & Beyond	Consumer	27.6	-8.12	2.00
Starbucks	Consumer	60.4	88.06	2.00
Jacobs Engineering Group	Business	19.9	-0.46	1.98
Certegy	Business	21.2	8.92	1.91
Harris	Hardware	27.4	64.22	1.82
Starwood Hotels & Resort	Consumer	33.9	64.71	1.80
Apria HealthCare Group	Health	13.9	15.74	1.79
OSI Pharmaceuticals	Health	—	132.09	1.74
Ambac Financial Group	Financial	12.7	19.13	1.72
T Rowe Price Group	Financial	25.6	33.16	1.71
DST Systems	Business	15.3	24.81	1.68
Noble	Energy	51.7	39.02	1.66
Getty Images	Business	37.9	37.34	1.65
Covance	Health	26.6	44.59	1.63
Cintas	Business	27.0	-11.91	1.62

Current Investment Style

Value Blnd Growth — Large Mid Small

Market Cap	%
Giant	0.0
Large	22.0
Mid	68.2
Small	9.8
Micro	0.0
Avg $mil: 4,164	

Value Measures		Rel Category
Price/Earnings	21.28	0.97
Price/Book	2.77	0.92
Price/Sales	1.69	0.95
Price/Cash Flow	11.29	1.16
Dividend Yield %	0.24	0.56

Growth Measures	%	Rel Category
Long-Term Erngs	15.35	0.97
Book Value	9.67	0.96
Sales	7.14	0.83
Cash Flow	14.51	1.19
Historical Erngs	14.68	0.92

Profitability	%	Rel Category
Return on Equity	12.96	0.90
Return on Assets	5.44	0.76
Net Margin	10.06	1.05

Sector Weightings	% of Stocks	Rel S&P 500	3 Year High	3 Year Low
Info	26.82	1.25		
Software	10.34	2.40	13	5
Hardware	11.81	1.16	15	10
Media	3.18	0.83	4	1
Telecom	1.49	0.47	3	1
Service	54.49	1.17		
Health	23.10	1.85	27	16
Consumer	11.27	1.24	15	9
Business	12.39	3.06	15	8
Financial	7.73	0.37	11	8
Mfg	18.68	0.58		
Goods	9.95	1.07	13	7
Ind Mtrls	2.62	0.21	5	2
Energy	6.11	0.85	7	3
Utilities	0.00	0.00	0	0

Composition

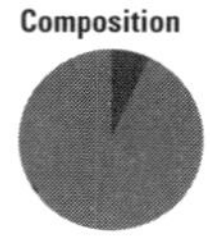

Cash	6.7
Stocks	93.3
Bonds	0.0
Other	0.0
Foreign (% of Stock)	1.7

Morningstar's Take by Karen Papalois 11-15-04

Westcore Midco Growth won't always be at the top, but it has strengths.

This fund stays true to its buy-and-hold approach. It likes buying mid-cap companies that have room to gain market share. Two types of stocks fall on its radar: the shares of firms with rapid sales growth and others that have taken a beating. In both cases, management keeps close tabs on valuation. In addition, the fund's average holding period is two years and that's longer than most. The funds longer-term view and attention to price keep it out of speculative stocks, which helps in downturns but can lead it to miss rallies.

The fund should retain that steady approach, too. It has worked hard to retain key analysts. That's important because five senior analysts pull the portfolio's trigger. On average, the fund's senior analysts have been with the advisor for more than 10 years, which is more than twice the typical four-year tenure for the category.

The fund also has a clear succession plan. Portfolio manager Todger Anderson, who has run the fund since its 1986 inception, has no specific retirement date, but he eventually will hand the lead manager duties to Will Chester, who has worked on the fund for 18 years. So, the portfolio isn't likely to end up in the hands of an inexperienced team.

That steadiness is also reflected in the fund's corporate governance. Westcore funds have been free of regulatory issues. Also, the board has an independent chairman, and it oversees few funds. Most directors have more than $100,000 invested in the fund. That helps keep their interests aligned with shareholders. Moreover, it has maintained a low 1.15% expense ratio.

At times, the markets will favor faster-moving growth offerings more than this one. Yet, this fund's reasonable approach has stood strong over the long haul. That combined with a steady team and healthy culture make it a good option.

Address:	1625 Broadway Denver CO 80202 800-392-2673
Web Address:	www.westcore.com
Inception:	08-01-86
Advisor:	Denver Investment Advisors LLC
Subadvisor:	None
NTF Plans:	Fidelity Retail-NTF, Schwab OneSource

Minimum Purchase:	$2500	Add: $100	IRA: $1000
Min Auto Inv Plan:	$1000	Add: $100	
Sales Fees:	No-load, 2.00%R		
Management Fee:	0.65%, 0.30%A		
Actual Fees:	Mgt:0.65%	Dist:	
Expense Projections:	3Yr:$359	5Yr:$622	10Yr:$1373
Income Distrib:	Annually		

Western Asset Cr Bd Inst

Analyst Pick

Ticker	Load	NAV	Yield	SEC Yield	Total Assets	Mstar Category
WATFX	None	$11.48	3.3%	3.47%	$2,359 mil	Intermediate-Term Bond

Governance and Management

Fiduciary Grade: B

Portfolio Manager(s)

Ken Leech, Western Asset's chief investment officer, oversees the management team, which has a fine record. Each member of the team manages the fund's holdings in a different market sector.

Strategy

In general, the fund is more aggressive than most of its peers. For example, management makes bolder duration adjustments (plus or minus 20% of its benchmark's duration) than many of the category's more conservative offerings. It also takes on added credit risk on occasion. Overall, though, it is a true core bond holding, with a focus on investment-grade bonds and a broadly diversified portfolio.

Historical Profile

Return: High
Risk: High
Rating: ★★★★★ Highest

Investment Style: Fixed Income

Income Rtn %Rank Cat: 59 33 45 49 10 29 28 39 62

▼ Manager Change
▽ Partial Manager Change

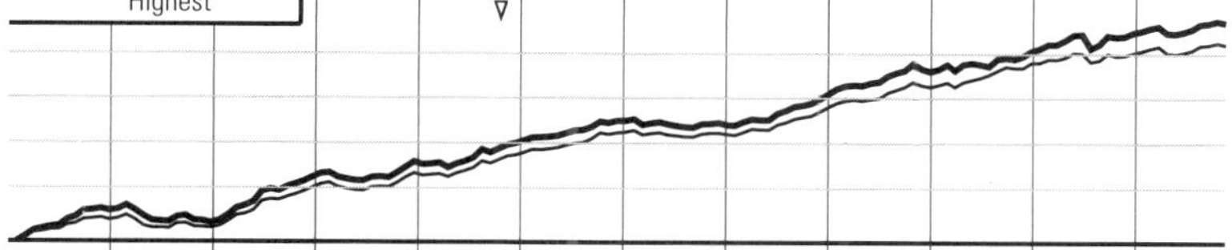

Growth of $10,000
— Investment Values of Fund
— Investment Values of LB Aggr

Performance Quartile (within Category)

History

	1993	1994	1995	1996	1997	1998	1999	2000	2001	2002	2003	12-04
NAV	11.20	10.04	11.40	11.14	11.41	11.12	10.28	10.87	11.10	11.37	11.59	11.48
Total Return %	13.87	-4.29	20.92	3.73	10.13	8.36	-1.70	13.34	9.48	8.70	7.77	5.30
+/-LB Aggr	4.12	-1.37	2.45	0.10	0.48	-0.33	-0.88	1.71	1.04	-1.55	3.67	0.96
+/-LB 5-10YR	1.63	0.22	-0.51	1.04	0.70	-1.78	1.18	0.90	0.66	-4.33	1.80	0.00
Income Return %	7.26	6.20	6.69	5.97	6.53	5.95	5.75	7.31	6.15	5.36	4.20	3.42
Capital Return %	6.61	-10.49	14.23	-2.24	3.60	2.41	-7.45	6.03	3.33	3.34	3.57	1.88
Total Rtn % Rank Cat	8	60	12	31	15	28	61	2	8	44	13	8
Income $	0.77	0.68	0.66	0.67	0.71	0.65	0.62	0.73	0.65	0.58	0.46	0.38
Capital Gains $	0.66	0.00	0.04	0.01	0.12	0.56	0.03	0.00	0.13	0.09	0.18	0.31
Expense Ratio %	0.50	0.50	0.50	0.50	0.50	0.50	0.50	0.50	0.50	0.50	0.49	0.49
Income Ratio %	6.00	6.00	6.98	6.30	6.40	6.00	5.70	6.30	6.80	5.60	4.90	3.50
Turnover Rate %	313	272	258	266	385	227	484	260	387	595	439	465
Net Assets $mil	185	228	398	539	624	682	683	740	883	1,271	1,990	2,193

Performance 12-31-04

	1st Qtr	2nd Qtr	3rd Qtr	4th Qtr	Total
2000	2.42	2.33	3.29	4.68	13.34
2001	3.66	1.28	4.69	-0.40	9.48
2002	0.51	2.44	2.68	2.82	8.70
2003	2.78	4.17	-0.50	1.17	7.77
2004	2.60	-2.21	3.58	1.33	5.30

Trailing	Total Return%	+/- LB Aggr	+/- LB 5-10YR	%Rank Cat	Growth of $10,000
3 Mo	1.33	0.38	0.35	20	10,133
6 Mo	4.95	0.77	-0.62	15	10,495
1 Yr	5.30	0.96	0.00	8	10,530
3 Yr Avg	7.25	1.06	-0.80	7	12,336
5 Yr Avg	8.89	1.18	-0.18	2	15,309
10 Yr Avg	8.46	0.74	0.00	2	22,527
15 Yr Avg	—	—	—	—	—

Tax Analysis	Tax-Adj Rtn%	%Rank Cat	Tax-Cost Rat	%Rank Cat
3 Yr (estimated)	5.15	5	1.96	72
5 Yr (estimated)	6.45	2	2.24	74
10 Yr (estimated)	5.77	3	2.48	82

Potential Capital Gain Exposure: 2% of assets

Rating and Risk

Time Period	Load-Adj Return %	Morningstar Rtn vs Cat	Morningstar Risk vs Cat	Morningstar Risk-Adj Rating
1 Yr	5.30			
3 Yr	7.25	High	High	★★★★★
5 Yr	8.89	High	High	★★★★★
10 Yr	8.46	High	High	★★★★★
Incept	8.68			

Other Measures	Standard Index LB Aggr	Best Fit Index LB. U.S. Univ. Bd
Alpha	0.1	-1.1
Beta	1.21	1.30
R-Squared	81	88
Standard Deviation	6.12	
Mean	7.25	
Sharpe Ratio	0.97	

Morningstar's Take by Paul Herbert 01-04-05

Western Asset Core Bond is home to our Fixed-Income Managers of the Year for 2004.

Fixed-income managers can get into trouble by making and then acting on bold predictions about macroeconomic trends. Many formerly intrepid funds that got burned by wayward rate bets at points in the 1990s are now sticking to making only slight duration and sector tilts. It's refreshing to come across a fund like this one, then, in which management will meaningfully reposition the fund based on top-down analysis. This team also rotates among bond sectors more confidently than many rivals, as it is backed by deep, experienced teams of specialists who can wring out inefficiencies in their areas of expertise.

The managers' willingness to stick their necks out has been evident recently. Late in 2003, they cut back the fund's long-held overweighting in corporate bonds and above-benchmark interest-rate sensitivity. They thought spreads on high-grade issues reflected improving fundamentals and were fearful that higher-than-expected inflation could sneak up on a napping Federal Reserve. They have also continued to favor inflation-protected Treasury bonds (TIPs) for this reason.

Outside of the TIPs stake, these decisions did not have a great impact on the fund's 2004 performance. Rather, moves to target specific maturities and credit tiers have paid off more than betting on sectors or rates. Overall, the fund turned in a 5.3% gain last year, which put it ahead of its benchmark and in the intermediate-term bond category's top decile for 2004.

That the managers stick to their convictions is laudable. Only time will tell if their stand on inflation is on the money, but, as the fund's longer-term record indicates, it's been better to bet with this management team than against it. For this reason and the firm's solid fiduciary standing, we've selected the fund as an Analyst Pick and recently awarded its bosses Fixed-Income Manager of the Year honors for 2004.

Address:	100 Light Street Baltimore MD 21202 888-425-6432
Web Address:	
Inception:	09-04-90
Advisor:	Western Asset Management Co Ltd
Subadvisor:	None
NTF Plans:	N/A

Minimum Purchase:	$1000000	Add: $0	IRA: $0
Min Auto Inv Plan:	$0	Add: —	
Sales Fees:	No-load		
Management Fee:	0.45% mx./0.40% mn., 0.10%A		
Actual Fees:	Mgt:0.42%	Dist:	
Expense Projections:	3Yr:$157	5Yr:$274	10Yr:$616
Income Distrib:	Monthly		

Portfolio Analysis 09-30-04

Total Fixed-Income:649	Date of Maturity	Amount $000	Value $000	% Net Assets
US Treasury Note (Fut)	12-20-04	307,400	342,870	7.31
EuroDollar (Fut)	09-19-05	292,500	283,696	6.05
US Treasury Bond (Fut)	12-20-04	146,500	164,400	3.50
Csfb Int Rate Swap Rec	09-14-07	132,510	132,492	2.82
Csfb Int Rate Swap Rec 0	09-14-07	132,510	132,492	2.82
GNMA 6%		113,890	118,019	2.52
US Treasury Note 3.375%	01-15-07	104,427	111,569	2.38
GNMA 5.5%		108,800	110,636	2.36
US Treasury Note 3.5%	08-15-09	99,230	99,831	2.13
Gs Int Rate Swap Rec Owr	09-22-07	96,800	96,790	2.06
Csfb Int Rate Swap Rec 1	09-21-07	88,000	87,989	1.88
US Treasury Note 4.25%	01-15-10	73,245	85,007	1.81
Residential Asset Sec 20	02-25-19	80,302	80,167	1.71
EuroDollar (Fut)	03-14-05	77,750	75,760	1.62
US Treasury Note 4%	06-15-09	72,160	74,263	1.58
Db Int Rate Seap Rec Owr	09-24-09	63,300	63,293	1.35
Csfb Int Rate Rec 1.91pc	09-21-07	58,700	58,693	1.25
GNMA 5%		46,865	46,601	0.99
US Treasury Note 3.625%	07-15-09	41,010	41,507	0.88
FHLMC 5%	08-01-33	32,522	32,306	0.69

Current Investment Style

Duration: Short Int Long
Quality: High Med Low

[1] figure provided by fund

Avg Eff Duration[1]	—
Avg Eff Maturity	—
Avg Credit Quality	—
Avg Wtd Coupon	3.47%
Avg Wtd Price	104.53% of par

Coupon Range	% of Bonds	Rel Cat
0% PIK	1.8	0.4
0% to 6%	79.3	1.2
6% to 8%	18.9	0.7
8% to 10%	1.7	0.3
More than 10%	0.0	0.0

1.00=Category Average

Credit Analysis	% bonds 09-30-04		
US Govt	—	BB	—
AAA	—	B	—
AA	—	Below B	—
A	—	NR/NA	—
BBB	—		

Sector Breakdown	% of assets
US Treasuries	11
TIPS	8
US Agency	0
Mortgage Pass-Throughs	14
Mortgage CMO	4
Mortgage ARM	0
US Corporate	19
Asset-Backed	4
Convertible	0
Municipal	0
Corporate Inflation-Protected	0
Foreign Corporate	1
Foreign Govt	0

Composition			
Cash	28.7	Bonds	60.1
Stocks	0.0	Other	11.2

Special Securities	
Restricted/Illiquid Secs	Trace
Exotic Mortgage-Backed	0
Emerging-Markets Secs	Trace
Options/Futures/Warrants	Yes

Westport Select Cap R

Ticker	Load	NAV	Yield	Total Assets	Mstar Category
WPSRX	Closed	$24.06	0.0%	$1,360 mil	Small Blend

Governance and Management

Fiduciary Grade:

Portfolio Manager(s)

Andy Knuth has been with Westport since the 1980s, serving as comanager at Managers Special Equity since 1985. Ed Nicklin had a good record managing Evergreen Growth & Income for 10 years before joining Westport in 1997. He also manages Westport.

Strategy

Comanagers Andy Knuth and Ed Nicklin look for stocks trading at modest price multiples relative to their long-term growth prospects. They aren't afraid to invest in companies that are out of favor as long as their long-term business models look strong. They typically have a long time horizon and keep turnover to a minimum.

Historical Profile

Return Below Avg
Risk Below Avg
Rating ★★★ Neutral

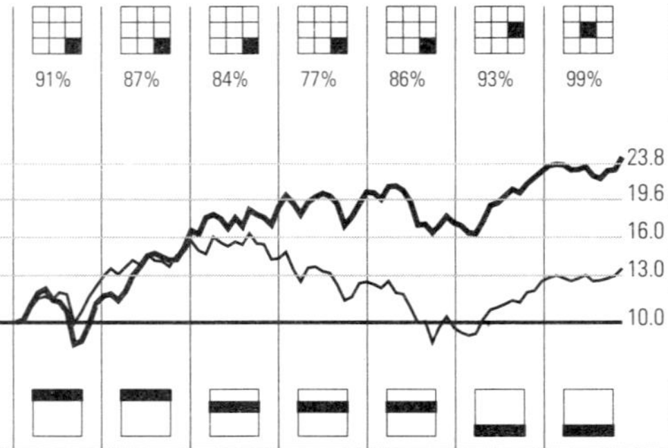

Investment Style
Equity
Stock %

▼ Manager Change
∇ Partial Manager Change

Growth of $10,000
▬ Investment Values of Fund
— Investment Values of S&P 500

Performance Quartile (within Category)

1993	1994	1995	1996	1997	1998	1999	2000	2001	2002	2003	12-04	History
—	—	—	—	10.00	11.54	16.47	18.23	19.45	16.49	21.79	24.06	NAV
—	—	—	—	0.00*	15.40	42.72	13.60	8.22	-15.22	32.14	10.43	Total Return %
—	—	—	—	—	-13.17	21.68	22.70	20.10	6.87	3.47	-0.44	+/-S&P 500
—	—	—	—	—	17.95	21.46	16.62	5.73	5.26	-15.11	-7.90	+/-Russ 2000
—	—	—	—	—	0.00	0.00	0.20	0.00	0.00	0.00	0.00	Income Return %
—	—	—	—	—	15.40	42.72	13.40	8.22	-15.22	32.14	10.43	Capital Return %
—	—	—	—	—	3	4	50	47	50	91	97	Total Rtn % Rank Cat
—	—	—	—	0.00	0.00	0.00	0.03	0.00	0.00	0.00	0.00	Income $
—	—	—	—	0.00	0.00	0.00	0.45	0.28	0.00	0.00	0.00	Capital Gains $
—	—	—	—	—	1.50	1.43	1.27	1.24	1.29	1.34	—	Expense Ratio %
—	—	—	—	—	-0.39	-0.33	0.13	-0.33	-0.74	-0.74	—	Income Ratio %
—	—	—	—	—	19	10	15	11	4	12	—	Turnover Rate %
—	—	—	—	—	21	80	110	210	314	456	467	Net Assets $mil

Performance 12-31-04

	1st Qtr	2nd Qtr	3rd Qtr	4th Qtr	Total
2000	8.93	-1.73	1.76	4.29	13.60
2001	-4.06	12.06	-15.92	19.71	8.22
2002	3.03	-7.83	-15.27	5.37	-15.22
2003	-5.52	17.78	5.71	12.33	32.14
2004	3.52	-0.99	-2.10	10.05	10.43

Trailing	Total Return%	+/- S&P 500	+/- Russ 2000	%Rank Cat	Growth of $10,000
3 Mo	10.05	0.82	-4.04	92	11,005
6 Mo	7.73	0.54	-3.10	89	10,773
1 Yr	10.43	-0.44	-7.90	97	11,043
3 Yr Avg	7.35	3.77	-4.13	90	12,371
5 Yr Avg	8.75	11.05	2.14	73	15,211
10 Yr Avg	—	—	—	—	—
15 Yr Avg	—	—	—	—	—

Tax Analysis	Tax-Adj Rtn%	%Rank Cat	Tax-Cost Rat	%Rank Cat
3 Yr (estimated)	7.35	87	0.00	1
5 Yr (estimated)	8.49	66	0.24	10
10 Yr (estimated)	—	—	—	—

Potential Capital Gain Exposure: 32% of assets

Rating and Risk

Time Period	Load-Adj Return %	Morningstar Rtn vs Cat	Morningstar Risk vs Cat	Morningstar Risk-Adj Rating
1 Yr	10.43			
3 Yr	7.35	-Avg	Low	★★
5 Yr	8.75	-Avg	-Avg	★★★
10 Yr	—	—	—	—
Incept	14.02			

Other Measures	Standard Index S&P 500	Best Fit Index Russ 2000
Alpha	4.2	-1.7
Beta	0.82	0.75
R-Squared	69	94
Standard Deviation	15.82	
Mean	7.35	
Sharpe Ratio	0.38	

Portfolio Analysis 09-30-04

Share change since 11-03 Total Stocks:75	Sector	PE	YTD Ret%	% Assets
⊖ Caremark RX	Health	32.8	55.67	5.26
Universal Health Service	Health	14.9	-16.59	3.61
Computer Associates Inte	Software	—	13.92	3.12
Unocal	Energy	11.4	19.85	2.62
Hilb Rogal & Hobbs Compa	Financial	15.0	14.30	2.42
Houston Exploration	Energy	10.6	54.19	2.42
Overnite	Business	—	64.67	2.39
BankUnited Financial A	Financial	20.0	23.89	2.36
Emmis Communications A	Media	—	-29.06	2.32
CACI International A	Business	25.8	40.13	2.29
Western Wireless A	Telecom	—	59.59	2.13
ITT Educational Services	Consumer	32.8	1.24	2.04
⊖ First National Bankshare	Financial	—	—	2.03
Darden Restaurants	Consumer	20.1	32.28	1.98
DeVry	Consumer	23.1	-30.92	1.96
Charles River Laboratori	Health	24.5	34.02	1.89
Pogo Producing	Energy	10.6	0.87	1.87
Ruby Tuesday	Consumer	14.5	-8.32	1.84
Perot Systems	Business	20.9	18.92	1.82
FNB	Financial	15.1	12.78	1.80

Current Investment Style

Value Blnd Growth — Large Mid Small

Market Cap	%
Giant	0.0
Large	11.5
Mid	50.8
Small	31.8
Micro	5.9

Avg $mil: 2,022

Value Measures		Rel Category
Price/Earnings	17.91	1.04
Price/Book	1.98	0.99
Price/Sales	1.25	1.32
Price/Cash Flow	3.62	0.62
Dividend Yield %	0.44	0.53

Growth Measures	%	Rel Category
Long-Term Erngs	12.72	0.94
Book Value	8.95	1.59
Sales	5.97	1.39
Cash Flow	17.91	3.63
Historical Erngs	10.76	1.44

Profitability	%	Rel Category
Return on Equity	11.89	1.14
Return on Assets	5.15	1.04
Net Margin	7.17	0.98

Sector Weightings	% of Stocks	Rel S&P 500	3 Year High	3 Year Low
Info	21.72	1.01		
Software	8.24	1.92	16	8
Hardware	3.39	0.33	5	2
Media	7.38	1.92	14	7
Telecom	2.71	0.86	3	1
Service	61.20	1.32		
Health	15.34	1.23	17	11
Consumer	13.51	1.49	16	11
Business	12.84	3.17	15	10
Financial	19.51	0.94	20	11
Mfg	17.08	0.53		
Goods	2.75	0.29	3	2
Ind Mtrls	4.78	0.38	8	4
Energy	9.55	1.33	10	6
Utilities	0.00	0.00	4	0

Composition

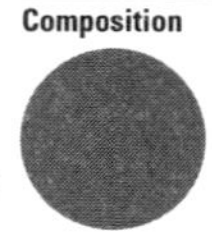

Cash	0.8
Stocks	99.3
Bonds	0.0
Other	0.0
Foreign (% of Stock)	1.2

Morningstar's Take by Karen Wallace 11-30-04

Westport Select Cap is not losing its touch.

At first blush, this fund's performance appears to be on a downward trend. After ranking in the small-blend category's top decile in 1998 and 1999, it has fallen into the category's basement in 2003 and for the year to date through Nov. 29, 2004.

Investors in this closed fund needn't fret, however: Much of the fund's recent underperformance owes to its managers' sensible strategy. Experienced managers Ed Nicklin and Andy Knuth buy firms in which they have high conviction, and continue to hold them as they move up the market-cap ladder or through bouts of poor performance. Indeed, the fund had more than 65% of its assets in small- and micro-caps in 1999 and 2000, compared with only 38% now. Consequently, the fund's mid-cap weighting has grown from around 20% of assets in 1999 to more than 50% now. Thus, as small-cap stocks have outperformed larger fare over the past five years, the fund has fallen behind category peers.

On the other hand, some of the fund's top holdings simply have struggled this year. For example, second-largest holding Universal Health Services has been roiled by bad debt, and radio broadcasting stock Emmis Communications hasn't rebounded as quickly as management had anticipated. In addition, several insurance brokers in the portfolio have been hit by "collateral damage" stemming from the SEC investigations of other top insurers. Turnarounds can take awhile to bear fruit, however, so management is patient with laggard holdings in which it has conviction. As such, we're comfortable that these struggles don't indicate a falloff in stock-picking ability.

We think investors should be patient with this fund. It has been a solid performer in absolute terms over the long term, rising about 8% and 10% per year over the trailing three- and five-year periods. In addition, owing to its low-turnover style, its tax-adjusted returns are impressive.

Address:	253 Riverside Avenue Westport CT 06880 888-593-7878
Web Address:	www.westportfunds.com
Inception:	12-31-97 *
Advisor:	Westport Advisers LLC
Subadvisor:	None
NTF Plans:	Fidelity Retail-NTF, Schwab OneSource

Minimum Purchase:	Closed	Add: —	IRA: —
Min Auto Inv Plan:	Closed	Add: —	
Sales Fees:	No-load, 0.25%S		
Management Fee:	1.00%, 0.12%A		
Actual Fees:	Mgt:1.00%	Dist:0.25%	
Expense Projections:	3Yr:$459	5Yr:$792	10Yr:$1735
Income Distrib:	Annually		

White Oak Growth Stock

Ticker	Load	NAV	Yield	Total Assets	Mstar Category
WOGSX	None	$34.06	0.0%	$1,545 mil	Large Growth

Governance and Management

Fiduciary Grade: B

Portfolio Manager(s)

Seasoned. Jim Oelschlager and comanagers Donna Barton and Doug MacKay have guided the fund since its 1992 inception. Barton is the firm's senior trader and MacKay leads the research effort and is also lead manager of Red Oak Technology Select.

Strategy

The managers practice a top-down, buy-and-hold approach that focuses on identifying market leaders from high-growth sectors--namely technology, health care, and financials. The team has stuck to its compact portfolio of mega-cap names through thick and thin, often adding to holdings when their prices dip. The upshot of this line of attack is that the fund tends to post big gains in bull markets, but it is also extremely vulnerable to market downturns.

Historical Profile

Return Average
Risk High
Rating ★★ Below Avg

Investment Style: Equity — Stock %

1993	1994	1995	1996	1997	1998	1999	2000	2001	2002	2003	12-04
	88%	95%	96%	97%	98%	100%	99%	100%	100%		

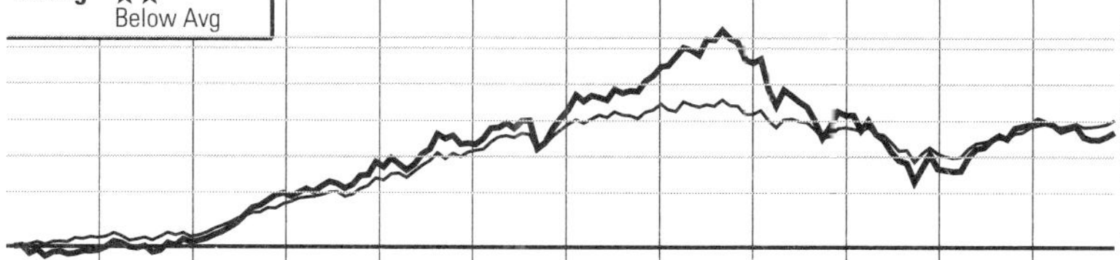

Performance Quartile (within Category)

1993	1994	1995	1996	1997	1998	1999	2000	2001	2002	2003	12-04	History
11.08	11.75	17.90	23.55	29.18	40.71	61.12	63.07	38.44	23.06	35.19	34.06	NAV
-0.26	6.29	52.70	32.27	24.30	39.51	50.14	3.60	-39.05	-40.01	52.60	-3.21	Total Return %
-10.32	4.98	15.17	9.33	-9.05	10.94	29.10	12.70	-27.17	-17.92	23.93	-14.08	+/-S&P 500
-3.13	3.67	15.52	9.15	-6.19	0.80	16.98	26.02	-18.63	-12.13	22.85	-9.51	+/-Russ 1000Gr
0.53	0.23	0.30	0.28	0.09	0.00	0.00	0.00	0.00	0.00	0.00	0.00	Income Return %
-0.79	6.06	52.40	31.99	24.21	39.51	50.14	3.60	-39.05	-40.01	52.60	-3.21	Capital Return %
93	3	1	4	63	21	21	5	97	97	2	99	Total Rtn % Rank Cat
0.06	0.03	0.04	0.05	0.02	0.00	0.00	0.00	0.00	0.00	0.00	0.00	Income $
0.00	0.00	0.00	0.07	0.06	0.00	0.00	0.28	0.00	0.00	0.00	0.00	Capital Gains $
0.97	0.97	0.97	0.95	0.98	1.00	1.00	0.96	0.95	1.00	1.07	—	Expense Ratio %
0.54	0.19	0.29	0.23	0.06	-0.22	-0.34	-0.38	-0.31	-0.32	-0.36	—	Income Ratio %
27	37	22	8	8	6	6	14	15	11	4	—	Turnover Rate %
6	6	11	40	392	1,092	2,725	5,503	3,487	1,804	2,165	1,545	Net Assets $mil

Performance 12-31-04

	1st Qtr	2nd Qtr	3rd Qtr	4th Qtr	Total
2000	20.12	8.00	1.00	-20.93	3.60
2001	-33.28	3.59	-29.04	24.28	-39.05
2002	-4.94	-25.78	-25.07	13.48	-40.01
2003	-2.21	25.32	8.46	14.81	52.60
2004	-0.40	-1.00	-12.10	11.67	-3.21

Trailing	Total Return%	+/- S&P 500	+/- Russ 1000Gr	%Rank Cat	Growth of $10,000
3 Mo	11.67	2.44	2.50	18	11,167
6 Mo	-1.84	-9.03	-5.31	99	9,816
1 Yr	-3.21	-14.08	-9.51	99	9,679
3 Yr Avg	-3.95	-7.53	-3.77	90	8,861
5 Yr Avg	-10.97	-8.67	-1.68	80	5,593
10 Yr Avg	11.39	-0.68	1.80	17	29,408
15 Yr Avg	—	—	—	—	—

Tax Analysis	Tax-Adj Rtn%	%Rank Cat	Tax-Cost Rat	%Rank Cat
3 Yr (estimated)	-3.95	84	0.00	1
5 Yr (estimated)	-10.98	75	0.01	1
10 Yr (estimated)	11.35	7	0.04	1

Potential Capital Gain Exposure: -158% of assets

Rating and Risk

Time Period	Load-Adj Return %	Morningstar Rtn vs Cat	Morningstar Risk vs Cat	Morningstar Risk-Adj Rating
1 Yr	-3.21			
3 Yr	-3.95	-Avg	High	★
5 Yr	-10.97	-Avg	High	★
10 Yr	11.39	+Avg	High	★★
Incept	10.59			

Other Measures	Standard Index S&P 500	Best Fit Index PSE Tech 100
Alpha	-6.9	-7.6
Beta	1.67	1.02
R-Squared	83	93
Standard Deviation	27.53	
Mean	-3.95	
Sharpe Ratio	-0.20	

Portfolio Analysis 12-31-04

Share change since 09-04 Total Stocks:21	Sector	PE	YTD Ret%	% Assets
⊖ eBay	Consumer	81.6	80.07	9.40
⊖ Cisco Systems	Hardware	24.5	-20.26	9.36
EMC	Hardware	41.5	15.09	7.44
MBNA	Financial	14.0	15.53	7.26
Charles Schwab	Financial	32.9	1.77	6.57
⊖ Medtronic	Health	30.7	2.68	6.23
⊖ Applied Materials	Hardware	20.7	-23.80	6.20
⊖ Juniper Networks	Hardware	NMF	45.56	6.10
⊖ Dell	Hardware	34.0	24.01	5.80
Citigroup	Financial	15.3	2.72	5.47
⊖ Linear Technology	Hardware	32.4	-7.10	5.13
Pfizer	Health	22.0	-22.31	4.48
⊕ Amgen	Health	37.7	3.82	4.01
☼ Rockwell Automation	Ind Mtrls	28.0	41.75	3.04
☼ Electronic Arts	Software	30.9	29.36	3.03
Microsoft	Software	36.1	8.95	2.75
☼ Qualcomm	Hardware	42.0	58.20	2.32
☼ United Parcel Service B	Business	28.5	16.40	2.13
☼ Symantec	Software	34.5	49.33	2.04
☼ Avid Technology	Software	30.9	28.65	0.64

Current Investment Style

Value Blnd Growth — Large Mid Small

Market Cap	%
Giant	52.0
Large	46.9
Mid	1.1
Small	0.0
Micro	0.0
Avg $mil: 48,965	

Value Measures		Rel Category
Price/Earnings	25.42	1.20
Price/Book	3.91	1.21
Price/Sales	4.69	2.18
Price/Cash Flow	11.41	1.04
Dividend Yield %	0.65	0.84

Growth Measures	%	Rel Category
Long-Term Erngs	15.80	1.12
Book Value	16.48	1.30
Sales	9.08	1.07
Cash Flow	15.24	0.92
Historical Erngs	16.24	1.12

Profitability	%	Rel Category
Return on Equity	16.82	0.94
Return on Assets	11.50	1.23
Net Margin	18.35	1.49

Sector Weightings	% of Stocks	Rel S&P 500	3 Year High	3 Year Low
Info	51.37	2.39		
Software	8.47	1.97	15	5
Hardware	42.90	4.21	47	30
Media	0.00	0.00	0	0
Telecom	0.00	0.00	0	0
Service	45.60	0.98		
Health	14.74	1.18	22	13
Consumer	9.41	1.04	9	0
Business	2.13	0.53	3	0
Financial	19.32	0.93	31	19
Mfg	3.05	0.09		
Goods	0.00	0.00	0	0
Ind Mtrls	3.05	0.24	3	0
Energy	0.00	0.00	0	0
Utilities	0.00	0.00	0	0

Composition

Cash	0.1
Stocks	99.9
Bonds	0.0
Other	0.0
Foreign (% of Stock)	0.0

Morningstar's Take by Christopher Davis 10-15-04

Despite White Oak Growth Stock's many virtues, most investors won't find it a redeeming investment.

This fund boasts many admirable qualities. For one, advisor Oak Associates generally acts with fund shareholders' interests at heart. Manager Jim Oelschlager invests a tidy sum in this and other Oak funds--$17 million by his count. Although expenses have ticked up in recent years, Oak deserves credit for keeping costs low, even when this fund and its siblings have had little in the way of assets.

We also like funds that stick to their strategies through thick and thin. On that score, it's tough to find fault with this fund. It concentrates its picks in what Oelschlager believes are the sectors with the best growth prospects--health care, finanicals, and most especially, technology. In the most recent bear market, when tech-related stocks suffered precipitous losses, Oelschlager left his heavy weighting in the sector virtually untouched. The fund's miniscule 4% turnover rate in 2003 reflects Oelschlager's long-term commitment to his picks.

While there's no doubting management's devotion to its strategy, we question whether its risks are worth taking. Not only is the portfolio heavily skewed toward tech stocks--hardware and software stocks account for a whopping 56% of assets--it is concentrated in just 20 holdings. To be sure, that mix can be quite rewarding, as the fund's 52% gain in 2003 made clear. The downside, though, can be brutal. In the March 2000 to October 2002 bear market, for example, the fund shed 58% of its value. And more recently, poor-performing tech holdings such as Cisco Systems and PMC-Sierra have dragged the fund to a 13% loss for the year to date through Oct. 13, 2004, one of the category's worst showings.

For those who share Oelschlager's conviction in high-growth areas, this offering could serve as an aggressive kicker for a well-diversified portfolio. However, for most folks, we think it's too risky to be worthwhile.

Address:	Oak Associates Funds Kansas City, MO 64121-9441 888-462-5386
Web Address:	www.oakassociates.com
Inception:	08-03-92
Advisor:	Oak Associates Ltd
Subadvisor:	None
NTF Plans:	Fidelity Retail-NTF, Schwab OneSource

Minimum Purchase:	$2000	Add: $50	IRA: $2000
Min Auto Inv Plan:	$2000	Add: $25	
Sales Fees:	No-load		
Management Fee:	0.74%, 0.20%A		
Actual Fees:	Mgt:0.70%	Dist:	
Expense Projections:	3Yr:$353	5Yr:$612	10Yr:$1352
Income Distrib:	Annually		

William Blair Intl Gr N

Ticker	Load	NAV	Yield	Total Assets	Mstar Category
WBIGX	Closed	$22.09	0.0%	$3,000 mil	Foreign Large Growth

Governance and Management

Fiduciary Grade: B

Portfolio Manager(s)

George Greig is in his second stint with this offering. He helped launch the fund in 1992 and has done well since returning in 1996. Before joining William Blair, he was a founding partner of PBHG.

Strategy

Manager George Greig looks for companies with good growth prospects, high returns on equity, and low debt. He also considers qualitative elements such as corporate culture and the strength of management. Although Greig isn't solely a top-down investor, he often uses themes, such as Asian economic growth, to help drive his stock picks. An emerging-markets stake of 10%-15% is not uncommon here. Greig looks across market caps for his picks, and multinationals often rub shoulders with tiny, unknown names in this portfolio. William Blair instituted a fair-value-pricing policy on this fund in 2003.

Historical Profile

Return High
Risk Average
Rating ★★★★★ Highest

Investment Style: Equity Stock %

100% 99% 93% 97% 92% 85% 85% 89% 95%

▼ Manager Change
▽ Partial Manager Change

Growth of $10,000
- Investment Values of Fund
- Investment Values of MSCI EAFE

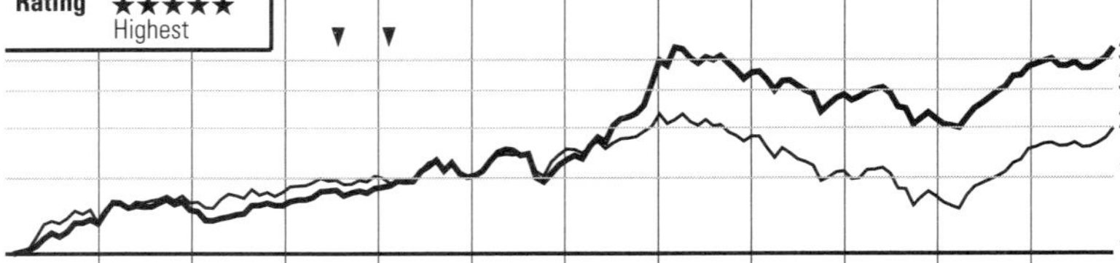

Performance Quartile (within Category)

1993	1994	1995	1996	1997	1998	1999	2000	2001	2002	2003	12-04	History
13.18	12.36	13.12	13.95	13.14	14.62	24.03	17.93	15.48	13.13	18.65	22.09	NAV
33.80	-0.04	7.21	10.20	8.39	11.46	96.25	-8.10	-13.66	-15.18	42.21	18.48	Total Return %
1.24	-7.82	-4.00	4.15	6.61	-8.47	69.22	6.09	7.76	0.76	3.62	-1.77	+/-MSCI EAFE
1.59	-7.39	-4.20	3.33	6.12	-7.23	68.27	5.26	7.73	0.62	2.79	-1.90	+/-MSCI Wd xUS
0.00	0.18	1.05	0.52	0.56	0.18	0.00	0.32	0.00	0.00	0.16	0.03	Income Return %
33.80	-0.22	6.16	9.68	7.83	11.28	96.25	-8.42	-13.66	-15.18	42.05	18.45	Capital Return %
78	36	66	72	38	66	3	2	7	23	15	24	Total Rtn % Rank Cat
0.00	0.02	0.13	0.07	0.08	0.02	0.00	0.08	0.00	0.00	0.02	0.01	Income $
0.36	0.79	0.00	0.43	1.86	0.00	4.49	3.97	0.00	0.00	0.00	0.00	Capital Gains $
1.71	1.51	1.48	1.44	1.43	1.36	1.35	1.59	1.60	1.51	1.50	—	Expense Ratio %
0.11	0.15	0.87	0.19	0.01	0.09	-0.43	-0.44	-0.11	-0.36	0.05	—	Income Ratio %
83	40	77	89	102	98	122	116	112	73	57	—	Turnover Rate %
40	71	90	105	129	140	40	116	189	527	1,355	2,062	Net Assets $mil

Performance 12-31-04

	1st Qtr	2nd Qtr	3rd Qtr	4th Qtr	Total
2000	7.70	-5.26	-4.00	-6.19	-8.10
2001	-11.21	3.20	-16.13	12.34	-13.66
2002	1.81	-0.82	-19.13	3.88	-15.18
2003	-5.71	17.85	11.79	14.48	42.21
2004	5.36	-2.29	-0.47	15.63	18.48

Trailing	Total Return%	+/- MSCI EAFE	+/- MSCI Wd xUS	%Rank Cat	Growth of $10,000
3 Mo	15.63	0.31	0.48	9	11,563
6 Mo	15.08	0.08	-0.29	14	11,508
1 Yr	18.48	-1.77	-1.90	24	11,848
3 Yr Avg	12.64	0.75	0.42	13	14,292
5 Yr Avg	2.54	3.67	3.30	6	11,336
10 Yr Avg	12.25	6.63	6.31	5	31,759
15 Yr Avg	—	—	—	—	—

Tax Analysis	Tax-Adj Rtn%	%Rank Cat	Tax-Cost Rat	%Rank Cat
3 Yr (estimated)	12.62	10	0.02	5
5 Yr (estimated)	1.49	6	1.02	65
10 Yr (estimated)	10.69	7	1.39	75

Potential Capital Gain Exposure: 25% of assets

Rating and Risk

Time Period	Load-Adj Return %	Morningstar Rtn vs Cat	Morningstar Risk vs Cat	Morningstar Risk-Adj Rating
1 Yr	18.48			
3 Yr	12.64	High	Avg	★★★★
5 Yr	2.54	High	Avg	★★★★★
10 Yr	12.25	High	Avg	★★★★★
Incept	12.65			

Other Measures	Standard Index S&P 500	Best Fit Index MSCI Wd xUS
Alpha	1.6	1.1
Beta	0.91	0.92
R-Squared	93	93
Standard Deviation	16.57	
Mean	12.64	
Sharpe Ratio	0.69	

Portfolio Analysis 12-31-04

Share change since 11-04 Total Stocks:130	Sector	Country	% Assets
Sanofi-Synthelabo	Health	France	2.71
⊖ Tesco	Consumer	U.K.	2.43
Carnival	Goods	U.K.	2.21
⊖ SAP	Software	Germany	1.88
BG Grp	Utilities	U.K.	1.87
⊖ Ericsson AB (publ)	Hardware	Sweden	1.84
Standard Chartered	Financial	U.K.	1.76
CNOOC Ltd	Energy	Hong Kong	1.58
☼ E.ON	Utilities	Germany	1.51
Erste Bank	Financial	Austria	1.51
Reckitt Benckiser	Goods	U.K.	1.49
Canon	Goods	Japan	1.45
Hoya	Goods	Japan	1.43
Samsung Electronics	Goods	Korea	1.43
America Movil S.A. de C.	Telecom	Mexico	1.42
ORIX	Financial	Japan	1.41
Hyundai Motor	Goods	Korea	1.38
Statoil Asa	Energy	Norway	1.38
⊖ Hon Hai Precision Indust	Business	Taiwan	1.33
Sharp	Goods	Japan	1.32

Current Investment Style

Value Blnd Growth — Large Mid Small

Market Cap	%
Giant	34.0
Large	34.3
Mid	28.5
Small	3.3
Micro	0.0

Avg $mil: 9,664

Value Measures		Rel Category
Price/Earnings	17.28	1.17
Price/Book	2.94	1.41
Price/Sales	1.48	1.41
Price/Cash Flow	8.76	1.59
Dividend Yield %	1.55	0.76

Growth Measures	%	Rel Category
Long-Term Erngs	15.66	1.31
Book Value	8.98	5.19
Sales	8.81	1.91
Cash Flow	5.14	0.68
Historical Erngs	20.48	2.46

Composition

Cash	3.0	Bonds	0.0
Stocks	94.9	Other	2.1

Foreign (% of Stock) 100.0

Sector Weightings	% of Stocks	Rel MSCI EAFE	3 Year High	3 Year Low
Info	9.98	0.60		
Software	3.87	3.58	6	0
Hardware	2.65	0.73	9	2
Media	0.47	0.21	3	0
Telecom	2.99	0.31	5	0
Service	53.96	1.21		
Health	8.03	1.11	13	4
Consumer	12.44	2.47	15	7
Business	9.26	1.70	18	6
Financial	24.23	0.90	28	16
Mfg	36.06	0.93		
Goods	17.00	1.24	26	17
Ind Mtrls	8.56	0.70	12	6
Energy	6.49	0.88	6	1
Utilities	4.01	0.75	6	1

Regional Exposure	% Stock		
UK/W. Europe	46	N. America	6
Japan	20	Latn America	7
Asia X Japan	17	Other	4

Country Exposure	% Stock		
Japan	20	Germany	7
U.K.	16	Canada	6
France	8		

Morningstar's Take by Arijit Dutta 11-30-04

William Blair International Growth continues to do well by opting for the road less traveled.

The fund's five-year streak of finishing in the foreign large-growth category's top quartile looked to be in severe jeopardy earlier this year, but it has recovered nicely. After trailing the category average up until midyear, the fund's 10.29% return through Nov. 16 now puts it solidly ahead of its typical rival.

A nearly 20% stake in emerging markets (which is more than twice the category average) largely explains the rebound. Undeterred by the correction that befell these stocks in the spring of 2004, manager George Greig held on, trimming only some of his Chinese holdings. His conviction paid off, as Greig's Egyptian and South African selections posted major gains. His continued reliance on indirect plays on Chinese growth, such as the U.K.'s Standard Chartered Bank (which provides financial and business services in the region), has also triumphed.

Greig's willingness to venture into emerging markets isn't the only indication of his self-assured, independent style. The fund's average market cap is about half that of its average peer and points to the alacrity Greig and his team have shown in detecting growth stocks off the beaten track. The decision to close the fund in March 2004 was dedicated to preserving this advantage. Even among blue chips, Greig has been fairly inventive: Picks such as Manulife Financial--a stock that appears in few rival funds' portfolios--have appreciated strongly of late.

Investors should keep in mind, however, that this fund's bold style does court significant risks, as its emphasis on smaller-cap and emerging-markets stocks makes it particularly vulnerable to a market downturn. Still, Greig's stock-picking has proved equal to the task, and the fund has posted impressive relative performance in virtually all market conditions.

Shareholders here should feel content.

Address:	222 W Adams St Chicago IL 60606 800-742-7272
Web Address:	www.wmblair.com
Inception:	10-01-92
Advisor:	William Blair & Company, LLC
Subadvisor:	None
NTF Plans:	Fidelity Retail-NTF, Schwab OneSource

Minimum Purchase:	Closed	Add: —	IRA: —
Min Auto Inv Plan:	Closed	Add: —	
Sales Fees:	0.25%B, 2.00%R		
Management Fee:	1.00%		
Actual Fees:	Mgt:1.00%	Dist:0.25%	
Expense Projections:	3Yr:$474	5Yr:$818	10Yr:$1791
Income Distrib:	Annually		

William Blair Sm-Cp Gr N

Ticker	Load	NAV	Yield	Total Assets	Mstar Category
WBSNX	Closed	$25.73	0.0%	$771 mil	Small Growth

Governance and Management

Fiduciary Grade: B

Portfolio Manager(s)

Michael Balkin and Karl Brewer have managed this offering since its December 1999 inception. This is their first stint running a retail mutual fund.

Strategy

Management uses a combination of bottom-up and top-down analysis to pick stocks. It looks for industry and sector trends that can spur growth and prefers companies that have strong catalysts for sustainable sales and earnings growth. The thing that sets it apart is its valuation consciousness and a contrarian streak that leads the team to jump in when a stock is promising but beaten down.

Historical Profile

Return High
Risk Above Avg
Rating ★★★★★ Highest

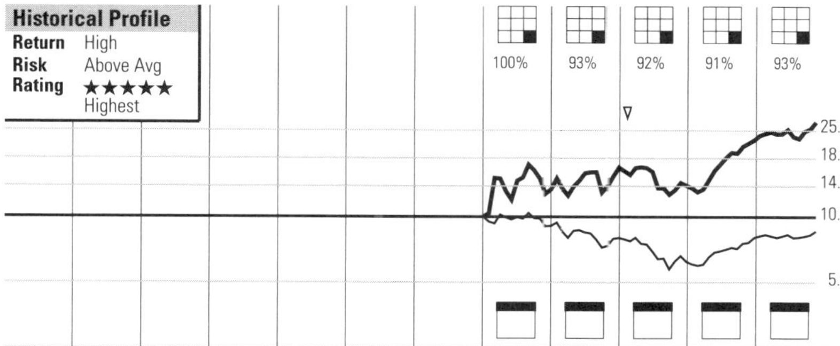

Investment Style
Equity
Stock %

▼ Manager Change
∇ Partial Manager Change

Growth of $10,000
— Investment Values of Fund
— Investment Values of S&P 500

Performance Quartile (within Category)

1993	1994	1995	1996	1997	1998	1999	2000	2001	2002	2003	12-04	History
—	—	—	—	—	—	10.19	13.16	16.58	13.72	21.83	25.73	NAV
—	—	—	—	—	—	1.90*	33.68	25.99	-17.25	61.87	27.29	Total Return %
—	—	—	—	—	—	—	42.78	37.87	4.84	33.20	16.42	+/-S&P 500
—	—	—	—	—	—	—	56.11	35.22	13.01	13.33	12.98	+/-Russ 2000 Gr
—	—	—	—	—	—	—	0.00	0.00	0.00	0.00	0.00	Income Return %
—	—	—	—	—	—	—	33.68	25.99	-17.25	61.87	27.29	Capital Return %
—	—	—	—	—	—	—	2	2	10	7	2	Total Rtn % Rank Cat
—	—	—	—	—	—	0.00	0.00	0.00	0.00	0.00	0.00	Income $
—	—	—	—	—	—	0.00	0.43	0.00	0.00	0.36	2.01	Capital Gains $
—	—	—	—	—	—	1.60	1.60	1.59	1.62	1.52	—	Expense Ratio %
—	—	—	—	—	—	-1.60	-0.75	-1.15	-1.37	-1.19	—	Income Ratio %
—	—	—	—	—	—	—	433	147	133	103	—	Turnover Rate %
—	—	—	—	—	—	—	3	12	24	328	476	Net Assets $mil

Performance 12-31-04

	1st Qtr	2nd Qtr	3rd Qtr	4th Qtr	Total
2000	49.66	-2.16	11.60	-18.19	33.68
2001	-6.38	26.70	-18.45	30.24	25.99
2002	-0.42	-3.94	-21.37	10.02	-17.25
2003	-3.94	30.20	12.35	15.19	61.87
2004	8.75	2.57	-1.81	16.22	27.29

Trailing	Total Return%	+/- S&P 500	+/- Russ 2000 Gr	%Rank Cat	Growth of $10,000
3 Mo	16.22	6.99	1.14	13	11,622
6 Mo	14.12	6.93	5.96	4	11,412
1 Yr	27.29	16.42	12.98	2	12,729
3 Yr Avg	19.47	15.89	13.68	1	17,052
5 Yr Avg	23.49	25.79	27.06	1	28,718
10 Yr Avg	—	—	—	—	—
15 Yr Avg	—	—	—	—	—

Tax Analysis	Tax-Adj Rtn%	%Rank Cat	Tax-Cost Rat	%Rank Cat
3 Yr (estimated)	18.73	1	0.62	45
5 Yr (estimated)	22.70	1	0.64	28
10 Yr (estimated)	—	—	—	—

Potential Capital Gain Exposure: 24% of assets

Rating and Risk

Time Period	Load-Adj Return %	Morningstar Rtn vs Cat	Morningstar Risk vs Cat	Morningstar Risk-Adj Rating
1 Yr	27.29			
3 Yr	19.47	High	Avg	★★★★★
5 Yr	23.49	High	High	★★★★★
10 Yr	—	—	—	—
Incept	23.88			

Other Measures	Standard Index S&P 500	Best Fit Index Russ 2000
Alpha	16.1	7.6
Beta	1.06	0.98
R-Squared	66	92
Standard Deviation	23.43	
Mean	19.47	
Sharpe Ratio	0.78	

Portfolio Analysis 12-31-04

Share change since 11-04 Total Stocks:81	Sector	PE	YTD Ret%	% Assets
Laureate Education	Consumer	32.0	53.14	3.17
⊖ ValueClick	Business	32.4	46.97	2.37
Integra LifeSciences Hol	Health	67.0	28.86	2.29
Kforce	Business	35.5	18.72	2.25
VitalWorks	Software	—	0.68	1.98
Optimal Group A	Business	—	47.25	1.92
Coinstar	Business	26.6	48.15	1.88
Insight Enterprises	Consumer	15.3	9.15	1.77
Affiliated Managers Grou	Financial	28.2	46.01	1.74
Jarden	Goods	27.5	58.89	1.61
4 Kids Entertainment	Goods	20.7	-19.22	1.60
Airgas	Ind Mtrls	21.8	24.36	1.53
Elizabeth Arden	Goods	—	19.18	1.51
⊖ Labor Ready	Business	23.5	29.16	1.49
Credit Acceptance	Financial	26.8	66.34	1.45
WebEx Communications	Software	14.8	18.07	1.45
Lions Gate Entertainment	Software	—	137.05	1.44
Gasco Engy	Energy	—	-42.47	1.41
Axcan Pharma	Health	29.4	23.45	1.40
⊖ Intermix Media	—	—	253.13	1.37

Current Investment Style

Value Blnd Growth — Large Mid Small

Market Cap	%
Giant	0.0
Large	0.0
Mid	17.8
Small	49.6
Micro	32.6
Avg $mil: 666	

Value Measures		Rel Category
Price/Earnings	24.76	1.14
Price/Book	2.45	0.93
Price/Sales	1.56	1.04
Price/Cash Flow	6.13	0.77
Dividend Yield %	0.04	0.13

Growth Measures	%	Rel Category
Long-Term Erngs	18.08	1.05
Book Value	6.21	0.96
Sales	6.17	0.96
Cash Flow	8.46	0.62
Historical Erngs	5.46	0.40

Profitability	%	Rel Category
Return on Equity	6.25	0.63
Return on Assets	3.14	0.72
Net Margin	6.53	0.95

Sector Weightings	% of Stocks	Rel S&P 500	3 Year High	3 Year Low
Info	17.75	0.83		
Software	9.64	2.24	14	3
Hardware	5.77	0.57	14	6
Media	2.34	0.61	7	1
Telecom	0.00	0.00	3	0
Service	65.18	1.41		
Health	18.02	1.44	23	14
Consumer	13.95	1.54	22	12
Business	27.23	6.72	28	15
Financial	5.98	0.29	11	3
Mfg	17.06	0.53		
Goods	8.08	0.87	8	1
Ind Mtrls	2.73	0.22	6	1
Energy	6.25	0.87	7	3
Utilities	0.00	0.00	0	0

Composition

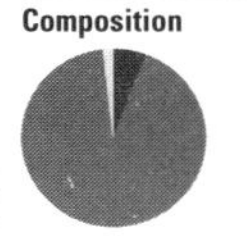

Cash	5.7
Stocks	92.5
Bonds	0.0
Other	1.8
Foreign (% of Stock)	5.6

Morningstar's Take by Kerry O'Boyle 12-14-04

This stellar offering continues to deliver.

At the expense of sounding like a broken record, William Blair Small Cap Growth is trouncing its rivals yet again. It's up 22.3% for the year to date through Dec. 13, 2004, roughly 13.5 percentage points better than its typical rival. If these results stand through the end of the year, it will mark the fifth consecutive year--basically every year since its inception--that it has landed in the top decile of the small-growth category.

Credit goes to managers Karl Brewer and Michael Balkin and their flexible, research-intensive stock-picking style. Balkin and Brewer spend a lot of time on the road meeting with company management teams, suppliers, competitors, and customers in an effort to gain an edge in sorting through underfollowed small-cap stocks. They're not afraid to go against the grain either, often buying the out-of-favor stocks of firms that they believe still have viable business models. Long-time holding and Internet advertising company ValueClick gained 225% in 2003, after a dismal 2001-2002, and is up another 40% in 2004. And underfollowed independent film producer Lions Gate Entertainment--up 143%--has been a top-10 holding for most of the year.

Shareholders of this closed offering should keep expectations in check, however. Balkin says that this is the second longest up cycle for small-cap stocks in history and that a number of big-picture issues--such as rising interest rates, a weakened dollar, and a heightened regulatory environment--could lead to continued choppiness in the markets. Still, he doesn't view small-growth stocks to be overvalued by any means, and is still finding attractive investment opportunities such as ocean-shipper OMI and packaging firm Jarden.

This offering's outstanding record speaks volumes, though. Superb stock-picking has kept it heads and shoulders above its peers in a variety of market conditions, and those fortunate enough to own it should hang on.

Address:	222 W Adams St Chicago IL 60606 800-742-7272
Web Address:	www.wmblair.com
Inception:	12-27-99 *
Advisor:	William Blair & Company, LLC
Subadvisor:	None
NTF Plans:	Fidelity Retail-NTF, Schwab OneSource

Minimum Purchase:	Closed	Add: —	IRA: —
Min Auto Inv Plan:	Closed	Add: —	
Sales Fees:	0.25%B, 1.00%R		
Management Fee:	1.10%		
Actual Fees:	Mgt:1.10%	Dist:0.25%	
Expense Projections:	3Yr:$481	5Yr:$830	10Yr:$1813
Income Distrib:	Annually		

WPG Core Bond

Ticker	Load	NAV	Yield	SEC Yield	Total Assets	Mstar Category
WPGVX	None	$10.81	2.9%	2.94%	$154 mil	Intermediate-Term Bond

Governance and Management

Fiduciary Grade: B

Portfolio Manager(s)

Dan Vandivort took over this fund early in 1995 and was joined by comanager Sid Bakst in 1998. A team of sector specialists conducts its own trading, and three credit analysts round out the team.

Strategy

Prior to 1998, this fund focused solely on government securities. Since that time, however, the fund has invested across the domestic, investment-grade spectrum. Lead manager Dan Vandivort doesn't make interest-rate bets and doesn't take on much credit risk. He keeps the portfolio's duration--a measure of interest-rate sensitivity--within 5% of that of the Lehman Brothers Aggregate Index. The fund rotates among the Treasury, mortgage, agency, and corporate sectors of the market and also concentrates on individual security selection and yield-curve positioning.

Historical Profile

Return High
Risk Average
Rating ★★★★★ Highest

Investment Style: Fixed Income — Income Rtn %Rank Cat: 67 84 45 36 27 76 78 84 79

▼ Manager Change
∇ Partial Manager Change

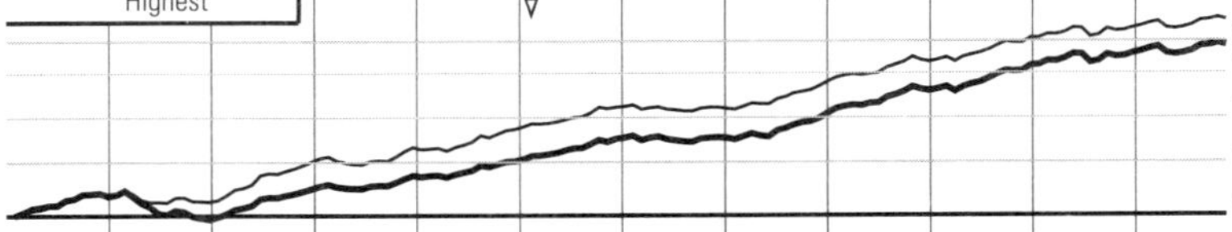

Growth of $10,000 — Investment Values of Fund; Investment Values of LB Aggr (20.5, 18.0, 15.0, 12.5, 10.0)

Performance Quartile (within Category)

1993	1994	1995	1996	1997	1998	1999	2000	2001	2002	2003	12-04	History
10.37	8.83	9.38	9.19	9.34	9.64	9.07	9.40	9.80	10.44	10.66	10.81	NAV
8.95	-8.71	13.26	3.85	7.37	9.26	-0.12	10.66	9.61	10.85	5.04	4.38	Total Return %
-0.80	-5.79	-5.21	0.22	-2.28	0.57	0.70	-0.97	1.17	0.60	0.94	0.04	+/-LB Aggr
-3.29	-4.20	-8.17	1.16	-2.06	-0.88	2.76	-1.78	0.79	-2.18	-0.93	-0.92	+/-LB 5-10YR
7.86	6.38	6.87	5.86	5.66	5.97	5.94	6.79	5.29	4.15	2.91	2.94	Income Return %
1.09	-15.09	6.39	-2.01	1.71	3.29	-6.06	3.87	4.32	6.70	2.13	1.44	Capital Return %
77	99	94	29	90	8	18	38	7	5	34	29	Total Rtn % Rank Cat
0.79	0.64	0.59	0.54	0.51	0.54	0.56	0.60	0.49	0.40	0.30	0.31	Income $
0.15	0.02	0.00	0.00	0.00	0.00	0.00	0.00	0.00	0.00	0.00	0.00	Capital Gains $
0.81	0.80	0.82	0.81	0.86	0.50	0.50	0.50	0.50	0.50	0.45	—	Expense Ratio %
7.43	7.18	6.52	5.87	5.56	5.71	5.98	6.58	5.04	4.02	2.81	—	Income Ratio %
98	116	375	333	330	685	531	448	432	539	562	—	Turnover Rate %
335	216	172	128	108	139	137	114	124	105	145	154	Net Assets $mil

Performance 12-31-04

	1st Qtr	2nd Qtr	3rd Qtr	4th Qtr	Total
2000	1.83	1.24	3.24	3.98	10.66
2001	3.39	0.89	4.69	0.37	9.61
2002	-0.30	3.88	4.75	2.17	10.85
2003	1.76	2.83	-0.10	0.48	5.04
2004	2.72	-2.65	3.27	1.06	4.38

Trailing	Total Return%	+/- LB Aggr	+/- LB 5-10YR	%Rank Cat	Growth of $10,000
3 Mo	1.06	0.11	0.08	38	10,106
6 Mo	4.37	0.19	-1.20	28	10,437
1 Yr	4.38	0.04	-0.92	29	10,438
3 Yr Avg	6.72	0.53	-1.33	12	12,155
5 Yr Avg	8.07	0.36	-1.00	8	14,741
10 Yr Avg	7.35	-0.37	-1.11	28	20,325
15 Yr Avg	6.86	-0.84	-1.46	73	27,054

Tax Analysis	Tax-Adj Rtn%	%Rank Cat	Tax-Cost Rat	%Rank Cat
3 Yr (estimated)	5.47	3	1.17	15
5 Yr (estimated)	6.34	3	1.60	19
10 Yr (estimated)	5.25	9	1.96	26

Potential Capital Gain Exposure: -2% of assets

Rating and Risk

Time Period	Load-Adj Return %	Morningstar Rtn vs Cat	Morningstar Risk vs Cat	Morningstar Risk-Adj Rating
1 Yr	4.38			
3 Yr	6.72	High	+Avg	★★★★★
5 Yr	8.07	High	Avg	★★★★★
10 Yr	7.35	+Avg	-Avg	★★★★
Incept	7.28			

Other Measures	Standard Index LB Aggr	Best Fit Index LB Aggr
Alpha	0.4	0.4
Beta	1.02	1.02
R-Squared	99	99
Standard Deviation	4.65	
Mean	6.72	
Sharpe Ratio	1.16	

Portfolio Analysis 10-31-04

Total Fixed-Income:113	Date of Maturity	Amount $000	Value $000	% Net Assets
FNMA	11-15-33	10,000	10,181	4.62
FNMA	11-01-32	9,775	10,132	4.60
US Treasury Note 2.375%	08-15-06	9,945	9,927	4.51
FNMA	11-15-33	9,020	8,986	4.08
FNMA	11-01-32	8,000	8,410	3.82
FNMA	11-15-18	7,805	7,825	3.55
US Treasury Note 2.75%	08-15-07	7,175	7,171	3.26
FHLBA 3.75%	08-18-09	5,700	5,750	2.61
FNMA 5.5%	07-01-34	5,065	5,164	2.34
US Treasury Bond 5.375%	02-15-31	4,745	5,154	2.34
FNMA	11-01-19	3,990	4,071	1.85
US Treasury Note 4%	06-15-09	3,630	3,748	1.70
FNMA	11-15-18	3,500	3,624	1.65
FHLMC 5.5%	09-01-19	3,336	3,456	1.57
US Treasury Note 2.25%	02-15-07	3,415	3,386	1.54
US Treasury Note 3.375%	12-15-08	2,975	3,005	1.36
US Treasury Note 1.875%	01-31-06	2,645	2,631	1.19
US Treasury Note 2.625%	05-15-08	2,450	2,423	1.10
FNMA 5.25%	06-15-06	2,235	2,326	1.06
FNMA 4.375%	03-15-13	2,105	2,114	0.96

Current Investment Style

Duration: Short Int Long — Quality: High Med Low

¹ figure provided by fund

Avg Eff Duration¹	4.7 Yrs
Avg Eff Maturity	7.1 Yrs
Avg Credit Quality	AAA
Avg Wtd Coupon	3.02%
Avg Wtd Price	102.60% of par

Coupon Range	% of Bonds	Rel Cat
0% PIK	31.1	7.7
0% to 6%	86.9	1.4
6% to 8%	10.8	0.4
8% to 10%	2.2	0.4
More than 10%	0.0	0.0

1.00=Category Average

Credit Analysis		% bonds 10-31-04	
US Govt	68	BB	0
AAA	4	B	0
AA	6	Below B	0
A	8	NR/NA	0
BBB	14		

Sector Breakdown	% of assets
US Treasuries	18
TIPS	0
US Agency	9
Mortgage Pass-Throughs	29
Mortgage CMO	3
Mortgage ARM	0
US Corporate	13
Asset-Backed	5
Convertible	0
Municipal	0
Corporate Inflation-Protected	0
Foreign Corporate	0
Foreign Govt	0

Composition			
Cash	22.3	Bonds	77.7
Stocks	0.0	Other	0.0

Special Securities	
Restricted/Illiquid Secs	3
Exotic Mortgage-Backed	0
Emerging-Markets Secs	0
Options/Futures/Warrants	No

Morningstar's Take by Paul Herbert 10-31-04

WPG Core Bond has much of what we like and only a bit of what we don't.

One of the things that we find most appealing about this fund is its measured approach to risk. Its managers believe that they can beat the pack by making slight bets on attractive issues, maturities, and bond sectors, with the help of quantitative models that look at valuations and technicals. However, they aren't willing to go out on a limb to take on excessive credit risk. They eschew below-investment-grade issuers altogether, and the fund's average credit quality is usually much higher than average for intermediate-term bond funds. Interest-rate bets are also off-limits here.

The managers' caution, along with their ability to eke out gains within their plain-vanilla framework, has been evident lately. With corporate bonds' valuations trading richly as a result of a strong run from late 2002 to early 2004, at mid-year comanagers Daniel Vandivort and Sid Bakst decided to slightly reduce the fund's stake in credit and invest the proceeds in Treasury bonds. This move helped as Treasury yields dropped decidedly during the third quarter. They have also been able to add value from security selection within corporate bonds, despite the low overall level of volatility in the sector, by identifying cheap 30-year bonds among the BBB tier. In all, the fund has gained 4.1% for the year-to-date period ended Oct. 29, 2004, ahead of more than two thirds of its peers.

This ability has also been apparent over the long haul, as the fund has outpaced the majority of its peers in each calendar year since 1998. Low fees also deserve some credit for the fund's success, as it charges just 0.45% per annum.

Our one knock on the fund is that Vandivort and Bakst have not signaled their alignment with shareholders' interests by investing substantial portions of their own money here. As a result, our recommendation of the fund must be a qualified one.

Address:	One New York Plz New York NY 10004 800-223-3332
Web Address:	www.wpginvest.com
Inception:	02-20-86
Advisor:	Weiss, Peck & Greer, LLC
Subadvisor:	None
NTF Plans:	N/A

Minimum Purchase:	$250000	Add: $5000	IRA: $0
Min Auto Inv Plan:	$250000	Add: $50	
Sales Fees:	No-load, 2.00%R		
Management Fee:	0.45%, 0.05%A		
Actual Fees:	Mgt:0.43%	Dist:	
Expense Projections:	3Yr:$144	5Yr:$252	10Yr:$567
Income Distrib:	Monthly		

Tables and Charts

This section breaks down the performance of the Morningstar Categories and lists the best- and worst-performing funds.

Performance Summary–Equity Funds

Morningstar's Open-End Fund Universe

Category	2004 Total Return % 1st Quarter	2nd Quarter	3rd Quarter	4th Quarter	2004	Annualized Total Return % 3 Year	5 Year	10 Year
Domestic Equity	**3.89**	**1.04**	**-2.43**	**11.54**	**14.32**	**7.35**	**4.13**	**11.77**
Large Value	2.40	1.12	-0.21	9.23	12.91	5.63	4.35	11.35
Large Blend	1.87	0.95	-2.19	9.35	9.96	2.93	-1.77	10.42
Large Growth	1.46	1.04	-4.59	10.10	7.64	0.01	-7.64	9.00
Mid-Cap Value	4.53	1.83	-0.39	11.19	17.90	11.13	11.41	13.40
Mid-Cap Blend	4.40	1.15	-1.81	11.82	16.00	9.81	7.18	13.16
Mid-Cap Growth	3.98	0.70	-4.61	12.95	12.93	3.68	-3.42	10.25
Small Value	5.96	1.82	-0.71	12.39	20.58	15.53	15.81	15.01
Small Blend	6.06	1.11	-1.85	12.94	18.86	12.51	11.84	13.10
Small Growth	4.39	-0.36	-5.47	13.86	12.09	4.89	-0.55	10.24
International Equity	**7.12**	**-3.03**	**1.36**	**14.52**	**20.47**	**14.47**	**0.58**	**6.44**
Europe Stock	3.30	0.59	1.15	15.08	20.94	13.40	2.25	10.07
Latin America Stock	7.70	-8.70	15.55	21.65	38.26	21.39	7.66	7.32
Diversified Emerging Mkts	8.67	-9.51	7.68	16.69	23.75	22.17	4.29	4.71
Diversified Pacific/Asia	10.75	-5.13	-1.49	13.07	17.09	11.66	-5.32	1.79
Pacific/Asia ex-Japan Stk	5.60	-9.78	6.22	11.92	13.22	15.95	2.30	3.07
Japan Stock	14.46	-1.19	-9.42	11.61	14.26	10.79	-8.72	-0.90
Foreign Large Value	5.18	0.94	0.55	14.09	21.77	14.62	4.67	8.52
Foreign Large Blend	4.07	-0.94	-0.08	14.19	17.59	9.42	-2.93	6.39
Foreign Large Growth	4.80	-2.17	-1.19	14.06	15.58	7.92	-5.72	5.18
Foreign Sm/Mid Val	8.34	0.29	-0.20	13.87	24.02	21.44	9.97	9.88
Foreign Sm/Mid Grth	8.55	-0.28	-1.17	15.35	23.97	17.29	-0.32	12.55
World Stock	4.07	-0.49	-1.34	12.70	15.16	7.59	-1.15	8.71
Specialty Stock	**4.96**	**-2.95**	**2.85**	**10.43**	**15.61**	**11.21**	**5.61**	**11.44**
Specialty-Communications	7.19	-0.85	-2.19	17.86	22.37	1.18	-12.35	9.83
Specialty-Financial	5.15	-2.75	1.12	9.91	13.70	10.75	11.70	16.67
Specialty-Health	5.04	0.85	-4.24	7.70	9.37	0.78	7.96	13.84
Specialty-Natural Res	6.63	3.33	10.87	4.77	28.37	17.82	14.40	13.22
Specialty-Precious Metals	-1.30	-18.37	14.69	-0.43	-8.05	33.57	18.27	3.25
Specialty-Real Estate	11.81	-5.56	7.85	15.73	31.88	23.62	21.36	15.10
Specialty-Technology	1.09	-0.49	-11.16	16.08	3.81	-2.88	-16.91	9.59
Specialty-Utilities	4.03	0.21	5.82	11.80	23.41	4.84	0.45	10.00
Hybrid	**2.66**	**-0.80**	**0.47**	**6.63**	**9.23**	**7.45**	**4.09**	**9.52**
Conservative Alloc	2.05	-1.27	0.78	4.12	5.71	5.12	3.80	7.87
Convertibles	3.36	-0.93	-0.80	6.86	8.72	8.22	3.54	10.30
Moderate Allocation	2.29	-0.31	-0.28	6.83	8.62	4.71	2.17	9.24
World Allocation	2.93	-0.70	2.19	8.69	13.88	11.75	6.83	10.67
Total Equity Fund Average	**5.18**	**-1.63**	**0.58**	**11.76**	**16.25**	**10.89**	**3.19**	**9.48**
Total Fund Average	**3.80**	**-1.85**	**1.64**	**7.71**	**11.61**	**9.14**	**4.52**	**8.31**

Index Benchmarks

Category	1st Quarter	2nd Quarter	3rd Quarter	4th Quarter	2004	3 Year	5 Year	10 Year
Domestic Equity								
S&P 500	1.69	1.72	-1.87	9.23	10.87	3.58	-2.30	12.07
Wilshire 5000	2.61	1.28	-1.79	10.33	12.63	5.47	-1.42	11.92
Wilshire 4500	5.84	-0.02	-1.68	13.96	18.57	11.89	1.36	11.96
Russell 2000	6.26	0.47	-2.86	14.09	18.33	11.48	6.61	11.54
S&P 400	5.06	0.97	-2.10	12.15	16.47	10.51	9.53	16.09
International Equity								
MSCI EAFE	4.34	0.22	-0.28	15.32	20.25	11.89	-1.13	5.62
MSCI World	2.62	0.87	-1.00	11.94	14.72	6.95	-2.45	8.09
MSCI Europe	0.89	2.13	1.21	15.92	20.88	10.98	0.06	10.54
MSCI Pacific	12.73	-4.03	-3.50	13.96	18.98	14.33	-3.71	-0.66
MSCI Latin America	6.24	-9.16	16.55	19.81	34.77	19.19	5.76	5.15
MSCI Emerging Markets	8.87	-10.34	7.39	16.81	22.45	19.54	2.09	0.98
Miscellaneous								
US 90-Day Treasury Bill	0.24	0.28	0.39	0.52	1.43	1.39	2.81	4.02
Consumer Price Index	1.68	1.23	0.11	0.58	3.64	2.63	2.56	2.47

Performance Summary–Fixed-Income Funds

Morningstar's Open-End Fund Universe

Category	2004 Total Return % 1st Quarter	2nd Quarter	3rd Quarter	4th Quarter	2004	Annualized Total Return % 3 Year	5 Year	10 Year
Specialty Bond	**2.05**	**-2.18**	**4.29**	**4.25**	**8.84**	**11.18**	**7.93**	**8.11**
Bank Loan	1.64	1.09	0.85	1.09	5.11	5.30	4.61	5.39
High Yield Bond	1.76	-0.62	4.05	4.14	9.88	10.56	4.89	6.45
Multisector Bond	2.03	-2.40	4.11	3.60	8.03	10.43	7.30	7.57
World Bond	1.80	-2.93	3.09	6.78	8.79	11.71	7.81	7.57
Emerg Mkts Bd	3.00	-6.06	9.34	5.63	12.37	17.88	15.04	13.59
General Bond	**1.84**	**-1.90**	**2.33**	**0.86**	**3.22**	**4.65**	**5.99**	**6.36**
Long-Term Bond	3.23	-3.69	4.62	2.14	6.28	8.07	8.63	8.18
Intermediate-Term Bond	2.41	-2.50	2.94	0.84	3.81	5.51	6.83	6.92
Short-Term Bond	1.20	-1.18	1.25	0.21	1.60	3.24	4.91	5.52
Ultrashort Bond	0.52	-0.21	0.52	0.25	1.17	1.79	3.60	4.80
Government Bond	**2.75**	**-2.91**	**2.89**	**0.86**	**3.89**	**5.68**	**7.00**	**6.85**
Long Government	4.80	-5.10	4.84	1.79	6.95	9.16	9.68	8.54
Intermediate Government	2.25	-2.17	2.51	0.67	3.39	4.71	6.31	6.47
Short Government	1.19	-1.45	1.33	0.13	1.32	3.16	5.01	5.53
Municipal Bond	**1.23**	**-2.06**	**3.15**	**0.90**	**3.36**	**5.17**	**5.88**	**5.78**
High Yield Muni	1.86	-1.45	3.36	2.22	6.37	6.46	5.98	5.86
Muni National Long	1.40	-2.45	3.65	1.01	3.78	5.64	6.35	6.12
Muni National Interm	1.18	-2.15	3.07	0.61	2.81	5.18	5.86	5.71
Muni Single ST Long	1.32	-2.18	3.35	1.01	3.65	5.44	6.29	6.08
Muni Single ST Inter	1.15	-2.16	3.14	0.62	2.86	5.15	5.93	5.91
Muni Short	0.62	-1.07	1.36	0.16	1.17	2.94	3.99	4.22
Muni NY Int/Sh	0.97	-2.14	3.11	0.55	2.57	5.23	5.98	5.80
Muni NY Long	1.27	-2.49	3.67	0.96	3.57	5.71	6.51	6.20
Muni CA Int/Sh	0.98	-1.93	2.84	0.69	2.56	4.51	5.42	5.49
Muni CA Long	1.52	-2.53	3.92	1.19	4.25	5.43	6.53	6.40
Total Fixed-Income Average	**1.73**	**-2.17**	**3.22**	**1.65**	**4.65**	**6.51**	**6.52**	**6.56**
Total Fund Average	**3.80**	**-1.85**	**1.64**	**7.71**	**11.61**	**9.14**	**4.52**	**8.31**

Index Benchmarks

Category	1st Quarter	2nd Quarter	3rd Quarter	4th Quarter	2004	3 Year	5 Year	10 Year
Government and Corporate								
Lehman Brothers Aggregate	2.66	-2.44	3.20	0.95	4.34	6.19	7.71	7.72
Lehman Brothers Government	2.93	-2.98	3.11	0.49	3.48	5.70	7.48	7.46
Lehman Brothers Mortgage	1.92	-1.13	2.61	1.26	4.70	5.48	7.14	7.56
Consumer Price Index	1.68	1.23	0.11	0.58	3.64	2.63	2.56	2.47
US 90-Day Treasury Bill	0.24	0.28	0.39	0.52	1.43	1.39	2.81	4.02
Specialty Bond								
First Boston High Yield	2.67	-0.19	4.50	4.56	11.96	13.88	8.17	8.62
Salomon Brothers World Government	1.86	-3.33	3.28	8.50	10.35	14.86	8.79	7.60
Municipal Bond								
Lehman Brothers Muni	1.73	-2.37	3.89	1.25	4.48	6.44	7.20	7.06
Lehman Brothers CA Muni	2.04	-2.23	4.10	1.59	5.50	6.26	7.30	7.26
Lehman Brothers NY Muni	1.64	-2.33	3.85	1.15	4.28	6.39	7.18	7.16

Performance Summary 1990–2004: Equity Funds

Morningstar's Open-End Fund Universe

Category	1990 TR%	1990 # of Funds	1991 TR%	1991 # of Funds	1992 TR%	1992 # of Funds	1993 TR%	1993 # of Funds	1994 TR%	1994 # of Funds	1995 TR%	1995 # of Funds
Domestic Equity	**-7.84**	**508**	**38.84**	**563**	**12.56**	**634**	**15.15**	**789**	**-1.03**	**1038**	**30.38**	**1321**
Large Value	-5.79	92	27.90	104	10.13	114	13.98	145	-0.59	184	32.61	244
Large Blend	-3.79	125	31.82	138	8.64	155	11.51	189	-0.54	251	32.85	315
Large Growth	-3.18	104	42.78	116	7.39	131	11.28	165	-1.64	216	32.41	260
Mid-Cap Value	-10.64	27	31.42	29	16.11	31	19.12	33	-1.36	41	28.00	47
Mid-Cap Blend	-5.94	26	34.61	27	14.52	30	16.09	33	-1.71	42	28.96	57
Mid-Cap Growth	-6.48	61	50.31	64	9.03	69	14.80	89	-1.38	118	33.88	160
Small Value	-16.60	14	38.60	15	20.80	19	16.74	25	0.19	33	23.84	40
Small Blend	-12.72	26	39.78	29	16.14	36	15.88	43	-1.60	60	26.10	75
Small Growth	-5.45	33	52.35	41	10.27	49	16.99	67	-0.66	93	34.81	123
International Equity	**-12.13**	**70**	**14.82**	**92**	**-3.25**	**120**	**46.62**	**163**	**-2.08**	**237**	**5.26**	**368**
Europe Stock	-6.09	6	8.00	11	-5.28	13	29.75	13	4.74	15	17.27	21
Latin America Stock	—	—	—	—	1.75	2	67.21	3	-15.92	5	-20.30	7
Diversified Emerging Mkts	-5.33	1	15.05	2	-0.92	3	77.76	4	-7.39	12	-1.21	40
Diversified Pacific/Asia	-13.84	4	16.80	5	-4.34	5	57.21	6	-3.98	7	6.42	12
Pacific/Asia ex-Japan Stk	-15.14	1	22.67	2	12.05	3	66.51	6	-18.40	11	-0.15	22
Japan Stock	-28.56	3	5.18	4	-20.66	5	23.27	6	18.06	6	-3.06	6
Foreign Large Value	-7.13	7	15.32	10	-3.96	12	38.09	17	2.34	22	11.64	29
Foreign Large Blend	-10.39	23	12.41	27	-3.97	34	34.68	51	-1.24	66	11.38	93
Foreign Large Growth	-10.71	8	15.46	8	-3.44	14	38.23	19	-1.82	26	10.07	48
Foreign Sm/Mid Val	—	—	—	—	-3.24	2	44.89	3	2.92	6	5.89	9
Foreign Sm/Mid Grth	-12.93	1	11.69	1	-9.08	1	49.48	2	-3.29	4	7.73	8
World Stock	-11.13	16	25.59	22	2.08	26	32.30	33	-1.02	57	17.41	73
Specialty Stock	**-8.28**	**77**	**32.98**	**84**	**9.40**	**87**	**26.78**	**96**	**-0.63**	**125**	**29.72**	**166**
Specialty-Communications	-16.71	3	38.32	4	16.61	4	29.81	5	0.48	7	29.18	8
Specialty-Financial	-17.21	9	60.24	9	35.11	10	18.47	11	-2.94	11	44.95	12
Specialty-Health	14.76	10	63.80	10	-4.69	11	3.03	14	4.14	16	48.25	19
Specialty-Natural Res	-8.13	14	5.59	16	2.83	16	21.13	17	-1.57	21	21.15	27
Specialty-Precious Metals	-22.48	16	-3.17	16	-15.66	16	80.97	16	-13.19	18	4.84	19
Specialty-Real Estate	-13.96	5	29.59	5	15.87	6	21.10	6	-0.62	11	15.20	21
Specialty-Technology	0.75	11	50.37	11	14.96	11	24.60	11	18.14	14	46.72	25
Specialty-Utilities	-3.28	9	19.10	13	10.13	13	15.14	16	-9.45	27	27.46	35
Hybrid	**-0.69**	**104**	**26.11**	**112**	**9.84**	**125**	**15.04**	**157**	**-3.59**	**224**	**22.20**	**305**
Conservative Alloc	2.04	10	22.88	13	7.90	14	12.67	18	-3.67	34	20.52	53
Convertibles	-5.68	15	33.54	15	14.89	16	16.46	18	-4.90	23	22.22	27
Moderate Allocation	0.18	74	24.80	78	8.13	89	11.84	114	-2.52	157	26.17	212
World Allocation	0.72	5	23.23	6	8.42	6	19.20	7	-3.25	10	19.90	13
Total Equity Fund Average	**-8.41**	**759**	**27.94**	**851**	**5.71**	**966**	**29.40**	**1205**	**-1.63**	**1624**	**20.09**	**2160**
Total Fund Average	**-2.73**	**1334**	**22.43**	**1492**	**6.59**	**1713**	**22.38**	**2169**	**-2.70**	**2924**	**18.49**	**3826**

Index Benchmarks

Index	1990	1991	1992	1993	1994	1995
Domestic Equity						
S&P 500	-3.12	30.48	7.62	10.06	1.31	37.53
Wilshire 5000	-6.18	34.21	8.97	11.28	-0.07	36.45
Wilshire 4500	-13.56	43.45	11.76	14.54	-2.65	33.39
Russell 2000	16.24	-19.51	46.05	18.41	18.91	-1.82
S&P 400	-5.12	50.07	11.90	13.93	-3.59	30.92
International Equity						
MSCI EAFE	-23.45	12.13	-12.17	32.56	7.78	11.21
MSCI World	-17.02	18.28	-5.23	22.50	5.08	20.72
MSCI Europe	-3.85	13.11	-4.71	29.28	2.28	21.62
MSCI Pacific	-34.42	11.30	-18.40	35.69	12.83	2.78
MSCI Latin America	-12.70	45.00	11.69	50.66	-0.99	-15.03
MSCI Emerging Markets	-13.55	55.68	9.03	71.66	-8.72	-6.91
Miscellaneous						
US 90-Day Treasury Bill	7.99	5.68	3.59	3.12	4.45	5.79
Consumer Price Index	6.11	3.06	2.90	2.75	2.67	2.54

Performance Summary 1990–2004: Equity Funds

Morningstar's Open-End Fund Universe

1996 TR%	1996 # of Funds	1997 TR%	1997 # of Funds	1998 TR%	1998 # of Funds	1999 TR%	1999 # of Funds	2000 TR%	2000 # of Funds	2001 TR%	2001 # of Funds	2002 TR%	2002 # of Funds	2003 TR%	2003 # of Funds	2004 TR%	2004 # of Funds
20.37	**1595**	**25.41**	**2055**	**10.11**	**2606**	**26.27**	**3160**	**5.02**	**3741**	**-3.63**	**4506**	**-19.80**	**5271**	**36.05**	**6079**	**14.32**	**6680**
20.06	286	27.44	349	11.53	418	5.49	495	9.96	559	-3.36	636	-18.54	781	28.45	926	12.91	1053
21.43	372	27.73	483	21.45	616	20.57	756	-4.44	901	-11.89	1049	-21.81	1216	27.24	1361	9.96	1485
19.65	313	26.41	396	33.01	516	37.98	603	-13.11	743	-21.42	929	-27.42	1039	28.70	1200	7.64	1306
18.93	53	26.62	71	2.49	91	8.56	115	19.85	128	6.67	148	-13.07	199	35.62	248	17.90	283
20.22	69	25.55	92	10.19	111	21.80	142	9.90	172	0.20	223	-16.27	283	36.50	331	16.00	362
17.28	195	19.44	257	17.79	303	59.54	364	-3.76	430	-19.34	563	-27.14	641	36.09	729	12.93	787
22.99	53	29.91	69	-6.44	96	6.66	132	17.77	154	16.59	173	-10.05	201	43.44	243	20.58	277
22.59	90	26.66	117	-4.66	173	14.30	212	14.06	252	8.80	294	-15.79	357	43.24	395	18.86	438
20.17	164	18.90	221	5.66	282	61.55	341	-5.05	402	-8.91	491	-28.09	554	45.14	646	12.09	689
13.73	**485**	**1.21**	**628**	**1.92**	**816**	**60.65**	**989**	**-17.42**	**1099**	**-15.59**	**1262**	**-13.12**	**1468**	**44.24**	**1644**	**20.47**	**1783**
24.92	24	21.21	31	16.87	40	31.87	56	-6.02	66	-17.65	83	-12.91	97	38.50	106	20.94	115
26.19	7	27.79	7	-37.07	7	60.18	12	-15.58	12	-5.91	13	-19.95	16	61.74	16	38.26	16
14.45	52	-1.40	74	-26.36	99	71.00	109	-30.37	116	-3.15	134	-5.72	155	55.47	173	23.75	179
3.80	12	-24.28	13	-4.05	18	91.62	20	-31.89	20	-19.47	20	-12.48	20	37.71	24	17.09	27
12.16	29	-30.71	33	-7.61	46	72.75	52	-23.59	58	-2.08	64	-9.32	68	52.76	70	13.22	76
-12.61	11	-16.14	12	6.29	16	111.88	28	-34.01	28	-30.41	34	-12.81	37	38.27	39	14.26	42
15.19	44	8.19	58	9.35	64	26.32	84	-2.32	94	-13.94	101	-11.36	124	39.48	135	21.77	146
12.88	122	6.79	165	13.68	216	39.28	249	-15.78	284	-21.72	324	-16.67	390	33.64	441	17.59	489
14.54	62	7.31	74	14.05	96	54.65	118	-20.08	131	-23.58	155	-19.23	175	34.69	191	15.58	203
15.88	11	-7.50	15	5.07	22	33.47	25	-5.39	26	-8.30	30	-3.04	39	50.08	46	24.02	52
20.76	12	9.12	20	19.28	36	92.81	45	-15.71	56	-24.57	70	-14.82	73	53.92	81	23.97	90
16.62	99	14.10	126	13.58	156	41.93	191	-8.29	208	-16.26	234	-19.07	274	34.66	322	15.16	348
20.71	**201**	**14.94**	**263**	**11.61**	**353**	**31.61**	**441**	**9.36**	**544**	**-10.10**	**778**	**-9.83**	**888**	**39.42**	**977**	**15.61**	**1058**
9.65	9	27.72	9	42.58	10	57.50	15	-29.54	15	-28.75	35	-38.15	40	42.26	40	22.37	40
31.97	12	47.38	20	6.30	38	-2.12	52	27.62	66	-2.70	84	-9.74	101	32.74	103	13.70	111
13.20	21	22.12	28	21.57	40	18.44	49	56.41	69	-11.60	120	-27.82	157	32.00	183	9.37	188
33.44	32	3.79	38	-25.22	50	30.32	58	31.33	60	-10.70	64	-3.49	74	32.34	81	28.37	92
11.54	24	-41.54	25	-10.49	25	6.72	30	-16.71	30	18.84	34	-32.76	39	59.17	43	-8.05	47
33.23	35	22.90	54	-15.75	77	-2.89	103	26.78	120	9.87	136	4.28	146	37.06	173	31.88	213
21.62	30	10.29	44	52.95	59	27.03	78	-31.91	125	-35.10	241	-42.63	265	56.71	279	3.81	289
11.02	38	26.82	45	20.96	54	17.89	56	10.89	59	-20.66	64	-23.82	66	23.06	75	23.41	78
13.80	**372**	**16.23**	**495**	**9.72**	**590**	**15.62**	**691**	**2.47**	**756**	**-3.61**	**847**	**-6.10**	**977**	**20.98**	**1161**	**9.23**	**1431**
10.57	75	14.52	111	10.43	126	6.34	153	4.77	164	-0.58	186	-3.12	228	12.33	282	5.71	394
15.75	34	18.80	41	5.05	45	29.68	53	0.91	56	-6.69	60	-7.96	64	26.64	68	8.72	75
14.16	250	19.83	324	13.66	399	10.85	464	1.98	515	-4.44	576	-11.62	654	20.09	764	8.62	905
14.70	13	11.76	19	9.74	20	15.62	21	2.23	21	-2.73	25	-1.68	31	24.84	47	13.88	57
17.24	**2653**	**12.96**	**3441**	**7.45**	**4365**	**38.78**	**5281**	**-2.40**	**6140**	**-9.54**	**7393**	**-13.29**	**8604**	**38.02**	**9861**	**16.25**	**10952**
12.92	**4570**	**11.29**	**5591**	**6.30**	**6838**	**23.27**	**8031**	**1.90**	**9138**	**-3.71**	**10689**	**-4.93**	**12224**	**25.79**	**13921**	**11.61**	**15332**

1996	1997	1998	1999	2000	2001	2002	2003	2004
22.94	33.35	28.57	21.04	-9.10	-11.88	-22.09	28.67	10.87
21.20	31.29	23.43	23.56	-10.93	-10.89	-20.85	31.63	12.63
17.25	25.69	8.63	35.49	-15.77	-9.30	-17.81	43.72	18.57
28.44	16.49	22.36	-2.55	21.26	-3.02	2.49	-20.48	47.25
19.18	32.24	19.11	14.72	17.49	-0.60	-14.53	35.59	16.47
6.05	1.78	19.93	27.03	-14.19	-21.42	-15.94	38.59	20.25
13.48	15.76	24.32	24.95	-13.19	-16.80	-19.89	33.11	14.72
21.09	23.80	28.50	15.93	-8.40	-19.90	-18.38	38.54	20.88
-8.58	-25.49	2.41	57.63	-25.77	-25.39	-9.29	38.48	18.98
18.87	28.34	-38.06	55.48	-18.38	-4.24	-24.79	67.06	34.77
3.93	-13.45	-27.67	64.09	-31.90	-4.68	-7.97	51.59	22.45
5.26	5.31	5.01	4.87	6.32	3.67	1.68	1.05	1.43
3.32	1.70	1.61	2.68	3.39	1.55	2.38	1.88	3.64

Performance Summary 1990–2004: Fixed-Income Funds

Morningstar's Open-End Fund Universe

Category	1990 TR%	1990 # of Funds	1991 TR%	1991 # of Funds	1992 TR%	1992 # of Funds	1993 TR%	1993 # of Funds	1994 TR%	1994 # of Funds	1995 TR%	1995 # of Funds
Specialty Bond	**2.40**	**68**	**21.61**	**77**	**9.13**	**89**	**13.92**	**111**	**-3.95**	**150**	**16.39**	**205**
Bank Loan	9.60	4	8.03	4	6.21	4	5.70	4	6.60	4	7.84	4
High Yield Bond	-9.48	44	37.02	47	17.35	47	19.12	52	-3.11	69	16.99	86
Multisector Bond	-2.78	11	25.89	14	9.37	17	15.48	25	-5.24	33	17.98	49
World Bond	12.27	9	15.49	12	3.60	21	15.36	30	-5.67	42	18.21	53
Emerg Mkts Bd	—	—	—	—	—	—	—	—	-12.31	2	20.91	13
General Bond	**6.64**	**126**	**14.46**	**140**	**6.63**	**178**	**9.34**	**249**	**-2.44**	**331**	**15.45**	**420**
Long-Term Bond	4.02	6	18.52	6	8.59	7	15.93	9	-7.19	16	25.20	18
Intermediate-Term Bond	6.80	88	16.89	97	7.29	119	10.52	160	-3.95	216	17.74	275
Short-Term Bond	7.60	24	13.51	29	5.94	40	6.81	64	-0.82	80	11.23	101
Ultrashort Bond	8.14	8	8.93	8	4.69	12	4.10	16	2.21	19	7.63	26
Government Bond	**7.37**	**106**	**14.92**	**111**	**6.62**	**130**	**10.84**	**163**	**-4.33**	**209**	**19.40**	**261**
Long Government	4.28	10	17.16	10	7.63	12	17.76	12	-7.82	15	29.40	16
Intermediate Government	8.99	67	14.65	71	6.36	81	8.20	97	-3.89	123	16.55	159
Short Government	8.85	29	12.94	30	5.86	37	6.55	54	-1.28	71	12.24	86
Municipal Bond	**6.04**	**275**	**11.11**	**313**	**8.43**	**350**	**11.31**	**441**	**-5.27**	**610**	**15.21**	**780**
High Yield Muni	5.40	16	11.60	17	8.66	17	11.75	19	-4.52	28	15.90	32
Muni National Long	6.12	70	12.01	78	8.92	80	12.46	90	-6.71	119	17.23	149
Muni National Interm	6.50	30	10.65	32	8.21	35	10.63	48	-3.76	76	14.14	95
Muni Single ST Long	6.11	45	11.24	49	8.54	64	12.46	81	-6.94	121	17.00	162
Muni Single ST Inter	6.23	28	10.72	40	8.55	47	11.76	65	-5.66	100	15.89	123
Muni Short	6.21	13	8.56	14	6.54	16	6.97	24	-0.58	32	8.13	42
Muni NY Int/Sh	5.72	9	11.99	10	8.95	13	11.19	16	-4.80	19	14.38	24
Muni NY Long	5.18	24	13.18	28	9.54	31	12.71	35	-7.48	39	16.89	54
Muni CA Int/Sh	6.46	5	10.03	7	7.75	8	10.68	16	-4.64	19	13.86	25
Muni CA Long	6.51	35	11.13	38	8.64	39	12.45	47	-7.56	57	18.66	74
Total Fixed-Income Average	**6.04**	**275**	**11.11**	**313**	**8.43**	**350**	**11.31**	**441**	**-5.27**	**610**	**15.21**	**780**
Total Fund Average	**-2.73**	**1334**	**22.43**	**1492**	**6.59**	**1713**	**22.38**	**2169**	**-2.70**	**2924**	**18.49**	**3826**

Index Benchmarks

Benchmark	1990 TR%	1991 TR%	1992 TR%	1993 TR%	1994 TR%	1995 TR%
Government and Corporate						
Lehman Brothers Aggregate	8.96	16.00	7.40	9.75	-2.92	18.47
Lehman Brothers Government	8.72	15.32	7.23	10.66	-3.38	18.34
Lehman Brothers Mortgage	10.72	15.72	6.96	6.84	-1.61	16.80
Consumer Price Index	6.11	3.06	2.90	2.75	2.67	2.54
US 90-Day Treasury Bill	7.99	5.68	3.59	3.12	4.45	5.79
Specialty Bond						
First Boston High Yield	-6.38	43.75	16.66	18.91	-0.97	17.39
Salomon Brothers World Government	11.98	15.81	5.53	13.27	2.34	19.04
Municipal Bond						
Lehman Brothers Muni	7.29	12.14	8.82	12.28	-5.17	17.46
Lehman Brothers CA Muni	—	—	—	—	-6.38	19.30
Lehman Brothers NY Muni	—	—	—	—	-5.02	17.24

Performance Summary 1990–2004: Fixed-Income Funds

Morningstar's Open-End Fund Universe

1996 TR%	1996 # of Funds	1997 TR%	1997 # of Funds	1998 TR%	1998 # of Funds	1999 TR%	1999 # of Funds	2000 TR%	2000 # of Funds	2001 TR%	2001 # of Funds	2002 TR%	2002 # of Funds	2003 TR%	2003 # of Funds	2004 TR%	2004 # of Funds
16.41	**258**	**9.37**	**315**	**-0.78**	**396**	**7.60**	**499**	**2.72**	**550**	**4.29**	**611**	**6.31**	**682**	**18.97**	**745**	**8.84**	**810**
6.75	5	7.21	5	6.26	7	6.08	10	5.32	19	1.58	33	0.65	45	10.36	46	5.11	49
13.51	107	13.17	129	0.06	178	4.60	248	-7.38	274	2.31	313	-1.35	347	24.39	388	9.88	428
10.52	62	9.21	72	1.21	85	3.06	98	1.40	108	3.79	108	6.74	118	16.24	125	8.03	139
10.65	66	3.60	86	9.67	96	-2.80	102	3.28	108	2.11	114	13.70	125	13.38	137	8.79	143
40.64	18	13.67	23	-21.12	30	27.07	41	10.97	41	11.64	43	11.83	47	30.48	49	12.37	51
4.44	**470**	**8.49**	**545**	**6.13**	**631**	**0.55**	**715**	**8.27**	**821**	**7.26**	**945**	**6.27**	**1081**	**4.65**	**1269**	**3.22**	**1410**
3.81	21	12.34	24	5.86	24	-3.25	37	8.92	39	8.46	48	8.94	55	9.53	58	6.28	66
3.33	310	8.94	359	7.47	423	-1.33	485	9.81	554	7.65	634	8.10	738	4.96	843	3.81	919
4.47	112	6.48	132	6.15	148	2.30	155	7.66	185	7.18	207	5.44	226	2.62	295	1.60	342
6.13	27	6.18	30	5.05	36	4.49	38	6.70	43	5.76	56	2.61	62	1.50	73	1.17	83
1.83	**290**	**10.27**	**320**	**8.47**	**362**	**-2.61**	**394**	**12.98**	**416**	**5.92**	**448**	**10.96**	**481**	**2.31**	**554**	**3.89**	**603**
-1.19	16	15.35	17	11.42	26	-7.64	31	19.60	32	3.69	33	16.70	38	3.40	45	6.95	52
2.88	175	8.63	194	7.47	217	-1.43	235	10.98	253	6.92	276	9.37	298	2.15	351	3.39	378
3.81	99	6.83	109	6.51	119	1.25	128	8.36	131	7.16	139	6.80	145	1.37	158	1.32	173
3.62	**899**	**8.21**	**970**	**5.44**	**1084**	**-3.24**	**1142**	**9.78**	**1211**	**4.24**	**1292**	**7.77**	**1376**	**4.35**	**1492**	**3.36**	**1557**
4.06	37	9.74	42	5.37	46	-4.47	53	5.52	61	5.11	71	6.01	73	6.84	77	6.37	79
3.38	172	9.13	184	5.32	203	-4.77	218	11.16	232	3.84	243	8.37	258	4.85	271	3.78	275
3.53	107	7.70	117	5.46	124	-2.44	134	9.34	141	4.29	157	8.59	182	4.15	205	2.81	225
3.44	188	8.96	189	5.36	216	-4.79	224	11.19	237	4.24	245	8.10	249	4.63	249	3.65	249
3.47	150	8.19	171	5.47	191	-3.09	195	9.86	202	4.28	215	8.42	228	4.11	249	2.86	256
3.80	47	5.18	50	4.60	59	0.59	64	5.93	68	4.80	74	5.19	79	2.41	89	1.17	107
3.53	27	8.15	31	5.72	36	-2.72	39	10.32	41	4.09	42	8.82	49	4.10	58	2.57	64
3.22	61	8.97	64	5.72	72	-4.73	73	12.02	76	3.63	79	8.80	84	4.89	94	3.57	95
4.00	26	6.81	31	5.53	36	-1.05	39	9.43	46	4.36	50	7.51	54	3.28	68	2.56	72
3.74	84	9.23	91	5.82	101	-4.90	103	13.01	107	3.74	116	7.87	120	4.19	132	4.25	135
6.43	**1917**	**8.80**	**2150**	**4.56**	**2473**	**0.00**	**2750**	**8.34**	**2998**	**5.03**	**3296**	**7.60**	**3520**	**7.45**	**4060**	**4.65**	**4380**
12.92	**4570**	**11.29**	**5591**	**6.30**	**6838**	**23.27**	**8031**	**1.90**	**9138**	**-3.71**	**10689**	**-4.93**	**12224**	**25.79**	**13921**	**11.61**	**15332**

1996	1997	1998	1999	2000	2001	2002	2003	2004
3.63	9.65	8.69	-0.82	11.63	8.44	13.25	4.10	4.34
2.77	9.59	9.85	-2.23	13.24	7.23	11.50	2.36	3.48
5.35	9.49	6.96	1.86	11.16	8.22	3.75	3.07	4.70
3.32	1.70	1.61	2.68	3.39	1.55	2.38	1.88	3.64
5.26	5.31	5.01	4.87	6.32	3.67	1.68	1.05	1.43
12.42	12.63	0.58	3.28	-5.21	5.78	3.11	27.93	11.96
3.62	0.23	15.30	-4.27	1.59	-0.99	19.49	14.91	10.35
4.43	9.19	6.48	-2.06	11.68	5.13	9.60	5.31	4.48
4.43	9.43	6.93	-2.79	12.68	5.21	8.45	4.86	5.50
4.74	9.84	6.88	-2.03	12.01	4.84	9.67	5.30	4.28

Domestic-Equity Funds

Morningstar Funds 500 Universe

Leaders

One Year (12-31-2004)

Cat	Fund Name	Total Return%*	Morningstar Rating	Style	Sales Charge%
SR	Morgan Stan Ins US R/E A	37.28	★★★★		None
SR	T. Rowe Price Real Est	36.82	★★★★		None
SR	Security Cap US Real Est	36.81	★★★★		12b-1
SN	Vanguard Energy	36.65	★★★★★		Clsd
SN	AIM Energy Inv	36.62	★★★★		Clsd
SR	Fidelity Real Estate Inv	34.15	★★★		None
SR	Columbia Real Est Eq Z	31.08	★★★		None
SR	Vanguard REIT Index	30.76	★★★		None
SG	FBR Small Cap	30.67	★★★★★		Clsd
SN	T. Rowe Price New Era	30.09	★★★★		None

Three Year (12-31-2004)

Cat	Fund Name	Total Return%*	Morningstar Rating	Style	Sales Charge%
MB	Fidelity Leverage Co Stk	33.89	★★★★★		None
SB	Bridgeway Ul-Sm Co Mkt	30.89	★★★★★		Clsd
SG	FBR Small Cap	25.04	★★★★★		Clsd
SR	T. Rowe Price Real Est	24.81	★★★★		None
SR	Fidelity Real Estate Inv	23.82	★★★		None
SR	Morgan Stan Ins US R/E A	23.69	★★★★		None
SV	N/I Numeric Inv Sm CapVl	23.37	★★★★★		Clsd
SR	Vanguard REIT Index	22.55	★★★		None
SR	Security Cap US Real Est	22.52	★★★★		12b-1
SR	Third Avenue RealEst Val	22.42	★★★★★		None

Five Year (12-31-2004)

Cat	Fund Name	Total Return%*	Morningstar Rating	Style	Sales Charge%
SV	N/I Numeric Inv Sm CapVl	26.63	★★★★★		Clsd
SV	Boston Part SmCp II Inv	26.10	★★★★		Clsd
SG	Wasatch Micro Cap	24.49	★★★★★		Clsd
SG	William Blair Sm-Cp Gr N	23.49	★★★★★	—	Clsd
SR	Third Avenue RealEst Val	23.21	★★★★★		None
SB	Bridgeway Ul-Sm Co Mkt	22.85	★★★★★		Clsd
SR	T. Rowe Price Real Est	22.80	★★★★		None
SR	Fidelity Real Estate Inv	22.25	★★★		None
SB	Wasatch Small Cap Value	22.07	★★★★★		Clsd
SR	Morgan Stan Ins US R/E A	21.80	★★★★		None

Ten Year (12-31-2004)

Cat	Fund Name	Total Return%*	Morningstar Rating	Style	Sales Charge%
MG	Calamos Growth A	23.42	★★★★★		4.75
MB	Meridian Value	21.00	★★★★★		None
SG	Fremont U.S. Micro-Cap	20.17	★★★★		Clsd
SH	Vanguard Health Care	20.15	★★★★★		None
SG	Baron Growth	19.25	★★★★★		Clsd
SG	Wasatch Core Growth	19.25	★★★★		Clsd
SH	Eaton Vance Wld Health A	18.89	★★★★		5.75
LB	Legg Mason Value Prim	18.58	★★★★★		12b-1
MG	Fidelity New Millennium	18.57	★★★★		Clsd
MV	Muhlenkamp	18.28	★★★★		None

Laggards

One Year (12-31-2004)

Cat	Fund Name	Total Return%*	Morningstar Rating	Style	Sales Charge%
ST	Fidelity Sel Electronics	−9.81	★★★		None
LG	White Oak Growth Stock	−3.21	★★		None
SG	Wasatch Ultra Growth	−0.82	★★★★		Clsd
LG	Atlantic Whitehall Growth	−0.46	★★★		None
SG	Brown Cap Small Co Instl	0.24	★★★		Clsd
ST	Fidelity Sel Technology	0.43	★★★★		None
SV	Tocqueville Sm Cap Value	0.78	★		12b-1
SG	RS Diversified Growth	1.48	★★		Clsd
ST	T. Rowe Price SciTech	1.60	★★★		None
LG	Fidelity Adv Eq Gr T	2.67	★★★		3.50

Three Year (12-31-2004)

Cat	Fund Name	Total Return%*	Morningstar Rating	Style	Sales Charge%
ST	Fidelity Sel Electronics	−8.47	★★★		None
SG	Brown Cap Small Co Instl	−5.37	★★★		Clsd
LG	Vanguard U.S. Gr	−4.67	★		None
LG	White Oak Growth Stock	−3.95	★★		None
SC	Scudder Flag Communic A	−3.30	★★★		5.75
LG	Gabelli Growth	−3.07	★★★		12b-1
ST	T. Rowe Price SciTech	−2.99	★★★		None
LG	Fidelity Adv Eq Gr T	−2.08	★★★		3.50
LG	ABN AMRO/Montag Gr N	−2.00	★★★★		12b-1
ST	Northern Technology	−1.77	★★★		None

Five Year (12-31-2004)

Cat	Fund Name	Total Return%*	Morningstar Rating	Style	Sales Charge%
ST	T. Rowe Price SciTech	−18.78	★★★		None
ST	Northern Technology	−17.49	★★★		None
SC	Scudder Flag Communic A	−16.04	★★★		5.75
ST	Fidelity Sel Technology	−14.37	★★★★		None
LG	Vanguard U.S. Gr	−13.93	★		None
MG	Janus Enterprise	−13.27	★★		None
ST	Fidelity Sel Electronics	−11.62	★★★		None
LG	Janus Olympus	−11.35	★★		None
SG	RS Emerging Growth	−11.24	★★		Clsd
LG	White Oak Growth Stock	−10.97	★★		None

Ten Year (12-31-2004)

Cat	Fund Name	Total Return%*	Morningstar Rating	Style	Sales Charge%
SB	FPA Paramount	5.52	★★		5.25
LG	Vanguard U.S. Gr	5.92	★		None
ST	T. Rowe Price SciTech	6.21	★★★		None
LG	Fidelity Destiny I	6.75	★★★		8.24
CA	Gateway Fund	7.40	★★★		12b-1
LG	AIM Constellation A	8.01	★★★		5.50
LV	Vanguard Dividend Growth	8.21	★★		None
CA	Merger Fund	8.38	★★★		Clsd
MG	Janus Enterprise	8.65	★★		None
LG	AmCent Growth Inv	8.73	★★★		None

*Three-, five-, and 10-year returns are annualized.

International-Equity Funds

Morningstar Funds 500 Universe

Leaders

Cat	Fund Name	Total Return%*	Morningstar Rating	Style	Sales Charge%
	One Year (12-31-2004)				
LS	T. Rowe Price Latin Amer	38.35	★★★★		None
EM	Oppenheimer Develop MktA	33.00	★★★★★		5.75
FV	Dodge & Cox Intl Stock	32.46	★★★★		None
FR	Vanguard Intl Explorer	31.77	★★★★★		Clsd
WS	Oppenheimer Glob Oppor A	29.88	★★★		5.75
FR	Fidelity Intl Sm Cp	29.43	—		None
FA	Oakmark Intl Small Cap I	28.95	★★★★		Clsd
FR	Columbia Acorn Intl A	28.91	★★		5.75
FA	Third Avenue Intl Value	27.70	★★★		None
EM	T. Rowe Price Emg Mkt St	26.98	★★★		None
	Three Year (12-31-2004)				
SP	AmCent Global Gold Inv	32.58	★★★		None
EM	Oppenheimer Develop MktA	29.32	★★★★★		5.75
FR	Artisan Intl Sm Cap	26.44	★★★★★		Clsd
EM	Templeton Devel Mkts A	25.01	★★★		5.75
FA	First Eagle Overseas A	24.69	★★★★★		Clsd
FA	Third Avenue Intl Value	24.26	★★★		None
EM	Dreyfus Prem Emerg A	24.05	★★★★		Clsd
FA	Oakmark Intl Small Cap I	23.09	★★★★		Clsd
PJ	Matthews Pacific Tiger	22.70	★★★★		None
EM	Vanguard Em Mkt Idx	22.55	★★★		None
	Five Year (12-31-2004)				
SP	AmCent Global Gold Inv	18.90	★★★		None
WS	Oakmark Global I	18.59	★★★★★		None
IH	First Eagle Glbl A	16.78	★★★★★		5.00
FA	First Eagle Overseas A	16.63	★★★★★		Clsd
EM	Oppenheimer Develop MktA	14.07	★★★★★		5.75
FA	Oakmark Intl Small Cap I	13.94	★★★★		Clsd
FV	Longleaf Partners Intl	12.62	★★★		Clsd
IH	Amer Funds CpIncBldr A	11.11	★★★★		5.75
EM	Dreyfus Prem Emerg A	10.38	★★★★		Clsd
FV	Oakmark International I	9.94	★★★★		None
	Ten Year (12-31-2004)				
WS	Oppenheimer Glob Oppor A	15.88	★★★		5.75
FA	First Eagle Overseas A	14.54	★★★★★		Clsd
FR	AmCent Intl Disc Inv	14.50	★★★★		Clsd
WS	Amer Funds CapWrldGI A	14.36	★★★★★		5.75
IH	First Eagle Glbl A	13.92	★★★★★		5.00
FB	Julius Baer Intl Eqty A	13.85	★★★★★		12b-1
WS	Oppenheimer Glob A	13.68	★★★★		5.75
FG	Fidelity Diversified Int	13.00	★★★★★		Clsd
IH	Amer Funds CpIncBldr A	12.81	★★★★		5.75
WS	Amer Funds New Persp A	12.55	★★★★		5.75

Laggards

Cat	Fund Name	Total Return%*	Morningstar Rating	Style	Sales Charge%
	One Year (12-31-2004)				
SP	AmCent Global Gold Inv	−8.17	★★★		None
WS	Janus Worldwide	5.54	★★		None
FV	Longleaf Partners Intl	10.21	★★★		Clsd
WS	Fidelity Worldwide	12.24	★★★		None
WS	Van Kampen Glob Val Eq A	13.04	★★★		5.75
FB	Fidelity Overseas	13.54	★★★		None
FG	T. Rowe Price Intl Stk	13.89	★★★		None
DP	Fidelity Pacific Basin	14.08	★★★★		None
FB	Oppenheimer Quest Intl A	14.10	★★★★		5.75
IH	Merrill Global Alloc A	14.27	★★★		0.02
	Three Year (12-31-2004)				
WS	Janus Worldwide	−1.01	★★		None
FG	AmCent Intl Growth Inv	5.30	★★★★		None
WS	Van Kampen Glob Val Eq A	6.04	★★★		5.75
FG	T. Rowe Price Intl Stk	6.95	★★★		None
FG	Artisan International Inv	7.24	★★★★		None
FG	Janus Overseas	7.27	★★★★		None
WS	AmCent Global Gr Inv	7.28	★★★		None
WS	Fidelity Worldwide	8.04	★★★		None
FB	Oppenheimer Quest Intl A	8.28	★★★★		5.75
WS	Atlas Global Growth A	8.45	★★★★	—	12b-1
	Five Year (12-31-2004)				
WS	Janus Worldwide	−9.06	★★		None
FG	AmCent Intl Growth Inv	−6.19	★★★★		None
DP	Fidelity Pacific Basin	−5.46	★★★★		None
FG	Janus Overseas	−5.02	★★★★		None
FG	T. Rowe Price Intl Stk	−4.58	★★★		None
FB	TIAA-CREF Intl Equity	−3.34	★★★		None
FB	Fidelity Overseas	−2.97	★★★		None
WS	AmCent Global Gr Inv	−2.85	★★★		None
FB	Fidelity Spar Intl Index	−1.52	★★★		None
FG	Artisan International Inv	−1.48	★★★★		None
	Ten Year (12-31-2004)				
SP	AmCent Global Gold Inv	2.31	★★★		None
PJ	T. Rowe Price New Asia	3.06	★★★		None
DP	Fidelity Pacific Basin	3.36	★★★★		None
FG	T. Rowe Price Intl Stk	5.07	★★★		None
EM	Vanguard Em Mkt Idx	5.20	★★★		None
EM	Templeton Devel Mkts A	5.58	★★★		5.75
FB	Fidelity Overseas	6.61	★★★		None
FB	Vanguard Intl Value	6.99	★★★★		None
FB	Vanguard Intl Gr	7.04	★★★★		None
PJ	Matthews Pacific Tiger	7.38	★★★★		None

*Three-, five-, and 10-year returns are annualized.

Fixed-Income Funds

Morningstar Funds 500 Universe

Leaders

Cat	Fund Name	Total Return%*	Morningstar Rating	Style	Sales Charge%
	One Year (12-31-2004)				
HY	Northeast Investors	14.38	★★★★		None
EB	Payden Emerging Mkts Bond	13.13	★★		None
EB	Fidelity New Markets Inc	12.50	★★★★	—	None
EB	PIMCO Emerg Mkts Bd A	11.79	★★★		3.75
IB	T. Rowe Price Intl Bd	11.41	★★★		None
IB	Amer Funds CapWrldBd A	11.38	★★★		3.75
MU	Loomis Sayles Bond Ret	11.02	★★★★★		12b-1
HY	Eaton Vance Inc Boston A	10.71	★★★★		4.75
HY	T. Rowe Price Hi-Yld	10.35	★★★★★		Clsd
HY	Amer Funds Amer H/I A	9.78	★★★★		3.75
	Three Year (12-31-2004)				
EB	Fidelity New Markets Inc	18.44	★★★★	—	None
EB	PIMCO Emerg Mkts Bd A	18.37	★★★		3.75
MU	Loomis Sayles Bond Ret	17.42	★★★★★		12b-1
IB	T. Rowe Price Intl Bd	17.25	★★★		None
IB	Amer Funds CapWrldBd A	15.52	★★★		3.75
EB	Payden Emerging Mkts Bond	13.69	★★		None
HY	Eaton Vance Inc Boston A	12.57	★★★★		4.75
MU	Fidelity Strategic Inc	12.40	★★★★★	—	None
HY	Fidelity High Income	12.37	★★★	—	None
HY	T. Rowe Price Hi-Yld	11.70	★★★★★		Clsd
	Five Year (12-31-2004)				
EB	PIMCO Emerg Mkts Bd A	19.29	★★★		3.75
EB	Fidelity New Markets Inc	15.17	★★★★	—	None
EB	Payden Emerging Mkts Bond	13.48	★★		None
HY	Pioneer High Yield A	12.56	★★★★		4.50
MU	Loomis Sayles Bond Ret	11.50	★★★★★		12b-1
GL	PIMCO Real Ret A	10.85	★★★★		3.00
CL	Vanguard Long-Tm InvGrde	9.92	★★★★		None
GL	Vanguard Long-Tm US Try	9.89	★★★★		None
IB	Amer Funds CapWrldBd A	9.69	★★★		3.75
MU	Fidelity Strategic Inc	9.50	★★★★★	—	None
	Ten Year (12-31-2004)				
GL	Vanguard Long-Tm US Try	9.25	★★★★		None
CL	Vanguard Long-Tm InvGrde	9.11	★★★★		None
HY	Amer Funds Amer H/I A	9.09	★★★★		3.75
MU	Hancock Strategic Inc A	8.94	★★★★		4.50
HY	Eaton Vance Inc Boston A	8.76	★★★★		4.75
HY	T. Rowe Price Hi-Yld	8.70	★★★★★		Clsd
CI	Fremont Bond	8.63	★★★★★		None
GL	T. Rowe Price US Try L/T	8.55	★★★		None
CI	PIMCO Total Ret Instl	8.54	★★★★★		None
CI	TCW Galileo Tot Ret Bd I	8.54	★★★★★		None

Laggards

Cat	Fund Name	Total Return%*	Morningstar Rating	Style	Sales Charge%
	One Year (12-31-2004)				
MS	Calvert Tax-Fr Res Lim A	0.62	★★		1.00
GS	Vanguard Short-Tm Trs	1.03	★★★★		None
UB	Payden Limited Maturity	1.09	★★		None
MS	Vanguard Sht-Tm TE	1.12	★★★		None
UB	Fidelity Ultra-Short Bd	1.32	—		None
GS	Vanguard ShtTm Fed	1.36	★★★★		None
UB	SSgA Yield Plus	1.44	★★	—	12b-1
MS	USAA Tax Ex Short-Term	1.52	★★★★		None
MS	Vanguard LtdTm T/E	1.53	★★★★		None
MS	T. Rowe Price T/F Sh-Int	1.61	★★★★		None
	Three Year (12-31-2004)				
UB	SSgA Yield Plus	1.31	★★	—	12b-1
UB	Payden Limited Maturity	1.56	★★		None
MS	Calvert Tax-Fr Res Lim A	1.87	★★		1.00
UB	Constel CIP Ultr Sh F/I I	1.92	★★★		None
MS	Vanguard Sht-Tm TE	2.08	★★★		None
CS	Metro West Low Dur M	2.91	★★★		12b-1
MS	USAA Tax Ex Short-Term	3.14	★★★★		None
MS	T. Rowe Price T/F Sh-Int	3.50	★★★★		None
MS	Vanguard LtdTm T/E	3.52	★★★★		None
GS	Vanguard ShtTm Fed	3.62	★★★★		None
	Five Year (12-31-2004)				
MS	Calvert Tax-Fr Res Lim A	2.91	★★		1.00
HY	Fidelity High Income	2.99	★★★	—	None
UB	SSgA Yield Plus	3.01	★★	—	12b-1
MS	Vanguard Sht-Tm TE	3.17	★★★		None
UB	Payden Limited Maturity	3.55	★★		None
UB	Constel CIP Ultr Sh F/I I	3.69	★★★		None
MS	USAA Tax Ex Short-Term	4.10	★★★★		None
MS	Vanguard LtdTm T/E	4.49	★★★★		None
MS	Strong S/T Muni Bond Inv	4.50	★★★★★		None
MS	T. Rowe Price T/F Sh-Int	4.60	★★★★		None
	Ten Year (12-31-2004)				
MS	Calvert Tax-Fr Res Lim A	3.48	★★		1.00
MS	Vanguard Sht-Tm TE	3.64	★★★		None
UB	SSgA Yield Plus	4.29	★★	—	12b-1
MS	USAA Tax Ex Short-Term	4.56	★★★★		None
UB	Payden Limited Maturity	4.59	★★		None
MS	T. Rowe Price T/F Sh-Int	4.63	★★★★		None
MS	Strong S/T Muni Bond Inv	4.63	★★★★★		None
MS	Vanguard LtdTm T/E	4.67	★★★★		None
MS	Fidelity Spar Sh-IntMuni	4.71	★★★★		None
MS	Thornburg Ltd-Tm A	4.82	★★★★		1.50

*Three-, five-, and 10-year returns are annualized.

Benchmark Averages

Category	Portfolio Statistics P/E Ratio	P/B Ratio	P/CF Ratio	Average Mkt Cap $Mil	Top Three Sectors % of Stock			Cash %	Turnover %	Yield %	Expense %	Potential Cap Gains Exp%	MPT Statistics Alpha	Beta	R^2
Domestic Equity	**25.2**	**4.1**	**25.2**	**21461**	**Financial 18**	**Ind.Materials 14**	**Healthcare 12**	**3.7**	**94**	**0.3**	**1.48**	**–1**	**7.5**	**0.96**	**72**
Large Value	20.1	3.2	20.1	33192	Financial 27	Ind.Materials 16	Energy 11	3.5	65	1.0	1.43	10	2.2	0.96	90
Large Blend	23.1	4.1	23.1	36987	Financial 21	Healthcare 13	Ind.Materials 13	3.5	73	0.6	1.25	–3	–0.5	0.95	94
Large Growth	28.9	5.3	28.9	33190	Healthcare 19	Hardware 16	Consumer 14	3.2	104	0.2	1.54	–39	–3.2	0.99	86
Mid-Cap Value	20.5	2.8	20.5	5996	Financial 24	Ind.Materials 19	Goods 9	5.3	66	0.4	1.56	16	7.8	0.88	77
Mid-Cap Blend	23.0	3.5	23.0	6008	Financial 18	Ind.Materials 13	Consumer 11	4.8	123	0.2	1.44	14	6.5	0.93	77
Mid-Cap Growth	30.0	4.9	30.0	5194	Healthcare 18	Consumer 14	Hardware 13	3.2	137	0.0	1.66	–35	0.6	1.00	72
Small Value	22.2	2.5	22.2	966	Financial 21	Ind.Materials 21	Consumer 11	4.9	71	0.2	1.58	21	12.4	0.86	60
Small Blend	24.1	3.1	24.1	1235	Ind.Materials 19	Financial 18	Business 11	4.6	98	0.1	1.48	20	9.4	0.94	63
Small Growth	30.2	4.6	30.2	1056	Healthcare 18	Business 14	Hardware 12	3.6	122	0.0	1.70	–15	2.0	1.09	65
International Equity	**21.0**	**4.3**	**21.0**	**16322**	**Financial 20**	**Ind.Materials 18**	**Goods 15**	**4.7**	**93**	**0.8**	**1.82**	**–23**	**5.3**	**0.78**	**54**
Europe Stock	19.3	5.2	19.3	24707	Financial 25	Goods 13	Energy 11	6.3	128	0.7	1.85	–28	1.5	1.03	84
Latin Amer Stock	27.6	3.1	27.6	8002	Media 27	Ind.Materials 24	Energy 13	2.8	60	0.8	2.24	–32	7.5	1.25	64
Div Emerging Mkts	18.0	3.3	18.0	5894	Ind.Materials 20	Financial 19	Goods 15	3.3	96	0.6	2.11	–10	10.4	0.94	70
Div Pac/Asia	21.5	2.6	21.5	8832	Financial 28	Ind.Materials 19	Goods 19	2.3	81	0.9	2.33	–62	3.0	0.70	56
Pac/Asia ex-Japan	19.3	3.4	19.3	5813	Financial 25	Goods 16	Ind.Materials 14	3.7	94	0.5	2.16	–31	6.7	0.78	47
Japan Stock	21.4	2.3	21.4	7341	Ind.Materials 26	Goods 24	Financial 16	15.9	168	0.3	1.72	–75	3.1	0.71	32
Foreign Large Value	18.8	3.6	18.8	17798	Financial 25	Ind.Materials 16	Goods 16	4.6	39	1.0	1.54	16	3.0	0.95	92
Foreign Large Blend	19.9	4.2	19.9	22065	Financial 25	Goods 16	Ind.Materials 13	4.3	81	0.8	1.70	–10	–1.9	0.97	95
Foreign Large Growth	22.3	5.2	22.3	17887	Financial 22	Goods 17	Ind.Materials 11	3.0	115	0.3	1.86	–22	–3.3	0.98	93
Foreign Sm/Mid Val	21.1	4.2	21.1	1557	Ind.Materials 25	Business 17	Financial 14	6.7	60	1.0	1.71	22	11.2	0.77	74
Foreign Sm/Mid Grth	21.9	5.1	21.9	1802	Ind.Materials 22	Financial 16	Business 13	4.0	132	0.3	2.05	–15	5.9	0.93	79
World Stock	23.4	4.6	23.4	20449	Financial 19	Goods 14	Ind.Materials 13	3.7	96	0.4	1.83	–15	–2.9	0.92	85
Specialty Stock	**29.1**	**4.2**	**29.1**	**12320**	**Financial 24**	**Ind.Materials 16**	**Healthcare 13**	**8.3**	**221**	**0.9**	**1.84**	**–47**	**1.4**	**0.63**	**52**
Communications	25.0	3.2	25.0	16919	Media 54	Hardware 20	Telecommunications 13	3.3	556	0.2	1.74	–84	–1.0	1.62	74
Financial	15.7	2.5	15.7	19361	Financial 96	Business 1	Ind.Materials 1	3.4	233	0.6	1.79	16	7.5	0.87	74
Health	28.6	5.7	28.6	15989	Healthcare 94	Financial 2	Ind.Materials 1	4.2	222	0.0	1.93	–7	–1.6	0.72	50
Natural Resources	25.9	3.4	25.9	10922	Energy 71	Ind.Materials 25	Business 2	6.6	267	0.5	1.71	11	16.0	0.69	32
Precious Metals	38.7	5.2	38.7	2450	Ind.Materials 100	— —	— —	7.3	120	1.6	1.75	1	32.5	0.50	5
Real Estate	31.8	2.9	31.8	3111	Financial 94	Consumer 5	Ind.Materials 1	2.9	82	3.1	1.64	23	21.9	0.34	14
Technology	36.4	5.3	36.4	13452	Hardware 48	Software 21	Business 8	3.6	232	0.0	2.07	–180	–5.0	1.78	74
Utilities	18.3	2.5	18.3	10476	Utilities 68	Media 20	Energy 9	4.5	196	2.3	1.62	–15	2.0	0.85	63
Hybrid Fund	**23.1**	**4.0**	**23.1**	**26370**	**Financial 25**	**Ind.Materials 13**	**Healthcare 9**	**9.7**	**83**	**2.2**	**1.29**	**–0**	**1.7**	**0.49**	**71**
Conservative Alloc	23.4	4.0	23.4	24415	Financial 23	Ind.Materials 13	Healthcare 12	14.8	74	1.8	1.34	1	2.9	0.28	62
Convertible	25.7	3.9	25.7	15385	Financial 34	Ind.Materials 12	Consumer 10	3.6	98	3.5	1.54	–2	5.4	0.52	66
Moderate Allocation	23.0	4.0	23.0	27307	Financial 21	Ind.Materials 13	Healthcare 12	7.9	86	1.4	1.25	–0	1.8	0.58	87
World Allocation	19.8	3.7	19.8	18888	Financial 24	Ind.Materials 14	Goods 12	13.7	49	1.9	1.53	7	4.3	0.54	79

Category	Portfolio Statistics Duration	Maturity	Average Credit Quality	Avg Wtd Coupon	Avg Wtd Price	Cash %	Turnover %	Yield %	Expense %	Potential Cap Gains Exp%	MPT Statistics Alpha	Beta	R^2
Specialty Bond	**4.3**	**7.1**	**BB**	**7.88**	**103.29**	**7.0**	**102**	**5.8**	**1.32**	**–25**	**0.3**	**0.27**	**13**
Bank Loan	0.3	2.8	B	2.50	100.40	12.5	74	3.2	1.44	–9	4.1	–0.03	1
High Yield Bond	4.2	6.6	B	8.35	103.87	5.4	101	6.7	1.31	–33	9.0	0.07	1
Multisector Bond	4.7	8.5	A	6.51	101.49	11.6	105	5.0	1.37	–17	5.7	0.68	39
World Bond	4.9	7.2	AA	4.86	92.34	16.6	181	4.7	1.34	2	5.4	0.98	51
Emerg Mkts Bd	5.8	13.0	BB	7.88	100.86	10.7	214	5.9	1.53	–18	11.7	0.98	15
General Bond	**3.6**	**6.6**	**AA**	**4.89**	**103.50**	**15.0**	**186**	**3.1**	**1.05**	**–59**	**0.1**	**0.52**	**50**
Long-Term Bond	6.6	17.5	A	6.34	106.06	4.2	110	4.9	1.10	2	0.3	1.35	77
Interm-Term Bond	4.4	7.0	AA	5.20	104.11	12.8	222	3.6	1.08	–1	–0.4	0.94	90
Short-Term Bond	2.0	3.1	AA	4.56	102.40	19.3	135	2.8	1.00	–3	–0.1	0.41	75
Ultrashort Bond	0.6	7.4	AAA	3.06	101.11	30.9	119	2.1	0.76	–6	–0.1	0.10	35
Government Bond	**3.9**	**6.8**	**AAA**	**4.57**	**103.23**	**11.9**	**243**	**2.8**	**1.07**	**–1**	**–2.3**	**1.26**	**82**
Long Govt	10.5	15.8	AAA	2.99	94.39	8.9	393	2.3	0.94	5	–3.2	2.40	88
Interm Govt	3.8	7.1	AAA	4.94	104.95	11.8	255	3.4	1.12	–3	–0.8	0.86	89
Short Govt	2.2	3.7	AAA	4.21	102.04	12.9	171	2.7	0.99	–4	–0.7	0.51	81
Municipal Bond	**5.7**	**11.5**	**AA**	**5.37**	**106.54**	**2.3**	**30**	**3.6**	**1.09**	**3**	**–2.4**	**0.93**	**72**
High Yield Muni	6.5	14.9	BBB	6.30	101.52	1.2	31	5.0	1.25	–17	1.7	0.65	77
Muni National Long	6.7	13.3	AA	5.51	106.67	1.2	46	3.8	1.15	4	–0.9	1.04	95
Muni National Interm	5.1	7.4	AA	5.34	108.69	3.0	46	3.3	0.99	3	–0.9	0.94	97
Muni NY Long	6.5	13.9	AA	5.39	106.74	1.4	22	4.0	1.13	8	–0.8	1.02	92
Muni NY Int/Sh	5.1	8.4	AA	5.19	108.51	3.3	42	3.[illegible]	1.03	3	–0.9	0.95	95
Muni CA Long	7.1	15.8	AA	5.38	103.87	0.9	29	3.9	1.09	4	–1.5	1.11	94
Muni CA Int/Sh	4.7	7.0	AA	5.20	108.11	3.6	41	3.1	0.91	5	–1.3	0.88	94
Muni Single ST Long	6.3	16.2	AA	5.32	105.45	1.0	17	3.9	1.18	5	–0.7	0.96	95
Muni Single ST In/Sh	5.2	9.9	AA	5.28	107.29	2.1	18	3.5	1.04	3	–1.0	0.94	96
Muni Short	2.4	3.4	AA	4.61	104.71	11.3	48	2.2	0.88	–2	–0.5	0.41	80

Sectors Legend: Software, Hardware, Media, Telecommunications, Healthcare, Consumer, Business, Financial, Goods, Ind.Materials, Energy, Utilities

Morningstar Manager of the Year Past Winners

Year	Manager of the Year	Winning Fund	Current Fund
2004	Brian Berghuis	T. Rowe Price Mid-Cap Growth	T. Rowe Price Mid-Cap Growth
	Ken Leech and Team	Western Asset Core Bond	Western Asset Core Bond
	Management Team	Dodge & Cox International Stock	Dodge & Cox International Stock
2003	Joel Fried Theo Kolokotrones Howard Schow	Vanguard Primecap Vanguard Capital Opportunity	Vanguard Primecap Vanguard Capital Opportunity
	Bill Fries	Thornburg International Value	Thornburg International Value
	Management Team	Fidelity Spartan Muni Income	Fidelity Spartan Muni Income
2002	Joel Tillinghast	Fidelity Low-Priced Stock	Fidelity Low-Priced Stock
	Management Team	Dodge & Cox Income	Dodge & Cox Income
	Rudolph-Riad Younes Richard Pell	Julius Baer International Equity	Julius Baer Intl Equity Heritage Intl Equity
2001	Jean-Marie Eveillard Charles de Vaulx	First Eagle SoGen Global	First Eagle Global First Eagle U.S. Value
	Robert L. Rodriguez	FPA New Income	FPA Capital
	William C. Nygren	Oakmark Select	Oakmark I, Oakmark Select I
2000	Bill Gross	PIMCO Total Return	PIMCO Low Duration, PIMCO Total Return
	Christopher Browne William Browne John Spears	Tweedy Browne Global Value	Tweedy, Browne American Value, Tweedy, Browne Global Value
	Jim Gipson Doug Grey Peter Quinn Michael Sandler Bruce Veaco	Clipper Fund	Clipper Fund
1999	EuroPacific growth team	American Funds EuroPacific A	American Funds EuroPacific
	Jerry Paul	Invesco High Yield	Retired
	Jim Callinan	RS Emerging Growth	RS Emerging Growth, RS Information Age
1998	Bill Gross	PIMCO Total Return	PIMCO Low Duration, PIMCO Total Return
	Bill Miller	Legg Mason Value	Legg Mason Opportunity, Legg Mason Value
	Mark Yockey	Artisan International	Artisan International
1997	David Baldt	Deutsche Fixed Income	Schroder Municipal Bond
	Helen Young Hayes	Janus Overseas Janus Worldwide	Retired
	Mario Gabelli	Gabelli Asset	Gabelli Asset, Gabelli Value
1996	Hakan Castegren	Harbor Intl	Harbor Intl
	Joe Deane	Smith Barney Managed & Calif Municipals	Smith Barney Mgd. Muni, Smith Barney Tot Ret
	Shelby Davis	Davis New York Venture Selected American Shares	Retired
1995	Dan Fuss	Loomis Sayles Bond	Loomis Sayles Fixed Inc, Loomis Sayles Bond Ret
	Jack Laporte	T. Rowe Price New Horizons	T. Rowe Price New Horizons, T. Rowe Price Div. Sm Cap
	Jack Mussey	Colonial Newport Tiger	Retired
1994	Robert L. Rodriguez	FPA New Income	FPA Capital, FPA New Income
1993	Jeff Vinik	Fidelity Magellan	Retired
1992	Bill Dutton	Skyline Special Equities	Skyline Special Equities
1991	Donald Yacktman	Selected American Shares	Yacktman, Yacktman Focused
1990	Martin Whitman	Equity Strategies	Third Avenue Value
1989	Tom Marisco	Janus Twenty	Marsico Focus, Marsico Growth
1988	Peter Lynch	Fidelity Magellan	Retired
1987	Jerry Palmieri	Franklin Growth	Franklin Growth

Best Five-Year Tax-Adjusted Returns

Morningstar Funds 500 Universe

Domestic Equity

Page	Cat		5-Year Tax-Adjusted Return %
		Highest	
91	SV	Boston Part SmCp II Inv	25.1
95	SB	Bridgeway UI-Sm Co Mkt	22.8
529	SG	William Blair Sm-Cp Gr N	22.7
413	SR	Third Avenue RealEst Val	22.1
300	SV	N/I Numeric Inv Sm CapVl	21.7
517	SG	Wasatch Micro Cap	21.1
391	SR	T. Rowe Price Real Est	20.7
519	SB	Wasatch Small Cap Value	20.6
180	SR	Fidelity Real Estate Inv	20.1
342	SV	Royce Special Equity Inv	20.0
48	SV	AmCent Small Cap Val Inv	20.0
35	SV	American AAdv SmCpVl Pln	19.7
97	SG	Buffalo Small Cap	19.6
292	SR	Morgan Stan Ins US R/E A	19.6
32	SV	Aegis Value	19.3
353	SR	Security Cap US Real Est	19.2
88	SG	Bjurman, Barry MicroCp Gr	18.8
394	SV	T. Rowe Price Sm Val	18.7
488	SR	Vanguard REIT Index	18.5
134	SG	FBR Small Cap	18.5
		Average 5-Year Tax Adjusted Return	**4.4**

Taxable Bond

Page	Cat		5-Year Tax-Adjusted Return %
		Highest	
327	EB	PIMCO Emerg Mkts Bd A	13.2
174	EB	Fidelity New Markets Inc	11.4
323	EB	Payden Emerging Mkts Bond	9.4
265	MU	Loomis Sayles Bond Ret	8.5
335	HY	Pioneer High Yield A	7.7
59	IB	Amer Funds CapWrldBd A	7.5
480	CL	Vanguard Long-Tm InvGrde	7.4
194	MU	Fidelity Strategic Inc	6.9
379	IB	T. Rowe Price Intl Bd	6.6
525	CI	Western Asset Cr Bd Inst	6.5
470	CI	Vanguard Intm Bd Idx	6.4
530	CI	WPG Core Bond	6.3
119	CI	Dodge & Cox Income	6.2
216	CI	Fremont Bond	6.2
396	MU	T. Rowe Price Spect Inc	6.1
227	CI	Harbor Bond	6.1
322	CI	Payden Core Bond	6.0
333	CI	PIMCO Total Ret Instl	6.0
404	CI	TCW Galileo Tot Ret Bd I	5.8
471	CI	Vanguard IntTm Inv-Gr Fd	5.8
		Average 5-Year Tax Adjusted Return	**5.4**

International Equity

Page	Cat		5-Year Tax-Adjusted Return %
		Highest	
40	SP	AmCent Global Gold Inv	18.5
308	WS	Oakmark Global I	18.2
201	IH	First Eagle Glbl A	13.6
202	FA	First Eagle Overseas A	13.5
311	FA	Oakmark Intl Small Cap I	12.8
314	EM	Oppenheimer Develop MktA	11.9
263	FV	Longleaf Partners Intl	10.3
310	FV	Oakmark International I	9.1
382	LS	T. Rowe Price Latin Amer	9.1
460	WS	Vanguard Global Equity	8.3
279	PJ	Matthews Pacific Tiger	7.8
58	IH	Amer Funds CplncBldr A	7.7
127	EM	Dreyfus Prem Emerg A	7.4
284	IH	Merrill Global Alloc A	6.5
295	WS	Mutual Discovery A	6.4
296	ES	Mutual European A	6.2
434	FA	Tweedy, Browne Glob Val	5.9
60	WS	Amer Funds CapWrldGI A	5.5
370	EM	T. Rowe Price Emg Mkt St	4.9
409	WS	Templeton Growth A	4.9
		Average 5-Year Tax Adjusted Return	**3.0**

Municipal Bond

Page	Cat		5-Year Tax-Adjusted Return %
		Highest	
439	ML	USAA Tax Ex Long-Term	7.7
191	ML	Fidelity Spar Muni Inc	7.5
481	ML	Vanguard Lg-Tm T/E	7.4
469	ML	Vanguard Ins L/T TE Inv	7.4
398	ML	T. Rowe Price T/F Inc	7.0
467	ML	Vanguard Hi-Yld T/E	6.9
438	MI	USAA Tax Ex Interm-Term	6.5
189	MI	Fidelity Spar IntermMuni	6.5
49	MI	AmCent Tax-Free Bond Inv	6.0
214	ML	Franklin Ins T/F Inc A	6.0
472	MI	Vanguard IntTm T/E	5.9
70	MI	Amer Funds T/E Bd A	5.8
210	ML	Franklin Fed T/F Inc A	5.7
399	MS	T. Rowe Price T/F Sh-Int	4.6
192	MS	Fidelity Spar Sh-IntMuni	4.6
365	MS	Strong S/T Muni Bond Inv	4.5
483	MS	Vanguard LtdTm T/E	4.5
418	MS	Thornburg Ltd-Tm A	4.5
440	MS	USAA Tax Ex Short-Term	4.1
493	MS	Vanguard Sht-Tm TE	3.2
		Average 5-Year Tax Adjusted Return	**5.7**

Lowest Expense Ratio

Morningstar Funds 500 Universe

Domestic Equity

Page	Cat		Expense Ratio %
		Actively Managed Funds	
511	CA	Vanguard Wellesley Inc	0.26
465	SH	Vanguard Health Care	0.28
456	LV	Vanguard Equity-Inc	0.32
484	MG	Vanguard Mid Cap Growth	0.34
512	MA	Vanguard Wellington	0.36
514	LV	Vanguard Windsor II	0.36
446	MA	Vanguard Asset Alloc	0.38
455	SN	Vanguard Energy	0.38
513	LV	Vanguard Windsor	0.39
453	LV	Vanguard Dividend Growth	0.40
462	LB	Vanguard Gr & Inc	0.42
421	LB	TIAA-CREF Growth & Inc	0.43
486	LG	Vanguard Morgan Gr	0.44
499	MB	Vanguard Strategic Eq	0.45
422	LG	TIAA-CREF Growth Eqty	0.45
487	LB	Vanguard Primecap	0.46
146	LG	Fidelity Destiny I	0.47
509	LV	Vanguard U.S. Value	0.49
449	MG	Vanguard Cap Opp	0.52
		Index Funds	
94	LB	Bridgeway Blue-Chip 35	0.15
500	CA	Vanguard Tax-Mgd Bal	0.17
502	LB	Vanguard Tx-Mgd Gr	0.17
501	LG	Vanguard Tx-Mgd App	0.17
504	SB	Vanguard Tax-Mgd SmCap R	0.17
445	LB	Vanguard 500 Index	0.18
188	LB	Fidelity Spar 500 Idx	0.19
507	LB	Vanguard Tot Stk	0.20
447	MA	Vanguard Bal Idx	0.22
464	LG	Vanguard Gr Idx	0.23
510	LV	Vanguard Val Idx	0.23
488	SR	Vanguard REIT Index	0.24
193	LB	Fidelity Spar Tot Mkt Ix	0.25
448	LG	Vanguard Calv Soc Idx	0.25
459	MB	Vanguard ExtMktIdx	0.26
485	MB	Vanguard Mid Cap Idx	0.26
420	LB	TIAA-CREF Equity Index	0.26
496	SB	Vanguard SmCp Idx	0.27
497	SV	Vanguard SmCp Vl Idx	0.27
495	SG	Vanguard SmCp Gr Idx	0.27
		Average Expense Ratio	**0.98**

International Equity

Page	Cat		Expense Ratio %
		Actively Managed Funds	
474	FB	Vanguard Intl Gr	0.45
424	FB	TIAA-CREF Intl Equity	0.49
475	FB	Vanguard Intl Value	0.56
473	FR	Vanguard Intl Explorer	0.57
58	IH	Amer Funds CpIncBldr A	0.65
40	SP	AmCent Global Gold Inv	0.69
67	WS	Amer Funds New Persp A	0.78
233	ES	ICAP Euro Select Eqty	0.80
60	WS	Amer Funds CapWrldGl A	0.81
120	FV	Dodge & Cox Intl Stock	0.82
229	FV	Harbor Intl Instl	0.86
61	FB	Amer Funds EuroPac A	0.87
460	WS	Vanguard Global Equity	0.90
253	WS	Janus Worldwide	0.92
381	FG	T. Rowe Price Intl Stk	0.92
249	FG	Janus Overseas	0.94
177	FB	Fidelity Overseas	1.00
387	PJ	T. Rowe Price New Asia	1.09
435	FB	UMB Scout WorldWide	1.10
409	WS	Templeton Growth A	1.10
		Index Funds	
452	FB	Vanguard Dev Mkts Idx	0.00
457	ES	Vanguard Eur Stk Idx	0.27
503	FB	Vanguard Tax-Mgd Intl	0.28
190	FB	Fidelity Spar Intl Index	0.47
454	EM	Vanguard Em Mkt Idx	0.48
		Average Expense Ratio	**1.15**

Lowest Expense Ratio

Morningstar Funds 500 Universe

Taxable Bond

Page	Cat		Expense Ratio %
		Actively Managed Funds	
468	GI	Vanguard Infl-Prot Secs	0.18
471	CI	Vanguard IntTm Inv-Gr Fd	0.20
461	GI	Vanguard GNMA	0.20
492	CS	Vanguard Sht-Tm Inv-Grade	0.21
491	GS	Vanguard ShtTm Fed	0.22
466	HY	Vanguard Hi-Yld Corp	0.23
494	GS	Vanguard Short-Tm Trs	0.26
482	GL	Vanguard Long-Tm US Try	0.26
480	CL	Vanguard Long-Tm InvGrde	0.28
426	CS	TIAA-CREF Short-Term Bd	0.30
423	HY	TIAA-CREF High-Yield Bd	0.34
324	UB	Payden Limited Maturity	0.40
330	CS	PIMCO Low Duration Instl	0.43
333	CI	PIMCO Total Ret Instl	0.43
530	CI	WPG Core Bond	0.45
119	CI	Dodge & Cox Income	0.45
525	CI	Western Asset Cr Bd Inst	0.49
164	GI	Fidelity Inflation-Protec	0.50
322	CI	Payden Core Bond	0.51
404	CI	TCW Galileo Tot Ret Bd I	0.51
		Index Funds	
470	CI	Vanguard Intm Bd Idx	0.20
490	CS	Vanguard Sh-Tm Bd Idx	0.20
505	CI	Vanguard Total Bd Idx	0.22
		Average Expense Ratio	**0.59**

Municipal Bond*

Page	Cat		Expense Ratio %
		Actively Managed Funds	
483	MS	Vanguard LtdTm T/E	0.14
472	MI	Vanguard IntTm T/E	0.14
493	MS	Vanguard Sht-Tm TE	0.14
469	ML	Vanguard Ins L/T TE Inv	0.15
467	ML	Vanguard Hi-Yld T/E	0.15
481	ML	Vanguard Lg-Tm T/E	0.15
428	ML	TIAA-CREF Tax-Exempt Bd	0.30
189	MI	Fidelity Spar IntermMuni	0.43
191	ML	Fidelity Spar Muni Inc	0.47
192	MS	Fidelity Spar Sh-IntMuni	0.47
399	MS	T. Rowe Price T/F Sh-Int	0.51
49	MI	AmCent Tax-Free Bond Inv	0.51
438	MI	USAA Tax Ex Interm-Term	0.51
398	ML	T. Rowe Price T/F Inc	0.54
439	ML	USAA Tax Ex Long-Term	0.56
440	MS	USAA Tax Ex Short-Term	0.56
101	MS	Calvert Tax-Fr Res Lim A	0.57
210	ML	Franklin Fed T/F Inc A	0.61
70	MI	Amer Funds T/E Bd A	0.61
214	ML	Franklin Ins T/F Inc A	0.63
		Index Funds	
		None	
		Average Expense Ratio	**0.45**

* There are only 23 municipal-bond funds in the Morningstar Funds 500 universe, none of which are index funds.

Lowest Turnover Rate

Morningstar Funds 500 Universe

Domestic Equity

Page	Cat		Turnover Rate %
		Actively Managed Funds	
96	SG	Brown Cap Small Co Instl	1
211	LB	Franklin Growth A	2
395	LB	T. Rowe Price Spect Grth	2
268	LB	Mairs & Power Growth	2
433	MV	Tweedy, Browne American	3
357	LV	Sequoia	3
157	MA	Fidelity Freedom 2020	3
478	CA	Vanguard LifeSt Income	4
260	LB	Legg Mason Value Prim	4
132	LV	Excelsior Val & Restruct	4
264	SV	Longleaf Partners Sm-Cap	4
391	SR	T. Rowe Price Real Est	4
156	CA	Fidelity Freedom 2010	4
123	LB	Dreyfus Appreciation	5
224	CA	Gateway Fund	5
477	LB	Vanguard LifeSt Growth	5
254	LG	Jensen J	5
502	LB	Vanguard Tx-Mgd Gr	5
476	CA	Vanguard LifeSt Cons Gr	5
359	LG	Smith Barney Aggr Grth A	5
		Index Funds	
507	LB	Vanguard Tot Stk	2
445	LB	Vanguard 500 Index	2
193	LB	Fidelity Spar Tot Mkt Ix	3
188	LB	Fidelity Spar 500 Idx	4
348	LB	Schwab 1000 Inv	5
94	LB	Bridgeway Blue-Chip 35	5
488	SR	Vanguard REIT Index	7
122	LB	Domini Social Equity	8
459	MB	Vanguard ExtMktIdx	8
448	LG	Vanguard Calv Soc Idx	8
420	LB	TIAA-CREF Equity Index	17
95	SB	Bridgeway Ul-Sm Co Mkt	19
504	SB	Vanguard Tax-Mgd SmCap R	21
447	MA	Vanguard Bal Idx	27
496	SB	Vanguard SmCp Idx	39
464	LG	Vanguard Gr Idx	44
510	LV	Vanguard Val Idx	48
485	MB	Vanguard Mid Cap Idx	73
495	SG	Vanguard SmCp Gr Idx	108
497	SV	Vanguard SmCp Vl Idx	109
		Average Turnover Rate %	**57.23**

International Equity

Page	Cat		Turnover Rate %
		Actively Managed Funds	
201	IH	First Eagle Glbl A	5
202	FA	First Eagle Overseas A	6
434	FA	Tweedy, Browne Glob Val	8
263	FV	Longleaf Partners Intl	10
120	FV	Dodge & Cox Intl Stock	11
412	FA	Third Avenue Intl Value	11
435	FB	UMB Scout WorldWide	12
279	PJ	Matthews Pacific Tiger	15
314	EM	Oppenheimer Develop MktA	15
460	WS	Vanguard Global Equity	19
67	WS	Amer Funds New Persp A	19
68	EM	Amer Funds New World A	20
229	FV	Harbor Intl Instl	21
473	FR	Vanguard Intl Explorer	21
102	FV	Causeway Intl Value Inv	21
40	SP	AmCent Global Gold Inv	22
315	WS	Oppenheimer Glob A	22
58	IH	Amer Funds CplncBldr A	24
61	FB	Amer Funds EuroPac A	25
408	FV	Templeton Foreign A	25
		Index Funds	
506	FB	Vanguard Total Intl Stk	3
452	FB	Vanguard Dev Mkts Idx	4
457	ES	Vanguard Eur Stk Idx	5
503	FB	Vanguard Tax-Mgd Intl	9
454	EM	Vanguard Em Mkt Idx	11
190	FB	Fidelity Spar Intl Index	31
		Average Turnover Rate %	**54.99**

Lowest Turnover Rate

Morningstar Funds 500 Universe

Taxable Bond

Page	Cat		Turnover Rate %
		Actively Managed Funds	
480	CL	Vanguard Long-Tm InvGrde	11
461	GI	Vanguard GNMA	26
436	CI	USAA Income	28
361	UB	SSgA Yield Plus	32
404	CI	TCW Galileo Tot Ret Bd I	33
492	CS	Vanguard Sht-Tm Inv-Grade	33
335	HY	Pioneer High Yield A	38
56	HY	Amer Funds Amer H/I A	39
379	IB	T. Rowe Price Intl Bd	39
304	HY	Northeast Investors	40
119	CI	Dodge & Cox Income	41
255	MU	Hancock Strategic Inc A	42
265	MU	Loomis Sayles Bond Ret	42
423	HY	TIAA-CREF High-Yield Bd	42
110	UB	Constel CIP Ultr Sh F/I I	44
400	GL	T. Rowe Price US Try L/T	52
466	HY	Vanguard Hi-Yld Corp	52
197	UB	Fidelity Ultra-Short Bd	53
471	CI	Vanguard IntTm Inv-Gr Fd	55
154	BL	Fidelity Float Rt Hi Inc	61
		Index Funds	
505	CI	Vanguard Total Bd Idx	66
470	CI	Vanguard Intm Bd Idx	98
490	CS	Vanguard Sh-Tm Bd Idx	111
		Average Turnover Rate %	**143.92**

Municipal Bond*

Page	Cat		Turnover Rate %
		Actively Managed Funds	
210	ML	Franklin Fed T/F Inc A	7
70	MI	Amer Funds T/E Bd A	8
483	MS	Vanguard LtdTm T/E	8
212	HM	Franklin Hi Yld T/F A	9
214	ML	Franklin Ins T/F Inc A	9
472	MI	Vanguard IntTm T/E	10
493	MS	Vanguard Sht-Tm TE	10
481	ML	Vanguard Lg-Tm T/E	11
469	ML	Vanguard Ins L/T TE Inv	18
418	MS	Thornburg Ltd-Tm A	21
352	MI	Scudder Interm T/A F AARP	21
440	MS	USAA Tax Ex Short-Term	22
191	ML	Fidelity Spar Muni Inc	23
439	ML	USAA Tax Ex Long-Term	23
438	MI	USAA Tax Ex Interm-Term	23
467	ML	Vanguard Hi-Yld T/E	24
397	HM	T. Rowe Price T/F Hi-Yld	27
398	ML	T. Rowe Price T/F Inc	27
101	MS	Calvert Tax-Fr Res Lim A	31
189	MI	Fidelity Spar IntermMuni	31
		Index Funds	
		None	
		Average Turnover Rate %	**29.54**

* There are only 23 municipal-bond funds in the Morningstar Funds 500 universe, none of which are index funds.

Manager Changes

Morningstar Funds 500 Universe

	Departing Manager/Team	Current Manager/Team	Date of Change
AmCent Ginnie Mae Inv	C. Casey Colton	Robert V. Gahagan	09/08/2004
AmCent Intl Growth Inv	Mark S. Kopinski	Creveling/Perelstein/Strabo	01/01/2004
AmCent Vista Inv	David Rose	Fogle/Hollond	03/22/2004
Columbia Acorn A	John H. Park	McQuaid/Mohn	04/30/2004
Columbia Acorn Select Z	John H. Park	Ben Andrews	04/30/2004
Fidelity Ginnie Mae	Thomas Silvia	William Irving	11/01/2004
Fidelity Inflation-Protec	Thomas Silvia	William Irving	11/01/2004
Fidelity Intl Disc	Penelope A. Dobkin	William J. Kennedy	10/04/2004
Fidelity Intl Sm Cp	L Kvaal	Paton/Sano	01/07/2004
Fidelity Invt Grade Bond	Kevin Grant	Jeffrey Moore	12/01/2004
Fidelity Pacific Basin	William J. Kennedy	Dale Nicholls	10/04/2004
Fidelity Sel Electronics	Samuel M. Peters	James Morrow	02/01/2004
Fidelity Sel Health Care	Steve Calhoun	Samuel M. Peters	02/01/2004
Fidelity Struc Mid Cap VI	Robert L. MacDonald	Ciaran O'Neill	02/01/2004
Fidelity Total Bond	Kevin Grant	Ford O'Neil	12/01/2004
Franklin SmMid Cap Gr A	Aidan O'Connell	Jamieson/McCarthy	04/15/2004
Gabelli Glob Telecomm	Marc J. Gabelli	Mario J. Gabelli	05/01/2004
Janus Growth & Income	David J. Corkins	Minyoung Sohn	01/01/2004
Janus Worldwide	Laurence J. Chang	Jason Yee	07/01/2004
Jensen J	Val E. Jensen	Hibler PhD/Millen/Zagunis/Schoenstein	01/31/2004
Legg Mason Spec Invt Pr	Lisa O. Rapuano	William H. Miller III	01/14/2004
MFS Mass Inv Trust A	Brooks Taylor	Beatty/Laupheimer Jr.	02/17/2004
MFS Total Return A	Lisa B. Nurme	Calabro/Adams/Baldini/Douglas et al	05/31/2004
Mairs & Power Growth	George A. Mairs III	William B. Frels	06/30/2004
Marsico Focus	James A. Hillary	Thomas F. Marsico	04/30/2004

Manager Changes

Morningstar Funds 500 Universe

	Departing Manager/Team	Current Manager/Team	Date of Change
Marsico Growth	James A. Hillary	Thomas F. Marsico	04/30/2004
Meridian Value	Kevin C. O'Boyle	Richard F. Aster Jr.	01/01/2004
Morgan Stan Ins US R/E A	Douglas A. Funke	Theodore R. Bigman	06/30/2004
Mutual Discovery A	Timothy Rankin	David J. Winters	10/08/2004
Mutual European A	Matthew T. Haynes	David J. Winters	11/30/2004
Mutual Shares A	Timothy Rankin	Winters/Turner	10/08/2004
Northern Technology	John B. Leo	Gilbert/Koch	07/31/2004
Oppenheimer Develop MktA	Rajeev Bhaman	Mark H. Madden	12/01/2004
Putnam Investors A	Paul Warren	Wiess/Brooks/Cervone/Yu	01/10/2004
Schwab 1000 Inv	Geraldine Hom	Jeffrey Mortimer	07/19/2004
Sentinel Small Company A	Scott T. Brayman	Charles Schwartz	09/17/2004
State St Res Aurora A	Caroline Evascu	Paul Haagensen	05/21/2004
T. Rowe Price Intl Disc	John R. Ford	Thomson/Dydasco/Edwards/Gunn	02/29/2004
T. Rowe Price New Asia	John R. Ford	Edwards/Dydasco	02/29/2004
TCW Galileo Select Eq I	Leigh Crawford	Blum/Burlingame	01/02/2004
Templeton Devel Mkts A	H. Allan Lam	Lim/Mobius/Wu	05/01/2004
Vanguard Capital Value	Charles T. Freeman	David Fassnacht	06/30/2004
Vanguard Windsor	Charles T. Freeman	Fassnacht/Fedak/Phillips Jr.	06/30/2004

Fund Name Changes

Morningstar Funds 500 Universe

Previous Name	Current Name	Date of Change
INVESCO Energy Inv	AIM Energy Inv	10/2004
PBHG Clipper Focus PBHG	Clipper Focus PBHG	07/2004
Turner Ultra Short Dur Fix Inc I	Constellation CIP Ultra Sh Dur Fix Inc I	05/2004
Turner Small Cap Value	Constellation Clover Small Cap Value	05/2004
Thompson Plumb Balanced Fund	Dreyfus Premier Balanced Opportunity J	02/2004
FBR Small Cap Value A	FBR Small Cap	03/2004
Fidelity International Growth & Inc	Fidelity International Discovery	10/2004
Janus Special Equity	Janus Contrarian Fund	09/2004
Oppenheimer Quest Balanced Value A	Oppenheimer Quest Balanced A	02/2004
PIMCO Foreign Bond D	PIMCO Foreign Bond (US Dollar-Hedged) D	05/2004
TCW Galileo Small Cap Value I	TCW Galileo Value Added I	02/2004
Thornburg Limited-Term Muni Natl A	Thornburg Limited-Term Muni A	06/2004
Vanguard Interm-Term Corp Bd	Vanguard Interm-Term Investment-Grade	08/2004
Vanguard Long-Term Corporate Bond	Vanguard Long-Term Investment-Grade Fund	08/2004
Vanguard Short-Term Corp	Vanguard Short-Term Investment-Grade	08/2004

Summary Pages

This section offers the essential risk and return data for all 500 funds in a table format, allowing you to make quick comparisons across funds.

Domestic-Equity Funds

Page		Cat	Style Box	NAV	Total Return % through 12-31-04 1Yr	Annualized 3Yr	5Yr	10Yr	Yield %	Morningstar Rating Statistics through 12-31-04 Performance	Risk	Morningstar Rating	Expense Ratio %	Sales Charge %
	S&P 500				**10.87**	**3.58**	**-2.30**	**12.07**						
31	ABN AMRO/Montag Gr N	LG		22.65	4.10	–2.00	–5.45	11.47	0.1	+Avg	-Avg	★★★★	1.06	12b-1
32	Aegis Value	SV		18.15	13.48	16.01	20.63	—	0.0	+Avg	Low	★★★★★	1.50	None
33	AIM Constellation A	LG		22.84	6.18	1.10	–6.68	8.01	0.0	Avg	+Avg	★★★	1.29	5.50
34	AIM Energy Inv	SN		27.83	36.62	17.01	16.09	15.64	0.0	+Avg	+Avg	★★★★	1.76	Clsd
35	American AAdv SmCpVl Pln	SV		19.91	23.19	20.16	21.31	—	0.3	High	+Avg	★★★★	1.16	None
36	AmCent Capital Val Inv	LV		7.09	14.25	8.12	8.18	—	1.0	+Avg	Avg	★★★★	1.10	None
37	AmCent Equity Growth Inv	LB		22.08	13.98	5.76	–1.28	12.50	1.1	+Avg	Avg	★★★★	0.69	None
38	AmCent Equity Income Inv	LV		8.11	12.53	9.93	12.51	15.34	2.3	High	Low	★★★★★	1.00	None
42	AmCent Growth Inv	LG		19.71	9.91	0.34	–6.87	8.73	0.0	Avg	Avg	★★★	1.00	None
43	AmCent Inc & Growth Inv	LV		30.67	12.98	5.70	–0.65	12.78	1.9	Avg	+Avg	★★★	0.69	None
46	AmCent Large Co Val Inv	LV		6.49	14.28	8.44	8.49	—	1.5	+Avg	Avg	★★★★	0.90	Clsd
47	AmCent Select Inv	LG		38.08	7.35	1.12	–5.03	9.50	0.2	+Avg	-Avg	★★★★	1.00	None
48	AmCent Small Cap Val Inv	SV		10.17	21.81	13.68	21.73	—	0.3	+Avg	Avg	★★★★	1.26	Clsd
50	AmCent Ultra Inv	LG		29.50	10.69	2.29	–6.05	10.40	0.0	+Avg	Avg	★★★	1.00	None
51	AmCent Value Inv	LV		7.39	14.36	8.82	11.46	14.05	1.0	+Avg	Avg	★★★★	1.00	None
52	AmCent Veedot Inv	MG		5.54	7.16	5.94	–1.32	—	0.0	Avg	-Avg	★★★	1.50	None
53	AmCent Vista Inv	MG		14.52	15.79	9.37	–1.27	9.72	0.0	Avg	Avg	★★★	1.00	None
54	Amer Funds Amcap A	LG		18.33	9.81	5.01	3.41	13.64	0.3	High	Low	★★★★★	0.73	5.75
55	Amer Funds Amer Bal A	MA		18.00	8.92	**7.84**	**9.47**	**12.15**	2.0	+Avg	Avg	★★★★	0.67	5.75
57	Amer Funds Amer Mut A	LV		26.48	10.74	6.25	6.90	11.94	1.7	Avg	Low	★★★★	0.62	5.75
62	Amer Funds Fundamen A	LV		32.25	13.91	7.50	3.22	13.27	1.7	Avg	Avg	★★★	0.66	5.75
63	Amer Funds Grth Fund A	LG		27.38	11.95	5.08	1.81	14.78	0.3	High	Avg	★★★★★	0.70	5.75
64	Amer Funds Inc Fund A	MA		18.56	12.92	10.59	9.42	12.10	3.5	High	-Avg	★★★★★	0.57	5.75
65	Amer Funds Inv Co Am A	LV		30.75	9.78	5.85	3.28	13.04	1.7	Avg	Low	★★★	0.59	5.75
66	Amer Funds New Econ A	LG		21.03	12.45	4.89	–4.38	10.52	0.4	+Avg	+Avg	★★★	0.89	5.75
69	Amer Funds Sm World A	SG		31.20	17.76	11.25	–0.79	9.87	1.0	Avg	-Avg	★★★	1.12	5.75
71	Amer Funds WashingtonA	LV		30.78	9.92	5.60	5.45	13.54	1.9	Avg	-Avg	★★★★	0.64	5.75
72	Ameristock	LV		40.54	5.52	2.44	5.61	—	2.6	Avg	Avg	★★★	0.77	None
73	Ariel	SV		53.17	21.97	13.98	16.84	16.24	0.0	Avg	-Avg	★★★★	1.07	12b-1
74	Ariel Appreciation	MB		47.67	13.10	9.91	12.90	16.15	0.1	+Avg	Avg	★★★★	1.15	12b-1
77	Artisan Mid Cap Inv	MG		29.56	14.66	4.65	7.16	—	0.0	+Avg	Avg	★★★★	1.19	Clsd
78	Artisan Mid Cap Value	MV		16.96	**26.20**	**18.41**	—	—	0.0	High	Avg	★★★★★	1.39	None
79	Artisan Small Cap	SG		16.76	22.10	7.72	6.70	—	0.0	+Avg	Avg	★★★★	1.27	None
80	Artisan Small Cap Value	SV		17.61	21.15	17.62	17.73	—	0.0	+Avg	-Avg	★★★★	1.18	Clsd
81	Atlantic Whitehall Growth	LG		14.54	–0.46	–1.47	–4.01	—	0.0	+Avg	+Avg	★★★	1.39	None
83	Baron Asset	MG		52.52	**27.13**	9.01	3.16	12.08	0.0	+Avg	-Avg	★★★★	1.34	12b-1
84	Baron Growth	SG		44.87	26.61	13.52	9.48	19.25	0.0	High	Low	★★★★★	1.33	Clsd
85	Baron Small Cap	SG		22.08	22.16	15.28	5.85	—	0.0	+Avg	Low	★★★★	1.33	12b-1
88	Bjurman, Barry MicroCp Gr	SG		30.75	3.42	12.48	19.89	—	0.0	High	+Avg	★★★★★	1.46	Clsd
89	BNY Hamilton SmCap Gr Is	SG		15.54	5.59	4.24	–0.28	—	0.0	Avg	Avg	★★★	1.06	None
90	Bogle Small Cap Gr Inv	SB		26.33	10.78	13.16	14.06	—	0.0	Avg	+Avg	★★★	1.35	Clsd
91	Boston Part SmCp II Inv	SV		23.31	16.47	14.40	26.10	—	0.0	+Avg	+Avg	★★★★	1.80	Clsd
92	Brandywine	MG		27.18	13.11	5.19	–0.19	11.12	0.0	Avg	-Avg	★★★★	1.08	None
93	Bridgeway Balanced	CA		11.57	7.61	6.95	—	—	0.7	+Avg	+Avg	★★★★	0.94	None
94	Bridgeway Blue-Chip 35	LB		7.18	4.79	3.45	–3.10	—	1.7	Avg	Avg	★★★	0.15	None
95	Bridgeway Ul-Sm Co Mkt	SB		17.77	19.13	**30.89**	**22.85**	—	0.2	High	Avg	★★★★★	0.67	Clsd
96	Brown Cap Small Co Instl	SG		29.80	0.24	–5.37	2.06	13.11	0.0	Avg	Avg	★★★	1.18	Clsd
97	Buffalo Small Cap	SG		27.65	28.82	13.10	20.47	—	0.1	High	Avg	★★★★★	1.01	Clsd
98	Calamos Convertible A	CV		21.20	7.54	8.66	5.67	13.73	2.5	+Avg	Avg	★★★★	1.15	Clsd
99	Calamos Gr & Inc A	CV		29.82	9.67	10.29	**6.95**	**16.94**	1.5	High	+Avg	★★★★★	1.14	4.75
100	Calamos Growth A	MG		52.98	18.65	12.41	10.67	**23.42**	0.0	High	Avg	★★★★★	1.31	4.75
103	Clipper	LV		89.68	5.87	6.08	12.58	16.93	0.6	High	Avg	★★★★★	1.13	None
104	Clipper Focus PBHG	LV		17.33	6.82	6.26	14.13	—	0.3	+Avg	High	★★★★	1.48	None
105	Columbia Acorn A	SG		25.93	21.05	14.76	—	—	0.0	High	Low	★★★★★	1.33	5.75
107	Columbia Acorn Select Z	MG		21.13	18.58	**12.60**	11.48	—	0.0	High	Low	★★★★★	1.12	Clsd
108	Columbia Acorn USA A	SG		24.77	20.12	12.49	—	—	0.0	+Avg	Avg	★★★★	1.65	5.75
109	Columbia Real Est Eq Z	SR		26.78	31.08	22.34	19.98	**15.67**	3.6	Avg	Low	★★★	0.97	None
111	Constel Clover Sm Cap Val	SV		26.96	20.14	11.43	14.28	—	0.0	Avg	+Avg	★★	1.27	None
112	Davis Appr & Income A	CV		27.50	**13.08**	**12.35**	5.36	11.76	2.4	Avg	Avg	★★★★	1.10	4.75
113	Davis Financial A	SF		41.00	12.11	7.53	8.34	**17.07**	0.0	Avg	+Avg	★★★	1.10	4.75

Bold numbers indicate *highest* return for the listed time period in each category.

Domestic-Equity Funds

Page		Cat	Style Box	NAV	Total Return % through 12-31-04 1Yr	Annualized 3Yr	5Yr	10Yr	Yield %	Morningstar Rating Statistics through 12-31-04 Performance	Risk	Morningstar Rating	Expense Ratio %	Sales Charge %
	S&P 500				**10.87**	**3.58**	**-2.30**	**12.07**						
114	Davis NY Venture A	LB		30.69	12.37	7.20	3.71	14.43	0.8	+Avg	Avg	★★★★	0.92	4.75
115	Delafield	SV		25.21	20.85	16.15	18.75	15.88	0.0	Avg	Avg	★★★	1.32	12b-1
116	Delphi Value Retail	MV		17.22	12.52	10.47	10.01	—	0.0	Avg	Avg	★★★	1.64	12b-1
117	Dimensional US Micro Cp	SB	—	15.12	18.39	18.17	14.32	16.39	1.8	+Avg	High	★★★	0.56	None
118	Dodge & Cox Balanced	MA		79.35	13.30	11.02	11.64	13.95	2.0	High	Avg	★★★★★	0.54	Clsd
121	Dodge & Cox Stock	LV		130.22	19.17	**12.16**	12.40	16.89	1.1	High	Avg	★★★★★	0.54	Clsd
122	Domini Social Equity	LB		29.54	9.26	3.28	−3.98	11.55	1.0	Avg	+Avg	★★★	0.95	12b-1
123	Dreyfus Appreciation	LB		38.69	5.57	1.74	−0.88	11.80	1.3	+Avg	-Avg	★★★★	0.96	None
124	Dreyfus Emerging Leaders	SB		44.23	14.23	8.35	4.64	—	0.0	Low	Avg	★	1.31	Clsd
125	Dreyfus Midcap Value	MB		32.45	17.53	7.27	13.00	—	0.0	Avg	High	★★★	1.18	Clsd
126	Dreyfus Prem Bal Opp J	MA		19.59	7.01	5.75	7.68	12.80	1.1	High	+Avg	★★★★	1.07	Clsd
130	Eaton Vance Utilities A	SU		9.79	25.11	**11.29**	**3.54**	12.64	2.4	High	Avg	★★★★★	1.15	5.75
131	Eaton Vance Wld Health A	SH		10.66	6.81	1.05	11.84	18.89	0.0	+Avg	Avg	★★★★	1.80	5.75
132	Excelsior Val & Restruct	LV		42.43	**19.36**	10.59	6.63	**17.47**	0.8	High	High	★★★★	0.99	None
133	FAM Value	MB		46.65	16.86	11.41	13.66	13.50	0.2	+Avg	Low	★★★★	1.24	None
134	FBR Small Cap	SG		41.81	**30.67**	**25.04**	18.78	—	0.0	High	Low	★★★★★	1.60	Clsd
135	Fidelity	LB		29.88	7.84	2.19	−3.35	11.18	1.3	Avg	+Avg	★★★	0.59	None
136	Fidelity Adv Eq Gr T	LG		45.71	2.67	−2.08	−7.43	9.92	0.0	Avg	Avg	★★★	1.32	3.50
137	Fidelity Adv Small Cap T	SG		24.63	23.52	11.02	1.63	—	0.0	Avg	-Avg	★★★	1.59	3.50
138	Fidelity Asset Mgr	MA		16.21	5.40	4.33	2.24	9.14	2.4	Avg	Avg	★★★	0.73	None
139	Fidelity Asset Mgr: Aggr	LG		11.31	11.05	2.40	0.88	—	0.5	High	+Avg	★★★★★	0.91	None
140	Fidelity Asset Mgr: Grth	MA		14.82	6.05	3.58	−0.11	9.09	2.2	Avg	High	★★	0.82	None
141	Fidelity Balanced	MA		17.82	10.94	9.19	6.99	11.02	1.4	+Avg	Avg	★★★★	0.66	None
142	Fidelity Blue Chip Grth	LG		41.71	6.26	−0.32	−5.86	8.82	0.9	Avg	-Avg	★★★	0.67	None
143	Fidelity Capital Apprec	LG		26.03	11.26	9.94	0.12	11.49	0.0	High	+Avg	★★★★	0.88	None
144	Fidelity Contrafund	LG		56.74	15.07	9.99	1.62	13.81	0.1	High	Low	★★★★★	0.98	None
145	Fidelity Convertible Sec	CV	—	21.60	10.21	6.79	5.58	13.20	2.6	+Avg	+Avg	★★★★	0.82	None
146	Fidelity Destiny I	LG		12.83	6.86	1.22	−7.27	6.75	1.3	-Avg	-Avg	★★★	0.47	8.24
147	Fidelity Destiny II	LB		11.92	10.60	4.01	−2.53	11.37	1.4	-Avg	Avg	★★★	0.55	8.24
148	Fidelity Discovery Fund	LB		11.30	10.62	3.69	−1.57	—	1.2	Avg	Avg	★★★	0.84	None
150	Fidelity Dividend Growth	LB		28.49	5.84	1.27	2.33	14.28	1.4	+Avg	+Avg	★★★★	0.89	None
151	Fidelity Equity-Inc	LV		52.78	11.29	6.21	4.31	11.94	1.5	Avg	Avg	★★★	0.70	None
152	Fidelity Equity-Inc II	LV		24.01	9.88	7.21	4.21	11.65	1.5	Avg	Avg	★★★	0.64	None
153	Fidelity Exp & Multinatl	LB		19.64	13.59	7.00	4.60	17.29	0.5	High	High	★★★★★	0.83	None
155	Fidelity Four-in-One Idx	LB		25.17	12.34	6.58	0.12	—	1.7	-Avg	-Avg	★★★★	0.08	None
156	Fidelity Freedom 2010	CA		13.62	7.24	5.37	2.41	—	2.1	Avg	+Avg	★★★	0.08	None
157	Fidelity Freedom 2020	MA		13.96	9.55	5.69	0.81	—	1.9	Avg	+Avg	★★★	0.08	None
160	Fidelity Growth & Income	LB		38.21	9.84	2.31	−0.99	11.05	1.4	Avg	Low	★★★★	0.69	None
161	Fidelity Growth Company	LG		56.07	12.12	1.80	−5.89	12.57	0.1	+Avg	High	★★★	0.83	None
163	Fidelity Independence	LG		17.83	11.65	5.14	−2.96	10.62	0.6	+Avg	+Avg	★★★	0.55	None
170	Fidelity Leverage Co Stk	MB		22.68	24.46	**33.89**	—	—	0.2	High	High	★★★★★	0.85	None
171	Fidelity Low-Priced Stk	SB		40.25	22.18	17.31	19.44	**17.83**	0.3	High	Low	★★★★★	0.97	Clsd
172	Fidelity Magellan	LB		103.79	7.49	0.80	−3.87	10.16	1.2	-Avg	Avg	★★	0.70	Clsd
173	Fidelity Mid-Cap Stock	MG		23.45	9.05	1.71	3.92	14.65	0.3	+Avg	Avg	★★★★	0.65	None
175	Fidelity New Millennium	MG		31.69	4.28	4.69	−2.47	18.57	0.0	+Avg	+Avg	★★★★	0.76	Clsd
176	Fidelity OTC	LG		34.69	8.12	4.05	−8.94	11.04	1.2	+Avg	High	★★	0.89	None
179	Fidelity Puritan	MA		18.95	9.28	7.14	5.57	10.41	2.3	+Avg	-Avg	★★★★	0.64	None
180	Fidelity Real Estate Inv	SR		29.54	34.15	23.82	22.25	14.98	2.2	Avg	Avg	★★★	0.83	None
181	Fidelity Sel Electronics	ST		37.78	−9.81	−8.47	−11.62	**16.45**	0.0	+Avg	+Avg	★★★	1.06	None
182	Fidelity Sel Health Care	SH		128.09	8.66	1.06	3.69	13.77	0.1	Avg	-Avg	★★★★	0.99	None
183	Fidelity Sel Technology	ST		60.19	0.43	−0.14	−14.37	13.07	0.3	+Avg	Avg	★★★★	1.14	None
185	Fidelity Small Cap Indep	SG		19.72	15.02	7.09	6.66	10.33	0.0	Avg	Low	★★★★	0.93	None
186	Fidelity SmCp Retirement	SG		15.88	14.99	6.88	—	—	0.0	Avg	Low	★★★★	0.99	None
187	Fidelity Small Cap Stock	SB		18.16	14.57	11.88	10.76	—	0.0	Avg	Avg	★★★	1.08	None
188	Fidelity Spar 500 Idx	LB		83.36	10.73	3.46	−2.42	11.85	1.7	+Avg	Avg	★★★★	0.19	None
193	Fidelity Spar Tot Mkt Ix	LB		33.05	12.11	5.15	−1.58	—	1.4	Avg	+Avg	★★★	0.25	None
195	Fidelity Struc Mid Cap VI	MV		14.35	21.87	12.05	—	—	0.3	Avg	Avg	★★★★	1.05	None
198	Fidelity Value	MV		71.29	21.21	13.93	12.40	13.38	0.2	Avg	Avg	★★★	0.98	None
200	First Eagle Fund of Am Y	MB		26.06	15.91	9.53	7.37	16.02	0.0	Avg	Low	★★★★	1.46	12b-1
203	FMI Focus	SB		34.75	7.05	7.23	9.30	—	0.0	-Avg	High	★★	1.43	None

Bold numbers indicate *highest* return for the listed time period in each category.

Domestic-Equity Funds

Page		Cat	Style Box	NAV	Total Return % through 12-31-04 1Yr	Annualized 3Yr	5Yr	10Yr	Yield %	Morningstar Rating Statistics through 12-31-04 Performance	Risk	Morningstar Rating	Expense Ratio %	Sales Charge %
	S&P 500				**10.87**	**3.58**	**-2.30**	**12.07**						
204	Forward Hoover Sm-Cp Eq	SG		18.45	22.77	10.96	10.92	—	0.0	+Avg	-Avg	★★★★★	1.83	12b-1
205	FPA Capital	SV		39.98	12.62	14.47	14.96	**17.76**	0.0	Avg	High	★★	0.83	Clsd
206	FPA Crescent	MA		23.55	10.21	12.97	**15.25**	**13.98**	0.3	High	+Avg	★★★★★	1.41	None
208	FPA Paramount	SB		13.93	15.89	12.82	9.24	5.52	0.0	-Avg	Avg	★★	0.99	5.25
209	Franklin Bal Sh Invmt A	SV		58.26	25.30	15.15	16.71	15.09	0.7	Avg	Low	★★★	0.91	Clsd
211	Franklin Growth A	LB		33.80	11.30	2.53	0.97	10.33	0.2	Avg	Avg	★★★	0.98	5.75
213	Franklin Income A	CA		2.52	**12.17**	**13.28**	**12.02**	10.71	6.2	High	High	★★★★★	0.68	4.25
215	Franklin SmMid Cap Gr A	MG		34.16	13.04	3.10	–4.71	12.47	0.0	Avg	+Avg	★★	0.98	5.75
217	Fremont U.S. Micro-Cap	SG		32.64	9.79	4.88	1.66	**20.17**	0.0	+Avg	+Avg	★★★★	1.64	Clsd
218	Gabelli Asset	MB		41.45	16.49	9.25	4.98	14.02	0.1	Avg	-Avg	★★★★	1.38	12b-1
219	Gabelli Glob Telecomm	SC		17.23	23.37	7.43	–5.69	11.71	0.5	Avg	-Avg	★★★	1.62	12b-1
220	Gabelli Growth	LG		26.12	4.69	–3.07	–9.17	10.25	0.0	Avg	+Avg	★★★	1.47	12b-1
221	Gabelli Sm Cp Growth AAA	SV		28.62	21.68	16.58	13.04	14.96	0.0	Avg	-Avg	★★★	1.42	12b-1
222	Gabelli Value A	MB		19.49	12.78	7.72	3.95	14.56	0.0	Avg	Avg	★★★	1.44	5.50
223	Gabelli Westwood Bal AAA	MA		11.95	8.84	5.01	4.54	11.03	1.8	+Avg	-Avg	★★★★	1.22	12b-1
224	Gateway Fund	CA		24.31	6.95	4.33	3.16	7.40	1.2	Avg	+Avg	★★★	0.97	12b-1
225	George Putnam of BostonA	MA		18.06	8.32	5.21	5.05	10.00	1.7	Avg	-Avg	★★★	1.00	5.25
226	Greenspring	MA		20.91	8.69	10.31	11.34	10.29	3.1	High	+Avg	★★★★	1.14	None
228	Harbor Capital App Instl	LG		28.67	9.34	–0.39	–7.57	11.32	0.4	+Avg	+Avg	★★★★	0.67	None
230	Harbor Large Cap Value	LV		16.33	14.77	5.18	5.36	12.28	0.9	Avg	+Avg	★★★	0.68	None
231	Henlopen	SG		30.47	16.78	15.10	4.58	17.14	0.0	High	+Avg	★★★★	1.38	None
232	ICAP Equity	LV		44.01	11.33	2.61	2.98	13.01	1.6	Avg	Avg	★★★	0.80	None
234	ICAP Select Equity	LV		34.35	17.98	7.79	6.18	—	1.6	+Avg	Avg	★★★★	0.80	None
235	ICM/Isabelle Sm Cap Invt	SV		16.30	18.12	11.28	10.07	—	0.0	Low	High	★	1.88	12b-1
236	Janus	LG		24.57	4.69	–0.04	–8.88	9.32	0.0	Avg	Avg	★★★	0.90	None
237	Janus Balanced	MA		21.25	8.71	4.93	1.43	12.01	1.9	+Avg	-Avg	★★★★	0.88	None
238	Janus Contrarian Fund	MB		13.24	22.61	12.76	—	—	0.2	+Avg	+Avg	★★★★	1.01	None
239	Janus Core Equity	LB		20.36	13.77	4.76	–1.27	—	0.4	Avg	-Avg	★★★★	0.96	None
240	Janus Enterprise	MG		37.62	20.69	5.54	–13.27	8.65	0.0	-Avg	+Avg	★★	1.03	None
241	Janus Global Life Sci	SH		17.99	14.95	0.79	2.26	—	0.0	-Avg	+Avg	★★	0.98	None
243	Janus Growth & Income	LG		32.19	11.89	3.06	–3.65	14.63	0.5	High	-Avg	★★★★★	0.91	None
245	Janus Mercury	LG		21.57	10.77	1.28	–10.84	11.86	0.1	Avg	+Avg	★★★	0.97	None
246	Janus Mid Cap Val Inv	MV		22.09	18.36	12.75	**17.08**	—	0.4	High	Avg	★★★★★	1.08	None
247	Janus Olympus	LG		28.63	8.74	0.92	–11.35	—	0.0	-Avg	+Avg	★★	1.03	None
248	Janus Orion	MG		6.94	14.90	5.09	—	—	0.0	Avg	Avg	★★★	1.08	None
250	Janus Sm Cap Val Instl	SV		29.98	13.80	9.74	15.14	17.42	1.1	+Avg	+Avg	★★★★	0.82	Clsd
251	Janus Twenty	LG		44.80	**23.89**	5.66	–10.81	13.81	0.0	+Avg	+Avg	★★★★	0.89	Clsd
252	Janus Venture	SG		58.59	17.56	10.03	–8.65	11.25	0.0	Avg	+Avg	★★	0.90	Clsd
254	Jensen J	LG		24.35	6.01	3.09	**5.64**	13.03	0.7	High	Low	★★★★★	0.88	12b-1
257	Kalmar Gr Val Sm Cp	SG		16.17	12.81	10.57	9.36	—	0.0	+Avg	-Avg	★★★★	1.26	None
258	Legg Mason Opp Prim	MB		15.67	13.80	17.32	10.11	—	0.0	+Avg	High	★★★	1.90	1.00
259	Legg Mason Spec Invt Pr	MB		46.48	13.05	16.78	7.46	16.51	0.0	+Avg	High	★★★	1.78	12b-1
260	Legg Mason Value Prim	LB		65.23	11.96	9.22	1.88	**18.58**	0.0	High	High	★★★★★	1.70	12b-1
261	LKCM Small Cap Equity Ins	SB		21.46	22.09	13.20	11.67	14.75	0.0	Avg	Low	★★★★	0.97	None
262	Longleaf Partners	LV		31.32	7.14	9.80	11.99	15.07	0.5	High	Avg	★★★★★	0.91	Clsd
264	Longleaf Partners Sm-Cap	SV		29.85	14.78	16.70	13.58	16.05	1.3	Avg	-Avg	★★★	0.95	Clsd
266	Lord Abbett Affiliated A	LV		14.78	12.60	6.17	4.89	12.89	1.3	Avg	Avg	★★★	0.84	5.75
267	MainStay MAP I	MB		34.20	16.69	9.08	9.20	16.41	0.3	+Avg	-Avg	★★★★	1.10	None
268	Mairs & Power Growth	LB		70.33	17.99	**11.05**	**13.02**	18.03	1.0	High	-Avg	★★★★★	0.75	None
269	Managers Special Equity	SG		90.41	15.19	8.59	2.78	13.93	0.0	+Avg	Avg	★★★★	1.43	None
270	Marsico 21st Century	LG		12.01	22.30	**17.68**	—	—	0.0	High	+Avg	★★★★★	1.50	12b-1
271	Marsico Focus	LG		16.61	11.70	6.89	–4.51	—	0.0	+Avg	Avg	★★★★	1.30	12b-1
272	Marsico Growth	LG		17.66	14.38	7.90	–3.38	—	0.0	+Avg	Avg	★★★★	1.30	12b-1
274	Masters' Select Equity	LB		15.26	13.54	6.62	4.03	—	0.0	High	+Avg	★★★★★	1.23	Clsd
276	Masters' Select Small Co	SG		13.84	21.01	—	—	—	0.0	— —	—	1.65	None	
277	Masters' Select Value	LV		14.90	14.70	9.24	—	—	0.0	+Avg	Avg	★★★★	1.28	None
278	Matrix Advisors Value	LB		54.41	3.90	5.99	7.63	—	0.8	High	High	★★★★	0.99	None
280	Merger Fund	CA		15.42	2.71	2.47	5.23	8.38	0.0	Avg	Avg	★★★	1.37	Clsd
281	Meridian Growth	MG		37.24	14.47	11.63	**15.40**	14.52	0.0	High	-Avg	★★★★★	0.88	None
282	Meridian Value	MB		38.09	15.10	10.34	15.53	**21.00**	0.7	+Avg	-Avg	★★★★★	1.09	None

Bold numbers indicate *highest* return for the listed time period in each category.

Page		Cat	Style Box	NAV	Total Return % through 12-31-04 1Yr	Annualized 3Yr	Annualized 5Yr	Annualized 10Yr	Yield %	Morningstar Rating Statistics through 12-31-04 Performance	Risk	Morningstar Rating	Expense Ratio %	Sales Charge %
	S&P 500				**10.87**	**3.58**	**-2.30**	**12.07**						
283	Merrill Basic Value I	LV		31.82	10.48	6.85	4.60	12.15	1.3	Avg	+Avg	★★★	0.56	5.25
287	MFS Mass Inv Grth Stk A	LG		12.36	9.63	−1.26	−7.65	11.79	0.4	Avg	Avg	★★★	0.95	5.75
288	MFS Mass Inv Trust A	LB		17.26	11.51	2.04	−2.38	10.42	0.9	Avg	-Avg	★★★	0.94	5.75
289	MFS Strategic Value A	LV		16.08	17.94	7.29	10.54	—	0.7	+Avg	High	★★★★	1.29	5.75
290	MFS Total Return A	MA		16.00	11.35	7.11	7.76	11.31	2.4	+Avg	-Avg	★★★★	0.89	4.75
291	MFS Utilities A	SU		10.99	**29.88**	10.14	1.41	**13.29**	1.2	+Avg	Avg	★★★★	1.19	4.75
292	Morgan Stan Ins US R/E A	SR		23.21	**37.28**	23.69	21.80	—	1.8	+Avg	Avg	★★★★	1.00	None
293	Muhlenkamp	MV		78.97	24.51	13.87	15.13	**18.28**	0.1	High	High	★★★★	1.18	None
294	Mutual Beacon A	MV		15.87	14.13	9.26	9.46	—	2.0	-Avg	Low	★★★	1.21	5.75
297	Mutual Financial Svcs A	SF		20.47	**15.17**	**14.12**	**17.00**	—	1.1	+Avg	-Avg	★★★★	1.48	5.75
298	Mutual Qualified A	MV		19.41	16.27	9.55	10.05	—	1.6	Avg	Low	★★★	1.20	5.75
299	Mutual Shares A	LV		22.94	13.44	8.32	8.84	—	1.3	+Avg	Low	★★★★	1.19	5.75
300	N/I Numeric Inv Sm CapVl	SV		19.30	23.80	**23.37**	**26.63**	—	0.4	High	Avg	★★★★★	—	Clsd
301	Needham Growth	SG		31.17	6.20	3.91	6.21	—	0.0	+Avg	Avg	★★★★	1.77	12b-1
302	Neuberger Ber Fasciano In	SG		42.86	12.55	10.07	7.21	12.51	0.0	+Avg	Low	★★★★	1.22	None
303	Neuberger Ber Genesis Inv	SB		29.84	18.76	14.92	17.66	17.15	0.0	High	Low	★★★★★	1.05	Clsd
305	Northern Technology	ST		11.82	3.05	−1.77	−17.49	—	0.0	Avg	Avg	★★★	1.25	None
306	Oak Value	LB		30.74	8.00	2.58	4.89	12.84	0.0	High	+Avg	★★★★★	1.25	None
307	Oakmark Equity & Inc I	MA		23.50	10.36	9.99	13.49	—	0.8	High	-Avg	★★★★★	0.92	None
309	Oakmark I	LV		41.77	11.73	6.22	9.64	11.79	0.4	+Avg	+Avg	★★★★	1.05	None
312	Oakmark Select I	LV		33.35	9.73	7.40	**14.46**	—	0.7	High	Avg	★★★★★	1.00	Clsd
313	Oppenheimer Cap Inc A	MA		12.46	10.28	7.26	7.55	11.48	3.9	+Avg	+Avg	★★★★	0.89	5.75
317	Oppenheimer Main St Sm A	SB		20.08	19.18	13.62	12.78	—	0.0	Avg	+Avg	★★★	1.17	5.75
318	Oppenheimer Main Street A	LB		35.46	9.39	3.82	−1.60	9.99	1.2	Avg	-Avg	★★★	0.93	5.75
319	Oppenheimer Quest Bal A	MA		18.04	10.29	4.86	5.13	13.77	0.1	+Avg	High	★★★★	1.38	5.75
321	Pax World Balanced	MA		23.22	13.39	6.62	3.09	11.74	0.9	+Avg	-Avg	★★★★★	0.99	12b-1
325	PBHG Mid Cap PBHG	MB		18.54	18.01	8.39	11.61	—	0.0	+Avg	Avg	★★★★	1.37	None
326	PIMCO CommRealRetStrA	SN	—	14.78	15.78	—	—	—	5.3	—	—	—	1.24	5.50
331	PIMCO RCM Glob Tech Instl	ST		36.31	**17.93**	**5.94**	**−9.17**	—	0.0	High	Avg	★★★★	1.36	None
334	Pioneer A	LB		42.06	11.63	3.51	−0.27	11.94	0.8	Avg	-Avg	★★★	1.09	5.75
336	Putnam Capital Opport A	SB		12.02	18.42	5.84	7.20	—	0.0	-Avg	High	★	1.19	5.25
337	Putnam Fund for Gr&Inc A	LV		19.40	10.97	4.51	2.90	10.76	1.2	-Avg	Avg	★★	0.90	5.25
338	Putnam Investors A	LB		12.59	12.76	3.11	−7.65	10.28	0.1	-Avg	+Avg	★★	1.05	5.75
339	Putnam Voyager A	LG		16.61	4.79	−1.35	−9.13	9.10	0.0	-Avg	Avg	★★★	1.04	5.25
340	Royce Opportunity Inv	SV		13.31	17.51	19.02	18.84	—	0.0	+Avg	High	★★★	1.15	Clsd
341	Royce Premier Inv	SB		15.12	22.82	16.27	15.08	14.75	0.0	+Avg	Low	★★★★	1.16	None
342	Royce Special Equity Inv	SV		19.61	13.91	18.80	20.59	—	0.9	+Avg	Low	★★★★★	1.19	Clsd
343	Royce Total Return Inv	SV		12.26	17.52	14.55	15.56	15.75	1.0	Avg	Low	★★★★	1.18	None
344	RS Diversified Growth	SG		22.69	1.48	−0.82	−6.19	—	0.0	-Avg	+Avg	★★	1.48	Clsd
345	RS Emerging Growth	SG		32.36	15.16	0.37	−11.24	13.20	0.0	Avg	High	★★	1.49	Clsd
346	RS MidCap Opport	MG		12.18	12.36	7.08	−0.21	—	0.0	Avg	Avg	★★★	1.53	12b-1
347	Salomon Bros Investors O	LV		20.52	10.83	4.69	4.85	13.79	1.6	Avg	High	★★★	0.67	Clsd
348	Schwab 1000 Inv	LB		34.59	10.82	3.99	−1.96	11.81	1.4	+Avg	Avg	★★★★	0.54	None
349	Scudder Flag Communic A	SC		16.80	21.21	−3.30	−16.04	8.87	0.0	Avg	Avg	★★★	1.34	5.75
350	Scudder Flag Val Bldr A	MA		24.28	8.74	4.87	3.44	12.48	1.7	Avg	High	★★★	1.15	5.75
353	Security Cap US Real Est	SR		17.82	36.81	22.52	21.74	—	2.8	Avg	+Avg	★★★★	1.18	12b-1
354	Selected American S	LB		36.87	11.97	6.73	3.38	15.14	0.7	High	-Avg	★★★★★	0.93	12b-1
355	Selected Special Shares S	MB		12.44	11.34	9.05	1.89	11.77	0.4	-Avg	+Avg	★★	1.21	12b-1
356	Sentinel Small Company A	SG		7.47	15.98	11.20	14.93	15.13	0.0	+Avg	Low	★★★★★	1.20	Clsd
357	Sequoia	LV		154.27	4.51	6.02	9.60	15.97	0.0	High	Avg	★★★★★	1.00	Clsd
358	Skyline Spec Equities	SV		28.64	16.61	15.01	16.57	13.29	0.0	Avg	Avg	★★★	1.48	None
359	Smith Barney Aggr Grth A	LG		95.17	10.61	0.53	2.83	**16.38**	0.0	High	+Avg	★★★★	1.19	5.00
360	Sound Shore	LV		36.70	15.34	8.72	8.90	14.21	0.3	+Avg	+Avg	★★★★	0.98	None
362	State St Res Aurora A	SB		40.48	14.95	11.35	16.98	—	0.0	Avg	+Avg	★★★	1.40	5.75
363	Strong Adv Common Stk Z	MB		22.65	9.96	7.18	3.64	13.47	0.0	Avg	Avg	★★★	1.40	Clsd
364	Strong Opportunity Inv	MB		46.40	17.62	5.70	4.07	13.31	0.0	Avg	Avg	★★★	1.40	None
366	T. Rowe Price Balanced	MA		19.70	10.32	7.08	3.78	10.11	2.3	+Avg	-Avg	★★★★	0.78	None
367	T. Rowe Price BlChpGr	LG		30.92	9.25	2.41	−2.17	12.03	0.5	+Avg	-Avg	★★★★	0.95	None
368	T. Rowe Price Cap Apprec	MA		19.49	**15.29**	**13.30**	14.40	13.95	1.5	High	-Avg	★★★★★	0.83	None
369	T. Rowe Price Div Growth	LB		22.92	11.90	4.52	3.90	11.33	1.1	+Avg	Low	★★★★	0.83	None

Bold numbers indicate *highest* return for the listed time period in each category.

Domestic-Equity Funds

Page		Cat	Style Box	NAV	Total Return % through 12-31-04 1Yr	Annualized 3Yr	5Yr	10Yr	Yield %	Morningstar Rating Statistics through 12-31-04 Performance	Risk	Morningstar Rating	Expense Ratio %	Sales Charge %
	S&P 500				**10.87**	**3.58**	**-2.30**	**12.07**						
371	T. Rowe Price Eq-Inc	LV		26.59	15.05	7.96	7.67	13.00	1.5	+Avg	Avg	★★★★	0.78	None
372	T. Rowe Price Fincl Svcs	SF		23.50	13.42	11.26	12.78	—	0.7	Avg	Avg	★★★	0.97	None
373	T. Rowe Price Glob Tech	ST		5.50	10.22	5.01	—	—	0.0	High	-Avg	★★★★★	1.50	None
375	T. Rowe Price Grth & Inc	LB		22.51	10.82	2.66	2.90	10.34	1.1	Avg	Avg	★★★	0.82	None
376	T. Rowe Price Gr Stk	LG		26.67	10.24	3.66	0.15	12.21	0.6	+Avg	Avg	★★★★★	0.76	None
377	T. Rowe Price Health Sci	SH		23.11	**15.84**	4.80	10.50	—	0.0	+Avg	+Avg	★★★	1.00	None
383	T. Rowe Price Med & Tele	SC		28.43	**26.30**	**12.16**	**–0.33**	**16.96**	0.0	High	Avg	★★★★★	1.10	None
384	T. Rowe Price Mid Gr	MG		49.88	18.39	8.83	6.52	15.73	0.0	High	-Avg	★★★★★	0.87	Clsd
385	T. Rowe Price Mid Val	MV		22.99	20.56	15.78	16.85	—	0.4	High	Avg	★★★★★	0.91	None
386	T. Rowe Price New Amer	LG		33.14	11.10	2.39	–3.28	8.96	0.0	+Avg	+Avg	★★★★	0.98	None
388	T. Rowe Price New Era	SN		33.68	30.09	17.52	13.32	13.01	0.7	Avg	-Avg	★★★★	0.72	None
389	T. Rowe Price New Horiz	SG		29.24	17.90	8.92	4.26	13.23	0.0	+Avg	Avg	★★★	0.91	None
390	T. Rowe Price Pers Inc	CA		14.84	9.95	8.00	6.27	9.81	2.4	+Avg	Avg	★★★★★	0.71	None
391	T. Rowe Price Real Est	SR		17.90	36.82	**24.81**	22.80	—	3.3	+Avg	Avg	★★★★	1.00	None
392	T. Rowe Price SciTech	ST		19.10	1.60	–2.99	–18.78	6.21	0.0	Avg	Avg	★★★	1.09	None
393	T. Rowe Price Sm Stk	SB		31.82	18.77	10.48	10.91	14.51	0.0	Avg	Avg	★★★★	0.96	Clsd
394	T. Rowe Price Sm Val	SV		35.68	**25.69**	18.99	19.73	16.21	0.4	+Avg	Low	★★★★	0.88	Clsd
395	T. Rowe Price Spect Grth	LB		16.87	15.16	7.45	2.70	11.21	0.7	+Avg	+Avg	★★★★	0.00	None
401	T. Rowe Price Value	LV		22.90	15.36	7.75	8.03	14.83	0.8	+Avg	+Avg	★★★★	0.97	None
402	TCW Galileo Opportunity N	SB		13.73	13.56	12.36	16.17	12.62	0.0	Avg	+Avg	★★★	1.50	None
403	TCW Galileo Select Eq I	LG		19.58	12.92	5.72	–2.20	12.69	0.0	High	High	★★★★	0.89	None
405	TCW Galileo Value Added I	SB		13.88	4.50	5.93	—	—	0.0	Low	High	★	1.61	None
406	TCW Galileo Val Opport I	MB		22.33	10.72	6.27	17.26	—	0.0	+Avg	High	★★★★	0.98	None
411	Fairholme	MB		22.77	**24.93**	15.09	**18.85**	—	0.3	High	Low	★★★★★	1.00	None
413	Third Avenue RealEst Val	SR		26.96	28.16	22.42	**23.21**	—	0.7	+Avg	Low	★★★★★	1.19	None
414	Third Avenue Sm-Cap Val	SB		22.57	21.27	14.55	15.21	—	0.4	+Avg	-Avg	★★★★	1.17	None
415	Third Avenue Value	SB		51.70	**26.60**	13.75	12.82	15.60	1.5	+Avg	Low	★★★★	1.11	None
416	Thompson Plumb Growth	LB		46.79	4.16	3.01	10.35	16.84	0.9	High	High	★★★★	1.07	None
419	Thornburg Value A	LB		30.88	7.20	2.84	0.77	—	1.0	Avg	-Avg	★★★	1.37	4.50
420	TIAA-CREF Equity Index	LB		8.59	11.68	4.62	—	—	1.6	+Avg	Avg	★★★★	0.26	None
421	TIAA-CREF Growth & Inc	LB		12.20	9.55	1.62	–3.37	—	1.4	-Avg	Avg	★★	0.43	None
422	TIAA-CREF Growth Eqty	LG		9.17	6.16	–1.69	–10.23	—	0.7	-Avg	+Avg	★★	0.45	None
425	TIAA-CREF Managed Alloc	MA		11.13	10.69	6.01	0.71	—	3.4	Avg	Avg	★★★	0.00	None
427	TIAA-CREF Soc Choice Eq	LB		9.19	12.46	5.01	—	—	1.3	+Avg	Avg	★★★★	0.27	None
429	Tocqueville Sm Cap Value	SV		17.92	0.78	11.98	12.39	16.13	0.0	Avg	High	★	1.36	12b-1
430	Torray	LB		41.08	6.90	5.18	2.27	14.86	0.5	+Avg	+Avg	★★★★	1.11	None
431	Turner Midcap Growth	MG		24.43	11.05	3.70	–5.98	—	0.0	-Avg	High	★★	—	None
432	Turner Small Cap Growth	SG		23.97	11.90	6.10	–3.66	15.30	0.0	+Avg	+Avg	★★★	1.25	Clsd
433	Tweedy, Browne American	MV		25.37	9.42	4.69	5.58	13.01	1.5	-Avg	-Avg	★★★	1.38	None
437	USAA Income Stock	LV		16.66	12.02	4.50	3.92	10.04	1.5	Avg	-Avg	★★★	0.79	None
441	Van Kampen Comstock A	LV		18.51	17.57	7.38	9.91	15.62	1.2	+Avg	+Avg	★★★★	0.90	5.75
442	Van Kampen Eq and Inc A	MA		8.62	11.77	7.77	8.03	13.66	2.1	+Avg	Avg	★★★★	0.83	5.75
444	Van Kampen Growth & IncA	LV		20.19	13.94	7.43	6.75	13.94	1.1	Avg	-Avg	★★★★	0.86	5.75
445	Vanguard 500 Index	LB		111.64	10.74	3.47	–2.38	12.00	1.8	+Avg	Avg	★★★★	0.18	None
446	Vanguard Asset Alloc	MA		24.56	11.09	5.92	3.38	12.01	2.0	High	+Avg	★★★★	0.38	None
447	Vanguard Bal Idx	MA		19.45	9.33	5.84	2.41	10.45	2.6	+Avg	Avg	★★★★	0.22	None
448	Vanguard Calv Soc Idx	LG		8.02	8.27	2.28	—	—	1.5	+Avg	+Avg	★★★★	0.25	None
449	Vanguard Cap Opp	MG		30.77	21.65	9.44	6.92	—	0.2	+Avg	Avg	★★★★	0.52	Clsd
450	Vanguard Capital Value	LV		11.75	15.38	5.56	—	—	1.1	Avg	High	★★★	0.53	None
451	Vanguard Convertible Sec	CV	—	13.29	7.20	8.54	5.25	10.26	2.8	+Avg	Avg	★★★	0.84	Clsd
453	Vanguard Dividend Growth	LV		12.15	11.02	3.29	1.07	8.21	1.8	-Avg	-Avg	★★	0.40	None
455	Vanguard Energy	SN		40.00	**36.65**	**22.03**	**19.29**	**16.18**	1.3	+Avg	-Avg	★★★★★	0.38	Clsd
456	Vanguard Equity-Inc	LV		23.50	13.57	6.23	5.86	12.66	2.4	+Avg	-Avg	★★★★	0.32	None
458	Vanguard Explorer	SG		74.57	13.75	7.36	6.33	12.32	0.0	Avg	-Avg	★★★★	0.72	None
459	Vanguard ExtMktIdx	MB		31.36	18.71	11.74	1.37	12.16	0.9	Avg	+Avg	★★	0.26	None
462	Vanguard Gr & Inc	LB		30.61	11.11	4.13	–1.80	12.46	1.4	+Avg	Avg	★★★★	0.42	None
463	Vanguard Growth Equity	LG		9.66	5.35	0.27	–10.86	9.28	0.1	Avg	+Avg	★★	0.61	None
464	Vanguard Gr Idx	LG		26.41	7.20	1.00	–6.94	11.52	1.1	+Avg	Avg	★★★★	0.23	None
465	Vanguard Health Care	SH		126.79	9.51	**7.11**	**12.93**	**20.15**	0.9	High	Low	★★★★★	0.28	None
476	Vanguard LifeSt Cons Gr	CA		15.26	8.02	6.22	4.31	9.48	2.8	+Avg	Avg	★★★★	0.00	None

Bold numbers indicate *highest* return for the listed time period in each category.

Domestic-Equity Funds

Page		Cat	Style Box	NAV	Total Return % through 12-31-04 1Yr	Annualized 3Yr	5Yr	10Yr	Yield %	Morningstar Rating Statistics through 12-31-04 Performance	Risk	Morningstar Rating	Expense Ratio %	Sales Charge %
	S&P 500				**10.87**	**3.58**	**-2.30**	**12.07**						
477	Vanguard LifeSt Growth	LB		20.04	12.58	6.79	0.97	10.55	2.0	+Avg	-Avg	★★★★	0.00	None
478	Vanguard LifeSt Income	CA		13.53	6.01	5.54	5.74	8.81	3.3	+Avg	-Avg	★★★★	0.00	None
479	Vanguard LifeSt Mod Grth	MA		17.91	10.57	6.67	2.82	10.22	2.5	+Avg	Avg	★★★★	0.00	None
484	Vanguard Mid Cap Growth	MG		16.05	11.38	4.36	–0.85	—	0.0	Avg	+Avg	★★★	0.34	None
485	Vanguard Mid Cap Idx	MB		15.64	20.35	11.30	10.15	—	1.0	+Avg	Avg	★★★★	0.26	None
486	Vanguard Morgan Gr	LG		16.32	10.47	4.16	–3.11	11.87	0.6	+Avg	Avg	★★★★	0.44	None
487	Vanguard Primecap	LB		62.30	**18.31**	7.13	2.16	15.78	0.7	High	High	★★★★	0.46	Clsd
488	Vanguard REIT Index	SR		18.79	30.76	22.55	21.18	—	4.7	Avg	+Avg	★★★	0.24	None
489	Vanguard Selected Value	MV		18.07	20.38	13.66	14.68	—	1.4	+Avg	Avg	★★★★	0.60	None
495	Vanguard SmCp Gr Idx	SG		15.16	16.06	11.94	7.17	—	0.1	+Avg	-Avg	★★★★	0.27	None
496	Vanguard SmCp Idx	SB		26.83	19.90	11.77	6.98	12.28	1.0	-Avg	+Avg	★★	0.27	None
497	Vanguard SmCp Vl Idx	SV		13.97	23.55	13.30	15.05	—	1.6	Avg	+Avg	★★★	0.27	None
498	Vanguard STAR	MA		18.74	11.60	7.27	6.60	11.61	2.4	+Avg	Avg	★★★★	0.00	None
499	Vanguard Strategic Eq	MB		21.43	20.49	14.61	11.27	—	0.6	+Avg	-Avg	★★★★	0.45	None
500	Vanguard Tax-Mgd Bal	CA		18.49	7.16	5.24	2.27	9.42	2.6	Avg	High	★★★	0.17	None
501	Vanguard Tx-Mgd App	LG		28.05	11.75	4.06	–3.03	11.72	1.3	+Avg	Avg	★★★★	0.17	None
502	Vanguard Tx-Mgd Gr	LB		26.36	10.83	3.60	–2.29	12.09	1.8	+Avg	Avg	★★★★	0.17	None
504	Vanguard Tax-Mgd SmCap R	SB		21.25	22.84	13.33	11.73	—	0.8	Avg	Avg	★★★	0.17	None
507	Vanguard Tot Stk	LB		28.77	12.52	5.32	–1.44	11.81	1.6	+Avg	+Avg	★★★★	0.20	None
508	Vanguard U.S. Gr	LG		16.18	7.03	–4.67	–13.93	5.92	0.3	Low	+Avg	★	0.53	None
509	Vanguard U.S. Value	LV		13.75	13.70	7.86	—	—	1.5	+Avg	Avg	★★★★	0.49	None
510	Vanguard Val Idx	LV		21.35	15.29	6.44	2.43	12.16	2.2	Avg	+Avg	★★★	0.23	None
511	Vanguard Wellesley Inc	CA		21.58	7.57	7.27	9.02	**10.84**	3.9	High	Avg	★★★★★	0.26	None
512	Vanguard Wellington	MA		30.19	11.17	7.72	7.53	12.34	2.8	High	Avg	★★★★★	0.36	None
513	Vanguard Windsor	LV		18.07	13.38	6.49	8.15	12.81	1.4	+Avg	High	★★★	0.39	None
514	Vanguard Windsor II	LV		30.73	18.31	8.56	7.63	13.71	1.9	+Avg	Avg	★★★★	0.36	None
515	Wasatch Core Growth	SG		43.23	21.65	9.11	18.11	19.25	0.5	High	Avg	★★★★	1.21	Clsd
516	Wasatch Heritage Growth	MG		11.14	—	—	—	—	—	—	—	—	0.95	None
517	Wasatch Micro Cap	SG		6.93	12.70	13.17	**24.49**	—	0.0	High	Avg	★★★★★	2.19	Clsd
518	Wasatch Small Cap Growth	SG		39.46	13.36	6.07	11.60	15.85	0.0	–Avg	Avg	★★★★	1.20	Clsd
519	Wasatch Small Cap Value	SB		5.53	21.58	16.28	22.07	—	0.0	High	+Avg	★★★★★	1.73	Clsd
520	Wasatch Ultra Growth	SG		26.84	–0.82	5.24	11.67	15.33	0.0	+Avg	+Avg	★★★★	1.50	Clsd
521	Weitz Hickory	SB		32.86	22.61	8.64	0.24	17.15	0.7	Avg	High	★★★	1.30	None
522	Weitz Partners Value	MV		23.90	14.99	6.17	7.51	18.05	0.3	Avg	-Avg	★★★	1.13	None
523	Weitz Value	MV		37.70	15.74	7.29	8.17	18.08	0.5	Avg	-Avg	★★★★	1.11	None
524	Westcore Midco Growth	MG		7.48	12.48	9.23	–0.76	11.23	0.0	Avg	Avg	★★★	1.14	None
526	Westport Select Cap R	SB		24.06	10.43	7.35	8.75	—	0.0	-Avg	-Avg	★★★	1.34	Clsd
527	White Oak Growth Stock	LG		34.06	–3.21	–3.95	–10.97	11.39	0.0	Avg	High	★★	1.07	None
529	William Blair Sm-Cp Gr N	SG	—	25.73	27.29	19.47	23.49	—	0.0	High	+Avg	★★★★★	1.52	Clsd

International-Equity Funds

Page		Cat	Style Box	NAV	Total Return % through 12-31-04 1Yr	Annualized 3Yr	5Yr	10Yr	Yield %	Morningstar Rating Statistics through 12-31-04 Performance	Risk	Morningstar Rating	Expense Ratio %	Sales Charge %
	S&P 500				**10.87**	**3.58**	**-2.30**	**12.07**						
40	AmCent Global Gold Inv	SP		12.00	**–8.17**	**32.58**	**18.90**	**2.31**	0.7	Avg	+Avg	★★★	0.69	None
41	AmCent Global Gr Inv	WS		7.79	15.11	7.28	–2.85	—	0.2	Avg	Avg	★★★	1.31	None
44	AmCent Intl Disc Inv	FR		13.47	16.26	15.33	0.58	**14.50**	0.0	+Avg	Avg	★★★★	1.57	Clsd
45	AmCent Intl Growth Inv	FG		9.06	15.31	5.30	–6.19	8.10	1.0	+Avg	Avg	★★★★	1.28	None
58	Amer Funds CplncBldr A	IH		53.26	17.40	12.83	11.11	12.81	3.4	+Avg	-Avg	★★★★	0.65	5.75
60	Amer Funds CapWrldGl A	WS		33.89	19.42	15.53	8.24	14.36	2.5	High	-Avg	★★★★★	0.81	5.75
61	Amer Funds EuroPac A	FB		35.63	19.69	11.18	–0.17	10.15	1.4	+Avg	-Avg	★★★★	0.87	5.75
67	Amer Funds New Persp A	WS		27.72	14.27	9.47	2.22	12.55	0.9	+Avg	Avg	★★★★	0.78	5.75
68	Amer Funds New World A	EM		32.27	20.79	18.21	4.64	—	1.7	-Avg	Low	★★★	1.31	5.75
75	Artisan International Inv	FG		22.14	17.76	7.24	–1.48	—	0.6	+Avg	+Avg	★★★★	1.22	None

Bold numbers indicate *highest* return for the listed time period in each category.

International-Equity Funds

Page		Cat	Style Box	NAV	Total Return % through 12-31-04 1Yr	Annualized 3Yr	5Yr	10Yr	Yield %	Morningstar Rating Statistics through 12-31-04 Performance	Risk	Morningstar Rating	Expense Ratio %	Sales Charge %
	S&P 500				**10.87**	**3.58**	**-2.30**	**12.07**						
76	Artisan Intl Sm Cap	FR		17.56	25.70	**26.44**	—	—	0.6	+Avg	Avg	★★★★★	1.57	Clsd
82	Atlas Global Growth A	WS	—	21.02	17.79	8.45	3.08	—	0.3	+Avg	+Avg	★★★★	1.54	12b-1
86	Bernstein Intl Port	FB		21.23	18.48	14.60	4.87	—	0.8	High	Avg	★★★★★	1.28	None
87	Bernstein Tx-Mgd Intl	FB		22.58	17.58	14.30	4.40	8.88	0.7	High	Avg	★★★★★	1.24	None
102	Causeway Intl Value Inv	FV		16.17	26.31	17.75	—	—	1.4	+Avg	High	★★★★	1.23	12b-1
106	Columbia Acorn Intl A	FR		28.75	28.91	16.53	—	—	0.5	-Avg	-Avg	★★	1.59	5.75
120	Dodge & Cox Intl Stock	FV		30.64	**32.46**	**19.81**	—	—	0.8	+Avg	High	★★★★	0.82	None
127	Dreyfus Prem Emerg A	EM		19.61	26.88	24.05	10.38	—	0.4	+Avg	-Avg	★★★★	1.86	Clsd
149	Fidelity Diversified Int	FG		28.64	**19.66**	**15.58**	**4.11**	**13.00**	0.5	High	-Avg	★★★★★	1.22	Clsd
167	Fidelity Intl Disc	FB		28.20	19.05	15.43	1.77	9.59	0.5	High	+Avg	★★★★★	1.11	None
168	Fidelity Intl Sm Cp	FR		23.28	29.43	—	—	—	0.3	—	—	—	1.51	None
177	Fidelity Overseas	FB		35.38	13.54	9.69	–2.97	6.61	0.5	Avg	+Avg	★★★	1.00	None
178	Fidelity Pacific Basin	DP		19.77	**14.08**	**13.38**	**–5.46**	**3.36**	0.4	Avg	Avg	★★★★	1.17	None
190	Fidelity Spar Intl Index	FB		32.02	19.86	11.68	–1.52	—	1.7	Avg	Avg	★★★	0.47	None
199	Fidelity Worldwide	WS		18.25	12.24	8.04	1.70	8.08	0.6	Avg	Avg	★★★	1.28	None
201	First Eagle Glbl A	IH		38.81	**18.37**	**21.55**	**16.78**	**13.92**	1.1	High	Avg	★★★★★	1.24	5.00
202	First Eagle Overseas A	FA		21.77	21.83	**24.69**	**16.63**	**14.54**	1.1	High	Low	★★★★★	1.25	Clsd
229	Harbor Intl Instl	FV		42.70	17.97	15.90	5.36	11.07	1.3	Avg	+Avg	★★★	0.86	None
233	ICAP Euro Select Eqty	ES		30.18	**26.87**	13.68	4.95	—	1.0	Avg	Avg	★★★	0.80	None
242	Janus Global Opps	WS		14.24	15.33	10.31	—	—	0.2	+Avg	High	★★★★	1.16	None
249	Janus Overseas	FG		24.26	18.58	7.27	–5.02	11.99	0.9	+Avg	High	★★★★	0.94	None
253	Janus Worldwide	WS		41.41	5.54	–1.01	–9.06	9.10	0.8	-Avg	Avg	★★	0.92	None
256	Julius Baer Intl Eqty A	FB		31.61	**23.22**	**17.31**	3.78	**13.85**	1.4	High	Avg	★★★★★	1.31	12b-1
263	Longleaf Partners Intl	FV		15.55	10.21	9.20	**12.62**	—	0.0	Avg	+Avg	★★★	1.68	Clsd
273	Marsico Intl Opp	FG		12.01	17.06	15.18	—	—	0.0	High	Avg	★★★★★	1.60	12b-1
275	Masters' Select Intl	FB		16.89	14.37	10.80	1.18	—	0.4	+Avg	+Avg	★★★★	1.10	Clsd
279	Matthews Pacific Tiger	PJ		15.90	**23.34**	**22.70**	**8.66**	**7.38**	0.6	+Avg	+Avg	★★★★	1.48	None
284	Merrill Global Alloc A	IH		16.47	14.27	12.67	9.61	12.41	2.6	+Avg	+Avg	★★★	1.13	0.02
295	Mutual Discovery A	WS		24.08	18.93	12.22	9.86	—	1.9	High	Low	★★★★★	1.46	5.75
296	Mutual European A	ES		19.50	21.18	**13.82**	**9.82**	—	2.7	+Avg	Low	★★★★	1.43	5.75
308	Oakmark Global I	WS		21.81	15.63	**19.03**	**18.59**	—	0.5	High	+Avg	★★★★★	1.26	None
310	Oakmark International I	FV		21.13	19.09	14.59	9.94	**11.56**	1.3	High	High	★★★★	1.20	None
311	Oakmark Intl Small Cap I	FA		20.03	**28.95**	23.09	13.94	—	1.3	+Avg	High	★★★★	1.49	Clsd
314	Oppenheimer Develop MktA	EM		26.88	**33.00**	**29.32**	**14.07**	—	1.4	High	+Avg	★★★★★	1.52	5.75
315	Oppenheimer Glob A	WS		60.77	18.67	9.61	3.86	13.68	0.6	+Avg	+Avg	★★★★	1.15	5.75
316	Oppenheimer Glob Oppor A	WS		33.25	**29.88**	14.25	3.63	**15.88**	0.0	+Avg	High	★★★	1.19	5.75
320	Oppenheimer Quest Intl A	FB		18.90	14.10	8.28	2.20	9.68	0.2	+Avg	Low	★★★★	1.59	5.75
370	T. Rowe Price Emg Mkt St	EM		19.41	26.98	22.51	5.01	—	0.2	Avg	+Avg	★★★	1.43	None
380	T. Rowe Price Intl Disc	FR		32.63	23.76	19.65	1.73	11.72	0.0	+Avg	Avg	★★★★	1.32	None
381	T. Rowe Price Intl Stk	FG		12.93	13.89	6.95	–4.58	5.07	1.2	Avg	Avg	★★★	0.92	None
382	T. Rowe Price Latin Amer	LS		15.95	**38.35**	**21.40**	**9.65**	**7.99**	1.3	+Avg	-Avg	★★★★	1.41	None
387	T. Rowe Price New Asia	PJ		10.04	18.60	18.18	0.56	3.06	0.0	Avg	Avg	★★★	1.09	None
407	Templeton Devel Mkts A	EM		18.52	25.45	25.01	4.64	**5.58**	1.4	Avg	-Avg	★★★	2.17	5.75
408	Templeton Foreign A	FV		12.30	18.14	12.10	4.55	8.75	1.8	Avg	-Avg	★★★	1.23	5.75
409	Templeton Growth A	WS		22.89	17.00	12.06	7.55	11.88	1.8	+Avg	-Avg	★★★★	1.10	5.75
410	Templeton World A	WS		17.75	15.63	10.65	3.64	11.07	1.7	+Avg	-Avg	★★★★	1.11	5.75
412	Third Avenue Intl Value	FA		18.41	27.70	24.26	—	—	1.2	Avg	Low	★★★	1.75	None
417	Thornburg Intl Value A	FB		20.40	17.73	13.86	**5.38**	—	0.4	High	-Avg	★★★★★	1.49	4.50
424	TIAA-CREF Intl Equity	FB		10.67	17.37	11.68	–3.34	—	1.6	Avg	+Avg	★★★	0.49	None
434	Tweedy, Browne Glob Val	FA		23.19	20.01	9.62	7.14	12.38	1.2	Avg	-Avg	★★★	1.39	None
435	UMB Scout WorldWide	FB		24.10	18.02	9.75	1.56	10.40	0.7	High	Low	★★★★★	1.10	None
443	Van Kampen Glob Val Eq A	WS		11.62	13.04	6.04	3.71	—	0.0	Avg	-Avg	★★★	1.64	5.75
452	Vanguard Dev Mkts Idx	FB		9.20	20.25	12.00	—	—	2.1	+Avg	Avg	★★★★	0.00	None
454	Vanguard Em Mkt Idx	EM		14.68	26.12	22.55	5.31	5.20	1.8	Avg	Avg	★★★	0.48	None
457	Vanguard Eur Stk Idx	ES		25.99	20.86	11.21	0.12	**10.79**	2.2	Avg	Avg	★★★	0.27	None

Bold numbers indicate *highest* return for the listed time period in each category.

International-Equity Funds

Page		Cat	Style Box	NAV	Total Return % through 12-31-04 1Yr	Annualized 3Yr	5Yr	10Yr	Yield %	Morningstar Rating Statistics through 12-31-04 Performance	Risk	Morningstar Rating	Expense Ratio %	Sales Charge %
	S&P 500				**10.87**	**3.58**	**-2.30**	**12.07**						
460	Vanguard Global Equity	WS		18.06	20.09	17.88	9.50	—	1.2	High	Avg	★★★★★	0.90	Clsd
473	Vanguard Intl Explorer	FR		16.34	**31.77**	21.33	**6.13**	—	1.4	+Avg	Avg	★★★★★	0.57	Clsd
474	Vanguard Intl Gr	FB		18.86	18.95	9.55	–0.52	7.04	1.7	+Avg	Avg	★★★★	0.45	None
475	Vanguard Intl Value	FB		30.93	19.77	13.77	3.22	6.99	1.6	High	+Avg	★★★★	0.56	None
503	Vanguard Tax-Mgd Intl	FB		10.33	20.25	12.06	–1.20	—	2.0	+Avg	Avg	★★★★	0.28	None
506	Vanguard Total Intl Stk	FB		12.60	20.84	12.93	–0.60	—	2.0	+Avg	Avg	★★★★	0.00	None
528	William Blair Intl Gr N	FG		22.09	18.48	12.64	2.54	12.25	0.0	High	Avg	★★★★★	1.50	Clsd

Fixed-Income Funds

Page		Cat	Style Box	NAV	Total Return % through 12-31-04 1Yr	Annualized 3Yr	5Yr	10Yr	Yield %	Morningstar Rating Statistics through 12-31-04 Performance	Risk	Morningstar Rating	Expense Ratio %	Sales Charge %
	LB Agg				**4.34**	**6.19**	**7.71**	**7.72**						
39	AmCent Ginnie Mae Inv	GI		10.45	3.12	4.44	6.19	6.76	4.6	+Avg	Low	★★★★	0.59	None
49	AmCent Tax-Free Bond Inv	MI		10.91	2.65	5.22	6.12	5.92	3.3	Avg	Avg	★★★★	0.51	None
56	Amer Funds Amer H/I A	HY		12.61	9.78	10.90	7.23	**9.09**	6.9	+Avg	+Avg	★★★★	0.67	3.75
59	Amer Funds CapWrldBd A	IB		20.01	11.38	15.52	**9.69**	**8.21**	3.9	Avg	Avg	★★★	1.02	3.75
70	Amer Funds T/E Bd A	MI		12.54	**4.37**	5.98	**6.63**	**6.68**	4.1	+Avg	Avg	★★★★	0.61	3.75
101	Calvert Tax-Fr Res Lim A	MS		10.61	0.62	1.87	2.91	3.48	1.8	-Avg	Low	★★	0.57	1.00
110	Constel CIP Ultr Sh F/I I	UB		10.10	**1.74**	**1.92**	**3.69**	**4.99**	2.2	Avg	-Avg	★★★	—	None
119	Dodge & Cox Income	CI		12.84	3.64	6.75	8.24	8.12	4.2	High	-Avg	★★★★★	0.45	None
128	Eaton Vance Fltg Rt A	BL	—	10.23	3.51	—	—	—	2.9	—	—	—	1.09	2.25
129	Eaton Vance Inc Boston A	HY		6.58	10.71	**12.57**	5.64	8.76	8.0	+Avg	Avg	★★★★	1.06	4.75
154	Fidelity Float Rt Hi Inc	BL	—	9.98	**4.47**	—	—	—	3.1	—	—	—	0.86	None
158	Fidelity Ginnie Mae	GI		11.08	4.20	4.99	6.56	7.00	4.1	+Avg	Low	★★★★	0.60	None
159	Fidelity Government Inc	GI		10.24	3.60	5.52	**7.15**	7.00	3.0	+Avg	+Avg	★★★★	0.63	None
162	Fidelity High Income	HY	—	9.09	9.69	12.37	2.99	7.42	7.5	Avg	+Avg	★★★	0.77	None
164	Fidelity Inflation-Protec	GI		11.41	8.24	—	—	—	1.3	—	—	—	0.50	None
165	Fidelity Interm Bond	CI		10.52	3.20	5.75	7.15	6.77	3.5	Avg	-Avg	★★★	0.61	None
166	Fidelity Interm Govt	GI		10.24	2.40	4.78	6.50	6.59	2.9	Avg	Avg	★★★	0.60	None
169	Fidelity Invt Grade Bond	CI		7.53	4.53	6.17	7.56	7.14	3.3	+Avg	Avg	★★★★	0.63	None
174	Fidelity New Markets Inc	EB	—	14.33	12.50	**18.44**	15.17	**14.45**	6.0	+Avg	Avg	★★★★	1.00	None
184	Fidelity Sh-Term Bond	CS		8.98	1.86	4.02	5.49	5.76	2.5	+Avg	Avg	★★★★	0.57	None
189	Fidelity Spar IntermMuni	MI		10.15	3.74	**6.00**	6.54	6.44	3.9	High	Avg	★★★★★	0.43	None
191	Fidelity Spar Muni Inc	ML		13.09	4.73	6.97	7.62	7.11	4.3	+Avg	Avg	★★★★★	0.47	None
192	Fidelity Spar Sh-IntMuni	MS		10.38	1.82	3.75	4.62	4.71	2.6	+Avg	Avg	★★★★	0.47	None
194	Fidelity Strategic Inc	MU	—	10.77	9.44	12.40	9.50	—	5.1	+Avg	Avg	★★★★★	0.80	None
196	Fidelity Total Bond	CI		10.63	5.47	—	—	—	3.4	—	—	—	0.65	None
197	Fidelity Ultra-Short Bd	UB		10.04	1.32	—	—	—	1.5	—	—	—	0.55	None
207	FPA New Income	CI		11.18	2.60	5.12	7.36	7.35	3.5	Avg	Low	★★★	0.62	3.50
210	Franklin Fed T/F Inc A	ML		12.16	5.39	6.14	6.62	6.42	4.6	+Avg	Low	★★★★	0.61	4.25
212	Franklin Hi Yld T/F A	HM		10.75	**6.88**	6.68	6.36	**6.55**	5.5	+Avg	Avg	★★★★	0.62	4.25
214	Franklin Ins T/F Inc A	ML		12.38	4.13	6.08	6.95	6.24	4.4	Avg	-Avg	★★★	0.63	4.25
216	Fremont Bond	CI		10.46	5.10	6.71	8.51	**8.63**	2.1	High	+Avg	★★★★★	0.61	None
227	Harbor Bond	CI		11.83	**5.47**	7.11	8.33	8.34	2.8	High	Avg	★★★★★	0.57	None
244	Janus High-Yield	HY		9.92	8.85	9.01	6.79	—	6.1	+Avg	Low	★★★★	0.95	None
255	Hancock Strategic Inc A	MU		7.18	8.75	10.90	7.67	**8.94**	5.1	+Avg	Avg	★★★★	0.90	4.50
265	Loomis Sayles Bond Ret	MU		13.80	**11.02**	**17.42**	**11.50**	—	6.7	High	High	★★★★★	1.00	12b-1

Bold numbers indicate *highest* return for the listed time period in each category.

Fixed-Income Funds

Page		Cat	Style Box	NAV	Total Return % through 12-31-04 1Yr	Annualized 3Yr	5Yr	10Yr	Yield %	Morningstar Rating Statistics through 12-31-04 Performance	Risk	Morningstar Rating	Expense Ratio %	Sales Charge %
	LB Agg				**4.34**	**6.19**	**7.71**	**7.72**						
285	Metro West Low Dur M	CS		9.43	**3.27**	2.91	4.71	—	4.0	Avg	+Avg	★★★	0.58	12b-1
286	Metro West Total Ret	CI		9.82	5.15	5.85	7.37	—	6.0	+Avg	High	★★★★	0.65	12b-1
304	Northeast Investors	HY		7.87	**14.38**	10.53	5.15	7.85	7.1	+Avg	-Avg	★★★★	0.67	None
322	Payden Core Bond	CI		10.61	4.51	6.63	7.94	7.47	3.7	+Avg	+Avg	★★★★	0.51	None
323	Payden Emerging Mkts Bond	EB		12.23	**13.13**	13.69	13.48	—	5.8	-Avg	Low	★★	0.86	None
324	Payden Limited Maturity	UB		9.90	1.09	1.56	3.55	4.59	1.7	-Avg	-Avg	★★	0.40	None
327	PIMCO Emerg Mkts Bd A	EB		10.86	11.79	18.37	**19.29**	—	3.9	Avg	+Avg	★★★	1.25	3.75
328	PIMCO Foreign Bond D	IB		10.47	6.17	5.49	6.85	—	2.3	Avg	Low	★★★	0.96	None
329	PIMCO High-Yield A	HY		9.97	9.02	9.88	6.59	—	6.4	Avg	Avg	★★★	0.90	3.75
330	PIMCO Low Duration Instl	CS		10.20	2.39	4.31	5.72	**6.48**	2.1	High	Avg	★★★★★	0.43	None
332	PIMCO Real Ret A	GL		11.49	**8.71**	**11.02**	**10.85**	—	3.4	Avg	-Avg	★★★★	0.90	3.00
333	PIMCO Total Ret Instl	CI		10.67	5.15	6.95	8.46	8.54	2.3	High	+Avg	★★★★★	0.43	None
335	Pioneer High Yield A	HY		11.61	6.75	11.13	**12.56**	—	6.2	+Avg	+Avg	★★★★	1.06	4.50
351	Scudder Hi-Yld T/F AARP	HM		12.79	4.96	**6.72**	—	—	5.2	+Avg	+Avg	★★★★	0.76	None
352	Scudder Interm T/A F AARP	MI		11.46	2.93	5.10	—	—	3.8	+Avg	Avg	★★★★	0.70	None
361	SSgA Yield Plus	UB	—	9.96	1.44	1.31	3.01	4.29	1.2	-Avg	Low	★★	0.57	12b-1
365	Strong S/T Muni Bond Inv	MS		9.84	**3.21**	**4.10**	4.50	4.63	3.1	High	Avg	★★★★★	0.70	None
374	T. Rowe Price GNMA	GI		9.66	3.82	5.03	6.72	6.99	4.5	+Avg	-Avg	★★★★	0.69	None
378	T. Rowe Price Hi-Yld	HY		7.20	10.35	11.70	7.43	8.70	7.6	High	-Avg	★★★★★	0.78	Clsd
379	T. Rowe Price Intl Bd	IB		10.69	**11.41**	**17.25**	8.57	7.15	2.3	+Avg	+Avg	★★★	0.91	None
396	T. Rowe Price Spect Inc	MU	—	12.09	8.06	9.94	8.32	8.68	4.0	+Avg	-Avg	★★★★	0.00	None
397	T. Rowe Price T/F Hi-Yld	HM		11.79	6.65	6.71	**6.58**	6.39	5.1	+Avg	+Avg	★★★★	0.71	None
398	T. Rowe Price T/F Inc	ML		10.06	4.33	6.20	7.02	6.62	4.3	+Avg	-Avg	★★★★	0.54	None
399	T. Rowe Price T/F Sh-Int	MS		5.44	1.61	3.50	4.60	4.63	2.7	+Avg	Avg	★★★★	0.51	None
400	T. Rowe Price US Try L/T	GL		11.86	5.79	7.54	8.90	8.55	4.3	Avg	Avg	★★★	0.67	None
404	TCW Galileo Tot Ret Bd I	CI		9.61	5.19	6.38	8.39	8.54	4.7	High	-Avg	★★★★★	0.51	None
418	Thornburg Ltd-Tm A	MS		13.78	1.74	4.08	**4.77**	**4.82**	2.8	+Avg	+Avg	★★★★	0.91	1.50
423	TIAA-CREF High-Yield Bd	HY		9.48	9.16	10.56	—	—	6.9	Avg	+Avg	★★★	0.34	None
426	TIAA-CREF Short-Term Bd	CS		10.55	1.72	**4.32**	—	—	2.9	+Avg	+Avg	★★★★	0.30	None
428	TIAA-CREF Tax-Exempt Bd	ML		10.93	4.58	7.02	—	—	3.5	+Avg	+Avg	★★★★	0.30	None
436	USAA Income	CI		12.42	4.52	6.00	7.75	7.84	4.4	+Avg	+Avg	★★★★	0.52	None
438	USAA Tax Ex Interm-Term	MI		13.34	4.27	5.70	6.48	6.43	4.3	High	-Avg	★★★★★	0.51	None
439	USAA Tax Ex Long-Term	ML		14.18	**5.60**	**7.43**	**7.72**	**7.16**	4.5	High	Avg	★★★★★	0.56	None
440	USAA Tax Ex Short-Term	MS		10.76	1.52	3.14	4.10	4.56	2.5	+Avg	Avg	★★★★	0.56	None
461	Vanguard GNMA	GI		10.44	4.13	5.39	7.04	**7.42**	4.6	High	Avg	★★★★★	0.20	None
466	Vanguard Hi-Yld Corp	HY		6.44	8.52	8.97	5.70	7.63	7.1	Avg	-Avg	★★★★	0.23	None
467	Vanguard Hi-Yld T/E	ML		10.83	4.98	6.21	6.92	6.84	4.7	High	-Avg	★★★★★	0.15	None
468	Vanguard Infl-Prot Secs	GI		12.57	**8.27**	**10.89**	—	—	4.5	High	High	★★★★★	0.18	None
469	Vanguard Ins L/T TE Inv	ML		12.82	3.93	6.55	7.46	7.07	4.6	High	+Avg	★★★★★	0.15	None
470	Vanguard Intm Bd Idx	CI		10.68	5.22	7.21	8.72	8.22	4.7	High	High	★★★★★	0.20	None
471	Vanguard IntTm Inv-Gr Fd	CI		10.07	4.75	7.08	8.26	7.98	4.7	High	High	★★★★★	0.20	None
472	Vanguard IntTm T/E	MI		13.58	3.23	5.18	5.95	5.94	4.1	+Avg	Avg	★★★★	0.14	None
480	Vanguard Long-Tm InvGrde	CL		9.55	**8.94**	**9.44**	**9.92**	**9.11**	5.5	+Avg	High	★★★★	0.28	None
481	Vanguard Lg-Tm T/E	ML		11.48	4.12	6.45	7.40	7.07	4.5	High	High	★★★★★	0.15	None
482	Vanguard Long-Tm US Try	GL		11.51	7.12	8.67	9.89	**9.25**	5.0	+Avg	Avg	★★★★	0.26	None
483	Vanguard LtdTm T/E	MS		10.92	1.53	3.52	4.49	4.67	2.9	+Avg	Avg	★★★★	0.14	None
490	Vanguard Sh-Tm Bd Idx	CS		10.14	1.70	3.71	**5.74**	6.26	3.0	+Avg	+Avg	★★★★	0.20	None
491	Vanguard ShtTm Fed	GS		10.41	**1.36**	3.62	**5.69**	**6.10**	2.8	+Avg	Avg	★★★★	0.22	None
492	Vanguard Sht-Tm Inv-Grade	CS		10.66	2.11	3.84	5.54	6.18	3.4	+Avg	Avg	★★★★	0.21	None
493	Vanguard Sht-Tm TE	MS		15.63	1.12	2.08	3.17	3.64	1.9	Avg	-Avg	★★★	0.14	None
494	Vanguard Short-Tm Trs	GS		10.47	1.03	**3.77**	5.56	5.98	2.7	+Avg	Avg	★★★★	0.26	None
505	Vanguard Total Bd Idx	CI		10.27	4.24	5.47	7.22	7.42	4.3	+Avg	Avg	★★★★	0.22	None
525	Western Asset Cr Bd Inst	CI	—	11.48	5.30	**7.25**	**8.89**	8.46	3.3	High	High	★★★★★	0.49	None
530	WPG Core Bond	CI		10.81	4.38	6.72	8.07	7.35	2.9	High	Avg	★★★★★	0.45	None

Bold numbers indicate *highest* return for the listed time period in each category.

User's Guide

User's Guide

The following is a complete alphabetical listing of the terms and features found in the pages of *Morningstar Funds 500.*

A

Actual Fees
see Expenses and Fees

Address
Usually the location of the fund's distributor, this address is where to write to receive a prospectus.

Advisor
This is the company that takes primary responsibility for managing the fund.

Alpha
see Modern Portfolio Theory Statistics

Analysis
see Morningstar's Take

Analyst Picks
We highlight a few of our favorites in each investment category. Funds that make the cut as Analyst Picks tend to have terrific long-term records, experienced managers, and moderate-to-low costs. However, we sometimes relax one of these criteria when a fund is truly superior in the other areas. For example, if a fund is supported by a number of talented, experienced analysts, we won't necessarily drop it from our picks list when there is a manager change. There is no upper limit on the number of funds that can be named Analyst Picks in a category, but in major groups such as large blend, there are normally five to seven. Smaller categories often have fewer picks. To be listed as an Analyst Pick, a fund must be widely available to new investors; when a fund closes, it is removed from the list. Other reasons a fund may be dropped from the list include the following: a shift in investment style, poor performance, a management change, organizational turmoil at the fund-company level, and an increase in costs.

Average Credit Quality
see also Credit Analysis

Average credit quality gives a snapshot of the portfolio's overall credit quality. It is an average of each bond's credit rating, adjusted for its relative weighting in the portfolio. For the purposes of Morningstar's calculations, U.S. government securities are considered AAA bonds, nonrated municipal bonds generally are classified as BB, and other nonrated bonds generally are considered B.

Average Effective Duration
Average effective duration provides a measure of a fund's interest-rate sensitivity. The longer a fund's duration, the more sensitive the fund is to shifts in interest rates. The relationship among funds with different durations is straightforward: A fund with a duration of 10 years is expected to be twice as volatile as a fund with a five-year duration. Duration also gives an indication of how a fund's net asset value (NAV) will change as interest rates change. A fund with a five-year duration would be expected to lose 5% of its NAV if interest rates rose by 1 percentage point, or gain 5% if interest rates fell by 1 percentage point. Morningstar surveys fund companies for this information.

Average Effective Maturity
see also Average Nominal Maturity

Average effective maturity is a weighted average of all the maturities of the bonds in a portfolio, computed by weighting each bond's effective maturity by the market value of the security. Average effective maturity takes into consideration all mortgage prepayments, puts, and adjustable coupons. (Because Morningstar uses fund-company calculations for this figure and because different companies use varying interest-rate assumptions in determining call likelihood and timing, we ask that companies not adjust for call provisions.) Longer-maturity funds are generally considered more interest-rate sensitive than their shorter counterparts.

Average Historical Rating
see Rating and Risk

Average Nominal Maturity
see also Average Effective Maturity

Listed only for municipal-bond funds, this figure is computed by weighting the nominal maturity of each security in the portfolio by the market value of the security, then averaging these weighted figures. Unlike a fund's effective maturity figure, it does not take into account prepayments, puts, or adjustable coupons.

Average Stock Percentage
see also Composition

For stock-oriented funds, we provide a yearly average stock position calculated by averaging all reported composition numbers for the year. These averages provide a valuable complement to the current composition numbers; investors can compare a fund's current level of market participation with its historical averages.

Average Weighted Coupon
see also Coupon Range
Average weighted coupon is computed by averaging each bond's coupon rate adjusted for its relative weighting in the portfolio. This figure indicates whether the fund is opting for a high- or low-coupon strategy, and may serve as an indicator of interest-rate sensitivity, particularly for mortgage-backed funds or other funds with callable bonds. A high coupon frequently indicates less sensitivity to interest rates; a low coupon, the opposite.

Average Weighted Price
Average weighted price is computed for most bond funds by weighting the price of each bond by its relative size in the portfolio. This number reveals whether the fund favors bonds selling at prices above or below face value (premium or discount securities, respectively) and can also serve as an indicator of interest-rate sensitivity. This statistic is expressed as a percentage of par (face) value. This statistic is not calculated for international-bond funds, because their holdings are often expressed in terms of foreign currencies.

B

+/- Benchmark Index
see Indexes

Best Fit Index
see also Indexes and Modern Portfolio Theory Statistics
The Best Fit Index is the market index whose monthly returns have correlated the most closely with a given fund's in the most recent 36 consecutive months. Morningstar regresses the fund's monthly excess returns against monthly excess returns of several well-known market indexes. Best Fit signifies the index that provides the highest R-squared, or correlation with a given fund.

Beta
see also Modern Portfolio Theory Statistics
Beta, a component of Modern Portfolio Theory statistics, is a measure of a fund's sensitivity to market movements. It measures the relationship between a fund's excess return over T-bills and the excess return of the benchmark index. Equity funds are compared with the S&P 500 Index; bond funds are compared with the Lehman Brothers Aggregate Bond Index.

C

Capital Gains $
Capital gains are the profits received and distributed from the sale of securities within the portfolio. This line shows a summary of the fund's annual capital-gains distributions expressed in per-share dollar amounts. Both short- and long-term gains are included, as are options premiums and distributions from paid-in capital.

Capital Return %
see also Income Return % and Total Return
Morningstar provides the portion of a fund's total returns that was generated by realized and unrealized increases in the value of securities in the portfolio. Frequently, a stock fund's returns will be derived entirely from capital return. By looking at capital return and income return, an investor can see whether the fund's returns come from capital, from income, or from a combination of both. Adding capital and income return will produce the fund's total return.

Category
see Morningstar Category

Composition
see also Average Stock Percentage
The composition percentages provide a simple breakdown of the fund's portfolio holdings, as of the date listed, into general investment classes at the bottom of the Portfolio Analysis section. Cash encompasses both the actual cash and the cash equivalents (fixed-income securities with maturities of one year or less) held by the portfolio. Negative percentages of cash indicate that the portfolio is leveraged, meaning it has borrowed against its own assets to buy more securities or that it has used other techniques to gain additional exposure to the market. The percentage listed as Stocks incorporates only the portfolio's straight common stocks. Bonds include every fixed-income security with a maturity of more than one year, from government notes to high-yield corporate bonds. Other includes preferred stocks (equity securities that pay dividends at a specified rate), as well as convertible bonds and convertible preferreds, which are corporate securities that are exchangeable for a set amount of another form of security (usually shares of common stock) at a prestated price. Other also includes all those not-so-neatly categorized securities, such as warrants and options.

Country Exposure
For each international portfolio, the country exposure information displays the top five countries in which the fund is invested. This information is gathered directly from the portfolios given by the fund companies.

Coupon Range
see also Average Weighted Coupon
Taxable-bond funds feature a table listing the breakdown of each portfolio's bond coupons, or rates of interest payments. The coupon range is designed to help an investor complete the picture suggested by the average weighted coupon statistic.

These ranges differ according to Morningstar Category and, due to changing interest rates, are subject to alteration over time. Whatever the breakdown may be, the first number is always exclusive and the second number is always inclusive. A range of 8% to 10%, for example, would exclude bonds that have a weighted coupon rate of exactly 8% but would include bonds with a weighted coupon rate of 10%. High-yield bond funds include PIKS in their coupon breakdown, which are payment-in-kind issues that make interest payments in the form of additional securities rather than cash.

The overall percentage of bond assets that fall within each coupon range is noted in the % of Bonds column. The Rel Cat column compares a fund with others in its Morningstar Category. The category average is set at 1.0.

Credit Analysis
see also Average Credit Quality
This section depicts the quality of bonds in a bond fund's portfolio. The credit analysis shows the percentage of fixed-income securities that fall within each credit-quality rating as assigned by Standard & Poor's or Moody's.

At the top of the ratings are U.S. government bonds. Bonds issued and backed by the government, as well as those backed by government-linked organizations such as Fannie Mae and Freddie Mac, are of extremely high quality and thus are considered equivalent to bonds rated AAA, which is the highest possible rating a corporate issue can receive. Morningstar gives U.S. government bonds a credit rating separate from AAA securities to allow for a more accurate credit analysis of a portfolio's holdings. Bonds with a BBB rating are the lowest grade that are still considered to be investment-grade. Bonds that are rated BB or lower (often called junk bonds or high-yield bonds) are considered to be speculative. Any bonds that appear in the NR/NA category are either not rated by Standard & Poor's or Moody's, or did not have a rating available at the time of publication.

Current Investment Style
see also Investment Style Box and listings of terms in table
For equity funds, this section lists a fund portfolio's current averages for various portfolio statistics, including price/earnings, price/cash flow, and historical earnings growth. To provide perspective, we compare these measures with the funds' category average.

For bond funds, this section lists a portfolio's current duration, as well as averages for effective maturity, credit quality, weighted coupon, and price. These numbers are helpful in determining how much interest-rate and credit risk the portfolio currently has. For example, funds with high durations typically are very sensitive to changes in interest rates, whereas those with durations of just a year or two tend to be relatively insensitive to interest-rate changes. Funds with AAA or AA average credit-quality rankings take on less credit risk than those with, for example, B ratings, which indicate the portfolio holds a lot of high-yield (or junk) debt.

Morningstar currently uses price/cash flow, price/book, and median market capitalization to categorize foreign funds. This section also compares international-stock funds' current valuations with those of the MSCI EAFE Index, which is the most widely used benchmark for international offerings. Funds with low valuations typically hold stocks that aren't expected to grow rapidly, and therefore land in one of the value style boxes. By contrast, portfolios with high valuations typically hold fast-growing issues.

D

Distributor
The distributor, also known as the fund underwriter, is the company that distributes the shares of the fund. This task usually includes promoting the fund and preparing and sending out fund literature.

Dollar-Cost Averaging
see Minimum Automatic Investment Plan

Duration
see Average Effective Duration

E

Emerging-Markets Securities
see Special Securities

Equity Style
see Investment Style Box

Exotic Mortgage-Backed Securities
see Special Securities

Expense Projections
see Expenses and Fees

Expense Ratio %
see also Average Expense Ratio and Fees
The annual expense ratio, taken from the fund's annual report, expresses the percentage of assets deducted each fiscal year for fund expenses, including 12b-1 fees, management fees, administrative fees, operating costs, and all other asset-based costs incurred by the fund. Portfolio transaction fees, or brokerage costs, as well as initial or deferred sales charges, are not included in the expense ratio.

The expense ratio, which is deducted from the fund's average net assets, is accrued on a daily basis. If the fund's assets, listed in the lower part of the History section, are small, the expense ratio can be quite high because the fund must meet its expenses from a restricted asset base. Conversely, as the net assets of the fund grow, the expense percentage should ideally diminish as expenses are spread across the wider base.

Expenses and Fees
see also Average Expense Ratio, Expense Ratio, and Load
Morningstar distinguishes among the myriad fees and expenses encountered with mutual funds. The different expenses and their characteristics are listed below.

Sales Fees
Also known as loads, sales fees list the maximum level of initial (front-end) and deferred (back-end) sales charges imposed by a fund. The scales of minimum and maximum charges are taken from a fund's prospectus. Because fees change frequently and are sometimes waived, it is wise to examine the fund's prospectus carefully for specific information before investing.

B (12b-1)
The 12b-1 fee represents the maximum annual charge deducted from fund assets to pay for distribution and marketing costs. This fee is expressed as a percentage. Some funds may be permitted to impose 12b-1 fees but are currently waiving all or a portion of the fees. Total allowable 12b-1 fees, excluding loads, are capped at 1% of average net assets annually. Of this, the distribution and marketing portion of the fee may account for up to 0.75%. The other portion of the overall 12b-1 fee, the service fee(s), is listed separately and may account for up to 0.25%. Often, funds charging a relatively low 12b-1 fee will allow shareholders to convert into a share class without the fee after a certain number of years. (These are normally deferred-load funds.) When this is the case, we note the conversion feature and the number of years after which it applies. Investors should check the fund's prospectus for full details.

D (Deferred Load)
Also called a contingent deferred sales charge or back-end load, a deferred load is an alternative to the traditional front-end sales charge, as it is deducted only at the time of sale of fund shares. The deferred-load structure commonly decreases to zero over a period of time. A typical deferred load's structure might have a 5% charge if shares are redeemed within the first year of ownership, and decline by a percentage point each year thereafter. These loads are normally applied to the lesser of original share price or current market value. It is important to note that although the deferred load declines each year, the accumulated annual distribution and services charges (the total 12b-1 fee) usually offsets this decline.

L (Front-End Load)
The initial sales charge or front-end load is a deduction made from each investment in the fund. The amount is generally based on the amount of the investment. Larger investments, both initial and cumulative, generally receive percentage discounts based on the dollar value invested. A typical front-end load might have a 4.75% charge for purchases less than $50,000, which decreases as the amount of the investment increases. For those with $1 million to invest, the entire front-end load is waived. Investors who have significant assets and work with a financial advisor are therefore better off buying front-load shares than deferred-load shares.

No-Load
This label denotes the fund as a true no-load fund, charging no sales or 12b-1 fees.

R (Redemption Fee)
The redemption fee is an amount charged when

money is withdrawn from the fund before a predetermined period elapses. This fee does not go back into the pockets of the fund company, but rather into the fund itself and thus does not represent a net cost to shareholders. Also, unlike contingent deferred sales charges, redemption fees typically operate only in short, specific time clauses, commonly 30, 180, or 365 days. However, some redemption fees exist for up to five years. Charges are not imposed after the stated time has passed. These fees are typically imposed to discourage market-timers, whose quick movements into and out of funds can be disruptive. The charge is normally imposed on the ending share value, appreciated or depreciated from the original value.

S (Service Fee)

The service fee is part of the total 12b-1 fee, but listed separately on the page. Capped at a maximum 0.25%, the service fee is designed to compensate financial planners or brokers for ongoing shareholder-liaison services, which may include responding to customer inquiries and providing information on investments. An integral component of level-load and deferred-load funds, the fees were previously known as a trail commission. Only service fees adopted pursuant to Rule 12b-1 are tracked. Despite the implication of its name, service fees do not act as compensation for transfer agency or custodial services.

W (Waived)

This indicates that the fund is waiving sales fees at the time of publication. A fund may do this to attract new shareholders. Call the fund's distributor to ensure that the waiver is still active at the time of investment.

Management Fee

The management fee is the maximum percentage deducted from a fund's average net assets to pay an advisor or subadvisor. Often, as the fund's net assets grow, the percentage deducted for management fees decreases. Alternatively, the fund may compute the fee as a flat percentage of average net assets. A portion of the management fee may also be charged in the form of a group fee (G). To determine the group fee, the fund family creates a sliding scale for the family's total net assets and determines a percentage applied to each fund's asset base. The management fee might also be amended by or be primarily composed of a performance fee (P), which raises or lowers the management fee based on the fund's returns relative to an established index (we list the maximum by which the fee can increase or decrease).

It might also be composed of a gross income fee (I), a percentage based on the total amount of income generated by the investment portfolio.

The letter A denotes an administrative fee, which is the fund's maximum allowable charge for its management-fee structure, excluding advisor fees. Costs associated with Securities and Exchange Commission compliance may also be included under this label. Administrative fees often operate on a sliding scale and include the costs of basic fund operations, such as leasing office space. Investors should note that there is not necessarily a total expense differential between funds with disclosed administrative fees and funds without. Most funds roll administrative costs into their management fees; other funds, especially those with out-of-house administration, prefer to break them out. For this reason, we include administrative fees in the Management Fee area.

Actual Fees

Taken from the fund's prospectus, this area qualifies the management and 12b-1 distribution and service fees. Actual Fees most commonly represent the costs shareholders paid for management and distribution services over the fund's prior fiscal year. If fee levels have changed since the end of the most recent fiscal year, the actual fees will most commonly be presented as a recalculation based on the prior year's average monthly net assets using the new, current expenses. Although contract-type management and distribution costs are listed in a fund's prospectus, these are maximum amounts, and funds may waive a portion, or possibly all, of those fees. Actual Fees thus represent a close approximation of the true costs to shareholders.

Expense Projections (Three-, Five-, and 10-Year)

The SEC mandates that each fund list its expense projections. Found in the fund's prospectus, these figures show how much an investor would expect to pay in expenses, sales charges (loads), and fees over the next three, five, and 10 years, assuming a $10,000 investment that grows by 5% per year with redemption at the end of each time period. Expense projections are commonly based on the past year's incurred fees or an estimate of the current fiscal year's fees, should a portion of the overall fee structure change as of the printing of the fund's most current prospectus. Newer funds are required to print expense projections for only one- and three-year time periods since longer-term projections may not be possible to estimate.

F

Fiduciary Grade

Morningstar's Fiduciary Grade for funds goes beyond the usual analysis of strategy, risk, and return. The Fiduciary Grade allows investors and advisors to assess funds based on factors that we believe influence the manner in which funds are run; the degree to which the management company's and fund board's interests are aligned with fund shareholders; and the degree to which shareholders can expect their interests to be protected from potentially conflicting interests of the management company.

We assign each fund a letter grade from A (best) to F (worst). Funds are graded on an absolute basis. There is no "curve."

Morningstar analysts' evaluation of five factors determine the grade for each fund: Regulatory Issues, Board Quality, Manager Incentives, Fees, and Corporate Culture.

Each factor is worth a maximum of 2 points, for a total of 10 possible points. Points for each component are awarded in increments as small as 0.5 point. With the exception of Regulatory Issues, the worst possible score a fund can receive in each component is zero. For Regulatory Issues, the minimum score possible is -2. We assign each fund's overall letter grade as follows:

A: 9 - 10 points
B: 7 - 8.5 points
C: 5 - 6.5 points
D: 3 - 4.5 points
F: 2.5 points or less

For ease of use, we translate funds' scores for each of the five individual factors into the following qualitative terms:

Excellent = 2 points
Good = 1.5 points
Fair = 1 point
Poor = 0.5 point
Very Poor = 0 points and below

Morningstar's Fiduciary Grade for funds is entirely different from the Morningstar Rating for funds, commonly known as the star rating. There is no relationship between the two.

Fixed-Income Style

see Investment Style Box

G

Growth

see also Investment Style Box and Value

Often contrasted with a value approach to investing, the term growth is used to describe an investment style in which a manager looks for equity securities with high rates of revenue or earnings growth. A company's valuations are generally not emphasized as much as they are in value-style investing.

Growth of $10,000

see Performance

Growth Measures

Long-Term Earnings Growth

Earnings are what are left of a firm's revenues after it pays all of its expenses, costs, and taxes. Companies whose earnings grow faster than those of their industry peers usually see better price performance for their stocks. Projected earnings growth is an estimate of a company's expected long-term growth in earnings, derived from all polled analysts' estimates. When reported for a mutual fund, it shows the weighted average of the projected growth in earnings for each stock in the fund's portfolio. This measure helps determine Morningstar's growth score for each stock and the overall growth orientation of the fund.

Historical Earnings Growth

Historical earnings growth shows the rate of increase in a company's earnings per share, based on up to four periodic time periods. When reported for a mutual fund, it shows the weighted average of the growth in earnings for each stock in the fund's portfolio. This measure helps determine Morningstar's growth score for each stock and the overall growth orientation of the fund.

Sales Growth

Sales growth shows the rate of increase in a company's sales per share, based on up to four periodic time periods, and is considered the best gauge of how rapidly a company's core business is growing. When reported for a mutual fund, it shows the weighted average of the sales-growth rates for each stock in the fund's portfolio. This measure helps determine Morningstar's growth score for each stock and the overall growth orientation of the fund.

Cash Flow Growth

Cash flow tells you how much cash a business is actually generating—its earnings before depreciation, amortization, and noncash charges. Sometimes called cash earnings, it's considered a gauge of liquidity and solvency. Cash-flow growth shows the rate of increase in a company's cash flow per share, based on up to four time periods. When reported for a mutual fund, it shows the weighted average of the growth in cash flow for each stock in the fund's portfolio. This measure helps determine Morningstar's growth score for each stock and the overall growth orientation of the fund.

Book Value Growth
Book value is, in theory, what would be left over for shareholders if a company shut down its operations, paid off all its creditors, collected from all its debtors, and liquidated itself. In practice, however, the value of assets and liabilities can change substantially from when they are first recorded. Book value growth shows the rate of increase in a company's book value per share, based on up to four periodic time periods. When reported for a mutual fund, it shows the weighted average of the growth rates in book value for each stock in the fund's portfolio. This measure helps determine Morningstar's growth score for each stock and the overall growth orientation of the fund.

H

Historical Profile, Star Rating, and Overall Assessment
see also Morningstar Category
The star rating displayed in the Historical Profile section is a fund's overall risk-adjusted star rating. The star ratings for the three time periods in the Rating and Risk section are combined here. In ascending order, these categories are Lowest (1 star), Below Average (2 stars), Neutral (3 stars), Above Average (4 stars), and Highest (5 stars). Funds less than three years old are listed as Not Rated.

History
see also individual listings of terms in History section
The History section is a table of annual information providing performance and expense statistics along with relative comparisons on a yearly basis. The Overview pages found at the beginning of each category list some of the same statistics, but these are calculated as averages for each fund category (with the exception of net assets, which is an aggregate figure).

I

Inception
The date of inception is the date on which the fund commenced operations. If an asterisk appears next to the date that indicates the fund's inception was not on the first business day of the year. Returns for that partial year appear in the History section of the page. (Those returns are also marked with an asterisk.)

Income $
Income reflects the dividends and interest generated by a fund's holdings. This area shows a fund's yearly income distribution expressed in per-share dollar amounts.

Income Distribution
Income distribution represents the number of times per year that a fund intends to make income payments (from either dividends or interest). A fund generally makes distributions monthly, quarterly, semiannually, or annually.

Income Ratio %
The fund's income ratio reveals the percentage of current income earned per share. It is calculated by dividing the fund's net investment income by its average net assets. (Net investment income is the total income of the fund, less expenses.) An income ratio can be negative if a fund's expenses exceed its income, which can occur with funds that have high costs or tend to emphasize capital gains rather than income. Because the income ratio is based on a fund's fiscal year and is taken directly from the fund's annual shareholder report, it may not exactly correspond with other calendar-year information on the page.

Income Return %
see also Capital Return % and Total Return
Income return is that portion of a fund's total returns that was derived from income distributions. Income return will often be higher than capital return for bond funds, and typically lower for stock funds. Adding the income return and the capital return together will produce the fund's total return.

Income Return Percentile Rank
This ranking shows how a fund's income distributions have stacked up against other funds in its category. Each calendar year features a ranking, with 1 being the highest percentile and 100 the lowest. We use the income-return figures printed in the History section to determine the rankings. This ranking is calculated off a trailing 12-month figure.

Indexes
see also Best Fit Index

Benchmark Index
A benchmark index gives the investor a point of reference for evaluating a fund's performance. In all cases where such comparisons are made, Morningstar uses the S&P 500 Index as the basic benchmark for stock-oriented funds, including moderate- and conservative-allocation funds and convertible-bond funds. The Lehman Brothers Aggregate Bond Index is used as the benchmark index for all bond funds. We also provide a comparison with a secondary, specialized benchmark. Because the S&P 500 Index is composed almost entirely of large-cap domestic stocks, it is a good performance measure for large-cap domestic-stock funds and the overall market, but other comparisons are less useful. Comparing a foreign large-value fund with the S&P 500 Index, for example, does not show how the fund has done relative to foreign stock markets, so a fund's total return in the History and Performance sections is compared with a more specialized index.

Investment Style Box
see also Current Investment Style, Growth, Investment Style History, Market Capitalization, Morningstar Category, and Value
To help investors cut through the confusion and profusion of fund types, Morningstar designed the style box, a visual tool for better understanding a fund's true investment strategy. Based on an analysis of a fund's portfolio, the Morningstar style box is a snapshot of the types of securities held by the fund. The style box is calculated with methodology similar to that used to assign the Morningstar categories. By providing an easy-to-understand visual representation of stock and fund characteristics, the Morningstar style box allows for informed comparisons and portfolio construction based on actual holdings, as opposed to assumptions based on a fund's name or how it is marketed. The style box also forms the basis for Morningstar's style-based fund categories and market indexes.

Domestic-Stock Style Box
The Morningstar domestic-stock style box is a nine-square grid that provides a graphical representation of the "investment style" of stocks and mutual funds. It classifies securities according to market capitalization (the vertical axis) and growth and value factors (the horizontal axis). Note: Fixed-income funds are classified according to credit quality (the vertical axis) and sensitivity to changes in interest rates (the horizontal axis).

Stock Style Box

Risk	Investment Style: Value	Blend	Growth	Average Weighted Market Capitalization
Low	Large-cap Value	Large-cap Blend	Large-cap Growth	Large
Moderate	Mid-cap Value	Mid-cap Blend	Mid-cap Growth	Mid
High	Small-cap Value	Small-cap Blend	Small-cap Growth	Small

Within the stock style box grid, nine possible combinations exist, ranging from large-cap value for the safest funds to small-cap growth for the riskiest.

How It Works
Style box assignments begin at the individual stock level. Morningstar determines the investment style of each individual stock in its database. The style attributes of individual stocks are then used to determine the style classification of stock mutual funds.

The Horizontal Axis
The scores for a stock's value and growth characteristics determine its placement on the horizontal axis of the stock style box:

Value Score Components and Weights

Forward-looking measures	
Price-to-projected earnings	50.0%
Historical-based measures	
Price-to-book	12.5%
Price-to-sales	12.5%
Price-to-cash flow	12.5%
Dividend yield	12.5%

Growth Score Components and Weights

Forward-looking measures	
Long-term projected earnings growth	50.0%
Historical-based measures	
Historical earnings growth	12.5%
Sales growth	12.5%
Cash flow growth	12.5%
Book value growth	12.5%

Growth and value characteristics for each individual stock are compared to those of other stocks within the same capitalization band and are scored from zero to 100 for both value and growth. To determine the overall style score, the value score is subtracted from the growth score.

The resulting number can range from 100 (for low-yield, extremely growth-oriented stocks) to -100 (for high-yield, low-growth stocks). A stock is classified as growth if the net score equals or exceeds the "growth threshold" (normally about 25 for large-cap stocks). It is deemed value if its score equals or falls below the "value threshold" (normally about -15 for large-cap stocks).

And if the score lies between the two thresholds, the stock is classified as "core."

The thresholds between value, core, and growth stocks vary to some degree over time, as the distribution of stock styles changes in the market. However, on average, the three stock styles each account for approximately one third of the total free float in each size category.

The Vertical Axis

Rather than a fixed number of "large cap" or "small cap" stocks, Morningstar uses a flexible system that isn't adversely affected by overall movements in the market to classify stocks as small, medium, or large. Large-cap stocks are defined as the group that accounts for the top 70% of the capitalization of the Morningstar domestic-stock universe; mid-cap stocks represent the next 20%; and small-cap stocks represent the balance. The Morningstar stock universe represents approximately 99% of the U.S. market for actively traded stocks.

Moving from Individual Stocks to Funds

A stock fund is an aggregation of individual stocks and its style is determined by the style assignments of the stocks it owns. By plotting all of a fund's stocks on the stock style grid, the range of stock styles included in the fund immediately becomes apparent. An asset-weighted average of the stocks' net value/growth scores determines a fund's horizontal placement—value, growth, or blend.

A fund's vertical placement is determined by its "market cap," which is defined as the geometric mean of the market capitalization (or average weighted market cap) for the stocks it owns, where:

Cap1 = the capitalization of stock 1 and W1 = the % weight in the portfolio and the geometric mean of market capitalization $=(Cap1^{W1})(Cap2^{W2})(Cap3^{W3})(Cap4^{W4})\ldots(CapN^{WN})$

For a simple example, consider a fund that owns just three stocks:

25% stake in Stock A, market cap = $1.85 Billion
35% stake in Stock B, market cap = $3.56 Billion
40% stake in Stock C, market cap = $8.58 Billion

Its geometric mean of market capitalization would equal:

$(\$1.85\text{ bil}^{.25})(\$3.56\text{ bil}^{.35})(\$8.58\text{ bil}^{.40}) = \$4.30\text{ Billion}$

Note that this number is larger than the fund's median market cap—the capitalization of the median stock in its portfolio. That's because stock C, with a relatively higher market cap, occupies the biggest slice of the portfolio. The geometric mean better identifies the portfolio's "center of gravity." In other words, it provides more accurate insight into how market trends (as defined by capitalization) might affect the portfolio.

Style box assignments for stocks are updated each month. Assignments for funds are recalculated whenever Morningstar receives updated portfolio holdings for the fund.

Using the Style Box

In general, a growth-oriented fund will hold the stocks of companies that the portfolio manager believes will increase earnings faster than the rest of the market. A value-oriented fund contains mostly stocks the manager thinks are currently undervalued in price and will eventually see their worth recognized by the market. A blend fund might be a mix of growth stocks and value stocks, or it may contain stocks that exhibit both characteristics.

Understanding how different types of stocks behave is crucial for building a diversified, style-controlled portfolio of stocks or mutual funds. The Morningstar style box helps investors construct portfolios based on the characteristics, or style factors, of all the stocks and funds that portfolio includes.

Recent Methodology Changes

We made significant changes to the Style Box methodology for domestic stocks and stock funds, effective June 30, 2002. Previously, a stock or fund's horizontal placement within the Style Box was determined by two factors—its combined relative price/book and price/earnings ratios. Our new system uses an enhanced 10-factor model, with separate scores for value and growth characteristics. The new methodology better measures the characteristics of individual stocks and is also more in line with the way portfolio managers look at stocks.

We also made changes to the way we determine capitalization bands and calculate a fund's market capitalization. Instead of basing the size breakpoints using a specific number of stocks, Morningstar now defines large-cap stocks as those that account for the top 70% of the domestic-stock market, mid-cap stocks as those that account for the next 20%, and small caps for the remaining 10%.

For mutual funds, we switched from using median market capitalization to the geometric mean of market capitalization (or average weighted market-cap). The latter method results in a number that better represents how market trends (as defined by capitalization) might affect the portfolio.

International-Stock Style Box

These style boxes are similar to the domestic-stock style boxes described above, although the methodology is different.

On the vertical axis, international-stock funds are grouped as small, medium, or large. Funds with median market capitalizations of less than $1 billion are grouped in the small-cap box. Funds with median market caps equal to or greater than $1 billion but less than or equal to $5 billion are labeled as mid-cap offerings. Funds with median market caps exceeding $5 billion are large cap.

On the horizontal axis, international-stock funds, like their domestic counterparts, are separated into value, blend, or growth funds. We take the stock portfolio's average price/cash-flow ratio relative to the MSCI EAFE Index and add it to the portfolio's average price/book figure relative to the MSCI EAFE Index. (The MSCI EAFE average in each case is set equal to 1.00.) If the sum of the relative price/cash flow and the relative price/book is less than 1.75, the fund is defined as a value offering; if the sum lands from 1.75 to 2.25, the fund is classified as a blend vehicle; if the sum is greater than 2.25, the fund falls into the growth column.

Bond Style Box

Domestic- and international-bond funds feature their own Morningstar style box, which focuses on two pillars of bond performance: interest-rate sensitivity and credit quality. Morningstar splits bond funds into three groups of rate sensitivity as determined by duration (short, intermediate, and long) and three credit-quality groups (high, medium, and low). These groupings graphically display a portfolio's average effective duration and credit quality. As with stock funds, nine possible combinations exist, ranging from short duration/high quality for the safest funds to long duration/low quality for the more volatile.

Bond Style Box

Risk	Duration: Value	Blend	Growth	Quality
Low	Short-term High Quality	Interm-term High Quality	Long-term High Quality	High
Moderate	Short-term Medium Quality	Interm-term Medium Quality	Long-term Medium Quality	Medium
High	Short-term Low Quality	Interm-term Low Quality	Long-Term Low Quality	Low

Within the bond style box grid, nine possible combinations exist, ranging from short duration or maturity/high quality for the safest funds to long duration or maturity/low quality for the riskiest.

Along the horizontal axis of the style box lies the interest-rate sensitivity of a fund's bond portfolio based on average effective duration. This figure, which is calculated by the fund companies, weights each bond's duration by its relative size within the portfolio. Duration provides a more accurate description of a bond's true interest-rate sensitivity than does maturity because it takes into consideration all mortgage prepayments, puts and call options, and adjustable coupons. Funds with an average effective duration of less than 3.5 years qualify as short term. Funds with an average effective duration of greater than or equal to 3.5 years and less than or equal to six years are classified as intermediate. Funds with an average effective duration of greater than six years are considered long term. (The duration ranges are slightly different for municipal-bond funds: Less than 4.5 years is short term; 4.5 to seven years is intermediate; greater than seven years is long term.)

If duration data are not available, Morningstar will use average effective maturity figures to calculate the fund's style box. Although duration is the more accurate measurement, maturity can also be used to gauge the amount of interest-rate risk in a fund's portfolio. Funds with an average effective maturity of less than four years qualify as short term. Funds with bonds that have an average effective maturity greater than or equal to four years but less than or equal to 10 years are categorized as intermediate, and those with maturity that exceeds 10 years are long term.

Along the vertical axis of a bond style box lies the average credit-quality rating of a bond portfolio. Funds that have an average credit rating of AAA or AA are categorized as high quality. Bond portfolios with average ratings of A or BBB are medium quality, and those rated BB and below are categorized as low quality. For the purposes of Morningstar's calculations, U.S. government securities are considered AAA bonds, nonrated municipal bonds generally are classified as BB, and all other nonrated bonds generally are considered B.

For hybrid categories, both stock and bond style boxes appear on the page.

Investment Style History

see also Investment Style Box

A fund's Morningstar style box can change over time, perhaps because of a manager or strategy change or because market forces affect a portfolio's price ratios. To give investors an idea of how a fund's investment style has varied, a row of style boxes is included above the Performance Graph section. Each style box shows where a fund placed at the end of the calendar year. This feature chronicles such aspects as consistency in investment style, or it may help explain why a stock fund did especially well or poorly during growth- or value-driven periods. It could also shed light on why a bond fund performed well or poorly in periods when lower-quality issues were in favor.

Investment Value

see Performance

IRA Purchase

see Minimum Purchase

L

Load

see also Expenses and Fees

Load denotes either a fund's maximum initial or deferred sales charge. For initial, or front-end, loads, this figure is expressed as a percentage of the initial investment and is incurred upon purchase of fund shares. For deferred sales charges (also known as back-end loads or contingent deferred sales charges), the amount charged is based on the lesser of the initial or final value of the shares sold. If the fund does not have a load and remains open to investors, None appears. We list 12b-1 only in this space if the fund has no sales fees, but does have a 12b-1 fee. If the fund no longer offers shares to new investors, Closed is listed here. A percentage followed by a W indicates that, at the time of publication, the fund is waiving its load for the general public.

Load-Adjusted Return %

For this statistic, total returns are adjusted downward to account for sales charges and are listed for the trailing one-, three-, five-, and 10-year periods. For funds with front-end loads, the full amount of the load is deducted. For deferred, or back-end loads, the percentage charged often declines the longer shares are held. This charge, often coupled with a 12b-1 fee, usually disappears entirely after several years. Morningstar adjusts the deferred load accordingly when making this calculation. For funds that lack a 10-year history, we provide an annualized load-adjusted return figure for the period since the fund's inception.

M

Management Fee

see Expenses and Fees

Manager

see Portfolio Manager

Manager Change

see also Portfolio Manager

It is important for investors to know how much of a fund's performance can be attributed to current management. We track manager changes by using two symbols, which indicate when a full or partial manager change has occurred. The symbol (▼) marks a total manager change, when an entirely new manager or team of co-managers assumed fund leadership. The symbol (▽) indicates a partial change, when at least one manager remains with the fund while another joins or leaves.

Market Cap

see also Market Capitalization

Shown for domestic-stock funds, this section gives investors a view of the different sizes of companies in a fund's portfolio. Every month, we break down a stock portfolio into five different sizes of companies by their market capitalization and show what percentage of a fund's stock assets is devoted to each. Instead of using stationary market-cap cutoffs, we base our boundaries on percentiles: We call the largest 1% of U.S. companies Giant, the next 4% Large, the next 15% Medium, the next 30% Small, and the bottom 50% Micro. The Market Cap section is designed to help investors complete the picture suggested by the median market cap statistic. While average weighted market cap pinpoints the size of the average holding, this section allows investors to see the whole range of companies held by the fund.

Market Capitalization (Average Weighted)
see also Market Cap and Relative Comparisons
For domestic-stock offerings, this measures the portfolio's "center of gravity," in terms of its market-cap exposure. A market capitalization is calculated for each stock. Its weight in the average weighted market cap calculation is then determined by the percentage of stocks it consumes in the overall portfolio. For example, a stock that is a 10% position in a fund will have twice as much influence on the calculation than a stock that is a 5% stake. See Investment Style Box for a more-detailed explanation.

Maturity
see Average Effective Maturity and Average Nominal Maturity

Mean
see Standard Deviation

Minimum Automatic Investment Plan
(Min Auto Inv Plan)
This indicates the smallest amount with which an investor may enter a fund's automatic-investment plan—an arrangement where the fund takes money on a monthly, quarterly, semiannual, or annual basis from the shareholder's checking account. Often, the normal minimum initial purchase requirements are waived in lieu of this systematic investment plan. Studies indicate that regular automatic investment (also known as dollar-cost averaging) can be a very successful investment plan for long-term investors.

Minimum Purchase
Minimum purchase indicates the smallest investment amount a fund will accept to establish a new account. Also noted is the smallest additional purchase a fund will accept in an existing account (this figure follows the designation ADD). None indicates initial or additional investments can be of any amount. In addition, we include the smallest permissible initial investment a fund will accept in an individual retirement account (IRA). If the fund does not offer an IRA program, N/A will appear.

Modern Portfolio Theory Statistics
Alpha, beta, and R-squared are components of Modern Portfolio Theory (MPT), which is a standard financial and academic method for assessing the performance of a fund, relative to a benchmark. To understand how to use MPT stats, readers unfamiliar with them may want to begin with the following explanation of R-squared, then move to beta, and finally to alpha. The three statistics should be used in combination with one another.

Morningstar bases alpha, beta, and R-squared on a least-squares regression of the fund's excess return over Treasury bills compared with the excess returns of the fund's benchmark index (the S&P 500 for stock-oriented funds and the Lehman Brothers Aggregate Bond Index for bond funds). These calculations are computed for the trailing 36-month period.

Morningstar also shows additional alpha, beta, and R-squared statistics based on a regression against the Best Fit Index. The Best Fit Index for each fund is selected based on the highest R-squared result from separate regressions on a number of indexes. (See also Best Fit Index for descriptions. If the standard index already has the highest R-squared, it will be shown again as the Best Fit Index.) For example, many high-yield funds show low R-squared results and thus a low degree of correlation when regressed against the standard bond index, the Lehman Brothers Aggregate. These low R-squared results indicate that the index does not explain well the behavior of most high-yield funds. Most high-yield funds, however, show significantly higher R-squared results when regressed against the CSFB High-Yield Bond Index.

Both the standard and best-fit results can be useful to investors. The standard index R-squared statistics can help investors plan the diversification of their portfolio of funds. For example, an investor who wishes to diversify and already owns a fund with a very high correlation (and thus a high R-squared) with the S&P 500 might choose not to buy another fund that correlates closely to that index. In addition, the Best Fit Index can be used to compare the betas and alphas of similar funds that show the same Best Fit Index.

Alpha
Alpha measures the difference between a fund's actual returns and its expected performance, given its level of risk (as measured by beta). A positive alpha figure indicates the fund has performed better than its beta would predict. In contrast, a negative alpha indicates a fund has underperformed, given the expectations established by the fund's beta. Many investors see alpha as a measurement of the value added or subtracted by a fund's manager.

There are limitations to alpha's ability to accurately depict a fund's added or subtracted value. In some cases, a negative alpha can result from the expenses that are present in the fund figures but are not present in the figures of the comparison index. Alpha is completely dependent on the accuracy of beta: If the investor accepts beta as a conclusive definition of risk, a positive alpha would be a conclusive indicator of good fund performance.

Beta

Beta is a measure of a fund's sensitivity to market movements. It measures the relationship between a fund's excess return over T-bills and the excess return of the benchmark index. Morningstar calculates beta using the same regression equation as the one used for alpha, which regresses excess return for the fund against excess return for the index. This approach differs slightly from other methodologies that rely on a regression of raw returns.

By definition, the beta of the benchmark (in this case, an index) is 1.00. Accordingly, a fund with a 1.10 beta has performed 10% better than its benchmark index after deducting the T-bill rate in up markets and 10% worse in down markets, assuming all other factors remain constant. Conversely, a beta of 0.85 indicates that the fund has performed 15% worse than the index in up markets and 15% better in down markets. A low beta does not imply that the fund has a low level of volatility, though; rather, a low beta means only that the fund's market-related risk is low. A specialty fund that invests primarily in gold, for example, will usually have a low beta (and a low R-squared), as its performance is tied more closely to the price of gold and gold-mining stocks than to the overall stock market. Thus, although the specialty fund might fluctuate wildly because of rapid changes in gold prices, its beta will remain low.

R-squared

R-squared ranges from 0 to 100 and reflects the percentage of a fund's movements that are explained by movements in its benchmark index. An R-squared of 100 means that all movements of a fund are completely correlated with movements in the index. Thus, index funds that invest only in S&P 500 stocks will have an R-squared very close to 100. Conversely, a low R-squared indicates that very few of the fund's movements are explained by movements in its benchmark index. An R-squared measure of 35, for example, means that only 35% of the fund's movements can be explained by movements in its benchmark index. Therefore, R-squared can be used to ascertain the significance of a particular beta or alpha. Generally, a high R-squared will indicate a more reliable beta figure. If the R-squared is low, then the beta explains less of the fund's performance.

Morningstar Category

see also Historical Profile and Investment Style Box

While the investment objective stated in a fund's prospectus may or may not reflect how the fund actually invests, the Morningstar Category is assigned based on the underlying securities in each portfolio. We assign categories based on three years of composition and style boxes. For funds that are not yet three years old we use an average of the portfolios since the fund's inception.

The Morningstar Category helps investors make meaningful comparisons between funds. The categories make it easier to build well-diversified portfolios, assess potential risk, and identify the top-performing funds.

The following is a list and explanation of the categories. We place funds in a given category based on their portfolio statistics and compositions over the past three years. If the fund is new and has no portfolio history, we estimate where it will fall before giving it a more permanent category assignment. When necessary, we may change a category assignment based on recent changes to the portfolio.

Stock Funds

Domestic-Stock Funds

Funds with at least 70% of assets in domestic stocks are categorized based on the style and size of the stocks they typically own. The style and size divisions reflect those used in the investment style box: value, blend, or growth style and small, medium, or large. Based on their investment style over the past three years, diversified domestic-stock funds are placed in one of the nine categories shown below:

Large Growth	Mid-cap Growth	Small Growth
Large Blend	Mid-cap Blend	Small Blend
Large Value	Mid-cap Value	Small Value

Morningstar also includes several other domestic-stock categories:

Communications, Financial, Health Care, Natural Resources, Precious Metals, Real Estate, Technology, Utilities, Convertible Bond (convertible-bond funds have at least 50% of their assets invested in convertible securities), Conservative Allocation (conservative-allocation funds invest in both stocks and bonds, with just 20% to 50% of assets in stocks), and Moderate Allocation (moderate-allocation funds invest in both stocks and bonds, with more than 50% in stocks).

International-Stock Funds

Stock funds that have invested 40% or more of their equity holdings in foreign stocks (on average over the past three years) are placed in an international-stock category, based on the following parameters:

Europe: at least 75% of stocks invested in Europe.

Latin America: at least 75% of stocks invested in Latin America.

Diversified Emerging Markets: at least 50% of stocks invested in emerging markets.

Diversified Asia/Pacific: at least 65% of stocks invested in Pacific countries, with at least an additional 10% of stocks invested in Japan.

Asia/Pacific ex-Japan: at least 75% of stocks in Pacific countries, with less than 10% of stocks invested in Japan.

Japan: at least 75% of stocks invested in Japan.

Foreign Large Value: a majority of assets invested in large-cap foreign stocks that are value-oriented (based on low price/book and price/cash flow ratios, relative to the MSCI EAFE Index).

Foreign Large Blend: a majority of assets invested in large-cap foreign stocks, where neither growth nor value characteristics predominate.

Foreign Large Growth: a majority of assets invested in large-cap foreign stocks that are growth-oriented (based on high price/book and price/cash flow ratios, relative to the MSCI EAFE Index).

Foreign Small/Mid-Cap Value: a majority of assets invested in small- and mid-cap foreign stocks that are value-oriented (based on low price/book and price/cash flow ratios, relative to the MSCI EAFE Index).

Foreign Small/Mid-Cap Growth: a majority of assets invested in small- and mid-cap foreign stocks that are growth-oriented (based on high price/book and price/cash flow ratios, relative to the MSCI EAFE Index).

World: at least 40% of stock holdings invested in foreign stocks, with at least 10% of stocks invested in the United States.

World Allocation: a fund with stock holdings of greater than 20% but less than 70% of the portfolio where 40% of the stocks and bonds are foreign. Also, must have at least 10% of assets invested in bonds.

Bond Funds

Funds with 80% or more of their assets invested in bonds are classified as bond funds. Bond funds are divided into two main groups for classification purposes: taxable bond and municipal bond. Note: For all bond funds, maturity figures are used only when duration figures are unavailable.

Taxable-Bond Funds

Long-Term Government: at least 90% of bond portfolio invested in government issues with a duration of greater than six years, or an average effective maturity of greater than 10 years.

Intermediate-Term Government: at least 90% of bond portfolio invested in government issues with a duration of greater than or equal to 3.5 years and less than or equal to six years, or an average effective maturity of greater than or equal to four years and less than or equal to 10 years.

Short-Term Government: at least 90% of bond portfolio invested in government issues with a duration of greater than or equal to one year and less than 3.5 years, or an average effective maturity of greater than or equal to one year and less than four years.

Long-Term Bond: focuses on corporate and other investment-grade issues with an average duration of more than six years, or an average effective maturity of more than 10 years.

Intermediate-Term Bond: focuses on corporate and other investment-grade issues with an average duration of greater than or equal to 3.5 years but less than or equal to six years, or an average effective maturity of greater than or equal to four but less than or equal to 10 years.

Short-Term Bond: focuses on corporate and other investment-grade issues with an average duration of greater than or equal to one but less than 3.5 years, or an average effective maturity of greater than or equal to one but less than four years.

Ultrashort Bond: used for funds with an average duration or an average effective maturity of less than one year. This category includes general corporate and government bond funds, and excludes any international, convertible, multisector, and high-yield bond funds.

High-Yield Bond: at least 65% of assets in bonds rated below BBB.

Multisector Bond: seeks income by diversifying assets among several fixed-income sectors, usually U.S. government obligations, foreign bonds, and high-yield domestic debt securities.

Bank Loan: invests primarily in floating-rate bank loans instead of bonds. In exchange for their credit risk, they offer high interest payments that typically float above a common short-term benchmark.

World Bond: at least 40% of bonds invested in foreign markets.

Emerging-Markets Bond: at least 65% of assets in emerging-markets bonds.

Municipal-Bond Funds

High-Yield Municipal: Municipal fund that over the past three years has kept an average of 50% or more of assets in issues rated

BBB or below. For the purposes of this calculation, nonrated issues are considered to be high-yield debt.

Muni National Long-Term: a national fund with an average duration of more than seven years or an average maturity of more than 12 years.

Muni National Intermediate-Term/Short: a national fund with an average duration of between 4.5 years and seven years, or an average maturity of between five years and 12 years.

Muni New York Long-Term: a fund with at least 80% of assets in New York municipal debt, with an average duration of more than seven years or an average maturity of more than 12 years.

Muni New York Intermediate/Short: a fund with at least 80% of assets in New York municipal debt, with an average duration of between 4.5 years and seven years.

Muni California Long-Term: a fund with at least 80% of assets in California municipal debt, with an average duration of more than seven years or an average maturity of more than 12 years.

Muni California Intermediate/Short: a fund with at least 80% of assets in California municipal debt, with an average duration of between 4.5 years and seven years.

Muni Single-State Long-Term: a single-state fund with an average duration of more than seven years or an average maturity of more than 12 years.

Muni Single-State Intermediate-Term: a single-state fund with an average duration of between 4.5 years and seven years, or an average maturity of between five years and 12 years.

Muni National Short-Term: focuses on municipal debt/bonds with an average duration of less than 4.5 years or an average maturity of less than five years.

Morningstar Risk-Adjusted Rating
see Rating and Risk

Morningstar Style Box
see Investment Style Box

Morningstar's Take
The analysis interprets and enhances the numerical data that appear on the page in an effort to provide an assessment of a fund's worth. To accomplish this, a Morningstar analyst scrutinizes past shareholder reports, puts historical performance into the perspective of market trends, and whenever possible, interviews the fund manager or another fund official. Although many people are involved in producing the Morningstar page, the analyst is ultimately responsible for its content.

N

NAV
see Net Asset Value

Net Assets
see also Total Assets
This figure gives the fund's asset base, net of fees and expenses, at year-end of past calendar years and at month-end for the current year.

Net Asset Value
A fund's net asset value (NAV) represents its per-share price. A fund's NAV is derived by dividing the total net assets of the fund by the number of shares outstanding.

No-Load
see also Expenses and Fees
This label denotes the fund as a true no-load fund, charging no sales or 12b-1 fees.

NTF Plans
This indicates which No Transaction Fee programs offer the fund. Wrap programs are not included in this section.

O

Options / Futures / Warrants
see Special Securities

Other Measures
see Modern Portfolio Theory Statistics, Sharpe Ratio and Standard Deviation

P

Partial Manager Change
see Manager Change

P/E
see Price/Earnings Ratio

Percent of Assets (% Assets)
see % Assets entry in Portfolio Analysis

Percentile Rank (% Rank)

see also Performance

Located in the Performance and History sections, these rankings allow investors to compare a fund's total returns with those of other funds.

In the Performance section, we compare the fund's total return for various time periods against the same Morningstar Category (% Rank Cat). In the History section, we compare a fund's calendar-year total returns with its category's (Total Rtn % Rank Cat). In both sections, a fund's total returns are ranked on a scale from 1 to 100 where 1 represents the highest-returning 1% of funds and 100 represents the lowest-returning funds. Thus, in the Performance section, a percentile rank of 15 under the % Rank Cat column for the trailing three-month period indicates that the fund's three-month return placed in the top 15% of all funds in its category for that time period.

Performance

see also Percentile Rank, Tax Analysis, and Total Return

The tables in this section display the fund's total return figures for various time periods. The trailing total returns are as of the date listed in the section heading above. The trailing total returns are accompanied by relative statistics that allow readers to compare the returns with appropriate indexes and category averages.

Investment Value Graph

The Investment Value graph line shows a fund's performance trend, derived from the fund's historical growth of $10,000. It provides a visual depiction of how a fund has amassed its returns, including the performance swings its shareholders have endured along the way. The growth of $10,000 begins at the date of the fund's inception, or if the fund has been in existence for more than 12 years, then growth of $10,000 begins at the first year listed on the graph. Also, featured in the graph is the performance of an index (S&P 500 or MSCI EAFE), which allows investors to compare the performance of the fund with the performance of the benchmark index.

Quarterly Returns

The first section provides the fund's quarterly and year-end total returns for the past five years. The quarterly returns are compounded to obtain the year-end total return shown on the right. (Calculating the sum of the four quarterly returns will not produce the year-end total return because simple addition does not take into account the effects of compounding.)

Total Return %

see also Total Return for more information about the calculation

This figure is calculated by taking the change in net asset value, reinvesting all income and capital-gains distributions during the period, and dividing by the starting net asset value.

+/- S&P 500

see also Indexes for a complete list of the indexes and their abbreviations

This statistic measures the difference between a stock fund's total return and the total return of the S&P 500 Index. A negative number indicates that the fund underperformed the index by the given amount, while a positive number indicates that the fund outperformed the index by the given amount. For example, a listing of -2.0 indicates that the fund underperformed the index by 2 percentage points. The difference between each stock fund's performance and the S&P 500 Index is listed. Bond funds are compared with the Lehman Brothers Aggregate Bond Index. The next column shows the same performance figure relative to another more specialized benchmark index.

% Rank All/Cat

See also Percentile Rank

Morningstar lists two total return percentile rankings for each fund for various time periods. The first compares a fund with all funds in the Morningstar database (% Rank All), while the second compares the fund's total return for that period against the funds in the same Morningstar Category (% Rank Cat). In both cases 1 is the highest or best percentile ranking and 100 is the lowest, or worst.

Growth of $10,000

This column shows the current value of a $10,000 investment made at the beginning of each of the time periods listed. These calculations are not load- or tax-adjusted.

Performance Quartile Graph

The Performance Quartile graph is a representation of the fund's calendar-year total-return percentile rank among funds in the same category. A more specific version of this information is presented numerically in the History section (Total Rtn % Rank Cat). The black bar on the graph represents the quartile in which the fund's performance ranking falls. If the top quarter of the graph is shaded, for example, the fund performed among the top 25% of its category that year.

Portfolio Analysis

Occupying much of the right side of the page is the Portfolio Analysis section. Prominent in this section are the fund's most recently reported top securities (excluding cash and cash equivalents for all but short-term bond funds), ranked in descending order by the percentage of the portfolio's net assets they occupy. With this information, investors can more clearly identify what drives the fund's performance.

Morningstar makes every effort to gather the most up-to-date portfolio information from a fund. By law, however, funds need only report this information four times during a calendar year, and they have two months after the report date to actually release the shareholder report and portfolio. Therefore, it is possible that a fund's portfolio could be five months old or more at the time of publication. We print the date the portfolio was reported. Older portfolios should not be disregarded, however; although the list may not represent the exact current holdings of the fund, it may still provide a good picture of the overall nature of the fund's management style.

Items that pertain to the fund's portfolio are detailed below:

Total Stocks/Total Fixed-Income

Total Stocks indicates the total number of stock securities in a fund's portfolio, and Total Fixed-Income denotes the number of bond securities a fund holds. These do not simply refer to the stocks or bonds listed on the page; rather, they represent all stocks and bonds in the portfolio. These listings can be quite useful for gaining greater insight into the portfolio's diversification.

Share Change

Applied only to common stocks, the share change entry indicates the change in the number of shares of each stock from the previously reported portfolio. The share change column is dated and represents the change from the portfolio received just prior to the current one on the page. For stock funds, we indicate whether a fund has enlarged, reduced, or initiated new positions with the following symbols: (⊕) for purchases, (⊖) for sales, and (☼) for new holdings.

Security

This column lists the names of the stock or bond securities held as of the portfolio date. For stock holdings, this line typically displays just the name of the issuing company. Other stock labels are included where appropriate, such as ADR, which distinguishes an American Depositary Receipt. Bond holdings, however, will usually include more information to differentiate among the many types of bonds available. For most bonds, the coupon rate is listed as a percentage figure after the name of the bond. Adjustable-rate mortgages and floating-rate notes will have ARM or FRN (or IFRN for inverse-floating rate notes) listed after the name of the bond to indicate that the coupon rate is variable. Some adjustable-rate bond listings will include the formula by which the coupon rate is calculated, which is usually a fixed percentage plus some benchmark value. Securities followed by the abbreviation IO are interest-only securities, or those that consist only of the interest portion of a security, not the principal portion. PO indicates a principal-only security that sells at a discount to par and carries a coupon rate of zero.

Sector

see also Sector Weightings and Subsector Weightings

The industry sector of each stock holding is reported in this column. This gives investors greater insight into where a fund's top holdings are concentrated and where its vulnerabilities lie. For specialty funds, we list each stock's subsector.

P/E

see also Price/Earnings Ratio

To add depth to the average P/E number for the entire portfolio (listed under Current Investment Style), the P/E ratio for each stock is reported here. NMF means the stock's P/E is 100 or more. A dash means the company has no earnings or the figure is not available.

YTD Return %

The year-to-date stock returns show whether one or two big winners (or losers) are driving fund performance, or a lot of little successes. In some cases, losses in top holdings can suggest a bargain-hunting strategy if a position in a losing stock is new or expanded.

% Assets

The % Assets column indicates what percentage of the portfolio's net assets a given security constitutes. Morningstar calculates the percentage of net assets figure by dividing the market value of the security by the fund's total net assets. If a given security makes up a large percentage of the fund's net assets, the fund uses a concentrated portfolio strategy, at least with respect to the security in question. If, however, the percentage figures are low, then the manager is simply not willing to bet heavily on a particular security.

Date of Maturity

Maturity, located in the portfolio section for bond funds only, indicates the date on which a bond or note comes due. This information can be used in determining the portfolio's basic fixed-income strategy. For example, if most of these dates are a year or two away, the fund is taking a conservative, short-term approach. The maturity dates listed here, however, are not adjusted for calls (rights an issuer may have to redeem outstanding bonds before their scheduled maturity) or for the likelihood of mortgage prepayments. Thus, they might not accurately state the actual time to repayment of a bond, and might overstate a portfolio's sensitivity to interest-rate changes.

See Average Effective Duration for a better measure of interest-rate sensitivity.

Amount

Found on bond-fund pages, the amount column refers to the size of the fund's investment in a given security as of the portfolio date listed above. The size is enumerated in thousands. For bonds, this figure reflects the principal value of the security in thousands of dollars.

Value

Value simply gives the market value of a particular security in thousands of dollars as of the portfolio date. The value column allows investors to gauge whether a fixed-income security is selling at a premium or a discount to its face value, as reflected in the amount column.

Portfolio Manager (s)

see also Manager Change

The portfolio manager is the individual or individuals responsible for the overall fund strategy; as well as the buying and selling decisions for the securities in a fund's portfolio. To help investors know who is running a fund, we detail management with a brief biography. We note the manager's background, experience, analytical support, other funds managed, and whether the manager invests in his or her own fund.

Potential Capital Gain Exposure

see Tax Analysis

Price/Book Ratio

see also Relative Comparisons

The price/book ratio of a fund is the weighted average of the price/book ratios of all the stocks in a fund's portfolio. Book value is the total assets of a company, less total liabilities. A company's P/B ratio is calculated by dividing the market price of its outstanding stock by the company's book value, and then adjusting for the number of shares outstanding. (Stocks with negative book values are excluded from this calculation.) In computing a fund's average P/B ratio, Morningstar weights each portfolio holding by the percentage of equity assets it represents; larger positions thus have proportionately greater influence on the final P/B. A low P/B may indicate that the stocks are bargains, priced below what the companies assets could be worth if liquidated.

Price/Cash Flow

see also Relative Comparisons

Price/cash flow is a weighted average of the price/cash flow ratios of the stocks in a fund's portfolio. Price/cash flow represents the amount of money an investor is willing to pay for a dollar of cash generated from a particular company's operations. Price/cash flow shows the ability of a business to generate cash and can be an effective gauge of liquidity and solvency. Because accounting conventions differ among nations, reported earnings (and thus P/B ratios) may not be comparable across national boundaries. Price/cash flow attempts to provide an internationally standardized measure of a firm's stock price relative to its financial performance. In computing the average, Morningstar weights each portfolio holding by the percentage of stock assets it represents; larger positions thus have proportionately greater influence on the fund's final price/cash flow ratio.

Price/Earnings Ratio

see also Relative Comparisons

The price/earnings ratio of a fund is the weighted average of the price/earnings ratios of the stocks in a fund's portfolio. The P/E ratio of a company, which is a comparison of the price of the company's stock and its estimated earnings per share, is calculated by dividing these two figures. In computing the average, Morningstar weights each portfolio holding by the percentage of stock assets it represents; larger positions thus have proportionately greater influence on the fund's final P/E. A high P/E usually indicates that the market will pay more to obtain the company's earnings because it believes in the firm's ability to increase its earnings. (P/E can also be artificially inflated if a company has very weak earnings, which may be temporary. For example, during recessions, cyclical firms' earnings fall and their P/Es rise.) A low P/E indicates the market has less confidence that the company's earnings will increase; however, a fund manager with a value investing approach may believe such stocks have been overlooked or undervalued and have potential for appreciation.

Pricing Service

Because the municipal-bond market contains a very large number of issues, many of which are small and obscure, it is common for muni funds to hold bonds that are rarely traded. In fact, some muni funds will buy up the whole supply of a municipal bond when it is issued and hold it to maturity, ensuring that the bond never trades at all. If a bond isn't traded, it has no current market price. Yet, mutual funds must calculate their net asset values at the end of every day. Most funds thus rely on an independent pricing service to estimate the prices of these bonds based on each day's market activity. Here we name the pricing service a fund uses, the most common of which are J.J. Kenny, Muller, and Interactive Data. A few funds simply estimate bond prices internally. In such cases, we designate those funds accordingly.

Profitability Measures

Return on Assets (ROA)

This measures how effectively companies use their assets to generate profits. The formula for an individual firm is net income divided by assets. Companies with high returns on assets include software firms and beverage companies. Both types of companies frequently generate high profits but have relatively small investments in plant, equipment, and other assets. Firms with low returns on assets are typically in manufacturing or other capital-intensive industries. Companies with low returns on assets tend to have low valuations and are mostly held by value funds; by contrast, growth managers favor firms with high returns on assets. A fund's ROA is equal to the weighted average ROA of its individual holdings.

Return on Equity (ROE)

This calculation reveals how effectively management has invested shareholders' equity, which is the amount of money initially invested in the business plus retained earnings. ROE is simply net income divided by average shareholder equity. A high ROE is often a sign that a company's management uses its resources wisely, and the company is often located in a growing industry with high barriers to entry. For example, thanks to its dominance of the software operating-systems market, Microsoft usually sports high ROEs. By contrast, companies with low ROEs frequently operate in stagnant industries where there is overcapacity. For example, automakers frequently earn low returns on equity. Companies with high ROEs generally have better business models, but as a reflection of that, their share prices are often expensive. Growth managers typically prefer companies with high and rising ROEs, while valuation concerns may lead value managers to buy firms with low ROEs. A fund's ROE is the weighted average of its individual holdings' ROEs.

Net Margin

We arrive at net margin by dividing a firm's net income (after all expenses, including taxes) by its sales. This measures how effective a company is at wringing profits out of each dollar of revenues. Companies with high net margins tend to have strong competitive positions, while those with low net margins often operate in highly price-competitive industries such as retailing. Companies that consistently earn high net margins include pharmaceuticals and successful software companies. Low-margin businesses include supermarkets and other retailers. High-margin firms earn superior returns but also garner premium valuations, so the stocks are often too expensive for value managers. At the fund level, net margin represents the weighted average of the individual stocks' net margins.

R

Rank

see Percentile Rank

Rating and Risk

see also Historical Profile

In this section, Morningstar includes load-adjusted returns and several risk measures and proprietary statistics.

Morningstar Return

An assessment of a fund's excess return over a risk-free rate (the return of the 90-day Treasury bill) in comparison to similar funds, after adjusting for all applicable loads and sales charges. In each Morningstar Category, the top 10% of funds earn a High Morningstar Return, the next 22.5% Above Average, the middle 35% Average, the next 22.5% Below Average, and the bottom 10% Low. Morningstar Return is measured for up to three time periods (three, five, and 10 years). These separate measures are then weighted and averaged to produce an overall measure for the fund. Funds with less than three years of performance history are not rated.

Morningstar Risk

An assessment of the variations in a fund's monthly returns in comparison to similar funds, with an emphasis on downward variation. The greater the variation, the larger the risk score. If two funds have precisely the same return, the one with greater variations in its return is given the larger risk score. In each Morningstar Category, the 10% of funds with the lowest measured risk are described as Low Risk, the next 22.5% Below Average, the middle 35% Average, the next 22.5% Above Average, and the top 10% High. Morningstar Risk is measured for up to three time periods (three, five, and 10 years). These separate measures are then weighted and averaged to produce an overall measure for the fund. Funds with less than three years of performance history are not rated.

Regional Exposure

All international-stock funds, as well as precious-metals funds, feature a regional exposure listing. This table displays the percentage of the fund's total net assets invested in the U.K./Western Europe, Japan, Asia ex-Japan, North America, and Latin America. Below the regional information on each page, we list the five largest country exposures. The information in this section is gathered from portfolios and is the most recent available.

Relative Comparisons

see also Market Capitalization, Price/Book Ratio, Price/Cash Flow, Price/Earnings Ratio, and Subsector Weightings

At various places in the Portfolio Analysis section, Morningstar shows how an individual fund compares with the average of all funds within its category (Rel Cat) or a benchmark index (Rel S&P 500). The category average (or index) is always set equal to 1.00. For example, a municipal-bond fund with a utilities weighting of 1.50 relative to its category has 50% more in utilities issues than its average peer. Stock statistics are displayed in comparison with the S&P 500 Index. In this case, 1.00 represents the index. A relative P/B ratio of 0.43, for example, indicates that the fund's P/B is 57% lower than that of the index.

Restricted/Illiquid Securities

see Special Securities

Return

see Historical Profile and Total Return

Risk

see Rating and Risk, Modern Portfolio Theory Statistics, and Standard Deviation

R-squared

see Modern Portfolio Theory Statistics

S

Sales Fees

see Expenses and Fees

Sector Analysis

For government-bond funds, which generally invest most of their assets in AAA rated securities, a Sector Analysis table replaces the Credit Analysis shown for other bond funds in the Portfolio Analysis section. The table indicates the percentage of bond assets held in various types of government bonds, including Treasuries, mortgage pass-throughs, adjustable-rate mortgages, and collateralized mortgage obligations. Because the government-bond market has become a virtual alphabet soup of acronyms, we've listed some definitions below.

Agency ARMs

These adjustable-rate mortgage securities are issued by the government agencies FNMA, FHLMC, or GNMA. All carry AAA credit ratings.

ARMs

These adjustable-rate mortgage bonds are backed by loans that reset periodically based on movements in market interest rates.

CMOs (collateralized mortgage obligations)

These derivative securities are created by chopping up mortgage pass-throughs or whole loans into various slices to redistribute the cash flows (both principal and interest payments) from the underlying bonds. The CMO category found on all government-bond pages except the adjustable-rate mortgage funds includes PACs (planned amortization class bonds), floating- and inverse floating-rate CMOs, and accrual or Z-tranche bonds, among other varieties.

Fixed CMOs

Collateralized mortgage obligations with fixed coupons.

FHLMC mortgages

These are mortgage pass-through securities issued by the Federal Home Loan Mortgage Corporation. Like FNMA issues, FHLMC pass-throughs are implicitly, but not explicitly, guaranteed by the U.S. government.

Fixed mortgages

These are bonds backed by a pool of mortgages. Coupon payments are established at the time of issuance.

Floating-Rate CMO
Collateralized mortgage obligations with floating-rate coupons that are reset to the movements in an index.

FNMA mortgages
These are mortgage pass-through securities issued by the Federal National Mortgage Association. FNMA mortgage pass-throughs are implicitly, but not explicitly, backed by the U.S. government.

GNMA mortgages
These are mortgage pass-through securities issued by the Government National Mortgage Association. These bonds are backed by the full faith and credit of the U.S. government.

IOs (interest-only securities)
These are mortgage-backed derivatives that receive some or all of the interest portion of the underlying mortgages, but no principal amounts. They typically sell at discounts and are very volatile. That's because when interest rates decline, homeowners may refinance and prepay their mortgages, which eliminates future interest payments on the mortgage principal, making the IO less valuable, if not worthless. When rates rise, however, these securities rise in value.

Other
For government-general or government-mortgage funds, this category includes holdings that don't fall into one of the six major categories (U.S. Treasuries, GNMA, FNMA, or FHLMC mortgages, CMOs, or ARMs). Typically, agency debentures compose the holdings in Other. These are bonds issued by FNMA and FHLMC to finance their activities and are not backed by pools of mortgages. For ARM funds, Other includes primarily U.S. Treasuries.

Private ARMs
These are adjustable-rate mortgage securities issued by an entity other than GNMA, FNMA, or FHLMC. They aren't necessarily riskier credits, but they can carry some liquidity risk.

U.S. Treasuries
This category includes any bond or note issued by the U.S. Treasury.

Fixed-Income Sector
The fixed-income sector illustrates the type of bonds a fund owns. These sectors help investors compare and understand the sector exposure of each mutual fund. This data is especially useful for comparing two funds that may be in the same Morningstar Category. The fixed-income sectors are calculated for all domestic taxable-bond portfolios. It is based on the securities in the most recent portfolio. This data shows the percentage of bond and cash assets invested in each of the 14 fixed-income sectors.

Morningstar groups all fixed-income assets into the following sectors:

U.S. Government
U.S. Treasuries
This sector includes all conventional fixed-rate debt issued by the Treasury department of the United States government (i.e. this sector excludes TIPS). Some examples of this type of debt are Treasury bonds and Treasury notes. Treasury bills are included under % Cash, because they mature in less than 12 months.

TIPS
TIPS are inflation-indexed debt issued by the U.S. Treasury. (The term TIPS derives from their former name, Treasury Inflation-Protected Securities.) These bonds have principal and coupon payments that are linked to movements in the Consumer Price Index. They are a defensive measure against expectations of inflation, which typically erodes the real yield of conventional bonds. Even if inflation fears are in check, these bonds can benefit when the yields fall on traditional Treasuries. These unique securities act very differently than any other fixed-rate bond, and their volatility can change over time, depending on the level of interest rates.

U.S. Agency
This sector includes debt securities issued by government agencies—such as the Federal National Mortgage Association (FNMA), also known as Fannie Mae, or the Federal Home Loan Mortgage Corporation (FHLMC), also known as Freddie Mac—to raise capital and finance their operations. These "debentures" are not secured by physical assets, so they differ from most of the mortgage bonds that are issued by these agencies.

Mortgage
Mortgage Pass-Throughs
These are fixed-income securities that represent a claim to the cash flows associated with a pool of mortgages. The bondholders are entitled to a share of the principal and interest payments paid by the homeowners. The majority of these bonds are issued by a government agency such as FNMA, GNMA, or FHLMC. A few private corporations and banks also securitize and package mortgages in this way, and those are also included in this sector.

Mortgage CMO

Collateralized mortgage obligations (CMO) are similar to pass-through mortgage securities, but investors have more control over whether they will be paid sooner or later. CMOs are structured by time, so that some investors can line up for the first series of cash flow payments, while others may choose to put themselves at the end of the line. A fund manager would buy a late-paying CMO if they believed that there would be a lot of mortgage refinancing in the near term. This would protect the fund from getting its money back too early, which would require it to be reinvested at a lower interest rate. Most CMOs are based on mortgages from government agencies, such as FNMA and GNMA.

Mortgage ARM

Adjustable-rate mortgage (ARM) securities are backed by residential home mortgages where the interest rate is reset periodically in relation to a benchmark. Most ARMs are from government agencies, such as FNMA and GNMA.

Credit

U.S. Corporate

This sector includes all fixed-income securities that are issued by corporations domiciled in the United States. Corporate bonds are issued with a wide range of coupon rates and maturity dates.

Asset-Backed

Asset-backed securities are based on the expected cash flow from such things as auto loans, credit-card receivables, and computer leases. The cash flows for asset-backed securities can be fixed (e.g. auto loans have a defined payment schedule and a fixed maturity) or variable (credit-card debt is paid at random intervals). These securities typically range in maturity from two to seven years.

Convertible

Convertible bonds give the owner an opportunity to convert the bond to a certain number of shares of common stock at a certain price. As the stock approaches that price, the option to convert becomes more valuable and the price of the convertible bond also rises. These securities usually provide lower interest payments, because the option to convert to stock could potentially be quite valuable at some point in the future.

Municipal

Local and state governments issue municipal bonds in order to raise money for operations and development. This financing is sometimes used to build or upgrade hospitals, sewer systems, schools, housing, stadiums, or industrial complexes. Some municipal bonds are backed by the issuing entity while others are linked to a revenue stream, such as from a tollway or a utility. Municipal bonds are exempt from federal tax and often from state and local taxes, too. The tax break allows municipal governments to sell the bonds at a lower interest rate, because the investor gets an additional tax benefit.

Corporate Inflation-Protected

Inflation-protected securities are similar to TIPS, but they are issued by a private entity rather than by the U.S. government. These bonds are linked to an index of inflation, and the principal and coupon payments increase when inflation increases. As with TIPS, these securities behave quite differently than conventional bonds.

Foreign

Foreign Corporate

These fixed-income securities are issued by corporations that are based outside of the United States.

Foreign Government

These fixed-income securities are issued by governments outside the United States.

Cash

Cash can be cash in the bank, certificates of deposit, currency, or money market holdings. Cash can also be any fixed-income securities that mature in less than 12 months. Cash also includes commercial paper and any repurchase agreements held by the fund. Because this data point is based on only the cash and bond assets in the fund, it can be different than the % Cash in the composition breakdown, which is expressed as a percent of total assets.

Sector Weightings/Economic Spheres

see also Subsector Weightings

Morningstar divides the stock market into three broad "economic spheres," each of which contains four specific industry sectors. Sectors are based on what companies actually do. That is, unlike some other sector classification systems, sectors aren't based on expected behavior of the stocks of these companies.

The economic spheres with their major inclusive sectors are as follows:

Information Sphere

Made up of the Software, Hardware, Media, and Telecommunications sectors.

Service Sphere
Made up of the Health Care, Consumer Services, Business Services, and Financial Services sectors.

Manufacturing Sphere
Made up of the Consumer Goods, Industrial Materials, Energy, and Utilities sectors.

The sectors with their major inclusive industries are as follows:

Software
Companies engaged in the design and marketing of computer operating systems and applications. Examples include Microsoft, Oracle, and Siebel Systems.

Hardware
Manufacturers of computer equipment, communication equipment, semiconductors, and components. Examples include IBM, Cisco Systems, and Intel.

Media
Companies that own and operate broadcast networks and those that create content or provide it for other media companies. Examples include Time Warner, Walt Disney, and Washington Post.

Telecommunications
Companies that provide communication services using fixed-line networks or those that provide wireless access and services. Examples include SBC Communications, AT&T, and Alltel.

Health Care
Includes biotechnology, pharmaceuticals, research services, HMOs, home health, hospitals, assisted living, and medical equipment and supplies. Examples include Abbott Laboratories, Merck, and Cardinal Health.

Consumer Services
Includes retail stores, personal services, home builders, home supply, travel and entertainment companies, and educational providers. Examples include Wal-Mart, Home Depot, and Expedia.

Business Services
Includes advertising, printing, publishing, business support, consultants, employment, engineering and construction, security services, waste management, distributors, and transportation. Examples include Manpower, R.R. Donnelley, and Southwest Airlines.

Financial Services
Includes banks, finance companies, money-management firms, savings and loans, securities brokers, and insurance companies. Examples include Citigroup, Washington Mutual, and Fannie Mae.

Consumer Goods
Companies that manufacture or provide food, beverages, household and personal products, apparel, shoes, textiles, autos and auto parts, consumer electronics, luxury goods, packaging, and tobacco. Examples include PepsiCo, Ford Motor, and Kraft Foods.

Industrial Materials
Includes aerospace and defense firms, companies that provide or manufacture chemicals, machinery, building materials, and commodities. Examples include Boeing, DuPont, and Alcoa.

Energy
Companies that produce or refine oil and gas, oilfield services and equipment companies, and pipeline operators. Examples include ExxonMobil, Schlumberger, and BP Amoco.

Utilities
Electric, gas, and water utilities. Examples include Duke Energy, Exelon, and El Paso.

Sector weightings are also calculated in-house for municipal-bond funds. Although they are generally listed in order of descending credit risk, the categories are not as neatly divided as the stock sector weightings. General obligation bonds, which garner income from the municipality's tax revenues, are listed first (though some perceive these as risky if the issuing municipality is shaky). Revenue-based municipal-bond sectors follow. Near the bottom of the list are lease-backed and industrial-activity bonds, which are generally considered more risky for investors to hold. Demand notes, however, are unrelated to the other types of municipal bonds and hold little credit risk due to their short durations.

The municipal-bond classifications are as follows:

General Obligation
General obligation bonds, which are repaid from general revenue and borrowings rather than from the revenue of a specific project or facility.

Utilities
Electricity, gas, nuclear power, dams, telephones.

Health
Hospitals, nursing homes, retirement facilities.

Water/Waste
Water, sewers, sanitation, irrigation, drainage.

Housing
Single and multifamily housing.

Education
Colleges and universities, independent and unified school districts, student loans, tuition.

Transportation
Transportation by air, water, road, or railroad.

COP/Lease
Certificates of participation and lease bonds, used to finance a variety of public endeavors.

Industrial
Economic and industrial development, pollution control, resource recovery, conventions, expositions, stadiums, hotels (typically backed by a business or corporation rather than by a municipality).

Misc Revenue
Miscellaneous revenue bonds.

Demand
Short-term municipal securities.

SEC Yield
see also Yield
SEC yield is a standardized figure that the Securities and Exchange Commission requires funds to use to calculate rates of income return on a fund's capital investment. SEC yield is an annualized calculation that is based on a trailing 30-day period. This figure will often differ significantly from Morningstar's other yield figure, which reflects trailing 12-month distributed yield, because of differing time periods as well as differing accounting policies. For example, SEC yield is based on a bond's yield to maturity, which takes into account amortization of premiums and discounts, while Morningstar's distributed yield is based on what funds actually pay out.

Share Change
see Portfolio Analysis

Sharpe Ratio
The Sharpe ratio is a risk-adjusted measure developed by Nobel Laureate William Sharpe. It is calculated using standard deviation and excess return to determine reward per unit of risk. First, the average monthly return of the 90-day Treasury bill (over a 36-month period) is subtracted from the fund's average monthly return. The difference in total return represents the fund's excess return beyond that of the 90-day Treasury bill, a risk-free investment. An arithmetic annualized excess return is then calculated by multiplying this monthly return by 12. To show a relationship between excess return and risk, this number is then divided by the standard deviation of the fund's annualized excess returns. The higher the Sharpe ratio, the better the fund's historical risk-adjusted performance.

Short Sales
Short sales are bets that a stock will fall. To sell short, a mutual fund borrows shares from one party and then sells them to another on the open market. The fund's managers hope the stock drops, because they would be able to buy the shares back at a lower price and then return them to the lender. The difference between the original price and the price management pays to buy the shares back is the profit or loss. Short sales can slow returns in a rising market, but reduce losses or even produce gains in a falling market. One of the risks of short sales is that the maximum gain is 100%, but potential losses are unlimited.

Special Securities
This section shows a fund's exposure to a variety of complex or illiquid securities, including derivatives. The percentage of total net assets represented by each type of security is listed to the right of each group. Some securities may fall under more than one type.

Restricted/Illiquid Securities
Restricted and illiquid securities are issues that may be hard to accurately price and difficult to sell because an investor may be unable to find a buyer quickly. Private placement issues and 144(a) securities are both included here. Both types have varying degrees of liquidity and are exempt from some of the cumbersome registration and disclosure requirements that public offerings usually face.

Emerging-Markets Securities
Debt or equity securities from emerging markets are listed here. These figures are calculated from the most recently available portfolio. Anything aside from the following developed markets is considered emerging: Australia, Austria, Belgium, Canada, Denmark, Finland, France, Germany, Ireland, Italy, Japan, the Netherlands, New Zealand, Norway, Singapore, Spain, Sweden, Switzerland, the United

Kingdom, and the United States. This list is subject to change as markets become more developed or vice versa.

Exotic Mortgage-Backed Securities
This section indicates how much of a fund's net assets are held in unusual mortgage-backed derivatives. Specifically, we delineate those securities that see their price changes magnified when interest rates or mortgage-prepayment speeds change. Because not all mortgage-backed derivatives have these traits, we include the following: interest-only (IOs) and principal-only paper (POs), inverse floating-rate securities (IFRNs), and Z-tranche collateralized mortgage obligation issues, all of which are fairly clearly labeled in a fund's shareholder reports. Kitchen-sink bonds—a complex mix of interest-only bonds, principal-only bonds, and cast-off CMO tranches—are also tallied here. For stock funds, which rarely hold mortgage-backed issues of any kind, we combine exotic mortgage-backed securities with structured notes. Municipal-bond funds do not have an exotic mortgage-backed section in the Special Securities box.

Options/Futures/Warrants
Options and futures may be used speculatively, to leverage a portfolio, or cautiously, as a hedge against risk. We don't show the percentage of assets devoted to options or futures because it is difficult to determine from shareholder reports how much of a portfolio is affected by an options or futures contract. We also include forward contracts and warrants in this area.

Standard Deviation
Standard deviation is a statistical measure of the range of a fund's performance. When a fund has a high standard deviation, its range of performance has been very wide, indicating that there is a greater potential for volatility. The standard deviation figure provided here is an annualized statistic based on 36 monthly returns. By definition, approximately 68% of the time, the total returns of any given fund are expected to differ from its mean total return by no more than plus or minus the standard deviation figure. Ninety-five percent of the time, a fund's total returns should be within a range of plus or minus two times the standard deviation from its mean. These ranges assume that a fund's returns fall in a typical bell-shaped distribution. In any case, the greater the standard deviation, the greater the fund's volatility has been.

For example, an investor can compare two funds with the same average monthly return of 5%, but with different standard deviations. The first fund has a standard deviation of 2, which means that its range of returns for the past 36 months has typically remained between 1% and 9%. On the other hand, assume that the second fund has a standard deviation of 4 for the same period. This higher deviation indicates that this fund has experienced returns fluctuating between -3% and 13%. With the second fund, an investor can expect greater volatility.

Mean
The mean represents the annualized average monthly return from which the standard deviation is calculated. The mean will be the same as the annualized trailing, three-year return figure for the same time period.

Star Rating
see Historical Profile and Rating and Risk

Strategy
While the Morningstar Category gives investors an idea of what sorts of investments a manager makes, it does not fully capture the nuances of a manager's approach to picking stocks or bonds. In this section, Morningstar analysts explain what criteria a manager uses in selecting securities and how risky a given approach may be. On the equity side, the strategy description often focuses on what size and type of company a manager prefers, along with a discussion regarding how he or she balances growth and value factors. With bond funds, the strategy section explains whether the manager makes interest-rate and credit-quality bets, or whether management attempts to add value with individual security selection.

Style Box
see Investment Style Box

Subadvisor
In some cases, a fund's advisor employs another company, called a subadvisor, to handle the fund's day-to-day management. If the fund employs a subadvisor, the portfolio manager probably works for the fund's subadvisor, not the fund's advisor.

Subsector Weightings
see also Relative Comparisons and Sector Weightings
For specialty funds (also called sector funds), we replace the standard sector weightings, which include broad industry classifications such as hardware, with a breakdown of the fund's weightings in the sector's subindustries, or subsectors. Each sector has its own breakdown of subsectors, which can help investors decide which specific areas of an industry

the fund invests in, and how pure its focus is. The subsector weightings show at a glance whether a fund is conservatively diversified across a sector, betting on just a couple of risky subsectors to charge up returns, or crouching defensively in the mildest corner of the specialty. The fund's weightings relative to its category average are also shown.

Each specialty's breakdown also includes an Other classification, but a large weighting there shouldn't be interpreted as meaning the fund is investing outside of its specialty. This is merely a catchall designation to classify the stocks that don't meet the exact criteria for any specific subsector. It's impossible to capture every nook and cranny of the sprawling technology category, for example, in the eight subsectors included on the page. Thus, a fair number of tech stocks fall into Other.

Systematic Investment $
see Minimum Automatic Investment Plan

T

Tax-Adjusted Return %
see Tax Analysis

Tax Analysis
The information provided in the Tax Analysis section can be used to evaluate a fund's aftertax returns and its efficiency in achieving them. Additionally, the potential capital-gain exposure figure can provide a glimpse at a shareholder's vulnerability to taxation. All these figures can help an investor judge which funds have used tax-friendly strategies. They can also aid in deciding which funds are best suited to tax-deferred accounts and which serve better as taxable investments.

Tax-Adjusted Return
The Tax-Adj Rtn % column shows an estimate of a fund's annualized aftertax total return for the three-, five-, and 10-year periods, excluding any capital-gains effects that would result from selling the fund at the end of the period. Consistent with SEC guidance regarding tax-adjusted returns, these figures reflect the maximum load paid by fund shareholders. To determine this figure, all income and short-term (less than one year) capital-gain distributions are taxed at the maximum federal rate at the time of distribution. Long-term (more than one year) capital gains are taxed at a 20% rate. The aftertax portion is then reinvested in the fund. State and local taxes are ignored, and only the capital gains are counted for tax-exempt funds, because the income from these funds is nontaxable.

The category percentile rank (% Rank Cat) for each fund's tax-adjusted return is also listed. This ranking helps investors compare a fund's estimated aftertax performance with that of other funds in the category.

Tax-Cost Ratio
This represents the estimated percentage-point reduction in an annualized return that has resulted from income taxes over the past three-, five-, and 10-year periods. The calculation assumes investors pay the maximum federal rate on capital gains and ordinary income.

Potential Capital Gain Exposure
Morningstar calculates potential capital-gain exposure to give investors some idea of the potential tax consequences of their investment in a fund. We cannot predict what a fund's taxable distributions might be, but we can offer some clues based on a fund's liquidation liability. The figure shows whether a fund has consistently distributed taxable gains or has been relatively tax-efficient.

A mutual fund's assets are composed of paid-in (investment) capital, appreciation or depreciation of this capital, and any undistributed net income. Paid-in capital is simply the monies investors have put into the fund (which can decrease should shareholders decide to redeem their shares). Any appreciation of this capital may eventually be taxed. Our potential capital-gain exposure figure shows what percentage of a fund's total assets represent unrealized (or at least undistributed) capital appreciation.

Capital appreciation can be either unrealized or realized. In the first case, the fund's holdings have increased in value, but the fund has not yet sold these holdings; taxes are not due until the fund does so. Realized net appreciation (commonly called realized gains) represents actual gains achieved by the sale of holdings; taxes must be paid on these realized capital gains, which the fund must distribute each year if it can't offset them with realized losses. Unrealized appreciation may turn into realized gains at any time, should the fund's management decide to sell the profitable holdings. Thus, our formula includes unrealized appreciation as part of the potential capital-gain exposure.

A negative potential capital-gain exposure figure means that the fund has greater net losses than it has gains. This likely indicates that the fund has or will have a tax-loss carryforward, which would mean that some amount of future gains could be offset by past losses. Given the severity of the bear market that began in March 2000, many funds sport significant tax-loss carryforwards. In some cases, the negative capital-gains exposure may equal many times the net assets of the fund. For example, a fund with negative capital-gains exposure that is five times as great as the current net assets would have a capital-gains exposure figure of -500%.

To keep our calculation current, we update the information between shareholder reports by accounting for a fund's market losses or gains, the sale or redemption of shares, and the payment of capital gains. This updated figure is not quite as precise as the one stated in the shareholder report, but it is more current and therefore more relevant to the investor.

Telephone Numbers
These are the local and toll-free (if available) numbers that an investor may use to contact the fund, call for a prospectus, or get marketing information.

Ticker
A ticker is the symbol assigned to the fund by the NASDAQ system. The ticker is commonly used to locate a fund on electronic price-quoting systems.

Top Five States
We display the five states or U.S. territories in which a municipal-bond fund invests most heavily and the percentage of the portfolio each state or territory represents. This information reflects the holdings of the portfolio on the page.

Total Assets
see also Net Assets
This figure reflects the total assets of all the fund's share classes at the end of the most recently reported month.

Total Cost
see Expenses and Fees

Total Return % Rank Cat
see Percentile Rank and Performance

Total Return
see also Capital Return % and Income Return %
All references to total return represent a fund's gains over a specified period of time. Total return includes both income (in the form of dividends or interest payments) and capital gains or losses (the increase or decrease in the value of a security). Morningstar calculates total return by taking the change in a fund's NAV, assuming the reinvestment of all income and capital-gains distributions (on the actual reinvestment date used by the fund) during the period, and then dividing by the initial NAV.

Unless marked as load-adjusted total returns, Morningstar does not adjust total return for sales charges or for redemption fees. (Morningstar Return and Morningstar Risk-Adjusted Ratings do incorporate those fees.) Total returns do account for management, administrative, and 12b-1 fees and other costs automatically deducted from fund assets. The quarterly returns, listed in the Performance section, express the fund's return for each individual quarter; the total shown on the right is the compounded return for the four quarters of that year. An asterisk next to the total return number indicates that the return is calculated for a partial quarter or partial year because the fund began operations during that time period.

Total Stocks/Total Fixed-Income
see Portfolio Analysis

Turnover Rate %
The turnover rate provides a rough measure of the fund's level of trading activity. This publicly reported figure is calculated by the funds in accordance with SEC regulations, and Morningstar gathers the information from fund shareholder reports. A fund divides the lesser of purchases or sales (expressed in dollars and excluding all securities with maturities of less than one year) by the fund's average monthly assets. The resulting percentage can be loosely interpreted to represent the percentage of the portfolio's holdings that have changed over the past year. The turnover ratio is most accurate, however, when a fund's asset base remains stable. A low turnover figure (typically less than 30%) might indicate that the manager is following a buy-and-hold strategy. High turnover (more than 100%) could be an indication of an investment strategy involving considerable buying and selling of securities.

V

Value $000
see Portfolio Analysis

Value
see also Growth and Investment Style Box
The investment style commonly referred to as

a value approach focuses on stocks that an investor or fund manager thinks are currently undervalued in price and will eventually have their worth recognized by the market. It is often contrasted with a growth-style approach to investing.

Value Measures

Price/Projected Earnings

Projected earnings are the consensus analyst opinion of how much a company will earn during its next fiscal year. Price/projected earnings represents the amount investors are paying for each dollar of expected earnings per share. When reported for a mutual fund, it shows the weighted average of the price/projected earnings ratio for each stock in the fund's portfolio. This measure helps determine Morningstar's value score for each stock and the overall value orientation of the fund.

Price/Book Value

Book value is, in theory, what would be left over for shareholders if a company shut down its operations, paid off all of its creditors, collected from all of its debtors, and liquidated itself. In practice, however, the value of assets and liabilities can change substantially from when they are first recorded. Many investors use the price/book ratio—the ratio of a company share price to its total book value per share—as a way to value a stock. If the share price is less than total equity per share, the company is selling for less than its break-up value. When reported for a mutual fund, it shows the weighted average of the price/book ratio for each stock in the fund's portfolio. This measure helps determine Morningstar's value score for each stock and the overall value orientation of the fund.

Price/Sales

Price/sales represents the amount investors are paying for each dollar of sales generated by the company. Price/sales is usually a less volatile measure than either price/earnings or price/book and can be especially useful when evaluating companies with volatile earnings. When reported for a mutual fund, it shows the weighted average of the price/sales ratio for each stock in the fund's portfolio. This measure helps determine Morningstar's value score for each stock and the overall value orientation of the fund.

Price/Cash Flow

Cash flow tells you how much cash a business is actually generating—its earnings before depreciation, amortization, and noncash charges. Sometimes called cash earnings, it's considered a gauge of liquidity and solvency. Price/cash flow represents the amount investors are paying for each dollar generated from a company's operations. When reported for a mutual fund, it shows the weighted average of the price/cash flow ratio for each stock in the fund's portfolio. This measure helps determine Morningstar's value score for each stock and the overall value orientation of the fund.

Dividend Yield

Dividends are the per-share amount taken from a company's profits and paid to shareholders. Dividend yield is equal to a company's annual dividend divided by its share price. It works as a kind of valuation measure—the lower the yield, the more investors have to pay for each dollar of dividends. Investors often consider stocks with high dividend yields potentially undervalued investments. When reported for a mutual fund, it shows the weighted average of the dividend yield for each stock in the fund's portfolio. This measure helps determine Morningstar's value score for each stock and the overall value orientation of the fund.

Y

Yield

see also SEC Yield

Yield, expressed as a percentage, represents a fund's income return on capital investment for the past 12 months. This figure refers only to interest distributions from fixed-income securities and dividends from stocks. Monies generated from the sale of securities, from options and futures transactions, and from currency transactions are considered capital gains, not income. Return of capital is also not considered income. NMF (No Meaningful Figure) appears in this space for those funds that do not properly label their distributions. We list N/A if a fund is less than one year old, in which case we cannot calculate yield. Morningstar computes yield by dividing the sum of the fund's income distributions for the past 12 months by the previous month's NAV (adjusted upward for any capital gains distributed over the same period).

Indexes

Manager Index